A NEW
CATHOLIC COMMENTARY ON
HOLY SCRIPTURE

A NEW
CATHOLIC COMMENTARY
ON
HOLY SCRIPTURE

Rev. Reginald C. Fuller D.D., Ph.D., L.S.S.
General Editor

Rev. Leonard Johnston S.T.L., L.S.S.
Old Testament Editor

Very Rev. Conleth Kearns O.P., D.S.S
New Testament Editor

With a foreword by
the Cardinal Archbishop of Westminster

NELSON

Nihil obstat: Nicholas Tranter, S.T.L.
Lionel Swain, S.T.L., L.S.S.
Censors
Imprimatur: + John Cardinal Heenan

WESTMONASTERII, die 25 Aprilis, 1969.

The *Nihil obstat* and *Imprimatur* are a declaration that a book or pamphlet is considered to be free from doctrinal or moral error. It is not implied that those who have granted the *Nihil obstat* and *Imprimatur* agree with the contents, opinions or statements expressed.

THOMAS NELSON AND SONS LTD
36 Park Street London W1
P.O. Box 336 Apapa Lagos
P.O. Box 25012 Nairobi
P.O. Box 21149 Dar es Salaam
P.O. Box 2187 Accra
77 Coffee Street San Fernando Trinidad

THOMAS NELSON (AUSTRALIA) LTD
597 Little Collins Street Melbourne 3000
403 George Street Sydney 2000

THOMAS NELSON AND SONS (SOUTH AFRICA)
(PROPRIETARY) LTD
51 Commissioner Street Johannesburg

THOMAS NELSON AND SONS (CANADA) LTD
81 Curlew Drive Don Mills Ontario

THOMAS NELSON, INC. PUBLISHERS
Nashville and New York

A Catholic Commentary on Holy Scripture

First published February 1953
Reprinted 1953, 1955, 1957, 1960
New and fully revised edition 1969
© Catholic Biblical Association 1969
Revised and updated July 1975

SBN 171220102
Printed in United States of America

FOREWORD

Never in the life of the Catholic Church have more people shown interest in biblical studies. For a variety of historical reasons the faithful have never been extensive readers of the Bible. Apart from the fact that the majority of our people were poor and often illiterate, Bible reading was at times regarded as hazardous to the faith. This was in part the result of the policy of the reformers in the sixteenth century who set the Scriptures against the authority of the teaching Church. Texts of Scripture were commonly used to discredit the claims of the magisterium.

This attitude began to change with increased educational opportunities and the rise of scriptural scholarship within the Church. During the last thirty years the laity has savoured the beauty of the written Word of God. Hitherto their familiarity with the Scriptures was limited to the readings they heard at Mass on Sundays and Holy Days.

It is sometimes said that the Second Vatican Council was responsible for the new enthusiasm for the Bible. This is not quite true. The earlier *Catholic Commentary* was published and eagerly acquired some years before the Council. It is easy to forget this, as well as the fact that Catholic scholars such as Abbot Chapman were encouraging Bible reading among the laity two generations ago. It is true, however, that the greatest impetus came through the Council, which insisted on the need for a more thoroughly biblical theology.

This new volume is therefore most opportune. The Catholic community is indebted to the editors who have persevered through many years of study and research to give us this authoritative work showing the place of the Bible in the life of the Church.

PREFACE

The appearance of the first edition of *A Catholic Commentary on Holy Scripture* was an event of some significance for English-speaking Catholics, and its wide distribution throughout the world showed that the work was not unsuccessful in achieving its aim of interpreting the Bible in the light of contemporary research.

The speed, however, of development in biblical studies since that time has been such that before many years had passed a new edition was seen to be urgently necessary. Initially, a moderate revision was planned and the work put in hand. As the work progressed, however, it became clear that a much more thorough revision was called for. As a result of this revised estimate, not more than one-fifth of the first edition material has been retained in the present volume.

Both editors and contributors have kept the original aim, namely to unfold the genuine sense of the Scriptures while making the fullest use of modern biblical research. In the years since the appearance of the first edition, Roman Catholic participation in biblical study has steadily grown and, in interpreting the Bible, the differences between them and other denominations have diminished in number and significance. This is a welcome result of the present biblical revival and the encouragement given to it by recent Popes. The word "Catholic" has been retained in the title of this *Commentary*, not to indicate the differences, such as they are, but to emphasize that this work is a contribution by Roman Catholic scholars to the spread of knowledge of the Word of God. So far from emphasizing differences, we believe this *Commentary* will show how much common ground there now is in the field of Bible study. For this reason we hope and believe that the work will prove of service, not only to Roman Catholics but also to readers of widely differing denominations or of none, and in this way make a real contribution to the ecumenical movement fostered by the Second Vatican Council and the World Council of Churches.

It cannot be too often stressed that a commentary is intended to be a companion to and not a substitute for the reading of the Bible. It is therefore presupposed that the reader has a Bible at hand when using this volume. As the *Commentary* is based on the original texts it is of secondary importance which English translation is used. Contributors have been free to make their own choice where specially desired. Such passages are printed in italics. At the same time the editors felt that it would be of value, for the sake of consistency in reference and quotation, to give prominence to one particular version. The *Revised Standard Version* commended itself for this purpose in view of its faithfulness to the original texts and its world-wide circulation. Thus, the RSV numbering of chapters and verses has been followed; and that of the Massoretic text, where this differs, has been added in brackets. Secondly, and indeed following from the feature just noted, the normal English spelling of Bible names has here been adopted, in preference to that based on the Latin Vulgate which obtained till recently in Catholic commentaries.

The general plan of the original edition has been retained. The Bible text is commented on, paragraph by paragraph according to the sense, rather than verse by verse. Lengthy treatment of particular points is relegated to articles of introduction; and a copious use of cross-references assists the reader to make the best use of both introduction and commentary. Though the principal views on any one question are given prominence, the contributor, has, where desired, expressed his personal point of view. Every endeavor has been made to complete the Bibliographies up to the time of printing. Contributors have been drawn, as for the first edition, from all parts of the English-speaking world. In addition we have to thank a small number of foreign scholars for some notable contributions. In particular we may mention the significant introductory article by His Eminence Cardinal Bea whose recent death is a heavy loss to the Church. Among the maps at the end of the *Commentary* may be mentioned those of Jerusalem, embodying the results of recent excavation, and a detailed map of archaeological sites. Lastly, a very full Index is added.

Though the Editorial Committee assumes full responsibility for the *Commentary* as a whole, it should be noted that, in the concluding stages of its preparation, the main burden of the work has fallen on the shoulders of the General Editor.

The Editorial Committee wishes to thank His Eminence Cardinal Heenan for writing a Foreword to the Commentary and likewise the many contributors whose willing co-operation and forbearance lightened the burden of preparation. Thanks are due also to the staffs of Thomas Nelson and Sons, and St Paul's Press, Malta, for their skill and patience in carrying out a long and difficult task. Finally, the Committee expresses its deep gratitude to the Abbot of Ealing for generous and unfailing hospitality during the years of preparation. Only those who took part can fully appreciate how much it meant to have so congenial a meeting-place as St Benedict's Abbey.

It remains to recall those contributors to the present work whom God has called to Himself, namely, the Revv. R. A. Dyson S.J., E. Power S.J., E. F. Sutcliffe S.J., Sebastian Bullough O.P., and, as already mentioned, His Eminence Cardinal Bea. Let us remember them in our prayers with gratitude.

BERNARD ORCHARD O.S.B.
R. C. FULLER
L. JOHNSTON
CONLETH KEARNS O.P.

CONTENTS

ARTICLES OF GENERAL INTRODUCTION

ARTICLES OF INTRODUCTION TO THE OT

COMMENTARIES

+ The sequence of sections is arranged chronologically throughout the volume, but the following numbers are not used: 76, 98—102, 128—9, 218—22, 321—35, 455—8, 639—40, 694—700, 920.

CONTENTS

ARTICLES OF INTRODUCTION TO THE NT

COMMENTARIES

LIST OF CONTRIBUTORS

ARBUCKLE, Rev. N., O.F.M., S.T.L., L.S.S.; Lecturer in Sacred Scripture, Franciscan Study Centre, University of Kent, Canterbury.

BARTON, Right Rev. Mgr. J.M.T., D.D., L.S.S., F.S.A.; Consultor of the Pontifical Biblical Commission; sometime Professor of Sacred Scripture, St. Edmund's College, Ware. President (1952) of the Society for Old Testament Study.

†BEA, His Eminence Cardinal Augustine; President of the Secretariate for Christian Unity.

BLENKINSOPP, J., B.A., D.Phil., L.S.S.; Assistant Professor of Old Testament, Notre Dame University. Visiting Professor, Divinity School, Vanderbilt University, and Chicago Theological Seminary.

BUCK, Rev. Fidelis, S.J., S.T.L., D.S.S.; Professor of Sacred Scripture, Toronto School of Theology, Toronto, Canada

†BULLOUGH, Rev. S., O.P., M.A., S.T.L.; Lecturer in Hebrew at the University of Cambridge.

BUTLER, Right Rev. Bishop B.C., O.S.B., M.A.; St. Edmund's College, Ware, Herts.

BYRNE, Rev., P., S.M., B.A., S.T.L.; Professor of Sacred Scripture, Mount St. Mary's, Milltown, Dublin.

CASTELLINO, Rev. G., S.D.B., D.D., D.S.S.; Professor of Assyriology at the University of Rome.

CODY, Dom Aelred, O.S.B., S.T.D., D.S.S.; Professor of Holy Scripture at the Collegio di S. Anselmo, Rome.

CONDON, Rev. K., C.M., B.A., S.T.L., L.S.S.; Professor of Sacred Scripture, All Hallows College, Drumcondra, Dublin.

CORBISHLEY, Very Rev. T., S.J., M.A.; sometime Master of Campion Hall, Oxford.

COUVE DE MURVILLE, Rev. M.N.L., M.A., S.T.L.; Catholic Chaplain at the University of Sussex.

DALTON, Rev., W.J., S.J., M.A., D.S.S.; Professor of New Testament Exegesis, Jesuit Theological College, Parkville, Australia.

DOCKERY, Rev. J.B., O.F.M., M.A., F.R.HIST.S.; Franciscan School, Stony Stratford, Wolverton, Bucks.

DUNCKER, Rev. P.G., O.P., S.T.M., D.S.S.; Consultor of the Pontifical Biblical Commission; Professor of Biblical Hebrew at the Pontifical Biblical Institute, Rome.

†DYSON, Rev. R.A., S.J., D.D., L.S.S.; Professor at the Pontifical Biblical Institute, Rome.

FANNON, Rev. P., S.M.M., D.D., L.S.S.; Montfort House, Blundellsands, Liverpool.

FOSTER, Right Rev. Mgr. R.J., S.T.L., L.S.S.; sometime Professor of Sacred Scripture at Oscott College, Sutton Coldfield, Birmingham.

FULLER, Rev. R.C., D.D., Ph.D., L.S.S.; Visiting Professor of Old Testament in the University of Nairobi, Kenya; sometime Chairman of the Catholic Biblical Association of Great Britain.

GIFFIN, Rev. P.R., S.T.L., L.S.S., B.A.; Lecturer in Sacred Scripture, St. John's Seminary, Wonersh, Guildford, Surrey.

GRAYSTONE, Rev. Geoffrey, S.M., D.D., D.S.S.; Professor of New Testament, Notre Dame Seminary, New Orleans, Louisiana, U.S.A.

GRECH, Very Rev. P., O.S.A., S.T.D., L.S.S.; Principal and Professor of New Testament at the Augustinian Theological Faculty, Rome.

GREEHY, Rev. J.J., D.D., L.S.S., B.A.; Professor of Sacred Scripture, Holy Cross College, Clonliffe, Dublin; Lecturer in Sacred Scripture at Mater Dei Institute, Dublin.

HANLON, Rev. T., S.T.L., L.S.S.; Lecturer in Sacred Scripture, Craiglockhart College of Education, Edinburgh.

HARRINGTON, Rev. W., O.P., S.T.L., L.S.S.; Professor of Sacred Scripture, Dominican House of Studies, St. Mary's, Tallaght, Co. Dublin; Lecturer in Sacred Scripture, Milltown Institute of Theology and Philosophy, Dublin.

HUESMAN, Rev., J.E., S.J., M.A., S.T.L., L.S.S., Ph.D.; Professor of Old Testament and Hebrew, Alma College, Los Gatos, California; Professor of Old Testament and Hebrew and Archaeology at the Graduate Theological Union, Berkeley, California.

JOHNSTON, Rev. L., S.T.L., L.S.S.; Lecturer in Divinity, Mary Ward College, Keyworth, Nottingham; sometime Professor of Sacred Scripture, Ushaw College, Durham.

JOYCE, Rev. E., C.PP.S., S.T.D., L.S.S.; sometime Associate Professor of Theology, St. Joseph's College, Rensselaer, Indiana, U.S.A.

KEARNS, Very Rev. Conleth, O.P., D.S.S., sometime Rector of the University of St. Thomas, Rome; Professor of New Testament in the same University; Consultor of the Pontifical Biblical Commission.

KEELER, Very Rev. R., O.F.M. Cap.; S.T.L., L.S.S., Professor of Sacred Scripture, The Friary, Crawley, Sussex; Lecturer in Divinity at Coloma College, West Wickham, Kent.

LEAHY, Very Rev. M., S.T.L., L.S.S.; sometime Professor of Old Testament at St. Patrick's College, Maynooth.

McKENZIE, Rev. J.L., S.J., M.A., S.T.D.; Professor of Old Testament, University of Notre Dame, Indiana, U.S.A.

McNAMARA, Rev. M., M.S.C., S.T.L., D.S.S.; Professor of Sacred Scripture, Sacred Heart Seminary, Moyne Park, Ballyglunin, Co. Galway.

McSHANE, Rev. J., S.T.L., L.S.S.; Lecturer in Religious Education, Notre Dame College of Education, Glasgow.

MARSH, Rev. A., O.C.S.O., S.T.L., L.S.S.; Professor of Sacred Scripture, Sancta Maria Abbey, Nunraw, Haddington, E.Lothian, Scotland.

MAY, Rev. E., O.F.M. Cap., D.D., L.S.S.; Professor of Sacred Scripture, Capuchin Theological Seminary, Garrison, N.Y., U.S.A.

MORAN, Rev. William L., Ph.D., L.S.S.; Professor of Assyriology, Harvard University.

MULCAHY, Rev. J., C.S.Sp., M.A., S.T.L., L.S.S.; Professor of Sacred Scripture, Holy Ghost College, Kimmage, Dublin.

MURPHY-O'CONNOR, Rev. J., O.P., S.T.L., L.S.S.; Professor at the École Biblique de St. Étienne, Jerusalem.

NORTH, Rev. R., S.J., M.A., D.S.S.; Professor of Biblical Archaeology, Exegesis and Semitic Languages, Marquette University, Milwaukee, and at the Pontifical Biblical Institute, Rome.

O'CURRAOIN, Rev. T., S.P.S., B.A., S.T.L., L.S.S.; St. Patrick's Seminary, Kiltegan, Wicklow, Eire.

O'HERLIHY, Right Rev. Bishop D.J., D.D., Ph.D., L.S.S., Bishop of Ferns, Wexford, Ireland.

O'ROURKE, Rev. J.J., M.A., S.T.L., L.S.S.; Professor of New Testament and Biblical Theology, St. Charles Seminary, Philadelphia, Pa.

ORCHARD, Dom J.B., O.S.B., M.A.; St. Benedict's Abbey, Ealing, W.5.

PENNA, Very Rev. A., C.R.L., D.S.S.; Consultor of the Pontifical Biblical Commission; Professor of the History of Christianity, University of Perugia.

POTTER, Rev. R.D., O.P., M.A., S.T.L., L.S.S., Blackfriars, Manchester.

†POWER, Rev. E., S.J., DOCT. LING. OR.; sometime Professor of Biblical Archaeology, Pontifical Biblical Institute, Rome.

REES, Dom D.D., O.S.B., M.A., S.T.L., L.S.S.; Professor of Sacred Scripture, Downside Abbey, Bath; Lecturer in Hebrew, Bristol University.

REES, Rev. William, M.A., B.Litt.; Nazareth House, Hammersmith, London.

† RUSSELL, Dom R.R., O.S.B., M.A., D.D.; sometime Lecturer in Divinity and Sacred Scripture, Downside Abbey, Bath, Somerset.

RYAN, Most Rev. Dermot, M.A., S.T.L., L.S.S.; Archbishop of Dublin, sometime Professor of Eastern Languages, University College, Dublin.

SAYDON, Right Rev. P.P., D.D., L.S.S.; Emeritus Professor of Old Testament in the University of Malta.

SCULLION, Rev. J.J., S.J., M.A., L.S.S., DOC EN THÉOL.; Professor of Old Testament Exegesis, Jesuit Theological College, Parkville, Victoria, Australia.

SIMSON, Rev. P., W.F., S.T.L., L.S.S.; sometime Professor of Scripture, White Father's House of Studies, London.

SMITH, Rev. A., C.P., S.T.L., L.S.S.; St. Gabriel's College, Blythe Hall, Ormskirk, Lancs.

†SUTCLIFFE, Rev. E.F., S.J., M.A., L.S.S.; late Professor of Sacred Scripture, Heythrop College, Chipping Norton, Oxon.

SWAIN, Rev. L., S.T.L., L.S.S.; Professor of Sacred Scripture, St. Edmund's College, Ware, Herts.

SWANSTON, Rev., H.F.G., M.A., M.Litt. Ph.D.; Lecturer in Systematic Theology, University of Kent, Canterbury, England.

THEISSEN, Rev. Dr. A., Professor of Sacred Scripture, Priesterseminar, Köln, W. Germany; sometime Professor of Sacred Scripture, Ushaw College, Durham.

VAWTER, Rev. B., C.M., S.T.L., D.S.S.; Professor of Sacred Scripture, De Paul University, Chicago.

WANSBROUGH, Dom H., O.S.B., M.A., S.T.L., L.S.S.; Professor of Sacred Scripture, Ampleforth Abbey, York.

WATSON, Rev. W.G.E., S.T.L., L.S.S.; St. Augustine's, Datchet, Slough, Bucks.

ZERAFA, Rev. P., O.P., S.T.D., L.S.S.; Professor of Old Testament Exegesis and History of Israel, Università di San Tommaso, Largo Angelicum, Rome.

ABBREVIATIONS

THE BOOKS OF THE BIBLE

Gn	Genesis	Wis	Wisdom		Mt	Matthew
Ex	Exodus	Sir	Sirach		Mk	Mark
Lv	Leviticus		(Ecclesiasticus)		Lk	Luke
Nm	Numbers	Is	Isaiah		Jn	John
Dt	Deuteronomy	Jer	Jeremiah		Ac	Acts
Jos	Joshua	Lam	Lamentations		Rm	Romans
Jg	Judges	Bar	Baruch		1, 2 Cor	1, 2 Corinthians
Ru	Ruth	Ezek	Ezekiel		Gal	Galatians
1, 2 Sm	1, 2 Samuel	Dn	Daniel		Eph	Ephesians
1 (3) Kgs	1 Kings	Hos	Hosea		Phil	Philippians
2 (4) Kgs	2 Kings	Jl	Joel		Col	Colossians
1, 2 Chr	1, 2 Chronicles	Am	Amos		1, 2 Thes	1, 2 Thessalonians
Ez	Ezra	Obad	Obadiah		1, 2 Tm	1, 2 Timothy
Neh	Nehemiah	Jon	Jonah		Ti	Titus
Tb	Tobit	Mi	Micah		Phm	Philemon
Jdt	Judith	Na	Nahum		Heb	Hebrews
Est	Esther	Hb	Habakkuk		Jas	James
Jb	Job	Zeph	Zephaniah		1, 2 Pt	1, 2 Peter
Ps	Psalms	Hag	Haggai		1, 2, 3 Jn	1, 2, 3 John
Prv	Proverbs	Zech	Zechariah		Jude	Jude
Eccl	Ecclesiastes	Mal	Malachi		Apoc	Apocalypse (Revelation)
Song	Song of Songs	1, 2 Mc	1, 2 Maccabees		Rev	Revelation (Apocalypse)

QUMRAN SIGLA

1QIs[a]	First Isaiah Scroll	4QSam[a]	1 and 2 Samuel MS
1QIs[b]	Second Isaiah Scroll	4QSam[b]	1 and 2 Samuel (a second MS from
4QTLevi	Testament of Levi		the same cave)
1QpHab	Habakkuk Commentary		
		2Q 13	Jeremiah scroll
1QS	Rule of the Community (Manual of	2Q 16	Ruth
	Discipline)	2Q 18	Hebrew Ecclesiasticus (Sirach)
1QSa	Rule of the Community (Appendix)	2Q 19—20	Book of Jubilees
1QM	War of the Sons of Light against	6Q 4	Kings
	the Sons of Darkness	11Q Ps[a]	Psalms scroll unrolled 1961
1QH	Psalms of Thanksgiving		
CD	Cairo Damascus Document;	6QD	'Damascus Document' from
	Fragments of a Zadokite Work		cave 6
1QApoc	The Genesis Apocryphon	4QDeut32	Deut ch 32 MS
4QpNah	Commentary on Nahum	4QOrNab	Prayer of Nabonidus. A
4QEx[a]	Exodus MS (in Palaeo-Hebrew		document from lost Danielic
	script)		literature

OTHER ABBREVIATIONS

AAS	Acta Apostolicae Sedis	CAP	R. H. Charles, Apocrypha and Pseudepigrapha of the OT, 1913
AASOR	Annual of the American Schools of Oriental Research	CAT	Commentaire de l'Ancien Testament
AB	Anchor Bible	CB	Corpus Berolinense, Leipzig 1897—
AI	R. de Vaux, Ancient Israel, E.tr. 1961.	CBEB	Cheyne and Black, Encyclopaedia Biblica
AJSL	American Journal of Semitic Languages and Literature	CBi.[1 and 2]	Century Bible, Old[1] and New[2] Series
Amb.	Ambrose	CBQ	Catholic Biblical Quarterly
AmER	American Ecclesiastical Review	CBSC	Cambridge Bible for Schools and Colleges
AmiCl.	L'Ami du Clergé	CCHS (1)	Catholic Commentary on Holy Scripture, 1st ed., 1953
ANEP	Ancient Near East in Pictures, 1954.		
ANET	Ancient Near Eastern Texts, 2nd ed., 1955.	CCSL	Corpus Christianorum, Series Latina
AOT	Gressmann, Altorientalische Texte, Berlin und Leipzig, 1926[2]	CGTC	Cambridge Greek Testament Commentary, ed. C.F.D. Moule, 1957—
Aq.	Aquila's version	Chrys.	St John Chrysostom
Aquin.	St Thomas Aquinas	CIL	Corpus Inscriptionum Latinarum
Aram.	Aramaic	CIS	Corpus Inscriptionum Semiticarum
ASS	Acta Sanctae Sedis	Clem.Alex.	Clement of Alexandria
ATD	Das Alte Testament Deutsch (Göttingen)	CleR	Clergy Review
		CNT	Commentaire du Nouveau Testament
Ath.	Athanasius	ColBG	Collationes Brugenses et Gandavenses
Aug.	Augustine	ConjNT	Conjectanea Neotestamentica
AV	Authorized Version (King James Version)	CS	Cahiers Sioniens
		CSCO	Corpus Scriptorum Christianorum Orientalium, Rome. Paris, etc., 1903—
BA	Biblical Archaeologist		
BabBa.	Baba Bathra	CSS	Cursus Scripturae Sacrae, Paris, 1890—
BASOR	Bulletin of the American Schools of Oriental Research	CSEL	Corpus Scriptorum Ecclesiasticorum Latinorum, Vienna 1866—
BaTal.	Babylonian Talmud	CV	Confraternity Version (See NAB)
BB	Bonn Bible series	Cyp.	St Cyprian
BBSAJ	Bulletin of the British School of Archaeology, Jerusalem	Cyr.Alex.	St Cyril of Alexandria
BDB	Brown, Driver, Briggs: Hebrew and English Lexicon, Oxford, 1906	DACL	Dictionnaire d'Archéologie chrétienne et de Liturgie
Bib.	Biblica		
BibOr.	Bibbia e Oriente	DbR	Dublin Review
BibSt.	Biblische Studien	DBS	Dictionnaire de la Bible, Supplément
BIES	Bulletin of the Israel Exploration Society	DBV	Vigouroux, Dictionnaire de la Bible
		dc	deuterocanonical
BiViChr.	Bible et Vie Chrétienne	DJD	Discoveries in the Judaean Desert, Oxford 1955—
BJ	La Sainte Bible de Jérusalem		
BJRL	Bulletin of the John Rylands Library	DOTT	Documents from Old Testament Times, ed. D. Winton Thomas 1958
BKAT	Biblischer Kommentar Altes Testament (Neukirchen)		
BNTC	Black's NT Commentaries	DowR	Downside Review
BZ	Biblische Zeitschrift	DSS	Dead Sea Scrolls
BZAW	Beihefte zur Zeitschrift für die alttestamentliche Wissenschaft	DTC	Dictionnaire de théologie catholique
		DV	Douay Version (Challoner's revision)
BZNW	Beihefte zur Zeitschrift für die neutestamentliche Wissenschaft	Dz	Denzinger-Bannwart, Enchiridion Symbolorum, editions 1—31
		DzS	Enchiridion Symbolorum, 32nd edition onwards, revised by Schönmetzer
CAH[1 and 2]	Cambridge Ancient History, old[1] and new[2] edition		

ABBREVIATIONS

EchB	Echter Bibel (Würzburg)	IrTQ	Irish Theological Quarterly
EHAT	Exegetisches Handbuch zum Alten Testament	JAOS	Journal of the American Oriental Society
EnchB	Enchiridion Biblicum, 2nd ed., 1954; 4th ed., 1961	JB	Jerusalem Bible
EOTInt.	Eissfeldt, The Old Testament, An Introduction, 1965	JBL	Journal of Biblical Literature
		JE	Jewish Encyclopaedia
EstBib.	Estudios Biblicos	Jer.	Jerome
EstE	Estudios Eclesiasticos	JJS	Journal of Jewish Studies
ET	Expository Times	JNES	Journal of Near Eastern Studies
EtB	Etudes Bibliques	Jos.Ant.	Josephus, Antiquities
ETL	Ephemerides Theologicae Lovanienses	JosBJ	Josephus, De Bello Judaico
E.tr.	English translation	JosCAp.	Josephus, Contra Apionem
Eus.HE	Eusebius, Historia Ecclesiastica	JPOS	Journal of the Palestine Oriental Society
EvQ	Evangelical Quarterly		
EvT	Evangelische Theologie, new series, München	JQR	Jewish Quarterly Review
		JRAS	Journal of the Royal Asiatic Society
Exp.	Expositor	JSS	Journal of Semitic Studies
		JTS	Journal of Theological Sudies
		Just.	Justin Martyr
Fs.	Festschrift		
GAB	Grollenberg, Atlas of the Bible	KAT	Kommentar zum Alten Testament (Leipzig-Gütersloh)
GB	Gesenius-Buhl, Handworterbuch 17th ed. 1915	KB	Koehler and Baumgartner, Lexicon in Veteris Testamenti Libros
GK	Gesenius, Hebrew Grammar, ed. Kautsch, Eng. edition revised by A. E. Cowley, Oxford 1910²	Kh.	Khirbet (ruins)
		KIB	Keilinschriftliche Bibliothek, Berlin 1889-1915
Gk., Gr.	Greek	KV	Knox Version
Greg.	Gregory the Great		
HAT	Handbuch zum Alten Testament (Tübingen)	LHNT	Lietzmann, Handbuch zum Neuen Testament, Tübingen
HDB	Hastings, Dictionary of the Bible, 1898	LTK	Lexikon für Theologie und Kirche, ed. Buchberger, Freiburg-im-Br., 1957²
HDCG	Hastings, Dictionary of Christ & the Gospels		
HERE	Hastings, Encyclopaedia of Religion & Ethics, 1908-1921	LumVi.	Lumière et Vie (et Alban-Lyss)
Heb.	Hebrew	LXX	Septuagint, (A) Codex Alexandrinus, (B) Vaticanus, (S) Sinaiticus
HeyJ	Heythrop Journal		
HibbJ	Hibbert Journal	LXXCam	Brooke, McLean and Thackeray, The Old Testament in Greek.
HKAT	Handkommentar zum Alten Testament (Göttingen)	Me.	Mélanges
HRCS	Hatch and Redpath, Concordance to the Septuagint	MGC	Moulton and Geden, Concordance to the Greek New Testament
HT	Hebrew Text	Misc.	Miscellanea
HTR	Harvard Theological Review	MMV	Moulton and Milligan, Vocabulary of the Greek New Testament, 1930
HUCA	Hebrew Union College Annual		
		MT	Massoretic Text
		Mus	Muséon
IB	Interpreter's Bible		
ICC	International Critical Commentary	NAB	New American Bible (See CV)
IDB	Interpreter's Dictionary of the Bible	NEB	New English Bible
IEJ	Israel Exploration Journal	NIC	New International Commentary on the New Testament
Ign.	Ignatius of Antioch		
Iren.	Irenaeus	NovT	Novum Testamentum (periodical)
IrER	Irish Ecclesiastical Record	NovTSuppl.	Novum Testamentum Supplements

ABBREVIATIONS

NRT	Nouvelle Revue Théologique	SB	Strack-Billerbeck, Kommentar zum
n.s.	new series		NT aus Talmud und Midrasch
NT	New Testament	SBib	Sources Bibliques
NTD	Das Neue Testament deutsch	SCat.	Studia Catholica
NTL	New Testament Library	ScE	Sciences Ecclésiastiques
NTS	New Testament Studies	ScotJT	Scottish Journal of Theology
		Scr.	Scripture
		SOr.	Studia Orientalia
OLF	Oxford Library of the Fathers	ST	Summa Theologica (St Thomas)
Ori.	Orientalia	StudT	Studia Theologica
Orig.	Origen	SvExÅb.	Svensk Exegetisk Årsbok
OT	Old Testament	Syn.	Synoptic (Gospels)
OTL	Old Testament Library	Syr.	Syriac
OTS	Oudtestamentische Studiën		
		T	Tell
pc	protocanonical	Tert.	Tertullian
PC(2)	Peake's Commentary on the Bible,	TGl.	Theologie und Glaube
	2nd ed., 1962	ThS	Theological Studies
PCSB	Pirot-Clamer, La Sainte Bible	TKNT	Herder's Theologischer Kommentar
PEF	Palestine Exploration Fund Quarterly		zum NT, 1953—
	Statement, 1855—1936	TLZ	Theologische Literaturzeitung
Pent.	Pentateuch	TPQ	Theologisch-Praktische Quartalschrift
PEQ	Palestine Exploration Quarterly,	TQ	Theologische Quartalschrift
	1937—	TRu.	Theologische Rundschau (neue Folge)
PG	Patrologia Graeca, ed. P. Migne	TSt.	Texts and Studies
PJB	Palästina Jahrbuch	TU	Texte und Untersuchungen zur
PL	Patrologia Latina, ed. P. Migne		Geschichte der altchristlichen
PW	Pauly-Wissowa, Realencyclopädie der		Literatur
	classischen Altertumswissenschaft	TWNT	Kittel, Theologisches Wörterbuch
			zum Neuen Testament
		TYD	J. T. Milik, Ten Years of Discovery
R.	Redactor; editor		in the Wilderness of Judaea, E.tr.
RA	Revue d'Assyriologie et d'Archéologie		1959.
	orientale	TZ	Theologische Zeitschrift
RB	Revue Biblique		
RBen.	Revue Bénédictine		
RevSR	Revue des Sciences religieuses		
RF	Robert-Feuillet, Introd. à la Bible	VDom.	Verbum Domini
RGG	Die Religion in Geschichte und	Vg	Vulgate (Sixto-Clementine edition)
	Gegenwart, 3rd ed., 1957—62	VgB	Vulgate, new critical Benedictine
RHE	Revue de l'Histoire ecclésiastique		edition, 1926—
RHPR	Revue d'Histoire et de Philosophie	VieInt.	Vie Intellectuelle
	religieuses	VieSp.	Vie Spirituelle
RHR	Revue de l'Histoire des religions	VigChr.	Vigiliae Christianae
RNT	Regensburger NT, ed. Wikenhauser	VL	Vetus Latina
	and Kuss, 2nd ed. 1956—	VS	Verbum Salutis series
RSPT	Revue des Sciences philosophiques	VT	Vetus Testamentum (periodical)
	et théologiques	VTB	Vocabulaire de Théologie Biblique,
RSR	Recherches de Science religieuse		Léon Dufour.
RSV	Revised Standard Version	VTS	Vetus Testamentum, Supplement.
RT	Robert-Tricot, Guide to the Bible		
RTh.	Revue Thomiste		
RV	Revised Version	W	Wadi or West
		WH	Westcott and Hort, The New
			Testament in the original Greek.
SacB	La Sacra Bibbia, ed. Garofalo	WV	Westminster Version
SamP.	Samaritan Pentateuch	WW	Wordsworth and White, Novum
SAns.	Studia Anselmiana		Testamentum Latine

WZKM	Wiener Zeitschrift fur die Kunde des Morgenlandes	ZKT	Zeitschrift für katholische Theologie
		ZLH	Zorell, Lexicon Hebraicum et Aramaicum Veteris Testamenti, 1940—
ZAW	Zeitschrift für die alttestamentliche Wissenschaft		
		ZNW	Zeitschrift für die neutestamentliche Wissenschaft
ZDMG	Zeitschrift der deutschen morgenlandischen Gesellschaft	ZThK	Zeitschrift für Theologie und Kirche
ZDPV	Zeitschrift des deutschen Palästina-Vereins		

A.D.	Anno Domini: 'in the year of the Lord'	ibid	ibidem: 'in the same place'
		id	idem: 'the same'
b.	born	i.e.	id est: 'that is'
B.C.	before Christ	lit	literally
c.	circa: 'about'	MS, MSS	manuscripts
cf	confer: 'compare'	op cit	opere citato: 'in the work named'
ch, chh	chapter(s)	St	Saint
d.	died	v, vv	verse(s)
e.g.	exempli gratia: 'for example'	viz	videlicet: 'namely'
f, ff	and following		

NOTE ON TRANSLITERATION

The method of transliteration used for both Hebrew and Greek should offer no special difficulty to the reader. For Hebrew words it may be noted that 'alep = '; ḥet = ḥ; ṭet = ṭ; 'ayin = '; ṣade = ṣ; śin = ś; šin = š. The letters without dageš are written thus ḇ, ḡ, ḏ, ḵ, p̄, ṯ. One or two contributors however have preferred the more usual style: bh, gh, dh, kh, ph, th, (e.g. in the Psalms). Vowels long by nature are written usually with a circumflex accent; those long by position with a horizontal line or bar over them, e.g. yôm, dāḇār.

A NEW
CATHOLIC COMMENTARY ON
HOLY SCRIPTURE

THE BIBLE IN THE LIFE OF THE CHURCH

PART I

BY AUGUSTINE CARDINAL BEA

1a Introduction—'The Church has always venerated the divine Scriptures as she venerates the very body of the Lord. For from the table both of the word of God and of the body of Christ she unceasingly receives and offers to the faithful the bread of life, especially in the sacred Liturgy. . . . For in the sacred books the Father who is in heaven comes to meet his children with great love and speaks with them; and the force and power in the word of God is so great that it remains the support and energy of the Church, the strength of faith for her sons, the food of the soul, the pure and perennial source of spiritual life' (Vatican II, Constitution, *Dei Verbum*, on Divine Revelation, n. 21). The first theme of this Introduction, in CCHS (1), (art 1. *The Place of the Bible in the Church*), could hardly be expressed more concisely and also more profoundly than by the words which we have quoted from ch 6 of *Dei Verbum*. In consequence, we shall here simply explain and comment in detail on this ch, but we shall insert it in the body of the Constitution, and complete and illustrate it with other conciliar documents. The Constitution on Divine Revelation was in fact among the last documents promulgated by the Second Vatican Council. But the practical consequences which derive from its doctrine for the various aspects of the life of the Church were fairly widely touched upon either in the documents promulgated before this Constitution (e.g. in that on the Sacred Liturgy and in the Decree on Ecumenism), or in those promulgated more or less together with it, as is the case for the documents on the Apostolate of the Laity, on Priestly Formation, on the Ministry and Life of Priests, and on the Missions. In this way the Council itself offers us copious examples of the place which Sacred Scripture occupies in the life of the Church.

b THE PEOPLE OF GOD GATHERED INTO ONE THROUGH THE PREACHING OF THE WORD OF GOD

First of all let us consider **in general** what Holy Scripture signifies for the Church. Here is the reason added, in the context of the words quoted above, why the Church has always venerated Divine Scripture and taken care to nourish herself upon it: 'The Church has always regarded the Scriptures together with sacred Tradition as the supreme rule of faith, and will ever do so. For inspired by God as they are, and committed to writing once for all, they impart without change the word of God himself, and they make the voice of the Holy Spirit resound in the words of the prophets and Apostles' (ibid). Various conciliar documents introduce us still more deeply into this purpose by indicating what may be called the existential position which the Word of God occupies in the life of the Church. For it is precisely **through the preaching of the Gospel that the People of God is gathered together**. The Decree on the Ministry and Life of Priests declares: 'The People of God is gathered into one first of all through the word of the living God' (n. 4). Similarly the Constitution on Divine

Revelation itself explains that the mystery of Christ 'had **1c** not been manifested to other generations as it was now revealed to his holy Apostles and prophets in the Spirit, so that they might preach the Gospel, stir up faith in Jesus, Christ and Lord, and gather together the Church' (n. 17). The dogmatic Constitution on the Church returns repeatedly to this thought: 'The Apostles by preaching everywhere the Gospel (cf Mk 16:20) which was received by their hearers under the influence of the Holy Spirit, gathered together the universal Church, which the Lord established on the Apostles and built on blessed Peter, their head, with Jesus Christ himself as the supreme corner-stone (cf Rev 21:14; Mt 16:18; Eph 2:20)' (n. 1, 9). Speaking in a similar way of particular churches, this same Constitution says that in them 'the faithful are gathered together by the preaching of the Gospel of Christ' (n. 26).

Then speaking of the divine mission entrusted by **d** Christ to the Apostles, the same Constitution says that it will endure to the end of the world 'because the Gospel to be handed down by them (the Apostles) is for all time the source of the whole of the life of the Church. For this reason the Apostles took care to appoint successors in this hierarchically structured society' (ibid n. 20). Concerning this same theme of the word of God as principle of life, the Constitution says that the bishops 'by the ministry of the word communicate God's power to those who believe unto salvation' (n. 26).

(1) But what is the meaning in this text of the term **e** 'the word of God'? Naturally by the preaching of the Apostles was meant in the first place the doctrine of Christ which they had received and had originally preached orally. Indeed the Constitution on Divine Revelation observes that the command of Christ 'was faithfully fulfilled by the Apostles who by their oral preaching, by example and by ordinances handed on what they had received from the lips of Christ, from living with him and from his works, or what they had learned through the prompting of the Holy Spirit. It was fulfilled also by those Apostles and apostolic men who under the inspiration of the Holy Spirit committed the message of salvation to writing' (n. 7). Therefore this same document adds 'Hence there exists a close connection and communication between sacred tradition and sacred Scripture' (n. 9), and 'they form one sacred deposit of the word of God which is committed to the Church' (n. 10). However the declarations of the conciliar texts that the People of God have been united by means of the word of God hold without any doubt also for Holy Scripture. Thus the Constitution on Divine Revelation says that the writings of the NT occupy a prominent place in the sacred deposit of the word of God. 'The word of God which is the power of God for the salvation of all who believe (cf Rm 1:16) is set forth and shows its power in an **eminent** way in the writings of the New Testament' (n. 17). The reason for this is that these writings are 'a perpetual and divine witness' of the fulfilment of the mystery which was hidden

1e before all ages in God, that is of the Incarnation, the Redemption and the foundation of the Church. Hence it is fully justifiable to interpret the texts mentioned above on the function and place which the word of God occupies in the life of the Church in a specially eminent sense of the written word of God, Holy Scripture.

f (2) What is the **deep meaning** of the doctrine expounded above that the Church is gathered together by means of the preaching of the Gospel and of the word of God? To understand it, we must remember the doctrine of the NT, recalled in the conciliar Constitution on the Church. According to this, just as Israel in its pilgrimage in the desert came to be called 'Church', Ecclesia, Qahal, that is assembly of God (cf Neh 13:1; Nm 20:4; Dt 23:1ff) so the New Israel, the Church of the NT, comes also to be called Church, or assembly of Christ. And the Constitution goes on: 'God has **gathered together** as one all those who in faith look upon Jesus as the author of salvation and the source of unity and peace, and has established them as the Church, that for each and all she may be the visible sacrament of this saving unity' (n. 9). So every time that the word of God rings out, there rings out this divine call which gathers together the people of God.

g We can however penetrate still **more deeply**, always following the doctrine of the Constitution of the Church; 'Christ instituted this new covenant, that is to say, the new testament in his blood (cf 1 Cor 11:25) by **calling together** a people made up from Jews and gentiles; they came together in unity not according to the flesh but in the Spirit and are the new People of God. For those who believe in Christ, being reborn not from a perishable but from an imperishable seed **through the word of the living God** (cf 1 Pt 1:23), not from the flesh but from water and the Holy Spirit (cf Jn 3:5f), are finally constituted "a chosen race, a royal priesthood, a holy nation, a purchased people, . . . who in times past were not a people, but now are the People of God" (1 Pt 2:9f)' (n. 9). So this is the way in which the People of God is gathered together, the Church is united by means of the word of God. The Decree on the Ministry and Life of Priests adds this significant and clarifying explanation: 'In fact through the saving word the spark of faith is struck in the hearts of unbelievers and fed in the hearts of the faithful. By this faith the community of the faithful begins and grows' (n. 4).

h A **confirmation** for all we have been saying on the function of the Word of God in the life of the Church comes from the repeated declarations of the Council that the duty of preaching the Gospel is among the principal duties both of Bishops and of Priests: 'Among the principal duties of bishops, the preaching of the Gospel has pre-eminence', says the Constitution on the Church (n. 25); and the Decree on Missionary Activity: 'The bishop should be first and foremost the herald of the faith, to lead new disciples to Christ' (n. 20). Then the decree on the Ministry and Life of Priests: 'Priests as co-workers with their bishops, have as their **primary** duty the proclamation of the gospel of God to all'. In this way they fulfil the Lord's command: 'Go into the whole world and preach the gospel to every creature' (Mk 16:15). 'Thus they establish and build up the People of God' (n. 4).

2a THE WORD OF GOD ENTRUSTED TO THE APOSTLES AND THEIR SUCCESSORS

What in more detail is the way in which **the word of God becomes source of the life of the Church**? This comes about through **preaching** and this was entrusted by Christ to **the Apostles and their successors, the**

bishops. This answer is contained in the texts already **2a** quoted. Christ entrusted the proclamation of this word to the **Apostles**. Then that the mission entrusted to them by Christ might endure until the consummation of the world, the Apostles entrusted it to their own successors, **the bishops**. This is an essential point of Catholic ecclesiology. As regards the function and place of the Apostles the thing is too clearly attested in the NT to be set in doubt. Hence it is admitted also by those Christians who do not share Catholic ecclesiological doctrine. The difficulty arises over the successors of the Apostles and in consequence over the hierarchical structure of the Church. Obviously we cannot treat it fully here. We shall content ourselves with adducing just one, but that an essential, conciliar text. The Apostles 'that the mission assigned to them might continue after their death, passed on to their immediate co-operators, as by way of testament, the duty of perfecting and consolidating the work begun by them. They charged them to attend to the whole flock in which the Holy Spirit had placed them to shepherd the Church of God (cf Ac 20:28). They therefore chose such men, and thereafter settled that when they died, other approved men should carry on their ministry' (n. 20). Who are principally their successors **b** of the Apostles? The Constitution answers: 'Among the various ministries which from the earliest times were exercised in the Church, as Tradition witnesses, the chief place belongs to the office of those who, appointed to the episcopate through a succession which comes down uninterruptedly from the beginning, possess the lineage of the apostolic seed. Thus, as St Irenaeus testifies, through those who were appointed bishops by the Apostles and their successors down to our own time, the apostolic Tradition is manifested and preserved in the whole world' (ibid). This text already contains in part the relevant proofs taken either from Holy Scripture or from the most ancient Tradition. So we have no need to add others.

(1) Rather than occupy ourselves further with these **c** ecclesiological foundations, it is important for us to see clearly what exactly is the **task of these Successors of the Apostles as regards the Word of God**, and in particular the written Word? It is the age-long problem of the relation between Sacred Scripture and Sacred Tradition, between Sacred Scripture and Teaching Authority of the Church. Here too let us start afresh from basic facts, that is from the beginnings of the Church themselves. The text we have already quoted from the Constitution on Divine Revelation stated that Christ's command to instruct all nations was faithfully carried out both by the Apostles through oral preaching, examples and institutions, and by these Apostles and men of their circle who through the inspiration of the Holy Spirit wrote down the tidings of salvation (cf n. 7). So we have a double way of proclaiming the message of salvation: oral and written. Now as to the latter, two cases have to be distinguished: if he who sets the message of salvation in **d** writing is an Apostle, it is clear that when he writes, as when he preaches, he draws upon his own knowledge and carries out his own mandate—always under the guidance of the Holy Spirit. On the other hand those who were not Apostles but only 'of the circle' of the Apostles proceed differently. St Luke puts it with his well-known precision in the introduction to his Gospel: they draw upon the testimony of those who were witnesses of the life and death of Christ and became ministers of the word: 'Inasmuch as many have undertaken to compile a narrative of the things which have been accomplished among us, **just as** they were delivered to us by those who were from the beginning eyewitnesses and became ministers of the

2d word, it seemed good to me also, having followed all things accurately from the beginning, to write an orderly account for you, most excellent Theophilus, that you may have exact knowledge concerning the facts of which you have been informed' (Lk 1:1—4). But let us add immediately that both the writers who were Apostles and the others all wrote 'under the inspiration of the Holy Spirit' through whom their writings 'have God as their author and have been handed on as such to the Church' (Divine Revelation n. 11).

e What are **the results** of this whole process, whether of oral preaching or of what is expressed in writing? First of all the fact that the apostolic preaching, besides being handed on to the successors of the Apostles orally, is also 'expressed in a special way in the inspired books' (Divine Revelation n. 8), that is in the books in which the principal author is God himself. There is further a practical consequence which concerns the members of the Church, and that is the **obligation** to hold fast what has been handed on by the Apostles whether orally or by writing: 'The Apostles therefore, in handing on what they themselves have received, warn the faithful to hold fast to the traditions which they have learned either by word of mouth or by letter (cf Thes 2:15) and to fight for the faith which has been handed down to them once for all (Divine Revelation n. 8). What is the **content** of the things handed on? It includes 'all things which contribute to the holiness of life and the increase in faith of the People of God; and so the Church, in her teaching, life and worship, perpetuates and hands on to all generations all that she believes' (ibid).

f It is undeniable that the explanation of the way in which the word of God becomes concretely the principle of the life of the Church and the consequences of this doctrine have revealed to us a number of elements determining a somewhat complex situation. The factors which taken together make up the transmission of Revelation, that is the word of God, are thus synthesized by the conciliar Constitution on Divine Revelation: 'It is clear that sacred tradition, sacred Scripture and the teaching authority of the Church are so linked and joined together according to God's most wise design, that one cannot stand without the others, and that all together and each in its own way under the action of the one Holy Spirit contribute effectively to the salvation of souls' (n. 10). So the relative factors are: Sacred tradition, sacred Scripture and the teaching authority of the Church. All three are so intimately united that no one of them can subsist independently of the others; each of them acts according to its own way and all together act under the determining influence of the Holy Spirit. Let us try then to grasp more deeply the way of acting proper to each of these factors and how they co-operate and converge to the same end of handing on the word of God to men and contributing to their salvation.

g (2) Let us start from a **psychological reflection**. Christ had to conceive and realize the way to transmit to humanity across the generations and by means of the Church the doctrine which he had brought from the Father. He found himself faced with the same fundamental problem which meets anyone who desires to transmit to posterity not only a certain number of facts, but especially a certain doctrine, still more a certain spirit. It is the specifically human difficulty met by all great founders in the social, political or religious fields. Two ways are open to them—and they are those which in fact have been followed in various ways in history: that of living transmission by means of men purposely formed, who would then form others, or that of the written word.

Naturally these two means or ways could also be combined **2g** and used together. In dealing with the aim to transmit a spirit, it was very natural to think that the better and more effective way would be to do it by means of men prepared for this work who would transmit this spirit to others in a living way. History shows how in the majority of cases if this method was used, there was needed, to give the transmission a minimum of stability, the support of a minimum of formulae, which could be transmitted either with the oral transmission or in writing. Here naturally there arose a new difficulty, that of transfusing and incarnating a spirit into formulae. Moreover from the very way in which they were preserved and transmitted, these had to be not too numerous. The gravest difficulty was the comprehension and interpretation of such formulae in successive generations with all the changes of mentality and sometimes also of language which such succession carried with it. Therefore to the formation of men who would transmit the spirit in question in a living way, there had to be added the transmission of the right **interpretation** of the formulae in which it had been incarnated. Thus little by little the formulae, whether **h** transmitted orally or by writing, came to be immersed in a living fluid of interpretations and transmitted together with this living stream which went on growing and increasing with the passage of time. This stream of living interpretation which accompanied the formulae across the generations, had to grow the more, the more the spirit in question acquired importance and influence on the life of men. This meant in fact that the men who had the task of transmitting the formulae had time and time again to give life to them, in order to be able to communicate the spirit to ever wider strata of men and make it operative in their lives. Moreover this could not be managed with the immobility in which the formulae by themselves had been preserved and, so to speak, mechanically transmitted, but only on condition that the spirit was ever more deeply understood and assimilated by whoever had to transmit it.

(3) Now let us see **how Christ acted** with the purpose **i** of transmitting his doctrine from generation to generation by means of the Church. He chose rather first of all **living transmission**, that is preaching, the proclamation by means of his envoys, the Apostles and their successors, as is expressed in his command: 'Go then and make disciples of all nations . . . teaching them to observe all that I have commanded you' (Mt 28.19f). That this way had to last till the end of the world is shown by the words which the Lord adds: 'And lo, I am with you always, to the close of the age' (ibid). Besides, living transmission is part of the divine pedagogy already practised in the OT and then continued in the New, as St Paul explains in his letter to the Romans: 'How are men to call upon him in whom they have not believed? And how are they to believe in him of whom they have never heard? And how are they to hear without a preacher? And how can men preach unless they are sent? . . . So faith comes from what is heard, and what is heard comes through the command [RSV 'by preaching'] of Christ' (Rm 10:14f, 17).

(a) Let us seek to determine more closely the nature **j** of this transmission. The first and essential element is the **authority** of those sent by Christ: Christ invested them with his own authority and so, in this sense, with a divine authority. In fact he assured them: 'He who hears you, hears me, and he who rejects you rejects me, and he who rejects me rejects him who sent me' (Lk 10:16, cf Mt 10:15). The Constitution on Divine Revelation is still fuller and more explicit in this respect. It speaks of the 'living teaching office of the Church, whose

2j authority is exercised in the name of Jesus Christ' (n. 10). And the Constitution on the Church specifies: 'Bishops are the heralds of the faith who lead new disciples to Christ. They are authentic teachers, endowed with the authority of Christ, who preach to the people committed to them the faith they must believe and put in practice. By the light of the Holy Spirit they make the faith clear, bringing forth from the treasury of Revelation new things and old' (n. 25). The Constitution continues with precision: 'Bishops when they teach in communion with the Roman Pontiff, are to be respected by all as witnesses to divine and Catholic truth. The faithful are to accept the judgement of their bishop, given in the name of Christ in matters of faith and morals, and adhere to it with religious respect. This religious respect of will and intelligence must be shown specially to the authentic teaching of the Roman Pontiff' (ibid).

k The divine guarantee of the truth goes, under determined conditions, even as far as the divine **charisma** of **infallibility**, as the same Constitution explains further on: 'The individual bishops do not enjoy the prerogative of infallibility. Nevertheless even when they are dispersed around the world, provided that they maintain the bond of communion among themselves and with Peter's successor, when in their authentic teaching on faith and morals, they concur on one judgement to be held as definitive, they proclaim the doctrine of Christ **infallibly**. This is still more clearly verified when, gathered together in an ecumenical council, they are teachers and judges of faith and morals for the universal Church. Their definitions must then be adhered to with the submission of faith' (ibid).

In the first of the texts quoted from the Constitution on the Church the expression that the Bishops make the faith clear 'by the light of the Holy Spirit' is to be noted (cf also Divine Revelation n. 10). The thought that the Apostles and their successors are assisted and supported by the Holy Spirit returns repeatedly in various forms in the same context of the Constitution on the Church. We shall speak of it more fully later, but it is important even now to have noticed this fact which is quite simply **decisive** for understanding the way in which Christ willed and realised the transmission of his doctrine.

3a (b) Let us also look at the **fullness of content** of what the Apostles preach and teach in this way. Jesus had given command in the text just quoted to teach and observe all that he had commanded. Now since the Gospel is not an ideology but aims at creating new life, the subject matter of preaching and teaching becomes also very extended. The Constitution on Revelation says on this matter: 'What was handed on by the Apostles includes everything which contributes to the holiness of life of the People of God and to the increase of the faith; and so the Church in her teaching, life and worship, perpetuates and hands on to all generations all that she is herself, all that she believes (n. 8). This fullness of content has consequences also for the way, that is the means, of transmission, which includes not only the word but also examples and institutions, as again the Constitution teaches: The Apostles 'in their oral preaching, in example and in ordinances, handed on what they had received from the lips of Christ, from living with him, from what he did, or what they had learned under the inspiration of the Holy Spirit' (n. 7).

b (c) But in his understanding of man and human nature, Christ has nevertheless not disdained the **help of the written word also**. 'Besides living preaching, some men, whether Apostles or men of their circle' 'under the inspiration of the Holy Spirit committed the message of salvation to writing' (ibid). This same Constitution underlines the advantages possessed by the written word of God. The divine Scriptures 'inspired as they are by God and committed once for all to writing, impart the word of God himself **without change**, and make the voice of the Holy Spirit resound in the words of the prophets and Apostles (ibid n. 21). Here we are dealing with human words, inasmuch as the preaching of the Apostles is that which has been fixed in these writings by themselves or by their collaborators; nevertheless as these writings have been composed 'through the inspiration of the Holy Spirit', in virtue of this divine inspiration, it is God himself who becomes their principal literary author; the human words are at the same time words of the Holy Spirit (cf art. 'The Inspiration of Holy Scripture'). **3b**

c (d) A further step: the divine written word does **not supplant** or render superfluous the **handing on and the living preaching** of the Apostles and their successors. The task assigned to the Apostles and their successors is the fundamental fact willed by Christ himself for the whole duration of his Church. Besides, the written word of God has need in various ways of the support of living preaching. Not that the Apostles are its 'masters' and can change it or do the like. The written word of God is something definitive which of itself is removed from subjection to any human authority; Sacred Scripture, as we have seen earlier, imparts the word of God without any modification and makes the voice of the Holy Spirit resound. But it cannot witness by itself to its own character as word inspired by God. The peremptory and divine value of its witness can be recognized only **after** its inspired character is certain. So it is living tradition which enables the Church to know the whole canon of the Sacred Books (n. 8), since these books have been entrusted to the Church as they are, that is as inspired (ibid n. 11). Further, this written word has need to be interpreted. The Apostles themselves show **d** that they are clearly aware of the need for an authentic interpretation of the word of God and know that this interpretation is their right and duty. St Peter, speaking of the epistles of St Paul, says that in them 'there are some things hard to understand, which the ignorant and unstable twist to their own destruction, as they do the other Scriptures' (2 Pt 3:16). And at the beginning of the same epistle he declares very energetically: 'First of all you must understand this, that no prophecy of Scripture is a matter of **private** interpretation, because no prophecy ever came by the impulse of man, but when men spoke for God it was the Holy Spirit that moved them (ibid, 1:21f). To the private and illegitimate explanation is evidently opposed the official interpretation of the 'ministers of the word', of the Apostles and their successors who constitute the living teaching authority of the Church willed by Christ himself. Hence the Constitution on Divine Revelation declares 'The task of interpreting authentically the word of God, whether written or handed on, has been entrusted exclusively to the living teaching office of the Church, whose authority is exercised in the name of Jesus Christ' (n. 10).

e (e) Moreover, the living tradition, or preaching 'makes the Sacred Writings unceasingly active' (ibid n. 8). Indeed the office of the Apostles of proclaiming the word of God should not and could not be exercised in a mechanical way. The handing on of revelation to living men who live in such various conditions with various mentalities and cultures, requires absolutely the explanation and interpretation of the gospel message, that it may be gradually assimilated and enter the life of men, in the concrete. Again, this living character requires that the office of interpreting the word of God in all its fullness, whether it is written or handed on by living people, be given and reserved to the Apostles and their successors. In fact the

3e Constitution on Divine Revelation declares: 'The Apostles after the Lord's Ascension handed on to their hearers **f** what he had said and done. This they did **with that fuller understanding** which they enjoyed after they had been instructed by the events of Christ's risen life and taught by the light of the Spirit of truth' (n. 19). The Constitution also speaks in the same way of the work of the sacred authors who wrote the four Gospels: 'Selecting some of the many things handed down by word of mouth or in writing, reducing some to a synthesis, elucidating some in view of the state of the churches, and retaining the form of proclamation, but always in such fashion that they conveyed the sincere truth about Jesus' (n. 19; the Instruction of the Biblical Commission 'Holy Mother Church', AAS, 56 (1964) 715 can be compared with this and also Augustine Cardinal Bea, *La Storicità dei Vangeli*, Brescia, 1964, 38ff).

g From this last requirement it appears clearly that Sacred Tradition, however faithful to the command and to the doctrine of Christ, is not and cannot be a thing without movement. There is in it a continuous progress, following upon **a continuous attempt to comprehend and penetrate** more fully what it contains. This agrees with Christ's word to the Apostles: 'I have yet many things to say to you, but you cannot bear them now. When the Spirit of truth comes, he will guide you into all the truth . . .' (Jn 16:12f). In this sense our Constitution affirms explicitly that the "Tradition which comes from the Apostles **progresses** in the Church with the help of the Holy Spirit' (n. 8). And elsewhere it explains: 'The Church, Bride of the Incarnate Word and taught by the Holy Spirit, progresses to attain an ever deeper understanding of Sacred Scripture so that she may unceasingly feed her sons with the divine word' (ibid n. 23). In this way 'there is growth in the understanding both of the things and of the words handed down. This comes through the reflection and study of believers, who meditate upon them in their heart (cf Lk 2:19, 51), through a deep understanding of the spiritual things experienced and through the preaching of those who have received together with episcopal succession, the sure gift of truth. For as the centuries succeed one another, the Church constantly moves forward to the fullness of divine truth, until the words of God reach their completion in her' (n. 8).

h (f) It will be said that everything that has been stated on the task of the teaching authority of the Church is thoroughly clear. And yet it leaves a doubt which is not trifling and can become a preoccupation: If the Church's teaching authority has the task of interpreting and explaining in a living way the word of God, written or handed on, and of rendering it operative, could there not perhaps easily come from all this the danger that the word of God remains at the mercy of men and their arbitrariness? The danger, humanly speaking, is there. But apart from the guarantee of the presence of Christ and the work of his Holy Spirit in the Church—of which we shall say more later—we must indicate also the **i very clear limits** set to the work of the successors of the Apostles. First of all it results from the NT that the Apostles—and in consequence their successors also— **are not masters** of the deposit of faith, but **only** and exclusively **administrators**. A very characteristic concept of the teaching of the NT is that of 'handing-on'. This involves knowing how to receive a doctrine, to preserve it and to transmit it faithfully (cf 1 Thes 2:13; 2 Thes 2:15; 3:6; 1 Cor 11:2, 23; 15:1ff; Rm 6:17, etc). We may recall in this connection the well-known formulae of St Paul: 'I received from the Lord what I also delivered to you' (1 Cor 11:23); 'I delivered to you what I received'

(1 Cor 15:3). Time and again the warning is repeated to **3i** keep the doctrine as it has been transmitted (cf 2 Thes 2:14; 1 Cor 11:2; 15:2). Indeed St Paul uses the very strong expression: 'Even if we or an angel from heaven should preach to you a gospel contrary to that which we preached to you, let him be accursed. As we have said before so now I say again, If anyone is preaching to you a gospel contrary to that which you received, let him be accursed' (Gal 1:80f). (Cf on this point, Augustine Cardinal Bea, **Storicità dei Vangeli**, Brescia, 1964, 26f).

The Constitution on Revelation speaks in the same **j** sense. It says very explicitly: 'The teaching office (of the Church) is **not** above the word of God, **but serves it**, teaching only what has been handed on, listening to it devoutly, guarding it prudently, and explaining it faithfully by divine commission and with the help of the Holy Spirit. Everything which it presents for belief as divinely revealed, it draws from this one deposit of faith' (n. 10). In other words the teaching authority of the Church— not less but in fact more than the faithful—must listen with faith to the word of God, accept it in its fullness, and keep it in its purity with the most absolute fidelity. Hence the Constitution on the Church says: 'When either the Roman Pontiff or the body of bishops together with him defines a judgement, they pronounce it **in accord with revelation itself. All are obliged to abide by and be k ruled by this revelation** which, whether written or preserved by tradition, is transmitted in its entirety through the legitimate succession of bishops and specially through the care of the Roman Pontiff. Under the light of the Spirit of truth it is thus religiously preserved and faithfully expounded in the Church' (n. 25). In order to be thus faithful to Revelation and to the sacred deposit confided to them, the members of the Church's teaching authority have a grave obligation to search out what is the doctrine of the faith with regard to particular points: 'The Roman Pontiff and the bishops, in view of their office and of the importance of the matter, give vigilant care and take appropriate means to inquire properly into that revelation and to give due expression to its contents' (ibid). This was done, for example at the dogmatic definition of Pius **l** IX on the dogma of the Immaculate Conception and for that of Pius XII on the bodily Assumption of the Blessed Virgin Mary into heaven (cf e.g. Vincenzo Sardi, *La Solenne definizione del domma dell' Immacolato Concepimento di Maria Santissima. Atti e documenti pubblicati nel 50 anniversario della stessa definizione, Roma, 1904*; G. Filograssi, 'L'Assunzione di Maria santissima, domma di fede', in *Civ. Catt.* 4 (1950) 281—92). This was done, using an enormous apparatus of Commissions and of experts, in interminable discussions with thousands of speeches of the Council Fathers both in the preparation and in the course of the development of the Second Vatican Council. And it is well known in what measure hundreds of theologians collaborated, without speaking of the fact that all this work rested on centuries of studies—exegetical, patristic, theological, etc. Of the collaboration of those who do not belong to the sacred hierarchy with the members of the hierarchy itself we shall speak again presently. And this will constitute a further complement to the concrete image of what is meant by sacred Tradition and the living teaching Authority of the Church and of its position with regard to the word of God in general and the written word in particular.

(g) Has what we have said so far completely described **m** the way in which Christ has provided for the transmission of his Word to humanity across the generations? No. There remains a highly important question: How could

3m Jesus pledge his own divine authority in everything taught by those he sent, the Apostles and their successors? They are and remain poor fragile human beings and as such they can so easily make mistakes, if not altogether abuse their authority. And Jesus certainly cannot cover with his authority either abuses or errors; still less can he demand that teachers who can thus abuse their commission and go wrong should be believed, as he is. And yet he requires that they should be believed as he is believed. How can he? He can do it because he is able to assure the absolute fidelity of his envoys to his doctrine and to the truth. It is for this that when he confers the mandate 'Go therefore and make disciples of all nations . . . teaching them to observe all that I have commanded you' he adds the assurance: 'Lo, I am with you always, to the close of the age' (ibid). Therefore the acceptance or not of the truth of the Teaching Authority of the Apostles and of their successors with all the prerogatives which belong to this Authority—as we have explained above—is a question of faith in Christ and in his promise. That promise is to assist those he sent, continually and even to the end of the world, in order that they may hand on his doctrine faithfully and without error. So faith can truly be put in them as in Christ himself.

4a How does Christ **fulfil these promises of his in the concrete**? Certainly they also signify that he himself is present and lives in his Church, he being 'the Head, from whom the whole body, nourished and knit together through its joints and ligaments, grows with a growth that is from God' (Col 2:19). All the same he himself assigns the task of assisting the Apostles and their successors, especially in the handing on of his doctrine, **to the Holy Spirit**, who is at the same time his own divine Spirit. This task of course does not concern only that presence whereby the Holy Spirit animates the whole life of the Church and all its members, so that St Paul can say: 'anyone who has not the Spirit of Christ does not belong to him (Rm 8:9). Nor does it concern only the presence whereby the Holy Spirit gives the baptized access to the Father (cf Eph 2:18), abides in their hearts as in a temple (cf 1 Cor 3:16; 6:19), prays in them, bears witness to their adoption as sons (cf Gal 4:6; Rm 8:15f, 26), and instructs and directs them through various gifts (cf 1 Cor 12–14). In the case of the Apostles and their successors we are concerned, besides all these gifts, with a new and quite special gift. Christ has promised the Apostles his own special assistance with regard **to their office as authentic**
b **teachers** of his doctrine. He made this promise in view of the coming of the Holy Spirit on the day of Pentecost: 'Behold I send the promise of my Father upon you; but stay in the city until you are clothed with power from on high' (Lk 24:49). And again: 'You shall receive power when the Holy Spirit has come upon you, and you shall be my witnesses in Jerusalem and in all Judaea and Samaria and to the end of the earth' (Ac 1:8). In the discourse at the Last supper he spoke repeatedly of the sending of the 'Spirit of truth' (cf Jn 14:17; 15:26) and in particular: 'These things I have spoken to you while I am still with you. But the Counsellor, the Holy Spirit, whom the Father will send in my name, he **will teach you all things**, and bring to your remembrance all that I have said to you' (Jn 14:25f) 'I have yet many things to say to you, but you cannot bear them now. When the Spirit of truth comes, he **will guide you into all truth**; for he will not speak on his own authority, but whatever he hears he will speak, and he will declare to you the things that are to come' (16:12ff). Hence St Paul can say that 'the Church of the living God (is) the pillar and bulwark of the truth' (1 Tm 3:15).

The Constitution on the Church makes this doctrine **4c** more specific and precise. Speaking of the office of the Apostles and of their successors, it says: 'For the discharging of such great duties, the Apostles were enriched by Christ with a special outpouring of the Holy Spirit coming upon them (cf Ac 1:8; 2:4; Jn 20:22f). **This spiritual gift they passed on to their helpers** by the imposition of hands (cf 1 Tm 4:14; 2 Tm 1:6f), and it has been transmitted down to us in episcopal consecration, (n. 21). A little further on the Constitution declares solemnly: 'It is clear that by means of the imposition of hands and the words of consecration, the grace of the Holy Spirit is so conferred and the sacred character so impressed, that bishops in an eminent and visible way undertake Christ's own role as Teacher, Shepherd and High Priest, and act in his person' (ibid). Only such assistance of the Holy Spirit can offer a valid foundation to the guarantee of truth and still more of infallibility.

We may conclude our rather long but fundamental **d** exposition on the tasks of the Apostles and their successors as regards the word of God with one last observation. It concerns the **spirit** in which these Shepherds ought to fulfil their own mission. Here is the problem: There is no doubt that the office entrusted to the Apostles and their successors is as lofty as it could be. So it is no wonder that in the course of centuries it has caused vertigo in one or other of the Hierarchy, and made him a victim of vainglory or pride; nor that in the history of the Church this office was sometimes repudiated as contrary to Christian humility and to the brotherhood which ought to exist between the disciples of Christ. Hence—while keeping intact the doctrine of the NT and of the Church on the point—it is important to underline the **spirit** with which this great office ought to be exercised. The spirit is that of humble service. The ministry of the Apostles and of their successors is not conceived as an exaltation of one over the rest, but as **humble service of the brethren**. Speaking of the office of the bishop the same Constitution declares that 'the office which the Lord committed to the shepherds of his People is a true **service**. In sacred Scripture it is significantly called 'diaconia' or ministry (n. 24; The Constitution adds in evidence a series of Biblical texts). And again: 'Those ministers who are endowed with sacred power are **servants** of their brethren, so that all who are of the People of God and therefore enjoy true Christian dignity, may work towards a common goal freely and in due order, and arrive at salvation' (n. 18).

SACRED SCRIPTURE IN THE CHURCH
5a

In The Liturgy—We have established the duties and the competence of the Shepherds with regard to the word of God. It remains to see, always in the light of the conciliar documents, how this duty is put into practice, or what practical measures are envisaged by the Council that the written word of God may become effectively the principle of the whole life of the Church. In this connection we have already seen the energetic declaration of the Constitution on Divine Revelation: 'Access to sacred Scripture ought to be wide open to the faithful' (n. 22). Now the first and foremost place where this access is opened and where the Church offers the faithful the bread of life, not only that of the table of the Body of Christ, but also that of the word of God (cf Divine Revelation n. 21) is the **Sacred Liturgy**.

(1) First of all the **deep spirit of faith** which **b**

5b inspires the use of Holy Scripture in the Liturgy is to be noted. The conciliar Constitution on the Liturgy, just as it professes its deep faith that Christ is present in the Sacrifice of the Mass, professes also its faith that in the Liturgy Christ 'is present in his word since it is he himself who speaks when the holy Scriptures are read in the Church' (n. 7). This principle is repeated in a slightly different form when speaking of the didactic and pastoral character of the Sacred Liturgy: 'In the Liturgy God speaks to his People and Christ still proclaims his Gospel' (n. 33).

c (2) Here then is **the general principle** which inspires the use of Holy Scripture in the Liturgy: 'Sacred Scripture is of paramount importance in liturgical celebrations'. Why? The Constitution answers: 'For it is from Scripture that lessons are read and explained in the homily and psalms are sung; the prayers, collects and liturgical hymns are Scriptural in their inspiration, and it is from Scripture that actions and signs take their meaning' (n. 24). In other words we are not dealing only with lessons from the Bible; the Sacred Liturgy is wholly— in lessons, chants, prayers, hymns, rites, actions and signs—permeated with Holy Scripture and hence makes it to permeate the liturgical community itself. From this arises the practical conclusion of the Council concerning liturgical reform: 'Therefore to achieve the restoration, progress and adaptation of the sacred liturgy, it is necessary to promote that warm and living love for Scripture to which the venerable tradition of both Eastern and Western rites gives testimony' (ibid).

d From the general principle are derived the following practical directives: (1) 'In sacred celebrations there is to be more reading from holy Scripture, and it is to be more varied and more suitable'. (2) 'The ministry of preaching is to be fulfilled faithfully and properly; moreover it should draw its content mainly from scriptural and liturgical sources; it should proclaim God's wonderful works in the history of salvation, that is, in the mystery of Christ, which is ever present and active within us, especially in the celebration of the liturgy'. (3) 'Bible services should be encouraged on the vigil of the more solemn feasts, on some weekdays in Advent and Lent, on Sundays and feast days, particularly in places where no priest is available . . .' (n. 35). (4) The general principle on the abundance and variety of the lessons from sacred Scripture in the Liturgy is applied also to the Divine Office: 'Readings from sacred Scripture are to be so arranged that the riches of God's word may be more easily accessible in more abundant measure' (n. 92).

e We have already heard mention in these texts of the Ministry of the word. In fact with regard to the preaching which takes place in the sacred Liturgy the Council declares that in the Liturgy of the word—that is the reading of sacred Scripture and its explanation 'the proclamation of the death and resurrection of the Lord is inseparably joined to the response of the listening people, and to the offering itself whereby Christ ratified the New Covenant in his blood. The faithful communicate in this offering both by their prayers and by their reception of the Sacrament' (Decree on the Ministry and Life of Priests, n. 4; on this deep union between the liturgy of the Word and the Sacrifice, cf Augustine Bea, 'The Pastoral Value of the Word of God, *Worship*, 30 (1956), 632—48. Of the use of sacred Scripture in preaching we shall speak later when treating of the priestly ministry and life.)

f **In the Preparation of Future Preachers**—It is obvious that the realization of the Council's intention to make the whole Church live in the greatest possible measure from the word of God depends decisively on the **5f preparation of priests** fitted for this work. For as things stand today, they are the principal preachers and heralds of the Gospel. In fact the council was much preoccupied, especially in the Decrees on Priestly Formation, on the Ministry and Life of Priests and on Missionary Activity, to ensure the Biblical preparation of priests.

(1) Speaking of the **spiritual formation** of future **g** priests, the Council says that this 'should be closely linked with doctrinal and pastoral training. Especially with the help of the spiritual director, this formation should be given in such a way that the seminarians learn to live in familiar and constant companionship with the Father through Jesus Christ his Son in the Holy Spirit. They are destined to be made like to Christ the Priest through sacred ordination. They should accustom themselves also to live intimately united to him as friends in their whole life. They should live Christ's Paschal mystery in such a way as to know how one day to initiate into it the people who will be entrusted to them. They should learn to look for Christ in **faithful meditation on the word of God**, in active participation in the most holy mysteries of the Church, above all in the Eucharist and the Divine Office' (n. 8). In saying that spiritual formation should be closely bound up with doctrinal and pastoral formation, the Council invites us to seek for the further explanation of the words we have quoted in the texts in which it speaks of the renewal of theological studies. In fact it is precisely in this part that there is traced out a whole vast programme destined and capable to give a new and profound orientation not only to the studies but to the whole life and activity of the future priest.

Speaking **in general** of the preparation of those who **h** 'are going to be sent to various nations', the Decree on Missionary activity says that 'they should be nourished with the word of faith of good doctrine' (1 Tm 4:6). Then it adds 'These they will draw principally from **Sacred Scripture**, as they study deeply the Mystery of Christ whose heralds and witnesses they will be' (n. 26). **Note:** similarly the same Decree, speaking of the formation of **catechists**, says it is necessary that they 'study Catholic doctrine, especially in the fields of Scripture and liturgy . . .' n. 17). Then speaking of the formation of priests in the territories of the missions, it says that what the Council has decided as regards priestly vocation and formation should be observed, and then adds: 'The greatest attention should be paid to what was said about joining spiritual formation closely with the doctrinal and pastoral formation, about living a life patterned upon the Gospel without concern for personal or family advantage, about deepening the sense of the mystery of the Church' (n. 16). From this arises the precise aim of the formation: 'From these principles they will learn a magnificent lesson of dedicating themselves without reserve to the service of the Body of Christ and the work of the Gospel, of remaining united with their own bishop as his faithful fellow workers, of offering their own co-operation to their brethren' (ibid). And here are **the means**. 'To achieve this general aim, the whole formation of the students should be ordered in the light **of the mystery of salvation as it is presented in holy Scripture**. This mystery of Christ and of man's salvation they should find present and should live in the Liturgy' (ibid).

(2) The Decree on Priestly Formation in its turn **i** speaks specifically: 'In the reform of ecclesiastical studies the first objective must be a better integration of the various theological and philosophical subjects. They should work together harmoniously to open the minds of the students progressively to the **Mystery of Christ**. That

5i mystery penetrates the whole history of the human race, is continuously active in the Church and is operative principally in the priestly ministry' (n. 14).

And here is **the way to carry out this task**: 'That this vision may be given to the students from the very start, ecclesiastical studies should begin with an introductory course of suitable duration. In this initiation the **Mystery of Salvation** should be presented in such a way that the students see the meaning of ecclesiastical studies, their order and their pastoral purpose. At the same time they should be helped to make faith the foundation and soul of their whole life and be strengthened to embrace their vocation with full personal commitment and a joyful heart' (ibid).

j (3) These **principles** are then **applied** to the various branches of the theological sciences. Let us notice so far as concerns **exegesis**: 'Special care should be taken over the **formation** of the students in the study of **sacred Scripture**, which ought to be the soul of all theology. After a suitable introduction, they should be initiated accurately into the method of exegesis, apprehend the principal themes of divine Revelation and take encouragement and sustenance from daily reading and meditation on the sacred books' (n. 16). Besides the expression that Sacred Scripture should be 'the soul of all theology'——an expression of which we shall speak later—we may also note the integration of the teaching with the daily reading and meditation of the sacred books, and that the teaching should encourage and sustain this personal work. In the same context we may also note that the decree requires 'a suitable knowledge of the languages of sacred Scripture (n. 13).

k Sacred Scripture ought also to exercise a profound influence on **dogmatic theology**: In this 'The biblical themes are presented **first**. Then the students should be shown what the Fathers of the E and W Church contributed to the faithful transmission and elucidation of the individual truths of revelation . . . '(n. 16). And this is not enough. 'Likewise **all the other** theological subjects should be renewed by a more living contact with the mystery of Christ and the history of salvation'. In particular the Decree requires: 'Special attention needs to be given to the development of **moral theology**. Its scientific exposition should be more thoroughly nourished by scriptural teaching. It should show the nobility of the vocation of the faithful in Christ and their duty to bring forth fruit in charity for the life of the world' (ibid).

l **Priestly Ministry and Life**—If it is true that the Mystery of Christ in the Church 'works principally through the priestly ministry' (Ministry and life of Priests, n. 14), it is clear that the plan of the Council concerning sacred Scripture must be realized above all through the work of priests. One of the principal fields of this work is **preaching**. In connection with this the Constitution on Divine Revelation establishes the general principle: 'All the preaching of the Church, like the Christian religion itself, must be nourished and ruled by sacred Scripture' (n. 21). Further on in the same chapter the Constitution turns once again to explain that these principles hold **for every kind** of the ministry of the word: 'The ministry of the word, that is pastoral preaching, catechetics and **all Christian instruction**, in which the liturgical homily should have a privileged place, takes wholesome sustenance and holy strength from Holy Scripture' (n. 24). Think of the place occupied in the life of the Church by the Sacred Liturgy—above all Holy Mass with preaching relative to it—and the Divine Office for those who share in it. Then perhaps it becomes possible to measure the vast and fruitful possibilities offered

through these conciliar dispositions for the knowledge of 5l Sacred Scripture in the Church. Even taken by themselves they already indicate a spacious long term plan to enable the Church to live from the written word of God.

Given that so much depends on priests in this matter, m the practical conclusion immediately drawn by the Council is also understandable: 'Therefore all the clergy must **keep constant contact** with the Sacred Scriptures through diligent sacred reading and careful study. This holds especially for the priests of Christ and **others**, such as deacons and catechists, **who** by reason of their office **are active in the ministry of the word**. It is required lest any of them become "an empty outward preacher of the word who is not a listener inwardly", while they must share the abundant wealth of the divine word, especially in the Liturgy, with the faithful committed to them' (n. 25).

This contact concerns in the first place the **spiritual n life** of the priest. Speaking of the life of priests the Decree on the Ministry and Life of Priests declares with regard to helps for their spirituality: 'Of all spiritual helps those acts come first by which the faithful receive nourishment from God's Word at the twofold table of sacred Scripture and the Eucharist. It is obvious how important is the energetic and frequent exercise of such means for the personal sanctification of priests' (n. 18). The same Decree **specifies** further, speaking of the way in which the priest can and should tend to holiness: 'Since they are ministers of God's Word, **they should every day read and listen to that word** which they must teach to others. If at the same time they are working to realize its message in their own hearts, they will become ever more perfect disciples of the Lord. So the Apostle Paul writes to Timothy "Meditate on these things, devote yourself to them, so that all may see your progress. Take heed to yourself and to your teaching; hold to that, for by so doing you will save both yourself and your hearers" (1 Tm 4:15f). For as priests search for a better way to hand on to others the fruit of their own contemplation, they will come to a deeper understanding of "the unsearchable riches of Christ" (Eph 3:8) and the manifold wisdom of God' (n. 13).

The **knowledge** also which the priest should possess o should be drawn in the first place from the reading and meditation of sacred Scripture: 'The knowledge of a sacred minister should be sacred, since it is drawn from a sacred source and directed to a sacred end. Hence it should be drawn **primarily from reading and meditating on sacred Scripture**' (ibid n. 19). In this spirit the Council requires that priests 'occupy themselves with perfecting their own theological knowledge suitably and ceaselessly' (ibid), while the Decree on Missionary Activity also speaks explicitly of 'biblical refresher courses' for the use of the clergy to be organized by episcopal conferences (n. 20). **Sacred Theology and Biblical Sciences**—The themes 6a of theology and biblical exegesis are essentially connected both with the preparation of future preachers of the word of God and with their further perfection. We have already seen how the Council begs Catholic exegetes and others concerned with theology to devote their energies 'to an exploration and exposition of the divine writings, using appropriate means. This they should do in such a way that as many ministers of the divine word as possible should be able effectively to provide the nourishment of the Scriptures for the people of God' (Divine Revelation n. 23).

(1) Not only the teaching of Theology but also the b work of theologians in general should be capable of making an essential contribution to this preparation of the

6b ministers of the word. How this is so appears clearly from the way in which theological work is conceived in the Constitution on Divine Revelation: 'Sacred theology is based on the written word of God, together with sacred Tradition, as its perpetual foundation. By that word it is most powerfully strengthened and constantly rejuvenated through examining in the light of faith all the truth hidden in the mystery of Christ. For the sacred Scriptures contain the word of God, and since they are inspired, are truly the word of God. Therefore the study of the sacred page should be like the soul of sacred theology' (ibid n. 24). It is impossible to stop and explain this profound text in detail. We will only underline its various elements: Sacred Scripture—obviously together with sacred Tradition in the sense we have formerly explained—is for theology a perpetual foundation, a source of solidity and a spring of ever fresh youth, and finally—and this is the thought of Leo XIII in the Encyclical 'Providentissimus', justly called the Magna Charta of biblical studies—like its soul.

c This is certainly a profound and an exigent vision of the tasks of theology. It is good that exegetes be conscious in what great measure the realization of this grand conception depends on the help which they can and ought to give to the teachers of dogmatic theology. For example it is for the exegetes to furnish the material necessary for this purpose, that is, an interpretation of sacred Scripture which is above all theological, as was required by the Encyclical 'Divine Afflante Spiritu' of Pius XII (cf EnchB 552ff). In particular they should provide a biblical theology to help those engaged on dogma in the difficult field of the so-called Scriptural argument, so that they can draw upon the fullness of the history of salvation set forth in sacred Scripture both of the New and also of the OT. Only thus will they be able to fulfil what is required, as we have seen above, by the Decree on Priestly Formation, that in dogmatic theology the biblical themes are to be set out in the first place.

d (2) The love of the Council for sacred Scripture appears also in the way in which it speaks of the **exegetes** and of their task. There are first of all the warm words of **encouragement** which it accords to exegetes and in general to those engaged in the biblical sciences: 'The Sacred Synod encourages the sons of the Church who are biblical scholars to continue energetically the work they have so well begun with a constant renewal of vigour and with loyalty to the mind of the Church' (Divine Revelation n. 23). Besides this the Council reminds the exegetes that it is for them to contribute to that profound understanding of the Divine Writings which is the great yearning of the Bride of the Incarnate Word: 'The task of exegetes is to contribute to the deeper understanding and exposition of the meaning of sacred Scripture' (n. 12). And here there opens a whole new important prospect for biblical science. It not only collaborates in the grand and highly important aim of forming the greatest possible number of ministers of the Divine Word; it **collaborates with the Teaching Authority of the Church itself**, 'furnishing the preparatory studies whereby the judgement of the Church is matured' (ibid). In this sense the Holy Father, Pope Paul VI speaking to those participating in the Biblical Week of the Lecturers in sacred Scripture in Italy, has recently said, that the office of interpreting the word of God 'in its decisive influence on the real value of this transcendent Word, is greater than man; it requires a grace, it requires a rule, a fidelity: "Propria interpretatione non fit" (2 Pt 1:20). You know it. That is, your office **shares in the teaching authority of the Church**' (Oss. Rom. 24 (Sept 1966), 1).

The Holy Father mentioned in the words just quoted **6e** that the words of sacred Scripture 'are not subject to private interpretation' (2 Pt 1:20); the Council too recalls the practical consequences of the truth that the preaching and hence also the explanation of the written word of God has been entrusted by Christ himself to the Apostles and their successors. Hence the **interpreter** must keep always present before him both **Sacred Tradition and the living Teaching Authority of the Church**. As regards the former element, the Constitution on Divine Revelation underlines repeatedly—as indeed the Supreme Teaching Authority of the Church had also done again and again, especially in the last ten years, that 'proper account must be taken of the living Tradition of the whole Church' (n. 12), that is of the teaching of the Church throughout the ages. And again: The Church taught by the Holy Spirit in her concern to attain an ever deeper understanding of sacred Scripture, 'rightly also encourages the study of the holy Fathers of both E and W and of the sacred Liturgies' (n. 23). These, moreover, are essential parts of sacred Tradition.

As regards the second element, the Constitution **f** admonishes that the work of the exegete should proceed 'under the watchful care of the **sacred Teaching Office** of the Church' (ibid), that is of the successors of the Apostles who rule the Church at a determinate moment. Indeed the interpretation of sacred Scripture 'is subject in the final instance to the judgement of the Church, which carries out the divine commission and ministry of guarding and interpreting the word of God' (n. 12). Both rules are a clear consequence of what we have explained on the mission and the tasks of the Hierarchy. It is enough to have mentioned them here. They will be dealt with further in the section which treats of Hermeneutics, the science of the rules for the interpretation of sacred Scripture.

In the Life of the Faithful—The aim of all that we **g** have said up to now is in the final reckoning that the **faithful** be really nourished and live from the written word of God. All the same this must not be understood as if the activity which leads to this objective should be only on the part of the Shepherds and of their respective collaborators—priests, theologians and exegetes—while nothing remains for the faithful except to receive this nourishment passively from them. The faithful themselves must **actively take in hand** the reading and meditation of the word of God. Indeed after having exhorted those who are concerned with the ministry of the word to keep an ever continuous contact with the Bible, the Constitution on Divine Revelation adds: 'Equally this Sacred Synod earnestly and insistently urges **all the Christian faithful**, especially religious, to learn by frequent reading of the divine Scriptures "the surpassing knowledge of Jesus Christ" (Phil 3:8). For "ignorance of the Scriptures is ignorance of Christ". They should therefore gladly put themselves in contact with the sacred text itself, whether it be through the sacred Liturgy, so rich in the divine word, or through devotional reading, or through instructions suitable for the purpose and other aids which in our days are commendably spread abroad thanks to the approval and active support of the shepherds of the Church' (n. 25). But the document immediately gives an admonition that the reading be accompanied by **prayer**: 'And let them remember that prayer should accompany the reading of sacred Scripture, so that God and man may talk together; for "we speak to him when we pray; we listen to him when we read the divine sayings"' (ibid).

(1) If the document when turning to the faithful **h** adds 'especially religious', it is doubtless thinking of

6h those members of the religious state who are neither clerics nor priests, since of these last it has already spoken. In the Decree on the Renewal of the Religious Life the Council exhorts **all religious in general** to draw for their own spiritual life in the first place upon **reading and meditating the Divine Books**: 'Therefore let the members of communities energetically cultivate the spirit of prayer and the practice of it, drawing on the authentic sources of Christian spirituality. In **the first place** they should have the Holy Bible in their hands daily, that from the reading and meditation of the Sacred Books they may learn "the surpassing knowledge of Jesus Christ" (Phil 3:8)' (n. 6).

i (2) Returning now to the theme proper to this section which concerns the simple faithful (who are neither clerics nor religious) it is to be noted that the Decree on the Apostolate of the Laity enumerates among aids to the apostolate 'a deeper knowledge of sacred Scripture' (n. 32). Speaking of the origins of the spirituality of the laity in connection with the apostolate, it says: 'Only by the light of faith and in **meditation on the word of God** is it possible always and everywhere to recognize God in whom "we live and move and have our being" (Ac 17:28), to seek his will in every event, see Christ in every man, whether neighbour or stranger, and judge rightly of the true meaning and value which temporal things have in themselves and in relation to man's final goal' (n. 4). As a kind of comment on these words, let us follow the conciliar description of the spirit which should animate the lay apostle. It is given us in the same chapter and is wholly pervaded with the spirit of the Gospel and of the NT in general: 'The charity of God, "poured into our hearts through the Holy Spirit who has been given to us" (Rm 5:5) enables the laity to express in their lives the **j** true spirit of the **Beatitudes**. Following Jesus who embraced poverty they are neither depressed by the lack of temporal goods nor puffed up by their abundance. Imitating the humble Jesus, they do not desire empty honours (Gal 5:26), but seek to please God rather than men, ever ready to leave all things for Christ's sake (cf Lk 14:26) and to suffer persecution for justice's sake (cf Mt 5:10). For they remember the words of the Lord: "If any man would come after me, let him deny himself and take up his cross and follow me" (Mt 16:24)' (ibid).

7a (3) It naturally falls to the **Shepherds to be guides and helpers of the faithful in this field** still more than in others, since it is such a delicate one. The first task is to provide appropriate **translations**: 'Since the word of God ought to be available to all at all times, the Church with maternal concern sees to it that suitable and correct translations are made into different languages, by preference from the original texts of the sacred books' (Divine Revelation n. 22). Further 'it devolves on sacred bishops, "who have the apostolic doctrine", to give the faithful entrusted to them suitable instruction on **the right use** of the divine books, especially the NT and above all the Gospels, through translations of the sacred texts. Such versions are to be provided with necessary and fully adequate explanations so that the sons of the Church may safely and **profitably** grow familiar with the sacred Scriptures and be penetrated with their spirit' (n. 25). The words 'safely and profitably' are to be **b** particularly noted. Already St Peter had remarked how so great a gift of God as is sacred Scripture, in the hands of people with little instruction and especially little solidity in the faith, can become from a nourishment of life an instrument of their own ruin (cf 2 Pt 3:16). How often this has been repeated through the history of the Church and is still repeated today! It is therefore the sense of her

own responsibility for the faithful and her love of souls **7b** which urges the Church to watch over the use of the word of God on the part of the faithful. If in certain periods and determinate circumstances she has believed through pastoral prudence that she should not simply give the whole of Scripture into the hands of the faithful——and these are cases about which we cannot deal in particular here——nonetheless even in these periods she continued to offer the faithful, above all in the sacred Liturgy, the bread of the word of God.

In Ecumenism and Missionary Activity——let us also **c** touch briefly upon two subjects in which the Council seeks to use the written word of God for the realization of the Kingdom of God: Ecumenism and the Missions. (1) For Ecumenism the Council establishes a general principle: 'In dialogue itself sacred Scripture constitutes a **precious instrument** in the mighty hand of God for attaining that unity which the Saviour offers to all men' (Ecum. n. 21). In a way the Council itself indicates to us the manner and the road for this dialogue. After having acknowledged that beyond the visible confines of the Catholic Church there can also be found many of the constituent elements out of which the Church is built and given life, as for example the written word of God (cf ibid n. 3), the Council describes this fact in more detail. It honestly recognizes the differences which exist in this field between us Catholics and the Christians of the Reform: 'When Christians separated from us affirm the divine authority of the sacred Books, they think differently from us——and differently among themselves——about the relationship between the Scriptures and the Church. In the Church, according to the Catholic faith, an authentic teaching office has a special role in explaining and proclaiming the written word of God' (ibid n. 21). This done, the Council **d** describes, as if to provide the basis of dialogue, how much there is in common in this field between us and them: 'A love, veneration and almost an adoration of sacred Scripture lead our brethren to a constant and expert study of the sacred text. For the Gospel "is the power of God unto salvation to everyone who believes, to Jew first and then to Greek" (Rm 1:16)' (ibid). And here is how they manifest this love and veneration in the concrete: 'Calling upon the Holy Spirit (these brethren) seek God in sacred Scripture as he speaks to them in Christ, the One whom the prophets foretold, God's Word made flesh for us. In the Scriptures they contemplate the life of Christ, as well as the teachings and actions of the Divine Master on behalf of man's salvation, in particular the mysteries of his death and resurrection' (ibid). [NOTE. It is well known that **e** the expression 'quasi sibi loquentem' of the Latin text in this passage has been interpreted in the sense of 'as if he were speaking'. Hence there has been seen in this text a denial that God really speaks to us in sacred Scripture. However, this is not the meaning of the expression in this context. The Latin 'quasi' is not the 'as if it were' of the Latin grammar in schools. But, as often in biblical and in fact also in classical Latin, it has the meaning 'in a manner', 'so to speak'. We meet for example the expressions 'philosophia laudatarum artium **quasi** parens'; 'aliquem philosophiae **quasi** heredem relinquere'. When God speaks to us in holy Scripture the meaning is not that of speech in the proper sense but rather in a metaphorical sense. Compare in this connection the Constitution on Divine Revelation: 'For in the sacred Books the Father who is in heaven comes with great love to meet his children and speaks with them . . .' (n. 21)].

Then this veneration for sacred Scripture among **f** our brethren bears its fruit also in their **Christian life**: 'The Christian life of these brethren is nourished

7f by faith in Christ. It is strengthened by the grace of baptism and by the **hearing of God's word**. It is expressed in private prayer, in **meditation on the Bible** ... (Ecumenism n. 23). On this point also, the Council, while honestly recognizing existing divergencies, affirms the possibility and the bases of dialogue: 'And if in moral matters there are many Christians who do not always understand the gospel in the same way as Catholics and do not admit the same solutions for the more difficult problems of modern society, nevertheless they share our desire to cling to Christ's word as the source of Christian virtue. ... Hence the ecumenical dialogue could start with discussions concerning the application of the gospel to moral questions' (ibid).

g Finally the Council opens the door to a **work in common** with non-Catholic Christians in the biblical field, when in the Constitution on Revelation it says of translations of the Bible: 'If, given the opportunity and the approval of Church authority, these translations are produced in co-operation with separated brethren as well, all Christians will be able to use them' (n. 22). It is well known that not a few initiatives in this sense have already come to light in different parts of the world and continue to develop rapidly with great spiritual advantage for the souls of many Christians.

h (2) Other interesting and fruitful suggestions have been given by the Council **in the mission field**. Especially well known is the preoccupation of the Council to prepare **editions** of sacred Scripture, **for the use of non-Christians**: 'Editions of sacred Scripture, provided with suitable notes, should be prepared also for the use of non-Christians and adapted to their circumstances. Both pastors of souls and Christians generally should see to the wise distribution of these in one way or another' (n. 25).

i A further profound suggestion has regard to the problem of **adaptation in the missions**. With the progress of evangelization in the missions there arises the well-known and most difficult problem of assuming elements of the culture proper to each people, purifying them and creating a culture permeated with the spirit of the Gospel. On this subject the Decree on Missionary Activity says: 'The seed which is the word of God sprouts from the good ground and is watered by divine dew. From this ground the seed draws sap, which it transforms and assimilates into itself so as finally to yield abundant fruit. Thus, as happens in the economy of the Incarnation, the young churches rooted in Christ and built up on the foundation of the Apostles have the wonderful capacity of absorbing all the riches of the nations which have been given to Christ as an inheritance (cf Ps 2:8). From the customs and traditions of their peoples, from their wisdom and their learning, from their arts and sciences these churches derive all those elements which can contribute to the glory of the Creator, the revelation of the grace of the Saviour and the proper shape of Christian life' (n. 22).

j And now what is the safe and fruitful way to realize this great synthesis? Here too the Council indicates the **7j** study of Revelation and in particular of the **written word of God**: 'To achieve this goal it is necessary that in each great sociocultural territory, as it is called, theological research should be set on foot. In this way, under the light of the tradition of the universal Church, there will be fresh scrutiny of the deeds and words in divine Revelation attested in **sacred Scripture** and explained by the Fathers and the teaching authority of the Church. Thus it will be more clearly seen in what ways faith can seek for understanding in the philosophy and wisdom of these peoples. A better view will be gained of how their customs, outlook on life and social order can be reconciled with the manner of living taught by divine Revelation. As a result, avenues will be opened for a more profound adaptation in the whole area of Christian life' (ibid). The happy result which will come out of this is thus described by the Council: 'Thanks to such a procedure, every appearance of syncretism and of false particularism will be excluded, and Christian life accommodated to the genius and character of each culture. Particular traditions, together with the individual patrimony of each national community, illumined by the light of the gospel, can be taken up into Catholic unity' (ibid). A result certainly hard to obtain, but all the more wonderful and important.

Concluding the vast panorama traced here on the **k** position which sacred Scripture occupies and must occupy in the life of the Church, we shall come to this realization. The Council has established first of all the deep doctrinal foundations on which arises all that the Church undertakes to make the word of God really the principle of her entire life from which she may be nourished and live at all levels. Besides, the Council has traced a spacious long term programme to attain this great goal by means of the use of sacred Scripture in the Liturgy, in every sort of preaching, in theology and exegetical science, in reading and meditation on the part of the faithful, in the ecumenical and missionary fields. It has suggested and offered specific measures in order that the ministers of the word may be prepared, be penetrated intimately by that same word and be the first to give impress to it. Certainly all these human measures would not suffice by themselves without the abundant dew of the grace of God. Nevertheless the Church trusts that the Spirit of Christ, the Spirit who inspired the divine writings, who has guided her in the Council, will guide, strengthen and grant her perseverance in the realization of this spacious programme also. In this sense the Constitution on Divine Revelation rightly concludes with the significant words: 'In this way, therefore, through the reading and study of Scripture, let "the word of the Lord speed on and triumph" (2 Thes 3:1), and let the treasure of revelation entrusted to the Church increasingly fill the hearts of men. Just as the life of the Church grows from continuous frequentation of the Eucharistic mystery, so we may hope for a new surge of spiritual vitality from intensified veneration of the word of God which "abides for ever" (Is 40:8, cf 1 Pt 1:23–25)' (n. 26).

THE BIBLE IN THE LIFE OF THE CHURCH

PART II: AN HISTORICAL SURVEY

BY DOM D. REES

8a Bibliography for Parts I and II of this article.—W. M. Abbott, *The Documents of Vatican II, with notes and comments by Catholic, Protestant and Orthodox Authorities*, 1966; *Commentary on the Documents of Vatican II*, in 5 volumes, by a group of scholars including H. E. Cardinal Bea, Karl Rahner etc. Vol 5 (containing 'Divine Revelation') 1968; G. Auzou, *The Word of God*, 1940; J. Bonsirven, *Exégèse rabbinique, Exégèse paulinienne*, 1939; C. Charlier, *A Christian Approach to the Bible*, 1958; J. Daniélou, *The Bible and the Liturgy*, 1960; M. Deanesley, *The Lollard Bible*, Cambridge, 1920; J. de Lubac, *Exégèse mediévale*, 1959; C. H. Dodd, *According to the Scriptures*, 1953; *The Bible Today*, Cambridge, 1946; S. L. Greenslade (ed.), *The Cambridge History of the Bible*, 1963; A. Harnack, *Bible Reading in the Early Church*, 1912; J. Levie, *The Bible: Word of God in Words of Men*, 1961; D. E. Nineham, *The Church's Use of the Bible, Past and Present*, 1963; H. Wheeler Robinson, *The Bible in its Ancient and English Versions*, Oxford, 1954²; B. Smalley, *The Study of the Bible in the Middle Ages*, Oxford, 1941; C. Spicq, *Esquisse d'une Histoire de l'Exégèse latine au Moyen Age*, 1944; T. W. Manson (ed.), *The Bible Today*, 1955; L. Bouyer, *La Bible et l'Evangile: Le Sens de l'Ecriture*; H. Daniel-Rops *What is the Bible?*, 1958; K. Rahner-R. Schnackenburg et al., *The Bible in a New Age*, 1955.

b Introduction—God's people in the Old Testament was constituted primarily to hear, remember and reflect upon his word ('Hear, O Israel . . .' Dt 5:1; 6:4), then to transmit it to succeeding generations (Dt 6:20) and even to the Gentiles (Jer 31:10). In the New Testament, too, God's people gathered together in the Church are commissioned to be both the recipients (Col 3:16) and the agents (Mt 28:20) of his word which had found perfect utterance in Christ, just as they are of his sacraments. The purpose of the following pages is to examine how the Church in practice carried out its function in regard to Scripture; and to consider in some detail the various ways in which at different epochs she has communicated the Word of God to the people.

c Method—In this survey we have to consider throughout the ages the Church's relation to the Bible from several aspects. First and foremost, **the Church realizes herself**, becomes most completely what she is, **in her official public worship**, the Liturgy. And in this activity, Bible readings, biblical chants, biblical commentary, besides the looser use of biblical formulae which pervades every rite, occupy such a major position that the Liturgy has been truly described as the 'Bible in action'. And it is a striking feature of Church history that those generations of Catholics which have been liturgically decadent have been precisely those whose **d** interest in the Bible has been flagging. Secondly, the liturgical experience of **the Scriptures** within the Church is prolonged **in the everyday lives of indi-**

vidual Christians by private reading of the Bible and, **8d** where illiteracy makes this direct access to the Scriptures impossible, by such means as popular devotions, iconography, sacred drama, musical oratorios and pilgrimages to holy places, all of which, though not formally the study of the written Bible, do engender a lively familiarity with the history of salvation which it contains. The limitation of these extra-biblical media is that very often, along with scriptural stories, they purvey much other edifying or hagiographical material without any means of distinguishing it from the inspired word of God. Thirdly, **Catholic scholars e and exegetes** bring to bear upon the contents of the Scriptures all the resources of the human intellect as well as the findings of secular sciences in order that the full potentialities, and the problems too, of God's word might be realized and made available to a wider public. **Exegesis** is a true science, **seeking** in the first place **to establish the objective meaning of the Scriptures** (rather than to read one's own meanings into it, which would be **eisegesis** and merely arbitrary), and, like all sciences, requires, and today more and more, a close association of efforts among its practitioners. Such a collaboration, both between scholars who are contemporaries and between the generations in the patient formation of schools and traditions, has always been one of the distinctive features of Catholic Scriptural scholar- **f** ship. Fourthly and finally, the attitude of the Church towards Scripture can be gauged from **the directives of her highest authorities, the Popes or the General Councils**. Such official pronouncements of the Church's Magisterium on Scriptural questions are far less frequent than is often imagined (cf § 50e).

Jesus and the Bible—Both in his teaching and in his **g** controversies our Lord made frequent appeal to the irrefragable authority of the Jewish Bible, the OT (Jn 10:35; Mk 7:9—13; Mt 5:18), often using with solemn finality the introductory formula 'It is written . . .'. In this his practice showed that the Scriptures, unlike some other Jewish institutions, had not been superseded by his coming, but rather had found the key to their fullest meaning in his Person, especially after the Resurrection (Jn 5:39; Mt 5:17; Lk 22:37, and especially Lk 24:25, 44), where the mention of all three categories of OT writings—Law, Prophets and Psalms—shows that the OT as a whole must be referred to Christ. The narrators of the Gospels, especially Matthew (2:15, 23), enthusiastically continued the application to Christ of the oracles of the OT, often with a cavalier disregard of their original literal sense. Such an exposition of the Scriptures, referring them all to his Person, was begun by Our Lord in the liturgical context of the public reading of the Bible in the synagogue services (Lk 4:16—30), an example which his followers were to imitate. This close unity of the two Testaments in a single history of salvation was throughout the succeeding centuries the pattern observed both

14

8g in the Liturgy and in Christian commentaries on the Bible.

h In the Apostolic Age—To the early Christian converts in Jerusalem their knowledge of Christ's saving events came to them not through documents, but through the oral preaching of the Apostles, the Kerygma (Ac 2:42; 4:4; 5:42). But even though they do not seem to have been a bookish community, nevertheless one of the first things to be proclaimed by this Apostolic preaching was that in Christ's work the Scriptures had been fulfilled (Ac 2:16, 31; 3:18, 24; 8:34; 10:43; 13:27), and one of the reasons why Jesus' Resurrection was 'good news' was that it charged with a new meaning all the ancient prophecies, since all Christ's acts were 'according to the Scriptures' (1 Cor 15:3, 4). The birth of the Church was followed therefore by a careful scrutiny of the OT in the light of these recent events, so intense that the LXX, the Greek version used most generally, soon became regarded and shunned by the Jews as a Christian preserve. It is possible also that many anthologies of Messianic texts applicable to Jesus, the so-called Books of Testimonies, circulated among the Christian preachers and their converts.

i St Paul, in his missionary journeys, continued Jesus' practice of proclaiming in the first place in synagogal asemblies the fulfilment of the Scriptures by Christ. He also demonstrated the organic unity of the two Testaments by occasional recapitulations of Israel's history which he led to its fruition in Christ (Ac 13; Rm 5; 1 Cor 10). His exposition of the Gospel, especially of the call of the Gentiles in Rm 9—11 was always preceded by very thorough and extensive Biblical research. In the NT, of 200 quotations formally cited from the Old and introduced by such a formula as 'It is written . . .', 118 are to be found in St Paul. He declared their inspiration (2 Tm 3:16) and urged his readers to study them **j** assiduously (1 Tm 4:13; 2 Tm 3:15). When he distinguished the understanding of the Bible 'according to the letter', that is the superseded interpretation confined within the perspectives of Judaism, from that 'according to the Spirit', namely with reference to Christ, St Paul was launching a principle that would have a mighty career in the history of biblical interpretation, one which would be repudiated by rationalist critics, interested only in the meaning of the OT for its contemporaries, and abused by those who would see arbitrary and fanciful typologies everywhere, but one which, if reasonably applied, can alone give the Christian meaning of the whole of Scripture (e.g. 1 Cor 10:1—10; Eph 2:20).

9a The Early Fathers—especially St Clement of Rome (fl. c. 96)—are very lavish with their quotations from the Bible, not only from the OT, for which they reserve the formula 'as it is written', but also, though often without acknowledgement, from most of the books of what subsequently became the NT Canon. They are therefore important witnesses to the slow crystallisation of the Christian Bible and to the dating of its component books. In the early Christian community the letters of St Paul were read at the Liturgy as were the Gospels, and often the practical norm of canonicity besides that of their Apostolic authorship was simply 'those books which are read at the liturgy'. The Great Prayer which concluded Clement's Letter to the Corinthians is woven from phrases borrowed from the OT, showing again the actualization of the Word of God in the Liturgy. The Epistle of Barnabas (between 70 and 100) purports to show that Christians, not Jews, are the true heirs and possessors of the OT which must be understood spiritually (in the Pauline sense). The unity of sacred history

was impugned by the heretic Marcion (d. c. 160) who, **9a** exaggerating the contradictions between OT and NT, and interpreting both in a strictly literal sense in accordance with his belief that God had dictated the Biblical writings syllable by syllable, the writers being merely passive instruments, denied that the Jewish Scriptures had any authority for Christians. Catholic resistance to the proposed Marcionite expurgations contributed much to the formation of the Canon. On the opposite extreme, the Gnostics, claiming to discern everywhere in the Bible a secret allegorical sense, were withstood by St Irenaeus (d. c. 200), rejoining that the spiritual sense of Scripture is best understood in the light of the Tradition of the Apostolic churches. That the Church is the real home of the Bible, where alone it can be understood fully, is the argument too of Tertullian (d. c. 220) who invoked the Roman legal principle of Prescription to deny heretics the right to use or comment upon the Scriptures. But **b** notwithstanding all the confusions arising from the heretical abuse of the Bible, the drastic step of denying the layman access to the Scriptures was never taken. In the times of persecutions, the first care of persecutors and oppressed alike was the fate of the Christian bibles. To hand them over to the heathen in order to be profaned was to earn the shameful title 'traditor', one of the worst forms of apostasy. And in his edict of 303, Diocletian thought he could best sap the life of the Church which he recognised to be, in a certain sense, 'a people of the Book', by ordering the destruction of bibles. In their sermons and homilies, the great Fathers of the Church all presuppose in their hearers an intimate acquaintance **c** with the sacred text. Even their frequent extravagances of allegorization spring from a feeling that everything should have its roots in Scripture, while on the other hand the great Antiochene preacher, St John Chrysostom (d. 407), was ever anxious to set Scripture in relation to the most homespun details of everyday life. Only the utterly destitute would he excuse from including a bible among his private possessions, a demand which presupposes that bibles were cheap and widely available. Clement of Alexandria (d. c. 215) speaks of Scripture readings at home before the chief meal of the day and wants married people to study the Bible together. Jerome (Ep. 107) urges that even children should play games devised on biblical themes and learn the Psalter by heart. Thus in the early Church Scripture offered a central place in popular life and piety, never, as in some other epochs rich in exegesis, becoming the preserve of academics.

Alexandria and Antioch—The most renowned **d** intellectual institution in the early Christian world was undoubtedly the Catechetical School (*Didascaleion*) of Alexandria, and its primary concern was the study of the Bible, giving its name to an influential tradition of scriptural interpretation. The preoccupation of this school of exegesis was to discover everywhere the spiritual sense underlying the written word of Scripture. This allegorical method of interpretation did not originate with Christians or Jews, but with Pagan philosophers, especially the Stoics, in order to explain away the absurdities of the fables concerning the Olympian gods. The Alexandrian Jew, Philo (d. c. 50), applied the same **e** method to those passages of the OT which would scandalize Gentiles, thus abandoning the prima facie historical assertions of the text in order to attain philosophical or ethical meanings, expressed in symbols. Christian allegorism differs from both these predecessors in that it does not have their typically Greek aversion to history, but finds the events and persons of one

9e historical epoch, the OT world, to be signs and reflections of events and persons in subsequent historical epochs, the Christian era and the eschatological days. In this way it was saved from the chameleon tendency endemic in allegorism whereby anything might be taken to mean anything else, so that lofty and ingenious human thoughts could be substituted for the humble words of the Scriptural text.

f The most lengthy exposition of this method of interpretation is found in Origen's (d. c. 254) *De Principiis*, Book 4. His scheme is to see in Scripture three different senses corresponding to the component parts of the human person according to the psychology current in Platonist thought, viz body, soul and spirit. The bodily (somatic) sense of Scripture is the straightforward historical meaning and was intended for those who lived before the Christian era, and still today for simple Christians. The soul of the Scriptures, the psychic sense, is the moral meaning implicit in this history and is directed at those living at the present time who were also proficient Christians. Finally the spiritual (pneumatic) sense is the allegorical meaning written for the benefit of future believers and for those Christians who are already perfect.

g Although Origen himself was occasionally guilty of excesses, seeking far-fetched mysteries in numbers, in proper names and even in the nomenclature of plants, animals and minerals, his method, as when used in the *Contra Celsum*, was a well-intentioned attempt to remove from the Bible as unworthy of God all that was absurd or impossible when taken in the literal sense. Only too often however among the Fathers this was to become a subterfuge which has been superseded in the modern era by the study of literary genres. But nevertheless the Origenist spiritual sense, in contrast to that of Philo, so far from excluding the literal explanation, presupposes it as its point of departure. Hence the monumental attempt of Origen's *Hexapla* to establish a text of the Scriptures which would be authoritative in theological discussion and controversy. The influence of the Alexandrian school was both widespread and enduring. Apart from such native scholars of the city as Didymus the Blind (d. 398), Athanasius (d. 313), and Cyril (d. 444), both the Latin and the Cappadocian Fathers were heavily indebted to this tradition.

h In protest against the allegoristic excesses of certain Alexandrians, there crystallized at Antioch a circle of biblical scholars which set a far greater store on the sober and erudite exposition of the literal and historical sense. It was reluctant, for example, to read 'Christ' into many of the portions of the OT, especially the Psalter, hitherto universally accepted as Messianic, but rather preferred to understand them in a contemporary context. Comparatively little is known of this school since not only was its sphere of influence far more restricted than that of Alexandria, but it had also fallen into a largely undeserved disrepute because of the part played by some of its leading figures in the Christological controversies that led to the Nestorian schism. Many of its productions have therefore perished because they were considered as

i heretical. Among the great names of this school were Theodore of Mopsuestia (d. 428), Theodoret of Cyr (d. c. 458), Diodore of Tarsus (d. c. 390), Methodius of Olympos (d. c. 311), Ephrem (d. c. 373) and the Syrian Fathers generally, with St John Chrysostom (d. 407) as its great populariser. One should not however set too sharp a contrast between the Alexandrian method, which satisfied an obvious spiritual need, and the Antiochene, devoted to scientific studies and therefore, as well as because of its reputation for heterodoxy, the darling

of many modern 'critical' Scriptural scholars. The **9i** Antiochenes too did not deny that for Christians the text could have very frequently a higher typological meaning which they called '*theoria*'.

The Latin Fathers—were less prone to speculative **10a** adventures than the exegetes of the East, and, perhaps for this very reason, they became more Bible-minded than their Greek counterparts. Most of them—Hilary of Poitiers (d. 367), Ambrose (d. 397), Augustine (d. 430) and Jerome too (d. 420) in his younger days—were addicted to the Alexandrian allegorical method, although with greater discipline, since orthodox theology was now more closely defined than it had been in Origen's time. Indeed the pre-Christian Augustine's aversion to the Bible because of its anthropomorphisms and poor style was dissipated by Ambrose's sermons on 'the letter that killeth and the spirit that quickeneth'. Thereafter Augustine saw in the minutest details of the OT prefigurations of Christ and his Church. '*In Vetere Testamento Novum latet, et in Novo Vetus patet*.'

It was the Origenist controversies in 393 that led Jerome to recoil from this allegorical preference and to concentrate on the historical meaning in which he believed the spiritual sense must be firmly grounded. To his quest for this primary meaning he brought to bear his ever-growing familiarity with rabbinical traditions, Palestinian topography and the Hebrew language, and, still more important and far ahead of his time, his recognition of the human element in inspiration, the differing personalities of the Scriptural authors, each with his own mentality, style and limitations. He was also the first to assert the need to return to the Hebrew text for a correct explanation of the Bible. For him indeed, 'Not to know the Scriptures is not to know Christ'.

The Dark Ages—A period of genius is not infrequently followed by a period of repetition. Such was the case even with the highly sophisticated Byzantine world, where exegesis henceforth consisted largely in repeating the sayings of the Fathers arrayed in Catenae and Florilegia. But this was even truer of the rude Christian West, where the book that had the greatest vogue was the not very original *Moralia in Job* of St Gregory the Great (d. 604). Yet even at this time the Bible remained the most studied book and Bible study represented the highest levels of learning. Bede the Venerable (d. 735) was far better known to his contemporaries for his commentaries on Scripture than for his *Ecclesiastical History of England*. These 'monastic centuries' were moulded too by the Rule of St Benedict (d. c. 540) which assigns a prominent place to the Bible, whether in the lengthy time allocated to '*lectio divina*', or in the almost exclusively Biblical components of the '*Opus Dei*', the Divine Office, which in the life of a monk should have priority over every other duty. In its original form this Office, which was soon to be adopted by others besides monks, comprised the recitation of the whole Psalter in the course of each week and the systematic reading of the whole Bible continuously, throughout the days of the year. This time too saw the beginnings of *vernacular*, or more truly, non-Latin *versions* of the Bible. *Partial translations* into Anglo-Saxon were the work of Caedmon (d. c. 680), Bede and Aelfric (d.c. 1020). German versions came from the hands of Notker Labeo (d.c. 1022), Abbot Williram (d. 1085) and the monks of Mondsee, but a French translation was not available until the 13th cent when one appeared under the auspices of the University of Paris.

The Middle Ages—may be described as the era in **11a** biblical studies when the literal sense progressively came into its own. In the 12th cent. when the intellectual

11a hegemony had passed from the monasteries to the cathedral schools, biblical study was not only still the crown
of all learning, but also was still characterized by a
servile fidelity to the Patristic heritage and by an exegesis
that was almost exclusively allegorical, having edification
rather than science as its object. Most prestigious among
the textbooks embodying this tradition was the famous
Glossa Ordinaria, a product of the school of Anselm of
Laon (d. 1117). But already people were becoming alive
to the difficulties of this approach. Abelard (d. 1142) in
the *Sic et Non* had shown how rarely the Fathers were
unanimous and demanded play for the reason, at least in
choosing between their contradictory opinions. Richard
of St Victor (d. 1173) also maintained that the Fathers
had neglected the literal sense, and therefore their work
must be completed, and indeed it was his Parisian
community of Augustinian Canons, especially Andrew of
St Victor (d. 1175), who were the pioneers in insisting on
the basic importance of the literal meaning. To know
better the OT as it must have been conceived in the minds
of its authors they conversed with Jewish rabbis and even
studied Hebrew.

b Such a tendency was strongly reinforced by the new
mental outlook engendered by the rediscovery of Aristotle.
For, just as in Aristotelian psychology the soul obtained
knowledge through the five senses and their objects rather
than through innate ideas, so analogously in Scripture
St Thomas (d. 1274) identified the true meaning as something not hidden behind but rather as shining through the
text literally understood. By the 'literal sense' he meant
that which was intended by the inspired writer himself,
while the 'spiritual senses' are those intended by God.

c St Thomas himself was not only a great commentator on
Scripture, but also in his *Summa* made the argument
from Scripture an integral, and often the crucial part,
the *sed contra*, of each article. Thus he both followed the
method of the Fathers and anticipated the programme of
Leo XIII's Encyclical *Providentissimus* by requiring that
Scripture should be the very soul of theology.

d After St Thomas there was a widespread revival of
recognition of the literal sense. His stand on its importance
was shared by Albert the Great (d. 1280) and even by
Bonaventure (d. 1274). The apocalyptic extravagances
of Joachim of Fiore (d. 1202) had done much to discredit
too exclusive a preoccupation with the spiritual sense.
To attain the minds of the sacred authors, the ancient
languages began to be studied by many—Greek by
Bishop Grosseteste of Lincoln (d. 1253) and his disciples,
Hebrew by Nicholas Trivet (d. 1328) and Nicholas of
Lyra (d. 1340) whose giant eighty-five volume work, the
Postillae, a work in which he has drawn very heavily from
the rabbinical commentaries, was to be so highly esteemed
by Luther just because of its freedom from allegorical

e pretensions. That such a mentality was not confined to
a few talented individuals is evidenced by the decrees of
the Council of Vienne (1311), requiring that chairs for
the study of Greek and the Oriental languages be established in all universities and monasteries, though,
because of the scarcity of qualified teachers, this decree
remained a dead letter, perhaps one of the reasons why
the biblical achievements of the later Middle Ages belied
the promise of the earlier years and returned to a riotous
and all-too-easy use of the 'spiritual sense'.

During these centuries when standards of literacy
were low, when the educated classes knew Latin and
books, before the invention of printing, were scarce and
expensive, there was no great demand for vernacular
versions of the Bible, though there were in fact a good
number of partial translations, as we have noted above.

Nor were there any special restrictions on their circul- **11e**
ation on the part of the Church authorities. The increased
demand and the imposition of restrictions which appeared
later were both part of a different historical context
namely that of the late 14th and 15th centuries.

There were many causes which contributed to the **f**
decline which then set in: the over-elaboration of scholastic
theology and its increasing separation from the Scriptures
to the point where the Bible was quoted only when a
'proof-text' was required to lend support to some proposition; the exaltation of 'Tradition' into something approaching a rabbinical science; the increasing ignorance
of the clergy, due partly to men entering the clerical state
for worldly reasons and without training, partly to the
ravages made in the ranks of the clergy by the Black
Death. There were other developments just as regrettable.
The introduction of portable breviaries to be used by
itinerant friars when they had perforce to say their Office
outside Choir necessitated an abridgement of the amount
to be recited; and the cuts were made in the provisions
for Bible reading where the continuous arrangement was
supplanted by one whereby only the initial chapters, or
even less, of each book were read in turn throughout the
year. The consequence of the waning familiarity of the
clergy with the sacred text was that popular preaching too
ceased to be biblical.

The Church was in a parlous state and there were many **g**
who protested about abuses, notably **John Wyclif and
John Hus**, but unfortunately these protests came precisely at the time of the Great Schism when most people
hardly knew which was the rightful Pope, and Church
authority was at a discount. In consequence the Council
of Florence, summoned by King Sigismund, was mainly
concerned with the question of whether Popes should
be subject to General Councils, rather than with the
practical and urgently necessary task of root and branch
reform. Thus the protests met with no effective response
on the part of authority; indeed rather the opposite. In
consequence of this, and of the unorthodoxy of doctrine
manifested by some of the would-be reformers, a bitterness of spirit entered in and a policy of repression was
adopted by Church hierarchies.

A prominent feature of the reformers' programme **h**
was the use of Scripture in which they sought to find the
authority and spiritual food which they looked for in vain
elsewhere. Thus it was that John Wyclif initiated a translation of the Bible into English, cf § 32*b*, and thereby
provoked a policy on the part of the Church authorities
quite different from that prevailing hitherto. The vernacular Scriptures were now being used as a vehicle for the
propagation of unorthodox teaching, apart from the fact
that the translation had not been made or approved by
ecclesiastical authority. Consequently at the Council
of Oxford in 1408 restrictions were imposed and unauthorized translations banned. To make it quite clear
that this measure was taken in relation to unorthodoxy
of doctrine the Council added the qualification that this
applied only to translations made in the time of Wycliffe or
after. Without in any way minimizing the claim of the
Wycliffite Bible to be the first complete one in English,
it may be observed that such a version could hardly have
been produced earlier in any case since English had only
just emerged as a national language. It should moreover
not be forgotten that between Wycliffe's time and the
outbreak of the Reformation many vernacular translations were produced by Catholics in other parts of Europe,
the total being estimated at over one hundred. 'It is not
sufficiently emphasized that the printing of vernacular
texts long preceded the Reformation in several countries',

11h *Cambridge History of the Bible*, 1,423. Again, the Protestant insistence on translating from the original tongues was not new. It had already been anticipated by scholars such aş Lorenzo Valla (d. 1457), Erasmus (d. 1536), Lefèvre of Etaples (d. 1536). One should also recall the team of Spanish scholars who, under the direction of Cardinal Ximenes, combined to produce the magnificent Complutensian Polyglot Bible.

i In the sixteenth cent., the linking of vernacular versions with the doctrines of the Reformers led inevitably both to the repression of such versions where this was possible and to a certain waning of enthusiasm on the part of the Church authorities for the translation of the Scriptures into the vernacular. While admitting that vernacular versions could be useful it was laid down by the Council of Trent that none should be allowed unless made under authority and accompanied by notes. Thus when the Douay emigrés (cf § 34) came to make their translation into English they openly declared that they did so not because they thought it necessary for Catholics to have such Bibles in themselves but because there were so many heretical translations around that it was important for Catholics to have an orthodox text. In the interests of strict orthodoxy moreover they made their translation from the approved Latin Vulgate and not from the original texts. The increasingly numerous divisions among Protestants all claiming to base their position on the Bible did nothing to reassure Catholics of the necessity of providing vernacular versions for everyone regardless of the state of his education and divorced from the control of authority.

j Nevertheless in spite of the attachment of the Reformers to the slogan *Sola Scriptura*, Catholics did not react with *Sola Ecclesia*, and abandon Scripture to the Protestants. The rejection of Church authority and of Tradition by the new votaries of Scripture eventually made them dependent instead upon the consensus of **k** scholarly opinion. On the other hand the Catholic reaction to the Reformers' emancipation of the Bible was for the most part defensive rather than positive, and most of the initiatives then taken within the Church in the scriptural field remained on the scholarly and academic level. Largely because of the influence of Cardinal Pole (d. 1558), the Council of Trent repeated and extended the enactments of Vienne requiring provision for lectureships in Scripture in all cathedrals, monasteries and convents. In 1546 it recognized the Vulgate as the Church's 'authoritative' text, 'authoritative' not in the sense that from a critical point of view it was superior to the extant manuscripts in Greek and Hebrew, but as a reliable source of dogmatic arguments for theological teaching or debate. This declaration led to the Vulgate's revision under Popes Sixtus V in 1590 and Clement VIII in 1592. As a compensation for withholding from the laity the use of the vernacular in the Mass, the Council ordered that sermons be preached in all churches on Sundays and Feastdays, an innovation which in its own way might have led to a wide diffusion of the love and knowledge of the Bible if the clergy themselves had been steeped in the Scriptures.

l And this indeed might have happened, if certain Council Fathers had not ferociously attacked the breviary revised in 1534 by Cardinal Francis Quiñonez (d. 1540) on the admirable principle of restoring to the clergy the continuous reading throughout the year of all the books of the Bible. This breviary had a phenomenal success, running through more than a hundred impressions in thirty-two years before it had to give place in 1568 to the Breviary of Pius V. In the meantime however, the very Bible-centred arrangement of Quiñonez's Breviary had made a powerful impression upon the compilers of the **11l** Anglican Book of Common Prayer which still reflects its influence. An interesting illustration of a widespread mentality in the Church regarding the Scriptures is furnished by a remark of de Arze, a Spanish opponent of Quiñonez's Breviary, that 'the Church has committed to her privileged servants (*potioribus ministris*) the task of studying Scripture, to the *rudiores clerici*, on the other hand, the office of Psalmody' (see J. Jungmann, *Pastoral Liturgy* (London 1962), pp. 200ss., J. Wickham Legg in *Henry Bradshaw Society* Vols 35 (1908) and 42 (1912).

The Post-Reformation Period—Such a professional **12a** note was dominant in the attitude of many Catholics to the Bible for the next three centuries, though it is hardly likely that the voluminous commentaries of so many learned Jesuits—Minocchius (d. 1555), Bellarmine (d. 1621), Maldonatus (d. 1583), Cornelius a Lapide (d. 1651) would have been published had no eager audience awaited them. These works too were largely intended for the use of preachers and revived the typological method, so beloved of Pascal, of explaining all the Scriptures by reference to Christ and his Church. This generation at least compares very well with their Protestant contemporaries who treated Scripture largely as a quarry of proofs in controversy against Catholics and, as was the case with Buxtorf (d. 1629), had an excessive esteem for rabbinical exegesis. With the beginning of the **b** Age of the Enlightenment and the application of rational criticism to the Bible there were Catholics in France ready to make use of the new knowledge and try to arrive at a harmony of Faith and Reason. Among these the French Oratorians were prominent and of that Order **Richard Simon** (1638–1712) deserves notice as the pioneer of biblical criticism in the modern sense of that term. Simon was endeavouring to show that the Protestants were wrong to ignore Tradition and he never wavered in his personal loyalty to the Church, cf 92a. His biblical criticism however was so far in advance of anything hitherto proposed by Catholics that it was condemned by the Church authorities. It was condemned because they had mistaken notions of the truth of Scripture (the full Mosaic authorship of the Pent was regarded as almost *de Fide*) and also because the newly evolving science of biblical criticism was being used by rationalist critics to empty the Scriptures of their supernatural content. In considering the condemnation of Simon it is well to remember that the other Christian Churches took a similar line at that period. In Britain traditional interpretation fought a rearguard action throughout the 18th cent. slowly withdrawing all the time, but the outbreak of the French Revolution had the effect in this country of fostering a conservative reaction in the field of biblical study and 'Higher Criticism' became taboo. Meanwhile, however, the rise of Wesleyanism had sparked off a renewed interest in religion and the Bible in particular. In all this however, Catholics who by now were very few in number had little part. In France the Church was torn asunder by Jansenism while in Germany the Bible both from the devotional and critical viewpoints was being more and more studied.

At the **beginning of the 19th cent.** the situation was **c** unpromising. Though higher criticism was at least temporarily banned in Britain by the tacit consent of the Churches, there was a great activity in spreading the knowledge of the Bible through the means of the newly formed Bible Societies. Unfortunately at that time, the diffusion of Bibles was not infrequently accompanied by proselytism and Roman Catholic countries were often chosen for that purpose. This provided yet another reason

12c for Catholics to have nothing to do with the Bible Societies and indeed prejudiced them against the idea of spreading the Scriptures in the vernacular.

In Germany biblical criticism was becoming more and more rationalistic, a trend which only served to strengthen the British reaction against criticism. Catholics in this country began to develop a mild interest in Bible reading and a number of family Bible editions were issued. But the circulation of such works must have been small. In the realm of scholarship there were few positive signs of life until the latter half of the 19th century. Even then substantial scriptural works like the joint commentaries of the learned Jesuits Knabenbauer, Corneley and Hummelauer and Vigouroux's *Dictionaire de la Bible* (1886) impressed more by density of information than boldness of spirit. At a lower level Cardinal Manning could sigh 'How I wish I could convince my flock that the Bible is not on the Index'—an attitude hardly surprising in view of the repeated Papal condemnations of the Protestant Bible Societies. (In fairness it should be added that if all colporteurs of these societies were men of George Borrow's temper (d. 1881) such reactions were understandable.)

d The Awakening—The period 1890–1914 was the most crucial since the Reformation for the Church's official attitude towards the Bible generally and the rights of biblical criticism in particular. The founding of the **Ecole Biblique in Jerusalem** with the approval and explicit encouragement of the Holy See marked a new era in Catholic biblical scholarship, in which loyalty to tradition was coupled with an open approach to and frank acceptance of the assured findings of biblical criticism (cf § 96*e*). But this happy state of affairs was short lived. The rise of Modernism began to compromise all real progress. The Encyclical Letter **Providentissimus Deus** (1893), the first authoritative statement on biblical studies and the place of the Bible in the Church, was a reaction to Loisy's unorthodox views. It dealt with the nature of Inspiration and Inerrancy and devoted much space to the question of the teaching of Scripture in seminaries. On the one hand Catholic professors should be well equipped in Oriental languages and the science of biblical criticism while, on the other, they should approach the Bible in a spirit quite different from that of Loisy and his associates. Leo XIII wanted Scripture to be so integrated with theology as to be its very soul, illuminated by the teaching of the Fathers and taking account of the spiritual or allegorical sense. The Pope also dealt with the Oriental manner of writing and explained how in Genesis the visible world is described as it appears and in the language and concepts of the writer. One should not expect them to make statements of a rigorously scientific character. In 1902 the Pope established the **Biblical Commission**, a body of learned Catholic exegetes to foster and guide Biblical studies generally and later to examine for and confer degrees in Scripture. Unfortunately for its reputation the early activities of the Commission coincided with the repression of Modernism, cf 96*e*–*i*, and to us today it may well seem to have severely limited the horizon for biblical investigation but its findings must be considered in the light of the situation at that time. No doubt Catholics were thereby saved from a number of unprofitable speculations potentially dangerous to the Faith though at the price of checking progress in other ways. Indeed the fear of Modernism which had been denounced by Pius X in the Encyclical *Pascendi* and in the Decree *Lamentabili* almost paralysed professional Scriptural study for more than two decades: exegetes tended to shun contentious issues and concentrate on ancient languages, archaeology and other scholarly specialities.

By the 1930s biblical activity was again reviving **12e** at a rapid pace **and** this increased **after the war** under the impetus of Pope Pius XII's Encyclical Letter *Divino Afflante Spiritu* in 1943, see 96*i*. Considerable developments took place both in the scholarly and in the popular spheres. Popular movements like the Jeunesse Ouvrière Chrétienne (Young Christian Workers) made it their practice to have 'Gospel Inquiries' at all their meetings. The Liturgical Movement, fast gathering momentum, aimed at this stage to equip every Catholic with an informative Missal for following the Mass, thus fostering a greater awareness of the Scriptures among the Catholic devout and a public for books on the Bible by such men of letters as Paul Claudel and Daniel-Rops. The infant **Ecumenical Movement** too was fast discovering Scripture as one of the principal theatres of co-operation between Catholics and other Christians, especially since during the inter-war years these latter had shed many of the more extreme biblical hypotheses which had characterized an earlier generation. In the field of biblical scholarship, *Divino Afflante Spiritu* was a landmark, the importance of which it would be difficult to exaggerate, cf § 96*i*. This Letter has sometimes been regarded as a complete reversal of policy on the part of the Church, but a closer study of it reveals a basic continuity of principle with *Providentissimus Deus*, reaffirming though with different emphases the main provisions of its predecessor, and setting them in a wider perspective.

An important new development since Vatican II has been **f** Catholic cooperation in the translation and editing of the Bible on an ecumenical basis, in such ventures as the American *Anchor Bible*, the *Revised Standard Version*, the French Ecumenical Bible and the projected new edition of the Welsh Bible. The increasing use of the Vernacular in the Liturgy, besides the spreading practice of Bible Services and Vigils, has helped to generalize among all Catholics that same biblical turn of mind which was so evident in all the arguments and phraseology of the official documents of Vatican Council II, as compared with those of Trent.

Prompted no doubt by the needs of the vernacular liturgy, **contact** has also been made in the mission fields **between the Catholic authorities and** the representatives of **the Protestant Bible Societies** with a view to cooperation in the production of Bibles. After a number of meetings in various countries the matter was referred to the Secretariate for Christian Unity and in 1966 it was announced that an American priest, Fr Walter Abbott S.J., had been appointed as secretary to Cardinal Bea with special responsibility for relations with the Bible Societies and to investigate the question of whether a common Bible text was a possibility. It was felt strongly that such an achievement would be of vital importance not only for the ecumenical movement but even for the future of Christianity as a whole. It may already be stated that in the view of the Church authorities there appears to be no insuperable difficulty on the question of text and that the outstanding problem is the difference of view regarding the canonical status of the deuterocanonical books known to Protestants as the Apocrypha, cf § 13. With the manifest goodwill now being shown by both sides progress towards a practical solution should be rapid, though agreement on the doctrinal issues will necessarily be a more distant prospect.

A few more recent interventions of ecclesiastical authority on scriptural matters should not be omitted. **g The Biblical Commission** has shown itself **in recent years** as firm a **defender of the liberties due to**

12g **scholars** as it was of the truth and divine origin of Scripture during the Modernist Crisis. In 1941 a letter to the Italian bishops (EnchB 522—33), which deplored a campaign accusing certain scholars and institutions of rationalism and modernism, anticipated most of the principles enunciated in *Divino Afflante*. In 1948, a famous letter of the Commission addressed to Cardinal Suhard of Paris (EnchB 577—81) assured him of the open character of many of the questions raised by the first eleven chapters of Genesis, though the subsequent Encyclical *Humani Generis* of 1950 (EnchB 611—20) corrected the misunderstanding that the genre of this primeval history was myth rather than history in the widest possible sense. In 1964 the Biblical Commission issued an *Instruction on the Historical Truth of the* **12g** *Gospels* (text and translations in CBQ 26 (1964), pp. 299ss.), enlarging upon *Divino Afflante's* recommendation of the study of literary genres, a method which in certain circles had fallen into disrepute because of the extremist views of certain members of the *Formgeschichte* school. This Instruction with admirable clarity and amplitude shows the possibility of a discriminating and fruitful use of the methods pioneered by this School without falling into any denial of the historical truth of the Gospel. Because of its reasoned and helpful explanations this document is indeed a model of the spirit of service which should animate authority in the post-Conciliar Church.

THE FORMATION AND HISTORY OF THE CANON

OLD TESTAMENT CANON

BY R. C. FULLER

NEW TESTAMENT CANON

BY R. J. FOSTER

13a Bibliography—*General*: J. Hölscher, *Kanonisch und Apokryph*, 1905; H. Höpfl, 'Canonicité', DBS 1 (1928), 1022—45 with ample bibliography; S. Zarb, *Historia Canonis Utriusque Testamenti*, 1934; F. Kenyon, *Our Bible and the Ancient Manuscripts*, 1958[5]; Barucq-Cazelles, 'Le Canon des livres inspirés', in RF 1957; J. H. Crehan, 'Canon' in *Dict. of Catholic Theology*, I (1963), 321ff

OT Canon: H. E. Ryle, *The Canon of the OT*, 1899[2]; B. J. Roberts, *The OT Text and Versions*, 1951; H. H. Rowley, *The Growth of the OT*, 1950; H. B. Swete, *Introd. to the OT in Greek*, 1914[3]; A. Jeffery, 'The Canon of the OT' in IB 1, 32ff; R. H. Pfeiffer, 'The Canon of the OT' in IDB, 498—530; H. F. Hahn, *The OT in Modern Research*, 1954; E. G. Kraeling, *The OT since the Reformation*, 1955; A. C. Sundberg, *The OT of the Early Church*, 1964; B. J. Roberts, *The OT Canon; a suggestion*, 1963; F. V. Filson, *Which Books belong to the Bible*, 1957.

NT Canon: B. F. Westcott, *A General Survey of the Canon of the NT*; K. Aland, *The Problem of the NT Canon*, 1962; F. W. Beare, 'The Canon of the NT' in IDB, 520—32; H. F. D. Sparks, *The Formation of the NT*, 1952; M.-J. Lagrange, *Histoire ancienne du Canon du NT*, 1933.

Articles: R. E. Murphy, A. C. Sundberg and S. Sandmel, 'A Symposium on the Canon of Scripture', CBQ, 28 (1966), 189—207; D. Barthélemy, 'L'Ancien Testament a muri à Alexandrie', TZ 21 (1965), 358—70; P. W. Skehan, 'The Biblical Scrolls from Qumran and the Text of the OT', BA, 28 (1965), 87—100; A. Jepsen, 'Kanon und Text des AT' TLZ 74 **13a** (1949), 65—74; F. Hesse, 'Das AT als Kanon?', *Neue Zeitschrift für Systematische Theologie*, 3 (1961), 315—27; E. Flesserman van Leer, *ZTHK* (1964), 404—20; P. W. Skehan, 'The Biblical Scrolls from Qumran and the Text of the OT' in BA 28 (1965), 87—100.

b Meaning of 'Canon'—The Greek word which we translate as 'Canon' originally signified a rod or bar and so it came to mean a measuring rod. Then it was used metaphorically for any rule or standard of excellence in art or literature,—thus the ancient Greek authors were called canons (*kanones*)—or for a rule of conduct as by St Paul, Gal. 6:16. Similarly, the rules, decisions and decrees enacted by the Church to be the standard of doctrine, discipline and worship were called canons, and for a like reason men talked of the canon of Scripture or the canonical Scriptures because they contained the rule or standard of faith and morals. But this is not the sense in which the phrase 'Canon of the Scripture' is commonly used. It is usually taken to mean the **collection or list of books acknowledged and accepted by the Church as inspired**, i.e. Canon is taken in the passive sense of the books conforming to the rule for their acceptance as inspired works. Hence, the list would serve to distinguish sacred from profane writings. Similarly, books are said to be canonical or canonized when they form part of the canon. The earliest certain evidence of this usage is from the works of Athanasius (c. 350) although there are some who believe (from indications in Latin versions of his works) that it was used much earlier by Origen (d. 254). This Scriptural Canon comprises the OT and NT.

Note. The inclusion of books in the Canon of Scripture, whether Jewish or Christian, was a long, and often unconscious, historical process. For the first Christians, "The Scriptures" were the OT, and that included the books current in both Palestinian and Alexandrian Jewish communities. But for a long time no attempt was made to determine precisely the limits of the collection, see 15 *bc*; 21*ab*. Regarding the NT Canon, Aland has pointed out that it should not be treated in isolation from the OT. The Christian Canon of Scripture is an indivisible unity and should be treated as such (*Problem of NT Canon*, p. 2).

THE OLD TESTAMENT CANON

BY R. C. FULLER

13c The OT was the official collection of the sacred writings of the Jews before it became part of the Christian Scriptures. But two things must be noted. The OT Canon recognized by the Catholic Church contains seven more books (and parts of two others) than are contained in the present Jewish Bible. Moreover, the order of books is different. The Heb. Bible arranges them approximately in the order of recognition as sacred writings. The Christian Bible following the LXX arranges the books roughly by subject matter (see § 14a). Thus the Heb. Bible comprises (according to our way of counting) 39; and the Catholic OT has 46. We follow the Jewish order of books in this art. so as to trace the process of 'canonization'. The Protestant Canon of the OT following the Jewish, is shorter and omits Tb, Jdt, Wis, Sir, Bar, 1 and 2 Mc, and parts of Est and Dn namely Est 10:4—16—24 and Dn 3:24—90, and ch: 13 and 14. These books and parts of books were not included in the Heb. Bible at the end of the 1st cent. A.D., and have survived only in the Gr. Bible adopted by the Christians.

d The books which are included in the Heb. Bible are known as **proto-canonical** (p.c.) and those which have survived only in Gr. are called **deuterocanonical** (d.c.). The terms were first used by Sixtus of Siena in 1566, but are somewhat unfortunate in that they suggest two distinct canons (see § 15a) whereas they are intended to indicate only chronological priority of the p.c. over the d.c. as regards recognition of their canonical status, and even then only in general terms.

It is not to be supposed that there was any *clear* idea of inspired literature at the beginning. There were official records, laws, oracles and patriarchal traditions. Nor was there any very obvious distinction between civil and religious records, just as there was no real distinction between 'Church' and 'State'. In the earlier stages God guided his people rather through the spoken word and the records were gradually collected as being the concrete and written expression of that word. Hence, all the records were in some sense regarded as prophetic, cf the 'Former and Latter' Prophets. The 'Former Prophets' comprise in fact historical books.

It has been suggested by Pfeiffer that the change in emphasis from Oracle to Book took place with the finding of the Book of the Law in the time of Josiah, 621 B.C. From that time onwards all the stress was on the Law and its observance.

e The following table may be useful for reference:

Hebrew Bible
The Law: Gn, Ex, Lv, Nm, Dt.
The Prophets: The Former Prophets: Jos, Jg, 1 and 2 Sm, 1 (3) and 2 (4) Kgs.
The Latter Prophets: Is, Jer, Ezek, and the Twelve (i.e. Hos, Jl, Am, Obad, Jon, Mi, Na, Hb, Zeph, Hag, Zech, Mal).
The Writings: Ps, Prv, Jb, Song, Ru, Lam, Eccl, Est, Dn, Ez, Neh, 1 and 2 Chr.

Christian Bible (Old Testament). **13e**
The Pentateuch: Gn, Ex, Lv, Nm, Dt.
Historical Books: Jos, Jg, Ru, 1 and 2 Sm, 1 (3) and 2 (4) Kgs, 1 and 2 Chr, Ez, Neh, *Tb, Jdt*, Est including *10:4—16:24*.
Wisdom Books: Jb, Ps, Prv, Eccl, Song, *Wis, Sir*.
Major Prophets: Is, Jer, with Lam and *Bar*, Ezek, Dn, including after *3:23 the Prayer of Azariah and the Song of the 3 Children, ch 13 Susanna, ch 14 Bel and the Dragon.*
Minor Prophets: Hos, Jl, Am, Obad, Jon, Mi, Na, Hb, Zeph, Hag, Zech, Mal,
Historical Appendix: *1 and 2 Mc.*

Deuterocanonical Books, The Apocrypha—The books and parts of books in italics above are included in the Canon by Catholics, who call them deuterocanonical. Others exclude them from the Canon and call them Apocrypha. Some Church of England Bibles print the Apocrypha apart, after the OT (or even after the NT) and include amongst them also 1 (3) and 2 (4) Esdras and the Prayer of Manasseh; works which Catholics likewise exclude from the Canon. The Letter of Jeremiah is included by Catholics as part of Baruch in the Canon; by others with the Apocrypha.

Formation of the Jewish Canon: Beginnings. It is to **14a** Moses, the Lawgiver of Israel, that tradition ascribes the beginnings of a collection of sacred literature (Dt 31:9); the earliest nucleus of law, together with the then scanty written records of the tribes, were gathered together by him, for transmission to posterity. But the first efforts on any large scale to collect together a literature are probably to be ascribed to the reign of Solomon. By that date, there were, of course, already in existence very varied records, genealogies, lists of places, chronicles of the previous kings, epic poems, legislative material including bodies of particular laws (e.g. the Book of the Covenant), the earliest psalms—but not yet a connected history. According to the prevailing view of Pentateuchal composition, this was the task now begun and in the succeeding centuries more than one narrative was composed incorporating earlier material. Thus we may consider the Yahwist and Elohist traditions to have been formulated and eventually united into one history which we now find in the Pent (cf § 136i). By the time of Hezekiah's reform (2 Chr 29) in the 8th cent. B.C. there were further additions of Psalms, collections of wise sayings or proverbs, many of these attributed to Solomon (cf Prv 25:1), and of course the court records. In addition there began to be collected prophetical books or written records of the outstanding prophets of the day such as Hosea, Micah and Isaiah. The Temple in Jerusalem would have been the depository for this literature, or at least for the greater part of it. We may note here the finding of the 'Book of the Law' in the Temple at the time of Josiah's reform, 2 Chr 34:14. It was in all likelihood the Book of Deuteronomy, or at least a substantial part of it, which

14a may well have been written at the time of, or soon after, Hezekiah's reform in the preceding century, (though incorporating earlier material), and lost during the reign of the wicked Manasseh. The Book had a profound effect on Israel's history, and it is noteworthy that the Books of Kings are permeated with the spirit of the Deuteronomist.

b **The Law, the Prophets and the Writings**—It was during the exilic and post-exilic periods, however, that the most thorough-going editorial work was done, and the books of the OT began to take the shape with which we are familiar. The 'priestly' editors as they are called, were largely responsible for codifying much of the ritual legislation and adding to it. Moreover, they were preoccupied with the worship of the Temple, and this theme dominates a great deal of their narrative which has been incorporated in the Pent. Certainly, by the time of Ezra's reform c. 450 B.C., the Pent was complete, and it is even possible that he had a hand in its final compilation. In a ceremony rather like that in which Josiah promulgated the Book of the Law (2 (4) Kgs 22–3) Ezra read out the Book of the Law of Moses (the Pent) 'from early morning until midday' Neh 8:3. It seems probable that at this date only the Pent was officially regarded as canonical, because the Samaritans, who set up their own separate religious organization soon after this time, recognized only those books as canonical Scripture. And indeed, even when other books were added to Israel's Canon at a later date, **the Law** continued to be regarded as in a class by itself. In contrast with pre-exilic times when people depended on a word or oracle from the Lord through his prophets, there was now a 'machinery' for the instruction of the people, namely, the synagogues which were springing up everywhere and in which the Law was expounded every Sabbath to the people (cf § 613d).

c So during the next two centuries a second group of books gradually took shape. The Pent contained much history interspersed with its law in order to show how God works through the history of his people and how law grows out of experience. In the historical books which follow (Jos, Jg, Sm, Kgs) the author is less interested in history for history's sake than in using the facts of history to illustrate certain religious themes, and to bring out the workings of God. This is why the Jews call these books **'the Former Prophets'**. There are later historical books of course, namely, Chr, Ez-Neh, written before the end of the 3rd cent. B.C. These books were not included in this second group possibly because the second group had already acquired a special status which they had not yet reached. Consequently we find them ultimately relegated to the third group of sacred books—'The Writings'. Those historical books called the Former Prophets, show evidence of later editing. Just as the Pent bears the marks of the priestly editors throughout, so these historical books display signs of a Deuteronomist stamp on top of the indications of composite authorship. It is unlikely that this editing could have taken place before the going into exile; moreover, the history of Kgs takes us later than this. We are probably correct in suggesting an exilic date for this work. It goes without saying that much of the historical material contained in the books dates back many centuries.

d To the earlier historical books ('the Former Prophets'), were added the books of the **'Latter Prophets'**, that is to say the collections of written prophecies gathered over the years since about the 8th cent. B.C. After 400 B.C., when the voice of prophecy seemed to have been silenced, the Jews collected together as much as they could of the written records of their prophets and eventually placed these beside the Law. Some prophets of course, left noth- **14d** ing in writing. Again we need not suppose that the records we do possess were all written down by the prophets themselves. Certainly, they did write at times; thus Jeremiah dictated some of his oracles to Baruch (Jer 45). Besides prophecy, these books contain not infrequently biographical material, and all this was woven into the book, together with the oracles. The title, 'Latter Prophets' includes Is, Jer, Ezek, and the 12 Minor prophets; and their final editing took place probably in the relatively short period of time towards the end of the 5th cent. B.C. Nevertheless, at that time the preoccupation was chiefly with the Law, and it was that which Ezra concentrated upon. Another century at least was to pass before 'the Prophets' attained an equivalent status. In the prologue to Sir, written by the grandson of the author about the year 130 B.C., we read of the existence of at least two clearly defined groups of sacred writings, namely, the Law and the Prophets, the latter title evidently referring to the Former and Latter Prophets, of which we have been speaking. This second group was probably complete about the year 200 B.C.

There also existed at this time a large quantity of other **e** sacred literature, some of it dating back a long way, the Psalms for instance, the Proverbs, and some of the later historical works. It is easy to see the unique position of the Pent, and why it was cut off from the rest, but it is more difficult to understand why and on what principle the 'Prophets' were cut off from the other books referred to above. Perhaps it was convenient to separate this second group from the rest of the literature for practical purposes. What remained was called by the general name of **'The Writings'** or simply 'The Other Books', and here we find the greatest variety of all. Into this collection were put those books which were recognized rather late, and others which perhaps had only just been written. The chief book in the group is of course the Psalms and, indeed, the group seems to be designated under this name by Christ, who speaks of 'the law of Moses and the prophets and the psalms', Lk 24:44. In the 2nd cent. B.C. a further gathering of Sacred Books took place. In 2 Mc 2:13 we read that as Nehemiah founded a library and collected books about the kings and prophets, so did Judas Maccabeus collect all the books which had been lost on account of the war.

The closing of the Jewish Canon.—At Jamnia **f** (Jabneh) towards the end of the 1st cent. A.D., the Rabbis included in this group Ps, Prv, Jb, Song, Ru, Lam, Eccl, Est, Dn, Ez, Neh, 1 and 2 Chr. To speak more exactly it was a question of excluding *other* books with claims to canonical status, rather than officially including the ones cited, which of course were already 'in possession'. But there does not seem to have been any such clear-cut view *before* that time. In fact, if there had been it is hard to see what the deliberations of the Rabbis were about. In the century before Christ, and indeed up to A.D. 70, we have the period of the apocalyptic writings which constituted a vast literature (cf § 454a–e). Besides this, there was an abundant output of moral or wisdom writing, such as Sirach, which achieved great popularity. Some of this literature was originally composed in Heb. or Aram.; but apart from the Sir. Heb. text found in the Cairo *Geniza* (cf § 441a), and the fragments from Qumran and Masada, nothing of these originals has survived. The rest of this literature was written in Gr. and this and the Gr. translations of the other books have survived largely because of their preservation by the Christian Church.

The evidence from Qumran and Masada shows **g**

14g that this literature circulated not only throughout the Dispersion but also in Palestine. Moreover it appears to have been read in Palestine not only in Heb. or Aram. but also in Gr.—a language which was familiar to a large proportion of the population.

Though there was no clear-cut view of the Canon prior to A.D. 70 there must have been at least some general ideas on the matter of the inclusion or otherwise of this literature. Clearly there were grades of status and though we have no direct evidence on the matter it is probable that certain books (i.e. those which survived in the LXX) were singled out from the rest in course of time as belonging to the Canon of Scripture. It was for this reason that they were copied in the MSS of the LXX by the Christian Church. After A.D. 70 controversy began between Christians and Jews, and arguments from Scripture were produced from both sides. **The Christians used the text of the LXX** whereas **their opponents**, though they may have used the LXX as well, **could always refer back to the original Heb.**; and not infrequently the LXX differed from the Heb. The Jews refused to consider the possibility that the Gr. might have a better reading, and decided that the LXX was wrong especially where it seemed to favour the Messianic interpretation. They turned more and more to the Heb. text until finally the LXX was (c. A.D. 130) condemned outright and became anathema to every orthodox Jew, cf § 26*j*. Already before this rejection of the LXX there was a narrowing of outlook with regard to the actual books to be regarded as sacred and canonical. It is not difficult to see why the apocalyptic literature lost face. Quite simply, after A.D. 70 it was discredited. For so long these books had been proclaiming the sudden and glorious manifestation of the Messiah and the confusion of his enemies. Then came the great revolt in A.D. 66 largely inspired by these explosive ideas and this was followed by the débâcle of A.D. 70, and the destruction of their hopes. As for the rest of the literature, its **exclusion was no doubt due to the greater insistence on the law and a turning away from the more liberal outlook of many of these books.** Perhaps also some of the contents was not to the liking of the Jews in that it seemed to favour the Christian Messianic interpretation. Besides this, it was necessary to exclude the new literature of the Christians which was beginning to accumulate, namely the epistles, the Gospels, and the Acts of the Apostles, and was being used against them.

h None of these reasons was however given for the rejection of this literature. Jos (C. Ap I, 8) says that the Jews have only 22 sacred books 'which are justly believed to be divine'. This is clearly an artificial number (the total of letters in the Heb. alphabet) but it included all 39 of the books referred to above § 13*e*. Josephus goes on to say that the period of prophecy lasted from Moses to the reign of Artaxerxes (Longimanus—465–424 B.C.) king of Persia, and that though Jewish history has been written since then it has not the same authority because 'there has not been an exact succession of prophets since that time'. The criterion that an inspired and canonical book had to be written not later than Artaxerxes, or (as it is implied elsewhere, *Talmud, Baba Bathra* 14b–15a) not later than Ezra, may now be seen as a move on the part of the Jewish authorities to exclude at one stroke the vast mass of apocalyptic literature which had gained such a hold on the people, as well as other books which were not to their liking. Sir and Mc were excluded by this; Dn and Jb were included because regarded as prophetic; Song, Prv and Eccl were ascribed to Solomon and so included; Wis and Psalms of Solomon were ex-

cluded perhaps because only in Gr. Est being in Heb., **14h** was (eventually) included but only after a long period of doubt based on its contents. It was presumably regarded at last as having been written before the death of Ezra. Lam was accepted as belonging to Jer; Bar was excluded because not written in Heb., cf IB, I, p. 32ff. This criterion of canonicity in fact bears all the marks of having been worked out *post factum*; it cannot have existed before A.D. 70. It is true that the traditional figure of the prophet had been absent, but the writers of the apocalyptic literature and indeed of the post-Ezra literature in general regarded themselves as in the prophetic tradition and were so regarded by the people. 'That Sirach, a book manifestly written after Ezra, came so near to being included in the Jewish Canon militates against the argument that the theory limiting inspired writings to pre-Ezra times was of long standing in Judaism', Sundberg, p. 116. D. S. Russell observes that the apocalyptists were convinced of their own inspiration as authentic successors of the prophets, (*The Method and Message of Jewish Apocalyptic*, 133, 158). Further it seems clear that the mention of the 'other books' in the prologue to Sir was not meant to indicate a closed group, because in 2 Mc 15:9 Judas Maccabeus encourages his men from 'the Law and the prophets' without mention of a third group.

At Jamnia about A.D. 90 the Rabbis rejected all 15a this literature including the d.c. books, but even then the matter was not so clear-cut as it seemed. The canonical character of Est—of which book no trace has been found at Qumran—was in doubt for a long time among both Christians and Jews. Doubts likewise were expressed about Prv, Song, Ru, Eccl and Ezek before they were eventually accepted everywhere. On the other hand books which were rejected continued to be used for a time. Thus Sir in particular was still read and quoted as Scripture though it was banned from public reading in the synagogue. It continued to be read for several centuries. No doubt it is due to the rejection of these books by the Rabbis that their Heb. or Aram. texts were not preserved except accidentally in one or two cases. **Was there an Alexandrian Canon?**—Did the Alexandrian Jews recognize as sacred certain books which were not so recognized in Jerusalem? It used to be argued that the books known as d.c. which are extant only in Gr. were recognized as inspired and canonical only among the Jews of the Dispersion and especially of Alexandria who read their Scriptures in Gr.; and the Christians took over this larger Canon from the Alexandrian Jews when they took over the LXX. But this is too simple a view. In the first place, we have seen that many of these books were originally written in Heb. or Aram. and many fragments of them have been found at Qumran in addition to fragments in Gr. The books were certainly known in Palestine before A.D. 70 though unfortunately it is not possible to say exactly what status they enjoyed throughout the country or even among the Qumran community. It is true that generally speaking biblical MSS found there are written in a formal book-hand and moreover on parchment or skin of some kind. Others are written on papyrus but the evidence does not allow us to state categorically that a book written in a book-hand on parchment was necessarily recognized as canonical Scripture or conversely that one which was not so written was therefore given no such recognition. In Cave 6 for example fragments of Kgs have been discovered written on papyrus and on the other hand a MS of the Book of Jubilees was found written in the book-hand normally reserved for biblical MSS. Moreover some of the Qumran

15a Community books seem to have been treated with a consideration at least equal to or even exceeding that accorded to the canonical books. But **is it antecedently likely that Alexandria would have consciously recognized books which were not regarded as sacred in Jerusalem?** Would Jews of the Dispersion have looked anywhere but to Jerusalem for guidance as to their canonical literature? Most certainly no one would have turned to Alexandria for guidance in preference to Jerusalem. Moreover it was because of the need to give authority to the LXX that the legend of its origin recorded in the Letter of Aristeas (§ 26*b*) was concocted. There a fanciful tale is related about how authority for the translation was received from Jerusalem. The point of the story is the necessity for asserting that the translation did have the approval of the Jewish authorities in Palestine. It seems logical therefore to conclude that there was no conscious difference between the two centres. Given the vague views on canonicity at the time a definite list of books was not to be expected, but we may be sure there was no obvious divergence in this matter of the Canon. Moreover, if there had been such a thing, it is improbable that the first Christians would have adopted the LXX and its extra books in conscious opposition to the Jews of Palestine. The first Christians, after all, were of Heb. or Aram. speech, though very soon outnumbered by Greek-speaking converts.

b **The Christian Canon of the OT**—It has often been said that the first Christians being largely Gr.-speaking took over the LXX Bible and that this Bible included the extra books. In this way the books came to be accepted as inspired by the Christian Church. We have seen however that many of these books were originally written in Heb. or Aram. and that there is no real evidence of any such distinction between Canons before the Fall of Jerusalem. The first Christians would have used the Scriptures which lay to hand. In the days before A.D. 70 there must have been some fluidity as to which books precisely were regarded as canonical. For most of the books there would of course have been no doubt at all. But some would have been marginal, though such differences of opinion as occurred would have been perhaps personal rather than territorial. Then came the great disaster of A.D. 70, followed by the bitter controversies between Christians and Jews leading to the rejection by the Jews of certain books as well as of the LXX itself. By this time of course the great majority of Christians were Gr.-speaking and their Bible was the LXX. It was not to be expected that any decisions taken now by the Jews and taken moreover (as it would appear to the Christians) out of hostility against them, would have any influence over their recognition of particular books. That is to say—the Christians continued to have the same rather vague attitude to the canon of the OT as the Jews had had before A.D. 70. They agreed about most of the books to be included but were uncertain about the precise limits of the Canon. Our earliest MSS of the complete OT (LXX) are of the 4th cent. A.D. and therefore an uncertain guide as to the Canon of the 1st cent. But negatively they reveal an interesting fact. There is no uniformity in the MSS as to the d.c. books to be included. Thus LXX (S) has Tb, Jdt, 1 Mc, 4 Mc, Wis, Sir. LXX (B) has not got Mc. LXX (A) has 1–4 Mc, Wis, Sir, Tb and Jdt. One 3rd cent. papyrus fragment

c has Wis and Sir (no Gr MS has 4 Esd.). It should be noticed that the d.c. books are distributed throughout the OT and not gathered into one place. We may conclude from this that they were placed on an equal footing, even if some books also seem to have been thought inspired

and canonical which were afterwards rejected. If this was **15c** the case in the 4th cent., we are fairly safe in assuming that the position was no less vague in the first. We must be clear on this point. **The first Christians did not accept their Canon from the Jewish authorities of Jamnia in A.D. 90.** They had already received—before A.D. 70—the books which were later to be listed as canonical. We can get some idea of the books they recognized by tracing quotations and references to particular books. In the NT itself there are no explicit references to the d.c. books but there are traces. Thus Mt 6:14 = Sir 28:2; Mt 27:39–40, = Wis 2:12–15; Rm 1:20ff = Wis 13–14; Heb 11:35–39 = 2 Mc 6:18–7 = 42; Jas 1:19 = Sir 5:11–13; 1 Pt 1:6 = Wis 3:3ff. When we come to the Apostolic Fathers and early Church writers there is no difficulty in finding quotations from the d.c. books and moreover quotations made in very much the same way as those from the p.c. books. 'Thus Clement of Rome places the story of Judith side by side with that of Esther; the Wisdom of Sirach is cited by Barnabas and the Didache and Tobit by Polycarp', Swete, op. cit:, 224.

The earliest lists and Jewish influence—In his **16a** *Dialogue with Trypho* 32, Justin Martyr says that he will use only those books 'which are esteemed holy and prophetic, among you (i.e. among the Jews). Justin's own views on the d.c. books are clear. He accepts them, but already the Jewish decision on the Canon is having its influence. It is when we come to the first lists given by Christians that we notice a distinct move in the direction of the Jewish Canon. Thus, Melito of Sardis (A.D. 175) writes to Onesimus 'when therefore I went to the East and came to the place where these things were proclaimed and done, I accurately ascertained which are the books of the OT and I send you the list as given below'. Then follows his list, which does not include Est and the d.c. books. (Eus. HE, IV, 26). The omission of Est may reflect Jewish doubts on its canonicity but the omission of the d.c. books shows that Melito is giving the Jewish Canon. He may have done this to provide Onesimus with a list of the books useful in controversy with the Jews; or he may have accepted the shorter Canon. The evidence for a conclusion is lacking. As against this, the Muratorian Canon from Ch 29, about the same time includes the book of Wisdom.

Origen of Alexandria (d. A.D. 254) likewise gives a **b** list of the OT Canon, according to the Jewish reckoning, but in this case he explicitly states that he is giving the Jewish Canon, or as he says 'according to the Hebrews', Eus. HE. VI. 25. This would be important in controversy with the Jews. But his own views were different. In his *Letter to Africanus* (PG. XI. 47ff), who rejected the story of Susanna because it was not included in the Daniel received by the Jews, Origen says that this and Bel and the Dragon and the d.c. parts of Esther should be accepted on the grounds that the Gr. Bible had been accepted by the Church. This Letter of Origen to Africanus is basic evidence of the attitude towards the d.c. books in the 3rd cent. It is nevertheless a matter for comment that there is no early list of the Christian Canon and one is drawn to the conclusion that no early complete list was possible. The final word had not yet been said as regards a few of the books. K. Aland says 'For the primitive Church there was no hard and fast Canon of the OT' (p. 3). but this needs qualification. There was indeed a contrast between the cut and dried Jewish Canon and the comparatively nebulous Christian Canon on which there had been no authoritative decision. On the other hand there was agreement on 90% of the Canon and the number of books on which there was any discussion was very small

16b indeed. It would hardly be surprising if some Christian writers came under Jewish influence. It is worthy of notice that the Syriac translation of the OT made about A.D. 200 omits the d.c. books. On the other hand, they were inserted later. It is difficult to avoid the conclusion that proximity to Palestine was not without its influence in this case. From what has been said it will be seen that there is a discrepancy in some writers between their acceptance of the d.c. books individually because the Church receives them, and their reluctance to draw up a list of the Christian canon: indeed it seems that they are over-influenced by the Jewish Canon. But in the long run, the practice of the Church prevailed.

From the beginning of the fourth century—It has been said above that Origen in his controversy with Jews used only the Hebrew Bible because this alone was recognized as canonical by his opponents. This meant in practice that these books were used to prove doctrine while the d.c. books were only to be used in Christian circles, or for the instruction of catechumens. It is easy to see how at a later date the idea could arise that there was a difference of authority in the books themselves. Thus *Athanasius* in his *Festal Letter* 39 (A.D. 367) PL 26, 1435ff calls the d.c. books non-canonical and to be read only to catechumens. But he puts Est among these, and also *Pastor* and the *Didache* while Bar is placed among the canonical. Besides the exigencies of controversy with the Jews as a possible cause of confusion, there was also the proliferation of apocryphal literature. Many of these works bore names similar to canonical books, and in fact were given such names in order to promote their acceptance, cf § 88c. Sometimes they were quoted by the Fathers as Scripture, but at no time were they accepted by the Church or read at public services. Their very multitude, however, made some Fathers over-cautious and inclined to be stricter than the situation warranted. This may have been a contributory reason for the too-ready acceptance by certain Fathers of the shorter Jewish canon. A number of Eastern Fathers besides Athanasius followed him in rejecting the d.c. books and classing them as non-canonical, e.g. Cyril Jer, Epiphanius, and Greg Naz; while Euseb classed them as disputed. Nevertheless, as with the earlier Fathers, many of these frequently quote the d.c. books as if on the same level as the Heb. Canon. The important thing to notice is that the Fathers with the exception of Jerome never class the d.c. books with the apocryphal or spurious books of heretical origin (the third group of Athanasius).

d In the West, both **Rufinus and Jerome have a divided witness on this point**. When they were in Rome, neither had any difficulty in accepting the d.c. as received by the Latin Church. It was when they went East that they came under the influence of the Jews, and rejected the d.c. books. Rufinus called them 'ecclesiastical' to be read with profit but not to prove doctrine. Jerome, more forthright than Rufinus, says that the d.c. books are apocryphal, thus using this word of these books for the first time. In his *Prologus Galeatus* he likewise says of them 'non sunt in canone', PL 28, 600—603. By using the term 'apocryphal' of these books, Jer is the first writer it seems, in the Western Church, to deny (implicitly) their inspiration, c. A.D. 390. He explicitly denies the canonical character of any book not found in the Heb. Bible. Nevertheless, as in the case of many other Fathers, even when he has declared himself in favour of the shorter canon, he goes on to refer to and use the d.c. books as if they were canonical. Moreover, when he is translating the OT he is well aware that his view is at variance with the prevailing view at least in the West. 'There is no book

or fragment of the deuterocanon,' says Cornely, 'which **16d** he does not use with reverence, and as a divine authority' (CSS, 1, *Introd. Gen.* 1885, p. 107). It was Augustine of Hippo who became the defender of the d.c. books against Jer, and very probably he was instrumental in having the question of the Canon discussed and pronounced upon at the African Councils. All this was not without effect on Jer. He tells us that he translated the d.c. books into Latin as a concession to the authority of the bishops (*Praef. in lib. Tob.*, PL 29, 24—25). Then in A.D. 402 he attempts to exculpate himself to Rufinus and says he did not really deny the inspiration of the d.c. books but was only giving the opinion of the Jews (*Apol. contra Ruf.* 11, 33. PL 23, 476).

St Augustine and the African Councils—Aug **e** accepts the longer canon on the authority of the Church (*De Doct. Christ.* 8; PL 34, 41), and defends individual books on the grounds that they are read in Church. Thus, Wis was found worthy of being read from the lector's pulpit in the Church of Christ (*Lib. de Praedest. Sanctorum*, c. 14). At the Council of Hippo, A.D. 393 a list was drawn up giving the longer canon, and this was repeated, and confirmed at the 3rd and 4th Councils of Carthage, A.D. 397 and 418. At the end of the decree there is a footnote: 'Let this also be made known to our brother and fellow priest, the holy Boniface, bishop of Rome, or to other priests of those parts, for the confirmation of this canon; for we have learned from the Fathers that we should read these in Church' (EnchB 16—20). In A.D. 405 Exsuperius, bishop of Toulouse, wrote to the Pope, Innocent I, asking him for a ruling on this question, perhaps worried by Jerome's statements. The Pope replied in his letter *Consulenti Tibi* (PL 20, 501) repeating the list drawn up by the Councils. These were the **first official professions of belief concerning the Canon**, although not involving the highest authority speaking *ex cathedra*. But they were enough to produce a virtual unanimity of view in the W during the 5th cent., though in the E, and in particular in Syria, general agreement was not reached until the 7th cent., when the E accepted the longer canon. Subsequent texts of the Latin Bible, of course, always included the longer Canon, until the period of the Reformation was reached. However, some editions included 3 and 4 Esd and the Prayer of Manasseh. When the Clementine Vulgate was printed after the Council of Trent, these books too, were printed, though at the end, apart from the Canon 'lest they altogether perish'—as the note adds.

Later History—After St Augustine, opinions again **17a** became divided. Even Pope Gregory the Great spoke of 1Mc as being amongst 'those books which, though not canonical were produced for the edification of the Church'. (*Lib. Mor.* 19, 21; PL 76, 119). Evidently the great prestige of Jer was not without its effect on posterity. Cardinal Cajetan, nearly a thousand years later, endorsed once more the view of Jer in calling these books apocryphal, i.e. not inspired, but added that they might be used for edification and even be called canonical, thus admitting that inspiration and canonicity are separable, (Cajetan, *Comm. Esther*, quoted in Cornely, *Introduction...* 1, 135). These views were expressed *after* the statement of the Council of Florence on the Canon of Scripture in the Decree *pro Jacobitis*, A.D. 1441 (Dz 1335), repeating exactly the list of the earlier Councils. When the Reformation came therefore, the adoption of the shorter Canon by the Reformers was not a breaking away from a unanimous position; still less, of course, a dissenting from the Council of Trent, which was itself, one should rather say, induced to make a pronouncement because of the views of

17a the Reformers. Nevertheless, speaking generally, one can say that the books finally accepted by the Catholic church were those which were quoted regularly by the Church Fathers and Writers as Scripture, and read as such in Church, and which appear to have been continuously copied into the MSS of the Greek Bible, and thence into the Latin Bible. Some books occasionally found in MSS of the LXX were eventually excluded in the W, e.g. 3 Esd, the Prayer of Manasseh, 3 and 4 Mc, Ps 151 and the Psalms of Solomon. External reasons may be found in the fact that these books are seldom, if ever, quoted by the Fathers and Church writers, or that they are a duplication of existing books (e.g. 3 Esd) or that their contents were considered to be unworthy, or because they were of too late origin (e.g. 4 Esd). But in the last resort one can only see the Spirit of God working through his Church.

b When the **Reformers** broke away from Rome they had to settle this question of the OT Canon. A number of considerations had to be borne in mind. There was, for example, the awkward fact that one of the d.c. books, 2 Mc, spoke of the intercession of the saints (15:14), and of prayers for the dead and so by implication, purgatory (12:43—45). Furthermore, since the books were not in the Heb. text, and the Reformers laid such emphasis on having Bibles from the originals, it was not surprising that they rejected these books, or at least placed them on a lower level. For there was a difference of view here. Whereas Luther and the Church of England regarded them as for edification, and on a lower level than the Heb. Canon, Calvin on the other hand and Calvinists generally, thought them of no account and not to be read in Church at all. The respective positions may be seen in the Thirtynine Articles on the one hand (1559) and the Westminster Confession (1647), on the other. The Reformers, having rejected the d.c. books, gave them the title of 'apocrypha'—a name which Jer had given them for the first time, and indeed alone among all Church writers of the early centuries. It should be noted that the Reformers included under this heading the extra books sometimes printed in Latin Bibles— namely, 3 and 4 Esd (which Protestants call 1 and 2 Esd) and the Prayer of Manasseh. Hence, the terms 'deutero-canonical books' and 'apocrypha' are not synonymous. **17b** Church of England Bibles continued to include the d.c. books amongst the 'Apocrypha' (as they were, and are, called), though at the back of the OT. The Archbishop of Canterbury even imposed a year's imprisonment for publishing Bibles without the 'Apocrypha'. This was in 1615. Nevertheless they were omitted more and more in subsequent editions of the Bible. In the early 19th cent. the Edinburgh Bible Society denounced the 'Apocrypha' as superstitious and absurd, and within a few years all the Bible Societies had decided not to publish them at all. It may be said, however, that among Protestants generally today the 'Apocrypha' are coming back into greater use.

The Council of Trent in 1546 declared that it **c** accepted all the books of OT and NT with equal feelings of piety and reverence. There follows the longer Canon, as originally enumerated by the Councils of Africa Dz 1501—1504 (EnchB 57—60). From the time of Trent, Catholics have regarded the d.c. as on the same level as the p.c. and equal in the degree of their inspiration. The declaration of Trent was reaffirmed at the First Vatican Council, (Dz 3006, 3029; EnchB 77).

The Orthodox Church throughout most of its history has kept the longer Canon, though not precisely the number held as canonical by Rome. But at the time of the Reformation, Cyril Lukaris, Patriarch of Constantinople, began a struggle against what he considered increasing Papal influence, and for this purpose inclined towards the Protestants. His Confession, published at Geneva in 1629, and distinctly Protestant in tone, was rejected by the other Orthodox. He published a Gr. Bible of an openly Protestant type, printed at Geneva, in which the d.c. were omitted. However, his attempted reforms gained little support, and the Sultan had him murdered eventually at the instigation of his enemies. In the years following his death, the Orthodox Church held a series of Synods, in which they affirmed the ancient Orthodox Faith in the most uncompromising manner, anathematized Cyril's Confession and rejected his Bible. Since that time, opinion in the Orthodox Church has fluctuated between the shorter and the longer Canon, but predominating in favour of the longer.

THE NEW TESTAMENT CANON

BY R. J. FOSTER

18a **Its Formation**—The formation of the NT Canon was, like that of the Old, a gradual process. The writings of which it is made up were, in the first instance, separate, independent writings, called into being at different times, in different circumstances, to meet various needs. There was no intention on the part of the Apostles and their disciples of collaborating in the production of a common work to be left as a legacy. Our Lord and his Apostles were teachers rather than writers; they taught and preached the word of God, for, in St Paul's words, 'Faith comes from what is heard' (Rm 10:17). The written word came to reinforce the oral Gospel (cf Lk 1:4). Each book of the NT was issued separately and has its own history. St Paul, for instance, would write a letter to a community to meet some practical need, to give further instruction, to exhort or to give warning against impending dangers. Such letters written to the different local churches throughout the Empire would be interchanged between them, sometimes at the request of the Apostle himself (Col 4:16). The letters would increase in number and each community would acquire a collection of them: we can already see how the germ of a Canon arose. This small collection of books would increase as further writings, which bore the unmistakable stamp or guarantee of apostolic origin, were added to it. In the NT itself there are clear signs of such a collection in process of formation, taking its place alongside the OT Scriptures: 'So also our beloved brother Paul wrote to you according to the wisdom given to him, speaking of this as he does *in all his letters*. There are some things in them hard to understand, which the ignorant and unstable twist, to their own destruction, as they do *the other scriptures*' (2 Pt 3:15).

b As the number of living witnesses gradually dwindled, and as the number of communities increased through the rapid spread of the faith, it became more and more apparent how valuable it would be for the instruction of future generations if there were written records of the teaching, life, death and resurrection of our Lord. At first, as Cerfaux remarks, 'We find ourselves on mixed ground between purely oral tradition and the first written schemes. St Luke tells us of many attempts at systematization which he had been able to consult (Lk 1:1). There must have been a pre-history, most probably not of purely oral tradition, preceding the final stage in which the memoirs were fixed in the canonical Gospels' (*The Four Gospels*, E.tr., 1960, p. 19f). The Gospels themselves, once composed, would pass from one community to another in the same way as the letters, and each community would add the new writings to its collection as soon as they came to hand. Striking evidence for the early circulation of Jn, for instance, is given by P 52, a papyrus fragment of Jn, which comes from Egypt and is dated as belonging to the first half of the 2nd cent. (C. H. Roberts, *An unpublished Fragment of the Fourth Gospel*, 1935). Collections were not made rapidly, for progress would be impeded by slowness and difficulty of communication and limited means for the multiplication of copies of writings. In fact, a considerable period of time must have elapsed before the widely scattered churches possessed all the writings in circulation. There were other difficulties too: it was, for example, sometimes hard to tell if a smaller letter, more private in character and of less important doctrine, really emanated from genuine apostolic sources. In addition, the circulation of spurious and tendentious works, claiming apostolic origin, would tend to make people wary of accepting anything which was not of proven and undoubted apostolic authority. In these circumstances, then, it is not surprising that there were several books, genuine and inspired, whose full canonical status was not universally acknowledged for a long time. These have become known to us as the **deuterocanonical books of the NT** (cf § 13*d*). They are Hebrews, James, Jude, 2 Peter, 2 and 3 John, and the Apocalypse (or Revelation). But there are no differences between Catholics and Protestants regarding the books which constitute the NT Canon: they are the four Gospels, the Acts of the Apostles, fourteen Epistles 'of St Paul', the seven Catholic Epistles (James, 1 and 2 Peter, 1, 2, 3 John, Jude) and the Apocalypse or Revelation.

History—It is reasonable to suppose that, quite early on, **19a** the more important churches, Rome, Alexandria, Corinth, Antioch and others would possess apostolic writings which they regarded as authoritative, though at this stage their lists might vary. Already we have seen that there is evidence in the NT of a collection of Pauline writings received as Scripture. The Apostolic Fathers further illustrate the unique place occupied by the Gospels and the writings of the Apostles. The careful line of demarcation between these writings and their own is quite noticeable. Clement of Rome, writing to the Corinthians (c. A.D. 96), says: 'Take into your hands the epistle of the Blessed Paul the Apostle. What did he write to you when the Gospel was first preached? Truly, under divine inspiration (*pneumatikōs*) he wrote to you concerning himself, and Cephas, and Apollo, because even then you had formed parties among yourselves' (*Ep Cor* 47:1; PG 1, 305). Ignatius of Antioch (d.c. 107–110) remarks to the Ephesians that St Paul makes mention of them in 'every epistle', a hyperbole which implies a collection of Pauline epistles of acknowledged authority, *Eph* 12:1; PG 5, 656. Eph 4:26 is quoted by St Polycarp (c. 70–156) together with Ps 4:5, as in the 'Scriptures', *Phil* 12:1 PG 5, 1014.

Quite apart from these explicit passages, there are many incidental references and coincidences of thought and language which betray a remarkable acquaintance with the writings of Paul, cf F. X. Funk *Patres Apostolici* (*Index Locorum SS.*). 'Elsewhere in the Apostolic Fathers', writes Westcott, 'there are clear traces of a knowledge of the Epistles of St Paul to the Romans, 1 and 2 Corinthians, Galatians, Ephesians, Philippians, and 1

19a and 2 Timothy, of the Epistle to the Hebrews, of the Epistle of St James, the first Epistle of St Peter, and the first Epistle of St John. The allusions to the Epistles of St Paul to the Thessalonians, Colossians, to Titus and Philemon, and to 2 Peter are very uncertain; and there are, I believe, no coincidences of language with the Epistle of Jude, and 2 and 3 John' (*History of the Canon NT*, p. 48). In fact their familiarity with the epistles is so extensive that we can hardly doubt that a collection of them was in wide circulation and commonly known.

There are allusions, too, to the written Gospels, although our Lord's life and teaching were still familiar from oral tradition, cf. Funk, loc cit Mt 22:14 is quoted by the Ep. of Barnabas (c. 100) with the scriptural formula *hōs gegraptai*, 'as it is written' (4:14, PG 2, 733). The judgement of the early writers is, therefore, clear, for they use the books as authoritative, accept them as apostolic and quote them as inspired.

b The Apologists—During the succeeding period in the life of the Church when she was faced by the persecution of the Roman Empire and the attacks of heretical false brethren, the Apologists came to her aid. In their works evidence for the canonical writings is abundant. Justin Martyr describes them as resting upon Apostolic authority: 'For the Apostles', he writes, 'in the memoirs composed by them, which are called Gospels, have handed down to us what Jesus had thus enjoined upon them' (1 *Apol* 1, 66; PG 6, 429). These 'memoirs' were read together with the Prophets when the Christians met for worship on Sundays (1, 67), thus bearing witness to a Christian collection of writings which had taken its place alongside that of the OT. That Justin is speaking of the four Gospels which we possess today, seems to be confirmed by the work of his disciple Tatian, who composed his *Diatessaron*, or harmony of the Gospels, exclusively from them. Justin also quotes Apoc as by St John. St Denis of Corinth (d.c. 176), in an interesting passage, complains of heretics corrupting his writings, but consoles himself with the thought that the same is done even to the Scriptures of the Lord (Eus HE 4, 23; PG 20, 389). The heretic Marcion (c. 150) also gives direct testimony to the existence and authority of a NT Canon by drawing up one of his own, which included a mutilated Lk and ten Pauline epistles.

By the end of the 2nd cent. all the NT books were generally known and the divine character of most of them was universally admitted. Irenaeus (d. 202), familiar with the traditions of Asia Minor, Gaul and Rome, and connected through his teachers with the close of the apostolic age, explicitly names and accepts the four canonical Gospels, rejects the claims of others which are apocryphal, quotes twelve epistles of Paul as Scripture, accepts Apoc as Johannine, and makes use of the Catholic epistle (*Adv Haer*. 3, 11; PG 7, 885). He has no reference to Phm and does not think that Heb was written by St Paul.

The witness of Tertullian in North Africa and Clement in Alexandria is the same. The former, writing against Marcion, reproves him for his treatment of the Gospels, and defends their authenticity and authority, *Adv Marcion* 4, 2. He quotes all the NT books except 2 Pt, 2 and 3 Jn, but ascribes Heb to Barnabas and excludes it from Scripture. Clement quotes all the undisputed books of the NT, and, according to Eusebius, gave concise accounts of all the canonical Scriptures, not passing over the disputed books, i.e. Jude and the other catholic epistles, and also the Ep. Barn., and Apoc. Pet. He regarded Heb as Pauline, written in Heb. for

Hebrews, and translated into Gr. by Luke (HE 6, 14; **19b** PG 20, 549).

The earliest **list** that has come down to us, though **c** it need be by no means the earliest written, is the Muratorian Fragment (c. 200) discovered by Muratori in the Ambrosian Library, Milan in 1740. It contains a catalogue of books which were recognized as authoritative at Rome at the end of the 2nd cent., viz. the four Gospels, Acts, the epistles of St Paul (except Heb), two epistles of St John, Jude and Apoc. It omits (in addition to Heb) Jas, 1 and 2 Pt and one epistle of Jn. There also seems to be a reference to the Apoc. Pet., which 'some of us do not wish to be read in the Church'. The Pastor of Hermas is excluded because of its recent date (text: EnchB 1–7).

The NT part of the Chester Beatty papyri, dating back to the first half of the 3rd cent. or earlier, comprises three codices which, when complete, would have covered the whole NT, except the Pastoral and Catholic Epistles. P 45 contains parts of the four Gospels and Ac; P 46, most of the Pauline Epistles with Heb in second place; P 47 part of Apoc.

It is generally admitted from the evidence that, from the beginning of the 3rd cent., the NT was composed essentially of the same books as our present Canon. This does not mean that there was no hesitation, discussion or examination of the claims of the d.c. books; this there was, but the outcome of it all was that the writings, acknowledged as authoritative at the end of the 2nd cent., retained their status. Other writings which were held in high esteem, occasionally quoted as Scripture, and sometimes added to NT MSS, as, for instance, Ep. Clem., Pastor Herm., Ep. Barn., Didache were excluded from the Canon. The pretensions of Marcion and the Edict of Diocletian (A.D. 303), which ordered the destruction of all sacred books, may have had some influence in furthering the final delimitation of the Canon.

The Position of the Deuterocanonical Books— 20a During the 3rd cent. some of the Fathers hesitated to accept some books because of doubts cast upon their authenticity. Some were short and not well known and, when their claims for full canonical status were considered, it is easy to understand that it might not be immediately conceded. Others, like Apoc and Heb, were suspect for more positive reasons. Apoc had been almost universally received from the earliest times but, during the 3rd cent., there was a reaction against it in the East. The occasion of the interruption of the long tradition seems to have been the use made of Apoc to support the Millenarian heresy. It was this that led St Denis of Alexandria to examine again the claims of the book to be the work of an apostle. He does not venture to deny its inspired character or canonicity— tradition was too strong—but the differences of style, thought and language led him to the conclusion that the fourth Gospel and Apoc were not written by the same person. Almost inevitably doubts regarding the authorship resulted in hesitation as to its canonical authority. In the 4th cent. this hesitation is illustrated by Euseb. who strangely classes Apoc both among the 'accepted' books and among the 'spurious' books, whereas in reality he calls in question only its authenticity. His writings are of interest because he actually undertakes to record any tradition which would throw light on the formation of the Canon (HE 3, 3; PG 20, 217) and gives a summary of his results (ibid 3, 25). The books which he here enumerates are grouped into four classes: (1) The accepted writings, viz four Gospels, Ac, fourteen Pauline Epistles, 1 Jn, 1 Pt, and Apoc 'if it seems right'. (2)

20a Disputed books, but accepted by the majority, Jas, Jude, 2 Pt, 2 and 3 Jn. (3) Spurious writings, Ac of Pl, Shepherd Herm., Apoc Pt, Ep. Barn. Didache and Apoc 'if it seems right. This last, as I said, is rejected by some, others place it among the accepted writings'. (4) Various heretical gospels and acts which are to be wholly rejected. In the first two classes, he has our present Canon, indicating, at the same time, the 'disputed' character of the d.c. books.

Apoc was not included among the canonical books by Cyr Jer, the Council of Laodicea, Greg Naz, Amphilochius and others in the E. In the W, however, the authority of Apoc was upheld by Jer, Aug and the other great Latin Fathers. Finally it was accepted in both E and W. Ath mentions it and receives it along with other NT writings as one of the springs of salvation (Ep 39; PG 26, 1438).

b Hesitation in the acceptance of Heb was due to similar circumstances, but in this case, it was in the W and not in the E that it persisted for any length of time. In the W the ep. was not regarded as Pauline, and, in consequence, its canonical character was called in question. In the E it was generally regarded as belonging to Paul, either directly or indirectly. Origen, for instance, suggested that the thought was the Apostle's but the style and composition were that of a disciple reproducing his master's teaching. Others followed this opinion and, though the immediate authorship of the book might be considered uncertain, it retained its traditional place amongst the canonical writings. Ath who lists all our present canonical books, enumerates 14 epistles of Paul, including, of course, Heb. From the 4th cent., though its authorship might still be disputed, its canonical authority was recognized and acknowledged in the W as well as the E. It was included in the lists of the African Councils and that of Innocent I, (cf § 16e). By the end of the 4th cent. the difficulties occasioned by certain books disappeared, and there was no further serious attempt to dispute the claims of the accepted books. The Canon then received was the one finally defined at Trent and is the NT Canon universally accepted today.

21a Criterion of Canonicity—Since the inspiration or divine authorship of any particular work can be made known to us only by the Divine Author himself, any criterion or principle by which we can judge the inspired or canonical character of a book must include a divine witness. Such divine testimony is to be found solely in **tradition coming, in one form or another, from Christ and his Apostles**, preserved in the Church and supported by her authoritative pronouncements. But the question arises: in what precise way did apostolic tradition guide the Church in determining which books to admit to the Canon of the NT?

As noted above (§ 19a), the first Christians gradually built up a collection of books which they regarded as specially sacred and authoritative because they bore the unmistakable stamp or guarantee of apostolic origin. They were at the same time wary of including in the collection any work which was not of proven and undoubted apostolic authority. Starting from this fact, Lagrange and others maintain that from the beginning the chief criterion of canonicity was the apostolic origin of the writings. Since the Apostles were sent to teach in the name of Christ and were his ambassadors, whatever they taught was to be received as the word of Christ, Rm 2:16, 16:25; 2 Cor 4:3. But why limit their teaching to the spoken word? Were they not just as much the ambassadors of Christ when they wrote as when they spoke? In this way whatever was written by an Apostle was inspired and, on this understanding, was accepted by the faithful. The writings of Mark and Luke were received because they **21a** were considered as coming from Peter and Paul respectively (cf Lagrange, *Hist. ancienne du Canon du NT*, 1933; RB 44 (1935), 216—18; Zarb, op cit 518ff). But, it is objected, is it right to make the transient charisma or gift of inspiration coextensive with the permanent office of apostleship, or to elevate Mark and Luke virtually to the status of Apostles? In fact it is possible to commit an Apostle's teaching faithfully to writing and yet not be inspired in the true sense of the word.

Other writers avoid these difficulties by maintaining that the Apostles pointed out the NT scriptural books equivalently or implicitly in the way they treated and regarded them: by setting them apart, by putting them on a level with OT books, by sanctioning their use in public worship. The Apostles, in the various regions where they preached the Gospel, would guide the faithful in their acceptances, and apostolic tradition thus formed would be handed down in the great apostolic sees. This would leave room for the later hesitation, when smaller books, written to more isolated communities, became known, and for variations in the number of accepted books in different communities. (Recently K. Rahner, *Inspiration in the Bible*, E. tr. 1961, has put forward the theory that the inspired nature or divine authorship of certain books was revealed to the Apostolic Church by the very fact that those Books emerged and were accepted, within the Church, as her genuine self-expression in normative written form. Further on this view, which belongs rather to the field of speculative theology, see J. H. Crehan S.J., *A Catholic Dictionary of Theology*, 1, 324.)

An Anglican view suggests that there may have been **b** three main criteria: the authority derived by a book from its author, the authority accorded to a book by the Church at large, and the authority which accrued to a book from its own inherent worth, H. F. D. Sparks, *The Formation of the NT Canon*, 1952, 149—50. There is also the view recently proposed by Kurt Aland, *The Problem of the NT Canon*, 15ff, who thinks that, when discussing the external principles which played a part in the choice of the canonical Scriptures, one can only speak of the 'Prinzip der Prinzipienlosigkeit'— the principle of having no principles. He does add, however, that by A.D. 200 five-sixths of the NT was complete and the norm by which these books were measured was the 'regula fidei' or rule of faith. It was, he says, the influence of the Church that closed the Canon formally at the end of the 4th cent. Since he does not admit an infallible magisterium, he adds that 'our task is the discovery of the correct principles of selection from the formal Canon and of its interpretation with the purpose of achieving a common, actual Canon and a common interpretation of its contents' (p. 31.)

In whatever way the apostolic teaching and guarantee regarding the Canon were conveyed to the Church, it was these which determined the acceptance of the books. The unerring precision of acceptance is remarkably demonstrated in the case of the small and almost private letter to Philemon which won universal recognition, while other writings, Ep. Clem., Ep. Barn., Pastor Herm., were rejected. In this regard, Jerome writes in the Prologue to Phm, 'Those who uphold its genuine character urge that it would never have been received by all the churches throughout the whole world unless it had been believed to be the work of Paul, the Apostle' (PL 26, 637).

Conclusion—If we turn our eyes back from the Canon, **c** as defined in the 16th cent., to the writings of the early Fathers, we find a striking coincidence of range between

21c their quotations and implicit references, and the limits of the present Canon. The reason is not far to seek. The scriptural Canon is a dogma, a revealed truth and as such has its history or development, not in the sense of addition or increase, for this is not possible after the Apostolic age, but in the sense of being more fully, more explicitly understood. Revealed truth is only gradually unfolded, and is not immediately understood in all its aspects, penetrated in all its depths, appreciated in all its richness and beauty, nor foreseen in all its implications. Newman, writing about the books of the NT Canon says: 'The first century acts as a comment on the obscure text of the centuries before it, and brings out a meaning, **21c** which with the help of the comment any candid person sees really to be theirs' (*Development of Christian Doctrine* 4:1, 3).

The truth made known by our Lord and his Apostles was received by the Church, was generally known in the 2nd cent., was made clearer by the opinions and controversies of the 3rd and 4th, and when occasion demanded was made explicit and final by definition. A later age holds more explicitly and, in this sense, more fully, what an earlier age accepted implicitly, but it does not possess a different doctrine or a new revelation.

THE LANGUAGES, TEXTS AND VERSIONS
OF THE BIBLE

RUDOLPH KEELER O. F. M. Cap

(For Greek text of NT, see §§ 601—4)

22a Bibliography: *Languages*: C. F. Jean, 'Inscriptions Semitiques', DBS (1943) 384—417; Vriezen-Hospers, *Palestine Inscriptions*, Leyden, 1951; G. R. Driver, *Semitic Writing*, 1954²; *Aramaic Documents*, Oxford, 1957; H. H. Rowley, *The Aramaic of the OT*, 1929; D. W. Thomas, 'The languages of the OT', in *Record and Revelation*, ed. H. W. Robinson, 1938; H. Birkeland, *The Language of Jesus*, Oslo, 1954; C. F. D. Moule, *The Language of the NT*, 1952; M. Black, *An Aramaic Approach to the Gospels and Acts*, 1967³; F. G. Kenyon, rev. A. W. Adams. *Our Bible and the Ancient MSS*. 1958⁵. *Hebrew OT Text*: C. D. Ginsburg, 'Introd, to the Massoretico-critical Edition of the Hebrew Bible*, 1897; P. Kahle, *Masoreten des Ostens*, Leipzig, 1913; *Masoreten des Westens*, Stuttgart, 1, 1927, 2, 1930; *The Cairo Geniza*, Oxford, 1959²; J. Coppens, *La critique du texte hébreu*, 1950; A. von Gall, *Der hebr. Pentateuch der Samaritaner*, Giessen, 1914—19; D. W. Thomas, 'The Textual Criticism of the OT', in *The OT and Modern Study*, ed. H. H. Rowley, 1951; F. M. Cross, *The Ancient Library of Qumran and Modern Biblical Studies*, New York, 1961; 'The History of the Biblical Text in the Light of Discoveries in the Judean Desert', HTR 57 (1964), 281—99; 'The Contribution of the Qumran Discoveries to the Study of the Biblical Text', IEJ 16 (1966), 81—95; H. M. Orlinsky, 'The Textual Criticism of the OT', in *The Bible and the Ancient Near East*, Garden City, 1961; P. W. Skehan, 'The Qumran Manuscripts and Textual Criticism', in VT Supp. 4 (1957), 148—60; 'The Biblical Scrolls from Qumran and the Text of the OT', in BA 28 (1965), 87—100. E. Würthwein *The Text of the OT*, E.tr. 1957.

b *Versions*. H. Swete-R. Ottley, *An Introd. to the OT in Greek*, 1914³; R. R. Ottley, *A Handbook to the LXX*, 1920; C. H. Dodd, *The Bible and the Greeks*, 1934; R. Devréesse, *Introd. à l'étude des MSS Grecs*, 1954; H.St. J. Thackeray, *Some Aspects of the Greek OT*, 1924; J. W. Wevers, 'Septuaginta Forschungen', ThRS 22 (1954), 85—138, 171—90; P. Katz, 'Septuagint Studies in the Mid-Century', in *The Background to the NT and its Eschatology*, ed. W. D. Davies, 1956; D. Barthélemy, 'Les Devanciers d'Aquila', Leiden, 1963. *Other Versions*: M. McNamara, *The NT and the Palestinian Targum to the Pent.*, Rome, 1966; M. H. Goshen-Gottstein, *Aramaic Bible Versions*, Jerusalem 1963; C. Peters, *Das Diatessaron Tatians*, Rome, 1939; A. Vööbus, *Peschitta und Targumin des Pent.*, Stockholm, 1958; 'Neuentdecktes Textmaterial zur Vetus Syra', in TZ 7 (1951) 30—38; 'Studies in the History of the Gospel Text in Syriac', in CSCO 128 (1951); G. Zuntz, *The Ancestry of the Harkleian NT*, London, 1945; S. Lyonnet, *Les Origines de la Version Arménienne et le Diatessaron*, Rome, 1956; W. Till, 'Coptic Biblical Fragments in the John Rylands Library', in BJRL 34 (1952) 432—58; W. S. Friedrichsen, *The Gothic Version of the Gospels, a Study of its style and textual history*, Oxford, 1926; F. C. Burkitt, *The Old Latin and the Itala*, Cambridge, 1896; B. Botte, *Versions Latines* **22b** *antérieures á St Jerome*, DBS Supp. 5 (1952) 334—47; A. Cordoliani, 'Le Texte de la Bible en Irlande du Ve au IXe siècle', in RB 57 (1950) 1—38; B. M. Metzger, 'Survey of Recent Research on the Ancient Versions of the NT', in NTS 2 (1955), 1—16. S. Jellicoe, *The Septuagint and Modern Study*, Oxford, 1968.

Languages of the Bible—The p.c. books of the OT, i.e. **c** those contained in the Heb. Bible, are all written in Heb. except parts of Dn (2:4*b*—7:28) and Ez (4:8—6:18; 7:12—26), one verse of Jer (10:11, most probably a later insertion) and two words in Gn (at 31:47), which are written in Aram. Bar, Jdt, Tb, 1 Mc and the d.c. parts of Dn and Est are extant only in a Gr. version. Sir. was known only in a Gr. version until the end of last century, when about two thirds of the Heb. text were discovered in the now famous Geniza (i.e. a room in a synagogue where worn-out copies of sacred books are kept) of Old Cairo. More recently fragments of this text have been found at Qumran, as have also fragments of Tb in Heb. and Aram. 2 Mc, Wis and all the books of the NT were composed in Gr. Heb., Aram. and Gr. are thus the languages of the Bible.

Semitic Languages—The chief characteristics of this **d** linguistic family are the following. The roots or ground forms from which the words are derived are usually composed of three consonants, though there are indications of biliteral roots in the earliest period. Vowels do not form part of the roots but merely help to express various modifications of the radical sense. They are thus of much less importance than in Aryan languages and are usually not expressed in alphabetical writing since a reader, familiar with the structure of the language, can supply them from the context. The simple form of the verb is modified by added letters, lengthened vowels and reduplicated radicals to express intensive, causative, reciprocal and reflexive action. The passive is distinguished from the active by a change of vowels. Person and number are indicated by prefixes and affixes derived from the corresponding personal pronouns. Abbreviated forms of these pronouns are also affixed to verbs and nouns when governed by them. The Semitic verb has no tenses in our sense of the word but modes of action. The perfect is the mode of completed, the imperfect of incompleted action, but both may express past, present and future time according to the context. The structure of the various nominal forms is in general similar to that of the verbal forms. Through the loss of short final vowels the cases of the nouns and the moods of the verbs, preserved in literary Arabic, have largely disappeared in Heb. and Aram. In syntax the relation between the various parts of the sentence and in particular the exact character of dependent clauses are not as definitely expressed as in Aryan languages and must often be determined from the context. In general

22d Semitic languages are defective in indicating delicate shades of meaning and are better adapted to narrative and poetry than to philosophical or scientific discussion. Finally they have some guttural sounds not easily pronounced by non-Semites. When the Greeks borrowed the Phoenician alphabet they used these unfamiliar consonants to express vowels.

e The **Semitic languages are usually divided** into South-Semitic—Arabic, Ethiopic and Sabaean; East-Semitic—Assyrian and Babylonian; and N-W-Semitic—Aramaic, Ugaritic, Canaanite, Phoenician, Hebrew and Moabite. Arabic is the most faithful to the ancient form of the original, conjectural, proto-Semitic tongue, has an extensive literature and is still spoken in many parts of the E. Assyro-Babylonian lost the peculiar Semitic guttural sounds when adopted by non-Semites, but like Babylonian civilization, was widely diffused in ancient times and appears as the diplomatic language of the Near E in the 14th cent. B.C. Canaanite and Aram., as the languages of neighbouring regions, Canaan and the Syrian hinterland, are most closely allied. Trade and commerce played a large part in the later diffusion of the languages; the Phoenician sea-traders spread their language around the Mediterranean seaboard after 1200 B.C., and the Aramean land-traders made their language international throughout the Near E in the Persian period. Syr. and the language spoken by Our Lord and the Apostles are respectively E and W dialects of Aram.

f **Hebrew**—The name is derived, through the Latin Hebraeus, Gr. *Hebraios*, from the Aram. *ebrāyā*, and primarily designates not the land but the people. Similarly, *'hebraisti'*, lit 'in Heb.', in the NT usually indicates not Heb. but Aram., the language then spoken by the Hebrew people. In the OT the language of the Hebrews is called 'the lip of Canaan' (Is 19:18) and *yehûdît* or Jewish (2 (4) Kgs 18.26, 28; Neh 13:24). That Heb. is a Canaanite language may also be inferred from the regular use of *yâm*, lit 'sea', for W and *negeb*, lit 'arid land', for S; Canaan is peculiar in having both desert for its S and sea for its W boundary. The Hebrews therefore when they settled in Canaan adopted the language of the country, to which however their ancestral language was closely akin.

g For the study of the Heb. language and script we have besides the biblical texts a number of inscriptions in Heb. and other Canaanite dialects. The earliest Heb. inscription is the agricultural **calendar of Gezer**, now dated about the 10th cent. B.C. It briefly enumerates the field labours associated with the different months of the year. Next come the 75 inscribed **ostraca** or potsherds, recording deliveries of oil and wine from various persons and places to **the royal palace of Samaria** in the late 9th cent. B.C. **The Siloam inscription** commemorates the building of a tunnel at Jerusalem in the reign of Hezekiah, by which the waters of its only spring, Gihon, were conveyed into the city. A palimpsest found at Murabba'at and dating from the same period—it is the oldest known papyrus—gives a list of four personal names. The numerous but laconic inscriptions on jar-handles found in various cities of S Palestine and most of the inscribed seals, whose owners can sometimes be identified with biblical personages, belong to the late monarchical period. Lastly the 18 inscribed ostraca discovered at Tell ed-Duweir and commonly known as the **Letters of Lachish** were written shortly before the exile. These letters are invaluable for the information they give on the character of popular literary composition in the late pre-exilic period.

h Ancient inscriptions in other Canaanite dialects begin with the pictographs on copper, dating from the 3rd **22h** millennium and found at Byblos on the Syrian coast. Next come the texts of the library discovered in 1929 at **Ras Shamra (Ugarit)** further to the north on the same coast. They are dated c. 1400 B.C. and are particularly important for their number and religious character. The Canaanite glosses of the **Tell el-Amarna** tablets belong to the 14th cent. B.C. The earliest text in the linear Phoenician script, from which the Greek and our own are ultimately derived, is the sepulchral inscription of **Ahiram of Byblos**, probably from the 10th cent. B.C. The Phoenician alphabet, here fully developed, is used in all the Heb. inscriptions mentioned above. Phoenician inscriptions are very numerous, cover a wide area and extend down to the 2nd cent. A.D. They consist chiefly of dedications and memorials on tombs, are brief in content, and rarely antedate the Persian period. More closely akin to Heb. is the long inscription of Mesha (c. 840 B.C.) discovered at Dibon in northern Moab, cf § 81*l*.

Pre-exilic and Post-exilic Hebrew. Though every **i** language evolves in the course of centuries, there is little trace of evolution in biblical pre-exilic Heb. The canticle of Deborah alone informs us of dialectical peculiarities in the language of the N tribes. The Shibboleth episode (Jg 12:5, 6) manifests diversity of pronunciation. Archaisms like *hay^etô* (Gn 1:25 etc) are rare and not easily explained. In general the early books of the Bible exhibit the same stage of the language as the Lachish letters. It does not follow from this that all these books are of late pre-exilic origin. Writing was in common use among the Hebrews at a much earlier period, and we have no reason to reject the tradition that even before the occupation of Canaan laws and historical records were written down (cf Ex 17:14; 34:28). The copy of the Law discovered accidentally in the reign of Josiah was presumably of earlier origin. Pre-exilic historical books attest the use of earlier sources (e.g. 'the book of the acts of Solomon', 1 (3) Kgs 11:41). The kings had their scribes (2 Sm 8:17; 20:25 etc). Hezekiah collected the Proverbs of Solomon. Isaiah and Jeremiah were ordered to write some at least of their prophecies. The conclusion to be drawn from the linguistic uniformity of earlier and later texts is therefore that the language of the earlier writings was modernized in the later period.

The **post-exilic Hebrew writers** are markedly in- **j** ferior in literary genius to their pre-exilic predecessors. There is a corresponding deterioration in the language which manifests itself principally in two ways. The niceties of Heb. idiom are often neglected and Aram. forms of expression are adopted into the language. Some examples will show the character of these innovations. The first is exemplified by abbreviations such as not repeating a preposition before a noun in apposition with its object or a governing noun before several succeeding genitives; double plurals in genitival combinations like 'men of names' for 'men of name'; use of the article as a relative; frequent substitution of the infinitive absolute for a finite verb. The second is illustrated by new forms of the infinitive with *m* prefixed, use of *hēn* 'behold' for *'im* 'if', anticipation of noun object by a pronominal suffix, prefixion of *l* to noun object when determined. The chief prose exponent of post-exilic Hebrew is the author of Chronicles, Ezra and Nehemiah.

Transition from Hebrew to Aramaic—It is clear from **k** 2 (4) Kgs 18:26 that the common people of Jerusalem did not understand Aram. in 701 B.C. That the change of language was made in Palestine between this period and the exile is excluded by the testimony of the Lachish letters written in Heb. It was most probably during the

22k exile when the Jews came into close contact with Aramaic-speaking peoples in S Babylonia that they began to speak that tongue; this had its effect on their own speech. When they returned to Palestine they found Aram. in possession and had to continue their bilingualism. Heb. however was still 'the language of Judah' in the 3rd cent. B.C. (2 Chr 32:18) though already there were some who could not speak it (Neh 13:22). The Aramaisms of the Chronicler and the use of Aram. in Ez not only in official documents but also in historical narrative bear witness to the pressure exerted by that tongue on Heb. speakers in the same period. Yet, at least among some sections of the middle classes of Judaea, Heb. seems to have continued to be a living language down to Christian times. Only after A.D. 135 and the almost complete depopulation of Judaea did it cease to be used colloquially, although it was preserved in rabbinic circles (cf J. T. Milik, TYD, 1959, 130–1).

l **Aramaic**—the simplest in syntactical structure of all the Semitic tongues, takes its name like Heb. from the people who spoke it, the Aramaeans. They were nomads who spread from Arabia into Mesopotamia and thence crossing the Euphrates founded a number of city-states in the region extending from Armenia in the North to Transjordania in the south. Thus controlling the international highway of the Near East, for which empires had fought at an earlier period, they exercised a preponderating influence in international commerce in the early first millennium B.C. It is owing to this fact and the adventurous spirit of the Aramaean traders that Aram. became so widely diffused as the language of trade and commerce.

m Our knowledge of **ancient Aram.** is derived from texts which range in time from the 8th cent. B.C. to well into the Christian era, and in space over all the countries of the Near East from Taxila on the Hydaspes to Elephantine on the Nile. The earliest and most important inscriptions discovered at **Zingirli** and in the neighbourhood of Aleppo in N Syria belong to the 8th cent. B.C. Then too, begin the Aram. inscriptions on weights and Aram. endorsements on Assyrian contracts. It was, however, in the Persian period that the language became most widely diffused, as the texts discovered in Iran, Mesopotamia, Asia Minor, Syria, Arabia and Egypt abundantly attest. The Aram. documents of Ez and the narratives of Dn belong to this period. For their better understanding and the solution of the vexed question of their date, the considerable number of Aram. papyri and ostraca discovered at the turn of the century at **Elephantine** are particularly important. These are dated in the 5th cent. B.C. The Aram. texts of the Bible, if authentic, must exhibit, at least in their original form, the same stage of linguistic development.

n Languages develop in two ways, structurally and phonetically. Structural development is exhibited by the disappearance of old and the appearance of new forms in the structure of the language. As these forms are usually too firmly fixed to be much affected by textual transmission, the structural stage of a language is easily discerned. Phonetic development appears in sound changes and assimilation of sounds originally distinguished. When our knowledge of the pronunciation of a language is derived from written texts, its phonetic stage is often difficult to determine. Writing is orthographical as well as phonetic, it sometimes fails to register sound changes, as in modern English and French, where spelling and pronunciation differ widely. There is a further difficulty in the case **o** of biblical texts frequently copied. The original writing may have been modernized and systematized. We may conclude therefore that structural forms rather than

alterations of letters, which may or may not attest phonetic **22o** development and in some cases can be definitely attributed to later copyists, are the best means of determining the original character of biblical Aram. Of these the causative forms of verbs, the prefix of the reflexive forms, the inner passives and the remains of the jussive attest a stage of the language at least as ancient as that of the Elephantine papyri. For the authenticity of the Ez documents it is important to note that they maintain the ancient final *m* of the 2 and 3 pl. pronominal suffixes. The Ez narrative and Dn have the later final *n*, while the Elephantine papyri have both forms. The systematic use of *d* in biblical Aram. to represent an ancient Z has been interpreted as a sound change completed in the 3rd cent. B.C. The sound in question, however, an aspirated *d*, which has no equivalent in the Phoenician alphabet, is expressed by *d* as well as Z in Assyria in the 8th cent. The omission or mode of expression of a final *a* is also a matter of orthography. These examples show that alterations of letters are less reliable indications of the date of biblical Aram. than structural forms, even in the very improbable hypothesis that the biblical texts, repeatedly copied, are exact reproductions of the original.

Biblical Greek—The Greek of the original texts and **23a** of the LXX version (see § 26*b*) of the Bible, recognized in the Renaissance period as a debased form of classical Gr., could not be satisfactorily explained as long as it remained an isolated phenomenon. The study of the numerous Gr. papyri discovered in Egypt during the last cent. has finally revealed to us its origin and character. It is not a biblical or Jewish or Alexandrian dialect of Gr. but the Koine or common Gr. which supplanted the classical form of the language and became international in the Hellenistic period inaugurated by the African and Asiatic conquests of Alexander the Great. The zeal of **b** Greek rulers for the hellenization of their eastern subjects and still more the exigencies of trade and commerce account for its world-wide diffusion. Attic Gr. had lost its purity even in Greece itself in the 4th cent. B.C. and was in any case, in its classical form, ill adapted to popular and international use. The Koine is the current Attic Gr. modified and accommodated to a new and wider sphere of utility. It was naturally used by the sacred writers as the language understood by their contemporaries, providentially designed and admirably adapted for the preaching of the Gospel to all nations.

The Koine was not merely a spoken language. It was **c** taught in the schools and was the ordinary medium of literary expression. It thus preserved a general uniformity despite the variations resulting from the nationality or lack of education of the writer and the colloquial or literary character of his composition. It differed from Attic Gr. mainly in aiming at a simpler and easier but at the same time clearer and more vigorous mode of expression. The vocabulary is less rich but more varied in its origin. In phonetics there is a tendency to reduce diphthongs to simple vowels. Declensions and conjugations are simplified and occasionally assimilated by analogy. There is a preference for longer and composite rather than shorter and simpler words. Co-ordination of dependent clauses is also preferred to subordination and direct speech to indirect. Prepositions are more frequently used not only in composition with verbs but also to strengthen the case endings of nouns and even pleonastically with adverbs. Pleonasm also appears in an excessive repetition of personal pronouns. The vocative is often accompanied by the article for greater emphasis. The infinitive is used loosely with or without the article in final, consecutive or explanatory clauses, but is preferably replaced on the

23c other hand by a *hoti* clause after verbs of saying and perceiving. The article is used more frequently and before clauses as well as nouns. Adjectives are often replaced by substantives in the genitive. The popular character of the Koine is manifested by sense construction, anacolutha and other grammatical irregularities.

d The Gr. of the Bible is distinguished from that of profane literature by the presence of semitisms, both hebraisms and aramaisms. The LXX interpreters of a Heb. and sacred text reproduced in Gr. some of the modes of expression and phraseology of the original Heb. These hebraisms vary in number according to the freedom or literalness of the different translators. They appear also in the NT owing to the influence exerted on the sacred writers by the language of the LXX which they consciously or unconsciously imitated. The aramaisms of the NT are explained by the fact that Aram. was either the native language of the inspired writers or the language of sources which they used.

e The discovery in the Egyptian papyri of nearly all the words previously considered peculiar to biblical Gr. established the **Koine origin of the NT vocabulary**. The semitisms discovered in Egyptian Gr. have been similarly interpreted as Koine idioms by many scholars. It should be noted, however, that semitisms in the Bible may appear as coptisms in the papyri. Coptic has many non-Gr. idioms in common with Heb. and Aram. Coptic writers would naturally reproduce their native modes of thought in their new medium of expression.

24a **The Hebrew Text of the OT**—Under this heading the Aram. texts are implicitly included. The d.c. parts (see § 13*d*) of the OT on the other hand, whether written originally in Gr. or only extant in a Gr. version, belong to the history of the LXX. By way of introduction to the history of the text some account must be given of the medium by which it was transmitted.

b **Papyrus** was the ordinary material used for writing in Palestine in biblical times. We learn from the narrative of Wen-Amon that it was imported in large quantities from Egypt to Canaan in the 11th cent. B.C. Its rapid disintegration in a damp climate explains why so few literary remains and biblical texts have been discovered in Palestine. It was too fragile also to be a suitable material for Babylonian script, for which fine clay, not easily procurable in Palestine, was required. We may conclude therefore that the sacred text was not originally written in cuneiform characters but in alphabetic script, especially since the inscription of Ahiram, discovered at Byblos in 1923, has shown that the Phoenician alphabet was fully developed by about 1,000 B.C. From the use of the **Phoenician script** in **ancient Heb. inscriptions** we may infer that it was the regular medium for the transmission of the Heb. text of the OT. This script, otherwise known as **palaeo-Hebrew**, is found at Qumran as an archaistic survival from the book hand of Israelite times. This palaeo-Hebrew script is found also in the Sam. Pent. text, which separated from the main stream of Jewish tradition in Hasmonean times. The **Aram. or 'square' script**, common throughout the Near E in trade until the late Persian period, also came into use for the biblical texts about the 3rd cent. B.C., and was the basis for the script used by the later rabbis and the Massoretes.

c The form of the book in OT times was the **roll or volume** (cf Jer 36). A long strip of papyrus was attached at one end to a support round which it was rolled. The writing was usually only on the inner side of the papyrus and began at the further end so that the volume would be unrolled as it was read. Papyrus was the more sophisticated material but there is no doubt that in Syria and Palestine *leather* was regularly used. The Talmud require- **24c** ment that all copies of the Law should be written on skins was no doubt only confirming the existing and traditional practice. At Qumran, both skins and papyrus have been found, but mostly skins. 'The scrolls', says Yigael Yadin, 'are all of animal hide and are written on the hairy side' (*The Message of the Scrolls*, 78). The codex form of the book was later admitted by the Jews for private copies but not for use in the synagogue.

The Phoenicians like the Greeks usually failed to **d** indicate the separation of words in their inscriptions. The Hebrews and Arameans on the other hand marked the end of each word by a point, like the Latins, in their inscriptions and by a short interval in the papyri. Errors in the division of words are of comparatively rare occurrence in the Heb. text. Moreover the earliest specimens of the square script exhibit the peculiar final forms of the Heb. letters. We may conclude, therefore, that the separate words were indicated, though perhaps not very clearly at times, certainly in the later and probably in the earlier period. Punctuation marks and vowel points are of later Massoretic origin (see § 25*c*).

History of the Hebrew text—Our present Heb. text **e** undoubtedly contains many corruptions of various kinds: omissions attested by the LXX, incorrect readings, alterations of numbers and dates, errors in orthography and lexicography, interpolated glosses and marginal notes. There are many indications on the other hand that this text has remained practically unchanged from c. A.D. 100 to the present day (see § 25*a*). The divergencies from the archetype belong therefore, for the most part, to the period of its gradual formation. The problem had been enormously complicated previous to the discovery of the DSS by the fact that with the sole exception of the Nash papyrus, containing the Decalogue and the Shema (Dt 6:4–6), and dated to the Maccabean period, all biblical Heb. MSS dated from the 10th cent. A.D. or later.

Period of formation—The evidence had always sug- **f** gested that before the standardization which began to take place about A.D. 100 there had been a great variety in the Heb. text—a variety which is reflected not only in the comparison of one quotation with another in the Heb. Bible itself but also in the text of the Sam Pent and the LXX. The Sam Pent, discovered in the 17th cent. A.D., was extant in some MSS dating back to the 7th cent. A.D., while the LXX existed mainly in the great 4th cent. uncials, as well as in some earlier fragments (cf §§ 26*a*; 26*g*); however, the authority of these texts compared with the MT was by no means settled. The rigid scribal practices for the copying of the HT made possible a high degree of fidelity to an early archetype even in late MSS; and the geniza practice, whereby old MSS were disposed of, often by burying, as soon as they had been copied out afresh, explains the paucity of the MSS until a comparatively later date. Now, however, the recent discoveries at Qumran of at least some part of every book of the Heb. canon, with the sole exception of Est and also of fragments of Sir, Tob and of the LXX of Ex, Lev and Num, all of which predate A.D. 68 at the latest and some of which are considerably earlier; and at Murabba'at of 2nd cent. A.D. materials, have given us a much clearer insight into the early history of the HT, as well as its relation to the LXX and the place of the Sam Pent. There can no longer be question of setting one text against the other and arguing as to which is superior; now each can be seen to take its place in a continuous history of development. The characteristically expansionist Palestinian text-type, where everything prophesied must be said to have been fulfilled, and hitherto known mainly from the Sam Pent,

24f is found at Qumran in 4QpaleoEx^m. This expansionist tendency, a feature of Palestinian editorial technique, and also observable in the 'proto-Lucianic' LXX recension (cf § 26d) and such MSS as 4Q Sam^{abc} have led F. M. Cross to posit a non-Palestinian point of origin for the MT of Sam and the Pent, as these texts are concise and unexpanded. He suggests Babylon as being the most likely place for this tradition. Thus the MT for these books represents a reaction from the normal Palestinian style and the reasons why this type of text became the standard form still remain mysterious. However the other books of the MT, as far as the evidence will take us, seem to show something of this expansionist harmonizing tendency, for example in the Isaiah scroll (1QIs^a) and in the book of Jer, where the shorter text of the LXX is also found in a Heb. MS (4QJer^b) at Qumran, and where the MT seems to be an expanded edition of this shorter text. This editorial activity differs from that of the scribes after standardization, for they were concerned with maintaining a scrupulous fidelity to the consonantal text; the earlier editors however regarded the text as sacred but not inviolate; as capable of internal expansion and fuller explanation.

g The **comparison of the MT with the LXX** (250—c. 100 B.C.), and the relationship between them can now be put in a much clearer light. While the individual books of the LXX must always be treated and evaluated separately, the results of this comparison have enabled scholars to reinforce conclusions that could only be held very tentatively prior to the Qumran and other discoveries. In particular, the evidence for different Hebrew recensions, hinted at by the existing LXX MSS, has been supported by the discoveries of similar reworked Heb. texts, and the new insights thus gained into the various sources of the different Gr. translations make it possible to control much more adequately the varied Gr. evidence for the individual books. No conclusions can be drawn as to the superiority or otherwise of the LXX as a whole, nor can it be considered as a merely popular translation compared to the MT, but each part of the evidence must be seen as fitting into some part of a continuous history of development. Thus there are in the LXX several books (Wis and 2 Mc) composed in Gr., while others, such as Dn and Est, have additions not in the MT. In Prv and Sir we have generally expanded texts in all MSS for the former and some for the latter, and for Sir this recension dates at least to the 1st Christian cent., as can be shown by the quotation of Sir 12:1 in the *Didache* (1:6). The same dating is also true for the reworking of the 1st 9chh of Prv, as Prv 2:21 in this recension is quoted in the works of Clem Rom (1 Clem. 14:4).

25a Standardization—The Massoretic Text—Versions made from the Heb. in the 2nd cent. A.D. and later, exhibit a remarkable agreement with MT against the LXX. This has been the chief reason for assigning the unification of the HT to c. 100 A.D. It is generally thought to be the work of the Hebrew Academy in Palestine, which was transferred to Jamnia after the fall of Jerusalem and thence later to Tiberias. A notice in the Talmud tells us that the single standard text was made by Majority vote from three different texts which had **b** been saved from the Temple. All texts differing from this standard text were officially banned. The virtual identity of the Isaian text referred to above (as also in other fragments from Qumran Cave 4) shows however that the text was already substantially in existence in pre-Christian times. It has also been suggested that in deciding which text was to be accepted as authoritative more weight was likely to be given to the authority of

particular scribes (e.g. Aqiba, 2nd cent.) than to the **25b** number of MSS.

The Heb. text received a further development after **c** its unification from the critical studies of the **Scribes (1st-6th cent.)** and the **Massoretes (6th-10th cent.).** The Scribes divided the text into vv, indicated the places where words should be altered or omitted or supplied by the reader, and marked with points doubtful or spurious readings. They are also supposed to have altered slightly some expressions which sounded irreverent. The euphemistic substitution of bless (God) for curse (God) may be cited as an instance. The Massoretes supplied the vowel points and the accents by which the pronunciation, the tone and the interconnection of the words were indicated. These innovations, at first very rudimentary in form, were most probably introduced in the 7th cent., and only in private copies of the text. It was not until c. 900 that the Massoretic school at Tiberias perfected the system which was later to be accepted by all. Massora **d** means tradition. The Massoretes also committed to writing traditions relating to the sacred text and handed down orally from the period of the Scribes. The Massora or textual tradition was usually written either on the lateral margins (*massora parva*) or at the top and bottom of the page (*massora magna*), or at the end of the papyrus roll (*massora finalis*). Such critical indications as the number of times a rare word occurred in the Bible, variations in the spelling of certain words, alterations of the written word to be made by the reader, were noted briefly in the *parva* but more fully in the *massora magna*. The *massora finalis* gave the number of vv in the different books or parts of books and other minute computations as well as various notes on peculiar words and expressions. The **e** Massoretic schools of Palestine and Babylonia differed not only in their method of expressing the vowels but also to a less extent in the traditions which they recorded. In Palestine itself the rival schools of Ben Asher and Ben Naphtali flourished in the 10th cent. Later, however, the Tiberian system was generally adopted and the Massora of Ben Asher prevailed over that of his rival. The present division of the text into chh is of Christian origin. It was first introduced in the Latin Vg in the 13th cent. to facilitate references and later adopted by the Jews in private but not in liturgical copies of the sacred text.

Until the discoveries of the Cairo Geniza, already **f** referred to, the Nash papyrus and the DSS, **the earliest known MSS of the Heb. Bible** belonged to the 10th cent. A.D. These medieval MSS were first collected in the works of B. Kennicott (Oxford, 1776—80) and G. de Rossi (Parma, 1784—88) based on the text of Jacob ben Chayim (Venice, 1525), which had become the *textus receptus*. Ginsburg also collected more than 70 MSS and 19 printed editions over the first quarter of this century. The main printed editions of the present day are the 3rd edition of Kittel's *Biblia Hebraica* (Stuttgart, 1937), based on the Leningrad MS B 19^A, a ben Asher text dated A.D. 1008; and the British and Foreign Bible Society's 1958 edition by N. H. Snaith. *Biblia Hebraica* has been widely criticized for its textual apparatus, but the text itself reproduces the ben Asher MT well. The Hebrew University in Jerusalem is preparing an edition based on the extant portions of the ben Asher Aleppo codex; the critical apparatus is well presented and extensive, as the preparatory publication of several chapters of Is has shown.

In the textual criticism of the OT, it must be recognized **g** that *Biblia Hebraica* cannot be used indiscriminately in its conjectural emendations and Greek evidence, although a new edition (now in preparation), may help to remove

25g many of these objections. The critical authenticity, or conformity of the MT with the originals may be inferred from its conformity with the ancient versions and from the scrupulous care of its custodians to preserve intact the sacred text. This authenticity is only substantial and does not exclude various corruptions which may often be corrected with the aid of the ancient versions more especially the LXX, taking into account the reservations noted above (cf § 24*g*). In such cases the authenticity of the rendering and its derivation from a different Heb. text must be proved. Proof has in some cases now been provided by the DSS. Corruptions which occurred before any versions were made may also be corrected by conjectural emendation. These corrections presuppose grave doubt about the genuineness of the text, and may only be admitted when the recognized rules for textual emendation have been fully observed.

26a **Versions of the OT—The Septuagint**—The ancient versions of the Bible give us valuable information about the original text and its traditional interpretation. Of these the Gr. version of the OT made at Alexandria and known as the Septuagint is by far the most important. It preserved for us the inspired d.c. parts of the OT, was generally used in preference to the Heb. text by the NT writers in their scriptural citations and was the Vg of the E and W Church for several centuries until it was superseded among the Latins by the Vg of St Jerome. The method of its transmission as regards writing, book-form etc was similar to that of the NT text with which it is sometimes associated in the codices. The uncials and minuscules in which it is contained are 1534 in number but rarely exhibit the whole OT. The earliest and most important uncials are described below (cf § 26*g*). Still earlier fragments of the LXX have been discovered in Egypt, of which the Chester Beatty papyri, Vols IV–VII of Kenyon's edition, are particularly important. Two short fragments of Dt, PRG 458, published by C. H. Roberts at the Manchester University Press in 1936, and P. Fouad 266, reproduced and studied by W. G. Waddell in JTS 45 (1944), 158 61, may also be mentioned as our oldest Gr. biblical texts belonging to the Maccabean period, together with those found at Qumran and mentioned above.

b **Origin and Character of the LXX**—The Gr. letter of Aristeas to Philocrates, composed at the latest in the 2nd cent. B.C., informs us that Ptolemy II Philadelphos (285–246), a great bibliophile, had the Heb. Torah translated into Gr for his famous library by 72 Hebrew scholars summoned from Jerusalem and domiciled in the island of Pharos where they completed the version of the Pent in 72 days. The segregation of the translators in different cells and the marvellous agreement of their different versions is a further embellishment of Philo. This tradition gave rise to the name 'Septuagint' (seventy), and the later assumption that the whole of the OT was then translated, caused this name to be given to the Gr. translation as a whole. But the letter is certainly a literary fiction. In fact the LXX was produced between 250 B.C. (Pent) and the 1st cent. B.C. by a number of translators who differed widely. The need felt by the Alexandrian Jews for a Gr. version is the most probable explanation of its origin and suggests also that the other sacred books were translated without much delay. The Prologue of Sir, written in 132 B.C., records the translations into Gr. of the Law, the Prophets and the 'rest of the books' as an accomplished fact. That the work was protracted over a considerable period may be concluded from the large number and different qualifications of the translators, revealed by internal evidence. It is generally supposed that the translators used texts written **26b** in Heb. characters. The ancient theory of Tychsen, more recently revived by Wutz, that the texts had been previously transliterated from Heb. into Gr. is unsupported by solid argument and generally rejected.

The **character of the translation** varies with the **c** translators. It is literal in Song, Ecc, Pss and the Prophets (except Dn); faithful in the Pent and the historical books; free in Jb, Prv, Dn and Est. The Gr. is good in the original works Wis and 2 Mc, and in Jb and Prv, fair in Pent, Is and 1 Mc, but poor elsewhere. The sense of the Heb. text is best indicated in Pent, least well in Is, Minor Prophets, Jb and Prv. Important variations from the MT due to the translators and to be distinguished from those already indicated as due to a different Heb. text, are the following: frequent omissions in Jb amounting to a sixth of the text; some additions and amplifications in Prv; a rendering of Dn so different from the original that it was rejected in the 3rd or 4th cent. A.D. and replaced by the version of Theodotion (see § 26*i*).

In view of the wide divergencies both of text and **d** style, the theory had been put forward by **P. Kahle** that the **LXX was never a pre-Christian collection of translations from Hebrew originals. It started**, he suggests, **as a Gr. Targum**, oral at first then written for synagogue use. Then the Pent was translated officially in Alexandria. That is the LXX properly so called. The rest of the Bible was translated by different hands at different times, and it was not till the 4th cent. A.D. when the Christian church selected and standardized this variety of translations that the LXX as we know it came into being. Kahle's position, disputed particularly by P. Katz and H. M. Orlinsky, was based on very real difficulties in the textual evidence, especially the variant readings in Philo, Josephus and certain of the Fathers. However, the work of **D. Barthélemy** on the Gr. minor Prophets scroll from the Wadi Khabra, dated to the 2nd half of the 1st Christian cent., has finally put paid to this theory of LXX origins. Barthélemy has shown that this scroll is a reworked form of the LXX minor Prophets, using accepted rabbinic hermeneutical practices in order to bring the text more into line with the Heb. texts then extant in Palestine. This recension Barthélemy **e** calls 'kaige' or 'proto-Theodotionic', and he shows that it is also found in the minor Prophets citations of Justin Martyr, as well as in parts of Sam-Kgs in Cod B and most printed editions, namely 2 Sam 11:4–1 Kgs 2:11 and 1 Kgs 22-2 Kgs. Research into the text of Sam-Kgs by F. M. Cross has also led him to posit the existence of an earlier 'proto-Lucianic' recension in the Pent and Sam. It has always been known that the 'Lucianic' recension predates Lucian of Antioch (d. 312), as it is found in the quotations of Josephus. Cross says that this is a reworking of a still older and therefore 'proto-Lucianic' recension, once again in order to bring it into line with the Heb. texts of Sam then extant in Palestine. This 'proto-Lucianic' recension is found in the MSS group b o c$_2$ e$_2$, Josephus, and the 6th column of the Hexapla, and was carried out in the 2nd/1st cents. B.C. Thus for the books of Sam-Kgs we have a fairly clear process of development—the earliest Alexandrian rendering, or 'Old Gr.', in the non-'kaige' parts of Cod B; then a gradual process of revision to fit the Palestinian Heb. texts in the 'proto-Lucianic' and 'kaige' recensions. Thus the divergencies in the LXX are probably to be explained by **different recensions** rather than by a variety of isolated translations.

Writing and Writing materials of LXX—It was **f**

26f usually written on papyrus until the 4th cent. A.D. when parchment was introduced (see § 601*f*), the writing used was uncial (see § 602*b*), the cursive script appeared about the 9th cent. As parchment was costly, old MSS were often rubbed out and used again. These are called palimpsests. Often the older and usually more valuable text is still visible under the later writing.

g **The MSS of the LXX**—Those from which our direct knowledge of the text is derived are estimated at about 15 uncials. 1560 minuscules and 200 papyri (see § 26*a*). Most of these are incomplete or fragmentary. Individual codices in each of these three classes are generally indicated by arabic numerals according to a system introduced by C. R. Gregory, but preceded by *p* when designating papyri. The earlier method of indicating the oldest uncials by Latin and Greek capitals is however generally retained. Both S and the Heb. *aleph* are used for the Cod Sinaiticus. The oldest and most important codices are the following: B—Vaticanus, 4th cent., probably of Egyptian origin, contains the whole Bible from Gn 46:28 to Hb 9:14; S—Sinaiticus. 4th/5th cent., discovered in the monastery of St Catherine on Mt Sinai, and now in the British Museum, contains the whole Bible with many OT omissions; A—Alexandrinus, 5th cent., belonged to the Patriarch of Alexandria, now in the British Museum, contains the whole Bible with occasional omissions; C—Codex Ephraemi rescriptus, 5th cent., palimpsest now in the Paris National Library, contains only fragments of the OT but nearly all the NT; G— Colbertino-Sarravianus, 5th cent., contains Gn 31:53 to Jg 21:12, Hexaplaric text (see § 26*k*) with many of the original diacritical signs, 130 leaves at Leyden, 22 at Paris and 1 at Leningrad; Q—Marchalianus, 6th cent., in the Vatican library, contains all the Prophets, Hesychian text (see § 26*n*) but with marginal readings from the Hexapla. Besides the Chester Beatty papyri already referred to (§ 26*a*), we now have a number of fragmentary MSS from Qumran, as has been noted above.

h **Later Greek versions**—For the better understanding of the history of the LXX some account must be given here of the Gr. versions made from the Heb. text in the 2nd cent. A.D. Disputes between Jews and Christians and the existence of a standard Heb. text emphasized the differences between the text recognized by the Jews and the versions to which the Christians appealed. The hellenistic Jews in particular needed a Gr. version of their official text for use in their synagogues and for polemical purposes. Three Gr. versions of the whole Heb. Bible were thus made by Jewish proselytes:

i Theodotion, Aquila, and Symmachus. *Theodotion* was until recently thought to be a late 2nd cent. Jewish convert, but it is now clear that his version precedes and in a sense prepares for that of Aquila. It was made in Palestine, and shows traces of rigidity and attention to minor Heb. particles. *Aquila* (c. A.D. 130) is even more rigid, and reproduces consistently words from the same Heb. stem with words derived from the same Gr. stem, even if these have to be invented; also every individual Heb. particle is given some Gr. equivalent, even if this is against Gr. usage. Patristic quotations, Hexaplaric fragments and palimpsests from the Cairo Geniza are the chief sources of our knowledge of the text, although the version of Eccl transmitted with the LXX bears many signs of his techniques, and may be an early piece of his work. *Symmachus* (c. 180) sought to express the sense of the Heb. exactly and in much better Gr. than his predecessors; his version was highly esteemed by Jerome. This is the least known of the three versions at the present time; a few quotations by the Fathers, marginal notes in Cod Q

and a few Hexaplaric remains are our only sources. Three **26i** other anonymous translators are mentioned by Origen who used them in the Hexapla for some books. All these translations were utilized by Origen in his revision of the LXX.

History of the LXX—(see § 26*b*) In the past the history **j** of the LXX was considered as beginning with Origen, who produced the first critical edition of the text in the fifth column of the Hexapla, and continuing through the recensions of Hesychius and Lucian in the following centuries. Now however, Origen is seen to stand at the end rather than at the beginning of a continual process of revision of the Gr. text to conform it more closely to the Palestinian Heb. text. This process began in the 'proto-Lucianic' and was continued in the 'kaige' recension, and was brought to its ultimate point in the translation of Aquila. With this understanding of the historical situation, it is possible to gain a much better picture of the original Heb. in the pre-Christian period, and so the value of the LXX for textual criticism is thereby enhanced.

Origen and the Hexapla—In compiling this monumental work c. A.D. 240 Origen's aim was twofold: to aid Christian apologists in their disputes with the Jews by indicating exactly what was and what was not contained in the Heb. text and to provide the Church with a uniform text by removing the variants found in the codices. The Hexapla is so called from the six corresponding columns into which it was divided and which contained respectively: (1) the Heb. text in Heb. letters; (2) the same in Gr. letters; (3) Aquila; (4) Symmachus; (5) LXX; (6) Theodotion. An edition containing only the four Gr. versions was called the Tetrapla. The words Heptapla and Octopla are used to indicate the occasional addition of a 7th and 8th column containing extracts from the anonymous Gr. versions mentioned above. The fifth column not only exhibited Origen's recension of the LXX text but also indicated how it differed from the Heb. original. Words or groups of words not in the Heb. were marked by an *obelus* (÷ or ⟶) while the deficiencies of LXX supplied from the other Gr. versions were marked by an asterisk. The end of LXX redundance or deficiency was also marked by a *metobelus* (: or / or ⫶). In establishing his LXX text Origen chose from the variant readings of the codices those which were supported by the later Gr. versions. Jerome rightly condemns this criterion as compromising the purity of the text. He also blames Origen for introducing into his fifth column passages from Theodotion's versions (marked by asterisks). Origen followed the Heb. order of the text in his Hexapla except in Prv, where however it was clearly indicated and Gr. transpositions were marked by a combination of *obeli* and asterisks.

The Hexapla, which must have numbered about **l** 12,000 pages, was too vast ever to be copied in its entirety. But the recension of the LXX text in the fifth column was widely diffused and highly esteemed. The use made of the later Gr. versions if critically questionable was practically advantageous for an ecclesiastical text thus brought into closer conformity with the inspired Heb. original. The textual confusion arising from Origen's recension must be attributed to the scribes who failed to reproduce the asterisks and *obeli* in their copies. Only two codices, G and 88—Chisianus (Prophets), exhibit marked texts. The recension is found without the marks in 376, 426 (Gn-Jg), A, 247 (Kgs), V, 253 (Wisdom books), Q (Prophets). The marks have also **m** been preserved in a Syr. version (see § 28*b*) and in Jerome's Latin recension of Jb, but are missing in

26m the Armenian version and in the Gallican Psalter. A fragment of the Hexaplaric Psalter lacking the first column was recovered seventy years ago in a palimpsest found in the Ambrosian library in Milan. The most complete collection of citations from the Hexapla is found in the critical apparatus of the Göttingen edition of the LXX (see § 26q).

n Recensions of Hesychius and Lucian—Jerome draws our attention (Praef. in Paralipom.) to the fact that the MSS of the LXX exhibit three types of text. These are all recensions (i.e. deliberate revisions of earlier texts assumed to need correction and therefore emended according to the corrector's idea of the original text), and were made, he says, by Hesychius at Alexandria, Origen at Caesarea, and Lucian at Antioch. We have no other direct information about Hesychius but he has been identified with the Hesychius martyred at Alexandria, although this can only be conjecture. The character of this recension, which became the common text in Egypt in the 4th and 5th cents., can be deduced from the citations of the Egyptian Fathers, especially Cyr Alex (d. 444)—and the Coptic versions. It is also presumably found, at least in part, in the biblical codices produced in Egypt during the above centuries or copied from them, as e.g. MV 39 121 198 233. Some authors have found this recension in B.

o Lucian was a priest of the Church of Antioch, where he died a martyr in A D 312; however, the recension that was formerly attributed to him is now known to extend back into pre-Christian times. The recension is used in the commentaries of the great Antiochene exegetes, Chrysostom and Theodoret, for the books of Ex to Dt; it is found in the 6th column of the Hexapla for the sections 1 Sam 11:2—1 Kgs 2:11 and for 1 Kgs 22 plus 2 Kgs, and in the MSS b o c_2 o_2 for this section also. Its chief characteristics are: clearness and elegance of language, conflation of readings from different codices, additions chiefly from Theodotion, harmonizing corrections from the Heb. The text which he revised was different from that used by Origen and Hesychius and less close to B. This recension though most widely diffused in Byzantine times did not however supplant the others like Lucian's NT recension. The chief difficulty in reconstituting the original text is the mixture of the recensions in the different codices.

p Editions of the LXX—The Polyglot Bible of Cardinal Ximenes (called *Complutensian* from the Latin name for its place of origin, Alcala, 1517), exhibits mainly a Lucianic text. The Aldine edition (Venice, 1518) is more doubtfully regarded as Hesychian. The Vatican edition of Sixtus V (Rome, 1587) is based on B, but other codices were also used to supply lacunae and correct errors. The resultant text was so highly esteemed and so frequently reproduced by various editors that it may be called *textus receptus*. Grabe's edition (Oxford, 1707—20) is based on A with various emendations, always expressly indicated, from the Complutensian and Sixtine editions. The first really critical edition was that of

q Holmes and Parsons entitled *VT Graecum cum variis lectionibus* (Oxford, 1798—1827). Though not always accurate it is still useful as a storehouse of materials. The edition of Tischendorf (Leipzig, 1869[4]) supervized by Nestle (ibid 1887[7]) has a revised Sixtine text with a critical apparatus derived from ASC. Lagarde's half-completed edition (Gn—Est, Göttingen, 1883) is a reconstitution of Lucian's recension. Finally, the Universities of Cambridge and Göttingen produced two minor editions of the LXX, Swete's in England (1894) and Rahlfs' in Germany (Stuttgart, 1935), and

inaugurated two major editions. Of the latter, Gn—Tb **26q** have already appeared in England (ed. Brooke, McLean, Thackeray, Manson) and Gn, Ru, Ps, Wis, Is—Mal, 1 and 2 Mc in Germany and last of all, Wis (1962) and Sir (1965). The critical apparatus, generally restricted to the earlier uncials in the minor editions, is elaborate and carefully selected in the major editions. The printed text is traditional, that of B supplemented when necessary from S and A in the English editions, but critical as reconstituted by the editors of the German. M. L. Margolis inaugurated a critical edition with Jos, but nothing more has been heard of this since.

Authority of the LXX—The substantial authenticity **r** of our LXX text is critically established by the number and antiquity of the codices, all in substantial agreement, in which it is contained. Its authority as an authentic version of the inspired OT may be critically deduced from its substantial conformity with the MT and is dogmatically established by its exclusive use as the OT of the Church for several centuries. The numerous critical studies of the codices during the last century, of which the fruits have now begun to appear, have for their object the restoration of the text in its original form. The older Heb. text on which the LXX version is based can then be determined with some degree of confidence and critically used to correct errors and clarify obscurities in the later MT.

The Targums—When Heb. began to pass out of use by **27a** the common people, the Palestinian Jews experienced the same need of an Aram. version of the Bible as their hellenistic brethren did of a Gr. version. They preferred, however, to retain the sacred Heb. text in their liturgy, but made it intelligible to all by adding an Aram. version. Targum means 'version'. The Targums were originally extempore because objection was taken to the use of written translations in the synagogue. They were however subsequently written down and have undergone inevitable modifications in the course of transmission. They vary in origin, date, character and dialect. Three Targums of the **b** Pent are extant in whole or in part; these are known as Jerusalem I (Palestinian, Pseudo-Jonathan), Jerusalem II (previously known only from fragments found in the Cairo Geniza, a complete copy was discovered in 1957 in the Vatican Library: Codex Neofiti I) and Onqelos. Both Jerusalem Targums render the sacred text quite freely, add explanatory glosses and contain later interpolations of a legendary nature. Jerusalem II is particularly important because it seems to have originated in pre-Christian times and to furnish us with an example of the Aram. spoken by our Lord and his disciples. The Targum of Onqelos (Aquila ?) is of Babylonian origin and renders the text as literally as Aquila rendered it in Gr., it came into general use after the 4th cent. and was so highly esteemed as to acquire an official character and be provided with a Massora. The Targum of the Prophets **c** (historical books and prophets) is attributed to Jonathan ben Uzziel, a disciple of Hillel, but belongs to the 5th cent. in its present form. It is not so literal as that of Onqelos especially in interpreting difficult passages and contains various explanations. The Targums show considerable variety. They are usually literal in Jb, Ps, Prv, but very free and diffuse in the five Megilloth (lit 'Rolls'—books used liturgically on certain festivals: Song—Passover; Ru—Pentecost; Lam—Day of Atonement; Eccl—Booths; Est—Purim). In Jb and Ps moreover double versions appear. In Prv the interpreter depends on the Syriac OT. Two Targums of Est are extant but none of Dn and Ez-Neh. The Targums are less important for

27c textual criticism than for the knowledge they give us of Jewish traditional interpretation. Quotations of OT in NT seem sometimes to have been influenced by Targumic versions. The latter will be found in the Polyglot Bibles and in the editions of P. de Lagarde (Prophets, Hagiographa, Leipzig, 1872–3), Ginsburg (Jerusalem I and II, Berlin, 1899–1903) and Sperber (Onkelos, Leyden, 1959).

d **Syriac Versions of the OT. The Peshitta**—The word *peshitta* literally means 'simple' and, when applied to the Bible, indicates either the text of the simple and ordinary people as opposed to that of the learned or the simple text not marked with critical signs. The name first appears in the 10th cent. and distinguishes the Syr. version made from the Heb. and in common use from later OT versions made from the Gr. and of interest to scholars. The Peshitta OT, as attested by the early Syriac writers Aphraates and St Ephraem in the 4th cent., contained all the p.c. books and Sir translated from the Heb. and the remaining d.c. books rendered from the Gr. The Heb. text used differed little from the MT and the translators were apparently Jewish Christians. The Jewish element predominated in the early Syriac church and the Targums exercised a considerable influence especially on the version of the Pent. The version is usually dated in the 2nd cent. A.D. Though more homogeneous than LXX it gives indications of different translators and different periods. The rendering is, however, generally clear and elegant, neither **e** too literal nor too free. The Peshitta has many readings, especially in Ps, Is and Minor Prophets, in agreement with the Gr. version where it differs from MT. This might be due to the original translators or to later revisers. The two hypotheses are not mutually exclusive but the second is by far the more probable. Greek culture penetrated among the Syrians when they became subject to Rome in the 3rd cent. and there is abundant evidence from the 5th cent. onwards of the efforts they made to conform their biblical texts to those of their highly esteemed Greek neighbours **f** of the school of Antioch. The codices of the Peshitta are remarkable for their antiquity: at least 15 are from the 5th/6th cent. Several of these are in the British Museum; Cod Ambrosianus, perhaps the most important, is at Milan. This contains the Sapiential and Prophetical books and was published by Ceriani in the last century. The chief editions have been those of the Paris and London Polyglots (17th cent.), those of Lee (London, 1823), of the missionaries of Urmiah (1852) and of the Dominican Press (I–III, Mosul, 1887–91). None of these have much critical value. **Critical editions** of a few books have appeared (cf W. E. Barnes, *Peshitta Psalter*, Cambridge, 1904; *Pentateuchus Syriace*, London, 1914; D. M. C. Englert, *The Peshitto of II Sm*, Philadelphia, Pa., 1949; etc). The latest (1967) to appear is a sample edition of Song, Tb and 4 Ez published in 1966 by the Peshitta Institute of Leiden University. This comprises the first books to appear of a new critical edition of the Peshitta OT inaugurated in 1959 by the International Organization for the Study of the OT. The direction of the undertaking was entrusted to Dr P. A. H. de Boer, professor of OT Studies at Leiden and apart from the staff of the Leiden Institute, about thirty scholars of other countries have been engaged to take part. Information about its progress is published in VT.

28a **Syriac Versions of LXX. 1. The Philoxenian**—This version of the whole Gr. Bible takes its name from Philoxenus, the Monophysite Bishop of Mabbug (Hierapolis on the Euphrates), at whose bidding it was made by a certain Polycarp, c. 508. Only fragments of Is and Ps are extant from the OT. They have been edited by Ceriani (*Monumenta sacra et profana*, 5, 1, Milan, 1873) **28a** and Mingana (Exp 46 (1920), 149–60).

2. **The Syro-Hexaplar**—Paul, Bishop of Tella (near **b** modern Urfa, a little E of the Euphrates), translated into Syr. the Hexaplar text of Origen in 615–17. The version is very literal, reproduces exactly the critical signs of the original and gives a number of variants from the later Gr. versions. It is thus of the greatest importance for the reconstitution of Origen's text. Ceriani published in 1863 the text of Ex 1:1–33:2, and in 1874 that of the Prophets and the Hagiographa (op cit 2 and 7), all from 8th cent. MSS. 2 (4) Kgs and other fragments from Paris and London MSS were edited by P. de Lagarde (*Bibliotheca Syriaca*, Göttingen, 1886–92).

3. **The Syro-Palestinian**—This version of the Gr. OT **c** and NT was probably made in the 5th cent. for the use of the Melkite Syrians of Palestine. Although written in Syr. characters the language is W Aramaic and the version is generally regarded as the best representative of the language used by Christ and the Apostles. It first became known from lectionaries of late date, but fragments were subsequently discovered in various codices, chiefly palimpsests, dating back to the 6th cent. and showing that the version was not restricted to merely liturgical texts. Of the d.c. books Sir and Wis are represented. The text is hexaplaric and is entirely unaffected by E Syriac tradition. The most complete collection of the texts is that of H. Duensing, *Christlich-palaestinisch-aramaeische Texte und Fragmente*, Göttingen, 1906.

Syriac Versions of NT. 1. The Diatessaron—The **d** first Syr. version of the Gospels was a harmonized narrative, called in Gr. *Gospel by means of the Four* (i.e. Evangelists) and in Syriac *Gospel of the Mixed* (i.e. Evangelists). It is still disputed whether the original harmony was written in Gr. or in Syr., but the discovery in 1933 of a Gr. fragment in the ruins of Dura-Europos in NE Syria dated c. 225 shows that it was used in the E in Gr. form at a very early period. Also the text is so close to the Gr. text of our Gospels that it is difficult to believe that it is a translation from a Syr. original, even though scholars like Kahle and Vööbus have been inclined to this opinion. The author of the work was Tatian, Syrian **e** by birth but Gr. by education. He was a disciple of St Justin, whom he accompanied to Rome and whose school he directed after his master's martyrdom (c. 166). Later he returned to the E, where he manifested heretical tendencies, condemning marriage and the use of wine and flesh meat, c. 172. Traces of these tendencies in his work confirm its traditional authorship and indicate its approximate date. Tatian's object was to provide his countrymen with a popular life of Christ, compiled from its four authoritative sources after the fashion of the oriental historians, and freed by harmonization from the difficulties encountered by ordinary readers in establishing the chronological order of events and reconciling the variations of the different evangelists. His skill in arranging his materials and the charm of his presentation of the Gospel narratives no doubt explain the success of his work, at least until the adoption in the 5th cent. of the Peshitta as the official version of the Syrian Church. Our knowledge **f** of it is chiefly derived from an Arabic 11th cent. version of the Syr. Diatessaron—in which however the later Peshitta text has been generally substituted for that of Tatian—from citations in the homilies of Aphraat the Wise and other Syrian Fathers, and from a 5th cent. Armenian version of Ephraem's Syr. homiletic commentary. An Old Latin harmony and its 13th cent. German, Dutch and Italian derivatives are also helpful. From these it is generally concluded that the original

28f order of the Diatessaron has been preserved in the Arabic version and that it contained some important passages attested by the W and the Antiochene, but not by the E recension. The text and sources of Tatian remain uncertain. There is an English version of the Arabic Diatessaron by J. H. Hill (Edinburgh, 1910²). The most recent critical edition with a French translation is that of A. S. Marmardji (Beirut, 1936). L. Leloir edited and translated Ephraem's commentaries into Latin (I Text, 1953; II Translation, 1954, CSCO, 137, 145). A 13th cent. Persian translation of a very interesting Syriac Diatessaron was published with an Italian translation by G. Messina (Rome, 1951; cf also Bib 24 (1943) 59–106 and B. M. Metzger, 'Tatian's Diatessaron and the Persian Harmony of the Gospels', JBL 69 (1950) 261–286).

g 2. Gospel of the Separated (Evangelists)—Two Syriac codices of the separate Gospels were discovered within the last century: one, called Curetonian (Syr^cur) from its discoverer and first editor, in a monastery of the Nitrian desert in Upper Egypt; the other, a palimpsest, called Sinaitic (Syr^sin) although of N Syrian origin, in the monastery of St Catherine on Mt Sinai. They have approximately the same date (end of 4th cent.) and are apparently two recensions of the same Syr. version, conveniently called the Old Syriac, dating from the beginning of the 4th cent. or a little earlier and exhibiting the western type of text (cf § 603d). Although both MSS are incomplete, together they provide us with nearly the whole of the four Gospels. Under the title *Evangelion da Mepharreshe*, F. C. Burkitt edited the Curetonian text with the variants of Sin. (Cambridge, 1904) and A. S. Lewis the Sin. text, which she discovered, with the variants of Cur. (London, 1910). With these Gospels may be associated the first Syr. version of the Ac and the Pauline Epistles, attested by Armenian versions of Ephraem's commentaries and exhibiting undoubtedly in the Ac, but less markedly in the Epistles, the same type of text. No trace remains of other books of the NT included doubtless in this early version.

h 3. The Peshitta NT—Rabbula, Metropolitan of Edessa (411–35), according to his almost contemporary biographer, made a fresh translation of the NT from Gr. into Syr. and ordered the separate Gospels to be read in the churches instead of the Diatessaron. This translation, or rather recension, has until fairly recently been identified with the Peshitta NT used by all Syr. writers, whether Jacobites, Nestorians or Catholics, after c. 450. The studies of Vööbus and Black have however shown that Rabbula regularly used a revision, presumably his own and certainly later than Syr^cur and Syr^sin, of the Old Syriac version. This revision is not yet the Peshitta with which we are familiar but marks a stage in the **i** process which gave rise to it. The Peshitta has often been compared to the slightly earlier NT recension of Jerome; it certainly obeys the canons the latter laid down for himself—fidelity, correctness of language, the retention of expressions consecrated by usage and the elimination of Western readings from the Gospels. (Many of these still appear in Ac). The original Peshitta omitted 2 Pt, 2–3 Jn, Jude and Apoc, added in the codices from later versions. As in the OT the codices are remarkable for their antiquity and their uniformity. *Tetraevangelium Sanctum*, edited by P. E. Pusey and G. H. Gwilliam (Oxford, 1901; reprinted 1950) is an excellent critical edition of the Gospels. Their text together with Gwilliam's edition of Ac, Pauline Epistles, Jas, 1 Pt, 1 Jn, and J. Gwynn's edition of the Philoxenian version of 2 Pt, 2–3 Jn, Jude, Apoc

make up the British and Foreign Bible Society's *NT in* **28i** *Syriac* (London, 1920).

4. The Harkleian NT—It is still disputed whether the **j** Harkleian version of Syr. tradition is identical or not with the NT of the Philoxenian Bible mentioned above. The latter was intended for the Monophysites and rendered the Gr. much more literally than the Peshitta. Thomas of Harkel in Syria, according to his own account, merely provided the Philoxenian NT text c. 616 with critical signs (*obeli* and asterisks) and marginal notes derived from a collation of three Gr. MSS. There is however some evidence that he actually revised the text. Further study of the question is called for. The marginal variants of the Harkleian NT exhibit a mainly Western type of text.

5. The Syro-Palestinian—To the remarks already **k** made on the OT version it may be added that the NT exhibits a marked dependence on Origenian tradition in the place names and seems to be based on a Caesarean text.

Coptic Versions—Coptic is the name given to the **29a** language of the Egyptians after it began to be written in Gr. letters with some supplementary characters, in the 2nd cent. A.D. Though it is less well adapted than either Lat. or Syr. to give an exact rendering of Gr. Texts, the Coptic versions of the Gr. Bible are nevertheless of great critical as well as historical importance owing to the types of text which they exhibit. They are written in several different dialects e.g. Sahidic (S or Upper Egypt), Bohairic (N or Lower Egypt), Fayumic, Achmimic and sub-Achmimic or Assiutic (Middle Egypt). Of these, Sahidic and Bohairic are the most important. All the NT except a few vv is extant in these two dialects and has been published with English translation and critical apparatus by G. Horner (*The Coptic Version of the NT in the Northern Dialect*, 4 vols., Oxford, 1898–1905; ... *in the Southern Dialect*, 7 vols., Oxford, 1911–24). Only parts of the less complete OT have appeared in scattered publications. The Sahidic version is usually assigned to the 3rd cent., the Bohairic to the 4th or 5th. The need of a vernacular rendering was felt earlier in **b** S Egypt than in N Egypt where Gr. was better known. The Bohairic exhibits moreover the greater precision and skill in translation which usually distinguishes later versions from earlier ones. A Sahidic papyrus codex of OT fragments and Ac (Brit. Mus. Or. 7594) belongs to the very beginning of the 4th cent., and several other (e.g. Bodmer) OT MSS are attributed to the 4th cent. Both Sahidic and Bohairic versions of the NT exhibit in the main an E type of text. The Sahidic has however many readings, but none of the manifestly spurious additions of the W text in the Gospels and Ac. It thus confirms the testimony of the papyri to the existence of a W type of text in Egypt in the 2nd cent., gradually replaced by the better E type. The change, begun in the N, took some time to reach the S. The Bohairic has a purer E text with some readings peculiar to itself. The Coptic versions of the OT were made from the Gr., not the Heb. and include the d.c. books. Though sometimes emended from other Gr. codices they generally follow B. Fragments of the Sahidic Jb in the Vatican library are uncontaminated by hexaplar additions.

Armenian and Georgian Versions—These versions **c** may be considered together since it is now fairly certain that the Georgians derived their version from that of their Armenian neighbours. The latter, when converted to Christianity c. 300, were unalphabetic and seem to have first used the Syr. Scriptures. Traces of a Syriac Diatessaron have been discovered in their liturgy. The invention

29c of their alphabet derived from the Gr. is attributed to a certain Mesrop and was immediately followed by the translation of the Scriptures into Armenian undertaken by the Patriarch Isaac (300–440). There are independent reasons for dating the practically contemporary Georgian version before 450. The Armenian version of the separate Gospels was made directly from the Gr. Its many syriacisms are best explained as due to the original translators who reproduced Syr. expressions from their Diatessaron. The Armenian language is an excellent medium of translation and the version is both faithful and **d** elegant. The critical importance of the Armenian and Georgian versions is derived from the Origenian text of the OT and the Caesarean text of the Gospels which they exhibit. A plausible explanation of the existence of such a text at Constantinople is provided by the 50 Bibles copied in Palestine for the Emperor Constantine by Eusebius of Caesarea. The earliest codices of both versions belong to the 8th–9th cent. The best edition of the Armenian Bible is that of J. Zohrab (Venice, 1805) which gives a collection of variant readings. The Georgian Gospels have appeared in an excellent critical edition in *Patrologia Orientalis*: Mk (1929) and Mt (1933) by R. P. Blake; Jn (1950) by Blake and M. Brière; Lk (1955) by Brière.

e Gothic Version—According to the historian Philostorgius the Gothic Bishop Ulfilas (d. 383) translated the whole Bible except Kgs into Gothic. More than half the Gospel text is extant in the 6th cent. Cod Argenteus now at Uppsala but of N Italian origin. There are fragments of other books in various MSS. The type of text that has come down to us has been considerably influenced by the Old Latin versions (cf W. Streitberg, *Die gotische Bibel* I: *Der gotische Text und seine griechische Vorlage*, 1950³; II: *Gotische-griechische-deutsches Woerterbuch*, 1950²; Heidelberg).

f Arabic Versions—There is no definite indication of an Arabic rendering of the Scriptures before the 8th cent. The Gospels and other books of the NT were then first translated from the Syriac Peshitta. The later version of the Syriac Diatessaron already mentioned is the only Arabic scriptural text of critical importance. The OT was translated from the Heb. by Saadiya Gaon in the 10th cent. Other and probably earlier versions were made from the Syriac Peshitta and the Greek LXX. The Arabic text in the Paris and London Polyglots is partly from the MT (Pent), partly from the Peshitta (Histor. Books and Jb), and partly from the LXX (Prophets and Wisdom Books).

g Ethiopic Version—As the Ethiopians or Abyssinians were converted to Christianity in the 4th cent., the version of the Bible in their native language called Ge'ez must have been begun at latest in the 5th. It was most probably based on a Gr. text of the B type and of Egyptian origin but not always correctly translated. This version was subsequently revised first from the Sahidic and later (c. 13th cent.) from Arabic texts. The revision is occasionally manifested by double translations. The codices do not antedate the 13th cent. The only complete edition of the OT and NT is that of the Italian Catholic Mission (Asmara, 1920–26). There are critical editions of parts of the OT by Dillmann (Leipzig, 1853–94), Bachmann (Berlin and Halle, 1893), Pereira (*Patr. Orient.*, 2.9.13), Loefgren (Paris, 1927; Uppsala, 1930), Mercer (London, 1931) and Gleave (London, 1951).

h Slavonic Version—This is the latest version made directly from the Gr. in the 9th cent., by the Slavonic Apostles, Cyrillus and Methodius, who provided their converts with an alphabet derived from the Gr. and a vernacular version of some of the sacred books. The **29h** version was generally believed to exhibit the Antiochene text then used in Constantinople. Of late, however, it is contended that the earlier codices (10th–11th cent.) differ from the later in presenting many Hesychian and Caesarean readings. The translators would then have derived their text from a codex of their monastery near Brussa. Gennadius of Novgorod completed the version from the Vg in the 15th cent.

The Old Latin Versions—The name indicates the **i** versions of the Scriptures used in the W Church before the introduction of the Vg of Jerome. The need of a Latin version was felt earlier in the provinces than at Rome where Gr. was better understood and more generally spoken. There is some indication of such a version in Gaul in 177 and the books and Pauline Epistles possessed by the martyrs of Scillum, who knew no Gr., attest the existence of a Latin version in Africa in 180. Tertullian confirms this attestation though he sometimes prefers his own renderings from the Gr. Aug and Jer sometimes speak of a multiplicity of Latin versions, but they may be referring rather to the multiplicity of 'corrections' which everyone who knew a little Gr. seems to have thought himself entitled to introduce into the Latin MSS. Most scholars are however agreed that there were at least two distinct Old Latin Versions, an African and a European, though some OT books were contained in only one of these and several translations have undergone revision. Recent research suggests a third Old Latin Version; this is Spanish and to some extent independent of the other two.

The numerous and consistent citations of Cyprian **j** point to the African version and enable us to determine some of the codices in which it is found. The earliest indications of a Latin version at Rome belong to the middle of the 3rd cent. Aug in a famous passage, the sense of which is disputed (cf Botte in DBS 4 (1948), 777–82), seems to prefer what he calls the Itala, which he found in Milan, to the African version he had previously used, as combining greater fidelity to the Gr. with clearness of expression. This preference may have been suggested by the version of the Pauline Epistles which he subsequently used and partially extant in Cod R (*Les fragments de Freising*, ed. De Bruyne, Rome, 1921).

Many of the fragmentary remains of the Old Latin **k** version were collected and edited by Pierre Sabatier, *Bibliorum sacrorum latinae versiones* (3 vols., Rheims, 1739–43; Paris, 1751). This great work was to be re-edited and considerably enlarged by Joseph Denk whose death in 1927 prevented completion of the project; it is now being carried on by the monks of Beuron Abbey, and numerous fascicules have already appeared under the title of *Vetus Latina, die Reste der altlateinischen Bibel* (Freiburg, 1949–). Other important collections supplementing Sabatier are being published in *Old Latin Texts* (Oxford, 1883–) and *Collectanea biblica latina* (Rome, 1912–). The British and Foreign Bible Society is sponsoring still another collection but none of this has yet appeared. Witnesses to the Spanish Old Latin version are being edited and published at Madrid by T. Ayuso Marazuela (*La Vetus Latina Hispana*, I: *Prolegomenos*, 1953; II: *Psalterium Wisigothorum Mozarabicum*, 1957).

Character and Value of the Old Latin Versions— **l** All the versions are from the Gr. and in popular Latin suited to the lower classes for whom they were intended. They are thus linguistically important for the study of the evolution of the Latin language. The early renderings, always literal but often inexact, have little exegetical

291 but much critical value as witnesses to the Gr. text of the 2nd cent. Unfortunately, however, the original versions are contaminated in the codices by the later Gr. recensions. The NT exhibits predominantly a Western type of text. Many codices have been revised from the Vg. The citations of the early Latin Fathers are the chief means of distinguishing in doubtful cases between Old Latin and Vg readings.

30a The Latin Vulgate Version—The ever-increasing number of variants in the MSS of the Latin Bible led Pope Damasus in 382 to commission Eusebius Hieronymus (St Jerome), his secretary and the greatest biblical scholar then in Rome, to produce a more reliable and consistent text. This was not to be a new translation but a revision of the Old Latin versions: Jerome had to adopt the best texts he could find and provide a new text only when none of those already existing did justice to the original Greek. In 383f he emended the Gospels, the Psalter (possibly that now known as the *Psalterium Romanum*) and, more probably, the rest of the NT. The Pope died in 384 and the following year Jerome left Rome for the E; in 386 he settled for good in Bethlehem. In the years that followed he emended some of the p.c. books of the OT with the help of the Gr. Hexapla; the work included a fresh emendation of the Psalter, that later known as the Gallican. Apart from Jb and Ps little remains to show for this work. He went on to produce a new Latin translation from the original Heb. of all the p.c. books of the OT, including the Psalter. He did not wish to translate the other OT books, doubting their inspiration (cf § 16d), but yielded to the importunity of friends with regard to Tb and Jdt and translated these from the Aram.; he translated the Dn fragments (from the Gr. of Theodotion) because they were so well known that he feared he would otherwise be thought by the unlearned to have mutilated the inspired book. The whole work was completed in 405.

b As Jerome himself had feared, his version—both revision and translation—was received coldly by his contemporaries; the translation particularly offended because of the frequent departures from the familiar diction and the new meanings often presented. Many of the objections arose from an exaggerated respect for the LXX whose faults were now frequently revealed by the accurate rendering from the Heb. originals. It was feared that people's faith in the Scriptures would not survive the shock of discovering that many words and phrases they had thought divinely inspired were merely man's corruptions of the divine original. Not even the more conservative revisions were adopted for liturgical use and the version as a whole was not officially accepted by the Western Church until the 16th cent. Already by the end of the Middle Ages Jerome's text had practically disappeared, but the many versions of what was thought to be his work, together with Old Latin texts of the books he would not translate were then collectively called by the title, given of old to the LXX, of the Vulgate or 'Common' version. The Heb. Psalter never succeeded in replacing the Gallican in popular favour and it is a version of this latter that is found in all editions of the Vg.

c History of the Vulgate Text—The keen opposition felt towards Jerome's version exercized considerable influence on those who made copies of it. For some 200 years readings from the more popular Old Latin versions were constantly being introduced into the text. Subsequent copyists selected the readings they preferred from the rich variety offered by the earlier MSS. Periodically attempts were made to remedy the evil by the production of what was hoped would become the standard text, but they did little to stem the tide of textual corruption. Moreover, the textual criticism employed by those who made them—Cassiodorus in the 6th cent., an unknown Spaniard in the 8th, Alcuin and Theodulf of Orleans in the 9th—was such as to give little certainty that their productions were anything like Jerome's original. In the 13th cent. Stephen Langton, then Chancellor of the University of Paris, tried to bring order out of chaos by obliging the students to use a uniform text produced by himself. This edition exhibits for the first time the division **d** into chh, a feature which made it popular throughout Europe, but the text itself could scarcely have been worse. Its corruptions produced many *correctoria*. The first printed Bible, produced by Gutenberg at Mainz in 1452, and those which immediately followed it exhibit the corrupt Parisian text. A better text based on Italian codices was edited by Leonardus Basileensis at Vicenza in 1476. Marginal corrections and variants first appeared in the edition of A. Castellanus (Venice, 1511). Critical editions based on a collation of various codices followed, of which those of R. Estienne (Paris, 1528f) and G. Hittorpius (Cologne, 1530) and that of the theological faculty of Louvaine (1547f) may be mentioned. The 4th edition of the Estienne Bible (Paris, 1551) is memorable as the first to contain the division of the whole text into vv indicated by marginal numbers. The edition of I. Clarius (Venice, 1542) sought to correct the Vg with the help of the original texts. Finally, entirely new Latin versions, like those of the NT by Erasmus (Basle, 1516) and of the OT by S. Münster (Basle, 1534) began to make their appearance.

The Vulgate and the Council of Trent—The con- **e** fusion and uncertainty produced by the number and variety of Latin biblical editions in the 4th cent. was, as we have seen, the occasion of the Church's commissioning Jerome to produce a text which could safely be used by all. And when in the 16th cent. she sought to remedy the same sad state of affairs, it was natural that she should think again of the same great Father of the Church and see in his work a version she could safely adopt as her own. The Council of Trent therefore, in the second decree of its fourth session in 1546, proclaimed the **authenticity of the Vg** and ordered the preparation and publication of a corrected edition of its text: *Haec* **f** *ipsa vetus et Vulgata editio, quae longo tot saeculorum usu in ipsa Ecclesia probata est, in publicis lectionibus, disputationibus, praedicationibus et expositionibus, pro authentica habeatur et ut nemo illam reiicere quovis praetextu audeat vel praesumat. . . .*

Sense of the Decree—The decree is not concerned with **g** the original texts or the various non-Latin versions but only with **Latin editions** of the sacred text. It does not judge or condemn any of these but prefers the Vg to the others and declares it **the official Bible of the Latin Church**. The essential requisite of an official Bible at all times and especially at the time of the decree was **freedom from doctrinal error**. The preference accorded to the Vg was based therefore not on its critical but on its doctrinal accuracy. The long use and approbation of the 'Vulgate' in all its variant forms throughout the Western Church suggested its substantial conformity with the original texts and its definite authority in matters of faith and morals. It was therefore declared authentic or authoritative in the sense that its testimony in doctrinal matters can never be legitimately rejected. Its accuracy in other respects is neither asserted nor implied. In *Divino afflante Spiritu* Pius XII stresses the fact that the decree applies only to the Latin Church and the public

30g use of the Scriptures and that it in no way diminishes the authority and value of the original texts in corroborating, confirming and elucidating Catholic doctrine (cf AAS 35 (1943) 309.

h **The Emendation of the Vulgate Text**—A reconstitution of Jerome's text according to modern canons of textual criticism could scarcely be expected at the time of the Council of Trent. Nevertheless the Commission appointed by Sixtus V to prepare the new emended text under the presidency of Cardinal Carafa in 1586, if we may judge by the record of their labours preserved in the Cod Carafianus, would at least have made good use of the available MS evidence had not the Pope, appalled by the number of changes they wished to make in their text (the 1583 edition of the Louvain Bible), rejected their proposals and himself prepared the Sixtine edition of the Vg, published by the new Vatican Press in 1590. This edition, recognized as needing correction even by Sixtus himself, was almost **i** immediately withdrawn from circulation. It was revised very hurriedly under Gregory XIV (d. 1591) and Clement VIII, Angelo Rocca and Francis Toletus being largely responsible for the work; only three months were given to the actual printing and the new edition appeared in 1592. A further revision appeared the following year and another in 1598, the latter together-her with an incomplete list of the many *errata* to be found in all three Clementine editions. It was left to scholars of a later age (as e.g. M. Hetzenauer, Regensburg, 1914) to produce editions more exactly in accord with the intentions of the Clementine editors. Only in 1604 was the name of Clement added to that of Sixtus on the title page of what is still the official Latin Bible text of the Catholic Church.

j The Sixto-Clementine edition of the Vg leaving much to be desired from the critical point of view, Pius X entrusted to the Benedictine Order in 1907 the task of comparing the ancient MSS and collecting the variant readings with a view to restoring Jerome's original text. The importance of this work is obvious: if we can recover Jerome's text we can, by its means, reconstruct to some extent the Heb. text used by him at the end of the 4th cent., viz a text much older than the work of the Massoretes. The MS tradition is chiefly represented by two families, the Italian and the Spanish; most of the oldest MSS are those of the Gospels. The Italian Cod Amiatinus is the oldest surviving codex of the whole Bible. It was copied c. 700 in a Northumbrian monastery from a codex of Roman origin; the text is possibly that of the recension of Cassiodorus. The Lindisfarne Gospels (6th/7th cent., now in the British Museum) have a similar type of text. Other important codices of the Italian family are the Sangallensis (Gospels, end of 5th cent.), Fuldensis (NT, early 6th), Mediolanensis (Gospels, early 6th), Claromontanus (Gospels—Mt is Old Latin, 6th), Harleianus (Gospels, **k** 6th/7th). Except for the Amiatinus and its derivatives, the early Anglo-Saxon and Celtic MSS have little critical but in some cases great artistic value, as e.g. the celebrated Book of Kells (Gospels, 7th/8th) and the Book of Armagh (NT, 8th/9th), both in Trinity College, Dublin. Alcuin's recension of the whole Bible is attested by Cod Carolinus (British Museum), Paulinus and Vallicellinus, all three from the 9th cent. The oldest and best representatives of the Spanish family are the Pentateuchus Turonensis (6th/7th), Cod Toletanus (whole Bible, 8th), Cavensis (whole Bible, 9th), Legionensis and Complutensis (whole Bible, but some books are in the Old Latin text, 10th). The recension of the Visigoth Theodulf, Bishop of Orleans (d. 827) is attested by Cod Theodulphianus, which was

made under his personal supervision; it is less popular **30k** than the Alcuinian recension which it contaminated and is based on Spanish tradition.

The revision of the Octateuch was entrusted to Dom. **l** H. Quentin, who in *Mémoire sur l'établissement de la Vulgate* (Rome, 1922) and other works explained the method followed. He divided the 70 relevant codices into three families—Spanish, Alcuinian and Theodulphian—and used what he considered the oldest and best MS of each family to form his text: when all three agreed he accepted their reading even if all other MSS disagreed and internal evidence was against it; when two agreed against the third he accepted the majority reading; when all three disagreed he had recourse to other important MSS but did not allow the Heb. original to influence his final choice. In this way he hoped to arrive at the archetypal text, ancestor of all three families, which would not necessarily be identical with Jerome's original but would be as near as the available MSS could take him to it. Only when the archetypal text was obviously corrupt would he have recourse to internal evidence.

Quentin was severely criticized by Catholic and non- **m** Catholic scholars alike for his classification of the codices, the too close dependence on Cod Amiatinus that he attributed to the Alcuinian family, the excessive authority he gave to his chosen MSS, and the derivation of these from a single archetype. More recently doubts have been raised as to the possibility of recovering anything like Jerome's text in view of the constant intrusion of Old Latin readings into this during the first 200 years of its existence (cf B. J. Roberts, *The OT Text and Versions*, p. 262). It seems safe to say that the Benedictine text which has so far appeared (Gn—Sir in 1965) is no guide to Jerome's original, but the excellent critical apparatus published with each book gives an accurate account of the state of the text towards the end of the vital 200 years. The Wordsworth-White edition (NT, Oxford, 1889— **n** 1954; *editio minor*, 1911) has two advantages over the above work: the text itself is allowed to show the full fruits of the editors' researches, and the better MS tradition of the Vg Gospels makes possible a nearer approach to the originals in their regard. More recently Pope Pius XII ordered the preparation of a new Latin version of the Psalter from the original texts; this appeared in 1945 and its use was permitted for the daily recitation of the Breviary. A new revision is now being made at Rome.

Vernacular Versions—Versions of the whole or of part **31a** of the Bible in European languages appeared first in England and Germany in the 8th cent., in France and Hungary in the 12th, in Italy, Spain, Holland, Poland and Bohemia in the 13th. After the Council of Trent, versions were naturally made from the official text of the Vg. The history of the English versions is treated elsewhere (§ 32); a word on the Welsh and Gaelic versions will not, then, be out of place here.

It is not known when parts of the Bible were first **b** translated into Welsh; the earliest extant MS, containing a version of Jn 1:1—14, is thought to date from the 12th cent.; others containing Gn 1, the Decalogue, some Pss, Lk 1:26—38 are from the 13th/14th cents. The version now in use among non-Catholic communions is that done by William Morgan, Vicar of Llanrhaeadr-ym-Mochnant and later Bishop of Llanelwy, assisted by the bard, Edmwnd Prys. It was published in 1588 and revised in 1620, under Richard Parry, Morgan's successor to the above See, by the great Welsh scholar, John Davies, Vicar of Mallwyd. Morgan's NT owed much to a version, largely the work of William of Salesbury, which had appeared in 1567. The orthography of the Morgan-Parry version was

31b modernized in 1955; in its older form it had already been reprinted 401 times by 1900. The text sometimes reveals the influence of the English AV and sometimes follows the Vg against both AV and Morgan. It also adheres more closely to the classical Welsh forms, often rejecting the colloquialisms adopted by Morgan. The Bible of 1620 has exercised as much influence on the Welsh language as has the AV on the English. New translations of books of the NT, sponsored by the Guild of Graduates of the University of Wales, appeared between 1921 and 1945, a Catholic edition of the Sunday Epistles and Gospels in 1941 and a version of Mt in colloquial Welsh by Islwyn Ffowc Elis in 1961. Work on a new version acceptable to all communions has been in progress since 1963.

c Not all the multitude of **Gaelic** MSS has been studied. It is therefore impossible to name the earliest biblical fragments extant. It has been thought that an **Irish** version of the Bible was made by Richard Fitzralph, Archbishop of Armagh, in the 14th cent., but there is no certain evidence of this. There are many biblical quotations in the 15th cent. translation of the pseudo-Bonaventurian *Life of Christ* but the version is almost certainly original. Protestant versions of the Bible appeared in Ireland in 1602 (NT) and 1685 (OT). In more recent times Catholics have had their own version of the Gospels since 1917 when Peadar Ó Laoghaire published that part of his rendering of the Vg. Since then there has been a version of the Gospels and Acts by P. Kerr (1943) and of the Psalms (new Latin Psalter) by Fr Colmcille O.C.S.O. (1961) and of Daniel by P.O. Fiannachta and W. Harrington O.P. (1966). An episcopal commission, headed by D. Ó Floinn, has for some time been preparing an authoritative version of the NT. This was to be based on the Vg text but done in the light of the Gr. originals; Lk, the first fruit of their labours, appeared in 1964. Future translations are now to be directly from the Gr

d Protestant versions of the Gaelic Bible used in Scotland were considerably influenced by the Irish ver- **31d** sion of 1602–85 a special edition of which had appeared in Roman characters in 1790. A translation from the originals, made under the auspices of the Scottish S.P.C.K., appeared between 1783 and 1801; it was revised in 1807, 1826 and 1860, much of the revision consisting in the removal of Irish idioms and the improving of the orthography. About 1835 a Catholic version of the NT was made from the Vg by Ewan MacEachern. Revised by Colin C. Grant (later Bishop of Aberdeen) with the help of other priests, it appeared in 1875. This version was independent of the Irish influence so obvious in the Protestant versions. It has been used to provide the Epistles and Gospels for the 1963 edition of the Gaelic Prayer Book. The Protestant version at present in use appeared in 1902. Prepared under the auspices of the S. P.C.K. and adopted by the National Bible Society of Scotland, this was virtually a new translation—though preserving as far as possible the diction and idiom of the Bible of 1826—by a commission of well-known Gaelic scholars representing both the Established and the Free Churches and under the chairmanship of Norman McLeod.

The progress being made in determining the original **e** form of the Heb. and Gr. texts and the desire to provide the faithful with scriptural versions, not only doctrinally sound like the Vg but also critically exact and accurately rendered, have produced **in recent years numerous Catholic vernacular versions from the original texts**. The use of these, previously restricted to private reading, was extended by Pius XII in a decree of the Biblical Commission in 1943, to public reading and instruction; an authoritative interpretation of the decree by the Secretary of the Biblical Commission will be found in Bib 27 (1946) 319. More recently, with the encouragement of the Second Vatican Council, active collaboration with other denominations in Bible translation has been taking place; cf § 12*f*.

THE ENGLISH VERSIONS OF THE BIBLE

BY JOHN BERCHMANS DOCKERY O.F.M.

32a Bibliography—The choice is very large. Only a selection of works which give a comprehensive treatment of the subject is offered here. The two classic works on the subject of English versions are: *The Cambridge History of the Bible: the West from the Reformation to the present day*, ed. S. L. Greenslade Cambridge 1963; H. Pope: *English Versions of the Bible*, revised and amplified by S. Bullough, St Louis, Mo. 1952.
Other General Works: F. F. Bruce *The English Bible*: *a history of translations* London 1961. A short, clear, up-to-date account of the history and development of· the Bible in England; T. H. Darlow and H. F. Moule *Historical Catalogue of Printed Editions of Holy Scripture* London 1903–11, vol I English Editions; J. R. Dore *Old Bibles: an Account of the Early versions of the English Bible* 1882[2]; F. Kenyon *Our Bible and the Ancient Manuscripts*, 1958[5] chs. X–XII; J. G. MacGregor *The Bible in the Making*, 1961; W. F. Moulton *The History of the English Bible*, last complete ed. 1911—abridged ed. 1937; E. H. Robertson, *The New Translations of the Bible*, 1959; H. W. Robinson (ed.) *The Bible in its Ancient and English Versions* Oxford 1940; Reprinted with appendix Oxford 1954; L. A. Weigle *The English New Testament from Tyndale to the RSV*. Nashville 1949, London 1950; B. F. Westcott *A General View of the History of the English Bible*, 1905, 3rd revision by W. A. Wright

b Earliest English Bible—Some paraphrases and translations into the vernacular were made in England of at least some parts of the Bible about the end of the seventh cent. and continued by Bede and others. In those days the standard of literacy was low, books, before printing was invented, very scarce, and educated people were able to read Latin. In the 9th cent. King Alfred translated or caused to be translated several books of the Bible, as did Aldhelm and Aelfric. But the Bible in general use was the Latin Vulgate 'In no part of the western world was this version studied more diligently and copied more lovingly and faithfully than in Great Britain and Ireland', F. F. Bruce, *The English Bible*, 1. Possibly the finest MS of this Bible, the Codex Amiatinus was made in England at Jarrow or Wearmouth. One early form of trans. was the interlinear gloss—i.e. a translation between the lines of a Latin MS. Thus the **Lindisfarne Gospels**, a magnificent MS in Latin, has an interlinear trans. in the Northumbrian dialect of the tenth cent. The Norman Conquest radically modified and slowed down the development of English as a national language and in consequence translations into the vernacular continued to be sporadic and partial until the fourteenth century, when English began to emerge as a national language, a blend of Norman French and the various Anglo-Saxon dialects. Some objected to the vernacular Scriptures and complained that 'the jewel of the clergy has become the toy of the laity'. Nevertheless the demand, inevitably, grew as English came to be more widely spoken by the educated classes. Hitherto they had been **32b** satisfied with either Latin or Norman-French Bibles. St Thomas More, Cranmer and even Foxe the martyrologist affirm the existence of English versions, at least of large portions of the Bible before Wycliffe's time and MSS have survived of English trans. of the Gospels (11th cent.) Mk, Lk, St Paul's ep. (14th cent.), Apoc (11th cent.)

John Wycliffe—However it is now generally accepted that the first complete English version of the Bible was made towards the end of the 14th cent. by Wycliffe and his followers. Wycliffe was perhaps the most eminent theologian of his time at Oxford and a great popular preacher who fiercely attacked the abuses of the age. Unfortunately in doing so he expressed unorthodox views concerning the sacraments of Penance and the Eucharist, the use of relics and against the celibacy of the clergy. He strongly advocated a translation of the Scriptures into English so that the poor people could read God's word for themselves. Such a version would also make it easier for him to propagate his teachings. Wycliffe and his companions made a translation of the NT in 1380, followed by one of the OT two years later, both of course from the Latin Vulgate and the latter including the deuterocanonical books. It is uncertain what part Wycliffe took in the translation. He may have translated the NT but most of the OT was the work of Nicholas of Hereford, one of his ardent supporters. Nicholas was vice-Chancellor of the University of Oxford but later retired to the Carthusian monastery at Coventry where he died. Hereford's work on the OT is scholarly and literal; that of his collaborators more free and colloquial. Many familiar phrases from the Wycliffite Bible are found in most later English versions, e.g. 'strait is the gate and narewe the way'; 'the beame and the mote'. In 1384, after Wycliffe's death, John Purvey, one of his followers revised the translation. In the general prologue Purvey expressed his indebtedness to Nicholas of Lyra the Franciscan scholar and expert in Heb. and rabbinical studies who represented the culmination of a long tradition in these fields of knowledge.

Wycliffe's teachings were condemned repeatedly in England during the latter part of the 14th cent. and at the **Council of Oxford, 1408** translations of the Scriptures into the vernacular were forbidden unless and until they were duly approved by Church authority. The reason for this was the use made of the Wycliffite Bible in spreading the doctrines of Lollardy. In fact there was nothing unorthodox in the translation itself though, in the prologue, novel views on the Eucharist were expressed, incompatible with the faith. Finally in 1415 at the **Council of Florence** all Wycliffe's works were condemned. The actual Bibles however continued in use, shorn of their heretical prologue, and were in the possession of both religious houses and those of the nobility. Many of these Bibles may now be seen in the British Museum—mostly copies of the second Wycliffite version.

32b The suggestion that these Bibles are really Catholic translations from the time before Wycliffe has now been abandoned. Once separated from the prologue there was no reason why they should not be used by Catholics and they came to be tacitly accepted. It should be noted that the Council of Oxford did not condemn vernacular translations. As Sir Thomas More said: 'It neither forbiddeth the translations to be read that were already well done of old before Wycliffe's days, nor damneth his because it was new but because it was naught; nor prohibiteth new to be made but provideth that they shall not be read if they be made amiss till they be by good examination amended.' *A Dialogue against Heresies.*

c First Printed Editions—The year 1525 saw the publication of the NT in Tyndale's translation and in 1530 there appeared his trans. of the Pent. from the Hebrew. This was soon followed by Jonah. Unfortunately, like Wycliffe, Tyndale made his translation a vehicle for bitter attacks on the Church.

Tyndale was put to death in 1536 but left his translation of the OT in manuscript. The English ecclesiastical authorities condemned his Bible because it was considered to be part of the Lutheran reform. In their view much of the wording of the text and the prefaces emphasized basic principles of the reformers, e.g. justification by faith alone. The real reason for the condemnation seems rather to have been himself than his Bible, for his leanings towards Lutheranism were well-known. It was on account of these opinions that he was compelled to carry out his work on the continent. His translation was a great improvement on that of Wycliffe, especially in literary merit, e.g. his translation of I Cor 13 has persevered through many versions. As regards orthodox Catholic teaching his translation gave some grounds for condemnation—his NT clearly reflects the influence of Luther's 1522 NT. The authorities objected to his rejection of 'priest' for 'elder', 'church' for 'congregation' and his notes were offensive to the Church. In 1543 Parliament banned it as a 'crafty, false and untrue translation'; yet it is estimated that 80% of the words in the RV stand as in Tyndale's NT, and his Pent. formed the basis of most subsequent English versions. Cuthbert Tunstall, Bishop of London, had never encouraged Tyndale's efforts and, being especially perturbed by the circulation of this Bible, had it condemned and burned.

d In the NT Tyndale used the Gr. text of Erasmus and compared it with the Vg In the OT he translated from the Heb., also comparing it with the Vg and Luther's German version. Tyndale's later corrections departed more from the Vg and from Wycliffe and his 1534 edition of the NT formed the basis for the AV, RV and RSV. When Cranmer became Archbishop of Canterbury in 1533 the making of a new translation was committed to **Miles Coverdale** (1488–1569). He had been an Augustinian friar who left his Order under the influence of the Reformation, repudiated Catholicism and became the first Protestant Bishop of Exeter. In 1535 his English Bible was published. He did not claim Tyndale's knowledge of ancient languages but he made use of Tyndale's translation, together with Latin and German versions, as the title-page says, 'translated from Douche and Latin'. He followed Luther's example of putting the d.c. books, (he called them *Hagiographa* but later they were named *Apocrypha* by non-Catholics), at the end of the OT (cf § 17b). Later English versions followed this example or omitted them. Coverdale's Bible was issued without royal authority but apparently there were no obstacles to its circulation. The second edition in 1537 received royal licence, 'set forth with the Kynges most

gracious licence'; yet in 1546 King Henry forbade anyone **32d** to have a copy of either Tyndale's or Coverdale's NT. Because Coverdale's translation was not made from the original languages, it did not satisfy scholars. It may have been tactful of Coverdale not to mention Tyndale's Bible, but his NT is mainly Tyndale. It was essentially a 'Protestant' version, e.g. 'congregation' for 'church', etc., but Coverdale was not a controversialist as Tyndale was. He was the first to introduce chapter summaries. One part of his Bible, the Psalter, has remained in the Prayer Book, as his English style has lent itself to singing.

In 1537 another English version appeared, known **33a** as the **Matthew Bible**. It was thought to be the work of a Thomas Matthew but now it is generally considered to be a composite translation edited by **John Rogers** (1500–55), a friend of Tyndale who became a Protestant under his influence. Some think that 'Matthew' stands for Tyndale's own name, but in any case the pseudonym was probably used to protect the translator from the fate that overtook Tyndale. In fact Rogers became one of the first of the Marian martyrs. His work was a revision mainly of Tyndale with emendations from Coverdale. The king gave it royal licence but did not authorize it for use in public worship. Numerous editions appeared; the last in 1551. This version welded together the best in Tyndale and Coverdale; his dependence on Tyndale is clear from his copious and offensive notes—it was the controversial nature of these that spoilt his work, though the Matthew Bible was an important influence on later versions.

The **Great Bible**, so called on account of its size, (11″ × 16½″) was an attempt to supersede the two existing Bibles, Coverdale and Matthew, both considered unsatisfactory for one reason or another. Thomas Cromwell, deciding that these two Bibles stood in need of revision, assigned the work to Coverdale. It was now generally accepted by the reformers that the English Bible should be translated from the original languages. For this reason Coverdale worked on the Matthew Bible rather than on his own; but he was influenced by Tyndale's translation especially in his retention of his ecclesiastical vocabulary. He used the last edition of Tyndale's NT of 1534–35, corrected by Sebastian Munster's Latin version of the Heb. OT, the Latin Bible of Erasmus and the Complutensian Polyglot, (cf § 26p).

The Great Bible, often known as Cromwell's Bible first **b** appeared in 1539 and though not considered heretical by Catholics, was defective in many places. It was the first English Bible to be authorized for public use in churches. In 1542 Convocation made an unsuccessful attempt to have it corrected by the Vg but a 2nd ed. had appeared in 1540, for which Cranmer himself had written the preface, (hence often known as Cranmer's Bible) which became the standard text. There were seven editions of it in the next two years and many more before the last edition of 1569. As the publicly-used Bible it remained unchallenged until the appearance of the Bishop's Bible in 1568. During Mary's reign no definite steps were taken to suppress it, though many English Bibles were burned. Neither Parliament nor royal proclamation denounced the Great Bible and when Elizabeth came to the throne, it was still in general use throughout the country.

Richard Taverner (1505–77) was a lawyer and a **c** Gr. scholar though he knew no Heb.; he was a layman, the only one to produce an entire Bible, but licensed to preach by Edward VI. He revised the Matthew Bible and from the standpoint of scholarship, the result was a great improvement, particularly in his accurate rendering of

33c the Gr. article. He aimed at compression and vividness often substituting a Saxon word for a Latin word, (e.g. 'spokesman' for 'advocate'), and did not hesitate to coin words. He also introduced many strange spellings, e.g. 'peax' for 'peace', 'hable' for 'able'. Owing to his lack of Heb., his standard of accuracy in the OT was not as high as in the NT; he merely polished up the text of Matthew's OT. His influence on later versions was slight but some of his words and expressions have survived, e.g. his use of 'parable' for 'similitude'. The first edition of 1539 is the most reliable as later editions contain many alterations by Bishop Becke. Taverner's own marginal notes were not controversial and the Bible might have had a better reception had it not appeared so short a time before the Great Bible which entirely eclipsed it. The last edition was in 1552. It is of interest to note that a certain A. Marler was granted permission to sell copies of the Great Bible in 1541, unbound for 10/— and bound for 12/— a copy. (In today's money about £30 and £36).

d During the reign of Edward VI when all restrictions on reading the Bible were removed, thirtyfive editions of the NT appeared and thirteen of the whole Bible. When the young king died and Mary Tudor succeeded, publications of the English Scriptures ceased and her reign witnessed only one edition, the NT from Geneva in 1557. It was at this time that a number of clerics left the country to join Knox and Calvin. Among these were Coverdale, Beza and William Whittingham, sometime Fellow of All Souls, Oxford, and related by marriage to Calvin. These exiles decided to produce another English version, which became known as the **Geneva Bible**. Several hands took part in its completion. The NT was a revision of Tyndale's by Whittingham, more specifically Matthew's version of Tyndale, with some changes based on Beza's Latin NT of 1556. It was apparently only an interim edition for in 1560 there appeared the full Bible with a dedicatory epistle to Queen Elizabeth. The OT was a thorough revision of the Great Bible. Instead of the usual black letter type, Roman and italic types were used which rendered it much easier to read and this won it a place never achieved by previous Bibles. Its phrases find an echo in Scripture-quotations from Shakespeare to Bunyan. It remained the family Bible until the outbreak of the Civil War in 1642. For the first time in an English Bible the text was divided into verses. Its widespread popularity was due also to its quarto size. It was appointed to be read in the Churches in Scotland, though never in England. At least 140 editions of the whole Bible or NT were printed. It superseded the Great Bible and also held its own against the Bishops' Bible and even against the AV for a generation. The notes for the original 1560 edition emphasize 'justification by faith alone' and make frequent attacks on Rome, thus making this first edition Protestant rather than Calvinistic. Later editions supply notes of a more Calvinistic nature; indeed this Bible played no small part in promoting English Puritanism. In spite of this, the AV was to benefit considerably from the scholarship of the Geneva translators. It formed a turning point in the history of the English Bible for it was more independent than the Great Bible which relied on Matthew, as Matthew relied on Tyndale. The Geneva Bible started afresh and a new way was opened for the later AV of 1611.

e The growing popularity of the Geneva Bible made it impossible to continue reading the Great Bible in church. Apprehensive of the Calvinistic tendencies of the Geneva Bible Archbishop Matthew Parker in 1561 submitted a plan for the revision of the Great Bible. The **Bishops' Bible**, as it came to be called, took seven years to complete. The Great Bible was checked by the **33e** Heb. text and the controversial notes were omitted; though it contained notes strongly Protestant in tone, these were neither anti-Catholic nor anti-Calvinist. On the whole the revision was inadequate and unsatisfactory, being little more than a safe and dignified compromise. It went through many editions until the last in 1606, but copies of the NT continued to be printed until 1619. In 1571 Convocation ordered this Bible to be used throughout the country and in 1572 there was a considerable revision of it, especially of the NT. Though not a work of high merit, it formed the official basis for the revision of 1611. It was the first text to be published in England by episcopal authority.

Catholic Bible—Meanwhile Catholics were considering **34a** a vernacular Bible and it was the professors of the English College at Douay who took up the work. Mainly from Oxford and exiled on account of their faith, even in Douay they were not left at rest; a storm on the political horizon threatened the existence of the college and caused its transfer to Rheims for fifteen years (1578—93). The chief names concerned with this translation of the Bible were: i) **William Allen** (1532–94) Fellow of Oriel College, Oxford, Principal of St Mary's Hall and Canon of York, who, refusing to conform in 1561 withdrew to Louvain. He opened the English College at Douay in 1568 and later founded a similar college in Rome. He was created Cardinal and appointed to the Sixtine commission for the revision of the LXX and the Vg. ii) **Gregory Martin** (d. 1582), scholar of St John's College, Oxford, poet, hebraist and Greek scholar. He too refused to conform to the religious changes in England and went to Douay in 1570. iii) **Richard Bristow** (1538–81) Fellow of Exeter College, Oxford, was a convert to Catholicism. He taught at Douay and went as its rector to Rheims. iv) **William Reynolds** (1544–94), another convert to the Catholic Church, from New College, Oxford, also went to Douay.

On 16th October 1578 Gregory Martin began an **b** E. tr. of the Bible in order to meet 'the heretical corruptions imposed upon the English nation'. He determined 'to translate two chapters a day with Dr Alanus and Mr Bristous as revisors'. In 1582 there was printed at Rheims the NT translated 'faithfully into English out of the authentical Latin ... diligently conferred with the Greek ... especially for the discovery of the corruptions of divers late translations and for clearing the controversies in religion of these days ...' The reason for the translation was 'not of necessity ... but upon consideration of the present time and condition of our country'; i.e. a vernacular version would not have been necessary in more peaceful times. The preface goes on to say that the Church 'never wholly condemned all vulgar versions' but gave warning against indiscriminate interpretation. The Council of Oxford, called by Thomas Arundel, Archbishop of Canterbury, in 1408, had demanded diocesan approval for the publication of Bibles. The translators of the Rheims NT went on to explain that, lest any doctrinal error should creep in or the true sense of the Holy Ghost be missed, they had followed the Fathers and Jerome himself 'in keeping religiously the very barbarisms of the vulgar Latin text', e.g. 'supersubstantial bread' (Mt 6:11); 'similitude of the prevarication of Adam' (Rom 5:14). The annotations, considerable in extent, were added 'to show the studious reader both the heretical corruptions and false deductions'. Then follow the reasons why the Vg was used for the translation: its ancient character, its tradition, its accuracy and its sincerity as well as the decree of the Council

34b of Trent. The Rheims translators set out to produce a literal translation as they clearly point out in their preface of 1582. Further light is thrown on the intentions of the translators by a book published in the same year, 1582, by Martin entitled, *A Discoverie of the manifold corruptions of the Holy Scriptures by the Hereticks of our dais, especially the English Sectaries and of their foule dealing herein by partial and false translations to the advantage of their heresies in the English Bibles used and authorised since the time of Schisme*. In this work Martin makes a careful study of a number of phrases in the English Bibles and comparing them with the Heb. or Gr. expressions establishes the accuracy of the recently published Catholic Bible; he also asserts that many of the inaccuracies have been due to the influence of the new religious teachings. The following year this expression of strong Catholic views was answered in equally strong language by William Fulke, Master of Pembroke Hall, Cambridge, in his *Defense of the Sincere and true translation of the holie Scriptures into the English tong against the manifold cavils, frivolous quarrels and imprudent slanders of Gregory Martin, one of the readers of Popish divinitie in the trayterous Seminarie of Rhemes*.

c The groundwork of the Rheims NT was supplied by the existing English versions from which Martin did not hesitate to borrow freely; his renderings often bear a striking resemblance to Coverdale's diglot of 1538. The translation also shows traces of a careful study of the Bishops' Bible and the Geneva Bible and through them of the earlier translators from Tyndale onwards. But generally speaking, the Rheims NT follows Wycliffe, whereas Protestant translations follow Tyndale. The notes in the first edition of this Catholic NT were most probably contributed by Bristow. The preface, termed 'ingenious' by its critics, gives reasons for publishing a new English translation. Many critics gratuitously suggested that the obscure style was deliberately adopted in order to prevent readers from understanding the Bible; the Catholic Church, they said, had been compelled by circumstances to produce vernacular Bibles but made it as difficult as possible to understand them! Later scholars, among them Carleton and Westcott, have praised the accuracy of the Rheims-Douay version. Among points to be specially noted is the careful treatment of the definite article arising from a study of the Greek text, as Taverner had shown. In 1589 William Fulke, continuing his controversy, published the Bishops' version and the Rheims NT in parallel columns. This secured for the Catholic NT a publicity which it would not have otherwise obtained and this publicity was indirectly responsible for the marked influence of the Rheims NT on the AV.

d It was not until 1609–10 that the Catholic OT was published, in two volumes. In the preface the editors declare that the work had been 'completed long since but lack of funds prevented its publication before'. Another reason for the delay may have been that this OT, based on an unofficial Louvain text, might be corrected by the Sixtine edition of the Vg, published in 1590. It is again stated in the preface that the real purpose of the translation was polemical: 'Now since Luther and his followers have pretended that the Catholic Roman faith and doctrine should be contrary to God's written word and that the Scriptures were not suffered in vulgar languages lest the people should see the truth and withal these new masters corruptly turning the Scriptures into diverse tongues, as might best serve their own opinions, against this false suggestion and practice, Catholic pastors have, for one especial remedy, set forth true and sincere translations in most languages of the Latin Church.' Criticisms were made against the OT such as had been launched against the NT, especially its too close adherence to the Latin text. There was a partial reversal of this attitude when many of the improved translations of the Rheims NT were introduced into the AV, (the Douay OT appeared too late to influence the AV), e.g. 'converted' (*convertantur*) for 'turn' (Mark 4:12); 'founded' (*fundata*) for 'grounded' (Eph 3:17); 'centurion' (*centurio*) for 'captain' (Ac 10:22); 'sign' (*signum*) for 'badge, token' (Mt 26:48); 'clemency' (*clementia*) for 'courtesy' (Ac 24:4). Not only did the Rheims NT introduce such Latin words into the English language but it also influenced the AV in the direction of modernization, e.g. 'moisture' for 'moistness' (Lk 8:6); 'what man is there' for 'what man is it' (Ac 19:35); 'distresses' for 'anguishes' (2 Cor 12:10). The Rheims-Douay gave a glossary ('explication') of new words and it is surprising how many have become well-established, e.g. acquisition, advent, allegory, assumption, calumniate, character, evangelize, neophyte, resuscitate, victim, etc. The Psalter was thought to be the weakest part of the translation: but this was because Jerome's Gallican Psalter, made from the LXX, had been included in the Vg and not his translation from the Heb. (see § 30b). In the Douay OT there were annotations of a doctrinal nature, most valuable at a time when the Catholic body in England was so short of pastors. The purpose of these notes was to interpret the text in conformity with the faith of the editors and the decrees of the Council of Trent, as well as to rebut the arguments of the reformers. The d-c books are found distributed among the other canonical books in the Catholic OT. At a time when there was almost no knowledge of the relative value of MSS of original texts, the Rheims-Douay Bible, based on the Latin, drew attention to an important fact. Since the Vg was made in the 4th cent. many readings contained in it might be more exact than those in very late and corrupt Greek MSS that were used to make translations in the sixteenth century. But obviously one must bear in mind the fact that the Vg MSS too were subject to error. No further edition of the Rheims-Douay version appeared for another hundred years.

Authorized Version (called in USA **King James 35a Version**)—The official authority given to the Bishops' Bible caused the Puritans to agitate for a new translation, to which James I agreed. Almost all existing English Bibles, including the Rheims NT were used as sources with the Bishops' Bible of 1572 as the main text. The translators were to keep the 'old ecclesiastical words' because it was feared that the Puritans would discard all ecclesiastical tradition. The completed work appeared in 1611 and became known later as the Authorized Version. It was in fact never officially authorized either by Church or State, though the King's 'speciall command' conferred considerable authority and it became the official Bible of the Church of England until modern times. It was favourably accepted by the non-conformist Churches. Being translated from the original texts, it claimed to be more accurate than a translation from the Latin, but (as has already been seen) this did not necessarily follow. Its notes do not stress differences in theological views, and scholarly marginal notes add much to textual criticism. The 'Apocrypha' were included as it was not until the Long Parliament of 1644 that the books of the Heb. canon only were directed to be read in the Church of England. After the Restoration this policy was reversed but the non-conformists continued for the most part to disregard the d.c. books. The AV weathered all attacks

35a and nearly a thousand editions of all or part were published between 1611 and 1800. Alterations are found in many editions: 'Thou art Christ' (Mt 16:16) became 'Thou art the Christ'; 'The words of Jesus' (Mt 26:75) became 'the word of Jesus'; 'For press' (Mk 2:4) became 'for the press'; 'He came and worshipped' (Mk 5:6) became 'He ran and worshipped'. The revisers were accused of being 'damnable corrupters of God's word' for making such changes. Though the AV received no approbation from Convocation or Parliament, it obtained a pre-eminent place on its own merits, 'the noblest monument of English prose.' It was published in Scotland in 1633, in Ireland in 1714, and in the American colonies in 1752.

b **Later Catholic Editions**—During the course of the hundred years following the publication of the only existing Catholic English Bible, its language became increasingly strange. 'In a number of places it is unintelligible and all over so grating to the ears of such as are accustomed to speak, in a manner, another language, that most people will not be at the pains to reading them.' As an example of the truth of this criticism by Dr Nary Nm 6:17 reads in the Rheims-Douay edition, 'The ram he shal immolate for a pacifique host to the Lord, offering withal the baskette of azymes and the libamentes that by custom are dew.' With the authority of the Archbishop of Dublin, **Dr Nary** published a modernized version of the NT in 1718. His sense of English rhythm was excellent and he had a high ideal of the translator's task, being probably ahead of his time in his understanding of it. He had another object in view, namely, to replace 'Bibles that are so bulky that they cannot conveniently be carried about for public devotion; and so scarce and dear that the generality of people neither have nor can procure them for private use'. In 1730 another President of the English College, Douay, **Dr Robert Witham**, published a revision of the Rheims NT. In his preface, having praised the work of the original translators for producing such a true and literal translation and not a paraphrase, Witham thought that 'the Rheims translators followed too scrupulously the Latin, even to the placing of words'. He changed almost every v in his revision **c** of the NT. The censor of this edition was **Dr Richard Challoner**, vice-president of the College at Douay. The same year Challoner returned to England to work on the mission and in 1738 a new revision of the NT appeared which was probably the work of Challoner, assisted by Francis Blyth, O.D.C. Both these men were converts from Protestantism and being familiar with the language of the AV did not hesitate to adopt many of its renderings. Thus, the young man who followed our Lord, (Mk 14:51), and, according to the Rheims translation was 'clothed with sindon upon the bare', became 'cloathed with linnen cloath over his naked body'. Challoner's wide pastoral experience made him familiar with the needs of the people for whom the English Bible was required. This qualification more than made up for any lack of the profound scholarship that adorned the previous translators. Challoner's aim was to give his people a Bible they would read and understand and carry about with them; and this he did in the further revision of the NT of 1749. In this edition further alterations were made towards the AV and the expressions so familiar to modern readers of the Catholic Bible were introduced, e.g. instead of 'But when I was made a man, I did away the things that belonged to a little one' Challoner wrote, 'But when I became a man, I put away the things of a child' (I Cor 13:11). The next year, 1750, the whole Bible was published, 'newly revised and corrected according to

the Clementine edition of the Scriptures'. It went **35c** through six editions in the lifetime of Challoner who died in his ninetieth year in 1781. His corrections in the OT almost amounted to a new translation. There must of necessity be a certain resemblance between any two Catholic versions, both translated from the Vulgate; but, this connection between the Douay and Challoner's being allowed for, Challoner's version is nearer to the AV than it is to the Douay in phraseology and diction. In the NT the Gospels are the best, the Epistles the least satisfactory part of his work. In the necessary simplifying of the English text, there was some loss of the dignity and rhythm of the original version of 1582; but Challoner produced what has been the Bible of English Catholics for nearly two hundred years. Nevertheless differing texts are found, due to the changes by different editors. For example, Bernard MacMahon produced a new edition in 1783 which professed to be a revision of Challoner and basically it is, but there are over five hundred variations and still more in an 1816 edition, known as Dr Troy's Bible. Dr Cotton maintained that the changes made in subsequent editions of the Rheims-Douay Bible produced a Bible further from the AV than Challoner's Bible ever was. (H. Cotton, *Rhemes and Doway. An attempt to shew what has been done by the Roman Catholics for the diffusion of the Holy Scriptures in English*, Oxford, 1855. On this work cf H. Pope, op cit 92–97).

Revised Version—In the course of time, the need was **d** felt for a revision of the AV as new sources of knowledge became available. In 1856 a petition for a royal commission was put before the House of Commons, but not until 1870 did the Convocation of Canterbury decide to undertake the work. A committee was formed of members of the Church of England as well as of other non-Catholic communions, (Cardinal Newman was invited but felt unable to accept). They published the NT in 1881, the whole Bible in 1885, and the Apocrypha in 1894. In the preface to the NT the debt of the AV to the Rheims NT was at last publicly recognized. Though possessing greater accuracy than the AV, the RV lacked its style and dignity. But all agree that its appearance was a milestone in the history of the English Bible and a greater landmark than early critics ever suspected. Its scholarship has never been disputed.

The revisers were 'to introduce as few alterations as possible into the text of the AV consistently with faithfulness', as the preface states. The Gr. text they used, based on LXX(B) and (S), was the work of B. F. Westcott and F. J. A. Hort, both occupying professorial chairs at Cambridge. For the OT the MT was employed. Towards the end of the 19th cent., revisers in America **e** were at work and produced in 1901 the **American Standard Version**, a recension of the RV in which were included words and phrases that were a matter of preference for Americans, e.g. 'Holy Spirit' for 'Holy Ghost'. In general the American revisers desired a more extensive elimination of archaic words than the English revisers wished, e.g. the American version of the Lord's Prayer reverted to the 'who art in heaven' of the Rheims NT. Perhaps the major defect of both the RV and the ASV of the NT is that they are too literal and follow the Gr. order of words rather than the natural English word order.

The International Council of Education appointed in 1937 a committee of scholars to revise the American Standard vrsion and their work was published as the **Revised Standard Version** of the NT in 1946 and of the OT in 1952. The revision is 'based on the consonantal

35e Hebrew text' for the OT, and for the NT the best available texts. 'The major reason for the revision of the King James' version ... is the change since 1611 in English usage'. Over twelve million copies of the RSV were sold within ten years.

Other Modern Non-Catholic Versions—Only briefly can mention be made of a number of modern English Protestant texts:- i) Richard Weymouth: NT in 1902, a careful, conservative and literary translation; ii) Twentieth Century NT (1898, revised 1904) changed the traditional order of books to the chronological order; iii) James Moffat: the whole Bible (1913—24) a one-man translation, the first for nearly four hundred years and a complete breakaway from the style of the AV. It became most popular; iv) Basic English Bible, 1949, (it uses only a thousand words), has a simple direct style; v) New English Bible, 1961 under the direction of Dr C. H. Dodd, aims at rendering the original into idiomatic English designed primarily for private use. vi) J. B. Phillips's version has achieved a very wide circulation, especially of its separate parts in paperbacks: Epistles (London, 1947), Gospels (1952), Acts (1955), Revelation (1958); NT in one volume (1958). His principles of translation are: use only language that is commonly spoken; expand if necessary to make the meaning clear; keep the style flowing and easy to read.

f Modern Catholic Versions—In 1811 a revision of Challoner's version, which became known as Dr Hay's version, went through a number of editions in Ireland. In the same year Thomas Haydock, printer and schoolmaster in Manchester, suggested that his brother, the Rev George Haydock of Ushaw College, should prepare a new translation. It was mainly Challoner and published in fortnightly parts. Other editions of Challoner appeared but when Bible Societies began to produce their cheap copies, Catholics felt they should do something similar, so the 'Catholic Board' inaugurated the 'Roman Catholic Bible Society'. After initial difficulties about the text and notes, the NT was published in 1815 'stereotyped from the edition published by authority in 1740' i.e. Challoner's revision, though the notes were abridged and the text modernized, ('said' for 'saith'; 'my' for 'mine'). Between 1816 and 1829 the text of Challoner's third revision was published in several editions. Dr John Lingard made a translation of the Gospels from the Gr., using the Vg wherever possible. In 1857 Cardinal Wiseman approached Newman about the possibility of a new translation but nothing came of it. It must suffice to say that during the next hundred years ninety different editions of the NT were published and fifty-six of the complete Bible; a figure that does not include the vast number of editions appearing in America (See H. Pope: *English Versions*, 719—46).

36a Twentieth Century Catholic Versions—The **Westminster Version** is an unofficial (i.e. not commissioned by the Hierarchy) English translation from the original languages. The NT under the direction of Cuthbert Lattey S. J. was completed in 1936; but the OT remains unfinished. The translation of both Testaments, though uneven, is good, and the version is accompanied by copious notes and commentaries. It is interesting to notice that in the OT proper names appear as in the AV and not as in the Vg. The **Confraternity Version** is a new trans. from the originals. It was begun before the 1939—45 war in the U.S.A. as a translation from the Vulgate under the auspices of the Confraternity of Christian Doctrine who published the NT in 1941 as a revision of the Challoner-Rheims version. The Committee then changed its policy; and its proposed new translation of the OT

from the Hebrew into modern English is nearing comple- **36a** tion,. at the same time as a trans. of NT from the Greek.

Knox Version—In 1939 Monsignor Ronald Knox was **b** asked by the English Hierarchy to make a translation of the NT from the Vg. Knox's aim, was to express the Bible 'in timeless English' in a style that was 'accurate, intelligible, idiomatic, readable'. He pointed out that a literal translation was not always accurate. The NT, authorized by the Archbishops and Bishops of England and Wales, appeared in 1945. The preface stated that it was not intended to displace the Rheims version of the NT, 'on the contrary we now have two official versions in the Church in this country'. The translation was completely new, breaking away from all previous translations and became popular both in England and America. It had the overwhelming advantage of being the work of a single author who was a master of English. In 1949 his OT was published for private use only, though it bore the *imprimatur* of Cardinal Griffin. It represented what Knox himself claimed to be 'my idea of how the OT ought to be translated'. This meant that his translation was written in a freer, more personal style than was found in the NT. In this edition of the OT the book of Psalms was a translation from the Vg Gallican Psalter, but Knox gave in an appendix a translation into English of the new Latin psalter made in 1943 from the Heb. by members of the Pontifical Biblical Institute. In the 1955 edition of Knox's Bible the Gallican Psalter is replaced by this new psalter.

RSV Catholic Edition—The whole story of the Bible **c** from Wycliffe to modern times has been one of divergence and differences in English versions, with the gap between Christians growing wider and wider. In our own days a change in this long tradition is being effected and there is a movement in the direction of a common Bible. Thus the Second Vatican Council commended the making of present-day versions from the original text of the Bible for the use of the faithful, and added: 'As opportunity offers, and with the approval of Church authority, such versions can be made in collaboration with our separated brothers and be available for use by all Christians' (*De divina Rev.*, 22). In England it was thought that one practical approach to this ideal would be to edit an existing version. The recently published RSV seemed to be the best starting point. The preliminary difficulties were surmounted and the NT was ready by 1956, but then Cardinal Griffin, who had approved the plan, died and things remained in abeyance until Archbishop Gray of St Andrews and Edinburgh gave his *imprimatur* to the NT of the RSV Catholic edition in 1964.

In 1966 the whole Bible in **the RSV Catholic edition** was published. In it: (i) the d.c. books (known to Protestants as the Apocrypha, cf § 13e) are included, and moreover in their traditional Catholic order as in the LXX and the Vg; (ii) in accordance with Canon Law, explanatory notes are supplied; (iii) a small number of changes of wording has been made, where the textual evidence is evenly balanced, (iv) some passages omitted in RSV have been restored. The publication of this Bible is a great step forward towards the ideal of a common Bible.

The **Jerusalem Bible** is a translation from the original languages following closely the critical text on which the well-known Bible de Jerusalem is based and providing an English version of the notes appended to the French translation. It thus provides for Catholics in English-speaking countries not only a version from the original languages but an annotated Bible for the first time in many years. The translation, the work of many hands, is

36c adequate, and effectively brings out the meaning. It attempts to render the originals into good standard English, which at times can be beautiful but at others pedestrian. The whole Bible was published in 1966.

Meanwhile in the U.S.A. a promising and significant
d step of another kind was taken when the production of *the Anchor Bible* was begun. This is described by its editors as a project of international and interfaith scope: Protestant, Catholic and Jewish scholars from many countries contribute individual volumes under the general editorship of William Foxwell Albright and David Noel Freedman. Each volume contains a new translation of the particular book concerned, together with introduction and notes; and whilst the work 'is aimed at the general reader with no special formal training in biblical studies, yet it is written with the most exacting standards of scholarship'.

e **APPENDIX**: As a matter of interest to show the development of the text in English versions of the Bible during six hundred years, a passage (Mt 13:3—4) has been chosen at random from each of the following Bibles:-

i. WYCLIFFE (1380): Lo! he that sowith zede out to sowe his seed. And the while he sowith, sum felden byside the weye, and briddis of the eyre camen, and eeten hem.

ii. TYNDALE (1525): Beholde / the sower went forth to sowe / and as he sowed / some fell by the wayes syde / & the fowles cã / and devoured it uppe.

iii. COVERDALE (1535): Beholde, The sower wente forth to sowe: and as he sowed, some fell by the waye syde: Then came the foules, & ate it up.

iv. MATTHEW (1537): Beholde, the sower wẽt forth to sowe. And as he sowed / some fell by ye wayes syde / & the fowles came & deuoured it up.

v. CRANMER (1539): Beholde, the sower wẽt forth to sowe. And whan he sowed, some sedes fell by ye wayes syde, & the fowles came & deuoured them up.

vi. GENEVA BIBLE (1560): Beholde, a sower went forthe to sowe. And as he sowed, some fel by the wayes side, and the foules came and deuoured them up.

vii. BISHOPS' BIBLE (1568): Beholde, the sower went foorth to sowe. And when he sowed, some seedes fell by the wayes side, and the fowles came, and deuoured them up.

viii. RHEIMS NT (1582): Behold the sower went forth to sow. And whiles he soweth, some fell by the way side, and the fowles of the aire did come and eate it:

ix. AUTHORIZED VERSION (1611): Behold, a sower went forth to sow. And when he sowed, some seeds fell by the way side, and the fowles came, & devoured them up.

x. CHALLONER (1750): Behold the sower went forth to sow. And whilst he soweth some fell by the way side, and the birds of the air came and eate them up.

xi. REVISED VERSION (1881): Behold, the sower went forth to sow, and as he sowed, some seeds fell by the way side, and the birds came and devoured them.

xii. MOFFATT (1913—14): A sower went out to sow, and as he sowed some seeds fell on the road, and the birds came and ate them up.

xiii. WESTMINSTER (1928): Behold, the sower went forth to sow. And as he sowed, some seeds fell by the wayside, and the birds of the air came and ate them up.

xiv. KNOX (1945): Here, he began, is the sower gone out to sow. And as he sowed, there were grains that fell beside the path, so that all the birds came and ate them up.

xv. RSV. (1946): A sower went out to sow. And as he sowed, some seeds fell along the path, and the birds came and devoured them.

xvi. BASIC ENGLISH (1949): A man went out to put seeds in the earth; and while he put them in, some seeds were dropped by the wayside, and the birds came and took them for food.

xvii. NEW ENGLISH BIBLE (1961): He said: A sower went out to sow. And as he sowed, some seed fell along the foot-path; and the birds came and ate it up.

THE INSPIRATION OF SCRIPTURE

BY LIONEL SWAIN

37a Bibliography—Standard and useful works: L. Alonso-Schökel, *The Inspired Word*, 1965; A. Barucq—H. Cazelles, *Les Livres Inspirés*, RF 1, 6—67; J. Beumer, *Die katholische Inspirationslehre zwischen Vatikanum I und II*, Stuttgart, 1967; P. Benoit, *Inspiration and the Bible*, 1965; W. Chillingworth, *The Religion of Protestants*, 1888; H. G. Gadamer, *Wahrheit und Methode*, Tübingen, 1960; W. B. Glover, *Evangelical Non-Conformists and Higher Criticism in the Nineteenth Century*, 1954; S. L. Greenslade (ed.) *The Cambridge History of the Bible*, Cambridge, 1963; P. Grelot, *La Bible, Parole de Dieu*, 1965; W. Harrington, *Record of Revelation*, Dublin, 1965; J. Levie, *The Bible, Word of God in words of men*, 1961; G. Loretz, *The Truth of the Bible*, 1968; J. H. Newman, *On the Inspiration of Scripture* (ed. J. D. Holmes and R. Murray) 1967; K. Rahner, *Inspiration in the Bible* (Quaest. Disp., 1, 1960); K. Rahner and others, *The Bible in a new Age*, 1965; R. Preus, *The Inspiration of Scripture*, 1957; A. Richardson and W. Schweitzer, *Biblical Authority today*, 1951; P. Synave and P. Benoit, *Prophecy and Inspiration*, 1961; D. M. Stanley, *The Concept of Biblical Inspiration*, 1958; B. B. Warfield, *Revelation and Inspiration*, 1927.
Articles: P. Benoit, 'Inspiration and Revelation' *Concilium*, Dec. 1965, 1—10; J. Coppens 'Comment mieux concevoir et énoncer l'inspiration et l'inerrance des saintes Écritures' NRT 86(1964), 933—47; W. Harrington, 'The Inspiration of Scripture', IrTQ 29(1962) 3—24; N. Lohfink, Über die Irrtumsösigkeit und die Einheit der Schrift', *Stimmen der Zeit*, 98(1964), 161—81; D. J. McCarthy, 'Personality, Society and Inspiration', ThS, 24(1963), 553—76; J. L. McKenzie, 'The Social Character of Inspiration' CBQ 24(1962) 115—24; I. de la Potterie, 'La Verité de la sainte Écriture et l'histoire du Salut d'après la Constitution dogmatique "Dei Verbum"', NRT 88(1966) 149—69; G. Schrenk, art. 'grapho' in *Theological Dictionary to the NT*, 1, 742—73; L. J. Topel, 'Rahner and McKenzie on the Social Theory of Inspiration' Scr 16—17 (1964—65), 33—44; P. Zerafa, 'The Limits of Biblical Inerrancy, *Angelicum* 39(1962), 92—119.

b 1 Introduction—An eminent work of literature, or, more precisely, a collection of literature, the Bible is also, and above all, the work of God, his Word, produced that is, under the divine influence. Since the 17th cent. this supernatural character of the sacred authors and, consequently, of their writings, has been called 'inspiration', a term derived from the Vg translation of 2 Tm 3:16. Prior to that date the more common expression used to designate this charism was 'Prophecy' or 'prophetical'. The most significant aspect of the word 'inspiration' is that it implicitly attributes the divine influence in the composition of the Sacred Scriptures to the Holy *Spirit*, the relationship between the *Spirit* and the *Scriptures* being a constant phenomenon throughout the whole history of inspiration.

As is the case with many other aspects of the Faith, **37c** it was only gradually that the Church came to a mature understanding of inspiration. It is the purpose of the present study to follow this development in its broad outlines from the peripheral position it occupied in the OT to the central place it holds in current theological discussion. Obviously attention will be concentrated on the influence exercised by the Holy Spirit on men *to write*, with all that this process involves, but it will be seen eventually that this particular action of the Holy Spirit is ultimately fully intelligible only in the light of the more general action of the Holy Spirit in the people of God, the Jewish people in the OT and the Church in the New.

2 The Old Testament—Although the Biblical religion **d** is not a 'religion of the Book' the phenomenon of writing appears quite early in its history. Nevertheless, nowhere in the canonical literature of the OT is there established an explicit relation between writing and the Holy Spirit. This absence is all the more striking in that the Spirit of God played such a vital part in the establishment and maintenance of God's people: Moses (Nm 11:16—17), Joshua (Nm 27:15—23), elders (Nm 11:16—17), judges (Ju 6:34), prophets (Hos 9:7: Is 42:1), artists (Ex 31:3), Kings (1 Sm 10:6; 16:13), sages (Sir 39:6: Wis 9:17), and the future Messiah (Is 11:1; 61:1) were all men of God's Spirit, and the prophets were also, and above all, men of God's word (Jer 1:9). The tablets of the testimony are ascribed to God's own handiwork (Ex 32:15; 34.1), and there are several records of divine commands to write (Dt 31:19; Is 8:1; 30:8; Jer 30:2—4; 36:2, 32. Ezek 43:11; Heb 2:2), but these involve only particular texts, not the whole corpus of Israel's literature. Even the expression 'sacred books' (1 Mc 12:9; 2 Mc 8:23) tells us no more than that Israel, as many other peoples, possessed books of a certain character. It is, however, possible to argue deductively and by analogy to the idea of the inspiration of the Scriptures in the OT. Granted that God chose to reveal himself to and through a people and that writing is a necessary part of that people's culture, it would seem to follow that its literature should fall under the divine influence in a way similar to its other natural components, e.g. its leaders. Such an argument is not very satisfactory since it leaves untouched the question as to why only a part, albeit the greater part, of Israel's literature was considered to be inspired. In any event, it must be admitted that the communication of God's word by writing held a minor position in the tradition of the OT and one entirely relative to the more dynamic and living forms of communication: God's action within the history of His people, especially as it was realized in and by its charismatic leaders, Moses, the Judges and the Kings, the spoken word of the prophet, priest and sage, and the song of the psalmists.

3 Inspiration in Judaism at the time of 38a Christ—Towards the end of the OT period, possibly as the dynamism and vitality which had created Israel's

38a faith began to wane, attention became increasingly fixed upon the *writings* which enshrined the old spirit. 4 Esdras 14:23—27 (written about A.D. 100) which presents God dictating to Esdras, during 40 days, two hundred and four books, of which only seventy were to be published, expresses this tendency very well.

At the time of Christ, both Palestinian and hellenistic Judaism attributed an absolute value to the Scriptures. For the Rabbis the phrase 'the Scripture says' or 'it is written' was clearly the equivalent of 'God says'. Even here, however, it would be a mistake to consider Judaism as a religion 'of the Book', since the text of the Scriptures was always interpreted in the light of Israel's living faith, officially voiced by Rabbi or priest. In particular, Rabbinical tradition attributed the whole of the Tora to God's dictation or even actual writing. Although the whole corpus of Jewish canonical writings was technically divided, in order of dignity, into: the Law, the Prophets and the Writings, these were all considered sacred and often grouped together under the one title of the 'Tora'.

b   It was **Philo of Alexandria** who first applied to the sacred authors and their writings the prophetical vocabulary of 'inspiration': '*epipnein*', '*katapnein*' (*De Monarch.* 9; *De Somniis* 2, 34; *Quis rev. div. her.* 249) expressions which, in Greek thought, were closely associated with the idea of ecstasy and rapture. Philo also mentioned the need for a corresponding inspiration of the readers of these writings if they were to grasp their meaning properly. **Josephus**, for his part, employed the similar word '*epipnoia*' of the prophets' literary activity (CAp 1.8).

c 4 The New Testament—As far as the literature of the OT is concerned, Christ, the Apostles and the NT authors in general reflected remarkably the contemporary Jewish attitude, speaking frequently of 'the Scriptures' (Mk 12:10; Mt 22:29: Lk 4:21; Jn 5:39; I Cor 15:3, 4) as authoritative sources and introducing many passages with the technical phrase 'it is written' (Mt 4:4—10; 21:13: Lk 19:46). Several passages present God actually speaking in the Scriptures (Mt 22:31: Rm 1:2). More important, the author of Hebrews ascribed this rôle to the Holy Spirit (3:7; 9:8; 10:15). Reflecting more the conceptions of hellenistic Judaism 2 Tm 3:16 and 2 Pt 1:21 expressed the influence exercised by the Holy Spirit, the first on the actual writings (*theopneustos*), the second on their authors (*hupo pneumatos hagiou pheromenoi*), although it is interesting to note that in the second case the action of the Holy Spirit is related explicitly not to the writing of the prophecy, but to its oral proclamation. 2 Tm and 2 Pt present the two main aspects of inspiration: the sacred authors are **inspired to write** (2 Pt), therefore their **work is inspired** (2 Tm). A possible, though in this context not very probable and not commonly accepted, translation of *theopneustos* as an active epithet: 'breathing in God' would suggest a third aspect: the Scriptures, because they are written under the influence of the Holy Spirit and, therefore, transfused with the Holy Spirit, exhale the same Holy Spirit, in other words present the reader with God's word.

d   Several passages of the NT evince the quite early recognition that the charism of inspiration also extended to certain of its own parts. This faith is clearly expressed in 2 Pt 3:16 where St Paul's letters are put on a par with the 'other Scriptures'. Similarly, I Tm 5:18 quotes a saying of Christ (Lk 10:7) as 'Scripture' alongside a quotation from Dt. Greater explicit emphasis is also placed in the NT than in the Old on the role of writing as a means for the communication of God's word. As such it was doubtless considered as an extension of the apostolic

oral preaching (Jn 20:30—31; 1 Jn 2:12—14; 5:13). The **38d** author of Apoc expressly records the order to write (1:10—11) and closely relates his 'prophecy' to the actual book (1:3: 22:7, 10, 18, 19). Even more clearly than the OT, the NT presents the Holy Spirit as the dynamic and vivifying principle at work amidst the New People of God (Ac 2:1—4; I Cor 12:4—11). It is difficult, therefore, to envisage the important function of writing not being attributed to the Holy Spirit, although such a connexion is not explicitly made.

5 The Fathers—In general, the Fathers considered the **e** Scriptures and the sacred authors under the aspect of prophecy. Much of their reflection was but a repetition of the data of the NT. On several scores, however, they contributed to a deeper understanding of the mystery of inspiration. It is in fact **Gregory of Nyssa** who applies the abstract term 'inspiration' both to the sacred authors and to their books for the first time. In their effort to discern more closely the actual mode of the Holy Spirit's action upon the sacred authors, they employed a varied vocabulary: the Holy Spirit 'spoke' (*legein*), 'suggested' (*upagoreuein*), 'dictated' (*dictare*) what the sacred authors were to transmit to their readers. As this terminology would suggest, the main interest was to emphasize the transcendent, divine action. Thus the human author was but an **instrument** (organon) at the service, usually of the Holy Spirit, but also of the Word. This instrument was variously compared to a harp, lyre or flute, played by the Holy Spirit. This is how **Hippolytus** summed up the whole tradition: '. . . prepared by the **prophetical Spirit** and fittingly honoured by the **Word** himself, united to the Word as instruments, they had him always within them as a plectrum, so that, under his movement they should announce precisely what God wished; because the prophets did not express themselves by their own power, and it was not what they themselves wanted that they preached' (*De antichristo, 2 PG 10, 728*). Such passages **f** as this founded the now common analogy between the Incarnation and inspiration: just as the human nature of Christ is the instrument of the Word, formed by the Holy Spirit, so the human authors of the Bible are the instruments of the Word formed by the same Holy Spirit. Nevertheless, this analogy is not without the danger, not always avoided, of extolling the divine influence at the expense of the human authors' natural freedom: 'Quis haec scripserit, valde supervacue quaeritur, cum tamen auctor libri spiritus sanctus fideliter credatur. Ipse igitur haec scripsit, qui scribenda dictavit', Gregory the Great, *Moralia in Job*. Praef. 1, 2 PL 75, 517. Implicit in the idea of the Holy Spirit **dictating** is the idea of his **authorship**, made explicit in the above passage from Greg. The original setting of the phrase '**God, the author of the Scriptures**' was the African councils of the fourth and fifth cent. where it occurs equivalently in the anti-manichean professions of faith, affirming that the one God is the author, in the sense of source or originator, of both the Old and New Testaments or dispensations. Already in the '*Statuta Ecclesiae Antiquae*' (5th cent., EnchB 30) there is possibly a reference to the actual books in which these were represented, but this is certainly the case in the Decree for the Jacobites at the Council of Florence (1442, EnchB 47), at the Council of Trent (1546, Ench B 57) and Vatican I (1870, EnchB 77).

It would be wrong, however, to suggest that the Fathers completely neglected the role of the human authors or failed to take their individual characteristics into account. Cyr. Alex., Chrys. and Aug. among others, drew attention to the style and idiosyncrasies of individual authors,

38f although Aug. makes a point of underlining that even these are God's gifts to the authors.

39a **6 The Middle Ages**—Although Hugh of St Victor and St Thomas drew the explicit distinction between the **prophets** and the **hagiographers**, it was not fully exploited by the theologians of the Middle Ages, who still approached inspiration as proper to prophecy, of which hagiography was an inferior kind. The real contribution of these theologians was most probably the closer scrutiny to which they subjected the precise relationship between God and the inspired. In doing this, they developed philosophically the main acquisitions of the Patristic age: God is the **author** of the Scriptures, the sacred authors are his **instruments**. Thus Albert the Great said that in the production of the fourth Gospel, God's wisdom was the 'first efficient cause' and John the 'immediate efficient cause' (*Enarrationes in Ioann*. Prol.). Henry of Ghent applying to the mystery of inspiration the theory of appropriation and thus bringing in all three divine Persons, distinguished between the principal author and the ministerial authors (*Summae Quaestionum Ordinariarum* a.9, q.2). According to **St Thomas**, the Holy Spirit was the **principal** author of Scripture and man was the **instrumental author** (*Quodl*. 7, art. 14 **b** ad 5). This application of the general theory of instrumental causality to the case in question was a stroke of genius to bear fruit only much later. St Thomas himself did not elaborate this application, the above passage being merely a fleeting reference to inspiration in a context explicitly concerned with the different senses of Scripture. Nevertheless, he expounded his ideas on instrumental causality in relation to **the Sacraments** in III*ᵃ*. q.61 art. 1, in corp. and ad 2; in relation to **Christ's humanity** in III*ᵃ*, q.13 art. 3, in corp.; q.19 art. 1, in corp.; q.45 art. 2, in corp. etc; and in relation to the **ministers** of the **Sacraments** in III*ᵃ*, q.62 art. 5, in corp. In the section of his work consecrated to inspiration (II*ᵃ*–II*ᵃᵉ*, q.171–4; cf also *De Verit*. 12–13) St Thomas dealt exclusively with the human agent's acquisition of knowledge, either by vision (prophecy) or illumination of the intelligence (hagiography). As P. Benoit has recently pointed out, this distinction does not coincide with the distinction between **revelation** and **inspiration**, since in several passages St Thomas uses these last two terms synonymously. The rigid dichotomy sometimes made between inspiration and revelation would not seem, therefore, to have St Thomas' backing. Nevertheless, he viewed both of these operations from the purely intellectual point of view, leaving out of question, or considering as merely accidental, the actual proclamation of the revealed message by the agent, either by the spoken word or in writing. In a later question (II*ᵃ*–II*ᵃᵉ* q. 177 art. 1) writing about the gift of utterance of wisdom (I Cor 12:8) he did, however, envisage the grace of communication and even compared the speaker's tongue to an 'instrument' of the Holy Spirit (in corp.).

c **7 From the 16th century to 1907**—From the 16th cent. onwards, the case of the divine influence exercised on the actual writing of the Scriptures, not envisaged in the previous periods, came to be examined in itself. Throughout most of this period, however, the problem was vexed by the implicit identification of inspiration with revelation, or the communication of divine truth. The Council of Trent itself added little to the debate, being more intent on defining the Canon of the Scriptures and their totality as sacred (EnchB 57–60). It did, however, consecrate the ancient formula: God the author of the OT and NT, (EnchB 57). Following the usage of preceding centuries it also applied the notion of dictation by the Holy Spirit to the reception of truth by the apostles **39c** (EnchB 56). The notion of dictation figured largely in the thought of the post-Tridentine theologians, especially **Melchior Cano** and **D. Bañez**. Both of these authors applied the idea, not to the communication of truth to the human authors, but to the divine impulse to write. It was understandable that the Protestants, committed to the principle of 'Scriptura sola', should exploit the idea of verbal dictation, the Holy Spirit thus being considered as dictating to the human author verbatim **d** exactly what he was to write. It was also natural that Catholic theologians, faced with this too exclusive appeal to Scripture, should extol the living voice of Tradition and, arguing against the Protestants' somewhat selective use of the Scriptures, should stress that *the whole Bible* was *inspired*, that is, in the contemporary terminology, dictated by the Holy Spirit: '. . . omnia scripta esse dictante Spiritu Sancto' (**Robert Bellarmine**); 'Scripsit tota Biblia Deus per homines quibus ea dictavit' (N. Sérier). Thus the prevalent use of the dictation idea among Catholic theologians was probably due to the influence of Protestantism. It is also probable that the much wider vision of revelation possessed by Catholic theologians enabled them to propose other explanations of inspiration. On the other hand, the narrowness of the Protestant view led to the extreme position of **J. Buxtorf** who maintained that the Hebrew codex of the OT was inspired (*theopneustos*) 'tum quoad consonas, tum quoad vocalia sive puncta ipsa, sive punctuorum saltem potestatem'.

The obvious inconvenience of the dictation theory **e** was that it minimized to an extreme the active role of the human author who was equivalently considered as a merely passive instrument in God's hand, a kind of human tape recorder. It was not long, therefore, before a reaction set in against this mechanical view of inspiration, in favour of other views which would take the manifestly human aspect of the Scriptures into account. N. Sérier, **E. Suarez** and **Cornelius a Lapide**, among others, distinguished between two kinds of inspiration, the one which consisted in a 'specialis motio antecedens', really equivalent to dictation, and the other which consisted in an 'assistentia et quasi custodia' (Suarez), in other words, in a purely negative safeguard against error. **L. Lessius** (1587) exaggerated this second kind, holding that a book would be inspired even if, having been written solely by human industry, it were merely guaranteed afterwards by the Holy Spirit as being free from error. A very similar view was propounded by succeeding authors. J. Bonfrère (1625), H. Holden (1655) and Haneberg (1852), the last two attributing to the Church the role which the others gave to the Holy Spirit. Carrying the view to its extreme, Chrisman (1798) and J. Jahn (1816) simply identified inspiration with the divine assistance which guaranteed **f** freedom from error.

Such views, while allowing more scope to the human authors than previous ones, hardly did justice to the constant datum of tradition: that God was the author of the Scriptures. They extolled the human aspect at the expense of the divine. Moreover, by having recourse to freedom from error as the essence of inspiration, they were in fact trying to explain 'obscurum per obscurius'. Since the rise and progress of textual criticism in the 16th cent., of literary criticism in the 17th, of rationalism in the 18th and of archeology, the natural sciences and the more scientific study of history in the 19th, it had become increasingly evident that the assertions of the Bible could no longer be taken simply at their face value. It appeared to many, even believers, that the Bible was frankly in

39f error on many points, while others resorted to various means devised either to whitewash the obvious discrepancies between the discoveries of the human reason and the Bible, or to reconcile particular errors found in the Bible with its overall veracity. Still others, ostrich-like, buried their heads in the biblical sands. In this context what was needed most was a reminder of the correct perspectives from which the whole problem should be reviewed. This was given officially by the **1st Vatican Council**.

40a Against the current rationalism of the time, the 1st Vatican Council, first re-affirmed the doctrine of Trent and then rejected the above-mentioned insufficient views: 'The Church regards them (the books of the OT and NT) as holy and canonical, not because, having been produced by human industry, they were then approved by her authority; nor even because they contain revelation without error, but because, **written by the inspiration of the Holy Spirit**, (Spiritu Sancto inspirante) they have God as their author, and as such have been handed over to the Church' (EnchB 77). The Council here clearly emphasized both the source of the Bible's sacredness and canonicity as residing in the charism of inspiration, and also the actual, continual assistance of the Holy Spirit at the writing of the books. It also marked a certain independence of the inspired books vis à vis the Church. Thus the Council introduced the doctrine of the 'inspiration' of the Bible explicitly among the tenets of the Faith for the first time: 'Si qui sacrae Scripturae libros ... **divinitus inspiratos** negaverit ...' (EnchB 79).

b After the 1st Vatican Council, the centre of the theological stage, as far as inspiration was concerned, was held by **J. B. Franzelin** who, in his *Tractatus de divina Traditione et Scriptura (1870)* distinguished in the Scriptures between a **formal** and a **material element**. The first, consisting in the **ideas expressed**, was the essential object of inspiration, whereas the second, consisting in **the words and the manner** in which the divinely inspired ideas were expressed was left to the character and initiative of the human authors, benefiting nevertheless from the divine assistance which guaranteed freedom from an erroneous presentation of the ideas. Attractive as this view seemed at first, and despite its wide following, its weaknesses soon became obvious. The dichotomy between the ideas and the words in a literary work was a false and dangerous one, evincing a Platonic anthropology. In reality words and the ideas which they express are as indissociable as the material actions and the soul in a human person. Thus, expressing the word, even the written as distinct from the spoken word, is not simply accidental to the idea, a mere appendage; it constitutes an aspect of the idea itself. Franzelin's view, therefore, hardly did justice to the traditional doctrine that God was the author of the books themselves. Also the divine assistance which he allowed to the actual writing of the books was little improvement on the views of the pre-Vatican authors.

c **Leo XIII** in his encyclical *Providentissimus Deus (1893)* rectified the unfortunate tendency of Franzelin's view by giving a definition of inspiration which was to become classic. After recalling the original contribution of Vatican I, quoted above, he continues: 'Therefore it is not relevant to maintain that the Holy Spirit assumed men as instruments for writing in such a way that any falsehood could be attributed not indeed to the primary author but to the inspired writers. For he so **aroused and moved them to write** by a supernatural power, so **assisted them as they wrote**, that they should con-

ceive with a **right mind, will to write faithfully** and **40c** aptly express with infallible truth, all those things and those alone which he ordered: otherwise he would not be the author of the whole of Scripture' (EnchB 125). In this dense passage, Leo XIII rejects any dichotomy between the principal author and his instruments, and affirms both the profound depth and the universal presence of the Holy Spirit's activity, thus applying to both man's will and external powers of execution what St Thomas had confined to the intelligence, and preparing the way for the approach to inspiration as an analogous notion.

Encouraged by *Providentissimus Deus*, several theologians, E. Levesque, **T. Pègues**, D. Zanecchia, **M. J. Lagrange**, sought to explain inspiration by recourse to the Thomistic notion of instrumental causality and, in reaction against Franzelin, to situate the charism of inspiration more in the practical execution of the sacred books than in their intellectual conception. Franzelin had taken as his starting point the traditional notion of God as the author of the Scriptures and had tried to see how it was verified. These last authors, however, began with a theology of inspiration and tried to show how the traditional notion was justified. Unfortunately, the modernist crisis, reflected in the official documents *Lamentabili* and *Pascendi* (1907), did not allow this new approach to the problem of inspiration to bear much fruit. The seed was sown, but the harvest was to come only much later.

8 Inspiration today—Already in 1920, Benedict **41a** XV in his encyclical *Spiritus Paraclitus*, after outlining St Jerome's witness to the traditional doctrine of inspiration, echoed the orientation of Leo XIII and subsequent theologians: 'But there is no doubt that each of the authors of the sacred books **freely** produced his work by God's inspiration **according to his own nature and intelligence**' (EnchB 448). It was, however, **Pius XII** who, in this respect as in so many others, both summed up a whole tradition and provided the impetus for further reflection in *Divino Afflante Spiritu (1943)*. Speaking about the recent contributions to the progress of biblical studies, he made a special mention of those theologians who had exploited the notion of instrumental causality in relation to inspiration, and explicitly recognized the deeper insight into this mystery which they afforded: 'Starting from this principle that the hagiographer in writing the sacred book is the **"organon"** or **instrument** of the Holy Spirit, **living and endowed with reason**, they rightly observe that, acted upon by the divine movement, he so uses his own faculties and abilities, that everyone is able to recognise easily the proper character, the marks and traits of each author (*Spiritus Paraclitus*, EnchB 448) in the book which has been produced by his work' (EnchB 556). Pius XII did **b** more than endorse a view of inspiration. He insisted that a sound view of inspiration was the necessary basis for a sound hermeneutic: since the human author is the living intelligent instrument of the Holy Spirit, it follows that the mind of the Holy Spirit, the ultimate meaning of the Scriptures, is attainable only through an increasingly deeper understanding of the human author's mind (EnchB 557). At last the human aspect of the Bible was seen in its right perspective and the relationship between the divine and the human clearly expressed in an official document. The **2nd Vatican Council** (*Constit. Dei Verbum*, III, 11) summed up the teaching of Pius XII and his predecessors in less technical language: 'For the writing of the sacred books, God chose men; he used them in allowing them the usage of their faculties and of all

41b their resources, so that, he himself acting in them and by them, they should transmit in writing, as real authors, all that he wished, and only that'.

c **Contemporary theological discussion** concerning inspiration revolves around three interconnected ideas: 1. the notion of instrumental causality 2. the complexity of the Scriptural data 3. the ecclesial aspect of inspiration. 1. **The notion of instrumental causality**—It is obvious that the notion of **instrument**, traditional as it is, cannot be lightly applied philosophically to the sacred writers, since a human being is not just a thing, as a pen or a knife, but a living, intelligent person. It is, therefore, difficult to understand how this creature can be 'used' without its natural freedom and consciousness being violated, and yet these are safeguarded by Leo XIII's definition of inspiration and subsequent official documents. This dilemma is not peculiar to the case of inspiration. It is common to all the instances of God's supernatural influence upon man and occurs even in the natural order when it is a question of reconciling human freedom with

d God's creative act. It can be resolved by recourse to the Thomistic notion of God's **transcendent causality**. God moves the creature according to its own peculiar nature. His movement is not juxtaposed to the creature's action but submerged within it. It is man's nature to act consciously and willingly. God can move him to act precisely in that way. If God does so he may be called the **principal cause** of the activity and man the **instrumental cause** the effect being entirely attributable to both causes, though on the two different levels of principal and instrumental causality respectively. In the case of inspiration, the effect produced is a literary work. Since the cause of a literary work is called an 'author' both God and the human agent are authors. The Bible is **entirely man's work and entirely God's work**.

e The concept of God's transcendent causality applied to inspiration is truly liberating. Once properly grasped, many false problems, not always evaded even in modern discussion, are seen in their true light. It facilitates the dissociation of the notion of inspiration from any one of its preconceived modes. Revelation affirms the fact of inspiration, but it is left for human research based on the data of the Scriptures themselves, to describe exactly *how* the Holy Spirit inspired the sacred writers. There is no dichotomy between faith and reason. A parallel might be drawn between the doctrine of inspiration and the doctrine of creation, particularly in the light of the last century's evolutionary theories. So many false problems were then raised and false solutions given simply because the affirmation of the fact of creation was identified with its mode. It is now possible to reconcile the fact with a great variety of modes. Similarly, it is for human research to show precisely how the Bible was produced. The principle of God's transcendent causality enables the theologian to relate scientific discovery to God's action: if *this* is how the Bible was produced, then *this* is how God produced it.

42a 2. **The complexity of the Scriptural data**—The application of the principle of instrumental causality to inspiration means that whatever elements have contributed to the production of the Bible were assumed by the Holy Spirit as his instruments, the divine influence coinciding exactly with the human aspect throughout. The consequences of this principle are many and far-reaching. Until the advent of literary and historical criticism, the composition of the sacred books was considered a fairly simple affair. But it is now seen increasingly how many and varied are the influences—personal, social, historical and cultural, which contribute

to the production of literature. And then there is the phenomenon of literature itself. How is the written word different from the spoken word? The philosophy of literature, as of language in general, is still in its infancy. To show how this complexity is embraced by God's transcendent causality is no mean task. Before all else, the temptation to tender a detailed a priori explanation of how a book came to be written must be resisted. Even as far as an individual author of the 20th cent. is concerned, the composition of a literary work is a highly complex operation not easily dissected into the **speculative judgements** concerning doctrinal or historical truths to be transmitted and **practical judgements** having objects other than the communication of these kinds of truth, for example, the means to be adopted in communicating the truth, the encouragement, amusement, annoyance of the readers. Man is a unity, b and something is always lost in the attempt to isolate his thought from the concrete circumstances in which it is expressed. On the other hand, there is an aspect of truth contained in those circumstances which will always escape even the speaker's or writer's full consciousness. Thus an author, by his choice of the subject for his book, his use of language, his judgement on persons and events etc often betrays his background, character and interests in a way which he himself would not suspect. This is part and parcel of the literary phenomenon which must also be taken into account in the consideration of the Bible, which, as all literature, **suggests much more than it affirms**. The Bible, however, is not a 20th cent. literary work, and the vast amount of oral tradition, documentation, editing, re-editing, adaptation, elaboration and interpretation, which modern literary and historical criticism discerns as having gone into its production, calls for a much more flexible application of the instrumental causality principle than has hitherto been suggested. It is true that, strictly speaking, the charism of c inspiration is ascribed to those human authors who were responsible for the production of the original texts as they now stand. But what about the sources used by the author or authors, say, of the Pentateuch, or the oral tradition behind the Synoptic Gospels? Are we to hold that the 'authors' concerned here did not enjoy the charism of inspiration? **P. Benoit**, who, since 1947 has consecrated several important studies to the problem of inspiration, provided the germ of an answer to this question in 1959 drawing attention to the **analogous character of inspiration**. He discussed three correlative kinds of inspiration, each related to a charism: the inspiration **to act**, the inspiration **to speak** and the d inspiration **to write**. P. Grelot has rightly suggested recently that these analogies of inspiration should be extended further to include the **action of the Holy Spirit among the people of God** both in the OT and in the NT, articulated by more charisms than just prophecy and apostleship, cited by P. Benoit. If this proposition is accepted, inspiration can be seen as far-reaching profound, and varied influence of the Holy Spirit at different levels of the people of God, from the living tradition, subsequent on God's historical activity and the prophetical preaching, to its crystallization in the Scriptures. Obviously scriptural inspiration applies only to the last but it is also clear that it is closely related to the other forms which prepare its way, including the inspiration, that is, the Holy Spirit's preparation of the sacred writers' sources, written or oral. In other words, what the early proponents of the instrumental causality explanation applied analogously to the sacred writer's intelligence, will and external powers of execution, can

42d be applied to the author's **social and cultural dimen-**
e **sions** as well. This view corresponds to what modern
criticism says about the complex genesis and development
of the Scriptures and avoids the two extremes of holding
either that certain well-defined authors of the sacred
books were alone inspired or that the people as a whole
was alone inspired, the books themselves being no more
than the concretization of their faith. All the data seems
to indicate that although the Holy Spirit was at work
among the people before anything was written, nevertheless the actual Scriptures were written under a specific
motion of the Holy Spirit related to certain charismatic
functions within the people and at the service both of
God and of the people. Moreover, the written word is
never simply a substitute for the spoken word or a mere
f concretization of a living faith. It has a specific cultural
value and meaning. Thus the consignment of the spoken
word or of Israel's or the Church's religious tradition to
writing was not merely accidental. It was an irreducible
contribution to that tradition, and itself a communication
of God's word, since the human authors, for all their
dependence upon tradition, were necessarily selective in
their treatment of it and wrote for the specific purpose
of communicating God's word. This word could have coincided with what had simply been said before (Is 30:8)
or could have been a new angle on traditional material
(Jn 20:30–31). In other words, the role of the sacred
writers was *creative* as well as *representative*. **J. L.**
McKenzie in his article on the '*Social aspect of In-*
spiration' (1962) emphasized too strongly the social
aspect, whereas the exposition of **D. McCarthy** in '*Per-*
sonality, Society and Inspiration' (1963) has given a
much more nuanced and satisfactory treatment of the
matter, allowing for the influence of society upon the
sacred writers, but at the same time defending their
g freedom of expression and personal contribution. Granted
the profound insertion of God's people within the context
of human history and culture, it is obvious that, on this
view of inspiration, the line of demarcation between where
natural forces alone end and inspiration begins becomes
much more blurred than in the view that the sacred author
alone is inspired. But precisely where does the natural
end and the supernatural begin? **K. Rahner** was right
when he suggested in his own contribution to this problem
that the criterion of the correct formulation of a theological point is whether it involves the most fundamental
of theological problems, and, in a sense the whole of
theology. In fact the mystery of inspiration is but one
specific aspect of the more fundamental mystery: the
relationship between the natural and the supernatural
order.

43a 3. **The ecclesial aspect of inspiration**—The contemporary concern with the social character of inspiration
raises the question of the relationship between inspiration
and the Church. The actual society in which the Holy
Spirit was active was the people of God, the Jews in the
OT and the Church in the NT. Further, those who committed the people's faith to writing and addressed God's
word to the people, were members of the people, endowed
with a special charism for this role. All the recent research into the nature of inspiration has converged on
this point: it is not possible to isolate scriptural inspiration
from the many other charisms of the Holy Spirit in the life
of the Church. To make it the most important charism is
b to mutilate Christianity. It must be seen in relation to
the general 'inspiration' of the Holy Spirit in the Church
(I Cor 12:4–11). This vision must be retrospective
and pro-spective. It must embrace the genesis and development of revelation up to the time of its concretization

in writing, but also the various ways in which the fixed **43b**
letter of the Scriptures is continually vivified by the
living Church, articulated in the liturgy and the charismatic magisterium, and assimilated by believers under
the influence of the Holy Spirit. It is only in this context
that the otherwise equivocal and misleading expression
'the Bible is the Word of God' has a meaning. K. Rahner **c**
has emphasized this point forcibly in his work on inspiration (1958) showing how the Scriptures are a constitutive
element of the Church formed totally by the influence of
the one Holy Spirit. They are the crystallization, the
objectivization of the Church's faith, and thus the
permanent norm of that faith. Rahner, however, was only
explicitly concerned with the NT. **N. Lohfink** (1964) has
stressed the role of the Church in the inspiration of the
OT. The charism of scriptural inspiration is attributed
to the last author or editor of the inspired text. According
to N. Lohfink the apostolic Church, taking up the OT
in its life, liturgy and preaching, could be compared to
an author using previous sources and therefore be seen as
the author of the OT. As P. Grelot (1965) has pointed out, **d**
the role of the apostolic Church in regard to the OT is
rather a matter of interpretation, albeit inspired, than
of authorship. Moreover, the apostolic Church explicitly
recognized the OT Scriptures as inspired (2 Tm 3:16).
It remains true, however, that with the advent of Christ
and the apostolic preaching the whole of the OT received
a new meaning which it did not contain explicitly. To
P. Grelot himself is due the most satisfactory placing of
the charism of inspiration in the context of the other
charisms in the life of the Church, as well as the latest
comprehensive treatment of the problem of inspiration
as a whole.

9 The Truth of Scripture—If the Bible is God's Word, **44a**
in the sense mentioned above, the essential effect of
inspiration is **God's communication to men**. But this
is a literary communication, and, in this connexion, the
observations of **H. G. Gadamer** are relevant: 'In written
form, everything handed down is contemporary with every
present moment. In it, therefore, there exists a unique
co-presence of past and present, to the extent that present
consciousness has the possibility of free access to all
that has been handed down in writing' (*Wahrheit und
Methode* (1960), 367) and 'What is fixed in writing,
has detached itself from the contingence of its origin and
author and is positively freed for new relationships' (ibid
373). Although the consignment to writing of a people's
religious tradition or the spoken word of God's messengers
has as its primary purpose to assure them of a permanent
and more general value and meaning, nevertheless this
value and meaning must always be measured by those
which the literature had when it was first written and
for the immediate people for whom it was produced.
Modern literary and historical criticism has disclosed **b**
that the Bible is the functional literature of God's people
and has drawn attention to its accidental, occasional and,
above all, social character. If by revelation we know that
the Bible is God's Word, that is, we are aware of its
vertical dimension, by human research we know that it is
man's word, that is, we are aware of its horizontal dimension. The question concerning the truth of Scripture must
be seen in this context. All forms of literature, as all
other forms of communication, can convey truth. Truth,
however, is an analogous concept. A joke, for instance,
has a truth, although this is not identifiable with the
material accuracy of all the details recounted. The human
authors of the Bible wrote for the wide variety of reasons
common to all human authors—to instruct, certainly, but
also to exhort, to comfort, to criticize, to record their

44b confessions of faith and prayers, even to amuse. Each of these aims, which can be couched in a variety of literary forms, has its own kind of truth.

c The history of inspiration has shown that the same tools which were originally used against this mystery—literary criticism, the discoveries of the natural sciences etc turned out eventually to be instrumental in the forging of a more flexible notion of inspiration. The same must be said about the truth of Scripture. This has always been a corollary of its inspiration, and it was not until the advent of the critical sciences and rationalism, especially during the 19th cent., that it was questioned with any poignancy. Naturally in a context of critical, scientific and historical immaturity, the truth of the Bible was identified with the information it appeared to give concerning the creation of the world, the origin of man and the **d** course of human history. The conflict between the discoveries of science and this naive view of biblical truth was, therefore, inevitable. It was also understandable that against this onslaught on the Bible, theologians should at first adopt a negative stance: 'the Bible is *free from error*'; and that a great deal of ink should have been spilt on trying to justify this assertion in a variety of ways, either by forcing the discoveries of science to fit into the biblical data (**concordism**), or by restricting inspiration to **matters of faith** (H. Holden 1655), or by narrowing it to exclude '**obiter dicta**' (**J. H. Newman 1884**), or by confining inerrancy to matters of faith and morals (*D.'Hulst* 1893), or by recourse to '**implicit quotations**' which were not guaranteed by the charism of inspiration. All of these attempts were vitiated by a negative, defensive attitude which implicitly identified, as did the views of the opponents, biblical truth with scientific and historical accuracy. It was in this context that the 1st Vatican Council saw the necessity of affirming that the sacred books contained 'revelation without error' (EnchB 77). In this, Leo XIII in *Prov Deus* (EnchB 120—5), Pius X in *Lamentabili* and *Pascendi* (EnchB 202, 273, 280), various decrees of the Biblical Commission, and Benedict XV in *Spir Par* (EnchB 461) followed suit.

e Already in *Prov Deus*, however, Leo XIII suggested another, although not entirely new, approach to the question of biblical truth. Still in a markedly apologetic strain, he pointed out, following *Aug.* and *St Thomas*, that the Holy Spirit, in speaking through the sacred authors, did not wish to teach men the interior constitution of visible things, which would not be beneficial to salvation. Rather, the sacred authors spoke of such things 'according to their appearances' (EnchB 121). This passage laid down a useful principle for those parts of the Scriptures which touched on matters common to the **f** natural sciences. It was thought for some time that the same rule could be applied to **the case of history**, but *Benedict XV* in *Spir Par* rejected such a theory of '**history according to appearances**' (EnchB 457). In fact the natural sciences and history are not in the same category. While salvation in no way involves the physical structure of the universe, it does involve its history, for God has revealed himself within, and by, human history. It was necessary therefore, to defend a certain **historical truth** for the Bible, although the question concerning the nature of this historical truth and the way it was conveyed by the ancient historians remains an open question. It was with this problem in particular in mind that **Pius XII** in *Divino Afflante Spiritu* exhorted scholars to explore the various literary genres, particularly in the field of history, which were current in the ancient middle East and which were used by the sacred authors (EnchB 560). A more recent decree **44f** of the Biblical Commission (April 1964) endorsed a **g** similar programme à propos of the Gospels. The Constitution *Dei Verbum* of the *2nd Vatican Council*, which insists throughout on the **salvific character of revelation**, speaks of the truth which God 'in view of our salvation, wished to be consigned to the sacred Scriptures' (Ch III, par. 11). **I. de la Potterie** (1966) has shown the importance of this particular formulation. It avoids the unfortunate material distinction, current at the end of the last century, between matters of faith and morals, which engage inspiration and, therefore, are taught without error, and other matters which are not covered by inspiration, and, therefore, are not necessarily taught without error. Further it places the reason for the Bible's truth in the divine intention to save. This means that biblical truth must be seen in relation to salvation, eventually effected in Christ. There is thus a notable **h** move here away from the Gk idea of abstract truth to the Heb. notion of dynamic, vital truth. In other words, the truth of the Scriptures is essentially salvific truth. This does not exclude historical truth or even other natural truths, but these are all put to the service of God's will to reveal to men both himself and his saving plan.

In view of the apparent discrepancies between the biblical data and the discoveries of the critical and natural sciences, is not this to suggest that God uses error to communicate truth? It is in this connexion that an intelligible view of biblical truth is seen to demand necessarily a healthy view of inspiration. The flexible notion of inspiration outlined above leads to the conclusion that God wanted to say through the sacred authors only what they wanted to say and said. This is what is meant by the literal sense of the Scriptures. Even granted that there are certain passages, say, of the OT, which eventually are seen to contain meanings unsuspected by their original authors, these are valid meanings only in so far as they are made explicit within the biblical tradition itself. This is what is meant by the '*sensus plenior*' or fuller understanding of such passages.

The all-important question is, therefore, precisely **45a** what did this particular author mean to say and in fact say? This question cannot be answered a priori, nor by a facile identification of what an author is saying with the way he says it. It is precisely the role of literary and historical criticism to establish, by patient research, what is the mind of the author in each individual case. In this respect the study of **literary forms** is of vital importance. But the 'mind of the author' is itself an analogous concept. Certainly the sacred author may wish to communicate a religious truth or record an historical event and here, obviously, the 'doctrinal' or 'historical' content of his words will be very high, although even in these cases it is necessary to take into account the conceptual apparatus of the author's own time and, particularly, the various ancient ways of presenting historical truth. Very often, however, the author intends to inculcate a religious or moral truth, to exhort, to comfort, to reprimand or to praise God, and in these cases the doctrinal and historical aspects will be subordinate to the author's practical purpose. The exterior form of each **b** book or part of the Bible is not an infallible criterion concerning the author's aim. Literary and historical criticism have repeatedly shown that books which appear at first to be historical can be, in fact, didactic stories. In strict loyalty to a sound view of inspiration, attention must also be paid to the author's **degree of affirmation** on any one point, since God affirms only what, and in so far as, the sacred author affirms. Doctrinal and historical

45b truth rest in the judgement. It is only when the sacred author judges a matter with certitude that his judgement can be considered under the aspect of doctrinal or historical truth. On many points he is entitled to express an opinion or even hazard a guess. These are inspired opinions and guesses and are worth only the degree of affirmation given them by the authors. This approach, far from undermining the notion of biblical truth, enhances it and places it in its right perspective. It avoids the now unnecessary pre-occupation with the negative 'inerrancy' of the Bible. But, above all, it highlights the **c** multiform character of biblical truth. Literature is not only expressive, it is also symptomatic and suggestive. An author expresses not only his own thought and intentions but also the conditions, ideas and aspirations of the society in which he lives. An aspect of biblical truth, suggested by the discoveries of modern criticism, is the way in which God has assumed for the communication of his revelation, not 'ideal' instruments but real, 'true' men, steeped in the culture and literary techniques of their time, with all the 'imperfections' and inaccuracies which, from the modern viewpoint, this entailed. In other words, he did not blind human nature with moral science **d** but educated it to receive the revelation of Christ. N. Lohfink has rightly emphasized the importance of this progressive aspect of revelation for an understanding of biblical truth. God is the author of the whole Bible. He revealed his mind only partially in the OT. The fulness of revelation came only with Christ and the NT. This means that the affirmations, ideas and aims of the OT authors are necessarily preparatory, incomplete and imperfect in relation to the NT. The Word of God in the OT is essentially relative to his Word in the New. This remark is particularly relevant to the question of OT morality. **The truth of the Bible** thus becomes **Christocentric**, not in the sense that the mystery of Christ is read into the OT events and personages, after the manner of Alexandrian allegory, but in the sense that the Word of God which was to be eventually manifested in human nature was at work in the OT, gradually assuming, purifying, educating, preparing human nature, in both its moral and its cultural aspects, in readiness for the fulness of time. The patristic intuition which drew the parallelism between the Incarnation and inspiration in this way receives a new dimension.

e The past too exclusive pre-occupation with a negative view of the truth of Scripture has tended to encourage the neglect of other important consequences of inspiration which are clearly noted in 2 Tm 3:15—17: '. . . the sacred writings which are able to instruct you **for salvation** through faith in Christ Jesus. All scripture is inspired by God and profitable **for teaching**, **for reproof**, **for correction** and **for training in righteousness**, that **45e** the man of God may be **complete**, **equipped for every good work**'. These sum up what is meant in the modern problematic by the positive truth of Scripture.

10 Conclusion—Several salient points appear through- **f** out this brief history of inspiration. The first is **the relationship between inspiration and the Holy Spirit**. Is this purely fortuitous or even merely a matter of accommodation? The Holy Spirit was the creative and directive force in the history both of Israel and of the Church, the principle of Mary's conception of the Word, and the truth giving Light promised to the disciples. The constant connexion between inspiration and the Holy Spirit thus suggests the importance of inspiration as a stage in the history of salvation. The second point is the essentially **relative character of inspiration**. Scriptural inspiration, that is, the influence of the Holy Spirit on certain individuals to write was but one among many other charisms bestowed by the Holy Spirit upon the people of God. Moreover, it is clearly secondary to the more important charism of prophecy in the OT and the apostolate in the New. The essential role of the sacred **g** writers was to crystallizé and concretize revelation, transmitted initially by word of mouth. It is true that in writing the sacred writers ordered their material in their own way and impressed their own personality upon it, acting as real authors, but they did this within the framework of the original revelation—inspiration to write was not inspiration to reveal, but to fix, and, in fixing, to make more explicit what had been revealed. It follows from this that the Scriptures are not God's Word in the strict sense, that is, God's revelation. Rather they **re-present this Word**, in so far as they relate to Christ, the Word, through the apostolic preaching. The oral transmission of revelation was obviously necessary in a society which was predominently illiterate. Even at the time of the NT, literature was far from being the normal means for the communication of ideas. This leads to the third point. **h** By the Incarnation, the Word assumed human nature. Previously he had been at work in the history of Israel assuming, as it were, all the instruments which creation afforded: history, nature, the minds, hearts and executive powers of men. Could it not be that the assuming of the literary phenomenon was another link in this chain, in which God used nature as an instrument of Grace, the working out of the **incarnational principle**? To communicate himself to men God has used, and continues to use, the whole of creation. Viewed in this light, scriptural inspiration is but one instance, albeit a unique and irreducible one, of the work of the Holy Spirit in creation, replete with powerful lessons for an understanding of God's action in the world today.

THE INTERPRETATION OF THE BIBLE

BY LIONEL SWAIN

46a **Bibliography—Official Documents**—Dogmatic Constitution on Divine Revelation of the Second Vatican Council, edit. Vatican Polyglot Press, 1965; E. tr. CTS, 1966. 'Instructio de historica Evangeliorum veritate', AAS, 1964. 172—8, E. tr. The Tablet, May 30, 1964, 617—19.

General Works—L. Alonso Schökel, *Understanding Biblical Research*, 1963; J. Bright, *The Authority of the OT, 1967*; J. D. Grant, *The Interpretation of Scripture*, 1961; J. Levie, *The Bible, Word of God in Words of Men*, 1961; A. B. Mickelsen, *Interpreting the Bible*, 1963; J. K. S. Reid, *The Authority of Scripture*, 1957; J. Wilkinson, *Interpretation and Community*, 1963; IB, 1, 106—41.

b **Special Points**—P. Anfeld, 'Exégèse critique et exégèse dogmatique', ETL 43 (1967), 405—419; Y. Congar, *Tradition and Traditions*, 1966; A. Deissler, *Das Alte Testament und die neuere katholische Exegese* Freiburg i. Br. 1965; H. de Lubac, *L'Écriture dans la Tradition*, 1966; R. M. Grant, *The Letter and the Spirit*, 1957; P. Grelot, *Sens chrétien de l'AT*, 1962; id 'Que penser de l'interprétation existentielle?', ETL 43 (1967) 420—443; R. Marlé. 'Le Problème théologique de l'herméneutique', 1963; id, *Bultmann et l'interprétation du NT*, 1966; id, 'Le Chrétien d'aujourd'hui devant la Bible', *Études*, Dec. 1964, 627—39; id, 'Le Dogme dans la Foi', *Études*, Jan. 1967, 8—22; J. L. McKenzie, 'Problems of Hermeneutics in Roman Catholic Exegesis', JBL 1958, 197—204; J. Muilenburg, 'Preface to Hermeneutics', JBL, 1958, 18—26; D. E. Fuchs, *Hermeneutik*, 1954; A. Richardson and A. Schweitzer, *Biblical Authority for Today*, 1951; C. Romaniuk, *Les Chemins de l'exégèse du NT*, 1963; J. C. Rylaarsdam, 'The Problem of Faith and History in Biblical Interpretation', JBL, 1958, 27—32; K. Stendahl, 'Implications of Form-Criticism and Tradition-Criticism for Bible Interpretation', JBL, 1958, 33—38; L. Steiger, *Die Hermeneutik als dogmatisches Problem*, 1961; J. Barr, *Old and New in Interpretation*, 1965; P. G. Duncker, 'Biblical Criticism', CBQ, 1963, 22—33; R. E. Brown, 'The Sensus Plenior in the Last Ten Years', CBQ, 1963, 262—85; id 'The Problems of the Sensus Plenior,' ETL 43 (1967) 460—469; L. A. Schökel, 'Hermeneutics in the Light of Language and Literature', CBQ, 1963, 371—86; R. E. Brown, 'After Bultmann, What?', CBQ, 1964, 1—30; B. Vawter, 'The Fuller Sense: Some Considerations', CBQ, 1964, 85—96; P. J. Cahill, 'Rudolph Bultmann and Post-Bultmann Tendencies', CBQ, 1964, 153—78; C. Westermann, *Essays on OT Interpretation*, 1964; G. Van Riet 'Exégèse et reflexion philosophique', ETL 43 (1967) 390—404.

c **Introduction**—The process and art of interpretation are by no means peculiar to the sphere of the Bible or, indeed, to the field of literature as a whole. Interpretation is the indispensable counterpart to all forms of communication, ranging from the banalities of the ordinary human conversation to the computerized transmissions of a lunar

probe. Biblical interpretation, together with the various **46c** problems which it involves, is but one example of a more vast and complex question—that of the meaning of language, understood in the wide sense to include all forms of communication, and, ultimately, of the meaning of existence. This question is a specifically philosophical one, which is receiving increased attention in these days, and any sound, realistic exegesis of the Bible must take cognizance of the fact. Clearly, the initial stance adopted in relation to any datum to be interpreted depends upon elements outside that datum itself. As social animals, for instance, we know by convention and education the rules which govern a conversation. To appreciate that conversation in a language other than our own an additional apparatus is required. The chemist must know the elementary significance of the reactions which he is analyzing. **d** Even a computer needs to be 'programmed'. Similarly, when we approach the undeniable phenomenon, or datum, of the Bible, it is necessary for our minds to be attuned to the object of their study. Obviously, such a conformity of subject and object is necessarily incipient and, in many areas, tentative, otherwise the whole question of interpretation is itself meaningless, but it is an absolute pre-requisite for a complete understanding of the Bible. In other words, a 'purely objective' knowledge of the Bible is as chimerical as a 'purely objective' knowledge of anything, all knowledge implying, of its very nature, a subjective element. In the last analysis, the criterion of the accuracy of an interpretation is not an objective datum but the reasonableness or justification of a subjective attitude which, by definition, will always defy 'objectiviation'.

The above remarks are intended as a necessary pre- **e** lude to, and justification of, the method of treatment followed in this study. **The Bible is a work of literature** or, more precisely, a collection of such works, and must be approached as such, according to all the currently accepted norms and procedures of literary criticism. In the case of the Bible, the task of appreciation is unusually complicated in that the body of literature concerned hails from the ancient Middle East and covers a period of nearly two thousand years. Moreover, the Bible manifestly makes certain **historical claims**. It is true that all literature is in some sense historical, in so far as it reflects and represents the culture and the conditions of the time in which it was produced, but the Bible is historical in the sense that it proclaims the occurrence of certain events within the course of human history. This fact demands that the Bible be viewed accordingly, attention being paid not to the merely artificial, positivistic criteria of historicity but to the meaning of history. Further, and this is possibly **f** the most neglected aspect of the Bible, this literary work makes a definite and absolute **claim to explain existence** and offers answers to the most pressing problems of the human mind. In a word, the Bible constitutes a philosophy, comparable, therefore, to all the other known philosophies. The Bible represents, no less

B✳

than all other literature, an attempt on the part of man to come to grips with the fundamental problems of his existence.

B✳

46f than these, the perennial quest of the human mind and heart for the meaning of existence. Finally, though still within the context of the explanation of existence, the Bible propounds a religion, the relation of man to a deity different from, and beyond, himself, who is responsible for existence. There have been, and are, many religions and there exists an organized study of the history and comparison of these religions. The biblical religion, from the merely natural or phenomenological point of view, enjoys the same respectability as all other religions, and deserves to be assessed by the recognized standards of the study of religions.

g The Bible, however, is not only a literary, historical, philosophical, religious phenomenon. It also claims to represent **God's Word to man**. In so far as this manifest assertion is merely observed from the outside, or even acknowledged as a phenomenon specifically characteristic of the biblical religion, it is confined within the bounds of religious criticism, but once it is accepted as true, as a fact, it enters the ambit of faith, the science of which is theology. There is therefore a vast difference between the study of religion and theology. For the one, merely natural powers of observation and judgement are sufficient, for the other faith is absolutely necessary. This does not mean that the demands of theology impede or limit the procedures of critical scholarship, since each discipline operates on a different level, the role of theology being to direct, pervade and inspire scholarship, to give it a new dimension, irreducible to any merely rational dimension. Further, theology, as any other science, has its own principles which must be applied to the Bible. Certainly, there is a sense in which every reality has a theological dimension, but this is particularly true in the case of the Bible which is specifically God's Word.

h God's Word to man is not the simple transmission of ideas about himself and about man to be grasped by a mere notional assent. It is the communication of himself to man, an invitation to participate in the divine life, which calls for a personal, vital response of the whole man. As St Augustine pointed out, the fullness and the purpose of the Scriptures are nothing more than the life of charity (*De Doct. christ.*, I, 35). Thus the Bible is understood fully not just on the notional plane, even though that were to include faith, but on the level of the heart, of Christian living. Any presentation of biblical interpretation which neglects this last aspect is, therefore, necessarily truncated and distorted. For an historical survey, see § 8.

The Critical Approach cf § 91*d*.

47a **(a) the Bible as literature**—The history of exegesis reveals that the vicissitudes through which the Bible has passed are not dissimilar to those through which the mystery of the Incarnation has passed throughout the history of the Church. The Bible, as Christ himself, is both human and divine—not partly human and partly divine, but wholly human and wholly divine. Moreover, the divine is expressed only through the human (cf Jn 1:14; 14:8–10). The mystery of the Incarnation implies that if we want to know who and what God is we must scrutinize the man Jesus. Similarly, the mystery of inspiration means that if we wish to know God's Word we must understand what the Bible says and in the way it is said. History has shown that it is extremely difficult to maintain the balance between the divine and the human, the necessary and the contingent. The opposing tendencies have been to stress the one aspect to the exclusion or minimization of the other. The only orthodox and sane approach is to face the reality, which is not without a certain scandal. God's Son, in becoming man, has taken upon himself human

nature with all that this involves by way of imperfection **47a** and weakness, in all but sin (cf Heb 4:15). Similarly, God, in choosing the human reality of literature, more specifically the literature of an insignificant group of ancient Middle Easterners, through which to reveal himself, has committed himself to all the imperfection and obscurity that this implies. It is this simple fact which forms the basis and the starting point of sound biblical interpretation which is inspired by the conviction that the more one understands the literary phenomenon of the Bible the clearer will be one's grasp of God's Word, just as the more one appreciates the meaning of human nature the better one understands the significance of the Incarnation.

(b) textual criticism—The first and most basic task of **b** biblical scholarship is to establish and define the actual object of its study, that is, the text of the Bible in the original languages—Heb., Aram. and Gr. This involves not only considerable proficiency in these languages, but also the ability to manipulate the huge mass of evidence for the original text buried in a multitude of manuscripts and versions. Only when the scholar is reasonably sure of the text before his eyes can his real task of interpretation begin, see § 602.

(c) literary criticism—A text does not make literature. **48a** This comes to birth only when the words express meaning, the ultimate object of the scholar's endeavour. The ways in which literature conveys meaning are many and varied. Doubtless it does this principally through the actual sense of the *words* used. Even in our modern languages the same word can have several meanings or nuances of meaning, and the taking of the intended meaning depends upon a complicated system of inbred convention. In the case of the Bible, we are separated from the language in which it is written by two thousand years and more. What would have been grasped spontaneously by the original readers or hearers of the biblical texts can now be appreciated fully only by painstaking research into the use of language in the Ancient Middle East. Moreover, as was pointed out above, the biblical texts themselves stretch over a period of nearly two thousand years. It is obvious that the use of the same words changed and developed during that time, and it would be wrong to attribute to a word in an early text the meaning which it has in a later one, or vice versa.

In order to establish the correct meaning of the words it is not enough to consult dictionaries and lexica. The *context* of their use must also be considered. In the case of the OT, the translation of the LXX can also afford valuable insights into way in which the words were understood in 3rd and 2nd cent. B.C.

The meaning of words varies also according to the **b** way or *literary form* in which they are used. Here again the Bible provides particular difficulties. We are familiar with the various literary forms in our own literature— the drama, the comedy, the novel, the poem, the historical work, and so on, but we are not so conversant with those of the ancient world. Nevertheless the close study of the ever increasing wealth of literature from the ancient Middle East is helping to fill the gaps. It is only when we understand, and in the measure that we understand, the ways in which the ancients expressed themselves that we will be able to grasp adequately the meaning of the sacred writers. The keen interest and attention given today to the literary forms of the Bible should not, however, obscure the fact that the Bible is a unity and that, considered as such, there is a sense in which it can be said to have one literary form, in so far as that unity is not accidental, nor willed by God alone, but is also seen and intended by the final editors of the Bible. Thus after the

47b analytic process of Form Criticism comes the study of the way in which all the various forms discerned have been integrated and synthesized into a greater whole, which, being the final result of the charism of *inspiration*, is the ultimate object of the scholar's research.

c Closely connected with the notion of literary form is the idea of *symbolism*. Literature conveys meaning not only linguistically but also symbolically, not only by instruction or information but also by evocation. Living in a highly mechanized, sophisticated society we are possibly less conscious of this aspect of language than our forebears, certainly less so than the ancient inhabitants of the Middle East. It is in this field, probably more than anywhere else, that the science of *ethnology* can contribute a great deal towards an understanding of the Bible. A close study of primitive peoples living in the world today reveals remarkable similarities between the thought patterns and forms of expression of these latter and what we know only indirectly of those of the ancient Middle East. In this way, it is possible to complete the cultural background picture to the Bible. In particular, it is through ethnology that the term *myth* has been delivered of its derogatory overtones and restored to respectability as a recognized mode of thought and expression.

d Language is not only expressive. It is also *creative*. Theoretically speaking, the word expressed should transmit and re-create in the mind of the hearer or reader the meaning *intended* by the speaker or writer. In fact it does this, and much more besides. The word once uttered is, in a sense, independent of its author. It is charged not only with the meaning *intended* by its author, but also with other possible meanings which could reveal the mind of the author in a way which he did not *intend*. In other words, language is *symptomatic*. Applied to literature this means that although an author does not in fact intend explicitly or consciously to describe himself or the times in which he lives, he cannot in fact avoid doing this, however indirectly and subconsciously. This observation is necessary for a correct appreciation of the *literal sense*, that is, the meaning which the sacred author intended to convey and which would have been taken by the people whom he addressed originally. It is this literal sense, corresponding to the mind of the author, which the critic must try to establish by means of all the technical tools at his disposal. Nevertheless, the expression 'the mind of the author' must be taken in a wide sense, to include the indeliberate and the sub-conscious. Human words are seldom an adequate, let alone a complete, representation of an author's ideas. Indeed they are themselves interpretations of these latter. On the other hand, the author's words often transcend his ideas, causing a variety of repercussions in the minds of others. Applied to the Bible, these two factors provide the basis for development and for what will be called later the '*fuller understanding*' of the literal sense.

e **(d) historical criticism**—The most characteristic literary form of the Bible is that of *history*. It purports to represent certain events which have occurred within the course of human history. Nevertheless the manner of presentation is quite unlike the techniques of modern historiography. The rôle of the historian in relation to the Bible is, therefore, threefold. Firstly, on the more general plane, with the aid of an increasingly precise knowledge of the history of the ancient Middle East, he must situate the Bible in its historical context, and see each of its parts, as far as this is possible, in relation to its particular historical background. It is only in this way that the precise tenor of the sacred authors' expressions can begin to be appreciated. Secondly, the historian must try

to illustrate, particularly with the help of *archaeology*, **47e** the historical truth of the Bible. Alternatively, he may show where, despite appearances, the text does not even contain historical truth. Thirdly, this time more from the point of view of the philosophy of history, he should explain and justify the sense in which the Bible contains history. Modern thinking tends to veer away from the idea of history as a mechanical, computerlike recording of past events, towards the idea of history as an interpretation of those events. Considered in this light, the history of the Bible is seen to be less a tabulation of past happenings than a clear affirmation of the intervention of God within human history.

(e) philosophical criticism—When the Bible is seen in **f** its eventual unity, it can be shown to present, despite its manifest diversity, a remarkable consistency of thought, which, although it could hardly be termed a 'system', nevertheless vies with the great philosophical structures of both the ancient and the modern world as an explanation of the universe and, more precisely, of man's place within it. Indeed it would be quite easy to illustrate how the biblical world outlook has influenced many such philosophies. A host of familiar concepts, such as the meaningfulness of history, the value of the material universe, human freedom, the dignity of woman, owe their origin predominantly to the biblical tradition. Faced with the Bible considered as a *philosophy*, the critic must pass from the process of mere description to that of *judgement of value*. He must judge it not simply on the basis of literary and historical criteria but also on the grounds of philosophy, and since the questions of philosophy concern the nature, meaning and destiny of man, as of the whole of existence, he can hardly remain indifferent to the biblical view. He must, however implicitly, either accept or reject it, and, needless to say, his decision will inevitably colour his whole subsequent approach to the Bible.

(f) religious criticism—Similar remarks could be made **g** regarding the relationship between the Bible and world religions, particularly those of the ancient Middle East. In fact the Bible did not come to birth in a vacuum, but in the cradle of human civilization, where religion played a dominant role. Many of the images and ideas displayed throughout its pages derive from the powerful religions of Egypt, Mesopotamia and Canaan, although they are purified and put to the service of the revealed religion of Israel. This means that to assess the quality and worth of Israel's religion it is necessary to view it against the background of those other religions. It is only then that the originality and transcendence of the biblical religion can be fully appreciated, and since religion, even more than philosophy, demands a response of acceptance or rejection, the critic cannot remain indifferent.

Although the value judgement involved in both philosophical and religious criticism remain completely within the realm of reason, it nevertheless prepares for or precludes, according as the judgement is one of acceptance or rejection, the perspective of faith, and, therefore, forms either the ideal bridge or the hiatus between the purely critical and the theological approaches.

The Theological Approach

(a) the Bible as God's Word—What has been said so **49a** far about the Bible would be appreciated by any careful student, be he believer in the biblical religion, agnostic or even atheist. The Christian, however, and, as far as the OT is concerned, the Jew and the Moslem, know by *faith* that the Bible is more than a mere book or collection of books, since in its pages it is God who speaks to man. This realization—it cannot be too emphatically stressed— pertains to the domain of faith. Sound criticism, under

49a its various aspects outlined above, could show that the Bible is superb literature, even that it propounds a unique and transcendent religious and moral message, but it could not of itself induce the critic to recognize in the Bible the Word of God. Faith is not the product of the Bible. On the contrary, the Bible is the expression of a people's faith—the Jewish people in the case of the OT, the Christian Church in the case of the New. It follows from this that it can be understood fully only in the light of that faith, that is, by persons who share that same faith. It can also be said, applying to the present case what was mentioned above as pertaining to all language, that the Bible, as an expression, does not exhaust the content or **b** meaning of faith. Clearly the approach to the Bible, even with faith, will vary according to one's idea of *revelation*. The view outlined below is that of the Catholic tradition, particularly as it is enunciated in the two most recent official documents on the question, the Encyclical Letter of Pope Pius XII, 'Divino Afflante Spiritu', and the Dogmatic Constitution on Divine Revelation of the Second Vatican Council. Both of these distinguish very carefully two different, though inter-related, levels of interpretation— that of scientific criticism and that of theology. While giving the fullest possible scope to the former, they maintain that, of itself, it is insufficient for a complete understanding of the Bible and needs to be integrated into a theological approach which corresponds to the basic structure of the Christian revelation. There is nothing substantially new in all this. It is essentially a recapture of the fundamental intuition of the whole of Christian, and indeed Jewish, biblical exegesis down to the late Middle Ages. The actual techniques of criticism may have changed, but it is the same marriage between Faith and Reason which is advocated.

c The basic structure of the Christian Faith demands that the critic, who wishes to understand the Bible in the light of that faith, take cognizance of three points in particular: firstly, the theology of revelation; secondly, the theology of inspiration; thirdly, the theology of the Church, Tradition and the Magisterium, or teaching authority within the Church.

50a **(b) theological aspects**—God's Word, that is, **revelation**, is not identified simply with the Bible, although this latter is the most direct means of coming into contact with it, and is the most privileged witness of it. In the OT, God spoke to persons and communicated himself to a people, long before this Word was crystallized in writing; and Christ himself did not write a book, but rather established a community, the Church, which bore his message, well before it was consigned to writing. Nevertheless, the Bible does constitute a unity which evinces a certain *development*, from a beginning to a completion, thus tracing the actual development of God's revelation. In fact God did not reveal himself and his plan of Salvation suddenly but gradually, over a period of time. Moreover, the *mystery of Christ* is both the *fulfilment* and the *centre* of this plan of Salvation. These two characteristics of revelation—its development and its Christ-centredness, form the basis of the Christian understanding of the Bible, particularly of the OT, as is clearly seen from a consideration of the NT witness itself (cf Mk 1:15; Jn 5:39).

b A sane theology of **inspiration** stresses the fact that God, the principal author of the Bible, uses the sacred authors, with all their individual characteristics, as instruments in the communication of his saving truth to men. This means that the main attention of the critic must be concentrated on the theological aspect, or truth, of the Bible. Only in this way will he avoid being sidetracked into a host of false questions concerning the inerrancy **50b** of the Bible.

As was pointed out above, an essential aspect of the **c** structure of revelation is that it has been communicated to a people, a **Church**. This ecclesial, or community, aspect has received particular emphasis in recent years, even on the part of the so-called independent scholars, in the study of the 'history of forms'. One of the most important contributions of this study has been the light which it has thrown on the role of the community, whether the Jewish people in the case of the OT, or the Church in the case of the New, in the elaboration of the biblical message into the form in which it is now presented. Accordingly, it is seen that the sacred authors depend to a large extent upon the living faith of the community which they represent and that they exercise a certain role, or charism, within that community. When to this observation is added the fact that much of the biblical material is itself interpretation, of one kind or another, of previously existing biblical passages, it can readily be grasped that there is little fundamental difference between the charism of writing scripture and that of interpreting it. If the sacred authors were ecclesially minded, it would seem to follow that an accurate and full appreciation of their 'minds' involves a sharing in the faith of the community, which gives the 'sympathy' required in any conversation—and interpretation is a kind of conversation. Likewise, in view of this consideration, 'private' interpretation is something of an anomaly.

This mentality of the sacred authors, or 'spirit' of **d** their writings, into which the would be interpreter must penetrate by faith, is substantially nothing more or less than what is commonly known as '**Tradition**', that is, the continuing spirit, or mind, of the Scriptures, without which they would be a dead letter (cf 2 Cor 3:4; Rm 2:29; 7:6), which is handed on within the Church. It is by having his mind and heart attuned to this Tradition that the Christian interpreter has a sense of the meaning of the Bible, a 'feeling' for its message, for which no amount of critical scholarship can compensate. The use of the term 'spirit' in this context is intentional and appropriate. Tradition does not add anything to the Scriptures considered as God's Word, no more than man's spirit adds something to his body. Spirit and body, or flesh, are two distinct, irreducible, but correlative, aspects of the one reality, man. Similarly, Tradition and Scripture are but two aspects of the one entity, God's Word. To attempt the interpretation of the Scriptures without recourse to Tradition would be like performing a surgical operation on a corpse.

It is impossible to separate God's Word from the **e** divinely appointed, instrumental authority, through which it is communicated to men, both in the OT and in the New. Scripture, as indeed Tradition, is not only the expression of faith, it is also a means of the presentation and of the communication of that faith, in so far as it is charged with the teaching authority, or **Magisterium**, of the Church, vested in the Apostolic College, and its successors (cf Mt 28:16—20). This point needs to be carefully understood. The authoritative interpretation in question here concerns not the Bible considered as an object of critical study, involving such complex matters as date, authorship, literary form, circumstances of composition, derivation and elaboration of ideas, and so on, but the Bible considered as a presentation of God's *saving truth*. The role of the Magisterium in this regard is twofold. Firstly, it positively presents the true doctrinal, moral and spiritual content of the Scriptures. It does this generally through a fairly wide interpretation of an accumulation of

50e texts, supported by many other arguments. The instances in which the Magisterium has intentionally and clearly pronounced on the meaning of individual passages are very rare, and even here it hardly goes beyond an easily recognizable meaning of the passage in question, and always leaves ample room for critical investigation. Secondly, it negatively defends the true meaning of the Scriptures by rejecting certain interpretations as appearing incompatible with sound doctrine and morals. Here again, however, it is important to underline both the rare and the historically relative character of such decisions.

f It would be false to deduce that the above-described theological stipulations serve to cramp the interpreter's style, as demands imposed from without. The whole point of this brief exposition has been to show that they flow from the interpreter's faith moulded according to the actual structure of God's revelation. The ideal expressed in the 'Scriptura Sola' of the Reformers is a Will-o'-the-wisp. The Scriptures demand a *principle of interpretation* corresponding to the level from which they are viewed, as is evidenced by the present preoccupation of even independent scholars with the search for a comprehensive hermeneutic principle.

g **(c) the literal and theological meaning**—As described above, the *literal meaning* of the Scriptures is that meaning which corresponds to the intention, or the 'mind', understood in the wide sense, of the sacred authors. The theological meaning is not added to this literal meaning, but is included within it. The sacred authors were aware at least vaguely, that their work was related to God and his plan of salvation, in other words, that they were his instruments. Moreover, their work receives full significance only as part of a larger whole, that is the entire Bible. It follows from this that the literal sense must ultimately be the theological sense. Indeed—and this is a point which is not always realized sufficiently—the sacred authors were themselves *theologians*. Theology does not begin where the Bible leaves off. The Bible *is* already theology. Paradoxically, therefore, to understand the literal meaning it is necessary to be a theologian.

51a **(d) further understanding**—According to the normal rules of psychology, a human author *intends* his meaning to be *one*, although there is no contradiction in saying that the 'one' meaning intended by the author comprises various elements. This applies also to the Scriptures where there is no possibility of a *multitude of meanings*, in the strict sense of the word, although certain passages contain, within the one meaning, **several levels of meaning**. The author of the Fourth Gospel, for instance, uses various expressions which are susceptible of a two-fold meaning, on the level, that is, of the literal, contextual, appreciation of the particular passages (cf Jn 8:28). The Scriptures, however, are unlike other writings in two most important respects. Firstly, they owe their claim to fame not simply to the fact that they are the work of this or that particular literary genius, as is the case, for instance with Hamlet, or Oliver Twist, but, more precisely, because they form part of the vast ensemble of Israel's, and the Christian Church's, literature. They are, in other words, much more the common property of God's People than most literary works. This explains the anonymity of many of the sacred authors, as also the frequent recourse to pseudonymity. It also accounts for the manifold re-readings, reinterpretations, re-writings and editorial manipulations of the scripture texts detected by modern biblical scholarship, which are governed by the charism of *inspiration*. Secondly, and obviously closely connected with this last aspect, the sacred authors are only *instruments* used by God, the *principal* author of the Bible. This means

that the ultimate meaning of the Bible, which involves the **51a** work considered as a whole, and towards which the individual sacred authors have contributed, transcends the meaning of any one of its parts. In the last analysis, the mind of the author to be grasped in the case of the Bible is the mind of God, made manifest *through* the minds of the individual sacred authors seen as a 'team'. These two **b** characteristics of the Scriptures, taken in conjunction with the fact of the unity and Christ-centredness of revelation, make for a deeper *understanding* of the various parts of the Bible in relation to the whole, or, more particularly, to their central and pivotal point, the mystery of Christ, according to which the OT is seen to be a *preparation for*, a *foreshadowing of*, a *divine pedagogy in*, the NT, its *'fulfilment'*. Considered in this light, many passages of the OT evince a content which would be unsuspected had the NT not been written. A classical example of this is Gn 3:15. Theologians, however, are by no means unanimous in their interpretation of this phenomenon or in the use of vocabulary to describe it. Some are reluctant to see in this light thrown on the OT by the New anything but an extrinsic relation to the literal meaning of the original, while others speak of a 'fuller sense' or 'fullness of sense' already implicit in the original passage as part of the literal meaning, but now made explicit with reference to the fullness of revelation made in Christ. It seems to do more justice to the data in question, however, to speak not so much of a fuller sense, or meaning, as a **fullness of understanding**. **c** This preference for a term which designates a subjective condition rather than an objective meaning fits better into the picture, described above, of a passage which has a determined meaning, even a theological one, being assumed into a much larger interpretative tradition and being applied to different historical or existential situations and thus receiving further understanding. It is the constant and repeated relevance of the original *meaning* to the different historical and existential circumstances which makes such an *understanding* of the text 'objective'. In this respect, it is important to point out the role played by biblical exegesis within the biblical tradition itself. Clear as the development of revelation within the Bible is, it did not come about as the result of a continual process of evolution, but through the constant re-interpretation of pre-existent biblical texts or traditions, as an explanation of a concrete event or condition. The Jewish exegesis of the OT, like that of Christ himself and the authors of the NT, was not the disinterested, objective, unbiased scrutiny of the text that much of post-Renaissance exegesis has unconvincingly claimed to be. It was the art of discovering an explanation of the present in the biblical tradition. In other words, the present is not so much an explanation of the text as the text of the present. Thus in the teaching of Christ and the preaching of the Apostles the Christ event was explained, in the most obvious way possible to their first audiences, in function of the Scriptures, used in a variety of contexts: kerygmatic, apologetical, homiletical, liturgical. There is little cause for wonder, then, that there is a remarkable impression of continuity between the OT and the New.

Strictly speaking, the only passages of the OT which **d** can be said to have a fuller understanding are those which have definitely received this, either explicitly or implicitly, in the NT itself. Subsequent theology, however, particularly that of the Fathers, made the 'Christian understanding of the OT' a universal principle of its interpretation, reading, wherever possible, the mystery of Christ back into the OT. Although this method is basically sound, being suggested by the procedure of the NT itself, it has been

51d nevertheless vulnerable to abuse, as indeed it is still today, and too often the 'Christian' or 'spiritual' meaning stressed at the expense of the 'historical' or 'literal' meaning, with unwarranted importance being attached to mere superficial similarities between the two Testaments. The general principle of fulfilment of the OT by the New can be particularized and exemplified legitimately only when it pinpoints a fundamental and profound similarity of *structure* as existing between the relevant passages of the NT and those of the Old. It is worthwhile pointing out here that the modern notion of literal sense, with all the knowledge of the cultural and religious background of the original texts that this entails, permits the critic to establish such relationships in a way inaccessible to the Fathers.

e It has become classical since the times of the Fathers to divide this fuller 'understanding', as distinct from the literal meaning, into what is called the allegorical, tropological and anagogical 'senses', according as the passages in question are understood to refer to the Christian mystery in the various phases of its historical installation in the life and work of Christ, including the Church, its moral and sacramental realization in the lives of the faithful, and the final accomplishment in glory, respectively. Here again, this distinction corresponds to a phenomenon within the Scriptures themselves where certain passages may be understood only in an allegorical, tropological or anagogical sense; but it is also open to abuse.

f Although the NT is the 'fulfilment' of the Old, and thus represents the final stage of God's Word to men, nevertheless a similar development has occurred within the ambit of the NT itself, the words and actions of Christ, in particular, being re-read, recounted and recorded in a way parallel to that in which the biblical material of the OT had already been elaborated. Thus it is possible to interpret Christ's words and actions on the various levels just mentioned above. The surest method of doing this is by trying to enter into the minds of the authors themselves in order to see how *they* understood Christ's words and actions. Modern Gospel studies emphasize the fact that the evangelists, in reporting their material, do this in an interpretative way. It is fairly easily recognizable, for instance, that the author of the Fourth Gospel interprets Christ's miracles as the actions of Christ efficacious in the Church here and now. In the classical terminology, this would be the 'tropological' interpretation.

g The above mentioned interpretation of the OT in the light of the New has had as its inevitable result that God's intervention into history in Christ is moulded after the fashion of his interventions in the course of Israel's history. Thus the fundamental structure of the NT corresponds to that of the Old. By this very fact the message and meaning of the OT is seen to refer beyond its immediate historical context to the future Christian message. It is this relative value of the OT which is exploited in the **typological** understanding of its message, according to which the leading persons, the main events, the principal institutions of the Old Law are seen as 'types', foreshadowings, blueprints of the New. Clearly there is a close relationship between the fuller understanding and typology. The former concerns more the actual texts of the Scriptures, the latter concerns more the realities described in those texts. The principle of typology is suggested by the NT exegesis (cf 1 Cor 10:6–12; Rm 5:14; Col 2:17). Great caution has to be exercised, however, in the use of this method. Only when a person, event or institution of the OT can be seen to correspond basically and structurally, and this on the level of the literal meaning, to the NT may it be considered to be a *type*. Moreover this typological character of an **51g** OT text should be seen less as an actual *meaning* of the passage, intended by the original sacred author, than as a further understanding of its import, in the light of subsequent history and experience within the biblical tradition.

Given the idea of development and unity within the **h** Bible, the search for a *fuller understanding* and the *typological method* are both legitimate approaches to the text, since they correspond to the literal meaning of the text. Many of the Fathers, however, particularly those in the Alexandrian tradition, and even some authors nearer our time, established correspondences between the OT and the New, or between the Christian life and the texts of the NT, without any such objective basis. This is known as the **allegorical** method and is to be discouraged as a method of exegesis. Certainly there are passages in the Bible which are themselves allegories, for example, the Song of Songs, and Gal 4:21–31, and thus need to be interpreted as such, but this is different from the case envisaged here. It is also worth pointing out that even in Gal 4:21–31 it is typology which forms the basis of the allegory.

It is possible to *deduce* from the literal meaning of **i** the Scriptures, with the aid of a minor premiss, a further 'meaning' which was neither explicitly contained within the literal meaning, nor shown by subsequent development within the biblical tradition to be implicitly involved in it. This is known as the **consequent meaning**. It is clearly more closely related to the literal meaning than the allegorical understanding, and scholars differ concerning its precise status. For some it is a mere theological deduction, for others it is part of the literal sense. In fact it is by this procedure that the Church's understanding of revelation has progressed. In the measure, therefore, that the Church's understanding is seen to be vital for the full, theological, therefore, *literal* understanding of the Scriptures, the consequent could be said to be related to the *fuller understanding*.

The accommodated understanding.—Where the **j** Bible is considered to be God's Word it tends to become also the privileged vehicle of expression, its words and images being used to describe persons and situations which have little or nothing in common with the original occasion of those words and images. In itself this is a perfectly natural and legitimate process, and is used a great deal in the liturgy, but it must not be seen as affording a meaning, or even an understanding of the original biblical text, in any sense of the word, and, above all, it should not be taken as a basis of theological argument.

The impression given of biblical interpretation so **k** far may be that of a kind of archeological research. The reality is far different. The whole point of biblical interpretation is to attain God's Word addressed to his people here and now. This is what is called the **existential interpretation**, or understanding. This is not a matter of *demythologizing* the content of the Bible, stripping it, that is, of what is considered to be merely relative to a particular historical situation or experience, and thus arriving at the 'kernel' of the biblical message, which can then be re-presented in more relevant contemporary idiom. It is rather a question of entering into the meaning of the biblical language and symbolism, with the more positive view to capturing their significance. Only then will it be appreciated that this significance has a permanent value amid the changing circumstances of history, and that, therefore, it has a relevance for the man of today.

(e) the significance of biblical realities—A discus- **l** sion of biblical interpretation is usually confined to a

511 consideration of the actual meaning of the text. In view of what has been said already about *typology*, however, it is clear that the hermeneutics of the **things** described by the text also needs to be taken into account. In fact, as St Thomas saw, this process belongs more to the realm of *biblical theology* than that of exegesis.

The revelation of the Bible is an historical revelation. The *events* there recorded are, therefore, of considerable importance. The greatest of them, for example the Exodus or the Exile and Restoration, not only evince the action of God within history on behalf of his people at a particular point of time. They also set the pattern for his future and final interventions. In this way, the events of Israel's past receive further understanding in the light of the Christ event.

m God has also used certain individual **persons** in his plan of salvation as it is developed throughout the OT—the Patriarchs, Moses, the Prophets, the Kings, the Priests, and so on. These form part of the essential structure of the OT religion. This explains why the mystery of Christ is expressed, both by himself and his Apostles, in these categories, thus making all these characters in some sense or other *types* of the Christian mystery.

n What has been said about persons applies also to the **institutions** of the OT. The Christian religion has its origins in the people of God of the OT. It is therefore only natural that the religious institutions of this latter—the Temple, the liturgy and so on, should be reviewed in the light of Christ who is seen to transform them without destroying their profound significance. Hence they too are seen to be *types* of the essential structures of the Christian religion.

52a The Spiritual Approach

(a) God's Word as a communication of the divine life—If God speaks to man, it is not simply to tell him something about himself and man's relation to him. On the most profound level all human language symbolizes a community of existence and of life. For God to speak to man means that there is a community of life in which God has had, and still has, the initiative. In other words, the **52a** ultimate aim of revelation is that God should enter into coversation, in the fullest possible sense of that term, with man, and man with God. It involves, therefore, a communication of, and a participation in, the divine life, and, consequently, on the part of man, a sincere spiritual life, an imitation of his heavenly Father, made manifest in Christ.

(b) the Bible and the liturgy—Seen as a communica- **b** tion of God's life, the Bible is thus comparable to the liturgy and the sacraments, not as separable from them, but as intimately related to them. On the one hand, the language and symbolism of Scripture are the privileged means of expression in the liturgy, while, on the other hand, God's Word in the Scripture is re-vitalized, actualized in the praying Church. In the last analysis, therefore, the *existential* understanding of the Bible corresponds eminently to the liturgical and sacramental presentation of God's Word, in which God acts in his Church here and now.

Conclusion

To ask the Bible critic how he operates is rather like **c** asking a man how he thinks or how he appreciates the beauties of nature. In the final analysis, there are as many ways of interpreting the Bible as there are interpreters. Nevertheless, there are certain objective norms, required by the very nature of the case, which have been outlined above. Some of these pertain to the rational order, others to the level of faith, there being no conflict of interests between these two areas, but rather interpenetration and supplementation. The Scriptures being addressed to the whole man, require the attention of the whole man, with his reason and his faith, to be properly appreciated. The various approaches to the Bible constitute a harmonious whole, from the most material aspect of textual criticism to the heights of existential understanding, with each having its particular importance. Thus biblical interpretation is but one example of the dialogue and cooperation which should exist between reason and faith, between science and theology.

THE GEOGRAPHICAL SETTING OF BIBLICAL HISTORY

BY ROBERT NORTH S.J.

53a Bibliography—F.-M. Abel, *Géographie de la Palestine*, 1933—8, has never been equalled. D. Baly, *Geography of the Bible*, 1957, gives an up-to-date, somewhat geological, orientation. George Adam Smith's *Historical Geography of the Holy Land* in its 26th ed. of 1935 is still fascinatingly readable. The pioneer works are C. Ritter, *Comparative Geography of Palestine*, 1866, and E. Robinson, *Biblical Researches*, Boston 1856²; *Physical Geography*, 1865. Recent summary of M. du Buit, *Géographie de Terre Sainte*, 1958 and DBS 6, 1021—66. See also Yohanan Aharoni, *The Land of the Bible*, an historical geography, E. tr. 1966; R. Brown in *Jerome Commentary* (1968) ch. 73, pp. 638—652.

b Among the Biblical **Atlases**, Grollenberg is enticing for a Catholic beginner. Special merits attach to each of Wright-Filson, May, Rowley, Smith, Lemaire-Baldi, Guthe, and Eretz-Israel. Among Palestine **Guide-Books**, on the contrary, none quite fits our need: in English I. Benzinger's Baedeker 1904, B. Meistermann 1928, E. Finbert or Z. Vilnay 1955. The French *Guide Bleu* 1932 was by Abel; 1956 by R. Boulanger (*Moyen-Orient*); also *Turquie* 1956; *Egypte* 1952 by M. Baud. The best exegetical approach is in the now-outdated Notre-Dame de France guide of 1932. Valuable specialization in C. Kopp, *Holy Places of the Gospels*, 1962. Source-material: D. Baldi, *Enchiridion Locorum Sanctorum*, Jerusalem 1955²; bibliographies of R. Röhricht and (continuing) P. Thomsen, *Die Palästina-Literatur*.

c Name and location—Our word Palestine is Hebrew *pᵉlištîm*, 'Philistines'. This applied directly only to the SW coast around Gaza. But the Greeks and Romans called *Syria Palaestina* that portion of vast Syria which lay SW of Damascus and corresponded largely to the Israelites' Promised Land. Eventually it became distinguished into *Prima*, Judea with capital at Caesarea; *Secunda*, Galilee and northern East-Jordan with capital at Beth-Shan; *Tertia* or *Salutaris* around Petra. Thus Palestine loosely included territories about Moab, which we will call E Jordan rather than Transjordan or Eastern Palestine. It also included the Negeb S from Beersheba to the eastern gulf of the Red Sea.

d Variant Names—Just as the Holy Land was called 'Philistia' or 'Syria' depending on the point of view from which it was approached by our Greco-Roman world, so it received other names from its nearer neighbours. The **Egyptians** called it *Retchenu*, which, strangely, was their way of pronouncing Lydda, the metropolis nearest to them. They also called it *Khâru*, doubtless because some Hurrians were located in Idumea (Gn 14:6; 36:20; Eleutheropolis = Bêt-Hôrìm).

e The **Babylonians** similarly called Palestine 'Hittite-Land', because some Hittites were installed there (Gn 23:10; also for Hiwwites 34:2; Ezek 16:3), far from their homeland around Boghazköy in central Turkey. Though *Phoenicia* is commonly understood as the territory north of *Canaan*, these two names both mean 'sea-growth

dye', and were applied coextensively to the coastland **53e** occupied by the pre-Israelite waves of Semites who had come from Babylonia, where they were named *Amorites* or 'Westerners': not because of where they were to end up, but because they *came from* the W, presumably the S-Arabian peninsula (or from NW, many now hold).

Syria itself, as Palestine's surname, historically has **f** meant the whole sixty-mile-wide coast of the eastern Mediterranean. It begins at the S with Egyptian Arîsh, then includes Philistia-Canaan-Phoenicia-Lebanon. Farther N comes the limited access to the sea, from Arwad to Ugarit, which the modern State of Syria has managed to keep for its vast desert and upper-Euphrates granary. In the N corner opposite Cyprus, even historic 'Antioch-in-Syria' has been detached and made a part of Turkey.

The **skeleton** of this coastal Syrian Holy Land is **g** constituted by two parallel ridges, most massive at Lebanon and Hermon. The valley between them, there called Beqa', extends northward as the Qrontes. Southward it becomes the deepest crevice of the earth's crust, at the Dead Sea, then extends less deeply to the 'Aqaba gulf and Aswan in Egypt.

The history of Palestine has been largely shaped by **h** the **four parallel bands** of Syria: coast, Lebanon, rift, Antilebanon. Along the west is the coastline itself, at some points several miles in width, but zero at modern Haifa and at the 'Ladder of Tyre' and Beirut's Dog-River. Next comes the Lebanon range. It is prolonged southward, dislocated in Galilee and at Gerizim, but betraying its skeletal origins in the N-S watershed of Samaria-Juda. Within the third band, the Jordan River trickles from the Beqa' slopes, through the vales of Hula and Tiberias, where its surface is 200 metres below sea level, to the Dead Sea twice as low; its structure is prolonged southward as the 'Araba desert, waterless down to 'Aqaba. The fourth or most inland parallel strip is the prolongation of Mt Hermon: northward as Antilebanon, southward as the flat plateaux of Gilead, Moab, Edom.

Fertile Crescent and Goshen-Horeb—Everything **i** E of these four bands is bleak desert as far as the Euphrates. Thus the transit between Babylon and Palestine-Egypt required an immense northern detour along the water-lines called the Fertile Crescent. These movements are exemplified in **Abraham's journey** from Ur (Gn 12:31), which puts the kingdoms of Sumer, Babylon, Hurrian Mitanni, and the Hittites, into the framework of biblical geography (on which see the splendid Elsevier-Nelson Atlas of Mesopotamia by Beek).

Equally momentous for the early biblical narrative is **j** the NE Nile Delta of Egypt, called the 'Land of Goshen'. At the site called Avaris which Asiatic **Hyksos** invaders had made their capital around the time of Joseph in 1700, slave-labour of the Israelites was used after 1300 to rebuild a city named Raamses (Ex 1:11), which still later became known as Tanis (Nm 13:22). The **Exodus-route** doubtless detoured southward near the modern Suez ferry, to a Horeb in the S of that peninsula today called

53j Sinai. The Horeb-Sinai was probably Mt Moses near St Catherine's Monastery, rather than (as Jerome thought) Serbal near the oasis of Feiran (?Rephidim). But noteworthy modern scholars claim that the Exodus took a more direct northward route (reference to the 'Philistines' in Ex 13:17 being somewhat anachronistic in any case), and some few of these even locate Horeb at Qadesh-Barnea', in view of undeniable similarities between Ex 17:7 and Nm 20:13.

k **Boundaries**—In generic or vaguely 'prophetic' terms, the Land Promised in Ex 23:31; Jos 1:4, included everything from the SW River of Egypt at Arîsh, to the 'entry of Hama' N (Nm 34:8; Ezek 48:1), and the Euphrates E. David actually occupied as far as Palmyra, but this occupation (despite 2 Chr 8:8 diverging from 1 (3) Kgs 9:18) refers to a trade-agreement protecting Zobah, his farthest outpost (2 Sm 8:3).

l The normal boundaries of biblical Palestine were considerably less than those fixed by the British Mandate, identical with those now occupied by Israel plus West-Jordan. **'From Dan to Beersheba'**, a strip of 156 miles, the same as from Liverpool to Dublin, describes well the smallness of this territory. To the SW of Dan lay 'Galilee of the Gentiles', where despite a few adventures around Megiddo the claims of 'Asher' or even of Zebulun were never fulfilled as far as we know. The heartland of Samaria and Juda, including the SW Shefela foothills, affords the setting for the bulk of the biblical narrative. SE of the Jerusalem-Beersheba line was desert-steppe. The Sharon coast from Carmel to Philistia seems never to have been Jewish before Herod. Nor was E-Jordan, really, despite the scenario of Joshua 13 and the 'Omri episode.

m The **area** thus effectively occupied by the biblical people was some 160 × 20 miles, say 3000 square miles. Even if we measure in straight E-W lines, we get a width of only 20 m. at Dan and 70 m. at Beersheba, average 45, or some 7500 sq m., the size of Wales. Official square mileage for Israel is 8000; to this add 2250 for W-Jordan. E-Jordan runs to 35,000 more; Lebanon is only 3500. Egypt's area is a twenty mile band along the thousand-mile length of its Nile.

n Some **distances** by road: Nazareth-Bethlehem direct is about the hundred-mile distance form Dublin to Armagh. Of this the direct Jerusalem-Nazareth road is 92 m. All the way from Dan/Metulla to Eilat/'Aqaba is only as far as from Sydney to Canberra, some 280 m. From Haifa to Tiberias is about the same 32 m. as from Gloucester to Bristol, or Limerick to Neenah. From Jaffa to Jericho, though straight up and down a mountain, involves no more mileage than the 70 from Manchester to Birmingham, or London to Southampton. From Jerusalem to Beirut is a five-hour drive, to Cairo seven. E-Jordan is a narrow band of 280 m. from Hermon to 'Aqaba.

54a **Population-Centres**—Demographic figures for biblical Palestine are discouragingly elusive. Josephus claimed a million in Jerusalem at Passover. Even if not preposterous, this could leave the normal as low as 100,000. Taking into account infant mortality, maturity of excavated skeletons, and relevant modern parallels, half a million for the whole of Palestine would seem to be an educated guess.

b The three major areas, Juda, Samaria, and Galilee, may be regarded as roughly **three 'squares'** of latitude. By coincidence, Shechem appears just as the centre of Samaria, and just N of it is Nazareth near the centre of Galilee. Due S of Shechem is Jerusalem, but it is closer to the NE corner of its box, because at this latitude the coast flares westward.

c Clustered **around Jerusalem**, clockwise from the noon position, are Saul's Gibeah, Rachel's Ramah, **54c** Jeremiah's Anathoth; then Bethany, Bethlehem, Battir, Me-Neptah. Somewhat farther N are Gibeon and Mizpah of Samuel; Bethel and 'Ay of Joshua; Ephraim-Rimmon and Michmash. E of Jerusalem is complete bleakness as far as spring-fed Jericho in the Jordan plain. S of Bethlehem is Amos' rugged wilderness of Toqoa'.

d W of Jerusalem the situation improves. 20 m. southward is the thriving metropolis of Khalil, '(Abraham) the Friend (of God)', successor to **Hebron**. Its suffragans are Mamre and Qe'ila NW, Debir (at Mirsim or near Dahiriyya) SW, and Ziph-Carmel-Ma'on S. Directly W of Jerusalem is 'Ayn Karim, today Bet-Kerem (but that name is now equated with the Ramat Rachel excavation called by others Netopha). NW of Jerusalem are three rival sites of the Easter **Emmaus**: Qiryat-Ye'arim, more justly famed for the Ark passage (1 Sm 7:1); then Qubayba near the E of Joshua's Ayyalon valley, at a normal walking distance from Jerusalem, the 60 stadia or 7 m. which is the better reading of Lk 24:13; finally at the westward lowland of Ayyalon near Gezer, at some 160 stadia or 18 m. from Jerusalem, the modern 'Amwas preserves the name and cathedral of Emmaus-Nicopolis.

e The population-centre of W Juda is the **Lachish** area, crossroads of the Jerusalem-Gaza and Joppe-Beersheba highways. A modern prefab metropolis, successor to Arabic Falûja, is called Gath; but its excavations are identified rather as Mamsht. E of Falûja run the N-S foothills called **Shefela**, with important settlements at the points where torrent-beds cut their way. At the N is Beth-Shemesh, with Zora and Eshtaol, and the modern railway in the valley of Soreq. S of that is the valley of Goliath, called Ela or Terebinth, between hills with tenuous linguistic claim to the names of 'Azeqa and Sokoh. Nearer to ancient Lachish in the S are Maresa and Eleuthoropolis, 'City of the Free/Hurrians/Cave-Dwellers': Hôrîm means all these things, and caves abound in the environs, though the Arab name suggests rather 'City of Giants', Bêt-Gibbôrîm (not Repha'îm as in the railway 'Valley of Giants' south of Jerusalem).

f The **coastland of Juda** was Philistine domain. It begins at the N near the Rubin River. Accaron/'Eqron is sought opposite the Iamnia of the Rabbinic Scripture-canon Council; but more likely both 'Eqron and Gath were near Batâsha, between coastal Ashdod/Azotus and Beth-Shemesh (1 Sm 5f). Of all the settlements of these Philistine 'Sea-Lords', only Ashkelon was really on the sea; it has retained an importance through the centuries. But it was always outshone by inland Gaza, which in the time of Jesus' infancy was under the Egyptian flag.

g Beersheba was the natural capital of 'Simeon', or rather of **Negeb**-Juda. Recent excavations show it to have been earlier a centre of the last Stone Age culture, called Ghassulian chalcolithic. W of Beersheba were Gerar and Sharuhen; far SW Qadesh-Barnea'; and far, far SE the town on the 'Aqaba gulf of the Red Sea which was called both Eilat and Esyon-Gaber.

h Separating **Juda from Samaria**, a vague natural border extended from seacoast Jaffa, via Lydda or Antipatris, to Shiloh. Yâfō or Joppe, 'the Beautiful', had immemorial importance as the only natural harbour of Palestine, though since 1909 it was eclipsed by the Zionist reception-settlement installed N of it at Tel Aviv. Sister-settlements radiate almost uninterruptedly as far as Iamnia, Lydda-Ramla, and Rôsh ha-'Ayin. This ras al-'ayn, from which gushes the perennial Yarqon River, is Paul's Antipatris, and less assuredly Aphek. In the nearby foothills are various sites of Gilgal, and the Modi'in of the Maccabees.

54i The towns of **Samaria** are almost wholly on the hill-tops. Shift of the capital from Shechem to Tirzah eastward marked an alignment with Syria and Assyria. Removal from there to Samaria-City (renamed Sebastē under Herod) symbolized realignment with the Mediterranean world. Northward on the fringes of Esdraelon were Dothan and Janîn/'En Gannim. **Sharon** Coast was virtually unoccupied, until Herod the Great by building an artificial harbour made Caesarea the 'Roman capital of Judea'. It eventually became a centre of the Easter-Date controversy and of related biblical studies under Origen and Eusebius.

j The plain between Samaria and Nazareth, left by the dislocation of Lebanon range, extends almost unbroken from 'Akko NW to Beth Shan SE. Its central portion is a natural unit, whose name **Esdraelon** is a Gr. form of its SE outpost Jezreel, near Gideon's spring. At its SW stood Armageddon or Mt Megiddo, which with nearby Taanak immemorially barred the 'Ara pass through Carmel. Esdraelon's NE boundary was Tabor and Mt Moreh, ill-named 'Little Hermon' by an inference from Ps 89(88):12. Actually from Naim or Endor on Moreh's NW slope, (Great) Hermon can be seen as a twin of Tabor, by a freak of perspective.

k Haifa was non-existent until a Sycaminos was founded toward the end of NT times. The Crusaders fancifully called it 'Caiphas'. In creating there a splendid port and metropolis, the British Mandate brought stone from Mughâra quarry in **Mt Carmel**, thereby opening a paleolithic skeletal deposit. Over against it on the sea stands the Crusader castle of Athlit, a little N of the hellenistic temple at Dor.

l Excavations at **Nazareth** show that though unmentioned in the OT, it began to be occupied about 600 B.C. The 'precipice-leap' or *Qafza* S of town, though too remote for Lk 4:29, yielded momentous paleolithic skeletons. Carpenters from Nazareth were undoubtedly called upon, when Jesus was a boy of ten, to rebuild Sepphoris as Antipas' capital six miles NW. Somewhat farther and NE stood **Cana**. A town called Chafr Channa was recognized by the Franciscan Quaresmi as a slightly more probable site for this town than a deserted ruin called Qâna. Consequent Franciscan ministries at Channa determined the course of the pilgrims' highway, now asphalt, from Nazareth to Capernaum. But geographers meanwhile came to agreement that Qâna was the site dictated by more ancient roadways. It is on the lowest slope of Yotpat mountain [where Josephus ingloriously turncoated: *BJ* 3 (340) 8], at the edge of the little Netopha plain north of Nazareth.

m Northward from the foot of Tabor, at a little mound called 'Horns of Hattin', the Crusaders' crucial defeat was inflicted by Saladin in 1287. From this lofty plain, preferred by some as site of the Sermon on the Mount, there opens a spendid view on the **Sea of Galilee**, and also the best pedestrian descent via Doves' Valley straight to Magdala. Northeast of Magdala is Genesareth plain with the cave of paleolithic *homo galileensis*, and the Minya ruin which may perhaps cover a west-shore Beth-saida. The superbly preserved synagogue of Telhum, dating from the third or perhaps partly late-first Christian century, is now agreed to be 'too good to be anything other than Capernaum'. Another impressive synagogue-ruin is visible at Chorazin. S of Magdala and the 'pagan metropolis' Tiberias stands a vast and long-lived settlement called Bet-Yerah.

n Tobit's Safed is the capital of **N-Galilee**, and nearby Mt Meiron (1200 metres) is the highest peak of Palestine. Eastward in the Jordan rift are Hazor and Dan, and at the edge of Hermon is Paneas rebuilt as Philip's Caesarea. **54n** Along the Mediterranean, Palestine merges with Phoenicia near the promontory called *niqra/naqûra* or 'Ladder' of Tyre.

Population-centres of **E-Jordan** are rare. In the N, **o** Edrei is at Der'a on the Syrian border; nearer the Jordan are Gadara, Pella, and Jabesh-Gilead. In the region of 'Amman/Philadelphia are Gerasa, Succoth, Penuel, Heshbon, and Nebo/Madaba. On the N and S brinks of Arnon gorge are Dibon and 'Ar-Moab; then Kerah/Qîr, Petra, and 'Aqaba/Eilat.

The system of wadis—Except for the Jordan, there are **55a** few perennial streams in Palestine. Stony slopes shuttle off the rainfall in flash floods. These 'torrents' cleave for themselves deep interweaving streambeds, which are then left dry as a bone. The dry watercourse, called *wadi*, serves as the least burdensome route of access for pedestrians heading from the lowland up into the mountains. Its strategic and commercial importance was thus very great.

The most impressive wadi-system opens out like a **b** broad fan, with funnel at Antipatris near Tel Aviv, and a dozen tributaries fingering down over the whole highland between Shechem and Jerusalem. Southernmost of these are the Ayyalon Valley where the 'sun stood still' (Jos 10:12), and the Natûf Valley which gave its name to Palestine's mesolithic age. Huge wadis draining Samaria westward are called Ballût and Qânâ. Near their confluence, these dry streambeds receive an unending gush from the *ras al-'ayn* 'Fountainhead'. This flows into the Mediterranean as the **Yarqon** River between the excavated mounds Qasîla and Jarîsha N of Tel Aviv.

Some minor but historic **Mediterranean streams: c** In the S are the Torrent of Egypt (Arîsh, Nm 34:5); excavators' Ghazza and Heṣi; Suqrayr or Goliath valley. The R. Rubin draws from Samson's Soreq valley, and from the 'Valley of Giants' where the railway downgrades S from Jerusalem. Along Carmel are the rivers Alexander, Hedêra (Dothan and Megiddo passes), and Crocodile; and near Haifa the cave-man wadis Mughâra and Fallâh. N of Haifa the plain of Esdraelon is drained by the sluggish trickle of Qîshôn: it must have been unusually swollen when it 'tumbled the bodies' of Jg 5:21. A natural northern boundary of Palestine is the river called Qâsimiyya, 'divider', though it empties north of Tyre. Its earlier course, called Litânî, cleaves majestically the crags around Beaufort Castle.

Into the Jordan from the W flow a few streams: **d** Jâlûd at Beth Shan, Far'a near Shechem, Qilt at Jericho. The 'scroll wadis' of Qumran, Qedron/Nar, Murabba'ât, and 'En-Gedi, empty into the Dead Sea. Opposite them from the E pour important streams Callirhoë, Arnon, and Zered. The NW tributaries of Jordan are the Jabbok famed in Jacob's history (Gn 32:32; now Zerqa), and the Yarmûk providing a total flow equal to that of the Jordan near Gadara.

The Jordan itself was providentially formed out of **e** tiny rivulets barely indenting the crags of Lebanon, as Smith's *Historical Geography* muses with delightful piety. The trickles flow together into a plashing stream called Hasbâni, northernmost arm of the Jordan, furnishing only an eighth of its volume. Where it enters the present boundaries of Israel it runs parallel with the outflow of two gushing springs. The Dan now furnishes five-eighths of Upper Jordan's flow. A source near Caesarea-Philippi, at Banyas—'the caves of Pan'—1000 feet above sea level, was formerly picturesque and mystic.

These streams crawl through the Hula area, which was **f** a swampy lake until Israeli engineers dried it up in 1957. Near Hula the Jordan Rift descends below the level of the

55f Mediterranean. By the time its streams flow near Capernaum into **the Lake** shaped like a pear or 'harp' (*Kinneret*), the surface-level is minus 680 feet. Oppressive lakeshore heat is relieved by sudden winds, which blow up violent storms out on the water. Fishermen still toil through the night and spread out their nets at Tiberias for mending by day. It is often remarked how here more than anywhere else in Palestine the memory and the presence of Christ are vividly recalled.

g Straight W out of Kinneret's southern tip flows a greenish but clear Jordan. But it gets rather muddy in meandering southward a full 200 m. to cover the 60 m. distance to the **Dead Sea**. It becomes so deeply sunken in its bed or *Zôr*, that the surrounding mud-flats or *Ghôr* are incapable of any agriculture. Seven million tons of water are fed into the Dead Sea every day and perish by evaporation! A Zionist scheme to save these waters by diverting them from Dan through Syria and Galilee is blocked on the grounds that the Dead Sea would dry up or become noxious. But its salt-ridden waters support no life even now, though bathing in them is buoyant and hygienic, if you can wash off the greasy film promptly afterwards. Along its banks are practically no settlements, and 'any change would be an improvement' in lowering the surface below its sulphur-springs.

h The 1300 feet **depth of the Dead Sea** equals the depth of its surface below the Mediterranean, or 2600 feet in all. This in turn equals the adjacent Judean summits' height. This means a rise of a full mile along a horizontal distance of only 10 m.! The normal 'Good Samaritan road' skirting Jericho spreads the gradient over some 20 m. The Dead Sea is about 8 m. broad, roughly equal to Kinneret; its length is 47 m., almost equal to the Jordan as far as Kinneret.

i **Climate**—Palestine is called in Dt a land 'flowing' (with milk and honey, 6:3), because of its gushing springs and streams (8:7) and especially the *rainfall* distinguishing it from irrigation-cultures like Egypt and Babylon (11:10). A decrease of rainfall since biblical times, due to both deforestation and natural cycles, seems undeniable.

j The **rain** is evenly distributed along averages of 2-6-10-12-10-9-5-2 days per month from October to May in Jerusalem, and rarely a drop from June to September. But the average total rainfall is 24 inches, the same as in Nazareth or London (though in 1949 Jerusalem got 35 inches in 68 days, attaining the norm of northernmost Galilee). In Beersheba annual rainfall is only eight inches, but the **dew** adds an equal amount. **Snow** is always visible on top of Mt Hermon, and occasionally on the Judean hills, but not enough to assure the soaking of the soil instead of its erosion.

k The hills of Jerusalem, Samaria, and Nazareth are livable in summer and winter, because the nights are cool and the days are warm. The intolerably hot days are not in midsummer but unpredictably in May or October through blasts of the parching *sharqi* or E wind, our 'sirocco'. Along the coastal plain the summer humidity of Jaffa and Haifa is hard to endure, and the lowering of **temperature** at night is only half of Jerusalem's. Fahrenheit averages at Jerusalem/Haifa are 75.2/82.4 in August and 47.2/57.2 in January; extremes are 23-99/39-100. The summer heat is even more intense and oppressive in the Jordan Rift, at Tiberias, Jericho, and Sodom; but these are winter havens.

l **Plants and Animals**—On one thing at least the pilgrim's surface-impression is correct: the olive-tree is cultivated all over Palestine. Olives are eaten by the bowlful, often making a full meal along with bread. But their importance is greater for cooking-oil and liniment.

In Arab areas grapevines are still widespread, though **55l** their exploitation for wine is limited by Qoran observance. Fig-trees are seen frequently enough, but their fruits are not so common or luscious as in Italy. Wheat abounds; but barley was so much more common in NT times that even Catholics are now heard claiming that Jesus would have used barley bread at the Last Supper.

The plant-world has seen four chief **intrusions** since **m** Bible times. Palestine's principal export-product is the orange, from huge plantations near Jaffa. Bananas of moderate size and some oranges grow at Jericho, but its palms never seem to have a date. The cactus was brought in chiefly as a cheap fencing-material, but its crude seedy 'prickly pears' taste good in hot weather. The gum-tree, as our eucalyptus is delightedly hailed by Australians, seems to have been introduced from there, for the purpose of anchoring down sand-dunes long enough to allow a topsoil to form; but some render as 'gum-trees' the site of the Philistine defeat in 2 Sm 5:24, where others prefer balsam or pear.

Occasional **lentils** keep the Palestinian aware of the **n** 'mess of pottage' of Jacob and perhaps Tamar (Gn 25:34; 2 Sm 13:7 Douay). There are peas, garbanzos, and beans. There is a coarse broad bean called *Ful* (from which comes Tell el Ful, the modern name of the mound of Saul's Gibeah). A Turkish delight is eggplant, along with cucumbers and variants like a tiny squash; and there are tomatoes. The Mediterranean array of spinach-cabbage greens is missing, but lettuce is prized amid heat and thirst, and the celery-like fennel gave its name of Shumra to Ugarit (Ras Shamra). Rice is an imported staple. No coffee grows here, though it was discovered at Mocha in Arab Yemen. Tobacco now flourishes at Naim. The Crusaders made sugar-cane flourish at Jericho, but it has now vanished.

The apricot is so common throughout the Arab world **o** that its name *mishmash* is a synonym for junk. Apples in W Palestine are rare, though gorgeous in Lebanon. The watermelon is called 'American', as distinct from honeydew cantaloup. There are almonds, still called as in Hebrew *lûz* (near Bethel, Jos 16:2; but *shāqēd* Jer 1:11). The Cedars of Lebanon are now found only on a few remote mountaintops. In Palestine **treelessness** is cause rather than effect of rainfall-diminution, but is being remedied by eager Arbor Day techniques inside Israel. Fascinating folklore about such biblical household words as the burning bush, Jonah's gourd, the mustard-seed, and lilies of the field, are available in the Moldenkes' *Plants of the Bible* (Waltham, Mass., 1958).

In the field and on the table a pilgrim sees **sheep and** **p** **goats**. He gets the impression, wrongly, that there are no cows. There are even pigs well screened in Jewish farms. The broad tails of the sheep, valued for a buttery substance called ghee, get so fat that sometimes a little cart is attached to keep them from dragging on the ground. Black-haired goats provide most of the milk and tenting-material, but ruthlessly devour newly-planted trees.

Donkeys are everywhere except in church, and get **q** some of the tenderness which the Englishman reserves for dogs—maltreated starvelings in Palestine. You are never very far from a camel but hardly ever on one. If you encounter a hyena at Qumran or a school of wild boar at Chorazin, you don't stop to argue. The bear, lion, and stag have disappeared. But there are wolves, also the 'little foxes' of Song 2:15; and the jackal, endearingly called 'Wowie!' in Arabic. Glimpsing a hare recalls the list of clean and unclean animals of Lv 11:6.

Field-life is preserved with arresting vividness in **r** mosaic floors of Nirim, Beth Shan, Madaba. But the

55r mosaic in the Capernaum 'multiplication of the loaves' church shows lush exotic **birds** which fit the visitor's impression of Egypt rather than Palestine. An owl will sometimes eye you, and clouds of storks pass overhead to or from the northland.

s There are an estimated 20,000 **insect**-species in Palestine. The scorpion is as repulsive as it is enticing. In 1952 occurred the last big locust-plague, grasshoppers really. More dangerous than occasional snakes are the fever-ticks lurking in caves where one seeks neanderthal or scroll remains. No crocodile has been seen in Palestine or even Egypt for almost a century. But some spoilsport is sure to cry 'sharks' or 'bilharzia' when the Red Sea or Nile beckons the pilgrim to a refreshing swim. F. Bodenheimer's *Animal and Man in Bible Lands* (E. J. Brill, Leiden, 1960), interestingly relates Palestinian fauna to geology, prehistory, cuneiform records, Egypt, and Greco-Roman classics.

56a Geopolitical Units—A realistic appraisal of OT narratives on Palestine soil must begin from the fact that they focus on two points, Jerusalem and Shechem. These were both venerable ancient sanctuaries. It has been plausibly maintained that the populations living about them were loosely associated after the fashion of the Greek **amphictyonies**. Their bond of unity was not federal or administrative. It would have consisted solely in sending votive gifts to the shrine, gathering there for recurring festivals like the Olympic Games, and defending each other from attack.

b The southland belongs to Juda, and was polarized at first around Hebron or Beersheba rather than the pocket of Canaanite resistance at Jerusalem (Jos 15:63). In the N, the lion's share of territory and population around Shechem belongs to Ephraim. By a helpful coincidence, **J and E** designate not only Juda and Ephraim, but also two detectable Pentateuch strands whose geographical partiality is unmistakably southern and northern respectively, (cf §§ 135—6).

c Ephraim is linked to Manasseh by a bond of relationship avowedly closer than that of the neighbouring tribes. Manasseh's territory is more sprawling, even off to the E and N of the Jordan. But it is less sharply delimited and less influential than Ephraim's, into which it is for practical purposes **absorbed**. Similar except for the claim of closer relationship was the absorption of Simeon and perhaps Reuben by Juda.

d The territory N of Jerusalem as far as Bethel had naturally the strategic significance of a **buffer** between two rival confederacies. Out of this territory emerged the first figure heroic enough to win acclaim as simultaneous leader of the two rival groupings: Saul, of the clan called Benjamin. To him are linked the origins of kingship, and thus of federal unity. Though he was territorially neutral, the northern amphictyony immediately asserted a possessive protectorate over him. This was an inevitable political reaction to the recorded fact that almost from the moment of his coronation, Saul found himself the puppet of a stronger young hero from the S: David of Bethlehem-Hebron. Saul's situation is portrayed as a nervous breakdown consequent upon tribal inability to adjust to a new administrative pattern, segregating permanent civil-military authority from priestly-prophetic functions.

e David shrewdly realized that his hope of a **united kingdom** would be greatly assisted by the seizure of the Jebusite citadel as a neutral fief from which he could impartially govern S and N. (Compliance of the Jebusite priest-king successor of Melki-Zedek was perhaps secured by assuring to his line the 'eternal priesthood' of Abraham's 'Most High God' within Israel, substituting (Melek-)

Zadok for Abiathar within the line of Aaron-Levi (1 Chr **56e** 16:39; 1 (3) Kgs 3:4).)

f Nevertheless the union of N and S effected under David and his son was uneasily personal. To give it a more objective juridical and sentimental stability, David had to give force to the bonds of kinship whereby the two realms could be brought to acknowledge an **underlying unity** deeper than their amphictyonic rivalry. It has been maintained even by such recent Catholic experts as J. de Fraine, *Atlas*, that the descendance of 'Twelve Tribes' from sons of a single father is a legal fiction, for federating clans of unconnected origin which had migrated into Canaan from different directions. The history of their united emigration from Egypt is characterized by de Fraine as the legitimate literary device of 'generalizing' the type-case of a single one among those clans.

g However, it remains just as scientifically tenable that there truly was a link of **blood-brotherhood** among the last wave of Semitic tribes invading Canaan. Even their predecessors, the Amorites, who for a thousand years had been preceding Abraham on the Fertile Crescent route from Ur into Canaan, were ultimately of the same stock, ethnically as well as linguistically Semitic. But no matter how loyally we take the biblical Twelve Tribes as literally historical, some enigmas continue to enshroud them. Tribes like Caleb and Machir, perhaps also Jerahmeel, Jair, and the Qenites, hold within the Israelite framework an importance far surpassing shadowy Asher, Simeon, and Reuben. If the tribal-brotherhood was an artificially fabricated link, it could easily have been better fashioned to fit the facts. We may prefer to say that Caleb, brought in secondarily by a juridical 'adoption' which is ultimately *fiction*, ended up quite naturally in possession of territory left unclaimed by a tribe (Simeon?) which had just shrivelled up into extinction.

57a Joshua 12—21 is universally acclaimed our chief source for biblical geography. There are over 600 topographical references, 180 for Juda alone in chapter 15. In CCHS (1) § 57*e-h* can be consulted Father Power's competent summary of the modern Arabic place-names linked with most of these toponyms. But Power's inventory is unconcerned with certain obvious features which today would have to be taken as point of departure for geographic delimitation:

b (a) For Juda at least there are lumped together **two separate lists**, one of frontier-towns (15:1—12), the other of *all* towns by *districts* (15:21—62), separated by a cadenza about Caleb indefinably linking 15:54 to 14:6—15. (b) Precision of detail in the lists is proportioned to **nearness to Jerusalem**. Practically the only assuredly-known point of Zebulun, Naphtali, and Issachar is Mount Tabor which they have in common. Fixing Asher on the shore N of Carmel is unsupported by Zebulun traditions or by a single place name certainly known from other evidence, (despite variant 'Akko for Umma of 19:30; and on Aphek see *Bib* (1960), 41—63). (c) A comparison of the Twelve Tribes **boundaries** printed in major atlases reveals irreducible disagreements amounting to 80%!

c In this situation the only rational procedure is a reappraisal of what the passage really *intended* to convey. There should be no hesitation in admitting that lists of names from the time of David or even later are **inserted** into the Joshua-framework, since even the narrative parts of Jos as contrasted with the more pedestrian course of events in Jd betrays a legitimate theological idealizing. It may further be soberly inquired whether a list like Asher is considered to correspond to any historical reality at all; there can be a certain value even in the faithful transmission of popular traditions about place-names.

57d Taken in this respectfully realistic perspective, here is approximately the **geographical content** of Joshua 12—21. **Juda** is by far the greatest and most important tribe, line of the anointed King David (and the) Messiah. Each of the twelve *counties* of Juda contains more precise toponyms than do any of the entire tribes farther N. **Benjamin** is associated with Juda in its greatness and nearness to Jerusalem. Its autonomy is asserted; yet unless its thin tongue of territory was regarded as a Juda-protectorate, it could neither survive nor allow Juda a frontier secure against encroachments from the N. **Dan** is acknowledged to have shared briefly the function of buffer-state, before it sought *lebensraum* in the far NE (Jg 2,34). The archaic name of **Simeon**, to which no political reality corresponded in David's time, is resurrected in Jos 19:1—9 as an afterthought to 15:21—32; but the real units of tribal organization federated into Juda from the S were 'Qen(izz)ite Caleb' (1 Chr 2:54) perhaps with Othniel, and Jerahmeel.

e Despite Juda's hegemony, **Ephraim** possesses the deepest-rooted importance of all the tribes. This is due to its immemorial connection with the Shechem-Gerizim and Shiloh shrines, but also to vague survivals in Dt 27:4 which link it with the crossing of the Jordan. Ephraim is acknowledged to be in some special way the heir of that Joseph-tribe to which the whole confederacy was most indebted when a crisis of famine and Hyksos-invasion bore them down into Egypt. Equality with Ephraim as son of Joseph, claimed for the far-flung northern neighbour **Manasseh**, is a form of 'legal adoption' of the Machir-tribe with which Ephraim had found it necessary to contrive a modus vivendi.

f Galilee plays almost no part in the OT narrative. It is expressly called 'Gentile territory' in Is 8:23 (=9:1); so Jg 1:9. To it are vaguely allotted some vaguely known archaic tribes. **Issachar** is nominated 'patron saint' of Esdraelon, in whose southern corners the Israelites had a few exploits to their credit in Jg 4:14; 7:1. Neither **Zebulun** nor **Naphtali** drove out the Canaanites, says Jg 1:30,33; and it was doubtless the ringing Messianism of Is 9:1 which would eventually make Naphtali seem very real as the land on which Capernaum lies and Zebulun as the land of Nazareth. In the far N of Naphtali's allotted domain, Hazor is associated with an early Israelite *geste* in Joshua 11. But the abrupt leap from the far southland of the preceding verse lends point to the surmise of some excavators that an encounter with the king of Hazor which actually took place later in S Esdraelon has been placed here in accordance with Joshua's system.

g It is probable that this concern to allot different parts of the country to one or other of the 'Twelve Tribes' dates from David's time, and was an essential of his empire-building. 'The census narrated in 2 (4) Kgs 25:5—8 reveals to us the boundaries of the land inhabited by Israelites in the reign of David, practically identical with the region divided among the tribes' (Power). Less apparent is **Solomon's** reason for weakening this needed tool by dragging in a system of twelve 'Taxation-Zones' which exempted Juda and cut sharply across the 'old' tribal frontiers; 1 (3) Kgs 4:8—19: 1. Mt Ephraim; 2. Western Benjamin; 3. Sharon inland from Caesarea; 4. Dor; 5. Esdraelon-Beth Shan plain; 6. Jair in northern East-Jordan; 7. central East-Jordan; 8. (in) Naphtali; 9. 'Asher and (B^e) 'alot' (= ? Qiryat-Ye'arim west of Jerusalem!); 10. (in) Issachar; 11. (East-)Benjamin; 12. another part of northern East-Jordan, for which the LXX B reads 'Gad'.

h Whatever may have been his intention, Solomon's reorganizing led to the **breakup of the coalition** he and his father had held together. Samaria's authorities did **57h** not in fact withhold the Northern Crown from Solomon's (Southern) successor in 1 (3) Kgs 12:1. They merely required him to sign a Magna Carta; and his refusal to do this was so scornful as to force open recognition of the primeval political duality. 'Only Juda' is said in 1 (3) Kgs 12:20 to have remained subject to Rehoboam; but in the next verse 'Juda and Benjamin': hence the rebels are called 'the Ten Tribes'.

The **frontier** between S and N fluctuated amazingly. **i** In the time of Amos 7:13 it was as little as ten miles N of Jerusalem, near Bethel. In Hasmonean times it was just as near to Gerizim, at Akrabeta [Jos BJ 3 (55) 3,5]. N-Israel, not Juda, held on to David's E-Jordan tributaries. We learn this concerning Moab when Mesha proclaims that he has thrown off the yoke. Without the Moab approach-roads, it is hard to see how Juda could have maintained effective hold on Edom: on the contrary, Edom in the person of Herod's father eventually engulfed Juda.

Breakup and Recombining of David's Realm— **58a** N-Israel was gradually absorbed by Syria and then **Assyria**, which proclaims it 'the house of 'Omri' even while accepting tribute from the usurping dynasty of Jehu in 841 B.C. In 733 its separate provinces are called by the Assyrians *Magidu*, *Gal'azu*, *Du'uru* (Gilead, Dor). In 721 the dismemberment extends farther S to *Sumerina*, and in 711 to *Ashdud* (Azotus, including the whole Philistine coastland).

Under Nebuchadnezzar in 586 Juda was demolished **b** and its territory incorporated into Samerina, as one segment of a vast colony which gradually became known as *Ebirnari*, 'Trans-Euphrates'. The **Persian** overthrow of Babylon left unchanged this arrangement so disadvantageous to the exiles returning in 538. Darius after 522 made Ebirnari one of the four major satrapies, but only in 438 was a measure of autonomy restored to Juda, or rather to Nehemiah as a protégé of Artaxerxes.

In turn the Persian structure fell to Alexander's dual **c** succession. Palestine was midway between the Ptolemies of Egypt, who from Gaza ruled until 198, and the Babylonian Seleucids who under Antiochus III took Palestine away. In Mc we find **Hellenistic** administrative names like *Galaaditis* and *Samaritis*. *Idumaea* represents the spread of Edom to the SW of Juda. The Philistine coast is called *Paralia*.

New Testament districts—At the death of Herod the **d** Great, his Roman 'allies' intervened to carve up for his (three!) 'tetrarch' sons the considerable territory his personal manoeuvring had amassed for Juda. The Philistines had kept their hold on his birthplace Ashkelon, and the Phoenicians held Galilee north of Dor. In E-Jordan, there was a sort of amphictyonic cluster of Greek city-states called the **Decapolis**. Its chief centres were 'Ammôn, renamed Philadelphia, and Gerasa and Gadara. But it included Scythopolis or Beth Shan opposite Pella, and enigmatically in some lists Damascus. As for the Nabatean claim on Damascus, see *PEQ* 87 (1955) 34.

Herod's son Philip received the NE tetrarchy, from **e** *Iturea* around Bethsaida-Julias, to Caesarea-'Philippi' and *Trachonitis*, including Gaulan, Bashan = *Batanea*, and (H)Auran (*itis*). Herod Antipas received Galilee and *Peroea* = 'Trans(jordan)ia'. Archelaus received Samaria and the eleven 'toparchies' of Juda, but governed so badly that he was displaced by a Roman '**Procurator**'. This was the situation existing when Jesus was condemned by Pontius Pilate, whose name carved in stone was recovered at Caesarea (Maritima) in 1960!

58f Herod Antipas was still ruling **Galilee** at the time of Jesus' trial. He had no official administrative position in Jerusalem, but it was natural that as the nearest reigning dynast of Judea he should reside and receive some tokens of honour there. After Christ's death, so much administrative ability was shown by Herod Agrippa I, the son of Philip, that to him were gradually committed Galilee from 39, then Judea from A.D. 41. But at his **58f** death in 44, the whole of Palestine was subjected to a Roman Procurator dependent upon Syria. Thus the Holy Land was more inexorably drawn into the superb Roman transit and communications system which was to be exploited for the spread of the Gospel by Paul and the other Apostles.

THE HISTORY OF ISRAEL

I. TO 130 B.C.

BY L. JOHNSTON

9a Bibliography—Besides the works given in the bibliographies of the articles referred to below:
W. F. Albright, *From the Stone Age to Christianity*, 1957[2];
J. Bright, *A History of Israel*, 1960; J. Bottéro, *Le problème des Habiru à la 4ème rencontre assyriologique internationale*, 1954; R. de Vaux, AI, 1961; G. Mendenhall, *Law and Covenant in Israel and the Ancient Near East*, 1955; M. Noth, *The History of Israel*, E. tr, 1958 (from 2nd German ed.); H. H. Rowley, *From Joseph to Joshua*, 1948.

b Introduction—The main source for the history of Israel is the Bible itself; the reader is therefore referred to the commentaries on the individual books for more detailed treatment of specific points which it would be pointless to duplicate here. No single book in the Bible, however, is simply 'history' in the modern sense of the word; the literary characteristics of the books must be taken into account, and for this the reader is referred particularly to the articles on *Introd. to the Pent.* (§§ 130—40) and *The Historical Books* (§§ 241—44). Archaeological discoveries have widened our perspective and contributed to our understanding of biblical literature, and these are dealt with in the article *Archaeology and the Bible* (§§ 77—84).

c Israel's Ancestors—Israelite traditions concerning their ancestors are recorded in Gn 12–50; they were at first handed down orally, with all the hazards normal to such a mode of transmission, and when they were eventually written down they were influenced by the interests, especially theological, of this later age (cf § 243e—f). Nevertheless, these traditions agree remarkably with certain archaeological information. Israel claimed descent from one Jacob, who was the son of Isaac, who was the son of Abraham. All of these are connected with Mesopotamia, Jacob in particular with the Arameans. There is archaeological evidence that in the Middle Bronze Age (c. 2000—1550), semi-nomadic Amorites made their way from the Syrian desert into the more fertile regions of Mesopotamia (where they eventually formed the Babylonian empire) and Canaan. Proper names such as Abram, Jacob, Levi, Ishmael and Benjamin are found in documents of this period. Many incidents in the Bible are illuminated by reference especially to **texts from** the town of **Nuzi**: the duty of a barren wife to provide a substitute for her husband (cf Gn 16:1—4); inheritance by a slave in case of childlessness (cf Gn 15:1—4); the importance of the teraphim as giving a title to inheritance (cf Gn 31:19). The manner of life of the patriarchs is exactly that of semi-nomadic wanderers whose flocks form the principal source of life and sign of wealth, but who gradually adopt some form of agriculture (cf Gn 37:5—17, Joseph dreams of ears of corn; but his brothers still lead their flocks some distance away from the camp).

d Israel's traditions, then, give us a fair picture of the sort of life lived by their semi-nomadic ancestors. As for the biographical form in which the stories are cast, we must take account of the tendency to describe a group in terms **59d** of an individual (Gn 10 is probably the best example of this—all the peoples on earth are described as 'sons' of Noah's three children). This does not mean that Abraham, Isaac and Jacob are merely fictional; but it does mean that we have to be aware also of the group of which they are representatives. This is particularly instructive when we reflect on the story of Jacob, with its strongly Aramean connexions (cf Dt 26:5, 'My father was a wandering Aramean'). Israel's origins are not quite as simple as might be suggested by the abbreviated formula 'Abraham begot Isaac who begot Jacob who begot twelve sons from whom are descended the twelve tribes'. Canaan received successive migrations from Aram Naharaim, the land of the two rivers, and all of them contributed something to the stock from which later Israel was made up. But it is not as a matter of family pride that these stories have their place in Israel's traditions, nor out of interest in ethnic origins; but because already amongst their ancestors the foundations of their faith was laid, faith in the living God who called Abraham to a covenant with himself (cf Rm 4:11f).
The Exodus—The Amorites were not the only people **60a** on the move in the Middle Bronze Age. Shortly after them the Hurrians, originating probably from the region of Armenia, came southwards; by the 15th cent. they had occupied a region of the NW borders of Babylonia which they called Mitanni, as well as towns such as Nuzi, and had moved also into Canaan. The successive pressure of Amorites and Hurrians led to a further movement south, into Egypt, which led eventually to the newcomers taking control of the country. The Egyptians called them the Hyksos, 'foreign rulers'; there were at least two waves of immigration, but the total period of **Hyksos control was c. 1720—1580**. The native Egyptian leaders who then drove them out followed up the campaign of liberation with aggressive action in Canaan which established Egyptian authority as far as the Euphrates, where they came up against the power of Mitanni.

Meanwhile, in Asia Minor the **Hittites** had been **b** growing in strength and became strong enough to threaten both Mitanni and, more remotely, Egypt. The Mitanni appealed for Egyptian help, but this was the period when Akhenaten, from his new capital at Amarna, was concentrating more on his religious reform than on political affairs. But the Hittites succeeded in conquering Mitanni, and Akhenaten's successors reversed his political (and religious) policy to face this new danger. Under **Ramesses II** vigorous action was taken to recover Egyptian control over Asia. This was partly successful, but the drawn **battle of Kadesh** was followed by a treaty with the Hittites. Ramesses II then turned his energy to building activities at home. His successor Merneptah also campaigned in Canaan—the record of one of his campaigns (c. 1230 B.C.) carved on a stele gives us the first mention of Israel outside the Bible: 'Israel is laid waste, his seed is not'.

60c This is the background to the account of the Exodus given in the Bible. The story of the Hyksos (as well as the biblical tradition of Abraham and the Beni Hasan wall painting, ANEP, plate 3) show that semitic immigration into Egypt was a not uncommon event. After the expulsion of the Hyksos and the Egyptian victories in Canaan, the number of semites was increased by captured prisoners. These captives, employed as slaves, were known in Egyptian as '*apiru*. (The term is almost certainly connected with the Mesopotamian *Habiru*, and both with the biblical 'Hebrews'; it is not, however, the name of a people but a description of social status with a fairly wide range of meanings—semi-nomads, mercenaries, slaves). The Bible tells us how a **group of these '*apiru* were led by Moses** (the name is Egyptian in form, as are Phinehas, Hophni, Merari) **out of slavery to mount Sinai**, where some striking experience bound them together into the nucleus of the nation of Israel.

d Many of the historical details underlying this account will probably always escape our grasp: for example the exact means by which the slaves achieved freedom, or the precise route they followed to Sinai (for further discussion, see § 180*j*). But the essential character of the experience is clear. It was above all a religious experience, associated with the worship of God under the name of Yahweh. This divine name may have been known before this time and may have been known amongst other nations; the exact etymological significance of the name too is open to dispute. But Israel interpreted the word as meaning 'He is'—not in a theoretical or metaphysical sense, but with dynamic and practical connotations: the God whose reality was unmistakably demonstrated in his action on their behalf. The manner of his action too distinguished Yahweh from other gods of the day. Worship was directed to these gods primarily as responsible for the phenomena of nature; their action—and therefore their nature—was inseparably linked with the cycle of nature. But Israel had now made contact with a God whose action took the form of historical intervention, and who was therefore outside and above the world of human experience.

e Israel was bound to Yahweh by a **covenant**. The form in which the covenant is expressed has much in common with contemporary treaties between an overlord and his vassals. By the covenant, Israel recognized Yahweh as their Lord, and accepted the obligation to his service. But this very fact puts Israel in a special relationship with him which implies the idea of election developed later by the prophets: 'You only have I known of all the families of the earth' (Am 3:2). God on his side guaranteed protection and assistance, which contains the roots of the theology of 'promise'. Yahweh is thus 'present' with Israel, and this concept is symbolized in the Tent where Yahweh and Israel meet. Moreover, this relationship with Yahweh is the basis of Israel's existence as a community; the stipulations of the covenant are the constitution of the nation. This great event—or complex of events—was ritually commemorated later, and it was in the context of this celebration that the account as we have it took shape (cf § 188).

61a The Twelve-Tribe League—The newly-formed community soon made their way towards the fertile land of Canaan. In their advance, they had to face not only the Canaanites, but the peoples who had recently (early 13th cent.) settled in Transjordan, and later the **Philistines**— part of the **Peoples of the Sea** whom Ramesses III drove off from Egypt and who gained a footing in Canaan early in the 12th cent. On the other hand, they were freed from the massive opposition which would have resulted from the

presence of any single power in the area. The infiltration of **61** Aramean tribes in Mesopotamia and the incursion of the Peoples of the Sea put an end to the power of the Egyptians and the Hittites and limited the expansion of Assyrian power. Canaan itself was occupied by a mixed population (we have already spoken of the Amorites and the Hurrians); and though these peoples had developed a uniform culture, politically there was no real unity; the country was composed of independent city-states. This certainly assisted the Israelites in their advance.

Israel at this stage is often described as an **amphi- b ctyony**—a group of tribes united by a covenant round a central shrine. But this raises the question of the origin of the tribes which traditionally constituted the amphictyony. The subject is extremely complex and there is not yet any agreed solution; but these are some of the factors which have to be taken into account. (a) First of all we must bear in mind a principle already mentioned, that the ancestor of the tribe sometimes stands for the whole tribe descended from him; a clear example of this is Gn 49, where Jacob's blessing is obviously aimed not at his sons as individuals but at the tribes as they existed in Canaan. (b) The birth of Jacob's sons narrated in Gn 30 expresses Israel's awareness that the tribes did not all stand in the same relationship to one another; they have one common ancestor, Jacob, but they have different mothers, thus dividing them into four groups. (c) One would expect the 'eldest sons' to represent the senior tribes; but in fact the tribes corresponding to the three eldest sons, Reuben, Simeon and Levi, played no important part in the post-Exodus period; therefore presumably they were important before that, in Canaan. (d) The term Hebrews is probably connected with the term Habiru; but the Habiru were active in Canaan in the 14th cent. and again a century later (ANET, 487, 255)—that is to say, at a time when the Israelite Hebrews were supposed to be in Egypt. (e) Ex **c** 12:38 speaks of those who came out of Egypt as 'a mixed multitude'; and certainly amongst those who entered Canaan there were Midianites (Nm 10:29—32) and Kennizites like Caleb (Jos 14:13); and after this they were joined by the family of Rahab, the Gibeonites and presumably many more of the Canaanites. This shows that it was not blood relationship which constituted membership of Israel, but acceptance of the covenant; but it shows also that the covenant could be accepted by those who had not taken part in the Exodus or the experience at Sinai. (f) The capture and renaming of the city called Horma is said (Jg 1:17) to be part of a campaign by Judah, Simeon and Caleb in the south of Canaan; but in Nm 21:1—3 the same incident is attached closely to the wandering in the desert; this duplication would be explained if there had been a **separate advance into Canaan by certain tribes from the S, distinct from the other invasion from the E.** (g) Joshua and Judges give two different pictures of the occupation of Canaan; these are not necessarily mutually exclusive (see § 255*f*), but certainly the picture in Jg, of a **laborious struggle by separate tribes**, seems more natural than Joshua's version of a swift, single successful invasion by all the tribes under one leader; and this suggests to us that there may be a large measure of idealisation and simplification in Jos.

But this, taken with the other points, leads us to **d** ask further questions: if this is true of Jos, might not the account of the Exodus too be a similar simplification? and might not then the story of the descent into Egypt under Joseph be yet another? With suitable hesitation, the present trend of opinion may be summed up by saying that it seems possible that the 'sons of Israel' who were

61d at Sinai joined forces with other groups who were already in Canaan either because they had never left there (the Reubenites?) or because they had entered earlier (Judah?). This 'simplification' is, of course, a perfectly legitimate literary procedure; all that we later call 'Israel' derives essentially from that group which, originally wandering in Canaan, were later enslaved in Egypt and made their way back to Canaan only after undergoing the decisive experience at Sinai. All other elements which go to make up the historical Israel do so only in so far as they too accept the essential covenant link and share, by proxy as it were, in the experience of Sinai. Indeed, it tells us a great deal about the strength of the covenant ideal that the group from Sinai should have absorbed the others, instead of themselves being lost in the population of Canaan.

e The Settlement—Although we have seen that there is some reason to suspect that Joshua's account of the invasion may be a simplification, nevertheless, archaeological evidence confirms that Canaan did suffer violent attacks in the late 13th cent. Cities which Joshua is said to have defeated were in fact destroyed about this time—Debir (Jos 10:38), Eglon (10:36), Lachish (10:31) and Hazor (11:10). It would seem, then, that there were a number of initial victories which enabled the tribes to gain a foothold in the land, but, as Jos itself points out, e.g. 13:2–6, leaving the main work of settlement still to be achieved. Jg gives us an account of this work. The nature of the book—a collection of **individual episodes under local leaders whose activities may have overlapped** or on the contrary may be separated by many years—makes it impossible to give a detailed history of the period. One fixed point is provided by the victory of Deborah and Barak in the plain of Esdraelon (Jg 4:4—5:31), which gave them entry to this rich plain and encouraged cooperation between the tribes in the area. Archaeological evidence from Megiddo suggests that this important victory took place about 1125.

f For the rest, we must be content to find in Jg a good general picture of the period, extending over two centuries from **1200 to 1000**. The initial victories had no doubt brought several Canaanite cities or clans over to the side of the invaders and as time went on, the numbers of the tribes were increased by others, especially those of Amorite stock who had been living in Canaan as Habiru; the unity of all these was sealed by a special covenant ceremony at Shechem (Jos 24). But this still left many to oppose the newcomers, and this opposition was backed by chariotry and strongly fortified cities. For much of the period the Israelites were hemmed into the hill country where the chariots could not advance (the victory at Esdraelon was said to be due to a storm which bogged down the chariots). In their struggle for possession the Israelites had to contend not only with the native Canaanites, but also with marauding bands from across the Jordan (3:7–30), semi-nomadic raiders like the Midianites (6:1–6), and later the Philistines (the stories of Samson).

g The amphictyonic organization of **Israel** at this time stands out clearly. They **form a sacred league**, their warfare is a holy war, and the men who are their leaders are not men of recognized official position but men endowed by God specially for this purpose. The tribal feature of the organization is equally evident; each of the tribes makes its own way, cut off by the mountainous terrain from any close communication with the others; the leaders are tribal leaders and though a group of tribes may collaborate in a particular campaign, sometimes too they are at war with each other (Jg 12:1–6). This tribal

independence eventually brought the amphictyony to the **61g** **brink of disaster**. The Philistines (a group of the Peoples of the Sea who had settled on the W coast of Canaan about 1150) were better organized than either Canaanites or Israelites and above all were better armed, having the secret of iron. Israel had not made much headway against the Canaanites; but against the Philistines they were even worse placed and were unable to resist their steady advance inland. The climax was reached with the **battle of Aphek about 1050**, when the Philistines not only achieved complete victory but even **captured the Ark** of the Covenant, the visible sign of the God of the Covenant. It was returned shortly afterwards, but the event was a serious blow to the idea of the amphictyony. Samuel succeeded in keeping alive the spirit of the covenant, but it was clear that some other form of organization was needed to deal with the Philistine threat. It was inevitable that the idea of monarchy should be proposed.

The Monarchy—The idea of a king over a tribal league **62a** bound together by a common loyalty to one God was subject to great sociological and theological objections. And Saul, the first appointed to fulfil the office of king, did not succeed in overcoming them. The two accounts of his rejection (1 Sm 13:3–14, 15:7 23) are both concerned with breaches of covenant law, illustrating his failure to reconcile the demands of his position as king with the demands of the covenant. He did give new vigour and cohesion to Israel's struggles, and even after his death there were many who were still loyal to his memory. Many others, however, were alienated by the fits of depression and suspicion to which he became subject, probably partly as a result of the strain of his difficult position; and when he died in a disastrous battle with the Philistines, the way was open for a new leader, David.

David was a man of great gifts who had already **b** distinguished himself as a soldier under Saul. This incurred for him the jealousy of Saul and he withdrew into the southern desert, putting himself and an increasing band of followers at the service of one of the Philistine kings. When Saul died he returned from exile and settled in Hebron, where he was recognized as king by the southern tribes. In the north, Saul's prestige won a following for his son Eshbaal; but after a few years he forfeited the support of the general on whom he relied, and David was then left without a rival.

David's **military achievements** may be briefly stated; **c** but the brevity must not blind us to the magnitude of the task so successfully carried out. First, he completely broke the power of the Philistines, confining them to a small area round their original settlement on the coast, subject to the Israelite king as overlord. Secondly, he brought the Canaanite population to accept his rule; in some cases no doubt this was done by force of arms (as at Jerusalem); but in many more it was simply the moral pressure of his success which led the Canaanite cities to realize that they had nothing to lose and much to gain by accepting his overlordship. Thirdly, he put an end to the attacks from outside Canaan which had plagued Israel in the struggle for possession—Edomites, Moabites, Ammonites and Arameans were not only defeated in battle but in varying degrees forced to accept the authority of David.

But the most significant achievement of David was **d** connected with his **capture of Jerusalem**. This city, which had successfully withstood all attack up till then, was captured by David early in his reign. He made it the capital of his kingdom, and had the Ark of the Covenant brought there. The situation of such a capital, so

62d difficult to attack, would obviously appeal to David as a soldier. He also appreciated the political advantages of the move; the unity of the twelve tribes under one leader was not yet an accepted fact; indeed, David's clash with Saul and then with Saul's son had introduced an even more dangerous partial unity in which one group of tribes was ranged together against another group, the north against the south; from a capital like Jerusalem, without previous associations with either north or south, the king could more easily look for the loyalty of both. Moreover, the unconquered Canaanite communities too could more easily accept David as ruler when he ruled from one of the ancient Canaanite cities. But far outweighing the military and political advantages of the

e move was the **religious significance** which was attached to it. The Ark of the Covenant had passed from sight and mind since the battle of Aphek; and by bringing this symbol of the covenant to his new capital, David declared his intention of ruling not as despotic king, but as guardian of the covenant traditions. By this he hoped to do precisely what Saul had failed to do, to persuade the people that he was not changing anything essential, but was simply giving their old ideals new form. David's supporters could show that the monarchy did not conflict with the covenant ideal, but that the king simply embodied the covenant. The bond between God and the nation which the covenant expressed was now realized in the king. With instinctive genius, contemporary ideas were adapted to this end. In Mesopotamia, the king was said to be God's adopted son; but Israel's king was son of God in this sense, that he represented the nation which was God's first-born son (Ex 4:22). As representatives of their gods, other kings brought fertility and prosperity to their countries; but Israel's king brought to the country the blessings of the covenant. The covenant with the people as a whole is now focussed on the king in particular (cf 2 Sm 7:5—16), and his anointing betokens his sacred position; he is a *messiah*.

f David's military success and political skill had made the principle of monarchy thoroughly acceptable; but it did not settle the question of who in practice was to be king, and the end of David's reign was disturbed by trouble with his sons concerned with this point. First there was a favourite son Absalom, who, having removed his elder brother on the grounds that he had violated their sister, took advantage of the lenient treatment he received to set on foot a campaign to win popularity among the people (perhaps especially the people of the northern tribes). When he judged that this had achieved sufficient progress, he had himself proclaimed king at Hebron and advanced on Jerusalem. David fled beyond the Jordan; but it soon become apparent that Absalom's support was not as universal as he had hoped, and David decided to make a stand. Absalom's army was routed and he himself was killed by David's commander Joab.

g This event had also a minor repercussion which showed that the old rivalry between north and south was never far below the surface. When the king returned across the Jordan, he was met by 'all the people of Judah and half the people of Israel' (2 Sm 19:41). When the people of Israel protested at this, the Judeans claimed the king as one of them; whereupon a Benjaminite named Sheba called the men of Israel to leave David to the Judeans. But the revolt was quickly quelled. After Absalom, David's son Adonijah thought that he stood next in line, and unlike Absalom he had official support for his claim. This was partly due to the fact that David's policy of conciliation and unification had left him with two priests and two commanders of the army; Abiathar and

Joab supported Adonijah, but Zadok the priest and **62g** Benaiah the general gave their support to Solomon, David's son by Bath-sheba whom he had seduced from her husband Uriah. Under their pressure and especially under the prompting of the prophet Nathan, David on his death-bed finally appointed Solomon as his successor, and this proclamation put an end to the hopes of Adonijah. Shortly afterwards, he and Joab were executed, and Abiathar was exiled to Anathoth.

Solomon entered into the inheritance which his **63a** father had won for him. Although he maintained a standing army greater than David's (including a strong force of chariotry and cavalry), we have no certain evidence that it was ever engaged in fighting. Solomon's reign was as outstanding for its diplomatic success as David's was for its victories. He linked his country by treaty (often accompanied by marriage alliance) with the Edomites, Moabites, Ammonites, and even the Egyptians and the Hittites and the Sidonians. This last was of great importance for the **commercial ventures** which Solomon also instituted; the Sidonians were great sailors and traders, and they initiated the Israelites into the arts of seamanship and helped to start trading voyages from the gulf of Aqaba. This in turn was connected with the **metal industry** from the deposits round Ezion-geber. On land too, he made himself master of the caravan trade, **importing horses** from Cilicia and chariots from Egypt, and exporting them again.

The wealth that resulted from this sudden surge **b** of economic activity gave rise to a great increase in **literary activity** too. The business of the kingdom called for the employment of skilled scribes, and this in turn led to the composition of works such as the History of the Succession to the Throne which was later incorporated into a larger history of the monarchy (2 Sm 9—1 (3) Kgs 2 cf § 241*d*). Oral literature, of course, already existed; but now it was recorded in writing and also reordered— as for example the stories which form the basis of the present book of Judges. But the most important literary composition of the period is the work of J (or perhaps the *Grundlage* from which both J and E were derived; cf § 135*a*). This was a national epic expressing the pride of a nation at the peak of its power, but it was also a deeply theological work, which tried to relate the national destiny to God's plan for the world as a whole. In addition to these historical works there was also the beginnings of a type of literature which was particularly associated with Solomon, the '**wisdom literature**' (1 (3) Kgs 4:29—33; cf § 357*b*). Finally we may mention the psalms which were composed at this time for use in the new temple.

For **building** too marked Israel's new prosperity. **c** Signs of this are to be found in many cities at this time— some of them ominous: the great houses of the rich, while the poor lived in hovels huddled together. But it was mainly in the **royal buildings** that the rising standard of living was to be seen. Archaeological evidence for this is provided most strikingly at Megiddo, with the palatial stabling for some 400 horses. Naturally, however, it was the king's own city of Jerusalem which benefited most. Not only had the population increased, but the bureaucratic regime called for much more space than David's modest palace could provide. The extension took place mainly to the north of the city, centring round the king's own palace and that for the queen. But the masterpiece of his achievement was the **construction of the temple** following the Canaanite pattern of rectangular building with closed sanctuary at the end, built largely of stone and richly ornamented.

63d But all of this had to be paid for, and not even the immense wealth flowing into the country from trade and tribute could keep pace with the lavish style of living which Solomon adopted. He had to cede some of his territory to Hiram of Tyre, to whom he owed so much for the materials and manpower used in building the temple. He also divided the country into twelve districts, each of which was responsible for the upkeep of the court for a month. He even imposed forced labour—previously confined to prisoners of war and non-Israelites—on the population.

e Israel was not the people to accept all this unquestioningly; nor were their objections simply economic, but ideological. It was only fifty years since the question of monarchy was first raised, and many people had then doubted whether it was reconcilable with the status of a league of tribes bound together by covenant with God. Saul had failed through lack of respect for the covenant law; and it had taken all David's skill and tact to show that the two concepts of government could be compatible. But now Solomon, having attained the throne by appointment and court intrigue rather than by clear divine designation, ruled like any other monarch, without any reference to the covenant status of the people he governed. He ignored the religious demands of the covenant by his toleration of idolatrous worship, and he ignored the political demands of the covenant by treating the people as his chattels. The division of the country into twelve departments each responsible for the upkeep of the court cut right across the tribal division of the country; it may have been justified from the point of view of administrative convenience, but it indicated a certain disregard for national traditions. During Solomon's reign, his success won toleration for his policies; but he was storing up trouble for his successors.

64a **The Divided Kingdom**—The trouble arose amongst the northern tribes who had always felt themselves less involved in the destiny of the Davidic dynasty. A certain Jeroboam had already voiced their discontent during the reign of Solomon and had been forced to take refuge in Egypt for it. He now returned and led a deputation to the new king, Rehoboam; and when the very **reasonable demands** of his party **were rejected**, he did more than threaten rebellion—he set up an independent state with himself as king.

b Rehoboam naturally refused to recognize the new state, and the first years were spent in warfare, to reduce the rebels on the one hand, to maintain independence on the other. But the two sides were not left to fight it out between themselves; external events intervened to complicate the situation. In Egypt the Libyan **Shishak** had overthrown the dynasty which was allied to Israel by marriage, and after the death of Solomon he made a victorious sortie into Israel, and imposed a heavy tribute on the land. Domestic difficulties prevented him from continuing his campaign, but he did enough to make both Judah and Israel forget their own wars for a while. To the N, the Aramean states (see **61a**), especially the **kingdom of Damascus** under the energetic new ruler Rezon, also intervened actively in the affairs of the two states. They were first called in by Rehoboam's son Abijam in a renewed attempt to subdue the N, and from then on they were a continual threat to Israel's northern and western frontiers.

c This, combined with certain theological difficulties, brought Israel to a state of **near anarchy**. For the northern state came into being as a protest against the centralized monarchy of Solomon; but once David's dynasty was rejected, there was no reason why Jeroboam's should be accepted. So that the incompetence of the rulers **64c** to deal with the Aramean threat led to exasperation especially in the army, and led to a series of assassinations and usurpations. Jeroboam's son Nadab was assassinated by one of his officers called Baasha; his son Ela was assassinated by Zimri; and Zimri ruled for a week before being faced by further insurrection.

It was in these circumstances that yet another **d** general, **Omri**, (885–874) came to power. But Omri succeeded in maintaining his power and gave the country stability. He did this as Solomon did it, by means of alliances; an alliance with the Phoenician kingdom of Tyre, where another usurper had recently seized power, and—an even greater tribute to his skill—an alliance with Judah, both alliances being sealed by marriages. Symbolic of the confidence of the new régime was the building of a new capital Samaria. Omri's conquest of Moab is recorded on the stele set up by Mesha king of Moab and discovered in 1868.

The effect of this new stability was seen in the military sphere during the reign of Omri's son **Ahab**, (874–53) who inflicted a surprise defeat on the Arameans still harassing his western territory. That this victory was not followed up was due to the threat of Assyria.

Assyria had been growing in strength since the **e** disappearance of the Hittites and the Mitanni two centuries previously, and had recently turned against the Aramean states settled along the Euphrates. At first, this left Damascus, freed of her rivals, in a position to intervene in the affairs of Judah and Israel, as we have seen. But when the Assyrians advanced still further westwards, the smaller nations realized that their only hope lay in combining their forces. Thus the Israelites, having just defeated the Arameans of Damascus, immediately joined forces with them as well as with other minor states, and the coalition succeeded in halting the Assyrians at the **battle of Qarqar**, 853 B.C. Once the immediate danger was averted, however, the alliance broke up and Israel and Damascus resumed their hostilities. This time, Israel was not successful; and once more this military failure combined with internal factors to produce revolution.

The internal factors were religious. When Israel **f** broke away from Judah, this was not intended to be a rejection of the Yahwist faith; in fact, the revolt was a protest against the secularization of the state by Solomon. Jeroboam set up two official centres of worship, one at Bethel and another at Dan, corresponding to Jerusalem, the official centre of worship in Judah. But several reasons led to a weakening of the traditional faith. First of all, although the national existence was based on the covenant with Yahweh, it was not to be expected that all the people, especially the late-comers to the covenant, should be equally clear on all that this involved; and on their entry into Canaan there was a great temptation to equate Yahweh with the gods of nature worshipped there; the story of Gideon, otherwise known as Jerubbaal, shows what must have happened fairly frequently. For many Israelites, therefore, the **g** bulls which figured in Jeroboam's shrines—innocent though they may have been in origin (cf AI, 333)—must have appeared no different from the idols which represented the Canaanite gods. And if this was so of the Israelites, it was even more so for the Canaanite population, large numbers of whom, having accepted David's rule without any real change in religion, were now subjects of the northern kingdom; for them too the Yahwist faith could not be expected to be a matter of any great concern. But the greatest harm was done by the marriage between

64g Omri's son Ahab and **Jezebel**, princess of Tyre; this brought paganism into the very court of Israel, and from there Jezebel used every effort to spread it throughout the country as a whole. The victory of her national religion would be a victory for her national way of life, a sign of Tyre's superiority to Israel. In particular it would mean that Israel's monarchy could be like Tyre's, unrestricted by the sanctions of a divine law to which the king too was subject.

h But there were still in Israel defenders of the old ways and of Israel's true faith; and one of these, **Elijah**, stirred up the national conscience against Jezebel. There was growing resentment against this pagan rule which insisted on trying to change things within Israel while failing to protect the country against attacks from without. Finally **Jehu**, (841—814) one of the generals in the field against the Arameans, started a revolt and with a bloody purge of all the old regime had himself installed as king. He had scarcely seated himself on the throne however before he had to face the threat of Assyria. Shalmaneser III invaded Phoenicia and laid siege to Damascus in 841. Among the cities and nations forced to pay tribute was Jehu who is depicted on the **Black Obelisk of Shalmaneser** kissing the feet of the Assyrian king. The accompanying text refers to the tribute paid by 'Jehu, son of Omri', cf ANET 280.

i Events in **Judah** meanwhile followed much the same pattern as those in the north. The split weakened the power of both kingdoms; and just as Israel was subject to the attacks of the Arameans, so Judah lost control of the Philistines and of Edom. The alliance with Omri brought about some improvement and **Jehoshaphat** (870—848) of Judah took advantage of this to restart the trading voyages from Ezion-geber, and to make internal administrative reforms (2 Chr 19:8—11, cf § 306p). But Judah was associated with Israel in the ill-fated Aramean war, and the king, Ahaziah, fell in Jehu's purge. His mother, **Athaliah**, then took over the government herself and wiped out the rest of the royal family except one child, Joash, who was hidden away by one of the priests. Athaliah was one of Omri's house, who had come to Judah as Jehoshaphat's wife as part of the alliance between the two kingdoms. She was a woman of the same stamp as Jezebel and tried to transform Judah into a pagan state under a despotic monarchy. But paganism had not made such deep inroads in Judah as it had in Israel, and there was a stronger tradition there of loyalty to David's dynasty and its ideals. Athaliah's reformation, then, was not as successful as Jezebel's; and its end, too, was a simpler matter than the end of the house of Omri. The boy Joash was brought forward at a suitable moment, the people rallied to his support, and Athaliah was deposed and put to death.

j The violence with which Jehu had acted against the house of Omri might have seemed to promise better things in the war against the Arameans. But in fact things went even worse, and soon the Arameans were in possession of the whole of Transjordan and were even able to make attacks on Judah. But this desperate situation was suddenly and completely reversed just before 800 B.C. This was none of Israel's doing, however. It was yet another Assyrian raid (one more foretaste of things to come). Adadnirari III invaded the West in 802 and received tribute from Sidon, Tyre, Philistia, Damascus and Edom.

The invasion from Israel's point of view was so happily timed that it severely crippled Damascus but petered out before reaching Israel. This brought immediate relief to the Israelites, and though they had not

been strong enough to bring it about themselves, they were **64j** quick to take advantage of it. Israel and Judah together were able to concentrate their forces on the much easier targets provided by the smaller nations around them; military success led to political success, and both in turn led to economic prosperity as the trade routes were opened up again and tribute from the vanquished flowed in. In a very short while the combined kingdoms of **Jeroboam II of Israel** (787—747) and **Uzziah of Judah** were almost equal in extent and influence to that of Solomon. The Deuteronomic historian however passes over them almost in silence, 2 (4) Kgs 14—15, because they did not keep the law of the Lord. The economic **k** prosperity was accompanied by **religious and moral degradation**. The nation was by now in a fair way to losing sight completely of the idealism on which it was founded; social injustice went unchecked, and there was oppression and exploitation of the poor by the rich. But Israel's religion had the internal vitality to produce men of sufficient spiritual insight and independence of thought to speak out against abuses such as these; and the 8th and 7th cent. were particularly rich in such men, the 'prophets' (see § 452a) who instituted an uncompromising critique of public and private morality and pointed out, often in language of great beauty and vigour, that conduct like this endangered the health and ultimately the very existence of the nation.

The message of the **prophets** found confirmation in **65a** the political events of the N kingdom after the death of Jeroboam II. The corruption of morality undermined the very structure of society and brought about a state of anarchy even worse than that which had existed at the beginning of the kingdom's history. Jeroboam's son Zechariah reigned for six months before being assassinated by Shallum, who lasted a month before Menahem seized power in a bloody civil war. He was succeeded by his son Pekahiah, who almost immediately fell to another of the same name, Pekah.

This situation was aggravated by—and partly caused **b** by—the **reappearance of Assyria**. Tiglath Pileser III had restored order in Mesopotamia and was now embarked on what was to be a definitive series of campaigns westwards. The western states tried to oppose the invader as usual by a coalition, led by king Uzziah of Judah, cf § 293d. But this time it was of no avail, and a crippling tribute was imposed on the defeated states; 738 B.C. There were some who thought that rather than suffer the beggary that this would involve, it was better to try once more recourse to arms. Pekah was the leader of this party, and having seized the throne from Menahem's son, he tried to reform the coalition against Assyria. Judah, now ruled by Uzziah's son Jotham, saw no prospect of success in this and held aloof. **Damascus and Israel** felt that they could not go forward with their plans while an uncommitted Judah menaced their rear, so they made plans to bring about a forcible change of regime in Judah and appoint one of their own nominees as king. At this stage Jotham died and his son Ahaz had to face this difficult situation (Edomites and Philistines too seem to have taken advantage of his difficulties to join in the attack). Rejecting Isaiah's advice, he appealed to the Assyrians for help. This was almost irrelevant since Assyria would certainly have intervened in any case. **The intervention (734 B.C.) of Assyria was decisive. The coalition was utterly broken**, Damascus was destroyed, its king killed and its territory annexed. Israel escaped more lightly through the death of Pekah who had instigated the rebellion and the prompt submission of his successor Hoshea; but even here many cities were

65b destroyed, some of the population was deported and part of the territory was annexed.

c But Israel had still not learned from this bitter lesson. Taking advantage of the death of Tiglath Pileser, and with a vague hope of help from Egypt, Hoshea rebelled once more. This time the Assyrians determined to end trouble once and for all. After a two year siege, the capital Samaria was taken; large numbers of the population were deported and replaced by others from different parts of the empire, and **Israel ceased to exist**. The fall of Israel was a salutary shock to the sister-kingdom of Judah. The religious and moral abuses which prosperity had brought to the northern kingdom had made their way into Judah also, and submission to Assyria had brought about an increase in pagan influence. It may seem paradoxical that this went hand in hand with an increased confidence in the covenant bond with Yahweh, but the paradox is only apparent—Yahweh was treated as a talisman, his oracle a magical formula which could be relied on regardless of the moral dispositions of his devotees.

d The economic hardship caused by the events already described (the invasion of Damascus and Israel, the rebellion of Edom cutting off the trade-routes south, the tribute to be paid to Assyria) and above all the extinction of a major branch of the covenant people, did something to bring Judah to a more realist attitude and produced a frame of mind which made it possible for **Hezekiah**, who had now succeeded Ahaz, to follow up the teaching of prophets like Isaiah with some **reforms**, particularly in measures against idolatry.

e Politically, this reform was assisted by the fact that Assyrian attention was diverted by more pressing troubles nearer home. There the **Babylonians** under a new leader, Merodach Baladan, were trying to organize the nations subject to Assyria with a view to rebellion. For many years Hezekiah was persuaded by Isaiah not to take part in this (and the fate of a Philistine attempt in 713 showed how right he was). But the death of the Assyrian king in 705 was the signal for a general revolt and Hezekiah could no longer resist. He prepared for war, strengthened the defences of Jerusalem and constructed a tunnel to bring the waters from the spring of Gihon to the pool of Siloam within the city walls. But the new **Assyrian king, Sennacherib**, reacted swiftly. He first subdued Babylon, then marched down the Mediterranean coast to deal with the Philistines, defeated the Egyptians, and then (701 B.C.) turned on Judah. **Jerusalem was besieged**, and eventually Hezekiah had to pay a huge sum of money to the Assyrians though the city was not itself destroyed. (Some details in this campaign—or perhaps there were two campaigns—are not yet clear, cf § 294a–h).

f For the next seventy years or so, Assyrian power remained strong enough to induce Judah to give up further thoughts of rebellion. Hezekiah's son **Manasseh** was indeed an all too faithful vassal and allowed paganism to run riot in the country. But religious feeling was not entirely dead and probably played some part in the movement which led to the assassination of Manasseh's son Amon. The new king, **Josiah**, could then take up and **extend the reform of Hezekiah**. This reform (622 B.C.) seems to have been based on, or fostered by, a document found in the temple at this time, probably the nucleus of the present book of Dt, a presentation of the covenant in the spirit of the prophets. One of the steps envisaged by this document and put into practice by Josiah was the **centralization of worship** at the Jerusalem temple. The experience of the N kingdom in particular had shown that without strict supervision it was very **65f** easy for the worship of Yahweh to degenerate into just another form of idolatry; and Josiah now adopted the very radical solution of abolishing all temples and shrines except the Jerusalem temple. Those who were in charge of such shrines and who had permitted idolatrous worship were put to death, and the rest were invited to Jerusalem to take part in the services there. Since this was obviously not practicable in every case, great hardship resulted, which is reflected in the Deuteronomic admonition to care for the Levite, along with the widow, the orphan and the stranger. At Jerusalem itself, the vast increase in numbers of the priests led to a differentiation in grade—the Jerusalem priests retained their rank, the others were reduced to a secondary grade and were known as 'levites'.

Josiah's reform was made possible by the growing **g** difficulties facing the Assyrian overlords. The Babylonians made themselves increasingly the focal point for rebellions all over the vast empire; and about 620, this pressure began to tell. **Nabopolassar** was proclaimed king of Babylon and advanced up the Euphrates while the Medes attacked from the north. Assyria fought stubbornly, but Nineveh fell in 612, and the Assyrian army withdrew westwards, where they held out for a few more years.

The Egyptian king, Necho, who owed his position to **h** the Assyrians, marched northwards during this final struggle, partly to come to the help of his overlord, but partly also to be in a position to challenge Babylon if Assyria should fail. Josiah of Judah thought that the fall of Assyria would be to Judah's advantage and tried (609 B.C.) to stop Necho, but lost his life in doing so, at **Megiddo**. The Pharaoh replaced his son and successor Jehoahaz by Josiah's son, Jehoiakim, thus implicitly claiming authority over the kingdom. But the Babylonians by now had consolidated their hold on the empire they had inherited from Assyria, finally defeated them at **Carchemish**, 605, and drove the Egyptians back as far as the borders of Egypt itself. The Babylonian prince **Nebuchadnezzar** was halted here, and returned home to regroup his forces, and to inherit the kingdom on the death of his father. Judah thought that this indicated a weakness in the Babylonian authority and declared independence. Nebuchadnezzar immediately ordered his vassal states in the district to attack, and then in 598 came to settle the revolt himself. Jehoiakim died at this moment; and his son Jehoiachin had to pay the penalty for his father's folly in the deportation of many of the important citizens and his own imprisonment at Babylon.

The Babylonians appointed his uncle as king under **i** the name of **Zedekiah**. With Jehoiachin still alive, though in exile, his position was undoubtedly difficult, but his own vacillating character did nothing to help matters. He swung from one extreme to the other between the two schools of thought in the country—those who were in favour of accepting Babylonian domination for the time being, and those who thought that the Egyptians could still be a match for the Babylonians and that an alliance with them might yet bring freedom.

To any clear-sighted observer of the time sub- **j** mission was obviously the only safe course. Spiritually, however, rebellion and inevitable disaster might be seen to be the more profitable. For Josiah's reform had not wrought a deep and universal effect; in one regard, it had even made matters worse. For a permanent failing of the established religion was formalism—attention to the external ceremonial of religious practices without

81

65j regard for internal dispositions; and since Josiah had given such prominence to the temple at Jerusalem, this superstitious attitude attached itself to this building in particualr. This was the house of God; Jerusalem was the city where God himself had his dwelling; it must therefore be inviolable, no matter what the conduct of its inhabitants may be.

k It was this distortion that gave particular poignancy to the preaching of **Jeremiah** at this time. Politically, he saw that rebellion was useless; but for the spiritual ills of the nation he saw that political disaster was the only adequate remedy. Matters in any case were taken out of his hands. Zedekiah rejected his advice, fell in with the wishes of the pro-Egyptian party and rebelled against Babylon. Reaction was swift and decisive. **The city fell in 587**, Zedekiah was taken to Babylon as a prisoner, and with him still more of the population. Judah was reduced to the status of a province of the Babylonian empire. But a further act of disobedience— the **assassination of the governor, Gedaliah**— resulted in the loss of even this degree of independent existence, and the country was incorporated into the neighbouring province of Samaria.

66a The Exile—Little is known of life in Judah during the next half-century. Life did continue; some form of worship was even carried out on the site of the ruined temple in Jerusalem. But leaderless in a ravaged land, it was simply a matter of existing, and the spiritual leadership which would lead to a revival of the nation was not to come from Judah.

For the **exiles in Babylon**, material conditions were not too difficult—they were able to settle down in self-contained communities, to earn their own living, to take part in the commercial and social life of the place in which they found themselves. But spiritually they had suffered a shock which could have been expected to drive them to forget their past, their history and their faith, and to settle down to make a new life for themselves

b with the Babylonians. But two great **prophets** appeared amongst the exiles, Second Isaiah (Is 40–55, cf § 461*d*) and Ezekiel. They not only found an explanation for the exile which saved the remnant of Israel from extinction, but pointed the way to a nobler road ahead. They saw in the disaster which had overtaken the people of Yahweh not a sign of God's failure but a sign of his power; for it was Israel which had failed, and their God was one who would not take such failure lightly; he was such, moreover, as could make use of all the peoples of the world to achieve his purpose. His purpose, however, was not rejection but purification. In suffering, the exiles would learn to be truly 'servants of the Lord', bearing the burden of Israel's years of infidelity.

c The exiles of Judah, then, did not lose their national identity. To help them to maintain their distinctness from the people amongst whom they lived, the **customs peculiar to themselves were stressed—the observance of the Sabbath, circumcision and the laws of ritual cleanliness**. But above all this, was the purest foundation of their faith—**the Word of God**. God had chosen them, God had intervened in their history, God had spoken to them by the prophets; and all of this was embodied in their national traditions. All of this, then, whether written or unwritten, was carefully collected and treasured, written and copied. The traditions of the priestly caste were of particular interest, not merely because the matters of ritual which were their concern were matters of principle at the time, but also because in their hands lay the continuity of worship; with touching piety they conserved the memory of the temple

ritual, against the day when the temple would again be **66d** used for worship.

For the prophets foresaw that the exile would be **d** temporary. Political events of the day gave them good grounds for this. **Cyrus of Persia**, having made himself master (549 B.C.) of the empire of the Medes, Babylon's old allies, was clearly preparing to attack Babylon itself. The king of Babylon, on the other hand, **Nabonidus**, showed no great interest in government, leaving it to his son **Belshazzar**. In 539 Cyrus's plans were mature and such was the thoroughness of his preparation and the lethargy of Babylon that the conquest was achieved with no great struggle.

The Return from Exile—One of the first acts of Cyrus **67a** was to proclaim freedom for the captive peoples in Babylon, thus opening the way for the Judeans to return home. There was not, however, a mass movement to return; many had lived in Babylon now almost all their lives, and many more had ties that could not be easily broken. But a small party (537 B.C.) did set off at once under **Sheshbazzar**, and there was a steady trickle over the years that followed. When they arrived in their home-land, they found that conditions were quite different from the hopes they had nourished in exile. Their old homes were not simply waiting to receive them. The land was still suffering from the Babylonian devastation, and where it was not a wilderness it was largely occupied by the people who had not been taken captive and by the Edomites who had moved in as the captives left.

The newcomers settled down as best they could, and **b** one of their first cares was to erect an **altar** on the site of the ruined temple and to start again the formal worship. The next step was to begin the rebuilding of the temple and the walls of the city itself, but great opposition was encountered from those who had occupied the land in their absence and the work ground to a halt. No further progress was made for many years. Then in 520 B.C. Zerubbabel, governor of Judah, and Jeshua a priest of the Jerusalem line, took up the work again. But above all it was two prophets, Haggai and Zechariah, who stirred the people to life and spurred them on with the work of rebuilding, until the **temple was finally finished in 515** B.C., cf § 310*h*.

This revival of national spirit coincided with a period **c** of upheaval in the Persian empire following the death of Cyrus's successor Cambyses in 522 B.C. which seemed to hold out even greater hopes for the Jews; the prophets began to speak of Zerubbabel in messianic terms. This hope was short-lived. Darius I quickly brought the empire under control again. But it gave grounds to the Samaritans to make trouble for them with the Persians. The **Samaritans**, in spite of their mixed origins, had shown themselves ready to welcome the returned exiles as brothers; but when these gestures were rebuffed, they did all in their power to resist the growth of a rival state on their borders. They drew the attention of the Persian authorities to the new temple, hoping that it would be treated as a sign that the Jews were claiming autonomy. Darius had enquiries made and found that the building was within the Jewish rights.

In spite of this progress conditions were still very **d** difficult and the future was doubtful; until, nearly a century after the first return, **Nehemiah and Ezra** came from Persia. (For the chronological problems connected with these two, cf § 311*a*). Nehemiah used his position as an official at the court to obtain personal authorization from the King, Artaxerxes I. Armed with this, he was able to counter the efforts of the Samaritan

67d authorities to repress the Jews. He considered his task to be primarily political. He rebuilt the walls of Jerusalem, made a start on the rebuilding of the city itself and the rehousing of the population, and encouraged people to move into the city from the districts round about. He was also concerned with religious matters such as mixed marriages—the marriage between the family of the High Priest and that of Sanballat, governor of Samaria was an outstanding scandal. But this was all directed mainly to the establishment of a properly Jewish state, a province of the Persian empire under its own governor, independent of Samaria.

e His work was complemented by that of Ezra, whose activity partly coincided with that of Nehemiah. He too had an official position, something like a 'commissioner for Jewish affairs'. It was the Persian policy to allow the various peoples of the empire to follow as far as possible their own way of life; and this 'scribe of the law of Moses' came to Judah with the commission **to see that the people followed this law**. What this 'law' was is not quite clear, but it must have been at least some form of the present Pent. He began with a solemn reading of this law, and then set about bringing practice into conformity with it. Sabbath observance, mixed marriages and temple worship all came under his reforming attention. By the end of the 4th cent., through the work of Nehemiah and Ezra, a Jewish state was firmly established on the soil of Palestine.

f Naturally this reform was not carried through unopposed. Many of the priests in particular felt the hardship of separating from their foreign wives, and some of these, including the grandson of the high priest who had married Sanballat's daughter, moved to **Samaria** and formed the nucleus of a **rival religious party** which was to have its own rites and temple on **mount Gerizim**. But how necessary the reforms were felt to be can be seen from the experience of the **Jewish colony at Elephantine in Egypt**. This colony had been in existence probably at least as long as the community in Judah; but the correspondence with Judah and Samaria about 400 B.C. shows that although they still considered that they had ties with Palestine, it was not quite so clear that they really held the same faith; divinities other than Yahweh appear to have been recognized in their temple.

g Nevertheless it is true that the reform involved a certain narrowing of horizons. **The importance of the priests at this time**, and especially the emergence of the **office of 'High Priest'** (reflected in the Pentateuchal accounts of the institution of the priesthood) is significant. These now, in the absence of a king of David's line, were the authorities in the state, which behind the walls of Jerusalem devoted itself to religious pursuits, cut off from the world and with little interest in the political events of the day. It is possible that some Jews were involved in the troubles which distracted the Persian empire about the middle of the 3rd cent. and which, according to one tradition, resulted in a deportation to Hyrcania. But if so, this was enough to teach them a lesson. They played no part in the great events of the war between the Persians and the Greeks, the world-shaking **conquests of Alexander the Great**, or the wars that split the empire after Alexander's death. The Jews meanwhile were concerned with their glorious past which was the testimony of their God; the sacred books in which that past was contained were given definitive form and a new account composed bringing the story up to modern times—the work composed of Chronicles-Ezra-Nehemiah.

But by no means all Jews were in Judah. The exile **68a** and the troubled events since then had resulted in a **diaspora—the scattering of the Jews into almost every country of the world**. These could not fail to be much more influenced by the world around them than their brethren in Judah. One indication of this was the increasing use of the Greek language rather than Heb. Even in Judah since the exile the use of Heb. had gradually dropped out and it had become customary to follow the reading of the Scriptures by a paraphrase in Aram., the common language of the day. Outside of Judah the same custom arose with the use of Gr. and from this *Targum* (as the translation was known) arose in Alexandria the Gr. version known as the **Septuagint**.

Gradually, Alexander's work of hellenizing the **b** world began to affect even Judah. Signs of the lively, questioning spirit which was abroad at this time can be seen in the books of Job and Qoheleth, both of which call into question the traditional dogma that misfortune is the result of sin. The **Wisdom literature** too in general shows an awareness of the world beyond the confines of Jerusalem. This resulted in two schools of thought within the nation; the conservatives who felt that the proper attitude of a Jew to the encroaching world was simply resistance, and the progressives who felt that if their faith was not to fossilize it would have to come to terms with the world. Political events brought these two schools into conflict.

The struggle for power following the death of Alexander **c** the Great left the eastern part of the empire shared between two dynasties, the Seleucids who ruled from **Antioch and the Ptolemies in Egypt**. Palestine fell within the domain of the latter; but in 198 Antiochus III, fired with larger ambitions especially in face of the rising power of Rome, incorporated Palestine into his empire. But at **Magnesia in 190** he was decisively defeated by Rome, a heavy tax imposed on his kingdom, and his son taken to Rome as a hostage. When this son returned to rule as **Antiochus IV** (175—163) he found himself desperately short of money and yet still intent on building up a strong empire united by a single hellenistic culture. The pro-Greek party in Jerusalem seemed to promise the hope of fulfilling both these ends together; a Jew who had adopted the Gr. name of Jason offered the king money in return for the office of high priest, in which he would further the king's plans for imposing Gr. customs on the country. This sparked off a sordid series of squabbles, between the progressives and the traditionalists whose feelings were deeply shocked by this, and between the pro-Greeks themselves, one outbidding another for the favour of the king. When this appeared to endanger his authority, Antiochus IV—already angered by his humiliation at the hands of the Romans in Egypt—intervened actively and tried to impose hellenization by force, cf § 587e.

This decided some of the traditionalists on resistance. **d The rebellion was led by the family of Mattathias of Modein**. His son **Judas** led a series of guerilla attacks which were so successful that they encouraged others to swell his forces. Antiochus IV was at this time engaged elsewhere, on the further borders of his empire, against the Parthians; but he was still able to send a strong force to deal with the rebellion. The defeat of this force was the first real victory for Judas and he was soon able to enter Jerusalem and **rededicate the temple** after its pagan defilement (this, **December 164**, introduced the new feast of Dedication into the Jewish calendar). He then pressed on with the liberation of the rest of Palestine and finally turned against the hellenist

68d citadel within Jerusalem itself, the Acra. This drew the attention of the Greeks to the urgency of the situation; a strong army now attacked from the S and would undoubtedly have crushed the rebellion if internal dissension in the empire had not forced them to call off the attack.

e In addition, the Greeks offered all that the Jews had rebelled to achieve—**religious liberty and a certain degree of political independence.** But Judas now determined on the wider aim of complete independence. He himself died in battle shortly afterwards (160 B.C.) and his brother **Jonathan** took up the struggle. His forces were completely unable to match those of the Greeks; but again internal events in the Seleucid camp came to his aid. There were at that time two claimants to the throne, and Jonathan played one off against the

other, until he found himself recognized as ruler of a **68d** Jewish state and high priest. He then played his part of supporting the side he had opted for and in the warfare which followed won the territory which went with his position. When he died, (143 B.C.) a victim of further treachery within the Greek camp, his brother **Simon** succeeded without any difficulty. During Simon's ten-year rule he succeeded in maintaining the independence of the state in the disturbed affairs of the Seleucid empire; but the power of this empire was rapidly waning and when Simon was assassinated in 134, his son **John Hyrcanus I** succeeded to his titles and position as undisputed ruler of an autonomous state. The Hasmonean dynasty, as his line was known, ruled with various vicissitudes, until Herod the Idumean became king with Roman backing.

For **Chronological Tables** see pp. 153—55.

THE HISTORY OF ISRAEL II

GENEALOGICAL TABLES

69a

THE HASMONAEANS

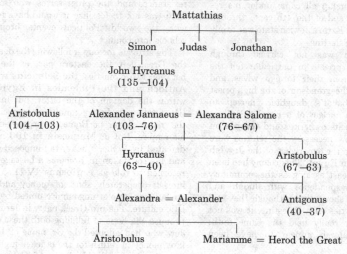

THE HERODIANS

b

(N.B.—These tables are not complete but contain all the names appearing in the accompanying text.)

RULERS OF PALESTINE

69c

JUDAEA + IDUMAEA   SAMARIA   GALILEE + PERAEA   ITURAEA, etc.

B.C.			
135	John Hyrcanus		
104	Aristobulus I		
103	Alexander Jannaeus		
76	Alexandra Salome		
67	Hyrcanus		
67	Aristobulus II		
63	Hyrcanus		
40	Antigonus		
37	Herod the Great		
4	Archelaus		Herod Antipas	Herod Philip
A.D.			
6	Coponius		
11	Ambivius		
14	Rufus		
16	Valerius Gratus		
27	Pontius Pilate		
34			(To Syria)
	Marcellus		Herod Agrippa I
37	Marullus		
39		Herod Agrippa I	
41	Herod Agrippa I		
44		Fadus	
46		Tib. Julius Alexander	
48		Cumanus	
52		Felix	Herod Agrippa II
59		Festus	
62		Albinus	
64		Gessius Florus	
66		Vespasian	
69		Titus	
70		Fall of Jerusalem	

THE HISTORY OF ISRAEL

II.   130 B.C.—A.D. 135

BY T. CORBISHLEY S.J.

70a Bibliography—*Ancient Authorities*: Josephus, Ant 13, 8–20, 11; BJ 1, 2–7, 11; Life. Tacitus, Hist. 5, 9–13; Annals, 2, 85; 12, 54. *Modern*: Schürer, *A History of the Jewish People in the Time of J.C.*, 1880 etc with bibliography; M.-J. Lagrange, *Le Judaisme avant J.C.*, 1931; J. Pickl, *The Messias*, 1946; A. H. M. Jones, *The Herods of Judaea*, 1938; W. Otto, *Herodes* (in PW); W. O. E. Oesterley, *A History of Israel*, 2, 1932; T. Corbishley, 'The Chronology of the Reign of Herod the Great', JTS 26 (1936); J. Bonsirven, *Le Judaisme Palestinien au Temps de J.C.* 1935; F. M. Abel, *Histoire de la Palestine*, 1952; Stewart Perowne, *The Life and Times of Herod the Great*, 1956; id *The Later Herods*, 1958; M. Noth, *The History of Israel*, E. tr. 1959[2]; Edwyn Bevan, *Jerusalem under the High Priests*, 1904; Bo Reicke, *Neutestamentliche Zeitgeschichte*, Berlin, 1965; F. V. Filson, *A NT History*, 1965; Y. Yadin, *Masada*, 1966. For **Tables** see pp. 84–5 and pp. 153–5.

This article deals chiefly with the main political events of the period. For other aspects of the life and thought of these times, the reader is referred to other articles, such as *The Jewish World in NT Times*, comm. on Mc, *Pagan World in NT Times*, *Pagan Religious Movements*.

The political changes that occurred in Palestine during this period are complicated, but the following main lines of treatment suggest themselves.

I The Hasmonaean dynasty	130—40 B.C.
II Herod the Great	40—4 B.C.
III Judaea under Archelaus and the Romans	4 B.C.—41 A.D.
IV Galilee under Herod Antipas	4 B.C.—39 A.D.
V Herod Agrippa I	37—44 A.D.
VI Palestine under the Romans	44—66 A.D.
VII The Rebellion	66—70 A.D.
VIII The Jews of the Diaspora	

b 1 The Hasmonaeans: 130—40 B.C.—At the end of the story of the Maccabees we are left with the impression that the great national uprising associated with the name of Judas Maccabaeus and the Hasmonaean family (deriving its title from its founder Hashmon) had spent its force. **John Hyrcanus** had been compelled to pay tribute once more to Antiochus VII of Syria, and this would imply the end of the hard-won independence of the Jews. But with the death of Antiochus in 129, his kingdom began to break up. Ptolemy VII of Egypt fomented civil war in Syria and a succession of claimants fighting for the remnants of power in Antioch reduced the once great kingdom of the Seleucids to a condition of pathetic impotence. Small principalities were established in independence of the central authority and the Jews returned to complete autonomy. The bronze coinage of John Hyrcanus reappears, bearing a Hebrew legend: 'John the High-Priest and the Jewish Commonweal', though the title of king does not yet occur. Not content with reasserting the independence of Judaea itself, John pushed forward the frontiers to the east, north and south. Beyond the Dead Sea, Madaba was annexed, whilst **70b** the power of Samaria was gradually worn down. The rival temple on Mt Gerizim was destroyed and later (108) the Greek city of Samaria was entirely obliterated, pits being dug so that water might undermine the foundations. The acquisition of Scythopolis (Beth-Shan), commanding the passage of the Jordan below the Sea of Galilee, paved the way for the annexation of Galilee itself. An event which was to be of unexpected significance was the conquest of Idumaea to the south. The inhabitants of the area were forcibly Judaized, being compelled to undergo circumcision, and it was from this half-Jewish, half-Gentile nation that the Herodian family sprang. The whole situation and outlook had changed radically from the days of the Maccabees. Then it had been a renewal of the fervour of Israel's early years in the desert—a passionate desire to worship their God in peace and freedom though not necessarily in independence. Desire for the latter came only later and was not shared by all. The Hasidim would have been satisfied to worship God freely and live according to his laws; the hellenising party, including many of the priestly class, no doubt were willing to accept foreign domination for other less commendable reasons. Nevertheless there must have been a considerable number who realized that, apart from any worldly considerations, freedom to worship could only be guaranteed by political independence. The trouble was that, as on previous occasions, political ambitions soon overshadowed religious aims. In establishing their power the Hasmoneans were lucky in finding Syria in decline; they aimed at a revival of David's kingdom and, for this purpose, embarked on a series of military campaigns which were often remarkable for their ruthlessness. Nevertheless John Hyrcanus, in spite of his military prowess, still did not call himself king. To that extent he paid lip service to the idea of a theocracy. He took the title of High priest, thus ousting the Zadokite line which had been in possession of that dignity since the time of David and Solomon. Yet he and many of his successors lived as secular rulers, thus arousing the hostility of the Hasidim and those who thought like them.

John Hyrcanus died in 104, being succeeded by his **c** son Judah (or Aristobulus), under whom the annexation and Judaization of Galilee were completed. After a brief reign, he was succeeded by his brother **Alexander Jannaeus** (103—76), who assumed the title of King and extended the frontiers of Israel, until it became practically co-terminous with the old kingdom of David. Campaigning beyond the Jordan, where he annexed Gadara and Amathus, he then turned SW and after a year's siege reduced Gaza on the Hellenized Philistine coast (96). But a later expedition beyond Gadara into Gaulanitis brought him into conflict with the Nabataean Arabs, a powerful tribe which had also wrested its independence from Syria. He suffered a severe reverse and almost lost his throne and life in a fierce popular revolt. But he succeeded in restoring his position and though he suffered

70c further defeat at the hands of Aretas III, he made more conquests in Transjordania.

d At his death, the throne was occupied by his widow **Salome** (76—67). Her first step was to secure her position at home by allying herself with the growing power of the Pharisees. This group, apparently the successors of those Hasidim who had proved such valuable fighters under Mattathias, 1 Mc 2:42, had been at loggerheads with both John Hyrcanus and Alexander Jannaeus. They represented the stricter and more nationalistic element and were growing in importance; over against them were the Hellenizing Sadducees, sceptical and worldly, including most of the priestly aristocracy. Salome, being a woman, could not hold the office of high-priest, so whilst she retained the royal title, her son Hyrcanus succeeded to the high-priesthood which had been held by his father. The Pharisees supported him against his brother Aristobulus, who was backed by the Sadducees. (In later times when the Pharisees were persecuted by Herod, the reign of Salome became for them a legendary golden age.) On her death, the quarrel between the brothers broke out into open strife and Aristobulus wrested kingship and high-priesthood from Hyrcanus.

e It is at this time that the power which was to grow into the Herodian monarchy first appears. An Idumaean, Antipater by name, son of one of the lieutenants of Jannaeus, espoused the cause of Hyrcanus, induced the Nabataeans to assist him and before long Aristobulus was besieged on the Temple site. But, more important still, Rome's power was now beginning to dominate the Levant. After the decline of Syria, the chief power in Asia Minor devolved upon Mithridates, king of Pontus. He soon tried conclusions with Rome and more than held his own until **Pompey** was sent by the Senate to end the threat to their interests in the E Mediterranean. Having defeated Mithridates, Pompey resolved to settle the whole E question by a definitive arrangement. In addition to other annexations, the important province of Syria, with its capital at Antioch and stretching from the Mediterranean coast to the upper waters of the Euphrates, was added to the empire. This province, one of the most important of Rome's possessions, was destined to play a predominant part in the defence of the E frontier. In it were normally stationed three legions, which, in addition to warding off the menace of Parthia, could be employed to overawe the turbulent peoples to N and S, including the ever-troublesome Jews. It was necessary, at the same time, to make arrangements for the government of Palestine and in 63 Pompey was in Jerusalem. A couple of years earlier his lieutenants had made a temporary settlement by persuading the Nabataeans to withdraw their support from Hyrcanus and handing over the power in Palestine to Aristobulus. This decision was reversed by Pompey, who made Hyrcanus once more ruler and high-priest. Aristobulus himself saw the futility of resistance, but some of his followers held out, and could only be persuaded to yield by the arrival of Pompey in person at the head of an army. We are told that after reducing the citadel, Pompey made his way into the Holy of Holies itself, thereby shocking Jewish sentiment. Unlike other conquerors, however, he did not lay hands on the treasures of the Sanctuary. When Pompey returned to Rome to celebrate his triumph, Aristobulus was taken along with him.

f Though the Jews nominally retained their independence, henceforward they would always have to reckon with Rome. Their territory was reduced, the Greek cities and the seaboard being lost. Over Judaea, Idumaea, Galilee and Peraea reigned Hyrcanus, with the title of *tetrarch*, though he was also high-priest. He was in **70f** immediate subordination to the Roman governor of Syria and through him to the central authority in Rome. By way of controlling still more effectively this turbulent folk, Gabinius, governor of Syria (57—54) split up the Jewish territory for administrative purposes into five districts, each with its local sunédrion, sitting at Jerusalem, Gaza, Amathus, Jericho and Sepphoris. The step was doubtless taken with a view to weakening the central government at Jerusalem, and preventing its becoming a threat to Syria as it had once been, but there were probably certain advantages to the Jews themselves in this devolution. At any rate we find traces of the survival of the local sunédria elsewhere than at Jerusalem, though of course in the NT it is only the Sanhedrin there that appears.

Theoretically then the destinies of the Jews at this **g** time were in the hands of Hyrcanus, high-priest and tetrarch. But the real power was wielded by **Antipater**, who was to play a role analogous to that of the Mayors of the Palace under the Merovingians. From now until the death of Herod the Great, the history of foreign affairs in Palestine is largely the story of the diplomatic relations between the Idumaean family and the successive claimants for supremacy at Rome. Pompey and Caesar, the 'liberators' and the triumvirs, Octavian and Mark Antony struggled in turn for the lordship of the world, and all the cunning of Antipater and Herod was needed to enable them to maintain their position.

In 54 B.C. Jerusalem received another visit from **h** a Roman army. Crassus, on his way to the Parthian war in which he was doomed to meet disaster and death, robbed the Temple of something like 10,000 talents. But this was only an isolated incident. In 49 war broke out between Pompey, defending the established government, and Julius Caesar, and in the circumstances there was only one possible choice for Antipater to make. Not only was Pompey the representative of lawful authority, but the E provinces were largely under his control, whilst Hyrcanus and Antipater owed their present positions to him. Naturally Caesar liberated Aristobulus to embarrass Hyrcanus, but fortunately for the latter his brother met his death at the hands of Pompeian troops whilst on his way to reclaim his kingdom. Pompey's death in Egypt created what might have been a very awkward situation for Antipater, but he won the favour of the dictator by assisting him with troops when fighting for his life at Alexandria (47). In the relieving force which marched to Caesar's rescue was a contingent of Jewish soldiers under the command of Antipater himself. By this means, he obtained from Caesar confirmation of Hyrcanus in his position and also the establishment of himself as administrator of Judaea, despite the protests and appeals of Antigonus, son of Aristobulus. Moreover, Joppa was restored to Judaea. On Caesar's assassination, Antipater characteristically transferred his allegiance to the party of Brutus and Cassius, who controlled the E provinces of the empire, but their defeat at Philippi raised no problems for him. He had already died of poison administered by a private enemy that same year (42).

2 Herod the Great (1) His Rise—When Antipater **71a** died, his two oldest sons, Phasael and Herod, the latter a young man just over 30, were already prominent in public affairs. Phasael had acted as his father's lieutenant in Idumaea, whilst Herod had held a military command in Galilee. Here he had come into contact with one of those outbursts of violence characteristic of the period. Whether they were genuine nationalistic uprisings, on the model of the Maccabaean effort, or whether the 'zeal' of these men was little more than a cloak for personal

71a aggrandisement and their activities not far removed from plain brigandage, we cannot decide. But we shall encounter a number of such incidents in the course of this review. The leader on this occasion was one Hezekiah. Herod suppressed the movement and killed the man himself, but he was summoned before the Sanhedrin at Jerusalem to stand his trial on a charge of killing a Jew unlawfully. The support of the Roman governor and his own high standing in the eyes of Hyrcanus resulted in his acquittal (47 B.C.), but the incident rankled and he later exacted vengeance on those who had thus humiliated him.

b Mark Antony came to Palestine in 41 and, despite attempts on the part of the Jews to set him against the sons of Antipater, the Roman, appreciating Herod's capacity to control the Jews, showed favour to him and his brother and both were appointed tetrarchs. Antony's shrewdness was soon borne out by events. In 40 B.C., the Parthians, Rome's traditional enemy in that region, invaded Syria and the Jewish aristocracy saw in them a means to rid themselves of the Idumaean intruders. Jerusalem received a Parthian army, Phasael was killed, Herod fled. The high-priest, Hyrcanus, was mutilated and deported, and his brother's son, Mattathiah Antigonus, installed in his place, resuming the title of king. It was a repetition of the events of 67 B.C., with the Parthians playing the role assigned on that occasion to the Nabataeans.

c This Parthian invasion of Syria and Palestine meant, of course, that the cause of Herod was identified with the interests of Rome. He was formally recognized by the Triumvirs and the Senate as king of the Jews. The expulsion of the Parthians from Palestine, essential to the security of the Empire, was the necessary preliminary to Herod's assumption of power. Even after the Parthians had retreated, Rome co-operated with Herod in the military events leading up to the siege of Jerusalem, where Antigonus was resisting desperately. In 37 B.C., Herod entered into full possession of his kingdom, including Samaria once more. The last Hasmonaean king perished under a Roman axe.

d **(ii) Herod as King**—Characteristically, Herod began his reign with a massacre. Of the members of the Sanhedrin who had brought him to trial ten years before, 45 were put to death, and the full quota of 71 was made up of Herod's own nominees. This broke the power of the aristocratic opposition, but at the same time left a rankling desire for vengeance. The situation was further complicated by domestic intrigue. Herod had married Mariamme, a member of the Hasmonaean family, whose mother Alexandra wanted her son Aristobulus to be made high-priest. For this purpose she intrigued with Cleopatra of Egypt, who was coveting some of Herod's territory. To placate her, Herod yielded. Soon afterwards, however, he solved the problem in his own way by having Aristobulus drowned. He escaped the effects of the anger of Cleopatra and therefore of Antony's displeasure because the latter could not afford an unstable Judaea at his back at a time when the final break with Octavian was looming ahead (c. 34 B.C.). Henceforth Herod kept the appointment to the high-priesthood in his own hands, nominating only those who supported his policies. The break with the Hasmonaean family was completed by the execution of Hyrcanus, the old high-priest (30) and the murders of Mariamme (29) and her mother Alexandra (28 B.C.).

e Into all the details of the political and domestic intrigues that made up the background of Herod's reign, it is impossible for us to enter. It will suffice to say that it was only by the most ruthless measures and the employ- **71e** ment of numbers of spies and informers that he could hope to maintain his throne. Parallel to this was his extensive work of fortification, beginning with the restoration of the walls of the capital and the fortress Hyrcania. Throughout his reign, we hear of cities founded or rebuilt and fortified, and the disposition of troops. Herod also established a string of colonies and fortified posts to protect his frontiers—we may mention Machaerus, the scene of John the Baptist's death—and apparently reorganized the local administration of the country. Of his army, we know that it was composed largely of mercenaries—Idumaeans, Thracians, Germans and Greeks (he received from Octavian Cleopatra's Celtic bodyguard)—though it included a number of Jews of the Diaspora, always more loyal to Herod than the Palestinians.

Many of Herod's measures were clearly directed to the repression of brigandage and other disturbances, and their success is proved by the almost complete absence of open rebellion during the reign. At the same time it should be said that his rule was manifestly efficient and prosperous, as is shown by the fact that he was able to make considerable reductions in taxation, even though his gifts were ostentatiously lavish.

Nor should it be thought that all his building was of **f** a military nature. Outstanding was **his work on the Temple**. Pagan and sceptical as he was, he was yet shrewd enough to appreciate his people's passionate concern for the worship of God, and vainglorious enough to desire the renown attaching to such a work. Side by side with an appreciation of his subjects' traditional religion went all those Hellenizing tendencies and practices by which he thought to assimilate himself to his fellow-princes and perhaps curry favour with Rome. The building of pagan temples and theatres, the establishment of games, in a word all those activities which had characterized the rule of Antiochus Epiphanes and led to the Maccabaean revolt, were repeated by Herod. But his knowledge of the Hebrew soul taught him where to halt.

The chief external events of the reign are naturally **g** concerned with his **relations with Rome**. The enmity of Cleopatra, due partly to her covetousness and partly to the intrigues of his household, turned out in the end to Herod's advantage. In the year before the battle of Actium, Herod had been on the point of associating himself with Antony's preparations against Octavian, when Cleopatra had him dispatched on a mission against the Arabs. This proved a more difficult task than he had expected and he did not complete his mission until after Antony had sailed to his disastrous defeat (31 B.C.). When therefore Octavian met Herod there was no reason why he should not confirm him in full possession of his dominion. In fact the Jewish king received from his Roman overlord certain territories (e.g. Jericho, Gaza, Azotus) which had been taken away from the Jewish kingdom either by Pompey or by Cleopatra. Later in the reign Augustus presented to Herod the districts of Trachonitis, Batanaea and Auronitis, and on the death of the tetrarch Zenodorus two years later (20 B.C.) the remainder of his former dominions, Ulatha and Paneas. This meant that the area of the kingdom ruled over by Herod was greater than it had ever been in the history of Israel, and though his brother Pheroras was nominated tetrarch of Peraea, Herod was his overlord.

According to Josephus, the relation between Augustus **h** and Herod was that of intimate friends. This seems hardly credible, but there is no doubt that Augustus took the greatest interest in the affairs of Palestine, which provides an excellent example of a 'client-kingdom'. Herod

71h was nominally free, but all his policy was subordinate to the decision of the emperor. On one occasion we are told that, suspecting too great independence of action on the part of the Jewish king, the emperor wrote a sharp rebuke saying that, whereas he had formerly treated Herod as a friend, henceforth he would deal with him as a subject. And in the closing years of the reign we are told of an occasion when the whole nation took an oath of loyalty to the emperor (the Pharisees manifesting their strong nationalistic feeling by refusing to take the oath).

i Some account must be given of the **family quarrels** which embittered the closing years of the king's life. The complete story is too involved owing to the complexity of interests causing the friction. Nor does the manifest bias of Josephus's sources help us to a clear picture. But in brief outline the facts seem to have been as follows. Alexander and Aristobulus, Herod's sons by Mariamme, stood high in their father's favour, a fact which aroused the jealousy of Antipater, a son by an earlier marriage, who hoped to succeed to the throne and now feared that he might be displaced. He alleged that he had discovered a plot of his two half-brothers to kill their father and usurp the throne. Whatever be the truth of the story, Herod was convinced by the evidence adduced and had his sons put to death, only to discover that the informer was not less guilty than they. Antipater therefore met with the same fate, very shortly before Herod himself died in agony. (On hearing the story of these executions Augustus is said to have remarked: 'I'd rather be a sow of Herod's than his son'.)

There were other instances of intrigue, fostered by the women of the court—Herod was married at least ten times—and involving the opposition of the Pharisees, which still further clouded the mind of the king, and in the end he was almost insane with suspicion and fear. He had waded to the throne through blood, he had maintained his position by assassination or judicial murder, and it is against such a background of ruthless and treacherous behavior that we must read the story of the visit of the Magi and the massacre of the Innocents.

72a 3 Judaea under Archelaus and the Romans— On the death of Herod (4 B.C.) the kingdom was partitioned between three of his sons—Archelaus (who received Judaea, Samaria and Idumaea), Antipas (who held Galilee and Peraea) and Philip (to whom went the territory north-west of Galilee—Gaulanitis, Trachonitis, Ituraea, etc). The settlement was not made without friction, as there had been some inconsistency in Herod's own arrangements. The Roman emperor, after appeals to him from the interested parties, decided on the division described above, conferring the title of tetrarch on the three rulers. This division of territory remained substantially unaltered until after the Crucifixion, the only alteration in status being that after ten years of rule, Archelaus was dispossessed and his tetrarchy incorporated into the full imperial system. In fact the chief importance of the reign of Archelaus is that it paved the way for this step. Even whilst the negotiations at Rome, following on the death of Herod, were still proceeding, various claimants to the title of 'king' made their appearance in b Palestine. One of these was Judas or Theudas, son of that Hezekiah who had been put to death by Herod in 47 B.C. (perhaps to be identified with the Theudas of Ac 5:36). The Roman governor of Syria, Quintilius Varus, dispatched two legions to repress these movements, and an uneasy peace prevailed for a time in Judaea. But the efficiency and strength of Herod had not been inherited by Archelaus who became increasingly unpopular, and in A.D. 6 two separate embassies, one Jewish and one

Samaritan, begged Augustus to abolish the monarchy. He **72b** decided that the only practicable solution was to make Archelaus's tetrarchy a Roman province and he accordingly instructed the governor of Syria, P. Sulpicius Quirinius (the 'Cyrinus' of Lk 2:2) to make the necessary arrangements. A census of the district was initiated (cf Ac 5:37) and a procurator, Coponius, was appointed. Another outburst of nationalistic feeling occurred, led by Judas the Galilean, who according to Josephus now founded the party of the 'Zealots'. If this last statement is true, he did little more than give formal character to a movement long in existence. Judas himself perished and his followers were disbanded, but he left sons who were to give trouble later. Archelaus retired into honourable exile in Southern Gaul.

Judaea a Roman Province—A succession of procur- c ators, nominated by the emperor for varying periods of office, now ruled Judaea, with their headquarters at Caesarea on the coast. Most of them have left little beyond their names on the page of history. The great exception is Pontius Pilate, the most famous governor in the history of the world. His governorship began in A.D. 27 and ended ten years later. During that period, apart from his share in the events culminating in the Crucifixion, he is known for his arrogance or, it may be, mere lack of tact in his handling of the Jews. Of the riots which his conduct occasioned, the most interesting for us is that which occurred when Pilate alienated some of the Temple funds to help to build an aqueduct to improve the Jerusalem water supply. It is probable that this incident is referred to in Lk 13:1, 2; and it is not at all unlikely that Barabbas took part in the movement. The final incident in Pilate's career was an unnecessarily brutal suppression of a Samaritan rising, leading to his removal from office by the governor of Syria, Vitellius.

Although the Qumran Community is dealt with elsewhere (§ 610) reference must be made to it here. Apparently at the end of the Maccabean rising this new sect appears to have established itself, perhaps in protest against what they regarded as an illegitimate priesthood, in the desert regions in the Dead Sea area. Their first occupation of the site came to an end probably in 31 B.C., as the result of an earthquake. Successors—or survivors—returned under Archelaus and were finally destroyed by the Romans in A.D. 68.

4 Galilee under Herod Antipas—As we have seen, **73a** on Herod's death, a separate tetrarchy was constituted of Galilee and Peraea, ruled by Antipas. He took the name of Herod, as a sort of dynastic title and it is he who figures in various passages of the narrative of the Public Life. Apart from the building activities recorded of him by Josephus, we know little of the external events of his reign. It is of some interest to note that an unsuccessful expedition which he undertook against the king of Arabia Petraea is attributed by Josephus directly to his conduct in divorcing his wife, daughter of the Arabian king, in order to take his brother's wife, Herodias. There had been some previous friction about a disputed boundary, but the king made the treatment of his daughter a casus belli and fought a successful engagement against the troops of the ruler of Galilee. The people believed, we are told, that Herod's lack of success was due to his murder of John the Baptist. Like Archelaus in Judaea, Antipas was eventually deposed by Rome (at the instigation of his nephew, Herod Agrippa I, as we shall see later), and in the year A.D. 39 retired into exile in Gaul. His tetrarchy was for a time ruled by Agrippa.

Meanwhile, a word must be said of the remainder of b

73b Herod the Great's kingdom, the region of Gaulanitis, etc. This passed into the hands of **Philip**, who also assumed the name of Herod. Like his father and his half-brother Antipas, he founded cities, notably Caesarea Philippi and Bethsaida Julias. He seems to have been an efficient and conscientious ruler and unlike most of the Herodians was universally regretted when the end came. He died in A.D. 34 and his tetrarchy was for a time attached to the province of Syria.

c **5 Herod Agrippa I**—When Aristobulus was executed by his father, Herod the Great, he left two sons and several daughters. Of these Agrippa was to lead the most successful life and he laid the foundations of his future prosperity during the years of his sojourn **at Rome**. He was sent there (c. 7 B.C.) when he was still quite a small boy by his mother Salome, whose own mother Berenice was a friend of the empress Livia. The boy, who was popular and attractive, was brought up in close association with the younger members of the imperial family circle, but after the deaths of Germanicus (A.D. 18) and Drusus (A.D. 23) his prospects seemed very gloomy and he returned to Palestine. At first he received a post at Tiberias, one of the new foundations made by his uncle, Herod Antipas, but after a time he attached himself to the governor of Syria, L. Pomponius Flaccus (32—35). (He was therefore almost certainly at Tiberias during the Public Life.) Eventually (A.D. 36) he returned to Rome, where he managed to curry favour with Gaius, shortly to become Emperor.

d When Gaius (Caligula) ascended the throne, one of his first acts was to make over to Agrippa the tetrarchy of Philip, who had died three years previously. Agrippa remained at Rome for the time being, setting sail for the East in the autumn of 38. His arrival at Alexandria, where he called on his way, began a disturbance which was to flare up into more serious riots, leading to the famous embassy to Caligula in which Philo took a leading part (cf § 75b inf).

Soon after Agrippa's arrival **in Palestine**, he managed by intrigue to obtain the deposition of his uncle, Herod Antipas, the tetrarch of Galilee. Antipas was exiled to Lyons, his dominions being added to the tetrarchy of Agrippa (A.D. 39). When, in 41, Claudius succeeded Caligula, he practically reconstituted the old Herodian kingdom, conferring on Agrippa the title of king. In other words, a fresh attempt was to be made to restore the old position of client-kingdom. But the death of Agrippa within three years put an end to this solution and once again the kingdom came under direct Roman control. Agrippa left a son of the same name, but he was too young to be trusted with power and he was given the small kingdom of Chalcis to rule. In A.D. 53 a new arrangement was made, Chalcis reverting to the province of Syria and Agrippa receiving the territory that had constituted Philip's tetrarchy, with the addition of Abilene and some outlying districts. Little of this territory was in any sense Jewish, but Agrippa's own descent and the part he plays in the story of Acts make it necessary for some mention to be made here of his kingdom. Moreover, on the accession of Nero (54) some portions of Galilee were added to his dominions.

There is little to record of the reign. Styling himself Marcus Julius Agrippa, he manifested his desire to associate himself closely with the Roman aristocracy, and it is not suprising to find him consorting with the Roman governor of Judaea. In other respects, his reign recalls some of the features of his great-grandfather's, especially in the liberality of his benefactions, particularly to the Greek city of Berytus, but he seems to have been blest with

a more placid disposition. At any rate, his long reign, **73d** which lasted until his death (probably in A.D. 93) was not marked by any serious internal or domestic troubles, despite the complexity of the matrimonial arrangements of the members of his family.

6 Palestine under the Romans—Tacitus's well- **74a** known sentence, *duravit patientia Judaeis usque ad Gessium Florum procuratorem*, aptly sums up the story of Israel between the death of Herod Agrippa I and the outbreak of the rebellion (A.D. 44—66). A succession of incompetent or rapacious governors inflamed the already irritated feelings of the Jews who, as a nation, never reconciled themselves to Roman rule.

It may be true that, as Josephus argues, the final breach was the work of a minority of extremists, but it is not less certain that those who were content with their position in the Roman system were still fewer. The story of Roman-Jewish relations is one of an irreconcilable cleavage of ideals. The Jewish tradition of an autonomous theocracy could not be squared with the cosmopolitanism of a regime in which everything, including religion, must be subordinated to the interests of a universal empire. Whilst the Romans did try to make all possible allowances for the idiosyncrasies of the people they governed, the peculiarity of the Jewish ethos was something they never understood. The Maccabees had carried the nation with them in their resistance to Hellenization by Syria; we cannot doubt that the nation as a whole was behind the final attempt to win independence of Rome.

The clash between **Fadus**, who took over the province **b** on the death of Agrippa, and another Theudas, was followed by an outbreak, led by James and Simon, sons of that Judas who had raised the standard of revolt in A.D. 6. The governor of the time was an apostate Jew, Tiberius Julius Alexander—a tactless appointment though one which doubtless commended itself to the central government as providing a ruler who might be expected to understand this difficult race. The ring-leaders were crucified. We hear of further troubles under his successor **Cumanus** due to the insolence of the occupying troops, though one serious outbreak occurred as the result of the chronic hostility of Jew and Samaritan.

We come now to the governorships of **Felix and** **c** **Festus**, known to us from the closing chapters of the *Acts*. The former is shown by Josephus to have been brutal and treacherous in his handling of the constant risings, and though his successor seems to have displayed more tact, the situation was getting rapidly out of control. Festus died in office and before his successor arrived the Sanhedrin attempted to reassert its authority and independence by putting to death the Apostle James, bishop of Jerusalem. The high-priest was deposed for this, but no other punitive steps seem to have been taken. **Albinus** (62—64) appears to have been conciliatory in his treatment of the Jews, but his policy of appeasement received its inevitable reward. Mildness was mistaken for weakness.

7 The Rebellion—The anti-Roman element became **d** ever more violent, and when **Gessius Florus** arrived (64) he doubtless came with orders to spare no effort to retrieve the situation. The temper of the Jews was everywhere inflamed, and it was perhaps beyond human ingenuity to avert disaster. But in A.D. 66 Gessius Florus repeated the action of Pontius Pilate in sequestrating Temple funds for administrative purposes and this provoked a riot. The governor marched in person to Jerusalem with a large force, demanded the production of the ringleaders, and when he received no more than an apology from the Sanhedrin, ordered his troops to clear

74d the Upper Market. Many casualties were inflicted on the people and much material damage done. The Sanhedrin seems to have been genuinely anxious to co-operate with the Romans in the preservation of order, but the conduct of the troops was too provocative. For a time Agrippa's intervention and appeals to the more responsible elements in the capital met with some success, but he could not persuade them to accept the rule of Florus and in the end he had to withdraw, baffled. The extremist Eleazar then precipitated a crisis by proposing the termination of the daily sacrifice which by custom had long been offered for the emperor. The pro-Roman party, or at least those who believed that their own interests and those of the nation would best be served by loyalty to Rome, resisted this proposal, but the majority sided with Eleazar. The sacrifice was suspended. The rebellion had begun.

e The Sanhedrin appealed to Florus and to Agrippa for military support, and though Florus did not think it prudent to risk his troops, a force was sent by Agrippa. Thus the rebellion began with a skirmish between the opposing parties amongst the Jews themselves. Passions rose higher, the whole city threw itself into the movement, the Roman garrison was besieged and when it surrendered on a promise that the lives of its members would be spared, they were all treacherously killed.

The inevitable sequel was an outbreak of anti-Semitism at Caesarea, where 20,000 Jews are said to have been massacred. The Jews in turn took reprisals and soon the whole country was aflame. The legate of Syria, Cestius Gallus, hastily led an army into Judaea, but after an unsuccessful siege of Jerusalem was compelled to withdraw to Caesarea.

f The details of the story are inextricably confused, partly because of the nature of the situation, partly because we have to rely on the rather disingenuous narrative of Josephus. Since he wrote his *Jewish War* chiefly with an eye to excusing his own conduct and that of his people, there are necessarily suppressions and evasions. Moreover, the Jews themselves were fiercely divided and much of the time were fighting amongst themselves. Nor do the details concern us here.

In the spring of 67, Nero sent out a new legate to conduct the operations—**Titus Flavius Vespasianus**, the future emperor. He set about reducing Galilee and the rebellious parts of Agrippa's kingdom. This occupied the whole of the campaigning season of that year and the following spring Vespasian began the task of methodically crushing the outposts of Peraea, Idumaea and Judaea, gradually closing in on the capital. But the death of Nero constitutionally terminated his commission and he waited for its renewal before laying siege to Jerusalem. Throughout the year of the Four Emperors operations were held up, and when Vespasian was himself proclaimed emperor by his troops, he left for Italy, leaving his son Titus to complete the task of suppressing the rebellion.

g The story of **the siege of Jerusalem** is sufficiently well known. All that need be said here is that the Jews were already considerably weakened by their own internal dissensions. Neither fanaticism nor the fear of reprisals could resist the methodical onslaught of the Roman army. The Temple was taken in August and (apparently deliberately) given to the flames. By the end of September all resistance was at an end and the city reduced to a heap of rubble. The prophecy of the rejected Messiah was terribly fulfilled. Judaea itself remained as a unit of the Roman Empire; but the Jewish national state came to an end with the destruction of Zion.

The revolt did not however end with the fall of **74h** Jerusalem. The strongholds of Herodium, Masada and Machaerus were still in rebel hands. One by one they fell to the Romans. The last and greatest—**Masada**—an almost impregnable mountain fortress, west of the Dead Sea, withstood a year's siege before it fell in A.D. 73, and even then it was not taken by storm. When all hope had disappeared, the Jewish garrison committed collective suicide. The only survivors were two women and five small children who had managed to hide themselves from the others. Recent excavations there have revealed many interesting details of the siege, cf Y. Yadin, *Masada*, 1966.

Judaea was now administered as an **imperial pro-** **i** **vince**, the procurators resided as before at Caesarea and the Tenth Legion (Fretensis) was garrisoned in the ruined city of Jerusalem. Gradually people came back to live once more in its habitable parts. Though the Temple had been destroyed, this was due to the hazards of war and not official policy. Judaism continued to be a *religio licita* within the Roman system. The Temple however, for many reasons, could not be rebuilt and consequently the rites of sacrifice were no longer carried out. Jewish worship centred more and more on the local synagogues, as in the Diaspora. It was these that kept alive a sense of national identity. With the end of sacrifice, the Sadducean priesthood lost its importance and the **Pharisees** held undisputed leadership, see § 613a c. In place of Jerusalem, **Jamnia**, on the coast, S of Jaffa, became the principal religious centre and a new council was formed to take the place of the Sanhedrin. Here began that meticulous study of the Scriptures which under the rabbis continued for many centuries. But Jamnia could never be a new Jerusalem; and consequently, hope for a restoration of the old Jerusalem lingered on. There were still Jews enough left in the country to foster and maintain this hope which led ultimately to the final insurrection of A.D. 132–5. Of the intervening years few details are available in contemporary records. Spasmodic rebellions broke out in different places which did nothing to endear the Jews to the Roman authorities. These occurred for the most part in the Diaspora but possibly also in Palestine.

The final revolt, as violent as that of A.D. 66–70, **j** appears to have been provoked, at least in part, by Hadrian's plan to build a pagan city, *Aelia Capitolina*, on the site of Jerusalem. The Jewish leader, Simon ben Koseba, took the name of Bar Kochba, 'Son of the Star', an allusion to Nm 24:17, thus giving himself a certain Messianic aura. Revolt broke out in A.D. 132 and spread rapidly. A new State of Israel was proclaimed, coinage minted, the priesthood resumed its functions and sacrifice began again. National enthusiasm knew no bounds and the rebels gained control of many areas of the country besides Jerusalem. The Roman reaction, after initial reverses, was slow and deliberate. Strongholds were encircled and starved into surrender. The last stand of the 'Son of the Star' was on a hill-top south of Jerusalem. The final surrender came in A.D. 135. Large numbers of the population were killed or sold as slaves and on the site of Jerusalem there rose, as planned, the splendid new Roman colony of *Aelia Capitolina*. The temple of Jupiter Capitolinus was erected on the site of the Temple and that of Venus over the Sepulchre of Christ. The Romans had not forgotten that 'sect of the Jews' known as 'Christians'. Jews were forbidden to enter the city on pain of death. The very land lost its ancient name and the crowning insult was that it became known by the name

74j 'Palestine'—derived from Israel's ancient enemies, the Philistines.

75a 8 The Jews of the Diaspora—cf J. Vandervoorst 'Dispersion ou Diaspora'. DBS 2 (1934) 433—45; E. Schürer, 'Diaspora' HDB Extra vol, 1904, 91—109. No history of Israel is complete without some mention of those communities of Jews who lived scattered throughout the civilized world beyond the frontiers of Palestine. After the Babylonian captivity, a strong Jewish element remained in Mesopotamia, and we know that in Egypt also there were such large numbers of Jews as to constitute a special administrative problem. They had presumably made their way there originally for purposes of trading, as also they had established themselves in Asia Minor and Greece, and as far as Italy and Gaul. But many also, especially in Alexandria and the West, had come under compulsion, either as prisoners of war or deported by conquerors such as Ptolemy I of Egypt. It was reckoned that, at the beginning of the empire, there were in Egypt a million Jews to eight million Egyptians. We are told by Strabo that the Jews in Alexandria had their own national head, who apparently presided in certain legal and judicial processes. They also resided in special quarters of the city, as they seem to have done in most places (e.g. Antioch and Rome).

b One or two incidents may be singled out as exemplifying the nature of the problem created for the Jews themselves no less than for their rulers. Thus at Alexandria in A.D. 38 a fierce pogrom broke out, occasioned it would seem by the visit there of Agrippa I, on his way to Palestine. Jews were maltreated, their property destroyed. The situation deteriorated still further when the governor of Egypt, apparently in attempt to curry favour with the emperor, ordered the statue of Gaius to be set up in the synagogues. In their distress and danger, the Jews appealed to Caesar. Two embassies, the Jewish one headed by the philosopher-exegete Philo, the Gentile one headed by Apion, dilettante and charlatan, appeared before Gaius. Needles to say, the emperor insisted on the carrying out of the prefect's orders, and went so far as to require the Jews at Jerusalem to set up a similar statue in the Temple. However, the intervention of Agrippa and the emperor's death relieved the situation. The incident is significant as indicating the **tension existing between Jew and non-Jew** in the empire, a tension liable to burst out into open rioting given the necessary occasion. At Rome itself, in A.D. 19, Tiberius expelled the Jewish community (though we are told that no less than 4,000 of them were drafted to Sardinia for police-work), ostensibly because of the trickery of four men, but we cannot doubt that the measure was taken as a means to keep the peace. Similarly we are told of constant riots in the capital, leading to a further expulsion in A.D. 49, an event having special interest for us because of the reference to it in Ac 18:2.

c The surprising thing is that, so long as no popular disturbance was caused, the Roman authorities as a whole seem to have treated the Jews with remarkable forbearance, granting them unusual immunities and dispensations. They were apparently exempt from military service, and their Sabbath law was respected. But with the growth and spread of Christianity, the occasions for disturbance in the empire multiplied, and there can be little doubt that this was one factor in the attitude of the government to the Christian body. How far the Jews were responsible, through Poppaea, for the turning of Nero's mind to the Christians after the fire of A.D. 64, we cannot be sure, but it is by no means an unlikely hypothesis.

It seems not improbable that in the eyes of the Roman authorities there was at first little to choose between Jew and Christian and it is likely that some of the early persecutions were due to disturbances between the two communities,—a state of affairs reflected in the prophecy of Our Lord (Mt 10:17—19).

ARCHAEOLOGY AND THE BIBLE

BY ROBERT NORTH S.J.

77a Bibliography—The easiest first orientation is C. McCown, *Ladder of Progress in Palestine*, 1943; also J. Finegan, *Light from the Ancient Past*, Princeton, 1959²; M. Burrows, *What mean these Stones?*, New Haven, 1941; with pictures, J. Gray, *Archaeology and the OT World*, 1962; B. W. Anderson, *The Living World of the OT*, 1967²; J. Thompson, *Bible and Archaeology*, Grand Rapids, 1962; H. Franken, *Primer of OT Archaeology*, Leiden, 1963; Most authoritative brief work is W. F. Albright, *Archaeology of Palestine*, 1966³; K. M. Kenyon, *Archaeology in the Holy Land*, 1965²; her *Beginning in Archaeology*, 1960³, gives techniques; Sir F. G. Kenyon, *The Bible and Archaeology*, 1940; Expert illustrated survey by G. E. Wright, *Biblical Archaeology*, 1057 and *Introduction*, 1960; indispensable are J. B. Pritchard, *Ancient Near Eastern Texts*, 1955²; and *Ancient Near East in Pictures*, 1954; *Archaeology and the OT*, Princeton, 1959. Lively and brilliantly illustrated, L. Grollenberg, *Atlas of the Bible*, 1956; cf P. Lemaire-D. Baldi, *Atlas Biblique*, Louvain 1960; G. Wright-F. Filson, *Historical Atlas to the Bible*, Philadelphia, 1956; lighter, A. Parrot, *Discovering Buried Worlds*, 1955, and in addition several works on specific sites; I. Price, *The Monuments and the OT*, Philadelphia, 1959; W. Williams, *Archaeology in Biblical Research*, 1965; N. Glueck, *The Other Side of the Jordan*, New Haven, 1940; id *Rivers in the Desert*, 1959; AASOR 23, 1951; D. Winton Thomas (ed.), *Archaeology and OT Study*, Oxford, 1967; M. Noth, *The World of the OT*, Oxford, 1966; Jerome Commentary, 1968; ch. 74.

b Very valuable now are: IDB articles by G. van Beek, 'Archaeology' 1, 195—207; J. Kelso, 'Pottery' 3, 846 53; S. DeVries, G. Caird, 'Chronology', 1, 580—599—607; R. Hamilton, 'Architecture', 1,209—15; O. Sellers, 'House', 2, 657. The briefer Black's (= Harper's) Bible Dictionary by J. Miller, 1952, relies on Albright but unevenly. Pertinent information can be gleaned from J. Steinmueller, *Catholic Biblical Encyclopedia*, 1962²; HDB, 1963²; J. L. McKenzie, *Dictionary of the Bible*, 1966.

c Though the bulk of archaeological literature, Israeli included, happens to be in English or available in translation, still these classics must be kept in the forefront of attention: A. Barrois, *Manuel d'archéologie biblique*, (1939—53); L. Hennequin, 'Fouilles' (outdated but a model of exposition), *DBS* (1936) 3, 318—524; C. Schaeffer, *Stratigraphie comparée* Oxford: 1948; C. Watzinger, *Denkmäler Palästinas* Leipzig, 1931—3; K. Galling, *Biblisches Reallexikon* Tübingen: 1937; M. Avi-Yonah, S. Yeivin, *Qadmoniyyot Arṣenu* Tel Aviv: Me'uhad, 1955. Indispensable for specific sites and topics is the documentation of *DBS*, *Religion in Geschichte und Gegenwart*, Tübingen: Mohr, 1958—62; and *Enṣiqlopediya Miqra'it*, Jerusalem: Bialik, 1950. L. H. Vincent—AM. Stève, *Jérusalem de l'ancien Testament*,

I: *Archéologie de la Ville,* ; II (i) *Le Temple,* (ii) *Evolution* **77c** *historique . . . de la Ville,* 1954—6.

Outside Palestine—For **Egypt,** J. Baikie, *Egyptian* **d** *Antiquities in the Nile Valley* 1932; I. E. S. Edwards, *Pyramids of Egypt*, 1947. We possess nothing like J. Vandier's *Précis d'archéologie égyptienne* 1952—5 and must rely on J. Wilson's *Interpreter's Dictionary* 2, 39—66 and the *histories* quoted there; also *JNES*, *Journal of Egyptian Archaeology, Chronique d'Egypte*; A. Scharff, *Agypten [und Vorderasien] im Altertum*, Munich: Bruckmann, 1950; the *Guide Bleu* by M. Baud (1950 edition maps best!) incorporates valuable archaeological information. For *papyri* see E. Power in CCHS (1) § 77; 81; now on Bodmer papyri, F. Filson, BA 20 (1957) 53—63; 22 (1959) 48—51; on Chenoboskion, R. North, CBQ 24 (1962) 154—70.

Babylonia—Again, there is nothing in English like **e** A. Parrot's *Archéologie mésopotamienne*, 1946—53 or G. Contenau's *Civilisation d'Assour*, 1951; but S. Lloyd's *Foundations in the Dust* and *Twin Rivers*, 1947, are breathtaking surveys of pathfinders' explorations. M. Beek, *Atlas of Mesopotamia*, 1962; colourful *National Geographic* reconstructions 'Daily Life in Bible Times'. R. Boulanger, *Guide Bleu: Moyen Orient*, 1956. For a survey centred about Warka, R. North, *Ori* 26 (1957) 185—256; also *Guide to Biblical Iran* (Rome: 1956). On Hurrians, R. O'Callaghan, *Aram Naharaim* (Rome: 1948—61).

Anatolia—Both Seton Lloyd's *Early Anatolia* (1956) **f** and O. Gurney's *Hittites* (1952) are priceless Penguin treasures. Romanticized, but skilfully, are C. Ceram's *Secrets of the Hittites* (= *Narrow Pass, Black Mountain*; New York: 1958) and *The March of Archaeology* (= *Gods, Graves, and Scholars*; New York, 1956) Boulanger's *Guide Bleu: Turquie* is weak on Pauline sites; see CBQ 18 (1956) 30; 276; 22 (1958) 81. B. Hrozny, *Early History of Western Asia* (London: 1950) is a humane archaeologist's unreliable theorizing. For Roman Turkey still unsurpassed are Sir William Ramsay's *St Paul the Traveller* 1925¹⁵, *Letters to the Seven Churches* 1904, *Cities and Bishoprics of Phrygia* 1897; on individual sites see *PW*; and also for the related sites in Greece.

1 Pre-Twentieth Century—Excavation has dynamical- **78a** ly re-ordered biblical research within our generation. Pius XII wrote (*EnchB²* 546): 'Conditions of biblical studies . . . have greatly changed since Leo XIII's [1893] encyclical, when hardly a single Palestine site had been excavated. Now . . . more precise techniques experimentally developed . . . have shed on exegesis a light recognized by all experts [and unearthed] valuable written documents'. The word *archaiología* itself, as introduced by Josephus Flavius A.D. 95, was simply 'science of the past' or history. As rendered 'Antiquities', it came to focus rather those concrete usages of daily life which can be

93

78a discerned between the lines in books really written about politico-cultural trends. More concrete antiquarian or museum interests also gradually contributed, ever since Babylonian Nabuna'id 550 B.C., Eusebius and Epiphanius A.D. 300, and especially the Italian Renaissance. Epoch-making compilations were made by Bochart 1653, Reland 1714, Ugolini 1744—69. The nineteenth-century 'Archaeologies' of Saalschütz, Keil, and Nowack, and some more recent ones by Volz and the Catholics Kortleitner and Nötscher, would nowadays be better entitled 'Culture History', notes A. Bea, *Bib* 23 (1942) 84; a more 'psychological' application of this technique is J. Pedersen's *Israel* 1926—47. More enriched with excavation-results are Barrois and the now-normative *Ancient Israel* of de Vaux.

b Archaeology as understood today has a parentage entirely distinct from literary sifting. It means 'reconstruction of the fabric of ancient daily life from surviving objects themselves, including unearthed writings in their material aspects.' Its first great milestone after Pompeii was the scholarly invasion accompanying Napoleon to Egypt in 1789. This resulted in Champollion's deciphering hieroglyphics by the aid of the **Rosetta Stone**. Analogously in 1837 H. Rawlinson broke the code of cuneiform by daringly copying the sheer-cliff **inscription of Behistun**. The third milestone was H. Schliemann's dream-come-true, the digging up of Homeric Troy from the ground. His claim to have verified 'successive complete cities roosting atop one another' lent other pioneers an unduly naive but basically valid notion of *stratification*. This was applied to Palestine by Sir William Flinders Petrie. After brilliant but erratic discoveries in Egypt at 'Amarna and Tanis, he established in 1890 near Gaza the principle by which biblical excavation was set on a solid footing. 'Broken pottery without inscription adequately keys chronological sequence'!

c Petrie worked for the Palestine Exploration Fund, an 1865 London project. This brought to a head and redirected the surge of intrepid rediscovery of 'Arabia' by Maundrell 1703, Pococke 1738, and Niebuhr, Burckhardt, Seetzen 1800. Following French explorers Guérin and de Vogüé, F. de Saulcy in 1863 had made the first excavation on Palestine soil at the Jerusalem tomb of Saddan-Helen. A Congregationalist missioner Eli Smith in a three-month tour of 1838 with Edward Robinson (*Biblical Researches*, Boston, 1856²) had recaptured from Arab folklore more OT localizations than all the centuries since Eusebius, as generous rival Tobler declared. This convinced the British that their major task was an accurate *Survey of Western Palestine*, executed 1881—8 by C. Wilson and C. Conder. The daredevil exploit of a third officer, Charles Warren, to get to the bottom of the Temple-pinnacle, still adorns the title-page of PEQ. The Fund also published epochal researches of German G. Schumacher and Frenchman C. Clermont-Ganneau.

d Within the year of Petrie's first stratigraphic excavation in Palestine, a sixteen-year-old Dominican named **L.-Hugues Vincent** began correlating and interpreting the results of Palestine digging. This task lasted uninterruptedly through excavation's Golden Age until his death in 1960. In 1890 also, pioneer exegete M.-J. Lagrange [1855—1938; see F. Braun, *The Work of Lagrange*, (Milwaukee; Bruce, 1965)] had founded in Jerusalem the Dominican *École Biblique* and its associated *Revue Biblique*, official organs of the French government since 1921 while actuating ever more firmly their title of 'international'. Meanwhile at Jerusalem was located also the German Lutheran *Palästina-Verein* with its masterful

Zeitschrift; while for the older German Orient-Society **78d** (*ZDMG*) H. Guthe's researches achieved a Bible-Atlas even today in some respects unsurpassed.

Palestine excavation thereupon fell into three natural eras separated by the two world wars. Before treating them systematically, it will be opportune to premise a brief summary of the finds relevant to exegesis meanwhile being ferreted out in Egypt, Syria, Babylon, and Anatolia. Each excavated site can be seen in the chart on pp. 96—97, which indicates tabularly the modern-Arab and alleged-biblical place-name, its location on Map 3, the excavators' dates, finds, and publications, and the paragraph of this article treating its biblical importance.

2 Survey—Egypt. Palestine was always the bridge for **79a** commercial-military interaction between the Assyrian or Hittite empires and Africa. Egypt's cultural developments before 3500 B.C. (Vandier) shared or paralleled those of Ghassulian Palestine. From 1900 B.C., 'Execration-Texts' (edited by Sethe and Posener), written on pottery in order to be smashed and thus by sympathetic magic damage enemy neighbours, survive to afford our earliest list of Canaan place-names. With Abraham's entry begins the saga compiled by A. Mallon, *Les Hébreux en Égypte* (Rome: 1921). Tomb-decorations, especially at Memphis-Saqqâra and **Thebes-Luxor**, furnish striking parallels to the Wisdom-Books (see § 357*b*) and to the court-experiences of Joseph and Moses.

In 1887 at **Amarna** were found some 300 clay tablets **b** in the international chancery-language: at that date Babylonian cuneiform even in Egypt! Many letters from rulers in Jerusalem and other Canaan city-states in 1370 B.C. ask help against marauders called *Habiru*. As a *word*, this is identical with 'Hebrews', whether it means 'dusty' (donkey-caravaneers)' or 'border-crosser' (southwest U.S. 'wetback'). If this identity of *name* warrants concluding to *some* identity of *groups*, then the Hebrews must either have entered Egypt after this time, or had their Exodus earlier, or remained partially installed in Canaan while their cousins were in Goshen. Independently of this, the palaces and tombs built for the Pharaoh Akhenaten show him to have moved the capital to 'Amarna from Thebes in order to spearhead a reform of realism in art, and of 'sun-disk monotheism' (renounced by his famed successor Tut-Ankh-Amon!), which may well have influenced the human terminology in which the Sinai covenant was formulated. See now E. Campbell, *Chronology of the Amarna Letters*, Baltimore, 1964; J. van Seters, *The Hyksos*, New Haven, 1966; R. North, *Archeo-Biblical Egypt* Rome, 1967.

Today in the Cairo museum may be inspected the **c** mummies of three Pharaohs likeliest to have been involved in the **Exodus**. Rameses II, 1301—1234, was an extensive builder all over Egypt as far south as Thebes and Abu-Simbel. His name is especially frequent on the monuments of **Tanis** in the NE Delta. Its excavator, P. Montet, holds it to have been the capital of the 'Hyksos' invasion about 1700, doubtless linked with the immigration of Joseph's brothers. The same urban-area perhaps included a 'royal residence' at nearby Qantir, according to A. Alt, *Kleine Schriften*, III, 176. Thus in the far-flung ruins of Tanis we are almost surely right in recognizing the city **Rameses** of Ex 1:11, built by slave-labour of Joseph's descendants. The earliest mention of Israel is on a pillar of Rameses' successor Me(r)neptah dating from 1230 B.C. (ANEP 342) and visible today under the same roof as his mummy. It enumerates among defeated Canaan towns a *ysr'r* 'obliterated and without seed'. This may quite plausibly be a 'slanted press-

79c release' about the Exodus, portrayed as Meneptah's own *ejection* of the Israelites from Egypt 'to die of hunger in uncultivated Sinai'. But the Albright school and the Jerusalem Dominicans interpret Meneptah's claim to imply that the Exodus had taken place at least forty years before Meneptah, under Rameses II, whose father Seti I would thus have been the 'Pharaoh of the Oppression'.

d Tanis is also rich in monuments of Sheshonq, Pharaoh about 930, who left on a wall of Luxor place-names of his Canaan invasion 1 (3) Kgs 11:40; 14:25; J. Simons, *Egyptian Topographical Lists*, (Leiden 1937); E. Vogt reporting B. Mazar, Bib 38 (1957) 234). The Tanis ruins include also a million mud-bricks stamped with the name of Psusennes. Either he or Sheshonq or a predecessor may have been the father-in-law of Solomon, 1 (3) Kgs 9:16.

South of Tanis in the Delta is Tumilat valley, a normal haven of Asiatic refugees as is shown in vivid portrayals like the 1800 B.C. Beni-Hasan cave near 'Amarna. Naville's excavation of Maskhuta in Tumilat yielded stones with the names of both **Pithom** Ex 1:11 and **Succoth** Ex 13:20; though one of these may have been located at nearby Retâba. Farther SW, at Yahudiyya, Naville excavated Hyksos-fortifications and typical 'juglets', and also the much later 'rival Yahweh-temple' of 200 B.C. which JosAnt 13(65)3,1 locates at **Leontopolis**. A similar temple of Jewish colonists 490 B.C. at **Elephantine** island opposite Aswan is attested by 80 important papyri found in 1898, edited by Cowley and probed theologically by A. Vincent after excavations by Jesuits S. Ronzevalle and Mallon. One papyrus is a Persian royal decree, minutely regulating what appears to be Jewish Passover rites.

e Other papyri-finds at Oxyrhynchus in 1897 and **Chenoboskion** in 1946 are 'logia' importantly related to the composition-procedure of our Gospels, as well as to the Gnostic heresy of the Copts, who are Christian Egyptians using a language like Greek. Our Gospels themselves are most remarkably vindicated by the Bodmer Papyrus, in which almost the whole of John was copied about A.D. 160. This surpasses even the Beatty papyri found in 1929 and published by F. Kenyon in London 1933-7, with portions of Gospels, Acts, and Paul, as copied before A.D. 250. From the same date are Gr. OT passages antedating Origen's Hexapla. Far more ancient still are three Fayum fragments of Dt. One, called the Nash Papyrus, found 1902, contains the Ten Commandments. Another was published by C. Roberts at Manchester in 1936. The third is 'Fuad 266' from Cairo 1939 [W. Waddell JTS 45 (1944) 158]. All three copies were made scarcely a century after the LXX had been produced. Numerous non-biblical papyri found within our century have shown for the first time the NT *koinē* as a genuinely-existing widespread dialect. The form and techniques of plebeian letter-writing are remarkably paralleled in Paul. At Cairo, finally, may be inspected the remains of a Roman settlement called Babylon at the time of Christ's birth (controvertedly echoed in 1 Pt 5:13); but alleged souvenirs of his 'Flight into Egypt' (Mt 2:15) are folklore.

f Syria—Since 1925 at Ras Shamra, ancient **Ugarit** on the North-Syrian coast, C. Schaeffer has found thousands of tablets in a previously-unknown cuneiform language, not syllabic as in Babylon but alphabetic. This 'Ugaritic' is the closest known language to biblical Heb. Its epics of religious mythology, most conveniently available in C. Gordon's Pontifical Biblical Institute edition, are dated about 1400 B.C., and exhibit Leviathan

and other biblical motifs. Reinterpretation of the whole **79f** Bible in the light of Ugarit is fostered by M. Dahood, especially in his Anchor Bible *Psalms* (1965). Farther S on the Phoenician coast is **Byblos**, whose name has given us the words 'book' and 'bible'. Excavations of M. Dunand here show a religious centre venerated already when Cheops was building his Great Pyramid about 2500 B.C. The stone coffin of Ahiram of Byblos about the time of Solomon affords data on art-syncretism and the origins of the alphabet. **Tyre** and **Sidon** harbours have been explored with the aerial-survey technique discovered by R. Poidebard; the remains relate rather to the Roman than to the prophetic age. The temple of **Ba'albek** in **g** the Beqa'-valley between the Lebanon and Hermon mountains, may, like Egyptian Idfu, be a late survival (200 B.C.) of sacral styles used by the (Phoenician) architect of Solomon's Temple. In the Syrian desert the extensive Roman ruins of **Palmyra** attest what had doubtless been a caravan-station since Solomon's day, though it was scarcely the Ta(d)mar built by him, 2 Chr 8:4(DV). Still farther E, at Harîri on the Euphrates, A. Parrot has brought ancient **Mari** to life. Its king Zimri-Lim was contemporary of Hammurabi, but his records leave debatable dates centered around 1750, 1700, 1650: in relation to which, Abraham is now generally dated around 1850 rather than the 2100 superficially implied by biblical figures. Thousands of Assyrian tablets at Mari mention places contemporary with the patriarchs. A few miles northward on the Euphrates is the Roman desert-fort called **Dura-Europos**. Its unique frescoed synagogue of A.D. 240, excavated by Yale in 1930 and completely rebuilt in Damascus, attests how the rabbinic prohibition of religious images worked out in real life.

Babylonia—The cradle not only of Abraham but of **h** all Occidental cultures was the Tigris-Euphrates valley. The unearthed cuneiform Creation and Flood epics afford striking insight into the literary techniques known to the author of Gn 1—10. From the excavations of Sumerian **Warka** (Uruk Gn 10:10) and Elamite **Susa** emerge our earliest attestations of the invention of writing, 3200 B.C. These non-Semitic Sumerians were overcome by Semitic invaders of Accad. The newcomers built at **Ur** a 'ziggurat' or terraced-pyramid, under Ur-Nammu about 2100 B.C., excavated by L. Woolley. It was of fired bricks and bitumen, unlike the numerous sun-dried brick ziggurats of the area. Hence it affords a better idea of the enterprise of Gn 11:3 than **Babel** itself, where the ziggurat has disappeared, though imposing palaces of Nebuchadnezzar survive. Hegemony of the Tigris valley Semites in the S half called Babylonia reached its zenith under Hammurabi about 1700. His famous 'Code' found inscribed on a heavy diorite pillar at **Susa** in 1902, in the light of cognate codes more recently unearthed, shows inescapably both the background and the superiority of the Mosaic Covenant-Code of Ex 21—23. Between Hammurabi and Nebuchadnezzar (600 **i** B.C.), the Tigris valley was ruled mostly from the N, (Assyria). Its monarchs, Shalmaneser, Sargon, and Sennacherib, after subjugating Palestine, left records helping to decipher the complex biblical chronology. One of the Assyrian capitals, **Nineveh**, was plundered rather than excavated by early adventurers; Nimrud-**Kalah** is being excitingly exploited by Mallowan, and **Assur** farther S and **Gozan**-Halaf farther W have been stripped down with German thoroughness. Abraham's route to **Haran** is illustrated by Assyrian tablets recently dug up there and especially at **Nuzi**, a Hurrian outpost

HUNDRED CHIEF BIBLICAL EXCAVATION SITES, DIRECTORS, PUBLICATIONS, DATES, AND FINDS

here	Site; IDENTIFICATION	Map	Campaigns	Excavators	Report-Title or Auspices-Periodical	Epoch B.C.	Finds
80d	'Afula	S-18	'26 '37	E. Sukenik	PalExpQ '36, 150; JourPalOrS '48	3500	Ghassul-Esdraelon link
80a	'Ajjul-ʿAGLAYIM	Z-16	1931	W. Petrie	Ancient Gaza (EgExF '31–50); AASOR '33, 55	2000–1200	B,C, Hyksos-fort
79b	'Amarna-AKHETATEN	S-7	'87 '38	Petrie, Peet, Davies	City of Akhenaten (L '51); Rock Tombs (NY '03)	1370	A(Habiru),B,J,P,T
80h	'Amid-GENESARETH	Q-18	1925	F. Turville-Petre	Researches in Prehistoric Galilee (Oxf '27)	180,000	F, neanderthal skeleton
79j	ANTIOCH [+] ALALAKH	H-12	'32 '49	Stilwell; Woolley	Antioch (Princeton '34–52); Alalakh (Lo '55)	300–A.D.400	H,M,T; R,T
80m	'Arad	N-11	'62–5	Y. Aharoni, R. Amiran	IsrExpJ '62, 144; '64, 280; RevBib '64, 393	3500–400	D,G,I,R,T
80d	'ASCALON-'Asqalan	X-15	1920	J. Garstang	PalExpQ '21–23; DictBibSup 1, 621	2500–A.D.400	R,S
58a	ASHDOD-AZOTUS	V-15	'62 '67	D. Freedman; M. Dothan	Ashdod (IsrExpJ Sup, 1967); BibArch '64	2500–A.D.400	B,C,D,I,J,M,P,R,S
144g	ASSHUR-Shergat	J-19	'03 '14	W. Andrae	Das wied.Assur (Lpz '38); WVDOG 10—#57	2500–400	B,G,R,S,T,Z
80d,k	'Atlit-Mughara	R-16	1930	C. Johns; D. Garrod	QDepAntPal '32, 111; '37, 137; Stone Age Carmel (Ox '37)	400; 180,000	B,M/F, neanderthals
84a	'Ay-Tell	V-18	'33 '64	Marquet-Krause; Yeivin	Fouilles d'Ai (Paris '49); BASOR 178 (1965) 13	3300 [] 1000	G,R,T; basalt; burrows
84a	Azor	U-16	1958	J. Perrot; M. Dothan	'Atiqot 3 (1961) 1–83	3500	house/face ossuaries
79h	BABEL-BABYLON	M-19	'99 '17	R. Koldewey	Excavations at B (Lo '14); WVDOG#2—#59	1200–300	C,G,H,R,S,T, faience
56b	BEERSHEBA-Matar/Safadi	N-11	'53 '60	J. Perrot; M. Dothan	'Atiqot 2 ('59) 1–71; IsrExpJ '55, 17 + 176; '60, 120	3200	D,F,J,S; basalt; burrows
	BET-ALPHA-Hepsi-Bah	S-19	1929	E. Sukenik	Ancient Synagogue of Beth-Alpha (Jerusalem '32)	A.D.500	mosaic zodiac
80e	BETHEL-Beitin	U-18	'34 '55	W. Albright; J. Kelso	BASOR 56 ('34) 2; 164 ('61) 5; BibArch '56, 36	2000–A.D.70	I,M,R; Ai-correlations
80f	BETHSHAN-Beisan/Husn	S-19	'21 '33	Fisher, Rowe, Fitzgerald	Beth-Shan Excavations (Philadelphia 1930–40)	3500–A.D.500	B,C,G,I,S,T; mosaic-church
80m	BETHSHEMESH-Burayq	R-17	'36 '56	B. Mazar; N. Avigad	B (Jerusalem '57); IsrExpJ '59, 205; Scrip '54, 169	A.D.150–500	B,G,I; Mishaa-centre
80a	BETHSHEMESH-Rumayla	X-16	'10 '33	D. Mackenzie; E. Grant	PEF Annual 1911f; Beth-Shemesh (Haverford '39)	1500–A.D.500	D,R,T; Philistine pottery
299e	BETHZUR-Tubayqa	Z-18	'31 '57	W. Albright; O. Sellers	Citadel of Beth-Zur (Phila '33); BASOR 150 ('58) 8	1800–300	C,I,M; Mcb citadel
79j	Boghazköy-KHATTUSHA	C-11	'06 '67	H. Winckler; K. Bittel	Bogazköy I–III (Berlin '52–7); WVDOG #19, #63.	1800–900	A,B,D,G,R,S,T
79f,	BYBLOS-Jubayl	K-12	'25 '67	P. Montet; M. Dunand	B-Egypte; Fouilles de B (Paris 1928; '29–55).	4000–A.D.200	B,D,G,H,I,R,T (Obelisks)
80m	CAESAREA-Qaysari	S-16	'55 '60	S. Yeivin; D. Levi	Lombardia-Oriente (Milan '63) 163; IIILoNNov. 2 '63	A.D.30–600	C,D,H,I,S,T; mosaics
80g	CAPERNAUM-Telhum/Tabgha	Q-18	'05 '21	Kohl; Orfali, Schneider	AntikeSyn (Lpz '16); Caph (Paris '22); ChMult (Pad '34)	A.D.200–500	Synagogue, S; mosaic-ch.
79j	CARCHEMISH-Jerablus	G-14	'14 '20	C. Hogarth; L. Woolley	Carchemish I–III (British Museum 1914–52)	2400–600	B,C,I,R,S, battlefield
79e	CHENOBOSKION + Oxyrhynchus	R-7	'47 '97	J. Doresse; B. Grenfell	Secret Books (Lo '60); Sayings of Jesus (Cam '20)	A.D.300	Papyri; early Logia
80l	Deir 'Alla-SUCCOTH	T-19		H. Franken	Vetus Testamentum 11 (1961) 361	900	D,R, industries
—	Dhiban-DIBON	Z-19	'50–56	Morton; Tushingham	BASOR 133 (1954) 6; AASOR 36 (1957)	2500–A.D.400	C,I(Mesha-stela!),R,S
80l	DOTHAIN-Dotan	T-17	'53–64	J. Free	BASOR 160 (1960) 6; BibArch 19 (1956) 43	3000–300	D,R, monumental stair
79g	DURA-EUROPOS-Salihiyya	J-16	'20 '35	M. Rostovtzeff	Excavations of Dura (Yale 1950–59)	A.D.100–300	C,P,R,T; Jewish cult-images
54g	EILAT-Khulayfa	Q-11	1938	N. Glueck	AASOR 15 (1935) 42; BibArch 28 (1965) 69	950	Solomon port; NOT refinery
79d	ELEPHANTINE-Aswan	Z-8	'04 '18	Rubensohn; Ronzevalle	ZtsÄgSr 1909; 14; AmnServAntEg 1919, 1	1400–400	A,D,R; Yahweh-temple
84c	EMMAUS [+] Qubayba	V+X-17	'32 '44	L. Vincent; B. Bagatti	Emmaüs (Paris 1932); E-Qubeibeh (Jerus '47)	A.D.200–1200	Mosaic-churches; D, road
80j	ENGEDI-'AynJidi	Z-18	1961	Y. Yadin; Y. Aharoni	IsrExpJ 12 (1962) 167–262	3500; A.D.130	A,B; Bar-Kokba war dispatches
79k	EPHESUS-Seljuk	E-5	1863, 1966	J. Wood; F. Miltner	Discoveries (London 1877); Ephesos (Vienna '58)	300–A.D.300	B,G,H,R,T (Council-Church)
80j	Far'a-TIRSA	T-18	1946 '64	R. de Vaux	Revue Biblique 54 (1947) 394; 68 (1961) 557	3500–600	B,C,D,G,R; 'Omri-palace
80a	Far'a-SHARUHEN	N-11	'27–29	W. Petrie	Beth-Pelet (Egypt Expl.Fund, 1931)	1800–400	B; horse/Hyksos origins
80j	Fashkha + Murabba'at	Z-18	1958	R. de Vaux	Revue Biblique 66 (1959) 215–55	100–A.D.500	D,M; ?tannery
80a	GEZER-Jazar	V-16	'02 '35	R. Macalister	Excavations of G (PEF An '12); PEQ '35, 19	3500–300	B,D,G,I; obelisk-T; cistern
80h	Ghassul	V-19	'29 '60	Mallon, Koeppel, North	Teleilat G (Rome '36–40); G 1960 (Rome '61)	3500	D,F; earliest frescoes
80e	GIBEA-Ful	X-18	1922	W. Albright	AASOR 34 (1960; L. Sinclair)	1400–A.D.70	C,I,M; Saul's capital
80l	GIBEON-Jib	X-18	'56–62	J. Pritchard	Winery. Defenses (Phila '64); BibAr '61, 19	1800–800	B,I; cistern, chaft
79j	GORDION-Yassihüyük	D-9	'00 '64	G. Koerte; R. Young	Jahrbuch 1904; AmJourArch '55, 1	750–250	C,R,S,T
79i	HALAF-GOZAN	G-16	'11 '39	von Oppenheim; Moortgat	Tell Halaf (London '33); 3 vols. German	3500–900	A
	HARRAN-SultanTepe	H-15	1952	S. Lloyd	Anatolian Studies 1954, 65; 1958, 245	1500	
80d, m	HAZOR-Qadah	P-18	'26 '58	J. Garstang; Y. Yadin	Joshua-Judges (1931); Hazor (Jm 58–60)	1800–700	B,C,G,R,S,T; Mycene-ware
80a	HEBRON/Rama-MAMBRE	Z-17	1932	E. Mader	Mambre (Freiburg 1957)	600–A.D.400	C,H,T; road
	Hedera	T-16	1934	E. Sukenik	JourPalOrSoc 17 (1937) 13–30	3500	domiform ossuary
80a	Hesi-'EGLON	Z-15	1890	W. Petrie; F. Bliss	Tell H-Lachish (EgExpF 1891); MoundMC ('98)	2300–400	Stratification-principle!

Pl.	Site	Grid	Years	Excavators	Publications	Dates	Features
80a	Jamma-SALTON	N-10	1927	W. Petrie	Gerar [conjecture] (Eg Exp F 1928)	1300–400	C,R, granaries
80f	Jerash-GERASA	U-20	'28 '34	C. Kraeling; J. Crowfoot	Gerasa (ASOR/Yale 1938); Churches (Lo '31)	A.D.100–500	H, amplest Gospel ruins
84b	JERICHO-Sultan/'Alayiq	V-19	'06 '58	Garstang; Kenyon/Kelso	J. Ergeb (Lpz '13); Story/J (Lc '42); DigJ (Lo '57); AASOR '55–8	4000–A.D.400	B,C,D,R,T; lacunal; villa
80k	JERUSALEM-Antonia/Probatica	M-11	'90 '56	Cré, Vincent; de Vaux	Le Lith (Paris '33); FB '52, 513; DBS 5, 938	30–A.D.8	Prison-games; Mary-house
80k	-Olivet		'49 '60	Bagatti, Corbo, Saller	Dominus Flevit (Jlem '58); Exc.Bethany (J '57)	A.D.50 (–500)	Judeo-Christian symbols
80h	KANISH-Kültepe	D-12	'24 '64	B. Hrozny; T. Özgüç	Ausgrabungen von Kültepe (Ankara 1950)	1800–400	A,B,C,D,R; Assyrian enclave
79j	Kara Tepe	F-11	'48 '56	H. Bossert; H. Cambel	Ausgrabungen von Karatepe (Ankara 1950)	900	C,R,S; bilingual I
79j	Kerak-BETHIYERAH	R-18	'44 '56	P. BarAdon; P. Delougaz	IsrExpJ 2 (1952) 165; Chicago OIP 85 (1960)	3000–A.D.400	C,D,R,H,T
80d	LACHISH-Duwayr	Z-17	'32–38	J. Starkey; O. Tufnell	Lachish I–IV (Oxford 1938–58)	1800–400	C,I,R,T; ostraca-A!
79k	LAODICEA + HIERAPOLIS	F-7	1890	W. Ramsay	PaulyRE 12, 723; 8, 1404; BibArch '55, 9; '50, 1	200–A.D.200	H; G R
79a, d	LUXOR-THEBES	V-9	1850–1967	L. Borchardt; J. Breasted	J. Baikie, Egyptian Antiquities (Lo '32) 351–623	1800–400	A,B,C,D,G,H,I,M,R,S,T
80g	Manshiyya [not GATH]	Z-17	'55 '60	S. Yeivin	IsrExpJ 10 (1960) 120; Frs. Report (Jm '61)	3500–400	D,R
80j, m	MARI-Harîri	K-17	'33 '67	A. Parrot	Mari (Paris 1960); Syria 1935–65	2500–400	C,S,T,Z; school; Hammurabi-A
80f	MASADA	N-12	'54; '65	M. AviYonah; Y. Yadin	IsrExpJ 7 (1957) 21 ff; 9 (1959) 13; 15 (1965) 1–120	100–A.D.400	A,R; Herod-C; cisterns, church
80e	MEGIDDO-Mutasallim	S-17	'03 '39	G. Schumacher; G. Loud	TelM (Lpz '08 '29); ChiOIP (29 '48); BibA '50, 28	3500–400	B,C,G,I,J,R,T; stables
80f	Metser	S-17	1957	M. Dothan	IsrExpJ 7 (1957) 21 ff; 9 (1959) 13	3200	apse houses; Ghassuloid
80m	Mirsim-?DEBIR	Z-17	'26 '32	W. Albright	AASOR 17 (1937); 22 (1943); ArchPalBib (NY '35)	1800–700	D, industries
79i	Nasba-?MIZPAH	V-18	'26 '35	W. Badé	C. McCown, Tell en Nasbé (Berkeley 1947)	2500–200	B,D,G,I,R,T
79i	Natûf	X-17	1928	D. Garrod	PalExpJ 1928, 182 JourExpAnthropl 1932, 257	12,000	F, mesolithic
79k	NAZARETH + Qafza	R-17	'54; '33	B. Bagatti; R. Neuville	SBF Liber Annuus '5; Paléolithique/Juda (P '51)	600–A.D.1200	mosaic-ch; caves; F. neandert.
79i	NEBO + Mukhayyat	X-19	1933	S Saller	Mem. Moses (Jm '41); Town Nebo ('49); BibA'48, 50	A.D.600	mosaic-churches (Map: Madaba)
80l	Nimrud-KALAH	H-19	1845; 960	A. Layard; M. Mallowan	Iraq 1954, 115	900	A,C,R,Z
79d	NINEVEH-Mosûl	H-18	1850; 930	A. Layard; R. Thompson	Monuments of Nineveh (London 1853)	900	A,C,S; Lachish frieze
80m	NUZI-Kirkuk/Yorgân	H-21	'27 '31	F. R. Starr	Excavations of Nuzi (Harvard 1937–58)	3500–1600	Abraham-era; A,D,T
80j	PERGAMUM-Bergama	C-5	'85 '27	C. Humann; T. Wiegand	Alterthümer/P (Berlin '85–23); R. Kaehler, P ('49)	400–A.D.800	C.H,R,S,T; Zeus-altar
80m	PERSEPOLIS Jamshîd	P-28	1935	A. Herzfeld; E. Schmidt	Persepolis, 2 vols. (Chicago OIP; 1953–58)	400	A,B,C,I,S
79i	Petra-SELA'	Q-12	'97 '67	G. Horsfield; D. Parr	G. Robinson, SarcophagusAC ('30); QDAP '38, 1; PEQ '61	200–A.D.400	B,C,G,H,I,S,T; high-place
80c	PITHOM-Mashkhûta	N-8	1883	E. Naville; L. Habachi	Store City Pithom (EgExpF 1885); RGG3 5, 389	1600–300	I,R,S; Goshen refugee-haven
79a	Qasila-JOPPE	U-15	'49 '52	B. Mazar-Maisler	IsrExpJ 1 (1951) 61 + 125 + 194	900–A.D.200	C,R, kiln, refinery, port
79k	Qumran-?TR-HA-MELAH	X-18	'49 '55	R. de Vaux	RevBib 63 (56) 53; 66 (59) 87; SchweichL 1961	800–A.D.100	Scrolls-A; cisterns; C,D,M
80b	RamatRahel-NETÔPA	X-17	'54 '62	Y Aharoni	IsrExpJ 6 (1956) 102 + 137; BibArch 24 (1961) 98	1000–A.D.600	T: casemates; aeolic capitals
80d	Sa'idiyya-ZARETHAN	U-18	'64–67	J. Pritchard	Illustrated London News, July 2, 1966, pp. 25ff	2500–100	B,D,H,I,J,R; bitumen-mummies
80b	SAMARIA-Sabastya	T-17	'08 '35	G Reisner; J. Crowfoot	Harvard Exc. Sam. (24); S.-Sebaste (Lo '38–57)	900–A.D.400	A,C,H,I,J,T
79c	Saqqara-MEMPHIS	Q-7	'80 '67	L. Borchardt; J. Lauer	Memphis I–VI (Lorton: Egpt Exp. F 1909–15)	2500–300	A,B,H,I,P,S,T, pyramids
79k	SARDIS-Sart	D-6	'10 '67	H. Butler; G. Hanfmann	Sardis (Princeton '22–32); BASOR 154 (1959) 5	1200–A.D.200	D,H,T, church, synagogue
78b	Sha'ar-ha-Golan	R-19	1948	M. Stekelis	IsrExpJ 1 (1950) 1–19	7000	herringbone-incised jars
79j	SHECHEM-Nablus/Balâta	U-17	'13 '67	E. Sellin; G. Wright	ZDPV 1926–8; 41: BibArch '57, 82; 63, 1–27	2000–300	C,G,H,I,R,T
79f	SHILOH-Seilun	U-18	'26 '32	H. Kjaer		1800–A.D.400	(Ark-shrine) mosaic churches
79h	SUSA-Shûsh	L-24	'97 '64	J. de Morgan; R. Ghirshman	Mémoires de la Délégation en Perse (40 vols)	3500–A.D.400	B,C,T, Hammurabi-code
79h	TAANACH-Ta'nak	S-17	'02 '63	E. Sellin; P. Lapp	Tell T (Vienna 1904–6); BASOR 173 (1964) 4	1600	C,D,R,I; cult-objects
79d	Tahina	Z-17	1927	D. Buzy	Revue Biblique 37 (1928) 558–78	8000	F, neolithic
80a	TANIS-Sân/AVARIS/RAMSES	M-8	'29 '52	W. Petrie; P. Montet	Én-gmes/Tanis: Drane/Avaris (P '52); RB '46, 75	2500–A.D.400	B,C,G,I,J,R,S, obelisks
	TARSUS + Mersin	G-11	1934	H. Goldmann; J. Garstang	Exc. GözlüKüle (Princeton '50–6); PrehM (Ox '53)	4000–A.D.300	D,H,F
	TROY-Hisarlik	B-5	'72 '36	H. Schliemann; C. Blegen	Troy (NY '75); Troy I–IV (Cincinnati 1950–8)	2500–A.D.200	C,H,R,T. Started it all!
	UGARIT-RasShamra	J-12	'29 '62	C. Schaeffer	Ugaritica (Paris 1939-49-1; Syria 1951–	4000–800	A,B,C,G,I,J,R,S
	UR-Muqayyar	N-22	'22 '34	Hall; Woolley	Exc. Ur (Lo '54); Ur-Exc. (Penn/BritMus '39–54)	3500–550	B,C,D,G,J,T,Z
	Warka-URUK/ARACH	N-21	'12 '60	Jordan; H. Lenzen	WVDOG 51; Uruk-Warka 1–14 ('30–57; Ori '56, 246	3500–A.D.400	A,C,G,T,Z; Gilgamesh-R
	Yahudiyya-LEONTOPOLIS	N-7	1887	E. Naville; W. Petrie	Mound of Jew; Hyksos/Isr. Cities (EgExpF '90; '06)	1800–200	R; juglets; Onias-T
	Zakariyya + MARESHA	X-15	1898	F. Bliss	Exc.Palest (PEF 1902; H. Thiersch, Rock Tombs ('05)	1600–A.D.300	B,C,M,P; ?Azeqa

ADDITIONAL ABBREVIATIONS USED IN THIS CHART

AnnServAntEg Annales du service des antiquités de l'Égypte   ChMut Church of the Multiplication   Chicago OIP Chicago Oriental Institute Publications

LeLith Le Lithostrotos   WVDOG Wissenschaftliche Veröffentlichungen der deutschen Orient-Gesellschaft.

79i about 1600 B.C. The modern Turkey border near Haran-Gozan was the homeland named Mitanni of the Hurrians, biblical Horites. E of the Tigris-valley, monuments of the Persian liberators of deported Juda (539 B.C.) are richest at Pasargadae, **Persepolis**, and Ecbatana-Hamadan.

j **Anatolia**—Assyrian merchants penetrated far to the NW, and in Abraham's day set up an enclave or *karum* at **Kanish** (Kültepe) near Kayseri, excavated since 1948 by T. Özgüç. All around them was the heartland of the Hittite world-power, hinted at obscurely in Gn 23:10; 15:20; but practically unknown until in 1906 H. Winckler excavated **Boghazköy**. Even pre-Homeric **Troy** turns out to have been a sort of western frontier-post of this empire, whose apogee lasted from 1700 to 1300. Hittite law-codes afford further insight into the setting of Ex 21—23. Later and much farther S the Hittites had an unexpected revival around 900 in a line of excavated forts from **Carchemish**, Alalakh, and Zencirli, to the recent find-site of a Phoenician-Hittite bilingual inscription at **Karatepe**. In 'Phrygian' or post-Hittite Anatolia the chief excavations were at **Gordion** and Sardis since 1950, linked with the names

k of Midas and Croesus. Besides **Sardis**, the other city 'condemned' in the Apocalypse, **Laodicea**, is also a completely abandoned field of monumental ruins at Eskihisar near Denizli. Philadelphia and Thyatira are the quiet villages Alashehir and Akhisar. The other three Apocalypse 'angels', **Pergamum**, **Ephesus**, and Smyrna, are today populous cities which have been the scene of excavations magnificently rich in Roman monuments known to Paul and John. Miletus also on the Ionian coast, and **Perga** on the S, like Corinth and Athens, abound in imposing ruins of the Apostle's Hellenic background. More meagre for our knowledge of Paul's toil are the results of soundings farther E at Lystra, **Tarsus**, and both Antiochs; and at Salamis and Paphos on the island of **Cyprus**.

80a **Palestine pioneering**—1890—1914 was a period of trial-and-error development of techniques. Petrie's over-eagerness to claim discovery of biblical cities mars the titles of the reports: *Hesy-Lachish* 1891, rather 'Eglon; *Beth-Pelet* 1930, rather Sharuhen dug 1927 at 'southern Far'a'; *Ancient Gaza* 1931—50, rather Beth-'Aglayim at 'Ajjul; *Gerar* or rather Jamma 1928. Petrie's mandate was continued by R. Macalister of Dublin with American F. Bliss at **Maresa** and several sites near Zakariyya-'Azeqa, then alone with conspicuous success at **Gezer**, despite some chronology-lacunas still being rectified. The British Fund also sponsored Duncan Mackenzie of Knossos in a 1910 excavation of **Beth-Shemesh**, which by happy coincidence turned out to be Palestine's richest deposit of Aegean-origin Philistine pottery; but his dating of the pre-Philistine masonry was somewhat lowered in a reopening of the site by American E. Grant in 1928.

b German pioneering revolves mostly around the great theologian Sellin, at **Ta'anak** 1901, Jericho 1907, Shechem 1913; his Jericho collaborator C. Watzinger also opened Megiddo with G. Schumacher in 1903. These sites were destined to frustrate even Anglo-American expeditions of much vaster scientific array in the thirties; but the publication of finds by the German Orient-Gesellschaft was admirably methodical. **Shechem**-Balâta was troubled in its postwar reopenings and less-felicitous publishing; but Sellin's 1934 collaborator Steckeweh was able to ensure a desired continuity in Wright's 1957 expedition. The unique cuneiform tablets and cult-objects harvested at Ta'anak have only since 1965 been

subjected to the stratigraphic revision which was the **80b** fruit of this pioneering.

German influence also underlay the first American **c** venture. The leader of Harvard's 1908—10 **Samaria** excavations was G. Reisner, trained in Egypt by Troy's Dörpfeld and Babylon's Koldewey. His Sabastiya 'palace of 'Omri and Ahab', containing ivory art-treasures and significant tax-receipt ostraca, was re-examined in a 1931—5 joint expedition with the British J. Crowfoot and K. Kenyon and the Jewish E. Sukenik. A synthesis of early results of Palestine excavation especially at Gezer was achieved in Vincent's 1909 *Canaan*.

The British Mandate has become known as 'the **d** Golden Age of Palestine excavation'. It undoubtedly established working-conditions ideally congenial to occidental scholarship. Its Antiquities Director J. Garstang in six campaigns at Jericho took a great step forward, though leaving something for further British ingenuity to unravel under Miss K. Kenyon. Garstang also made important soundings at Hasor, taken up by Yadin in 1955—8, and at **Ascalon** (Ashkelon). But the greatest British achievement of this era was at **Duwayr** in South-Juda. Its leader, J. L. Starkey, fell a martyr to the science of biblical exploration and the Anglo-Zionist mistrust aroused in local Arabs by the Mandate. But he had succeeded in discovering in 1931(-8) the city-gate with 21 jar-fragments bearing messages written in ink to **Lachish**. From these 'ostraca' we draw our most vivid corroboration of Nebuchadnezzar's campaigns in the time of Jeremiah. For an earlier dating, see N. R. Ganor, 'The Lachish Letters' in PEQ 1967, 74—77. Another scarcely less tragic accompaniment of rising Zionism was the (natural) death of French Jewess Judith Marquet-Krause shortly after her 1933 excavation had proved the vast ruin of **'Ay** to have been uninhabited for a thousand years when Joshua attacked it. Meanwhile Zionist research was climaxed by E. Sukenik at the mosaic synagogue of **Bet Alpha** and at chalcolithic Afula and Hedera. Among other nations special mention is merited by the Danish expedition of **Shiloh** 1923—32 under Hans Kjaer.

British-American amity in Mandate-research involved **e** chiefly the revitalizing of the American Schools of Oriental Research (ASOR) by William Foxwell Albright from 1920 to 1935 and by his continuing influence after his return to Baltimore. Beginning with Saul's citadel of **Gibea** at Fûl in 1921, then **Bethel** in 1927 with Kelso and Bet-Sur in 1931 with Sellers, Albright culminated in 1926—32 at **Mirsim** south of Hebron. It is the acknowledged masterwork of efficiently-economical excavation-technique and interpretation, though not all accept its identification with Debir-Qiryat-Sepher. But the real measure of Albright's achievement is rather his fostering of the Palestine Oriental Society and its *Journal*, his correlating of dig-results throughout the Middle E in *BASOR* through 1963, and the leadership attained by such disciples of his as Nelson Glueck, G. Ernest Wright, Roger O'Callaghan, and John Bright. The Albright appraisal became paramount in rectifying dating-results of the two major American excavations of this era, at Beth-Shan and Megiddo, both in Esdraelon plain. Near **f** the Jordan, the **Beth-Shan** temple complex from which allies rescued the dishonored body of Saul, had gone through various rebuildings. But apparently its origin was not as early as 1300, date assigned by Pennsylvania University's 1921—33 excavation under C. Fisher and A. Rowe. At **Megiddo**, the Chicago University Oriental Institute's most grandiosely-budgeted of all Palestine excavations reduced Schumacher's 'pillar-temple' to the famed 'Solomon's stables', and unearthed Solomon's

80f city-gate. The dating of that Solomonic stratum by G. Loud and P. Guy was revised, first drastically by Albright (G. Wright, BA 13 (1950) 28—46) and then in some details by Yadin's work at Hasor. But the opulent many-volumed publication of Megiddo, and the present-day condition of the excavated surface, remain undoubtedly the most splendidly instructive achievement of the 20th cent. Excavation Era. The most imposing of standing monuments in Palestine are at **Jerash**, excavated also by the Americans in 1933; and Badé's work at Nasba-Mispa also merits notice.

g Catholic participation in the excavation-field was throughout and worthily represented by the Jerusalem Dominicans, but not alone. And first of all it must be loyally recognized that although American pioneer Robinson had a blinding bias against the Franciscan 'monkish traditions', the presence of these friars' 'Custody' at **Calvary** since the 1300s had stored up a treasury of precious topographical observations and useful contacts with the local population. Though a certain tension attended incursion of modern critical outlooks, still in the long haul the Franciscan Custody has shown itself brilliantly equipped by its traditions and administrative machinery to forge to the fore. G. Orfali's work at **Capernaum** has been monumental; and the *Liber Annuus* and *Publications* of the Flagellation Studium Biblicum embody the researches and excavations especially of Italian B. Bagatti and American S. Saller at **Nebo** and other Byzantine sites. Meanwhile the Jerusalem Assumptionists, under Germer-Durand, and the Betharram Fathers did notable work in collecting and classifying flints. Buzy's Tahunian finds became normative h for Palestine neolithic. Thus was laid the groundwork for that stratified 'prehistory' (Turville-Petre at **Amud**) of which the Catholics René Neuville (French consul) and Dorothy Garrod became outstanding experts. Miss Garrod is famed for the neanderthal '**Carmel Man**' found by her and McCown. But her chief site, mesolithic **Natuf**, was ceded to her by its discoverer, A. Mallon, who after a training in Coptology had been called to found from 1913 to 1926 the Jerusalem branch of the Pontifical Biblical Institute. He directed its 1929—34 excavations at **Ghassul** NE of the Dead Sea, and with Neuville and M. Stekelis was the first discoverer of that transition-period from Stone to Bronze Age which has since become known at more than a hundred Palestine sites by the name 'chalcolithic' coined by Albright. Though Mallon was disappointed in his aim of finding artifacts contemporary and relevant to Abraham, it is perhaps providential that the brilliant fresco-art of Ghassul is a token of the Holy See's disinterested support of scientific archaeology.

In Jerusalem, at the NE corner of the Temple area, the Sisters of Sion erected their beautiful basilica over the Roman stone pavement claimed by Vincent to be the '**Lithostrotos**' and outset-point of the Way of the Cross, contested by Vincent's confrères Abel and i Benoit. Slightly farther E, the White Fathers' Melchite seminary has long fostered a significant biblical museum at the site where Cré's excavations (continued by de Vaux) corroborate ancient traditions juxtaposing the **Probatic Pool** and the tasteful Crusade church over the spot where St Anne is believed to have given birth to the mother of Jesus. An imposing Benedictine basilica was built by gift of the German emperor at Jerusalem's most dominatingly-strategic point. It was called 'Dormition', but more significantly it rises over the excavated Byzantine monument perpetuating the site of the **Cenacle**: though the Crusade-masonry currently-called 'Cenacle' is misleadingly regarded as an 'adjacent' site, and is pre-empted by the later 'David's Tomb' tradition dear to Muslims and **80i** Jews. Explorations at the stone stairway near the 'house of Caiaphas', Gethsemane, Olivet, Bethlehem, Bet-Jimal, and Nazareth, further attest the vigour of Catholic participation in the excavation-movement.

Partitioned Palestine—Since the creation of a **state j of Israel** in 1948, factors both national and religious have provoked an unparalleled boom in archaeological research. This reached its climax in Yigael Yadin's acquisition of the original Qumran scrolls in 1955, his related 1960 discoveries at '**En-Gedi**' and the sensational excavations at **Masada**. But the **Qumran** cave-find itself was in 1947 in what presently became the 'Jordan' half of Palestine; and in the Jerusalem Rockefeller Museum are treasured the thousandfold fragments and four complete scrolls of later discovery, while the two bronze treasure-scrolls are kept in Amman. This uneasy situation reflects not only the fratricidal tension of Palestine, but shows also the constructive scientifically-mediatorial role which Christian leaders of unconquerable persistence have been able to play. The Dominican Roland de Vaux was not only invited to accept the leadership of all the Scrolls-acquisition and editing activities; he also effectively guided the excavations of both Qumran 1952—5 and **Fashkha** 1958. Between times, 1946—59, he discovered the palace of 'Omri's **Tirsa** capital at Far'a in E Samaria, the most extensive excavation of the Jordan Kingdom of those days.

Meanwhile British fostering of **Arab Palestine k** excavation was no less vigorously reasserted by Kathleen Kenyon at Jericho and Ophel. The situation at **Jericho** Sultan mound was chaotic when she took over in 1952. An outer stone wall and varying phases of an inner two-width brick wall had all been ascribed to the Joshua-siege, at dates fiercely controverted: Garstang 1385, Albright 1315, Vincent 1250 B.C., all had come to link the *brick* wall with Joshua. Miss Kenyon showed that the *latest* masonry of this wall antedated 2000 B.C.; and that *nowhere* on the mound was there any sufficient artifact deposit to prove occupation at any date between 1500 and 800. Though she and the Albright school seemed willing to ascribe this dearth to erosive factors, the whole history of Palestine methodology forces us to acknowledge rather that a biblical episode cannot be localized where there are no corresponding artifacts. An identical situation exists at Joshua's '**Ay**, cf above, 80d. Though it would be overhasty to conclude with Martin Noth that 'excavation has proved the Joshua-account fictional', still neither can we answer this charge by ignoring the stupefying convergence of evidence from the two excavations most concerned with Joshua 1—8. Nor does it seem possible to maintain that either biblical Jericho or 'Ay was located at some nearby mound other than Sultân and et-Tell. Jericho has thus become a classic proof of what experts have tried to warn the public all along. Excavation is not a bargain 'proof of the truth of the Bible'. Rather the truth of the Bible rests on techniques of normal historical testimony (even apart from the claim of inerrant divine authorship), in which excavation plays its solid part but all in all 'has raised as many problems as it has solved'.

For Miss Kenyon's British School of Jerusalem, **l** explorations have also been made at **Petra** by P. Parr and Diana Kirkbride, while Jericho collaborator H. Franken has gone on to head the Netherlands Society for Near E. Research in its 1960 excavation at Deir'alla-**Succoth**. Several ASOR sites have been reopened like Bethel and Beth-Sur, and chiefly Balâta-Shechem under G. Ernest Wright. J. Free of Wheaton-Chicago at **Dotan** in Samaria

80l since 1953 has found extensive masonry from the Joseph-era and a crowded Iron Age urbanism illustrating 2 (4) Kgs 6:13. J. Pritchard after editing the double thesaurus of excavated exegetic materials ANET-ANEP, went on since 1956 to dig at Jîb N of Jerusalem an imposing water-storage complex fitting biblical data on **Gibeon**, and since 1962, Sa'idiyya (Zarethan) near Deir'alla.

m In Israel proper (pre-1967), the most grandiose enterprise since Megiddo has been the 1955—8 excavation of **Hasor**, N of Lake Tiberias, by Hebrew University specialists Y. Aharoni, R. Amiran, T. Dothan and others captained by Y. Yadin. Also conspicuous has been the work correlated for the University by Joseph Aviram: at the Dead Sea **Masada** fort under M. Avi-Yonah then by Y. Yadin, at Beth-Shearim under N. Avigad, at Ora and Ramat Rahel under Amiran and Aharoni, at **Khirbet Karak** under P. Bar-Adon, and at Stone Age sites of Carmel and **Yarmuk** by M. Stekelis. University Rector B. Mazar(-Maisler) in 1948 at **Qasîla** N of the Yarqon River near Tel Aviv dug up the Solomonic settlement corresponding to Jaffa. Meanwhile government agencies have sponsored excavations of S. Yeivin at **Caesarea** and the site prematurely renamed with Albright 'Gath'; also M. Dothan at Meser and Azor, and Y. Kaplan about Tel Aviv, sites which together with the Negeb work of American Nelson Glueck and French prehistorian Jean Perrot have multiplied Ghassulian deposits. Since 1965 have emerged conspicious results from Aharoni's excavation of Arad, and from David Freedman's cooperation with Dothan at Ashdod. Israeli explorers have also dutifully cleared Muslim remains at Acco and the splendid Byzantine church of seacoast **Shavey Sion** farther N; while at **Nazareth** the erection of a new Annunciation Basilica occasioned Bagatti's significant excavation.

81a 3 Exegetical Results—The fruits of all this excavation-fervor may now be summarized under three heads: chronology, technology, and architecture. Palestinology passed to the level of an exact science with Petrie's discovery of the **stratification**-principle, implying the importance of unmarked broken pottery. The 'strata' sought in imitation of Schliemann at Troy were at first naively flat, homogeneous, and monolithic. Only gradually was asserted the realistic view that continuing occupation results in contemporaneous deposits at widely differing 'levels', sometimes separated by lacunas or depressed areas where occupation may have been interrupted for centuries. We should reserve the term 'level' for any homogeneous and more or less horizontal patch of occupation-remains, 'layer' for any apparently-contemporaneous and continuous complex of such patches ranging over various altitudes. 'Stratum' itself will have to be defined 'all the materials of the site, however remote from one another or multiple in layers, which subsequent analysis and comparison show to have constituted a single continuous period of recognizable homogeneous culture.' It must be strongly insisted that this **stratum**, as proper unit of scientific chronology, is not an objective empirical reality dug up out of the ground and subject to no cavil or controversy; it is rather a *working hypothesis* produced by the excavator's intellect and insight from a multiplicity of such concrete realities, plus the data of literary documents and common-sense, therefore subject at all points to the sources of error and possibilities of revision inherent in all creative scientific hypotheses. The now-normative Wheeler-Kenyon technique, presumed above, may be found explained in Bib 34 (1953) 2 and more fully in IDB 1, 197.

b Stratification in Palestine depends almost exclusively on **pottery**. This must remain mysterious to a modern until he forces himself to realize that 'mud-pies' performed **81b** practically all the domestic functions which we parcel out among the supermarket-complexity of 'usable things' made of brick, wood, paper, porcelain, glass, tin, aluminium, iron, plastic, transistors, and literally everything we see about us in our houses except textiles. The houses and fences were built of that same mud from the front yard, casually moulded into blocks. There were no chairs or bedsteads; the tables were reeds woven into mats, and these may have supplemented the piling of cloaks or blankets which afforded all desirable comfort and warmth for repose. The furnace was a jar with coals in it. Light was provided by a jar with oil and a wick in it. The plumbing was a water-jar in the corner. The refrigeration was a porous jar whose perspiration cooled the contents. The canisters, plates, skillets, spoons, glasses, were jars. The brief-case and library-shelf was a jar. But not all the useful 'mud-pies' were receptacles. They provided the statuary or pictures on the wall, loom-weights, wheels for carts, toys for baby. Letters were written for centuries on a mud tablet, even with a pencil of mud, and enclosed in an envelope of mud; casual notes were jotted down on a sherd; and even for those who could afford writing on skins or papyrus, the inkstand and penwiper and writing-table were of clay, as recently found at Qumran.

When baked, this universality of mud-utensils **c** became paradoxically the most **destructible and** the most **indestructible** of realities. Smashing whenever dropped or colliding, the vessels had so little value and were so immediately replaceable that they were left to lie around in profusion. Indeed, a genuine usefulness of broken pottery lay in raising the floor-level, adding bulk and strength to the mud-bricks, serving as poor Job's knife or squeegee, or taking notes at Lachish. Because of the rapid turnover, styles in pottery became as ephemeral and as tyrannical as our own modern taste in teacups or millinery. Families moving to another town or quarter found it cheaper to smash the pottery they could not sell, rather than cart it expensively to be smashed along the way. In contrast, **coins** are transported easily and preserved through generations of displacements, which seems overlooked when Kelso in IDB 3,848 calls coins a better dating-agent than pottery, against Albright in the Wright-Filson *Atlas* p. 10. But pottery *survives* even when and where it is destroyed. The components of these pottery utensils simply *could* not lose their tell-tale form, unless by unthinkably futile systematic grinding down to powder. Inevitably, then, **d** pottery has survived for thousands of years to attest inexorably the date at which that 'level' of Palestine soil was occupied. Not that every single sherd betrays this information: that is a common misapprehension, due doubtless to some experts' whimsical glee at mystifying the populace. A broken jar, smashed into the number of pieces which will make least trouble, consists of perhaps twenty sherds whose form is too small or nondescript to identify it, unless it happens to bear painting or similar adornment. But it will have about ten pieces, mostly of the neck, also of base or handle, which not only identify its style and date but even suffice to give the exact dimensions and often (at least in combination) make possible a reliable drawing of the complete original. From these ugly-duckling sherds, by the insight of a Vincent, an Albright, a Mazar, and a Kenyon, has grown up out of nothing within our century the **science of chronology**. Naturally this science takes into account coins and literary attestations of earthquake or conflagration; also such by-products of nuclear research as the radiocarbon dating technique invented in 1946 and

81d applicable to only very bulky deposits of expendable organic materials untouched by other organic materials in course of extraction. From these techniques has been put together the following accurate yardstick or clock of Palestine chronology (photo in Sellers, IDB 2, 847).

e For the debate regarding transit from Early to Middle Bronze around 2000 B.C., see P. Lapp reported in *Jerome Commentary*, 1968, p. 663 (¶74:52) or *BASOR* 184, 1966, 26—35.

f From this newly-scientific table results an entirely revised—though by no means as yet assured—base for the **pivotal dates** of biblical chronology. Abraham is now universally dated some two centuries later than the 2100 B.C. to which fragmentary allusions within the Bible add up. Hammurabi, though the equation of him with Amraphel is discredited, bounds in 1700 the horizon of some two centuries of Abraham-tribe migrations. We cannot read any modern background-book without getting clearly in mind *which* of the three tenable Hammurabi-dates is being followed (see **79g** above). The Hyksos invasion of Egypt about 1700 B.C. seems plainly to reflect the saga of Joseph's brothers; and the Habiru Semitic marauders known to be in Canaan in 1370 possess the same name as the Hebrews, though this leaves untouched the question of *how many* 'Hebrews' were in Egypt. Rowley's hypothesis (*From Joseph to Joshua*, 1952) that the Jacob-tribes emigrated to Egypt only after this Habiru-uprising is as unnecessary as the former view (maintained as recently as 1933 in Cardinal Bea's *De Pentateucho*) that the Exodus took place in 1500 with the expulsion of the Hyksos. Universally now

g the Exodus is linked with Rameses II, 1301—1234. The majority opinion (Albright, Dominicans) considers him the Pharaoh of the **Exodus about 1270**, and regards his father Seti I as the Oppressor. But since the Oppressor in Ex 1:11 built the town named Rameses, we support CCHS (1) in the view that Rameses II was the oppressor, and the Exodus itself took place under Meneptah and is slantedly described in his 1228 stela proclaiming 'Israel defeated and without seed' (see **79u** above). The soil of

Palestine must be counted upon to add evidence for solv- **81g** ing this dilemma; if total absence of relevant artifacts at both Jericho and 'Ay be honestly acknowledged to have been so far the major defeat and frustration of archaeological exegesis, this merely heartens us to redouble our efforts both of reappraisal and of further search. Only with David's succeeding Saul do we have finally a firm bed-rock date, conveniently 1000 B.C. despite variants of a couple of years. Excavation has provided four concrete extra-biblical datings for biblical events, helping to anchor (though not yet solve!) the thorny problem of 'pre-or-post-dated' Kings chronology. No excavation-find has yet helped to unravel the tangle of Seleucid-Maccabee chronology (see now Bib 36 (1955) 430). But the Qumran jars and coins, and Olivet ossuaries, mark a first step toward narrowing down the dating-criteria of the NT era, which through all previous excavation-results remained almost indistinguishable from the two hundred years preceding and following.

Technology—Palestine chronology rests on the un- **h** contested universality of terracotta for the utensils of daily life, especially among the common folk. None the less, excavation has revealed a noteworthy progress in the use and manufacture of other commodities. **Beads**, even perhaps of rudimentary glass as early as the pyramids, and similar decorative trifles were made into necklaces as early as Ghassul 3500 B.C. A whole industry of bracelets, rings, and brooches grew up alongside. Scarabs for signature-seals (some naming Israelite kings) were carved out of porphyry and diorite; obsidian served for the tinier flints. Flint-tools themselves improved little, at least aesthetically, after the fan-scraper, so that their presence at the side of pottery betokens mostly stagnation. An exception of course would be the increasingly artistic use of **stone** instead of clay for figurines, but in the image-hating Jewish religion this repugnant trade never got a foothold. Some tent pins, mortars, and brayers are of stone; while of bone or ivory we have both statuettes and practical objects like combs and awls. Isolated objects **i** of meteoric **metal** are found from earliest times, and even

81e

Period	Begins	Typical artifacts
Old Stone	600,000	Fist-size flints, not retouched
Neanderthal	180,000	Willow-leaf flints, retouched; cave art (outside Palestine)
Mesolithic	12,000	Tiny flints curved to fit in sickle; agriculture-beginnings
Neolithic	B.C. 8,000	Polished flints; earliest pottery quite 'advanced', painted
Chalcolithic	4,000	Cornet-cup, churn, lug-handle, mat-base, rope-moulding; gray beaded ware, wall-frescoes; fan-scraper flint; basalt brazier
Early Bronze	3,200	Ledge-handle, hole-mouth, button-base; orange crisscross; wheel
Middle Bronze	2,000	Carination, maximum graceful body; tripod or parabola-base; black juglets with white pinpoints in bands (Yahudiyya)
Late Bronze	1,600	Chimney-bilbil, metallic ware; milk-bowl with wishbone-handle; Megiddo metope-painting; Mycenean glaze-like imports
Early Iron	1,200	Pinched lip; double handle; strainer spout; pilgrim-flask; Philistine swan-metope
Late Iron	900	Red ware, ring-burnish; dumpy heavy form; sand-stand pointed base
Persian etc.	600	Dearth of artifacts; Attic, Rhodian imports; sand-stand; coins!
Hellenistic	300	Eggshell-grey; fusiform unguentaries; sand-stand becoming Qumranoid
Early Roman	B.C. 50	Petra red eggshell; Qumran jars; flat ribbing; spout-circle lamps
Late Roman	A.D. 200	Sigillata, inimitably smooth red with maker's stamp; ribbing
Byzantine	500	(Style lags behind politics!) Cross! sharp-ridge metallic ribbing
Muslim-Crusade	800	Glaze

81i copper seemingly alloyed with subliminal proportions of tin; but genuine bronze appears in widespread use only after 2000. Thus the names of both Chalcolithic and Early Bronze eras are misnomers; the former could easily be revised to ceramolithic, but then it would be far more natural to lump into one archaeological era *all* the period involving earliest pottery sans metal, 6000–2000 B.C. Metal refineries dated under Solomon 950 B.C. by Glueck at Eilat (but retracted in BA, 1966.) and Mazar at Qasila (utilizing ceramic crucibles!) have prompted reappraisal of similar enigmatic installations at earlier excavations. Naturally the chief use of metal (and indeed, alas, all technological progress of all times) was chiefly in the armaments-race; Yadin has combined his archaeological and military competences into a study of the weapons known to us from excavated discovery— *The Art of Warfare in Biblical Lands* 1963. Ponderous stone presses for oil or wine and mills for grain (Capernaum!) must have utilized **wood** and metal for their functioning in a way that is not easy to reconstruct.

j Scarcely any wood object survives in the climate of Palestine; the discovery of some in a very charred state of slow-oxidation was hailed by Miss Kenyon at Jericho as a triumph. Presence of wood roof-beams over houses or sapling-trunks to uphold them is inferred mostly from stone plinths within the room; also from ash-chunks or simple holes, within a buried heap of fallen masonry. The invention of **glass** is associated by classic authors with biblical Acco and Tyre shortly before the Christian era; this is an oversimplification but doubtless due to production-conditions then current. Minting of **coins** after 500 B.C. quickly became a major industry of Antioch and other Near E centres.

k It is important to bear in mind that both archaeology and technology are intensely concerned with the production of **written records**, but strictly on their material side. The *content* of these records, whether a single word scribbled on a pebble or the fifty-thousand densely-written clay tablets of Mari, pertains to the same class of historical documentation as Homer or Plutarch or our daily newspaper; assembled in ANET-ANEP or more usably in D. Winton Thomas *Documents from OT Times* (London, 1958). But the chronological context in which unsigned undated writings were first unearthed is archaeology's tenderest care, as has appeared massively in Qumran research. The **writing-materials** too are concrete monuments which speak a language different from that which is incised upon them; see A. Lucas, *Ancient Egyptian Materials*, 1962[4]. This includes the rudimentary pencils, styli, nails, brushes, quills; paints and inks of vegetable or metallic base; granite, in Egypt's obelisks, wall-plaster in her tombs; limestone at Lachish; clay at Babylon and 'Amarna; papyrus conserved for 4,000 years in Egypt's dry climate; goatskin and its transformation into parchment at Pergamum; transit from rolled-up scrolls (our word 'volume') to the codex of turned pages, doubtless called 'book' (*bíblos*) because of some hitherto-undiscovered pre-eminence of Egypt's Syrian coastal enclave at Byblos.

l Also the type of **alphabet** used may be considered the archaeologist's domain, even if more properly assigned to the kindred sciences of epigraphy and palaeography. Byblos again and the Sinai mines provide the oldest evidences, from 1500 B.C., both undeciphered really, yet agreed to reflect the order of our Semitic alphabet, first clearly recorded in a tablet of Ugarit found 1949 (ANEP 263). Brief cuneiform writing has appeared, syllabic at Ta'anak and alphabetic at Beth-Shemesh. The earliest Palestinian writing which survives is relatively

late, since the Lachish ostraca do not really antedate the **81k** Babylonian Exile. The Gihon tunnel ('Siloam') inscription of King Hezekiah dates from 700 and is long and well preserved (now in İstanbul). The **stela of Mesha** king of Moab ('Moabite Stone') discovered at Dibon in 1868 recounts the 840 B.C. revolt against the 'Omri dynasty implied in 2 (4) Kgs 3:5. Oldest of all is the brief Gezer calendar of 1000, cryptic even if we agree it is a schoolboy's agricultural reminder. The other epigraphic material consists mostly of laconic or abbreviated tax-receipts scribbled on potsherds. To claim that any of these finds attest the use of whatever we mean by the 'Hebrew' language as distinct from Canaanite (-Ugaritic) and Aramaic must seem unrealistic in the light of Rosen's proof that biblical Hebrew differs more from the Mesha dialect than from Aramaic!

Architecture—Early Palestine excavations relied **82a** understandably upon architectural-styles as a dating-criterion. Re-reading the debate about the 2000 year range assigned by sober analysis to the walls of Jericho or Mamre-Hebron warns us post-factum of the utter futility of the assumption that aesthetic or even technological superiority implies later date. Even the so-called Herodian masonry criterion transferred from the Jerusalem wailing-wall to other contested sites seems to fit centuries earlier or later at Sebastiya and Beth-Shearim. This is not to deny that certain more specific manifestations such as the casemate-wall, headers-stretchers masonry, and proto-Aeolic capital (all identified at Solomonic Megiddo) afford genuinely valid chronological indications. The diagonal ribbing of Nabatean stonework at Dibon seems uncontestable. But the Greco-Roman pediment décor resolutely dated to the century of Jesus at Qedron or Capernaum has been displaced to two centuries earlier at the one by Vincent, and later at the other by Orfali. Criteria proving Roman masonry at the Antonia Lithostrotos or Gallicante stone-stair are severely assessed by Benoit, though he defends the stone threshold over which Jesus walked to execution. We must therefore firmly agree that the architecture of Palestine will interest and help exegesis *only* insofar as its dating is *antecedently* established by reliable external criteria, chiefly pottery, found *within the bricks themselves* and especially in the *foundation-trenches* whose relation to apparently-adjacent debris can and must be rigorously observed and determined.

It is chiefly the **Walls of Jerusalem** that have **b** clamored with tragicomical frustration for the application of such criteria, in order to yield their indispensable contribution not only to that city's history but to the very origins and nature of Davidic Israel. Though massive independent (not to say antagonistic) researches of Vincent and Simons tend to agree that the SW hill was enclosed between 950 and 700 B.C., the clarion voice of Albright holds out for as late as 30 B.C. (Avi-Yonah and Galling also postexilic), while Dalman makes it part of the Jebusite settlement prior to David in 1000! Similarly the two recent Catholic rivals agree to reject the well-substantiated Robinson-Sukenik North Wall of A.D. 50, which Vincent claims to trace along the present Herod-Damascus-gate line. More cogent is their agreement, now shared by most Protestants, that the Robinson objections do not invalidate the traditional (Orthodox-Franciscan) Calvary outside the W wall. Other Roman tombs are significantly visible within that building, while a mile N and W are tombs still containing a man-size stone, round and fitted into a groove to roll in front of the tomb-opening (Mk 16:3). On Miss Kenyon's more recent work at the Ophel and Damascus Gate walls, see PEQ

82b 98, 1966, 82; and E. Vogt, *Bib* 78, 1967, pp. 337–358.

c The best surveys of Palestine architecture are in Hebrew: M. Avi-Yonah's in *Qadmoniyyot Arsenu* (Tel Aviv: Me'uhad, 1955), and S. Yeivin's in *Ensiqlopediya Miqrait* (Jerusalem: Bialik, 1954) 2, 179–262; cf R. Hamilton IDB 1, 209–215. The only references to architecture in de Vaux's *Ancient Israel* are under Religion and War. Reconstruction of the Jerusalem **Temple** has been a pastime of experts in every era; currently one must guard against Schick and even take into account reserves of the Albright school against the otherwise admirably up-

d to-date Howland-Garber model. Despite Bagatti, *Bib* 43, 1962, p. 1, the 'Rock' enshrined in 'Omar's Dome' is the threshing-floor of Ornan and the sanctuary of the Crusade *Templum Domini*; but experts are so far simply unable to agree whether David located over this rock the Holy of Holies or rather the Altar of Sacrifice of the temple-forecourt. Ultimately more useful than juggling the cryptic measurements of Chronicles, Ezekiel, Josephus, and Pierotti, is the simple gaze at an undoubted 'parallel' such as the (Hittite!) ground plan of Hasor. Also, though notably antedating Solomon, the Idfu design incorporates elements identical to others surviving from pre-Solomonic Egypt; and the blueprints of Solomon's Phoenician architect are overtly recognizable at Syro-Hellenistic Ba'albek.

83a Urbanism—like technology is a by-product of the armaments-race. The normal mode of habitation would be each family under its own vine and fig tree, surrounded by its own plot of land and constituting with its neighbours an unwalled village, like Ghassul or the towns given the name *haser*. Under threat of raid, however, not only did the larger agglomerations have to be defended by a wall; but the smaller groupings had to run helter-skelter to the nearest refuge. The forts of Rehoboam in 2 Chr 11 are so spread about that they must be regarded as a *civil defence* of existing population-centres, rather than a frontier 'Maginot Line'; the forts of 'Uzzîyâ 2 Chr 26:10 are more like outposts, including Qumran! The allegedly typical-Hyksos sloping or battered rampart style involves in fact wholly disparate structural characteristics at various sites; and the Albright-Kenyon reasons for linking them with the rise of horse-chariot warfare are highly

b controvertible (Y. Yadin). The excavation of 'Ay is best interpreted as showing how under the menace of Joshua's invaders, villagers from Bethel and its environs took refuge for defence behind the long-mouldering ramparts which had come to be known as simply 'the ruin' ('Ay = tel). Like farmers on the slopes of Vesuvius, villagers gradually came to feel that life would be more organized and serene if they just resided permanently within a rampart, trekking to their farm-chores at increasingly greater distances, or abandoning them in favour of lucrative urban pursuits. The jubilee of Lv 25 and the disconnected social legislations which it recapitulates reflect an effort to stem this flight from the farm by making small family landholdings inalienable in perpetuity. But the increase of urbanism had its advantages, too. Where many are clustered densely together and desperately in need of turning an honest penny, experts in specialized techniques forge to the

c fore, and ingenuity spawns new industries. Thus the mammoth **town-walls** excavated at Jericho, Hasor, Tirsa, and even those surviving uninterruptedly in the Jerusalem of our own day, are a symbol of technological progress too.

d Like other armaments, the town-wall was cannily publicized as having uses for peace too. To climb up and walk along the parapet was not only the ancient

equivalent of entertainment for young people, it also **83d** brings Jerusalemites even today a refreshing breeze and beautiful view. Moreover where strategy dictated a double line of wall, as at Jericho, it was a natural step to filling the insulation-space with rooms called **casemates** as at Megiddo, suitable for storing weapons and boilable oil, but also eventually for housing-projects. There was normally only one **city gate**, consisting of e several mammoth portals facing various directions swerving from the ramp of access (Megiddo, Lachish). This is most strikingly the case with the city-gates of modern Jerusalem; but the large number of gate-names attested in Neh 2:13ff and the allusions of the prophets are implausible, and must refer to purely internal passages. (In Damascus even today the word for *gate* means simply 'street'.) The city-gate as excavated at Balâta or Mirsim contained numerous rooms, suitable for lodging guests of the government like a sort of Blair House. At Lachish these rooms served as **archive** or Record-Office; while the use of the city-gate as tribunal and parliament is attested in 2 Sm 15:2; Am 5:10 and throughout the Mediterranean world (J. Gray, PEQ 85 (1953) 118; C. Wolf JNES 6 (1947) 98; G. Evans, Jour Rel Hist 2 (1962)1). Hence we should really translate the word for *gate* in peacetime contexts as '**Courthouse**'.

Before the advent of the automobile, there was very f good reason for building the houses close together and even terraced on top of one another over the narrow winding streets. This assured a maximum of warmth in winter and of coolness in summer, and convenient nearness of points of interest at all times. Tourists who find repellent the crowded irregular hill-towns of Palestine or Italy need only recall how without a car our broad avenues would be interminable and comfortless in the blasts of winter wind or blanketed in humid summer sun. Albright's Mirsim probably gives us the fullest data regarding domestic architecture. At Tirsa de Vaux found not only 'Omri's palace but also a narrow street separating the well-built solid houses of the rich from rickety shacks of the poor, exactly as blasted by Am 5:10; 3:15. Since de Vaux doubtless intends to gather his extensive g experience of excavated architecture into a separate volume, his *Ancient Israel* index includes 'house' only as equated with family, a significant insight, though Sellers IDB 2, 657 notes it means 'abode' 2000 times in the Bible. Houses in the plain as at Beersheba were made of mudbrick; samples from Jericho and Ghassul show finger-indentations for taking the mortar (also of mud); also traces left by the needed straw thickener (Ex 5:7). A slanting roof of boughs or reeds kept the infrequent rain from seeping down too destructively; and when a wall fell over it was simply fused with the womb of mother earth again and moistened to raise the ground level or provide new bricks for rebuilding. On mountaintop-sites from Hebron to Samaria stone was cheaper than dirt! Tooled stonework reproved in Ex 20:25 (at least h for those monumental structures where it would seem most in place) begins in Canaan only shortly before the Israelites' arrival, but reaches a peak at Sabastiya—both under 'Omri and in Herod's time. We must beware of statistical inferences from the proportion of stone houses which survive at least in groundplan; brick houses are attested too, though their reconstruction is more problematical. Round or apsidal brick houses, a Stone Age characteristic at Jericho and Meser, seem thereafter unheard-of till Parthian Warka. Houses on the city wall with a window opening on the great outdoors play an important role in the salvation of Rahab Jos 2:15 and Paul 2 Cor 11:33. The inn of Lk 2:7 was a caravanserai or khan as

83h still visible in Sidon or Damascus: a rectangular enclosure where families set up their pavilions near the wall and let animals huddle together in the middle; since more warmth and privacy could be found in a cave, we should render the Gospel words rather 'since the inn was no place for them' and praise instead of blaming the Bethlehemites who made such a hillside cave available for Mary's parturition.

84a Our information about house-structure is magnificently illumined by the discovery of numerous house-shaped **ossuaries** or small bone-caskets, all from chalcolithic times; chiefly from Hedera and Azor, but never at Ghassul; though in clay, they show bolts and projecting beams most realistically imitating wood-construction. From this same period, or at least from its Beersheba manifestation, are attested underground houses of burrowing type connected by tunnels as for sepulchral architecture. This too is of the burrowing type in the OT period, especially at Middle Bronze Jericho, though generally not connected catacomb-fashion. Limestone-hollowed **tombs** of slightly architectural character must have been known during the period of the Kings, though in searching for them we are hindered by uncertainty as to how late or literally-taken was the rabbinic prohibition against burial near habitations. Frequent child-burials under floors, though doubtless Canaanite, cannot surely *all* be regarded as

b horrid sacrifices detested in 1 (3) Kgs 16:34. With the Hellenistic era at Maresa is inaugurated a conspicuous new fashion of rock-hewn catacombs involving a genuine architectural facade, with loculi (Hebrew *kokim*), sometimes combined with a sort of arched-over altar called **arcosolium**; this style reaches its peak in the Jerusalem Synedria tombs from the century before Christ, to which may be ascribed also Queen Saddan's tomb (called by de Saulcy 'Tombs of the Kings') and the three conspicuous free-standing monuments still visible in Kedron valley. The fantastic dream-world of **Petra** consists almost exclusively of such rock-hewn tombs. Also contemporaneous is the pleasing multiplication of columns in avenues as at the **Jerash** oval forum or at Palmyra. Use of the 'vault' or genuine **arch** as an architectural element seems

to have come into Palestine only with Herod (so Hamilton **84b** IDB 1,210 despite adjacent blueprint of 5th cent. Lachish arches!), but the 'false-arch' of horizontal doorway-stones gradually projecting as they go up until they meet overhead is noticeable in a tunnel of Hasor imitating this frequent Bogazköy style.

Since the OT era lasted some twenty times as long as **c** the period from Herod's birth to John's Gospel, it is natural that excavation hits upon far more strata of that era and thus gives the whole of archaeology an OT flavour. But the real anguish of NT spade-research is something quite different. Localities associated with the life of Jesus, being few in number and concentrated in area, have prompted a feverish zeal of exploration. As a result, we are confronted in almost every case with two or three 'rival' sites clamorously validated by 'facts' of excavation which upon closer look may appear to be rather wishful devotion. There are two Canas, two or three Emmauses, three 'houses of Jesus' at Nazareth, two Lithostrota, two houses of Caiaphas, two Transfiguration-sites, two Ascensions and Gethsemanis, two Mounts of the Sermon or three or none. There was even a brief American-born flurry for a variant Calvary; and if none of the alternatives for Capernaum are now considered, that is due more to asphalt access-roads than to research. These rivalries **d** are annoying and may eventually quite alienate the hopeful inquirer. But he must realize that this very wrangling is the concrete exemplification of scientific laws. The emulation is a guarantee that no relevant data will pass unnoticed for lack of interest, and each claim of 'fact' however biassed may in due course turn out to embody some usable grain of truth. At any rate, one genuine emphatic 'Witness' of Christianity is the fact that its enthusiasm for the soil where Jesus walked has unloosed pursestrings and multiplied progresses in excavation-technique. The result has been a vast background-documentation for the biblical era. Even beyond that, search for traces of the 'Man of Galilee' has brought us *homo galileensis* and other Stone Age attestations of man's earliest origins more numerous than in any comparable area of our planet.

MEASURES, WEIGHTS, MONEY AND TIME

BY ROBERT NORTH S.J.

(For **85a-d** see Table on p. 106)

e **Bibliography—(a) General**: G. Barrois, IB (1952) 1, 152—57; A. E. Berriman, 'A New Approach to the Study of Ancient Metrology', RA 49 (1955) 193—201; R. Bratcher, 'Weights, Money, Measures and Time', *Bible Translator*, 10 (1959) 165—74; R. de Vaux, AI, 178—209. **(b) Weights and Measures**: H. Lewy, 'Assyro-Babylonian and Israelite Measures of Capacity', JAOS 64 (1944) 65—73; A. Oxé, 'Kor und Kab', *Bonner Jahrbuch* 147 (1942) 91—126; R. Scott, 'Weights and Measures of the Bible', BA 22 (1959) 22—39; id, 'The Hebrew Cubit', JBL 77 (1958) 202—14; A. Segré, 'Documentary Analysis of Ancient Palestinian Units of Measure', JBL 64 (1945) 357—75; id, 'Babylonian, Assyrian and Persian Measures', JAOS 64 (1944) 73—81; O. Sellers, 'Weights and Measures' IDB 4, 828—39; F. Skinner, 'Measures' in *History of Technology* (1955) 1, 774; Y. Yadin, 'Ancient Judean Weights', *Studia Hiero-* f *solymitana* (Jerusalem Bialik, 1960) 0, 1 17. (c) **Money**: F. Banks, *Coins of Bible Days*, 1955; H. Hamburger, 'Money', IDB 3, 423—35; R. Loewe, '(Hag 1, 6) The Earliest Biblical Allusion to Coined Money?' PEQ 87 (1955) 141—50; A. Reifenberg, *Ancient Jewish Coins* (Jerusalem, 1940); D. Schlumberger, *L'argent* g *grec dans l'empire achéménide*, 1953; **(d) Time**: S. De Vries, 'Calendar', IDB (1962) 1, 483—88; S. Gandz, 'Studies in the Hebrew Calendar' JQR 39 (1949) 259—80; 40 (1950) 157—72, 251—77; A. Jaubert, *La date de la cène*, 1957 (see P. Skehan, CBQ 20 (1958) 192—99; H. Cazelles, Bib 43 (1962) 202—12; J. Obermann, JBL 75 (1956) 285—97); E. Jenni, 'Time', IDB 4, 642—49; J. Morgenstern, 'The Three Calendars of Ancient Israel', HUCA 1 (1924) 13—78; 10 (1935) 1—148; 20 (1947) 1—36; 21 (1948) 365—496 [17 (1942) 1—52 by J. and H. Lewy] J. Naveh, IEJ 12 (1962) 27—32; R. North, 'Maccabean Sabbath Years', Bib 34 (1953) 501—15; id, 'Derivation of Sabbath', Bib 36 (1955) 182—201; id, *Sociology of the Biblical Jubilee*, 1954, 122—92; R. Parker, *Calendars of Ancient Egypt*: Chicago University, 1950; R. Parker and W. Dubberstein, *Babylonian Chronology*, 1956[3]; E. Thiele, *The Mysterious Numbers of the Hebrew Kings*, 1965[2].

86a Length: Measurement among the Jews as among all other peoples was in origin a comparison with parts of the body. Systematization fixed by law in Egypt and Babylonia was borrowed, but eclectically. Values assigned here in our chart are shown by recent research to have varied within certain limits.

The '**Elbow** (-to-fingertip)', called **cubit**, occurs at Ugarit and a hundred times in the Bible. Three computations are known. The Egyptian, 24 finger-widths of each 0.8 inch or 1.8 cms, was 'common' (Dt 3:11: Og's bed 162 inches long). This fits the Siloam tunnel inscription: 1200 cubits = 533.1 metres (or 1749 feet, which by coincidence gives 17.49 inches per cubit). The Temple was thus rather small: 90 × 30 ft., 45 ft. high (1 (3) Kgs 6:2) according to the 'common' cubit (2 Chr 3:3). But **86a** the Temple blueprints in Ezek 40:5 used the 'Great Cubit' of 28 finger-widths, 20.39 inches or just a half-metre. This equals the 'Royal' cubit of Egypt, but that was 27 finger-widths in Mesopotamia, says Herodotus, 1, 178. This fits two 'graduated' statues of Gudea of Lagash, 2000 B.C. The sword-length *gomed*, only in Jg 3:16, is 'cubit' in RSV but 'span' in Gr. Four cubits of water make a fathom (Ac·27:28). The 'reed' (our 'rod') was common in Sumer in Ezekiel's sense of 6 cubits. But a rod or reed normally meant a measuring-stick; the opulent Egyptian example pictured in IDB 4, 836 is one cubit long.

The **palma** or four-fingers is some three inches, and **b** the maximum extension or 'span' of the fingers is seven to nine inches. The ratio of *palma* to span is given as 3:1 by de Vaux, 2:1 by Sellers. We suggest 5:2 as more realistic. At any rate the hand-width is one-sixth cubit. The Vg confuses span and *palma* under the one term *palmus*. 'Finger' as a unit occurs only Jer 52:21, but often in the Talmud.

Distances were commonly measured by walking-time; **c** a 'day's journey'. Neither foot nor pace (even in 2 Sm 6:13) served as a unit of distance, but 'mile' (Mt 5:41) is the Roman 'thousand (paces)', 1477.6 metres or 4860 feet as compared with our 5280. The more ordinary distance-unit was the **stadion**. Its computation at Alexandria as 606 ft. was normative. Since variants of 576 and 630 were in use, it may very aptly be rendered 'furlong' (660 ft.). Just by chance the 606-ft. stadion turns out to be almost exactly ten thousand 'finger'-units. The 60 stadia from Emmaus to Jerusalem in Lk 24:13 is 6 miles (11 km), corrected by Origen to 160 stadia or 18.4 miles (30 km). The *schoenus* of 2 Mc 11:5 is forty stadia in Pliny, though 60 in Herodotus; and the geometer Hero reckons both 48 and 30; this last would best fit the 5 schoeni from Jerusalem to Bet-Sur (actually 18 miles, 29 km, some 157 stadia).

Area. Not a single unit of surface occurs in the whole **d** Bible. A 'yoke' of land (Is 5:10; 1 Sm 14:14) is perceptively rendered by Jerome *iugerum*, which comes from *iugum* but means a half-acre: what a pair of oxen could plough (in a day, Arabic *faddân* implies rather in a season). In Babylonia, land-area was reckoned by its growth: oddly, by bushel of *seed* rather than of yield; so 1 (3) Kgs 18:32. In Egypt the linear measure was used ('squared' to be supplied): a hundred 'cubits' (Gr. *arourá*) amounted to 2/3 acre. Today land in Palestine is measured by the *dunam*, 1000 m² (some 32 × 32 m), about one-tenth hectare or a quarter-acre, needful for reading excavation-reports. The hectare is 100 metres sq or 10,000 sq metres, equivalent to 2,471 acres. An acre is 208 feet square, more exactly 43,560 square feet (0.4047 hectare), half a U.S. city block (one house and lot is about an eighth-acre). The mound of Jericho measures 150 × 300 metres, some four hectares or eleven acres; Megiddo and Lachish are each 12 hectares

85a Length

measure	Finger *'eṣba'* *daktylos*	Palm *ṭepaḥ* *palaistē*	Span *zeret* *spithamē*	Cubit *'ammâ* *pēchus*	Reed *qaneh* *kálamos*	Furlong *stádion*	Mile	Schoenus
in units	1	4	10	1 / 24	6 / 144	416.4 / 10,000	3331.2 / 80,000	16,656 / 400,000
ft/inches	0/0.728	0/2.915	0/7.28	1/5.47	8/8.33	606/0	4860/0	24,300
metres	0.0185	0.074	0.185	0.444	2.664	184.7	1477.6	7388

Conversion factors (to next column): ×4, ×2.5, ×2.4, ×6, ×69.4, ×8, ×5

b Volume (* = liquid)

	Finger *log**	Palm *qab*	Span *omer* *'issaron*	Cubit *hin**	Reed *se'â*	Furlong *'epa* *bat**	Mile *letek*	Schoenus *homer* *kor (*?)*
in units	1	4	[0.1] 7.2	12	24	[1.0] 72	360	[10] 720
British (imperial gallon = 277.2 cu. in.)		1.07 qt	2 qt	3.22 qt	6.4 qt	0.6 bushel 19.2 qt 4.83 gallons	96 qt	192 qt
U.S. (gallon = 231 cu. in.)	0.62 liquid pt.	1.1 dry qt	2 dry qt	3.86 liquid qt	6.4 dry qt 0.2 bushel	0.62 bushel 19.97 dry qt 23.25 liquid qt 5.8 gallons	3.1 bu	6.4 bu 58.1 gal
litre = 10 cm³	0.3	1.2	2.2	3.6	7.3	22	110	220

Conversion factors (to next column): ×4, ×1.8, ×1.6, ×2, ×3, ×5, ×2

c Weight (* Attic; £ as money)

in units	Finger *gera* (£ *as*)	Palm **obol*	Span *beqa'* *drachm (£) £ denarius	Cubit *pym* (? *nsp*)	Reed *sheqel* (£) (£ stater)	Furlong *mna* (*) (£)	Mile	Schoenus *talent* (*) (£)
in units	1	6	10	13	20	1000		60,000
grams	0.57	3.8	5.71	7.6	11.4	571.2		34.2 kg
ounces	0.02	0.13	0.2	0.27	0.4	20		75.6 lbs
£	1d		10d		4s 2d	£5		£300
$	1¢		10¢		50¢	$12		$718

Conversion factors (to next column): ×6, ×1.3, ×1.3, ×1.3, ×50, ×60

d Calendar

	Babylonian	Canaanite	Maccabean
January	Shebat		Peritt(-os)
February	Adar		Dystr(-os)
March	Nisan	Abib	Xanthik
April	Iyyar	Ziw	Artemisi
May	Siwan		Daisi
June	Tammuz		Panem
July	Ab	Sak	Loi
August	Elul		Gorpiai
September	Tishri	Etanim	Hyperberetai
October	Marḥeshwan	Bul	Dioscor
November	Kislew		Appellai
December	Tebet		Audynai

86d (30 acres), and the circumvallation at the foot of Haṣor mound is 240 acres!

e **Volume**, or **capacity**, was then as now based upon a unit applied to both **liquid and dry** commodities. The dry multiples of our *quart* are incommensurate with the liquid. But there is reason to maintain that the **ephah**, (Heb. *'epâ*) was called **bath** (Heb. *bat*), for liquids, and could be integrated into the same continuous system. At least the fragmentary information we possess cannot exclude this working hypothesis. Variability of measures of capacity is due to the fact that they are just the names of utensils used in commerce or in the home: some Egyptian (*'epâ, hin*), some Phoenician (Ugaritic *homer, leket, log;* Aramean *bat*), some Babylonian (*kor, se'â, qab*).

Reduction of the ephah (*'epâ*) to litres was laboriously attempted by Barrois, at first on the basis of JosAnt 8 (57) 2, 9 equating *log* and *xestēs/sextarius* (0.54 litre; 0.96 pint), whence the bath (*bat*) would be 39 litres (8.6 British imperial gallons; 10.3 U.S.): this is the estimate adopted by Power in CCHS[1]. Two jar-fragments discovered at Duwayr-Lachish marked *bt* seemed to Inge reconstructable as 45 litres, and another from Nasba-Mispa held 40. But when another jar marked *bt* found at Mirsim-Debir was judged to be only half that large (22 litres according to Albright), Barrois in IB took as his bath '(one half) the average' of previously-reconstructable jars: surely a very arbitrary and narrow basis for so

f swooping a conclusion. Albright's figure, though precarious, is at least a concrete empirical datum, which was worked out into a whole metrology by Scott, and which our chart adopts merely as a concrete plausibility. The IDB article by Sellers rates the bath as 5.5 gallons, lower than Albright or Barrois; the ephah he makes exactly sixteen quarts as against Albright's 19.2. De Vaux ends up denying the validity of all assumption that the bath is even roughly univocal in early and late Jewish history, though he notes a Qumran charcoal-scrawl of '2 se'â 7 log' on a 35-litre jar, which would fit Inge's maximal 45-litre bath. However de Vaux admits that the application of this norm to the *homer* proves absurdly high, though Milik strongly defends it.

g The bronze laver or 'Sea' of the Temple was ten cubits in diameter. Its radius was thus 2.22 metres and its area 15.48 m². Its depth was equal to its radius, thus giving volume 34.37 m³. This is declared in 1 (3) Kgs 7:23 equal to 2000 *bat*, whereby the *bat* would be 17 litres. But 2 Chr 4:5 for the same dimensions gives 3000 *bat*, or 11 litres each. Clearly both alternatives are hyperbolic, and do not exclude our chart's 22-litre *bat*. In Zech 5:6 a woman can fit inside an *'epâ*-measure; but it is a vision, in which one could also see a woman inside a medicine-bottle. Sellers estimates the *'epâ* as we do, at about a half-bushel; but his table varies unexplainably for the multiples, and he claims only 'somewhere sometime some of these estimates would be good'!

h The equation *'epâ* = *bat* = one-tenth (*homer* = *kor*) is from Ezek 45:11. Comparing Ex 16:36 with Nm 15:4, we learn that *'omer* = *'issaron* = one-tenth *'epâ*. From Babylonian records we learn that 1 *gur* = *kor* = 30 (*sutu* = *se'â*) = 180 (*qa* = *qab*). The earlier Assyrian equation *imêru* (*homer*) = 10 *sutu* does not equate *gur* with Ezekiel's *kor*; there may have been a devaluation, but even the larger figure falls short of our chart. *Homer* is a donkey-load, for grain-quantities large but scarcely much over 6 bushels or 50 gallons; Nuzi portrays it as less than four bushels. Even this amount is absurdly large both for the quails per man in Nm 11:32 and for the seed needed per *'epâ* of crop in

Is 5:10; but these are hyperboles inculcating a moral **86h** lesson. *Letek* in Hos 3:2 and Ugarit is smaller than a *homer;* following Jerome we reckon it as half. Jerome renders both '*omer* and the hundred-times-larger *homer* as *gomer!* The Egyptian *hnw* was only a seventh of our Heb. *hin*-estimate. The *artaba* of Dn 14:3 is a Persian measure short of two bushels. The *metrētēs*, 9 gallons (Jn 2:6); *choenix*, one quart (0.9–1.2 litres; Apoc 4.6); *modius*, less than a peck (in Mt 5:15 'light under a *bushel*' metaphorical for the *container*); *xestēs* (Mk 7:4, also a container); and other NT measures are Hellenistic.

Weight. Throughout ancient western Asia, the **sheqel** **87a** was the unit for both weighing and paying (really the same verb even in Latin!). In the Babylonian 'sexagesimal' computation, the notation 'unit written in front of zero' represented the next number after *five* instead of after *nine* as in the Egyptian and modern 'decimal' system (or after *one* in electronic brains). Thus as the U.S. has 100 cents to the dollar and 100 dollars to the basic large banknote, so the Babylonians reckoned 60 sheqels to the mna and 60 mnas to the talent. (This system has survived in our time-computation of minutes and seconds.) Ezek (45:12) seems to have tried to impose this norm, but the more common usage of Bible and Ugarit devalues the mna to 50 sheqels, doubtless under influence of the decimal system, like the Palestine British pound divided into 100 *grush*.

Excavation has revealed some fifty **marked weights** **b** in the Palestine of Jeremiah's day, chiefly at Duwayr-Lachish. The units 1, 2, 4, and 8 are accompanied by the sign for sheqel, a truncated 8. The unit weight averages 0.41 ounces or 11.5 grams. This equals roughly the weight of half-a-crown or a half-dollar. Strangely, the weight from Gezer marked 'royal' weighs *less*. It may have been lightened by oxidation. There was a 'heavy' sheqel at Ugarit, assumed to be somewhat greater than the normal (9.5 grams) even if not actually *double* like the Babylonian 'royal' units (8.4/16.8 grams: de Vaux). Sellers claims this 'royal' weight was only 5% above the respective 'normal' and 'heavy' counterparts, indicating 'payments to the royal treasury were slightly larger than the same sums used in ordinary transactions' (compare 2 Sm 14:26). The 'sanctuary sheqel' (Ex 30:13 and often) may have been simply a *standard* kept by the priests (though de Vaux rejects inferences from Germer-Durand's 'Caiphas-house' weights), or possibly the 20% markup of Lv 27:13. Naturally the 'official heavy sheqel' had nothing to do with the ineradicable human trait of keeping two sets of weights according to whether you are buying or selling (Dt 25:13; Prv 20:23).

Several weights marked **pym** 'two mouths' or two- **c** thirds, do in fact weigh some 8 grams, as against the sheqel-average 11.4. This is now claimed to be the meaning of 1 Sm 13:21, 'it cost a *pym* to sharpen'. Other excavated weights are marked *nsp*. This corresponds to the Arabic *nusf*, 'half', and the name appears as a half-sheqel at Ugarit; but the Palestine weight averages 10 grams, and is thus a sort of heavy *pym*. 'It would be gratuitous to say that the average represents the standard; doubtless the average will be changed as more inscribed weights are found' (Sellers). Some *pym*-samples are heavier than *nsp*, and others lighter than *beqa'*.

Talent is a Greco-Roman word meaning originally **d** 'balance-scale'. It represents the older Ugaritic-Hebrew *kikkar*, 'round (-stone-weight)'. The 'balance', *moznayim*, is also often attested in the Bible; it functioned with weights instead of with the modern 'graduated scale'. The weights were called 'stones'. Excavation has revealed thousands, often stamped with the amount; sometimes

87d they were in metal or in artistic forms (photos IDB 4, 831). **Mna**, in Heb. *māneh*, means simply 'counting'; its occurrence is rare, being generally replaced by '*n* sheqels'. The fine of 30 sheqels in Ex 21:32 is a half-mna in Hammurabi. The *qesita* of Gn 33:19 seems to have been two or three mnas (Greek *amnós*, which may however refer to the price or weight of a lamb).

e **Coinage** was invented only with the Lydians about 600 B.C.; in 500 the earliest international coin is named after Darius the **daric**, worth £2 or $5, *adarkon* in Ez 8:27. The daric is probably meant also by *darkmon* of Ez 2:69, though this properly means the later Athenian 'owl'-**drachma**. Mention of the daric in 1 Chr 29:7 is anachronistic, but the use of fixed weights as money-equivalent must have been gradually gaining ground (Gn 20:16, 37:28). The normal value of the **sheqel** was its weight in silver, but gold was sometimes specified (*both* in 2 (4) Kgs 18:14 = Sennacherib ANET 288), rated at sixteen times the price of silver instead of thirteen as today. Coins marked YHD about 350 B.C. were apparently minted by 'Juda' as Persian province. In practice the Jewish sheqel-coin was equated with such neighbouring units as the stater, tetradrachm, or argenteus. Though the argenteus officially weighed twenty grams more, this eight percent was far less than the variation due to deterioration, alloy, and 'business methods'. The Gospel 'penny' or **denarius**, though rated at a dime or shilling, should realistically be regarded as a guinea or $3, a minimum daily wage in English-speaking countries; perhaps $1 for underdeveloped areas. Our own modern penny, negligible small-change, stands roughly between the *as* (*sárion*) of Mt 10:29 and its double, the *dipondius* of Lk 12:6. The *leptón* of Mk 12:42 or its double in Mt 5:26 may be reckoned at a mill, Arabic *fils*.

f **In Maccabean times**, the government mints were at 'Akko, Sidon, Tyre, Joppe, Gaza. Over 500 fine silver coins from Tyre dated to what would be 8 B.C., were found cached at Qumran. Other coins minted by the Jewish high-priests beginning 110 B.C. are the chief dating-criteria of the Qumran excavation. The Herods have left us a considerable coinage, though Jesus shows familiarity with Caesar's minting in the immortal Mt 22:21. Coins struck by Pontius Pilate do not bear his name but that of Tiberius (IDB 3, 428; picture 433). The majority of Jewish coins in modern collections are from the Bar-Kokba rebellion, A.D. 135.

g **Calendar.** Biblical months are mostly specified by number instead of name. The older books use Canaanite names: Passover-month is Abib in Ex-Dt; and three **87g** others occur in the Temple-dedication 1 (3) Kgs 6—8. Of these names, only Etanim and Bul (says De Vries; de Vaux adds Ziw) occur in Phoenician inscriptions, along with some names of other months. In the Arad excavation Ṣak has now been found as the name perhaps of a summer month, cf Is 18:4: PEQ 95 (1963), 3. In post-exilic biblical books occur seven Babylonian month-names, and the other five are attested in contemporaneous Jewish Elephantine papyri.

The calendar was lunisolar. The word and the very notion of month imply the moon's phases. But to keep these synchronized with solar-seasonal variation, eleven days per year have to be added. This was not done annually, nor by lengthening some months as among us (Leap Year was decreed ineffectually in Egypt 237 B.C., effectively only by Caesar). Instead, a whole extra month Adar was inserted every third year or so. This is known from Talmudic practice; there is no hint of it in the Bible, unless Nm 9:11 refers to postponing Passover from Second Adar to Nisan rather than from Nisan to Iyyar. Cappadocian and Arab-farmer hints of a 350-day year of 7 calendaric units of 50 days (and/or years) may account for the sabbath/jubilee year styliz-ing of Lv 25.

'Postdating' versus 'predating' enigmas of Israel's **h** regnal years arise partly from the fact that New Year (not a solemnity of royal-divine enthronement as in neighbouring empires) was celebrated varyingly in Sept. and March, cf § 125d. These two months (Tishri and Nisan), involving important festivals of agricultural origin, are mentioned more often in the Bible than all the others together. The Gezer 'Calendar' is a schoolboy agriculture-almanac, our earliest surviving sample of Palestine writing.

The Seleucid era year-numbering beginning in October, **i** 312 is followed in 1 Mc—the system followed in 2 Mc cannot be determined. Later, in apocryphal Jubilees and at Qumran, a calendar was used in which every annual occurrence falls always on the same weekday, with major feasts on Wednesday to preclude sabbath journeying. This usage has been invoked to account for the sequence of Ez 8, and the Passover in Lk 22:15 preceding that of Jn 18:28.

Strangely, the OT has no word for hour or minute. Aramaic *sha'â* in Daniel is a vague 'point of time'. The famed sundial of Is 38:8 has turned out to be just a staircase. But in Gezer of 1200 B.C. was found a sundial of an Egyptian type in use since 2000.

THE APOCRYPHA OF THE OLD AND NEW TESTAMENTS

BY R. J. FOSTER

88a Bibliography—F. Amiot, *Evangiles apocryphes* 1953; J. Bonsirven, *La Bible apocryphe*, 1953; CAP, 1913, reprinted 1963; R. H. Charles, *Between the Old and New Testaments*, 1914; W. O. E. Oesterley in *A Companion to the Bible*, ed. T. W. Manson, 1939; M. R. James, *The Lost Apocrypha of the OT, their titles and fragments*, 1920; id *The Apocryphal NT*, Oxford, 1953; E. Kautsch, *Die Apokryphen und Pseudepigraphen des AT*, 2 vols, Tübingen, 1921²; C. Tischendorf, *Acta Apostolorum Apocrypha*, Leipzig, 1851; id *Apocalypses Apocryphae*, Leipzig, 1866; S. Szekely, *Bibliotheca Apocrypha*, Freiburg i. B. 1913; E. Schürer, *The Jewish People in the time of J. C.*, 1900; C. Dimier, *The OT Apocrypha*, 1964; J. Hervieux, *What are Apocryphal Gospels?*, 1964; H. H. Rowley, *The Relevance of Apocalyptic*, 1963³; C. C. Torrey, *The Apocryphal Literature*, 1945; R. H. Pfeiffer, *History of NT Times with an introd. to the Apocrypha*, 1949. E. Hennecke—W. Schneemelcher, *Ntl Apokryphen*, I, 1050³.

b The name **Apocrypha** is applied to writings of a religious character which at one time claimed or were regarded in some places as of divine authority and part of the inspired Scripture but which were eventually excluded from the Canon by ecclesiastical authority. But Catholics and Protestants are not agreed on the Scriptural Canon and hence differ on the question as to which books should be considered apocryphal. A number of books considered apocryphal by Protestants are regarded as canonical by Catholics and called deutero-canonical. In addition, Protestants give the name apocrypha to the Prayer of Manasseh and 3 and 4 Esdras, cf 13*e*. Catholics on the other hand reserve the name Apocrypha for a large selection of works of uncertain or spurious origin, which appeared, sometimes anonymously, but usually under assumed names, from about 200 B.C. to the second or third century A.D. In the case of 'New Testament' apocrypha the works often assumed names of various patriarchs, prophets or apostles. For all these the Protestants introduced the name *Pseudepigrapha*.

c Meaning of the Name—Etymologically the name is a neuter plural from the Greek *apokruphos*, which means hidden or secret. When first applied to writings, it was used in a laudatory sense of books kept secret because they contained esoteric doctrine too sacred to be revealed to any save the initiated. Thus the disciples of the Gnostic Prodicus boasted that they possessed the secret books, *Biblous apokruphous*, of Zoroaster, Clem. Alex. *Strom.* i, 15; PG 8,773. In this way, too, Gregory of Nyssa refers to the NT, speaking of Rev as *en apokruphois, In suam ordinationem* PG 46, 594; cf also JE 2, 1; 4 Esd 14:45f. By degrees the original meaning became obscured, giving way to the unfavourable sense which it still retains, partly, no doubt, because esoteric literature flourished most amongst heretical sects and partly because the books themselves were pseudonymous.

Origen used it in a derogatory sense of questionable works which contained 'much that is corrupt and contrary to the true faith', *Prol. Cant.* PG 13, 83. It eventually connoted writings which were false, spurious or heretical. 'Let us omit, then, the fables of those scriptures which are called apocryphal, because their obscure origin was unknown to the fathers from whose authority the true Scripture has been transmitted to us . . . ' writes St Augustine, and again 'Many writings are produced by heretics under the names both of other prophets, and, more recently, under the names of Apostles, all of which, after careful consideration, have been set apart from canonical authority under the title of apocrypha'. *The City of God*, E. tr., 1934, 2, 95f. And so the name came to be applied to certain Jewish and Christian writings, outside the Canon, composed about the beginning of the Christian era, of doubtful authority, and ascribed to various patriarchs, prophets or apostles. In this way we understand the expression today. The Apocrypha are spoken of as OT or NT Apoc according as their subject matter refers to the OT or NT. The former are usually of Jewish, the latter of Christian origin, though many of the Jewish Apoc contain Christian interpolations.

It was not until Jerome's time that the word was used **88c** of the d.c. books, and he was the first to do so (cf PL, 22, 877); his practice was followed by others, and in the 16th cent., when the Protestants adopted the Jewish Canon, they designated as 'Apocrypha' the books they rejected (cf § 17*b*).

THE APOCRYPHA OF THE OT

Their Origin and Purpose—Their origin was due to **d** the unfortunate plight of, and the depressed state prevailing amongst, the chosen people just before and during the commencement of the Christian era. Despairing of the times in which they lived, conscious of their enslavement to the hard yoke of foreign domination, they felt keenly the disparity between their present state and the ideal future which was assuredly one day to be theirs. With no prophetic voice to guide, encourage and console them, the writers of the Apocrypha strove to turn the eyes of the nation to a time, not far distant, when Israel would realize its destiny as a nation chosen apart. They gloried in painting a vivid picture of the triumphant reign of the Messiah, soon to come, in which all God's promises would be fulfilled and the triumph of the just would be evident to all. Hope is the keynote of the Apocrypha and, it has been well said, hope is the main underlying motive power which prompted the writing of many of them. This apocryphal literature served, in various ways, to rekindle in the Jews their intense faith in their own inevitable glorious destiny. It thus afforded them comfort in their trials, satisfied the demand for prophetic guidance and helped to solve the perennial problems of the suffering of the just and the apparent hopelessness of any fulfilment of the prophetic utterances of the past. It served also to drive home the pre-eminence of the Law and the

88d need for its strict observance, whilst throwing light on many of their theological questions, such as the prosperity of the wicked, the certainty of judgement and retribution, and the resurrection of the dead. On the development of doctrine in the Apoc and in the Apocryphal period cf HDB, extra vol. 272—308 W. Fairweather, 'Development of Doctrine'.

To bring about this transformation of outlook various methods were adopted. At one time the writers would modify the sacred text of the Scriptures, as it were rewriting it to suit their purpose; at another they would select one of the great characters of old and set him before their readers with added fictitious details and embellishments to inspire enthusiasm and provoke imitation, (cf Schürer, Div. 2, 3, p. 133f). Most frequently they adopted the prophetic or **apocalyptic** method, peering into the hidden future and, in mysterious and enigmatic form, revealing its supposed secrets (cf § 454a). To accomplish their purpose more surely, they chose to compel the attention of their contemporaries by assuming the names and guise of the men of the ancient and classic past. They wrote as though from the early days of Israel's history, but foretelling to their own generation what was shortly to come to pass. In this way they could effectively issue warnings and inspire hope. How well they succeeded has been summed up by Schürer, 'If we find that, from the date of the tax imposed by Quirinius, whereby Judaea was placed directly under Roman administration, revolutionary tendencies among the people grew stronger and stronger year by year till they led at last to the great insurrection of the year 66, then there cannot be a doubt that this process was essentially promoted if not exclusively caused by the apocalyptic literature', op cit p. 48.

e Division of Apocrypha—Although no division of the Apoc is entirely satisfactory nor completely free from criticism since many might be said to belong to more than one category, we may group them into three classes according to their character. We give a selection only. For a very full list, see CAP.

f Apocalyptic Apocrypha—Ethiopic and Slavonic Enoch, Assumption of Moses, 4 Esdras, Syriac and Greek Apocalypses of Baruch, Apocalypse of Abraham, Apocalypse of Elijah, Testament of Abraham, Apocalypse of Zephaniah, Sibylline Oracles.

g Historical Apocrypha—Book of Jubilees, 3 Esdras, 3 Maccabees, Life of Adam and Eve (or Apocalypse of Moses), Ascension of Isaiah, History of the Rechabites, Zadokite Fragment, Book of Asenath, Testament of Job, Testament of Solomon, Genesis Apocryphon.

h Didactic Apocrypha—Testaments of the Twelve Patriarchs, Psalm 151, Psalms of Solomon, Odes of Solomon, Prayer of Manasseh, 4 Maccabees. Considerations of space preclude a detailed treatment of them all, but it is possible to give a short description of some of the more important of them.

Apocalyptic Apocrypha

i The Ethiopic Enoch, perhaps the most important of the Apoc, is an apocalyptic work, composite in character, whose various parts range from c. 200 B.C. to late in the 1st cent. B.C. The whole of it has only been preserved in an Ethiopian version. It is known as 1 Enoch to distinguish it from the later Apocalypse, 2 Enoch; or, alternatively, as Ethiopic Enoch to distinguish it from the Slavonic 2 Enoch after the earliest extant versions of each. The original language of both of them is thought to be Heb. or Aram.

The book falls into 6 parts: 1—36, **The Angelic 88i Book**, which recounts the judgement and punishment of the angelic 'watchers' who fell on account of their love for the daughters of men, Gn 6:1—4, Enoch's intercession for them, and finally his journeys through the earth and Sheol. It is an attempt to explain the origin of sin and evil in the world.

37—69: **The Book of Parables** contains three parables or similitudes: the first reveals the secrets of heaven, the second the Messiah, the Elect One, the Son of Man, and the third tells of the Great Judgement and the happiness of the Just. In a passage remarkable alike for its doctrine and beauty of expression, the second parable describes the Son of Man: 'And before the sun and the heavenly signs were created, before the stars of heaven were made, his name was named before the Lord of spirits. He shall be a staff for the just, that they may lean upon him and not fall; he shall be the light of peoples, and he shall be the hope of those who suffer in their hearts. All those who dwell upon the dry land shall prostrate themselves and adore him, and they shall bless and sing praises to the Lord of spirits', cf § 676i.

72—82: **The Book of Astronomy** which comprises the revelations of the angel Uriel to Enoch concerning the heavenly bodies. 83—90 **The Book of Visions**, which is Enoch's vision of the Flood and of Israel's history up to the establishment of the Messiah's reign. 91—105: **The Book of Exhortation**, which is a warning foretelling the doom of sinners and the blessings of the just. 93 + 91:12—17: **Apocalypse of Weeks**, which stresses the final triumph of the just, their reward, and the final damnation of the wicked. Portions of Enoch have been discovered at Qumran, cf TYD, 33f.

The Slavonic Enoch—is an apocalypse which is some- **j** times known as the *Secrets of Enoch*. From its sacrificial references one may conclude that the book was written before A.D. 70, and it probably belongs to the 1st cent. of the Christian era. Enoch in his 356th year is said to have been taken up by angels through the seven heavens to the throne of God. He sees the angels who rule the stars and keep the storehouses of dew and snow. The apostate angels ask him to pray for them. The main interest of the work is the light it throws on some scriptural allusions such as the seven heavens, the presence of evil spirits 'in heavenly places', and Ezekiel's creatures 'full of eyes'.

The Assumption of Moses—This work typical of the **k** apocalyptic apocrypha was first edited in 1861 from a 6th cent. Latin MS found in the Ambrosian Library, Milan. The first few lines, which probably contained the title, and the end of the book are missing. It was written in Heb. or Aram. by a Palestinian Pharisee shortly after the deposition of Archelaus in A.D. 6. In character it is something like a *Testament* or *Farewell-Speech*. Indeed the text as we now have it may well be the result of a fusion of two separate works, the *Testament of Moses* and the *Assumption of Moses*, both known to the ancients. Much of the latter would seem to have been lost, though its title has survived. The work relates how Moses after appointing Joshua his successor, foretells the entry of the Israelites into Canaan, the subsequent schism of the ten tribes, the ever-increasing religious corruption, the Captivity, the impiety of priests and kings, but, in the end, the final heavenly judgement by which Israel would be raised to the stars. It is a good example of the attempts made to halt the growing secularization of religion and to inculcate strict obedience to the Law.

The Fourth Book of Esdras is one of the most widely **l** circulated, read and translated of the Apocrypha. It is

881 a composite work: chh 3—14 were the Jewish original, to which the Christians added chh 1—2; 15—16. The Jewish part, originally written c. A.D. 100 in Heb. or Aram. now exists only in versions of which the chief is the Latin. It contains seven visions made to Ezra in Babylon during the Exile. The ever-present problems of human life form the subject of these visions: the trials of the just, the prosperity of the wicked, and the apparent greatness of the number of the damned.

The author finds his answer in the inability of the limited human intellect fully to comprehend the plans of God, owing to the immensity of divine wisdom. In the last vision Ezra is bidden to write some books of instruction for future generations, because the Law had been burnt and the people had become ignorant of it. Ezra then dictated to five scribes 24 books which were to be for all, and, in addition, 70 books which were esoteric or reserved for the wise.

Several antiphons and liturgical texts, including the famous Reproaches on Good Friday, the Easter antiphons for martyrs, and the *Requiem Aeternam* of the office of the Dead, may be traced to this book. Their presence in our liturgy may be due to Byzantine influence, (cf I. Schuster, *The Sacramentary*, 1924 I, 80f, 405. For a full account of the Book, see CAP, 2, 542—624).

m **The Syriac Apocalypse of Baruch** is so called from the Syriac form in which it has come down to us. Though written towards the end of the 1st cent. A.D., it professes to describe revelations made to Baruch at the time of the destruction of Jerusalem by the Babylonians. Charles describes it as 'almost the last noble utterance of Judaism before it plunged into the dark and oppressive years that followed the destruction of Jerusalem', CAP 2, 470. It is noteworthy for its treatment, from the point of view of the Pharisees, of such important doctrines as the Messiah and his kingdom, original sin and freewill, the future judgement and the resurrection.

The Greek Apocalypse of Baruch is of Jewish origin, and relates the journey of Baruch through the five heavens. It belongs to the 2nd cent., and shows signs of having been edited by a Christian writer.

n **The Apocalypse of Abraham** belongs to the end of the first or the beginning of the 2nd cent. A.D. and is of Jewish origin. It was originally written in Heb. or Aram. Chh 1—8 tell of Abraham's conversion from idolatry to monotheism: the remaining chapters, which are apocalyptic, comprise visions concerning the future of the Jewish race.

o **The Sibylline Oracles** in their present form consist of twelve books numbered 1—8; 11—14; an enumeration which does not represent any single MS but is the result of the fusion of three different types of text, cf H. N. Bate, *The Sibylline Oracles*, 1918, 16. The oracles and predictions ascribed to the Sibyl, the oldest of the Gr. prophets, enjoyed great popularity and veneration through the Graeco-Roman world. In the capital itself they were jealously guarded and consulted in times of serious crisis. Her prophecies, marked by no fixed sequence or form, spoke of doom and disaster. Because of their awe-inspiring influence in moulding the religious thought and outlook of the time, the hellenistic Jews of Alexandria enlisted the support of this kind of literature during the 2nd cent. B.C. as a powerful means of propagating Jewish doctrine and faith. This practice continued down to Christian times and was borrowed by Christians themselves who, in their turn, brought into existence Christian Sibylline Oracles. In some cases Christians revised or interpolated the Jewish sibylline writings, and it is now almost impossible to determine exactly what is Christian and what is Jewish. Arendzen writes, 'Probably a dozen

880 different Jewish hands, if not more, worked at the Sibyllines from 160 B.C. to A.D. 240. The varying fortunes of the Jewish race for four hundred years are thus mirrored in this collection of oracles. They are mostly oracles of doom on Israel's foes, and rather poor copies of the *Burdens* against the nations of Isaiah, Jeremiah, and Ezekiel. The destruction of the world by water, fire, war, pestilence, earthquake and famine, and the subsequent happiness of Israel in the Messianic kingdom are commonplaces which grow monotonous', J. P. Arendzen, *Men and Manners in the Days of Christ*, 1928, 166. So it is that in the *Dies Irae* the Sibyl and David are quoted as testifying to the terrors of the judgement day, *Teste David cum Sibylla*, cf F. J. E. Raby, *A History of Christian Latin Poetry*, (Oxford, 1927) 446f.

Historical Apocrypha

89a **The Book of Jubilees** derives its name from its dividing the history of Israel of which it treats, from the Creation to Moses and the Law-giving on Sinai, into 'jubilee' periods of 49 years. It is really a free reproduction of the biblical narrative, interspersed with legendary additions, with special emphasis on the greatness of the Law and its abiding validity, and upon the divine origin of certain legal practices, the strict observance of which it is concerned to inculcate. The author was desirous of a reform in the rules concerning the regulation of the calendar and festivals. It is also known as the *Little Genesis* and the *Apocalypse of Moses*, to whom the revelation was supposed to have been made on Sinai by the Angel of the Presence, 1, 27; it may belong to the 2nd cent. B.C. and its authorship is uncertain. Some fragments of it have been found among the Dead Sea Scrolls at Qumran, cf TYD, 32.

The Genesis Apocryphon is an Aram. work discovered **b** at Qumran. So far only five of its 22 columns have been published chiefly because it is in a poor state of preservation, cf G. Vermes, *The Dead Sea Scrolls in English*, 215f. Text: 216—24. The first editors of the MS regarded it as a sort of apocryphal version of stories from Gn. Other critics think that it may be an early specimen of a written Aram. Pent. Targum from Palestine. 'At this stage with the bulk of the scroll unpublished, one can do no more than raise the question whether the so-called Genesis "Apocryphon" is, in fact, an old Aramaic Targum, and give some reasons for thinking it may be', M. Black, *The Scrolls and the Christian Origins*, 193—4. Its date may be 1st cent. B.C.

The Third Book of Esdras must be distinguished from **c** the canonical books of Ezra and Nehemiah. Confusion is apt to arise since 3 Esd is sometimes called 1 Esd from its position in the LXX, the VL and Syr. versions, while Ez Neh, which follow it are called 2 Esd. In the Vg it is set apart from the canonical books in an appendix under the name 3 Esd. For the most part the book corresponds with Ez Neh with the exception of the added section, 3:1—5:6, which is taken from elsewhere and describes an intellectual competition between three members of Darius' bodyguard in which Zorobabel, one of the three, was successful. 3 Esd, even for what it has in common with Ez Neh, seems to be independent of the MT of those books, and some maintain that it is a direct translation of a Heb. Aram. original which differed in many ways, notably in the historical sequence of events from the MT (cf Frey in DBS 1, 431f). This question is connected with that of the claims of 3 Esd to be admitted to the Christian canon of the OT. It is alleged that the African

89c Councils included it in the Canon in the phrase 'Hesdrae libri duo' (EnchB, 16, 19), but that Florence and Trent through a misunderstanding failed to include it, (cf Howorth, JTS, 1906, p. 343ff; reply by H. Pope, ibid, 1907, p. 218ff. For a defence of the attitude of Trent: Frey, art cit 433—42). For a full account of the Book, see CAP, 1, 1—58.

d The Third Book of Maccabees—This is a strange title for a book in which Maccabean history finds no place, but is due, no doubt, to its position in MSS after 1 and 2 Mc. The author writes of events in Egypt during the reign of Ptolemy Philopator. Enraged by the High Priest's refusal to allow him to enter the Holy of Holies, Ptolemy had the Jews living in his domains brought to Alexandria and cruelly tormented. The king finally ordered that they should be trampled to death by infuriated elephants. At the prayer of Eleazar, a priest, angels rescue the Israelites by turning the elephants against their keepers. As a result Ptolemy becomes their friend, issues a letter proclaiming their loyalty, grants them a seven days' feast, and allows them to return home and take vengeance upon apostates. The purpose behind the story is obviously to stimulate the enthusiasm of the Jews for their religion, to encourage them in adversity, to warn apostates, and to vindicate Jewish loyalty to civil authority. Events similar to those recounted in 3 Mac are to be found in Jos c. Ap. 2, 5, but in a different context. Both accounts are based upon events of which the time and circumstances cannot now be determined. 3 Mc moreover contains legendary details of uncertain extent. The book was written in Gr. and belongs to the 1st cent. B.C. or the beginning of the 1st cent. A.D.

e The Life of Adam and Eve or **Apocalypse of Moses**— The Latin *Life of Adam and Eve* and the Gr. *Apocalypse of Moses* are both based upon the same Heb. or Aram. original. These works embody a mass of legend about the life of our first parents. They serve to show later Jewish teaching, especially on the resurrection and future life, at the end of the 1st cent. A.D. when they were written.

f The Ascension of Isaiah is a composite work comprising three originally distinct writings: the Martyrdom of Isaiah 1:1—3:12 and 5:1*b*—14, which is of Jewish origin; a Christian apocalypse, known as the *Testament of Hezekiah* 3:13—51*a*; and the *Vision of Isaiah*, also of Christian origin, 6:1—11:40.

In its present form it seems to date back to the 2nd cent. A.D., but the first part is more likely to be earlier, probably belonging to the 1st cent. A.D., if not to pre-Christian times. We are introduced in the earlier section to Isaiah the prophet foretelling his own death at the hands of Manasseh, the king 'in whose heart Beliar dwelt'. He is later denounced to the king for his alleged prophecies against him and against Jerusalem. The outcome of it all is the martyrdom of Isaiah, told in the story, so familiar to Jews and Christians, of his being sawn asunder with a wooden saw. cf ch 5. But meanwhile the so-called *Testament of Hezekiah* has explained the reason for Beliar's hatred of Isaiah, namely because he had foretold the destruction of Satan's power by Christ. The third part, the *Vision*, describes the prophet's journeys through the seven heavens where he is allowed to contemplate many hidden secrets. The chief value of the work is the light it throws upon the life of the early Church.

g The Book of Asenath is a romance woven round the references to Joseph's marriage to Asenath in Gn 41:45ff. It is Jewish in character, but has been subjected to Christian revision. Its date is probably 2nd cent. A.D. Kohler says it belongs to 'the hellenistic propaganda literature by which Jewish writers endeavoured to win the non-Jewish world for the Jewish faith, while at the same time representing their Hebrew ancestors as physical as well as moral heroes'. JE 2, 176. **89g**

Didactic Apocrypha

The Testaments of the Twelve Patriarchs—The **h** general theme of this work is ethical. The twelve sons of Jacob are represented as giving their last words to their children, as Jacob himself had done to his son in Gen 49: 1—27. Each discourse falls into three parts, a brief autobiographical sketch of the Patriarch with emphasis on his characteristic vice or virtue, then a moral lesson and exhortation based upon it, and finally a prophecy regarding the future of his descendants. The original language was either Heb. or Aram. and its date was the second half of the 2nd cent. B.C. Some portions were discovered at Qumran, cf TYD p. 34f, and F. M. Braun, RB 67 (1960) pp. 516—49.

The Psalms of Solomon—These psalms, eighteen in **i** number, were written about the time when Pompey captured Jerusalem in 63 B.C. Their author, a Palestinian Pharisee, expresses his confidence in God and the future, his contempt for wrongdoers, his sorrow at his country's misfortunes, and his opposition to the Hasmonean dynasty. His hope is fixed on the glorious reign of the Messiah. 'They are very close to the Psalms in their form and spirit, and express the best aspects of the Jewish mind, in its faith and hope in Jahweh, its patriotism and messianic hopes'. C. Dimier, *The OT Apocrypha*, p. 21. The work is now extant only in Gr. and Syr. though it was originally composed in Heb., probably by Palestinian Jews, in the 1st cent. B.C. Certain features of the Psalms are similar to the religious outlook of the Qumran community. The reason for their ascription to Solomon is not known and the title may, of course, be a later scribal addition.

The Prayer of Manasseh owes its origin to 2 Chr 33: **j** 11—13; 18f. It is an attempt to supply the prayer to which the passage refers. Though short the prayer is beautiful: it opens with praise of God, vv 1—7; then follows an earnest prayer for pardon of sin vv 8—18; it concludes with a short doxology. This prayer is found in the appendix to the Vg. The text of the prayer appears for the first time in the *Didascalia*, 2, 22, but its composition is probably 1st cent. A.D. The Prayer, written by a hellenistic Jew, probably owes its survival to inclusion in the *Didascalia*.

The Fourth Book of Maccabees is a hellenistic work, **k** written at the beginning of the Christian era, to show that right reason, under the guidance of the Law, is the complete master of all the passions—it is an attempt to blend the orthodox Jewish faith and Stoic philosophy. The theme is illustrated from Jewish history, especially from the heroic sufferings of the Maccabean martyrs; hence the title of the book. It has been argued that it was primarily a lecture or address for the synagogue.

Psalm 151 is found as an additional psalm in the LXX **l** with the title, 'This Psalm was written by David with his own hand, though it is outside the number, composed when he fought Goliad (sic) in single combat'. It is a short psalm of eight vv, in which David boasts that though the least of his brethren, he was chosen to fight and overcome Goliath. Its origin is uncertain, and it has no claim to be considered genuine. Part of it, however, is to be found in the second responsory of Matins for Sundays and Thursdays after Pentecost: 'He it was who sent his angel and took me from my father's sheep, and anointed me with the oil of his anointing', cf text HDB 4, 146.

THE APOCRYPHA OF THE NT

90a We do not include under this heading those books, produced during the 1st and 2nd cent., now grouped together under the name *Apostolic Fathers*, some of which, for a short time, seemed to linger on the edge of the Canon before being finally excluded, such as the Ep. of Clement to the Corinthians, the Ep. of Ignatius, the Ep. of Barnabas, and the Pastor of Hermas. We confine ourselves to those writings which seem to make a false claim to be considered canonical and part of the NT, and of which some were tendentious or heretical. They may be conveniently grouped, analogously to the NT, as Gospels, Acts, Epistles and Apocalypses.

b **Apocryphal Gospels**——The Gospels according to the Hebrews, according to the Egyptians, of the Ebionites. The Protovangelium of James, the Gospels of Peter, Thomas, Bartholomew, Nicodemus and Philip. The Arabic Gospel of the Infancy, the History of Joseph the Carpenter, and the Assumption of Mary.

c **Apocryphal Acts**——Acts of Peter, John, and Paul. The Preaching of Peter, Acts of Andrew, Thomas, Philip, Matthew, and Barnabas.

d **Apocryphal Epistles**——Letters of our Lord and Abgar; Letters of Paul and Seneca; Correspondence between Paul and the Corinthians, the Epistle to the Laodiceans, the Epistle of the Apostles or Discourses of our Lord with the Apostles.

e **Apocryphal Apocalypses**——Apocalypses of Peter, Paul, Thomas, Stephen, John, The Blessed Virgin Mary and others.

f In addition to these there are **Agrapha**, i.e. deeds or sayings of our Lord which find no mention in the Gospels, (cf Jn 20:30; 21:25), but which have been preserved and handed down to us by tradition. They are to be found here and there in the writings of the Fathers, in some biblical MSS, and a few papyri fragments, but not many of them are considered authentic, cf L. Vaganay, DBS, 1 (1928), 159–98; J. H. Ropes, *Agrapha*, HDB extra vol. pp. 343–52.

g **The Origin of the NT Apocrypha**——The NT Apocrypha owe their existence, in part, to the fact that the narratives given to us in the canonical Scriptures are short and often undetailed. People were anxious to know more about our Lord's birth and early life and about his Mother and other characters who played a part in the Gospel story. They wanted to know where those apostles, who are not mentioned in Ac, exercised their missionary zeal. They were curious, too, about the future life and what happens after death. The Apocrypha set out to supply these apparent omissions. Many legends were woven round the hidden life of our Lord, the life of Mary and the later activities of the Apostles, and more apocalypses appeared to satisfy popular desire. Most of this apocryphal literature is ill-founded, but some has been found worthy of credence and a small amount has been absorbed into the Church's liturgy and played its part in popular devotions and Christian art. We will now consider some of the more important works:

h **The Protoevangelium of James** is a very popular and widely read story of our Lady's life and the birth of her Son. It is based on the Gospel narrative which it fills out with many legendary and imaginative details, often of a puerile character. It tells how Mary was miraculously born to Joachim and Anna (incidentally, the first mention of the names of Mary's parents), and how, when three years old, she was presented in the Temple. Nine years later Joseph was miraculously singled out to be her spouse by a sign given to the High Priest—a dove coming forth from Joseph's rod and resting on his head. The account of the birth of Christ is embellished with all kinds of un- **90h** restrained and unimpressive details. The book is of interest, however, as an indication of the early veneration for the Blessed Virgin Mary and was probably written between A.D. 150 and 180.

The Gospel of Thomas (i) is another infancy gospel **i** belonging to the 2nd cent. but of heterodox origin. It recounts extravagant youthful miracles of our Lord between the ages of five and twelve, as, for instance, when he formed clay birds on the Sabbath, and on being rebuked clapped his hands and caused them to fly away. The Child is represented as petulant, bringing sudden death to another child who collided with him, and when the bystanders blame him for such action, he strikes them with blindness. Such a picture stands in marked contrast to the quiet dignity of St Luke's story.

The Gospel of Thomas (ii) belongs to a collection of 13 **j** leather-bound volumes of papyri, written in Coptic and belonging to the 4th cent., discovered in 1945–6 by peasants in an old cemetery tomb near **Nag Hammadi** in Upper Egypt, (cf W. C. van Unnik, *Newly discovered Gnostic Writings*, E. tr. 1960). This Gospel of Thomas bears no relation to the infancy gospel (i) just mentioned. It is a Gnostic work largely based on the canonical Gospels. It consists of more than 100 sayings of our Lord introduced by the words 'These are the secret words which Jesus the Living spoke and Didymus Judas Thomas wrote. And he said "He who will find the interpretation of these words will not taste death"'. Among the Gnostics there was a strong emphasis on secrecy and their idea of salvation through 'knowing' something (in this case the interpretation of Jesus' words) is expressed in this introduction to the Gospel of Thomas. It has been suggested that originally this Gospel may have been a sort of harmony of our Lord's sayings, and was then edited and enlarged by Gnostics to suit their own purposes. In this Gospel which may go back as far as the 2nd cent., our Lord has been transformed into a Gnostic revealer of secret wisdom and saving truth. (cf A. Guillaumont and others, *The Gospel according to Thomas: Coptic text established and translated*, 1959; R. M. Grant with D. N. Freedman, *The Secret Sayings of Jesus according to the Gospel of Thomas*, 1960; J. Doresse, *L'Evangile selon Thomas*, 1959; id *The Secret Books of the Egyptian Gnostics*, E. tr. 1960). Also among the Nag Hammadi MSS is a **Gospel of Philip** which contains nothing but Gnostic speculations, (tr. by C. J. de Catanzaro, JTS, 1962, 35–71) and the so called **Gospel of Truth** previously known from allusions in the early Fathers. This is a meditative, homiletical treatment of themes partly derived from the canonical Gospels and partly from heterodox Jewish speculation. It deals with the meaning of salvation as revealed by our Lord, but is completely unlike the Gospels.

The Assumption of Mary——The many translations and **k** various forms of this work attest its wide popularity. In its Gr. form it is introduced as 'The narrative of St John the Theologian concerning the Falling Asleep of the Holy Mother of God', but the Latin version ascribes it to Melito of Sardis. In all probability it belongs to the fourth cent. It tells of the death of Mary and how the apostles were summoned to mount upon the clouds and assemble from all parts of the earth round her deathbed. Those who had died were raised to life in order to be present. For three days after her death the 'voices of invisible angels were heard glorifying Christ our God which was born of her. And when the third day was fulfilled the voices were no more heard, and thereafter we all perceived that her spotless and precious body was translated into paradise', M. R. James, *Apoc NT*, 208.

90k The interest which centred round the early tradition of Mary's Assumption is further illustrated by the added legendary details.

l **Letters of our Lord and Abgar**—Eus HE 1, 13 (PG 20, 119ff) records the story of Abgar, king of Edessa, who wrote to our Lord asking him to come and cure him of the terrible disease from which he was suffering. Jesus sent back a written reply, praising his faith and assuring him that although he could not come in person he would certainly send one of his apostles, after his Ascension, to heal him. This legend, which belongs to the first part of the 3rd cent., became popular during the Middle Ages and has left its mark on the Syrian and Celtic liturgies.

m **The Letters of St Paul and Seneca**—There are 14 letters, written in Latin, which were known to Jer and Aug and were therefore in existence in the 4th cent. The contents of the letters are rather commonplace and the style is poor. Seneca tells Paul that he had been much refreshed by reading his epistles, but expresses his anxiety lest 'polish of style' be wanting to 'his majesty of thought'. He mentions Nero's favourable reception of his views. In his reply the Apostle shows appreciation of the philosopher's goodwill, but warns him against bringing the Christian religion any more to the notice of Poppaea and Nero. Seneca then sends Paul a book on 'eloquence of expression', and sympathises with the sufferings of the Christians. In conclusion Paul expresses the hope that he may become a 'new author, by showing forth with the graces of rhetoric the unblameable wisdom of Jesus Christ, which you, having wellnigh attained it, will instil into the temporal monarch, his servants, and intimate friends.' James, *Apoc NT*, 484.

n **The Acts of Peter** were written in Gr. c. A.D. 200. It is said that when Paul left Rome for Spain, Peter was summoned to the capital from Jerusalem to combat the errors of Simon Magus. It is these acts which give us the famous and familiar 'Quo Vadis' story and the description of Peter's being crucified head downwards. Traces of Gnostic influence are found here and there. One interesting example occurs quite early, in the description of the Eucharistic sacrifice offered by Paul before he sets out for Spain. We notice that bread and water are brought for the sacrifice in accordance with the Gnostic Encratite practice, for they regarded wine as evil, cf Epiphanius, *Adv. Haer.*, 2, 1, 47 (PG 41, 853).

o **The Apocalypse of Paul**—The author pretends that the work was discovered in the foundations of St Paul's house at Tarsus. The Apostle is represented as urging the world to repent of its crimes because the forces of nature are crying out against the wickedness of the human race and calling for punishment of sinners. He witnesses the ultimate fate of just and unjust, and sees the torments of the wicked in hell. The terrible scenes so vividly depicted were known to Dante, who made use of them in his *Inferno*. The work is generally assigned to the 4th cent., but some authors place it much earlier (cf Pope, op cit 293). The work was widely read in the Middle Ages, despite Augustine's severe condemnation.

p **The Church and the Apocrypha**—In the earliest period little objection seems to have been made to the Apocrypha. The book of Enoch and the Assumption of Moses had been quoted in the canonical epistle of Jude, and there was in places a lingering hesitation about the inspired character of some of these books, such as the Esdras apocrypha. But with the rapid increase of Christian apocryphal literature and its widespread use **90p** by heretical sects amongst whom some of it arose, the Fathers began to examine it more carefully. Their verdict was highly unfavourable, and they frequently warned the faithful against such writings. Irenaeus denounced the heretics because 'They adduce an unspeakable number of apocryphal and spurious writings, which they themselves have forged, to bewilder the minds of foolish men, and of such as are ignorant of the Scriptures of truth'. *Adv. Haer.*, 1, 20. Origen was outspoken in his condemnation and Eus no less severely wrote, 'We have been compelled to make a catalogue . . . in order that we might know these same writings and those which have been put forward by the heretics in the name of the Apostles, whether as containing Gospels of Peter, Thomas, or Matthias or of some others besides these, or as containing Acts of Andrew and John and other apostles. None of these has been thought worthy of any kind of mention in a treatise by any member of the successive generations of ecclesiastical writers. The character of their style, also, is far removed from that of the apostles, and the thought and tenor of their contents is so much out of harmony with true orthodoxy as to prove that they are certainly the forgeries of heretics. For this reason they ought not to be placed amongst the spurious writings, but rejected as altogether monstrous and impious', HE 3, 25.

The first official declaration about them comes from the Council of Hippo, A.D. 393, which said that apart from the canonical Scriptures nothing was to be read in the Church under the heading 'Sacred Scripture', EnchB 16, 17. This enactment was repeated at Carthage in 397, Dz 186. The so called Decree of Gelasius, variously ascribed to Damasus, Gelasius and Hormisdas, but, as now seems almost certain, of much later origin, (cf JTS 14 (1913) 321ff; 469ff) contains a list of about 40 books which it condemns as apocryphal, Dz 354. Innocent I in his letter to Exsuperius also condemns them, EnchB 22. In the course of time these condemnations were forgotten, the apocrypha came to enjoy once again great popularity, and in the Middle Ages exercised no small influence on devotion, art and literature.

The Value of the Apocrypha—Their theological value is small, for they contain little that could deepen our understanding of divine revelation. But both Jewish and Christian Apocrypha serve to throw light on the times in which they were written. The former reveal the doctrines which were to the forefront and commonly accepted at the time of our Lord; the latter make known to us what interested the early Christians. We learn what held their attention, what attracted their veneration, and devotion, what ideals they cherished for this life and what they expected to find in the next. Nor must we overlook the part they played in the liturgy and in the literature and art of the Middle Ages. To them we owe the feast of the Presentation of our Lady, (cf Schuster, op cit 5, 290) and the names of Joachim and Anna. Some of the masterpieces of art and literature drew their inspiration from them, (cf DBS 1, 468; E. Male, 'L'Art religieux en France', 1923, ch 3). And finally, even where they fail, they are not without their value, for a mere cursory reading of the legends, marvels and aberrations of the Apocrypha intensifies our appreciation of the true Scriptures, setting in gratifying relief the quiet simplicity and unassuming majesty of the inspired Word of God. (cf further J. Hervieux, *What are Apocryphal Gospels*? 179 ff.)

THE CRITICAL STUDY OF THE OLD TESTAMENT

BY ROBERT NORTH S.J.

91a **Bibliography**—T. K. Cheyne, *Founders of OT Criticism*, 1893; A. Bentzen, Introd OT, 1952², 2, 10—61; J. Coppens. *The OT and the Critics*, 1942; id *Histoire critique de l'AT*. 1938; O. Eissfeldt, *Hexateuch-Synopse*, Leipzig, 1962-1922; EOT Int, 1965; E. Kraeling, *The OT since the Reformation*, 1955; H.-J. Kraus, *Geschichte der historisch-kritischen Erforschung des AT*, Neukirchen, 1956; (here referred to as KG); H. Hahn, *The OT in Modern Research*, 1966²; H. Höpfl-S. Bovo, *Introd. Specialis in VT*, 1963⁶, 32—149; S. Mowinckel, *Erwägungen zur Pentateuchquellenfrage*, Oslo, 1964; C. North, in: H. H. Rowley (ed.) *The OT and Modern Study*, Oxford, 1951, xv-xxxi, 48—83; M. Noth, *Überlieferungsgeschichte des Pentateuch*, Stuttgart, 1948; J. Prado, *Propaedeutica*, Turin, 1954, 409ff; D. C. Simpson, *Pentateuchal Criticism*, 1924⁷, A. Weiser, *The OT, its Formation*, 1951; J. Steinmann, *Biblical Criticism*, 1958². S. L. Greenslade, *Cambridge History of the Bible II*, 1963; G. Fohrer, *OT Introduction*, 1968.

Articles—A. Bea Bib 16 (1935) 175—200; H. Cazelles, DBS 7 (1964), 708—858; id RF 1, 121—161, 278—343; S. DeVries, IDB, 1, 407—18; N. Lohfink, *Stimmen der Zeit*, 177 (1966), 330—44; 174 (1964), 161—81; R North, AmER, 126 (1952), 241—57, 150 (1964), 314—45; C. Sant, *Melita Theologica*, 10 (1958) 52—63, 3 (1951) 16—21; J. Coppens, 'La Critique textuelle de l'AT', ETL 36 (1960), 466—75.

b **Introduction**—The first edition CCHS § 43—46 contained an informative and reliable defence of 'Higher Criticism'. Since then, the whole movement has been made the subject of an excellent research-volume by H.-J. Kraus (above; herein KG). He shows remarkable fairness and originality in emphasizing Catholic leadership in a critical scholarship which for good reason had come to be considered almost exclusively Protestant. At the same time Kraus shows clearly the extent to which the critical movement tended to counter the principles of the Reformation and even sweepingly reject some of them. The resulting tension and conflict were salutary. Especially after the progressive welcoming of Catholic voices back into the discussion, there resulted a healthy combination of rationality with devout submissiveness to God's Word. This acceptable and flattering Protestant presentation greatly helps Catholics today to study dispassionately the penetration of critical methods into our Church.

c Moreover Kraus wrote his volume for the late 20th cent. Literary dissection linked to the symbols JEDP and Wellhausen has rightly yielded the stage to an intense concern for the oral and liturgical origins of our biblical traditions. But we cannot raise our edifice without the stones that support it. 'Our problem here is precisely that ever-clamorous difficulty of the Younger Generation. In current scientific OT research, scholarly youth has lost all awareness of the continuity of the investigative process. Form, Cult, Tradition-history are now the popular terms: and the methods and problems of documentary criticism **91c** are widely ignored. . . . But there is a cultural development here to be analyzed and understood and it would give a new vitality to our education centers', KG 2. It may be noted that PC (2) has an article on Form Criticism but none on literary source-analysis or its history.

Biblical Criticism—A critic is one who passes judge- **d** ment, assesses. Criticism may be of various kinds— textual, literary and historical, cf § 47b—e. **Textual** criticism is concerned with the transmission of the text, and usually manuscript transmission. Its aim is to eliminate errors in transcription and to try to restore, as far as possible, the original text. **Literary** criticism analyses the work, investigating its origin and composition, the author or authors, the influences which contributed to its formation and its subsequent editing. Lastly, **historical** criticism seeks to place the work in a historical setting, to see its effect on its contemporaries and later history. These principles apply to the Bible in much the same way as to other literature. At one time the term 'criticism' was held in evil repute by Catholic scholars as almost synonymous with 'unorthodox'. This was partly due to a misunderstanding of the nature of the Bible, a feeling that its divine origin somehow exempted it from the normal rules of human authorship, cf §§ 47b, 49a—d. But it was also partly because some critics themselves went to the opposite extreme and thought it part of their task to exclude any possibility of supernatural reference in the text.

There has always been critical bible scholarship. Early rabbis and Christian Fathers noted some 'discrepancies' and tried to explain them, generally by concordism. Theodore of Mopsuestia was called rationalistic because he took the Canticle for what it plainly purports to be, romance lyric (PG 66, 699). Hugh of St Victor denied Solomonic authorship of Wisdom and referred Daniel 11 to Maccabees (PL 175, 9). Rabbi Abraham Ibn Ezra in Spain before 1150 queried the Canaanite reference of Gn 12; 6. But modern critical exegesis is rightly dated from 1500. Not without reason it coincides with the emphasis on 'Scripture Alone' in nascent Protestantism.

Luther, in his demand for more active and submissive **e** use of the Bible in the vernacular, did not aim to promote a critical attitude towards it. On the contrary, he equates 'Scripture alone' with 'the (grammatically) literal and historical sense' (*De servo arbitrio* 700; O. Clemen 1959 ed. 3, 194). But he applied this rule rationally, rather than inconsistently as KG 13 finds Calvin saying: 'Luther is not meticulous in seeking out what the text is actually saying in its historical background; he contents himself with any fruitful truth it may yield.' At any rate it was the Reformers' *focusing of attention* on the Bible which led inevitably to the rise of critical questioning.

Modern Criticism—Among the Reformer Andrew Karl- **f** stadt doubted Mosaic authorship, though rejecting earlier rabbis who like Jerome (PL 23, 190) had

91f cautiously eyed Ezra as an alternative. Karlstadt also subjected the Canon to rational criticism. But he began again the pre-Aquinas patristic tendency to set typology ahead of the 'literal (historical) sense'. The first really original key-words of criticism, Compiler and Redactor, were introduced by Catholic jurist Andrew Maes in a 1574 commentary on Joshua, though it was put on the Index because he ascribed to Ezra the redaction of this work along with Judges and Kings. Maes did equally valiant work on the Syriac text and on LXX (B). His Jesuit pupil Bento Pereira in a 1600 commentary on Gn defended Mosaic authorship, but with critical reflections bringing the spirit of Maes to the attention of Simon.

g Meanwhile Louis Cappellus became the real founder of Textual Criticism; his 1624 *Arcanum punctationis Revelatum* refuted the notion that Heb. vowel marks came into our Bible (under divine inspiration!) before A.D. 500. Against Hugo Grotius' striving toward a purely historical explanation for everything in Scripture, echoed in the deist Herbert of Cherbury, John Cocceius fathered the portentous formula 'Salvation-History'. The *Leviathan* of Thomas Hobbes in 1651 declared that to know the author or at least the date of each biblical book, 'the light that must guide us [is] that which is held out to us from the Bookes themselves' (3, 33). Calvinist Isaac LaPeyrère in Paris abjured the 'heresy' of his 1655 Pre-Adamite hypothesis, which is in fact against no Catholic dogma and marked a momentous step bringing exegesis along into the world newly opened out by science. And with the 1670 *Tractatus Theologico-Politicus* whose ch 7 maintains the growth of the Pent. by accretion during all the time between Moses and Ezra, Baruch Spinoza laid a philosopher's groundwork for modern hermeneutics (and stimulated Simon to refute him, says R. Deville NRT 73 (1951) 724).

92a **Richard Simon** (1638–1712) in 1678 had brought through to the eve of publication his *Histoire critique du Vieux Testament*, when the copies were confiscated through Bossuet's intervention, because of Simon's views on the Mosaic authorship. Simon's biography by Jean Steinmann (Paris, 1960; p. 8) claims to be nothing other than a reopening of the dossier of the lifelong conflict between these two men. Bossuet triumphed then, Simon now. (Steinmann allows no weight to Jesuit hostility, mentioned pp. 320 and 397, which KG 59 with no indication of sources holds to have been paramount.) Of the 1300 printed copies of the *Histoire Critique* almost all were burned; one which escaped went through several editions in Amsterdam. But it was a century later in 1776 on the appearance of the German translation that Simon was acclaimed and overnight made 'the Father of Biblical Criticism'. (KG attributes the translation to Semler; but G. Hornig rejects this, see his *Die Anfänge der historisch-kritischen Theologie: Semler. . . und Luther*, Lund, 1961, 185 and n. 34; he further cites Semler's warning against 'Simon's cheap Catholic ideas about

b tradition', 187, n. 41). Meanwhile Simon was promptly expelled from the Oratorians in whose Paris library he had thriven on valuable oriental manuscripts and rabbinic grammars. But until his death he remained a priest in good standing, for all his sharp-tongued obstinacy not unlike Jerome's. Kraeling, 43, declares him 'a Protestant who had reverted to Catholicism'; while Lohfink (*Stimmen der Zeit*, 177 (1966) 331) sees his achievement growing out of a Jewish-Calvinist-Catholic ferment 'from which the Lutherans stood aloof encased in their verbal inspiration'. Simon went on to write industriously on varied subjects, anticipating the modern ecumenical and litur-

gical movement in many of his works. Inter alia, he also **92b** attacked Vossius' modern-sounding claim that the only *real* Bible from the beginning was the LXX (D. Barthélemy, TZ 21 (1965) 358) even for the Jews. Simon rightly mocks the preface of Brian Walton's admirable Polyglot for its divinizing of the Heb. language. In his turn, Simon was attacked uncomprehendingly by skilful Protestant exegete Jean Le Clerc.

Simon's *Histoire Critique* (E.tr. by W. Davis, *Critical* **c** *History of the OT*, 1682), contains three parts. The first, on the history of the Heb. text, not really proceeding methodically from hard facts to working hypotheses, plunges at once into his most original and undying innovation. Simon supposes the existence of a bureaucratic corps of 'public secretaries' whose gradual accretions 'according to their respective plan' up to the time of Ezra produced the biblical books which have come to be thought the work of unitary authors. Diversities of style in the Creation and Deluge narratives show that Gn could not have been written by that Moses who was author of the Laws. Simon then further evaluates the Masoretic techniques for the transmission of our Heb. text. His Second Part gives a history of the Versions. Here he boldly anticipates Pius XII in 1943 by reacting against undue respect for the vulgate, resulting from Trent's declaration of its 'authenticity'. The Third Part is a history of exegesis.

Simon, recapitulating Maes and alongside Astruc, says **d** KG 36, 'was the fountainhead of new ideas destined to flood Protestant biblical scholarship under Semler (KG 62ff) by **his concept of a continuous chain of tradition** [admittedly not distinguishing nicely between handing-down-process and thing-handed-down: a vagueness which has been criticized also in Vatican II, Revelation ch 2]. Simon had grasped that the **history of a literature must be based on a history of its** *Überlieferung* **(handing down, tradition)**. This notion of "Tradition" suddenly takes on a fearful importance. . . . The Reformers in taking up OT questions had shunned any whisper of tradition, much less *oral*. They could never have tolerated the assumption of such a Catholic-sounding process operative in the very origins of our Bible. Orthodox notions of inspiration as mechanical dictation also raise problems. . . . Simon explicitly defends his critical findings about Tradition as Trent's own newly-retrieved Catholic insistence: "only prejudiced or uninformed Protestants could balk at it!". It is stupefying that these momentous theological premisses have to this day never given pause to Protestant scholarship in its taking over of Simon bodily via Semler (who though drawing mostly from this Catholic, yet taxed Protestant orthodoxy with 'papistic authoritarianism' for emphasizing God's word as *present*, while for Semler it is largely to be identified with a vanished situation in the *past*: KG 98). Simon's notion of 'critical' is **e** the decisive starting point of exegetical scholarship: not only the obviously-recognizable Wellhausen kind; but today's much more favoured *Überlieferung* researches of Martin Noth; and '(the Form Criticism and Sitz im Leben of) Gunkel only finally comes to grips with the Tradition challenge flung down by Richard Simon' (KG 318, cf 97). To cite another Protestant witness: 'precisely the pre-eminence of Scripture ("Scripture only"!) inhibited Protestant theologians from candid scrutiny of their highest authority, whereas the Roman scholar (Simon), with tradition as highest authority, could be relatively free towards Scripture' (IDB 1, 411).

Valuable as were his general observations and theories, **f**

92f Simon did not actually provide a concrete key on verifiable factual data to open out Bible origins. This achievement was left for **Jean Astruc** (1684–1766). He wrote eighty years after Simon but his influence was quicker and more decisive. He was a Catholic, following the transfer from Protestantism of his father, a clergyman of Jewish origins. His impact doubtless owed much to his post as court-physician to the king of France (and/or the Polish king August the Strong of Dresden). He wrote widely on different subjects but was not a biblical scholar—de Vaux rightly calls him 'a stowaway among the Argonauts of exegesis' (VTS 1 (1953) 182). His septuagenarian masterpiece was published anonymously in Paris, though the title-page says explicitly Brussels, Fricx, 1753. He claims only to have found further justification for our assurance that Moses is the author of the Pent, as is shown by the title, 'Conjectures on the original records which it seemed Moses used to write Genesis' (E. O' Doherty, CBQ 15 (1953) 300).

g The really great discovery of Astruc was that the **alternation between YHWH and Elohim** as name of God comes in blocks so compact that it **cannot reasonably be ascribed to caprice or to the motivation of a single author**. He further concluded that some ten other blocks could be similarly distinguished but without the help of the divine names. Moreover he claimed that Moses compiled his narrative by distributing these dozen source documents neatly among four columns, but a later un-perceptive scribe mingled them all into a single continuous work. These mechanical details do not greatly affect the essential YHWH-Elohim criterion, which itself is not fully adequate but was and remains the best opening to get into the problem. (Objections have been made to this criterion but de Vaux, VTS 1 (1953) 189, holds that those of Dahse for example have been refuted by J. Skinner, *The Divine Names in Genesis*, 1914.) The hypothesis was incorporated into Eichhorn's Introduction to the OT in 1780, and when two years later Astruc's own work was translated into German a real avalanche was begun. In Eichhorn's own words: 'Astruc did what no exegete had ever ventured to do, namely to dissect the whole of Genesis into separate components'. Dissection became a long-glorious and eventually a dirty word.

h German Critical School—Astruc's work was actually anticipated by Henning Witter in his *Jura Israelitarum* (1711), but this became known only in 1924, in A. Lods's 'Astruc', RHPR 4 (1924) 109 and 201; see also his ZAW 42 (1925) 134 and H. Bardtke, ZAW 66 (1954) 153. Witter explicitly enunciated the principle that our Pent is made up of preexisting oral compositions of which one never contains the name YHWH 'used ordinarily by Moses'. But this German and Protestant discovery went totally unnoticed long after Astruc's independent expression of it had given the distinctive character to two centuries of German Protestant Bible research. This was meanwhile dominated by the conservative giant **Johann David Michaelis** (1719–91), who by his expert use of improved philological and antiquarian techniques was sowing and cultivating for a harvest which he did not foresee. For Michaelis, the Pent was a highly personal achievement of Moses, just as the Psalms speak of Jesus so plainly that no open-minded Jewish reader could fail to recognize this.

93a Pentateuchal criticism, however, was not the only subject of concern in biblical studies, nor were these isolated from the theological and philosophical trends of the day. **Johann Herder's** *Briefe das Studium der Theologie betreffend*, 1790 (see also his *Vom Geist der Ebraischen Poesie*, 1782, in dependence on the **93a** Anglican bishop Robert Lowth) introduced a modern-sounding strain into biblical studies. Characterized by what he would call 'naturalness', what others would call 'the romantic strain', it is akin to current notions of humanism and existentialism. It means breaking away from academic categories to try to relive what an ancient writer is saying, in the total human emotional experience of the real world around us. **Gotthold Lessing's** *Die Erziehung des Menschengeschlechts*, 1780, also follows this trend. It characterizes 'God's revelation in and through the human race' as the divine *economy*, a Gr. term meaning originally housekeeping or management (interestingly, the Second Vatican Council debated whether to adopt this more patristic term instead of what Protestants had been calling 'Salvation-History'; the term, however, has misleading connotations today). Lessing's dismay at 'hanging of eternity on a spider's web' anticipates Kierkegaard's gnawing anxiety which lies at the roots of existentialism.

b Lessing was also responsible indirectly for an even greater influence in biblical studies. Spinoza's work (see above § 91g) in applying the principles of historical criticism to the Bible was only part of his general aim, namely, to show that there was no special revelation to Israel and that Nature was God's only manifestation. The deists continued this line of thought in varying degrees and with very partial success. It was left to **Hermann Reimarus** to take it up once more, this time with an effect which can only be described as cataclysmic. By applying his principles to the Bible narrative, he aimed to destroy its supernatural character along with its historical reliability, and left the reader with the impression that the narrative was either pure myth as regards the OT or largely imposture as regards the NT, cf § 633c. Reimarus did not dare publish his work (*Apologie oder Schutzschrift für die Vernünftigen Verehrer Gottes*), and it was only after his death that Lessing published anonymous extracts from it—the famous **Wolfenbüttel Fragments**, 1774–78.

c Reimarus's views met with violent opposition, and even the most progressive critics rejected his position decisively. J. G. **Eichhorn** (1752–1827), a student of Michaelis and other eminent philologists, was strongly influenced by Semler and Herder's 'naturalness' and passionately denounced the 'Reimarus Lessing' as inconsistent with the 'Herder Lessing'. Critics such as Eichhorn and Semler countered Reimarus by rejecting indeed the supernatural in the narrative of the OT on the whole, but interpreting it as **an account written by primitive peoples who were ignorant of secondary causes and tended to ascribe everything they did not understand to the direct action of God** as First Cause. Eichhorn spoke often of the *infantia generis humani*. (For the influence of this on NT criticism, see § 633c). KG 124 sees in this a momentous turning point of biblical criticism: 'the rationalistic pattern of a man-centred or nature-phenomenological interpretation of historical development is pressed into service to parry attacks on the OT'.

d In the field of **Pentateuchal studies**, Eichhorn was responsible for preserving Astruc's theories from oblivion. But he also added much to Astruc's surgical and unprofessional analysis; with more precise scholarship he was able to define more clearly the **two main sources** which Astruc had proposed. Like Astruc, too, Eichhorn presumed that it was Moses who was responsible for compiling these sources; though in the 4th ed of his

93d introduction he allowed a greater part for a later redactor.

The next indispensable development came when Karl Ilgen in 1798 recognized that the name Elohim is used in two separate documents (one of which would later be called P). Thus already there appeared the three basic sources recognized in Gn even today. This (Wellhausen) 'documentary theory' in essentials retains its full validity even though (or *because*) like all hypotheses of modern science it is being continuously rectified and improved. Hence it seems inopportune to perpetuate any longer the tags 'Supplement/Fragment/Neo-Documentary' Hypothesis by which at their first appearance certain modifications to Genesis source-criticism were considered to rival or threaten the Astruc-Eichhorn

e line. Notably the Scots Catholic **Alexander Geddes** in his Hexateuch translation (1792) and **Critical Remarks** (1800), indeed maintained a plurality of 'fragments'; but his observations as developed in Germany by **Johann Vater's** 1802 Pentateuch-Commentary were chiefly influential in making Dt a compilation of such fragments under Josiah as hinted in 2 (4) Kgs 22 (E. Nestle ZAW 22 (1902) 170; 621 B.C. Vater held this to have been the nucleus of our Pent; a foredoomed assumption. But with his discovery the main line of inquiry possessed the completed roster of sources whose symbols have become JEDP.

f Again, the tag 'supplementary hypothesis,' was expressly rejected by its foremost bearer, **Heinrich Ewald**, *Theologische Studien und Kritiken* 4(1831) 595. He maintained that both Elohists (E and P) were before the Yahwist or J-narrator. His eight-volume History of Israel in 1863 represented the first consistent synthesis based on the new critical source-analysis, in a work whose sweep and insights make it a useful reference work even today. But the 'supplementary' alternative had really been propounded—explicitly as a device for salvaging valid features of the 'fragment' hypothesis while maintaining the basic 'documentary' lines—by **Wilhelm De Wette** (1780–1849) in his *Lehrbuch der historisch-kritischen Einleitung . . .* 1829[3] (KG 147). De Wette is considered by Eissfeldt (*Introduction* 171) to have liberated Pentateuch criticism from dogmatic shackles by his pronouncements on Dt (already

g in his university *Dissertatio critica* 1805). Actually what De Wette adds to Vater is chiefly wrong: namely that D as an autonomous entity was *later* than all the other sources including P. But he accompanied this verdict with a claim that the deuteronomic style could be followed through Joshua and as far as Kings. This is rightly seen to be a clairvoyant anticipation of Martin Noth's post-Wellhausen dominance, and is linked with an equally grandiose anticipation of the essential lines of Gunkel's post-Wellhausen 'Sitz im Leben categories'. This research fills De Wette's 1823 Psalm-Commentary, as shown by KG 162f; 166; see 171 for further paradoxes of De Wette's 'new critical dogmatism' replacing the research-barrier of church orthodoxy. 'De Wette in New England', as title of S. Puknat's *Proc Am Phil* 102 (1958) 376, refers only to the influence his translated works had there. See also R. Smend *De Wettes Arbeit* (1958) and TZ 14 (1958) 107.

h At any rate the focal point of Pentateuch analysis was now shifted from Gn to Dt, thanks to De Wette and also to Eduard Riehm's 1854 *Die Gesetzgebung Mosis im Lande Moab*. We insist, therefore, that the state of affairs as surveyed in Hermann Hupfeld's 1853 *Die Quellen der Genesis* was no Neo-Documentary 'New Phase' (*EOT Int* 164) but a mere straightening out of

tangled strands. Though he still made the two Elohist **93h** documents precede J, he marked an advance in postulating a fourth hand or post-J Redactor who combined them. This stage of inquiry dominated the important Gn commentaries by August Dillmann 1875 and Franz Delitzsch 1887[5].

But a Copernican revolution was yet needed to shift **i** J into the most primitive position and P into the sophisticated latest stage: features which to current scholarship seem the most obvious of all the attainments of Genesis criticism. The shift seems due to the cooperative researches of **Eduard Reuss** (in an 1834 lecture putting the Levitical cult laws *after* the prophets) and his student **Karl Graf**, especially after Graf's excited rediscovery of Richard Simon (*Strassburger Beiträge* 1847; KG 223). In 1862 Graf wrote to Reuss: 'The whole midriff of the Pentateuch is postexilic'; and he further elaborated in *The Historical Books of the OT*, 1866.

At this juncture the Netherlands' **Abraham Kuenen** **j** (1828–91) produced *Historisch-Kritisch onderzoek* (English almost simultaneous: 1865[1], 1886[2]), spelling out the details of the now-complete JEDP-sequence with a lucidity which brought conviction to many devout pastors hitherto mistrustful of the New Learning. Kuenen saw '*real history*' as a thing to be recaptured by reassembling the separate stones dismantled by scholars from the edifice of tendentious 'salvation history' offered to us in the present form of our Bible.

Julius Wellhausen (1844–1918), surpassing even **94a** the lucidity of Kuenen, has rightly gone down in history as responsible for a definitive scientific formulation to which he contributed chiefly its definitiveness. He did this first by his *Die Composition des Hexateuchs* (1866), then mostly by his 1878 *History of Israel*, more modestly called in its next six editions *Prolegomena* (1905[6]). He holds that Pent and Jos reached their present form after the Exile, perhaps under Ezra after 450; thus their legal and rubrical materials stem from the *latest* phase of Israel's cultural development, though (contrary to what is often imputed to him) Wellhausen expressly states that these legal materials embody very ancient usages to a degree which is not always easy to determine exactly. Within this P framework may perhaps be distinguished **b** a basic Priestly theologian-archivist from a final R(edactor) who combined the framework itself with the other sources. We may distinguish also, as preliminary-P, an H, some author akin to Ezekiel who composed what A. Klostermann had recognized in Lv 17–23 as the 'Holiness-Code'. Before P, at or near the time of Josiah 621 B.C., Dt was composed as a unit entirely separate from the Gn-Nm sources, though continued in Jos. The combined JE document is earlier, and its separate parts earlier still; the date hazarded for the earliest written form of J, 850 in Wellhausen, is now rather linked with Solomon's 'wisdom' around 950, though neither dating is alleged on the basis of any concrete facts. Wellhausen insists that the Book-Prophets beginning around 750 reflect very clearly a cultic situation preceding both D's limitation to a single (Jerusalem) sanctuary, and P's variegated sacrifical system; but J and E show nothing essentially at variance with prophetic religion.

However, Wellhausen's service to the JEDP theory went much farther than ironing out the details of its hypothetical chronology. In the wake of De Wette and Ewald he concentrated on **reinterpreting the alleged events of Israelite history in the order and motivation in which they had really happened.** In doing this, he was largely influenced by Hegel's dialectical evolutionism mediated to him by Wilhelm Vatke's 1835

94c *Religion des AT.* The recent research of L. Perlitt (BZAW 94; 1965) aims to disprove this Hegel-Vatke influence by showing that Wellhausen examined all his facts carefully in themselves and built up his reconstruction of Israelite history out of them alone. But the formulations of KG 178 against which Perlitt (p. 3 n. 7 and p. 162f) is plainly arguing, make full allowance for the fact that 'Wellhausen's end-effect is far from Hegel'; and Wellhausen called Vatke's 'the most important contribution ever made to the historical understanding of ancient Israel' (Kraeling 73). Hegelian evolutionism is by Catholic evaluators even today almost universally held to be the unpardonable flaw in Wellhausen's re-

d construction of history. Some conclude that the whole JEDP fabric is thereby vitiated (as Cardinal Bea in his published works, though he expressly stated to me that not everything contained in them is in the form which research progress around 1950 would warrant); others feel that, with this defect isolated and expunged, the system is basically sound (cf de Vaux in VTS 1 (1953) 195 and in his introduction to Gn in JB, along with reserves on the dissection of *written* sources). But it would seem that the time has come to recognize that what Catholic authorities were afraid of in 1906 (Dz 1997) was not Hegel but *evolution*. Now that biological evolution has been explicitly admitted (Dz 2327; the wider extension of its principles in an evolutionism like that of Teilhard de Chardin is today intensely controverted), **much of what has been written against Wellhausen's 'Hegelian evolutionary postulates' might well be searchingly re examined.** Perlitt could at least claim validly that Wellhausen does deal primarily with *facts* whatever may be his more general philosophical tendencies. Before surveying his results we must also add that no defence can be attempted of another great and factual flaw in Wellhausen's work: he throve at a time when archaeological research was just beginning, and as a distinguished Arabist he seemed totally unable to recognize the mammoth importance of newly-unearthed cuneiform literatures from Babylon; and Amarna and Ugarit were presently to dominate even more the history he was striving to objectivize.

e Taking the JEDP source-analysis and the late dating of P as a working hypothesis, Wellhausen builds his synthesis on historical rather than literary-dissecting evidences. **He divides the history of Cultus** into five sections: place, victims, feasts, priesthood, paraphernalia. For each section elements *dependent* on earlier elements or unmentioned in provably early accounts are dated with P. The other elements by similar criteria are apportioned to D or JE. Wellhausen's technique for posing the questions for each epoch and answering them out of the sources, and thus tracing Israel's religious evolution, is unexampled in its methodical exactness (KG 241). Before the 7th cent. no limitation of cultus to a single sanctuary was ever advocated by the authorities shown acting in the Bible. After the 6th cent. this centralization is not only presumed, but the whole of earlier history is written in such a way as to make Mosaic institutions like the Ark-Tent an anticipation of this tardy cult-monopoly.

f The sacrifices of the earliest phase are held to have been rather primitive in their superstitious veneration for blood as a sort of animism. The strongest criticism of Wellhausen is directed against his assurance—allegedly preconceived, or borrowed from sociologists like Tylor—that human religious practices go through an evolution from the more primitive to the more refined. Such preconceptions were thirty years ago widely held to have been disproved by

Wilhelm Schmidt's scholarly anthropological verification **94f** of monotheism as the most primitive observable tribal stage. But even sympathetic experts now discount an element in Schmidt's evidences as being due to prior penetration of missionaries. And in the last analysis, history tells us only too plainly that the whole achievement of religion in its growth has been progressively to *liberate* men from ignorantly attributing to the caprice of autocratic gods those natural phenomena discoverable and controllable by science. **The extent to which God's revelation condescendingly conformed to the stage of cultural and scientific advance already attained by its recipients**, though already recognized by the early Fathers, **has latterly been vindicated** by the painful breaking down of a resistance on the supposed authority of the Bible, to heliocentrism and evolution.

The validity of Wellhausen's tracing of an evolving **g** Levitical priesthood to its latest stage in Chr can be inferred from the similar development outlined in de Vaux AI 345—465. Moreover the chh devoted to 'History of Tradition' and to the deuteronomic re-working of Sm-Kgs make somewhat unrealistic the claim of even de Vaux that Wellhausen was insufficiently concerned with oral strands or Noth-style *Überlieferung*-history. Of course not everything in Wellhausen is right. Even much of what is right is expressed with a bitterness against prevailing orthodoxies which cannot fail to antagonize. But not everything which is cynical is wrong. the P-strand *does* 'skip over what is interesting, and go into great detail on what is dull'. We shall be nearer to a balanced and just assessment of his enduring contribution to biblical study if (as CCHS[1] § 44*j* recommends) we advert primarily to the positive aspect and not expect him to have risen above the limitations of his own scientific and cultural background in a way we would not require of the Church Fathers or the inspired biblical authors themselves.

The **book-prophet** movement, partly in its alleged **h** kinship to D, becomes ultimately the pivot of a source-analysis originally concerned with the historical books. Amos in 750 is held to have been the first to link social morality with monotheism, which Moses indeed introduced to replace the equivocal (henotheist? monolatrous?) attitude of Jacob toward the various locally-venerated beings all called El. Sweeping denial of ethical character in the monotheism of Moses is impossible without rashly rejecting recent researches which maintain his personal responsibility for the lapidary formulations of the ('natural law'!) Decalogue. But here again we must not be **i** so wedded to tags or slogans as to refuse a grain of truth to indisputable evidences of progress. The monotheism of Adam or Jacob is not *exactly* the monotheism of Moses, nor this *exactly* the monotheism of Amos, just as it is not *exactly* the monotheism of Jesus or Paul or Aquinas or of each separate individual professing it today. What my total existential commitment to a single true God means is a thing which I could not even express, much less harmonize exactly with that of any other one man or teacher living even today. What monotheism means to Amos and in the age of Amos is doubtless a somewhat more refined and ethical doctrine than in the age of Moses. And this involves no implication that revelation itself has changed or the revealing God was untrue to himself; he has simply communicated to his chosen people as much of the total truth about himself as they were in a given age sufficiently educated to receive.

Prophetism, as it now began to be called, moves **j** toward the centre of attention because of influences other than Wellhausen. His sympathizer **Bernhard Duhm** produced in 1875 *Theology of the Prophets as basis for*

94j *the history of inner evolution of Israelite religion.* Here he recaptures that re-living of the individual prophet's total emotional life in its realistic historical background which Herder had already luminously advocated (KG 251; 131). Prophetic insight is now seen as an advance not only over the 'God of armies' mentality but also over an excessive concern for the 'God of storms and mountains'. Duhm's numerous commentaries on the individual prophets showed a skill symbolized in his emending of 'Chaldaeans' to *Kittim* in Hb 1, 6: which though a conjecture without authorization in any then-existing text, turned out to be confirmed by the Qumran Habakkuk scroll discovery. **Bernhard Stade** pursued similar aims by his *Biblische Theologie des AT* in 1905 and especially by founding in 1881 the still-unequalled *Zeitschrift für die Alttestamentliche Wissenschaft*.

k But sociology and psychology as newly-invented sciences were now to contribute the decisive impulse to research into the prophets. **Wilhelm Wundt's** influential 'Ethnic Psychology' 1906[2] (E. *Elements of Folk Psychology*, 1916) treats of visionary phenomena in a way that led Gustav Hölscher to attempt in *Die Profeten* (1914) a sort of psychoanalysis. The seers and prophetic guilds akin to Babylonian *baru* or *mahhu*, described in the books called 'Earlier Prophets' in the Heb. canon, were henceforward known as 'mantic' with full awareness that this derives from *mainō* and madness. They are often given the title *nabi*. Amos (7:14) dissociated himself from *nabi*-guilds. Yet there has been some point in the effort made to reserve the name of *nabi* for the Book-Prophets as an advance on mantic frenzy. Meanwhile the unique genius of **Max Weber** flashed out in the third volume of his *Religionssoziologie* (1921). It was translated as *Ancient Judaism* only in 1952. Analyzing the Israel plebs as a 'guest'-populace, he chose the term *pariah* for this and thus antagonized some of their descendants whom his overall insights should rather have flattered. He undyingly characterized the 'Judges' and Prophets as *charismatic*. This term is skilfully analyzed in other researches of Weber's as antithesis of the also-useful 'bureaucracy'. See Hahn 166–184 on the furthering of biblical sociology by A. Lods, A. Causse, and the Americans Louis Wallis, William Graham, and Salo Baron.

95a Gunkel—Religious sociology and religious psychology thus become genuine sciences alongside 'Comparative Religion'. To their data may be added the Herder 'naturalness', and the evolving notions of history and text-tradition. Out of all this now emerges a momentous school or rather dimension of all further biblical research, frustratingly called **Religionsgeschichte**. Rather than 'history of religions', it corresponds to that 'recapturing of the total real-life authorship situation' which is an ideal of the best modern practitioners of Form-Criticism. Presuming here what we have contributed above on the origins and boom of the Excavation-Movement (78a-80m; also Hahn 185–225), we have now truly reached the post-Wellhausen phase of biblical scholarship, with the meteoric rise of **Hermann Gunkel** (1862–1932).

b Actually Wellhausen and De Wette, and even Simon, had promoted quite explicitly a type of research oriented toward the *Gattung*, 'form-category', and *Sitz im Leben*, 'concrete situation in real life', both of which are rightly considered Gunkel trademarks. Far from 'dismantling' the existing edifice of recorded salvation-history in order to reconstruct 'what really happened', Gunkel's urge (*TLZ* 1906; KG 311) was to recognize and isolate the 'literary forms' *as they actually exist* within our Bible, and then with sociological imagination retrieve the real-life

situation from which such forms must have evolved. A **95b** sample of the extent to which his achievement has dominated OT research may be seen in the very outset of Eissfeldt's *Introd.* (1965), where 120 pages are devoted to 'The Pre-Literary Stage: the Smallest Units and their Setting in Life'. Even more momentous is the controversy raging about Bultmann under the name of 'Demythologizing', but really concerned with tiny oral units of tradition about Jesus and their vital situation in the earliest Church.

Though his Gn comm. (1910[3], 1922[5]) was Gunkel's **c** most masterful enrichment of exegesis with sociological saga-research, he is today perhaps more widely identified with his even more pioneering work on **the Psalms** (*Die Psalmen*, 1926[4]). He rejects as point of departure the emphasis of Carl Steuernagel on the fact that Heb. lyric poetry did have a kind of organic continuity through epochs of varying piety. Rather we should start from distinguishing the 'kinds' which within the text itself are recognizable as principal. These are **hymns, pilgrimage-chants, didactic verse; then Plaints and Thanks**, each in both individual and communitarian forms; then two types of **King-psalms**, those about the human king's crises, and those in which God is enthroned as king. Equally recognizable is claimed to be the fixed position of the respective types in an ancient **situation of public worship**. Worshippers in that situation are seen as having tended naturally to use a stock of prayerful motifs common not only as to the content but even as to the formulation. The exegete's function is simply to re-express in remote and modern cultures what the real living worshipper once felt in the depth of his heart. The exegete tries not to say something about the Pss from outside, but to express their piety by experiencing it from within.

Gunkel's approach to the Pss was carried forward **d** by **Willi Staerk and Rudolf Kittel**. His peremptory claims for the liturgy as matrix of our Bible formulations were set off on a significant new line by Paul Volz, *Das Neujahrsfest Jahwes* (*Laubhüttenfest*) in 1912, followed up by Sigmund Mowinckel's resoundingly successful *Psalmen-Studien* (1922; not = 1962, *The Psalms in Israel's Worship*). A long preface Gunkel wrote for Hans Schmidt's 1914 *Prophets* extended his insights to this sphere. In a broader range Gunkel's Saga research was promoted by **Hugo Gressmann**, especially as editor of ZAW after 1924. Gressmann in 1914 under the title 'Albert Eichhorn and the *religionsgeschichtlich* School' endeavoured to assign some credit to this obscure exegete. This (not Johann) Eichhorn re-focused on the *thing*-handed-down some of that attention which 'tradition research' had been monopolizing for the handing-down-*process*. We are concerned not so much with traceable influence of other religions from outside as with traceable continuity of the religion we are investigating—as somehow our own—from its own origins (KG 298). Gressmann's 1905 *Der Ursprung der israelitisch-jüdischen Eschatologie* and 1929 *Der Messias* afford interesting parallels in techniques to an early work of Gunkel's ranging far throughout Scripture, from Genesis 1 all the way to Apocalypse 12: *Schöpfung und Chaos in Urzeit und Endzeit*, (1895, 1931[2]).

'Programs' for future OT research began now to be **e** fashionable and we may with KG 329–58 (Hahn 103–9) fruitfully compare the three by Gunkel ('Aims and Methods', 1913), Kittel ('Future of OT Scholarship', ZAW 1921), and Gressmann ('Duties', ZAW 1924). For Gunkel all exegesis must deal with history, but in the sense of *Religionsgeschichte* without dogmatic fetters. Kittel fully approves the furtherance of all that Gunkel had

95e done, and insists even more on the exploitation of recently excavated evidences. But he holds out hopes of regaining the genuine religious *values* traceable within a merely descriptive religious phenomenology, so that somehow exegesis can be enriched by a right guidance from that living religious tradition which some see as a dogmatic straitjacket. Systematic and even religious philosophy cannot forever be left outside the pale of the exegete! Gressmann, while clinging closer to Gunkel's historicizing aims, insists that our research should bring to light not only what Israel borrowed from outside, but even more 'its own soul; its own originality and distinctiveness within the Near East; producing with the help of Weber-style sociology a 'Culture-History of Israel within the Culture-History of the Ancient Near East'. This plea was already partially satisfied by **Alfred Bertholet's** *Kulturgeschichte Israels* in 1919, and even more remarkably by the original outlooks of **Johannes Pedersen,** *Israel, its Life and Culture* (I 1920; II 1934); see Hahn 66—79.

96a Wellhausen 'won over the **English-language** public by his article "Israel" in *Encyclopaedia Britannica*[9]; it is his article "Hexateuch" in the *Encyclopaedia Biblica* (1901) which best summarizes his positions', RF, 1, 297. The ninth *Britannica* contained noteworthy contributions of its editor, **William Robertson Smith,** translator of Wellhausen's *Prolegomena*. Smith's *Lectures on the Religion of the Semites* (1894[2] — 1956) and other researches akin to James Frazer's *Golden Bough* were perhaps the most original and appreciated British con-

b tribution to biblical studies at this time. Another influential outlet for German critical theories was James Hastings' *Dictionary of the Bible* in four volumes (Edinburgh 1898) and in one volume (1909 re-edited 1963). But perhaps the most momentous boost to Bible study in our language was the adaptation of the *Hebrew Dictionary* of Wilhelm Gesenius by **Francis Brown, Samuel Driver, and Charles Briggs.** Driver was a great leader of this time. His perceptive *Introduction* is still used, and his son Godfrey has become one of the leading Semitists of our day. **John Skinner** ably defended the Gn. sources and was a leader in Prophets research. Both the prestigious **International Critical Commentary** and the compact **Cambridge Bible** did much to consolidate the JEDP position. The *Schweich Lectures* held annually since 1908 and skilfully published constitute one of the richest sources of biblical lore.

c The British **Society for Old Testament Study** was founded in 1917 and the collaboration of Cuthbert Lattey S. J. and Mgr. J. M. T. Barton was conspicuously in advance of the ecumenical era. This Society in addition to an annual book-list, has edited surveys of its scholarship in 1925, 1938, 1951, 1967. Perhaps the most distinctive contribution, though not necessarily the most universally appreciated, is the **'Myth and Ritual Pattern'** of **S. H. Hooke** (1933; *The Labyrinth* 1935; *Origins of Early Semitic Ritual*, 1938), finding in Israelite cultus a New Year's re-enactment of Near Eastern mythic resurrection of the dead life-cycle by a 'sacred

d marriage' of the divine king. This line of inquiry dovetails with **Scandinavian emphasis on divine kingship,** queried by M. Noth and J. de Fraine, but not without a continuing fascination. Related researches into cult-prophecy by **Aubrey Johnson** and Alfred Haldar have been favoured with wider acceptance. Another and more universally accepted British achievement is the notion of Corporate Personality worked out by **H. Wheeler Robinson** (BZAW 66, 1936) and pursued by de Fraine and F. Spadafora. The veteran OT scholar

H. H. Rowley has been in the forefront of British **96d** exegesis by his numerous densely-documented and judicious researches and his re-editing of classic or foreign works.

Catholic re-entry into the main stream of critical **e** scholarship must be linked with the great name of **Marie-Joseph Lagrange,** Dominican founder of the Jerusalem École Biblique (see § 80g). The misadventures attending his efforts to open Catholic eyes to the merits of JEDP and related researches have been set forth in *AmER* 126 (1952) 241—57. The 1893 Encyclical *Providentissimus Deus* of Pope Leo XIII shortly after Lagrange's Jerusalem initiative seemed to give it encouraging support. But presently troubles arose out of the 'Modernism' of Alfred Loisy, professor at the Institut Catholique in Paris, and British Jesuit George Tyrrell; (see *Continuum* 3 (1965) 168; 145—209; and M. de la Bedoyère's life of Baron Friedrich von Hügel, one of Lagrange's early contributors to *Revue Biblique*). In R. Grant's *Bible in the Church* 1960, 149, a chapter on the Catholic Church stops dead at 'Modernism'. As is known, Lagrange was discouraged from diffusing his OT views, and providentially turned to produce his **masterful gospel commentaries;** his article in RB 47 (1938) 163—83 is posthumous.

The founding of the **Pontifical Biblical Institute f** of Rome (periodicals *Biblica, Orientalia, Verbum Domini*) in 1909 was expressly intended to 'refute by scientific means' the critical trend in exegesis. The Jesuits to whom it was committed feared not being adequately prepared for this enterprise; but the organizer, Leopold Fonck, advanced with great assurance. He intervened with Pius X against Merry Del Val on behalf of progressive exegesis at America's Catholic University; but in establishing a Jerusalem branch of the Biblical Institute he voiced a mistrust of the Dominican enterprise which long rankled (see RB 47 (1938) 347).

The Biblical Institute is not an organ of the Vatican, **g** though it is officially approved and along with the Biblical Commission has had a monopoly of granting degrees in Scripture studies. **The Pontifical Biblical Commission** was founded in 1902 as an official Vatican organ to regulate questions of exegesis. From 1906 onwards this body issued a number of 'Replies' (as they were called) on a variety of subjects—against the theory of a Second Isaiah, late Psalms, the two-source theory in gospel criticism; and against acceptance of the JEDP sources on the basis of proofs thus far adduced. Such decrees are not 'irreformable' (and in fact one Holy Office decree rejecting scholarly consensus on 1 Jn 5:8 was dramatically repealed in 1927, DzS 3628); but their influence was great. J. Touzard's cautious defence of JEDP positions was stigmatized as 'unsafe' (AAS 12 (1920) 158), and Brassac's *Manuel Biblique* was declared so full of defects that it was incapable of emendation (AAS 15 (1923) 616). Nevertheless some progress was evident in the work of such writers as Sanda, Nikel, Heinisch and Goettsberger; and Albert Vaccari, professor at the Biblical Institute, admitted JE-style sources and was publicly approved by Pius XI in 1937 (see RB 47 (1938) 169—72). Divergent but parallel critical views were set forth by Louvain's J. Coppens in *The OT and the Critics* (1942[3]) and in his edition of van Hoonacker's Hexateuch analysis after the latter's death.

Two serious factors outside the Church must be **h** recognized as legitimately encouraging the Catholic opposition to prevailing critical theories: (a) sweeping denials of the Wellhausen theory by scholars such as Orr,

96h Wiener, Eerdmans, Jacob, Cassuto, Young and Robertson (see Hahn, 22—41), together with the querying of the Elohist by Volz, Rudolph, von Rad and Mowinckel; and on the other hand (b) the excesses of other critics in sub-dividing JEDP into a whole alphabet of minor strands (as C. Simpson's *Early Traditions of Israel*, Oxford, as late as 1948). Such excesses must be distinguished from the almost-acceptable recognition of a subdivision of J; Smend's J^2, Eissfeldt's L(ay source), Pfeiffer's S(eir) or K(enite), Fohrer's N(omad).

Seminary manuals such as Höpfl-Gut, Simon-Prado and Steinmueller's *Companion* (1942) continued therefore to be dominated by conservative positions such as those expressed by A. Bea, rector of the Biblical Institute, in his *De Pentateucho*, 1933, rejecting all basis for JEDP (see also his article in Bib 16 (1935) 177). But Bea, though remaining loyal to the Popes he served, admitted that the critical position was altering and eventually he became a worldwide leader in the related
i struggle of ecumenism. But **the decisive moment for Catholics was the publication in 1943 of** *Divino Afflante Spiritu* in which Pius XII not only **encouraged freedom and charity for biblical research** but also explicitly recognized the necessity for a critical approach. Then in 1948 Cardinal Suhard of Paris, pressing for the repeal of obsolete decrees, received instead an important letter stating that such decrees had never been intended to fetter research, and that in the Catholic world 'no one doubted' that large blocks of rubrics in the Pent in fact came from long after Moses (DzS 3863). This was soon followed by de Vaux's *Genèse* (JB, 1951), attaching the tags JEP with genuine acceptance 'even to the extent of breaking up a single verse into parts due to the separate strands'. De Vaux emphatically qualified his strands as oral rather than scissors-and-paste recombining of written documents, and he subscribed to the customary rejection of Wellhausen's philosophical presumptions. De Vaux's position soon dominated the whole of Catholic research. His influence and that of the Dominican École Biblique and of Catholic scholarship in general, thereupon came to be a massive and dominating force in world exegesis, thanks chiefly to the leadership he has assumed in archaeology. His excavation at Fara' (-Tirzah) was followed by his general direction of all the **Qumran** excavation, manuscript handling and publication, cf 80j.

A final tranquilizing of consciences in regard to un-repealed replies of the Biblical Commission is recognized in the unofficial but impressive comment of two Commission officials, A. Miller (*Benediktinische Monatschrift* 31 (1955) 49) and A. Kleinhans (*Antonianum* 30 (1955) 63—65): see E. Siegman, CBQ 18 (1956) 23, to the effect that the Commission's Replies were provisional norms shaped by the state of knowledge and the peculiar dangers of the time in which they were issued and certainly not closing the way to further investigation. Indeed many of the positions then viewed askance as not proven have since been accepted by Catholics in the light of subsequent research, while others have been abandoned by most scholars as being too extreme.
j We have seen above (93*b*,*c*) the close link between OT criticism and gospel researches. NT criticism is dealt with elsewhere in this volume (633—40). But even compartmentalized research has to recognize the validity of the question to what extent the OT can be judiciously evaluated apart from the New. Attention has been insistently drawn to this question by scholars such as Wilhelm Vischer, Karl Barth, H. H. Rowley and Norbert Lohfink. These honourable scholars are far removed from the anti-Semitic overtones faced frankly and contritely by

KG 393. But for purely scientific and exegetic reasons **96j** (apart from any incidental ecumenism), other Christians hold that they will always have a legitimate field of inquiry into the extent to which God's OT message was and remains valid, and remains in some way a patrimony which they hold in common with today's worshippers of Jewish faith.

American archaeological and ecumenical study 97a of the Bible background has come into prominence about the great figure of **William Foxwell Albright**. Born 1891 in Chile of Methodist missionary parents and early mastering Semitic and other languages he came to Jerusalem in 1920 as director of ASOR. This 'American School of Oriental Research' owed its origin to the **Society of Biblical Literature** which was founded at New York in 1880 and began publishing JBL in 1882. In 1895 J. Thayer as president called for an ASOR and appointed the committee which founded it in 1890. Its publications BASOR, AASOR, and BA, and the researches which they reported, were long guided by Albright. Meanwhile **James Breasted's Oriental b Institute of the University of Chicago** furthered the relevance of the Near East to Biblical research. Though increasing Jewish leadership in Bible study has revolved largely about Israel excavation, American Jewish experts like **Nelson Glueck** and **Harry Orlinsky** have extended their influence to more textual and theological areas. Glueck's East-Jordan and Negeb surface-exploration; **G. Ernest Wright's** Shechem excavation, archaeological synthesis, and 'God who Acts' theology; **Mitchell Dahood's** Ugaritic-Hebrew philology; **Joseph Fitz-myer's** Aramaic and Qumran research; **Raymond Brown's** ecumenical and Johannine studies; linguistic discoveries of **Frank Cross** and **David Noel Freedman**; **James Pritchard's** ANET, ANEP, and excavations; **William Moran's** Assyriological and Deuteronomic work at Chicago, Rome, and Harvard; and the **Anchor Bible** and (Catholic) **Jerome Commentary**—all these owe much to Albright's influence. Albright and archaeological movements related to him, though formed on German models, have constituted a sort of antithesis to German leadership traced above; and have earned much sympathy from Catholics as well as among Jews and Protestants. Yet as Père de Vaux pointed out to the 1964 meeting **c** of the Society of Biblical Literature, the apparent iconoclasm of Martin Noth and the current German scholarship identified with him is in fact based on a profound direct acquaintance with the text, in the production of commentaries and textual studies in a way which has never characterized Albright's school, despite its newly launched and uneven Anchor Bible.

We need not hesitate to admit, therefore, the extent **d** to which current **Form-Critical Studies**, under the aegis of **von Rad** and **Bultmann**, carry forward the main line of critical research from Simon through Wellhausen to Gunkel, cf § 133. **Albrecht Alt's** 'Leipzig school' has dominated the scene since his 1929 *Gott der Väter*. It holds that separate and personal nature-deities of the Patriarchs became fused with many a Canaanite place-bound divinity called 'El of the respective locality'. Alt's remarkable application of excavated-place names to determine the historical adjuncts of Israel's occupation of Canaan and eventual 'State-Structure' fills thirty years of research articles now felicitously gathered up in three volumes of *Kleine Schriften*. Here also we find Alt's discoveries on casuistic versus apodictic legal formulations, which have inspired the broader and more original researches, especially from **Henri Cazelles'** leadership of exegesis in homeland-France. Many of Alt's mantles fell **e**

97e on the broad shoulders of **Martin Noth**, who far surpassed them by his *History of Israel* synthesis, ZDPV-editing, active guidance of research in Jerusalem, and commentaries on Joshua, Exodus-Numbers, and Kings. Yet Noth's most central influence will doubtless remain his 'history of the traditions' in Pent and Chr, the 'etiologies' of Jos, and (despite recent impugning) the 'amphictyony' structure of bi-polar Judah and N-Israel. Noth only gradually came round to supporting von Rad's claim that our Pent derives from two separate 'cult-dramas': Tabernacles at Shechem concerning the Sinai event ('credo' of Dt 5,2), and the Gilgal 'Feast of Weeks' concerning the Canaan takeover ('Credo' of Dt 26, 5—9). If to these we add Noth's Egypt-preliminary as a third (Passover) cult-drama; and then with **Walter Beyerlin** recognize how the formulations of all three point back to a *unitary* event earlier in Israel's recollection: we are not far from a culmination which may well enlist the support of all partisans of literary-dissection, form-criticism, cult-pattern, and Catholic tradition!

Not that the end of a road has been reached. It **f** would seem that the next decisive battleground will be Hermeneutics or semantics. Prized researches of **Luis Alonso-Schökel** reflect the extent to which Catholic exegesis is now ripe for entry into the areas outlined in RGG³ (1959) 3, 243—62. We have not yet sounded all that was implied when Kuenen's 'what really happened' as the exegete's goal was replaced by Gunkel's 'what the writer *means*' (KG 330). 'God is Dead' and Bonhoeffer's 'fringe-area religious crutch' compel ever-renewed appraisal of Quintilian's view that 'every statement we ever make is metaphorical' along the lines of Ch 17 in Bernard Lonergan's 1957 *Insight*, and the Existentialist researches of Eduard Schillebeeckx and Karl Rahner.

THE RELIGIOUS INSTITUTIONS OF THE OLD TESTAMENT

BY A. SMITH C.P. AND W. WATSON C.R.L.

103a Bibliography—W. F. Albright, *Archaeology and the Religion of Israel*, Baltimore, 1953; J. Bright, *A History of Israel*, 1961; W. Eichrodt, *Theology of the OT I*, 1961; J. Pedersen, *Israel, Its Life and Culture*, *III–IV*, 1959; R. de Vaux, O.P., AI, 1961; Hans-Joachim Kraus, *Worship in Israel, A Cultic History of the OT*, Oxford, 1966. E. tr. from German 2nd ed. by G. Buswell; H. Ringgren, *Israelite Religion*, 1967 H. H. Rowley, *Worship in Ancient Israel*, 1967; R. E. Clements *God and Temple*, the idea of the divine presence in Ancient Israel, Oxford 1965; H. Renckens, *The Religion of Israel*, E. tr. 1967.

b Introduction—'I am the Lord your God' (Dt 5:6). Israel's relationship with God was such that there was little if anything in the national life which did not have a religious aspect. Birth, death, marriage; law, government; even warfare—all of these had their appropriate religious ceremonial and could validly be dealt with in an article on Israel's 'Religious Institutions'. Here, however, only those institutions which directly concern the formal and public worship will be treated.

c Desert Shrines—The original prescriptions of the Covenant were inscribed upon two tablets and kept within a costly wooden chest called **the Ark** (Dt 10:1ff; Ex 25:16, 21). The fullest description of it is given in Ex 25:10—21 but most commentators agree that this is a late text and includes objects which were added later to the description of the Ark. Nevertheless, it does reflect authentic traditions going back to the days in the desert. The Ark was both the **container of the Decalogue** and the **throne of the invisible God**. We find corroboration for this twofold purpose in the custom of other ancient religions of keeping contracts and laws at the feet of their gods in a chest. Hittite treaties (c. 1450—1200 B.C.) whose structure and formulas are so strikingly reflected in the Mosaic Decalogue were also kept beneath the feet of the gods of the covenant parties (cf G. E. Mendenhall, *Law and Covenant in Israel and the Ancient Near East*, Pittsburgh 1955). Being the visible sign of God's presence the Ark also preceded the people in their journey (Nm 10:35f; Dt 1:33; Jos 3:3; 1 Sm 4:3—4, 7; 2 (4) Kgs 19:14f). During the period of the settlement it was moved from sanctuary to sanctuary (Shechem, Bethel, Gilgal) until it was finally set up and housed at **Shiloh**. This place then became the **central sanctuary** since where the Ark was there was the place where God dwelt in a most intimate way. It was here that Israel would renew the covenant whose laws were contained in the Ark. During the time it dwelt at Shiloh it was called, 'Ark of the Covenant of the Lord of Hosts' (1 Sm 4:4; 2 Sm 6:2). The tribes assembled there for war since the Ark was also regarded as the palladium of God. When it was brought into battle Israel's enemies could say 'a god has come into the camp' (1 Sm 4:7; cf also Nm 10: 35—36; 14:43—44). It was captured by the Philistines at the disastrous battle of Aphek in 1050 B.C. (1 Sm 4:1—11).

Its presence proved unfortunate and unwelcome so they **103** returned it to Israel at Beth-Shemesh whence it was taken to Kiryath-Jearim (1 Sm 5:1—7:2). David brought it to Jerusalem (2 Sm 6:1—19). It seems to have been lost with the Babylonian destruction of Jerusalem in 587 B.C. It is not heard of again and no new Ark was built (Jer 3:16). The Ark is characteristic of Israelite religion and shows one basic difference from the belief of the Canaanites: God is not connected to a specific place but to certain groups of people. The members of the clan worshipped one god, irrespective of where they happened to be, and so remained closely knit, cf A. Alt, *Essays in OT History and Religion*, Oxford 1966, pp. 1ff.

The text in Ex 25 speaks also of a golden plate above **d** the Ark of the same width and length called the **Kapporeth** or **Mercy Seat** which had a golden cherub at each end. Both these sacred objects belong to Israel's later history. Neither is mentioned in the description of Solomon's Temple (1 (3) Kgs 6:1—8:8). We only read of the Mercy Seat again in the post-exilic Chronicler who describes the Holy of Holies as 'the room for the mercy seat' (1 Chr 28:11). The two cherubim in Solomon's Temple stood on their feet facing down the Temple. Their name is from the Akkadian word '*Karibu*' which describes a spirit who advised the gods and interceded with them for the people. Israel saw them as spirits of perpetual prayer and adoration who ministered for her at the throne of Yahweh (cf 2 Sm 22:11; Ps 18(17):11). In appearance they probably looked like winged lions with human heads as did their Babylonian and Syro-Phoenician counterparts. The cherubim represented Yahweh's cloud-chariot (cf 1 Chr 28:18, Hb 3:8 etc), a throw-back to Baal's epithet 'Rider of the Clouds'. Their form goes back to the sphinxes of Egypt, but the representation of a throne supported by cherubim has its origin in Phoenicia. In the Temple one wing of these mighty figures touched the side wall of the Holy of Holies. With their other they overshadowed the Ark (1 (3) Kgs 6:27). One suspects that both the Mercy Seat and its cherubim were made after the Exile, the former as the substitute for the lost Ark as the throne of God, the latter as smaller imitations of the first cherubim. They rested on the ends of the Mercy Seat, facing each other and overshadowing the Mercy Seat with their wings.

Besides the Ark, the throne of the invisible God, the **e** Israelites also had in the desert a tent-shrine or sanctuary, known usually as the **Tabernacle** from the Latin for 'tent', (the term used in the Vg). It is usually held that the original purpose of the Tent was for consulting Yahweh: it was the Tent of Oracles where Moses met and spoke with God 'face to face'; and it was pitched outside the camp. Thus it is recounted in Ex 33:7—11; which is probably to be ascribed to the Elohist, our oldest source on this subject. It was known as the **Tent of Meeting**, Heb. *'ōhel mô'ēd*. The people used Moses as their intermediary with God.

The later Priestly tradition interwoven with the **f**

03f earlier, developed the idea of God's presence in the Tent and preferred to use the name of *Dwelling*, Heb. *miskan. Origins and History of the Oldest Sinaitic Traditions*, E. tr, implied in the earlier title. In keeping with this later idea we read in ch. 35ff very elaborate instructions for the making of the Tabernacle—the mishkan. We are also told that the Ark was kept in it, Ex 40:3 and in keeping with the idea of God dwelling among his people, the Priestly tradition envisages the Tent as being in the centre of the camp, Nm 2:2, 17, cf de Vaux, AI, 294—5; N. H. Snaith, *Leviticus-Numbers*, CBi², 28—29.

W. Beyerlin however, gives a different picture. Ex 33:7—11, though belonging to the E-source, is not a unity and includes diverse traditions not always compatible: e.g. vv 8, 10 assume the tent to be in the middle of the camp, v 7 states it to be well outside. He concludes that the earlier tradition held that the Tent was in the middle and that everyone could approach and consult Yahweh. Later the Elohist editor separated it from the people and forbade people to approach Yahweh except through Moses. Beyerlin asks 'Why cannot P, which often goes back to old traditions in its picture of the camp, have followed an old tradition which places the Tent in the centre of the camp?', *Origins and History of the Oldest Sinaitic Traditions*, E. tr. 1965, 112—13. Whatever the way its character developed, we can at least be sure that both Tent and Ark date back to the desert period. As M. Noth observes: 'By its very nature a tent sanctuary belongs in the milieu of men who are not firmly settled and themselves live in tents; thus everything is in favour of the tradition of a tent-sanctuary going back to the time before Israel became settled in a cultivated land', *Exodus*, E. tr. 1962, 255. The names of Hophni and Phinehas, sons of Eli and priests of the Ark in Shiloh are ancient and of Egyptian origin.

Before the tribes crossed into Canaan they set up the Tent for the last time outside the Promised Land on the Plains of Moab (Nm 25:6). Some texts speak of the Tent at Shiloh (Jos 18:1; 19:51) although some scholars regard them as of a later tradition. According to 1 Chr 21:29f and 2 Chr 1:3 it was kept at the high place of Gibeon.

g **The Sanctuaries of Israel**—When Israel began to settle in Canaan they used various places for the worship of Yahweh. Their choice was not arbitrary. The place selected had to be a 'holy place', i.e., Yahweh must in some way have made himself known there, it must possess the divine presence. Hence a 'holy place' could be a piece of land (Sinai in Ex 19:12), a sanctuary (foundation of Ophrah in Jg 6:11—24; 25—32) or a 'high place' (1 Sm 9:13, 14, 19). The origin of some of the sanctuaries was traced back by tradition to the Patriarchs. The establishing of the sanctuary of **Shechem**, for example, is attributed in the J Tradition to Abraham (cf Gn 12:6—7) and in the E Tradition to Jacob the ancestor of the twelve tribes (cf Gn 33:19; 48:22). These sanctuaries were old Canaanite cultic centres. This illustrates the assertion 'There is no element in the cultic tradition of the OT which is not in some way connected with the world of Canaanite religion. The worship of Israel did not fall down complete from Heaven, but arose out of a keen struggle with the powerful religious forms and practices of the country' (Kraus, op cit 36; cf 169—170). Thus the stories of patriarchs founding these shrines really recount attempts by Hebrews to take over the Canaanite-founded sanctuaries or at least share the worship there. It was **at Shechem that the tribes became a federation united by the bond of Covenant** (Jos 24). Here the Covenant was recited and renewed yearly at the Feast of Tents (Dt 31:9—13) while it remained the central sanctuary.

Various elements of this renewal ceremony are scattered **103g** through the works of the Deuteronomic redactors (cf Dt 11:26—32; 27:1—6; Jos 8:30—35). The system of twelve tribes grouped together around a central sanctuary is regarded as 'the central religious institution of Israel after the Conquest' (Albright, p. 102). But more than any other it was the sanctuary of **Shiloh** which fulfilled this important place in the nation's life. It was here that Joshua set up the Tent of Meeting (Jos 18:1; 19:51; 22:12). Yearly pilgrimages were made there (Jg 20: 26—28; 21:19—21; 1 Sm 1:3ff). A 'house of God' was built there for the Ark which was brought there (Jg 18:31; 1 Sm 1:7, 9; 3:2—3, 15), and its chief priest was held in high esteem. This great sanctuary was destroyed by the Philistines around the year 1050 B.C. (Ps 78 (77); I Sm 4:10ff; Jer 7:14). The temple was a Canaanite innovation and involved fixed cultic personnel. Thus sacrifice ousted prophecy (1 Sm 3, 1). The Philistine destruction was considered divine punishment for this pagan mould of worship (Jer 7:12ff). Its successor became the sanctuary of Jerusalem when David moved the Ark there from Kiryath-Jearim.

Closely linked with the patriarch Jacob was the **h** sanctuary of **Bethel** (Gn 28:18f; 31:13). This was originally Canaanite; the pagan tradition comprised three important elements: the god 'Bethel' worshipped there, the *maṣṣebâ* ('sacred pillar') and the stairway, perhaps a symbol of the mountain top on which such shrines were usually built; cf Gn 28:12—13. The Ark was probably taken there during the time of Israel's war against the Benjaminites (cf Jg 20:18, 26, 31; 21:2). After the division of the kingdom in 922 B.C. Jeroboam I made Bethel with Dan in the N a rival sanctuary to Jerusalem and set up there one of his golden bulls as the symbolic throne of God (1 (3) Kgs 12:28—30). Another interpretation is that the actual image was venerated. In the texts from Ras Shamra El is called 'bull' (*tr* and Baal appears as a bull in the mythological texts. The golden calves would then represent the true God; there was never identification of image and deity. It was 'the king's sanctuary and it is a temple of the kingdom' (Am 7: 13). Bethel and Dan were most probably chosen because there were already temples there (Gn 28:22; Jgs 17). It was destroyed by the Assyrians during the years of their siege of Samaria (724—722 B.C.) We learn from 2 (4) Kgs 17:28 that the Assyrians sent a priest to re-establish worship at Bethel but this revival was short-lived. The sanctuary was finally desecrated and destroyed under the reforming zeal of Josiah (2 (4) Kgs 23: 15—20).

Another sanctuary, **Gilgal**, was near Jericho (J. **i** Muilenburg, 'The Site of Ancient Gilgal', BASOR 140 (1955) 11ff) and hence the first sanctuary after the entry into the Promised Land (Jos 4—5). Its name means 'a circle' of stones and here Joshua set up twelve stones to commemorate the crossing of the Jordan (Jos 4:20), which shows the amphictyonic nature of the sanctuary. It was a great political and religious centre under Saul who was made king there, 'before the Lord in Gilgal' (1 Sm 11:15). Many sacrifices were also offered there (1 Sm 10:8; 13:7f; 15:21, 33).

After the destruction of Shiloh and the capture of the Ark the sanctuary of **Gibeon** became the central tribal sanctuary. Set on a mountain (2 Sm 21:6, 9) it was 'the great high place' of the time of Solomon which he visited and where he offered sacrifice (1 (3) Kgs 3:4—15). It was one of many 'high-places' which were considered as legitimate holy places of worship in early Israel (1 (3) Kgs 3:3; cf also 1 Sm 9:12f).

103i Throughout her long history Israel used other sanctuaries of diverse origin, antiquity and importance. Such were Mamre near Hebron (Gn 13), Mizpah, Ramah (1 Sm 7), Beersheba (1 Sm 8:1f; Am 5:5, 8:14), Ophrah (Jg 6) and Dan (Jg 17—18).

j The greatest of all the sanctuaries was the **Temple of Jerusalem**. David had captured the city of the Jebusites and set up a tent there for the Ark (2 Sm 6:17; 7:2; 24:16—25). In the fourth year of Solomon (c. 959 B.C.) a Temple was begun where the name of Yahweh could dwell (1 (3) Kgs 8:29). It was finished seven years later (1 (3) Kgs 6:38). Most of its raw materials, architects and craftsmen were supplied by the Phoenician King of Tyre, Hiram (1 (3) Kgs 7:13f). It stood for 400 years until its destruction by Nebuchadnezzar king of Babylon in 587 B.C.

The texts from which we draw a description of this Temple have been through many hands. Details of structure and lay-out have been omitted. Glosses are added and technical terms used whose precise meaning still escapes final clarification. However, from a union of what knowledge these texts provide with extra-Biblical information about other Near Eastern Temples we can form a fairly good idea of what Solomon's Temple might have looked like. The temple and its furnishings possessed a cosmic symbolism, the building on earth corresponding to the temple in heaven.

k If we had entered the Temple area from the E and begun to walk towards the Temple we would have had to skirt round an Altar of Sacrifice which lay immediately in front of the Temple. Over on our left would be the 'Sea of Bronze', a large water holder where the priests purified themselves (1 (3) Kgs 7:23—26). This 'Sea' symbolized the vast primeval ocean, the *Apsû* of Babylonian cosmogony. Climbing the steps to the entrance we would pass the ten wheeled water pedestals, five on either side, for the washing of the sacrificial victims (1 (3) Kgs 7:27, 38). Going through the Temple doors between the two great, free-standing bronze columns (1 (3) Kgs 7:15ff), we would have entered the *Ulam* or entrance hall of the Temple. A few yards further on we would go through the opening of an inner wall into the *Hekal* or Holy Place where we would see the golden altar of incense (1 (3) Kgs 6:22), the table of sanctified bread before the Holy of Holies and the ten candelabra (1 (3) Kgs 7:48f; cf Is 6). (The seven-branched candlestick was not part of Solomon's furnishings but a later addition). Finally, we would see the costly curtain falling before a raised section of the floor. Beyond this was the *Debîr*, the Holy of Holies, in which the Ark of the Covenant was enshrined under the shadow of the wings of the Cherubim (1 (3) Kgs 6:23ff). In front of the porch were two pillars, variously interpreted as *maṣṣēbôt* ('sacred pillars'), as symbols of the cosmic pillars through which the sun passes daily, or as cressets. Their names, Jachin and Boaz, are the first words of dynastic oracles promising permanence to the royal line.

l Centralization of Worship—But the multiplicity of 'high places' and other sanctuaries apart from the Temple in Jerusalem was not regarded with favour either by the kings of Judah or by the prophets. The dangers of political disunity, especially after the division of the kingdom, and of religious syncretism from the influence of foreign religions were great. Hence in the reign of Hezekiah (718—687) the 'high places' of Judah were suppressed and the people told, 'you shall worship before this altar in Jerusalem' (2 (4) Kgs 18:4, 22, cf Is 36:7). This movement towards reform and centralization suffered a setback under his impious son Manasseh (2 (4) Kgs 21:3)

but was carried on with greater vigour than before under **103** Josiah (640—609). His reform is fully described in 2 (4) Kgs 22:3—23:25 and 2 Chr 34:1—35:19). He was inspired by the previous efforts of Hezekiah and by the laws of Dt which had been found during his reign. These laws had crystallized in legislation a tendency already present in the very structure of the nation as a system of tribes grouped round a central place of worship and which the Deuteronomic editors wished the nation to accept and conform to by the recognition of Jerusalem as 'the place which the Lord your God will choose, to make his name dwell there' (Dt 12:11). After the tragic death of Josiah there was a slipping back into the old ways (Jer 7:1—20; 13:27). Then there was the Exile when the nation had no sanctuary at all and Jerusalem lay in ruins. After their return Israel never had any other sanctuary but the Temple which they then rebuilt.

The Ministers of Religion cf H. Ringgren, 204—219— **104** Like other nations Israel had a priesthood for the service of God. These ministers were called, 'priests, the sons of Levi' (Dt 31:9). However, the earliest traditions in the OT do not suggest there was a regular priesthood. It was for the father to perform acts of worship; this is especially true of the patriarchs. Priests are not mentioned till the period of the Judges (Jg 17). The term for 'priest' in Heb. is *kōhēn*, as in Ugaritic, Phoenician and Nabatean. No satisfactory etymology has been proposed and the Arabic cognate *kāhin* has more the meaning of 'soothsayer'. In the Ugaritic texts the *khn* is a general cultic official at a sanctuary and the usual name for the priest (cf also 1 Sm 5:5; 6:2).

The priesthood was not a vocation but **an hereditary office** which passed from father to son (Jg 18:30; 1 Sm 1:3). The granting of priesthood was called 'filling his hand' (cf Ex 32:29; Jg 17:5—12), a term which seems best explained by the right which his office gave the priest to a share in the revenues of the sanctuary which he served and the sacrifices offered there. Noth compares this with the equivalent rites described in the Mari texts; 'Amt und Berufung im Alten Testament', *Bonner Akademische Reden* 19 (1958) 6—8. Some were installed as priests to a particular sanctuary while others were a type of 'unattached cleric', wandering and seeking installation at a sanctuary or living by the charity of the people (Dt 12:12; 18:6—7; Jg 17:7—9). Because of their status as ministers of the altar they were 'sacred' and set apart from the profane world (1 Sm 2:28; Nm 1:50; 3:6ff). While they had no territorial rights in Israel (Jos 13:14, 33; 18:7), David had plans to assign to them certain cities which are listed in Jos 21 and 1 Chr 6:54ff. It is disputed whether these plans ever got beyond the planning stage. What is certain however is that many Levites did actually live in many of the cities mentioned in the lists such as Shechem, Anathoth, Gibeon etc.

The origin and development of **Israel's priesthood b** is a complex question. The opinion followed here is not, therefore, to be regarded as the only one possible. Texts quoted to show that this priesthood was instituted by the direct intervention of God and that the Levites were the divinely appointed assistants of Aaron and his sons (Nm 1:50; 3:6ff), are contradicted by other texts. Compare, for example, Nm 3:6ff where the Levites are appointed to minister to Aaron and his sons with Ex 32:25—29 where the Levites stand with Moses in opposition to Aaron and by their obedience to him gain for themselves instalment 'for the service of the Lord' (Ex 32:29).

In pre-Mosaic times the tribe of Levi was simply a **c** secular tribe and in Gn 49:4—7 it is condemned with the tribe of Simeon for its violence. We must presume that it

04c became a peaceful tribe and began to specialize in cultic worship. One is tempted to see in the account of Ex 32 the traces of a tradition that Moses installed them as the official tribe for the performance of Israel's worship. While it is true that in the early period of Israel's history we still find non-Levites exercising priestly functions, such as Samuel who was an Ephraimite (1 Sm 1:1; 2:18), and the sons of David (2 Sm 8:18), it appears that by the 8th cent. only those who could claim membership of the tribe of Levi were regarded as legitimate priests. Some authors would hold for a distinction between the actual tribe of Levi and the priesthood of 'Levites'. But this would be to go against the strong Scriptural tradition which links the priesthood with this tribe.

d **In the early days there was no distinction drawn between priest and levite.** Both were equally ministers of the altar with the same rights and powers. But with the establishment of a priesthood by David in his new capital of Jerusalem and the building of a magnificent Temple by his son, the seeds of future discrimination between this priesthood and that of the lesser sanctuaries were sown. This would receive further impetus from the centralization policies of Hezekiah and Josiah in the 8th and 7th cent. Although the priests of the other sanctuaries were entitled to come to minister in Jerusalem if and whenever they desired, enjoying the same rights and privileges as the 'Levitical priest' (Dt 18:6–8), in practice however (as we see reflected in the Books of Kings, cf 2 (4) Kgs 23:9) a distinction was made by the Temple clergy between the 'Levitical priest' and 'Levite'. When Ezekiel wrote in the 6th cent. the distinction is a recognized fact (Ezek 44:10, 31).

e The post-exilic priesthood of Jerusalem, which traced its pedigree back to Aaron through his sons Eleazar and Ithamar, became powerful with the total and effective centralization of cult in the Second Temple. Therefore this Priestly Tradition would read back into the Exodus situation much of their own: of Aaron as the chief priest and his sons to whom perpetual priesthood was granted by God (Ex 29.9, 44, 40.15, Nm 25:7–13; 3:3) and of the Levites as the divinely appointed assistants to this priesthood (Nm 3:6ff).

To the Levites was confided charge of the Tent and the Ark (Nm 1:50–53). They were also to act as advisers (1 Sm 14:41–42) and as teachers to give instruction or 'torah' concerning worship and the interpretation of the laws (Dt 33:10; Jer 18:18; Ezek 7:26; Mi 3:11) They were to be present during sacrifices to assist and to carry the blood of victims to the altar (Ezek 44:11). Some sacrifices were their privilege alone (Lv 4:3ff; 16).

f In the performance of the Temple worship there were **five main officials.** The highest official was the 'chief priest' (1 (3) Kgs 4:2; 2 (4) Kgs 25:18). After the Exile this office grew in importance and the title of 'High Priest' was assumed. Beneath him was the 'second Priest' (2 (4) Kgs 23:4; 25:18; Jer 52:24). The remaining three officials were called the 'three keepers of the threshold' (2 (4) Kgs 25:18). Other lower-ranking ministers included door-keepers (1 Chr 26:1–19), a keeper of vestments (2 (4) Kgs 22; 14) and twenty-four classes of singers whose institution is attributed by the Chronicler to King David himself (1 Chr 25, cf § 303a).

The financial support for all the clergy came from the offerings made to the sanctuary and their share of taxes (2 (4) Kgs 12:5–17; Nm 18:8–32; Lv 6–7). They also received a share of the various sacrifices and of the offerings of first-fruits and the tithes on corn, cattle, oil and new wine etc (cf Am 4:4; Tb 1:6–8). On priests and Levites see also § 253i–j.

Sacrifice cf R. de Vaux, *Studies in OT Sacrifice*, **104g** Cardiff, 1964——Sacrifice to the deity is of the essence of cult. From earliest days Israel expressed her worship of Yahweh in various types of sacrifice. It is difficult to trace the origin in time of many of them since our main source of information in Lv chh 1–7 is, according to the common opinion, the mirror of the sacrificial rites performed during the time of the Second Temple. One permissible assumption nevertheless, is that sacrifices involving first-fruits, oil, flour etc could only have become a part of her ritual when Israel became a settled and agricultural society after the Conquest.

Each sacrifice can be looked at from three points of view: (a) the material offered—animals, cereals, spices, liquids; (b) the action of offering—burning, either completely or partially, pouring, sprinkling; (c) the purpose for which it was offered—thanksgiving, expiation, etc. It was this third aspect which determined the other two; but the descriptions given in the Bible and the names used for the sacrifices (holocaust, sin-offering, etc) slip from one aspect to another.

Two types whose origins can certainly be traced back **h** to Israel's **beginnings** were the Sacrifice of Burnt Offering or Holocaust and the Sacrifices of Peace Offerings (cf Ex 10:25; 18:12; 20:24; 32:6; Jg 20:26; 1 Sm 6:15; 13:9; 1 (3) Kgs 3:15). The Canaanites knew both forms of sacrifice. The OT attests this in 1 (3) Kgs 18 (holocaust) and Ex 34:15ff (sacrificial meal). The Moabites also offered holocausts (Nm 23; 2 (4) Kgs 3:27); Naaman, a Syrian, offered both holocausts and communion sacrifices (2 (4) Kgs 5:2 (4) Kgs 5:17). The Phoenician colony of Carthage has yielded two 'tariffs' which list these sacrifices as well as other types. True these documents are later than the OT passages referred to, but they are confirmatory evidence. Religious practice in pre-Israelite Canaan is documented in the Ras Shamra texts. There both burnt-offering (*šrp*) and peace-offering (*šlm*) are mentioned; one of the duties of Danel's son was to eat a communion sacrifice in the temple of Baal (Aqhat legend). It is noteworthy that these W Semitic sacrifices were unknown in both Mesopotamia and Arabia; however they were practised in Greece. Because of this de Vaux proposes that the Canaanites borrowed holocaust and communion-sacrifice from a pre-Semitic civilization, before the 14th cent. The Israelites in their turn took over these religious rites, but with adaptation. None of the lean meat was burned, which blurred the pagan idea of a meal for the god as well. More important still, a blood rite, an essential part of Hebrew sacrifice missing from the cults of Ras Shamra, Phoenicia and N Africa, was added. (de Vaux op cit p. 50).

'olāh or 'that which ascends' is the name given to the Sacrifice of **Burnt Offering** whose smoke rose to God. If the offering was a bird its head was wrung off by the priest. Animals of the herd or flock were killed by its offerer. The blood of the offering was taken by the assisting priest and poured round the Altar of Sacrifice. The bird was burnt and the animal was first skinned, then cut into pieces which were then placed on the altar by the priest (the entrails and legs were first washed) to be burnt (Lv 1:1–17). After the settlement in Canaan additions were made to the rite: an offering of flour mixed with oil was also burnt and wine poured out at the foot of the altar (cf Lv 23:12f). Nothing was kept from this sacrifice either by the offerer or by the priest. God received all. It was regarded, therefore, as the most perfect of all sacrifices (Lv 1:9b). Many ancient sacrifices of burnt offerings were made in Thanksgiving or Intercession (cf Gn 8:20; 22:1–13; 1 Sm 6:15; 7:9). In time this must have

104h assumed a more expiatory significance which we see reflected in Lv (cf Lv 16). The use of blood is significant. It was in its blood that the soul or life of the victim was regarded as especially present. The blood of the offering was the symbol of the blood and life of the offerer and the action of pouring it out around and on the altar was the expression of the man's interior desire to offer himself totally to the Lord.

i *Šelāmim* or **Peace Offerings** were joyful sacrifices in which an important part of the ritual was a meal to be taken from certain parts of the offering. There were three kinds. It could be offered as a token of gratitude and thanks for divine favours (Lv 7:12—15). This was called *tôdah*. It was a sacrifice of joy as can be seen from the hymns composed to accompany it, for example, Ps 56 (55):12b—13a, 'I will render thank offerings to thee, for thou hast delivered my soul from death' (cf also Jer 17:26; 33:11; Am 4:5; Ps 50 (49):14, 23). The meal that followed the sacrifice had to be finished on the same day (Lv 7:15). The Votive Offering or *neder* was a sacrifice offered to fulfil a vow, 'I will come into thy house with burnt offerings; I will pay thee my vows . . .' (Ps 66 (65):13; also see Ps 22 (21):26; 116 (114—115): 14, 18). With this sacrifice the meal could be eaten on **j** the following day if any remained over (Lv 7:16). The Freewill Offering or *nedābāh* like the thank offering was a voluntary act of gratitude whereby a man expressed his inner wish to submit himself to the service of the Lord (Lv 22:18; Nm 29:39; Dt 16:10; 23:23; Am 4:5). The remains of the meal after this sacrifice could also be finished on the next day. In these three sacrifices only the fat from the entrails, kidneys, and the lobe of the liver were burnt and the fat of a sheep's tail. The rite of sacrifice is similar to that of Burnt Offering and is described in Lv 3. Two parts of the offering were to be given to the priest, the breast and the right thigh (Lv 7:30—33). An offering of cereals also went with these sacrifices (Lv 7:12—14). Because of the meal which formed part of these rites they are also called 'communion sacrifices'. Those who participated were to be legally clean since the meal was part of the ritual and the flesh of the victim had become holy because of its contact through its blood with the sacred altar.

The **Cereal Offerings** which accompanied all animal sacrifices in which blood was shed could also be offered by themselves in sacrifice (Lv 2). We read also of oil being used by itself, being poured over the Altar of Sacrifice (Mi 6:7) and of frankincense (Is 43:23; Jer 6:20; 17:26; 41:5).

A word may be added on **Human Sacrifices**. This practice is a mark, not of savages, but of civilized peoples. Of Israel's neighbours neither Arabs, Sumerians nor Assyrians accepted this mode of sacrifice. Exceptions are due to Phoenician influence; even in Moab this rite was a last resort in dire emergency (2 (4) Kgs 3:27). Again, the texts of the OT recording human sacrifice in Israel stress that it was considered extraordinary, e.g. Jephthah's vow (Jg 11, 30—40); and Abraham's obedience (Gn 22, obviously an outright condemnation of such sacrifice). A related problem is that of sacrifices to Moloch. These are condemned by the Bible as unlawful and due to the influence of Canaanite religion (e.g. Dt 12:29—31). *molk* in Punic and Neo-Punic inscriptions of N Africa is a term for child-sacrifices (though sometimes lambs were substituted); *mlk* (whatever its vocalization) is used in the same connection in Ezek 16:21; 23:37—39; Is 30:33. Latin and Greek texts witness to the same type of sacrifice at Carthage: dead or alive the victim was always burnt. We know that much earlier this custom obtained

in Phoenicia, but the Ras Shamra tablets do not offer **10** strong enough evidence for Ugarit (de Vaux, *Studies*, pp. 52—90). See W. Albright, *Yahweh and the Gods of Canaan*, 1968, 209ff.

Two other sacrifices in Israel's religious life were **k** those of *Hattā't* or **'Sacrifice for Sin'** and *'Ǎšām* or **'Sacrifice for Guilt'**. The whole question of these two sacrifices is very complex and is treated excellently in L. Moraldi, *Espiazione Sacrificale e Riti Espiatori nell' ambiente biblico e nell'antico testamento*, Rome 1956. There is no clear indication of expiatory sacrifices in W Semitic texts. The Marseilles sacrificial tariff [ANET pp. 502—3] from Carthage) lists a sacrifice termed *kll*, erroneously interpreted by some as an act of expiation; (see D. M. L. Urie, 'Sacrifice among the W Semites', PEQ 1949, pp 67—68). Similarly *klli* in a Ras Shamra poem (II AB (viii) line 19 = ANET p. 135c.) can only mean 'like a lamb'. Further, there is no corroboration for equating Ugaritic *atm* with Heb. *'ašām*, as the word occurs only in fragmentary texts and appears to be Hurrite in origin. However there are indications that the concept of sacrifice for expiation was not unknown to the Canaanites; cf A. De Guglielmo, 'Sacrifice in the Ugaritic Texts', CBQ 17 (1955) 212—3. In Sacrifice for Sin the 'Sin' spoken of was treated more objectively than subjectively. Imputability was secondary. What was essentially at stake was legal and cultic impurity which cut the person off from the worshipping community of God's holy people. Thus, we find that the sacrifice has to be offered for the consecration of altars (Ex 29:1—37; Lv 8:1—36), of Levites (Nm 8:5—21), in cases of contact with corpses (Ezek 44:25ff), of leprosy (Lv 14:10—31) and so on. The 'sins' were therefore treated as 'material rather than formal' (Moraldi, op cit p. 147). The purpose of the sacrifice was the removal of whatever separated a person from God's holy people and the consequent reunion.

In the Sacrifice for Guilt this guilt was regarded as **l** there, regardless of inadvertence or ignorance. When a person became aware of this 'guilt' he must offer the appropriate sacrifice. (Lv 5:14—26; 7:1—10). The emphasis in this sacrifice was upon the necessity to 'make amends' when the rights of God or of one's neighbour had been violated unwittingly. Of the two elements involved in this rite, the sacrifice and the action of restitution, it was the latter element that was primary (cf Lv 5:14—16, 20—26).

The rites for these sacrifices were similar. The victim used was determined by the social status of the offerer. For the High Priest it was a bull (Lv 4:3—12) and the same for the whole people (Lv 4:13—21). A male goat was to be the victim for a prince (Lv 4:22—26), while a female goat or a lamb was to be that of the ordinary Israelite (Lv 4:27—35; Nm 15:27—31). The ritual is given in Lv 4—7; Ex 29:10—14; Lv 8:14—17; 9:7—11, 15.

We can be sure that there were **stages in the m development of the regular use of sacrifices in worship**. In the time of the second Temple there were sacrifices in the morning and evening of a lamb with an offering of flour mixed with oil and wine (Ex 29:38ff). Incense also was burnt in the morning and evening (Ex 30:7—8). On each Sabbath the twelve pieces of the 'bread of the Presence' (Nm 4:7) which probably represented the twelve tribes were to be renewed. They were kept on a table before the veil of the Holy of Holies. The old loaves were to be eaten only by the priests (Lv 24:5—9; Nm 4:7; 1 Sm 21:5, 7; 1 (3) Kgs 7:48).

05a Feasts—In dealing with the feasts of Israel we must remember that the two oldest liturgical calendars of Ex 23:14—17 and Ex 34:18—23 fix the times of their feasts according to the Autumnal Year, i.e. of a year reckoned from Autumn to Autumn. Subsequent texts edited after the Babylonian Conquest follow the Babylonian method of reckoning the year from Spring to Spring. The Babylonian names were also gradually adopted. The cultic calendars are discussed in Kraus, op cit 26—92.

The Feast Day *par excellence* was the **Sabbath**. The custom of observing the seventh day was a very old institution and is mentioned in all the traditions of the Pent: Ex 23:12 (E); Ex 34:21 (J); Dt 5:12—14 (D); Ex 31:12—17; 35:1—3 (P). The day was to be sanctified (Dt 5:12) and those who could would visit the Temple. This would explain why the Temple guard was doubled (2 (4) Kgs 11:7). The daily sacrifices were doubled (cf Nm 28:9—10). Men ceased from work even in the time of ploughing or reaping (Ex 34:21). In the time of the Exile the legislation became stricter and the violation of the Sabbath could mean death (Ex 31:14; Nm 15:32—36). The Sabbath had become the symbol of Israel's status as God's own people (cf Ezek 20:12f; 22:8, 26; Neh 10:32; 13:15; Is 56:1—7; 58:13f). Its strict observance was the mark of the pious Jew and distinguished him amid his pagan surroundings.

b Attempts are made to see its origin in the Babylonian moon-day or *šapattu*. While much cannot be reconciled with the practice of the Sabbath as found in Israel nevertheless certain similarities are not lacking. A pre-Mosaic institution, it must originally have been due to the humanitarian need for a day of rest. But religious motives were sought. The seventh day was fixed upon as the mystic number whose dual gave the 14th day which was the day of the full moon. Like the Babylonian *šapattu* it was a somewhat sombre day because of its various prohibitions. Yet, in Israel, it was primarily a day of joyful rest (Is 58:13) cf R. North, 'The Derivation of Sabbath', Bib 36 (1955), 182—201. Apart from this Babylonian influence a more specific contribution was made by Syrian-Canaanite religious practice where the number seven was sacred. Periods of 'seven years' are often mentioned in the Ras Shamra texts. In two religious poems seven years of drought (ANET p. 153, line 43 = AQHT C) and seven years of plenty (ANET p. 141b = I AB (v)) appear, reminiscent of Gn 41·1ff. Thus 'seven years' is a unit of time; this is reflected in the Israelite Sabbatical Year. Again, in Syria and Canaan a self-contained sequence of seven days was used. In fact rites lasting seven days, where the desired effect occurred on the seventh day, are common to both Ugarit (ANET p. 150 = AQHT A (i)) and Israel (Jos 6:6ff). The origin, then, of the seven-day week was probably the festival week. This the Israelites borrowed from their neighbours, celebrating it, however, *lyhwh*, 'for Yahweh' (Ex 20:10; Lv 23:3); cf Kraus, op cit pp 85—87.

c Drawing their inspiration from the Sabbath were the two religious institutions of the **Sabbatical Year** and **Year of Jubilee**. Every seventh year land was to lie fallow, its produce given to the poor, and slaves to be freed. Its aim was to remedy the social evils of poverty and slavery. The legislation for it is found in Ex 21:2—4; Dt 15:1—18; Lv 25:2—7, 18—22. It is in Lv 25 that we find the law of the Jubilee Year every fifty years. Ideally it was a general releasing of land, property, slaves and a remission of debts. In practice there seems no evidence that it was ever kept, 'a Utopian law and it remained a dead letter' (de Vaux, op cit p. 177). See also R. North, *Sociology of the Biblical Jubilee*, Rome, 1954.

On the appearance of the crescent of the new moon **105d** when each month began, the **Feast of the New Moon** was held. A holocaust was offered of two bulls, a ram and seven lambs. Other offerings and libations were made and a goat sacrificed as an offering for sin (Nm 28:11—15). It was an old feast and often mentioned with the Sabbath (Is 1:13; Hos 2:11). It went back at least to the days of Saul (1 Sm 20:5, 18, 26). On the first day at the beginning of the seventh month (the month of the great feasts) a solemn Feast of the New Moon was kept. It is described in Lv 23:24f; Nm 29:1—6. Its commencement was signalled by the blowing of trumpets hence it is sometimes called the 'Day of Acclamation'. The Feast could also, because of its solemnity, preserve the memory of the old civil and religious year which had begun in the autumn. Celebration of the first day when the moon becomes visible is common to ancient Sumerian and Babylonian religion; 'the day on which the moon is renewed' is mentioned in the Ugaritic texts as well (e.g. Text III D I, 9), when very probably a *hieros gamos* ('sacred marriage rite') was enacted. This feast (minus the fertility rite) was first observed by families in Israel, (1 Sm. 20:5ff), but eventually the ceremonies were restricted to the temple.

The three great Feasts mentioned in the oldest **e** liturgical calendars were the Feasts of Unleavened Bread, of Weeks, and of Ingathering of Tents. They were Pilgrimage feasts when 'all your males shall appear before the Lord your God at the place which he will choose' (Dt 16·16). To the first of these we must add the **Feast of Passover**. It was not originally a pilgrimage feast and is not mentioned as such in the oldest calendars. But, because of its desire to centralize worship in Jerusalem, the Deuteronomic Tradition made this popular, local feast into one of pilgrimage uniting it with the Feast of Unleavened Bread: 'You may not offer the passover sacrifice within any of your own towns . . . but at the place which the Lord your God will choose, to make his name dwell in it . . .' (Dt 16:5f). This Passover Feast with its characteristic blood-ritual and links with the Spring and full moon belongs to a nomadic and pastoral society, cf J. B. Segal, *The Hebrew Passover from the Earliest Times to A.D. 70*, 1963. This is amply borne out by the indications of the rites. The victim was a male from the flock (of sheep or goats), but not necessarily the first-born. Its blood was smeared on jambs and lintels; originally perhaps on the tent pole and fabric of the nomads' tents (as among the Bedouin today); this blood-rite was apotropaic. This is the only sacrifice where the victim is roasted and not boiled in a cauldron. Nomads would have no encumbering cooking utensils; there was no need, then, to break the animal's bones as it did not have to fit into a cooking-pot. Later this simple practical detail was made into a prohibition (Ex 12:46). Bitter herbs merely added flavour to the meal, eaten at twilight after the flocks had been led back from pasture. The dress prescribed was that of nomad shepherds. De Vaux defends the view that the Passover Feast celebrated the seasonal moving of flocks when the shepherds left winter pastures for the summer grazing grounds; later the feast was historicized as a commemoration of the deliverance from Egypt (R. de Vaux, *Studies*, 1—26. The idea was first proposed by L. Rost in ZDPV 66 (1943) 206 ff). It was probably kept as a religious rite even in pre-Exodus times and after the Exodus, tradition linked this Spring Feast with the memory of that mighty work of God in the deliverance of the tribes.

The Passover was held after sunset on the 14th day **f** of the month Nisan which was the first month of the year. The day was counted from morning to morning. The **Feast**

105f **of Unleavened Bread** (cf § 180*b*) began on the next morning, the 15th day of Nisan and was to last seven days (Ex 23:15; 34:18) from one Sabbath to the next (Ex 12:16; Dt 16:8). But the full moon required for the Passover Feast did not always occur on the day before a Sabbath so, in practice, the Feast of Unleavened Bread had to be held immediately afterwards irrespective of whether it was a Sabbath day or not. It coincided with the putting in of the sickle to cut the barley crop (cf Dt 16:9) and the unleavened bread was made with the new grain. On the day following the start of the feast a sheaf of the new crop was to be offered to God (Lv 23:11, 15). This feast, therefore, probably arose when Israel settled in Canaan and became a crop-raising people (Lv 23:10).

g This feast opened the harvest season and was used to count the time until the next great feast which was to bring the wheat harvest time to a close: the **Feast of Weeks** (Ex 23:16; 34:22; Dt 16:9—10). Seven full weeks were to be counted from the day when the first sheaf was offered. On the following day which was the 50th day the Feast of Weeks was to be held (Lv 23:15ff). It was limited to only one day but was the occasion of great rejoicing (Dt 16:10, 11, 17). Sacrifices were made of leavened bread, animals, cereal and drink offerings (Lv 23:17—19).

h After all the harvesting including that of fruit, was over it was time to give thanks. This was the occasion for the great Autumn Festival of the **Feast of Tents**, or **Booths**, (Ex 23:16; 34:22; Dt 16:13ff). It was *the* feast (Ez 45:25) and lasted for seven days. Lv 23:39 calls it 'the feast of the Lord' and Josephus, 'the holiest and the greatest of Hebrew fests' (Ant VIII, iv, I). It had first been vaguely fixed for the time 'when you gather in from the field the fruit of your labour' (Ex 23:16) but later legislation commanded its celebration on the 15th day of the seventh month, i.e. of Tishri (Sept.—Oct.) for seven days until the 22nd day when there was to be a solemn day of rest (Lv 23:39ff). Nm 29:12—38 gives in detail the kind and number of sacrifices to be offered on each of the days of the feast. The other calendars of Ex 23 and 34 place it at the end of the year since they follow the older reckoning. A number of scholars see in this feast an ancient New Year festival which was developed under the monarchy into an enthronement festival of Yahweh or of the king as his representative. Apart from such facts as that this Feast of Tents was essentially an agricultural feast and kept on the 15th day *after* the start of the New Year, there is no trace of such a feast in the liturgical or historical texts. Similarities

between certain feasts of Israel and Babylonian counter- **105i** parts should not be exaggerated. At the Feast of Tents Israel renewed its covenant with God (Dt 31:9—13). It was probably the yearly feast celebrated at the central sanctuary of Shiloh in the time of the Judges (Jg 21:19ff; 1 Sm 1:3, 21). There was dancing and drinking of the new wine (Jg 21:21). At Shiloh, Eli rashly supposed that Hannah was drunk (1 Sm 1:13, 14). The booths which were built were to remind Israel of her nomadic life in the wilderness and of her nature as the convenanted community of the Lord of Hosts, at his disposal, ready to dwell in the tents of war in loyalty to him.

i This same month of Tishri was also chosen after the Exile for the celebration of the most Solemn Feast of the **Day of Atonement** on its 10th day (Lv 23:27—32. Nm 29:7—11). Some do not favour such a late origin but a strong argument for this is the fact that in its ritual neither the Ark nor the Cherubim are mentioned although this was the only time during the year that the High Priest entered the Holy of Holies. We know that the Ark was lost during the Babylonian conquest. In the 4th cent. the Holy of Holies was called 'the room for the mercy seat' (1 Chr 28:11). The reckoning of the day from evening to evening used in Lv 23:32 dealing with the Day of Atonement is that of later Judaism which was also used in NT times. Sacrifices in expiation did exist in Israel from her earliest days, but no actual feast for such a sacrifice can be traced in preexilic texts. The rite is fully described in Lv 16:1—34. Its purpose was to destroy, to eliminate what was contrary in the people to their calling as God's holy nation and to re-consecrate them to the service of the God of the Covenant.

j A new feast was created by Judas Maccabeus: Hanukkah, the **Feast of Dedication**. This was in 164 B.C. and the date was to be the 25th Kisleu (Nov.—Dec.) to commemorate the purification and re-dedication of the temple which Antiochus Epiphanes had desecrated three years before (1 Mc 4:36—59; 2 Mc 10:5). Josephus calls it 'the Feast of Lights' (Ant. XIII, vii, 7). It was a joyful occasion and lamps were lit in front of the houses. It lasted for eight days and on each successive day the lamps were increased by one.

A later non-religious Feast mentioned in 2 Mc 15:36 was that of **Purim** (cf Est 9:17—19). It was the occasion for a carnival and was held on the 14th and 15th of Adar (Feb.—Mar.), but the joyful feast was preceded by three days of fast and lament.

THEOLOGY OF THE OLD TESTAMENT

BY W. WATSON C.R.L.

06a Bibliography—*General*: W. F. Albright, *From the Stone Age to Christianity*, 1957²; M. Burrows, *An Outline of Biblical Theology*, Philadelphia 1946; W. Eichrodt, *Theology of the OT*, I 1961 (E. tr. of 1959⁶ revised to 1960), II 1967 (E. tr. of 1964⁵); **A. Gelin,** *Les Idées Maîtresses de l'AT*, 1959⁶; P. Heinisch, *Theology of the OT*, Collegeville, Minnesota 1950; P. vam Imschoot, *Théologie de l'AT*, I: *Dieu* 1954; II: *L'Homme* 1956 Tournai; E. Jacob, *Theology of the OT*, 1958 (E. tr. of 1955); G. A. F. Knight, *A Christian Theology of the OT*, 1964²; L. Köhler, *OT Theology*, 1957 (E. tr. of 1949²); T. Maertens, *Bible Themes I*, II Bruges 1954; O. Procksch, *Theologie des AT*, Gütersloh 1950; G. von Rad, *Theology of the OT* I, 1962; II, 1965; L. Roth, *God and Man in the OT* 1959; H. H. Rowley, *The Faith of Israel*, 1956; N. H. Snaith, *The Distinctive Ideas of the OT*, 1944; T. C. Vriezen, *An Outline of OT Theology*, Oxford 1958 (E. tr. of 1954⁷), G. W. Wright, *God Who Acts. Biblical Theology as Recital*, (Studies in Biblical Theology 8) 1952.

b *The Problem of OT Theology*: J. Barr, 'The Problem of OT Theology and the History of Religion', Canadian Journal of Theology 3 (1957), 141—9; G. Ebeling, 'The Meaning of "Biblical Theology"', JTS 6 (1955), 210—25; P. Fannon, 'A Theology of the OT', Scr 19 (1967), 46—53; P. Wernberg-Møller, 'Is There an OT Theology?', HibbJ 59 (1960—1), 21—29.

07a There is no agreement among scholars as to the scope, method and task of a theology of the OT. Certainly the a priori approach of Ceuppens and Heinisch, who tried to force the beliefs of the OT into an alien scholastic framework, is no longer possible. Some idea of the present situation in this field can be gained from T. Vriezen (op cit 118—26) who considers the term 'theology of the OT' itself ambiguous. It can mean a theology contained in the OT; in this case it would be a descriptive historical science, largely concerned with the religion of Israel. Or else the discipline would be theology which has the OT as its object. T. Vriezen prefers to see OT theology as 'the connecting link between dogmatic and historical theology'. As a theological science, it differs from a study of the history of Israel's religion, and should examine the message of the OT itself as well as in relation to the NT. **The task of OT theology is to define the characteristic features of the OT message, with special regard for the element of revelation.** Ultimately, evaluation of this message must be made from a Christian standpoint.

b With regard to the theology of the OT and OT religion there is general agreement that they are distinct, though necessarily related disciplines. But there is a sharp division between scholars who think that a systematic presentation of OT theology is not possible and those who think that it is. According to the former the OT is a dynamic living record of the acts of God (this point will be considered later) and cannot be adequately reduced to a static system of cut and dried beliefs. Those who accept systematization of OT theology have used one of several lines of approach. Some still follow the classical synthesis: God, Man, God who saves Man; (e.g. P. van Imschoot). Other scholars have posited **one concept as central to OT revelation** and made that the basis of their presentation of theology. For E. Sellin it is the holiness of God; for L. Köhler, God as Lord. W. Eichrodt **c** continues to maintain that **the Covenant is central to the OT**. In his preface to the English edition of his *Theology* he wrote (1960): 'The concept of the covenant was given this central position in the religious thinking of the OT so that, by working outward from it, the structural unity of the OT message might be more readily visible. Notwithstanding many alterations in detail . . . this overall orientation of the work has been deliberately retained. For the concept of the covenant enshrines Israel's most fundamental conviction, namely its sense of a unique relationship with God. . . . All crucial statements of faith in the OT rest on the assumption, explicit or not, that a free act of God in history raised Israel to the unique dignity of the People of God, in whom his nature and purpose were to be made manifest' (op cit I, 17—18). Eichrodt's work still remains the best survey of OT theology and his insistence on the importance of the Covenant has been borne out by recent studies on just this subject in relation to treaties of the ancient Near East.

A third school of thought prefers the **historical d presentation of OT theology**: God revealed himself in his saving acts on behalf of the people of Israel. G. Wright, in fact, writes that biblical theology is 'the confessional recital of the redemptive acts of God in a particular history, because history is the chief medium of revelation' (*God Who Acts*, 13). Other exponents of this view are C. H. Dodd, H. P. Robinson and H. H. Rowley.

On the basis of the unity of the two Testaments, **e** Old and New, a further group see **OT theology as Christology**. While defining OT theology as 'the systematic account of the specific religious ideas which can be found throughout the OT and which form its profound unity' E. Jacob also holds that 'a theology of the OT which is founded . . . on the OT as a whole, can only be a Christology, for what was revealed under the old covenant, through a long and varied history, in events, persons and institutions, is, in Christ, gathered together and brought to perfection' (op cit 11—12). O. Procksch and W. Vischer hold similar views, while G. Knight goes one step further in his *Christian Theology of the OT*, where he tries to establish the meaning of the OT for the present Church. P. Wernberg-Møller (loc cit), in sharp contrast to the Christological approach, would grant an OT theology as possible only as long as it does not take its starting-point in the NT and, moreover, understands the OT in its pre-Christian setting exclusively.

108a By far the most important work on OT theology today comes from the pen of G. von Rad. The first volume, subtitled 'The theology of Israel's historical traditions', appeared in 1957; the second, with the subtitle 'The theology of Israel's prophetical traditions', in 1960. Both have now been translated into English. W. Eichrodt writes that this work 'opens a new phase in the discussion of the problems and methods of OT theology. It provides us with a theologically profound and artistically accomplished handling of the leading concepts and homiletic aims of the biblical writers such as could only be the product of a thorough-going absorption into the whole world of their ideas and beliefs' (op cit 1:512). G. von Rad emphasizes the discrepancy between the picture of Israel's history as reconstructed by critical study and the portrayal of salvation-history by the OT itself. The OT writers do not pretend to present a true history of Israel; the repeatedly mentioned acts of God in history simply glorify the God of Israel. OT faith is on a different plane to historical truth. **For G. von Rad, then, the historical books proclaim Israel as the people of God**; the **sapiential writings** and the **psalms constitute the response of Israel** (Vol I). The **prophets pronounced the criticism of that faith** (Vol II).

b That the proclamation of the OT witnesses can be incorporated into a self-contained system of belief is denied by von Rad. This is because the various confessions of faith in Yahweh are sharply distinctive in character. It is not the people of God which forms the subject of theological study, but the more important confessions of belief in the God of Israel, organized round the religious concept of a people of God. Consistently enough he approaches the relation of the two Testaments through typology, in a very limited sense. He admits of no methodical understanding of the OT as pre-figuring Christ; not even NT usage is recognized as a norm for the typological interpretation of the Old. The exegete is free to choose or create connections between the Testaments, as he wishes.

c W. Eichrodt considers von Rad as guided by 'the conviction that the existentialist interpretation of the biblical evidence is the right one' (op cit 1:515), a principle to be rejected as invalid. 'The one task which OT theology can never abandon' is 'that of pressing on from the OT evidence to a system of faith which shall, by virtue of its unified structure and consistent fundamental attitude, present a character unique in the history of religious' (op cit I. 520). The summary of the teaching given in the OT to be presented here is **a synthesis of the attitude of the whole bible to each of the subjects treated**: God as one, as creator, as present to Israel etc. There is no space available to trace out the historical developments of doctrine which took place, though these are taken into account. This approach has been adopted because, although the OT contains several different 'theologies', the book as we now have it is a whole. It is for the commentaries on the individual books to point out the various schools of theology in the text. But, before this overall view of the OT can be outlined, some problems related to OT theology must be considered.

d Hebrew and Greek Thought—In connection with OT theology must be mentioned the exaggerated contrast alleged to exist between semitic and hellenistic thought. An extreme subscriber to this common view is T. Boman (see op cit) The main points of contrast usually indicated are as follows. Hebrew thought is dynamic whereas among the Greeks it was static; the Semitic conception of reality was almost exclusively concrete: there was no abstract thinking till Greek influence was experienced **108** by the Jews. Finally, among the Hebrews man was viewed as a unit, composed of soul and body, a unit which was itself part of a totality, such as a family or tribe. The Greeks, on the other hand, held that man was an individual, an immortal soul imprisoned in a corruptible body. In short it is a 'contrast between the divisive, distinction-forming, analytic type of Greek thought and the totality type of Hebrew thought' (J. Barr, *Semantics* 13). The dichotomy, however, is not so sharp as is generally thought; similarities between the two cultures have been collected by C. Gordon (*The Common Background of Greek and Hebrew Civilizations*, New York 1965) on the basis of archaeological and linguistic evidence. Further, J. Barr (op cit 8—20) has shown some of the proofs offered in support of the contrast to be very slender. Also, abstract ideas with concrete meanings were used in ancient Hebrew poetry, as is clear from the findings of M. Dahood (cf his *Ugaritic-Hebrew Philology*, Rome 1965, 44), which blurs somewhat the line of demarcation commonly assumed.

Current methods of biblical theology are constructively **e** criticized by J. Barr in his *The Semantics of Biblical Language*, Oxford 1961. Put briefly, his main contention is that words, by themselves, cannot be bearers of thought. This means that arguments drawn from etymologies are not so strong as many authors would like to think. The connection between biblical language and biblical theology must be made firstly at the level of larger linguistic complexes, such as sentences, speeches and poems. It is the sentence, not the individual word, which is the linguistic bearer of theological statements. The various 'theological word-books' of the bible must, therefore, be used with care because they tend to give a false picture of biblical theology and biblical thought. Barr suggests as well that the linguistic training of many theologians is not deep enough for the theological structures built by them. 'It is probable that a greater awareness of general semantics, of general linguistic method in all its aspects, and an application of such awareness in biblical interpretation, would have valuable and important results for theology' (op cit 296).

The Names of God—To a certain degree it is true **109** that Semitic names are indicative of the character of their bearers. This is especially so for gods; E. Jacob goes so far as to term divine names 'expressions of the living God'. A further point is that these names were used by Israelite worshippers and so epitomize the belief of the ordinary man. The names to be discussed here were, many of them, common to many gods in several religions of the ancient Near East. But the God of Israel, again like the pagan gods, had his own proper name, which has only recently been reconstructed in its complete form. God's own name is Yahweh-El, written accurately in Hebrew: *yahweh-'ēl*. That such is the full original form of the later hypocoristic Yahweh is accepted by many scholars today. Among those who put forward this opinion are W. Albright (e.g. *From the Stone Age to Christianity* 259—61) and D. Freedman, 'The Name of the God of Moses', JBL 79 (1960) 151—6. The vocalization of the first part of God's name has been established by syllabic spellings in Amorite names as well as by late Greek transcriptions (e.g. *Iabē*). Yahweh is the third person **b** masculine form of the verb 'to be', in the hiphil; cf P. Haupt JBL 43 (1924) 370ff. Thus the whole formula, Yahweh-El, means 'God causes to be', 'God creates'; El is common Semitic for 'God', see below. The phrase is very probably part of a litany recited in praise of God; it is well known that the babylonian god Marduk

09b had fifty names. It must be mentioned that other scholars prefer the meaning 'he is' or 'he exists' for Yahweh, on the rather tenuous grounds that nowhere else does the Hebrew verb 'to be' occur in the hiphil or causative form. There is evidence that a god *Yaw* was part of the Ugaritic pantheon, worshipped as a son of the high god El. The suggestion was first made by C. Virolleaud (*La Déesse 'Anat*, Paris 1938, 98) and, as C. Gordon comments, 'like many of Virolleaud's pioneer insights, this one (*yw* = Yahwe) has been brushed aside too hastily ... Yahwe with -h-corresponds to (Ugaritic) Yw' (*Ugaritic Textbook*, Rome 1965, 410). See also R. de Langhe, 'Un dieu Yahweh à Ras Shamra?', Bulletijn voor Geschiedenis en Exegese van Oude Testament, 14 (1942) 91—101.

c *yahweh seba'ôt*, or sometimes *yahweh 'elohê (has) s^eba'ôt*, first appears in 1 Sm 1:3 and is very common in the prophetical writings. This expanded title of Yahweh is closely connected with the Ark of the Covenant. Literally it means **'Yahweh of the Armies'**, but it is not clear whether the armies of Israel or of the heavens (i.e. the stars or the angels) are intended. Both are probably true, the connection with the Ark of the Covenant, which was the palladium of war, suggesting the original meaning of 'Armies' to be the men of Israel; later, theological thought extended or transferred the term to include the angels.

d The title 'Most High' appears in Hebrew consonantally as *'l*, *'ly* and *'lyn*; the first two forms have only lately been identified. It is used rarely in the OT, mostly in poetic texts. The same epithet occurs also in Ugaritic, South Arabic and Aramaic, where it is not the name of a god but designates the chief god of the pantheon. Similarly in Israel Yahweh is called 'the Most High', because he is superior to all other powers. Sample texts are Ps 16 (15): 6; 2 Sm 23:1 and Nm 24:16.

e El, like its cognates in other Semitic languages, means simply 'god'. However the god El was head of the Canaanite pantheon; his function was implied, in a transferred sense, when the God of Israel was also called El. In early pre-Mosaic texts El is sometimes further defined as El of the Heavens (Ps 136 (135): 26); El of Israel (Gn 33:20) etc. This has led to the suggestion that Israel once worshipped a god El. The name Elohim was also used by the worshipping community. It is the plural of the word El, which has another plural: Elim. The relationship between Elohim and Elim is not clear. When designating pagan gods, the plurality is obviously intended. Applied to Yahweh they are plurals of majesty and therefore singular in meaning. Another word for 'god' is *'elôah*, possibly of Aramaic origin.

f There is a whole range of names used for God in the OT. Some of the more important have been discussed here; the others can be found in dictionaries and lexica. However, several 'new' titles have been recovered from the biblical text in the light of modern philological discoveries. The psalms, being the ancient prayers of Israel, are especially rich in divine appellatives and the following treatment borrows much from M. Dahood, *The Psalms I*, AB 1966, xxxvi-xxxvii and *passim*.

Corresponding to Canaanite *aliyn b'l*, 'Baal the Victor', God is called 'The Victor' in Ps 22 (21):29; 27 (26):13; 100 (99):3 etc. A variant of Most High is 'The Exalted One' (Heb. *mārôm*) in Ps 7:7; Jer 31:12. Punic *magon*, 'emperor', gave the clue to the title 'Sovereign' in such texts as Ps 7:10; 47 (46):9; 84 (83):10. 12. Previously *mgn* had been translated 'shield' wherever it occurred, regardless of context. Many of the psalms appeal to God's justice, so it is not entirely unexpected to find him

addressed as 'The Just One': Ps 14 (13):5; 129 (128):4 **109f** or 'The Ancient Just One': Ps 31 (30):18.

God as Personal—The very high value the Israelites **110a** attached to God's name early on in their history, as well as their use of it are indications of the personal nature of God. In fact by the act of revealing his name (Ex 3) God declared himself an individual. He was present where his name was pronounced (Ex 33:19); by making known his name God made himself accessible to his worshippers. However there was no danger of religion here being reduced to mere magic: Yahweh made no secret of his name and, further, punished heavily any misuse of it. The many and varied names of Israel's God show him to be a person. As A. Alt has pointed out (*Essays in OT History and Religion*, 1—66) these names reveal God as regulating the lives of those who worship him; they do not reflect his action in Nature. An exception is, perhaps, the epithet 'Rider of the Clouds' (e.g. Ps 68 (67): 4) borrowed from Canaanite mythology. Yahweh refers to himself as 'a jealous God' (*'el qannā'* **b** Ex 20:5) which strongly denotes his character as a person. The personal aspect of God shown forth in his names tended to represent him as too human. To counteract this God was depicted as spiritual, though this was never explicitly stated. He was considered infinitely superior to man and in no way equal to him. Many of his titles are indicative of his superhuman personality; as the 'Living God' he is the source of all life (Dt 30.20) whereas the gods of pagans do not even exist (Is 40—43). Another indication of God being regarded as spiritual is the prohibition of images of Yahweh (Ex 20:4): he cannot be adequately represented in any form at all.

God is One—We now have a large amount of evidence **c** that the religious community of ancient Israel did not come into being at the beginnings of history, but at the end of a very civilized, sophisticated and cosmopolitan era. There is no basis for J. Wellhausen's hypothesis of an evolution from primitive animism to ethical monotheism. During the Amarna Age (c. 1350 B.C.) there was a general tendency to monotheism everywhere. Men of different backgrounds and origins met and a universal religion was produced. In Egypt, for instance, Amenophis IV (1361—1345; XVIIIth Dynasty) tried to purify the near-monotheism which had developed since Old Kingdom times. He changed his name to Akhenaten, proscribed worship of the God Amun, and thus antagonized the established clergy. Palestine was the hub of exchange in this age and there the monotheistic spirit took permanent root. 'Palestine was sufficiently international to digest universal monotheism and make of it a permanent factor in the future of mankind; Egypt could not digest it because of deep nationalistic institutions' (C. Gordon, *The Common Background of Greek and Hebrew Civilizations* 119). Gordon sees 'monotheistic trends' even in Homer's *Iliad* (21:103) and Herodotus' *Histories* (3:40) (op cit 234). W. Albright shows how 'the evidence of ancient Oriental religious history, combined with the most rigorous critical treatment of Israel's literary sources', agrees with the tradition of Israel representing Moses as a monotheist' (*From the Stone Age to Christianity* 400). In Israel there was no problem of theoretical atheism: God's existence was never questioned. The polemic of the prophets was directed against polytheism, and more specifically, against the gods of Canaan.

God who Acts—The God who revealed himself in the **d** OT is the God who acts; thus, what W. Eichrodt terms 'affirmations about the divine activity' are more sharply

110d delineated than those concerning his being. These affirmations regard his power, lovingkindness, justice, love, wrath and holiness. Ancient poetry in Israel celebrates Yahweh as a powerful warrior (e.g. Ex 15:21). The epithet 'Yahweh of the Armies' has been discussed above. The idea is reflected in chants such as 'The Lord, strong and mighty, the Lord, mighty in battle' Ps 24 (23):8. But, no matter how terrifying the power of God might be, there is no suggestion of uncontrolled forces being unleashed. Powerful as he is, God is a person, in cõmplete command. The concept of God's lovingkindness stems from the Covenant; for the Covenant, as in any political alliance contracted in the ancient Near East, implied the duty of loyal mutual service. Men turn to God's 'steadfast love', (Heb. ḥesed) when in difficulties (e.g. 1 (3) Kgs 3:6). The imagery and title of Yahweh as 'Shepherd' are also based on the notion of covenantal loyalty.

e God and Justice—The title 'The Just One' (see above § 109f) attests to Israelite belief in God as just. In the early period of Israel's history God's being just was manifested in the protection he gave against her enemies (cf Jg 5:11). Within Israel Yahweh lived up to his title by preventing any perversion of justice, in accordance with the belief in the ancient world that the deity safeguards justice. The divinity in question was usually the sun-god, which explains, possibly, the invocation 'The Lord God is a sun' (Ps 84 (83):11). The rise of prophecy in Israel initiated a new approach to the justice of God. Yahweh is to enter a new covenant with his people, when his dowry will be righteousness and true judgement (Hos 2:19) to re-establish the inner life of Israel to godliness. W. Eichrodt sees the essence of the original biblical concept of God's righteousness in 'a loyalty manifested in the concrete relationships of community', 'a personal quality that transcends all laws and standards' which 'remains an essentially religious conception' (*Theology* I, 249).

f God's Love—Hebrew is a language rich in terms to express the concept 'love'. Yet in the early period of Israel full use was not made of them to refer to God's dealings with men. Words such as 'lovingkindness' were preferred as founded in the Covenant. The prophets began using a wider vocabulary, the earliest and most notable among them being Hosea. Yet, however many words might be available, the paradox of **God's love for errant man could never be rationalized**. Jeremiah preached how God's love had not been recognized by Israel and had turned to wrath (cf Jer 12:7—9). The most important teaching on the love of God is contained in Dt. It is generally agreed that there are distinctive features in the deuteronomic teaching, in many places original. The idea of mutual love between God and his people goes back to Hosea. But, while the prophet intentionally avoids speaking of Israel's love for Yahweh (mentioning, of course, God's love for his people) the reverse is the case in Dt. Again, Dt does not use marriage as an image of divine love. W. Moran in 'The Ancient Near Eastern Background of the Love of God in Deuteronomy', CBQ 25 (1963) 77—87, affirms 'on the basis of biblical and extra-biblical evidence, the existence of a conception of a profane love, analogous to the love of God in Dt. This profane love is also one that can be commanded, and it is a love too that may be defined in terms of loyalty, service and obedience. It is, like the love of God in Dt, a covenantal love' (loc cit 81—82). The language of prayer shows how divine love is related to individuals, cf 2 Chr 30:9.

g The Wrath of God—Predicated of God, anger emphasizes his personal character. Anger is simply the opposite **110** of God's good pleasure. He vents his wrath not so much directly as indirectly: when angry he turns his face away from his covenant people. See, for instance, Ps 60 (59):1 'O God, thou hast *been furious with* us, broken our defences; thou hast been angry; *thou hast turned away from* us'. Hence the prayer 'Turn back to us' repeated in times of misfortune. The reason for God's anger was transgression on the part of man, or more precisely, an offence against the covenant or even God himself. His wrath was never arbitrary but the legitimate reaction to the breaking of stipulations he had made known. In cases when there seemed to be no reason for God's angry intervention, the mysterious divine displeasure was accepted philosophically (e.g. 2 Sm 15:26). Wrath was not considered one of God's permanent attributes, for the God of Israel was no capricious despot. Occasionally God's anger was aroused by sins of which men were unaware, especially in times of national calamity. The immediate task was to discover the guilty party and exact the punishment God required (Jos 7:1ff; 1 Sm 14:37ff; 2 Sm 21). The old Israelite attitude is unique in that God's anger is also considered as operating in individual acts of punishment.

The Holy God—Whatever the etymology of the word **11** qādôš, 'holy', its use suggests the idea of separation, i.e. the isolation of the sacred from the profane. E. Jacob insists rather on the idea of power as the essential aspect of holiness, a power which communicates itself to bestow life. True, holiness in God is the power to make others holy, but the texts in the bible insist more on his being 'wholly other', a sacred person to an extreme degree. So holy is he that man cannot approach him, cf Gn 28:10—19; man's first response is fear and even terror Gn 15:12. Holiness is primarily predicated of God: he is separate from and above creation; so he is transcendent and differs totally from false gods (Ex 15:11). God is also ethically holy and thus the standard of moral excellence for his creatures (Lv 19:2). The prophets reshaped the terminology of holiness to enhance the idea of moral perfection. God is holy because he makes his people holy, cf Is 6. He is 'The Holy One of Israel'. To appear in his presence the Israelites had to obey complex ritual laws, cf Lv 17—26.

Theophanies—J. Jeremias would classify the appear- **b** ances of God under two heads: Yahweh comes either to bless or to punish. When he appears as judge to inflict punishment, his form is never described; there is only an account of what happens as a result of his coming. The form of God is, however, more or less recognizable on those occasions when he appears in order to bless. Only the first type are real theophanies which have a literary form all their own and often occur as independent insertions in larger contexts, mostly in poetry (e.g. Ps 77 (76):17—20). The original form comprised two elements: a description of God's coming and a portrayal of the corresponding reaction in nature and among God's enemies. The marvels accompanying him show his majesty and are at the same time God's weapons (e.g. thunderbolts) used to strike down the enemies of Israel. An ancient Israelite belief is that of **Yahweh's self-manifestation in human form**. Apart from Gn 2, which **c** is a special case before the dawn of history, there are old folk-sagas telling of meetings with God in human form (Gn 18f; 32:24ff). Again, we read of Moses 'whom the Lord knew face to face' Dt 34:10 (but see Ex 33:23). Such passages retain their force even when compared with others where God's voice was heard, but no form was seen (Dt 4:12.15—18). At different stages in her religious

11c history Israel made differing statements about God in relation to the world. It is noteworthy, however, that despite the anthropomorphisms used there was never any suggestion of God being visible in animal form.

d Alongside such concrete imagery attempts were made at a progressively spiritual presentation of God's self-manifestation. The first of these is the *mal'āk yhwh*, the messenger or angel of God. This emissary is an agent of God in the role of helper (2 (4) Kgs 1:3,15) or destroyer (2 Sm 24:16f). Possibly the spheres of activity of different divine beings were attributed to the 'angel of Yahweh'. Passages such as Gn 16, where the angel is practically identified with Yahweh, express the presence of God in the angel phenomenon. God operated indirectly through his angel thus safeguarding his transcendence. Another such attempt at making the theophany more spiritual is the use of *kābôd*, the glory or majesty of Yahweh, comparable to Akkadian *melemmu*, a fear-inspiring splendour. It was a dazzling radiance which accompanied Yahweh and enhanced the gulf between him and man. No one could see it and live; even Moses was only allowed to see it from a distance (Ex 33:18). Later, the prophets consider revelation of Yahweh's glory part of the hope of salvation (cf Is 40:5; 59:19).

e The Spirit of God—*rûah* always means 'wind' or 'breath', as the bearer of life, proceeding from God and giving life to creation. Belief in the divine breath of life helped Israel away from polytheism much as the personal view of Yahweh prevented an explanation of the world on pantheistic lines. The OT concept of the Spirit of God has significance only in connection with historical experience. The Israelites saw the spirit acting in the charismatic leaders (judges, prophets, liberators). Such men were in contact with the divine world and acted to establish the kingdom of God in Israel. With the institution of the monarchy there was no further need for spontaneity of charismatic leadership. The spirit also equipped men to be spokesmen and messengers of Yahweh: a man of the spirit was marked out by his function. Apart from exceptions like Moses and Elijah, the spirit was usually erratic in its manifestations. The OT subordinated to the punishing God the power of the spirit for evil. For the prophets the Spirit of God is a consummating power in the New Age.

f God's Word—Man's word was considered by both the ancient Israelites and her neighbours to be very potent. Proof of this is the efficacy ascribed to blessings and curses. The word of God, then, was depicted as even more powerful; this is shown clearly in the Priestly account of creation (Gn 1). Israel had experienced the divine word in history, which in her case at least, regulated life (cf Ex 20:1 etc). Further, when occasion demanded, the covenant was enforced by the word of the prophets, whose oracles, because they were the word of Yahweh, were enunciated in poetry. Gradually however the dynamic concept of God's word was restricted to existing only in the laws of Scripture: the Law was even called 'the word of the Lord' (Nm 15:31). The Word never became fully static because it was linked with the Spirit of God. Statements about the activity of the Word and that of the Spirit overlapped, though there was never actual merging.

g The Wisdom of God—Situated at the crossroads of many cultures, Israel was open to the influence of international wisdom literature. Much of the OT teaching, therefore, on God's wisdom derives from the lore of other nations. God instructed the farmer (Is 28:24—26), the king (1 (3) Kgs 3:9) and the judge (2 Sm 14:17) in their respective skills; so he must be supremely wise. That wisdom is God's prerogative is stated in Jb 12:13ff; Is 31:2 and Dn 2:20—23. He knows life in all its forms (Jb **111g** 10:4) and effects whatever he has planned. In his wisdom he created man and the universe. He alone is wise enough to distinguish good from evil and so repay the just man and the sinner (Ps 1). One of the main lessons of Jb is that man cannot fathom God's wisdom except by revelation (cf 28:12—21). In the later books the Wisdom of God is identified with the Law. To receive the wisdom of God one had merely to obey the law; cf Sir 15:1—6. It was but a step from such a view to the personification of wisdom (cf Prv 8) though it is difficult to draw the line between hypostatization and mere poetic imagery.

God, the Creator—The idea of creation is subordinate **h** to that of covenant. The OT stresses faith in the covenant-God rather than in the creator of heaven and earth. In the Gn account, God remains independent of his creation, to which he grants autonomy, an autonomy which makes the Covenant possible. God created the world because of his plan of salvation and love for humanity, a plan in which Israel was to be his instrument.

The OT shows the influence of many different **myths of i creation**; yet no actual myth has yet been found which refers explicitly to the creation of the universe. Those so far discovered dealing with the creation of man and the ordering of the universe, also recount theogony and theomachy. The Sumerian paradise myth of Dilmun has strong affinities with the first chh of Gn, and may even be the origin of the now unrecognizable word-play between the 'rib' and Eve as 'the mother of all living' (Gn 2:22 and 3:20). More famous is the Babylonian myth *enûma elish*, which relates the making of man from the blood of the god Qingu (Tablet 6), but is more concerned with the battle for supremacy among the gods. Various myths **j** were current in Egypt from the second millennium ascribing man's creation to different single gods. Common to these ancient Near Eastern legends is that man was formed to serve the gods by the direct intervention of one or more of them. **In sharp contrast the OT teaching is monotheistic. God's direct and personal intervention in creation is described with anthropomorphisms.** He is the architect who sees to the laying of the foundations of the world and the various stages of its construction (cf Am 9:6); or the potter moulding clay (Is 45:18). Not too much can be made of the statistics for the verb *bārā'*, 'to create', as J. Barr has adequately shown (*Semantics* 281f). The clearest reference to creation from nothing is 2 Mc 7:28.

Creation is a beginning; it has a sequel: the con- **k** servation and continuance of the universe. From the Ugaritic tablets, for example, it is apparent that El is the creator of gods and men; but it is Baal who, as the god of vegetation, maintains creation and on him life in the world depends. Similarly the OT distinguishes between creation and conservation (cf Ps 136 (135):5—9; Dt 26), both predicated of God.

God in Heaven—Yahweh is the God of heaven where he **112a** has a court of **celestial beings with the general name of angels**. Originating in pre-Mosaic popular belief, this multitude has collective names such as 'the army of Yahweh' (1 (3) Kgs 22:19), 'the assembly of the holy ones' (Ps 89 (88):7) or 'the council of El' (Ps 82 (81):1). Singly they are termed *mal'āk*, 'angel'. Belief in these spirits arose from a need to picture God as powerful, with a heavenly court. This ancient pagan idea of the king of the gods enthroned with his court around him, as in the Ugaritic myths, is reflected in 1 (3) Kgs 22:19. The army of heaven also functioned as a choir to praise the King in song (Ps 29 (28):2). Relevant also is Jb 38:7 'when the morning stars sang together, and all the sons

112a of God shouted for joy', showing that angels derive, perhaps, from the starry heaven; cf Is 14:12. Confirmation of the astral origin of angels is the Canaanite poem 'The Birth of the Beautiful and Gracious Gods',

b i.e. Dawn and Dusk; cf Is 60:19. An angel is a messenger of Yahweh, higher in order than man, but still a creature. The messenger function of angels is exemplified in Jg 6:11—23. More often they act on God's behalf (2 Sm 24:16f). The angels of nations (Dt 32:8) are degraded national deities, now completely under Yahweh's universal rule. They appear mostly in writings of the Persian and Greek periods. The idea of an angel mediating between man and God is ridiculed by Eliphaz (Jb 5:1), possibly as a polemic against the Mesopotamian belief in a personal god who would intercede in the assembly of the great gods. In Tb, on the contrary, personal guardian angels play a prominent part (cf 12:15) and even have special names (3:17; cf Dn 8:16). The angel concept is ancillary to Yahwism, used to show God's exaltedness (Ps 103 (102):20f) his power to help (Jg 5:20) and to punish (Gn 19). Another member of the heavenly court, and hence not a demon, was 'the Satan', a secret agent who roamed the world looking for victims to accuse before God. The ancient idea of man's public prosecutor (Jb 1—2; Zech 3:1—2) later became simply 'satan' who tempted men to do evil (cf 1 Chr 21:1) and was eventually considered to personify evil, in order to stress that only good can come from God.

c **The Presence of God**—The idea of God's presence is linked with his dwelling place and theophanies. 'Far from conveying a restricted notion of God, or denying his lordship over the whole creation, the Jerusalem temple, more than any other institution of Ancient Israel, was the centre of a faith which asserted that Yahweh, the God of Israel, was lord of the whole earth' R. Clements, *God and Temple, The Idea of Divine Presence in Ancient Israel*, Oxford 1965, ix. This can only be appreciated against the background of ancient Near Eastern religion and culture. In Mesopotamia, where cosmic gods were worshipped, some symbol was needed **to localize the active divine presence**. Such were **statues and sacred mountains**; local gods could also symbolize the great high gods. **God's presence was never linked, in Israel, to any sort of images**.

d But he was considered present, in some way, in the ark and the tent of meeting. The ark was the permanent symbol of his presence (cf Nm 10:35—36), in the manner he appeared on Sinai. The tent of meeting was a shrine for receiving oracles; God was not always present there, but only when inquired of (Ex 33:7—11), cf § 103e. After the institution of the monarchy the temple was the place of God's appearing; and his presence was always an active coming to his people. Mount Sion represented Palestine, and theoretically, the whole earth. After the division of the kingdoms, sanctuaries arose in the N

e and Yahweh was believed to be present there as well. It was the prophets, from Amos on, who decried false ideas of the presence of Yahweh in Israel's cult, insisting more on the demands of the Covenant. With the deuteronomic reform, theology replaced mythology: Yahweh would maintain his relationship with his people only if they respected the Covenant. Eventually, as foretold by the prophets, the temple was destroyed, an act of wrath by the very God who dwelt there. During the Exile it is no longer a place but a cultic community which is associated with Yahweh's presence. After the Return there were varying beliefs regarding God's presence with his people. Some clung to the pre-exilic concept of God in his temple (Jl 2:27; 3:16f); the Chronicler refrains from giving an

opinion, merely listing current ideas (2 Chr 6:18). How- **11** ever, the dominant belief is in God's transcendence (Ez 1; Dn 2:18f), possibly due to Persian influence.

The Covenant—The notion of the covenant is central to **f** the OT, and of the many covenants God made with his people over the course of the history of salvation, the most important was contracted **at Sinai**. In recent years study of the covenant has intensified, based mainly on analysis of documents recording state treaties brought to light by excavation in the Near E. The **literary form of the OT covenants has been found to be closely related to that of such ancient treaties**, especially the Hittite vassal-treaties. Comparison has also aided a reconstruction of the rite carried out in the drawing up of such treaties. There were two copies of the document which was read out before the assembled people, with the gods as witnesses. The curses invoked on those who ever broke the covenant were probably acted out, for effect, and some sort of religious ceremony terminated the proceedings. One of the stipulations was that a copy had to be deposited in the sanctuary of the vassal. The whole document was read out in public at stated intervals, to remind the people of their obligations. The details of the rite varied over the centuries, thus affording us a criterion with which to date the covenants of the OT.

The **paradise-narrative** has all the elements of a **g** covenant, and is theoretically the first which God ever made with man; cf L. Alonso-Schökel, 'Motivos sapienciales y de aleanza en Gn 2—3,' Bib 43 (1962), 295—316). The Pact made with Noah is more explicit: God established his covenant on condition that Noah and his family entered the Ark (Gn 6:18). **After the deluge** God made another one-sided **agreement with Noah** and his descendants (Gn 9:8ff), universal in scope and perpetual. **With Abraham** God's covenant had many of the same features, but with slight differences. The promises are again of a saving character (Gn 15:18f) and universal (Gn 17:7—8), though their fulfilment depends on Abraham and his children keeping the covenant. The **h** **Sinai covenant** was bilateral according to W. Most (loc cit 1—9) for the following reasons: a condition is required for the exercise of 'lovingkindness', namely fidelity to the covenant; in texts such as Dt 26:17—18, Yahweh and Israel are set parallel to one another. Further, the imagery used for the covenant relationship is marriage, which is a mutual contract. Comparison with other treaties of the ancient Near East shows the Sinai Covenant to be more like those of the late second millennium, suggesting strongly a thirteenth century date for the actual making of the covenant; cf K. Kitchen, *Ancient Orient and OT*, 1966, 99—100.

At Sinai Yahweh revealed binding commandments to **i** his people, as part of the pact, and through them life with God was possible. These ordinances covered three different fields simultaneously: they were laws for everyday human life, legal prescriptions and rubrics for the cult. Here was initiated a special relationship of the People of Israel with Yahweh. In fact here Israel became the people of Yahweh: 'For you are a people holy to the Lord your God; the Lord your God has chosen you to be a people for his own possession, out of all the peoples that are on the face of the earth' (Dt 7:6). For Israel the Sinaitic Covenant is the basic one: all other Covenants (the Paradise stipulations, the pact with Noah etc.) are really projections of it into the past.

Election—The election of Israel by God, like the **11** Covenant, are expressions of the special relationship between Yahweh and his people. There can be no understanding of the meaning of the OT without a study of

13a God's mysterious election. Election shows God's majesty and holiness, and implies the right to make decisions which transcend man. **Election means that someone has been called to carry out a special task** and this implies responsibility. The emphasis is not on being loved, but on the task to be performed. In the bible 'both the election in Abraham and the election through Moses figure' (H. Rowley, *The Biblical Doctrine of Election*, 1950, 31); cf Gn 12:2; Ex 3. There is no contradiction: Moses led out of Egypt the same nation which before, in

b Abraham, had left Haran. The divine election, like the covenant, is never merely automatic; it had to be renewed by each generation of those inheriting it. The **chief purpose of the divine election of Israel was service**. Israel was free to choose, but in repudiating the Covenant she repudiated her election, which was failure to give God service. The service was to receive and treasure the revelation of God given to her at the Exodus. She was called to reflect the character of the God who was revealed to her. Her election was ultimately for service to the world: she had a mission to the nations. 'The only God is the God of all men, and the Israel that truly beholds his glory must proclaim his glory to all men, that he may worthily be praised until the earth is filled with that glory'. (H. Rowley, op cit 94).

c **Messianism**—Messiah is not a technical term in the OT, as it was to be in later Judaism and in Christianity. It is simply the Hebrew for 'anointed (one)'. The heads of kings, priests and prophets were anointed with oil, thus signifying their consecration to act in Yahweh's name. Only in Is 45.1 is it used of someone not part of the covenant community. It was an essential part of Israel's thought to hope for better things to come, and these hopes—found in the patriarchal promises and in the covenant of Sinai—can be called 'messianic' in the broad sense. With such hopes, a 'Messiah', a specially consecrated person, is often associated. Through the books of the OT this Messiah is presented as an antitype of great persons in Israel's past. Prophecies depicting the messianic age as a return to paradise (Am 9:13ff; Is 9:6—9) hark back to Adam before the fall. Other

d texts refer to a new Exodus (Is 52:12) through 'a prophet like me (i.e. Moses)', Dt 18:15. But these hopes came to be associated with the king especially. During David's reign the vexed question of kingship received theological support. True, the rise of the davidic dynasty is a historical event, as is clear from the account of David's accession to the throne (1 Sm 16:14—2 Sm 5:12). Also, the actual choice of David as king was due to the requests of the men of Judah and the elders of Israel. Nevertheless, the election of David and his successors goes back ultimately to God. The acclamation of the people was recognition of a charismatic leader already appointed by God. The Dynastic Oracle (2 Sm 7:12—17) was the clearest expression of God's approval of the monarchy, at least for Judah. This approval is expressed in the form of a covenant, an eternal covenant (cf Ps 89 (88) and 132 (131). As each new king came to the throne, the promises once made to David were reaffirmed and with each new king, hope burned anew that he would be the ideal king, ruling with justice and righteousness. The chief features of the oracle, permanence and security, gave rise eventually to the Messianic hope, a hope which remained with the Jews even during the exile

e and blossomed in the intertestamental years. There is some dispute among scholars as to whether the hope for a Messiah developed during the period of the monarchy or later. According to S. Mowinckel, for example, the Messiah belongs to the last times, he is not a figure of the future hope; so-called 'messianic' passages appearing **113e** in the times of the kings are due to re-editing. The hope for a Messiah belongs to the post-exilic age. Others, e.g. J. L. McKenzie, 'Royal Messianism', CBQ 19 (1957) 25—52, suggest that with the institution of the monarchy 'royal' messianism evolved, which included the promise of an eternal dynasty connected with the covenant, set in a kingdom of righteousness and justice, where there would be safety from enemies as well as internal security and prosperity. Yahweh would intervene to extend this kingdom over the whole world. The messianic hope was also conveyed by other figures. Among these perhaps the most famous is the Suffering Servant of Yahweh described by Isaiah, in which the notion of vicarious suffering was introduced into the OT. The enigmatic 'son of man' described by Dn (7:1—28) is very probably to be identified with the Messiah and lies behind much NT teaching about Christ. From these texts the Messiah emerges as prophet, priest and king.

Morality—Although OT religion is not primarily a **114a** moral system, and although its ideas of morality were conditioned by historical circumstances, nevertheless, it has already been shown that it was not a-moral: cf 111a, 112i.

Morality in the OT is concerned with man's heart (Prv 4:23; 23:7), even though the commandments prohibit actions that can be seen. **God did not reveal truth to man all at once, but in stages**. Therefore behaviour tolerated or even praised in the early part of Israel's history was later proscribed as men learned more about God. Man's Fall necessitated a revision of God's plan for men and a corresponding change in his requirements. For instance, the prohibition regarding the tree of the knowledge of good and evil makes no sense for fallen man. These requirements were altered yet again after the redemption had been effected. Many practices and deeds related in the OT are not necessarily thereby to be slavishly imitated simply because they are mentioned, or God makes use of them (e.g. Gn 30:37ff) A distinction must be made between what is actively approved and what is merely tolerated or permitted, cf § § 216f, 225d, 246g, 353c.

The basic **norm of man's behaviour is his like-** **b** **ness to God**: for man was created in God's image (Gn 1: 26). Thus the laws regulating man's conduct rest on God's own perfection and are consequently unchangeable. Intended as it is to meet every situation in which man may find himself, the content of moral teaching in the OT is vast and complex. However, the various series of different regulations are grounded in a set of principles: the Ten Commandments. Even though some scholars consider the number ten to be less primitive than the ubiquitous grouping into three or six, the Decalogue is important enough for OT revelation to be examined as a whole. It regulates the two fundamental spheres of man's action: his relations with God and with his fellow-men. The laws given to man at Creation are, to some extent, continued in the Decalogue; these were to procreate and fill the earth and hold dominion over it; to observe the sabbath, work for a living and marry only one partner. It may be noted, incidentally, how much higher Israelite sexual morality was than that of her contemporaries. In Israel, sex was connected with God, the author of all life; and sexual relationships were such that they could eventually be considered a model of God's relationship with man; cf Hosea and Eph 5:23. For Israel, the revelation of the commandments was a highly important saving event. The commandments themselves are, of course, only part of the larger whole which is the Covenant. They were

114b never thought of as being in any way an absolute scale of prescribed ethics. Rather, the Sinai event was a revelation given at a specific time in history offering Israel the gift of life, a gift she was free to accept or not by obeying or disobeying the commandments. Most of the ten precepts are, in fact, negative and make no attempt to cover every aspect of life; they are Yahweh's minimum demands. And they are called in the OT not 'the Law' but 'the Ten Words'. Older than these 'Words' is the series of twelve curses pronounced at Shechem, protecting the community against secret crimes (Dt 27:15ff). As old, if not older, is Ex 21:12.15−17; while Lv 19:13−18 is very like the Decalogue in outlook. The priests drew up these sets of injunctions in order to put before men, in short mnemonic form, God's will for Israel.

c **Righteousness**—The most important concept in the OT for man's relationship to God and man is that of righteousness, *ṣedāqâ*. It is the highest of life's values: all properly ordered life depends on it. But 'righteousness' was no absolute ideal norm of ethics: Israel did not measure deeds against any such norm. What counted were the various relationships a man had, and to which he was bound to keep true. The norm, then, is the specific relationship affected by the line of conduct a man follows. Every man has a set of relationships: to his family, his tribe, to his profession or trade etc. Above all these is the loyalty he owes Yahweh, fulfilled chiefly in worship. If a man is true to the claims his different relationships make on him, then he is just. Often a judge had to decide whether a man was just or not on precisely this basis (Ex 23:7); cf also 1 Sm 26:23. Under the monarchy community life developed, with sharp differentiation between its members. Men began to realize the chief ends of social righteousness. The king, as supreme judge, represented God as king and judge. The prophets saw that God's purpose extended beyond a mere kingdom to a reign of universal peace and righteousness. The monarchy ensured God's cooperation only when fighting injustice and violence.

d **Sin**—Hebrew is rich in terms for expressing the concept of sin and sinning. Here two of the more important will be mentioned. *ht'* and its derivatives mean missing the mark, i.e. a failure in relationships between men and between man and God. *pš'* is the strongest word for sin and indicates rebellion. In general it can be said that sin is conduct contrary to the accepted norm. The OT rarely mentions sin in theoretical terms; much more frequently definite sins of various people are described or referred to. Sin is not often reflected on theologically, see for instance Gn 6:5; Jer 17:9; Jb 14:4. More in line with OT thought and practice is the **confession of sin**. Before the cult developed into a separate sphere of activity, sin was possible in every aspect of life, though in general it implied breaking God's law. Thus it was regarded as a direct offence against God. Further, sin **114** affected adversely the whole community. Order could only be restored by the death or banishment of the sinner (and his family). Every evil act did not remain isolated but had continuing effects; there was no sharp distinction, then, in the OT, between sin and penalty. The use of e the words *'āwon* and *hēṭ'* bears this out; e.g. Nm 32:23. The community was liable to suffer the penalty of an individual's sin unless it dissociated itself from the sinner. No investigation of motive or error mattered; what did matter was that a sin had been actually performed. Offences committed in error must have been frequent; deliberate sin was viewed with horror. The conflict arising from this objective theology of guilt and individual culpability is reflected in many parts of the OT (cf Gn 20:3ff; 1 Sm 14:24ff). The teaching of prophets like Ezekiel and Jeremiah were stages in the solution to the problem, but the true answer was not forthcoming until the revelation of the New Testament.

Immortality and Resurrection—The **reticence f maintained by the OT** regarding life after death is explained by the conflict experienced with worship of the dead in neighbouring religions. Also, man's hopes were centred on the joys of life on earth: the next life was left to Yahweh. By original sin man forfeited the privilege of immortality, symbolized by 'the tree of life' (Gn 2:9). Man is born to die, and death was accepted as the moment when Yahweh determined to end his gift of life (cf 2 Sm 12:23). Nevertheless, belief in an eternal life of bliss with God, after death, is very ancient as shown by many passages in the psalms. The psalmists appeal to the assumption of Henoch (Gn 5:21−24) and of Elijah (2 (4) Kgs 2:1−12) and confidently expect the same privilege after the final judgement. True these two men never actually died; yet the tradition remained in Israel and was voiced more explicitly in later books (e.g. Wis) and in the Apocrypha.

The Underworld—According to the OT one descends g under the earth to the realm of the dead, referred to mostly as *šeʾôl*. Existence in Sheol is a shadowy copy of life on earth; rank, even, is respected (Is 14:9ff), but everywhere reigns silence, stillness and dust. This idea of the underworld appears also in the Babylonian myth of Ishtar's Descent into Hades and in parts of the Gilgamesh Epic. There are some thirty poetic names for the realm of the dead in the bible, among them 'the Pit', 'Destruction' and 'Eternal Home'. The survival of a dead person in this abode was considered dependent on what happened to his corpse, which explains why such pains were taken for decent burial (Tb 1:17). Belief in survival after death, in the actual grave, continued even after the idea of Sheol as a communal dwelling for the dead was current. There was never any worship of dead heroes as gods. Contact with dead people rendered one incapable of worshipping Yahweh (Lv 21:1).

THE GENTILE NEIGHBOURS

BY H. F. G. SWANSTON

This article attempts to expound briefly something of the character of the societies bordering upon Israel in the OT period. In such a small compass it seems more useful to concentrate on the cultural and religious attitudes of these societies, and to deal with historical events only in so far as these affect the cultural assumptions of the societies. For fuller information about purely historical events, the reader is referred to the article on **History** in the present volume and to the comm. on the individual historical and prophetical books as well as to the works listed in the respective bibliographies.

1 EGYPT

115a Bibliography—I. E. S. Edwards, *The Pyramids of Egypt*, 1961; id, *The Early Dynastic Period in Egypt*, CAH² fasc. 25, 1964; W. B. Emery, *Archaic Egypt*, 1967³; H. Frankfort, *Ancient Egyptian Religion*, New York, 1948; id, *Kingship ana the Gods*, Chicago, 1948; T. Lambdin, 'Egypt: its Language and Literature in *The Bible and the Ancient Near East*, ed. G. Ernest Wright, 1961; W. S. Smith, *The Old Kingdom in Egypt*. CAH² fasc. 5, 1962; J. A. Wilson, *Egyptian Culture and Religion*, in *The Bible and the Ancient Near East*, 1961; A. Gardiner, *Egypt of the Pharaohs*, 1966⁷; E. Otto, *Egyptian Art and the Cults of Osiris and Amon*, 1968.

b The theology of Egypt—It is difficult for us to set Egyptian theology in order because at no time did the Egyptian scribes produce a set of structured definitions of what they meant by God and creation and the world. The very language of Egypt is so replete with concrete terms that it is immediately apparent that the Egyptians had little occasion for abstract thoughts. They employed instead of abstract terms groups of various and unrelated concrete descriptions which could be placed alongside one another without embarrassment at their incongruities. This situation is made the more complex for us by the Egyptian delight in syncretism. Almost any new story could be happily placed by the side of those already established for centuries and become part of the accepted legend-pattern. This allowed new theologians to reorganize the old orthodoxies in revolutionary ways without causing any disquiet. An example of this is the Memphite theology in which an effort to handle abstractions in a new way resulted in a new god, Ptah, being credited with creating the universe. Contrariwise, we may suppose that the heresy of Akhnaton was not that he was an innovator but that he supposed his innovations to supplant rather than complement the system of the old imperial gods.

c The emphasis on order, harmony and reconciliation in Egyptian thought—this derives from the Egyptians' realization that their society was a coming together of opposites. The geography of Egypt, a fertile valley between deserts, brought home to them the fact that they existed only by the tension of opposites. The differences

between the delta of Lower Egypt opening out onto the **115c** Mediterranean, and the Nile valley surrounded by desert, were not merely of geography but of very disparate dialects and cultures. This was recognized by the royal administration which worked through two viziers and two treasurers. There were periods when there were even two capitals. Politically the people were aware of themselves as men of two lands, Lower and Upper Egypt; the Pharaoh was often called 'Lord of Two Lands', and, because he was Wadjet, the cobra-goddess of Lower Egypt, and Nekhbet, the vulture goddess of Upper Egypt, he was also called 'the Two Ladies'. Cosmologically the Egyptians thought of themselves as protected by the combined forces of Horus, the bright son of Osiris, and Seth the dangerous furious power. One account of creation puts the very existence of Egypt in these terms: the 'Memphite theology' text presents the emergence of Egypt as part of the divine ordering of the universe from oppositions. Ptah, the creator of all. . . He who unified this (land) has appeared as King of Upper Egypt and as King of Lower Egypt', and 'It happened that sedge and papyrus were put at the two outer gates of the temple of Ptah. That means: Horus and Seth, who bore with each other and united in friendliness so that their quarrel is ended wherever they may be. They are united in the temple of Ptah, "the Balance of the Two lands" in which Upper Egypt and Lower Egypt have been weighed'

The Nile—The great sign of recurring life was the **d** return of the Nile waters after the great summer drought. The dominance of the Nile in all matters Egyptian is manifest in the Egyptian language. 'To go northwards' is, in Egyptian, the same word as 'to go downstream', and since everything in Egypt is right and according to the fixed decree of the gods, this situation holds everywhere; so when they spoke of the Euphrates it was of an unnatural river which went 'downstream by going upstream', and when they spoke of the land of the dead and prepared men for their travels there, they provided two boats, one with sail down for going N with the river and one with sail up for going S against the stream. The Nile was the paradigm for foreign lands and other worlds. Nations that did not have the Egyptian Nile had to have another Nile: one worshipper remarked to his god: 'Thou hast put a Nile in the sky so that it may come down for them' (Aton-hymn, 9, ANET 370) The two Niles are represented on a tomb at Abydos bringing papyrus, lotus and many varieties of food and drink to all people. Everything everywhere is uniform and symmetrical. There is an echo of this Egyptian praise of the Nile in the doxology fragments of Amos 8:8; 9:5, together with, as in Ps 104, adaptations of the Egyptian notion of perfect divine control of the elements of light and dark.

A static world—Egyptian culture arose within the static **e** symmetrical context of the land, within the facing banks of the great river, the desert on either side and in the distance the facing E and W hills. This symmetry of

115e geography is influential both in the balance of Egyptian artefacts and in the parallelism of Egyptian hymns. It may be that Hebrew doublets derive their impulse from this source. Certainly some Egyptian influences are discoverable in Heb. literature. For example, the creation story of Merikare, 130—4 (ANET 417), is much like the Genesis narrative and much unlike other Levantine creation myths in making creation purposeful and anthropocentric—the world is made for man. This story leads, like the Genesis narrative, into a flood story. Again, the Memphite text suggests that the Creator's response to his work was one of Genesis-like satisfaction: 'And so Ptah was satisfied, after he had made everything'. Once created the world remains the same. The universe has an order which, however menaced by Seth and the forces of disruption, is always kept under the control of Horus, the Pharaoh. We may think of this as a reconciliation of distinct forces, an amity of distinct gods, but it is questionable whether the many gods of the cosmogonies and the statues were thought of as totally distinct.

f Polytheism?—The Egyptians knew that a single representation of a god in one place did not suffice to express the presence of the divine in the universe. They therefore spoke necessarily of 'the gods', but were not necessarily making a dogmatic proposition in favour of a polytheistic scheme. The various temples of the various gods were not entirely distinguished by the scribes, however much they may have been by the people. Each temple, for example, shared in the character of the Primeval Hill, was the Primeval Hill in that place. Again, the divinity represented by the statue was present to the worshipper in the shrine but was not himself localized in the shrine; only in the act of the cult were the god and the man present to one another. We should be in a bad way if we supposed that those villagers who speak of 'our Madonna' and compare 'your Madonna' unfavourably with her, were making 'polymarianistic' remarks, or if we supposed those who speak of the Trinity are not monotheist. Theologies always look a little odd from the outside. The Egyptians spoke in plurals and knew in the singular. On each Primeval Hill the sun-god, Atum, sits to become all things, each morning the triumphant sun pushes away the forces of darkness, each New Year the world of divine order triumphs over chaos; these were spoken of as distinguishables but were known to be the only way in which human beings could express their several awarenesses of the one victory. The Pharaoh was not simply 'the god', he was also 'the gods', as the Tell el-Amarna letters (c. 1411—1358) evidence. If we can justify 'Elohim' we ought to be patient with some Egyptian expressions.

g For most modern readers 'Egypt' has connotations of Exodus and pyramids, of an epic escape from persecutors and a preoccupation with death. This popular view is the result of highly successful OT teaching. We have inherited the Hebrews' view of their enemies. We are prepared to accept Isaiah's description of a treaty with Egypt as 'a covenant with death', (Is 28:15). To the Egyptians it seemed as if their religion was concerned not with death but with the fulness of life. We look with curious and unsympathetic eye at the huge tombs and tiny shrivelled mummies and see only death. For the Egyptian all this was a sign of life to come. As the new grain rose each year from the dead seed, so men would rise from the tomb in the customary harmonious order managed by the gods. From the power of Geb (or Ptah), the Earth, and Nut, the Sky, came the rising lord of the dead, Osiris. In the Memphite theology, and in the Mystery Play of the Succession, Osiris *is* the new grain, in the **115** Ptolemaic temple of Philae ears of grain grow from the supine body of the god, and seeds were sown in the tombs of the XVIIIth Dynasty and watered until they grew to show the resurrection of the dead through the power of Osiris. Osiris was also the fertility power of the Nile water which made it possible for grain to grow in the fields.

Egyptian Society—If we systematize Egyptian theology **11** we have systematized also the Egyptian social theory. Both have as their pivot the person of the Pharaoh. The ruler was not merely the head of the political structure and leader of human order, in his own person he was the principle of harmony in the universe. In him the divine and the human order came together. Each Pharaoh as he put on the Red Crown of Lower Egypt and the White Crown of Upper Egypt, and ascended the throne of Horus, *was* the god Horus, and each Pharaoh as he was wrapped in mummy-cloth and placed in the tomb to enter the land of the god of the dead, *was* the god Osiris. The Pharaoh acted in the world of god as much as in the world of man. Through him the divine was in the world. The Pharaoh is the order of the universe. He makes the Nile to rise, the corn to grow and the sun to shine. He is responsible for *maat* in the cosmos, for truth and right order. In many texts he is called 'the god' (netjer) or 'the good god' (netjer nefer). He is always Horus, 'the great god'. In tombs the dead describe themselves as 'honoured before the Great God' referring to their service of the dead Pharaoh. On the other hand, despite some popular assumptions on this matter, the Pharaoh was never identified with the Sun, he is *like* his father Re, the Sun. In the Turin Papyrus and in the History of Manetho (who lived in the Greek period), the sun god is said to have been the first king of Egypt. All succeeding rulers were reflections of Re. In popular, non-Memphite, theology, the Sun is the creator god, father of Maat, and the procreating virile power whose force is manifest in the cattle of Egypt, hence the Pharaoh is sometimes called 'strong bull' and ordinary men are described as 'the cattle of god'.

The Pharaoh was the priest of all the gods. Although **b** he himself rarely took part in the ordinary duties of the daily cult, nothing was done except in his name and on his behalf. The Pharaoh was the commander of the army and victor at all battles undertaken by his generals. The Pharaoh is the instigator of all policies and is given credit for all civil administration. No man else has power of his own. The Pharaoh was a living witness to the communion that man had with the divine. He is, after the fusion of the cults of Osiris and Re at Heliopolis during the period of the Old Kingdom, most often called 'Son of Re' because the god had taken the place of his human guardian and father in order to lie with the Pharaoh's human mother. The Pharaoh, therefore, could not be resisted by anyone who had a merely human father, nor by the material elements which were at his sword. In the Pharaoh's will was the peace of the land. The emphasis on order gave the Pharaoh the support of an established way of doing things, a ritual and a court tradition which took charge of almost every act. The title 'pharaoh' is an instance of this ceremonial. It derives from '*per-aa*', which means 'the Great House' and was an impersonal reference to power and authority, rather like 'the Sublime Porte' or 'Downing Street'. This provision for most occasions only made the more exacting those times when the Pharaoh had to decide himself, knowing that his will was effective in the whole universe and his actions produced repercussions all over the cosmos. The Pharaoh must remain a lonely god. The sculptures of the Middle King-

6b dom recorgnize this in portraits of tired Pharaohs weighed down by responsibility.

c Such a figure in so near a culture could not but impress the men of Israel. When they came to establish the royal ritual the Hebrew liturgists turned for their model to the courtly ceremonial of Egypt. The Pharaoh on his accession went through a series of intricate ceremonies at various important town-shrines in the two lands. These were his coming out of obscurity, his progress from incubation, not his birth. He was suddenly seen as the living Horus, son of Osiris. He went through lustrations to be pure before his father, and was then taken in a litter to the chapels of Horus of Efdu and Seth of Ombos who presented him with four arrows to be discharged against his enemies at the four cardinal points, until after many other rites he was proclaimed with all his titles before his own people. The influence of these impressive rituals upon the neighbouring Israelites is the subject of debate but it does seem likely that the incubation of Solomon, 1 (3) Kgs 3:5ff, the arrow incident of Elisha and King Joash, 2 (4) Kgs 13:15—19, and Ps 18:34 where God teaches the king to use the bow, the protocol list of titles of Is 9:6—7 (cf Lk 1:32—33), and the coronation anthem of divine sonship, Ps 2:7ff, derive something from Egyptian courtly ceremonial (cf K. H. Bernhardt, *Das Problem der altorientalischen Königsideologie in AT*, Leiden, 1961).

d **The Collapse of the Pharaonic power**—The Old Kingdom of the III—IV dynasties, (c. 2778—2263), collapsed because the Pharaohs could not control the growing independence of the nobility and provincial administrators. During the period of building the great pyramids the self-sufficiency of the nobles is marked by the manner in which they set up their tombs far from the Pharaoh's pyramid. The society gave way to internal anarchy; little barons set up administrations of their own and refused to acknowledge the rights of the central authority. At the same time, and for the same causes, the country was invaded by barbarian Asiatics, and the Egyptians themselves plundered the tombs of the dead because they were too dispirited to earn a living from the Nile fields. Stability, so prized in Egypt, was lost in a whirligig of social changes. Customary respects were no longer paid, and no one knew whence he came or whither he was going. The country was disturbed by the debilitating rivalry of Koptos, Herakleopolis and Thebes.

e Hope and expectation in this world seemed useless and the grave was now spoken of as a welcome haven. The Egyptians began to take a more 'spiritual' view of realities which was sometimes mere escapism and sometimes a call for the individual to have a more responsible relation with other men which would enable him (and not the Pharaoh alone) to become Osiris at his death. Menthuhotep II (2065—2060) finally reunited the country but his dynasty did not produce any significant changes in Egyptian life. The accession of Amenemhet I, (2000—1970), XIIth Dynasty, led to a long period of great energy and achievement; the capital was moved 300 miles northwards because Thebes was not positioned properly for a strong centralized government, Nubia was colonized as far as the Second Cataract, Phoenicia given an Egyptian governor, vast schemes of agricultural reform and irrigation put into effect, and the literary work of this Dynasty is more impressive than of any other time in Egyptian history. The famous Execration Texts, curses of Asiatics written on pottery which was immediately smashed, belong to this period; the names in the pots demonstrate that many semites were living in Egypt at this time.

Then came an even more decisive change in Egyptian **116f** life. The central government of the XIVth Dynasty collapsed in the 18th cent. before the onslaught from outside the country. The Asiatic Hyksos princes with their horses and chariots of war occupied the two lands and ruled 'in ignorance of Re' (ANET 230). The Egyptians, led by the princes of Thebes, XVIIth Dynasty, summoned up enough frightened energy to evict these semitic invaders (who may have included ancestors of the Hebrews who later came out of Egypt; it has been suggested that Jacob-el is a Hyksos name), but from the 16th cent. onwards they never again felt relaxed and secure within the divinely ordered frontiers. Ever after they had to take note of what the barbarians were doing. In order to keep Egypt safe the gods went to war against Hittites, Sea Peoples (Philistines), and Assyrians, and the Egyptians discovered that they were a nation among the nations and no longer the kin of the gods.

The Empire Ahmosis of Thebes (1580—1558), the **g** first Pharaoh of XVIII Dynasty, with great energy reconquered Nubia and his family pushed the Egyptian frontiers outwards until Thutmosis I (1530—1520) erected his stele announcing victory on the Upper Euphrates. Though during the reigns of Thutmosis II and of Queen Hatshepsut (1505—1483), the Asiatics rebelled with some success, Thutmosis III (1483—1450) reconquered the Asian provinces at Megiddo, (1483) and Kadesh, (1463), and set up an Egyptian-dominated civil service in the lands W of the Euphrates to organize the incoming tribute. During the reign of his indolent grandson Amenophis III, (1400—1370) and great grandson Amenophis IV, (1372—1354), as the Amarna letters from the Asiatic princes demonstrate, the vigorous Hittite power overran the territories of Syrians, Phoenicians and Mitanni. Amenophis IV changed his religious allegiance from Amon the old state god, to Aton (the sun disk), removed the capital from Thebes to the Tell el-Amarna site where he built a new city of Akhetaton, and renamed himself Akhenaton (Splendour of Aton). The change was against the interests of the priests of Amon and in 1350 his grandson Tutankhamon returned to traditional forms at Thebes. Meanwhile the internal administration had collapsed and the Hittites were preparing for further conquests. But by 1278 the Egyptians under Rameses II (1301—1235) and the Hittites of Hattusil were more worried by the Assyrian menace than by each other, and made a peace which lasted two whole generations. It seems likely, despite the general acceptance of Rameses as the Pharaoh of the Exodus, that this event is to be placed in the reign of his successor Merneptah, (1234—1224) cf 81f, g and 175d. Rameses' successors had to deal also with the Sea People, who having defeated the Hittites were making raids on Egypt itself. In 1194, 1191 and 1188 they were thrust back by Rameses III, (1198—1166), but those who had settled on the Palestinian coast were able to remain. These are the Philistines of the OT.

From this time on Egypt has to engage in diplomatic **h** activity to obtain what before would have been taken by force. The encouragement given by Sheshonq I, (950—929) to Jeroboam (1 (3) Kgs 11:40) was effective, the army sent into Asia when the Assyrians were besieging Jerusalem was not (2 (4) Kgs 18:21). By the reign of Tanutamon (663—656) Egypt's weakness is total. The old imperial city of Thebes, whence Pharaohs had ruled from Nubia to the Euphrates, was sacked by the Mesopotamian Army. The Egyptians dreamed of the restoration of the Empire, and Neco, (609—594) XXVIth Dynasty, almost managed it; he defeated Josiah at

116h Megiddo and put a puppet, Jehoiakim, (608—598) on the throne of Judah, (2 (4) Kgs 23:29—35), but was defeated (605) by the Babylonian prince, Nebuchadrezzar at Carchemish, (Jer 46:2). These events demonstrated that once Egypt's Pharaoh accepted that he was a king among kings the whole fabric of Egyptian culture, based as it was on the Pharaoh as the divine presence within the world, must collapse.

2 MESOPOTAMIA

117a Bibliography—J. Bottéro *La religion babylonienne*, 1952; E. D. van Buren, 'Building of a temple tower', RA 46 (1952) 65—174; 'Sacred Marriage in Early Times in Mesopotamia', Ori 13 (1944) 1—72; E. Dhorme, *Les religions de Babylonie et d'Assyrie*, 1949; H. Frankfort, *Kingship and the Gods*, 1948; 'State Festivals in Egypt and Mesopotamia', Journal of the Warburg and Courtauld Institutes, 15 (1952) 1—22; C. J. Gadd, *Ideas of Divine Rule in the Ancient East*, Schweich Lectures 1945—8; S. H. Hooke (ed) *Myth and Ritual*, 1933; *Myth, Ritual and Kingship*, 1958; T. Jacobsen. 'Formative Tendencies in Sumerian Religion', in *The Bible and the Ancient Near East*, 1961; M. E. L. Mallowan, *Early Mesopotamia and Iran*, 1965; S. A. Pallis, *The Babylonian Akitu festival*, 1926; H. F. W. Saggs, *The Greatness that was Babylon*, 1962; G. Widengren, *The King and the Tree of Life in Ancient Near Eastern Religion*, 1951. T. Jacobsen, 'Early Political Development in Mesopotamia', ZA 52 (NF 18) 1957, 91ff; E. Strommenger, *The Art of Mesopotamia*, 1964.

b The character of Mesopotamian society—Confidence in the stability of the social order was not part of the Mesopotamian's outlook. He had little trust in anything here and now. The great powers which directed his life and the movements of the cosmos were out of his sphere. He lived in the valley of the Tigris and Euphrates where dozens of cultures had sprung into being and fallen into dust; in the Proto-literate period the rulers of Uruk discovered that a society could be properly based on a series of great canal complexes irrigating the plain, and this gave hope of permanency, but even then the Mesopotamian never lost the sense that everlastingness could not be inherited by man. Too often, despite the work of the Gugallu canal inspectorate, the **river banks burst at the spring floods** and swept away the boundary marks which set the limits of a man's property. **Nothing seemed permanent**. Everything seemed unpredictable. The Sumerians never discovered how to estimate the coming rise of the rivers. They knew nothing of the snow melting in the Armenian mountains and the spring rains in the Zab river drainage area, upon which the height of their rivers depended.

The characteristics of the two great rivers influenced the settlement on their banks. The 1700 mile long Euphrates had low banks and was subject to less violent floods than the Tigris. It became a most effective carrier of civilizing ideas. The civilization of Brak was the same as that of Uruk, 800 miles down stream, and that of Mari in the middle reaches was the same as that of Sumer. The towns grew together because men travelled up and down the river with some ease. The Tigris, whose old name, Idiglat, means 'swift as an arrow', was more difficult to navigate, and therefore communications were not developed between the towns on its banks and these show great differences of culture.

c However, with his canals at work the Mesopotamian's villages grew prosperous and large, and, if, as seems sensible, despite the criticisms of A. Falkenstein, we accept the theory of primitive Sumerian democracy advanced by Thorkild Jacobsen, they turned into cities while still retaining the village habit of asking all adult men for their opinion on matters affecting the future of the community. Sometimes these assemblies voted in a leader to deal with particular crises, sometimes, while keeping the pretence of a popular voting system, electing a more permanent leader who could organize the labour necessary for the erection of the massive brick mountains, ziqqurats, that were built at this time. In this society of interacting free men with an elected leader it was thought that the rulers of the world who sat in the heaven acted within a similar social structure. The cosmos was thought to be a large Mesopotamian village where rule was in the hands of adult free-gods, where order was arrived at after hard debate of interests and the balancing of opposing wills.

The Council of the Gods—Both the references to the **d** matter in the OT and the Gr extracts from the late Babylonian writer Berossus (c. 340—275) tell us of a Mesopotamian society ruled by a pantheon of chthonic city gods. The elements of the universe, Anu, (sky), Enlil, (storm), Ki, (earth), Enki, (water), had to be lobbied to press at the divine assembly for the interests of their worshippers. The natural forces were conceived as being totally anthropomorphic and therefore were quarrelsome amongst themselves and spiteful towards men. They had to be wooed. The elements had wills and made judgements. Gibil and Gira, the firegods, were particularly invoked against witches. One man cast an image of his enemy into the flames saying to the fire: 'Scorching Fire, warlike son of Heaven, Thou fiercest of thy brethren, Who like Moon and Sun decidest lawsuits; Judge thou my case, hand down the verdict. Burn the man and woman who bewitched me' (*Before Philosophy* 147 Mrs. Frankfort's version of Maqlu, Tablet II, 104ff). Water was also asked to decide lawsuits. The ordeal was thought of as water seizing the perjurer, the adulteress, or witch; Hammurabi's laws assume that 'if the Holy River clutches him' the accusation is proven.

The Pantheon—The gods were headed by Anu under **e** whose arch all their debates were held. Anu survived as chief of the gods even after the suppression of the city states by the imperialist national powers. His great shrine was at Uruk (biblical Erech). He was seconded by Enlil whose storm could put an end to everything under heaven. Anu gave the orders and all things bowed, not automatically as neutral objects, but personally as engaged wills.

Mesopotamian Cosmogony—Creation is the assertion **118a** of divine order. For the Mesopotamians it was an assertion which had to be fiercely backed by force against the inimical power of chaos. The great epic *Enuma elish* describes how the hero Enlil (there can be no doubt that the storm god was the original hero of the epic though his name has been removed in favour of others' at various stages in the poem's telling) was chosen by the gods to be their champion and how he defeated the chaotic Tiamat by his stormy power. Though Anu has authority he has to enlist Enlil's force to keep the cosmos going. The Mesopotamian realized the need for compulsion if peace were to be preserved. He realized also that sometimes the storm is sheer violence, unrestrained tyranny, and that every authority employs violence at its own risk. However, given an authority backed by force the ordinary village life can proceed. Hence he thought that, given Anu backed by Enlil, the Earth (Ki, or Ninhursaga or Ninmah) can produce the food needed by

18a men, in peaceful harmony with the sweet water, Enki. The world within which human society can exist is ordered by Enki, who sets divine deputies to administer the two rivers, the sea, and the rainwinds, appoints gods to oversee the plough, the furrow and the granary. He is thought of as the lord of an estate.

b **The temple**—The Mesopotamian temple was a building among other buildings, a sign of the god committing himself to the society of men, and in an almost exclusive sense to the society of men in that particular city. The god made himself one with the worshippers. The gods, therefore, had a real interest in the economic and military survival of their chosen cities. The fortunes of their city were linked to their own prestige in the assembly of the gods. Ningal, goddess of Ur, is represented in one poem as going begging for her city at the doors of Anu and Enlil, and weeping at the assembly as the doom of Ur is pronounced and the Elamitic barbarians clamber among its ruins.

Since the temple was the home of a member of the city-society there was no word for 'temple' in Sumerian, it was simply a house (é), and was built at first according to the plan of a house, and run as a home by the god's wife and his servants: the worshippers and tenants. The Mesopotamian shrine of modest proportions that characterized the early period of a city was generally replaced, on the emergence of the city as a power in the land, by the distinctive Sumerian-Akkadian ziqqurat. This stepped pyramidal building of three to seven stages could be as much as a hundred and fifty feet high. The most acceptable explanation of the significance of the ziqqurat architecture is that of Andrae, though this has been subject to a great deal of criticism, notably from H. Lenzen. However, Andrae's theory does account for many features of the ziqqurat and may be accepted as the best theory we have so far. He suggests that the ziqqurat was designed as a stairway between heaven (signified by the temple at the top of the Structure) and earth (signified by the temple at ground level). The god came from the divine assembly in the vault of heaven and alighted at the top, descended the stairway and met his people in the lower temple, (cf Gn 11:3—5 and 28:12).

c The Temple priests owned a vast proportion of the land under cultivation, and an equally large proportion of the grazing flocks. The temple shepherd was a quite important member of the Mesopotamian society until the very end of the empire. Men worked either as direct servants of the temple community or as tenants of temple lands. The Mesopotamian land tenure system of dependence on the temple may well be an example of what Jacobsen (*Bible and Near East*, 'Formative tendencies in Sumerian Religion', 274) refers to as 'the strong urge to tender allegiance and therein to achieve security and salvation', and which leads to a more and more anthropomorphic view of the numinous. Reversewise, the powers of evil in the world were thought to be opposed to any social obligation and allegiance even among themselves, and to be totally lacking in human characteristics, 'neither males are they nor females . . . they have not wives, engender not children'.

Besides their commitment to their own citizens the urban gods were committed to the leading gods of the assembly. The lesser gods held their city and temple as tenants or feudal dependents of the greater gods. Enlulim, the divine herdsman, cared for the flocks of the other gods, and is described in terms used of human temple herdsmen like Amos (cf Arvid S. Kapelrud, *Central Ideas in Amos*, Oslo, 1961) and Doeg the Edomite, (1 Sm 21:7). In Ugarit the chief priest is called 'leader of herdsmen',

while in the late kingdom of the Assyrians the king was **118c** called 'the great shepherd'. Evidently the divine work was later carried through by priests and kings.

The King—That all men, including the free citizen and **d** the magistrate, were servants of the gods was obvious to every Mesopotamian man. The king himself was made aware of his servile position before the god in a ceremony at the New Year festival (which took place on the first eleven days of the first month, Nisan, which included the day of the spring equinox) in Babylon, when he gave up all the royal regalia and presented an account of his stewardship. This is sometimes referred to as 'the negative confession' because the king denied his guilt of one offence after another. At the end of his report the king was punished by non-too-symbolic blows on the face and lugs at his ears until the tears came, and was then given back his royal dignity. On occasions of national calamity the king was conscious that disaster had come by his negligence and performed a penitential ceremony of great rigour. There was no assurance given to the Mesopotamian king that he was kin to the gods.

One of the main services demanded of the king was **e** the erection of the temple, its continual repair, and the performance of the ritual within it. There are many representations of the kings performing actual building jobs: the British Museum bronze of a Sumerian king bearing the building materials to the site, and the Pennsylvania limestone stele of Ur Nammu of Ur, in which in several scenes the king is shewn as receiving the insignia of justice and the mason's rod and line from the moon-god Nanna, and then shown carrying the builder's axe and adze; and in the celebrated dream of Gudea the gods present him with a ritual hod as a sign of the task assigned him. By omens the divine plan for the temple was discovered and then the king himself moulded the first brick. When the labourers had finished and the artisans had completed the decoration of the structure, the king led the statue of the god into his temple.

Ritual substitution—So important was the king and so **f** accepted the power of omens that when a portent showed that calamity was about to come upon the crowned man sometimes a poor substitute was set upon the throne for a while to receive the blow, when the moment of catastrophe was passed the king would resume his state. The substitute was so complete that when (c. 1860) despite this precaution a king of Isin died the substitute who escaped the omen remained to rule as total king.

The gods were treated to this kind of charade on other occasions. There exists among many other magic charms, which constituted the major part of Assyrian popular religion, one from Ashur which enables a sick man and his priest to dress up a goat in the man's clothes and so deceive the goddess of death when she comes for the sick man. Further, the gods themselves were sometimes **g** impersonated by ritual substitutes whose actions bound the god. Since the old gods were the forces of nature it was possible for the people to ignore at times the anthropomorphic myths (and even these were often based on the character of the natural force being personalized, for example the story of Enlil the rapist is a story of the uncontrollable outburst of dark and stormy forces in the world) and to personalize these forces in the ritual of the sanctuary. In the festivals those who cultically performed the part of the god and goddess *were* the god and goddess, they *were* the natural forces, the foci of the elemental powers in the cosmos. When the king of Isin went in to the priestess at the spring festival he was the creative power of spring, the shepherd god Tammuz, coming to the fertile earth, the goddess Inanna. The grain rose *because*

118g *of the rite.* Similarly when the king of Babylon performs the ritual against Kingu, the evil husband of Tiamat (she married him after the death of Apsu and, incongruously, he it was who stirred her to avenge his predecessor), the flood waters of spring are held back by Marduk, who knew that his city depended on the crops in the fields around it.

h Fertility Rites—Even at their most urban, Mesopotamian states still were dominated by the primitive demand for fertile fields. The chief festival of imperial Babylon was still the New Year renewal of the soil. The 'royal tombs' of the First Dynasty of Ur, (the treasures dug up by Woolley and now in Philadelphia), seem somehow to be connected with the New Year festival of Tammuz performed to restore the fertility of the land and to 'fix the destiny' of the king. It may be that 'Queen' Shub-Ad (tomb PG/800) and another lady (tomb PG/1054) were priestesses who, with their kings, were ritually murdered when they had grown too old to celebrate the fertility cult. To suggest this is not to choose between Woolley's second theory of the burial of the god-king, and A. Moortgat's theory of the sacred marriage. The whole matter demands slow judgements since much confusion has risen from the rhetoric of those who too-readily discern patterns of kingship, fertility, and dying gods. We have to be particularly careful to have in mind the limits of our material. It is not proper to assert, for example, that because certain phrases occur in both Mesopotamian and Heb. poems there must have been identical ceremonies for the employment of the songs in which the phrases occur. Nor can we with any certainty say how large a part ritual prostitution played in Heb. cult on the evidence of the use of *Qᵉdēšā* (obviously in some close way associated with *Qadishtu*) in Dt 23:17 and 2 (4) Kgs 23:7. We simply have not on these and other matters enough evidence to speak of the influence of Mesopotamian rites on Heb. religion.

119a The Instability of Mesopotamian Society—The New Year festival was supremely important because everything in Mesopotamian life was so uncertain. There had to be an ordered beginning of the year. To the worshippers it seemed that the seasons would certainly not be given unless the ritual was performed. Everything in their lives depended on the assembly of the gods who established with an arbitrary vote, that arose from their free will, the destinies of the city and each individual citizen.

The democracy of divine society combined with the dangers of their own geography to make change ever-present to the Mesopotamians. They therefore, in their insecurity had a worship of petition and a reliance on prophecy and astrology as ways of discovering what was about to occur. So important were omens in everyone's life that a great deal of the surviving literature is concerned with them. About one third of more than twenty-thousand tablets recovered from the library of Ashurbanipal at Nineveh record omens and their significances. The interest in magic spells was not confined to the uneducated. Ashurbanipal sent his provincial officials lists of magic works required for his library.

b Since the gods were free and the elements dangerous, and since magic was difficult to control, the Mesopotamians were led to put enormous emphasis on obedience in the state. Only total service to the word of the *lugal*, the 'great man', could keep the forces of chaos beyond the city. As the gods greet Marduk as their king with the loyal acclamation 'Thy word is Anu'. So men must obey the word of the king: 'soldiers without a king are sheep without their shepherd' (RA 18, 123, rev. ii, 14'–5').

Gradually in the second millennium there grew up a sense that men must work through reason to justice. With **119** the breakdown of the system of land-tenure dominated by the temples there were more and more cases for the courts to judge and so more and more amendments to the old laws. The second year of Hammurabi, (c. 1790–1750) was known as the year 'in which he set forth justice in the land', and throughout his reign this king was continually creating a body of law in the form of decisions to act as precedents. It may be that even the famous 'Code' was a collection of such individual decisions.

Men began to ask why the gods should give law to men and not acknowledge the claims of justice themselves. This is the dominant thought behind the literature of which *Ludlul bel nemeqi* is the most famous example, and is one of the motifs of the epic of **Gilgamesh** which is concerned with the injustice of death coming to the good and the innocent. After all his efforts towards immortality and the gross hardships of his quest, the plant of immortality is by an unlucky chance eaten by a snake. Gilgamesh wept. Mesopotamian thought comes to disillusion with the order and justice once thought to be at work in the world, and thus concludes that moral action has no lasting value.

Enuma elish—This myth is later than many other **c** Mesopotamian stories. It appears about the first half of the second half of the second millennium. The version we have is written in Akkadian (a language which for a long time was spoken in Mesopotamia alongside Sumerian and, by the end of the third millennium was spoken by the whole population), and is the cultic epic of the hero-god Marduk. The history of the various versions of the poem is an indicator of the power-centres of Mesopotamia. The poem was first about the hero Enlil of Nippur. He was replaced by Marduk of Babylon, and then, on Assyria replacing Babylon as the focus of Mesopotamian power, Assur replaced Marduk as the hero of the epic. Of course such changes did not occur immediately upon political change. Not until Babylon had for some time been the political leader was Marduk accepted as leader of the divine warriors. Marduk (Amar-utuk, 'young bull of the sun') is the undisputed hero of the extant recension of the epic.

Just as the land of Mesopotamia itself grows from the **d** silt where the rivers meet the sea so in this epic Lahmu and Lahamu, the founders of the divine race grow from Apsu and Tiamat the sweet and salt waters of chaos. The divine progenitors are characterized by ordered activity—they perform a dance on the belly of Tiamat, and make her so uncomfortable that Apsu and Tiamat decide to destroy the new gods. In a great fight Apsu is defeated by Ea-Enki, the father of Marduk. Tiamat, taunted by the powers of evil, rises to avenge her husband Apsu. Ea, even when backed by the authority of all the gods in assembly, cannot overpower the full force of chaos. His virile young son, Marduk, is chosen to be champion of the gods. He accepts the responsibility on the condition, to which they all agree, that he is proclaimed ruler of the gods. Marduk raises his mace, climbs into his chariot, and hurtles against Tiamat. The goddess opens her dragon mouth to devour him and he drives the storm-winds down her maw so that she cannot shut her jaws. Marduk then shoots his arrows between her teeth and pierces her heart. He next slits the dead Tiamat in two like a flat fish and hangs half to be the vault of heaven and spreads half to be his footmat below. On the vault he builds his royal house, setting locks and guards to ensure that the waters of the vault shall not escape. He fixes the planets and constellations so that their recurring paths mark out the pattern of the calendar, and then, amid general

19d divine rejoicing, he invents man to do the hard work of the world, leaving the gods free for feasting. The shout of the sons of God in Job 38 may echo the rejoicing of the gods at the victory of Marduk in the Akkadian creation epic.

e We can recognize the assimilatory process at work in Mesopotamian theology in the litany of Marduk that the gods chant at the feast. The last acclamation of Marduk is to name his as 'Fifty' (the numerical designation of Enlil) while Ea, the old leader, himself cries out: 'Let his name be Ea', and Marduk is given the Sumerian title *Lugaldimmirankia*, (King of the gods of heaven and earth). Later, in 714, Sargon II addressed Ashur, the god of the city of Ashur, as 'father of the gods, the great lord'. Such are the chances of power.

Since the universe is the coming together of free wills after the manner of a village assembly, it is evident that at different times different gods will be the elected leader of the divine assembly, and that therefore at different times different cities and their kings will lead the Mesopotamian world. The theology provided the theory of history. In turn Kish and Agade, the cities of Inanna, were eclipsed by Ur, because Nanna had succeeded to leadership among the gods. When Hammurabi of Babylon subjected Isin and put the rest of Mesopotamia under his rule this was an effect of the election of Marduk as leader of the gods in the place of Nininsina of Isin. Marduk was in his turn replaced by Assur in the government of Mesopotamia. The coming of a new power was accounted for by supposing a change of will in the assembly of the gods. It was therefore a simple matter to accommodate a victory or a revolution in the general view of Mesopotamian theory.

f At such times of change Sumerian ritual found the perfect word and expressed the unhappiness of the god and his city in **laments of great beauty**. In the song of despair the worshipper and the god became one in their sharing the collapse of hope. In a delicate reversal of duties the worshipper comforts the god in order that the god may find courage to rebuild the city. (For examples concerning Ur and Nippur cf Kramer, *Assyriological Studies*, Oriental Institute, University of Chicago, 12; ANET (1), 455–63). A related lament is that for Tammuz the dead shepherd god, killed, like so many shepherds on the grassy steppe of S Babylonia, by the mountain men, and, being found, came back to give fertility to the land. By the middle of the first millennium the **lament for Tammuz** was being sung by the women of Jerusalem to the outrage of Ezekiel (Ezek 8:14). (For a list of extant laments ranging from less than fifty to more than two hundred lines consult M. Witzel, *Tammuz-liturgien und Verwandtes*, Analecta Orientalia, 10). Sometimes the town did not sing a lament but demanded vengeance against the aggressor god. At Lagash, after Lugalzaggisi of Umma had sacked the town, the citizens called on the divine assembly to punish the crime of Nidaba, goddess of Lugalzaggisi.

g The lament of Lagash was not long in having its satisfaction. In 2300 or so Sargon of Agade conquered the whole of Mesopotamia, parts of Syria and Asia Minor, and put troops on Crete. This vast empire lasted until 2250 going under to the Gutian barbarians from the eastern hills who were in turn pushed back by the III Dynasty of Ur (c. 2120–2010), which itself collapsed with the capture of Ur by the Elamites. In this hectic swapping of supremacies Babylon emerged.

It would seem that Babylon's influence grew by the energies of those of the invading semitic Amorites ('westerners') who settled in the town, culminating in the enthronement of Hammurabi (c. 1790–1750) as lord **119g** of Sumer, Akkad and of the **Mari** region on the Middle Euphrates. The tablets found here and those of Kanish in Cappadocia speak of Haran, whence came Abraham, as a flourishing city at this time, and provide not inconsiderable linguistic support for the antiquity of the patriarchal narratives. Again the **Nuzu** tablets present a picture of Mesopotamian society in the middle of the second millennium which is often in detailed harmony with that presupposed in the patriarchal narratives. This is a strong argument for these narratives' substantial historicity.

Though Shamshi-Adad I, (c. 1815–1780), was per- **h** haps even more imposing than Hammurabi, on his death the Assyrian empire went gradually into decline until Tukulti-Ninurta I (1256–1233) defeated the Kassite princes and occupied Babylon. Assyria had then to put every effort into resisting the Aramean invasion of semitic Syrian tribes. The vigour of Tiglathpileser I, (1098–1068) gained the Assyrians some respite, and but not until Ashur-nasir-apli II, (884–859) was the empire free to engage in wars of aggrandisement. At this point Israel, a neighbour of the Arameans and Phoenicians, began to feel the Assyrian pressures which led to their defeat with the Arameans at **Qarqar**, (853), and the submission of Jehu to Shalmaneser III recorded on the 'Black Obelisk', now in the British Museum.

The Assyrians never quite managed to contain Baby- **i** lonian local patriotism and through the reigns of Tiglathpileser III (745–727), Sargon II (722–705) and Sennacherib, (705–681) the Assyrian kings had to beat down the revolts of the Babylonians led by Merodach-baladan. Hezekiah of Judah allied himself with them in 701 but later had to pay tribute to Sennacherib. The Babylonian irritations seemed to be at an end with the burning of the city in 648, but the citizens enlisted the support of the Indo-European Medes, captured Ashur, 614, and in 612 Nineveh fell. Under the prince Nebuchadrezzar II (605–561) they defeated the Egyptians at Carchemish (605) and took over the land of Hatti, including Syria and Palestine, (2 (4) Kgs 24:7). The Egyptians rebelled in 601, and the men of Judah in 597, (King Jehoiachin and 3,023 citizens were transported) so when Judah relying on Egyptian aid, rebelled again in 589, Nebuchadrezzar decided to destroy Jerusalem which resisted his siege until July 586.

Such a history could not but confirm the Mesopotamian in his view of a changing world where no value counted but strength of will.

3 CANAAN

Bibliography—Y. Aharoni, *The Land of the Bible*, **120a** 1966; G. R. Driver, *Canaanite Myths and Legends*, 1956; J. Engnell, *Studies in Divine Kingship in the Ancient Near East*, 1943; C. H. Gordon, *Ugaritic Textbook*, 1965; *Ugaritic Literature*, 1949; J. Gray, *Legacy of Canaan*, VTS V, Leiden, 1965[2]; *The Canaanites*, 'Ancient Peoples and Places', 1964; A. R. Johnson, *Sacral Kingship in Ancient Israel*, 1955; A. S. Kapelrud, *Baal in the Ras Shamra Tablets*, 1952; C. F. A. Schaeffer, *Reprise des Fouilles de Ras Shamra-Ugarit*, 1955; W. Schmidt, 'Königtum Gottes in Ugarit und Israel', BZAW, 80, 1966[2]; R. de Vaux, 'Le cadre géographique du poème de Krt', RB, 46 (1937) 362–72; 'Les textes de Ras Shamra et l'Ancien Testament', RB, 46 (1937) 526–55. W. F. Albright, *Yahweh and the Gods of Canaan*, 1968.

120b The early history of Cannan—The agriculture of the rich alluvial soil of the coastal plain and the Jezreel Valley, the oak trees of the Sharon Plain, the olives of the Shephelah, the grain crops of the Philistine Coast down as far as Gaza, the fruit trees and vines of the Judean hill country, the farms of Chinnereth, made the Canaanites very aware of the importance of the annual divine renewal of fertility. Their gods are the farmer's gods. Their history is the history of invaders coveting their farm-lands. The Israelites were not alone in their description of this as a land flowing with milk and honey. Sinuhe, an Egyptian nobleman, travelling in the Levant as a refugee from Sesostris I (1980–1935), wrote of Canaan: 'It was a good land . . . figs were there and grapes. It had more wine than water. Plentiful was its honey, abundant its olives'. The name derives from Kinahhu, a purple dye made from shell-fish of the Syrian coast (the Greek term for the area, Phoenicia, is simply the translation of this word), and it is this coastal region, supplemented later by the plain of Megiddo and the Hazor region, which is generally meant by 'Canaan', (cf Jg 5:19).

The early history of the area is one of tough local communities rejecting many attempts to bring them into one state and accepting without much enthusiasm elements of the cultural developments of Mesopotamia and Egypt. The great advance came with the native invention of the consonantal alphabet. It was in developed forms of this script that the royal scribes of Israel and Judah kept their chronicles and it was taken by the Phoenicians to Greece and became the usual script of Greek letters. In it, in Canaan, a great body of literature, much larger than we have in the great finds of Ras Shamra, was composed. It is possible from the Egyptian Amarna tablets, Akkadian tablets from Atchana, Amorite sources, the linear inscriptions from Sinai, Lachish, Byblos, the calendar of Gezer and the collection of cuneiform tablets from Ras Shamra, to construct a highly detailed picture of the social, political and literary life of Canaan in the Middle and Late Bronze Ages.

c   The interest of the great powers in Canaan was motivated by the timber resources of Lebanon. Thus Sargon of Akkad (c. 2500) in his Omen texts speaks of his conquest of the land of 'the mountains of cedar', and the Gilgamesh epic tells of an heroic struggle with Huwawa, the guardian of the cedars, and the Egyptian Papyrus 'Golenischeff' (ANET 25ff) speaks of vast amounts of timber being exported from Byblos. The trade was both ways. Many of the gold objects in the royal tombs of Byblos were evidently gifts of the Pharaohs to the rulers of this harbour city. Something of what the Canaanites took from the great powers can be seen in the imitative designs of their famous ivories (cf 1 (3) Kgs 22:39 and the denunciations of Am 3:15; 6:4). They employ Mesopotamian or Egyptian motifs and hardly ever invent even a new stance for the sphinxes and gods they have borrowed. Trade went on with other powers; and Mycenean and Anatolian designs are frequent among the ivory panels which decorated Canaanite furniture.

d **The coming of the Phoenicians**—The harbour cities of the Phoenicians lie along the coastal strip from the Gulf of Alexandretta to Carmel. The economy of these cities was mainly maritime, and their trading-ships went out to distant ports in the Mediterranean and, during the alliance of Hiram of Tyre and Solomon of Jerusalem, to the Red sea and perhaps the E African coast. With trade went customs and religious practices. Jezebel, the Tyrian princess who came to Israel to marry Ahab, brought not simply a commercial advantage but also an opportunity for Baalism to be respectable again in Israel. The Tyrian sailors founded Carthage, c. 814, **120** and hence the child-sacrifices to Moloch were offered along the N African coast.

The Ras Shamra tablets from ancient Ugarit demonstrate that the second millennium Phoenicians of the coastal region lived in a society very much like that described as Canaanite in the OT. Ugarit fell to the Philistines (*Pulusatu*, as the Egyptian chroniclers called them) and other 'Sea Peoples' moving S, c. 1200. The progress of the invaders (who seem to have been related to the Mycenaeans, may have fought at Troy, and certainly had spent time in Crete, cf Am 9:7) was halted by Rameses III. The Egyptians could not dislodge the Sea Peoples from the coast of Palestine and so made a show of allowing them to remain as officially dependent tenants. This fiction did not last long. The Philistines settled down in the old cities, adopted a modified form of the old feudalism, organized their armies and, because of their succeeding to the old Hittite monopoly of iron, became the most feared of Israel's enemies. This society survived even the campaigns of David and throughout the monarchical period in Israel the Philistines remained in possession of the coast between Jaffa and Gaza. David had greater success in subjugating the Jordan peoples of Ammon and Edom.

Saul had made great efforts to destroy the men of Ammon, who, raiding from their high moors, had been a menace since the time of the Judges; after David's attack the Ammonites contented themselves with forays against the Israelites beyond Jordan, (Am 1:13f). To the S of these tribes and to the E of the Dead Sea were the people of Moab who were with Ammon the traditional enemies of Israel: the story of their incestuous generation was a ribald piece of Heb. folk lore (Gn 19:31ff), and that Ruth was a Moabitess (Ru 1:22) went only to show how Yahweh could bring good out of anything, and that the king of Moab, when rebelling against Jehoram of Israel (2 (4) Kgs 3:4ff), should offer human sacrifice to his god was typical of the people. These two peoples invaded Judah in 602, (2 (4) Kg 24:2) and took part in the Babylonian attack on Jerusalem, (Ezek 25:1–11).

Canaanite Society—If we are ready to take the legend **121a** of Keret as informative (though we have to remember that four centuries separate the Keret story and the administrative texts), we shall see that at first the king was primarily the channel of natural fertility (*mt rp'e*) and of supernatural revelation (cf 2 Sm 14:20, 1 (3) Kgs 3:3). Later the **introduction of horses** created a feudal hierarchy of barons, *mrynm*; and the king, because the amount of civic administration increased rapidly, had to leave priestly functions in the cult, and the transmission of the divine message, to others. The feudal organization of society may have been influenced by the structures of the kingdom of Mitanni, where the mainly Hurrian population was ruled by a Indo-aryan chariot aristocracy called *maryannu*. The feudal system of the Canaanites was adopted by the invading Sea Peoples (cf David at Ziglag, 1 Sm 27:6:28:1), and then by Saul (1 Sm 22:7) and his successors. The king was, thus, the owner of all the land and disposed of it to his servants as tenants-in-chief. He was, however, more than the owner of the land; he was the guardian of the people. The Aqht text about king Danel and his son is a source, besides the Egyptian ritual already mentioned, of understanding of the incubation of Solomon (1 (3) Kgs 3:4ff). Danel emerges (2 Aqht V, 6–8 1 Aqht, 21–5) from the cultic incubation to perform the kingly acts of justice for the widow and the orphan, (cf the woman of Tekoa's appeal to David, 2 Sm 14, with the climax in verse 17).

21a People were protected by a complex set of laws administered by local elders which could not be abrogated except perhaps by the unanimous will of interested parties and permission of the king, (cf 2 Sm 14:4f), and by an equally rigorous set of popular customs, like the vendetta and its complement, the sanctuary. These laws and customs, together with a procession of ceremonies at crucial times in a man's life, such as birth, puberty and marriage, led towards inexorable and total death beyond which there was no hope.

b Canaanite religion—Little direct evidence has been found of the religion of the pre-Hebrew Canaanites, but quite a deal may be learned from such indirect evidence as the Egyptian Execration Texts from Luxor and Saqqara (c. 1850 and 1800), and the Ras Shamra Texts (c. 1300), and, even more indirectly, from OT references to Canaanite practices. The **Luxor Execration Texts** list the enemies of Egypt, and include among these the wild tribes of Syria and Palestine whose leaders have Amorite theophoric names very similar in form to those of the heroes of the patriarchal narratives of Hebrew tradition. In these names the gods are described as near relations of men: uncle (*'ammu* or *ḥaluh*), brother, (*'aḥu*), showing that the earliest Canaanite society was one of small family groups, and this, together with the divisive geographical factors of the area, explains the rise of small city-states. Such divided small states were obviously not well prepared to withstand the Hebrew invaders. Some indeed welcomed the foreigners as recruits in their efforts against the neighbouring cities Lahaya of Shechem allowed the early Hebrews to settle in his territory with every sign of friendliness, (cf Gn 33:18ff).

In the second group of Execration Texts, probably from Saqqara, the kin-names are fewer, and the god Hadad is obviously thought of as the chief protector of the people. Hadad is the storm-god of the winter rains which, at the beginning of the farmers' year, break the soil for the plough to be driven across the fields. He was a fertility god (like the lost Tammuz, and like Tammuz was wept for by cultic girls particularly at Meggido, cf Zech 12:11). The names on these tablets suggest that the people are primarily interested in Hadad as protector of the crops which form the basis of their livelihood.

c At the head of the pantheon was *El*, the Father of Men, (*'ab 'adm*), and the Bull, (*tr*), who sits where the two streams meet (cf Gn 2:10–14; Ps 46:5; Ezek 47; Jl 4:18). Second to El came Baal, the Prince, (*zbl*, cf Baal-zebul, god of Ekron), and rider of the clouds (cf Ps 68:5; 104:3; Dt 33:26), god of thunder and life who lived on Baal-Saphon, the Mountain of the North (cf Is 14:13; Ezek 28:14, and the home of Yahweh in Ps 48:3). Baal is a typical Near E divine hero, like Enlil or Marduk in Mesopotamia, conquering the watery goddess *ym* (cf Ps 74:12–19; 89:10–15; 93; 104:9 Ezek 29:5; 32:4–5; Na 1:15), despite the set-backs of drought and death, and building his house in the clouds where he may control the trap door which lets the rain fall through upon earth (cf Gn 7:11). At the final triumph of Baal the people cry out 'Let Baal be King!', and it would seem, likely that the myth was recited at the cult (cf Heb. 'enthronement psalms', e.g. Ps 10:16; 29:10; 47:7; 68:24; 74:12; 98; 6).

d The building of Baal's house is preceded by a great blood-bath, the work of the goddess Anat, to encourage the life-force to spread abroad. The blood of Baal's enemies is to bring fertility to the soil, (cf perhaps the sacrifice of human life at the beginning of the barley harvest, 2 Sm 21:1–9). The coming of Baal to his worshippers is heralded by a similar blood-letting in the Carmel drama

(1 (3) Kgs 18:44–45). Perhaps the building of the house **121d** for Baal was to provide a setting for the *hieros gamos* (Gray: *The Legacy of Canaan*, Leiden, 1965[2], 51, note 3). Gray (op. cit., 53) suggests that the myth of the building of Baal's house has certain essential features which have their counterpart in the dedication of Solomon's temple in Jerusalem which was celebrated at the time of the rain festival of Canaan, and included a hint of Canaanite imitative fertility magic in the water-drawing at the feast of Tabernacles. Certainly Amos (2:7) condemns ritual prostitution at the Feast, and in the Mishnah there are directions for keeping the women apart from the men during the dancing.

This myth is continued in the story of Baal's attempt **e** to conquer death and sterility in the person of the god Mot and of Baal being lost in the underworld. Uniting Tammuz and Osiris elements in the myth (this syncretism is typical of Canaanite culture) the Canaanites instituted a ceremonial weeping for the dead god (cf Jg 11:40) in which girls tore their hair and put dust on their heads, (cf the sarcophagus of King Ahiram of Byblos, and Jer 2:37), and followed this with the finding of the body and a ritual feast for the dead Baal (cf Dt 26:14 which reflects the struggle against these fertility cults), until at last Baal rises again. The festival of Baal's return and the outburst of fertility which accompanied him gave full rein to the *qᵉdēšim* and the *qᵉdēšôt*, those cult prostitutes so often denounced by the Hebrews. Mot has a resurgence of power every seven years when the fields had to lie fallow (cf Ex 23:10–11; Lv 25:3–7). Gray (*Legacy of Canaan*, 8) connects the fallow year with the punishment of Baal's fratricide and sees here a parallel with the sterility of the ground that is part of the curse on Cain, (Gn 4:11–12). A similar sterility occurs in the Aqht Text (1 Aqht 34–48) when the goddess Anat has the hero killed. These and other incidents in the Krt Text have been over-eagerly compared to the Joseph story in Gn, which has been claimed as a fertility saga (Bo Reicke, *Analogier mellan Josefberattelsen*; *Genesis och Ras Shamra-texterna*, SvExÅb, 1945, 27ff). More likely is Gray's conjecture (*Legacy of Canaan*, 131) that the myth is reflected in the account of the drought after the massacre of the Gibeonites (2 Sm 21:1ff). The whole fertility cult was designed to ensure that life went on in an ordered sequence, but of course it did not contain a moral imperative for right action: everything was done because it was expedient to be done.

Among many other Canaanite gods, besides El and Baal, there ought to be some mention of **Shalem**, since his name survives in 'Jerusalem', and in 'Absalom' and 'Solomon', he seems to have been identical with Moloch, who was worshipped in Jerusalem (1 (3) Kgs 9:7, Zeph 1:5, et al.), by the sacrifice of children. He was worshipped in Moab (2 (4) Kgs 3:27, and an inscription of Tiglath Pileser III concerning the 8th cent. Salamanu, king of Moab) and, probably, under various titles in most Canaanite cities.

Canaanite Ritual—The Temple of Baal at the Cana- **f** anite capital, Ugarit, is built on the same tri-partite plan as the temple of Solomon in Jerusalem. The sanctuary at Gezer, which had a similar plan, with its monoliths on a raised platform or 'high place' (*bāmāh*, cf Albright, 'The High Place in Ancient Palestine', VTS IV, 1957, 243–58) and its socket for the symbolic 'green tree' of the fertility ritual of Baal-Hadad and the goddesses Asherah, Astarte and Anat, who were all concerned with procreation and harvest, (cf also the shrines at Bethshan and Byblos), show us what was meant in the denunciations by the orthodox of Jerusalem of the country cults.

121f One of the most frequent themes of Canaanite art is the Tree of Life with caprids reaching up; sometimes the goddess Asherah herself takes the place of the Tree. Gray's theory of the Tree myth's intimate relation to the agricultural year seems to stand despite some objections by Gordon (*Ugaritic Literature*, 1949, 3—5) and Cassuto ('Baal and Mot in the Ugaritic Texts', IEJ 12, (1962) 77—86), and he seems right too in his relating the triumph of Baal to the Enthronement Psalms and the Kingship of Yahweh. Mowinckel suggests ('Psalm Criticism between 1900 and 1935', VT 5 (1955) 25) that the Heb. Enthronement Psalmists found the theme of creation linked with that of kingship in Mesopotamian **g** rather than Canaanite sources. Gray (*Legacy of Canaan*, 157) and W. Schmidt (Königtum Gottes in Ugarit und Israel, BZAW 80 (1961)) think that the ideology of the kingship in the cult of El Elyon in Jerusalem was the most important influence after David's occupation of the city. The New Year festival of the Canaanites was, of course, adapted for Hebrew purposes. While the Hebrew scribes would have none of Baal (as early as the book of Judges there are denunciations of the 'men who go awhoring after Baal' and fertility cults, Jg 8:33), Yahweh very early assimilated the creative and kingly characteristics of El, who was it seems once the High God, suzerain of Yahweh and his tribal worshippers, (cf Dt 32:8—9, where El appears to give Israel to Yahweh), and there is something of truth in F. Lokkegaard's remark, ('A Plea for El, the Bull, and other Ugaritic Miscellanies', SOr, Joanni Pedersen Dicata, 1953, 232) that El is 'the special contribution of Canaan to the world'. Gray (*Legacy of Canaan*, 190ff) and Eissfeldt (ThLZ, LXXIX, 1954, cols 283ff) suggest that some Canaanites in the Late Bronze Age did come to a monotheism of El.

The gods were worshipped in an elaborate ritual whose Ugaritic technical terms, literary forms, and cultic practices are parallelled in Hebrew texts, and the possibility of the elaborate ritual of Lv being primitive is again tenable, but similarities of rite are not so significant as differences of theology.

The mythical lordship of Baal had always to be won again in cyclic patterns. Fertility had continually to be defended. Yahweh's acts might be celebrated again and again in a liturgical year, but his acts themselves were performed in history. He had created the fruitful earth once and for all.

4 THE HITTITES

122a **Bibliography**—E. O. Forrer, 'The Hittites in Palestine', PEF, 68, (1936—7) 190ff; 69, 100—115; O. R. Gurney, *The Hittites*, 1961[2]; H. G. Guterbock, 'The Hurrian Element in the Hittite Empire', Cahiers d'Histoire Mondiale, II, 1954; D. R. Hillers 'Treaty Curses and the Old Testament Prophets.' Bibor 16 (1964); D. J. McCarthy, *Treaty and Covenant*, Analecta Biblica, Rome, 1963; C. L. Woolley, et al., *Carchemish, Report on the Excavations at Djerabis on behalf of the British Museum*, I, 1914; II, 1921; III, 1952.

b **The People**—Two groups are referred to as 'Hittites' in the OT: inhabitants of the hills of Judaea, and inhabitants of Syria. The first group died out early in the Hebrew occupation of Palestine. The redaction of the text of Jos 1:2—4 evidences to the disappearances of these Hittites. The original text described the Hebrews in the land of Moab on the E bank of the Jordan determining to grab the Hittite hills 'over this Jordan'. The later editor did not know of these Hittites. In order to make **122** some sense of the reference to Hittites he added a note saying that they lived 'in Lebanon, even unto the great river, the river Euphrates'. For this editor the only Hittites were the Hittites of Syria, who were known at Hebron at the time of Abraham.

'Hittite' may in the OT sometimes refer generically **c** to the Hurrians. For example, Uriah, the 'Hittite', (2 Sm 11:6ff), almost certainly has a Hurrian name, (cf M. Vieyra, RHA 5 (1938) 113f; W. Feiler, ZA, 45 (1939) 216ff; H. G. Ginsberg and B. Maisler, JPOS 14 (1934) 243ff). In other contexts 'Hittite' refers to the imperial power of Anatolia but there seems to have been no time when the Hebrews related either of the Hittite groups they knew to the great empire in the NE. Various suggestions have been presented to explain how the Hittites of Palestine were related to those of the Anatolian plateau whose conquests never reached further than Damascus. E. Farrer (PEQ, 1936, 190—203; 1937, 100—115) suggests that the Mursilis II (c. 1330) account of the men of Kurustamma in the NE part of the empire being sent into Egyptian-ruied territory, might refer to the settlement in Palestine of fugitives from Hittite conquests. O. E. Gurney (*The Hittites*, Pelican, 1952[2], revised 1961, 61) agrees that this may be the case but says that a 'reference to the weather-god of Hatti as the instigator of the move is in favour of a deliberate act of state rather than a flight of fugitives from the Hittite conquest.' Gurney (op cit 62) interestingly suggests that the Hattian language, which is the earliest known among the inhabitants of Anatolia, was once spoken by the occupants of the Palestinian hills, and that the 'Hittites' of the Bible were oddments left in their settlements by the invading Hurrian and Semitic peoples. He further suggests that the Syrian Hittites of the Bible were originally inhabitants of Kizzuwatna.

The Neo-Hittite kingdoms—In Syria and the Taurus **d** mountains the Hittite way of life went on for five hundred years after the old Anatolian empire collapsed during the turbulent times of the Sea Peoples' invasions. This outlying province took over the title of the old empire which had been centered at Hattusas (near the modern village of Boghazköy) and had been capable of defending itself against Tutmosis III and later Rameses II. Syria, ruled from Carchemish, is called by the Assyrians the 'land of Hatti' and its many princes are referred to by the Hebrews as 'Kings of the Hittites', (2 (4) Kgs 7:6; 2 Chr 1:17).

It is difficult to know and not easy to guess how much of the old society and its customs and attitudes survived the political and social upheavals which followed upon the fall of Hattusas. The towns were given new names, always a sign of significant social change, and their importances were juggled. Aleppo became Halman and lost prestige while Arpad became one of the chief cities. The society, in which these neo-Hittite kingdoms of Syria existed, was neither Anatolian Hittite nor of the earlier Syrian Hittite or Hurrian form, but was characteristic of a new people who came to Syria in the general movements of people from some provinces of the old Hattusan empire. After the upheavals contemporaneous with Rameses III the Syrian Hittites became highly prosperous (witness the tribute required of them by the Assyrians in 876). Their military men were sought after as mercenaries, (cf 2 Sm 11:3ff; 1 Sm 26:6), and their ladies served in Solomon's harem, (1 (3) Kgs 11:1). In 853 the kings of Hamath and Damascus actually forced Shalmaneser III at Qarqar to give up his expedition,

22d but between 738 and 709 Syria was annexed to form Assyrian provinces.

It is not likely that after so many upheavals much of the original way of life should have survived in its pristine form, but religious customs and beliefs deriving from the early Hattusan way of life must in some transmuted form have survived to the end of the Hittite kingdoms.

23a Hittite Religion—The Anatolian empire never aimed at religious uniformity within its frontiers. Local gods were left on the sanctuaries of conquered or assimilated towns, but gradually these merged with one another and with the metropolitan gods. In this easy acceptance of foreign ways they were behaving in just the manner of their worshippers who accepted native cultures newly found as part of their tradition.

b In Hittite Anatolia the great god was the storm-god, and his Syrian representations show him with a destroying axe and a flash of lightning. In the Taurus region and N Syria he is called by his Hurrian name, Teshub, and is depicted as a human-headed and winged lion. The storm-god myth is related to the Babylonian creation myth. It is a story of the god fighting the dragon Illuyankas, at first unsuccessfully, and at last saved by a human being who in turn comes to grief. This myth-ritual was recited at the great spring *purulli* festival. This celebration, like most others in the Hittite ceremonial, was dominated by the king as chief priest of the gods. Though he was also commander of the army it is as priest that the king is most usually depicted on royal monuments, generally, as at Alaca Hüyük and Malatya, as priest of the storm god. Some later kings had other patrons: Hattusilis III (1275–5) worshipped the Hurrian goddess Shaushka/Ishtar, and his son Tudhaliyas IV (1250–1220) is shown in the side gallery at Yazilikaya in the arms of the storm-god's son, Sharruma; but generally the royal house remained the chief priests of the storm-god himself. Another myth having parallels in Babylonian literature, but readily adaptable to Syrian circumstances, was the tale of the lost god. The earth loses its fertility because the god in a temper has left the soil to its own devices. After a series of high adventures and the casting of strong spells (always a major element of Hittite religious practice), the god is brought back to invigorate the earth.

c Hittite treaties This aspect of Hittite life has made an impact on modern discussions rather greater than others for two reasons: i) most of the extant texts are of treaties between nations and are therefore written in an already known diplomatic language, mostly in the Akkadian of Mesopotamia, and these were therefore more quickly available than the rest of the Boghazköy texts; and ii) the treaty texts were thought to have elements in common with Hebrew covenant forms and therefore to assist in the interpretation of OT difficulties.

Hittite treaties have been employed in OT discussions

since the publication of Viktor Korošec's monograph in **123c** 1931, and the studies of George Mendenhall (1954) and Klaus Baltzer (1960). Korošec's analysis of the general shape of these treaties has held its own. He divided them thus: i) prologue; ii) description of the historical situation within which the treaty was being framed; iii) contractual terms; iv) safeguards for the text of the treaty to prevent tampering with the clauses; v) an invocation for the gods to witness the treaty; vi) curses upon the breaker and blessings on the keeper of the treaty terms. It will be seen immediately that there is some degree of correspondence between this formula for feudal and international treaties and the Sinai covenant of Ex 20 and its renewal in Jos 24, and more particularly, in the framing of the Deuteronomic tradition.

Despite the fact that very little is known of treaties **d** between 1200 and 850, it used to be almost universally maintained that the Israelite covenant with Yahweh derived its form from the old Hittite feudal treaties between king and vassal. But there are certain differences which need to be emphasized at least as much as the similarities: i) the Hittite treaty might have been negotiated by a minister or deputy but this officer's name never occurs in the account or in the treaty text; among the Hebrews Moses is always to the fore as the mediator between people and Yahweh; ii) in the languages of Sumer and Hatti the treaty is always spoken of in terms of an oath-making *māmītu* or *adê*, whereas the Hebrew *berît* derives from the rite of animal sacrifice and this puts the emphasis not on the word given but on the acting of the ritual of treaty-making, which was probably in itself cultic. It would seem that the sources of covenant language (and therefore probably of covenant significance) are not Akkadian but Amorite. Mari documents use 'killing an ass' as a term for 'making a treaty', (cf Jos 24:32). This seems nearer Hebrew usage than the **e** Hittite terminology. Certainly there are ceremonies in Hittite religion which recall the ritual of the covenant in Gn 15:9–18, but these Hittite ceremonies are concerned with purification rather than with the making or renewal of treaty. The language shows, what is apparent from the whole context of the covenant passages, that the covenant is not thought of by the Hebrews as merely an exchange of oaths for a contract. The Sinai covenant tradition, which is older than the deuteronomic tradition, demonstrates that the covenant is a ritual act rather than a pledging of a word. The covenant is brought into being by *šelāmîm* sacrifices, uniting the worshipper with Yahweh, and not by the *šalimu* exchange of oaths. Even the contractual elements of the deuteronomic tradition are part of the ritual representation of the original Sinai covenant at which Yahweh revealed his will for those who would take part in his service. The contractual elements do not constitute the covenant, they are the expression of the effects of the relationship which the covenant has already brought about.

THE CHRONOLOGY OF THE
OLD TESTAMENT

BY E. F. SUTCLIFFE S.J.

REVISED BY R. C. FULLER

124a Bibliography—(1) *General*: F. K. Ginzel, *Handbuch der mathemathischen und technischen Chronologie*, 3 vols, Leipzig 1906—14; H. R. Hall, *Ancient History of the Near East*, London 1950[11]; D. D. Luckenbill, *Ancient Records of Assyria and Babylonia*, 2 vols, Chicago 1926—7; A. Deimel, S.J., *Vet Test. Chronologia Monumentis Bab.-Assyr. illustrata*, Romae 1912; J. B. Pritchard, *Ancient Near Eastern Texts* 1955[2]; F. X. Kugler, S.J., *Von Moses bis Paulus*, Münster in Westf. 1922; L. Pirot & V. Coucke, DBS 1 (1928), 1244—79; CAH, 1 & 2, revised ed. 1963; J. Bright, *A History of Israel*, 1960; J. Finegan, *Handbook of Biblical Chronology*, Princeton, 1964; D. Winton Thomas, *Documents from OT Times*, 1958;

(2) *Maccabean Age*: J. Hontheim, S.J., 'Zur Chronologie der beiden Machabaerbüchen' ZKT 43 (1919) 1—30.

(3) *Ezra-Nehemiah*: A. Van Hoonacker, *Nouvelles Etudes sur la Restauration juive après l'Exil de Babylone*, Louvain 1896; RB 10 (1901) 5—26, 175—99; 32 (1923) 481—94; 33 (1924) 33—64; W. M. F. Scott, 'Nehemiah-Ezra' ET 58 (1946—7) 263—7; H. H. Rowley, *The Servant of the Lord and other Essays*, 1952, 131—159.

(4) *Period of the Kings*: J. Begrich, *Die Chronologie der Könige von Israel und Juda*, 1929; E. Vogt, S.J., 'Nova Chronica Babylonica de pugna apud Karchemish et expugnatione Jerusalem (597)', Bib. 37 (1956), 389—97; S. Smith, *Babylonian Historical Texts relating to the Capture and Downfall of Babylon*, 1924; C. Schedl, 'Textkritische Bemerkungen zu den Synchronismen der Könige von Israel und Juda', VT 12 (1962) 88—119; E. R. Thiele, JNES 3 (1944) 137—86; id *The Mysterious Numbers of the Hebrew Kings*, 1965[2]; C. J. Gadd, *The Fall of Nineveh*, 1923; D. J. Wiseman, *Chronicles of the Chaldaean Kings, (626—556 B.C.), in the British Museum*, 1956; A. Poebel, 'The Assyrian King-List from Khorsabad' JNES, 1, (1942), 247—306, 460—92, 2 (1943) 56—90; J. McHugh, 'The Date of Hezekiah's Birth', VT 14 (1964) 446—53; J. Hontheim S.J., ZKT 42 (1918) 463—82; H. Hänsler O.S.B., Bib 10 (1929) 257—74; J. Gray, *1 & 2 Kings*, 1964 55—74; W. F. Albright, 'The Chronology of the Divided Monarchy of Israel' BASOR 100 (1945) 16—22; 'New Light from Egypt on the Chronology and History of Israel and Judah, BASOR 130 (1953) 4—8. C. Schedl, *Geschichte des AT*, 1962[4].

(5) *Judges and Exodus*: J. Hontheim S.J., 'Die Chronologie der Richterzeit in der Bibel und die ägyptische Chronologie' ZKT 37 (1913) 76—132. On the date of the Exodus: R. de Vaux, ZAW 56 (1938) 225—38; L.-P. Vincent, RB 48 (1939) 579—83; W. F. Albright, BASOR 74 (1939) 11—23; H. H. Rowley, PEQ (1941) 152—7; id., *From Joseph to Joshua*, 1950, gives an exhaustive bibliography. See also references in the text.

The OT provides very imperfect information about **124** relative chronology and none at all about absolute chronology. Though the broad sweep of the story is in chronological sequence this is not always the case with regard to particular events. In some cases events apparently successive in time were actually contemporaneous as in Judges; the story itself is not complete, witness the gap of unspecified length between Ezra-Nehemiah and Maccabees; the numbers given are not always correct, they and proper names being most exposed to corruption in transmission. Numbers accurately transmitted are sometimes intentionally vague as in the frequent use of the number forty, and sometimes difficult of interpretation through ignorance of ancient methods of computation, literary forms and editorial procedure.

Thus, in Gn, the chronology of the patriarchs is not historical but symbolical and theological. The material for an exact chronology was in any case lacking to the author and if this is true of the Patriarchal period it is even more the case with the ages which stretched back to the beginnings of the human race. On this see § 145a. Not surprisingly the ground becomes firmer the farther one advances in time and it will be convenient to start at the end of the OT with the books of Maccabees.

Though the idea of an absolute chronology is foreign **c** to the OT, it does contain information which renders possible the determination of definite dates for certain events around which others may be grouped with greater or less probability. The history of the Maccabees is reckoned by the Seleucid era, called in 1 Mc 1:11 'of the kingdom of the Greeks'. This era was computed by the Greeks from Sept.—Oct. 312 B.C. There were, however, local variations, Ginzel 3, 41f. The author of 2 Mc, writing in Greek, also begins the year in the autumn (Tishri). 1 Mc, on the other hand, puts the beginning of the era in spring six months *earlier*, reckoning from 1 Nisan. The two systems thus overlap by half a year. This is the clue to apparently conflicting statements. In 1 Mc 6:16 Antiochus Epiphanes is said to have died in the year 149, whereas in 2 Mc 11:33 a letter of Antiochus Eupator, the son and successor of Antiochus Epiphanes, is dated the 15th of the month Xanthicus (Nisan) in 148. The half-year Tishri to Nisan is the 2nd half of a year in 1 Mc and the 1st half of a year in 2 Mc. Thus Tishri to Nisan 148 is the 2nd half of that year in 1 Mc and the 1st half in 2 Mc. The following 6 months from Nisan to Tishri are the 1st half of 149 in 1 Mc and the 2nd half of 148 in 2 Mc.

A discussion of the chronological order: Ezra-Nehemiah or Nehemiah-Ezra, will be found in § 311 a—d.

The second great help in fixing the absolute chronology of the OT is **the Canon of Ptolemy**, a celebrated **d** mathematician and astronomer who lived in Egypt in the 3rd cent. A.D. The Canon, which begins with the Babylonian king Nabû-nasir (Nabonassar), 747 B.C., after the

24d Babylonian and Assyrian kings continues with the Persian and Greek monarchs, and ends with the Roman emperors in the Christian era. The year according to Egyptian custom is reckoned as beginning on the 1st day of the month Thuth. As the Egyptian year consisting of 365 days was a quarter of a day shorter than the solar year, the 1st Thuth moved through the course of the solar year returning to the same day of the solar year in a period of 1,460 years, the Sothic cycle. The regnal years are all given as full years. This method means that the year in which a king dies is reckoned wholly either to the deceased king or to his successor, i.e. either according to the system of **post-notation** by which a king's regnal years were counted from the 1st Thuth following his accession, or the system of **pre-notation** according to which they were counted from the 1st Thuth preceding his accession. Calculation has shown that the Canon post-dates up to Alexander exclusively and predates from his reign onwards, Hontheim ZKT 42 (1918) 465f.

e The dates of this Canon partly coincide with those of a series of Assyrian documents which are of great importance for our purpose. These are the **Assyrian eponym lists**, the eponym (*līmu*) being the official after whom each year was named. The lists are printed in Deimel 5ff and, with the results of later research, in Luckenbill II 427—9 and ANET, 274—301. In one form of those lists a brief historical note is attached recording some outstanding event of the year, generally a military campaign. For the eponymate of Bur-Sagale it is an eclipse of the sun, which astronomers have shown to have taken place in 763 B.C. By means of this entry the absolute date of all others can be fixed with the reservation made § 124i. The lists are thus found to extend from 893 (892) to 040, and in a partially fragmentary state from 1103 to 933. On the use of these Canons in fixing the dates of Assyrian monarchs see Deimel 19 and 32. In Assyria the kings reckoned their regnal years from 1 Nisan of the year following their accession. The period between the date of accession and the following 1 Nisan was called *rēš šarrūti* 'the beginning of my reign' and is followed by 'the first regnal year'. For an example from the Obelisk of Shalmaneser III see Deimel 24; Luckenbill I, §§ 557ff; ANET 278. Similarly Nebuchadnezzar ascended the throne in the spring of 605, but counted his 1st regnal year from 1 Nisan 604.

Fortunately for our chronology the contacts of the Hebrews with Assyria and Babylonia provide certain synchronisms which afford a basis for the determination of the absolute dates of many of **the kings of Israel and f Judah**. It is convenient to begin with Josiah. He fell in battle near Megiddo attempting to prevent the march north of Pharaoh Necho. The date of this encounter is fixed by the Babylonian chronicle which gives an account of the last years of the Assyrian empire and was published by C. J. Gadd, *The Fall of Nineveh* (London 1923). This shows that Necho's march to the Euphrates took place before Tammuz (the 4th month) (June—July) in Nabopolassar's 17th year, which began Nisan (March—April) 609. See B. Alfrink, Bib 8 (1927) 385—95. This fixes the 3 months reign of Josiah's son Jehoahaz from before the 4th month to before Tishri, the 7th month, 609. Hence Jehoiakim, his successor, came to the throne before Tishri, and that month 609 began his 1st regnal year (post-dating, § 125c). This is supported by the addition in Jer 25:1 which equates the 4th year of Jehoiakim with the accession year of Nebuchadnezzar.

g The chronology of 2 (4) Kgs 15—19, which is of first importance for the interpretation of Is, see § 475, is extremely complicated. For a good summary of the various positions, see H. H. Rowley, 'Hezekiah's Reform **124g** and Rebellion', in BJRL 44 (1962), 409—412. Some authors work back from the battle of Megiddo in 609, and by adding up the data given in the Bible, they reach the following conclusions. Josiah's 31-year reign ended in 609; therefore it began in 640—639. Amon reigned for 2 years before this, i.e. from 642/1. Manasseh reigned 55 years, i.e. from 697/6 to 642/1. Hezekiah reigned 29 years, i.e. from 726/5 to 697/6. The most obvious objection to this chronology is that 2 Kgs 18:13 explicitly places Sennacherib's invasion in the 14th year of Hezekiah's reign; and from Sennacherib's account, we know this was in 701, cf § 294a, and Pritchard, ANET, 287f. Several writers therefore conclude that the 55 years attributed to Manasseh (2 (4) Kgs 21:1) should read 45. This would place *Hezekiah's accession in 716 or 715*, and (allowing for a certain overlapping because of post-dating and ante-dating, accession years etc) 701 could have been his 14th year.

This solution, however, does not harmonize with the synchronisms between the reigns of Israel and Judah in chh 15—18, where the Fall of Samaria (18:10) is placed in the 6th year of Hezekiah. Many solutions have been proposed (see Rowley art cit). J. McHugh, in VT 14 (1964) 446—53, has argued that we must distinguish between dates extracted from the Temple archives in Jerusalem, and dates worked out by different editors from these. He concludes that Ahaz reigned from 732/1 to 716/5, when Hezekiah succeeded. The synchronisms with Israel in 2 (4) Kgs 18:1, 9—12, he suggests, come not from the archives but from the editors, see § 125c. For a similar chronology cf Albright BASOR 100 (1945); Thiele op cit 99—135.

The **fall of Samaria** marked the end of the N King- **h** dom, 2 (4) Kgs 17:6f. Shalmaneser V began the siege and took the city shortly before his death in Dec. 722, 2 (4) Kgs 18:9f. This is borne out by Sargon II's own inscriptions. They prove that he waged no war before the second year of his reign which began in April 720. The 'Annals of Khorsabad', for the purpose, it seems, of crediting Sargon II with military fame from the very beginning of his reign, place his capture of Samaria in 722, whereas it actually occurred in 720. Owing to Shalmaneser's death and to Sargon as a usurper being forced to consolidate his position on the throne, the settlement at Samaria in 722 was not thorough. When trouble broke out again, Sargon was obliged in 720 to take the town a second time. For detailed proof see C. J. Gadd in *Iraq* 16 (1954) 173—201 and E. Vogt, S.J., 'Samaria a. 722 et 720 ab Assyriis capta' Bib 39 (1958) 535—41.

Two remaining synchronisms with Assyrian history **i** are the **payment of tribute by Jehu to Shalmaneser III** recorded on the latter's Black Obelisk, see § 291a on 2 Kgs 9:1—14, and the **Battle of Qarqar**, in which the same Shalmaneser defeated Ahab and his allies according to his own account, Pritchard, ANET 277—9, see § 290a. These two events used to be dated in reliance on what has been rashly styled 'the infallible Assyrian eponym-list'. But the fact is that above 786 dates will differ by one year according as Balatu who is given in one list as eponym for 767 is considered an erroneous insertion in that list or an accidental omission elsewhere. Here the shorter chronology is followed and the two events are dated 841 and 853 respectively. In either case the important fact remains that they are separated by an interval of just 12 years.

Further information is provided by the **synchronisms 125a between the kings of Israel and of Judah**. Jeroboam and Rehoboam, the first rulers of the divided kingdom,

125a came to the throne almost at the same time. Jehu gave Jehoram of Israel and Ahaziah of Judah their death-wound on the same day, 2 (4) Kgs 9:24—27. Moreover, the biblical story provides a whole series of cross-references between the reigns of the two kingdoms. These synchronisms of each kingdom in terms of the regnal years of the other fit into a consistent scheme down to the death of Azariah in 740—739 if due account is taken of the time of year when the regnal years began in each kingdom and of their methods of treating a sovereign's accession year. Thiele's study has rendered a service to chronology in these matters; but see J. McHugh above, § 124g.

b To discover the method of computing regnal years it is necessary to bear in mind the Hebrew custom of counting a part of a year or a day as a whole year or day. Thus Abijam came to the throne of Judah in the 18th year of Jeroboam, and is said to have reigned 3 years though he died in the latter's 20th year, 1 (3) Kgs 15:1f, 8f. Similarly Nadab became king in the 2nd and was murdered in the 3rd year of Asa, but is said to have reigned 2 years, 1 (3) Kgs 15:25, 28.

c The **method of computing regnal years was from Tishri in Judah and from Nisan in Israel**. Solomon began the building of the temple in the 2nd month of his 4th year, and completed it in the 8th month of his 11th year, 1 (3) Kgs 6:1, 37f. It would therefore seem that the building occupied $7\frac{1}{2}$ years. Actually it was $6\frac{1}{2}$ years recorded as 7 according to the custom of counting a part as a whole, 1 (3) Kgs 6:38. The months were counted from Nisan, Ex 12:2, and, if Solomon's regnal years had also been reckoned from Nisan, then the building would have taken $7\frac{1}{2}$ years. They must have been counted from Tishri, for in that case the building began in the 8th month (not calendar) reckoned from the beginning of his 4th regnal year, occupied the next 6 years reckoned from that month, and was concluded in the 2nd month reckoned from the beginning of his 11th year. Rehoboam and the other kings of Judah naturally followed the same system. Jeroboam and the other northern kings, on the other hand, adopted the system of reckoning their regnal years from Nisan. An indication of the change may be seen in the fact that on this basis of computation the synchronisms between the two kingdoms fit in harmoniously down to the death of Azariah.

d These synchronisms also reveal the method followed for dealing with the accession year of each sovereign. In Judah the accession year of a king was reckoned to his predecessor and the new king began the enumeration of his regnal years with the month Tishri following his accession. This is called **post-notation** or the accession-year system cf above § 124d. The opposite system by which the accession year was counted as the first year of the new sovereign was adopted in Judah from 848 with the accession of Joram down to the accession of Amasiah in 796. This would be explained by Athaliah's desire to follow the custom of the northern court where she had been born, for there the system of **pre-notation** was followed. In this system the sovereign's accession year was reckoned both to himself and to his predecessor, and it was followed in Samaria from the dividing of the kingdom down to the **accession of Joash in 798**. From this time the **post-notation** system was **followed in both kingdoms** to the end of their history, in this agreeing with the practice of Assyria and perhaps reflecting its influence, cf § 87h.

As the beginning of the regnal year in the two kingdoms was separated by the six months between Nisan and Tishri, it may happen that the synchronisms fix the accession of a new ruler between either Nisan and Tishri or between Tishri and Nisan. In the former case the calen-**125c** dar year is fixed as both months fall in the same Julian year. In the latter case it remains uncertain whether the accession took place in the closing months of the preceding calendar year or the opening months of the following. Thus Joash of Judah came to the throne in 835 (between Nisan and Tishri) whereas Jehoahaz of Israel began his reign in 814—813 (between Tishri 814 and Nisan 813).

The **chronological indications in Kings** occur **e** consistently at the beginning of the reigns and it is difficult to know to what extent these details depend on ancient sources. As they stand they **clearly belong to the editorial framework** of a later age, and scholars are divided as to their reliability. While some ascribe them to the editors themselves, others hold that they are based on ancient annals, though in some cases they have undergone a certain manipulation. If there were evidence of a schematic chronology, doubt would obviously be cast on the system as a whole. Gray (56), thinks that there is such evidence: 'The foundation of Solomon's Temple 480 years after the Exodus is represented as the middle point of the period visualized, which thus ended in the return from exile of certain influential elements among the Jews and the resumption of worship and perhaps limited restoration of the ruined Temple soon after 539. Less the 50 years of exile, the period of the monarchy from Solomon's foundation of the Temple to the Exile thus occupies 430 years, and into this artificial scheme the various reigns are made to fit. This fact must qualify any effort to arrive at a firm chronology on the basis of the data in Kings alone'.

The chronological data of Kings may be divided into (a) **f** the duration of reigns, and (b) synchronisms between Israel and Juda. The fact that there is a schematic arrangement does not of itself indicate clearly what one may ascribe to later editorial manipulation and what to ancient sources. Thus, synchronizations with the reigns of neighbouring kings were a feature of ancient annals, e.g. Assyrian and Babylonian, and may well have been a characteristic of the early sources on which the compiler of Kgs drew. But equally clearly they might have been the work of a later editor and in some cases evidently were. Each case must be examined on its own merits, Gray, 56—57.

The **hypothesis of co-regencies** as a solution of **g** the apparent discrepancies is rejected as a desperate expedient by certain authors, e.g. Mowinckel, 'Die Chronologie der israelitischen und judäischen Könige', *Acta Orientalia*, 10 (1931—2) 161—275, except of course where there is Scriptural evidence for such, as in the case of Jotham, 2 (4) Kgs 15: 5, 32, and, according to de Vaux (A I, 101), Solomon, 1 (3) Kgs 1:32. Nevertheless it is indubitable that the existence of the practice of co-regency 'gives us a reasonable justification for assuming that in certain other instances of apparent discrepancy in the chronology of Kings the practice of co-regency similarly solves the difficulty ... Moreover, in a polygamous society, as the case of David's family indicates, the designation of an heir-apparent and his association with the reigning king was a natural measure to obviate civil strife', Gray, 58.

The chronology of **the undivided kingdom** is only **126a** vaguely indicated in Sm and Kgs. Solomon is said to have reigned 40 years, 1 Kgs 11:42; so is David, 2 Sm 5:4; 1 (3) Kgs 2:11, his reign being divided into 7 years at Hebron and 33 in Jerusalem; Saul likewise is stated, in Ac 13:21, to have reigned 40 years. It is clear that the number 40 is used to indicate a reign of considerable length but the exact duration of which is unknown. In the

26a case of Solomon however it would seem to be very close to the mark. Synchronisms based on the reign of Hiram, king of Tyre lead to about the year 970 for the beginning of Solomon's reign, Jos. *C.Ap.* 1, 18; J. Hontheim, ZKT 36 (1912) 50—5, while Kgs suggests 931 as the year of his death.

b For **the period of Judges** no accurate chronology is possible. The round number 40 occurs constantly, indicating periods of rule of a Judge during which the land rested and periods of oppression by Israel's enemies. Even in the unlikely hypotheses of these figures being exact, there is no means of knowing whether they follow one another chronologically. The rule of the Judges did not extend over the whole country and it may well be that some of them were contemporaries. It is probable that a proportion of the chronological data is to be traced to early sources but the general framework is more likely to be the work of a later editor. The 480 years given in 1 (3) Kgs 6:1 as the period from the Exodus to the 4th year of Solomon is probably an artificial computation, see § 125*e*.

c **The date of the Exodus** has been variously reckoned to be either in the late 15th cent. under the XVIII dynasty of Egypt or in the 13th under the XIX dynasty. The **earlier date** (see Bibliography) would seem to be **abandoned** by most authorities today in favour of the later. The Tell el-Amarna Letters were once thought to favour an early date inasmuch as they provide evidence of local conditions and tribal movements which seem to suggest the likelihood of such an invasion at about that time, see § 196. Again, the fall of Jericho, dated by Garstang c. 1400, seemed to be strongly in favour of the early date, PEF (1936) 170. Nevertheless, Père Vincent was advocating the later date already, PEF 63 (1931) 104—5; RB 44 (1935) 583—605 Miss K Kenyon writes 'It had been believed in the earlier excavations that the defensive walls of the Late Bronze Age town had been discovered and that they had been destroyed by earthquake and fire. It became clear in the course of the recent excavations that those walls had been mistakenly

identified. They actually belonged to the Early Bronze **126c** Age . . .' *Archaeology in the Holy Land*, 1960, 210. In other words, what had looked like first-hand evidence of the destruction of Jericho by Joshua was in fact to be ascribed to a much earlier date. There was a Late Bronze settlement on the site about 1400 B.C. but this was abandoned within a century, and later erosion has removed nearly all trace of it. This would have been the 'town' in existence at approximately the time of the Exodus. The biblical account says that after destroying the city, Joshua laid a curse upon any man that should rebuild it, Jos 6:26. 'Certainly, no fragment of the walls of the Late Bronze Age city . . . survives', Kenyon, *Digging up Jericho*, 1957, 170; and no rebuilding was attempted until the time of Ahab, 1 (3) Kgs 16:34.

The later date for the Exodus is supported by the **d** fact that whereas little is known about the building activities of the Pharaohs of the XVIII dynasty in the Delta area, there are many remains of the constructions of Rameses II in that locality during the 13th century. Moreover the name of one of the store cities built by the Israelites was Ramses, Ex 1:11, thus pointing to the same conclusion; though it is possible either that the name is older than the XIX dynasty (being compounded of that of the god Ra) or that the city was named thus at a later date. Iron is mentioned as in use at the time of the conquest of Canaan, Jos 6:19, 24; 17:16, 18. But though the beginnings of the Iron Age in Palestine were about 1200 B.C., this again is not a conclusive proof. 'As early as the 14th cent. B.C. iron began to be used rather extensively for weapons,' Albright, *The Archaeology of Palestine*, 1949, 110. In general, 'the weight of evidence from the OT regarding conditions in Egypt, Palestine and Transjordan implies a date in the XIX dynasty in the 13th cent. for the Exodus, with the main phase of the Hebrew settlement in Palestine after the campaigns of Rameses II, (1289—1224)'. J. Gray, PC (2) 70.

For the patriarchal period and earlier ages, see above 124*b*.

CHRONOLOGICAL TABLE

127a

Hebrew History
c. 1050—1012 Samuel; Saul
c. 1012—972 David
c. 972—931 Solomon

Judah	Israel	Notable Events
931—913 Rehoboam	931—910/9 Jeroboam	925 Shishak (Sheshonk I) invades Judah
913—911/10 Abijam		
911/10—870/69 Asa	910/9—909/8 Nadab	
	909/8—886/5 Baasha	
	886/5—885 Elah	
	885 Zimri	
	885—874/3 Omri	
	874/3—853 Ahab	
870/69—848 Jehoshaphat		
		858—824 Shalmaneser III
		853 Battle of Qarqar in Ahab's last year
	853—852 Ahaziah	
	852—841 Jehoram	
848—841 Jehoram		
841 Ahaziah	841—814/3 Jehu	841 Jehu kills Jehoram of Israel and Ahaziah of Judah on the same day; he pays tribute to Shalmaneser III

127a Judah	Israel	Notable Events
841—835 Athaliah		
835—796 Joash	814/3—798 Jehoahaz	
	798—782/1 Jehoash	
796—768 Amasiah		
	782/1—753 Jeroboam II	
768—740/39 Azariah		
	753—752 Zechariah	
	752—752/1 Shallum	745—727 Tiglath-pileser (Pul)
	752/1—742/1 Menahem	743 (?) He receives tribute from Menahem
	742/1—740/39 Pekahiah	
740/39—732 Jotham	740/39—730/29 Pekah	
732/1—716/15 Ahaz		734 Tiglath-pileser's expedition against Philistia
		733 and 732 His campaigns against Damascus
	730/29—721 Hoshea	
		727—722 Shalmaneser V
	722 Capture of Samaria; end of the Northern Kingdom	
		722—705 Sargon II
716/15—687/6 Hezekiah		
b		705—681 Sennacherib
		701 He invades Judah
687/6—643/2 Manasseh		
		680—669 Esarhaddon who names Manasseh among his subject kings
643/2—641/0 Amon		
641/0—609 Josiah		
		628 Jeremiah begins his mission
		625—604 Nabopolassar, prince of Babylon
		623/2 The finding of the book of the Law
		612 Destruction of Nineveh by the Medes and Babylonians
609 Jehoahaz		609 Death of Josiah defeated at Megiddo by Necho of Egypt (610—594)
609—598 Jehoiakim		
		605—561 Nebuchadnezzar
		604 Nebuchadnezzar's 1st regnal year from 1 Nisan
598 Jehoiachin		598 Captivity of Jehoiachin
598—587 Zedekiah		
		589 Jan. 15. Beginning of the siege of Jerusalem
		588 Imprisonment of Jeremiah
587 End of the Kingdom of Judah; deportation of Zedekiah		587 Fall of Jerusalem; Babylonian captivity
		574/3 The 25th year of Jehoiachin's captivity and 14th from the fall of Jerusalem, Ez 40:1
		561—560 Evil-Merodach (Awel-Marduk)
		561 Jehoiachin is released from prison
		560—556 Neriglissar (Nergal-sharusur) of Babylon
		556—539 Nabonidus; Belshazzar

The Persian Empire

127c 538/7 Decree of Cyrus permitting the return of the Jews

537/6 The foundations of the temple are laid

520/19 Work is resumed on the temple
515 Dedication of the temple

458 Return under Ezra
445 Return of Nehemiah
433 Nehemiah goes back to Susa
433/2 His second visit to Jerusalem
398 Return under Ezra (van Hoonacker's view)

559—529 Cyrus
539 The beginning of the attack on Babylon
538 Cyrus captures Babylon;

529—522 Cambyses
521—486 Darius I Hystaspes

485—465 Xerxes I (Ahasuerus)
464—424 Artaxerxes I Longimanus

424 Xerxes II
424 Sogdianus
423 404 Darius II Nothus
404—358 Artaxerxes II Mnemon
358—338 Artaxerxes III Ochus
338—336 Arses
336—330 Darius III Codomannus
333 His defeat by Alexander

d The Earlier Seleucid Kings

312—280 Seleucus I Nicator
280—262/1 Antiochus I Soter

261—247 Antiochus II Theos
247—226 Seleucus II Callinicus
226—223 Seleucus III Soter
223—187 Antiochus III the Great
187—175 Seleucus IV Philopator
175—163 Antiochus IV Epiphanes
163—162 Antiochus V Eupator
162—150 Demetrius I Soter
150—145 Alexander Balas
145—139/8 Demetrius II Nicator
145—142/1 Antiochus VI Epiphanes
139/8—129 Antiochus VII Sidetes

The Earlier Ptolemies

323—283 Ptolemy I Soter
285—246 Ptolemy II Philadelphus (partly co-reign)
246—221 Ptolemy III Euergetes
221—203 Ptolemy IV Philopator
203—181/0 Ptolemy V Epiphanes
181/0—145 Ptolemy VI Philometor
145—116 Ptolemy VII Euergetes

Note 1—The first year given for the Hebrew kings is that of their accession, for the Persian kings that of their first regnal year. Two dates separated by a slanting line mean that the accession or other event occurred between Tishri of the first-named year and Nisan of the following year.

Note 2—For the detailed chronology of the Maccabean age see § 587.

Note 3—The dating chosen by contributors of the individual articles in this commentary does not necessarily coincide with that given in the above Table.

INTRODUCTION TO THE PENTATEUCH

BY P. G. DUNCKER O.P.

130a Bibliography—J. P. Bouhot-H. Cazelles, 'Pentateuque', DBS 8, 687–858; A. Bentzen, *Introduction to the OT*, 1952; J. E. Carpenter-G. Harford, *The Composition of the Pentateuch*, 1902; U. Cassuto, *The Documentary Hypothesis and the Composition of the Pentateuch*, 1953; H. Cazelles, 'La Torah ou Pentateuque', in RF I 278–382; A Clamer, in PCSB, I, 9–76; J. Coppens, *The OT and the Critics*, 1943; C. Kühl, *Die Entstehung des AT*, 1953; H. J. Kraus, *Geschichte der historisch-kritischen Erforschung des AT* . . . 1969²; S. Mowinckel, *Le Decalogue*, *Études d'histoire et de philosophie religieuses*, 1927; C. R. North, in *The OT and Modern Study*, ed, H. H. Rowley, 1951, 48–83; G. Rinaldi, 'Pentateuco', in *Enciclopedia Cattolica*, 9, 1952; R. de Vaux, 'A propos du second centenaire d'Astruc', VTS 1 (1951) 7–23; id, in JB 7–14; A. Weiser, *Introduction to the OT*, E.tr., 1961; EOT Int, 155–241. G. von Rad, *Studies in Deuteronomy*, E.tr. 1953; id. *The Problem of the Hexateuch and other Essays*, E.tr. 1966; W. Beyerlin *Origins and History of the Oldest Sinaitic Traditions*, E.tr. 1965. M. Noth, *The Laws of the Pentateuch and other Essays*, E.tr. 1966.

b Names—'Pentateuch' is a transcription and anglicization of the corresponding word in the Gr. expression *hè Moséos pentateuchos biblos* = 'the fivefold book of Moses', which occurs for the first time in Ptolemy's 'Letter to Flora', 2nd cent. A.D. (PG 41, 560); its Latin transcription 'Pentateuchus' is already used by Tertullian (PL 2, 257 [282]).

The 'Pentateuch' denotes what the authors of the OT and NT called 'The Book of the Law of Moses' (Neh 8:1); according to the so-called Lucianic recension of the LXX also in Neh 13:1); 'The Book of the Law of Yahweh' (2 Chr 17:9); 'the Law of Moses' (2 Chr 23:18; Lk 24:44); 'the Book of Moses' (Neh 13:1); 'the Book of the Law' (Gal 3:10); 'the Law' (Neh 8:2; Rm 3:21).

The division of this work, ascribed to Moses, must date from at least about the 3rd cent. B.C., for the LXX supposes it.

c Contents—The Pent contains the ancient records of Israel's history from the very beginning till the time they were on the point of taking possession of the Promised Land. Thus it contains narrative as well as law. Yet it has always been called by the Jews the 'Law' (Tôrāh) or rather 'the Law' (hattôrāh), because they considered the narratives as leading up to the laws and forming their historical setting, but principally because the narratives themselves, just like the laws and together with them, were looked upon as divine 'instruction' or 'teaching', which is the general meaning of the word 'tôrāh'.

d The narrative sections are chiefly found in Gn, Ex and Nm; they are practically absent in Lv and only partly contained in Dt, by way of sermons delivered by Moses. The legislative part begins in Ex 20, and covers the rest of this book, apart from a few historical notes and Ex 32–34; it embraces the whole of Lv (8–10 on the institution of the priesthood intends to give the ritual of the ordination of priests), and occupies a number of sections in Nm and a large part of Dt (12–26).

Literary Composition—The conviction of Jews and **e** early Christians alike that the Pent had to be considered as the work of Moses was taken over by the Fathers and ancient Christian writers as well as by the post-biblical Jews, and generally maintained right up till the 16th cent. There were a few exceptions. Ptolemy, a gnostic, considered it a Jewish apocryphon; the Jew Eben Ezra (12th cent.; cf A. Lods, *Histoire de la littérature hébraïque et juive des origines à la ruine de l'État Juif, 135 après J.-C.*, 1950, 86) contended that the Pent in its present form could not be from Moses; and Hugo a St Caro (13th cent.; *Opera omnia* 1, Venice 1754, 151), thought the attribution of Dt to Joshua at least probable.

Critical Questioning—Since another article is devoted **f** to the whole question of critical scholarship (91*a*), it will suffice to give a brief outline here of the history of Pentateuchal criticism.

It had always been assumed that the distinction of sources on the basis of the divine name was the discovery of J. Astruc. In 1925, however, A. Lods published his discovery that H. B. Witter, *Jura Israelitarum in Palaestinam*, 1711, was the first to notice the different names used for God suggesting different oral sources in Gn 1:2–3:24. But J. Astruc was the first to divide Gn into various documents partly on the basis of this distinction (*Conjectures sur les mémoires originaux dont il paroit que Moise s'est servi pour composer le livre de la Genèse*, 1753): an Elohistic document which calls God Elohim, a Jehovistic which uses the name Yahweh (or Jehovah or Jahvé, etc, as the name used to be spelt: thus the symbol J), another dealing with the history of non-Israelite peoples, one in which God is not mentioned, etc. J. G. Eichhorn, *Einleitung in das AT*, 1780–83, accepted Astruc's distinction of the main sources and established it in detail up to Ex ch 2. Like Astruc he maintained the Mosaic authorship of the Pent but later allowed the hand of a redactor in the time of Joshua. K. D. Ilgen (*Die Urkunden des Jerusalemischen Tempelarchivs*, 1798) divided E into E¹ and E². E¹ bears some resemblance to the document later known as P though Ilgen's division of material differed widely from that of later scholars. He also recognized D as a separate document.

This gives us the **Older Documentary Hypothesis.**

Alexander Geddes (*The Holy Bible* . . . 1792; **g** *Critical Remarks on the Hebrew Scriptures*, 1800) remained unconvinced of the reality of these documents and contended that their contents were independent fragments put together by an editor of the time of Solomon or Hezekiah. This **Fragment Hypothesis** was further developed by J. S. Vater, *Commentar über den Pentateuch*, 1802–5, who distinguished 39 such fragments in Gn alone and said the Pent. was composed partly in

30g the time of Moses, partly during the reigns of David and Solomon, and finally put together about the time of the Exile. W. M. L. de Wette, *Beiträge zur Einleitung ins AT*, 1806, largely concurred with Vater, but thought the E fragments might originate from an *Urschrift Elohim*. He was also the first to connect Dt with Josiah's reform, thus joining historical criticism to literary criticism of the Pent.

h As a reaction against this increasing fragmentation of the Pent. H. Ewald reviewing Stähelin's *Kritische Untersuchungen über die Genesis*, in *Theologische Studien und Kritiken*, 1831, maintained that it consisted of one fundamental Elohistic document (*Grundschrift*) composed towards the end of the period of Judges or the beginning of the monarchy but that gaps in this were supplemented from a Jehovistic source in the times of Saul, Solomon and Ezekiel. This **Supplementary Hypothesis** was supported by F. Bleek, *De libri Geneseos origine . . .*, 1836, with the qualification that the supplements were all due to one author, developed by F. Tuch, *Commentar über die Genesis*, 1838, and adopted later by de Wette, *Lehrbuch der historisch-kritischen Einleitung in die . . . Bücher des AT*, 1845.

i Later however Ewald redivided E and further critical studies, especially by H. Hupfeld, *Die Quellen der Genesis . . .*, 1853, tended to show that J and E^2 were not merely supplements to E^1. Thus with D solidly established as a separate document by E. Riehm, *Die Gesetzgebung Moses im Lande Moab*, 1854, the original documentary theory was restored in a new form.

131a **Wellhausen's Theory**—Meanwhile a new direction was introduced by scholars such as E. Reuss, *L'histoire sainte et la loi*, 1879; *Geschichte der Heiligen Schriften des AT*, 1890²; K.H. Graf, *Die geschichtliche Bücher des AT*, 1866; A. Kuenen, *Historisch-kritisch onderzoek nar het ontstaan van de verzameling van de boeken des Ouden Verbonds*, 1893³. They pointed out that most of the laws in the Pent belonged to a late date since the older historical and prophetical books show hardly any trace of them. Dt 12—26 was, they thought, the oldest collection and was to be identified with the 'Book of the Law' found in the Temple in 622 B.C. (cf 2 (4) Kgs 22:3); Josiah's religious reform appeared to correspond to the prescriptions of this code. Many laws of Ex-Nm appeared to be very similar to those found in the book of the prophet and priest Ezekiel, so these—contained in P—were ascribed to that prophet and other priests of the time of the exile. This suggested the chronological order J, E, D, P.: the **New Documentary Hypothesis.**

b This theory was particularly maintained by **Julius Wellhausen** and is still connected with his name because of the clear, simple, persuasive and masterly way in which he presented it. His principal works are *Die Composition des Hexateuchs . . .* 1899³; *Prolegomena zur Geschichte Israels*, 1905⁶ and his own account of his theory in Cheyne's *Encyclopedia Biblica* and in the *Encyclopedia Brittanica*. With great learning and skill he developed the various linguistic and historical arguments for the theory, and especially those concerning the religious ideas of the four documents. He applied Hegel's philosophy to the OT (following W. Vatke, *Die Biblische Theologie wissenschaftlich dargestellt*, 1835) and traced the whole process of evolution of religion in the Pent: traces of the animism, fetishism, totemism and polydemonism of premosaic religion in J; Moses's monolatry or henotheism (putting Yahweh above all other gods) in J and E; the pure monotheism of the prophets in D; and the nomism of the dominating priesthood with their ever-increasing insistence on the Law (*Nomē*) in P. J, therefore, must be

regarded as the oldest document; and this was also sup- **131b** ported by its vivid, colourful, anthropomorphic language. As it showed particular interest in all that concerned the **c** tribe of Judah, it was taken to have been composed in the kingdom of Judah between 850 and 750 B.C. E is less anthropomorphic, more sober and severe, of deeper theological reflection, seeing everywhere a more direct influence of God (who is always called Elohim until in Ex 3 the name of Yahweh, used from the beginning in J, was revealed to Moses) and insisting on persons and places of interest for the other tribes. This document therefore was regarded as a little later than J and composed in the kingdom of Israel. After the destruction of the northern kingdom in 722 B.C. both documents must have been united to form JE, before D was joined to it towards the end of the monarchy or the beginning of the Exile. When P was completed this document was added by Ezra, who moulded the whole work into the Pent as we know it.

Further Developments—Wellhausen's theory won **d** wide acceptance but not without opposition. The Biblical Commission in particular drew attention to the fact that much of it was based on aprioristic prejudices and preconceptions and did not pay sufficient regard to the text itself. (See 96g, h). Others, while accepting the theory in general, brought to light differences in the documents themselves, to such an extent that at one time a return to the 'Fragment Hypothesis' seemed possible. But the only subdivision which eventually gained some measure of acceptance was O. Eissfeldt's theory (*Hexateuch-Synopse*, Leipzig, 1912) that J seemed to contain a source less influenced by cultic tendencies and which could therefore be distinguished as a 'Lay Source' (Laienquelle, L).

But by this time other factors had given a different direction to research and put the problem in a different perspective.

Archaeological Research—As the Biblical Commis- **132a** sion had justly noted, Wellhausen's theory was largely conjectural, unsupported by objective evidence. But archaeological research had just been coming into its own while Wellhausen was popularizing his theory, and objective evidence for testing it was now becoming available. Excavations brought to light numerous objects and texts which made known the religious ideas, prescriptions and practices of the nations surrounding Israel; as also their moral, social, juridical, matrimonial, political and commercial relations, regulations, manners and customs. Since these are all anterior to Moses and show a much higher standard of culture and civilization than that of the Israelites, the latter must obviously have been influenced by them either directly or indirectly. Particular- **b** ly a great many legislative texts have been found, such as the Code of Hammurapi (18th cent. B.C.), the Hittite (14th cent.) and Assyrian (12th cent.) collections of laws, the centuries older Babylonian and Sumerian codes, Hittite treaties and a great number of matrimonial and commercial contracts from Nuzi and Kerkuk. These have illustrated and confirmed what Gn tells us about the mentality, ways and doings of the Hebrew Patriarchs. These fit in very well with what we now know of the Ancient Near Eastern world in the first half of the second millennium B.C.; but they are completely different from the social, juridical and political structure of the time when, according to Wellhausen, the story of the Patriarchs must have been conceived and thought out, and should therefore have been composed and described according to the mentality and customs of this later age, since Wellhausen did not know the old documents we are now acquainted with. Moreover, the existence of so many ancient laws

132b proves that a body of legislation originating from Moses is at least possible; especially since the Mosaic law presented in the Bible undoubtedly contains very ancient prescriptions and specific modes of expression similar to those found in ancient profane legislation.

c Value of Tradition—In addition to archaeological discoveries and partly influenced by them, another line of research which makes the situation today very different from what it was in Wellhausen's time is the attention to the value of oral tradition. This is particularly stressed by the so-called 'Scandinavian school'. They insist on the importance of oral tradition in the transmission of old stories, laws, songs, proverbs, sayings, etc. Some have gone to the extreme of saying that these oral traditions were for the most part not written down before the Exile. One of the principal champions of this theory is J. Engnell (*Gamla Testamentet: en traditionshistorisk inledning*, I, Stockholm, 1945). Against this, G. Widengren (*Literary and Psychological Aspects of the Hebrew Prophets*, Uppsala, 1948) rightly maintains that oral and written tradition must have existed side by side, and thinks that in urban surroundings written tradition may even have preceded oral; cf E. Nielsen, *Oral Tradition. A Modern Problem in OT Introduction*, London, 1954. This line of thought continues to attract the attention of scholars. But it is partly a development of and partly a contribution to another line of research which is already well-established and has already borne good fruit, namely, form-criticism.

133a Form Criticism—The knowledge of ancient oriental literature revealed by archaeology led to a more general recognition of the historical substratum of the Pentateuchal narratives and laws, and induced scholars to examine these from a literary point of view in the light of that literature. This line of research was initiated by H. Gunkel (*Schöpfung und Chaos in Urzeit und Endzeit*, 1895; *Die Sagen in Genesis*, 1901; *Die altisraelitische Literatur, Kultur der Gegenwart*, 1906, 1925[2]; *Genesis*, HKAT, 1924[4]; cf his *Einleitung in die Psalmen*, completed by J. Begrich, 1925), continued and developed by others such as H. Gressmann (*Die Anfänge Israels, Die älteste Geschichtbeschreibung und Prophetie Israels*, 1921–22); J. Hempel (*Die althebräische Literatur und ihr hellenistisch-jüdischer Nachleben*, 1930; 'The Literature of Israel: The Forms of Oral Tradition', *Record and Revelation*, 1938, 28–44); and especially with regard to the various formulations of Pentateuchal laws first applied by A. Alt (*Die Ursprünge des israelitischen Rechts*, 1934 = *Kleine* **b** *Schriften* I, 1954, 278–322). This method of critical research aims at discovering the primitive units or elements which go to make up the narratives and laws of the Pent, whether they were proper to Israel or borrowed from others, to what extent they were influenced by foreign forms; and finally their *Sitz im Leben* (a German technical term which may be rendered 'situation in life')—that is to say, their precise meaning and original significance in the social, cultural and religious life of Israel before being integrated into the great documents or traditions of the Pent. This later development of Form Criticism has been called 'Tradition Criticism' (*Traditionsgeschichte*). The main names to be mentioned are G. von Rad, 'Das Formgeschichtliche Problem des Hexateuchs', *Beiträge zur Wissenschaft vom AT*, 78 (1938), 46–68; 'Der Anfang der Geschichtsbeschreibung', *Archiv für Kulturgeschichte*, 32 (1944), 1–42; *Deuteronomium Studien*, 1947 (E. tr *Studies in Deuteronomy*, 1953); *Das erste Buch Mose*, ATD, 1956 (E. tr OTL, 1961); and M. Noth, *Ueberlieferungsgeschichte des Pentateuchs*, 1948;

Das zweite Buch Mose, ATD, 1959[2] (E. tr OTL, 1962). **133** It may be noted here that von Rad strongly advocates the old idea of an original Hexateuch, whereas Noth is the principal promoter of the theory which has since been gaining ground that Dt should be regarded as the introduction to a large historical work comprising Jos, Jg, Sm and Kgs, later detached from it and added to the Tetrateuch Gn-Nm on account of its similar historical background in the narrative sections.

Form criticism has undoubtedly shed new light on the gradual composition of the Pent and furthered its proper understanding.

Legal Sections—In studying the legal parts of the **c** Pent, form critics have singled out a body of 'case law' (e.g. Ex 21:2ff)—all in prose, introduced by '*ki*' ('when . . .') and often continued by "*im*' ('if . . .'). These appear to be similar to Sumerian, Babylonian, Assyrian and Hittite laws both in form and in subject matter, generally dealing with civil ordinances. They presume Israel's settlement in Canaan and were probably taken over from the Canaanites. So for example, it seems, the bulk of Ex 21:2–22:16. Quite different in literary form and subject matter are many other legislative precepts and regulations, more rhythmic in style, beginning with an address to man in the 2nd person (e.g. Ex 20:13ff) or with either a participle (Ex 21:15ff), a relative pronoun (Lv 20:2) or a curse (Dt 27:15ff). These are of an apodictic-categorical type and chiefly concern man's relations to God and his fellowmen. This kind of law, rarely to be found in profane oriental legislation, seems more proper to Israel and basically older than the casuistic prescriptions adopted from the Canaanites.

In the course of time laws from these two main cate- **d** gories were linked together, amplified and adapted to later conditions, before receiving their present place in the great bodies of law which have long been distinguished in our Pent—namely, the Book of the Covenant (Ex 20:22–23:33), the Deuteronomic Code (Dt 12–26), the Law of Holiness (Lv 17–26) and the Priestly Code (e.g. Lv 1–16). Some scholars maintain that individual laws may first have been joined in groups of ten or twelve, since we have the well-known Decalogue (Ex 20:3–17 and Dt 5:6–21 though in expanded and adapted form), and also a Dodekalogue (Dt 27:15–26 containing twelve interdictions each beginning with 'Cursed be . . .'). This contention remains hypothetical, but certainly a number of small originally independent collections have been identified within the above-mentioned corpora. So for **e** instance Lv 18:6–30 and 20:10–26, giving more or less the same precepts about purity and matrimony, have surely been taken over as they were found by the redactor of the Law of Holiness. Another originally independent section in this code must have been the one on priests and sacrifices (Lv 21, 22). Another section of this code, Lv 23 dealing with various festival days, is obviously an adaptation of an earlier text to later circumstances, and it is even possible to ascertain that Lv 23:18–19 has been amplified from Nm 28:27–30 belonging to the chronologically later Priestly Code. In this Code too the section about sacrifices (Lv 1–7) and legal purification (Lv 11–15), as well as that dealing with the sanctuary (Ex 25–31 and 35–40), undoubtedly existed separately at first. In the Book of the Covenant one collection of civil law can easily be singled out (Ex 21:1–22:17) through its special heading: 'Now these are the ordinances (*mishpāṭîm*) which you will set before them'; while the laws immediately following this section (Ex 22:18ff) give an example of the way that civil and moral-religious laws have been joined together. Again,

33e in the Deuteronomic Code the section of laws in casuistic form, Dt 21—25, must originally have existed separately from the foregoing section on cult. Of great importance, finally, is the recent comparison between the ancient E (particularly Hittite) vassal treaties and the Sinaitic Covenant, bringing to light striking similarities and offering new possibilities of understanding the constitution of the Pent.

f **Narrative Sections**—Here too form criticism tries to determine the original elements and specify their precise nature and meaning, their *Sitz im Leben*. The forms distinguished are myths, fairy tales, sagas, legends, anecdotes, tales (Novelle), dream-stories, etc—all parts of the literary composition of the biblical history from the beginning to Moses and Joshua. These terms have to be taken as they are understood in our day, though are not defined by all in exactly the same way and are often overlapping. Modern scholars are commonly agreed there are no **myths** in the Bible in the old popular sense of the term; the term is generally taken by scholars to denote biblical narratives about the origin of the world and of man and other prehistoric situations in terms and imagery manifestly derived from ancient mythology familiar to the people the authors were primarily writing for; the authors adapt them to their own religious viewpoint and sometimes make use of them to counteract its pernicious influence. Something of a **fairy tale** may perhaps be seen in Balaam's talking ass (Nm 22:22—35).

g The term **saga** (originally Scandinavian) has been adopted to mark off the primitive units of a more secular character from those in which the religious significance of persons, places or events was more marked; the term **legend** has been restricted to these latter. In particular sagas are often etiological, composed to satisfy man's quest for explanations: why are the Canaanites (Gn 9:20 27), Moabites and Ammonites (Gn 19:30—38) so detestable? why Jacob's (= Israel's) pre-eminence (Gn 25:21—26; ch 27) and Ephraim's superiority among the tribes of Israel (Gn 48)? why that particular shape of mountain near the Dead Sea, like a person in flight (Gn 19:17—26)? Many sagas are only a popular etymological explanation of names, e.g., of Jacob's children (Gn 29—30). As examples of legend may be cited the narrative about Bethel (Gn 28:10—22), the Passover (Ex 12:1—14), Korah's and Dathan-Abiram's rebellion (Nm 16). Myths, fairy tales, sagas and legends recall the more unusual, striking, marvellous aspects of the remote past, explaining them in order to instruct; **anecdotes** or **tales** present persons and events even of the past according to the normal happenings of everyday life, and are intended to entertain. The former are akin to the sagas and present man in a passive light, reacting to what happens to him; the latter are akin to fairy tales and show him taking an active, dominant part in what concerns him.

All of these are simply names to denote specific aspects of what is generically called 'ancient popular history', based on real facts or truths but presenting them in a way that is coloured, magnified or amplified by the imaginative power of successive generations inquiring into their ancient past.

h **Tradition Criticism**—This development of form criticism has led some to distinguish two fundamental traditions—the Exodus, and the conquest of the Promised land; or three if the Journey through the desert is considered a separate one, each of these being made up from the material just considered and preceding the four main traditions compiled in the present Pent.

134a **Modern Position**—In the light of archaeological discovery and other research just dealt with, to which 134a Catholics contributed, Catholic scholars as well as others are in a better position to judge what out of Wellhausen's original theory appears to be well-founded and to form a sound basis for further investigation. Official recognition of this fact was signalled in a letter of the Biblical Commission in 1948 (EnchB⁴ 577—81) and in the encyclical letter *Divino Afflante Spiritu* (EnchB⁴ 538—68). This has led to a large measure of agreement and it will be appropriate to outline the generally accepted position here (cf Cazelles, DBS 8, 736—858), leaving particular points to the commentaries on the respective books.

Objective critical study of the text of the Pent has b brought to light undeniable differences of language, style, ideas, mentality and viewpoint; many repetitions and doublets; various contradictions; a number of anachronisms; a great diversity of religious, cultic, moral, social, juridical and commercial aspects and conditions; and a manifest development in thought and expression. This has brought universal agreement on the basic literary division of the Pent into at least four main documents or traditions still designated for want of better names as J, E, D and P. These correspond to Wellhausen's four documents, but their literary and historical background is nowadays better understood and taken account of. They appear to be simply gradual and relatively late fixations of much older oral and also written traditions which seem to have been originally conserved, elaborated and developed at local shrines or sanctuaries where, in the liturgy, God's mighty dealings with his Chosen People were remembered and celebrated and his divine ordinances were first presented and inculcated.

The different codes of law of the four documents or c traditions are merely the ultimate collections of pre-existing prescriptions, considered to be essential and fundamental and therefore to be maintained and insisted upon as inviolable and unchangeable. Whereas their final fixation in the various codes clearly shows the peculiarities of the document or tradition they belong to, they still betray their original forms, partly specific to Israel and partly common to the juridical norms of the higher civilizations the Israelites had come into contact with.

The entire **Pentateuchal legislation** is presented as d based on the alliance God made with Israel, delivered by him from Egyptian bondage, at Mt Sinai (Horeb). In connection with it mention has already been made (Form-History) of the ancient Mesopotamian, and especially Hittite, vassal-treaties. These numerous texts from the middle of the third millennium till the end of the 7th cent. B.C.—with unfortunately a break for the period corresponding to the time of David—are mostly treaties between unequal parties: the superior imposes his stipulations in a direct style, different from the ones used in the codes, and adds curses and blessings called upon those who shall prove themselves either disloyal or faithful. It is still a matter of dispute how far this general scheme has been used in the Pentateuch's record of God's alliance with Israel at Sinai (Horeb). Its influence appears more clearly in the whole structure of Dt than in the Code of the Covenant with its actual historical setting (E)—besides in both cases the stipulations have already received the form of codes—and far less in the yahwistic tradition with its predominating narratives; it must moreover be noted that in all those profane texts the deity occurs only as witness, whereas in the biblical text God himself is the principal contracting party. The vassal-treaties, however, do make us better understand why God's particular relation to his Chosen People came to be expressed in terms of a Covenant.

134e It is commonly admitted that the Pent contains a **history of salvation**, and that the Israelites realized that Yahweh was the God of their fathers Abraham, Isaac and Jacob and the one who with his mighty power saved them from the Egyptian bondage, and was ready to rescue them from all further miseries. But, again, very ancient Mesopotamian and also Egyptian and Ugaritic texts already dealt with the idea of salvation—a basic problem to mankind realizing its own insufficiency—and voiced man's desire and hope to be delivered from distress and to obtain happiness. They expected this from the deity, particularly by means of its representative, the king, with whom the people were considered to be more or less identified (corporate personality); he had to assure outward peace and internal prosperity, whereas personal bliss was implored and hoped for through cultic rites and hymns. This whole ancient historiography is of great importance in order to understand how the idea of salvation was conceived and expressed in Israel, already from the time of the Patriarchs, and came to be written down during the monarchy, first of all in the Yahwistic (Jehovistic) tradition, when the undoubtedly pre-existing traditions began to receive their proper fixation.

135a Yahwistic Tradition (J)—This is generally looked upon as the first and oldest synthesis of pre-existing oral and written traditions, practically all narratives, since the only legislative section ascribed to it is Ex 34, the so-called Yahwistic Decalogue. These narratives form an almost continuous story, beginning with Gn 2:4^b, further dominating in Gn and continuing, though to a far lesser extent, in Ex and Nm. Its lacunae are probably to be explained by the interrelation of texts taken from the other main traditions and preferred to corresponding passages in J by the one who inserted them.

b The criteria by which J can be recognized are many and must be taken together to have convincing force. There is first the use of the name Yahweh (this name is used by other traditions only after it is said to be revealed by God to Moses (Ex 3)). Then a special vocabulary, e.g. the merchants to whom Joseph was sold are called Ishmaelites, the inhabitants of the Promised Land, Canaanites; the mountain of God is always named Sinai and a maidservant, '*šifhāh*'.' The style is very simple, clear, vivid, imaginative, with colourful dialogue, apt to keep the reader in suspense, as in the narratives about Paradise, man's Fall, Sodom and Gomorrah, the preparations of Isaac's marriage. Only a few lines suffice to characterize Abraham's magnanimity, Jacob's cunning, Laban's avarice. The accounts are of an aetiological kind, intending to give an explanation, often playing upon words, of institutions and usages, and above all of the great problems of man's death and all the other miseries as a result of sin, the dispersion of mankind into many nations and their mutual antagonism.

c But this story of man's wickedness is then transformed into the story of his salvation by the ever more patent interventions of God's mercy as well as by his hidden providence, saving Noah, calling Abraham into Canaan, bringing back Jacob, making Joseph powerful in Egypt, rescuing Israel from Egyptian bondage by Moses, leading the people through the desert and from there right up until they stood on the threshold of the Promised Land. God's relations with man are intimate, concrete and described in anthropomorphic terms: Yahweh appears in human shape, acts in a human way, experiences human emotions, associates himself with man; but through the anthropomorphic veil one perceives a very lofty idea of God, who always remains Yahweh, the Lord, occupying himself with his creatures without lowering his dignity,

unalterably preserving his holiness and greatness, **135** standing out far above all the deities of the other peoples of the Ancient East.

And here we touch the principal point of J's theology. **d** As we have already observed, outside Israel, too, man was convinced that his life and fate were subject to mysterious, higher, divine powers, which communicate fecundity, fertility, prosperity; that his sufferings and miseries are the results of some fault of his own towards the deity, and that only this deity could liberate him from evil and procure him happiness. Whereas, however, the ancient profane historiography, though one god is usually preferred to the rest of the pantheon, shows hesitations and incertitude by admitting the adverse power of other deities, J is firmly convinced and has the unswerving faith that Yahweh has in fact proved himself to be the real and true God, capable of saving his people.

J's history of salvation is further characterized by the **e** importance it gives to the **legitimate heir of the divine promises** of salvation given to the patriarchs. This heir is not the firstborn (Isaac not Ishmael, Jacob not Esau, Judah not Reuben), but the one designated by Yahweh; and it must be noted that in an Ugaritic text of the 15th–14th cent. B.C. not the eldest, but the youngest (eighth) son of Keret receives the first born's blessing. Hence the importance of the respective mothers: Sarah, Rebekah and even Eve (Gn 3:15). The legitimate heir is also the one primarily referred to by the Messianic texts (Gn 3:15; 49:10; Nm 24:7, 17), all proper to J. Moreover, by mentioning the acts of cult at the ancient local shrines (Shechem, Ai, Beersheba, Jerusalem), where Canaanite dynasties had reigned, J apparently tries to adopt local, possibly pre-Israelitic, Canaanite cultic traditions, in order to legitimate their later possession by the heir it had in view.

The intended heir, though never named, was un- **f** doubtedly David, who first gathered the various Israelitic tribes under his sceptre and as king was to be the 'Anointed of Yahweh,' receiving the guarantee of all Yahweh's blessings, in which the people, his so-called 'corporate personality,' would participate. These blessings, however—to counteract the monarchic ideology of the time—came to him not automatically, but through Yahweh's promises to the patriarchs and lastly through the mediation of Samuel. Hence Moses appears in J as the last patriarch. He is first the great liberator, who though not himself a king, is the adopted son of Pharaoh's daughter, gives the people food and drink (a royal function of the Pharaohs) and also holds out to them the prospect of a land flowing with milk and honey, promised to Abraham. Just as God appeared to the patriarch when he made a Covenant with him (Gn 15:17), so likewise he appears to Moses in fire, first in the burning bush, then at Sinai. Moses is also the great mediator, bringing the people into contact with God, the same Yahweh the patriarchs and even Seth had already invoked and who is now manifesting with mighty power his ascendancy and predominance over the Egyptian deities and their king with all their renowned wisdom. Already Joseph's cleverness had appeared to surpass **g** the sagacity of the wise men of Egypt; but when J exalts him, calls him the prince of his brethren, secures him the best part of Canaan, it is not on account of his wisdom, which J does not entirely approve of, but because Jacob imparts to him God's blessing. And Joseph cannot prevent his younger son being preferred to the elder by Jacob, who assigns the sceptre not to him nor to Ephraim, but to Judah. Though Moses is the great mediator between God and his people, yet, just as the Pharaohs and the

135g later Davidic kings had their prophets and priests, so Moses does not directly communicate God's will: he had the divine ordinances written on tables of stone (Ex 34) and Aaron to speak for him (Ex 4:13ff); in J, therefore, Moses is not a prophet, nor is he a priest in the functional sense of the word, but he is invested with the priesthood belonging to the prerogatives of the Pharaohs and the Davidic kings.

h Taking account of the above observations—and many more could be made—it seems clear that J intended to legitimize, according to the prevailing ideas of the time, the sacred kingship, but insisting on the rights of Yahweh, the God of the Patriarchs and of Moses: the Davidic king is Yahweh's representative, not because he is the first born or next in succession, but as designated by Yahweh himself; in him, therefore, the people can safely put their religious faith and hope.

i J shows an outspoken **preference for the tribe of Judah**: its territory (Hebron, Mamre, Beersheba, Kadesh, even Jerusalem), its founder (Judah is the man who wanted to save Joseph and took the responsibility for the safety of Benjamin), its future kingdom (Gn 49:8—12; Nm 24:3—9. 15—24); it must therefore have originated from Judah. The people appears to be well settled in Canaan with organized agricultural feasts (Ex 34) and still united, since all Jacob's children are equally mentioned and blessed (Gn 30 and 49), whereas Abraham and Jacob peacefully pass through sanctuaries of the N and all honour is still given to Joseph. On the other hand, what we know about David's and Solomon's accession to the throne, about Solomon's building a temple in honour of Yahweh at Jerusalem and as the man who brought in the wise men and the wisdom of Egypt, corrupting the ancient traditions of Israel, is quite in accordance with J's whole tendency and interest. Moreover, Edom and Moab appear to be subjected (Gn 27:30, Nm 24:17f), though there may be a hint at Edom's proximate freedom (Gn 27:40, cf 1 (3) Kgs 11:25), and Ephraim as the prince of his brethren could be an allusion to the political schism. For these and similar reasons it is thought that the Yahwistic traditions were fixed towards the end of Solomon's reign, the 10th cent. B.C.

136a Elohistic Tradition (E)——It is to be expected that after the schism, separating Israel from Judah, Israel would have its own tradition, presenting its proper outlook upon the past. This supposition is borne out by the critical study of the Pent, recognizing this Israelite tradition first of all in E. This too consists mostly of narratives, but woven up with them are two legislative sections, the Decalogue (Ex 20:1—17) and the Book of the Covenant (Ex 20:22—23:33). E's narratives too may originally have formed a more or less continuous story, but only parts of it are to be found in the actual Pent. It is commonly accepted that E starts with Gn 20—though traces of it may be recognized in Gn 15 (e.g. v 16, in contradiction with v 13 and using the term Amorites)—is further met with in the rest of Gn, particularly in the Joseph-section, increasingly in Ex and Nm and very likely, as we shall see later on, in some sections of D.

b Here again the **criteria** by which E can be discerned are manifold: God is always called 'Elohim' until E narrates the revelation of the name Yahweh (Ex 3:13—15), though P also uses this name in the same way; Canaan's inhabitants are named Amorites, Joseph's purchasers, Midianites; instead of '*šifḥāh*' we find "*āmāh*" and Sinai is always Horeb. Though the style is more sober and severe, less vivid, picturesque, dramatic

than in J, it must be admitted that from this point of view **136b** the two traditions cannot always be clearly distinguished (e.g. Gn 22, ascribed to E, but with a few Jahwistic insertions of minor importance, is a very colourful and impressive narration). E marks a greater distance between God and man: divine revelations have a more immaterial aspect; God himself remains invisible, speaking through dreams or visions or in the midst of clouds, often acting through his agents (angels); to see God would mean man's death (Ex 33:20); images of God are strictly forbidden (Ex 20:4). One also observes a **c** higher standard of morality in E, e.g. Abram's proposal in J that Sarai should present herself not as his wife, but as his sister (Gn 12:11ff) is explained in E's parallel text by saying that she was the daughter of his father though not of his mother (Gn 20:12); Jacob's cunning (Gn 30:37—43) is differently interpreted, viz. as something coming from God (Gn 31:6—13).

E's main characteristic, however, is the special **d** viewpoint from which he deals with the same general subject matter as that of J. The very separation between Israel and Judah was caused by the **deficiencies, failings and blunders of the monarchy**. These began to manifest themselves during the reign of Solomon and were first sharply denounced by the prophet Ahijah (1 (3) Kgs 11:29ff), who rebuked the king for having followed other deities and for not having kept God's commandments and statutes; they had become worse and ever more patent since then, both in Judah and Israel. E's concern is to conserve the heritage promised to the Fathers, to return to the ancient premonarchic, Mosaic traditions of the desert. Hence E's interest in the providential way in which the people came into Egypt through Joseph and were led out again through Moses; as God's spokesman or prophet Moses arranged God's alliance with the people, the Sacred Covenant, of which the stipulations were laid down in the Decalogue and the Book of the Covenant, that the people might always and exactly know what they had to avoid and what to observe in order to please God and to be blessed by him. It is with E that the Pent began to receive its form of **e** an alliance between God and his people after the example of the ancient treaties, possibly to counteract the tendency to seek security in pacts with other nations. It has moreover been suggested that E's view is based on the supposition of the confederation of the various tribes in a kind of 'amphictyony' expressed in a treaty of alliance at Shechem under Joshua (Jos 24). Whereas, however, in this treaty God still appears rather a divine witness than one of the contracting parties, in E the treaty-structure is already transformed into an alliance between God and his people.

That **E originated from N Israel** can be confirmed **f** by the fact that it appears to have the N tribes in view: their cities such as Shechem and Bethel are frequently mentioned, as also Deborah's and Rachel's sepulchres in Israel's territory; great prominence is given to Joseph and to his sons Manasseh and Ephraim; Reuben is here the man who tries to rescue Joseph; the people of Israel at large comes to the fore (Nm 23:7—10, 18—24); and there are no messianic texts in E.

The fixation of E must be **attributed to the old g prophetical circles in the kingdom of Israel**. It is in E that Abraham is called a prophet, intervening with God on behalf of Abimelech (Gn 20:7—17). Though this name is not expressly given to Moses, yet God says to him: 'I will be with your mouth and teach you what you shall speak' (Ex 4:12), also 'with him I speak mouth to mouth' (Nm 12:8); and the prophet Hosea calls Moses

136g a prophet (Hos 12:13). E's teaching is precisely what the earlier prophets were insisting upon in the kingdom of Israel. Elijah went to Horeb to be comforted (1 (3) Kgs 19). Amos exhorts the people to seek the word of the Lord (Am 8:12), to hate evil and to love good, to establish justice (5:14ff), pointing to the moral obligations of the Covenant, which also Judah has transgressed by not keeping its statutes (2:4), and without which cult was of no value (5:21—27). Hosea understands and presents the Covenant of the desert as a matrimonial union between God and Israel, his spouse, broken by Israel's infidelity, but to be restored, if she repents, in righteousness and in justice, in steadfast love and in mercy (Hos 2); he turns against the monarchy as not from God (8:4) and warns against political treaties with other nations like Egypt and Assyria (7:11; cf Is 30:1); the Covenant with Yahweh must suffice and alone gives security.

h Having its origin in Israel, E must have been composed before the fall of the N Kingdom in 722 B.C. As a reaction, however, against the monarchy, which had appeared to be a disappointment, E is to be dated after J, and not before the 9th cent., if the mention of 'Ur of the Chaldeans' (Gn 15:7) belongs to E, as many now think; for the name 'Chaldeans' occurs in Mesopotamian texts only from that century onward. The name of Elisha has been proposed as E's redactor, since this prophet appears as a mediator of salvation, like Moses (2 (4) Kgs 13:14).

i All agree that **E's legislative texts**, the Decalogue and the Book of the Covenant, belong to E's oldest part and may substantially go back to Moses' time; but it is also commonly admitted that these texts and the other E sections are not only based on ancient material, even older than that which J had made use of, but were very much influenced by their being amalgamated with J into a new entity, and even more by the later Deuteronomic Tradition, which itself seems to be a further development of E and also originating from the N, as will now have to be explained.

137a Deuteronomic Tradition (D)—So called because it is chiefly to be found in Dt and, in the Pent, almost restricted to it. D is easily distinguished from the other main traditions by its characteristic expressions: 'with mighty hand and outstretched arm', 'to adhere to Yahweh your God', 'to keep his commandments', 'to do what is good in his eyes', 'to exterminate the evil in the midst of you', constantly repeated; and particularly by its oratorical, paranetic, moralizing style, on the one hand apparently influenced by sapiential literature, noted for its exhortations to disciples, and on the other hand manifesting the prophetical concern already shown in E, not to have any other alliance than the one with Yahweh.

The critical analysis of Dt leads to the conclusion that its apparent unity (a number of sermons by Moses to the people at Moab, surrounding the so-called Deuteronomic Code and followed by texts related to Moses' death) is only the final result of its long and complex history, of which a brief outline is here given.

b The **oldest part of the book** is to be found in Dt 5—30, and precisely in those passages where the people are addressed in the 2nd pers. sing., with elimination of all verses and pericopes in which they are spoken to in the 2nd pers. pl. This very valuable criterion cannot, unfortunately, be checked in the English (and several other) versions which indiscriminately translate both by 'you'. In the RSV e.g. Dt 5 begins thus: 'And Moses summoned all Israel and said to them, "Hear (sing.), o Israel, the statutes . . . which I speak in your (plur.)

hearing . . . and you (plur.) shall learn them. . . ."' In **137b** vv 2—5 Israel is further spoken to in the plural, in vv 6—21 (the Decalogue) always in the singular, in vv 22—33 again in the plural. In the following chh the same distinction can be made.

The entire basic section of Dt 5—30 appears to be **c** composed, like E, on the model of the ancient treaties, but without the historical introduction which is a later addition, and the tone is here moralizing. As in E we have in D Horeb, the Decalogue (Dt 5:6—21), the Deuteronomic Code as a parallel to the Book of the Covenant, the insistence on God's commandments and the ordinances prescribed in the law through the mediation of Moses, and the strict observance of these to show one's faithfulness to the only alliance which will procure true salvation; emphasis is laid on the prophetical office (18:9—22) and, when kingship is accepted as a matter of fact, the king is severely warned not to go into excesses (as Solomon), but to observe the law (18:4—20). But E's ideas receive **d** a further development in D. God appears more emphatically as the only one (6:4), the supreme Lord not merely of Israel but of all the nations even mightier and greater than Israel, which he conquered in order to give his people the Land promised to the Patriarchs. The Covenant is presented in D as an engagement of Yahweh's gratuitous free will, of his love, by which Israel has become God's Chosen People, the sacred community of God. As a jealous God, Yahweh does not tolerate other gods and demands fidelity and loyality, not merely as required in the old treaties of vassality, but with the deeper sense of true and sincere love (6:5). It is in this spirit of love that God has given his law, containing all his precepts and statutes, and it is in this spirit that these must be carried out. Israel's whole history is now centered around Moses, who made known God's law to the people and put it next to the Decalogue into the Ark of the Covenant, where it is to remain as a testimony, pointing out that it should have force forever.

The fundamental **similarity of structure, outlook e and teaching between E and D** makes it very probable that Dt's basic section which we have been speaking about originates, like E, from the N; and the same is suggested by what we read in D about the Levites. They are the priests, but supposed to live in the various cities of Israel and in poor circumstances, for the Israelites going up in pilgrimage to 'the place which Yahweh your God chooses' will have to support them (12:12; 14:27); those Levites may, however, take permanent abode in that place and are then allowed to minister there like the other priests (18:5—8). But the latter apparently did not admit this regulation (2 (4) Kgs 23:9); the priests of the high places (very likely those Levites), were not allowed to come up to the altar of the Lord in Jerusalem—the clergy of Jerusalem would not permit the Levites, having come there from the kingdom of Israel after its fall to exercise their priestly functions in Jerusalem's temple. It must have been those Levites who took the religious inheritance of the kingdom of Israel, not only preserved in E but also in the other levitical traditions, with them to have it revived round the one sanctuary left, the temple of Jerusalem. And this must have happened at the time of King Hezekiah, known for other literary activity (Prv 25:1) and also for his action against the high places (2 (4) Kgs 18:4). From all this we may conclude that Dt's basic section must have been composed at that time and corresponds to 'the book of the law' found in the house of the Lord in the reign of King Josiah (2 (4) Kgs 22:8), where it may have been hidden during the reign of the far from religious kings, Manasseh and Amon.

137f It is commonly admitted that Josiah's religious reform, insisting on centering all cult round Jerusalem's temple, is founded on Dt's basic section; but the opposition of the local clergy to the Levites from the N, as expressed in 2 (4) Kgs 23:9, may be an indication that this 'book of the law' met with opposition. In the meantime the Levites from the N tried to have the Elohistic Tradition, already composed and presenting a more ancient legislation (the Book of the Covenant) amalgamated with J. The 'Jahwist', who is responsible for this fusion of J and E, is very likely himself of the Deuteronomic school, since a number of passages in E have a typical Deuteronomic character; cf e.g. Ex 12:25—27 with Dt 6: 20—25; Ex 23:21—25 with Dt 7: 1—6; Ex 34:13—14 with Dt 6:14—15.

g Dt's basic section is chiefly legislative. The present form of Dt, longer and more historical in aspect, is due to the addition of chh 1—4 and 31—34, and to the insertion of the 'you' (plural) passages and, as some maintain (Cazelles, col. 816), of several Elohistic texts. The precise date of those additions and insertions cannot always be stated with certitude. Some parts, like 4:29—40; 28:47—69; 30:1—10, suppose the exile; and others point to an even later time, e.g. 32:48—52, betraying the style of P.

It seems quite probable that Dt was first intended as a preface to a large historical work in which the ancient, already written, traditions about the conquest of Canaan (Joshua, Judges), Samuel, David and the other kings, were rewritten from a Deuteronomic viewpoint during the exile, when Kgs received its final redaction (2 (4) Kgs 25:27—30). Dt was then later, still during the exile, separated from this work and added to J E. This fusion into J E D may also have occasioned other changes giving Dt its present form—the insertion of the E texts into D and also of the 'you' (plural) passages after the example of Dt 27 (this too is supposed to belong to E and contains the plural form in its addresses to Israel), and finally its concluding chh.

138a Priestly Tradition (P)—The name is explained by the particular interest shown in this tradition in cult and the priest as its minister, who moreover appears to be the most important person in the national life of the people. Beginning at the very first page of the Bible, this tradition runs through Gn, Ex and Nm, embraces the whole of Lv, has traces in Dt, and is by many supposed to continue in Jos.

P has a vocabulary not to be found outside this tradition in the Pent; e.g. *'miškan'* and *'miqdas'* for 'tabernacle', *'minhāh'* only in the sense of 'oblation' or 'cereal offerings'; *''ēdāh'* as denoting the Jewish community; *'qorbān'* as a general term for sacrifice. The style is monotonous, dry, schematic, repeating over and over again the same stereotyped formulas like: 'These are the generations of ... (in Gn); 'The Lord said to Moses' (introducing laws). But it can nevertheless be very impressive, e.g. in the account of creation (Gn 1:1—2:4 ᵃ).

b God is transcendent, high above man, unapproachable. Hence, the repeated admonition only found in P: 'You shall be holy, for I the Lord your God am holy' (Lv 19:2; 20:26); the rigorous distinction between holy and profane, pure and impure; its insistence that man must worship God; the prominence of the levites as entirely dedicated to God's service and out of whom only the sons of Aaron may be taken as God's priests and special ministers, the proper mediators between him and his people. As to the mutual relations between men, P safeguards their matrimonial and social aspects against all irregularities, considered from a cultic point of view. P alone has the precept of loving one's neighbour as oneself (Lv 19:34).

With the exception of the Yahwistic Decalogue **138c** (Ex 34), the Elohistic Decalogue (Ex 20:1—17) and Book of the Covenant (Ex 20:22—23:33), and the Deuteronomic Decalogue (Dt 5:6—21), all the **other numerous laws of the Pent belong to P**. Introduced by the already mentioned stereotyped formula to denote their intimate relation with Moses' initial legislation, they do contain very old elements, showing traces of ancient, archaic ideas, manners and customs, and vestiges of the primitive nomadic life of the people, e.g. the regulations about purity and impurity, and the notion of sin underlying the ritual of expiation on the day of atonement. But most of these laws in the actual Pent suppose and concern a sedentary life with an urban civilization and culture, with agricultural feasts and an amply developed and minutely regulated temple cult.

It is very difficult to retrace the exact **history of d this priestly legislation**. The 'Law of Holiness' (Lv 17—26), so called on account of its insistence that man should be holy before God, is now generally considered to be its oldest section and even as something apart, usually designated as H. It is itself undoubtedly a compilation of pre-existing legislative texts and collections of law, for there are many repetitions and doublets, the same precepts are differently formulated in either apodictic (18) or casuistic (20) style, the latter occurring also in Assyrian State-letters of the 7th cent. B.C.; they have apparently been subject to special adaptations when inserted in H, which itself appears to have received some later additions when it became integrated into the rest of P.

H has much of the structure of the Deuteronomic **e** Code: both are presented in the form of a discourse, start with a regulation on sacrifice, terminate with blessings and curses, and inculcate the centralization of cult. In this regard H may be looked upon as the counterpart of the Deuteronomic Code, though rather a collection of laws than a proper code, containing the legislative tradition of priestly circles towards the end of the Judean monarchy, as is now commonly held. This opinion is based on the intimate contact between H and Ezek. This prophet, himself a priest, cannot be the author of H in its present structure—he undoubtedly contains later elements, and when Ezek refers to pre-existing laws (Ezek 20:11—18), he appears to have those of H in mind—nevertheless the whole mentality and even literary construction of both is so very much the same, that they must be of about the same time with a slight priority of H. Moreover, the striking similarity between H and Ezek in those texts in which the priest-prophet denounces the faults of the priests and the court, first brought to the fore by J. G. Vink (*Leviticus*, in *De Boeken van het Oude Testament*, Deel II, Boek 1, Roermond en Maaseik, 1962, 67; cf also his explanation of Lv 8:3f), justifies his conclusion that H might have been intended as a prophetical criticism of the court and of the temple-clergy so intimately connected with it.

The next and principal part of the Priestly legisla- **f** tion is woven into the history of the past as understood and interpreted with regard to the future by the Priestly Tradition, and generally dated towards the end of the exile, when Cyrus allowed the Jews to return to their homeland. After the collapse of the Judean monarchy and the deportation of the people to captivity in Babylon, the clergy formed a rallying point for the exiles in a pagan country, under a pagan ruler and faced with the enticement of a pagan cult. They found it necessary to foster and reanimate religious belief and national consciousness, and to reorganize the life of the people

138f on the general principles of common blood, common traditions and an authentic clergy, so that the nation could continue under quite new circumstances (Cazelles, col. 828). With this end in view P drew up a general history of the past, with a continuous chronology, directed and commanded by God, on whom alone all depend and who is therefore entitled to impose his will on

g man. By creating the world with man as its center and God's representative on earth, God entered into a first bond with man, referring to the Sabbath as sacrosanct because observed by himself, and taking care that life, originating from him, would pass from generation to generation. During the Flood God made life continue in Noah, with whom he concluded a second pact, binding all men and marking the importance of blood as the seat of life and therefore as something essential in the sacrifices to be offered to God as the supreme Lord. With Abraham, singled out from all other men, God entered upon a third alliance, characterized by circumcision as token and pledge of one's belonging to God's Chosen People. Leading them in a providential way through various vicissitudes and even from Canaan to Egypt, God rescued them from the Egyptian bondage and established the central cultic revelation at Sinai through the mediation of Moses the Levite and Aaron the priest, the faithful observance of which would be the only guarantee of security and happiness in the restored Jewish community after the second return to the Promised Land.

h A characteristic of P is the **prominence he gives to the Aaronic priesthood** for the custody of the religious life of the people. This has been explained (de Vaux AI, 394—97) by the hypothesis that after the exile a compromise was arrived at between the two main priestly families which originally served together at the ark of the Covenant, brought by David to Jerusalem, viz. those of Abiathar and Zadoc (2 Sm 15:24—29). After Abiathar's expulsion by Solomon (1 (3) Kgs 2: 26f; cf 1 Sm 2:27—36; 3:11—14), Zadoc's family had become the sole official clergy at the temple of Jerusalem; but both families, legitimizing themselves as descended from Aaron, the one through Ithamar and the other through Eleazar (Pinehas), appear again together in the service of the restored temple (1 Chr 24:1—6; cf 16: 3—8, 50—53).

i As to the previous history of the P-tradition much work has still to be done; though this is undoubtedly the more recent and easily to be recognized, its provenance and development have up till now been far less studied than those of the other main traditions. They seem, however, to have been collected and brought up to date that they might constitute the law of State for the restored Jewish community in its homeland under Persian hegemony, when they were united with the other ancient traditions contained in J E D.

j Conclusion—Comparing the above critical view of the literary composition of the Pent with the old traditional one, we may say that in the old conception stress was almost exclusively laid on the providential, divine way in which the Pent came about; it was regarded as the result of God's direct action on the one human author, Moses, who also played the principal part in it, with only a few later additions, e.g. about his death; while the **modern approach**, struck by the diversity of language, style, culture, mentality, and outlook in the Pent, has come to place more emphasis on its complex human authorship as rooted in the common faith of individuals and community (corporate personality), without, however, denying God's special action in and through them. The study of this complex human author-

ship, marked by the four main traditions, brings us into **138** closer contact with the essential strands of Israel's life and aspirations: the significance of the Judean kingship in J; the purity of faith of the prophets and their struggle for it in E; the high moral and religious standard of the priestly families in D; and in P, Israel's universalism and theocratic organization under Persian sovereignty, when cult had become its only distinctive characteristic.

Religious teaching—Various religious and doctrinal **139** aspects of the four main traditions or documents composing the Pent have already been touched upon and those proper to each of the five books will be dealt with in the articles dedicated to them; only a general view can be given here.

It has already been pointed out (cf 'Contents') that **b** the Pent was called 'the Law', because both its legislative and historical parts aim at conveying a divine teaching: the essentials of the Chosen People's religion. For Israel's religion is an historical religion, based on God's revelation as given to definite persons, in determined places and circumstances, at certain moments of its history. This history, which was not conceived and written down according to modern historical principles and which varies in character according to the successive periods concerned, (primeval times, Patriarchal age, Moses) has not been recorded for its own sake. It retraces God's relations with mankind and particularly with his Chosen People, and thus presents the basis, nucleus and summary of Israel's religion. The Pent consequently has always been for the Jews their principal sacred book, to be read and meditated upon in their religious gatherings and, up to the present day, in their synagogues. It is the Law, their main teaching.

The very first page of the Pent offers at once an **c** extremely **high notion of God**: the sole supreme, transcendental, almighty Being, calling the whole visible world into existence by a mere word, the expression of his sovereign will. This **pure monotheism**, not to be found in any other ancient people, even those with a far higher standard of culture, cannot be explained merely by Israel's own reflexion, but necessarily postulates divine revelation. Man is considered as entirely depending on God, who created him as his representative on earth and for man's own happiness, which primarily consists in his right relation to God. All the miseries, death included, which nevertheless befall man, are consequently explained as ultimately due to man's own fault, to his turning away from God, and are therefore understood as divine punishment for man's sin. Though evil increases, God's plans in creating mankind cannot **d** be frustrated. He not only called man into being, but takes a continuous interest in him during the whole of his life. He reveals his omniscience by showing that he knows the secrets of the human heart, his justice by blessing and saving the righteous and chastising and condemning the wicked, his merciful love by being always ready to accept the sinner on his repentance, his divine Providence by leading mankind according to his own designs towards the end he has in view. In spite of man's original fall, which deprived him of God's familiar companionship, and notwithstanding man's subsequent sins, God's love and mercy impelled him to come again into close contact with man, first with the whole of mankind by saving Noah from the Flood and making him the new Adam of the new world; and then with one particular people, which of his own free will and predilection he singled out by calling Abraham from pagan surroundings, that he and his posterity

39d might enter into a very special relation with the one true God.

e This principal theme of the Pent, that **Israel had been picked out by God** and so became his Chosen People, finds its realization in a second: that **God contracted an alliance with Abraham**, the first ancestor of the Chosen people which was repeated with succeeding Patriarchs. The bond with Noah was its remote preparation and led up to it. It was confirmed by the solemn Covenant God established between himself and his people at Mt Sinai through the mediation of Moses. But divine election resulting in a Covenant necessarily requires its observance by the contracting parties; and this brings us to a third main Pentateuchal theme, that of **the Law**. In his bond with Noah God had only prescribed some very general conditions to be carried out by man, and in his alliance with Abraham and the following Patriarchs he merely insisted that they should **f** be faithful to it. But in concluding his Covenant with his Chosen People, God gave it his precise law with all its civic as well as its religious obligations, that man might know exactly what the Covenant demanded, in order to get all the benefits attached to its strict observance. Then God too, as the other contracting party, by freely proposing the Covenant and entering on it, was by this very fact himself bound to meet his own obligations; for divine justice, avenging transgressions of the Law, had equally to recompense its loyal observance. Hence the fourth and last chief theme of the Pent: **God's promises**. Immediately after man's fall and its severe punishment, he announced a final victory in man's struggle against evil, and to Noah he pledged that mankind would never be destroyed again. To Abraham, however, and the other Patriarchs, God promised continuous and lasting blessings, which found their concrete realization in the fact that his Chosen People, in spite of vicissitudes and delays, would nevertheless possess, a land 'flowing with milk and honey' (Dt 31:20).

140a In the Pent these four main themes cannot be separated; they are interwoven, completing one another. They together express the firm conviction that the one true God, the Creator of the world and of all mankind, was yet in a very special way, which no other people could boast of, the God of Israel, Yahweh; that Israel was God's 'own possession among all the peoples', to him 'a Kingdom of priests and a holy nation' (Ex 19:5, 6). This conviction was the result of Israel's own reflection, corroborated by divine revelation and matured through the ages down to the time the Pent received its present form. All the earlier misfortunes, the complete destruction of the kingdoms of both Israel and Judah, and finally the hard reality of the Babylonian Captivity had made the people understand that the loss of the Promised Land was due to their own fault, since they had not lived up to their character as God's Chosen People, had been utterly disloyal to his Covenant, had grievously transgressed his Law now testifying against them (Dt 31:26) and had consequently made

themselves altogether unworthy of his promises. But in **140b** repentance and penance they had also understood that God in his unbounded love and mercy would take them back again, restore the Covenant and lead them back to the Promised Land as in Moses' time 'by a mighty hand and an outstretched arm' (Dt 4:34), if only they would now be faithful to his Law. They realized now that its later precepts were but a necessary sequel to those made known to them through Moses, an adaptation to the ever changing circumstances of subsequent centuries, whereas all that had come to pass from Moses right up to their own time could be considered as a reflex of what had happened from the very beginnings of their becoming God's people down to the time of Moses. They expressed this religious conception of their ancient history and legislation in what is now called the Pent, as this was gradually composed and was finally presented and accepted by all as their principal 'Tôrāh' or Teaching.

Since in the meantime the Davidic dynasty, not- **c** withstanding God's solemn assurance that it would stand for ever (2 Sm 7:16), had fallen, the Jews began to realize that the various prophetical texts concerning Yahweh's anointed, the Messiah, indicated not so much one of David's successors previous to the destruction of his kingdom, as rather **a future ideal King of his race**. They also began to understand better similar passages in the Pent about the one who would gain the final victory over evil (Gn 3:15), the sceptre not passing from Judah until he comes to whom it belongs (Gn 49.10), the star coming forth from Jacob and the sceptre rising out of Israel (Nm 24:17), etc, as referring to that same Messiah, the ideal King to come, who would completely fulfil all their expectations of the divine promises.

The Pentateuch's teaching concerning the fundamental **d** relations between God and man holds good for us as well, inasmuch as God's Providence ordering all to the benefit of the Chosen People, notwithstanding all their aberrations and apostasy and in virtue of their repentance and conversion, has only to be extended to his ways with the whole of mankind through **Christ**. God's final revelation to man, in whom the Pent finds its fullest and ultimate meaning. Our Lord himself told the Jews that their Sacred Scriptures bore witness to him (Jn 5:39) and that they should believe Moses (= the Law, the Pent), who had written about him (Jn 5:45). For Christ had not come to abolish the Law (= Pent) and the Prophets (the second Jewish section of the Sacred Books), but to fulfil them (Mt 5:17). The Law (Pent) is to be looked upon as a mere pedagogue or custodian, leading to Christ by educating and protecting the Chosen People till he himself came (Gal 3:24). He would establish, by his own sacrifice on the Cross (of which all the sacrifices of the Law were but a faint shadow) the New Covenant with all those who believe in him and thus become members of his new Chosen People, Abraham's offspring by faith, heirs according to promise (Gal 3:29).

GENESIS

BY B. VAWTER C.M.

141a Bibliography—(A) Commentaries. (For patristic commentaries and down to the 19th cent., see DTC 6, 1206–8) H. L. Strack, Munich, 1905[2]; J. Skinner, ICC, 1912[2]; H. Gunkel, HKAT, Göttingen, 1922[5]; O. Procksch, KAT, Leipzig, 1924[3]; E. König, Gütersloh, 1925[3]; S. R. Driver, 1926[12]; P. Heinisch, BB, 1930; J. Chaine, 1948; H. Junker, EchB, Würzburg, 1949; G. von Rad, ATD, Göttingen, 1949–53; E.tr. OTL 1961; R. de Vaux, BJ, 1951; C. A. Simpson, IB, New York, 1952; A. Clamer, PCSB, 1953; F. Michaéli, Neuchâtel, 1957–60; E. A. Speiser AB, 1964.

b (B) Background and General—I. Guidi, 'L'historiographie chez les Sémites', RB 3 (1906), 509–19; A. Robert, 'Historique (genre)', DBS 4, 9–12; H. H. Rowley, *From Joseph to Joshua*, Oxford 1950; R. C. Dentan (ed.), *The Idea of History in the Ancient Near E*, New Haven, 1955; B. Vawter, *A Path Through Genesis*, 1956; G. L. Guyot, 'Messianism in the Book of Genesis', CBQ 13 (1951) 415–21; O. Eissfeldt, *Die Genesis der Genesis*, Tübingen, 1958; D. Bonhoeffer, *Schöpfung und Fall*, Munich, 1955: E. tr. *Creation and Fall. A Theological Interpretation of Genesis 1–3*; 1959; J. L. McKenzie, 'Myth and the Old Testament', CBQ 21 (1959), 265–82; A. M. Dubarle, *Le péché originel dans l'Écriture*, 1958: E.tr. *The Biblical Doctrine of Original Sin*, 1964; J. de Fraine, *Adam et son lignage*, Tournai, 1959; G. E. Wright, 'Archaeology and Old Testament Studies', JBL 77 (195), 39–51; H. Cazelles, 'Patriarches', DBS 7, 81–156; W. F. Albright, 'Abram the Hebrew; A New Archaeological Interpretation', BASOR 163 (1961), 36–54; G. A. Mendenhall, 'Covenant Forms in Israelite Tradition', BA 17 (1954) 50–76. H. Haag, *Biblische Schöpfungslehre und kirchliche Erbsündenlehre*, Stuttgarter Bibelstudien, 1966. H. Gunkel, *The Legends of genesis*, 1964; I. Hunt, *The World of the Patriarchs* 1967.

142a Name—By the Jews, Genesis is called *Bereshith*, 'in the beginning', the Heb. word with which the book begins. Our title is derived, as are practically all our titles for the biblical books, from the LXX. In using the word *genesis*, 'beginning', 'origin', the LXX translators doubtless had in mind primarily the narrative of creation with which the book opens, summarized in 2:4 as *hē Biblos geneseōs*. The same expression occurs in 5:1, however, again to translate the Heb. catchword *tôledôt*, which is repeated in 6:9; 10:1; 11:10; 11:27; 25:12; 25:19; 36:1; 37:2 and translated in each case *hai geneseis*. Gn was recognized, therefore, as a book of many origins.

b Plan and Purpose—The tenfold *tôledôt* of Gn represents the 'outline' given it by its final author. This Heb. word means, when used in the construct as here, 'the-generations-of', that is to say, 'the-ones-generated-by', or, more freely, 'the history-of'. In 2:4 it is retrospective, of the 'generations' of the heavens and the earth, i.e., their denizens, whose creation has just been described; in the other instances it is prospective, of the descend-

ants of Adam (5:1), Noah (6:9), the sons of Noah (10:1), **142b** Shem (11:10), Terah, that is to say, Abraham's family (11:27), Ishmael (25:12), Isaac (25:19), Esau (36:1), and Jacob (37:2). This schematism, especially as it involves the number ten, is a characteristic of the Priestly tradition to which all of these passages belong. Since the *tôledôt* of Esau (36:1) is repeated in 36:9, it may be that the original ten of the Priestly tradition did not include the aberrant and retrospective 2:4; the final author of Gn. could have added this for symmetrical reasons.

From a Western point of view, at least, a more satisfying outline is provided by the **Contents** of the book itself—an outline which, obviously cannot be in conflict with the author's intentions. (I) Genesis 1–11, **c** or, perhaps more precisely, down to 11:26, is **the story of human origins**. The story of human origins is, in turn, divided into the following parts: (a) the six-day creation narrative (1:1–2:4*a*); (b) the story of paradise and the fall of man (2:4*b*–3:24); (c) the story of Cain and Abel: the first murder (4:1–16); (d) the history of the Cainites (4:17–24); (e) the history of the Sethites (4:17–5:32); (f) the flood narrative and the covenant with Noah (6:1–9:17); (g) the blessing and cursing of Noah's sons (9:18–29); (h) the peopling of the earth from Noah's sons (10); (i) the tower of Babel (11:1–9); the Semites (11:1–26). (II) **The patriarchal History** begins with 11:27–32, the genealogy of Terah, leading to Abraham, the ancestor of the Israelites. The Patriarchal History is divided into three major cycles corresponding to the three major personages with which the history is concerned: (a) the story of Abraham (12–25), to which is attached the story of Isaac (26); (b) the story of Jacob (27–35), with the supplementary genealogies of Esau (36); and (c) the story of Joseph (37–50), in which is embedded a variant story of Judah (38).

The purpose with which the author of Gn ordered this **d** material cannot be separated from the purpose of the larger unity of which Gn is a part, namely the **Pentateuch** (or Hexateuch). Though the division of the Pent into separate books of fairly equal length is very ancient (far older than the LXX) and responds to divisions present in the text itself, the individual books are not adequately understood apart from the complete history to which they contribute. Specifically, Gn is the introduction to a history whose function it is to tell of the Covenant made by God with the people of Israel, to detail the Law of Moses which was the result of the Covenant, and to describe the concession of the Promised Land which was its fulfilment. In this introductory capacity Gn narrates the origins of the people Israel and the preliminaries to the Covenant.

It is in this light that we must understand the meaning that the story of human origins in Gn 1–11 had to the author. Though these chapters are rich in a theological content of perennial worth, they appear in

Gn as the prologue to a *history* of the divine economy and **142d** are conditioned by this historical perspective. Creation of the universe and of man are taught by Gn not as isolated theological truths, but as the first in a long series of God's beneficent acts that has culminated in the election of a people. Two associated themes run throughout the entire narrative, to which all its details are related and contribute. The first of these is the theme of *selection*, with its corollary of the opposition of good and evil; the second is the theme of *divine grace*, which continues its good providence for man despite all human folly and sin.

e Thus man, created by God and placed by him in an earthly paradise, rebels against the divine dispensation and seeks autonomy, introducing sin into the world. Expelled from the earthly paradise, man continues and increases in his sin, while mastering the various arts and crafts that are necessary to him in a world no longer passively subject to his dominion. The progress of sin is marked in the history of the wicked Cainites, rejected in favour of the Sethites who have replaced the murdered Abel as the object of divine choice. By the time of the flood, however, the whole of mankind has become a mass of corruption, save only the just man Noah. The flood follows as God's repudiation of his creation, the return of the primordial chaos from which the world was formed. Here, too, however, grace and election remain, for while evil is punished, the innocent are spared, from which a new creation can begin. After the flood, with God now having reconciled himself to deal with man as a sinful creature and no more to destroy the world because of man, the world is repeopled in many races, nations, and tongues: the Japhethites, Hamites, and Semites. Of these, the Semites alone speedily occupy the centre of the stage as the objects of divine predilection. Finally, with a last glance at man's persistently futile attempt to master his own destiny (the Tower of Babel), the author of Gn directs his attention to the family of Abraham, to whom the Lord will consign his promise.

f The same themes continue in the **Patriarchal History**. Abraham, himself alone out of all his father's house the object of the divine choice, begets the Ishmaelites through Hagar, and through Keturah various other peoples; but only Isaac and his descendants are the children of God's promise. The opposition between the chosen and the rejected continues, and it is especially manifest in the story of the two sons of Isaac, Jacob and Esau, from whom spring, respectively, the Israelites and their most bitter enemies, the Edomites. The conclusion of the Patriarchal History is the **story of Joseph**, that son of Jacob through whom the children of Jacob, or Israel, went down into Egypt to be made into a people, whence God would call them forth to become his covenant people.

Throughout the Patriarchal History God's providential intervention in protecting and safeguarding his elect and the promise committed to them is repeatedly stressed. This is brought out in the various incidents that are told of the patriarchal families, and also in the history itself. In one sense the Patriarchal History is what it is often called, a kind of anticipation of the possession of the Promised Land by the Patriarchs' descendants, the Israelites. In another sense, it is just the opposite. The Patriarchs do not possess the Promised Land; they merely sojourn there as aliens and strangers. Only in God's good time, and in the fulness of this time, will the land come into the possession of Israel. Not through any virtue of its own, not even in virtue of its great

ancestors, did Israel come into the destiny which God **142f** had designed for it. Genesis is, then, throughout a testimony to grace.

Composition and Literary Character—As noted in **143a** CCHS (1) § 137*h*: 'That the whole book is not from the pen of one author is clear from the differences of style to be met in it. Were these confined to the treatment of different themes, the change of style might be explained as due to the requirements of the subject-matter. But in the sections 1:1—2:3 and 2:4—25, which provide a case of this kind, the former having the grandiose theme of the creative power of God and the latter the more personal theme of man's first earthly home, the difference of style is accompanied by the more subtle difference of mental outlook. In the second section this is more intimate, more personal, more simple. But even within this latter section there is one passage, 10—14, that describing the four rivers, which the reader feels to be out of harmony with the tone and spirit of the rest of the account and to be therefore from another mind,' cf Letter of the Biblical Commission to Cardinal Suhard 16 Jan 1948, EnchB 577. See also §§ 130*f* and 135*a*.

In determining the sources used in Gn, we must **b** consider first the phenomenon of the **doublets**, or even **triplets**, that are so frequently encountered in the text. Here we are not referring to the normal repetitiveness of Semitic style, aided by the tendency towards parallelism, but to the **frequent repetition of the same episode**, often with varying or conflicting details. There are, for example, two narratives of creation, as noted above; there are two genealogies of the descendants of Adam, most of the names of which are repeated in chh 4—5; two stories of the flood have been woven together in chh 6—8, in which the flood arises from different sources and has different chronologies, in which Noah takes different numbers of animals into the ark, himself enters the ark twice (7:7 and 7:13), and so forth; twice Abraham risks Sarah's honour in making her pass for his sister (12:13—20 and ch 20), and the same story is later told of Isaac and Rebekah (26:6—11); twice Abraham expels Hagar (chh 16 and 21); the story of Joseph is told in two ways: he is taken away by Midianites, with Reuben's help, or by Ishmaelites, with Judah's (37:18—35), and there are similar discrepancies throughout the rest of the narrative. These are but a few of the duplications that point to a variety of source material.

Added to this phenomenon is that of the **variety of c language and style**. The most striking instance of this is doubtless in the titles that are used for God, in the **different usage between Elohim (God) and Yahweh** (usually rendered LORD in our English Bibles). In the first creation story God is called *Elohim*, in the second *Yahweh-Elohim*, and simply *Yahweh* in ch 4 which follows. In the story of Abraham and Hagar of ch 16 God is called *Yahweh*; in the other story of ch 21 he is called *Elohim*. The same ambivalence appears throughout the combined story of the flood. One series of texts is quite schematic and monotonous in its use of formulas, showing an affection for numbers and technical terms. It also tends to be consciously theological, avoiding anthropomorphisms and stressing the transcendence of God. Another is refreshingly ingenuous in its expressions, marked with a vivacity of style that betrays the true story-teller's art. Still another series stands somewhere in between the first two extremes and has proper characteristics of its own.

It is from the patterns which these textual phenomena **d** form, what de Vaux has called their 'constants', that

143d the critics have been able through painstaking research to discern the sources that have gone to make up Gn. There is now a fairly general agreement that these sources are basically three—a fourth, the 'D' of the critics, appears elsewhere in the Pent, but has not entered into Gn. Known variously throughout the history of Pentateuchal criticism, since the 19th cent. the three sources have been called 'J' (for *Jahwist* or Yahwist), 'E' (for *Elohist*), and 'P' (for *Priesterschrift* or 'priestly writing'). It was formerly the tendency to distinguish further subsidiary sources (J_1, J_2, J_3, etc), but though it is obvious that the three major sources have themselves made use of more ancient material of various kinds, whether written or orally transmitted, today there is no claim that the necessary 'constants' can be found to distinguish continued sources in the proper sense of the word. The single noteworthy exception to this rule in modern criticism is that of Otto Eissfeldt, who adds a source 'L' (for *Laienquelle* or 'lay source') which he considers to be an older stratum in the material assigned to 'J'. On the relative ages acribed to those sources as *written* components of the Pentateuch, see § 94. The properties, preoccupations, and specific theology of the several sources as these affect Gn will be dealt with in their place in the commentary.

e Our concern with Gn is mainly and pre-eminently with the text in its final form; it is in this form that the text is canonical and inspired, given to the Church as such and as such presented by the Church to us. It is no less obvious, however, that the distinction of the final author's sources is a necessary step in interpreting his meaning. In every case, it is the *use* to which the author put his source material that is the key to what he intended to communicate as an inspired writer. We cannot properly understand this until we have understood the sources themselves. The author's meaning may at times be as apparent in what he has omitted or combined or changed as in what he has left unaltered. Furthermore, it is certainly of more than passing interest for the understanding of Gn to recognize that in the ancient Yahwistic source that has served as the framework for the finished work of Gn. there was already contained the substance of what is now in the canonical book, both as to content and as to its theology of history. As a written work, the Yahwistic source may be as early as the time of Solomon, in the 10th cent. B.C. Since it in turn gives evidence of the long oral and written transmission that made it possible, our examination of the sources of Gn is not irrelevant to its historical as well as to its religious character. What really becomes of less relevance in this connection is the time of the final compilation of the book.

144a Genesis and History—Gn is **presented by its author as a history**, not simply as a collection of religious truths in narrative form. This is an important fact for us to bear in mind. We are not being faithful to the author's intent when we ignore his historical purpose or attempt to allegorize Gn to extract from it transcendent religious teaching that no longer has a reference to historical fact. For the author of Gn history was the record of the deeds of God, the sphere in which he had revealed himself to man: the writing of history was, therefore, the only theology he knew. A recognition of the author's historical purpose must be our first principle of the interpretation of Gn, a principle that applies, even though in different ways, to the history of origins in Gn 1–11 as well as to the Patriarchal History.

It is no withdrawal from this principle, however, to remind ourselves that the concept of history is not a univocal one, whether in the abstract or in Gn itself. **144** We must, in the first place, judge the history of Gn by the **historical standards that were recognized by its author** rather than by our own. Likewise, we must bear in mind that not all the elements in the history of Gn as the author found them in his sources and as he intended to use them have an equal historical value. As the Biblical Commission pointed out in their letter to Cardinal Suhard (1948), *the very notion of historical truth itself* possessed by the ancient biblical authors ('et leur notion même de la vérité historique') is one of the factors that must be weighed in our determination of their inspired judgements and thus of their literal meaning in their writings.

It has become common in biblical circles to use **b** the German term **Heilsgeschichte** to apply to biblical history in general. Unfortunately, there is no equivalent English expression for this word that so aptly epitomizes the Bible's historical conception. *Geschichte*, 'history', in the first place, is not precisely the same as *Historie*: while the latter term refers to the concept of documented, statistical history, the historical positivism or 'scientific' history that is scarcely two centuries old, the former is **the history that is actually the possession of the ordinary man**. The ideal of *Historie* is, as it was expressed by the 19th cent. positivists, to reconstruct the past *wie es eigentlich gewesen*, 'as it actually happened', in exact statistical detail by the sifting of sources, rigorously excluding from the reconstruction any interpretation of its events or any selection of them on the basis of their relative worth. Whether this ideal ever was or is fully achieved in practice, may be questioned. It is, nevertheless, what we think of today in the abstract as 'history', despite the fact that it obviously escapes the control of anyone but the academic historian working with primary sources. The history that we actually know is *Geschichte*, that is, our communication through popular transmission with the ethos and meaning of our past, whether of our religion, our nation, or even of our family or local community. **Geschichte is concerned with transmitting significance in preference to statistical detail**. This is the biblical idea of history, and it would obviously be improper to measure this idea against another historical ideal that it did not share and that was unknown to it.

Biblical history is a *Geschichte* devoted to and **c** conditioned by *das Heil*, i.e., salvation, redemption, the beneficent dispensation and economy of God. This is the formality under which it viewed the history of the people of God. It should be evident how imperfectly the English 'salvation history' captures the idea of *Heilsgeschichte*.

If all biblical history is *Heilsgeschichte*, this is nevertheless a form that is subject to many variations. Biblical history is as much subject to variations as any other, depending on the nature of the subject with which it is dealing, the character and content of the sources used, and the author's specific purposes in writing his history. It is on the basis of these considerations that we must distinguish the different kinds of history that we find in Gn.

The Patriarchal History can be called a **tribal, d** or perhaps better, a **family history**. What is certain is that older opinions that regarded the stories of the Patriarchs as disguised myths or the fictitious accounts of eponymous ancestors can no longer be critically held. While it is true that the narratives have picked up many popular traits in the centuries of their telling and bear witness to the art of their transmitters, there can be no doubt that they perform the proper function of history, to

144d put us in authentic contact with the past. The geographical and political data supposed in this history agree substantially with what archaeology and the recovery of Ancient Near E texts have told us of this era. Many of the social and legal customs observed by the Patriarchs are in keeping with what we know from independent sources to have been practised in those days—which were not known to the Israelite authors who handed on this history, and which, therefore, could not be composed by them. The record of the patriarchal migrations and activities can be fitted reasonably into the larger history of the other ancient peoples of the Near E. The Patriarchal History has awaited the modern age of scientific archaeology, when the exact reconstruction of vanished cultures and societies is now possible, for the proof of its remarkable and tenacious memory of the past. 'Abraham, Isaac, and Jacob no longer seem isolated figures, much less reflections of later Israelite history; they now appear as true children of their age, bearing the same names, moving about over the same territory, visiting the same towns (especially Harran and Nahor), practising the same customs as their contemporaries. In other words, the patriarchal narratives have a historical nucleus throughout, though it is likely that long oral transmission of the original poems and later prose sagas which underlie the present text of Gn has considerably refracted the original events. This process of handing down the ancient tradition by word of mouth from generation to generation led to the omission of many details which would have interested a modern historian, but it also brought about a recasting of tradition in more dramatic form, emphasizing its religious and pedagogical values. Our gain is thus far greater than any possible loss' (Albright, *Archaeology of Palestine* 236f).

e From what has been said already, some of the peculiarities of the history of Gn that differentiate it sharply from modern history will be obvious to the reader and ought to cause him no difficulty. He should not be surprised, for example, to find **anachronisms** in matters of geographic or historic detail. In ch 26 Abimelech, the king of Gerar, and his people are called Philistines, though it appears that the Philistines did not inhabit this region until Israelite times, centuries later. (For a contrary view, see A. Pohl, *Historia VT* 72–75.) This is precisely the kind of anachronism that is proper to popular history, as when we commonly say that Caesar invaded England or that Columbus discovered America. What is surprising in Gn is that there is relatively so little of this anachronistic view of the past, and that the ancient traditions employed by the author have retained so much of the authentic colouring of their origins.

f **Folk etymologies** are likewise a common characteristic of popular literature. In Gn they are particularly evident in the J tradition. The Semites set great store by the significance of names, not the philological significance but the significance which the name had acquired in some connection that had meaning for them. Throughout Gn the names of persons or places are continually related to the events told about them through the use of folk etymologies. Thus in 17:5 the change of Abram's name to Abraham, which historically was doubtless due to a dialectical change, is related by the author to the new life which Abraham began in the covenant with Yahweh, and the new name is explained by the title *'ab-hāmôn*, 'father of a multitude', which Abraham was to enjoy in virtue of the covenant. The morphological explanation of this change of spelling would have held no interest for the author of Gn.

g The **genealogies** of Gn are intended to show the relationships of peoples (not necessarily blood relationships) and to connect together various parts of the story **144g** rather than to record historical generations. In place of individuals, whose names were generally unknown, the names of tribes or their geographical locations were frequently substituted. Intervening generations, furthermore, might be simply subsumed in a single 'he begot' or 'she bore'. Thus with the children of Keturah in 25:1–4, we have the names of places, e.g., Midian, Sheba, and of peoples, e.g., Asshurim, with whom the Israelites recognized relationship and which they therefore derived by a genealogy from Abraham.

Anthropomorphisms are the rugged and familiar **h** ways of speaking about God which are particularly noteworthy in the J tradition but also are common to all the traditions. Actually, anthropomorphisms are virtually a necessity if one is to speak of a personal God at all in terminology other than the purely metaphysical. We use anthropomorphisms as does Gn; but they are likely to be different anthropomorphisms. 'In reality, the statement that "God is spirit" (Jn 4:24) is no less anthropomorphic than "the just shall behold his face" (Ps 11:7). The difference is merely that the one uses a spiritual part of man, the other a physical, as a *primum analogatum* for expressing a truth about God. In each case a word and a concept are used which originate in analysis of man himself; they necessarily combine similarity with dissimilarity when they are predicated of God. In other words, they are both analogies' (R.A.F. MacKenzie, 'The Divine Soliloquies in Genesis' *CBQ* 17 (1955) 158). In Gn God is found walking in the garden of Eden in the cool of the evening (3:8), he is grieved to the heart (6:6), takes counsel before acting (11:7), is entertained with food and drink in Abraham's tent and bargains with him for the city of Sodom (chh 18—19), etc. These are bold anthropomorphisms, taken straight from the familiar life of man, and there should be no difficulty in recognizing that they are not straight historical reporting. These popular accounts are the product of a people of rudimentary theology, though not of a rudimentary knowledge of God. With all their naïveté and simplicity, they hold up an image of God that is essentially true.

The **chronology** used throughout Gn is not historical **145a** but symbolical and theological. An integral part of this chronology is found in **the ages assigned the Patriarchs** and especially the fantastic ages attributed to the generations before the time of Abraham. The patriarchal traditions arose in a milieu that made no attempt to relate this family history to contemporary world affairs or to preserve an accurate relative chronology among the various elements of the traditions. The stories about the Patriarchs have been arranged with an eye more to their topical content than to their relative chronology. Since a chronology of the patriarchal era was lacking to the author of Gn, and he had even less a possibility of imagining the course of the ages that had preceded patriarchal times, he made use of the symbolic chronology found in the P tradition. The fact that the chronology of P has, in the final editing of Gn, been combined with the other traditions that did not know of it, has given rise to the well-known improbabilities of the text relative to the ages of the persons involved—Sarah a woman 'beautiful to behold' in chh 12 (J) and 20 (E), capable of arousing the passions of the Pharaoh and the king of Gerar, when according to the P chronology she would have been, respectively, 65 and 90 years old; Hagar carrying about the infant Ishmael in her arms (21:9—21 E) who, according to previous indications (16:3 P; 21:5 P), would have been about 16 years old; etc. The chronology of P possesses, in part, a theological symbolism, but appears to have at times no

145a justification other than its author's interest in arranging numbers schematically. The following analysis of the P chronology is that of Johannes Schildenberger, as published in his *Vom Geheimnis des Gotteswortes* and elsewhere.

b The chronology begins with the two series of the generations of the 'patriarchs' before and after the flood, in chh 5 and 11:10—26:

	1. Adam	2. Seth	3. Enosh	4. Kenan
Year at begetting	130	105	90	70
Rest of life	800	807	815	840
Total years	930	912	905	910

	5. Mahalalel	6. Jared	7. Enoch	8. Methuselah	9. Lamech	10. Noah
	65	162	65	187	182	500
	830	800	300	782	595	450
	895	962	365	969	777	950

	1. Shem	2. Arpach- shad	3. Shelah	4. Eber
Year at begetting	100	35	30	34
Rest of life	500	403	403	430

	5. Peleg	6. Reu	7. Serug	8. Nahor	9. Terah
	30	32	30	29	70
	209	207	200	119	135

The number 365, taken from the solar year, occurs three times in the P chronology of Gn: Abraham comes into Canaan in his 75th year, 365 years after Shem begot Arpachshad, therefore one age since the flood. By this numerical device the author signifies that a new epoch in world history has begun with Abraham. Enoch's lifespan is 365 years: one age of brightness in an evil generation. Finally, in P the flood lasts 365 days, the separation between the two ages begun by Adam and Shem respectively.

The genealogy of ch 5 falls into two halves. In the first half the year of each generation at the begetting of the following is always divisible by 5 and descends in multiples of 5 from 130 to 65, that is, to half the first. Beginning the second half of the list, Jared's age is 32 more than Adam's, or Adam's age plus half the 65 of the preceding and the following generation. Thus Jared is related to the preceding series and to the following most important person in the series, Enoch, who appears in the symbolic seventh place. Enoch has been made the centre of the whole list. In his lifespan of 365 years, 65 years was a proportionate age for begetting a new generation; and to begin the list, this number was simply doubled for Adam, the first father. After Enoch the numbers are again related in multiples of 5: between Jared and Methuselah is a difference of 25 years, between Jared and Lamech a difference of 20. The product of these is 500, the year of Noah. Jared, who begins the second half of the list, has like Adam, who begins the first half, 800 years of life after begetting the following generation.

c The list of ch 11 begins with 100 years, 30 less than Adam's. This is also the age of Abraham at the birth of Isaac, and thus the line of Shem is related both to the **145c** Sethites and to the new era begun by Abraham. The 30 years' minus that separates Shem's age from Adam's is the characteristic of this list: it turns up again with Shelah, Peleg and Serug. Terah's age is 70, twice that of Arpachshad. All the numbers divisible by 10 when added together (100 + 30 + 30 + 30 + 70) equal twice the age of Adam; all the numbers not divisible by 10 when added together (35 + 34 + 32 + 29) equal the age of Adam. Then, as already noted, there are 365 years from Arpachshad's begetting till the entrance of Abraham in Canaan.

Abraham is 75 when he comes to Canaan, 100 at Isaac's birth, and has a total lifespan of 175 years. The 75 years before his call by Yahweh correspond to the 75 after the birth of the promised Isaac; thus for 100 years, a 'generation' (Gn 15:13, 16), his life in Canaan consecrates it for his descendants (even as the J tradition represents him consecrating the shrines of Canaan). Israel was to be in Egypt 430 years (Ex 12:40): the Patriarchs are in Canaan just half that time, 215 years. The temple of Solomon, finally, comes 480 years after the Exodus from Egypt (1 (3) Kgs 6:1), that is, 12 man-ages of 40 years (as in Jg 3:11; 4:3; 5:31, etc), or 1200 years after the birth of Abraham (cf Gn 21:5; 25:26; 47:9; Ex 12:40; 2 (4) Kgs 6:1).

Joseph lives 110 years (Gn 50:26): it is known from **d** Egyptian sources that this was considered an ideal, full life. Similarly, Joseph's descendant Joshua has 110 years: through Joseph the Israelites descended into Egypt, and through Joshua they entered into Canaan. The same kind of relation surrounds Moses: Levi, the ancestor of Moses's tribe, and Amram, Moses's father, both live 137 years, ten years less than Jacob, the ancestor of them both. Kohath, the second son of Levi through whom Moses was descended, lived 4 years less than Levi (Ex 6:18). The differences of 10 and 4 are both even numbers; similarly, Jacob's age is the product of 2 × 70 with an added 7 years. Moses lives 120 years, a number certainly related to the 12 tribes, which is divided into three periods of 40 (man-ages): the first spent in Egypt, the second in preparing to lead his people, the third in the wilderness. His 'early' death is a punishment (Nm 20:12, etc): had he lived the 137 years of his father and of Levi, he would have spent 17 years (10 + 7) in Canaan just as Jacob spent 17 years in Egypt (Gn 47:9.28). The number 17 is a special characteristic of the patriarchal ages. Note the schematism:

Abraham 175 = 7 × (5 × 5)   7 + 5 + 5 = 17
Isaac   180 = 5 × (6 × 6)   5 + 6 + 6 = 17
Jacob   147 = 3 × (7 × 7)   3 + 7 + 7 = 17

In ch 5 the declining total lifespans bring out **e** that death, or the shortening of life, is the punishment of sin. After Adam all the ages are smaller except those of Jared, Methuselah, and Noah and all are said to have died except Enoch. Enoch, the just man, is the great exception, for 'righteousness is immortal' (Wis 1:15). Enoch's justice accounts for the elevated ages of his father and son, and Noah too has a longer life, for he also is just. Methuselah dies in the year of the beginning of the flood; the flood begins on the 17th day of the second month of Noah's 600th year, and all of Methuselah's dates (187, 782, 969) are multiples of 17; thus Methuselah connects the flood with Enoch, and shows that the justice of the latter had now run its course. Jared's age, as just noted, is longer because the father of a just man must also have been just; but on the other hand Lamech, the father of the just Noah is given a highly symbolic age of 777, while his other years (182,

145e 595) are also multiples of 7. He died five years before the flood, lived with Adam 56 years (8 × 7), with Seth 168 years (24 × 7), with Enosh 266 years (38 × 7), with Kenan 361 years (51 × 7 + 4), with Mahalalel 416 years (59 × 7 + 3), with Jared 548 years (78 × 7 + 2) and with Enoch 113 years (16 × 7 + 1). Lamech explains Noah's name by folk etymology as referring to the Sabbath rest (Gn 5:29, probably J); correspondingly, the flood ends at the beginning of Noah's 601st year, i.e., the seventh century of his life, and Noah lives an additional 350 years, i.e., seven jubilee periods (50 years marks the jubilee or special Sabbath year). Seven is the 'sacred' number and 10 is the number of completeness; their sum is the 17 that is so prominent in these lists.

f The chronology allows, as did the Babylonian flood traditions, for 10 generations before the flood and 10 after it: Abraham is the 10th generation after the flood, corresponding to Noah in the first genealogy. The fantastic ages are also part of the Babylonian pattern, where they are reckoned in the tens of thousands in contrast to the comparatively modest figures of Gn, which never exceed 1000. There was doubtless a theological symbolism involved here, since a thousand years was associated in the Hebrew mind with divine existence (Dt 7:9; 1 Chr 16:15; Ps 90 (89):4), and thus denied to any man. When Adam has begotten the following generation, he lives another 800 years; this number is increased by 7 (the number of the week) for the next generation; then by 15 (a half-month); then by 40 (an indefinite time, cf Gn 7:12; Ex 24:18; Nm 14:33); finally by 30 (a month), and the next generation is of Jared, again with 800, who begins the second half of the list, the symbolism of whose numbers we have seen above.

There are unquestionably many other symbolisms and interrelations of these numbers that still escape us. That they were always recognized as symbolic and not historical seems to be evidenced by the freedom with which they were handled in Sam Pent and LXX. While the Samaritan text tends to diminish the numbers, to make them more 'realistic', the LXX adds to them, assimilating one to another.

146a What of the remainder of **the primaeval history**, the vast ages of man on earth covered by the passages from ch 4 down to the beginning of the Patriarchal History? If history is the remembered past, to what extent can the sources used in Gn be said to have preserved authentic recollections? Formerly, of course, no difficulty was felt in imagining an unbroken tradition that could easily have preserved such recollections in view of the biblical chronology. As Pascal wrote in the 17th cent.: 'Shem who saw Lamech, who saw Adam, at least saw Abraham, who saw Jacob, who saw those who beheld Moses.' If Adam died in the year of creation 930, Methuselah was already 56 years old, and when Methuselah died in the year 1656, Noah was 600 years of age; Noah in turn, survived Abraham's birth by 60 years. However, as we have just seen, the chronology of Gn does not correspond to historical reality. Furthermore, despite the extraordinary ages that Gn assigned to the generations which it used to bridge the gap between creation and the historical times of Abraham, we now know that the age of man on earth is far vaster than Genesis could possibly have imagined. The age of man is to be reckoned not in thousands of years, but in hundreds of thousands; the oldest fossil remains of man may go back as far as a million years. It obviously surpasses belief that merely human tradition could span this vast age with any accurate information.

Could it be, then, that God provided miraculously **146b** for the accurate transmission of such reliable information, or that he revealed it to the author of Gn? The possibility, of course, no believer in revealed religion would deny. All the evidence, however, indicates that he did nothing of the kind. The names that we encounter in these chh are all Hebrew, and Heb. is a relatively late language in the development of human cultures. The first men on earth were certainly not Hebrews, nor were they even Semites. The various inventions that are mentioned, such as agriculture, the developments of the arts and crafts, such as metalworking, the founding of cities,—all these, which Gn puts at the very beginnings of mankind, we know to have been fairly recent accomplishments of the human race when measured against its total lifespan. It does not appear possible, in other words, to effect a strict concordism between the data of Gn and what scientific archaeology and anthropology have made known to us concerning human prehistory.

This certainly does not mean that there is no **c** history of any kind in these chh. As Chaine wrote, *Genèse* 99f, 'There remain certain recollections: the pastoral life had not always existed; there had been a period when men did not know music or use metals. Since bronze is mentioned before iron (4:22), perhaps it was recalled that the former had been the first in use. The author accounts for the principal inventions that existed in his time. "A strict history was impossible", as Lagrange observed, "yet it was necessary to bring out the continuous chain that unites the history of salvation. The Bible avoids absurd and unfitting stories. . . . It even refrains from unrelated stories. It attaches itself to the tangible, to the then existing inventions, speaks of their origin and progress, and leaves them in a twilight which does not even pretend to be a documented history" (*La méthode historique* 212f)'. Certain stories, such as that of the flood, certainly go back to some factual event, even though the details could not be recovered today on the basis of scientific history. The homogeneity and continuity of the narrative is artificial; it is a composite of heterogeneous materials. But it is a sober reconstruction, dominated by an historical sense. There is nothing in it that borders on the fantastic, frivolous tales with which other ancient peoples supplied for their ignorance of the past. Unlike the origins-myths of other ancient peoples, Gn frankly makes Israel a late-comer, lost among the countless families that make up world history. This realism is otherwise unheard of in antiquity.

As the Biblical Commission wrote in the *Letter to* **d** *Cardinal Suhard*, in 1948, 'These literary forms do not correspond to any of our classical categories and cannot be judged in the light of the Greco-Latin or modern literary types. It is therefore impossible to deny or affirm their historicity as a whole without unduly applying to them norms of a literary type under which they cannot be classed. If it is agreed not to see in these chapters history in the classical and modern sense, it must be admitted also that known scientific facts do not allow a *positive* solution of all the problems which they present. . . . To declare a priori that these narratives do not contain history in the modern sense of the word might easily be understood to mean that they do not contain history in any sense, whereas they relate in simple and figurative language, adapted to the understanding of mankind at a lower stage of development, the fundamental truths underlying the divine scheme of salvation, as well as a popular description of the origins of the human race and of the chosen people. In the meantime it is necessary to practise patience which is part of prudence and the wisdom of life.'

146e Much of what has been said applies to the narrative of **creation and the fall of man, Gn 1–3**. Certainly these are not accounts that depend even remotely on eyewitnesses. Some of the elements in these narratives can be duplicated in the creation-myths of other Near-Eastern peoples, though in Gn they have been assimilated thoroughly into formulations that are completely and originally Israelite in inspiration, cf § 152*d*. Thus Gn 1 is a word picture contrived in order to affirm the creation of the visible universe by one supreme God. It is in no sense a scientific or historical account of the actual course of events in the beginning of time but is adapted to the mentality of a primitive people and embodies a number of contemporary ideas in its description of the visible world. Here and in the two succeeding chh we have an account of the beginnings of the human race and the origin of sin. Similar accounts in the Babylonian myths have often been pointed out but there is no close likeness. Certainly, there is Oriental imagery in plenty, which the Hebrews shared with their neighbours, but here it is purified and serves merely as a vesture for the religious teaching far surpassing anything contained in the traditions of other nations, cf R. de Vaux, *Genèse*, BJ, on ch 2. The account in Gn 3 is evidently intended to provide an explanation of the origin of sin and the consequences for the human race. De Vaux suggests that Gn is concerned with the transmission of the punishment rather than the guilt. At the same time however, it should be added that Gn underlines the moral deterioration of the posterity of Adam and at least hints at a parental responsibility in this respect on the part of our first parents. Apart from the fact that Gn 3 belongs to the oldest stratum of tradition in the Pent there is little to guide us in tracing the account further back towards its origin, cf § 153*a*, *b*.

147a **The Theology of Genesis** is the greatest gift that this great book has to give us. It will be the function of the commentary to bring out this rich theology, cf § 106*f*. It is, in fact, impossible to interpret Gn accurately without recognizing the priority of its author's theology in every line of its narrative. We cannot repeat too often that history to the author *was* theology, the means whereby God had revealed himself to man, making known to him his attributes and his sovereign will. The history had to be true as the condition of a true theology, but history that had no theological import was of no concern to the author. It would not have occurred to him to ask, for example, as a modern reader will ask, who was the wife of Cain. His use of the story of Cain and Abel had nothing to do with speculations on how the human race was propagated; rather, he intended to show that the sin begun by Adam and Eve was continued in their descendants and that this fact was of significance to all mankind in its relationship to God. When he recalled the story of the flood he was not disturbed by the conflicts of detail that were in the two Israelite versions of the story that he combined, nor did he wonder about any of what we might be tempted to consider the historical problems that are connected with it. He told the story to show how a provident God and not chance rules the universe, and that this God is equally just and merciful. Even the Patriarchal History, whose authentic historical colouring means so much to the modern critical reader, was not included by the author simply for its historical reliability, which, for that matter, he had no way of checking. The Patriarchal History is the history of God's grace.

b That the God of Gn is the God of Israel, that Gn is concerned with Israel's ancestors, and that Israel and its privileged position in the plans of God are the *Leitmotiv* of the history of Gn, do not in any way lessen its transcendent and perennial value as a theological **147b** work. It has been said that the story of Israel is that of mankind itself. This is true, not merely in the sense that the universal religion of Christianity is the fulfilment and realization of the Israel of the OT. It is true as well because the history of Israel mirrors the activity of the God of the universe. What God did with Israel, 'the light to the nations', is the pattern of his salvific will for all mankind. Alike in their response to divine grace and in their rejection of it, in their following out of high aspirations and in their betrayal of divinely revealed human destiny, the people of Israel show forth the relation of man to his God, the telling of which is theology.

1:1–11:26 THE BOOK OF ORIGINS

1:1–2:4a The Priestly Story of Creation—In the **148a** beginning of all things, God creates the heavens and the earth, which as yet lacks form, covered over by a watery chaos. Over the waters moves the spirit of God, his creative power, ready to bring forth order and life, 1–2. After this summary statement, the creation of the visible universe in its present form is described as a work of six days, the first three days being concerned with the determination of the various areas or regions of the universe, the other three with the peopling or adornment of these regions (2:1 *ṣebā'ām*, 'their host').

The first day sees the creation of light and the separation of light from darkness, 3–5. On the second day the solid vault of the heavens is raised above the earth to separate the waters on the earth from those which are above the vault and which come down upon the earth through openings in the vault as the seasonal rains, 6–8. The work of the third day is to collect the waters of the earth into seas and to bring forth the dry land. Plant life is brought forth on the land, 9–13. On the fourth day the heavenly lights are created and placed in the heavens, 14–19. The work of the fifth day is the creation of fish and birds, corresponding to the waters and the airy heaven of the second day, 20–23. On the sixth day animal life is created to inhabit the dry land educed on the third day. Lastly, man is created in the image and likeness of God and given dominion over the earth. The plant life is also given him as his food, 24–31. On the seventh day, the Sabbath, God rests from all his labours and sanctifies this day as the day of rest for man, 2:1–4*a*.

'That the first two chapters of Gn reproduce two **b** distinct accounts of creation and not a single one in which the second part would be only the necessary complement of the first, is indicated not only by the difference in divine names, Yahweh and Elohim, but also by many divergences in content and form: the succession of events is quite different in 1:1–2:4*a* and 2:4*b*–25; the order of creation is quite different: in the first the world with its constitutive elements, earth, sea, firmament, celestial bodies, fish, birds, and animals, exist before the appearance of man and women; in the second, on an earth dry from the first there is no plant before the formation of man: after him, God forms the trees, the animals, and, last of all, woman. While Elohim in the first chapter speaks and acts as the sovereign master of all things whose word is creative and whose orders are immediately executed, Yahweh Elohim of the second chapter works with his hands to realize his designs, shapes man and the animals out of earth, plants trees, takes a rib from man's side to make woman, fashions tunics of skin: such an incompatibility in the representation of divinity appears incompatible with literary unity. Furthermore, we have confirmation

148b in the use of different expressions to denote the same things, and especially the same action of God, rendered in the first account by the verb *bārā'*, create, *'āśâ*, make, and in the second by *yāṣar*, fashion; not to speak of the rhythm produced by the repetition of identical formulas in the first chapter, which does not appear at all in the second' (Clamer, *Genèse* 103).

c The **schematism** of the Priestly narrative is evident, and must be taken into account in evaluating the artistic nature of the literary form adopted by the author. There is, first of all, the balance of the six days already observed in part: (*see table at foot of page.*)

We have noted the correspondence that IV-V-VI have to I-II-III, the *opus ornatus* corresponding to the *opus distinctionis*, as was already remarked by the Fathers, We note also the special correspondence that VI has to III: the creation of the animals to inhabit the dry land, on the one hand, and of man to feed on plant life on the other. A certain imbalance, however, is recognized in this last correspondence, and this has led some to postulate a pre-existence of the six-days' outline in which there was originally a single work assigned to each day. Originally, the creation of man *and* the animals was the work of the sixth day, corresponding to the eduction of the dry land only on the third day. In order to give added prominence to man, his creation was first separated from that of the other animals by the P author. Then, to restore the balance, at least in part, an additonal work was assigned to the third day and this creation was in turn related to man. See A. Deimel, *'Enuma eliš' und Hexaëmeron*, 1934, 78ff.

d The schematism has even more subtle variations when the work of the six days is examined according to the various recurring elements that run throughout the entire narrative. These elements, which are seven, may be determined by the following formulas:

a—introductory: 'And God said . . .' (*wayyō'mer'elōhîm*)

b — the creative word: 'Let there be . . .' (jussive of the verb)

c — fulfilment of the word: 'And there was . . .' (indicativo of the verb)

d — a description of the act of creation in question

e — a name-giving or blessing: 'And he called . . . blessed . . .'

f — the divine commendation: 'And he saw that it was good' (*wayyare' kî-ṭôb*)

g — the concluding formula: 'And there was evening and morning, the—day.'

e When these elements are inspected in relation to each of the six days, the following additonal symmetry is revealed:

I a–b–c–f–d–e–g   a–b–c–d–f–g   IV
II a–b–d–c–e–g   a–b–d–f–e–g   V
III a–b–c–e–f   a–b–c–d–f   VI
    a–b–c–d–f–g   a–b–d–e–c–f–g

(For the proper appreciation of this symmetry, it should be observed that LXX has altered the order of II to abcdeg and has added to that of V to make abcdfeg; LXX

rather than MT is followed in some modern translations.) **148e** We find that there are seven c's, d's and f's, that is, seven fulfilments of God's creative word, seven descriptions of creative act, and seven declarations of the divine satisfaction with creation. Furthermore, throughout 1:1—2:4a the verb *bārā'*, create, appears in various forms exactly seven times; the divine name Elohim occurs 35 times (5 × 7); and the total number of Heb. sentences in the passage is 49 (7 × 7), or, with the inclusion of 2:4a, 50. If the twice repeated *wayyō'mer 'elōhîm* of 1:28.29 are added to the computation above, we find that God has been directly quoted 10 times, in the number of completeness. The number three is also featured: besides the pairing of three work-days, the formula *wayyiqrā'*, 'and he called', occurs three times in the first series, and in the second series together with the instance in 2:3, *wayebārek*, 'and he blessed', occurs three times. The verb *bārā'* is also used, exceptionally, three times in relating the creation of man. See Schildenberger, 'Der Eingang zur Heilsgeschichte', Benediktinische Monatschrift, 28 (1952), 193—204, 371—88.

With this artistic framework in mind, we may proceed **f** to the interpretation of the text. **1.** 'In the beginning': *berē'šit* may be taken as an absolute, thus the traditional translation, 'In the beginning God created'; or as a construct introducing a temporal clause, whereby the main verb would appear only in 3: thus Moffat's translation: 'When God began to form the universe, the earth was void and vacant. . . . God said, "Let there be light!"' This second translation is syntactically justifiable, and the MT punctuation of *bārā'* (rather than *berō'*) is no argument against it, cf GK § 130*d*; Joüon § 129*p*. It has long been recognized as an alternative to the traditional rendering but was given added encouragement in modern times because of the supposed similarity of this opening verse to the *Enuma eliš*. Neither is the traditional rendering absolutely justified by appeal to the Jewish tradition inherent in the translations of LXX and Vg, since this could be due to later Jewish thought that insisted on an explicit *creatio ex nihilo* (cf 2 Mc 7:28). In favour of the traditional translation the following may be urged: (1) The remainder of the passage, consisting in short categorical sentences, would be strangely out of harmony with the proposed long introductory adverbial clause. (2) The author, who is a master theologian, would be guilty of a gross theological anticlimax unless 1 is considered as his initial assertion of God's creative activity, which is then spelled out in the following vv. This would be especially true, were his main assertion considered to be found in 2; but even the 'Let there be light!' of 3 is extremely weak if it follows a statement of unexplained coexistence of God and chaos. This is hardly credible for an author who insists throughout on the divine omnipotence. (3) The creation theology of P, in its terminology and conceptual background is that of the Second Isaiah. Gn 1:1 is to be related to such passages as Is 44:6; 48:12f, from which it is evident that it is of the very nature of God to be *first* outside the sphere of any other

I	II	III	IV	V	VI
separation of light and darkness = creation of *light* (good)	separation of *water* by the *firmament*	eduction of the *dry land*	creation of the *heavenly lights*	creation of *fish* and *birds*	creation of the *animals*
		creation of the *plants*			creation of *man*

D

148f being (cf W. Foerster, *ktizō*, in TWNT, 3, 1011). See C. Stuhlmueller, 'The Theology of Creation in Second Isaias', CBQ 21 (1959) 429—67. In this connexion, it may be added that the author, who certainly knew *Enuma eliš*, could very easily include *berē'šîṯ bārā'* in his polemic against the untranscendent gods of the Babylonian epic: in the beginning God already *is*, while **g** *everything* else comes to be. Nevertheless, we must still reckon with the possibility that *berē'šîṯ* is to be taken as in Moffat and that the author does not explicitly affirm (though neither does he deny) that the material out of which the universe is formed is also God's creation. We would hold as more probable that he does make this affirmation, and we would consequently give to *bārā'* the meaning of creation in the true sense. It is often remarked that this word does not mean of itself to create out of nothing; but it must be added with equal justice that neither *creare* nor *ktizein* nor any of the equivalent terms in our modern languages signifies of itself **creation** from nothing. This meaning depends on usage, on association, and on context. The word always appears in the OT with God as its subject; it can refer to the divine activity in history as well as in creation, but it is always reserved for the production of something that is essentially new in virtue of a sovereign exercise of power. While we hardly expect a treatise on *creatio ex nihilo sui et subiecti* from our Hebrew author, since this would demand a philosophical development to which his age had not attained and of which it felt no need, neither should we exaggerate the difficulty of the conception of true creation. Given the author's purpose and context, it is not at all extraordinary that he should have used this word to signify the coming into being of *all* things as the work of God's power. 'The heavens and the earth' means the cosmos, the universe; Hebrew lacked a single word for this idea. Thus this initial assertion of the author is a summary statement of what is to be explained *per partes* in the following verses. In view of the description found in 2, there is an hypothesis that this expression was originally 'the waters and the earth' (i.e., *mayim* rather than *samayim*: the more familiar combination would have displaced the less familiar), cf E. Vogt in Bib 34 (1953) 261f. This is certainly possible, but not too likely. If it should be correct, there could hardly remain any doubt that the interpretation of *berē'šîṯ bārā'* proposed above **h** is the correct one. The word that we translate **'God'** (*'elōhîm*) has the form of a plural in the MT vocalization. This is certainly not a vestige of polytheism in Israelite usage, though the word is also used in the OT as a true plural to refer to the gods of the Gentiles. Ordinarily it is constructed with a singular verb when it means the God of Israel. The plural form is usually explained as an intensification to stress the category of being rather than the individual, thus to mean 'godhead' rather than simply 'God'; certain analogies to such usage can be found in other Semitic languages. However, it is likely that the word is not a plural at all, but rather a singular that has preserved the ancient case ending in *m* found in other venerable words (*terāpîm, 'ûrîm, tummîm, sanwērîm*) that were similarly vocalized by the massoretes as plurals. See A. Jirku, 'Die Mination in den nordsemitischen Sprachen und einige Bezeichnungen der altisraelitischen Mantik', Bib 34 (1953) 78—80. The 'singular' form *'elôah* (mainly restricted to the book of Job) has the appearance of being late and may be a back-formation or an Aramaism.

149a 2. Objection has often been made to this v as interrupting the natural flow from 1 to 3 and as negating the majestic effect of 1. Although it might be conceded that

the author inserted this v into a previously existing **149** framework, however, there is no doubt that it forms an integral part of his teaching, and it cannot be separated from the rest of his theology. In the perspective of P, God stands between man and chaos; God has first saved man from this chaos through the work of creation, and at any time can allow it to return. In the P version of the flood story, the flood is caused by the return of this initial chaos. **'Waste and void'**: *tōhû wābōhû*, the combination ex- **b** presses the utmost in chaotic formlessness, as in Jer 4:23 describing the devastation of war. The creative work of God is not only to bring into being, but also to order. 'Darkness covered the abyss' is in parallel. Darkness to the ancients was the unknown, the abode of evil; in the same significance the word appears in the NT. The abyss (*tehôm*) is the watery chaos that was conceived to have engulfed the earth at the time of creation. As God's first creative word will dispel the darkness with his light, so the second will drive back the primordial waters. It is precisely in this v that we have the closest resemblance to the creation myth represented not only by *Enuma eliš* but also by the Canaanite literature certainly known to the author. Poetic allusions to the myth are frequent enough in the OT (cf Jb 3:8; 9:13; 26:13; Pss 74 (73):13f; 104 (103):26; Is 27:1), where it is used metaphorically much as parts of classical mythology have been used in the Christian liturgy. The allusions to the myth in Gn are slight: *tehôm* doubtless corresponds to the Tiamat of the Babylonian myth, the primordial monster of the chaos, and *bōhû* may be related to the Canaanite Baau, the goddess of night (cf Euseb., *Praep. evang.* 1, 9; PG 21, 76); but in Gn there is no trace of any mythical significance to these words, which rather were simply terms long associated with the common cosmological conceptions that Israel shared with its neighbours. Similarly, **c** 'the spirit of God' here doubtless is to be understood precisely as *God's* breath, conceived as the source of life and order. Cf Ps 33 (32):6: 'By the word of Yahweh the heavens were made; by the breath of his mouth all their host' (cf Ps 104 (103):30; Jb 33:4; 34:14; Sir 24:3); thus, too, in the NT Christ is called the 'life-giving spirit' of the supernatural life, 1 Cor 15:45. It is true, *rûaḥ* means also 'wind,' and the figure here does appear to be of God's breath as a mighty wind soaring over the abyss; but *'elōhîm* does not appear to be here or elsewhere in the OT *merely* a superlative epithet, cf D. W. Thomas, 'A Consideration of Some Unusual Ways of Expressing the Superlative in Hebrew,' VT 3 (1953) 209—24. *Soared* rather than *brooded* (the interpretation of the rabbis: the spirit of God incubating life) appears to be the meaning of *meraḥepet* on the basis of the Ugaritic evidence.

3. Light is the first and necessary work of creation, **d** the condition of life and order. In the Heb. conception, light had an existence of its own, not causally connected with the heavenly bodies, just as the heavenly bodies were independent of one another in their production of light (cf Jb 38:19). The formula, 'God said, "Let there be"'. . . And it was', expresses God's omnipotence and transcendence, in contrast to the creation myths in which creation was a laborious fashioning from divine material. 4. 'And God saw how good the light was' (Albright). Seven times it is reiterated that God's creation is a work of his goodness, directed by his good purposes, not like the adventitious and brainless production of *Enuma eliš*. Only the light is called good: darkness to the Hebrew was not merely the absence of light, but that which was opposed to it. 5. What God 'calls' by the same token he appoints and ordains; hence the equivalence of the parallel formula:

49d 'God blessed'. The Hebrew day began with the evening. Now that light has been created, there is the possibility of evening and morning, and therefore, as it were, God's creative work is renewed with each changing day, cf Ps 19(18):2f. In choosing to divide the work of creation over six days, the Priestly author glorifies the Mosaic Sabbath and represents God as the ideal worker who carries out his allotted tasks on six days and rests on the seventh. **6.** The 'firmament' is the vault of heaven, the sky, which the ancients conceived as a great hollow bowl inverted over the earth. The Heb. word *rāqîa'* means something hammered out, like shiny metal (cf Jb 37:18). This primitive idea of the sky as a firmament supporting the waters 'above the earth' is found also in the NT (2 Pt 3:10; Apoc 6:14). **9—10.** The dry earth was thought of as a flat disk floating on a subterranean sea, kept stationary by pillars (Jb 9:6). The waters of the sea washed the land on all sides and, through apertures in the land, formed its seas and rivers and springs. **11.** Three kinds of plant life are distinguished: the apparently seedless herb-life, the grains whose substance is their seed, and the fruits which enclose seed. Similarly, three types of animal life are distinguished in 24. **14—19.** Ancient man lived close to the stars, on which he depended to regulate his times, seasons, and directions. The temptation to divinize the stars was irresistible at times, even for Israelites. In *Enuma eliš* the stars are all represented as deities. The biblical author, however, goes out of his way to emphasize that they are mere creatures, fixed by God on the firmament and allotted their courses for man's use. Probably for the same reason he does not use the words 'sun' and 'moon', both of which were divine names in Semitic religions. Obviously no distinction is made between stars and planets, and the relative sizes are as they appear to the terrestrial eye. **20.** Probably LXX is to be preferred to MT in making both the swimming creatures and the flying creatures swarm from the sea (LXX *petomena = mᵉ'ôpēp* in place of *yᵉ'ôpēp?*). The two were associated by the ancients, who saw birds apparently rising from and descending into the sea at the horizon. God uses the sea as his instrument of creation here, and in 24 he uses the land to bring forth animal life, but man is made directly by him in his image and likeness. **21.** The sea monsters, which ancient man put at the extremities of the seas, which in the Gentile myths were represented as rivals to the gods, are merely among the creatures which God has made for his own purposes. **24.** 'Cattle and creeping things and beasts of the earth': that is, domestic animals, reptiles, and wild animals. We think of domestic animals as primitively savage; the Heb. thought the opposite: that animals originally domesticated had later become wild.

f **26—28.** That man is the crowning achievement of God's creation is brought out by (1) his creation put at the end, in the place of climax and emphasis; (2) his creation as a personal act of God, who makes him in his image and likeness; (3) the explicit statement of purpose in this creation; (4) the representation of divine counsel taken before creation. 'Let us make': with whom is the divine counsel taken? One thing is certain, that there is no 'relic of polytheism' in this carefully monotheistic narrative. **The plural** has been explained as a 'plural of majesty' as used in contemporary royal protocol (Chaine), though it is usually denied that Heb. possessed such a usage. God could be represented as taking counsel with the heavenly court of angels (Jb 1; 1 (3) Kgs 22:19f; Is 6); they, together with God himself, would form the *'elōhîm* is whose image and likeness man is made, as in Ps 8:6 (von Rad). There is, however, no indication of the heavenly court in this context. Is it not rather **to** express the fulness of God's being? 'If God uses the **149f** plural, this supposes that he possesses in himself such a fulness of being that he can deliberate with himself just as several persons deliberate among themselves' (Lagrange, 'Hexaméron', RB 5 [1896] 387). The Hebrew had no way of expressing analogy of being, but he certainly knew that there was a difference between God's existence and ours. 'Man' (*'ādām*) is a collective **g** noun possessing no plural. Mankind in general is meant, as is shown by the plural verb and pronominal object. **'Image and likeness':** the two words are not precisely synonyms. Image (*ṣelem*) is rather an exact reproduction, a duplicate, whereas likeness (*dᵉmût*) denotes only a resemblance. Man is said to have been created as one who is a 'copy' of God; yet this statement is immediately modified, since no one can be a precise image of the transcendent God. There is a superficial resemblance to this narrative in *Enuma eliš*, according to which man was made (partly) from the blood of a god. Here, however, a completely transcendent God freely creates man like to himself. In what, in the author's mind, did man's God-likeness consist? According to our psychology, we have no difficulty in finding the likeness to consist in man's spiritual nature, his intellect and will which separate him from the rest of animal creation and make him analogous to God. Our psychology, however, was not the author's, who did not have our conception of the rational soul and its spiritual faculties. It is to be noted that it is man himself, not merely his nature, that is in the image and likeness of God: the author's conception is existential rather than essential. The second part of 26 complements the first. Read with Syr., 'the cattle and all the beasts of the earth'. Man's dominion over creation makes him like God, who has dominion over all: he has a share in God's lordship, autonomous in his own sphere though subordinate to God's supreme rule. See D. T. Asselin, 'The Notion of Dominion in Genesis 1—3', CBQ 16 (1954) 277—94. The creation of man and woman together is the viewpoint of the Priestly creation story. There is no indication that the author thought of this first creation as of one man and one woman, but doubtless he did think of it in this way. **29—31.** All plant life is given as man's food, while to the animals the herbal life is given. After the flood (9:3 P) man will feed on flesh, though without blood. This represents what is developed far more extensively in the J narrative of chh 2—3, the ideal, paradisaical peace which reigned at the beginning of God's creation. The same idea is inherent in the divine satisfaction with all of creation in 31. Similar ideas of a lost golden age that had preceded the historical era in which flesh was eaten turn up in other literatures (cf Ovid, *Metamorphoses* 15, 96f).

2:2—3. With the evening and morning of the sixth day **h** (1:31), the seventh day has already begun, hence the 'seventh' of 2 (MT) is not to be changed to 'sixth' with LXX; the perspective of 'finished' is pluperfect (cf 17:22; 49:33). The word *šābat* means 'desist', not 'rest': this narrative continues to avoid all but the necessary anthropomorphisms to insist on the difference between the Creator and the created Man rests on this day which God has sanctified, it is God's gift to him to rest from his labours. God, however, does not rest, for he is always in act; he has only desisted from his work of creation: it is a completed, historical fact. There is, accordingly, no 'evening and morning' ascribed to the seventh day.

'The text about God's creation of the world has no **150a** author in our sense of the word.... To write out these 35 vv, Israel's faith required centuries of carefully

150a collected reflection. Such cosmological and theological knowledge, even that in the "table of nations", Gn, ch 10, was nourished in ancient Israel at the sanctuaries. The final form of the material as we have it may date from the exile, but its roots and beginnings certainly lie hidden in the bosom of the oldest Yahweh community' (von Rad, *Genesis* 61f). From what has been seen above, it should be evident how thoroughly Israelite, through and through, is this narrative, and that it has in its substance **nothing to do with the mythologies of other ancient peoples.** That the Israelites were familiar with the mythologies and could even make use of them in their poetry (Jb 7:12; Is 27:1, etc), we have seen. Both from the patriarchal traditions of the Mesopotamian origins of Israel and subsequently, the Israelites were accustomed to the ways in which the Gentiles thought of their gods and the connexion of the universe with the gods. Sharing with them a basically common culture, it was inevitable that they should at times use some of the same language and figures (this is much more the case with the Yahwistic than with the Priestly narrative). But it is no less true that this language and these figures have all been re-thought in the context of Israelitic religion and revelation, leaving no contact with mythopoeic thought. See *Bibliography* and also J. L. McKenzie, 'Mythological Allusions in Ezek 28:12—18', JBL 75 (1956) 322—27.

b At the turn of the present century, the *'Babel und Bibel'* school, in the first flush of enthusiasm sparked by the new cuneiform discoveries, attempted to find a **direct dependence of Gn on the Gentile myths,** specifically on the Babylonian (originally Sumerian) creation myth *Enuma elis* (ANET 60—72), which has been called 'the Babylonian Genesis'. Some of the undoubted superficial resemblances of Gn to *Enuma eliš* have been noted above in the commentary. Modern criticism that has survived the earlier extravagances, however, would agree that these resemblances need no further explanation than **the more or less common view of the cosmos** shared by *Enuma eliš* and Gn, which the one explained mytho-poetically, the other theologically. 'Doubtless there are some terms which obviously were common to ancient Oriental, cosmological thought; but even they are so theologically filtered in P that scarcely more than the word itself is left in common' (von Rad). It can also be added, as we have suggested before, that Gn may have multiplied the points of contact by its deliberate polemical attitude to the myth. In *Enuma eliš* there is no real beginning: before the gods there existed already Apsu, the personified abyss of sweet water, the male principle, and Mummu or Tiamat, the personified abyss of salt water, the female principle. There is, obviously, **nothing of a transcendent God, nothing of a true creation.** There is, rather, a theogony, of which there is no trace in Gn the divine principles of light and darkness, the upper and nether worlds, etc, emanate from the commingling of the primordial waters. Once the gods have been formed, their clamouring disturbs their divine progenitors. Apsu and Mummu (the latter now separate from Tiamat) resolve to slay them, but instead Nudimmud (or Ea, the earth-god) slays Apsu and forms from his body the underworld. Tiamat now engenders various monsters and sends them against the gods under the leadership of Kingu, a new husband whom she has brought forth. The gods elect Marduk (the god of Babylon) as their chief to do battle with Tiamat's array; Marduk drives a hard bargain, demanding and receiving supremacy among the gods (this was propaganda for the Babylonian temple). Marduk succeeds in killing Tiamat, after which he splits her body 'like a shellfish' into two

parts. The upper part he arches into the firmament, and **150** he posts guards to see that her waters do not escape. On the firmament Marduk fashions dwellings for the star-gods. From the lower part of Tiamat's body the dry earth is formed. Last of all, Marduk creates man, from the blood of Kingu (who is now executed) and the dust of the earth. Man is characterized as a 'savage', whose purpose is to work for the gods. This brief description exhausts the true parallels between *Enuma eliš* and Gn; we have passed over many of the other contrasts. It is scarcely necessary to underline the impossibility of the dependence of the lofty theology of Gn on the Babylonian myth.

The explanation that we have given above has tried **c** to recapture the thought processes of the original author and the information that was at his disposal: this is to interpret according to the author's **literary form,** cf § 133*f*. It recognizes the profound theology of Gn and its dependence on the historical revelation of Israel, but no less its author's lack of knowledge concerning the exact process through which the universe was actually formed through countless aeons, the true physical construction of the cosmos, and other such information as mankind has gained only in subsequent centuries through the painstaking study of the natural sciences.

Prompted by the laudable intention of defending the **d** inerrancy of the Scriptures, another form of interpretation, called **concordism,** appeared with the advent of modern scientific discovery. Concordism tried to safeguard inerrancy without turning its back on indubitable scientific facts by positing a harmony between biblical and scientific thought. That is to say, the six 'days' of Gn in this explanation, are actually the geological periods, perhaps of millions of years, during which the earth was gradually formed. The 'waters above the earth' are the mists in the clouds, and so forth. It should be obvious that concordism satisfies neither science nor Gn. There are not six geological periods, but four, and this is but one of the minor discordances between the scientific view of the universe and that of Gn. It is true that the Biblical Commission in 1909 made a gesture towards the concordists by stating that there was nothing contrary to faith in taking the word *yôm* to refer to an indefinite period of time. However, it is contrary to good Heb. grammar so to take it. Furthermore, the Commission on the same occasion rejected the basic premise of concordism in its affirmation that 'it was not the mind of the sacred author in the composition of the first chapter of Genesis to give scientific teaching about the internal constitution of visible things and the entire order of creation, but rather to communicate to his people a popular notion in accord with the current speech of the time and suited to the understanding and capacity of men'; see Dz 2127; EnchB 342.

Because of the obvious unreality of concordism, other expedients of interpretation have been devised, all, however, prompted by the same illusory intention: **restitutionalism, diluvianism, periodism,** as well as the **visionism** of F. Hummelauer, cf Ceuppens, *Historia Primaeva* 46—64. Graphic representations of the non-scientific Hebrew cosmology can be found in Schedl, *Urgeschichte und Alter Orient* 26; Vawter, *A Path Through Genesis* 40, etc.

The basic error that lies behind these sallies into **e** bad science and bad exegesis is a confusion as to the nature and the purposes of inspiration. The words of Gn 1 are all divinely inspired, but they are the **inspired words of an ancient Israelite author speaking to the men of his age as one of them and in their language.** For him to have anticipated the discoveries of modern science, divine revelation would have been a necessity, and there

50e is not the slightest indication that any such revelation was given, just as there is no reason that it should have been. The Holy Spirit, as Aug taught in this connection, had no purpose to instruct men in things which are of no significance for salvation (*De Genesi ad litteram* 2, 9, 20 (PL 34, 270); cited by Leo XIII in the encyclical *Prov. Deus* (Dz 1947; EnchB² 121)). The Fathers generally understood these principles very well. Augustine's norms of interpretation, for example, written down in *De Genesi ad litteram* 1, 18—19 (PL 34, 260f) over 1500 years ago, need little adjustment in principle for use today by a modern exegete. Concordism was a much later development, influenced by the 'fundamentalist' or 'literalistic' approach to the Scripture with its consequent confusion of the roles of revelation and inspiration.

51a **2:4b—25 Man and Woman in the Garden**—This passage is often called 'the second creation narrative of Gn', and in a sense it is, since at least the essential doctrine of creation as detailed in 1:1—2:4a is repeated here. It speedily becomes apparent, however, that the author is only secondarily interested in creation as such; his theme is *man*, and he treats other aspects of creation only insofar as they directly relate to man. To the extent that he does offer a creation narrative, he does so in a style and with a procedure quite different from those of the Priestly narrative. He begins with a representation of the earth at creation as a dry waste, as yet untilled by man (though a mist is said to have watered the ground), **4b—6.** God's first act was to shape man from the dust of the ground and to make him a living being by breathing into his nostrils the breath of life, **7.** Next God planted a garden where he placed the man whom he had formed, **8.** In the garden grew every type of tree whose fruit may be eaten, and especially the tree of life and the tree of the knowledge of good and evil, **9.** A parenthesis describes the garden in more detail, especially mentioning its wonderful water-supply, **10—14.** Once again it is stated that man was placed in the garden by God to till it and keep it, and to live from its fruits, **15.** The condition of man's continued existence in this ideal state, however, was that he should on no account eat of the tree of knowledge of good and evil, **16—17.** Man was as yet alone: there was no creature like to himself, **18.** This was only emphasized when God had created the various kinds of animal life and brought them all before man to be named; none of them was like man, **19—20.** Now, therefore, God made woman from man's side, and when man had seen woman, he recognized that at last there was another creature sharing his own nature, **21—23.** From this fact the narrator also concludes to the divine purpose in human marriage, **24.** In complete control of their lower natures, neither man nor woman experienced any shame at their nakedness, **25.** This last v sets the stage for ch 3, of which this story is really the introduction.

It is evident to what purpose the final author of Gn included both these accounts of creation. The theology of the Priestly narrative (P) we have already seen. If it contains much that is lacking in this Yahwistic narrative (J), it soon becomes plain what additional values this story contains which were not explicit in P.

b The literary form of J is ancient traditional narrative which has doubtless been formed from the threads of pre-existing stories reaching back to times far more remote. The unevennesses in the narrative have always encouraged literary critics to try to disengage the strands of the original components of the story. One of the more recent attempts is that of H. Haag (see 'Die Themata der Sündenfall-Geschichte' in Fs H. Junker, Trier, 1961, 101—10), who finds two originally distinct themes, (a)

that of the tree of life with man in the garden, and (b) **151b** that of the fall of man on earth through eating the tree of knowledge. He would distinguish the vv in chh 2—3 according to these themes, allowing for editorial vv (indicated in parentheses) that have connected the two parts, and also for later additions to the combined text (indicated in square brackets), as follows: (a) 2:8.9bα [10—14]; 3:(22a) 22b 23a(23b)24. (b) 2:4b—7.9abβ.15—17 [18] 19f [21—24] 25; 3:1—15.[16] 17—19. Other authors do not believe that a convincing division can now be made in a narrative that has passed through so many centuries of integrating tradition. At all events, we are justified in taking it as a unity, and in fact we must do so. It was in this form that it was used by the Yahwist to introduce his great historical work, and in this form it was accepted and made a part of our canonical book.

4b. '*When Yahweh God made earth and heaven*': **c** what in P is the substance of its story is in J merely an introduction: his concern is with man on the earth. **5.** In its own way, this narrative speaks of the formlessness of earth at its beginnings, but to an entirely different purpose. There was no plant life on earth because Yahweh had not yet brought rain upon it *and because there was no man to till it.* **6.** This is a difficult v to understand in context, and in the minds of some authors is one of the anomalies that the Yahwist did not bother to remove from his narrative (Chaine). It appears to be related to 10—14, concerning a marvellous supply of water coming from *under* the ground, and therefore does not contradict 5 which speaks of no rain falling upon the earth. The word *'ēd* can hardly mean 'mist' here (RSV, CV), whatever the meaning in Jb 36:27. LXX, Vg, and Onqelos translated 'fountain' or 'spring'. On the analogy of Akkadian use, the word can mean the underground sea, or a tributary therefrom, which would seem to be meant here. The verse seems adversative to the sense of the foregoing. does it mean that the earth was blest, in that it was watered from below and did not have to depend on the seasonal rains? One may point to the analogous condition in Egypt, hence 13:10 'well-watered, like the garden of Yahweh or like Egypt'. In this acceptation, such was the earth prepared for man before his sin, but after his fall he had to be at the mercy of the rains. In P the *tehôm* is a quasi-enemy of creation that must be vanquished by God; but *tehôm* can also be represented as beneficent, cf 49:25. **7.** This is the climax toward which the author has been **d** working: 'Then Yahweh God formed man of dust from the ground and breathed into his nostrils the breath of life, and man became a living being'. Heb. anthropology, unlike the Gr., did not distinguish the body from the soul: there is in Heb. no separate word for body, and what has sometimes been translated 'soul' (*nepeš*) is actually the *person*, the *being* itself. 'The Hebrew idea of the personality is an animated body, and not an incarnated soul' (H. W. Robinson, 'Hebrew Psychology', *The People and the Book*, 1925, 362). Like all the 'science' of its day, the Heb. conception was based exclusively on appearances. The difference between the living and the dead was marked by the presence or absence of *breath*, which, of course, could only come from God (Eccl 12:7). The Hebrew did not consider plant life to be true life. That which was animated by the breath was variously called, as here, '*āpār*, 'dust', or *bāśār*, 'flesh' (Jb 10:9—12). Withdraw the life-breath, and the creature reverts to the dead matter from which it was formed (Jb 33:4; Pss 104 (103):29; 146 (145):4). Neither from the standpoint of 'dust' nor from that of 'breath' is there any distinction between man and the beasts (Eccl 3:18—20).

151d Thus there is nothing in Gn 2:7 concerning the immortality of the soul of man. The author knows well, as he goes on to show, that man is quite distinct from the beasts; but the basis of the distinction is not rooted here. J begins a long series of word-plays in stating that man ('ādām) was formed of dust from the ground ('adāmâ).

e 8. In his description of the garden, its furnishings, and man's condition there, J employs a series of figures, most of which were common coin in Near Eastern literature, some of which occur elsewhere in other biblical contexts, with variations (cf Is 14:12—15; 51:3; Ezek 28:12—16; 31:4.8f 18). The garden which Yahweh is said to have planted was evidently conceived as a park of trees. Eden ('ēden) is an Akkadian word meaning 'plain'. This was a frequently occurring geographical term referring to various places, but here it is located only vaguely in the mysterious and remote east. The Yahwist is more concerned with the significance of the garden than with its location (in Jer 51:34 'ēden means 'delights'); that Yahweh *put* man whom he had formed into this garden signifies the extraordinary favours which he lavished on his creature. 9. These favours included, among others, the tree of life (cf Prv 11:30; 13:12; 15:4). The tree of the knowledge of good and evil we shall see again later on. 10—14 interrupt the flow of the narrative (15 recapitulates 8—9 after this parenthesis) and are somewhat at variance with 8, which does not attempt to localize Eden. Of the four rivers named, the last two are certain: the Tigris and the Euphrates, the two great rivers of Mesopotamia. About the other two we cannot be equally sure. Ancient opinion identified them with the Ganges and the Nile, the other two great rivers known to the classical world. But the first is said to encircle ḥawîlâ, which to the author evidently meant all or a part of the Arabian peninsula. The second may, indeed, refer to the Nubian Nile. 'Four' is a universal attribution to describe the world: 'the four rivers of the world' is cognate with 'the four corners of the world'. The author intends to say that the marvellous river that emerged from Eden was of such size that it was the source of the rivers that encompassed the world. His geography was as rudimentary as his other science, and he doubtless thought of all the great rivers as having a common source. This source to him, and therefore his location of Eden, was doubtless 'in the north' (cf Is 14:13; Ps 48 (47):3). In the Ugaritic myths, El, the chief god, also dwells in the north, at the source of

f the waters of the earth. 15. The narrative of man in the garden resumes, with an added note as to God's purpose in placing man there. We see from this v that Gn does not teach that human work is only a punishment consequent on the fall. 16—17. Man is made free of all the trees in the garden with the exception of the tree of the knowledge of good and evil; this last is forbidden under pain of death. *Knowledge* to the Semite is never anything abstract or extrinsic to the knower: knowledge is experience. A man 'knows' his wife; to 'know' the Lord is to live the life ordained by the Lord, even, in a true sense, to live the Lord's life (cf Jn 14:7, 15—17). What experiential knowledge is signified by eating of this tree? *Good and evil* is not disjunctive in sense but cumulative: just as 'going and coming' to the Hebrew meant movement in general, 'good and evil' involves the entire moral order. Without the experience of sin, man could not be said to know good and evil, that is, to experience the entire moral order. In its broadest acceptation, then, man is proscribed under pain of death from committing sin. Is it possible to determine more precisely what, in the author's mind, was the object of this proscription? There is some undeniable sexual imagery that occurs in connexion with 'the

knowledge of good and evil' (cf *infra*); however, it is to **151** be noted that in the perspective of this narrative woman has not yet been created. For the moment it will suffice to see that Yahweh has imposed upon man in the garden some prohibition as a test of his obedience.

18. Also important to the author was the nature **g** and role of woman. Therefore he now begins to tell of her creation, and by protracting the story deliberately he brings out better just what her nature is. First, it is noted that man is social by nature and has the need of his own kind. 19—20. Then Yahweh proceeds to the formation of the animals (from the earth, as in the case of man) which are given their names by man. Thus is expressed the dominion that was attributed explicitly to man in the Priestly narrative of creation. Name-giving was the mark of ownership. The animal life, therefore, is integrated into man's life and assigned its role. Yet in none of the animals did man find one like to himself. Without explaining in what the fact consists, the author states the fact itself, that man is different from the other animal creation. Of course, this has been evident throughout the entire story with its emphasis on man and on Yahweh's solicitude for him. 21—22. Finally, one is made like to man: woman. Woman's creation is fittingly solemnized. The man is put into a deep sleep (*tardēmâ*, as in 15:12 J), in which Yahweh's wonders are performed; from his side some human part is taken (*sēlā'*, 'a rib', as traditionally translated), and from this Yahweh 'builds' woman. Bringing her now into man's presence, 23, the significance of all this Yahweh allows to be expressed in the man's words of greeting: she is flesh of his flesh and bone of his bone, that is, she possesses the same nature with man (cf 29:14). Cf Aug 'Natura quippe mulieris creata est quamvis ex virili quae iam erat, non aliquo motu iam existentium naturarum' (*De Gen. ad litt.* 9, 15, 26 (PL 34, 403)). This may seem a commonplace to us, but it was important to the author to insist, against contemporary opinions to the contrary, that woman was not an inferior being to man. Rather, man and woman complement each other in the same human species. Cf Amb, 'Bene "aedificavit" dixit, ubi de mulieris creatione loquebatur, quia in viro et muliere domus videtur quaedam plena esse perfectio' (*De paradiso* 11, 50 (CSEL 32, I, 307)). A word-play reproducible in English underlines the relation of woman ('iššâ) to man ('îš). 24. The **h** author further explains this principle in relation to human marriage. There is no doubt that the inspired author, though he lived in a society that permitted both polygamy and divorce, taught that monogamous, indissoluble marriage was what Yahweh had intended in the creation of man and woman (cf Mt 19:4—6 and the use of this text by the Council of Trent, Dz 969). Like the inferior status of women in human society (cf *infra*), polygamy and its attendant evils were the result of sin and its consequences, not of the divine intention. 25. Man and woman were as yet without sin and the consequences of sin; they had, therefore, none of what a later theology would call the concupiscence of the flesh. That along with their other exceptional gifts man and woman in the state of first innocence also possessed sanctifying grace is not stated in Gn. Our doctrine of grace is dependent on NT revelation. However, they are represented as being on terms of great intimacy with God, and it is shown how this intimacy is destroyed by their sin.

The theory of evolution or transformism is not strict- **i** ly, and certainly not exclusively, a question to be raised in commenting on Gn. The author obviously knew nothing of any such theory, and he can be enlisted in its favour or in opposition to it only by applying a concordistic

51i interpretation to his text. Doubtless he believed, as he had no reason to believe otherwise, in a direct creation by God of all existing species, human or non-human; but this is far from saying that he intended to affirm this belief as part of his inspired teaching.

No Christian, of course, could accept a purely blind or mechanical evolutionism or one that would derive the spiritual human soul from merely material causes. A scientific hypothesis, however, which envisages a gradual development of the human body need not be in conflict with the doctrine of divine creation any more than is the undoubted fact of the gradual development of the physical universe through its many aeons. In the encyclical letter *Humani Generis* (1950) Pope Pius XII stated that the question of the evolution of the human body might be freely discussed by those competent in such a discussion, reserving to the Church the right of a final decision in such a matter that concerns the truths of Christian faith as well as the natural sciences (AAS 42 (1950) 575f; EnchB² 615f). The encyclical, further, makes no distinction between the body of the first man and the body of the first woman in referring to evolution; and indeed the text is concerned to stress identity of nature rather than distinction of origin.

j As regards **polygenism**, the Pope went on to say, the position is not quite the same: 'For the faithful cannot embrace that opinion which maintains either that after Adam there existed on this earth true men who did not take their origin through natural generation from him as from the first parent of all, or that Adam represents a certain number of first parents' (EnchB² 617). He based this opinion not on the narrative of creation but on the traditional understanding of the nature and transmission of original sin: 'It is in no way apparent (*cum nequaquam appareat*) how such an opinion can be reconciled with what the sources of revealed truth and the documents of the teaching authority of the Church propose with regard to original sin, which proceeds from a sin actually committed by an individual Adam and which through generation is passed on to all and is in everyone as his own' (the encyclical cites here Rm 5:12—19 and canons 1—4 of the Fifth Session of the Council of Trent, Dz 788—91).

We should not, however, exclude the possibility of a subsequent development in Catholic theology. With regard to the words of Pius XII A. M. Dubarle writes: 'More than once it has been pointed out that there is a difference between declaring a reconciliation impossible and stating that we cannot see how it can be reconciled. In the second case it is possible to envisage a later modification of the intellectual situation. This is not, therefore, excluded by the encyclical, which is in any case not an irrevocable document. In fact studies in exegesis and conciliar history lead us to ask whether the intention of the author of Gn, of St Paul and of the Fathers of the Council of Trent was really directed to the strict unity of origin of the human race and not rather at the universality of sin' *The Biblical Doctrine of Original Sin*, E. tr. 1964, 228; see also K. Rahner, s.v. 'Monogenismus' in LTK). In the view of some theologians, such a reconciliation is not only possible already but necessary as well. So, for example, A. Hulsbosch, *God in Creation and Evolution*, E.tr. 1965; M. Hurley S.J. 'The Problem of Original Sin' CleR 52 (1967), 770—86.

k It must be repeated that the biblical text is making a theological statement, not a scientific one—basically, the same as that made by St Paul in Rm, that all men have sinned and all need redemption. We cannot appeal to the text for scientific information which it was in no position to give; on the contrary, it can and must **151k** be understood in the light of scientific findings.

The particular problem of polygenism is of course connected with modern discussion of other aspects of original sin, in the light of the Council of Trent's teaching about an inherited state of sin. But here again factors are involved which lie outside the scope of the exegete. In the treatment which follows we restrict ourselves to the interpretation of the mind of the inspired writer.

3:1—24 The Fall of Man—After the narrative of **152a** man's constitution in paradisaical happiness, the author proceeds to the account of man's temptation and fall and the introduction of sin into the world. The Yahwistic narrative continues through this ch, which falls into three parts: the temptation and fall, 1—7; the divine decrees passed in judgement on the fall of man, 8—19; and the consequences of the fall for mankind, 20—24.

1. Throughout the story of the fall, the tempter of man is consistently called 'the serpent'. Later Jewish understanding of the problem of evil identified the serpent as the devil (Wis 2:24), and it was to insist on this identification that the Bib. Comm. ruled that what appears in Gn as 'the serpent' (*sub serpentis specie*) is really the devil (see EnchB 338). In the time of Gn there was as yet no developed notion of a personal devil; 'satan' appears for the first time in Jb 1, and then not as a malign spirit but one of the heavenly court of Yahweh. What prompted the author to select the serpent to signify the power of evil will be discussed below. The present narrative shows a keen awareness of the psychology of temptation. The serpent first deliberately exaggerates the divine prohibition, to put the woman on the defensive from the outset. **2—3.** The woman rises to the bait: while she corrects the serpent's insinuation, her own reply somewhat exaggerates the divine proscription and leaves her open to further suggestion. **4—5.** The suggestion is now overt: God's motive in the prohibition is really a mean and jealous one, to prevent men from enjoying his divine prerogatives. We are not obliged to accept the serpent's exegesis as to the true meaning of 'the knowledge of good and evil' which we have discussed above; but his words formulate the temptation to which our first parents succumbed: 'to be like gods', that is, to be a law unto themselves. **6—7.** The serpent withdraws, true to the craft that was ascribed to him in 1, and allows his suggestion to do its work. The woman gives in to the temptation and in turn seduces the man. Then the half-truth that the serpent had uttered is revealed in all its irony: they have not become like gods, but they have now experienced good and evil. The consequence of this is immediately manifest. No longer innocent, they recognize their nakedness and all that it implies.

8. Another consequence: the ease and familiarity with **b** which man had lived with Yahweh is now gone. Man is ashamed in the presence of his Creator and flees from 'the sound' of his approaching footsteps in the garden. **9—13.** If sin has estranged man from God, it has also estranged one man from another. The man tries to place the blame on the woman, or even on God himself, insinuating as a reproach 'the woman that you gave to be with me'. The woman in turn blames the serpent, which also was a creature of God. Yahweh inquires no further; it is evident how thoroughly the work of disorder has been done. **14.** In the divine sentence pronounced on the serpent, our text speaks on two levels, on the level of the serpent itself, chosen to represent the tempter, and on the level of the tempter that is represented.

152b Hence there is a twofold meaning in such an expression as 'to eat dust', which both refers to the actual posture of a serpent (Is 65:25; Mi 7:17) and is a figure of speech for abasement (Is 49:23; Mi 7:17; Ps 72(71):9). There is no reason to believe that the author thought that serpents had once walked; however, that Gentile myths sometimes featured walking serpents may be part of the explanation of his use of the serpent-symbol. **15.** See the discussion of this v below. **16.** The harsh reality of woman's servile state in ancient society is explained as the consequence of sin. Woman's hard lot is epitomized in the pains of childbirth; yet to this she will be continually drawn through the desire for her husband, in whom she will find not an equal companion but a master. Note that these words are not a 'curse', and far less are the pains of childbirth represented as the divinely ordained destiny for woman. Like disease and other physical evils they are the result of sin, and like disease they may be alleviated without scruple. **17—19.** Not labour, but the hardness of labour, is man's punishment. Not man but the land is 'cursed', that is, it is cursed as far as man is concerned, no longer yielding him his food willingly but with reluctance. No longer is creation passively subject to man as was the original intention. Yahweh had threatened death as the price of eating the fruit of the tree (2:17). That death is not instantly inflicted may be taken as a gesture of divine mercy; nevertheless, at the end man must die, after a life of wresting his existence from the earth.

c **20.** An abrupt transition. However, it can be taken as exemplifying the subjection of woman to man. Eve (*hawwâ*) is frequently taken as having some relation to 'living' (*hay*), and this appears to be the etymology the author is suggesting. However, there are Aram. and Arabic cognates that mean 'serpent', which is suggestive in this context. If Eve was given a name reminiscent of what had taken place in the garden, additional poignancy would be attached to the note that she is 'mother of all the living'. This is the first use of a proper name for either of our first parents. Adam appears as a proper name only with 4:25; up to that point we have invariably *hā'ādām*, 'the man' (the massoretic punctuation ignoring the article in 2:20; 3:17,21 is doubtless erroneous). **21.** As in 8:21 (J), Yahweh reconciles himself, so to speak, to dealing with man in his changed condition. His loving protection continues despite man's infidelity. **22.** This is usually translated 'Man has become like one of us', i.e., like one of the heavenly court or, simply (cf 1:26), like God. In this case, the statement is taken as one of irony, echoing the lying promise of the tempter. The chief difficulty for this interpretation (which is at least as old as Amb) is that the text gives no indication that any part of it is to be read ironically. 'Like one of us' (*ke'ahad mimmennû*) can also mean 'like one of his own', hence some understand the text: Man and all those born of him are now alike, knowing good and evil (cf 8:21). No more, therefore, may he partake of the tree of life. **23—24.** Man is driven from the garden, the entrance to which is protected by Cherubim and a flaming sword. Cherubim were winged creatures, later identified with angels, which were conceived as accompanying the Deity and serving as his ministers (cf Ps 18(17):10f). In the Bible they are sometimes represented as human in form and sometimes as animal-like (in Ezek 1; 9; 10, for example). In Assyro-Babylonian art, they were invariably animal in form. The flaming sword, on Assyro-Babylonian analogy, is doubtless a thunderbolt, stylized in art as a zigzag lightning flash. The text seems to think of a cherub on either side of the gate to the garden with the lightning flashing between them, **152** barring the entrance.

Such elements in the story of Gn 2—3 as the Cherubim **d** and flaming sword necessitate a consideration of **mythological parallels** to the biblical story. Gn has many specific details which are common in Eastern folklore. In the *Myth of Ea and Adapa* (ANET 101—3) we find 'water of life' and 'bread of life'. Adapa, fashioned by Ea, is warned against a certain food that will be offered him by the gods. Adapa declines the food and loses his chance to become immortal, but this is due to a trick of the gods rather than to his own fault. Furthermore, Adapa is not a man, but a demi-god. 'Even if our author did have such traditional lore in mind (i.e., of the Fall), it was only by way of vague remembrance' (T. H. Gaster, *The Oldest Stories in the World* (New York, 1952) 90f). In the *Epic of Gilgamesh* (ANET 96) Utnapishtim directs Gilgamesh to a 'plant of life' that lies at the bottom of the sea. Gilgamesh obtains this plant, but it is stolen from him by a serpent. Other superficial similarities can easily be found, and this is not at all surprising in view of the fact that the Gn account was doubtless of ultimate Mesopotamian origin and employed figures that it had taken from the Mesopotamian cultural world.

However, there is no true parallel to the story of the Fall of Man in Mesopotamian literature, which, in fact, excludes the possibility. Cf Heidel, *The Gilgamesh Epic and OT Parallels* 138: 'In the realm of the gods, death existed even prior to the creation of the universe. . . . The death-god, called by the Sumerian name Uggae, already existed and ruled before the creation of man. As for death among humankind, it was not attributed to some fall into sin on the part of man. On the contrary, according to the main Babylonian creation story, man was formed from the blood of the wicked Kingu and therefore was evil from the very beginning of his existence'. The biblical narrative contains a theology, and supposes a revelation, which in all its essentials was unknown to the Gentiles.

The nature of the sin of our first parents as it was **153** represented by the biblical author may, however, have some connection with the Gentile mythology, which the author certainly knew very well. He was writing for men and women who not only lived in the same times as he did, but shared a similar cultural background even if perhaps they were not so learned and well-read as he was most probably was. It cannot be denied that the author, in presenting his account, had consciously or unconsciously (though the first alternative is more than apparent) to allow for the knowledge which his readers had of the myths and legends of their neighbours. Like the good narrator that he was, the author may very well have so described the temptation and fall as to make them an object lesson for his contemporaries, by suggesting a sin to which they were all too prone. This is the basis of the 'sexual' interpretation of the sin proposed by Coppens, among others.

The serpent was a sex symbol in the Canaanite **b** religion of Palestine as well as in other Semitic religions. By the Canaanites it was associated with the god Baal and the goddess Asherah, both fertility deities. In view of such an association, one may readily see how to an Israelite audience the serpent could be an apt symbol of temptation to diabolical rites. Throughout their entire history in Canaan, Baal worship held a peculiar fascination for the people of Israel, against which the Law and the Prophets continually inveighed, and frequently enough in vain. While 'the knowledge of good

53b and evil' concerns the moral order in general, the expression was often used with specific reference to sexual knowledge (Dt 1:39; 2 Sm 19:35). The eating of 'the forbidden fruit' might have been expected to evoke a similar association, as with the raisin cakes which were used in the worship of Asherah (Hos 3:1). We recall, finally, that it is of their sex that the man and woman are made immediately conscious after their sin, and it is in the sexual order that punishment is decreed for the woman. Certainly the sacred author would not be suggesting that there was anything wrong in sex itself or that in the ideal order as intended by God for man there would have been no sexual intercourse; on the contrary, as we have seen (2:24), he taught that monogamous marriage was of divine institution. Rather, he would be thinking of some sexual abuse which was a danger to the Israelites from the contaminating influence of Canaan, such as the invocation of a fertility deity or a seeking of sexual experience contrary to its intended purpose. See also Lagrange, 'L'innocence et le péché', RB 6 (1897) 341ff.

c Gn 3:15 has been traditionally called **the Protoevangelium**, that is, the first proclamation of the good news of salvation. In this text there is that which is certain and that which continues to baffle the interpreter. Firstly, it is certain that the 'enmity' of which the text speaks does not refer simply to the natural repugnance of woman for the serpent. 'I shall place' determines the enmity as one in which God plays a part. The enmity, then, is a moral one divinely willed between the woman and what the serpent represents. The 'woman' in the context can only be the woman who appears throughout and who is addressed in the following verse, Eve, 'the mother of all the living' (3:20). The 'seed' of the woman is collective, referring to her descendants in general (as the 'seed' of Abraham in 13:15; 17:7, etc.), therefore the entire human race. This is evident, since the 'seed' of the serpent is also collective, that is, the powers of evil who will continue the work of the tempter throughout the history of the human race. 'It': since the 'seed' is collective, this should be the translation of the Heb. pronoun *hû'*. LXX, however, has *autos*, 'he', instead of the expected *auto*. This is not necessarily due to dittography (*autos sou tērēsei*) nor to a slavish rendering of *hû'* (which is masculine, to agree with the masculine *zera'*, 'seed'), nor does it testify to a personal messianic interpretation on the part of the LXX. The identical *constructio ad sensum* appears in the LXX of 2 Sm 7:12; 1 Chr 17:11, where, as in Gn 3:15, the word *sperma*, 'seed', though neuter, is followed by a masculine pronoun: the translator could not forget that a *human* 'seed' was in question whether collective or individual), and he therefore thought of *anthrōpos*, 'man', or *huios*, 'son', as the antecedent of the pronoun. On the Vg reading *ipsa*, 'she', see below.

d 'It will *crush* your head, and you will *crush* its heel'; alternatively, 'It will *watch for* your head, and you will *watch for* its heel'. What is certain is that the same verb *šûp* is used in each case, and hence the translation should be the same. What is not certain is the translation. The verb appears elsewhere only in Jb 9:17 'he crushes me with a tempest' (RSV), or 'with a tempest he might overwhelm me' (CV), and in Ps 139 (138):11 'darkness shall overwhelm me' (RV; corrected in other versions to *yᵉšukkēnî*, 'cover me'). The verbal idea is evidently something of a malign, overwhelming action. LXX translated as though the verb were *šā'ap*, 'watch for' (which can also have the malign connotation of 'lying in wait for').

VL reproduced the LXX: *Ipse servabit caput tuum, tu* **153d** *servabis eius calcaneum*. Jer compromised, as he often did, with popular opinion, translating the verb in the first instance *conteret* (with the Heb.) and in the second *insidiaberis* (with LXX). However, in his *Liber hebraicarum quaestionum in Genesim* he observes, having noted the VL translation, '*Melius habet Hebraeo: Ipse conteret caput tuum, et tu conteres eius calcaneum, quia et nostri gressus praepediuntur a colubro. et Dominus conteret Satanam sub pedibus nostris velociter*' (PL 23, 981). Whatever the precise meaning of the Heb. verb, we have in this passage an announcement of the continuous struggle that must exist between mankind and the evil that will try to dominate man, a struggle in which God is very much concerned.

Do we also have an announcement of the eventual **e** victory that mankind will win? Everyone will agree that the text contains 'less a promise of victory than of perpetual strife' (McKenzie, *The Two-Edged Sword* 104). However, probably most commentators will also find a prediction of victory implied both in the figure that is employed (a human foot crushing the head of a serpent whose fangs, in turn, are imbedded in its heel) and in the fact that this is a struggle willed by God, the outcome of which, in view of *Heilsgeschichte*, can only be victory (so Driver, de Vaux, Chaine, Clamer, *et al.*). Thus we have a basis for finding the '*Reparatoris futuri promissio*' of which the Biblical Commission spoke in 1909 (see EnchB 3.38). The soteriology of this passage, however, was not to be fully grasped until the NT had revealed the manner in which man's victory over the serpent was attained; and even then, the Fathers are by no means in agreement as to how the text was to be fitted into the messianic history. There is no recognizable allusion to Gn 3:15 elsewhere in the Hebrew Bible, and it was not interpreted messianically by either pre- or the post-Christian Jewish exegesis. It is unlikely that there is any reference to it in Gal 4:4; Rm 16:20, or even in Apoc 12. Irenaeus, following Justin, appears to have been the first to see in the text a personally messianic reference to Christ; but more than half of the Fathers, including the greatest Doctors of the East (Basil, Greg Naz, Chrys) and the West (Amb, Aug, Jer, Greg), did not take it as messianic at all. This, of course, does not mean that it is illegitimate for us today to employ sound exegetical principles to discern such a messianic sense in the light of NT revelation and the development of Christian doctrine, as has been done by Coppens, Rigaux, and others.

The *mariological* sense of the passage followed once **f** it was recognized to have a personally messianic application. The Vg reading, however, does not seem to be an early Christian testimony to a mariological interpretation. The *ipsa* reading is found in most of Vg mss, and even the relatively few that have *ipse* have mainly been 'corrected' to *ipsa* by a subsequent hand; but in view of St Jerome's statement cited above, it is doubtful that he translated *ipsa*. This reading was known to him and to Aug, however. It appears to have come from Amb who was in this dependent on Philo Judaeus. Philo, arguing from a supposed rigid law of parallelism, maintained that the pronoun should pair with 'woman' rather than with 'seed', since the opposition in this member of the v returned to that of the woman and the serpent. Neither Philo nor Amb interpreted 3:15 messianically; to both of them 'she' was the woman of the context, Eve. The bulls *Ineffabilis Deus* (Dec. 8, 1854) of Pius IX and *Munificentissimus Deus* (Nov. 1, 1950) of Pius XII respectively defining the dogmas of the Immaculate Conception

153f and the Assumption of our Lady make use of the messianic and mariological interpretation of Gn 3:15 that later developed in Christian tradition.

154a **4:1—16 The Story of Cain and Abel**—After the expulsion from the garden, two sons are born to the man and his wife, **1—2**. On the occasion of their offering sacrifice, the favour of Yahweh for the younger son and his displeasure with the elder son are made manifest, **3—7**. Thereupon Cain, the elder son, commits the first murder, killing his brother Abel, **8—10**, for which Yahweh condemns him to a life of wandering upon the earth, **11—12**. On Cain's protestation, however, that this banishment has doomed him to a hopeless existence, **13—14**, Yahweh guarantees him his own protection, **15—16**.

Chh 4—5 of Gn have a twofold function. On the one hand, they bridge the gap between the creation narrative and the story of the flood: the flood stands at mid-point in this salvation history between creation and the historical times that were introduced by Abraham, and the genealogies of 5 and 10 serve to tie the parts together. Even more theologically, these chh also are used to show that the sin introduced by our first parents also claimed their descendants, who even surpassed their father in his rebellion. As this truth appears much more explicitly in ch 4 than in the genealogy of 5, the final author of Gn has continued the story of the Fall with the history of Cain and the Cainites, which is part of the same original Yahwistic history. The story of Cain and Abel brings out mankind's need of salvation in its struggle with evil (cf 4:7 with 3:15). Further, in v 10f the divine sentence passed on man in banishing him from the garden is repeated and intensified.

b **The literary form** of this narrative (J) becomes apparent when it is closely examined. 'This narrative did not originally treat of the sons of the first man, for it supposes a developed civilization (v 2), that ritual has been already instituted (v 3f), that there are other men who can kill Cain (v 14), and that there is an entire clan which will protect him (v 15). It may refer to the traditional ancestor of the Kenites (see Jg 1:16; 4:11; 1 Sm 15:6), perhaps the same as the Kenan who figures in the genealogy of Seth (Gn 5:9). At all events, J has detached this narrative from its historical context and, in relating it to the origins of humanity, has given it an eternal value—after the revolt against God (the sin of paradise) comes the struggle of man against man, to which is opposed the twofold commandment which sums up the Law, the love of God and the neighbour (cf Mt 22:40)' (de Vaux). Lacking historical records of the earliest human beings who had lived countless centuries and even millennia before, the author has used an ancient narrative which doubtless had to do originally with contrasting the life of the peasant and the shepherd, to the advantage of the latter.

c **1—2.** J delights in popular etymologies. 'I have *created* a *man* with Yahweh', i.e., Eve exults that she has been allowed to share in the creative work of Yahweh, who made the first *man*. Cain (*qayin*) means 'smith', but the primary meaning was probably 'fashioner', derived from *qānâ* 'make', 'fashion': *qānîtî*, 'I have created'. On this meaning of *qānâ* cf 14:19.22; Prv 8:22. Abel (*hebel*) is a 'breath', doubtless an allusion to his very short life. **3—5.** No explanation is given why Yahweh accepted Abel's sacrifice and rejected Cain's. Though later Jewish tradition (reflected also in Heb 11:4; 1 Jn 3:12) explained this on the basis of merit, the

author doubtless intended a further illustration of the **15** gratuity of God's choice, who also in the case of Isaac, Jacob, *et al.*, passed over the eldest son in favour of another. **6—7.** In rejecting Cain's sacrifice Yahweh has not thereby rejected Cain himself. 'If you do well, *there is lifting up*', i.e. Cain can hold his head high (Castellino, von Rad). Sin is personified as an animal (the serpent?) crouching at the door of Cain's heart ready to pounce if he gives in to his evil inclination. Though prone to evil, man is free to choose or to reject it. **9.** Cain's answer to Yahweh contains his own sentence: he is brotherless by his own choice (Bonhoeffer). **10.** Blood, as the seat of life (Lv 17:11) was sacred to God; it could not be eaten, but must be poured out on the ground and covered with earth (Lv 17:13f). But the earth will not receive and cover over this innocent blood that has been slain. **11—12.** In 3:17ff it was said only that the earth would yield man its fruits reluctantly; here, in the face of this other sin, the earth is Cain's total enemy. The rootlessness of nomadic life was seen as a further punishment of sin. **15—16.** The 'mark of Cain' is not, as in the popular acceptation, the brand of a murderer, but a sign to protect Cain. The reference is probably to a tribal marking which was to give warning that anyone who did harm to Cain would have to fear the blood-vengeance of his clan (the Kenites?). Blood-vengeance was a deterrent against total lawlessness; it was at the same time, however, a sign of the existence of such lawlessness, just as the giving of the Law with its stated provisions of retribution (Ex 21:12ff, etc) would mark the end of this lawless period and be a signal favour from God. *Nôd* means 'wandering' (Ps 56 (55):9), cf v 14.

17—24 The Cainites—J has joined this genealogy **d** to the story of Cain and Abel chiefly because of v 23f, 'the song of the sword': in Lamech's savage boast he saw a further enlargement of man's lawlessness represented in one of Cain's descendants. From simple murder, man 'progressed', in Cain's case, to sevenfold revenge, and now to seventy times sevenfold killing even for less grievous offences than murder. The genealogy may have been originally a Kenite tradition which ascribed the beginnings of the various arts and crafts to their ancestors. On the Kenites and their mysterious connection with Israelite history, see de Vaux, AI 478f; Anderson, *Understanding the OT* 36. The biblical author was less interested in the popular story of the origins of human institutions than in the religious use he could make of the story. Originally it had nothing to do with the story of Cain and Abel. Here Cain is no longer a wanderer, but a founder of cities. Jabal (20) is the 'father' of those who tend flocks, though Abel according to 4:4 was a tender of flocks. This genealogy, too, evidently had no original connexion with the flood story which follows in the Yahwist's narrative.

17. The name of Enoch (*hᵃnôk*) is associated with the **e** fact that Cain dedicated (*hānak*) to him the city he founded. The city and city-life often figure pejoratively in the Bible, and especially in Gn (10:11f; 11:1—9; 18:16—19:29, all J); hence it is probably not by chance that the author attributes the origin of cities to the first murderer, though the original sense of the attribution in the genealogy was not pejorative. **19.** Polygamy is mentioned for the first time, contrary to the Yahwist's teaching in 2:24. Possibly there was a significance for the author in the fact that Lamech's first marriage gave rise to the 'peaceful' crafts, the second to those which are 'warlike'. **20.** Jabal is the 'father' of those who lead (*ybl*) flocks. **21.** Jubal is

54e the father of musicians: *yōḇēl*, whose etymology is disputed, the Heb. word for the jubilee year, was connected with the idea of music, either originally or by association. Cf R. North, *Sociology of the Biblical Jubilee* (Rome, 1954) 103f. **22.** Tubal-cain: that is, Tubal the Cainite, Kenite, or 'the smith'. The Kenites were, it is thought a tribe of nomadic smiths: in ancient times smithing was traditionally a craft of itinerants. Cf F. W. Robins, *The Smith* (London, 1953) 13–18. **23–24.** Lamech is not content with the protection promised to Cain but must arrogate to himself the right to fix the laws of life and death. Our Lord's words in Mt 18:22 may have been uttered with this episode in mind.

f 25–26 The Sethites—Having shown the progression of evil through the genealogy of Cain, the Yahwistic author now brings history down to the flood with the genealogy of Seth, the ancestor of the just man Noah. However, in the canonical text of Gn the Yahwistic genealogy of Seth has been truncated in view of the Priestly genealogy that follows in ch 5. The name of Noah originally appeared in the present list, but the author of Gn has transferred it to 5:29 lest he spoil the effect of his history by a premature introduction of the hero of the flood. It is obvious that 5:29 interrupts the even flow of P's formulaic procedure. It is rather wholly in the tradition of J: the name Yahweh is used, allusion is made to the curse of the ground (3:16), and a popular etymology is found for Noah's name in that 'this one will bring us relief' (*yᵉnahamēnû*). **25.** Adam is used for the first time as a proper name. God *appointed* (*šāṯ*) Seth as another *seed* to replace the murdered Abel. **26.** Enosh ('*enôš*) also means 'man'. 'At that time men began to call upon the name of Yahweh': so in J, which puts the origins of Yahweh cult in prehistory. In the other Pentateuchal traditions the name of Yahweh is a Mosaic revelation. However, both viewpoints defend a truth: J insists that the Yahweh of Israelite revelation was the same God worshipped by Israel's ancestors.

55a 5:1–32 The Pre-Flood Patriarchs—It becomes immediately evident that basically the same traditional names were available to those responsible for the genealogy of ch 4 and the Priestly one we have at hand. The names have been used quite differently and in a different order, but they correspond almost exactly:

	J		P
	Adam		Adam
[Abel]	Cain	Seth	Seth
		Enosh	Enosh
	Enoch		Kenan
	Irad		Mahalalel
	Mehujael		Jared
	Methushael		Enoch
	Lamech		Methuselah
Jabal, Jubal, Tubal-cain			Lamech
	[Noah]		Noah

b **The literary form** of the P genealogy owes much to Babylonian influences. The Babylonians also customarily counted ten generations from creation to the flood, to which they assigned fantastic ages. On the ages in this biblical genealogy, see above § 145*b-f*. The Babylonian genealogies, however, made all the names refer to kings of Babylonia, creating the fiction of an uninterrupted Babylonian domination since the time of creation. The biblical names are rather of 'patriarchs', shadowy figures of the past. The exact meaning of most of the names escapes us, but they all appear to be Heb., and

therefore, relatively speaking, recent. Another point **155b** of contact with the Babylonian lists lies, probably, in the name assigned to the final generation, the man who is also the hero of the flood story. In Sumerian he was called Ziusudra, in Akkadian Utnapishtim, and both these names mean 'one of extended life'. It is very likely that the Heb. name Noah had much the same meaning according to its true etymology **The theological purpose** of the Priestly author, which can be better seen when this genealogy is compared with that of 11:10ff, is without doubt expressed in the declining lifespans ascribed to these men of ancient times. As the genealogies approach historical times, the ages become more 'realistic'. Long life was a sign of divine favour. In his own way, and in this instance a much less theological way, P conveys the truth contained in the J story of creation and fall, that man in his present state has fallen from a divine favour that he once enjoyed.

3. Like Adam, created to the image and likeness of **c** God, Seth is created in the likeness of Adam; thus the divine resemblance in which man was constituted is, by implication, transmitted to the entire human race that is to follow. P had only this genealogy of mankind through Seth. However, we must also remember that as it stands in the present text of Gn, this remark follows the Yahwistic story of the fall of man. Therefore the author of Gn doubtless saw an additional significance in Adam—now a fallen man—generating sons in his own likeness. **21–24.** The figure of Enoch was one of extreme fascination for later Jewish writers, cf Sir 44:16; 49:14; Wis 4:10–14; Heb 11:5. On the centrality of Enoch in the schematism of this list, see above § 145*b*. Here the author appears to allude merely to a tradition already well known to his readers and therefore needing little elucidation. What that tradition precisely was is somewhat uncertain; evidently, however, it had to do with a man of ancient times who had never died, who had, instead, been 'taken' by God. In view of the Heb. lack of knowledge concerning an afterlife, it is not difficult to see why Enoch became an object of curiosity and speculation, as did Elijah, of whom the same expression is used in 2 (4) Kg 2:10. Some of the culmination of this speculation is to be found in the apocryphal Book of Enoch, an apocalyptic work which had some influence on the NT; cf § 88*i-j*. The later extravagances of the Enoch speculation are completely lacking in Gn, however, whose author has dealt with the tradition quite laconically. There may be an additional influence of the Babylonian genealogies here. In Gn, Enoch appears in the symbolic 7th place, and his total years are 365, the number of days in the solar year. In a Sumerian version of the antediluvian king-lists, as also in the Babylonian king-list as reproduced by Berosos in hellenistic times, a certain En-men-dur-Anna of Sippar is found in the seventh place. Sippar was the city sacred to the sun-god. Though the relation of these ideas to those of Gn would not seem to be due to pure chance, it should also be plain that the relation is a superficial one that hardly touches on the essence of the biblical author's message.

6:1–4 Sons of God and Daughters of Men—This **156a** is one of the most disputed passages of Gn, and the determination of **its literary form** is consequently difficult. It seems opportune to note at the outset: (1) the story appears to be truncated: the author has selected only a part of the story that he wished to use; (2) the *biblical* significance of the story that the inspired author wished to attach to it appears in the following v 5: the story is, for him, a further illustration of

156a the wickedness of man that necessitated the divine intervention represented by the flood; (3) we must, therefore, distinguish the *theological use* made of the story in Gn from the original sense that it may have possessed in its pre-biblical state: this same distinction we made in respect to the story of Cain and Abel and the genealogy of the Cainites, and we shall need to make it again in regard to subsequent episodes. The interpretation given here mainly follows the analysis of Johann Fischer, 'Deutung und literarischer Art von Gen. 6:1–4', *Alttestamentliche Studien Nötscher*, 1950, 74–85.

b Firstly, as to **the biblical meaning**. J joined this ancient narrative fragment to his genealogies of the Cainites and Sethites in 4:17–26. The Cainites he represented as a wicked race of men, whereas it was from among the Sethites that men began to call upon Yahweh (4:26). Because of this last fact, the Sethites might, in a true sense, be termed 'sons of God', that is, those who stood in a special relationship to God: the Semitic 'son' need imply simply a pertinence, as in the case of the 'sons of the prophets' 1 (3) Kgs 20:35, 'sons of thunder' Mk 3:17, 'sons of darkness', 'sons of light', 'sons of wrath', etc. As opposed to these, the Cainites could be termed 'sons of men' and 'daughters of men', since man is evilly inclined (8:21). Therefore 6:2 could mean to J (and be the sense that he intended to convey in this passage), that in time all mankind became hopelessly corrupt, since even the good Sethites were corrupted through their intermingling with the Cainites; and thus the verdict passed on the story in 6:5. A further intention that may have been contained in the expression 'men of renown' (v 4), we shall consider below.

c This interpretation which identifies the 'sons of God' with the Sethites and the 'daughters of men' as Cainites is quite ancient in Christian tradition: Julius Africanus *Quae supersunt ex quinque libris Chronographiae* 2 (PG 10, 65); Chrys, *Expos. in Ps. 49:1* PG 55, 240f); Theodoret, *Quaestio 47 in Genesim* (PG 50, 148f); Aug, *De civitate Dei* 15, 23 (CCSL 48, 490f). It very likely expresses the sense both of J and of the final author of Gn. However, we do not have an adequate appreciation of what Gn has done with this text until we see what its original meaning was. 'Sons of god' in Heb. (*b^enê hā'elōhîm, b^enê 'elōhîm*, or *b^enê 'elîm*), lit. 'sons of the gods' (in Dn 3:25 (92) the Aram *bar-'elāhîn*, 'son of the gods') customarily means 'angels': the monotheistic equivalent of the heavenly host of deities for which this identical expression was used in the Canaanite and Phoenician religions. This is the meaning of 'sons of god' in Pss 29 (28):1; 89 (88):7; Jb 1:6; 2:1; 38:7. There would appear to be no doubt that the same was meant in Gn 6:2, for these 'sons of god' are contrasted with 'daughters of men' (*b^enôt hā'ādām*), and it has just been said that 'men (*hā'ādām*) began to multiply on the face of the ground, and daughters were born to them'. The 'daughters of men', in other words, are simply human women, while the 'sons of god' pertain to the order of *'elōhîm*: gods in the polytheistic religions, or angels in the monotheistic religion of Israel. This interpretation of Gn 6:2 is ancient in Judaism: The Book of Enoch 6–7; Jubilees 5, 1f; Philo, *De Gigantibus* 6ff; JosAnt 1, 3, 1. A secondary reading of LXX for 6:2 has *hoi aggeloi tou theou* for *hoi huioi toû theou*. Early Christian writers also accepted this interpretation: Clem. Alex. (cf J. Quasten, *Patrology* [Utrecht, 1953] II, 17); Just, *Apol.* 2, 5 (PG 6, 452); Tert., *De virginibus velandis* 7, 2 (CCSL 2, 1216).

Ancient angelology was quite primitive in ascribing human **156** capabilities to the angels.

Gn 6:1–4 appears to have been originally a legend **d** which told of the cohabitation of angelic beings with human women, from which union was born a race of giants. Here and in Nm 13:33 these giants are called *n^epîlîm*; elsewhere they are termed *'anāqîm* (Nm 13:33; Dt 1:28; 2:10f 21; 9:2) or *r^epā'îm* (Dt 2:10f 20). In common with other ancient peoples (doubtless through a misinterpretation of massive archaeological remains) the Israelites believed that some of the aboriginal inhabitants of the earth had been giants. Jewish tradition also represented these giants as rebels against God (Sir 16:7; Wis 14:6). With rare exceptions that were sometimes encountered, the race of giants had perished from the earth and were now in Sheol; hence the terms *r^epā'îm* ('shades') and *n^epîlîm* ('those who have gone down'?). Ezek 32:27 also speaks of the *gibbōrîm* ('mighty men', 'warriors') as resident in Sheol: this is the word used for the giants in Gn 6:4; cf Is 14:9. This story is similar to the Gr. and other legends of the Titans, as in the Prometheus myth, who challenged the ruling gods of heaven and earth, cf Eus., *Praep. evang.* 5, 4. In insisting that the *gibbōrîm* were '*men* of renown' J may have had a polemical purpose against the Gentile myths which had made them rival gods.

In 6:3 Yahweh says, 'my spirit shall not remain in **e** man forever, for he is flesh, but his days shall be a hundred and twenty years'. The original sense of the story: apart from this divine decision, the *n^epîlîm* could have been immortal, as pertaining to the order of *'elōhîm*; but God resolved that their human nature ('flesh') should prevail, and limited the duration of his life-breath in the *n^epîlîm* to 120 years. In his 'demythologized' use of the story J also may have considered the 120 years as a limitation placed on the life of man in token of man's now general corrupt state. It is more likely, however, in view of the story of the flood which he connected with this episode, that he made the 120 years signify a period of grace bestowed on mankind before the coming catastrophe. This is almost certainly the meaning of the final author of Gn, since ages longer than 120 years are later ascribed to individual men in P. 120 is a conventional number: one system of Babylonian computation, which we preserve in geometry and in counting time, dealt in multiples of six.

If we are to do justice both to the content of **f** these vv and the context in which they are now placed, it seems necessary to adhere to the distinction we have made between the original sense of the story and its biblical use. In the article we have followed, Fischer has shown how unconvincing are all the alternative solutions that ignore the prehistory of the text. Recently J. B. Bauer has attempted to make 'sons of God' = all men (created in God's image and likeness) and 'daughters of men' = all women (as taken from man), cf VDom 32 (1953) 95–100. This interpretation disregards the source analysis of Gn, however, and does not adequately explain either the theology or the ancillary details of 6:1–4.

5–8 Preparation for the Flood—In a vivid anthropomorphism J passes judgement on the tale of human degeneration. There is no recourse but that Yahweh must 'repent' what he has done and now undo it by destroying man and all that was created for his sake. Yet there is a ray of hope: 'Noah has found favour in the eyes of Yahweh'.

6:9–8:22 The Flood—The tradition of a great, **157** world-destroying flood has been handed down in at least

57a ten separate Babylonian sources. The most complete and the best known of these is in the Gilgamesh epic, tablet 11, lines 1—196 (ANET 93—95). Basically the *narrative* of the Babylonian story is the same as that of Gn having the following points of close contact: (1) as in Gn, the *occasion* of the flood depends on a divine decision; (2) the *principals* are the same: one man and his family are the survivors of the flood; (3) a *revelation* of the coming flood is divinely made; (4) a ship of refuge is *constructed* according to divine specifications; (5) *animals* as well as men are taken aboard; (6) *the end* of the flood is determined by the flight of birds; (7) the ark of refuge comes to rest on a *mountain*; (8) a *pleasing sacrifice* concludes the story. At the same time, there are so many variations in inconsequential detail that no one today would argue for a direct dependence of Gn on any extant Babylonian version of the flood story. Rather, both the Babylonian story and Gn go back to some common Mesopotamian tradition, a tradition which both have transmitted with more than the normal retention of detail.

b The flood-tradition has been recorded by many other peoples. Its appearance in the mythology of ancient Greece and Rome is thought to be due to Oriental influence, but no one has satisfactorily accounted for the uniformity with which it consistently turns up in the literatures of more remote and unrelated peoples. 'As for the natural and historical aspect of the Flood problem, theology is not competent to express an independent opinion. It may be said, however, that even natural scientists have not considered the prevailing explanation—that the numerous Flood stories in the world arose from local catastrophes—to be sufficient (e.g., E. Dacqué). On the one hand the distribution of the saga (among Indians, Persians, Africans, Melanesians, and Australians, among the Eskimos, the Kamchatkans, Indians of the Americas, etc), on the other hand its remarkable uniformity (flood caused by rain), require the assumption of an actual cosmic experience and a primitive recollection which, to be sure, is often clouded and in part brought to new life and revised only later by local floods' (von Rad). There doubtless was, therefore, an ancient cataclysm that gave rise to these stories which have preserved its recollection. What the dimensions of that cataclysm were, however, and when it occurred, it is impossible for us to say. It was once thought that archaeology had uncovered evidence of the biblical flood in Mesopotamia. However, while there is such evidence for various floods of generous proportions in ancient times, it is now recognized that there is none for a single flood that extended throughout the entire region.

c Now that we know the provenance of the flood story in Gn, we have a better insight into **its literary form**. It is no longer necessary to ask ourselves how the details of the story could be literally true, or to devise ingenious explanations to make the Scripture say what is acceptable to modern scientific knowledge rather than what it obviously does say. The author of Gn did not compose this story; he took it ready-made from his cultural ambience. It is a story that was told by men who had no conception of the vastness of the universe and of its physical laws, who therefore certainly had no intention of suggesting the countless miracles that would be necessary to bring about precisely what the story describes. By the time the story reached Gn, it had become an account which told of the covering of the entire earth by flood waters and of the preservation of all the species of animal life in one vessel that survived the cataclysm. The author of Gn, who had **157c** no intention of transmitting other than a *popular* history, certainly did not and could not submit the story to the principles of historical criticism. His is a citation from sources, in which he did not necessarily intend to affirm the truth of each individual detail.

We are further enlightened on his attitude to these **d** details when we see that the story in Gn itself is a **compilation of two separate traditions** which have been combined to the disregard of their conflicts in detail. Virtually all modern commentators have accepted the evidence for this composite character of the flood story; Cassuto stands practically alone in having advanced any new arguments against the evidence, and his series of alternative hypotheses must be adjudged, in the balance, less probable than the theory of compilation. The evidence consists, first of all, in the manifold repetitions of the story: twice God recognizes the human depravity necessitating the flood (6:5; 6:12); twice he announces its coming (6:13.17; 7:4); twice he orders Noah to enter the Ark (6:18—20; 7:1—3); twice Noah obeys (6:22; 7:5); twice Noah's entrance into the Ark is described (7:7; 7:13); twice the flood is said to have begun (7:10; 7:11); twice the waters increase and raise the Ark from the ground (7:17; 7:18); twice all living beings are said to die (7:21; 7:22—23); twice the waters abate (8:1a; 8:3a); twice God promises that there will be no more floods (8:20—22; 9:8—17). It is true that there remain other repetitions beyond these and that Semitic storytelling delights in repetition; but Semitic repetition never went to the length of duplicating every significant detail in a single story. Additional repetitions in the Gn story, as a matter of fact, may point to still other sources that underlie the two that we can now determine.

Furthermore, the combination of *discrepancies* with **e** the repetitions is decisive in favour of the theory of compilation. In 6:19—20 and 7:15—16 the animals which are taken into the Ark are mentioned simply as a pair of each species. In 7:2, however, we read of seven pairs of the clean animals and one pair of the unclean. Characteristically, 7:2 appears to belong to J which dated the beginnings of Yahwism in prehistoric times (cf §154f), whereas the other traditions begin the distinctive observances of Yahwism only with Mosaic times. Characteristically, too, it is J (8:20ff) that has Noah offer a sacrifice to Yahweh at the end of the flood story. In 7:4.12 and 8:2b the flood is caused by rain (*gešem*). In 7:11 and 8:2a it is caused both by rain and the return of the primordial sea: 'the fountains of the deep and the floodgates of heaven'; the mention of the *tehôm* recalls the P account of tradition. Furthermore, the *gešem* of J is the winter rain (Am 4:7; Song 2:11; Ez 10:9.13), whereas in P the flood began on the 17th day of 'the second month' (7:11), that is, the month Iyyar, which extended from mid-April to mid-May. It was at this season—the end of spring and the beginning of summer—that the flood occurred in the version according to Berosos. We shall mention only one other major conflict: that of the chronology. In J the rain lasts for 40 days and 40 nights (7:4; 7:12). The total duration of the flood, therefore, the rising of the waters and their abatement, is 61 days (the seven days of 8:8 together with 8:10, 'another' seven days, and 8:12). This is quite modest in comparison with P. In P the floodgates of heaven and the sources of the deep are open for 150 days (7:24; 8:2a.3b). The waters disappear entirely in the 601st year of Noah, the first month, the first day of the month (8:13).

157e Since the flood began in the 600th year of Noah, the second month, the 17th day (7:11) and the earth was not dry until the 601st year, the 2nd month, the 27th day (8:14), the entire process took one year and 10 days. Many other discrepancies, perhaps more important ones, could also be noted.

f The author of Gn was as well aware of these discrepancies as we are. The fact that he combined the conflicting details into a single narrative should tell us of itself that such details were not his reason for telling the story. His reason was, rather, **theological**. It is this theology, too, that completely distinguishes the story in Gn from its Babylonian counterparts. The Babylonian flood story is completely amoral if not anti-moral. The decision of the gods to destroy the world and man is motivated by nothing more noble than pique and caprice. One of the gods saves his human client from the disaster for his own selfish ends and because of his rivalry with the other gods. The magnitude of the catastrophe unleashed by the gods surprises them and frightens them at the same time that it carries out its work of destruction. When the gods smell the odour of sacrifice after the flood has receded, they are vexed to learn that mankind has not been utterly destroyed. Only after long wrangling is an acceptable solution devised: the human survivor must himself become one of the gods. It should be evident from what unlikely materials the author of Gn, and the Israelite storytellers before him, have constructed the supremely theological narrative that we have in the Bible. In using this ancient story to bring out the justice and mercy of God and as illustrating his perennial dealing with mankind, Gn may be said to have adapted a popular tradition **parabolically** to its religious purposes.

g Unlike his previous practice of setting integral parts of J and P side by side, here the author of Gn has woven the two together into a continuous narrative. He was able to do so in this instance because of the relatively minor divergences in the two narratives. Also, in this instance he has relied more heavily on P than J. The former was more detailed and more explicit in its theology, and thus better suited to carry the burden of the biblical story. J has been used more as a supplement, and apparently parts of it have been omitted. The distribution of these chh according to the two sources is usually determined in this fashion: P: 6:9–22; 7:6.11.13–16a.17a.18–21.24; 8:1–2a. 3b–5.7.13a.14–19. J: 7:1–5.7–10.12.16b.17b. 22–23; 8:2b.3a.6.8–12.13b.20–22.

h 6:9. 'Noah walked with God': said also of Enoch in 5:24. This allusion distinguishes Noah most perfectly from the general corruption described in 11. Of no one further will it be said that he walked *with* God; Abraham, too, was blameless, but Abraham walked *before* God (17:1 P). **11.** 'The earth was filled with **violence**': this word (*ḥāmās*) appears frequently in the prophetic writings to express moral depravity. **12.** 'All flesh' is an expression that occurs throughout P, sometimes, as here, meaning all mankind, sometimes all life without exception. **13.** 'The end has come for all flesh': another prophetic expression (Am 8:2; Lam 4:18; Ezek 21:30.34) which refers to God's eschatological judgement. **14–16.** The ark (*tēbâ*) is a kind of box, as is evident from its dimensions; outside the present narrative the word is used (not by chance) only in Ex 2:3.5 for the 'basket' in which Moses was saved from death. In the Gilgamesh epic the dimensions of the ark are different and it is even more box-like, yet it is called by the ordinary word for a boat. The meaning of *gōper* wood is unknown; CV has 'resin-wood', which

doubtless expresses the idea. The word *qinnîm*, 'nests', is **15** usually taken to mean rooms in the ark. Some correct the text to *qānîm*, 'reeds' (CV 'make it tight with fibre'); in the Gilgamesh epic the ark seems to have been made partly of reeds. The cubit was the length of the forearm from the elbow to the fingertips, therefore about one foot and a half. 'A *sōhar* make for the ark, and finish it to a cubit upward' (or, 'from the top'): the word is variously taken to mean an 'opening' (perhaps a kind of lattice-work running round the top of the ark for light and air) or a (gabled?) 'roof'. **17.** 'The (not 'a') flood' **i** ('waters' is a gloss): the *mabbûl* is the heavenly sea above the firmament which was formed on the second day of the P creation story. In the perspective of P, the flood is more than a mere punishment of man; it is a withdrawal of God's creative act, a reversion of the entire cosmos to the chaos from which God formed it. **7:2–3.** On the distinction between clean and unclean animals, see § 200*a–j*. **16.** In J Yahweh himself shuts Noah up within the ark: another anthropomorphism that brings out the divine solicitude. If God is utterly just in punishing wickedness, he is no less merciful in saving the innocent. **8:1.** 'God remembered': though God allows chaos to return as the consequence of human misdeeds, yet he is always prepared to intervene and save to show forth his mercy. **4.** Ararat is the Urartu of the Akkadian cuneiform texts, the classical Armenia. The mountainous region about Lake Van to the N of Mesopotamia is meant. **7–12.** Mariners in ancient times often used birds to discover the direction of land when they had been driven off their course. **20–22.** J concludes with a sacrifice: it is fitting that man's first action on an earth purged of its evil should be to erect an altar to God. In turn, Yahweh is represented as reconciling himself, as it were, to man the sinner. Nature will be permitted to follow its regular course in a world made imperfect by man, and never again will Yahweh attempt to cope with sin in the radical manner of the flood. Rather, his grace will continue to pursue good and evil alike.

Typology of the Flood—We have already seen that the **j** biblical word *tēbâ*, 'ark', is found elsewhere only in Ex 2:3.5, where it is used of the vessel in which Moses was saved from death. There is no doubt that the connection between the two instances is an intentional one—the instrument of salvation for Israel on the one hand, of salvation for mankind on the other. Here, however, the direction of literary influence is doubtless from Ex to Gn rather than the other way round. The term is not the normal one that would be expected in reference to the vessel of the flood story, and it is entirely without precedent in the Babylonian parallels. Moreover, *tēbâ* appears to be an Egyptian word, as might be expected in the Moses traditions. At the same time, the two events have evidently been seen in relation to each other. The flood, and the salvation obtained from it, show up as types of later disasters in which God's mercy is made manifest along with his justice. Thus especially with regard to the exile and the salvation and restoration of the remnant of Israel (cf Is 54:6–10). Also the final judgement is described in the cosmological terms found in the flood story (cf Is 24:17–23). The comparison of the heedless generation of Noah's time with that of the eschatological future was also one made by our Lord (Mt 24:36–39). It is not surprising, therefore, that the NT sees the ark as a type of Christian baptism, which has saved from eternal destruction and made possible the new life of Christ (1 Pt 3:20–22). The Fathers adopted and developed this typology, seeing in the ark now a symbol

57j of baptism, now of the Church ('Peter's barque'). For the same reason, the ark of Noah is one of the favourite representations in the art of the catacombs.

58a **9:1—17 God's Covenant with Noah**—A sequel to the flood story in P. It is the first in a series of patriarchal covenants that will serve as the preparation for the great Covenant of Sinai with the Israelite people. In keeping with the fact that the flood signified a return of the primaeval chaos, this covenant appears as a kind of new creation and repeats some of the language of the creation story. As in 8:21, however, God recognizes as the *status quo* fallen man in a disordered world that has replaced the paradisaical peace of the first creation. Therefore, permission is given for the eating of flesh, provided that the sanctity of life is still recognized.

b 4. Blood was recognized to be the seat of life, and therefore something sacred and reserved to God. Even when not involved in sacrifice, the blood of an animal could not be consumed but must be poured out on the ground (Dt 12:16, etc). The prohibition of blood became one of the dietary laws of the Mosaic code, but because of its inclusion within the provisions of this covenant with Noah the later Jews considered it to be binding on all mankind. Hence the concession made to their feelings in the regulation imposed on Gentile Christians living in a Jewish environment according to Ac 15:20, 29. From this apostolic precedent, the custom of abstaining from blood was observed in some parts of the early Church. 5—6. The sanctity of human life is upheld, since man is created in God's image. To underline this sanctity, even a brute animal that slays a man must be killed and not eaten (Ex 21:28). For the same reason, permission is given to take the life of a murderer; but only he must be slain, not another. Unrestricted blood vengeance is checked, pending the more precise regulations of the Law. 8—17. The covenant with Noah is an engagement by which God binds himself to all creation, with the promise never again to destroy the world by flood. To every covenant some external sign was attached as its memorial and reminder. The rainbow is aptly chosen to signify the present covenant since it was one of the phenomena associated with the flood: when men look up at the clouds and see that God has placed his 'bow' there, they are to remember that God has promised not to use this instrument of destruction (Hb 3:9) against their earth.

c **18—29 The Blessing of Shem and the Curse on Canaan**—This passage was in J in its present place, between the story of the flood and the table of the nations that follows; however, as in other instances, J has not harmonized all its minor details with the surrounding context but has concentrated on the theological use to be made of the passage itself. Here Shem, Ham, and Japheth are represented as sons still living in their father's tent rather than, as in the flood story, married men who were heads of families of their own. Furthermore, despite the designation of 19, the passage is not concerned with Shem, Ham, and Japheth as ancestors of the peoples of the world, the character which they have in the table of the nations. Rather it is concerned with Canaan, the descendant of Ham, in relation to Shem and Japheth; secondarily, it shows an additional relationship of Japheth to Shem. The perspective, therefore, is Palestinian throughout (Canaan). The biblical author has seen in the story the explanation of the fact that the Canaanites lost possession of their land and became subject to, first of all the Semites (Israel), but also to the Japhethites, 'who

dwell in the tents of Shem'. It has been generally **158c** thought that Japheth refers to the Philistines, who throughout all Israelite history maintained an enclave within the promised land; however, in the Yahwistic 10:14 the Philistines are Hamites. Others think that the 'Hittites' are meant, the non-Canaanite peoples who appear in the Patriarchal stories and in later Israelite history. Whoever may have been meant precisely, it is the author's intention to show that the blessings reserved to the Semites have also, in some fashion, been extended to some non-Semites. The final 28—29 are a conclusion taken from P.

20—21. The planting of the vine by Noah is in fulfil- **d** ment of the prophecy of 5:29: vineyards and wine were counted among God's choicest blessings (Ps 104 (103):15; 1(3) Kgs 4:25; Hos 2:15; Mi 4:4; Am 9:13). The effects of wine had to be learnt through its use, hence the Fathers excused Noah's drunkenness on the ground that he was the first to try it. **22—24.** Since Noah learns of what Ham/Canaan has *done* to him, it may be that the biblical author has deliberately passed over some more distasteful details of the story. Just as reverence for one's father and mother was a supreme moral duty (Ex 20:12), words or deeds directed against them were crimes punishable by death (Ex 21:17). **25—27.** In the Semitic mind, blessings and curses were not mere formulas, but produced the effect they pronounced. See below, 27:1—45. The Hebrew *dābār*, 'word', is also a thing, a fact. Cf J. L. McKenzie, 'The Word of God in the OT', ThS 21 (1960) 183—206.

10:1—32 The Table of the Nations—Here again the **159a** author of Gn has combined his sources that contained similar data, and once more it is P that has furnished the substance of the account while J has been used to supplement it. The two can be separated fairly easily as follows: P: 10:1*a*.2—7.20.22—23.31—32. J: 10:1*b*.8—19.21.24—30. It is easy for the modern Western reader to skip over lightly such lists as this and fail to recognize the importance they had to the author of Gn. This list is an integral part of the history of salvation, which is a history of divine grace. It will be noted that Israel plays no part in it, save in the most obscure manner possible. Rather, the very obscurity of Israel, from all natural points of view, is the point of emphasis. Before embarking on the Patriarchal History which will bring out the origins of Israel in the extraordinary grace vouchsafed to Abraham and his descendants, the author shows how complex were the relations of the families of men and how, consequently, Israel and its ancestors were, from a detached point of view, insignificant and lost in a sea of nations.

It is easily seen that the **genealogical form** adopted **b** here actually relates peoples and regions more than it does individuals. Some of the names are frankly eponymous, much as though, in more familiar terms, it might be written: 'Britain became the father of America, and America begot Virginia, Vermont, Massachusetts. . . .' This, however, was not an artificial device to the ancients as it would be to us, for peoples were then much more readily conceived of as persons and as having a corporate personality. The relationships contained in the genealogies are based on geography and historical considerations rather than on race or true blood connections. The latter may be present, but they are only incidental to the author's purpose. In general, the peoples most remote from Palestine are listed as Japhethites; the Hamites tend to be those Gentile peoples with whom the Israelites had had unpleasant relations; and the Semites are those with whom the Israelites

159b recognized some kind of kinship. Because of the historical considerations involved, the same name may be variously categorized, cf Sheba in 6 and 28.

c 2–5 Japhethites—**2**. Gomer: Cimmerians. Magog: unidentified. Madai: Medes. Javan: Greeks (Ionians). Tubal and Meshech: the Tabali and Mushki of the Assyrian texts, Tibarenoi and Moschoi in Herodotus; inhabitants of the S shore of the Black Sea. Tiras: probably island dwellers of the Aegean Sea. **3**. Ashkenaz: Scythians. Riphath: unidentified. Togarmah: Tegarama in the Hittite texts; a region in Asia Minor between the upper course of the Halys and the Euphrates rivers. **4**. Elishah: perhaps Crete. Tarshish: perhaps Tartessos on the S coast of Spain, but it is the name of several places and Spain seems far away, in the context. Kittim: Cyprus (Sam P). Rodanim (so MT MSS; LXX; Sam P): the inhabitants of Rhodes.

d 6–20 Hamites—Cush: Ethiopia. Mizraim: Egypt. Put: usually identified with the Egyptian Punt, the present-day Somaliland. Canaan: the Israelite designation for the pre-Israelite inhabitants of Palestine. **7**. All these names probably refer to localities in the Arabian peninsula. **8–12**. Nimrod was a semi-legendary Near E figure who has never been satisfactorily identified. He appears to have been put in relation to Ninib or Ninurta the Babylonian god of war and hunting, patron of the city of Calah. In Mi 5:5 Assyria is called 'the land of Nimrod', and the Arabic name of Calah, the Iraqi site that has yielded spectacular Assyrian remains, is Nimrûd. Here, with the Yahwist's interest in origins, he is considered the first warrior and a mighty hunter: 'before Yahweh' is a superlative. All the sites connected with him are Mesopotamian: Babel (Babylon), Erech (the modern Warka in S Iraq), Accad (Sargon's capital which gave its name to the entire region of N Mesopotamia and to the Assyro-Babylonian language), Shinar (Babylonia), Nineveh (probably 'the great city' of the gloss in 12), and Calah. Rehoboth-Ir ('city squares') and Resen refer to unknown cities in the same region. Nimrod may have been associated with Cush because of the similarity of the Babylonian name *kaššu*, the Cassites, who dominated Babylonia for several centuries. In 11 prob. 'from that land he went forth to Ashur (Assyria)'. **13–14**. Most of these names are unknown. Lehabim: Lybians? Pathrusim: inhabitants of Pathros, upper Egypt.

e Caphtorim: Cretans. **15**. Sidon: the city of Phoenicia by whose name the N Canaanites were known (Jg 18:7). Heth: eponym of the Hittites. In the Bible 'Hittites' does not usually refer to the people of the great empire of Asia Minor but to pre-Israelite inhabitants of Canaan whom it distinguishes from the Canaanites. But see below § 165*g*. The Assyrians also referred to Phoenicia-Syria-Palestine as '*Ḫatti*-land'. **16–18**. In the E tradition the generic name for the aborigines of Canaan tends to be Amorites, in J Canaanites, and in P Hittites (cf Ezek 16:3). D (cf Nm 13:29; Dt 1:7) makes the Canaanites the inhabitants of the seacoast and the plains, while the Amorites (together with the Hittites, Hivites, Horites, Jebusites, and Girgashites) are residents of the hill country. Other names are Amalekites, inhabitants of the Negeb, and Perizzites (cf Jos 3:10). For the significance of most of these distinctions we have only conjecture. Arka, Sin, Arvad, Zemar: cities on the Phoenician coast. Hamath: city on the Orontes frequently mentioned in the Bible. **19**. The W and S limits of the land of Canaan. Gaza: one of the cities of the Philistine Pentapolis. Lesha: otherwise unknown, identified by the Jerusalem Targum and Jer (*Quaest. in Gen*. 10, 19; PL 23, 1004) with the later Callirrhoe on the E coast of the Dead Sea. The other sites are featured in the later narratives **159** of Gn.

21–32 Semites—**21**. Eber: eponym of the Hebrews, cf **f** *infra* § 161*e*. Here and in 24ff appears the J version of the Priestly genealogy of Shem found in 11:10–26. **22**. Elam: nation to the E of Babylonia, part of modern Persia, racially non-Semitic. Ashur: Assyria (Hamite in 11 above?). Arpachshad: perhaps the final consonants *kšd = kaśdîm*, the Chaldeans; in 22:22 Chesed the son of Nahor, Abraham's brother, is the eponym of the Chaldeans. Lud, Hamite in 13; uncertain, but not the Lydians. Aram: roughly equivalent to modern Syria. **23**. These names all refer to Aramaean sites, location unknown. Uz: not that of 22:21, which is Edomite. **24–25**. These are intended as personal names. 'In his days the earth was divided' (*peleg* = 'division'): perhaps a reference to 11:1–9; others think of the great network of irrigation canals (Akkadian *palgu*) dating even from Sumerian times by which Mesopotamia was watered. **26–29**. Some of these Joktanite names are unknown, but all seem to refer to regions of the Arabian peninsula. The same is to be said of the Mesha and Sephar of 30.

11:1–9 The Tower of Babel—It is evident that the **16** original purpose of this story was to tell of a divine intervention in the affairs of men by which the varied languages of the world arose. Ancient man found the phenomenon of foreign languages as surprising to him as it can be to the uneducated today, and he naturally thought of them as being deformations of some once common tongue. It is equally evident that this aetiological interpretation was attached to an event that had actually occurred, though it is doubtful that we can determine today what that event was in terms of scientific history. The event took place in Mesopotamia—the story itself places it in 'the land of Shinar', and what is described is obviously something peculiarly Mesopotamian, the construction of one of the huge stepped towers or ziggurats that were the characteristic of every ancient Babylonian town. The story itself has associated the event with Babylon for the sake of a popular etymology, and certainly the ziggurat of Babylon was a famous one. However, the famous ziggurat of Babylon was not left uncompleted, as the story seems to suppose. Perhaps the story had in mind the ziggurat of Borsippa, the present-day Birs-Nimrûd a few miles SW of Babylon, which was restored and completed by Nebuchadnezzar II (cf J. Plessis, 'Babylone et la Bible', DBS 1, 773). The massive ruins of this site remain among the most spectacular of Mesopotamia.

Gn has not used this story to teach anything about **b** the origins of languages, as Greg. Nyss. recognized long ago (*Contra Eunomium* 12; PG 45, 996f). The explicit references in ch 10 to the distribution of the various peoples over the lands 'each with his own language' (5, 20, 31) are from P, while this story was originally in J. However, even though not explicit, such a distribution was probably already taken for granted also in the J sections of ch 10. At all events, it was certainly taken for granted by the final author of Gn who combined the two sources. 'Language' in ch 11 meant something different in his teaching, therefore, than simply the national speech proper to a distinct people: he was helped in making this distinction by the fact that 11:16f, 9 used a word for 'language', *śapâ*, lit. 'lip', different from the *lāšōn*, lit. 'tongue', of ch 10. He has taken the common speech of the men in question to mean their common intentions and plans, which were opposed to those of Yahweh. Following J, he has recognized in the story of the tower a manifestation of human pride, man's continued

0b determination to work out his destiny on his own terms to the disregard of the divine economy. The Mesopotamian ziggurat was not in intention a work of rebellion, but the expression of the desire to draw closer to the gods. Nevertheless, as the biblical author viewed it, this was a continuation of the human proclivity for taking an initiative ('to be like God') which must be left to God himself. It is on this somewhat negative note that the Yahwistic prehistory concluded. Yet the note is not really negative in view of what follows it. For what follows is the history of salvation begun in the election of Abraham. If we must reach the melancholy conclusion that man of himself can only mismanage his affairs, the other side of the coin is the salvific will of God, which now begins to manifest itself in an ever more apparent way.

c **2.** This commemorates the migration of some ancient people into the plains of Babylonia: perhaps the Sumerians, the first inhabitants known in historical times (who, however, dispossessed an earlier, unknown people). **3.** A Palestinian author describes the, to him, exotic building methods of Mesopotamia: 'they had brick for stone and bitumen for mortar'. The sun-dried or baked mud-bricks of Mesopotamian construction resulted in structures that have weathered the ravages of time down to the present day. **4.** The words quoted of the builders of the tower are reminiscent of statements made by the Mesopotamian kings who built the ziggurats (cf Plessis, loc cit 774). **5—7.** Yahweh is represented quite anthropomorphically, as he is so often in J. Also, as in 1:26, etc, we have the use of the first person plural, cf *supra* § 149*f*. **9.** 'Yahweh confused (*bālal*) the language of the whole earth': the author finds a popular etymology for Babel, the Heb. equivalent of the Akkadian name Bab-ili or Bab-ilâni ('gate of the god(s)'), which we know by its Gr. form 'Babylon'.

d **10—26 The Postdiluvian Patriarchs**—On the numbers and generations involved, see above § 145. Arpachshad, Shelah, Eber, and Peleg appear in the genealogy of 10:22—25. Reu: an Aramaean tribe, the Ru'ua, is mentioned in Assyrian inscriptions as inhabiting the region along the Tigris and Euphrates. Serug: a city and region of Sarûgi existed midway between Carchemish and Haran. Nahor: this name appears in Babylonian inscriptions as that of a city and also as a personal name. In 26 another Nahor appears as Abraham's brother. Abraham's other brother, Haran (*hārān*) is not the same as the Haran (*hārān*) of 31. On the names Terah, Abram (Abraham), Haran, see below.

31a **11:27—50:26 THE PATRIARCHAL HISTORY**
11:27—25:18 The History of Abraham
11:27—32 The Terahites—We are now introduced to the Terahites, the clan from which the Bible derives the

Israelites and other related peoples of the environs of **161a** Palestine: (*see table at foot of page.*)

The Bible identifies this family as originally **pagan** (cf Jos 24:1—4) and as **deriving from Mesopotamia**. Archaeology and our widened knowledge of the ancient Near E have confirmed this picture. Most of the clan names, at least, are E Semitic (Akkadian) rather than Heb. and some of them are definitely to be related to the worship of the Semitic moon-god Sin. Among the latter are to be counted Sarai = Akkadian *šarratu*, 'queen', appelative of Nin-gal, Sin's consort; Milcah, 'princess', another appelative of Nin-gal; Laban, 'white', referring to Sin; possibly also Terah ('month') and Abram (of disputed etymology, but having some reference to the 'father' (*abu*), that is, Sin). The name Haran, as far as can be determined by analogy from the Beth-haran of Nm 32:36 (Beth-haram in Jos 13:27), was also the name of a deity. As we have already seen, there are countless indications in the earliest of the traditions employed in Gn to show their Mesopotamian origin. We shall see below the evidence for the correspondence of the laws and customs observed by the Patriarchs to the law and custom of contemporary Mesopotamia.

In 28 the first particular site associated with the **b** Terahites is **Ur**. Here and in 31 as well as in 15:7, therefore in both P and J, the MT qualifies this Ur as 'of the Chaldees'. This can only have reference to the ancient city of lower Mesopotamia which at various times, since about 2500 B.C., dominated the religious and political life of the ancient Near E. Since lower Mesopotamia became the land of the Chaldeans only many centuries after the Terahites, 'of the Chaldees' is certainly an anachronism. Is it also a gloss? It has been noted that elsewhere in the Bible the origins of the Patriarchs are put simply 'beyond the River' or are specifically located about Haran in N Mesopotamia; a postexilic text such as Neh 9:7 evidently depends on the Pentateuchal account in its present form, and therefore does not necessarily argue against a gloss here. There were, as now known from cuneiform texts, other cities named Ur or Ura. Hence some authors believe the Ur of Gn was originally without qualification, referring to some N site, and was later glossed to identify it with the most famous Ur of all. However, this appears to be an unnecessary conjecture, for there is ample reason to connect Ur with Haran, and the migration of the Terahites from the one to the other city is perfectly understandable in the light of the history of the times. During the zenith of Ur's power as chief city in Mesopotamia (Ur III, c. 2065—1960 B.C.) Haran appears to have been founded as a daughter city, part of its extensive trading empire. 'The Old-Assyrian **c** trade with Cappadocia can be traced back to the reign of Ibbi-Sin, last king of Ur. Harran on the Balikh was

31a

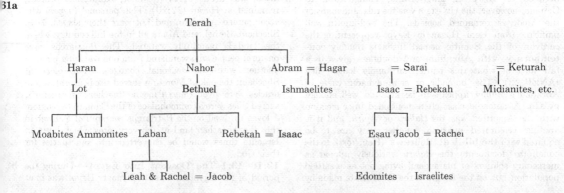

161c probably the N base of operations for this trade, as well as for commerce between Assyria and Iran to the E and Syria-Egypt to the W. So far there have been no deep operations on the site, and the name first appears in the Cappadocian tablets of the 19th cent., as well as often in the Mari texts. Its meaning is "caravan city" (*āl ḥarrānim*) like the name of Arabic Qayruwàn (Kairouan) in Tunisia. As is now well known, the names of Serug and Nahor, as well as probably of Terah, are found attached to towns in the neighbourhood; "the town of Nahor" (Gen 24:10) is mentioned in the Mari documents almost as often as Harran under the name *āl Naḥur*. There can, accordingly, be no doubt as to the importance of the Harran region for the caravan trade of the 19th cent. B.C. In view of the close trading relation between Ur and Harran, it is quite likely that the great temple of Sin (still called in later times by the old Sumerian name *Eḥulḥul*) was founded by the kings of Ur III, whose chief god was Sin' (Albright, 'Abram the Hebrew' 45f). Sometime after 1960 Ur was captured by the Elamites and ceased to have any importance until the 18th cent. when the Elamite kings of Larsa, Warad-sin and Rim-sin, made it a holy city for the moon-god. It is during this period that many authors would place the Terahite migration to Haran. Hence there seem to be good grounds for holding that Gn has preserved here an authentic tradition linking Heb. origins to lower Mesopotamia. As already noted, 10:22 and 22:22 also suggest this link.

d **The identity of the Terahites** in relation to the known peoples of the time is a celebrated question. The Bible refers to them as Aramaeans (Gn 25:20; Dt 26:5), though possibly in a geographic rather than an ethnic sense. They were, at all events, W Semites, and it is most likely that the Terahite migration from Ur to Haran and from Haran to Palestine must be connected with the Amorite invasions of the Fertile Crescent between 1900—1700 B.C. The Amorites, W Semites who came originally from the Syrian desert, are mentioned for the first time in a stele of Gudea of Lagash now in the Louvre (ANET 269), on which it was recorded that alabaster was brought from Tidanum in the land of Martu. Martu is Sumerian for 'Western land': the Akkadian equivalent was Amurru. The stele makes it clear that this Western land was Syria/Cilicia (in the centre of which was Haran). According to A. Poebel in JNES 1 (1942) 257f, this Tidanum is the Dedan of Gn 25:3, there represented as a descendant of Abraham through Keturah: if this is true, then Gn also connects the Amorites with the Terahites.

The Amorites who poured into Mesopotamia adapted themselves to the highly organized political life that had existed there since Sumerian times: the Amorite dynasty of Babylon is famous even to the casual reader because of its great lawgiver-king Hammurabi. In Canaan, however, the city-state was the rule, and many of the Amorites remained nomads. The well-known wall painting from Beni Hasan in Egypt representing the caravan of the Semitic nomad Ibsha is roughly **con-temporary with Abraham** and doubtless gives us a fair idea of what this patriarchal family looked like

e (ANEP 2f). The nomadic or semi-nomadic caste of Abraham's family appears to be attested well enough by Gn. A nomadic class often mentioned in connection with the Amorites was the *Ḥabiru* or *'Apiru*, and it is another celebrated question whether they are to be equated with **the biblical 'Hebrews'** (Heb. *'ibrî*). In the cuneiform documents the *Ḥabiru* variously appear as mercenary soldiers or marauders, living not as a settled population but on the fringes of the settlements made by Amorites and others; only from 14th cent. texts from Ras **161** Shamra do they appear at last as a settled population, and from these same texts it is clear that the word *Ḥabiru* is W Semitic. The word 'Hebrew' is used in the Bible of Israelites by Egyptians (Gn 39:14.17; 41:2; Ex 1:16; 2:6); of Israelites by Israelites when speaking to Egyptians (Gn 40:15; Ex 1:19; 2:7; 3:18; 5:3; 7:16; 9:1.13); of Israelites by Philistines (1 Sm 4:6.9; 13:3.19; 14:11; 29:3); of Israelite slaves (Ex 21:2 = Dt 15:12 = Jer 34:9.14); of Abraham in Gn 14:13 (cf *infra*); only once, in a late text, simply to mean 'Jew' (Jon 1:9). The cumulus of evidence seems to be that the term was originally applied to the Israelites by foreigners and designated them as outsiders, a class apart. In this the usage would correspond to that of *Ḥabiru* in the cuneiform literature. The eponymous derivation of 'Hebrew' from Eber (Gn 10:24) is doubtless artificial: originally the term was probably social (like 'Bedawin') rather than ethnic.

If the migration of the Terahites is probably to be placed within the period of the Amorite incursions, 1900—1700 B.C., there is no agreement as to whether it would have been toward the beginning or the end of this period. **The age of Abraham** is placed at the beginning of the second millennium by probably the majority of authors (Albright, de Vaux, Glueck, et al), but others (Pohl, Gordon, Rowley, et al) would make the date much later. In part, the decision depends on the later chronology of the Exodus and Conquest, cf § 126c. At all events, between 1700—1600 B.C. the Transjordan and the Negeb lost their sedentary populations that are supposed in the Patriarchal History, hence a date later than this could hardly be presumed.

12:1—9 The Call of Abraham—In the preceding **162** section, **28—30** are considered to be the beginning of this Yahwistic story of the call of Abraham; the rest of the section complements the Priestly list of Postdiluvian Patriarchs.

1—3. As the barrenness of Sarai was already mentioned in 11:30, Yahweh's initial promise to Abraham is already a test of his faith. The verb *weníbrekû* can be translated 'they shall be blest' or 'they will bless themselves'. As Abraham himself is called *a blessing*, the passive sense of the verb is recommended. At all events, it is clear that the blessing promised to Abraham is to extend to others. This blessing is that of a great 'name': that which the men of Babel tried to achieve for themselves independently of Yahweh (11:4). With the story of human origins and human rebellion now told, Yahweh intervenes in history to choose one man through whom his designs will be fulfilled. What were the secondary causes through which Abraham was called out of paganism into the worship of the true God, the sacred writer does not tell us. **4—5.** Only a part of the Terahites migrated to Canaan with Abraham. Lot's father was dead (11:27f); Nahor, Abraham's brother, remained at Haran (22:20). The 'persons' (*nepeš*) who accompanied Abraham and Lot were their slaves. **7—9.** Shechem, Bethel, and Ai are all in the hill country, where the land is plentifully watered. The Patriarchs were pastoral people who wandered from one watering place to another with the seasonal changes. 'The *place* at Shechem: the oak of Moreh: a sacred site is meant, where oracles were given (*môreh* means 'teacher', 'instructor'); sacred trees were a commonplace of the Canaanite religion. J loves to dwell on the Patriarchs' worship of Yahweh in this then heathen land at the very sites which later, in Israelite times would be converted into sanctuaries for their God.

12:10—13:1 The Descent into Egypt—During the **b** period of the Egyptian Twelfth Dynasty Egypt was in at

162b least nominal control of Canaan and there was free transit between the countries; archaeology has shown a prevalence of Amorite names in Egypt during this time (1900—1700 B.C.). As noted above, the caravan of Ibsha doubtless gives us a visualization of Abraham's appearance in Egypt. This continuation of the Yahwistic narrative has, therefore, an intrinsic probability. Abraham's conduct appears shabby to us, but according to the moral standards recognized in his day he was acting prudently, and it would be a false issue to attempt to judge him by Christian standards. On the repetition of the theme of this story in chh 20 and 26, see below. Obviously its lesson was an important one for the author of Gn: Yahweh is faithful in safeguarding his promise, protecting it from the interference of Pharaoh and even of Abraham himself! In **16** the omission of horses is not accidental. It is generally held that horses were introduced into Egypt only in the time of the Hyksos, cf § 170*i*; the nomads of Abraham's time had the ass (donkey) in place of the horse, cf the picture of Ibsha's caravan. However, the skeleton of a horse was discovered in the archaeology of Twelfth Dynasty Buhen, near Wadi Halfa in the Sudan, cf W. B. Emery in the *Illustrated London News* for 12 Sept. 1959, 250. According to one widely credited view, the camel was not domesticated until the 13th cent. B.C., and consequently references to the camel here and frequently throughout the Patriarchal History are anachronisms. This view, however, is disputed by various authorities. **18.** The author tells his story without irrelevant detail. No explanation is given how Pharaoh recognized the plagues as a divine visitation and how he discovered the truth about Abraham's wife.

c **13:2—18 The Separation from Lot**—J. 2—7. The term 'Perizzites' in 7 sometimes substitutes for 'Amorites' in the coupling 'Canaanites and Amorites' to designate the sedentary inhabitants of the land of Canaan. Abraham and Lot were nomadic herdsmen, not inhabiting the cities of Canaan with which they are brought in contact, but living on their fringes. **8—9.** This action by which Abraham and Lot reach agreement and avoid family strife is typical of the covenants which regulated the practical affairs of everyday life in nomadic society. Though Abraham would have had the right of choice as the elder to Lot, he magnanimously cedes this right to his nephew. **10—13.** On Sodom, Gomorrah, and Zoar, see below § 164*e*. In 10 by 'Egypt' is meant the Nile Delta. In 13 preparation is made for the story of ch 19. **14—17.** Abraham does not simply choose the land of his sojourn on his own authority; rather, he is told to traverse its length and breadth in token of its later possession by his descendants. As in 12:7, we have here the tradition of the promised land, which was especially dear to Israelite historians who had seen the fulfilment of the promise in the Exodus and Conquest. **18.** The 'oaks' (or 'terebinths', so also in 12:6) of Mamre: another sacred site. Mamre was in the heights overlooking Hebron, today called Râmet el-Khalîl, 'heights of the Friend': Abraham is known to the Muslim Arabs as 'the Friend of God' (cf 2 Chr 20:7).

d **14:1—24 The Expedition of the Kings**—This ch is unique in the book of Gn (it belongs to none of the three traditions recognized elsewhere in the book) and indeed in the whole annals of Israel. 'Almost every sentence is full of antiquarian information, and nowhere in the patriarchal stories do we find such a mass of historical and geographical detail' (von Rad, 170). Not all of this information is equally credible. It might be just possible to find an explanation for a coalition of four great kings from Mesopotamia against five very insignificant Canaanite townships, and for the curious route the expedition took;

it may have been a joint attempt to clear a trade-route to **162d** the Red Sea, and the incident described here a minor detour of importance only in the local traditions of the people involved. But then what about the Rephaim, Zuzim and Emim in v 5—names used elsewhere only in a quasi-legendary context? (cf § 156*d*) Mamre, a place name in 13:18, appears here (v 13) as a personal name, along with Eshcol (a place name in Nm 13:23f, JE). Most striking of all is the fact that Abraham ('the Hebrew'! see § 161*e*) is introduced so late into the story, and that when introduced is portrayed in a way different from that of the other patriarchal traditions (though it does not necessarily contradict them). It seems that Abraham was introduced later into a story of uncertain date and origin. Moreover, the incident concerning Melchizedek (17—20) appears to be from yet another source; notice how smoothly 21 takes up after 16. But it is probably the Melchizedek incident which explains the importance of the whole passage in the mind of the compiler, and the reason why it was included in the story of Abraham.

The only other place in the OT where Melchizedek is **e** mentioned is the royal Ps 110 (109). This can hardly be accidental and must be taken into account in trying to understand the present passage. The great difficulty faced by the monarchy was the apparent conflict between this form of government and the amphictyonic ideal of the independent tribes bound together by covenant with God (see 1 Sm ch 8 with comm. and § 62). This difficulty was not lessened when David began to rule as king of the Canaanite town of Jerusalem. The transfer of the Ark, palladium of the amphictyonic league, to Jerusalem was one way of reassuring the people that their ideals were safe in the hands of David. But both Ps 110 (109) and the present passage may be seen as propaganda to the same end. The Israelite king, ruling from Jerusalem, was to be regarded as rightful successor of the ancient priest-kings of Jerusalem represented here by Melchizedek (who already recognized in some way the God of Israel, v 18f) and whom Abraham himself treated with great respect. It is also possible that the passage contains a plea in favour of Zadoc, chosen by David to be priest of the Jerusalem shrine. He may have been originally priest of the pre-Israelite shrine of Jebus, later legitimized and adopted into the line of Aaron. Cf H. H. Rowley, 'Zadoc and Nehustan', JBL 58 (1939) 113—41; id, 'Melchizedek and Zadok', in *Fs Bertholet*, 1950, 461—72. This interpretation does not necessarily conflict with the former 'By linking Abraham with the future capital of David, the text is trying to justify Israel's very ancient connections with Jerusalem, and the rights which the king and the priesthood held over Israel' (de Vaux, AI, 310).

1—4. Though we cannot identify any of the kings who **f** appear in this ch with known Mesopotamian rulers, the names all ring true. After the collapse of Ur III and until c. 1830 B.C. (the rise of the Amorite dynasty of Babylon) Elam exercised control throughout the Fertile Crescent: in this story it is an Elamite king who is in charge of the expedition and to whom the kings of Canaan had been subject. His name, Chedorlaomer, (*Kudur-Lagamar*, 'servant of Lagamar' [an Elamite deity]), is authentically Elamite. Amraphel (*'āmar-pî-'el*, 'the mouth of [the] god has spoken'), the king of Shinar, bears a W Semitic name, in keeping with the Amorite domination of Babylonia. The once popular identification of Amraphel with the Amorite king Hammurabi must now be abandoned, for philological as well as chronological reasons. Arioch (*Arriwuk* or *Arriyuk*) was the name of several Mesopotamian rulers; Ellasar has not been

162f satisfactorily identified, but it was probably *not* Larsa in S Babylonia. Tidal is the Heb. version of the Hittite royal name *Tudhalia*; he is called 'king of *Goiim*', 'nations', a title that was sometimes given the Hittites. These vv also introduce us to all five cities of the pentapolis of which we shall hear more in chh 18—19: Sodom, Gomorrah, Admah, Zeboiim, and Bela (Zoar). The Valley of Siddim doubtless refers to the entire region in which these cities were once situated, now submerged by the Dead Sea S of the Lisan.

g **5—7**. This route of conquest would hardly have been possible after c. 1700 B.C., when these regions were without sedentary populations. Ashteroth-karnaim ('the two-horned Astarte') is today Tell 'Aštarah in the Hauran. Ham, further S, is still called Ham. Shaveh-kiriathaim ('plain of the twin cities') is in the vicinity of Khirbet el-Qaryetein, E of the Dead Sea. Hazazon-tamar, elsewhere simply Tamar (Ez 47:19; 48:28), is at the extreme S of the Dead Sea, on the Cisjordan side. The other geographical indications are well-known in the Bible. Biblical tradition regarded the Horites (Hurrians) as the aborigines of Edom, later driven out by Esau and his descendants (cf 36:20ff).

h **10**. Bitumen still rises in large quantities from the Dead Sea bed. Evidently the kings of the Valley of Siddim had chosen to join battle on their own terrain, hoping to benefit from its treacherous character, but instead they were defeated. **12**. Up to this point the story has been uncharacteristically concerned with world history. Only now is the connexion made with Patriarchal History: after parting from Abraham, Lot had moved towards Sodom (13:12). **13—16**. Abraham appears here as a powerful chieftain with 318 warriors under his command, allied with other chieftains of the region and at the disposal of the five kings to serve as mercenary troops. The Ḥabiru are represented in this capacity in the Mari tablets. According to Albright ('Abraham the Hebrew', 52) the *hapax legomenon* used for Abraham's troops (*hănîkāyw*) is an Egyptian word used in the 20th cent. and later for the retainers of Asiatic chieftains. **17**. 'The Valley of Shaveh, that is the King's Vale': *shaveh* itself means 'valley' or 'plain' (cf 5 above). Hence it may be assumed that the original reading of the text was *šāweh hammelek*, 'King's Vale', and the present 'King's Vale' of the text (*ēmeq hammelek*) is an interpretative formula taken from 2 Sm 18:18 (Vincent, de Vaux, Simons). The latter was certainly a site near Jerusalem. Whether the same may be said for the valley of this v depends on the
i original character of the source material. **18—20**. See above. Salem is probably a deliberate truncation introduced in Israelite times (so also in Ps 76 (75):3), since the Amarna tablets give the name as *Urušalim*, the E Semitic equivalent of the biblical Jerusalem. *Yᵉrusalem* would mean 'Salem (a deity) has laid (the foundations of the city)'. The deliberate shortening of the name would have been to remove these pagan connotations; probably the MT vocalization *yᵉrušālayim* is also intended to conceal the connexion with the pagan god Salem. This deity is known from the Ras Shamra and Amarna tablets: he possessed a temple in 'the country of Jerusalem'. The priest-king Melchizedek fits into a pattern that was common in the city-states of Canaan and throughout the Near E. His name associates him with Zedek (*malkî-sedeq* = 'Zedek is (my) king') who was doubtless another deity worshipped in Jerusalem; cf Adonizedek ('Zedek is (my) lord'), the king of Jerusalem in Jos 10:1. He is described as priest of El-Elyon (the 'Most High God'), a divine title which we know to have been used among the Canaanites. Many of these titles were later applied to

Yahweh by the Israelites. But what is remarkable here **162** is that the author allows Abraham to accept Melchizedek's **God** as his own (**22**; LXX, Syr. Sam P, omit Yahweh; it has probably been introduced by a later Israelite writer to avoid scandal). The whole tone manifests an approval of Canaanite religion unique in the Bible. See above. The bread and wine that Melchizedek 'brought out' may have been something more than a common meal for Abraham and his followers: eating together can have a religious significance, as in the consummation of a covenant (cf Ex 24:11). But even the Epistle to the Hebrews, which exploits the typology of Melchizedek's priesthood at great length, finds no symbolism relating to Christ in the bread and wine. In their recognition of Melchizedek's priesthood as **a type of Christ's**, the NT and Christian tradition depend on the messianic Ps 110 (109) which sees in Melchizedek a type of the messianic king in that he was both *king* and *priest* in *Jerusalem*. Heb. further developed the typology, but Clem. Alex. was the first to see in the bread and wine a figure of the Eucharist, while Cyprian in the 4th cent. was the first to consider Melchizedek's offering to Abraham a real sacrifice. It is in the final development of this typology that Melchizedek appears in the Canon of the Mass. Cf P. F. Cremin, 'According to the Order of Melchizedech', IrER 51 (1938) 469—87; 52 (1938) 37—45; 53 (1939) 487—500.

21—24. Abraham's refusal to accept any share of the booty underlines his disinterestedness. His refusal to receive any benefit at the hands of the king of Sodom also contrasts with his willing involvement with Melchizedek. Both these facts were, of course, significant to an Israelite author.

15:1—21 Yahweh's Covenant With Abraham—This **163** ch gives evidence of being a compilation from sources: to cite only one example, in 5 Abraham is able to count the stars, so that the 'vision' of 1—6 appears to have been one in Abraham's sleep at night, yet in 12 the sun is only going down, and not until 17 does it become dark. The ch is mainly J, but another source has been interwoven with it so thoroughly that it is impossible to make a convincing separation. The other source is commonly thought to be Elohistic, which thus appears in Gn for the first time. **1**. 'Fear not' is a reassurance often reiterated in divine communications (Gn 21:17; 26:24; Lk 1:13; 1:30, etc). The 'reward' that is promised to Abraham appears, in this context as in others, to mean rather God's free gift. Reference is to the promise of numerous offspring (12:2), which in view of Sarai's barrenness (11:30) appears to be impossible of fulfilment. **2—4**. 2b is obscure and possibly corrupt; however, the meaning seems to be that Abraham, in default of natural heirs, had adopted as his heir Eliezer, the trusted slave who was steward of his possessions (24:2). Under the Mosaic Law there was no provision for such arrangements. Abraham appears to have been following the contemporary Nuzi laws of adoption (cf § 167d): another testimony to the reliability of these patriarchal traditions. **6**. In the face of the probabilities to the contrary, Yahweh repeats his promise. Abraham makes an act of faith in God, who thereby accounts him 'just'. 'Justice' (*sᵉdāqāh*) or 'righteousness' **b** signifies a right relationship with God. Later Christian theology would refer to this condition as that of sanctifying grace. The significance which St Paul attached to this text as implying the gratuitousness of justification is well known, cf Rm 4:1ff; Gal 3:7ff. **7**. The other promise to Abraham involved the future possession of the land of Canaan (12:7; 13:14ff). This promise is solemnized in a covenant ritual, the preparations for which are described

63b in **9—10**. The Heb. for 'make a covenant' is *b^erît kāraṭ*, lit. 'cut a covenant'. Doubtless the expression derives from some rite similar to that described here. Cf also Jer 34:18: at Mari (cf § 79*g*) 'slaughter an ass' meant 'make a covenant'. The animals were slaughtered and divided (except the birds, which were too small), and the contracting parties took their covenant oath between the divided parts, the signification being that they called down a similar fate upon themselves if they should violate their oath. In the text of a treaty between Ashur-nirari VI of Assyria (753—46 B.C.) and Matti-ilu, king of Bit-Agusi, we read: 'This head [of an ox] is not the head of the ox, but the head of Matti-ilu, his sons, his nobles, his people, and his country. If anyone sins against these vows, just as this head is removed, so may he be removed' (cf Clamer 265). **11**. Birds of prey were an ill omen. **12**. 'Deep sleep':
c *tardēmāh*, as in 2:21. In this state divine revelations are often given (Jb 4:13; 33:15). **13—16** interrupt the dramatic story. These vv explain the patriarchal promise of the land as fulfilled in the Israelites, as elsewhere in the Pent. Nowhere else, however, does a generation (16) equal 100 years (13). In Ex 12:40 (P) the duration of the Israelite sojourn in Egypt is given as 430 years. 'Go to your fathers' in 15 can hardly mean simply burial in the family tomb, for Abraham has broken with his family and will die in another land than theirs. **17**. The oven (*tannûr*) and torch signify the divine presence: throughout the Bible fire indicates the presence of divinity. In this instance, God alone passes between the divided animals, for the covenant is unilateral, a gratuitous promise (Chaine). **18—21**. The 'ideal limits' of the promised land are given, asserted at least in principle in Solomon's time (1(3) Kgs 4:21). The 'river of Egypt' is the Wadi el-'Arîsh which divides Palestine from the Sinaitic Peninsula. On the Kenites, cf above § 154 *b,d*. The Kenizzites are elsewhere related to the Edomites (36:11); some of them, at least, were later incorporated into Israel. Caleb (Jos 14:6ff, etc) was a Kenizzite. Kadmonites appear only here; they may be the same as the 'people of the east' (*b^enê qedem*) of 29:1, that is, Arab peoples living to the east of Palestine (cf also Kedemah among the Ishmaelites in 25:15). The other names we have seen.

d **16:1—16 The Birth of Ishmael**—J, with the exception of 3 and 15f, a brief parallel version of the story from P. Having recalled Yahweh's promise to Abraham which is to be fulfilled in the birth of Isaac, the author shows how Abraham and his wife attempted to anticipate the divine blessing through their own devices, not entirely successfully. As St Paul would later say, Ishmael was born according to the flesh, but Isaac according to the promise (Gal 4:23). The arrangement supposed in **1—6** is not provided for in the Mosaic Law, but seems to have a parallel in Nuzi legislation (cf ANET 220, also the Code of Hammurabi 144). Legally, the child of Hagar would have been Sarai's, since the purpose of the arrangement was to provide a legitimate heir. On the other hand, what is supposed in 4—6 seems to be provided for in the Code of Hammurabi 146. The laws in this code refer explicitly to certain restricted classes, but they certainly are based on more general legal principles. Sarai did not have the right to send Hagar away, since Ishmael was Abraham's heir, but she could treat her as the slave she was. **7**. The action of 1—6 presumably occurred at Mamre (13:18), from which Hagar fled to the S, towards her homeland. Shur, 'wall', refers to the defensive wall on the Egyptian frontier built to control the immigration of 'Asiatics'. Here and in 9f reference is made to the 'angel of Yahweh', while in 13 the Person who speaks to Hagar is identified with Yahweh himself. By some this is explained by assuming that in the

most primitive form of the story the speaker was Yahweh **163d** himself, and only later out of reverence the word 'angel' was inserted in some places. In other traditions besides J, the process seems to have been extended, so that Yahweh speaks more and more mediately to his creatures. However, it is doubtful in these ancient times whether the Israelites thought of the 'angel of Yahweh' as a personage distinct from Yahweh himself. The 'angel' (*mal'āk*), lit. 'messenger' was rather Yahweh himself made manifest to man. See below, in ch 18.

9—10. Yahweh also has a blessing for Ishmael because **e** of Abraham, though he is not to be the bearer of the promise. Therefore he insists on Hagar's return. **11**. Ishmael = 'God hears'. **12**. What is being described is the life of the Bedawin Arab, whose way of life simultaneously attracted and repelled the later Israelite. **13**. 'The God of vision': *'ēl ro'î*. Probably this was another divine title used in Canaan later appropriated to Yahweh. The sense of the rest of the verse is obscure. Perhaps: 'Have I actually seen God, yet lived after my vision?' (cf Ex 33:20; Jg 6:23, etc). **14**. The conjectural reading of 13*b* is based on the popular etymology intended for Beer-lahai-roi, in which *lahay* has some relation to 'life'. Its precise meaning is unknown, as is its location and that of Bered. Clamer suggests as the site the Biyar Mayin between Ain Qedeis (Kadesh) and Jebel Umm el-Bared.

17:1—27 The Covenant of Circumcision—P 164a version of the covenant made with Abraham, paralleling the JE account in ch 15. It was important to the author because of the religious interpretation given to the practice of circumcision, a usage prevalent among many other peoples, ancient and modern, for various reasons. Since circumcision was not practised in Mesopotamia but had been adopted by the Hebrews after their entry into Canaan, it could rightly be seen as a sign of the covenant of grace which God extended to Abraham. So also the change in spelling of the names of Abraham and Sarah, which doubtless had as its historical explanation the dialectical variations between Mesopotamian and Canaanite use.

1. 'God Almighty': El Shaddai, a divine name of disputed origin. In P Shaddai is the proper name of God as known to the Patriarchs, and the name Yahweh is restricted to the Mosaic revelation (cf Ex 6:3). To 'walk before' God is to live consciously in God's presence; this formula is characteristic of the Patriarchal covenant (cf 24:40; 48:15) and is distinguished from the relationship of the just men of the pre-Abrahamic age who 'walked with' God (5:22,24; 6:9). Like Noah, however (6:9), Abraham must be 'blameless'. **2—4**. No covenant ritual is described as in ch 15: P speaks of no sacrifice before the time of Moses. **5**. 'Father of a multitude (of nations)': *'ab hamôn*, is the popular etymology invoked to explain the change of Abram into Abraham. J also sees in the call of Abraham a blessing that was to extend to other nations besides Israel (12:3). **8**. The land in which the Patriarchs live as sojourners (21:23; 28:4; 35:27; 36:7; 37:1; 47:9; Ex 6:4) will be given to Abraham's descendants in fulfilment of this covenant. **9—14**. For the Israelites circumcision signified the consecration of the source of life to God. It was to remain for them a sign of their belonging to the people of God, and could be neglected only at the cost of excluding oneself from this people. **15**. No religious explanation is given for the change of Sarai's name to Sarah. **17**. Abraham's reaction to the promise, as yet unspecified, of the birth of Isaac is a good psychological study in which reverence for the word of God is mingled with natural incredulity. Abraham

164b 'laughed' (*yiṣḥaq*), a word-play on the name Isaac, repeated in 18:12 and 21:6. **18—21.** As before (cf 16: 1—16), Abraham suggests what to him appears the most likely means for the fulfilment of God's promise of a numerous posterity, which, however, is overruled by a reiteration of the divine provision just announced. Ishmael, too, is to be blessed as the father of a great nation, but the covenant made with Abraham will find its continuation in Isaac.

c **18:1—15 Yahweh visits Abraham**—The J passages of chh 18—19 contain some of the most anthropomorphic representations of God to be found in Gn, yet they also manifest a profoundly true conception of the divine nature and of God's attributes of justice and mercy. The present story is told with great artistry: Abraham and Sarah at first perceive in their guests only distinguished men; Sarah's reaction in 12 is the natural one of a woman who thinks her husband's guest has expressed a conventional politeness in ignorance of her advanced age; in 15 fear follows on her realization that the visitors are not ordinary men. The description of the hospitality offered, the manner of serving, Sarah's seclusion from the men, and the rest, are all true to desert life.
1. It is difficult to determine whether Yahweh himself appears accompanied by two angels ('men', 2), or whether all three 'men' are 'angels of Yahweh'. See on 16:7. **3.** 'My lord' (*'aḏōnî* in place of MT *'aḏōnāy*): a conventional title of respect. Abraham addresses the one who appears to be the leader of the party. Syr., however, read the plural (*'aḏōnay*) throughout the verse, and perhaps correctly. **6—8.** Abraham acts the part of the lavish and deferential host in the best tradition of Oriental hospitality, the virtue most prized by the ancient Semite. **10.** The J version of the announcement of Isaac's birth. **12.** Sarah's laugh is again a play on the name Isaac; see on 17:17. **14.** The identity of the heavenly visitors is now explicitly revealed.

d **16—33 Yahweh's Dialogue With Abraham**—**17—19** stress the special relationship between Yahweh and Abraham, according to which the latter could be called 'the friend of God'. They also bring out (as in 17:1 P) the moral obligations of the covenant, something not mentioned in ch 15. **20.** The sinfulness of Sodom cries to heaven for divine punishment. **23—32.** The scene is Hebron (1), on the heights overlooking Sodom and Gomorrah. Yahweh and Abraham are represented as 'bargaining', in Oriental fashion, concerning the future of Sodom. In part, the lesson of this colloquy is to condition the rigidity of the OT doctrine of collective retribution. God does not destroy the just along with the wicked. Even more important, perhaps, is its insight into the nature of righteousness: for the sake of the few just (who are not to be found in Sodom), God will even avert retribution from the wicked. The just man is truly the life of the community.

e **19:1—29 The Destruction of Sodom and the Deliverance of Lot**—Israelite tradition related that four of the cities of the Pentapolis mentioned in ch 14 had perished and now lay beneath the Dead Sea. Wis 10:6 (a summary of all the traditions) speaks of the destruction of the Pentapolis cumulatively; Hos 11:8 may be an E tradition (mentioning only Zeboiim and Admah) corresponding to this J tradition which mentions only Sodom and Gomorrah; Dt 29:22 has all four cities destroyed. Zoar alone is spared. The traditions have preserved an historical fact: the S region of the Dead Sea coast is known to the Arabs today as Jebel Sdum or Usdum, in which the name of Sodom may be found. The ancient destruction could have taken place through

sinkage and ignition of the asphalt and sulphur with which **16** the Dead Sea is saturated: there was a similar occurrence in Roman times. The S shore of the Dead Sea is still receding; present-day Arabs are said to recall that their immediate ancestors could wade from El-Lisan to the opposite bank, a thing no longer possible.
1. Here and in 15 the heavenly visitors are called **f** angels (*mal'āḵîm*, 'messengers'); the text may have originally read 'men' as in ch 18. Lot had pitched his tent near Sodom (12:13); here we see that he had taken up residence in the town. **4—5.** The unnatural vice which has been named after this biblical incident was widespread in the ancient world. It was regarded as an abomination by the Israelites, punishable by death (Lv 18:22; 20:13; Dt 23:18f); but the Code of Hammurabi 187, 192, 193 protected its 'votaries'. **8.** Lot proves to be a better host than father. His action can hardly be praised; however, he chose what he thought the lesser of two evils. His gracious hospitality, like Abraham's, is set in contrast to the boorish conduct of the men of Sodom. **9.** Lot's plea is contemptuously rejected on the score that he himself is a sojourner in Sodom with no civic rights. **12—13.** The men of Sodom have failed the test proposed by Yahweh (18:20f), therefore Sodom must be destroyed. Yet divine judgement cannot fall upon the innocent (22), and for the sake of the just others may be spared. **18—22.** Lot's reference to his proposed refuge as a 'little place' (*miṣʿār*) prepares for the popular etymology of Zoar (*ṣōʿar*). The site of Zoar is unknown, but it was a city that existed in later Israelite times (Dt 34:3; Is 15:5; Jer 48:34) and apparently in mediaeval times as well. **26.** Lot's wife disobeys the command in 17 and becomes a pillar of salt. One of the salt formations resembling stalagmites that surround the Dead Sea doubtless suggested this description of the fate of her whom tradition had said perished in the ruin of Sodom. The religious meaning is obvious: 'where God intervenes in a direct act on earth man cannot adopt the stance of a spectator; and before divine judgement there is only the possibility of being smitten or of escaping, but no third alternative' (von Rad). **29.** This seems to be a summary parallel tradition from P. Here the salvation of Lot is ascribed to Abraham's intercession.

30—38 Origin of the Moabites and the Ammonites— **g** Lot is presented in ambivalent character: faced with a dilemma involving the sanctity of his roof, he made a decision that did him little credit; told to flee to the hills he secured an alternative refuge from God; now he has decided to reside in the hills after all. Finally, he is associated with an act which, however well motivated, was an abomination in Israelite eyes (Dt 27:20.23; Lv 18: 6—8). The Israelites acknowledged relationship with the Ammonites and Moabites, but they could not have failed to look with horror on the source of that relationship as related in this (possibly polemic) tradition. Like the story of Tamar in ch 38, however, this narrative illustrates the fierce Semitic desire for offspring. Moab and Ammon are given popular etymologies: *mēʾāḇ* (32.34.36), 'by [our] father'; Ben-ammi (28) means 'son of the parent'.
20:1—18 Abraham and Sarah in Gerar—This is an **h** Elohistic parallel to the J tradition of ch 12 which localized the event in Egypt. A third version of the story follows in ch 26. The same religious teaching is involved: God's protection of his elect. Here we see that Abraham's fault is attenuated by the mention that Sarah was in fact his half-sister. Also, it is made clear that Abimelech had not actually approached Sarah. This story has been incorporated into the author's work without regard to the Priestly chronology: if this chronology were historical,

164h Sarah would have been ninety years old (cf 12:4 + 17:17 + 21:5) when she attracted the attention of Abimelech. **1.** 'From there': in the present text of Gn Abraham understandably departs from the region of the events of ch 19. **3–7.** This narrative is remarkable in showing a Canaanite king on familiar terms with God and also in vindicating the purity of his motives. **4.** Why Abimelech had not approached Sarah is doubtless explained in 17—18. In the OT view sin is an objective fact, an offence to God, regardless of a lack of malice on the part of the offender. Similarly, a man's sin affects all that he owns, all that constitute with him a corporate person (cf Jos 7:16—26). **7.** 'A prophet': in the sense of a man of God's special protection. **9—18.** In his honourable and generous treatment of Abraham and Sarah and complete shouldering of the blame in this matter, Abimelech displays a fear of God more singleminded than Abraham's. This lesson of humility would not have been lost on the Israelite reader.

165a **21:1–7 The Birth of Isaac**—In this passage the critics usually assign 1*a*,2*a*,6*b*—7 to J, 1*b*,2*b*—5 to P, and 6*a* to E. The three traditions all told of the birth of Isaac. E also has the word-play on Isaac's name (cf 17:17; 18:12), but here (**6a**) the laughter is that of joy. Since we do not have the Elohistic account of the promise of Isaac, it is not clear whether this tradition contained the detail of Sarah's advanced age.

8–21 The Dismissal of Hagar and Ishmael—Elohistic: originally a doublet of J, ch 16. There was sufficient disparity of detail, however, to make each version important in its own right. Once again we see how such a story is independent of the P chronology: here Ishmael is evidently considered to be an infant (cf 15), whereas in its present context and presupposing a consistent chronology Hagar's son would have had to be upwards of fifteen years old (cf 16:3; 21:5).

b **8.** The age of weaning was up to three years, cf 1 Sm 1:22ff; 2 Mc 7:27. **9.** 'Playing': *ṣāḥaq*, another play on the name of Isaac ('with her son Isaac' is lacking in MT supplied from LXX and Vg). Later Jewish tradition, on which St Paul is dependent in Gal 4:29, considered this play to have consisted in Ishmael's contemptuous treatment of Isaac. The verb may have such a meaning. However, for a jealous mother, it sufficed to see her son together with the slave-girl's on a position of equality for her to demand the expulsion of Hagar and her child. **10.** If the situation presupposed is that which seems to underlie ch 16, then Sarah did not have the right to drive Hagar away; see on 16:1—6. As contrary to established social custom, therefore, the expulsion would have to be authorized by way of exception, in view of God's larger plans, as we see in **12—13.** **17.** 'God heard': a play on the name Ishmael. In the Elohistic narrative the angel of God does not appear as a man but speaks as a voice from heaven. **19.** 'A well'; cf 16:14. **21.** The region of the Ishmaelites, cf 25:17—18.

c **22–34 Abraham's Covenant with Abimelech**—This account is a good example of the way in which parallel traditions have been combined in compiling this ancient history. The two versions were so alike that they could be welded together without difficulty, yet they tell two different stories. E related simply a covenant of friendship. In it, Beer-sheba is given a popular etymology from *beʾēr* (well) + *šāba* (swear). In J the covenant results from a dispute over a well, and Beer-sheba is so called from *beʾēr* (well + *šeba* (seven), that is, the seven lambs which Abraham sets apart. In ch 26 another version of this story will be found associated with Jacob.

E

(22) At that time Abimelech and Phicol the general of **165c** his army said to Abraham: 'God [Elohim] is with you in all that you do. **(23)** Swear therefore to me that you will not use deceit against me or against my children; that you will exercise the same kindness towards me and the land in which you dwell that I have always exercised towards you.' **(24)** Abraham said: 'I will swear.' **(27)** Abraham took sheep and oxen and gave them to Abimelech, and the two of them made a covenant. **(31)** Therefore the place was called Beer-sheba, because both of them took an oath there.

J

(25) Abraham reproached Abimelech because of some wells which Abimelech's servants had taken by force. **(26)** Abimelech answered: 'I do not know who did this thing. You did not tell me of it, and I did not hear of it until today.' **(28)** Abraham set aside seven ewe lambs from the flock. **(29)** Abimelech said to Abraham: 'What do these seven ewe lambs mean that you have set aside?' **(30)** But he replied: 'You will take these seven ewe lambs from my hand as a testimony that I dug this well.' **(32)** And they made a covenant at Beer-sheba. **(33)** And he planted a tamarisk tree at Beer-sheba, and he invoked there the name of Yahweh, God eternal.

22—23 presupposes the story of ch 20. Abimelech **d** recognizes the special protection which Abraham has from God and therefore seeks his sworn friendship. **25—26.** The importance of wells in these dry regions made them an inevitable source of conflict among pastoral peoples. **30.** By accepting a gift, the recipient acknowledges the truthfulness of the giver. **33.** 'A tamarisk tree': as a witness to the covenant. 'God eternal': El-Olam, another divine name of the Canaanites appropriated to Yahweh. As usual, the Yahwistic tradition associates the sacred sites of Canaan with the Patriarchs. **34.** Only here is Beer-sheba located 'in the land of the Philistines'; the J part of ch 26 also identifies Abimelech as 'king of the Philistines', but the locale is Gerar as in ch 20. Most authorities agree that the Philistines were not in Palestine prior to 1200 B.C. Cf above § 144*e*. Abimelech's name is Semitic, and the Philistines were not Semites.

22:1—19 Abraham's Obedience—Mostly E— **e** despite the fact that in the present text the name Yahweh appears in 11 and 14. By some, 15—18 are judged to be a parallel account from J, but this is not the common view. The vv do seem, however, to represent a subsequent addition to the original story. This narrative is one of the most sublime of the Patriarchal History, of inimitable pathos that 'can hardly be read without tears' (Skinner). The event is commemorated in the NT in Heb 11:17—19, and especially by St Paul in Rm 4, where Abraham is shown to be the type of all who have their salvation through faith in God. **1.** 'God tested Abraham': the reader is told from the beginning that what is to follow is a test of Abraham's faith and obedience. The Patriarch himself, however, discovers this only subsequently: for the moment, the Author of life is commanding him to destroy all his hopes of progeny and thus the fulfilment of God's promise to him. **2.** The greatness of the sacrifice is emphasized. 'The land of Moriah' has never been identified. The original text may have been 'land of the Amorites' (so Syr.) and later revised by a scribe in view of 2 Chr 3:1. **12.** The true essence of sacrifice consists in purity of heart and inward disposition. **13.** There may have been some religious or

165e other significance attached to this representation which now escapes us: the statue of a ram in a similar position was found in the excavations of Ur (cf Woolley, *Ur of the Chaldees* pl. 6; ANEP 218, text 329). **14**. The name which Abraham gives the place, *Yahweh yire'eh*, doubtless originally appeared as a popular etymology of Moriah. However, the interest of this story for the Israelite did not lie in the connexion of any specific Palestinian sanctuary with the Patriarchs, but rather in contrasting Patriarchal (and Israelite) sacrificial practice with the human sacrifices, and in particular the sacrifice of infants, common among the Canaanites. Under heathen influence human sacrifice was later practised in Israel (cf 2 (4) Kgs 16:3, etc), contrary to Israelite law and over the protests of the prophets. **16**. Only here in Gn is God said to swear 'by himself'. **18**. See on 12:3.

f **20—24 Nahor's Sons**—This genealogy (J) serves to relate the Hebrews to various other peoples. P represents some of the relationships differently: Aram is the son of Shem in 10:22, and Uz is the son of Aram in 10:23. The particular purpose in inserting the genealogy here appears in 23: Bethuel, the father of Rebekah, whose story will be told in ch 24. Milcah and Nahor: see above § 161*a*. **21**. Buz: in the region of Dedan (cf Jer 25:23); *Bâzu* in Assyrian inscriptions. Kemuel is otherwise unknown. **22**. Chesed: see on 10:22. Hazo: in Assyrian inscriptions *Hazu* is associated with the *Bâzu* of 21. Pildash and Jidlaph: unknown. **24**. Tebah: a city near Damascus (2 Sm 8:8), later captured by David. Gaham: unknown. Tahash is possibly the *Tahši* of the Amarna letters: a site somewhere in the Lebanon, therefore fittingly associated with Maacah, a region S of Mt Hermon (Jos 13:11).

g **23:1—20 The Death and Burial of Sarah**—P. **2**. Kiriatharba: 'city of the four'; Hebron is divided into four quarters to this day. The Priestly tradition consistently calls Hebron by its Canaanite name. **3**. 'Hittites': see on 12:15. There is no extrabiblical evidence that this Indo-European people was ever in Palestine; Hittite records, which are voluminous, indicate that the Hittites never penetrated S of Damascus. P seems to use the terms 'Hittite' and 'Canaanite' interchangeably (cf 36:2). However, **4—20** contain some details that have caused this question to be examined afresh; cf M. R. Lehmann, 'Abraham's Purchase of Machpelah and Hittite Law' in BASOR 129 (1953) 15—18. Hittite law differed from the common Mesopotamian law in attaching obligations to things rather than persons (§§ 46—47 of the Hittite Code, ANET 191). If a man acquired a whole field, certain feudal services were owed by him to the king; if he acquired only part, the services would be owed by the major owner. Abraham seems to have tried to avoid acquiring these feudal obligations, which Ephron was just as eager to be rid of; hence the offer was first made to acquire burial rights only, but without success, as Ephron refused to sell the cave apart from the whole field. If the Hebronites were observing Hittite law, something must have connected them with the historical Hittites. Woolley in *A Forgotten Kingdom* 32ff has theorized that these 'Hittites' were part of a migration from the Caucasus which produced not only the Hittite kingdom of Anatolia and Asia Minor but also various settlements in Palestine. If this tradition has actually preserved a recollection of Hittite law, it is of great antiquity, for with the passing of the Hittite kingdom after 1200 B.C. the knowledge of this law was lost until its recovery in modern times. **6**. This is conventional politeness: the Hebronites offer Abraham the free use of any of their sepulchres, but that, after all, is not what he has requested. Thus the way is left open to the negotiation that follows. **9**. 'Give': as this

v makes clear, the meaning is 'sell'. **10**. The transaction **165g** takes place in the city gate, the customary gathering place for matters of public record. **16**. There was no coinage of money at this time: the shekel was originally a weight. **17**. A characteristic of Hittite contracts as known through archaeology is that the number of trees in a field are always accurately enumerated. **20**. Though the Patriarchs lived in Canaan as strangers and sojourners (4), their Israelite descendants were consoled to know that they had been buried in their own ground. The cave of Mach-pelah according to tradition lies beneath the mosque in modern Hebron, a site that has not been made available to archaeology.

24:1—67 A Bride for Isaac—This J tradition almost **166** amounts to a novelette. A wife is sought for Isaac among Abraham's own kindred in order to avoid contamination with the religions of Canaan. At the same time, it is required that the girl should come to Canaan, for there must be no return to the heathen conditions from which Yahweh had called Abraham and his descendants. **1—9**. This reads like a deathbed commission. J probably originally recorded Abraham's death during the servant's journey to Aram Naharaim (cf 62—67); see below on 25:7—11. **2**. 'Under my thigh': a euphemism for the organ of generation. An oath in this form (again in 47:29) signified reverence for the source of life and the Author of life. **10**. Nahor: see above § 161*a*. **12—14**. The sign which the servant asks of Yahweh is not arbitrarily chosen, but will also be an indication of the girl's character. **28**. 'Her mother's household': an unusual expression, probably signifying that Rebekah's father was dead. In **29** and the following vv Laban appears to be the head of the family. **29b** logically follows **30a**. **50**. MT has 'Laban *and* **b** *Bethuel*'. In view of the surrounding context *ûbetû'ēl* is either an addition to the text or a corruption of *ûbêtô*, 'and his household'. **53**. These are the bridal gifts. The nose-ring and the bracelets that the servant had previously given Rebekah were a reward for her courtesy and a means of introducing himself to Laban's household. **55**. Oriental hospitality decreed lengthy negotiations and celebrations. By these standards, the servant's return is precipitate; however, he explains his haste as due to his desire to bring to a successful conclusion this commission on which God has so obviously set his seal of approval. **57—58**. The marriage has already been arranged, according to custom, without the consultation of the bride (51). Now Rebekah's consent is asked. Nuzi marriage contracts indicate that when a brother rather than a father gave a girl in marriage her consent was required. Assyrian law protected a woman's right to stay in her homeland: she could not be married to a foreigner against her will. One or other of these provisions may have been the custom of Aram Naharaim. **62**. Abraham is no longer mentioned, and Isaac is now the servant's master (65). See above on 1—9 and cf 25:11. **65**. The veiling of the bride was part of the marriage ceremonial. **67**. 'The tent': the nuptial tent. MT adds '(of) Sarah his mother', which is deleted by most commentators as a gloss. 'For the loss of his mother': originally the text may have had 'father'.

25:1—6 Keturah's Children—This genealogy is **c** usually assigned to J; some of the relationships appear differently in the P genealogy of 10:7. No attempt has been made to reconcile this rather casual reference to progeny with the previous narrative according to which Abraham had despaired of having a son; however, the purpose of the genealogy is rather to relate peoples to the Hebrews than to add to the history of Abraham. **2**. Zimran: LXX Zebran, is possibly Zabram, an Arab village W of Mecca. Jokshan: probably the Joktan of 10:26—28

66c (J), there also the father of Sheba. Medan: unknown. Midian: the best known of these Arabian peoples, frequently associated with the Israelites (cf Ex 2:15ff; 18, etc). Ishbak: there is a *Yasbuk* mentioned in Assyrian monuments, referring to a region in N Syria; however, this appears to be an Arabian genealogy. Shuah: in Edom, cf Jb 2:11. **3.** All these names doubtless refer to Arabian tribes and localities. **4.** Ephah: a country in N Arabia, cf Is 60:6. Abida: appears in Assyrian texts, designating the name region as Ephah. Epher, Ephah, and Hanoch later appear as Israelite names (1 Chr 2:46f; 4:17; Gn 46:9, etc), which may mean that they were among the Midianite peoples incorporated into Israel. **6.** Concubines: Hagar is also meant? Cf the Lipit-Ishtar code § 25: 'If a man has taken a wife and she has borne him children and these children remain alive; and if a slavegirl has also borne children to this man her master, and the father has given freedom to the slavegirl and her children; the slavegirl's sons shall not divide the inheritance together with the sons of her master' (ANET 160).

d 7–11 The Death of Abraham—Recorded only in P. **8.** 'Gathered to his kinsmen': this does not mean here simply that he was buried in the ancestral cemetery, since Abraham was not. On the Hebrew idea of the condition of the dead, see § 617*k-l*. **9.** P does not seem to have known of the expulsion of Ishmael (21:8–21). **12–18 Genealogy and Death of Ishmael**—P. All the names which can be identified are those of nomadic and sedentary Arab tribes. Twelve tribes are mentioned, as in the later Israelite federation. **13.** Nebaioth and Kedar are mentioned in Assyrian records; cf Is 60:7. Mibsam: later given as an Israelite clan (1 Chr 4:25). **14.** Mishma likewise appears as a Simeonite clan in 1 Chr 4:26. All three names in this v are associated in ancient records with Tema (15), a city in NW Arabia which may have been the cultic centre of the Ishmaelite federation. **15.** Jetur and Naphish appear together in 1 Chr 5:19 as tribes defeated by the Reubenites in the time of Saul.

o 25:19–26:35 The History of Isaac—We are told very little about Isaac independently of the histories of Abraham and Jacob.

25:19–26 The Birth of Esau and Jacob—The chronological framework of this passage (19–20, 26*b*) is, as usual, from P. The rest of the vv are from J. **20.** Paddan-aram is the P equivalent of the J Aram Naharaim. **22.** This struggle in the womb typifies the future contention of the two sons. Rebekah evidently took her question to some sanctuary of Yahweh, receiving the oracle recorded in the following v. **23.** Israel (Jacob) is to be a mightier people than Edom (Esau). **25.** Esau is 'red' (*'ad*e*mônî*), a play on the name Edom; he is covered with hair (*sē'ār*), a play on Seir, the country of the Edomites (36:8). In Arabic a word cognate to the Heb. Esau means 'hairy'. **26.** The name Jacob (*ya'aqōb*) probably means 'may he (God) protect'; here it has been given a popular etymology in relation to the word 'heel' (*'āqēb*): 'one who supplants'.

27–34 Esau sells his Birthright—A mingling of J and E. The possibility of an elder son's selling his first birthright is known from a Nuzi contract. In the eyes of the Hebrews the one most at fault in this story was not Jacob, who admittedly took advantage of his brother's weakness, but Esau, who set such little value on his birthright (cf 34). **27–28.** The two boys typify the two ways of life that co-existed in Palestine; this as well as the partisanship of their parents is to divide them. **30.** 'Let me gulp some of the red, that red there!' Esau merely sees red food (*'ādōm*), the nature of which has not yet been made known (*nāzîd* in 29: 'something cooked'). His

folly is thus compounded, in that he is willing to trade **166e** his birthright for what he finally discovers (34) is only common lentils. His uncouth and shallow character is also brought out in **32**: exaggerating his need, he can think only of satisfying his present hunger without reckoning the consequences.

26:1–35 Isaac and Abimelech—This ch contains **f** the only stories about Isaac that are not also part of the Abraham or Jacob histories. With the exception of 34–35 (P: the introduction to 27:46ff) the content of this ch has the characteristics of J.

1–5. The promises descend to Isaac. On the Philistines, see 21:34. **6–11** is a doublet of the story told in ch 20 (E). In this version the theme is handled quite briefly and gingerly, and Rebekah is never in any actual danger. In **8** the verb translated 'fondling' is *sāhaq*: another play on the name Isaac. **12–16** contain the first mention of agriculture in connexion with the Patriarchs (cf 30:14; 37:7. **17–22.** On the importance of wells, see on 21:25–26. **20.** Esek: 'contention'. **21.** Sitnah: 'enmity'. **22.** Rehoboth: 'broad places', 'spaciousness'. In the original form of the source used in ch 21 apparently the digging of these wells was ascribed to Abraham; here 15 and 18 are glosses inserted to harmonize the two versions of the account. **23–25** connect Isaac with the cultic centre at Beer-sheba even as 21:33 did Abraham. **26–33** is a variant version of 21:22–33. Here a covenant meal is mentioned, lacking in the earlier version. However, the name given the well in 33, *šib*e*'â*, is closer to the 'seven' (*šeba'*) of the J part of 21:22–33 than to the 'swear' (*šāba*) that is featured in the present version. Hence some authors believe that 33 of the present ch originally followed 21:30. **34–35:** see below on 27:46ff.

27:1–29 The History of Jacob **167a**

27:1–45 Jacob by Fraud wins Isaac's Blessing—J. One of the most vividly told stories in Gn. There should be no attempt to excuse the malice of the lying and deceit practised, even though these, too, must be judged according to the standards of the times. The author, though he had little or no sympathy for Esau, himself recognized that what Rebekah and Jacob did was wrong and shows that it was punished: Rebekah lost her beloved son, and Jacob had to leave his homeland.

1–4. Death-bed blessings and prophecies were customary and considered as especially effective (cf 49:1ff; Dt 33:1ff; 2 Sm 23:1ff). Isaac asks for food to rally his strength before blessing his eldest son. **5–17.** Rebekah acts throughout the part of the over-fond mother, ruthless in her aim to further the future of her favourite son. The plan is entirely hers, but Jacob concurs in it completely. His momentary objection in 12 is only pragmatical. **20.** This is the worst of Jacob's lies, invoking the name of Yahweh himself in his deceit. **27–29.** The blessing extends both to Jacob and to his descendants. Israel is promised a fertile land and dominance over Edom. **33–38.** In the Semitic mind, a word once uttered was both causative and irrevocable; even though he had done so in error, Isaac had given a blessing to Jacob that could not be recalled. **36.** Esau plays on the name Jacob with the verb *'āqab*, 'overreach', 'supplant'. Despite Esau's unadmirable qualities, it is impossible not to feel sympathy for this rather stupid man who finds himself frustrated by his shrewd mother and brother. **39–40.** The 'blessing' of Esau (Edom) is hardly a cheerful one. The relative infertility of the Edomite soil is referred to; in 40 is figured the long struggle of Edom for independence from Israel (cf 1 (3) Kgs 11:14ff) after its conquest by David (2 Sm 8:12–14). **41–45.** Esau cannot keep his plans secret, and Rebekah hears of them. She thinks

167a that a short absence by Jacob will suffice to cool the anger of the impulsive Esau. Actually, however, Jacob will be gone for twenty years, and mother and son will never see each other again.

b **46—28:9 Jacob's Departure for Paddan-aram**—This P narrative continues the account begun in 26:34—35. It contains another explanation of Jacob's departure from the family of Isaac. P apparently said nothing about the rivalry of Jacob and Esau or the fact that Jacob had supplanted Esau. Rather, the occasion of Jacob's departure is Esau's marriages with women of the land of Canaan, which are displeasing to both Isaac and Rebekah. Therefore Isaac sends Jacob away to get a wife in Paddan-aram even as his father had obtained Rebekah for him. When Esau learns that Isaac has sent Jacob away with a blessing for this purpose and that his marriages with Canaanite women displease his parents, he imitates Jacob to the extent of taking another wife who is an Ishmaelite, thus one of his father's relatives.

c **10—22 Jacob at Bethel**—Mostly E, with 13—16 and 19 inserted from J. Delorme, 'A propos du songe de Jacob', Mémorial A. Gelin, 1961, 47—54, has brought out the way in which the present narrative has combined the best features of E and J.

11. '*The* place' (three times with the article): a holy place. **12.** The exact nature of the visionary 'ladder' (or 'stair' or 'ramp') is debated, but the significance of the vision is plain enough and is adequately explained in 17: here is the meeting place of heaven and earth, between God and man; cf Jn 1:51. **13—15.** The promises made to Abraham, then to Isaac, now descend to Jacob. **17.** At least by popular etymology, Bethel means 'house of God'. **18.** An earlier story associated the sanctuary of Bethel with Abraham; cf 12:8 (J). Here it is connected with Jacob. The 'pillar' (*maṣṣēbāh*) was a commonplace object found in both Canaanite and Israelite sanctuaries. In Canaanite use it was a fetish, which explains the frequent condemnation of *maṣṣēbôṯ* in the OT. The Israelites interpreted them as memorials of God's appearances. 'When the later Israelites went to the sanctuary of Bethel to offer their sacrifices and pay their tithes (Am 4:4), they recalled there the memory of Jacob. Perhaps there was pointed out the sacred monolith erected by the Patriarch, just as for centuries at Mamre there have been pointed out the well and the tree of Abraham' (Chaine). **19.** According to Jos 16:2; 18:13 Luz was a distinct place near Bethel, but the two sites were later identified. **20—22.** As formulated by Jacob, the covenant with God is conditional and not entirely disinterested. However, in the following episodes Jacob is shown to have matured spiritually. **22.** This and Am 4:4 are the earliest references to tithes as a regular practice of religion (cf 14:20).

d **29:1—14 Jacob meets Rachel**—JE: continued through chh 29—30. These introductory vv which set the scene appear to be Yahwistic throughout. **2—3** and **7—8** accurately reflect contemporary practice: wells were possessed communally and were blocked with rocks whose size would prevent an individual from diverting the waters to his purely private use. Jacob, however, wants the shepherds to be done with their business and depart so that he may be alone with Rachel. **10.** Jacob displays unusual strength: so also in his handling of the *maṣṣēbāh* (28:11.15), which was usually a massive stone.

15—30 Jacob's Marriage to Leah and Rachel— Through a parallel is denied by various authors, there seems to be a striking correspondence between the Jacob-Laban relationship in Gn and the following adoption contract from Nuzi (in which the OT names **167** have been substituted for the original ones of the contract): 'Tablet of adoption whereby Laban, the son of Bethuel, has adopted Jacob, the son of Isaac. As long as Laban lives, Jacob will assure him food and clothing. When Laban dies, Jacob will be his heir. If Laban fathers a son, the latter will divide his inheritance equally with Jacob, but it is the son of Laban who will take Laban's gods. Further, Laban has given his daughters Leah and Rachel as the wives of Jacob. If Jacob takes another wife, he loses all right to Laban's goods, land, and buildings' (cf ANET 219f). From the text of Gn we see that (1) Laban apparently had no sons at the beginning of his arrangement with Jacob: they appear only later (31:1); (2) after these sons were born, the household gods belonged to them: this explains Laban's concern and the wrongfulness of Rachel's theft (31:19, 30ff); (3) Jacob's secret flight with Laban's daughters is an acknowledgement that both he and the daughters still belonged to Laban, even as Laban claims (31:31, 43); (4) Jacob was not to marry outside the family (31:50) and hence was given the handmaids of the two daughters (29:24, 29).

15. Ostensibly prompted by family feeling and **e** generosity, Laban is laying plans to further his own designs on Jacob. **17.** Leah's eyes lacked the lustre prized by the Oriental: 'She must have . . . eyes as black as those of a gazelle', E. Daumas, *La femme arabe* (Alger, 1912) 30f. **18.** Whether or not the arrangement between Laban and Jacob was as outlined above, Jacob's labour takes the place of the customary *mōhar* or bridal 'purchase' (cf 34:12). **23.** Jacob the overreacher finds himself outthwarted by one shrewder than himself. The substitution was made possible by the custom of having the bride veiled from her husband (cf 24:65). **26.** Laban's answer is doubtless truthful, despite the injustice that he had done Jacob. **27.** The marriage celebrations lasted a week; cf Jg 14:12. **28.** Jacob obtained Rachel in advance of the additional seven years of labour for which he contracted.

29:31—30:24 Jacob's Children—This story gives an **f** insight into the conditions of a polygamous household. The names of Jacob's sons are those of the later Israelite tribes, which are derived in this view from the Patriarch's immediate descendants. Other texts of the OT indicate that Israelite origins were not quite so homogeneous, and some of the tribal names were probably more ancient than Israel itself. Despite these facts, authentic traditions had been preserved concerning Israel's eponymous ancestors, as will be seen.

31. 'Hated' is too loose a word: the term is a legal one, cf Dt 21:15ff. Leah who, after all, was not at fault for being less favoured than Rachel receives her compensation from God. Leah becomes the ancestress of two of the greatest Israelites, Moses (Levi) and David (Judah). Thus divine providence is seen to be at work despite Jacob's own preference. **32—35.** The names of Leah's four children are given popular etymologies in each case corresponding to her utterance at their birth. **30:1—5.** See on 16:1—6. 'Bear upon my knees': signifies that Bilhah's children will be Rachel's legally. It may be noted that here Rachel (and in 9—13 Leah) names the handmaiden's children: a sign that she is the legal mother. **6—8.** Popular etymologies as in 29:32—35 (so also in 11—13, 18—20, and 23—24). **14—16.** The mandrake (*mandragora vernalis* or *officinarum*) or love-apple (U.S.: the May apple), a herb possessing a root resembling a man, was popularly thought to be an aid to conception. The biblical text,

67f however, ascribes the birth of all of Jacob's children to the intervention of God. **21.** No etymology is offered for Dinah's name: she did not figure in the history of the Israelite tribes.

g 25—43 Jacob's Wealth—25—26. Having completed his term of service, Jacob seeks to sever his relationship with Laban. **27.** Anxious to retain Jacob's services, Laban confesses that he has learnt by divination (*nāḥaš*) that Jacob's God has been responsible for his prosperity. He is therefore amenable to an arrangement more to Jacob's profit. **31—36.** Two cunning men attempt to outwit each other. Jacob's request is disarming: he asks for the animals less likely to be found in the flock, since black goats and white sheep are the rule. Laban accordingly removes by a three days' journey the animals which would be likely to produce the kind that would fall to Jacob's lot. **37—43.** Left alone with the greater part of Laban's flock, Jacob now proceeds to get the better of the wily Aramaean. The physiological principle involved was and still is widely credited, cf Pliny, *Hist Nat* 7, 10; Jer, *Liber hebraicarum quaestionum in Genesim* (PL 23, 985).

68a 31:1—32:3 Jacob's Flight and the Covenant with Laban—Mostly from E with a few vv from J. **1—3.** Both Laban and his sons, mentioned here for the first time, resent the prosperity that Jacob has achieved while in Laban's employ. **4—13.** The *apologia* of Jacob to his wives presupposes a somewhat different salary arrangement than that contained in the composite story of ch 30. The E narrative apparently did not know of Jacob's stratagem in connexion with Laban's flock. **14—16.** Laban has lost the respect of his daughters, who raise no objection to accompanying Jacob to his homeland. Lit. 'he has entirely *eaten up* the money given for us': this expression is also found in the Nuzi documents. **19.** Jacob chooses a time to depart when Laban and his household would be busy with the shearing and diverted by the feasting customary on such occasions (1 Sm 25:1ff; 2 Sm 13:23ff). On the household gods (*t*e*rāpîm*), see above on 29:15—30. For another view, cf Moshe Greenberg, 'Another Look at Rachel's Theft of the Teraphim', JBL 81 (1962) 239—48. Rachel's motive in this theft is not clear, but presumably she regarded the idols as a protection for her family (cf 35:2). **26—30.** Laban's speech on overtaking Jacob is a mixture of bluster, of just grievance over the violation of certain of his rights, and of frustration at being unable to use his superior force against Jacob in view of the divine prohibition he has received (24). **32—42.** At least on the question of the theft of the household gods Jacob believes himself to be in a strong position, not knowing of Rachel's action. Thus, after Laban's fruitless search, he is able to return Laban's righteous reproaches with interest. **34—35.** The Israelite reader, for whom household gods were a superstitious thing of the past, could not miss the irony of this scene: women in their menstrual periods **b** were legally unclean (Lv 15:19ff). **42.** 'The Fear of Isaac', i.e., 'the God whom Isaac feared': one of the pre-Israelite names by which God was known to the Patriarchs (cf 53). **43.** Laban brushes aside Jacob's elaborate protestation with a reassertion of his right; see above on 29:15—30. However, he also becomes more conciliatory and decides to make the best of the inevitable. **44.** 'covenant': an agreement by which Laban definitively recognized Jacob's independence from his household but also guaranteed the continued protection of his daughters' rights. The biblical account has also apparently remembered and associated with this

event an ancient boundary covenant between Israel and **168b** Aram (Laban is several times called 'the Aramaean' in this ch), concerning which a memorial existed in the region of Gilead. The story seems to be composite: the memorial of the covenant is both a pillar (45) and a heap of stones (46ff), and the covenant meal is mentioned twice (46 and 54). **47.** *Y*e*gar śāhadûtā'* is the Aram. for 'the heap of witness'; *gal 'ed* is the same in Heb. The latter term here and in 48 serves as a popular etymology for Gilead. **49.** Mizpah means 'watchpost'; the Mizpah of Jg 10:17; 11:11, 34 is meant, but its location is unknown. **51.** The text of 45ff may have originally ascribed the erection of the memorial witness to Laban. **32:2—3.** A story is begun here that is never completed: perhaps it was similar to 23—33 below. Mahanaim means 'camps' or 'armies'.

32:4—22 Jacob prepares to meet Esau—There **c** are here two separate traditions of Jacob's preparations to meet Esau. (1) The first, 4—14a, is from J. Having sent messengers from whom he learns that Esau is on the way to meet him with 400 men, for safety's sake Jacob divides his entourage into two camps (another popular etymology for Mahanaim), then rests that night at the Jabbok ('Jordan' in 10 should be 'Jabbok'). (2) The parallel account is from E, **14b—22.** According to this, Jacob divided his followers into several droves, the forward droves carrying presents, so that Esau would meet Jacob himself only after this 'conditioning'. Again it is recorded that he spent the night in the camp.

23—33 Jacob's Wrestling—This narrative is by some attributed to J, by others to E or to a combination of J and E, and by still others to an independent source. It seems to differ from both the preceding accounts in that Jacob does not spend the night at Mahanaim after all, but fords the Jabbok and sends everything on ahead, remaining behind alone. (1) In part the story exists to explain the change of Jacob's name to Israel, i.e., the ancestral name of the Israelites. Also a popular etymology is given (31) for the name of the nearby Penuel, later an important Israelite city (Jg 8:8ff; 1 (3) Kgs 12:25). Likewise it accounts for a dietary law seemingly observed by the early Israelites (33), which, however, was not adopted by the Mosaic law. (2) The sense of the story seems to be that Jacob struggled not with 'an angel' but with God himself; cf 29 and 31 and the meaning of Penuel, 'the face of God'. (3) What, then, is the meaning of the story? See, e.g., J. Schildenberger, 'Jakobs nächtliche Kampf . . .', *Misc. Biblica Ubach*, 1953, 69—96. It may be pointed **d** out that this episode has a certain parallel to the preceding encounter with Laban. In both instances there is a night vision of God before a crisis coming on the morrow, and whereas in the other story Jacob triumphed over a man, here he prevails with God (cf 29). Thus perhaps the significance of the change of names: as Jacob the Patriarch was an overreacher, a supplanter (cf 27:36), but as Israel he stands in a new relationship to God, having received a blessing that, in a sense, validates what he had previously obtained by conniving.

25—26. Jacob's opponent is called 'a man'; see on 18:1—15 and 16:7. **27.** The spirit world was thought to be particularly active at night, and the Bible frequently represents theophanies as occurring at night (cf 15:5, etc). This request of the 'man' reveals to Jacob his true nature, and he demands a blessing. **28—29.** The blessing consists in Jacob's new name: for the Semite the name was the reality that it signified. The name

168d Israel is of uncertain etymology, but here it is made to mean 'strive with God (and prevail)'. Gn, which consistently teaches that God is the Lord and Master of all history, also insists on the role of human activity and initiative in the work of life: man must 'contend with God'; cf Mt 11:12.

169a 33:1—17 Jacob meets Esau—J. **2.** Jacob's fear of Esau causes him to deploy his party by groups, the children under their mothers, in the reverse order of his affection for them. **3.** Here and in the following conversation with Esau, Jacob's conduct strikes one as excessively obsequious. Partly this is conventional Oriental politeness, but mainly it must be taken as evidence of Jacob's justified fear of Esau's continuing enmity. **4.** Esau greets Jacob with an affection that is unexpected, but seemingly unfeigned. **8.** Cf 32:8f. **9.** Oriental politeness dictates the preliminary refusal of a gift. **12.** Esau takes it for granted that Jacob will come with him to the Edomite region of Seir. Jacob, however, who has not forgotten his brother's mercurial character, has other plans in mind. In Edom he could be at best the pale shadow of Esau the warrior-chieftain. **15.** For the same reason that he has put off Esau's proposal to travel together, feigning his intention of joining him later in Seir, Jacob declines the offer of an Edomite armed guard. **17.** Succoth: cf Jos 13:27; Jg 8:5ff. Jacob's settlement in this place is described as a semi-permanent one; the sheds for his stock provide a popular etymology of its name ('huts').

b 18—34:31 The Rape of Dinah—In **18**, probably from P, Jacob returns to Shechem in Palestine rather than to Succoth. In 12:6f, (J), the holy place of Shechem was associated with Abraham; here in **19—20** (E) it is associated with Jacob. In Israelite times, of course, this holy place was converted from Canaanite to Yahwistic worship. According to Jg 9:4 the god of Shechem was Baal-berith (in 9:46 El-berith), that is, 'lord (or god) of the covenant'. Here the inhabitants of Shechem are called 'sons of Hamor', that is, Hamorites or *benê ḥamôr*, even as Israelites are *benê yiśrā'ēl*, 'sons of Israel'. In other words, the tradition had preserved no true proper names of the principals in question and used simply names applicable to all Shechemites. In Heb. *ḥamôr* means 'ass'. Note the relevance of these facts in connexion with the covenant rite known from Mari and mentioned in the commentary on 12:9—10 above.

c In the story of the sons of Jacob and the Shechemites two traditions have been woven into one: (1) In **J** Shechem sees Dinah, violates her, and carries her away to his house. Wishing to marry her, he accepts the condition imposed: circumcision. Then Simeon and Levi kill him and his father, pillage his house, and carry away their sister. Jacob reproaches them. This is the story of 34:2*b*—3.5—7.11—12.14.19.25*b*—26.29*b*—31. It is a simple family drama. (2) In E Shechem notices Dinah and asks for her through his father. The condition proposed is general circumcision for all the Shechemites: it is a question of the fusion of two peoples. The Shechemites accept the alliance, but through treachery all the sons of Jacob pillage the city and kill all the men. This is the story of 34:1—2*a*.4.6.8—10.13.15—18.20—15*a*. 27—29*a*.

Similarly, two different facts seem to be represented: the story of a family quarrel and also some tribal history. In the later history of the conquest of the promised land by the Israelites nothing is said of a capture of Shechem, though this important town was certainly in Israelite hands at the time (cf Jos 24). Archaeology which has

verified the conquest of so many of the other sites **169** mentioned in the Bible has repeatedly confirmed the fact that Shechem remained undisturbed during this period; G. E. Wright, 'Archaeology and OT Studies', JBL 77 (1958) 48. Therefore it has been plausibly suggested that this story may have remembered an earlier, pre-Exodus conquest by some of the ancestors of the Israelites.

33:20. El Elohe-Israel, that is, El, the God of Israel. **34:1.** This is the only story in Gn involving Dinah, who is named elsewhere only in 30:21 and 46:15. **2.** 'Hivite' should probably be read 'Horite' with LXX: that the Shechemites did not practise circumcision indicates that they were non-Semitic. **30.** Jacob condemns the folly rather than the treachery of the deed. In 49:5—7 the ferocity of Simeon and Levi is repudiated. However, **31,** Simeon and Levi's proud reply doubtless indicate what would have been the reaction of the average Israelite on hearing the story; cf Jdt 9:2ff; *Jubilees* chh 30—32.

35:1—15 Jacob returns to Bethel—The final ch of **d** the history of Jacob gathers together the author's remaining material concerning the Patriarch. The present passage is the Elohistic sequel to the preceding story, into which, however, a narrative from the Priestly tradition (9—13) has been inserted.

1. A reference to Jacob's vow in 28:20—22 (E). **2.** Jacob's family must lay aside all the relics of the religion of Mesopotamia and embark upon a new life in the service of the God of the Patriarchs. Ritual washing and the change of clothes further signify this new state. **4.** Ear-rings, probably crescent-shaped in honour of the Semitic moon-god, were common heathen amulets; cf Jg 8:24ff; Hos 2:15. **7.** MT has 'he called the place El-bethel', i.e., 'the God of Bethel'. The ancient versions omit the 'El'. In 28:19 the naming of Bethel is from J, but E elsewhere seems also to have presupposed the name as already given (cf 31:13 and here in 3). **8.** Rebekah's nurse was mentioned in 24:59. Her presence in Jacob's entourage at this time is unexplained. Allon-bacuth: 'oak (or terebinth) of weeping'. The mention of this incident is made probably in view of the more famous Deborah of Jg 4:5. **9—13.** P's version of the story of 32:23—33: only its position in the present context of Gn would localize it at Bethel. **14—15.** Jacob fulfils his vow.

16—20 Benjamin's Birth and the Death of Rachel— **e** E. According to it, Benjamin was born near Bethel; according to P (cf 26 below), he was born in Mesopotamia; according to the material incorporated into the history of Joseph, as will be seen, Benjamin's birth evidently occurred much later.

16. Ephrath: an unknown site near Ramah, N of Jerusalem (cf 1 Sm 10:12; Jer 31:15). **17.** The midwife seeks to console Rachel in her pain by reminding her of her prayer in 30:24. **18.** Rachel calls Benjamin 'son of my pain', but such an unlucky name would never be seriously given to an infant. The popular etymology of Benjamin is 'son of the right hand', the right hand being the sign of happiness and good fortune. **19.** 'That is, Bethlehem': this is a late, and incorrect, gloss. The 'tomb of Rachel' pointed out to the visitor at Bethlehem depends on this glossed text; the tomb is an ordinary Muslim mausoleum. **20.** The text is laconic concerning Jacob's grief over Rachel; cf 48:7.

21—22a Reuben's Incest—J. The story is incomplete, doubtless intentionally so; reference is made to the incident in 49:4. The tower 'of Eder' means 'of the flock', i.e., a tower set up to facilitate watching the flocks.

39e Since there were doubtless hundreds of these in the region, the site is unknown. From this point on, J generally calls Jacob Israel.

22b–29 Jacob's Sons and Isaac's Death—P. As in the case of Ishmael (see on 25:9), this tradition does not seem to have known of Esau's living apart from Isaac and Jacob. In the main history of Jacob, Isaac was presumed to have died while Jacob was in Mesopotamia (cf 27:1–4). Both 25:9 and 35:29 are conventionalized summations inculcating filial piety.

f 36:1–43 Esau and the Edomites—This ch is a miscellany which has been assembled from various sources, some of them doubtless Edomite. In **1–5** there is a list of **Esau's wives and sons**, taken from some independent source. The names of the wives differ from those given by P in 26:34; 28:9. **6–8** is from P, which like J and E recorded that Esau settled in Edom. However, in this version Esau's departure was peaceable, after his father's death and Jacob's return to Canaan, and was prompted by a motive similar to that which separated Abraham and Lot (13:5ff). The list in **9–14** derives from the same source that produced 2–5, here giving **Esau's sons** according to his several wives. The names are mainly those of Arabian tribes, and there are twelve tribes as in the case of Israel and Ishmael (25:12–18). The list in **15–19** is a doublet of 9–14, from a different source. **Two Horite (Hurrian) name-lists** appear in **20–30**. In the Israelite perspective, the Horites were the aborigines of Edom who had been driven out by Esau. Actually, the names in these lists are Semitic, not Hurrian: they are for the most part **geographical designations** written up in the form of a genealogy. In **31–39** the list of **Edomite kings** prior to the conquest of Edom by David seems to be an authentic Edomite document. It is interesting to note that it testifies to an elective monarchy. The final **40–43** are from P. Here we find a list of Edomite villages and clans which presuppose relationships sometimes differing from those of the preceding lists: Oholibamah (41), for example, is now a chieftain rather than a wife of Esau (2).

'0a 37:1–50:26 The History of Joseph—This is not only the most extensive of the Patriarchal histories, it is also the one that consistently maintains the highest literary standards. With the exception of a relatively few vv from P, the Joseph story found in Gn has been compiled from two versions, which we may continue to call J and E. As will be seen, however, the J and E strata in the Joseph story differ in some respects from their counterparts in the rest of the Patriarchal History. Apparently in their dealing with this story both of these traditions had to accommodate themselves to a **narrative with strong historical roots** that had organized its material without too much reference to the rest of the Patriarchal traditions. A recent and intensive study of this history from the standpoint of Egyptology has led to the conclusion that its original source, which produced both of the versions joined in Gn, is a history dating from the 18th Egyptian dynasty, to which, the author believes, Joseph should be related (cf J. Vergote, *Joseph en Egypte*, Louvain 1959). If this conclusion is correct, it would appear that **the original Mosaic structure** of the Pentateuchal tradition has been modified less in the Joseph story than in any other part of Gn.

b 37:1–36 Joseph sold into Egypt—Aside from 1–2 which are a standard Priestly introduction, this ch is about equally divided between J and E: this is the only explanation consistent with the discrepancies of detail in the passage. **J** consists of 3–4.12–17.18b.

21.23.25–27.28b.31–33a.33c.34b–35a. According to **170b** this story, Joseph's brothers hated him because his father preferred him; when he comes to them at Dothan, they plot to kill him. Judah tries to rescue him (the 'Reuben' of 21 was probably originally 'Judah'), but the brothers strip him of his tunic and, at Judah's continued plea, rather than kill him they sell him to a caravan of Ishmaelites. Then the brothers deceive Jacob with Joseph's bloody tunic, and Jacob mourns for him. The E version is in 5–11.18a.19–20.22.24.28a.28c.29–30. 33b.34a.35b.36. According to it, the brothers hate Joseph because of his dreams of grandeur. They decide to kill him and throw his body in a cistern, but Reuben persuades them to throw him into the cistern alive, hoping to rescue him later. The brothers leave, and in their absence Midianite traders pass by, draw Joseph from the cistern, and take him to Egypt. Reuben returns to find Joseph gone; meanwhile, while the brothers report him dead and Jacob refuses to be consoled, Joseph is sold in Egypt to Potiphar.

2. Still a third reason for the hatred of Joseph **c** by his brothers is given by P: Joseph had informed on them in some matter. **3.** The difference in age between Joseph and the other sons of Jacob is more pronounced in this story; cf 29:31–30:24. **5–11.** Dreams as the means of divine revelation are featured in the E story of Joseph; cf chh 40f. The content of Joseph's first dream evidences the semi-sedentary aspect of the life of the Patriarchs as does 26:12–16. **10.** Apparently Rachel is presumed to be still living, despite 33:16–20 (also E). **17.** 'Dothan is N of Shechem, S of the plain of Esdraelon, where there are excellent pasturages. The caravan route which went from Gilead into Egypt passed by Beisan, Jezreel, round the foot of the mountains of Gilboa, and by the S of the plain of Esdraelon reached the defiles of Carmel to attain the coastal plains of the Mediterranean and descend towards the Nile delta. The Ishmaelites are coming from Gilead; whence the Midianites are coming is not said' (Chaine). **21.** 'Judah' should be read here for 'Reuben' in view of 25–27. In the J story of Joseph Judah is specially featured, cf ch 43. **22.** The E story of Joseph features Reuben, cf 42:22ff. **25.** Spices were much in demand in Egypt for liturgical and medicinal use and for embalming. **26.** 'Conceal his blood': blood spilt and left uncovered cries to heaven for vengeance; cf 4:10; Jb 16:19. **35.** 'All his daughters': the preceding history of Jacob told of only one daughter, Dinah. On the concept of Sheol, the nether world, see § 617k. **36.** Potiphar is an authentically Egyptian name: 'that which Ra has given'.

38:1–30 Judah and Tamar—Scarcely has the **d** dramatic story of Joseph begun when it is interrupted by this ch which has no connection with it. The ch exhibits most of the characteristics of J, but it varies from the other Patriarchal traditions in having Judah settle permanently apart from his brothers. Apparently the author of Gn inserted the story here for lack of a better place. The tradition was too important to omit because of the significance of Judah, the tribe to which David belonged; likewise Tamar is related through Perez (Nm 26:21) to David (Ru 4:18), and thence to Christ (Mt 1:3). The separation of the tribe of Judah from the rest of the tribes is an historical fact: cf Jg 1; the absence of Judah from the Song of Deborah (Jg 5); Dt 33:7. The Adullam where Judah settled is in the Judaean Shephelah W of the Dead Sea; it later appears in the story of David, where Judah's isolation from the other tribes is also manifest.

170e 1. The chronology of this episode in relation to the rest of the Patriarchal History cannot be determined; see above. 2. Judah shows none of the antagonism to Canaanite marriages manifested by his ancestors (24:3; 27:46—28:1). 5*b* is obscure, as are the ancient versions. Possibly: 'She was in Kezib [= Achzib, Jos 15:44] when she bore him'. 7. The sense is that Er died a premature death because of his wickedness. 8. The custom of levirate marriage is supposed, which was later incorporated into the Mosaic law (Dt 25:5ff). 9—10. Onan's sin consisted both in his mean disregard of family duty and in the unnatural means which he used to avoid this duty. 11. Judah was at fault in evading the levirate responsibility, as he later admits (26). 12. The Timnah is probably that S of Hebron (Jos 15:57). 14. Tamar disguises herself as a prostitute (cf 21). 17. A kid seems to have been a conventional exchange in such transactions. 18. The signet seal worn around the neck and the staff were the signs of a man of importance. Tamar chooses tokens that will make Judah's later identification absolutely certain. 21. The word used for 'harlot' here is q^{e}dēšāh. This term, lit. 'consecrated woman', has its origin in the institution of cult prostitution practised by the Canaanite and other contemporary peoples. It is doubtful that Tamar so represented herself to Judah. The expression is used only by the Adullamite Hirah. 24. The double standard recognized in sexual relations is apparent in this story. Tamar would have been dealt with as an adulteress since she was considered to be bound to Shelah. The penalty of burning was preserved in the Mosaic law only for the wives of priests (Lv 21:9), other adulteresses being punished by stoning (Dt 22:20, 21, 24). 26. That Judah had no further relations with Tamar may indicate that he now did his duty in recognizing her rights as his daughter-in-law. Tamar was considered worthy of praise by the Israelites (cf Ru 4:12) in view of her devotion to the principle upheld by the levirate law. 29. Perez means 'breach' or 'break through'.

f 39:1—23 Joseph is cast into Prison—The J history of Joseph continues. 1. Ishmaelites: cf the Midianites of 37:36. Since the two versions originally told parallel stories, doubtless 'Potiphar, one of Pharaoh's officers, the captain of the guard' has been inserted to harmonize the two stories into a single one. Similarly, 'where the king's prisoners were kept' in 20 harmonizes the present ch with the following. Originally the J story told only of Joseph's experiences in the household of 'an Egyptian' who bought him from the Ishmaelites. 7—20. An Egyptian story having some superficial resemblances to this biblical tradition is the *Story of Two Brothers* (ANET 23—25). 9. Adultery would not only be an injustice to Joseph's master, but also a great sin against the God whose law is supreme in Egypt as well as in Palestine.

g 40:1—23 Joseph interprets the Dreams of Two Prisoners—The E narrative continues. Once more the 'captain of the guard' of this ch was originally the Potiphar of 37:36, whose name may have been suppressed here in order to harmonize the stories into a consecutive narrative. It was in the house of such an official that important political prisoners were detained. The harmonization has been completed by the addition in 3, 5, 7, and 15 of references to Joseph in prison with the butler and baker.

1. These men were high court officials, not simply menials. 5. Two dreams as in 37:5—11 and in 41:1—8 (also E). 8. The Egyptian preoccupation with dreams and their interpretation is well attested; cf ANET

495. Joseph insists that if God sends dreams only he **170** can reveal the meaning. 13. 'Pharaoh will lift up your head', i.e., restore him to favour. The same expression is used in 2 (4) Kgs 25:27 of Jehoiachin's release from prison by Evil-merodach. 15. In the E version of the Joseph story, Joseph was stolen by the Midianites. 19. Again 'Pharaoh will lift up your head', but this time as an executioner.

41:1—36 Joseph interprets Pharaoh's Dreams— With the exception of a few doublets in the latter part, this ch is E. 16. Joseph again insists that only God can make known the meaning of dreams which are prophetic. 32. The repetition of the dream's message signifies its urgency. 33—36. Provisions of this kind were both feasible and customary in bureaucratic Egypt during times of famine.

37—57 Joseph appointed Viceroy of Egypt—40—1. h The elevation of a commoner to the highest positions in Egypt, even to that of Pharaoh itself, was not unheard of; see below. 42. The word used for 'linen' here is Egyptian. The gold chain was a decoration of Egyptian dignitaries (cf ANEP 135). 43. 'Bow down' is a traditional rendering of the Egyptian word *abrek*, of uncertain meaning, found here. 45. Joseph's Egyptian name is thought to mean 'God speaks: he lives'. Asenath is a name having some reference to the Egyptian goddess Neth. Potiphera is a fuller form of the name Potiphar, already seen. On was the city later known as Heliopolis, the holy city of the sun-god Amun and seat of his all-powerful priesthood. 51—52. Popular etymologies are suggested for the names Manasseh and Ephraim from the words 'forget' and 'fruitful'. Joseph does not mean that he has forgotten his ancestry but that he has found happiness to cause him to forget what he had suffered. 53—56. Famine occurred when the Nile failed to inundate. An inscription on the island of Suheil in Upper Egypt speaks of a seven-year famine more ancient than the one described here (cf ANET 31f).

While **the period of Egyptian history** into which **i** the story of Joseph should be fitted is a matter of some debate among scholars, it has long been thought that **the age of the Hyksos** provides the most likely setting. The Hyksos, whose name probably means 'foreign princes', were a governing class which completely dominated Egypt and Nubia between 1720—1580 B.C., a period of native Egyptian impotence. They left the civil administration of Egypt intact and ruled the country as its Pharaohs. They are thought to have introduced the chariot into Egypt (cf 43 above) and also the use of horses (in 47:17 horses are mentioned for the first time in Gn). Their capital was not the traditional Memphis or Thebes but at Tanis in the Nile delta (see chh 46—47 below). Some, at least, of the Hyksos were Semites. In such a situation the rise of Joseph the Semite might become more understandable. See on the chronology of the Exodus, § 126*c*.

42:1—38 Joseph's Brothers come to buy Food— **17** Gn continues to join the two versions of the history of Joseph to explain how the Israelites came to Egypt through his agency. The two versions were virtually the same, differing only in minor details. E features Reuben (42:37f) as before, and J features Judah (43:3ff) as before. E relates that Simeon was kept as a hostage for Benjamin (42:18ff), a detail that is lacking in J. In E the brothers find their money in their sacks only after returning to Canaan (42:35), while in J it is found on their way home (43:21). The present ch is mainly E.

1—2. Cf 41:57. 3—5. Though the Joseph story has retained the tradition of the twelve sons of Jacob (cf also

1a 37:9), here and throughout the remainder of the story Benjamin is evidently supposed to be a very young child who has replaced Joseph as Jacob's favourite. **9**. The brothers bowing before Joseph fulfils the dream of 37:9. The preoccupation with spies that is featured in this story is another detail consistent with the Hyksos rule in Egypt. **15**. Joseph seizes on his brothers' mention of a living but absent brother as a pretext to test their veracity. Actually he is testing them in a far more important matter, to see whether they are still ruled by the same passions as before. His treatment of his brothers is not vindictive but is designed to teach them through a measure of the suffering which he underwent at their hands. The lesson is not lost on them (cf 21). **24**. Simeon is chosen as hostage since he is the oldest of the brothers who were faithless to Joseph; Joseph has only now learnt that Reuben had tried to save him (22). **27—28**. These vv have been inserted from J in view of the fact that it is used to continue the story in ch 43.

b 43:1—34 Jacob's Sons take Benjamin to Egypt— At the middle point of the story, the offer of Reuben to go surety for Benjamin, the author continues from J, repeating the one detail so that now Judah also intervenes. **7**. These questions do not appear in the E version of the story used in ch 42 but were doubtless in the first part of the J version. **11**. Jacob sends some of the delicacies of Palestine as a gift of homage. **12**. Joseph's return of the money was an act of delicacy to signify that the brothers had been his guests. Together with the rest of his conduct, however, this has further mystified Jacob and his sons. **14**. 'Your other brother', the summary mention made of Simeon in 23 appears to be an addition to harmonize the two versions; so also here. **32**. In view of the strict Egyptian dietary laws, Egyptians did not eat together with foreigners. The Jews themselves later practised the same kind of exclusiveness, cf Dn 1:8. **33**. Joseph's evident knowledge of their family history adds to the mystery. **34**. 'Five times': the number five is repeatedly connected with matters Egyptian (cf 41:34; 45:22; 47:2.24; Is 19:18).

c 44:1—34 Joseph's Final Test of His Brothers— The same version of the history continues. **1**. 'And put each one's money in the mouth of his sack' is thought by many to be a later addition to the text, patterned on the account of the first journey. **5**. 'Is it not by this (cup) that he divines?': water-divination, 'reading' the pattern of drops falling from a cup, was much practised in Egypt. As one of the wise men of Egypt, Joseph would be expected to be a diviner. See on 15. **9**. The penalty for stealing the cup, a sacred object, would normally be death. **15**. 'Do you not know that such a man as I can divine?' Joseph does not actually say that he practised divination, and doubtless the biblical author did not mean to imply that he did. The source of Joseph's superior knowledge concerning all the events regarding his brothers is soon to be revealed. **18—34**. Judah's plea is a model of tact and eloquence which succeeds at last in breaking down the barriers which Joseph had erected against his emotions. In Judah's words Joseph sees that the salutary lesson he intended for his brothers has indeed been taken.

d 45:1—15 Joseph reveals himself to his Brothers— Gn concludes the story of Joseph and his brothers by thoroughly weaving together the endings of both J and E. This explains the occasional repetitions and slight unevennesses such as Joseph's question in 3 following on the lengthy speech of Judah in the preceding ch. **5**. Magnanimously, and as a man of faith, Joseph sees the evil done by his brothers as an unconscious furthering of the providence of God. **8**. 'A father to Pharaoh':

Joseph's title as vizier. **10**. Goshen is the modern **171d** Wadi Tumilât in the fertile Nile delta. The history of Joseph supposes the Egyptian capital to have been nearby.

16—28 Jacob invited to Egypt—16—20. The general esteem in which Joseph is held is extended to his father and brothers. **24**. Joseph tells his brothers not to dispute over the responsibility for their treatment of him in the past (cf 42.22), but to let bygones be bygones. **28**. The gifts convince Jacob of the truth of his sons' report, but it is at the fact that Joseph lives that he rejoices.

46:1—48:12 Israel settles in Egypt—1—5 mainly **e** E. **1**. Before setting out, presumably from Hebron (cf 35:27; 37:14), Jacob wishes to consult the will of God at Beer-sheba, where Isaac had built an altar (26: 23—25). **3**. This final reiteration of the promises made to the Patriarchs reveals that the nation that is to descend from them will be formed in Egypt. **4**. 'I will bring you up again': the reference is to the Exodus. **6—7** is the P summary of the migration of Israel. **8—27**. This P genealogy is late and artificial: it is a traditional list of Jacob's descendants that has been inserted here despite its disagreement with its context. It is not a list of those who came down with Jacob to Egypt, since Er and Onan were already dead (12), the ten sons of Benjamin (21) could hardly have been born as yet, and Joseph's sons (27) were born in Egypt. The total of the numbers given does not tally with the seventy of 27. Probably the list has been revised several times in the process of its transmission. Compare the lists in Ex 6.14ff, Nm 20.5ff, 1 Chr 2—8, which differ from this in some of the names and degrees of relationship. **28—47:5** are J. **28**. Judah is again featured. **31—34**. Joseph urges his family to stress the aspect of their life most distasteful to the Egyptians so that the Pharaoh will settle them in the land of Goshen near himself and apart from the heartland of Egypt. This detail is also consistent with the assumption that the rulers of Egypt at the time were the foreign Hyksos. Why the Egyptians detested shepherds is not explained. **47:5—6** read in the order of LXX: 'Pharaoh said to Joseph, "Let them live in the land of Goshen. And if you know of any able men among them, place them in charge of my own stock" (J). Jacob and his sons came into Egypt to Joseph; and Pharaoh, king of Egypt, heard of it. And Pharaoh said to Joseph, "Your father and your brothers have come to you. The land of Egypt is at your disposal: settle your father and your brothers in the best land"' (P). In P, which concludes this episode, Pharaoh takes the initiative and makes the announcement to Joseph. **7**. Jacob greets Pharaoh by invoking upon him the blessings of God. **11**. 'The land of Rameses' is the P equivalent of 'the land of Goshen'. Rameses is the city of Tanis, originally built by the Hyksos, but not called Rameses until rebuilt by the Pharaoh Rameses II in the 13th cent B.C.

13—26 Political Effects of the Famine in Egypt— f This passage from J, which likes to explain the origins of things, reflects an historical fact, that Egypt passed from a feudal state of private property into a despotism in which all the land belonged to the Pharaoh and the powerful nobles. It was a situation which interested the Israelites, who had a tradition of private property and personal freedom. The main point of the story, however, does not consist in its archaeological interest but in the acknowledgement made by the people of Egypt in 25: Joseph's administration saved the people from starvation. **17**. The first mention of horses in the Bible; cf above § 170i. **22.26**. The exemption of the priests is quite

203

171f historical: the powerful priesthood of On was virtually immune from control by the Pharaoh.

27—31 Jacob's End draws Near—This first tradition of 'Jacob's last words' is Yahwistic with the exception of the chronology of 28, which is from P **29**. For this form of oath see on 24:2. **31**. Jacob bows in gratitude to God for the favour that will be granted him at Joseph's hands. LXX, followed by Heb 11:21, read 'staff' for 'bed'.

g **48:1—22 Jacob adopts Ephraim and Manasseh**—The second tradition of 'Jacob's last words' is mainly E but also contains elements drawn from the other sources. It explains for the Israelites why there was no tribe of Israelites bearing the name 'Joseph', while the two Joseph-tribes, Ephraim and Manasseh, ranked along with the others as derived from sons of Jacob. It also explains Ephraim's dominance as due to the blessing of Jacob. During a great part of Israelite history Ephraim was the most important of the tribes. **7**. This apparently pointless reference to Rachel's death and burial has suggested to some that there was a variant tradition, contrary to that of ch 50, according to which Jacob was to be buried in Rachel's tomb. 'Bethlehem': see on 35:19. **13**. According to custom, Joseph put the eldest son in a position to be reached by Jacob's right hand. **16**. 'The angel who has redeemed me': God himself as he appears to men; see above § 163d. **18**. Joseph thinks that Jacob has made an understandable mistake. **20**. The blessedness of Ephraim and Manasseh will be proverbial. **22**. 'I have given to you rather than to your brothers one *š^ekem*': this is the name of the city of Shechem. See above § 169c. After the conquest of Canaan Shechem was in the territory of Ephraim.

172a **49:1—28 The Destiny of the Tribes of Israel**—The title 'Jacob's Blessings' is derived from 28, which thus represents this third tradition of 'Jacob's last words' as a conventional death-bed blessing. In the main, however, we do not find blessings here, but pronouncements of various kinds regarding the tribes of Israel as they existed in the period of the Judges and the early monarchy. It is agreed that this passage (it could hardly have been uttered by the dying Jacob in its present form) represents a tradition that has been developed and recast in its transmission. Actually, the poetry appears to be some of the most ancient that we possess in the OT, having relations with other passages such as Dt 33 and Jg 5. In the form in which we have it, not all the parts seem to be of the same age. It is not clear whether the compiler of Gn found this poetic collection in any of the three Mosaic traditions which he usually employed; it may have been independent of all three.

3—4 Reuben. The first-born, Reuben, should have inherited the leadership of the Israelites. However, he forfeited this right by the crime narrated in 35:22. The tribe of Reuben was still important in the days of the Judges (Jg 5:15—16), but it soon declined (cf Dt 33:6) and eventually disappeared.

5—7 Simeon and Levi. These two brothers are condemned for their savagery toward the Shechemites as described in ch 34. The tribe of Simeon was 'dispersed' by being absorbed into that of Judah (cf Jos 14:6—16; 19:1—9; 15:26—32.42); it is not mentioned in Dt 33 or Jg 5. The tribe of Levi also disappeared as a political unity; it had to depend on the charity of the other Israelites among which his was 'scattered' (cf Dt 12:12, 18,19; 14:27.29). However, nothing is said here of Levi's priestly privileges, which are extolled in Dt 33:8—11.

b **8—12 Judah**. The first three sons having been passed over for various reasons, Judah, the fourth, is given

pre-eminence and described with royal attributes. The **172** tribe of Judah came into prominence with the monarchy under David and achieved a dominance that rendered it quite unique thereafter, despite the partition of David's kingdom after the death of Solomon. In **10b** occurs one of the most celebrated passages in Gn: 'until *šylh* comes, and to him the obedience of peoples'. The italicized word, or words, is anomalous in biblical Heb. and has never received an explanation that has obtained general agreement. One of the most recent, and perhaps most successful attempts to explain the v (cf W. L. Moran, 'Gn 49:10 and its use in Ez 21:32', Bib 39 (1958) 405—25) understands the words as *šay lōh*, 'tribute to him'. There is probably an allusion here to the oracle of Nathan (2 Sm 7:11—16; Ps 89(88):30—38) concerning **the messianic character of the tribe of Judah in the Davidic line**; cf J. L. McKenzie, 'Royal messianism', CBQ 19 (1957) 25—52. This prophecy of the establishment of God's kingdom through Judah which is so fundamental to the messianic expectation of Israel and Judaism found its ultimate fulfilment in the kingship of Jesus Christ. In keeping with this interpretation are **11—12**: the messianic age is often represented in terms of exaggerated material abundance (cf Am 9:13—14; Hos 2:24).

13 Zebulun. The fortunate geographical position of the tribe of Zebulun is singled out. This maritime position (so also in Dt 33:19) does not correspond with the determinations of Jos 19:10—16, but the tribal boundaries must have varied at different periods.

14—15 Issachar. This tribe inhabited fertile farm- **c** land. **15** may be a patronizing reference to the ease and security which Issachar found by bending its back to sedentary labour: the nomadic spirit which prizes unattached freedom still lives in some of this poetry.

16—18 Dan. During the period of the Judges the tribe of Dan had to fight for survival, but eventually it gained an advantageous position where it could dominate the trade routes. The half-verse **18** may be a pious gloss or an insertion to mark the middle of the poem. **19 Gad**. The Gadites settled in the Transjordan, where they were raided by and raided the nomads of the region (cf Jg 10—11; 1 Chr 5:18—22). **20 Asher**. The territory of Asher was very fertile. **21 Naphtali**. MT is corrupt and the ancient versions differ widely; cf CV, RSV, BJ. Probably something was said similar to the statement on Asher; cf Dt 33:23. **22—26 Joseph**. This is the only **d** blessing properly so-called in this collection of poems. **22**. MT has Joseph called *ben-pōrat*, lit. 'son of a fruitful one (fem. part.)'. After the Targums, *pōrat is taken to* mean a tree or vine, and hence the *bānôt*, lit. 'daughters', of the second part is rendered 'tendrils' or 'branches'. The text is ungrammatical and probably corrupt, and various emendations are proposed. Probably, however, the v was concerned with the flourishing state of the Joseph-tribes, specifically Ephraim (*prt*, fruitful, probably alludes to *'prt* = Ephraim). **23**. This v evidently refers primarily to attacks on the Joseph-tribes, the precise circumstances of which are unknown. **24**. 'The Mighty One of Jacob': Yahweh's title in Is 1:24; 49:26; 60:16; Ps 132 (131): 2.5. Yahweh is here also called 'the Shepherd, the Rock of Israel' (Syr. 'the Shepherd of the Rock of Israel'); the latter title is found in 2 Sm 23:3; Is 30:29. **25—26**. The blessing is chiefly an agricultural one; cf 27:27—28; Dt 33:13—16. These vv are probably older than 8—12 and reflect a period when Ephraim was the dominant Israelite tribe. **27 Benjamin**. The tribe of Benjamin was noted for its warlike qualities; it was important during

72d the late period of the Judges and the early monarchy. **28—33 Jacob's Death**—These vv, together probably with the prose introduction in 1 above, are from P. This last will of Jacob, that he should be buried in the family tomb at Mach-pelah (ch 23), is shown to have been fulfilled in 50:12f below.

e **50:1—11,14 The Burial of Jacob**—As noted above on 48:7 (probably E), there is the beginning of a reference that may have originally placed Jacob's burial with Rachel (cf the mention of Leah in 49:31). The present passage, J, originally placed it in the Transjordan: such is the evident sense of 10f, as otherwise the route that is followed would make no sense. But at this point the final author of Gn inserted 12—13 from P: out of all the traditions he selected the one that located the burial at Mach-pelah.

2—3. Mummification was unknown to the Israelites and was regarded by them as a curiosity. It was practised here and in the case of Joseph (26) as a means of preserving the body until a definitive burial could take place. Herodotus (*History* II, 86—88) speaks of various kinds of mummification, the most thorough of which required 70 days. According to Diodorus, the Egyptians mourned a king for 72 days. Here the Egyptians mourn Jacob in deference to Joseph. **5.** 'In the sepulchre that he dug for himself' does not correspond to the burial cave of Mach-pelah. Cf Ac 7:16 (a mingling of two traditions?), according to which Jacob was buried in Shechem. **7—8.** The repeated 'all' in these vv obviously is an exaggeration

to stress the great solemnity of Jacob's funeral. **10—11.** **172e** Goren-Atad ('threshing-floor of Atad' or 'of the bramble') and Abel-mizraim ('field of Egypt', here given a popular etymology as 'mourning [*'ēbel*] of Egypt') were presumably the same place. The text insists that the site, which is otherwise unknown, was beyond the Jordan.

12—13 The Burial at Mach-pelah—These vv from P conclude the account begun in 49:28 33.

15—21 Joseph's Magnanimity—The conclusion of the **f** history of Joseph is Elohistic. **16.** This dying request of Jacob is not elsewhere recorded, but there is no reason to conclude that it was invented by Joseph's brothers. Joseph evidently accepts it as authentic. **19—21.** Joseph's reply is that God has already ruled in this case. Their action, though evilly intended, has through divine providence resulted in a great saving of life. For him to move against the lives of his brothers now would be to move against God's manifest design.

22—26 Joseph's Last Days—**22.** 110 years represented the Egyptian ideal of human life (cf ANET 414). This is another indication of the Egyptian coloration of this history. **23.** To see one's children's children was accounted a great blessing (cf Ps 128 (127):6; Prv 13:22; 17:6). Joseph lives to see his great-grandchildren. Machir became a clan in the tribe of Manasseh (Jg 5:14; Jos 17:1). That Machir was 'born on Joseph's knees' implies his adoption by Joseph; see on 30:1—5. **24.** A reference to the Exodus; so also in 48:21. **25.** Cf Ex 13:19; Jos 24:32.

EXODUS

BY P. ZERAFA O.P.

173a Bibliography—*Commentaries*: P. Heinisch, BB 1934; G. Beer, HAT 1939; E. Kalt-N. Adler, Herder's Bibel-kommentar 1948; J. C. Rylaarsdam-J. E. Park, IB 1953; A. Clamer, PCSB 1956; B. Couroyer, BJ 1958²; H. Schneider EchB 1958³; M. Noth, OTL, 1962; D. M. G. Stalker, PC (2), 1962.

b *Chronology*—E. Drioton, 'La Date de l'Exode' RHPR 35 (1955) 36–50; R. North, 'Date and Unicity of the Exodus', AmER 134 (1956) 161–82; H. G. Asmussen, *Zur Datierung des Auszuges*, Dis. Kiel 1960; *Topography*—P. Montet, 'Tanis, Avaris et Pi-Ramses', RB 39 (1930) 5–28; J. Gabriel, 'Wo lag der biblische Sinai?' WZKM 39 (1932) 123–32; H. Cazelles, 'Donneés géographiques sur l'Exode', RHPR 35 (1955) 51–60; id 'Les localisations de l'Exode et la critique littéraire', RB 62 (1955) 321–64; J. Simons, *The Geographical and Topographical Texts of the OT*, Leiden, 1959; B. Rothenberg, *God's Wilderness: Discoveries in Sinai*, 1961.

c *Covenant and Law*—A. Alt, *Der Ursprung des israelitischen Rechts*, Leipzig, 1934; A. Eberharter, 'Décalogue', DBS 2 (1934) 341–51; H. Cazelles, *Le Code de l'Alliance*, 1946; J. Lewis, *The Ten Commandments*, 1946; H. H. Rowley, 'Moses and the Decalogue', BJRL 34 (1951) 81–118; J. A. Fitzmyer, 'The Aramaic Suzerainty Treaty from Sefiré in the Museum of Beirut', CBQ, 20 (1958) 444–76; I. Fransen, 'L'Alliance du Sinai, (Ex 19ss)', BiViCh 26 (1959) 19–28; J. L'Hour, 'L'Alliance de Sichem', RB 69 (1962) 5–36, 161–84, 350–68.

d *The Name Yahweh*—A. M. Dubarle, 'La Signification du nom de Iahweh', RSPT 35 (1951) 3–21; E. Dhorme, 'Le nom de Dieu d'Israël', RHR 141 (1952) 5–18; G. Lambert, 'Que signifie le nom divin YHWH?', NRT 74 (1952), 897–915; M. Allard, 'Note sur la formule "ehyeh ašer ehyeh"' (Ex 3:14), RSR 45 (1957), 79–86; D. N. Freedman, 'The Name of the God of Moses', JBL 79 (1960), 151–6; R. Abba, 'The Divine Name Yahweh', JBL 80 (1961), 320–8; E. C. B. McLaurin, 'YHWH. The Origin of the Tetragrammaton', VT 12 (1962) 439–63.

174a Name—The Hebrews had no special name for the second book of Moses. They considered it as a part of a larger whole, the Torah, and indicated it by its serial number *hômeš šēnî* 'The Second Fifth' (Sotah 36*b*) or by its opening words *we'ēlleh šemôt* 'These are the Names' (Orig., *Comm. in Ps*, PG 12, 1084). The hellenistic Jews coined the Gr. name *Exodos* 'Departure', which was taken up by the early Christian writers and the extant MSS of the LXX. In its latinized form, Exodus, it passed through the VL and Vg into the modern Christian translations.

b Contents—The whole Torah deals with God's plan of forming the Chosen People and leading them to the Promised Land. Gn expounds the preparatory phase in the story of the Patriarchs. Ex introduces the fulfilment of this plan. It starts with an important historical turning-point which marks the very birth of Israel (cf Hos 11:1). **174** After a long sojourn in Egypt, the people have multiplied and are suffering under Egyptian oppression, seemingly abandoned by God. When a prospective deliverer appears in the person of Moses, the oppression becomes harsher and the hope of salvation fainter. The supreme might of God prevails over all obstacles, punishes the godless Egyptians and leads the people through sea and wilderness to the mountain of Sinai. Here the straggling troop of Israelite clans are moulded into a theocratic community by the Covenant with Yahweh, based on the observance of the Sinaitic law, contained in the Decalogue, the Book of the Covenant and the Ritual Legislation. The loyalty of the people is immediately put to the test and they sink into idolatry. The Covenant is renewed and God's orders about the construction and consecration of the Tabernacle are carried out. God's descent on the Tabernacle signified by an enveloping cloud marks the end of Ex whose limits are determined by the practical division of the Torah into five rolls.

Authorship—See § 130*e*. The divine plan of salvation **c** was a continuous unfolding of sacred history and revelation, of which the Bible was the living witness and instrument. The inspired words never became a dead letter; under divine inspiration they were adapted to the changing vicissitudes of the people and acted as a sure guide all through the history of Israel. It is not surprising therefore that Ex betrays a marked note of diversity. The outstanding figure that dominates both the historical and the legislative texts is Moses, and tradition is right in considering him as author of the whole in a real sense. But the events here narrated do not constitute a hermetically closed historical period. They are the foundation stone of a long chain of divine interventions that follow as a natural sequel. So also the Mosaic legislation was not intended exclusively for the time of Moses; it was to command the religious and sociological structure of Israel in all the subsequent historical periods. Whatever happened after Moses was a re-enactment of his original work, and all later legislation was a re-promulgation of the primitive Mosaic institutions. This homogeneous development of the divine plan ensured the continuity of the genuine Mosaic tradition. It is difficult to separate in Ex the underlying Mosaic layer from later modifications and additions. All the book contains the work of Moses as it shines forth in undiminished vitality through the various periods of Israel's history.

Structure—Critics distinguish different phases in the **d** growth of Ex and have arrived at a sufficiently reliable distribution, if not of single lines, at least of the main passages among the Pentateuchal sources known as J E D P. The result is a rather disconcerting mosaic composed of many literary fragments. In the narrative sections J supplies the fundamental text, completed and repeated by E and P. The legislative part is based on E, with minor contributions from J and longer contributions of P in the cult sections. The D style is discernible only

74d in short and rare pericopes. This dependence on different sources explains some overlapping and repetition both in the narrative and in the legislative passages. For this reason the exegete must sometimes split up a text and study its various components before dealing with the general meaning of the whole.

e This approach to the study of the sources is not always free from danger, for it is mostly based on literary peculiarities and could easily end up with the establishment of four geographically and chronologically independent doctrinal units, which is a historical fallacy. There never existed four independent doctrinal traditions in Israelite history. When Israel became one people in pre-monarchic times, the concept of its religion based on the idea of the Covenant was also fully developed and became the perennial and common heirloom of all the tribal sections of the people. After the consolidation of the monarchy, the great figure of David, the God-sent saviour, greatly influenced Israel's theological thought, so that the Jahwistic source which was fixed in writing around that time presents itself as a covenantal theology reinterpreted in the light of the messianic promises attached to the Davidic dynasty. With the separation of the two kingdoms after Solomon the Davidic myth faded into secondary importance while the pure covenantal theology again asserted itself and materialized in the Elohistic source, to be further developed by the Deuteronomist. The Priestly source also falls back on the Sinaitic Covenant, and interprets it according to the special viewpoint of the Jerusalem clergy. The successive elaborators of Israel's doctrinal inheritance never rejected the legacy received from their forbears. They added their own contribution and somehow fitted the whole into one rather awkward frame. This is why we have e.g. different fragmentary accounts of the Sinaitic theophany, and two different decalogues combined together by the device of a re-

f promulgation of a rejected code. The final arrangement of the whole material comes from the Priestly tradition and this fact has to be taken into consideration in order to catch the general meaning of Ex. The clergy of Jerusalem placed the temple service at the centre of all theological speculation and therefore interpreted the events at Sinai as a liturgical Covenant. The chronological reckoning of the march to Sinai begins with the feast of the Passover, and is led on by different stages to the erection and consecration of the Tabernacle a year later. This source does not attach too much importance to the decalogue and Book of the Covenant, which it accepted from the older traditions; its attention is continuously fixed on the singular significance of the desert Dwelling. The older sources mentioned the Tabernacle as the meeting-place of Moses with Yahweh, and their information has been given a convenient place in the book (33:7–11), but this was not enough for the Priestly narrator. He elaborated his own solemn account of the whole affair, furnishing detailed divine commands about its construction (25:1–31:17) and describing minutely the execution of the work (35:1–40:33), ending up with the presence of Yahweh in the Tent after its erection (40:34–38). In its present state therefore, the whole book is planned as a gradual preparation for the erection of the Tabernacle of the desert, conceived by the Jerusalem clergy as a reduced replica of the temple, cf §103e–f.

175a Historicity—The theological speculations of the Pentateuchal sources are firmly anchored in two basic events which constitute the nucleus of all Israelite ancestral traditions: the **presence of Israel in Egypt** as forced labourers and the **formation of a theocratic commun-ity at Sinai through the mediation of Moses**. It is **175a** not necessary to embark on a lengthy discussion about the historical character of these events. If they are not historical the subsequent unfolding of Israel's history would be inexplicable. The very fact that it was deemed necessary to attach somehow or other all later accretions to these basic facts goes to prove that they are well grounded in very old and sound traditions. The formation of these traditions, coinciding with the origin of the people itself, naturally follows the general trend of all ancestral traditions of the Ancient E. Usually expressed **b** by the device of various genealogies, they represent the actual situation of a group at a given time, and are easily adaptable to the changing vicissitudes of the group itself. A split in the group gives rise to new traditions, while the amalgamation of different groups entails the fusion of their respective traditions. So also with Israel's ethnic groups and their traditions. The homogeneous picture of one people sojourning in Egypt and moulded into a theocratic community at Sinai dates from the time when all Israel was definitively united on Palestinian soil and its various traditions fused together, the whole traditional patrimony thus becoming the common possession of all the people. A close study of the old ethnic and traditional reminiscences of the Bible proves that before this fusion some partial traditions circulated independently. It is therefore not necessary to suppose that every single Israelite was in Egypt and witnessed the Sinaitic theophany. The important thing is that all Israel by its unification in pre-monarchic times is the spiritual heir of the promises made to the Patriarchs and the divine favours deriving from the events of the exodus and the Sinaitic Covenant.

Date—The figures supplied by the Bible have a theolo- **c** gical rather than a mathematical value. Taking the construction of the Solomonic temple (c. 966 B.C.) as the central event of Israel's history, the Bible calculates back 12 generations of priests (480 years) to the erection of the Tabernacle of the desert, which corresponds to the 12 generations of priests that intervene between the Solomonic temple and its reconstruction after the exile. A purely chronological consideration of the scanty information available indicates the 13th cent. B.C. as the most probable date of the exodus, for the following reasons. On their way to Palestine the Israelites clashed with the Edomites and Moabites. The former established their kingdom at the end of the 14th or the beginning of the 13th cent. B.C., the latter during the 13th cent. B.C. The Israelite archeological stratum in Palestine belongs to the Iron Age which appeared there at the beginning of the 12th cent. B.C. Moreover it appears from the Bible **d** that at the time of the exodus the Pharaohs had their royal residence in the Delta and undertook extensive building programmes. The Hebrews too dwelt in the Delta and were pressed into Pharaoh's service, helping to build the store cities of Pithom and Ra-amses. It is now well known that while the XVIIIth dynasty resided at Thebes in Upper Egypt, the XIXth dynasty dwelt in the Delta. In Pithom (Tell Artabi) has been found the temple dedicated to the god Atum by Ramses II (c. 1301–1235) who also built Ra-amses (probably Qantir), his Delta residence. All this points to Ramses II as the Pharaoh of the oppression and to his successor Mernephtah (c. 1235–1223) as the Pharaoh of the exodus. It is true that Mernephtah mentions the presence of Israel in Palestine along with the feats accomplished in his fifth year, but it is easy to suppose that this could refer to a clash with one of the diverse roaming groups that finally constituted the unified Israel on Palestinian

175d soil. Starting therefore from Egypt in the second half of the 13th cent., Israel infiltrated into Palestine at the beginning of the 12th cent. B.C.

e Teaching—Exodus teaches us, in the first place, that God chose the Hebrew nation as his special instrument in the execution of his plan for the redemption of mankind. The freedom of this choice is clearly manifested. *I will be gracious to whom I will be gracious, and I will be merciful to whom I will be merciful* (33:19). He first makes known to them his identity by the revelation of the divine name, Yahweh. He then shows his goodness and his omnipotence by the prodigies through which he delivers them from the bondage of Egypt. The same attributes are manifested in his solicitude for their temporal needs by the provision of water, quails, and manna in the desert. He manifests to them his majesty at Sinai and makes a Covenant with them, securing them his constant favour and protection and exacting from them special holiness of life and obedience to his commands. His wisdom and holiness appear in the ethical and religious precepts which he imposes on them, surpassing immeasurably the laws of other ancient peoples. When they revolt from him he manifests his detestation of their sin and threatens punishment, but finally, when they show repentance, yields to the intercession of Moses and admits them to pardon.

f St Augustine's pronouncement on the relation between the OT and the New: *Novum in Vetere latet, Vetus in Novo patet*, 'the New is hidden in the Old, the Old is manifest in the New', is particularly true of Exodus. The Sinaitic Covenant or Testament is a type of the NT. Its mediator, Moses, is a type of Christ. The *kingdom of priests and holy nation* of Israel (19:6) is a type of the members of the Church, the holy priesthood (1 Pt 2:5), who enjoy the fulfilment of the promise. The sacrifice of the Passover is a type of the sacrifice on Calvary. Its sacrificial commemoration is a type of the Eucharistic sacrifice. The manna is a type of the sacrament of the Eucharist, also pre-figured by God's visible presence among his Chosen People. The typical character of the Tabernacle and the various ceremonies connected with it is developed in Heb. Many rites of the old revealed religion are incorporated in our liturgy.

But once more it must be remembered that if the events described in this book have this 'typical' value in relationship to the NT, it is because this was the real beginning of a new relationship between God and man; and the work of Christ was the completion of the work here inaugurated. Covenant, redemption, grace—these are the fundamental qualities of religion and of life for a Christian; but it is in the Exodus that these qualities are revealed in operation. The God we worship is here made manifest; and it is his love and his truth which are laid down as a 'way' for men today, called to be one people as 'sons of God'. The principles of justice and charity inculcated in the Book of the Covenant still cry out for application to heal the wounds of the world.

176a (A) Departure from Egypt (1:1—15:21).

1:1—2:10 Oppression of the Israelites and Birth of Moses—The sorry plight of the Israelites was commonplace in Egypt. The Ramessides undertook extensive building programmes in the Delta, and as was customary in that country they relied on forced labour to recruit an enormous mass of man power, far exceeding the limited possibilities of their prisoners of war. The Israelites had been living under privileged conditions. Occupying fertile pasture-land, away from the Egyptian urban centres, they had managed to maintain their freedom of movement, so cherished by semi-nomadic pastors. Now they lost their liberty: they were pressed into service by **176** the king and allotted a task not according to their liking. As long as the authority of Egypt ruled supreme in the E Mediterranean, the king fostered no sinister intentions in their regard. It was only later that an abrupt turning-point in the political situation brought about a complete change in his policy regarding Israel. Egyptian supremacy waned, Canaan was in turmoil, Libya threatened invasion, Pharaoh felt insecure. The Israelites began to be considered a menace to the security of the state, and the killing of newborn males was decided upon as a means of gradual extinction. Old Israelite traditions insist more on the bondage than on the death of the infants; here both measures are used to illustrate the danger of extinction and serve as an introduction to the birth of Moses.

1—7. Although rather complex and varied, the whole **b** Israelite nation was equally heir to the divine promises made to Abraham, and beneficiary of the marvels of the exodus. All the Israelites are therefore traced back, in a spiritual line of descent, to Abraham through the 12 sons of Jacob who had settled in Egypt and mightily increased in the Delta region. **8—10**. A new king came into power, who did not acknowledge the good services rendered by Joseph to his country: probably Ramses II, famous for his vast constructions in the Delta. He no longer followed the benevolent policy of his predecessors towards the people of Israel, but initiated a series of restrictive measures which, under his successor, culminated in the order to kill the newborn males. **11—14**. First restrictive measure: forced labour. Common in Egypt, but new to Israel, it entailed the loss of freedom; they were employed in the back-breaking brick industry. Thus they helped in the building of Pithom and Ra-amses, store cities in the eastern Delta. Pithom occupied the site of Tell Artabi in W. Tumilat. Further N, Qantir probably represents the site of Ra-amses, the Delta residence built by Ramses II.

15—21. Second oppressive measure. Political instabil- **c** ity rendered the presence of Israel on Egyptian soil undesirable, and Pharaoh tried to enlist the help of the midwives who served the Hebrew women to curb the growth of the people. When they assisted at a childbirth they were to kill the male infants, leaving alive the females. The Egyptian midwives, with Heb. names traceable to Egyptian prototypes, were God-fearing people. They let live the males, and explained that the Hebrews were sturdy women who gave birth before the midwife came to their help. Fear of God is a very common biblical expression and stands for the fulfilment of all the duties of man towards God. As a reward for their rectitude, God granted them a numerous posterity. The use of the term 'Hebrews' here is probably significant. Egyptian records **d** speak of *'aperu*, people who roamed all over the Middle E and poured over the Egyptian frontier as captives, mercenaries, labourers and fortune seekers. The Israelites formed part of this roving element. The Bible itself does not reserve the title of 'Hebrew' to the descendants of Abraham, for it places Eber, the eponym of the Hebrews, a long way up in the family tree of Abraham (Gn 10: 10—26). In biblical narratives however, only the history of the Israelite branch of the Hebrews is taken in consideration. **22**. Third measure: Pharaoh ordered his people to throw the Hebrew male children into the river: the Nile and its many branches. This may well refer to some acts of violence committed by the Egyptians in the Hebrew settlements.

2:1—10. The birth of great men in ancient times is **e** regularly marked by some spectacular sign of divine providence which defends the helpless child from the

76e mischief of man and nature. A very popular theme represents the child exposed on the waters of a river or in the deep recesses of a forest where it is eventually rescued and reared into a hero. The legend of Sargon I is a typical example (ANET² 119). The birth-story of Moses, built on the same lines, stands out for its complete lack of mythological elements. The common theme is developed within the framework of a very moving narrative, in which everything is treated quite naturally and no effort is made to explain any incongruities that may arise from the special rank of the characters involved. Moreover it is firmly anchored in such reliable facts as Pharaoh's attempt to curb the increase of the Israelites,

f and Moses' own Egyptian name and upbringing. 1—4. The story is centred exclusively on Moses; what may have happened to other children is not said. He was born in the house of Levi, one of the tribal groups of Israel. No details about parents, sister and brother are available here: these occur only later (6:20; Nm 26:59). Full of faith in God (Heb. 11:23), the mother braved Pharaoh's fury

g and protected the child, by a ruse. 5—10. Moses is an Egyptian name meaning 'child', an abbreviation of a longer form like Thutmosis 'son of Thot', Ahmosis 'son of Ooh', with the name of the Egyptian god dropped off. Biblical tradition explains the name as 'drawn out of the water': a popular etymology based on assonance to the Heb. word māšāh 'draw', which only partially bears out the meaning attached to the name.

177a 2:11—7:7 Flight and Call of Moses. General Remarks—This section provides the norm for all biblical history and typology. Moses left Egypt and took refuge in the desert there to meet God. The Israelites also witnessed God's theophany in the desert after leaving Egypt, and there too Elijah encountered God (1 (3) Kgs 19:8—18). The prophets considered the solitude of the desert as the ideal background for God's action on the soul (Hos 2:16; Jer 2.2), and the pious Qumranites actualized this ideal in their refuge by the Dead Sea. Moreover the flight from Egypt is a pattern for all further deliverances (Is 40:3; Jer 16:14—15; Mi 7:14—15) and a model for the baptismal liturgy of the primitive Church (cf M. E. Boismard, VieSp 94 (1956), 339—52).

b The narrative may seem overcharged and clumsy, for it stitches together two great events in the history of the Chosen People: the revelation of Yahweh to Abraham and the subsequent revelation to Moses and his followers. It is here that Moses and the Israelites were introduced to the intimacy of Yahweh, the God of Abraham. So that while we feel the novelty of God's revelation and the creative work of Moses, the whole theme of the exodus is linked up to the ancient revelation and initial promises of patriarchal date. This explains the apparent antinomy in the description of the revelation of the divine name. The Patriarchs had known and adored Yahweh, but it is only in the desert that the followers of Moses caught up with the relatively advanced stage of Abraham's knowledge of God.

In the desert Moses lived with the Midianites, and this may have contributed to his religious formation. In the early stages of Israel's history, some Midianites must have been on very familiar terms with the Abrahamites, for the Midianite tribes are presented in biblical tradition as the descendants of Abraham by Keturah (Gn 25:1—4). In later times some oriental Midianites periodically harassed the Israelite settlements in N Palestine and Transjordan by their sudden raids, and consequently in Israelite traditions Midian took the

place of a dreaded foe. They were expected to adhere to 177b Yahweh in messianic times (Is 60:6).

Midian is a political not a geographical term: it c indicates the land inhabited by the people of that name. The bulk of the Arabian tribes mentioned in the Bible had their rallying point E of the Gulf of Aqaba, but furnished as they were with camels, they were very mobile, and we have testimony of Arab infiltration all over Palestine and Transjordan (Nm 24:22—24; 1 Chr 4:25; 5:19; Neh 4:1). The Midianites, an Arab tribe, also had their centre of activities on the Arabian Peninsula, where a tract of land S of Edom is generally called Midian. The Midianite clan of the Kenites, among whom Moses passed his desert years, must have wandered W of Aqaba, for the biblical description of Israel's wanderings in the desert of Sin, more or less identifiable with the place of Moses' sojourn, suits best the S part of the Sinaitic Peninsula, which therefore stands for the Midian of this narrative. In fact the Israelites arrived there after skirting the Red Sea coast, and before heading for the region of Kadesh, which they reached after an eleven days' journey through Seir (Dt 1:2). The wanderings of the Kenites are well known to the Bible which speaks of them both in the N (Jg 4:17; 5:24) and in the S of Palestine (Jg 1:16; 1 Sm 15:4—7; 27:10; 30:29).

Moses received his mission at the **Mountain of God** d in Midian, identified in old biblical traditions with the mountain where Israel later made the pact with Yahweh. This identification is perhaps the reason for the double name of the mountain. Sinai in the tradition of the S tribes and Horeb in the N literature. Owing to very fragmentary information, one cannot locate the mountain with certainty. The best arguments still tell in favour of the massive block of granite in the S reaches of the Sinaitic Peninsula called **Jebel Musa**, with a towering peak of 7,647 ft. It fits well in the itinerary of the Israelites who travelled S along the coast until they struck into the interior at Debbet er-Ramleh and made their last halt before Sinai at W. Refayed. This localization dates from the 4th cent. A.D. and has a good chance of being due to a much older tradition. Nabatean pilgrims frequented this sacred ground and left numerous inscriptions in the neighbourhood. Moreover Elijah's flight to Horeb (1 (3) Kgs 19:8—18) shows that the site of the mountain was not unknown in the 9th cent. B.C.

Much less probable are some **alternative sites** e proposed by different authors for different reasons. **Jebel Serbal** is one of them. It was chosen because of its proximity to the oasis of Feiran, where some ancient writers preferred to locate the last halt before Sinai. The discovery of old inscriptions on Serabit el-Khadim attracted the attention of some scholars to this mountain, but this identification fell into oblivion when it was ascertained that the inscriptions had nothing to do with Sinai. The possibility of locating Sinai in the region of **Kadesh** has been considered and rejected, for it would upset the established direction followed by the Israelites in their wandering. Other authors look for the mountain **E of the Gulf of Aqaba**. This is the most likely ground for a Midianite settlement and is rich in volcanic peaks, non-existent on the Sinaitic Peninsula, which would provide the natural background to the imposing descriptions of fire and smoke in the theophany. Moreover it was outside Egypt's sphere of influence and provided a secure hiding place to Moses. Reasonable though it may seem f at first sight, this opinion is not very convincing. It has already been noted above that the Midianites were not tied down to their E area of activities. The

177f description of the theophany does not necessarily postulate any volcanic phenomena; it simply brings into play the accepted signs of God's presence, fire, smoke and cloud. Moreover in the S of the Sinaitic peninsula, Moses was as much out of reach of Egypt's influence as he would have been E of Aqaba. The Egyptians controlled the mining areas in the NW of the Peninsula, but did not permanently occupy its lower end. Petra has also been singled out as a possible site for Sinai because of its vicinity to Kadesh and supposed cult of the moon-god, that would render it a likely goal for Israel's pilgrimage. This hypothesis has not gained ground, for it places the arrival at Sinai after the events of Kadesh, and the presence of the moon-god cult is not supported by weighty arguments.

g 2:11–22 The Flight—11–12. In Pharaoh's court Moses remained a Hebrew at heart, and on reaching maturity (translated into figures in Ac 7:23), he began to visit the labour gangs. In striking the Egyptian Moses acted according to the sacred tribal law of retaliation. A wrong done to a member of a community has to be avenged by some other member, and so justice is established. Among nomad peoples tribal law takes the place of our civil codes, and is no more unchristian than our civil sanctions. **13–22.** Moses had to seek refuge in Midian. He was introduced to Midianite life at a well, the most important asset and usual meeting place of desert settlements. After a dispute over precious water, Moses was admitted into the household of a priest and married one of the girls, named Zipporah, 'bird'. By her he had a son, Gershom, 'outcast', explained in popular etymology as 'stranger there'. The name of the priest is here given as Reuel 'friend of God', while in other places he is called Jethro 'abundance' (cf 3:1; 4:18; 18:1, 2, 5, 6, 9, 10, 12). The Midianites appear in the story of Moses both before and after the exodus. This probably explains the double form of the name.

h 23–4:18 The Call—23–25. Introduction to the call of Moses. Ramses II died and a feeling of hope swept over the oppressed people. **3:1–6.** Moses was driving the flock of his father-in-law away from the desert towards higher and grassy ground, when he wandered onto the Mountain of God, probably an ancient cultic site. Here the God of the Patriarchs appeared to him. 'Angel of Yahweh' is a circumlocution meaning Yahweh himself (cf Gn 16:7, 13). In the OT the presence of Yahweh is generally signified by some spectacular natural phenomenon; here it is indicated by a ball of fire settling about a bush. The narrative enhances the inviolable sanctity of God: those who trespass upon God's sacredness, by coming too near or casting intrusive glances, expose themselves to death (cf 19:21).

i 11–12. Moses has misgivings. This is a usual device for developing the description of an apparition. He first pleads his unfitness, and God assures him of his assistance. Similar assurance is given to other people chosen for a special mission (Jg 6:12; Lk 1:28). The actual arrival at the Mountain of God was to the Israelites sign enough of Moses' divine mission. **13–15.** Moses then objects to God's anonymity. Whenever God is about to make an important promise he identifies himself (Gn 15:7; 17:1; 28:13) so that the beneficiaries will know to whom the favour is to be ascribed. Here God discloses his name, Yahweh (discussed in next paragraph), which will for ever identify him as the God of the exodus. The sacred author avails himself of this occasion to explain its meaning. **16–22.** A forecast of what really happened afterwards, according to the biblical method of presenting events first in project and then in fact. The pretext of a

sacrifice in the desert is a veiled way of demanding final **177i** release, which did not deceive Pharaoh. The precious objects appropriated by the Israelites were spoils of victory retained as a just recompense for their toils (Wis 10:17). **4:1–9. 6.** Leprosy can mean all kinds of **j** ills that putrefy the outside of a body, a house (Lv 14:34) or clothing (Lv 13:47). **10–18. 14.** The figure of Aaron appears here for the first time. The narratives that deal with his activity constitute a secondary theme in the story of the deliverance, and intermingle with the primary theme dealing with Moses. A connection ensues from the fact that Aaron is Moses' brother and spokesman. In some texts the activity of Aaron overlaps that of his brother; the old traditions about Moses were recast in view of Aaron's participation in the events of the exodus.

The Divine Name Yahweh (3:13–15)—The origin **178** and meaning of this name are still shrouded in mystery. The text is difficult to interpret, because it has undergone some retouching. The primitive theme developed here was the identification of God. This is what Moses asked for (13) and got (15), according to the normal procedure of patriarchal revelations (Gn 15:7; 17:1; 28:13). The narrative therefore originally consisted of 13 and 15 (minus the redactional 'again'). The inspired author inserted the explanation of the name, based as usual on popular etymology, to show us what it stood for in the mind of the Israelites.

From the corresponding first person sing. 'I am', it appears that the name was understood as an impf. third person sing. masculine Qal of the verb 'to be', and interpreted as 'he is'. The meanings of popular etymologies always correspond to some concrete event or fixed situation, which in our case must have been the campaign against the lure of idols who seem to be, but in reality are not, gods; only Yahweh is God (Dt 32:17, 21; Is 44:6; 45:5). By attaching the origin of the name to the verb 'to be', the hagiographer expresses the unique position of Yahweh as God. As in the case of Moses' own name, the etymological reference does not cover the full import of the theological significance intended by the author.

Other interpretations have been proposed by dif- **b** ferent authors. A very popular one understands the enigmatic 'I am who I am' as a refusal to disclose the real name, or an impossibility to define it. Taken by itself it could be so interpreted, but the context shows that a real name was actually communicated. Moreover Moses was not to tell the people 'who (ever) he is', but 'he is', which is not void of meaning. A reference proposed by some scholars to an action of God such as bringing into existence, blowing, loving, felling, etc is unsupported by text and context. Nor is it easy to read in the text the idea of God's true existence or the plenitude of his being. This interpretation would hang in the air without a fixed historical context such as popular etymologies postulate.

The **scientific etymology** and origin of the name have **c** not yet been ascertained; one can only mention the different forms in which it was known through the ages. Towards the end of the Jewish era, in sign of reverence, the Hebrews refrained from pronouncing the name and substituted for it the Heb. word for Lord. To ensure this substitution the massoretes pointed the name in the consonantal text with the vowels of 'Lord', thus giving rise to the hybrid form Jehovah (Yehowah) adopted by European authors since the 12th cent. A.D. It is now more or less certain that the Hebrews read it Yahweh. This pronunciation possibly coincided with its interpretation in popular etymology as a verbal form from the verb 'to be'. There are also some reasons to believe that in earlier times it was read Yahwoh (W. Vischer, 'Eher Jahwo als

78c Jahwe', *Theol. Zeits. Basel* 16 (1960), 259—67). The Bible contains some other shorter forms: Yah, used independently, and Yeho-, Yo-, -yahu, -yah as elements of proper names. If the same name is detected in the Ugaritic Yaw (c. 15th cent. B.C.) and Accadian Yaum-, -yaum (20th cent. B.C.) the genuineness of revealed religion remains unimpaired: to Abraham Yahweh is the God of the promises, to the followers of Moses the God of the exodus.

d **4:19—31 Return of Moses to Egypt—19—23.** Another and more popular account of Moses' departure (cf 4:18), with a theological evaluation of the coming events. The slaying of the first-born sons in all Egyptian households is a punishment for the oppression of Israel, who is the first-born of God (Jer 31:9; Is 19:25). The hardening of Pharaoh's heart is not considered here as a moral fault but as a misfortune inflicted by Yahweh on the enemy of his people, which entailed the subsequent national disasters. **24—26.** As in the case of Jacob (Gn 32:23—33), before Moses is qualified for his mission he has to undergo a mysterious ordeal of an unknown kind. Old traditions bracketed this event with the circumcision of Moses, (probably carried out when he married Zipporah) and of his son. The rather enigmatic text which carries these traditions could be explained as follows. Because his son is uncircumcised, Moses is defiled before God and incurs his wrath. Aware of her husband's plight, Zipporah circumcises the boy and touches Moses with the **e** blood. He is thus cleansed and reinstated. **27—31.** The events forecast in the apparition begin to unfold themselves. Moses returns to Egypt, performs the signs and is accepted by the Hebrews as their deliverer. The part of Aaron is here definitively dovetailed into the story of Moses (cf note on 4:10—18). To do this the narrative leads us back to the Mountain of God where Aaron meets his brother, receives his instructions, follows him into Egypt and acts as his spokesman before the people.

f **5:1—6:1 Unsuccessful Appeal to Pharaoh 15.** The old Hebrew traditions contain traces of initial negotiations with Pharaoh conducted by the representatives of the people. This is why after Moses and Aaron present their demand, the negotiations are continued by the Heb. foremen. But as the story develops Moses and Aaron are recognized as the sole negotiators for the people. The bricks were made from the black alluvial soil kneaded into a pasty mass, shaped in wooden moulds and allowed to dry in the sun. Straw was added to increase consistence. In Egypt the harvesters collected only the ears of corn, the stalk was left on the fields where it was gathered by the brickmakers.

g **6:2—7:7 A Reassessment of the Call of Moses—** Thus far the narrative has proceeded by fits and starts, leaving some obscurities. The Priestly redactor of the pent. traditions rearranged the older material into a more logical order, and took special pains to locate the family of Moses within the great genealogical framework that serves as a background to the unified patriarchal traditions. No new element is brought forward. The author insists however on the continuity between the exodus and the promises made to Abraham; he enhances the role of Aaron as co-liberator of Israel, and tries to explain the apparent incongruity of **h** the gradual revelation of the divine name. **2—3.** It is difficult to imagine that P was unaware of a pre-Mosaic revelation of the divine name. The S (J) traditions traced back the cult of Yahweh at least to Enosh (Gn 4:26). In P the name of the mother of Moses, Jochebed (6:20; Nm 26:59), begins with the shorter form of Yahweh. Moreover the vision of Moses in the genuine N (Elohistic) tradition (3:13, 15) did not contain exactly a revelation

of a new name, but only an identification of God. In a **178h** later period the etymological explanation of the name was also attributed to Moses and inserted in the narrative. To this etymological explanation P alludes when he declares that the name was not known before Moses. **4—9.** God **i** explains that the liberation will take place in view of the promises made to the patriarchs, thus establishing a link between the two periods. The Israelites turned a deaf ear to Moses. This is not expressed in the first narrative, but a possible rejection is there envisaged by Moses who asks for a sign (4:1) which is granted by God (4:2—9). **10—13, 26—27.** Moses is not alone to receive his mission from God; with him Aaron also is commissioned by Yahweh to lead the Israelites out of Egypt. This reflects the importance attached to the priestly race in the late monarchy. **28—8:7.** Here the figure of Moses is again in the foreground and Aaron is relegated to the office of a prophet, i.e. spokesman, of his brother. Moses was 80 years old. This number is a conventional translation of two more or less lengthy periods: the time he spent in Egypt and his sojourn in Midian.

The Genealogical List (6:14—25)—Semitic genealo- **j** gies indicate the respective social position of correlated groups, and are liable to change if something interferes with the established order. The present genealogy reflects the outstanding position of the Aaronites, who in the opinion of P are the exclusive titulars of the priestly office. It is inserted into the genealogical scheme of the whole people by the mention of Reuben and Simeon, always placed first among the sons of Jacob (Gn 46:8—10; En 1:2), and traces the descent of Levi down to Phinehas, the grandson of Aaron. The Gershomites are included among the sons of Levi (cf also Gn 46:11; Nm 3:17; 26:57), but are not attached to Moses as in the N traditions (2:22; Jg 18:30). They were in charge of the sanctuary of Dan, which was not at all acceptable to the Jerusalem priesthood. The relation between Amram and Jochebed, being part of a genealogical scheme, should not be judged in the light of the law that prohibited marriage between nephew and aunt (Lv 18:12 13; 20:19).

7:8—12:16 The Plagues of Egypt — This section **179a** forms a literary whole which by different stages leads to the actual liberation of the Israelites. Before introducing the plagues the author recounts another interview with Pharaoh in which Moses and Aaron perform a sign. When Pharaoh refuses to obey the accredited messengers, God enforces his will by means of the ten plagues. More or less the same pattern runs through the plagues: Moses presents himself before Pharaoh and demands the release of Israel threatening divine punishment. Pharaoh refuses, is punished, but holds fast till his stubbornness is broken by the tenth plague. The narrative gathers momentum: Moses becomes more outspoken, Pharaoh more ready to negotiate; and the plagues increase in vehemence: the first four produce annoyance and distress, the next four inflict serious damage to property and person, the ninth is ominous of outraged divinity and the last portends extinction. But for all this schematic apparatus the **b** narratives betray evident signs of dependence on flexible and **independent traditions** which maintained their peculiarities when they were inserted into the present context. The role of Aaron is eloquent in this connection: sometimes only Moses appears on the scene; at other times Aaron is introduced as a spokesman or companion of Moses. Moreover a different number and order of plagues appears in Pss 78 (77) and 105 (104). The tenth plague fits well within the scheme, but it has a pattern of its own because of the liturgical prescriptions attached to it. The plagues refer back to some natural disasters that afflicted

179b Egypt in such a manner and with such intensity as to manifest the omnipotence of Yahweh whom Pharaoh had dared to brave and despise.

c 7:8—13 A Preliminary Sign—Moses had obtained the power of performing wonders by means of his staff as an authentication of his divine mission (4:1—5). **11**. The insertion of the magicians in the story is a rare piece of subtle polemics. By confronting the power of Aaron with the craft of the magicians, who at first try to compete, but afterwards are forced to give up, the author furnishes an indisputable proof of the might of Yahweh and the authentic character of his wonders. For this reason he does not wholly discredit the magicians from the very beginning, but lets them slowly exhaust all their magic resources in two other competitions with Aaron. Jewish tradition gives the name of the magicians as Jannes and Jambres (2 Tm 3:8).

d 14—24 First Plague: Water Pollution—We need not suppose that all the waters of Egypt were turned into real blood. The narrative fuses together two sources of pollution. In the older tradition, when Yahweh struck the river the fishes died and poisoned the water, so that the Egyptians had to look for drinking water in wells dug around the Nile. A further expansion of the story deals with the theme of the water turned into blood: a wonder imitated by the magicians. It is not very probable that the author is thinking about the reddish colour of the river during inundation. This phenomenon hardly affects the Lower Nile, and presents no danger to animal life. Perhaps the story foreshadows the bloody epilogue of the plagues.

e 25—8:15 Second Plague: Frogs—In flooded Egypt frogs are a common phenomenon; Egyptian mythology even endows them with a life-giving power. This supposed source of life was turned by divine will into a source of pestilence, which was all the more annoying because of the number and ubiquity of the frogs. **7**. The timing of the magicians' intervention, immediately after Moses' action, follows a logical, not a chronological sequence.

f 8:16—19 Third Plague: Gnats—The narrative marks an important stage in the development of the story, but is very simple in structure. The presence of gnats is no rare occurrence in Egypt, but here it is exceptional for they are produced at will and in great numbers. Their great number is expressed by the mention of dust, a proverbial figure of an innumerable multitude (Gn 13:16). The finger of God does not refer to the miracle produced by Aaron but to the failure of the magicians which they attributed to a sinister intervention of Yahweh. Second Isaiah, chronologically very near to P, uses the finger as a symbol of oppression (Is 58:9).

g 20—32 Fourth Plague: Vermin—The author does not specify the nature of these noxious creatures; the Heb. term indicates only their overwhelming number, which eventually produced some result: Pharaoh is forced to negotiate. This time the narrative is more developed than usual: the exact timing of the beginning and end of the plague is mentioned beforehand, and a discrimination is made between the Egyptian and Hebrew settlements as a sign of Yahweh's control of the situation. The land of Goshen is set apart (22), the people of Yahweh is saved (23); most probably the author is here influenced by the tenth plague.

h 9:1—7 Fifth Plague: Murrain—A grievous pestilence which played havoc among the Egyptian domestic animals while the possessions of Israel were spared. Of these animals the horse was introduced in the Hyksos period and the camel was known but not in common use. The enumeration simply indicates that all kinds of domestic animals were stricken. The death rate was very high. The

author says that 'all the cattle died': totality is the usual **179** biblical substitute for a high percentage. The narrator does not take into consideration the appearance of domestic animals in other plagues; the plague stories are basically independent units.

8—12 Sixth Plague: Boils—Skin diseases were not **i** rare, but this epidemic was exceptional for it afflicted man and beast, and was caused by Moses at Yahweh's command. The author does not pinpoint the nature of the disease with the accuracy of modern medical diagnosis; this would add nothing to the significance of his narrative; he only mentions a general external infection of everybody. The effect of his description is heightened by the fact that the magicians themselves were stricken.

13—35 Seventh Plague: Hail—The author describes a **j** terrific storm of thunder and hail, fatal to every kind of life: a rather exceptional phenomenon in Egypt. **14**. There is a new development in the theological evaluation of the plagues. In 7:3—5 the author explained why God hardened the heart of Pharaoh; here he explains why his stubbornness was not immediately punished by death: the manifestation of God's might is the answer to both problems. The loose rendering of 9:16 quoted by Paul (Rm 9:17) combines both perspectives, and serves to illustrate the supreme liberty of God, creator of all things. The narrative supposes that those Egyptians who took Moses' threat seriously were also spared. This agrees well with the universalistic viewpoint of the Jahwist who lived at a time when the star of David was spreading its light over the conquered gentile neighbours.

10:1—20 Eighth Plague: Locusts—A rare but very **k** dreaded calamity, harbinger of wide-spread famine. This narrative is closely linked with the preceding one: the note about the wheat and spelt which survived the hailstorm (9:32) is a preparation for the description of the locust plague, where it is again said that these insects ate up what remained after the storm (10:5, 15).

21—29 Ninth Plague: Darkness—A short narrative **l** that marks the transition from the recurring drama to the final act. **22**. Three days is a conventional expression for a period of expectancy often found in the Bible (Hos 6:2; Jon 2:1; Ac 9:9 etc). If we require a natural phenomenon for a precedent, we could explain the darkness as an intensification of the khamsin, a SE wind which fills the air with sand and darkens the atmosphere. It is however more probable that the author is enlarging on the feeling of dark expectation that settled over Egypt—but not on the Israelite settlements—just before the final blow. Darkness is a common biblical expression for despondency and distress.

11:1—13:16 Liturgical Institutions and the Tenth 180a Plague: Preliminary Remarks—Around the description of the tenth plague are centred some prescriptions relating to three different institutions, viz the Passover, Unleavened Bread and the Offering of the First-born, and all of these have influenced the description of the plague. The **Passover** was an old pastoral feast consisting of a springtime night sacrifice to secure protection against evil powers. It was probably celebrated just before the shepherds moved out of their winter grazing-grounds into greener regions which provided pasture during the dry season. The travelling attire of those taking part in the meal was well fitted for the occasion. The rites of the sacrifice stress its nomadic origin. It was roasted over a fire and eaten with unleavened bread and bitter herbs: the nomad does not employ kitchen utensils to cook his meat, and unleavened bread and wild plants form his normal diet. In Israel the Passover became a memorial of the fateful night when the blood of the sacrifice pro-

180a tected them against the Destroyer who played havoc among the Egyptian families. Because of its connection with the exodus, Passover signified also the release from Egyptian bondage and was a type of Christ's redeeming sacrifice on the cross.

b Originally **Unleavened Bread** was not connected with Passover. It was an agricultural pilgrimage feast celebrating the beginning of the barley harvest. Unleavened bread was prescribed, so that the product of the new harvest would not be contaminated by any remnant from the old crop. It lasted a whole week, with a cultic assembly at the beginning and end. Israel adopted this feast after occupying Palestine, and later on the Deuteronomic reformation linked it with Passover which occurred more or less at the same time of the year. An old tradition referred this feast back to the exodus. In their haste to leave Egypt, the Israelites carried with them and baked the dough which had not been mixed with leaven. This circumstance is perpetually commemorated in the feast of Unleavened Bread.

c The **Offering of the First-born** is an ancient Israelite practice of returning the first fruit of the womb to God, the giver of all life. The usual way of dedicating something to God was by sacrificing it, but the Israelites never allowed human sacrifice, and their children were ransomed instead of being sacrificed. The dedication of the first-born is here connected with the plague: it is a reminder of the extermination of all the first-born of the Egyptian households.

d 11:1 10; 12:20 12 Tenth Plague: Death of the First-born—The description of the final and decisive battle for liberty is more imposing than usual, but originally it must have followed the simple plague pattern, now hardly recognizable. From 11:7—8 it appears that the plague was originally introduced by the usual announcement before Pharaoh, but this has been partially dropped because of the final break in negotiations inserted in 10: 28—29, and instead we have a briefing of the Israelites, which does not fit very well with their lack of preparedness transparent in 12:39. After this introduction there is a general conclusion to the preceding plagues (11:9—10), not postulated by the original form of the narrative, and placed here as a transition to the final act of the dramatic event. This time the plague affected the people themselves.

e 12:37. Succoth, Heb. form of the Egyptian Tjeku whose ruins are to be found in Tell Maskhuta. They are said to have been 600,000 able-bodied men (cf also Nm 1:46) apart from their families and other ethnic groups that joined them in the march. This figure does not have a numerical but a **symbolic value**: it shows God's exceptional protection under which the Israelites prospered and flourished notwithstanding the Egyptian oppression. Some secondary details, originating from the liturgical institutions, have embellished the original narrative. We are thus informed that Yahweh's plan was executed during the night by the Destroyer who passed over the Hebrew households because their lintel and door-posts were touched with the blood of the sacrifice. The victims were the first-born of man and animals. The fleeing Israelites had only unleavened cakes to eat, for they had no time for leavening their dough or gathering other provisions for the journey.

f 12:1—28 Institution of Passover and Unleavened Bread—1—14. General rules for the annual celebration of Passover. These were not fully observed on that eventful night as everything is supposed to have happened immediately after God's instructions were communicated. Passover was celebrated at the full moon of the first month, and P specifies that the animal should be sacrificed

at twilight on the 14th of the month. This first month is **180f** Nisan, corresponding to our March—April according to Babylonian terminology and calendar, adopted by the Hebrews after the death of Josiah. In the earlier Israelite calendar the year began in autumn, and this month was called Abib. Passover was a family feast and everybody celebrated it at home with the traditional nomadic rites. In the Deuteronomic reformation Passover was transformed into a pilgrimage feast; the animal was to be sacrificed in Jerusalem and cooked by stewing (Dt 16:7). But these innovations did not take root, and were abandoned soon after. **15—20.** General instructions **g** about Unleavened Bread, not necessarily connected with the liturgical observances of the exodus. Unleavened Bread and Passover are linked together: both begin at the same time. This presupposes the amalgamation of the two feasts, in force since Deuteronomic times. Seven days of unleavened bread, i.e. uncontaminated by the old leaven, are prescribed as a sign of the new era ushered in by the early harvest. The first and last days were the most important; they were days of rest with a cultic assembly. **21—28.** Another description of the Passover ritual in **h** which the mention of the Destroyer is a clear reminiscence of the ancient pastoral sacrifice. Popular etymology explained the name by a supposed Heb. verb meaning to pass, for the Destroyer passed over the Hebrew settlements when he smote the Egyptian households. The real meaning of the name is still obscure. Perhaps originally it was connected with the shepherds' annual move from the steppe into the more fertile pastures of the dry season.

For 12:29—42, see **d** above.

12:43—13:16 Passover, Unleavened Bread and i First-born—43—51. Additional prescriptions dealing principally with the conditions for participating in the Passover sacrifice. The author has in mind Israel already settled in Palestine. The order not to break the bones of the victim, here first recorded (cf also Nm 9:12), was fully accomplished in the Antitype (Jn 19:36). **13:3—10.** Same regulations as before about Unleavened Bread, but here only the last day is proclaimed a feast (cf 12:16). This ritual should be 'a sign on the hand and a memorial between the eyes'. This is evidently a metaphor based on the tattooing of hands and ornaments hung on the forehead. Originally these signs and ornaments were marks of religious attachment. Metaphorically they signify a remembrance: this ritual is a permanent remembrance of the exodus. **1—2, 11—16.** It is specified that only the male first-born are to be returned to Yahweh (cf also 34:19—20; Dt 15:19). Like the holocaust, this offering expresses the supreme dominion of God, and so only the best, the male first fruit of the womb is chosen for the purpose. Human first-born are ransomed. So also the first-born of the ass, not eligible for sacrifice, are ransomed or otherwise unceremonially killed (cf also Nm 18:15—16). A later theological development considers the consecration of the Levites as a substitute for all the first-born of Israel (Nm 3:12—13; 8:16—18).

13:17—14:31 The Crossing of the Sea—The flee- **j** ing Israelites bound for Palestine could follow either of two routes. The shorter one led straight to Gaza all along the Mediterranean coast. This was the usual way, and was well controlled and guarded by the Egyptians. The longer route crossed the isthmus at its S end, skirted along the shore of the Red Sea on the Sinaitic Peninsula, then striking E and N ended up at Elath on the Gulf of Aqaba. It was the route of the Egyptian miners who dug metal on the Sinaitic coast. Two other routes, passing straight across the desert to Kadesh and Elath, were essentially

180j camel tracks and almost impassable for a large number.
k Notwithstanding the fragmentary state of the old traditions, there is enough evidence to show that all agree in leading the Israelites to Sinai, and therefore all of them favour the S route. The difficulty consists in locating the point of the crossing. Our narrative is a patchwork of partial data and obscure place-names gleaned from different traditions.

l Both P (14:2) and E (13:17—18) indicate that the people first set off in a northerly direction, but then turned S to 'the sea'. E specifies that this is the 'Reed Sea'— surely somewhere in the vicinity of the Red Sea (cf 10:19; 1 (3) Kgs 9:26). P does not mention the name of the sea, but since immediately after the crossing the people struck deep into the desert, a place in the vicinity of the Red Sea would suit his version too. J does not mention the detour N, but has the Israelites march straight from Ramesses to Succoth (12:37) and thence to Etham (13: 20); and though he too does not specify the name of the sea and although Etham cannot be identified with certainty, the southerly direction of the march and the fact that immediately after the crossing the Israelites make their way to Sinai imply that he too has in mind an area near the Red Sea.

m The P text provides something of a problem. Here (14:1), the Israelites were ordered to 'turn back' from the direction they had originally intended, and to 'encamp in front of Pi-ha-hiroth, between Migdol and the sea, in front of Baal-zephon'. Pi-ha-hiroth, an ancient name of Egyptian origin, may well be original but is unknown. Modern research has identified Baal-zephon with the Greek Casios, to be located on the sand bank which separates the Sirbonian lagoon (Sebkhet Bardawil) from the Mediterranean. Migdol means 'a fortress', and could refer to any of the Egyptian forts that lined the coast and the isthmus; but, writing at the time of the exile, the author must have had in mind the famous Migdol which at that time represented the N frontier of Egypt (Jer 44:1; 46:14; Ezek 29:10; 30:6) and which survived as Magdolum in the Roman itineraries. This most probably stood at the present Tell el-Heir, near the Mediterranean and a long way from the Red Sea, but also some fifty miles from Baal-zephon.

The P narrative, however, is clearly overcharged (14:2; Nm 33:5—8), and it is hardly likely that the place-names are all original. Most probably he accepted the rather vague indications given in the older sources, and supplemented them by adding two names representing well-known sites at the borders of Egypt, without intending to describe their precise location nor to state that the Israelite crossing took place at these geographical locations.

n We may reconstruct the sequence of events as follows. When the Israelites abandoned their original route, Pharaoh thought that something was amiss, and plucking up courage he led an expeditionary force to subdue them. He overtook them by the sea, and as they had no easy way of escape, he leisurely waited for their surrender. They were in fact panic stricken. Moses calmed them down, and the presence of God, represented by a pillar of cloud, protected and shaded them from the Egyptians. Yahweh pushed away the waters by a strong E wind and secured an easy crossing for the Israelites. At the same time he clogged the wheels of the pursuing Egyptians, and accomplished their defeat by hurling them into the waters returning to
o their former flow. This description fits in very well with the old topographical features of the Red Sea. At the time of the exodus this sea communicated with the Bitter Lakes from which it was separated by a shallow bank of sand

and extensive marshes. A ford, which the Israelites intend- **180c** ed to cross, provided a passage across the marshes. The use of the ford much depended on the flow of the waters, which were tidal and influenced by the elements. By God's providential act the marshes were fordable at the right time for the Israelites, while the Egyptians could not avail themselves of this opportunity. P is responsible for some poetical touches added to the old story (22, 26— 29). It specifies that Moses rent the sea asunder so that the Israelites could proceed dry shod between two towering walls of water. When the Egyptians stepped on the sea-bed in pursuit, Moses brought back the waters and drowned them all.

15:1—21 Canticle of Victory—The last line of this **181a** canticle (21) is an ancient hymn and probably contains the oldest literary formulation of the miracle. It was a cultic hymn, and in practice it would be supplemented by a more detailed narrative of the event. Its introduction (20) links it to the immediate sequel of the crossing. Miriam and the other women would have sung it to the Israelites returning from the ordeal of the crossing. This note hardly fits the historical context in which it is inserted; it reproduces a scene from the later battle stories in which the women acclaim the returning victors (1 Sm 18:6—7). Miriam was a prophetess (cf also Nm 12:2, 6), and must have been a woman of authority among the Israelite tribes, but very few traces of her activity have survived the vicissitudes of Israel's history. She is given as a sister of Aaron, but her relation to Moses is not expressed. We are yet far from the Priestly schematization of Moses' family.

Upon this short hymn is built the double canticle **b** placed in the mouth of Moses and the Israelites. It is preponderantly hymnic in form, celebrating as it does God's glory and might, but it has also marked traces of the thanksgiving style, in which the worshipper acknowledges God's bounty. The first part (1b—10) enlarges on the theme of the miraculous crossing which illustrates God's care for the Israelites and especially his almighty power. He is the awesome warrior who crushes his enemies just as they are about to pounce confidently on an easy prey. No one source has furnished the cast of the picture. The older tradition is represented by the overthrow of the enemies, and the later poetical elements supplied the idea of the waters piling themselves up like a dam. Then **c** comes a transition strophe (11—13) beginning with a hymnic refrain about Yahweh's excellence above all objects of heathen worship. The people engulfed by the earth are the Egyptians. Swallowed up by the waters, they fall into the deep recesses of the underworld, abode of the dead. The reference to God's assistance in the journey is an introduction to the following section. The 'holy abode' means Canaan in general, the land chosen by Yahweh for his dwelling. The second section (14—18) sings of Yahweh's accomplishments during the journey towards Palestine. Edom and Moab are here mentioned because of the detour made by the Israelites around their territory. It is more difficult to assess Philistia's role in this canticle. Perhaps it is singled out because later on the Philistines were a great danger to Israel's survival. In this context the mountain and the sanctuary are not specific references to Jerusalem and its temple, but general references to Palestine, sanctified by God's presence. A prose addition (19) appended to the canticle refers back to the miracle of the crossing, described earlier.

(B) The Journey to Sinai (15:22—18:27) **182a**
22—27 March to Marah and Elim—Old traditions containing a series of anecdotes, illustrating God's care for his people in the desert, some of which were connected with particular stopping-places. These anecdotes have

182a been woven into a continuous itinerary by P who is responsible for the overall order of the march. He begins by leading the Israelites from their camp by the Red Sea down the Sinaitic coast to Elim which could well be located in W. Gharandel. Within this section of the narrative the author places the event of Marah in the desert of Shur (called also desert of Etham, Nm 33:8) which extends from Kadesh to the frontiers of Egypt and the Red Sea. In Israel's tradition this anecdote explains the providential presence of fresh water in an unidentified spot of that dry and salty region. It is presented under the form of one of the numerous grumblings of the people, and illustrates the sovereign will of Yahweh that executes the plan of salvation notwithstanding the recalcitrance of the people and the adversity of the elements. The episode permits the author to introduce a Deuteronomic reflection about the benefits of obeying the divine laws (25b—26): Yahweh can and will look after the welfare of his faithful followers.

b **16:1—36 From Elim through the Desert of Sin; Quails and Manna**—No halting-place is mentioned here for the narrative does not depend on local traditions. After a short journey along the coast, the Israelites struck E into the desert of Sin that spans the distance between Elim and the approaches of Sinai. P explains here God's providence with regard to Israel's nourishment in the desert. Their food was certainly varied, but the author singles out and brackets together two special items, quails and manna, which in other traditions are treated separately. They are presented in the form of a story of Israel's 'murmuring'; they grumbled for lack of richer food and God sent them quails in the evening and manna in the morning. In Nm 11:31—34 the story of the quails depends on a local tradition and the people's greed is illustrated in the name of the place. In this section the quails appear as a providential food sent by God's bounty. The phenomenon was connected with the springtime migration of quails from the interior of Africa over the Sinaitic Peninsula, and offered a very welcome change

c of diet to the wandering Israelites. The Manna is described at greater length. From the biblical description (cf also Nm 11:7—9) we conclude that it is a viscous substance exuded by some trees, especially the tamarisk (*tamarix mannifera*), at the sting of an insect. It falls to the ground in clear and soft yellow-brown drops that harden in the cool of the night and dissolve in day-time heat. Once gathered they do not normally rot. They are therefore collected in the morning and eaten with bread or cooked. The substance is sweet and is still a favourite food of wandering tribes. The present annual output in Sinai is rather meagre, but it was more abundant at the time of the exodus when the peninsula had a denser vegetation. For the Israelites it was a godsend: ready-made food, spontaneously provided by the forbidding wilderness. It was also a novelty, for as forced labourers they had been living on the products of cultivated land. The novelty of the food is the basis of the popular etymology that derives the name from an otherwise unrecorded Heb. form meaning 'what'. The real origin of the word is not known.

d Manna must have been exceptionally plentiful for in Israelite traditions it represents the staple food of the desert. God's providence in sending a bountiful nourishment at the right time has been expanded in poetical descriptions which specify the time of its arrival, the quantity gathered and its short life. An omer (16) is a dry measure, c. 6½ pints. The divine origin of this bread makes it a most fitting type of the true bread from heaven, the sacrament of the Eucharist, our spiritual food during the

journey to the promised land. To the story of the manna 182d is attached the sabbath legislation concerning the food (22—30). It is not easy to determine how the observance of the sabbath was introduced in Israel, but it figures in all the Pent. sources, and J already attaches it to the manna narrative. We can therefore reasonably assume that this custom dates back to the very origins of Yahwism. It is also possible that the origin of the sabbath is to be looked for outside and before the Yahwistic religion. The e ban on work on the sabbath applied also to the preparation of food. P enlarges upon the same prescriptions, explaining that manna was not available on the sabbath (27). He further informs us that a jar with an omer of manna was placed as a remembrance in front of the Testimony (the tables of the law in the Ark), before Yahweh (in the Tent). Tent, Ark and law have not yet appeared in the history of the desert wandering; this information possibly relates a later practice.

17:1—7 Rephidim—7. The place was named Meribah f 'strife' and Massah 'temptation'. The redactor passes over two other halting-places, Dophkah and Alush, placed before Rephidim in Nm 33:12—14. On the other hand, in association with Rephidim he discusses two anecdotes about Meribah and Massah that depend on local traditions. In Nm 20:1—13 Meribah is located near Kadesh and this is probably the best geographical location for the name as appears from the compound Meribah-Kadesh (Nm 27:14; Dt 32:51; Ezek 47:19; 48:28). The anecdote of Meribah probably illustrates some surprising feature of one of the springs around Kadesh. Popular etymology explains the name by Israel's strife against Moses (2) or Levi (Dt 33:8). Originally it could have been connected with some strife of which this particular spring was the scene. The name of Massah is dovetailed in our text g because its anecdote was similar to the story of Meribah. For this reason also the two place-names are mentioned alongside each other in Dt 33:8; Ps 95 (94):8. Massah appears alone in Dt 6:16; 9:22. It is not possible to determine its site or the real origin of the name. Popular etymology explains it as a tempting of Yahweh (7) or Levi (Dt 33:8). Rephidim can be conveniently located in W. Refayed, at the approaches to Jebel Musa. The reference to Horeb (6) is difficult to explain in this context, and is probably an interpolation.

8—16 Battle with the Amalekites—The Amalekites h were a confederation of tribes, largely concentrated in the S of Palestine and roaming over the Sinaitic Peninsula. This is the first of a series of hostile actions that highlight the relations between Israel and Amalek. David finally overcame them, and most probably their remnants were later assimilated by the Israelite tribes. In fact P includes the Amalekites among Esau's descendants (Gn 36:12, 16). Joshua led the Israelites against Amalek, and defeated them after a long and hard-fought battle. **15.** The altar's name reproduces Israel's battle-cry against the Amalekites, Yahweh's perpetual enemies (16).

18:1—27 Jethro visits Moses; Institution of i Judges—This narrative is a complete whole by itself and is located at the Mountain of God, Sinai (cf Dt 1:9—19). The redactor received it from older traditions and refrained from giving it his finishing touch that would have inserted it harmoniously in the Sinaitic itinerary which he picks up again in 19:1. He simply places it side by side with the other events of Sinai that follow in its wake. Unlike J (4:20), E had not expressly mentioned the departure of Moses' family from Midian. The remark in 2b smooths out the difference. The Mountain of God was a holy place also to the Midianites. **13.** Among the j Israelites, contentions were settled either by the sentence

182j of qualified elders or by the decisions of Yahweh, obtained by various means. Moses had been exercising both functions. He now delegated to others the civic powers, reserving to himself those problems that had to be solved by divine decision. The role of communicating divine decisions does not exactly include the function of teaching the law to the people.

183a (C) Sinaitic Covenant (19:1—40:38)
19:1—20:21 Theophany on Mount Sinai—Much light has been shed upon the Sinaitic Covenant by recent studies about the so-called suzerainty treaties, by which the Hittite overlords used to bind their vassals to perpetual subservience. A constant pattern is observable in the agreement. It begins with the formula 'So speaks' followed by the personal particulars of the lord. A historical review of the benefits rendered by the lord to his vassals establishes a legal basis for the treaty, and then the stipulations are laid down. The lord promises his assistance, while the vassal has to observe various conditions including unflinching loyalty and an annual tribute. The gods of both parties are called upon as witnesses. Blessings are proclaimed on the vassal for his faithfulness, curses for unfaithfulness. The treaty is put down in writing and placed in the temple. The same basic pattern can be discovered in the Sinaitic Covenant. But the successive re-enactments of this Covenant have left their mark on the original narrative, which moreover was handed down by different traditions, so that it is not easy now to arrive **b** at the bare chronicle of the event. **1—2a.** The usual indications of time and place from P. Although very few topographical details are available, the site of the camp could be reasonably located in the plain of Er-Raha, NW of Jebel Musa (see general remarks on 2:2—7:7). The date of the arrival is fixed in the third month of the exodus, on the very day of the departure, i.e. the 15th of the month. **2b—3a.** Fragments of an Elohistic introduction to the theophany: 'Israel encamped before the mountain **c** and Moses went up to God'. **3b—9a.** The fruits of the Covenant are described with some Deuteronomic touches. God's love and care (the eagle metaphor is more fully developed in Dt 32:11) calls for faithful service from Israel. A faithful response to the Covenant would make Israel the peculiar possession of Yahweh. They would become a kingdom of priests, a holy nation: two synonyms that enhance the special relationship of Israel to Yahweh. The people signified their compliance. Yahweh promised a visible sign of his presence to increase the people's confidence in Moses. **9b.** An awkward interpolation to separate two different speeches of Yahweh. **10—15.** A Jahwistic introduction to the theophany. Moses is supposed to be on the mountain and the theophany is announced for the third day. The people have to undergo ritual cleansing and abstain from sexual relations in view of the holy meeting with God. Moreover they have to observe the strict sanctity of God by keeping at a respectful distance from the mountain. Any transgression on this point entails the penalty of death (see also 21—34; but cf commentary on 24:9—11). In 13a the author describes the traditional Israelite penalty for such offences. 13b supposes that some were to accompany Moses upon the mountain (cf also 24:1—11), but the relative instructions **d** are no longer available. **16—17, 19.** The theophany is here presented under the form of a great storm, with thunder, lightning and thick cloud (E). **18, 20.** Another version of the theophany (J) rather evokes the image of a volcanic eruption: the mountain smoked and trembled as Yahweh settled upon it in a flame, so as to resemble a heated kiln with smoke bursting from its cone. The phenomena described in both accounts of the theophany are conven-

tional signs of God's presence and a proof of Moses' **183d** divine mission. **21—25.** A later expansion on the theme **e** of Yahweh's inviolable sanctity: people and priests alike are to keep away from the mountain under the penalty of death. The mention of priests, who have not yet appeared in Israel's history, enhances the difference between God's sphere and man's. The special caution required of the priests in 22 is an allusion to the priestly demeanour in the temple services. Aaron is abruptly introduced as Moses' companion in his intercourse with God (cf 24:1). The announcement in 25 has remained without a sequel because of textual disturbance.
20:1—17. The decalogue; see below. **18—21.** Elohistic sequel to the theophany.
The Decalogue (20:1—17)—The present order of the **f** text implies the following sequence of events: Yahweh signified his presence on the mountain in a special way and delivered the decalogue; the Israelites were terrified and begged Moses to act as intermediary; Moses received and communicated to them the Book of the Covenant (20:22—23:33), and concluded the alliance 24:1—11). The Deuteronomist found the decalogue already in its present place and it presented him with the theological problem that normally it is not allowed, under penalty of death, to come in close contact with divinity. He explains that although the Israelites have heard the voice of Yahweh, in the future they will communicate with him through Moses and thus avoid the death penalty (Dt 5:23—27). It is evident however that the decalogue does not stand **g** in its right place. It is not connected with what immediately precedes or follows it, and 20:18—21 is the natural sequel to 19:19. Moreover, the Book of the Covenant (20:22—23:33) is not only a late arrival in the text, but it did not yet occupy its present place in the time of the Deuteronomist, for this redactor does not give any sign of its presence. The insertion of the Book of the Covenant cannot therefore be given as the reason for the transfer of 20:18—21. Nor was this transfer carried out with the intention of establishing a direct contact between God and the people in the delivery of the decalogue, for although the present order of the pericopes gave this impression to the Deuteronomist, the text does not expressly say that God had already spoken to the people before they were terrified. E's account of the theophany **h** (19:16—17, 19) was surely followed by a list of stipulations. This is postulated by the fact that Moses was chosen as a mediator. These stipulations were most probably the decalogue itself, originally placed by E at the end of his theophany. When the E narrative was absorbed into the J account, the decalogue was placed after J's theophany that ends in 19:20 (expanded in 19:21—25), and E's sequel to the theophany (20:18—21) found itself in its present place after the decalogue.

The decalogue has come down to us in two slightly **i** different texts: a Deuteronomic recension in Dt 5:7—21, and an Elohistic text with Priestly touches in Ex 20:3—17. The two texts are based on the original Sinaitic stipulations, with later additions according to the necessities of time and place. These additions give the text the appearance of a rather heterogeneous collection of laws, some containing a bare prohibition, others expanded into lengthy prescriptions. Most probably the original text was more homogeneous. It is not certain however that the shorter form is the older one. The cultic laws which belong more properly to the Sinaitic context remain rather long even when the evidently late expansions are set aside, while the shorter ones betray signs of abbreviation with didactic intent. The conventional number of the com- **j** mandments is also a didactic offshoot. The Deuteronomist

183j (Dt 4:13; 10:4), on which Ex 34:28 depends, presents a list of ten precepts. As the older text was not based on this number, he split the last precept into two. Once this number was established, it was also applied to the older text by considering the introduction to the decalogue as a separate commandment. Thus two separate enumerations (here considered with reference to 20:2—17) came into being, viz the Deuteronomic list (3—6, 7, 8—11, 12, 13, 14, 15, 16, 17a, 17b) and its application to the older **k** tradition (2, 3—6, 7, 8—11, 12, 13, 14, 15, 16, 17, or 2—3, 4—6, 7, etc). St Augustine's exposition of the Deuteronomic division secured its universal acceptance in the Latin Church, while the Greeks followed the other system. At the Reformation the Lutherans kept the Latin, the Calvinists adopted the Greek division. English Protestants took the Greek division from the Calvinists. Though the decalogue is strictly related to the Sinaitic Covenant, it is not nationalistic but universal in its outlook and sets forth the fundamental principles of all religious and moral obligation. First it deals with man's duty to God, and then with his duty to his neighbours.

184a **2.** Historical prelude to the stipulations of the Covenant, laying down the basis of Yahweh's right to demand absolute obedience from Israel—the deliverance he had worked in love and mercy. **3.** The basic demand made of Israel is the adoption of Yahweh as their God, to the exclusion of other objects of worship. The wording bears the mark of Deuteronomic times, the worship of other gods along with Yahweh in the period of the monarchy. **4—6.** In its present state this precept is a continuation of the preceding one (but cf 34:14—17). It does not concern the representation of Yahweh or the adoption of other gods, but the making of other objects of private worship, considered as a source **h** of protection by family groups. **7.** All misuse of the divine name is forbidden, but perjury seems to be especially intended for vain speech generally means deceit. The later Jews exaggerated this precept into a prohibition of even a reverent use of the sacred name. **8—10.** The observance of a recurring date as a day of rest from customary work was very common among ancient peoples. The peculiar trait of the Israelite institution is the religious significance given to this custom: the sabbath is consecrated to Yahweh as a sort of tithe on time. **11.** The example of Yahweh, who worked six days and rested on the seventh, is the reason given here for consecrating to him every seventh day. The use of the scheme of creation as a justification of the sabbath is a rather late contrivance. The more ancient tradition in Dt 5:15 explains the observance of the sabbath as a right due to God because of his intervention in favour of Israel at the time of the exodus. The social aspects mentioned elsewhere (23:12; Dt 5:14) reflect the usual significance **c** of the day of rest among ancient peoples. **12.** This precept covers obligations regarding human relationships. It is especially intended for adults who are to show due honour to their aged parents in need of protection. **13.** The terminology indicates an unwarranted killing, but it does not distinguish between premeditated and unpremeditated murder. **14.** An essential condition for adultery in Israelite custom was the married state of the female partner. In this matter betrothal involved the status of marriage. **15.** All kinds of robbery are envisaged here, including theft of men (cf 21:16). **16.** This precept is best explained in a juridical setting; it forbids false deposition before the legal assembly at the gates of Israe-**d** lite settlements. 'Neighbour' means anybody with whom one comes into contact. **17.** The Israelite is forbidden to covet his neighbour's possessions, indicated by the general term of house. The second part of the precept

singles out the principal components of this house; there **184d** is no sign however of it being a later expansion of the first part. In Dt 5:21 the wife has been separated from the other elements of the house and is the object of a separate precept.

20:22—23:33 The Book of the Covenant—So **e** called because of 24:7, it contains a development of the old juridical customs of Israel, and as such it dates back to Moses. The present formulation of these customs betrays the beginning of a transition from nomadic life to stable settlement and organized juridical procedure. A confrontation with the prophetic and deuteronomic literature shows that it already existed as a self-contained entity at the beginning of the monarchy. Most probably it represents the legislative code of the tribal federation formed under Joshua and sanctioned by the Covenant of Shechem. It was inserted in its present place after the deuteronomic epoch, for D does not know it in this place. No strict logical order is discernible in the code: it is just a collection of legal customs handed down by old traditions. Some laws **f** are expressed in apodictic style (a direct command) others are casuistic in form —they express what has to be done in particular cases: 'If so-and-so . . . then so-and-so'. It is now agreed that the apodictic style is not proper to Israel, but is found in ancient non-biblical documents. The difference between the two is purely one of form. In Israel both kinds are equally binding and sacred, but the casuistic prescriptions bear the marks of legal procedure. A great similarity has been noted between the **g** Book of the Covenant and other ancient legislations, such as the Code of Hammurabi, the Assyrian Lawbook and the Hittite Code. The similarities are very striking, and it is not at all improbable that some Israelite groups had experience of foreign legislative codes, but a real dependence on these codes is not proven. On its way towards a settled life, Israel naturally developed a juridical corpus similar in some points to the legislation that for centuries had already regulated the sedentary life of the nearby nations. Moreover two important differences distinguish **h** the Israelite legislation from its neighbouring counterparts. The other codes are chiefly concerned with the maintenance of property rights, show little regard for the poor, and favour the rich as the important members of the community. In Israel the legislation has a higher standard of religion and morality, because the religious spirit pervades the civil enactments, as appears in particular from the rights accorded to slaves and the special consideration shown to the poor and oppressed. The foreign codes are real collections of laws or jurisprudence, based on the accepted sociological situation of each nation. The Israelite prescriptions are essentially stipulations laid down by God as the overlord and saviour of his people.

22—26 Public worship—This is a very old ordinance, **i** but it was only later attached to the Book of the Covenant which has its natural introduction in 21:1. **22—23.** A general prohibition of the cult of idols motivated by the fact that Yahweh spoke to the people from heaven, and not through any material image. **24—26. 25.** The stones should be unhewn, so as not to loose their natural integrity through human trimming. Old tradition had imposed on the priest a simple loin-cloth as the sole sacrificial garment. Public decency therefore did not permit the altar to be placed in an elevated position. It was to rest on the ground so as not to be approached by steps (but cf 28:42—43; 39:28). Any place indicated by God (through theophanies, visions etc) as convenient for the cult was eligible for the erection of an altar. The deuteronomic reformation, bent on centralizing the cult, later restricted all cultic activities to the sacred site of Jerusalem (Dt 12:2—7).

184i After settlement in Canaan the bare rock (Jg 6:20) or a block of stone (1 Sm 14:33) would serve as an altar. The altar material mentioned here indicates an epoch when the roaming tribes periodically moved onto cultivated soil for summer pasture.

k **21:1—11 Slaves—1.** Original introduction to the Book of the Covenant, before 20:22—26 was added. **2—6.** Various kinds of slavery were current in Israel as in the other ancient countries. Here, only the case of the Hebrew male slave (pertaining to the confederation of the Israelite tribes) is considered, who could sell himself or be sold by his family or pressed into slavery because of insolvency. His service lasted only six years, after which period he was free to leave his master. A similar disposition in the Code of Hammurabi (§ 117) prescribes that a wife, son or daughter given into servitude by an insolvent head of **l** family should be freed after three years. If the man preferred an easy slavery to a stunted liberty, he could give himself up for ever to his master. **6.** The ear indicates obedience and the nailing to the door permanent attachment. Originally this rite could have taken place before a domestic deity placed at the door, but in its present state as part of the Book of the Covenant, which regulates public relations in a historical atmosphere hostile to material images of the deity, the reference must be to a public act performed at a sanctuary. **7.** A female Israelite once sold into servitude remains a slave for ever. This condition was improved later, when the same status was decreed for females as for males (Dt 15:12). **8—11.** She obtains special rights if the master takes her as wife for himself or his son. Any infraction of these rights sets her free.

m **12—17 Capital Offences**—Whoever strikes to death or kidnaps a man is punished by death. Same penalty is prescribed for those who strike (not necessarily to death) or curse their parents. In primitive societies private blood vengeance is a substitute for the non-existent public juridical apparatus. This was the rule in Israel, where the avenger would be a near kinsman of the offended. Later social evolution reduced this practice but did not totally extinguish it. It was commonly accepted that an involuntary offence was not punishable. An innocent offender was protected against a hasty blood vengeance by the right of asylum enjoyed by the sanctuaries. While on sacred ground the offender could not be molested unless his guilt was duly established. It is not said here how his guilt or innocence were ascertained. A later organization of the juridical procedure singled out six towns which obtained the right of asylum once reserved to the sanctuaries. The elders of these towns (Jos 20:4) or of the offender's residence (Dt 19:12) are to establish his innocence or guilt. Some supplementary details added after the exile (Nm 35:13, 28; Jos 20:6) were never observed in practice. The Code of Hammurabi (§ 14) lays down the penalty of death for kidnappers of children.

n **18—32 Bodily Injuries**—The talion (*lex talionis*), here loosely attached to a particular casuistic enactment, is the basic rule of the whole Book of the Covenant. In ancient times justice was ensured through the practice of blood vengeance, which required every injury to be paid back. The talion regulated this act of justice. While blood vengeance knows no limits, the talion restricted the punishment in kind and degree in proportion to the injury. As such it was quite humane and laudable. But its strict application led to some less commendable results. An example of this is furnished by the Code of Hammurabi (§ 116) which ruled that if somebody caused the death of a free man's child, committed to him as a pledge, his own child should be put to death. The talion never became **184m** a dead letter in Israel, but it changed its aspect in the course of time. In some cases, especially in death penalties, **o** it still bore the character of an act of retaliation. But more often it became an act of reparation; the judges applied the principle in order to determine the amount of indemnity due to the injured. In our text the talion is mentioned with reference to a retaliatory measure, but the context insists more on the equality of offence and sanction than on retaliation. The Book of the Covenant often applies the reparatory sanction, and it is possible that satisfaction by recompense was generally applicable also to capital offences (cf 30). In this section we have only sample rules which could guide the judges in solving similar cases. An exhaustive list of juridical cases is not to be sought for in Israel's legislation.

18—19. A clear example of the application of the talion **p** to reparation. Stone and fist are just two examples of a large range of minor acts of violence which temporarily incapacitate the injured. No bodily penalty is inflicted on the offender; he has only to defray the medical expenses and compensate for loss of work. Similar cases are contemplated in other collections of laws. The Code of Hammurabi (§ 206) lays down that whoever strikes another man unwittingly, must pay the surgeon. For a bodily injury the Hittite Code (§ 10) enjoins the supply of equal man labour, defrayal of medical expenses and a compensation of ten silver shekels. **20—21.** The death of a slave who **q** succumbs to his master's blows has to be avenged. The nature of the penalty is not specified. The Heb. text could mean blood vengeance, which would entail the death penalty, but it seems that blood vengeance was not applicable to the offence of a free man against his slave (cf 26—27). Apparently the law called upon the judges to inflict a convenient punishment, perhaps a fine, on such offenders. If the slave survives two days, the connection of the death with the beating is not evident, and the loss of the master's property is considered sufficient punishment. The Code of Hammurabi (§ 282) also, by punishing a slave's disobedience with ear-mutilation implies that a master could not put his slave to death at will. **22—25.** **r** Too short to be completely clear. Injuries inflicted on a pregnant woman, during a fight resulting in miscarriage, are punished by a fine determined by the husband and paid in the presence of judges, who apparently have to pronounce on the reasonableness of the husband's demand, and see to its fulfilment. The foetus is not regarded as a person, but if the woman dies the talion is applied. It is not said however what the law would require in this circumstance. The Code of Hammurabi (§§ 209—214) imposes various penalties according to the status of the pregnant woman. If she is a free man's daughter and dies, the offender's daughter is to be put to death. The Assyrian Lawbook has a long discussion on various cases of miscarriage and their peculiar penalties which include the miscarriage of the offender's daughter. **26—27.** Although **s** blood vengeance was not applicable to the offences of master versus slave, the master was not allowed to inflict unwarranted punishment on his slaves. Unjust treatment was amended by setting the slave free. It is possible however that some distinction still remained between a free man and a freed one. This law, which endows slaves with specific rights, does not have any counterpart in foreign legislations; here only the master is indemnified if the slave is injured by another man. **28—32.** In the Code of Hammurabi (§§ 250—2) the ox is not subject to punishment, but the responsible owner has to pay a fixed fine that varies according to the victim. If the owner is not responsible no action is taken.

184t 21:33—22:16 Damage to Property—33—36. 33. Cisterns for the preservation of rainwater are common on Palestinian soil, so poor in fresh-water springs, and constitute a continuous threat to the life of man and beast. **35.** The word for 'price' is 'silver', the commonest instrument for business transactions at that time. It was however still considered as an object of barter, not as currency. It is here supposed that the dead animal could be eaten; later restrictions appear in 22:30; Lv 17:15—16; Dt 14:21.

u **22:1—4** (MT, 37—22:3; throughout the chapter MT is one verse less). The Book of the Covenant takes a very serious view of cattle stealing for it not only requires indemnification, but in punishment multiplies the fine according to the guilt. Particularly incriminating is the thief's haste to render the stolen animal irrecoverable. If insolvent he is sold as a slave. In parenthesis it is noted that the life of a thief (probably any thief) caught in the dark is not protected by blood vengeance, because in this case deliberate murder cannot be proved. On the contrary the daytime thief is protected by blood vengeance, but he has to undergo the punishment prescribed for theft. Foreign laws required greater compensation, and in some cases imposed the penalty of death for cattle stealing. **5—6.** Negligence is presumed in both cases. Foreign codes have similar dispositions, but are more precise in estimating the damage and compensation in the first case.

v **7—8.** The usual means of safeguarding property during the absence of the owner was to leave it in someone else's care. The text implies that the innocent depositary is not bound to indemnify the owner. In the Code of Hammurabi the case of an inculpable depositary is not discussed; he is always held responsible and must indemnify the owner. On his part he might seek indemnification from the thief (§ 125). For the validity of the deposit it requires a written contract attested by witnesses (§ 123). A depositary who refuses to return the deposit, must double the deposit to the owner (§ 124). An owner who claims indemnification for non-existent damage is disproved before the god and fined double his claim (§ 126). **9.** A general axiom appliable to all property disputes. It is not said how God signifies his decision; the Bible mentions such means as sacred lots, ordeal, oath, oracle, etc. Nor is it clear whether the plaintiff, if guilty, should pay double his claim.

w **10 13.** The old law that exonerated the innocent depositary (cf 7) is here modified as applied to animals injured or lost in a neighbour's keeping.

x **15b.** The price of hire is supposed to cover also the dangers incurred by the animal during work. The text however is not very clear. It could mean that the labourer using the injured animal is a hireling, and compensation is taken out of his wages. In the Code of Hammurabi (§§ 244—9) injury done to a hired animal must be compensated, unless it is killed by a lion or perishes by an act of god. In the latter case innocence is ascertained by an oath. The Hittite Code (§§ 75—76, 78) requires compensation for damage or ill-treatment of hired animals, unless caused by the hand of god. More primitive and humane, the Israelite legislation favours the free lending of property.

y **16—17.** Before betrothal the girl is counted among the belongings of her father. In Dt 22:29 the case of a father's refusal is not contemplated; the marriage price is fixed at 50 shekels and the seducer is denied the right to repudiate the violated girl.

185a 22:18—23:9 Religion and Charity—18—20. In the OT sorcery means trafficking with strange powers, rivals of Yahweh. It was similarly punished in the Code of Hammurabi (§ 2) and the Assyrian Lawbook (§ 47) **185a** because of the damage caused by its malignant influence on person and property. **21—24.** The law in favour of the stranger who does not enjoy the protection of his kin is motivated by the exodus theme. The rights of the widow and orphan are protected by the talion. **25—27.** Financial **b** enterprises were not commonly undertaken by the early Israelites; here the case is contemplated of a poor man who is forced to borrow money for his personal needs. When commercial activities became more common it was permitted to charge interest to foreigners, but the sacred law of brotherhood still prohibited interest exacted from fellow Israelites (Dt 23:21).

25. His garment is the poor man's only coverlet. The Code of Hammurabi (§§ 49—50, 94—103) allows interest in all cases of loans but seeks to regulate its rate and forbids exploitation of the temporary needs of a poor debtor. **28.** Cursing God or the prince is a capital offence (cf Lv 24:16). Here the prince may well be a tribal head, responsible for and guardian of the Covenant. **29—30.** **c** A very general rule requiring the offering of the produce of the land and first-born of man and beast, without any detail about the amount and method of offering. The fulness (wine, cf Nm 18:27; Dt 22:9) and outflow (oil) represent agricultural product in general. It is explained elsewhere that the first-born of man and some animals are ransomed (13:11—16; 34:19—20; Nm 18:15—16). The eighth day does not designate the exact timing of the offering, but the beginning of a period within which it was made (Lv 22:27) as in Gn 2:17. **31.** In earlier times (21:33—36) the carcass of a dead or lacerated animal was allowed for human consumption. This custom was later restricted (Lv 7:24; 17:15; Dt 14:21) by legislation requiring a ritual killing of all animals slaughtered for food. **23:1—9.** General instructions for the equitable **d** functioning of justice in judicial assemblies. (cf Lv 19:15). By an association of ideas, a call for charity to one's enemy by helping him in difficulties (4—5) is inserted among the rules about contentious cases. This precept is not opposed to the words of Christ on the character of the Old Law (Mt 5:43). He refers to the generally stern spirit of the legislation based on the talion as compared with the New Law of universal charity and forgiveness.

23:10—19 Holy Days and Seasons—10—11. The **e** object of the sabbatical year (more fully described in Lv 25:2—7; Dt 15:1—18) was not economic, to increase the fertility of the soil, but religious and sociological, to restore the balance of nature disturbed by human devices leading to alienation of property, forced servitude and enslavement of the soil itself. It was not widely observed. The sabbatical repose probably applied at first at different times for different items, but was later synchronized (Dt 15:9), and P begins a universal reckoning of the sabbatical year from the occupation of Canaan (Lv 25:2). **12.** The repose of the sabbath day has a different motiva- **f** tion: a general rest from daily fatigue (but cf 20:11). **13.** This prohibition explains the substitution of *bōšet* 'shame' for *ba'al* 'master' in proper names. The originally inoffensive *ba'al* became notorious as a designation of alien gods. **14—17.** The three annual pilgrimage feasts in their agricultural setting. Adopted by Israel on Palestinian soil, they celebrated Yahweh, lord and giver of all blessing. **Unleavened Bread** (cf 12:15—20; 13:3—10) marked the beginning of the barley harvest, and represented the new life, undefiled by any remnant of the older leaven. It is here attached to the exodus theme, but not yet connected with Passover. **The Feast of the Harvest g** **(Feast of Weeks,** 34:22) was connected with the wheat

185g harvest and occurred on the 50th day (hence Pentecost) from the offering of the first-fruits of the barley harvest. The **Feast of Ingathering (Feast of Tabernacles,** Lv 23:34; Dt 16:13) celebrated the gathering of the fruit harvest, of which wine and oil were the more important. It was held in autumn and lasted 7 days. Later on an eighth day was added and the beginning was fixed on the 15th of Tishri (Lv 23:34—36). **18.** As a rule leavened bread could not be offered, probably because changed from its natural condition; cf similar prohibition of hewn stones in 20:25. It was however prescribed for the sacrifice of Praise (Lv 7:13; cf also Am 4:5) and the Feast of Ingathering. **19.** The cooking of a kid in its mother's milk was a pagan sacrificial rite, now known from the Ras-Shamra tablets as pertaining to the cult of Ashera, goddess of fertility.

h 20—33 Promises and Warnings for the March to Canaan—This passage connects the Book of the Covenant with the future stay in Canaan, and thus **i** anchors the latter firmly in the Sinaitic tradition. **20.** The angel is here a sort of guardian, distinguished from Yahweh. **24.** The steles (pillars) in question were symbols of the male divinity. **28.** The hornets (cf Dt 7:20; Jos 24: 12; Wis 12:8) are most probably a metaphor meaning discouragement. **29—30.** One of the biblical explanations of the slow progress of the conquest. Another explanation is given in Jg 3:2. **31.** The ideal boundaries of the Promised Land, based on the traditional extent of Solomon's sovereignty (1 (3) Kgs 5:1, 4; Ez 4:20), from the Red Sea (Gulf of Aqaba) to the Sea of the Philistines (Mediterranean), and from the desert (boundaries of Egypt) to the River (Euphrates). More realistic boundaries are indicated in Jg 20:1.

186a 24:1—11 The Making of the Covenant—1—2, 9— 11. Continuation of J's account of the theophany. **11.** They saw clearly the manifestation of God's presence, as appears from the description of their vision (10). As the general OT axiom has it, no one can see God and live. This rule is not based on Yahweh's invisibility, but on his sanctity, whose violation entails the penalty of death. This is why the beneficiaries of the OT apparitions expected to die (Jg 6:23; 13:22; Is 6:5). They were however spared: only those who illegally trespass upon God's **b** sanctity incur the penalty (cf 2 Sm 6:7). **3—8.** This section contains a different account of the Covenant. It is intimately related to the Book of the Covenant, and most probably shared its vicissitudes in textual tradition. The attribution of the liturgical role to the young men instead of to the official priesthood proves its great antiquity. **8.** The blood of the victim sprinkled both on Yahweh's altar and on the people is the essential rite of the Covenant in this tradition. The sacrifice of Christ was also a covenant sacrifice by which the New Covenant was ratified. It is in the consecration of the chalice that this character is emphasized in its Eucharistic continuation.

c 12—18 Moses on the Mountain—Two different traditions. In the first one (12—15a) Moses is called to the mountain and remains there for some time to receive the tables of stone. He goes up accompanied by Joshua, leaving Aaron and Hur to look after the people in his absence. The natural sequence of this account is found in 31:18ff which recounts the deeds of the people during Moses' absence. The second (15b—18) is an introduction to the ritual prescriptions in chh 25—31, which in the mind of P are the basis of the Sinaitic legislation. The glory of Yahweh settled on the mountain in the form of fire shrouded with cloud. In this context the glory of Yahweh is the manifestation of his presence. In other places it could mean his majesty or the honour due to him. Moses ascend-

ed on the seventh day, and stayed there 40 days, i.e. a **186c** fairly long period.

25:1—31:17 Ritual Legislation—This section **d** contains the legislation concerning the Tabernacle and its utensils. Another account of this legislation appears again in 35:1—40:38 under the form of an execution of orders. In the Bible, facts and events are not presented in a simple straightforward narrative, but are woven together into a harmonious order that offers an explanation for their coming into being. They appear as the result of an order (cf 3:22; 12:35), a prediction (3:21; 12:36), a question (3:13—15), an objection (4:10—12), or some other introductory formula. The important element is the fact itself, while the introductory formula is only a literary device, fashioned according to the requirements of the reality it has to introduce. This procedure is observed in the first tablet of the Legend of Keret (14th cent. B.C., cf ANET² 143—5) where an order and its execution are a simple repetition of each other. The same **e** applies to the ritual legislation of Sinai. The liturgical objects are presented first in project and then in execution. The two accounts develop more or less the same themes, but differ in the order of the texts. The LXX, probably depending on a different Heb. text, has an order of its own and lacks some passages. The second account is more elaborate, and some prescriptions which are evident additions in the legislation (e.g. chh 30—31) are properly found in the account of the execution. This shows that the second section was recast, the first only retouched. The **f** legislation is discussed together with the commentary on the execution of the work, in the following order:

25: 1—9	see on 35, 4—36, 7
10—22	see on 37, 1—9
23—30	see on 37, 10—16
31—40	see on 37, 17—24
26: 1—37	see on 36, 8—38
27: 1—8	see on 38, 9—20
9—19	see on 38, 9—20
20—21	see after 37, 17—24
28: 1—5	see on 39, 1
6—14	see on 39, 2—7
15—30	see on 39, 8—21
31—35	see on 39, 22—26
36—38	see on 39, 30—31
39—43	see on 39, 27—29
29: 1—46	see after 40, 1—38
30: 1—10	see on 37, 25—29
11—16	see after 38, 9—20
17—21	see on 38, 8
22—38	see on 37, 25—29
31: 1—11	see on 35, 4—36, 7
12—17	see on 35, 1—3

31:18—32:35 The Golden Calf—We have here **187a** a very old anecdote with additions evidently due to the influence of later events. **4.** The image represented a bull, probably intended as the pedestal of God, which secures God's presence among the people. Aaron tried to make their action conform as closely as possible with the requirements of Yahwism, and proclaimed a feast to Yahweh which included sacrificial banqueting and gave rise to sexual orgies. **20b.** This was a kind of ordeal (cf Nm 5:11—28) by which God punished the guilty members of the community.

Later touches have expanded the original anecdote. **b** The role played by Aaron is hard to define. It seems that in the old narrative the fault was attributed to the people while Aaron was presented as the last mainstay of Yahwism. Later on he became involved in the general backsliding; his activity was mentioned in the account

187b of the casting (reported again in 21—24) and his name was clumsily introduced in 25 and 35. The episode however does not impair his position and reputation, and may have been influenced by some event in which some priests were

c reproached with idolatrous worship. The image most probably represented a **bull**, symbol of divinity in the Ancient Orient. The Sacred author treats it disdainfully as a calf perhaps because of its small stature. Its description reminds us of the bulls (also called calves) erected by Jeroboam I in his northern sanctuaries to discourage the people from frequenting the temple of Jerusalem (1 (3) Kgs 12:26—33). The reference to the episode of Jeroboam I explains why the narrative speaks about god in the plural, while it is clearly stated that only one bull was moulded; the same declaration is made about the image here (4) and that of Jeroboam I (1 (3) Kgs 12:28). Another secondary theme attached to the

d anecdote is the **intercession of Moses**. It contains some refined theological thinking. It illustrates the real guilt of the rebellious people who avoid total destruction only because of Moses (9—14). On the other hand it insists that the guilt will not go unpunished; God did not accept the substitution of Moses for the people: he only reserved his punishment to the appointed time (30—34). One could perhaps discover here a hint of the punishment awaiting the worshippers of the golden calves of Jeroboam I. In 32 human destiny is described as a book written by Yahweh in the manner of city registers (cf Ezek 13:9). A short anecdote about the Levites (25—29) has also been inserted into the bull story. They are said to have stood by Moses and punished all offenders regardless of family ties (cf Dt 33:8—11). The episode served as a justification of the Levites' disputed right to the priesthood.

e **33:1—23 Yahweh's Presence among the People**—Following Yahweh's instructions to leave Sinai (32:34), we have a series of texts loosely connected together by the common theme of Yahweh's presence, away from the mountain. **1—6.** The general sense is that Yahweh refuses to accompany the people personally, lest he be obliged to exterminate them because of their stubbornness; he would only send his angel with them. When the people agreed to strip themselves of their ornaments in sign of continued repentance, God's

f relation to the people took a new turn. 4 anticipates 5—6. **7—11.** Moses used to pitch the Tent of Meeting some distance from the camp, and to have there familiar conversation with Yahweh, cf § 103e. The terms used here indicate a great intimacy but do not imply that Moses used to see Yahweh himself. This intercourse was the source of oracles for the people. It is not said when the use of the Tent was introduced, nor is the Tent connected with the Ark of the Covenant in the older texts, but most probably it did house the Ark which was the visible sign of Yahweh's continued presence. While the Ark probably lasted till the destruction of the Solomonic temple, the Tent disappeared with the adoption of sedentary life. It was set up in the Plains of Moab (Nm 25:6), but it is not certain that it was ever fixed on Palestinian soil, where the Israelites had the local sanctuaries at their disposition. In 1 Sm 1:7, 9; 3:15 the Ark is evidently housed in a building. Such texts as Jos 18:1; 19:51; 1 (3) Kgs 8:4; 1 Chr 16:39; 21:29; 2 Chr 1:3—6, which mention the presence of the Tent after the occupation of Palestine, are rather late and betray the author's intention of enhancing the continuity of Israel's cult with the Sinaitic institutions, cf § 103e, f; R. de

g Vaux, AI, 297. There is no reason whatever for questioning the historicity of the Tent during the desert wandering.

(A similar cultic object is recorded in the history of **187g** pre-Islamic Arabs). P sometimes calls it the Abode or Dwelling (26:1, 6, 12, 13, 15; Nm 1:50, 51, 53; etc) and locates it in the centre of the camp as a sign of God's presence among the people. He deals with it at great length when he relates the ritual prescriptions and their execution, to be discussed later. **12—17.** Israel's privileged state of intimacy with Yahweh, ever present in the sanctuary, is here illustrated by a rather bold dialogue between Moses and Yahweh which seems to take place on the mountain (cf 21). **18—23** 'glory' i.e. Yahweh himself. The author is **h** perplexed by two apparently conflicting facts. On the one hand, as the general principle has it, nobody is allowed to come in close contact with divinity (20); on the other hand tradition attributed to Moses a direct vision of God (Nm 12:6—8). He solves the problem by explaining that Moses had a direct, but not unqualified, vision: he saw God from behind. Similar perplexity appears in Dt 5:24—27. Moses' privilege is unique: God in fact is gracious and merciful with whom he pleases (19). This means that man has no claim to the gratuitous gifts of God, such as the favours accorded to Moses and the forgiveness accorded to the people, which he gives to whom he wills. St Paul cites this text to prove that the Jewish nation had no claim to the gift of an efficacious call to the faith of Christ (Rm 9:15).

34:1—35 The Sinaitic Covenant—This section **188a** presents some almost insoluble problems. The various elements that compose it can roughly be divided into two parts: the Covenant (10—27), and its literary framework (1—9, 28—35). The literary setting is closely connected to the anecdote of the bull, with its story of the stone tables broken by Moses. It thus presents the Covenant as a renewal of an annulled pact. But the original nucleus was an independent narrative of the Covenant whose stipulations were fixed in writing by Moses. The literary setting was arranged later to give **b** it a historical context. The stipulations here are often called the **Jahwistic decalogue**, although they were not intended to be divided into ten commandments. Everybody agrees that our present decalogue (20:3—17; Dt 5:7—21) is a development of an older one whose exact wording cannot be fixed with certainty; it is probable that these Jahwistic laws, centred around cultic practices, present an earlier state of our decalogue. A confirmation of this could be found in 34:1 where they are identified with the laws of the original tables. The description of the Covenant is not complete; it is not said how the stipulations were accepted and the pact concluded. These details should be looked for in the description of the Sinaitic theophany (24:3—8), where they remained when the Jahwistic laws were transferred here to give place to a more elaborate form of the decalogue.

5. Some themes from the preceding sections are **c** again taken up. (cf 33:18—23). **13.** The Asherim were sacred poles, emblems of the goddess of love and fertility, Asherah, from which they derive their name. **14—27. d** There is no evident logical order in these Jahwistic stipulations. The prescriptions generally regard the people as settled on Palestinian soil. All of them, except Yahweh's assurance that their property would be protected during their absence on pilgrimage feasts (24), appear also in the decalogue and Book of the Covenant discussed above. Alien gods and other objects of worship, here separately prohibited (14—17), appear as the object of one proscription in 20:3—6. The three pilgrimage feasts (18, 22—23) are dealt with in 23:14—17 (cf also 12:15—20; 13:3—10). God himself ensures that no harm befall the belongings of his followers during these

188d pilgrimages (24). The author does not explain how. The offering of the first-born (19—20) was treated in 13:1—2, 11—16. The sabbath (21) forms part of the decalogue (20:8—11) and reappears in the Book of the Covenant (23:12). On unleavened bread as material for sacrifice (25*a*) cf 23:18; on 25*b* cf 12:10. Same rules in 26 as in 23:19. Moses is instructed lastly to put in writing

e these covenantal stipulations (27). 28—35. The second part of the literary frame of the Jahwistic stipulations. Moses remained on the mountain forty days and forty nights (cf 24:18) and he wrote the words of the Covenant on the tables of stone. Coming as it now does after the order given to Moses to write the stipulations, this writing on the tables should normally be attributed to Moses. But this section is only loosely connected with the stipulations, and forms a natural sequel to 1—9 where Yahweh declares that he wants to write the words himself. The subject of the writing in 28 is therefore not Moses but Yahweh. The face of Moses was all shining when he returned to camp. This brightness, produced by intimate and prolonged intercourse with Yahweh was unsupportable to the Israelites and had to be concealed by a veil which he only removed when he spoke with God. The religious lesson conveyed is that the greater our union with and our knowledge of God the more like to him we become.

f **Chh 35—40 (25:1—31:17) The Tabernacle and its Utensils**—The ritual legislation was an essential element of the Sinaitic Covenant. Israel could not become God's holy people by mere observance of a legal code which made no provision for an organization of cult. To the ancients in general and Israel in particular religion without ritual was inconceivable. Excavations have revealed to us highly developed rituals in Egypt and Mesopotamia in the third millennium B.C. and in Syria in the middle of the second. It is therefore natural to suppose that Moses, who established the Yahwistic cult at Sinai, handed down also his instructions for the liturgical expression of this cult which remained for ever the basis of all liturgical action in Israel. The liturgical institutions never lost their original Sinaitic aspect, because they were firmly grounded on the revealed cult instituted by Moses, but they had to be adapted to the ever changing circumstances of the chosen People, so that by the time of the exile the Israelite liturgy had acquired a new look; but this renewed liturgy was justly attributed to Moses as its author, for it was nothing

g but an adaptation of the institutions of Moses. The liturgy of the desert Tabernacle, later superseded by that of the temple, is no exception to this general rule. The older texts (33:7—11) call it the Tent of Meeting, but do not describe it or its furnishings. The descriptions contained in Ex, supplied by P, come from the time when an elaborate temple ritual had for centuries supplanted the desert liturgy. No wonder therefore that the narrator imagines the Tabernacle of the desert as a collapsible temple, and together with older reminiscences he introduces some details derived from the Solomonic construction. The liturgical institutions did not figure in the pre-Priestly text of Ex. They were introduced by the P who imposed the liturgical scheme on the exodus theme and construed all his narrative as an introduction to the erection and the consecration of the desert Tabernacle.

h **35:1—3 (31:12—17) Sabbatical Repose**—This prescription is placed here as a prelude to the liturgical institutions that begin with the next section. In this context the kindling of a fire is a general term for cooking.

i **4—36:7 (25:1—9; 31:1—11) Material and Artisans**—6. Bluish and reddish purple dyes, manu-

factured mostly in Phoenicia, were obtained from shell- 188i fish, the *murex trunculus* and the *murex brandaris*, scarlet from a species of cochineal, the *coccus ilicis*. The fine linen was of Egyptian origin; the Heb. term used to indicate it is also derived from an Egyptian word. Goats' hair is still woven into material for tent covering. The word *tahas*, RSV 'goatskin', probably means a kind of dolphin.

36:8—38 (26:1—37) The Tabernacle—The Tent j of Meeting (cf 33:7—11) is here simply called a Dwelling by P. He describes it as a complicated structure, half tent, half building, thus uniting reminiscences of the desert Tent and the pattern of the temple which superseded it. The overall result closely resembled the Solomonic construction, but the surface measurements were only about half as big. 8—19. For a correct inter- k pretation of the text it has to be noted that the author distinguishes a Dwelling, a tent, and two other coverings. Then comes the description of the wooden framework. The Dwelling is not the wooden framework, but the first covering spread over it, while the tent is the second covering. The other coverings are the third and fourth. 20—34. The sacred author imagined a tent that by its l special shape would prefigure the pattern of the Solomonic temple, and therefore he combined the coverings of a tent with the fixed, though collapsible, framework of a temple. As the shape of a normal tent and the plan of a temple cannot be easily fused into a harmonious unit, some incongruities are naturally to be expected. These however do not in any way impair the symbolic value of the construction that the author envisaged. Note also that neither the figure of a tent nor the pattern of the Solomonic temple require a sloping roof. The temple was flat-topped, and the gentle slope of the bedouin tents flows down in an almost unbroken line.

35—38. The inner space was divided into the Holy m Place and the Most Holy Place (Holy of Holies) by a veil, similar to the first tent-covering in material and ornamentation. Except for the notes about the table and lampstand, this plan reproduces the interior arrangement of the Solomonic temple which was also divided into the Holy Place and the Holy of Holies. In the Solomonic n model the first two-thirds of the temple were assigned to the Holy Place and the rest was occupied by the Holy of Holies whose exact position is still doubtful. In order to ensure a cubic space measuring 20 cubits on each side (1 (3) Kgs 6:20) and an even roof, one may suppose that the Holy of Holies was not on the same level with the Holy Place, but stood on elevated ground. Our text does not say where the veil was hung to mark the separation between the Holy Place and the Holy of Holies. Most probably the latter occupied the rear third of the Tent, consisting of a cubic space measuring 10 cubits on each side and located on the same level with the Holy Place. It is worth noting that this internal arrangement of the Tent and the Solomonic temple is very similar to the arrangement of the Egyptian temples which consisted of the Holy of Holies, with its furnishings of cultic objects, and the temple hall. They were also provided with a court as in the Solomonic model and the Mosaic construction.

37:1—9 (25:10—22) The Ark—6. 'Mercy-Seat'— 189a or propitiatory. On this the blood of the victims was sprinkled on the Feast of the Atonement to expiate the sins of Israel. The word is used of Christ (Rm 3:25) who by offering satisfaction for our sins made God propitious to us. The position of the cherubim on the ends b excludes the view of Heinisch that they were worked in relief on the Mercy-Seat so that their heads nearly met in the centre; it suggests rather standing or kneeling

189b figures of winged youths (since angels appear in human form in the Pent). Semitic parallels of these angels are not lacking. Tutelary winged deities flanking the entrances of temples and palaces were commonplace in Mesopotamia, and Syria has produced divine thrones flanked by winged sphinxes.

c This general description, stemming from P is a collection and reassessment of old traditions about the Ark. Originally the cherubim were not attached to it. These originated at the time of Solomon, who placed them in the Holy of Holies (1 (3) Kgs 6:23—28) and set the Ark beneath their wings (1 (3) Kgs 8:6). From then onwards Ark and cherubim became inseparable. The highly ornamental lid of the Ark is the repository of the post-exilic traditions about the mercy-seat. The Ark was not reconstructed after the exile (cf Jer 3:16), but there was a mercy-seat on which and in front of which the priest sprinkled the blood of the victim (Lv 16:14—15) on the Feast of the Atonement. This ritual is not connected with either the Ark or the cherubim. In 1 Chr 28:11 the Holy of Holies is called the room of the mercy-seat, so that one can safely conclude that in post-exilic times this played the former role of the Ark. This justifies its insertion in the description of the Ark.

d The Ark served a two-fold purpose. It was the throne of Yahweh sitting on the cherubim (1 Sm 4:4 etc) who there manifested himself to his people, received their prayers and offerings and led them in their expeditions, and was therefore called Ark of God. It also contained the decalogue, permanent testimony of the Sinaitic Covenant, and was therefore called Ark of the testimony and Ark of the Covenant. In some texts this second purpose obtains more prominence than the first. In Dt 10:1—5 it is even the only purpose mentioned, as if the Ark was simply a coffer expressly constructed to contain the tables of the law. It does not seem however that this was the original purpose of the Ark. The proper abode of the legislative codes in the Ancient Orient was the sacred area where the law obtained the protection and sanction of the deity at whose feet it was deposited. If therefore the tables of the law were placed in the Ark, this was only because it carried with it the presence of Yahweh.

e The connection between the Ark and the Tabernacle does not derive from the Solomonic usage, but must go back to the very origins of the two objects. The older texts are not clear enough about this connection because they are very fragmentary. 33:7 could be quoted in its favour if *lô* referred to the Ark, but this interpretation is anything but certain. However, this connection is self-evident, for Moses must have had some symbol of God's presence and instrument for communicating with God in the Tabernacle. The non-Israelitic parallels of this Tabernacle also contained sacred objects, symbols of the deity. After the occupation of Canaan and the disappearance of the Tabernacle, the Ark remained the only

f palladium of the tribes. It was with the people at their camp in Gilgal (Jos 4:18—19) and then it appears in Bethel (Jg 20:26—27). Later on it found a permanent dwelling at Shiloh (1 Sm 3:3), but having been taken to the battle of Aphek (1 Sm 4:4), it was captured by the Philistines (1 Sm 4:11). When God harassed them because of the Ark, they hastened to return this terrible object to the Israelites at Bethshemesh (1 Sm 6:12). Thence it passed on to Kiriath-jearim/Baale-judah (1 Sm 7:1; 2 Sm 6:2), and finally David brought it to Jerusalem

g and covered it with a tent (2 Sm 6:12, 17). Solomon built his temple to house it (1 (3) Kgs 6:19) and there it probably remained till it was destroyed together with

the temple, although no text says expressly that it lasted **189g** all that time. According to an old legend, recorded in 2 Mc 2:1—12, before the destruction of Jerusalem Jeremiah hid the Ark together with other cultic objects on Mount Nebo.

10—16 (25:23—30) The Table—According to the **h** representation on the Arch of Titus in Rome which bears a model of the table of the Herodian temple, the frame was fixed about half-way up the legs. Our text however requires the frame to be put higher, just below the surface. **16.** 'Salvers and cups', probably for bread and incense respectively, flagons and bowls with which to pour libations, presumably on the ground near the table. According to Lv 24:5—9 (cf also Ex 25:30) twelve loaves **i** of bread were placed on the table as an offering to Yahweh on the eve of the sabbath and after a week were replaced by fresh loaves and eaten by the priests. The incense was also renewed each week-end. The bread was called presence bread or showbread, because it was placed before the presence of Yahweh. Other names for it were holy bread, continual bread and loaves of proposition or setting-out. The custom of setting bread before the deity was very common in the Ancient Orient, especially in Mesopotamia and Egypt, and represented the feeding of the deity, as appears from some magical texts and ritual tablets. In Israel the loaves were regarded as a sacrificial offering. This is confirmed by the fact that they were accompanied by incense, burned at the week-end. Its antiquity is attested by the episode of David and the priest of Nob (1 Sm 21:2—7). It presupposes however the conditions of sedentary life and therefore was not in use among the Israelites before the occupation of Canaan.

17—24 (25:31—40) The Lampstand—From our **j** rather incomplete description we gather that the lampstand was a conventional representation of a flowering almond tree, as appears from the almond blossoms that adorn it. The seven blossoms on the top were the lamps, in the form of containers with a pinched edge for the wick. *peraḥ* 'flower' means a lamp-tray in the Mishna. This description agrees in general lines with the representation on the Arch of Titus in Rome, based on the lampstand of the Herodian temple.

In the Solomonic temple there were ten lampstands, **k** obviously with one lamp each, placed in front of the Holy of Holies, five on each side (1 (3) Kgs 7:49). It does not seem that they had any specific symbolical meaning; they were needed to illuminate the dark interior, and were used only as needed: no trace of a perpetual vigil-light can be found in the old texts (cf 1 Sm 3:3). After the exile the ten Solomonic lamps were replaced in the second temple by the seven-branched lampstand which served as a pattern for our text. It was a vigil-light, and therefore had to burn perpetually all through the night before Yahweh (27:20—21; Lv 24:2—4). This new sig- **l** nificance of the light is expressed by the very shape of the lampstand, modelled as a stylized almond tree. The Hebrews called the almond tree *šāqēd* 'vigilant' because it awoke so early in the spring from its winter sleep, and thus aptly symbolized the vigil kept by the lights in the temple. As this symbolism appears elsewhere (Jer 1:11—12; Eccl 12:5) and explains adequately the shape of the lampstand it is superfluous to connect it with the ancient veneration of sacred trees. In Zech 4:1—14 a seven-light stand, which has no relation to any particular existing form, symbolizes the omniscience of God. The seven-branched lampstand of the second temple was carried off by Antiochus IV Epiphanes (1 Mc 1:21). Judas Maccabeus later replaced it by a new one (1 Mc 4:49).

(27:20—21) The Lamp—This is understood as the **m** sum of the lights burning on the lampstand. The

189m prescription, which reappears in more or less the same wording in Lv 24:2—4, belongs to the institutions of the second temple which supplied the pattern for the preceding description of the lampstand.

n **25—29 (30:1—10, 22—38) The Altar of Incense, Anointing Oil and Incense**—The redactor who recast the account of the execution of God's orders united together and fitted into this convenient context the description of the anointing oil, incense and altar of incense, which in the relation of God's orders appear only as appended additions. As usual, the redactor limits himself to the manufacturing of objects without mentioning their actual use (but cf 40:16—33). Moreover he reduces to a minimum the lengthy description of the anointing oil

o and incense contained in God's instructions. **The Altar**—In Heb 9:4 it is idealistically combined with the Ark and located with it in the Holy of Holies. The order to purify the altar of incense (30:10) is not expressly mentioned in the ritual of the Day of Atonement (Lv 16: 15—17) but it is included in the general purification of

p the Holy Place. The description of the altar of incense is based on the altar set up in the Holy Place of the temple of Jerusalem. The desert sanctuary did not actually possess such an altar. It is not mentioned among the furnishings in 26:33—37, and it is known that at that time offerings of incense were made with censers (Lv 10:1; Nm 16:6—7, 17:18; 17:11—12). We do know that the second temple had a golden altar which was taken away by Antiochus IV Epiphanes (1 Mc 1:21). Some scholars have doubted the existence of an altar of incense in the Solomonic temple, but all the evidence that we possess suggests that there was one. Incense altars with four horns have been found in Canaan at Shechem and Megiddo (8th–7th cent. B.C.) and Tell Beit Mirsim (11th cent. B.C.). Moreover a clear reference to this altar is found in 1 (3) Kgs 6:20; 7:48 and perhaps in 2 Chr 26:16.

q The **anointing oil** consisted of pure olive oil, mixed in determined proportions with four spices, myrrh, calamus, cinnamon and cassia. Myrrh was an Arabian gum exuded by the *balsamodendron myrrha* and is described as flowing, i.e. spontaneous, and therefore of choice quality. The three other spices were obtained from aromatic shrubs indigenous to SE Asia and imported by Sabaean merchants. The mention of the altar of incense and the laver (30:28) shows that the instructions for

r the preparation of this oil are of late origin. The **incense**, a gum imported by the Sabaeans (Jer 6:20), was also mixed with other ingredients, stacte, onyx, galbanum, and was seasoned with salt. The stacte and galbanum were gums exuding from trees not yet definitively identified. The onyx was provided by a shell-fish gathered in the Red Sea. The addition of salt to the various ingredients could have a symbolic significance unless it was simply employed to obtain a more abundant smoke. In rabbinical times this mixture was enriched by many other substances, and the penalty of death was meted out to those who omitted some of these ingredients.

190a **38:1—7 (27:1—8) The Altar of Burnt Offering**— It is simply called 'the altar' in 27:1 because the original instructions did not contain the description of the altar of incense, inserted later. The existence of this altar at the time of Moses needs no proof. The Israelites offered sacrifices, and therefore they must have made use of some kind of sacrificial altar. Its shape however cannot be determined with absolute certainty, because the description is scanty and obscure. Old biblical tradition represented the altar of nomadic life as a simple heap of

b earth or pile of stones (20:24—25). The altar of the

Tabernacle would have been much more elaborate. Its **190b** shape is best explained as a reduced and portable replica of the altar set up by Ahaz in Jerusalem (2 (4) Kgs 16: 10—16) which also served as a model for the altar of the second temple. Ahaz's altar must have been quite large, and was approached by a flight of steps or a ramp. Its dimensions are not given, but most probably we can obtain a fair idea of its form from the traditional measurements of the Solomonic altar in 2 Chr 4:1 (20 × 20 × 10 cubits) which seem to refer to the altar of Ahaz or the one that succeeded it. Solomon's altar was made of bronze (1 (3) Kgs 8:64) and its shape is still a matter of discussion. Later altars were made of stone. The **c** desert replica is described as a chest of acacia wood overlaid with bronze, five cubits in length and breadth and three in height. The idea of steps or ramp was reproduced in a grating of bronze network placed all around the ornamental base of the altar, so as to cover the altar's lower half, while its ornamental base reached a little higher up.

27:2. Horns are also found on the altars of the Assyr- **d** ians and other ancient peoples. They are symbols of strength. The portable character of the altar required it to be hollow. The narrator does not explain how this hollow chest of wood overlaid with bronze could actually be used for holocausts. Some scholars have suggested that it was **e** filled with earth, so as to obtain the kind of altar acceptable to the Book of the Covenant (20:24). Others think that it was covered by a bronze grating that supported the fire and the victim. The explanations are in no way demanded by the text. The narrator described the desert Tabernacle and its furnishings as a reduced replica of their Solomonic or post-exilic counterparts, and took everything else for granted, without stopping to consider how his objects would function. The importance of the cultic objects of the desert did not lie in their actual performance but in their theological significance as a preparation for the real thing, the temple and its utensils. Nor is it necessary to combine 20:24 with 27:1—8; 38:1—7: the two prescriptions belong to two quite different historical situations, and do not refer to each other.

8 (30:17—21) The Bronze Laver—No description of **f** this is given and it is clearly a late addition since it does not figure among the cultic objects mentioned in chh 25—27. Moreover a constant supply of water for the priests' ablutions would be difficult to procure in the desert. The prototype was the modest bronze laver which must have been set up in the second temple in place of the impressive Sea of Bronze constructed by Solomon (1 (3) Kgs 7:23—26). The installation of a laver in sanctuaries for ritual ablutions was common in the Ancient Orient. Some of them were also of great dimensions. In fact the laver of the temple of Lagash was called an Ocean, and that of the temple of the Sun at Babylon was called a Sea. Female ministers are not mentioned in the cultic **g** institutions of Israel. They do appear in some cultic situations, such as processions, and the caravans of the exiles returning from Babylon carried with them many female singers, but they did not exercise any real cultic function. It is possible however that the second temple already began to attract the attention of pious women (cf Lk 2:37). Mirrors were made of polished bronze.

9—20 (27:9—19) The Court of the Temple—God **h** dwelt in the Holy of Holies, gave audience to his ministers in the Holy Place, and received the homage of his people in the Court.

(30:11—16) The Poll-tax—On the occasion of a **i** census all males over twenty had to pay a tax of half a

190i shekel for the upkeep of the sanctuary. This prescription contains a theological justification of the temple-tax instituted after the exile (Neh 10:33—35): the tax is explained as an atonement money to appease God's wrath after a census. The ancient Hebrews like the Romans considered a census as an encroachment on God's domain (2 Sm 24:10), but a sacred poll-tax, imposed on rich and poor alike, would legitimate it. The narrator has in mind the census recorded in Nm 1:1—47, which was of course undertaken and carried out under God's orders.

j Weights and measures did not always have a standard value in Israel, since they were mostly based on some natural object or activity that fluctuated according to the circumstances (cf **87**). Moreover, individual honesty was no more guarantee against fraud at that time than it is nowadays. It is therefore specified that the half-shekel is to be reckoned according to the measurement of the temple.

k 21—31 Inventory of Metal Offerings—After describing the construction of the sanctuary and its furnishings, the narrator draws up a reckoning of all the gold, silver and bronze employed by the artisans. It is a very late section, and presupposes the most recent additions in the preceding account of God's instructions. The poll-tax is already gathered and is not used for the upkeep of the sanctuary but furnishes the material for its silver fittings. The sacred author is obviously anticipating and re-interpreting the poll-tax discussed above (30:11—16) and the census which finds its natural setting in Nm 1:1—47. There it is expressly ordained by Yahweh and carried out by Moses. It is not necessary to take the amount of metals collected by Moses at its mathematical value.

l The Israelites were surely not lacking in precious materials, but taking into consideration the fact that a talent weighed about 75 pounds, it is hardly possible that they could muster at that time the great amount of gold, silver and bronze indicated by the text. The text however does signify the great willingness of the Israelites to contribute bountifully for cultic purposes. It also indicates the awe inspired by the splendour of the temple and its utensils which served as a model for our narrator. The temple complex may not have been exceptionally rich and awesome when compared with its Egyptian and Mesopotamian counterparts, but for the poor Israelites it was a nonpareil, and the myth of Solomon's richness and magnificence continued to grow after the exile when the joint efforts of the returning exiles could produce only a poor replica of his achievements.

191a 39:1 (28:1—5) Ceremonial Vestments of the High-Priest—The narrator has in mind the various elements that somehow or other belonged to the ceremonial dress of the high-priest after the exile. They all have an old and independent history, and it is not easy to explain how they can be combined into one uniform. Israel's priesthood is attached to Aaron and his four sons. Nadab and Abihu died childless (Lv 10:1—3). Eleazar and Ithamar were the official ancestors of the Zadokites and Abiatharites, two rival priestly families. In the time of David both families shared the priestly function, but under Solomon Zadok ousted his rival and the Zadokites retained the exclusive right to the Israelite priesthood till after the exile, when the Abiatharites regained their priestly rights and exercised them alongside their rivals. The sons of Aaron are mentioned here because some of the vestments were common to all priests.

b 2—7 (28:6—14) The Ephod—In the early Israelite period the ephod was the only ceremonial garment of the priests. It was a sort of loin-cloth worn on the naked body (cf 2 Sm 6:14, 20) and fastened by a belt. Originally it had been just the ordinary clothing of men, but when the **191b** dress fashion changed the archaic custom was perpetuated in cultic usage. A simple linen ephod was worn by the young Samuel during his service in the sanctuary of Silo (1 Sm 2:18) and by the priests officiating in the cultic place of Nob (1 Sm 22:18). David also wore it when he took part in a religious ceremony (2 Sm 6:14). More refined customs later added other items to the priestly apparel, and the ephod was retained only as an external ornament on the priestly dress. The ephod described **c** here belongs to the particular apparel of the high-priest. It resembled the older ephod in shape but was made of more precious material. Moreover it was furnished with braces which passed over the shoulders and joined together on the edge of the ephod in front and at the back. Two gems set in gold and inscribed with the names of the twelve tribes were attached to the braces. Because of its association with the priestly functions the ephod was sometimes regarded as a cultic object used for oracular purposes (1 Sm 30:7—8), and could easily degenerate into an object of worship (Jg 8:27). It is however difficult to ascertain how the oracles were obtained from the ephod. cf AI, 350—2.

8—21 (28:15—30) The Breast-Plate—The narrator describes an ornamental pouch worn on the **d** breast and attached to the shoulder-pieces that supported the ephod. Originally it must have been a simple purse containing the sacred lots called by the obscure names of Urim and Thummim. These were sticks or dice signifying conventionally the one an affirmative, the other a negative reply to a question asked, or the one approval, the other disapproval of a course of action proposed. Sometimes no answer was obtained (1 Sm 14:37, 41), perhaps because no lot or both lots together were extracted from the purse. They were operated by the priests and belonged to the pre-Israelite sanctuaries of Palestine. The Israelites adopted this device and employed it till the time of the early monarchy. There is no recorded instance of such a consultation after the time of David. It was in fact superseded by the prophetic oracles, and remained only as an ornamental sign of Yahweh's judicial power, worn by the high-priest. It was therefore called the breast-plate of judgement. **10.** The **e** twelve precious stones have not been identified with certainty. All translations of their names, both old and modern, depend on the interpretation of the LXX. The inscriptions on them and on the two gems of the ephod braces were to remind Yahweh of his people whom the high-priest represented.

22—26 (28:31—35) The Robe—It was of a single **f** piece extending to the knees with apertures, one for the head, around which it was strengthened by a band, and two for the arms. No sleeves are envisaged. It was not a specifically priestly dress but an apparel of distinction, worn by kings (1 Sm 24:5), princes (Ezek 26:16) and other prominent people (Jb 1:20). The high-priest wore it as a sign of his high rank. **24.** The sacred writer does not tell us what the pomegranates on the high-priest's dress stood for. They could be interpreted as a simple ornament; Phoenician art offers numerous examples of pomegranates used as an ornamental motif. They could also have a symbolical significance. The pomegranate embodies the idea of fecundity and opulence, and could well signify the plenitude of priestly power wielded by the high-priest. The bells were to protect the **g** life of the high-priest from the insidious evil spirits by their ringing as he went into and came out from the Holy Place. It was a common belief in the Ancient E that evil spirits beset the entrance of the sanctuaries to molest

191g the worshippers. For this reason the doorposts of the Babylonian temples were flanked with representations of tutelary deities to counteract the lethal activity of the evil spirits; and it was also believed that the ringing of bells routed these spirits. This popular belief formed part of Israel's folklore too, and was concretely expressed in the ornamentation of the high-priest's dress. In later times the meaning assigned to the inscriptions on the precious stones of the ephod braces (28:12; 39:7) and the breast-plate (28:29) was extended to the bells: they were to remind Yahweh of his people, represented in the person of the high-priest (Sir 45:9). This vestment is called 'the robe of the ephod' obviously because the ephod was worn over it, although by its nature the robe was an outer garment.

h 27–29 (28:39–43) Tunic, Head-dresses, Breeches and Girdle—These were intended for Aaron and his sons, i.e. all the priests. The **tunic** was a common dress worn by all the Israelites next to the skin. It reached down to the ankles and was provided with sleeves. The priestly tunic was made of fine linen. The narrator mentions two **head-dresses** which in 28:39–40 are ascribed to Aaron and his sons respectively. Both were wound round the head like a turban. Aaron's head-dress however was of a special kind, similar to that worn by royalty (cf Ezek 21:31). The post-exilic i high-priests coveted the royal insignia. The common Israelites did not wear **breeches**, but the priests had to wear them while officiating in the sanctuary or at the altar of holocausts. Public decency, which motivated the prohibition of altar steps in 20:26, does not seem to be especially intended here. The priests had to wear breeches even when they were already sufficiently covered by tunic and robe, and when they were not in an elevated position. The priests had rather to hide that part of the body from Yahweh, under penalty of death. The dark mystery of sex, so prominent an element in other ancient cults was not deemed fit for the holy liturgy of Yahweh. In 28:42–43 the mention of breeches is clearly an addition, but in 39:28 it forms an integral part of the text recast later. The ornamental **girdle** (29) was a symbol of high rank j (cf Is 22:21). According to tradition it encircled the body several times and had lengthy extremities which were thrown over the shoulders during ceremonies. As all served barefoot in compliance with the oriental reverential custom (cf 3:5) there is no mention of footwear. In 28:41 (cf also 30:30; 40:15) it is said that the sons of Aaron, i.e. all the priests, are to be anointed. This note anticipates the lengthy instructions about the installation of the priests that follow later on, and does not quite agree with them for in 29:9 the anointing of the priests is not mentioned. It was in fact a very late innovation introduced long after the exile. See commentary on 29:4–9, (192 f, g).

k 30–31 (28:36–38) The Diadem—It carried the inscription 'Holy to Yahweh' and served to avert any danger arising from ritual faults committed by all the Israelites during sacrificial offerings. Originally it was a royal badge; the high-priest took it over after the exile.

l 32–42 Inventory of the Cultic Objects—A list of all the objects manufactured in view of the liturgical service in the desert. In 42 the manufacturing of the sacred objects is attributed to the Israelites in general, because all the people had sponsored the work by their bountiful offerings. But Moses' appreciation and blessing were naturally intended in a special way for the selected artisans who by God's election and under his guidance m executed the work. In this section the two names for the desert sanctuary, Tent of Meeting and Tabernacle are

coupled together. In the older narratives (33:7–11) the 191m sanctuary was indicated by the former name, while the latter is generally used in the previous sections containing Yahweh's ritual instructions and their execution (but cf 38:30). In our passage the author obviously wants to combine together the older traditions about the Tent of Meeting and his elaborate description of the Tabernacle, which in the present state of the text could by misunderstood as applying to two different objects, cf § 103f. In the following section (40:1–38) the two names are again coupled together, or are used indifferently to indicate the same sanctuary erected by Moses under God's orders.

40:1–38 Erection and Consecration of the Taber- 192a **nacle**—In the mind of the Priestly narrator who recast the account of the execution of God's orders, this is the climax of the Exodus theme. Before his intervention there was neither the detailed description of the erection and consecration of the sanctuary nor the relative divine instructions (but cf 29:43). All his editorial work, however, was directed towards this event. In his interpretation, the events of the exodus were given a liturgical significance; the importance of the Sinaitic legislation is now derived from the instructions about the building of the Tabernacle, and its actual erection and consecration concludes the Sinaitic cycle. Once the Tabernacle is erected a new era begins: Yahweh speaks with Moses in the Tabernacle and lays down the disposition for the institution of the priesthood and the actual conduct of the services. For this reason he does not describe the b installation of the priests, the special consecration of the altar of holocausts and the legislation about the daily sacrifice. These have been mentioned previously in God's instructions (29:1–46), and the present author actually presupposes them (40:29, 31), just as he introduces the mention of the installation of the priests among his instructions (40:12–15); but the real description of the consecration of the priests and the detailed instructions about the daily sacrifice are left for a later moment (Lv 6:2–6; 8:1–36; Nm 28:3–8) because they belong to the epoch of the erected sanctuary. On his c part he supplies both the description of the erection (and consecration) of the sanctuary and God's instructions to justify it. His chronological sequence is also anchored firmly on this event. The last chronological note had been given in 19:1 with reference to the arrival at Sinai. Now he picks up again his chronological sequence and places the erection and consecration of the sanctuary on the first day of the first month of the second year. A whole year was required for the march to Sinai and the execution of God's orders regarding the erection of the Tabernacle. Once it is completed, God takes possession of his dwelling by means of a cloud which is a conventional figure signifying the presence of Yahweh. This figure has already been employed in the description of the Sinaitic theophany (19:16; 20:21), and is used again to indicate Yahweh's presence in the account of the consecration of Solomon's temple (1 (3) Kgs 8:10–12). The exodus theme is thus d brought to its final conclusion. A short note appended to this theme gives another explanation of the cloud: it regulated Israel's starts and halts along their journey to Canaan. This note serves as a link between the exodus theme and the subsequent wanderings in the desert.

(29:1–46) Instructions about the Consecration of e Aaron and his Sons—This section is based for the most part on the post-exilic ritual of the priestly consecration. It lays down God's instructions about the ritual to be followed in the installation of the priests, but the express

192e order to put these instructions into effect only appears after the erection and consecration of the Tabernacle in Lv 8:2, where it properly belongs according to the redactor who is responsible also for the overall arrangement of the actual text of Ex. Once the express order is given, the installation of the priests follows without any f loss of time as is described in Lv 8:3–36. **4–9.** The washing of the body secures ritual purity which was required not only of the high-priest but also of all Israelites who approached the presence of Yahweh. A ritual bath was similarly prescribed in Egypt for the investiture of the priests. **6.** The golden object fixed to the head-dress is here called a diadem (nêzer) while in 39:30 it is called a flower ṣîṣ, RSV 'crown' in both). In fact it was a royal badge shaped like a flower. Breeches are not mentioned because they were not part of the ceremonial dress, but a protection against the dangerous holiness of Yahweh. It is more difficult to explain the absence of the ornamental girdle mentioned also in Lv 8:7. Perhaps the author identifies it with the belt of the g ephod. For the anointing oil cf 37:29. In this way Moses was to fill the hands of Aaron and his sons, i.e. install them in office. There are some examples in the older texts of priests being installed in office, but there is no instance of any anointing or consecration of a priest before the exile. The priest was holy not because of an initial ceremony, but by virtue of his sacred functions. Anointing was reserved to the king, and was transferred to the high-priest only after the exile when the high priest claimed for himself some royal prerogatives. Later still the anointing was extended to all the priests (Ex 28:41; 30:30; 40:15; Lv 7:36; 10:7; Nm h 3:3). **10–42.** The sacrificial ceremony which concluded i the consecration of the priests. The ritual follows the general rules for sin-offerings prescribed in Lv 4:1–12. j **26.** The waving was probably a movement of the offering towards the altar, but its exact significance is obscure. k In the case of the priestly consecration the sacrificer

receives only the breast. In **27** the (right) thigh is also 192k assigned to him, but the narrator is here referring to the priest's customary right in peace-offerings. The cultic meal concludes the sacrificial ceremony, which is to be repeated on seven successive days. To this account of the sacrifice some secondary material has been added. In **29–30** it is ruled that the vestments of Aaron should be used in the investiture of future high-priests, that will also last for seven days. In Nm 20:28 it is actually narrated that after Aaron's death Moses passed his vestments on to Eleazar his successor. This narrative is very old, and does not mention any anointing or consecration. In **36–37** the l consecration of the altar of holocausts is made to coincide with that of Aaron and his sons while in 40:9–10 it goes with the general consecration of the sanctuary where it properly belongs. In Lv 8:3–36 the consecration of the sanctuary with its utensils and the altar of holocausts is combined with the consecration of Aaron and his sons which immediately follows it (Lv 8:10–11), but the seven-day ritual for the special consecration of the altar of holocausts is not mentioned. This combination of sanctuary and priests has been dropped by our redactor because he places the erection and consecration of the sanctuary as the climax of the Sinaitic events, and the consecration of the priests as a natural sequel to the erection of the sanctuary. The ruling about the daily m sacrifice (**38–42**) is also attached to the priestly consecration, as if both would start at the same time. The narrator describes the post-exilic daily service. Morning and evening a lamb was offered as a holocaust accompanied by meal mingled with oil and a libation of wine. Older texts attest an animal sacrifice in the morning and a vegetable offering in the afternoon. **43–46.** General remarks about the benefits proceeding from the consecration of cultic persons and objects: it ensures the presence of Yahweh among his people and serves as a perpetual reminder of the divine election and liberation of Israel.

LEVITICUS

BY P. P. SAYDON

193a Bibliography—*Commentaries*: N. H. Snaith, CBi², 1967; A. T. Chapman—A. B. Streane, CBSC, 1914; P. Heinisch, BB, 1935; A. Clamer, PCSB, 1946; H. Cazelles, BJ, 1951; H. Schneider, EchB, 1955; N. Micklem, IB, 1953; M. Noth, ATD, 1962, E. tr. OTL 1965. *On sacrifice*: A. Médebielle, 'Expiation' in DBS 3 (1938); G. B. Gray, *Sacrifice in the OT*; 1925; *Other subsidiary works*: W. Kornfeld, *Studien zum Heiligkeitsgesetz (Lev 17—26)*, 1952; R. North, *Sociology of the Biblical Jubilee*, 1954; R. de Vaux, AI, 1961; *Studies in OT Sacrifice*, 1964. H. H. Rowley (ed.), *The OT and Modern Study*, 1956. A. Edersheim, *The Temple, its ministry and services*, n.d.

b Title—Leviticus, the title of the third book of the Pent, is derived through Vg from the LXX *Leueitikon*. It is certainly very old and probably of pre-Christian origin (H. B. Swete, *An Introduction to the Old Testament in Greek*, 215). In the Hebrew Bible it is called *wayyiqra* (St Jerome *Vaicra*) from its opening word. Leviticus is an appropriate title descriptive of the contents of the book which deals mainly with the Levites' duties in connection with the sacrificial worship. It was the liturgical book of the Israelites and may be compared to our Ritual.

c Contents—The contents of Leviticus fall into two main parts corresponding to the two aspects of God's relation to his people. Yahweh was the God of the Israelites whom he had called out of Egypt and adopted as his firstborn. He was a God infinitely holy, unapproachable by man (Ex 19:21; 24:2) and yet dwelling amidst his people (Lv 22:32; 26:12). As the supreme Lord of Israel he had the right to their obedience, reverence, love and worship, while his divine presence demanded of them such sanctity of life as would make them his worthy children (Lv 11:44f; 19:2; 20:26). Sacrificial worship and sanctity of life are therefore the two leading motives of Leviticus and a general description of its contents which are exhibited more particularly in the following paragraphs.

d Analysis and Structure—The book of Exodus carries the history of Israel down to the erection of the Tabernacle.

The liturgical and ceremonial legislation implementing the narrative of Exodus is contained in Leviticus which opens with a detailed description of all the forms of sacrifice (chh 1—7). Then follows an account of the priestly ordination of Aaron and his sons and their solemn entry upon office (chh 8 and 9). A short appendix stressing the necessity of sacerdotal sanctity is added (ch 10). Chh 11—15 deal with the distinction between cleanness and uncleanness and the ritual purification from uncleanness. Ch 16 describes the ceremonial of the Day of **e** Atonement. Chh 17—26 constitute a well-defined body of laws to which the title '**Law of Holiness**' has been appropriately given. Although the various groups of laws in this collection, and sometimes even the several laws, appear to be independent, their character is determined by the principle that holiness must be the distinguishing

mark of Israel. They differ notably from the laws **193e** contained in the preceding chapters. Their outlook is broader, their range of application more extensive and more varied. Although the priesthood and the sacrificial worship are clearly in view, they do not occupy a central position as in chh 1—16. Ch 17 contains prescriptions on the slaughtering of animals for sacrifice and for food. Ch 18 deals with unlawful sexual intercourse. Ch 19 is a miscellaneous collection of ordinances of a religious, domestic, and social character. Ch 20 gives a punitive sanction for the offences specified in chh 18 and 19. Chh 21 and 22 extend the Law of Holiness to priests in their domestic life and in the performance of their sacerdotal duties. Ch 23 is a festal calendar indicating the days on which religious assemblies are to be held and prescribing the manner in which these days are to be observed. Ch 24 is an erratic block of miscellaneous ordinances interrupting the logical sequence of chh 23 and 25. Ch 25 relates the institution of the Sabbatical Year and of the Year of Jubilee. Apparently it is the sequel to ch 23; but on a closer examination the character of the institutions in the two chapters will be found to be completely different. The Sabbatical Year and the Jubilee Year are a social and an economic, rather than a liturgical, institution. No sacrificial offerings, no holy convocations, no abstention from work are enjoined. Ch 26 is a hortatory speech cast in the style of Dt 28, and concluding the section chh 17—26. Ch 27 contains two appendices on vows and tithes respectively.

It appears from a first reading that Lv is not a **f** complete and systematic exposition of the various laws regulating divine worship and the domestic and social life of Israel. It is rather the result of the combination of **various partial collections of laws**. The Law of Sacrifice (chh 1—7) formed certainly one collection with its proper superscription (1:1) and subscription (7:37). Chh 8—10 formed another collection. It relates the consecration of Aaron and his sons to the priesthood, their first offering, their sin and their death. Chh 11—15 consist of minor collections logically, but not necessarily chronologically, related to each other. Ch 16 may have originally followed ch 10, but its position after chh 11—15 is more appropriate. Chh 17—26 formed one collection of laws made up of smaller groups characterized by a common style and phraseology and by the frequent insistence on holiness as the distinguishing mark of Israel. Ch 26 is probably the work of the compiler who closed the collection 17—25 with a hortatory discourse. The last chapter was added when the rest of the book had already been completed.

It is clear from the above analysis that Lv is a book composed of widely varying material of different dates of origin. Moreover the question of its composition has to be considered in the context of the origins of the Pent as a whole, see §130e. It is generally agreed that apart from the Law of Holiness, **the book belongs to the P tradition or Priestly stratum**. The **narrative**

193f portion, chh **8—10**, may perhaps be regarded as the **original nucleus** around which the other material, though not necessarily later in origin, gradually gathered. Chh 1—7, the comprehensive instructions on sacrifice, fit suitably into the book before the narrative nucleus. The chh on cleanness and uncleanness, 11—15, come well before the cleansing ritual in 16. The last considerable section, the Law of Holiness, clearly had an independent existence for an appreciable time before inclusion in the book, and being of a mixed character was appropriately placed after the other material. 'To fix the place of origin' says M. Noth, 'is at least as important as to arrive at a date. For traditional cultic material does not live in a vacuum, nor is it theoretically formulated to be practised here and there, but grows out of the worshipping life of a particular holy place', p. 15. He is of opinion that the **bulk of the book**, chh 1—7, 11—15, **17—25 originated in Jerusalem and that the** *final* **form of the non-narrative portions of Lv probably dates from the end of the Kingdom of Judah or the beginnings of the Exile**, ibid. It may be added that **some of the laws in the book appear to be of very great antiquity**. Thus the prescriptions for various kinds of sacrifice (1:2; 3:1—17; 5:14—26) have their counterpart in the Ugaritic texts of pre-Mosaic times. The sabbatical year and the Jubilee year were also known before Moses as they occur in Nuzi sacrificial texts.

194a **Sacrificial Terminology**—An explanation of the more frequent sacrificial terms is given here in order to relieve the commentary of useless repetitions. On the sacrifices see also §104*g*.

(*a*) The **holocaust** or **burnt offering**. A word of Greek origin (holocaustos LXX *holokautōma*) meaning literally 'a whole burnt-(offering)'. The corresponding Hebrew word, '*ōlāh*, is commonly derived from the verb '*ālāh*, 'to go up', hence 'that which goes up' (BDB s.v. '*ōlah*), the victim being considered as going up in the flames of the altar to God and so expressing the ascent of the soul in worship (ibid). The holocaust symbolized man's recognition of God's universal sovereignty and was therefore the noblest form of sacrifice (St Thom. 1, 2 q 102, a 3 ad 8 et 10). It had a great part in the Levitical liturgy. Besides the daily morning and evening holocaust (Ex 29:38—42; Nm 28:3—8; etc), others were offered on festal days and other specified occasions (Lv 12:6—8; 14:13; etc).

b (*b*) The **peace offering**; Heb. *šelāmîm* (Lv 3:1—17). It is difficult to say what the exact meaning of the Hebrew word is. Some link it with *šillēm* 'to requite', hence *šelāmîm* is a sacrifice offered for favours bestowed by God (St Thom. loc cit). Others connect the word with the verb *šālēm* 'to be sound, safe', and the noun *šālôm* 'peace, soundness'. Hence *šelāmîm* would denote peaceful, friendly relations with God. Though this meaning may not be the original one, it applies very well to all forms of peace-offerings, the distinguishing feature of which is the sacrificial meal of which the offerer has the right to partake. Peace-offerings were prescribed on the fulfilment of a Nazirite vow (Nm 6:14) and on the Feast of Weeks (Lv 23:19).

(*c*) The **sin-offering**; it is subdivided into two forms: the sin-offering (Vg 'pro peccato') and the trespass-offering (Vg 'pro delicto'). Both were intended to expiate sin and to re-establish friendly relations with God, but the difference between them is not clear. It is commonly believed that 'trespass' was an offence consisting in the unlawful withdrawal or retention of what was due to God or man, hence an offence involving material damage (Médebielle, 61; Gray, 58; and the dictionaries by BDB, Buhl, König, Zorell s.v. '*āšām*) and 'sin' was any other **194b** ordinary sin. A slightly different distinction is proposed here. 'Sin' was any ordinary offence committed through human frailty or passion. 'Trespass' denotes fundamentally a state of culpability, imputability, indebtedness, cf P. Joüon in Bib (1938) 454—9. The sense of indebtedness is evident in 6:4. The sense of culpability is also apparent as it is inseparable from sin, but it may not be so evident when the sin is said to have been committed through ignorance or inadvertence, as in the cases contemplated in 4:2, 3, 13, 22, 27; 5:2, 3. These unintentional sins **c** constituted a real, though involuntary, transgression, and were therefore legally imputable and were to be expiated when the offender became conscious of his offence. 'Trespass' was therefore a material sin or, in some cases, a formal sin involving material damage to one's neighbour. In both cases the offender is guilty. Sin-offerings were very common in the Levitical liturgy, cf e.g. Lv 8:2; 12:6; 14:19; Nm 6:11, 14; 28:15.

(*d*) **Cereal-offerings**, Heb. *minhāh*, originally 'a **d** gift', then a sacrificial term, designating an oblation which consisted of uncooked flour, unleavened bread and parched grain.

(*e*) **Libations** of wine, as a part of the sacrificial **e** ritual, are mentioned only once in Leviticus (23:13), more frequently in Numbers (15:5, 7; 28:7; etc).

(*f*) '**To expiate**', Heb. *kippēr*. This verb occurs **f** frequently in the liturgical terminology, (cf 4:20, 26, 31, 35, 5:6, 13, 16, 18; etc). Some interpreters, especially E. König, ET 22 (1910—11) 232—4, defend the meaning 'to cover' on the grounds of biblical usage and Arabic affinities. Expiation would then mean a covering or a non-imputation of sins. Others, however, prefer to link up the verb *kippēr* with Assyrian *kapāru* 'to destroy, to wipe away'. An allied meaning is 'to be bright', according to C. F. Burney, JTS, 11 (1909—10) 437 footnote, brightness being the effect of wiping and polishing. According to this interpretation, which is preferable both philologically and exegetically, expiation implies the destruction of sin and the consequent cleansing of the soul. For a fuller discussion, see Médebielle, 69—83; Gray, 67—76.

Religious Value—As literature Lv is not one of the **g** more readable books of the Bible. The legal nature of its contents, the queerness of many of the liturgical regulations, the monotonous repetition of stereotyped forms and expressions combine to make the book unattractive to the average reader. But its apparent dullness is counterbalanced by the religious significance and the moral teaching which the book conveys and will ever retain throughout all ages. The following are some of the more important doctrinal points:

(*a*) **The importance and sanctity of the liturgical h service**. The law of sacrifice emphasizes the importance of the external cult based on the recognition of God's universal sovereignty and man's need of expiating his sins and thus re-establishing normal relations with God. The liturgy of the sacrifice is calculated to impress on us, as on the Israelites, the idea of the sanctity of God to whom alone sacrifice is offered. The sacrifice is offered through the ministry of a special caste—the priests; the victim must be without blemish, and those who partake of the sacrificial meal must be free from any ceremonial uncleanness. Moreover, the sacrifice of the OT foreshadowed the sacrifice of Christ, and the sacrificial meal symbolized the sacramental communion of the New Law; cf the allegorical interpretation of the Aaronic priesthood and sacrifice in Hebrews.

(*b*) **The sanctity of priests**. The priests, God's **i**

194i ministers, must be holy. Their duty of holiness is clearly expressed in Lv 21:6: 'They shall be holy to their God.... For they offer the offerings by fire to the Lord, the bread of their God, therefore they shall be holy'. The whole ceremonial of their consecration was expressive of the high degree of sanctity that was inherent in their office. See also ch 21.

j (c) **Imitation of God.** The imitation of God's attributes, especially his holiness, is an indispensable condition for fellowship with God. The Israelites must be holy because their God is holy (11:44; 19:2; 20:26). This is a fundamental principle of Christian life enunciated in almost the same words by Christ (Mt 5:48). Although the Levitical holiness was, to a large extent, external, it was by no means restricted to mere ceremonial cleanness irrespective of internal dispositions. In 19:2 the duty of holiness is further determined by such injunctions as respect towards one's parents, the worship of one God, which are religious and ethical precepts.

k (d) **The observance of God's commandments and temporal happiness.** The observance of God's commandments is a source of temporal happiness (26:3—13), while the transgression of his law carries with it severe punishment in this world itself (26:14—39). This is always true, provided, however, temporal happiness and calamities are viewed in their relation to eternal life.

l (e) **Bodily cleanliness and religion.** Bodily cleanliness is not without relation to religion. If life is the gift of God, all that contributes to its preservation may form the object of a divine enactment and thus become a religious practice. Thus the seclusion of lepers and certain ablutions were sanitary prescriptions with a religious significance.

A. Cult Institutions—Sacrifice and the Consecration of Priests (chh 1—10).

195a 1 Various Kinds of Sacrifice and their Ritual (chh 1—7). Some general regulations had already been given (Ex 28; 29), but in this book a fuller exposition of religious institutions and liturgical regulations is added. The Law of Sacrifice, on account of the central position which sacrifice holds in divine worship, heads the list of ritual prescriptions.

All the Levitical laws are represented as communicated directly by God to Moses, but the expression 'the Lord spoke to Moses' introducing the several ordinances must be understood as expressing continuity in the compilation and adaptation of existing laws and practices.

b 1:1—17 The Holocaust and its Ritual—The victim could be of the bovine or ovine species, provided it was male and without blemish. Other domestic animals and wild animals could not be offered. For a list of disqualifying physical defects of the victims, see Lv 22:17—25; cf also Dt 15:21, 22; 17:1; Mal 1:8. The offerer laid his hands on the head of the victim thus symbolically identifying himself with it and signifying his adoration, gratitude, etc, which made the sacrifice acceptable to God (4). The opinion held by St Thomas (1, 2, q. 102, a. 3 ad 5), Médebielle, 142, and others that the imposition of hands represented symbolically the transference of the offerer's sins to the victim which consequently incurred the death penalty (penal substitution), is less probable. Expiation was common to all forms of sacrifice (Lv 17:11), though it was more strongly felt

c in connection with sin-offerings. The victim is burnt entirely, except the hide which is assigned to the officiating priest (Lv 7:8). The sacrificial burning is expressed in Heb. by the verb *hiqṭîr* which, used in a liturgical sense, means 'to burn the victim in such a way as to make it exhale an odour of incense' (C. Lattey, *The Book of*

Malachy, in WV, xx f). A. van Hoonacker, RB, 1914, **195c** 171—4. God's acceptance of the sacrifice is expressed anthropomorphically by the sweet agreeable odour rising up from the burnt victim; cf Gn 8:21. The expression 'a sweet savour', originally 'a soothing odour', has become a technical term denoting the divine pleasure or the divine acceptance.

The Levitical law allowed the offering of birds only in cases of poverty; cf 5:7—10; 12:6—8. Even a small offering is accepted by God when it comes from a sincere heart.

2:1—16 Bloodless Offerings and their Ritual— d These were brought as an accompaniment to animal sacrifice, cf 8:26—28; 9:17; 23:13, 18; Nm 6:15; 28:5; etc. They consisted of fine flour and oil prepared in different ways, and frankincense put on, but not mixed with, them. Fruit and vegetables were not offered except as first fruits, see vv 12—16. The sacredness of these offerings made it unlawful for laymen to partake of them (6:14—18). It is not without significance that bread was the commonest material of bloodless offerings in the Hebrew ritual. Oil and salt were used as ingredients in the sacrificial offering, while wine was generally offered with an animal sacrifice or bread (Hos 9:4). No other meal offerings were brought on the altar. The typical relation of the sacrificial meal of the OT to the Eucharistic meal of the New Law is obvious.

It was forbidden to make an offering of leavened **e** bread or of honey on the altar. Fermentation was associated with corruption and putrefaction, and honey is liable to ferment. Moreover, honey was used in the sacrifices of the Canaanites, the Egyptians and the Assyro-Babylonians. In the NT leaven is the symbol of evil (Mt 16:6—12; Mk 8:15; Lk 12:1; 1 Cor 5:6—8; Gal 5:9). Leavened bread and honey could be presented to God only as offerings of firstfruits and, in the case of leavened bread, as a part of the sacrificial meal, but were never burnt on the altar, cf 7:13; 23:17; 2 chr 31:5. **Salt** was an indispensable ingredient in all sacrificial offerings. It had a twofold use: it rendered the sacrificial meal, as any ordinary meal, more palatable, and it symbolized the inviolability of God's covenant with his people, hence the expression 'a covenant of salt' to designate a permanent and inviolable bond, cf 2 chr 13:5 and Nm 18:19. The origin of the expression goes back to the nomadic custom which regarded those who have partaken of the same meal or taken salt together as united by a bond (W. R. Smith. 270f).

Cereal-offerings could be made not only as an accompaniment to an animal offering but also as an offering of firstfruits. This was their ritual. The ears of the new corn were dried at the fire and rubbed till the grain was separated from the husks. The grain was then ground and sifted, oil was poured upon it and frankincense added. The 'memorial' was burnt upon the altar and the rest was eaten by the priests. Though the law here mentions only the firstfruits of corn, in Nm 18:13 and Neh 10:37 it covers all the land produce. In the latter cases the ritual was different.

3:1—17 The Peace-offering and its Ritual—Of all **g** forms of sacrifice this bears the closest analogy to the Sacrament of the Eucharist. Its distinguishing feature was the sacrificial meal of which both the priest and the offerer partook after a portion of the victim had been burnt on the altar (Lv 7:11—21).

The victim could be of the ox, sheep or goat kind, male or female, but without blemish. The first part of the ceremonial is similar to that of the holocaust. **5.** The reason for the burning of these parts was either that

195g they were regarded as a special delicacy and therefore to be reserved to God, or because the intestines, especially the kidneys and the liver, were considered by the Hebrews as the seat of life and emotion and therefore to be reserved to God like the blood. The first opinion is preferable. The Heb. *ḥēleḇ* 'fat' is used not infrequently to designate the choicest part of the products of the land (Gn 45:18; Nm 18:12, 29; Dt 32:14; etc). Moreover although the kidneys and the liver are sometimes considered as the seats of emotion (Jb 19:27; Ps 16(15):7; 73(72):21; Lam 2:11; cf E. Dhorme, *L'emploi métaphorique des noms de parties du corps en Hébreu et en Akkadien* [Paris, 1923] 128—33), these internal organs become the symbol of an insensible and unresponsive heart when they are represented as enveloped by fat (Ps 17 (16):10, 119 (118):70).

h **4:1 6:7 Expiatory Sacrifices and their Ritual**— Sins are either expiable or inexpiable. Expiable sins are those committed through human frailty or through ignorance or inadvertence; these are atoned for by a sin-offering if they are sins of human frailty, and by a trespass-offering if they are sins of ignorance; cf P. P. Saydon, 'Sin-offering and trespass-offering', CBQ (1946) 393—8. Inexpiable sins are punishable by death or excommunication (Lv 7:25; 17:9, 10; 19:8; 20:3; etc). See also § 183c.

196a **4:1—12 Expiatory Offerings for the High-Priest**—The characteristic features of the ritual of this sacrifice are the disposal of the blood and the consumption by fire of the victim outside the camp. Since blood was regarded as the seat of life (Lv 17:11), the sprinkling of blood towards the veil, which concealed the inaccessible throne of God, and the smearing of the horns of the altar were a symbolical representation of the sinner crying before God for mercy and forgiveness and for the re-establishment of friendly relations with him. No part of the flesh could be eaten either by the priest or by the people, everyone being ceremonially unclean (2). Nor could the victim be burnt on the altar because it was not a holocaust. A parallel between the victim of the expiatory offering burnt outside the camp and Christ who suffered outside the gate of Jerusalem is drawn in Heb 13:12.

b **13—21 Expiatory Offering for the Community**— This is a material transgression of the law which must be expiated when it becomes known to the offender. The only difference in ritual from that described in 3—12 is that the rite of the imposition of hands is performed by the elders as representatives of the people. The identity of the ritual is a clear indication that the sin of the high-priest and that of the community were considered to be of equal gravity. **20b.** Some sort of prayer may have formed part of the expiatory ritual.

c **22—26 Expiatory Offering for a Ruler**—The sin of a chief of a tribe being considered to be of a lesser gravity than that of the whole people the expiation is obviously simpler. The victim is a he-goat without blemish. The ritual is like that in 13—21. But no blood is brought inside the sanctuary.

d **27—35 Expiatory Offering for an ordinary Israelite**—The victim is either a she-goat or a ewe-lamb. The ritual is the same as that described in 24—26.

e **5:1—13 Expiatory Sacrifices for Special Sins**—This section specifies some particular offences for which an expiation is required. In ch 4 the expiation is considered in relation to the social condition of the offender; in 5:1—6:7 it is considered in relation to the offence. It is possible that all the sins enumerated in this section are sins of ignorance, though this is not expressly stated for all.

The first case (1) is that of a person who, having **196e** heard the curse uttered on an unknown offender, fails to reveal what he knows (cf Jg 17:2 and Prv 29:24). He is guilty because he hinders the execution of justice. But as such reticence is generally due either to fear of vengeance or to an imperfect sense of duty, his sin is practically comparable to an unintentional sin.

The second case (2, 3) is that of a person who inadvertently touches the dead body of an unclean animal or an unclean person or something which man has rendered unclean. In all these cases such a person is really unclean and besides purifying himself, must offer a sacrifice to expiate the sin of omitted purifications. On unclean animals, see Lv 11 and on human uncleanness Lv 12—15.

The third case (4) is that of a person who swears **f** rashly. A rash oath is a sin and needs expiation. The ritual is that prescribed in 2:2, 3. A characteristic feature of the ritual of these expiatory sacrifices is the confession of the offender's sin accompanying the rite of imposition of hands. The confession of sins is expressly prescribed in this case (cf Nm 5:7) and in the ceremonial of the Day of Atonement (Lv 16:21), but very probably it was a feature common to all expiatory sacrifices; cf F. Zorell in VDom 1 (1921) 35.

5:14—6:7 Expiatory Sacrifices for Sins of Fraud g against God and Man—When a person unlawfully retains or withholds what is due to God or to man, he shall offer an expiatory sacrifice, make good the damage caused to God or man and moreover pay a fine amounting to one-fifth of the value of the property unlawfully retained or withheld.

17—19. It does not appear to what particular case of fraud this article of law refers. A. Vaccari, 156, distinguishes between sins of omission (15) and sins of commission (17). But in this case the offering of a ram would hardly be enough. It is probable that 17—19 do not refer to any particular case, but contain a general statement which receives further determination in the cases contemplated in 6:1—7.

6:8—7:38 Supplementary Regulations concern- 197a ing the Various Sacrifices.

8—13 The holocaust or **burnt offering**—Apart from private holocausts and those offered publicly on festivals, the law prescribed that two holocausts should be offered daily, one in the morning and the other in the evening (Ex 29:38—42; Nm 28:3—8). It is the daily evening holocaust that the law refers to in 6:9. It was offered 'between the two evenings' (Nm 28:4), that is, according to later Jewish practice, between the afternoon and the evening (Jos.Ant 14, 4, 3 'about the ninth hour' i.e. 3 pm; cf also Edersheim, 116). This holocaust is to be kept burning on a slow fire all night. As many sacrifices were offered during the day, the law, by this prescription of a night-long sacrifice, provided that there should not be a single moment in which a sacrifice was not offered to God, foreshadowing in this manner the sacrifice of the New Law which is offered at all times in all parts of the world. The sacrifices are dealt with here from the point of view of the *priests'* part in these rituals. **12.** According to 9:24 this perpetual fire had a miraculous origin. It signifies God's perpetual presence among his people and has its Christian counterpart in the oil lamp continually burning in our churches before the Blessed Sacrament.

14—18 Meal Offerings—Cf ch 2. They are presented **b** through the ministry of the priests but not necessarily on their own account. The ritual is that prescribed in ch 2. As holiness is considered to be communicable through contact, any person or thing that touches the sacred

231

197b oblations becomes holy and must have the holiness washed out by means of certain ablutions before returning to the ordinary business of life (cf M.-J. Lagrange, 149; W. R. Smith, 446).

c 19–23 The High-Priest's Oblation—According to later Jewish practice the high-priest, at his own expense, offered an oblation twice a day. It was made of flour mingled with oil and gently baked by the fire; he brought the half of it to the fire in the morning, and the other half at night (Jos.Ant 3, 10, 7). The words '*in the day of their anointing*' (**20**) very probably must be taken in the sense of 'On that day and onwards'. For a similar meaning of the expression 'in the day of', cf 7:35. Vaccari, 157, restricts the meaning of the word 'perpetual' (Heb. *tāmîd*) to the seven days of the priestly ordination ceremony (Ex 29:35; Lv 8:33). But the word *tāmîd* is a technical term denoting the daily perpetual sacrifice. As this oblation was made by the high-priest, it could not be consumed either by himself or the priests, who were inferior to him, and therefore it had to be entirely burnt.

d 24–30 The Sin-offering—It was a most holy offering and was therefore to be eaten in a holy place, i.e. in the court of the tabernacle. The officiating priest naturally called other priests to share in the sacred meal, as is implied in **29**, because it was impossible that any one man could consume such a quantity of meat in one meal. Its holiness could be communicated through contact; see § 197*b*. The regulation concerning the sacred meal did not apply to the cases when blood was brought inside the sanctuary (4:1–21) and to the expiatory sacrifice on the Day of Atonement.

e 7:1–7 The Trespass-offering—There is a close similarity between the ritual of the sin-offering and that of the trespass-offering. The words 'the same shall be the law of both these sacrifices' (**7**) must be restricted to the concluding part of the verse, that is, in both sacrifices what remains of the victim belongs to the officiating priest.

f 8–10 Priests' Dues from Other Offerings—The skin of the burnt-offering belonged to the ministrant. In the Carthaginian table of sacrificial fees the skin is also assigned to the priest (G. A. Cooke, *A Text-book of North Semitic Inscriptions*, Oxford, 1903, 123), but at Marseilles it went to the offerer (Cooke, 112). As regards the meal-offerings a distinction is made between cooked offerings, as those mentioned in 2:4–10, and uncooked offerings, whether mingled with oil or dry, as those specified in 2:14–17 and 5:11. The former went to the officiating priest, the latter were divided between all the sons of Aaron in equal portions. The reason for this different assignment was that the uncooked offerings were usually so abundant that they could not be consumed by one man, Clamer, 2, 67.

g 11–21 The Peace-offering—The Levitical liturgy distinguishes three kinds of peace-offerings, or rather three reasons for which peace-offerings are brought: (i) thank-offerings or 'sacrifices of praise' (Ps 50(49):14, 23; Ps 107 (106):22); (ii) vow-offerings made in fulfilment of a vow (Ps 61 (60):9; 66 (65):13, 14); (iii) free-will offerings (Ps 54 (53):8). There are some slight differences in the ritual of these various offerings. **15**. After the sacrifice has been offered, that is, after the portions reserved for the Lord have been burnt on the altar and the priest has taken his share of the flesh and the cakes, the offerer together with his relatives and friends sits at meal in the neighbourhood of the sanctuary. The whole of the flesh must be consumed on that day. In the case of vow- and free-will offerings the flesh may be eaten also on the following day. Only one day was allowed for the consumption of the thank-offering probably because the occasion

being certainly a happy one, the offerer had to invite a **197g** number of guests such as would consume the whole of the flesh in one day and at the same time add to the festive character of the sacred meal. But vow- and free-will **h** offerings were more of a private matter; there was no special reason for rejoicing and the flesh therefore could be consumed by fewer guests and in a longer time. But in no case was it permissible to eat the flesh on the third day. If any flesh was left over after the second day, it was to be burnt. Any eating on the third day rendered the sacrifice unacceptable, and in the case of a vow-offering the offerer would have to offer another sacrifice. Sacrificial meat could not be eaten after the second day because after the second day the flesh begins to go bad and becomes unfit for consumption. **21**. The expression 'to be cut off from one's people', used in a religious sense, is a technical expression for excommunication or exclusion from all the privileges and blessings granted by God to the Israelites. But in some cases the death penalty is meant.

22–27 The Use of the Fat and Blood of Animals— **i** This is an abridged repetition, with some new details, of the regulations in ch 3 concerning the use of fat and blood. Here it is forbidden to eat them. Any person who transgresses either of these laws shall be excommunicated; cf 21. See also Lv 17:10–14.

28–34 The Priests' Share of the Peace-offering— **j** It has been said above (12–14) that a portion of the oblation accompanying the peace-offering went to the priest. Now the law specifies which parts of the peace-offering itself fell to the priest. **29–32**. These verses supplement the ritual prescribed in ch 3. Whether some ritual was prescribed for the presentation of the fat is not apparent, but in 8:26f the fat is said to be waved before the Lord.

The **rite of waving**, which is certainly prescribed **k** for the breast of the victim, consisted in swinging the offering towards the altar and back again with the hands of the offerer resting upon the hands of the priest. The forward motion was a symbolical declaration that those portions were given to God, while the backward motion signified that the gift was returned by God and assigned to his representative, the priest. This ceremony was so characteristic of certain offerings that the word *tᵉnûpāh* 'waving' became a liturgical term denoting a wave-offering in general, or, in particular, the breast of the wave-offering (10:15). Another due of the priests was the right thigh of the victim, Heb. *tᵉrûmāh* 'lifting up', hence what is separated from the rest and raised up as a contribution. Probably the *tᵉrûmāh* was a liturgical rite with a religious significance analogous to that of the waving rite. Compare the analogous rite of the Offertory in the Mass.

Although the Levitical law expressly assigned **l** to the priests the breast and the right thigh of all peace-offerings, usage may have varied from time to time. The Deuteronomic law gives the priest 'the shoulder, the two cheeks and the stomach' (18:3). From 1Sm 2:13ff it appears that priests claimed more than the shoulder and the right thigh.

35–36 Conclusion—This is the conclusion of the sec- **m** tion 6:8–7:34 dealing with the priestly dues. The Heb. word for 'anointing' in **35** (AV and RV *anointing-portion*) should very probably be rendered 'fixed or measured portion', the Heb. word *mišḥāh*, which literally means 'anointing', being probably related to Assyrian *masāḥu* 'to measure', *masīḥu* 'specific measure' of grain, dates, etc. (Muss-Arnolt, *A Concise Dictionary of the Assyrian Language*.) The word occurs again with the same meaning in Nm 18:8. This right the priests begin to enjoy from the

97m day of their priestly ordination, and they will continue to enjoy it for ever as the Lord has commanded; see chh 8—10.

n **37—38 General Conclusion**—These verses are very probably a general conclusion of the whole section dealing with sacrifice (chh 1—7), though the order in which the various sacrifices are enumerated in **37**, holocaust, oblation, sin-offering, trespass-offering, consecration-offering and peace-offerings agrees with 6:8—7:34 more than with chh 1—6.

198a **2 Institution of the Aaronic Priesthood (chh 8—10)**—The ritual here described is that of post exilic times. On the whole subject see §§ 104, 192e. The Israelites, even before the Sinaitic legislation, had their own sacrificial system (Ex 3:12, 18; 5:1, 3; etc) which was further developed when the priesthood became a permanent institution.

b **8:1—36 The Consecration of Aaron and his Sons**—The instructions given in Ex 29 are here carried into effect. As the account of the consecration agrees almost verbally with Ex 29, we shall limit ourselves to a brief exposition of the ceremony referring the reader to the commentary on Exodus for a fuller explanation.

c **1—4 Introduction** = Ex 29:1—3—The anointing oil is not mentioned in Ex 29:1—3 but in 7. The congregation has no part in Ex 29.

d **5—6 The Washing** — Ex 29:4—Bodily cleanliness as a sign of internal purity is an indispensable condition before approaching the altar.

e **7—9 The Vesting** = Ex 29:5, 6—The Urim and Thummim are not mentioned in Ex 29:5, 6 but in Ex 28:30.

f **10—12 The Anointing of the Tabernacle and Aaron**—The anointing of the tabernacle and the sacred vessels is prescribed in Ex 30:26—28 and 40:9—11, but not in Ex 29. There is hardly any reason for rejecting 10b, 11 as an interpolation. The anointing of the tabernacle and that of Aaron are probably independent of each other and may have been prescribed on different occasions, but in point of fact they can hardly be separated as we cannot conceive of a consecrated tabernacle without consecrated priests and *vice versa*. For 12 cf Ex 29:7.

g **13 The Vesting of Aaron's Sons** = Ex 29:8, 9.

h **14—17 The Sin-offering** = Ex 29:10—14—The ritual is that prescribed in Lv 4:4—12, with the omission of the sprinkling of blood against the veil and the smearing of the horns of the altar of incense. In 15b it is expressly stated that the smearing of the horns of the altar of holocausts with blood had the effect of purifying, literally 'removing the sin from', the altar and sanctifying it. This sin-offering, unlike that of Lv 4:1—12, is not intended to expiate any particular sin or sins of Aaron's, but only as an indispensable requisite of holiness demanded of all the ministers of the altar.

i **18—21 The Holocaust** = Ex 29:15—18—The ritual is that prescribed in Lv 1:10—13.

j **22—32 The Ram of Ordination** = Ex 29:19—34—This sacrifice is called 'ordination offering' (22, 28, 29) on account of the occasion on which it was offered. The Heb. word for ordination here is *millû'îm*, which is derived from the verb *millē'* 'to fill', which gave rise to the expression *millē' yād* lit. 'to fill the hand' and as a liturgical expression 'to confer the power, to institute to a priestly office' hence 'to ordain'. Therefore *millû'îm* is 'institution to the priesthood, ordination'. But the fundamental idea conveyed by the word is the conferment of a certain power; cf P. Joüon in Bib 3 (1922) 64—66. Though the occasion of the sacrifice gives it a special

character, certain features, such as the apportionment **198j** of the priestly dues, make it resemble a peace-offering. **23**. The smearing of these organs with blood signified **k** that 'the ear must be attentive to the commands of God, the hand ready to do his will, the foot prepared to walk in his ways', Chapman—Streane, 48. **30**. The sprinkling **l** with oil, though in strict conformity with the injunctions of Ex 29:21, raises some difficulties. There is no apparent reason why Aaron should be sprinkled with oil after having been anointed (12), nor is it clear whether there was only one sprinkling with blood and oil mingled together, or two separate sprinklings. The difficulty would disappear if we removed from the text of Ex 29:21 and Lv 8:30 the words 'the anointing oil' as an interpolation, but the excision is hardly justified.

33—36 Duration of the Ordination Ceremony—Cf **m** Ex 29:35—37. The ceremony described above was to be repeated for seven consecutive days. During this time they were to abide at the entrance of the tabernacle performing the special service prescribed to them.

9:1—24 The Inauguration of Aaron's Priestly **n Service**—Cf § 104e for its significance. Aaron first offered his own expiatory sacrifice with the ritual prescribed in 4:4—12, with the exception of the imposition of hands and the sprinkling of the blood against the veil. It must be remarked that Aaron had not yet been solemnly introduced into the inner sanctuary. After the holocaust, offered with the same ritual as in 1:10—13, there followed the sacrifices of the people. The oblation was burnt upon the altar (**17**). The last words of the v are an allusion either to the holocaust which had been burnt that very morning or to the daily perpetual holocaust (Ex 29:38—42; Nm 28:3—8). The account was written when the morning sacrifice had become a regular feature of the divine service.

God's acceptance of the first sacrifices was manifested **o** by a heavenly sign. Aaron, having performed all the sacrificial service, lifted up his hands and blessed the people, probably in the manner prescribed in Nm 6:22—26, descended from the altar and went into the tabernacle with Moses. Probably Moses by introducing Aaron into the inner sanctuary, but not into the Holy of Holies, vested him with further priestly rights. This ceremony may be compared with the solemn entry of a new bishop into his Cathedral Church and his enthronement. When they came out, they blessed the people and the glory of the Lord appeared in the sight of all in the form of a fire consuming all the offerings upon the altar. For a similar manifestation of God's acceptance of a sacrifice cf Jg 6:21; 1 (3) Kgs 18:38; 1 Chr 21:26; 2 Chr 7:1.

10:1—7 The First Priestly Transgression and its **199a Punishment**—It is not clear what the sin of Aaron's sons was considered to be. It was certainly irreverence connected with fire and incense-offering. It is commonly held that Nadab and Abihu made use of fire that was not taken from the altar. But the expression 'a strange fire' probably means a fire-offering made against the regulations, therefore an irregular fire-offering, a fire-offering made not in the manner that was commanded. The story is told to stress God's infinite holiness. For similar punishments cf Nm 11:1; 16:35; 2 (4) Kgs 1:12. God being holy, those who approach him must be holy. Moses here quoted God's words, but we cannot say on what occasion God pronounced them. The dead bodies of Nadab and Abihu were instantly removed and buried outside the camp. Aaron and his surviving sons, Eleazar and Ithamar, were strictly forbidden to show any sign of mourning, which, however, was allowed to other relatives and the whole people. The reason for this prohibition is given in

199a Nm 19:11—22. Later legislation was less strict as it permitted the priests, but not the high-priest, to mourn for their closest relatives; cf 21:1—6, 10—12.

b 8—11 The Priests forbidden to drink Wine—The close connexion between this prohibition and the episode of Nadab and Abihu gave rise to the tradition that drunkenness during the divine service was the sin of the two priests. The priests, the only persons who could approach God and who were the recognized teachers in Israel, had to be perfectly sober both out of due reverence and in order that they might be able to discriminate between what was holy and what was not holy, between what was clean and what was unclean, and to teach the people all the laws given by God to Moses.

c 12—15 The Portions reserved to the Priests—This passage is supplementary to the narrative relating the offering of Aaron's first sacrifice (ch 9). Only the sons of Aaron had a right to a portion of the oblation (6:18), his daughters being allowed to share in the peace-offerings only. For the persons who were entitled to a share in the priestly portions, see 22:11—13.

d 16—20 The Sin-offering not eaten by the Priests—Moses is angry with Eleazar and Ithamar and rebukes them because they have not eaten the holy portion in a holy place. He puts forward two reasons: (i) God has given you a portion of the sin-offerings that you might, by eating it, expiate the sins of the people. The eating is a complementary part of the whole sacrificial ritual which is acceptable to God only if the several constituent actions are properly performed. (ii) No blood was brought into the sanctuary, a portion of the victim was therefore to be reserved to the priest (6:26). Aaron answers for his sons as the only person responsible. He justifies his action by expressing his doubts about God's acceptance of his partaking of the sin-offering. His sons' sin-offering and their holocaust could not avert the calamity which had befallen him. How could he therefore hope that his eating the victim would propitiate God?

**200a B. Laws of Purification and Atonement (chh 11—16).
1 Uncleanness and its Removal (chh 11—15)**—In the Levitical legislation uncleanness denotes the state of a person who, on account of certain actions not necessarily sinful, cannot approach God. Both this person and the cause of his condition are said to be unclean. Uncleanness is generally external, not necessarily involving any transgression of the moral law, and therefore its removal too was an external ceremony reinstating the unclean person in his former condition. The study of anthropology has shown that the distinction between cleanness and uncleanness and the religious notions underlying the distinction are very widespread and far older than the Hebrew people. Some of these ideas and practices were taken over by the nomadic Israelites and were later sanctioned by God in so far as they were not inconsistent with monotheistic belief and as a means to train the Israelites to higher standards of moral cleanness. The moral and religious motive of the cleanness-laws is clearly stated in 11:44: 'Be holy because I am holy'. On the subject of Cleanness and Uncleanness, see M.-J. Lagrange, 141—57; W. R. Smith, 446—56; cf § 232*i*.

b 11:1—47 Clean and Unclean Food—The distinction between clean and unclean animals is based on sanitary grounds, on a sense of natural aversion and, to some extent, on religious considerations, certain animals having idolatrous and superstitious associations. A parallel list of unclean animals is given in Dt 14:3—20. For a comparison, see Driver, *Deuteronomy*, in ICC, 156—9.

c 1—8 Beasts = Dt 14:3—8—The criterion whereby animals are judged 'clean' is that they must 'have the hoof divided and chew the cud'. According to this criterion **200c** the camel is pronounced unclean because it chews the cud but has not the hoof divided. For the same reason the rock-badger and the hare are unclean because they do not divide the hoof although they move the jaws like ruminants. The pig is unclean for the opposite reason. The swine was forbidden food to the Semites and an abomination to the Jews (2 Mc 6:18f). Uncleanness, like holiness, could be transmitted by contact, and an unclean person had to be temporarily separated from all social intercourse until he was purified. Contact with a living unclean animal was not forbidden, otherwise the Israelites would have been deprived of their ordinary means of conveyance, the camel and the ass.

9—12 Fishes = Dt 14:11—18   **d**

13—19 Birds = Dt 14:9f—The principle underlying the **e** classification of these birds as unclean is that they are mostly birds of prey feeding on carrion. Some of the birds enumerated are of doubtful identity.

20—23 Winged Insects = Dt 14:19, 20—cf Mt 3:4; **f** Mk 1:6.

24—28 Uncleanness by Contact—As uncleanness is **g** communicable by contact, whoever carries or touches, even inadvertently, the carcass of an unclean animal defiles himself and remains defiled till the evening. Contact with a dead unclean animal was believed to be dangerous whereas contact with a living unclean animal was not: cf § 200*c*.

29—38 Uncleanness caused by Reptiles, etc—The **h** uncleanness produced by reptiles is restricted to contact with their corpses as they were never used as food. Three ways of dealing with such uncleanness are here indicated. (i) The uncleanness adheres to the surface and can be washed away by water (**32**). (ii) The uncleanness penetrates into the thing itself which must therefore be destroyed (**33—35**). (iii) The uncleanness cannot be removed and may therefore be disregarded (**36, 37**).

39, 40 Contact with the Corpse of a Clean Animal— **i** This rule is meant to supplement the law concerning the contact with dead animals (24—28). By 'dead animal' is meant an animal which dies a natural death.

41—47 Conclusion—This is a regulation supplementary **j** to 29—31 and the conclusion of the whole section on the prohibition of unclean food. The ultimate reason why the Israelites must guard themselves against any uncleanness is the Lord's holiness and his relation to the Israelites. Yahweh is the God of the Israelites, and the Israelites are his people. Fellowship with God implies a certain likeness to him, or imitation of his perfections. The Israelites must be holy because their God is holy.

12:1—8 Purification after Childbirth—The origin **k** of life, which could not be explained naturally, was attributed by all primitive peoples to mysterious powers acting on woman. Generation was therefore always looked upon with superstitious awe, and women after childbirth were tabooed all the world over (cf J. C. Frazer, *Taboo and the Perils of the Soul*, 1914[3] [*The Golden Bough*, III] 147ff). But the Levitical law has also a religious significance. God is the source of life, and a holocaust is accordingly offered him in recognition of the origin of a new life from him. The sin-offering (**6, 8**) does not imply that childbirth or conjugal intercourse were considered morally sinful. The only inference is that the mother after childbirth is ceremonially unclean, and atonement has to be made by a sin-offering. Sin-offerings were also prescribed for other ceremonial uncleannesses; cf 14:19, 22; 15:15, 30.

1—4 The Birth of a Male—If a woman gives birth to **l** a male, she is unclean for seven days, as in her courses,

200l and is therefore subject to the restrictions specified in 15:19—24. For the next thirty-three days she continues to purify herself, the only restriction being abstention from holy things and the sanctuary. The number thirty-three has no other value but that of a remainder of forty after subtracting seven. Seven and forty are two symbolical round numbers indicating two stages in the period of recovery from childbirth.

m **5 The Birth of a Female**—In this case the two periods of seven and thirty-three are doubled. The reason may be either the popular belief that the birth of a girl is physiologically more dangerous for her mother and therefore requires a longer period of convalescence, or the opinion that, as woman was the first to bring sin into the world, the birth of a female should impose on her mother a longer seclusion.

n **6—8 The Purification**—At the end of the purification period the mother had to bring a lamb in its first year for a holocaust and a pigeon or a turtle-dove for a sin-offering. If she was poor, the law allowed her to bring two turtle-doves or two pigeons, one for the holocaust and the other for the sin-offering. The Virgin Mary offered the sacrifice allowed to a poor woman (Lk 2:24).

201a **13—14 Leprosy**—Leprosy was a fairly common disease in ancient times. References to it occur in both the OT and the NT, cf Ex 4:6; Nm 12:10; 2 Sm 3:29; 2(4) Kgs 5:1, 27; 7:3; 15:5; Mt 10:8; 11:5; Lk 7:22; etc. But it is doubtful whether the Heb. word šāra'at, LXX and Vg lepra denote always what is now known as leprosy, or are also applied to other skin diseases. In ch 13 various forms are described. The Hebrews always regarded leprosy as a contagious disease and perhaps as a punishment by God, and this explains both the isolation of the diseased and the necessity of ceremonial purification. On leprosy, see A. R. Bennett, *Diseases of the Bible* (1887), 15—53; HDB, 2, 95—9; DBV, 4:175—87.

b **13:9—17**—If there is only a white efflorescence covering the skin from head to foot, it is not leprosy but some form of psoriasis or scaly cutaneous disease which is neither contagious nor incurable, and the priest shall therefore pronounce him clean. But if there is an ulceration ('raw flesh'), which must be distinguished from a temporary sore, it is a case of leprosy, and the person affected must be declared unclean.

c **29—37 Leprosy in the Hair**—It is a contagious disease, and the person affected is unclean. Suspicious cases are to be re-examined after a week's quarantine.

d **38—39 White Spots on the Skin**—The disease described here is a form of eczematous, cutaneous affection distinguished by spots of a dull white colour. It is not contagious and produces no uncleanness.

e **40—44 Baldness**—Baldness is not infectious and produces no uncleanness except when it is complicated by the usual leprous symptoms. Such complicated cases are to be treated as the other cases of leprosy.

f **47—59 Leprosy in Garments**—What is meant by this form of leprosy is not clear. The opinion that leprous garments are those worn by lepers is not probable. It is commonly believed that the word 'leprosy' is applied to certain greenish and reddish spots in garments caused by mildew on account of their similarity to the leprous symptoms and of their corrosive action and insanitary effects. The treatment is more or less the same as in the case of leprosy in man including isolation of the infected garment, washing and in some cases destruction.

g **14:1—32 The Purification of the Leper**—Although true leprosy is an incurable disease and no purification will therefore be required, some of the varieties described in ch 13 can be cured. When a diseased person is cured, he must be formally readmitted into the community according to a prescribed ritual. The cleansing ceremony consists of two parts, the removal of the uncleanness (**2—9**) and the readmission to the community, and consequently to fellowship with God (**10—20**). **201g**

2—9. The symbolism of this ceremony is obvious. The **h** sprinkling cleanses; the blood, and the water from a spring, not from a cistern, symbolize the new life which is being imparted to a person hitherto regarded as dead; the setting of the bird free represents release from confinement and reinstatement in civil rights; the cedar is noted for its soundness and medicinal powers; the hyssop, not the *hyssopus officinalis* L. which does not grow in Palestine, but the caper (*capparis spinosa* L.) or a kind of marjoram (*origanum marjorama* L.) was selected for its cleansing properties; the scarlet colour of the band represents the blood of a new life.

10—20. The first lamb is to be offered as a trespass offering. The reason for such an offering is that the uncleanness of the leper is considered as an involuntary guilt which has to be atoned for as a sin of ignorance or inadvertence; cf Saydon, CBQ 8 (1946) 307.

The guilt is of a lesser gravity in comparison with **i** those specified in 5:14—6:7, and this is the reason why a lamb and not a ram is offered. The ritual of the sacrifice is substantially identical with that of other trespass-offerings, but is accompanied by additional ceremonies which give the sacrifice its distinguishing feature. The priest, not the offerer as in 7:29—34, waves the lamb together with the log of oil. It may be however that the waving ceremony is performed by the offerer himself assisted by the priest; see note to 7:28—34. The lamb is then slain in the court of the sanctuary as the holocaust and the sin-offering. The smearing of the leper with blood has the same symbolical significance as in the consecration of priests (8:23), the purification of a leper being regarded as a reconsecration to the Lord's service.

33—53 Leprosy in Houses—Certain greenish and **j** reddish patches in the inner walls of a house are called leprosy on account of their similarity to macular leprosy. Their natural cause is damp or decay, but they are represented as a plague inflicted by God. The infected house is examined by the priest who is to order the necessary repairs or its destruction or declare it clean according to the nature and gravity of the infection. It is a sanitary regulation with a religious significance.

49—53 Purification—The rite of purification is similar **k** to that prescribed for the leper (3—7). The setting of the bird free lends support to the opinion that this rite expresses symbolically the carrying away of the uncleanness by the fleeing bird (W. R. Smith, 422).

15:1—53 Sexual Uncleanness and its Purifica- **202a** **tion**—Although hygienic considerations and the practice of many ancient peoples may lie at the root of these regulations, it cannot be reasonably doubted that their informing principle is eminently moral and religious. The immediate reason for such purifications is not the sinful character of the actions nor the pathological affections specified in this chapter, but the holiness of God which excludes from his service anything that offends decency. Cf 200a.

1—18 Uncleanness in Men—This is produced: (i) by **b** abnormal seminal emission (**2—3**); (ii) by a normal emission as in the case of a nocturnal accident (**16**) [Dt 23:10]; (iii) by lawful sexual intercourse (**18**). **19—30 Uncleanness in Women**—This is produced: (i) **c** by normal periodical discharges. A woman during her courses is unclean and communicates her uncleanness by contact. The apparent contradiction between **24** and

202c 20:18 is readily removed by supposing that the former deals with lawful conjugal relations and the latter with unlawful sexual relations during the prohibited time. (ii) By abnormal discharges, that is, those occuring outside the ordinary course or lasting longer than usual. Purification is required on account of God's presence among his people. The tabernacle is his dwelling-place and anyone approaching the tabernacle with an 'uncleanness' upon him defiles God's dwelling and deserves punishment.

d **2 Ritual of the Day of Atonement (ch 16)**—This day holds a prominent place in the Jewish calendar. Both its ritual and its religious significance mark it off from all other festival days and give it a special character which has earned for it, in later Judaism, the name *Yoma* 'the Day', or *Yoma Rabba* 'the Great Day'. As regards its religious significance suffice it to remark that the public and solemn expiatory sacrifice is offered by, and for, the whole people collectively. The Israelites are considered as one moral person asking forgiveness for all past offences. And Yahweh thus propitiated continues to look upon his people favourably, although he may be wrathful with individual persons for their private unexpiated sins. Additional regulations are laid down in 23:26—32 and Nm 29:7—11. On the ritual and meaning of the festival see Médebielle, 89—114, and art. *Expiation* in DBS, especially the bibliography 259—62. The literary problems are discussed by S. Landersdorfer, *Studien zum bibl. Versöhnungstag*, Münster, 1924; de Vaux, AI.

e **16:1**—The institution is connected with the death of Aaron's sons, Nadab and Abihu. But it is difficult to see what this connection really implies. Many consider the feast to be post-exilic. See § 105*i*. Some believe that ch 16 deals 'in reality with two subjects, viz (1) the conditions under which the high-priest might enter the Holy of Holies (see 2), and (2) an atoning ceremony, to be enacted once annually, on behalf of the nation' (cf Driver, 47), and that the two ceremonials were imperfectly combined together when the entry into the Most Holy Place came gradually to be restricted to the single annual Day of Atonement. Without denying the possibility of such development we prefer to consider that the entry into the Holy of Holies and the atoning ceremony were two complementary parts of a single institution. Now considering the close relation between these two actions and the expiatory virtue connected with the blood ritual performed within the Holy of Holies, one can easily understand why the legislator has combined together two apparently distinct ceremonials beginning with the more important one, namely, the entry into the Holy of Holies.

f **2—28 The Ritual**—It was only on the annual recurrence of this occasion that the high priest was allowed to enter the Holy of Holies; cf the symbolical interpretation in Heb 9:6—12. Supplementing the biblical narrative by later traditions recorded in the Mishnah (tractate *Yoma*, English trans. by H. Danby) we can easily reconstruct the ceremony. Two buck-goats were presented (**5**), one for a sin-offering on behalf of the people, the other for the atoning ceremony. Two lots bearing the inscriptions 'For Yahweh' and 'For Azazel' respectively were placed in a casket. The high-priest then shook the casket, drew the two lots, and bound a scarlet thread of wool on the head of the goat for Azazel and another thread about the throat of the goat for Yahweh. The true meaning of the word Azazel, which occurs nowhere else in the OT, is doubtful. Early Jewish tradition identified it with one of the fallen angels (cf CAP II, 191ff). Christian writers protest against this interpretation on the ground that what has been presented to the Lord cannot belong to anyone else. LXX

and Vg break the word up into two parts, '*ēz* 'goat' and **202f** '*āzal* 'to go away' and translate [*chimaros*] *apopompaios*, 'caper emissarius', whence DV 'emissary goat' and AV '[e]scapegoat'. But whatever the etymology, the symbolical meaning is clear; see further on.

What follows is the most solemn part of the ceremony **g** and one of its most distinctive features. **12—14**. Within the veil he burned the incense thus raising a cloud of smoke that concealed the majesty of God from human sight, 'for man shall not see the Lord and live' (Ex 33:20). Then after a short prayer outside the veil he returned within the veil with a bowl of the slaughtered animal's blood and sprinkled it upon the propitiatory and in front of it once upwards and seven times downwards. This blood ritual is the essential part of the whole service. Blood has a special expiatory virtue which becomes still greater when it is brought before the presence of God.

18—19. These blood aspersions had the effect of cleans- **h** ing the sanctuary, the tabernacle and the altar from the defilement of the priests and the people. The sins of the people, their ceremonial uncleannesses, the transgressions of the priests themselves were considered as contaminating God's dwelling-place among his people and thus rendering the sacrificial worship unacceptable. A purification was necessary that would restore the temple to its sanctity and secure the forgiveness of sins and fellowship with God.

20. After the expiatory and purificatory rites the **i** forgiveness and complete destruction of sins was represented dramatically by a characteristic ceremonial. While the scapegoat stood before the people, the high-priest laid his hands on its head and confessed the sins of the people, thus laying them symbolically upon the goat. Then a man appointed for the purpose took the sin-laden goat to an uninhabited place in the wilderness and there let it go, or, according to the Mishnah, pushed it over the rocks from the top of a mountain. There is a similar symbolism in the purification of the leper (14:7). See the spiritual application to Christ made in Heb 9.

26. The man who led the scapegoat into the desert had **j** to wash himself and his clothes, probably because the goat laden with sins was regarded as unclean and producing uncleanness by contact. For a complete description of the ceremonial at the time of Christ see A. Edersheim, 263—88.

29—34 Additional Ordinances and Annual Celebra- k tion—The ceremonial described above was instituted as an annual festival to be celebrated on the tenth day of Tishri, the seventh month (= Sept.—Oct.). The reason for this date is not stated. The two numbers ten and seven had a certain sanctity attached to them (E. König in HDB, III, 565). Besides attending the service in the temple the Israelites and all resident foreigners had to 'afflict themselves' and 'to abstain from work'. The expression 'to afflict oneself' used in a liturgical sense, means 'to fast' (Is 58:3—5). This is the only occasion for which **fasting** is prescribed, although fasting is a very ancient custom and is frequently referred to in the OT; cf 1 Sm 14:24; 2 Sm 1:12; 12:16; Jer 36:6, 9; etc. An allusion to the fasting of the Day of Atonement is made in Ac 27:9. Abstention from work is not restricted to any particular kind of work. The prohibition is general, 'thou shalt do no work' (cf 23:28—30), and is emphatically expressed in **31** by the alliterative assonant expression *šabbat šabbātôn* 'absolute rest'.

C. The Law of Holiness (chh 17—26). Cf § 138*d*. **203a** **17:1—16 Regulations concerning the Slaying of Animals for Food and for Sacrifice**—These regulations are a fitting introduction to the collection of the laws

03a of holiness. The underlying principle of the whole collection is that the people must be holy because their God is holy. Now the basis and root of holiness is the recognition and exclusive worship of the one true God, and therefore the avoidance of all practices that may lead to idolatry.

b 3–7 The Slaughter of Animals fit for Sacrifice—Private slaughter of animals was forbidden. This may point to a time when all slaughter of domestic animals was connected with sacrifice. Lagrange, 254, remarks that with the Arabs every immolation was in some way a sacrifice. The reason was that blood, considered as the source of life and as possessing a special atoning efficacy (**11**), belonged to God alone. Man therefore had no right over blood and consequently animal bloodshed was a crime, punishable by civil excommunication. The animal therefore must be killed at the tabernacle, the blood poured out at the base of the altar and the fat portions burnt on the altar. **7.** Another reason for the prohibition of domestic slaughter of animals was the danger of idolatrous and superstitious practices. If the Israelites had been allowed to kill their animals anywhere, they would hardly have resisted the inclination to offer sacrifices to the desert gods in the shape of goats (now called 'satyrs') whom they worshipped so often. (Idolatrous worship, generally involving prostitution, is called in the OT 'fornication'; cf Ex 34:15, 16; Dt 31:16; Jg 2:17; 8:27, 33; etc). This was a temporary regulation meant for the time of the desert wanderings. When the people settled down in Canaan, it became impracticable and had to be modified, making the killing of an animal at home permissible (Dt 12:15). The words 'a statute for ever' mean as long as possible and necessary.

c 8–9 The Place of the Sacrifice—All sacrifices, whether holocausts or otherwise, must be made in the tabernacle, and transgressions are punishable by excommunication. This law, unlike the preceding one, binds resident foreigners also and was never abrogated nor modified, but was further developed in Dt 12:5–14.

d 10–12 The Use of Blood—On the prohibition to eat flesh with blood cf Gn 9:4; Ac 15:20. It is based on primitive physiological conceptions and on religious grounds. Blood is the seat of life, and as such is best suited for expiation. The relation between expiation and the blood or life of an animal is commonly explained by the substitution theory according to which the blood of an animal is accepted by God as a substitute for man's life. There is a *penal substitution* and a substitution which we may call simply *symbolical*. The supporters of the penal substitution theory explain the expiatory virtue of blood by the supposition that the animal is killed instead of the death-deserving sinner, and the blood of an animal is accepted by God for the blood of man (see Médebielle, 114–65, and more recently in DBS art. *Expiation*). According to the non-penal or symbolical substitution theory the victim stands before God not as a substitute of a death-deserving man but as a concrete expression of the offerer's internal sentiments of repentance, love, adoration, etc, and the victim's blood or life is accepted by God as the expression of these sentiments. It is in view of these internal sentiments transferred symbolically to the victim by the imposition of hands that the blood or life becomes an efficacious means of re-establishing normal relations between God and man; see A. Metzinger, *Die Substitutionstheorie und das alttestamentliche Opfer* in Bib 21 (1940) 159–87, esp. 176f, 247–72, 353–77. The latter theory seems to me preferable because it can be applied to all forms of sacrifice; but it is by no means excluded that in particular cases an offerer may have expressed by his sacrifice and

especially by the imposition of hands his sense of death- **203d** guiltiness which he transferred to the victim.

It should be remarked, however, that the theory of **e** penal substitution has no support in **11** which in MT reads thus: 'Because the life of the flesh is in the blood, and I have given it to you (to be brought) upon the altar that you may make atonement (by it) for your lives, because the blood makes atonement by means of the life (which is in it)'. LXX has wrongly translated the phrase 'by means of the life' as 'instead of life', i.e. 'of your lives'. The offering of blood, therefore, represents the offering of life, and the offering of an animal's life symbolizes the offering of man's life. In this sense we may say that the blood of an animal is a substitute for human life.

15–16 The Eating of Dead Animals—This law binds **f** both the Israelite and the resident foreigner, but according to Dt 14:21 these foreigners are allowed to eat of an animal which dies a natural death.

18:1–5 Prohibition of Unlawful Marriages—On **g** the whole subject see E. Neufeld, *Ancient Hebrew Marriage Laws* (1944) 191–212. The immoral practices of the Egyptians and the Canaanites are condemned, and God's will is to be Israel's only guide. Life and temporal prosperity (though spiritual rewards are not excluded) are promised to those who walk in the way of the Lord. **5b** is cited in Rm 10:5 and Gal 3:12. The expression 'I am the Lord your God' at the beginning and at the end adds solemnity to the enactments which follow and may be compared with similar formulas in royal decrees.

6–18 Forbidden Degrees of Kinship—No man shall **h** have sexual intercourse with a woman who is near of kin to him. This is a general prohibition specified by the following list of degrees of relationship: (i) a son and his mother (**7**); (ii) a son and his step-mother (**8**); this must have been a common case in polygamous families, cf Gn 49:3; (iii) a brother and his paternal or maternal half-sister (**9**); the case of a marriage of a brother with his sister, though not expressly mentioned, is implied in this; (iv) a father and his granddaughter (**10**); (v) a brother and his step-sister (**11**); this case is already contemplated in **9** unless we read there 'and' instead of 'or' thus making the half-sister a full sister and supplying the missing case; (vi) a nephew and his paternal aunt (**12**); (vii) a nephew and his maternal aunt (**13**); (viii) a nephew and his uncle's wife (**14**); (ix) a father and his daughter-in-law (**15**); (x) a brother and his sister-in-law (**16**); see however the exception in Dt 25:5ff; (xi) a father and his step-daughter (**17a**); a father and the daughter of his stepson or his stepdaughter (**17b**); (xii) a husband and his living wife's sister (**18**); but marriage with a deceased wife's sister was not prohibited. Jacob's marriages with the two sisters Leah and Rachel were not in conformity with this law. On the whole the Levitical marriage legislation is stricter than that of the patriarchal age, thus pointing to a more developed social organization.

19–23 Certain Cases of Unchastity and Molech i Worship—Sexual relations with one's lawful wife during the menstruation period are forbidden; see also 15:24; 20:18. Molech worship consisting in sacrificing children as burnt-offerings is severely condemned; cf 2 Kgs 23:10; Ezek 20:31; and E. Mader, *Die Menschenopfer der alten Hebräer*, in Bib St XIV, 5, 6; A. Bea, *Kinderopfer für Moloch oder für Jahwe?* Bib 18 (1937) 95–107.

24–30 Parenetic Conclusion—In the introduction, **j** 1–5, life and prosperity are promised to those who keep God's commandments, the conclusion threatens transgressors with the loss of the land which God is about to give them.

E

203k 19:1—37 A Miscellany of Laws—This is a heterogeneous collection of laws regulating the domestic and social life of the Israelites and inculcating the necessity of holiness as a condition of fellowship with God.

1—4 Introduction—Parental respect, the observance of the sabbath and prohibition of idolatry; cf the decalogue Ex 20:1—12.

l 5—8 Peace-offerings—Cf 7:16—18.

9—10 Gleaning in the Cornfield and the Vineyard—The corn was not to be reaped up to the corner of the field, but a strip was to be left for the poor, and the ears that slipped out of the reapers' hands were also to be left for them. Cf the story of Ruth. Some bunches of grapes were also to be left to be gathered by the poor. Cf 23:22 and Dt 24:19—21.

m 11—14 Duties of Justice towards One's Neighbours—Unjust dealing is forbidden. The poor hireling must receive his wages daily. Unkind treatment of helpless persons is forbidden; cf Dt 24:14, 15.

n 15—18 Righteousness and Love for One's Neighbour—Justice must be administered irrespective of social positions. One interpretation of **16b** is: You shall not stand by when your neighbour's life is in peril. Another: You shall not withhold your true witness against a murderer. Or: You shall not endanger your neighbour's life by slander. Mutual love and fraternal correction are commanded, and feelings of hatred and vengeance must be uprooted from the heart. **18**. Note that the OT conception of 'neighbour' was restricted to one's fellow-nationals. Love was first limited to fellow-Israelites, and then extended to the resident aliens (33, 34). But the grand commandment of universal love was first proclaimed by our Lord; cf Mt 5:43, 44 and WV ad loc.

o 19 Unlawful Mixtures—The breeding together of cattle of different species, the sowing of a field with two kinds of seed, the wearing of garments woven of two sorts, wool and linen, are forbidden. The prohibition in a slightly modified form occurs again in Dt 22:5, 9—11. 'The motive of the prohibition', writes S. R. Driver, 'appears to be the preservation of natural distinctions: species . . . are designed by God to be distinct (cf Gen 1:11, 12, 21, 24, 25); each possesses its own characteristic features; and a principle thus visibly impressed by the Creator upon nature is not to be interfered with by man' (*Deuteronomy* in ICC, 252). This principle of individual existence applied to religion was meant to safeguard the integrity of the Israelite religion against any foreign heathenish infiltrations.

p 23—25 Firstfruits—The fruit of trees newly planted in the land of Canaan shall for the first three years (**23**) be considered as uncircumcised infants and consequently unconsecrated, unclean, unfit to be offered to God. In the fourth year the fruit must be offered to God, and in the fifth the people are permitted to eat of it. The reason for this injunction is that fruit trees must be allowed to attain their full development before their fruit is offered to God or eaten by man.

26a Blood Eating again forbidden—See 17:10.

q 26b—31 Magic and Superstition—Divination and augury so very widely practised in the E are forbidden. The cutting off of the hair or a part of it was, with certain Arab tribes, a superstitious practice. Cuttings in the flesh or lacerations as a sign of mourning, and tattooing are condemned on account of their heathenish associations (W. R. Smith, 334). In **29** the reference is probably to sacred prostitution although the prohibition as worded comprehends all prostitution. The Israelites must not consult those who conjure *ghosts* (cf 1 Sm 28), nor those who pretend to receive extraordinary knowledge from

their 'familiar' spirit. Any connection with diviners 203 would be a source of moral defilement.

32—34 Rules of Behaviour—Old age deserves respect and resident foreigners must be treated with affection.

35—36 Righteousness in Judgements and Honesty in Trade—Cf Dt 25:13—16. The bushel is the approximate equivalent of the Heb. *ephah*. The *hin* is about $1\frac{1}{2}$ gallons.

20:1—21 Punitive Sanction of the Preceding r Laws—This is a penal code supplementing the criminal code contained in ch 18. Certain penalties may appear disproportionate to the gravity of the offence, but they must be estimated according to the standards of the times. In the Code of Hammurabi many similar offences were punished by death (C. H. W. Johns in HDB, V, 584—612).

2—5 Molech Worship = 18:21—Stoning is the penalty inflicted on the offender. If the people take no heed of the offence, God himself will punish the offender by cutting him off from among his people. This divine punishment is not banishment from one's city, but death in some unspecified manner. Fornication in **5** and very often in the OT denotes unfaithfulness to God, idolatry.

6 Consulting Diviners = 19:31—Death is inflicted by God himself as above.

9 Cursing a Parent is punished by death; cf 19:3; s Ex 21:17. And the offender is held responsible for his own death. In § 195 of the Code of Hammurabi a man who struck his father had his hands cut off.

10 Adultery—The penalty is the death of both parties. Cf 18:20; Dt 22:22 and § 129 of the Code of Hammurabi.

11—21. The cases contemplated correspond to those in 18:8, 15, 22, 18, 23, 10, 19, 12, 14, 16 respectively.

22—26 Hortatory Conclusion—The ultimate reason for keeping these laws is God's holiness on which the writer insists so strongly and so often; cf 19:2; 20:7f. If God is holy, his people must be holy. The holiness of the people demands their separation from other peoples considered as unholy. The discrimination between clean and unclean food was also meant to emphasize the idea of Israel's separateness from other nations.

27 Against Witchcraft—This precept is supplementary to 19:31 and 20:6, where the Israelites are forbidden to consult magicians.

21:1—22:16 The Holiness of Priests—(i) In their t domestic life (21:1—15) and (ii) in the discharge of their priestly duties (21:16—22:16).

1—9 Regulations concerning Priests in general—As contact with a dead body produces uncleanness lasting seven days (Nm 19:11), priests, who must always be ceremonially clean in order to be fit to offer the offerings of the Lord, are forbidden to mourn for any person except those who live in the same house. 4 is obscure in Heb and still more so in Vg. Probably the sense is: If he is married, he must not defile himself for his wife's relatives. The shaving of the head or, more precisely, of the forehead (Dt 14:1), the cutting of the corners of the beard, the scratching of the body were signs of mourning and superstitious practices; cf 19:27 f. The character of their wives must be above suspicion, because the priest is consecrated to God.

10—15 Analogous Regulations concerning the High- u Priest—These were stricter and significant of the higher degree of sanctity inherent in the dignity of the high-priest. It was not permitted to him to mourn even for his parents. He was not to depart from the sanctuary where he resided or where he was officiating, because on his return he would defile it. He must marry a virgin, otherwise his children would be unholy.

03v 16–24 Physical Disqualifications for the Priesthood—The following blemishes were considered as canonical irregularities: blindness, lameness, hare-lip (?), congenital malformation, leg or hand fracture, to be crook-backed, dwarfness (or perhaps, emaciation), defective sight (?), scab, scurvy, crushed testicles. The persons affected were not unclean and therefore were not excluded from a share of the sacred offerings.

w 22:1–9 Ceremonial Disqualifications in Priests to partake of a Sacrificial Meal—The priests must be careful not to touch the holy offerings when they are in a condition of ceremonial impurity. Any transgression will be punished by degradation. On the impurities mentioned in **4–7** see chh 11 and 13–15; on **8** see 17:15.

x 10–16 Those Permitted to eat of the Priests' Portion—The general rule is that only the members of a priests's family and those considered to belong thereto have the right to eat of the sacred offerings. Strangers have no right because they do not form part of the priest's household. A person living with a priest for a short time and a priest's hireling are not considered as members of his family.

y 17–25 Animals Disqualified for Sacrifice—Animals offered for sacrifice must have no blemish in order that they may be acceptable to God. Such tainted victims are never accepted, not even if they are offered by a foreigner. On this general prohibition see Mal 1:8, 13.

z 26–30 Further Regulations concerning Sacrificial Victims—These directions rest on humanitarian motives and are meant also to develop a stronger sense of parental affection. **31–33 Hortatory Conclusion.** Cf 20:22–26.

04a 23:1–44 A Festal Calendar—This is a popular liturgical calendar regulating divine worship and prescribing the religious observances of each feast day; cf Nm 28 and 29; Dt 16.

1 3 The Sabbath—The mention of the Sabbath is very probably an insertion made by a reviser desiring to make a complete list. Note the repetition of the introductory formula: 'These are the feasts of the Lord' in **2** and **4**; cf 184b.

4–14 The Passover—For its institution see Ex 12. The paschal observances were: attendance at the sanctuary on the first and the seventh day; abstention from servile work, but not from ordinary domestic work, during these two days; offering of sacrifices during the seven days of the festival. A ritual feature consisted in presenting a sheaf, the first-fruits of the harvest, to be waved by the priest before the Lord. On the waving ceremony see 7:30. This was done 'the next day after the sabbath' (**11**), the sabbath here denoting the first day of the paschal week, or, more probably, the sabbath falling during that week. The offering of the sheaf was a communal, not a private, offering. The consumption of the new crop became lawful only after the offering of the first sheaf. But bread could not be eaten before Pentecost (**17**).

15–22 Pentecost or the Feast of Weeks—Its date fell seven weeks or fifty days after the offering of the first sheaf. This chronological relation between the Passover and Pentecost still survives in our liturgy. On this day a *new offering* is made by the whole community. In Nm 28:27 the victims are slightly different. This may be due to textual corruption in either text. Attendance at the sanctuary and abstention from servile work are obligatory. **22** is an insertion from 19:9.

b 23–25 New Year's Day—There were at least two ways of reckoning the year. The religious year, which regulated the annual cycle of festivals, commenced with Nisan (= March–Apr.) in the spring (Ex 12:2), and the civil year

commenced with Tishri (= Sept.–Oct.) in the autumn, **204b** as is still the Jewish practice today (Mishnah, tr. *Rosh ha-shanah*). Therefore the first day of the seventh month was the beginning of the civil year. The religious observances were: blowing of trumpets (cf Ps 81 (80):4), attendance at the sanctuary, abstention from servile work and offerings as specified in Nm 29:1–6.

26–32 The Day of Atonement—See ch 16, especially 29–34.

33–36 The Feast of Tabernacles—Its date is fixed for the full moon day of Tishri, the seventh month. The celebrations last seven days and include abstention from servile work, attendance at the sanctuary and sacrifices. The eighth day was a supernumerary day marked by an '*aṣeret* which is commonly taken to mean 'assembly', but is probably a technical term denoting abstention from work. The expression 'you shall do no servile work' would then be a popular way of expressing abstention from work. Supplementary instructions are given in 39–43. See also Nm 29:7–11; Dt 16:13–15, § 105h.

37–38 Subscription to the Calendar.

39–43 Supplementary Regulations concerning the c Feast of Tabernacles—This seems to be an addition made when the calendar had already been closed. Here the festival is associated with the gathering of all the crops, though elsewhere it is connected with the wanderings in the desert. Its characteristic feature was that during the seven days the Israelites were to dwell in booths. On the first day they carried in their hands fruits of beautiful trees, identified by a later tradition with the *ethrog* or citron, branches of palm trees, boughs of thick trees or, according to tradition, boughs of myrtle and willows of the brook. See Edersheim, 232–49. **44** is another conclusion which became necessary after the insertion of 39–43.

24:1–9 Instructions respecting the Lamps of the d Tabernacle and the Shewbread—This section forms an erratic block apparently detached from Ex 25–28. The reason for its actual position here and its relation to the law of holiness are matters of conjecture. **1–4** on the oil for the lamps are almost a verbal repetition of Ex 27:20f.

5–9 The Shewbread—See Ex 25:30. Twelve cakes made of fine flour were to be placed in two symmetrical rows or piles on the golden table outside the veil of the sanctuary. Frankincense was put upon them in order with its sweet odour to remind God of the offering. They were a communal offering, not a sacrifice (**9**), and were most sacred. As they belonged to God, they could not be eaten except by the priests. Later references to the shewbread occur in 1 Sm 21:3–6;1(3) Kgs 7:48; cf also Mt 12:3f.

This practice of placing loaves upon a table before the deity was wide-spread and reflected the popular belief that gods, like men, needed daily nourishment (W. R. Smith, 225f). But though the Israelitic practice may be a survival from an earlier stage of religious development, it acquired a higher significance. The bread was placed before God not for his nourishment but as a concrete expression of the nation's gratitude to God, the Giver of bread and all good things.

10–16, 23 The Blasphemer—Blasphemy was always e regarded as one of the gravest offences. Later Judaism went so far as to forbid any mention of the Sacred Name substituting Adonai 'the Lord' for Yahweh in the reading of the Scripture. This is a divine ruling to the effect that a blasphemer should be put to death. The witnesses then laid their hands on the offender's head thus signifying that he must bear the burden of his sin, and the whole congregation stoned him to death.

17–22 The Law of Talion—The provisions here laid down are based on the principle of criminal law current

204e among the Babylonians and the Arabs of the desert, namely, the law of retaliation ('lex talionis'); cf Ex 21:23—25 and the Code of Hammurabi, §§ 116, 200, 210, 219, 229, 232, 245, 263.

25:1—55 The Sabbatical Year and the Year of Jubilee—Two different institutions, which at certain times coincided, form the object of the regulations in this chapter. For the sake of clarity we will deal with the two institutions separately.

f **1—7, 20—22 The Sabbatical Year**—This law is parallel to the law of the Sabbath (Ex 20:8—11). As a period of six days is followed by a day of rest, so a period of six years is followed by a year of rest. The two laws have a religious and a humanitarian motive. After six days' work man must have a day's rest and turn his mind to God; in the same manner the land, after having for six years exerted its full powers, must have a year's rest. Periodical fallow years were, and are still, normal in the agriculture of many countries, but the fixing of the fallow year permanently in the seventh year and the relation between the rest day and the rest year mark off the Hebrew institution from similar practices. In the seventh year it was not permitted to sow or to prune the vine. The spontaneous growth of the land could not be stored, but could only be gathered when needed for food by the owner of the field and his dependants (6) as well as by the poor people of the country (Ex 23:11). An assurance of divine providence in the shape of an abundant yield in the sixth year was intended to remove any apprehensiveness as to the sufficiency of the means of subsistence during the seventh year (20—22). The produce of the sixth year was to last not only for that year, but also for the following year and till the harvest time of the eighth year; therefore practically for three years (21).

g **8—19, 23—55 The Year of Jubilee**—This institution is but another form of the week-institution based on the same principle of a period of seven time-units the last one of which is consecrated to God, the time-unit in this case being a seven-year period and the day of rest being transferred to the year following the seven septennial periods. This year, which was the 50th year, was called the year of jubilee from Heb. *yôbēl* which passed into our languages through Greek and Latin. The word *yôbēl* means 'a ram's horn used as a cornet' hence 'the blowing of cornets' and metonymically 'a festival or an extraordinary occurrence announced by the blowing of cornets' (BDB s.v.). The jubilee year was an institution of a social and economic character based on religious considerations. Its characteristic features were: (i) a fallow year; (ii) the reverting of property to its former owners; (iii) the emancipation of slaves; (iv) the suspension or, perhaps, the remission of debts. Some of these features were known to other peoples (see C. H. Gordon, RB 1935, 38—41; R. North, *Sociology of the biblical Jubilee*, 1954; R de Vaux, AI. The relation of meaning between the Hebrew jubilee and the Catholic jubilee is obvious; cf also Lk 4:19.

8—12 Institution of the Jubilee—The year of jubilee began on the tenth day of the seventh month (Tishri), that is, on the Day of Atonement and was announced by the blowing of trumpets. At the same time a proclamation went round that general release was granted, namely, that all landed property that had been sold, reverted to its original owners, and slaves were sent free to their families. It was also a fallow year, 11f.

h **13—19, 23—24 Alienation of Land**—The law regulating the purchase of land was based on the fact that God was the sole owner and man had only the use thereof. Consequently no one could sell his property outright; all

he could do was to sell the usufruct, and even this sale 204 was valid only to the next jubilee. In the jubilee year the usufruct thus acquired would expire and the land revert to its original owner. This law involves another social-economic principle, namely, that property is inseparably attached to the family.

25—28 Redemption of Land— This is a general provision of law based on the last-mentioned principle and contemplating, amongst other cases, one to which the jubilee concessions are applicable.

35—38 Prohibition of Usury—It was forbidden to i receive any sort of interest on money or on food from an Israelite. An impoverished Israelite must be given such help as is accorded to anyone who receives hospitality at one's house.

39—55 Emancipation of Slaves—An Israelite who has j sold himself to another Israelite is set free in the jubilee year. Permanent servitude and ill-treatment are forbidden. God is their only master. Slaves were to be bought from other nations, and these were to be bond-servants for life. This different treatment was in accordance with the privileged position of Israel as God's chosen people.

The apparent discrepancy between the Levitical law on slavery and the parallel law in Ex 21:2ff and Dt 15:12 is easily explained. Slaves were to regain their liberty in the sabbatical year. As the interval between two consecutive sabbatical years was six years, a six-year service was the maximum period for which a Hebrew slave could be made to serve. The six-year servitude, therefore, of Ex and Dt is to be taken as a maximum period, not as an invariable duration. The sabbatical year being a year of release, and the jubilee year being for all legal purposes a sabbatical year, it is evident that the same concessions are accorded to both. If an Israelite is a slave of a resident foreigner he must be set free in the year of jubilee. But he may be redeemed before that year, the price of redemption being proportionate to the number of years intervening before the jubilee, as in the case of land (25—27).

26:1—2 Prohibition of Idolatry—This is a repetition of precepts which are found in other parts of the law of holiness; cf 19:3f. k

3—46 Hortatory Conclusion—For similar exhortations see Ex 23:24—33; Lv 20:22—27; Dt 28.

3—13 The Blessings of Obedience—Blessings for this life are promised to those who obey God's law. These blessings must be taken in their literal and proper sense in accordance with the spirit of the OT religion which had to be adapted to the mentality of a primitive people in order to train them up to higher ideals of an unseen world by means of promises of material blessings. Spiritual blessings, however, are not excluded.

14—39 The Curses of Disobedience—These are l arranged in groups, each one being introduced by a statement of the people's obstinacy. 34. Then after the people's deportation the land will enjoy a rest, the sabbatical rest to which it is entitled and which it had not enjoyed on account of the people's disregard of the law. In this manner the land will pay back its due to God. And those who survive this terrible ordeal will drag on a miserable existence in the land of their enemies on account of their iniquities and those of their fathers.

40—46 Repentance and Restoration—God's temporal m punishments are corrective not vindictive. When their purpose is achieved forgiveness is granted. If the Israelites in the land of their exile confess their sins which have provoked God's anger, if they humble their insensible hearts acknowledging their punishment as an expiation for their sins, God will remember his covenant

4m and will take them once more for his people. No mention of the return from the exile is made here as in Dt 30:3—5; here the restoration is represented as an accomplishment of God's promises to the patriarchs and not merely as a return to the land of their fathers.

n **D. Appendix. Commutation of Vows and Tithes (ch 27).**

27:1—29 On Vows—The general law is that man is not obliged to make a vow; but if he does, he is under an obligation to fulfil it (Dt 23:21—3). The Levitical legislation deals only with the commutation of vows and contemplates the cases of a person, cattle, houses and lands being offered to God by vow.

14—15 Houses—The regulations for unclean animals apply also to houses.

o **16—25 Fields**—Two cases are contemplated. **16—21.** As no inherited land can be alienated in perpetuity, the consecration of a field to God is only of temporary duration lasting till the next year of jubilee. Its price therefore will have to be lowered according to the number of years since the last jubilee. The person consecrating a field has always the right of redemption as in the case of unclean animals and houses. If he fails to redeem it, his right will lapse, and in the jubilee year the field, instead of reverting to its original owner, will fall to the priests as sacred property. **22—25.** If a field belongs to its owner by purchase, as the purchase is only temporary (25:14—17), the consecration is also temporary, and in the year of jubilee the field will revert to the vendor. All these transactions must be made on the basis of the sacred shekel which is worth 20 *gerahs* or obols, the gerah or obol being equivalent to about ¾d. **26—27 What may not be vowed**—According to Ex 13:13 the firstling of an ass, a non-sacrificial animal, must be redeemed by a lamb.

28—29 Things interdicted—The technical Heb. word **204p** expressing religious interdict is *herem*, Vg and DV *anathema*. The fundamental meaning of *herem* is 'separation, seclusion' and, in a religious sense, the separation of a thing from ordinary use and its dedication to God. Hence the biblical notion of *herem* is 'a thing or person irrevocably withdrawn from common use and entirely devoted to God'. This general notion may be split up into two apparently opposite, though closely related, notions. A thing may be devoted to God either because it is agreeable to him, or because it is dangerous to the religious life of the people and therefore disagreeable to him. The first meaning naturally involves the idea of consecration, the other that of destruction. What is irrevocably devoted to God, whether a man, animal or field, can neither be sold nor redeemed. If it is a thing consecrated to God, it goes to the priests for their maintenance or for the temple-service (Nm 18:14; Ezek 44:29); if it is harmful to the religious interests, it must be utterly destroyed (Ex 22:20; Nm 21:2f; Dt 7:2; Jos 7; 1 Sm 15; etc.).

30—33 Tithes—One-tenth of all the agricultural produce **q** went yearly to the Lord and was given to the Levites for their maintenance (Nm 18:21). Tithes however were redeemable on payment of an additional fifth part of their estimated value. But the tithes of cattle were not redeemable nor commutable. Every tenth animal passing under the rod, while the flock or herd was being counted on entering or leaving the fold, was separated from the others and consecrated to God. Though the animals were counted daily, tithes were paid once a year only.

34 Conclusion—This is a conclusion not of the appendix only but of the whole book.

NUMBERS

BY P. P. SAYDON

205a Bibliography—*Commentaries*: H. Cazelles, BJ, 1952; H. Schneider, EchB, 1955; J. Marsh and A. G. Butzer, IB, 1953; G. B. Gray, ICC, 1903; A. McNeile, CBSC, 1911; L. E. Binns, *Westminster Comm.* 1927; P. Heinisch, BB, 1936; A. Clamer, PCSB. N. H. Snaith, C Bi.[2] 1967. *For reference*: F. M. Abel, *Géographie de la Palestine*, 2 vols 1933—8; W. R. Smith, *The Religion of the Semites*, 1927[3]; A. Clamer, art. *Nombres* in DTC; P. van Imschoot, *Théologie de l'AT*, 1956.

b Title—Numbers, the title of the fourth book of the Pent, is derived from the Gr. *arithmoi* through the Latin *Numeri*. It occurs in our oldest MSS B and S and may probably be referred to a pre-Christian origin (H. B. Swete, *An Introd. to the OT in Greek*, 1914, 215). In our modern editions of the Heb. Bible it is called *bᵉmidbār* 'in the wilderness', which is the fifth word of the book, but in older times it was called *wayᵉdabbēr* 'and [Yahweh] spoke', the opening words of the book (Jer, *Praef. in libros Sam. et Mal.*, PL 28, 552).

c Contents—The Gr.-Lat. title fails to convey any idea of the contents. The chh relating the numbering of the people, occupy a very small and not very important part of the book. The Heb. title is more indicative of the wanderings of the Israelites in the wilderness from the Sinaitic region to the plains of Moab. The Israelites had been for about one year in Sinai where they had received a religious and a social constitution. After being thus socially and religiously organized they moved northwards in the direction of Canaan. On arriving at Kadesh they attempted to invade the country from the S, but were defeated and had to turn back. For many years they wandered in the wilderness. Balaam the magician was called by the king of Moab to curse the Israelites, but God turned the magician's words into a blessing and a promise of further conquests. The Midianites were conquered, and the land E of the Jordan allotted to the tribes of Reuben and Gad and the half-tribe of Manasseh. Instructions were given for the division of the land of Canaan. Interspersed among the various episodes are a few groups of laws which are loosely connected with the narrative and can hardly be classified under headings.

d Structure and Analysis—The Book is made up of narratives and legislation. The historical narrative has many wide gaps which render the reconstruction of the history of the wanderings impossible. But this lack of unity and proportion is often exaggerated. On closer examination it is not difficult to discover at least the main lines and the leading ideas of the whole narrative. The book falls into three main sections: (1) (1:1—10:10) relating the last events in the Sinai region; (2) (10:11—22:1) relating some of the events which took place during the desert wanderings; (3) (22:2—36:13) relating the events in Moab.

e Part 1 is apparently an appendix to Ex and Lv, but it is also, at least in its general lines, an introduction to Part 2. The establishment of the tribal divisions round the tabernacle was a practical means to ensure a regular march **205** (10:5f). Part 2 is the main part of the book but it is not a continuous narrative; only a few isolated events are picked out. Rather than a history of the wanderings in the desert we have a few selected narratives illustrating the people's ingratitude and lack of faith, and the justice and fidelity of God who punishes the ungrateful people, but in such a manner as not to render his promises void. Part 3 is an account of the end of the journey, the first conquests and the arrangements concerning the occupation and the division of the land of Canaan.

In each part there is a group of laws interrupting the **f** development of the narrative. They are generally very loosely connected with the context and with each other. Some of them supplement previous laws, as 5:5—8 and Lv 6:1—7; 9:6—14 and Ex 12; 15:1—15 and Lv chh 1—5. Others introduce completely new matter as the Nazirite regulations in 6:1—21.

The book appears to be of a highly complex composition **g** containing as it does materials of widely differing character and date, some of great antiquity. The generally accepted analysis of the book ascribes the contents to the strata J, E, and P, the greater part being from P, see § 134*b*. J and E furnish the narrative with ancient stories and sagas dating from the period of the desert-wanderings and the early days of the occupation of Canaan. Of particular interest are the Balaam stories, ch 22—24, which have come down to us from more than one source. All these diverse materials have been worked over subsequently and edited on more than one occasion. We notice the tendency here as elsewhere to read back into the days of Moses, religious and social developments of a later age. In some instances, moreover, we can discern an idealization and magnifying of what was in all probability a smaller and more ordinary occurrence. The whole narrative is presented by the latest editor as a record of events that took place during the wanderings in the wilderness.

Religious Teaching—Some of the religious truths of **h** Lv, such as the holiness and unapproachableness of God, the sanctity demanded of his worshippers and particularly of his ministers are common to Nm. In addition, this book is concerned to bring out the following: 1. The Institution of ecclesiastical hierarchy. The divine service was to be performed by one tribe alone chosen by God (1:51; 3:5—13; 16). Divine vocation was absolutely necessary, and any usurpation of rights was severely punished (1:51; 16; 18:7). The hierarchy consisted of three grades: the high-priest, the ordinary priests and the Levites. They had different rights and different duties. As they served at the sanctuary, they derived their maintenance from the sanctuary. 2. God's presence with his people, his care of, and love for, them. This is illustrated by the cloud ever present amidst the people (9:15—23) and God's explicit declaration (35:34); by his responsive attitude to the needs of the people (11:31f; 20:2—13); by the assistance given to them to defeat their enemies and to conquer their lands (chh 21—31). 3. God's punitive justice and unchangeableness of purpose. Sin is always punished **05h** irrespective of the condition of the sinner. The people are punished (11:1—3, 33; 21:6; 25:1—5, 6—13); tribal chiefs are punished (14:36f); the Levites are punished (ch 16); Mary is punished (12:10); Moses and Aaron are punished (20:12). But the people are not totally exterminated, and so God's promises stand firm; cf Ez 20:18—22. 4. The power of intercession. 'The continual prayer of a just man availeth much' (Jas 5:16). Moses, the faithful servant in the Lord's house (12:7; Hb 3:5) repeatedly and successfully interceded with God for his unfaithful people (12:11—14; 14:11—24).

Part 1. 1:1—10:10 LAST EVENTS AT SINAI

06a **1—4 Before the Departure from Sinai. 1 The Census of the Twelve Tribes**—The reason for this census is not stated. Allusions to a census in view of a religious tax occur in Ex 30:12; 38:25. The total number of Israelites under the leadership of Moses is given on three most important occasions: when they set out from Egypt to Palestine (Ex 12:37), when they marched off from Sinai towards Palestine (Nm 1), and when they were about to enter Palestine (Nm 26). There appears therefore to be in the mind of the writer a relation between the number of Israelites and the ultimate destination of their journey. This relation accounts for the numbering of the people better than any supposed motive of taxation and military service.

b **1—19 The Appointment of 12 Tribal Representatives**—The census was to be carried out on the basis of military fitness or, better, on the principle that the age of 20 marked the beginning of manhood and that the real strength of a nation was represented by its fully-grown male members. Each tribe was to be numbered clan by clan and family by family. The tribe of Levi was not to be included (47).

c **20—46 The Numbers of the Several Tribes**—The order of the tribes is slightly different in LXX The historical accuracy of the numbers given for each tribe can hardly be maintained (Gray, 11—15). A total of 603,550 males from 20 years upwards represents a population of well over 2,000,000, including women and children. There are other instances of similar numerical inflations (cf 1 Sm 6:19), which are best explained, sometimes as part of the literary form and sometimes as textual corruptions.

d **47—54 The Levites not Numbered**—The sacred duties of the Levites, as specified in 50f, account for their not being numbered with the other tribes. They had no civil duties and therefore, constitutionally, they did not form part of the civil population, but were, so to say, an independent unit, a religious group under ecclesiastical jurisdiction. No one but Levites had the right to approach the tabernacle. Intruders were punished by death. This unapproachableness of God symbolized the unbridgeable distance between God and man. On the priesthood and the Levites, see § 104b—f.

e **2 The Arrangement of the Camp**—The encampment was a vast quadrilateral with the central quadrangle occupied by the tabernacle, cf § 103e. The Israelites were to pitch their tents on the four sides of the tabernacle, three tribes on each side, and everyone with his own company and under the ensign of his family. Judah was to encamp on the eastern side. This position of honour was a sign of the pre-eminence promised to Judah by his father (Gn 49:8ff). The ch reflects later religious developments.

f **3—4 The Levites, their Numbers and Duties**—

The sacerdotal legislation of Lv makes no mention of the **206f** Levites, all priestly duties being performed by the sons of Aaron. The institution of the Levitical order is first narrated here. The genealogical relation between the priests and the Levites was as follows: the priests were the direct descendants of Aaron, the son of Amram, son of Kohath, son of Levi (Ex 6:16—20); the Levites were the descendants of Levi by other branches. The priesthood was reserved to the sons of Aaron, who were assisted in their duties by the Levites, cf AI, 387—400.

3:1—4 The Priests—The Aaronic priests were Eleazar **g** and Ithamar and their offspring; Nadab and Abihu having died without issue (Lv 10:1f). Moses' name in 1 is unnecessary because his descendants had no right to the priesthood, but were simply Levites. On the concept of the Aaronic priesthood, see § 138 h—i.

5—10 The Order of the Levites—The Levites are **h** appointed to assist the priests in their service, such as the offering of sacrifices, and the community in their duties towards the sanctuary, to do all the work of the tabernacle and to take care of its furniture (cf 1:50). They are given to Aaron and his descendants as a gift from the children of Israel, but the priesthood will be the exclusive right of the Aaronites, and any encroachment on their rights will be punished by death.

11—13 The Substitution of the Levites for the **i** **Firstborn**—All the firstborn of Israel, representing as they do the first reproduction of life by a married couple, belong to God, the source of life. They became peculiarly his when he smote the firstborn of Egypt (Ex 13). They must therefore be devoted to his service. As this however was hardly practicable, God substituted the males of the tribe of Levi for the male firstborn of the other tribes. Thus the Levites became 'sanctified', i.e. separated from the rest and dedicated to the divine service.

14—39 The Census of the Levites, their Stations and **j** **Charges**—The Levites were divided into three main divisions descending from the three sons of Levi, Gershon, Kohath and Merari respectively (Ex 6:16). They were to be numbered from the age of one month, because the firstborn were not redeemable before that age (Nm 18:16). They camped on three sides of the Tabernacle. The eastern side was reserved to Moses and the priests. The camp of the Levites was between that of the Israelites and the tabernacle. The total number of the Levites was 22,000. The priests were not included. On the value of these numbers see note to 1:20—46.

40—51 The Substitution of the Levites—The substitution enjoined in 3:11—13 is carried into effect. The **k** census of the redeemable firstborn yielded a total of 22,273 with an excess of 273 over the number of Levites. As there were no more Levites to substitute for the surplus firstborn, these were redeemed by the payment of 5 shekels (c. 12s 6d) apiece. The proceeds were handed over to the priests.

4:1—49 The Numbers of the Serving Levites and **l** **their Duties**—In ch 3 the Levites were numbered in view of their substitution for the firstborn; here they are numbered in view of their special duties. In ch 3 their service is described in a general way; here it is defined more particularly. On account of the heavy work of transport of the ark, the tabernacle and its furniture they entered upon their service at the age of 30 and were released at 50. In 8:23—26 the period of Levitical service is from 25 to 50, and in 1 Chr 23:24—27 from 20 and upwards; cf also 2 Chr 31:17; Ez 3:8. The difference may be easily explained by the nature of the duties they had to perform; see on 8:23—26. As the Levites could not touch these sacred objects, the priests did all the

206l preliminary work of wrapping them up, fitting them with staves and placing those which could not be so fitted upon a sort of wagon.

207a **5:1—10:10 A Miscellany of Laws and Narratives**—Some of these regulations and narratives, e.g. ch 7, would have had a better place in Ex; others, as 5:5—6, 27 belong to the Levitical legislation; a few, as 5:1—4, 10:1—10, are supplemental to chh 1—4.

b **5:1—4 The Removal of Unclean Persons from the Camp**—The camp, God's dwelling-place among his people, had to be kept clean by the removal of lepers (Lv 13), those who suffered from a discharge (Lv 15) and those who were defiled by contact with the dead (Nm 19). Lepers were always excluded from cities (2 Kgs 7:3; 15:5); natural discharges too involved exclusion from the military camp (Dt 23:9—11).

c **5—10 Reparation for Certain Offences, and Sacred Gifts**—The regulation contained in **6—8** contemplates the case when the person to whom compensation for damages is due is dead and there is no relative to represent him. If a person commits a sin that causes material damage to another person (**6**), he will incur a guilt involving a duty of compensation; cf Lv 6:1—7. But if the wronged person is dead and has no relative to receive the compensation, this shall be paid to the priest as God's representative.

d **9f** are supplemental to Lv 7:28—38. The word *terûmāh* is used in its liturgical sense of anything 'lifted off a larger mass, or separated from it, for sacred purposes' (Driver, *Deuteronomy*, ICC, 142). This portion is assigned to the officiating priest, but the rest belongs to the offerer.

e **11—31 Trial by Ordeal**—This was a widespread practice in antiquity. It was known in Babylonia long before Moses (cf *Code of Hammurabi* § § 2 and 132; HDB, V, 599—608) and was common among many Semitic peoples (W. R. Smith, 179ff). It survived down to the Middle Ages, and the Church repeatedly expressed disapproval. From the 14th and 15th cent. the practice was gradually discontinued.

f Although this practice rests on the universal belief that no one guilty of any sin may appear before God with impunity, and that God will never permit an innocent person to be punished as guilty, with the Hebrews it had no superstitious associations nor any presumptuous call for a divine intervention. It does not subject the suspected person to any dreadful hazard such as walking over red-hot bars. An innocuous potion was the only means used as a test of innocence. Moreover, with other peoples this practice was intended to detect a secret sin; with the Hebrews, on the contrary, it was intended to prove one's innocence by washing away all suspicions of conjugal infidelity.

g **12f** are a description of the sin which a woman is suspected of having committed. When the suspicious husband has no legal proof against his wife, he has the right to bring her before the priest carrying with him an offering called 'the offering of jealousy' or 'the offering of remembrance (of a real or supposed sin)'. Then follows the most impressive part of the ceremony. The woman swears her innocence, calling down upon herself a divine punishment if she is really guilty. The punishment very probably was miscarriage or sterility or something similar. In order to express the entrance of the imprecations into the woman's bowels more forcibly, the curses were written down on a piece of skin or some other writing material and washed off into the bitter water (**18**) which was then given to the woman to drink. Then the offering was brought to the altar. For the waving ceremony see Lv 7:30. It was not usual to wave cereal offerings. Although an instantaneous divine response was naturally expected, it appears **207** that the result was not so speedy (**28**). Pregnancy and normal childbirth were infallible signs of innocence, but miscarriage would convict the unfortunate woman.

The concluding **29—31** must be interpreted in the **h** same sense as 12f viz whether the woman is guilty or not, the husband has the right to bring her to the priest and call upon God to decide. If she is innocent, the husband is not to blame for having suspected his wife's fidelity; but if she is guilty, she will have to bear the consequences of her sin.

6:1—21 The Nazirite Vow—A Nazirite is a person **i** who submits himself by vow to certain restrictions. The Heb. word is *nāzîr* from the verb *nāzar* which implies the idea of a religious separation, hence dedication to God (cf BDB *s.v.*). The Nazirite vow was, as a rule, of temporary duration. Lifelong Nazirites were exceptional; we know only of Samson (Jg 13:5) and Samuel (1 Sm 1:11), in both cases the vow being made by the mother. The institution survived into NT times. John the Baptist was probably a Nazirite (Lk 1:15); cf also Ac 18:18; 21:23—25. Considering the prominent part which hair plays **j** in the Nazirite regulations, one feels inclined to consider the Nazirite vow as a hair-offering or as a consecration of one's hair to God. Hair is certainly an appreciable element of man's natural perfection, and its offering to God involves on the part of the offerer a loss which not many people may be willing to sustain. Hence the religious significance of the hair-offering does not lie in a symbolical union of the worshipper with the deity (W. R. Smith, 325—35), but rather in giving up to God, the Giver of all one has and is, a part of one's self. This consecration of one's hair renders the whole person in some way sacred, and it is in this sense that a Nazirite may be considered as a person consecrated to God.

2—8 Regulations to be Observed by the Nazirite— **k** The Nazirite is to observe these regulations: (i) He shall abstain from all intoxicant liquors and from all the products of the vine. This may be considered as a secondary feature meant to render the consecration more agreeable to God; (ii) The most important regulation is that the Nazirite must not cut his hair during the term of his vow. The reason is that his hair has already been promised to God and therefore cannot be cut until the day when it is actually offered on the altar. The period of the vow may therefore be regarded as a preparatory sanctification of one's hair before it is given to God. (iii) He must avoid any contact with a dead body. Not even for his closest relatives is he allowed to defile himself, because he has 'the consecration of his God upon his head', i.e. he has on his head not only the mark of his consecration to God, but the thing itself that is consecrated to God.

9—12 Involuntary Violation of the Vow—These **l** regulations were so stringent that if a Nazirite happened to defile himself unintentionally, his vow was considered violated and was therefore to be undertaken afresh. On the seventh day, when he purified himself, he shaved his head, his hair being no longer worthy to be offered to God, and the day after he brought to the priest two turtledoves or two pigeons for a sin-offering and a holocaust. He brought also a lamb for a trespass offering. The reason for this sacrifice was that the defilement of the Nazirite, though unintentional, constituted a real transgression which had to be expiated by a special sacrifice; see P. P. Saydon, CBQ (1946) 397. On that day he recovered his sanctity and had to commence the period of his vow afresh.

13—21 The Conclusion of the Vow—On the expiration **m** of the period of the vow, the Nazirite was presented at the

7m entrance of the tabernacle. Various sacrifices were offered with their accompaniments of cereal-offerings and libations. Then the Nazirite shaved off his hair and burned it over the fire on the altar. The ceremony might now be considered terminated; what remained was the waving of the portions due to the priest and the sacred meal. On the waving ceremony see note to Lv 7:30. Although the law prescribed only three sacrifices, the Nazirite might bind himself to more (21*b*). The original significance of the ceremony, which was the offering of a part of one's self to God, was, to a great extent, obscured by the preponderant part played by the sacrifices which formed the central part of all the liturgical ceremonies.

n **22—27 The Form of the Priestly Blessing**—This is obviously out of its context. Its original place was probably after Lv 9:22 where the first mention of Aaron's blessing occurs. It is a short poem of three vv with two members each: bless—keep; shew his face—have mercy; turn his countenance—give peace. It is a prayer for material prosperity and safety from enemies, divine pleasure symbolized by the brightness of the face and bestowal of divine favours, divine protection and security against all misfortunes. Thus the name of the Lord invoked upon the people will be for them a source of blessings. There is an echo of this form of blessing Ps 67(66); cf also Sir 50:22. The analogy of this triple benediction with the Christian form of benediction in the name of the Father and of the Son and of the Holy Ghost has already been noticed by the Fathers. Cf also 2 Cor 13·13.

208a **7:1—89 The Gifts of the Princes**—Chronologically this ch should come after Ex 40 or after Lv 8—9 where the consecration of the tabernacle is referred to (Lv 8:10f). Stylistically, however, it is related to chh 1—4, having in common with them the same love for classification, numbers, and names.

The heads of the twelve tribes made two offerings. The first consisted of six wagons and twelve oxen for the transport of the tabernacle. Moses received the gifts and assigned them to the Gershonites and to the Merarites who had to carry the tabernacle (4:21—33). To the Kohathites he gave nothing as they had to carry the sacred objects on their shoulders (4:15).

The other offering (10—83) was a dedication gift of the same amount for the several tribes and was to be presented on separate days. Each gift consisted of one silver dish of c. 60 oz Troy, one silver bowl of c. 33 oz, both full of fine flour tempered with oil, one golden mortar or saucer weighing c. 4⅔ oz full of frankincense, one bullock, one ram and one lamb for a holocaust, one he-goat for a sin-offering, and two oxen, five rams, five lambs for a peace-offering. The concluding verse records the fulfilment of the divine promise contained in Ex 25:22, but it has hardly any relation to what precedes.

b **8:1—4 Instructions concerning the Setting of the Lamps upon the Candlestick**—For a detailed description of the candlestick and the manner in which the lamps were to be set up, see Ex 25:31—39.

c **5—22 The Institution of the Levites**—This section supplements the parallel passage in 3:5—13 where their institution is enjoined. The ritual comprehends two parts: purification and presentation, besides the usual sacrifices.

The Levites were first sprinkled with the water of purification, so called because it was intended to remove any ceremonial uncleanness (Nm 19); cf the rite of aspersion with holy water in the Catholic Church. Then they shaved themselves all over the body and washed their garments. 'The complete shaving comes at their original

purification and it is similar to that of the Nazirites; the **208c** idea being that the whole growth of hair, new from the dedication shall continue untouched and holy', PC(2) in loc. This outward cleanness symbolized inward purity. They were not anointed like priests, hence their sanctity was merely negative. On the distinction between priests and Levites, see § 104*d*.

When so cleansed, the Levites were brought before **d** the tabernacle where the representatives of the people laid their hands on them. The imposition of hands, which in NT times became a rite of the ordination of presbyters and deacons, here meant that the Levites were set apart and appointed for a certain office; cf Ac 6:6; 13:3. Then followed the 'waving ceremony' which consisted, probably, in a forward movement of the Levites towards the tabernacle and back again to their original position. The waving ceremony is expressed in Heb. by the verb *hēnîp*. The offering of the sacrifices was the last part of the ceremonial, after which the Levites entered on their duties.

23—26 The Age Limits of the Levitical Service—The **e** period of Levitical service was from the age of twenty-five until fifty. This apparently contradicts 4:3, but **26** gives the clue to the solution. At the age of fifty the Levites were released from compulsory service, but were allowed to give voluntary assistance or to do light work compatible with their age. We may therefore assume that the Levites entered upon their duties at the age of twenty-five, but the heavier work of transport was not compulsory before they were thirty.

9:1—14 The Institution of a Supplementary f Passover—This section may be divided into three parts: celebration of the Passover on the appointed day (1—5); a case arising out of the impossibility of unclean persons keeping the Passover (6—8); supplementary paschal regulations (9—14).

1 5. On the celebration of the Passover, see Ex 12:6ff. On defilement through contact with a corpse, **6 8**, see Lv 21:1; Nm 19:11. Implicitly these men asked for a modification of the existing law.

Supplementary regulations are given in **9—14**. The petition was granted and a new law was given providing also for the case of those who happened to be on a distant journey. The second Passover must be kept exactly according to all the prescriptions of the normal Passover; cf 2 Chr 30:1—27, 11*b* = Ex 12:8; 12*a* = Ex 12:10, 46. Those who without any reason fail to keep the Passover on the appointed day are to be punished by civil excommunication or banishment. **14** = Ex 12:48, 49.

15—23 The Cloud Directing the Israelites—This **g** and the following section (10:1—10) close the Sinai period and are an introduction to another period of the history of the desert wanderings. The cloud has already been mentioned in Ex 40:34—38, but here a detailed description is given of its functions. It rested over the tabernacle all day and all night. It looked dark by day and bright by night. When it was lifted up, the people would march off, and where it stopped, they would halt and remain camped until it moved again. The cloud therefore served as a symbol not only of divine protection but also of divine guidance through the desert.

10:1—10 The Silver Trumpets—The silver trumpet is **h** described by BDB as 'a long, straight, slender metal tube, with a flared end like those that can still be seen represented on the Arch of Titus at Rome. Their purpose was to summon the community when the camp was to break up. They were also to be blown in battle and on all the festivals; cf 31:6; Jos 6:4—20; 2 Chr 13:12, 14; 2 Chr 29:27; Ps 98:6.

PART 2. 10:11—22:1. DESERT WANDERINGS

209a A 10:11—20:21 From Sinai to Kadesh—This part covers a period of about 38 years, which with the one-year sojourn in the Sinaitic wilderness and the three-month journey from Egypt to Sinai (Ex 19:1) make up the forty fo.etold (14:34). Although the number 40 may not have an exact mathematical value, the time of the wanderings was certainly much longer than the events related suggest. Of the whole period very little is known, and all attempts to reconstruct the history must necessarily involve much guesswork. J and E traditions are used in this section, edited and supplemented by P.

10:11–36 The Departure from Sinai
11–28 The Order of the March—The cloud of smoke rose up and the people marched out of Sinai by successive stages. After several days of journeying they reached the wilderness of Paran which lay N of Sinai and S of the wilderness of Kadesh and is commonly identified with the E part of the desert of *et-Tih* (Abel, I, 434).

b The order of the march corresponds exactly with that described in ch 2. The order of the Levites is seemingly different. But in 2:17 the Levites are mentioned collectively as one body, while in 10:17 they are mentioned separately according to their various duties. It is but natural that those carrying the framework and the hangings of the tabernacle should march in front in order to have time to set up the tabernacle before the arrival of the ark and the sacred objects.

c **29–32 Hobab requested to accompany the People**—Moses' father-in-law is called Hobab here and Jg 4:11, while in Ex 3:1 and 18:1 his name is Jethro. Moreover in **29** and Ex he is described as a Midianite, but in Jg he is called a Kenite. Finally Moses' request to Hobab is inconsistent with God's promise to lead the Israelites through the desert, Ex 32:34. It has been suggested that Hobab was the real name of Moses' father-in-law, and Jethro an honorific title, while Reuel (Ex 2:18; Nm 10:29) may have been the name of a remoter ancestor. It is more likely however that we have here two divergent traditions, J and E. The Midianites and the Kenites were two racially related nomadic tribes whose centres of radiation were the E side of the Gulf of Aqabah and the rocky land SW of the Dead Sea respectively.

d **33–34 The Departure from the Mount of the Lord**—They started on a three days' journey with the ark going before them. We are not to understand that they never halted during this time, but the halts were short. The position of the ark in front of the host signified the Lord leading them along a safe path. Probably a detachment of Levites carrying the ark marched in front of the people while other Levites carrying the sacred objects marched in the middle, see v 21.

e **35–36 The Song of the Ark**—These two vv are probably the beginning of two songs composed after some victory; cf 35 and Ps 68(67):1. For the martial tone of these, cf de Vaux, AI, 259.

f **11 Incidents at Taberah and Qibrōt hatta' ᵃwāh**—The incidents related here are: the punishments of the murmurers; the lust for flesh and the quails; the appointment of the 70 elders.

g **1–3 The Murmurings at Taberah**—Taberah is not mentioned elsewhere in the OT except in Dt 9:22. The locality is unknown. After long months of sedentary life in the Sinaitic region the march through 'the terrible and vast wilderness' (Dt 1:19) must have been far from pleasant, and soon produced an outburst of complaints. The Lord punished their lack of faith by fire, probably caused by lightning, which destroyed a part of the camp. Through Moses' intercession the fire was extinguished and the **20** place was called *Tab'ĕrāh*, i.e. 'a burning'.

4–15 The Lust for Flesh—The people led by Moses **h** were to some extent a mixed multitude (cf Ex 12:38). There were some who had joined the Israelites without being particularly attached to the religion of Yahweh. As their chief interest was their material well-being, they asked for flesh as a change of diet. They were dissatisfied with the manna, and their dissatisfaction soon spread. The Israelites began to voice their discontent, remembering their varied diet in Egypt. In **6** Heb. *nepeš* (often 'soul') means 'throat' (P. Dhorme, *L'emploi métaphorique des noms de parties du corps en hébreu et en accadien*, 1923, 18f). The mention of the manna called for a parenthetic digression (**7–9**) supplementing the scanty information given in Ex 16:14, 31. The narrative then returns to v 6.

Moses must have been sorely grieved at the people's **i** ingratitude, and his state of mind is clearly reflected in his expostulation with God which reaches its climax in his petition for a sudden death as a means of deliverance from a desperate situation. Moses' words, strong though they are, do not reveal any lack of confidence in God (11–15). On the contrary they express an unshakeable conviction in God's power and a sense of filial attachment to him. For similar outbursts of apparent despair cf Ex 32:32; 1 (3) Kgs 19:4.

16–17, 24–30 The Appointment of the Seventy j Elders—In his expostulation with God Moses raised two points: he was unable to carry the burden alone and he was unable to feed the people with meat. God's answer covers both points. For the sake of clarity however we separate the two, dealing first with the appointment of the elders and then with the feeding of the people.

17. Though the spirit was conceived of materially as **k** something that could be multiplied and divided (cf 2 (4) Kgs 2:9f), the words 'taking away of the spirit that was in Moses' (**25**) must be taken in the sense of a communication of a divine spirit from the spirit that was in Moses, a communication which would involve no diminution of the spirit of Moses. Spirit here means a power enabling one to perform extraordinary deeds. On the appointed day a divine spirit descended upon the 70 elders who immediately began to prophesy. 'To prophesy' does not mean 'to predict the future', but 'to act and speak in the name of God, on his authority, as his delegate and spokesman' (E. Tobac-J. Coppens, *Les Prophètes d'Israël*, I, Malines, 1932, 3–9). Therefore the seventy elders were to be God's representatives but subordinate to Moses. The exercise of the prophetic office may have involved the performance of certain actions which were intended to manifest the powers communicated to them by God and to enhance their authority over the people and thus to render their assistance to Moses more effective.

26. Eldad and Medad. Nothing is known of these two, **l** not even whether they were two of the 70 prevented by some unknown reason from going to the tent or another two besides the 70. Their manifesting by means of certain external actions the reception of the prophetic gift which was not a communication from the spirit of Moses, was therefore considered as placing them in a position of independence in regard to Moses. Joshua was too much concerned for Moses' honour and pre-eminence which, he thought, would be seriously jeopardized if similar prophetic outbreaks were permitted outside the control of his leader. But the latter was far more concerned for the good of the people than for his own honour. The story besides illustrating the principle that the prophetic gift is not restricted to any class, reveals also a fine trait

91 of Moses' character. Cf Christ's reply to the sons of Zebedee, Lk 9:54—56.

m **18—23, 31—34a The Quails**—God granted the second request. The people were to be ceremonially clean on the following day when God would manifest his power before them. God fulfilled his promise. A wind blowing in a NW direction from the Gulf of Aqabah drove a huge flight of quails over the camp. It is a well-known fact that quails in springtime migrate in enormous flocks from the E, cross the Mediterranean and in autumn return to the S. In their long flights they are sometimes exhausted and fall to the ground so that they can easily be caught. See the ch on 'Quail Netting' in *Yesterday and To-day in Sinai*, by Major C. S. Jarvis, 1933 and cf Ex 16. They were cured by drying and eaten without cooking. The people's lust for flesh was thus satisfied, but they had to pay a terrible penalty. They had not yet exhausted the whole supply of dried quails when an epidemic broke out. Intemperance may have been one of the causes of the mortality. Those who died were buried outside the camp, and the place was called *Qibrôt hatta'awāh* or 'the graves of lust'. The locality is generally identified with a site called *Rweis el-Ebeirig*, a ten hours' march from Jebel Musa (Abel, II, 214).

n **34b—12:15 At Hazeroth: Moses Vindicated**—Hazeroth, the modern 'Ain el-Hadra (Abel, II, 214). Whether this narrative relates a domestic incident originating in female jealousy or expresses a widespread feeling of opposition to marriages with foreigners, such as we meet with in the time of Ezra, it is certainly intended to vindicate Moses' supreme authority and his lawful right to speak for Yahweh. Mary, Moses' sister, has the leading part. The motive of her murmuring was that Moses' wife was a Cushite. Cush, which usually denotes Ethiopia, is here probably the name of a N Arabian tribe to which reference is made in 2 Chr 14:9, 12f; 16:8, cf Hb 3:7. According to Ex 2:15—21 Zipporah, Moses' wife, was a Midianite, and Midian is in NW Arabia. It is possible that Moses married another woman besides Zipporah. Moses' wife may have enjoyed some special privileges on account of her husband's position. In any case the proud sister of the great leader would never tolerate that a man allied with a foreign woman should have pre-eminence over her and over her brother who had preserved unstained the purity of their race. She herself was a prophetess (Ex 15:20), and claimed equal authority and equal rights to leadership.

o Mary's complaints were not unnoticed by Yahweh. This anticipates the impending divine judgement. In a parenthetic remark Moses is said to be 'a man exceeding meek above all men'. Though he was attacked by his sister, he suffered silently and did not ask God to vindicate his honour. This laudatory statement is commonly toned down by modern commentators who give to the Heb. word translated 'meek' the meaning 'afflicted, ill-treated, bowed down' (E. König, *Hebr. und aram. Wörterbuch*, 338; Gray, 123). Yahweh himself took up the defence of his servant.

p The ordinary mode of prophetic revelation is by means of visions and dreams (cf Jl 2:28), but with Moses, who was Yahweh's most trusted servant (Heb 3:2), God dealt with greater intimacy speaking to him mouth to mouth or face to face (Ex 33:11; Dt 34:10), plainly and not enigmatically. It was a common belief in OT times that no one could see the deity and remain alive (Gn 32:30; Ex 33:20; Jg 6:22f; 13:22), but Moses was allowed to see the form of the Lord though not the Lord himself. The form of God was a human, though perhaps indistinct, appearance of God. It must be remarked, however, that

209p the purpose of the writer is to illustrate the familiarity of intercourse between Yahweh and Moses, and consequently Moses' superiority over Mary and the other prophets rather than to express any definite theological conception of God.

q After this vindication of Moses' privileged position Yahweh punished Mary with leprosy, the white leprosy, which was a milder form of the disease. Aaron was not punished, either because of his dignity as high priest or because he had only an unimportant part in the complaint. This story is instructive as illustrating the necessity of repentance, confession, and satisfaction—the three elements of the sacramental confession of the New Law—for the forgiveness of sin.

210a **13—14 The Exploration of the Land of Canaan**
b **13:1—17 The Selection of the Spies**—This geographical indication is so wide that the locality of the halting-place cannot be determined. In 27 the general designation 'wilderness of Paran' is further defined by the indication 'which is in Kadesh'. It is therefore legitimate to infer that the place reached by the Israelites was the northernmost part of the wilderness of Paran. This bordered on the wilderness of Kadesh which lay south of Canaan. At the end of the list of spies it is added that Moses changed the name of Hoshea, the representative of the tribe of Ephraim (9), into Joshua. Hoshea, Heb. *hôš'ēa* means, 'salvation'; Joshua, Heb. *y'hôšūa'*, means 'Yahweh is salvation'. Jesus is a Gr. form of Heb. *y'hôšūa'*.

c **18—21 The Mission of the Spies**—The mission was both military and economic. They were to consider the fortifications of the land and its natural resources. They were directed to pass through the Negeb, the wilderness stretching along the S boundary of Palestine, and to go up as far as the hill-country, which was later known as the mountains of Judah. There are many redundancies in these vv.

d **22—25 The Journey of the Spies**—Two narratives seem to be here interwoven usually ascribed to P and JE (cf § 134b). In 22 the spies traverse the whole country from the wilderness of Zin, properly Sin, which lies NE of Kadesh, up to Rehob in the north of Canaan, SW of Mt Hermon. The wilderness of Zin must be distinguished from the apparently homonymous place mentioned in Ex 17:1 and Nm 33:11f. The expression 'the entry of Hamath' is the name of a valley between Lebanon and Hermon, but as a topographical expression it denotes very often the N boundary of Palestine (34:8; Jos 13:5; 1 Sm 8:65, etc). But in 23 the spies come to Hebron which lies about 19 miles S of Jerusalem and 70 miles N of Kadesh. Thence they advance as far as the valley which was later called Wady Eshcol (24f) and which is generally identified with one of the valleys round Hebron (Abel, I, 404). It is possible that the spies were divided into two **e** or more groups who were to explore different parts of the country. Their separate reports were then amalgamated into one. The Hebron group met three Anakite chieftains of gigantic stature. The writer adds parenthetically the historical remark that Hebron was built seven years before Tanis (Heb. *Ṣô'an*) of Egypt. Tanis was built probably before 2000 B.C. It is often mentioned in the OT (cf Is 19:11, 13; Ezek 30:14; Ps 78 (77): 12, 43). This is easily explained if Tanis is identified with the city of Ramesses where the Hebrews lived for many years.
26—34 Conflicting Reports—It was a land flowing with **f** milk and honey, a proverbial expression denoting great fertility of soil and exquisiteness of food; cf Ex 3:8, 17; 13:5; 33:3, etc. and E. Power, VDom 2 (1922) 52—8. But the country was invincible. The report which promised

210f to be very encouraging ended on a dismal note. The people began to murmur against Moses. Although in 31 and in 14:24 Caleb alone is represented as opposing the majority report, in 14:5, 30, 38 he is supported by Joshua. Considering that the 'Caleb sections' acknowledge Moses as the only leader, while the 'Caleb-Joshua sections' associate Aaron with Moses, we do not hesitate to recognize another reason for the existence of two narratives and two reports combined into one story.

g 14:1–10 The Sedition—The people proposed to return to Egypt. They had completely forgotten the wonders wrought by God for them in the land of Egypt. When Caleb and Joshua remonstrated with them, the people prepared to stone the two men. Then the glory of Yahweh, i.e. the fiery cloud, appeared over the tabernacle.

h 11–25 The Punishment—Moses very ably pleaded for his people in the same manner as in Ex 32:11–13.

i After Moses' intercession God pardoned the people, but inflicted on them, as his justice demanded, the punishment of exclusion from the land of promise. Caleb alone, in reward for his wholehearted attachment to Yahweh, was to enter into the land and inherit his portion (Jos 14:12). Joshua is not mentioned with Caleb as this passage is a

j Caleb-section. God immediately executed his sentence. You think, he says to the people, that you are unable to conquer the Amalekites and the Canaanites; well, therefore, turn back southwards in the direction of the Red Sea, i.e. towards the Gulf of Aqabah.

k 26–38 The Forty Years' Wandering—This is a duplicate account of the punishment of the people and is really the sequel to v 10. Joshua is associated with Caleb, and Aaron with Moses. In 11–25 the punishment consists in the exclusion of the murmuring people from the land of Canaan; in 26–38 it is described as a 40 years' wandering in the desert until the death of all the living generation from the age of 20 years upwards. Their children under 20 years and, it may be reasonably assumed, the Levites together with Joshua and Caleb will survive to enter the land of Canaan. Even these will share, to some extent, the lot which will befall the people. The number 40 is a round number. The spies who had spread a false report were struck by the Lord and died on the spot.

l 39–45 The Israelites defeated—Hormah, so called on account of the facts related in 21:3, is generally placed in the vicinity of Beer-sheba (Abel, II, 350).

211a 15 A Miscellaneous Collection of Laws—This ch contains various disconnected regulations mostly concerning the sacrifices. No reason for their present position can be assigned. **1–16 The Quantities of Oblations and Libations accompanying the various Sacrifices**—Every public sacrifice was to be accompanied by an oblation and a libation according to the table given, in which it will be noticed that the quantities increase in proportion to the size of the animal. A different scale is given in Ezek. 46:5–7; 11, 14. For private and voluntary

b oblations no fixed measure is prescribed. **17–21 The Dough-offering**—After their settlement in the land of Canaan, the Israelites, before eating of the bread of the land, were to take a portion of the cereal produce, knead it into a cake and offer it to the Lord in the same manner as the contribution of the threshing-flour. **19.** The Heb. word '*arîsôt*, which may be approximately rendered 'dough', is of uncertain meaning.

c 22–31 Unintentional and Intentional Sins—22–29 are probably a more primitive form of the parallel legislation contained in Lv 4 and 5. The law here contemplates two cases only, a sin of ignorance committed by the community, and a sin of ignorance committed by an individual. **30.** Sins committed with a high hand, in **21** defiance of the law, cannot be expiated, but the offender is to be punished with excommunication. In IQS it is prescribed that no-one who persists in walking in his evil ways may be admitted into the community. **32–36 d The Sabbath-breaker**—Though Sabbath-breaking was a capital offence (Ex 31:14; 35:2), the present case may not have appeared of sufficient gravity to deserve the death penalty. A divine pronouncement was considered necessary. **37–41 The Tassels**—The custom of attach- **e** ing fringes or tassels to a garment is very old and probably connected with superstition (W. R. Smith, 437). The Israelites may have known and adopted this practice. Instead of rooting it up God impresses it with a new religious significance making it serve as a reminder of his commandments. The tassels were to be attached to the four corners of the mantle by a blue cord; cf Dt 22:12. References occur also in the NT; cf Mt 23:5. Christ himself wore a 'tasselled' cloak (Mt 9:20 and parallel passages). This Jewish custom has survived down to modern times. For illustrations see DBV art. *Frange*.

16:1–20:21 The Journey to Kadesh—The P **f** tradition is again resumed here, but with elements of JE.

16:1–40 The Rebellion of Korah and its Punish- g ment—The narrative shows signs of being composite. Moses addresses Korah and his party, and Dathan and Abiram separately. Korah was a Levite; Dathan and Abiram were Reubenites. Korah's grievance was that the Levites had not the same rights as the priests; Dathan and Abiram complained that Moses and Aaron exercised full powers over the whole community. It is not improbable that two stories, Korah (P) and Dathan-Abiram (JE), relating similar incidents have been amalgamated into one narrative. Korah and his followers claimed the same priestly privileges as the sons of Aaron, while Dathan and Abiram, descendants of Reuben, Jacob's firstborn, may have claimed for themselves the primacy over the other tribes and consequently the leadership and supreme authority over the people. The sedition was therefore an attack on the religious rights of the priests and on the civil rights of Moses. In Sir 45:22 the three rebels are mentioned together, but in Ps 106 (105):17 Dathan and Abiram are mentioned alone, and in Jude 11 only Korah. A Levite and three Reubenites, one of whom **h** however has no part in the narrative, rose up against Moses and Aaron challenging their authority. 250 of the leading personalities made common cause with the rebels. Their main grievance was that all the congregation being holy (Ex 19:6) Moses and Aaron should have no superior rights. Moses replied first to the Levites. Then he tried **i** to appease the Reubenites (12). **15.** Moses' request cannot be referred to any sacrifice being offered because the Reubenites were in their tents away from the tabernacle. Either something has fallen out of the text or Moses' words are to be taken in a general sense expressing a wish that God may never accept any offering made by the rebels. The narrative now reverts to Korah (16). For the **j** doctrine of individual responsibility cf Ezek 18. There **k** is some inconsistency in **24.** Korah, Dathan and Abiram are described as being in or around their tent or dwelling, cf 27. But in 19 it was stated that 'Korah assembled all the congregation against them (Moses and Aaron) at the entrance of the Tent of Meeting (the Tabernacle). A possible explanation is this: the Hebrew word used in 24, translated in RSV as 'dwelling', is *miškan*. But this word is never elsewhere used of human habitation; it always refers to the divine Tabernacle. It is possible that for 'Korah' one should read 'Yahweh', cf 17:13 (MT 17:18), and delete 'Dathan and Abiram' as an interpolation.

1k Alternatively one might read with LXX, 'the *congregation of Korah*'. The punishment of Korah would then have taken place before the *Tabernacle*, cf v 35. The addition of the names 'Dathan and Abiram' in 24 may have been motivated by the following account, vv 25—34, from JE, of their revolt against Moses' authority and the retribution meted out. The original Korah story would have ended with the death of Korah and his supporters by the fire that came out from the Tabernacle; in place of which we have his fate linked with that of Dathan and Abiram in the earthquake, **27, 32**, and only his supporters (the censer-bearers) destroyed by fire (35), cf 26:10. In confirmation of the distinction between the two stories, see Dt 11:6 where there is a reference to Dathan and Abiram being swallowed up by the earth but no mention **l** of Korah. **36—50.** The P narrative continued. The altar had already been covered with bronze, according to Ex 27:2, nevertheless, the censers, beaten flat, are suggested as a further covering, evidently not because the altar needed such a covering but as an appropriate way of disposing of them, sacred as they were yet illegally used. Eleazar was the successor of Aaron as High Priest, cf 20:26, and according to the P tradition was the ancestor of the Zadokites, cf 1 Chr 6:1—8. The task of gathering the censers was entrusted to Eleazar because Aaron, the high priest, was not allowed on any occasion to defile himself by contact with a dead body (Lv 21:11). Both the fire and the censers which had been brought before God had contracted holiness and had therefore to be **m** removed from any profane use. **41—50 Another Sedition**—Aaron's propitiatory action (48) is expressed in Heb. by the verb *kipper* 'to expiate', which, though generally used in connection with sacrifice, is connected occasionally with other actions (cf 8:19; 25:13; 31:50). For the meaning of *kipper*, see S. Lyonnet 'Expiation et intercession. A propos d'une traduction de St Jerome', Bib 1959, 885—901. The expiatory smoke of the incense may be considered as symbolizing man's prayer rising up to God (Ps 141(140):2).

n **17:1—13 The Blossoming of Aaron's Rod**—This story is intended to vindicate the superiority of the tribe of Levi over the secular tribes and to quash their pretentious claims to the priesthood. The tribe of Levi was represented by Aaron. The superiority of the tribe of Levi was thus vindicated, as against the other tribes. This was the corollary to the suppression of the Levites' attempt to usurp the powers of the priesthood, ch 16.

12f are the introduction to ch 18 and a connecting link between chh 16 and 18.

12a **18 The Duties and the Dues of the Priests and the Levites**—The sons of Aaron alone are authorized to approach the Lord, and they are assisted by the Levites in the performance of their duties. The correct hierarchy has now been established beyond dispute.

b **1—7 The Duties of the Priests and of the Levites**—The priests and the rest of the house of Levi shall be responsible for all the sins committed in connexion with the sanctuary, such as any unlawful approach thereto; and the priests shall be responsible for all the offences committed by them and by others in connexion with the priestly functions. The tribe of Levi ('the tribe of thy father' **2**) is to assist the priests during the divine service and take care of the tabernacle and the sacred vessels (3:7; 4:15). No layman may interfere; transgressions are to be punished by death. The Levites have been chosen from amongst the children of Israel as a gift to the Lord to serve in the tabernacle. But it is the exclusive right of the priests to serve at the altar and within the (outer) curtain of the tent. In **7** the

priesthood is considered, as it really is, a gift bestowed **212b** by God.

8—20 The Priestly Dues—As the priests possessed no **c** landed property, God assigned to them certain offerings made to himself. In a general way it is laid down that what is left over of all the contributions made to the Lord (i.e. those portions of the offerings which have not been burnt) belongs to the priests cf Lv 7. To the priests are assigned also the best of the oil, wine, and corn, and all the first fruits. **14.** Things devoted to God i.e. under the *herem* or ban go to the priest (Lv 27:28). **19.** For the meaning of 'covenant of salt' see note to Lv 2:13. **20** winds **d** up the whole section of the Levitical and priestly dues. As the priests and the Levites were the only persons authorized to approach the sanctuary, they had to direct all their care to its service rather than to the cultivation of the land. They had to depend chiefly on the sanctuary for their means of subsistence. In this sense, God was their possession. A similar, though far loftier, idea is expressed by David in Ps 16(15):5 and applied by the Church to clerics on the reception of the tonsure.

21—24 The Levitical Dues—cf Nm 35:3—8. On tithes **e** see Lv 27:30—33; Dt 14:22—29; 26:12—15.

25—32 A Tithe of the Tithes—(cf Neh 10:38), all the **f** Israelites, the Levites included, were obliged to offer to the Lord a contribution of their land produce. The tithe paid by the Levites must be the best of the tithes received from the people. What remains of the tithes may be eaten by them in any place, as the tithes are not holy things. By failing to pay the priests their due the Levites will incur guilt and become liable to the death penalty.

19 The Water for Purification—Many primitive **g** peoples have considered contact with a dead body to be a source of uncleanness, and various purificatory rites have been practised to avert the dangerous influences which such contact was believed to exercise; see Gray, 243—44 and references. The Hebrew rite rests ultimately on this widespread belief, its scope however is not personal safety from dangerous influences, but the necessity of safeguarding the holiness of God's dwelling. In NT times it furnished ample matter for allegorizing, cf Heb 9:13; Ep. Barn. 8, 1—7; Aug. *Quaest.* 33 in *in Num*, PL, 34, 732—7.

1—10 Preparation of the Water—(i) The officiating **h** minister is Eleazar, not Aaron, as the ceremony involves a contamination of all who take part. The reason why the cow is, contrary to custom, slain away from the tabernacle is the avoidance of any possible contamination of the camp and especially of the tabernacle. (ii) the priest dips his finger in the blood and sprinkles it seven times in the direction of the tabernacle (cf Heb 13:11), expressing thus the relation between the cow which has been slain and the Lord; (iii) the cow is entirely burnt, and while it burns the priest throws a piece of cedar wood and hyssop and a scarlet thread into the fire. As these ingredients are used in the purification of the leper (Lv 14:4), it is probable that they are used in this case with a similar, though perhaps weaker, symbolical meaning; (iv) when the cow has been burnt to ashes, the ashes are collected and deposited in a clean place outside the camp and kept there for the preparation of the water 'of impurity' i.e. destined to remove sin. All who take part in the ceremony become **i** unclean. The reason is either the similarity of the burning ceremony to the burning of the sin-offering outside the camp (Lv 4:12, 21), or the sanctity of the rite which is communicated to those who take part and who must therefore submit to an 'unsanctifying' action before entering again into intercourse with the rest of the people.

212j **11—22 Cases requiring Purification**—**16** Walking over a grave, hence the need for whitewashing the graves as a warning to passers-by to keep away (Mt 23:27; Lk 11:44).

k **20:1—21 Events at Kadesh**

l **1 The Death of Mary**—As the events related after Mary's death belong to the last period of the wanderings, it is probable that the year of her death was much nearer to the end than to the beginning of the desert wanderings. It is strange how briefly Mary's death is narrated. Neither her brother's grief nor the people's mourning is recorded.

m **2—13 The People's Murmuring for Lack of Water**—Shortage of water being an ordinary feature of the desert, no wonder that the Israelites with their large flocks suffered from it more than once. Unmindful of past benefits they assembled and expressed their complaints against Moses and Aaron in their usual aggressive manner **n** (cf Ex 16:2f; 17:3; Nm 11:4, 6). **9** In Ex 17:6 Moses was commanded to strike the rock, and obviously a similar action was intended here. Moses obeying God's command summoned the people and addressed them with these words: 'Can we bring you forth water out of this rock?' These words have been interpreted as an expression of Moses' ill-temper (Corn. a Lap. *ad loc.*), or impatience and unbelief. The text is probably corrupt. In Ps 106 (105):33 Moses is charged with uttering rash words while in a state of excitement. The charge of lack of faith is hardly admissible especially after the events of Ex 17. But Moses' unbelief may have been restricted to God's willingness to provide an ungrateful people with water, independently of any consideration of his power (Heinisch, 78; Clamer, 365). A certain degree of impatience, due to human imperfection, can hardly be excluded from Moses' words and action. In the same way is to be explained **o** the double striking of the rock. Water soon gushed forth from the rock, but Moses and Aaron were condemned, on account of their unbelief, not to enter into the land of promise. They thought, or may have thought, that God would no longer listen to their prayers. They believed in his punitive justice, not in his goodness, mercy, and fidelity. They expected a punishment rather than a manifestation of these attributes before the people. The place came to be called *mê merîbāh*, 'water of strife,' because there the Israelites strove with words against the Lord, and he vindicated his holiness. On the name *meribah* see Ex 17:7.

p **14—21 The Embassy to the King of Edom**—After the failure of the attempted invasion of Canaan from the S (14:44f) the Israelites had to reach the land from the E. From Kadesh to the eastern side of the Dead Sea the way was through the land of Edom which stretched along the Arabah depression from the southern end of the Dead Sea down to the Gulf of Aqabah. Before crossing the land of Edom Moses sent messengers to the king requesting his permission and assuring him of his good intentions. In order to gain his favour he addressed him as 'brother'. The Edomites were in fact descendants of Esau, Jacob's brother, Gn 36:9–19. But mistrusting these assurances they refused the request, and the Israelites had therefore to make a detour to the south.

213a **B. 20:22—22:1 From Kadesh to Moab**—This section relates military campaigns against peoples whose territory lay on the way of the Israelites towards the approaches to Canaan.

b **22—29 Death of Aaron and Investiture of Eleazar**—The site of Mt Hor is unknown. It was certainly on the borders of the land of Edom. In Dt 10:6 the place of Aaron's death is called *Mōserāh*. This may be the name of a range of mountains one of whose peaks was Mt Hor.

21:1—3 The Victory of Hormah—The topographical **21** names Arad, identified with Tell Arad some 50 miles N. of Kadesh and some 15 miles S. of Hebron, and Negeb, the wilderness in southern Palestine, take us to the southern borders of the land of Canaan, a position which is hardly consistent with the itinerary indicated in 14:25 and 20:21. Moreover it is not conceivable that the Israelites should not have exploited their victory **(3)** and developed their conquests from the south. The narrative may either be out of its chronological context or relate a campaign led by a single tribe while the bulk of the Israelites marched in a southern direction. References to Hormah occur in Jos 12:14; Jg 1:17. The expression 'the way of the spies' **(1)** is scarcely helpful to determine the geographical position. Heb. *'aṭarîm* may be a place-name of impossible identification, or a common noun of doubtful meaning. Vg rendering 'spies', which is based on the reading *tārîm* for *'aṭarîm* must not be overlooked. In fulfilment of a vow the victorious Israelites placed the city under a ban, i.e. they utterly destroyed it and called the place Hormah, which means, as Jerome adds by way of explanation, 'anathema' or destruction. On the *herem* or ban see Lv 27:28f and A. Fernandez in Bib 5 (1924) 3–25.

4—9 The Bronze Serpent—The story is an illustra- **d** tion of God's power, for he alone could heal a deadly bite by using means that were absolutely inadequate for the purpose. There is an echo of the serpent story in 2 (4) Kgs 18:4. See also Wis 16:6f. In Jn 3:14 it is a type of Christ's crucifixion.

10—20 The Journey to the NE of the Dead Sea—In **e** their detour round the territory of Edom the Israelites reached Oboth E of Edom, and afterwards Iyeabarim, SE of the Dead Sea (Abel, II, 26) and E of Moab. Then they camped in Wady Zered which flows into the southern end of the Dead Sea from the SE. Having departed from W Zered they halted at the northern side of the river Arnon (= Wady el-Mojib), at a place in the wilderness to the E of Moab and on the borders of the Amorites. **14**. A fragment of a popular song is cited from a collection of epic poems, called 'the Wars of Yahweh', celebrating the victories of the Israelites over their enemies. The meaning of the fragmentary lines is obscure. From Arnon they journeyed to Beer, a word meaning 'a well'. The site is unknown. The name is perhaps an abbreviation of an original form such as 'the well of God'. **17**. Another popular song is given here which was probably sung when water was being drawn. Then following a NW direction they came to a valley in the land of Moab, which is described by the appositional clause 'the top of Pisgah', NE of the Dead Sea.

21—32 Defeat of King Sihon and the Occupation of f his Country—The Israelites sent messengers to the king, as they had done to the king of Edom (20:14—21), requesting permission to pass through his territory. Apparently the embassy was despatched from the place reached in 21:20. It is preferable however to make the mission of the messengers follow immediately after 13 as all the sites mentioned in 14—20 are in Sihon's territory. The Amorites refused the request and marched with arms to meet the Israelites at Jahaz. They were defeated, and Israel occupied all their territory from the Arnon to the river Jabbok (= *Nahr ez-Zerqa*) which flows into the Jordan from the east. The writer remarks that Jazer was on the borders of the Ammonites, and this statement would account for Sihon's limitation of territory. Heshbon (= the modern *Hesban*) was the capital of Sihon's kingdom and had been captured from the former king of Moab. A popular song is again cited **g**

3g celebrating the Israelites' victory. Heshbon has been burnt down, who will build it up? Moab, the former lord of Heshbon, has been forsaken by Chemosh, their national god, and gone into captivity. The Israelites have conquered all the land.

h 33–35 Defeat of King Og and Occupation of his Country—The Israelites continued their victorious march northwards, defeated Og, king of Bashan, at Edrei some 32 miles E of the southern end of the Sea of Genneseret, and occupied all his territory.

i 22:1 Israel's Encampment in the Plains of Moab— The plains of Moab, the scene of the last events before the crossing of the Jordan into Canaan, cover an area not more than 7 miles wide, N of the Dead Sea and E of the mouth of the Jordan.

4a PART 3 22:2–36:13 EVENTS IN MOAB

The contents of this section are the story of Balaam, a second census and a miscellaneous collection of laws and narratives.

b 22:2–24:25 The Story of Balaam—The narrative is usually ascribed to the double source JE (see § 135), which would explain certain inconsistencies in the account. Thus at one moment Balaam appears to be Israel's friend, at another her enemy: on one occasion he acts on God's command (22:20) and the next is rebuked for contravening the Almighty's wishes (22:22). A noteworthy feature of these stories is the proportion in verse. Almost all the text of **Balaam's Oracles** in fact is in poetry 23:7–10, 18–24; 24:3–19, 15–24, as befits the ecstatic nature of his visions and praises of Israel. On the other hand, **the episode of Balaam's ass** has more of the character of folklore, not without its element of humour. Doubtless it acquired additional features in the course of the retelling.

c Theologians throughout the ages have debated the **character of Balaam** and reached different conclusions—on the whole unfavourable. The point however would seem to be of no particular importance. The stories are preserved for the sake of the oracles and these retain their significance whatever the character of the seer may have been.

d 2–14 The First Embassy to Balaam—One would expect 'Moab' instead of 'Midian' (4). But the Midianites are mentioned again together with the Moabites in **7**. The presence of the Midianites in Moab may be due to the migratory movements of the nomadic tribes; cf Abel, RB 40 (1931) 225. Feeling themselves unable to resist the enemy the Moabites resort to a peculiar form of strategy, that of cursing the enemy in order to render them powerless. It was a common belief shared by the Israelites themselves (Gn 9:25–27; 27:27–40; 49:3–28) that the blessings and cursings of a person living in close relations with the deity were never ineffective. The king, accordingly, sends for Balaam, requesting him to curse the Israelites. Balaam lived at Pethor (**5**) which is commonly identified with *Pitru* of the Assyrian inscriptions, a city on the Euphrates some 400 miles from Moab. His country is called 'the land of Amaw' which may mean 'the land of his people', a meaning preferred by many interpreters, E. Palis in DBV art. *Balaam*; E. Sutcliffe in Bib 7 (1926) 9–18, 31–9 and 18 (1937) 439–42. This fits in with the preceding text which states that Balaam lived at Pethor.

e Balaam promised the messengers to give them an answer the following day according to the revelation which God would make to him that night. The name of Yahweh has been put on his lips by later scribes, who on more than one occasion have interchanged the divine names, **214e** God and Yahweh. Most probably Balaam was a heathen magician who sought revelation from *his* own god, but the response was given by Yahweh himself.

15–20 The Second Embassy—Balak, not at all **f** discouraged by Balaam's refusal, sent another embassy with the promise of richer presents, Balaam, believing that his god might have changed his mind, sought his advice once more. This time God granted him the permission to accept Balak's invitation, on condition however that he would speak under his direction.

21–35 Balaam's Journey—**21**. The next morning **g** Balaam set out with the messengers. But the journey displeased Yahweh. **22**. To explain the apparent contradiction (see **20***b*) it has been suggested that God disapproved of Balaam's evil intention, not of the journey, cf Sutcliffe, Bib 7 (1926) 23 but see 214*b*. Balaam's intention was certainly perverse (**32**); he believed that God had permitted him to curse the Israelites and that he would even suggest the words for the cursing, cf 'do what I shall command thee' (**20**) i.e. 'speak what I shall command thee' (**35**). This however was not God's intention. God intended to turn evil into good.

23–35. The dialogue between **Balaam and the ass h** may be a dramatic representation of an unusual incident which occurred in the journey. See also 214*b*. The writer's main concern is made manifest from **35**: 'see that thou speak no other thing than what I shall command thee'. Balaam was to act as an instrument in the hands of God independently of Balak's instructions.

36–40 Balaam's Arrival at Moab—Balak went to **i** meet Balaam at Ir (*a city of*) Moab which lay on the river Arnon, on the extreme border of his kingdom. After having explained to Balak the conditions of his mission, Balaam went with him to *Qiryat ḥūṣôt*, a place of unknown situation, where numerous sacrifices were offered and substantial portions were given to the honoured guest.

41–23:12 Balaam's First Oracle—On the following **j** morning Balak took Balaam to Bamoth Baal, N of the Arnon, whence he could see an extremity of the Israelite camp and so pronounce his curses in sight of the enemy.

Balaam's first parabolic utterance consists of seven **k** couplets cast in synonymous parallelism. The general thought is this: I have been called by Balak to curse this people; but how can I curse a people which is not cursed by God? There are unmistakable signs that this people is blessed by God. It is a people dwelling by itself, segregated from other nations. Who can count these descendants of Jacob who are innumerable as the dust of the earth? (cf Gn 13:16; 28:24). Who can count even a fourth part (or, according to LXX, the myriads) of the Israelites (**10**)? At the end, Balaam expresses the desire of a happy end like that of the Israelites. Some commentators have seen in these words an allusion to the belief in a future life which, for the righteous people, will be a life of happiness. It is preferable however to interpret Balaam's words in the light of OT conceptions of future life as a desire for a happy end after a prosperous life.

23:13–26 Balaam's Second Oracle—Balak, believ- **l** ing he could obtain a favourable response from God if the curses were pronounced in the presence of another part of Israel, took Balaam to the top of Mt Pisgah which commanded an extensive view of the Israelites' camp.

Balaam's second utterance is cast in the same poetical form as the first. Its general thought is the immutability of God's purpose and the irrevocability of his blessings. 'God will not change his mind like us mortals. I have been instructed by God to bless and I have no power to recall God's blessings. There are no evil-doers among

214l the Israelites (or, there is no calamity in Israel). Yahweh is in their midst, and they proclaim him their king with joyful shouts. They are invincible because God, who brought them out of Egypt, is as strong as the wild ox. Living in such familiarity with God they need no divination, because God announces to them in due time what he intends to do'. Balak seeing that all his endeavours to get a curse from Balaam had the contrary effect of stressing the privileged position of the Israelites stopped Balaam blessing.

m **27—24:13 Balaam's Third Oracle**—Balak tries once more to obtain a curse from Balaam. His persistence is easily explained by the analogous heathen custom of consulting the oracle repeatedly until a favourable response is obtained. Balak, accordingly took Balaam to the top of Mt Peor which overlooks the waste land stretching out E of the mouth of the Jordan. Balaam inspired by God delivers his third oracle which differs from the others both in form and contents. It is introduced by the title: The oracle of Balaam, the oracle of a man whose eye is closed, of a man who hears the words of God, who sees the vision of the Almighty, whose eyes are opened when he falls down. The general sense of these words seems to be this: The seer, while receiving a divine communication, has his eyes closed; after receiving the communication, he opens his eyes and falls down in a state of exhaustion. The description of the seer with closed eyes has a parallel in the magical practices of the Arabs. The seer, while in communication with god, has his eyes covered, but after the divine communications the covering falls down and his eyes are opened to the reality of the world (see I. Guidi, in *Acts of the XIV Congress of Orientalists*, II, 8—12, Algiers, 1905). Others translate: the oracle of a man whose eyes are opened.

n **5—9** form the body of the oracle. Israel's prosperity will be like water overflowing from a bucket, 'and his seed shall be in many waters'. These last words hardly make any sense. A slight emendation based on LXX gives this sense: his seed, i.e. Israel's posterity, will be spread among many nations. If we read $z^e r\bar{o}'\hat{o}$ 'his arm' for $zar'\hat{o}$ 'his seed' a still better sense is obtained: his arm, i.e. Israel's power, will be over many nations. Their king is mightier than Agag, king of the Amalekites (who was conquered by Saul, I Sm 15), and his kingdom will be exalted. King Balak, sorely disappointed, sends Balaam away.

o **24:14—25 Balaam's Last Oracles**—Before leaving for home Balaam foretells what the Israelites would do to the Moabites in the future. For **15f** see note to 3f. Balaam is contemplating, in an ecstatic vision, the Israel of the future. He beholds a star rising out of Jacob, and a sceptre coming out of Israel. 'Star' and 'sceptre' are used here metaphorically, as symbols of royal power. For the use of the term 'star' as a royal title in the Assyrian and Egyptian literatures, see L. Dürr, *Ursprung und Ausbau der israelitisch-jüdischen Heilanderwartung* (Berlin, 1925), 105—9; and for the metaphorical use of the word 'sceptre' cf Gn 49:10. This mighty king will smite the temples (i.e. the inhabitants) of Moab and will lay waste all the sons of tumult, this being a designation of the Moabites, cf Is 16:6; Jer 48:29, 39. He will conquer Edom and Seir, the land of his enemies. Edom and Seir are synonyms, cf 36:8; Jg 5:4. In IQM Moabites and Edomites are included in the 'army of Belial' or 'enemies of God'. Domination will come out, or will be exercised, from Jacob, and he will destroy all the survivors from the cities.

p Commentators have endeavoured to identify this powerful king of Israel. David, naturally, was generally considered as possessing the strongest claims. He defeated **21** the Moabites (2 Sm 8:2), the Edomites (2 Sm 8:13, 14; 1 (3) Kgs 11:15) and all the neighbouring hostile peoples. From very early times Jewish and Christian interpreters have applied this prophecy to the Messiah (Just. *Dial. cum Tryph.* 106, PG 4, 450f; Iren., *Contra Haer.* III, 9, 2, PG 5, 782; Theodoretus, *Quaest. in Num.* 44, PG 80, 394; Hier. *Ep. ad Oceanum*, PL 22, 695) and the Messianic interpretation has remained general in the Christian Church. The Messiah is represented here as a victorious king crushing all opposition and ruling over Israel and the conquered nations. The Moabites and the Edomites are, politically, the peoples conquered, though not permanently (cf the Moabite stone, § 290h), by David, and are mentioned out of other nations conquered by David on account of the historical circumstances of the prophecy. But at the same time they represent all the nations that will have to submit to Christ. The prophecy, though applicable to David in a limited sense, had its complete fulfilment in Christ. It is interesting to note that the nativity of Christ was announced by a star (Mt 2:2) and Christ is called the morning star (Apoc 22:16). See F. Ceuppens, *De Prophetiis messianicis in Antiquo Testamento* (Rome, 1935), 84—101.

Three more oracles are added which have no con- **q** nexion with the Moabites. The first (**20**) refers to the Amalekites who are described as 'the beginning of the nations', i.e. the first who fought against Israel (Ex 17:8ff) or, with a poetic exaggeration, the most powerful of the nations, but whose end was to be utter destruction (I Sm 15). The second (**21f**) refers to the Kenites. The general sense is: though the Kenites dwell in rocky, inaccessible and therefore unassailable places (note the assonance of *qēn* 'nest' and *qēnî* 'Kenite'), they will be led into captivity by the Assyrians. What particular deportation is here referred to we are unable to say. The last oracle (**23f**) is very obscure and seems to refer to the period of Greek domination. Ships will come from *Kittîm*, i.e. Cyprus, or, according to later usage, from the western maritime countries (e.g. Italy). The Kittim will conquer Assyria and Eber who will perish for ever. A detailed explanation is impossible.

25 The Events at Baalpeor—The Israelites were **215** encamped in Shittim E of the Jordan and not far from its mouth. There they mixed with the Moabites and had immoral intercourse with their women. As a result of this intimacy they partook of the sacrificial meals to which they were invited by the Moabite women. By this idolatrous worship the Israelites attached themselves to the Moabite deity Chemosh, called here Baalpeor or 'the Lord of Peor'. This idolatry provoked God's anger who commanded Moses to execute all the chiefs responsible for this act of infidelity. The execution of this order is not related.

6. A chief of the tribe of Simeon publicly led a **b** Midianite woman to the camp. This act suggests either a mixed marriage or immoral intercourse. On seeing this, Phinehas, the grandson of Aaron, followed them to their tent and stabbed them with his dagger. Phinehas' zeal became proverbial; cf Ps 106 (105):30; Sir 45:28; I Mc. 2:26. Phinehas was rewarded by the promise of the (high) priesthood which was to remain perpetually in his family. God had already chosen Eleazar for Aaron's successor (20:25), but now the right is given to Phinehas' posterity to succeed their fathers as high-priests. The Ithamar line is therefore excluded from holding the office of high-priest, in perpetuity.

The Midianites seem to have acted at the suggestion of Balaam; cf 31:16.

5c 26 The Second Census—After so many disastrous events during forty years' wanderings in the desert it was necessary to number the people again, now that they were about to enter the land of Promise (see note to 1:1).

d 1—51 The Census—It is taken according to the same general directions as in ch 1. The order of the tribes is the same, except that Manasseh and Ephraim change places. For each tribe the main clan divisions are given. For the value of the numbers see the remarks on ch 1. 3. 'Spoke with them', (MT and Vg) should probably be corrected to *numbered them*.

e 52—56 General Directions concerning the Division of the Land—The land was to be divided among the tribes according to their numerical strength, and each portion assigned by lot. In other words the extent of the several portions was determined by the size of the several tribes, but the situation of each portion was determined by lot. See Jos 13—19.

57—62 The Census of the Levites.

63—65 Conclusion.

f 27:1—11 The Law of the Inheritance of Daughters—Hebrew custom did not give women the right to inherit. Hence if a man died without male issue his property would go out of his family. The levirate marriage was an inadequate provision against this forced alienation of the family property (Dt 25:5—10; see also the *Book of Ruth*, WV, xx—xxix by C. Lattey). The present law gave daughters an equal share of their father's inheritance.

g The daughters of Zelophehad, putting their case before Moses and the assembly, state that their father had no part in the revolt of Korah, otherwise his property would probably have been confiscated, but died for his own personal sins. As one's name was inseparable from one's land-property, their father's name would die out if his property passed into other hands outside the family circle. Their claim was recognized and a general law promulgated giving daughters the right to inherit their father's property in default of male issue. A similar practice prevailed in the ancient Near East long before Moses; cf C. H. Gordon, *'Parallèles Nouziens aux lois et coutumes de l'A.T.'* in RB 44 (1935) 38. The law contemplates also other cases of succession to a father's property.

h 12—23 Joshua Appointed Moses' Successor—Moses' request to be allowed to enter the Promised Land (Dt 3:25f) was rejected for the reason stated in **14**, but he was given, before his death, a view of the land from Mt Nebo, a peak of the range of Abarim, E of the Dead Sea and the Jordan. The punishment may appear disproportionate to his fault, especially considering his faithful service for so many years. 'But the divine majesty had to be vindicated, and a public failure atoned for, by a striking and impressive punishment: moreover there was another Land of Promise from which Moses was not excluded by his offence' (Binns, 189). It may be added that the divine punishments are proportionate not only to the gravity of the offence in itself but also to the position of the offender and to the degree of sanctity demanded of him.

i Moses humbly submitted to God's dispositions and asked him, the author of life (16:22), to appoint a successor who would lead the people into the Promised Land. Joshua was chosen, a man endowed with spirit, i.e. the spirit of wisdom (Dt 34:9), or, in a general sense, ability for leadership. Moses was then commanded to lay his hands on Joshua. The rite of imposition of hands in the O and NT has more than one significance; cf see J. Coppens, *L'Imposition des mains et les rites connexes dans le NT et dans l'Eglise ancienne*, 1925,

esp. 162f. Here it symbolizes the transference of power **215i** and may be compared with the analogous rite in the ordination of the Levites (8:10). Moses was further commanded publicly to declare him to possess authority over the people and therefore to have the right to their obedience. Joshua would stand before the priest, i.e. he would have an inferior position; the priest would consult God for him by the use of the Urim (Ex 28:30), and both Joshua and the people should abide by the instructions communicated to them by God through the priest. The secular authority was thus subordinated to the ecclesiastical.

28—29 A Liturgical Calendar—In Lv 23 a list of **216a** the yearly feast-days is given, here we have a table defining the sacrifices which are to be offered on each festival.

1, 2 Introduction—The Israelites must regularly present to God the offerings due to him which are anthropomorphically represented as God's food.

3—8 The Daily Offerings—See Ex 29:38—42; Lv 6:8—13.

9, 10 The Sabbath-Offering—This was of equal value to the daily offering, and offered in addition to it.

11—15 The Offerings of the First Day of each Month—In 13 read: one-tenth part of an *ephah*.

16—25 The Offerings of Paschal Week—Liturgical prescriptions taken from Lv 23:5—8 with additional instructions.

26—31 The Offerings of the Day of the Firstfruits, called also the feast of Weeks (Lv 23:15—22).

29:1—6 The Offerings for the Day of Trumpets— **b** See Lv 23:23—25. Since this festival fell on the first day of the month the offerings prescribed here were in addition to those prescribed in 28:11—15.

7—11 The Offerings for the Day of Atonement—See Lv 23:26—32 and Lv 16.

12—38 The Offerings for the Feast of Tabernacles—See Lv 23:33ff.

39 Conclusion—These are public offerings made on behalf of the whole community. In addition any person may present freewill and vow-offerings on any of these festivals.

30 On Vows especially those made by Women— **c** The following regulations are based on the principle that women are subject to their fathers or husbands, and therefore, without their approval, cannot promise to God anything that will interfere with the management of the house.

3 General Principle—If a man makes a vow to the Lord, or binds himself by oath to some abstinence, he shall keep his promise.

4—6 The Vows of an Unmarried Woman—If a marriageable girl makes a vow, the vow will be valid if the father, on becoming aware of it, does not express his disapproval. If he disapproves, her vow is annulled.

7—9, 11—16 The Vows of a Married Woman—A **d** husband has the right to veto his wife's vows, whether these were made before marriage or, inconsiderately, during marriage. God has no delight in hasty vows, Eccl 5:4. If a husband, after having tacitly approved his wife's vows, pretends to annul them, he will be guilty of a breach of promise, but his wife will be guiltless.

The vows of a widow and those of a divorced woman are **e** valid, **10**, as these women are no longer subject to their husbands.

31 The Extermination of the Midianites—This story **f** appears to be a midrashic narrative inserted mainly to illustrate certain principles of the 'holy' war. It may be based on an historical event but the details are inserted for a didactic purpose, i.e. to teach separation from

E✳

216f their gentile neighbours. On the holy war, see §§ 225*d*, 246*g*.

g **1–10 The Expedition**—The incidents which caused this war are related in ch 25. Moses organized an expedition of 12,000 men under the command of Phinehas. The reason why Phinehas, the priest, not Joshua, the future leader of the people, is chosen as commander may be the zeal displayed by him for Yahweh's honour on another occasion (25:7f). He carried with him 'the holy vessels and the trumpets to sound'. On the trumpets see 10:1–10. What is meant by 'holy vessels' is not clear. The phrase 'the trumpets to sound' must perhaps be read in apposition to 'the holy vessels'.

h **11–18 Slaughter of Prisoners**—When the warriors returned with prisoners and booty Moses disapproved of their sparing the women and the children and ordered that all the women who were either married or de-flowered, and all the male children should be slain, the former for having seduced the Israelites into idolatry and immorality, the latter in order to ensure a total extinction of the Midianite race. The virgins alone were to be spared and given as a prize to the combatants (cf Jg 21:11). The possibility of the girls seducing their husbands or masters was disregarded, but mixed marriages were, as a rule, prohibited; cf Ex 34:16; 1 (3) Kgs 11:2.

i **19–24 Purification of the Warriors and the Spoil**—The warriors owing to their state of defilement (Nm 19:16–19) had to stay outside the camp until they purified themselves and the spoil according to the rite prescribed in Nm 19:14–22.

j **25–54 The Division of the Spoil**—David acted in the same way (I Sm 30:24, 25). Out of each moiety a tribute was to be paid to the Lord. The contribution of the warriors consisted of 1/500th of their entire portion and was handed over to Eleazar; that of the rest of the people was fixed at 1/50th of their share and was assigned **k** to the Levites. Thus, although the booty was divided into two equal portions, the individual shares of those who fought were in reality greater than those of the non-combatants. Then the officers of the army brought to Moses and Eleazar articles of gold from the spoils as an offering to the Lord.

l **32 The Transjordanic Region is granted to the Tribes of Reuben and Gad and the half-tribe of Manasseh**—The tribes of Reuben and Gad, with whom the half-tribe of Manasseh is later (**33**) associated, asked Moses to be allowed to settle down in the land E of the Jordan. The request was granted under certain conditions.

m **1–5 The Request**—Seeing that the land of Jazer and the land of Gilead were lands of pasture the Reubenites and the Gadites asked to settle there. The 'land of Jazer' is the city of Jazer and its adjacent pasture-land. 'The land of Gilead' sometimes denotes the whole region E of the Jordan (Dt 3:12f); sometimes it is restricted to the country, S of the river Jabbok, or N of it, the river Jabbok being considered as dividing the land of Gilead into two halves (Jos 12:2). In this ch it is used in both these restricted senses. As the places mentioned in **3** are all situated S of the Jabbok, the land of Gilead in **1** designates southern Gilead.

n **6–32 The Request first Refused and then Granted**—The request, if granted, would have encouraged the other tribes to stay where they were and give up all prospects of further conquests. This would frustrate God's promise and thus provoke his wrath, as on the occasion of the mission of the spies (ch 13f). In order to avert both consequences Moses strongly opposed their demands. The representatives of the two tribes explained to Moses that

their request did not imply a refusal to take part in the **21** conquest of the land W of the Jordan. After assuring adequate protection for their wives, children, flocks and herds in the territory allotted to them, they would pass over the Jordan to fight together with the other tribes. Their explanation was accepted by Moses who directed that southern Gilead be assigned to them.

33–42 The Territory of the Reubenites, the Gadites o and the half-tribe of Manasseh—The 14 cities mentioned in **34–38** are all situated in a strip of land E of the Dead Sea and the Jordan, measuring c. 800 sq. miles. No line of demarcation between the two groups of cities can be drawn. It appears that each city was provisionally assigned to either tribe, the definite demarcation being made later by Joshua (See comm. on Jos 13:8–28).

Of the tribe of Manasseh some clans only had their **p** territory E of the Jordan. The clan of Machir conquered northern Gilead. Jair, another Manassite clan, took the tent-villages (Heb. *ḥawwôt*) and called them after its name. This district was, very probably, in Gilead itself (Jg 10:3–5; 1 (3) Kgs 4:13; l Chr 2:22) and SE of the lake of Genneseret. Nobah, another clan, took the district of Kenath, which was probably E of Jair and on the western slopes of the Hauran.

33:1–49 The Itinerary from Egypt to Moab—This **217** is a summary of the forty years' journeyings in the desert from Egypt to Moab through the various stages of the journey. The list of the stations is not complete. Many places cannot be identified with any degree of probability. Most of them have already been mentioned in Ex or Nm, but a few occur here for the first time. For the whole section see Abel, II, 208–17.

50–56 Directions respecting the Occupation of the b Land of Canaan—The Israelites are commanded: (i) to drive out and dispossess (**53**) all the inhabitants; a partial extermination will have for its effects retaliation by the Canaanites, seduction into idolatry, and punishment by God; (ii) to destroy all idolatrous representations carved on stone, and the molten images of their deities; (iii) to demolish all their high places, or places of worship (for a description of Canaanite high places see S. R. Driver, *Modern Research as illustrating the Bible*, 1908, 60f); (iv) to divide the land by lot as prescribed in 26:55.

34 The Boundaries of the Promised Land W of the c Jordan—Cf Ezek 47:13–20. A distinction must be drawn between the boundaries promised by God and those actually possessed by the Israelites. The description given here is an ideal one representing the extension of the territory, which the Israelites had the right to conquer, but which in point of fact they never completely conquered. Thus the western border, which is represented as running along the Mediterranean coast, was never in the hands of the Israelites, save for a small stretch in its central part, and even that for a short time only. The reason for this is that God's promise was conditional, i.e. subject to the faithful observance of his law by the Israelites; cf Jos 23:12f; Jg 3:1–4. The territory of Israel reached its greatest expansion during the reign of David.

3–5 The Southern Border—This is described in a **d** general way as running from the wilderness of Zin (13:21) along the side of Edom. More particularly the southern line started from the southernmost extremity of the Dead (or Salt) Sea on the east, turned to the south of the ascent or pass of *Aqrabbim*, passed through Zin, an unknown place, reached the south of Kadesh Barnea and followed its course to the Mediterranean Sea along the

7d torrent of Egypt (= Wady el-'Arish) after passing through Hasar Addar and 'Asmon.

e 6 The Western Border ran along the coast of the Mediterranean Sea.

f 7—9 The Northern Border extended from an undefined point on the Mediterranean coast, reached Mt Hor, of uncertain identification but certainly different from that of Aaron's death (20:22), went to the pass of Hamath (13:21) and ended at Ḥaṣar 'Enan, probably between Damascus and the Hauran, after passing through Zedad and Ziphron.

g 10—12 The Eastern Border started from Ḥaṣar 'Enan to Shepham, then it descended to Riblah east of an anonymous spring, flanked the eastern side of the lake of Chinnereth and followed the course of the Jordan down to the Dead Sea.

13—15 Conclusion

16—29 Appointment of Twelve Superintendents for the Division of the Land—Cf Jos chh 14—19.

h 35:1—8 The Levitical Cities—As no territory was assigned to the Levites, provision was to be made whereby they could possess at least some cities to dwell in and the surrounding land for their flocks. The several tribes were therefore commanded to cede to the Levites some of their cities in proportion to the size of their respective territories. The execution of the command is related in Jos 21. The Levitical cities were 48 in all including the 6 cities of refuge (cf 9—15). It is difficult to form a correct idea of the geometrical disposition of the Levitical possessions. In 4 the pasture-land extended 1,000 cubits, or 1,500 feet, from the wall of the city, and each side of the pasture-land was 2,000 cubits long (5).

i 9—34 The Cities of Refuge—Primitive social organization considered every individual as an inseparable part of his clan. Hence an offence against an individual was regarded as an offence against the whole clan and demanded adequate reparation. The Hebrew law modified this ancient custom by distinguishing between voluntary and involuntary manslaughter, and giving the right of blood-revenge to the next-of-kin only.

The right of sanctuary was common almost down to modern times when it had to be abolished on account of the abuses to which it led.

j 9—15 The Appointment of Six Cities of Refuge— If a man kills anyone he becomes liable to be slain by the nearest kinsman of the murdered person. Hebrew legislation modified this custom by establishing the principle that accidental killing cannot be punished by death. But the acquittal of an unintentional homicide is subject to certain conditions. He must appear before the assembly or popular council who will decide whether the killing was wilful or not, and, in case of an unintentional killing, the homicide will take refuge in an asylum where he will be safe from the blood-avenger. For the purpose of this law six cities were to be selected, the names of which are given in Jos 20:7f.

16—23 Distinction between Wilful and Unintention- 217k al Killing—The killing was to be presumed wilful: (i) when the death was caused by an instrument the use of which was likely to be fatal, such as an instrument of iron, a heavy stone, a wooden instrument or staff; (ii) when, failing this evidence, the relations between the homicide and the dead person were unfriendly, or when the death was premeditated. On the contrary the death was to be presumed to have been unintentional when, though it was caused by a murderous instrument, the relations between the two persons were friendly, and still more when the instrument was not in itself lethal. Therefore four cases may be distinguished: 1. Wilful murder: (i) death premeditated and caused by a murderous instrument; (ii) death premeditated and caused by a non-murderous instrument. 2. Unintentional homicide: (i) unpremeditated death caused by a murderous instrument; (ii) unpremeditated death caused by a non-murderous instrument.

24—32 Legal Procedure—All cases of killing must be **l** decided according to these principles. If it is legally proved that the death was wilful, the murderer is delivered into the hands of the murdered person's relatives. But if the death was accidental, the innocent man-slayer is taken to his city of refuge where he must remain till the death of the high-priest.

Further laws are added. 32 Detention in a city of refuge **m** was not only a deliverance from the hands of the blood-avenger, but also a sort of punishment for the shedding of human blood.

33—34 Hortatory Conclusion—The land of the Israel- **n** ites is the habitation of Yahweh, and therefore must be kept free from defilement. Bloodshed defiles the land, and this defilement cannot be expiated except by the blood of him that shed the blood.

36 The Marriage of Daughters possessing Landed o Property—It had already been decided that daughters had the right to inherit their fathers' property when there was no male issue (27:1—11). This concession now raised an important case. If an heiress married outside her tribe, her property would go to another tribe which would consequently have its territory increased, while that of the wife's tribe would be diminished. Such a transference of property not being made by sale, was unaffected by the Jubilee concessions (Lv 25:13ff), and was therefore likely to produce a certain fluctuation and instability of the tribal possessions, and perhaps even an extensive absorption of one tribe by another. In order to prevent this inconvenience the principle was laid down that the tribe and its possessions were inseparable and therefore no property of one tribe could be transferred to another. According to this principle it was decided that the daughters of Zelophehad should marry whom they pleased but within their own tribe.

DEUTERONOMY

BY W. L. MORAN S.J.

223a Bibliography—*Commentaries*: P. Buis–J. Leclerq, 1963; G. Henton Davies, PC (2), 1962; G. von Rad, ATD VIII, Göttingen, 1964 E.tr. OTL, 1967; G. Ernest Wright, IB II, New York, 1953.
Other literature: A. Alt, 'Die Heimat des Deuteronomiums', *Kleine Schriften zur Geschichte des Volkes Israel*, II, München, 1953, 250–75; R. E. Clements, 'Deuteronomy and the Jerusalem Cult-tradition', VT 15 (1965), 300–12; Frank M. Cross, Jr., and David Noel Freedman, 'The Blessing of Moses', JBL 67 (1948), 191–210; EOT Int 219–33, 299–301; J. A. Emerton, 'Priests and Levites in Deuteronomy', VT 12 (1962), 129–38; Fr. Horst, *Das Privilegrecht Jahwes*, Göttingen, 1930 = *Gottes Recht*, München, 1961, 17–154; A. Jepsen, 'Die Reform des Josia', Fs F. Baumgärtel, Erlangen, 1959, 97–108; N. Lohfink, 'Darstellungskunst und Theologie in Dtn 1, 6–3, 29', Bib 41 (1960), 105–34; id, 'Der Bundesschluss im Land Moab', BZ NF 6 (1962), 32–56; id, *Das Hauptgebot, Eine Untersuchung literarischer Einleitungsfragen zu Dtn 5–11*, Romae, 1963; G. T. Manley, *The Book of the Law, Studies in the Date of Deuteronomy*, 1957; Dennis J. McCarthy, S.J., *Treaty and Covenant, A Study in Form in the Ancient Oriental Documents and in the OT*, Romae, 1963; M. Noth, *Überlieferungsgeschichtliche Studien*, Halle (Saale), 1943; G. von Rad, Studies in Deuteronomy, E.tr., 1953; id, 'Deuteronomy', IDB I, New York-Nashville, 1962, 831–8; H. W. Wolff, 'Das Kerygma des deuteronomischen Geschichtswerk', ZAW 73 (1961), 171–186; G. Ernest Wright, 'The Lawsuit of God: A Form-critical Study of Deuteronomy 32', *Israel's Prophetic Heritage*, ed. Bernard W. Anderson and Walter J. Harrelson, New York, 1962, 26–58.

b Name—Among the Jews, who have retained the very ancient practice of referring to a literary work by its opening words, the last book of the Pent is known as *'ēlleh haddᵉbārîm* ('These are the words'), or simply *dᵉbārîm* ('Words'). The name Deuteronomy goes back to the Gr. (LXX) translation of a phrase in 17:18, where 'a copy of this law' was misinterpreted as 'this second law' (*deuteronomion*). The error, however, was not altogether unhappy, for at least in its final form Dt is presented as the text of a new covenant (29:1 = Heb 28:69), with a law which is distinct from, though intimately connected with, the law of Sinai-Horeb (4:13f; 5:31ff).

c Contents and Structure—Dt is Moses' farewell address to the people, delivered in Moab east of the Jordan, probably on the day of his death (1:1–5; cf 34:1–12). He first recalls the principal events from their departure from Sinai until the present (1:6–3:29), then exhorts them to observance of the law, stressing particularly the prohibition of images in the Decalogue (4:1–40). After a new introduction (4:44–49) parallel to 1:1–5, he reminds the people of the Sinai covenant and of their request, accepted by God, that he be their mediator and pass on to them any additional laws that **22** God might reveal to him (5:1–31); God did reveal other laws, and these laws are now promulgated. They are laws to direct the people's lives in Canaan, and their quintessential expression is the demand for absolute, undivided loyalty and commitment to Yahweh, which Moses passionately urges Israel to observe (6:1–11:25). In 12:1ff the law becomes more specific; in 12:2–18:22 it concerns the centralization of the cult at a unique sanctuary, its consequences, some other rules of worship (distinction of clean and unclean animals, apostasy), debtors, and offices (judges, king, priests, prophets); chh 19–26 are much less homogeneous and the various laws on cities of refuge, false witnesses, war, family rights, humanitarian customs, etc, exhibit no systematic arrangement. Ch 27 requires the erection of an altar on Mt Ebal and the performance of a ceremony of blessings and curses on this mountain and on Mt Gerizim; ch 28 announces the sanctions of blessing or curse attached to the law of Dt. In 29:1 (Heb 28:69) a third discourse of Moses is introduced; in chh 31–32 Joshua is installed to replace Moses as the leader of Israel's troops, the covenant text is written down and deposited next to the Ark, and the Song is recited as a witness against the people. Finally, Moses blesses the tribes, dies and is buried (chh 33–34).

The general structure of Dt exhibits four parts, dis- **d** tinguished by a late, perhaps the final, redactor through the alteration of *'elleh* and *wᵉzô't* in four superscriptions: I. 1:1–4:43 (superscription 1:1–5, beginning *'elleh*, 'These are . . .'), II. 4:44–28:68 (superscription 4:44–49, beginning *wᵉzô't*, 'And this is . . .'), III. 29:1 (Heb. 28:69)–32:52 (superscription 29:1, beginning *'elleh*, 'These are . . .'), IV 33:1–34:12 (superscription 33:1, beginning *wᵉzô't*, 'And this is . . .'). Other structural pointers are, for example, 'Hear/And now, O Israel" in 5:1; 6:4; 9:1; 10:12, which articulate the section 5:1–11:32; 'And now' in 4:1, which divides I. into 1:6–3:29 and 4:1–40; 'These are the statutes' in 12:1, which serves to distinguish 5:1–11:32 from 12:2ff, etc. The structural division into sections and subsections of course corresponds to differences of content (sometimes of authorship, too), which by and large are those of history, law, and sanctions (see §224a).

Literary Criticism—The evidence for several hands in **e** the composition of Dt is beyond cavil; it consists in the repetitions, the differences of language, the breaks in unity, and the competing, even contradictory, views which with all due allowance made for ancient, diverse norms of composition and for the combination by the same writer of various sources, cannot be explained except as the work of two or more authors. We cite only a few of the most obvious examples. Repetitions: the superscriptions of 1:1ff and 4:44ff (and in 5:1 Moses convenes the people as if he had not been speaking to them from 1:6ff). Differences of language: 32:48–52 exhibits the vocabulary of the Priestly Tradition, absent in general in Dt (and

3e contrary to 1:37; 3:26; 4:21, Moses is excluded from the Promised Land because of personal sin). Breaks in unity: 27:1–8, 11–26 is a jarring interruption in both form (narrative against direct discourse, departure from covenant formulary) and content (Dt leaves the location of the unique altar unnamed, ch 27 mentions Mt Ebal explicitly). Competing views: 12:15f permits non-sacrificial meat to be eaten in any town, 12:20f adds the restriction that the central sanctuary must be fairly distant (see also above on 32:48–52).

f Since the *Dissertatio critica* of De Wette in 1805, who in the first critical analysis of Dt demonstrated that Dt is a source distinct from the other Pent traditions and confined to this book, the goal of literary criticism has been to isolate the 'original Dt', which, it has been generally held, is to be identified, or virtually so, with 'the book of the law' discovered in the temple in the time of Josiah (2 (4) Kgs 22:8; see below, § 224e). This would be the core of Dt, and insofar as its discernment is possible and not a pseudo-problem based on false premises, it is commonly agreed that it is to be found in chh 5–26; 28.

g Chh 1–3 are best explained with M. Noth as the introduction to the Deuteronomic History, a work which extends through Jos-2 (4) Kgs. They do not really duplicate chh 5–11, from which they are quite different in form and content, and they are not therefore, as was once held, evidence of a second edition of the laws in chh 12ff. Rather, they were written to introduce a history which follows the people of God from Sinai-Horeb down to its sad latter days of imminent or actual exile. For the links between chh 1–3; 31; and Jos, cf Jos 1:2ff/Dt 1:38; 31:7f: Jos 1:12ff; 22:1ff/Dt 3:18ff; Jos 14:6ff/Dt 1:36.

4:1–40 is a later addition to chh 1–3 (see commentary). Its author was a revisor of the Dt History, from which he derived or, perhaps, into which he introduced, the message to the exiles that a return to Yahweh, that is, repentance and renewed community with God was still possible (4:29–31, Wolff). He is also the author of 30:1–10, where the same theme is developed, and similar contacts with ch 4 in theme and diction make it probable that the rest of ch 30 is also his work. Tracing him further and distinguishing him from the author of chh 1–3 in chh 29; 31–34, are difficult; to the latter we would assign at least 31:1–2, 3b, 7–10, 24–26, 34:1–6, and to the former at least 29:22–28 (Heb 29:21–28), and the incorporation of the Song (32:1–43) with its prose introduction (31:16–22, 28–30; also 32:44).

h Another stage in the growth of Dt, if it is not identical with the addition of 4:1–40, etc, is the joining of Dt-Dt History with the other Pent sources in Gn-Nm. Here belong 1:3 and 32:48–52; 34:1, 7–12; also, if it does not belong to an earlier stage, 33:1–29 (incorporating the Blessing) with the addition of 4:44 to create the four-part division of the book. To this stage too should perhaps be assigned the insertion of 27:1–8, 11–26 (and therefore 11:29–31).

In the analysis of chh 5–26; 28, an important distinction is to be made between previously existing sources and the various additions which accrued to them in their incorporation into Dt. Most of the regulations in chh 12ff were drawn from various earlier collections; apart from the law on centralization and its application to earlier rules of worship, there is little specifically Dt legislation. The blessings and curses in ch 28 also derive in part from traditional, fixed formulas, and similarly, the material in chh 5–11 had, in part at least, taken form before finding a place in Dt.

Among the 'legal' sources one is the group of 'removal' **i** laws (13:1–18; 17:2–7, (8–13); 19:(1–10), 11–13, 16–21; 21:1–9, 18–21; 22:13–27; 24:7; probably, too, 22:28f; 24:1–4; 25:5–10; perhaps 21:15–17, 22f; 24:5; 25:1–3, 11f; J. L'Hour, 'Une législation criminelle dans le Deutéronome', Bib 44 (1963), 1–28). They are characterized by the recurring formula, 'so you shall purge the evil from the midst of you' (13:5; 17:7, etc; in some cases slightly modified), and they are largely homogeneous, most of them being transparent casuistic formulations ('If . . .') of an earlier or related form of the Decalogue. Similarly, one may distinguish the laws on war (20:1–10; 21:10–14; 23:9–14), on membership in the sacred assembly (23:1–8 = Heb. 23:2–9), on the 'abominations' to Yahweh (16:21–17:1; 18:9–12; 22:5; 23:17f; 25:13–16; perhaps 14:3; J. L'Hour, 'Les interdits to'eba dans le Deutéronome', RB 71 (1964), 481–503). The parallels, the exact extent of which is hard to define, between Dt and the Book of the Covenant (Ex 21–23; cf also 34) suggest dependence, direct or indirect, on a related collection of laws (cf Dt 14:21a/Ex 22:30; Dt 14:21b/Ex 23:19b; 34:26; Dt 15:1–11/Ex 23:10f; Dt 15:12–18/Ex 21:2–6; Dt 15:19–23/Ex 22:28b–29; Dt 16:1–17/Ex 23:14–17; 34:18ff; Dt 16:18–20/Ex 23:2–3, 6–8; Dt 22:1–4/Ex 23:4f; Dt 23:20f/Ex 22:24f; Dt 24:10–13/Ex 22:24f; Dt 24:17f/Ex 23:9; 22:20–23). Another source of course, and cited as such in Dt, is the Decalogue in 5:6ff.

The presence of sources shows that in large part **j** the question of authorship concerns the work of combining them in a deeper unity, and on closer examination this unity is seen to derive from that urgent, hortatory tone which pervades Dt and gives it its special character. Exhortation, however, is primarily the task of the preacher, and its proper setting is an assembly of worshippers. Recognition of this fact, due largely to von Rad, is the basis for the current view that, beginning with a body of tradition, Dt in chh 5–26; 28 is the result of a gradual process of growth as in repeated liturgical gatherings the law was preached and its proclamation introduced by a short sermon. Earlier efforts, therefore, to separate literary strata and eventually arrive thereby at the original nucleus of the book are considered to have been in large part badly misconceived.

One norm, however, is still widely accepted for **k** distinguishing earlier and more recent levels in the text, namely, the use of the sing. or pl. in addressing the people; the sing. passages are considered the older. (Unfortunately this fluctuation between sing. and pl. is concealed in a modern English translation; for example, in 6:4ff Israel is regularly addressed as 'thou', but in vv 14, 16–17—until the last word—as 'you'). This norm, however, has only some validity in the laws of chh 12ff, in which the shift in number is very rare; and when applied rigidly to chh 5–11, in which the shift is fairly frequent, it seems to rend real unities and to result at times in an implausible text (for example, read the sing. 7:25b–26 without the pl. prohibition in 7:25a). Certainly the phenomenon is pre-dt, since it appears in the Book of the Covenant in a clearly earlier stage of its development (e.g. Ex 22:23; 23:9b). In Dt the rule seems to be that in passages recalling the past (5:1ff; 9:8ff) the pl. prevails, in hortatory passages the sing., with the shift to the pl., at least originally, a stylistic device for securing emphasis; later, the combination of sing. and pl. seems to have become a feature of style in such discourse with no particular significance (Lohfink).

223l However, even if chh 5—26 be a collection of exhortations and preached law, some redactional work comparable to literary authorship is not excluded and in fact is required by the evidence, especially in chh 5—11. Apart from minor later interpolations and redactional retouches, 5:1—6:25 and 7:1—5, 13b—24 were probably originally independent units, which were joined by a redactor in 7:6—13a. 8:1—18 is based on 6:10ff, but the divergent conception of the satiety foreseen in the Promised Land argues for a different author; since 8:19 harks back to 7:12 and supplies the expected allusion to the covenant-curse, the author of 8:1—18 and 7:6—13a is probably the same. (This implies that the exhortation of ch 8 is a 'closet-sermon'). In chh 9—11 it has already been indicated that 11:29—31 assumes the interpolation of 27:1—8, 11—26; 11: 26—28 is perhaps from the same hand. 11:22—25 is rather loosely connected with the previous vv, and in view of the extremely close parallel in Jos 1:2ff (Dt—History) it seems to be the work of the historian in chh 1—3 or 4. Similarly, 9:22—24, which is intrusive, echoes ch 1 (cf especially 9:23a/1—21; 9:23b/1:26, 32); moreover, 9: 1—7, which cannot be separated from 9:22—24 (see commentary), also harks back to ch 1 (cf 9:1f/1:28). It seems, therefore, that the author of chh 1—3 or 4 is the one who inserted 9:8ff along with additions of his own, which reflect his concern to show that the sin of Horeb was only the beginning of a history of sin culminating in the events of Kadesh-barnea. Moreover, since 8:19—20 provides the transition to 9:1ff, and since the vocabulary of the oath in 9:5 and 8:18 is unparalleled elsewhere in Dt, it appears that the author-redactor of 7:6—3a; 8:1—20; 9:1—7, 22—24 is one and the same, and hence the historian of chh 1—3 or 4. What his contribution may have been in the following chh remains to be established.

224a Form—Dt is presented as the text of a covenant or pact between God and Israel. In broad outline, this covenant begins by alternating recollections of the past (5:1ff; 9:7ff) with a call to total dedication to Yahweh (6:4ff; 10:12ff), then specifies more exactly the implications of the dedication (chh 12ff), briefly refers to an exchange of commitments between God and people (26:16—19) and to a cultic silence (27:9f), and concludes with a declaration of the covenant sanctions, blessings and curses (chh 28:1ff). The text of this covenant is committed to writing (31:9), the document is deposited next to the Ark, a portable sanctuary (31:26), and it is to be read to the entire people every seven years (31:10). Though it is to serve as a witness against the people (31:26), reference is also made to calling upon heaven and earth as witnesses (31:29; 4:26; 30:19).

b The significance of this outline and of other practices associated with the covenant in Dt is grasped only if, together with parts of the Sinai-tradition and Jos 24, they are examined in the light of ancient Near E international treaties. For these treaties, the texts of which have come down to us in sources from the latter part of the second millennium and from the 8th—7th cent. B.C., show a remarkable similarity in both structure and usage. The closest OT parallels seem to be found in the vassal treaties of the second millennium from Asia Minor (Hittites) and N Syria. Their normal structure is: 1. Preamble (suzerain introduced by name and title); 2. historical prologue (suzerain addresses vassal and recalls his or his predecessors' gracious deeds in favour of the vassal kingdom); 3. general stipulation (demands for vassal's undivided loyalty); 4. particular stipulations (military assistance, etc, but also visit to suzerain's court, payment of tribute, reading of treaty text to

vassal's subjects at fixed intervals); 5. list of gods **22** witnessing to treaty (among them heaven and earth); 6. curses and blessings. The treaty text was written, and the copies of the suzerain and the vassal deposited in a temple.

The influence of this treaty formulary on Dt is evident. **c** It explains much in the outline of chh 5—26; 28 and the practices noted above; in particular, the exhortations of chh 5—11 are seen to correspond in theme and structural position to the general stipulation of the treaties. Structurally, this influence is also evident in chh 1—4, in which after the history of the events from Horeb to Moab, in a transition typical of the biblical formulary ('And now . . .', 4:1; cf 10:12; Ex 19:5; Jos 24:14), we pass to the obligations of obedience, and, as in the Hittite treaties, one obligation is singled out as the 'great commandment', the essential expression of the suzerain's will and the basic norm of the subject's complete devotion and loyalty, which additional, particular stipulations apply to concrete, historical circumstances. 4:25—31 also add the sanctions of curse and blessing. In chh 29—30, we find history (29:2—8 = Heb 29:1— 7), allusions to the general stipulation and curses (29:16—21, 22—27 = Heb 29:15—20, 21—27), blessings (30:1—10), and invocation of witnesses (30:19).

Behind Dt, therefore, there is an institution which in **d** our reference to a liturgical setting we have already hinted at, but can now define more sharply; it is the institution of the covenant between God and his people, handed down in the living tradition of Israel's worship. It is this institution with its ancient formulary which permeates Dt and with the strong, hortatory tone already noted imparts to it a profound unity. The use of the formulary, it is true, varies. Its potentialities may be exploited for redactional purposes, as in the addition of 4:1ff to chh 1—3. A part of the formulary may be adapted with considerable modification; for example, the historical prologue becomes in 5:1—6:3 a proof from history of the essential continuity between the covenants of Horeb and Moab, and of the legitimacy of the Mosaic office in the promulgation of the law that follows. Parts too may be expanded, repeated, or merely touched upon in a passing allusion (see the exhortations); here we see the formulary serving as a basic pattern with formulas, themes and their inner relationships, while remaining open to quite different elaborations or adaptations to various literary genres. Nevertheless, this wide diversity illustrates rather than contradicts the fundamental importance of the covenant and its tradition in Dt.

Tradition—The origins of the dt tradition are very **e** ancient; they probably go back in some sense to the earliest days of Israel's occupation of Canaan, and even to Moses himself. The latter's role, it is true, is hard to assess, since even the earliest traditions on the Mosaic covenant (Ex 19ff) exhibit considerable development and reflect the circumstances and concerns of intervening centuries. However, we may with some confidence attribute to Mosaic influence the covenant institution, though not necessarily the covenant formulary described above, and the substantial concerns of the dt covenant, namely, the exclusive cult of Yahweh (general stipulation) extended and translated into terms of daily life through obedience to Yahweh's will for justice towards fellow-Israelites (cf Decalogue, particular stipulations).

In the account of the covenant concluded at Shechem **f** (Jos 24), which certainly reflects one of the earliest traditions of the occupation period, we probably have the oldest evidence for the influence of the same covenant

24f formulary found in Dt. The parallels in Ex 21—23 (see Literary Criticism), which date from around 1100 B.C., reveal the ancient roots of many dt laws, though the latter reflect frequently the adaptations necessary in a more advanced social and economic context. An equally ancient, or perhaps even earlier, body of stipulations lies behind the indirectly related series in Ex 20:23—26 + 23:14—19 and Ex 34:17—26, the dt contacts with which, again frequently in a later form, are also clear (see Literary Criticism). Moreover, it seems probable that the common source underlying the Ex texts extends to Ex 23:20—33 and Ex 34:11—16, which consequently would reflect the historical prologue and general stipulation of the ancient covenant text. It would be from this part of the source that Dt 7:1—5, 13*b*—24 derived; perhaps, in fact, in this passage of Dt and in the related stipulations in chh 12ff the earliest level of Dt is reached.

g Dt, therefore, is a later stage of a very ancient tradition. A *tempus ante quod* for the substance of chh 5—26; 28 is provided by the 18th year of Josiah (622), when 'the book of the law' was discovered in the temple. Though we should not attempt to reconstruct Dt from the general description of Josiah's reform, which had already been under way for some six years before the 'book' came to light (cf 2 Chr 34:3ff), nevertheless the celebration of the Passover in Jerusalem (2 (4) Kgs 23:21ff), an evident consequence of the 'book's' discovery, can hardly be explained except as based on Dt 16:1ff, the only evidence we have for the break with tradition requiring the Passover to be celebrated at the central sanctuary.

h However, there are many indications in the narrative of 2 (4) Kgs 22—23 that the document discovered had earlier been not a mere private program of reform, as is generally held, but the text of a covenant considered binding upon king and people. This being true, we must look for the occasion of such a covenant. Josiah's two predecessors, Manasseh and Amon, are clearly excluded by the religious syncretism which flourished in their reigns with their support and blessing; Hezekiah, however, was not only one of the most pious Judahite kings, but he is reported to have carried out a program of centralization of the cult (2 (4) Kgs 18:4), which accords perfectly with the demands of Dt 12. And if one accepted the historicity of the Chronicler's statement that Hezekiah also had the Passover celebrated in Jerusalem (2 Chr 30), the influence of Dt in his reign would be clearer. We may therefore trace Dt back to a covenant renewal in the late 8th cent. B.C.

i What of the centuries intervening between the premonarchical period, where we found the beginnings of the specific form of the dt tradition, and the late 8th cent., where the tradition has reached substantially its present form? The prevailing view is that this process of transmission was carried on in the N Kingdom, probably at some sanctuary (Shechem itself? For the problem, cf. G. E. Wright, *Shechem: the Biography of a Biblical City*, 1965, 138) and the final formative stage was reached not long before the downfall of Samaria in 722 B.C.; it is also proposed that it was particularly the Levitical priests fleeing to the S who were primarily responsible for introducing the 'dt reform' in Judah. This view may be right, but the facts it would explain admit of another interpretation; and its implication that, in the S, the Sinai tradition was for around two centuries virtually forgotten in favour of the Davidic covenant seems especially questionable.

25a Theology—Dt is a *summa theologica*, an original synthesis, and in many respects a bold one, of Israel's sacred traditions, customs and institutions. The **225a** patriarchs and God's promise to them of progeny and land, the exodus, the revelation of Sinai-Horeb, the desert wanderings, the taking of Canaan, sacred festivals, ritual and worship, the law of sanctuary and city-gate, judge, priest, prophet, king, holy war, covenant—Dt brings them all together, stripping many to their barest essence, refracting others in the prism of its special concerns, but despite the development of centuries and the several strata of authorship, imparting to all a profound unity in its vision of God and his people. It is a theology rooted in the present, a theology of reform, born in a crisis of faith. Though it is strongly traditional, it is not antiquarian; it reasserts the validity of ancient beliefs and practices, but it does not hesitate to adapt, change, even boldly innovate.

Yahweh is unique (6:4; 4:35; 4:39; 7:9), the lord of the universe (10:14; 4:32; 32:8), yet he has chosen Israel to be his people, sacred to him, his personal possession, his inheritance (4:20; 7:6; 10:15; 14:2; 26:18f; 27:9; 28:9; 29:13 = Heb 29:12; 32:9). This privilege, shared by no other people (4:19f; 32:8f), is absolutely gratuitous; it is explained by nothing in Israel, the most insignificant of peoples, but only by a love hidden in the mystery of God (7:7; 10:15).

This love first manifests itself in God's oath to the **b** patriarchs, which becomes the bed-rock of salvation-history. On this oath rest the exodus, the victories in Canaan and the possession of the land (4:37f; 7:8); because of it God forgives a sinful people and bestows on it a gift of which it is deeply undeserving (9:5, 27). It is this word of God which creates the bounty of Canaan and in which, indeed, every blessing is rooted (7:12; 8:18). Dt removes the slightest grounds for self-complacence or for urging any prior claim on God. And when God's purpose for Israel will seem to have ended only in the bitter frustration of exile, his people will not be without hope, for the merciful God who swore to the patriarchs will never abandon them, indeed he will gently call them to repentance with the promise of a future surpassing anything they had known in the past (4:29—31; 30:1—10).

One Yahweh—one place of worship, one altar. The **c** law of centralization was revolutionary. In pre-monarchical days of the Twelve Tribe League, Israel undoubtedly came together for common worship of its God; in fact, many scholars believe that the Ark functioned as a kind of central sanctuary for the League. Though this latter point is somewhat questionable, even if true it does nothing to diminish the truly revolutionary aspects of the Dt law, which had as a necessary result a radical secularization of Israelite life in terms of conventional religious categories; sacred space was drastically restricted, and sacred time in a sense concerned only this unique area. But adopting with modification the Sion election-theology and, perhaps, the Ark tent-theology, Dt sees in the presence of Yahweh's name in one place of his choosing an expression and the necessary consequence of his uniqueness. A God apart and of another order, Yahweh cannot be worshipped as were the gods of Canaan, who were many, with many cult-centres, or, like Baal, one god, but present and therefore worshipped in a plurality of manifestations (12:2ff). Undoubtedly, centralization was intended to solve the problem of syncretism which had long exercised, and often fatally, its fascination and had led to the assimilation of Yahweh to a Baal.

In its rejection of all that was Canaanite, Dt revived **d** the institution of the holy war and called for total,

225d pitiless destruction (7:1–5, 16; 20: 16ff). Perhaps, as has been proposed, the revival was inspired by the practical consideration of the necessity of conscripting a popular army, as in pre-monarchical days, after the king's professional army had been wiped out in the deportations of Sennacherib in the late 8th cent. But the motives Dt expressly proposes are purely religious; Canaanites in the people's midst would be a snare and an enticement to imitate the abominations of their cult. This bellicose fanaticism, it is true, was in the time of Dt largely theoretical; not only were the Canaanites as holders of the land a situation long past, but even if we see behind them Assyrians or any other contemporary Israelite enemy, the chances of annihilating them were extremely small. And it is this theoretical aspect which has been appealed to in order to diminish the horror of Dt's demand for total war, and to reconcile it with a course of revelation which culminates in the imperative of a universal love. Yet this is no solution of the problem; bad theory, be it capable of being put into practice or not, remains bad theory. Rather, here, as in the narrow nationalism of Dt which does not allow for even a hint of God's salvific design for all men—a slight exception may be 4:19— we must see a limitation of Dt theology, valid insofar as it honours God's absolute claims which brook no compromise, but severely time-conditioned by its historical context and ultimately requiring the correction of a fuller and final revelation, cf §§ 246g, 216f, 353c–e.

e It is in the holy war that Dt sees—and who would fault it?—the occasion for the expression of man's fundamental disposition towards God: absolute trust. The idea was not new; it was rooted in the institution itself. But Dt gives it a new emphasis and a new, more comprehensive, theological dimension. The holy wars of the past were initiated by a divine oracle or some other sign indicative of God's favouring the war and promise of support. In Dt the oracles and signs are replaced by the fact of the exodus, the perennial proof of God's power and the enduring assurance that this power will never fail his people (7:17ff; 20:1ff). And the trust which this sign is to evoke is antecedent to all law; to refuse it is, in effect, to reject the exodus, the very foundation of Israelite law (cf 1:29ff).

f For Dt, which here follows traditional covenantal theology, Israelite law is covenantal law. This is to say that antecedent to all service on Israel's part are Yahweh's free choice of this people and his saving intervention in its history; the law, therefore, defines Israel's response to grace, a response it owes in justice and gratitude. In fact, the law is unintelligible in any other terms (see especially 6:20–25), and it could not therefore be further removed from the charge of introducing a *do ut des* relationship with God. Nor is it a yoke imposed on a people constrained to serve willy nilly. It is freely accepted (26:17), and because it is, it requires more than mere external conformity (6:5), and is not only commanded, but is proposed (4:44), explained, and constantly motivated.

The service required by covenantal law is, first of all, a dedication of one's whole being to God (6:5), but one cannot honour God's exclusive claims if one ignores justice to fellow-Israelites (Decalogue, the 'removal' laws, 16:19f, etc) or the plight of the poor and helpless (12:12, 19; 14: 27–29; 15:1–18; 24:6, 10–15, 17–22; 26:12ff). In fact, in 10:19, in a context devoted to the general stipulation, love of the sojourner is by implication virtually raised to the same dignity and importance as the love of God.

g Dt, at least in its final form, is haunted by the awareness

of the people's radical sinfulness (9:6ff; 31:16ff) and **22** of consequent imminent disaster, and in some parts (cf 4:25ff; 28:47ff) one senses the presence of a tragedy no longer threatening but lived. The whole course of salvation-history is undone (28:58ff), the people is once more in Egypt, offering themselves as slaves, 'but no man will buy you' (28:68). Yet if the history is undone, it is not ended. God will gather Israel again, bring them back to the land, himself circumcise their hearts and thus insure that love which is the very substance of the law (30:1–10). Ultimately, therefore, Dt, which began as a covenant declaring Israel's obligations ends as a prediction of its restoration; law yields to prophecy. And the Dt history, which frames the law, is probably in final analysis intended as Israel's confession of its sins and the admission of the justice of the punishment of the exile. They are written down and laid before God, as the period of expectation begins until the prophecy is fulfilled. That it was fulfilled, and in a way Dt could not foresee, is of the essence of Christian faith.

1:1–5 Superscription—The original text probably **22c** included only 1a, 4–5 in the concentric structure:

    A 'These are the words' (1a)
      B the speaker (1a)
        C where (1a)
          D when (4)
        C' where (5a)
      B' the speaker (5b)
    A' 'this *teaching*' (5b).

This structure, with D in the centre, stresses the victories in Transjordan, which in the author's mind are of the greatest importance, for they are a prelude to, and a sign of, the conquest of the Promised Land (see 2:24ff; cf also 4:46f; 29:7f (Heb 29:6f); 31:4; Jos 2:10; 9:10; 12:2ff; 13:10ff). *Tôrāh* (5) is teaching, instruction, and its object may be history (cf Ps 78 (77):1) as well as law. Here, as is evident from 1:6ff, it is concerned **b** with history. **3** is a later addition to place Dt in the priestly chronology of the Pent and Jos (cf Ex 12:3, 6, 41, 51; 16:1; 40:1ff; Nm 1:1; 9:11; 10:11; 33:38; Jos 4:19). According to this chronology, which follows a calendar also employed in the Book of Jubilees and some Qumran documents, the discourses of Moses in Dt were delivered on a Friday, one of the three most important liturgical days in this system. Dt is thus incorporated into the 'desert liturgy': its movements regulated by the religious calendar, the people of God advances as in a great liturgy towards the possession of the home and blessings promised by God. Significantly, once they have entered the Promised Land, the dating of events, like the manna (Jos 5:10ff), ceases. With this addition, a new structure emerges, emphasising the divine authority behind Moses' words: A–C as above, D when (3a), E discourse according to previous divine command (3b), D' when (4), etc. **1b–2**, **c** as commonly agreed, is intrusive, with the probable exception of 'in the Arabah'; 2 seems quite out of context, and 1b seems to refer to a region in Moab considerably removed from the Jordan (cf Suphah in Nm 21:14 and the LXX Zoob instead of Waheb). However, our ignorance of the location of the other places mentioned in 1b renders any proposal for the scene of Moses' discourse quite conjectural. Apparently there was another tradition on the site of Moses' last address to the people. Some scholars have interpreted the various places in 1b as successive stations in the crossing of the desert, and consider the entire verse as the conclusion of Nm rather than the beginning of Dt; however, there are serious objections against this view. 'Beyond the Jordan' (1a) reflects the viewpoint of the writer in W Palestine.

226d **1:6—4:40 First Covenant Discourse**
1:6—3:29 History
1:6—8 (9—18)—2:1 The Anti-Holy War and Anti-Exodus—Yahweh hands over the Promised Land to Israel and at the same time initiates a holy war against its inhabitants, but Israel, faced with danger and lacking the necessary disposition of trust in God's help, refuses to attack. Accordingly, those of military age are excluded forever from the Promised Land. The author follows the J tradition in Nm 13—14, but makes significant changes. He stresses, for example, motifs of the ancient institution of the holy war and of its first greatest example, the exodus from Egypt. But he inverts these motifs, and what results is an anti-holy war and anti-exodus (cf the anti novel and anti-hero of contemporary literature); the motifs are present, but their **e** sense is profoundly transformed. This literary technique of inversion reveals the inner meaning of the events: the deep perversity of the people's sin, which contravenes God's gracious designs for them. This also emerges from the structure of the passage, which is determined by order of the speakers (on the omission of 9—18, see below):

> A Yahweh (6—8)
>   B Moses (20f)
>   C people (22)
>   D scouts (25)
>   C′ people (27f)
>   B′ Moses (29ff)
> A′ Yahweh (35f).

The turning point is the report of the scouts, after which begin the inversions and the opposition to what has gone before. C′ contradicts the readiness to engage in battle expressed in C; B′, though superficially so much like B, after the refusal of the people in C′ means something quite different and now only serves to establish more clearly the people's deep lack of trust (see below); A′ retracts the gift of the land in A. As a kind of appendix follow A (37—40), C (41), A′ (42), which open up new depths of perversity. Urged to conduct a holy war, Israel had refused; now, most solemnly warned against it, Israel goes forth to battle—and to bitter defeat. In the end we find it in banishment, circling in the desert. Such was the end of the first generation, such in all essentials will be, and for the same lack of trust (2 (4) Kgs 17:14), the **f** Israel in exile centuries later. **6.** 'The Lord our God' (cf especially 5:2 and 6:4): Yahweh is Israel's God through the bond of the covenant (Dt 26:17f; 29:13; Ex 6:7; Lv 26:12, etc). **7.** For the location of the various regions, see §§ 53h—54o; they are properly divisions of Judah, but are here extended, as occasionally elsewhere (Jos 9:1; 12:8), to embrace all of Palestine. 'The hill country of the Amorites', an expression found only in this ch (19, 20), probably refers to Palestine in general rather than, as some scholars maintain, to merely the S part. This view is supported by grammar; in the Heb. text, the verb 'go' has two direct objects, 'the hill country of the Amorites' and 'Lebanon', and what intervenes can therefore only specify the extent of the hill country and the peoples to be dispossessed. Confirming this analysis is 3:25, where the Promised Land consists of 'that goodly hill country, and Lebanon'. The stress on Palestine as mountainous is probably to be explained, in part at least, by the influence of Ex 15:17, the ancient hymn which guides the author in 2:2ff (see below); in this verse too Palestine is 'thy own mountain' (cf also Dt 32:13, Ps 78 (77):54). Yahweh's order therefore sends the people from 'this mountain' (6) to another, and the **g** fulfilment of Ex 15:13ff has begun. **8.** 'I *hereby give* the land over to you'. These words are both a grant of title to the land and a holy war oracle (cf 2:24, 31; **226g** 3:2; Jos 6:2; 10:8, etc). God is faithful to his oath to the patriarchs, and nothing remains for the people to do but to take possession of the land with the divine assistance assured by the oracle. This is a most solemn moment in salvation-history. **9—18**, see below. **19.** The terrors of the desert contrast with the goodness of the land of promise (25; cf 8:15); they are safely traversed because Israel obeys the divine word. The power of this word to save is also clearly implied in Israel's march in 2:2ff, each stage of which is introduced by a divine command. **20—21.** Moses repeats the holy war oracle, and adds the typical exhortation not to fear (cf 3:2; 7:18; 20:1ff; Jos 8:1; 10:8, 25, etc). **22.** The march **h** into battle is delayed by the people's proposal, which is, on the surface at least, a reasonable one, and as such it is accepted by Moses. However, the author probably intends it as a hint of the lack of trust which will soon become painfully evident, for in J, his source, it was probably Moses (Nm 13:17b), in P certainly Yahweh (Nm 13:2), who took the initiative. The author, therefore, apparently wishes to shift all responsibility for what follows on the people. **25.** Similarly, whereas in the source (Nm 13:27f) the scouts speak of the difficulties the conquest faces, here their report is simply favourable. In Dt it is only the perversity of the people which accounts for the distortion of the report in 28. **27.** **i** Now begins the anti-holy war! A holy war ends with the people in their tents, this war begins there; in a holy war the people go forth with a war-shout (Jos 6:5; Jg 7:20; 1 Sm 17:20, 52), in this war they murmur without making a move; and in their blasphemous denial of the primary article of Israelite faith, they employ terminology of a holy war oracle, 'to give into the hand', and in effect declare that Yahweh is warring not with them, but against them. **28.** The admission of melted hearts disqualifies them for participation in a holy war (cf 20:8; Jg 7:3). The Anakim, which bear a tribal name already attested in the Egyptian Execration Texts of the 19th cent. B.C., are usually associated with the area around Hebron (Nm 13:22, 28, 33; Jos 14:12, 15, etc), but they occupy a good part of the hill-country according to Jos 11:21f. Their renowned size may rest on more than popular imagination; the Egyptians were awed by the height of the bedouin ('some of them are four or five cubits', ANET 477b). **29—31.** The people disqualified, **j** this holy war exhortation of Moses comes *post festum*; cf the order of exhortation and testing for qualifications in 20:1ff. In this context, therefore, it is really an inversion of such an exhortation; Moses is like a general urging into battle an army of dead men, his efforts necessarily futile and grotesque, their only possible effect being to make even clearer the nature of his audience. These and the following vv pick up the reference to the exodus already made by the people (27), and by numerous allusions to the old tradition stress the exodus particularly as a holy war; cf 29 and Ex 14:13; 30 and Ex 13:21; 14:13, 14, 25; 32 and Ex 14:31; 33 and Ex 13:21; 14:19—21, 24f. Both here and by the shores of the sea Moses exhorts the people, but here his plea issues, not in trust (Ex 14:31), but the very opposite (32)—an anti-exodus.

35—40. Structure: A people (35), B Caleb (36), **k** C Moses (37), B′ Joshua (38), A′ people (39f). Note that B and B′ correspond as exceptions to the punishment of 35 (on Caleb's loyalty, see Nm 14:24; Jos 14:6ff). A′ restates A in other terms and shows its immediate consequences. **37**, because it interrupts Yahweh's speech to the people, is usually considered a later addition

226k along with the following v. However, Moses' plea in 3:23ff is most easily understood in the light of 1:37. The punishment of Moses confronts us with a mystery, for it is not due to any personal sin (see also 3:26–28; 4:21); if the author knew of such a sin (cf Nm 20:7ff, 23ff; 27:12ff; Dt 32:51; Ps 106 (105):32f), he makes no reference to it and does not use it to explain Moses' exclusion from the Promised Land. Rather, for him, Moses is innocent, and yet he suffers with, and because of, the guilty. The author perhaps intends to console the innocent among the exiles, and, in the silent acceptance by Moses of the divine will (3:29), to provide an example (N. Lohfink, 'Wie stellt sich das Problem Individuum-Gemeinschaft in Dt 1, 6 bis 3, 29', *Scholastik* 35 (1960), 403–407). We thus approach the idea of the Suffering Servant, whose passion is not only unmerited, but a source of salvation for sinners (Is 53:4ff). **39.** Ignorance of good and evil, that is, of everything, seems to characterize here those under the military age of twenty (cf 2:14; Ex 30:14; Nm 14:29), who were also excluded from the community's council.

l 41. After the command of 40, there is deep irony in 'just as the Lord our God commanded us'. **44.** Without the divine assistance, defeat is inevitable. **45.** Penitential rites are unavailing, Yahweh is unheeding. The author's description of the people's situation is very sombre; by omitting in 1:29ff all reference to Moses intercession as found in his source (Nm 14:13ff), he implies the absence of all effective human intercession for his contemporaries in exile, and now he stresses the ineffectiveness of ritual. **46.** It is difficult to reconcile this v with 2:14, which in putting 38 years between the departure from Kadesh-barnea and the crossing of the Zered indicates the people left almost immediately after the defeat at Hormah; besides, only in 1:46 is the place called simply Kadesh. This v seems, therefore, to be a later addition and an attempt to bring Dt into line with the older tradition of a long stay at Kadesh-barnea (cf Nm 14:45; 20:14ff). The failure to follow this tradition was probably dictated by theological considerations: to have remained at Kadesh-barnea would seem, after the command of 40, to constitute another sin and require additional punishment, for which there was no evidence.

m 9–18 Appointment of officials—This section seems based on a combination of Ex 18:13–27 and Nm 11:14, 16–17. In 18 the reference is probably to Ex 24:3–8. The entire passage is probably a later insertion: (1) it does not fit the context, which is elsewhere exclusively concerned with the entrance into Palestine, the holy war, etc; (2) since in this part of the ch the people is proposed as still obedient to God (19), we expect the same scheme of command—execution we find in 2:2ff (see below); (3) elsewhere Dt knows nothing of a legislative activity such as 18 ascribes to Moses at Horeb; (4) the structure which emerges from the removal of these vv (see above), is a strong confirmation of their secondary character. However, what inspired their insertion, the combination of Ex 18 and Nm 11, and other discrepancies from the **n** sources, is a problem. The insertion seems to be dictated in general by a desire to take some account of the Sinai-Horeb traditions neglected by Dt, especially those regarding the communication and the administration of the law. The distinction of the military and the judges evident in 15f, but absent in Ex 18, probably reflects the later practice of the author's times. Perhaps the allusions to Nm 11 are to be explained simply by the similarity of the situation of the overburdened Moses; this could lead an author depending on memory to use

phrases here and there of a quite different tradition. **22** Note that the burden of Ex 18 and Nm 11 is here reinterpreted as a sign of divine blessing.

2:2–3 17 Sacramentum Futuri—Author's sources: **22** Nm 20:14ff; 21:2ff; Ex 14–15. In content and style this section contrasts sharply with 1:6–2:1. The people move ahead steadily, they wage holy wars, they conquer, they take possession of and distribute the land—and they obey. These happy events, however, are only a beginning (2:25, 31; 3:24); they foreshadow in broad outline the wars, conquest and distribution of the Promised Land itself (cf Jos 11:23–12:8). Stylistically, the author appropriately avoids a concentric structure which brings us back, so to speak, where we began, and employs instead a rhythm of command and execution which hurries on, pausing only when the most solemn moment is reached, the oracle opening the war against Sihon (2:24f). To be noted are the later accretions, most of them of the same learned character and probably all from the same hand: 2:10–12 (12 speaks of the entire Promised Land as already possessed); 2:20–23 ('even to this day' in 22 betrays a perspective quite alien to the context); 3:9, 11, 13*b**b*–17 (15 'as it is to this day' as in 2:22; 16f is a doublet of 12f). **2–7 b** With only a slight modification, 3 repeats 1:6, and once more God starts his people towards the land. Exile is not the final word! 'Pass through' (4) introduces the *Leitwort* in this ch (Heb. '*ābar*, with various translations in RSV, in 4, 8 (bis), 13 (bis), 14, 18, 24, 27, 28, 29, 30); it is taken from Ex 15:16*b*. The fear of the Edomites the author also found in Ex 15:15. He does not follow Nm 20:14ff, but combines phrases from this tradition with Nm 21:21ff in the message to Sihon (27ff). He could not follow Nm 20:14ff because for him it was inconceivable that, except as a punishment for sin, Israel could be resisted. Rather, God has assigned the Edomites, Moabites (9), and Ammonites (19) their respective territories (cf Gn 36:43; 13:11f; 19:30ff; Dt 32:8); he is the universal lord. **8.** Contrary to the **c** route of Nm 33, it seems that the author has the people skirt the Edomite territory to the E, bearing E–NE from the Gulf of Aqaba at Elath (later name, probably Ezion-geber). They thus come directly into 'the wilderness of Moab'. **9.** The exact location of Ar is unknown. **10–12.** Cf Gn 14:5f. **13.** The Zered is commonly identified with the Wādī el-Hesā; others locate it as a branch of the Arnon. **14–16.** Before the decisive oracle of 17–19. 24–25, the fulfilment of the oath in 1:35 is carefully noted. The inversion of holy war and exodus motifs in ch 1 reappears. The death of at least some part of the condemned generation is described in terms drawn from the traditions on the holy war (15): the panic inspired by Yahweh is properly reserved for Israel's enemies in a holy war ('For indeed the hand of the Lord was against them, to *drive them in a panic* from the camp'—the same verb in Ex 14:25; Dt 7:23; Jos 10:10; Jg 4:15). The war which the people rejected is turned and waged against them, who in their terror repeat the experience of the Egyptians in the exodus (Ex 14:25). The anti-holy war and anti-exodus ended, the holy war against Sihon can begin (W. L. Moran, 'The End of the Unholy War and the Anti-Exodus', Bib 44 (1963), 333–42). **24–25.** A holy war oracle, with 25 **d** paraphrasing Ex 15:14; the conquest which the author finds predicted there, now begins to be realized. **26–29.** After the oracle the request sent to Sihon appears quite superfluous, but this provides the author with the opportunity, while adhering to the older tradition (Nm 21:21ff), to add the theological explanation for the refusal and thus to emphasize God's special providence for his

7d people (30). According to 23:4, the Moabites were hostile, which is probably much closer to historical fact; it seems that the author in 29 has again sacrificed history for theological concerns. Kedemoth's exact location (Jos 13:18) remains a matter of dispute; Heshbon, Sihon's capital, lay about 15 miles from the Jordan. **31—37.** Jahaz is mentioned by Mesha, king of Moab, in his famous inscription (the 'Moabite Stone') recounting his war with Israel (ANET 320); it was located somewhere between Medeba and Dibon. On the anathema or holy war see § 225*d*.

e 3:1—7, Sihon conquered and the territory between the Arnon and the Jabbok rivers in their hands, the Israelites move farther northwards to engage Og. Here the author seems to depend on an otherwise unknown tradition, for Nm 21:33—35 is a later addition based on Dt 3:1ff. In the Targums Argob is identified with Trachonitis. **10.** The 'tableland' extended from the Arnon to approximately Heshbon. **11.** Popular tradition seems to have identified a megalithic dolmen near Rabbah (modern Amman) as Sihon's bed, by which perhaps a sarcophagus is meant; the 'iron' is probably basalt, which, as Pliny attests, in this area had the colour and hardness of iron (actually 20%). **12.** The border separating Gad and Reuben remains undefined (cf Jos 13:15ff). **13—17** Geshur and Maacah were Aramaean territories, in the 10th cent., between Lake Tiberias and approximately Mt Hermon. The villages, however, of Havvot-jair were in Gilead (Nm 32:41; 1 (3) Kgs 4:13; Jg 10:4), and 14—17 is an unsuccessful attempt to harmonize Dt and Nm 32:39ff.

f 3:18—29 Preparations for the Future—The author returns to 1:37—39 (Moses, Joshua, people), but in inverse order. **18—20** seems to reflect the author's concern with the apparent anomaly of tribes who live outside the borders of the Promised Land (cf 1:7) and yet are Israelites. He solves the problem by having Yahweh give them their land (18), and by having them co-operate in the conquest of W Palestine (18—20), a duty which they will carry out perfectly (Jos 1.12ff, 4.12f, 22.1ff), cf Nm 32. **21.** Joshua, Moses' successor, is addressed and encouraged, but before Moses carries out the command of 1:38, he makes one last touching plea in 24f that Yahweh reconsider the stern decision of 1:37. Is not the fact that he has seen Ex 15:14—16 begin to come true before his eyes grounds for hoping that Yahweh has relented and will allow him to 'go over' (25, Heb. *'āḇar*; see above on 2:4) to 'that goodly hill country' (25, cf Ex 15:16*b*—17)?

g 26—28. No! He is the leader caught in the guilt of his people, but he is conceded the grace of beholding 'the good land' from afar. It has been proposed (David Daube, *Studies in Biblical Law*, Cambridge 1947, 24—39) that in an earlier form of this tradition this vision was the way in which Moses took possession of the land; cf Gn 13:14ff and the Roman practice of transferring property called *demonstratio finium*. **29.** This brief notice poignantly emphasizes Moses' silence before God's decision. Peor was a valley near Mt Nebo, which from the S dominated the Jordan valley (cf 4:46; 34:6).

28a 4:1—40 The Law and Its Demands—'And now' links 1—40 to 1:6—3:29 as covenantal stipulations, etc, to historical prologue (cf 10:12; Ex 19:5; Jos 24:14). The connexion, however, is weak and, in our opinion, secondary: (1) the motivation from history for obedience is drawn, not from 1:6ff, but from 4:9—14, 20—22 and the events at Baal-peor (cf Nm 25:1ff), which are not mentioned in 1:6ff; (2) the interpretation of 1:6ff as an historical prologue requires the removal of 3:18—29, and overlooks how intimately these vv are connected with

1:37—39 and, through theme and allusions to Ex 15, with **228a** 2:2ff; (3) the transition between the end of ch 3 and the beginning of ch 4 is very abrupt and quite unprepared for. 1—40, however, is in our opinion a unity and not, as is held by many scholars, a conglomerate of pre-existing pieces or a combination of two discourses. The basic structure is provided by the covenant-form (9—31).

1—8. Introduction: the excellence of the law. Two **b** motives are immediately presented to urge perfect obedience to the law ('statutes and ordinances', which are not clearly distinguished in Dt). First, the law is a source of life (1, 3f; cf Lv 18:5). Second, it is a teaching divine in origin, and a source of wisdom (5—8, 'Behold, I *teach* you . . .'), which bestows on its possessors a blessed life (Prv 1:32f; 7:2; 8:35f). In fact, the distinction of Israel in the eyes of the world will be its wisdom and discernment derived from the law. The prohibition to add to, or subtract from, the law (2), has many parallels in ancient Near E documents, treaties included (cf also 12:32; Jer 26:2; Eccl 3:14; Prv 30:6; Apoc 22:18f). In context the point of the prohibition is apparently that life and wisdom belong only to the law as taught by Moses; this, however, it must be admitted, is easily open to the misinterpretation that the law in its smallest detail is a complete and eternally valid expression of the divine will.

9—14. History: the Horeb experience. Given the **c** importance of the law, it is therefore crucial for Israel that it never forgot what happened at Horeb. For there, in a solemn liturgical gathering ('stand before the Lord'), not only was the Decalogue revealed and the laws of Dt given to Moses, but in the very experience itself the nature of the cult to be given God and, by implication, the basic expression of covenant-law were disclosed: no form seen, therefore no images; the heavens shrouded in deepest darkness, therefore no cult of heavenly bodies.

15—19a. General stipulation: the prohibition of d images. Here begins a commentary on the beginning of the Decalogue by way of citation, paraphrase and allusion: cf 16—18 with 5:8; 19 'worship and serve' with 5:9; 20 with 5:6; 24 with 5:9. It is remarkable that the prohibition against having other gods in 5:7 is ignored; this is certainly not an accident. The omission can be partly explained by the author's strong and explicit monotheistic faith (35, 39); the recognition of the existence of other gods possibly implicit in the first commandment of the Decalogue was intolerable. It can also be explained by the author's historical perspective, which is that of the exilic period, and his reflection on the abuses leading to the destruction of Jerusalem and the whole tragedy of 587 B.C.: (1) cf Ezek 8:3—18 (the same rare word 'image' in 3, 5 as 'figure' in Dt 4:16; the 'creeping things' in 10, perhaps secondary and an allusion to Dt 4:18, but then certainly an early interpretation of Dt; worship of the sun in 16); (2) the cult of heavenly bodies under Assyrian influence (2 (4) Kgs 21:3; 23:4; Jer 8:1ff, etc); (3) theriomorphic images, which point particularly to Egyptian influence, especially strong c. 600—587 B.C. 15—18, therefore, would regard, at least primarily, **e** images of other gods, not of Yahweh. This also makes sense in the historical context of the 6th cent. B.C., for the aniconic character of Yahweh's cult had at that time been long established. It also fits the replacing of 5:7 by 5:8 as the general stipulation—not other gods, but their images. The inclusion of the heavenly bodies along with images has not only the historical basis mentioned above, but reflects the author's belief that, unlike the 'other gods' of 5:7, they not only exist but have a certain divinity in the Hebrew sense of a supra-human, numinous quality.

228f **19b—22. History**. Therefore, in God's providence they have been allotted to the other peoples of the earth. Nothing in the author's way of speaking suggests that he finds the cult of heavenly bodies among Israel's neighbours reprehensible. He seems here to have been influenced by 32:8f, which assigns the nations to 'the sons of God'; elsewhere we find 'the sons of God' very intimately associated with the heavenly bodies as their visible manifestation (Jb 38:7; cf also Ps 148:2f). This admission, however, of a providential 'natural' religion, which the early Church Fathers Justin and Clement also found in this passage, only serves to throw into higher relief the privilege of Israel, which is Yahweh's very own.

g **23—24. Repetition of general stipulation with motive.**

25—28. Curses. Contrary to the earlier covenant-form, curses here precede blessings. This reflects the historical situation; the curse in its direct form, exile, is a fact, and hence curse and blessing no longer present two equally possible alternatives, but are now related as present and future.

h **29—31 Blessings**. But exile need not be the last line of Israel's history; Yahweh can be sought and still found, even outside the Holy Land (Jer 29:13; cf also Is 55:6; 65:1; 1 Chr 28:9; 2 Chr 15:2, 4). The people need only to turn to him in complete sincerity. This possibility of conversion is the kerygma, the proclamation, of the Deuteronomic History (Wolff); in fact, the conversion of the people is even predicted (see 30:1ff). This conviction, however, rests, not on the jealous God of Horeb (24), but on the merciful God who swore to the patriarchs.

i **32—40 Proof and final exhortation**. That the oath to the patriarchs should ground this conviction is argued in these vv. Our vision is now extended back to creation and across the entire world to verify that the Exodus and Sinai experiences are absolutely unique in all history. A unique God, a unique revelation—'*for* he loved your fathers . . .' (37). This love and the intention of giving the Promised Land (38) lie behind the unparalleled events of Israel's history. Therefore, this love—this seems implied by the author—could not permit that a curse undo, finally and forever, such a glorious past. **39—40** Now, therefore, this unique God must be acknowledged, and his will done according to Moses' commands, the law of Dt; we thus return to the exhortation of 1—8.

j **4:41—44 Cities of Refuge**—Narrative in style and very loosely connected with the context, these vv are an addition (cf 19:1ff). The purpose of the addition is probably to remove the difficulty of Moses' failure to set up the cities in Transjordan, once it had been taken.

229a **4:44—28:68 The New Covenant (Second Discourse).** **4:44—49 Superscription**—Probably the original superscription, but with some later additions (44, 46ab—b, 47—49). The 'testimonies' (45, also 6:17, 20) are properly stipulations of the covenant agreed to under oath; this meaning is urged by related nouns in Akkadian and Aramaic treaties. **48**. Heb. Sion, not to be confused with 'Zion', is probably a dialectal form of Sirion (3:9). **5:1—11:32 The 'Great Commandment'**—Though its formulations are many, changing with new conditions and in the face of new problems and dangers, the 'great commandment' of total commitment to God is a constant of the law (see above 225f). It is this commandment which is now so passionately urged and supported by every possible motive—justice, gratitude, repentance, fear of punishment, hope of reward.

b **5:1—6:3 Historical Introduction**—The primary purpose of this section is to establish Moses' authority **22** in the rôle of mediator he plays in Dt. Just as the Horeb covenant was in every way valid and binding (2—22), so is the law about to be promulgated by Moses (23—31). **2—5** recalls the fact of the covenant along with the place, contracting parties and other circumstances. **3** seems to contradict 2:14, but in the cultic setting which re-presents salvation-history, every Israelite becomes one with the people at Horeb. **5** is very difficult, apparently contradicting 4 and 22ff, which speak of a direct hearing of Yahweh's words (cf also 4:12). However, according to 23ff Moses stood apart and already occupied a special position; perhaps, therefore, the author conceived of the people as hearing Yahweh's voice in the thunder, but distinct words only through the mediation of Moses (cf Ex 19:9, 19). **6—21**. The covenant text. See Ex 20:2—17; we comment here only on the most important differences of the Dt edition. **12—15**. In Ex the Sabbath rest is **c** associated with the divine rest after the work of creation. In Dt one begins——this we consider the meaning of the slightly ambiguous Heb.——by recalling the slavery of Egypt and God's liberating intervention, and so one observes the Sabbath, and thereby continues God's saving work, by granting rest especially to the *personae miserabiles*, the slaves and aliens. An object of God's mercy, one must show a similar mercy to others. Ultimately, therefore, according to Dt, it was the divine pity which moved God to prescribe the Sabbath rest. **16** 'as the Lord your God commanded you', a clause also found in 12, is very difficult, for the covenant-text is *cited* in 6ff, whereas this clause looks back to the time of Horeb as past. Two explanations seem most likely: either these two commandments are later additions to the Decalogue, or they are the two commandments wherein Ex and Dt differ the most ('that it may go well with you' in 16 is not in Ex), and in either case they had to be justified as enjoying divine authority. **21**. Unlike Ex, the **d** wife enjoys in Dt a place apart. This probably reflects the relatively higher status of women in the time of Dt; 15:12ff (contrast Ex 21:2ff) implies that a woman could at the time own real estate, and 21:19 is clear evidence of legal recognition of a mother's position in the family. Whereas, moreover, Ex retains the same verb 'covet' for all the objects mentioned, Dt distinguishes coveting another's wife and desiring his house, etc. The distinction is commonly explained as that between an imperious desire which implies the act of seizure ('covet') and a purely internal desire without such an implication ('desire'); hence, Dt represents a more advanced view of the attitude required towards another's property. It is interesting to note that the list of house, field . . . 'or anything that is your neighbour's' also appears in a legal text from Ugarit (but see now CBQ 29 (1967), 543— **e** 54). **22**. The covenant's stipulations are proclaimed, two written copies made and handed over to Moses; these are conditions of a valid covenant. Actually, the copies were written and handed over only after the events of 23ff (cf Ex 20:18—21; 31:18), but chronological order is abandoned in order to bring together all of the juridically relevant facts regarding the Horeb covenant. **23**. Official representatives of the people approach Moses. **24—27**. Man and God, flesh and the living God—the one is too weak to bear the vision of the other (cf Jg 13:22), and hence the proposal of the representatives. **28—31**. God accepts it, and therefore what we may call the new order of Moses' mediatorship is established and binding. **32— 6:3**. In this parenetic transition to 6:4ff we almost imperceptibly pass from the laws of Horeb (32f, 'the Lord our God commanded' in the past at Horeb) to the

29e laws now to be promulgated (6:1ff) but revealed at Horeb (31, 6:1).

f 6:4—25 The 'Great Commandment' of the Decalogue—Basic to Israelite existence, even in the profoundly different conditions of life in Palestine, is the revelation of Horeb—hence this commentary on 5:6—10, which reaffirms the fundamental obligation of rejecting all other gods (5 'love' and 17 'keep the commandments' allude to 5:10; 12 cites 5:6; 14 alludes to 5:7; 15 cites 5:9b). We note, however, a certain shift of emphasis; the love of God has become the first, great imperative. And of course the Decalogue is no longer the only law; there are also the words of Moses 'this day' (6). It is this totality of law, old and new, whose claims on obedience 20—25 grounds on bed-rock, 'We were Pharaoh's slaves . . .'

g 4—5. Heb. of 4 is ambiguous, but RSV seems most probable. The statement is at once polemical, opposing Yahweh to the plurality of Baals in the popular mind, and deeply theological, for Yahweh is used virtually as a category—he is 'one Yahweh'—as if this name alone were capable of expressing what Yahweh is, a God unlike other gods, a God of another order. It should be remembered that 'god' was in Israel's general religious context a vague word embracing many levels of being; even silver of extraordinary quality could be called 'god'. The term, therefore, was singularly inept for the expression of a monotheistic faith. It is to this unique God that Israel must devote its entire being (heart, soul, might) in absolute, undivided loyalty. This is the meaning of love **h** in Dt. Its context is always one of faithful adherence to God (11:1, 22; 30:20), walking in his ways (10:12; 11:22; 19:9; 30:16), keeping his commandments (10:12; 11:1, 22; 19:9) or doing them (11:22; 19:9), heeding them or his voice (11:13; 30:16), serving him (10:12; 11:1, 13). This is neither parental nor conjugal love; it is covenantal love (W. L. Moran, 'The Ancient Near E Background of the Love of God in Deuteronomy', CBQ 25 (1963), 77—87). And in committing a man without reservation to the 'one Yahweh', Dt separates a man from all that is of this world as radically as Yahweh is distinct from any other god. **6—9.** 'these words' refer to the whole law of Dt; the transition from the particular precept to the totality is not without parallel (6:24; 12:28; 28:14), and was facilitated by the view that a general stipulation like 5 includes implicitly all particular laws. A metaphorical interpretation of 8—9 seems more probable (cf Ex **i** 13:10, 16), though the Jews took them literally. They inscribed Dt 6:4—9; 11:13—21 and Ex 13:1—16 on parchment and bound it on the hand and forehead at the daily recitation of the Shema (the first word in 6:4); these are the phylacteries of the NT, which at Qumran also include Dt 5:1—6:3. Cf the advice of a Sumerian sage: 'The instructions of a father are precious, put them about your neck'. **10—19.** The commands of 13f, 17f are not made until they are placed against the background of the utterly gratuitous gift of the land (10f) and of freedom from the Egyptian yoke (12). In **13** the object is stressed: 'Yahweh, not Baal or any other Canaanite god, you must fear . . .' Fear is a general term meaning worship, honour and reverence; it is not dread of the numinous, much less a servile attitude. Service refers to cult, and the oath is perhaps to be understood of a solemn asseveration of fidelity to God required before admission to the cult (cf Hos 4:15b; Jer 4:1f; 44:24ff, and in context, Jos 23:7; **j** Is 48:1; Zeph 1:5; cf F. Horst, 'Der Eid im Alten Testament', *Gottes Recht*, Munich 1961, 297f). **14.** 'to go after' is frequently used outside the Bible of a subject serving a king, a vassal his suzerain. **16.** Cf Ex 17:1—7; Ps 95 (94):8f. The 'testing' of God questioned whether God was present and effective (Ex 17:7; cf Dt 6:15a), **229j** and, worse still, in accusing God ('fault-finding') the people virtually denied the nature of their covenantal relationship, for they treated God as an equal who could be brought to justice and made defend his actions. This is the sheerest hybris and apostasy. **19.** The promise referred to is perhaps Ex 23:27ff; 34:11. **20—25.** It must be stressed again that the meaning of the law, which 20 inquires after, derives from its relation to salvation-history. The people were slaves (juridical status) of Pharaoh (owner) in Egypt (place, foreign land). Then Yahweh acted: he brought the people out (a freed slave 'goes forth'), 'with a mighty hand' (by force, not by purchase), dispossessing the Pharaoh 'before our eyes' (witnesses, no escaping the claims God can make on the basis of the exodus), to give the land (additional ground for a claim to service). Then, and only then, does God **k** command (24). Contingent on obedience are prosperity ('our good'), life and righteousness (that on the basis of which God judges the community favourably, keeps it in communion with himself, and bestows on it his blessings; cf 24:13, and for the connection of life and 'righteousness' especially Ezek 18:5ff). According to the 'vassal-treaties' of Esarhaddon, king of Assyria in the 7th cent., one of the obligations of vassals was the instruction of their children on the duties of the vassal relationship; an analogous practice is presupposed by 20—25.

7:1—25 Another Formulation of the 'Great Com- 230a mandment'—In 1—5, 13—24 we find numerous parallels to Ex 23:20—33 and Ex 34:11—16; the relationship, however, between the three texts does not seem to be that of direct dependence, but rather one of derivation from a common source, another ancient covenant text. In Dt 7 this text is commented upon, expanded, and in 17ff adapted to the form of a Holy War exhortation. Into this commentary are woven 6ff with allusions to the Decalogue. In this way two traditions with their general stipulations are united and ch 7 linked with 5:1—6:25.

1—5 Law—It is Yahweh who gives the victories over the **b** inhabitants of Canaan (cf Gn 15:19f). In return the people are to separate themselves completely from the Canaanites, granting them neither treaty (Ex 23:32; 34:12, 15) nor ties of marriage (Ex 34:16). This general stipulation was inspired by the same absolute rejection of other gods we find in the Decalogue. The effects of marriage are expressly noted (4), and it should be recalled that a treaty with another people involved accepting their gods as in some sense partners and protectors of the agreement. A Dt expansion is the anathema (2), which renders otiose the prohibitions which follow. The destruction of all Canaanite cultic installations is also derived from the old source (Ex 23:24; 34:13).

6—11 Motivation—This radical separation from the **c** Canaanites is a consequence of Israel's special status. It is holy to Yahweh, set apart for him, bearing his name (28:9f), and chosen to be his personal possession (Ex 19:5f). This is the mystery of divine election, which can be explained by nothing in Israel. It is a mystery of love, manifesting itself in the oath to the patriarchs and in the exodus. And so—here is the transition to 12ff— Israel must acknowledge Yahweh as the faithful God, rewarding (5:10) and punishing (5:9b, but note the insistence that the individual sinner is punished). Therefore, obedience!

12—15 The blessings on obedience—The covenant to **d** which God is faithful is that made with the patriarchs; the blessings therefore are absolutely gratuitous. On the diseases of Egypt cf Ex 15:26; 23:25.

16—26 Do not fear—In 16 we return to the law in 1—5,

230d in 17ff to the problem implied there in the admission that the Canaanites would enjoy an overwhelming superiority. But all fear should be dispelled at the memory of the exodus (cf 20:1ff). God will break all resistance by sending discouragement (rather than 'hornets') into the ranks of the enemy (20) and throwing them into a panic (23, cf 2:15). **25—26** are probably later additions. Statues with wooden cores (which therefore can be burned) and covered with silver or gold have been found in excavations.

e **8:1—20 The Heart of Man**—In 6:11 'to eat and be full' is proposed without further discussion as a blessing of God. It reappears in this ch (10, 12), but now, perhaps under the influence of 32:14f (cf also Hos 13:4ff), the ambiguity from which it suffers through human malice, is exposed. For such is the heart of man that in the midst of gifts he can forget the giver, and in blessings he can sow the seed of curses: 'My power . . .' (17). Therefore deep in his heart must be the conviction that like a father God trained him in the desert (**2—5**). To admit this long period was one of training is to concede it contained a lesson, which in view of the most striking feature of the desert days, the manna, can only be that ultimately man is sustained by the creative word of God (**3**); cf Egyptian parallels on the word of Ptah, for example, 'one lives on what proceeds from his mouth' (cf H. Brunner, 'Was aus dem Munde Gottes geht', VT 8 (1958) 428—9). It is this word which brings bread, manna or any other sustenance into existence, and therefore it is this word which gives life. The implications are clear: not only should the abundance of Palestine be attributed to this word, but if a man would live (1) he must also obey this word (6)—'it is your life' (32:47). Within the dread alternatives of life (1) or destruction (19f) with which 'this day' (1, 19) of revelation confronts the people, the author structures his discourse to the barest essence of his message, 'Take heed lest you forget the Lord your God . . .' (11).

f   A Exhortation (1)
          B Desert (2—4)
            C Palestine (7*b*—9)
              D Exhortation (11)
            C' Palestine (12f)
          B' Desert (14*b*—16)
     A' Curse (19f)

g Similarly, in **7—10**, which are so important for grasping the problem of prosperity in its full proportions, the author hymns the glories of the land:

     A 'good land' (7)
       B 'land of brooks . . . hills' (7)
         C 'land of wheat . . .' (8)
           D 'land of olive . . .' (8)
         C' 'land in which . . . bread' (9)
       B' 'land whose stones . . . hills' (9)
     A' 'good land' (10).

To us this praise may seem exaggerated, but not to a man coming in from the steppe or the desert. W Palestine is quite without iron and copper; iron deposits exist N of the Jabbok in Transjordan, while both metals were available in the S along the Aqaba and in the N in the Lebanon valley. The 'fiery serpents' (15) remain obscure (Nm 21:6). In **19—20** we have a curse corresponding to the blessing of 7:12ff; the last clause of **20** repeats the opening phrase of 7:12. The curse concludes the first of the two major divisions of 5:1—11:32.

231a **9:1—11:32 Sin and Covenant**—In 5:2—8:20 the dominant view of sin is that of a possibility in the future. That it is also a fact of the past is only briefly alluded to (6:16). Yet there is no full understanding of the coven-

ant, either of the history in which it is grounded, or 2: therefore of the law which it imposes, unless due account is taken of the sombre fact of sin. Only sin reveals the true dimensions of God's merciful intervention in the history of Israel and the full measure of his claims to obedient service.

9:1—10:11 Sin.

1—6 Introduction—As elsewhere in the OT, and com- **b** monly in the ancient Near E, war is here conceived as an ordeal in which God reveals through victory his judgement on who is right with justice on his side, and who is guilty ('wicked'). But the holy wars by which Israel will come into the possession of Palestine will present an anomaly: though the enemies are defeated and therefore judged guilty, this does not imply, as might be expected, that Israel is therefore 'righteous'. Actually, neither side is 'righteous', and, humanly speaking, there can be no case or judgement. But nevertheless God will intervene—because of his promise to the patriarchs. The grounds for self-complacency could not be denied more vigorously. All are sinners, Israelites and Gentiles alike. St Paul could hardly have written a more 'Pauline' passage. **3**. 'Quickly' should be understood of the victories over the Anakim (**2**), not over all the nations; it does not contradict 7:22. On the Anakim cf §226*i*.

7ff Horeb—The author now proves his concluding state- **c** ment in 6, that Israel is a 'stubborn people' (perhaps better, 'unsubmissive people', lit. 'hard-necked', since the image seems to have been taken from draught animals sufficiently powerful to resist the yoke borne on the neck or the goad stuck there). From Egypt to the present moment they have been rebels (**7**), even at Horeb, the very scene of revelation and covenant (**8ff**). 9:8—21, 25—29; 10:1—5, 10—11 seems to have existed independently before its use here. 9:22—24 are in the immediate context and in the general structure intrusive, and 7 is linked with these vv by theme and vocabulary. Moreover, 1—6 alludes to the Kadesh-barnea incident through the reference to the Anakim and the promise of victory; this connects these vv with 7; 22—24. 8ff therefore lacks an introduction. That it constitutes a unit in itself will be apparent from the structure, which is articulated by repeated references to the intercession of Moses. The ordering of events is not chronological (cf Ex 32; 34), but determined by juridical considerations; each section takes up the relevant facts in a broken and renewed covenant:

(1) a. **9:8—17**, sin and broken covenant; the broken **d** tablets imply juridically that the covenant was no longer in effect, for without a written document there was no covenant. b. **9:18f** intercession of Moses. (2) a. **9:20***a* sin of leader of people. b. **9:20***b* intercession of Moses.

(3) a. **9:21** the necessary rite of purification. b. **9:25** intercession of Moses.

(4) a. **9:26—29** intercession of Moses. The order is reversed now that we come to the renewal of the covenant. b. **10:1—5** the renewal (written document, handing over of document, deposit of document in portable desert santuary). (5) **a. 10:10** allusion to period of intercession of Moses. b. **10:11** leader of forces again placed in his post—on to the land of promise.

10:12—11:25 'And now, Israel'—The sad history of **e** Horeb, with its gracious renewal of the covenant, leads to a new appeal for total commitment to God. There are seven parts, the first six in an alternating rhythm of precept and motive, the last (11:13—25) a complex blessing and curse formula. (1) **12f** command, **14f** motive (lord of the universe, God has loved and chosen Israel alone); (2)

1e **16** command (interior purification, not just an external sign of being a covenant member), **17f** motive (Yahweh, God the king—warrior and judge—his justice and power especially concerned with the defenceless); (3) **19a** command (love the resident-alien, which after 18b becomes an imitation of God, and is remarkable for raising the love of the neighbour to the same level as the love of God, for both loves become an expression of total commitment), **19b** motive (cf Ex 23:9); (4) **20** command (cf 6:13; 'cleave to' means to be loyal, cf 2 Sm 20:2), **21f** motive; (5) **11:1** command, **2—7** motive (on Dathan and Abiram, cf Nm 16, which combines the stories of two rebellions); (6) **8a** command, **8b—12** motive **f** (complex, beginning with the hope of entrance into the land and long life on it, then the glories of the land itself; the watering with the feet refers to a device still in use among the Arabs and called a *shâduf*; somewhat tendentiously, the automatic rise of the Nile each year is compared unfavourably with Israel's water supplies, which require God's constant attention); (7) **13—15** conditional blessing on life in the land, **16f** warning against incurring the curses of the covenant and losing the land, **18—21** repetition of 6:6—9 with slight modifications, and motivation, **22—25** conditional blessing on the conquest (cf Jos 1:3—5; the desert is the S border, the Lebanon and Euphrates the N, the Mediterranean the W, while the Jordan is in context understood to be the E).

g **11:26—32 Transition** The subjects to be treated in ch 12ff are now announced: the blessings and curses of ch 28 (26—28), the ceremonies prescribed in ch 27 (29f), the laws of chh 12ff (31f); in other words, in inverse order to their actual treatment. 29f is secondary; it prepares the way for the intrusive ch 27. One place is localized, Shechem, and the author moves towards an increasingly precise localization, the oak of Moreh, a famous landmark (Gn 12:6; Jos 24:26; Jg 9:6); at the same time he very skilfully brings in Gilgal to prepare for 27:2.

2a **12:2—28 The Unique Sanctuary**—This section, with its far-reaching consequences for the people's life of worship, is the most distinctive in the dt corpus of laws. The repetitions, the partly conflicting viewpoints, and the differences in terminology are clear evidence of the text's complicated history. We should probably distinguish at least three strata: 12:13—19 (the earliest); 12:8—12; 12:2—7, 20—28 (+ 29—31). All agree in restricting worship to one sanctuary; there alone may any type of sacrifice or ritual offering be made. They are alike, too, in associating the sacrificial meals with joy, a making merry before the Lord (7, 12, 18). Twice (15f, 20—25) the problem raised by centralization, whether as a result the meats previously enjoyed at local sanctuaries may now be taken only at the one sanctuary, is treated and given basically the same answer: apart from the sacrifices and offerings mentioned, one may with no concern for ritual purity eat these meats as if they were non-sacrificial wild game (e.g., the hart and gazelle; **b** cf 14:5). The secularization, however, is not quite complete; though the blood, which in a sacrifice is reserved to God and poured on the altar (26), has in these circumstances no genuine sacral character ('like water', 16, 24; cf 15:23), nevertheless it may not be consumed, but must be poured on the ground. However, whereas 15f makes no further distinctions, in 20ff it is also required that the central sanctuary be too distant to be reached conveniently. A last common feature of the various expressions of the law is the stress on God's choice of the place of worship. Unlike the Canaanite gods, Yahweh was not a personified force of nature, and so no place in nature

was of itself sacred or enjoyed special contact with the **232b** divine. If a place was to have God's special presence, at which he would be more accessible and, therefore, should be worshipped, it must be the object of God's sovereignly free choice. This emphasis on divine transcendence is reaffirmed, in the opinion of most scholars, by attaching God's presence to his name, while his proper dwelling place remains in the heavens (26:15; cf 1 (3) Kgs 8:27ff).

2—7. Centralization (5) is introduced by a virtual **c** citation of 7:5 (3a), and is thus presented as an additional implication of the earlier law, which in requiring that the many places of Canaanite cult and the names of Canaanite gods be wiped out, prepares for the legislation on the one place of the presence of Yahweh's name. Hills and shady trees (2) were chosen both for their coolness and their numinous quality; they were the sites of sanctuaries, often quite simple, where fertility in field and flock was sought through rites and other practices often lascivious. On the hills too were the funerary shrines, the 'high places'. These were the scenes of Israel's infidelity, condemned by the prophets and chronicled by the Deuteronomic History (Hos 4:3; Jer 2:20; Ezek 6:13; 1 (3) Kgs 11:7; 14:23; 2 (4) Kgs 16:14; 17:10, etc). On the Asherim and 'pillars' see 16:21f. 5 speaks of Yahweh 'putting his name' (also 21 and 14:24); this is the formula used in the Dt History to designate Jerusalem (1 (3) Kgs 9:3; 11:36; 14:21; 2 (4) Kgs 21:4, 7). Moreover, 5 employs the expression 'out of all your tribes', which also recurs in the Dt History in connection with Jerusalem (1 (3) Kgs 8:16; 11:32; 14:21; 2 (4) Kgs 21:7); it implies that the choice regards not only the place but the tribe. 5, therefore, is a clear statement, and the only one, of the claims of the Jerusalem temple.

8—12. Centralization is here conceived as a stage of **d** salvation-history. The period of the desert wanderings is contrasted with the rest God will give in the land, which perhaps refers to the *pax Davidica* (cf 2 Sam 7:1, 10a); the Davidic ideal, it may be recalled, seems to have inspired the reforms and political expansion of Josiah. The election formula in **11** is 'to make his name dwell' (also 14:23; 16:2, 6, 11; 26:2; in 12:5 it is a gloss), or, perhaps more exactly, 'to make his name tent'. Elsewhere in the OT 'tenting' is frequently predicated of God (33:16; 1 (3) Kgs 8:12; Is 8:18; 33:5; Ps 74(73).2, etc) and the term may ultimately derive from the housing of the Ark in a tent (Ex 25ff; 2 Sm 7.0). It suggests mobility, the possibility of moving from place to place, as the Ark actually did before its installation at Jerusalem. This would explain why, though 'to make his name tent' is the more common expression in Dt, it is avoided by the Dt History; note, too, that it is used in Jer 7:12 for Yahweh's presence at Shiloh, not at Jerusalem.

13—19. This section, like the rest of the laws in Dt, **e** is couched in the 2nd pers. sing., a fact which favours its being the earliest part of ch 12. The Levites, who through centralization are now deprived of their sources of support, become a primary concern of Dt (12:12; 14:27ff; 16:11; 18:6ff; 26:11ff).

20ff. The possibility of territorial expansion (cf also 14:24ff) foreseen here may be connected with Josiah's movement into the N kingdom.

29—31 Rejection of Canaanite Rites—We return to the viewpoint of 12:2—7, and in **30** reference is made again to the old covenant text of ch 7 (7:16; cf Ex 23:24, 33; 34:12). The sacrifice of children, which is appended as a specific instance of Canaanite abominations, is first

232e mentioned in the 8th cent. (2 (4) Kgs 16:3) and apparently became a fairly widespread abuse only in the reign of Manasseh and later, cf § 104*j*.

f 12:32—13:18 (Heb 13 1—19). 'Other Gods'—Within a parenetic introduction (32, cf 4:2) and conclusion (13:18) three applications of the first commandment of the Decalogue are made in the form of case-law ('if'). These are the first of the 'removal' laws (cf § 223*i*), which are here considerably expanded by Dt.

1—5. Dreams as well as prophecy were recognized channels of divine revelation. The original law (1—2, except 'which you have not known', 5 up to '. . . put to death') does not discuss how a sign in apparent confirmation of an invitation to apostasy could come to pass; it is sufficient that the invitation be made—the man is to be put to death. The Dt additions are more critical and in a different tone. God allows such things to test the people (cf 8:2, 16); these signs and wonders therefore are not really a problem. Besides, the people have no experience of these other gods (2), but they have experienced the saviour and redeemer from Egypt (5). And once more the urgent appeal for total commitment (4). The faith which inspired the old law is thus made explicit and defended, the charged emotions against the culprit are diverted and directed rather towards Yahweh.

g **6—11.** Nor can ties of family and closest friendship be respected. In 6 read probably with SamP and LXX 'your brother, *son of your father or* son of your mother', that is, both half-brother and full brother. The Dt additions (last clause of 6, 7, 10*b*—12) add little to those of 1—5 except to defend the harshness of the law on the grounds that its observance will provide strong motivation against recurrence of the crime.

12—18. For apostasy even a whole city must be wiped out completely, for its guilt involves the whole people (cf 17). Distinctive of the original law (12—13 except last clause, 14 except last clause, 15*a*(*b*?), 16 except 'and multiply you . . .') is the primitive view of the anathema as a sacrifice to Yahweh.

h 14:1—2 Forbidden Mourning Rites—Two widely practised customs are here rejected (cf Lv 19:27f) on the grounds of Israel's filial relationship (cf 1:31; 8:5; 32:5, 19, 20) and its consecration to Yahweh. If the rites concern a dead human being, it must be remarked that they are referred to by prophets without rebuke (Jer 16:6; Ezek 7:18, etc), and it would probably follow that this prohibition is quite late. If the one dead, however, is a god (cf Baal in the Ugaritic myths, Adonis of Byblos, Sumerian Dumuzid), the law could be quite ancient (cf 26:12—15).

i 3—21 Clean and Unclean Animals—4—20, with its fine distinctions and technical, priestly learning, is in sharp contrast with the rest of Dt, and is a later addition drawn from a source common to Lv 11:2ff. Like its neighbours, Israel regarded certain animals as unclean and therefore their use as food prohibited. The origin of these taboos was very ancient and their basis at times quite obscure. Hygiene, natural aversion, and old superstitions were undoubtedly factors. Another, at least in some cases, was a strong reaction to Canaanite customs, in the face of which Israel grew in consciousness of its own distinctive calling and rejected whatever was sensed as incompatible with its 'holiness' (2, 21). An example of this is 21*b* (Ex 23:19; 34:26); its Canaanite background is clear from a Ugaritic mythological text, and though the exact significance of the rite remains obscure, it was evidently such as to be judged repugnant to true Yahwism. The criteria, therefore, in 4ff for distinguishing clean from unclean are not the ultimate grounds on which the animals (the identification of many of them is uncertain) **23:** were judged acceptable or not. **4—8. Land animals**. **j** Ruminants are determined by appearances, and therefore do not agree at times with the classifications of modern zoology. Contact with the carcass of an unclean animal was forbidden; if touched alive, no impurity resulted. **9f. Aquatic animals**. 'Fins' is uncertain. No concrete examples are given; Lv 11:10 is slightly more explicit. **11—20. Winged animals**. No general criterion is given, but those forbidden seem to be all birds of prey or scavengers. **21.** Deriving the prohibition from Israel's special relationship to Yahweh (cf also Ex 22:30), Dt quite consistently permits the alien non-Israelite to eat such meat (contrast Lv 17:15).

22—29 Tithes—The original law (22), which in 23ff is **k** adapted to the exigencies and effects of centralization, prescribes annual tithes on the fruits of the earth, not on animals (contrast Lv 27:30ff). This is the earliest form of tithing, which is attested on the profane level at Ugarit; there, a landowner receives tithes in grain, beer, oil and probably wine, which are carefully distinguished from animal payments attached to pasture land. The tithes were paid to Yahweh at some local sanctuary in acknowledgement of his ownership of the land (cf Gn 28:22; Am 4:4). Of course, in Dt the payment must be made at the central sanctuary; the first-born are also mentioned, probably because they were offered on the same occasion (cf 15:19ff). 23ff should not be understood as if the tithes were completely consumed in the banquet, which would rob the payment of all sense. Since the tithes originally constituted a large part of the revenues of the Levites at the local sanctuaries, it is provided that, if they can make the journey, they should share in the feast (27), and triennially the tithes were not to be paid, but turned over to the Levites and other *personae miserabiles* (28f; cf 26:12ff).

15:1—6 Year of Release—The oldest stratum (1) im- **23:** posed the release of Ex 23:10f (Lv 25:1ff): every seven years the land must be left fallow, an observance orginally intended to express recognition of Yahweh's ownership of the land, but already in Ex directed more immediately to the social purpose of helping the poor. There follows (2) a later, but pre-deuteronomic legal interpretation of the agrarian law, which has its application extended in terms of a more complex economy. The type of loan involved was one in which a person was pledged as security, and failure to pay allowed the creditor to seize the pledge and use his services as compensation. The release revokes this right; in the 7th year such a pledge could not be seized and those seized in the past were now freed. Probably, too—so at least 3*b*—the debt itself was cancelled. (RSV must be revised accordingly.) 3 is a further clari- **b** fication of the law, establishing who may not benefit from it (3*a*; cf 14:21), and excluding any payment, probably even if freely offered, a point which was not clear in 2. The idealism of **4—6** witnesses to a faith which sees in foreign domination and the economic straits which occasion such contracts, the effects of sin. **7—11 Loans**—With more realism on poverty (7, 11), and therefore from a different hand than 4ff, this law requires that no fellow-Israelite be refused a loan when he really needs it; the word used for loan allows for some security being given in exchange. **9—11** attempts to avert evasion of 2, but it speaks somewhat loosely and has in mind 7f, too. It is not interested in precise distinctions in types of loans, but in urging ready and generous help to the poor. The cry to the Lord (9) is an appeal to the ultimate protector of the law (cf Ex 22:22f; 22:26; Dt 24:15).

c 12–18 The 'Hebrew' Slave—This is a thorough reworking of the law in Ex 21:2ff (cf Jer 34:14; Lv 25:39ff). As is evident from the context, the 'Hebrew', whatever its meaning in Ex 21, is an Israelite who, unable to pay his debts, has been forced to enter the service of his creditor or sell himself to a third party. Ex 21 is a much more precise and comprehensive legal statement, while Dt is rather concerned with motivation (15, 18b) and with providing for the difficult period between legal and economic independence (13f). The procedure for becoming a perpetual slave (16f) is, as a consequence of centralization, also completely secular-
d ized (cf Ex 21:6a). **18** refers perhaps to the custom of hiring a man for three years (cf Is 16:14), and argues that six years' service has given the creditor twice that of a hireling and, therefore, adequate compensation. The Sumerian Lipit-Ishtar code (ANET 160, para 14) seems to provide for the release of a debtor after he has given in services the equivalent of double his debt; the Code of Hammurabi (ANET 170f, para 117) requires his release after three years. (H. Tsevat, 'Alalakhiana', HUCA, 1958, 125f, maintains that the Heb. word in question means, not 'double', but simply 'equivalent'.)
e 19–23 Firstlings—Cf Ex 13:2, 11–16; 22:28b–29; 34:19; Lv 22:26f; 27:26; Nm 18:15–18. The old law is in 19; 20ff is Dt expansion. In accordance with central-ization, the firstlings are to be presented at the central sanctuary (cf 12:6f, 17f; 14:23), and because of the journey this offering need not take place within a week after birth (so Ex 22:28f), but any time within the year, perhaps most often together with that of tithes (see above on 14:23). As sacred to the Lord, firstlings may not be put to profane use, nor be defective. Note that in Dt nothing is said about first-born children.
f 16:1–17 Festal Calendar—The ancient calendar of Ex 23:14ff; 34:18ff, which stipulated the celebration of three 'feasts', properly pilgrimages, each year, is adapted and expanded in accordance with the law of a unique sanctuary, cf § 105.
1–8 Passover-Unleavened Bread—Since the Pass-over (Pasch) was a sacrificial meal (Ex 12:1ff), as a result of centralization it could no longer be celebrated locally and within the private household; this aspect of the reform may have enjoyed some precedent (cf 2 (4) Kgs 23:22; 2 Chr 35:18). Celebration of the Passover at the sanctuary also affected the ritual. The door-posts are not smeared with the lamb's blood; any sacrificial animal is acceptable, not only a baby lamb or kid, and it is to be boiled (cf 1 Sam 2:12ff), which is expressly forbidden by Ex 12:9. The feast takes place in Abib (March-April, 'ripened ears (of barley)'); 'month' (1) is perhaps better taken as 'new moon period' of seven or even fourteen days, but there is no fixed date. A later stage of the text (at least 3ab–4a, 8) combines the Passover with the ancient agricultural feast of Unleavened Bread (Ex 23:15; 34:18; 13:3ff; Lv 23:6), a development that was almost inevitable because of their celebration within the same month and their common feature of the use of unleavened bread.
g 9–12 Weeks—Earlier called 'the feast of harvest' (Ex 23:16), this feast was the solemn conclusion of the offering of first-fruits begun at the feast of Unleavened Bread (cf Ex 23:15; Lv 23:9ff). First, the seven days of Unleavened Bread, which marked the beginning of the harvest (Lv 23:15); then, seven weeks to complete the harvest, with a feast on the fiftieth day (Pentecost). Since the harvest did not begin at the same time each year, the feast has no fixed date. In Judaism, if not earlier, it was historicized as the commemoration of

the giving of the Law; in Christianity, it celebrated **233g** the outpouring of the Spirit.
13–15 Tabernacles (Booths)—'The feast of in- **h** gathering' (Ex 23:16; 32:22) concluded the agricultural year and was the most joyful of all feasts, the feast par excellence (1 (3) Kgs 8:2, 6: Ezek 45:25). Here, for the first time, we find the feast called that of sukkôt, 'huts', which became its accepted name (Lv 23:34; Ez 3:4; Zach 14:16, 18, etc). The usual explanation is that it refers to the huts erected in the vineyards and orchards for dwelling purposes during the harvest; another proposal is that, since in the period of the early monarchy Israel's armies were housed in 'huts' (2 Sam 11:11), behind the name lies the conception of the people of God as Yahweh's army gathered round the Ark, the ancient palladium in Israel's wars (A. Alt, 'Zelte und Hütten', Kleine Schriften zur Geschichte des Volkes Israel, III, Munich 1959, 233–242). Certainly the explanation in Lv 23:42f is anachronistic; before the settlement in Palestine, the Israelites lived, not in huts, but in tents.
16–17 Summary—The omission of any reference to **i** the Passover is striking; perhaps these vv, and even 9–15, were added together with those which combine the Passover and Unleavened Bread. Only adult males are mentioned, since they alone as legally responsible persons were obliged to make this recognition of divine sovereignty; this does not exclude the larger circle of 11, 14.
16:18–20 Appointment of Judges—16:18–18:22 **234a** is for the most part concerned with the principal author-ities (judge, king, priest, prophet). The judges here are not the elders who elsewhere in Dt are so frequently concerned with the administration of justice (19:12; 21:3, 81, 19; 22:15; 25:7f), but are professionals, either local, as here (cf also 19:17f; 25:2), or at a central tribunal (17:9, 12). It is difficult to dissociate them from the institution established in the judicial reform of Jehoshaphat (2 Chr 19:4–11). The precise function of the 'officers' is not clear (cf the Levites as 'officers' in 2 Chr 19:11); their role in levying the army in 20:5f indicates a connection between the military and judiciary powers (cf also Ex 18:13ff; Dt 1:9ff). 19f, which incorporates a series of apodictic laws, is to be under-stood as directed to the entire people (cf Ex 23:1ff; Dt 1:17; 24:17; Ps 15 (14):5, etc).
16:21–17:1 'Abominations'—The first two regard **b** Canaanite practices (12:3). An Asherah was a sacred tree, or a wooden pole, dedicated, originally at least, to the Canaanite goddess of this name and the consort of Baal at Tyre; it undoubtedly had some association with fertility rites, and its presence next to Yahweh's altar would have assimilated him to Baal. The 'pillars' were of stone and commemorative steles, which originally were considered unexceptionable in orthodox Yahwism (Ex 24:4; cf also Gn 28:18, etc), but eventually as symbols of divinity were classified among idols (7:5; 12:3; Lv 26:1, Mi 5:12). They were a regular feature of the 'high places', where they at times at least were associated with dead ancestors. The context of the third law (cf Lv 22:20) has been taken to suggest that Canaanites offered defective animals to their gods, but this does not seem likely; rather, the three prohibitions are grouped together simply because they all regard 'abominations' of Yahweh.
17:2–13 Local and Central Tribunal—A 'removal' **c** law on apostasy (2–7), which as the most general case may have introduced the more specific cases of 13:1ff, is placed here with the addition of 6, which

234c lays special emphasis on procedure (cf 19:15). In this context apostasy is only an example of a crime; interest is shifted to the requirements of proof. Should these be lacking for one reason or another, the case is to be referred to the lay and religious authorities at the central sanctuary, whose decision is binding on the local judges (8–13). It is disputed whether this law spoke originally only of a lay judge, or only of priests (case beyond rational proof, recourse therefore to ordeal, etc), or of both. In the light of 2 Chr 19:8–11, which provides a very close parallel to this law and whose substantial historicity there is no reason to doubt, the last view seems the most probable.

d 17:14–20 King—The central authority of 17:8–13 provides the occasion for laying down some fundamental norms for kingship in Israel. The attitude towards the institution is one of reserve, if not positive hostility. Kingship is of foreign origin (**14** cf 1 Sm 8:5) and is acceptable only under a number of conditions: the king must be divinely chosen (**15***a*); an Israelite (**15***b*); he must shun the trappings and the political devices of the rulers of 'world powers' (a huge chariotry **16***a*; a great royal harem of which many of the members would come from marriages to cement foreign alliances **17***a*; vast crown properties of which the revenues would serve in part to maintain a professional army **17***b*); and, above all, he must be completely subjected, like any Israelite, to the covenant-law, the study of which is the only positive duty given to him (**19***f*). Since none of the modalities of either divine choice or popular will is indicated, the divine and human are not necessarily mutually exclusive. The prohibition against choosing a foreigner is puzzling. Neither the S nor, so far as we know, the N kingdom ever had a foreigner as a king or was in real danger of having one. Perhaps there is an allusion here to Israel's first and bitter experience of kingship under Abimelech, whose half-Shechemite origin encouraged revolt (Jg 9:28f). Equally obscure is the reference to the return to Egypt in 16. 28:68 suggests that it means the enslavement of Israelites in exchange for horses, but again our sources are silent about such an abuse of royal power. In view especially of 1(3) Kgs 10:28f and 11:3ff, Solomon's reign seems to have provided the author with a negative norm.

e 18:1–8 Priests—These laws inform the laity of what is due to the priest, and hence their brevity in comparison with the more detailed laws of Lv and Nm, which were destined for the instruction of the priests themselves. The nucleus is the old impersonal law of **3** on the priest's share of animal sacrifices (cf Lv 7:28ff; Nm 18:18). The rest is Dt expansion: **1** establishes the priests as propertyless, a consequence of their separation from their families (cf 33:9), and hence their dependence on offerings to God (**2**); **4f** refers to their claims to 'the best part' (not 'first fruits' or 'the first') of grain, etc (probably the tithes of 14:22 besides an offering of wool); **6ff** establishes the rights of the Levites dwelling apart from the central sanctuary to share equally with the others stationed there if the former performed priestly functions, though these rights were not always honoured (cf 2 (4) Kgs 23:9); the end of 8 is extremely obscure in the Heb text.

f 9–22 Prophets—In its desire to know the divine will and designs Israel is to have recourse, not to the means used by its neighbours (9–13), but to the prophets, who continue the work of Moses (14–19); however, even a prophet's message must be tested (20–22). In **10** various mantic techniques, all performed by professionals, are listed;' child-sacrifice is an exception, and an

obvious addition (cf 12:31). In **15**, not one prophet but a line of prophets is promised ('. . . will *continually* raise up . . .'), as the context demands (cf also 2 (4) Kgs 17:13). The messianic interpretation (Ac 3:22ff; Jn 6:14; 7:40) developed after the Exile in the light of Israel's eschatological hopes (R. A. F. MacKenzie, 'The Messianism of Deuteronomy', CBQ 19 (1957), 299–305). Some scholars maintain that **15** concerns a prophetic office with the authority to interpret the old and declare new law in the cult. The problem of false prophets is treated somewhat differently from 13:1ff. Open apostasy (**20**), as in 13:1ff, is punishable by death, but short of this a new norm for discernment is introduced: only the true prophet's prediction comes true (cf 1 (3) Kgs 22:28; Jer 28:9; Ezek 33:33). The possibility seen by Jer 18:7–10 is not considered.

19:1–13 Homicide—In line with an old tradition (Ex 21:12–14), two types of slaying are distinguished. **1–11 Involuntary.** The earliest law permitted refuge in any legitimate sanctuary (Ex 21:12f); later, six cities were assigned this function (Nm 35:9ff; Jos 20:1ff), three in Transjordan, and three in Cisjordan. Since this distribution ignores tribal boundaries and is based purely on geographical considerations, it could not have arisen before the time of David or Solomon, but not much later either, since the region of one of the Transjordanian cities was lost shortly after Solomon's death (de Vaux). Dt provides for three cities, but allows for the possibility of three more; at the time this law was composed Transjordan was clearly not part of Israel, and the way in which the possibility of future expansion is expressed is quite vague, and does not clearly refer to Transjordan. (4:41ff, of which 8f is unaware, is based on Jos 20.) The law is also vague on the procedure for establishing the refugee's innocence and the duration of his stay in the city of refuge. Inadequate as legislation, 1–10 is primarily interested in enunciating the fundamental requirement of the avoidance of shedding innocent blood (10, cf 13; also 21:8).

11–13 Voluntary. This 'removal' law has been re- **b** worded slightly in terms of the previous law. The murderer is executed, not by local authorities, but by the kinsman of the murdered man; the demands of vengeance, though controlled, are still honoured. Distinctive of biblical law is that, contrary to general custom in the ancient Near E, the family was not permitted to accept any form of compensation (cf Nm 35:31ff); a human life was invaluable and could not be assessed in shekels. **14 Family Land**—Cf 27:17; Job 24:2; Prv 22:28; 23:10. Throughout the ancient world great respect attached to the boundaries defining family property; even Plato, no friend of private property, revered Zeus Herkeios, the protector of boundaries, and considered the border lines between estates as divine (cf also the Roman god Terminus). The Dt expansion puts the possession of the land in the future and recalls the ultimate giver.

15–21 Witnesses—The necessity of two or more **c** witnesses to sustain a charge, which is without clear parallel in the ancient Near E, is a law of evidence intended to afford greater protection to the innocent. It is here extended to any charge, not only to one involving capital punishment (17:6; Nm 35:30). The 'removal' law in **16ff** has undergone a Dt reworking in view of centralization; judges, and probably the priests too, have been added to bring the appearance 'before the Lord' in line with 17:8ff. The inquiry of the judges (18) secularizes the entire procedure and in effect transforms the original law, which dealt with

5c non-rational methods of proof at a local sanctuary. In its original form—*mutatis mutandis*, this is also true of the present form—the law assumes, without explanation, that after the accusation both parties have appeared at a sanctuary and, again without explanation, the accusation has been shown to be false; this being the situation, the culprit is to suffer the punishment due the wrong-doing the other was charged with, a d principle well attested in Mesopotamian law. In other words, 16–18 should be read as a long description of the case, 19 as its solution (so also 13:12–14, then 15ff; 17:2–4, then 5). The explanation of the appearance in the sanctuary is probably that the falsely accused party appealed for an ordeal to establish his innocence. The ordeal was most likely an imprecatory oath to be taken by the accuser, in which case the presumption would be that the false accuser will refuse; this presumption is borne out by many cuneiform documents, an oath before the divinity being a terrifying experience which was avoided even by the innocent. In the context of 15, 16ff in the mind of Dt is probably an example of a case too difficult for the local tribunal to handle (cf 17:8ff after 17:6). The punishment of 19 is interpreted as an application of talion (cf Ex 21:23ff; Lv 24:18, 20; also Code of Hammurabi).

e 20:1–20 (Holy) War—Procedures to be followed in levying an army (1a*a*, 5–7, 9), before starting a siege (10–12), and during the siege (19–20) become those of a holy war after the Dt expansions (1a*b*–4, 8, 13–18). The exemptions in 5–7 (cf also 24:5) are ancient and paralleled in Ugaritic epic; they are intended to ensure a man progeny and some use of his property, the deprivation of which was a curse (28:30). The additions in 1a*b*–4 and 8 stress the inner dispositions and the religious significance of the war. Forced labour (11) and siege-works (20), in the context of Israelite history, point to the monarchical period. The mitigated anathema in 13f is duly qualified by 15–18, which adheres to the demands of 7.1ff. 19 can be illustrated by Assyrian texts, which often speak of the wanton destruction of orchards.

f 21:1–9 Unknown Murderer—The blood of the innocent cried to God (Gn 4:10), and therefore the case of an unknown murderer posed a most grave problem, since responsibility fell upon the community. The law adds a special circumstance, namely, the dead body has been found, not within a city or village, but in an open field; hence, the community responsible must first be determined by establishing which city or village lay closest, a procedure paralleled in Mesopotamia and Ugarit. The law prescribes a spoken formula which denies both personal guilt and knowledge of the culprit's identity (7), and a rite in some way symbolical of the removal of blood, which is carried off by the stream (6). 5, 8, 9*b* are secondary: 5 is otiose, since the Levites do nothing at all; 8 turns the slaughtering of the animal in 6 into a religious sacrifice of atonement; 9*b* is Dt parenesis.

g 21:10–14 Marriage to a Captive—The prescriptions of 12f and the right of the husband to dismiss the woman at his whim and without bill of divorce (contrast 23:1–4) are quite ancient and reflect the pitiful plight of the captive. The shaving of the head, etc, are probably not part of the mourning; rather, the hair, finger-nails and clothes being extensions, as it were, and symbols of the person, their removal or trimming signifies the captive's new status. Perhaps an innovation is the humane provision that, whether she has borne the husband children or not, she cannot be treated as a mere chattel;

she is given some legal status, which approximates to, 235g if it is not identical with, that of a concubine (cf Ex 21:7–11). The assumption in Dt is that she falls under the women mentioned in 20:14, and therefore this law does not contradict the prohibition against taking Canaanite wives.

15–17 Right of Primogeniture—'If a man has two h wives, *of whom he prefers one to the other*', this preference has no bearing on the rights of the first-born; cf Gn 48:13ff; 49:3f, 8; 1 Chr 5:1f and texts from Nuzi, Ugarit and Alalakh, which show that earlier custom permitted otherwise. The double portion, if this is the right translation, is well attested in Mesopotamian sources. However, the Heb. expression, which is also found in 2 (4) Kgs 2:9 and Zech 13:8, means rather two-thirds, and this extraordinary privilege of the first-born is paralleled in a legal text from Mari.

18–21 Rebellious Son—In this 'removal' law the reverence due parents is the heritage of a patriarchal society, but the mother now shares the father's dignity, and the *patria potestas* is limited; the father must bring the son before the elders for punishment.

22–23 Exposed Corpse—Special infamy was attached i to a corpse hung for public exposure after execution (cf Jos 8:29; 10:26f; 2 Sm 4:12). Of the two motive-clauses the first is pre-Dt (simply 'God'), the second is Dt and integrates the law within the general theme of the land.

22:1–12 Miscellaneous Laws—1–4 is an expanded 236a form of Ex 23:4f, which stresses that even one's opponent in a law-suit is to be helped; Dt speaks more generally of all fellow-Israelites. An individual could not raise an ass without undoing the pack, or an ox without removing the yoke. 5 refers to practices in Canaanite cults (transvestism with accompanying unnatural acts); in one Akkadian text they are especially associated with Amorites, that is, W Semites. The prohibitions of 9–11 probably reflect very ancient taboos (cf Lv 19:19). The original significance of the tassels in 12 is obscure; the explanation in Nm 15.37ff is a later rationalization.

22:13–29 Marriage—These are 'removal' laws which b have undergone only the slightest retouches.

13–21. In the first part (13–19) the wife is protected against a husband who seeks an easy way out of an unpleasant union. The husband is punished in three ways: a beating, a very heavy fine paid to the father of the girl, loss of all rights to divorce her. The primitive means of proving her innocence are not without parallel elsewhere. Without this evidence, however, the presumption is that the girl was not a virgin at the time of marriage (20–21); she had done 'a *shameful* thing in Israel', an expression which with one exception refers to a sexual crime; it means here that the girl between engagement and consummation of the marriage had committed the equivalent of adultery (cf 23ff). Probably, though this is not mentioned, the father had to restore the 'bride-price' paid by the husband at the espousals (cf the fine imposed on the husband).

22. Adultery, when the parties are caught *flagrante* c *delicto*, is handled very easily and quickly (cf Lv 20:10). The type of execution is not specified, but stoning is probably understood (24; cf Ezek 16:38, 40; 23:45, 47; Jn 8:5). No provision is made, as in Mesopotamian and Hittite laws, for condonation by the husband, though Prv 6:32–35 suggests that this was theoretically possible. Later Jewish law expressly excludes it.

23–27. An 'engaged' girl was considered legally

236c married; the suitor had paid the bride-price and therefore had a claim on the girl, even though the consummation of the marriage might come much later. Intercourse with her, therefore, was equivalent to adultery. Legal presumptions based on circumstances (time, place, etc) are attested in Assyrian laws on adultery.

d 28–29. After rape (cf Ex 22:16) the possibility that the father may refuse his daughter to the man is not considered; because of the obvious difficulty of marrying off such a daughter, such a consideration was probably no longer practical. Fifty shekels is too high simply for the bride-price and so must include a penalty (cf 19).

30. (Heb 23:1), since it deals with marriage, is appended to the preceding laws. Marriage or intercourse with a step-mother is declared incestuous (cf Lv 18:8; 20:11 adds the death penalty for intercourse; cf also Dt 27:20). The first part of the law attempts to suppress the custom of a son's inheriting his father's wives along with the rest of the property (cf 2 Sm 16:22; 1 (3) Kgs 2:22; Ezek 22:10).

e 23:1–8 (Heb 2–9) Membership in Assembly—A member was a male citizen, who bore arms and participated in the cultic and political assemblies. The date of composition, the Dt and pre-Dt additions, and the extent to which political relationships are reflected in 3 and 7f, are all highly controversial. **1.** The mutilation was deliberate. It was practised by priests in Syria, Asia Minor and Mesopotamia, but also pertained to the harem system; the former seems the more probable original motivation of this law. In the post-exilic period eunuchs were no longer excluded (Is 56:3ff). **2.** 'Bastard' is perhaps, more specifically, the offspring of an incestuous union. **3–6.** The historical motivation (4–6, cf Nm 22–24) is secondary; the censure of the Moabites and Ammonites rests on a different tradition from that of ch 2. In the context of 2, 3 should be compared with Gn 19:30ff, which of course reflects rather than explains the same hostility. **7f,** with its different style and explicit classification according to ritual purity ('abhor' is to treat as ritually impure), derives from another source; the benign attitude towards the Edomites and especially the Egyptians is hard to understand.

f 9–14 Purity of the Camp—This law deals in 10f with temporary exclusion from the people and therefore is placed after the laws of 1ff. Engaged in a Holy War, the army must be ritually pure; the impurity contracted by a nocturnal emission, for which there are parallels both in (cf Lv 15:1ff) and outside the Bible, is only one example (cf 1 Sm 21:6; 2 Sm 11:11). The anthropomorphism in 14 is quite un-Dt.

15–16 Fugitive Slave—Fugitive slaves were common in the ancient world (cf 1 Sm 25:10), and if from a foreign country, they were usually extradited (cf 1 Sm 30:15; 1 (3) Kgs 2:39f); extradition is a common stipulation of international treaties. It is such a slave who is treated here, with perhaps the additional implicit qualification that the slave was a native Israelite, first a slave in Israel, and then somehow sold to a foreign master; for this there would be parallels in Babylonian law.

g 17–18 Sacred Prostitution—Male and female prostitutes were part of the temple staff; they were 'consecrated ones' and the implications of this 'holiness' are suggested by Asherah's title 'Holiness' when she is depicted in her most erotic form. 2 (4) Kgs 23:7, especially in the light of contemporary Assyrian texts, indicates their more prosaic place in the temple-economy. 'Harlot' (18) could be a common prostitute, but the

parallelism with 'dog' favours her being part of the temple personnel; the latter term is attested as a designation of temple personnel on Cyprus, and in all probability refers to a male prostitute (cf also Phil 3:2; Apoc 22:15). In itself, however, the term was simply one of humility and could describe the relation of a servant to his master, subject to his king, etc.

19–20 Usury—Cf Ex 22:24; Lv 25:35ff. Originally **h** at least, the word used for interest referred to a loan with the interest deducted in advance; if then the loan was not paid in due time, further interest 'increase' (Lv 25:36), accrued to the debt. Since loans carried exorbitant interest rates, they were sought generally only in distress; the law therefore is primarily concerned with people in this situation. The theoretical basis of the prohibition against such loans may have been the familial relationship which, at least in theory, bound together all Israelites; possibly too the conception attested in Ugaritic documents that free-men did not impose interest on loans to each other, may also have been of some influence.

21–23 Prompt Payment of Vows—Cf Nm 30:2; Eccl 5:13f. Failure in this regard is frequently mentioned in Mesopotamian omen literature. **24–25** provides for the satisfaction of the immediate needs of the wayfarer or poor man while protecting the owner against abuses.

24:1–4 Remarriage to same woman—The existence **i** of divorce is assumed but is not the object of the legislation; rather, a very special case with all the conditions of 1–3 is treated. The meaning of 'indecency' (same expression 23:14) is obscure and gave rise later to rabbinic disputes (cf Mt 19:3). Why the woman was considered defiled and remarriage to her an abomination is equally obscure. Jer 3:1ff uses this law to show the legally impossible situation Israel has put herself in by her infidelity to God. **3.** 'And the latter husband *rejects* her'. **5.** For the exemption of the newly-wed, cf 20:7.

6–16 Varia—**6.** Pledges were taken by creditors not **j** so much as real security but rather as means of exerting pressure for payment of debts. Here is prohibited taking a vital necessity, the mill-stones with which the grain of daily bread was ground each day. **7.** A 'removal law', cf Ex 21:16. **8f.** The injunction to obey the Levites seems secondary; the reference to Miriam then becomes more meaningful (cf Nm 12:9ff). The original form would read, 'Be on your guard against an attack of leprosy'. The addition seems to allude to Lv 13–14. **10–13.** The loan is of the type involving a personal pledge (15:1ff); the pledge to be fetched is only a symbol. Any semblance of seizure is forbidden. Cf Ex 22:25f; Am 2:8; Ezek 18:12. **16.** This is often regarded as an innovation due to prophetic influence (cf Jer 31:29; Ezek 18:2), and a departure from the conception of solidarity we find in passages like Jos 7:24. Actually, it is quite traditional, and merely restates the judicial norms of criminal law found in Ex 21:31, where the customary law of the ancient Near E, which allowed for the punishment of children for their father's negligence, is unequivocally rejected.

17–22 Personae miserabiles—As far back as the **k** third millennium the legal tradition of the Fertile Crescent was guided by concern for widows, orphans and other defenceless persons. **19ff** finds close parallels in Babylonian harvest customs. However, what is new is the motivation which inspires these laws: remembrance of the past—slaves freed by God, who now through Israel would extend the divine pity to others.

25:1–3 Corporal Punishment—The intention of

k the law is to protect a man from excessively cruel punishment, probably by the bastinado, and therefore the beating is to be administered in the judge's presence, with the strokes being strictly proportionate to the crime and never exceeding forty (cf 2 Cor 11:24). 4. Comparable in spirit to 22:6f.

l 5–10 Levirate Marriage—An ancient custom, with parallels in Assyrian and Hittite laws and observed at least by the royal family at Ugarit, is here restricted to brothers living together on the same domain; this restriction seems designed to prevent alienation of the family property (cf also Ru 4:5f). Earlier (Gn 38), the sanctions were much more severe and the obligation might devolve even upon the father-in-law; Ru 3:12; 4:5 go further, the next-of-kin whether of the same family or not coming under the obligation.

11–12 Indecent Assault—This is the only instance of mutilation as a punishment prescribed by biblical law; an exact parallel is found in Middle Assyrian laws, and analogous cases in the Code of Hammurabi. In all it is the offending member which suffers.

m 13–16 Honesty in Commerce—Cf Lv 19:35f; Am 8:5; Prv 11:1. 13f prescribes the same weight or measure for buying and selling; 15 requires conformity to some commonly accepted standard.

17–19 Amalekites—Ancient enemies of Israel, the Amalekites are heard of from the desert period (Ex 17:8ff; Nm 14:43) until the time of David (Jg 6:3; 1 Sm 15; 30:1ff), then disappear from history. The charge made in 18 is not mentioned elsewhere.

n 26:1–15 Two Rituals. 1–11 Offering of First-fruits—Cf Ex 23:19; 34:26. The repetition of the ceremony in 4 and 10*b* and the double declaration in 3 and 5ff are clear evidence of a complex tradition; perhaps 3f is a revision reserving the ceremonial action to the priest. The relation between this offering and that of tithes is not clear; the fact that 1–11, like the law on tithes (14:22), is followed by the requirements for the triennial tithe (12–15 cf 14:28f) suggests a connection. The 'wandering Aramaean' of 5 is probably Israel's common ancestor, Jacob; a wanderer, he is without land and the rights which come with the possession of land. The beautiful declaration of faith and expression of gratitude in 5–10 instantly and profoundly transform an old agricultural feast; the offering is referred, not to the rhythm of nature and a god inherent in this nature, but **o** to historical events and the God behind them. **12 15 Triennial Tithes**—There are to be no deviations from the observance prescribed in 14:28f. The declaration of 13ff is made at the central sanctuary ('before the Lord your God'), but there are indications that a rite practised previously each year at a local sanctuary has here been adapted to centralization. The negative confession of 14 implies that the offering of tithes was associated by some with a cult of ancestors, who were mourned and then, perhaps by placing food and drink at their graves, were given a share in the feast. Other scholars see here allusions to rites in honour of a dying and rising god (cf 14:1f).

p 26:16–19 Exchange of Covenantal Obligations—16 concludes the promulgation of the laws, and harks back to the introduction in 12:1. **17–19**. Moses acts as intermediary between Yahweh and the people, and in this rite, which with its overtones of a parity relationship may have been modelled on the pact between king and people, the essence of the covenant-bond is reaffirmed: Yahweh is Israel's God, whom they will obey, and Israel is his people, whom he will cherish and bless in a most special way. 'As he promised' (18) and 'as he has spoken'

(19) are either an allusion to Ex 19:5f or refer back **236p** to similar statements in the covenant-liturgy.

27:1–26 Ceremonies at Shechem—This entire **237a** section, with the exception of 9f, is a later insertion: the references to Moses in the third person in 1, (9), 11 are unparalleled in chh 5–26 and 28; the content is completely different; the explicit reference to Shechem ill accords with the silence Dt elsewhere maintains about the place for Yahweh's worship. And the insertion itself presents many difficulties for literary criticism. Many explanations have been proposed of the following facts: 12 speaks of blessings, but no blessings follow; according to 12 the Levites are on Mt Gerizim, but in 14 they lead the liturgy for the entire people; in 13 only six tribes participate in the cursing, in 15ff, the entire people; 1–8 is quite redundant, and 4 is very ambiguous (are the stones those of 2f? 5 cf Jos 8:32). 4–8, 12f, 15–25 seem to be the nucleus of an old tradition, which is here incorporated by a late redactor intent upon associating Dt with the covenant of Shechem (Jos 24). **2f**. The stones **b** are those erected at Gilgal (Jos 4:20); thus Gilgal is also drawn into the Shechem tradition (cf 11:30). **4–8**. Cf Ex 20:24f; 24:4f. Writing on plastered surfaces is known from Egypt. **9f** follows 26:17–19; Israel is God's people, and before moving on to the blessings and curses which this covenantal union involves, it is ordered to pause in silence in the presence of this mystery. **12f**. On the slopes of the two mountains overlooking Shechem the people face each other: on Gerizim, the sons of Rachel and four of Leah's; on Ebal, two of Leah's (Reuben and Zebulun) and those of Jacob's concubines. **15–26** is a list of some of the gravest crimes, of which the common denominator is the secrecy with which they are committed. To reach the hidden sinful members guilty of any of them and to separate them from the community so that the divine wrath fall on them alone, the people gives its solemn 'amens' to the curses and thereby lets loose their awful power. **26** is an addition, which draws the entire law of Dt within the Shechem liturgy.

28 Blessings and Curses—Concluding the covenant **c** are blessings (1–14) and curses (15–68); cf Ex 23:20–33; Lv 26:3–45. Both parts have undergone some expansion, especially the curses. **1–14**. The totality of blessings is expressed in 3 and 6 (cf 16 and 19) by the union of opposites. 'Called by the name of the Lord' (10) means that Israel is Yahweh's possession, which of course he will protect, and hence the fear of the world.

15–68. The curses strike field and flock (17f, 22ff, 38ff, etc), family (17, 30, 32, 41, etc), body (21f, 27, 35, etc) and spirit (20, 28, 34). They bring the horrors of war, invasion and defeat (25f, 47ff), devastation (31, 33, 51), siege and its terrible consequences (51ff), deportations (32, 36, 41). Destroyed is the work of God promised to the patriarchs: the great nation is virtually annihilated (62), the few that are left alive are not in the Promised Land, but scattered among the nations, and—surely one of the saddest lines of the Bible— once again Israel is in Egypt, hoping only for the subsistence of slaves (68). These are the consequences of rejecting a God who asks only to be served in joy and gladness (47). **23**. This curse is found almost verbatim **d** in an Assyrian treaty. **24**. '. . . and dust from heaven shall come down . . .' **27**. The identification of the Egyptian disease is unknown. In **47ff** the style changes, close contacts with Jeremiah become very frequent (48/Jer 28:13; 49/Jer 4:13; 5:15; 52/Jer 5:17; 53/Jer 19:9), and the law is already written, not just spoken by Moses (58, 61). **49**. 'The Lord will *muster*'. **53**. The eating of

237d children during a siege is attested both in the Bible (2 (4) Kgs 6:28ff; Lam 4:10; cf Lv 26:29) and in Assyrian documents. **68.** Cf Hos 8:13; 9:3, 6. The ships are probably a reference to slave-trade.

e **29:1 (Heb 28:69)—32:52 Concluding Discourse and Ceremonies 29:1 Superscription**—This v is better taken as introducing, in the final redaction of Dt, the discourse and ceremonies which follow rather than as the conclusion to 5:1ff. 'Words of the covenant' refer, therefore, not to laws, but to the following instruction. The emphasis on the distinction between the covenants of Horeb and Moab is new; 5:1ff stresses rather their continuity.

29:2—30:20 Final Covenant Instruction
2—9 History—The purpose of salvation-history is that 'you may know that I am the Lord your God'. Knowledge here involves more than the mind; it is an acknowledgement engaging the whole person. This, we are told, is impossible even for eye-witnesses of the wonders of the exodus and the desert, unless God gives 'a mind to understand . . .' (4). For this penetration into the mystery of faith the author is probably dependent on Jeremiah (Jer 24:7; cf Is 6:10; Ezek 12:2). 9 is a parenetic formula of transition to 10ff.

f **10—15 Covenant**—The basic covenant relationship (12, cf 26:17ff) and those bound by it are defined— not only those present (10), but all Israelites and therefore all future generations (13f).

16—21 Warning—The experience of the past, with an allusion to the prohibition of images, is recalled (16f), and its purpose, the prevention of apostasy, driven home with the warning that neither individual nor family nor tribe can escape punishment under cover of the entire people (18ff).

22—29 Curses—The perspective suddenly widens to the entire people, who are in exile (28) and their land a waste. These curses are not threatened, they are explained (24ff). A strikingly close parallel in an Assyrian inscription (ANET, 300) indicates that those who put the question in 24 also answer it (25ff, therefore 'Then they will say . . .'). 29 is a parenthetical remark, perhaps a later insertion. The future, it seems to say, lies in the hand of God, and therefore our task is not to speculate on the future but to concentrate on what has been revealed, the demands of obedience. Perhaps the promise of restoration in 30:1ff, which goes back to Jer and Ezek, had aroused premature hopes among the exiles.

g **30:1—10 Blessings**—The proclamation of 4:29—31 is elaborated. Curse can never be the final word on God's people; exile can only be a means God uses to effect a conversion of heart. In fact, it is he himself who will circumcize the heart (cf 10:16) and make it capable of that total love which gives life. Thus the exile prepares for a New Exodus and a future even more glorious than anything Israel has ever known. This kerygma is strongly reminiscent of Ezek (36:24ff; 37:21ff), but especially of Jer and his new, interiorized covenant of the future (31:31ff; 32:39ff; on the restoration of fortune, cf Jer 29:14; 30:3, 18, etc; gathering the people, 23:3; 29:14; 32:37; the Lord's delight, 32:41). The covenant in Moab thus becomes, in its final expression, a prophetic prediction of restoration, and in the author's mind this was perhaps what distinguished it from the covenant at Sinai (cf 29:1).

h **11—20 Final Appeal**—Observance of the law is not beyond the people's powers. The law, like its protector (4:7), is near; it is not a remote, esoteric wisdom, but something that can be spoken, placed in the heart, and put into action (11—14). This day of revelation is decisive; the people are confronted with life and death, 23 and choose they must.

31:1—32:52 Seven short speeches accompanied by 23 certain ceremonial acts introduce the Song of Moses (32: 1—43). They are so ordered that the divine message and theophany in 14f provide the turning point from the three speeches which look to a happy future and obedience, to the concluding three which foresee sin and its punishment: (1) Moses—approaching death, conquest, divine aid (2—6); (2) Moses—Joshua installed in office (**7f**); (3) Moses—after conquest *tôrāh* to be read every seven years, obedience (**10—13**); (4) Yahweh— approaching death of Moses, Joshua to be confirmed in office (**14**); (5) Yahweh—on death of Moses rebellion predicted, Song to serve as witness against people (**16—21**); (6) Yahweh—Joshua confirmed as war-leader (**23**); (7) Moses—deposit of written *tôrāh* as witness against people ordered, leaders to be convoked to hear Song (**26—29**). Moses then recites the Song, after which in a final brief word, referring to both the *tôrāh* and the Song, he makes a last plea for obedience (46f). **48—52** is a transition to the blessing and death of 33:1ff.

Unquestionably the author has combined various **b** sources. The Song was originally an independent composition; 31:14f, 23 is a fragment of an older tradition, probably JE ('tent of meeting', never mentioned in Dt tradition), while 32:48—52 is a virtual doublet of Nm 27:12—14 (P). Yet there is a deep unity, which is provided by the institution of the covenant. Written covenant document, periodic reading, placing of document in sanctuary, witnesses—these all belong to this institution. Moreover, when supreme authority was transferred, the foundation of Israelite life, the covenant, was recalled (cf 1 Sm 12), and so the installation of Joshua is quite in context.

31:1—8, 14f, 23 Installation of Joshua—The ideal **c** age of an Egyptian sage was 110 (cf Gn 50:26; Jos 24:29); indicative therefore of the divine favour enjoyed by Moses is his age of 120. The reference to Joshua in 3 is abrupt and probably secondary. In **7f** Moses finally executes the order of 3:28. **14f, 23** are the divine confirmation of the new leader, but only in his rôle as war-leader; in Jos 1:2ff, in another theophany, he is confirmed as distributor of the land.

9—13 Text and Tradition—Levites and elders (cf 27:1, 9), clergy and official representatives of the laity, receive the written document. The year of release is designated, probably on the basis of an old tradition, as the occasion of the public reading. With the cancelling of debts (cf 15:1ff), in the joy of the autumn festival, life began anew, and fittingly therefore Israel returned to its origins, the saving deeds of God and his demands of service.

16—22 Prophecy—The sins of the future will not catch **d** God by surprise. He is the supreme lord, and so he predicts, in language drawn largely from the Song, which will be written proof of his prediction, the history of Israel that will follow. Dt thus becomes a dark prophecy. It should be noted that account is taken only of the first part of the Song (1—25).

24—30 Deposit of Tôrāh—The text of the covenant in Moab is deposited next to the Ark. Like the Song, it too is a witness against the rebellious people, and thus the *tôrāh* itself becomes prophetic.

32:1—43 The Song—The basic structure of this **e** baroque poem is provided by the literary form of a covenant lawsuit: summons to witnesses (1), accusation in form of a question (6), recounting of plaintiff's benefits to the accused (7—14), affirmative statement of breach

8e of covenant (15—18), judgement (19ff). This form has some parallels in documents of the second millennium (J. Harvey, 'Le "Rib-Pattern", réquisitoire prophétique sur la rupture de l'alliance', Bib 43 (1962), 172—196). It is clearly related to the covenant formulary: history of benefits, the crime corresponding to the stipulations of the covenant, covenant witnesses, punishment based on the curses of the covenant. However, as used here it is profoundly transformed. Not only is the lawsuit an event of the past (19f, ch 5), a source of reflection and teaching (2), but instead of being addressed to the accused, the judgement becomes a soliloquy (20—25), and then is suddenly turned against the very ones who in 25 are the instruments of divine justice; it is their guilt which is declared, and it is they whom God will judge and punish. The judgement against Israel becomes an oracle of salvation. The covenant lawsuit could conclude with either a condemnation or a mocking request to seek salvation from the gods for whom the people had abandoned Yahweh (Jgs 10:14); the latter seems to have left open the possibility of God's withholding his final judgement, provided the people repented (cf Jgs 10:15f). Both conclusions appear in this poem, judgement (19ff) and request (37f). In brief, this poem is a highly sophisticated piece of literature which subtly and effectively inverts an old literary form.

f The difficulty of dating its composition is evident from the wide range of scholarly opinion (12th—4th cent. B.C.!). The historical allusions are so vague that the 'no people' of 21 has been identified with Canaanites, Philistines, Aramaeans, Assyrians, or Samaritans. The failure to mention the exile among Israel's punishments rules out an exilic or post-exilic date; the differences from demonstrably ancient poetry of the pre-monarchical or early monarchical period, together with the sophistication just noted, make a date before the 9th cent. improbable.

g **1—5 Introduction.** 'Give ear—hear' (1) inverts the order of a traditional parallelism and is perhaps intended as an indication of the inversion of form in the entire poem. On heaven and earth as witnesses, cf §224*b*. 2 is a prayer that the speaker's words penetrate his audience (Israel, cf 6) and win their acceptance and understanding (cf Jb 29:22f). 'Our God' (3) is probably addressed to the witnesses of 1; it is to them too that Israel's guilt is announced (5), before Israel is spoken to directly (6). **6 Accusation.** 'Creation' refers to the bringing of Israel into existence as a people.

h **7—14 History.** As the universal God who separates the nations, he is the Most High, but as the one who keeps Israel for himself, he is Yahweh (8). 'The sons of God' are the angelic host, a demythologized form of the sons of El in the Canaanite pantheon, who numbered 70 (cf the 70 peoples in Gn 10, the 70 sons of Jacob in Dt 10:22). Their relationship to the nations is not stated; in the author's mind it was probably one of rule subordinated to Yahweh (cf 4:19; Sir 17:14). In any case, from creation itself God has chosen his people. Striking by its absence is any reference to the exodus; Israel is found in the desert, which is hardly Egypt, led to, and finally established in, the Promised Land (13, 'he made him *mount* the high places . . .'). This scheme of salvation-history, which is paralleled in Hos 9:10 and Ezek 16:3ff, probably goes back to a group which joined Israel only after the exodus. The land is a kind of paradise, full of sweets and fats, which are so lacking in the ordinary diet of the (semi-) nomad. The honey (13) is natural wild honey; 'mountain honey' is mentioned in Akkadian sources.

15—18 Sin. Despite God's having brought them from a **238h** terrible desert to a virtual paradise—and he alone did this (12)—Israel, fat with his gifts, rejects him for other gods (cf ch 8). The origin and meaning of Jeshurun, an ancient name for the twelve-tribe league, are unknown.

19—42 Judgement. This long section is articulated by **i** the catch-word 'say': 'And he said' (20), 'I *said*' (26), 'he will say' (37), 'I will say' ('swear', 40); note the alternation of person. Only in this section does Yahweh speak; up to this point the poet has been the only speaker. This is to be explained through the influence of the early prophetic form in which the prophet himself makes the accusation, quoting Yahweh only when the punishment is to be declared or threatened ('Therefore, thus Yahweh has spoken; . . .'). **20—25.** Talion determines the punishment of **21**. Note how we move back in these vv, with sin and the curse attached to it undoing, almost step by step, the work of grace: jealousy and anger (21/16), foolish and scoffing (21/15), same stem *nbl*), mountains and earth devastated, famine, etc instead of plenty (22—24/13f), sword and terror instead of the divine protection and gentle affection (25/10—12). Only one step remains, utter annihilation, for sin to undo the divine election itself (8f), and in a masterpiece of suspense, which can only be brought out in English by a free translation, in 26 this step seems to be reached: 'I said, "I will scatter . . . from among men. But no! I fear provocation . . ." '. Cf 9:28; Is 13:25; 48:9—11; Ezek 20:9, 14, 22, etc; note also the general structure of Jer (in the LXX) and Ezek, according to which the oracles against the nations succeed the condemnation of Israel.

28—30 refers to the enemies, not to Israel; the same **j** accusation can be levelled against them as against Israel—their conquest is to be explained, not by their numbers, but by Yahweh's having handed over his people for punishment. **31** is the poet's own reflection. In **32—35** Yahweh speaks once more. **37—39.** This part of the judgement is better understood as directed to Israel (cf Jer 2:28; Jg 10:11ff). In their utter helplessness they must see that the other gods are no gods at all, Yahweh is God, and he alone. Then the oath of **40—42** assures that Israel will be freed from its oppressors.

43. Conclusion. This short concluding hymn has **k** undergone much editorial activity, as the variants of LXX and Qumran prove. The original form is difficult to reconstruct, but almost certainly it was the 'sons of God' who were addressed, not the nations (cf 8).

44—52 Last words—Moses finishes his recitation of the Song (Joshua is associated with him to indicate his position as Moses' successor), and speaks one last word of exhortation. The covenant, with its long discourses and ceremonies, is concluded, the work of Moses is completed, and hence the word from God in 48ff, which forms the transition to 33:1ff. As already remarked above, the vocabulary is characteristic of P; also, Mt Nebo replaces the nearby Mt Pisgah (3:27). For the day in 48 cf 1:3; on Moses' sin, cf 1:37.

33:1—34:12 Blessing and Death—This final section, **239a** introduced by the last of the editorial notes dividing Dt into four parts, has a complex literary history due to the uniting of Dt and the Dt History with the rest of the Pent. **33:2—33 The Blessing**—This poem probably belonged to the JE tradition on the death of Moses. The individual blessings (6—25) are incorporated within an introduction (2—5) and a conclusion (26—29). 2—3, 26—29 are an originally independent poem; the opening vv have strong affinities with Jg 5:4f; Ps 68 (67):7f (HT 8f); Hb 3:3ff.

239a 4f is probably the earlier introduction to the blessings; 21b, which seems out of context, probably belongs here. The entire poem, both as a whole and in its individual parts, is one of the earliest pieces of Heb. poetry. The evidence drawn from spelling, diction, verse structure, contacts with Canaanite poetry, and the historical situations presupposed by the blessings, points to a date in the 11th cent. B.C. (cf F. M. Cross, Jr. and D. N. Freedman, 'The Blessing of Moses', JBL 67 (1948), 191—210). As is to be expected in so ancient a document, a number of parts remain obscure either because of faulty trans-**b** mission or because of our ignorance. **2f** describes a theophany of Yahweh the Warrior-God (cf 26f), accompanied by his heavenly court (he came *with* the ten thousands . . .'). **4f** is a new beginning, unfortunately obscure. Though 'the Lord' is not in the Heb text of 5, he is almost certainly the subject. The obscurity of 4b and the lack of an adequate context do not allow us to determine when Yahweh became king, though the revelation of Sinai is the most likely occasion; for other early references to Yahweh's kingship, cf Ex 15:18; Nm 23:21; Ps 68 (67):25; 24 (23):9. Some scholars see in 2—5 the reflection of an enthronement festival of Yahweh. **6** is lacking an introduction. Reuben is apparently an almost extinct tribe; Simeon, it may be noted, is not even **c** mentioned in the Blessing. **7**. Judah is in difficulty, possibly from the Philistines. **8—11**. The original blessing is in 11; 8—10 shows no sign of the archaic features which distinguish the rest of the poem. The content is also different from that of 11; it describes the priestly office of the Levites, the giving of oracles (Thummin and Urim were perhaps dice; cf Ex 28:30; Nm 27:21; 1 Sm 14:41f), teaching, and sacrificing. In 8—11, therefore, we have the later and earlier (11) stages of the tribe. Ex 17:1—7 and Nm 20:2—13 do not mention the Levites at Massah or Meribah (8f); 9 is strongly reminiscent of Ex 32:25—29. There were probably several traditions among the Levites explaining their priestly office. **12**. There is some doubt on the subject of the last clause. If it is Yahweh, then this must be an allusion to a sanctuary in Benjamin; if it is the tribe, then dwelling between the shoulders is an image of protec-**d** tion. **13—17**, Joseph, clearly the most important of the tribes, is favoured by God with rich crops (13—16) and military strength (cf Gn 49:22ff). In 16, rather than an allusion to the burning bush (Ex 3:3), we should read 'who

tented on Sinai'. **17**. 'The first born of the Bull is glorious, **23** indeed his horns are the horns of the Wild Ox'. The 'Bull' and 'Wild Ox' is El (-Yahweh); the same appellatives are used of El in Ugaritic texts. Yahweh therefore is El, an identification for which there is a mass of evidence, but his first-born is not a god—it is Joseph! **18f**. The contiguous tribes of Zebulun and Issachar are blessed together. The mountain where sacrifice is offered is probably Tabor. The seas must be the Mediterranean and the Lake of Galilee; according to Gn 49:13 Zebulun reached the former (contrast Jos 19:10—16). **20f**. Gad dominates Transjordan; on the displaced 21b, see above. **22—24** joins three Galilean tribes; Dan has by now moved to the N (cf Jos 17:40ff; Jgs 18:1ff). **26—29**. It is the Warrior-God who has given the victories and then security and prosperity. The image of 26 is familiar from Ugaritic mythological literature, where it is applied to the Storm-god Baal.

34:1—12 The Death of Moses—With the exception **24** of 'from the plains of Moab to Mt Nebo' and 'which is opposite Jericho' in 1, which are harmonizations with 32:48, 1—6 is to be attributed to the Dt historian. The detailed description of the land in 1b—3, which may be a later expansion, follows a N to S line; 'the Plain' is the Jordan Valley (Gn 13:10f), and Zoar was at the SE end of the Dead Sea. 7—9 derives from 'P' (cf Nm 27:15—23). The vigour of Moses at such an advanced age is evidence of God's favour. The mother of Nabonidus, **b** the Babylonian king, boasts in her funeral inscription of the sharpness of her faculties until her death at the age of 104. Aaron was also mourned thirty days (Nm 20:29). On the assumption that, like Aaron, Moses died on the mountain, and therefore in the final redaction of Dt on the same day as the Moab covenant was concluded (32:48; 1:3), then according to the calendar employed in 1:3, seventy days elapse between Moses' death and the crossing of the Jordan (Jos 4:19), or forty days after the mourning period is finished. 10ff is editorial and serves, by contrast, as a transition to the 'Former Prophets' (Jos-2 (4) Kgs). Distinctive of Moses are the intimacy of his union with God (10b; cf Nm 12:6—8) and his role as God's instrument in the events which brought the people of God into existence. 'Faithful in God's house' (Heb 3:2), he would yield this distinction only with the arrival of 'the Prophet who is to come into the world' (Jn 6:14), not the servant of the Lord, but his son.

THE HISTORICAL BOOKS

BY J. BLENKINSOPP

a Bibliography—A. Robert, 'Historique (Genre)', DBS 4, 7—23; C. R. North, *The OT Interpretation of History*, 1946; O. Eissfeldt, *Geschichtsschreibung in AT*, 1948; N. H. Snaith, in *The OT and Modern Study*, (ed. H. H. Rowley) Oxford, 1951, 84—114; J. Schildenberger, *Vom Geheimnis des Gotteswortes*, Heidelberg, 1950; J. Bright, *Early Israel in Recent History Writing*, 1956; B. S. Childs, *Memory and Tradition in Israel*, 1962; H. W. Wolff, 'Das Kerygma des deuteronomischen Geschichtswerkes', ZAW 73 (1961) 171—86; R. Davidson, *The OT*, 1964, 21—39.

b The Historical Books in the Scriptural Canon—The titles correspond closely to those listed under the same heading in the LXX. This version, unlike the Hebrew text, adopted a subject classification which was taken over into the Christian versions of the OT, of which the Latin concerns us most nearly, cf § 13øø. In the Jewish Canon, Jos, Jg, Sm and Kgs comprise the Former Prophets, Ru and Est are respectively the second and fifth of the five rolls or megillot and Ez, Neh and Chr are the last of the Writings or Hagiographa. Tb, Jdt and Mc are found only in the Greek canon.

Thus the Jewish canon makes no explicit reference to a historical category. In classifying the great historical corpus which goes from the Conquest to the Exile as prophetic, it was moved directly by a tradition of prophetic authorship, as witnessed in *Baba Bathra* 14b, 15a and Jos CAp. 1, 8, and by the fact that cycles of narrative which deal with prophetic figures feature in it (e.g. 1 Sm 1—15 Samuel; 1 (3) Kgs 17—2 (4) Kgs 13 Elijah and Elisha). Indirectly however there was also the profoundly prophetic i.e. religious point of view from which the history was seen to be written.

The LXX canon places Ru after Jg and 1—2 Paralipomenon ('the things omitted') immediately after the four Books of Kingdoms (Kings in Vg). Then follow 1 Esdras, 2 Esdras (= Neh). After Sir come Est, Jdt, Tb and 1—2 Mc follow Dn. Of the books which are classed here as historical some parts of Est and 2 Mc were composed originally in Gr. and Tb very probably in Aram. The rest are in Heb.

For text and versions see Introduction to each book.

c Survey of the Contents of the Historical Books—These books were composed over a period which goes roughly from the 10th cent. to the middle of the 1st cent. B.C. and cover the history from the Conquest (c. 1250 B.C.) to the accession of John Hyrcanus (134 B.C.). This coverage, however, is very uneven and the contents of the books should be regarded more as material which can be used, together with other sources, for writing a history of Israel than as itself constituting a history of Israel.

Our survey will, therefore, consider them purely as **source-material** in this sense. The story of the Conquest in Jos is deeply coloured theologically but includes genuine ancient material including detailed lists of towns and frontier stations from the time of the early monarchy or **241c** even before in some cases. The Judah town-list in Jos 15 may be connected with the administrative reform of Josiah in the seventh century (see A. Alt, 'Judas Gaue unter Josia', PJB 21 (1925) 100—116 and in *Kleine Schriften zum AT*, II 1953, 276—88). The account of the Conquest in Jos has to be supplemented by the earlier references in Jg 1. A fair part of the narrative in Jg is of either epic or popular character and has been assembled according to an artificial and stylized chronology. With regard to Jg 19—21, the crime of the Benjaminites of Gibea, we would have to bear in mind the polemical background against which the Judaean author is writing and this will also be true, in varying degrees, of the account of the rise to supremacy of David. Ru is set 'in the days of the judges' (1:1) but comes, in all probability, from a much later period.

The **historical character** of the material which has **d** been brought together in 1 Sm 1—15 is very difficult to evaluate. The stories about the ark (1 Sm 4—6; 2 Sm 6) seem to have arisen in a liturgical situation attached first to Shiloh then to Jerusalem. There are at least two distinct accounts of Samuel, of the translation to monarchy and the rise to power of David in which the question of his claim as against the Saulites plays a dominant role. With the so-called History of the Succession (2 Sm 9—20 + 1 (3) Kgs 1—2) we have a genuinely ancient source, written very soon after the events it relates and of the greatest historical value (see Introduction to 1—2 Sm). 2 Sm 7, the oracle of Nathan, is generally considered an introduction to this history though some follow Rost in taking the David source further back to include 6:16—23, the rejection of Michal, since this is relevant to David's claim. Others, especially, T. C. Vriezen and A. Weiser, connect all the history from 1 Sm 16 with the new Jerusalem cult-centre while Budde, finally, takes the whole history from 1 Sm 4 to 1 (3) Kgs 2 as a single corpus. It will be appreciated that there is still a great deal of uncertainty in this sector.

The reign of Solomon is well covered on the whole and **e** based on original sources—1 (3) Kgs refers to 'the book of the History of Solomon'. The long description of the building of the temple is obviously of central importance for the religious interpretation placed on the events by the author but introduces some disproportion. All of the period from the division of the kingdom to the Exile is covered, though here again the distribution of emphasis and space is dictated by the religious point of view of the writer. Thus the narrative-cycles about Elijah and Elisha cover a good part of the space dedicated to the N kingdom and thus link up with the writing prophets beginning with Amos. Omri, founder of a dynasty and known from the cuneiform inscriptions is dismissed in a few words (1 (3) Kgs 16:23—28) while Ahab, chiefly because of his matrimonial alliance with Tyre and the religious crisis which this provoked, has more than six chh dedicated to him (1 (3) Kgs 16:29—22:40). 2 (4) Kgs takes the

241e narrative down to the accession of Amel-marduk of Babylon, 562 B.C. (2 (4) Kgs 25:27).

f There is no comparable coverage for the exilic period for which we have to fall back almost entirely on extrabiblical sources. Tb purports to tell a story set in the captivity of the N kingdom but in fact reflects the situation of a later age. For the immediate post-exilic age we have Ez and Neh which take us to about 440 B.C. Est is set in the Persian period during the reign of Xerxes (486—465) but has little independent historical value. Finally, 1—2 Mc provides a wealth of information on the Seleucid persecution and the early Hasmonaeans (164—134 B.C.).

g Sources used—The question of historical evaluation is concerned principally with access to and use of sources. In some cases the historical books make explicit reference to sources used, in others the existence and use of these have to be inferred from the narrative itself.

As in the Pent. so in the historical books **ancient poetical compositions** or fragments of such have been preserved. Jos 10:13 quotes, in connexion with the battle near Gibeon, an heroic couplet from an epic collection called 'the book of yašar' from which 2 Sm 1:18, David's lament over Saul and Jonathan, and possibly also the enigmatic vv pronounced at the dedication of the temple (in some LXX MSS, 1 (3) Kgs 8:12—13) are taken. It is reasonable to suppose that there are other quotations elsewhere in the OT from this and similar ancient collections, see S. Mowinckel, 'Hat es ein israelitisches Nationalepos gegeben?', ZAW 53 (1935) 130—152; J. Dus, 'Die altisraelitische amphictyonische Poesie', ZAW 75 (1963) 45—54. Certain poetical, or at any rate fixed, forms such as blessings and curses also generally preserve their ancient identity e.g. Jos 6:26. It is, moreover, being increasingly realized that many of the narratives of a popular or 'heroic' character (e.g. Jg 14—16) are in fact prose redactions of what was originally verse or recitative, and in some cases we have the same event described both in verse and in prose e.g. Jg 4—5; Jos 10:10—15; 1 Sm 31 + 2 Sm 1:5—27.

h There are here and there in the historical books various **topographical lists and lists of personal names** some of which antedate the early monarchy. In Jos 12 there is a summary of the conquest with the names of the defeated kings and many follow Alt in tracing most of the town lists of Jos 13—20 to the early monarchy or even before (see above for the Judah list). For a recent examination Z. Kallai—Kleinmann, 'The town list of Juda, Simeon, Benjamin and Dan', VT 8 (1958) 134—60. The date of the list of levitical cities is uncertain, though there is no need to doubt its substantial antiquity. With the establishment of the monarchy and the creation of a court we have for the first time the prerequisites for the production and conservation of official records and a court literature. There are several texts which refer to the *mazkîr* = official recorder or archivist—of David, Solomon, Hezekiah and Josiah (2 Sm 8:17; 1 (3) Kgs 4:3; 2 (4) Kgs 18:18; 2 Chr 34:8) and a certain Shaphan *hassōper*—secretary—is mentioned in the story of the finding of the law-book in the temple during

i the reign of Josiah, 2 (4) Kgs 22:3. The *šoter* mentioned often in the Northern narrative strand and Dt may have had a similar function though his office was certainly more extensive than that of a scribe (cf akkadian šaṭāru = to write). There are several examples of records and lists from the royal archives e.g. David's children (2 Sm 3:2—5; 5:12—16), his officials (20:23—26), his campaigns and warriors (21:15—22 cf 1 (3) Kgs 4; 9:10—14) etc. The account of the building of the temple would very

likely have been preserved in the temple archives as also **2** the exchange of correspondence with Hiram of Tyre (1 (3) Kgs 5—7).

Sm, Kgs and Chr refer several times to **annals and j chronicles** which had been consulted in the redaction of these works. These include: the Annals of king Solomon, 1 (3) Kgs 11:41; the Annals of the kings of Israel, 1 (3) Kgs 14:19 etc; the Annals of the kings of Judah, 1 (3) Kgs 14:29 etc; the Chronicles of king David, 1 Chr 27:24; the Acts of king David, 1 Chr 29:29. Chr refers independently to prophetic compositions which some think may in fact be included in the canonical Sm and Kgs: Chronicles of Samuel, Nathan and Gad (1 Chr 29:29); the History of Nathan the prophet, the Prophecy of Ahijah the Shilonite and the Visions of Iddo the Seer (2 Chr 9:29); the Chronicles of Shemaiah the prophet and Iddo the Seer (2 Chr 12:15). This may well be significant for the canonical designation of *Former Prophets* and reminds us that the Court History of David is sometimes ascribed to a prophetic hand.

1 Mc provides us with a narrative which all agree has **k** high historical value though not all recognize the authenticity of the documents which are transcribed in 8:22—32; 10:22—47; 12:1—23; 15:15—24. It is likely that the author had recourse to earlier Jewish historical writings for the Maccabees, possibly also to some part of the work of Jason of Cyrene which is the basis for 2 Mc (see 2 Mc 2:23), though he only once refers to his sources, in 16:24, the Annals of the pontificate of John Hyrcanus. 2 Mc opens with two letters addressed to the Egyptian diaspora from Jerusalem. The second contains references to writings of Jeremiah (2:1), Memoirs of Nehemiah (hypomnēmatisma, 2:13) and various older works which Nehemiah and after him Judas Maccabeus gathered together. The author himself informs us that his work is an abridgement of a longer work by Jason of Cyrene (2:23) a Jew of the Dispersion who wrote in Gr. as did the anonymous author of 2 Mc. The four letters reproduced in ch 11 may have been added from a source other than Jason.

Do the Pentateuchal sources continue through the 242 historical books?—Assuming some form of the documentary hypothesis for the Pent the question arises whether and to what extent the same 'sources' can be traced in the historical books down to 2 (4) Kgs. This has been discussed for over half a century but so far no solution has been proposed which commands the overwhelming assent of scholarly opinion.

The attempt to trace J and E throughout the history at least to the time of Solomon was first made systematically by Cornill (1887) and Budde (1890) and was supported by some linguistic and stylistic analysis, though in a rather desultory way, by T. Klähn and others. In this attempt some were more confident than others. G. Hölscher, *Die Anfänge der hebräischen Geschichtsschreibung*, Heidelberg 1942, takes J down to 1 (3) Kgs 12 and E to 2 (4) Kgs 25. R. Smend and O. Eissfeldt add their primitive and secular pre-J source (L = *Laienquelle*) and trace L, J and E down into the David narratives. Others such as E. Jacobs claim to find these sources only as far as Jos while others again admit some similarities in the historical books with the earlier narrative strands of the Pent but do not think it possible to disentangle J and E. This is roughly the position of A. Weiser. Of recent years, **b** however, there has been a reaction against the whole attempt and a tendency to question its legitimacy especially with regard to 1—2 Sm where source criticism seems only to have added to the confusion. Many scholars prefer to speak only of various types of pre-deuteronomic

2b material here or distinct narrative-cycles which have been joined together or written-up versions of oral traditions which were attached to one or other of the local sanctuaries which enjoyed special prestige. The views of von Rad, for whom J ends with the completion of the conquest (Jos 21:43—45), of Noth with his Deuteronomist historical work (see below), and the emphasis on the role of oral tradition have all been influential in sapping the confidence of documentary critics in applying rigid criteria of source division especially in 1—2 Sm.

c A brief and very general review of the historical books from this point of view might be useful at this stage—omitting mention of Dt for which see the next section. In Jos 1—12 there are no absolutely clear affinities with the earlier sources of the Pent though there are, of course, abundant signs of very ancient traditions and writing, e.g. Jos 10, the battle near Gibeon (which some ascribe to the E corpus). In Jos 13—24 there is evidence here and there for sacerdotal redaction (P) of ancient material. In Jg, which has been edited by Dt, there are several ancient hero-sagas which are composite e.g. that of Gideon, 6—8, though the evidence for a conflation of J and E is not as strong as it is sometimes said to be (though the 'annunciation-scenes' of Jg 6:11—24 and 13:2—7 are similar in style and presentation to some passages ascribed to J in the Pent e.g. Gn 18:1—15). The story of Abimelech (Jg 9) certainly has some connexion with the N tradition though that is all we can say for certain. The 'appendices' of 17—21 are ancient as is generally recognized but here again it is going beyond the evidence to allocate them to J as is sometimes done,

d though they come from a Judaean hand. As regards 1—2 Sm at the present stage of enquiry, it would be better at the most to speak of a pre-E and pre-J stage evidenced in some of the narratives with the balance of antiquity in favour of the latter. Thus, the narratives concerning Shiloh and Gibeon have definite affinities with the Elohist source in the Pent though they antedate this latter. In the same way, there are some striking stylistic affinities between the David narratives in 1—2 Sm and the Yahwist in the Pent. It is clear, finally, that in 1—2 (3—4) Kgs quite distinct sources have been used, some of them referred to in the narrative itself (see above), which have been taken up into the deuteronomist history of the monarchy.

e The Deuteronomist History—It has long been noticed how the history of the monarchy comes to us in a theological framework which is found also in Jg and which informs the whole of Dt. This led Noth to the view that we should consider Gn—Nm separately and take Dt to be the introduction to a great historical corpus reaching to the exile, though the result of successive (at least two) editions. All the leading ideas on which historical judgement is based are found in Dt, especially that of covenant-fidelity. Since Dt itself is clearly the result of at least two editions it would appear that Dt 1:1—4:43 could well be the original introduction to the whole historical corpus. (See especially M. Noth, *Überlieferungsgeschichtliche Studien* 1957²; *Gesammelte Studien zum AT*, Munich 1957, 34—40. For Noth's historical method see his *History of Israel*, E.tr. 1960², 42—50 and for a criticism J. Bright op cit, 79—110.) Whether or not with von Rad we regard the deuteronomist historian as the founder of salvation history (Heilsgeschichte) it is clear that he sees the history of the monarchy as illustrating a religious principle—that of election, rejection and retribution.

f The problem remains, however, of the relation of the Dt redaction of the historical books to the sources which

it incorporates. The amount of editorial activity has to **242f** be decided on the basis of an examination of each section undertaken separately. Thus, Jos 8:30—35 is clearly deuteronomic as can be seen by comparison with the ceremony of covenant-making or covenant-renewal in the book of Dt itself. The covenant with the Gibeonites also finds some echoes in Dt, see CBQ 28 (1966) 207—19. Jos 23 is stylistically very similar to Dt and Jos 24, parallel to 23, also betrays signs of Dt retouching. Jg has been edited at least twice and one of these editions is clearly deuteronomic, the pattern being most evident in 2:11—19. It is probable that 17—21 were omitted from the Dt edition and then were added later. There are occasional signs of Dt in 1—2 Sm especially where religious comment is made on the course of events, though some authors tend to exaggerate in this respect, as, for example, in the study of R. A. Carlson, *David, the Chosen King*, Stockholm 1964.

With Solomon and the history of the divided monarchy **g** the evidence for deuteronomic thought and style is on every page. The history is taken forward by reigns in two parallel lines, N and S, until the destruction of Samaria. The history of each reign is composed on a formulary basis: name of the king and synchronization with his opposite number in the other kingdom—he did what was pleasing/displeasing to Yahweh—the history—reference to sources for what is omitted as not being religiously important for the writer—his death, burial and successor. The judgement on the monarchy is, on the whole, decidedly unfavourable, in keeping with the unfavourable view expressed in the later account of the origin of the monarchy in 1 Sm which is certainly akin to Dt (see commentary on 1 Sm 8:1). This is especially true of the kings of Israel in the N, none of whom receives a favourable verdict. Of eight of the Judaean kings it is said that 'they did what was pleasing to Yahweh', two of whom were Hezekiah and Josiah in whose reigns the author shows particular interest. This is not surprising in view of the historical connexion between the Dt law-book and the religious reforms of the latter and indeed probably of both.

The Work of the Chronicler—In 1—2 Chr and Ez-Neh **243a** we have a historical corpus comparable in design to the deuteronomist work, going from Adam to the post-exilic period and put together probably towards the end of the 4th cent. B.C. This work is not only a continuous whole, as can be seen in the overlap between 2 Chr 36:22—23 and Ez 1:1ff, but is homogeneous in style and outlook and was almost certainly composed by one author, probably a Jerusalem levite (for Albright's view that the author was Ezra himself see his *The Biblical Period from Abraham to Ezra*, New York, 95). Its affinities with the Dt history—and we should note that Dt also gives an important rôle to the levites—and the priestly traditions is also marked. The historical reliability of this composition has to be **b** assessed with regard not only to the sources used (see above) but also to the intention of the writer. His interests are centred in the historical genesis of the post-exilic 'church' of Israel identified with the community newly installed in Jerusalem and Judah, in the ordering of worship and sacred music, in the various duties of the cult functionaries attached to the temple especially the levites. All of these he traces back to David whose kingdom was the one perfect embodiment of the theocratic ideal and who is portrayed in the language of hagiography, in marked contrast to the realist description which we find in the David sources in Sm and 1 (3) Kgs, cf § 298f.

In the pursuit of these religious aims and the 'rational, **c** theological pragmatism' (A. Weiser) which he expounds, he allows himself considerable freedom in dealing with the

243c sources at his disposal. Not only are incidents omitted which would not fit in to his somewhat idealized presentation of the national past (e.g. David's adultery and murder of Uriah, 2 Sm 9), but often the religious institutions of his own age are read back into the past (e.g. in the description of the passover celebrated by Josiah, 2 Chr 35:1—19). This also may explain the confusion in the chronological order of the autobiographical notes of Ez and Neh. One of the basic theological principles according to which the history is written and which is inherited from Dt is that of retribution—'the soul that sins shall die'

d (Dt 24:16; Ezek 18:4). In keeping with this, it seems that his account of the conversion of the bad king Manasseh, 2 Chr 33:11ff, which is not found in 2 (4) Kgs 21 and which we would hardly have expected, has the object of explaining why this king who did evil lived so long. Later on he gives his own explanation why good king Josiah died young, namely, that he had stubbornly refused to heed the divine oracle communicated to him by Neco (2 Chr 35:21—22). We also find that he uses the greatest freedom in dealing with numbers which are often increased enormously beyond the bounds of credibility (though this is not confined to Chr); that he feels constrained to interpret theologically what seemed too artless in the sources he followed—e.g. where 2 Sm 24:1 attributes the temptation of David directly to Yahweh he attributes it to the adversary, Satan, 1 Chr 21:1, and that he never misses an opportunity to mention miraculous interventions as in 2 Chr 20:22—23.

e A study of these characteristics and in particular careful attention to the way he has used the earlier canonical writings as sources give us some idea of the writer's attitude to his work and what his intentions were. He evidently did not aim at presenting an exact reconstruction of the national past but rather at explaining certain aspects of the present in terms of the past seen from a particular point of view. It is hardly accurate to describe this freer kind of historiography as midrash as some do and we do not know in what sense the word is used in the reference which he makes to *the midrash of the prophet Iddo* (2 Chr 13:22) and *the midrash on the book of Kings* (2 Chr 24:27). As a consequence, those incidents which he narrates and which are not in the corresponding part of Sm—Kgs may just as easily come from sources unknown to us as be midrashic embellishments.

f **Historiography in Israel and the Ancient Near East**—It will be evident from what we have said so far that history in the context of the Ancient Near East and the OT in particular cannot be studied within the canons of classical historiography (Herodotus, Thucydides), much less those of the modern historian as laid down and practised by writers like Gibbon, von Ranke and Mommsen. We cannot determine *a priori* the kind of history with which we are faced since 'the ancient peoples of the East, in order to express their ideas, did not always employ those forms or kinds of speech which we use today, but rather those used by the men of their times and countries. Precisely what these were the commentator cannot determine in advance, but only after a careful examination of the ancient literature of the East' (*Divino Afflante Spiritu* 1943, par. 36). Therefore before discussing the question of historical truth in general 'one should examine closely the literary processes of the early oriental peoples, their psychology, their way of expressing themselves and their very notion of historical truth; in a word, one should collate without prejudice all the subject-matter of the sciences of palaeontology, history, epigraphy and literature'. (Letter of the Secretary of the Pontifical Biblical Commission to Cardinal Suhard Archbishop of Paris, Jan, 16th 1948). On this see especially 24 § 144.

The most common milieu for history, that is, historical g records, in the Ancient Near East is the court. A considerable volume of **royal annals**, lists of campaigns, inventories of different kinds, inscriptions and other 'archival' material has come to light in the course of the last century in Mesopotamia, Egypt and Asia Minor. (see in J. Pritchard, *Ancient Near Eastern Texts*, Princeton 1955[2]). We have already seen several examples of this class of material in the OT and occasionally we have a link-up with extra-biblical data (e.g. 2 (4) Kgs 3:6 the revolt of Mesha king of Moab and the **Moabite stele** which refers to the same event; the decree of Cyrus allowing the exiles to return, 2 Chr 36:22—23; Ez 1:1ff and the Cyrus (cylinder). But these brief records brought to light by archaeology hardly ever merit the title of historical narrative and there is, outside the field of the OT, hardly any evidence for the historical sense in the ancient Near East. Small-scale comparison is possible to some extent between the Egyptian *Königsnovelle* ('royal legend') and some episodes of the early monarchy but it is universally admitted that there is nothing elsewhere to match the continuous historical narrative of the OT (see E. Meyer, *Die Israeliten und ihre Nachbarstämme*, Halle 1906, 486). Parallel with these historical records written by trained h recorders and scribes employed by kings are temple records found everywhere in the semitic world at that time. We can with great probability place the description of the building of the temple (1 (3) Kgs 6—7) and the account of the finding of the law-book during the reign of Josiah in this category. We also have to reckon with the possibility that a certain type of narrative may reflect *directly* **liturgical usage** and only *indirectly* the event itself e.g. the taking up of the ark to Jerusalem, 2 Sm 6, may come to us by way of a liturgical celebration of this event, see A. Bentzen, 'The Cultic Use of the Story of the Ark', JBL 67 (1948) 37—53. Another possible source of historical narrative will be the circle or guild of disciples which grows up round a prophet e.g. Am 7:10—17, the account of the meeting between Amos and Amaziah told in the third person, the biographical passages in Jer which are generally attributed to Baruch, but especially **the great cycles of stories concerning Elijah and Elisha** which we find in Kgs, cf § 289.

Over recent years great importance has been given to i the rôle of **oral tradition** in the formation of many historical accounts found in the OT though this of course applies more to those of the Pent than the historical books (for the methods of study of oral tradition see E. Nielsen, *Oral Tradition*, London, 1954). In this respect we have to remember that a much more extensive use was made of memory in traditioning narratives especially of a popular or 'heroic' type, due partly to the fact that writing was a specialist and expensive occupation. This has been emphasized in different ways by scholars like H. Gressmann and G. von Rad. There is clear evidence for the use of techniques of oral composition in several narratives in Jos and Jg, and here and there in 1—2 Sm, which can be discovered by means of literary and stylistic analysis.

What, in sum, is asked of the reader of the historical j books is some sensitivity to the way of writing so different from ours today and to the purposes and attitudes of the writer of a bygone age, together with some knowledge of the milieu in which they came into existence, the need which they were intended to fill and the audience to which they were addressed. Thus, it should be clear that

3j the **deuteronomist history** is written from a **specifically religious** rather than purely historical point of view, that it is educative in intent and paranetic in character and that its native element is the theology of the covenant and the liturgy in which it was celebrated and renewed. This can be seen at once in the fact that the history narrated in Dt 1:1 3:29 comes to us in the form of a sermon by Moses addressed to *kōl-yiśra'el*, the liturgical plenary assembly, and that all the rest of the history down to the exile is nothing else than an extension of this. This is the indispensable approach to the further questions of historical truth and theological relevance.

4a History and Theology—For the Israelite, Yahweh is, above all, 'the living God'. This does not imply so much a statement about his nature as about his activity, his efficacious intervention in the course of events as distinct from the dead gods of the countries around Israel. The fundamental conviction was that **God revealed himself in and through events** and it is the perception of this presence within the course of history which OT writers wish to convey. Thus the **event is the medium of revelation and the writing of history the inspired perception of this**. Biblical inspiration, however, affects the writer as a member of a community which saw itself as the beneficiary of God's power and grace in the Exodus and the whole course of its history. His consciousness is therefore a reflexion of that of the whole social group. This consciousness of a special relationship, a unique vocation in history, brings it about that Israel 'appears a stranger in the world of its own time, a stranger wearing the garments and behaving in the manner of its age, yet separate from the world it lived in' (M. Noth, *History of Israel*, 2–3).

b It is possible to trace a progressive deepening of this consciousness in the development of Hebrew historiography but the progress is made possible only by surviving a series of crises of faith. Thus the promise to Abraham of land and posterity is at last fulfilled (Jos 21:43–45) but there emerges the mortal danger of the Philistine attack which precipitated the transition to monarchy which, in its turn, provoked a crisis of faith leaving its mark on the early chapters of 1 Sm. This crisis is overcome in principle by means of the covenant with David (2 Sm 7) understood as part of God's abiding covenant with his people, but the monarchy itself becomes a means of leading **c** the people into apostasy. It is this situation which faced the deuteronomist who applied to it the teaching of the great prophetic figures of the 8th cent.: that the covenant gave no automatic guarantee of national success or even survival and that Israel no less than the nations stood under the divine judgement. This can be seen clearly in his meditation on the causes of the fall of the N kingdom in 2 (4) Kgs 17:7–23. The exile provided the greatest crisis of all which could only be overcome by the exilic community identifying itself with the **purified Remnant of Israel** of which the prophets had spoken and seeing itself as having a redemptive mission to the world. This sense of uniqueness, apartness was intensified even more after the exile and is apparent in post-exilic writings. So, for example, in recording the insulting words of the emissary of Sennacherib under the walls of besieged Jerusalem—'No god of any nation or kingdom has been able to deliver his people from my hand or from the hand of my fathers. How much less will your god deliver

you out of my hand?'—the Chronicler adds a comment **244c** of his own: 'They spoke of the God of Jerusalem as they spoke of the gods of the peoples of the earth, which are the work of men's hands' (2 Chr 32:15, 19 cf 2 (4) Kgs 18:33—35).

OT history is part of the life-giving dialogue between **d** the covenant-God and his people. In keeping with the structure of covenant-making in the ancient Near East (see G. Mendenhall, *Law and Covenant in Israel and in the Ancient Near East*, Pittsburgh 1955) we find an historical declaration preceding covenant narratives in the OT, either in its simplest form—'I am the Lord your God who brought you out of the land of Egypt' (Ex 20:2) or much more extensive, e.g. Jos 24 which goes from Abraham to the Conquest. In this way history is the means of God's self-proclamation. Corresponding to this, we find in Israel a unique concept of history as *confession of faith*. Events are seen as *sidqot* = saving deeds, *po'alôt* = miracles, *gebûrôt* = mighty deeds, or are described simply as *hesed* = the revelation of the steadfast love of the covenant God. This confession of faith takes on the form of a liturgical recital in the historical psalms e.g. Ps 78 (77); 105 (104); 106 (105) and, in an adapted form, in the Wisdom literature e.g. Prv 10—15; Sir 44.

A Note on the Literary Character of Tb, Jdt and Est e (See also the comm. on these books.)—It is evidently impossible to consider these three books, especially Tb and Jdt which are d.c., in the same category as the other books which we have classed here as historical. If the intention of the authors was to write history then we can only conclude that they have failed: in Tb 1:15 Sennacherib is the son of Shalmaneser, the author of Jdt states that Nebuchadnezzar was king of Assyria 1:2, the temple is there immediately after the exile, 4:3; 5:19, we hear in Est of a decree to exterminate the Jews which goes against all that we know of the Achemenids, etc. It is **f** far from certain however, that history was the aim of the writers of these books. The very carelessness about history and topography in Tb—for example, the young man and the angel cover nearly 200 miles in two days!—warns us away from this and it is clear that though the setting is historical in a vague sense the events are fictional and the purpose is to edify by means of an entertaining story. The background of Jdt is also historical but we are disconcerted to find Persian names and Gr. customs intruding and the outlook has a great deal in common with the apocalyptic and legalist writings of the intertestamentary period. As regards Est, in spite of the Persian background being well filled in, e.g. the sensual and impulsive character of Xerxes, the author seems to have deliberately weakened the sense of history by means of hyperbole: a banquet lasting 180 days, Esther prepared for four years for her meeting with the king, a scaffold fifty cubits high etc. This has led many to follow Gunkel in describing the book as a historical novel. In addition to this, however, we must bear in mind in assessing its character the evident intention to explain the origin of and therefore justify the feast of Purim (3:7; 9:24, 26). This has led others, e.g. A. Weiser, to see in it the cult-legend of this late Jewish feast. The use of the term legend, *legendum* (liturgical reading) does not of itself prejudice the question of historicity but, taken with what we have seen above, would suggest caution in not claiming too much.

JOSHUA

BY E. J. JOYCE C.PP.S.

245a Bibliography—1 Commentaries: C. Steuernagel, NKAT, 1923[2]; A. Schulz, BB, 1924; A. R. Whitham, London, 1927; J. de Groot, Groningen, 1931; J. Garstang, 1939; M. Noth, HAT, 1958[2]; F. Abel, BJ, 1950; M. DuBuit, BJ, 1958[2]; J. McKenzie, Englewood Cliffs, 1966; B. Alfrink, Roermond, 1952; F. Noetscher, EchB, 1950. J. Gray, CBi[2], 1967.

b **2 Special subjects:** W. F. Albright, *The Conquest of Palestine*, Munich, 1953; J. Garstang, *The Story of Jericho*, 1948; N. Glueck, *The River Jordan*, Philadelphia, 1946; K. Kenyon, *Digging up Jericho: the Results of the Jericho Excavations 1952—56*, New York, 1957. J. Marquet-Krause, *La Résurrection d'une grande cité biblique: les fouilles de l'Ay (et Tell)*, 1949; G. Mendenhall, *Law and Covenant in Ancient Israel*, Pittsburgh, 1955; H. H. Rowley, *From Joseph to Joshua*, London, 1950. G. Von Rad, *Studies in Deuteronomy*, trs. D. Stalker, London, 1953; Y. Yadin, *Military and Archaeological Aspects of the Conquest of Canaan in the Book of Joshua*, Jerusalem, 1960; E. Kaufman, *The Biblical Account of the Conquest of Palestine*, trans. M. Dagut, Jerusalem, 1955; F. M. Abel, 'L'apparition du chef de l'Armée de Yahweh à Josué', SAns (1951) 109—113; id 'Les stratagèmes dans le livre de Josué' RB 56 (1949) 321—39; id 'Galgala qui et aussi le Dodecalithon', *Mémorial J. Chaine*, Lyon, 1950; A. George, 'Les Récits de Gilgal en Josué', *Mémorial J. Chain*, Lyon, 1950; H. Cazelles, *Etudes sur le Code de l'alliance*, Paris, 1946; E. Nielsen, *Shechem*, Copenhagen, 1955; J. L'Hour, 'L'Alliance de Sichem' RB 69 (1962) 5—36, 161—84, 350—68.

c **Contents**—The book of Joshua narrates the fulfilment of the promise made by God to Abraham that his descendants should possess the land of Canaan (Gn 12:7; 13:15; 15:7; 17:8). The book consists of three major sections: *1:1—12:24* the conquest of Canaan; *13:1—21:45* the division of the holy land among the twelve tribes; *22:1—24:33* final events and covenant renewal. The **early events** are described in detail: the crossing of the Jordon, the capture of Jericho and Ai, the treaty with the Gibeonites, and the defeat of the five Amorite kings who attacked them. Only one subsequent campaign is recorded, the defeat of the great Canaanite coalition in Galilee. A list of the kings slain by Joshua concludes the narrative. The incompleteness of the narrative is due both to the author's theological preoccupations and the variety of source material available to him at the time of writing.

d The second part is more complete, but is the occasion of a considerable number of difficulties which at the present time can only be solved by theorizing. The **land to be divided** and the land already divided are first described and the boundaries and chief cities of the transjordanic tribes are indicated. The allotment of Hebron to Caleb is then narrated. The first distribution at Gilgal follows, in which the most powerful tribes, Judah and the sons of Joseph, receive their lots. The remaining **24** territory is next surveyed and divided into seven portions which are assigned by lot to the seven remaining tribes in a second distribution made at Shiloh, the new headquarters. Six cities of refuge and the forty-eight Levitical cities are then enumerated. The description of the boundaries and the cities are not always presented in the same way, generally because the author is compiling source material reflecting different traditions.

In the final section of the book the **bond between** **e** **the Israelites** on both sides of the Jordan is manifested by the Altar of Testimony. In a very important account, the covenant renewal at Shechem, the people repledge their fidelity to God who has done all things for them. Many of the events of the book of Joshua are also narrated in Jg in a more primitive and historically more accurate manner. The content and message of Joshua can be understood best if the two books are studied in conjunction.

Literary History—Joshua, Samuel, Ezra, and Eleazar **f** have all been credited at one time or another with writing the book of Joshua. Modern scholarship, however, has demonstrated that the origin of Joshua, as of most OT books, is far too complex to be attributed to any one author. One of the characteristics of the book that leads to this conclusion is its composite character. Some of the raw materials used in the work are the following: ancient oral (later written) traditions associated with and preserved at such sanctuaries as Gilgal and Shechem; popular stories explaining the origin of customs, shrines, and ruins (etiological stories) collected possibly around 900 B.C.; geographical lists of boundaries and cities drawn up in the period of the early monarchy and periodically amended. Successive editors reworked and combined such materials, often not too adroitly, to give us the final work with its theological insight and its historical problems.

In the middle of the last century scholars such as Graf, Wellhausen and Kuenen regarded the book a product of the Pentateuch tradition and coined the word 'Hexateuch' ('six books') to express the unity of Gn, Ex, Lv, Nm, Dt, and Jos. Elements of the various traditions (JEPD) can be recognized in Jos, but not with the precision this theory demands; so it is generally abandoned by modern scholars.

As will become obvious in the course of this commentary, Joshua is thoroughly permeated with the spirit **g** of the Deuteronomic school. Accordingly, another theory has been proposed (Martin Noth, 1930) which is growing in popularity and which, when used with the necessary reservations, provides an excellent working hypothesis. In this approach Jos—Kgs constitute a deuteronomic history of Israel to which Dt itself forms the preface. As the theology of Israel was influenced by its history; so the telling of that history is now influenced by its theology, particularly the conditional nature of God's free election. This process of editing would be the work

45g of centuries; so that Jos appeared in its final form around the time of the Exile (587 B.C.). The general condition of the text of Joshua is good. The Heb. and Gr. texts do contain a number of variations by way of additions and explanations, but the best and latest translations have taken these into account so there will be no special need to consider them here.

46a Literary Form—Because of its composite character this book cannot be adequately classified under any one literary form. In the Heb. Bible Jos is the first of the 'Early Prophets'. This title has merit for it was under the inspiration of Yahweh that Joshua guided Israel. Elsewhere Joshua is classified as an historical book, but it certainly cannot be regarded as 'pure history' in the modern sense of the term.

If any general classification of the book can be given, it is that of *religious epic*. A frequent command in the bible is to learn from the past: 'Remember the days of old, consider the years of many generations; ask your father, and he will show you, your elders, and they will tell you' (Dt 32:7; Dt 6:20; Ex 12:26; 13:14; Jos 19:21—24; 22—28). Mindful of such admonitions the editors were concerned with history, but they were concerned as men of faith. For them the conquest of Canaan was the fulfilment of Yahweh's promise to the patriarchs. If the greatness of Yahweh, his power and generosity could best be brought out by epic exaggeration of the conquest, by magnifying the power of the enemy, or by minimizing the role of the Israelite, the editors, if the question ever occurred to them, would have felt perfectly justified in doing just these things. The entire narrative has been simplified in places, embellished in others in order to emphasize moral and especially religious values. J. L. McKenzie sums it up: 'in Joshua and Judges we have monuments of the most primitive faith of Israel, primitive both in the sense that it is early and in the sense that it is less developed. The books should be read as the first stages in Israel's religious adventure of faith, to read them in any other way is to evaluate them by a false standard.'

b Historical Value—A number of serious problems have arisen regarding the historical value of the book. Detailed descriptions of the destruction of Jericho and Ai are given; archaeology has demonstrated, however, that neither of these cities was occupied at the time of Joshua, at least not by any number of people. At Bethel evidence has been found of a conflagration which Joshua does not mention. We learn from Jg that many of the conquests attributed to Joshua actually took place after his death, sometimes many years after. To these difficulties others can be added by literary analysis. We have already seen that the complex structure of the book points to the presence of different sources, and Alt and Noth argue that a great number of independent events have been artificially united by attributing them to Joshua. Further it is suggested that the people of Israel entered the land only gradually and without any battles at all (see § **254e-g**).

c The problems presented are real, and as pointed out above, the editors 'theologize' history. Schematization, reducing a narrative to basic elements——in this case Yahweh, Joshua, and Israel——is obvious throughout the book. In this process the conquests of an individual tribe, or one that really took place later could be attributed to Joshua because he was a figure of the occupation. Such a theory would explain the overall coherence of the work and the lack of coherence in details.

Admitting that the editors' primary concern was theological and that they used sources with a freedom that would scandalize the modern historian is by no **246c** means the same as saying that the book is historically worthless. The period described in the book is dated today with great certainty as the end of the Bronze Age and the beginning of the Iron Age (c. 1200 B.C.). Significant in this dating are the following: (1) Bronze is used in the construction of the tabernacle (Ex 25:3) while iron is mentioned only later (Jos 6:24; 22:8; 17:16). (2) The Israelites were probably still in Egypt under Ramses II (c. 1298—1232 B.C.), but were established in Canaan by the time of Mernepta (c. 1232—1224). (3) Evidence has been found of a general cultural decline in the 13th cent. B.C. accompanied by the destruction of such Canaanite cities as Lachish, Debir and Hazor.

Archaeological investigation of this period in the history of Canaan has established that it was an age of confusion and unrest. Canaan itself was composed of numerous small city states at war with one another and beset with internal revolution against oppressive rule. Invaders from the West, the People of the Sea who included the Philistines in their number, appear at this time. In general, the book of Joshua reflects just such conditions.

The Man Joshua—Joshua, the hero and unifying **d** personality of this religious epic was the son of Nun of the tribe of Ephraim (Nm 13:8, 16; 1 Chr 7:27; Jos 19:49 but cf Nm 26:35—37). Originally called Hoshea 'he saves' (Nm 13:8), he was renamed Joshua 'Yahweh is Salvation' (Nm 13:11). The close relationship of Joshua and Moses is constantly emphasized. From his youth he was a servant and aid of Moses (Nm 11:28), they were together on Mt Sinai (Ex 24:13) and in the work of apportioning the land (Nm 33:28; 34:17). When Moses died, Joshua, the defender of his authority (Nm 11:28), was at his side (Dt 31:14; 32:44). At the death of Moses he began to function as the new leader of the people, an office that Moses himself had given him (Nm 27:15). More important and perhaps more reliable than these individual details——Noth maintains that the relationship of Joshua and Moses is entirely artificial——is the deuteronomist's emphasis on the theological fact that Joshua carried on the work entrusted to Moses. Yahweh promised to be with him as he was with Moses (Dt 31:23). It was on Yahweh's authority that Joshua depended (Jos 1:5, 17) and in Yahweh's power he found strength (Jos 7:10). This identification of Joshua in role of covenant mediator (cf Jos 24) is extremely important in an attempt to appraise his role in the conquest. In a number of instances Joshua's connection with military exploits is nebulous e.g. he is mentioned among the spies in Nm 13—14 and 26:65 but is not so mentioned in Jos 14:7 or Dt 1:36; the conquest of Hebron attributed to Joshua (10:36) is probably more accurately reported as the work of Caleb (15:13—17). Joshua's role as mediator of the covenant would make him tower over the history of his time and draw fragmented narratives into some semblance of unity.

Religious Teaching—Yahweh, the lord of the universe, **e** is the true hero of the book as even the people of the land confess (2:11; 9:9—10). The attributes of this great God are not expressed in the abstract language of the theologian but in concrete terms of the good things he has done for Israel. The attribute of Yahweh that stands out in almost every page of the book is his fidelity (justice). Long ago he had made a promise to Abraham that his descendants would possess the land of Canaan and no power of fortified cities or massed armies could impede the fulfilment of that promise. It is to bring out clearly

246e this attribute of God, for example, that the triumphal crossing of the Jordan (Jos 3) is described as a great liturgical procession with Yahweh, represented by the ark, leading the way.

Yahweh is faithful to his promise, but still the actual fulfilment of the promise is conditional, dependent upon Israel's fidelity in keeping the covenant. Hence the necessity of renewing the covenant (Jos 8:30—35; 24) and the observance of such religious, covenant **f** ceremonies as circumcision and the passover (15:2—11).

The anger of God, a fundamental concept throughout the OT, also is clearly demonstrated, particularly in the story of Achan (7:1ff). In biblical thought the justice and anger of God are clearly distinguished. God's justice is his salvific activity manifested in triumph. God's anger is made known in punishment. Justice and anger affect not the individual but the whole nation, therefore the entire people are punished when one man or family breaks the covenant. Such action is treason.

g Even ban or **total warfare**, *herem*, which was a common enough practice in antiquity, is presented in such a way as to communicate a religious message. The election of the Israelites at Sinai made them truly a chosen people, a people apart. Total destruction, which was by no means always carried out, was to preserve their religious integrity. As subsequent history makes abundantly clear, contact with pagan peoples occasioned many violations of covenant obligations. Total warfare, then, is presented as a means of protecting the covenant and the holiness of Yahweh. It might be noted here that there is no necessity to 'moralize' or justify the actions of these men of antiquity in terms of modern morality. Their actions and customs reflect the harsh moral codes of the primitive times in which they lived. After all, they had just begun the long journey that would lead to the perfect law of Christ, cf § 225*d*.

Joshua (Hebrew for 'Jesus') is often presented as a type of our Lord. As Joshua led the people through the waters of the Jordan into the promised land thus completing the great liberation of the Exodus; so Jesus leads the new people of God through the waters of baptism into the new promised land, the eternal kingdom, completing the liberation from sin.

247a **1—12 The Conquest of the Promised Land**
1: 1—9 Order to invade Canaan—Joshua, appointed the successor of Moses by Yahweh (Nm 27:17—23) and charged with the conquest of Canaan (Dt 3:28; 31:3), is now after the death of Moses (Dt 1:36; 3:27; 4:21) commanded to lead the people into the promised land. God promises him success in his mission, exhorts him to be courageous and diligent, and above all to be faithful to the law, the condition of divine assistance.

b This entire ch is deuteronomic in thought and spirit. Vv 1—9 provide a key for understanding the entire book. It is to be read not as history in the modern sense of the word nor merely as great literature; but as the history of salvation, the story of God through his special providence leading his chosen people into the promised land fulfilling his promise (Gn 15:18; 12:7; 13:15; 17:8; 26:4; 35:12; Dt 31:6; 28:7; 11:24—25; 1:7—8). To highlight this Joshua is presented as receiving his commission directly from Yahweh (cf Nm 27:17—23). **4.** The boundaries of the promised land are briefly described. Ideally they were to be the wilderness, the desert, on the S, the Mediterranean on the W, the Lebanon and Anti-Lebanon ranges to the N and the Euphrates on the E (Nm 34:1—10; Ezek 47:13—20; Jos 13—21). Actually they were never realized, but the point emphasized here is the generosity

of Yahweh. The phrase 'all the land of the Hittites', if it **247** is not a gloss, would refer to the land of Canaan (Gn 23:3; 27:46). **5.** Joshua has authority because Yahweh is with him as he was with Moses (Dt 7:24; 11:25; Ex 3:12). **6—9.** Emphasis is placed on necessity of fidelity (cf Dt 31:7, 23).

10—18 Preparation for the Invasion—Joshua orders **c** the people to collect supplies and be ready to cross the Jordan within three days. He reminds those already in possession of their territory E of the Jordan (Reuben, Gad and Half-Manasseh, Jos 13) of their obligation to take part in the conquest. 'Three days' usually an indefinite and short period of time (Hos 6:2; Est 4:16) is the same period of time spent in preparation to receive the law (Ex 19:11); perhaps it is used here to invite a comparison of the Sinai event and the invasion. **16—18.** The Heb. of these vv reveals a definite rhythm and parallelism and may be a formula, a military oath that could be shouted by the people.

2:1—24 The Spies and Rahab—At first reading this **d** ch is both chronologically and logically confusing. 1:10 sets three days till invasion, but the spies hide for three days (2:22). Rahab knows the intention of the men and describes the action of God in deuteronomistic style. The spies sleep in a moment of danger and carry on a conversation with Rahab after they have been lowered outside the wall. The most plausible explanation for these inconsistencies is not thoughtless compilation but careful editing on the part of the deuteronomic author to minimize the role of man and emphasize the work of Yahweh (2:24). **1.** Shittim refers to an area in the plains of Moab, the last transjordan stopping place of the Israelites about 5m. from the Jordan. Jericho, excavated most recently by Kathleen Kenyon (1952—1958), provides no sign of habitation at the time of Joshua and was almost certainly in ruins at the time of his entry, cf § 126*c-d*. It has been suggested that in true epic style the imposing ruins of this city were later associated with the conquests of Joshua. Attempts have been made to whitewash the profession of Rahab the harlot, but the Bible feels no such necessity. She is praised for her faith and good works (Heb 11:31). **8—13.** Rahab's plea for protection, containing a direct **e** quotation from Dt 4:39 and recognizing the God of Israel as the true God has certainly been edited if not totally created by the deuteronomic editor. **10.** The Amorites, a semitic people, founders of Mari and of the dynasty of Hammurabi, occupied Canaan as early as 2200 B.C. Sihon and Og (Nm 21:22; Dt 1:4; 3:3; 3:1) were totally destroyed by the Israelites (Dt 2:34; 3:6). **11.** A direct quotation of Dt 4:39, this is a primitive profession of monotheism. **14.** The spies bind themselves by oath which called upon God to punish them if they did not carry out their promise. **18.** The scarlet cord, perhaps an amulet of one of the spies (Gn 38:18), serves as a sign by which Rahab's house could be identified. That it is a valid type of Christ's redemptive blood is extremely unlikely. **24.** The ch closes with a typically deuteronomic statement: It is Yahweh who is delivering the land to them. It has been suggested that this story is etiological; a later, popular attempt to explain the presence of the descendants of Rahab among the Israelites.

3:1—4:24 Crossing of the Jordan—Even the most **248a** casual reading reveals several inconsistencies in the narrative of the crossing. In **6** it seems the procession is underway, but in **7** Yahweh speaks to Joshua again and he addresses the people again. In 3:17 and 4:1 the crossing seems complete, but in 4:4; 5:10 the people have

48a not yet crossed. The two piles of stones 4:3,9 add to the confusion. Obviously two and possibly more traditions have been preserved in the narrative. This very untidiness indicates that the concern of the author is other than historical. A number of parallels between this story and the Exodus can be detected and seem significant. The people prepare themselves for participation in a cultic act, a theophany (Ex 19:10—15); the water is separated so that the people can cross (Ex 14:21ff; Ps 114 (113):3); the ark at the head of the procession and at the end of the procession recalls the pillar of cloud and fire (Ex 13:21—22; 14:19—20). The manna which began with the exodus ceases with the entry into the promised land (Ex 16). At Gilgal through the rite of circumcision the covenant made at Sinai is renewed; the passover is celebrated at the end of the journey as it was at the beginning (Ex 12). As the story stands today (possibly part of the latest evolution of the book) it presents a grand liturgical procession, the completion of the Exodus. Yahweh triumphantly leads his people into the land he had promised them so many centuries before. It is this fact that the narrative wishes to dramatize.

b The concern of the editor to present a liturgical procession does not explain the seemingly confused narrative. There are indications that each of these chh is designed to bring out a particular climax. Each ch seems to have a definite center of gravity. In ch 3 there is a gradual build up to the words spoken to Joshua by Yahweh then a tapering off. In ch 4 the center of gravity is in the words of Yahweh— they are fulfilled. Perhaps this can best be presented as follows:

A. *3:1* introduction—the approach to the Jordan
  B. *2; 3; 4* the officials instruct the people
    C. *5* Joshua talks to the people
      D. *6* Joshua talks to the priests
        E. *7* Yahweh talks to Joshua (the climax)
      D' *8* Joshua talks to the priests
    C' *9—13* Joshua talks to the people
  B' *14* People follow out his instruction
A' *15—17* the crossing of the river

Ch 4 is more difficult to pattern since there seem to be a number of disrupting additions. Roughly it would look like this:

A. *1—10a*—orders concerning the stones
  B. *10b—13*—The ascent from the Jordan
    C. *14*—The fulfillment of the words of Yahweh that were the climax of ch 3
  B' *15—18*—ascent from the Jordan
A' *20—24*—The stones are set up and their significance explained

The author perhaps used various materials to fashion a *catechesis*, a religious instruction (3:6; 4:21 Dt 6:20; Ex 12:26; 13:14).

c 3:1 Joshua leads the People to the bank of the Jordan. **2** 'at the end of three days' seems to refer to the three days of 1:11. **3**. 'Levitical priests' is a frequent deuteronomic term (Dt 17:9; 18:1; 24:8). It has been suggested that this term may be a polemic against a non-levitical priesthood but its origin may be quite different; cf § 253j. The ark, the symbol of God's presence, is to lead the way (Ex 25:10). **4**. The space between the ark and the people—half a mile—seems exaggerated perhaps to bring out the holiness of Yahweh. **5**. The cultic character of the march is clear: Yahweh leads, priests carry the ark, the people are ordered to sanctify themselves. This rite of sanctification involved ritual washings of one's clothing and person, and sexual continence, all symbolic of separation from all that was not God who is wholly other and transcendent (Ex

19:10—15; Lv 11:44; 1 Sm 21:5). **10**. Seven groups of **248d** people are mentioned. The Canaanites were the principal inhabitants of Palestine, the LXX frequently translates the term as Phoenicians. The *Hittites* are associated with Asia Minor and N Syria. In the Bible the name is often applied to the inhabitants of Canaan in general. Of the *Hevites, Perizzites, Girgashites* and *Jebusites* little is known. (For Amorites cf 2:10) **11**. Yahweh is the real leader. **12**. This v interrupts the narrative and certainly seems to be out of order. Some omit is as a late gloss, others place it between 4:7 and 8. Still others suggest that it is in the present narrative to whet the reader's curiosity in preparation for the account in 4:1—9. **14—17**. Much of the language of the narrative **e** of the crossing of the Jordan is identical with that of the account of the crossing of the Sea of Reeds (Ex 14:21ff), and it seems quite obvious that the author wished to compare the two events (Ps 114 (113)). For all its fame, the Jordan is a small river that even in flood stage (March-April) would hardly present an insurmountable barrier. Three explanations can be distinguished for this event. The first, the traditional interpretation, holds that we have here the account of a miracle, the historical fact narrated is that Yahweh dried up the river so the people could cross on dry ground. An intermediate explanation holds that the historical fact narrated here is not a miracle except for the matter of timing. According to this explanation a landslide at one of the narrower parts of the river dammed up the water. Similar landslides have been noted in the not too distant past. In 1207 a landslide blocked the river for sixteen hours; another in 1927, for 21½ hours. The third explanation seems to remove any trace of the supernatural. It is suggested that the people simply crossed at one of the fords (the spies sent by Joshua crossed in such a manner 2:7). Because the river was at flood stage the crossing might still have been difficult, especially when not only men but women and children, animals and possessions also had to be brought across. Therefore stones were placed along the ford to mark the way and make the crossing less difficult (the twelve stones of ch 4). None **f** of these explanations can be rejected *a priori* as impossible or unworthy of Sacred Scripture. The fact of the matter is that we are dealing here with an account that is primarily theological, a *catechesis*, undoubtedly heightened and embellished in the telling to teach the saving power of Yahweh, a message that shines through as clearly today as it ever did. **4:2**. Two distinct traditions of the twelve memorial stones are in evidence. The present v indicates that the stones were taken from the river and placed on the land while **9** indicates that the stones were placed in the midst of the Jordan. Again, whatever the exact historical fact behind these two traditions might have been, the basic purpose of the stones was to serve as a constant reminder to the people of their debt to Yahweh (7, 21—24; cf Ex 24:4; Dt 6:20—21; 29:22 Jos 22:24). **g** **13**. The number of people, 40,000, seems to be an exaggeration, especially if it refers only to the tribes of Reuben, Gad and the half-tribe of Manasseh. **19**. The date is given as the tenth of Nisan in view of the Passover that will be celebrated. (Dt 11:30; Jos 15:7; 12:23). At least three towns called Gilgal are mentioned in the Bible: One near Shechem (Dt 11:30), one on the S boundary of Judah (Jos 15:7) and the most important one near the Jordan which is the one discussed here. The precise location of this Gilgal is disputed, Khirbet en Nitleh and Khirbet Mefjer have been suggested. Likewise, the explanation of the name (5:9) is uncertain. The term *gilgal* which means circle could refer to the circle

248g of stones, or the cutting around of circumcision. Gilgal remained the headquarters of Joshua for about five years (14:10) and was one of the favourite sanctuaries of the Israelites (1 Sm 7:16; 10:8; 11:14; 13:4; 15:33). **5:1.** The account is brought to a close by noting the terror the entry inspired in the inhabitants of the land.

249a 5:2—15 The events at Gilgal—This ch is composed of three closely related events: 2—9 the circumcision; 10—12 the celebration of the Passover; 13—15 the apparition to Joshua. Throughout the ch the author seems to be drawing a very close parallel between the events narrated here and the events narrated in Exodus (cf Ex 12—13).

2—9 The Circumcision—2. The rite of circumcision was very ancient, predating the bronze age (3000—1200 B.C.) as witness the use of flint knives in the ceremony. Just when it was introduced as a religious rite among the Heb. cannot be determined, but it seems very unlikely that Noth is correct in suggesting this episode at Gilgal as the introduction of the rite. Circumcision was a rite of initiation, a quasi-sacrificial offering of the first born to God, not through actual sacrifice, but by the symbolic offering of the foreskin. Among the Hebrews it was a sign of the covenant relationship to Yahweh (Gn **b** 17:9—14; 21:4; Ex 12:43—48; Lv 12:3). **3.** Gibeath Haaraloth, literally 'hill of foreskins', may have been the site near Gilgal where circumcision was practised. **5.** It is difficult to explain why the important rite would be omitted in the desert period, often considered a time of close intimacy with Yahweh (Dt 2:7; 8:2; 29:4), and restored now when it would incapacitate the fighting men for several days. The emphasis is again theological. All the men who had come out of Egypt had been circumcised. In the completion of Exodus with the entry into Canaan the promise of Yahweh has been fulfilled, therefore the covenant is reaffirmed. The story may also preserve the memory of people who had not participated in the exodus and desert wanderings being incorporated into the people of God. **9.** 'The reproach of Egypt' may refer to ritual uncleanness contracted in a foreign land, to the lack of circumcision, or to the condition of slavery.

c 10—12 Celebration of the Passover—The Passover was celebrated on the 14th Nisan (March/April). As the Israelites had celebrated the Passover on the day they left Egypt; so they now celebrate it when they enter the promised land—the great work of liberation was perfected and brought to completion. The religious stylization of this section is further brought out in the details of the food. The prescribed unleavened bread was eaten (Ex 12:6) and the parched grain (Lv 2:14). The manna, symbol of the desert wandering, ceased and they ate the 'produce of the land', symbol of agriculture and settlement. Yahweh had now given them rest from their wanderings.

d 13—15 The Apparition of the leader of Yahweh's Army—Here again the account is connected with the first Passover. In Exodus the angel went by on the very same day the Passover was celebrated (Ex 11:11), here he appears on the same day. In Exodus the angel was threatening (Ex 11:11), here the first appearance of the angel is threatening 'with drawn sword in his hand'. The angel in both accounts is the 'commander of the lord's army' (Ex 12:17), the true leader of Israel (Ex 23:20—23). In both instances the 'angel of Yahweh' is God himself. The point of this vocation-apparition is that Joshua is a second Moses, carrying on the work of Moses (Ex 3).

e 6:1—27 The conquest of Jericho—Various suggestions have been made to account for this chapter's lack of

order and conflicting statements. Just one example of **249** the conflict may be found by comparing 4, 5, 16a, where it seems the trumpets were sounded only after the city had been circled in silence, with 8, 9, 13 where the trumpets are sounded continually. One theory suggests that two traditions were handed down, one military, the other liturgical, and later fused. Another school holds that one oral account was transmitted with the gradual additions to which oral transmission is subject. Whatever the origin of the present story might be, (neither theory solves all the problems) it is primarily theological in purpose. What is described is not so much a battle as a ritual cultic act. Note how the priests predominate; how the sacred number seven recurs. It is Yahweh who prevails.

1. As pointed out above (2:1) Jericho was almost **f** certainly in ruins when the Israelites entered Canaan. Possibly the memory of another conquest has been associated with the more imposing ruins of Jericho. **2—5.** Instructions are given by Yahweh. Both the circling processions and the battle cry seem to play an essential rôle in placing the city under a curse which guaranteed the conquest of the city (Ex 19:13). **6—16.** The ark was often carried into battle (1 Sm 4:1—9; 2 Sm 11:11) to strike terror into the enemy (Nm 10:35). The ram's horn was used in battle (Jg 3:27; 7:18) and for divine worship (Lv 23:24; 25:9; 2 Sm 6:15). **17—19.** 'Ban warfare' was total warfare. **g** The Heb. word designating this, *herem*, indicated something removed from profane use, consecrated to God. The annihilation of the populace and the destruction of the booty was considered—repugnant as it seems to the modern reader—an act of religion, a means of preserving the integrity of religion (Dt 7:1—5; cf § 246e). **20—21.** Given the condition of the entire narrative it seems fruitless to speculate on the precise manner of the victory e.g. a well-timed earthquake, tunnelling into the walls while the defenders were distracted and so on. The story as it has come down to us defies historical analysis and it is better to read it for what it is: a grand statement of Yahweh's mighty intervention on behalf of his people. **22—25.** The promise made to Rahab is carried out. **26—27.** The curse of Joshua was violated in the time of Ahab (869—50) by Hiel of Bethel (1 (3) Kgs 16:34). It is possible that this curse originated after the time of Joshua.

7:1—8:29 The sin of Achan and the capture of Ai— h Three dominant theological ideas appear in this section: the notion of the ban; the angel of God; collective guilt. (cf above § 246e). The episode stands in sharp contrast to the capture of Jericho. There obedience brought victory; here disobedience brings defeat. There a strong fortress lost heart before nomad tribes; here Israel flees in panic from a smaller force.

7:1—26 Achan violates the ban—2. The name Ai **i** means 'the ruin' and is generally identified with the modern et-Tell. Archaeological information on this site presents us with another riddle for it was not occupied from 2200 till 1000 and was, therefore, literally 'a ruin' at the time of Joshua. L. H. Vincent has suggested that since the defenders are reported to be few in number (3) the ruins served as an outpost for Bethel (Bethaven), a city about a mile and a half to the W. W. F. Albright suggests that the destruction-narrative of another city, possibly Bethel (Jg 1:22), was later associated with the impressive ruins of Ai. Noth suggests an etiological story to answer the question 'whence came these ruins'. Whatever the historical event behind the story, it clearly

9i illustrates the correlation between guilt and punishment. **6–9**. The prayer of Joshua is desperate since God has abandoned his people (Ex 32:11–14). The answer attributed to Yahweh makes the nature of the crime explicit. The anger of God affects not the individual but the whole nation. Because of their solidarity the whole people is guilty of sin and punished accordingly. Later this idea will be somewhat modified (Jer 21:29–30; Ezek **j** 18:1ff). **16–18**. The guilty member is discovered by casting lots, a duty reserved to the Levitical priests (Nm 7:21; Dt 33:8). The casting of lots was basically a process of elimination. The Urim and Thummim, possibly different coloured sticks or stones, were placed in a container called the Ephod. A basic 'yes or no' situation was then set up and one of the lots was drawn (1 Sm 14: 40–42). **19–21**. Achan 'gives glory to God' by confessing his sins. **22–26**. The booty is confiscated and together with Achan, his entire family and possessions, is destroyed (burned and/or stoned). The name given to the valley is a play on words since the Heb. word for 'trouble' is from the same root as the word Achor.

k 8:1–29 The campaign against Ai resumed—The hand of the deuteronomist is again detectable. (Compare 8:1–2 with Dt 3:2–3; 1:21; and 31:8.) **2**. Surprisingly the ban is now mitigated and the Israelites are permitted to retain booty. **3**. The figure 30,000 seems greatly exaggerated since even in the time of the monarchy the army numbered only 30,000 (2 Sm 6:1), cf § 206c. **18**. Joshua is again presented as the successor of Moses in the stretching out of the javelin (Ex 17:8–13), a gesture that is not merely a sign but is effective in itself.

0a 8:30–35 Altar and Religious Celebrations on Mt Ebal—Joshua executes the commands of Moses (Dt 11:29–32; 27:4–7) by erecting an altar on Mt Ebal, writing a copy of the law on stones, arranging the people half at the foot of Mt Ebal and half at the foot of Mt Gerizim with the priests and ark between them and ordering the law read aloud, particularly the blessings and curses related to the observance or non-observance of the law. This passage has no intrinsic connection with the events just narrated—LXX places it after 9:2. The location, Shechem, would seem to indicate that it was originally associated with the events described in ch 24. Ch 8 and 9 are related to the territory around Gilgal. It may have been placed here as representative of ceremonies that took place both at Shechem and at Bethel. The covenant renewal will be discussed in detail in ch 24. **31**. In keeping with the instruction of Ex 20:25 and Dt 27:6 the altar is made of unhewn stones. **32–35**. Joshua in this renewal of covenant is again presented as a second Moses.

b 9:1–27 Covenant with the Gibeonites—**1–5**. A confederation of four important cities in the center of S Palestine, terrified by the victories of Joshua, send a delegation to Gilgal seeking an alliance. **7–15**. They obtain their request by pretending they have come from a distant place. **16–27**. With a story teller's fine ironic touch the Gibeonites' polite 'your servants' becomes the literal truth. At least two traditions seem to stand behind this story since at times Joshua is in command, and at other times the 'leaders of the congregation'. Noth has suggested that the only thing historical in the narrative is the presence in the temple of hewers of wood who were not Israelites that needed explanation. This opinion, however, is difficult to accept in view of the difficulty later encountered by Saul precisely because he violated a primitive pact with the Gibeonites (2 Sm 21:1). **c 1–2**. For the peoples mentioned cf 3:10. **3**. The

Gibeonites were a non-Canaanite enclave in Palestine **250c** sometimes identified with the Hevites (9:7; 11:19). Their home was in Gibeon, modern el-Jib, five m. N of Jerusalem. **7**. The Israelites are hesitant since they were forbidden to make covenants with Canaanites (Dt 7:2). **8–13**. Large segments of this address parallel almost exactly the words of Rahab (2:8ff) and betray the hand of the deuteronomist. **14–15**. Partaking of the Gibeonites' provisions automatically formed a pact. **17**. Chephirah is usually identified with Tell el Kefireh a few miles W of Gibeon in the valley of Aijalon. Be-eroth, el Bireh, is about 5 m. N of Jerusalem. Kiriath-jearim, the modern Tell el Azhar, is about 8 m. W of Jerusalem.

10:1–15 Defeat of an Amorite attack on Gibeon— **d** **1–5**. Five Canaanite kings united under Adonizedek, king of Jerusalem, attack the Gibeonites. **6–10b**. The Gibeonites appeal to Joshua for aid. The Israelites make a forced night march and defeat the coalition. **10c**. The victory is really won by the might of Yahweh. In addition to Jerusalem, the cities of the coalition were: Hebron, 20 m. S of Jerusalem; Jarmuth, Khirbet Yarmuk, in the Shephelah, 15 m. W of Bethlehem; Lachish, Tell ed Duweir, 25 m. SW of Jerusalem; and Eglon, Tell el Hesy (?) 8 m. W of Lachish. Familiarity with the book of Judges will alert the reader to the fact that the report of the conquest in this and in the following chh is highly stylized. The union of the five kings accords poorly with the general historical picture of the time, and Joshua's role in the events is uncertain (cf 13:1–6; 14:6–13; 15:13–19; 17–12, 16). **1**. 'and were in the **e** midst of them' though in MT, these words are absent from the LXX and are probably a gloss. **2**. For 'he' read 'they' (the king and his subjects). **10**. The enemy is put to flight via Beth-horon as far as Azekah. *Makkedah* is probably inserted in the text to prepare for the account in 16–27 which obviously comes from a different tradition. **11**. Neither the demoralizing effect of the unexpected arrival of the Israelites nor the panic engendered by the evil omen of a storm on the day of battle (1 Sm 7:10) is emphasized. Typically, it is Yahweh, the lord of the universe, who uses the forces of nature— hailstones (Jb 38:22)—to terrify the enemy (Ex 23:27), who is the real victor in the battle. For the last part of **f** the v compare 2 Sm 18:8. **12–14**. Undoubtedly the most famous passage of the entire book, the vv have a long history of exegesis. The 'miracle of the sun' has been taken as literal fact or pseudo-scientifically explained, e.g. the passage means that the sun ceased to give heat that would debilitate the men of Israel; or, the sun did not actually stand still, but its light was refracted by the hailstones thus prolonging daylight. It is generally recognized today that all such interpretations are unnecessary. These vv are in fact a second description of the victory at Gibeon, this time in poetic language. This is indicated both by the fact that the Heb. text itself has a poetic structure and that it is a quotation from the book of Jashar, an ancient collection of poetry (2 Sm 1:18). In such poetry the action of God is often described and highlighted by striking natural phenomena (Ps 68 (67); 18 (17); Wis 5:21–23; Hb 3:11; Jg 5:4–5, 20–21). This is soaring, imaginative language and one does an injustice to the poet by interpreting it in a wooden, literal way. Particularly pertinent here are Jg 4 and 5. The battle of Barak and Sisera is described in prose (4) then repeated in poetic language in the ancient canticle of Deborah where God is pictured as advancing before his armies and 'the earth quaked and the heavens were shaken, while the clouds sent down showers, mountains trembled in the presence of the lord' (4–5)

250f and 'from heaven fought the stars, from their courses they fought against Sisera' (5:20). **14.** This verse prosaically states the central point: the lord fought for Israel. **15.** It is most unlikely that Joshua would return to Gilgal, 20–25 miles away, then return to the pursuit of the kings. The Makkedah episode was obviously added from a different tradition.

g 16–43 Conquest of S Palestine—16–27. The five Amorite kings kept prisoners in a cave at Makkedah are brought forth and put to death. **28–39** Various cities are captured and destroyed one by one in the following order: Makkedah, Libnah, Lachish, Eglon, Hebron, Debir. **40–43** On the completion of the campaign Joshua returns to Gilgal. **17.** The site of Makkedah is unknown. **24.** The ceremony of placing one's foot on a conquered enemy is often depicted in ancient art and is mentioned in Ps 110 (109):1. It signifies both the humiliation of the enemy and his loss of power. **28.** Libnah is listed among the priestly cities (Jos 21:13) and the cities of Judah (15:42). The excavations of Bliss and Macalister (1899) indicate a destruction **h** around 1200. **31.** It is obvious that a very stereotyped pattern is followed in the narratives of conquest. Excavations carried on at Lachish by J. I. Starkey confirm the destruction of the city at the time of Joshua. **33.** No claim is made of the conquest of Gezer, and as a matter of fact, it was not taken by the Israelites. **34.** Eglon, excavated by Sir Flinders Petrie (1890), gives evidence of violent destruction at the end of the 13th cent. **36.** The destruction of Hebron and Debir **38** is in other traditions referred to Judah (Jg 1:10) or Caleb (15:13–17). We have here, in all probability, an artificial unification of the conquest by attributing all of it to Joshua (cf Jos 24). **40–43.** An exaggerated summary of the conquest is given which emphasizes again that Yahweh is the real hero.

251a 11: 1–15 Defeat of the N Canaanite League and the Completion of Conquest of Canaan—1–9 With the S conquered, Israel turns its attention to the N defeating a coalition under the leadership of Jabin, king of Hazor. **10–15** Hazor and the neighbouring cities are conquered and destroyed. It should be noted that nothing is said of any conquest of central Palestine, and only this brief, inadequate account is given of the conquest of the N. In the previous chh the material used was from the Gilgal traditions. Here the material is from a different source but still betrays the hand of the deuteronomist. **1.** Though the defeat and death of Jabin is narrated here as the work of Joshua, Jg 4:24 affirms that he was finally vanquished only after the defeat of his general Sisera by Barak. Hazor, excavated by J. Garstang (1926) and Y. Yadin (1955–58), was a very important city located about 10 m. N of the Sea of Galilee. Explorations of the site have established that it was almost certainly destroyed by the Israelites. Madon, modern Madin just S of Qarn Hattin, was a strong position W of the Sea of Galilee. Shimron is the Shamhuna of the Amarna tables, the modern Sem'uniye W of Nazareth. Achshaph, modern **b** Tell Kisan (?), was located 8 m. NE of Haifa. **2.** Chinneroth was located on the shore of the sea of Galilee. JB correctly translates 'the Arabah S of Chinneroth' as 'the valley S of Chinneroth'. The region of Dor was in the N part of Sharon. **3.** cf 3:10. **4–5.** The size of the enemy army is magnified to sweeten the victory. The 'waters of Merom', sometimes identified with Lake Huleh, more probably are to be located near modern Meirun NW of the sea of Galilee, hill country that would impede the use of chariots. The general area described here is the territory from the Mediterranean coast to the sea of Galilee.

6–9. With Yahweh's assurance of victory the battle is **25** joined and the enemy put to flight. The Israelites did not use chariots till the time of Solomon; so here the horses and chariots are destroyed. The cities named here indicate that the enemy scattered in all directions. **11–15.** The mopping-up operation is described and the ban is carried out (cf § 246e).

11:16–12:24 A Summary of the Entire Conquest— c 16–20 After the conquest of the territory of Galilee, a summary statement of the conquest of the whole of Canaan is presented. **21–23** The legendary Anakim are conquered. **12:1–6** These vv are a repetition of Moses' conquest of E Palestine related in Nm 21. It was probably inserted here to round out the picture. **7–24** A list of kings and cities taken by Joshua and the Israelites brings the first part of the book to a close. As was the case throughout this section this conclusion contains much that is idealistic—boundaries never achieved, cities never conquered (cf 13:1; Jg 1:1ff)—in an attempt to bring home one fundamental point: God had fulfilled all his promises. **16–17.** Mount Halak is identified with modern Jebel Halaq about twenty-five m. S of Beer-Sheba. Seir is the territory SW of the Dead Sea (Gn 32:4; 36:8). Baal-Gad even though it cannot be more accurately located than it is in the text—'at the foot of Mount Hermon'—marks the boundary to the N. **18–20.** The conquest took considerable time because Yahweh had (interpretatively) hardened the hearts of the Canaanites so that each area had to be taken by force of arms. **21–23.** The conquest of the Anakim, often described along with the Nephilim and Rephaim as a race of giants (Nm 13:22, 32–33; Dt 2:10; 9:2; 2 Sm 21:16–22), is here attributed to Joshua. Elsewhere Caleb is associated with this victory (Jos 15:13–14). Archaeology has found no evidence for a race of giants and it would seem that the legend grew from the impressive size of their cities and monuments rather than from actual physical size, (but cf note on Dt 1:28, § 226i).

12:7–24 The list of cities and kings here generally **e** follows the account of Jos 2–11. Some of the cities mentioned in this list, however, are not mentioned in the previous chh. **13b.** Geder is unknown unless it is to be identified with Beth-geder (1 Chr 2:51). **14.** Hormah is located in the vicinity of Beer-sheba; its conquest attributed to all Israel (Nm 2:3) or to Judah and Simeon (Jg 1:17). **14b.** Arad is possibly Tell Arad, 16 m. S of Beer-Sheba. Nm 21 attributes the conquest of this city to all Israel. Adullam (Gn 38:; 1 Sm 22) was probably in the Shephelah but its exact location is unknown. **15b.** Bethel was located about 14 m. N of Jerusalem. In Jg 1:22 the conquest of this city is associated with the tribe of Joseph. **17.** Tappuah is located between Shiloh and Shechem. **18.** Aphek is located on the coast. In Roman times this would be the location of the city of Antipatris. **21.** Taanach and Megiddo are situated in the pass which connects the coastal plain with the fertile land of Esdraelon SE of Mt Carmel. **22.** Kedesh of Naphtali, identified with Qades, was far to the N, beyond the former lake Huleh. **23b.** Goiim, literally 'nations' is a very uncertain reading. Listed among these cities are several which were not taken at the time of Joshua: Jerusalem, Taanach, Dor, Megiddo and Gezer (Jg 1). **13:1–21:45 The Division of the Land among the 252 Twelve Tribes.**

Introduction—Because the land was the gift of Yahweh, it was treasured by the Israelites. Thus, descriptions of the land, even though they might be simply lists of boundaries and cities tedious to the modern reader, were precious and were diligently preserved. At the same time,

52a geographic lists are extremely susceptible to change through addition or the conflation of similar material. It should be no surprise, therefore, that this section of Joshua presents a fair number of problems. The identity and relation of the various tribes discussed in this section are also the object of much theorizing. Any attempt to discover the actual historical picture must take into account not only the narrative of occupation as presented in the first section of this book but also the possibility of a gradual occupation of the land by independent groups and the possibility that the federation of the tribes was a gradual and growing thing. To understand this portion the use of maps is indispensable and will be presumed. On these chh, see § 57a-f.

b **13:1–33 Land to be Divided and the Land Already Divided**—1–7 The land to be divided is specified. 8–14 The territory already divided by Moses is defined and some provision is made for Levi. 15–33 The boundaries and chief cities of the transjordanic tribes are indicated. **1–7.** This section is editorial; its purpose is to introduce the geographical document that follows. The territory described represents the ideal boundaries of Israel which were never actually realized (Jos 1:4; Nm 34:1–10). Here the land reaches from Shihor (probably a branch of the Nile near Tanis) in the S all the way to Mt Hermon in the N (cf Jg 1:27–36; Jg 2:20–23; 3:1–6; Dt 7:22). **2.** The Philistines originated in Asia Minor or Crete and settled in the coastal plains of Canaan about 1200 B.C. (the name Palestine is derived from these people). Non-semitic, they were the bitter enemies of Israel and were never effectively subdued (Jg 13; 16; 1 Sm 4; 2 Sm 5·17-25). The Geshurites inhabited the territory **3** of Gerar. They were conquered only at the time of David (I Sm 22:8). The Avvites were a pre-Israelite tribe in the neighborhood of Gaza (Dt 2:23). The Canaanites, a semitic people, are here pictured holding the coastal lowlands. Sidonians were the inhabitants of the Phoenician coast. The Amorites seem to be distributed over the entire area of Canaan (cf Jos 3:10; 5:1; 10:1b). The Gebalites inhabited the territory around Byblos. **7b.** 'from the Jordan . . . boundary' is not in the Hebrew. An adequate idea of the land described in **8–14** can be obtained by consulting a map.

c **15–23 The Tribe of Reuben**—Though associated with Reuben, the firstborn of Jacob and Leah, the tribe of Reuben is one of the least known. Though still important at the time of Deborah (Jg 5:15), it must be supposed that it disappeared from the history of Israel rather early. The blessing of Moses suggests that the tribe was in some sort of trouble (Dt 33:6). Just what this was is not clear, though the invasion of Eglon (Jg 3), famine, and internal strife (Nm 16) have all been suggested. Gn 49:3 and I Chr 5:1 present the decline as a punishment for Reuben's sin of incest (Gn 35:22). The territory assigned to the tribe here is usually associated with the tribe of Gad. It has been suggested that the tribe of Reuben did not enter Palestine from Egypt.

d **24–28 The Tribe of Gad**—The eponymous ancestor of this tribe was Gad the son of Jacob and the slave girl Zilpah (Gn 35:26). Their claim to their land is here based on a grant from Moses (Nm 32), but there is some indication that they were already in the territory when the other Israelites arrived. The Moabite stone of Mesha describes the conquest of this land that the men of Gad had 'occupied for ages'. If the Gilead of Jg 5:17 is identified with Gad, one would have some slight confirmation of this idea. Aside from the fact that the tribe was warlike (Gn 49:19; Dt 33:20) little

is known about it. Hazael ravaged the area (2 (4) Kgs **252d** 10:33) and it was taken over by the Ammonites (Jer 49:1).

29–33 The Half-Tribe of Manasseh—Manasseh, **e** the oldest son of Joseph (Gn 41:51; 6:20) and his brother Ephraim were adopted by Jacob (Gn 48) and thus take their place among the tribes of Israel (cf 16:1–17:18 below). In the present discussion the 'sons of Machir' figure prominently. This, plus the fact that Machir is mentioned in the canticle of Deborah (Jg 5:14b) while Manasseh is not, gives rise to the suggestion that the 'sons of Machir', like the tribe of Gad, occupied this territory before the Exodus. If this is so, then the account of the adoption of Machir (Gn 50:23) would be a later attempt to explain the prominence of this group.

14:1–19:49 The Portion of the Tribes W of the f Jordan—This section draws on several documents: a pre-monarchical description of tribal boundaries, lists of towns and cities—particularly detailed in regard to Judah and Benjamin. These documents are joined together and annotated to give a picture of the occupation under Joshua.

14:1–15 Caleb Requests and Receives Hebron— **g** 1–5 This introduction explains that the land is to be distributed by lot (7:16). The omission of Levi and the double portion given the house of Joseph are also explained. 6–15 Caleb receives Hebron. **1.** According to priestly tradition, the Eleazar mentioned here is the third son of Aaron (Ex 6:23) and his successor (Nm. 20:24). According to Nm 26:2f he assisted Moses in the taking of the census. He was buried in the mountain region of Ephraim (24:33). **6.** Here and in 1 Chr 4:15 Caleb is called the son of Jephunneh, the Kenizzite. In I Chr 2:9, however, he is the son of Hezron of the tribe of Judah. Since the Kenizzites were of Edomite origin this latter text seems to be an attempt to explain the close relationship between them and Judah, a relationship that is attested by the fact that the conquest of Hebron is attributed both to Caleb (15:13–19) and to Judah (Jg 1:10; cf above 11:21). **15.** A popular interpretation of Kiriath-arba is given; a more likely meaning: 'city of the four clans'. Caleb received his land in virtue of the promise of Moses (Nm 14:24; Dt 1:36) not by lot.

15:1–63 The Portion of Judah—1–12 The bound- **h** aries of Judah are described. 13–19 Caleb's occupation of Hebron is reported in some detail. 20–63 A list of cities in the territory of Judah is incorporated. **1–12.** Judah, the eponymous ancestor of the tribe of Judah, plays a noble role in the Joseph story (Gn 37:26ff; 43:3ff; 44:1–14; 46:28). Nonetheless, the exact relationship of this heterogeneous tribe with Israel and with the Egyptian sojourn is the subject of much speculation. The absence of Judah from the narrative of Jgs 3–13 would seem to indicate that Judah was not closely allied with the other tribes. Dt 33:7 also refers to the separation of Judah from his brothers, but this text may refer to the period of the divided monarchy. The separation is most obvious from the history of the monarchy where Judah and Israel are only briefly united under David and Solomon. If the tribe of Judah entered Canaan as part of the people of Israel, if it shared the Egypt-Exodus experience, this separation is historically inexplicable. Such indications favour the theory that this tribe never went into Egypt. The description of Judah's **i** part in the conquest in Jg 1 would seem to rule out such an idea, but it is at least possible that the original document of that ch was reworked to glorify Judah because of its later prominence. Certainly the praise and blessing of Judah in Gn 49:8–13 (written during the united

252i monarchy) is an attempt to explain the tribe's importance in the time of David. **15—19.** A Kenizzite captures Debir and receives Achsah, daughter of Caleb, as a reward. This account of the conquest of Debir would seem more authentic than the stereotyped account of 10:38 (cf Jg 1:12ff). **20—63.** This list of cities is certainly of late origin, probably from the time of the monarchy.

j **16:1—17:18 The Portion of the sons of Joseph**— 1—4 Territory is assigned to Joseph as a single tribe. 5—10 Land is assigned to the tribe of Ephraim. 17:1—13 A portion is assigned to the tribe of Manasseh. 14—18 A reason is given for assigning Ephraim and Manasseh each a portion when together they constitute the 'house of Joseph' (cf Gn 48). **1—4.** The 'house of Joseph' conquered the city of Bethel and the surrounding area (Jg 1:22—26). It should be noted that it is precisely about the conquest of the land of Joseph and Benjamin (13:11—20) that we have the greatest amount of detail in Jos. Whatever may be said about the pre-exodus history of the other tribes, it seems certain that these two tribes were involved in the Egypt-Exodus experience, did enter Canaan through conquest, and were the core tribes of the covenant (cf 24:1ff). In Gn 49:22—21 the importance of the house of Joseph is brought out by the long blessing and mention of Yahweh's special protection. Dt 33:17 assigns the primacy once given to Judah (Gn 49:8) to **k** Joseph. **5—10.** The territory assigned to Ephraim is practically identical with the territory just assigned to Joseph. Ephraim, therefore, retains the original grant. Even though the 40,500 members attributed to the tribe (Nm 1:33) seems exaggerated, Ephraim was the largest and most powerful of the tribes and the name is often used as a synonym for Israel. There is a possibility that the name Ephraim was originally a place name that became a tribal name when the house of Joseph was divided. The preeminence of Ephraim, the second son of Joseph (Gn 41:52; 46:20) receives an imaginative explanation in Gn 48:17—20. **17:1.** Manasseh was second only to Ephraim in size (Nm 1:34; 26:29—34) and importance. (For details of Manasseh in transjordan cf 13:29—33 above). **3—6.** Five portions are assigned to the clans of Abiezer, Helek, Asriel, Shechem, and Shemida; another five to the subclans of Hepher (Nm 26:29—33). **7—13.** The territory assigned to Manasseh is described with the statement that the tribe was not strong enough to defeat the Canaanites in many of the cities. **14—18.** The hill country was first occupied, then the wooded area. (This may possibly include an allusion to the territory of Gilead across the Jordan.) This aggressive house is to meet its own need for expansion northward where no clear boundary is indicated.

253a **18—19:51 A Second Division of the Territory Worked out at Shiloh**—1—10 Joshua gives orders for a survey and division of the lands. This introduction, not in harmony with that noted in 14:1—5, indicates that the following material depends on a different source. The tribes receive their land in the following order: 11—28 Benjamin; 19:1—9 Simeon; 10—39 Zebulon, Issachar, Asher and Naphtali; 40—48 Dan. Joshua's personal inheritance is mentioned 49—50, and the section is concluded 51. **1.** As the conquest progressed, the sanctuary was transferred from Gilgal to Shiloh, modern Seilun 9 m. N of Bethel (Jg 19:21). Possibly the transfer took place when the transjordan tribes were dismissed (Jos 22). Shiloh remained the principal sanctuary during the time of the Judges (Jg 18; 21) and was probably destroyed around 1050 B.C. by the Philistines (1 Sm 4:3—4; Jer 7:12; 26:6, 9; Ps 78 (77):

60). The tent of meeting was the place where Yahweh **25:** met Moses (Ex 25:22), the place where God dwelt with his people (Ps 78 (77):60; Ex 40:34; 24:16; 29:42—43). For a detailed description of the tent cf Ex 26; 33:7—11; and 36:8—38: see also § 103e. The words of Joshua might indicate a reluctance on the part of the people to settle down.

11—28 The Portion of the Tribe of Benjamin— **b** The tribe of Benjamin described as a 'ravenous wolf' (Gn 49:27) and as the 'beloved of the Lord' (Dt 33:12) is associated with the youngest son of Jacob and Rachel (Gn 35:18). The precise relationship of the tribe of Benjamin to that of Joseph is the subject of dispute. Noth suggests that Benjamin was a part of the Joseph tribe which broke off and was named from its geographical position to the S of Ephraim ('Benjamin' can be interpreted as 'southerner'). This is by no means certain. Benjamin is mentioned as an individual tribe in the ancient canticle of Deborah (Jg 5:14) and it is the conquest of the land of Benjamin that is told in greatest detail. In the complex discussion about which tribes entered Canaan at the time of Joshua and which ones were already there, Benjamin stands out as the one that most certainly entered. The territory of Benjamin, though small, contained the important sanctuary of Bethel (Gn 35:8; 12:8; Jg 20:18; 1 (3) Kgs 12—13:32) and the city of Jebus (Jerusalem 2 Sm 5:5—9). Devastated by an inter-tribal war (Jg 19—21) Benjamin survived to give Israel its first king, Saul (1 Sm 10:20).

19:1—9 The Portion of Simeon—The eponymous **c** ancestor of this tribe was Jacob's second son by Leah (Gn 29:33) who is mentioned in the story of Joseph in Egypt (Gn 34:25,30; 42:24,36). The tribe of Simeon helped Judah in the conquest of S Canaan (Jg 1:3—17) or at least settled in the territory of Judah (cf discussion of Judah, 15:1—12 above). Simeon disappeared as a tribe very early becoming, apparently, a clan of Judah. In favor of this opinion is the fact that the territory of Simeon was within that of Judah (19:9) and that the cities here associated with Simeon are elsewhere assigned to Judah (15:2). This disappearance of the tribe of Simeon is explained as a punishment (Gn 49:5—9) for the treachery of Simeon and Levi at Shechem (Gn 34: 25—31). The absence of Simeon from Dt 33 suggests that the assimilation had already taken place by the time of David. An account of David's battle in the very area assigned to Simeon (1 Sm 31:1—30) would seem to confirm this for there is no mention at all of the tribe.

19:10—39 The Galilean Tribes—The pattern **d** followed in describing the land of the S tribes—the statement of the boundaries then a list of cities—is abandoned in the discussion of the N tribes. Instead one finds a list of cities interspersed with a few vague statements about boundaries. It is possible that more detailed information about the N tribes was unavailable to the editors. It is possible also that they simply were not as interested in N tribes and were content to work with a list of cities already compiled and easily available. **10—16 The Portion of Zebulun**—This tribe is associated with Zebulun, son of Jacob and Leah (Gn 30:19; Ex 1:3; 1 Chr 2:1). The description of the tribe as a sailor and voyager (Gn 49:13; Dt 33:18) presents a problem since the land assigned here, the W hills of S Galilee, does not reach to the sea. The tribe must have entered into some sort of agreement with the Canaanites who did occupy the sea coast. **17—23 The Portion of Issachar**—The eponymous **e** ancestor was a son of Jacob and Leah (Gn 30:17). The list of cities—no boundaries at all are given—would

3e indicate that the territory of Issachar was the plain of Esdraelon. This fertile area was very heavily Canaanite, and Gn 49:14—15 describes the tribe as slaves bowing to the Canaanites. Issachar could not have been completely dominated by the Canaanites, however, for it took part in the struggle against Sisera (Jg 5:14). Whatever the relations between the Canaanites and the tribe, they seem to have been profitable to Issachar (Dt 33:18).

f 24—31 The Portion of Asher—The eponym of this tribe was a son of Jacob and Zilpah, the slave of Leah (Gn 30:13). The territory assigned to the tribe is the coastal land N of Carmel. The prosperity of Asher is reflected both in Gn 49:20 and in Dt 33:24. Asher answered the call of Gideon (Jg 6:35; 7:23) and representatives of the tribe appear during the reign of Hezekiah (2 Chr 30:11). The impression is, however, that Asher contributed little to the history of Israel and generally 'stayed by the sea' (Jg 5:17). This independence of Asher and the fact that they lived among Canaanites (Jg 1:31—32) have led to the suggestion that the tribe actually consisted of Canaanites who had attached themselves to the Israelite confederation.

g 32—29 The Portion of Naphtali—Naphtali was the son of Jacob and Rachel's maid, Bilhah (Gn 30:8). Assigned the E part of Galilee, the tribe had difficulty in actually taking the land (Jg 1:33). Still it did become a fairly prosperous tribe (Gn 49:21; Dt 33:23) and an important military force (Jg 4:10; 5:18; 7:23).

40—48 The Portion of Dan—The ancestry of Dan is traced to Jacob and Bilhah (Gn 30:7), perhaps because of the close association with the tribe of Naphtali. Despite the fact that Dan is praised for its warlike qualities (Gn 49:16), the opposition of the Amorites (Jg 1:34) and the Philistines (Jg 13—16) made it impossible for them to occupy their assigned territory in the S, the Shephelah. Forced to look elsewhere for land, the tribe moved through the territory of Naphtali to the N uplands and settled in the vicinity of Leshem (= Laish, later named Dan) (Jg 17—18). This migration is regarded as an accomplished fact in Jg 5:17.

49—50 The inheritance of Joshua—Joshua received the city of Timnath-serah (Jos 24:30; Jg 2:9) in the territory of Ephraim.

h 20:1—9 The Cities of Refuge—In accordance with instructions given Moses (Ex 21:13; Nm 35:9—34) six cities, three in transjordan and three in cisjordan, are set up as places of asylum. These cities offered refuge only to persons who had killed unintentionally (Ex 21:14; Nm 35:11—14; Dt 4:41—43; 19:1—13) and were a means of avoiding unnecessary and unjust bloodshed. 3. The 'Avenger of Blood' (Heb. go'el) is the victim's nearest relative (Gn 4:15; 9:6; Nm 35:19; 2 Sm 14:11). The blood avenger is primarily the protector of the rights of his relative (Lv 25:23—25). This term was later used of God, the Go'el of Israel (Is 41:14; Jer 50:34; Ps 19 (18):14) with the same basic meaning of protector.

i 21:1—42 The Levitical Cities—The data on the tribe of Levi is so diverse as to defy harmonization. Like the eponymous ancestor of Simeon, Levi belongs to the Leah tribes (Gn 29:34; 35:23). The two were involved in the treachery at Shechem (Gn 34) and for their violence were cursed to be landless and scattered among the tribes of Israel (Gn 49:7). Dt 33:8—11 reflects none of this tradition. The Levites are a tribe faithful to Yahweh, with priestly duties reminiscent of Ex 32:25—29: 'Today you have ordained yourselves to the service of the Lord.' The fact that the Levites receive no land in Israel seems to be connected with both these traditions. In Dt the Levite is mentioned

with the widow and the orphan as an object of charity 253i (Dt 12:12,18; 14:18; 16:11; 26:12—13; Jg 17:7—13). How can this be harmonized with the present ch where 48 cities are assigned to the Levites (cf Nm 35:1—8; 1 Chr 6:39—66; Dt 14:28—29; 26:12; Lv 25:32; Ezek 48:12)? How would a lowly condition reflect on the words: 'You shall not have inheritance in the land. I Yahweh will be your inheritance' (Nm 18:20—24)? To complicate the picture even more, the adventures of Levi took place very early, quite possibly before the other tribes entered Canaan. But how can one separate the tribe of Levi, the tribe of Moses and Aaron, from the story of Egypt and from the Exodus? Still the problems do not end. The priesthood is a reward for the fidelity of the tribe (Ex 32:25—29; Dt 33:8—11), but when the Levites claim equality with the priests their claim is rejected (Nm 16—17), and in a number of passages the priesthood is limited to the Levitical clan of Zadok (Ezek 40:46; 43:19; 44:15). To do com- j plete justice to all these variant details is impossible, but one theory seems to come close. According to this suggestion the tribe of Levi and the Levites or Levitical priests were two distinct entities. Minean inscriptions have been found containing the South-Arabic word lw' designating some sort of cultic minister. The Heb. word lēwī has been taken to mean 'priest' or 'temple slave'. One who served in this capacity, regardless of his tribal affiliations, would then be known as a Levite. When the priesthood of Israel developed into an organized group, its members would be known as the 'sons of Levi'. Originally the term 'sons' in this phrase would simply have meant 'belonging to the group or class' as in the phrase 'sons of the prophets' (1 (3) Kgs 20:35). Identifying these 'sons of Levi' with the tribe of Levi was a very easy step. The result was the confusion we have been discussing. On the priesthood, cf § 104a-f. 4. The sons of Levi, in the strict sense, were Kohath, Gershon, and Merari (Ex 6:16; Nm 3:17; 4:1—33; 1 Chr 5:27). The cities are distributed to the clans that bore these names. The clan of Kohath, to which Moses and Aaron belonged, was in charge of the tent of meeting and the most sacred things (Nm 4:4). The 48 cities were not the exclusive possession of the Levites but places where they lived among others. Though the editing of this section may date from the time of David, the institution of these cities seems older (cf Nm 33:1—8; 1 Chr 6:54—81). 43—45. This section is brought to a close and once more the editors' theological preoccupation is made clear: 'not one of all the good promises which the Lord has made to the house of Israel had failed, all came to pass'.

22:1—24:33 The Final Events and Discourses 254a

22:1—34 The Departure of the Transjordan Tribes to their Territory—1—8 Joshua dismisses the transjordanic warriors after commending their obedience and exhorting them to remain faithful to Yahweh. 9—10 They depart and on reaching the Jordan erect an altar. 11—12 The Cisjordan tribes hearing of this apparent violation of the law prepare a punitive expedition. 13—20 A delegation is sent to investigate the significance of the altar. 21—29 The transjordan tribes explain that the altar is a symbol of unity. 30—34 The ambassadors and the people of Cisjordan accept this explanation of the altar of testimony. 1. The dismissal of the two and a half tribes is in keeping with earlier promises (1:12—18; Nm 32:6—32). 5. Emphasis is placed on keeping the covenant because it is the true bond between the tribes of Israel (1:7; Dt 6:5—7; 10:12; 11:13; 19:9; 28:9; 30:6).

254b 9—34 Misunderstanding over the Altar—Throughout the period of the Judges, sacrifice was offered at various places (Jg 6:26; 14:16). In fact the law on the unity of sanctuary seems to have originated only very much later; cf § 224h. This section with its concern for the unity of the sanctuary based on Dt 12:13—14 comes, therefore, from a later priestly tradition. It does emphasize that the unifying element of the various tribes was religion and cult. **10.** The wording of the Heb. text is ambiguous as to the location of the altar. Strictly speaking the land of Canaan is to the W of the Jordan which would indicate that the altar was built on the W bank. 19 however, seems to imply that the altar was put on the E bank of the river to cleanse the transjordan area. **12.** The cisjordan tribes prepare to wage war over the incident, because such an action might jeopardize the covenant with Yahweh and was an act of treason that could bring the entire nation to **c** disaster (cf 7:1—26). **13.** Phinehas, the son of Eleazar (Ex 6:25) had taken bloody vengeance on the Israelites who worshipped the Baal of Peor, an action for which he and his descendants received the covenant of perpetual priesthood (Nm 25). He presided at the sanctuary of Bethel (Jg 20:26—28). **14—20.** The delegation, citing the incident at Peor (Nm 25) and the story of Achan (7) emphasized that the action of the transjordan tribes put the entire confederacy in danger. **21—29.** With an oath the transjordan tribes protest they had no intention of turning away from the one God or of destroying the unity of the tribes. On the contrary, the altar is to be a witness to the future that the transjordan tribes are truly a part of Israel. **30—34.** The delegation, satisfied with the answer, departs; the purpose of the altar is again stated.

d 23:1—16 Joshua, Near his End, Exhorts Israel to be Faithful to Yahweh—This discourse of Joshua is the first of two conclusions to the book, probably of later origin than the second conclusion. **1—13** Joshua summons the representatives of the people and, after a general reference to the benefits received from Yahweh, reminds them that enemies still remain to be subdued in the territory allotted to them and that Yahweh will continue to give them victory in the future as in the past if they remain faithful to him. **14—16** The conditional nature of God's gifts is stressed. If the people are not faithful to their part of the covenant, they will perish. **1.** It is obvious from 13 that all the land has not yet been captured. **3.** Joshua introduces his discourse with the same words as Moses (Dt 29:1; 7:19), another implication by the editor that he carries on the work of Moses. **4.** Vg rightly omits 'along with all the nations I have already cut off' since 5 makes it clear that the topic is peoples not yet conquered. (Dt 11:23). **6—13.** The danger of associating with foreigners is emphasized. To appreciate the deuteronomic character of this speech cf Dt 5:32; 7:2—3; 10:20; 11:23; 3:22.

e 24:1—32 The Covenant Renewal at Shechem and the Death of Joshua—This ch is extremely important for an understanding of Jos and the entire history of Israel. The account of the distribution of the land (13: 1—21:45) indicates a very complex picture of tribal relations. It seems that the notion of the traditional twelve tribes entering Palestine as a unit is historically untenable. The facts seem to indicate that some of the tribes arrived in Canaan before the time of Joshua and some had never left the territory at all. Note the words of Joshua (24:14) 'Put away the gods which your fathers served beyond the river'. If Israel is viewed as a homogeneous group with the experience of the desert and the

conquest behind it, this reference to the service of false **25** gods would be very difficult to understand. A careful analysis of Jos has led M. Noth to suggest that before the event of Shechem Israel was not a people at all; that the land had been occupied gradually without any sort of military occupation. When the last tribes arrived under the leadership of Joshua, they brought a new vitality which attracted and united the people already there. Archaeological evidence of military action and new occupation of various sites in Canaan precisely at the time of Joshua weakens this theory considerably, but it does seem to be on the right track. The history **f** of Canaan before and during the period of occupation under Joshua was one of unrest and upheaval. The people of the land were rebelling against the decadent structure of Canaanite city-states. The 'habiru' of the Amarna tablets, for instance, might well indicate those who had dissociated themselves from the existing political structures, cf § 79b. When the core tribes—Joseph, Benjamin, Reuben and Simeon—arrived, they found large groups of people waiting precisely for the type of message they brought: an end to Canaanite serfdom; the dignity of each individual as a member of God's people. This theory would at least explain why there is no mention of the conquest of Shechem since it might very well have come to the Israelites peacefully by the federation of the people who occupied the territory. Whatever else might be said, such a theory makes the events of Shechem extremely important. Here the election of Sinai which had already constituted the core tribes the people of Yahweh was extended to embrace all those who were willing to accept the one true God.

Mendenhall's studies on suzerainty treaties are per- **g** tinent here. There can be little doubt that this treaty form influenced the writing of this ch. The suzerainty treaty is one between a superior and an inferior or subject power. The elements of this type of pact can be presented as follows: (1) the sovereign is named—Jos 24:2; (2) historical prologue, a free form narration of all the superior king has done on behalf of the subject people—Jos 24:2—13; (3) stipulations concerning the obligations which the inferior power takes upon itself— Jos 24:14; (4) the treaty is to be preserved at a shrine, it is a sacred thing, and read periodically—Jos 24:26 (cf Dt 31:9—13); (5) confirmation of the pact by the invocation of witnesses—Jos 24:22, the people and 26—27 the stones; (6) sanctions, blessings and curses, are listed. These are implied in this ch and mentioned expressly in 8:34 which is very closely related to the present account.

Death of those who had made the treaty would neces- **h** sitate its renewal (Jos 5:4—5) as would the incorporation of Israelites who had never gone to Egypt or who had returned before the general exodus. Not included in the Sinai experience, these people would enter the covenant relationship with Yahweh for the first time.

The basic material of the ch seems very ancient and presents Joshua in the important role of mediator of the covenant. While his connection with the narrative of conquest is often problematic, his role as the new Moses through whom the covenant is renewed and extended is not. It would be precisely because of his eminence here that scattered details of the occupation were associated with his name.

1. Shechem, modern Tell Balatah, was situated bet- **i** ween Mt Gerizim and Mt Ebal (cf 8:30ff) 40 m. N of Jerusalem. This was a very ancient shrine associated with Abraham (Gn 12:6ff) and Jacob (Gn 33:18ff). The principal temple at Shechem was called 'El-Berith', 'God

254i of the Covenant' (Jg 9:46) and 'Baal-Berith', 'Lord of the Covenant' (Jg 9:4). These names and the revenge of Simeon and Levi on the men of Shechem (Gn 34) may suggest that Israel had gained possession of Shechem in patriarchal times through some sort of pact. The decline of Shechem as a shrine seems to be associated with the story of Abimelech (Jg 9). The phrase 'they presented themselves before God' is a sacred formula **j** connoting cultic action. **2—13.** Here the deeds of Yahweh are related in a covenant symbol, that is, certain historical actions are narrated which symbolize all the good things God has done for his people. At later covenant renewals this section would be brought up to date by adding further blessings of God. **12.** The 'hornets' (Ex 23:28; Dt 7:20) might possibly indicate the terror that afflicted the Canaanites, another sign of divine intervention. **14—15.** The basic obligations of the covenant are presented, obligations which are spelled out in greater and growing detail elsewhere (Ex 20:1—23:19; 34:14—26; Dt 5:6—18; 12—26). **16—18.** These vv do not really indicate a free election on the part of the **254j** people. After a description of the great things done by Yahweh there is no choice left to the people but to give up false gods and follow Yahweh always. The initiative in the covenant comes from Yahweh. **19—28.** Basic sanctions are invoked and the people and the stones become witnesses to the covenant.

29—33 Traditions Concerning the Tombs of Joshua, k Joseph and Eleazar—29—30. 110 years was considered the perfect lifespan according to Egyptian standards. It is, therefore, a symbolic statement that Joshua was greatly blessed by Yahweh. Joshua was buried in his own territory (19:50; Jg 2:9). **32.** The burial of Joseph fulfils the command he had given while in Egypt (Gn 50:25). We are told that the Israelites brought his remains with them (Ex 13:19) so they could bury them in the territory of Shechem purchased by Jacob (Gn 33:19). This item of information fits nicely here for it brings out again the notion that Israel's wanderings are over, God had brought them to the promised land.

JUDGES

BY JOHN HUESMAN S.J.

255a Bibliography—Commentaries: G. F. Moore, ICC, 1895; K. Budde, Freiburg, 1897; W. Nowack, HKAT, 1902; B. Neteler, Münster, 1900; M. J. Lagrange, EtB, 1903; G. A. Cooke, CBSC, 1913; V. Zapletal, EHAT, 1923; A. Schulz, BB, 1926; C. F. Burney, 1930²; J. Garstang, 1931; J. Keulers, Brugge, 1932; C. J. Goslinga, Kampen, 1933—8; R. Tamisier, PCSB, 1949: A. Vincent, BJ, 1952; J. M. Myers and P. P. Elliott, IB, 1953; J. N. Schofield, PC (2), 1962; H. W. Hertzberg, ATD,
b 1959².—**Other Literature**: O. Eissfeldt, *Die Quellen des Richterbuches*, Leipzig, 1925; E. Auerbach, 'Die Einwanderung der Israeliten', ZAW 48 (1930) 281—95; G. T. Manley, 'The Deuteronomic Redactor in the Book of Judges', EvQ31 (1959) 32—38; C. A. Simpson, *The Composition of the Book of Judges*, 1958; M. Noth, 'Das Amt des Richters Israels', *Fs Bertholet* 404—17; H. Haensler, 'Der historische Hintergrund von Richter 3:8—10', Bib 11 (1930) 391—418; 13 (1931) 3—26, 276—96; W. F. Albright, 'The Song of Deborah in the Light of Archaeology', BASOR 62 (1936) 26—31; C. F. Whitley, 'The Sources of the Gideon Stories', VT 7 (1957) 157—64; A. Mallon, 'Chronique des fouilles: Sichem', Bib 8 (1927) 377—81; L. H. Vincent, 'Fouilles allemandes à Balata-Sichem', RB 36 (1927) 419—25; G. Welter, 'Stand der Ausgrabungen in Sichem', Archaeologischer Anzeiger (1932) 313f; E. Kalt, *Samson*, Freiburg (Breisgau) 1912; J. Blenkinsopp, 'Some Notes on the Saga of Samson and the Heroic Milieu', Scr 11 (1959) 81—89; J. Bewer, 'The Composition of Judges, chh 17—18', AJSL 29 (1913—14) 261—83; A. Fernandez, 'El Santuario de Dan', Bib 15 (1934) 237—64; C. Hauret, 'Aux origines du Sacerdoce Danite' (Jdg 18, 30s)', *Me A Robert*, 1957, 105—13; J. A. Bewer, 'The Composition of Judges, chh 19—21', AJSL 30 (1914—15) 81—93, 149—65; W. F. Albright, 'Excavations and Results at Tell el-Ful (Gibeah of Saul)', AASOR 4 (1924), 1—89; L. H. Vincent, 'Fouilles américaines à Tell el-Foul', RB 32 (1923) 426—30; W. F. Albright, 'The Role of the Canaanites in the History of Civilization', *Studies in the History of Culture*, 1942, 11—50.

c Name—The book of Judges is so called from the title given to the national heroes whose exploits form its main theme. The term Judge, however, is not to be narrowed down to our own modern legal category. For the author of our present book it took on a far wider connotation. *Deliverer, Champion, Vindicator, Charismatic-leader* are a few of the terms employed by modern writers to catch the flavour of the biblical Judge. Men chosen by God, in fact seized by the spirit of God, theirs was the task to save their tribe or their clan. Never do we find them exercising jurisdiction over the whole of Israel in the capacity of King. This came only later with Saul.

d Contents—The present book of Jg contains a religious history of Israel from Joshua to Samuel in the form of detached episodes. It begins with an account of the efforts of the tribes in Canaan to secure complete possession of their lots. Then comes an appropriate **255** introduction to the narratives of the great judges raised up by God to deliver the people from their various oppressors. Israel's history throughout the period is depicted under the form of recurring cycles of sin, punishment, repentance, and deliverance. The victorious struggles of Othniel with the Edomites, Ehud with the Moabites, Deborah and Barak with the Canaanites, Gideon with the Midianites, Jephthah with the Ammonites, and Samson with the Philistines are then described. Between Ehud and Deborah is a brief reference to the exploits of Shamgar against the Philistines. After Gideon the episode of Abimelech and the Shechemites is related apparently by way of appendix. Immediately before and after Jephthah the five minor judges are recorded. After Samson come the episodes of the origin and institution of the sanctuary of Dan and the outrage at Gibeah and war of the tribes against Benjamin.

Composition and Authorship—No competent **e** authority today accepts the Talmudic tradition that Jg is the work of a single author, Samuel. Rather is it very clear that oral traditions as well as early written materials have found their way into the composition of this work. Some of these traditions, the narratives e.g. dealing with Ehud, Deborah, and Gideon stem from the N, while those dealing with Jephthah and Othniel reflect a S background. Each area of Palestine clung jealously to the stories that shed light on its own beginnings. As the fall of the N kingdom in 722 was to lead to the union of the JE Pentateuchal sources, so too did it result in the compilation of the N — S stories to be found in Jg. This first compilation may well have taken place during the reign of Hezekiah (715—687). Still later, in the late 7th cent. a deuteronomic redactor reworked the product of the first compiler, this time unifying his materials around the theological theme of sin, chastisement, penance, and deliverance. With this redactor we have the basic framework of our present book. Later editors, moreover, were to introduce additional narratives, independent of the above-mentioned theological theme, but considered worthy of preservation. This was the manner in which stories such as the history of the sanctuary of Dan and the sorry tale of the Levite found their way into the book. Most authorities place the final redaction in the time of Ezra. For other analyses cf A. Bentzen, *Introduction to the OT*, Copenhagen 1952, Vol 2, 87—91 and EOT Int 258—67. The **f** book deals broadly with the period subsequent to Joshua, but it is widely held that it overlaps the earlier book and, in its first section 1:1—2:5, repeats to some extent the events of the conquest from a rather different angle. In the book of Joshua we have the official epic narrative of the conquest, with the victories emphasized and reverses played down, in order to bring out clearly the guiding hand of God and the fulfilment of his promise in respect of his people. But there was another side which was to become increasingly familiar as time passed, namely the shortcomings of Israel and their frequent backslidings

55f followed by military reverses and material hardships which God allowed to come upon them as punishment. In the opening chh of Jg we already see something of this. In support of the view that we have here a return to the time of Joshua some critics point out that in Jg 1:16 the Israelites are still at Jericho, and in 2:1 Gilgal is the headquarters as was the case in Joshua 4:19 and 14:6. But later (Jos 18:1) they appear to have moved to Shiloh and eventually to Shechem (Jos 24:1). The suggestion is that in Jg we have a rather more realistic account of part of the conquest with greater emphasis on the human side and the gradual nature of the advance. Traces of this indeed are already discernible in Jos itself. The opening words of Jgs 'After the death of Joshua' would therefore, in the view of these critics, apply to the book in general but without excluding the insertion of a certain amount of material, especially in the first section of the book, which dealt with earlier history.

g **Chronology of the Period**—The chronology might be considered defined in the text by the years of oppression (8 + 18 + 20 + 7 + 18 + 40 = 111) and of rest (40 + 80 + 40 + 40 + 6 + 20 = 226) under the six great judges, the years (23 + 22 + 7 + 10 + 8 = 70) of the five minor judges and the years of Abimelech (3) which make a total of 410 years. We cannot assume, however, that these periods are successive. As they refer in all cases only to a part of Israel some of them may well have been contemporaneous. The numbers are also more commonly formulated in terms of a generation (40) or half a generation (20) or two generations (80), and thus useless for an exact chronology. The period of oppression in 10.8 is clearly a later addition. In 11:26 we are informed that the period between Moses' conquest of Sihon's kingdom and Jephthah's victory over the Ammonites was 300 years. Here again we have apparently a later addition, artificially calculated, since the numbers previously recorded in Jg make a total of 301, and no account is taken of Joshua's long leadership. The period given would, moreover, transfer Jephthah to the period of the divided monarchy. We are thus forced to determine the chronology of the Judges' period by other data more solidly established, the invasion of Canaan c. 1250 B.C. (cf § 61e), and the enthronement of Solomon c. 960 B.C. Making due allowance for the reigns of David and Saul and the judgeship of Samuel we are left with about 170 years (c. 1220—1050 B.C.) for the period covered by Jg. The narratives of the six great judges seem to be arranged in chronological order. Othniel, a younger contemporary of Joshua, is the first, and Samson, who began the deliverance from the Philistines completed by David, is the last. Deborah is expressly indicated as the successor of Ehud. It is very likely and suggested in 10:7 that the oppressions of the Ammonites in the E and Philistines in the SW were more or less contemporaneous.

h **Character of the Period**—We have no information on the Judges' period from external sources. The empires of the Hittites and Hurrians no longer existed. Babylonians, Assyrians, and Egyptians had troubles of their own and were not interested in Palestine. The Israelites could thus increase and develop, if not without interference from neighbouring peoples, at least without danger of permanent subjection and deportation. The oppressions were temporary and local. The great judges, chosen naturally from the oppressed, all belonged to different tribes. As they were not always rulers, the statement that they judged Israel implies at most that any Israelite might seek justice from them. The first editor is chiefly concerned with the N tribes. Judah engrossed in her struggle with the Philistines and separated from her brethren by the

Hivite cities is rarely mentioned. Mt Ephraim is the **255h** centre of Israel as in the days of Joshua. A great judge, Deborah, and a minor judge, Tola, both Issacharites, reside there. Ephraim is the most powerful of the tribes, but his claim to leadership is resisted successfully by Jephthah. The rival claims of Judah are set forth by the second editor (1:2; 20:18). The tribes follow their own ways, but the consciousness of national and religious unity appears clearly in the Canticle of Deborah and still more in the war against Benjamin. The Israelites readily desert Yahweh to worship idols. They live in harmony with the Canaanites at Shechem and elsewhere. The crimes of Abimelech, the human sacrifice of Jephthah, the outrage of Gibeah are characteristic of a lawless period. Throughout the lengthy period of the Judges one factor, the cult of Yahweh, provided the sole centripetal factor for the Israelites. For during this time Israel may be likened to the amphictyonic situation of the early Greeks, i.e. numerous tribes linked together by use of a central sanctuary. If religion constituted the sole centripetal force welding the chosen people together, numerous elements served as centrifugal forces disrupting that unity. Most prominent among these centrifugal forces were religious syncretism, the adoption of divisive Canaanite cultic practices, and the very topography of Palestine itself. A glance at a contour map of Palestine will graphically illustrate that her topography in no way favours unity.

Religious Teaching—Jg teaches in particular the religious interpretation of the history of the chosen people. The facts are presented, not as the natural result of human causality, but as the execution of a divine plan. God uses the neighbouring nations to punish the sins of his people, and this punishment is an invitation to repentance, the indispensable condition of deliverance. His wisdom is manifested in the plan, his justice and holiness in the punishment of sin, his mercy in the pardon of the repentant sinner, and his goodness and omnipotence in the deliverance of the oppressed. That deliverance is the work, not of man, but of God, is particularly emphasized. The great judges are divinely appointed and divinely inspired. Gideon must diminish his forces, Barak must descend from Tabor to the plain that the real author of the victory may be known and glorified. Divine intervention is clearly manifested by the inadequacy of natural means. We thus learn that divine providence rules the world's history, that God intervenes miraculously in human affairs, that national calamities are usually the punishment of sin, and that amendment of life is the best guarantee of the restoration of national prosperity. The religious teaching includes also the exemplary chastisement of grave crimes, such as idolatry and disobedience to God's commands in the dealings of the tribes with the Canaanites, lack of good faith in Abimelech and the Shechemites and flagrant violation of the sacred law of hospitality at Gibeah. Prominent throughout Jg is the theme of God's use of weak human instruments. Ehud was a common man, Deborah and Jael women, Gideon an unknown youth, Jephthah a bastard outlaw, and Samson an amoral giant. The whole Bible, and particularly Jg hammers home the truth that God does not depend on human means for the fulfilment of his designs. And finally for the Christian who finds some of this book quite disturbing one must reiterate the important truth that the Bible describes certain Heb. practices without endorsing them. Some of their convictions were valid, e.g. trust in God's protection, belief in a fundamental moral law which forbade ultimate victory to the unrighteous, but in many practices they remained children of their day.

256a **1:1—2:5 War of the Tribes in Canaan**—Jg begins with a summary account of the efforts of the individual tribes to complete the conquest of Canaan. The exploits and failures of Judah and Simeon are first narrated (**1—21**), then the capture of Bethel by the house of Joseph (**22—26**), and finally the failures of Manasseh (**27—28**), Ephraim (**29**), Zebulun (**30**), Asher (**31—32**), Naphtali (**33**), and Dan (**34—35**). The account provides a very realistic picture of the gradual take-over. The final vv (**2:1—5**) are from a later redactor. 1:1—31 tells us that the Israelites did not defeat the Canaanites because the latter were stronger. Our later redactor puts religious faults as the basis of their failure.

b **1:1—3**. The beginning of the campaign is assigned by Yahweh, consulted through the Urim and Thummim (cf Ex 28), to Judah (cf 20:28), whom Simeon joins since his lot is within Judah's lot. **4**. To 'go up' means 'attack' without necessarily implying an ascent. They defeat the Canaanite and the Perizzites, a Hurrian clan, with great slaughter at Bezek. Some point to modern Ibziq, 11 m. SW of Beisan, as the site of this village, but others maintain that this is too far N and prefer Khirbet Bezqa in the vicinity of Gezer. **5—7**. Adonibezek, whose personal name is unknown since a title, Lord of Bezek, has been substituted for it, was king of Jerusalem. He is represented as a powerful ruler subsequently brought by his followers to that city. The Heb. cut off his thumbs and his big toes (**6a**), not to incapacitate him for military service, but as a degrading mutilation in which the sufferer sees an application of the *lex talionis*. **8**. A scribe, incorrectly supposing that the Heb. brought him to Jerusalem, interpolated an account of the capture and destruction of Jerusalem, an event only realized in David's time (cf 1:21; 19:12; Jos 15:63; 2 Sm 5:7). On 10—15 cf Jos 15:13—19. The capture of Hebron is mentioned (**10**) as an episode of the tribal war and (**20**) as an exploit of Caleb. Debir (**11**) is Tell Beit Mirsim, 13 m. SW of Hebron, and was excavated by Albright (cf AASOR I–II, XIIf, XVII, XXIf). Albright **c** dates the present destruction c. 1200. The Kenite nomads, kinsmen of the father-in-law of Moses, who had accompanied the Israelites as guides (Nm 10:29—32) and fixed their tents temporarily near Jericho, famous for its palms, went with the invaders (**16**) into the wilderness of Judah in the Negeb of Arad. This Arad is 17 m. S of Hebron. Here they dwelt with the Amalekites (cf 1 Sm 15:6). **17**. Zephath, renamed Hormah (*anathema* or *devoted to destruction*) is probably Khirbet Hora, 10 m. NE of Beersheba. Its capture is narrated proleptically Nm 21:1—3, **18**. For 'took' read 'did not take' (LXX), required by 3:3 and the context, since exclusion from the maritime plain (**19**) implies exclusion from the cities. In Jos 15:63 Judah replaces Benjamin. The situation is different here where Benjamin is blamed for neglecting to capture her chief city. **22**. Bethel, modern Beitin, was very prosperous and strongly fortified in the Late Bronze Age. This explains why it was not captured by Joshua. Its destruction by fire towards the close of the Late Bronze Age is attested by the excavations (cf BASOR 55 **d** (1934), 56 (1934), 137 (1954); BA 19 (1956). The success of the house of Joseph, like that of Judah, is attributed to Yahweh. **26**. The land of the Hittites was N of Kadesh on the Orontes. **27—29**. Beth-shean (modern Beisan), Taanach (modern Tell Ta'annak), Dor (modern El Burj), Ibleam (modern Tell Bel'ame), and Megiddo (modern Tell Mutesellim) were not wholly conquered until the time of the monarchy (cf 1 (3) Kgs 9:15—22). **30—33**. The three tribes of Galilee were particularly negligent and unsuccessful in extirpating the Canaanites.

34—35. The Amorites after dispossessing Dan were them- **25**. selves in course of time subjected to forced labour by the house of Joseph. Harheres most probably indicates Beth-shemesh, elsewhere associated with Aijalon and Shaalbim. **36**. Amorites should be read 'Edomites' (cf LXX). Since the ascent of Akrabbim was at the E end of the boundary between Israel and Edom (Jos 15:1—3) the Rock (Sela) indicates the W end at or near Kadesh. **2:1a**. The Angel of Yahweh is Yahweh himself, who reminds Israel of his past benefits, promise, and threat. The ascent is made from the E border at Gilgal. In 5:4 Yahweh comes from the S border, out of Edom. **5**. Bochim, lit *Weepers*, is a place near Bethel, probably identical with the terebinth of weeping (Gn 35:8). The sacrifice offered where Yahweh appeared attests repentance.

2:6—3:6 Introduction to the History of the e Judges—**2:6—9**. Jg is first attached to Jos by repeating the contents of Jos 24:28—31. **10—19**. Then the religious interpretation of the subsequent narratives is indicated. Israel's history appears as recurring cycles of sin, punishment, repentance, and deliverance. **20—3:6**. The domestic enemies are finally discussed: who they were, why they were left in the land, and how they led Israel astray. **2:13**. 'Baals' is found in the pl. to include all the various Baals, e.g. Baal-berith (8:33), Baal-peor (Num 25:3), Baal-zephon (Num 33:7), etc. Ashtaroth indicates the consort of Baal and goddess of fertility or in the pl. may represent all the goddesses. **20—23**. To punish violations of the covenant and to test Israel's fidelity to Yahweh the Canaanites were not all extirpated. The trial motive and its result are indicated **3:4—6**. Benevolent motives are also attributed to Yahweh, that future generations of Israelites might be trained to fight (**3:2**) and that the land might not be injured by depopulation (Ex 23:29; Dt 7:22). Since God's justice and goodness work together harmoniously there is no difficulty in this multiplicity of motives. **3:3**. Mt Baal-Hermon indicates the S end of the Lebanese chain.

3:7—1 Othniel—As the oppressions are local and the **f** deliverer is usually one of the oppressed, it is improbable that Othniel, lord of Debir in S Judah, would be chosen to repel invaders from Aram Naharaim, Aram of the two rivers (Euphrates and Khabur), in N Mesopotamia. The second part of the oppressor's name 'rishathaim', *of double wickedness*, is probably a Heb. qualification of the oppressor. Cushan has an Arabic termination and appears (Hb 3:7) in parallelism with Midian as an Arab tribe. There is question therefore of an Arab or Edomite invasion of S Judah. The original 'Edom' was read 'Aram'—a common error. As there were several Arams, Naharaim was inserted in 8, but not in 10, notwithstanding its remoteness from Palestine. The efforts of Jack and Haensler to introduce as the oppressor Tushratta (c. 1390—1360 B.C.), king of Mitanni (geographically identical with Aram Naharaim), fail to identify the names and antedate the event by two centuries.

12—30 Ehud—This judge, a Benjaminite, delivered his **g** people from the Moabites and their allies, Ammon and Amalek. He seized the opportunity offered by the payment of tribute to slay Eglon, king of Moab, and raise the standard of revolt in Benjamin and Ephraim. **13b**. The city of palms is Jericho. **15**. Ehud was left-handed, lit disabled in his right hand. The tribute, paid in kind, required many bearers. **16**. The sword of Ehud was a double-edged poniard with a short hilt so that its whole length was a short cubit (from elbow to knuckles). It was worn on the right thigh for a movement of the left hand towards the right would not arouse suspicion. **19**. Ehud accompanied the departing bearers as far as *the sculptured*

56g *stones near Gilgal*. The reference is obscure. Thence he returned and announced a secret message for the king who dismissed his attendants with the word *silence* and received Ehud, sitting alone in the *cool roof chamber*. This was built on the flat roof of the house and had several windows to allow the free passage of air. When Ehud declared that the message was from God, the king rose out of reverence and Ehud drew forth his poniard and thrust it into him. **23**. The action is easy to visualize. Once Ehud had murdered the king, he locked the door from the inside, slipped out by a window, descended by the usual outside stairway, and made good his escape. **28**. The fords of the Jordan were seized to prevent escape of fugitives and arrival of reinforcements. Eglon's palace was E of the Jordan.

h **31 Shamgar son of Anath**—This hero in the present text bears the name of an oppressor of Israel through a misunderstanding of 5:6. The v moreover is a late insertion, since 4:1 closely attaches the Deborah to the Ehud narrative. Anath, a goddess, appears also as a man's name.

57a **4:1–24 Deborah and Barak**—The two accounts of the deliverance from Canaanite oppression differ in one essential particular, the name of the oppressor. He is Shamgar son of Anath in the contemporary poem (ch 5) but Jabin king of Canaan reigning at Hasor in the later prose narrative (ch 4). Jabin was slain and his capital Hasor burnt by Joshua (Jos 11). The city, moreover, if rightly identified with Tell el-Qeda, was uninhabited in the Judges' period. It follows that some of the contents of Jos 11 have been interpolated into Jg 4. There is one indication that the interpolation was made after the narrative was written, namely the description of Jabin as king of Canaan, since all scriptural writers agree with profane records in assigning not one but many kings to Canaan. A foreigner like Shamgar might vaunt this title but not the king of a Canaanite city. We exclude therefore from ch 4 Jabin and Hasor as interpolations.

b **1–3**. Sisera, general of Shamgar, resided at Harosheth of the Gentiles at the W extremity of the plain of Esdraelon, and possessing 900 iron chariots oppressed Israel. **4–7**. Deborah, prophetess and judge, residing in Mt Ephraim, orders Barak, a Naphtalite, to assemble an army of 10,000 men on Mt Tabor ready to meet Sisera's army at the river Kishon. **8–11**. Barak obeys after stipulating that Deborah must accompany him. **12–13**. Sisera hearing of the revolt leads his army to the Kishon in the centre of Esdraelon. **14–16**. Barak, ordered by God through Deborah, descends to meet him in the plain, but Yahweh throws the enemy into confusion and gains a complete victory. **17–21**. Sisera in his flight enters the tent of Jael, wife of Heber the Kenite, who slays him as he sleeps by hammering a tent-peg into his brain. **22**. Barak views the dead Sisera. **23–24**. Israel gradually overpowers the oppressor.

c **2**. For 'Jabin' read *Shamgar* and omit 'who reigned in Hasor'. Harosheth is identified with Tell 'Amor, occupying a strategic position at the entrance to the plain of Esdraelon, near the village of Haritiye and inhabited in the early Iron Age. **4**. Deborah was a prophetess in the strict sense of the term, as her communications to Barak show, and also a judge as distributor of justice to the people. The palm-tree or possibly pillar (cf Jer 10:5) of Deborah between Bethel and Ramah has no connection with the terebinth of weeping (Gn 35:8), but merely indicates the site of her tribunal. Her residence in Mt Ephraim makes Barak's stipulation intelligible and explains the participation of Ephraim and Benjamin in the liberation of the N tribes. Barak recalls the Punic Barca 'lightning'. **6**. Kedesh in Naphtali, modern Tell

Qades, is about 5 m. NW of Lake Huleh. **7**. Omit the **257c** gloss 'general of Jabin's army'. LXX has an addition probably authentic after **8**. *For I know not on what day Yahweh will give me success*. **10**. Vg omits 'to Kedesh' after 'Naphtali'. MT supposes a muster at Kedesh in Naphtali, but does not mention the subsequent march to Tabor. Some hold that Kedesh in Issachar between Megiddo and Taanach, mentioned in **11**, is meant, but that locality was most unsuitable for a muster of the forces of Naphtali and Zebulum confined to the highlands by the iron chariots of the Canaanites. **11**. Heber is mentioned before the battle to explain the presence of Jael. The terebinth in Za-anannim was in the SW of Naphtali (Jos 19:33), and therefore near Tabor which is 10 m. NE of Kedesh in Issachar, here indicated, but 30 m. S of Kedesh in Naphtali. The battle was fought on the bank of the Kishon between Megiddo and Taanach (5:19). Barak's descent into the plain to meet the chariots on their own ground was humanly unwise but ordered by God to show that he alone could turn defeat into victory. Omit **17b** owing to the mention of Jabin and the fact that **d** Sisera did not enter the tent spontaneously but by invitation (**18**). **20**. The giving of curdled milk instead of water was probably a Bedouin ruse perhaps to induce sleep. While Sisera sleeps Jael takes a tent-peg and a mallet and drives the peg into his brain. Many prefer LXX reading *and he moved convulsively between her knees, gave up the ghost, and died* to our present version 'as he was lying fast asleep from weariness'. **23–24**. Omit Jabin.

5 The Triumph-Song—In addition to the prose account **e** (ch 1), Jg provides us also with a far older poetic rendering of the same event. This poem, one of our oldest pieces of Heb. verse, was composed about 1125 B.C. The depth of feeling that penetrates it throughout marks it as the work of one who participated in the fray. Though frequently called the Song of Deborah, it is clear from references such as those in 7 and 12 that it is rather about her than by her. The sequence of thought seems to be: Introduction (**1–2**), Coming of Yahweh to help his people (**3–5**), Oppression of Israel before the rising (**6–8**), Invitation to all to praise Yahweh (**9–12**), Praise of the patriotic tribes (**13–15a**), Reproach of the recreant tribes (**15b–18**), Battle (**19–21**), Flight (**22–23**), Exploit of Jael (**24–27**), Anxiety and hopes of Sisera's mother (**28–30**), Conclusion (**31a**).

1–2 Introduction—A more literal version of **2a** would **f** be 'When the hair was worn loose in Israel', an allusion either to a vow or to the practice, still in vogue among the Bedouins today, of removing the caffiyeh when entering combat.

3–5 Strophe 1—The rendering 'quaked' is supported **g** by LXX. Natural phenomena are frequent accompaniments of a theophany. In early Israel Yahweh is often linked with Sinai. The storm then moves from the S. **6–9**. The Shamgar of **6** is not to be confused with the Shamgar of 3:31. The mention of Jael in the same v should be considered a gloss. She came to fame as a result of the incident later described in this ch. **8a** provides an enigma; no satisfactory emendation or solution has as yet been proposed. **8b** alludes to the iron monopoly that excluded Israel. **10–11**. All are to join in praise and thanks to Yahweh, the rich who ride and the poor who walk. **12–18**. In poetic fashion Deborah and Barak are summoned to meet the enemy. Next, praise is meted out to Ephraim, Benjamin, Machir (Manasseh), Zebulun, Issachar, and Naphtali for their ready response, but bitter taunts to Reuben, Gilead, Dan, and Asher. 'The heights of the field' (**18**) may be simply figurative language for the fiercest

257g part of the fray, or it may suggest that the battle eventually moved from the plain to the nearby slopes. **19—21**. 'They got no spoils of silver' (**19**) indicates that in spite of their efforts the Canaanite coalition was to return empty-**h** handed. The fighting of the stars is poetic. All nature sides with Yahweh. **23**. Meroz is modern Khirbet Marus. **24—27**. Omit the prosaic gloss 'the wife of Heber the Kenite' after 'Jael' (MT 24). Some commentators object that Sisera is lying down in 4:21 but standing here when he receives the death-blow. In both cases however a wooden tent-peg is driven through his temples with a wooden hammer which could only be done as he lay prostrate. Nor could he fall between her feet if he received the blow standing. The description supposes not an erect posture but a convulsive movement before the final collapse. Jael's weapons are naturally those of a tent-dweller. She is praised like Rahab for siding with Yahweh and his people. Her **ruse de guerre** would be considered legitimate by herself and her primitive contemporaries and is not to be judged by modern standards of morality. **28—31**. The scene shifts to the Canaanite palace, and from the vigorous action of Jael the author turns to the solicitude of Sisera's mother as she awaits her warrior son. The Mesha inscription confirms the version 'maiden' (**30**).

258a **6:1—8:35 Gideon—6:1—10**. The Israelites again abandon Yahweh and are oppressed by the Midianites. Gideon is called by God to deliver them. He destroys the altar of Baal at Ophrah, erects an altar to Yahweh in its stead and receives a new name Jerubbaal 'Baal-fighter'. With a few men he wins a great victory, but refused the kingship. After his death Israel again wor-**b** ships false gods. The narrative is clear and consistent, but evidently derived from more than one ancient source. This appears especially in the double account of the erection of the altar. In the second account the immediate occasion is narrated to illustrate the teaching that conversion must precede deliverance. The fact only is related in the first account (**6:24**). The vague word 'there' may have indicated in the source the place where Yahweh appeared, but the subsequent narrator must have referred it to 'at Ophrah' in the second part of the v.

c 6:1—10 The Oppression—The cycle of sin and its consequent punishment is once again under way. This time the Israelites are pictured as established agricultural inhabitants of the land, beset by the incursions of the marauding Midianites. According to Gn 25:2ff Midian had Abraham as his father, but was sent eastward lest he interfere with the inheritance of Isaac. Elsewhere (8:24 and Gn 37:25—28) the Midianites are associated with Ishmael. **3** emphasizes the frequency of the Midianite raids. Mention of Gaza (**4**) indicates the wide scope of the attacks. On their prayer to God for help (**6**), a prophet (**8**) rises to challenge the people with their idolatrous practices.

d 11—24 Call of Gideon—Gideon was a Manassite of the clan of Abiezer (cf Jos 17:2), dwelling in Ophrah, et-Taiyibe, 5 m. SE of Endor. He is threshing corn, not with oxen on a threshing-floor, but 'in the wine-press, to hide it from the Midianites', when the angel of Yahweh appears to him under a terebinth and gives him his mission. He pleads incapacity, but is promised aid and success. The 'I will be with you' (**16**) is reminiscent of the help assured to Moses on his mission (Ex 3:12), and became a salient theme for divine help throughout the OT, culminating in the final use of the formula for the mission of the Apostles in Mt (**28:20**). When Gideon offers his guest a kid and unleavened cakes, the latter converts the loaves and flesh into a holocaust and disappears. Gideon now realizes who his visitor is and fears death. He is reassured by Yahweh, **25** invisibly present. He erects there an altar called 'the Lord is peace'.

25—32 He contends with Baal—'That night', the **e** night after the theophany, Gideon receives the order: 'Take your father's bull . . . and pull down the altar of Baal.' **26**. The altar to Yahweh is built 'on the top of the stronghold'. Joash refuses to surrender his son to his idolatrous townsmen, saying: 'Will you contend for Baal? Or will you defend his cause? . . . If he is a god, let him contend for himself, because his altar has been torn down. Gideon's new name Jerubbaal means therefore 'let Baal contend' and thus implicitly designates him as a Baal-fighter.

33—7:15 He prepares to Attack the Midianites—On **f** the occasion of a Midianite raid into the plain of Esdraelon, 'the spirit of the Lord took possession of Gideon' who assembled a large army and received assurance of victory by a double sign. The threshing-floor, usually on a flat, rocky hill-top, would not absorb the dew like the fleece, so that the first sign is inconclusive and consequently a second is asked and granted. Gideon now pitches his camp at the foot of Mt Gilboa, having the fountain of Harod—today known as 'Ain Tuba'un—between his forces and the Midianite camp in the valley, 'by the hill Moreh', modern Jebel Dahi. His forces, however, are too numerous for a God-given victory to be manifested by the inadequacy of the natural means used. The departure of the timorous reduces the number from 32,000 to 10,000 men. The numbers are surprisingly large and represent typical Semitic exaggeration. A further reduction of the army to 300 men is effected by rejecting those who bend the knees in drinking and choosing those who drink like a dog, conveying the water with the hand to the mouth. Various explanations have been offered for this principle of selection. Some authors see in the lapping technique a greater sense of alertness and watchfulness, and for this reason they were chosen. Others, on the contrary, see in this technique a far less effective means of absorbing water. In this case then it would be a further instance of God's choice of unlikely instruments to emphasize the divine character of the coming deliverance. **7:11**. By order of God Gideon reconnoitres the enemy camp with Purah his servant where he hears the Midianite's dream, a presage of victory.

7:16—21 The Battle—Gideon divides his forces into **259a** three bands to assail the camp at three different points and make the enemy believe that they are surrounded. The Israelites had pitchers containing torches in their left hand and trumpets in their right. **19**. As the early Hebrews divided the night into three watches, the attack took place about 10 p.m. It was only later that the Jews borrowed the Roman usage of four watches (Mt 14:25). The difficulty of carrying simultaneously trumpets, torches, and pitchers is imaginary. By passing the handle of the torch through a hole in the bottom of the pitcher both could be carried in one hand. The trumpets could be inserted in bandoliers.

22—8:21 The Pursuit—Of the places mentioned in **22 b** Beth-shittah lies in the valley of the Jordan, E of the river, perhaps at Tell-Slihal. Zererah, modern Tell es-Sa'idiyeh, is also E of the Jordan, about 10 m. N of the mouth of the Jabbok. Abel-meholah, modern Tell Abou Sifri, lies 12 m. S of Beisan, and Tabbath, modern Ras Abou Tabat, is E of the Jordan, about half-way between Jabesh-gilead and Succoth. The flight of the Midianites was then directed towards Transjordan. Control of the fords of the Jordan was essential at this juncture. Beth-barah (**24**), probably modern Tell Far'a,

9b S of Beisan, was occupied by the men of Ephraim with effective results. The fords near Beisan would have been held by the neighbouring Naphtalites, also summoned to join in the pursuit. With a soft answer (**8:2**) Gideon assuages the hurt pride of the Ephraimites. 'The gleanings of Ephraim'—allusion to their successes at the **c** ford of Beth-barah—were, he states, more fruitful than the vintage of Abiezer, the number slain by Gideon's own force. Succoth,—modern Tell Deir 'Alla'. That fellow-Israelites should refuse food to the famished warriors of Yahweh was a grievous crime. The punishment threatened and later inflicted was to tear the flesh from the bones as the chaff is torn from the grain in threshing. The names of the Midianite kings (**5**) Zebah and Zalmunna are obviously derisive changes of their real names, for Zebah means *sacrifice*, i.e. in this instance a victim of sacrifice, and Zalmunna means *a shortened* **d** *shadow*. **8.** Penuel, modern Tulul ed-Dahab, is about 5 m. E of Succoth on the Jabbok. **10.** Karkor, a small plain S of Succoth. The crescents (**21**) were probably worn as amulets (Is 3:20).

e 8:22—35 Subsequent History of Gideon—Having already erected by divine order a Yahweh-altar at Ophrah, Gideon now determines to establish there also a Yahweh-oracle, and uses for the purpose the golden earlets of the Midianites, his share of the spoils. The reasons alleged for interpreting the ephod as an idol are well refuted by Burney. It may be added that establishment of idol worship would be inconsistent with peace in the land (**28**) and fidelity to Yahweh (**33**) during Gideon's lifetime. These texts also imply that the institution of the Yahweh-oracle was not disapproved by the original writer. It follows that **27b** is a later addition since 'to play in harlot' or infidelity to Yahweh, the true spouse of Israel, by worshipping other gods or using foreign religious rites, cannot be reconciled with the fidelity implied in **33**. Ephods like altars outside the sanctuary would be tolerated originally, but later condemned as a Canaanite cult incompatible with Yahweh worship. The ingratitude of the people to the house of Gideon was shown in their toleration of the slaughter of his seventy sons by Abimelech.

260a 9:1—57 Abimelech—Gideon refused the rulership offered to him and his descendants after his victory, as being a usurpation of the rule of Yahweh (8:23, cf 1 Sm 8:7). Abimelech, his son, abandoned Yahweh for Baal and secured kingship for himself through his kinsmen in Shechem, then inhabited by a mixed population of Israelites and Canaanites. He was the offspring of a union between Gideon and a Shechemite, whose nationality, Israelite or Canaanite, is not indicated. The female partner in this union lived with her own people, not in her husband's house, and the children were regarded as hers. Abimelech was therefore supported by the Shechemites **b** against the Abiezrite sons of Gideon. Shechem, the modern Balata, about a mile E of Nablus, had very great importance in ancient Palestine owing to its central position and command of all the trade routes. Recent excavations on the site have clarified the references to it in ch 9. There was a lower city on the E side, and an upper on the W, each with its own gate. The upper city was artificially elevated above the plain and numbered among its edifices the palace of the ruler and the temple of Baal-berith. It is twice called Beth-millo (**6** and **20**). The Millo at Jerusalem, lit *filling*, was an earthwork strengthening a weak point in the fortifications, and had a *bêt* fort or tower (2 (4) Kg 12:20). The corresponding Assyrian *mulu* designates similarly a raised terrace on **c** which a tower or fort was built. The lower city was first

captured and those in the upper, informed by fugitives, **260c** took refuge in the fortified temple. Baal-berith, Baal of the Alliance, also called El Berith, God of the Alliance (9:46), was the principal god of the Canaanites of Shechem. The Canaanite sanctuary on the side of Mt Gerizim near Schechem cannot be the temple of El Berith in the tower of Shechem, since it was destroyed by fire at the close of the Middle Bronze Age.

9:4. A temple had always a treasury and was some- **d** times the repository of public treasure. Seventy silver shekels sufficed for the hiring of *worthless and reckless fellows*. **5.** 'Upon one stone' has no religious significance, but indicates the slayer's ruthlessness. The parable of Jotham contrasts Gideon and his sons who have worked for the common good with the selfish adventurer Abimelech and indicates the evil results to be expected from the foolish choice of the Shechemites. **14.** 'The bramble' is a low and straggling bush. **15.** The invitation to its shelter shows the absurdity of the choice and the fire the misfortunes which will result from it. **16—20.** The application of the parable is **e** indicated. The fundamental lack of good faith of the Shechemites in their dealings with Gideon and his house will appear also in their dealings with Abimelech and result in the ruin of both parties. Beer (**21**), the city to which Jotham fled, is modern El-Bire, N of Beisan and E of Tabor. **22.** Israel is a stereotyped expression. Abimelech ruled over a part of Israel. **23.** 'And God sent an evil spirit between Abimelech and the men of Shechem'; the evil acts of men are often attributed to God, because, though forbidden by him, they are part of the divine plan. **25.** The ambushers sought **f** to rob caravans which Abimelech owned or taxed. **28b.** The appeal of Gaal, a newcomer, is to the Canaanites of Shechem against the half-breed Abimelech. **31.** Arumah, modern Khirbet el-'Orma, 9 m. SE of Shechem. **37a.** 'Centre, lit navel, indicates the central point of the Palestinian mountain range. **44.** The sowing of salt, also recorded in Assyrian inscriptions, was a symbolical act indicating a barren region. Here as frequently the account of one event is completed before that of a second is begun without regard to chronological sequence. **50.** Thebez is probably the modern Tubas, 10 m. NE of Shechem. **53.** The upper, revolving stone of the handmill is indicated. It appears from **55** that Abimelech was supported by Israelites. The sacred writer concludes that Abimelech and the Shechemites were justly punished for their sins.

10:1—5 Tola and Jair—**1.** Shamir has not been **g** identified. LXX has Samaria. Tola, like Deborah, was an Issacharite residing in Mt Ephraim. Jair was a Manassite, living in Gilead. This comprised the area bounded on the N by the Yarmuk, on the S by the Arnon, on the E by the desert, and on the W by the Jordan. **4.** Havvoth means tent-villages, and their conquest by Jair is related in Nm 32:41. **5.** Kamon is the modern Qamm, E of the Jordan, $2\frac{1}{2}$ m. N of Taiyibeh.

10:6—12:7 Jephthah—The Jephthah narrative con- **261a** tains a few later additions and may be composite, though apparent discrepancies in the text are easily explained. The sins, oppression and repentance of Israel are first narrated (**10:6—16**), then the early history of Jephthah (**10:17—11:11**), his negotiations with the Ammonite king (**11:12—28**), his war against Ammon and his vow (**11:29—40**), and lastly his fight with the Ephraimites (**12:1—7**).

10:6—16 Sin, Oppression and Repentance—In this **b** introd. to the narratives of Jephthah and Samson, the

261b gods of Aram (Syria), Sidon, and Moab are out of place and probably a later addition. According to **8** the oppression was limited to the Transjordan area, but the following v indicates the tribes to the W of the river as well. **12.** For 'Maonites' LXX reads Midianites. The Sidonian oppression is probable though not recorded.

c 10:17–11:11 Early History of Jephthah—The Mizpah of Jephthah (**17**) is most probably the Khirbet Jal'ud of today, S of the Jabbok on the W border of Ammon. **11:3.** Tob, Dubu—now et-Taiyibeh NE of Gilead.

d 11:12–28 Negotiations with the Ammonite King—The territory in dispute was that between the Arnon and the Jabbok. The Ammonite was directly interested probably only in the N part, but the argument used suggested a wider claim. **24.** This *argumentum ad hominem* does not imply that Jephthah put Yahweh on the same level as the Ammonite god as a merely national deity. He next argues that Balak, king of Moab, did not contest Israel's right even though the region between the Arnon and Heshbon was ancient Moabite territory, and concludes by asking why the Ammonite reclamation was so long delayed. The references to Moab in the dispute are quite natural and do not suggest a quarrel with the Moabites. The only difficulty is the mention of the Moabite god Chemosh (**24**) instead of the Ammonite Malik. This is probably due to an alteration of the text through a misinterpretation of Moloch as king. Heshbon (**26**) is probably modern Tell Hesban, 20 m. E of the Jordan opposite Jericho. Aroer (**26**) is 12 m. up the Arnon on the King's Highway.

e 29–40 Campaign and Vow of Jephthah—**31.** The terms used clearly indicate not an animal but a person, not a mere dedication but a sacrifice. **33.** The Ammonite Aroer is identified above (**26**). Minnith is 4 m. from Hesban, and Abel-keramim is 4 m. from modern Amman. **39.** After two months Jephthah fulfils his vow. 'She had never known a man'; lack of offspring made her death more tragic to the Israelites. Jephthah's religious earnestness and religious ignorance in making and fulfilling his vow are equally apparent. The narrator informs us that he was inspired in his war measures but relates the other events of his career, including his early lapses and his barbarous vow, quite objectively without dissimulation and without comment.

f 40. 'year by year'. It has been suggested that underlying the annual commemoration of this event there is an ancient nature festival of the Canaanites which has been transformed into a celebration of a heroic Israelite legend. Some critics refer to the rite of mourning for Tammuz the fertility god who died each year, cf Ezek. 8:14, and suggest that Jephthah's daughter has been substituted for Tammuz, and that the tears shed for him have been transferred to her. It is certainly true that there are several seasonal laments in pagan mythology and ritual and it cannot be entirely excluded that details of some more ancient rite have been introduced into the ceremony for Jephthah's daughter. It is however unlikely that there has been any substitution of the one subject for the other. Can it really be supposed that the mourning for a god would be transferred to a virgin in Israel? cf Médebielle, DBS, 3, 11. Still less could one envisage the mere substitution of one myth for the other. It seems more reasonable to suppose that there is a historical basis for the event. While therefore the annual recurrence of the festival suggests links with some unidentified nature ceremonial we must regard its close association with the Tammuz cult as unproved.

g 12:1–7 Jephthah and the Ephraimites—The haughty Ephraimites, again (cf 8:1–3) offended at a **26** victory won without their intervention, 'were called to arms, and they crossed to Zaphon'. Zaphon associated with Succoth is Tell Sa'idiyyeh, guarding a Jordan ford near the mouth of W Kefranjeh. Jephthah's reasonable reply to their challenge does not avert a conflict in which Ephraim is defeated. **6.** Shibboleth means *ear of corn* or *stream*. A scribe has exaggerated the number of Ephraimites slain. In World War I Turks were similarly detected by Arabs at the crossing of the Jordan through their incorrect pronunciation of the emphatic s in basal.

8–15 Ibzan, Elon, and Abdon—These are the last minor judges. There was a Bethlehem in Judah and in Zebulun. The former is more probably intended as better known and elsewhere (19:1) explicitly indicated. **13.** Pirathon is the modern Far'ata, six miles WSW of Shechem.

13:1–16:31 Samson—Samson is portrayed as a **262** popular hero, dedicated to the service of Yahweh from his mother's womb and charged with the mission of beginning to deliver Israel from the oppression of the Philistines. As a Nazirite and a warrior he may never shear his locks since his dedication and his warfare are lifelong. Victory over the Philistines was reserved to David. Samson has the three characteristics of the popular hero, bravery, weakness towards women, and mother-wit. His superhuman strength, conditioned by the observance of the essential obligation of his state, is repeatedly attributed to the spirit of Yahweh, and Samson himself when he prays for its restoration recognizes it as a gift of Yahweh. His weakness towards women provides the opportunity for his exploits by bringing him into conflict with the Philistines. It has its place in God's designs but leads eventually to infidelity and betrayal. His mother-wit appears in his riddle and aphorisms and the humorous aspect of some of his exploits such as the destruction of the harvests of the Philistines. The historical and geographical situation is clear and consistent. The remnant of Dan, described as a clan, occupies the region of Zorah and Eshtaol as in 18:2ff, the scene of the events narrated, and is subject to the Philistines. The neighbouring men of Judah, as elsewhere attested (1:19), are under the same yoke and obediently hand over Samson to their oppressors.

The interpretation of the Samson narrative purely **b** as a solar myth is no longer proposed by critics. It is recognized that the Hebrew historians are not concerned with mythology as such but with sacred history and that Samson is manifestly represented as a popular hero. Our present text suggests the existence of a real person, in this case a Danite peasant of great physical strength, who carried on a private feud with the Philistines. This basic historical fact has accommodated itself to numerous folk-lore accretions, and has possibly accumulated some mythological detail in the course of ages.

13:1–25 Vocation and Birth of Samson—**2.** Zorah **c** modern Sar'ah, 14 m. W of Jerusalem.

The law of the Nazirite (Nm 6) involved abstention **d** from wine, strong drink, and unclean foods, allowing the hair to grow uncut, and avoidance of contact with the dead. Of these three requirements, it seems evident that Samson observed only the second. **15.** Manoah's offer of hospitality is courteously turned to a suggestion for a burnt offering. And in the midst of the sacrifice Manoah recognized the superhuman character of his guest. **25.** Eshtaol lies in the Shephelah area of Judah, two miles E of Zorah. Mahaneh-Dan, *the camp of Dan,*

262d was most probably a temporary site in the same general area. The spirit of Yahweh is manifested apparently by feats of strength.

e 14:1–20 Samson marries a Philistine, slays a Lion, and proposes a Riddle—1. Timnah, a village four miles SW of Zorah. **3.** The dissent of his parents, who object to Philistines as uncircumcised, obliges Samson to conduct the negotiations himself and to **f** contract a *sadika* marriage, the wife remaining with her people. 'His father and mother' (**5**) and 'his father' (**10**) seem to have been interpolated to regularize the marriage. If they had been with Samson they would have known that he slew the lion, and his father would have conducted the negotiations. **6.** Samson was inspired by Yahweh in his feat of strength, but not in his courtship. Returning to Timnah for the wedding, he interrupts his journey to take back the honey to his parents, which is surprising though the way was short. The carcass of the lion would dry up quickly in the hot climate, and the jackals would pick the bones clean. **11.** For 'when the people saw him' LXX reads 'and because they feared him', which provides a very different flavour to the episode. **18.** 'Before the sun went down' should probably be rendered 'before he (Samson) entered the bridal-chamber.' As Samson departs in anger, his bride is given to the best-man. The spirit of the Lord also inspires his feats in Ashkelon.

g 15:1–20 Samson burns the Harvests and slays Warriors—1. The husband usually brought a present **h** when visiting his *sadika*-wife. **3.** So sure is Samson of his future vengeance that he regards his obligation to avenge himself as already fulfilled. His words 'when I do them mischief' thus become intelligible. **4.** By foxes are probably meant jackals, which live in packs and are easily caught. **8.** 'And he smote them hip and thigh'; this is most probably a wrestling term, corresponding to the English cross-buttock, when a party, advancing his right leg and thigh, closes with his antagonist, and catching him with his right arm, or giving a round blow, throws him over his right hip upon his head. Etam is probably the rock, called 'Araq Isma'in, and containing a cave, over two miles ESE of Sarar. **15.** A 'fresh' jawbone would provide a suitable weapon; an old one would have been too brittle. **17.** 'Ramath-lehi' certainly means the height or hill of the jawbone. If the name existed before Samson's exploit, as is suggested by its mention in **9** and **14** (which may however be proleptical), it would be derived from the shape of the hill like Golgotha *skull*, or Luhith *little jawbone* (Is 15:5 and CIS Aram 196), and would be only **i** punningly associated with his weapon by Samson. In the alternative hypothesis the name would be derived from the weapon. **19a.** 'And God split open the hollow-place'; from this circular depression in the rock came the spring, not from the jawbone. It is named Spring of the Caller because Samson called to God who miraculously produced it. In a different context Caller would be interpreted Partridge, so named from the clear notes of its cry.

263a 16:1–31 Samson at Gaza and with Delilah: his b Capture and Death—1. Samson's passion leads him into an ambuscade. **2.** The watch was by day while the gate was open, the silence by night. The gate was of one piece when locked. Hebron is 38 m. from Gaza; hence it is much more reasonable to suppose some hill to the E of Gaza, in the direction of Hebron. **4.** The ancient name Sorek is preserved in Khirbet Suriq, 2½ m. from Zorah. Delilah was a Philistine, and her name means *amorous*, *flirt*, or *informer*. **5.** She was to discover wherein his great strength lay and inform

the five lords of the Philistines, who agreed to pay her **263b** 1100 silver shekels each. **7.** The first binding was 'with seven fresh bowstrings which have not been dried'. The Philistines lay in wait in another room. **11.** The second binding was with new ropes as in 15:13. **14b.** Samson on awaking 'pulled away the pin, the loom, and the web' to which his hair was attached. The pin was a flat piece of wood by which the web was pressed together. The mention of the hair marks an approach **c** to the secret, revealed at the next attempt. Delilah sees that no test is necessary and summons the lords of the Philistines. **20.** 'Shake myself' means free myself from my bonds. **21.** Grinding corn, the work of women, was an ignominious imposition. **24a** 'And when the people saw him' apparently refers to Samson, and thus **25** originally preceded **24**. The scene suggested is a banqueting-hall opening on to a courtyard.

17:1–18:31 The Sanctuary of Dan—With ch 17 **d** begins a series of appendices to the actual history of the Judges. First the establishment of an idolatrous sanctuary at Dan in NE Palestine is narrated. The facts are objectively recorded, but the sacred writer evidently disapproves of the erection by private authority of a new religious centre in Israel. The sordid origin of the sanctuary, the high-handed usurpation of the Danites, the idolatrous form of worship speak for themselves. The sanctuary is contrasted with the House of God in Shiloh and its origin is explained by the general lawlessness of the period. It contained a molten image of Yahweh and an ephod like that of Gideon. The image of molten work (cf the calf of molten work Ex 30:1) became a (graven) image and a molten (image) by the insertion of 'and'. In a second source the image is called 'teraphim'. This obscure word seems to designate an image (one substituted for the sleeping David, 1 Sm 19:13). It is associated with ephod in Hos 3:4 and with divination Ezek 21:26 (RSV 21:21). The multiplication of objects of cult in ch 18 is clearly due to interpolation, since it supposes the duplication of the Yahweh-image. The institution of the sanctuary of Micah on Mt Ephraim and his installation of a Levite priest are first related (ch 17), then the Danite discovery of a new home at Laish, their seizure of Micah's sanctuary on their journey thither, their conquest of Laish, re-named Dan, and their sanctuary and priest (ch 18).

Micah is an abbreviation of Micay^ehu 'who is like **e** Yahweh?' **2.** The curse enjoined on the robber brought prompt restitution. The mother had a molten image made from part of the silver, and set it up in the house of Micah. To this he added an ephod for a Yahweh oracle. **7.** The Levite of the clan of Judah must have been adopted into that tribe or placed under the protection of some patriarch. Micah's satisfaction in having a Levite for priest shows the antiquity of the levitical institution.

18:1. A territory was in fact assigned to the Danites, **f** bounded on the N by Ephraim, on the S by Judah, and on the E by Benjamin. The Amorites and the Philistines, however, restricted them to such a small portion of it that they sent out scouts to search for more likely quarters. **3.** The scouts 'recognized the voice of the young Levite', perhaps by the priestly intonation of his chanting, or perhaps because of an earlier acquaintance with him. **5.** While there the scouts avail themselves of the opportunity to have the Levite consult the Lord as to their mission, and they learn it will be favourable. **7.** Laish is probably Tell el-Qadi, 3 m. W of Baniyas, near the sources of the Jordan, and well-isolated from the coastal cities and the Aramaean states to the

F

263g E. **12.** Kiriath-jearim in Judah is the modern Abu-Ghosh, 8 m. from Jerusalem on the main road to the coast. **14–20. 24.** The *'elōhay* of MT should be rendered 'God', since it stands for the Yahweh-image, not a plurality of gods. **31.** The author points to the co-existence of the Danite shrine and that at Shiloh. The latter was destroyed by the Philistines (1 Sm 4), but the former remained in existence until late in the 8th cent.

264a 19–21 Origin, History, and Consequence of the War against Benjamin—The historicity of this narrative is wholly or partially denied by many critics. They argue that the united action of the tribes is out of harmony with the history of the period, and that the references to Jabesh-gilead, with which Saul had friendly relations, manifest the intention of the narrator to denigrate the tribe and friends of Saul. Exaggeration of numbers and adaptation of the narratives of the crime of the Sodomites and the capture of Ai are also urged as suggestive of fiction. It may be answered that the disunited activity of the tribes in the Judges' period is explained by the fact that the troubles were local. The crime at Gibeah was a religious matter of universal importance, and particular measures were taken to secure the co-operation of all. There is no trace of special animosity to Saul or Benjamin in the other historical books. The disaffection of Jabesh-gilead is paralleled by that of Meroz in Deborah's and Succoth and Penuel in Gideon's time. Exaggeration in numbers, no greater here than in 12:6, is not uncommon in the present text of the OT

b The stereotyped character of much historical narrative in the OT may account for similarities in recording distinct occurrences. The crimes of the Sodomites and the men of Gibeah are different. The failures of the early attacks on Ai and Gibeah are not similarly explained. Hosea on the other hand attests the outrage when he twice refers to 'the days of Gibeah' as the depth of depravity (Hos 9:9; 10:9). Recent excavations attest its punishment, the burning of the city in the period of the Judges. Saul attests its consequence when he calls Benjamin the least tribe of Israel (1 Sm 9:21); note how Gideon deprecating a similar honour does not belittle Manasseh (6:15). Would a post-exilic inventor attribute such depravity to the lack of a king or completely disregard the law of unity of sanctuary?

c 19:1–30 The Crime at Gibeah—**3.** The hospitality of the Bethlehemite is contrasted with the action of the men of Gibeah, whose crime, an abominable breach of the sacred law of hospitality, is thus foreshadowed. **12.** Gibeah, modern Tell el-Ful, lies 3 m. N of Jerusalem. It was partially excavated by Albright 1922–3. The original fortress was 'built toward the end of the 13th cent. B.C. and burned near the end of the twelfth' (Albright in AASOR 4 (1924) 8). It was subsequently rebuilt, and was fortified and prosperous as Saul's capital c. 1020 B.C. **13.** Ramah, today known as er-Ram, is 2m. further

d N. **22.** 'Base-fellows', lit sons of Belial. Belial may be understood as without profit in which case it should be translated 'worthless persons' or it may be interpreted as referring to Belial 'the abyss', in which case it would signify abysmally wicked persons. According to the present text the men of Gibeah are first Sodomites, later adulterers and murderers. The Levite accuses them **(20:5)** of intentional murder and adultery—not sodomy. This fact has led some to maintain that the mention

of sodomy here is an intrusion from Gn 19. Those who **264d** take this position hold that the men of Gibeah sought the Levite's concubine, and in this situation the old man offered his daughter instead. To save his host's virgin daughter, the Levite would then have turned his concubine over to the men. **30.** With the LXX insert: '*And he commanded the men whom he sent out saying, Thus shall you say to all the men of Israel. Has such a thing as this happened from the day when the children of Israel came up from the land of Egypt until today? Consider it, take counsel, and speak. And all who saw said: Never has a like thing happened or been seen since the Israelites came up from the land of Egypt until this day.*'

20:1–48 The War against Benjamin—**1.** Mizpah, **e** modern en-Nasbeh, lies 8 m. N of Jerusalem. Dan and Beersheba are approximately the limits of the territory occupied by the Israelites. **18.** Bethel is an hour's journey from Mizpah. As the ark was there **(27)**, the Israelites sought an answer from the Lord. The description of the battle is confused by the presence of two accounts and some textual corruptions, but the general sense is clear. The simulated retreat, the ambuscade, the fire-signal, and the simultaneous attack on front and rear in some way recall the capture of Ai (Jos 8). To draw the Benjaminites into the open country, the retreat was made along two highways, the first to Bethel being the northern road from Jerusalem to Shechem, the second not to Gibeah (MT) but more likely to Gibeon, branching off from this to the NW a half mile from Gibeah. The presence of caves assisted the secrecy of the attack. The fire-signal indicated the capture of the city to both parties. The Benjaminites fled to the desert, but only 600 of them reached Rimmon, modern Rammun, three miles E of Bethel. **48.** The execution of the herem, not explicitly commanded, on the cities, inhabitants, and beasts of Benjamin is described.

21:1–24 The Survival of Benjamin—**5.** The reference to the second oath perhaps originally belonged to **8**, where **5a** reappears more appropriately. Jabesh-gilead is known today as Deir Halawa, and is located about 6 m. W of the Jordan, SE of Beisan. **11b.** '*But the virgins you shall save alive. And they did so*' (LXX, not in MT) is required by the context. **19.** 'the yearly feast of the Lord at Shiloh'. Evidently a well known one. What was it? During the period of Judges Shiloh had eclipsed Gilgal and it became the central sanctuary of the tribal federation, cf de Vaux, AI 304. The feast referred to may well be the one mentioned in 1 Sm 1:3, but beyond that there is very little that one can say for certain. One may surmise however that it was the Harvest Festival which took place each autumn. This was the feast held when all the harvests had been reaped, all the fruits of the earth gathered, and the olives and grapes pressed. Heavy drinking of the new wine was not unknown, de Vaux, op cit 496. Naturally it was an occasion for popular rejoicing. In later times it was the moment for young men to choose their brides. In Dt. 16:13–15 the feast is called the Feast of Tents or Huts and is one of the three great national feasts; the other two of course being Passover and Pentecost or 'Weeks'. It may be that the original harvest feast was at a later date given a historical framework, that of the Exodus, and the whole dedicated to a commemoration of the wanderings in the wilderness. **22.** The plea is that the middle course adopted avoids the two extremes of seizure in battle which causes a blood feud and voluntary concession which would violate an oath.

RUTH

BY J. McSHANE

265a Bibliography—C. Lattey WV, 1935; P. Joüon, 1953; J. H. Myers, *The linguistic and literary form of the book of Ruth*, 1955; L. P. Smith, IB, 1955; G. Gerleman, BKAT, 1960; W. Rudolph, KAT, 1962; A. S. Herbert PC (2) 1962. J. Gray, CBi², 1967. *Articles*: R. E. Robertson, *The plot of the book of Ruth*, BJRL 32 (1950), 207—288; H. H. Rowley, *The Servant of the Lord and other Essays*, 1952, 161—168; G. S. Glanzman, *The origin and date of the book of Ruth*, CBQ 21 (1959), 201—207; O. Loretz, *The theme of the Ruth story*, CBQ 22 (1960), 391—399.

b Place in the Bible—In Gr. and Latin bibles, Ruth is inserted between Jg and Sm: this is doubtless due to the fact that the story is set in the period of the Judges (Ru 1:1) and provides a natural lead-in to Sm and Kgs through the genealogy of David which forms its conclusion. In the Heb. bible, Ruth is placed among the 'writings'; it is one of the five Megilloth for festal occasions, Ruth being read on the feast of Pentecost.

c Subject matter—After the death in Moab of Elimelech her husband and her two married sons, Mahlon and Chilion, (who had both married Moabite women), Naomi returns to her native Bethlehem accompanied by Ruth, one of her widowed daughters-in-law. Ruth works as a gleaner in the field of Boaz a wealthy landowner, who proves to be a kinsman of Elimelech. Boaz subsequently marries Ruth after a nearer kinsman has renounced his claim. Obed the child born of this union is the father of Jesse, himself the father of king David.

d Date of composition—Opinion is sharply divided on this question. BJ prefers a pre-exilic date as does Rudolph who favours the later period of the monarchy, but a post-exilic date seems to have the majority verdict today. Myers considers that there was an original poem orally transmitted for centuries before being rewritten in prose form in the exilic or post-exilic period, while Glanzman postulates several stages of composition.

e Purpose and literary character—The theme of the story is clear, viz the extraordinary survival of the family of Elimelech through the marriage of Ruth and Boaz, grandparents of David. There seems no reason to deny that the shorter genealogy (4:17) belonged to the original work. Ru is edifying history, an historical novel, extolling the virtue of piety which God rewards even when practised by a stranger. 'The book of Ruth, an account permeated with the most popular and the purest Israelite ideal, is entirely built up on the theme of *hesed*' (J. Guillet, *Themes of the Bible*, 38). There may also be a polemic purpose as held by those who favour a late date of composition, Ru being written as a corrective. Like Jon, Ru is 'universalist' in its outlook: just as God is interested in the salvation of the hated Assyrians, so also Ru makes the point that non-Jews are included in God's plan. Even David's birth can be traced to a 'mixed marriage'! Despite its brevity Ru is a literary gem much admired by Goethe. It is a charming story with its colourful scenes and minimal narrative providing the **265e** setting for the 'script' or dialogue.

The 'go'el' or redeemer—a term used for a kinsman, **f** the next-of-kin who was the protector of the clan or family. His obligations included blood vengeance, redemption from slavery, and the purchase of property in danger of being sold outside the family. The law is stated in Lv 25:25ff while Jer 32:6f provides us with a concrete example of the law in operation. (In Is 40—46 God is frequently referred to as the go'el of Israel). In Ru there is the added complication of a levirate type of marriage. The go'el is faced with a two-fold obligation, one part of which he is prepared to fulfil by buying back the property of Naomi to prevent its alienation. But he is unwilling to marry Ruth to provide a child for Naomi's widowed daughter-in-law. The child born of such a union would inherit the property redeemed by the go'el. Accordingly the go'el renounces his title and Boaz who is the next-of-kin-but-one steps in to purchase the land and marry Ruth. Rowley suggests that Boaz may have been childless in which case there was no question of his own children's inheritance being affected. The nearer kinsman on the other hand may have had children already: had he married Ruth, the property bought would then belong to the child of that union—as being heir to Mahlon, the deceased husband of Ruth. Dt 25:5—10 makes it clear that the law of levirate is of strict obligation and that failure to comply involves disgrace. 'Then his brother's wife shall go up to him in the presence of the elders and pull off his sandal off his foot and spit in his face'. But it must be remembered that the law of levirate in Dt is restricted to the case of a brother-in-law. Ru refers to an earlier period, perhaps to the time when the obligation belonged to the clan. Neither the next-of-kin nor Boaz was a brother-in-law; such is excluded by the story. Moreover in the earlier period a refusal to fulfil the law implied no stigma: the ceremonial removal of the sandal in Ru is much milder than in Dt, involving no disgrace but merely the renunciation of one's rights or duties.

Nm 27:9—11 seems to exclude widows from inherit- **g** ance. Yet Naomi puts up for sale the parcel of land which belonged to Elimelech. Her title to the land is difficult to explain, though the case is rather exceptional since both her sons are also dead. A further development takes place in the 2nd cent. B.C. Judith is said to own a considerable amount of property (Jdt 8:7).

The marriage of Mahlon and Chilion to Moabite women need not surprise us: Esau, Joseph and Moses were married to foreign women: David, Solomon and Ahab had foreign wives or concubines. Such marriages were subsequently forbidden by law (Ex 34:15—16; Dt 7:3—4). After the exile Ezra and Nehemiah were still attempting to enforce this law; cf Mal, § 583 c.

Does the book of Ruth represent Boaz as purchasing **h** his wife? Herbert (PC 2) answers in the affirmative: de Vaux, AI 27 disagrees—'This obligation to pay a

265h sum of money or its equivalent, to the girl's family obviously gives the Israelite marriage the outward appearance of a purchase. But the *mohar* seems to be not so much the price paid for the woman as a compensation given to the family, and, in spite of the apparent resemblance, in law this is a different consideration'.

266a 1:1—22 Emigration to Moab and Return—The story is 'set in the period of the Judges. A well-to-do family is driven from Bethlehem ('the house of bread') to seek refuge in Moab which lies to the E of the Dead Sea. The names are probably fictitious, chosen on account of their symbolism. Elimelech means 'God is king', Naomi 'My amiable one': Mahlon and Chilion suggest 'weakness' and 'consumption' respectively. The derivation of Orpah is difficult (BJ proposes 'the one who turns her back' cf 1:4): Ruth means 'friendship'. The marriage of Mahlon and Chilion to Moabite women (4) is noted without disapproval. Elimelech dies and within the space of ten years both Mahlon and Chilion are dead, leaving Naomi with two Moabite daughters-in-law who are childless widows. **6.** Naomi decides to return home advising the women to return each to her 'mother's house' (8)— the women's quarters allotted to their respective mothers in their paternal homes. Her motive becomes clear: she wishes God to bless these Moabites by providing partners for them in reward for their loyalty to their deceased husbands and to Naomi herself. In a further effort to dissuade them she speaks of a levirate marriage as the only possible way in which they could find a second

b Israelite husband (11—13). The possibility of Naomi providing further sons is presented as a forlorn hope. 14*b* is concise and pregnant with meaning 'Orpah kissed her mother-in-law, but Ruth clung to her' (RSV and CV against BJ, which adds with the Gr. that Orpah returned to her people). Naomi persuades Orpah to remain behind and worship Chemosh the god of Moab (15). **16, 17.** Ruth speaks to us as a model of heroic loyalty and piety; she confirms her declaration with an oath. **18—22.** Ruth accompanies Naomi on her return to Bethlehem. **20*a*.** 'Can this be Naomi?' (CV). '(This question) speaks paragraphs. It is doubtful if any scene in Ruth or elsewhere is superior in force, vitality, pathos. All changes which time and sorrow had wrought are expressed in this three-word explanation' (Jacob M. Myers, *The linguistic and literary form* ..., 20). **20.** Naomi ('amiable') wishes to be called 'Mara' ('bitter') to express her change of fortune; she had left Bethlehem in prosperity and now she returns a widow and childless. **22.** Naomi and Ruth arrive at the beginning of the barley harvest in April. We note how this detail prepares us for the events which follow.

c 2:1—23 Ruth in the field of Boaz—1. Straightaway we are introduced to Boaz a kinsman of Elimelech and a man of substance. **2.** Ruth exercises the right of the poor to glean at harvest time (Lv 19:9; 23:22; Dt 24:19—22) with the owner's consent.

4—17 The kindness of Boaz—He is a man of character, of religious conviction, a just employer, as we learn from the exchange of greetings. **7*c*.** The reply of the overseer is uncertain. RSV has 'she has continued from early morning until now, without resting even for a moment'. Similarly CV. BJ reads 'she has been on her feet etc'. **8.** Boaz is a man of advanced years (cf also 3:10). He tells Ruth to keep close to his maidens (this seems preferable to BJ emendation 'male servants' here as in 2:22, 23 and 3:2). **12.** 'under whose wings'. There is probably a later allusion to this in 3:9 where Ruth asks

Boaz to spread his wing (or 'skirt') over her. **17.** In **266c** such favourable circumstances Ruth's gleaning is highly successful—an ephah or bushel of barley being the total collected.

18—23. Return to Naomi—20. The living are Ruth and Naomi, the dead Mahlon and Elimelech. The reference to the latter 'shows that already Naomi's plan is in her mind' (L. P. Smith). Boaz is a kinsman, a 'go'el', though not the next-of-kin (cf 3:12).

3:1—5 Naomi plans the marriage—In many ways **d** Naomi, not Ruth, is the leading character in the book: she is the moving spirit behind this levirate type of marriage. The advice given to Ruth involved a certain amount of moral risk, but Naomi was convinced of the virtue of both Boaz and Ruth.

6—18. Ruth's petition and the reply of Boaz—9. Ruth asks Boaz to fulfil the duty of kinsman and marry her. **12.** There is a nearer relative whose claims have priority. **16—18.** Ruth reports to Naomi.

4:1—12. Transaction at the gate—The gate was **267a** the place where legal business was conducted. Boaz summons the nearer relative, whose name is not given. **2.** Boaz invites ten of the city's elders to sit down at the gate, leading citizens who were to hear the case and witness the settlement (cf Gn 23:10, 18; Jb 29:7; Prv 24:7; 31:23). **3.** cf § 265*f*. Naomi's title to property is not explained but simply stated. **5.** Redemption of the property is linked with the hand of Ruth in marriage. **6.** The go'el declines. Cf § 265*f*. The redeemed property would be inherited by Ruth's son who would legally be the son of Mahlon (in fact the legal son of Elimelech as we see from 5 where Ruth is said to be the widow of Elimelech). **7.** Here perhaps is an indication of the late date of Ru. **8.** Contrast ceremonial removal of the sandal with Dt 25:9. In Ru it merely symbolizes a contract (cf Ps 60 (59):10). **11.** The transaction over and officially witnessed, the elders and people congratulate Boaz and express the wish that God will make their union fruitful. **12.** The author recalls the story (Gn 38) of Judah and Tamar his daughter-in-law of whom was born Perez (and Zerah his twin) who continued the line of Judah. Judah was tricked by Tamar whereas Boaz willingly accepts his responsibilities towards Ruth.

13—17 Birth of Obed—It is Naomi not Ruth who **b** receives the congratulations of the women. BJ proposes a correction (14) 'Blessed be Yahweh who has this day seen to it that the deceased should have a kinsman to perpetuate his name in Israel'. The son of Ruth will continue the line of Elimelech; Naomi will be the child's legal mother. The child will be a comfort to Naomi in her old age; Ruth will mean more to her than seven sons (cf 1 Sm 2:5; Jer 15:9 etc.). Naomi takes the child as her own to nurse him. **17.** At the suggestion of the neighbours (cf Lk 1:59) his name is called Obed, 'one who serves' i.e. 'servant (of God)' though L. P. Smith thinks this name ill accords with the words of the women. Obed is the father of Jesse, himself the father of David.

18—22. The genealogy of David—This is strictly a **c** *second* genealogy; the book could have concluded with v 17. These vv seem out of harmony with the rest of the story. Obed is said to be the son of Boaz which seems against the theme of the book (cf 4:10, 17). Probably this concluding section is a later addition. But even the shorter genealogy reminds us of Mt 1, ' . . . and Boaz the father of Jesse, and Jesse the father of David the king . . . and Jacob the father of Joseph the husband of Mary, of whom Jesus was born, who is called Christ'.

1 AND 2 SAMUEL

BY J. BLENKINSOPP

268a Bibliography—*Commentaries*: For early Church writers and thereafter down to the modern epoch of critical exegesis see H. P. Smith, ICC 1904, latest impression 1961, still indispensable. Still useful are P. Dhorme, Et B, 1900 A. R. S. Kennedy CBi[1], 1905, influential; A. Schulz, EHAT, 1919; W. Caspari, KAT Leipzig 1926; A. F. Kirkpatrick CBSC 1930[2]; K. L. Leimbach BB 1936. More recently Caird, Schroeder, Little IB 1953; M. Rehm *EchB*, 1954[2]; G. Bressan, Turin 1955; H. W. Hertzberg, ATD 1960[2]; DTL, 1964; A. Van Der Born, De Boeken van het OT, Roermund 1956; R. de Vaux, BJ 1959; G. W. Anderson, PC (2).

Studies—L. Rost, *Die Überlieferung von der Thronnachfolge Davids*, Stuttgart 1926; E. Robinson, 'Samuel and Saul' BJRL 20 (1944), 175—206; M. Buber, 'Die Erzählung von Sauls Königswahl' VT 6 (1956), 113—173, A Weiser, 'Samuel und die Vorgeschichte des israelitischen Königtums' ZThK 57 (1960, 141—161; R. A. Carlson, *David the Chosen King*, Stockholm, 1964. Studies and articles on particular passages and problems will be given in the commentary.

b Place in OT Canon and Title In the Heb. canon, 1, 2 Sm are included in the Former Prophets, namely, the historical corpus Jos—2 (4) Kgs. It is likely that the title arose on the grounds that Samuel is himself the subject matter of the opening chh of 1 Sm, though he is hardly ever mentioned after 1 Sm 7 until the notice of his death in 25:1. We should bear in mind, however, the talmudic tradition which ascribed these books to prophetic authorship (*Baba Bathra* 14*b*), based, no doubt, on the reference to 'the chronicles of the prophet Samuel' in 1 Chr 29:29, though the identification is quite impossible. As a descriptive label the title is, in fact, inadequate from either point of view.

c For the Jews there was only one Book of Samuel. The division into two first occurs in the LXX for the purely practical reason that a vocalic script necessitated two rolls instead of one. The LXX, in fact, divided the whole corpus from the birth of Samuel down to Jehoiachin in exile into the four Books of Kingdoms (*basileiai*). This was taken up by the Heb. Bible in the 14th cent. and appears in the 2nd ed. of Daniel Bomberg's great Bible in 1517. The Vg, following but modifying LXX, has *libri regum* and this has resulted in the 4 Books of Kings division in most Catholic translations, a usage which is discontinued in this edition.

d Text—Together with Ezek and Hos the text of Sm is the most corrupt of the Heb. Bible. There is the added difficulty of a wide discrepancy between MT and LXX; this usually takes the form of a longer alternative text in the latter rather like D in relation to the Received Text in Acts, though there are also cases of the contrary e.g. in the Goliath episode (1 Sm 17:1—18:5). The textual critic must make use of all the means at his disposal in reconstructing the original text; there are, in the first

place, the passages with parallels in Chr, and 2 Sm 22 is **268d** paralleled in Ps 18 (17). Codex B representing the Egyptian recension is the main witness for LXX since A shows signs of harmonisation, and the prestige of this text, or rather of the Heb. text which it translated, has been greatly enhanced since the publication of two of the three Qumran Sm fragments (4QSam[a], 4QSam[b]). **e** These, dating from the 1st and 3rd cent. B.C. respectively, reveal a greater fluidity in the Heb. text tradition than hitherto suspected, and, above all, support LXX against MT decisively in the great majority of cases. Examples will be given in the commentary. See J. Wellhausen, *Der Text der Bücher Samuelis*, Göttingen 1871, a classic of OT text criticism and S. R. Driver, *Notes on the Hebrew Text of the Books of Samuel*, Oxford 1890, still a fundamental work. For the Qumran fragments see F. M. Cross, 'A New Qumran Biblical Fagment', BASOR 132 (1953), 15—26; 'The Oldest Manuscripts from Qumran' JBL 74 (1955), 147—72; *The Ancient Library of Qumran and Modern Biblical Studies*, 1958; M. Burrows, *More Light on the Dead Sea Scrolls*, 1958, 139—41.

Contents—1 Sm begins with the infancy and prophetic **f** vocation of Samuel (1—3) which is interrupted by an account of a further phase of the Philistine wars in which the Ark figures prominently (4—6). This section and the following ch (7) in which Samuel is described no longer as prophet but as 'Judge' is reminiscent of Jg. There follows a rather complex and difficult section on the transition to monarchy and the king-making of Saul (8—12), leading up to the story of his uncertain achievement and rejection by Yahweh (13—15). The highly complex and at times detailed description of David's introduction to the Court and the jealousy which his immediate popularity awoke in Saul (16—21), his subsequent flight from the king and career as a mercenary in Philistine pay (22—29), is followed by an account of a punitive campaign against the Amalekites and the subsequent defeat and death of Saul (30—32 Sm 1).

After an initial rather unsettled period (2—4), David **g** establishes himself as undisputed king, captures Jerusalem and makes it the new cult centre by bringing up the Ark and installing it in the city (5—6). The great dynastic oracle of Nathan the court prophet (7) and a short summary of internal and external affairs (8) introduce the long curial history of David's reign told chiefly in function of the all-important question of succession. (9—20 cont. in 1 (3) Kgs 1—2). This could be regarded as a prologue to the reign of Solomon the Magnificent. It is interrupted by an appendix (21—24) consisting of six supplementary notices inserted, no doubt, at this point when canonical Sm and Kgs were divided.

Composition and Literary History—A careful **h** reading shows that the narrative of 1, 2 Sm is not always consecutive and could hardly have been composed by one hand and at one time. The reader is puzzled by a number of discrepancies: thus Saul is made king but

268h some time later we find him working on his farm (1 Sm 10:17; 11:5ff); in 1 Sm 7:13 we are told that the Philistines never again entered the territory of Israel, but in 2 Sm 8 David is still busy subduing them; after the death of Agag we are informed that Samuel never saw Saul again until the day of his death (1 Sm 15:35), yet they meet later on at Rama (19:22). We may also find some difficulty in discovering who really killed Saul (1 Sm 31:4 cf 2 Sm 1:10) or whether it was David after all who killed Goliath (1 Sm 17:51 cf 2 Sm 21:19). In addition, the same person or event is viewed often from two or more mutually exclusive angles. Samuel himself is presented both as prophet (1 Sm 1—3) and as 'Judge' (1 Sm 7), and the monarchy is seen on the one hand as a legitimate extension of the charismatic office of 'Judge' and on the other as the product of apostasy and rebellion and the chief agent of the destruction of the community (see the explanation of national failure **i** in 2 (4) Kgs 17:7—23). Later on, David is offered the daughter of Saul in marriage and makes a pact of friendship with Jonathan three times, while the story of his flight from Saul, his betrayal, his taking refuge with the Philistines and his sparing of Saul are all duplicated. There is also considerable inequality in the style of writing; side by side with passages of obscure and rather inept writing such as 2 Sm 7 we have the so-called Court History of David (2 Sm 9—20) which has been justly described as 'the unsurpassed prose masterpiece of the Hebrew Bible' (R. Pfeiffer, *Introd. to the OT*, 1948², 341).

Since the very beginning of source analysis with J.G. Eichhorn, *Einleitung ins AT*, 1780—83, 2, 450ff, some at least of these difficulties have been known, but although some progress has been made much still remains uncertain. Our first task should be to state what is now generally held to be certain in the study of the literary history of Sm.

j All recognize the existence of a continuous work, the Court History of David (2 Sm 9—20 continued in 1 (3) Kgs 1—2), which forms the nucleus of the history of these books. Its main concern is with the succession of Solomon to David's throne in spite of opposition from the Saul dynasty and the claims of his brothers Amnon, Absalom and Adonijah whose deaths are recorded. It is generally assumed that the so-called prophecy of Nathan (2 Sm 7) formed a preface to this work and there are some who think such an introduction can be traced even further back (T. C. Vriezen in *Orientalia Neerlandica*, **k** 1948, 167—89). All are agreed in praising the remarkable psychological awareness and historical fidelity of this earliest extant piece of continuous historical writing in Israel. On the basis of the rather tenuous data which can be extracted from the narrative, some have attempted to identify its author. Duhm, followed by Budde, suggested Abiathar, David's priest afterwards exiled by Solomon; others have thought more probable Jonathan his son, though an earlier guess of Klostermann (1887), taken up after a long interval by Rost and later by Pfeiffer, pointed to Ahimaaz son of Zadok, whom the last-named scholar went so far as to designate 'the father of history'—in preference to the much later Herodotus. More recently Vriezen has suggested Zabud son of Nathan, but whether it was one of these or another we shall never know for certain. The importance of this narrative, written during Solomon's reign at such little distance from the events it records, can hardly be exaggerated, not only for what it tells us but for its relation to the rest of OT literature especially the problem of the identity of the so-called Yahwist in the Pent.

The difficulties are much greater in the earlier part of **l** Sm. Most scholars would accept the existence of two strands or traditions, one later than the other, before this material was absorbed into the great deuteronomist corpus. This would seem to be the case at least for the two distinct representations of Samuel as prophet and judge and for the two attitudes to the monarchy, though E. Robertson has argued against the need for this duality ('Samuel and Saul' BJRL 20 (1944), 175—206). When we try to go further and identify these two strands with the two oldest literary *corpora* in the Pent. we are on much more uncertain ground. That we have in Sm a continuation of **m** J and E was first proposed by Karl Budde and taken up by Wellhausen, Dhorme, Cornill and others more recently. Some have even wanted to take these two narratives right down to the fall of the kingdoms—in particular Hölscher and Eissfeldt, the latter adding L, an early secular source predating J. This position is now generally abandoned. There are, indeed, certain traits which remind one of the earliest literary ensemble in the Pent., and this would fit in with the view now gaining ground which assigns the Yahwist to Solomon's reign; but there are also more evident affinities with Jg in the early chh. In short, it is unlikely that any simple solution will fit the facts.

More in favour today would be a less schematic and **n** inflexible explanation, one able to recognize a wider diversity of material: narrative going back to the rhapsodic guilds at the shrines, worked by later editors into the overall scheme, oracular utterances, archival material, editorial comment, and so on. From the time of Kennedy (1905), an increasing number of commentators speak of several units or cycles in Sm: a Samuel cycle, an Ark cycle, a Saul cycle, and so on down to the Court Chronicle. Hertzberg (1960²) takes up an old suggestion and connects the different and at times conflicting traditions with different sanctuaries—Mizpah, Gilgal, Bethel and Gibeah—which, whatever our judgement in detail, contains a commonsense approach to the question of literary origins. This collection of ancient and venerable traditions must then have been edited at least once by the deuteronomic school, though we can have only the roughest idea of what they omitted or added or in what way they modified the raw material at their disposal. Finally, other additions were made somewhat in the manner of Jewish midrash: the canticle of Hannah (1 Sm 2), probably the account of the delirium of Saul at Ramah (1 Sm 19:18—24) and the feigned madness of David (21:10—15), and no doubt others.

Literary Genres—An indispensable condition for **269a** further investigation of any kind, but especially in the matter of historicity, is an awareness of the literary character of the document one is studying. Without pretending to give an exhaustive treatment, some idea of the remarkable diversity of literary forms in Sm can here be provided, dividing the material for convenience into three categories: courtly, popular and cultic. In the **Court History** itself we have chronologically the first letter in the OT—a very brief one (2 Sm 11:15). There are also here and there what we could describe as fragments of protocol—the cry at the accession (1 Sm 10:24 cf 1 (3) Kgs 1:25) and the royal *acclamatio* (2 Sm 15:10); it is also possible that the reference to the king as 'like the angel of God' (1 Sm 29:9; 2 Sm 14:17; 19:28) is a formal honorific address like those in the Amarna lists—of his children (2 Sm 3:2—5; 5:13—16). his officers (8:16—18; 20:23—26 and ch 23) and especially summaries of campaigns of the type familiar from

69b contemporary or near contemporary cuneiform inscriptions (1 Sm 14:47−52; 2 Sm 5:17−25; 8:1−14). The two poetic laments or *qînôt* (2 Sm 1:19−27; 3:33−34) inspired by the death of Saul and Jonathan in the first case and Abner in the second, are ascribed to David and there is no reason to doubt this ascription in view of the tradition of his literary and musical skill (see Ps 22 (21):4; 2 Sm 23:1; in 1 Sm 16:18 he is *n^eḇôn dāḇār*—

c 'a skilful reciter'). The 'Last Words' of David (2 Sm 23:1−7) form a *genre* in themselves, familiar elsewhere in the OT (e.g. Gn 49). Of **popular origin** are the **snatches sung by women after a battle** (1 Sm 21:12; 18:7 cf Ex 15:20−21) and the **proverbs and current sayings** brought in here and there (1 Sm 10:11; 24:12; 2 Sm 5:8); no doubt also oral, popular tradition has influenced the form in which many of the striking stories told have come down to us. There are **two psalms** (1 Sm 2; 2 Sm 22 cf Ps 18 (17)) added probably at a late stage of recension; there are also examples of the **prophetic oracle** in verse (1 Sm 15:22−23; 2 Sm 12:1*b*−4—in the form of a parable) comparable with those found in the prophetic literature and the familiar prophetic imperative; *koh 'āmar Yahweh*, 'Thus Yahweh

d has spoken!' (1 Sm 15:2−3). It is also likely that the **stories about the Ark** (1 Sm 4−6; 2 Sm 6, cf Ps 132 (131)) were composed for the benefit of pilgrims who visited the shrine. Finally, there are, as we should expect from what we know of the literary history of Sm, editorial or recensional passages, **homiletic expansions of the earlier material** especially in the deuteronomic vein and occasional explanatory notes (e.g. 1 Sm 2:25*b*). We should also be prepared to reckon with the probability that discourses, especially on key occasions, have been expanded, a literary practice common in antiquity e.g. David before the combat with Goliath (1 Sm 17:45−47), Samuel on the royal prerogatives (1 Sm 8.11−18).

e **Religious Significance**—What must strike and please a modern reader of Sm—perhaps not so much in the earlier chh which on account of their cultic origins or epic flavour or general discontinuity might prove somewhat difficult or uncongenial, but certainly at least in the long history of David—is its compelling realism and closeness to life. Even allowing for source division, there comes through in the story of Saul a frightful **picture of psychological disintegration contrasted with the strong and tender friendship between his son and the young David.** In the Court History itself what is at once striking is its marked secular character—the only explicitly religious note is struck in Nathan's admonition given in the form of parable (2 Sm 12:1*b*−4) and most commentators would not see this as part of the

f original narrative. This can be seen more clearly if it is compared with the idealistic portrait which emerges from Chr in which the central place is taken by the promise of God made through Nathan (2 Sm 7) and where David emerges as a paradigm rather than a real person of flesh and blood. We do not read there of his sin which begins in momentary passion and is rounded off in cold deliberation, nor of the strange, chill logic of his behavior when the child is born, nor of his despairing grief when the news is brought of Absalom's death. That the narrative is compounded to so large an extent of adultery and murder, rape and treachery, pride and folly makes it imperative that we look for the reason why it has been introduced into sacred history.

g In the first place, Sm traces the **transition from the sacred federation of the Tribes to monarchy**. The reaction to this crucial passage of history was twofold: an earlier group still close to that troubled time and writing under a monarchy still in full flower, **269g** saw it as a natural extension of the God-bestowed office of charismatic leader; Saul was another Gideon, but leadership had to be on a wider front and of longer duration on account of the greater danger which threatened, but it is the same God who directed the steps of the unaware son of Kish to his anointing (1 Sm 9:10) and there is no trace of what was to become the habitual opposition between king and prophet. Later, however, the eclipse of the monarchy and of the nation with it provoked a deeper meditation on the role of divine providence in human affairs, and the prophetic truth that 'the soul that sins shall die' (Ezek 18:20) was seen to be worked out on the larger scale of social and political affairs. David, with all his faults, was exempt from this negative judgement. He was the depository of the divine promise which through his dynasty was to be the guarantee of God's plan for Israel and the world coming to fruition in the future (2 Sm 7). **The Oracle of Nathan h is the starting-point of royal messianism in the OT**, a principle which can be demonstrated from Chr, Pss and the prophetic literature. In Jewish religious thought he is always connected with the messianic age and a visit to his tomb on Mt Sion shows the veneration in which he is still held. In the gospel, Jesus' descent from the great king is stressed in the genealogies, he is born in the city of David, he claims to be the true Son of David, and this contention plays an important part in the early *kerygma* (Ac 2.25−31; Rm 1:3 etc). It should be noted that the position of the king in the **i** divine economy has to be seen within the already existing framework of the covenant relationship, so that there was really no room for a divine-king figure in Israel, despite occasional borrowings from rituals of sacred accession to the throne and theologically high sounding protocol. But the reigning monarch always remained within the sphere of the sacred; he was the intermediary between God and the people, he in a sense recapitulated the people, was their spokesman before God and on great occasions also their sacrificing priest (2 Sm 6:13ff cf 1 Kgs 8:62). He was *māšîaḥ Yahweh*, Yahweh's Anointed.

This **recapitulation of the sacred community in j the person of the king** is of capital importance in the OT since it continues the forward movement already implicit in the original Sinai covenant (*b^erît*). For the Christian, this movement is determined in advance by its *terminus ad quem*, its fulfilment in the new reality in Christ, a community which, while bound up with the past (the church is the 'Israel of God' Gal 6:16) is brought into existence to be a perfect instrument of the divine will. In Sm we have a partial account of this community or kingdom in the making, one vital stage in the history of God's saving act.

We should note finally that this development is reflected, **k** as we might expect, in worship and liturgy. The passage from amphictyony to kingdom resulted in the taking of the Ark from Shiloh up to the newly captured Jerusalem where it was solemnly installed (2 Sm 6). This was an event of enormous significance since Jerusalem, 'city of the great king' (Ps 48 (47):3; Mt 5:35) was to become the symbol of unity, centrality and universality. It was to make possible, almost 400 years later, the centralization of worship based on the prophetic superimposition of Sinai—Sion, and it was, finally, to Jerusalem that the 'good news of God' was proclaimed.

1−4:1a Samuel's Infancy and Prophetic Call; the 270a Shiloh Priesthood—This section narrates the conception and birth of Samuel to Hannah who was barren but

270a whose prayer at the shrine of Shiloh was answered. She vows to consecrate him to Yahweh and in consequence Samuel passes his early youth in the sanctuary where he receives his prophetic call. In style, vocabulary and motif this story is strongly reminiscent of the birth of Samson (Jg 13) and, to a lesser extent, the call of Gideon (Jg 6), as also of other annunciation and conception scenes in the Pent. (Gn 16; 18; 28). It may well have been an introduction to a history of Samuel as charismatic leader of which only fragments remain in the canonical text. He was certainly considered as the last of the Judges in one tradition at least, as can be seen from the familiar formula in 1 Sm 7:15 and his rather surprising inclusion in the list of Judges in 12:7. The close similarity in conception of this chapter to Jos 24 points to a definite stage of recension of the Judges period. This narrative has been amplified in various ways as we shall see, especially by the reference to the corrupt priesthood of the shrine for the purpose of discrediting the local shrines and legitimizing the Zadokite priesthood which took the place of Eli's line during Solomon's reign.

b **1:1–2** Familiar introduction to this type of narrative cf Jg 13:2. The geographical situation: Ephraim is the central hill country; Ramathaim-zophim ('The Two Ramas Gazing') probably Rantis NW of Jerusalem just on the Jordan side of the 1948 armistice line rather than er-Ram 5 miles due N of the city. Elkanah ('El has acquired') has two wives: Hannah (Grace) and Peninnah (Pearl) in accordance with usage going back to the patriarchal period. The whole situation which the narrator describes is illuminated by Dt 21:15–17; cf also the situation of Abram with Sarai and Hagar (Gn 16) and Jacob with Leah and Rachel (Gn 29).

c **3–8 Shiloh** was at this time the central shrine, well situated in the heart of Ephraim, a pilgrimage centre sanctified by the presence of the Ark, the palladium of the tribes. The cult occasion forming the background of this scene was most probably the feast of Tents (cf Jg 21:19): this emerges from the fact that it was an agrarian feast, combining a harvest festival and great rejoicing (hence the suspicion that Hannah had drunk too much (1:14), cf § 105h, also the object of worship was Yahweh of

d hosts (cf Zech 14:16). What this latter title meant *at that time* is disputed, though it seems best to take the origins back to the early days of the Holy War of the tribes, connecting it with the Ark and translating: 'Yahweh (God) of the armies' (understood, of Israel). Later on, it was applied to the hosts of heaven and, chiefly through the use of Is 6:3 in the *Sanctus* of the Mass, has passed into Christian imagery. For Shiloh and the veneration of the Ark see R. de Vaux, AI, 297–302, 304–5. **4–7.** Refers to the sacrifice of communion concluded by the sacrificial meal taken together cf 9:22–24; 13:9 etc.

e **9–19a Hannah's Vow**—The vow, *neder*, is a well-attested act of piety in the OT (Nm 21:2; Jg 11:30ff; 13) often made, as here, conditional upon some favour being granted. Though not explicitly stated, the vow is that of the nazirate which involved abstention from strong drink, letting the hair grow and avoidance of contact with a dead body. These rules are found in Nm 6:1–21 though the formulation belongs to the Priestly edition and there is intermingling with laws of ritual purity. Comparison with Jg 13 is inevitable, where abstention from wine is enjoined on the mother during the period of gestation (Jg 13:4). **9.** For 'In Shiloh' MT, which is difficult to accept, it is usual to adopt Klostermann's emendation, based on 9:22, 'in the apartment' (reserved for the sacrificial meal) cf 1:18 in LXX. **12.** Eli's sup-

position was natural enough since it was not the custom **270c** to pray silently; drunkenness, moreover, would no doubt have been only too common on the occasion of a harvest feast cf. Ac 2:13. **16.** literally 'daughter of Belial' a characteristic Heb. use of the genitive, cf 2:12; 10:27; 25:17, 25 etc.

19b–28 The Namegiving and Dedication of f Samuel—Her prayer is answered and it remains for her to fulfil her vow. The great importance attached to namegiving is seen in the fixed, almost formulaic way such scenes are described cf Gn 16:11 (Ishmael); 21:6 (Isaac). The etymology is of a popular sort meant to bring out something striking about the child or be a good omen for the future. It has been pointed out that *šeʾiltîw*, 'I have asked for him', explains the name Saul much better than Samuel; but Saul is of Benjamin not Ephraim and most of the narrative of these early chh would not fit him. Samuel may mean simply 'the name of God'. **21.** The vow was, of **g** course, Hannah's but there was a solidarity in regard to responsibility for its fulfilment. **22.** Even today eastern women breast-feed much longer than is common in the W. From this v down to 2:6 we have the valuable help of the leather fragments found in Cave 4 at Qumran (4Q Sam^a). Here we read the addition (reconstructed): 'I will give him as a *nazir* for ever, all the days of his life' **24.** The thanksgiving sacrifice consists of an animal, cereal offering and wine for the libation, cf Jg 6:19. That this is the pattern of Canaanite sacrifice, indirectly attested by Ugarit (e.g. KRT A, 159ff in ANET 1955² 144) raises the important question of the origins of the Heb. sacrificial system. See R. Dussaud, *Les Origines Cananéennes du Sacrifice Israélite*, 1941.

2:1–10 Hannah's Psalm—See G. Bressan, 'Il Cantico **h** di Anna' Bib 32 (1951), 503–21; 33 (1952), 67–89. Apart from 2:5 the reference of this psalm to Hannah's condition is rather tenuous. It was quite normal for older poetic texts to be worked over by later editors, e.g. Ex 15 and Jg 5, and there are clear signs of the same here, especially the reference to the anointed king at the end. Comparison with similar psalms in the Psalter would lead us to classify it as a royal psalm, especially 2:1, 4, 10. Just as Luke has used the story of Samuel's infancy as a literary model for that of Jesus so this psalm provided a model for the *Magnificat*. **1.** The ox's or buffalo's horn as a symbol of power is **i** a commonplace in Heb. poetry. **2.** God as the Rock— another expressive and seminal image. **4.** This idea of turning the tables on human values and resources explains why this psalm finds a place in the history; it illustrates and emphasises the way God acts within the human predicament. **5a.** Textually difficult; LXX has 'The weak (or, hungry) have forsaken the land'. 4QSam^a is unfortunately defective here. **6.** cf Hos 6:2 Note that *šeʾôl* is parallel with 'death' as normally in Ps. **8b.** The 'pillars of the earth'—upon which the flat disc of the earth rests, like a platform above the waters, in the imaginative and profound but unscientific Heb. cosmology cf Ps 75 (74):4; Jb 9:6. **10.** The first occurrence of *mašîaḥ* in the OT, referring to the anointed king, the one actually reigning—but pointing forward to the ideal king of the future.

2:11–17 Conduct of Eli's Sons—**11.** Read with LXX **271a** '*She left him there before Yahweh and went to Ramah*'. This is a recapitulation-verse, cf 18, 21b, 26; 3:1, 19, which serves to keep Samuel before our minds and prepare for the prophetic call. This procedure is also followed by Luke in the Infancy Gospel—1:80; 2:40, 52. **12.** The use of *yādaʿ*, 'had (no) regard for', for prophetic, religious experience would suggest prophetic

271a influence in the composition of this passage, especially in view of the bitter polemic of the prophets against a corrupt priesthood, cf Hos 6:6 and 1 Sm 15:22—23 where such influence is certain. **14.** 4QSam^a gives only two words for the vessels, which reads better, cf 2 Chr 35:13 (LXX); it has a long addition at 2:16. **17.** The annual sacrifice concluded with a quasi-sacramental meal: the fat of the quartered animal—the rich, vital element according to the Heb. view—was offered to God by burning, the priest had the right to the breast and right leg and the rest was divided out among the offerer's family or associates in accordance with Lv 7:29—34. The priests' conduct is therefore described as sacrilege.

b **18—26 19.** A charming touch—she follows his growth year by year bringing him on each visit a new *me'îl*, outer garment. The linen ephod is the distinctive priestly garment (22:18; 2 Sm 6:14) worn also by the high-priest (Ex 28:6), different from the cult object of the same name (Jg 8:27) **22b.** Missing in LXX and 4Q Sam^a—a gloss inspired by Ex 38:8 (P); cf 2 (4) Kgs 23: 7. The Tent would have disappeared long before this. **25.** According to the OT one can sin against a neighbour, against the king, against God. Here sin in the strict theological sense is set apart, different from any other kind. The hardening of hearts (cf Ex 4:21ff; Is 6:9ff) is part of the mystery of grace and the possibility of its withdrawal; freedom is not impaired.

c **27—36.** Prophetic Revelation made to Eli—This oracle from the man of God duplicates that given to Samuel later, 3:11ff. This latter could be merely a confirmation, but there are other indications of a later date for this passage: a message brought by a special emissary from God beginning with a reproach based on sacred history, especially the Exodus, is elsewhere an indication of the deuteronomic hand (Jg 2:1—5 from the angel of Yahweh; 6:8ff from a prophet; 1 (3) Kgs 13:1ff from a man of God, as here); moreover, the concern with the Zadokite line and the condition of the priests of the local shrines at the time of the centralization of worship under Josiah is evident. **27.** 'Thus Yahweh has spoken!'—the prophetic formula cf 30. For an example of the same form of address and oracular utterance see Am 2:9— 13. **28.** We have no means of deciding whether the ephod here is a garment or an object used for consultation of the divine will. See § 191b and de Vaux, AI, 349—52.

d **29.** MT has 'kick (against)'; LXX 'look evilly upon'— the latter seems preferable. Eli is judged according to the clear proscription of the deuteronomic law in regard to parental obligation Dt 13:7; note 13:14 'sons of Belial' cf 1 Sm 2:12. **31.** The oracle concerns the suppression of the Aaronite priestly line in favour of the Zadokite. **33.** 1 Sm 22:17—20 the slaughter of Eli's descendants and escape of Abiathar: later in 1 (3) Kgs 2:27 he is deposed by Solomon in favour of Zadok, the 'faithful priest.' **36.** Refers to the plight of the priests of the high places who came up to Jerusalem after the Josian reform in search of employment 2 (4) Kgs 23:8 cf Dt 12; 18:6—8.

e **3—4:1a Samuel's Prophetic Call**—not dissimilar from the call which the later writing prophets received cf Is 6 which takes place in the Temple before Yahweh of the Hosts and therefore in the presence of the Ark as here. Where, however, Isaiah sees Yahweh (though indeed he does not describe him), Samuel hears only a voice. In both cases the prophetic career begins with an oracle of doom. See M. Newman, 'The Prophetic Call of Samuel' in *Israel's Prophetic Heritage* ed. Anderson, Harrelson, 1962, 86—97. **1.** What follows is a vision, *hazôn*, i.e. in the widest sense of the word i.e. a revelation—Samuel does not see anything; nor is he favoured with an inspired

dream of the kind so evident in the Northern literary **271e** tradition (E) e.g. Gn 28:11ff, for he goes and reports to **f** Eli. **3.** In the sacerdotal prescriptions for Temple liturgy the 'lamp of God' is kept alight from dusk to daybreak; see Ex 27:20; Lv 24:2—4; 2 Chr 13:11. A light shining in a house signifies that the owner is present; so too Yahweh is present in his 'house'. This explains the symbolism of the sanctuary lamp. That Samuel was lying in front of the Ark does not necessarily imply a sacred 'temple-sleep' to obtain a revelation, as practised among many primitive peoples and by Moslems (cf various interpretations of Ps 17 (16):15). **4.** Stylistically, the call is described dramatically by means of repetition: the voice is heard three times and only then does Samuel answer. This 3 + 1 structure is common in OT dramatic prose e.g. Jg 16; 1 Sm 5— the vicissitudes of the Ark; 2 (4) Kgs 2 the Taking up of Elijah. **9.** 'servant' also no doubt contains a cultic connotation. This answer to the divine call contains the essence of prophetic religion—to listen to the Word and obey. Here and in 15:22 where sacrifice is contrasted **g** with obedience (literally 'listening') we have the strong and evident influence of the 8th cent. prophets in the N Kingdom with their intransigent opposition to a corrupt priesthood and monarchy. **11.** The oracle in the form familiar in writing prophets e.g. 'on that day' for an oracle of judgement 'at which the ears of all that hear it will tingle' cf Jer 19:3 and 2 (4) Kgs 21:12. **13.** RSV loyally keeps to MT but LXX gives better sense. 'cursing themselves' is *tiqqun sopherim* (theological correction) for 'cursing God'. For Eli's condemnation see note on 2:29. **17.** The familiar form of imprecation; the precise form adopted was left to the speaker.

4:1b—7:17 The Philistine War and the Ark h Cycle—Samuel is represented as 'Judge' in the deuteronomic edition: in 4:1 he is listened to by 'all Israel', used technically of the plenary or representative assembly of the tribes; the Philistine ascendancy corresponds to the 20 years of oppression of 7:1 (cf Jg 4:3) and 7:3—17 is a direct continuation of the series in Jg ending with the usual formula, except that Samuel's judge-ship lasts his whole life and is thus a decisive extension of charismatic leadership and the transition to monarchy. The inclusion is completed by reference to the unworthy sons of Eli at the beginning and of Samuel at the end, which helps to prepare for the monarchy. The Philistine war is continued from Jg 13, but the centre of interest is the Ark, the cycle of the latter is continued in 2 Sm 6 and 1 Kgs 8:1—11. See R. Press, 'Der Prophet Samuel: eine traditions-geschichtliche Untersuchung', ZAW 56 (1938) 177—225; A. George 'Fautes contre Yahweh dans les livres de Samuel', RB 53 (1946) 161—84; N. H. Tur-Sinai, 'The Ark of God at Beth-Shemesh and Peres 'Uzza,' VT 1 (1951), 275ff.

4:1—11 The Defeat of Aphek—By skilfully blending **i** the narrative of the corrupt Shiloh Priesthood and the Ark cycle the author shows how national defeat is due to the working out of the divine oracle and the corruption of cult. From 1b the rhythm and style are quite different from what precedes and highly reminiscent of Jg 14—16. **1.** Ebenezer means 'Help-stone'; near Aphek but site unknown. The latter probably Rosh-Ha'ayin SE of the site of Antipatris. **3.** The Ark is here the palladium or aegis carried into battle, a common practice; the theological question was to explain *why* it proved ineffective, to which the answer was that Yahweh was no longer present, cf Ezek 10:18ff. **4.** Many of the refer- **j** ences to the Ark are expanded and glossed as here; for

271j terminology and theology of the Ark, see above, note on 1:3—8. **6.** 'ibrîm used only by non-Hebrew cf 13:7; 29:3. The rhythmic element is very strong here; the 'oy lānû ('woe to us') may have been a liturgical dirge and may be connected with the legendary Linus of the Greeks. The words would appear to have been expanded by the addition of the favourite deuteronomic theme of the mighty act of God in the Exodus.

k **4:12—22 Death of Eli and his daughter-in-law—18.** The number is part of the ideal divisioning of sacred history; cf Samson, Saul, David. **21.** The child's name 'î-kābôd means 'Where is the Glory?'—used in the theological sense of the divine presence; we must remember that the climax of the Ark cycle is to be its solemn establishment in the Jerusalem temple, the centre of cult.

l **5:1—12 The Ark with the Philistines**—The story is told artistically in the ternary pattern common in OT prose: three stages with the Philistines (Ashdod, Gath, Ekron), three stages in its triumph (Beth-shemesh, Kiriath-jearim, Jerusalem). **1.** Ashdod was one of the five Philistine 'city-states' which formed a rival amphictyony to that of the Hebrew tribes (see 6:17) **2.** Dagon (cf Jg 16:23) was the Amorite god of the grain, like Ceres. **5.** An etiological note, but this was a common way of avoiding evil spirits cf Gn 4:7. **6.** The affliction might have been bubonic tumours or pneumonic plague or just piles. See S. H. Blondheim, 'The First Recorded Epidemic of Pneumonic Plague', Bull. Hist. Medicine 19 (1955) 337—45; G. Driver, 'The Plague of the Philistines', JRAS 1950, 50—2. **8.** The five Philistine seranîm (cf Jg 3:3; Jos 13:3) probably correspond to the five towns (1 Sm 6:17). A similar system of rule is found in Carthage and the Gr. word turannos is probably connected with it. Gath may be the mound just N of Kiryat-Gat in the Shephelah but the soundings of 1957—9 uncovered no Philistine remains. Ekron is about 20 m. due N of Gath.

m **6:1—7:1 Return of the Ark**—It will be easy to understand the place which this narrative has in the general plan if we remember how important was the central Jerusalem sanctuary for the deuteronomic editors and their polemic against the local shrines (Dt 12; 2 (4) Kgs 23:8ff). In keeping with Heb. prose style the command (1—9) and the execution (10—16) are more or less parallel. 15, 17—18 are later additions.

n **1.** LXX adds 'their land swarmed with mice' cf 4; this could be original. **3.** MT. 'It will be known to you . . .'; LXX 'You will be atoned for'; one conjectural reconstruction is: '*Then shall rest be granted to you*' see D. W. Thomas in JTS 10 (1960) 52. **4.** This type of expiatory ex-voto was common in antiquity; the mice may be connected with the pestilence, especially if it was bubonic, but see 1 (LXX). **6.** A typical Dt expansion on the Exodus theme cf Ps 95 (94):8. **7.** The stipulations were in view of the sacred use to which the cart and oxen are to be put cf 2 Sm 6:3, 2 (4) Kgs 2:20; Mk 11:2. The calves are left behind to make the portent more difficult and therefore more striking cf 1 (3) Kgs 18:33—34. **12.** Beth-shemesh: a conspicuous mount near the busy little town of that name in the centre of the Valley of Sorek; a key-point for penetration into the Judaean uplands. As the name suggests, this was a Canaanite sanctuary to the sun-god (Shemesh) **15.** Probably added at the time of the priestly redaction to avoid the scandal of profane hands touching the Ark and of an unauthorized place of sacrifice. See H.

o Smith, op cit 47. **17—18.** A note added later giving the list of towns in the Philistine Pentapolis; the number of mice is greater than that stipulated above (4). The field of Joshua and other landmarks in that region, e.g.

Samson's cave, are still shown to visitors. **19.** MT is cor- **271o** rupt and reconstruction with aid of LXX must be conjectural. LXX reads: 'The sons of Jechonias did not rejoice when they saw the Ark of Yahweh, and he struck down 70 (50,000) of them . . .' The larger figure is, of course, a gloss. For an over-elaborate attempt at reconstruction see J. Bewer, 'The Original Reading of I Sam 6:19a', JBL 57 (1938) 89—91. **20.** The title 'This Holy One' expresses the absolute 'Otherness' of God, a concept basic to the Priestly writings of the OT and used often as divine title in Isaiah. **21.** Kiriath-jearim: 'Town of Forests' within the Gibeonite confederation (Jos 9) of the Conquest period. The Ark was not taken back to Shiloh because the latter had meanwhile been destroyed by the Philistines; this is clear from the excavations and from Jer 7:12.

7:2—17 Samuel the 'Judge'—This ch does not follow **272a** on consecutively from the preceding in which Samuel was not mentioned. It represents him as a theocratic ruler like Moses (cf Jer 15:1) and Joshua (cf Jos 24 and 1 Sm 12!) and like one of the 'Judges', only on a higher level of mediation. This can be seen in the mention of the fixed period of oppression in 2 (cf Jg 4:3; 15:20; 16:31 etc.); the pattern of distress—crying to Yahweh—intercession—victorious outcome; the final formula 7:15. It further represents the theocratic ideal in opposition to the profane institution of monarchy and points to the crisis of faith which the passage from one to the other implied. It can therefore be taken as a preface to the next chapter's anti-monarchical account of how that change came about.

2. A typical 'Judges' opening—'mourned' does not **b** give good sense; LXX (Lagarde) has 'turned to' which fits better. **3—4** '*If your conversion to Yahweh is really sincere . . .*' This repudiation of the local fertility gods was basic to the deuteronomic reform (2 (4) Kgs 23:4ff) and recurs constantly in Jg (2:1—5; 6:7—10; 10:10—16). **5—6.** Mizpah has generally been identified with Tell en-Nasbeh, excavated by Badè (1926—35), c. 8 m. N of Jerusalem on the Ramallah road, though there are good arguments for Nebi Samwil, a dominating height 5 m. NW of the city, not least of which is the name itself. Samuel is here the intercessor like Moses cf Ps 99 (98):6; Jer 15:1. 'All Israel' warns us that this is an amphictyonic meeting, and in Jg 20 Mizpah was the rallying point for the holy war, which would explain well the sequel here—7:7ff. Fasting and water-libation (not elsewhere **c** attested outside of 2 Sm 23:16 and the Feast of Tents, Zech 14:7) seem to express contrition, though some have supposed the account to be incomplete and presuppose a drought or famine (cf Jl 1:14 etc). Samuel 'judged' them in the same way as Deborah (Jg 4:4ff) and the Minor Judges. **8—12.** Samuel plays the same role in battle as Moses in Ex 17:8ff. The narrative speaks of some meteorological intervention under the direction of providence; thunder is often spoken of as the 'voice' of God in Pss cf also Jos 12, a battle fought in the same region, and Jg 5 the battle of Ta'anak. Beth-car; otherwise unknown; Klostermann's emendation to Beth-horon has much to commend it especially in view of topography. The nar- **d** rative ends with the usual etiological note explaining a local landmark, here 'The Stone of Help' cf 4:1. **13.** This is the usual 'Judge' conclusion cf Jg 3:30; it is evident that the Philistines did return, and often, but this literary tradition keeps within its own scheme. **14.** The Davidic conquest of the Philistines is also anticipated. **15—17.** Illustrate the semantic confusion in the use of 'to judge'; for while 15 tells us of the spatial (all Israel) and temporal (not 20, 40 years but all his life) extension of charismatic leadership 16—17 uses it in the more res-

272d tricted sense in which in Jg it is used of Deborah (Jg 4:4—5); Samuel goes round the sanctuary centres in annual assize. See for *šāpaṭ* O. Grether in ZAW 57 (1939) 110—21.

e **8–12 Transition to Monarchy**—This section is important in that it traces the transition from the sacred amphictyony to a secular pattern of government. The basic cause was the increasing precariousness of the tribal federation subjected as it was to constant pressure: from Moab (Jg 3:12), Hazor (4:2), Midian (6:1), the Ammonites (10:7) and now above all the Philistines. The immediate cause was the breakdown of Samuel's hereditary judgeship (1 Sm 8:1—3). The process was more gradual and uneven than might at first appear; Gideon, despite his overt refusal, seems to have accepted the kingly office (Jg 8:22—3), there was the abortive attempt of Abimelech (Jg 9), both of which experiments were viewed unfavourably, and on the other hand Saul's kingship is evidently transitional and very precarious; there is still the tribal call to arms (1 Sm 11) and as yet no professional or mercenary army and no organized administration. It is also described as charismatic (e.g. 10:10) in the same way as the leadership of the

f 'Judges'. This transition provoked a deep religious crisis in Israel; could this new thing, the monarchy, be absorbed into or adapted to the existing pattern of faith? See, in addition to items in bibliography, W. Irwin, 'Samuel and the Rise of the Monarchy', AJSL 58 (1941), 113—34; A. Weiser, 'Samuel und die Vorgeschichte des isr. Königtums', SThKirche 57 (1960) 141—61; G. Buccellati, 'Da Saul a Davide, Le Origini della Monarchia israelitica alla luce della storiografia contemporanea', BibOr 1 (1959) 251—82; E. Osswald, in TLZ 85 (1960) 145; I. Mendelssohn, 'Samuel's Denunciation of Kingship in the Light of Akkadian Documents from Ugarit' BASOR 143 (1956) 17—22; H. Wildberger, 'Samuel und die Entstehung des isr. Königtums', *Theol. Zeit.* Basle 13 (1957), 442—69.

g **8:1–10 The Demand for a King**—This ch together with the election of Mizpah (10:17—27) and the homiletic expansion of the Gilgal convention (12:6—25) is inspired by prophetic and deuteronomic opposition to the monarchy (cf the judgements passed on individual kings e.g. 1 (4) Kgs 13:34; 16:25—26) in the light of experience. **1.** Samuel's hereditary judge-ship breaks down; succession is always the crucial problem. Note that the prime duty of a king in the Ancient Near East was always to establish, not to pervert, justice, a concept which deeply influences the royal messianic texts. **2.** Both 'judging' at an out of the way place like Beer-sheba is strange; Jos. (Ant VI, 32) has one in Bethel, the other in Beer-sheba. **5.** Meeting of the clan sheiks at Ramah; they demand a king 'to judge us like all the nations'—they are thinking of the Canaanite city-states and neighbouring Aramaean kingdoms like Damascus; the theological implications of the request, assimilation in religion and cult, can be seen by reading 2 (4) Kgs 18:32—35 and its parallel in Chr. **7.** The answer of Yahweh: monarchy is a form of apostasy of the refusal of Gideon, though it seems, in fact, that he accepted, with the results as detailed (Jg 8: 23ff). **8.** Again the Exodus theme.

h **8:11—22 'Le Droict du Roi'**—Often compared with the passage on kings in Dt 17:14—20, written out of an experience of monarchy in Israel especially apropos of Solomon, 1 (3) Kgs 5; the similarity, however, apart from the phrase 'a king like all the nations round about' is not striking. A similar outlook can be documented from Ugarit and elsewhere. See Mendelssohn, art. cit. **16.** 'cattle' with LXX against MT 'young men'. **18.** 'You will cry

out' as in the time of the Judges, but now he will not hear **272h** you. **22.** The meeting is disbanded.

9:1–13 The Search for the Asses—de Vaux ap- **i** propriately entitles this finely-told story 'How Saul set off in search of his Father's asses and found a Crown'. Although the unity of the whole section on the kingmaking of Saul has been defended by Robinson and Buber (see articles above), this story comes almost certainly from an earlier source betraying a quite different attitude to monarchy. It may be closely related to 1 Sm 1—3—the style is similar and Samuel is prophet or seer (not judge) in both—and may even have aimed at presenting the call of prophet and king as parallel. For an interesting parallel see F. Dornseiff, 'Archilochos von Paros und Saul von Gibea', TLZ 80 (1955) 499f. **4.** Saul's itinerary **j** is hard to reconstruct: Shalisha (Kefr Thilth SW of Shechem) is well to the NW; Shaalim is unknown; then back to Benjamin and to Zuph which may be the birthplace of Samuel in 1:1. The purpose of such a devious journey may well be to emphasize the providential nature of the eventual encounter. See H. J. Stoebe, 'Noch einmal die Eselinnen des Kis', VT 7 (1957) 352—70. **6.** The title 'man of God' for prophet seems to have become frequent in the N about the time of Elijah (cf Jos 14:6; 1 (3) Kgs 12:22 and 2 Chr 11:2; 1 (3) Kgs 13:1ff; 17:18—24; cf also 'man of the Spirit' Hos 9:7). **7.** The custom of bringing a gift to a prophet is attested in the N at the same time e.g. Jeroboam's wife visiting Ahijah (1 (3) Kgs 14:3) and the man of Baal-Shalishah to Elisha (2 (4) Kgs 4:42). **9.** An important gloss which, however, **k** would appear to fit in better after 11 where the *rō'eh* is first mentioned. It looks back from the time of the 'classical' or writing prophets to the first period of ecstatic prophecy of 10:5; 19:20. (For the *rō'îm* and *nᵉbî'îm* see W. Eichrodt, *Theology of the OT*, 1961, 296—303 and W. F. Albright, *From the Stone Age to Christianity* (1957²) 289—309. **11.** The meeting at a well outside the city is a familiar motif in the OT and elsewhere cf Gn 29; the indications given are particularly long-winded. **12.** The high places (*bāmôt*) were built outside the town. They went against the old idea of Yahweh as abiding on Sinai alone, to which later Sion was assimilated (Gal 4:24—5). The practice was Canaanite and bore with it the constant temptation to assimilate Yahweh to the ba'alim, e.g. in Jg 6:25ff. Ex 20:24 admits plurality of sanctuary and 1 (3) Kgs 3:2 provides the excuse for the period down to Solomon, but they were definitely excluded in the Josian reform 2 (4) Kgs 23:8 and Dt 12:5.

9:14–10:1a Meeting with Samuel—**16.** Saul is **1** *nāgîd*, prince; it is sometimes supposed that this was a stage preparatory to the kingmaking (10:24; 11:14) but 16 speaks of the 'Matter of the kingship' and the anointing denotes royal status; but the series of charismatic saviours is carried on smoothly from Jg, and Saul later leaves his farm to fight the war of Yahweh. Noth's title of 'king-designate' seems best. For anointing in Israel see de Vaux, op cit 103—6. **21.** The choice of the least, the most insignificant, the younger son is a constant motif in biblical literature cf David 1 Sm 16; the initiative belongs always to God (1 Cor 1:27—29). **22.** The sacrifice of communion and sacred meal was the bond of solidarity between God and people with the king as intermediary. The choice portion (the 'leg and upper portion' RSV) which expresses his overlordship is similar to if not identical with that reserved for the priests (Lv 7:28—34; 10:14—15).

10:1b—16. The Sign—Again the ternary pattern: a **m** threefold sign with command and execution narrated parallel, though only the third sign is mentioned in the

272m latter, the first and second possibly being omitted as unnecessary. There are three men, three kids, etc. **1.** 'The Lord ... the sign to you' (RSV) supplied from LXX, missing from MT through haplography. **2.** Rachel's tomb was at Ramah according to the earlier tradition (Jer 31:15), changed later to Bethlehem (Gn 35:16) where it is now Moslem property. Zelzah may be a proper name but is more probably a corruption. **3.** Not Tabor in Galilee. Here as in 1:24 the sacrificial material is the same as in the Canaanite, Ugaritic sacrificial system. **4.** The giving of two out of three pieces of bread is reminiscent of the double portion given to Elisha (2 (4) Kgs 2:9 cf Dt 21:17)—a pledge of the
n prophetic spirit to come? **5.** nᵉṣîb can mean either 'garrison' (RSV) or 'pillar' (JB). This incident is significant for the history of the prophetic movement; one notes in particular the use of external stimuli and the connexion of these ecstatics with cult. See § 451b. It is evident that this earlier and sympathetic account regards the monarchy as charismatic. **8.** This command is at the root of Saul's rejection, though in fact he waited the stipulated period (13:7). **12.** The question 'And who is their father?' may be construed as an answer to the saying (but this is difficult) or an implicit rebuke for Saul mixing with men of low birth and, for some, doubtful reputation, or an enquiry as to who was their leader cf 2 (4) Kgs 2:12. The proverb is repeated 19:24.

273a 10:17–27 The Public Designation of Saul at Mizpah—Follows on ch 8 and continues in the deuteronomic vein: Exodus theme (18), the book with the royal prerogatives and duties (25 cf Dt 17:14–20) etc. For the view that Mizpah is secondary and the ceremony localized here on account of this city being the religious centre during the Exile, see de Vaux, op cit 304–5. **26.** Gibeah, already mentioned, is Tell el-Ful 3 miles N of Jerusalem. **27.** The mention of opposition links up with 11:12 and leads to the ceremony at Gilgal.

b 11:1–15 The Jabesh-Gilead Campaign and its Sequel—This account has much in common with Jg: it follows the Jg scheme for narrating God's saving acts (the phrase 'to do salvation' in 13 means to give victory, cf Zech 9:9); the Ammonite attack defeated by Jephthah in Jg 6 is in some ways similar; they attacked Gilead and the Israelites were at Mizpah, the men of Gilead attempted unsuccessfully to come to terms and then send for Jephthah to deliver them and the spirit of God fell on both heroes (Jg 11:29; 1 Sm 11:8). Since Jg 21 also deals with Jabesh Gilead—in this case its failure to be represented in the assembly at Mizpah— it is possible, as has been surmised, that we have here a Mizpah tradition.

c 1. The last two words of ch 10 are corrupt; they probably belong to this ch; 'about a month later ...' Nahash ('Serpent', doubtless after an Ammonite serpent-deity) is still there during David's reign (2 Sm 10:1ff). For the origins of Ammon E of the Jordan (Amman is the Jordanian capital) see Gn 19:38. Jabesh-Gilead: the name is probably preserved in wadi Jabis SE of Beth-Shan. They seem to have been closely connected with Benjamin and show their gratitude by burying the remains of Saul (1 Sm 31:11). **2.** This practice of putting out one eye is attested in the Ugaritic Legend of Aqht. **7.** The tribal call to arms and the holy war, cf the grim symbol in Jg 19:29, 'and Samuel' probably added. **8.** The review takes place at Bezek (Khirbet Ibziq S of
d the Gilboa range). The enormous and impossible figures, even greater in LXX, betray an editor with no interest in historical exactitude of detail; the division into N and

S indicates in general the date of composition. **14.** 'to **273** renew the kingship' an unusual phrase unless we take 12–14 as a later addition inserted to connect this event with the earlier Mizpah proclamation; otherwise read ûnᵉqaddeš 'let us sanctify'—by a special religious ceremony.

Ch 12 The Gilgal Assembly—Gilgal, near Jericho, was **e** the central sanctuary and therefore political centre of Benjamin and must have been the source for many of the traditions about Saul and this period, cf 13:4, 7. The political debut of Saul seems to have been modelled on that of Joshua, Dt 29–31; cf also the valedictory discourse of Joshua himself on the occasion of the Covenant renewal as prescribed every seven years at the feast of Tents (Jos 24 cf Dt 31:10). In general, this ch shows every sign of being of late redaction (see Smith op cit 82–3) and may have closed the Judges period at some redactional stage before the formation of the canonical book.

1. 'All Israel'—see above. **3.** In this avowal of **f** innocence, cast rhythmically and in rhyme as most prophetical oracles (cf 15:22ff), Samuel establishes his own covenant—fidelity to the Mosaic 'form of doctrine', cf Dt 29–31 and Nm 16:15. **6–13.** The profession of faith associated with the feast of Covenant renewal, cf Dt 26:5–9; 6:20–24; Jos 24. These are 'the great sacred facts that constitute the community' (G. von Rad, *Genesis*, 1961, 14) and begin here with Jacob the 'wandering Aramaean', leading to the Exodus. The mention of four Judges in the deuteronomic style (for MT Bedan read LXX Barak) ends with Samuel himself and thus leads into the sinful act of demanding a king. **14–15.** Paranetic section. **16–18** A portent—thunder **g** and rain during the dry season—is given to authenticate Samuel as true prophet, cf Moses and the prodigies preceding the Exodus (Ex 7–11); Elijah and the prodigy of Mt Carmel (1 (3) Kgs 18). **19–25.** The theme of election; the monarchy is permitted by God but must come under the Covenant with its moral demands. The deuteronomic history always regards the monarchy as bearing chief responsibility for national catastrophe (see 2 (4) Kgs 17:9). See K. Möhlenbrink, 'Sauls Ammoniterfeldzug und Samuels Beitrag zum Königtum des Saul', ZAW 58 (1940–1) 57–70.

Chh 13–14 Saul and the Philistine War—This **h** section ends with a summary 14:47–51, cf 2 Sm 8:15ff which makes it plain that ch 15 is an account of Saul's rejection of different provenance. It is, in substance, an account of Saul's part in the Philistine war, later aided by his son Jonathan, and may well be continuous with 9–10:16. Ch 13 contains in addition Samuel's proclamation of Saul's rejection at Gilgal (7b–15²) and a note explaining the comparative failure against the Philistines (19–22).

1. MT 'Saul was one year old when he became king and **i** he reigned two years over Israel' is impossible to reconstruct; later tradition gave him the stereotype 40 years (Ac 13:21). **2ff.** The story is put together from sometimes isolated pieces of tradition as in Jg, mainly dealing with skirmishes disputing control of the valley of Achor and the wadis leading down towards Jericho and the Jordan. For topography see G. Lombardi, 'Alcune questioni di topografia in I Sam 13, 1–14, 15', Studi Franciscani Liber Annuus, 9 (1959) 251–82. The reduction of the number—eventually to 600—has theological significance, as with Gideon's 300 (Jg 7:8). **3.** nᵉṣib can mean governor, garrison or monument; the context and verb would suggest the first, being an assassination meant to lead into the holy war, cf Jg 3. Read with LXX 'Saul blew the trumpet through all the

273i land, *and the Philistines heard it and said: "The Hebrews have revolted"'*. Saul would not have spoken of 'Hebrews'. **4b** together with **7b** seems to be a preparation for the rejection scene at Gilgal; leaving the uplands for the plain would be suicide and in fact in 16 they are still on the heights. **5**. One notes again here the preference for multiples of 3; numbers are schematic not realistic. Beth-aven may be an opprobrious nickname for Bethel common in the N prophets (Am 5:5; Hos 4:15 etc) or the Beth-aven E of Bethel mentioned in Jos 7:2.

j **7b**. The next 8 vv are from a different source and the introductory **7b** is meant to link them. The commentators have been hard put to it to discover Saul's fault; he waited the stipulated time (10:8), and his acting as priest was quite in order, as later with David and Solomon. But Samuel was Saul's charismatic partner, his point of contact with the divine will; the account, coming from prophetic circles, served to illustrate the prophet's essential function in society—Yahweh could only be reached through him.

k **13:15—23. 15**. Mention of the people with him in LXX is omitted in MT through homeoteleuton. The description of the Philistine attack is an introduction to the exploit of Jonathan. **19—22**. Text corrupt and difficult. For **21** see notes in JBL 61 (1942) 45—46; BA (1953) 33—36; *Arch. für Or.* 15 (1945—51) 68. The technique of smelting came from Anatolia and was for long a closely guarded secret. The *šeḳel* was the standard measure.

l **14:1—23 Jonathan's Exploit**—cf J. Blenkinsopp, 'Jonathan's Sacrilege' CBQ 26 (1964) 423—49. The Philistine war was characterized by this type of exploit, cf Jg 14—16; 1 Sm 17 etc. For topography see Lombardi art cit and G. A. Smith, *Historical Geography of the Holy Land*, (1806⁴) 250ff. **2**. For Gibeah read Geba (cf 13:15) Migron (MT) may be a place name (Is 10:28) but seems too distant; read 'threshing floor', a place traditionally sacred to king as mediator for the people cf Ugaritic Aqhat IA 19—23 (ANET 151); 2 Sm 24:19 25; 1 (3) Kgs 22:10. **3**. Ahijah is probably the same as Ahimelech in 21:2; 22:9. For the priest and the ephod see M. Tsevat, 'Studies in the Book of Samuel', HUCA 32 (1961), 191—216. Both in Ugarit and in the Mari letters there is evidence for a baru-priest or seer accompanying the army. **13**. Seeking a sign, *'ôt*, is an integral part of the holy war and, if a procedure little to our taste, shows at least the conviction of providence stemming from the idea of covenant loyalty. **14**. MT corrupt after '. . . twenty men'; if the word 'furrow' is correct it may refer to the dead lying in a long line. **16—19**. This abortive consultation of the ephod (MT 'ark') gives another insight into Saul's temperament. **23**. For 'Beth-aven' (MT) read 'Beth-horon' (LXX).

m **24—46. Two Ritual Faults**—A primitive story incorporating religious ideas in an early stage of development and almost untouched by editorial correction e.g. the fast as part of the holy war; the concept of an oath (cf Jg 11:31) and of sin which can even be involuntary; urim and thummim. There are also some rather curious parallels with Gn ch 3, the curse, the effect on the eyes after eating, the question 'What have you done? and the excuse etc. **31**. This is the scene of Joshua's spectacular victory (Jos 10). Life, contained in the blood (Dt 12:23) belongs to God and must be libated. **36**. Consultation of Yahweh, probably again by ephod though we are not told, was an inseparable part of the holy war (cf 23:2, 12). Before viewing this as a piece of moral irrelevance we should remember that what motivates it is the desire to conform to the will of the Covenant God and

that conscience is the proximate norm of morality. **273m** **45**. *pādāh*, redeem, is used metaphorically (cf Ex 13:13).

47—52. A summary of the reign which would normally **n** come at the end and perhaps once did so cf 'Judge' formulae and 2 Sm 3:2—5; 5:13—16; 20:23—6; but where this section recapitulates his successes ch 15 relates his rejection. The lists were copied from archival material. **49**. For MT 'Ishvi' read 'Ishyo' who is the Ishbaal of 1 Chr 8:33.

15 The Amalekite Campaign and Rejection of o Saul—Duplicates the earlier rejection (13) and comes from a different prophetic source hostile to the monarchy. Samuel is still theocratic leader and prophet in the style of those common during the later monarchy—Nathan, Elijah and others. It also prepares for the reign of David (28).

1—3 The Command The king owes the prophet **p** absolute obedience because the latter is the voice of God for him; the account here is written out of prophetic experience down to the time of Dt (Dt 18:9—22) cf 2 Sm 12: 1 (3) Kgs 20:40; 22:13ff; 2 (4) Kgs 9 etc. **2**. '*Thus Yahweh (Ṣᵉbā'ôt) has spoken!*' the introductory form familiar from the writing prophets. **3**. 'Amalek': Beduin nomads in the Negeb and Sinai peninsula, traditional enemies. See Ex 17:8ff; Nm 14:45. Samuel's command implements Yahweh's own words to Israel in the Dt Code (25:17—19); this and the fact that Saul's campaign remained unknown and without effect for David in his own troubles with the same enemy (1 Sm 30) has led to doubts on the historicity of this episode; but while remaining a prophetic paradigm, the incident has details (the campaign, name of the king etc) which are too circumstantial to admit this extreme view. For the *herom* see de Vaux, op cit 258—67.

4—9 Execution—The fault for the writer is not so much **q** violation of *herem* as disobedience to the prophet's voice. **4**. *Tᵉlā'im*—a town in the Negeb (Jos 15:24). For numbers see note on 11:8. The ensuing description is extremely vague; nomads do not live in cities and Havilah (cf Gn 2:11) and Shur (meaning wall, perhaps a defensive line facing Egypt) cannot be located with certainty and were probably equally nebulous for the author. **6—7**. The sparing of the Kenites, closely connected with Israel (Nm 24:10; Jg 4:11, 16) and the destruction of Amalek follow closely the oracles of Balaam (Jg 24) and Saul seems to be the 'hero' or king referred to (24.7). It is not clear why Saul left Agag alive after the campaign.

10—31—Samuel appears here as typical prophet and **r** man of God. **12**. *yad* 'monument', in the light of comparative material, would be a phallic symbol. **15**. Rather than a miserable subterfuge or an act inspired by avarice (19) this should be seen as a sincere act of religion, but Saul had already lost his point of contact with Yahweh through the prophet. **22**. This is the real prophetic oracle and it is rhythmic, composed of three short couplets (3b excluded). This opposition between the pervasive, false idea of sacrifice and obedience to God's word is thematic in the 8th cent. prophets of the N e.g. Am 4:4ff; 5:5ff; 5:21; Hos 4:12 and especially 6:6. See also 9:15 where Gilgal is condemned. **23**. 'divination', is parallel with *tᵉrāpîm*, idols, false gods. Dt and the deuteronomic historians connect divination and apostasy constantly with the monarchy (Dt 18:9; 2 (4) Kgs 17:17 cf Hos 3:4); they were eliminated together with necromancy during the Josian reform (2 (4) Kgs 23:24). **24**. The suggestion that 24—31 is a prophetic expansion, first made by Stade, is not improbable. For the symbol of the

273r torn cloak cf 1 (3) Kgs 11:11, 30ff. **29.** Another clear reminiscence of Balaam (Nm 23:19).

s **32—35 Death of Agag**—*ma'ªdannôt* is obscure, (RSV 'cheerfully'). LXX presupposes *me'odannit* 'trembling and omits *sar*, giving a consistent reading, cf JB 'reluctantly'. Less probable versions: bound, pampered, very fat (Vg). How he met his death is uncertain since the verb *sasap* occurs only here, but it is conceived as a ritual act, 'before Yahweh'. We can only see Samuel as labouring under an erroneous conscience; many of these ideas had still to be purified in the crucible of religious experience and suffering. For the textual problem see J. de Fraine, 'Le Roi Agag devant la Mort' EstE 34 (1960) 537—45; S. Talmon. 'I Sam 15, 32*b*, A Case of Conflated Readings', VT 11 (1961) 456ff. For the whole cf A. Weiser in ZAW 54 (1936), 1—28.

274a **16:1—18:5 David's Anointing and Political Debut**—The literary history of this section is particularly complicated. Thus 16:13 is only the first of three anointings of David and he is brought to Saul's attention on two different occasions (16:18; 17:55). Later on, the king's attempt to eliminate David and the latter's magnanimity is recorded several times. In addition, these two chh appear in a considerably shorter form in LXX which Kennedy and others think ought to be followed.

b **16:1—13 David's Anointing**—In many ways told parallel to that of Saul e.g. investiture by the Spirit (10:10; 16:13); both had to be fetched; the height of Saul and of Eliab (10:23; 16:7); the sacred meal. The vital point is that the Spirit of God comes upon David and deserts Saul, and it is upon this contrast that the ch is based. For 1—11 we have the help of the oldest Qumran MS, 4QSam[b] (see Introd.). **1.** Jesse and his sons mentioned also in Ru 4:17—21 and 2 Chr 2:12—17. Bethlehem (from Beth-Lahmu, sanctuary to the local god of war) a prominent centre of Judah about 7 m. by road S of Jerusalem. **2.** For MT 'you will take', LXX, supported by 4QSam[b], has '*take*', a small but significant, because typical, example of renewed confidence in LXX. The sacrifice and sacrificial meal is parallel to that with Saul (9:19). **4.** Add, with LXX and 4QSam, '. . . *oh seer*?' **10.** Here Jesse has eight sons; later (17:13) there are only four while in 1 Chr 2:13 there are seven in all. **13.** First mention of David. The name is certainly the name of the person, not of the office, but its origins are obscure. Perhaps from *dôd*, love, beloved. He is further described in 18. He is anointed later by the men of Judah (2 Sm 2:4) and of Israel (5:3). It is strange that in 17:28 Eliab knows nothing of this anointing.

c **14—23.** Saul's contact with God is through Samuel and this is now lost through disobedience; his seizing Samuel's garment is symbolic of this conviction. Later, after the death of the prophet, the only recourse left to him is necromancy (23:8). This is the theological theme. The 'evil spirit of God' which produced bouts of intemperate violence found, it is evident, the ground prepared by Saul's psychological instability. He has already had 'ecstatic' experience (10:6) and more than one fit of delirium is later described (18:10; 19:24). His love—hate relationship to David (16:21; cf 24:17; 26:21) and to Jonathan (20:23ff) should also be noted. **14.** No theological distinctions are made here cf Jg

d 9:23; 1 (3) Kgs 22:23. **18.** It seems clear that there are at least two distinct traditions about David which have been amalgamated: the young shepherd lad who gets mixed up in the fighting; the warrior—musician who is called to the king's service. The end of 19 brings them together. **23.** For the role of music in predisposing

to certain abnormal mental states cf 10:5; 2 (4) Kgs **274d** 3:15. For a psychological discussion on Saul's temperament see R. Scharf, 'Saul und der Geist Gottes', *Fs C. G. Jung* (1955) 209—38.

17:1—18:5 The Single Combat—There are several **e** difficulties in this passage, thus, (1) codex B, our principal LXX witness, omits 17:12—31, 41, 55—18:5 leaving what appears to be a coherent story. We do not know whether this is in fact an omission made on account of the evident difficulty of harmonizing with other traditions or whether MT has been expanded with the help of another source related to 16:1—13. On the whole, the latter would appear more probable. See H. J. Stoebe, 'Die Goliathperikope und die Textform der LXX', VT 6 (1956), 397—413. The two traditions on the political debut of David (see note on 16:18) are certainly continued and the final editor has striven to produce a harmonious and coherent presentation, though signs of his activity can be found in the text. (2) There is also **f** no unanimity as to who actually killed Goliath. The name occurs here only in 17:4 and 23 but in the latter verse it has been inserted later as is plain from the syntactic arrangement. The usual designation, starting from 17:8 and often repeated, is '*the* Philistine'. In 2 Sm 21:19 we are told that a certain Elhanan killed Goliath though the text is corrupt and interpreted differently in the parallel 1 Chr 20:5 where we read that Elhanan killed Lahmi brother of Goliath. There are three possible approaches to a solution: (i) either 1 Chr 20:5 represents the original text of 2 Sm 21:19 in which case there is no discrepancy (or) (ii) the name has been added to the story of David's single combat at a later stage, the Elhanan tradition being older (or) (iii) Elhanan is in fact David's personal name before he became king. See R. de Vaux, 'Les Combats Singuliers dans l'A.T.', Bib 40 (1959) 495—508 and note to 2 Sm 21:19. This last, however, is based on highly questionable arguments.

1. Another phase in the Philistine war cycle, cf 4:1; **g** 28:1. Socoh and Azekah are in the approaches to the Judaean uplands just S of the Samson country; the Valley of Elah (the Terebinth) is Wadi es-Sant. **4.** *îš habbēnayîm* could mean 'man selected for single combat' (lit 'man between two'), and 8 would therefore contain a formal challange. See H. W. Hertzberg, in JPOS XXI (1948) 110—16. His height (at least ten feet) evidently owes much to folklore (cf Gn 6:4; Jos 11:21 etc) but his armour is curiously similar to that of the Achaeans of the Homeric poems. **13** seems to come from a source different from 16:1—13, which knew of four not eight sons cf 1 Chr 2:13 where there are seven. **15—16.** Would appear to be added by a redactor in order to harmonize the two traditions on David and give him time to arrive. **29.** *dābār* being ambiguous, David meant either 'May I not even speak?' or 'Was it not a question of importance?' **32.** Continues smoothly from 11 without the difficult delay of 40 days. **37.** Both here and in David's speech of defiance, 45ff, the editor is at pains to bring out the theological implications of the episode. **40.** The sling was not a child's toy cf Jg 20:16. **54.** **h** Added at a later stage by a redactor who has forgotten that Jerusalem is not yet taken (2 Sm 5) and that David has no tent of his own in the camp. **55.** This account of Saul's first meeting with David is quite different from the preceding. **18:1—5.** The account of the beginnings of the David-Jonathan friendship is attached to the preceding narrative. The exact nature and implications of the covenant which Jonathan makes with his friend (cf 23:18) and of the gift which accompanies it escapes

74h us; it is Jonathan who acts throughout on the conviction that David, not he himself, is the heir-apparent. For one explanation see J. Morgenstern, 'David and Jonathan' JBL 78 (1959) 322—5.

i **18:6—19:7 Saul's Jealousy**—Here again the shorter LXX text (without 6a, 8b, 10—11, 12b, 17—19, 21b, 26b, 28b, 29b—30) offers in the main a more coherent narrative than MT. The LXX text fits in well after David's promotion to the position of Saul's squire and his fight with the Philistine and enables us to take 10—11 as an anticipated duplication of 19:9—10; probably David's engagement with both Merab (17—19) and Michal (20—22) represents a similar case of parallel traditions. **6a.** an editorial link-phrase. The womenfolk greeting the warriors after a fight with song, music and dance is well attested, cf Ex 15:20—21; Jg 11:34. The short couplet would have been repeated antiphonally as in Ex 15; see also 21:12; 29:5. **12b.** This is the theological **j** theme which the editor wishes to emphasise. **17.** The offer is made in fulfilment of the promise made in 17:25 but with evil purpose. 20—22 is quite different since it is nowhere linked with 17—19 and Michal falls in love with David. **18.** The difficulty was providing the *mōhar*, marriage present (cf 25), see de Vaux, op cit 26—29. **21b.** Absent in LXX, this would appear to be a harmonizing gloss. Klostermann's reading 'in two years' is unnecessary and hard to reconcile with 'today'. **27.** 'one hundred' in LXX. **29.** cf 12; Saul moves a step nearer to the tragic climax. **19:1—7.** This seems to be parallel to 20:1—39. If we suppose that Jonathan had already accepted David as successor to the throne (cf 18:3—4), a claim consolidated by his marriage to Saul's daughter, this would further explain his determination that David should survive in the face of the opposing design of his father.

75a **19:8—21:16 The Flight of David**—Here again a continuous narrative has been put together out of different and often parallel traditions. **8—10.** The same situation as 18:10—11—a feat of war by David followed by the insane attempt on his life by Saul. The divine name used is different. **11—17.** It is difficult to see this account of the Blockade of David's House as consecutive—in the circumstances the latter would hardly have gone home and the distance was minimal. The night chosen might well have been Michal's bridal night, as Smith suggests (op cit 179). **13.** *terāpîm* cf Gn 31:34; Jg 17:5, household idols; possibly from *rāpu* bearing the meaning 'to bring fertility'. It becomes a prophetic code-name for idolatry 1 Sm 15:23; abolished in the Josian reform 2 (4) Kgs 23:24. **14—15** seem to imply two **b** journeys. **18—24.** Here again this is not directly continuous with the preceding; it has much in common with the ecstatic experience at Gibeah (10:10—12) and provides occasion to repeat the same proverbial taunt as there. It also contradicts the statement made in 15:35. It could well be in direct continuity with 10. **18.** Naioth, a place-name in RSV, could mean 'dwelling-place', the *coenobium* of the prophetic guild (see Smith 181). There is evidence in the OT of such groups connected with local cult (cf 10:5) as also of right of sanctuary (1 (3) Kgs 2:28—30; 2 (4) Kgs 11:11). For the sending of three lots of messengers cf the story in the Elijah cycle 2 (4) Kgs 1:9—16.

c **20**—The main narrative here in which Jonathan denies that Saul is seeking David's life (2, 9) is not in harmony with the tradition preserved in 19:1—7. There are, in addition, two accounts of Jonathan's plan to save his friend: one which implies direct contact between them (11—17) and another in which this is excluded (18—23,

35—39). These have been brought together in a later **275c** recension. **1a.** This is meant to provide the nexus with the preceding incident. **5.** This was an ancient and important feast when a sacrifice was offered; often mentioned in the prophets (e.g. Am 8:5; Hos 2:13). See de Vaux, op cit 469. **13—17.** This certainty that David would succeed to the throne despite Saul's determination to establish an hereditary monarchy (v 31) is an important theme in the author's scheme of providential history. **23.** E. Finkelstein, 'An Ignored Haplography', JSS 4 (1959) 356, reads 'The Lord *is Witness* between you and me forever'. **24.** The king **d** sat 'at the meal' MT (literally, 'at bread'), cf 27; LXX has 'at the table'. **26.** MT is overloaded here and in general the text is not well preserved. David had committed an involuntary ritual fault. **30.** a common type of opprobrium; the exact translation is no longer possible—means 'son of a profligate' or something of the kind. Saul's wife was Ahinoam (14:50) but she does not appear to be Jonathan's mother. **31.** Again, the case of the reluctant heir-apparent! cf 13—17. **40—42.** As practically all the commentators agree, this is an addition which accords ill with the second plan of Jonathan; the whole point of the arrows stratagem was to communicate without running the risk of personal contact.

21:1—10. This is the first stage of David's flight; Nob, **e** on the E slopes of Mt Scopus, twin to the Mt of Olives and NE of the city, lies on the direct route to Bethlehem. This must have been an important religious centre—it had OG priests (22:18, 20), the ephod and the 'show bread'—since the Ark at Kiriath-jearim seems to have been under Philistine control. Despite the confusion in the priestly genealogies in 1 Chr, it seems certain that Ahimelech is the Ahijah of 14:3; the father is Ahitub in both cases (cf 22:9, 20) and the prophecy of 2:33 is fulfilled in Abiathar. The name Ahimelech reminds us of Melchizedek, priest-king of Salem, and the rites to Moloch practised nearby. **3.** David allays his fears with a plausible story. **5.** This is the *lehem happānîm*, 'Bread of the Presence' placed on a gold-faced table in the Inner Sanctuary, eaten and replaced every sabbath by the priests. See Lv 24:5—9 and Ex 25:23—30 (P). This confirms that Nob was the central sanctuary served by the priests who had fled from Shiloh. **4.** 4QSam[b] **f** here again supports the longer reading of LXX. **5.** David's answer is rather difficult; military operations undertaken in the course of the Holy War were sacred; and sexual intercourse rendered one ritually impure. 'Vessels' could refer to weapons (cf 9) or else be a euphemism for the sexual organs. **6.** See 12:3 and parallels. **7.** Prepares for the massacre of the next ch. For 'chief of the herdsmen' (*rōʿîm*) MT read '*of the messengers*' (*rōṣîm*) **10.** The sword had been left there as an ex-voto.

11—16. A humorous interlude which really belongs **g** to the cycle of stories about David as mercenary with the Philistines (ch 27) where Achish is his overlord. **14.** For MT 'made signs' read with LXX 'drummed' cf Vg: *impingebat*. See M. Biç, 'La Folie de David', RHPR 37 (1957) 156—62.

22—26 Narrow Escapes—There follows a group of **h** incidents mostly concerned with David's narrow escapes from the king and localized for the greater part in the Shephelah or the Arabah around Hebron. They promote the theological sense of the history by working out the doom of the king and the inevitable ascendancy of the blessed and anointed David, through whom God's purposes are to be realized. The two main threads in this latter are the progress to Jerusalem (where the

275h Ark will be solemnly installed) and the establishment of the messianic dynasty in the face of the contrary plan of Saul. These preliminary chh illustrate the tribulations through which the Christian must pass before entering the Kingdom. Coming to the literary question, there is evidence of parallel traditions in the Treachery of the Ziphites (23:19—24 and 26:1—25) and the Sparing of Saul by David (ch 24 and 26). Those commentators who divide according to personalities call this the 'Saul and David' section (Kennedy, Hertzberg etc). Budde advanced the interesting but undemonstrable hypothesis that the author of this section was Abiathar the priest.

i We divide it here into eight stories distinguished on the basis of subject-matter and topography: (i) 22:1—2 In the Cave of Adullam, (ii) 3—5 David sends away his parents, (iii) 6—23 Massacre of the Nob priesthood and escape of Abiathar (iv) 23:1—13 Narrow escape at Keilah (v) 14—28 Narrow escape in the Desert of Ziph (vi) 24:1—22 David spares Saul at Engedi (vii) 25:1b—43 David and Abigail (viii) 26:1—25 David spares Saul in the Desert of Ziph.

j **22:1—5** Adullam is about 12 m. SW of Bethlehem. David's clan was probably also proscribed with him. His career at this stage is similar to that of Jephthah (Jg 11). **3.** Mizpeh in Moab is unidentified. David had an admittedly tenuous claim on the Moabites, later to be conquered by him, in that his great-grandmother, Ruth, was from there (Ru 4:17). **5.** Gad and Nathan are to be the voice of God for David during his long reign.

k **6—23.** Another step towards Saul's spiritual dissolution. He has lost Samuel and the Ark, now he disposes of the Shiloite priesthood and thereby loses the ephod, last remaining contact with the divine will. Note also that it is made clear that the tragedy is the result of David's lie. The account follows on after 21:2—10. **7.** This was standard treatment for liegemen (cf 8:14—15) especially when, as here, they belonged to the same tribe as the king. There is always an undercurrent of hostility between the ten tribes and Judah in OT history which is exploited here. **8.** The victim of paranoia suspects everyone, even his closest associates. **17.** The couriers, equivalent perhaps to modern outriders, could not bring themselves to do sacrilege. It was left to a foreigner, Doeg, to be the instrument of fulfilling the prophecy made to Eli (2:32—3). **20.** cf 14:3.

l **23:1—13.** Keilah is 3 m. S of Adullam in the Shephelah; this exploit is therefore closely connected with 22:1—2. Before relieving the town David seeks an oracle—by ephod, as we are told later. **3.** Keilah is in Judah but may have been considered at that time as in the Philistine sphere of influence. **8.** Saul calls out the militia to profit by what he considers a providential occasion. **11.** This exchange is awkward. MT has two questions to which only one answer is given until the first question is repeated. In LXX only the first question is answered. 4QSam^b alone gives a clear reading with the two questions asked and answered separately.

m **14—28.** Another narrow escape, this time in the desert of Ziph, 5 m. S of Hebron. The strongly topographical character of these stories stands out; this one, like other etiological narratives in the OT, is designed to explain the origin of an unusual local feature, the 'Rock of Escape' (28). **14.** This v is overloaded; the midbār refers to the hilly and desert land E and S of Jerusalem. **15.** Horesh is about 2 m. S of Ziph. **18.** A confirmation of the berît of 18:3; 20:8; this strengthens the conjecture that the covenant concerned David's succession to the throne. **19.** The betrayal. Their action was understand-

able, as was that of the men of Keilah and, to a lesser **275i** extent, that of Nabal, since David's maquis force evidently lived off the land. This v is also overloaded; so much detail would have made Saul's injunction to enquire further superfluous. Jeshimon may have been used locally as a topographical name, but means 'wasteland', 'steppeland'. **24.** Maon is Tell Ma'in S of Ziph.

24. This is the first of two accounts of David sparing **n** his rival, the second of which is in ch 26; this strengthens the hypothesis of two parallel sources or traditions for this period. The purpose of this narrative which gives a strong impression of immediacy and factuality was to bring out the contrast between the king and David; Saul, as he himself implies (19), would not have acted so and in fact his massacre of the priests showed that he no longer distinguished in practice between profane and sacred. Moreover, the basic function of the king concerned justice and morality. The point is made once again that God has withdrawn from Saul and is with David; the theme of election and rejection. **1.** Ein Gedi ('Goat **o** Spring'), well-known oasis near the Dead Sea in the Judaean Desert, practically on the 1948 armistice line. **4.** 'cover one's feet' was a current euphemism for relieving oneself cf Jg 3:24. **5.** Clothing was considered among the ancient Semites as a kind of extension of personality, especially in the case of the royal regalia. **7.** šāsa', 'rend', 'tear' is inappropriate here; read with LXX 'persuaded'. **11.** 'my father' Though David was in fact Saul's son-in-law, this was a quite common form of address to a king or leader cf 2 (4) Kgs 5:13. **13.** It is generally thought that this proverb, inappropriate because in no way calculated to help the reconciliation, has been inserted by a later glossator. **21.** The 'Kingdom of Israel' is now the form and ideal, the central issue. Compare the oath which follows with that made to Jonathan (20:14—17); it will not be forgotten and will have important consequences for the future.

25. Gives a valuable glimpse into the social life of the **p** 11th—10th cent. in that region—the relation between nomads and the sedentary centres, the demand for protection money etc—a condition in some ways still prevailing today. Its vivid characterization, its touches of grim humour and remarkable psychological truth e.g. in the cool resourcefulness of the women (cf Rebekah, Jael, Batsheba . . .) and the long and skilful apologia of Abigail are characteristic of this writer. **1a.** a note on its own, cf 28:3 where it prepares directly for the Endor scene. Saul is now completely cut off. **1b.** For MT 'Paran' which is too far S read with LXX **q** 'Maon'. Carmel (cf 15:12) is just S of Ziph. Here we have the typical beginning of a good story cf Jg. 13:1; 1 Sm 1:1 etc. **3.** Caleb was a S tribe absorbed by Judah. According to the Alt-Noth reconstruction Mamre near Hebron was the centre of the 6 S tribes i.e. Judah, Caleb, Cain, Othniel, Jerahmeel, Simeon. The kingdom is founded on David's ascendancy over this federation (M. Noth, History of Israel, 178—203). **4.** This was a festive occasion, yôm tôb (8) when everyone was generous and hospitable cf 2 Sm 13:23. **6.** Follows epistolary form attested at a later period; according to G. R. Driver, 'A Lost Colloquialism in the OT', JTS 8 (1957) 272, this is paralleled by an Arab greeting still common. **11.** For MT 'water' read with LXX 'wine'—more con- **r** sonant with what follows. **22.** 'They who urinate against the wall' (Heb.) stands for males; see also 1 (3) Kgs 14:10; 16:11; 21:21; 2 (4) Kgs 9:8. **25.** nābāl means fool but with an undertone of wickedness; used in OT prayer often as a euphemism for 'sinner'. Paraphrase 'Fool by name and fool by nature' or (with

75r Smith 225) 'His name is Brutus and he is a brute'. **29.** The 'bundle or satchel of the living' may refer to pebbles used for counting sheep or goats which were kept in a small bag; the same expression occurs in the Qumran hymn 12. See O. Eissfeldt, *Der Beutel der Lebendigen*, 1960, who explains it with reference to one of the Nuzi tablets. **37—38.** possibly an apopleptic fit. **43—44.** cf what happened to Merab, 18:19. His firstborn Amnon was the son of Ahinoam; see the list in 2 Sm 3:2—5.

s **26.** Similar in many ways, as we have seen, to the sparing of Saul in ch 24, even in detail e.g. Saul has 3,000 men; he himself assures David of success; etc. There is also no reference here, as we might have expected, to the former case. We should note that two accounts seem to have been conflated here: in 5 David goes alone while in 7 he is accompanied by Abishai; in 9 and 10 we have juxtaposed reports of what he said and although he tells his companion to take the spear and jug, he in fact takes them himself; in 13 he goes back alone. **1.** cf 23:19 couched in the same words. **7.** A lance stuck in the ground was used to indicate the sheikh's tent among the Arabs. **12.** This *tardēmāh*, preternatural sleep, occurs in the Yahwist story of Adam, (Gn 2:21) and Abram (Gn

t 15:12). **19.** Interesting for the history of religious ideas in OT. Yahweh was conceived as the god of his land as, for example, Kemosh in Moab. When one went abroad one came under the jurisdiction of another god. This explains the great insistence on Israel as the land of Yahweh not of the *ba'alîm* previously in possession. See also the touching gesture of Naaman, 2 (4) Kgs 5.17. This popular conception helps to explain the crisis of faith at the Exile—see Ps 137 (136):4.

76a **27—2 Sm 1 The Last Act in the Tragedy of Saul**— It is fairly easy to grasp the literary structure of this section. Two strands have been skilfully interwoven: one, already anticipated in 21:11—16, of David as mercenary of Achish king of Gath; the other, which comes to us in two forms which can be partially reconstructed, speaks of the death of Samuel, Saul's search for an oracle through necromancy, the giving of the oracle and his subsequent death in battle, with what followed. The following scheme giving the two versions of the main narrative may help:

David spares Saul	Death of Samuel	Spirit of Samuel	Death of Saul
a) 24:1—23	25:1	28:3—25	31
b) 26:1—25	28:3		2 Sm 1.1—16

b **27:1—28:2 David, Mercenary of the Philistines**— The chronological sequence is uncertain: David's initial reception by Achish has already been told, and there seems little ground for pessimism at this point. Here he plays the age-old role of the *hapiru*. **6.** Ziklag, mentioned in Jos 15:31; 19:5; 1 Chr 4:30, possibly Tell el-Khuweilifeh c. 20 m. SE of Gath in the direction of Beersheba, was a good point from which to carry on the double game of defending Judaean centres while pretending to police the desert beduin for Achish. The chronological indication seems to mean that it was a royal borough some time during the divided Monarchy. Very likely a later gloss. **7.** cf 29:3 LXX has '4 months', which is certainly too short. **8.** Here David shows himself as a supreme opportunist; but he sees everything which happens to him as under the providence of God. The moral situation must be assessed in the context of a different milieu both social and psychological; the narrator moreover does not always feel called upon to comment by either approving or reprobating. **10.** Three of the six S tribes are here mentioned, cf 30:14 Chereth and Caleb and note on 25:3 above. **28:1—2.** Achish places him in a critical position; David gives an ambiguous

answer; and is promoted to the position of personal **276b** bodyguard of the king.

28:3—25. This account is closely connected with ch 15; **c** the oracle, which the spirit of Samuel gives, follows in 15:27—8, and it is possible that the notice that Samuel did not see Saul till the day of his death (15:35) may refer indirectly to what we read here. **3.** This is in the pluperfect; Saul violates his own proscription of necromancy. The reference to 'mediums and wizards' is found in the account of the Josian reform (2 (4) Kgs 23:24) following Dt 18:11. The prohibition is repeated in the levitical legislation (Lv 18:21; 20:6, 27). The Chronicler gives the seeking of knowledge from an undue source as a basic cause of Saul's failure (1 Chr 10:13). It is clear that this sin plays a great part in prophetic theology and history writing (cf 1 Sm 15:23). **4.** Shunem is in the centre of the great plain of Esdraelon half-way between Mt Gilboa to the S and Tabor to the N; Endor is a small village between Shunem and Tabor. Saul therefore had to make a wide detour to avoid the Philistine lines. **6.** Saul's spiritual isolation is complete. **13.** The witch says: 'I **d** saw an *elohim* coming up from the *earth*'. The primitive sense of *elohim* is 'a supernatural being', cf Ps 8:6 and probably Gn 3:5, cf *'ilib* in the Ugaritic religious texts which may come from *el* and *'ôb*, the word used here for 'spirit', *'ereş*, earth, can also mean 'underworld' (e.g. Is 29:6) as in other semitic languages (cf accadian *erşetu*, ugar. *arşu*); this is required here. Later she identifies it with Samuel on account of his mantle cf 15:27 and that of Elijah 2 (4) Kgs 2.13. Saul hears but does not appear to see. **17.** 'Yahweh has *torn* the kingdom . . .' the same verb, *qāraᶜ* as in 15:28. **18.** For comparative material on the anger of Yahweh see M. Vieyra in RHittAs, 19 (1961) 47—66. The story ends quietly as does ch 16.

29—30 David leaves the Philistines—We take up **e** again here the story of David's vicissitudes with Achish. The reference to the Philistine army on its way to Jezreel, 29:11, links up skilfully with 28:4 and prepares for the tragic finale at Gilboa. **1.** For Aphek see note to 4:1. The 'Fountain which was in Jezreel' (i.e. in the Plain of Esdraelon) very probably Ain Jalud just E of the town of Jezreel, though LXX (A) has Endor. The depth of Philistine penetration can be seen in the fact that they already had Beth-shan (31:10). What was at stake here was full possession of the great and fertile plain. **5.** Cf 21:12; for the *serānîm* see note to 5:8. **6.** The form of this oath, as also the appellation used in 9 (it will be used later by the woman of Tekoa, 2 Sm 14:17, 20, and by Mephibosheth 19:28) is due of course to the redactor. **8.** It is **f** difficult to believe that David had not his tongue in his cheek in making this protestation! 30:1. For the Amalekites see the note to 15:2; they knew how to time their raids well. **7.** cf 23:6. **9.** Wadi Besor cannot now be identified; the journey from Aphek to the region of Ziklag must have taken three days and it was not surprising that some fell out. This incident gives us a good insight into this type of mobile desert warfare. **14.** 'Cherethites' is practically synonymous with 'Philistines'; consonantally identical with Crete, generally taken as place of origin or at least of dissemination of the Sea Peoples (in Ezek 25:16 and Zeph 2:5 LXX has 'Cretans' for MT 'Cherethites') cf also the Ugaritic Legend of KRT (Keret?). They made up the bodyguard of David as David and his men had that of the Philistine Achish (2 Sm 8:18). **21.** The distribution of the captured booty gives another **g** example of David's strong sense of justice, an indispensable attribute of royalty. **24.** This *mišpaṭ*, rule based on precedent, is in the usual form of a couplet in trimeter, it being customary to put tags of this kind in verse for

276g easy learning. The same principle laid down in the sacerdotal rule for the Holy War, Nm 31:27. **26.** This was evidently a political move to prepare for his return by binding of S clans more closely to him. The list should be checked with lists of place-names in Jos; they are all in the region just S of Hebron. For 'Bethel' read 'Bethul' (Jos 19:4 which may be identical with the Bethuel of 1 Chr 4:30), for 'Ramoth-Negeb' read 'Rama' (Jos 19:8 LXX^A), for MT 'Rakal' read with LXX '*Carmel*' (cf 25:2 etc).

h **31 Battle of Gilboa**—for the military situation see 28:4. The story is told in what is practically a rhythmic recitative. **2.** For Saul's sons see also 14:49 and 1 Chr 8:33; 9:39. The fourth is Ishvi (14:49) or Ishbaal, elsewhere Ishbosheth. **4.** This is the self-inflicted death canonized by the literature of every heroic age, cf in the OT Abimelech (Jg 9:54), Zimri (1 (3) Kgs 16:18) and Razis (2 Mc 14:41). 2 Sm 1 contains a different tradition since it is improbable in the circumstances that the Amalekite would have invented the story. **7.** 'The men of Israel who were on the other side of the valley and on the other side of the Jordan' is in both MT and LXX; the correction to 'in the cities' in both phrases is graph-

i ically easy (*b'ry* for *b'br*) but conjectural. **8.** They would probably have sent the head and armour around with the messengers. The armour finishes in the temple of Ashtaroth, a deity taken over by the Philistines, like Dagon, from the natives. This would probably have been at Ashkelon (cf 2 Sm 1:20) where a bas-relief of the goddess has been discovered; later Derketo was worshipped there. According to 1 Chr 10:10 his head was stuck up in the temple of Dagon. This dishonouring of the dead is forcibly reminiscent of some incidents in the Homeric poems. **11.** The act of *pietas* performed by the citizens of Jabesh-gilead was in return for the prompt assistance given them by Saul, see ch 11. Beth-shan, now Beisan, notable for its immense *tell* and well-preserved amphitheatre, is just over the other side of the Jordan from Jabesh. This unique case of cremation was no doubt due to the cruelly disfigured state of the mutilated trunk; later the bones are given burial in Saul's own tribe (2 Sm 21:12). Burning, that is, desecrating the *bones* of the dead was considered a great crime cf Am 2:1. We can form an idea of what the funeral rites must have been like from later cases of royal obsequies e.g. 2 Chr 16:14; 21:19; Jer 22:18; 34:5, in the latter cases the ritual lamentation is mentioned, 'Woe, Lord'.

II SAMUEL

277a **2 Sm 1:1–16 Another Account of Saul's End**—This account differs in some significant points from the preceding. Saul does not commit suicide but is killed by an Amalekite who *happened* to be there; he is unwounded (9) but hard pressed not by the archers but by the enemy chariots (on Mt Gilboa!). It might be thought that the Amalekite was lying, but this is nowhere suggested by the author or suspected by David despite some inherent improbabilities in the story (the mention of chariots, the absence of reference to Saul's retinue, to the extent that he had to rely on a chance Amalekite to kill him). It has been proposed to divide this section into two separate traditions: in 1–4 + 11–12 the news is brought by one of Saul's men; in 5–10 + 13–16 by an Amalekite, the 'young man bringing the news' (5, 6, 13)—but this does not seem to be necessary. **1.** An evident continuation from

b 1 Sm 30:31. **2.** His condition already a sign of bad news. **3.** The scene is described in a way reminiscent of 1 Sm 4. **10.** *nēzer*, usually translated 'crown' or 'diadem', is the

symbol of the king as a consecrated person (from the same **277** root as *nāzîr*, 'consecrated one'). The *nēzer* of the high priest of a later age was something fastened with blue lace to the 'turban', made of gold and inscribed 'Holy to Yahweh' (Ex 29:6; 39:30; Lv 8:9). It was the custom for kings to go into battle in full regalia. **15.** The same fate overtook Ishbaal's murderers 4:10.

17–27 David's Lament over Saul and Jonathan— **c** This *qînāh*, lament, as the later one over Abner (3:33–4) is certainly authentic and is inserted from the 'Book of Yashar' which is quoted also in Jos 10:13 and possibly 1 (3) Kgs 8:13 (LXX). The text is not always well-preserved and little help is forthcoming from LXX. Since the refrain occurs at the beginning, at the end and in 25, it is not impossible that there were originally two *qînôt*, the second, equal in length to that over Abner, dedicated to the memory of Jonathan. **18.** 'and he said' should immediately precede the dirge, cf Jos 10:12. 'To teach the sons of Judah "The Bow"' is difficult. It is not likely that it refers literally to military expertise, with reference to the cause of Saul's downfall (1 Sm 31:3). It may be a title of a traditional song; or it may refer to Israel or the men of Judah as the Bow of Yahweh (as in Zech 9:13 and probably Hos 1:5); Yahweh being re- **d** presented in these old poems as a warrior (e.g. Ex 15:3); this especially if Yashar is the same as Yeshurun, the poetical designation of Israel (Dt 32:15; 33:5). **19.** 'The Glory of Israel'; perhaps 'Alas, the Glory! . . .' or 'Has the Glory . . .'? **21.** The same curse is found in the Ugaritic Aqhat and on the basis of this latter we can restore: 'Let there be neither dew nor rain upon you, nor upsurging of the deeps'. See H. L. Ginsberg, 'A Ugaritic Parallel to 2 Sam 1.23', JBL 57 (1938) 209–13; E. Speiser, 'An Analogy to Aqhat', JBL 69 (1950), 377. **24.** Compare the words of Sisera's mother, Jg 5:30.

2:1–5:5 David King of Judah—This section begins **e** with the anointing of David as king of the S tribal federation under Judah and ends with the extension of his kingship over the N tribes after the elimination of Abner and Ishbaal. It covers a period of 7½ years, but the writer skilfully selects the essential events and carries on the sweep of the narrative leading to the final triumph of David which centres on two points: the establishment of his dynasty; the setting up of a religious centre in Jerusalem (ch 5–6). These two motifs are basic to the Nathan oracle (7) and prepare for the Court History which follows.

2:1–11 The Situation after Gilboa—A decisive stage **f** in the development of political power; David's long wait is almost over, even though the Philistines evidently controlled both David in the S and Abner in the N. **1–4a.** David is still at Ziklag. Despite his *Lament*, the first and greatest obstacle to his progress was now removed, cf later the death of Abner 3:22ff; of Ishbaal, 4; the remainder of Saul's line except Mephibaal, 21. His achievement of suzerainty over Judah and the other partly incorporated S tribes is similar to that of Gideon and Abimelech. **3.** the 'cities of Hebron'—those which acknowledged Hebron as their centre. The name means 'League' and it was hallowed by the tombs of the Patriarchs; formerly Kiriath-Arba (City of the Four), Jg 1:10, a Calebite town. **4a.** No mention is made of the prophetic anointing at Bethlehem (1 Sm 16:13). **4b–7** **g** links up with 1 Sm 31; David once again shows his fine sense of opportunity by seizing the occasion to invite them to recognize his kingship. **6.** *hesed we'emet* 'steadfast love and faithfulness' (RSV), the fundamental expression of Covenant commitment. **8–11.** Here we are informed as to what happened to the kingdom of Saul

277g after the defeat. Abner ('My father is a Lamp' cf 2 Sm 21:17) holds it together by making Ishbaal king. MT 'Ishbosheth' ('Man of Shame') is theological correction for Ishbaal ('Man of Baal'), made at a time when it was no longer remembered that Israelite names containing the theophoric element 'Baal' (Lord) for Yahweh had been common especially in the N e.g. Jg 7:1 (cf Hos 2:18—19). Later *baal* was taken as applying exclusively to Baal Hadad, god of the storm. **8.** Mahanaim (The Two Camps), see also Gn 32:3 and 2 Sm 17:24. Probably Tell el-Hajjaj just S of the Jabbok. **10***a* and **11** are redactional glosses which interrupt the narrative. **40** is a conventional figure and 'two years' may be meant to correspond to the length of Saul's reign as given in the now corrupt 13:1.

h 12–3:1 North and South drift into war—the account which follows is written from a point of view highly favourable to David; not everything can be interpreted with certainty since the writer is often allusive.

12–17. This grim story of single combat by the Cistern of Gibeon has been differently interpreted. Some see it as a series of friendly wrestling bouts that got out of hand and ended in tragedy. See Y. Sukenik in JPOS 21 (1948), 110—16 and, for a conjecture on the technique involved, C. Gordon, 'Belt-Wrestling' in HUCA 23, 1 (1950), 131—6; others as an attempt to settle the issue by single combat. It is not, however, certain that Abner's coming to Gibeon (el Jib) was hostile, and the reference to the sitting on either side of the cistern looks like an attempt to negotiate in the course of which this initially friendly bout took place. See O. Eissfeldt, 'Ein gescheiterter Versuch der Wiedervereinigung Israels'. Nouv. Clio 3 (1951), 110—27; 4 (1952), 55—9. The great cistern of spectacular depth and with steps cut into the side has been cleared by Prof. Pritchard and his team J. Pritchard, *Gibeon where the Sun Stood Still*, 1962. **16.** Helkath-hazzurim—literally 'Field of Rocks' but probably corrupt, since it does not fit the context; read 'Field of Sides' or 'of Rivals'.

i **18–3:1** Only the first incident of a long war between David and the remnant of Saul's dynasty is recorded; the author emphasizes that this war came about more by tragic accident than design on David's part. Abner kills Asahel, David's nephew, in self-defence thus bringing on himself the blood-feud which ends in his own death (3:27). **24—28.** A truce is proclaimed and the pursuit of Abner called off. Note that the writer bases his story upon good local tradition and tells it with interest and verve. **3:1** A summary which links up directly with 3:6.

j 3:2—5 David's Sons at Hebron—these are divided from the other part of an archival list preserved in 5:13—15 in consequence of the decisive break constituted by the occupation of Jerusalem; in 1 Chr 3:1—4*a* they are continuous and there is one discrepancy—Daniel for Chileab, which latter reflects the Kalebite origin of Abigail. Daughters are not counted. **5.** For 'wife' read 'sister'. Marriage with a half-sister was not uncommon. The list is given in view of David's dynasty and the question of the succession.

k 3:6—21. First Steps to Union—Abner is evidently the real power in the disorganized and tributary Saulite kingdom. His taking Rizpah from the harem of the dead king had an obvious political significance as can be seen from the similar action of Absalom at the suggestion of Ahithophel (16:21). In 12:8 we are told that Saul's harem passed with the title to David. **9.** the *hubris* of Abner in setting himself up as Yahweh's agent without a call ends with his death. **13.** Another example of the amazing political acumen of David. This condition is vital since Michal had been given to David as wife

(1 Sm 18:27) and stood for the legitimacy of his claim; **277k** it implied also a repudiation of any irregular transaction—to his own advantage—which Abner might have come prepared to offer. **15.** A shorter form of the same name is given in 1 Sm 25:44. See H. J. Stoebe, 'David and Mikal', BZAW 77 (1958). **19.** Benjamin was Saul's tribe and therefore, presumably, the most difficult to persuade.

22–39. Murder of Abner—The inevitable outcome of **l** the blood-feud aided, no doubt, by jealousy and self-interest since Abner certainly expected to gain by the negotiations. The author is at pains to emphasize David's innocence, see especially 22, 26, 28, the lament and subsequent fast; there is no need to question this since his death meant the breakdown of negotiations which had promised well for David, even though Abner would have certainly been an obstacle later on. The impression this callous and treacherous act made on David can be gauged by the fact that he has it in mind on his deathbed (1 (3) Kgs 2:5) enjoining Joab's execution upon his son, which the latter carries out at once (32–34). It is not clear why David did not proceed against Joab at once, as he did against the slayer of Saul (1:15) and Ishbaal (4:12). **39** which in MT provides an explanation difficult to accept is textually uncertain and may originally, as in LXX, have referred to Abner not David.

4. Murder of Ishbaal—A decisive step towards absolute **m** power; the author emphasizes that this comes about not through violence or injustice but *within* the divine will. David is blameless whereas the murderers—they come from Saul's own tribe (2)—blasphemously pretend to act in the name of Yahweh, 8; yet their deed is objectively the means of the divine will being realized of the murder of Abner. 'The figures are pieces on God's chessboard' Hertzberg, ATD. 211. **2***b***–3.** A redactional note reminding the reader that Beeroth ('Wells'—now el Bireh about 10 m. N of Jerusalem) which belonged originally to the Gibeonite League was really Benjaminite cf Jos 9:17; 18:25. The site of Gittaim (cf Neh 11:33) is unknown; it may be the Gath of 1 Chr 7:21; 8:13; 2 Chr 26:6. **4.** Another insertion taken doubtless from **n** the later history of Mephibosheth (Meribbaal) ch 9 16:1—4; 19:25—31; 21:7. It was interpolated here to emphasize that now only this cripple was left of the Saul dynasty. The name is correctly given in 1 Chr 8:34; 9:40 Meribbaal = 'Baal is Advocate, Champion'; Meribaal = 'Hero of Baal'(?). The form here may be from *mippi ba'al*, 'from the mouth of Baal' or 'by order of Baal'. The treacherous act takes place in Mahanaim though all the circumstances are not clear in MT. V 6 in LXX followed by RSV reads: 'And the doorkeeper of the house was cleaning wheat, and she grew drowsy and slept; so Rechab and Baanah his brother slipped in'. **12.** cf 1 Sm 31:10.

5:1–5 David King of Israel—This corresponds to **278a** the anointing of David as king of Judah (the Hebron amphictyony) in 2:1—4*a* and close the period of 7½ years, cf 2:11. 1 Chr 11:1—3 simply transcribes this passage adding that the anointing was the fulfilment of the divine choice revealed through Samuel (1 Sm 16). The N–S unity depended however upon expediency and the personality of the king more than inner coherence, always threatened to come apart e.g. 19:41—20:3 and did in fact disintegrate after the death of Solomon. There are signs here of literary composition: 1—2 and 3 may be complementary. 4—5 is added as a familiar 'statistical summary' cf 1 Sm 4:18; 13:1; 14:47—51; 2 Sm 8:15—18 and the deuteronomic summaries in 1—2 (3—4) Kgs.

278a **1**b. cf Jg 9:2 Abimelek; this relationship was through David's marriage to Saul's daughter, hence the importance of her return. **2.** 'shepherd' a familiar metaphor for kingship cf Mi 5:3 and *passim* in Prophets and Psalms; also the homeric *poimēn* for ruler.

b **3.** It is now David not the Saulites (cf 3:21) who makes the covenant which must have included an oath of allegiance and possibly laid down some principles for preserving the balance between Israel and Judah. **6–16 Jerusalem: the End of the Road**—David's overlordship is at last crowned by the capture of the Jebusite city and its occupation as the new capital. The reality of kingship and political power is emphasized by the building of a palace and setting up the royal harem; this event is given theological significance even at the expense of chronology. In fact, the capture of the city probably took place after the Philistine war (17–25; 21:18–21) and, even on the basis of the schematic 40 years, the bulding of a palace by Hiram, whom we meet again in Solomon's reign (1 (3) Kgs 5:15), would have been much later. With the setting up of a new capital and cult centre (ch 6), roughly equidistant from the two centres of power, the nation first emerges recognizable as such; 'For the first time in their history they were taking part in a great historical movement, not as victims and sufferers, but creatively'. (M. Noth, *History of Israel*, 197). The origin of the city is obscure; it may be named after the god *slm* who figures in the Ugaritic texts. It occurs as *ursalim* in the Luxor texts (c. 2000 B.C.) and in the Amarna letter from prince Abdu-Heba (c. 1400–1370 B.C.). See ANET²487; DOTT 39; J. Simons, *Jerusalem in the OT*, 1952.

c **6–10.** The text is heavily glossed: 6b explains the Jebusite taunt, 7b explains Sion, 8b explains Lv 21:18 with reference to this event. Sion was S of the Temple Area' built on Ophel (The 'Hump'); a breached wall was found during the excavations. The 'water-shaft' (RSV) mentioned in the obscure v 8 (1 Chr 11:6 gives a quite different reading) may refer to the tunnel, discovered by Charles Warren, which brought the water of Gihon (the Virgin's Spring) into the city, but *ṣinnôr* remains uncertain. See also H. J. Stoebe 'Die Einnahme Jerusalems durch David' in ZDPV 73 (1957) 73–99. The name *Millo* suggests that it was the earth rampart built up to support what was to become the Temple Area of 1 (3) Kgs 9:15.

d **11–16.** The building of both palace and temple by Tyrian workmen in the Jebusite city suggests two sources of influence on the idea of kingship in Israel. Eleven children are here named, whereas in 1 Chr 3:5–8; 14:3–7 there are thirteen; for Eliada read Baalyada.

e **17–25 Two Victories over the Philistines**—These have been narrated here separate from other notices (8:1–14; 21:15–22; 23:8–39) on account of topography which makes it probable that the capture of Jerusalem followed soon after. The theological sense is powerfully emphasized—the decision, the victory comes from Yahweh cf 1 Sm 23:2, 4; 2 Sm 2:1. With the retreat of the Philistines back within their own frontiers the promise of the Land made to the patriarchs is to a great extent fulfilled. **17.** The 'Stronghold' is certainly not Jerusalem; probably the same as in 1 Sm 22:1–5 cf 2 Sm 23:13. The *casus belli* is the anointing by the Saulites. **18.** Valley of Rephaim cf Jos 15:8 is between Jerusalem and Bethlehem, SW of the city; Baal-Perazim probably Ras en-Nadir to the NW. The incident described in 23:13–17 has the same strong local colour. **21.** The taking of the Philistine gods is the reversal

of the Ark story, 1 Sm 4:11, and implies that Yahweh **278e** has brought about the victory. In 1 Chr 14:12 they are ordered to be burned.

22–25. A second campaign, not necessarily following **f** the preceding at once. The colourful episode of the sound of marching in the juniper trees (DV, following Vg 'pear trees'; others 'balsam' or 'mulberry') represents Yahweh in poetic, even epic fashion in terms of the autochthonous weather-god cf 22:10–11. The incident is commonly explained as an oracle from a sacred grove (Hertzberg 225). Reminiscent of the divine intervention in Jos 10:10–14 which took place in the same region. **25.** For 'Geba' read, with LXX and I Chr 14:16, 'Gibeon'.

6 The Ark brought to Jerusalem—This narrative **g** belongs to an original *Ark cycle* which probably arose in a liturgical context; it continues from 1 Sm 4–6. The inspired editor has skilfully positioned it after the previous ch: Jerusalem is to be not only the political but also the religious centre—leading up to the climax in the Oracle of Nathan (ch 7). This is the starting point of that momentous development in OT and NT which sees **Jerusalem**, 'city of the great king', as **the centre**, both in reality and in type, **where man meets his God**—in the prophets (e.g. Am 9:11), in Dt and the deuteronomic history, in the Priestly theology, in Psalms and the apocalyptic writers. It is possible that the Michal incident belonged earlier to the section on the Succession to the Throne of David 2 Sm 9ff (see L. Rost. *Die Überlieferung von der Thronnachfolge Davids*, 1926), but, if so, it has been skilfully integrated into the present narrative and serves the theological purpose which the history presents. The parallel account in 1 Chr 15 is freely adapted to illustrate themes dear to the Chronicler.

2. The various amplifications which occur when- **h** ever the Ark is mentioned suggest liturgical usage cf Ps 132 (131) and 1 Chr 16. Baale-judah is the Kiriath-jearim of 1 Sm 7:1 (cf Jos 15:9) about 7 miles from Jerusalem. **3.** a new cart, cf note to 1 Sm 6:7. Here we have Uzzah and Ahio instead of Eleazer whom we should have expected. LXX supposes 'his brothers'; Budde suggests '*ahiyw* 'his brother' and refers it to Zadok cf 8:17. **6.** Nacon—site unknown. LXX has Nodab, 1 Chr 13:9 Chidon. **6–8.** The whole Ark cycle stresses the radical holiness of Yahweh (see note and bibliography to 1 Sm 4:1b–7:17) and the impossibility of reducing the self-revelation of God to an ethical philosophy cf 1 Sm 6:19. What the whole incident illustrates is the feeling of Awe, *Schaudern*, Self-abasement as the beginning of true religion. **8.** a popular etymology; an experience calculated to remain in the memory, cf 5:20. **9–11.** The tragedy of Uzzah **i** resulted in David committing the Ark to Obed-Edom, a foreigner living in Gath (see note to 4:3); when it brought him not disaster but blessing—fertility, good fortune—the procession could continue after a three-month break. **14.** the manner of the procession, dancing, music, sacrifices etc, has suggested a parallel with the canaanite New Year Festival; see J. R. Porter, 'The Interpretation of 2 Sam 6 and Ps 132', JTS 5 (1954), 161–73. David wears the priestly *ephod* (see note to 1 Sm 2:19) and acts in the same way as the Jebusite and Canaanite priest-kings cf Gen 14:18ff.

20–23. The exchange between Michal and David **j** is full of psychological as well as religious truth—humility and realistic self-appraisal—and is, for the editor, the last episode in the history of the decline and fall of Saul's dynasty and intimately connected with the question of the succession. **21.** David's answer is

278j rhythmic. **23.** This seems to be attributed directly to Yahweh rather than to the aversion of the king.

279a 7 The Oracle of Nathan and Prayer of David— In addition to the commentaries and the study, still not superseded, of L. Rost quoted above, the following more recent studies may be consulted: Van den Bussche, *Le Texte de la Prophétie de Nathan*, Louvain, 1948; J. L. McKenzie, 'The Dynastic Oracle', ThS 8 (1947) 187–218; M. Noth, 'David and Israel in 2 Sam 7' in *The Laws in the Pentateuch and other Essays*, 1966, 250–59, and *Mélanges A. Robert*, 1957; E. Kutsch, 'Die Dynastie von Gottes Gnaden', ZThK 58 (1961) 211–23; A. H. J. Gunneweg, 'Sinaibund und Davidbund', VT 10 (1960) 335–41. From Cave 4 at Qumran comes an interesting midrash on 7:14 which can be compared with the Christian actualization of this ch e.g. in Ac 2:30; 13:22. '"I will be his father and he will be my son": he is the shoot of David who will stand with the Interpreter of the Torah who will rise in Sion in the end of days'. It also provides comparative material for the polemic against the Temple in NT, e.g. Ac 7, which owes much to this ch. See articles by Y. Yadin and D. Flusser in IEJ 9 (1959) 95–109.

b This narrative, which owes much to later theological reflection and shows signs of deuteronomic revision, is the climax to all that has gone before and the direct introduction to the Court History dealing with the davidic dynasty and the question of the succession. David proposes to build Yahweh a *house* (i.e. a temple) but Yahweh reveals that it is he who will build David a *house* (i.e. a dynasty). The old patriarchal promise is taken up, recapitulated and projected into a future which envisages the immediate succession of Solomon but also events in the more distant future. This sense, which we may legitimately call messianic, was so understood by David himself (7:19), by the author of Ps 89 (88) and 1 Chr 17 written after the Exile when the monarchy was no more. It is also assumed, as we have seen, in the NT, and is based directly on the meaning of *zera'*, seed, and *'aḏ-'ôlām*, for ever (13, 16). There are clear signs of rhythmic arrangement beneath the present form of the narrative, sometimes curiously similar to that in Gn 3.

c **1.** We cannot be certain that this event is chronologically in place. **2.** Nathan is first mentioned here; he is to figure prominently in the reign of David as court prophet, cf Isaiah and his dynastic oracles. **3.** 'The Lord is with you' cf 9. This is what the writer is at pains all the time to emphasize throughout the history of David—the *Emmanuel* idea. **4–5.** Introductory formulae familiar in the prophets, the first especially in Jer and Ezek. **6–7.** This is, in effect, a repudiation of the idea of the divinity as *tied* to a particular place, an idea which can feature only in a materialistic and naturalistic cult such as that of Canaan. Shiloh is therefore deliberately omitted from this historical summary. This should be seen in the same context as the prophetic denunciations of such a concept of worship **d** e.g. Am 5:21ff; Hos 8:11ff; Is 1:10ff; Jer 7; also 1 (3) Kgs 8:27 in Solomon's dedication prayer. For the eighth cent. prophets, the desert period was the ideal, as also here. **8.** Here the divine oracle begins. **9.** *'asîtî* = consecutive perfect therefore: 'I will make . . .', not past as in Vg and DV; see O. Loretz, 'The Perfectum Copulativum in 2 Sm 7, 9–11', CBQ 23 (1961), 294ff. The promises refer from this point to the future. 'A great name' seems to refer to the name acquired at accession to the throne, as in Egypt and elsewhere. See H. Bietenhard in TWNT 5 242ff and cf the name acquired

by Christ in his glorification, Phil 2:9. **10.** 'plant them' **279d** reminiscent of the Vineyard metaphor in the prophetic literature e.g. Is 5:1–7; Ezek 19:10–14. From here the individual and collective are practically indistinguishable, possibly due to redactional activity. As promise, it is an extension of the patriarchal promise; as covenant it **e** continues and extends that of Sinai. **12.** the centre of the prophecy, generally taken to refer to posterity, *zera'*, rather than to Solomon in particular. If this is so, 13 must be an addition to the original oracle in keeping with the idea expressed in 1 Chr 22:7–10. But it is not at all certain that *zera'*, 12, cannot refer directly to Solomon as the direct pledge of fulfilment in the distant future, in which case 13 can remain. **14.** This is the formula of divine adoption of the king as son, part of royal theology in the Ancient Near E cf Ps 2:7; 110 (109):3, and behind the messianic title 'Son of God'. **15.** *ḥesed*, 'steadfast love', is, on Yahweh's side, the great covenant quality wherein he reveals his inner nature; *passim* in the Prophets. Note finally how the whole structure of the oracle reveals the divine initiative from which salvation history comes into existence: 'not you . . . but I . . .'.

18–29 David's Prayer—He recognizes God's **f** hand in his own progress through many trials to the kingdom and in the history of his people. God is with him and with his people cf Emmanuel Is 7:14 etc **18** 'Sat'—an acceptable posture for prayer as can be seen from the monuments. **19.** 'shown me future generations'. MT 'this is the law of man', is usually amended or omitted. 1 Chr 17:17 'you show me as it were a series of men and he who brings it up is Yahweh God' shows that the text was not well understood even then. R. de Vaux compares with accadian *terît nišê* and suggests: 'This is the destiny of man'. There may have been a reference to Gn 3:17 added later as a gloss cf Am 4:13. **22.** The language in this praise of the Covenant-God is strongly reminiscent of Dt; **23** is textually confused, no doubt on account of the implied henotheism, cf Dt 4:7ff.

8:1–14 Lists of Campaigns—Drawn up in an almost **g** formulaic way—'he defeated . . ., they became servants to David and brought tribute'—may come in part from the royal archives. Historically, David's empire was made possible by a period of stagnation in the struggle for power in the Fertile Crescent in the 10th cent. Theologically, this section shows that the final fulfilment of the promise of the Land made to the Patriarchs is almost reached; the Land whose frontiers were to be 'from the Euphrates to the land of the Philistines and to the border of Egypt' (1 (3) Kgs 5:1 MT) cf here *Qere* to v 3 and the reminder that it was Yahweh's doing 6, 14. See A Alt in TLZ 75 (1950) 213–20.

1. *meteg hā'ammāh* obscure; a metaphorical ex- **h** pression about the control of power (*meteg* = bridle) or from accadian *meteg ammati* with the meaning 'the highroad of the mainland' (Sayce) cf 1 Chr 18:1 'Gath and her daughters' (i.e. dependencies, as perhaps in 1:20). **2.** This arbitrary disposal of prisoners of war was no better and no worse than current practice anywhere else in the world at that time (or later). **3.** cf 10:15–19. Zobah was a city-state in the Beqa' between Lebanon and Antilebanon. **12–13.** For MT 'Aram' read 'Edom' due to common scribal confusion between *r* and *d*, cf title of Ps 60 (59) and 1 (3) Kgs 11:15. According to the parallel 1 Chr 18:12 it was Abishai who fought this campaign in the Salt Valley, below the Dead Sea.

279i 15–18 Administration of the Kingdom—There are several such lists which punctuate the history of the monarchy, no doubt archival in origin—see especially the double of these vv in 20:23–26. **15.** To do justice and equity is the supreme function of the king in the ancient Near E, an idea basic to the understanding of the royal messianic texts e.g. Is 11:3–5. The significant accusation levelled against David by Absalom (15:2–4) can be compared with the words of the usurping Yassib, son of Keret, in the Ugaritic bronze-age epic (H. L. Ginsberg, BASOR Suppl. Studies 2–3, 1946, 32). **16.** The recorder had an important function; we might translate 'Chancellor'. **17.** This important v is unfortunately suspect cf 20.25; 1 Chr 18:16. Zadok could hardly be the son of that Ahitub who was grandson of Eli (1 Sm 14:3) when it was he who supplanted Abiathar of the Eli priesthood (1 Sm 2:30–6; 22:20; 1 (3) Kgs 2:26) in fulfilment of the prophecy made to Samuel. Zadok is sometimes represented as the link with the indigenous Jebusite priesthood—his name has the same theophoric element as Melchisedech and Adonisedek, both kings of pre-Israelite Jerusalem.

j 9 Jonathan's Son—Here begins the **Court History** concerned chiefly with the succession question, of vital importance in sacred history. See § 268g. The story of the lame Meribbaal (Mephibosheth), prepared for in 4:4, is the first ch of the history and opens, in its present state, rather abruptly. We hear of him and of Ziba his servant later on once more (16:3; 19:27–31; 21:7–8); David's kindness, primarily in fulfilment of the oath to Jonathan (1 Sm 20:15–17, 42), also served the purposes of this supreme political realist in rendering this last possible claimant to Saul's kingdom innocuous. It forms part of this history because it is the first but not the last of the obstacles placed in the way of the fulfilment of the promise made to David.

k 1. This *hesed* (kindness) (also 3, 7) is the covenant quality and is therefore explained by David's covenant with Jonathan; *hesed 'elōhîm*, 3, should be interpreted in this context. **3.** Ziba later figures as the calumniator of Meribbaal (16:1–4; 19:27–31). **4.** Near Mahanaim over the Jordan cf 17:27. **8.** We can imagine Meribbaal's feelings at receiving this call cf the situation of Jothan after the extermination of his kinsmen by Abimelech (Jg 9). **12–13** may well be an appendix added later.

280a 10–12 The Ammonite War and David's Sin— That this series of campaigns is not simply listed with the others outside the dynastic history (ch 8) is due to the fact that it serves as framework for David's sin which results indirectly in the next and vital stage of promise fulfilment—the birth of Solomon. Historically, it shows the 'Peasant King' (Smith op cit 313) on a par with the surrounding nations and threatening in fact to upset the precarious balance of power—hence the Ammonite-Syrian coalition. This type of warfare among these states was endemic so long as the great powers of the Crescent remained dormant.

b 1–5. For Ammon, Rabbah and Nahash see note on 1 Sm 11:1. The *hesed* again implies some treaty obligation acquired doubtless during the period of Saul's war against Ammon (1 Sm 11). The unfavourable reaction to the embassy of the advisors of the young king could perhaps be explained by David's message to Jabesh-gilead (cf 1 Sm 11:1ff) and the untimely deaths of Abner and Ishbaal; it would not be difficult to interpret these as acts of treachery. The shameful treatment of the ambassadors was in the same spirit as the *ḥerpāh* of 1 Sm 11:2, a gross violation of their sense of decency **280** and manhood.

6–14. The first campaign against Ammon and its **c** Aramaean allies: Beth Rehob, Zobah, Maacah and Tob, small states in the Beqa or Hauran regions. **7.** the *gibbōrîm* were the professional army as opposed to the old tribal militia (e.g. in 17); its creation and gradual predominance, composed as it was of mercenaries most of them foreign, is a significant aspect of the change to an ostensibly secular order introduced by the monarchy. **12** omit 'the cities of' as probably dittography with usual confusion of *r* and *d* (*beʿad ʿarê*) cf the Philistine army 1 Sm 4:9. The Ark would probably have been carried into battle as the national *palladium*.

15–19. Probably parallel to the summary in 8:3–9 **d** and inserted here because of the part it played in the Ammonite war through the coalition; this is brought out even more clearly in 1 Chr 19:16. In fact, David's N expansion was of decisive importance even theologically, as a step towards realizing the ideal frontiers of the Promised Land. **16.** This implies the existence of Aramaean groups in Assyrian territory. The site of Helam is unknown. **18.** For these numbers cf 1 Chr 19:18 where the number of chariots is ten times greater and the 40,000 refers to infantry; also 8:4 where 1,700 cavalry and 20,000 infantry are mentioned and its parallel in 1 Chr 18:4 which is again different; cf also § 206c. Apart from the evident freedom which the Chronicler allowed himself with numbers, there is some textual confusion here. See D. R. Ap-Thomas, 'A Numerical Poser' JNES 2 (1943) 198–200.

11:1–27a David and Bathsheba—The great prose **e** masterpiece contained in chh 11–12, of a type very familiar to the modern reader cf Tolstoy's 'The Kreutzer Sonata', is told with amazing psychological insight and truth. It is remarkable for what it omits more than for what it says explicitly; there is no moral comment, the doomed child remains without a name and the crime, as far as we are told, is never discovered by anyone except Nathan and Joab the accomplice. The theological profundity of the author can be judged indirectly by the astonishment and even scandal which its inclusion in sacred history has caused, beginning with the Chronicler who, in fact, omits it as not serving his purpose. It shows that God's purpose is fulfilled despite the disastrous reality of sin and the death that sin brings, for from this ruinous liaison was born Solomon, depository of the Promise. It illustrates also, what is too often forgotten, that the Israelite monarchy fell under a covenant which was in existence long before it and imposed obligations especially of justice which could not be ignored. In the case of any other king of 'the nations round about' taking the wife of a foreign mercenary, this drama could never have arisen; see also David's purchase of the threshing-floor from Araunah another non-Israelite 24:18–25.

2. It is possible and in keeping with what we learn **f** of her elsewhere that Bathsheba was not entirely innocent in exciting the king's lust and perhaps they had already met, as might be implied in the answer to David's enquiry. **3.** Uriah could be a Hebrew name—'Yahweh is my Light' though the man was a foreign mercenary—Hittite is often a generic term for one or other of the indigenous racial groups. **4b.** A note inserted with reference to Lv 15:19; this was the most favourable time for conception. **8.** David's object is to get Uriah back to his wife in time to avert suspicion in view of her pregnancy, a plan which is thwarted by the soldier's unexpected refusal of this furlough granted in the middle of an important

280f campaign and his insistence on sleeping in the palace barracks. Whether out of religious scruple (cf 1 Sm 21:4–5) or incipient suspicion he does not relent even when drunk. **11.** 'in booths'; or 'at Succoth'—in the Jordan valley on the Jabbok, prob. *Tell Deir 'Alla*. **19.** The exact anticipation of David's words (the interesting reference to the Ahimelech story, Jg 9) is explained by the common biblical literary procedure whereby command and execution are recorded in identical words. **26–27.** Mourning and fasting for the dead were the rule; from 1 Sm 31:13 the time appears to have been 7 days.

g **11:27b–12:15a The Parable of Nathan**—This simple, direct parable ending with the dramatic denunciation 'You are the man!' makes its point perfectly. The chief function of the king is to do justice, to protect the weak, the poor and socially depressed classes; David's condemnation is more on account of injustice than unchastity, as the parable makes clear. It is in verse (dimeter) and in a form familiar elsewhere in the historical books (the woman of Tekoa 14:4) and especially in the prophetic literature (e.g. Is 5:1–7; Ezek 16; 17; 19; 23 etc). It seems to have been added to the original narrative though it can hardly be proved from the conduct of David later on that he did not know of the condemnation.

h **6.** In accordance with the law, Ex 21:37, David pronounces his own sentence. **7.** 'Thus Yahweh has spoken!'—introducing the prophetic oracle. Its repetition at v 11 suggests an extension to the original oracle dealing with the abortive *Putsch* of Absalom (16:22) signalized by the appropriation of his father's harem. **13.** Both the spontaneous indignation of David at hearing Nathan's story and his immediate repentance show us at once the kind of man he was. His attitude to religious observance to which he brought a sincerity and spontaneity which many found disconcerting is well illustrated in the eating the Showbread (1 Sm 21:4) his dancing before the Ark (2 Sm 6) and his refusal to continue fasting and mourning after the death of his child (22–23). The great Ps 51 (50) is, according to the rubric, attached to this moment in David's career. **14.** MT has 'the enemies of the Lord' due to a theological scruple in the use of this verb.

i **12:15b–25 Death of the Child**—the reiteration of the fact and finality of the child's death (8 times in 4 vv) and the repetition in 21–22 give force and emphasis to this poignant narrative. **24–25.** The double name was not uncommon. Jedidiah means 'Beloved of Yahweh' and could be from the same root as David's own name. We should recall that love in this kind of context implies the divine choice. The designation of Jesus as 'the Beloved' (Mt 3:17) depends on the Isaian text about the 'Chosen one' (Is 42:1). Despite sin and the death it brings, the promise will be honoured.

j **26–31. Second Ammonite Campaign**—carried on from 10:6–14; 11:14–21, cf 1 Chr 20:1–3. **26.** 'the royal city'—perhaps a part of Rabbah (Amman). **30.** Milkom, the Ammonite God (cf 1 (3) Kgs 11:5), mentioned also in the Ugaritic texts, is altered to 'their king' *malkām* due to theological scruple. David was victorious also over the god of his enemies, cf the words of the Assyrian officer 2 (4) Kgs 18 and the crisis provoked at the Exile by the apparent victory of Marduk over Yahweh (Is 40ff). **31.** Not torture but forced labour—see 1 Chr 20:3.

k **13–14 The Crime of Amnon and its Sequel**—We have already learned that the throne of David is not to be occupied by a descendant of Saul (6:23), whose line is now represented by the insignificant Meribbaal. **280k** We read now of the elimination of three of David's sons in genealogical order: Amnon (13), Absalom (14—19) and Adonijah (I Kgs 1—2) leaving the way free for the child of promise—Solomon. Each of the three comes to his death through the sin of *hubris*, self-realization under different forms but outside the divine purpose and the terms of God's covenant with David (7). The sense of realism, factuality and immediacy of these stories is at once apparent though here and there are signs of their having been worked over.

13:1–37 Tamar dishonoured and avenged— **l** Amnon was the son of Ahinoam, Absalom and Tamar of Maacah; Tamar therefore was Amnon's half-sister. This kind of marriage, common in Egypt and Canaan and practised during the patriarchal period (e.g. Gn 20:12) was later forbidden by law (Lv 18:9, 11; 20:17; Dt 27:22) and reprobated (Ezek 22:11). **9–10** can be understood only if there was an outer and inner apartment. **18a.** This looks like an explanatory gloss; for the tunic, cf Gn 37:3. **21.** add with LXX '*yet he did not vex the soul of Amnon his son for he loved him, because he was his first-born*'. David always gave way to his sons, cf 27. **22.** 'neither good nor bad' cf 14:17—'nothing at all'.

23. Baal-hazor very probably *Jebel el-'Asur* N of **m** Ephraim *et-Taiyibeh* about 11 m. N of Jerusalem. Sheep-shearing was (and still is) a time for feasting and wassail cf 1 Sm 25:4. **28.** Absalom's *coup* was the result of 2 years' deliberation; it is impossible to avoid seeing the motive for the killing as not just vengeance but ambition; Absalom himself now becomes heir-apparent. **34.** This v has been imperfectly preserved; LXX has the people coming on the Beth-Horon road. The emendation suggested by Eissfeldt and Alt to Bahurim, a village NE of the Mount of Olives, is widely accepted. **37.** Absalom's mother, Maacah, was daughter of Talmai king of Geshur, a small Aramaean kingdom E of the Upper Jordan.

38—14:33 Temporary reconciliation of David n with Absalom—the narrative continues with the same mixture of realism, subtlety and even humour in the ruse of Joab and the parable of the woman of Tekoa. **38.** This repetition seems to point to the beginning of a new section. David's sorrow and resentment are somewhat blunted and, after all, Absalom is now the crown prince. **14:2** Tekoa is in the Judaean wilderness, S of Bethlehem, home of the prophet Amos (1:1). Compare her parable with that of Nathan 12:1ff. The Hebrew kings, as successors of the Judges, took over the supreme function of *mišpāṭ*, judgement, and remained always accessible to their subjects in this respect (see note to 8:15); the classes mostly in need of royal protection were widows and orphans (i.e. fatherless) cf 15:22f; 1 (3) Kgs 3:16ff; 2 (4) Kgs 6:26ff; 8:3ff etc. The incident is also a good example of the principle of collective responsibility of the *mišpāḥāh* or clan and the kinsman as blood-avenger. **11.** And yet, an ironical touch, it will be Absalom's hair that will cause his death! (18:9). **12.** Here begins the *dénouement*, cf 12:7. **14.** Amnon is **o** dead and no severity towards his murderer will bring him back again. **17.** 'good and evil'—everything as in v 20 cf 13:22; Gn 2:9ff; a reference to the almost divine knowledge and insight of the king. **25–27.** A eulogy of Absalom's beauty: in this, as in his impetuous and intemperate nature (14:30ff), he took after his father; the weight of his hair—perhaps about 5 lb, though LXX halves this—seems, like the description of the unique circumstances of his capture for which the present note

280o prepares (18:9), to report a popular tradition in vogue. **27.** Yet in 18:18 he has no son; of course, they may have died young. **28—33.** 'coming into the king's presence', lit. 'seeing the face of the king' is part of royal protocol, cf the Amarna letters, and is developed as a rich metaphor in Heb. prayer e.g. Ps 4:7; 80 (79):4. **33.** the kiss of reconciliation as in the liturgical *Pax*.

p 15:1—12 The Rebellion of Absalom—The second of the three sons now attempts to decide the course of the future even though not chosen by Yahweh to succeed. **1.** Not in accordance with Israelite custom; even the word for 'horse', *sûs*, is a loan word. His taking over judgement is an implicit claim to kingship. **7.** Hebron, Absalom's birthplace (3:2), must have resented David's change of capital, though his rebellion aims at the centrifugal N tribes (2, 6, 10). For MT 'forty' read *four*. **12.** Ahithophel ('My Brother is Folly') looks like a contemptuous nickname obtained by changing the original consonants. He came from Giloh, probably *Khirbet Jala* NW of Hebron and may have been the grandfather of Bathsheba (11:3; 23:34) which would suggest another reason for his treason.

q 15:13—16:14 Flight of David—This sudden reversal and plunge into the depths show David at his best: a great deepening of character through experience, humility and abandonment to the divine will at a moment when it must have seemed that the covenant mediated through Nathan had been either nullified or disproved by experience. We also see his ability to handle men and how he instinctively inspired confidence and loyalty. **r 16.** Caught between the centrifugal N tribes and Absalom to the S, David made no attempt to defend the city. He evidently did not foresee Absalom's treatment of the concubines left behind (16:21—2; 20:3). **18.** This parade of David's 'Foreign Legion'—including Cretans, Philistines and very likely Achaians (this is roughly contemporary with the Trojan War) prepares for the attestation of loyalty of Ittai of Gath—in marked contrast to the disloyalty of his own son and former associates. **23.** They left to the E, over Kidron, Mount of Olives, along what was later to be the Roman road to Jericho and the Jordan. **24.** This is the only mention of Levites in this early period and may well be a later **s** addition. **25.** A great sacrifice on David's part; he was in effect cutting himself off from every visible religious support and truly casting his bread upon the waters. At the same time he is already taking prudent measures against his return. **28.** 'fords', or the wadis which lead down to the Jordan (de Vaux). **30.** This v is strongly rhythmic and shows signs of careful stylistic composition, pointing perhaps to a cultic origin. Cf the account of the 'Glory' leaving the city and resting on the Mount of Olives in Ezek chh 10—11. It was probably a sacred place long before the setting up of the sanctuary of Nob (1 Sm 21:2) and its sacred character remained down to NT times. **32.** The Archites, mentioned in Jos 16:2, had their territory on the S limits of Ephraim.

t 16:1 Here occur two incidents a propos of men closely connected with the dynasty of Saul. Not even David seems to have found out whether Ziba had calumniated Meribbaal, judging by the outcome (19:27—28). **5.** Bahurim, NE of Mount of Olives, on the road to Jericho; it was evidently in Benjaminite territory, though even so Shimei's conduct was suicidal. **8.** Saul, Abner, Ishbaal certainly; but also very probably the ill-fated sons handed over to the Gibeonites (21:1—14).

281a 16:15—17:14 Absalom and Ahithopel—Absalom comes to the capital and is greeted by Hushai who ingratiates himself by flattery and thus prepares the usurper's downfall. **21.** The purpose of the suggestion is to lead **281a** Absalom, by publicly taking possession of his father's harem, to cross the Rubicon and proclaim himself as king in his father's stead. See note on 3:6. It may also have been an act of revenge for David's taking of Bathsheba, if Ahithophel was indeed her grandfather. The tent was the bridal tent (cf Ps 19 (18):6 and the Kuppah or canopy still used in Jewish weddings) and has suggested to some scholars that Absalom was re-enacting the pagan *hieros gamos* or sacred marriage which was the culmination of the accession ritual in the New Year Feast. **17:1** Ahithophel's plan for prompt action was the obvious one to follow and would probably have succeeded; there is some suggestion of personal animosity and hate in the old man's feverish haste. **3.** MT is confused and has to be completed from LXX—'as a bride comes home to her husband' (RSV), an early instance of this seminal metaphor to be taken up and developed in particular by Hos and Jer. **8.** Hushai has prepared his speech in advance and presents the case for delay skilfully; David needs time. He ends with a flourish of bravado, **13.** 14*b*. A concluding theological note. **17:15—29 David Saved by Hushai**—the machinery **b** set up by David before his departure goes into operation and saves him from almost certain destruction. **17.** Enrogel ('The Fuller's Spring') now *Bir Ayyub* ('Job's Well) S of Jerusalem in the Kidron. **18.** Not all in Bahurim (see note 16:5) were of the same persuasion as Shimei! **20.** The topographical indication given by the woman is uncertain (perhaps it was intended to be); 'over the brook of water' may be the outcome of textual corruption. **23.** The death of David's betrayer is similar in this respect to that of the betrayer of the Son of David as recorded in Mt 27:5. Apart from Ahithophel, we know of only Abimelech, Saul, Zimri and Razis (2 Mc 14:41) who commit suicide in the Scriptures. **25.** For MT 'Israelite' read 'Ishmaelite' (cf 1 Chr 2:17) and for Nahash very probably Jesse. The reference to Amasa's coming to Abigal (MT) implies the *sadîka* or *be'ena* marriage of the nomad beduin in which the wife stays with her own family and receives visits from her husband (e.g. Jg 15:1—3).

18:1—19:8 Defeat and Death of Absalom—Another **c** study in failure and spiritual disintegration not unlike that of Saul. The failure of Absalom is not due to the fortuitous play of circumstances; his attempt to bring about a kingdom of his own making and on his own initiative is at variance with the divine purpose and comes to nothing because God is present in the unfolding drama e.g. 17:14; 18:19, 28.

1. David's counter-attack is now ready; ironically, he operates from Mahanaim the former base of Abner and the Saul party. **3.** cf 21:17—an account which is earlier than this. David was now quite old and may not have been in full personal control as formerly, cf the brutally frank remonstrance of Joab, 19:5ff. **5.** The author is at pains to stress here, as so often, that David was not responsible for his son's death. **6.** 'the forest of Ephraim'—S of Mahanaim in the *Jebel Ajlun* district. For a description of the area and an evocation of this period of David's life see Nelson Glueck, *The River Jordan*, 1946, 93—101. **9.** In describing Absalom's death the author makes much of the shameful and even absurd circumstances which led to it; see also the contrast between the sepulchre he had himself prepared and the summary disposal of the disfigured corpse (17—18). **14.** 'into the heart of Absalom' perhaps not literally cf 'in the heart of the oak'; he still had to be finished off. **17f.** *Gal* is a heap or circle of stones cf Jos 7:26; 8:29; **d**

81d the *maṣṣēbāh* 'pillar' in the King's Valley (cf the gloss in Gn 14:17) near Jerusalem may have been erected after the premature death of a son (we are told he had three in 14:27), though the word *yad* suggests it was phallic cf 1 Sm 15:12; Is 57:8. The so-called Absalom's Tomb in the Kidron Valley has nothing to do with Absalom. **19.** The question now is: who is to break the news of Absalom's death? Joab, mindful of the king's order and of what happened to messengers sent to David on similar occasions (1:13ff; 4:9ff!) insisted on sending an expendable African slave whose colour would be a ready indication of bad news—messengers generally bearing on their persons indication of the nature of the news they brought e.g. 1:2; 2 (4) Kgs 9:17ff. Despite his pathetic eagerness to arrive first, Ahimaaz dared not tell the truth when face to face with the old king. The narrator is fully conscious of the pathos and emotional intensity of the scene.

e **19:9—40 The Return of David**—A new beginning in setting up the kingdom though trouble is soon to follow in the renewed breakaway of the N tribes and the usurpation of Adonijah. The story of the Return is built up in conscious parallelism with that of the Flight: encounter with Shimei (19:16—24 cf 16:5—13); Ziba and Meribbaal (25—31 cf 16:1—4); Barzillai (32—40 cf 17:27); the concubines (20:3 cf 16:20—23), though we cannot be certain that these episodes are in historical order. This was for David a period of intense political activity in which he shows himself still the supreme opportunist and realist.

f **11.** The end of the verse: 'The word of all Israel came to the king, to his house' should come at the beginning; the call for the king's return began in the N and was taken up by the sheiks of Judah only after some skilful diplomacy on the king's part. **12.** cf Jg 9:2; 2 Sm 5:1. Kingship is closely connected with kinship; note how this idea of 'bone and flesh' kinship is extended to the whole human race in Gn 2:23. **13.** Amasa was David's nephew 17:24. Joab had compromised himself by his brutal frankness but he was to dispose of his rival treacherously as he had of Abner (20:10; 3:27) and survive the death of his master, though not for long. **20.** Shimei was a Benjaminite and therefore not strictly of the Joseph clan which comprised Ephraim and Manasseh, but the three were closely connected both geographically

g and in origin (children of Rachel). **22.** 'What have I to do with you', of 16:9 10, a real rebuke; relevant for the NT use of the same expression Mt 8:29; Mk 1:24; Jn 2:4 etc 'an adversary'—literally 'a *satan*'. **24.** The condition of Meribbaal expressed mourning for the absent king; David did not go further into the real reason for his failure to go away with him. **30.** 'The whole proceedings down to the kiss and blessing at their leave taking is in the best style of Oriental culture and throws a particularly pleasing light on the bearing and person of David *post tot discrimina rerum*' Hertzberg, op cit 303. **36.** 'know good and evil' is explained by what follows cf Gn 2:9ff; I (3) Kgs 3:9; Dt 1:39; Is 7:15. **37.** Chimham was evidently his son.

h **41—20:22 Sheba and the Northern Secession**— The purely personal union between N and S achieved by David was under continual strain right from its inception and fell apart completely after the death of Solomon. **41—43.** There is some oscillation between sing. and plural here (in RSV plural is used throughout) which is interesting as a first stage towards personification of the tribes. **43.** '*I am the firstborn*' with LXX. Reuben was the firstborn of Jacob (Israel); in the tribal poem in Gn 49, which comes from the time of the early monarchy,

Reuben is seen as dispossessed in favour of Judah. **20:1.** **281h** Sheba was another Benjaminite (Gn 46:21) and may have been a kinsman of Saul. His call to Israel (in verse) signifies the end of the N levy; cf 1 (3) Kgs 12:16. **3.** This note, interrupting the narrative, connects up with 16:20—23. **4.** David decides on prompt action to crush the attempt at secession. Amasa does not succeed in raising the tribal militia in the stipulated time so his brother Abishai is sent northwards with the conscript force. Joab is passed over but is already planning his *revanche*. **8—10.** Another grim deed at Gibeon, cf 2:13. **i** Joab, like Ehud the left-handed Benjaminite (son of the right hand!) in Jg 3:15, succeeds, because of the unexpected side from which the blow is struck, aided by the Judas kiss which makes it impossible for Amasa to see his left hand. Either his sword fell while he was transferring it to the other side and he then picked it up, or he dropped it purposely to disarm the suspicions which Amasa must have entertained and then struck with another, shorter weapon. **11.** Joab's second move towards having himself re-instated; people, seeing the corpse in the middle of the road, would begin to ask awkward questions. **14.** Joab soon extinguished Sheba's opposition. Abel of Beth-maacah is modern *Tell Abil*, in 2 Chr 16:4 called 'Abel of the Waters', near the sanctuary of Dan at the Jordan sources N of where Lake Hule used to be. **18—19.** The woman seems to be **j** referring to the *kudos* of the Danite shrine (Jg 18; 1 (3) Kgs 12:30) which played an important part in the preservation of Israelite tradition. If 'mother in Israel' refers to the city it is the only such case in the OT. Jg 5:7 would suggest that it refers to the woman, though the verse is corrupt. **22.** What happened to Joab? 1 (3) Kgs 2:5ff suggests that he was protected by a royal pardon which however promptly expired with the king.

At this point the court history is interrupted and resumes at 1 (3) Kgs 1. As yet there is no answer to the Oracle of Nathan: who is to be 'the seed'? and on this uncertain note the story of blood and guilt is for the moment suspended.

20:23—26 David's Administration—The discre- **k** pancies between this and 8:16—18 (see note) may be explained either by the fact that this is a later edition of the one given earlier or that both are versions of a lost original; cf 1 Chr 18:14—17 and 27:25—31. **23.** Joab's return to power is the reason for the repetition of the list here at the close of the reign. **24.** Adoram cf 1 (3) Kgs 4:6 Adoniram during Solomon's reign; during the reign of Rehoboam his death is reported, 1 (3) Kgs 12:18 which throws some suspicion on the authenticity of this notice here. **25.** Sheva cf 8:17 Seraiah, 1 Chr 18:16 Shavsha—restoration is impossible. **26.** Jair—of the tribe of Manasseh in Gilead S of the Yarmuk; Nm 32:41; 1 (3) Kgs 4:13.

21—24 Six Appendices—A further interruption of **282a** the story of the succession. The six appendices put here by the final redactor are in symmetrical, chiastic order, a common OT stylistic feature, and therefore not necessarily an indication of serial composition and redaction as generally stated (e.g. Smith, op cit 373): 1. 21:1—14, Three year famine; 2. 15—22, Four Combats against Philistine giants; 3. 22, Psalm of David; 4. 23:1—7, Last Words of David (verse); 5. 23:8—39, David's heroes and their Exploits; 6. 24 Three day Plague. The exclusion of these passages from the main history is variously explained: either they contained material which was considered irrelevant or (as in 1 and 6) casting too much shadow on David, or, in the case especially of the archival

282a 2 and 5, they may have been unknown to the original historian.

b **21:1—14 The Three Year Famine**—This incident seems to have occurred fairly early in the reign, probably before 9:1ff which may have followed immediately after it. It seems also to be presupposed in Shimei's reference to 'the blood of Saul's dynasty', 16:8. Whether or not it was omitted from the Court History on account of religious attitudes deemed suspect, it is of great interest as documenting religious thought and practice at that time. There is the idea of blood-guilt and collective responsibility; the absolute binding force implied in a covenant—that made between Joshua and the Gibeonites (Jos 9:3ff)—and the terrible efficacy of the curse; the ritual sacrifice carried out on the high place to end drought and promote fertility, the efficacy of which is not in question for the writer. From the political angle, it illustrates David's policy, carried on and intensified by Solomon with, for the sacred writer, disastrous religious results, of tolerating and even assimilating non-Israelite enclaves. See for this last H. Cazelles, 'David's Monarchy and the Gibeonite Claim', PEQ 87 (1953) 1—14; 89 (1955) 165—75.

c **1.** 'sought the face of Yahweh' no doubt at the great sanctuary at Gibeon, later the scene of a revelation made to Solomon, 1 (3) Kgs 3:4ff; see also 1 Chr 16:39; 2 Chr 1:3. We have no mention of this deed of blood in our records, unless it refers to the slaughter of the priests of Nob, which is unlikely (Hertzberg 315). **2b.** an explanatory gloss. **6.** Seven indicates perfection and totality and occurs often in ritual acts of this kind cf Gn 4:24; 1 (3) Kgs 18:43. The blood-vengeance is in the form of a religious act 'before Yahweh' on a high-place (cf 1 Sm 15:33). Gibeon, now el-Jib, though the high place is probably Nebi Samwil, a prominent height about a mile S, named after the great prophet. **7** seems out of place before

d 8—9. The method of execution has led several scholars to see in it the re-enactment of a Canaanite seasonal fertility rite, a comparison based chiefly on a passage in the Ugaritic Baal and Anath cycle in which the goddess dismembers Mot and sows the remnants in the field, the birds descending on what is left of her prey (ANET 140; cf G. R. Driver, Canaanite Myths and Legends, 1956, 111). The verb used, however, is bq', to cleave, whereas in our text we have yq' which should be translated 'impale' or 'hang up'. See A. S. Kapelrud, 'King David and the Sons of Saul' Numen, Suppl. 4 (1959) 294—301 and ZAW 67 (1955) 195—205. **9.** The execution was carried out towards the end of April, at the time of the ritual offering of the first barley sheaf (Ex 23:15; Dt 16:1—9). The rains, which ended Rizpah's vigil, were evidently regarded as an extraordinary sign of Yahweh's answer to prayer and not the 'former rains' of Nov.—Dec. cf 1 (3) Kgs 18:40ff. **10.** Rizpah has not unjustly been compared to Antigone; she had already figured in the story of David's ascendancy (3:7). The whole of the present episode could be compared, from the point of view of the History of Religion, to other cases of human sacrifice both extra-biblical and biblical, e.g. 1 (3) Kgs 16:3ff, Hiel of Bethel; 2 (4) Kgs 3:27ff, the king of Moab. **14.** See 1 Sm 31:10—13. Zela of Benjamin (Jos 18:28) is probably Khirbet Salah near Nebi Samwil.

e **15—22 Four Combats against Philistine Giants**— These notices are heavily stylized; they begin in the same way and follow the same pattern. Their chronological situation cannot now be established, though in the parallel 1 Chr 20:4—8 they occur after the events narrated in 2 Sm 11—12. They deal in the main with heroes from Bethlehem, David's country. **16.** 'Ishbi-benob'

(RSV). MT was as much a puzzle to early translators **282** as it is to us. For the suggested correction 'iš benāyîm, single combat champion, see note to 1 Sm 17:4. The singular Rapah (giant) is generally taken to refer to the rephaim of Canaanite folklore, an early ethnic group (Gn 14:5; 15:20; Dt 2:11) in one series of texts and 'shades of the departed' in another (e.g. Is 14:9; 26:19; Jb 26:5); in which latter sense they also occur in the Ugaritic texts. See J. Gray, 'The Rephaim', PEQ 84 (1949) 127—39. According to a recent suggestion, the phrase (bîlîdê hārāpāh) should be translated 'of the corps of the arpe or scimitar' designating a determined fighting group distinguished by their arms. See F. Willesen, 'The Phoenician "Corps of the Scimitar" 2 Sm 21, 20' JSS 3 (1958) 327—35. For weight of spear and description of weaponry cf 1 Sm 17:4—7. **18.** Gob, if correct, is unknown cf LXX Geth and 1 Chr 20:4, Gezer. Sibbecai is one of the Thirty in 23:27. **19.** For the difficulties of this v see note to 1 Sm 17:7. The view of L. M. von Pakozdy, 'Elhanan—der frühere Name Davids?' ZAW 68 (1956) 257—9, namely, that Elhanan is the personal name, David the nomen officii, is based on a too hasty identification of the name 'David' with the dawidum of the Mari texts which appears to be a military title. **20.** 'îš mādôn is uncertain and was not understood at the time of LXX. 'îš middāh 'of great stature' is suggested. **21.** In 13:3, 32 he is called Jonadab.

22 Psalm of David—finds its place here as a theo- **f** logical commentary on the events of David's reign, with particular reference to his renown in war and his being saved by Yahweh from death. The language confirms an early date and there are signs of literary affinity with the royal psalms of thanksgiving and with 1 Sm 2:1—10. It is reproduced, with variations, in Ps 18 (17) the rubric of which attaches it to events in David's life. See there for commentary, also F. M. Cross and D. Freedman, 'A Royal Song of Thanksgiving' JBL 72 (1953) 15—34. **23:1—7 Last Words of David**—a poem in five strophes **g** in trimeter with variation, as is often the case, in the last strophe. The genre can be studied by comparison with the Last Words of Jacob (Gn 49) and of Moses (Dt 33) the latter following as here, a psalm attributed to the great man in question. David is here the spirit-invested prophet-king and the poem consciously imitates the Oracles of Balaam (Nm 23—24) especially in the opening ne'ûm. . . . Theologically, the poem is built around the idea of the divine choice and covenant (4th strophe), though some vv are too corrupt to yield a certain meaning. See, among various attempts at interpretation, S. Mowinckel, 'Die letzen Worte Davids' ZAW 45 (1927) 30—58; P. A. H. de Boer, 'Texte et Traduction des Paroles à attribuer à David en 2 Sam 23, 1—7' VTS 4 (1957) 47—56.

1 (first strophe). The last of these four titles is **h** diversely interpreted. Egregius psaltes Israel of Jerome commends itself less than 'favourite of the songs of Israel' in view of the psalms about David which have come down to us and incidents like 1 Sm 18:7; 21:12; 29:5. Ugaritic zmr = warrior has suggested the reading: 'Beloved of the Warrior of Israel', namely, Yahweh, cf Ex 15:3, 15 and passim in early Heb. literature. This would fit in even better with the context. **2—3a** (2nd **i** strophe). cf Is 11:1ff. For ṣûr, Rock, as divine title see passim in Dt 32; also 22:3. **3b—4**. (3rd strophe). The king gives light and fertility—both ideas common in royal ideology at that time and here transferred to David as ideal king. **5** (4th strophe). Refers back to the covenant announced through Nathan. Here we find the roots of

282i the messianic titles *Emmanuel* and *ṣēmāḥ*, Branch (Jer 23:5; 33:15; Zech 3:8; 6:12). **6—7** (5th strophe). 'Men of Belial' i.e. 'worthless men' cf 22:5 and often in the earlier narratives, 1 Sm 1:16, 2:12 etc. Here the lot of the unrighteous is described, as so often in the OT, in terms of the disposal of refuse.

j 23:8—39 David's Heroes and their Exploits—This section, which continues 21:15—22, gives a list of the Thirty, a special élite corps; of the Three of even greater fame; and of some of their exploits, and, in particular, of a well-remembered feat of daring at Bethlehem. Some of these 'archival' notices are not dissimilar from those of the 'Minor Judges' e.g. Jg 3:31.

8. Here begins the list of the Three. The textual difficulties of this v, and indeed of the whole section, can well be seen from Vg and DV. Read here 'Ishbaal the Hakmonite'. According to the parallel 1 Chr 11:11 the number is 300, one of several discrepancies. **9.** Eleazar may have been brother of Elhanan, cf 23:24. For MT 'When they defied the Philistines' read '*at Pas Dammim*' cf 1 Sm 17:1. **11.** 'a plot of ground full of lentils' (1 Chr 11:13 has 'barley'): it is the vivid detail which stays in the mind in the handing down of these old stories, cf the Samson cycle.

k 13—17. Water from the Bethlehem well—for an interesting parallel see E. Hull, 'David and the Well of Bethlehem: an Irish Parallel', *Folk-Lore* 44 (1933) 214—18. For the 'stronghold', cf 1 Sm 22:1. Apart from 1 Sm 7:6 this is the only water libation mentioned in OT.

18—24a. The two sons of Zeruiah and Benaiah and their exploits. Joab, the third son, is not mentioned as already playing a major part in the history. MT confuses three and thirty here; the Three have already been mentioned. Benaiah from Kabzeel in the Negeb, army commander in 8:18; 20:23; 1 (3) Kgs 2:29, is on record as smiting 'two ariels of Moab'. The word, usually understood as synonym for 'heroes or warriors', means 'lions of God' and more probably refers to animals of exceptional size and strength. The fall of snow, a quite unusual circumstance, would have enabled him to track down the lion in the pit or cistern. Cf Jg 14:5—6; 1 Sm 17:34—36.

24b—39. A list of thirty warriors. The final reckoning of 37 seems to include the three sons of Zeruiah, Benaiah and the Three. **27.** MT Mebunnai, read Sibbecai (1 Chr 11:29) known from 21:18. **34.** Eliam son of Ahithophel, cf note of 15:12. **39.** Uriah cf 11:3ff. See K. Elliger, 'Die 30 Helden Davids' PJB 31 (1935) 29—74.

l 24 The Census and the Three Day Plague—Originally connected with 21:1—14, as can be seen from the beginning and end of the two accounts, this narrative was separated on account of the stylistic arrangement of the appendices to the Court History and in order to lead on to the building of the Temple (on the site of Araunah's threshing floor) as the result of Yahweh's blessing. **1. 282l** In the parallel 1 Chr 21:1 Satan is the agent, cf Jb 1:6ff, in accordance with a later and more sophisticated theological approach. Here we find a very simple idea of divine causality. See A. Malamat, 'Doctrines of Causality in Hittite and Biblical Historiography: a Parallel' VT 5 (1955) 1—12. No clear reason is given why the king's action was sinful. It could be represented as another stage in the secularization of Israelite institutions with the creation of a native conscript army and the dissolution of the clan militia and with it the end of the Holy War; or perhaps the author regarded it as a ritual offence on account of the omission of the stipulated 'ransom payment'—though the texts where this is laid down seem to be later (Ex 30:12, cf Nm 1—2). **3.** Joab pronounces a blessing to offset in advance the expected curse. **5.** The **m** assessors begin in Transjordan Reuben territory—Aroer is present-day *Khirbet Araʻir* just N of the Arnon, with 'the city in the wadi' a well-known boundary mark (Dt 2:36). Jazer is about 40 mile due N. **6.** MT 'Hodshi' should read '*Kadesh*', well-known town on upper Orontes at the extreme N of the Beqaʻ. This and the coastal cities of Tyre and Sidon were beyond the true limits of David's kingdom. The circuit ended in the Negeb. **9.** These figures are different from the Chronicler's and are evidently far too high; OT numbers of this kind are more often either symbolical or stylized than realistic and factual. It is significant that the figures for Judah and Israel are separate; political unity never became a reality even at the apogee of the United Kingdom. **10. n** David's confession, cf 12:13. Here it is Gad (already mentioned 1 Sm 22:5) who brings the prophetic message. The three possibilities decrease in length of time but increase in intensity. They have already experienced three years famine (21:1ff), David positively excludes the second; so there is left only the third. **15.** add with LXX 'It was the time of the wheat harvest'. **16.** the angel is the *mašḥit*, the Destroyer—see the last Egyptian plague (Ex 12:23) and the rout of Sennacherib (2 (4) Kgs 9:35) also 1 Cor 10:10; Hb 11:28. The owner of the threshing floor has a Hittite or Hurrian name, Araunah (1 Chr 21:15 Ornan; LXX Orna). The threshing floor was connected with seasonal rites throughout the ancient Middle E. The site was above the old Jebusite city to the N, on what was to be later the Temple Area. **22.** Here again the *ad hoc* sacrifice was successful (cf 1 Sm 6:14). **24.** 50 shekels cf 1 Chr 21:25 '600 shekels of gold'. The cave of Machpelah bought by Abraham cost 400 shekels of silver (Gn 23:15)—the stories are somewhat similar. David's insistence draws our attention to the great purpose to which the site is to be put, cf the more solemn and expanded form in the Chronicler's account. With the conclusion of this last appendix, the story of the succession is finally resumed and concluded (1 (3) Kgs 1—2).

1 AND 2 KINGS

BY P. FANNON S.M.M.

283a Bibliography—Commentaries: J. Gray, OTL, 1964; J. Mauchline, PC (2), 1963; A. Médebielle, PCSB, 1955; J. H. Montgomery and H. S. Gehman, ICC, 1951; M. Noth, BKAT, 1964–5; M. Rehm, EchB, 1956; A. Šanda, EHAT, 1911–12; N. Snaith, IB, 1954; A. van den Born, 1958; R. de Vaux, BJ, 1949. **Other Works**: W. F. Albright, *Archaeology and the Religion of Israel*, 1953[3]; id, *The Archaeology of Palestine*, 1960[2]; id, 'Further Light on Synchronisms between Egypt and Asia in the Period 935–685 B.C.', BASOR 141 (1956), 23–27; J. de Fraine, *L'aspect religieux de la royauté israëlite*, 1954; A. Jepsen, *Die Quellen des Königsbuches*, 1953; M. Noth, *Überlieferungsgeschichtliche Studien*, 1943; E. R. Thiele, *The Mysterious Numbers of the Hebrew Kings*, 1951; E. H. Maly, *The World of David and Solomon*, Englewood Cliffs, 1966.

b Introduction—The Books of Kings are the continuation of Sm (the first two chh are the conclusion of the great document which began in 2 Sm 9; and the LXX groups Sm–Kgs together under the title of 'the four books of the kingdoms'). They begin with an account of the last days of David and Solomon's accession, and continue the history until the fall of Jerusalem and the exile—a period of more than 400 years. For a general view of the period see §§ 62–65.

c Formation—These books form part of the great **deuteronomic history** (see § 242*e*) and like the rest of this history were compiled from **previously existing material**. Three are mentioned in the text itself: the Acts of Solomon (1 (3) Kgs 11:41), the Chronicles of the kings of Israel (1 (3) Kgs 14:19) and the Chronicles of the kings of Judah (1 (3) Kgs 14:29).

The first of these appears to be a **varied collection** of different materials which was in turn derived from older sources. The other two must have been something like the **annals of the kings**. Besides these, the editor also used other sources of various kinds, **archives, records, legends**, etc, which will be discussed at the appropriate place in the commentary.

d The deuteronomic editor has firmly set his mark on all this material. His handling of it is marked by the two principal tenets of the deuteronomic school: that Yahweh **rewards fidelity to the Covenant and punishes infidelity**; and that **Yahweh must be worshipped at his one and only sanctuary in Jerusalem**. This can be seen first of all in the **formulae with which each king's reign is introduced and concluded**, and which forms a framework for the work as a whole. These formulae include a moral evaluation of the reign of each king; and the standard of judgment is obviously inspired by the deuteronomic law on the single legitimate sanctuary. All the kings of Israel are condemned with the phrase: 'And he did evil before the Lord', the evil being 'the sin of Jeroboam' who estalished shrines at Bethel and Dan (1 (3) Kgs 12:29) to rival Jerusalem. In Judah, eight kings merit approval, but even there the praise

of six of them is qualified by a reference to the fact **283c** that they too tolerated shrines of Yahweh outside Jerusalem.

This deuteronomic 'theology of history' further **e** shows itself in a presentation of material within the framework just noted. A constant recurrence of deuteronomic phrases is characteristic of the work. (A full list of parallels may be seen in Driver, *Literature of the Old Testament*, 200–2). The fullest formulation of this theology is given in the **long comment on the fall of Samaria**, 2 Kgs 17:7–23. A comparison between the Heb. (1 Kgs 14) and LXX (1 Kgs 12:24) texts on parallel matter show how the editor was able to interweave deuteronomic considerations with his sources. Whence it was also that the **story-cycles of Elijah, Elisha and the other prophets**, contrasting so oddly with the annalistic data from the royal archives, are essential to the writer's purpose. They establish the **existence and survival of the Isaian remnant** which gave hope for the future, despite the moral bankruptcy of the two monarchies: the prophets were right, the kings mostly wrong. In the very employment of prophetic sources a decisive verdict was passed on the political and nationalistic strivings of God's people. The books of Kgs were composed for the specific purpose of inculcating this religious teaching. By repeatedly referring the reader to historical records for further information on the victories, wars, and buildings of kings, the writer showed that his own object was not to give merely a secular narrative.

This becomes even more obvious in the **omission, f** or compression into a passing reference, **of much** that must have been **of great historical importance**. This is most apparent in the treatment of Omri and Jeroboam II. They were the greatest of Israel's kings, yet because the prosperity their kingdom enjoyed under them could not be accounted for by a writer concerned with affirming the deuteronomic principle of retribution, they were summarily dismissed and the reader referred to the 'History'. Solomon's idolatry is recounted only at the end of his reign in connection with his loss of territories (1 Kgs 11:4, 14ff). A similar loss by the reformer, Jehu, is minimized (2 Kgs 10:32f) and the Assyrian devastation of Judah under the pious Hezekiah is not mentioned, while Jerusalem's deliverance is recorded (2 Kgs 18–20). The final insolent prosperity under Manasseh is ignored.

There is strong evidence that the deuteronomic **g** redaction took place before the exile (cf W. Nowack, BZAW 41, 1925, 221–31) and even before the death of Josiah; the account of this king's death, 2 (4) Kgs 23:26–25:30 seems to come from another hand. But there are indications of a second redaction, also deuteronomic, dating from after the exile. This redaction, for example, mentions the release of Jehoiachin from prison, 2 (4) Kgs 25:27; and the same editor would also be responsible for some modifications in the text

83g which allude to the disaster of the exile, such as 2 (4) Kgs 17:19ff; 20:12—19; 21:11—15; the oracle of Huldah in its present form, 2 Kgs 22:15—20. Finally when, after the Exile, the various historical books underwent some influence of priestly editing, Kgs would receive some retouching.

h The **deuteronomic evaluation of the fall of a nation**, an evaluation made **by members of that nation, is without parallel in the Near E.** That fall was due to corruption in religion, belief and cult, stemming from the monarchies, and it has been suggested (A. van den Born, *Koningen*) that any edition of the work before 587 B.C. is ruled out since the destruction of the S Kingdom is the essential climax of the book and that its whole composition was carried out with this judgement expressly in view. But Yahweh was still god, despite the ruin of his people and their sanctuary. The fall of Jerusalem was not a failure but his success since Israel learned the nature of his demands through it. The work closes with the grace given to Jehoiachin as if a sign of salvation for his race, confirming the permanence of the Davidic line in conformity with the divine promises and keeping alive the OT messianism nourished on the image of an ideal king.

i Text—The Heb. (MT) text preserves well the original work, better than in the prophetic books, but not so well as in the Pent. The Gr. (LXX) text is important, not so much for the reading or explanation of difficult passages in the MT, as for the elimination of interpolated matter. The most remarkable features of the LXX are its changes in the order of the text and in the addition of some large sections. The chief **variations** are (1) 1 Kgs 4:20—28; (2) ch 7; (3) 16:28a-h (LXX) where the reign of Jehoshaphat appears before that of Ahab, contrary to MT. In (1) LXX gives a better order of vv, in (2) it describes the furniture of the temple before the palaces; (3) results from a difference in chronology. according to the LXX Jehoshaphat had come to the throne in the 11th year of Omri. The chief **additions** in the LXX are (a) 1 Kgs 2:35a-o; (b) 2:46a-l; (c) 12:24a-z. In (a) and (b) there is practically nothing contained that does not occur somewhere in the Heb. of ch 3—11. (c) seems to have come into the LXX independently of the canonical Heb., from sources similar to those of Kgs (see Skinner, *1 & 2 Kings*, 1904, 443ff). The LXX contains matter which is historically helpful but which itself has been worked over and glossed according to the MT.

j Chronology—It has been noted above how Kgs attempts to synchronize the reigns of the kings of Israel and Judah. However **the synchronizations of parallel kings do not agree** and whether the absolute data or the synchronizations are preferred, there are difficulties (the discrepancies being three years one way from Jeroboam to Jehu, and twenty-one years the other way from Jehu to the fall of Samaria). Much energy has been spent on this problem without any definitive solution being arrived at. J. Begrich (*Die Chronologie der Könige von Israel und Judah und die Quellen des Rahmens der Königsbücher,* 1929) thought that the writer employed as many as five different chronological computations, but there are evidently errors in the sources used. The latest attempt to establish a concordance seems to be W. F. Albright's in BASOR, 100 (1945), 16—22, cf §§ 124f to 125g.

THE FIRST BOOK OF KINGS

84a **1:1—2:46 The Succession to the Throne**—The two opening chh of 1 Kgs are a continuation of the magni-ficent 'court history' of 2 Sm. 11—20 (see 268j). Their **284a** realism indicates that they stem from contemporary documents. The monarchy was not established as hereditary and primogeniture was not yet an adequate title—whence the court intrigues which mark the time of David's senility.

1:1—4 David was bedridden (v 47), though only about 70 years of age (2 Sm. 5:4; 1 Kgs 2:11), whence the occasion for the crisis of the succession. Abishag was provided for the king both as nurse and mistress (cf 2:17) but David did not respond to her services. This lack of vitality in the king could be seen as an omen for weakness in the nation with whom he was bound up (cf A. R. Johnson, *The Vitality of the Individual in the Thought of Ancient Israel,* 1949). Shunem, the home of Abishag, was on the N rim of the plain of Jezreel. For the relation—whether of identification or distinction—between this Shunammite and the Shulammite of the Song of Solomon, see § 429c, and H. H. Rowley, 'The Meaning of the Shulammite', in AJSL 56 (1939), 84ff. **5—10** Adonijah was the eldest surviving son of David **b** (cf 2 Sm 13:28f; 18: 14; 3:3), personally attractive and the leading candidate (2:15). Joab, the military commander, and Abiathar, the only survivor of the priests of Nob (1 Sm. 22:18—23), were with Adonijah. The fact that others, including Solomon, were not asked to assist him would indicate Adonijah's knowledge of a court intrigue to place Solomon on the throne. The break which was to come between the N and the S is hinted at in the support which Adonijah (like Absalom before him, cf 2 Sm. 15:10) found in Judah (9). En-rogel is a spring on the S side of Jerusalem. The Stone of Zoheleth, 'the Serpent's Stone', may well have been a symbol of a serpent cult later introduced into the Jerusalem Temple or simply have meant 'the rolling stone.' **11—27** give the first indication that a promise of the succession for Solomon has really been made to Bathsheba and confirmed by an oath not previously mentioned (13). Nathan worked on David's pride and affection by main- **c** taining that his royal authority was being flouted and that his best loved wife and her son were in danger of being treated as rebels. David was stunned into a belated sense of duty. **28—40** Nathan was successful: Solomon was anointed and made co-regent at Gihon in the Kidron valley and acclaimed by the crowd. The palace guard, consisting of royal mercenaries, was a decisive factor (32—40). 39 states that Zadok alone anointed Solomon but 34 says that Nathan the prophet was associated with him. For Cherethites and Pelethites, see the comment on 2 Sm. 8:18. **41—53** Solomon having now been anointed co-regent, the forces at En-rogel became automatically a rebellion. It had to disband. Adonijah was treated (now) with a royal but cold magnaminity by Solomon (50—53) and undertook to be loyal to the throne and to retire to private life. **2:1—12.** It is doubtful whether this passage formed part of the original 'succession history'. Certainly it has been at least strongly edited by the deuteronomic redactor—for the tone of David's admonition in the opening verse, for example, cf Jos 1 and Dt 31:7.

5—11. Joab's crimes had stained the military honour **d** of David (LXX), leaving him open to the accusation of being their instigator, 2 Sm 16:7. A blood feud weighed heavily on the king and his descendants; it could only be extinguished by striking the real culprit. This commission to Solomon of the execution of personal vengeances reflects the current OT ideas on blood feuds. The curse of Shimei (v 8) was to weigh upon the descendants of David, since a curse (like a blessing) remained

284d efficacious. To render it void it must be returned against its author (44—45). David was hindered from doing this by his oath, but Solomon was not so bound. David died c 971. The 'City of David' was on the SE hill, running along the Kidron valley towards the pool of Siloam. Here David's descendants were also buried, at least until Ahaz, 2 Kgs 17:20. **12.** There is no indication in the biblical text that Solomon's accession was due to God.

e 13—46 Removal of the King's Opponents—The vivid narrative style indicates the resumption of the 'succession' document. **13—25.** The Queen Mother, who had an official title (*gᵉḇîrāh*, 15:13) was an important and influential personage in the ancient east (cf 15:13; 2 Sm 10:13; Jer 13:18; 29:2; de Vaux, *AI* 117—19). Married to Abishag, supported by Joab and Abiathar, Adonijah would be a danger to Solomon. Solomon treated the request as a renewal of his claim to the kingship itself: to take over the women of a ruler was looked on as an exercise of the royal power, 2 Sm 16:21 ff; cf 3:7; 12:8. He replied sharply to Bathsheba and decisively for Adonijah. **26—7.** Anathoth, the home of the prophet Jeremiah, today Anata, was some 4 m. NE of Jerusalem. Banishment excluded Abiathar from priestly functions. Here appears the deuteronomic principle that worship could be offered only at one central shrine. The line of priests descending from Aaron's younger son, Ithamar, **f** was closed. **28—35.** Solomon's plea, in killing Joab, was that either the general or the royal house had to expiate his crimes. Sanctuary covered manslaughter, but not murder, Ex 21:14. Zadok, though proposed in 1 Chr 24:3 as a priest of the Aaronic line of Eleazar, installed by Samuel after the massacre of the priests of Nob who were of the priestly line of Ithamar, may well in fact have belonged to the ancient Jebusite priesthood in Jerusalem, being priest king when David occupied the city. (Rowley, *The Discovery of the OT*, 1945, 52; de Vaux, *AI* 372—74). **36—46.** Solomon commanded Shimei under pain of death to reside in Jerusalem, and bound him by oath. Shimei, having perjured himself, was later 'justly' executed; but Solomon revealed the real reason (**44**): the curse formerly pronounced against David. 'Blessed be King Solomon' (**45**) is added by Solomon lest the curse he had just pronounced revert on him (cf v 33). The text shows no sympathy for Solomon and his questionable treatment of Adonijah.

285a 3:1—11:43 The Reign of Solomon—This section is made up of various kinds of material drawn from different sources—archives, temple records, etc. The main source, as the text itself indicates (11:41), was the 'Acts of Solomon'—not a chronicle, but a description of the wisdom, riches and magnificence of Solomon, a memoir after the oriental pattern. But this document too was drawn from earlier sources and it is not clear to what extent the redactor used them independently. The form and content of this varied material was not fixed till much later as can be seen from the repetitions and interruptions, and from the fact that the Gr. offers a different and sometimes better arrangement of the material. What is clear is the deuteronomic interest—the temple (compare for example the brief account of the much bigger palace buildings, 7:1—12, inserted in the account of the temple buildings).

b 3:1—15 The Dream at Gibeon—The first section, 4—15, is preceded by two short notes. **1** is probably an attempt at chronology; 9:24 says that Solomon's wife had lived in the city of David until the palace was finished, and since this was in his 4th year (6:37), it would appear suitable to mention his marriage here after the incident of Shimei which took place in his 3rd **285** year (2:39). **2—3** are two deuteronomic glosses—one mildly disapproving, the other excusing—preparing for the editor's main interest, the building of the temple; but preparing also for the next section where Solomon sacrifices at Gibeon—an action of which, in view of his thesis, he must disapprove. **4—15.** The purpose of this section is to legitimate Solomon's succession after the unusual circumstances in which he came to the throne. The basis of legitimation is the choice of the Davidic house (6,7). It also prepares for the character of the reign, and perhaps originally formed an introduction to the history of Solomon later displaced by the conclusion of the 'succession history'. The passage has many expressions—justice, wisdom, counsel, etc—which are associated with the messianic king in Is (9:6; 11:2, 4, 5). Gibeon, modern el-Jib, 6 miles NW of Jerusalem, was a pre-Israelite holy place. Dreams were a recognized vehicle of divine communication in Israel, especially in the Elohistic tradition. Egyptian Pharaohs too used the dream to authenticate the character of their rule (cf *ANET* 448ff). Solomon's youth (7), like the number of victims in 4, is the hyperbole characteristic of this kind of literature; but it may also contain a reference to the fact that the king's accession to the throne was regarded as the day of his birth as a son of God, cf Ps 2:7. **15.** The feast, the common meal, signifies the unity that exists between king and people and the blessings which flow to the community from the king. Absalom's revolt (2 Sm 15:11) and Adonijah's (1 (3) Kgs 1:9) also began with such a sacred meal.

16—28——A practical illustration of Solomon's wisdom follows. The motif is fairly common in other literature.

4:1—19 Administration—The source of this passage **c** was an archival document. On the ministers of state (1—6), see de Vaux, AI, 127. The continuity with David's administration is clear; Solomon retains his herald and the sons of his priest, secretary, prophet and commander of the army. **3.** The secretaries attended to official documents; the recorder was annalist and, in practice, Prime Minister. **4.** The reference to Zadoc and Abiathar is an error; it contradicts v 2 and has perhaps come from the similar list in 2 Sm 20:25. **5.** One of Nathan's sons was over the provincial *governors* (MT); and was aide-de-camp (omit 'priest' with LXX). **6.** A chamberlain presided over the palace, and a minister for public works over the conscript labour. **7.** For taxation, Israel, as distinct from Judah, was divided into 12 districts. The palaces and store-houses excavated at Lachish, Beth-Shemesh and Megiddo show how the provincial capitals were equipped. **8.** The administrative lists of Ugarit show that appellation by pat-**d**ronym alone was regular in families in the service of the king. The first district was based on Mt Ephraim, and ran from Joppa to the Jordan. **9.** The second, SW of the first, comprised the hill-country of the S settlement of Dan **10.** The third, N of the first, embraced the coastal plain of Sharon. **1.** The fourth ran NW of the third to Carmel. **12.** The fifth ran in from Carmel across the plain of Esdraelon to the Jordan. **13.** The sixth, N and S of the Yarmuk, was transjordanian Manasseh. **14.** The seventh ran S of the sixth to the Jabbok. **15.** The eighth was E Galilee, along the lake and upper Jordan. **16.** W Galilee, marching with the kingdom of Tyre was the ninth. **17.** The tenth was S of Galilee, around Mount Tabor. **18.** The eleventh was the E part of the territory S of the province of Ephraim, to the NW of Jerusalem. **19.** The twelfth was the most southerly of the three provinces E of the Jordan, Gad

285d (LXX), between the Jabbok and the Arnon. 'The Land', without further specification, designates the royal territory of Judah as distinguished from the provinces of
e Israel. Judah had then a special administration, and seems to have had a different administrative, organization—its exemption was not by privilege. Districts eight to twelve followed old tribal divisions; the rest natural boundaries. But the organization maintained fundamentally the dualism of N and S, Judah and Israel being separate and independent: see A. Alt, 'Israels Gaue unter Salomo' in *Kleine Schriften* II 76—89; F.-M. Abel, *Géographie de la Palestine*, II, 79—83; R. de Vaux, AI, 133ff.

f **20—28 (20—5:8) The Prosperity of the Kingdom**—This passage, in which the Gr. order is different from the Heb., interrupts the archival document; 'these officers' in v 27 refers back to 7—19, of which it is the continuation. The phrase 'Judah and Israel' (20) even suggests that it may belong to the post-exilic redaction; cf the use of this phrase in Jer 23:6, 2 Chr 16:11 etc. **21.** There is some basis for this exuberant description of Solomon's empire (so different in tone from the sober archival list above) in the fact that traders from these countries paid transit dues. **22—23.** 30 cors = c.340 bushels; the quantities, enough for 14,000 people, have probably been touched up by a scribe. **26.** *4,000* stalls is the number given in 2 Chr 9:25, and this corresponds with the 1,400 chariots of 10:26, allowing two horses and a reserve to each chariot. The strength of the cavalry too is suspect; at the battle of Qarqar in 853, Ahab contributed none and Damascus only 1,200 (ANET, 278). But Solomon's horse-trade may perhaps explain it. Stables of Solomon's time excavated at Megiddo held at least 450 horses, and others have been found at Taanak, Gezer, Tell el-Hesy and Hazor. **29—34 (5:9—14) The Philosopher King**—From a late popular source. **30.** The bent of the wisdom of the desert tribes and of the Egyptians was moralizing; Egyptian collections of maxims go back to 2000 B.C. **31.** Of the four sages only the fame is known. **32.** On the idea of 'wisdom', see

286a **5:1—9:9 (5:15—9:9) § 432 The Building of the Temple**
5:1—18 (15—26) Preparations—This is drawn from some archival source, though with deuteronomic glosses as in 3—5.

The embassy was to congratulate Solomon on his accession. Hiram had supplied materials and skilled workmen to David, 2 Sm 5:11. The historians Menander and Dios spoke of Hiram's great constructions at Tyre (Jos Ant 8, 5, 3; C Ap 1, 18). **4—5.** Settled conditions called for a temple to Yahweh, Dt 12:9. **6.** Sidon, the N partner of Tyre, had lost the hegemony of the Phoenicians, but they were still called Sidonians (cf 16:31) as late as Antiochus IV, 175—164 B.C. **7—8.** The famous voyage of the Egyptian Wen-Amon in 1100 B.C. was to obtain cedar-wood from Lebanon. In spite of continual exploitations it was still 'full of cedars, pine and cypress, marvellous in size and beauty' when Diodorus was writing, 1st cent B.C. *Beros* 'fir' is often rendered 'Cypress'. **9—11.** The rafts were beached at Joppa, 2 Chr 2:16. Wheat (20,000 *cors*, 230,000 bushels) and olive oil (20 *cors*, 18,000 gallons; LXX 180,000) were articles of commerce, not the workmen's food. This 'purest' oil was won by hand-pressure in a mortar. **12—14.** Work on sub-alpine Lebanon and raft-transport by sea were confined to the three summer months; thus each draft had two of the working months free. **15—16.** The second group were Canaanites, 2 Chr.

2:17, and worked in the hills of Judaea, where there **286a** was excellent marble (cf 'costly stones' 17) and limestone, Abel 1 181ff. Their lot was permanent slavery, 9:20ff. **17—18.** The skilled foreign workmen included the Phoenicians of Gebel (Byblos) famous shipwrights, Ezek 27:9.

6:1—38 The Building of the Temple—The source **b** for this was probably the temple archives; but almost equally clearly, these are not reproduced exactly, or not understood. The difficulties, both of text and of interpretation, make it almost impossible to give an exact description of the building with any certainty. cf A. Parrot, *The Temple of Jerusalem*, 1957; G. E. Wright, 'Solomon's Temple Resurrected', BA 4 (1941), 17ff; R. de Vaux, AI, 312—29. The nearest analogy to the temple of Jerusalem is that discovered in 1936 at Tell Tainat in N Syria. The tripartite division of the building (porch, nave, Holy of Holies) was a Syrian development which the Phoenicians adopted and spread; cf Albright, *Archaeology and the Religion of Israel*, 142ff. **1.** A late gloss; the LXX has here the simpler **c** dating given in v 37. The number 480 is either arrived at by 12 (the number of the tribes) multiplied by 40 (an average generation); or by reckoning back from the return from exile—50 years for the exile plus the 430 years which is the total of the duration of the reigns given in Kgs. **2.** On the basis of the 'ancient' cubit (see § 86a) the temple was approximately 103 ft. by 34 ft. by 51 ft: a modest size and much smaller than the House of the Forest of Lebanon (7:2). But its primary function was to house the ark; the congregation assembled in the large court-yard surrounding the building. **3.** The porch was as wide as the main building and was 17 ft. deep. **4.** The windows were high up on the walls. **5.** Built onto the outside was a cincture of rooms to serve as sacristies. **6.** This addition was 9 ft. wide on the ground-floor; the floor-beams of the two upper storeys did not pierce the walls of the temple, but rested on the ledges formed by the walls where they were stepped in twice. **7.** The use of dressed stone did not exclude carpenters' work at the actual building. **8.** The entrance to the ground-floor of the side-buildings was on the S. **9.** The ceiling of the temple was of cedar, the joists and beams forming compartments (MT), visible from beneath. The roof was flat, since altars could be erected on it, 2 Kgs 33:12. **10.** Cedar was used to roof the side buildings also, each storey of which round all the House was 9 ft. high. The three ceilings rested on the wall of the house by means of cedar beams. **11—14.** An addition **d** of the redactor, inserted here between the account of the building itself and the furnishings which follow. **15—22.** The main internal features described are the woodwork, the division into sanctuary and nave, the altar of incense and decoration. **15.** The temple was lined with cedar and floored with fir (or cypress; see on 5:8). **16.** The rear wall, to the height of 34 ft., formed the back of the innermost shrine, 'the oracle' (debir-from a root meaning hinder part; St Jerome connected it with *dabber* 'to speak'). It was a perfect cube, 20*a*, so there was a space of 17 ft. between its ceiling and the roof. **17.** The main hall, the nave, was 52 ft. long. **18.** There were carvings on the cedar walls. These probably linked the cherubs and palm-trees of 29. **20b—22.** To the cedar facings and the carvings a third element of decoration was added: goldleaf, probably used only on the low relief of the carvings. So understand the generalization of 22, which says that 'everything' was covered with gold. The text of these vv is badly confused, partly because of the glosses of scribes who felt the urge to exaggerate

286d the richness of the gilding. So too 30, where the interpolator is betrayed by the meaningless 'within and without'. From 21b it may be gathered that the doors of the Holy of Holies (cf 31) had golden bolts (MT); and from 22, that there was an altar (for incense) in the nave, in front of the Holy of Holies, and that its cedar was embellished with gildings. **23—30 The Cherubim**—See P. Dhorme and L-H. Vincent, *Les Cherubins*, RB 35 (1926), 328—58, 481—95. Sentinel figures with wings outstretched to shelter it stood over the Ark, 19. The work *kerub* derives from the Babylonian where *karibu* 'intercessor' was used anciently of minor gods who presented the prayers of suppliants. Later these *karibu* appeared with human head on winged bodies of lions, etc., and were associated with the guardianship of temples and palaces from Mesopotamia to Egypt. The small figures which flanked the Ark in the Mosaic Tabernacle were in human form, cf § 189*b*. Reproduced here on a gigantic scale, they must also be supposed to be human in form. Hence Ezekiel's address to the king of Tyre, 28:14: 'Thou, Cherub, anointed protector'. In 7:29 cherubs are distinguished from lions and oxen. Though they no longer formed the throne of Yahweh as in the ancient Tabernacle, they still manifested his presence and evoked reverence for his majesty; cf Gn. 3:24; Ps 17 (16):11. Since they were offered no cult and were not thought of as intercessors, they derive only in name and form from non-Israelite figures. On **f** 29f, see 18 and 22. **31—35 The Doors of the Sanctuary and Nave**—The descriptions of 6:31—6 are difficult to interpret; besides the uncertain meaning of many technical terms, the text is in need of emendation. 32*a* repeats 31*a*; for 32*b* see on 35*a*. **33.** On the door from the porch into the nave, the lintel was flat, so the ordinary rectangular opening resulted. Each of its two main leaves was of two sections, turning upon pivots, the two centre pieces provided a convenient entrance for daily use. **35a.** The decorations are the same as those on the inner door; the gilding was confined to the carvings, as elsewhere in the temple. **35b** shows how all the gold overlay is to be understood. The idea that the temple was walled and floored with plates **g** of gold is a late fantasy. **36. The Inner Court**—The court in which the temple stood was within the great court, 7:12, which embraced all the king's buildings. Every three courses of stone were succeeded by one course of wood, a reinforcement once necessary in brick walls. **37—38. Duration of the Work**—This ancient record preserves two Canaanite names of months; cf Phoenician *Zib*, *B-1*. Bul was Oct.—Nov. The regnal year began in Tishri, Sept.—Oct. Thus the work lasted from the 8th month of Solomon's 4th year to the 2nd month of his 11th, 6½ years, roughly 7. In the parenthesis, the months are reckoned from Nisan, March—April; see on 1. **h 7:1—12 Palaces**—Possibly from court archives. The palaces were begun only when the temple was finished; cf 9:10. **2.** Furthest S from the temple was a great hall, intended for ceremonial occasions; cf 10:21. Larger than the temple, it was 172 ft. by 86 ft by 52 ft. Three (LXX) rows of lofty pillars, fifteen to a row, gave the impression of a cedar forest, hence the name. **3—5.** It was not an open portico, for MT and LXX mention doors and windows facing each other in sets of three. Details are uncertain, for the text is corrupt. **6.** Next came a smaller hall of pillars, possibly the antechamber, **7,** to the Throne-room, where Solomon dispensed justice. **8.** Closest to the temple were the royal palaces. **9.** The stone was dressed on all faces, 'within and without'.

10—11. 17 ft. blocks went into the lower courses: larger **286h** are still to be seen in the 'Wailing Wall' of Jerusalem. **12.** The whole complex of buildings was enclosed in the **i** 'Great Court', whose walls were of the type described 6:36. The position of the Great Court was too well known to be mentioned. Today it is the Haram esh-Sherif, the 'Noble Sanctuary' of the Mohammedans, an esplanade some 550 yards long and 320 yards wide, on the NE hill. The site of the Temple is occupied by the paved platform which surrounds the so-called Mosque of Omar, really the 'Dome of the Rock'. Inside this is a rock, some 60 ft. long and 40 ft. wide, rising nearly 6 ft. above floor level. On this was erected, as is generally agreed, the Altar of Holocausts; cf 2 Sm 24:25; 1 Kgs 8:64. The Temple was a little to the W, its facade looking E over the altar towards the Mount of Olives.

13—51 Temple Furnishings 13—22. Jachin and j Boaz—Tyrian architects had built the temple after their own models, and a Tyrian craftsman supplied the standard fittings. **15—16.** Standing free before the porch were two columns, 40 ft. high, 6 ft. in diameter, of hollow copper ore bronze 3½ inches thick (4 fingerbreadths, LXX, Jer 52:51). Their capitals were crowned with bowls, upon which were gratings ('network, chainwork'— 'seven' comes from a scribal error). These features, and the 'lilywork', if understood as knobs, 19, 22, suggest that the columns were stylized reproductions of the tall incense-stands or cressets (firealtars) before many ancient temples. So W. F. Albright, 144ff; usually they are compared with the stone columns or obelisks of Egypt etc. **18, 22.** Two necklaces of metal pomegranates decorated each capital; cf 42. **21.** The names suggest inscriptions like 'May Yahweh establish (*yākîn*) the temple' or dynasty and 'In the strength (*be'ôz*) of Yahweh.' **23—6. 'The Sea'.** From the 3rd **k** millennium a reservoir known as Apsu, the primeval fresh-water ocean, was usual in the temples of Lagash, Eridu, Ur, Babylon etc.; basins on stands of oxen are pictured on the reliefs of Nineveh. Such decorations became common in the early Iron Age. 'The Sea' was at the SE corner of the temple, (39), of metal nearly 4 inches thick, with castings of gourds; to hold 2,000 *baths* (18,000 gallons) the sides must have curved outwards.

27—39 Stands—Water for ablutions, 1 Chr 4:6, was carried from the 'Sea' in wheeled stands, also common in ancient temples. The obscure and confused texts have been illustrated by archaeological finds such as the tiny model, probably an ex-voto, of the 2nd millenium found in Cyprus, DBV IV fig 260. The sides were panelled and decorated, and a small basin was set in a round opening in the top. **32—36** give a slightly varying account of the same thing. **40—51. Other Furniture. 40** adds utensils used in sacrifices, **41—45** recapitulate the objects described in 15—39. They were of polished bronze, an alloy of copper and tin, or pure copper; brass, an alloy of copper and zinc, was not known. **46.** The foundries were near the mouth of the Jabbok. **47—51.** The Altar of Incense was of cedar, 6:20, but it was finished in gold-foil like most of the larger objects; see on 6:35. For the loaves of proposition see 177*d*; for David's votive offerings, 2 Sm 8:11f.

8:1—66 The Dedication—This passage is based on **l** an actual account of the dedication, but expanded in deuteronomic style; and the hand of the post-exilic redactor can be seen in such passages as 41—51. **1—11 The Installation of the Ark**—This was the central rite, by which Yahweh took possession of his temple, his presence being in a special manner attached

861 to the Ark. **2.** It was ten months after the completion of the building. Ethanim ('perpetual streams', the only ones flowing, the wadis having dried up) was the old name for Sept.—Oct. later Tishri, the first month in the old reckoning; see on 6:1 and 37f. **2b** not in LXX (B. Lucian), reckons from Nisan. **3—9.** The precise details of the placing of the Ark suggest the record of an eye-witness which was quoted literally (cf 'unto this day') though all had disappeared when the book was written. The staves by which it was carried ran out sideways from the Ark; cf Ex 25:13—14. The door of the oracle being narrow, they were visible from the nave only when one stood close to the oracle. **10—11.** A dark storm-cloud (cf 12) testified to Yahweh's acceptance of his new dwelling; a similar miracle had sanctified the Mosaic Tabernacle, Ex 40:32ff).

m 12—13 Solomon's Hymn—The abrupt change to direct address shows that this is only an excerpt from the whole psalm, which the LXX says was preserved in a collection called 'The Book of the Just'; cf Jos 10:12; 2 Sm 1:18; though LXX here mistook *yāšār*, 'just', for *šîr*, 'canticle'. The hymn is not merely one of thanksgiving; it rather marvels at Yahweh's deliberately choosing darkness as the mode of his presence: his mysterious nature is thus better expressed than by the brightness of the heavens. Further, it sees in the temple a permanent bond between Yahweh and the dynasty.

n 14—61 Inaugural Address— **14.** The blessing here is a greeting as 2 Kgs 4:29; the strict sense in 55; cf 57. **15—21.** For the prehistory of the temple see 2 Sm 7; Dt 12. Since the name of Yahweh is attached to the temple he watches over it as his property; cf Dt 28:10; Is 4:1 his personal being is there, ruling and working; cf Is 30:27; 40:26. **22—30.** The author develops, after the style of Dt, the ideas of 15—21. He begins by stating the principle of mutual fidelity, **23:** divine benevolence results from the covenant of Sinai but it is conditioned by the loyalty of the people. This is the whole theology of the covenant, the central doctrine of the OT. Then two applications are made: Yahweh has kept his promise regarding the Temple, **24,** and he is equally held to his promise of maintaining the dynasty for ever, **25. 31.** The temple is to be the theatre of God's judgements: cf Nm. 5:21f. **33—40.** Calamities are the punishment of sin; the efficacy of prayer depends on sincere repentance. **41—51.** These supplements, added after the Exile, envisage a universalist hope (41—43), the custom in prayer of turning towards Jerusalem, 44 (cf Dn. 6:10), the concern for those of the Diaspora, 47ff. **51.** The furnace is a metaphor for a dreadful fate, Dt 4:20, possibly because of its use as a death penalty; cf Dn 3. **54—61.** The king is ideally an 'Everlasting Father', Is 9:6, hence the paternal blessing, 57; cf Ru 2:4. Praise of God precedes it; cf 15ff.

o 62—66 Inaugural Celebrations—The numbers are not correct: 1,800 an hour, 12 hours a day for 7 days! **64.** On holocausts, *meal* and peace-offerings see § 104 §195. **65.** The seven days coincided with Tabernacles, cf § 105h. The plain about Riblah and Kadesh on the Orontes was the 'Entrance of Hamath', Abel II 78; the 'River of Egypt' was the Wady el-'Arīsh, c. 50 m. S of Gaza.

9:1—9 Concluding Vision—The substance of the revelation has been elaborated by the inspired writer to meet a difficulty of the exiles. If the temple has perished, it is not because Yahweh was too weak to protect his own, but because he was too holy to tolerate evil in them.

287a 10—28 Finance and Public Works—**10—14.** Solo-

mon had to borrow to build, and ceded temporarily, **287a** 2 Chr 8:2, part of E Galilee with its revenues. Hiram's discontent was echoed in the name of the chief town, the most easterly of the tribe of Asher, Jos 19:27. Cabul perhaps suggested *kebal* 'like nothing at all'. **15.** A *record* follows of how conscript labour was used. The Millo (cf 11:27) seems to have been a massive fortification on the W, between Sion and the temple area; cf L.-H. Vincent, *Jérusalem*, 1, 171—87. Hazor (Heser; prob. Tell el-Qedah, where great stables have been excavated; cf on 4:27) SW of Lake Huleh, guarded the N approaches. Megiddo, Tell el Mutesellim, commanded the plain of Esdraelon. **17.** The rebuilding of Gezer signified that Solomon was to be sole master in Palestine. Relations with Egypt were henceforth less friendly; cf 11:14ff. The events of 16 were early in the reign. **19. b** Solomon fortified all the towns where he stored provisions and the cavalry depots; cf 4:7—26. There were iron mines as well as forests to be exploited on Lebanon. **20—22.** The data of the ancient records of 5:27; 11:8— which are to be preferred to the present data—include Israelites also as slaves. **23—28.** David's conquest of Edom had given Solomon command of its copper and iron mines, as well as access to the Red Sea. Copper refineries of Solomon's time have been found at Tell el-Kheleifeh, the ancient Ezion-Geber, now ½ m. inland on the Gulf of Aqaba. The site of Ophir is still debated: Somaliland, supposed to correspond to the Egyptian Punt, is credited with exports like those of 10:22, cf W. F. Albright, 133; the most ancient tradition (LXX, Josephus etc) says India; more probably S Arabia, a gold-producing country (cf Jb 22:24) inhabited by the Jectanides; cf Gn 10:29. For 420 talents, LXX has 120.

10:1—29. Prestige and Wealth—A historical inci- **c** dent (a trade mission) elaborated in popular style to show how Yahweh fulfilled his promise to Solomon, 3:12ff. **1.** The later Sabaean kingdom was in the Hadramaut, SW Arabia. But the Sabaeans are constantly met with along the EW trade route in N Arabia before 700 B.C. See Tiglath-pileser's inscription of 728, ANET, 284 and Gn 10:30; 25:3; Ex 38:13 etc. The name may still persist in the Wady esh-Shaba, near Medina, Abel, I 293. Possibly the N Sheba was a set of outposts of the S. Tiglath-pileser mentions five Arab queens. The 'hard questions' of the queen of Sheba were riddles and allegorical proverbs, of which Samson's, Jg 14: 12—19, are examples. **2—10. 13.** Solomon's wisdom was proved as much by his riches as by his answers: poverty would have been no recommendation of his prudence. **11—12.** The sources and display of Solomon's wealth follow in a series of disconnected notices. One great source was the joint naval expeditions with Hiram (cf 22), exporting iron and copper, 9:26ff. 'Almug' is probably citron wood: another conjecture is sandalwood—impossible if found on Lebanon, 2 Chr 2:8. **14— 15.** The figures have suffered. **16—17.** His guardsmen had ceremonial shields which, between parades, hung in the Lebanon Hall; cf 7:2. About 8 lb of gold (LXX) was used on each large shield, about 4 lb on the small: in 17 read '3 minas' (MT) for '300 lb'. **18—21.** Ebony thrones, inlaid with gold and ivory, were carried off from Megiddo by Thothmes III c. 1480. **22.** The **d** traders sailed either ocean-going ships to Tartessus in Spain, or refinery (*tarshish*) ships carrying ore from the refinery port of Ezion-geber on the Gulf of Aqaba. The Phoenicians had such ships to transport cargo from their copper-refineries in Spain and Sardinia. 'Peacocks' (*tukki*, Malabar *togai*) is doubtful. Better 'baboons' (cf

287d W. F. Albright, *Archaeology and the Religion of Israel*, 212). **26.** See on 4:26. **28—29** give another source of wealth. Cilicia was a great horse-breeding country; Egypt manufactured chariots; see Albright, ibid, 135. There is no need to substitute *Musri* (Cappadocia) for *Misraim* (Egypt), as is often done; besides, Solomon's middlemen could hardly have established a monopoly in a merely northern trade.

e 11:1—43 The End of Solomon's Reign—A good example of the deuteronomic method: basically historical information is retold and arranged in such a way as to point a moral.

1—13 Solomon's sin—The harem was originally a sign of Solomon's magnificence. It was customary for kings to send their daughters to one another's harems; Amenhotep III received from Naharina the princess Giluhipa with 317 ladies (Breasted, *Ancient Records*, II, 867). But these foreign contacts endangered the purity of Yahwism (Ex 34:16) and Dt 7:1—4, which forbade marriage with Canaanites, is here authentically interpreted to exclude all foreigners. The pagan shrines were for the wives and visiting businessmen. Astarte was the fertility goddess of the ancient E; there were local Astartes like local Baals. Milcom was the Ammonite form of Malik or Muluk (Moloch), a god common to the semites. Religious infidelity is chastised by enemies from without (14—25) and from within (26—40) the nation. But unlike Saul who lost all, Solomon will retain one tribe, Judah (which was to absorb Benjamin, perhaps by force).

14—22, 25b Revolt of Edom—**17—18.** The direct route being barred, the refugees gained Egypt via Midian, E of the gulf of Aqabah, and Paran, N of the Sinai Peninsula. The young prince was of marriageable age; the same term was used of Solomon at his accession, 3:7. **20.** 'Genubath', cf Egyptian genbt, 'lock of hair'; that of a crown prince was characteristic. As long as the Pharaoh was friendly to Solomon (see on 9:17) he detained Hadad. 25b. Hadad later set up an independent state in *Edom* (LXX), which must eventually have hampered Solomon's trade.

23—25a. Revolt of Rezon—Solomon maintained his hold over Coele-Syria, 2 Chr 8:3, but a new power arose in Damascus, which was to be the terrible enemy of Israel for 200 years.

f 26—40 Rebellion and Flight of Jeroboam—**26—28.** That the first sign of internal dissension came from an Ephraimite is significant. Jeroboam was in a position to share and exploit the resentment of the northerners under forced labour. For Zeredah cf the valley of Serida, in the centre of the hill country E of Joppa, Abel II 457. For the Millo, see on 9:15. **29—31.** The prophet from Shiloh, long the resting place of the Ark, supported Jeroboam, while affirming the divine choice of Jerusalem, 32, and David, 34. For the symbolic action cf I Sm 15:27; Is 8:1; Jer 19:10. **32—35.** The count, *ten* tribes and one, disregards one tribe; cf 13. Jerusalem lay in Benjamin, and Judah was to include also Simeon and part of Dan. **36.** The lamp corresponds to 'hearth and home'. The metaphor means that the family of David would not become extinct. **37—38.** Jeroboam is placed on an equality with David, but with the same obligations. **40.** *Shishak* (or Sheshonq), the founder of a new dynasty, had no ties with Solomon. At 12:24 LXX adds a variant account of Jeroboam, from which may be retained the fact that he began his abortive rebellion by seizing the fortress which he had just constructed for Solomon at Zeredah.

g 41—43 Death of Solomon—One of the author's sources is given: 'the Annals of the Reign of Solomon'. For the compilers see 2 Chr 9:29. He died c.931; LXX here adds that Jeroboam returned at once from Egypt to his native

city. Under Solomon, Israel had advanced rapidly to its **287f** greatest power and prosperity. The international situation was favourable, with Assyria and Egypt passive, and the genius and energy of Solomon seized the opportunity to build up a great political and commercial empire. Initially, 8:66, S and N were united in enthusiastic loyalty to his person. But he failed to weld them into an organic whole. Instead, he used his powers to submit his people, and not impartially, to oppressive taxation and conscription. Some of the fruits of the empire went to strengthen its defences, but much went to maintain the magnificence of his court.

12:1—14:20 The Reign of Jeroboam—This is the **288a** beginning of the second main section of the book, the synchronistic history of the divided monarchy. The main source is the Chronicles of the kings of Israel and Judah (see § 242e) treated in the deuteronomic manner; but a large section, 13:1—14:18, comes (like 11:29—32) from prophetic traditions. See § 453a.

12:1—24 Secession of Israel—**1.** Shechem, near Nablus, was central and revered because of its religious associations, Gn 12:6; 33:18; Jos 24:32. Its choice as a place of assembly shows that the northerners were insisting on consideration. In principle they recognized the right to the throne of David's heir. **2—3a.** Omit with LXX (B and Lucian); cf 20. **3b—14.** The delay and the answer to the reasonable request must have caused resentment. The whip was not just a metaphor; forced labour came under the lash, and the scorpion was a scourge with hooks. **15.** The rashness of Rehoboam was a turning point in the history. **16.** The old cry of the discontented northerners was revived; cf 2 Sm 20:1. Their land did not lie in Judah. Why then should they recognize David as king? Here it was a refusal to remain under Rehoboam's orders. In future, 'David' must confine his attentions to his own tribe. **17—24.** The king's bodyguard failed to protect *Adoniram* (LXX, Syr.; cf 4:6), and it is doubtful if even the full muster of the S, though equipped with Solomon's armaments, could have imposed his will on the N.

25—32 Religious Schism—Jeroboam fortified **b** Shechem and made Penuel on the Jabbok his base to protect the provinces E of Jordan. **26—27.** Jerusalem still drew pilgrims, 2 Chr 11:16. **28.** The young bulls were two images of the one Yahweh, as the appeal to Ex 32:4 shows; the verb 'brought' is in the plural in MT, but was originally in the singular; cf Neh 9:18. The Decalogue, Ex 20:4 etc forbade images designed for worship, including in fact those of Yahweh (cf Dt 4:15) but could possibly be interpreted as forbidding only images of false gods. The cult was not idolatrous, but the way was open for confusing Yahweh with his image, and his cult with that of the Phoenician and Canaanite Baals, also represented as bulls. The bull was the symbol of strength and life-giving force. It has been maintained (cf W. F. Albright, *From the Stone Age to Christianity*[2], 229f) that the bull was merely the pedestal of Yahweh, like the cherubim of the Mosaic ark. But the Bible makes it clear that it was an image, and therefore the great sin and scandal of Jeroboam—not a mere 'rubrical' innovation. **29.** Bethel (Beitin) 10 m. N of Jerusalem, was rich in the memories of Abraham, Gn 12:8; 13:3; and of Jacob, Gn 28:10—22; 35:1—16. Dan (Tell el-Qādi) near the source of the Jordan, had been the shrine of a famous image, Jg 18: 1—31. Thus the law of the one sanctuary was violated. **31—33.** But in restoring the ancient shrines, Jeroboam could present himself as the upholder of ancient traditions; cf 2 Kgs 18:22. Priests were recruited from all classes, the Levites having migrated to Jerusalem, 2 Chr 11:13. The feast of Tabernacles was a month later than

38b in Jerusalem. cf 8:2, 65. Bethel became the Chapel Royal, Am 7:13.

c **13:1—10 Threat to Bethel**—Three prophets condemned the impiety of Jeroboam, first a Judean, then a northerner, 32, then Ahijah, 14:7ff. **2.** The gravest ritual impurity was from contact with corpses, Nm 19:18. The unexpected precision of 2 would indicate an addition to 3, the primitive oracle. **3—10.** The prophet's aloofness marked the 'excommunication' of the cult.

11—34 The Northern Prophet—11—15. His motives are obscure. This 'nabi' was a primitive and inferior type of ecstastic (cf § 451b). **16—19.** The Judean, though he had a revelation to the contrary, accepted his mere word. **20—22.** The rest of this markedly popular account teaches that the divine commands are to be absolutely obeyed; the man of God may not doubt them—even in such circumstances as the present. The Judaean had, publicly at least, disavowed the mandate of Yahweh; the judgement on him had to be public (cf 25) to restore the impression made by his sign. Burial among strangers was abhorrent cf Gn 47:30; 50:25. **23—28.** Lions were native to Palestine, 1 Sm 17:34 etc, and, it is said, did not become extinct there till the 12th cent. A.D. **29—32.** Add with LXX, 'that my bones may be undisturbed with his', at 31b. For the fulfillment of his hopes see 2 Kgs 23:18. 'Samaria' is an anachronism, one of several signs of the late redaction of the story. 'To fill the hands', a technical term, is to give the insignia or rights of priesthood; cf P. Jouon, Bib 3 (1922) 64. **33.** Conclusion of the deuteronomic redactor. Not merely the calf-worship but the non-Levitical priesthood was the sin of the N.

d **14:1—20 Doom of Jeroboam's House—1.** The link with the foregoing is vague; it is probably late in the reign; cf 10. **2.** Ahijah was no longer friendly. The disguise sought to avert the worst. Jeroboam regarded the prophet as a magician who could sway the future, but could be tricked into giving a favourable verdict. **3.** The modest presents, which were in keeping with the disguise, included 'cakes', perhaps 'raisin bread'. **4—6.** The failing sight of Ahijah heightens the miracle of his inspiration. **7.** This with 12—14, is the original kernel of the sentence pronounced against Jeroboam's ingratitude. The rest, 8—11, 15f, is an expansion of the theme in conventional terms. **8.** See 11:6, 31; Dt 12:35; 13:19; 21:9. **9.** 'Above all that were before' can hardly refer to Solomon; the phrase is part of the style; cf 16:25, 30, 33. **10.** refers to all male descendants; cf 16:11; 21:21 etc. **11.** Is again conventional, cf 16:4; 21:24. **12—14.** Honourable burial was to be denied to the house of Jeroboam, but not to Jeroboam himself, 20, nor to the innocence of youth. The prophet looks beyond the brief reign of Nadab to Baasha, 15:27. **15—16.** The exile of 721, beyond the Euphrates, was the last of a series of staggering blows. For 'Asherim' see on 23f. **17.** Tirzah was the capital of Israel before Samaria (cf 16:24). **18—20.** The wars of Jeroboam included (a) the defence of Transjordania, 12:25, possibly against the Ammonites; (b) skirmishes with Rehoboam, 14:30; (c) open war with Abijam, 2 Chr 13:2ff; (d) possibly war with Damascus (cf 15:19); (e) the invasion of Shishak; cf on 25ff. These formed part of the Annals. He died c. 910.

e **21—31 Rehoboam of Judah—21.** He reigned c.931—913. For the kings of Judah, the mother is regularly named; cf on 2:12; 15:9f. Her influence no doubt furthered the idolatry which Solomon had favoured. **22—23.** In the Canaanite cults, stone pillars and wooden posts flanked the altars. The pillars represented Baal, the posts Asherah, his consort; MT passim, uses the proper names of the goddess, in the plural, 'ašerîm, for the wooden posts.

The Greeks used the name Hermes both for the god and for **288e** the pillar surmounted by his head. For the tree trunk, supposed to be an ashera, excavated at Ai, see L. H. Vincent, RB 54 (1947) 248f. Asherah, originally perhaps a sea goddess (cf Albright, 77f), was now more or less interchangeable with Astarte, goddess of fertility, of which green trees were the emblems. **24.** Sacral prostitution, involving both sexes, was a permanent feature of these cults; cf Herodotus 1.199; Lucian, de Dea Syra. Not all the country shrines were idolatrous. The high places tolerated by even good kings (cf 15:14; 22:44 etc) were shrines of Yahweh. But they were against the law of one sanctuary, and their installations were apparently modelled on the Canaanite. Stone pillars could be legitimate (cf Gn 28:17f with 35:7 and Ex 24:4) but their associations were pernicious. Hence the drastic action of Hezekiah and Josiah against them. **25—29.** Sixty N towns are included in the inscription of Karnak which records the Palestine expedition of Shishak (Egyptian Shoshenq or Sheshonq) c. 926. Possibly Jeroboam's neglect of promised tribute (cf 11:40) was the cause of the raid; it is placed here as the chastisement of Judah's impiety. **30—31.** Border skirmishes were frequent, the new boundaries still being fluid. Full-scale war had been averted, 12:19.

15:1—8 Abijam of Judah—1—2. He reigned c. 913— f 911. Daughter stands for grand-daughter here, as in 2 Kgs 8:26. Maacah's father was Uriel of Gibeah, 2 Chr 13:2, husband of Absalom's daughter Tamar, 2 Sm 14:27. **3—7a.** With the continued religious decline, the dynasty would have gone the way of Jeroboam's, but for David's merits. **7b.** Abijam even maintained the cult at Bethel, after capturing this and other towns from Jeroboam; cf 2 Chr 13:9; 15:8.

9—24 Asa of Judah, 911—870—9—10. After the early death of Abijam, Maacah, Asa's grand-mother, retained the dignity of queen-mother; cf on 2:12; 14:21. In Babylon and Assyria also the king's mother received special honours, witness the legendary fame of Semiramis (Sammuramat, whose son, Adad-Nirari III, called her 'Queen of the palace, his Lady'; cf E. Schrader, KIB, 11, 193). **13.** The image was apparently not the plain wooden post, but probably an Astarte, usually represented naked. **14.** The country shrines of Yahweh were left undisturbed, in spite of the law of one sanctuary. They were not as yet contaminated with heathenism, hence Asa's heart could be said to be perfect. **15.** Abijam had won booty from Jeroboam, and Asa from the Ethiopians, cf 2 Chr 14:12. **16—17.** When the Israelites re-took Bethel, g they advanced to within 5 m. of Jerusalem. **18—19.** Asa inaugurated the policy of foreign alliances with which the prophets ceaselessly reproached Judah (cf Is 7:4—9; 8:6—8 etc). **20.** Ijon (Tell Dibbin), Dan and Abel-beth-Maacah (Abil), lay round the source of the Jordan; Chinneroth (Tell el-Oreimeh), from which the Lake of Galilee took its ancient name, was the most southerly point of Syrian invasion. The territory was not permanently occupied (cf 2 Kgs 15:29) but Israel hardly regained it without making concessions of the type indicated in 20:34, as it covered the trade routes to Tyre and Egypt. All later wars had this prize in view. **21.** Tirzah, probably Tell el-Far'ah, near Nablus (R. de Vaux, RB 59 (1952) 551—83). **22—24.** Asa's new fortresses fixed the frontier a few miles N of Ramah. At Mizpah (Maspha; Tell el-Nasbeh) walls of this period have been found up to 26 ft. in width.

25—16:14 Dynastic Changes in Israel—25—26. Dur- h ing the long and happy reign of Asa in Judah, six kings, involving three dynasties, were to succeed each other in

288h Israel. **27—28.** As Nadab (910—909) was with the army, his slayer must have been a general. Gibbethon (Tell el-Melāt, between Jerusalem and the coast) was left in Philistine hands; cf 16:15. **29—16:6.** Baasha (909—889) disappointed the orthodox and led the people to defeat; cf 15:21. The prophet's denunciation spurred the discontented to action. **7.** Jehu outlived Ahab and Jehosaphat, 2 Chr 19:2; 20:34. **8—14.** With Elah (886—885) perished all the connexions who were bound to avenge him, his *'go' elim'*; cf Nm 35:19—27.

15—20 Death of Zimri (885)—Though energetic and brave, he was not a good organizer, and had not time to muster his supporters. These were numerous, as the subsequent civil war shows, and probably represented the Ephraim-Manasseh group of tribes, from which Jeroboam came. Omri had land in Issachar (cf ch 21) and so represented the more northerly group of tribes, like his patron Baasha, under whom he had conquered and governed Moab (Mesha Stone, § 81*l*). **17.** 'All Israel' is the army, 15. Contrast 'the people of Israel', 21, whose division later split the army.

i **21—28 Omri, 885—874—21—22.** LXX (B, Lucian) shows that Joram, brother of Tibni, continued the civil war. **23.** It lasted four years, as Zimri died in Asa's 27th year (15) and Omri's undisputed reign began in Asa's 31st. The twelve years are reckoned from Zimri's death (cf 16) ending in Asa's 38th (29). **24.** Samaria (see § 80*c*) for fortifications, palaces and ivories), re-founded by Herod as Sebaste (now Sebastiyeh), was a central and strong position, on an almost isolated hill which dominated its neighbourhood by almost 300 ft. **25—26.** The severe blame (cf Mi 6:16) is for introducing Phoenician worship and giving it state establishment which he did when he married Ahab to Jezebel. **27—28.** The marriage was one of his earliest political moves (Ahab's grand-son was 22 years old in 841, 2 Kgs 8:26) and one of his ablest, since the Tyrian alliance kept Damascus in check. He was a great ruler, and the Assyrians knew Israel henceforth as 'the Land of the House of Omri'.

289a **16:29—2 Kgs 13:21**—This section covers the following reigns: in Israel, Ahab, Ahaziah, Jehoram, Jehu, Jehoahaz, Jehoash; in Judah, Jehoshaphat, Jehoram, Ahaziah, Athaliah, Jehoash. The deuteronomic formula is still used to provide a framework, see 283f (except for Jehu and Athaliah, where it is not appropriate); but the matter within the framework is very different from that used previously. Very little of it is drawn from a properly historical source: 1 Kgs chh 20, 22; 2 Kgs 8:16—29; 9:1—10:14. The rest, apart from easily recognizable deuteronomic additions, is taken from **the prophetic cycles of Elijah and Elisha** (cf 283*g*). But the prophetic material itself is mixed. There is first of all **legend** (§ 241*j*) which is most easily recognized in the Elisha cycle, in which the miraculous element is prominent and the prophet is associated with the guilds of Gilgal, Bethel and Jericho, from whom no doubt the stories came. Other material may be classed as **saga**, in which again interest is focused on the person of the prophet, but without any exaggerated account of miracles: such would be 1 Kgs 18; 2 Kgs 5. Others again represent the prophet in the context of **historical events**—in such a way that in fact it is difficult to distinguish such stories from those purely historical narratives in which prophets intervene; compare, for example, 2 Kgs 3:3—20 where Elisha assists the Israelites in the war against Moab, with 1 Kgs 22:5—28, which deals with the Aramean war but in which prophets play an important part. It seems probable that an Elijah cycle and an Elisha cycle were compiled from originally independent stories of various kinds before being used as the basis for an account of the period. 'Evidently the attempt has twice been made to group round an eminent personage the tremendous events which shook Israel about the middle of the 9th cent. B.C., namely the prophetic revolutionary movement directed against the dynasty of Ahab . . . and the Aramean wars which pressed so terribly upon Israel' (EOTInt 292). These two cycles may already have been combined when the redactor used them for his history.

16:29—34 Ahab 874—853—Two enormities, the **b** Baal temple and human sacrifice, heralded the religious crisis which Elijah was to meet. **29—31.** Ethbaal had become king of Tyre and Sidon (cf on 5:6) by killing his predecessor, according to Menander (in Josephus, C. Ap. 1, 18, 23). The new dynasties supported each other. Ahab apparently paid a state visit to worship Melqart ('king of the city') the Baal ('lord') of Tyre. He was however also a worshipper of Yahweh, as the names of his children show (Ahazyah, Jehoram, Ataly*ah*). Prophets of Yahweh will be found in his entourage. **32—33.** Beside the altar, he set up an Asherah (cf on 14:23) and naturally, other Asherahs and massebahs (pillars) throughout the land, 2 Kgs 3:2. **34.** Excavations have shown that Jericho, was rebuilt at this era; cf § 126*c-d*. The sacrifices, common at such undertakings (cf L. H. Vincent, *Canaan*, 199), were to avert calamity; the orthodox looked on them here as the fulfilment of the curse of Jos 6:26.

17:1—24 Elijah and the Drought—The editorial **c** method can be seen here. The sin of Ahab introduces the drought, a punishment for idolatry and a challenge to Baal, god of fertility (1—7); this in turn leads to the miracle described in 8—16; and this then serves to introduce the raising of the dead child, which is not actually connected chronologically with the foregoing. On the name Elijah ('my God is Yahweh') see H. H. Rowley, BJRL 43 (1960—1) 190ff. Zarephath, now Sarafand, on the sea coast until the time of the crusades, is now 1 mile inland. **18.** The exclamation *māh lî walāk*, literally 'What (is there) to me and to thee', has various nuances; cf Jn 2:4. Here it expresses surprise and concern. The prophet's presence had seemed a blessing, but in the end it only called attention to her sins. **19—23.** The rite which accompanied the prayer (cf 2 Kgs 4:34, Ac 20:10) signified that the warmth of life should pass from the prophet to the child. **24.** The mother reaffirms her faith in the divine mission of the prophet (cf Lk 4:25) and further that Yahweh had been faithful all along to his first promise of blessing.

18:1—15 Return of Elijah—1—6. The new year had **d** come round twice in the drought, which lasted probably from after the March rains of one year till the November rains of the following year. The 3½ years of Lk 4:25, Jas 5:17 seems to be idiomatic, like the 'three days and three nights' of Mt 12:40. U. Holzmeister, VDom (1939) 167ff, takes it literally. But in such a spell, all vegetation and cattle would have been destroyed. The expeditions hoped to find wells and watered valleys where green fodder still grew. Ahab does not seem to have been personally hostile to the true religion, since his chamberlain was a 'strict servant of Yahweh', as his name implies; the persecution is ascribed to Jezebel. **7—10.** Ahab was on good terms with the neighbouring kings of Tyre, Syria, 20:34, Judah 22:5; he was ruler of Moab; hence he could make them swear that Elijah was not to be found. **11—14.** The spirit of Yahweh was considered as an external force (cf 46), which transported the prophet. These sudden disappearances seem to have been characteristic of the

89d history of Elijah, 2 Kgs 2:16, until his final taking up, 2 Kgs 2:11ff. **15.** Elijah was the servant of him who was about to reveal himself as 'Yahweh, (God) of hosts': i.e. lord of all earthly and heavenly forces; cf Gn 2:1 (nature), 1 Sm 4:4 (armies), Dt 4:19 (stars), Jos 5:14 (angels).

e 16—24 Challenge on Carmel—17. Ahab's anger died away with the prospect of relief. **19.** The majestic wooded range of Carmel was naturally sacred in the eyes of pagans (Tacitus, *Hist.* 2, 78; Suetonius, *Vespasian* 5; Iamblichus, *Pythagoras* 3:15) and was the site of the shrine of Yahweh, like Mt. Nebo (Mesha Stone). Tradition placed the meeting at the height El-Muhraqa, 'Burnt Offering', at the SE end of the range, close to the Kishon, 40, and Jezreel, 46. A lower point near by, Bir el-Muhraqa, with a spring, 34f, suits the place and text much better, as the sea was not visible without a climb, 43f. **21.** The reproach, 'How long will you limp from side to side?' suggests that the people were already familiar with the exigencies of monotheism; but no doubt the prophets—and precisely in situations such as described here—were responsible for making clearer what was involved: 'Yahweh is all or nothing'. There had been a certain co-existence between the cult of the local Baal and the worship of Yahweh. But now a conflict was developing between two opposite cultures. Phoenician culture under its national Baal Melkart was established in Samaria (16:32f) and this threatened to swamp Israelite culture under Yahweh. Whence the clear and peremptory message of Carmel ranks with that of Sinai in the history of Revelation. **22—24.** The ending of the drought might have been attributed to chance, lightning was decisive, especially as Baal, Hadad, 'Lord of Heaven', was the great storm-god.

f 25—49 Fire from Heaven—26. 'They *danced by* the altar': the Baal Marqod 'lord of the dance' had a shrine on Lebanon, and the ritual dances of Cybele and the *Dea Syra* were well known to antiquity. **27.** According to R. de Vaux, ('Les prophètes de Baal sur le mont Carmel' in *Bulletin du Musée de Beyrouth*, 1943), Elijah mocked four aspects of Baal: (1) the philosopher-inventor ('he is meditating'); (2) the patron of Phoenician merchants ('he is busy'); (3) the patron of his sailors; (4) the winter sleeper, for whose awakening, a feast was held in Tyre and Carthage, Jos, Ant 8, 5, 3. The last trait shows Baal as the vegetation-god. **28.** As a mourning-rite at least, self-wounding was prevalent, Dt 14:1; Jer 47:5. Originally based perhaps on the idea of blood alliance with the god, it was here an intense mode of prayer. **29.** 'raved on', cf 1 Sm 19:23f, 2 Kgs 9:11, like dervishes, who also wound themselves. **29—31.** The time, 3 p.m., was fixed according to the temple ritual, and the twelve tribes are represented as the twelve stones of the altar. Elijah seems to have wished for the united prayers of Israel and Judah, just as he acted in the interests of both. **33—35.** The drenching was not to produce rain by 'sympathetic magic', but to heighten the effect of the miracle. **36—39.** As on Sinai, Yahweh revealed himself by fire, the one God in the past who had converted to himself the people's fathers. **40.** In the 'war' between Yahweh and Baal, the servants of Baal underwent the fate reserved to the vanquished.

41—46. Miracle of the Rain—41—42. Hearing its approach in spirit, Elijah crouched down in an attitude of intense prayer. **44—46.** The prophet's solicitude for the king was friendly, with a final demonstration of his superhuman power, cf Ps 19 (18): 5. Jezreel (Zerin) was c. 15 m. away.

g 19:1—8 Flight to Horeb—1—2. Jezebel did not dare to kill Elijah but, to uphold her authority, she banished him

with threats. **3.** He could not long rely on Ahab and the **289g** fickle public. He fled without pausing in Judah because since c. 865, Jehoshaphat's son, Jehoram, was married to Athaliah, daughter of Ahab and Jezebel. **4.** The hardships and disappointments of his fugitive life wrung from him a plea for release. **5—8.** Wishing to safeguard the Covenant and re-establish purity of faith, Elijah undertook a 300m. pilgrimage to Sinai where the covenant was first established. He thus attached his work directly to that of Moses. Both experienced a theophany at Sinai, and both were to be present also at Christ's transfiguration, the theophany of the NT (Mt 17:1—9).

9—14. Theophany—9—12. Yahweh's coming was heralded by hurricane, earthquake and lightning. But he was not in this storm—contrast Ex 19:18; Ps 18 (17): 7ff. His presence was felt only in the quiet of a gentle breeze, thus intimate. Yet, terrible commands are given in 15—17.

15—18. The Divine Plan—Elijah's life-work was nearly over, but God had other instruments. **15.** The desert of Damascus is here probably the pasture-land E of the Sea of Galilee, then held by Syria. Hazael was a dignitary of Benhadad III, 2 Kgs 8:7f, who was yet to succeed Benhadad II. **16.** Similarly, before Jehu, two kings were to succeed Ahab. Thus, according to the immediate meaning of the text, Elijah was to anoint Hazael and Jehu c. 13 years before they came to the throne. In fact, it was only through Elisha that Elijah carried out his mandate. The prophecy was fulfilled substantially but the terms were not modified to suit the event exactly. **18.** The 'Remnant' (this is the first instance of an idea common in the 8th cent. prophets) is given in a symbolic number. Perhaps however the actual number of the orthodox in the N is indicated. For kissing as a religious rite, see Hos 13:2; Jb 31:27.

19—21. Vocation of Elisha—19. The homeland of *'elîsâ* 'God has saved', was Abel-Meholah, 16, probably Tell Abu Sifri, near the Jordan S of Beisan. The gesture with the distinctive mantle of the prophet (cf 2 Kgs 1:8; Zech 13:4; Mt 3:4) intimated the call. **20.** Elijah's answer seems to be a concession. **21.** For Elisha seems to have understood that Elijah demanded an immediate break with past; cf Lk 9:62. The anointing—metaphorical (since prophets were not anointed)—as prophet came later, probably just before the events of 2 Kgs 2. Meanwhile, Elisha was considered merely the servant of Elijah, 2 Kgs 3·11.

20.1—21 War with Syria LXX (B, Lucian) puts ch **h** 21 before 20, leaving the connexion between 20 and 22 unbroken. **1.** It was probably c. 858, before the drought; for the causes see on 15:20. Benhadad II (c. 875—845) at the Battle of Qarqar, 853 B.C., put into the field 1,200 chariots, 1,200 horse, 20,000 foot (ANET 278). There, against Assyria, 11 kings were allied; the 32 here must be the chiefs of the Syrian tribes. **2—9.** Ahab was prepared to pay a certain contribution but not to submit to an inspection in view of a general confiscation. **10.** Benhadad, threatening to raze the city, claimed to have so many soldiers that its dust would not make a handful for each. **13.** Jezebel's persecution had not started. The prophet is not Elijah, for popular traditions are inclined to ascribe rather more than less to an outstanding figure. **14—21.** Ahab, a brave and devoted leader (cf 18:6; 22:35) headed a sortie of picked troops, so few that the Syrians did not anticipate serious fighting. A full-scale attack routed them. The tactics are not made clear. The writer's intention was simply to show that the victory came from Yahweh, 13.

22—34 Another Campaign—22—23. The heart of **i**

289i Israel's territory was upland; Yahweh was compared to the Baal Hermon or Baal Lebanon. The principle that chariots and cavalry could be better employed on plains than among hills was clothed in religious form. **24—26.** The undisciplined or untrustworthy sheikhs were replaced by regular officers, and Benhadad advanced along the E of the Sea of Galilee (cf on 10:15) basing his forces on Aphek (Fîq, a few miles N of the Yarmuk). **27—30.** Yahweh was proved God of the plains as of the hills, therefore universal lord, since the battle was fought probably on the plateau SW of Fîq. Popular history lies behind the fantastic figures of 29—30. **30.** The walls were undermined, and house to house fighting followed. **31.** A burden on the back could be slung from a band around the forehead; hence the rope on the head to signify submission. Jos, Ant 8, 14, 4, explains it as a custom of Syrian suppliants. **33.** Vassals of Assyrian kings spoke of themselves as running beside the chariots of their overlord; cf inscription of Bar-Rekub of Sam'al, Bonkamp, *Die Bibel im Lichte der Keilschriftforschung* 402. **34.** Ahab regained what Omri had lost in an otherwise unknown war, and his merchants set up their own bazaars in Damascus. Ahab fought on the side of the Syrians at Qarqar, cf **h** above and also § 127*a*.

j **35—43 Condemnation of the Treaty**—In attacking twice against odds, Ahab had obeyed Yahweh and been rewarded; in making terms he had been guided only by politics and was punished. **35—36.** The 'sons of the prophets' were disciples grouped round sanctuaries of Yahweh; cf § 452*c*, and on 2 Kgs 2:3. In 38 and 41 they are simply 'prophets'. The story is in the popular style of 1 Kgs 13:24 and with the same warning. **37—38.** The object of the wound which presumably could be seen bleeding, was to distract attention from the bandage round his forehead, which merely concealed (tattoo-) markings by which a prophet could be known; cf Ezek 9:4ff. **39—41.** Like David before Nathan, 2 Sm 12:5, Ahab passed sentence on himself. **42.** The captive was not his to dispose of, but Yahweh's cf Jos 6:17 etc. The misplaced clemency of Ahab involved Israel in foreign commitments which in the end brought ruin. **43.** The true prophets aimed at preserving Israel as a people apart, Dt 33:28 etc. It was probably for their stand at this stage that Jezebel was allowed to proceed against them, 18:4.

k **21:1—16 Murder of Naboth**—After the Syrian wars, the events of chh 17—19 are probably to be inserted before this episode. **1.** The coveted vineyard was in Jezreel, as follows from 2 Kgs 9:21—25; from 19 and 22:38 it might have been thought to have been in Samaria. **2—3.** Ahab's request was not against Lv 25:23—28, for Naboth would not be left landless, nor against Nm 36:7, since the land would not pass from the tribe of Issachar; cf on 16:16. Naboth was obstinately conservative. **4—8.** It was the sharpness of the refusal that angered Ahab. Hence the repetition in 4 and 6, to contrast with the courtesy of the offer. The pagan despot, Jezebel, was ruthless. Her irony stung Ahab into delivering to her the royal seal. The scene is characteristic of her power over Ahab. **9.** The fast, suggesting impending disaster, Jl 1:14, Jg 20:26, built up an atmosphere of tension in which the people would be swift to punish an evil-doer. **10.** The two witnesses (cf Dt 17:6; 19:15) were 'sons of worthlessness' (*belîya'al*), scoundrels; P. Joüon, Bib 5 (1924) 178 explains the term as 'devil'; cf 2 Cor 6:15. The double blasphemy was against Lv 24:16, Ex 22:28. **11—13.** Naboth was stoned on his own land (cf 19), property outside Jezreel, to which the kings rode out to meet Jehu, 2 Kgs 9:21—26. The vineyard was in the town beside the

palace. His sons were killed too, 2 Kgs 9:26, to leave no 289 heirs to dispute the confiscation of property. There was no legal pretext for their death. But a king's enemies were often destroyed root and branch, 1:21 etc. **14—16.** Ahab must have learned the details and certainly sanctioned the murders.

17—29 Condemnation and Repentance—19. The 1 prophecy was fulfilled vaguely in 22:38, but more precisely, as Jehu understood, in 2 Kgs 9:25f. Ahab's blood flowed in Jehoram's veins. **20.** Ahab confessed that he was caught in the act. His misgivings show that he still had a lively sense of justice. Elijah's 'sold' is apt; Ahab had sold himself to Jezebel for the price of a vineyard. **21, 22, 24,** are a conventional interpretation of the prophecy by the writer; cf 14:10f; 16:2ff. **23.** is original but awkwardly placed; a fuller form in 2 Kgs 9:10, 36f. **25.** The mention of Jezebel's influence is not to excuse but to explain Ahab's conduct; a similar remark was made about Solomon, 11:3f. **26.** The Amorites are a prototype of Canaanite Baalworshippers as in Am 2:9; Ezek 16:3. Ahab had noble traits; cf 20 and on 20:14, which are faithfully recorded in spite of the writer's unsympathetic attitude. There is an unmistakable ring of triumph in the pardon which reminds us of the parables of Lk 15; and perhaps the fiercely zealous Elijah needed the lesson there taught by the father to the elder son. This episode is taken from a different source than that of chh 17—19; there the official cult of Baal is the chief factor in the downfall of the dynasty; here, as in 2 Sm 2, the contribution of the king's personal sin is stressed.

22:1—28 Micaiah and the False Prophets—1—3. 290. Israel probably regained territory E of the Sea of Galilee after the victory of Aphek, 20:34, but Syria still held the border town of Ramoth (Tell Ramith), on the trade route from Damascus to N Arabia. The battle of Qarqar (spring of 853) had not appreciably weakened the Syrians, for the Assyrians had to return to the attack four times in the next twelve years. But Ahab had been able to put 2,000 chariots into that battle, compared to Damascus' 1,200, Pritchard, ANET, 277—9. He was therefore strong enough to take the offensive (autumn 853). **4—5.** Jehoshaphat was allied both politically and by marriage to the house of Omri; cf on 19:3. **6.** The prophets who had survived the persecution (18:4; 19:14) had bowed the knee to Baal, 19:18, but still claimed to speak for Yahweh. **8.** This Micaiah, who had kept up the menaces of 20:42, was confused with the 8th cent. author of the prophetical book by the glossator of 28*b*. **9—14.** The false prophets counted for little, since the verdict of Micaiah could outweigh theirs. He had not as yet received a revelation; it came while he was on his way; cf 17, 'I saw'. **15—17.** After echoing sarcastically the words of the false prophets, he foretold defeat, without stating clearly that Ahab would die. The flight or capture of the king might have explained the leaderless state of the army. For the terms cf Nm 27:17 (Mt 9:36). **18.** The king sought to nullify the effect of his words by ascribing them to his personal malice. **19.** Micaiah therefore gave details of his revelation. **20.** The reference to Ahab's death was still veiled. **21.** The spirit of prophecy was to be transformed into a spirit of lying. **22—23.** The false prophets were branded as conscious liars, though Micaiah granted that in some way, God was responsible; cf 2 Sm 24:1; 1 Sm 26:19; Ex 4:21; 2 Sm 16:10. The Israelites were satisfied that Yahweh was the ultimate cause of every event and did not ask how precisely he was the cause both of good and of evil. **24—28*a*.** Having warned the false prophets that they would have to fly for their lives some day (cf 2 Kgs 20:26) Micaiah finally

90a stated clearly that Ahab would die in the battle. **28b.** Cf Mi 1:2.

b 29–40 Ahab's Last Campaign—29–30. Ahab was determined, if the end was come, to die among his soldiers, but he did not mean to make it easy for his destiny to overcome him. The Syrians were not to recognize him. He cannot have known their order of the day. Jehoshaphat was in no special danger; the silence of Micaiah in his regard was reassuring. **31.** With possible future alliances against Assyria in view, the king of Syria planned to end the war with as little loss as possible on either side. **32.** Jehoshaphat gave the Judaean war-cry to rally his men. **35–37.** Ahab did not allow himself to be taken to the rear, but, to avoid disheartening his troops, remained upright near the front till he bled to death. **38.** See on 21:19. **39.** Jericho was one of Ahab's undertakings. For the fortifications and ivories of Samaria, see DBS 3, 386–8 or W. F. Albright, *Archaeology of Palestine*, 137. His palace was decorated with ivories, Am 3:15; Ps 45 (44):9; they appear mostly as inlay for furniture. See § 80c.

c 41–50 Jehoshaphat of Judah, 870–848—41–46. Continuing the reform of Asa, he eliminated ritual prostitution; cf 15:1. **47.** Edom had been re-conquered; cf 11:14–25b; a deputy ruled probably with Israelite ministers. **48–50.** After a set-back, the Red Sea trade was apparently resumed. To bring 2 Chr 20:30 37 into line with this passage, 'Ahab' may be read here for 'Ahaziah'; the enterprise was hardly delayed till the end of Jehoshaphat's long reign. **50.** Some idea of the importance of Jehoshaphat as an administrator may be gathered from 2 Chr 17:19. His measures included fortification of towns, re-organization of the army, re-distribution of provinces, provision of religious instruction and division of the judiciary.

51–53 Ahaziah of Israel—An indication of the unity of the work now divided into 1 and 2 Kgs; Ahaziah's career is given here on a Chronicler's summary, cf § 283f, and continued on the Elijah-source which follows.

THE SECOND BOOK OF KINGS

90d 1:1–2 Ahaziah of Israel, 853–852: Invocation of Baalzebub—1. The loss of Moab and the illness or injury of the king are seen as chastisement for provoking Yahweh, 1 Kgs 22:54. **2.** Baal-zebub 'lord of flies' (cf LXX and Jos.Ant. 9, 2, 1). Zebub however is probably a contemptuous alteration of the original Zebul 'lofty mansion', 'high place'. The true form and meaning survived in the NT, Mt 10:25 etc., though the later Jews associated it with *zibbul* 'dung'. The Ras-Shamra texts mention *Z-b-l B-'-l*, from which the sense of 'sublime, lordly' cannot be excluded. Baal-zebul would not, then, be a local Ekron god but the Syrian god of life, similar to the Melkart of Phoenicia. Ahaziah disavowed Yahweh as the true God and as the God of Israel.

e 3–18 Intervention of Elijah—3–7. It is remarkable that he was not known to the soldiers. But he had always held aloof from the capital; cf 20:13; 22:8. **8.** His hairy mantle was distinctive; cf on 1 Kgs 19:19. **9.** The command was to 'come down' to Samaria; cf 15; Elijah was not on an inaccessible crag. **10–12.** The answer involved a grim pun: not the man ($'\bar{\imath}\check{s}$) of God, but fire ($'\bar{e}\check{s}$) of God was to come down. **11–16.** Why the destruction? (1) Elijah was defending his life; cf 15 and 1 Kgs 19:2f. (2) Disrespect for the prophetic office was visited with the extreme penalty; cf 2:23ff; 1 Kgs 20:36. The soldiers were executing an evidently sacrilegious order and the captain's 'man of God' was sarcastic. (3)

The people needed to be deterred from the sensual cult **290e** of Baal by the fear of God. Hence the prophet's appeal to motives of fear, 1 Kgs 17:1; 21:21; 22:17. It was not a prophet's duty to preach but to convey God's message **17–18.** This dating, which does not agree with 3:1, belongs to a secondary chronological system.

2:1–12 Assumption of Elijah—1. We may conclude **f** only that Elijah is no longer of this world, his destiny a mystery which Elisha will not explain. The text does not say that Elijah is not dead, but one may easily conclude this. On the return of Elijah cf Mal 3:25. There were several Gilgals, 'circle of stones', the simplest type of shrine. This one, to the N of Bethel, is different to that of Jos 4:19. **2–8.** Elijah paid a last visit of encouragement to the prophetic colleges (see § 452c) though he was not their head; cf 'your master'. **3.** They did not foresee his permanent disappearance (cf 16) and they were not to witness his passing. Moses too had passed away alone, with no one to know his grave, Dt 34:6. Elijah and Elisha must have returned to the Jordan somewhere above Jericho, for there was a ford lower down, 2 Sm 19:40f. The miracle (cf Ex 14:21, Jos 3:13) prevented the others following, and the bush then hid the pair from view. **9.** A double share was the portion of the firstborn, Dt 21:17; Elisha wished to inherit, with the office, the miraculous power and primacy of Elijah. **10.** Elijah doubted whether such extraordinary signs as he had wrought would be repeated in favour of an ungrateful people; cf 1 Kgs 19:14ff. **11.** The vision granted to Elisha, however, was one withheld from ordinary men; cf 6:17. Elijah ascended in a storm, like that in which Yahweh descended, Ex 1:4; Jb 38:1. **12.** Elijah, Israel's chariots and cavalry, had been worth an army to his people. The event took place probably in 851, after the death of Ahaziah and before the Moabite campaign; cf 3:11, and 13:14 below.

13–18 The Mantle of Elijah—13–15. After re- **g** peating Elijah's miracle, the former servant was acknowledged as master. **16–18.** The prophetic group had only a vague idea of what was to happen to Elijah. Apparently Elisha did not enlighten them.

19–22 Healing of the Waters—20–22. A new vessel was required for a sacred action, cf 1 Kgs 11:30; the salt signified preservation from foulness (cf Lv 2:13 etc). **23–25 The Bears—23.** The hostility at Bethel suggests that the prophet inveighed against the calf-worship. 'Baldhead' was possibly a current sneer against the distinctive 'tonsure' worn by the prophets, and familiar from the college at Bethel. For the idea of the collective responsibility of parents and children see § 139e. **25.** Elisha's own home was in Samaria, 5:9; 6:32. But he toured the country giving instruction. In the following narrative he is found at Carmel, Shunem, Gilgal, Jericho and Dothan.

3:1–3 Jehoram of Israel, 852–41—1. For the **h** dating, see § 283j. **2.** Jehoram started well, impressed by the events of 1:2ff. But he did not interfere with Jezebel's installations in the capital, and later there was a recrudescence of Baalism throughout the country; cf 10:21. Hence Elisha's sharp reproof, 13, and his support of Jehu, 9:1ff.

4–8 Campaign against Moab—4. Mesha recorded his successful revolt on the stele found at Dibon in 1869, now in the Louvre, and known as the **Moabite Stone** or **Stele of Mesha**, cf § 81l; see M.-J. Lagrange RB 10 (1901) 522ff. The sheep-rearing is referred to on the stone, l.30. It also speaks of '40 years' subjection'; see on 1 Kgs 16:15–20. **5–8.** Mesha had seized the fortresses N of the Arnon, Medeba, Qiryathayim, Ataroth,

290h Nebo and Yahas. The attack was therefore launched from the SE, after a march round the S of the Dead Sea and across the plateau of Edom. In vv 6, 11, 12, 14, Jehoshaphat is given as king of Judah, but chronology proves that the war took place only under his son, Jehoram of Judah. Jehoshaphat seems to have been named in consideration of his piety and the similar role he played in 1 Kgs 22. Here, the king of Judah, in contrast to the king of Israel, is shown as a fervent Yahwist (vv 11, 13–14).

i 9–20 Water in the Desert—9–10. For the vassal king of Edom see on 1 Kgs 22:48. On the border of Moab, 21, the army was exposed to attack when weakened by thirst. **11.** Elisha was not well known. This places the campaign c. 851. The Orientals did not dip their hands into a basin, when washing before and after meals: a servant poured for them. **13.** Jehoram's plea, 'Say not so! For it is indeed Yahweh' etc., was a confession of faith. Yahweh alone could help. **14–15.** The ritual music (cf. § 451*b*) was to induce ecstasy. **16–17.** Rains over the plateau, too far away to be remarked, could fill the wadis lower down. Elisha's foresight was supernatural. **18–20.** The order to devestate Moab was of exceptional severity; cf Dt 20:19f.

j 21–27. Invasion of Moab—21–22. The coloration was due to the sands of W. el-Hesa. There is a pun on *'ăḏōm* 'red', *dām* 'blood' and *Edom*. **23–24.** The Moabites could easily suppose that the king of Edom had turned on the others. **25.** Only the capital, Kir-haresheth (Kerak) cf Is 16:7, 11) resisted the invaders. **26.** Mesha tried to break through to the Edomites, to make common cause with them. **27.** Then he had recourse to human sacrifice, the Crown Prince probably offering himself freely, like Marcus Curtius in the Roman Forum or the Carthaginian general Hamilcar, who made himself a holocaust at Himera in 480 for the success of his army. Thus Mesha thought to avert the wrath of his god Kemosh (cf Mesha Stone, lines 5, 6) and to render his ramparts inviolable. Then 'there came great indignation (of Yahweh) upon Israel'; cf Jos 9:20 etc. Some calamity, probably a pestilence, forced the Israelites to retire. According to Stade, Sanda, Kittel, etc the original narrative said 'the indignation of Kemosh'. But this would be at variance with ancient ways of thought, especially Israel's; the Assyrians attributed a reverse to the anger of Nana, the Babylonians to the anger of Marduk. Mesha rebuilt his towns and remained unsubdued (Mesha Stone, lines 21–33).

k 4:1–7 Miraculous Multiplication of Oil—This and the next three chh are chiefly concerned with the miracles by which Elisha continued the extraordinary mission of Elijah, cf § 289*a*. **1–2.** Insolvent debtors could be sold as slaves, Lv 25:39; Am 2:6; a father could sell his children, Ex 21:2–7. Loyalty to Yahweh had been costly under Ahab. The widow had therefore special reasons for hope. **3–7.** The miracle was less lavish than that of Elijah, 1 Kgs 17, which was worked to avert the more enduring menace of famine.

8–10 Hospitality of the Lady of Shunem—8. For Shunem see on 1 Kgs 1:3. **9–10.** 'Holy' here is not so much 'good' as 'sacred'; hence Elisha was lodged apart, in a walled chamber on the roof. Such installations were sometimes only huts or leafy branches, 2 Sm 16:22; Neh 8:16. The furniture was a further mark of respect. Poor people sat and slept on the floor.

11–16 Promise of a Child—11–12. The prophet held himself notably aloof, treating with the lady only through his servant. This may be understood also in 16. **13.** His influence at court is understandable after the Moabite campaign. But the lady had clansmen to defend **290l** her interests.

17–37 The Dead Child restored to Life—17–19. l The child died of sunstroke; cf Jdt 8:2f; note the simple pathos of the original 'Oh, my head, my head!' **20–23.** It was evidently the custom to visit the prophet on holy days to seek instruction and counsel. The father's question was indifferent. He did not know that the boy was dead, and further discussion was cut off by a curt 'He will be well.' **24–28.** As the return journey was made the same day, 32, Elisha may have been at El Muhraqa (cf on 1 Kgs 18:20), about 15 m. from Shunem. Out of politeness, he sent Gehazi to meet the lady. She countered the conventional inquiry with an evasive answer. **29–31.** Two explanations of the mission of Gehazi are possible. Elisha mistakenly thought that his staff would work a miracle, like Moses', Nm 20:11. But earnest prayer was indispensable; cf Mk 9:28. Or Gehazi, who was crude and officious (cf 27; 5:20ff), presumed that he was to be the agent of a miracle (31). **32–34.** Elisha had thought to send the lady back with Gehazi; that he yielded to her insistence is perhaps a proof that he had not expected his staff to work a miracle. He followed the procedure of Elijah, 1 Kgs 17:21. **36–37.** The mother's gratitude, like her faith, is admirable; she paused before the prophet before turning to her son.

38–41 'Death in the Pot!'—38. The famine is per- **m** haps that of 8:1ff. **39.** Kohler suggests Dwarf Mallow for 'wild herbs' (*'ōrōt*). The creeping plant from which the gourds (*paqqu'ōt*) were gathered was probably the colocynth (Vg). It abounds in the Jordan valley (Hagen, *Lexicon Biblicum*). **41.** The meal would not make the dish edible without a miracle.

42–44 Multiplication of Bread—42. Baal-shalisha may be Kefr Thilth on the coastal plains (Abel II 250f). A hundred were fed by the miracle, more than 'the great pot' could cater for. The scene is therefore different, in spite of the resemblance of 'the people' in 41 and 42f. The prophet perhaps took the place of the priest as the recipient of the offerings of first-fruits, Lv 2:12ff; 23:14–20. **44.** The fragments recall Mt 14:20.

5:1–14 Naaman the Leper—1. The king of Syria **n** was probably Benhadad II, whom the Assyrians attacked without success; cf on 1 Kgs 22:1. Yahweh is represented as universal Lord, even of the Syrians, as in 1 Kgs 19:15–17. Naaman's disease was not real leprosy, for he remained at court, 18, whereas it was understood that lepers were segregated, 7:3. **2.** Syria, though at peace with Israel, 5–7, could not control all its restless frontier tribes. **4.** As a high official Naaman needed leave of absence. **5–6.** The courteous opening and ending of the letter have been omitted. The request was not so peremptory as it now reads. Naaman's gifts were princely, as befitted his state; contrast 1 Kgs 14:3. It was universally recognized that one should not approach a 'man of God' with empty hands; cf 1 Sm 9:7. But the bulk of the presents was probably for the king, who was supposed to have the prophet at his beck and call like a court magician. **7.** The king was probably Jehoram, who had already received the rebuff from Elisha—'Go to the prophets of thy father and thy mother', 3:13. He had therefore no illusions about his standing with Elisha. But his demonstration of alarm was meant to reach the prophet's ears. **8–10.** Elisha did not abate his customary reserve (cf 4:12) even for the great lord. **11.** Naaman however expected personal attention from the prophet, and some familiar ceremony, such as to wave his hand. Against LXX and Jerome, some modern commentators translate further, 'towards the (Holy) Place'. But the

90n hands were raised or outstretched in prayer, not waved; cf Ps 28 (27):2. **12.** The Jordan is narrow and turbulent; the great rivers of Syria, the present Nahr Barada and Nahr el-A'waj, are broad and clear. **13—14.** Naaman was loved and respected by his servants; cf 3. Like the favour bestowed on the Phoenician, 1 Kgs 17:9ff, the miracle was to have great significance in religious history, prefiguring the call of the Gentiles to the Messianic blessings, Lk 4:27.

o **15—19a Naaman's Faith—15.** Naaman recognized in Yahweh the one true God. He begged Elisha to take a farewell-present. **16.** Elisha refused. The holiness of Yahweh was reflected in his prophet's detachment. The prophets took presents from Israelites (cf on 5—6); but they were better instructed than this neophyte as to the nature of Yahweh. **17.** Naaman's desire to have Israelite earth for an altar does not mean that he had returned already to the pagan notion that gods were powerful only on their national territory. He recognized that the one God had special relation with the people and land of Israel. **18.** The ancient Semitic storm-god, Hadad, became the 'Lord' (Baal) *par excellence*. As national god of Syria he was known as Rimmon. To refuse to conform, at least externally, to his worship would have been looked on as rebellion. **19a.** What Naaman proposed to do was unlawful, but Elisha let the matter rest.

10b **27. Punishment of Gehazi—20—21.** While Gehazi thought with contempt of 'this Syrian', Naaman was so respectful, even towards the servant, that he alighted hastily (*wayyippōl*, cf Gn 24.64). **22.** To show that the request was not unwelcome, he insisted on giving more than asked. With two talents of silver Omri had bought the site of Samaria, 1 Kgs 16:24. **24.** 'When he came to the hill'. This was apparently a well-known part of Samaria. The term, which the versions confused with a similar word meaning darkness, is used elsewhere only of the SE spur of the temple hill in Jerusalem; but it is found on the Mesha Stone. **25—27.** Greed met with poetic justice; but the story also inculcates reverence for the prophet (cf 1:2ff; 2:23ff; 1 Kgs 20:36ff), whose standing had been endangered by the abuse of his name. The leprosy was like Naaman's. Hence Gehazi too could still move about freely, even at court, 8:4.

p **6:1—7 The Floating Axehead—1—2.** The group from Jericho, 2:5, or Gilgal, 4:38, is involved in this homely incident, which shows the kindness and power of the prophet and the affectionate regard in which he was held. The richly-wooded banks of the Jordan supplied tamarisk, wild olive, poplar etc., Abel I 213. **3—7.** What part the piece of wood played in the miracle is not clear.

8—23 'There are more with us than with them'—8—10. This incident was perhaps part of the campaigns which led to the re-capture of Ramoth-Gilead, 9:1, some time before 841. The Syrians were harrying Israel by a series of raids, 23, possibly in the hope of seizing the king; cf 1 Kgs 22:31. **12.** They knew of Elisha since Naaman's cure; if the incident is connected with 24—7: 20, which was probably much later, he had also figured in the anointing of Hazael, ch 8. **13.** Dothan (Gn 37:17) was c. 12 m. N of Samaria. **14.** It was illogical to hope to surprise the far-sighted prophet; they did what they could. **15—17.** The fiery escort (cf 2:11) did not intervene directly; the vision was only for the believers. **21—23.** Elisha saved their lives on the ground that they were not the king's prisoners. So Vg: 'Non percuties, neque enim cepisti eos gladis et arcu tuo, ut percutias'. The custom of killing prisoners, widespread in antiquity, apparently extended to Israel. MT, followed by RSV, avoids this. But Vg (cf LXX, Lucian) is surely correct.

The ending of the raids was not a mark of gratitude 290p towards Elisha, but a recognition of his powers.

24—33 Siege and Starvation—24. The weakness q of Israel, 7:13 (cf 13:7) points to a date much later than 841; cf on 8—10. After that date, Hazael reigned in Syria till c. 800. The Benhadad is therefore the third of the name. The king of Israel was Jehoahaz, 814—798, rather than Jehoash, 798—83, who loved and respected Elisha, 13:24; contrast 31ff. **25.** The coarsest food reached fantastic prices. MT's *ḥarê yōnîm*, 'pigeons' dung', seems to be a scribal error for *ḥarṣōnîm*, the edible tubers of the Star of Bethlehem, so I. Löw, *Die Flora der Juden* I 601, cf Vaccari, Bib 19 (1938) 198f. Among other conjectures are *ḥarûbîm* 'carob-pods' (cf Lk 15:16) and *ḥarṣannîm* 'unripe grapes'. **26—29.** Cannibalism was not unheard of; see Dt 28:53—57, Lam 2:20, Ezek 5:10; it is recorded of Ashurbanipal's siege of Babylon (Schrader, KIB II, 190) and of Titus' siege of Jerusalem (Jos BJ, 6, 3, 4). **30—31.** Elisha was held responsible. He must have encouraged resistance, when it was possible to come to terms, by holding out hopes of divine aid (cf 33); the king's penitential garb suggests the influence of the prophet. **32—33.** The role of the messenger is not clear. The attempt on the life of Elisha may be re-constructed as follows: the king first sent an executioner, then came himself when the officer returned to say that he could not enter. By this time the king's anger had died down, and he (not the messenger; cf 7:2) made what was really a last plea for aid, though he professed to despair.

7:1—20 Unexpected Deliverance—1. Sufficient r though not abundant relief was promised; the prices were still high, at least according to later reckoning (Mishnah, 'Erubin 8, 2). But a whole city had to be fed. **2.** The adjutant granted that Yahweh could send rain, but doubted the food. In other words, Yahweh directed the ordinary course of nature, but could not or would not intervene miraculously. **3—4.** The lepers were allowed to live in the no-man's-land between the city and the besiegers. **5—7.** Hittite states, now mostly Aramaean in population, survived in N Syria; they included Patin, Samal, Gurgum and Karchemish. Samal was allied later with Tiglath-pileser against Damascus, Bonkamp, 401f. North of these states lay Musri, which figured at Qarqar (ANET, 279) and this may be intended here by 'Egypt' (Misraim). Since it is a question of panic, there is no point in asking how these invaders could have traversed Syria, or how Egypt, if that be the original reading, could have put an army in the field, in view of her weakness at this period. The historical situation remains sufficiently thinkable. **7.** The horses left behind were re-mounts; the asses were pack-animals. **8—12.** The king was not over-cautious; Ai had been captured by the stratagem which he feared, Jos 8:2—21. **13.** 'Five horses' seems to be vague, like 'half a dozen'; cf 1 Sm 5:3; Is 30:17. **14.** If 'five' is to be taken strictly, there was an outrider with the two chariots. **15.** It was about 30 m. to the Jordan near Bethshan, from which a highway ran E of the Lake of Galilee to Damascus, Abel II 219. **16—17.** It is hardly likely that an officer was stationed at the gate merely to keep order while the people rushed out. Nor have the fixed prices much sense in a general pillage. Probably the king impounded the provisions while the people seized the rest of the booty. Then he set up a market in the usual place, the gate. The adjutant was knocked down accidentally; he was weak from hunger. **16—20.** The moral of the story is again reverence for the prophet; see on 5:25—27.

8:1—6 Power of the Prophet's Patronage—1. The s

290s famine was due to a series of poor harvests; the land still produced something; cf 6. **2.** The plain round Gaza was fruitful in corn. **3.** Some 14 years had passed since the miracle of 4:8—39. The lady had probably migrated under Jehoram, and returned under Jehu; the tenant thought to profit by the revolution. Her family was no longer influential; contrast 4:13. Her aged husband, 4:14, was dead. **4—6.** But Gehazi had apparently prospered on Naaman's money and had a place at court, which his type of leprosy did not forbid him; see on 5:1, 25ff. It is hardly likely that the healing of Naaman had not taken place. Jehu's contemporary in Syria was Hazael, and their relations with Elisha would have been different from those described in ch 5; see the following. The lady had asked only for her property and rent; she was granted her revenues in addition.

t 7—15 Elisha in Damascus—7. Elijah had left to Elisha the task of anointing Hazael, 1 Kgs 19:15. Perhaps it was the report of Benhadad II's illness that showed Elisha that the time was come. His fame is easily explained if the healing of Naaman had already taken place (though the influence of popular narrative style must be borne in mind as in all the stories of Elijah and Elisha). **8—10.** Wishing to spare a doomed man Elisha told Hazael to soothe the king with conventional re-assurance. The *ketib* is: 'Say: thou shalt not recover'. This is to avoid the semblance of a lie in the prophet's mouth; but then the Heb. negative would not be in its normal place (P. Joüon, *Grammaire de l'hébreu biblique*, p. 352) and one would expect 'for' to introduce the next sentence. It is best to keep the more difficult reading, with the *qere*, 18 Heb MSS, and the Versions. **12.** Horrified, but not reproachful, war being what it was, Am 1:13, Ps 137 (136):9 etc, he proclaimed Hazael as the scourge of God; cf Is 10:5; 45:1—7. **13.** 'Thy servant a dog' is conventional humility, 2 Sm 9:8, Lachish Letters RB 48 (1939) 250ff. Some hold that the king died unexpectedly under a cold compress intended to ease the fever. But it was not the business of a great official like Hazael to nurse the king. Rather, the words of Elisha worked on Hazael 'like the witches' prophecy in Macbeth' (Skinner). Shalmaneser, his contemporary, calls him 'the son of a nobody' (a usurper), (ANET 280).

u 16—24 Joram of Judah, 848—841.—18—19. It is generally assumed that his wife Athaliah, 26, was the daughter of Jezebel. Under her influence Jehoram allowed a temple of Baal to be erected in Jerusalem, 11:18. There was a reaction which he suppressed bloodily, 2 Chr 21:4,13. **20.** See on 1 Kgs 22:48. The success of Moab, ch 3, encouraged Edom; cf 2 Chr 20:1—10. **21—22a.** The text may be in disorder. The army which fled home must be the Judaeans. Apparently Joram was surrounded in the Zair, 5 m. NE of Hebron, but cut his way out. **22b.** Libnah (Tell es-Safi), a Canaanite town not far from Gath, probably allied itself with the Philistines, who, with Arabians, Moabites, and Edomites, formed a hostile block in the S, 2 Chr 21:16. **23—24.** His defeats were attributed to his impiety, and he was denied burial in the royal tombs, 2 Chr 21:20; see on 1 Kgs 2:10. The second 'with his fathers' is to be taken vaguely or omitted.

v 25—29 Ahaziah of Judah, 841—25—27. His reign actually lasted only 2 or 3 months. The youngest and only surviving son of Jehoram, 2 Chr 21:17, he was dominated by his mother, the grand-daughter of Omri, 2 Chr 22:3. The Baal-cult was maintained in Jerusalem, 11:18, and his political advisers were northerners,

2 Chr 22:4. **28.** Ramoth-Gilead had been returned to **290** Israel some time after 853 (cf 1 Kgs 23), probably as payment for help against Assyria. Hazael had been beaten off, but the army remained in the field to forestall any surprise attack. **29.** Joram's wound was slight (cf 9:21); the kings had left the field because victory seemed secure. Relations between the two courts had perhaps never been closer; cf 10:13. The destinies of the kings were linked together.

9:1—14 Anointing of Jehu—1—2. The work of **291a** Elijah and Elisha was about to bear fruit. The strict worshippers of Yahweh now formed a strong party (cf 1 Kgs 19:18), which was doubtless also opposed to the costly anti-Assyrian policy of the house of Omri; see on 1 Kgs 20:34—43. One of Jehu's first moves was to send tribute to Shalmaneser III (ANET 281). **3—10.** As in the case of Hazael, 8:13, it was through Elisha that Elijah executed his mandate of anointing Jehu, 1 Kgs 19:16. The secrecy left Jehu with the choice of the moment to strike. **11.** 'Madman' was popularly applied to prophets, Hos 9:7, Jer 29:26, with reference to their ecstasies; cf 1 Sm 1:10 etc. Jehu was evasive, till he sensed that his fellow generals had guessed the truth and were with him. **13.** In recognition of his kingship. The army was won over at once.

15—26 Death of Joram—15—19. Suspecting bad news **b** from the front, Joram sent horsemen, who could arrive with tidings faster than chariots. **20.** Jehu must have been known as a dashing leader of a division of chariots. **21.** The field of Naboth was not the vineyard, which was beside the palace, 1 Kgs 21:1, but some land E of Jezreel. The kings hurried out to hold a council of war at once if necessary. **22.** Jehu proclaimed himself as the champion of the religion of Yahweh. The 'harlotries' and 'sorceries' of Jezebel were the idolatrous practices which she promoted. They were in fact often licentious. **23.** Joram himself was driving; in his haste he had not taken a charioteer nor put on armour. **24—26.** Jehu, as adjutant of Ahab along with Bidkar, had been present at the meeting with Elijah, 1 Kgs 21:19—20. He made himself responsible for the fulfilment of the prophecy, which he knew had been transferred to Joram, 1 Kgs 21:29; cf 10:10. Two striking details are added to the oracle as given in 1 Kgs 21:19. (1) 'Yesterday': Ahab had gone to claim the vineyard the very next day; (2) the death of Naboth's sons. The oracle was felt to justify Jehu's action and confirm his claims to the throne.

27—29 Murder of Ahaziah—27. Beth-haggan, the En **c** gannim of Jos 19:21 (modern Jenin). Ahaziah had made about 7 m. when his pursuers came within bow-shot, at the rise of Gur, near the modern Belameh. They gave up the pursuit after wounding him; they had already driven over 50 m. since leaving Ramoth. He was followed later and killed, according to 2 Chr 22:9, where 'Samaria' may be understood as 'the land of Samaria'. Jehu's attack on Ahaziah is explained by the closeness of his relations with Joram; see on 8:25—29. In the event of a war with Judah, the adherents of the house of Omri would have declared against Jehu. But after Ahaziah's death, at the age of 22, there was no heir to the throne who could threaten Jehu.

30—37 Death of Jezebel—30. Jezebel did not lack **d** courage, and made no attempt to placate, still less to charm Jehu. She was over sixty; cf on 1 Kgs 16:27ff. Her attitude was: 'Show me, my women, like a queen; go fetch my best attires' (*Antony and Cleopatra*, V, 2). **31.** Her sarcastic 'Hail, you Zimri, murderer of your master' branded Jehu as a treacherous upstart destined to perish quickly, 1 Kgs 16:8—16. **32.** Jehu answered

91d the taunt with contempt (Vg, LXX); according to MT, he cried out, 'Who is on my side? Who?'. The chamberlains declared for him at once. **33.** Jezebel's gruesome end was characteristic of Jehu's cruelty. **34.** He did not wish, however, to give extreme offence to her royal kinsmen of Tyre. **35—37.** But the scavengers of eastern cities had been at work (cf Ps 59 (58):6, 15) and the once feared and famous lady had been utterly disgraced.

e **10:1—10 Slaughter of the Israelite Princes—1.** 'Sons' stands here for all the male descendents of Ahab; cf 'daughter' 8:26. Not all were minors. The challenge was addressed to the civil and military governors, the elders (cf 1 Kgs 21:8) and the guardians of the young princes. They controlled the chariots and garrisons of the capital and other fortress-towns. **3.** But there was probably no competent leader in the royal family, and Jehu's combination of aggressiveness and sarcasm completely intimidated Samaria. **6.** 'Rosh' meaning chief' or 'head' was interpreted by Jehu's correspondents in its most brutal sense (which may have been foreseen by Jehu). He placed the responsibility for the murders on them (v 9). **7—8.** The heads arrived in the dark, and were piled in a pyramid, as in Assyrian monuments. **9.** Jehu disowned the deed. **10.** But he asserted that in overstepping his mandate, the responsible agents were Yahweh's instruments; cf 1 Kgs 21:29. The people dared not disagree, and Jehu, under the cloak of zeal, could go on to further enormities.

f **11 Massacre at Jezreel—**The scene was the hometown of the Omri family, see on 1 Kgs 16.16. The object was to eliminate all possible avengers; see on 1 Kgs 16:11. Read therefore 'his kinsmen' (gōʾalāw) for 'his chief men' (gᵉdōlāw) with LXX (Lucian) and Old Latin. **12—14 Murder of the Judaean Princes—12.** Betheked of the Shepherds is generally identified with Beit Qad, 4 m. E of Jenin. But it did not lie on Jehu's route. Kefr Qud W of Jenin is more suitable. **13.** The kinsmen of Ahaziah were distant relatives; see on 8:25; 2 Chr 21:4. The sons of the queen are distinguished from the sons of the other ladies in the royal harem. It is surprising to find the princes N of Samaria four or five days after the revolution. Possibly they had gone on to Megiddo and attended the dying Ahaziah; cf 9:27. On their way back they gave the original reason for their journey. **14.** Jehu killed them as a further measure of security.

g **15—17 Jehonadab: Further Massacres in Samaria—**These two incidents may have been displaced in the text. **15.** The Rechabite clan, whose austere nomadic way of life is described in Jer 35, looked on Jehonadab as their second founder. At a time when Baalism threatened the S as well as the N, he made the separatism of his clan the defence of monotheism. Jehu feared that he would see through his facade of zeal. Hence his distrustful question. But Jehonadab pinned his faith in him, as Elisha had done. The history of the N shows prophet after prophet entrusting the work of God to candidates who deceived them once they were helped to power. **16.** Jehu's language reminds us of what the historian von Pastor called 'Cromwell's revolting Puritan jargon'.

h **18—28 Elimination of the Cult of Baal—18—19.** It seems that Jehu first gathered the official ministers who were in Samaria. They had to prepare the feast. **20—21.** Then he gathered the worshippers from the country shrines. They feared the worst, but dared not refuse the invitation. The worshippers of Baal in general were too numerous to be summoned, unless perhaps there was question only of those who worshipped Baal exclusively. It is hardly possible to restrict the number to those

whom fanaticism blinded to their danger (Médebielle). **291h** **22.** Special dress was often prescribed for religious ceremonies; see Ex 19:10, Gn 35:2; M. J. Lagrange, *Études sur les religions sémitiques*, 149. **23.** The main gathering was in the court of the temple. **24—25a.** Soldiers guarded the exits while Jehu and a bodyguard entered the temple proper. Jehu himself offered sacrifice, then sent his guards back into the court. **25b—27.** The text has suffered. For *massēbôt* 'pillar', 'statue', (26), 'aᵃšērāh may be read; cf 1 Kgs 16:33. The wooden pole could be burnt, but not the stone pillar. The destruction of the latter is mentioned in 27: 'And they demolished the pillar of Baal'. 'To this day' shows that the original account was written when the locality was still well known. It was the end of Baalism as an official cult, but remnants of it survived; cf 1 Kgs 19:17.

29—36 Reign of Jehu—28—31. Jehu was praised for **i** this and for destroying the house of Ahab, but the divine approval of his conduct ends there. Hence his dynasty was promised only a limited duration. Contrast the conditional promise of perpetuity made to Jeroboam, 1 Kgs 11:38. His mass murders were not condoned. He himself recognized that he was going too far, 10:9; and a hundred years later, the memory of his crimes was still appalling; Hos 1:4. **32.** Meanwhile Israel was punished for its long apostasy; cf 1 Kgs 19:17. Jehu had estranged Judah and Tyre, and the Assyrians, in spite of his tribute, gave him no help. After attacking Damascus in 841, they appeared in the W only once, in 838, in the next forty years. **33.** The Israelites lost, therefore, all their possessions in Transjordan. The V is overcharged with glosses inspired by Dt 3:12 f. **34—36.** Jehu died in 814, after reigning from 841.

11:1—3 Usurpation of Athaliah—Two accounts have **j** been combined in the history of Athaliah. The first, 1—12, 18b—20, attributed her fall to the priesthood supported by the royal guard. The second, 13—18a, incomplete, indicates it as coming from a popular movement. **1.** Joram, Athaliah's late husband, had killed all his brothers, 2 Chr 21:1. Ahaziah was the only one of his sons to survive the Arab invasion, 2 Chr 21:17, and he, with the 42 princes, had been killed by Jehu, 9:27; 10:14. There was no one to oppose Athaliah. What her intentions were with regard to the succession is hard to say. Possibly, as grand-daughter of Ethbaal (cf 1 Kgs 16:31), she meant to hand over the kingdom of David to her kinsman Mettenos of Tyre. **2.** Jehosheba hid Joash in the bedchamber, probably that of the high-priest Jehoiada (her husband, 2 Chr 22:11). **3** suggests that the high-priest had a house attached to the temple; cf 1 Sm 3:3ff. Priests had quarters E of the Great Court of the temple at a later date, Neh 3:28.

4—12 Coronation of Joash—4. 'Carites' (cf 19) may **k** be a scribal error for 'Cherethites', 2 Sm 8:18 etc. The loyalty of these foreign mercenaries was traditional, 2 Kgs 15:18ff; 1 Kgs 1:38. **5—6a.** The execution of the plot was planned for a Sabbath, when the changing of the guard took place. **6b** seems out of place, and is obscure; perhaps it is a gloss, giving the ordinary stations of the temple guard. The gate of Sur was possibly the E or main entrance. The gate of the Guards (cf 19) was on the S, since it led to the palace. The guards were in three battalions, two in the palace during week and one in the temple. On the Sabbath, the ⸋ battalion was to stand firm, instead of retiri⸋ palace, when the other two marched in t⸋ Thus the palace would be stripped of soldi⸋ soldiers were already armed; the offic⸋ were given the venerable trophies ⸋

291k of the occasion. **12.** The ceremony included a renewal of the covenant, which was both religious and political, **17:** hence the imposition of the 'testimony' (*'ēdût*), the Book of the Laws; cf Dt 17:18f. A common but unnecessary emendation for *'ēdût* is *ṣe'ādōt* 'bracelets'; cf 2 Sm 1:10.

l **13—21 Death of Athaliah—14.** There was a special place for the king (cf 23:3), by the pillar, Jachin or Boaz; cf 1 Kgs 7:21. His most enthusiastic supporters were 'the people of the land', the common people or the countryfolk (cf 18, 19, 20); they played an important part in a similar situation, 21:24. **16.** Athaliah was brought back to the palace by an entrance on the East, corresponding to the Gate of the Horses; cf Jer 31:40. **18.** She and Tyrian cult must have had followers among the city-folk. Hence the temple was guarded. **20.** If 'the people of the land' means the country-folk, there is special point in the remark that the city was quiet; it submitted. **21.** Jehoiada became regent, 12:3.

292a **12:1—5 Jehoash of Judah, 835—796—1—5.** By the time the king was about 25 years of age (cf 6), the temple had been built for nearly 150 years, and was in need of repairs. Moneys prescribed were, e.g. the 5 shekels paid for each first-born male, Nm 18:16; payments on the occasion of certain vows, Lv 27:2—9; the poll-tax, Ex 30:13. **5.** Each priest was to take the money from his acquaintance; possibly each dealt with his clansmen, and the 'acquaintance' would be his 'parishioners'.

b **6—16 Restoration of the Temple—6—8.** The priests were not conscientious; perhaps they resented the king's interference. **9.** Their role was then confined to seeing that each man paid his due. **10.** The administration of the money was supervised by a high court official; cf 18:18; 1 Kgs 4:3. **11—13.** Each contractor received a lump sum, and worked on an estimate, not on what we call a 'time and material' basis. **13.** New utensils came later, 2 Chr 24:14. **14—15.** The contractors gave satisfaction, and had not to give an account of their expenses and profits. **16.** Money accompanied or perhaps replaced certain sacrifices; two are mentioned: 'trespass' (*'āšām*), offered on the occasion of restitution for damage, Lv 5:14; 6:1—7; 'sin' (*ḥaṭṭā'at*), offered in reparation, Lv ch 4.

17—21 Troubles and Death of Jehoash—17. Jehoash may have sent help to the Philistines, who interfered with the Egyptian trade of Damascus. **18.** The two preceding kings had enriched the temple, in spite of their support of Baalism. **19—21.** According to 2 Chr 24:17—25, there was a reaction against the priestly party after the death of Jehoiada; cf 2. Foreign cults were brought back, and Jehoiada's son was stoned. The king paid for it by defeat, illness and a violent death.

c **13:1—9 Jehoahaz of Israel, 814—798—1.** It was the **22**nd year of Joas; cf 10:36; 12:1. **2—4.** Syria had a free hand against Israel (see on 10:32) till Adad-nirari of Assyria attacked Damascus c. 800. **5.** He may be the 'saviour'; preferably Jeroboam II, 14:25ff. **6.** The ungrateful people re-introduced even an *asherah*; see on 10:26. **7.** Ahab had had 2,000 chariots at Qarqar; Israel was brought very low.

10—19 Jehoash of Israel, 798—783; Last Prophecies of Elisha—14. Elisha was now nearly 90; see on 1 Kgs 17:1. The king mourned the loss of the champion who was worth an army; see on 2:12 and 6:8—7:20. **15—16.** With the laying on of hands, to signify the passing of the supernatural power from one to the other, cf 4:34f. Aphek was the scene of a former victory, 1 Kgs 20:26—30. **18—19.** Elisha's anger shows that the king was at fault; would be too negligent to press home his victories.

20—21 Death of Elisha—20. He was buried with his **292c** fathers at Abel-Mehola in the Jordan valley; cf 1 Kgs 19:19. With Israel so weak, the border foray is understandable. **21.** Cf Sir 48:14f. From Elisha, the chain of prophets went back through Elijah, Jehu and his father Hanani, 1 Kgs 16:1, 2 Chr 16:7, Ahijah, 1 Kgs 11:29, and Nathan to Samuel. Within 30 years, Hosea was at work. The prophetic tradition was therefore unbroken in Israel till the Exile.

22—25 The Promised Victories—The editor here **d** resumes his use of the annals of Israel. **22.** If this statement is present, Hazael survived Jehoahaz; but 25 suggests that Benhadad III had succeeded him before the death of Jehoahaz; see on 6:24. It is hardly possible to refer 'which he had taken' to Hazael. **24.** Adadnirari's inscriptions (ANET, 281) call the king of Damascus in 802 'Mari'. This is a title ('my lord'), not a proper name, R. de Vaux RB 43 (1934) 514—8; probably Benhadad is meant. **25.** The cities must have been W of the Sea of Galilee, as the land E of Jordan had been lost under Jehu 10:33.

14:1—6 Amaziah of Judah, 796—781—1—4. The **e** verdict on Amaziah is interrupted by an unusual restriction in 3 *b* ('but yet' etc), which reads like a gloss based on 2 Chr 25:12 (his idolatry). **5—6.** He could not condone the action which had given him the throne; cf 2 Sm 1:1—16; 4:1—12. The principle enunciated in Dt 24:16 was not always put into practice; cf 9:26, Ezek 18:20.

7 War with Edom—The trade route to the Red Sea, closed since the revolt of Edom over 50 years before, 8:22, was at stake; cf 22. The Valley of Salt, E of Beersheba, 2 Sm 8:13, may be the present Wady of Milh. Sela, a natural fortress, c. 40 m. S of the Dead Sea, became famous as the capital of the Nabataean kingdom, 100 B.C.—A.D. 100. Amaziah made it a military outpost; the new name, Yoqte'el 'God destroys', refers to the slaughter of Edomites, 2 Chr 25:12.

8—16 War with Israel—8. Jehoash probably demand- **f** ed the return of territory annexed by Judah during Israel's decline. **9—10.** The fable pointed out the folly of Amaziah's offers to fight it out. There does not seem to have been any request for the hand of an Israelite princess; that could not have been treated as presumptuous. **11—12.** Bethshemesh, now 'Ain Shems, was c. 25 m. W of Jerusalem; Jehoash took the initiative; cf on 8. **13.** According to Jos.Ant. 9, 9, 3, the breach was made for the entry of the victors. It was in the N wall, starting from the W corner, at the present Jaffa Gate. **17—22 End of Amaziah—17—19.** His apostasy was the **g** cause of the revolt, 2 Chr 25:14—27. The stronghold of Lachish (Tell ed-Duweir) was c. 36 m. SW of Jerusalem. **21.** Azariah was also known as Uzziah, the only name used of him in Chr, Hos, Am, Zech, Is. 'Azariah may have been used in the Annals of the kings of Judah, while 'Uzziah' was the popular name. **22.** He followed up Amaziah's victory over Edom by fortifying the terminus of the trade-route, at the head of the Gulf of Aqabah.

23—29 Jeroboam II of Israel, 783—743—23. During **293a** the long and prosperous reign of Jeroboam, Damascus, defeated by Zakir of Hamath c. 785 and invaded by Shalmaneser IV in 772, was no longer a menace. **24.** The prophets Amos and Hosea attest the decline of religion. **25.** For the 'Entrance of Hamath', see on 1 Kgs 8:65; the Sea of the Arabah was the Dead Sea. Jeroboam attacked the Ammonites, Am 1:13, and as Azariah shared the spoils, 2 Chr 26:8—10, it seems that Israel and Judah were allies again. To the prophet who foretold Jeroboam's conquests has been attributed, by way of

3a pseudepigraphy, the Book of Jonah (written in the 5th cent.). Gath Hepher, Jos 19:13 (now El-Meshed or Khirbet ez-Zurra) was a few miles N of Nazareth. **26—28a.** For the last time, Israel was experiencing the divine favour, under perhaps the greatest of her kings.

b 15:1—7 Azariah of Judah 781—740—1. Read 'the 2nd year of Jeroboam'. The chronology in chh 15 and 16 has been systematically glossed. Corrections are indicated in the commentary; for their basis, see 283*l*. **2.** His reign lasted some 42 years. **5.** Read possibly 'he dwelt in *his house free from duties*' (MT). The regency did not last long, as Jotham was only 25 when Azariah died; cf 7:33. **6.** His reign was prosperous, Is 2:7—16. 2 Chr 26 recounts his organization of army, armaments and fortifications, his successful maintenance of the trade route to the Red Sea against Philistines and Arabs, his promotion of agriculture and sheep-rearing.

c 8—12 Zechariah of Israel, 743—10. Jabesh suggests Gilead, 1 Sm 11, where Syria must have gained partisans during her long occupation of the land. The dynasty of Jehu had probably remained pro-Assyrian; see on 9:1f. The revolt may have been a move in international politics; but the social injustice described by Amos and Hosea must have counted. **12.** The house of Jehu was being punished for the 'blood of Jezreel', Hos 1:4.

13—16 Shallum of Israel, 743—14. Possibly Menahem led an Ephraimite party; he was pro-Assyrian; cf 19. Is 9:20 speaks of strife between Ephraim and Manasseh. Menahem's base, Tirzah, was in Ephraim; see on 1 Kgs 15:21. **16.** Tappuah was a few miles to the east.

d 17—22 Menahem of Israel, 743—738 Assyrian Invasion 738 B.C.**—17.** As the avenger of the dynasty of Jehu and upholder of its foreign policy, Menahem had a solid backing. Read possibly '6 years' instead of 'ten'. **19. Tiglath-pileser III** (cf 29) bore the name Pulu in his quality of king of Babylon. In 738 he marched against a league headed by Azriyau, king of Yaudi, possibly a small, otherwise unknown, state in Syria; but more probably Judah. Azriyau would then be Azariah (Uzziah), cf § 65*b*. He pressed on S to Raspuna, probably the hellenistic Apollonia, now Arsuf, c. 12 m. N of Joppa. Among the kings who paid him tribute were Resin of Damascus (cf 37) and Menahem, ANET, 282—3 **20.** If the talent was 3,000 shekels, 60,000 rich men paid about 80 dollars each.

23—26 Pekahiah of Israel, 738—737—23. Read 'the 2nd year of Jotham'. The new year occurred once in the reign. **25.** The dynasty supported by Assyria did not last long. The party which Shallum had represented was at work again, for Pekah had with him a picked force of 50 Gileadites; hence the alliance with Syria, 37. Heb. adds Argob and Arieh—which probably belong to the list of places in 29— the latter being read as Havvoth-jair (cf 1 Kgs 4:13). The treason and turbulence which heralded the ruin of Israel is vividly described by Hos 7:3—7.

e 27—31 Pekah of Israel, 737—732—The chronological difficulties in the dating of this and the following reigns are notorious, see § 124*h*; the suggested emendation of the text is one way of solving them. **27.** Read 'the 3rd year of Jotham' and '5 years'. **29.** By 734 the king of Damascus, looking, like Israel (cf Hos 7:11), to Egypt, organized an **anti-Assyrian league** which included the Arabs and all the southern states of Palestine except Judah; Rezin and Pekah attacked Ahaz to force him to join the league, cf v 37. Ahaz appealed to Assyria and **Tiglath-pileser invaded at once.** His own records state that he annexed 'the city of Gal'aza, the city

of Abillakka on the border of Bit-Humria (= Israel, **293e** the land of Omri), the broad land of Naptali', Bonkamp, 391. Gal'aza is Gilead (*z* for *d* as in the inscription of Zakir of Hamath, Bonkamp 395*n*); Abillakka is Abel Beth Maacah (cf 1 Kgs 15:20); Janoah was E of Tyre; Kedesh, N of Lake Huleh; for Hazor, see on 1 Kgs 9:15. Israel thus lost all her western territory N of Mt Tabor, and the whole of her transjordanian land. Of the deportations Tiglath-pileser writes: 'I carried away to Assur the people of Bit-Humria, all its inhabitants'. This was in 734 B.C. Deportation was standard Assyrian policy, cf §293*i*. **30.** In 733 Tiglath-pileser attacked Damascus, and some time later a revolt in Samaria spared him another siege. 'They overthrew their king Paqaha; I established Ausi (Hoshea) as king over them.' This inscription (ANET, 284) connects the change of rulers with the fall of Damascus in 732. Another inscription (Bonkamp, 397) speaks of a further invasion of Israel, Is 8:23. We may date Hoshea's installation in 730. To return now to follow the fortunes of Judah.

32—38 Jotham of Judah, 740—736—32. Read 'the 2nd year of *Menahem*'. **35.** Jotham was a great builder, 2 Chr 27:19. He added a third entrance, from the N, Ezek 9:2, to the inner court of the temple. There was already one on the east, Ezek 11:1, and one on the south, 2 Kgs 11:6, 19. **37.** This refers to the preparation for the war which developed under Ahaz, 16:5—9.

16:1—4 Ahaz of Judah, 736—716—1. Read '*the* **f** second year of Pekah'. **2.** For the decline in religion under Ahaz, see Mi 5:9—13; 6:16. **3.** Child sacrifice, especially that of the first-born son, was always common among the neighbours of Israel, 3:27; 17:31. It was forbidden to Israel, Lv 18:21, Dt 12:31. **4.** See on 1 Kgs 14:22f.

5—9 The Syro-Ephraimite War and Appeal to Assyria—5. Ahaz, having refused to be drawn into the anti-Assyrian league (see on 15:29), was to be deposed, and a nominee of the league put in his place, Is 7:1—9. He was attacked from all sides, cf § 293*e* and see 2 Chr 28:16f. **6.** Elath was restored to Edom. **7—9.** In 734 Tiglath-pileser overran Galilee and Gilead, 15:29 (as stated above § 293*e*). Then he marched S and plundered Gaza. Ashkelon, Ammon, Edom and Moab paid tribute, and with them is named Yauhazi of Yauda, AOT 348. 'Ahaz' therefore was a popular form of the theophoric name 'Yahweh possesses'. Damascus was invested in 733 and fell in 732. The inhabitants were deported to Kir, a region originally Aramaean, Am 1:5; 9:7, probably in S Mesopotamia, near Elam, Is 22:6. By placing himself under the protection of Tiglath-pileser, Ahaz prepared the ruin of his kingdom, Is 8:5f.

10—20 The New Altar—This notice on the liturgical **g** innovation is probably due to the deuteronomist's special interests. **10.** It was Tiglath-pileser's boast that 'in every country which I conquered, I set up a temple for the god Assur; and in every country I made an image of my royalty, and set it up as a sign of victory, and of the dominion which I held over the nations, by the command of Assur, my god', (Bonkamp, 393f). The altar which Ahaz dutifully admired was therefore in several tiers, the ziggurat-form common in Assyria and Babylonia; see on Ezek 43:13—17. **12—13.** Inaugural ceremonies included all the types of sacrifice mentioned at Solomon's dedication, 1 Kgs 8:64. **14—15.** King Ahaz ordered the ancient altar to be put aside '*until I can attend to it*'. **17—18.** It probably shared the fate of the other bronze installations, 1 Kgs 7:23—29, and of the Mussach ('covered walk'?), and the royal door, which were removed at the same time. Their costly metals went towards the tribute to the king of Assyria. He was

293g Chr 28:20. Ahaz meant to convey to Tiglath-pileser that he acknowledged the gods of Assyria. But the actual introduction of Assyrian cults (cf 21:3ff 23:4, 11; Jer 44:17; Ezek 8) may also be ascribed to him, as well as the fostering of Baalism, 4. Neither Hezekiah nor Josiah could undo his work.

h 17:1–4 Hoshea of Israel, 732–724—1. Read *'in the 4th year* of Ahaz'. **2.** The last king was not the worst. There was a strong party of Yahweh-worshippers in Samaria, 2 Chr 28:9–15, and Hoshea favoured them. **3. Shalmaneser V** became king in Jan. 726. Menander (cf Jos.Ant. 9, 14, 2) records a **campaign against Phoenicia**, which ended in Elulaeus of Tyre and his allies paying tribute. War was renewed when they fell away. This fits in with the Bible. **4.** Hoshea paid tribute in 725 (the Assyrian lists state that there were no campaigns in 726, Bonkamp 412). He withheld it in 723, having paid it for two years at the most. 'So' (to be read '*Sewe*', cf *ketib*) the 'Sib'e' of Sargon's inscriptions (ANET, 285), was commander-in-chief of Musri (Egypt) under its king Pir'u, possibly the Pharaoh Piankhi. As Sib'e had power to make war or peace, his popular designation as king is justified. Some hold that Musri here is an Arab state. But a king in the background with a viceroy in the Delta suits Egyptian conditions; and Egypt was certainly involved, Hos 7:11. Shalmaneser held Hoshea when he came to excuse himself. Josephus however, Ant. 9, 14. 1, says that Hoshea was taken when the city fell, and the long resistance certainly suggests the presence of the king during the siege. Thus 4 b may anticipate events to round off the career of Hoshea. On the other hand, Sargon nowhere mentions Hoshea. Ordinarily the Assyrian annals mention the names of kings captured with their cities. It is best therefore to keep to the primary sense of the text and take it that Hoshea was captured before the siege. This would account for the 9 years' reign (cf 1)—732–724.

i 5–6 Siege and Capture of Samaria—5. The only land left to Israel lay between the N rim of the plain of Jezreel and the boundary of Judah. The rest had been annexed between 734 and 732. Samaria was well placed for a siege; see on 1 Kgs 16:24. The Assyrians could winter in their new province of Damascus. **6.** Shalmaneser died at the end of 722, before the end of the siege. His brother, **Sargon**, who succeeded him in January 721, **actually took Samaria**, as he claims in four of his inscriptions, ANET, 284–5. It was in the interval before his official enthronement in Nisan. He states that he deported 27,290 captives, placed a governor over the land, and imposed on the inhabitants the same taxes as they had paid to their former kings. The city became the capital of an Assyrian province. Some of the deportees were settled at Halah, on the western slopes of the Zagros mountains; others in Gozan, by the river Habor (Khabur), which flowed into the Euphrates near Carchemish; others S of the Caspian Sea.

j 7–23 Reflections by the Deuteronomic Redactor on the Ruin of Israel—'The philosophy of sin and retribution is characteristically Deuteronomic as is the language of the whole section (7–17) which recalls Jeremiah's indictment of the apostasy of his contemporaries', J. Gray, *1 and 2 Kgs* 588. One new grief is adduced, star-worship, **16;** see on Amos 5:26. **18.** The long preparatory 'because' culminates here in a 'therefore'. **19–20** repeat 18, inserting an anticipatory verdict on Judah, and give perhaps an afterthought. **21–23** retrace cause and effect for the third time. The exile is the penalty of the calf-worship. The 'sin of Jeroboam' dominated the author's thought throughout his history of Israel. **21–23** contain perhaps

the original verdict, of which 7–18 is an elaboration **293** reminiscent of Dt and Jer.

24 New Settlers—The usual transfer of rebellious populations followed. It was not completed all at once. Cuthah, the Sumerian Gudua, lay c. 20 m. NE of Babylon. Possibly the Cuthaites and Babylonians migrated freely. Sargon had no reason to deport them. But 'the king of Assyria' may be taken as a general term. Sennacherib may have deported Babylonians to Israel after sacking Babylon in 689. They were among the strangers sent by his successors Esarhaddon and Ashurbanipal, Ez 4:2, 9f. The deportations from Syria followed the defeat of Hamath in 720. Avva is perhaps the Phoenician town called Ammia in the Tell el-Amarna letters; Sephar-vaim, the Syrian Shomeriya on Lake Homs (cf 18:34; 19:13;). In 715 Sargon settled Arabs in Israel, AOT 349. But Cuthaites predominated, for later Jews called the Samaritans simply Cuthaites, Jos.Ant. 9, 14, 3 etc.

25–28 The Cult of Yahweh—25. From 734 to 721 **k** cultivation had suffered; wild beasts could no longer be kept down. **26.** After Assyrian custom, Sargon had carried off the golden effigy from Bethel and abolished the cult; Tiglath-pileser had done the same at Dan. **27–28.** Sargon's concession was based on the belief that each country was under the control of a national god, whose goodwill was essential to the country's well-being. The restored cult bound new and old inhabitants together, 32; it was still flourishing in the time of Josiah, 23:15.

29–41 Samaritan Religion—29. Yahweh was of course not worshipped exclusively. And it must be supposed that most of the Israelites, to whom syncretism was no novelty, joined the new-comers in worshipping their gods. **30.** In Succoth-benoth may be recognized the Babylonian Sakkuth and Sarpanit; cf LXX Banit. Allowance must be made throughout for textual corruption of strange names. Nergal, god of the underworld, had a temple in Cutha. Ashima, probably the goddess-consort of Eshmun, was worshipped in Hamath, cf M. Lidbarski, *Ephemeris*, 2,323f. She occurs perhaps later in Ashim-Bethel, see A. Vincent, *La Religion des Judéo-Araméens d'Eléphantine*, 654–80. **31.** The Babylonian Nebo may be seen in Nibhaz; he was worshipped in Syria, cf Šanda, 2, 230. The Eblazer of LXX however suggests 'Baal the Helper'. Tartak is perhaps the Syrian Atargatis, the Ator (Astarte) of Attis. Adrammelech identifies Milk (biblical Molech), the deity of child-sacrifice in Syria etc, with the storm-god Hadad. Anammelech may identify him with Anu, one of the supreme Babylonian triad, Anu, Marduk and Ea. Anu and Adad had a joint temple in Assur at this time, Albright, 163. But Anammelech may represent the goddess Anath, consort of Hadad. **32–41.** After this fusion of religion and races, Jerusalem came ultimately to disown the northerners, Ez 4:3. The kingdom of Israel had perished spiritually as well as politically.

18:1–20:21. Hezekiah of Judah, 716–687—In his **294a** account of this reign the redactor had access to a prophetic source dealing with Isaiah which he uses to fill out the account of the reign in much the same way as the Elijah and Elisha cycles were used for the reign of Ahab, see § 289a. As was the case with those, it seems probable that here too the material is of different kinds. Thus 18:13–19:7, a first account of Sennacherib's invasion, may come from a historical source in which Isaiah plays a secondary part, while 19:8–35 may derive from a source dealing directly with the prophet. Similarly the apparent unity of ch 20 is made up of three stories, 1–8, 9–11, 12–19, the last of which certainly cannot belong here historically. If the king had 15 more years to reign

94a this would make it the year 701 B.C., whereas the embassy took place about 711. The events selected for detailed treatment reflect the special interest of the deuteronomic compiler; thus while an account is given of the king's religious reform and the invasion of Sennacherib which failed, silence is observed concerning Hezekiah's attempts—so fully described in Assyrian records—to secure allies against Sennacherib. Again, though the payment of tribute to the Assyrian king is duly recorded, the loss of territory is not mentioned.

18:1–2—The speeches attributed to Hezekiah in the beginning of his reign, 2 Chr 29–30, besides suggesting that Samaria had already fallen, indicate that the motives for the reform of Hezekiah had already provoked reflexion. This suits the date, 716, (cf § 283*l*) proposed as the year of accession. The synchronization with Hoshea is from a confused chronology, cf § 124*g*.

3–12 Reforms—3. The prophets Isaiah and Micah found a strong and zealous champion. The fall of Samaria, recounted 9–12, re-inforced their message, Mi 1:9; 3:12; cf Jer 26:18f. **4.** Not only the pagan shrines of Ahaz, 2 Chr 28:25, but shrines of Yahweh outside Jerusalem were abolished. This follows (1), from the absence of the formula, 'but the high place he did not destroy', used even of pious kings; (2) from 22. Even the memorial of the miracle of Nm 21:9 was destroyed. 'It was called Nehushtan'. The name seems to express both the material (*neḥōšet* ('bronze') and the object (*nāḥāš* 'serpent'). For the serpent as emblem of vegetation-deities, see J. Coppens, *La Connaissance du Bien et du Mal et le Péché du Paradis*, 1948, 99–107. It is attested in Palestine, DBS I, 952; II, 361; on the bronze serpent of Gezer, see L. H. Vincent, *Canaan* 174ff. Since Hezekiah was combating fertility-cults, his action against the apparently harmless object is understandable. **7–8.** The campaign against the Philistines was probably connected with the revolt against Assyria after the death of Sargon in 705. Ashdod, Ekron, Ascalon and Gaza were then ruled by nominees of Assyria, (Bonkamp 433 n. 4).

b 13–16 Invasion of Sennacherib. See § 65*e*. Sargon's son was detained in the E till **701. Then he turned against the W**, where Phoenicia, Philistia, Edom, Moab and Judah had formed, with Egypt, an **anti-Assyrian League. 14–16.** The capture of the great fortress of Lachish is depicted on the famous bas-relief of Sennacherib in the British Museum. Hezekiah pleaded for peace, and Sennacherib agreed to withdraw at the price of a **crushing indemnity.** Some of it no doubt was paid at once, but the rest was sent after Sennacherib to Nineveh; see his own account, ANET 287–8, where the figures tally with the Bible, except that the silver is given as 800 talents. Probably the Heb text has suffered; the cuneiform was never copied. Judah was almost beggared. Subsequently, it could pay only 10 silver minas yearly as tribute, while Ammon and Moab paid 2 and 1 gold minas respectively (R. H. Pfeiffer, JBL (1928) 185f). There were cogent reasons for paying what was demanded. Excavations at Lachish which Sennacherib stormed reveal, along with evidences of destruction a huge pit into which the remains of some 1,500 bodies had been dumped . . . J. Bright, *A History of Israel*, 269. Judah barely escaped the fate of Samaria and Lachish. Thus **13–16 summarize the campaign. The details of it**, and the event which forced Sennacherib to be content with less than surrender, **are told in 17–37; 19:1–36.** The supplementary account is from other sources whose style and interests are different; the king's name is written Hiziyyahu throughout. Contrast *Hizqiyyah*, 13–16.

17–37 First Summons to Surrender—17. The **294c** besieging army surrounded Jerusalem, as Sennacherib relates, and the commander-in-chief (the Turtan or Tartān), the general (the *Rab-šāqē*) and the royal chamberlain (the *Rab-sarîs*) came to parley. At the SE of the city, the aqueduct from the Upper Pool (Gihon, 1 Kgs 1:33 = 'Ain Umm ed-Daraj or 'Ain Sitti Miryam) debouched into the Lower Pool (Siloah = Birket el-Hamrah). The 'Way of the Fuller's Field' ran along a crest almost as high as Gihon. See Vincent, DBS, 942ff. and Is 7:3; 22:9. **18.** For the Israelite delegates, see on Is 22:15–22. **19–20.** Hezekiah, as a rebel, 20, is given no title. He had not yet humbled himself and paid tribute; cf 14f. **21–25.** The prospect for Jerusalem was hopeless according to the Assyrians. Egypt was of no avail, 21, nor Yahweh, firstly, because he was angry with Hezekiah, 22; then, because, he was on the side of Sennacherib, 25. This was based on Sennacherib's conquest of the country. **26–28.** Aramaic was then becoming the common language of business. The tactics of driving a wedge between king and people had been used successfully by Ashurnadirpal (Schrader, KIB 1, 64) and Tiglath-pileser, 15:30. The crude expression of 27 means that the people faced starvation. **29–32.** The **d** alternative was a truce for refreshment, followed by the gift of fine lands abroad. The fundamental object of the deportations was not so much to punish the common people, as to mingle the elements of the empire in a harmonious whole. In their own way, the Assyrian anticipated the policy of Alexander. **33–35.** The ultimatum culminated in the blasphemous statement that the real reason why Yahweh did not help, 22–24, was that he could not. Arpad, N of Aleppo, is added to the states of 17:24. **36–37.** The actual terms of the military ultimatum are not given. But the fine rhetorical gradation of 19–34 does not alter the negotiations substantially. Assyrian soldiers chanted hymns to Ashur and Ishtar when marching to war; the king's inscriptions attribute every victory to their gods. The analysis of the situation into confidence in Yahweh on one side, blasphemy on the other, prepares for the miraculous interventions of ch 19.

19:1–7 Anguish and Hope—1–2. Isaiah was another **c** Elisha; cf 13:14. He had constantly opposed Hezekiah's policy. **3.** The king, through his own fault, was in a painful and dangerous situation. **4.** He based his hopes rather on Sennacherib's excesses than on his own merits. **5–6.** It was precisely the blasphemy that was answered. **7.** Yahweh was to induce a spirit, a mood (of anxiety) in Sennacherib (cf Nm 5:14, 30, Is 61:3, Hos 4:12, Rm 8:15). Under its influence, disturbing news from home would induce him to return. The message could not be news of the Egyptians, 9; that rather delayed his return. We know from the Assyrian records that he did not meet his death till 681. But prophecy gives causal, not chronological connexions.

19:8–34. An account derived from another source, f see § 294*a*. **8–19 Summons to Surrender—8.** The siege and the campaign continued. Perhaps the general took back with him an offer of tribute. For Libnah, see on 8:22. **9.** Tirhakah, son of Piankhi (see on 17:4), last Pharaoh of the 25th (Ethiopian) dynasty, was the great power in the Delta since 715, under the Pharaohs Shabaka and Shabataqa. His title 'king' may refer to this or anticipate his coregency, c. 600. According to Herodotus, 2:141, Sennacherib advanced to meet him, and Tirhakah did not venture across the border. However, the **battle of Eltekeh**, where Sennacherib states he routed the kings of Musri, may have taken place at this juncture (ANET 287). **12.** The countries, named from E to W, lay

294f around the Upper Euphrates. On Gozan, see 17:6; on Haran, Gn 11:31; Telassar may represent Til-baseri in the Aramaean principality of Bit-Adini. **13.** See on 18:34. This is the real turning-point of the narrative: Sennacherib himself blasphemed, not merely his delegates. **14—19.** But instead of bringing up all his forces for a full-scale assault he had merely sent a letter. Hezekiah took it as the first sign of the promised relief. Hence he addressed Yahweh directly; contrast the penitential approach to Isaiah, 3—5.

g 20—34 Prophecy of Deliverance—21—28. Before the message, (32ff), a poetic elaboration of it, perhaps by Isaiah himself or from his circle, is inserted. **23.** Sargon and Sennacherib used similar phrases (Schrader, KIB II, 40, 86). **24.** The Assyrians invaded Egypt for the first time in 673. **25—28.** Yahweh had really performed the feats which Sennacherib ascribed to himself. The theme is Isaian; cf Is 10:6ff; 45:1ff. **29—31.** An oracle of reassurance (in prose). The promise would appear as a sign, or miracle, in the light of its unexpected fulfilment; cf Ex 3:12. **31.** Note the reference to a Remnant, so typical of Isaiah. **32—34.** The message makes explicit what was only implicit in 7. **32.** Sennacherib claimed that he threw up earthworks around the city but the denial of this in 32 is hardly sufficient grounds for ascribing this oracle to a later campaign.

h 35—37 Retreat of Sennacherib—35. Some catastrophe struck the invaders. This is known also from Herodotus, whose version (2:141), suggests bubonic plague. The angel of the Lord struck through pestilence, 2 Sm 24:15ff. 2 Chr 32:31 gives no figures; those given here are probably exaggerated in order to magnify the providential deliverance. **36.** Sennacherib, already anxious to close the campaign, 7, gave up all idea of conquering Jerusalem and accepted tribute instead, 18:14—16. The miraculous deliverance is celebrated in Pss 46 (45) and 48 (47); Is 31:8. Hezekiah could not but send the tribute on to Nineveh. His losses had been severe, and Assyrian governors threatened him in Damascus and Samaria. To explain the payment of tribute and the double summons to surrender, it has often been suggested that we have here a conglomerate account of two or more expeditions of Sennacherib. But there seems to be no compelling reason to suppose two campaigns, though 19:8—34 may well include a repetition by a later hand of details already recorded in the earlier passage 18:13—19:7, but stressing the terms of surrender and Hezekiah's prayer. The Assyrian annals do not give any grounds for postulating further invasions. Another explanation of the course of events is that Sennacherib first accepted tribute, 18:13—16, and then demanded unconditional surrender. Treachery however was not an Assyrian trait. They made harsh demands but contented themselves with their fulfilment. Besides, this explanation does not take into account the difference of sources, nor the statement of Sennacherib that the tribute was sent after him to Nineveh. See further Šanda II 242—96; Bonkamp 428—54. **37.** Nisroch is inexplicable, unless it is a corruption of (*mat*) *an-Assur-ki*, (the land) of the god Assur, the consonants correspond (Bonkamp, 457). Read probably 'Adrammelech his son and Nabosarusur'; the latter was an officer of Sennacherib. The Assyrian and Babylonian accounts (AOT 359f) then tally with the Bible.

i 20:1—11 Illness and Miraculous Healing of Hezekiah—1. Hezekiah's illness and the embassy of Merodach-Baladan are certainly **before Sennacherib's campaign of chh 18—19.** The prophecy was comminatory, not irrevocable; cf 1 Kgs 21:19ff. **6.** About

this time, Hezekiah was threatened by Sargon, AOT **294i** 351. **7a.** For the plaster see Pliny, *Hist. Nat.* 23, 7; Jerome, PL 24, 396. **8—10.** Hezekiah, naively enough, did not think that the acceleration of the sun's shadow, in its normal direction, was a sufficient phenomenon. **11. The symbolism** (cf Ps 102 (101):1) has been often remarked—the shadow of death turned back from Hezekiah. This is in fact the probable meaning of the 'sign', which admirers of the prophet later heightened to the level of a miracle. One may perhaps compare this with Jos 10:12—14 when 'the sun stood still'.

12—19 Embassy from Babylon—12. Merodach- **j** Baladan (Marduk-aplu-iddin 'Marduk gave an heir'), ruler of the Aramaeans of Bit-Yakin on the Persian Gulf, was master of Babylon from 720—710, till he was driven out by Sargon. A tenacious enemy of Assyria, he returned in 703, to be driven out finally by Sennacherib in 702. The embassy was a move against Assyria. **13.** Hezekiah's parade of his resources was both a promise of support and a boast of what he could do. **14—17.** Isaiah, 7:4; 30:15, always insisted on neutrality; to rely on foreigners was to doubt Yahweh; cf on 1 Kgs 20:43. The prophecy was all the more striking since Babylon was then unimportant. **18.** The time of its fulfilment was not determined; cf 19:7. Sons could mean descendants in general. At the time, Hezekiah had apparently no son; cf 21:1. **19.** A good example of '*Après moi, le déluge*'; but the king knew that a prophecy could be revoked. See on 1.

20—21 Tunnel of Hezekiah—20. From the time of **k** Solomon, a canal had brought the waters of Gihon, Jerusalem's one spring, on the W slope of the Kidron valley, to the gardens in the SE of the city. Ahaz had turned the canal westward, at its southern end, and collected the waters at the base of the rampart across the Tyropoean valley; cf on 18:17. The canal remained within the reach of a besieging army. To remedy this Hezekiah cut a tunnel, 560 yards long, through the rock, under the ancient acropolis, which terminated in a great reservoir in the Tyropoean Valley, known as the Pool of Siloam, above the old pool. In the tunnel, the **Inscription** was found last century cf § 81*l*. When this aqueduct was completed, the source was covered in, and the older canal blocked; cf 2 Chr 32:30; L. H. Vincent, *Jérusalem*, DBS 943—9; A. G. Barrois, *Manuel d'Archéologie Biblique*, I, 228ff. **21.** For Hezekiah's other achievements, see 2 Chr 29—32.

21:1—25:30—For the rest of the book the editor **295a** certainly has access to the 'Annals of the kings of Judah'. 23:4—20 are probably from this source. But the events described are so close to the time of the first redactor (see § 242*e*) that it is difficult to distinguish between his own account and his edited use of sources.

21:1—9 Paganism under Manasseh, 687—642— 1—2. The tendency towards Baal-worship curbed under Hezekiah was now given free rein. Micah, 6:6—8, had complained that the reform was only superficial. **3—5.** The predominance of the Assyrians explains the worship of their gods; see on 16:10ff.

10—16 Opposition of the Prophets—13. The measuring-line (cf Lam 2:8) and the plummet (cf Am 7:7) were builders' instruments. They refer here to demolition; cf Is 34:11. **16.** Reprisals followed protests. The later Jewish tradition (cf Justin, *Dial. c. Tryph.*, 120) was that Isaiah was sawn in two under Manasseh; cf Heb 11:37.

17—18 End of Manasseh—Esarhaddon names Manasseh among the 'kings of the sea-coast' who paid him tribute after the fall of Sidon, c. 671; Ashurbanipal names him among the vassals who supplied him with auxiliaries for his conquest of Egypt, 668 (ANET, 291, 294). He

295a fell foul of the Assyrians later; see 2 Chr 33:11—19. His subsequent conversion to Yahweh did not change the general trend of religion. Hence the verdict here ignores it.

19—26 Amon, 642—640—19—22. He favoured the anti-Yahwistic party, reintroduced foreign cults into the temple, 23:6, 12, and thus undid the repentant efforts of Manasseh; cf 2 Chr 33:15 **23—24.** Still the revolt was not the work of the Yahwistic party. But they seized the chance to stir up the people against the civil and military authorities and put their own candidate on the throne.

b 22 Josiah, 640—609—1. Read '18 years old;' cf LXX. He was c. 45 at his death (cf 23:36), therefore at least 14 at his accession. **2.** Some efforts at reform in the first part of his reign were not very successful, Jer 2:1ff; Zeph 1:2ff. **3—7 Repair of the Temple—3.** Thoroughgoing reforms began in the winter of 622, to culminate in the Passover 23:23. **4—7.** The system was that of Joash, 12:10ff.

c 8—11 Discovery of the Book of the Law—Its substantial identity with Dt is probable: (1) The title is found exclusively in Dt 28:61; 29:30; 30:10; 31:2, 6. The 'Book of the Covenant', 23:2, is found only in Ex 24:7, but the Covenant is mentioned frequently in Dt. (2) It held threats of exile against king and people, 11:16, 20; see Dt 4:25f.; 28:36f., 63; 29:23—27; 30:3ff. (3) The centralization of the cult, 23:8f, corresponded to its prescriptions; see Dt 12 etc. This holds good even if the events of 23:4—14 (whose 'statistical' style indicates a new document) preceded the finding of the book; cf 2 Chr 33:4ff. Dt is the only book which could initiate or ratify the centralization. It was an ancient possession, rescued from oblivion, not a recent fiction, composed to justify the reform: (1) the name was familiar. Note the articles, pointing to a definite authority, which Hilkiah, Shaphan and the king acknowledged at once. (2) All recognized that its prescriptions had bound their forefathers, 13. Even if the author invented the words attributed to Josiah, he expressed his conviction that the book was available before Josiah; see further § § 137; 224g—h. (3) A recent invention would not have commanded universal acceptance, especially on the part of the country clergy, who suffered thereby; see on 23:8f. (4) The threats of the book moved everybody deeply. But contemporary prophets left the people cold. The reigns of Manasseh and Amon account for its neglect. It was the custom to deposit sacred documents in shrines, Dt 31:26; 1 Sm 10:25.

d 12—20 Consultation of the Prophetess Huldah— 12—13. The king feared that the end was near. The Scythians were then a menace, Herodotus 1:105; see Jer 1:13 etc. **14.** Huldah was asked if and how disaster could be averted. From their previous threats, the answer of the prophets Jeremiah and Zephaniah could be guessed. The Second Quarter (cf Zeph 1:10) was the extension W of the temple, which Hezekiah had enclosed by a new outer wall, 2 Chr 32:5. **15—17.** The fall of Jerusalem was only 35 years distant. **18—20.** The king died in peace (cf 23:29) in the sense given in 20b.

23:1—3 Renewal of the Alliance—1. Like David praying for his doomed child, 2 Sm 12:14—23, Josiah stormed heaven. Huldah's prophecy could be revoked; see on 21:1. **2.** Jer 11:1ff probably refer to this assembly. **3.** For the king's place by the pillar, see on 11:14. The people answered 'Amen'; cf Jer 11:5.

e 4—14 Reform of the Cult—Possibly drawn from the Annals of Judah. **4.** The work had been going on for years, 2 Chr 34:3. This section seems to catalogue the results without regard to chronological sequence; hence it cannot

be said that the whole reform was inspired by the newly-discovered book. 'Keeper of the threshold' was the honorary title of a high order of priests, 12:10; 25:18. The actual duties of doorkeepers were performed by Levites, 1 Chr 9:17 etc. **5.** Possibly the idolatrous priests were killed, according to Dt 17:2ff. Assyria was in decline. Hence Josiah could proceed against Shamash ('the sun'), Sin ('the moon'), the Mazzaloth (*lit.* stations (of the sun)); 'the twelve signs' of the Zodiac, or perhaps the planets; (cf Jer 7:8). **6.** The common cemetery was considered little better than a dung-heap, Jer 26:23. **7.** See on 1 Kgs 14:24. **8.** These priests were orthodox, except that they functioned outside Jerusalem; contrast 5 and 20. Geba, 1 Kgs 15:22, and Beersheba indicate the N and S limits of Judah. **9.** The priests transferred to Jerusalem were not admitted to the sacred ministry. It is not clear what provision was made for them. 9b can mean (1) they kept the Passover, 21ff, with their families (cf Ex 12:15, 18); (2) they lived on their portion of the sacrifices, like priests excluded from office by a legal blemish, Lv 21:21ff. Eventually some at least were given minor functions; **f** see however on Dt 18:6—9. **10.** Topheth, 'place of fire', lay S of Jerusalem, at the junction of Ge-bene-Hinnom (the present Wady er-Rababi) and the Kidron valley. Gehenna Mt 5:22 etc corresponds to the short form Ge-Hinnom, Jos 15:8 etc. For child-sacrifice, see on 16:3; 17:31; Jer 7:31f; 19:4ff; 32:35. **11.** 'Horses and chariots of the sun' were cult-objects, lodged in a building or quarter called Pharurim. The name may be connected with E-Barbar (cf 1 Chr 28:18), the temple of the Sun-god in Babylonian Sippar. **12.** Roof-altars were for sacrifices to the heavenly bodies, Jer 19:13; 32:29; Zeph 1:5. **13.** The pagan shrines which had been restored each time after being suppressed by Jehoshaphat, Hezekiah etc, lay either on the S shoulder of Mt. Olivet, or on the Jebel batn el Hawa, opposite the SE hill of Jerusalem. As the common burial place lay between the two, there were materials enough to defile the shrines; cf Nm 5:2f; 19:11.

15—20 In the North—15. With Assyria, hard pressed **g** by the Medes and Babylonians, losing her grip on the provinces, Josiah could extend his zealous efforts beyond his own frontiers. Bethel was only a few hours to the N, but he reached even Naphtali, 2 Chr 34:6; cf 19. **16—18.** The prophecy of 1 Kgs 13:31f was fulfilled. **20.** He followed the examples of Jehu, 10:18ff and Elijah, 1 Kgs 18:40; and see Dt 17:2ff; these priests were treated as idolaters. Contrast 8.

21—23 The Passover—In addition to the ancient ritual prescriptions of Ex 12, the precept of Dt 16:1ff was enforced. Never before had the Passover been celebrated only in Jerusalem, and therefore never with such solemnity, 2 Chr 35:1—19. This was the 14th Nisan, within a fortnight of the events of 22:3ff, if the year began on the 1st Nisan. Either the year began with Tishri (see on 1 Kgs 6:1), or the account of the reforms is not chronological. This passage is to be ascribed to the Deuteronomist but the motive for the celebration is obscure. Egypt was once more at this time a power to be reckoned with and a possible danger to Judah. The Passover recalled the deliverance from Egypt.

24—28 Verdict on Josiah and Judah—24. Josiah **h** tried to stamp out even private superstitions. **25.** His zeal for religion, like Hezekiah's confidence in God, 18:5, was unrivalled. **26—28.** But idolatry had gone too deep to be eradicated by human efforts, as the next reigns showed; cf Jer, Ezek.

29—30 Death of Josiah—Nineveh had fallen in 612, but the Assyrians fought on till 608 in the western

295h province of Harran. See § 65*g*. Neco II 'went up to (aid) the king of Assyria', AOT 362, JosAnt. 10, 5, 1 (reading *'el* 'to' for *'al* 'against'; these Heb. prepositions are constantly confused in MT). Megiddo commanded the passage from the coastal plain to the plain of Jezreel and the north. Josiah was mortally wounded at the first encounter. His intervention in international conflicts was fatal, not only to himself, but to Judah.

i 31—35 Jehoahaz, 609——31—33. Neco's attitude shows that the popular movement which placed Jehoahaz on the throne instead of his elder brother was anti-Egyptian. Checked before Harran, Neco had returned to Riblah on the Orontes in the land of Hamath. Jehoahaz, opposed by the upper classes at home, dared not disobey his summons. He must be the son of Josiah called Shallum, whose fate was more miserable than his father's, Jer 22: 10—12. **34.** The change of name presented his successor as the creature of Neco, and possibly Neco as the instrument of Yahweh; Jehoiakim 'Yahweh raises'; cf 18:25. **35.** Jehoiakim apparently paid for his throne out of the pockets of his opponents, not out of the treasury.

296a 36—24:7 Jehoiakim, 609—598—36—24:1a. In 605, the 4th year of Jehoiakim (see Jer 25:1; 46:2), Neco suffered a crushing defeat, Jer 46:1ff, at the hands of Nebuchadnezzar, who became king of Babylon on the death of his father shortly after. Neco retired for good behind his frontiers, 7, and Nebuchadnezzar annexed Syria and Palestine. It is uncertain whether at this time he entered Jerusalem, cf Dn 1:1; Jos.Ant. 10, 11, 1 (citing the historian Berossus).

1b—2. Jehoiakim kept up the friendly relations with Egypt, Jer 26:22f, which were to be the ruin of Judah. As a result, he withheld tribute from Nebuchadnezzar in 602, when some Syrian states revolted against their new master (Bonkamp 513). Nebuchadnezzar marched against Syria, but sent only punitive expeditions, composed of troops of his loyal vassals, against Judah. Thus Jehoiakim could hold out for four years. **3—5.** He was an impious and tyrannical ruler, the circumstances of whose death are mysterious. The omission of the usual notice of burial seems deliberate; see Jer 22:13—19, 2 Chr 36:6.

b 8—12 Jehoiachin, 598——8. The new year occurred during his brief reign. Elnathan was a high official under Jehoiakim, Jer 26:22; 36:12, 25. **9—10.** The siege was the outcome of the state of war which had lasted since 602. **11.** The arrival of Nebuchadnezzar in person convinced Jehoiachin that resistance was rash. **12.** His voluntary surrender spared Jerusalem the worst. According to Jer 52:28, it was the 7th year of Nebuchadnezzar. This was the Babylonian reckoning, which did not count the *rēššarrūti* (after Nisan 605 to Nisan 604; see § 124*e*) whereas the author of Kgs, using the Israelite system, counted the *rēš šarrūti* as Nebuchadnezzar's first year. So too in 25:8, where the 19th year corresponds to the 18th of Jer 52:29.

c 13—16 Pillage and Deportation—13. 'All the treasures', and 'all Jerusalem', 14, are wide terms indicating a general calamity. They are not to be understood in the light of the more precise details which follow. The temple was only partially despoiled, 25:15; Jer 27:18. The gold and silver utensils were very numerous, Ez 1:11. Some had been carried off in 605, Dn 1:2, more were taken in 598, the rest in 587. Nebuchadnezzar had as yet no intention of eliminating the Judean kingship and its official cult. **14—16.** The relation of the figures of 14 to those of 16 is not clear. The more general and acceptable view is that the total is given in 14, and some of the details in 16. The 10,000 was made up of 7,000 warriors

(of the richer classes, 15:20), 1,000 skilled tradesmen, **296** and 2,000 others ('princes', 14, officials, 15, 'ancients', priests and prophets', Jer 29:1f). Another view is that 14 gives the total of important persons, including the 7,000 warriors of 16, and that 1,000 skilled tradesmen must be added on, making 11,000 in all. 3,023 were deported from the countryside, Jer 52:28. Since wives and children went also, well over 30,000 persons must have been deported. Among them was the prophet Ezekiel, Ezek 1:2. Jehoiakin died in exile, Jer 22:20—30. Nebuchadnezzar left the poorer classes to take over the property of the exiles in the hope of creating a loyal population.

17—19 Zedekiah, 598—587—17. Mattaniah was a son **d** of Josiah, and brother of Jehoahaz, 23:31, and Jehoiakim. For the change of name, see on 23:24. Zedekiah 'justice of Yahweh' was to recall the 'just' punishment which Nebuchadnezzar had inflicted on Jerusalem in 598; cf Jer 40:2f. Jeremiah gave the name a different meaning, when he based on it the hope of a happier future, Jer 23: 5ff. **18.** The parallel accounts in Jer 52 begin here. Hamutal is the lioness of Ezek 19. **19.** Idolatry in the temple is described vividly in Ezek 8—11; and see Jer 23; 2 Chr 36:14. Zedekiah's guilt is compared with Manasseh's, 21:20. The fall of Jerusalem was, it is implied, due to the wickedness of her last kings, Josiah excepted.

20 Last Revolt—Zedekiah was a weak character and he **e** destroyed his people by wavering in his allegiance to Yahweh. Disregarding the warnings of Jeremiah, the inspired spokesman of the orthodox, he threw himself into the arms of the anti-Yahwistic party, whose pro-Egyptian policy brought on the conflict with Babylon, Jer 27:2ff; 37:2ff; 38:17. Only the general trend of events is known. Zedekiah had sworn allegiance to Nebuchadnezzar and sent two missions to Babylon to affirm his loyalty, Jer 29:3; 51:59. At the same time he was intriguing with the enemies of Babylon, especially Tyre and Egypt, Ezek 26; 29:17f, Jer 27:2ff, JosCAp. 1, 21. Psammetichus II of Egypt visited Palestine in 592 (A. Alt, ZAW 30 (1910) 288ff), and it was probably then that Zedekiah committed himself to revolt, which began in 589 with an appeal for Egyptian aid, Ezek 17:15.

25:1—3 Siege of Jerusalem—1. It began on 25 Jan. **f** 589. The **Lachish Letters** give an idea of the mounting pressure against Jerusalem, L.-H. Vincent, RB 48 (1939) 250ff. Nebuchadnezzar, who had to deal with the Phoenicians also, was not always present; cf Jer 38:17. The blockade wall, *dāyēq*, is to be distinguished from the mounds, *sōlelāh*. The former ran round the city at some distance from the walls (cf JosBJ 5, 12, 2), the latter, like the Roman *ager*, were built up against the walls where an assault could be launched. **2—3.** The siege lasted till the 9th day of the 4th month (June-July) 587, 30 months in all. The number of the month, missing in MT, can be supplied from Jer 39:2; 52:6. The siege however was not continuous. Psammetichus died before he could attempt to relieve Jerusalem. But some time before Jan, 588, Ezek 29:17, his son Hophra advanced and the Chaldeans broke off the siege to meet him, Jer 37:4—10. He retired without effecting more and the siege was resumed. He attacked again in the course of 588 and 587, Ezek 30:20ff; 31:1ff; but was no match for the Chaldeans, Ezek 17:7. Herodotus, 2:161, says that Apries (Hophra) sent an army against Sidon and a fleet against Tyre. They must in fact have operated against Nebuchadnezzar, but they were too weak to impede him seriously, Ezek 17:7. In Jerusalem, famine and pestilence, Jer 38:2, 9, weakened the defenders, and this time no 'angel of the Lord', 18:35, came to the rescue.

296g **4 Fall of Jerusalem**—The breach was made probably in the N wall (cf 14:13) where the terrain was most suitable for attackers. Zedekiah and the garrison escaped at the opposite end of the city. There an ancient wall enclosed the SE hill, and the more recent wall of the SW hill ran across the Tyropoean valley to join it. Jer 39:4 speaks of a gate and Is 22:11 of a pool 'between the two walls'. The latter would be the lower pool of Siloah, the modern Birket elhamra at the mouth of the central valley. The 'king's garden' was to the SE, Neh 3:15. The refugees made for the Jordan valley, sometimes known as 'the Wilderness', though the name is mostly given to the valley S of the Dead Sea. They were making for Moab. The Chaldeans (*Kasdim*) were Aramaeans of the extreme S of Babylonia, who, after many unsuccessful efforts, had succeeded in becoming masters of Babylon, under Nabopolassar (625—605). They formed the backbone of the Babylonian army.

5—7 Capture of Zedekiah—**5.** Controlling the good routes, the Chaldeans soon came up with the king and his bodyguard. The rest of the army had already scattered and escaped, 23. Nebuchadnezzar was at his head-quarters at Riblah (see on 23:33); Jer 39:3 therefore speaks only of his officers at the fall of Jerusalem. **7.** According to Jer 52:10f, the princes were killed at the same time. These were probably the officers of the body-guard. Zedekiah was kept a captive till his death. The blinding of captives by a thrust of the lance is depicted on Assyrian monuments. Jer 34:3 prophesied that Zedekiah would go to Babylon; Ezek 12:13 that he would never see it.

h **8—10 Destruction of Jerusalem**—**8.** For the dating, see on 24:12. The day of the month is given as the 7th in MT, the 9th in Syr., LXX (Lucian), the 10th in Jer 52:12—July 20th to 28th. The fate of the city was decided after the trial of Zedekiah. Nebuchadnezzar then determined to replace the Judean state by a province with its capital at Mizpah, 23. **9—10.** The walls were completely dismantled only in parts, Neh 4:1; hence they could be repaired in 52 days, Neh 6:15.

11—12 Deportations—**11.** Cf Jer 52:15. No doubt many of the poor, who had nothing to lose but their lives, fled after the fall of the city; cf Jer 40:11f. Still the number of the deported, 832, as given in Jer 52:29 is remarkably small. It refers probably only to the upper classes, most of whom had been already deported in 598. **12.** Since the countryside was depopulated as well as the capital, the total must have been more like the 200,150 whom Sennacherib carried off in 701; see on 18:13ff. Hence Judah went into exile, 21*b*.

i **13—17 Stripping of the Temple**—**13.** 'Stands': '*cauldrons*'; cf Syr. The stands had been removed by Ahaz, 16:17. **14.** See on 1 Kgs 7:50. The bronze altar of holocausts, 1 Kgs 8:64, had been replaced by a stone structure (see on 16:17f); hence it is not mentioned here. Massive pieces were broken up for transport. The utensils were carried off intact; cf Jer 27:21f. **16.** 'Stands': '*cauldrons*', as in 13. **17.** Jer 52:21—23 gives a more

complete description of the pillars (cf 1 Kgs 7:15ff); the **296i** text here has suffered.

18—21 Execution of the Ringleaders—**18.** The Chaldeans knew the inner history of the revolt, as their treatment of Jeremiah shows, Jer 40. Seraiah was grand-son of Hilkiah, 22:4; his own son was not killed, but deported; cf 1 Chr 6:13ff. Ezra was of this family, Ez 7:1. Zedekiah had relied much on Zephaniah, Jer 21:1; 37:3; 29:25, 29. The doorkeepers were ranked next to the high-priest and his vice regent; see on 23:4. Some of Jeremiah's bitterest enemies were among the priesthood, Jer 20. **19.** The 72 were arrested in consequence of the enquiry held at Riblah, 6.

22—26 Fate of the Remainder—**22.** Jer 40—43 gives **j** a fuller account of what followed. Nebuchadnezzar tried to conciliate the remaining Israelites by giving them a fellow-countryman as provisional governor; cf Jer 40:10. Ahikam had been Josiah's envoy to Huldah, 22:14, and the defender of Jeremiah, Jer 26:24. The family was loyal to the policy of submission to Babylon which Jeremiah had urged, Jer 27:6ff. Gedaliah was entrusted with the command of a small detachment of Chaldeans, 25; Jer 41:3. **23.** For Mizpah, see on 1 Kgs 15:22. The generals had returned after the departure of the Chaldean army and seized some towns, Jer 40:10. On promise of amnesty, they submitted to Gedaliah, and the rest of the army and many refugees returned, Jer 40:9—12. **25.** It was now autumn, for the summer fruits and grapes were being gathered, Jer 40:12. The kings of Ammon planned the murder, Jer 40:14; it is not clear why. **26.** See Jer 41:16ff. Ishmael tried to lead the Israelites to Ammon, but was put to flight by the other leaders as soon as they learned of Gedaliah's death. Jeremiah and Baruch, protesting against the migration to Egypt, were forced to go with the refugees. Few, if any, foreign settlers, were transplanted to Judah; the only opposition on the return of the exiles came from Samaria, Ez 4.

27—30 Hopeful Signs in Babylon—**27.** Amel- **k** Marduk (562—560) was son and successor of Nebuchad-nezzar. Evil-Merodach, suggesting 'a fool is Merodach', is a tendentious alteration of a name meaning 'the man of Marduk'. Possibly he thought of making Judah a buffer-state against Egypt. The brevity of his reign prevented further developments. **28.** Jehoiachin was given pre-cedence over other vassals detained in Babylon. Many of the exiles were now prosperous business men; no doubt their money had something to do with Jehoiachin's honours. **29—30.** Nobles ate occasionally at the king's table (Schrader, KIB II 140). Jehoiachin did not dine every day with the king; but his needs were supplied by the court. The change of status was not unheard-of; Ashur-banipal had restored the captive Neco of Egypt to a greater power and dignity than he had before his revolt. To the Israelites it must have seemed that the wrath of Yahweh was at last appeased. Jehoiachin's good fortune lasted 'till the day of his death', Jer 52:34, which apparently took place before the end of Amel-Marduk's reign.

1 AND 2 CHRONICLES

BY J. MULCAHY C.S.Sp.

297a Bibliography—*Commentaries*: F. de Hummelauer, CSS 1905; E. L. Curtis and A. A. Madsen, ICC 1910; N. Schlögl, Vienna 1911; J. W. Rothstein and J. Hänel, KAT 1927; J. Goettsberger, BB 1939; L. Marchal, PCSB. 1949; M. Rehm, EchB 1954²; W. A. L. Elmslie, IB, 1954; W. Rudolph HAT 1955; E. Dhorme, Bible de la Pléïade, 1957; K. Galling, ATD 1958; A. van den Born, *Kronieken*, Roermond 1960; H. Cazelles, BJ 1961²; A. S. Herbert, PC (2) 1962; J. M. Myers, AB 1965. **Other Works**: P. Vannutelli, *Libri Synoptici VT seu Librorum Regum et Chronicorum Loci Paralleli*, Rome 1931–34; M. Rehm, *Textcritische Untersuchungen zu den Parallelstellen der Samuel-Königsbücher und der Chronik*, Münster 1937; G. von Rad, *Das Geschichtsbild des chronistischen Werkes*, Stuttgart 1930; A. C. Welch, *The Work of the Chronicler. Its Purpose and Date*. London 1939; M. Noth, *Ueberlieferungsgeschichtliche Studien*, Tübingen 1957²; C. C. Torrey, *The Chronicler's History of Israel*, New Haven 1954; G. Gerleman, *Synoptic Studies in the OT*, Lund 1948. **Articles**: A. Noordtzij, 'Les Intentions du Chroniste', RB 49 (1940) 161–8; A. Bea, 'Neuere Arbeiten zum Problem der biblischen Chronikbücher', Coll. Gand. 33 (1950) 205–27; S. Mowinckel, 'Erwägungen zum chronistischen Geschichtswerk' TLZ 1960 1–7; H. Neil Richardson, 'The Historical Reliability of Chronicles', Journal of Bible and Religion 26 (1958) 912; *G. J. Botterweck, 'Zur Eigenart der chronistische Davidsgeschichte', TQ 136 (1956) 402–35; R. North, 'The Theology of the Chronicler', JBL 82 (1963) 369–381; A. M. Brunet, 'Paralipomènes', DBS 1960; Idem, 'Le Chroniste et ses sources', RB 60 (1953) 481–508 and 61 (1954) 349–386; B. Mazar, 'The Campaign of the Pharaoh Shishak to Palestine', VTS IV, Leyden 1957, 57–66; D. N. Freedman, 'The Chroniclers' Purpose', CBQ 23 (1961) 438ff.

b Name—The work is known by the two names of Paralipomenon and Chronicles. The former was taken over by the Latins from the Greeks; this name is the genitive of the Gr. participle with the meaning 'the book of what was omitted'. As Theodoret explains, the author of the book put together 'whatever the compiler of Kgs has passed over'. This was until recently the title normally used in Catholic Bibles but it is yielding place to the second which was given currency by Jerome. After mentioning the Heb. title *Diḇᵉrê hayyāmîm*, lit. 'the events of the days', he says 'quod significantius *chronikon* totius divinae historiae possumus appellare', Prol. Gal. PL 28, 554. This second title, which Luther accepted from Jerome, has always been used in Protestant Bibles. It is more suitable in that the work can be described as historical, but it does not clearly state its special aim. 'The Annals' is probably the best approximation to the meaning of the Heb. title. The ancient authors did not give titles and still less sub-titles to their works. Otherwise the author might have chosen to write at its head:

'*Throne and Temple, the Pillars of God's Kingdom*'. The **297** division of Chr into two books is not original but has been taken over from LXX; this division passed from the LXX to the Vg and thence to modern translations. **Relation to Ez-Neh**—The opinion that Ez-Neh is the **c** continuation of Chr and forms one book with it is now very widely, though not universally, accepted. Rabbinical tradition (cf Brunet, DBS, art cit, 1228) suggests that these books arose in the same literary milieu. The literary arguments can be summarized as follows: a) the diction common to both books in regard to vocabulary, use of prepositions and syntax, b) the other books of the OT are used in the same way, the same method of quoting the Mosaic Law, the same mode of dealing with sources whether canonical (Sm-Kgs in Chr) or uncanonical (the memoirs of Ezra and Nehemiah in Ez-Neh), c) the functions of the Levites are described in the same diffuse style and almost in the same words, d) the same frequency of genealogies and public lists, e) both works centre on Jerusalem, the temple and public worship, f) in both there is the same solicitude for the divine law, g) the same diligence in setting down information about the priests and Levites. These arguments seem to prove at the very least that both works came from the same circles and possibly from the same pen. Identity of authorship, even proved, does not, it is plain, prove unity of composition. In favour of the unity of the two works it is pointed out that Ez-Neh begins precisely at the point where the story is left by Chr, and that Chr ends with part of the decree with which Ez opens. This repeated v 2 Chr 36:22, 23; Ez 1:1, 2, cannot be removed from Ez without rendering the subsequent passages meaningless nor from Chr since it forms the perfect completion of 2 Chr 36:21. This argument for unity seems very strong. On the negative side it may be urged that the only historical evidence for this hypothesis is a very nebulous Jewish tradition and that there is no trace in Ez-Neh of the Messianic hope although it would have been so easy to introduce it from the writings of the postexilic prophets. On this see below, § 298p. In the commentary it will be assumed that Chr-Ez-Neh form one work having a single author and a single theme.

Contents—The work begins with Adam and ends with **d** the decree of Cyrus permitting the exiles to return from the Babylonian captivity. But the history is not treated in the same way throughout. The first nine chh are given, for the most part, in the form of bare genealogical lists. The author's predominant interest is in the genealogies of the tribes of Juda and Levi, the ancestors respectively of the Davidic dynasty and of the Levitical priesthood. The death of Saul is narrated, not for its own interest, but because the account of his rejection by the Lord was required to explain the divine choice of David to be the ruler of Israel. In ch 10 the author enters directly on his theme: God's founding of his kingdom on earth by his choice of the Davidic dynasty as his representative and of the temple of Jerusalem as his

297d unique dwelling place. This theme runs through Chr-Ez-Neh. Chr can be divided into four parts: Introduction 1 Chr 1—9, The reign of David 1 Chr 10—29, The reign of Solomon 2 Chr 1—9, The other Davidic kings 2 Chr 10—36. The story is thus carried down to the destruction of Jerusalem by the Babylonians when the temporal rule of the dynasty ceased, but the book ends with a suggestion of the restoration which is to be described in Ez-Neh.

e Purpose—The purpose of the book, to prove the legitimacy of the claim of the Davidic dynasty and of the temple of Jerusalem to be the unique embodiment of the kingdom of God on earth, is especially manifest in the deliberate exclusion of the history of the N kingdom. This belongs to the history of Israel, but not to that of the dynasty of David and is consequently only recalled when it has bearings on the latter. Similarly the reign of Athaliah is hardly recognized because she was a usurper who was not of the line of David. The Davidic kings themselves, in whom interest centres, were heirs of the promise, not as individual persons, but in their official position as heirs of the Davidic throne. The Chronicler consequently omits incidents of their private lives. He omits the history of David's youth, of his glorious exploits in the reign of Saul, the story of his adultery and its consequences, for these are matters which are of no importance to his central theme of Throne and Temple. On the other hand, the religious activities of David and his choice of God as the founder of a dynasty which is to last forever are stressed. Even David's military exploits are given a relatively minor position in Chr as having no direct contact with the main theme of the book. The omission of direct reference to Solomon's idolatry is more striking, for this was punished by God by the rending of the kingdom and the removal of the greater part from the rule of Solomon's successors, 1 (3) Kgs 11:29—36. The manner in which the Chronicler refers to the fulfilment of the prediction of the Prophet Ahijah recorded in this passage of Kgs shows that in his opinion it was so familiar to his readers as not to require explicit repetition. But he will not stress the fault of the son of David.

f The divine promise—The Davidic dynasty being one of the principal elements in Chr, the divine promise to 'build David a house', to grant him posterity, could not but be given prominence, ch 17. Now, when the Chronicler wrote, these great promises seemed to have been rendered void. The Holy City with its temple had been destroyed; the dynasty had been swept away; the people lay in poverty and weakness under the rule of a foreign power. The Chronicler sets out to give the people new heart. The divine promises are not forgotten and God is not powerless to fulfil them: 'the word of the Lord endures for ever'. He therefore shows how God in the history of the kingdom blessed right-doing with prosperity and punished evil with calamity. This is a recurrent theme of his work, 2 Chr 12:1—2; 13:4—16; 14:11—13; 16:9; 19:2; 20:37; 21:10; 22:4—9, etc. In particular the final disaster of the destruction of Jerusalem is traced to the divine sentence provoked by the iniquities of kings and people, 2 Chr 36:5, 8, 9, 12—16: 'they kept mocking the messengers of God, despising his words, and scoffing at his prophets, till the wrath of the Lord rose against his people, till there was no remedy'. By such considerations the Chronicler attempts to move the people to a whole-hearted return to God. If that condition were fulfilled, they would again experience the happiness of the divine favour. The promise to David's dynasty might be in abeyance, might even seem to have lapsed, but God is faithful, his promise to David is of an everlasting house, he will not **297f** abandon his people and David's line forever. Let them only observe the Law and he will bring all his promise to fulfilment. (On the postexilic line of David cf 1 Chr 3:19—24).

The Temple—The claim of Jerusalem to be the only **g** place where legitimate worship of Yahweh is possible is the second principal element in the Chronicler's theme. Hence he wove into his story all that his sources recorded of the planning, building, inauguration, renovations, and general history of the temple, together with the arrangements prepared by David for the due and solemn celebration of the temple worship by the distribution of offices among the courses of priests and Levites, and the renewal of such arrangements by Jehoiada under Joash, by Hezekiah, and by Josiah. There can be no doubt that he wishes to stress the illegitimate character of the Samaritan cult which claimed independence from Jerusalem, God's chosen dwelling place. This point is made even more clearly in Ez-Neh but in Chr also we find the constant anti-Samaritan polemic at work. We cannot properly understand Chr unless we realize that its principal aim is to affirm the God-given rights of the Davidic dynasty and the Jerusalem temple and that the incentive to write almost certainly came from the persistent claim of the Samaritans to be God's people equally with the Jews, in spite of their rejection of both the line of David and the cult of Jerusalem.

More than a polemic—But the Chronicler intended to **h** produce a book with a purpose that was more than merely polemical. Since obedience to God's law was the duty of God's people and the way to prosperity, while disobedience led to disaster, and since an essential part of loyalty to God and obedience to his law was the whole-hearted observance of the (temple) ritual and worship, the Chronicler attempted to arouse the enthusiasm of his readers for this religious part of their national and individual responsibilities. As is manifest from the reproaches of the prophets Haggai and Malachi the postexilic Jews had been very negligent in this part of their religious duty. It was then not merely the Chronicler's personal interest in these religious matters that prompted him to devote so large a part of his book to them, but his realization of their importance for the nation and of the need to arouse in the people a vivid sense of their obligations in this regard.

Canon—If Chr-Ez-Neh originally formed one work, we **298a** should expect to find it in the Bible as one work and in proper sequence. While this is the case in the Gr. and Latin Bibles, in the printed editions of the Heb. Bible Chr is placed last among the Hagiographa and so occupies the last place of all. And this position is sometimes said to have obtained in the time of Christ on the strength of Mt 23:35, 'from the blood of innocent Abel to the blood of Zechariah'. As the murder of Zechariah by Joash took place as early as the 9th cent. and so was by no means the last in OT history, it is pointed out that, as the murder of Abel is recorded in the first book of the Bible, so that of Zechariah must have been recorded in the last, 2 Chr 24:21. But this argument is doubtful (cf comm. on Mt 23:35). We are not sure when Chr was received into the Heb. Canon. The book was certainly in the Jewish canon of Josephus (Jos. C. Ap. I, 8). It seems that Ez-Neh alone was canonized first for it is difficult to explain the repetition of Ez 1:1, 2 at the end of 2 Chr if Ez were received at the same time or added to an already canonized Chr. Probably the reception of Chr into the Heb. canon was delayed because it seemed to be a mere repetition of Sm-Kgs, while Ez-Neh, on the other hand,

298a offered entirely new material. When it was finally received, it was simply added at the end of Ez-Neh. But Jewish tradition and early Christian evidence of the Jewish canon do not permit a definitive statement. It appears that the Palestinian canon put Chr before Ez-Neh while the Babylonian which has prevailed put it at the end of the Hagiographa.

b Text—Except in the genealogical preface, where mistakes in transcription and omissions sometimes cause insuperable difficulties, the Heb. text of Chr has been well preserved and offers little difficulty.

c Date—That the work was not written till after the return from the Babylonian captivity is indicated by the excerpt from the decree of Cyrus, 1 Chr 36:22—23; and even with the possibility of this being a later addition the same conclusion follows from the mention of the establishment of the Kingdom of Persia in 2 Chr 36:20. If, as is probable, the Persian daric is the coin named in 1 Chr 29:7, the date would be sufficiently long after its introduction by Darius I, 521—486, for its use and name to have become familiar in Palestine. The strong anti-Samaritan bias also indicates the postexilic period and the stress on the right of the temple of Jerusalem to be the only legitimate place of worship seems to postulate that the book was written at a time when the Samaritans had already erected a temple of their own. Unfortunately, we do not know for certain when this happened but it was certainly after the time of Nehemiah. (Cf Jos. Ant II, 7, 2—II, 8, 7 and Neh 13:28). Eupolemus about the year 157 B.C. used the Gr. translation of 2 Chr 2:2 ff. (EOT Int 540) while Sir 46:8—10 (c. 190—180) presupposes the David of Chr. The evidence of the list of Davidic descendants in 1 Chr 3:19—24 is inconclusive partly because of the possibility of additions having been made to the text and partly because of its state and the difficulty of interpretation. Zerubbabel was the first governor of the Jews after the return from the exile in 538, Hag 1:1. Various emendations and interpretations have been offered, but Mt seems to give 6 generations after Zerubbabel and LXX + Vg 11. If Hananiah, the son of Zerubbabel was already an adult at the time of the return, with the allowance of 20 years to a generation, MT would point to a date some century later. On the reading of LXX + Vg Shemaiah the son of Shecaniah was in the 7th generation after Zerubbabel, and he was one of those who assisted Nehemiah in the rebuilding of the wall of Jerusalem in 445, Neh 3:29. If this is correct, each generation must have married very early as Zerubbabel could not have been much more than 40 in 438, as his grandfather Joachin was 18 in 598. The remaining generations of LXX + Vg would carry the date down to about the middle of the 4th cent. Finally, if, as seems likely, Chr-Ez-Neh originally formed one work, the date of the latter must be taken into account. It appears that the book could have been written any time between 400 and 200 B.C.

d Sources—In his work the Chronicler frequently names one or more works where further information may be obtained. The sources with historical titles are the following: (1) 'Book of the Kings of Israel and Judah', 1 Chr 9:1 (registration of the people); 2 Chr 27:7 (Jotham); 35:27 (Josiah); 36:8 (Jehoiakim); (2) 'The Book of the Kings of Judah and Israel', 2 Chr 25:26 (Amaziah); 28:26 (Ahaz); 32:32 (Hezekiah); (3) 'Book of the Kings of Judah and Israel', 2 Chr 16:11 (Asa), the title differing from (2) in grammatical construction only; (4) 'Book of the Kings of Israel', 2 Chr 20:34 (Josaphat); (5) 'Acts of the Kings of Israel', 2 Chr 33:18 (Joash). (6) 'Study (Midrash) of the Book of Kings', 2 Chr 24:27 (Joash).

As books used not to have titles, a fixed and definite **298** nomenclature is hardly to be expected, and there is no reason to doubt that (1), (2) and (3) represent the same work, and they are probably identical with (4), (5) and (6).

The sources named after prophets and seers are the following: (1) 'The Acts (or Words) of Samuel the Seer', 1 Chr 29:29 (David); (2) 'The Acts of Nathan the Prophet', 1 Chr 29:29 (David); 2 Chr 9:29 (Solomon); (3) 'The Acts of Gad the Seer', 1 Chr 29:29 (David); (4) 'The Prophecy of Ahijah the Shilonite', 2 Chr 9:29 (Solomon); (5) 'The Vision of Iddo the Seer concerning Jeroboam the Son of Nabat', 2 Chr 9:29 (Solomon); 'The Acts of Iddo the Seer', 12:15 (Rehoboam); 'The Study (Midrash; or, Investigation) of the Prophet Iddo', 13:22 (Abijah); (6) 'The Acts of Shemaiah the Prophet', 12:15 (Rehoboam); (7) 'The Acts of Jehu, the Son of Hanani', 20:34 (Jehoshaphat); (8) 'The history of Uzziah was written by Isaiah the prophet, the Son of Amoz', 26:22; 'The Vision of Isaiah the Prophet, the Son of Amoz', 32:32 (Hezekiah); (9) 'The Acts of Hozai' or 'The Acts of the Seers', 33:19 (Manasseh). Opinions differ considerably about the number and independent existence of these writings. Of (7) 'The Acts of Jehu' the text says explicitly that they were recorded (or incorporated) into the book of the Kings of Israel. In the case of (8) the history of Uzziah' could be a separate record now lost or perhaps part of the 'Vision of Isaiah' (2 Chr 32:32) which itself may have been part of the Book of the Kings of Judah and Israel. Furthermore, there is an opinion which holds that all these works were known to the Chronicler as parts of one large history to be identified with that called 'The Book of the Kings of Israel and Judah'. This is very likely because of the common Jewish opinion that Jos-Kgs was written by prophets who lived at the time of the events described in these books.

The genealogies in 1 Chr 1:1—9:44 are taken from unnamed sources. 1:1—2:5 is from Gn and the subsequent information could in part be derived from Ex, Nm, Jos, Ru and Sm-Kgs, but other parts as 2:14—15, are from non-canonical sources.

The historical work called 'The Book of the Kings of **e** Israel and Judah' etc cannot be identified with our Sm-Kgs as the former contained various facts not to be found in the latter: 1 Chr 9:1, the genealogies; 2 Chr 27:7, victories of Jotham; 33:18, the prayer of Manasseh. Whether Sm-Kgs was itself a source is controverted. The affirmative has been asserted on the grounds of the close verbal resemblance, the common textual errors, the grouping of facts, the order followed and in particular by comparison of parallel passages where mistakes of Chr can only be explained by misunderstanding of Kgs. These facts make it difficult to accept the hypothesis of a common source used both by Kgs and Chr which is proposed by Rothstein-Haenel, Goettsberger and Rehm. The fact that Chr adds many details not recorded in Kgs makes it clear that Kgs was not the only source at the Chronicler's disposal. The similarities and differences are best explained by the use of Sm-Kgs as a basic source which was supplemented by other sources which were available to Chr. Rudolph suggests that a later expanded edition of Kgs was at the disposal of Chr for the post-Salomonic history.

Reference is also made to genealogical registers drawn up in the time of Jotham and Jeroboam, 1 Chr 5:17, to 'The Annals of King David', 27:24, and to a collection of Lamentations, 2 Chr 35:25, different from that still extant. There is no reason to doubt that Chr also used oral traditions.

298e Granted that Chr did use Sm-Kgs as a source, as most modern scholars hold, it is evident that the manner in which Chr uses this source gives us a clear insight into his literary method and consequently enables us to form a reasonable judgement on his value as a historian and his purpose as a writer.

f Literary genre—The determination of the kind of literature to which Chr belongs will determine the message which God wishes to convey to us through the human author (cf § 48b). The Chronicler is, like all biblical authors, primarily a religious author; Chr is a theological rather than a historical work, written primarily to foster religion not to tell the story of the past. It is nevertheless true that many biblical works, while written to foster religion, intend to do so by narrating facts, even though they do not and could not deal with their materials in the manner of a 20th cent. historian. We must try to discover what the author wishes to convey to us, for that is what God, the Eternal Truth, wishes to convey. The Chronicler intends, as do the other authors of the historical books of the Bible, to face and interpret the history of God's action in his people. He tells us this history of the kingdom of God from Adam to the fall of Jerusalem and his purpose in doing so is, as we have seen, to show that the Davidic dynasty and the Temple of Jerusalem are the divinely chosen and sole legitimate incarnation of the kingdom of God and to encourage his fellow Judeans in obedient and joyful service of this kingdom and its God. To do this he uses materials which he found in various sources, canonical and non-canonical, written and oral. Since his purpose is not primarily to relate the past but to prove a thesis and to encourage his fellow countrymen, he feels himself free to use these materials as they seem helpful for the purpose he has in mind. We are fortunate in that, by comparing his text with that of Sm-Kgs, we can examine rather closely the way in which he uses his sources and seeing him at work understand the kind of book he intended to produce and consequently the kind of truth he wished to convey.

g Interpretation of sources—The Chronicler and his readers had a profound knowledge of and a deep reverence for the scriptural books upon which he drew. There could be no question of his wishing to deceive his readers. Yet he does alter these books by omissions, additions, qualifications, interpretations etc. In fact, while reverencing these works, he does not hesitate to interpret them, or to add to them in such a way that his work is, in great part, rather a theological meditation on and development of the facts than a presentation of the facts themselves. It appears then that here we have a special kind of literature, primarily theological, and only in a very qualified sense historical, which is moving towards that kind of literature that was later known as Midrash: a meditation sometimes sober, sometimes fanciful on the biblical text with a view to drawing some lesson for the practical life of the reader.

h Use of Sm-Kgs—How then does he use his sources, in particular Sm-Kgs? Sometimes his treatment of Sm-Kgs suggests that he had in general no more information than his source (2 Chr 36:3 betrays the same ignorance of the number of talents of gold imposed on Judah as tribute by Neco as 2 (4) Kgs 23:33 on which he clearly depends). This would seem to indicate that, while he had other sources besides Sm-Kgs, he did not possess a complete work covering the period from David to the exile and more extensive than the canonical work. If this be the case, we must assume that, where he is describing events which are paralleled in Sm-Kgs, we

are not entitled invariably to suppose that he had other **298h** sources and we are justified in making the general statement that his changes of Sm-Kgs are based on literary and theological grounds rather than on historical information. His use of the text of Sm-Kgs is, therefore, of the highest importance in assessing the personality and purpose of the Chronicler. He can be seen to be a highly intelligent writer, master of the other OT works and a skilled interpreter of them. Wellhausen's assessment of him in his *Prolegomena*, in which he treats the Chronicler almost as an imbecile, is no longer accepted by scholars. Besides it has been shown (e.g. Mazar art cit) that where the Chronicler has additional information and there is no reason to suspect any theological intention, he is an extremely reliable witness whose statements can occasionally be supported by archaeological or other extra-biblical evidence.

Where he modifies his sources the reasons are theological and can usually be discerned rather easily. The treatment of Manasseh, for example, is to be explained by his strong faith in short term retribution for good and evil. Because of this theological belief, he knew that Manasseh's long reign must be a reward for virtue. But the Manasseh of 2 Kgs 21 is the very type of evil. Therefore 2 Chr 33 explains that he was exiled in punishment for his sin and that as a result of his exile he repented, was restored to God's favour and rewarded with a long and happy reign. It is probable that the historical fact behind this theological explanation is that Manasseh was involved in the widespread revolt against Assyria about 650 and was in fact called to account by Ashurbanipal.

Liturgical emphasis—In the postexilic period, when **i** the Chronicler was writing, liturgical life and religious chant had become the very heart of the life of the people of God. The Chronicler saw in this a true fulfilment of the work of David and Solomon and so referred the full glory of the cult of his own time to the time of his hero, David. Here again there is a certain historical foundation for this in that David was the inaugurator of the cult of Yahweh in Jerusalem and was known to have been a composer of music and chant, Amos 6:5. It is at least not unlikely that he did organize systematically the liturgical worship that reached such splendour in the postexilic period. It is probable too that the Chronicler saw in the great importance which the office of high-priest attained in the postexilic period a fulfilment to a great extent of the promises made to David. For David and his successors are rightly seen by him to be theocratic rulers and their failure had for him to some extent been redeemed by the establishment of a theocracy under the high-priest. It was probably to indicate the legitimacy of this succession of priest to king that he shows David principally as the great fosterer of priestly and liturgical splendour. It is for this reason also that he gives such great prominence to Abijah, Jehoshaphat, Hezekiah and Josiah.

In judging the historical value—therefore of the **j** Chronicler's account of pre-exilic Judah, we must distinguish between those passages in which his theological preoccupations are evident and those in which the matter described is, as it were, theologically neutral. In neutral passages e.g. the account of Rehoboam's fortification of Judah, there seems to be no reason to doubt the strictly historical character of his narrative. In the other passages, however, we should be doing an injustice to him, were we to judge him merely as an historian. Since, for him, history is a handmaid of theology, it is the theological understanding that is

298j important for him, not the naked historical fact. If he clothes this naked fact with somewhat imaginary adornments, we must accept this as his method of teaching theology and not reproach him for the lack of an historical exactness which a comparison between his text and that of Sm-Kgs shows that he never intended. On other matters, which were not affected by the Chronicler's special point of view and purposes, historical value is recognized in his traditions. Thus M. Noth, in *Überlieferungsgeschichtliche Studien* is of opinion that Chr had preexilic sources for the history of the kings only for Hezekiah's tunnel, 2 Chr 32:30, for the last battle and death of Josiah, 35:20—24, and for various reports about the defensive works of the kings of Judah and their wars. But, as pointed out by A. Bea, in Bib 27 (1946) 145—6, if these reports are from ancient and reliable sources, there is every likelihood that other reports are similarly derived, and that the contrary must not be assumed but requires proof, which is not forthcoming.

k **The numbers** given are sometimes incredibly high. Thus Abijah had an army of 400,000 men and Jeroboam of 800,000, 2 Chr 13:3. Taken alone this could mean the total number of men who could be called up. This would avoid the difficulty of such vast armies being engaged at one and the same time, but the difficulty would remain that the figures would suppose a total population larger than the small country of Palestine could support. Actually the explanation is ruled out by 13:17, which says that 500,000 of Jeroboam's army were victims of the battle. Another suggested explanation is that 'thousand' stands for a fighting unit of that nominal number, though in fact it might be much under strength. But Jehoshaphat is credited with 1,160,000 fighting men, or on this explanation 1,160 regiments of nominally 1,000 men, 2 Chr 17:14—18. Even on the supposition that no unit was at more than half strength, the figures still leave an army of over 500,000 men. The problem is not confined to Chr, and seems to be a characteristic of Heb. historiography, a literary convention, understood and admitted as such by these ancient writers and their readers.

l **Doctrine**—The doctrine about God, as is customary in the Bible, is mostly concerned with his relations with man, but has some important lessons about God as he is in himself. The Chronicler is a strict monotheist who knows no god but Yahweh. God's universal presence is adumbrated in that 'heaven, even highest heaven, cannot contain him', 2 Chr 2:6. Nothing escapes his knowledge because 'the eyes of the Lord run to and fro throughout the whole earth', 2 Chr 16:9. In his hand is 'power and might', 1 Chr 29:12, and 'none is able to withstand' him, 2 Chr 20:6. 'All that is in the heavens and in the earth is' his, 1 Chr 29:11, so that man can give to God only what he has received from the divine bounty, 1 Chr 29:14.

But God does not live in glorious isolation in heaven; he is *the omnipotent ruler of the world*. His rule is based on perfect knowledge, for 'the Lord searches all hearts and understands every plan and thought', 1 Chr 28:9, and it extends to 'all the kingdoms of the nations', 2 Chr 20:6. His will prevails 'for God has power to help or to cast down', 2 Chr 25:8. Theologically the doctrine of God's providential government of the world is inchoate, since the problem of the harmonious working of God's rule and man's free will had not yet presented itself and no distinction is made between God's absolute and his permissive will. In fact an even greater stress than in Sm-Kgs is laid on the divine activity as opposed to

and almost as excluding human causality. Thus it was **298l** the will of God that Rehoboam should not condescend to the people's petition, 2 Chr 10:15. So too Ahaziah's visit to Joram that resulted in his death, 2 Chr 22:7, and of Amaziah's disastrous decision to make war on Joash of Israel, 2 Chr 25:20.

Retribution—As the just ruler of the world and **m** guardian of the moral order God must punish evil and reward good. But as the doctrine of retribution in the after life had not yet been revealed, this could be envisaged only in terms of prosperity and disaster in this world. In this Chr merely reflects teaching that had been handed on from the Pent. Jg, Kgs, and various Psalms. The doctrine has frequent application in our book. In the matter of punishment, from the death of Saul for his iniquities, 1 Chr 10:13—14, to the final destruction of Jerusalem and end of the kingdom, 2 Chr 36:13—17, and in the matter of reward, from the promise of David, 1 Chr 12—13, to that of Hezekiah, 2 Chr 30:8 f. But Chr presents the doctrine of retribution in a strictly mathematical and short term manner. It is not enough for him that sins be punished and virtue rewarded in this life. Justice must not merely be done, it must be seen to be done. Prosperity is always the immediate reward of virtue, suffering is always the immediate punishment for vice. If necessary, he will find reasons for prosperity and misery, even when the reasons are not given in his original source. The cases of Rehoboam, 2 Chr 12:1ff, Asa, 2 Chr 16:7ff, Uzziah, 2 Chr 26:16ff, and especially Manasseh 2 Chr 33 are symbolic. All the later biblical writers were faced with this problem of the reconciliation of God's justice and human wickedness. They knew that God was not mocked. It is this basic teaching that Chr conveys in this rather too rigorous manner. 'His retribution comes with a promptness and mathematical proportion which would be justly ridiculed if taken as assertion of historical fact. But as enunciations of the transcendental relations of a Big Being to little beings they are profoundly valid' (North art cit). He also wished to show that each man and each generation must face God and his revelation and that no one can escape the personal responsibility for his personal choice. But though God is just, 'his mercy is very great', 1 Chr 21:13, and in his mercy he is always ready to forgive, 2 Chr 30:9. He hears and answers the prayers of men, 2 Chr 7:12—16, even to the extent of granting a miracle, 2 Chr 32:24. Even one like Manasseh, whose iniquities had provoked God to anger, is heard and forgiven in answer to repentant prayer, 2 Chr 33:6, 12f. For though the service of God is light compared to the service of earthly princes, 2 Chr 12:8, man is very frail and 'there is no man who does not sin', 2 Chr 6:36, and a perfect heart to keep God's commandments can come only from him, 1 Chr 29:19; 2 Chr 30:12.

Covenant—Though God rules the whole world, yet he **n** deigned to establish an intimate divine relationship to Israel. He chose it out from all others and called it 'my people', 1 Chr 11:2. The covenant which he made with Abraham remained as 'an everlasting covenant' with Israel 1 Chr 16:16f. It is remarkable that Chr makes no reference to the great covenant with Moses but, like St Paul, stresses the choice of the people in Abraham. He passes on then to the choice of David which he also describes as a covenant as well as a promise 2 Chr 7:18; 13:5. This covenant is also a grace not due to any merits of Israel or David 1 Chr 17:7—15. It was he who chose David to be king, 1 Chr 11:2—3; 14:2; 17:7; 28:4; 2 Chr 6:6. He chose Solomon to be his successor, 1 Chr 17:11—12; 22:9; 28:5—7; 2 Chr 1:8; 6:10. More than

298n that, God promised David a dynasty that should rule for ever, 1 Chr 17:17, 13—27. Sometimes this promise is accompanied by the condition of fidelity, 2 Chr 6:16; 7:17—22. Sometimes it is unconditional, 2 Chr 13:5; 21:7.

o **Messianism**—The reality and content of the Messianic hope of the Chronicler causes considerable difficulty, if we believe that Chr-Ez-Neh form one book. Were Chr considered by itself there could be no doubt but that it is full of the messianic hope. The book is written at a period when the Jews formed an infinitesimally small part of the immense Persian Empire, and yet it treats of the history of the whole human race beginning with Adam as finding its meaning in this obscure city and people hidden in the hills of Judah. Having described and stressed God's choice of and eternal promise to David and his sons, Chr concludes with a passage which points directly to the restoration of God's people after the apparent annihilation of the Babylonian exile. He shows that the temple cult, the levitical priesthood and the sacred song which now form the heart of the life of God's people are the result of God's choice of David. For Chr the outstanding messengers of God are the prophets, whose teaching is full of the messianic hope in the Davidic line. He raises the promise to David and his sons to the level of a covenant and seems to hint by his omission of the Mosaic covenant that in the Davidic line rather than in the Mosaic law is to be found the fulfilment of the everlasting covenant made with Abraham. By narrating the glorious works of God through David in the past, he surely intends to remind his readers of the glorious promises to the new David of the prophets which are to be fulfilled in the future. Surely he could not have believed that the high-priestly rule and the temple services of his own day were the accomplishment of all that God had promised to David's line and that in these Jewish institutions there was no place for the house of David except as a glorious but long past memory; that the theocracy established in David had reached its fulfilment in the hierarchy of post-exilic Jerusalem. So far is this from being the case that he looks back with nostalgia to the days of David and of his faithful descendants e.g. Hezekiah and Josiah, and holds these wonderful days up as a model and therefore presumably, since God is faithful to his word, as an ideal that must yet be attained. To sum up, it is quite unbelievable that the Chronicler, who of all biblical writers is the most attached to David and his line, should believe that the promise made to David and his line by a 'covenant of salt' should be broken so as never to be accomplished.

p   Yet there is, at least at first sight, very little if any messianism in Ez-Neh, which is part of the same book. On closer examination however, we find hints of hope of a future restoration in these books particularly in the prayers. In Ez 9:7—9 and Neh 9:36 the Chronicler shows that he realizes the humble state of the Jews in the Persian Empire as bondsmen and slaves and implies a prayer for liberation. Surely this means that he does not consider their present situation as the full and perfect realization of the 'everlasting covenant, my steadfast, sure love for David' Is 55:3 which is the whole theme of Chr. We may explain the reticence of the Chronicler about the Davidic hope in Ez-Neh by the fact that he is writing under a foreign government which, while it might tolerate a description of the past glories of a subject race such as we find in Chr, was not likely to look with favour on any indications that this subject race was living in the hope of a return of these past glories or rather in the hope of a far greater liberty and glory in the future. The foreign ruler could certainly **298p** permit an admission that the present lowly state of Judah was a punishment for past sin but he would regard as treason any suggestion that this lowly state was to be ended by a glorious restoration to independence under a native and ancient line of kings. Nevertheless, we do find an interesting hint of the messianic hope in 2 Chr 6:42, where the Chronicler makes a significant addition to the text of 1 Kgs 8 in the prayer of Solomon at the dedication of the temple. He adds a quotation from Ps 132 (131), a clearly messianic psalm, in which God is insistently reminded of his promise of loyalty to David and his people: 'O Lord God, do not turn away the face of thy anointed one! Remember thy steadfast love for David thy servant'. This discreet but significant addition to the text of Kgs is surely significant of the hopes of the Chronicler as he writes his book under a foreign yoke.

The conditional promises referred to the temporal rule that came to an end through prolonged infidelity, 2 Chr 36:13—17. The unconditional promises referred to the spiritual rule of Christ, the second David, of whom it was foretold that 'he will reign over the house of Jacob forever', Lk 1:32. Herein lies the true fulfilment of the messianic hope of our book.

Faithful to his promise, Dt 18:18—22, God raised up q a **long succession of prophets** to guide, warn and rebuke his people: Nathan, 1 Chr 17:1, and Gad, 1 Chr 21:9 (David); Ahijah, 2 Chr 10:15 (Solomon); Shemaiah, 11:2; 12:5 (Rehoboam); Iddo, 13:22 (Abijah); Azariah, 15:1, and Hanani, 16:7 (Asa); Micaiah the son of Imlah, 18:7ff. (Ahab and Jehoshaphat); Jehu, the son of Hanani, 19:2, Jahaziel, 20:14, and Eliezer, 20:37 (Jehoshaphat); Elijah, 21:12 (Jehoram); unnamed prophets, 24:19, and Zechariah, the son of Jehoiada, 24:20 (Joash); an unnamed man of God, 25:7, and a prophet, 24:15 (Amaziah); Oded in Samaria, 28:9 (Ahaz); seers, 33:18 (Manasseh); messengers of God and prophets, 36:15—16 (Zedekiah).

Despite the vivid consciousness of Israel's privileged election our book is not hostile in principle to other nations, though it rigorously defends the unique position of the Jerusalem shrine as the only place where true sacrifice is to be offered. The praise of God is put in the mouth of Hiram, king of Tyre, 2 Chr 2:11—12, and of the queen of Sheba, 9:8. Appeal is made to the nations to come and adore God's presence symbolized by the ark, 1 Chr 16:28—29. The renown of the temple is to spread to all nations, 1 Chr 22—25. Solomon prays that the prayer of strangers who adore in the temple may be heard from heaven, 'that all the peoples of the earth may know' the name of God and serve him, 2 Chr 6:32—33.

Worship of the heart—It would not be fair to the r Chronicler to overstress, as some critics do, the ritualistic nature of his religion. It is true that external sacrifice according to the prescribed rites is of great importance to him but his stress on the special place of the levites to whom he shows himself much more favourable than to the priests and in particular his description of their vocation as 'to invoke, to thank and to praise the Lord, the God of Israel' 1 Chr 16:4, his love for sacred music and his stress on the virtue of humility reveal him as more than a mere ritualist but a worshipper in spirit and truth. This stress on the worship of the heart shines out especially in the prayer of Hezekiah 2 Chr 30:18, 19: 'The good Lord pardon everyone who sets his heart to seek God, the Lord God of his fathers, even though not according to the sanctuary's rules of cleanness'. In fact, the remarkable omission of the Mosaic covenant

298r and his stressing of the covenants of Abraham and David show him to be not nearly as much under the influence of the theology of P as at first sight appears. The main influence on his theology is rather D with its stress on localization of worship at Jerusalem and its strong teaching on retribution which Chr tends to develop even more systematically, as we have seen in the case of Manasseh. This inclination to D, so much less ritualistic than P, so much more inclined to the religion of the heart, is revealed also in the truly spiritual concept that Chr has of the relationship of God in cult.

s **Author**—In the Babylonian Talmud, Baba Bathra 15a, Ezra is listed as the author of the book that bears his name (= Ez-Neh) and of the genealogies of Chr. Nicolaus Lyranus extended this authorship to the whole of Chr, and in this view found many adherents down into the 19th cent. But it is incompatible with the common authorship and the lower date of Ez-Neh advocated by many. Very few modern authors agree with Albright in JBL XL (1921), 104—24 who holds for the authorship of Ezra on the grounds of similarity of style and manner between Chr and the Memoirs of Ezra. The question arises as to whether Chr is the work of one author or of two. Quite a number of scholars e.g. Galling, Rothstein-Haenel and Welch refer to two authors, one who wrote relatively early in the postexilic era and another who wrote fairly close to the Maccabean period. Their arguments, which are essentially based on textual and literary criticism have not won the assent of the majority of scholars. All modern commentators admit the existence of additions to the one original work, particularly in 1 Chr 1—9 and 23—27. Nevertheless the book as a whole shows a unity of outlook and style that can be explained only with difficulty if we assume the existence of more than one author. It should be pointed out that this question is not of major importance since it is the book as contained in the Bible in its final form, whether written by one or by many authors, that is the inspired work and that communicates to us the Word of God. The prevailing view is that no more can be said than that the interest manifest in the Levites, including the singers and the doorkeepers, suggests that the author was a Levite and probably one of the latter classes.

THE FIRST BOOK OF CHRONICLES

299a **1:1—10:14 Genealogical Introduction**—The purpose of this section is to show the preparation of the Davidic kingdom towards which all human history is directed. The Chronicler uses mainly biblical sources but he uses them with a freedom which we do not always understand though his general aim is clear: to emphasize that through the tribes of Judah and Levi God was and is working to establish his kingdom on earth. Sometimes we can make a guess at the reason for variations from the source e.g. it has been suggested that some otherwise inexplicable omissions are due to a certain prudishness which the Chronicler occasionally reveals. An example of this would be the omission of Onan's sin in 1 Chr 2:3 as compared with Gn 38. Sometimes the variations are due to a confusion in the original text between different but similar letters (e.g. *Hadar* Gn 36:39 = *Hadad* 1 Chr 1:50). Sometimes we must simply confess our ignorance. The names are partly personal and partly territorial. The genealogy is a literary form which was much used by biblical authors (cf Gn 5; Lk 3) but with whose laws we are not fully acquainted. It is a natural form in a people whose religion was closely linked with membership of the race. One fairly regular characteristic of

this literary form is what we may call the method of **299** exclusion. Thus in 1 Chr 1:5—23 we find the genealogy of the sons of Noah. The sons who are of no great interest to the author viz Japheth and Ham and their descendants are dealt with first and thus cleared out of the way and we hear no more about them. Then Chr goes on to deal with the important son Shem and his descendants.
1:1—27 From Adam to Abraham—1—4. The **b** antediluvian patriarchs. Gn 5:1—31. **5—23.** The Table of the Nations from Gn 10. **17.** After 'Aram' insert with one Heb. MS and LXX (A) 'and the sons of Aram', Gn 10:23. The form 'Meshech', which may be due to a reminiscence of the name in 5, is replaced by *Mash* in some Heb. MSS and Syr. in agreement with Gn 10:23. **24—27.** The postdiluvian patriarchs from Gn 11:10—26. **27.** For the change of Abram's name see Gn 17:5.
28—34 From Abraham to Israel—28. For the birth of Isaac see Gn 21:1—4, and of Ishmael, the elder but named second as of less importance, Gn 16:15. The list of Ishmael's descendants, **29—31**, is from Gn 25:13—15. 'Hadad' not the 'Hadar' of Gn 36:39. These two final letters are often confused in Heb. and the textual evidence varies in both places. The names of the sons of Keturah in **32—33** are taken from Gn 25:1—4. **34.** The sons of Isaac, unlike those of Abraham in 28, are given in the order of birth, Gn 25:25, and Jacob, Israel's original name, Gn 32:28 is not mentioned. Here as always Chr uses the sacred name Israel and never the natural name Jacob. Jacob's importance consisted solely in his covenant with God, 1 Chr 16:17 by which he became father of God's people. **35—54. The sons of Esau—35—37**, from Gn 36:10—13. **38—42.** The sons of Seir. Seir is the country of Edom. The names in this series seem to be collectivities and this explains **42** where 'the sons of Anah' is followed by only one name. We may presume that in other passages where the same phenomenon occurs the reference is to a tribe or clan rather than to a person. **43—50.** The kings of Edom, Gn 36:31—39. **51—54.** The chiefs of Edom, Gn 36:40—43. Edom is developed to show that Abraham is the father of many nations, Gn 17:5. The series is brought down to David who ended the native Edomite kingdom; thus even in the non-Israelite line attention is drawn to the great hero.
2:1—8:40 From Israel to David—'Having in ch 1 **c** brought humanity to Israel, the father of the promise, the author now faces the question—a very important one in his day—as to which elements of the people still belonged to the people of God's promise. This people in his time consisted of Judah, Benjamin and Levi and strove by interior and exterior loyalty to the Law and by care for the purity of the race (cf Ez-Neh) to bring to fulfilment the promise in a theocracy. This was especially important for Judah which had absorbed in the course of its history many elements which were not originally of Israelite origin. He had to legitimize these elements as true recipients of the promise' van den Born op cit p. 22. In these sections it is not always easy to follow the methods and purpose of the Chronicler in detail. The omission of Zebulun and the double genealogies of Benjamin; the fact that sometimes he follows and sometimes ignores the biblical sources especially Gn 46:8—25 and Nm 26:5—51; that sometimes he adds narrative passages and sometimes sticks strictly to genealogy; all these facts cannot be explained fully. Sometimes we must presume that he had a defective source and at other times we must suppose that other hands have been at work adding to and editing the original draft. While uncertainty remains, the main stresses are clear.

299c David and Levi, Throne and Temple receive the lion's share of the author's attention. While the historically important tribes of Ephraim and Manasseh are handled very briefly because of their links with the N kingdom and with the Samaritans, Benjamin receives special attention as the tribe that remained loyal to the Davidic line and came after the exile to form with Judah and Levi the true Israel of God's promise.

d 2:1–4:23 The tribe of Judah—Judah naturally comes first and receives most attention. As there was relatively little material about Judah in the biblical sources, Chr is obliged to use other sources, oral and written, and the combined result is not always easy to follow. There are probably also later additions and transfers. **3–4** come from Gn 38. The theme of God's retribution for sin appears even here in the genealogies. The sin of Onan is omitted in Chr probably from natural delicacy, which appears to be a trait of the Chronicler. **5.** Gn 46:12. **7.** Again a reference to punishment for sin. As Carmi has not been mentioned previously the words 'and the son of Zabdi: Carmi' have probably dropped out; see Jos 7:1. For 'Achar' read 'Achan' with some MSS here and Jos 7:1, MT Vg. **8.** Azariah, only here. **9.** Jerahmeel, only in this ch. Ram (Variant, Aram), Ru 4:19. Chelubai appears in 18 as Caleb. **10–17.** The sons of Ram **10–12.** Ru 4:19–22. **13.** 1 Sm 17:13. **14–15:** except David only here. **16.** Zeruiah only here mentioned as sister of David; her sons, 2 Sm 2:18. Abigail is called the daughter of Nahash in 2 Sm 17:25 and will have been David's stepsister. **17.** 2 Sm 17:25. **18–20.** The sons of Caleb; cf 9. This genealogy may be an allegory of the movement of the Calebites from a semi-nomadic to a sedentary life. For Azubah the name of Caleb's first wife means 'the deserted one' and probably refers to the semi-nomadic life in the Negeb, while Ephrath probably refers to the area around Bethlehem where the Calebites eventually settled. The other names are otherwise unknown except Hur and Uri, Ex 31:2, and Ephrath, the daughter of Machir, 21, 24. The interest of the list for the Chronicler centres in Bezalel, the craftsman responsible for the tabernacle and its furniture. **21–24.** Further on Hesron, **23** Geshur: a territory in N Transjordania; Kenath **e** prob. the modern Qanawat, W of the Hauran. **24.** 'Ephrathah, the wife of Hezron his father', a marriage forbidden by Lv 18:8. Ashhur = Hur, 19; 4:5. **25–41.** The descendants of Jerahmeel, 9; cf 1 Sm 27:10; 30:29. **31.** As Sheshan had no son, 34, Ahlai will have been a daughter. The Jerahmeelites lived in the Negeb and so in proximity to Egypt, 1 Sm 27:10. **36.** Zabad, 11:41. **42–55.** The sons of Caleb, 9, 18. **42.** Some of the descendants of Caleb are presented as the fathers or founders of towns in Judah. Ziph = modern Tell Zif, S. of Hebron. Some names seem to have fallen out after 'Mareshah'. **43.** Tappuah, a town, Jos 15:34. **45.** Ma'on, Jos 15:55, today Tell Ma'in, S of Hebron. Beth-zur, Jos 15:58, N of Hebron. **47.** Jahdai's name, which occurs here for the first time, must have dropped out from the previous list. **49.** Madmannah, Jos 15:31. A name has prob. fallen out before 'the father of Gibea'. As only those women are included in genealogies who played some part in history, it is hard to resist the conclusion that this Achsah is the daughter of Caleb, the son of Jephunneh, Jos 15:16, Jg 1:12. Probably, therefore, the sentence is an interpolation here, for Caleb, the son of Jephunneh, is called a Kenizzite, Jos 14:6, 14, though closely connected with the tribe of Judah, Jg 1:10–12, while for Chr he is a pure Judean. **50.** Kiriathjearim, a city of Judah, Jos 15:60. **51.** Bethgader, perhaps Kh.

Jedûr, NW of Hebron. **52.** 'Shobal the father of **299e** Kiriathjearim had sons: Rea'ya. Half of Manahath and the families of Kiriathjearim were the Ithrites . . . .' **53.** Of the clans of Kiriathjearim the Ithrites are mentioned 2 Sm 23:38. Sor'a, now Sar'a, near Beth-Shemesh; Eshtaol, Jos 15:33. The clans are the inhabitants of the neighbouring localities. **54.** Netopha, SW of Bethlehem. Manahath and Sor'a had mixed populations, 52, 53. **55.** The Kenites were a non-Israelite tribe that came to be closely associated with Judah. As Hammath is clearly a place name, Beth Rechab 'the house of Rechab' is clearly a place name also.

David was introduced in 2:15. **3:1–4.** The sons **f** of David born in Hebron, 2 Sm 3:2–5. The second son is called Daniel in Chr, and Cheleab in Sm. Possibly he had two names. **5–8.** David's sons born in Jerusalem, 2 Sm 5:14–16 and repeated in 1 Chr 14:4–7. **5.** Shimea, differently vocalized in Sm and 14:4. Ammiel is called Eliam in 2 Sm 11:3, with inversion of the two elements of the name; cf the inversion in Ahaziah, 3:11, and Jehoahaz, 2 Chr 21:17. **6.** Elisama is the name of a brother, 8, and is here a scribal error for Elisua, the form given in the other lists. **7.** Eliphelet appears here by dittography from 8 as in 14:5, but not in Sm. Nogah also is given in 14:6, but not in Sm. Two of the letters are the same as in Nepheg, of which it is prob. a duplicate. **8.** Eliada, which corresponds to Baaliada in 14:7, is an altered form with elimination of Baal which came to be associated with pagan worship. The number '9' which is additional to the '4' in 5, was added after the list had received accretions. **9.** 2 Sm 5.10, 10.1. **10 21.** The descendants of David. This section is probably secondary as Chr never elsewhere uses the form Azariah for Uzziah. **10** picks up the thread from 5. **15.** Johanan does not occur in Sm and prob. died before or with his father. Shallum, Jer 22:11, was also called Jehoahaz, prob. as a throne-name. On the evidence of the ages and length of Jehoiakim's reign given in 2 (4) Kgs 23.31, 30, 24.18, Shallum was born before Zedekiah and is mentioned last here perhaps as a sign of degradation, Jer 22:10–12; Ezek 19:3f. **16.** Zedekiah, otherwise unknown. **19.** Zerub- **g** babel is styled the son of Shealtiel, 17, in Ez 3:2 etc. Prob. Pedaiah was his true father and Shealtiel only in the legal sense, Dt 25:5f. **20.** Either the number '5' has been wrongly copied or names have been wrongly added to the text or, more probably, the words 'Sons of Meshullam' have been omitted at the beginning of the verse. **21–22.** Zerubbabel returned from Babylon shortly after the decree of Cyrus, 538 B.C., and Shemaiah, the son of Shecaniah, worked on the building of the wall of Jerusalem, Neh 3:29, with Nehemiah, who returned from exile in 445 B.C. In this interval of time it is difficult to fit all the generations supposed by RSV. However the text is uncertain and is understood by some in the sense that Hananiah was the father of all named in 21. Shemaiah would thus be in the third generation from Zerubbabel. Hattush seems to be called the son of Shecaniah, Ez 8:2f. **23.** Elioenai returned with Ezra, Ez 8:4. **24.** According to the suggestions made on 21–22 it is not certain that this list allows more than six generations inclusive of Zerubbabel.

4:1–23. Further Judahite genealogies—1. Carmi, **300a** 2:7. If this name is changed from Chelubai = Caleb we have a list of descendants in the direct line, 2:4, 5, 9, 19, 50. **3–4.** Text seems to be corrupt here. Etam, 2 Chr 11:6, Jezreel, Jos 15:56, Gedor, Jos 15:58, are towns in Judah. Ephrathah, 2:19. In 2:51 Salma, the son of Hur, is called father of Bethlehem. Such a

300a metaphorical fatherhood could well be predicated of both father and son. **5—7.** Ashhur; see on 2:24. **7.** 'And Koz' should be added at the end of this verse. **9—10.** Jabez in 2:55 a local, here a personal, name. 'Jabez' is associated with the root '*ʂ'b*, which means 'pain'. As the Hebrews attached great importance to the meaning of names, a prayer is inserted here to avert the effect of an unlucky name. **11—12.** The identification of this Chelub as the brother of Shuhah seems to distinguish him from the Caleb of 2:42. **13—14.** Othniel Jg 1:13; 3:9. Ophrah was a city of Benjamin, Jos 18:23, to which tribe belonged also the valley of craftsmen, Neh 11:35. **15—20.** These vv are very fragmentary. **15.** This Caleb, son of Jephunneh, may be the same as the Chelub of 11. **17.** Eshtemoa: a city of Judah, Jos 15:50. MT has 'she begot Miriam', suggesting that a mention of the Egyptian wife, 18, has fallen out. This explains also in 18 the distinction made: 'his Jewish wife'. Gedor; see on 4. There were two places named Soco in Judah, Jos 15:35, 48, also two called Zanoah, Jos 15:34, 56. **19.** opens with an uncertain text. Keilah, Jos 15:44; Maacathite a region SW of Mt Hermon. **20.** Another unconnected fragment. **21.** Shelah, 2:3. Mareshah, Jos 15:44.

b **4:24—43 The tribe of Simeon**—Simeon is dealt with here because of ancient links with Judah, which tribe eventually absorbed Simeon to a great extent. **28—33.** The territory of Simeon, Jos 19:1—9. Bethberi in 31 is prob. corrupted from Bethlebaoth in Jos. On Ziklag in David's time see 1 Sm 27:5f. Etam: in the territory of Judah as noted Jos 19:9. **34—38.** Leading men of Simeon. The tribes were divided, 38, into clans and the clans into families. **39—43.** Territorial conquests. **39.** 'And they went to the confines of Gerara', LXX. As the former inhabitants were non-Israelite, they felt justified in seizing their lands, Dt 7:2. **41.** 'and destroyed ... the Meunim who were found there'. Ma'on was the place SE of Petra whence they had wandered. The time indicated, 'to this day', is that of the Chronicler's source which cannot be fixed. So too in 43. **42—43.** The mountainous country of Seir (Edom) extended S of the Dead Sea. Saul's war against Amalek 1 Sm 15:7f, and David's, 2 Sm 8:12. The names of the captains occur only here and do not help to fix the date of this event.

c **5:1—26. The Transjordan tribes**—**1—10.** The tribe of Reuben. **1.** Reuben's crime, Gn 35:22. **2.** Joseph, reckoned as the firstborn, had the privilege of a double portion of the inheritance, Dt 21:17. Hence the double territory of Ephraim and Manasseh the two tribes descended from him. **3.** Gn 46:9. **6.** Tiglath-pileser's expedition against Galaad, 2 (4) Kgs 15:29, prob. 734 B.C. **8.** Aroer, Jos 13:16, Nebo and Baalmeon, Nm 32:38, fell to Reuben. **10.** The Hagrites, called in the Assyrian inscriptions Hagaranu, lived in NE Arabia. In Syr. the name came to be used as a designation of Arabs in general, Curtis 20.

11—17 The Tribe of Gad—**11.** The Gadites' territory ran N from that of Reuben. Bashan had been given originally to Manasseh, Jos 13:30. **17.** Jeroboam II 782/1—753 and Joatham 740/739—736/5; but the numbering will have been made while Joatham was acting as regent for his father Uzziah. Shortly after this the history of the trans-jordanic tribes came to an end with the invasion and deportation carried out by Tiglath-pileser, 734 B.C.

d **19—22. War against the Hagrites and their Allies**—This is a fuller account of the war briefly noticed in 10 as waged in the time of Saul. **19—20.** For the Hagrites

see on v. 10. In Gn Jetur and Naphish are the eponyms **300c** of Arab tribes. Nodab: only here. It is explained that God helped them because of their prayer and trust. Here we have a prominent point of Chr's theology. All man's work is in vain without the aid of Yahweh the Almighty. **21—22.** 'and a hundred thousand men alive. For many fell slain'. These men were not taken captive, and are loosely attached to the main verb. That this is the meaning is shown by the particle 'for'. The deportation of the Israelite tribes: see on v. 17.

23—24. The Half-Tribe of Manasseh—23. Bashan was inhabited by Gad; see on 11. The Manassites had the land on its N boundary. Baal-Hermon: perhaps modern Banias. Senir was the Amorite name for Hermon, Dt 3:9, but in Heb. usage was distinguished as part of the range; so also Song 4:8.

25—26. The Transjordanic Tribes are punished for Idolatry—Tiglath-pileser, king of Assyria 745—727, effected the union of Babylonia with Assyria by setting himself on the throne of the former country under the name of Pulu. Both names occur separately in 2 (4) Kgs 15:19. The name of Pulu is not mentioned in Syr. and is prob. a gloss. This is confirmed by the fact that the invasion here spoken of, 734 B.C., is that of 2 (4) Kgs 15:29 where the king of Assyria is named Tiglath-pileser. In these two vv we have a number of the keynotes of Chr's theology: the exile is a punishment for their sins, and God directly caused the destruction of the previous inhabitants: these two theses come from deuteronomic theology. The direct stirring up of the spirit of the Assyrian by God is also prominent in the theology of the prophets.

6:1—81 The Tribe of Levi (MT 5:27—6:66)—**Ex e** 6:16. **2—15 The descendants of Kohath chiefly of Aaron—2.** Ex 6:18. **3a.** Chr adds Miriam to the children of Amram, Ex 6:20. **3b.** Ex 6:23. **4a.** Ex 6:25. The genealogy of Ezra, Ez 7:1—5, is the same as far as Zadok, 8, except that an Azariah is inserted between Maraioth and Amariah, 7. From Zadok, 8, the Ezra list passes to the son of Zadok, 12. Names were traditional in families and there is nothing surprising in various generations having the same name. **8.** Zadok, high-priest under Solomon, 1 (3) Kgs 2:35. Ahimaaz, 2 Sm 15:27. **9.** Azariah high-priest under Solomon, 1 (3) Kgs 4:2. **11.** Amariah high-priest under Jehoshaphat, 2 Chr 19:11. **13.** Hilkiah, high-priest under Josiah, 2 Chr 34:9. **14.** Seraiah, high-priest at the fall of Jerusalem, 2 (4) Kgs 25:18. **15.** Jehozadak, Hag 1:1, Ez 3:2.

The list is given as that of the descendants of Aaron, not as that of high-priests, though some in the list are known to have held that office. Others known to have done so are not mentioned, Jehoiada, 2 Chr 22:11, Azariah under Uzziah, 2 Chr 26:20, and the number of generations given could not cover the interval of time between Aaron and the 6th cent. B.C. Jos. Ant. 5, 11, 5, states that the line of Eleazar retained the high-priesthood till Uzzi, 6:5, after whom it passed to Eli of the line of Ithamar to return to the line of Eleazar under Solomon. It is probable that the office did not always pass in the direct line of descent. It is remarkable that the Chronicler with his interest in the temple and public worship nowhere gives a list of high-priests as such.

The sons of Levi, 16—30, repeat 1 in 16 and 2 in **f** 18. **17.** Ex 6:17; Nm 3:18. **19.** Ex 6:19. **22—23.** Amminadab is not mentioned above, and the father of Korah, according to 37f and Nm 16:1 is Izhar. This passage clarifies Ex 6:24 where Assir, Elkanah and Ebiasaph might be taken for brothers. **24.** Uriel, of

300f David's time, 15:5. **25—28.** Should perhaps be read: 'The sons of Elkanah: Amasai and Ahimoth and Elkanah. The sons of (this) Elkanah: Zophai his son, etc'. This list of Samuel's ancestors gives the same names as in 33—35 and 1 Sm 1:1, but in altered forms. The sons of Samuel were Joel and Abijah, 1 Sm 8:2. The first name has fallen out here both in MT and LXX, and the Heb. expression for 'the second' appears as a proper name 'Vasseni'. This section is almost certainly secondary. Samuel is inserted as a great Levite although he was in fact an Ephraimite but he served at the altar and therefore must have belonged to the tribe of Levi, according to the Chronicler. Chr succeeds in his aim of making Samuel a Levite by identifying Elkanah, the father of Samuel 1 Sm 1:1, with the Levite Elkanah of the line of Kohath.

g 31—47. David's arrangement of liturgical singing—The importance that Chr attaches to that offering of the heart in sacrifice which must accompany and give meaning to the external offerings reveals itself in the unusual interest he shows in the music of the temple cult and in the levites to whom this duty of the worship of Yahweh was in a special way entrusted. He devotes more space in his book to the organization of the levites than to that of the priests. Since this temple song plays so large a part in his concept of true cult he attributes to David not merely an original organization of the levites but a developed organization which was in fact found only in his own time. David's removal of the ark, 2 Sm 6; his establishment of the three guilds of Levitical singers under Heman, Asaph and Jeduthun, 1 Chr 25. The list runs parallel to 22—28, but with omissions, scribal deformations (Joel, 36 = Saul, 24), and different names of the same person (Azariah 36 = Uzziah 24). **39.** Asaph was related to his 'brother' Heman through their common descent from Levi, being descended from Levi's sons Gerson and Kohath respectively. The position of Asaph's choir was 'at the right hand' of Heman's in the temple services. From Zerah, **41**, the names begin to agree with those in 20—21, with discrepancies usual in these ancient and imperfectly copied lists. **44.** It is not stated that Ethan changed his name or had two, but after 15:19 he is called Jeduthun, 16:42 etc. Other OT personages have two names e.g. Abraham, Sara, Jacob. **50—53.** The list of Aaron's descendants is repeated as far as Ahimaaz, 3—8, as he was of the time of David, 2 Sm 15:27. **54—60.** The cities allotted to the priests, Jos 21:1—4; 10—19. **54.** 'their dwelling-places according to their districts' **55.** 'and the pasture-lands thereof'. **57.** According to Jos 20, of these cities only Hebron was a city of refuge. **59.** Ashan, mentioned as a city of Judah in 4:32, appears as Ain in Jos. Before 'Bethshemesh' insert 'Juttah' with LXX, Syr. **60.** Read 'Gibeon and Geba', the former having fallen out by **h** haplography. **61—81.** The cities of the Levites. **61—65.** A summary, Jos 21:4—8. **66—81.** Jos 21:20—38. **67.** They were given Shechem, the city of refuge, with its pasturelands. **68.** Jokmean: in Jos Kibzaim. **69.** Elteke and Gibbethon, Jos 21:23, have fallen out of Chr. These were both in Dan, as were Aijalon and Gath-rimmon. **70.** Taanach (Jos 21:25) and Ibleam. **71.** After 'Gershomites' insert 'according to their families'. **72.** Kedesh: prob. read Kishion, Jos. **73.** 'Anem' has arisen out of En-gannim, Jos; today Jenîn. **75.** Hukok: Jos Helkath. **76.** Hammon: today el-Hammi, S of Tiberias. **77.** Jokneam and Kartah, Jos, must have fallen out as 63 reckons 12 cities to Merari. Tabor: in Jos, Nahalal. It is prob. that in some at least of

these cases of divergency Chr gives the actual practice **300h** as opposed to the original intention registered in Jos, but it is much more reasonable to assume that the text has suffered in transmission either between Jos and Chr or between Chr and us. Places such as these where we can compare two clearly parallel texts must warn us of the danger of two great readiness to fault a biblical author on the grounds of defective text, or too great eagerness to explain away all discrepancies. Often we simply have not enough information to give a definitive judgement.

7:1—5 The tribe of Issachar—In this and the **i** following section 6—12 it is probable that Chr is not using biblical data but military documents which are no longer extant. **2.** The numbering, 21:5. This number excludes the descendants of Uzzi, 3f. **5.** Previous numbers: Nm 1:29 = 54,400; 26:25 = 64,300.

6—12a The Tribe of Benjamin—Benjamin occurs again in ch 8 whereas there is no account of Zebulun, to which tribe it is therefore possible that the following list should really belong. But it cannot be simply transferred to Zebulun as a comparison of 6 with Gn 46:14 and 21 indicates. See also the very different list in Nm 26:38—41.

12b The Tribe of Dan—The text is corrupt but it is probable that this half-verse is a remnant of the lost Danite list. 12b is not linked with 12a and Hushim is the one Danite name in Gn 46:23. It appears with inversion of consonants as Shuham in Nm 26:42.

13 The Tribe of Naphtali—Gn 46:24; Nm 26:48f.

11 10 The Tribe of Manasseh Nm 26:29—34; Jos 17:1—3. The text has suffered considerably. **14.** Asriel was the son of Manasseh's grandson Gilead, Nm. **15.** Maacah was the name of Machir's wife, 16. The true text is lost. Zelophehad was the son of Hepher, Nm. Chr speaks as 'the second (son)' and therefore had an independent source. **16—17.** The names of these descendants are not in Nm.

20—27 The Tribe of Ephraim—Nm 26:35—37, where **j** the names as elsewhere do not exactly agree, does not make it plain that the names form a line of descent. **21.** The names of ancestors were often given to children of the same family. As the Philistine city of Gath was not captured by Joshua, Jos 11:22, the Hebrews would be likely to make a raid on their cattle. That the men of Gath are said to have been born in the land suggests that the Hebrew invaders had not. Ephraim was born in Egypt, Gn 41:52, and raiders from Egypt would not be said to 'come down' to Canaan. The difficulty of placing the raid in or after the time of Joshua is its connexion with the genealogical table. But this is also a difficulty against putting it in the lifetime of Ephraim on account of various intervening generations. The difficulty is not removed by the suggestion that Ephraim in 22 is used figuratively as is Rachel in Jer 31:15. A fragment of history seems to have become connected with the genealogy, but out of its chronological setting. **24.** Beth-horon: see on Jos 10:10. Uzzensheerah: today Beit Sira, W of the Beth-horons.

28—29 The Territory of Ephraim and Manasseh—**28.** Gezer and Shechem were levitical cities. **29.** cf Jos 17:11.

30—40 The Tribe of Asher—**30.** cf Gn 46:17; Nm 26:44. **31.** Birzaith is today Birzet NW of Beitin = Bethel. **35.** Helem—given as Hotham in 32. **38.** Jether—given as Jethran in 37. **39.** Ulla may be the same as Ara, 38.

8:1—40 The Tribe of Benjamin—7:6—12a; Gn 46: **k** 21; Nm 26:38—41. In 3 read 'Gera the father of Ehud' Jg

300k 3:15. The phrase 'These are the sons of Ehud' should be transferred from 6 to the beginning of 4. The text of 6—7 seems to be fragmentary; the words about deportation may be corruptions of proper names, though the deportation is supported by the otherwise unexplained sojourn in Moab, 8. 8. Sharaim is mentioned abruptly without introduction. 12. Ono: today Kefr Ana; Lod: today Ludd (Lydda) SE of Tel Aviv. 14. Read 'Their brothers were Elpaal, Shashak and Jeremoth'. 28. Jerusalem allotted to Benjamin, Jos 18:28, was a border city and was shared with Judah, Jos 15:63, Jg 1:21. In fact it was the city of David and his house and in practice was royal property and extratribal. 29—40. The family of Saul = 9:35—44. A special interest is taken in Saul as the great hero of Benjamin, the loyal tribe, but above all as the first choice of God for the Kingship and the fore-runner of David. 30. After 'Baal' supply Ner from 9:36. 33. Eshbaal = Ishbosheth 'man of shame', 2 Sm 2:8. The name of Baal was replaced by an opprobrious word to signify hatred of pagan cults. Chr alone uses the form Eshbaal, evidently reproducing an ancient source. The same holds, 34, of Meribbaal, elsewhere always called Mephibosheth, 2 Sm 4:4. Micah, 2 Sm 9:12. 35—40. Micah's posterity: only in Chr.

9:1a Conclusion of chh 1—8. Similar conclusions are found in 1 Chr 29:29 and 2 Chr 9:29. The book referred to is not the canonical book of Sm and Kgs for much of the material is taken from the Pent., Jos and other unknown sources.

l 9:1b—34 List of Dwellers in Jerusalem—The list gives laymen, 3—9, priests, 10—13, Levites, 14—34, among whom are porters, 17—27, and other officials, 28—34. The insertion of the list may have been suggested by 8:28—the families who 'dwelt in Jerusalem'. It is generally considered to be post-exilic and substantially identical with that in Neh 11. 2. The Israelites here are the laymen. 5. Shelah, the half-brother, 2:3f, of Perez and Zerah 4, was the eponym of the Shilonites. 10—13. The Priests. 10. These three stand here perhaps for the respective 'courses' of which they were the heads in the time of David, 24:7, 17. 17—27. The door-keepers, a separate group of Levites. 19—20. They had this office under Phinehas, Nm 25:7, in the days of the wonderings. He succeeded his father, Eleazar, in the office, Nm 3:32. 22. Samuel's regulations are mentioned only here; David's in ch 26 'for seven days' when their turn came round. 26. The four are named in 17. 28—34. Other officials. 30. 'Others, of the sons of the priests, prepared the mixing of the spices'; see Ex 30:34—38. 32. For the showbread see Lv 24:5—9. 33. The expected list of singers is not given, either here or Neh 11:22f. 35—44. The family of Saul. See 8:29—36.

m 10:1—14 Failure of Saul as king—Cf 1 Sm 31:1—13. The account serves the purpose both of introducing David's succession to the throne and of illustrating the theme that neglect of God's service is punished by adversity. Only at the end of the ch is there a reference to Saul's kingship and then only to say that God turned the kingdom over to David. The Chronicler sees in Saul a sinner rather than a king and his death not as the tragedy of the first king of Israel but as the just punishment of a great sinner. 1—5 = 1 Sm 31:1—5. 6. compresses 'his armour-bearer and all his men' to 'all his house'. This change is stylistic and theological. Even though Chr knows that Ishbosheth survived cf 2 Sm 2:8ff and that Saul had other descendants 1 Chr 8:33ff, 9:39ff, he sees no contradiction in saying that

his whole house died. 8—10. Sm is precise in recording **300n** that the weapons were laid up in the temple of Astarte, Chr in recording that the skull was put in the temple of Dagon. 12. They took the bodies from the wall of Beth-Shan where the Philistines had exposed them, Sm. 12 omits the burning of the bodies, which is mentioned in Sm, but supposes it by saying that they buried the bones. Sm says the spot was under an '*ēsil* = tamarisk, Chr under an '*ēlāh*, a tree of uncertain identification. In LXX and Vg it is called an oak and a terebinth, and according to Gesenius-Buhl it signifies any large tree. The similarity of the words may indicate a textual error. The bones were finally laid to rest in the sepulchre of Saul's father, 2 Sm 21:12—14. 13—14. These theological reflections are not in the parallel passage but are additions of Chr. Saul's death is a punishment for sin and it was God who slew him; human agencies such as the Philistines and the armour-bearer are not considered. According to 1 Sm 28:6 Saul did seek guidance from the Lord but the Lord would not answer him. The Chronicler knows that Saul's terrible end must be due to some great crime and so he says that he was punished among other things because he did not seek guidance from the Lord.

11:1—29:30 The Reign of David—The Chronicler has **301a** at last reached the point to which the whole of human history has been directed by God: the Kingdom of David. It is in the comparison between the treatment of David in Sm-Kgs and his treatment in Chr that the purposes and theological outlook of the Chronicler are most clearly seen. The David of Sm-Kgs though undoubtedly a great religious figure is painted in the round and is a man of flesh and blood with all the weaknesses to which flesh and blood are heir. In Chr he has become above all the canonized saint whose only interest and importance are in his religious and liturgical activity. But before accusing the Chronicler of falsification we must consider the long period of meditation on the meaning of the Davidic kingship that intervened between the Court history of 2 Sm 9ff and the composition of Chr. The prophets of the pre-exilic and exilic periods had developed a Davidic theology which became a central theme of post-exilic thinking, cf Is 2:1—5; Jer 23:5; Ezek 34:23ff. Their ideas had been formed under the influence of the vicissitudes through which the Davidic line had passed and had been accepted into the great deuteronomic theology. The psalms had also celebrated in high poetry the promises made to David and his line and the Chronicler is merely expressing the natural harvest of this long period of developing tradition. Just as Moses grew in stature as the ages passed and the Jews saw more and more clearly how much they owed to the mediator of the covenant of Sinai, so did David develop into a national hero as the Jews realized how much they owed to his establishment of court and temple in Jerusalem. Thus David in Chr is 'the ideal king who could **b** scarcely be considered otherwise than as a pious man who above all fostered the service of Yahweh, ruled his people justly in Yahweh's name and came to be so reverenced by Israel that all that was merely anecdotal and all that was human and faulty in him was pushed into the background'. (van den Born op cit p. 65) Ezekiel in particular had stressed the theocratic nature of the future restoration of Israel after the exile Ezek 34:23ff. Yahweh will be the God of Israel and David will be its leader. This picture of Ezekiel is the crystal through which Chr sees the historical Davidic age. For Chr Israel is a theocracy and its king must be uniquely theocratic as king. Everything therefore that is not directly religious and whatever is faulty or vicious in David must

301b be left out of the picture. The Chronicler does not deny the other facets of David's character and life for these were well known to him and to his readers from Sm-Kgs, but he is not interested in them as they have no special reference to his aim: to present the model of a theocratic king. This section of Chr is divided as follows: chh 11—12 the rise of David to power; 13—16 the sanctification of Jerusalem by the transport of the Ark; 17 the establishment for ever of the dynasty of David; 18—20 Wars of David which explain why he did not build the temple; 22—27 David's preparations for the Temple (23—27 are secondary); 28—29 Choice of Solomon as king.

c 11:1—3 David is anointed King over all Israel—2 Sm 5:1—3. The immediate sequence in the narrative of David's accession to the throne of all Israel does not of itself indicate that it followed immediately in time. The readers of Chr were well acquainted with the long war between David and the house of Saul, and the fact that it was the murder of Ishbosheth which gave him control over all Israel, 2 Sm chh 3—4. Chr supposes and does not disguise these facts, 3:4. Chr adds in 3 'according to the word of the Lord'; see 1 Sm 16:1—13. Comparison with the parallel passage in 2 Sm shows the addition of 'the Lord *your* God' to stress the special relationship of David with Yahweh, and the omission of 2 Sm 5:4—5 as Chr wants to stress only the link of David with Jerusalem, the centre of the theocracy.

d 4—9 David makes Jerusalem the Capital—2 Sm 5:6—10. The first thing to do was to capture the city in which God willed to establish his temple as the centre of divine cult. The Davidic choice of Jerusalem was astute politics for as it was conquered by himself it became a royal domain and could never be claimed by either Judah or Benjamin. But this was not the Chronicler's interest in it. In his eyes it was chosen by David as the centre not of an earthly but of a strictly theocratic kingdom. In becoming the city of David it became the city of God. Hebron was too southerly to be suitable as capital city. Jebus, on the SE hill of present Jerusalem, had also the advantage of being almost impregnable. **4.** Sm: 'the king and all his followers went to Jerusalem'. 'All Israel' went in the same sense as 'all Israel' (v. 1) had assembled at Hebron, viz in the persons of their representatives. 'All Israel' went to Jerusalem with David for this was a sacred public act and not a mere private act of David and his followers. **6** adds the promise to Sm's account. Joab was David's nephew by his sister Zeruiah, 2:16. Abner had been in command of Saul's forces, 1 Sm 26:5, but was treacherously slain by Joab to David's sorrow and indignation, 2 Sm 3:27—39. The king now found himself obliged by his promise to promote the murderer to the chief command. **8.** Chr adds that 'Joab repaired the rest of the city'. David's first thought was to strengthen the fortifications of his new capital.

e 10—46 David's Chief Supporters—2 Sm 23:8—39. Exploits of 'the three' are recounted, 10—14, then those of three other heroes, 15—25. There follow two lists of valiant men, 26—41*a* and 41*b*—46. **10—14.** The Three. **10.** not in Sm. Chr stresses the divine choice of David and the unity of the people in his support. **11** introduces the list of the heroes. Jashobeam (see also 27:2) killed three hundred at one time. **12—13***a***.** Eleazar was the son of Dodai; see 27:4. For the occasion of his exploit at Pas-dammim, see 1 Sm 17:1ff; for the exploit itself, 2 Sm 23:10. It has been lost here by homoeoteleuton, the scribe's eye passing from one mention of the Philistines gathering for battle to another. Both

mentions are preserved in 2 Sm 23:9 and 11. **13***b***—14. 301e** The same scribal error has caused the omission of the name of the third hero, given in 2 Sm 23:11 as Shammah. He was the hero who defended a field of barley or lentils. **15—19.** An exploit of three valiant men—other than the three mentioned above. Two are mentioned in 20, 22. **15.** 'The rock'—*hasûr* may be a corruption of *qāsîr*, 'harvest' giving 'at harvest time' as in 2 Sm 23:13, thus explaining David's thirst. **18.** cf 1 Sm 7:6, another water-libation. **20—25.** Abishai and Banaiah. Jashobeam, Eleazar and Shammah were 'the three' without further qualification, 11—14. **22—25.** Benaiah, captain of the army and son of Joiada the priest, **22.** 'He slew the two sons of Ariel of Moab'; so with Sm (LXX). Ariel; otherwise unknown. **26—41***a***.** A list of valiant men = 2 Sm 23:24 39. Both lists have suffered textually. Many are mentioned as high officers of the army: Asahel, 26, Shammoth and Helez, 27, Ira and Abiezer, 28, Sibbecai, 29, Maharai and Heled, 30, Banaiah, 31; see 27:7, 8, 10, 9, 12, 13, 15, 14. **32.** Hurai came from the ravines of Mt Gaash, Jos 24:30. Azmaveth of Bahurim was David's treasurer, 27:25. **41***b***—47.** A further list of valiant men. Not in Sm. Chr does not wish to end his list, as Sm does, with Uriah the Hittite as this would call to mind the sin of David which he avoids.

12:1—22 Further lists of the supporters of David— f 1—22 seems to break the connexion between 11:47 and 12:23. This section which is found only in Chr is probably a later addition and is itself not in good order as it moves from Ziklag 1—7 to the stronghold in the wilderness 8—18 and back to Ziklag again 19—22. It is not easy to see the purpose of this addition to Sm. **1—7.** Men of Benjamin abandoned their fellow-tribesman, Saul, and espoused the cause of David. It was two of the tribe who even murdered Saul's son Ishbosheth, 2 Sm 4:2. The insertion of the passage here implies that many at least of these supporters later helped David to win the kingship over all Israel. **1.** David's retirement at Ziklag, 1 Sm 27:6, a town presented to him by the Philistine king Achish. The Benjaminites were famous for ambidexterity, Jg 3:15; and 20:16 where skill with the sling is also lauded. Their skill with the bow, 8:40; 2 Chr 14:8; 1 Sm 20:20; 2 Sm 1:22. **4.** For 'the thirty', see 11:15. Of these Ishmaiah was one of the bravest and he had under him a group of thirty warriors. **14.** It is not said that they brought such large contingents of men with them. **15.** They were not deterred by the fact that the Jordan 'was overflowing all its banks'. This was caused by the melting of the snow on Hermon in March-April and by unusually heavy rains. Rudolph suggests an emendation that would give the meaning 'when it was overflowing its banks and made all the eastern and western valleys impassable'. The purpose of narrating this episode is to show God's special providence for David. **20.** It is noteworthy that Chr inserts something in praise of Manasseh, the ancestor of the Samaritans. This incident shows that all who accept the line of David are approved even if they come from the accursed stock of Manasseh.

23—40 David's supporters at Hebron—These lists **g** are given to stress the unanimous recognition of David by the people as their divinely ordained king. The numbers given are in most cases unbelievably high as frequently in Chr; and no adequate explanation can be found for them; no doubt they are part of the literary form. **39—40.** The unity of the people under their God-given king is expressed in a great feast. Joy at the feast especially at the liturgical feast is a characteristic of

301g Chr. This joy is a recollection of that of 1 (3) Kgs 4:20 and is essentially eschatological e.g. Ps 36:9; 17:15; Lk 12:37; Mt 26:29.

h 13:1—14 David's Attempt to bring the ark to Sion—1—4. A consultation is held; not in Sm. **2** introduces a general assembly after the private consultation with the leaders. Chr frequently mentions that the king takes counsel with others. He wishes to stress that *all* are members of the people of God and have responsibility for God's kingdom. Perhaps he is idealizing the behaviour of the kings in contrast to the dictatorial behaviour of the high priests of his own day. The necessary participation of all Israel especially in cult is stressed in 2 Chr 30; 2 Chr 34:33; 35:18. **3.** 'for we neglected it in the days of Saul'. How much more fervent in the service of God is David. **5—14.** The abortive attempt, 2 Sm 6:1—11. The limits of Israel are indicated by the S and N boundaries. The Shihor sometimes is the Nile but here more probably represents the Wadi el-'arish, which separates Palestine from Egypt. Once again Chr stresses that all Israel and not merely a chosen band took part in this great liturgical act. **7.** The cart was newly made so that nothing profane had touched it. **8.** 'Before God', the ark being the symbol of his presence, 6. **9.** 'To the threshing-floor . . . for the oxen stumbled'; the exact sense is uncertain. **10.** The ark should by law have been carried on its bars, Ex 25:12—14; the right to touch it was allowed only to the priests, Nm 4:15. During the troubled times of the Judges the Law was in general neglected, Jg 21:25, and so largely forgotten. David did not make the same mistake a second time, but insisted on the ark being carried by Levites, 15:2, which shows that Uzzah and Ahio were not Levites. Although Uzzah acted in good faith, the Israelites, so prone to idolatry through failure to understand the unique majesty of God, had to be taught the reverence due to him and his Law. **13—14.** Obededom, a man of Gath, and not an Israelite, was blessed by God for his care of the ark. When David heard this, he took heart, 2 Sm 6:12, and brought the ark into his own city, 1 Chr 15.

i 14:1—17 David's Palace; his Sons; Trouble with the Philistines—The interval between chh 13 and 15 was three months, 13:14; and the events here narrated occurred partly earlier (the legation from Tyre and the building of a palace, 1, trouble with the Philistines, 8—16) and partly later (the birth of David's sons, 3—7). **1—2.** 2 Sm 5:11—12. The ambassadors probably brought congratulations on David's elevation to the throne of all Israel. According to Sm the Tyrian craftsmen actually built the palace. **3—7.** David's sons. **8—16.** Encounters with the Philistines. 2 Sm 5:17—25. **12.** David took the idols away (Sm) and burnt them (Chr) in accordance with Dt 7:5, 25. Chr is most anxious to avoid any suggestion that David could have kept the idols and so he adds 'and they were burned'. **17** is not in Sm. The fear of David's power extended to 'all nations' near which heard of his exploits—a case of relative universality. To David is given the same glory as 1 (3) Kgs 3:28; 10:24 attributes to Solomon. Ps 2 may have influenced the formulation of this verse.

j 15:1—24 Introduction to the Procession with the Ark—1. David will have started this building soon after capturing the city from the Jebusites, 11:7f; 14:1. The place for the ark will have been prepared before the first procession to bring it to Jerusalem, ch 13. It is a question why a new tabernacle was constructed, according to 2 Chr 1:3 the mosaic tabernacle was at this time at Gibeon; but cf § 271*b*. **2—24.** The priests and Levites; not in Sm. This long section is added in

Chr to stress the strictly liturgical character of the **301j** transfer of the Ark to Jerusalem. In fact it was a stroke of political genius also to associate the central object of Jewish religion with the city of David. **2.** See on 13:10. David had now discovered his error. **5—7.** Kohath, Merari, Gershom, 6:1. Uriel, 6:24. Asaiah, 6:30. **8.** Elizaphan was also a Kohathite, Ex 6:18, 22, but his clan had become independent. **9.** Hebron, also a Kohathite, Ex 6:18. **10.** Uzziel, another son of Kohath, 6:2. Aminadab, 6:22. **11.** Zadok of the line of Eleazar, 6:8. Abiathar of the line of Ithamar, 6:3. The Levites are those of 5—10. **12.** For various means of Levitical purification, see Ex 19:10,15; 30:19; Lv 10:9. **13.** '. . . because we did not consult him as was fitting'. **20—21.** 'Alamoth' and 'Sheminith' are musical terms. They may refer to pitch—high and low respectively— or to melodies—'the maidens' and 'the eight'; or they may refer to modes of singing—'like the Elamites' and 'like the Shemeonites'. The whole question is obscure. **22.** The translation is probable but not certain.

25—16:3 The Procession with the Ark to the City of k David—2 Sm 6:13—19 in substance. Chr omits that David learnt that the anger of God had ceased by the divine blessing given to the house of Obededom, v 12 of Sm. It was not from a selfish desire to get all the blessings he could but from pure zeal for God's glory that the David of Chr brings the ark to Jerusalem. **29.** Chr omits the sequel given in 2 Sm 6:20—23, which is surprising as the punishment which befell Michal would have illustrated his doctrine of retribution. Perhaps the reason is that Michal describes David's behaviour in rather unbecoming language. **16:2.** Blessing was not an exclusively priestly function any more than it is today. **3.** 'A loaf of bread, a date-cake and a raisin-cake'; see L. Kohler, TZ 1948 397f.

16:4—6 Fresh Ordinances of Levitical Service— 302a only in Chr.

7—36 David's Psalm—8—22. The hymn = Ps 105 (104):1—15. **15—18.** Note that the covenant in which Chr is interested is the original covenant with Abraham; he passes over the covenant with Moses without mention but moves on to the covenant with David 2 Chr 13:5. **22.** The whole earth and all its potentates must reverence the people of God. This is an extraordinary claim for a nation as insignificant as the Judah of Chr to make and this universal claim continues in the following section with the call to all nations to praise Yahweh.

23—36 Later Additions to the Hymn—23—33 = Ps b 96 (95):1—13. **34—36** = Ps 106 (105):1 and 47. These, the first and last vv, seem to be set down as an indication that the whole Ps was to be sung. **36** is the doxology at the end of the 4th book of Psalms. As this Ps is post-exilic (see **35**) and therefore a later liturgical addition to David's ordinance, it is prob. that 22—33 is a similar addition.

37—42. Arrangement for Divine Service with the ark and the Tabernacle. **38.** there is some corruption in the text. **43 Conclusion of the Transference of the Ark—** 2 Sm 6:19*b*—20*a*. David returned to greet his household; see on Gn 47:7. The religious ceremony was no doubt followed by a domestic feast. This v is the immediate continuation of 16:3, from which Chr has separated it by the long insertion about David's cultic arrangements.

17:1—27 The Eternal Dynasty of David—This ch is **c** the very heart of Chr. The promise made by God to David (v 12) determines the construction of the whole work. To this event he looks back as the foundation of all that he hopes and prays for; from this promise he looks forward to a future that is to be a glorious fulfilment

02c of which the theocratic state in which he lives is the pledge. Note that this promise becomes in 2 Chr 13:5 and 21:7 a covenant like that made with Abraham and Jacob-Israel and apparently surpassing that made with Moses. **1—6.** David's desire to build a temple is not accepted— 2 Sm 7:1—7. 1 Chr omits 'The Lord had given him rest' because of what is to follow in chh 18—20 but it adds 'of the covenant' to stress the bond of God with His people and with David.

7—15 Glorious Promises to David: his Throne to stand for ever—2 Sm 7:8—17. **9.** Chr uses a stronger term than Sm probably because of the experience of the exile. **13** omits the words of Sm about the sins of the descendant of David as unbecoming. The prophecy received its full explanation from the words concerning Jesus Christ: 'he will reign over the house of Jacob for ever; and of his kingdom there will be no end', Lk 1:33. **14.** Chr makes a change that stresses the unbreakable link between God and the house and kingdom of David.

16—27 David's Prayer of Thanksgiving—2 Sm 7:18—29. **16.** David 'sat before the Lord': in the tabernacle in presence of the ark, which symbolized God's presence. **17.** The last sentence represents a corrupt Heb. text.

d 18:1—13 David's Successful Wars—2 Sm 8:1—14. The reason for the insertion of this account at this point seems to have been that it illustrates the divine favour enjoyed by David, explains the source of much of the wealth used in the preparation of the temple and shows David as a man of blood who is not to build the temple cf 22:8; 28:3. **1.** Conquered kings were often left in office as vassals and Gath had a king in the time of Solomon, 1(3) Kgs 2:39; cf 2 Chr 9:26 = 1 (3) Kgs 4:21. **2.** Chr omits the bloody scene of Sm as something that did not redound to David's credit. **4.** The figures here given are supported by LXX both of Chr and Sm. **9.** The name of Tou's son, Hadoram, supported by LXX both here and in Sm, is prob. a corruption of Hadadram 'Hadad is exalted'. **12.** Abishai, 2:16. As he won this victory for the king, it is in Sm attributed to David. The valley, today Wady el-Milh, runs SW from the Dead Sea.

14—17 David's Officials—2 Sm 8:15—18; cf 2 Sm 20:23—26. **17.** Chr's source may have had that they were *kohᵃnîm* or 'ministers' (of the Crown) as in Sm. By the time of Chr this word had only the sense of 'priests' and would be changed to a contemporary equivalent. It thus appears that the semantic development to 'minister' in the secular sense became obsolete, and that to 'priest' or minister in the religious sense became permanent. At any rate it would be quite impossible for Chr to allow that members of David's family were priests for this privilege was reserved to the tribe of Levi.

e 19:1—19 David's Defeat of the Ammonites and their Confederates—2 Sm 10:1—19. It is to be observed that Chr omits entirely ch 9 of 2 Sm as of no interest to his theme of Throne and Temple, and in the story of the Ammonite war he leaves out the whole story of David's adultery with Bathsheba and his murder of Uriah as darkening the character of his hero and this even though his omission of Bathsheba entails the omission of the birth of Solomon. Besides, the private family affairs of David are of no interest whatever to Chr. **4.** Sm: 'he shaved off half the beard of each'; Chr, he 'shaved them'. The indecent cutting short of their garments suggests that the hair was shaved off one-half of their bodies. **6.** Chr adds 'a thousand talents of silver'. Mesopotamia: Aram Naharaim, prob. the land on both sides of the Euphrates where it flows nearest to the Orontes. Zobah: see on 18:3. **7.** Sm gives a total of 33,000 men in agree-

ment with the 32,000 of Chr + 1,000 from Maacah **302e** (numbered in Sm but not in Chr). But in Chr by a textual error the number has become attached to 'chariots', to which it cannot refer. Medeba: a city E of the N end of the Dead Sea. The city is not named in Sm leaving the geographical situation obscure, as this encampment would be too far from Rabbah to be useful. We should probably read 'the waters of Rabbah' cf 2 Sm 12:27. **18.** Sm with more probability has 700 chariots.

20:1—3 Capture of the Ammonite Capital—2 Sm **f** 11:1; 12:30—31. **1.** It is strange that Chr has kept the remark that David remained at Jerusalem. In his source, as in Sm, it introduced the story of David's adultery with Bathsheba. With this omitted it has no purpose; and David was present at the final capture of Rabbah, today Amman, 2 Sm 12.27ff, though the victory was really that of Joab, his commander-in-chief. **2.** *Milcom*, the chief god of the Ammonites, was represented by a large image capable of bearing a golden crown weighing a talent. The name of this divinity has been erroneously vocalized in MT as *malkām* 'their king'. From this crown 'a precious stone', and no doubt part of the gold were utilized to make a diadem for David. **3.** David 'set them to labour with saws and iron picks and axes'. This is widely recognized to be the true meaning here and in 2 Sm 12:31. The instruments named suggest task work, not torture; and had David been guilty of unmitigated cruelty Chr would have omitted the passage as it omitted 2 Sm 8:2 and the account of David's deliberately procuring the death of Uriah. Chr now omits 2 Sm 13—20, the story of the family troubles of David. These would tarnish the fame of his hero and have no importance in his eyes as they have nothing to do with the essential role of David in the divine plan of establishing the kingdom of God and his worship in the city and line of David.

4—7 Exploits against the Philistines—2 Sm 21:18— **g** 22. **4.** Sm has 'at Gob': otherwise unknown; a scribal error. **5.** For the death of Goliath at the hand of David, see 1 Sm 17:49; 19:5; 21:9; 22:10. Textual corruption has occurred in both Chr and Sm. 'the Bethlehemite' of Sm (*bēt-hallaḥmî*) has become 'Lahmi' in Chr (MT) ('*et-laḥmî*), thus providing a name for Goliath's brother. Vg + DV may have kept the true text. And '*aḥî* (Chr) 'the brother of' has become in Sm '*et* (sign of the definite object) with the result that Elhanan has been credited in this text with killing Goliath. The name of Goliath's brother was either not known or not considered worth preserving, as was the case also with the Philistine of **6—7.** He, like the other two, was of the ancient race of the Rephaim, famous for their stature. It is however more likely that Chr has deliberately altered the text of 2 Sm 21:19 as he could not see how to reconcile the tradition given in this verse with the wellknown story recorded at length in 1 Sm 17.

21:1—22:1 The Census and its Punishment lead to h the Choice of a Site for the Temple—2 Sm 24:1—25. Chr and Sm cover the same ground but the differences, especially in language, are marked; and the two accounts are prob. not from the same immediate source. Chr may well depend on 'the book of Gad the seer', 29:29. Chr omits of Sm's matter 4*d*—7 and adds 6, 16, 26*b*—22:1. Chr has included this account of David's census, though displeasing to God, because its sequel was the choice of the site for the temple, the building and arrangements of which occupied so prominent a place in the Chronicler's interests. Therefore he stresses the calamity less than the good that came from the calamity. The purpose of the census is indicated in 5; those numbered were only the fighting men. The sinfulness of the census is indicated, 3,

G

302h 7, but not the ground thereof. It was known to readers that, according to the conscience of Israel, to number the people was to trespass on the supreme rights of God; see Ex 30:12. The sin may be the pride of David or perhaps his intrusion into a realm that is specifically the realm of Yahweh. In early Israel Yahweh had been known especially as the Lord of Hosts, the leader of the armies of Israel. The army had assembled freely and spontaneously at the call of the charismatic leader. Now this census foreshadowed a different outlook in which the king was the leader and called his army together by human calculation and planning. The sin then was rather that of counting God's blessings and assuming control of the wars of Yahweh.

i 1 reflects the more developed theology of Chr. In Sm it is God who stirs up David to number Israel in accordance with the broad concept that whatever happens in the world is attributable to the divine power that rules the universe. In this simple stage of theological development no explicit distinction was made between God's absolute and permissive will. The elements of the distinction were, however, already present, as God was known to be holy and to hate evil, of which he could not therefore be the true cause whether physical or moral. There is thus no contradiction but only clearer statement when Chr represents David as yielding to the instigation of a created cause. Later 'Satan' came to designate an evil spirit, Mk 3:23, and often, and it may well already have that sense here. In itself it means 'an adversary'. Note that Chr reads 'Israel' instead of 'Israel and Judah'. For him the only real Israel is the kingdom of David and his line. The later kingdom of Israel of the N is simply not Israel at all. **5.** The figures in Sm are 800,000 and 500,000. Either set of numbers gives a surprisingly high total population of about 6,000,000, and neither is likely to be correct. The textual tradition may be at fault; cf also § 206c. **23.** The blessing of Ornan is omitted in order that David may not be blessed by a heathen. **25.** Sm seems to say that the price of threshing-floor and oxen was 50 silver shekels, Chr that of the site alone 600 gold shekels. The much larger price of Chr is intended to enhance the prestige of David and the value of the holy place. **26.** Yahweh sends fire to stress the consecration of the place to himself. **22:1.** This v is obviously inserted for polemical reasons. God's chosen king rejects any centre of worship but Jerusalem. The N kingdom and its golden calves and, still more, the Samaritans and Mt Gerizim are not the dwelling place of Yahweh.

j 22:2—19 Preparations for building the Temple— **2—5.** Material preparations. **2.** David first took a census, 2 Chr 2:17, of the resident aliens, the survivors of the conquered inhabitants. He did not use the forced labour of native Israelites as the Solomon of 1 (3) Kgs 5:13 did. **6—16.** David's charge to Solomon. **8.** The shedding of blood as a ground for David's unsuitability to build the temple has not been previously mentioned in ch 17 or 2 Sm 7. It was not in harmony with the complete Levitical purity required in everything closely connected with the divine cult. **9.** There is a pun here on Solomon's name 'Šelômoh' and 'Šālôm' the word for peace. **14.** No ancient reader would have thought of taking literally the amount of treasure here mentioned. The hyperbolic character of the statement is more obvious in the Heb.: a hundred thousand talents of gold and a thousand thousand talents of silver. It recalls the statement that silver was as plentiful as stones in Jerusalem, 1 Kgs 10:27.

303a 23:1—27:34 The Temple Service the Work of David—It is generally accepted that 23:3—27:34 is a **303** later addition as it breaks the sequence of thought and events which is only resumed in 28:1. This addition has as its purpose to stress an idea dear to the original Chronicler: the perfect and complete organization of the Temple service as the work of David. The organization of Temple service here attributed to David was in fact the organization as it existed in the time of the hagiographer. But the author of Chr wishes to stress that the cult of his own day is the true expression of God's mind as revealed to David and so he directly attributes to the founder of the Temple all the legitimate development that took place in the centuries which followed. That David and the other kings of his line organized the service in the Temple for better (Hezekiah and Josiah) or for worse (Ahaz and Manasseh) is certainly true and that the king in pre-exilic times was the great master of liturgical worship is equally true. We may compare the attitude of Chr to that of the final editor of the Pent who attributes directly to Moses many laws and statutes which date from much later times. This attitude is based on the perfectly legitimate idea that a man is ultimately responsible for what his legitimate successors do in making explicit what is implicit in his own prescriptions for his own times. It is to be remarked also that cult is essentially conservative and therefore much that was done in Chr's own time could very easily be an exact survival of the earliest practices of that Salomonic Temple for which David is making arrangements in these chh cf § 104e—f.

23:1—32 The Courses and Offices of the Levites— **b** **1—2** anticipate ch 28. The mention of the Levites is the only link with what follows. **3—5** The numbers and offices of the Levites. **3.** From the age of 30 as in Nm 4:3, 23. But this is perhaps a scribal error, as when more help was required this age limit had been reduced to 25, Nm 8:24, and it is reduced still further to 20, 23:27. Or these variations may simply represent the inevitable conflict between theory and practice over the centuries. **4.** As there were 24 courses of priests, ch 24, and 24 of the musicians, ch 25, and 24,000 Levites are here allotted to the general work of the cult, it seems clear that they too were divided into 24 courses. As the names in 6—23 do not yield this number, we may suspect some defect in the text. The Levites as judges, 26:29 and 2 Chr 19:8—10. **5.** David's musical instruments, Am 6:5; 2 Chr 29:26; Neh 12:35. **6—24** The distribution by courses. **9a**, as the text stands, must be read after **9b. 10.** *Zizah.* N and Z are very similar letters in Hebrew. **12** = 6:2. **13.** It was a priestly function 'to bless in his (God's) name', Nm 6:23—27; but see on 16:2. **25—32.** Further Levitical ordinances.

24:1—19 The Twenty-four Courses of the Priests— **c** **1—6** Preliminary explanations. **1.** 6:3. **2.** Lv 10:1f; Nm 3:4. **7—19.** The heads of the twenty-four priestly courses. **7.** Names were traditional in families; hence these names recur, 9:10. Josephus, *Life* 1, belonged to the first priestly course. **10.** The course of Abijah, Lk 1:5. **19.** Chr wishes to stress that though the arrangement and division of courses is due to David, the actual ministry goes back to the time of Aaron. **20—31 The heads of the Levitical families—**This list comes from a different source from that of 23:6—24 and is fragmentary for some of the sons of Amram were the priestly descendants of Aaron, and these have already been dealt with, 1—19. The list begins with the Kohathites; see 23:15f; 6:2f, and proceeds with the Merarites, 26—30. The Gershomites have fallen out. **21.** Rehabiah, 23:17. **22.** See 23:12, 18. **23.** The text is here defective. These are the sons of Hebron; see 23:12, 19. **24.** See

303c 23:12, 20. **26.** See 23:21. **28—29.** See 23:21f. **30.** See 23:23.

d **25:1—31 The Twenty-four Courses of the Musicians**—The interest that Chr shows in liturgical chant and in the Levitical order of Singers has suggested to some that the author was himself a member of this group. But it is to be remembered that liturgical words, if divinely sanctioned, are just as important as liturgical actions in sacramental or quasi-sacramental liturgies cf Eph 5:26. Chr naturally therefore takes great interest in solemn liturgical language which of course is normally in the form of song and naturally accompanied by musical instruments. For this reason the use of the word 'prophecy' to describe it as in 25:1 is appropriate. In the organized cult of pre-exilic times there was a place for the cultic prophet and it would appear that in the post-exilic times of Chr, this role of cultic prophet was played by the authorized, and therefore inspired, singer of the liturgical texts.

e **1.** The three families represented respectively, Asaph the Gershomites, 6:39—13. Heman the Kohathites, 6:33, and Jeduthun (= Ethan), the Merarites, 6:44. That their function was to 'prophesy' to the sound of music is explained in 3 as singing the praises of God. The music and singing was in general loud and enthusiastic; see Ps 33(32):3, § 386m. **4.** The form and order of the last nine names suggest, with certain changes, a prayer which Curtis translates thus: 'Be gracious unto me, Oh Yah, be gracious unto me, Thou art my God whom I magnify and exalt. Oh my help (or: Thou art my help) when in trouble, I say, He giveth (or: Give) an abundance of visions'. **5.** Heman's large family would win him great respect among the Israelites who would see in it a signal blessing of God; See Ps 127 (126):3. **7.** The number of those 'instructed in the songs of the Lord, each one an expert' was 24×12, as enumerated 9—31. **8.** The phrase 'the teacher and the pupil' is not happily chosen in this connexion. It is an example of the Heb. idiom by which a totality is expressed by the conjunction of opposites, and does not imply against 7 that any were not expert. **9—31** gives the order in which the names of 2—4 came out by lot. It illustrates the difficulty of the accurate literary transmission of names. Although both lists occur in the same chapter, 10 differ more or less in MT. 9, 10, 12, 14 give the courses that fell to Asaph; 9, 11, 15, 17, 19, 21 those of Jeduthun, and the rest those of Heman. These highly trained singers and musicians were assisted by the 4,000 of 23:5.

f **26:1—19 The Courses of the Porters**—These were a special section of the Levites as were the musicians; and they will have taken their turn of office in the same way as the courses of priests. As with the other groups only the heads of families are named here. They were assisted by the 4,000 of 23:5. There were two main groups only among them, Kohathites represented by the sons of Korah, 6:22, and the Merarites, 10. The Gershomites had other functions, 26:21.

1. Meshelemiah: the name occurs in various forms, 26:14; 9:21; 9:17, 19, 31. Asaph: '*Ebiasaph*'; see 9:19. **4.** Obededom: 15:18, 24; 16:38 (not 13:14). **10.** Hosah: 16:38. Shimri's eldest brother must have died childless. **16.** Omit 'Sephim' (dittography). 'To Hosa (the gate) towards the W together with the gate of Shalleketh (otherwise unknown) by the rising causeway'. This may reflect a time later than David's. The temple-hill was on a higher level than the ground to S and W. The remains of two causeways have been discovered on the W named Wilson's Arch and Robinson's Arch. **17.** 'Towards the E were six (guards) a day ... and for the storehouse two

and two': two for each entrance, unless it is meant that **303f** there were two storehouses. **18.** The nature of the Parbar is uncertain, the name possibly being derived from a Persian word denoting some structure admitting light, perhaps colonnade.

20—32 Other Functions of the Levites—**20—28.** **g** Guardianship of the treasuries. **20.** Ahijah had charge both of the valuable properties required for divine worship, 9:26—29, and over what the faithful had dedicated to the sanctuary, 26:26—28. **21—23.** The text here is defective and no reasonable emendation is completely satisfactory. Those in 24—25 are Amramites; the Izharites and Hebronites are mentioned **29—31**, but the Uzzielites are omitted. **24—25.** See 23:14—17. Jeshaiah = Isshiah, 24:21. **29—32.** Secular functions. **29.** These Izharites were employed in the capacity of civil servants.

27:1—15 The Captains of the Army—The list dates at **h** least in part from an early period of David's reign; see on 7. Nearly all the commanders were heroes of David's early days and are taken from the list in 11:10—47. **1.** 'Who came on and went off duty'. **2.** 11:11. **3.** He owed his position in part to his descent from Judah through Perez, 2:4. **7.** Asahel, 11:26, was killed while David was still at Hebron, 2 Sm 2:18—23, and was succeeded by his son.

16—22 The Chiefs of the Tribes—The text is incomplete, Gad and Asher being wanting. **18.** David's brother, Elihu, is not otherwise known; his eldest brother was Eliab, 2:13; 1 Sm 16:6; 17:13, 28. **21.** Abner, prob. the celebrated commander of the army.

23—24. A Fragment on the Census—This seems to **i** take up the reference to a census in 1. **23.** The census being a measure of preparation in case of war, according to Nm 1:3 David did not number those under the conscript age of 20. The point of the reference to the prophecy of Gn 22:17 may have been clear in Chr's source. It cannot give the reason for the omission to count the younger members of the community, as this is sufficiently explained by Nm 1:3; and if it was a valid reason for the young, it would be equally so for all. In the original context it prob. gave a reason for the census as a whole, not to test but to illustrate the fulfilment of the divine promise. **24.** Joab was opposed to the census from the beginning, 21:3. He reported the result to the king, 21:5, but when David realized his error, he forbade it to be entered in the official chronicle.

25—31 The Stewards over David's Property— **32—34 David's Ministers**—The only officials in common with the earlier list in 18:15—17 are Joab and Abiathar. **32.** David had also a nephew named Jonathan, 20:7. The uncle and Jehiel, son of Hachmoni, 11:11, were guardians of the king's numerous sons, 3:1—9. **33.** 'The king's friend' seems to have been an official title. **34.** Ahithophel killed himself in Absalom's rebellion, 2 Sm 17:23. He was replaced by Jehoiada, the son of Benaiah. Jehoiada named his own son Benaiah after the boy's grandfather, 18:17. It is possible, however, that the names have been accidentally inverted.

28:1—29:20 David in Solemn Assembly proclaims **304a** **Solomon King**—The Chronicler's interest in the temple has led him to give such prominence to the plans for its construction as rather to obscure the main purpose of the assembly which was to proclaim Solomon as David's successor. The assembly has been already introduced, 23:1f. The enumeration of those summoned led to the long digression, 23:3—27:34, with its lists of the important persons belonging to the various classes. **1** gives a further list of those summoned with the omission of the leading priests and Levites already mentioned in 23:2. **2—10.**

304a First part of David's speech. **2.** '"My brethren and my people"; Whatever may have been the intentions of individual kings towards absolutism, this is at the heart of the teaching on monarchy in the OT. He occupies a unique position in Israel, religiously as well as politically, and may even be called Yahweh's son (cf v 6) but he is a human and not a deified being, *primus inter pares*'. (PC (2) 315*a*) The people not the ruler is the primary object of God's loving call, cf the Vatican Council Constitution, *Lumen Gentium* on the Church in which the ch of the People of God comes before any consideration on the manner in which the people of God is to be ruled. **4.** The choice of Judah, Gn 49:8—10; the choice of David's house, 1 Sm 16:1; of David, 1 Sm 16:13. God has certainly chosen irrevocably and for ever the line of David but the fate of the individual kings of that line depends on their personal b acceptance of this choice and all that it entails. **9.** 'Know God' in the pregnant sense of knowing with veneration and love; cf Ps 1:6. **11—19.** Plans for the temple. **11.** The house for the mercy-seat is the Holy of Holies. **16.** 1 (3) Kgs 7:48 mentions only one table of show-bread, but Solomon made 10, 2 Chr 4:8, 19, though the others will have been used, e.g. as stands for lights. **18.** God is poetically spoken of as riding on the cherubim, Ps 18 (17):10; 99 (98):1. **19.** Text is obscure. RSV renders best. This does not mean that David received revelations about all the details, but that he worked them out under the guiding Providence of God.

c **20—29:5** Continuation of David's address. **20** repeats the exhortation of 10, where the speech was interrupted. **29:1.** Solomon was yet 'young and inexperienced' (repeated from 22:5). **2.** 'onyx stones *with (their) settings, carbuncles* (?; reading *nōpek*) *and stones of variegated colour . . . and alabaster in abundance*'. **4.** The mention here of gold of Ophir, prob. in S Arabia, is not an anachronism. The expeditions which Solomon sent to obtain gold from there, 2 Chr 8:18; 9:10, show that Ophir was already known as an important source of supply, and David will have obtained his gold from intermediaries. 3,000 talents of gold would exceed 300,000 lb. in weight. The walls of the temple are recorded to have been overlaid with gold, 2 Chr 3:4f; 1 Kgs 6:20, but overlaying with silver is mentioned only here. It may be that Solomon found his supply of gold to be ample and used only the more precious metal for the purpose, cf § 286*d*. **5.** The words translated 'consecrating himself' mean literally 'Fill the hand'. This was the rubrical word for consecration. Though most authors do not take it in this sense here and understand it to mean 'offer a gift' it seems more likely that in a rubrical or liturgical book such as Chr the technical sense would be preserved. RSV trans. should therefore be accepted. Every gift offered to God receives its meaning from the fact that it is an expression of self-consecration to him. **6—9.** Offerings for the Temple. **7.** 'solids'; in MT *ᵃdarkōnîm*, by some identified with the Persian daric, a coin first struck by Darius I, 521—486, but a coin called the *dariku* occurs already in an inscription of Nabonidus, the last Babylonian king, 555—539 (W. Muss-Arnolt, *A Concise Dict. of the Assyrian Language*, s.v.). Others connect the word with the Gr. drachma. Whatever its derivation, it is used here to denote the smaller offerings in coin. Note that the numbers are all round; the precise figures were unknown. **8.** The precious stones were confined directly to Jehiel, who was in charge of the sacred treasury, 26:21f. **9.** This attitude of joy on the part of the people in the service of God is constantly stressed by Chr. Joy in service— especially liturgical service——is one of his essential d themes. **10—19. David's prayer.** David is described by

Chr, in harmony with all Heb. tradition, as an outstanding 304 man of prayer; in this prayer he expresses all the fundamental attitudes of Heb. prayer as we know them from the psalms: blessing, praise, thanksgiving, humility, confidence in God's promises and consequently confident prayer for his favours. **10.** Prayer for the Jew is primarily 'Blessing God' and David begins with a doxology which takes up a large part of the whole prayer. The glory of God moves him to praise and thanksgiving, to recognize the fragility of the creature and only in 19 to the direct object of his petition. The 'upright heart' of 17 which is the proper disposition in one who approaches God in prayer is the same as the 'whole heart' of 19. **11.** Possibly source of doxology added to the Lord's Prayer in some MSS of M. **15.** Men on earth are like strangers sojourning in a foreign land only for a short time. But there is no suggestion here yet of the glorious immortality to which we know ourselves to be called. **20— 22*a*.** Sacrifices and a sacrificial banquet. In addition to holocausts they sacrificed also peace-offerings of which the offerers partook in a sacred meal, Lv 7:11—16. **22*b*—25.** The inauguration of Solomon's reign. The e turbulent background to this peaceful scene is given in 1 (3) Kgs 1. **22*b*.** 'They made Solomon king', not (RSV) 'the second time' (wanting in LXX [B]) as added by a glossator with an eye on the anticipatory statement of 23:1. It was Zadok who anointed Solomon, 1 (3) Kgs 1:39, and when the new sovereign banished Abiathar, 1 (3) Kgs 2:27, Zadok remained as high priest, ib. 35. There are two interesting differences between the account of 1 Kgs and our text. Here Solomon is anointed *prince* and not king as in 1 (3) Kgs 1:34 and he sits on the throne of *the Lord* and not on my i.e. David's throne 1 (3) Kgs 1:35. These slight but undoubtedly deliberate changes stress once again the position of the theocratic king. He is not the true king; Yahweh alone reigns and the Davidic ruler is merely his earthly representative who sits, not on a throne that he can claim as his own, but on a throne that has meaning and true power only in as far as it is the throne of the Lord. **26—30.** The death of David. **27** shows David as reigning over all Israel throughout his reign even in Hebron. This is contrary to the undoubted facts as they are given in 2 Sm 5:5. For Chr Israel is that part of the Jewish people who accept David and his line as king; no other group, Jewish or not, has any right to the title Israel. He makes this very clear in 2 Chr when he simply ignores the N kingdom as non-Israelite because it rejected David in his heirs. **29.** These writings are probably the books of Sm and Kgs under other names. This fashion of describing books by the principal prophets who are mentioned in them is found elsewhere in Chr. These three prophets were personally acquainted with David, Samuel 1 Sm 16:13, Nathan 2 Sm 12:1, Gad 1 Sm 22:5.

THE SECOND BOOK OF CHRONICLES

1:1—9:31 The reign of Solomon—1 (3) Kgs 2:12—11: 305 43. In this section Chr uses the text of Kgs as his principal source. In his use of this source he follows the same principles and methods as he did in dealing with the reign of David. All stress is laid on the religious and liturgical elements of Solomon's life; the political background——a very lively one in fact as we can see from Kgs——is left out of account. We hear nothing therefore of the intrigues that led up to and followed from Solomon's ascent to the throne, nothing about the rather shocking deathbed wishes of David and their equally shocking fulfilment by Solomon;

305a above all, nothing about the polygamy and idolatry of Solomon or about the political unrest that troubled the last years of his reign. Solomon is an ideal king like David, his father. In Chr we find the early stages of that idealization of Solomon which we see in its developed state in Eccl and Wis 6—9. Solomon is a religious giant and is rewarded for his religion with immeasurable wisdom and riches.

b **1:1—6 Solomon's Sacrifices at Gibeon**—1 (3) Kgs 3:4. The ark of the covenant was now in the city of David, 1 Chr 15, but the tabernacle, which had housed it from the time of Moses till its capture and return by the Philistines, 1 Sm 7:2, together with the altar of holocausts are here stated to have been at Gibeon. David had appointed Zadok and his brethren priests at Gibeon, 1 Chr 16:39f. Through their ministry Solomon offered his numerous holocausts in thanksgiving for his elevation to the throne. This concept of the separate location of ark and tent, the ark at Jerusalem and the tent at Gibeon, is characteristic of Chr (cf 1 Chr 16:39; 21:29). It may be doubted however if the original Tent of the desert period survived the Philistine destruction of Shiloh where it had been placed Jos 18:1, cf § 103g. The Chronicler reasons that if Solomon offered sacrifice, 1 (3) Kgs 3:4, at Gibeon, the tent must have been there, even if the ark were already located under another tent which David had pitched for it in Jerusalem, 2 Sm 6:17. The first act of Solomon's reign is a religious and liturgical act in which all Israel joins. He carries out the essential function of the Davidic king: he leads all the people of God to God.

c **7—13 Solomon's vision at Gibeon**   1 (0) Kgs 0.5 15. Chr omits the fact that it was in a *dream* that God appeared to Solomon for in later times this was considered a very inferior means of divine communication. Chr omits the conditional promise of length of days, 1 (3) Kgs 3:14, perhaps because Solomon fell away and did not fulfil the condition, 1 Kgs 11:4. Though God also gives Solomon power and wealth, Chr lays stress on the wisdom which Solomon receives. And the great manifestation of this wisdom is in his religious activity: the building of the temple. Consequently he omits all worldly wisdom and power as they are described in 1 (3) Kgs 3:16—5:14. **14—17 Solomon's Military Power and Wealth**—1 (3) Kgs 10:26—29. **15.** Gold is not mentioned in Kgs. **17.** Solomon's wealth was greatly increased by this trade in horses and chariots.

d **2:1—18 Preparations for the Temple; Hiram's promise of help, Forced Labour**—Comparison of this ch with 1 Kgs shows that the role of Solomon is deliberately enhanced and that of Hiram diminished. Thus the omission of 1 (3) Kgs 5:1 leaves the initiative of the relationship with Solomon and not with Hiram. Building the temple is the best proof of the wisdom of Solomon and the best use of his riches. The great programme of profane building that Solomon carried out is only referred to in a very passing way by Chr, 7:11, 8:1. Yet we know from 1 (3) Kgs 7:1 that he spent 13 years building his own palace while he only spent seven on the house of the Lord, 1 Kgs 6:38. **1.** The completion of Solomon's own palace is mentioned in 7:11. **2.** is repeated but more fully in 17f. **3—16.** Negotiations with Hiram. 1 (3) Kgs 5:1—14. The purpose of the temple is above all the worship of God by sacrifice rather than to be a house for the Lord to dwell in. Chr suggests that God dwells in heaven and that the temple is a house for his name or as in 1 Chr 28:2 a footstool for Yahweh. We can see in this concept of the Temple a greater awareness of the transcendence of God than is to be found in Kgs' concept, cf also Ps 99 (98):5; Mt 6:34—35. **5.** The

exaltation of Yahweh above all gods would not be diplo- **305d** matic in a letter to a pagan king and suggests that the Chronicler did not have the actual wording of Solomon's missive, unless Chr wishes to suggest that Hiram was merely a vassal king of Solomon's. The tone of Solomon's letter to Hiram is more haughty than in 1 Kgs while the reply of Hiram is more submissive. In v 12 he refers to Yahweh as Maker of Heaven and Earth—a phrase not found in Kgs—and in v 14 he refers to David as 'my Lord'—where 'my brother' would be more normal in correspondence between equals. A subject king would naturally admit the supremacy of the god of his overlord. In v 10 Solomon determines the amount he is prepared to give the Tyrians; in Kgs it is Hiram who decides this matter. **13.** Huramabi is a much more important figure **e** in Chr than in Kgs. Chr who sees in the Temple of Solomon the fulfilment of which the Tabernacle in the desert was the type (compare 1 Chr 28:19 with Ex 25:9) models Huramabi on Bezalel and Oholiab, the craftsmen who worked on the Tabernacle, Ex 31:1ff, 35:30ff. The comparison with Oholia*b* may explain the suffix *abi* which Chr adds to the name Huram and the fact that Chr attaches Huramabi to the tribe of Dan like Oholiab rather than to the tribe of Naphtali as his source in Kgs does. (cf Brunet, RB 61 (1954) 359). **16.** Chr omits the treaty of 1 (3) Kgs 5:12. Apparently he considers that a treaty implies equality apart from the added reason that there should be no unnecessary contacts even with friendly non-Israelites. In this implication he is reflecting the outlook of post-exilic Judaism. **17—18.** The labour gangs. 1 (3) Kgs 5:15 **16. 17.** Solomon took a census of all the non-Hebrews resident in Israel, that is the remnants of the conquered inhabitants, whom his father had already numbered, 1 Chr 22:2. As the total equals the sum of the separate gangs spoken of in 18, it is evidently that of the able-bodied only. Kgs in MT + Vg, prob. through the accidental addition of one letter, has 3,300 overseers, but LXX (B) in agreement with Chr has 3,600. If the 30,000 sent by Solomon to help on Lebanon are added to the 150,000 mentioned here, we have the proportion of 180,000 workmen to 3,600 overseers, that is 1 to every 50. Solomon in Chr does not put Israelites to forced labour but only resident aliens.

3:1—17 Measurements and Adornments of the **f** **Temple**—**1.** Mt Moriah was the scene of Abraham's sacrifice of Isaac; see on Gn 22:2. On it was the threshing floor of Ornan, 1 Chr 21:15ff. See on 2 Chr 6:11. **2—4.** Time and Measurements, 1 (3) Kgs 6:1—3. **2.** On the relation of months to regnal years, see § 125d **3.** The length of the sanctuary (Holy Place and Holy of Holies) was 60 cubits *by the ancient measure*, cubits, that is, of 7 handbreadths; see § 86a. **4.** The porch or vestibule was 10 cubits deep, Kgs, and 20 cubits, the same as the Holy Place behind it, in width. This width is here called its 'length' as being its longer measure. 120 must surely be a mistake for 20. **5—7.** The Holy Place, 1 (3) Kgs 6:15—18. **5.** The Holy Place is 'the greater house' as being 40 cubits long, whereas the Holy of Holies was 20. **6.** The floor was made of planks of fir, overlaid with gold, 1 (3) Kgs 6:15, 30, and is not mentioned here. 'He adorned the house with precious stones'. In many respects Chr and Kgs mutually supplement each other. **7.** The gold was 'of the finest': 'of Parvaim', perhaps from Parwa in the Yemen. **8.** The Holy of Holies, 1 (3) Kgs 6:19—20. Chr adds the weight of gold used. **9.** Prob. only the heads of the nails, 1 (3) Kgs 6:21, were covered with gold. 50 shekels = c. 20 oz. The meaning suggested by RSV is prob. the best: that there was a goldplated nail of 1 shekel for every 50 shekels of gold used. The upper

305f chambers, 1 (3) Kgs 6:10. **10—13.** The cherubim, 1 (3) Kgs 6:23—28. **14.** The veil, not mentioned in Kgs, will have been hung against the partition separating the Holy Place from the Holy of Holies, 1 (3) Kgs 6:16. **15—17.** The two pillars, 1 (3) Kgs 7:15—22. Hiram made the pillars, Kgs; here the work is attributed to Solomon who had commissioned it. They were 18 cubits high, Kgs, Jer 52:21; and so Syr. here also. **16.** 'Chains like a necklace' surrounding each pillar (*rabîd* misread as *debir*).

g 4:1—22 Other Appurtenances of the Temple—1 supplies the dimensions of the bronze altar, mentioned 1 (3) Kgs 8:64. The height of the altar implies an approach to it by steps. This deviation from the prescription of Ex 20:26 may be explained by a change in the form of the dress worn. **2—5.** The Molten sea, 1 (3) Kgs 7:23—26. **3.** The word 'oxen' here is a slip due to the oxen, 4, on which the sea rested. What are here described are gourd-shaped ornaments under the brim, Kgs, 'compassing it, ten to a cubit, surrounding the sea, the gourds being in two rows, cast together with the sea'. **5.** The divergence as to its capacity, here 3,000 baths, in Kgs 2,000, is prob. to be explained by the accidental omission of 'three' in Kgs, the Heb. consonants for 'thousands' and 'two thousand' being the same. **6.** 1 (3) Kgs 7:38f. **7.** Ex 25:31—40 speaks of one 'candlestick' only. 1 (3) Kgs 7:49 has ten, as here. **9.** 'The great court' outside the court of the priests. **11—22.** 1 (3) Kgs 7:40—51. **17.** 'In a clay ground': some emend to 'at the ford of Adamah'. Chr puts the place between Succoth and Zereda, Kgs between the former and Zarethan, the similarity showing that there is a clerical error. **19.** 2 Chr 13:11 and 29:18 speak of only one table of show-bread. One of the ten, 8, therefore was for this purpose; the others perhaps supported the golden and silver, 1 Chr 28:15, candlesticks. The parallel passage, 1 (3) Kgs 7:48, has one table of show-bread only. **20.** A light was to burn before the Holy of Holies according to the *ordinance* of Ex 27:20f.

h 5:1—14 Transference of the Ark to the Temple— In chh 5—7 Chr has certainly retouched his source to bring it into harmony with the cultic practices of his own day. Thus he lays a special stress on the musical part of the ceremony and on the role of the Levites in general. **1.** 1 (3) Kgs 7:51. **2—11a.** 1 (3) Kgs 8:10,10a. It is to be noted that the whole people took part in the celebration; this is a characteristic feature of Chr. The king is merely the leader of the people, who must all as individuals take their part and personally seek God. There is no mere ritualism or sacerdotalism in the religious outlook of Chr. **3.** 'The solemn day' was the Feast of Tabernacles. **4.** In Chr the Levites, not the priests, Kgs, carry the ark. **7.** The Levites could not enter the Holy of Holies, and therefore the priests carried the ark on this last stage of its journey. **11b—13g** is not in Kgs. It is characteristic of Chr to add the musicians and singers from his love of liturgical music and song in joyful praise of Yahweh. **13h—14.** Kgs 10b—11. This is an anticipation of 7:1f.

i 6:1—42 Solomon's address and prayer at the Dedication of the Temple—1—11. The address. 1 (3) Kgs 8:12—21. **1—2.** Chr simply takes over this mysterious text directly from his source without giving any interpretation. The idea behind it seems to be that just as God had chosen darkness as the mode of his manifestation on Horeb Ex 20:21 so it is fitting that he should dwell in the darkness of the Holy of Holies. **5f—6b.** Not in Kgs and is obviously an addition of Chr to emphasize the unique position of Jerusalem as the only true

temple and throne of God, and of David as prince over **305** his people. Yet, in fact, others had been chosen by God, Shiloh before Jerusalem, Jer 7:12, and Saul before David, 1 Sm 10:1.**-11.** A comparison with the parallel passage in 1 (3) Kgs 8:21 shows that Chr has changed 'our fathers when he brought them out of the land of Egypt' into 'the people of Israel'. There seems to be a deliberate playing down of the Sinai covenant, and this suspicion is corroborated when we find that the references to the Exodus in 1 (3) Kgs 8:51, 53 are similarly omitted from the prayer of Solomon in Chr. A similar phenomenon occurs in 2 Chr 3:1 where the reference to the exodus of 1 (3) Kgs 6:1 is omitted and stress is laid only on the link with David and, through Mt Moriah—the scene of the sacrifice of Isaac—with Abraham. It would appear then that for Chr the great events in the history of Israel are the covenant with Abraham, which receives all the attention in 1 Chr 16:14—18 and the promise to David. Indeed Chr even prefers to call God's relation to David a covenant-relationship rather than a promise. For him the promise and covenant made to Abraham, the father of Israel, reaches its climax not in Moses, who is hardly mentioned at all, but in David the Messianic king, (cf Brunet art. cit. 1954, 368f). This point is of some importance as showing that Chr is not so exclusively loyal to the Mosaic institutions by which his contemporaries live as to forget the greater dignity of the original free promise of God to Abraham, who believed in God and was justified, or the fact that the great one to come, the Messiah, will be a new David to establish anew the kingdom of God. We seem to see here a foreshadowing of Pauline theology.

12—42. The prayer. 1 Kgs 8:22—50a. **13.** This bronze platform is added by Chr, perhaps under the influence of conditions of his own time, to make it clear that Solomon did not stand at the altar like a priest. **20.** 'where thou hast promised to set thy name', which practically means to manifest thy presence. **21.** Solomon prayed, turned 'towards it' (the sanctuary), that whosoever should pray 'towards this place' should be heard in heaven. So also in 26, 29, 32. This applied whether the suppliant was in the temple precincts or even in a distant country; see Ps 5:8; 138 (137):2; Dn 6:10. **23.** If an oath of accusation is met by an oath of denial, God Almighty is begged to judge between the two parties. **40—42.** The borrowing from Ps 132, which is not in Kgs, is discreetly but clearly Messianic for this psalm is entirely country; see Ps 5:7; 138 (137):2; Dn 6:10. **23.** If an 'Remember, O Lord, in David's favour all the hardships he endured etc'. In the circumstances of the postexilic writer these promises are only to be fulfilled in the Messiah. The Messianic interpretation seems to be corroborated by the change which Chr makes in Ps 132 (131):10. 'For the sake of David thy servant' is intensified to 'Remember thy steadfast (convenantal) love for David thy servant'. **42.** To turn away the face of a suppliant is to reject his petition, 1 (3) Kgs 2:16. Solomon prays that God will remember the favours he showered on David and treat his posterity with the same love.

7:1—22 God's Sign of Acceptance of the Temple; k Other Details; God's Assurance to Solomon—1—3. Fire from heaven and a cloud filling the temple. **1.** The fire is a sign that Yahweh as truly approves and hallows the temple and the sacrifice as he did the sacrifice of Aaron, Lv 9:24. The story is perhaps influenced by the story of Elijah, 1(3) Kgs 18:38. **2.** Similarly at the dedication of the tabernacle, Ex 40:34f. **3.** Quotes the words of the antiphon chanted by the people which occurs in Ps 136 (135):1 and elsewhere. **4—7.** The

05k sacrifices. 1 (3) Kgs 8:62—64. Rawlinson points out here that 'profusion was a usual feature of the sacrifices of antiquity. Three hundred oxen formed a common sacrifice at Athens. Five hundred kids were offered annually at the Marathonia. (Böckh's *Athens* I 283, E.tr.). Sacrifices of a thousand oxen were not infrequent. According to an Arabian historian (Kotibeddyn) the Caliph Moktader sacrificed during his pilgrimage to Mecca in the year of the Hegira 350, 40,000 camels and cows, and 50,000 sheep. Tavernier speaks of 100,000 victims as offered by the King of Tonquin. (See Milman's 'Gibbon', IV 96, note)'. **6.** Not in Kgs; note again the addition of Levites, music and song, and the repetition of the antiphon from 3. This antiphon sums up the fundamental lesson of the whole of Chr. **8 11.** The Feast of Tabernacles; conclusions. 1 (3) Kgs 8:65—66. **8.** 'the solemnity': the Feast of Tabernacles was distinguished by being called simply 'the feast'. **9.** On the solemn assembly following the feast, see §§ 105*h*, 204*b*. 'Because' begins a new sentence. Because the dedication had lasted 7 days and the feast 7 days, followed by the solemn assembly on the 8th day, the people could be dismissed, 10, on the 23rd. The feast began on the 15th. **12—22.** God's assurance to Solomon, 1 (3) Kgs 9:1—9. **12.** The purpose of the temple is to be a house of sacrifice rather than a dwelling-place of God; see on 2 Chr 2:4. **13—15.** Not in Kgs.

l 8—9 Other activities of Solomon—These two chh give the concrete proof of God's blessing on Solomon. Kgs is used as a source but all the shadows on the glory of Solomon are omitted. **1—6.** Building operations. See 1 (3) Kg: 10—19. **1.** The time indicated is 'at the end of the twenty years in which Solomon had built' the temple and his palace. **2.** Hiram gave these cities *back* to Solomon. For the prehistory of this event, see 1 (3) Kgs 9:11—13. Hiram had been disappointed with the cities. But perhaps Chr does not wish to think of Solomon being obliged to give anything to Hiram and consequently alters the account in Kgs. **7—10.** Labour Gangs 1 (3) Kgs 9:20—23. **8.** This is taken literally from Kgs even though the words 'to this day' are meaningless in Chr. **10.** 'And these (the officers of 9) were Solomon's chief overseers' of his labour gangs. The subordinate overseers were chosen from among the non-Israelites forced to work. In number they were 250, Chr, 550, Kgs. The discrepancy may be due to a copyist's error or to a difference in the basis of the computation. **11.** Pharaoh's daughter. Cf 1 (3) Kgs 9:24. It was not merely because she was a foreigner that she could not live in the royal palace: 'No wife of mine shall dwell . . .'. Chr presupposes the reader's knowledge of the marriage, 1 (3) Kgs 3:1; 7:8. 11*b* is not in Kgs. **12—16.** Solomon's care for the cult. 1 (3) Kgs 9:25. **17—18.** Expedition to Ophir. 1 (3) Kgs 9:26—28. Solomon went to Ezion-geber to supervise the construction of his ships there, Kgs. In this work he was no doubt assisted by Hiram, who sent his experienced seafaring men with Solomon's in these ships, Kgs. The text of Chr has been understood by many, as in RSV, to state that Hiram sent Solomon ships for the expedition, which could only be explained if the Phoenicians already had in the Persian gulf the trading stations mentioned by Strabo, 16, 3, 4 (ed. I. Casaubon, 1587, 527). But it is more likely that the text says that Hiram sent ships not 'to him' but 'for him': 'and Hiram assisted by sending ships (those built by Solomon at Ezion-geber) manned by his men, men familiar with seafaring'. Hiram's men were helped by Solomon's, who were only novices in the art of navigation. The amount of gold obtained was

450 talents, MT, 400, Syr., 420 Kgs, MT; 120, Kgs, **3051** LXX (B).

9:1—31 Solomon's Wisdom and Wealth; his m Death—**1—9** and **12.** The Visit of the Queen of Sheba. 1 (3) Kgs 10:1—10 and 13. **4.** Literally, she was 'out of breath' with astonishment. **8.** Comparison with Kgs shows that Chr has altered the text to emphasize that Yahweh is the true king of Israel and that the object of his love is Israel rather than Solomon.

10—11; 13—28 Solomon's Wealth and Glory—1 n (3) Kgs 10:11—12; 14—26. **21.** The destination of this expedition cannot have been Tarshish (Tartessus) in Spain both because of the products acquired and because in the similar passage, 20:36—37, the vessels were constructed at Ezion-geber at the head of the Gulf of Aqaba on the E side of the Sinaitic peninsula. These were damaged (in a storm) and 'could not go to Tarshish'. Moreover, in the parallel passage in 1 (3) Kgs 22:49 these ships were destined for Ophir, prob. on the S coast of Arabia or the E coast of Africa. It therefore appears that the Phoenicians will have given the name Tarshish to some distant trading-place perhaps on the Persian Gulf. There Strabo (see on 8:17—18) reports the existence of such stations adding that the Phoenicians gave their familiar names to new localities. But the term 'Ships of Tarshish' seems to have been used of any large ship built for long distance voyages, ocean-going liners in fact. Albright BASOR 83, 21f suggests that 'Tarshish' means 'metal refinery' and that the Tarshish-ships were ore-carriers originally and not ships that sailed to Tartessus in Spain. **26** – 1 (3) Kgs 1:01a. **27** repeats 2 Chr 1:15. **28** repeats in part 2 Chr 1:16. For the other countries, see 14, 23f. **29—31.** Conclusion on Solomon. 1 (3) Kgs 11:41—43, which as source names only Solomon's chronicles. Nathan, 1 Chr 17:1; Ahijah, 2 Chr 10:15; Iddo, 12:15.

10:1—36:21 The History of Judah from Reho- 306a boam to the Fall of Jerusalem. In this section the Chronicler confines his attention entirely to the kingdom of Judah since he considers that the N kingdom has fallen away from the Kingdom of God in rejecting the line of David. Even among the kings of the Davidic line he devotes by far the greatest part of his writing to the three kings—Jehoshaphat, Hezekiah and Josiah—who are in their religious zeal the outstanding successors of the ideal kings, David and Solomon. Another characteristic of these chh is the prominent part played in them by the prophets. At every important occasion in the history of Judah a prophet appears to give God's message which is always the same: trust in Yahweh alone. The famous phrase of Is 7:9 'If you will not believe surely you will not be established' is the leitmotiv if all this section. **10:1—12:16 Rehoboam** 931—914 B.C. b

10:1—19 Secession of the Northern Tribes—1 (3) Kgs 12:1—20. **15** supposes knowledge of the event described in 1 (3) Kgs 11:26—40. **16.** The king is spoken of as a shepherd who 'feeds' or pastures his flock. **11:1—4 War against the Northern Tribes forbidden**—1 (3) Kgs 12:21—24. **3.** Chr makes a very significant change in his source: 'all the house of Judah and Benjamin and the rest of the people' becomes '*all Israel* in Judah and Benjamin'. Chr omits everything about Jeroboam; consequently 1 (3) Kgs 12:25—14:20 is entirely omitted, but he gives other material about Rehoboam from other sources whose high quality we have no reason to doubt. **5—12 Fortifications**—Not in Kgs. Following close upon the threat of war with the newly established N Kingdom this account might suggest that the fortifications were a defence measure against that

306b state. But the cities best situated for that purpose (those in the frontier area of Benjamin) are not named. The position of the towns fortified in the S and W shows that they were directed against a threat from Egypt. The account thus prepares for the invasion of the Pharaoh in ch 12 and underlines the lesson that no human efforts can avert punishment designed by God, 12:5. **10.** As no towns in Benjamin are listed, the expression 'Judah and Benjamin' designates the S Kingdom.

c 13–17 Refugees from the Northern Kingdom— Not in Kgs. All decent elements left the realm of Jeroboam and turned to Jerusalem where alone was the true Israel with God's king and temple. Thus God brought good out of evil. The religious innovations of Jeroboam made men turn to the line of David and strengthened the loyalty of Judah to Yahweh. That such a movement did take place is not impossible; something similar certainly happened in the reign of Hezekiah after the fall of Samaria. In this passage Chr clearly has his own contemporaries, the Samaritans, in mind. **13.** The Levites were living scattered throughout Israel in the cities assigned to them according to the law, Nm 35:2–8; Jos ch 21. **15.** 'Satyrs': lit. 'he-goats', a contemptuous appellation based on mythology. Jeroboam himself introduced an illegitimate cult of Yahweh under the image of calves, Ex 20:4, but under his 'sons', 14, or successors the cult became debased by idolatrous contamination.

18–23 Rehoboam's Family—Not in Kgs. **21.** cf Dt 17:17 a first sin of Rehoboam. **22.** As Abijah was not the eldest, who was prob. Jeush, this preference of him was against Dt 21:15–17. **23.** 'He dealt wisely, and distributed some of his sons through all the districts of Judah... and procured wives for them'. His motives will have been further to guard against the threat of invasion and to diminish the possibility of the brothers taking action against the elevation of Abijah.

d 12:1–12 The Invasion of Shishak—1 (3) Kgs 14:25–28. Shishak I, c. 945–c. 924, founded the XXII (Bubastite) dynasty. He has left a record of this Palestinian expedition on the walls of Karnak. **1.** The name 'Israel' is used of the S Kingdom alone. The details of the idolatry are given 1 (3) Kgs 14:22–24. **2.** Chr brings out clearly the link between sin and immediate punishment which is only implicit in Kgs **3.** Sukkim were foreign troops in the service of Egypt. Cf *OT and Modern Studies*, ed. H. H. Rowley, 1951, 18. **5.** Here appears Shemaiah, the first of the series of prophets mentioned in intro. to ch 10. **6–7.** The theme of humility and of God's giving grace and forgiveness to the humble is one of Chr's favourite themes. Cf 7:14, 12:12, 33:23, 34:27, etc. As the wrath of God was not poured out on Jerusalem, the city was not captured by storm; and, **8,** the treasure carried away by the Pharaoh will have been voluntarily surrendered to save the city. Solomon's golden shields, 9:15f.

13–16 Conclusion—1 (3) Kgs 14:21–22, 29–31. **15.** Add after 'the seer', 'this is true also of the genealogy'. This is a reference to 11:18ff.

e 13:1–14:1a Abijah 914–912/11.

13:1–2a Introductory—1 (3) Kgs 15:1f. **1.** This is the only case in which Chr indicates a synchronism between the two kingdoms, prob. as leading up to the war with Jeroboam, 2b. **2.** Micaiah is a deformation of Maacah, 11:20, whose father was Uriel and whose grandfather was Absalom, 11:20. Her mother was Tamar, 2 Sm 14:27, and she herself received the name of her great-grandmother, 1 Sm 3:3.

2b–20 War with Jeroboam—1 (3) Kgs 15:7c. **3.** Chr omits here the condemnation of Abijah by 1 (3) Kgs 15:3. It would seem to clash with the character of Abijah **306** as it emerges from his speech in 5–12. **5.** Salt being incorruptible, 'a covenant of salt' is a perpetual covenant, Nm 18:19. This speech is, of course, an address to the Samaritan contemporaries of Chr as much as to Jeroboam the son of Nabat. Once again Chr stresses the importance of the covenant with David rather than the promise to David. **7.** To call the adherents of Jeroboam 'worthless scoundrels' is special pleading in view of the account in ch 10. The contrast with Kgs is even more striking for there the breakaway is approved by a prophet of God, Ahijah the Shilonite, 1 (3) Kgs 11:31ff. Rehoboam was inexperienced, lit. 'a youth', much as we sometimes speak of a grown man as a child. He was 41 years old at his accession, 12:13. **9.** See 11:13–15. **14.** For the priests with their trumpets in war, see Nm 10:8f. **20.** The circumstances of Jeroboam's death are unknown.

21–14:1a Conclusion—1 (3) Kgs 15:7–8. **22.** For **f** further information about Abijah, Chr refers to 'the *Midrash* of Iddo the prophet'. A Midrash is an enquiry or study, and so a commentary. Centuries later the rabbinic commentaries treated their material with great freedom and the word took on a corresponding shade of meaning, but there is no ground for reading that meaning back into earlier centuries. Chr omits a comment on Abijah's sins such as is given 1 (3) Kgs 15:3, but indications that 'his heart was not perfect with the Lord' are not wanting. His son Asa had to abolish the idolatrous altars, 14:2, and the false worship of Maacah is mentioned in 15:16. But Abijah did not wholly abandon the worship of Yahweh. On the contrary, he made offerings to the temple, 1 (3) Kgs 15:15.

14:1b–16:14 Asa 912/11–871/70—If we grant **g** that the Chronicler is prepared to admit impossibilities to support his teaching on divine retribution, the career of Asa can be explained as follows: Tradition told the Chronicler that Asa had a long reign which ended in sickness. This meant that he must have been a good king by Chronicler's religious standards who yet committed some fault. The virtue for which he was rewarded with a long reign was his reforming zeal. This was so great that it deserved the reward of a very long and peaceful reign. Therefore any lack of success that Asa suffered could have come only at the end of the reign and was immediately punished by dropsy. The Chronicler **h** now fits the facts to this schema by making his war with Baasha, which he knew of from tradition, break out in the 36th year of his reign, when Baasha was already ten years dead. This altering of the facts for a theological purpose seems to be too much to allow, even to the Chronicler. The best solution to the problem seems to be to assume that the occasion of the war with Baasha was Asa's great religious reform in his 50th year. This was, of course, a threat to the peaceful development of the still struggling N dynasty and Baasha naturally took the steps described in 2 Chr 16:1 to ward off this threat. War ensued in the 16th—not 36th year—of Asa. It ended in a victory for the S kingdom but Asa's sins in the conduct of the war and especially his ill treatment of a prophet met their merited punishment in the dropsy which affected Asa's last days and seems to have necessitated a regency of his son Jehoshaphat for the last two years of his reign. This interpretation would also explain the statement of 1 (3) Kgs 15:16 that there was war between Asa and Baasha all their days and yet leave room for a reign of Asa that was on the whole peaceful.

14:1b–5 Religious Reform—1 (3) Kgs 15:11f. **1b.** **i** The 10 years of peace are generally understood to be

306i the opening years of the reign before the invasion of Zerah. **2.** Chr changes the condemnation of Asa by Kgs into praise. Asa must have been a good king as he had a long reign. Besides for whatever reason, political or religious, he did what was most important in the eyes of Chr: he organized the true worship of Yahweh. **6—8 Military Preparations** 1 (3) Kgs 15:23; Jer 41:9. **8.** These are the numbers of fighting men who could be called on, not the numbers of a standing army, but **j** grossly exaggerated. **9—15 The Invasion of Zerah**— Not in Kgs. **9.** Zerah the Cushite. A comparison with Nm 12:1 and Hb 3:7 shows that the Cushites came from Cushan, apparently a district associated with Midian, and that they were therefore nomadic bedouin raiders like the Midianites of Jg 6ff who 'were like locusts for number'. Chr is actually more moderate in his estimate of a million men. This interpretation of the *raid* (rather than *invasion*) is corroborated by the fact that the headquarters of Zerah is Gerar, now Umm Jerar, in the desert steppeland S of Gaza. **15.** 'And they smote the tents of those who had *flocks*'.

k 15:1—7 Warning of the Prophet Azariah—Not in Kgs. **1.** Azariah is otherwise unknown. **2.** This is the basic theme of all prophecy and of prophecy in Chr in particular. **3—6.** The reference is to the lawless period of the Judges; see Jg 2:10—20. It was a time of repeated cycles of idolatry, affliction, repentance and forgiveness. In **5—6** the reference is to the tribes and cities of Israel. The war against Benjamin, Jg chh 20f; the destruction of Shechem, Jg 9:45. Van den Born points out that **5—7** are an example of the anthological style that is so popular among the later books of the Bible. The post-exilic authors make very wide use of the works and words of their predecessors. (v d Born op cit 168).

8—18 Religious Reform—**8.** The reform in 14:2—5 is an anticipatory mention of that recorded here but from another source. Here too the statement that he removed the idols (lit. abominations) out of the cities of Ephraim he had taken (see 17:2) seems to be an anticipation as till now Asa seems to have had no war with the N Kingdom. He also *renovated* the altar before the vestibule of the sanctuary. **12.** These covenant renewals dot the pages of Chr, cf Abraham, David, Asa, Jehoiada, Hezekiah and Josiah. **15.** All Judah rejoiced at the oath. Joy in the cult of Yahweh, in the observance of his covenantal law is a characteristic of Chr, as is the music of the preceding v. **16 18.** 1 (3) Kgs 15:13—15. **17.** These high places were not for idolatrous cults but for the illegitimate worship of Yahweh. **18.** Abijah had prob. made these offerings at such illegal high places. **19 Reward for Fidelity**—cf supra. That the report of the war in 16:1—5 is very incomplete is shown by the reference in 15:8 to the cities of Ephraim captured by Asa.

l 16:1—6 War with Israel—1 (3) Kgs 15:17—22, **7—10.** Reproof and Prophecy of the Seer Hanani—not in Kgs. One of the central themes of all the prophets is their opposition to foreign entanglements. **11—14.** Asa's Death and Burial—1 (3) Kgs 15:23f. **12.** It is possible that the physicians were rather 'medicine men' (a suggestion of van Selms).

m 17:1—21:1a Jehoshaphat 871/70—848— Jehoshaphat was a very pious king and therefore receives great attention from Chr, far more than he would merit as a political figure or than Kgs in fact gives him. It is noteworthy that all the wonderful stories of the Elijah cycle are omitted by Chr. Even Elijah, the great prophetic defender of Yahwism is omitted because he had no connexion with David or Sion.

17:1—19 His care for religion; Success; Military 306m preparations—Not in Kgs except 1a = 1 (3) Kgs 15:24b. But Chr uses another written source which he follows faithfully. This is shown by the use of 'Israel' to mean the N kingdom while in Chr's normal use of the word it means Judah and Benjamin only. **1b—2.** Military preparations necessitated by the late war with Israel. **3—5.** Religious spirit and consequent divine blessing. **6—9.** Religious reform and instruction of the people. **6.** The people were so prone to idolatry that fresh measures were already necessary after the action of Asa, 14:3. He did not remove the high places dedicated to the unlawful worship of Yahweh, 20:33. In **9** note the book of Mosaic law. **10—11.** Salutary respect of the neighbouring nations. **12—19.** Military strength. **17.** The Benjaminites were celebrated for their skill with the bow. Each archer, whose two hands were required to shoot with the bow, was protected by a companion holding a shield.

18:1—34 War with Ahab against Syria—It is **n** surprising to find this narrative preserved by Chr. For Jehoshaphat collaborates with the wicked Ahab and does not follow what he recognizes to be a prophetic oracle. Nevertheless he is such a contrast to Ahab in insisting on an answer from a true prophet that the story is left in. 19:2—3 does, however, point out that he did wrong. Even Jehoshaphat, that supremely pious king, cannot escape the strictures he merits according to Chr's retributive scheme. 1a repeats verbally 17:5b. **1b.** Jehoshaphat's son Jehoram married Athaliah the daughter of Ahab, 21:6; 22:2. **2—34.** Consultation and War, 1 (3) Kgs 22:2b—35. **27d** is a marginal gloss from Mi 1:2. **31.** 'And the Lord helped him' etc is not in Kgs.

19:1—3 Jehu's Rebuke to Josaphat—Not in Kgs. **o 2.** Jehu: see 20:34; 1 (3) Kgs 16:1. It is not indicated that any punishment followed.

4—11 Religious and Legal Reform—The section is **p** possibly introduced to show how Jehoshaphat lived up to his name which means 'Yahweh is judge'. Not in Kgs. The legal reform was itself religious in that Israel was a theocratic state, and its law was enshrined with divine sanction in the sacred books. **5.** Dt 16:18 ordered the appointment of judges in all the cities. David had already appointed judges, 1 Chr 23:4, but the system required reorganizing and may have fallen partly into disuse. **10.** This court at Jerusalem was to be a court of appeal to which cases would be sent from the provinces. It was to decide 'between blood and blood', i.e. in cases of homicide to adjudicate whether there was accident or guilt, Ex 21:12—23. And its functions were concerned with 'the law, the commandments, the statues and the judgements', or legal decisions of the courts. Unwitting transgressions of the law had to be atoned for, Lv ch 4. **11.** The court had two departments, the strictly religious and the civil, and the secular judges, 8, had the help of Levites as *assessors*, who would be experts in the law.

20:1—30 God grants Victory over Invaders—Not **q** in Kgs. **1.** cf 17:10. This must be a different source which Chr preserves as it stands because of the moral lesson. The Moabites and Ammonites were accompanied by Meunites, whose name seems to be preserved in El-Ma'an, E of Petra; see 10 and on 1 Chr 4:41. **2.** The Moabites were from E of the Dead Sea and the Meunites from Edom. Engaddi is the modern 'Ain Jidi on the W coast of the Dead Sea. **3.** Previous general fasts, Jg 20:26; 1 Sm 7:6. **5.** As Jehoshaphat stood in the midst of the people 'before the new court', the court in question would be that of the priests, 4:9, but unless some unrecorded renovation had taken place, it would hardly be called the new court. Some think that the

306q Chronicler is using a term current in his own day. **9.** Recalls the answer given to Solomon's prayer, 6:24—35 and 7:12—16. **10.** Dt. 2:4, 9, 19. **11.** The land of Israel is not the possession of the Israelites but the possession of God. **14.** Note that it is a Levite that prophesies. Perhaps Chr's emphasis on Levites is intended to suggest that they replace in post-exilic times the pre-exilic prophets, especially the cultic prophets. He uses the Hebrew root *nb'*, which is that used for prophetic action, in describing their temple function of song. **16.** The gully would be dry in summer. Jeruel, only here, but part of the wilderness of Judah. **19.** The sons of Korah were also sons of Kohath, 1 Chr 6:22, but for some reason it was wished here to give them special prominence. **20.** Tekoa: S by E of Bethlehem. For the words of the king cf Is 7:9. **21.** Note the refrain. The singers were clad 'in holy array', see on 1 Chr 16:29. **22—23.** No miracle is implied in the defeat of the invaders. They destroyed themselves. 'The Lord set an ambush against' the invaders, by inspiring Jehoshaphat to do so. In the confusion that perhaps ensued in the early morning light the Moabites and Ammonites suspected the Edomites of treachery and the final result was mutual massacre.

r **31—21:1a Conclusion; Death of Jehoshaphat**—1 (3) Kgs 22:41—51a. **33.** He did not abolish the high places where sacrifice was offered to God against the prescription of Dt 12 as he had those established for idolatrous worship, 17:6. The people were not fully loyal. He omits the statement in Kgs that he made peace with the king of Israel. For Chr there is only one king of Israel: Jehoshaphat. Besides he has no interest in the N kingdom. **34.** Here and elsewhere Chr omits all reference to male prostitutes, probably from a certain natural horror of such an abominable religious practice. The account in **35—37** of the proposed mercantile expedition to Ophir and Tarshish supplements and is supplemented by that in Kgs. See on 9:21. It is however more probable that to explain Jehoshaphat's bad luck in his shipping ventures, the source is changed and Jehoshaphat is made the prime mover in the alliance with the godless Ahaziah of Israel.

307a **21:1b—20 Jehoram** 848—841—Chr now omits everything in 2 Kgs down to Kgs 8:45 even the cycle of Elisha is of no concern to the true kingdom of God. **2—4 Slaughter of his brothers**—Not in Kgs. **3.** Jehoshaphat in putting his sons in command of fortified cities had followed the policy of Rehoboam, 11:23. **4** suggests that so far from Jehoram's rule being accepted by all, his brothers aided by some of the leading men had conspired against him, and 13 indicates that their opposition was due to his idolatrous practices. **5—7.** Summary of the reign = 2 (4) Kgs 8:17—19. **7.** Chr changes Kgs' 'The Lord would not destroy Judah for the sake of David his servant' into 'The Lord would not destroy the house of David because of the covenant he had made with David'; there is characteristic stress on David and on his *covenant*, not his promise. **8—10b.** Revolt of Edom and Libnah, 2 (4) Kgs 8:20—22. **9.** He was unable to crush the revolt, but though surrounded by the Edomites he managed to break through and escape. Kgs adds that his men fled. **10c—20c.** Not in Kgs. **10c—11.** His evil-doing. Idolatry was called fornication as Israel was considered to be the spouse of God. **12—15.** Epistle from Elijah. The order of the narrative in Kgs might suggest that Elijah had already been rapt into the skies, 2 (4) Kgs ch 2, but the Hebrew historians often do not follow the chronological sequence of events, and this passage shows that he was still working in the N Kingdom. Hence he communicates with Jehoram

by letter. **16—17.** Invasion of Judah. It is unlikely that **307** the Ethiopians (Cushites) across the Red Sea would here be styled neighbours of the Arabs, and there were prob. Cushites in N Arabia. Cf 14:9. His sons had promoted the worship of Baal, 24:7. Jehoahaz is another form of the name Ahaziah, that of the next king, 22:1. **19.** For the ceremonial fire, see on 16:14. **20a** repeats 5. **20d.** His burial, 2 (4) Kgs 8:24b. He was buried in the city of David, where his fathers were buried, Kgs, but not in the royal sepulchres, Chr.

22:1—9d Ahaziah 841 B.C.—**1—2 Introductory.** 2 **b** (4) Kgs 8:24b—26. The invasion in which his brothers were killed, 21:17. His father was 40 at the time of his death, 21:20, and Ahaziah was 22 years old at his accession, Kgs. Athaliah was the daughter of Ahab, 21:6, and the grand-daughter of Omri. Brunet (R. B. art. cit. 1954 385) suggests that the age of Ahaziah is increased by Chr from 22 to 42 to leave room for the various murders of his descendants. **3—4.** His wickedness. 2 (4) Kgs 8:27. **5—6.** Expedition with Jehoram. 2 (4) Kgs 8:28f. **7—9c.** His death. 2 (4) Kgs 9:21—27. **8.** Ahaziah may have had nephews old enough to be his pages, but perhaps LXX is right reading 'brothers', i.e. '*relatives* of Ahaziah'. **9.** When Ahaziah was brought to Jehu 'they (Jehu's men) killed him'. Chr and Kgs supplement each other, but the succinctness of the accounts does not permit certainty as to the course of events. Ahaziah, seeing that Jehu had killed Jehoram, fled by way of Beth haggan (Jenin), pursued by Jehu, Kgs. (Ahaziah, however, succeeded in escaping. Whereupon Jehu caused him to be searched for, and his men captured him in Samaria, where he was in hiding and brought him to Jehu, Chr. The verb may be conative. In this case, he never reached Samaria, as his attempt to take refuge there was frustrated.) Then Chr's terse statement that they killed him is amplified in Kgs. When Jehu saw him, he ordered his men to kill him in his chariot. They struck and wounded him at the ascent of Gur near Ibleam, but he managed to escape to Megiddo, where he died of his injuries. Though this reconstruction of events is possible, it seems a little forced and it might be better to presume that Chr is following a different tradition which he finds preferable to that given in Kgs. **22:9e—23:15 Athaliah** 841—835. **c**

The memory of Athaliah as a usurper who was not of Davidic descent was so hateful to the Chronicler that he contents himself with a bare mention of her six years' reign. Nothing is recorded of it except the bloody measure by which she secured the throne, 10, the means by which the future king was secured from her murderous purpose, 11—12, his eventual coronation, 23:1—11, and her ignominious death, 12—15.

9e—10. Athaliah seizes the throne. 2 (4) Kgs 11:1. **11—12.** Joash is saved. 2 (4) 11:2f. Chr adds that Jehoshabeath was married to the high-priest. This enabled the boy to be concealed in the priest's quarters in the temple; and the danger of discovery was the less that Athaliah, as a worshipper of Baal, would not frequent the temple. **23:1—11.** The conspiracy and coronation of Joash. 2 (4) Kgs 11:4—12. Chr changes the military coup in the temple supported by the priests—this is Kgs' concept of the conspiracy—into an entirely priestly and levitical move supported by the people. He certainly could not admit that the royal guards, who were foreigners, could enter the temple. **2.** The name 'Israel' is used of Judah as in 21:4. **3.** God's promise to David, 2 Sm 7:16. **5.** The priestly and Levitical courses, 1 Chr chh 23—26, changed offices on the Sabbath. That day was suitable for the conspirators as larger numbers

07c would not attract attention. The 1st division of Chr corresponds to the 3rd of Kgs, and the 2nd and 3rd to the 1st and 2nd of Kgs. The 'foundation' gate is called 'the gate of Sur' in Kgs, the similarity of the two names in Heb. being of evidence of textual corruption. **11.** The word 'testimony' should probably be changed to 'armlets', part of the royal regalia. It is specified by Chr that the king was anointed by Jehoiada and his sons. **12—15.** Death of Athaliah. 2 (4) Kgs 11:13—16. **13.** As so often in Chr the singers lead the celebration.

d **23:16—24:27 Joash** 835—796. **16—19 The Covenant Renewal—16.** Comparison with 2 (4) Kgs 11:17 will show that a change of text makes the covenant entirely centred on the Lord in Chr. In Kgs there is a separate covenant between the king and the people. **18** joins together three of Chr's favourite themes: levites, joy and song.
20—21 Enthronement of Joash. 2 (4) Kgs 11:19f.
  24:1—3 Introductory. 2 (4) Kgs 12:1—3. Repair of the temple. 2 (4) Kgs 12:4—16. The two accounts supplement each other on various points. **6.** The contribution appointed by Moses, Ex 30:11—16 and 38:25. **7.** Kgs implies that the money was appropriated by the priests. Chr omits this. **8.** The chest will have been placed on the outside of the gate leading into the inner court. The text in Kgs, 9, which says the chest was placed 'by the altar' has been corrected in Chr, since the people had no access to the court of the priests. **14.** No money was spent on utensils for the temple while the work of repair was in progress, Kgs 13, but when it was finished it was found that there was a considerable sum still in hand and this was used for the provision of precious vessels for use in divine worship.
15—16. Death of Jehoiada. Not in Kgs. He lived to a very advanced age. If the figures are correctly transmitted, he must have been in his eighties when he married Jehoshabeath, the daughter of Joram, 22:11, who died at the age of 40, 21:20; and consequently the mar-
c riage could not have taken place many years before. But it is very probable that Chr is using here the Heb. convention that associates a long life with great virtue. 'He had done good to Israel, for God and for his house', the temple. **17—22.** Idolatry and consequent murder of Zechariah. Not in Kgs. This section is added to explain the Syrian invasion; it was a punishment for the sin of Joash in sacrilegiously murdering the son of his benefactor. The religious reform after the death of Athaliah had not been whole-hearted. **21.** If the Syrian invasion was already threatening, the king may have considered that the prophet's announcement that the people could not prosper after forsaking God, would discourage them. According to Mt 23:35, Zechariah was killed between the sanctuary and the altar. **23—24.** Invasion of Syrians. 2 (4) Kgs 12:17f. They did not capture Jerusalem, as Joash bought them off with valuable treasure, Kgs. Chr stresses the punitive character of the invasion. The real sufferers were Joash and the princes who had led him astray. **25—27.** Death of Joash. 2 (4) Kgs 12:19—21. **25.** The time-link with the invasion suggests that Joash's sickness was due to wounds. **26.** No pure-blooded Israelite but children of mixed marriages raised their hands against God's anointed. This probably had contemporary point in the mixed marriage struggles of post-exilic Jerusalem and Samaria.
f **25:1—28 Amaziah** 796—767—Amaziah had a long reign and so must have been a good king. Therefore Chr leaves out 2 (4) Kgs 14:3b—4
  1—2. Introductory. 2 (4) Kgs 14:1—4. He did not abolish the high places, Kgs, and later fell into idolatry,

14. 3—4. Punishment of his father's murderers. 2 (4) Kgs **307f** 14:5f. They were *his courtiers.* **5—10.** Preparations for war. Not in Kgs. **7.** Characteristically a prophet appears and administers a reprimand for partnership with idolatrous Israel. **10.** The anger of the hired Israelites will have been due in part to the loss of the expected booty. Their reprisals are related in 13. **11—12.** War with Edom. Kgs 14:7. **13.** Revenge of the Israelite mercenaries. Not in Kgs. They took advantage of Amaziah's absence during the Edomite campaign, and, starting from Samaria, made a raid against the cities of Judah as far as Bethhoron, a border town at this time belonging to Judah. But the suggestion offered by Dhorme (*La Bible de la Pléiade*, 1,423) is very tempting, namely: As one would have expected Amaziah's dismissal of the northern mercenaries to be rewarded by God rather than punished, the v should be translated: 'but they (the people of Judah) killed three thousand of them and took much booty'. **14—16.** Amaziah is reprimanded for idolatry. Not in Kgs. This is inserted to explain Amaziah's defeat by the northerners; it was a punishment for idolatry. **17—24.** War with Israel. Kgs 14:8—14. **20.** The mention of the gods of Edom refers to 14. **24.** The house of Obededom had retained the charge of the treasury since the time of David; see 1 Chr 26:15. **25—28.** Conclusion and death of Amaziah. Kgs 14:17—20.
26:1—23 Uzziah (Azariah) 767—739—The details **g** given by Chr about Uzziah indicate that he had other material at his disposal taken from sources generally recognized as reliable.
  1—4 Introductory. 2 (4) Kgs 14:21—22; 15:2f. That the people made him king does not signify their choice of a younger in preference to an elder brother, but that the unpopularity incurred by his father on account of the foolish and ruinous war undertaken against Israel led to his deposition. Otherwise the remark in **2** that his reconquest of the Red Sea port of Ailath took place after his father's death would be meaningless. Uzziah had probably been regent for his father Amaziah from the time of the latter's unsuccessful campaign against Joash of Israel. He would have been sixteen in 792/1 and this would explain the 52 years of the documents. **4.** He acted rightly as Amaziah had done in the first part of his reign before he fell into idolatry. **5.** His goodness not lasting. Not in Kgs. **6—15.** Military preparations and successful wars. Not in Kgs. **6.** Jabnia or Jabneh was later called Jamnia, 1 Mc 4:15. **7.** For the Meunites see on 1 Chr 4:41 and 2 Chr 20.1. Gurbaal is otherwise unknown. **9.** The corner-gate, also 25:23, at the NW of the city; the valley-gate, prob. at the SW leading from the valley of Ge-hinnom. The third was by the angle, of uncertain location. **16—21.** Usurpation of sacerdotal functions and chastisement. 2 (4) Kgs 15:5 records that God struck the king, but omits the reason. **16.** He was false to the Lord God by disobeying his law, Nm 16:1—40; 18:1—7; 1 Sm 2:28. **20.** A leper was levitically unclean, Lv 13:11. **21.** Lv 13:46 gives the law of isolation. **22—23.** Conclusion. Kgs 15:6f. Isaiah's call to the prophetic office fell in the last year of Uzziah, Is 6:1.
27:1—9 Jotham 739—734/3—Jotham's 16 years of **h** rule can only be explained if we assume that he became regent for his father when Uzziah contracted leprosy in 750.
  1—2. Introductory. 2 (4) Kgs 15:32—35b. The transgression of the people, Chr, was the frequenting of the illegitimate high places, Kgs. **3—4.** His buildings. Kgs 15:35c. Ophel: the S projection of the hill on which stood the temple. **5—6.** Successful war against the

307h Ammonites; piety rewarded. Not in Kgs. The Ammonites had paid tribute to Uzziah, 26:8, but now again asserted their independence. The subjugation by Jotham was also temporary as tribute was paid for only three years. The Ammonites prob. took advantage of the Syro-Israelite invasion, Kgs 15:37. **7—9.** Conclusion. Kgs. 15:36—38.

i 28:1—27 Ahaz 734/3—728/7—Ahaz is the worst king in the whole line of David. Chr can find nothing good to say of him. Even the Israelites of the N were more generous and noble than he! Here we see Chr's elevated idea of the call of God. All good men can be called if they show love for the people of God, and a member of the line of David can be rejected even though the line itself must stand.

1—4. Introductory; idolatry. 2 (4) Kgs 16:2—4. **1.** Hezekiah is said to have been 25 when he succeeded his father Ahaz, 29:1. Either this number is corrupt, or Ahaz must have been over 20 at his accession. According to the existing figures he died aged 36. **2.** The Baals are the various divinities known as 'Lord' in their respective localities. **3.** *The valley of Bene-hinnom* is that now called Wady er-Rababi S and W of Jerusalem. **5—7.** Punishment by invasion. Kgs 16:5f; Is 7:1. **8—15.** Israel returns the captives. Not in Kgs. This is a remarkable passage for a post-exilic Jerusalemite to write. It is in the line of the parable of the good Samaritan. **10.** It was forbidden to make bondservants of fellow-Israelites, Lv 25:39—43. **15.** Jericho belonged to the N Kingdom already in the time of Ahab, 1 (3) Kgs 16:34. **16—21.** Appeal to Tiglath-pileser for help. Kgs 16:7—9. Chr deliberately stresses the black side of Ahaz's foreign policy. **17.** The Edomites, ruthless enemies of the Israelites, took many captives. **21.** The statement that the appeal to the Assyrian availed him nothing is based on the long view that in the end Ahaz was no better off for it. Kgs records the immediate relief afforded by Tiglath-pileser's attack on Damascus in the years 733—32. **22—25.** Ahaz gives himself entirely to idolatry. Kgs 16:10—18. The two accounts differ in their selection of material from the common source, in such a way that Chr darkens the picture that Kgs gives of Ahaz. What appears in Kgs as an altar to Yahweh after the model of the Damascus altar has become in Chr unmitigated idolatry. Chr also gives the impression that Ahaz destroyed the vessels of the temple out of hatred for Yahwism while Kgs says that he did all these sacrilegious acts 'because of the king of Assyria'. **23.** The gods of Damascus 'struck' Ahaz. The sacred writer accommodates his words to the impious king's belief instead of saying 'whom he believed to strike him'. **26—27.** Conclusion. Kgs 16:19—20. Ahaz was buried with his fathers in Jerusalem, Chr, in the city of David, Kgs, but not in the royal sepulchres, Chr.

j 29:1—32:33 Hezekiah 728/7—699—For Chr, as for Kgs, Hezekiah is one of the great kings of Judah, but the treatment of this important figure differs very much in the two accounts. While for Kgs the great event is the invasion of Sennacherib, and to it he devotes two thirds of his attention, in Chr our attention is directed to the cultic activity of Hezekiah and Sennacherib occupies a relatively minor place.

29:1—2 Introductory. 2 (4) Kgs 18:1—3. **3—19.** The purification of the temple. Not in Kgs. **3.** Chr shows that Hezekiah's first and overriding interest is in the temple. 'In the first year of his reign, in the first month' he reopens the temple which his wicked father Ahaz had closed. **4.** Note the stress on the Levites. **5.** The Levites were to make sure that they were in a state of Levitical purity. Then they were to remove all the 'filth' **30** of idolatry from the temple. **9.** This phrase suggests that Chr is putting post-exilic ideas into the mouth of Hezekiah. **10.** The *Covenant* is the basis of union with God and sincere covenant renewal is an infallible means of averting God's wrath. **11.** This affectionate address of the Davidic king is made to the *Levites*. **13.** And among these Levites the singers occupy an equal place. **20—30.** Inauguration of the renewed temple-worship. Not in Kgs. **21.** The he-goats were for sin-offerings, 23, the other victims for holocausts. They were offered for the royal house, for the ministers of the temple, and for the people. **22.** For the sprinkling of the blood round about the altar, see Lt 1:5, 11. **23.** Laying the hand on the victim, Lv 1:4, 4:4. **24.** Again Israel stands for the S Kingdom, which Chr considered the true Israel as ruled by the divinely appointed Davidic dynasty. **25.** The celebrations would not be complete without the musicians, and, **30,** the glad songs of the Levites.

31—36. Further celebration of the reopening of k the temple. Not in Kgs. **31.** The king said 'You have consecrated yourselves to the Lord'. After the long neglect of the temple the sacrifices offered had been equivalent to a re-consecration to God's services. To 'fill the hand' is a technical term for consecration. In holocausts, as in sin-offerings, no part of the victim was returned for the use of the offerer. So it was those of generous heart who offered holocausts. **33.** The number of other victims was nearly ten times as large. On the sacrificial meal following peace-offerings, Lv 7:11—17. **34.** The priests were inadequate in number, in part at least because comparatively few were in a state of Levitical cleanness 'for the Levites were more earnest in purifying themselves than the priests'. MT of Lv 1:6 with sing. verb assigns the task of flaying the victim to the offerer, but SamP, LXX (and Vg) to the priests. It would certainly expedite matters that the ceremonial act should be entrusted to men skilled by long practice. It is difficult to understand this great praise for the Levites and this gratuitous insult to the priests if it were not occasioned by the relations between priests and levites in the Chronicler's own period. **36.** And all rejoiced '*that God had re-established it for the people, for it had been effected in a surprisingly short time*'.

30:1—27. Solemn Celebration of the Passover. Not l in Kgs. The circumstances of the celebration will of course vary somewhat according to one's choice of date for the death of Ahaz and accession of Hezekiah. The feast appears to have been celebrated in the first year of his reign, 2 Chr 30:2. On the early dating of Hezekiah's accession the celebration took place a few years before the invasion of Samaria by Shalmaneser when Hoshea was still on the throne, and a helpless vassal of Assyria, paying a heavy tribute. On the late dating the celebration would have taken place some years after the Fall of Samaria at a time when the Assyrians were settling foreigners in the captured territory to replace the thousands of Israelites deported to other areas. 2 Kgs 15:29 and 17:24. Furthermore these settlers from distant lands were bringing their gods with them. Some commentators hold that this Passover never took place. 'The significance of this account seems to be that Israel has been born again. It is a dramatic re-presentation of the first Passover at the Exodus. It is to be for all Israel although only a few responded from the northern tribes ... It is clear that what is described in this chapter is not a historical event but a remarkable irenical hope in the Chronicler's day ... It seems clear that we must read this chapter against the background of the Samaritan

3071 schism of the 4th cent. B.C., A. S. Herbert, PC (2), in loc. It does not however seem necessary to deny all historicity to the event. The political situation in both alternative periods, though troubled, need not have altogether precluded such an approach from the people of Judah to their blood relations and co-religionaries in the N kingdom. The attempt was in any case a failure, 2 Chr 30:10—11. Only a few pilgrims came and those from the far N. What does however appear to be clear is that the description of the event is written in terms more suitable to the situation in the days of the Chronicler himself after the Samaritan schism had taken

m place, J. Bright, *History of Israel*, 266. **2.** The celebration of the Passover in the 2nd month is an extension of the permission given Nm 9:10f. **6.** This address of Hezekiah is of course intended by the Chronicler to be read by the Samaritans of his own time. Tiglath-Pileser had carried many of the N kingdom into exile in 734, 2 (4) Kgs 15:29. **13.** On the relation of the Passover to the feast of unleavened bread, see §§ 105*d*, 180*a—b*. **14.** Jerusalem where the feast was to be celebrated was first purified by the destruction of idolatrous shrines; see 28:24. After the feast the good work was extended throughout the land, 31:1. **17.** Normally it was the duty of the heads of families to kill the paschal victim, Ex 12:3—6. On this occasion the duty was undertaken by Levites 'for every one who was not clean, to make it holy to the Lord'. This and the following vv illustrate what we should now call the ecumenical spirit of Chr. **20.** To such the Lord was merciful and did not punish, Lv 15.31, 20.14—10.

n **31:1—21 Various religious reforms—1.** Destruction of idolatrous shrines. 2 (4) Kgs 18:4. At the end of the Paschal festival by a spontaneous movement 'all the Israelites present went forth (from Jerusalem) to the cities of Judah', and destroyed the pillars and Asherim. It is possible that Chr has transferred to the reign of Hezekiah an event that is more likely to have occurred in the reign of Josiah. **2—3.** The king's care for the temple worship. Not in Kgs. The neglect of the days of Ahaz rendered necessary a fresh assignment of duties to the members of the different courses. **4—19.** Provision for the needs of priests and Levites. Not in Kgs. This provision for the support of the clergy was probably necessary in a special way after the fall of the N kingdom which left many faithful clerical followers of Yahweh among a pagan people. There can be no doubt that many of these returned to the centre of Yahwism when their own shrines were laid waste. **7.** The harvest began in the 3rd month and the fruits were gathered in the 7th. **14.** Note that a *Levite* is in charge. **16—19.** The sequence of thought is not clear and seems to have been disturbed by the insertion of clauses regarding conditions for participating in the distributions. **20—21.** Praise of Hezekiah's religious zeal. Not in Kgs. Since Hezekiah was good he prospered. This will be shown clearly in ch 32.

o **32:1—22 Sennacherib invades Judah—**2 (4) Kgs 18:13—19:37; Is 36:1—37:38; Sir 48:19—24. Chr reduces the invasion to very little compared with his enormous development of the liturgical and ecclesiastical activities of Hezekiah. **1.** That the invasion occurred 'after these events and this manifestation of fidelity' to God prepares the reader for the providential deliverance. **2—8.** Defensive measures. Not in Kgs. **4.** The water from Gihon joined the brook Kidron. The immense labour of cutting the underground tunnel which later brought its waters within the city of David to the Pool of Siloam, 30, could not have been accomplished in the time allowed by war conditions. **5.** Millo; see on 1 (3) Kgs 9:15.

9—16. Sennacherib's officers call for surrender. 2 (4) **307o** Kgs 18; 17—37. **16.** There seems to be a Davidic and Messianic reference here to Ps 2:2. **17—20.** The blasphemies of the Assyrian move Hezekiah and Isaiah to prayer. 2 (4) Kgs 18:28ff.; 19:15—19. **17.** The reception, but not the writing of this letter, is mentioned in 2 (4) Kgs 19:14. **21.** Rout of the Assyrian army. 2 Kgs 19.35—37. **22—23.** Subsequent international fame of Hezekiah. Not in Kgs. **22.** The Lord 'gave them rest on every side'. **24—31.** Various supplementary information. **25—26** allude to the display of self-satisfaction and pride manifested 2 (4) Kgs 20:12—19, a passage which is rendered more intelligible by the mention of the king's humbling himself and the postponement of punishment. **27—29.** The king's riches. Cf Kgs 20:13. **29.** 'And he acquired flocks' (*ᵃḏārîm* for *'ārîm* 'cities'); but the word is prob. to be omitted as due to dittography. **30.** See on 4 and 2 (4) Kgs 20:20. The king blocked up access to the spring from without the city, and from this *higher* level led the water *underground* to the Pool of Siloam. **31.** 2 (4) Kgs 20:12—19; also 25—26 above. 32—33. Conclusion 2 (4) Kgs 20:20f. **33.** Hezekiah seems to have been honoured by a special sepulchre.

33:1—20 Manasseh 699—643/42—This is the **308a** classic example of Chr's retribution theology. Manasseh had a very long reign and this must have been a reward for virtue. Yet he is known to Kgs and Jer as the worst of the Davidic line. To develop his teaching Chr uses a tradition that Manasseh had to do homage to the king of Assyria. This homage must have followed a revolt and in his defeat Manasseh turned to God, was forgiven and rewarded with a long life, cf PC (2) 319*b*.

1—9. Introduction; Manasseh's wickedness 2 (4) **b** Kgs 21:1—9. **10.** Warning Kgs 21:10—15. **11—13.** Punishment and pardon. Not in Kgs. **12.** In his tribulation 'he humbled himself exceedingly' before God. Manasseh is known from the Assyrian inscriptions to have been a vassal of both Esarhaddon, 681—669, and of Ashurbanipal, 669—626. His recorded tribute to the former was paid in 676/675, and the revolt prob. took place after this, followed by captivity at Babylon, of which city Shamashshum-ukin, one of Esarhaddon's sons, was prince-regent. The return was prob. under Ashurbanipal, who is known to have restored conquered kings in the hope of securing their continued allegiance. **14—17.** Fortifications; rejection of idols. Not in Kgs. **14.** The wall ran from the Fish Gate, prob. in the N wall, along the W slope of the Kidron valley down to the hill of Ophel at the SE corner of the city. Gihon: see on 32:4. **15.** 'The idol'; see v 7. **17.** The conversion of the king and people can have been neither deep-rooted nor long continued. Amon, 22, must have learnt his idolatry during his father's lifetime, and the final destruction of Jerusalem is attributed to the wickedness of Manasseh's reign, 2 (4) Kgs 23:26, Jer 15:4. **18—20.** Conclusion. 2 (4) Kgs 21:17—18. **18.** A prayer of Manasseh, is printed at the end of editions of Vg. **19.** 'The seers': perhaps to be emended and read as a proper name: Hozai. **20.** That Manasseh was not buried with his fathers is thought by some to indicate his relapse into idolatry. On the other hand, that would not have displeased his idolatrous successor.

34:21—25 Amon 643/642—641/640. **c**
21—25. Introduction; idolatry, conspiracy and death. 2 (4) Kgs 21:19—26.

34:1—35:27 Josiah 641/640—609—Josiah though a great king in the eyes of Chr is not as great apparently as Jehoshaphat or Hezekiah. This may be because of

308c his sad end which implies some fault in his behaviour. **34:1—2.** Introductory. 2 (4) Kgs 22:1f. **3—7. Destruction of idolatrous shrines.** Not in Kgs, but with 4, 5 and 7 cf respectively 2 (4) Kgs 23:6, 16, 19f. Chr is more exact chronologically in setting part of Josiah's reforming activity before the finding of the book of the law in his 18th year of reign. The order of narrative in the Bible is frequently not the chronological order. **3.** The beginning of the reform in Josiah's 12th year may have been due to the influence of Jeremiah. The 13th year of Josiah in which Jeremiah received his mission, Jer 1:2, reckoned by the pre-notation system would be the same as the 12th reckoned by the post-notation system; see § 124f. **6.** 'In their ruins round about' i.e. 'ruinous though they were'. These cities were nominally in the Assyrian province of Samaria, but the Assyrian empire was no longer able to exercise effective control so far from the capital. **8—19. The finding of the book of the Law.** 2 (4) Kgs 22:3—11. § 295c. **9.** The Jerusalem temple is the real symbol of the unity of the people of God. All subscribe to it. This is written with contemporary conditions in mind. **12—13.** Chr's favourites, the musicians, seem a little out of place here unless their function was to give the beat

d for work in common. **14.** Chr probably understands this book to be the whole Pent. **18.** He read passages before the king (lit. 'read in it'). **20—28.** God's answer through the prophetess. 2 (4) Kgs 22:12—20. **28.** Josiah died on the field of battle at Megiddo in 609, but the words of the prophetess had a restricted meaning. The king's peace was not to be disturbed by the final catastrophe of the destruction of Jerusalem. It is, however, a testimony to Chr's fidelity to its sources that the passage has been reproduced without alteration to make it more obviously fit the king's end. **29—32.** Renewal of the covenant. 2 (4) Kgs 23:1—3. **30.** This was not the whole book of the Law that had been found. The king's purpose was to renew the covenant of Sinai, Ex 24:4—8. The suitable procedure was consequently to read 'the book of the covenant', which Moses had read when the people had first entered into the solemn pact with God, Ex 24:7. This suggests that the book found was the Pent. The loss of the book was due to the idolatry that reigned even in the temple under kings like Amon, Manasseh and Ahaz. In the list of those who attended the reading of the book, Chr changes the 'prophets' of Kgs into 'Levites'. Probably his teaching in this is that the Levites took over in post-exilic Jerusalem the function and honour that belonged to the prophets, especially cultic prophets in the pre-exilic period. **31.** Chr shows a final renewal of the covenant before the great catastrophe. **33.** Abolition of Idolatry. 2 (4) Kgs 23:4—20, which in part belongs chronologically to the period before the finding of the book of the Law; see 2 Chr 34:3—7.

e **35:1—19. Solemn celebration of the Passover.** 2 (4) Kgs 23:21—23. Chr loves the feasts and celebrations of the temple and obviously considered the very brief account of 2 (4) Kgs 23:21—23 quite inadequate. In this account we find Chr's characteristic predilection for the Levites once again, vv 3, 14—5, 18. **3.** The teaching office of the Levites, also 17:8f. The removal of the ark from the Holy of Holies has not been mentioned. Some think it was removed during the repairs to the temple fabric; others that the profanations of Josiah's predecessors had not spared the most holy spot of all. Once the ark was restored to its proper place in the Debir, the Levites would not again have to carry it as they had done during the wanderings in the wilderness. **6.** The Levites had to kill the paschal victims.

What had been a concession to necessity in 30:17 becomes **308** normal practice here and in v 11. Perhaps this is a justification of the practice of Chr's own day. **7.** The lambs and kids, Ex 12:5, were to be killed as paschal victims, the oxen as peace-offerings, Dt 16:2. **11.** The sprinkling of the blood, also 30:16. 'The Levites flayed them'. **15.** Jeduthun is here called 'the king's seer'; see 29:30; 1 Chr 25:5. **17.** On the relation between the Passover and the feast of the unleavened bread, see §§ 105d, 180a—b. **18.** See on 30:26. The Passover of Josiah was made the more solemn and memorable by the discovery of the book of the Law, and, perhaps, by the more prominent part the Levites played in it.

20—24e. Death of Josiah in battle. 2 (4) Kgs f 23:29f. **20.** In 609, the year of his accession, Neco marched to the Euphrates to fight against the Medes and Babylonians, Jos, *Ant.* 10, 5, 1, who had practically destroyed the Assyrian empire, the capital having been lost in 612. Neco wished to secure at least Syria and Palestine for himself. Signs of the Egyptian occupation of Carchemish at this period have been discovered there. The Babylonians, however, under Nebuchadnezzar put an end to the Asian dominion of Egypt in the expedition of 606—605. Josiah, now free from the fear of Assyrian domination and misjudging the rising strength of Babylon, thought that the only danger to his independence lay with Egypt. **21.** It seems that Chr's reasoning was as follows: Josiah died a tragic death in defeat. Therefore he must have committed some fault. But the tradition at Chr's disposal made no reference to any fault of Josiah, but did refer to the words of Neco. These words, whose historicity there is no reason to doubt, are understood by Chr to be a true divine oracle so that the sin of Josiah for which he was so severely punished was the rejection of the words of a prophet, even though in this case the prophet was a pagan and an enemy. Rather than admit that suffering and untimely death are not always the result of sin, Chr is prepared to find a sin in something which few others would regard as such. **22.** Megiddo: at the entry to the plain of Esdraelon and a position of considerable strategic importance. **24.** They moved him from his war-chariot into one more comfortable, built for civilian use. **24f—25.** Mourning for Josiah. Not in Kgs. These lamentations of Jeremiah for Josiah have perished. It became a law or custom to sing these dirges every year on the anniversary of his death. 'Behold, they are written in the Lamentations'. There used to be other collections besides that still extant. **26—27.** Conclusion. 2 (4) Kgs 23:28. The source is indicated where might be found his other acts 'and good deeds'. **36:1—3 + 4b Jehoahaz** 609—The story is told g rather more fully in 2 (4) Kgs 23:30d—33 + 34c—d. The deposition took place at Riblah on the Orontes, Kgs 33. Kgs 3 reads lit. 'and the king of Egypt deposed him in Jerusalem', but a word has perhaps been omitted and the true text would be 'deposed him from reigning in Jerusalem'; see Kgs 33.

36:4a + 5—8 Jehoiakim 609—598/97—Chr adds to 2 (4) Kgs 23:34—24:5 the information of 6b—7. The text does not say that he was actually carried away to Babylon, but he 'bound him in chains to take him to Babylon'. In Kgs this incident would come after 24:1a. Nebuchadnezzar satisfied himself that he would be a loyal vassal if treated generously and reinstated him on the throne, but he again rebelled after three years. The Babylonian showed his magnanimity also in carrying away only *part* of the temple treasures. The date will have been not long before the 3rd year of Jehoiakim ended with Tishri 606 in the 20th year of Nabopolassar.

08g Nebuchadnezzar was on his way to the invasion of Egypt from which he was recalled by the news of his father's death.

h **36:9—10b Jehoiachin** 598/97—597—Chr is much more summary than 2 (4) Kgs 24:8—16. **9.** Jehoiachin was eighteen when he began to reign, Kgs. Perhaps there has been some corruption in the textual transmission of Chr and the numeral 'ten' has been displaced from the age of the king to the length of his reign.

i **36:10c—20a Zedekiah** 597—596.

10c—13a. Introductory; Revolt. 2 (4) Kgs 24:17—20. **10c.** Zedekiah was Jehoiachin's uncle not his brother, Kgs; but the tradition on this point seems to have wavered cf 1 Chr 3:15, 16. In the account of the fall of Jerusalem, theology occupies a much more prominent part than historical detail. **12.** He did not humble himself before Jeremiah the prophet. Here we have two of Chr's favourite themes: humility and prophecy. **13a.** Ezekiel dilates on the sinfulness of violating this oath, 17:18—19. **13b—16.** Wickedness of king and people. **17—19.** The destruction of Jerusalem. 2 (4) Kgs 25:1—21; Jer 39:1—9; 52:4—27. **20—21.** The Babylonian captivity a fulfilment of prophecy. Not in Kgs. Jer 25:9—12. The law had been persistently neglected and among its other provisions that of the rest of the land every seventh year, Lv 25:4. The Chronicler recalls that an enforced sabbath of the land should come when the people were scattered among **308i** the nations, Lv 26:33—35. Note the constant stress all through here on the prophets, for the Chronicler sees in the exile and return the fulfilment of Jeremiah's prophecy Jer 25:9—12. He probably understood the 70 years of the prophecy as referring to the period from the fall of the temple in 586 to its restoration under Darius (520—515) cf Ez 5—6. This in itself is a refutation of the idea that Chr is entirely a priestly book. Those who remained behind in Judah are entirely ignored by Chr for they are ancestors of the present Samaritan enemies. The true remnant of Israel was carried off to Babylon and came back only after Israel had been sanctified by the exile. Nothing is said of the fate of Zedekiah for the line of David did not continue through him but through the captive Jehoiachin and the line of David is the only interest of Chr.

22—23 Decree of Cyrus permitting Return from j Exile—This passage is verbally the same as Ez 1:1—3b. The explanation of this double occurrence is that, when Ez-Neh was separated from Chr, the passage was left at the end of Chr as well as at the beginning of Ez to indicate that the books in fact belonged together. But see § 298a. The concept of Cyrus as the instrument of Yahweh is characteristic of Deutero-Isaiah e.g. 41:25; 45:1—7.

EZRA—NEHEMIAH

BY P. SIMSON W.F.

309a Bibliography—*Commentaries:* A. Bertholet, Freiburg-Tübingen, 1902; L. W. Batten, ICC, 1913; G. Hölscher, Tübingen, 1923⁴; W. Rudolph, HAT, Tübingen, 1949; M. Rehm, EchB, 1950; A. Fernandez, Madrid, 1950; V. A. Médebielle, PCSB, 1952; A. Gelin, BJ, 1953; K. Galling, ATD, 1954; H. Schneider, BB, 1958; J. M. Myers, AB, 1965; F. Michaeli, CAT, 1967.
Special Works: C. C. Torrey, *Ezra Studies*, 1910; A. van Hoonacker, 'La Succession chronologique Néhémie-Esdras', RB 32 (1923) 481—94; 33 (1924) 33—64; H. H. Schäder, *Ezra der Schreiber*, Tübingen, 1930; id 'Esra', Iran. Beit. I, 212ff; W. O. E. Oesterley, 'The Early Post-exilic Community', ET 48 (1935—6) 341—5; 394—8; E. Würthwein, *Der 'amm ha'arez im A. T.*, Stuttgart, 1936; K. Galling, *Syrien in der Politik der Achaemeniden bis 448 v. Chr.*, Leipzig 1937; R. de Vaux, 'Les décrets de Cyrus sur la reconstruction du Temple', RB 46 (1937) 29—37; K. Galling, 'Kronzeungen des Artaxerxes', ZAW 63 (1951) 66—74; id 'The Gola-List according to Ezra 2 and Nehemiah 7', JBL 70 (1951) 149—58; N. H. Snaith, 'The Date of Ezra's Arrival in Jerusalem', ZAW 63 (1951) 53—65; H. H. Rowley, 'The Chronological Order of Ezra and Nehemiah', in *The Servant of the Lord and other Essays*, London 1952; H. Cazelles, 'La mission d'Esdras', VT 4 (1954) 113—40; A. Jepsen, 'Nehemia 10', ZAW 66 (1954) 87—106; W. Rudolph, 'Esras und Neh mit 3 Esra', TLZ 79 (1954) 144ff; H. H. Rowley, 'Nehemiah's Mission and its Background', BJRL 37 (1955) 528—61; id 'Sanballat and the Samaritan Temple', BJRL 38 (1955) 166—98; P. Grelot, 'La dernière étape de la rédaction sacerdotale', VT 6 (1956) 174—89; V. Pavlovsky, 'Die Chronologie der Tätigkeit Esdras', Bib. 38 (1957), 275—305, 428—56; M. Rehm, 'Nehemias 9', BZ, NS 1 (1957) 59—69; A. Lefèvre, 'Néhémie et Esdras', DBS 31 (1958) 393—424; J. S. Wright, *The Building of the Second Temple*, London 1958; J. Morgenstern, 'The Dates of Ezra and Nehemiah', JSS 7 (1962) 1—11; M. W. Leeseberg, 'Ezra and Nehemiah: a Review of the Return and Reform', *Concordia Theol. Monthly* 33 (1962) 79—90.

b Name and Place in the Canon—In the early Heb. Bible Ez and Neh formed one book entitled 'The Book of Ezra' (cf JosCAp., I, 8; Jer, Ep 53 ad Paulinum, n. 7, PL 28, 1403). In LXX MSS they also formed one book with the title Ez B and were placed immediately after the apocryphal book called Ez A. The division into two books is first found in a Heb. MS of 1448, but Origen already attests to a division in the LXX version; cf Eus., HE, 6, 25, PG 20, 581. The presence of a title in Neh 1:1 may explain why this division was made.

In HT Ez-Neh are found among the Kethubim or Hagiographa, immediately before 1 and 2 Chr; in LXX and Vg they are placed among the historical writings after the books of Chr.

c Text and Versions—Apart from two Aramaic frag-ments, the books were written in Heb., but the language **309** is shot through with Aramaisms. One also finds expressions of Persian origin. The Aram. is that spoken in the 5th cent. B.C., as is evident from comparison with the Elephantine papyri written in the same language. The HT on the whole is in a poor state, especially in the genealogical lists the transcription of which is subject to errors.

In LXX there are two **Gr. Versions.** These are the **d** two texts, Ezra A and B. Ez B corresponds to the canonical Ez-Neh, while Ez A is the apocryphal 3 Ez to be found in the Vg Appendix. According to most scholars, the latter is probably due to a compiler who wished to describe the history of the temple and divine worship from the Passover of Josiah to the full restoration at the time of Ezra, Neh 8. It seems to have been compiled before the LXX version, Ez B, was made. It was used by Josephus and was cited by not a few Fathers as inspired, but from the 5th cent. it was considered by all as apocryphal.

For the **Syriac** Version, cf Walton, *Biblia Polyglotta*, IV 1—29, and C. A. Howley, *A critical examination of the Peshitto version in the book of Ezra*, N.Y., 1922.

Canonicity—The books of Ez-Neh are not quoted either **e** in OT or NT. The passage about Neh. in 2 Mc 1:18—2:13 is drawn from another source. But Jewish tradition has always inscribed them among the canonical writings and, apart from some hesitation on the part of the Antiochean school, Christian tradition sanctioned this verdict. The Council of Trent has defined them as canonical.

Contents and Division—Ez-Neh deal with the period **f** from the return of the exiles after the Decree of Cyrus, 538 B.C., to the second mission of Neh. in 433 B.C., but the history of this period is by no means complete. There are comparatively long periods of which nothing is related, e.g. between 538 and 520; between 486 and 448. The books actually deal with a few episodes, and may be divided into four parts: Part I: The Return of the Jews under Sheshbazzar and its immediate sequel (ez 1:1—6:22):

- (*a*) The edict of Cyrus and return under Sheshbazzar with the sacred vessels belonging to the temple, 1:1—11.
- (*b*) A list of the exiles who returned and of the cities they occupied, 2:1—70.
- (*c*) The building of the altar of holocausts, 3:1—7.
- (*d*) The laying of the foundations of the temple, 3:8—13.
- (*e*) Samaritan opposition, 4:1—24.
- (*f*) The completion of the temple under Zerubbabel and Jeshua, 5:1—6:15.
- (*g*) The dedication of the temple and the celebration of the Passover, 6:16—22.

Part II: The Return under Ezra (Ez 7:1—10:44):
- (*a*) The return of the exiles, 7:1—8:36.
- (*b*) The dissolution of mixed marriages, 9:1—10:44.

309f Part III. The Rebuilding of the Walls by Nehemiah (Neh 1:1—7:73):

(a) In the 20th year of Artaxerxes I (445) Neh. asks permission to return to Jerusalem, 1:1—2:8.

(b) Neh. returns and inspects the walls by night, 2:9—20.

(c) The rebuilding of the walls under difficult conditions, 3:1—6:19.

(d) The appointment of watchmen, 7:1—3, and a census of the people, 7:4—73.

Part IV. Religious Reforms and Political Organization (8:1—13:31):

(a) The Renewal of the Covenant, 8:1—10:33.

(b) The population of Jerusalem is augmented, various lists, 11:1—12:26.

(c) The dedication of the walls, 12:27—42.

(d) Provision for the support of priests and Levites, 12:43—46.

(e) Neh. returns to Jerusalem a second time and corrects various abuses, 13:1—31.

10a **Origin of the Books: their Author, Date and Literary Character**—Originally Ez-Neh formed with Chr a large historical work often called today 'The Chronicler's History'. The whole work is governed by the same theological point of view, is written in the same style, and displays such an over-all unity that it undoubtedly came from the hand of a single author. But the identity of this author is unknown; his writings suggest that he was a member of the temple staff.

The Chronicler's history belongs to the latter part of the 4th cent. B.C.; for the list of high-priests (Neh 12:11) stops with Jaddua, a contemporary of Darius (12:22) who was according to JosAnt. 11, 7, 2 and 8, 2ff, Darius III Codomannus (336–331). Other indications reinforce this conclusion. Ezra and Nehemiah are spoken of as persons who have long since disappeared from the historical scene, Neh 12:26, 46. The frequent use of the expression 'The King of the Persians', Ez 1:1, 2, 8; 3:7; 4:3, 5, 7, 24; 7:1, insinuates that the Persians were no longer masters of Palestine. There are many Aramaisms.

There already existed another major historical work, the Deuteronomic history (Dt to Kgs, cf § 242e). The Chronicler's intention is not only to complete this history by carrying it down to the 4th cent. B.C., but also to stress, in the light of the priestly interests of post-exilic Judaism, what we might call the 'liturgical vocation' of God's people. This standpoint is clearly present in Ez Neh.

b That the author of Ez-Neh made use of a variety of **sources** is evident. Some parts are in Heb., some in Aram.; some parts use the first person, some the third; the style changes abruptly from one passage to another. The number of sources is uncertain, but the following can be detected without difficulty: (1) The Memoirs of Ezra and of Nehemiah which constitute the two main sources. Ezra's Memoirs appear in Ez 7:1—10:44 and also in Neh 7:73b—9:37, though it is difficult to determine how much of the Ezra narrative belongs to the Ezra Memoirs as sometimes Ezra speaks in the first person and sometimes he is spoken of in the third person. These Memoirs were probably originally a report on Ezra's mission, destined to the Persian authorities who had sent him 'to make enquiries about Judah and Jerusalem' (Ez 7:14), and to the Jewish community in Babylon who had financed at least partly the work of the restoration. The Memoirs of Nehemiah are quoted almost verbatim in Neh 1:1—7:73a; 11:1—2; 12:27—43 and 13:4—31. They describe the many services rendered by Neh. to God's people, to Jerusalem and the temple; but their tone and the frequent prayers scattered through the text give them an air of **310b** 'autobiography'. (2) Over and above these two main **c** sources, the following documents will also be found: (a) Aram. documents, Ez 4:7—6:18 and 7:12—26. The first contains the protest of Rehum to Artaxerxes I against the rebuilding of the walls, 4:7—16; the king's reply, 4:18—22; the letter of Tattenai to Darius concerning the reconstruction of the temple, 5:7—17, and Darius' answer, 6:1—12; the dedication of the temple, 6:13—18. The second has the edict of Artaxerxes to Ezra, Ez 7:12—26; (b) Heb. documents from the state archives: the decree of Cyrus, 1:2—4; the lists of those who first returned, Ez 2:1—70 = Neh 7:6—72; who returned with Ezra, Ez 8:1—14; who contracted mixed marriages, Ez 10:18—44; who helped in the building of the walls, Neh 3; who signed the covenant, Neh 10; who inhabited Jerusalem, etc, Neh 11:3—35, and who as priests or Levites returned with Zerubbabel, Neh 12:1—26. All these are first-class sources that give to the Books a character of historical credibility.

It belonged to the Chronicler to organize his sources **d** into a historical synthesis. He dismembered the Memoirs of Ezra and inserted the section which should have followed Ez 8:36 into the book of Neh, Neh 7:73b—9:37, so as to synchronize the activity of Ezra and Nehemiah. But if he is to be held responsible for Ez 7:1—11, which constitutes a sort of prologue to Ezra's Memoirs, he seems for the rest to have limited his personal contribution to quoting his source. The Memoirs of Nehemiah, and the various documents they include, show equally very few traces of redaction work, but one will easily recognize the Chronicler's hand in Neh 12:33—36, 41—42. As to the Aram. source, the names of kings quoted show clearly that the author uses it in the reverse order of the events: the opposition provoked by the rebuilding of the walls, Ez 4:7—24, is evidently posterior to the rebuilding of the temple, Ez 5:1—6:18; this modification allowed the Chronicler to present a severe charge against the Samaritans.

Historical Background—1. **Israel in exile**. The **e** exiles, whose number is estimated at 60,000—80,000, were settled in various districts near Babylon, e.g. Tel-abib, Ezek 3:15, Tel-melah, Tel-harsha, Ez 2:59, and Casiphia, Ez 8:17. In their new home they came to enjoy considerable freedom. Many continued to lead an agricultural life, others followed commercial pursuits and gradually acquired wealth, Ez 2; Zech 6:10ff. Excavations at Nippur have unearthed ledgers of the Jewish banking family of 'Murashu and Sons', 450—400 B.C. The ancient position of the elders of the people seems to have been recognized by the Babylonians, Ezek 8:1; 14:1; 20:1. They resisted religious apostasy, Ezek 14:1—11, despite the temptation in the popular mind to feel that Yahweh was showing himself less powerful than the Babylonian Marduk.

2. **Israel in Judah.** Of the life of those who remained **f** in Judah (30,000—40,000) little is known. After the destruction of Jerusalem, the Babylonians had organized Judah into the provincial system of the empire. As a province the land was placed under the charge of a governor. But the first and only governor appointed by the Babylonians was murdered, Jer 41:1—2; 2 (4) Kgs 25:25. As a consequence, the province of Judah was probably abolished and at least the bulk of its territory incorporated into the neighbouring province of Samaria. Only the cream of Jewish leadership had been taken into exile, and the poorer elements of the population were left behind to harvest the crops (see Jer 29:10; 2 (4) Kgs 25:12). Lam describes the distress of these

310f people, and Jer 44, Ezek 33:23—26 show that religious syncretism, idolatry and immorality increased, furthered, no doubt, by infiltration into the empty land from Moab, Ammon, and particularly from Edom.

g 3. **The Return.** The Jews owed their liberation to one of those recurring surprises which make the course of history, humanly speaking, unpredictable. Cyrus the Great (559—529), son of Cambyses of the Achaemenid family, was a member of a Persian tribe—the Pasargadae. The little kingdom of the Achaemenids, in the district of Susa, placed itself at the head of a coalition of Persian tribes. By 549 Ecbatana, the capital of the Median overlords, had fallen and Cyrus declared himself 'king of Persia'. The attention of the world was now focused on this extraordinary individual in whom the prophets had already seen an anointed of the Lord who 'gives up nations before him (Cyrus) so that he tramples kings under foot', Is 41:2; 44:28; 45:1. With the collapse of its Median partner, Babylonia took fright and its king Nabonidus (556—539) made league with Lydia and with Egypt. By 546 Sardis, the capital of Lydia, had fallen to Cyrus. He was then ready to strike at Babylonia, and in 539 he defeated the Chaldaean army and entered Babylon without opposition. In 525 Egypt was added to the Persian Empire by Cyrus' son Cambyses. Later, repeated attempts were made to conquer Greece. One expedition sent by Darius I was defeated at Marathon, 490 B.C.: another, in 480, was led by Xerxes I who was defeated in the naval battle of Salamis. Unable to subdue Greece, the Persians nevertheless kept a firm hold over the interior of Asia for about two centuries.

h **Cyrus the Persian** had none of the ruthlessness of Semitic conquerors. His faith (Zoroastrianism) and his political foresight made him broad-minded, and he came to exiled Judah as a **liberator rather than a conqueror.** Within a short time of his occupation of Babylon, Cyrus issued the edict, Ez 1:2—4, which was to restore the fortunes of Israel.

The first group of returning exiles was led by Sheshbazzar who immediately laid the foundations for a new temple on the site of the one destroyed, Ez 5:16, but the Jews were unable to complete it because of **opposition from hostile neighbours.** The aristocracy of Samaria in particular still considered Judah as part of their territory and they naturally resented any limitations of their prerogatives there. As to the Jews resident in the land, they did not all welcome the influx of immigrants. They had considered the land as theirs, Ezek 33:24, and probably still did; they would scarcely have been eager to give place to the newcomers or lend them a helping hand. It is not surprising, therefore, that **work on the temple** soon ground to a halt. It was not until 515 B.C. that Zerubbabel as governor of Judah with the help of the high-priest Jeshua and the encouragement of the prophets Haggai and Zechariah finally finished the building.

i Little is known of the situation in Judah between 515 and 450. The position of the community was most insecure: not only were relations with Samaria as strained as ever, but **Edomites and Arabs** who occupied most of S Palestine, proved to be **a permanent danger.** Lacking adequate protection, the Jews found their position intolerable. It was for this reason that in the reign of Artaxerxes I, Ez 4:7—23, they took matters into their own hands and began to rebuild the fortifications of Jerusalem. This initiative was immediately countered by Samaria; a first complaint was sent to Xerxes in 486, Ez 4:6. A second and a third reached Artaxerxes Ez 4:12—13, 16, who ordered the work to be stopped, Ez 4:21—23.

But in 445, a Jew named Nehemiah, Artaxerxes' **310** cupbearer, obtained from the king a rescript authorizing the **building of the walls of Jerusalem**, and was appointed governor of Judah, Neh 5:14; 10:1, which was made a separate province independent of Samaria. In spite of incredible difficulties, Nehemiah was able to carry out his mission: he restored the city-walls, thus giving the community physical security, and arranged for a portion of the people to come and live in Jerusalem, Neh 7:4; 11:1f; he also showed himself a devoted administrator who protected the poor, Neh 5. Nehemiah's term of office lasted twelve years (445—433), after which he returned to the Persian court, Neh 13:6. But we find him again in Jerusalem some time later, certainly before 424, Neh 13:6, trying to remedy the many abuses which spoilt the inner life of the community, Neh 13.

In the meantime, however, another leader had appeared on the scene, Ezra 'the scribe'. Ezra probably came to Jerusalem about the year 427. According to his Memoirs, he did not come alone but, in accordance with the permission given him, Ez 7:13, at the head of a group of exiles. His commission was quite different from that of Nehemiah. It concerned religious matters only. He was armed with a copy of the Law, together with a rescript from king Artaxerxes granting him extensive powers to enforce it, Ez 7:12—26. Ezra's work transformed the Jewish community from a nation into a law community.

Chronology—(This study follows closely John Bright's **311** *History of Israel*, p. 356—86). Ez-Neh offers a major critical problem: Who came first to Jerusalem, Ezra or Nehemiah? 1. Some, accepting the date of Ez 7:7 as the seventh year of Artaxerxes I (458), place Ezra's arrival some thirteen years before that of Nehemiah; this is the traditional view. 2. Others, e.g. van Hoonacker, believe that the Artaxerxes of Ez 7:7 is Artaxerxes II; they therefore bring Ezra on the scene long after Nehemiah's work had ended (398 B.C.). 3. Still others, seeing in the 'seventh year' of Ez 7:7 an error for either the 'thirty seventh year', or the 'twenty seventh year', place Ezra's arrival either after Nehemiah's but before the latter's term of office had ended, or between Nehemiah's two terms of office. Each of these positions has its merits; but the last one seems to be open to the fewest objections.

In the first place it is certain that Nehemiah came **b** to Jerusalem c. 445, for he is found there together with Eliashib, the high-priest, Neh 3:1, and Jehoiada his son, Neh 13:28; moreover his Samaritan contemporary was Sanballat, Neh 2:19, etc. Now from the Elephantine papyri (Sachau I) we know that the sons of Sanballat and Johanan, the son and successor of Jehoiada in the office of the high-priest, were living in 408—407 B.C. This fixes the activity of Nehemiah during the reign of Art. I (465—424).

A number of reasons make it difficult to believe that **c** he had been preceded by Ezra: (*a*) the disturbed early years of Artaxerxes I do not furnish a very likely setting for Ezra's unprotected journey from Babylonia to Palestine, Ez 8:22; (*b*) Ezra's mission concerned religious matters only: he was commissioned to teach and impose the Law of the God of Israel, Ez 7:25—26, and he had hardly reached Jerusalem when he set to work, Ez 8:32ff; yet according to Neh 8, it was only in 445 that he read the Law to the people and they wept when they heard it (v 9); (*c*) what is still more serious—the sequence Ez-Neh leads to the conclusion that Ezra's mission was a failure, since Nehemiah had to repeat the reforms Ezra had undertaken, Neh 13. But neither the

1c Bible nor Jewish tradition so paint the father of Judaism; (d) arguments could also be taken from several situations described in the books of Ezra and Nehemiah: for instance, Nehemiah found the city of Jerusalem largely in ruins, Neh 7:4, but when Ezra arrived it seemed to be inhabited and relatively secure; moreover if Ezra did precede Nehemiah, it is strange, to say the least, that Nehemiah does not refer in his Memoirs to the work of his predecessor, and in particular to the Law he had read to the people; (e) the Chronicler, it is true, places Ezra before Nehemiah, but various indications in his text, suggest that this is not necessarily a chronological sequence: for example, Neh 12:26 lists leaders of the Jewish community between the building of the temple and the writer's day and these are: Joshua, Joiakim (the father of Eliashib, Nehemiah's contemporary), Nehemiah and Ezra—in that order; Neh 12:47 passes from Zerubbabel to Nehemiah, with no Ezra in between.

d For all these reasons, we hold that **Ezra came to Jerusalem between Nehemiah's two terms of office.** Nehemiah having gone back to the Persian court in 433 may have told Ezra about the urgent need of the Palestinian community for a religious reform, and Ezra was able to undertake this important task in 427.

Taking into account the chronological data scattered through the text, this is how one will view the sequence of events narrated in the books of Ezra and Nehemiah:

538: The edict of Cyrus and the return of Sheshbazzar (Ez 1).

538—525: successive caravans of exiles return to Judah. Sheshbazzar lays the foundations of the temple; and starting in 520, Zerubbabel builds it. In 515, solemn Passover (Ez 2—4:5; 4:24—6:22).

400. Samaritan intrigues against Juda (Ez 4:6)

465—448: By order of the Persian authorities the work of reconstruction in Jerusalem comes to a halt (Ez 4:7—23).

445: Nehemiah arrives at Jerusalem. The walls are rebuilt and dedicated, and the city is peopled (Neh 1—7:72, except 5; 11:1—20; 12:27—43).

445—433: Nehemiah's first term of office (Neh 5).

427—424: Ezra's mission: journey to Jerusalem (Ez 7:1—8:36); public reading of the Law (Neh 7:72b—8:18); the affair of mixed marriages (Ex 9:1—10:44); public confession of sin (Neh 9:1—37).

Before 424. Nehemiah's second mission (Neh 13:4—31); the community promises to keep the Law (Neh 10). (cf A. Gelin, BJ, Introd. 19—20).

e Historical Value—Based as they are on reliable sources the books of Ezra and Nehemiah constitute historical records of great value. Archaeological discoveries confirm the picture of Cyrus drawn by the Chronicler; they show him as a monarch very tolerant in religious matters, who allowed all deported people to return to their native lands, and who showed respect for their local sanctuaries, restoring, e.g., the temple of Marduk in Babylon. The **Chronicler** shows himself also **well informed about** the administrative structure of **the Persian State**, Ez 4:7—23; 5:3—17; 6:1—13; the Elephantine papyri, discovered at the beginning of this century, confirm the historical framework of the books. From them we learn, e.g., that Samaria was the governor's seat, that his name was Sanballat, Neh 2:19, etc; that there was in Judah a twofold authority, civil and religious. As to the Samaritan opposition on which the author has so much to say, Ez 4:1—23, it certainly reflects the mentality of the former N Kingdom whose population had been partly taken into exile in 721 B.C. and replaced by colonists from Mesopotamia who had nothing in common with Judah.

Finally, the activity of the returned exiles is confirmed by **311e** the prophetic books of Haggai and Zechariah.

But however well informed and accurate the Chronicler **f** may be, history is not his only concern. His aim is to write the history of Israel's vocation; and, a member of a community whose spirit had been shaped to a great extent by the prophets of the exile, Ezekiel in particular, he sees Israel as the holy nation consecrated from its origins for the service of God: his liturgical interest is one of the main motifs of his work; David becomes for him the one who organized Israel as a church. It was David who made Jerusalem his religious capital; who planned the building of the temple; who organized the music of the temple and gave the Levites their duties. But David was of the tribe of Juda; and the Chronicler almost makes the history of Israel coincide with the history of Judah and Benjamin; he hardly mentions the events of the N Kingdom and if he does mention the N tribes, it is to associate them with the two privileged tribes of Judah and Benjamin in the liturgical festivities of the temple of Jerusalem, 2 Chr 15:9; 30:1, 5, 11, 18; 34:6, 7, 9, 13.

The books of Ezra and Nehemiah reveal the same **g** preoccupations: Judah and Benjamin constitute the true Israel, Ez 1:5; 4:1; Neh 11:4; whereas elements from the N arouse suspicion. The life of the community is focused on the temple and the Chronicler takes pleasure in describing the activities of priests and Levites, Neh 12:44ff. Israel has come back from exile, not as a nation, but as a church, and in the Chronicler's mind, this profound change in Israel's life is not just a response to the political vicissitudes of the period. Rather, it is a return to the charter of Judaism handed down from David.

The Significance of Ez-Neh—With the return from **h** exile there began a new phase in the history of Israel. Israel was no longer an independent nation, but a Persian province. From the political standpoint all was lost. One thing alone remained, **its religious patrimony**. Second Isaiah (Is 40—55) had imagined the return from exile in terms of a new Exodus, Is 41:17—20; 49:7—26; rescued from the servitude of Babylon, Israel could now freely serve its Lord, and be to him in all truth a 'kingdom of priests, a holy nation', Ex 19:5—6. Worship, the highest possible form of service, was its main preoccupation: even before the foundation of the new temple had been laid, sacrifices were offered and feasts celebrated in Jerusalem, Ez 3:1—7; and if the second temple did not compare in splendour with the temple of Solomon, it was the place where Yahweh was enthroned in the midst of his people; just as the congregation of Israel in the Sinai desert, the post-exilic community had no king except Yahweh himself. Worship, however, is not simply a matter of sacrifices offered to God in his temple; to serve God finally means to obey **his Law.** Ezra had brought with him from Babylonia the law that priests had compiled in exile, Ez 7; he made it **the charter of the post-exilic community**, Neh 8:1—2, 18; 9:3, 13—14, 29, 34. The solemn proclamation of the Law, described in Neh 8—10, the repeated 'Amen' of the people, Neh 8:6, the promise made by the whole community to keep the Law, Neh 10, echo the ceremony of the Sinai covenant, Ex 24. A genuine reform in Israel could not but be a return to the spirit of the desert. It could not have lasting results either unless Israel agreed to live in the desert, cut off from the rest of the world: the wall which Nehemiah built around the city of Jerusalem was a symbol of his work for the racial and therefore religious purity of his people.

The restoration undertaken by Nehemiah and Ezra **i**

311i had its weaknesses: the rituals of the temple often became empty forms; the cult of the Law could easily degenerate into cold legalism; and the danger of ostracism always threatened a community so intent on preserving its patrimony. But in spite of many disorders against which the post-exilic prophets never failed to protest, Mal 1: 8, 12—14; 2:10—16; Zech 7:8—12; 8:16—17, the elite of Israel lived up to their vocation. The psalms of 'the poor' reflect their deep sense of God, Ps 116 (115), 120 (119), 123 (122), 124 (123), 130 (129), etc, whereas other poems bear witness to the missionary spirit which animated the community, Ps 96 (95):7—8; 98 (97):4—6.

j Finally, **the Mosaic institutions** themselves **received several additions** the importance of which was to grow with the last centuries of the OT: the **'scribes'**, many of them laymen, devoted to the study and explanation of the law; the **Sanhedrin** or council of elders, which during the Greek domination was the chief administrative authority in matters both spiritual and temporal; the **synagogue.**

Judaism was born; the community of Israel was now equipped for the last stage in the economy of the Promise. The day was not far off when Christ, in whom 'all the promises of God find their Yes', 2 Cor 1:20, would come not to abolish but to fulfil the ideal of the post-exilic community. The Church born of him would then be in all truth 'a chosen race, a royal priesthood, a holy nation', 1 Pt 2:9.

EZRA

312a Section 1: Ez 1—6: The Return of the Jewish Exiles to Jerusalem: the Re-establishment of Worship and Rebuilding of the Temple.
This opening section manifests very clearly both the Chronicler's intention and the mentality of the post-exilic community. Cyrus, 'Solomon redivivus', felt called by God to build him a house at Jerusalem, 1:2; he therefore gave the exiles their freedom so that they might go back to Jerusalem and rebuild the temple of the Lord, 1:3—5. Nothing is said of the circumstances of the return of the first caravan, except that the exiles brought back the many vessels of the house of the Lord carried away by Nebuchadnezzar, 1:7—11; among the members of this caravan, the ministers of the temple, priests, Levites, singers, doorkeepers, occupied an important place, 2:36—43. Shortly after their arrival in Judah, the returned exiles set to work in order to restore the altar of God, 3:2, and thus be able to devote themselves to the service of God, 3:3—6. Chh 3—6 deal with the rebuilding of the temple and the difficulties it entailed; the section ends on the description of the Passover which, in the eyes of the community, was now the 'memorial' both of the Exodus from Egypt and of their return from Babylonia; they had been made free 'to serve God', 6:19—22; cf Ex 3:12; 7:16, etc.

b 1:1. The Edict of Cyrus—The book begins with the last words of 2 Chr, vv 1—3a occurring in 2 Chr 36:22—23. 'first year': i.e. of Cyrus' reign over the conquered Babylonian empire (538 B.C.). As king of Persia he had ruled since 559; cf 5:13. 'the word of the Lord': cf Jer 25:11—12; 29:10 where the period of captivity was predicted as 70 years, a round figure, the meaning of which may very well by symbolic; the actual duration of the captivity from the Fall of Jerusalem in 586 was about 50 years. The sacred writer makes clear that the purpose of the book is to demonstrate the fulfilment of prophecy; cf Is 44:28; 45:1—4. 'the Lord stirred up . . . Cyrus'; cf Is 45:1 where Cyrus is styled **312** 'Yahweh's anointed'. He was the instrument chosen for the fulfilment of the divine plan. 'proclamation': the Cyrus cylinder in the Brit. Museum shows that Cyrus gave similar permission to all subject and deported peoples, cf ANET pp. 315—16. The announcement would be in a special form (and language) for promulgation to each separate group. The writer gives the particular form in which it was announced to the Jewish people. This was not the decree cited 6:2ff but the 'proclamation' by which heralds made that decree known. 'in writing'; cf 6:2ff.

2—4 The Proclamation—2. 'The Lord, the God of **c** Heaven, has given me': 'the Lord' represents, as always, the divine name 'Yahweh'. Although not a monotheist, Cyrus had great regard for the religious beliefs of his subjects, and claimed the patronage of each local divinity; e.g. his capture of Babylon is ascribed to the favour of Marduk. So here his success is attributed to Yahweh. **3.** If the permission to rebuild the temple was an act of political insight, it was also a fulfilment of the divine plan for the restoration of Israel. 'Whoever is among you of all his people, may his God be with him'. The words are a common form of greeting. 'among you': all the subjects of the Persian empire. 'of all his people': the proclamation has in view the Jews of the S kingdom who had been deported by Nebuchadnezzar; perhaps also the Northerners taken into exile in 721 B.C. **4.** 'let each survivor': 'whoever is left': a typically biblical expression meaning the messianic remnant, the holy seed through which salvation will finally come, Is 10:20—21; 49:13; 51:7. 'let each survivor . . . be assisted by the men of his place': non-Israelites (6) as well as those Jews who would not wish to return themselves. 'besides freewill offerings': gifts of money, etc, towards the expenses of rebuilding the temple.

5—11 The Return of the Jews—5. The Effect. 'the **d** heads of the fathers' houses': the heads of the families or clans. 'everyone', etc, implying that many did not avail themselves of the opportunity of returning. The lot of many of the exiles was not unhappy; for the prophets, the remnant coincides with the Poor, Zeph 3:11—13. **6.** The return from exile will be a new Exodus, Ex 3:22; 11:2; 12:35.

7—8. Cyrus **restores the vessels** taken from the Temple. **7.** Cyrus was sending back to the various cities of Babylon the statues of idols carried off by his predecessor Nabonidus to Babylon, and rebuilding temples for them when necessary. The God of the Jews had no image that could be returned, Ex 20:4—6, but his temple could be rebuilt and some of its furniture restored. 'Nebuchadnezzar had carried away': cf 2 (4) Kgs 24:13; 25:13—17. **8.** 'Sheshbazzar': his identity is puzzling, as he is named only here and in 5:14, 15, whereas throughout the rest of this section Zerubbabel appears as the leader. Some scholars think that Sheshbazzar and Zerubbabel are two names for the same individual. In favour of this view are the facts that (a) the foundation of the temple is ascribed to both, 3:8; 5:16; (b) Sheshbazzar is 'a prince (nāśî') of Judah', and Zerubbabel is of the Davidic line, 1 Chr 3:18; (c) the title of governor (pehāh) is given to both, 5:11 and Hag 1:1. Yet (a) it is strange to find the same person, a Jew, called by two Babylonian names; (b) in Ez 5:14f, the Persian Satrap quotes the statement of the Jewish leaders, Zerubbabel and Jeshua, who seem to refer to Sheshbazzar as a different individual. More probably then, Sheshbazzar was the predecessor of Zerubbabel.

9—11. The number of the vessels. **9.** 'censers': or knives, 'liturgical knives' (Zorell). The enumeration of

2d 9—11 may be meant to impress: the exiles did not leave Babylonia empty-handed. But above all it bears testimony to the great care with which objects pertaining to divine worship were gathered, cf Ex 25—31; 35—40.

e 2:1—70 The Register of the Jews who returned— The list is repeated in Neh 7:6—73 and 3 Ez 5:7—45 with some differences in names and numbers due to the mistakes of copyists. It belongs to the Memoirs of Neh, and probably groups together several successive caravans of exiles. Placed where it is in Ez, it constitutes a fitting introduction to the narrative that follows; compare 3:2 and 2:2; 3:9 and 2:40. The title (1), the mention of Babylonian localities from which certain families came (59), the need of establishing one's genealogy (62f), the numbering of the singing men and women (65) and the mention of transport animals only (66f) suggest that the document was composed shortly after the Return.

f 1—2a Introduction. 1. 'the people of the province': the Jews inhabiting the Persian subprovince of Judaea, the district of which Jerusalem was the centre and of which Zerubbabel was governor after Sheshbazzar. 'returned': the return was chiefly a migration to the land of their fathers by Jews born in Babylonia. The majority of Nebuchadnezzar's deportees would have died during the intervening years. 'each to his own town': to the city to which his clan belonged, in so far as this was practicable. The Persian province of Judaea was smaller in area than the kingdom of 50 years before. 2. 'Zerubbabel': the descendant of Jehoiachim, he was of royal blood; cf 2 (4) Kgs 24:8—15; Ez 1:8 and 3.2. The Chronicler sees him essentially as the builder of the temple, but seems to ignore the messianic titles granted to him by Haggai and Zechariah; cf Hag 2:23; Zech 6:12f. 'Jeshua': he was the high-priest of the Return, Hag 1:1—12; Zech 3:1, the son of Jehozadak and grandson of the high-priest Seraiah whom Nebuchadnezzar put to death at Riblah after the destruction of Jerusalem; cf 1 Chr 6.1 15; 2 (4) Kgs 25:18—21. 'Nehemiah': not to be confused with Nehemiah, the son of Hacaliah, Neh 1.1. The names number 11, but the list in Neh 7:7 has 12, naming also, after Re-elaiah, a certain Nahamani, omitted here by an error in transcription. They are probably intended to be symbolic of the 12 tribes of Israel.

g 2b—19. A list of 'the men of the people of Israel', the laity as distinct from the priests and Levites. The names are those of clans.

20—35. Another list according to localities (except 30—32) which are all within a radius of 25 m. from Jerusalem. The numbers are much smaller than those of the families in 3—19. It has been suggested that this second list included the proletariat whereas the first one gave the families of the upper class.

36—39. Of the four priestly houses mentioned here, one, Pashhur is not among the 24 enumerated in 1 Chr 24:7—18; it was probably a branch of the house of Malchijah (cf 1 Chr 9:12; 24:9; Neh 10:3).

40—42. The families of the Levites. These include the Levites proper, 1 Chr 24:30—31, the singers, 1 Chr 25:1—7, 9—31, and the doorkeepers, 1 Chr 26:1—19. The number of Levites (74) is surprisingly small; humiliated by the Deuteronomic reform and by Ezekiel, Ezek 44:9—14, they may have felt little inclined to go back to Jerusalem; unless of course very few of them went into exile at all because they were too poor to attract Nebuchadnezzar's attention in 587 (cf A. Gelin, BJ, ad loc). 40. 'the sons of Jeshua and Kadmiel, of Binnui, of Hodaviah', reading binnûi for benê with Neh 12:8 and 3 Ez.

h 43—54. 'The temple servants': Nethinîm. The name

means 'given' to the temple service; cf 1 Chr 9:2. They **312h** formed a distinct class and assisted the Levites in the discharge of the more menial tasks, and were originally captives of war, Jos 9:23; on the return from exile they were reckoned as members of the Israelite community, Neh 10:29: cf M. Havan, VT 11 (1961), 159—69. 50. 'Me-unim': inhabitants of Maon, they were an Arab people subjugated by Uzziah, king of Judah, 2 Chr 26:7. 'Nephisim': an Ishmaelite tribe, Gn 25:15; hence also Arab (cf 1 Chr 5:18—22).

55—58. 'Solomon's servants': the descendants of the native Canaanites conquered by Solomon and employed on his buildings, 1 (3) Kgs 9:21. They formed a subdivision of the Nethinim, Neh 7:28; cf 7:60; 11:3.

59—63. Israelites and priests of uncertain origin. **i** 59. 'Telmelah', etc: localities in Babylonia. 61. 'Barzillai', the Gileadite, benefactor and then favourite of David, 2 Sm 17:27. His estates were inherited by his daughters, one of whom was married to a priest who thereupon received the family name; hence, probably, the difficulty about his genealogy. 62 bears witness to the care taken of family registers and to the genealogical lists in the sacred writings. 63. 'the governor': Tirshatha, Persian tarshata, 'he who is feared', is here applied to Sheshbazzar. It is roughly equivalent to 'His Excellency'. 'the most holy food': the priest's portion of the sacrificial meat, Lv 7:31—34. 'Urim and Thummim': cf Ex 28:30; the high-priest had not yet been re-installed in his function.

64—67 A Summary—The total of the returned exiles **j** (42,360) agrees with that given in Neh 7:66 and 3 Ez 5:41. The items, however, in all three lists fail to produce the sum. Perhaps the 12,000 persons unaccounted for were women and children.

65. 'male and female singers': not the temple singers of 41, but those employed to sing at feasts and funerals, etc, 2 Sam 19:35, Eccl 2:7. Some commentators liken the singers to camp-followers (cf Ex 12:30; Nm 11:4).

66—67. The animals enumerated are beasts of burden. The horses and mules would be ridden by the wealthier, the asses by the poorer classes. The camels and asses would carry the baggage.

68—69. The gifts for the construction of the temple. 69. 'darics': the Persian daric was worth about 5 dollars; a 'mina' of silver about 30 dollars. Neh 7:10ff breaks down the totals given here into contributions from 'His Excellency', from the chiefs of the clans and from the people.

70. The verse sums up the whole list and matches 2:1. 'lived in Jerusalem and its vicinity', is absent from Heb.

3:1—13 The Renewal of Worship and the Beginning **313a** of the New Temple—1—3 The Building of the Altar—1. 'the seventh month' of the religious year (Tishri, presumably Sept.—Oct.), the first of the civil. Compare with Neh 7:72b—8:1; the Chronicler has already in mind the meeting organized by Ezra in the autumn of 427. 2. 'Jeshua': cf 2:2. Zerubbabel's 'kinsmen' are the heads of the families (2:2). 'son of Shealtiel': in 1 Chr 3:19 Zerubbabel is called the son of Pedaiah, the brother of Shealtiel. The discrepancy may be explained by the suppositions (a) that he was the real son of Pedaiah and the legal son of Shealtiel (Pedaiah having married Shealtiel's childless widow, according to the law of Dt 25:5f), or (b) (following some MSS), the son of Pedaiah and the grandson of Shealtiel. 'built the altar': the chief purpose of the Return was to restore to Yahweh his due cult in Sion 'which he had chosen'. Both love and duty to God required

313a the exiles to make the venture. Ps 137 (136) pictures the desolation of Israel in its inability to perform the temple liturgy. Ezek and other prophets, had, during the exile, filled them with longing enthusiasm for the Day of Yahweh, associated often with the Messianic coming, when a purified remnant of God's people would rebuild the temple more glorious than before; and though in face of innumerable obstacles, their fervour slackened (as Haggai trenchantly reminded them) we see here the first enthusiasm of the Return, when they were able to renew the sacrifice on Mt Sion, the symbol of a reunited people, and make plans for the re-erection of the temple.

b 3. 'they set the altar in its place': i.e. where it had formerly stood. An effort seems to have been made to continue the worship on the site of the temple after its destruction, Jer 41:5, but the present situation demanded a new altar. 'fear . . . because of the people of the land': an allusion to the opposition mentioned in 4:1—5.

4—6 The Feast of Tabernacles—cf Nm 29:12—39 and Sv 23:39—43; see also note on Neh 8:14. 5. 'and after that': after the celebration of this feast, the use of the prescribed daily sacrifice (a lamb every morning and evening, Nm 28:3—8) as well as the offerings of the first of the month (new moon) and of all the set feasts were resumed, together with the sacrifices dictated by private devotion; cf Nm 28:11—15; Lv 23:1—44.

c **7—13 The Laying of the Temple Foundation**—This event marked the beginning of a new era for the community. The destruction of the temple in 587 had been a death blow to the Israelites; it meant that Yahweh had abandoned his city, Ezek 11:23—25, and his people. The exiles, it is true, had felt God's protecting presence in Babylonia, Ezek 11:16; but even then, how could they have forgotten that Jerusalem was the place which Yahweh had chosen for 'His Name' to dwell there, cf Ps 137 (136): 1—6? Encouraged by their prophets, Ezekiel in particular, they had clung to the hope that one day Yahweh would lead them once again out of servitude into his land where they could serve him. This day had now come, and with the offering of the first sacrifices and the laying of the temple foundations, the words of Ezekiel came true at long last, 'the name of the city henceforth shall be, The Lord is there', Ezek 48:35.

d 7. 'to the sea, to Joppa': the operation, as in the case of the first temple, 1 (3) Kgs 5:6—11, involved hauling timber from Lebanon down to the coast, then floating it in rafts to Joppa, whence the Jews undertook its further transport to Jerusalem. 8. 'the second month': Apr.-May, 536 B.C. 'Zerubbabel . . . and Jeshua': according to 5:13—16 and 6:3—5, the re-building of the temple had been entrusted to, and was actually carried out by, Sheshbazzar; the mention of Zerubbabel and Jeshua here may be redactional. 8b. 'they appointed the Levites': the promotion of the Levites is one of the characteristic features of the Chronicler. 9. 'Jeshua': not the Jeshua of 8 (who was high-priest), but a Levite, 2:40. 'Kadmiel and his sons, the sons of Judah': read with Ez 2:40; Neh 12:8, 'Kadmiel, Binnui and Hodaviah', i.e. the heads of the Levites. 'Henadad and the Levites' seems to be a marginal gloss for Hodaviah which crept into the text. 10. 'according to the directions of David': cf 1 Chr 16. 11. 'responsively': antiphonally. The words of praise which follow are the refrain of Ps 136 (135). 'foundation': this was a promising beginning but the work was shortly abandoned to be resumed again only after 16 years. Haggai blames the community's inertness and lack of zeal; the present book speaks only of vague opposition, 4:4—5, but it is easy to fill in the details.

e According to Ez 3:8 the foundations of the temple

were laid in the 2nd year of the Return, whereas Hag 2:1 **313i** and Zech 8:9 seem to imply that the work did not begin until the 2nd year of Darius (520 B.C.). But the statements of the prophets are sufficiently explained if it is assumed that a commencement was made in 536, that the progress of the work was suspended because of opposition, and that the renewal of it in 520 was practically a fresh start, as indeed the book of Ezra itself declares it to have been, 5:2. 'wept': cf Hag 2:3.

4:1—24 The Record of Opposition—(1) from the reign **314** of Cyrus to the reign of Darius, 4:1—5; (2) during the reign of Xerxes, 4:6; (3) during the reign of Artaxerxes I, 4:7—23. 1. 'the adversaries': the descendants of the immigrants, who, to replace the Israelite population that had been deported after the fall of Samaria (721 B.C.), had been introduced, first of all by Sargon from Babylon and the East, 2 (4) Kgs 17:24, then by Esarhaddon (2) and Ashurbanipal (10). 2. 'we worship your God': literally, 'we seek your God': this is an expression often used by the Chronicler, cf 2 Chr 15:1—15. To seek God means to seek his presence in particular through participating in the liturgy of the temple, cf Ps 24 (23):6; Zech 8:21; it also means 'to worship God in accordance with the law', cf Dt 4:29. The Samaritans' claim to cooperate in the work of building the temple is based upon common worship. An Israelite priest had been brought back from captivity to teach them the worship of Yahweh, 2 (4) Kgs 17:28. 'Esarhaddon': 681—668, the successor of Sennacherib. 3. 'nothing to do with us': the Samaritans **b** had made of their own pagan religion and of the Israelite worship a hybrid syncretism which was the principal reason for their repulse by the Jews; the official reason offered was the fact that the exiles were not authorized to extend to others the privileges conferred upon them by Cyrus. 4. 'the people of the land' ('am hā'āres): the expression meant at first 'the landowners', cf 2 (4) Kgs 23:30, 35, as opposed to the poor who have nothing (dalat hā'āres). Here it refers to the half-pagan Samaritan settlers. The expression is no longer purely sociological; the people of the land are those who do not even understand the law and are unclean (cf A. Gelin, BJ, ad loc). 'discouraged': the Heb. construction gives the idea of a continuous policy of hindering, terrifying and bribing. 5. 'hired': 'were bribing' the local Persian officials. The effect of this opposition was the interruption of the building of the temple up to the 2nd year of Darius, from 536 to 520.

6—23 deal with much later history. Having mentioned **c** that the opposition of hostile neighbours prevented the Jews from speedily building the temple, the author collects from his sources three later instances of similar opposition in which recourse was had to the Persian court. 6. Of the first, to Xerxes in 485, we know neither the author nor the objects. 7. Of the second, to Artaxerxes I, the authors are named but not the object; perhaps because the accusation was without effect. 'written in aramaic': Aram. was the language of Syria and N Palestine at this time, and soon to be adopted by the Jews themselves. It was the *lingua franca* of the Fertile Crescent and regularly used in Persian administrative documents dealing with lands W of Euphrates. This v like the preceding, is apparently a citation from a larger document.

8—23. The third recourse (also to Artaxerxes I) **d** is reported extensively (11—16) and is followed by the reply of the king (17—22). The writer probably drew from an Aram. source, since the text continues in Aram. till 6:19 where Heb. is abruptly resumed. The charge made in this section is not the building of the temple

4d (the subject of which is resumed in 24 and ch 5) but the fortification of Jerusalem (12). **8.** 'commander', i.e. governor of the province of Samaria in which the district of Judah was included, cf 4:17. 'scribe': the governor's secretary. The greater part of 9—11 is a parenthesis to explain who the colleagues were that associated themselves to Rehum in the accusation. The names of the nationalities to which the Samaritans belonged, show their non-Jewish origin; the identification of most of them is uncertain. **10a.** 'Osnappar': Ashurbanipal (668—626), successor of Esarhaddon. Following the Assyrian practice of transferring captured populations, he used central Palestine as a convenient dumping-ground for the peoples mentioned. It is curious that the petitioners should qualify an Assyrian king as 'great and noble' when writing to a Persian monarch. 'beyond the river': the regions west of the Euphrates which formed the Syrian satrapy of Abar-Nahara ('beyond the river').

e 11—16 The Letter—12. 'and now': as in 17, it is an epistolary form, marking a transition. **14.** 'because we eat the salt of the palace': because we are in the king's pay; cf *salarium*, money given to provide salt. **15.** 'the book of the records': records kept by Artaxerxes' predecessors.

17—22 Artaxerxes' Reply—17b. 'greeting': *peace*. **18.** 'plainly': the allusions, etc, of the letter had been faithfully explained. **20.** 'mighty kings': as David, Solomon, Menahem, etc. **24.** 'the second year of the reign of Darius'. 520 B.C. The narrative of Neh shows how utterly the attempt to restore Jerusalem had failed. We may infer that the enemy destroyed what work had been accomplished; for it seems to have been on this occasion that 'its wall was broken down, and its gates destroyed by fire', Neh 1:4. With 24b the writer returns to the history of the previous century, repeating 5b.

f 5:1—17 The Building of the Temple recommended—1—2. The narrative of 4:5 is resumed. There is silence regarding the period 536—520. The hostility of their neighbours had so discouraged the Jews that they said: 'The time has not yet come to rebuild the house of the Lord', Hag 1:2. Out of this despondency they were roused by the prophets Haggai and Zechariah. **1.** 'who was over them': i.e. inspired them; cf Dt 28:10; Jer 7:10, etc. **2.** 'began to rebuild': the earlier attempt had failed so completely that the resumption of the work could be considered as a new undertaking.

3—5 The Complaint against the Jews—3. 'Tattenai': he is named in a Babylonian document of 502 as governor 'beyond the river', i.e. satrap of Abar-Nahara; cf JNES 3 (1944) 46. 'Shetharbozenai': Shethar is the name, Boznai perhaps an official title of unknown meaning. We may assume that complaints from the Samaritans led the satrap to inquire what authority the Jews had received to undertake the work. That authorization was required to rebuild the temple under Persian rule is evidenced by the Elephantine papyri; cf § 79d. **4.** 'They also asked': MT reads, 'we asked'; but the third person, adopted by LXX, is more natural.

g 6—17 The Letter of Tattenai to Darius—Tattenai could not venture to arrest a work which was alleged to have the sanction of Cyrus (13), but cautiously decided to refer the whole matter to Darius. The tone and contents of this report are studiously fair and dispassionate. **8.** 'we went': the satrap's residence was in Samaria. 'huge stones': lit 'stones of rolling', so large that they had to be moved on rollers. **11.** 'a great king': Solomon, 'the great king', 1 (3) Kgs 6:8. **13.** 'Cyrus

king of Babylon': the king of Persia was also master of **314g** the Chaldaean capital. **14.** 'governor': of the district of Judaea, under the authority of the satrap of 'Beyond the River'. **16.** 'from that time': from 536 to 520 B.C. **17.** 'archives': lit 'house of treasures', which was apparently the repository of important documents as well as of treasures.

6:1—22 The Persian King approves the Rebuilding h of the Temple: its Completion and Dedication.
1—5 The Finding of the Decree of Cyrus—1. 'Babylonia': as in 5:17 the word is used loosely by the Jewish writer as meaning not the city alone, but the kingdom of Babylonia, including Persia. **2.** 'Ecbatana': the capital of Media and the summer residence of the Persian kings. It is the modern Hamadan in Iran. Cyrus had remained in Babylon, after its capture, from Dec. 539 to Mar. 538. In the summer of 538 he was in Ecbatana, and a decree of his 'first year' would naturally be dated there and preserved there. This detail is interesting evidence of the reliability of the writer's sources: Ecbatana was deserted after Alexander's conquests, and the Jewish writer of the Gr. period would never think of locating Cyrus' archives there. 'a scroll': of leather or parchment. The use of these materials, rather than clay tablets, was favoured by the adoption of the Aram. script in the Persian chancellery. Cuneiform could not well be written on parchment. 'on which this was written', etc. It refers to the 'minute' of an oral decision taken by Cyrus. There is no need to suppose that this and 1:2—4 are different versions of a single document. The 'proclamation' was public; the 'record' here given is a memorandum notifying the royal pleasure to the officials whose duty it was to put in force. Its curt and business-like style is natural to such a document. **3.** The memorandum of Cyrus is now quoted. 'its height', etc. The length of the temple is not given, and the other dimensions are twice those of Solomon's temple; cf 1 (3) Kgs 6:2. The figures seem wrong, for the new temple was inferior to the old one; cf Hag 2:4. **4.** 'three courses of great stones and one course of timber': the meaning is not clear: perhaps (a) three storeys of stone surmounted by one of wood; (b) each three layers of stone was followed by one of wood (cf 1 [3] Kgs 6:36). The 'cost' was to be defrayed from the royal revenue, i.e. probably from taxes gathered locally for the king's court (cf E. Dhorme, *La Bible*, ad loc). For the fulfilment of this decree, cf 1:7—11.

6—12 The Decree of Darius to Tattenai—6. 'Now i therefore': an abrupt transition to the decree of Darius to which there is no introduction. Probably the sacred writer had before him the complete text of Darius' reply to Tattenai in which the rediscovered edict of Cyrus was quoted. The first part of the reply he merely summarized (1:2); the Cyrus record he quoted in full (3:3—5); then he continued copying in full the last part of Darius' letter. **10.** 'pray for the life of the king' etc: cf Jer 29:7; Bar 1:10—12; 1 Mc 7:33, where the Jews are bidden to pray for the welfare of pagan rulers; cf also Rm 13:1—7; 1 Pt 2:13—17. There is no indication, however, that the Persian kings had a special reverence for the God of the Jews. Similar directions for prayers and sacrifices for the king were issued to the Babylonian and Egyptian polytheists.

In view of the detailed knowledge of the requirements for Jewish ritual (9), it has been questioned whether this is a copy of a Persian decree, and not rather a digest of it by the Jewish writer in his own words. It seems likely that the decree was drafted by a Jewish secretary, for we know from the narratives of Neh that Jews did occupy

314i posts of importance at the Persian court. And if such friendly intervention was possible, it would be highly desirable for Zerubbabel and his companions to get as detailed a commission as possible, which would leave little scope for restrictive interpretations of the king's will by local officials.

j **13—18 The Completion and Dedication of the Temple**—**14.** 'through the prophesying' etc.: i.e. strengthened by the inspired words of Hag and Zech. 'Artaxerxes': the temple was completed in the reign of Darius. The name is a gloss added through misunderstanding of the documents in 4:7—23. **15.** 'the third of Adar' which fell between Feb. and March. 'the sixth year': 515 B.C. The work, resumed in the 2nd year of Darius, 5:2, had taken more than four years to finish. **17.** The relatively modest number of the sacrificial beasts contrasts with the numbers given in 1 (3) Kgs 8:5—63, but at the same time, in consideration of the poverty of the community, it is impressive. 'all Israel': the 'remnant' that returned is conscious of representing the whole people of God. Hence the sin-offering for the twelve tribes, although ten had been swallowed up in the Assyrian empire. **18.** 'as it is written in the book of Moses': 1 Chr 23:26 distinguishes various groups of Levites and other temple-servants, but the Pent (the book of Moses) ignores such a priestly organization. With this v, the Aram. document comes to an end. The Chronicler is responsible for 19—22.

k **19—22 The Celebration of the Passover**—**20.** 'all of them were clean': ritual purity, but also a symbol of the purity of heart on which Ezekiel had so much insisted, cf Ezek 35:22—26. 'So they killed the Passover': originally the paschal lamb was immolated by the head of each household, Ex 12:3—7; here, as in the days of Josiah, according to the Chronicler, 2 Chr 35:14, by the Levites. **21.** 'everyone who had separated himself': Israelites left in the country when the rest were deported, who having mixed with the surrounding pagans, now threw in their lot with the new community. **22.** 'with joy': liturgical celebrations are a source of joy, cf Ez 3:12; they remind the Israelites of 'the day which the Lord has made, so that they may rejoice and be glad in it', Ps 118 (117):24. The Passover of 515 B.C. actually counts among the major 'Days' in the history of Israel; cf 2 Chr 30:21—26; Neh 8:10 (cf X. Léon-Dufour, 'Joie', in VTB). 'the king of Assyria': the Persian empire included the former one of Assyria.

315a **Section II: The Work of Ezra, 7—10.**

With the coming of Ezra, the history of the post-exilic community took a decisive turn. It was not sufficient for God's people to be a 'kingdom of priests'; it was also its vocation to be 'a holy nation', separated from the rest of the world. Ezra, 'a scribe skilled in the law of Moses', 7:6, put all his energy in erecting around the Judaean community the protecting wall of the law. Sent by the Persian king to teach and to enforce this law, 7:25—26, he knew too well where compromise in this matter had led the nation, 9:6—15, not to show himself inflexible, ch 10. His attitude, however, was not inspired by cold legalism, but by his great **love for God and for his people**. His character and his methods were, no doubt, controversial, but Jewish tradition has done him justice by seeing in him the father of Judaism.

b **7:1—11 Introduction**—from the Chronicler who makes use of Ezra's report. **1a.** Artaxerxes is Artaxerxes I. In the early years of this king an effort was made to surround Jerusalem with a wall (4:12), though with no success. **1b—5.** For the genealogy of Ezra, cf 1 Chr 6:4—14. In 1—5 it is schematic; only 16 generations are given for a period of 800 years. Possibly it is arranged to give prominence to the three leading figures, Aaron, **315** Azariah (Solomon's high-priest), and Ezra, with seven generations between each pair. **6.** 'a scribe skilled in the law': in later Judaism and in NT 'scribe' has the technical sense of an official interpreter of the Law. Before the Exile it meant a writer or copyist, and in particular a royal secretary, 1 Sm 8:17; 1 (3) Kgs 4:3, etc. The change in meaning dates from the application of the term to Ezra. We cannot tell whether he began as a scribe for the Persian government (which is likely, in view of his favour with the king), or as a copyist (of the Sacred Books) for the Jewish community. In any event he devoted himself to the study of the law, and his authority is based largely on his intimate acquaintance with its prescriptions. What exactly this 'Law' was is not quite certain; most probably it was a version of the Pent, though probably not in the form that we now know it. 'all that he asked': i.e. as contained in the letter in 12—26. **7.** 'the seventh year of Artaxerxes': as explained in the introduction, we read 'the 37th year', i.e. 428 B.C. **8.** 'fifth month': Ab, July—Aug. **9.** 'first month': Nisan (Mar.—Apr.). 'he began to go up': i.e. 'he fixed the departure' for the first day. Because of difficulties, the actual journey was not begun till the twelfth day, 8:31. The journey occupied nearly four months and the distance travelled was about 900 miles. **10.** Though Ezra led a body of settlers his mission appears to have had purely religious ends in view. His purpose 'to study the law, to do it and to teach it' to his countrymen is an epitome of the ideal scribe's career; cf Ac 1:1.

12—26 The Letter of Artaxerxes—It is written in **c** Aram. Two points are particularly worth noting in this document, (1) the law is promoted to the rank of state-law and made obligatory for all the Jewish communities of 'Beyond the River', 25—26; (2) the financial dispositions detailed in 15—24 bear witness to the extraordinary liberality of the Persian monarch. **12.** 'king of kings' and 'God of heaven' are authentic Persian phrases. **14.** 'seven counsellors': cf Est 1:14. 'make enquiries' (with authority to correct abuses): the norm of the enquiry is to be 'the law of your God, which is your hand'. **16.** 'all the silver and gold': Ezra has a roving mission to raise money. In 15—16 three kinds of offerings are mentioned: (1) from the king and his counsellors; (2) from the people of Babylonia (cf 1:4, 6); (3) from priests and people—free will offerings. **22.** 'talents . . . measures . . . baths': cf §§ 86—87. In 701 B.C., the Assyrians claim to have received 800 talents as only part of the ransom paid by Hezekiah. **23.** 'lest his wrath be against the realm': we have here the familiar oriental conception of the local divinity who will be offended if his rites are not duly performed in a given place; and who, if offended, is capable of punishing the offenders in that same place. Palestine, which guarded the route to Egypt, was of great importance for the Persian control of that country; and by these measures Artaxerxes meant to win the good will of the local divinity as well as of the inhabitants. **25.** 'the wisdom of your God': an allusion to the law; law and wisdom are often associated particularly in the Wisdom Writings (cf Dt 4:6—8; Sir 24). 'those who do not know': to know the law means 'to obey its precepts'. The acquaintance with the Jewish ritual and the temple personnel displayed in this document, the 'biblical' vocabulary it uses, suggest that it was drafted by a Jewish secretary, or is in response to a petition of Ezra.

27. Here begins in Heb. a verbatim extract from **d** the personal Memoirs of Ezra, extending to the end of

5d ch 9. 'Blessed be the Lord': Ezra appreciates perfectly well the interested motives of the Persian, but he understands that God is using Artaxerxes, as he had used Cyrus earlier, to further his plans for Israel. Nor should we underestimate the providential character of the Return. The stubborn resistance of the Jews to assimilation during the captivity, their mass return to their ancestral land against every worldly advantage, and the astonishing cooperation given them by the Persians, are without parallel in the history of the E.

e 8:1—36 The Journey to Jerusalem—1—14. A list of those who accompanied Ezra. The number given, of men only, is 1,496. With women, children and a small number of slaves, the caravan comprised about 6,000—8,000 persons. **2.** Gershom and Daniel represent respectively the senior and cadet lines of the Aaronic priesthood; Hattush, the line of David. These have the place of honour. Then come the laymen grouped in twelve families. Most of these families appear (with some variations) in Ez 2 as having contributed to the first group of immigrants under Cyrus.

15—20 The Rendezvous at Ahava—15. Ahava is an unknown locality; but it is also the name of a canal (cf 21, 31). Ezra ordered the clans to gather near its confluence with another canal. 'sons of Levi': only 74 Levites had accompanied the first expedition, 2:40. They were indispensable for the revival of the temple worship. **17.** 'Casiphia': unidentified, but presumably near Babylon. There appears to have been a colony of Levites and Nethinim there, **18.** 'Sherebiah': he seems to have been the 'learned man'; cf Neh 8:7; 9:4, etc. **20.** 'mentioned by name': it probably means that a list was made.

f 21—23 The Fast at Ahava—21. 'a straight way': i.e. a prosperous journey. Apart from the ordinary difficulties of organization, there was a real danger of attack from brigands or Bedouins. A large caravan, including women and children, and bringing treasure, would be a tempting prey without the protection of a military escort. **22.** To seek protection by human means seemed to Ezra a sign of little faith in the power and goodness of God; cf Ps 118 (117):8—9; 146 (145):2—6.

24—30 The Offerings—24. Ezra appoints 12 priests and 12 Levites to take charge of the treasure. **26.** '650 talents of silver': at least £1,250,000; '100 talents of gold': about $2,800,000. The surprisingly large amount suggests textual corruption or exaggeration by copyists. **27.** 'darics': cf 2:69. 'two': 3 Ez '12'; LXX with a change of vowels, 'diverse', which is a better reading. **28.** 'holy to the Lord': i.e. consecrated, set apart. **29.** 'the chambers': the rooms adjacent to the temple where the objects and treasures needed for worship were kept.

g 31—36 The Arrival in Jerusalem—31. 'twelfth day': they had set out from Babylon on the 1st day and assembled at Ahava on the ninth. **32.** The journey lasted about 110 days. 'remained': rested. **33.** The vessels were counted and the bullion weighed. 'into the hands of' the two priests charged with receiving gifts made to the temple. 'Meremoth, son of Uriah': he is not yet recognized as priest in Neh 3:21; it must have taken some time before his family was able to assert its priestly title. **36.** 'satraps ... governors': the satrap ruled over a province; the governor administered a small district. 'they': the last two vv summarize this part of Ezra's Memoirs.

16a 9 The Question of 'Mixed Marriages'—As has already been explained in the introduction, the Chronicler has dismembered Ezra's Memoirs and inserted the section which should follow Ez 8:36 into the book of Neh.

1—5 The Sin of the People—Reason and experience **316a** had shown that marriages with idolatrous people were a grave danger for the religion of Israel, because the pagan consort, especially the woman who is more inclined to be tenacious in the practice of religion, could draw the Israelite partner to pagan superstitions; hence the rigorous measures adopted by the deuteronomic legislation: cf Dt 7:1—4; 23:4ff; 1 (3) Kgs 11:7—13. The reason given is always religious (cf 9:1, 11), but a new motive begins to appear after the Exile: the purity of the Jewish race must be safeguarded (cf 9:2). **1.** 'peoples of the land': non-Jews, not only the communities bordering on Jewish territory. At this time a proportion of the inhabitants of Judaea itself must have been Gentiles. The list combines names familiar in the older writings, with those of countries which were the chief source of more recent corruption (Ammon, Moab, Egypt). **2.** 'holy race': a people set apart and consecrated to God; cf Lv 20:26; Is 6:13. 'faithlessness': cf Mal 2:11. **3.** Oriental demonstrations of great sorrow; cf Lv 10:6; Jos 7:6; Jb 2:13ff. **4.** 'trembled at the words of the God of Israel', i.e. the divine punishments threatened in the Law. 'the returned exiles': they constitute the most dynamic part of the community, and in that sense they are the community. **5.** Ezra stood before the people assembled in the temple at the time of the evening oblation (cf 10:1) and united them with him in his confession.

6—15 Ezra's Prayer—This prayer is a genuine confes- **b** sion of sin, but it is also meant to impress upon the community the gravity of the situation. God has spared the returned exiles, Is 1:9; Jer 31:1—2, and they now form the 'Remnant' through whom Israel lives on; the Israel of the Promise, destined to become a great multitude, Is 60:21ff, channel of life for the whole world, Jer 5:1; Ex 19:6; their sin is a betrayal of their mission; it endangers the very existence of God's people. **8.** 'but now for a brief moment'. from the time of the edict of Cyrus, 538 B.C. 'remnant', the survivors of the nation's shipwreck; cf Ezek 14:22. 'a secure hold': 'a nail' driven into the wall or a 'tent-peg' which holds up or supports. 'brighten our eyes': grant well-being; cf 1 Sm 14:29. **9.** 'bondmen': subjects of the Persian king. 'protection': lit. 'a wall', but in the figurative sense of 'divine protection' (cf Ps 80 (79):13) or as referring to the royal edict forbidding interference with the Jews in Jerusalem; cf 7:26. **11.** 'prophets': principally Moses in the Pent; Dt 7.1—3 and Lv 10.24ff are cited according to sense. 'pollutions ... abominations ... uncleanness': these three words characterize idolatry. **12.** 'never seek their peace'; cf Dt 23:6; Ezek 23:32. **15.** 'thou art just': just and good; the term ṣaddîq expresses God's saving and merciful activity. With this humble confession, full of trust in the goodness of God, Ezra ends and crowns his prayer.

10 The Expulsion of the Foreign Wives—1—5. The c People's Confession and Pledge. The narrative is resumed in the third person; from now on the sacred writer presents the Memoirs of Ezra in a summary form. **1.** 'a very great assembly': presumably the same group as in 9:4 but increased in numbers. **2.** 'Shecaniah': his own father, Jehiel, had married a foreign wife; cf 26 (if it is the same Jehiel). **3.** 'let us make a covenant': God's covenant stands for ever, for God is faithful; but the resolution which the community is about to take will allow the Israelites to make up for the treason of which they are guilty. 'the counsel of my lord': this is the first time we have heard of Ezra's counsel to expel the foreign wives; 2—4 appear to summarize a debate in which

316c various speakers, including Ezra, had taken part; the final resolution may have been proposed by Shecaniah, but it was certainly inspired by Ezra himself. 'according to the law': either (a) the general law forbidding such marriages is now to be enforced; or (b) the 'putting away' is to be performed in accordance with the regulations for divorce contained in the law, Dt 24:1–2. **4.** 'it is your task'; Ezra has, by his commission from the king, both power and responsibility to enforce the law. 'we are with you': an assurance of support against anticipated opposition. 'be strong and do it'; cf Jos 1:6, 7, 9, etc.

d **6–8 The Proclamation—6.** 'chamber': one of the rooms adjacent to the temple. **7.** The men alone were summoned; cf 9. **8.** 'forfeited': 'devoted', i.e. put under a religious ban. Property so 'devoted' was to be destroyed or confiscated to sacred uses; cf Dt 13:13–17. 'banned': excommunicated. 'congregation': Heb. *qāhāl*; a fairly frequent term in the Chronicler's writings, it usually qualifies Israel as the worshipping community; cf 1 Chr 13:2f; 28:2f; 2 Chr 6:2f; 20:5; 29:23f; 30:2f. The word was used for those who shared in the covenant at Sinai; and it will be used for those who renewed their devotion to the Law under Ezra, Neh 8. It connotes those to whom belong the covenant and the promise. In the NT this 'congregation' is the 'Church' (cf K. L. Schmidt, *The Church*, London 1957, p. 57ff).

e **9–14 The Assembly—9.** 'the ninth month' of the religious year began towards the end of Nov. and hence fell in the rainy season. **11.** 'make confession': *give glory*. It was used as an invitation to a culprit to speak the truth and acknowledge his fault; cf Jos 7:19; Jn 9:24. **13.** Time was needed to straighten out the involved question of mixed marriages; meanwhile the people who had come in from a distance could not, in the rainy weather, live and sleep in the open air. **14.** 'let our officials stand for the whole assembly': a committee of the leading men will handle the matter. The 'divorce court' sat in Jerusalem. The elders and judges would be required to give evidence concerning the marriages and afterwards to see that the decision was carried out.

f **15–17 The Commission—15** should stand in parenthesis since it breaks the connection between 14 and 16. **16.** The Heb text reads, '*and there were selected Ezra*'. etc. But read with 3 Ez and some LXX MSS: '*and Ezra the priest selected men*', etc. 'tenth month': Tebeth (Dec.–Jan.). This first sitting was held 13 days after the announcement of 9:1 and the hearings were terminated within 90 days, i.e. by the first day of Nisan (Mar.–Apr.). The harsh measures here described were adopted by Ezra in order to keep the worship of God from being contaminated by, and finally lost in, the surrounding paganism. A small and feeble community was peculiarly exposed to external influences, and Ezra might well fear the results, if marriage alliances were permitted with the neighbouring peoples, whose women were 'the daughters of a foreign god', Mal 2:11.

g **18–44 The List of the Offenders**—It falls into five groups of 17 priests, 6 Levites, 1 singer, 3 porters and 86 laymen—113 in all. The Nethinim are not named, perhaps because, as slaves of alien origin, they were not at that time looked on as part of the Jewish community. **25.** 'of Israel': as distinct from the preceding, who were dedicated to the temple service. The list that follows goes by the name of the heads of families mentioned in 2:3–20, but in a different order. The text, especially towards the end, is badly copied and uncertain. **44.** The text is particularly obscure. 3 Ez 9:36, adopted by RSV, may represent the original text.

With the list of 18–43 the activity of Ezra comes **316** abruptly to an end, to be resumed in an unexpected fashion in Neh 8:1ff. Chronologically speaking, however, the affair of the mixed marriages was followed by the expiation ceremony described in Neh 9:1–37; cf § 318c.

NEHEMIAH

1–6 The Governorship of Nehemiah and the Re- 317 building of the Walls. In the eyes of the Chronicler, the post-exilic restoration amounted to a new creation: when the exiles returned to Juda they were faced with complete chaos; but God raised up three great leaders who, in turn, shaped the community into a people after his own heart. **Zerubbabel** built the temple and thus secured God's protection over the land; **Ezra** taught and enforced the Law which gave the new Israel its spiritual autonomy. It belonged to **Nehemiah** to restore the ruins of the city of Jerusalem. His work was by no means less important than that of Zerubbabel and Ezra. For not only did it bring to the Israelites a much needed material security, but it also marked a decisive step towards the fulfilment of the words spoken by the exilic prophets, Ezekiel and Second Isaiah. One must read such texts as Is 52; 54; Ezek 40–48, to understand the full meaning of Nehemiah's achievement.

1:1a. Introduction—'The words': as originally **b** compiled, the Memoirs of Nehemiah followed Ezra without a break; this introduction was inserted by the sacred writer to indicate that another source (the Memoirs of Neh.) is being quoted. The abruptness of the second sentence shows that the extract does not start with the beginning of Nehemiah's story.

1b–4a Evil Tidings from Jerusalem—1b. 'Chislev': the ninth month, Nov.–Dec. 'twentieth year': of the reign of Artaxerxes I, 445 B.C. This phrase is probably a later insertion taken from 2:1, but really contradicting it, for the 20th year of Artaxerxes began, 2:1, with Nisan (Mar.—Apr.), 445 B.C., and Chislev was the ninth month of that year. Yet the events of ch 1 obviously preceded the interview with the king in ch 2. 'Susa': the winter residence of the Persian kings; cf Ez 6:2. **2.** 'brethren': kinsmen. Hanani introduced to Nehemiah some new arrivals from Jerusalem, with their sad story, very likely in the hope that Nehemiah would use his influence with the king; in fact, this may have been the purpose of the Judaeans' long journey. 'the Jews that survived'; so too in 3. The reference is to those descendants of the exiles who had migrated to Palestine; the Remnant, saved by God, as the prophets had foretold; cf Is 10:20–21; Jer 23:3; 31:7. **3.** 'the wall ... its gates': very likely this destruction occurred on the receipt of Artaxerxes' letter (cf Ez 4:7–23), which had not ordered the destruction of the work done, but that would almost inevitably follow; cf § 313e.

5–11 Nehemiah's Prayer—It follows the pattern of **c** many OT prayers; cf Ex 32:11–13; Ez 9:15–18; Dn 9:4–19; it consists of a call to the God of the Covenant (5), a confession of sin (6–7), an appeal to God's promise (8–9), and an entreaty for help in the undertaking Nehemiah contemplated (10–11). Covenant, Law, sin, punishment, mercy, fidelity, are its main themes; they are also the themes which sum up the history of salvation. Nehemiah's fidelity to the Persian king cannot be questioned; but far from cutting him off from his people, it gave him greater opportunities for taking a leading part in the restoration of the post-exilic community. This twofold fidelity, political and religious, marks him as one of the great figures of Israel's history.

17c **5.** 'who keeps covenant and steadfast love': Nehemiah's confidence is based solely on God's fidelity; cf Ex 34:6–7. 'thy servants': one of Israel's titles, since the time of Exodus; cf Ex 3:12. **8–9.** Cf Lv 26:27–45; Dt 4:25–31; 30:1–5. **8.** 'remember': when God remembers, he intervenes and saves; cf Ex 2:23–24. **10.** The liberation from Egypt is a frequent motif in Israel's prayers; cf Ex 32:11ff. **11.** 'Now I was cupbearer to the king': this is added to show that the words 'of this man', 1:11, refer to Artaxerxes, and that this prayer was in the heart of Nehemiah while serving the king, 2:4. 'a cupbearer': therefore, not the only one or the chief one. The cupbearers of the Persian court were generally non-Persian eunuchs. It was their duty to pour out and taste some of the wine as a precaution against an attempt to poison the king.

d **2:1–20 Nehemiah's Appointment as Governor and Arrival in Jerusalem—1–8 The Commission of Nehemiah—1.** Nisan (Mar.—Apr.), 445 B.C. 'before him': LXX has 'wine before me', implying that it was Nehemiah's turn to act as cupbearer. 'sad': HT is uncertain—perhaps, *I had not been out of favour with him*, i.e. Nehemiah regarded himself, with some reason, as the king's favourite, and hoped, therefore, that his petition would be granted. 'very much afraid': since sadness was a breach of court etiquette (cf Est 4:2) and Nehemiah's petition would be for the exact opposite of the king's recent decision (cf Ez 4:7–23), he had reason enough to be apprehensive. **3.** Nehemiah makes his appeal on the ground of filial piety, saying nothing of building fortifications which would have an ominous sound to an E ruler, only too accustomed to periodical revolts in outlying provinces. **5.** This is the crucial request, and the double introduction conveys the intense earnestness with which Nehemiah made it. 'rebuild it': the request implied authority over the people, independence of local Persian officials, a certain financial control—in short, the office of governor. **6.** 'the queen': the Heb. implies 'a favourite member of the harem'. 'I set him a time': Nehemiah was governor for 12 years, 5:14. **7.** 'governors': besides the satrap who governed all the province of 'Beyond-the-River', there were Persian governors of its various districts. It was such an appointment that Nehemiah received for Jerusalem. **8.** 'forest': the Persian word is *pardes* from which is derived the English 'paradise'. 'The royal park' is the nearest equivalent.

e **9–10 The Journey to Jerusalem—9.** 'the king's letters': of safe-conduct (7). 'officers of the army': Nehemiah as governor, 8:9; 10:1, was invested with civil and not, like Ezra, ecclesiastical authority; and consequently was attended by a bodyguard; contrast Ez 8:22. **10.** 'Sanballat': an Assyrian name meaning 'Sin [the lunar god] gives life'. He is named the Horonite probably because he was from Beth-Horon, rather than from Horonaim in Moab, for in this latter case, Nehemiah would have expressed his contempt by calling him the Moabite. He was governor of Samaria. In a document among the papyri fragments of Elephantine, dated the 17th year of Darius II (407 B.C.) we read that the sons of 'Sanballat governor of Samaria' have great authority. 'Tobiah the Ammonite' was perhaps of the lineage of the family of the Tobiads, which as we know from Josephus (Ant. 12, 5, 1) and from recently discovered papyri was famous about 300 B.C. for its wealth and power in the region of Ammon. 'the servant': the word means 'slave', Ex 21:1–7, but it is also a title of honour, 1 Sm 29:3; 2 (4) Kgs 22:12. Here Tobiah certainly has a part in the government of the province. 'heard this':

of Nehemiah's arrival, not of his purpose. It was a **317e** sufficiently disturbing idea that a strict and zealous Jew, backed by the king's authority, should be governor in Jerusalem.

12–16 The Inspection of the City Walls by Night— **f** Nehemiah's manner was remarkable; he had drawn out from the start the main lines of his program; but he was prudent enough not to speak about it; he wanted to see by himself in detail what had to be done, 2:11–15. When he did tell the community about his intentions, he held all the winning cards. **13–14.** The topography of ancient Jerusalem is too obscure to admit of the various parts of its walls being identified with certainty, but Nehemiah began his tour from the SW and pursued his course, first along the S wall, then along the E wall up the side of the 'torrent', i.e. 'the Kidron'. **17–20 Nehemiah's Appeal: the Derision of his Enemies—**Nehemiah having satisfied himself as to the practicability of his plan, called an assembly. The Chronicler is utilizing, not transcribing, Nehemiah's Memoirs. Nehemiah's appeal is based on three convincing arguments: the pitiful state of Jerusalem, God's favour, the king's permission. **17.** 'disgrace': by reason of our inability to defend ourselves. **19.** To the two adversaries already mentioned is added Geshem the Arab, perhaps governor of the province of the Arabs, which included Edom. **20b.** 'you have no *portion* or *right* or *memorial* [i.e. nothing by which to remember you] in Jerusalem': these words resemble the declaration in Ez 4:3 and imply a claim on the part of the Samaritans to share in the fortunes of Jerusalem.

3:1–31 A List of the Builders of the Wall—This **g** ch was taken from some official record of the repairing of the wall and inserted in Nehemiah's narrative. The workers were organized according to families, localities, or professions, into 42 groups, each headed by one or two men. Those dwelling in nearby villages—Jericho, Tekoa, etc—were also summoned. Each group was assigned a certain gateway or section of wall—the lengths of the latter varying considerably, according as the need of repair was greater or less. This list does not mention any of the names of Ezra's caravan (cf Ez 8:1–14), an omission which suggests that Nehemiah came to Jerusalem before Ezra. The Heb. text is in a poor state and many of the plentiful topographical details are quite obscure. It is clear, however, that the description starts at the E and the N wall and proceeds counterclockwise (cf § 82b).

1. 'Eliashib': cf Ez 3:2; Neh 12:10 and 13:4, where his close connexion with Tobiah shows that he did not sympathize with the policy of Nehemiah. 'the Sheep Gate': in the NE section of the wall. Through it the sacrificial animals were led to the temple; cf Jn 5:2. 'consecrated it': *qiddešûhû* has been substituted out of respect for the priesthood for *qērûhû*, 'laid its beams' of the other gate-building accounts (cf 3:6). 'the Tower of the Hundred': the origin of the name is unknown. 'Hananel': cf Jer 31:38; Zech 14:10. **3.** 'the Fish Gate': about the middle of the N wall. **5.** 'their lord': i.e. Nehemiah; the chiefs of Tekoa refused to join in the work.

6. 'the Old Gate': probably so called either because **h** it gave access to the old part of the city or because it belonged to a part of the wall older than the repaired wall of Hezekiah, 2 Chr 32:5. It was probably on the N side of the city to the W of the Fish Gate. **7.** 'who were under the jurisdiction of the governor of the province Beyond-the-River': HT is obscure: perhaps it denotes the limit of the restoration undertaken by the men of Gibeon and Mizpah: i.e. 'up to' the place where the satrap

317h of 'Beyond-the-River' held court on his visits to Jerusalem. **8.** 'as far as the Broad Wall': the portion between the Gate of Ephraim, 12:38, and the Tower of the Ovens, 11, on the W (?) side of the city. **9.** 'ruler of half the district': the province, ruled by a governor, was divided into districts, and these often into two parts, each of which was ruled by a 'prefect'. So also in 12, 14, 15, 16, 17. **11.** 'another section': either 'a further portion' of the same section or 'undertook another piece of restoration work'; compare 3:21, 27 with 3:3, 5; 18 with 24. 'the Tower of the Ovens': between the Gate of Ephraim and the Valley Gate. **12.** Shallum shared with Rephaiah (9) the prefecture' of the district of Jerusalem'. 'he and his daughters': perhaps it [the half district] and its villages'; cf 11:25, 27 Heb. But it is quite possible that even women joined in the work. **13.** 'the Valley Gate': cf 2:13. This was the main entrance on the W side. 'the Dung Gate': cf 2:13. The wall, having passed due E from the Valley Gate to the Dung Gate, then turned in a northerly direction.

i   **15.** 'the stairs': at the S extremity of the E hill. A similar flight of steps was unearthed in 1895 near the pool of Siloe and another in 1913—14 at the S point of Ophel. 'the City of David': the Jerusalem that David captured from the Jebusites. It embraced the E hill, (Ophel). **16.** 'the sepulchres': according to this text they should be on the SE slope of Ophel, 2 Chr 32:3, where, in fact, they were found (1913—14). 'the pool': distinct from the lower pool of Siloe, it is probably the pool of Solomon mentioned above under 2:14; cf Is 22:11. 'the house of the mighty men': probably barracks for the royal bodyguard.

       19—24. The places here indicated cannot be exactly identified, but we find ourselves on the E wall, approaching the temple and so we meet the houses of the 'priests' (21ff). **22.** 'the men of the Plain': the technical name given to the plain of the Jordan valley near Jericho; but the same term also means 'the surroundings', which would make better sense here (cf E. Dhorme, La Bible, ad loc). **26.** The first part of the v, 'and the temple servants were living on Ophel', is a parenthesis, probably a later addition to be read after 27. The servants' quarters adjoined the temple on the S. 'Ophel': the S section of the temple hill. 'the Water Gate': leading to the spring of Gihon in the ravine of the Kidron (?). **28.** 'the Horse Gate'; cf Jer 31:40; 2 (4) Kgs 11:16. **32.** With the Sheep Gate, the circuit is complete.

j   **4:1—23 Opposition**—This ch in the HT does not begin until v 7.

1—6 The Samaritans ridicule the Work—**1.** Here Nehemiah's Memoirs are resumed; 1—3 narrate an incident similar to that of 2:19—20. 'Sanballat': his irritation at Nehemiah's arrival, 2:10, increased after work on the wall was begun. **2.** 'will they restore things?': HT reads, 'will they leave to themselves?', which does not make any sense. RSV offers as good a version as any. **3.** 'their stone wall' is a phrase of contempt; the building of a wall adequate for defence is a laborious task. **4—5.** This is the first of the parenthetical prayers which characterize Nehemiah's writings; cf 5:19; 6:9; 13:14, 22. It is based on Jer 18:23; 12:36, 17, 18; 18:2—22. The insults addressed to the Jews are finally directed against God whose honour is at stake. **5.** 'they have provoked the builders to anger'. **6.** As the different parties worked simultaneously on the wall, it was quietly restored up to one half of its height, and this success was a stimulus to greater effort.

7—12 Threats—**7.** An early inspection had satisfied the foe that nothing effective would be accomplished by the Jews; now they hear that an essential part has been done **317** 'the Ashdodites': the people of Ashdod, one of the principal Philistine cities. **10.** A rhythmic song; similar popular refrains are not uncommon in the historical books; cf 1 Sm 18:7; 2 Sm 20:1; 1 (3) Kgs 12:16; 2 Chr 18:16. Besides the hostility of the Samaritans, the Jews themselves were becoming overwhelmed by fatigue. **12.** The text is not clear; RSV follows LXX and Syr. Jews living in Samaritan cities heard of the plot and came to warn Nehemiah.

13—23 Measures for Defence—**13.** HT is very dif- **k** ficult; the verb 'I stationed' appears twice, the first time without complement; RSV suppresses one of them and the sense is fairly clear: Nehemiah takes counter-measures which will discourage the Samaritans. **19—20.** Because of the great extent of the wall, the defenders were scattered; hence the need of collecting all available forces quickly to any threatened point. **21.** 'half of them held the spears' is probably a copyist's repetition from 16 and to be omitted. **22.** The Jews dwelling in the suburbs used to return home for the night. Because they were needed for defence, Nehemiah made them lodge in the city. **23.** HT is hopeless; the last word 'water' is certainly an error; it is omitted by LXX; RSV is clear.

5:1—19 Difficulties within the City: Nehemiah's l Governorship—This ch can hardly be in its right place; there was neither occasion nor leisure for such complaints and proceedings during the 52 days of feverish activity that marked the rebuilding of the wall. Moreover the date in 5:14 shows that we are at the end of Nehemiah's rule. The ch appears to belong to a later period and describes later acts of Nehemiah's administration.

1—13 Social Abuses—**1.** 'against their Jewish m brethren': i.e. the rich and the nobles (7). The story of the oppression of the poor by the rich is a familiar one with the prophets. It is distressing to see how quickly in a poor and struggling community avaricious 'capitalism' had revived. **2.** 'with our sons and daughters, we are many': most scholars, since the 18th cent. read 'ōrebîm instead of rabbîm, and translate, 'we are giving in pledge our sons and daughters, in order to get corn to eat and live'; this would be an allusion to a fairly common practice in antiquity; cf 2 (4) Kgs 4:1; Am 2:6; 8:6; Is 50:1. The ancient laws in Israel tried to control it; cf Ex 21:7; Lv 25:39. **4.** 'upon our fields and our vineyards': a repetition from 3 and probably a gloss. This social-economic crisis was due to a bad harvest and consequent famine. The poor had no resource but to borrow from wealthy money-lenders, and, as a security, to give either their property, when they had any, or their children. Deprived of the profits from their holdings and the labour of their children, there was little hope of ever paying off the debt; hence their children would remain slaves and their vineyards be seized. 'the king's tax': the royal tax was one that Nehemiah dared not fail to collect, although he did his best to lighten the burden (14). **5.** 'our flesh', etc; we and our children are Jews just as they are; such oppression should have no place among brethren of the same blood. **7.** 'you are exacting interest, each from his brother': in fact there is no question of interest of usury in this case; perhaps one should read, 'burden', massā' with several Heb. MSS, instead of usury, interest, maśśā: you impose a burden each one on his brother. **8.** Nehemiah and other pious men had, out of their own purses, redeemed Jews who had been enslaved for debt by their pagan creditors. **9.** 'taunts': such cruel treatment of fellow-Jews makes the nation and its religion a byword to the pagans. **10.** 'let us leave off this debt': in the

7m spirit of Jer 34:8—22 and Dt 15:1—11, Nehemiah invites his hearers to release purely and simply what they have lent. (cf E. Dhorme, op cit ad loc). **11.** 'the hundredth': some critics read '*debt*' in conformity with 10*b*. **12.** 'the priests' were called not to take the oath but to administer it. **13.** 'lap': 'the fold of my garment': the action is symbolic, after the manner of the prophets.

n **14—19 Nehemiah's Governorship**—This is Nehemiah's apologia for his administration, particularly on the financial side. In the E high political office has been fatally accompanied by corruption, oppression, and self-enrichment; from all these evils Nehemiah refrained 'for love of God'. More than that; out of pity for his people's poverty, he waived his own salary as governor and bore the expenses of the office out of his own pocket. Evidently he was rich enough to afford it; but such generosity is no less remarkable in the rich than in the poor. **14.** His governorship lasted from 445—433 B.C. 'the food allowance': a proportion of the taxes was allotted to the governor and his establishment for their maintenance. This allowance Nehemiah forewent. **15.** 'forty shekels': about $30—with much greater purchasing power. **16.** 'acquired no land': an allusion to 10; Nehemiah did not take advantage of his position to buy up the land of the poor. **17.** He regularly entertained 150 officials and welcomed Jews from the Dispersion to his table.

o **6:1—19 The Wall completed**—The narrative about the rebuilding of the walls, which was broken by ch 5, is here resumed.

1—9 Opposition from without—**2.** The wall proper was now finished, therefore the opportunity for attack had gone by; so Sanballat and his confederates seek to allure Nehemiah to a conference in order to get him into their power. 'Ono': now Kefr Ana, some 7 m. E by SE of Jaffa. **3.** Nehemiah refuses to go on the ground that he is too busy with the work on hand. **5.** 'an open letter': that its content might reach and intimidate others. **6—7.** In the letter Sanballat pretends to give friendly information of the dangerous gossip which is so widespread that the Persian king is sure to hear of it, and suggests a conference that they may find a way of extricating Nehemiah from his perilous situation. **9.** 'thinking', etc: 'saying'.

p **10—14 A Further Attempt to entrap Nehemiah**—This section is very compressed and the text corrupt. The general sense is that Sanballat had hired a fake prophet to persuade Nehemiah that his life was in danger and to induce him to seek safety in the inner sanctuary of the temple, where no layman was permitted to enter. Such an impious act would have gravely discredited him in the eyes of the people. **10.** 'Shemaiah': not known otherwise. 'who was shut up': obscure; the most likely explanation is probably that the prophet could not, for some reason or other, go to Nehemiah, and therefore asked him to come to his house; cf Jer 36:5, where the same expression is used. 'within the temple': in the Holy Place, which corresponded to our modern nave. **11.** 'and live': it was forbidden to a layman to enter the inner sanctuary under pain of death; cf Nm 18:7. **14.** 'the prophetess Noadiah': not found elsewhere; but there is no reason why one should read with LXX 'the prophet'; there were prophetesses in Israel, cf Jg 4:4; 2 (4) Kgs 22:14.

q **15—16 Completion of the Work**—**15.** 'Elul': the sixth month, Aug.—Sept. of 445. For another instance of the rapid erection of walls under patriotic impulse, cf the action of Themistocles and the Athenians. **17—19 Enemies within**—During the whole of this period a treasonable correspondence was carried on

between Tobiah and the disaffected Jewish nobles. **317q** **18.** 'were bound by oath to him', etc: Tobiah's connexion by marriage ensured him the support of many leading Jews. He was the son-in-law of Shecaniah and the father-in-law of the daughter of Meshullam. He was also related by marriage to the high-priest Eliashib, 13:4.

7:1—73 Arrangements for the Protection of the **318a** **City: A List of the Returned Exiles.**
1—4 Nehemiah's Precautions—**1.** 'the singers and the Levites': probably a gloss; singers and Levites had nothing to do at the gates of the city. **2.** 'governor of the castle': captain of the fortress (probably connected with the temple and doubtless the military headquarters as well as the seat of government). **3.** City gates were usually opened at sunrise and closed at sunset. 'still standing guard': i.e. before they went to bed. Every precaution was taken lest the citizens be surprised by an assault at a time when they could not promptly defend themselves. **4.** 'no houses had been built': some exegetes understand, 'the offspring of the returned exiles was not yet numerous'; cf Ex 1:21; but the use of the verb 'to build' seems to rule out this figurative interpretation.

5. As a preliminary step to increasing the population of Jerusalem, Nehemiah proposed to take a census of all persons of Jewish descent. 'those who came up at first': during the reign of Cyrus. This record must have been found in the archives of Jerusalem. Original in Neh 7, it is also found in Ez 2:3—58, but with variants in the names and sometimes in the numbers.

6—73 The List—**21.** 'Hezekiah': i.e. of the subdivision which took its name from Hezekiah, probably not the king of that name. **68.** This v is omitted in some of the oldest Heb. MSS, probably through an oversight but found in Ez 2:66.

8:1—9:37 Religious Reform—A number of modern **b** scholars believe that this section belongs to the Ezra narrative. Their reasons are: (1) chh 8—9 interrupt the story of Nehemiah's plan to find inhabitants for Jerusalem, Neh 7:4, which is resumed only in 11:1; (2) the unexpected re-appearance of Ezra in this section; (3) the change in the narrative of Neh 8—9 from the first to the third person.

There is no agreement however as to the place Neh 8—9 should be given in the Ezra narrative. Some scholars insert it after Ez 10 where it would fill a gap. Others are inclined to the view that Neh 8—9 originally followed Ez 8; actually this view fits much better with the chronological data offered by the text: (1) Ez 7:1—8:36, Ezra's journey to Jerusalem, 427 B.C.; (2) Neh 7:72*b*—8:18, the reading of the Law, two months after Ezra's arrival, on the 1st day of the 7th month, cf Ez 7:9 and Neh 7:72*b*; (3) Ez 9:1—10:44, the affair of mixed marriages raised in the 9th month, cf Ez 10:9, 16, and the end of the commission on the 1st day of the 1st month, 426 B.C., cf Ez 10:17; (4) Neh 9:1—37, a public confession of sin on the 24th day of the same month, cf Neh 9:1.

8:1—18 The Reading of the Law and the Feast of **c** **Tabernacles.**
1—12 The Reading of the Law by Ezra—**1.** The opening words of this section are very similar to those in Ez 3:1 after the list of names. When the Chronicler described the first gathering of the returned Exiles, Ez 3:1ff, he gave it the colour and solemnity of the ceremony which took place later with Ezra. 'Ezra': this is the first time Ezra is mentioned in Nehemiah. 'the book of the law of Moses': cf 315*b* on Ez 7:6. **2.** 'assembly':

318c cf Ez 10:8. 'the first day of the seventh month' of Tishri, the Feast of Trumpets. Before the Exile, this month opened the new year; cf Ex 23:16; 34:22; Lv 23:24ff; Nm 29:1. **3.** 'he read from it' selected passages. **4.** Nehemiah is not mentioned. **6.** 'lifting up their hands': in token of approval and solidarity. **7.** 'the Levites helped the people to understand the Law': the Chronicler insists on the role played by the Levites. **9.** Omit 'Nehemiah' with 3 Ez; the verbs that follow are in the singular, as if Ezra alone was the subject; omit also therefore 'the Levites'. 'wept': when they saw how they had broken the Law; cf 2 (4) Kgs 22:11ff. The solemn assembly of Neh 8 must be compared with the convocation of Sinai, Ex 19ff, and with the ceremony of the renewal of the covenant under King Josiah 2 (4) Kgs 23; these texts deal with three vital moments in the history of Israel, and they present a striking parallelism: (1) in each case the people are called together to a convocation by God's word; (2) then they hear a solemn proclamation of the Law; (3) after which they are led to agree, by praise and prayer, to the word thus expressed. But whereas the ceremonies of Ex 19 and 2 (4) Kgs 23 were crowned by a sacrifice, the convocation of Neh 8 comes practically to an end with the people 'making great rejoicing' in a community-meal. Even if the synagogue type of worship, limited to Scripture readings and prayers with no sacrifice is not precisely a product of the Exile, there is no doubt that we find in Neh 8 a first instance of a new type of worship which gained its importance for God's people as a result of the impossibility of carrying out a sacrificial worship after the destruction of the temple. It is there that the service of the Word in Christian worship finds its deepest roots (cf Louis Bouyer, *Life and Liturgy*, 1956, 23—27).

d 13—18 The Feast of Tabernacles—13. 'the second day': of the 7th month. **14.** 'written in the Law': the text nearest to Neh 14ff is Lv 23:33—36, 39—43. But a comparison between the two texts makes it clear that the law alluded to in Neh does not exist as such in the Pent as it is today; cf § 204*b*—*c*. **17.** 'since the days of Jeshua the son of Nun' they had not celebrated the feasts with such joy and festal pomp; for previous celebrations, however, cf Hos 12:9; the author is evidently quoting Ezra's Memoirs, cf Ez 3:4. **18.** 'the 8th day': cf Nm 29:35; Lv 23:36.

e 9:1—37 A Public Confession of Sin—This ch follows Ez 10:44; the affair of mixed marriages was concluded by an expiation ceremony; compare Neh 9:2 and Ez 9:1*a*, 2*a*; 10:11*b*.

1—5 A Day of Fasting and Sackcloth—1. 'the 24th day' of the 1st month, 426 B.C. 'fasting . . . sackcloth . . . earth': penitential rites derived from the mourning ritual; cf Jl 1—2. **2.** 'confessed their sins': as a nation; the penitential liturgy included a 'lamentation' given here in 6—37; cf Pss 74 (73); 79 (78); 83 (82). **3.** 'they read': the Levites, while the people listened; 'a fourth of the day': i.e. 3 hours. **4.** 'the stairs': platform; cf 8:4. **5.** 'At the invitation of the Levites': 'bless the Lord', etc, the people (though it is not expressly stated) responded, joining in the divine praise and in the confession which followed.

f 6—37 The National Confession—This prayer is one of the most beautiful and complete liturgical prayers to be found in OT outside the psalter; it expresses the piety of a community whose trust in God was all the greater as it was based on genuine humility. After an act of faith in one God, the creator of heaven and earth, it first recalls God's early mercies to Israel, the nation's

unworthy return, the divine forbearance, the people's **318** renewed disobedience, and their consequent punishment; it then acknowledges the justice of their chastisement and concludes abruptly with a picture of Israel's present plight, which is, in itself, an appeal. There are no compelling reasons for asserting that this prayer is a later insertion.

6. 'And Ezra said': omitted by HT. 'the heaven of heavens': cf Ps 68 (67):34. 'the host of heaven': probably the angels; cf Ps 103 (102):21. Ezra goes on to recall the main lines of Israel's history: (*1*) the call of Abraham, 7—8. **8.** Cf Gn 15:18—21. 'righteous': therefore faithful to his promises; (*2*) the servitude of Egypt and the liberation through the waters of the Red Sea, 9—11. **9.** Cf Ex 3:7; 14:10. **10.** Cf Ex 7—12. 'name': reputation; cf Ex 9:16. **11.** Cf Ex 14:21; 15:4, 5, 19; (*3*) Israel's wanderings in the desert under God's guidance, 12—21. **12.** 'a pillar of cloud . . . of fire': **g** the symbol of God's presence, cf Ex 13:21. **13—14.** The Sinai Covenant, cf Ex 19—20. **15.** The gift of manna and water, cf Ex 16:4ff; 17:6. But God's generosity was answered by Israel's sins. **17.** Rebellion. 'appointed a leader': or 'set their heads to return to their bondage in Egypt', cf Nm 14:4. 'thou art a God ready to forgive': cf Ex 34:6—7. **18.** The Golden Calf, cf Ex 32:1—4. And yet, God did not abandon his people. **19.** Cf Ex 40:34—38. **20.** 'good spirit': 'thy favourable breath', i.e. thy help; perhaps the figure contains an allusion to the sending of quails carried by the wind, Nm 11:31. 'to instruct them': to make them prosper. **21.** Cf Dt 8:4; 29:5; (*4*) The conquest of Canaan, 22—25. **22.** The kingdoms of Transjordan were not included, in the strict sense, in the land promised to the fathers, Gn 12:7; Nm 32:7; Dt 2:30—3:20; (*5*) The period of the Judges, 26—28. The text sums up in a few words the theology of the book of Judges, cf Jg 2:6—3:6; (*6*) The prophets and successive invasions, 29—31. **30.** Cf Zech 7:12. 'spirit': divine revelation made to the prophets; (*7*) Present distress, 32—37. **32.** 'Assyria': the domination by Assyria had been succeeded by that of Babylon and Persia. **36***b*. 'slaves': subjects of Persia. **37.** The taxes were excessive. 'we are in great distress': God will, no doubt, see this distress, and just as in the past, he will perform signs and wonders in order to save his people.

9:38—10:39 The Renewal of the Covenant—The **h** relation between 10:31ff and 13 is evident. During his second term of office, Neh corrected a number of abuses in the service of God. In order to prevent them from recurring, he probably invited the community to promise solemnly to keep the Law, and the record of this 'new covenant' was deposited on the temple archives. The Chronicler may have found it there, unless it had already been added to Nehemiah's Memoirs; and he connected it with the reading of the Law narrated in chh 8—9.

9:38—10:29 The List of Signatories—9:38 is 10:1 **i** in MT, and in fact it belongs to ch 10. **1.** 'those who set their seal': the names include priests, Levites and the families whose heads signed on behalf of their houses.

30—39 The Obligations of the Covenant—30. No intermarriage with non-Israelites; cf 13:23—27; see also Ex 34:16; Dt 7:3; compare with Ez 10:44. **31.** No trading on the Sabbath day: cf 13:15—22; see also Ex 31:12—14; 23—12; Dt 5:12; Lv 19:3; and the observance of the sabbatical year by allowing the land to lie fallow, Ex 23:10f; Lv 25:2—7, and by not exacting the payment of debts, Dt 15:1—6. **32—33.** Payment of the temple tax. This is a modification

18i of the half shekel prescribed in Ex 30:11—16 (cf Mt 17:24). Perhaps this change was due to the straightened circumstances of the community. **33.** 'showbread': 'bread of the setting forth': cf § 189*i*. **34.** Provision of wood for the altar. 'cast lots': to determine the time and order in which each family was to supply wood. 'as it is written' refers to the burning not the fetching of wood; cf Lv 6:12. **35—37.** The offering of first-fruits, Ex 23:19; Dt 26:2—10, first-born, Ex 13:13; Nm 18:16—19, and of tithes, Lv 27:30; Nm 18:21—32; Dt 14:22—29; cf Neh 13:10, 14, 31. **37.** 'coarse-meal' in the form of a paste, Nm 15:21. 'contributions', lit. 'something separated', i.e. the portion of first-fruits and sacrifices set apart for the priests. The Levites received a tenth from the people and gave to the priests a tenth of all they received; cf Nm 18:25—28. This was placed in the storerooms that stood around the temple.

9a **11:1—12:26. The City peopled**—This section takes up the thread that had been dropped at 7:4—72*a*. The inhabitants of Jerusalem were few in proportion to the area of the city, 7:4. Chiefly the official classes dwelt in Jerusalem; the mass of the people lived in the surrounding villages, 11:1. Nehemiah decided to select by lot one man in ten to reside in the city. For this purpose a census was required; Nehemiah used a list of the returned exiles already drawn up, 7:5—73*a*. His 'Memoirs' were then interrupted by a description of the feast of Tabernacles and the covenant (chh 8—10). The text now returns to the subject of repopulating Jerusalem and briefly describing the method adopted. **1.** 'the holy city': this expression goes back to Is 48:2; 52:1; it appears again in Neh 11:18; Dn 9:24; Tb 13:9; Mt 4:5; 27:53; Apoc 11:2. But it was when God chose Jerusalem as 'the place where his holy name would dwell' that it became the holy city. **2.** Some, apparently, over and above the tenth selected by lot, volunteered to dwell in Jerusalem. 11:3—12:26 contains lists taken from the state archives with abridgments and necessary adaptations.

b **3—9 The List of the Residents of Jerusalem**—The same list is found in 1 Chr 9:2—19 with variations. **3—9.** The chief laymen. **8.** The text seems corrupt. A suggested emendation is *we'ehā(y)u gibbôrê ḥayīl*, 'and his kinsmen were mighty warriors'. **9.** 'their overseer': of the Benjamites. 'second over the city': second in charge.

10—14 The List of the Priests.

15—18 The Levites. 19. The Porters. **20** interrupts the account of the residents of Jerusalem. It would be more appropriate before 25. **22—24.** Notes about officers and the singers. **23.** 'the king': Artaxerxes. **24.** Pethahiah' seems to have been an official representative of Jewish interests at the Persian court. **25—36.** The towns and villages occupied by the Jews. **25—30.** The Judaean towns. **30.** 'the valley of Hinnom' ran along the SW wall of Jerusalem. **31—36.** The Benjamite towns.

c **12:1—26 A List of Priests and Levites** arranged by periods; it carries us down to the times of the sacred writer. **1—9.** A list of priests and Levites who came with Zerubbabel and Jeshua, the high-priest. The names in 1—7 also appear with some variations in 10:3—8; 12:12—21; see also Ez 2:36—39. **9.** 'stood opposite them in the service': for antiphonal singing. **10—11.** The succession of high-priests is carried down from Jeshua (c. 520) to Jaddua who was contemporary with Alexander the Great (c. 333). Eliashib was high-priest at the time of Nehemiah. **12—21.** The list in 1—7 was of the contemporaries of Zerubbabel; this list gives the heads of those same families 'in the days

of Joiakim', the successor of Jeshua as high-priest. **319c 17.** 'Minianim': the name of the representative of this family has fallen out. **22—26.** Further lists. **22.** 'Darius the Persian': either Darius II who died in 405, or Darius III (Codomannus), defeated by Alexander. **23.** 'the Book of the Chronicles': not the Chronicles of the OT. **24.** 'Jeshua, *Binnui*, Kadmiel': cf Ez 2:40, Neh 12:8*l*. 'over against them': 'opposite them' in the choir. 'watch corresponding to watch', for antiphonal chant.

27—43 The Dedication of the Walls—One would **d** naturally expect this event to follow closely upon their completion on the 25th of Elul (cf 6:15). But the Chronicler wanted to make it match the dedication of the temple, Ez 6:13—18. Thus two dedication ceremonies crown two historical periods; the first marked by Zerubbabel, and the second—in the Chronicler's view— by Ezra-Nehemiah. The description is taken in the main from Nehemiah's Memoirs (cf the use of the first person), but for 33—36 and 40—43 the writer probably had recourse to a temple or priestly document. The dedication was a symbolic handing over of the walls to the possession and guardianship of Yahweh. The high-priest is not mentioned as taking part in the procession because he awaited its arrival at the temple.

27—30 The Preparation—**28.** 'the sons of the singers': **e** merely 'singers'. 'Netophathites': Netophah was about 15 m. S of Jerusalem. **30.** 'purified themselves' for the solemnity by ceremonial purification; cf Ez 6:20.

31—39 The Procession—The description of this great event must be read against the background of Is 10—66. The post-exilic Jerusalem had not yet been completely rebuilt, and its population was still small; jealous neighbours threatened its very existence. But it remained the 'holy city', a sign of the New Jerusalem sung by the prophet of the Book of Comfort, Is 54:1—3. Nehemiah's procession prefigures the Day when all nations flock to Jerusalem, Is 60:1ff; cf François Louvel, 'Les Processions dans la Bible', Maison-Dieu 43 (1955) 5—28.

The procession was marshalled in two great choirs; starting from the W side of the city, one choir went round the S half of the wall, and the other round the N half. They joined in the open space before the temple. **32—33.** Behind the singers and musicians came one half of the chiefs of Judaea with Hoshaiah, otherwise unknown, at their head. **34—35.** They were followed by seven heads of the priestly families with trumpets, and eight of the Levitical order with accompanying instruments, while Ezra walked at the head of the priests. **34.** 'the priests' sons' = priests; cf 28. The presence of Ezra is probably an interpolation of the Chronicler.

The Route of the Procession—From the Valley Gate **f** the two columns moved in opposite directions. Along the S route of the first column were the Dung Gate, the Fountain Gate, the Stairs of David and the Water Gate at the E of the temple. Along the N course of the second column, the Tower of the Ovens, the Broad Wall, the Gate of Ephraim, the Old Gate, the Fish Gate, the Tower of Hananel, the Tower of Meah, the Sheep Gate, and the Muster Gate.

35b—36. If the Valley Gate be either the Gate of the Essenes or that found in the Tyropoeon Valley, the distance travelled by each column was about the same (c. 1600 and c. 1300 yards). **43.** The two columns met in the open space before the temple and songs of rejoicing were sung and sacrifices of thanksgiving offered. See Map 9A.

12:44—13:3 An Ideal Period—During his second term **320a** of office, Nehemiah was obliged to intervene in order to

320a correct a number of abuses, 13:4ff. The present section, on the contrary, describes Israel as the ideal community in which the service of the temple was perfectly organized, 12:44—47; and where foreigners had no part, 13:1—3. The Chronicler probably intended to conclude the book by thus summing up some of the most important achievements of the restoration under the leadership of Zerubbabel and Nehemiah; in which case, 13:4ff would only be an appendix. **44.** 'on that day': at that time; see also 13:1; the author does not think of a precise date; he has in view a general description of the post-exilic community at the time of Zerubbabel and Nehemiah. **45.** HT is obscure. The priests, Levites, singers and porters discharged the duties of their office. **47.** 'they set apart': the people set apart a tenth portion for the Levites who in turn gave a part to the priests according to Nm 18:25—32.

b　**13:1—3. Foreigners are excluded from the community.** The event contrasts with the abuse which Nehemiah had to correct; compare 13:1—3 and 13:4—9, 28. **1.** 'was found written': the rest of this v and 2 is almost integral citation of Dt 23:3—5. **3.** 'all those of foreign descent': well in line with Ezra's reform, this measure goes beyond the requirements of the law; cf Dt 23:7—9.

c　**13:4—31 Nehemiah's Second Mission**—Nehemiah remained in Jerusalem for twelve years (445—433 B.C.) and then returned to Susa. He followed anxiously the life of the people of Jerusalem, and when informed of alarming symptoms in their spiritual state, once more obtained permission to visit the city. The date of this second mission is uncertain; it must have taken place before the death of Artaxerxes (424 B.C.). It concerns abuses that had arisen in Judaea during Nehemiah's absence.

4—9 The Expulsion of Tobiah from the Sacred Precincts—Nehemiah's intervention both to expel Tobiah from the temple precincts and to enforce measures against mixed marriages, 23—29, has only one aim: to safeguard the holiness of God's people. **4.** 'before this': before the excommunication of the non-Israelites narrated in 13:1—3. 'Eliashib': not the high-priest of 3:1, 20ff; 10:22; 13:28. 'Tobiah': one of Nehemiah's chief enemies, 2:10. He persuaded Eliashib to give him a room inside the temple precincts, doubtless offering the priest some percentage. This room became a branch office of the Bank of Tobiah whose head office was in Ammon. **5.** In the rooms about the temple courtyard were stored whatever was needed for divine worship and for the maintenance of the sacred ministers; cf 12:46. **6.** Neh returned to Babylon at the end of the period for which he had asked leave of the king, 2:6. **6b—7.** Tobiah was an Ammonite, 2:10; 4:3, and, as such, his presence in the temple precincts, apart from his business, was

an affront to the holiness of the place. **9.** 'they cleansed **320** the chambers' made unclean by Tobiah's presence; cf Hag 2:13.

10—14. Nehemiah, finding that the contribution for **d** the support of the Levites had been neglected with the result that they had to seek a livelihood in the country to the detriment of the temple service, brought them back to Jerusalem, insisted on the payment of tithes, and appointed a commission of two priests and two Levites to supervise the distribution; cf 12:44, 47. **14.** One of the parenthetic prayers of Nehemiah: he prays that he may be remembered for his zeal on behalf of the temple.

15—22 The Observance of the Sabbath—Throughout the OT fidelity to the sabbath is considered as a sure test of Israel's dedication to God. The sabbath is this part of time which man offers as a tithe to God the creator, Gn 2:2—3; Ex 20:11, and it serves also as a weekly reminder of the liberation from Egypt, Dt 5:14—15. By enforcing the sabbath legislation Nehemiah obliged the Israelites to remember that they were a people created and saved by God. **15.** 'I warned them on the day when they sold food': MT is not clear; perhaps should one read, '*bāhem* '*against them*', instead of '*b*e*yôm*', '*on the day*', 'I protested against them when they sold food'. **16.** The Tyrians, sailors and fishermen, as pagans, were not interested in the Mosaic Law. **17—19.** Nehemiah rebuked the leading citizens and ordered the gates to be shut on the eve of the Sabbath and the law of rest to be observed. **19.** 'when it began to be dark': the sabbath began at sunset. **20.** The merchants, for a week or two, set up a market outside the walls. **21.** Nehemiah promptly used his authority as governor to put down this evasion of his regulations.

23—29 Measures against mixed Marriages—The **e** question of mixed marriages was again giving trouble. Nehemiah found Judaeans married to Philistines, Ammonites and Moabites, and their children unable to speak Hebrew. The guilty were punished and an oath exacted against the repetition of the offence. Even the high-priest's family was involved in guilt. **23.** Cf 13:1—3. **26.** Cf 1 (3) Kgs 11:3. **28.** One violation of the law gave particular offence; a grandson of the high-priest had married the daughter of Sanballat (cf 2:10). The offender was banished and, according to Jewish legend, he set up a schismatic priesthood in Samaria, and later had a temple built on Mt Gerizim. **29.** 'defiled the priesthood': the family of the high-priest was contaminated by the incident.

30—31 A Brief Recapitulation—Cf 12:44—13:3. **31.** 'The offering of wood': cf 10:34. As already explained, Nehemiah, in order to ward off for good the abuses mentioned in ch 13, probably invited the community to promise solemnly to keep the law, ch 10. We do not know when Nehemiah died. He is praised in Sir 49:15.

TOBIT

BY P. GIFFIN

336a Bibliography—*Commentaries*: R. Galdos, CSS 1930; M. Schumpp, München, 1933; A. Miller–J. Schildenberger, BB, 1940; A. Clamer, PCSB, 1952; G. Priero, SacB, 1953; R. Pautrel, BJ, 1957²; F. Zimmermann, New York, 1958; *Other literature*: D. C. Simpson, *Tobit*, CAP 1. 174–241; R. H. Pfeiffer, *History of NT Times with Introd. to the Apocrypha*, 1949; L. Pirot, 'Ahikar' DBS 1 (1928) 198–207 with earlier bibl.; A. Clamer, 'Tobie (livre de) DTC 15 (1946) 1153–76 with earlier bibl.; J. O'Carroll, 'Tobias and Achikar' DbR 93 (1929) 252ff; R. Pautrel, 'Trois textes de Tobie sur Raphael', RSR 39 (1951) 115ff; J. Hennig, 'The Book of Tobias in the Liturgy', IrTQ 19 (1952) 84ff; P. Saydon 'Mistranslations in Codex Sinaiticus of the Book of Tobit', Bib 33 (1952) 363ff.

b The Text—The basic and unsolved problem of Tb is concerned with the text. The book exists in several recensions of a Gr. version and in Latin, Heb., Aram., Syr., Ethiopic and Coptic. All these differ in so many details that, while there is no doubt that they represent the same original story and that many of them are interdependent, the textual critic is faced with problems in every verse and the relationships of the various textforms remain uncertain. It is difficult therefore to avoid an element of the arbitrary in making choice of a text.

c The three Gr. recensions are represented by (a) the majority of MSS including LXX (B) and (A); this is the textus receptus with which coincide the Syr. version in 1:1–7:9 and the Ethiopic version; it was preferred by Swete, provided the text for RV and RSV and is the primary text in the opinion of some scholars. (b) LXX (S), presenting a longer text than (a) and having close affinity to VL; Simpson, Zimmermann, Pautrel, Clamer and others consider that this form best represents the original; it is however defective, especially in 4:7–19 and 13:8–11, and the readings of S elsewhere clearly require correction; Milik, TYD, 1959, 31f reports fragments of three Aram. and one Heb. MS of Tobit, all following this recension. (c) Minuscules 44, 106, 107 (Holmes-Parsons)—44, p, d, (Brooke-McLean-Thackeray) for 6:8–13:8 of the book; this form is the basis of the Syr. from 7:9 onwards and is represented by a fragment of the 6th cent. containing 2:2–8, cf Simpson, op cit 176.

d Of the other versions (d) VL is contained in several MSS of different types printed by Sabatier, cf Brooke-McLean-Thackeray, *The OT in Greek* III part I, Cambridge 1940, p. ix–x. (e) An Aram. text has been edited by A. Neubauer, *Book of Tobit*, Oxford 1878. (f) In Heb., we have the Munster Hebrew, cf Neubauer op cit and two texts in Gaster, *Two Unknown Hebrew Versions of the Tobit Legend*, London 1897, including the 'London' Hebrew, and also the Heb. of Fagius in Walton, *London Polyglot* IV. (g) Last but not least is the Vg Latin made by Jer. at the insistence of his friends; an Aram. text was translated orally into Heb. by a rabbi, re-translated

into Latin by Jerome and written down by a secretary; **336d** the whole was done with speed—'unius diei laborem arripui'—and without much enthusiasm on the part of Jerome for whom Tobit was an apocryphal work, cf his prefatory letter in PL 29, 23.

This highly intricate textual situation, the versions **e** varying in a multiplicity of details, is discussed at length by Simpson, op cit and in JTS 14 (1912–13) 516–530, and by Zimmermann, op cit 32ff and 127ff. The basis of this commentary is the RSV translation of the textus receptus (a), but it would appear that the best supported conclusions of this complex textual debate are as follows: (a) represents a later, abbreviated edition of (b); (b) is itself a translation and is in places corrupt, yet it brings us as close as we can get to the original; (c) is a more polished and refined form of (b) with some conflation with (a); (d) is of the same family as (b) and is a valuable witness to the original but is not necessarily translated from S as Zimmermann would have; (e) was made not before the 4th cent. A.D. and, although it shares with Vg the singular characteristic of using the third person throughout when speaking of Tobit, even in **f** chapters 1–3, yet it does not represent Jerome's 'Chaldee' text; the Heb. versions (f) are all secondary—the Munster text betraying connections with both (b) and (e), the London Heb. appearing to depend on Vg, the Fagius Heb. being a very free translation based on the (a) form; the Vg (g) is again a very free rendering, containing theological and ascetical additions peculiar to itself which are the work of Jer. cf 3:16–21; 6:17–22; 2:12–18; 14:15–17, together with the surprisingly charming touch of 11:9, and manifesting also certain omissions where Jer. seems to have deliberately abbreviated cf (in S) 1:4, 6–8, 19–25; 5:14; 14:1–7. Vg also in places closely follows VL, doubtless used by Jer. in the process of translation or editing. Characteristic of the Vg is the name Tobias for both father and son. In fact, most modern commentators have taken form (b) as the basis of their work, correcting from (a) and (d) when Sinaiticus fails.

The Vg text must be treated as a secondary witness. **g** To this point the 'authenticity' of the Vg as explained in DAS presents no difficulty. The Council of Trent, however, defined (DzS 1502–5; EnchB 58–60) the canonicity of books of OT and NT, which it recited, 'wholly and with all their parts . . . as they are contained in the old vulgate Latin edition'. Nevertheless, Trent certainly did not intend to enter the arena of textual criticism and it does not appear that this decree covers those parts of the Vg of Tobit which we have characterized as 'Jerome's additions'. Trent formally considered only the deuterocanonical books and sections of books of OT and certain passages of NT which at that time were controverted among Catholics and Protestants; it was these books and passages which the Council intended its decree to touch. Cf Vacant, *Études sur le Concile du Vatican*, I 399–400 and EnchB 526–9.

336h In dealing with the book of Tobit we are therefore in the unusual position of having to interpret a book whose original text is lost and whose translations, if they agree in the substance of the story, vary enormously in detail. Even if one accepted the inspiration of the LXX translation, the difficulties would hardly be eased. One may even query whether it is correct to speak of an 'original text' of this book and may envisage the possibility that our present welter of textual forms may have descended from independent presentations of the same story.

337a Canonicity—The book of Tobit was not accepted into the Heb. Bible and was the object of the same Patristic hesitations as the other d.c. books. Jer. was firm in excluding it from the Canon as was, explicitly, Ath PG 26, 1177. Cyr Jer, Epiphanius and Greg. Naz. omit it from their lists of canonical books. On the other hand, besides quotations from Tobit in Polycarp, *Ep. ad Phil.* 10:2 (Tb 4:11) and Hermas, *Mand.* 5:2 (Tb 4:19, Vaticanus), we find the book cited as scripture in Clem Alex PG 8, 1089; 9, 324, in Orig PG 11, 448 and in the *Testimonia* of Cyprian PL 4, 728. Amb. has a series of brief homilies on the book, PL 14, 759ff. The canonicity of Tobit was recognized by the local councils of Hippo (393) and Carthage (397); in the E, the Council in Trullo (692) seems implicitly to have accepted the book in accepting the canons of Carthage. Tobit was included in the lists of Florence and Trent. By the Reformers it was placed among the apocrypha.

b Original language—Gr., Heb. and Aram. have each been favoured by competent scholars whose differences of opinion themselves suggest that objective evidence on which to base a generally acceptable solution has hitherto been lacking. While the discovery of Heb. and Aram. fragments at Qumran has tipped the balance in favour of an original in one of these two languages—as had already been indicated by the Semitisms of the Gr. e.g. in LXX (S) 1:11; 3:6; 11:4; 12:8, 15; 13:13—the choice between them remains less clear. Neither Jerome's use of an Aram. MS nor Origen's remark (*Ep. ad Africanum*, PG 11, 79) that the Jews did not possess the book in Heb. is at all decisive, so that arguments can be drawn only from the internal evidence **c** of the extant Versions. It is notoriously difficult to reach a lost original through a translation; we may cite difficult passages of the Gr. or the variations between the Gr. versions as pointers to an underlying Heb. or Aram. text which translators have mis-read or misunderstood and which we may now reconstruct, but unless the examples quoted are both numerous and themselves not the result of mere inference, we shall have to be content with only probable solutions. This line of research has been most vigorously and most convincingly pursued by Zimmermann, op cit Appendix II; he reaches the conclusion that the Gr. version was made from a Heb. text which was itself a translation of an original Aram. This is attractive, especially as one would expect such a work as Tobit to appear first in the language of the people; we may take it as an adequate working hypothesis.

d Place and Date—There is complete uncertainty as to the place where Tb was written. The author is not personally acquainted with the setting of his story; one might forgive even an inhabitant of Mesopotamia for failing to realize the relative altitudes of Ecbatana and Rages, 5:6 in Sin, but he should know that the distance between these towns is some 200 miles, very much more than could be covered in two days' journeying, ibid, and that a journey from Nineveh to Ecbatana would lead one away from, not towards, the Tigris, 6:1. Whether, however, the author wrote in Egypt (Simpson, op cit

185) or in Palestine (Pautrel, op cit 9 with some hesita- **337e** tion; Pfeiffer, *History of NT Times*, 1949, 275 with enthusiasm) or in Antioch in Syria (Zimmermann, op cit 15ff) cannot be known.

As to date, Tb appears to have been written well **e** after the Exile. The author's knowledge of Assyrian times is sketchy; he gives the royal line of succession as Shalmaneser, Sennacherib, Esarhaddon in 1:15, 24 (the names appear in a variety of forms in the MSS) with no mention of Sargon, the true father of Sennacherib; it was not Shalmaneser but Tiglath-Pileser III who deported the tribe of Naphtali, Tb 1:2 and 2 (4) Kgs 15:29; the destruction of Nineveh is quite mistakenly attributed to Ahikar (!) in LXX (S) and to Nebuchadnezzar and Ahasuerus in LXX (B) 14:15. On the other hand, the similarity between large sections of Tb and the mainly post-exilic Wisdom literature, especially Sirach, indicates a date after the Exile for Tb. Tb 1:6—8 gives details of tithes for priests and Levites, a practice highly developed in the period of the 2nd Temple, while Tb 14:5 surely refers to the 2nd Temple, possibly quoting Hag 2:3, 9. Moreover, it is just tenable that the **f** emphasis on Tobit's courage and piety in burying the dead, 1:17f; 2:3f was pointed at an inferred ban on burial enacted by Antiochus IV in Maccabean times, 2 Mc 9:15. There is, however, no other sign of the Maccabean persecutions or of the sects among the Jews which appear to derive from that time, nor is there any reference to the doctrine of the resurrection which came to the fore in that era and which might well have been mentioned in the context of say Tb 3:6, 10, 13. On the whole, it is best to place the writing of Tb tentatively at about 200 B.C.

Influence on Tobit—It is impossible to overemphasize **338a** the strongest and all-pervading influence discernible in the book—that of Judaism and the earlier OT. The author of Tb is utterly a Jew, steeped in the literature of his people. The Law is explicitly mentioned in 6:12 and 7:13, but its regulations and its narratives form the background of the whole book onwards from 1:6, with which compare Dt 16:16. Compare also 1:7 on tithes with Nm 18:24ff and Dt 18:3—5; 1:8 on care for the poor with Dt 14:28—29; 1:11 on food laws with Lv 11 and Dt 14; 2:1 on Pentecost with Ex 23:16 etc; 4:14 on prompt payment of wages with Lv 19:13 and Dt 24:15. While 4:12 recalls the marriages of the Patriarchs in Gn 24:3f and 28:1f, the whole section of Tb dealing with the wedding and the homecoming of Tobias and Sarah leans very heavily on Gn 24. Of the prophets, Amos 8:10 **b** is quoted at Tb 2:6; Jonah or Nahum is named at 14:4, and Jon 4:3, 8 is possibly quoted at 3:6; the sections 13:9ff and 14:4ff are a tissue of prophetic phrases. Especially in 4 and in 12:6—10 are to be found echoes of the Wisdom books of the OT. Compared with the profound and ubiquitous influence of the OT itself, any other influences visible in the book are pale and insignificant. Yet a number has, with varying degrees of probability, been discovered by the scholars' eagle eyes. Persian influence may be seen in one major item and some minor references. Insistence on next-of-kin marriage **c** in 3:15 and 6:12 extends the Mosaic Law on the marriage of heiresses and may be an echo of Magian doctrine that between relatives of the first degree marriage was not only right but eminently meritorious. Nm 36:8 requires that heiresses should marry within their own tribes, but we have no knowledge of law or custom which demanded the death penalty from a father who failed to marry his daughter to a blood relation; nor was it apparently necessary that an heiress marry her nearest relation. Yet

338c Raphael states firmly that Raguel would deserve death if he failed to marry Sarah to Tobias. Such a notion may have come from Persian sources; it may however have been introduced simply as part of the plotting of the story
d (cf *infra*). The name of the demon, Asmodeus, 3:8, is very likely derived, in the opinion of some, from that of the Persian Aeshma-Daeva; nevertheless the name may be derived from the Heb. root *smd* = to destroy, and the character of the demon be a development of that of the Satan of Job. Finally, the dog of Tobias is a novelty in the OT. The OT thinks generally of the dog as a pariah, a scavenger, a half-wild beast of which there is little good to be said. Only here in Tb and in a few grudging references to shepherds' dogs and to watch-dogs, Jb 30:1; Is 56:10, is there any hint that a dog is useful or friendly to man. In Persia, on the other hand, the dog was protected by numerous instructions in the Vendidad. The scanty remarks in Tb 5:16; 11:4 may reflect these. The suggestion strongly supported by Simpson, op cit 185, 187f, that the Egyptian *Tractate of Khons* was also in the mind of the writer of Tb is even less capable of proof. The Tractate tells the story of a princess possessed by a devil who is exorcised by the intervention of Khons, the god of Thebes. The similarities between this tale and that of Tb are not such as to presuppose any interdependence and are as likely to be the result of a vague coincidence of theme as of direct borrowing or even half conscious recollection.

e But in the Gr. of Tb there are several mentions of one Ahikar; in 1:21 he appears as the vizier of Sennacherib, re-appointed by Esarhaddon, and the patron and kinsman of Tobit; in 2:10 he goes to Elymais; in 11:18 he and Nadab, kinsmen of Tobit, attend the wedding celebrations; in 14:10 his previous good works are said to have delivered him from the machinations of his adopted son Nadab. We must surely see here references to
f the well-known story of the wise man Ahikar. According to a tale *The Wisdom (or The Book) of Ahikar* which can be traced in Aram. as far back as the 5th cent. B.C. among the Jews of Elephantine and which is known also in Syr., Arabic and Gr., Ahikar was the minister of Sennacherib; he adopted as his heir and successor his nephew Nadab who, proving utterly ungrateful, plotted against and brought about the downfall of his benefactor; Ahikar, however, after a period in hiding (Tb 2:10?) was providentially restored to his former position (Tb 1:21—22) and his nephew perished miserably in prison
g (Tb 14:10) The story includes a number of aphorisms attributed to Ahikar of which some are paralleled in Tb 4; it had wide currency and popularity. It is a priori likely that the author of Tb knew the tale; the references he makes to Ahikar are illuminated only on this supposition. He appears to have introduced the sage into his account of Tobit as his kinsman both to link his story with one already well-known and well-liked and also to stress the prestige of his own hero. Perhaps even, the author saw Tobit as a Jewish Ahikar and intended in his work to translate the moral of the older tale into the language and thought forms of his own people. For the story of Ahikar cf CAP II, 715—784 and ANET 427ff.

339a The nature of the **Book of Tobit is clearly didactic**; here we are given, with the implied exhortation that we too go and do likewise, a picture of Jewish piety in action, a portrait of Jewish wisdom as it was to be lived. And most attractive it is. It is the thought of God that dominates the book; upon him all depends; he it is who is served when justice and charity are used towards other men; to him his servants turn naturally and readily in
b prayer. There is little in this book which is foreign to Christianity, though obviously much that needs to be complemented. Tobit is entirely faithful to the Law; he **339b** alone of his tribe has worshipped in Jerusalem, the place of God's choice, where he offered first-fruits and tithes as the Law commanded. It is worth noting that, dutiful as Tobit was in visiting the Temple, there is not the slightest indication of that blind superstition against which the prophets inveighed e.g. Jer 7:4ff. In exile, Tobit keeps **c** himself from the contamination of the Gentiles 1:6; 4:12 yet again with no sign of that hatred or contempt for the Nations which at times grew out of this precautionary measure. He spends himself in unselfish charity and risks his life in burying Jews executed by the tyrant 1:19f; his tribulations he bears with resignation in prayer 3:1—6; his advice to his son is a pot-pourri of the later Wisdom writings in which Wisdom, international and secular in its origins, has become steeped in Jewish theology; his prayer of rejoicing in chapter 13 is one of the minor peaks of the OT. Tobias the son is a worthy scion of his devout father; he illustrates the deep feeling of the good Jew towards his parents, he is alive to the reality of God, he recognizes the hand of God in his marriage 8:5ff. The **d** feeling of family love, unity and stability is one of the most obvious and attractive traits of the book. The warmth of love between husband and wife, between parents and children, delights the reader; and this is all of God's ordering. The passages which are peculiar to the V (Vg 3:16—19; 6:16—22; 8:2) merely draw out ideas already contained in the Gr. texts—the total difference between animal lust on the one hand and married love, in God, on the other. It is in the context of marriage that love, fruitfulness and mutual help are integrated cf P. Grelot, *Man and Wife in Scripture*, 71—74. It is not surprising that the Nuptial Mass has used the text and reminiscences of Tobit or that some marriage customs of Christianity (blessing the marriage-bed, three nights of abstinence after marriage) have reflected its advice.

All this is for our instruction, still very relevant **e** and topical. But the real hero of the book is Divine Providence. We are meant to see clearly in this story the all-embracing wisdom and power and kindliness of God—a power which is exercised over all things, over individuals and over nations alike in love and mercy for those who serve him. The later Jewish tendency to stress the separateness of the Holy One is clear in the words of Raphael 12:12f and indeed throughout the book in which God acts through his servant-angel; and Christian belief in the Guardian Angel, through whom God's loving providence may be effective, is developed from the similar doctrine which this book so vividly illustrates. Neverthe- **f** less, the great prayers of praise and petition which stud the book and underline its message make equally clear the Jewish and our realization of God's immediate bonds with and nearness to his people. The God to whom angels and demons are subject is the God who does not hide his face from men, 12:15; 6:17; 13:6.

The problem of reconciling God's goodness and justice **g** with the sufferings of the good Tobit and the innocent Sarah, a problem which exercised so many Jewish minds in the last centuries before Christ, is here hardly touched upon. In Anna's taunt of 2:14 and in Tobit's prayer in 3:35 are echoes of the traditional notion that all suffering was punishment for sin and the sins of the fathers were visited upon the children; the prayers of Tobit and of Sarah 3:6, 13 exemplify too the limited understanding of life after death which was one of the factors in the problem—yet the book of Tb sets out not to debate this burning question but rather to show what is the good man's attitude in suffering and to assure the reader that virtue, somehow, will be rewarded in the end. The

339g book is an exhortation to perseverance and confidence; it is, as has been suggested, a sermon on the text of Ps 40 (39):2—3 or Rom 8:28.

340a To what extent the story of Tobit is **historical** in the usual modern sense of the word we cannot say. Nor is this a matter of great importance; didactic myth or historical narrative, the story of Tobit and his son is equally effective as a reminder of what we owe to God, of God's care for his own and as a call to do manfully and wait upon the Lord. And that surely is what the book is intended to be. Doubtless the story of Tobit has some sort of factual basis, if only the basis of its general setting in the period of the historical Exile, but the impression conveyed by the book is that its author was little interested in the bare events of his story. So much is the book dominated by its desire to preach man's true relation to God and to his fellows that it is neither possible nor necessary for us to give a firm answer about **b** its historical character. We have noted above the points which indicate the author's ignorance of or lack of interest in history and geography; we may note again that though the story is set in 8th and 7th cent., the ideas and religious practices described are those which were especially stressed well after the Exile. The book combines a studied parallelism (Tobit, Anna, Tobias neatly correspond to Raguel, Edna, Sarah; the trials and prayers of Tobit are matched by those of Sarah; Raphael balances the demon Asmodeus) with an irritatingly loose and patchy narration. Why was it so heinous an offence to bury the dead? Must Anna work to support the family, while Tobit can afford to hire a companion for his son? Were Tobit and Tobias ignorant of the existence of their kinsman Raguel as 6:9 suggests or did Tobias know all about Sarah's unhappy situation? Were marriages really arranged in such haste as is depicted in ch 7? It seems that the episodes of the narrative are manipulated by the writer merely as a means to an end; he is more interested in having us imitate Tobit, serve the omnipotent merciful God of Tobit than in vouching for the historicity of his story. So, Christian tradition has found in this small book a rich mine of theological and ascetical treasures; in so doing, Christian tradition has effectively seen the point of this inspired story of Tobit and his son.

341a 1:1—2 Title—The personal and geographical names appear in different forms in the Gr. recensions and versions. The Gr. forms of the father's name are anglicized as 'Tobit', of the son's name as 'Tobias'. The members of the genealogy are otherwise unknown; LXX (S) adds 'son of Raphael, son of Raguel'. The geographical names indicate the area of Upper Galilee, NW of the Sea of Galilee. On Shalmaneser cf § 337e; he reigned 727—722; the name appears in the Syr. and VL where the Gr. has Enemessaros. There is no MS support for reading 'Sargon' here, even though the latter was in fact the father of Sennacherib, cf 15.

b 3—22 The Pious Tobit—**3.** The metaphor is frequent in all sections of OT, cf Ps 119 (118):30 where 'following the way of truth' is paralleled by 'I have set forth thy ordinances before me'. The true way of God is indicated by the Law, Ps 119 (118):1; Dt 8:6 which is the expression of wisdom, Sir 24:23ff, denied to the Gentiles Tb 4:19b. In this Tobit excelled. **4.** Written from the point of view of the S kingdom of Judah; despite the schism of the N tribes 1 (3) Kgs 12 he is devoted to the Jerusalem Temple, Dt 16:16, where he presented his first-fruits and tithes. The laws controlling what was to be tithed and to whom the tithes were due varied in the course of OT history; here we are shown Tobit to be meticulously devoted to the Law without the writer's sorting out its

variants; legislation is in Lv 27:30ff; Nm 18:12ff; **341** Dt 14:22ff; 18:1—5; 26:12ff. **8.** At the back of author's mind may have been memories of Deborah the prophetess in Jg 4:4—5. **9.** On marriage within the family cf § 338c and 4:12 below. **11.** As in Dn 1:8; Jdt 12:1—2; Est 14:17. **14.** 'Gabael son of Gabrias' appears in 4:20. **c 15.** Sennacherib was in fact Sargon's son. LXX (B) reads 'Acheriel'. The roads might well be dangerous until the new king had imposed his authority. **17.** The lack of burial was a crowning horror, Is 14:18—20; Jer 8:1f; 14:16 and conversely 1 Sm 31:11ff; 2 Sm 2:4ff; 21:8ff. **18.** In place of RSV read '*And if Sennacherib the king, when he came fleeing from Judea, put any men to death, I buried them . . .*'. The reference is to 2 (4) Kgs 18:13—19:37. **21.** Cf 2 (4) Kgs 19:37; Esarhaddon reigned 681—669. For Ahikar see § 338e. According to LXX (S) Ahikar was vizier also under Sennacherib and was re-appointed by Esarhaddon.

2:1—3:6 Trials of Tobit—**1.** Pentecost cf Ex 23:16; **d** Lv 23:15ff; Dt 16:9ff. **4.** Because such burials were still illegal cf 1:17ff or merely in respectful preparation for burial? **5.** Not a legal purification which according to Nm 19:11ff would not be so easily performed. **6.** Amos 8:11. **10.** Little hope of providing a clinical diagnosis of Tobit's malady. Elymais = Elam. The Vg here inserts 3:12—18, a comment on the patience and faith of Tobit. **11ff.** An episode which is intended to provide further illustration of the justice of Tobit now reduced to a nadir of humiliation and recrimination, cf Jb 2:9. **14b.** That misfortune and suffering were always to be equated with punishment for sin was a notion that died hard among the Jews (cf §339g). For RSV 'You seem to know everything', read with some support in VL '*Everything is known about you*' i.e. the present sufferings of Tobit show that he was not as pious as he had appeared to be; much of the argument of the book of Job is on the same lines. **3:1ff.** Illustrated in passing in this prayer of Tobit are many OT ideas—the mercy and truth and justice of God, the possibility of 'unwitting offences', the hand of God shown even in the disasters which afflict his people, the vague understanding of an after-life. The prayer for death is paralleled in that of Moses Nm 11:15, of Elijah 1 (3) Kgs 19:4, of Job Jb 7:15, of Jonah 4:3, 8. Similar acknowledgements of God's justice and Israel's sins are in e.g. Ez 7:6f; Neh 9.

3:7—17 Trials of Sarah: Prayers answered. More **342a** than 350 miles away to the E, another sufferer prays for death at the same time. Jdt 1:1—4 extols the greatness of Ecbatana. **8.** A demon, Asmodeus, is in love with Sarah and has killed her seven husbands on their wedding night 6:13f; 7:11. It is strange that while the reader is let into the secret by the author and Tobias appears to be aware of Asmodeus' activities, neither Sarah nor her parents nor her household show any knowledge of the demon's responsibility for her troubles. This looseness of plotting, the use of the common round number seven, the inherent unlikeliness of the story (even for those who accept with certainty the existence of evil spirits), the secondary role of Asmodeus—all suggest that we are here in the realm of fiction. Jewish interest in demons grew *pari passu* with **b** their interest in angels; it was only late in OT times that the spirit world came to be recognized by Judaism (cf§616a—c) and much was made of it in extra-biblical literature, not always with a full appreciation of its complete immateriality. For the writer of Tobit, Asmodeus is a mere means by which the almighty God, lord of all, manifests his providence to bring Tobias and Sarah together 6:17; he is a lay figure erected only to be demolished as an example of the great God's redeeming his servants from their troubles. **9b.** As unpleasant a fate as **c**

342c one could wish for a Jewish woman, to die childless. **10.** Vg typically omits the intention of suicide and elaborates three days and nights of Sarah's praying. **11.** Doubtless facing towards Jerusalem, cf 12 and Dn 6:10; the prayer is very like that of Tobit—deliberately so, so that God's answer to each may stand out boldly in the reader's mind. **15.** Replaced in Vg by six vv on the purity, high ideals and trust of Sarah. **16.** Glory of God = 'the radiant power of his being' in the phrase of Vriezen, *Theology of OT*, 150. **17a.** On Raphael cf. Theol of OT.

343a **4:1—20 Wisdom of Tobit**. His prayer for death will be granted, he thinks, so he sets about settling his affairs. Why, in his poverty, did he not recall his money before?—because the plot and hence the moral of the tale requires an economy of divine intervention; many birds are to be killed by one divine stone. Much of this ch is reflected in other Wisdom writings. **3—4.** Respect for parents, Prv 23:22; Sir 7:29. **5—6.** Loyalty to the God of Israel. **6—19** are missing in LXX (S). **7—11.** The duty of almsgiving, cf 339*a—c* and 16; almsgiving was to be one of the common religious practices of Judaism. **10.** RSV uses 'charity' here in the modern sense of almsgiving; its reward is granted in this life in the length of days—so often is OT esteemed as a great blessing. **12—13.** 'Immorality' again in the narrower modern sense of sexual misconduct. To marry within one's own kith and kin is stressed in Gn 24:3f; 28:2; as did Abraham according to Gn 20:12
b and Noah according to Jubilees 4:33. Tobit quotes the traditional blessing of children and the land which is still used in Mt 5:5 of the Messianic kingdom. **14.** See Lv 19:13; Dt 24:15. **15.** A version of the Golden Rule which is found also in *Ahikar*. **17.** The Gr. reads 'pour out' not 'place' and some recensions have an easier reading, 'Pour out wine and (break) your bread on the tombs of the just...'. The verse appears to refer to the offering of sacrifices or of food to the dead, but this is a practice foreign to Jewish thought and Sir 30:18 speaks of its pointlessness. The MSS evidence supports the difficult word 'tomb' despite the suggestion that 'tomb' is due to a mistaken reading of an original Heb. bqrb (= among) as if it were bqbr (= on a tomb). Perhaps the likeliest explanation of the command here is that it refers to the rites of consolation as are mentioned in Jer 16:7; Ez 24:17. The verse is also in Ahikar.
c **5:1—21 Preparations for the journey**; the power of God begins to make itself felt. **3.** LXX (S) speaks of two bonds and the dividing of one or both of them between the depositor and the trustee—a not unusual procedure for identification later. **4.** The first statement of the nature of Raphael. How God's providence rules all! **12.** The names are significant, 'God-helps, son of God-favours'. The problem of the angel's lie does not really arise; we are in the field of story-telling and the plot must be developed to a denouement of revelation later; meanwhile, the reader enjoys his private information about the angel and rejoices at the merciful ways of God.
d **13.** The names vary considerably in the versions. We know nothing of these (fictional?) characters. **16.** The reader, but not Tobit, realizes how truly the angel of God goes with Tobias cf 21 and already praises God for it. **19.** The precise sense is doubtful but the general intent is clear—'What is money, that our son's life be risked for it?'. **20.** 'Sister' was a loving term of address to a wife cf 8:4, 7 and Song 4:9ff; it was perhaps of Egyptian origin.

344a **6:1—18 On the Way**. **1.** From Nineveh to Ecbatana and Rages they should be moving away from the Tigris. **2.** One need not imagine a monstrous fish; that it would have swallowed Tobias is T's own thoughts on the subject;

once his first panic is allayed, he is able without much **344a** trouble to land the fish. **6.** The demon is thought of as causing trouble but as unable to tolerate the fumes of the burning heart and liver—a common enough notion of the day. Against a background of profound faith in the omnipotent God such as fills this book, there is no more of 'magic spells' here than in the Christian use of holy water in exorcisms. The idea of repelling evil spirits by merely material rites was to be found also outside Jewish circles and was borrowed and adapted in the light of the Jewish understanding of their unique God. **9—12.** See § 338*c*. There is an application of some form of the **b** Levirate Law here, Dt 25:5f, but of the strict sense in which it is enjoined by the angel we have no further information. It seems that Tobias is strangely ignorant of Raguel and his family, whereas 13—14 suggest quite the opposite; there is untidiness in telling the story. **16.** Vg gives to the angel a series of remarks implying that the earlier bridegrooms had been killed by the demon because of their brute lust and exhorting to three nights of continence. The sentiment may be salutary, but the author is Jerome.

7:1—9:6 The Wedding of Tobias and Sarah. **2.** The **c** writer is fond of the effective technique of allowing his reader to enjoy the ignorance of others and to watch the gradual revelation cf 8:9. **9.** The marriage negotiations are brief; Sarah is given to Tobias 13 and the marriage contract (of which we have a number of examples e.g. from the DSS) is signed. **13.** The Vg at 7:15 provided the **d** blessing of the Nuptial Mass. **8:3.** We can discern the thought of the author. Sarah is released from her trials; the demon's power is broken and he is removed far away from the possibility of harming Sarah any more—to the furthest ends of the earth, to the desert which is the proper abode of demons, to the pagan darkness of Upper Egypt, where he is kept safely out of the way. All this is achieved invisibly by means suggested by and the personal action of the angel who is God's minister in all this. **5.** Vg 8:4—10 considerably enlarges the prayer of Tobias. **9b—18.** One of the most delightful and half humorous examples of the writer's skill in story-telling, enshrining a gem of a prayer. These vv might be taken as typical of the whole book, with its lesson that heaven is very close to earth. **19.** Drawing upon other biblical accounts of weddings e.g. Gn 24:54—5; 29:32. **Ch 9.** The collecting of the money left with Gabael is now a matter of minor importance; yet it too will be happily achieved, for the Lord God is lavish in blessing his children. Again Vg elaborates the blessing of Gabael.

10:1—11:19 The Happy Return. **1—7.** see the remarks **345a** on 7:2. **11:1** LXX (S) and VL mention that the caravan come to Kaserein, Charran which we cannot now identify. **4.** It is a pity that the tail-wagging dog of Vg 11:9, made famous as an example of Newman's obiter dicta, must be considered purely Jerome's insert. **8—13.** The recensions differ as to how precisely Tobit is cured: in LXX (B) the gall is merely an irritant: in LXX (S) and VL the gall itself causes the 'white films' to loosen and they are peeled away by Tobit or Tobias. **14.** But cured Tobit is—and his immediate reaction makes the point that this is the work of God with (the addition is meant to be significant to the reader) his angels. **18.** The joy and also the prestige of Tobit are increased by his famous kinsman's visit cf 1:21.

12:1—22 Raphael revealed. **1—5.** We are to note the **b** active gratitude and generosity of father and son. **6—10.** The words of the angel sum up the thesis of the book; on 6 are based the introit and communion of the Mass of the Trinity; the praise of alms-deeds echoes Tobit's own words

345b in ch 4. **11—15.** The angel as intermediary; in LXX (S), Raphael is also God's instrument in the trials of Tobit. Here is probably the origin of the tradition of the seven archangels, though the word is used in the Bible only in 1 Th 4:16 and Jude 9. For the source of the 'seven', we need not look to the seven spirits of Ahura Mazda in Persian mythology or to the seven high court officials of Persia Ez 7:14; Est 1:10; it is sufficient to recognize the common OT use of the term as a significant number. These angels are among the beings closest to God—and his servants 18, 20. **19.** An indication of what we would call the spirituality of angel nature. **22.** 'The angel of the Lord' is in the earlier strata of OT hardly distinguished from the Lord himself; in these later writings, the gulf between the Holy One and his servants is made quite clear.

c 13:1—18 A hymn of praise, exceedingly fine, put into the mouth of Tobit and used in the Roman Breviary in Lauds of Tuesday. It is divisible into two sections: 1—8 is a call to the exiles and the Diaspora; 9—18 makes particular application of the first part to Jerusalem, echoing the era of the aftermath of the Babylonian Exile rather than the exile of the ten N tribes. The chant has no explicit reference to the tribulations and the deliverance of Tobit but it suits his situation and illustrates the keen sense of community felt and lived by OT Jews—the individual's fate being bound up with and an expression of that of his people. It well delineates the piety of Tobit and of all Jews; to do so it uses earlier Biblical books.

d 2. Cf Dt 38:39; Is 38:10ff; Hos 6:1; Wis 16:13. **4.** Mt 23:15 refers to later Jewish zeal for proselytes; Ac evidences the favourable impression made by Judaism on many an earnest God-seeker. On God our Father cf Is 63:16; Jer 3:4; Sir 23:1; Wis 14:3. **6.** Addressed to the sinners of Israel. **8—11** are missing in LXX (S) the scribe having been misled probably by the homoioteleuton in the phrase 'King of heaven'. **10.** The Temple will be rebuilt. **11.** See Is 60:1—7; Ps 74 (73):7 'the dwelling place of thy name'. **12.** Ps 122 (121); 137 (136):7ff. **13.** cf Ps 126 (125). **16.** Is 54:11, 12; Apoc 21:18ff; so, meta- **345** phorically, is described the glory and richness of the future Jerusalem.

14 This Epilogue briefly describes the remaining **346** happy and saintly years of Tobit (and Tobias) who dies peacefully in a good old age surrounded by son and grandsons. The writer could imagine no greater reward than this—a long and prosperous life with many descendants to preserve one's memory cf Gn 50:22ff; Jb 42:14ff; this insight into the happiness of a good life spent in loving obedience to God is by no means to be despised even in the light of fuller, later revelation, Lk 18:30. The ages allotted to Tobit and Tobias are different in almost every version of the story. Within this framework there are noted, as if foretold by dying Tobit, some of God's saving acts which are known to the writer from the past history of his people. A similar device is adopted in Gn 49; Dn 7—11 and, characteristically, in much apocalyptic writing which derives from Dn. So, the continuity of God's working in history is demonstrated; what is time and its succession to God! **4.** Nineveh, the Assyrian capital, fell **b** before the assaults of Medes and Babylonians in 612. For 'Jonah', whose foretelling of the end of Nineveh was to his chagrin rendered null by the mercy of God, LXX (S) substitutes 'Nahum' whose three chapters form a tauntsong on the city's destruction. Jerusalem, too, and the Temple were, to be desolate (587) but **5**, God was to bring back his people from exile, 538, and the Temple was to be rebuilt, by 515. The author adds his own vision of the future; in future ages there will be a yet more glorious Temple—in the time of the Messiah—having in mind e.g. Is 2:2—3; Hag 2:6—9 and resuming the theme of Tb 13:11 whose passing reference to the nations is here enlarged. **10.** On Ahikar see § 338e. **15.** Cf § 337e. The LXX (S) version of this verse is even more vengeful about the end of Nineveh; a Jew would see in the collapse of Assyrian imperialism not merely the downfall of a cruel tyranny but the triumph of the just God.

JUDITH

BY P. GIFFIN

347a Bibliography—Commentaries: L. Soubigou, PCSB 1949 with earlier bibl.; A. Miller, BB 1940; F. Stummer, EchB 1950; H. Bückers, Herder's Bibelkommentar, 1953; A. Barucq, BJ 1959²; G. Priero, SacB 1959. **Other Literature**: F. Stummer, 'Geographie des Buches Judith', Stuttgart 1947; A. Lefèvre, 'Judith' DBS 1949; A. Dubarle, 'Les textes diverses du livre de Judith' VT 8 (1958) 344ff; id 'La mention de Judith dans la littérature ancienne juive et chétienne', RB 66 (1959) 514ff; H. Cazelles 'Le personnage d'Achior dans le livre de Judith', RSR 39 (1951) 125ff; P. Skehan, 'Why leave out Judith?' CBQ 24 (1962) 147ff; id 'The Hand of Judith', CBQ 25 (1963) 94ff; A. Dubarle, *Judith: formes et sens diverses traditions*, Rome, 1966. And see the Bibliography for Tobit.

b Contents—The story falls into two clear sections. The first **1—7** describes the exploits of Nebuchadnezzar and his general Holofernes,—the victory over Arphaxad of Media **1**, Holofernes' campaign against the western nations **2—3**, the resistance and plight of the Israelites at Bethulia **4—7**. The second **8—16** narrates the deliverance of Israel by Judith,—her excellence and her rebuke of the faint-hearted **8**, her prayer **9**, her preparations and her acceptance into the Assyrian camp with the climax of the murder of Holofernes **10—13:11**, the triumph of Judith **13:12—15:13**, the canticle of Judith **16:1—17**, the epilogue **16:18ff**.

c Text—Our earliest text is the Gr. which exists in four recensions cf J. Schwartz, 'Un fragment grec du livre de Judith', RB 53 (1946) 534ff. These are not nearly so different among themselves as are the recensions of Tb and Est and present no special textual difficulty. This version is dependent on a lost Heb. original which is still apparent beneath the sufficiently pliable Gr.; examples may be found in R. H. Pfeiffer, 298f. The standard Gr. text is that of the codices LXX (S, B and A). The Syr. and the VL are derived from the Gr., probably from the form in codex 58, = LXX (Cam)k. The VL is judged by Cowley op cit 243 to be a fairly close translation from the Gr. but to be 'rough, often merely latinized hebraistic **d** Greek'. The Vg of Jer represents a hasty translation from a now lost Aram. text with an eye to the VL. In the preface to his version (PL 29, 39) Jer. states that he reluctantly undertook this work only because he understood, *legitur*, that the Council of Nicaea considered the book canonical. In his *Prologus Galeatus*, PL 28,600f, he himself excludes Jdt from the canon, so that he wrote of his translation, 'huic unam lucubratiunculam dedi, magis sensum e sensu quam ex verbo verbum transferens' PL 29, 40. It contains inversions of order, some omissions amounting to about one-fifth of the Gr. and a number of additions. Compared with the Gr. standard text, the Vg represents a paraphrase. The Heb. MSS we possess represent either a free re-translation from Gr. or Lat. or entirely separate versions of an oft-told and popular story.

The Message—It is manifest that Jdt sets out to teach; **348a** to remind Israel of the nature of her God and of its consequences. The book is steeped in the thought of God, in severe contrast to the MT text of Est, and it is a noble picture which this often maligned book presents to us. Perhaps it is the power of God which is most stressed; he is the creator 13:18; 9:12, by his word 16:14, so that to man he must be incomprehensible; nothing can bind him; it is for God to act as he sees fit, to deliver or to destroy; it is for man to plead with God and to wait his good pleasure 8:14—17, for it is God who knows and actually designs all that happens 9:5—6. Yet this God is the God of Israel 9:13—14 for whom he has done great things in the past (for special parallelism between the Exodus and the Judith stories cf Skehan, art cit CBQ 25 (1963) 94ff), whose whole history he has moulded 5:6—19, whose destiny for good or for evil he holds in his hands 7:25, with whom he has made his covenant 9:13, so that Israel is God's inheritance 13:5, consecrated to him 6:19. Since Yahweh is a God who cannot **b** tolerate sin, he will at times visit his people in wrath at their unfaithfulness 5:17—18; 7:28; 8:19, but even in the greatest peril his people should bless the Lord in thanksgiving 8:25, for his scourge is a warning 8:27. When Israelites are faithful to God 5:20—21; 8:18, though great nations rise against them 16:4, yet they can trust him with all confidence 7:30. It is here that Jdt manifests similarities with apocalyptic writing. They differ obviously in manner of presentation, but their basic ideas are the same—the wicked in self-confident power confront the saints of God with apparently overwhelming might; nevertheless it is the saints who will surely triumph for with them is God almighty cf Ez 38—39; Dn 7—8; among the Qumran scrolls, *The War Rule* 1:15—19. They therefore do well to pray in penance 4:8ff; 6:19; **c** 9.1 and they are heard 4:13; naturally when they see their deliverance, they at once react in praise of the merciful omnipotence of the Lord 13:14, 17; 16:11, 13. This view of the God of Israel is the basis of the worship that is offered him; his sanctuary is the Temple in Jerusalem 4:2, 12, 13; 5:19; 9:8 which must at all costs be protected from profanation 4:12; 8:21, for there precisely God's name rests. It is there that through the ministering priests 4:14; 11:13 God is adored in petition and sacrifice 4:14; 16:18—sacrifice which expresses a true fear of the Lord 16:16. But if the hub of worship is in Jerusalem, petition and praise resound through all the land, intensified in fasting, sackcloth and ashes.

It is perhaps surprising that in so strongly nationalistic **d** a book the door to Judaism is gladly thrown open to outsiders. Achior 5:5ff is, of all peoples, an Ammonite cf 1 Sm 11:2; Jer 40:14; Dt 23:3, but he is welcomed into the company of the chosen people and the blessings of the Covenant 6:20; 14:6—9 on the basis of his faith and circumcision. Cazelles, art cit, discusses and favours the identification of Achior in Jdt with Ahikar in Tb (338e); he suggests that the writer of Jdt used the

348d well-known but indistinct figure of this sage and ruler as a type of the Gentile 'saved by sharing the persecutions and the suffering of the Chosen People' and moreover 'saved by that same act of divine power which saves the Chosen People'.

e **Judith herself** is described as an ideal of later Jewish piety; she is an individual indeed but her name ('Jewess') is not without significance—she is a pattern of what all God's servants should be 11:17. Her chastity in widowhood is remarked upon 8:4; 16:22. She observes not only the sabbaths and the feasts but their eves as well 8:6. She is meticulous about the rules governing clean and unclean foods and the laws of ritual cleansing 12:2, 9, 19; 16:18; 11:12. In this she is a model of Pharisaic religion. It is no wonder that her devotion is blessed—she is rich, she is beautiful, she is held in high repute by all 8:7–8—though it may be noted that there is no mention of her having children. The story centres round her courage, her initiative, her selflessness 13:20; she exemplifies the dictum, 'Pray as though all depended on God; labour as though all depended on yourself'.

f Commentators have sometimes toiled to apologize for or allowed themselves to sneer at the actions of this paragon—the use of feminine wiles, the lies, the murder itself. They have surely failed to see that a cardinal aim of the book is to illustrate God's reaction to sin and to sanctity; the just, Israel and Judith, may confidently rely on God's omnipotent support; the sinner, Holofernes and Nebuchadnezzar, inevitably come to ruin. In this instance, God deals with overweening pride through human agency, by the hand of a woman 13:12, 18; 16:6. It is the justice of God which slays Holofernes and routs the Assyrians. If Judith lies and parades her beauty to gain her end, the writer of the book sees in this only a wily, bold and justifiable stratagem; after all, the People are at war. He would not, being a good Pharisee, normally permit deceit and seduction; in the circumstances, he views with some complacence the enemies of God destroyed by their own lust and blindness. He, inspired though he is, lacks the delicacy of the fully Christian conscience which denies that the end justifies the means. He is a man of the OT, limited in many ways, who for all his appreciation of God and his holiness is not given to understand as profoundly as the Christian what that holiness calls for in human conduct.

349a **Historicity**—Granted that the didactic features of the book predominate, to what extent is the narrative based on fact? The indications given by the book itself suggest that the factual content is slight. Any Jew with knowledge of the OT alone would know that Nebuchadnezzar was king of Babylon not Assyria; that the return from Exile 4:3; 5:19 took place under the aegis of the Persians; that the 18th year of Nebuchadnezzar 2:1 was the year of Babylon's destructive campaign in Juda and the fall of Jerusalem cf 2 Kgs 25:1, 8; that the years following the return were years of distress and disorganization (cf Ez and Neh *passim*) with nothing approaching Jewish control **b** over Samaria to the borders of Esdraelon 4:4–7. In the very perpetrating of his 'howlers' the Jewish writer shows his mind; he is making no attempt at all to relate an event which has a real historical setting. One might even go so far as to say that the writer, a Jew by no means ignorant of the OT, is deliberately prescinding from any particular period of the history of Israel, is of set purpose and consciously producing a timeless tale with ingredients drawn from many centuries. For example—the Assyrian domination based on Nineveh was a fact in the late 8th cent. and for most of the 7th; Nebuchadnezzar ruled in Babylon and the Medes were a

power to be reckoned with in the first half of the 6th cent.; **349** the period of Persian strength extended from about 540 to **c** about 330 B.C. and from this age the writer draws the names of Holofernes and of Bagoas (they are mentioned elsewhere as generals of Artaxerxes III in his W campaigns) as well as certain technical phrases such as 'to prepare earth and water' 2:7 and 'akinakēs', the sword of Holofernes, 13:6. The piety of Judith and the people, with its emphasis on fasting, on food laws, on payment of tithes 11:13, on ritual purity, certainly coincides, as we have seen, with the spirituality of the Pharisees, spiritual descendants of the Hasidim of the 2nd cent.; the role of the High Priest 4:6; 15:8 and of the 'Senate' (Gr. 'gerousia'), wielding supreme secular power in Israel, directs attention to the post-Maccabean era. If we are to give the writer credit for *any* knowledge of **d** his people's history, we must allow that he has drawn on his acquaintance with the past and with his own age simply to illustrate an eternal truth—that God protects those who are faithful to him and overthrows the self-sufficient sinner. The most obvious source of the story is the brief reference to Jael in Jg 4:17ff; 5:24ff. We have no knowledge of any other similar episode in OT history. Cf Skehan, art cit CBQ 25 (1963) 94.

It should be noted, however, that some commentators **e** see in this book an account of an actual event, distinct from the episode of Jael and Sisera; the account would have been embellished to a greater or less extent; the names of the persons and/or places would be pseudonyms, but behind them lie identifiable characters and settings. There is nevertheless the greatest variety of opinion as to when this event took place and what real oppressor of Israel is hidden under the name Nebuchadnezzar. See for example G. Brunner, *Der Nabuchodonosor des Buches Judith*, Berlin 1959, commending as the invader one Araka who rebelled against Darius I in 521. Pfeiffer, op cit 295, gives a list of seventeen identities suggested for Nebuchadnezzar; this list is not exhaustive! One might hazard the opinion that such a welter of differing views indicates a false premiss and that the writer's intention was to typify rather than conceal.

The **date** of the writing of Judith, from what has been **f** said above, appears to be the 2nd cent. B.C. Its general atmosphere, though less belligerent than that of Est, would still be appropriate to Maccabean times and later. It may be necessary to distinguish between the date of the writing and the date of the origin of the story. *Prima facie* the book derives from Palestine. The suggestion that the book originated in Egypt is made by J. E. Bruns, CBQ 16 (1954) 12ff and ibid 18 (1956) 19ff but must remain only a suggestion. On the **canonicity** of Jdt opinions have varied on a par with Tb. It was not accepted into the Jewish (Palestinian) canon; it is regarded as apocryphal by non-Catholics; for the opinions of early Christian writers cf Tobit. It is numbered among the d.c. books, cf § 13*d–e*.

1 Campaign against Arphaxad—The scene is being **350a** set; the power, the ability and the success of those who will eventually attack Israel are here demonstrated. Nebuchadnezzar ruled in Babylon 604–562; his father, with the help of Cyaxares of Media, took and destroyed Nineveh in 612 and wiped out Assyrian domination. Of Arphaxad, king of the Medes we have no knowledge: possibly the name is a corruption of Phraortes, a Median king of mid 7th cent. possibly it is drawn from Gen 10:22 which mentions also Asshur and Elam (Babylon). Ecbatana was in Media near modern Hamadan, a great city in its day though its defences are exaggerated here; a cubit would be very roughly the equivalent of 18

350a inches. The battlefield is to be S of the Caspian Sea, in the region of Ragae not far from Teheran. Each king gathers his allies; Arphaxad is supported by the men of the Iranian plateau and by the plain dwellers of the river valley (Hydaspes = R. Karkheh in SW Persia) as well as by the unknown king Arioch of Elymais which lay E of these rivers. All these are summed up as 'Chaldeans' which interprets the reading of the Gr. MSS having 'Cheleoul' with many variants.

b Nebuchadnezzar issues a general summons to all the westerly nations as well as to Persia, the mention of which with Assyria and the Chaldeans completes the roll of the great empires. From Cilicia in SE Asia Minor, all Syria and Palestine and Egypt is called to the colours; the nations are recorded roughly in order from N to S. Gilead is N Transjordan; Bethany, variously spelt in MSS, is near Hebron; Chelous is probably SE of Beersheba, while Kadesh is the oasis of Kadesh-Barnea which figures largely in the story of the desert-wandering after the Exodus. The 'river of Egypt', the traditional frontier, was the Wadi el-'Arish, S of Gaza; the Egyptian names are all biblical and mainly in the Delta; Tahpanhes cf Jer 2:16, Raamses cf Ex 1:11, Tanis appearing elsewhere as Zoan or Avaris; Memphis, the capital of Lower Egypt, is S of the Delta. The summons to the armies of Nebuchadnezzar goes throughout Egypt to its southern frontier with Ethiopia. It evoked no response for Nebuchadnezzar was 'only one man', i.e. isolated and without actual allies or, with Cowley, 'a man of naught'; the Gr. uses the difficult 'isos' where RSV has 'only one'.

c The king therefore vows vengeance not only on the lands already mentioned but also on the Transjordan kingdoms of Moab and Ammon cf 5:2, traditional neighbours and enemies of Israel (an ominous note is sounded here with the mention of their names) and all nations to the 'two seas'—the Mediterranean and the Red Sea most probably.

d 2–3 Holofernes in the West—2. Or with BJ 'decided with his own lips the annihilation of all this region'. 4. Holofernes is the name given in Diodorus 31:19 to a Cappadocian ally of Persia operating in the W in the time of Artaxerxes III Ochus, 358–338. 5. The title 'Great King, Lord of all the earth' is from Persian court language. 7. 'Prepare earth and water', Persian idiom for 'surrender' which occurs often enough in Herodotus e.g. 6:48. 12. 'As I live', not dissimilar to the phrase put on the lips of Yahweh himself e.g. Nm 14:21, 28 and occurring frequently in the form 'as the Lord lives'. The presumption of Nebuchadnezzar is stressed cf 3:8; 6:2. 21. The march of Holofernes and his incredible host takes him in three days, according to the standard text, some hundreds of miles W from Nineveh to the borders of Cilicia. Bectileth itself cannot be identified. 22ff. The passage is intended to describe a punitive expedition in the area of Cilicia and the desert

e borders of the Syrian desert as far S as Damascus. We can identify few of the places named; Put and Lud appear from OT usage to be generally associated with Egypt and Ethiopia, Gn 10:6, 13; Jer 46:9; Ez 30:5; Na 3:9; Rassis, if it is not Tarsus in Cilicia, is unknown; Ishmaelites Gn 21:21 represent the desert nomads, as do the Midianites, though their region of Japheth would appear from Gn 10:1–2 to be in Asia Minor and only distantly 'fronting toward Arabia'. It is 24 which disturbs the account: although the brook Abron is unknown and the variants for this name in the MSS are startling, yet, as the text stands, Holofernes is supposed to have passed naturally from near Upper Cilicia to Cilicia and Damascus

f by way of Mesopotamia! Either this v is out of place in

our text or the writer is utterly ignorant of even the **350f** framework of geography of the Near E or he is quite indifferent to the route of the expedition. The last seems most likely: there is no evidence of displacement of the text in the MSS; he could scarcely be so abysmally ignorant of elementary and widely known topography as his arrangement implies. The writer is portraying a blitzkrieg, a vast horde advancing inexorably and rapidly, crushing all opposition, until it stands on the borders of Israelite territory. As the history is an amalgam of different periods to represent a timeless enemy, so the topographical survey is an amalgam of different regions, all conquered and ravaged, to represent the omnipotence of that enemy. One is reminded of Is 10:28–32 the impact of which is in on way lessened by the fact that the Assyrians' route was quite other than the prophet had described. **28.** From Damascus the fear of Holofernes **g** spread S along the coast: Sur is either a doublet for Tyre or represents Dor, S of Carmel; Ocina is Acco (Ptolemais); Jamnia is Jabneel, a little N of the Philistine cities. All surrender. **3:8a** is reminiscent of e.g. 2 (4) Kgs 18:4. **3:8b** again notes the folly of Nebuchadnezzar at the precise moment when his armies face Israel; will Israel too accept or be forced to accept this claim as had other nations? Dothan is Tell Dothan, some 12 m. SW of Gilboa, and has been excavated cf RB 69 (1962) 266; BASOR 160 (1960) 6 with references to earlier reports. Geba is not identifiable; Scythopolis is the Hellenistic name of Beth-shan at the SE end of the valley of Jezreel which runs from the E side of the great plain of Esdraelon.

4 Reaction in Israel—3a must refer to the return from **h** the Babylonian exile from 538 onwards cf 5:19. The Temple was then built anew 5:18b, so that the 'profanation' may refer to a much later event—the desecration by Antiochus IV Epiphanes in 167. **4.** Of the places recorded, only Samaria, Beth-horon (a few miles NW of Jerusalem) and Jericho are known. **6.** Though it is apparent that the High Priest had some secular authority by about 200 B.C., the combination of this office with supreme civil and military responsibility can be said to begin only with Simon Hyrcanus 143–134, 1 Mc 14:41. The two towns are said to be of the utmost importance and something of their situation can be deduced from 6:11; 10:10 but we cannot now identify them. It has been suggested that Bethulia may be a pseudonym for Jerusalem or Shechem; this is scarcely likely. **8.** A 'senate' appears in 1 Mc 12:6, **i** a development of a body of advisors which must have existed informally in all ages. **9ff.** The prayers of Israel are intensified by the wearing of sackcloth, an ancient practice, though the covering of the altar is unique. Fasting was prescribed by the Law only on the Day of Atonement Lv 23:27 but became increasingly common after the Exile. **11.** 'Spread out . . . sackcloth'; better to read 'hands' for 'sackcloth'—on the basis of a mistranslated Heb. original.

5–6 Achior—2–3. The conscripted allies of 3:5 might **351a** be expected to know local conditions. 'Canaanite' was an ancient term not much used in later biblical writing except in reference to the period of Israel's settling into their land. 'Governors' translates what is a Persian word 'satraps'. **5.** Achior, cf § 348d. He appears as a non-Jew bearing impressive witness to the great acts of Yahweh in the election of Abraham, the Exodus, Conquest, Exile and Return. **6–9.** cf Gn 11:21ff. Mesopotamia = Haran. Various embellishments are added here to the account in Gn. **15.** Amorite was one **b** of the general biblical terms for the peoples of Canaan and thereabouts, Nm 21:21–25. **16.** Similar lists are traditional e.g. Jos 9:1. **17.** The Deuteronomic concept

351b that prosperity is the fruit of fidelity to God and the Covenant, Dt 7:12ff; the counterpart is to be seen in vv 18 and 20 *infra*. **18.** The first part refers to the annihilation of the N kingdom of Israel in 721, the second to the Babylonian Captivity of Judah in 587. **21.** Judith uses the same argument later, 11:10. **6:1ff.** For the writer, this invasion has religious significance; Nebuchadnezzar's pretensions put him into direct opposition to the Lord and represent the perennial madness of human pride. **2.** Ephraem—one would expect 'Ammon' as some MSS read, but the phrase is a quotation from LXX Is 28:1. **4.** recalls the apocalyptic picture of Ez 38—39. **5.** Holofernes sneers at the servile origin of Israel coming out of Egypt; the reader will remember that this exodus was a God-sent deliverance. **14.** It is not possible to define the role, powers or origin of these magistrates.

c 7 The Attack Begins—3. Here and in 18 we are in ignorance of the whereabouts of the places named; in each case the general movement is clear. The Assyrians deploy in a show of strength; the local levies maintain a closer blockade of Bethulia. Springs are mentioned in 3, 7, 12, 17—either there were many or there is confusion in the account. **8.** Esau=Edomites, Gn 36:9. **28.** The people prefer slavery to death; may God not let them die of thirst. Uzziah waits for help from the S to raise the siege or rain from God to fill the depleted cisterns.

d 8 Reaction of Judith—1. Sarasadai is mentioned in Nm 1:6 as a Simeonite, to which tribe Judith belonged, 9:2. **3.** Balamon presumably = Balbaim 7:3 = Belmain 4:3. **4f.** We are to understand that Judith's energy, courage and high patriotism derived from her outstanding piety. **5.** 'Tent', cf 2 Sm 19:1; 2 (4) Kg 4:10. **11—17.** The Vg version of Judith's speech differs considerably from the Gr. She acknowledges amply the over-riding supremacy of God. **18—24.** Yet, Israel being now faithful to him (in fact there is little evidence of idolatry between the Exile and the Seleucid persecution) may confidently expect his help; in any case, Bethulia, vital to the defence of Judea must hold fast. **26—27.** Testing of Abraham in Gn 22, of Isaac perhaps in Gn 26:1—16, of Jacob in Gn 29:21—30; 32:3ff. Here is a view of suffering which outmodes the older view that all suffering was a penalty for sin.

e 9 Prayer of Judith—1. The connection with the Temple worship is made clear. **2—4.** Cf Gn 34 where a certain blame attaches to Simeon. 'To loose the girdle' is a Gr. rather than a Heb. phrase. **5—6.** A fine portrayal of God's foreknowledge and effective providence. **7—11.** It is the pride and presumption of Assyria which calls for Yahweh's intervention; it will be brought about by a mere woman, supported by him. Cf Ex 15:1—18; Ps 33 (32):16f. **12—13.** For it is God's chosen whom Holofernes now attacks. There is no attempt to hide the deceit which Judith plans, 10, 13.

f 10—13:11 Safety achieved—The story is told dramatically in vivid detail; suspense is admirably built up to the climax; if there remain some loose threads, some unanswered questions in the mind of the reader, the general effect is of verisimilitude and the awkward corners are skilfully turned. **10:4.** cf Is 3:18—23. **5.** 'Fine bread' is bread that is legally pure, according to later Pharisaic

scruples. **7—8.** The beauty and the self-possession of Judith are to be her only weapons. **20.** A very elaborate tent in sections. **11:6.** The equivocation here is paralleled in 11:16; 12:4, 18. **13.** It is not necessary to suppose that this was planned by the citizens of Bethulia—or that Judith in fact considered it a heinous offence. **17.** Artful arrangements with a view to future escape from the camp. **23.** The most one might expect of Holofernes was that Yahweh of Israel would be admitted into his pantheon with other gods. **12:11.** Bagoas, a common enough name and found e.g. in Diodorus 16:47 of a eunuch general of Artaxerxes III. **13:2.** Holofernes was *sodden* with wine. **11.** Judith's cry might be taken as the motif of the whole book, cf Ex 15:1—2.

351f

13:12—15:7 Rout of the Assyrians—Emphasized in **g** the section and basic to the whole book is the recognition that it is God who has saved Israel through a woman, 13:14—18; 14:10. **13:14.** 'Praise God' represents a threefold Alleluia. **18—20.** Applied to Our Lady in several of her feasts, cf Lk 1:28, 42. **19.** 'Thy hope' i.e. thy confidence in God. **14:10.** We are meant to note the contrast between the believing Achior and the arrogant Assyrian. **14.** 'Knocked at the door' or 'clapped his hands at the door'. **15:4.** cf 4:4, 6. A general assault made by all Israel—from Samaria, Judea and Transjordan. The author apparently thinks of the Galileans as untouched by Holofernes' advance down the coast 3:6, 9 though they now lie behind his front line.

15:8—16:25 Triumph of Judith—Salutations to the **h** heroine from the leaders of the people 15:8ff, from the women 15:12ff, from all Israel 15:13, but above all, salutations to God. **9.** Used of Our Lady. **12.** Such dances as in 1 Sm 18:6, but the crowns of leaves and the branches, 'thyrsoi', are in the Gr. rather than the Jewish manner. **16:2ff.** The Canticle can be divided: 2—3 God the Warrior; 4—12 The danger and the delivery; 13—17 Universal praise of the Creator God of Israel. **2.** 'Begin a song to God' translates the present Gr. which probably misrepresents an original Heb. meaning 'Praise my God'. **5.** Note the 'my': Israel speaks through the mouth of Judith the Jewess. **7.** 'Sons of Titans' presents in Gr. idiom the Nephilim of Nm 13:32f. **8—9.** The writer sees **i** no reason to hide the fact that Holofernes was dazzled and deluded by Judith's deliberate art. **10.** The Assyrians are here metamorphosed into another great pagan power. It matters little for the author's purpose. **11.** Translate: My oppressed people shouted their war cry and they (the enemy) feared; my weak ones (shouted) and they (the enemy) trembled; they (my people) lifted up their voices and the enemy turned back. **13—16.** A mosaic of phrases **j** from many psalms with a firm statement on prophetic lines that fear of the Lord must underline all outward observance, cf Hos 6:6; Ps 51 (50):18. **17.** The language of apocalyptic e.g. Jl 4:12—16; Is 66:24. It is not safe to use the vague language of this v as evidence of the writer's belief in rewards and punishments after death. **18ff.** The national days of thanksgiving for the victory and peace brought by Judith as by Deborah and Jael Jg 5:31. The long, happy and blessed life of Judith in highest repute, her death at a ripe old age, her decent burial with her family, the mourning of all Israel for her—what greater blessings could a good Israelite imagine or deserve?

ESTHER

BY P. GIFFIN

352a **Bibliography**—*Commentaries*: L. B. Paton, ICC 1908; L. Soubigou, *Esther*, PCSB 1947 with earlier bibliography; F. Stummer, EchB 1950; H. Bückers, Freiburg 1953; A. F. Knight, Torch, 1955; A. Barucq, BJ 1959[2]; *Other Literature*: S. Talmon, 'Wisdom in Esther' VT 13 (1963) 419ff; H. Ringgren 'Esther and Purim' SvExAb 20 (1955) 5ff; A. Robert 'Historique (Genre) BDS IV 22; R. Hanhart ed., *Esther, LXX, gött*; 1966; and see bibliographies for Tb and Jdt. Further literature listed in EOT Int.

b **Contents**—There are two interwoven plots, the defeat of the machinations of Haman against his personal enemy, the Jew Mordecai, and the deliverance of the exiled Jews from massacre by the courageous intervention of the Jewess Esther in the king's harem. The setting is Persia; the period is that of Xerxes I, 486—465 B.C.

c **Text**—The Heb. is consistent in all MSS. The Gr. text is much longer than the Heb. Of the Gr. recensions, two are worthy of note: The standard text in most cursives and in LXX(S, B and A); according to the last verse of the version, this is a translation made in Jerusalem by one Lysimachus and published in Egypt in the '4th year of Ptolemy and Cleopatra'. We may ask 'Which Ptolemy?' (there were 14) and 'Which Cleopatra?' (there were half-a-dozen). It is most probable that the text refers to Ptolemy VIII and his wife, so that the book reached Egypt in 115—114. The other Gr. recension is the Lucianic text extant in some cursives; it differs in very many details of phrasing, tends to expand and is even more rhetorical than the standard Gr. Both texts are in Brooke-McLean-Thackeray, III.

d The VL is from the Gr. of the standard text but adds and omits many details. The Vg was claimed by Jer to be a sufficiently literal version of the Heb.; as his trans. exhibits a number of minor additions to and omissions from our present Heb., it may be that he worked from a Heb. text slightly different from that now in our hands. Jerome translated the Heb. to where it ended in his 10:3; he then found in the Gr. MSS a further passage which he translated and left at the end of his version 10:4—11:1. Finally he went back over the Gr. text; he did not bother to translate all the scattered phrases which the Gr. had supplementary to the Heb. up and down the book, so that these phrases appear now neither in

e Knox nor in RSV. But he found certain large sections of new matter in Gr. and these, together with the pericope mentioned above Vg 10:4—11:1, are the **deuterocanonical** parts of Esther. Jer translated them in the order in which he found them, adding them to the end of the translation from Heb. and Gr. which he had already completed. These translations from the Gr. alone form 10:4—16:24 of the Vg and Knox; they appear too in the apocrypha of RSV; they appear in the order in which they occur in the Gr. MSS, save that Vg 10:4—11:1 should be at the very end and, naturally,

they make no coherent story as they stand. These major **352f** sections are: **A.** Vg 11:2—12:6 Dream of Mordecai, to be placed before 1:1. **B.** Vg 13:1—7 Edict of Xerxes against the Jews, to be placed after 3:13. **C.** Vg 13:8—14:19 Prayers of Mordecai and Esther, to be placed after 4:17. **D.** Vg 15:1—3, Advice of Mordecai to Esther, parallel and expanded version of 4:8, not appearing in RSV apocrypha. **E.** Vg 15:4—19 (RSV 15:1—16) Esther's appeal to Xerxes, parallel and much expanded version of 5:1—4. **F.** Vg 16:1—24 Decree of Xerxes on behalf of the Jews, to be placed after 8:12. **G.** Vg 10:4—11:1 Interpretation of Mordecai's dream, to be placed at the end of the book. With this rearrangement a coherent, if not always consistent, tale is unfolded.

What is the **relationship** between these d.c. passages **g** found in the Gr. and the shorter Heb. text? These passages are to be regarded as inspired, but they are most probably additions to an earlier Heb. text and were originally written in Gr. (i.e. they are not translations); the reasons are manifold: 1. There is no sign of Heb./Aram. original of these sections; Aram. versions mentioned in CCHS (1), 310g depend on the Gr. of Josephus and others and were made in 10th cent. A.D. 2. These passages show no signs of having been translated from a Semitic language, though of course they have the stock OT phraseology; contrast for example the Gr. of Jdt which is full of literally translated Heb. idioms. 3. It is alleged that these parts do not come from the **h** same hand as the rest of the Gr. of Esther and that they are therefore interpolations in the Gr. itself. Here one may wonder whether the evidence at our disposal is sufficient to discriminate between varying styles. 4. A number of remarks in these pericopes do not square with the narrative in the Heb.: contrast MT 6:3f with Vg 12:5 on Mordecai's reward; MT 3.5 with Vg 12:6 on reason for Haman's hatred; Mt 2:15—18 with Vg 14:15f on Esther's behaviour at court; MT 3:1 with Vg 16:10 on ancestry of Haman. 5. These passages repeat **i** material in the body of the book: the genealogy of Mordecai is in the Gr. at both 2:5—6 and 11:2—4 (Vg); the plot against the king is detailed in 2:21—3 and 12:1—3 (Vg). It seems from their very nature that these additions in Gr. are intended to introduce or at least to make explicit some religious elements. There is in the Heb. very little indeed which would indicate any sort of religious approach or teaching; we are given a story of racial triumph on an almost purely secular level, the story of any minority vindicated in any empire. Of the religious practices of the Jews, even of God **j** himself, nothing is said; only in 4:3, 14—16 is his providence and his openness to prayer briefly and vaguely implied; otherwise, the tale is entirely secular—a group of exiles in the Persian Empire is put in danger of extinction by the injured pride and caprice of a potentate but is able to turn the tables on the villain by the happy chance of its having a more powerful advocate at court. Nothing more. The book is not in opposition to Jewish

352j religious thought; it can be fitted into that thought; it is in fact illumined by Jewish belief——but it does not display much evidence of it.

353a The **Greek version** alters the character of the book; occasionally this is done by expanding the translation of the Heb.; cf 2:20 where Mordecai had charged Esther 'to fear God and to obey his commands' and 6:1 where 'The Lord drove sleep away from the king'. But it is the added sections which decisively re-orientate the story. Mordecai's dream at the beginning and its interpretation at the end establish clearly that the whole episode is part of God's controlled planning Vg 11:10ff; 10:4,9ff. the prayer of Mordecai acknowledges and powerfully preaches the universal rule of God the creator to whom a unique service is due; this is the God who acted among the Patriarchs and manifested himself at the Exodus; he has chosen Israel for himself as his heritage and portion and he will save Israel by his mercy for his own **b** glory. These are themes familiar in OT. So also in the prayer of Esther—the garments of mourning and her fasting are explicitly part of her turning to God who alone is able to save as he has so often saved Israel in the past; God himself has afflicted the people because of their apostasy, but they are his people whom he has chosen as the instrument of his glory and he will not allow their total destruction; he will not abdicate his position in the face of those whose victory would apparently be the victory of no-gods; his own nature requires that he show himself clearly as 'king of all gods' by saving his own. Compare, among literature of a similar type or period, Dn 9; Neh 9:6ff; Jdt 9:5ff,11ff; Tb 13:1–6; Sir 36:1ff; for the assertion of one's own innocence cf Ps 17 (16); 18:21ff; 26 (25); 59 (58):4–5.

c It is the Gr. form of Esther which has been received by the Church; yet this form as much as the Heb. is liable to shock the Christian reader by the account of the Jews' retaliation in ch 9. That the unjust decree of the king against Jews should be rescinded, that Haman should be punished, even that the Jews should forcefully defend themselves against actual attackers as appears in 8:11—with that the Christian might agree. But the story envisages the Jews attacking and slaying their enemies indiscriminately, 9:5, apparently taking the offensive, and Esther is represented as asking for renewed opportunity for further slaughter 9:13—all **d** that is quite unacceptable. And so it should be. A number of valid points may be made in defence of the morals of Est but it is idle to pretend that the conduct of the Jews here narrated measures up to the Christian ideal. It would be surprising if it did; the OT abundantly evidences the patience of God, his gradual revelation of ever purer ideals, his willingness to take men as they are and to build on what appears to be meagre foundations; this has been God's way of acting in the history of the Chosen People and in the lives of individuals, and we cannot quarrel with it. The very men whom he chose to record his message were burdened by the limitations of their age, as we are burdened by ours. See **e** CBQ 17 (1955), 128ff. But to be fair to Est, we must allow that the story accepts the undebated standards of its day (perhaps a later generation will look back in amazement on our unrealized cruelties). We must recognize that dominant in the thought of the Jews was the correct realization of their status as God's chosen and privileged instrument, so that, though they might take a rather exclusive view of their own importance, they nevertheless desired vengeance not as a purely and always personal matter but as a vindication of God's honour. We must admit as a corollary of this Jewish role

that opposition to the Chosen of God was in a sense **353** opposition to God and his working in the world. Finally, in this desire for vengeance there is a very real sense of justice, a keen sense of sin and God's reaction to it, which is to be preferred to a lazy and spineless indifference to evil. These points may be exaggerated or interpreted too narrowly, but they are not without foundation and value. On this 'morality' see §§ 216f, 225d, 246g. Indeed, to read Esther today is to be reminded of the **f** inadequacies of the past—and of our inadequacies; to acknowledge the power and the wisdom of God in action among and for the Jews—and among and for us; to recall that the complete dependence of the Jews on their God mirrors ours; to recognize that the prayer of the suffering People of God is no less effective today than in OT times; and to be encouraged that, precisely because the Lord is righteous and is 'King of the gods and master of all dominion', he will have mercy upon his inheritance Vg 14:7, 12; 13:17.

To what extent the story of Esther is factual is debated. On the face of it, not many people would give much credence to Est as history but for the fact that it is a biblical book and 'the Bible is true'. The evidence we **g** have suggests strongly that we have a tale set against an historical background, embodying at least one historical character (Xerxes) and some accurate references to actual usages of Persia, but a tale making no serious attempt to chronicle facts, aiming rather at producing a certain moral attitude in the reader. Such a genre is entirely to be expected in the inspired books and is designated 'haggadic midrash' cf Bloch, 'Midrash' DBS 5,1263ff. Some factors in the setting accord with **h** fact—separation of palace from city of Susa, the council of the seven princes 1:13ff, the excellent courier service at the command of the king 3:13; 8:10, the exclusion of mourning garb from the palace 4:2 etc. Yet it appears that Xerxes's queen was neither Vashti nor Esther but Amestris; we have no further information inside or outside the Bible (e.g. Sir 44ff) of a Jewish queen who saved her people or of a pious Mordecai who rose to such heights in the Persian court. Mordecai himself taken into exile by Nebuchadnezzar in 597, is still fit to be Prime Minister in Xerxes's time, 486–465; the proposed massacre of the Jews contradicts all we know from the Bible of Persian tolerance, while the planned massacre of Persians by permission of the Persian king is rather unlikely. The delays decreed before the massacres seem pointless and unreal 3:12ff; 8:12; the 10,000 talents of silver offered by Haman is an impossibly large sum, 3:9; and the king's prolonged debate before divorcing Vashti 1:13ff is in surprising contrast to the readiness with which he orders the killing of Jews or Persians. There are inconsistencies in the story also: could **i** Esther conceal her Jewish race when Mordecai-the-Jew is known to be so interested in her? Did Haman approach the king at night to beg the execution of Mordecai, 6:4? Would Esther, in a position of dire emergency, have postponed her request to a king found unexpectedly to be so amenable, 5–7? The book bears moreover some of the traits of a mere story—all the officials of the Empire are banqueted for months, the royal concubines are prepared for a whole year, 75,000 Persians are slain in a single day, a towering gallows is prepared for Mordecai; here is the effective exaggeration which adds colour to an E tale. And the story is carefully ordered **j** in pointed contrasts—Mordecai, the descendant of Benjamin and of Saul's kinship 2:5, overcomes Haman the descendant of Agag 3:1, just as Saul had overcome Agag 1 Sm 15; Esther replaces the Gentile Vashti; the

353j Jews in general turn the tables on their Gentile enemies—the drama is artistically and tellingly worked out. One may guess that the success of Joseph at the court of Pharaoh, Judith's deliverance of her people from mortal peril, the stories in Dn 3 and 6 may have contained the germ from which Est grew, but that can be **k** no more than a guess. One may wonder whether there is significance in the similarity between the name Esther and the name of the Babylonian goddess Ishtar, between the name Mordecai and the name of the god Marduk, so that one would have to look for the source of the tale among the myths of Elamite gods. But one can only wonder. At least one may note the similarity of situation provided by the non-canonical 3 Maccabees. All these and analogous lines of thought indicate that Est itself proclaims its nature as didactic fiction.

354a How the book came into its **present form** must remain a matter of conjecture. It is reasonable, however, to propose that there originally existed, its derivation unknown, an old, highly patriotic and nationalistic tale of Jewish dangers and triumphs in quite secular a mood, 1:1—9:19; to this was added later a passage in rather different a manner 9:20ff which would justify and explain the feast of Purim as the Jews kept it. This again, the Heb. form of the book, was taken over and considerably re-edited with additions, now found in the Gr., so that it became a profound expression of God's providence over his people and demonstrated the virtue of prayer and fasting. That is to say, an inspired midrash was written on an older profane tale.

b The institution of the **feast of Purim** is recounted in Est at 9:20—32 with a reference back to 3:7 where Pur is said to mean 'lot'. If Est is not to be considered a book of history, the story cannot really explain the feast as a commemoration of the Jews' escape, though the feast itself was a reality. There are many theories about the origin of the feast (cf Lefèvre in RF, 1.692) and about the connection between the feast and the book. Theories they must remain until further evidence is forthcoming. Meanwhile the suggestion of Lefèvre loc cit slightly emended will suffice as a reasonable working **c** hypothesis. This is as follows: a spring festival of Babylonian origin was taken over by the Jews and kept in the month of Adar (Feb.-Mar.) in a secular and not at all religious fashion with which perhaps one might compare the pre-Lenten Carnival; on this day Est in Heb. form was read as an example of Jewish triumphs and as a composition not unsuited to the mood of the day; the feast came to be thought of as celebrating the deliverance of the Jews in Persia as is described in Est, the 'festival legend' of the day, and came also to be called the 'Day of Mordecai' as in 2 Mc 15:36; so the feast and the celebration were justified and explicitly explained by the postscript to the book found in 9:20ff.

d For the **date** of the book we are dependent on the writing itself. If the dates in the colophon are to be trusted and are correctly interpreted, it is not later than about 115; if the silence of Sirach is significant, it is not much earlier than about 180; 2 Mc 15:36 is the earliest reference to the feast of Purim. The vigorously nationalistic tone of the book would coincide well with the upsurge of patriotic feeling in the time of the Maccabees, as would the correspondingly harsh attitude to the Gentiles. Probably it is safest to date the writing simply within the 2nd cent. before Christ. For the age of the tale which it enshrines we have no evidence at all.

e The **canonicity** of Est has at times been called in question. The Jews themselves hesitated over its admittance to the canon and no fragments of it have as yet been found at Qumran. It is nowhere quoted in the NT. **354e** However, it was generally accepted in the Christian church in the extended form, though at times its position was queried—most explicitly by Ath. PG 26, 1176 who sees in Est no canonical book but a work which is to be read with profit for instruction. Other early lists **f** simply omit the book e.g. Melito of Sardis PG 5, 1221 with Greg Naz in PG 37, 472. Jer would appear to accept only the Heb. form—judging from his notes appended to his translation of the Gr. additions. The evidence of Jewish and early Christian writers is collected and discussed by A. C. Sundberg, Harvard Theological Studies XX, *The OT of the Early Church*, 1964. The purely Gr. sections of the book are relegated to the Apocrypha by non-Catholics. The whole book in its traditionally Christian form is accepted definitively by Trent, DzS 1502—4.

NB—The commentary follows the Gr. order; references to the purely Gr. sections accord with the RSV numeration.
11:2—12:6 Dream of Mordecai—Artaxerxes the **g** Great (465—423) is the name consistently applied to the king in LXX (B, S and A), but the Lucianic recension has Assucrus = xerxes (486—465) = MT Ahasuerus. Nisan is the opening month of the Jewish religious year in the Spring. Susa was the site of the winter palace of the king. There dwelt Mordecai whose Judaism is stressed throughout the story, though the name appears to be connected with Marduk, the god of Babylon ; it occurs again in Ez 2:2 and Neh 7:7. For the Benjaminite ancestry cf 1 Sm 9:1 and 2 Sm 16:5. MT 2:6 makes him definitely a contemporary of King Jeconiah of Judah, taken to Babylon in 598; chronology sits loosely on the writer who is merely sketching in a background for his narrative. **5.** The dream has affinities with the visions of Dn 7ff; it is explained only at the end of the Gr. version 10:4ff and it is typical of the apocalyptic style and content, insisting on the ultimate deliverance and triumph of the now sorely afflicted people of God. **12:1.** Another and disparate account of **h** the conspiracy and of Mordecai's service is in MT 2:23ff; 6:2ff. **6.** Haman, the villain of the piece, is introduced rather abruptly; apparently we are to understand that the executed conspirators were in some way connected with him, even that Haman was party to the plot (?). The cause of his hatred for Mordecai and the Jews is otherwise described in MT 3:6. In MT 3:1 he is called an Agagite, either with reference to Agag a region of Media or with reference to the old enmity of the Benjaminite Saul in 1 Sm 15:7—9, an Amalekite denounced in Ex 17:14; Dt 25:17—18. 'Bougaean' here and in the Gr. of 3:1 and 9:10 is most probably a corruption of an original 'Agagaios'.
1:1—22 The King's Feast—2. For 'Susa the capital' **i** read here and elsewhere 'the citadel of Susa'. At times, e.g. MT 3:15; 8:14, 15, the writer seems to distinguish correctly between the city proper and the fortified quarter, but he appears also to identify, wrongly, the citadel and the royal palace. Throughout this section an attempt is made to paint a picture of magnificence and luxurious splendour to contrast with the plight of the exiled Jews. **8.** The verse is intended to illustrate the benignity of the king—again in contrast with his later attitude to the Jews. Jos.Ant. 11:6, 1 notes the contrast between **j** the consideration of the king on this occasion and the usual Persian practice of forcing drink on guests; whether Josephus knew of the custom or is merely deducing its existence from this verse is a moot point. **11.** There is a similar tale in Herodotus I, 8 of the Lydian king Candaules. **19.** The unalterable laws of the Medes and

354j Persians are a pleasant fiction, cf Dn 6:8, 13 and Dn 6:25; Est 8:5, 8 where they are in fact changed. What human act, suggests our writer, is irrevocable if God lays his hand upon a matter?—as he is going to do as the story unfolds. **22.** 'Speak according to the language of his people' is omitted in the Gr. and seems irrelevant in the Heb., it may be a corrupted repetition of the sense of the first half of the verse.

355a **2:1—23 The Advancement of Esther—1.** The king, according to the Heb., regrets at leisure the hasty decree promulgated in his cups; the Gr., however, pictures him indifferent and forgetful of Vashti. **5.** Here the Heb. introduces Mordecai for the first time of comment on Gr. 11:2. **7.** The name Esther would appear to derive from that of the Babylonian goddess Ishtar; the girl's Heb. name means 'Myrtle'. The account of Esther's success is in many ways parallel with the story of Dn 1:3ff though the omission of any mention of God in the MT of the former is notable. **10.** There seems to have been no reason why Esther should have concealed her origins at this stage; presumably it is done in order to heighten the effect of Esther's plea in 7:3. **19.** Only the MT has this account of a second gathering of virgins. Many possible emendations of the text have been proposed so as to produce the sense 'when the many virgins were gathered together' or 'when Esther went with the maidens into the second harem' cf 14 above. That Mordecai sat at the king's gate indicates that he was in the royal service. **21.** Compare 12:1ff in the Gr. The Lucianic revision tidily omits 2:19—23 entirely.

b **3:1—15; 13:1—7 Royal decree against the Jews—** The first mention of Haman in the Heb. cf Gr. 12:6. No reason is here given for Mordecai's refusal to offer due reverence to Haman; in Gr. 13:13 the refusal is explained as due to unwillingness to derogate from the glory which is the right of God alone. If anything, 3:4 indicates a racial basis for Mordecai's independence, even though Haman is not yet declared to be an enemy of the Jews. Haman's resentment is to vent itself on all Jews. **7.** According to Gr. 3:7 the favourable day for Harman's vengeance is the 14th Adar; MT 3:13 proposes the 13th of the same month. The Gr. has slightly expanded the Heb. brevity of this verse in explaining why Haman cast lots. It is not unlikely that the verse is a gloss in the Heb. added with the section 9:20—32 to link the story of Esther **c** explicitly with the feast of Purim. **8.** These are familiar grounds of resentment against Jews cf Dn 1:8; 3:8ff. **11.** The king disdains the proffered inducement or recompense for the loss of Jewish industry and leaves the Jews freely at Haman's mercy. The Gr. addition 13:1—7 gives the text of this decree; it is more drastic than but expresses the same policy as that in 1 Mc 1:41—50. Strange indeed that so much warning of the day was tolerated; what were the Jews expected to do meanwhile? **d** **4:1—17; 13:8—18 Mordecai's Reaction—1ff.** Sackcloth and ashes were the traditional signs of penitence and means of satisfaction as well as the accompaniment of the most earnest prayer cf Jdt 4:9—12. Fasting was decreed even before the Exile at times of public calamity; it was only in later Judaism that it became a regular practice of Jewish piety. These gestures indicate a turning to God 4:16; it is notable that the writer refrains from saying so, even here. **8.** The Vg 15:1—3 adds from what Jer calls the 'editio vulgata' Mordecai's reminder to Esther of her former low estate and dependence on him; he urges her to pray to the Lord and to intercede with the king for her people against Haman, (RSVCE Est 4:8b). The passage echoes 4:8 of the Heb. and represents the same verse in the Gr., but

it does not appear in RSV 'Additions to the Book of **355e** Esther'. **14.** 'Another quarter' is of course God, but mention of his name is avoided; the phrase was later to become a Rabbinic paraphrase for 'God'. This is as close **e** as the MT gets to proclaiming faith in God's direction of his people's history; the reticence is astonishing. **17.** Here the Gr. adds 13:8ff the prayer of Mordecai; in a splendid supplement to the untheological MT there is acknowledgment of his supreme power, vindication of Mordecai's attitude to Haman and a moving plea that God should intervene on behalf of those who belong to him, whom he made his own in the Exodus from Egypt, who are the witnesses to his praise on earth. Ps 18 (17):21—24 and 26 (25):4ff are to be compared with the protestations of innocence in this prayer.

5:1—8; 14:1—19; 15:1—16 Esther's Intervention— f The MT 5:1—3 gives a brief, straightforward account of how Esther, without any further appeal to God, successfully approaches the king and is welcomed by him. The Gr. greatly adds to and expands this passage with a much longer account of her great fear, of her penance and prayer and of her approach to the king; the story is told much more dramatically and underlines the risk which Esther took and her high courage in endangering her own life for the sake of her people's—a courage all the greater in that she mastered extreme and justified terror. **14:1—2.** In this version Esther's natural reaction is to turn to God; penance and prayer complement each other; Lv 10:6 mentions the custom of letting 'the hair of one's head hang loose' as a sign of mourning, which is what Esther does also, though the Gr. versions vary. **3—19.** Her prayer recapitulates the past acts of God—his election of Israel, his promises, his reaction to Israel's sins in the exile; now, in this even more pressing danger, she begs the Lord to keep his own, to demonstrate his true power against those who in attacking his people attack him, to help her who is otherwise without help; like Mordecai, she reiterates her own innocence and her loathing of her position, entailing as it does commerce with gentiles. In such straits, Esther may be pardoned for exceeding a prayer for deliverance and asking too for the punishment of Israel's enemy in verses 11, 13. **15:10.** The Gr. is mystifyingly epigrammatic, 'common is our ordinance'; the RSV translation which is surely correct might be justified by reading 'koinōn' rather than 'koinon'. **5:4—8.** The postponement of Esther's request increases the tension of the tale and allows time for Haman to be hoist with his own petard.

5:9—7:10 The Fall of Haman—The writer's art is **h** considerable as he sets the scene for the denouement; Haman at the height of his power contrives his own fall. **14.** The gallows is over 80 ft high. **6:3** contrasts with Gr. 12:5. **7.** On the honours to be paid to the king's favourite compare Gn 41:42f; Dn 5:29. **13.** The writer's national self-confidence is put in the mouth of Zeresh; the Gr., typically, names the help of God as its basis. **7:4.** Esther makes the same point as did Haman in 3:9—that the destruction of the Jews will mean a loss to the royal treasury. **8.** Veiling the face must be presumed to be the token of a judgement already implied in Xerxes' outraged exclamation.

8:1—9:19 with 16:1—24 The Vengeance of the i Jews—On the ethics of the following narrative, see § 353d. Fortunes are completely reversed; Esther is given the property of Haman; Mordecai succeeds to the position of Haman and becomes ever more influential, 9:4; the new decree (as irrevocable as the former!) formalizes the king's already implied consent; the narrative of its writing deliberately parallels the account of 3:12ff. After

355i 8:12, the Gr. adds the text of the new decree in 16:1—24. This stresses machinations of Haman which have not been mentioned in the story; he is now accused of treason, 16:12—14 and is termed a Macedonian, intriguing against Persia cf 16:10. One can only surmise that the term is here used as a synonym, from the Persian point of view, of 'deadly enemy'; it is an expression that would have meaning only after the campaigns of Alexander the Great, in 334 at the earliest, when he was on the point of threatening the Persian Empire. The decree contains such attestations of the power of the Jewish God as are put in the mouths of other monarchs, Dn 4:34; 6:26.

j **9:2.** It seems inescapable from this verse, as from 5 and 14, that the Jews used the opportunity not to defend themselves against actual attack but to slay potential enemies and to pay off old scores. It is not a pretty picture; nor are we bound to think it is. **7.** The names vary greatly in form in the different versions. They appear printed in vertical columns in MT, in the manner (says the Targum) in which the men were hanged or their corpses exposed. **10:15.** The refusal to take plunder indicates that the Jews acted from no sordid desire for gain but only from a strict sense of justice— a somewhat redeeming trait. **13.** Even if one allows a distinction between 'Susa the capital' (= the citadel of Susa) in 6 and 'Susa' (= the residential area) in 13, one cannot admire Esther's determination. **16.** The standard Gr. gives 15,000 as the number killed.

k **9:20—10:3 Establishment of the Feast of Purim**— This passage would appear to be a later addition differing in style and matter from the preceding chh; the previous vv suggest 15 Adar as the feast-day for the Jews of the city and 14 Adar for Jews of the provinces; this passage commands both days to be kept by all. It is likely that the short ch 10 is to be judged a separate footnote. **355k** In the modern Jewish calendar, 13 Adar is the fast of Esther; 14 Adar is Purim; 15 Adar is Shushan Purim, kept by Jews living in walled cities. Whatever the provenance of this section, it maintains the secular atmosphere of the rest of the Heb. book. **27.** 'And all who joined them', cf 8:17b. **29ff.** The MT seems to require correction, there being confusion of subjects (Esther and/or Mordecai) and the number of letters; yet any correction must be conjectural. It is probably best, with Barucq, to suppress the mention of Mordecai at the beginning of the passage and to amend the verbs so as to make Queen Esther the sole subject of these vv. There is difficulty in the reference to 'this second letter'; which was **l** the first letter sent? Altogether, this appendix from 20 onwards betrays a composite character; materials from different sources have not been perfectly dove-tailed; this is apparent also in the abrupt and unexpected introduction of 'fasts and lamentations' which must refer back to 4:16 but which have hitherto been entirely lacking in the regulating of Purim. The final ch records the prosperity of the king who dealt justly with the Jews in a formula which is obviously imitated from the books of Kings e.g. 1(3) Kgs 14:29; we need not deny the reality of this 'Book of the Chronicles..', which may have been a Jewish writing, but we know nothing of it.

10:4—11:1 The Dream Explained and the Colophon—This passage, the last of the Gr. additions, refers **m** back to the very beginning of the Gr. version The deliverance of the Jews through Esther and Mordecai is seen to have been the planned providence of God remembering his people; that providence, we are reminded, is still active. The Colophon is dealt with in § 354d.

THE POETICAL AND WISDOM LITERATURE

BY R. A. DYSON S.J.

REVISED BY G. CASTELLINO S.D.B.

I OLD TESTAMENT POETRY

356a Bibliography—R. Lowth, *De sacra poesi Hebraeorum*, Oxon. 1753; E. König, *Stilistik, Rhetorik, Poetik in Bezug auf die bibl. Literatur*, Leipzig 1900; V. Zapletal, *De poesi Hebraeorum in VT conservata*, Frib. Helvet., 1909; N. Schlögel, *Die echte bibl. -hebr. Metrik*, (*Bibl. Stud.*, 17, 1); A. Vaccari, S.J., *De libris didacticis*, Romae, 1935; A. Condamin, S.J., *Poèmes de la Bible*, 1933; F. Zorell, S.J., *De forma quadam carminum hebraeorum frequenter adhibita parum explorata*, *Misc. Bibl.* II (Romae, 1934) 297–310; W. H. McClellan, S.J., 'The Elements of OT Poetry', CBQ 3 (1941) 203ff; G. B. Gray, *The Forms of Hebrew Poetry*, 1915; T. J. Meek, 'The Structure of Hebrew Poetry, J Rel 9 (1929) 523–50; T. H. Robinson, *Poetry and Poets of the OT*, 1947; G. Castellino, *I Salmi*, Torino 1954, 17–24; St. Segert, *Problems of Hebrew Prosody*, VT Suppl. VII, Leiden, 1960, 283–91; A. Schökel, *Die Stilistische Analyse bei den Propheten*, ibid, 154–64; H. Kosmala, *Ancient Hebrew Poetry*, VT 14 (1964), 423–45; C. H. Gordon, *Ugaritic Manual*, 1955, 107–20; R. E. Murphy O. Carm, 'The Wisdom Literature of the OT', *Concilium* 1 (1965), 68–75.

b The Poetic Books—The OT contains all that we know of the poetry of Israel. As with other peoples, poetry seems to have been the **earliest form of literary expression** in Hebrew. Several fragments and some complete poems are embodied in the narrative books, all of them very old. The more notable are: the sword-song of Lamech (Gn 4:23f); the blessings of Isaac (27:27–29, 39–40); the blessings of Jacob (49:1–27); Moses' song of triumph (Ex 15:1–18); the song of the well (Nm 21:17–18); the prophecies of Balaam (Nm 23:7–10, 18–24; 24:3–9, 15–24); the song of Moses (Dt 32:1–43); the death-bed blessings of Moses (Dt 33:2–29); Joshua's command to the sun and moon, taken from the book of Jashar (Jos 10:12–13); the song of Deborah (Jg 5:2–31); Samson's proverbs (Jg 14:14, 16). Specimens from the later books are: Hannah's prayer (often compared with the Magnificat) 1 Sm 2:1–10; the maidens' acclamation of David (1 Sm 18:7); David's lament over Saul and Jonathan (2 Sm 1:19–27), and Abner (2 Sm 3:33–34); the song of David (2 Sm 22:2–51); David's last words (2 Sm 23:1–7); and the song of David when the ark was placed in the tent (1 Chr 16:8–36).

c Of the prophetic writings some books or portions of books are in prose, e.g. Hag, Jon (except ch 2), much of Jer, chh 40–48 of Ezek, and parts of Is, Hos and Zech. Others (Jl, Obad, Mi, Hb, Zeph, Mal) are definitely poetic, with the same kind of metrical structure which is used in Pss and the other poetical books.

d The didactic books which are wholly versified form a consecutive group of seven. The book of Job is a didactic poem arranged in the dramatic scheme of a dialogue; the Psalms are devotional prayers and hymns; **356** Prv and Sir are didactic compositions of varying length, and Eccl a reflective work in prose intermixed with passages in poetry; Song is a series of nuptial hymns with the dramatic form of a dialogue; Wis is of a religious and philosophical content in poetical form.

External Form—The technique of Heb. poetry is by no **e** means fully understood, but some things seem to be clear. Thought in a particular form and, therefore, sentence patterns are its external feature. The line or verse, usually composed of two shorter units (stichs), occasionally of three (tristich), is the fundamental unit, as was clearly expressed by Origen (see Card. Mercati, in 'Studi e Testi' 142, 19 and G. Castellino, *Salmi*, 18f). The lines are knit together by **parallelism**, i.e. by an equal distribution or balance of thought so that the individual lines correspond with one another. This parallelism is called **synonymous** when the second line merely echoes the first with some modification (e.g. Ps 2:4; 37 (36):1–2; 51 (50):9; 70 (69):2; 76 (75):2; Prv 3:13–18); **antithetic** when it is in sharp contrast with the first line (e.g. Ps 1:6; 20 (19): 8–9; Prv 10:1–4, 16, 28; 13:9); **synthetic** or progressive, when the idea expressed in the first line is developed and completed in the following lines (e.g. Ps 1:1; 3:5, 6; 19 (18):8–10; Prv 26:3). Sometimes, too, we find four lines so connected that the first corresponds to the third and the second to the fourth (e.g. Ps 127 (126):1), or the first with the fourth and the second with the third (e.g. Ps 137 (136):5–6).

This pairing of similar thoughts is often an aid **f** to the correct exegesis of an ambiguous word or phrase: e.g. 'the *breath* of his mouth' in Ps 33 (32):6*b* is simply the 'word' of line *a* by which the heavens were made: cf also Ps 88 (87):11. It should also be noted that in a couplet the phrasing is often so distributed that only from both lines do we get the adequate subject and predicate; e.g. Ps 92 (91):3 means 'to praise thy mercy and fidelity day and night'; cf also Ps 19 (18):1–2; 42 (41):9; Gn 49:27.

Rhythm—Heb. poetry is rhythmical, i.e. there is a **g** recurrence of stressed and unstressed syllables in a relatively regular succession. Usually the v has from two to four accents to a stich, and the two (three) stichs that go to make a v may have a different number of accents. So that various combinations are possible: $2+2$; $3+3$; $4+4$; or $3+2$; $2+3$; $4+3$; etc. To obtain this effect some of the monosyllabic particles lose their accent to the next word, and the construct state forms one unity with its following noun. These and other peculiarities help to determine the number of accents or beats within each verse. As an example we cite Jg 5:4.

> *Yahwéh, beṣēʾtekắ miś-śéʿír,*
> *beṣaʿdekā miś-śédēh ʾedôm,*
> *ʾéreṣ rāʾăśāh, gam-šămáyim nâtápû,*
> *gam-ʿăbîm nāṭepû máyîm.*
> *'Yáhweh, at thy márch from Séʿir,*

356g *thine attáck from the field of Édom,*
éarth was sháken and héaven collápsed,
and the clóuds póured down wáter.'

Sometimes we find parallelism and rhythm in perfect agreement, each word having a stress:

ya'arṓp kammātắr liqhî́,
tizzal kaṭṭal 'imrātî́.

'May my teáching dróp as the ráin,
my spéech distî́l as the déw' (Dt 32:2a).

A line of five accents regularly has a caesura or pause after the third; this type of verse is called the **qinah** because it is used in the *qinoth* or Lamentations of Jeremiah to produce a plaintive melancholy cadence. It is also found in the Psalms, e.g. Ps 19 (18):9:

The feár of Yáhweh is púre, endúring foréver
the júdgements of Yáhweh are trúe, júst altogèther.

h Metre—It was the opinion of the ancients (Jos. Flavius, Philo, and some Fathers of the Church like Orig, Jer, Euseb) that Heb. poetry, like classical poetry, was governed also by metre, i.e. by a regular succession of long and short syllables; and specific metrical denominations are applied by them to some of the Psalms. But probably their sayings are to be interpreted analogically, to mark a certain correspondence between the Heb. accented syllables and the syllables on which the arsis occurs in the classical metres (see G. Castellino, Bib 15 (1934), 505—16). In reality, although the number of accented syllables is fixed to produce the rhythm, this is not true of the intervening unaccented syllables, which seem to be governed only by the law of pronunciation and euphony. The expression 'metrical structure' is, therefore, analogous rather than precise.

i Strophe or Stanza The sense itself often demands the division of the poem into strophes. As the lines are related to each other by parallelism, so the strophes themselves are often connected by a higher echo of the same.

j The strophic arrangement of a poem may also be identified by various stylistic devices used in the construction of a strophe: e.g. the refrain or intercalary verse: cf Ps 42 (41): 5, 11 and 43 (42):5 which form one poem; 46 (45); 49 (48); the *anaphora* or the repetition of a word or expression at the beginning of several successive verses: cf Ps 13 (12):2—4; the *epiphora* or repetition of the same words at the end of successive lines: cf Ps 118 (117):10—12, the *symploce* or repetition of one word or expression at the beginning and of another at the end of successive vv: cf Ps 118 (117):2—4.

k The *acrostic* or *alphabetical poem* may also help in the reconstruction of the strophic unit: cf Pss 9—10 (9); 25 (24); 34 (33); 37 (36); 119 (118); 145 (144); Prv 31:10—31; Sir 51:13—29; Lam 1—4. On the Heb. word *selãh* cf § 381o.

l Some scholars believe that nearly all Heb. poems can be divided into strophes in such a way that the second (antistrophe) corresponds to the first, the third (epode or alternative strophe) differing from the first two both in matter and form. It is worth noting that the Rãs-Shamra poetry comes from a cultural and literary setting more closely allied to Heb. poetry than either the Babylonian or Egyptian, and that there are points of contact in their structural forms, e.g. in Ps 29 (28) and 70 (69); cf Gordon, op cit 108—20.

m Internal Qualities—These are determined by the age, condition of life and environment in which the writers lived. Although the OT is of divine authorship, it comes also within the scope of literature, and is to

be appreciated as such. For the Holy Spirit poured the **356m** flood of his exalted message into the mould of oriental minds, leaving clearly impressed upon it the peculiarities of style of each writer and his time. The substance of the message remains unchanged, but its shapes are various. Using a simple but vigorous diction, profuse figures of speech and rhetorical devices the sacred writers left as a heritage a sublime imagery of religious thought and a great wealth of deep feeling. Thus we find:

(a) simile, i.e. an expressed resemblance between **n** two objects of unlike classes: e.g. man's transient existence (Ps 103 (102):15; 129 (128):6; Jb 7:6; 9:25, 26; 14:2, 11); (b) metaphor, i.e. an implied comparison (Ps 18 (17):4; 71 (70):3; Gn 49:3—27); (c) allegory, i.e. a developed and continued metaphor (Ps 80 (79); Is 5:1—7; Ezek 17:1—10; Prv 24:30—34); (d) personification (Ps 19 (18):5; Is 44:23; 49:13; Prv 8:12—36; Wis 8:2; Jb 28:14, 22); (e) hyperbole (Ps 109 (108):6—15) where the author prays for retribution upon his enemies in the 'fine frenzy' of the poet; (f) irony (Is 5:22; 47:1, 5, 8—9, 13—14; 14:9—20; Am 4:4—5); (g) word-play (cf the Heb. of Mi 1:8—16; Am 5:5; 6:13; Hos 6:8—10; 12:12; Is 10:28—29). An example from Is 5:7 will illustrate its effectiveness:

'*And he looked for judgement* (mišpāt); *but, lo!*
bloodshed (mišpah),
for justice (sᵉdāqāh); *but, lo! a cry* (sᵉ'āqāh)'

Summing up: the technique of Heb. poetry is made up of rhythm and not of metre; the verse consists of a fixed number of unstressed syllables. Each v is usually divided into two (more rarely, three) members (stichs) knit together by the law of parallelism. Vv can be grouped to form strophes. It is however essential to keep in mind that the poet was not bound to absolute regularity either in parallelism or rhythm or in strophic construction. He wrote because of the inspiration within him and in its expression he was fettered by no poetic structure that was meticulously exact or regular in form.

II THE WISDOM LITERATURE

Bibliography—A. Vaccari, S. J. *De libris didacticis,* **357a** 1935; *id* 'Sapientiaux (Livres)', DAFC, IV, 1182—1214; H. Duesberg, *Les Scribes inspirés,* 1938; A. M. Dubarle, *Les Sages d'Israël,* 1946; W. O. E. Oesterley, *The Wisdom of Egypt and the OT,* 1927; O. S. Rankin, *Israel's Wisdom Literature,* Edinburgh, 1936; G. von Rad, *Josephgeschichte und ältere Chokma,* VT Suppl. I, 1953, 120—7, and, *Gesamm. St. z. A. T.,* Munich, 1958; E. Murphy, *The Seven Books of Wisdom,* Milwaukee 1960. Id 'The Concept of OT Wisdom Literature', in *The Bible in Current Catholic Thought,* 1962, 46—54; M. Noth and D. W. Thomas, Ed., *Wisdom in Israel and in the Ancient Near East,* VT Suppl. III, Leiden 1955; Leclant, Edit., *Les Sagesses du Proche-Orient ancien,* 1963; H. Cazelles, *Les Débuts de la Sagesse en Israel,* ibid, 27—40;—For the connection with Egypt see especially, Helmuth Brunner, *Weisheitsliteratur,* in *Handbuch der Orientalistik* 1/2, 1952, 90—110; W. von Bissing, *Altägyptische Lebensweisheit,* Zürich 1955; J. A. Wilson, in ANET, 1955, 405—24; H. Gese, *Lehre und Wirklichkeit in der alten Weisheit,* Tübingen 1958; B. Gemser, *The Instructions of 'Onchsheshonqy and Biblical Wisdom Literature,* VT Suppl. VII, 1960, 102—28; E. Würthwein, *Die Weisheit Ägyptens und das AT,* Marburg 1960. For the connection with Mesopotamia see mainly: J. J. van Dijk, *La sagesse suméro-accadienne,* Leiden 1952; E. Gordon, *A New Look at the Wisdom of*

357a *Sumer and Accad*, BiOr XVII (1960), 131—52, with full bibliography; W. G. Lambert, *Babylonian Wisdom Literature*, Oxford 1960; G. R. Castellino, *Sapienza Babilonese*, Torino 1962 (especially for the interpretation of Mesopotamian conceptions); G. Couturier, 'Sagesse babylonienne et Sagesse israelite', in ScE 14 (1962) 293—309.

b The Wisdom Books—Wisdom literature is the general name given to those books of the OT whose main theme is wisdom, ranging from God's wisdom personified to the practical philosophy of life. They are written, for the most part, in a proverbial or aphoristic style which today we call gnomic, and in form and subject-matter they find a parallel in the gnomic poetry of classical literature. These books are Prv, Jb, Eccl, Sir and Wis, to which are sometimes added Song and Ps. Yet the last two books are not, strictly speaking, Wisdom literature. The former is a lyrical poem, and most of the Psalms are not, in the precise sense of the word, sapiential, although several psalms (Ps 1, e.g.) belong to this class. Job, though not gnomic in form, merits a place among the sapiential books because of its speculative discussions on the origin and moral value of suffering and its hymn to Wisdom (ch 28). Typical of wisdom literature are Prv, Sir, and, to a lesser degree, Eccl. They consist of sententious sayings that are independent, or, at most, grouped about a definite subject. The book of Wisdom, written in Gr., is more philosophical and less gnomic.

These seven books, both in the Heb. Bible and in Vg, where they are placed in the middle, form a special group, to which we may add the eulogy of Wisdom in Bar 3:9—4:4. In the Roman Missal they have, with the exception of Ps, the collective title of 'Liber Sapientiae', when read as Epistles in the Mass.

c Origin—The proverb is the standard form of folk wisdom. Every people has its own collection and the proverbial style of utterance is popular among Orientals. These proverbs pass from lip to lip and embody the wisdom or practical philosophy of life gained by experience. They express, in short pithy sayings, something that common experience has shown to be true. A proverb is 'the wisdom of many and the wit of one'. Among the Hebrews such popular sayings often took a religious form, and a number of proverbs, both secular and religious, are found in the early literature of Israel: e.g. 'Is Saul also among the prophets?' (1 Sm 10:12 and 19:24); 'From the wicked shall wickedness come forth' (1 Sm 24:13); 'the strength of a man is according to his age' (Jg 8:21). Other early forms of wisdom are the riddle (e.g. Jg 14:14); the fable (e.g. Jg 9:8—15) and the parable (e.g. 2 Sm 12:1—6).

d In the OT the golden age of proverbial utterance is associated with the name of Solomon, the wise king *par excellence*. 1 (3) Kgs 4:29—30 states that 'God gave to Solomon wisdom and understanding exceeding much and largeness of *mind* as the sand that is on the seashore'. According to 1 (3) Kgs 4:32 he 'spoke three thousand proverbs'. There is no reason to deny that he possessed an acute power of observation, a shrewd insight into human nature and the faculty of expressing himself in pointed sayings, a number of which are preserved in the older portions of 'Proverbs' (10:1—22; 16; 25:1—28; 27).

e The Heb. word for proverb is *māšāl*. Originally it seems to have meant 'likeness', then a short saying containing a comparison. Eventually, however the word acquired an extended sense and became an expression for a sententious saying or authoritative utterance in figurative and poetic form (Nm 23:7, 18; Is 14:4—6). It was in this popular form of expression that the Wisdom literature **357** was chiefly written.

The Wise Men—a number of proverbial sayings in the **f** Wisdom literature of the OT may have come at first from the lips of the people, but if so, they have been altered and modified so that the stamp of the professional teacher is upon them. The prophets speak of the existence of 'wise men'. In Jer 18:18 they are clearly marked off from the other two great classes of religious teachers: 'the law shall not perish from the priest, nor counsel from the wise, nor the word from the prophet'. The wise men, therefore, occupied a definite position in the religious community and the study and teaching of wisdom was a recognized pursuit. It is frequently stated that the prophets often condemn wise men and wisdom (Is 5:21; 29:14; 44:25; Jer 4:22; 8:9; 9:23), but a study of these texts shows that the abuse, not the use of wisdom, is the object of the prophets' invective. Moreover it is clear from other texts that they greatly valued true wisdom. For Isaiah it is a gift of God (33:6), and upon the Messiah shall rest the spirit of wisdom (11:2). In fact it is a prophet who calls God himself for the first time by the name of Wisdom (Is 31:2; cf 28:23—29), and Jeremiah, in full agreement with the sapiential books, proclaims in a formula dogmatically significant, that God in his wisdom created the universe (10:12; 51:15). The wise men base their teaching on revelation and human experience, the one illuminating the other, but they regard revelation as the ultimate foundation of wisdom and the fear of God as its beginning and characteristic quality.

Wisdom in the Historical Books—In the earlier OT **g** writings 'wisdom' generally means the professional skill of craftsmen or administrative ability. The makers of the tabernacle (Ex 35:31—35) and of the priestly garments (Ex 28:3) received the gift of wisdom. Joseph possessed such political foresight as to win from Pharaoh the encomium of 'the wisest man' (Gn 41:39); Joshua, Moses' successor, was divinely filled with the spirit of wisdom (Dt 34:9) and Solomon's wisdom ranged from political acumen (1 (3) Kgs 5:12) and keen jurisprudence 1 (3) Kgs 3:28) to the solution of riddles (1 (3) Kg 10:1—4) and knowledge of natural history (1 (3) Kg 4:33). This wisdom, however, is an intellectual, not a moral quality; it is practical ability, not a religious virtue.

Wisdom in the Sapiential Books—Among these **h** books, Prv, Sir and Wis are of chief importance. Of lesser value for our study are Jb, Eccl and Bar (3:9—4:4). Prv hold perhaps the highest place among the sapiential books. It is a composite work that gets its name from the two oldest and longest portions (chh 10—22:16 and chh 25—29) which are entitled 'The Proverbs (*mišlê*) of Solomon', and in it we may trace the development of wisdom literature from its earliest forms to the most evolved. Sir was written, like Prv, in Heb. *māšāls*. It was composed about 180 B.C. and translated into Gr. by Ben Sira's grandson shortly after 132 B.C. It is a practical moral guide and praises particularly the divine wisdom manifested in the Law. Although written in the heyday of Hellenism, its author remained uninfluenced by Grecian culture and exhorted his readers to remain faithful to the Law and true wisdom (24:1—34; 36:1—17; 44:1—50:29). Wis was written in Egypt, probably at Alexandria, 150—50 B.C. It praises the divine wisdom as manifested in the history of Israel. In the clarity of its doctrine on immortality (chh 3—5) it far excels other OT writings. Its language is Gr. like certain of its ideas, but its doctrine is Jewish. Its purpose was to console the Jews in Egypt and to put them on their guard against the false wisdom of Hellenism.

357i Job is a book apart. Its author is a Hebrew, but the characters of the drama, even Job himself, are not; Wisdom, then, in the mind of the Jews, though bound up with religion, can be independent of revelation; but its principles, drawn from reason and experience, shine forth in greater relief beneath the light of revelation. Eccl is a difficult book. Whatever be the solution to the problem of its literary composition, it teaches the vanity of earthly things and the value of true wisdom. It condemns the search for pleasure when it is absorbing and divorced from the fear of God (2:1; 7:14—15), and its final conclusion is 'Fear God and keep his commandments, for this is the whole duty of man' (12:13). The alleged influence of Gr. philosophy has been much exaggerated. By showing the insufficiency of earthly joys, Eccl prepared the Jewish mind for a fuller revelation of the future life.

358a **The Notion of Wisdom**—It is from the above mentioned writings that we gather the Heb. notion of wisdom. In order to arrange this matter more conveniently we propose, with A. Vaccari, S. J., *Greg* I (1920) 218, the following division:

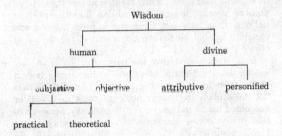

b **Human Wisdom**—In the older portions of Prv that elementary *practical* wisdom which consists in knowing how to live rightly plays a notable part. In the connotation of shrewdness it has a special name, *'ormāh* ('discernment', 'shrewd insight') and its contrary is *peti or petayyût* ('simplicity', 'inexperience') cf Prv 14:15; 22:3; 27:12. Further, by wisdom (*hakmāh*) may be indicated the technical ability that goes together with 'intelligence' (*bînāh*), cf Ex 28:3; 35:30ff. Prudence itself according to its purpose may be good or bad (Ex 1:10; Is 5:21; 29:14). But true prudence cannot be disconnected from religion, so that the real wise man is he who accepts God's will as manifested in his Law. In Jer (4:22; 5:21; 8:9) 'pious' and 'wise' interchange. Therefore it is not surprising that religious wisdom itself (*hokmāh*) is constantly stressed. It is to this form of wisdom that the first 9 chh of Prv exhort us and their doctrine is epitomized in the axiom that is the keynote of the book: 'the fear of God is the beginning of wisdom' (Prv 1:7; cf 9:10; 15:33; 30:3; Jb 28:28; Sir 1:16). This fear is synonymous with reverence and filial devotion. It is 'the fullness of wisdom' (Sir 1:16); 'the crown of wisdom' (1:18); 'the root of wisdom' (1:20). In the concrete it is the practice of religion.

c **Theoretical Wisdom**—The intellectual curiosity which gave rise to speculations about nature, man and God, is not characteristic of the Heb. mind. Hence it is that speculative wisdom has little place in the sacred books. Eccl, which so highly stresses and recommends practical wisdom, declares vain that wisdom which would know the ultimate reason of things, especially in the divine government of the world (1:12—18). The author of Job proposes a profound theological problem, the divine Providence in the government of the world (28:12—14), with special regard to the question of the sufferings of the righteous,

to which, however, no one but God can give an adequate **358c** answer (28:23). As far as man is concerned, he concludes tersely:

> 'Behold the fear of the Lord, that is wisdom;
> And to shun evil, that is understanding' (28:28)

The starting point, then, of the Heb. sage is not a question but a creed. Given that there is a Supreme Being, Creator, Sustainer, Ruler, Judge of all, then wisdom is to understand, so far as may be, God's words and ways and to turn that knowledge to practical account. Wisdom is, in all the complex relations of life and conduct, to do the will of God.

Objective Wisdom—Since the practice of religion is **d** essential to true wisdom, it follows that the observance of the revealed Mosaic Law is a prominent element of objective wisdom. Actually the sapiential literature, especially the older part, does not seek either the basis or the formulas of morality in the letter of the Law, i.e. in something that is specifically Hebrew. It transcends all that is local and temporary, giving to its teaching an absolute, rational foundation based on the psychological observation of the human heart and human life. Cradled in the stronghold of exclusiveness, it overleaps the barriers and reaches forth to the whole family of man. Hence its precepts have a universal application. They are the patrimony of all mankind.

Still, revealed Law is a manifestation of divine **e** wisdom; hence the two, the Law and Wisdom came to be identified. This identification is emphasized in Baruch (3:10—4:1) and Ben Sira expresses the same idea in a more dramatic and poetical fashion when he pictures wisdom as proceeding out of the mouth of the Most High, seeking a dwelling-place among the nations (Sir 24:1—12) and receiving an abode in Sion, where she found her full expression in the Book of the Law (24:23—24). In thus identifying the Law with wisdom, Baruch and Ben Sira only gave greater relief to the idea already expressed in Dt 4:5—8: 'I [Moses] have taught you *laws* and statutes as the Lord my God hath commanded me ... observe and fulfil them; for this is your *wisdom*', etc. It is not difficult, therefore, to understand how the Hebrews came to give the name of Wisdom to the revealed Law.

Wisdom as a Divine Attribute—To the writers of the **359a** sapiential books 'all wisdom is from God' (Sir 1:1). He is its source and he alone can give it to man (Prv 2:6). Wisdom, then, is an attribute of God whose clear reflection is seen in the never-ending marvels of nature (Ps 104 (103):24, Prv 8:19—20; Jb 28:12—28; Wis 13:1—9), and in the ordering of human events (Sir 17:14—15; 18:12—14). God therefore is all-wise; in fact he is Wisdom personified. Conversely Wisdom is God himself.

Personified Wisdom—Wisdom as a principle of moral **b** life regulating human actions is personified in Prv 1:20—28; 8:1—3, 12—15 and 9:1—5. But in the mind of the poet wisdom is more than a practical virtue. In Prv 8:22—31 he places on her lips those sublime and familiar words:

> 'God possessed me as in the beginning of his
>   ways, before his works, of old;
> I was set up from everlasting,
>   from the beginning, before the earth was.
> When there were no primeval waters, I was
>   conceived, . . .
> When he established the heavens, I was
>   present, . . .
> I was by him as a master-workman,
>   and I was daily his delight,
>   exulting always before him,

Exulting in his habitable earth,
and my delight was with the sons of men.'

The Wisdom that speaks here is in God; but it is also conceived as distinct from God, proceeding from him by way of generation, and subsistent, though working with him as an architect or an artist ('*āmôn*'). It is more than a poetical personification, though not yet a clearly defined personality. Meanwhile it prepares the way for and prefigures the doctrine of the distinction of persons in God.

c In Sir 24:1—7, Wisdom, again speaking in the first person, presents herself under another aspect. In this passage Wisdom is a personification of the Law. The truth revealed by God and Law imposed by him are properly conceived as outward manifestations of the eternal divine Wisdom, as the word (*logos*) of God, as something that goes forth from God and comes to man, and on the journey takes on, as it were, a personality all its own; then, deposited in writing, is concretized in the books of the Law. The same mental process may be observed in Baruch.

d If, lastly, we turn to Wis, its abstract thought and philosophical speculation tell us that, without having left Israel, we are on the terrain of Hellenism. In his description of Wisdom the author exhausts the rich philosophical dictionary of Greece. For him, too, as in Prv, Wisdom is the artificer of all, but he prefers to describe her, not in the act of creating the universe, but as continually active in penetrating (7:24), ordering (8:1) and renewing (7:27) all things. Yet though she fills the universe, she is intrinsic to God; for 'she is a breath of the power of God, a pure emanation of the glory of the Almighty ... a reflection of eternal light, a spotless mirror of the working of God and an image of his goodness' (7:25—27); words so sublime and profound that St Paul appropriated them to describe in human language the ineffable mystery of the divine generation of the Word (cf Heb 1:3; also Col 1:15, 17). From this portrayal of Wisdom to the definitely Personel Wisdom (*Logos*) of the NT was but a step.

e **Foreign Influence**—Analogous collections of gnomic poetry were in existence in Babylonia and Egypt before the Heb. sapiential books were composed. In Babylonia many collections of proverbs, sayings, fables, etc, as well as more theoretical compositions, are in existence in the Sumerian and in the Akkadian language (see § 357*a*). The specifically Sumerian productions have only become known of late, and the Akkadian ones are now fully published so that their comparison with the Biblical wisdom literature is both instructive and easy. From Egypt are known seven wisdom compositions that range from 2800 down to 100 B.C.; of other five compositions we have fragments, and of other seven only the titles. All this wisdom literature throughout the E and through all periods of its history shows that 'wisdom' is first of all a spontaneous creation of the human spirit; and it testifies also to the wide circulation of this type of literature.

It is against this background that the specifically biblical wisdom is to be seen. As regards Babylonian influence, two examples may be mentioned; the poem 'I will praise the Lord of Wisdom', to be compared with Jb; and the 'Babylonian Theodicy' in connection with the more theoretical problem of 'the righteous sufferer'. As regards Egyptian influence, of special interest is the Egyptian hieratic text of 'The Teaching of Amenemope' published by Sir Wallis Budge in 1923—4. **359e** There is a curious resemblance between the thirty chapters of this work and the thirty quatrains (read *šelôšîm* = 30 in Prv 22:20) which compose Prv 22:17—24; 22, as well as between the thought-content and verbal expression as far as Prv 23:11. The relation between them is more than fortuitous, but scholars differ in determining it. P. Mallon (Bib 8 [1927] 3—30) admits the dependence of Prv upon the Egyptian sapiential book; others affirm a common dependence upon an older Egyptian or Heb. source.

Since the 'Teaching of Amenemope' is variously **f** dated between 1000 and 600 B.C., chronology cannot settle the question of dependence. It is to be noted, however, that the thirty quatrains in Prv run consecutively, but in Amenemope they are scattered throughout the work. This would be difficult to understand in the case of a direct dependence of the Heb. work on the Egyptian, but is intelligible if the compiler of Prv made, more or less, a copy of an older Heb. writing, while Amenemope took a number of its ideas and elaborated them in his own way, inserting them in his text wherever he thought it suitable. In any event, wherever the inspired authors have made use of the wisdom literature of other nations, they have put their own impress upon it and carefully left out all that might savour of polytheism or offend the majesty of God.

It is often stated that the personification of wisdom **g** in the later sapiential literature is due to the impact of Gr. thought. It is, however, a canon of sound criticism not to explain by foreign influence what may well be accounted for by indigenous factors. Actually, personification of the divine attributes is not at all alien to the Heb. mind (cf Ps 85 (84):13; 89 (88):14—15; 94 (93):15); and it was quite natural that the revealed word (*logos*) of God should be graphically personified (Sir 24:1—22). There is no doubt that the author of Wis was acquainted with Gr. philosophy and adopted in part its logical classifications. Deeply versed in the OT doctrine, his aim was to prove to his fellow-Jews the superiority of Heb. wisdom and to win the gentile reader to his view. To this end he clothed old truths in new formulas that were understood and appreciated by those familiar with Gr. philosophy. Hellenism, however, does not enter into the texture of his thought. The closest resemblance is found in 7:22—24, but the 'spirit of understanding' that 'pervades and penetrates all things' (24*b*) is not the world-soul (*logos*) of the Stoics, immanent in all things, the active principle of a pantheistic all, but is as distinct from the world as a workman from his work, intrinsic to God and transcendent.

In a word, the speculations of Hellas had a purely **h** metaphysical origin and were born from the search for a rational explanation of the world and its phenomena. The wisdom of the Heb. sages springs from morality and religion. It is a divine plant with its roots in the rich soil of revelation. It is offered, not as the scientific explanation of the essence of things, but as a guide of virtue. Its personification played a great part in evolving and formulating the NT doctrine of the Word of God. In the OT all the essential elements were there. Finally the name alone was wanting. St John supplied that when, in his prologue, he proclaimed to the world the Word as the only begotten Son of God, the second Person of the Blessed Trinity.

JOB

BY R. POTTER O.P.

360a **Bibliography—Commentaries**: S. R. Driver and B. J. Gray, ICC, 1921; P. Dhorme, EtB 1926; E. tr. 1965; E. J. Kissane, 1939; C. Larcher, BJ, 1950; A. B. Davidson rev. by H. C. C. Lanchester, CBSC, 1951; A. Weiser, ATD, 1968[5], J. Steinmann, 1956; F. Horst, BKAT, 1960; P. Dhorme in *La Bible* (Bibliothèque de la Pléiade, 1959); C. J. Ball, *The Book of Job*, a revised text and version, 1922; E. G. Kraeling, *The Book of the Ways of God*, 1938; V. E. Reichert, Soncino Bible, 1946; W. E. Stevenson, *The Poem of Job*; 1947.

b **Articles**: A. Lefévre DBS 4 1073–1098, 1948; H. H. Rowley, 'The Book of Job and its meaning', BJRL 41 (1958–9), 167–207; P. Humbert, 'Le Modernisme de Job', VT Supp. 3 150–161; G. R. Driver, 'Problems in the Hebrew text of Job', ib. 72–93; P. W. Skehan, 'Strophic Patterns in the Book of Job', CBQ 23 (1961) 125–142; W. A. Irwin, 'Job's Redeemer' JBL, 81 (1962) 217–229; M. B. Crook and S. A. Eliot, 'Tracing Job's Story', Hibb. J. 60/239 (1962) 323–9; D. S. Shapiro, 'The Book of Job and the Trial of Abraham', Tradition 4/2 (1962) 210–20; R. A. F. Mackenzie, 'The Purpose of the Yahweh Speeches in the Book of Job', Bib 40 (1959) 435–45; L. J. Kuyper, 'The Repentance of Job', VT 9 (1959) 91–94; R. Tournay O.P., 'L'Ordre primitif des chapitres 24–28 du livre de Job', RB 64 (1957) 321–4; N. M. Sarna 'Epic Substratum in the prose of Job', JBL 76 (1957) 13–25; W. Vischer 'God's Truth and Man's Lie; A study of the message of the Book of Job', *Interpretation* 15 (1961) 131–46; B. H. Kelly, 'Truth in Contradiction: a study of Job 20–21', *Interpretation* 15 (1961) 147–56.

c **Introduction**—Besides being the name given to the literary and spiritual masterpiece now under consideration, 'Job' also refers to an age-old hero of tradition both in and outside Israel. And finally by this name we often designate the author of the book of Job who more than once would seem to have undergone in his own person something of the agonies of body and mind which are described in these vv of sublime beauty. Job taken in these three senses provides us with headings for part of the introduction.

d **The Book**—Jb opens with a prose prologue in a patriarchal setting. Job is depicted as a great sheikh, comparable almost to Abraham, cf Gn 12:16; 13:6 and 24:35. Yet the author is not consistent (nor need he be), for in this prose prologue, which covers the first two chh, we are shown Job's sons going from house to house to feast (Jb 1:13), and not gathered nomad-like under one or more tents (cf de Vaux, AI, 22–23). Job the great wealthy sheikh is a man of integrity, whole and perfect. Linked to the patriarchal background is a heavenly court scene. Then, quite naturally and simply 'the Adversary' or Satan comes on to attack Job and call in question his integrity and disinterestedness. God then allows Satan to attack Job and put him to the test. Soon Job loses all—family, possessions, and the esteem of **360d** others which he both expected and valued (cf Jb 2:9 and 30:9). Yet he retains his integrity of character, and to that extent Satan has failed. Then Satan is allowed by God to test Job yet more, and Job is struck with a particularly loathsome disease which some would label elephantiasis or tubercular leprosy. The author is probably simply trying to convey the most terrible disease possible. Yet Job comes through this too, patient and enduring.

Three friends then arrive from afar to comfort him. They hail from widely different quarters, but are represented as all arriving together to comfort Job. But for several days they simply sit beside him, silent in their sympathy.

The silence is broken by Job's soliloquy (ch 3) which **e** wells forth as a cry of anguish leading him to curse the day he was born. Each of his friends then speaks in turn, three times over; and each, at least at first, is answered by Job. The first cycle of speeches lays down the principal points at issue, and Eliphaz's first speech (Jb 4 and 5) is the classic statement in impressive vv of an orthodox Hebrew outlook at its best, and as such, in great part, rings true even to a Christian today. As sin is universal, so suffering must be the necessary accompaniment wherever human beings are to be found. But God is Supreme Right, and so the good must prosper and the wicked must perish. The sufferings of the good must be for a time only; God will wipe away all tears and put an end to evil. But the majestic and severe statements of Eliphaz, true in their own order, theologically and theoretically, convey nothing to a Job or any sufferer who is distraught with pain of body and soul and, like Job, hounded by God himself, 'the terrors of God are arrayed against me' (Jb 6:4).

Bildad principally appeals to past experience; God **f** will not reject an innocent man, but the guilty only (cf Jb 8:13 and 8:20). But, argues Job, God 'destroys both the blameless and the wicked' (Jb 9:22). Zophar is stung to the point of accusing Job of some grievous sin. Job is suffering much; therefore argues Zophar Job must have sinned. It is as obvious as that. Job's friends subsequently make more and more of this point. Job counters in the first cycle, their arrogance and lack of sympathy (Jb 12:5) and specious arguments, 'your maxims are proverbs of ashes; your defences are defences of clay' (13:12). The further speeches of the second and third cycles add little that is new, but do accentuate the issues and the tensions which are mounting between Job and his friends. There is no progress in thought any more than in action for Job is not a drama. But there is an intensification of poignancy and feeling between Job and his friends as the dialogue proceeds. And indeed the accusations of the friends go far: Eliphaz reaches a point in which he accuses Job of abuse of power and heartless indifference to the wants of others (22:5–11). These may well be the temptations of a wealthy man:

360f but the charge is fully and magnificently answered in Job's apologia (ch 31).

g The third cycle remains uncompleted, but this in itself is no imperfection. It may well be that it is only the modern reader who expects regularity of structure, i.e. three sets of three speeches, each answered by Job. We have then irregularity in structure, but nowhere any diminution in the sublimity of the poetical form. Job consistently protests his innocence; without claiming to be perfect (though equivalently called so in the prologue 1:1), he maintains that he has never merited such grievous misfortunes. To some extent he agrees with his friends in holding that merits and deserts should be better matched, and at the same time he casts himself upon his 'Vindicator', whom Job's faith has ever sought, despite momentary lapses of tongue and mind in the midst of excruciating agonies. Job's faith, elicited from the innermost being of his better self, remains untarnished all through the dialogue; and of God he says:
Would he contend with me in the greatness of his power?
No: he would give heed to me.
There an upright man could reason with him,
And I should be acquitted for ever by my judge. (23:6—7)
The faith of Job is even more striking than the patience of Job which has become proverbial.

h Up to this point, prologue (1 and 2) and dialogue (3—27) are for the most part consistent and hold together unquestionably as a unity. When we come to ch 28, some would suggest that there is a break. It can no doubt be taken as a poem on its own in the best sapiential tradition. It is a magnificent composition on the remoteness and elusiveness of wisdom. God alone knows where wisdom is to be found. Only by reverence and obedience may a man attain to wisdom and to God. It remains quite tenable that the author of Job inserted this poem because he wanted a meditative pause precisely at that juncture.

Next follows (chh 29—31) a long, and final, 'the words of Job are ended' (31:40), monologue in which Job surveys his life with its happiness in the past, its suffering and miseries in the present, and then, despite these last, a solemn oath and renewed protestation of innocence. All this section is most impressively moving, adding much to the total build-up of the book of Job, and at the same time furnishing us with much more about the person of Job who appears here human, alive, suffering. These chh may also serve to tell us about the author of Job. Could it not be, at this point, the author who is describing deeply-felt personal memories and feelings? cf 29:2ff.

i Next come the Elihu chh (32—37), introduced by a short prose prologue. Elihu is depicted as a young man who bursts upon the scene and leaves it equally suddenly, and seemingly quite independently of the rest of the book. He simply makes four speeches, expects, and gets, no answer, and disappears. Many scholars look upon these chh as adventitious and not part of the original book of Job. This is the more common attitude of critics. But we can also hold that the Elihu speeches, which had many qualities of thought and diction, may be a supplement added by the author himself, or, possibly, a contribution added to the debate by another author. After some bombastic self-introduction, and virtually talking to himself, Elihu tries to re-state the arguments of the friends in a more appropriate form and with a shift in emphasis. Elihu also adds to the discussion when, for example, in ch 35 he puts forward a view which is a criticism both of Job and his friends, for both are really seeking to get something out of their service of God, Job by complaining, the friends by clinging to

their orthodoxy of belief. In fact God is so great that **360i** he is not 'changed' by our goodness or wickedness. God can be attained, by those who are utterly sincere and seek him for his own sake. Suffering is simply a part of God's educative process, and we are to accept it as such, and sing the praises of God in good days and bad equally.

With ch 38 God appears, and in this theophany shows **j** himself to Job. There is no argument, no explanation of the innocent's suffering, simply God present, the God of Abraham, Isaac and Jacob, the great I AM. And God puts before Job the wonders of creation which surpass his understanding. Job submits, humbly, prayerfully, faithfully. God is then represented as re-enforcing his lesson with a detailed description of the monsters Behemoth and Leviathan. These are made yet more monstrous by a vivid and vigorous poetic imagination. Job submits once again: '*I have heard of you by word of mouth, but now my eye has seen you. Therefore I disown what I have said and repent in dust and ashes*' (42:5—6).

The poetry of our book ends here, and then finally we have a prose epilogue which in some ways balances the prologue. It definitely seals the vindication of Job's faith and point of view, for his friends are roundly condemned by God and sacrifices as well as the prayers of Job are asked of them (42:7—9). Last of all comes a restoration of Job and all his substance and a rebuilding of his family, the whole described with a certain extravagance and rather in the manner of classic fairy tales (42:10—16).

Job, as hero of ancient tradition—It is reasonable **361a** to hold, and there is ample evidence, that Job was the name of an ancient patriarch, sage or hero both in Israel and in yet older traditions of Mesopotamia and Egypt. It is reasonable too to hold that there was an historical person behind the book as we have it and to that extent we may rejoin patristic tradition which never had any doubt that Job was other than an historical character, and the book of Job an historical narration. But we must also recognize that the book as we have it 'is the artistic creation of the author who used the ancient figure of Job as the vehicle for his message' (Rowley in BJRL Sept. 1958, 172).

This ancient figure of Job is certainly referred to **b** in two passages of Ezek (14:12—14, and 19—20) where we read of Noah, Danel (RSV Daniel) and Job. We should read with the consonantal text of Ezek 'Danel', and more so as Danel appears in Ras Shamra texts from about 1400 B.C. The Phoenician Danel and Edomite Job seem to be associated, and both were no doubt historical figures, Danel being introduced into Ras Shamra mythology while Job was introduced into Heb. wisdom literature. A further point of interest is that the Danel of Ras Shamra is outstanding in virtue and wisdom, and also unfortunate for he loses his son—as Job lost his children (cf *The Legend of AQHT*, ANET 149—55).

The theme of Job or of a just man suffering is found **c** in ancient Mesopotamia as in Egypt. Thus the text Ludlul bēl Nēmeqi, sometimes called the Babylonian Job, is a long monologue in which a certain nobleman relates how he had met with every conceivable calamity, and then was eventually restored to health and prosperity by the Lord Marduk. The writing is attributed to the Kassite period 1500—1200 B.C., and the writer, like Job, is perplexed: how can the world be ruled by the Lord Marduk whom all expect to be just. Yet Marduk allows even the most devoted to suffer. The author of Ludlul finds no answer to the problem: he can

361c only state: the Lord Marduk has smitten, yet it is he who shall heal (cf W. G. Lambert, *Babylonian Wisdom Literature* 21—62). Another text termed 'The Babylonian Theodicy' has a Job-like dialogue between a sufferer and his friend. Specially striking are the lines: (Lambert p. 87).

> 251. How have I profited that I have bowed down to my God?
> 252. I have to bow beneath the base fellow that meets me;
> 253. The dregs of humanity, like the rich and opulent, treat me with contempt.

which can be compared with Jb 30:1, 8, 9 (for the text of W. G. Lambert, op cit 63—89).

d The Sumerians too had turned their minds to the problem of human suffering. A text of c. 1700 B.C. gives us another ancient parallel to the book of Job (cf Kramer, VTS, 3 *Wisdom in Israel and the Ancient Near E*, 170—82). Sumerian teaching was that man's misfortunes were the result of his sins or misdeeds. They even taught that 'never was a sinless child born to its mother', so that there cannot be any cases of unjust suffering. The victim of unjust suffering simply has to keep on praying and continually 'glorifying his god and keep wailing and lamenting before him until he turns a favourable ear to his prayers' (op cit 171).

Of about the same period is an Akkadian text dealing with the same problem of human suffering [cf Nougayrol, *Une Version Ancienne du Juste Souffrant*, R B 59 (1952) 239—56].

e For Job like traditions in Egypt, the Dialogue of the Despairing One with his own soul, dating from 1800 B.C. is usually cited. It is interesting that this text was written apparently when the Hebrew patriarchs lived nomadwise in Egypt. Parallels in numerous details with the book of Job have been adduced by P. Humbert (*Recherches sur les sources égyptiennes de la littérature sapientiale d'Israël*, Neuchâtel, 1929) but he has overstated his case. It remains very uncertain whether the author of Job knew the Dialogue. There is simply a very general kinship in the writings and some affinity in ideas.

f How assess these parallels in the literatures of Mesopotamia and Egypt? It seems clear that there is, all through, a constant theme or tradition about an innocent sufferer. We would conclude (cf J. Steinmann, *Le Livre de Job*, 43) that there is no direct dependence of our Heb. Job on these ancient texts but simply an identity of theme and sometimes of literary style. The author of Job did not proceed from a vacuum nor create the whole content of his book. He echoed a tradition and an anxiety which went further back than Yahwism and which had found some expression in Mesopotamia and Egypt. And he knew that in the Heb. tradition there was an innocent sufferer called Job, whose life and experiences had been in some ways lived before in older and wider traditions.

g To be complete a note should be added on the person of Job in Christian tradition. The Epistle of St James (5:11) tells of the blessings of those who endure, and cites the endurance or patience (*hypomenē*) of Job. The association of Job with lasting patience has lingered on in the Christian mind.

h **The author of Jb** knows about life in towns (19:13ff; 24:10, 12, 16; 29:7ff; 30:28; 31:2), but also knows desolate wadis where wretchedly poor folk live precariously on thorny roots and growths (cf the vivid passage in 30:4ff). He has certainly experienced a desert-crossing (38:26—27), and knows about bedouin razzias and pillage (1:15, 17). He apppears to be familiar with Edomite territory (1:1ff) and with oases in vast solitudes **361h** (cf e.g. 6:19).

Yet in the finished book of Jb, the nomadic and patriarchal life serves simply as a back-cloth skilfully woven out of a number of real experiences of the poet in the course of his travels. Thus he remembers, and conveys vividly, the gazelle giving birth in the sand (39:1ff), the wild-ass in the steppes (39:5—6), and the habits of ostriches (30:29 and 39:13) and jackals (30:29).

Our author has been farther afield yet. He is informed **i** about mines and mining. This would mean the Sinai region, or possibly the copper-mines near Aqabah (cf 28:1). He has very clear recollections of Egypt, and knows of pyramids and burial places (3:14, 18, 21), and of palaces stuffed with wealth (3:15), of slaves and their warders (3:18 and 7:1—2), of reeds and papyrus (8:11), of the Nile and its canals (9:26), of the fall of the flooded river to the point of drought (14:11). Travels in this far-away land no doubt prompted the author to depict the hippopotamus and crocodile more than emphatically, in almost make-believe dimensions (40:15ff and 41:1ff).

The influence of Egyptian ideas appears in expressions **j** such as 'the balance of divine justice' (31:6), 'the weighing of hearts' (6:2), and in the negative confession (31:1—40).

All these travel-impressions are unusual in Heb. literature which is for the most part bounded by a Holy Land horizon. There is thus an exotic and cosmopolitan note about Job the author, cf P. Humbert, *Le Modernisme de Job* VTS, 3, 150 61. He is a much travelled and thoughtful Jew, furnished in mind in the way suggested, before becoming a supreme poet and poetic genius.

It can reasonably be argued that the poet in some **k** measure suffered as Job suffered, and 'the spiritual history too is that of the author himself' (T. H. Robinson, *The Poetry of the OT*, 73). Robinson even maintains that the author of Jb was a leper, and that in the main dialogue it is Job who is the hero (no one would deny this). But then Job, it is suggested, *is the author himself* at least in feeling and in thought. This can be further supported by comparing chh 3—31 with 32—37. The author of 3—31 is certainly sympathetic to Job, that of 32—37 is critical or hostile. This argument may not convince. More effective is an argument from chh 29—31, which, it could be argued, are in part personal reminiscences of one who has known and deeply felt good and bad days and who is inwardly convinced of his innocence before God.

Date of writing—Job 7:17ff is a bitter parody of Ps. **l** 8:4. Therefore Jb is later than Ps. 8. But the dating of Psalms is notoriously difficult. We might say that it is not late in the post-exilic period.

Other evidence is from the text itself, from the aramaisms, etc. This is not very conclusive. The main theme of the poem supposes or implies a fully mature prophetic teaching and the kind of monotheism which was developed during the exile. Nothing more definite would seem to be possible so we must date the writing of Jb end of 5th cent. or beginning of 4th cent. B.C.

The text of 15:19 is sometimes cited for the date but it is vague and at best a scribe's gloss (cf Steinmann, *Job* p. 245). Ezekiel 14:14—20 refers *not* to the book but to a popular tradition about Job.

Doctrine and Theology—The prose narratives and **362a** the poetic dialogue and speeches are quite different in literary style. It is however possible to look upon Jb as the work of a poetic genius who built his masterpiece on the basis of two prose narratives. Even if the date of

362a the book can only approximately be determined still something can be established from the text as we have it about the author's beliefs about God and man and the interplay of the two.

The author lays the scene outside Israel. The characters are all Arabs or Edomites. Thus the term Eloah for God is said to be Edomite (cf Ben-Yehuda, *The Edomite Language* in JPOS, I (1921), 113ff). And yet, despite the background assumed and supposed, Job and his friends talk and reason as people formed in the traditions of Israel. Their 'foreign' names and background are little more than a literary fiction. But they may just serve to show that the wisdom and general teaching of the book stem from something wider than the school of those who claimed to be in the line of Abraham, Isaac and Jacob.

b On one point the author is consistent with the assumed literary setting: none of the characters in the poetic sections use the sacred name Yahweh (12:9 is an apparent exception cf commentary in loc.). The names used are El, Eloah, Elohim (rarely) and Shaddai, sometimes separately and often in conjunction. In the Prologue and Epilogue the sacred name Yahweh occurs *passim*.

From Ex 6:2—3 it can be shown that Yahweh, Elohim, El-Shaddai are names designating the one same God whose attributes are universal. This too can be shown from many texts in our poem cf 27:2—4, 8—11 etc. Much of the dialogue is in splendid doxologies coming most appropriately from the lips of a true Israelite. They are in fact the creation of the author who was through and through a Hebrew (cf 5:8—18, 9:4—13, 11:7—9, 12:13—25, 26:5—14).

c The whole poem is permeated and dominated by **the idea of a unique God** (5:9, 9:10, 37:5), **Creator and Lord of all** (12:13), **inaccessible** (23:8—9) and **beyond all human reckoning** (11:8—9). The Will of God is omnipotent, God does what he wills (9:12, 11:10, 23:13—14). All comes from him, suffering, joy, wound and healing (5:18, 22:18). Something of an oriental resignation to God's will appears in 1:21, cf 1 Sm. 3:18. God dwells in a heavenly court (1:6, 38:7) surrounded by 'sons of God' who are the angels his attendants and messengers. These angels are above men and can serve as intermediaries between God and mankind (5:1, 33:23—24). Yet God can find faults in these (4:17—19, 5:1, 2, 8, 15:14—16), as indeed in the very heavens and the stars (15:14—16, 25:4—6). Among the mysterious heavenly beings is 'the Satan' or Accuser (1:6) cf Mt. 16:23. Satan's role is to query the disinterestedness of Job (1:9—11).

d **Life is one of God's most mysterious gifts. It is a source of all good, as also of utter misery**; thus ch 3 is a long protest against life. Yet life is God's gift, as is the light (3:4—5, 20). God fashions man in his mother's womb (10:8—12). In 2 Mc 7:22 we find a continuation of the tradition of Job on this. The breath of life is from God (12:10, 33:4) and without it death comes about (34:14—15). God is Author of life as of death (8:8—9, 34:14—15). Job curses the day of his conception (3:3) with intense feeling. But never is there any question of suicide. Death is looked upon as good in the light of present excessive sufferings (cf 3:11—12, 16, 21, 22; 6:8—9; 10:18—19). **Death indeed brings a rest** (3:17, 18, 19) which contrasts with the pains and agitations of this life (3:20—26). Death is a leveller of **e** all men in every position (3:14—15, 19). There is a certain stress on the fact of **no return after death** (14:7—12, 18—22), and for the modern reader of Jb,

imbued with the Christian idea of resurrection, the **362e** adaptation or transposition of mind to Job's viewpoint does not come easily. For Job **life and death are utterly apart** (14:21—22 cf Lk 16:26). Sheol, death, the tomb, and Abaddon (28:22) loom large in the poem, and they are fatal and final. Man is a very small thing in the face of death's grim reality (cf 7:17—18, 13:28, 14:1—2). Man's life is likened to harsh military service (7:1—2), and life is fleeting (9:25—26). Life is further made sombre by the abandonment and deceit of friends (6:15—17, 19:13—17). Job has if anything a pessimistic view of men and the society of men (cf 24, *passim*, 36:7—12 etc).

God exercises a rigorous control over men (34:21—22) as over nations (34:25—30); yet God is not always fault-finding. There is a **kindly solicitude** on God's part (10:12, 29:2—5). God wants man's betterment, and chastises him for that purpose (5:17, 33:19ff). This last idea is the one more particularly developed in the Elihu speeches. God, is Judge and justice governs **f** his relations with men. He is a **just Judge** (9:14—16, 10:13—15, 37:23) and weighs the deeds of men (31:6). In harassing pain and acute distress of mind, Job inveighs against the divine justice (16:11—18; 19:6—12; 27:2—3). Yet more basically, he has confidence in the showing forth of divine justice 'I know that my Vindicator lives . . .' (cf 19:25—27; 31:35—37).

The 'fear of the Lord' is paramount and characterizes Job (1:1, 8; 2:3) and it is wisdom (28:28). In the same text we get 'departing from evil' and 'fear of the Lord' in parallelism and as correlatives. Similarly in Prv. 3:7, 16; 16:16; 23:11—12. Then note how 'justice' or righteousness is sublimated to become charity in the beautiful passages 29:12—17, and 30:25, and finally in 31:16—21, 29—30, 31—32.

Sinners, the wicked, and the unbelieving **are shown g up by their deeds**. Eliphaz's characterization of wickedness (22:6—9) is based on the Law and the Prophets. Thus parallels can be found in Ex 22:25—26; Is 58:7; Ezek 18:7; Dt 24:17, etc. Throughout ch 24, Job denounces sins as they are in the world of his day: e.g. moving boundary stones (24:2) which was strictly forbidden in Dt 19:14; 27:17 (cf Hos 5:10; Prv 22:8). Theft too is denounced, especially as it affects the orphan and widow (24:3); and there is reference to the maltreating of children (24:9), slavery and forced labour (24:4—11), manslaughter, murder and adultery (24:12, 14, 15). Later on, in the 'negative confession' Job comes back to adultery (31:9—12), injustice to inferiors (31:13—15), harshness towards the poor (31:16—18, 21). It is the language of the Psalms, especially e.g. Ps. 50 (49):7—8. And the cult of stars and constellations is condemned (31:26—28) as it is in the Law and Prophets, cf Dt 4:19; 2 (4) Kgs. 21:3; Jer. 8:1—2.

Job's friends take their stand on *traditional teaching* **h** *in Israel* or what has been handed down from father to son through the ages, cf Eliphaz in 15:9—10, 17—19, and Bildad in 8:8—10. That doctrine involves a thislife reward, something to be got here and now (4:6—7, 8—11). Job in ch 12 satirises and probes their pretensions, cf especially 12:2—3. The appeal to the knowledge of those who have travelled is something new (21:29). A door is opened 'to a wider understanding'. Yet wisdom and understanding are not an individual's privilege nor that of a whole nation: they are hidden *in God* (cf ch 28). Job himself, approved by God (42:7), admits that he has spoken of what outstrips him (42:1—6). How much the more must his friends be charged with

62h error. And anyway the traditional arguments of Job's friends partly break down in face of the stark reality of suffering, and are in part answered by Job's protestations of innocence (cf 6:10; 9:17; 13:16; 16:17; 27: 2–10).

63a **The Type of Literature**—The prose passages, introduction, epilogue and the introduction to Elihu's speeches, cannot be used to decide the literary type of the book as a whole. They are simply a necessary basis or taking-off points for the theme of a book which is substantially poetical and which in sublime v thrashes out the agonizing problem of how a man may be wholly innocent and yet be the victim of calamity. The sublimity of the thought and poetry makes us hesitate to say that the book belongs to Wisdom literature. We need to say more: **it belongs to Wisdom literature in its most poetic and sublime form**. In this respect it has nothing in common with the homely and often pedestrian elements in Prv, Eccl, etc. Wisdom in Jb is seen to be ceaselessly touching upon the **mysteries of God's action and God's Being.**

b The book can also be said to teach: it is **didactic**, with the lesson that **even great suffering is no proof of antecedent iniquity**. It is also hortatory in that it proposes an example, if not of consistent patience, at least of final resignation and humble **submission to the divine will**. This aspect of the teaching of Jb seems to have made a lasting impress on the Christian conscience, which, since the Ep. of St James, has so often spoken of the patience of Job. (Jas 5:11. RSV, 'steadfastness'.)

The adjectives 'epic' and 'dramatic' are sometimes applied to the book. An epic of the mind and heart we might call it, despite the loose-knit structure—which some critics would see as discontinuity and lack of structure. But Jb was never a drama. Drama implies action as well as dialogue, and there is no action except in the prose narratives of the Prologue and Epilogue. **Jb is first and foremost a poem, mainly in the form of a dialogue**, predominantly reflective, but with outbursts of intense feeling. There is an ebb and flow of thought about human suffering and God's attitude: but there is no 'solution', no explanation beyond the inscrutable will of God. Jb remains a problem book.

c **Poetic Form**—The metrical forms of Jb are often varied and no doubt this was of set purpose. The characteristic metre of the book is that of **two vv in equal parts**, each containing three significant words or stresses, and with parallelism of thought. It is the commonest metre in Heb. poetry generally. In Jb cf eg. 18:16, 28:1 + 2, 30:9, etc. Also in Jb are found 2:2, 4:3 and other metres. Cf 17:1, 11 and 3:19. **On occasion** we find the famous qinah or **lamentation rhythm** (3:2) cf Jb 2:9, 19:1, 21:11. We can discern a 4:4 rhythm in Jb 3:3. Most critics would agree about the varied metres in Job.

More problematical is the question of strophes and stanzas. About these there is no agreement. Dhorme Le Livre de Job, Introd. cl, admits that he has had to give up his avowed intention of trying to divide the poem into regular strophes. Kissane, The Book of Job, L–LIX, has perhaps made most of the theory of strophes. More recently the subject has been confidently revived by P. W. Skehan in CBQ 23, (1961) 125–142. This author goes so far as to urge that 'strophic structure is integral to the poem in Job so completely that any literary analysis that does not come to grips with this feature is a failure'. His analysis of Jb 3:3–24:11 is cogent but when he comes to the third cycle of speeches, the attempt to find strophic patterns seems to break

down and Skehan admits that his effort there is but **363c** tentative.

Texts and Versions—Jb employs many words which **d** are not found elsewhere in the OT. Many of them can only be explained by reference to Akkadian, Aram. or Arab. The difficult vocabulary did not make for an accurate transmission of the text which has an unusually large number of erroneous or dubious readings. It is estimated that only one third of the vv have escaped the attention of 'correctors'. However the hey-day of ingenious emendations has gone, and with a generally better knowledge of kindred languages and Near E lore, there is no doubt that we can often have more convincing explanations of the hapax legomena.

As to the **order of the text**, an extreme view was taken by authors who worked on the assumption that an editor had composed the book as best he might from torn fragments. Without going as far as this, many would agree that there have been dislocations in the text: thus 27:13–23 is now printed as part of Job's discourse, but its tenor is all the reverse of what Job has been maintaining, and it expresses the attitude of his friends. The passage is commonly thought to be part of the third speech of Zophar.

The **LXX version** in its primitive form was consider- **e** ably shorter than the Heb. It is now generally agreed that the Gr. translator omitted passages which already existed in the Heb., and not that there was a subsequent expansion of the Heb. text by the addition of matter which was not in the original. The LXX has omitted more than one fourth of the whole text. Why he did so is uncertain. But the unequal distribution of passages suggest deliberate shortening.

According to Swete, (Introd. to the OT in Greek, 256) the LXX of Jb was made by an Alexandrian Jew for the general reader rather than for the synagogue. The translation is free and sometimes lapses into paraphrase, so that it is no longer possible to recover the exact reading of the original. The Gr. text needs to be used with great caution for purposes of textual criticism; but it can on occasion help to the restoration of the Heb. original.

Even more caution is required in the use of the **Latin Vulgate**. St Jerome certainly strove to make the translation as accurate as possible. In fact his version of Jb has a rhythm and beauty of language which makes it supreme among all ancient versions. But Jer, while giving the correct meaning often treats the original text with considerable freedom. Note, for example, how he changed the whole import of 19:25 by his translation 'in novissimo die de terra surrecturus sum'. In the Heb. nothing corresponds to 'die'; 'de terra' is represented by 'on the dust', and the verb is in the third person, not the first. Moreover Jer was influenced by the LXX which he had himself translated. From all this it is clear that still greater reserve is required in the use of the Vg for the reconstruction of the text.

The Place of Job in the history of Revelation— **f** In the rich diversity of that library which is the Bible, Jb stands alone and supreme, utterly sui generis. Yet it was composed at a point in time, and even if that point can be determined only approximately, we can still establish relationships with other books and trends of thought. **To read Jb after reading Prv** makes us realize that we have passed from a world of wisdom, reflection and queries based on everyday observation, and **from a conventional moral code** with often facile solutions, **to a book which in every respect plunges deeper into realities.** Though the

363f conventional and traditional moral code is set out impeccably and more profoundly by an Eliphaz, still it fails to cope with the reality of acute suffering of body as of mind. All is brought into question, and the questioning takes the form of long and moving plaints, and indeed of cries of anguish (as in ch 3). The easy optimism of Prv is no more, and in Jb there is something much more akin to the groans and pains of Jeremiah 'man of tears' and those prophets who first broached **the problem of suffering and particularly that of**
g innocent suffering. Thus Habakkuk provides a first statement of the problem:

'Thou who art of purer eyes than to behold evil,
and canst not look on wrong,
Why dost thou look on faithless men,
and art silent when the wicked swallows up
the man more righteous than he?' (Hb 1:13)

Jeremiah takes up the same theme and asks 'Why does the way of the wicked prosper?' (Jer 12:1). The catastrophe of the fall of Jerusalem added point to what was already sensed in the prophetic tradition of Israel. It was then by-passed and arrested in the later tradition of Eccl which takes up the attitude of a disillusioned sage and so blocks the way of any further seeking or deeper experience. For Eccl man is alone in a senseless world 'abandoned like a monad to a process eluding all theological logic' (Von Rad, *OT Theology I*, 458), and faith is well-nigh dead.

h In Jb, however, the problem is faced in all its intensity. 'Seldom, if ever, has a great poet ventured on so ruthless an exposure of the futility inherent in beliefs which rest on too shallow foundations' (T. H. Robinson, *The Poetry of the OT*, 68). With his facing of the problem goes a profound faith and that pure monotheism which emerged particularly after the Exile. Job's particular contribution has been termed 'an apotheosis of justice' (Pedersen) or of that Utter Rightness which is God himself and infinitely above the capacities of a created mind. The more a man seeks to grasp something of that Righteousness transcendent, the more he realizes that human righteousness or justice is a thing of naught. There is indeed a *leitmotiv* discernible throughout the poem (cf 4:17 7:20 9:2–3 15:14–16 22:3 25:4–6 33:8 35:5 36:9 40:4–5 and 42:6) telling how man's righteousness is brought to nothingness: God alone remains, Infinite, Utter Right, Lord of all. This truth remains unquestioned but also unfathomable. In this sense there is no 'solution' to the problem of Job. **The outcome of the harrowing and sublime work is a demand for faith and yet more faith.**

i Something of a solution was to emerge from another tradition which was also post-exilic. The songs of the **Servant of Yahweh** were to teach the redemptive and vicarious value of the just man's suffering (cf Is 53). Later a fuller consideration of this linked to next-life teaching was to come in the book of **Daniel** (12:1–3) as also in Wisdom (3–5). The trials and sufferings of a just one are there related to and will indeed be exchanged for an eternal beatitude, while the temporal prosperity of the wicked only prepares for eternal loss.

But these findings of a later Jewish tradition were hidden from Job. We need to force ourselves to realize that his sublimities and his faith remain unmistakably throughout the poem on the side of a curtain which drops, inevitably and finally, at death.

364a **1:1–2:10 Prologue**—The author of the poem of Jb has retained the style and characteristics of an age-old popular tale in this prose 'prologue' which can be divided into two scenes, thus: prelude, 1:1–5, two scenes in **364**
heaven 1:6–12; 2:1–6, and two scenes of consequences upon earth 1:13–22 and 2:7–10.

1:1–5 Prelude—'There was a man', or as we would say 'Once upon a time'. Nathan's parable in 2 Sm 12:1 starts in this way. 'Job' or Iyyob. No satisfactory etymology is known. Some have argued to a parallel in the arabic name Ayyabah. 'in the land of Uz' (Us) said **b** to be S of Edom cf Gn 36:28, Lam 4:2. Abel, *Géographie de la Palestine* 1, 284, locates it at the extreme NW of Arabia. cf also Dhorme in RB 8 (1911) 104 'Le pays de Job' who suggests (i) el Iṣ, S of Et-Tafileh, (ii) a site S of Ma'an; this is better as it would in fact be exposed to Bedouin incursions, as recounted in our narrative. In LXX Uz becomes 'in the land of Ausatis'. An extant local tradition places Job's country at Deir Eyyoub, 40 miles SSW of Damascus, cf Abel *Syrie-Palestine*, 449. Certainly however the country of Job, according to our prologue, is in the Edomite region or definitely S.

'Blameless and upright'. These are forceful words in the Heb. The LXX translators sensed this and represented the underlying reality by four terms 'genuine or true, blameless, just and God-fearing'. From the beginning it is emphasized that Job was a good man. Yet was he to suffer excruciatingly in body and mind. Besides conforming to the OT ideal of perfection Job is also represented as patriarch-like in his family and possessions. He was a great personage, a great sheep-owner like Mesha of Moab, 2 (4) Kgs 3:4.

3. 'sheep' RSV and CV—should really be 'sheep and **c** goats' or small cattle. Not one English term corresponds to Heb. ṣ'n. 'Three thousand camels' is often said to be an anachronism, but there is difficulty in determining when the camel was domesticated in the ancient Near E, cf W. F. Albright, *From the Stone Age to Christianity*, 1946, 120, and De Vaux RB 56 (1949) 7ff 'Les Patriarches Hébreux et les découvertes modernes', and De Vaux in RB 72 (1965) 'Les Patriarches hébreux et l'histoire', especially 15–17. 'She-asses' cf Gn 32:15. These were always more valuable than the male and cost three times as much. Our scene in general opens with an impression of a well-to-do pastoral society, with perhaps some kinship with the patriarchal narratives of Gn 12–50, yet without the nomadic traits. Jews of the monarchical and later periods tended to refer to and to idealize their pastoral and nomad life beyond Jordan. This was ever a recall of their origins whose high point was the Exodus. 'people of the E' or beyond **d** Jordan, with some reference to a tradition of wisdom stemming from the E. This is one of the ways in which the character of Job presented to us; the whole book of Jb has reference to a wisdom tradition, and wisdom traditionally came from the E. **4.** We are then introduced, seemingly, to the picture of a care-free, opulent, leisured society, in which Job was outstanding precisely because of his deeply religious spirit. **5.** He would 'sanctify them, rising early', making them undergo some rite of purification before the sacrifice. 'cursed God'; the text has thus been restored by all modern editors. From a very early period scribes could not face the material blasphemy, and the text came to be written as 'bless God'. LXX seems to mitigate or paraphrase '*lest my sons in their intent should have devised anything evil before God*'.

6–12 First scene in heaven's court—There is now a **e** sudden passage to heaven's court which is suggestive of the grand courts of oriental monarchs. Yahweh receives the sons of God, i.e. the angels, in audience; cf the prophetic vision of Micaiah son of Imlah, in 1 (3) Kgs 22:19: 'And Micaiah said, "Therefore hear the word

364e of the Lord: I saw the Lord sitting on his throne, and all the host of heaven standing beside him on his right hand and on his left . . . " ' Satan in Job's prologue plays the same part as the lying spirit in Micaiah's vision. **6.** 'the sons of God' are the angels or beings superior to man who constitute Yahweh's court and council cf 38:7. 'While the morning stars sang in chorus and all the sons of God shouted for joy', and cf Ps 29 (28); 82 (81):1; 89 (88):7. 'Satan' or the adversary (as RSV and CV note) or the tempter. Later the word developed pejoratively into meaning a fundamentally evil being, the Devil, cf Ps 109 (108): 6; Zech 3:1—2; 1 Chr 21:1. **7.** Yahweh is represented as talking with familiarity and ease to Satan, who in turn is quite unabashed. Satan's answer recalls Zech 1:10—11 where horses stand for those whom Yahweh has sent to 'patrol the earth'. **8.** Yahweh himself endorses the estimate of Job's character, and thus are prepared more effectively the changes in Job's fortune which are soon to come. **9.** 'Is it for nothing that Job is God-fearing?' Job's piety being undeniable, his motives are attacked. **12.** Job and 'all that he has' i.e. his outward properties and all who are associated with him, family, friends, etc. But his own person, for a time, is to be respected. The trial or testing of Job is to be progressive, and finally attacks his innermost being. The emphasis on God's permissive Will here has been adduced as a sign of later Jewish theology.

f 13—22 Disaster upon disaster falls upon Job
15. 'Sabeans' are bands of pillaging nomads. Neither this term nor 'Chaldeans' of v 17 should be taken too literally; cf 6:19: 'the companies of Saba have hopes', The terms used here are very generic. Job lived on the edge of the desert, and in the ordinary course of events might expect raids, without such disastrous results.

Sabeans of Sheba (a town name given to a region) were a S Arabian people whose capital was at Marib 45 m. E of Sana. Sabean inscriptions were discovered and deciphered in the 19th cent. The following OT texts allude to the wealth and trade of Sheba: 1 (3) Kgs 10:1; Is 60:6; Jer 6:20; Ezek 27:22; Jl 4:8; Ps 72 (71) 10:15 **20.** 'robe': the outer garment or *me'il* is meant, worn over a tunic, and seemingly the attire of men of rank (1 Sm 18:4; 24:4). Tearing the upper garment is said to be still a mourning custom among the Jews of Persia. It was the first sign of great mourning, cf Gn 37:34; Jos 7:6; Ezek 9:3—5. Est 4:1. Cutting the hair was the second stage; cf Jer 7:29; Mi 1:16.

g 21. cf Gn 2:7 and 3:19; Eccl 5:14, 18; Sir 40:1 This last text effectively relates mother's womb and the womb of mother earth. The idea is latent in Job's words here. Job's disasters were certainly profoundly felt; yet the expressions of his grief were partly conventional, almost liturgical, using the approved rites of torn clothes and cut hair. For mourning usages cf Barrois, *Archéologie Biblique*, 2, 317; Contenau, *Manuel d'archéologie orientale*, 1056. The poignancy of Job's words is further impressed upon us if we remember that in ancient Heb. thought a full life on earth was to be followed by a thin unsubstantial existence in Sheol, an existence which scarcely differed from that which precedes a man's birth, cf 3:13—16 which plays upon these two states. **22.** 'In all this Job did not sin or charge God with wrong.' A first triumph of Job's faith and enduring patience; there has been no wavering in spiritual resolution and integrity.

h 2:1—6 Preparing for further onslaughts upon Job—The section is almost, but not quite a repetition of 1:6—12 and in this respect very hebraic. **4.** 'skin for skin' an idiomatic phrase whose precise force was already

lost at the time of the Targum paraphrases which suggest **364h** a readiness to sacrifice a lesser member for a more important. Dhorme in *L'Emploi métaphorique des noms de parties du corps en hébreu et en Akkadien* RB 29 (1920), especially 470—1, argues further that in v 5 Satan asks God if he may afflict Job in 'bones and flesh'. Now 'bones and flesh' are the intimate, inward parts of man in Heb. psychology, as opposed to 'skin' which is external. 'Skin for skin' would then seem to mean that up to then Job's affliction was but superficial. In effect, says Satan, just wait till we strike him in 'bone and flesh'. **7—8.** 'loathsome sores', cf 'the grievous boils of which you cannot be healed from the sole of your foot to the crown of your head' (Dt 28:35). The impression of loathsome purulent sores is heightened progressively with a wealth of detail in 7:5; 19:7; 30:17; 30:30. Anyway, Job's affliction renders him 'unclean' in the Levitical sense (cf Lv 13—14). Hence he returns to his village dung-heap or mazbula, 'among the ashes'.

9—10. Job's wife, like Adam's in Gn 3, becomes, in **i** the words of Augustine, *diaboli adjutrix*. 'bless God' of MT is here again, (as in v 5 and 1:5 and 11) to be read as 'curse God and (then) die'. **10.** Job sinned not with his lips, and so confounded the expectation of Satan as expressed in 2:5. **11—13.** A link-passage serving as a *mis-en-scène*, and for the presentation of the characters of the dialogue which is to come. An 'action' passage in the poem of Job, where generally there is little action, and scant progression of thought until the climax which is in the Theophany. **11.** Temanite. Teman or Teiman is often mentioned in the OT; cf Gn 36:11, 15, where are listed Edomite chieftains. Edomites and Temanites had a reputation for wisdom. This was perhaps the reason for Eliphaz's speaking first. Eliphaz, cf Gn 36:4 where Eliphaz is son of Esau, that is Edom. For the association of Edom and Teman cf Jer 49:7. 'Bildad' etymologically, perhaps simply 'city' or 'region'. 'Shuhite' Shuah is in Gn 25, 21. 'Sophar' possibly related to sipper or sparrow. 'Naamathite' either Dj. el Na'ameh or en-Na'emi. **12.** 'They did not recognize him': illness and misfortune had so transformed or disfigured him. 'tore his coat' 'tossed dust' i.e. the conventional mourning usages cf note on 1:21. **13.** 'Seven days and seven nights' or the recognized time for mourning cf Gn 50:10; Is 31:13; Sir 22:12. (*days* in all these texts). Grief calls for silence cf Lam 2:10.

3:1—26 Job's anguished plaint—which we can **365a** take as the first 'act' of this tragedy. Job curses the day of his birth and wishes that he had never been born. The whole is one 'plaint', but we can sub-divide into 1—10, Job curses his day of birth; 11—19, Job wishes that he had been still-born; 20—26. Why does God prolong life for the wretched of this world? The whole passage is a wild and profound explosion of anguish, and has been likened to the roar of a wounded beast. Antecedent to this curse is Jer 20:14—18. Job derived his theme from Jeremiah and perhaps a commonplace of poetic tradition and re-wrote it in his own way. This 'lament of a sick man' (Gunkel) is like chh 29—31, addressed neither to God nor directly to his friends. Rather is it a monologue on his wretchedness and a prayer for an oblivion that has never been.

3:3 'the night which said'. This rendering makes **b** the night personified so as to bear witness about what happened in it. 'a man-child is conceived', or as LXX 'See, a male boy'. Hence perhaps CV 'the child is a boy'. **4.** Job's cry represents the opposite of God's command in Gn: 'let there be light'. If Job's birthday cannot be blotted out, may it at least be a day of blackness uncared

365b for by God. **5.** *Ṣalmawet* black gloom: the strongest Heb. word to express deep darkness. 'claim it' (reading *yegā'aluhû*, Kittel's correction). The root meaning is that of effectively claiming property or redeeming it; the right or duty of doing this usually devolved on the owner's nearest relative or the 'goel'. 'barren'—*galmûd* means stony, sterile, unproductive. 'no joyful cry', contrasting, for instance, with the joyful cries of bride and bride-

c groom cf Jer 25:10; 33:11. **8.** Those who curse the day are necromancers or spell-binders who can cast a blight on certain days or seasons. Another way is to make it refer to the wicked who pursue their nefarious deeds under cover of night. This idea is paralleled in 24:13 and 38:12. Leviathan is no doubt a mythological sea-monster supposed in many parts of the world to swallow the moon, etc, at a time of eclipse; and days on which occurred an eclipse were considered ill-omened. Leviathan or the primitive sea monster is known in many mythological texts, e.g. Baal and Anat epic ANET 138*b*; and there are striking allusions to it in the poetry, e.g. of Is 27:1, as also in Ps 74 (73):13 and 104 (103):26. (But in 40:25 Leviathan stands for the crocodile, cf 41:1). Finally, casting down Leviathan or the Dragon is an apocalyptic image of the triumph of God's cause cf Apoc

d 12:3, 4, 9. **9.** 'stars of its dawn', *of its twilight* CV. The Heb. term *nešep* sometimes means twilight, as in 7:4; 24:15; Prv 7:9 etc, and sometimes dawn or sunrise Ps 119 (118):147. The context here would seem to favour dawn star, for this star or stars will not appear to announce the dawn. The eyelids of the morning is a poetic figure which has parallels in classical literature, e.g. Sophocles *Antigone* 103 'eyelid of the golden dawn', cf also Homer's 'rosy-fingered dawn'. **10.** Steinmann makes this the last v of a strophe as giving a reason for the cursing of that day—which in fact did not prevent the birth of the unhappy man.

12. Either his father's knees, on which a new-born child was laid as a sign of legitimation, or those of the wet nurse. (Steinmann). **13.** A powerful poetic picture of Sheol which is depicted as a land of eternal sleep and untroubled rest. **14.** Death is the great leveller; all human conditions meet in Sheol. 'waste places' *horābôt*. Some would read *harāmôt* and render 'pyramids'. Certainly the pyramids were mausoleums and monuments in waste places.

e **15—19.** Represents fairly free criticism of the social order. Job rejoices that the poor, the slaves and the submerged tenth are all at last to be freed in Sheol. There is no discrimination in the kingdom of the dead. Thus we can say that Job no longer speaks as an imagined sheik in an Edomite patriarchal society; here the author's personality breaks through and we are given a glimpse of a well-informed citizen of a large empire, of one who is awake to its social ills. And we are in fact more in the line of Wisdom literature in this as in several other passages of our poem. **16.** Cf the *ektrōma* of 1 Cor 15:8. **18.** '*captives*' CV, who had been employed on forced labour. 'prisoners' RSV, like the Israelites in Egypt.

f **23.** Job's way is hid, so that he cannot see which way to escape from the harrowing difficulties which beset him. The image is a familiar one e.g. Hos 2:6; Jb 19:8; Lam 3:7. **24** *'for sighing comes more readily to me than food'* CV. This is better than RSV's 'as my bread', but cf note there. The thought is familiar to us from Ps 42 (41):3 and Ps 80 (79):5. **25.** He has only to think of something disastrous and it comes upon him. Job's plaint should be compared with Ps 88 (87). Many similarities in thought, particularly in the idea of a descent

into Sheol, 'friends and neighbours gone, a world of **365f** shadows is all my company' (18).

4—14 FIRST CYCLE OF SPEECHES

4:1—5:27 Eliphaz's first speech; God's universal 366a goodness—We now embark upon the dialogue. Eliphaz has been stung by Job's plaint (3). He is the oldest of the three, and now, after a long silence (2:13) sets out in magnificent terms a very conventional theology wholly in line with the tenets of the period—all true enough, yet somehow failing in the face of bitter suffering and anguish. Analysis: Eliphaz begins gently with a word of apology (4:2) and surprise (3:5), recalls Job's perfect life (6); then come some general truths: the righteous man never perished in afflictions, whereas the wicked are punished (7—11). He has learnt in the course of a mysterious revelation that no man is righteous before God (12—21). He then turns to Job: resentment against God is disastrous (5:1—7) take to God (8), whose government is wonderful and good (9—16), whose chastisements lead to ultimate blessing (17—26); let Job take heed (27).

4:1. Eliphaz opens with a question. A common way of **b** opening the discussion; cf Eliphaz's questions in 15:2 and 22:2; Bildad's in 8:2 and 18:1; Zophar's in 11:1. **3—4.** 'You have instructed many', i.e. 'physician heal yourself!' The true force of *Yāsar* is to instruct morally, and here, to teach people to look upon their afflictions as a father's chastening. 'weak hands' . . . 'feeble knees' contrasting with the radiant messianic hope of Is 35:23. **5.** At the first taste of trouble, so it seems to Eliphaz, the onlooker, Job has broken down entirely. **6.** Eliphaz admits that Job has been 'perfect' and governed by the fear of the Lord, in the fullest Heb. sense cf 1:1.

7—9. 'Who that was innocent ever perished?' is the **c** assertion of a convinced and orthodox Jew. Then if the righteous do, in effect, suffer, it can only be disciplinary suffering. 'Eliphaz's theodicy is that of the old fashioned school, represented by Ps 37 (36)', Driver and Gray, ICC, 43. This psalm should be read as a parallel to our passage here. **8.** 'who plough iniquity'. This well represents *'awen*; the root idea is that of something empty, valueless, disappointing. **9.** The image is of a hot blast coming up from the desert, cf Hos 13:5; Is 40:7. **10—11.** A graphic figure describing the sudden break-up of the wicked in terms of the dispersion of a den of lions. In English we can say lion, lioness and lion-cub, but Heb. poetry has five words!

12—21. A mysterious vision in the night. This is **d** added to produce a certain impressiveness and awe in Eliphaz's utterance. 17—21 give the content of the revelation granted to Eliphaz. **12.** 'To me'. The Heb. emphasizes this. **13.** 'amid thoughts' (*se'ipîm*) meaning tangled, divided; BDB have 'disquietings' or excited thoughts. Render: *Amid worrying thoughts from visions of the night.* **19.** Human beings whose bodies are compounded of clay. The notion came into being from Gn 2:7; and cf 2 Cor 5:1. Man is even more fragile than a moth. **21.** The end of life is like a collapsing of a tent which occurs as soon as the pegs or stakes holding it in place, are plucked up. Note the parallel in Is 38:12. Other figures for the end of life are, the cutting of a thread (Jb 6:9); cutting the cord to which a lamp is suspended (Eccl 12:6).

5:1. 'Call now . . .' is not ironical, but simply an ani- **e** mated way of putting a supposition. 'holy ones' are the angels cf 15:15. The favourable intervention of angels was an article of faith in Judaism cf Zech 1:12; Tb 12:12; Test. of Levi 3:5. **2.** Since no man is just

366e before God, it is foolish to nurse resentment at misfortune. *Kā'as* is vexation or a feeling of chagrin, cf Prv 12:6. **4.** 'crushed in the gate' does not refer to a horrible accident, but to lawsuits or before magistrates who sat in judgement outside city gates, and could on occasion crush weakling and friendless folk. **5.** Corrupt v whose original sense can scarcely be recovered. RSV is as good as any. Targum paraphrases 'robbers will make spoil of their wealth', paralleled in Ps 109 (108):11; this furnishes a clue for the rendering of 5c. No emendation seems satisfactory.

6. Eliphaz's principle: travail and affliction are not from causes external to man; they are as natural as the upward flight of sparks. **7.** Literally 'as the sons of flame fly upward', i.e. sparks. A poetical figure for what cannot be otherwise. **8—16.** God's correction is for our good. **f** This passage forms a wonderful hymn of faith: God is great in his works, and alongside that Job's troubles are nothing, says Eliphaz. **11.** In the face of all manner of injustice, Eliphaz affirms his faith in a God who redresses wrongs. **13.** The only passage of Job cited in the NT (1 Cor 3:19). LXX read here '*He catches the wise in their thoughts*'. Thus St Paul either had another version, or made his own rendering. **14.** The perplexity and bewilderment of those whom God thwarts. They are like blind people groping about in the bright light of day cf 12:24—25. **17—26.** The happiest possible expression of trust in God. 'An idyllic and engaging picture of the happiness awaiting Job if he will receive God's **g** chastisement aright', Driver and Gray in ICC. **19.** 'From six troubles . . . in seven' . . . An ascending numeration of type common in OT, especially in proverbial literature. The meaning is that six would be a large number, but it is increased to seven. And the use of seven to denote the consummate character of things is quite frequent in the Bible and in ancient literature, cf Prv 6:16—19. Other figures in Sir 25:9; 50:27—28; Prv 30:18 and Amos 1:3—11. **23.** 'in league with the stones of the field'. Retain this reading with MT. Kittel's note suggests reading *benê* or *'adōnê*, meaning spirits or impish beings harmful to husbandry; a needless correction. To be 'in league with the stones of the field' is explained by Driver-Gray in ICC as a poetical figure, implying that stones will not accumulate to mar the field. Better explanation is to take it not of the many stones on almost any Palestinian field, but of the *boundary stones* or limit protectors.

367a 6—7 Job's answer to Eliphaz—Job starts by justifying his plaint which is caused by an excess of suffering (6:2—3) and which comes directly from God (4). Why be surprised if he moans (5—7). He makes a fresh appeal to death (8—10) for life is no longer worth while (11—13). Friends are unreliable and deceptive (15—21) and avoid giving help (22—23). Job invites them to give real reasons not empty speculations (24—26). Even the words of Job are just (28—30). He is unhappy because subject to life's conditions, a veritable mercenary (7:1—12), suffering day and night (3—5). He is heading for death and the land of no-return, (6—10). He cannot keep silence (11) and asks God directly, why these harrowings by day and by night? (12—14). Death is something desirable (15). Should fleeting man be dogged by God? (16—19); even if he sins, why not a little patience? (20—21). There is a striking contrast between the quiet masterlike, self-sufficient thesis of Eliphaz, and the very personal, pathetic and deeply felt answers of Job.

b **6:2** 'O that', *lô* in contrast to *'îm*, for wishes which cannot be fulfilled. *ka'as* 'vexation' (RSV) 'anguish' (CV) in parallelism with *hawāti*, (Kittel emendation) i.e.

'what has befallen me', or 'calamity'. **3.** Cf Prv 27:3. 'my **367b** words have been rash'. *Lā'û* is from a root (Heb. and Arab) meaning to speak too fast or without control. **4.** 'for the arrows of the Almighty are in me'. The '*immādî* is literally 'with me'. Used with varying nuances in 9:35; 10:12, 17; 13:19, 20 etc. In 28:14 it is used in parallelism with *bî* 'in me'. This is the meaning here. cf Hamlet's 'slings and arrows of outrageous fortune'. 'their poison', *hāmāh* is a poison of arrows and the venom of serpents cf Ps 58 (57):5; Dt 32:24, 33. **5.** Job again argues from the immensity of his pain to justify his plaint. He uses a proverbial phrase. The *dĕse'* (grass) cf Gn 1:11, is purposely contrasted with *belûl* or nourishment of domestic animals, cf Is 30:24, **6.** *tāpēl* is that which is tasteless. New (or late) Heb. of 'unsalted fish'. *rûr*, 'slime', only occurs again 1 Sm 21:13 for 'saliva'. Here the meaning is 'juice'. *hallāmût*, either (a) a name of a plant 'mallows', 'purslane' (RSV) or (b) with Dhorme, Jewish commentators, (e.g. Sa'adia) and CV 'the white of an egg' (So too AV RV).

7. 'appetite', literally 'my soul' as in Prv 10:3; 13:25; **c** 27:7; or it simply = 'I' as in CV. **8—10.** Cf Ps 119 (118): 50. **10.** 'of the Holy One': *qādôš*. The attribute *par excellence* of the thrice holy God in Is 6:3. Used as a substantive to designate God in Is 40:25; Hb 3:3; Sir 45:6—7. **13.** 'Advice' CV, 'resource' RSV. Neither strong enough; sense of *tušiyyāh* is '*sound counsel*'; almost a technical term of proverbial literature. As in 5:12; 11:6; 12:16. Admittedly the etymology and meaning are both uncertain. **17—19.** Metaphors are taken from the experience of Arab traders who return in summer to find dried up wadis instead of rushing streams. So the sympathy and understanding which Job expected have evaporated.

7. Ch 6 had remained on the plane of personal **d** grief; Ch 7 gives Job's more generalized view of human life. **1.** 'days of a hireling' cf 14:6. *Sākû* is used not only of a day's wage but also of the soldier or mercenary, cf 2 Sm 10:6; Jer 46:21. **3.** 'of emptiness'; RSV catches the force of *šau'*, cf Sir 30:17. 'a life of deception'. **6.** 'Without hope'. We can also render 'for lack of thread *tiqewâh* cf Jos 2:18, 21. So Dhorme. **7.** Job is addressing God directly (cf v 11). God in fact breathed the breath of life into man's nostrils Gn 2:7. Cf Ps 78 (77):39, where God remembers that sinners are 'flesh and a wind that goes and comes not back'. We need, as we read this, ever to bear in mind Job's complete ignorance of the reality of a future life. **8** 'behold', *šûr* is a word which **e** is characteristic of Job cf 17:15; 20:9; 24:5; 34:29; 35:5, 13, 14. Without going outside the book of Job, we can learn from it that Sheol is: a land of no return, 10:21; deep down, 11:8; hidden, 14:13; 24:19; 26:6; clouded with dust, 17:16; thick darkness, 10:21; 17:13; *rendez-vous* of all the living, 30:23, whatever their condition on earth 3:13—19.

Thus **9** he who goes down to Sheol shall not come up again. **16.** *mā'astî* 'I loathe it', ellipsis for 'I loathe my life' (RSV). Full phrase in 9:21. **17.** Evident recall of Ps 8:5 'but uttered in a mood of bitterness and not reverential wonder' (V. Reichert). Note '*enôš* or 'man' in the widest sense, 'human being'. **18.** 'visit': *pāqad* is not simply 'remember' or 'observe', but 'harass', 'pursue', 'weigh down upon'. The date of Ps 8, if this could be determined, would help towards determining the date of Job. There is, however, no certainty about the psalm date. **20.** 'Watcher of men'. Uttered by Job in wretchedness of soul. At the same time we are furnished with a true title of God who alone knows the secrets of men's hearts, who alone sees every moment of our lives.

367f **8:1—22 Bildad answers Job**—Bildad is more outspoken than Eliphaz, but with no new argument condemns Job's words as *mighty wind*, and holds firmly on to a traditional belief in commutative justice. God is Justice itself and would make Job prosperous if he were righteous; and if Job deserves joy, he will receive it. We can divide up the speech thus: 1—7 God is just, 8—10 the experience of former generations, 11—22 it is the godless who perish.

8:2. Bildad interrupts Job with an impatient cry, thinking no doubt that he had spoken too long. **3.** Bildad fires off a number of questions which set the stage for his developments. '*iwwet* is 'bend', 'curve', or 'pervert' as here. Used of falsifying a balance in Am 8:5. **4.** Bildad separates the case of Job from that of his sons. Each is responsible for his own deeds, as in Ezek 18:10, cf Dt 24:16. **5.** Bildad's arguments are as Eliphaz's: all is not lost for Job; he can modify the rigours of divine justice and recover his first prosperity. **6.** Bildad cannot bring himself to believe in Job's protestations; 'rightful habitation', cf Jer 21:23; 50:7; CV, 'rightful domain'; literally 'abode of your righteousness'. **8—10.** Brevity of life is a constant theme of Scripture writers, cf 14:2; Ps 102 (101):12; Ps 144 (143):5; Eccl 6:12.

g **8:13. 9.** Is a parenthesis, in part ironic. **11.** *Gōme'* the rush or papyrus, cf Ex 2:3; Is 18:2; 35:7. '*Aḥû*—reed-grass, ('Achu' is the demotic Egyptian word), cf Gn 41:2, 18 and perhaps in Hos 13:15. The Egyptian imagery here may serve to show that Bildad looked upon Egyptians as possessors of the most ancient wisdom, and more certainly suggests the poet's acquaintance with Egypt. **19.** 'this is the joy of his way' is the sense obtained without altering the text. '*there he lies rotting beside the road*' CV is based on Dhorme's reconstruction, reading m^esôs (for m^eśôś) from the root *sûs*, with the meaning 'rot' or moth-eaten. This gives a better adversative parallelism. If we retain RSV reading, Bildad is speaking sardonically; this is all the joy the wicked can have—green for a moment before the sun comes. **20—22.** These vv are very psalm-like in style. For 'they that hate you' cf Ps 9:14; 18 (17):18; 21 (20):9; 35 (34):19 etc. 'clothed with shame', cf Ps 25 (24):26; 132 (131):18 etc. 'tent' of the wicked—the supposedly nomad *milieu* of the Job story explains the use of *tent* for dwelling place or family.

368a **9—10 Job's reply to Bildad**—Job agrees with Bildad that God does not pervert justice, and with Eliphaz that no man can be just before God. How indeed can a man stand up against the Creator of the universe or meet him in judgement? Innocent or guilty he would lose his case. He who has received so much from God is being mysteriously and wantonly destroyed. Better would it have been to have died in the womb. At least let him have a brief respite before going to the eternal gloom of Sheol. Divide up thus: 9:1—3, Job's helpless nothingness before the mind of God: 9:14—35, faced with God himself he cannot have justice: 10:1—7, why indeed should God afflict him? 10:8—12, God's wonderful care in fashioning him and endowing him: 10:13—7, was this simply that he might afflict him?

b **9:2—4.** There is no arguing with God 'wise in heart and mighty in strength'. **5.** The great poetic themes are now developed, mountains, earth, stars, heavens, oceans, and finally the very minions of Rahab the mythological monster (v 13). *Mountains* just because of their association with the divine, cf the part played by Sinai, Horeb, Carmel, Sion, Olivet. Shaddai as a title of God originally perhaps meant 'mountaineer'. The Siqqurat of Assyro-Babylonian temples was in principle a sanc-

tuary. The great altar in the Temple of Solomon was on **368b** a mountain, cf Vincent RB 55 (1948) 444. **6.** 'pillars' are, in the common ideas of Heb. cosmology, considered to be supporting the world over Sheol and emptiness. A trembling or shaking of the pillars would be the earthquakes which are not unusual in Palestine. **7.** Even the sun is at the mercy of God. 'It rises not', not because of mist or fog, but because of eclipses. Amon of the Egyptians and Shamash of the Assyro-Babylonians also came to be considered as servants of God. 'seals up the stars' which are God's writing in the sky contrasts with Bar 3:34 of the joyous shining of the stars. Cf Ps 19 (18):4.

V. 9. The constellations are picturesque and mythologi- **c** cal in Heb. terminology as in modern speech. Ayiš is the Bear; Cimah is Arcturus or the Pleiades, Cesil, 'the fool' is Orion. 'Chambers of the South' RSV or '*constellations*' CV, are supposedly a group near the S Cross. *ha-ḥeder* the 'room' or 'chamber' designating the S occurs in 37:9. A poetic expression for the place where the winds are stored up. **13.** 'Rahab' is the chaotic ocean. The 'helpers of Rahab' are a demoniacal horde from E mythology. Cf ANET 62. Subject to God indeed; but the implication is, God might unleash them on Job.

14—24. A powerful tirade, which comes near to **d** blasphemy on Job's part. The imaginative language and background is that of the legal world and courts. Job is depicted as one 'in dock' and whose case is worse than hopeless ... **20.** 'my own mouth would condemn me' suggests (Steinmann) confessions extracted under torture. But '*Piv*' might be read (cf Kittel's note) and so we would translate *his* (God's) mouth would condemn me. **26.** 'like skiffs of reeds'. A reminiscence of Egypt and its Nile craft. **30.** 'cleanse my hands with lye' (bor or borith), soda or soap made from ashes of certain plants. Oil with soda soap was known in Babylonia before 2000 B.C.

10:1 Literally 'my soul loathes my life'. We could compare the Egyptian Dialogue of a dead man with his soul. ANET 405. **2.** 'do not condemn me', '*do not put me in the wrong*' CV, that is without formulating charges. The terminology is juridical. **3.** 'seem good to you', '*a pleasure for you*' CV, literally 'is it good for you?' i.e. have you some profit in acting thus? cf 13:9 for the turn of phrase. **4.** 'eyes of flesh' cf Is 31:3; 1 Sm 16:7. **5.** Another supposition. Only needs to be stated to be rejected. **6.** Job distinguishes 'iniquity' ('*guilt*' CV) arising from inadvertence, and wrong-doing or sin which is a deliberate violation of God's law. **10.** 'poured me out like milk'; of the formation of the foetus in primitive ideas of biology. **11—2.** The physical and spiritual gifts **e** which make up a whole man. The poet has no thought of the sinfulness of human flesh. The human body is a noble work of God; and behind and in the human functions of procreation and gestation lies the activity of God. **13.** 'your purpose' i.e. to chastise Job who was not a sinner. **17.** New witnesses, because God will charge him with new crimes. **18—22.** 'Why was I ever born?' A return to the theme of the original plaint, 3:11; cf 6:8. **19.** Cf Jer 20:17. **21.** Cf 7:10; 16:22 for the 'land of no return'. The same idea occurs in the Babylonian Descent of Ishtar *ll* 4—5; ANET 106—9. Our author was conversant with the great literature of his time and before.

Ch. 11 Zophar's first speech—Pitiless in respect of **f** Job's physical and spiritual torments, Zophar can only find it in him to rebuke Job for what he considers his boasts of innocence. He repeats the arguments of Eliphaz and Bildad cf e.g. 11:18—20 with 8:20—22. References to the 'empty man' and 'wild asses colt' (*jackass*, CV) serve to castigate Job's folly and unrepentant obstinacy.

368f **1.** Zophar 'the Naamathite' (*Naamaite*, CV) is less sensitive than the dignified Eliphaz and gentle Bildad. These differences in disposition or character bring variety and relief into the dialogues. **2.** 'full of talk'. Literally 'a man of lips' insinuating that Job, ventriloquist-like, makes words rise from his throat and not from his heart. cf Is 29:13. 'your babblings' cf Is 16:6; 48:30. **4.** *leqaḥ* is literally what one receives by tradition and so 'doctrine'

g or 'teaching'. **12.** Note the assonance *nābûb* ('stupid') with *yillābēb*, which last (in niphal) means *possession* of understanding. *pere' 'ādām* is borrowed from Gn 16:12 where it is said of Ishmael that he will be 'a wild ass of a man'. So with Dhorme (147—8) we would render this v, which would seem to be a proverbial saying:

'Thus a stupid man becomes wise,
Just as a wild ass's colt becomes a master ass.
(E. tr., p. 163.)

15. 'without blemish'; ('*in innocence*' CV). mûm is a physical or moral blemish; both here. **19.** 'entreat your favour'. Usually with reference to God. When used of men it means to win them over by favours, flatteries or caresses, cf Prv 19:6; Ps 45 (44):13. **20.** Literally 'the outbreathing of the soul' or death. Hence CV '*they shall wait to expire*'.

369a **12—14 Job's third reply—to Zophar**—Divide up thus: 12:1—6, Job rebukes his friends' wisdom; 7—25, God is omnipotent, what of his justice? 13:1—12, his friends are poor advocates for God's cause; 13—19, Job challenges God; 20—28, pleads with God. Finally comes a *qinah* or plaint. 14:1—6, man's frailty; 7—22, is there life after death? **12:1.** Job's word is bitter and biting: 'you are the intelligent folk, and when you die there will be no more wisdom!' **3.** Literally 'to me then is a heart'; 'heart' standing for understanding as usual in Heb. thought. **4.** Job expected sympathy from his friends; and

b this is the result. **9.** The use of the sacred name Yahweh for God here is anomalous. Kittel's text notes that several MSS read Eloah, and this may well have been the original reading. **10.** Note this recall of Gn 1, and cf Ac 17:28. **15.** A reference to the crossing of the Red Sea in the Exodus epic. **16—22.** God's infinite power as affecting individuals. **18.** 'the bonds of kings' ('*imposed by kings*', CV); *mûsar* properly denotes control, moral discipline or teaching. Kings are autocrats, but God could put an end to their rule and power over people. The waistcloth is the distinctive mark of a captive. God turns rulers into lowly prisoners. **19.** 'the mighty'. The meaning is literally 'the permanent ones' or those established in rank or authority, cf Am 5:25; Dt 21:4; Nm 24:21. 'Priests', a particular illustration of an established class. This was specially true of the Israelite priesthood of later times, which was hereditary. **20.** God overthrows the very basis of the sapiential tradition in Israel. **21.** 'loosens the belt' = incapacitates. Flowing garments would normally be gathered up for strenuous action. Cf 1 (3) Kgs 8:46; Is 5:27; Is 45:1. **24—25.** A climax in the utter collapse of wise and prudent counsellors or leaders.

c **13:1—5.** Resumes 12:3 'I have understanding as well as you'. **3.** 'I would speak to the Almighty'; '*I wish to reason with God*'. CV. Strongly emphatic. In 13—15 Job puts his resolution into practice and resolves to speak freely while maintaining his integrity. **4.** Literally '*plasterers of lies*' cf Ps 119 (118):69. **5.** Silence can be golden. Cf Prv 17:18. **7.** Heb. word order stresses contrast between their words and their object: 'Is it for God . . .' **14.** '*I will take my flesh between my teeth*' means 'I am at death's door'. The breath of life is conceived of as slipping out between the teeth. Job is simply saying that he may pass away

d at any moment. **15.** '*Slay me though he might*'. CV. Job

expresses his sense of the nearness of death. This was **369d** often borne in upon him, cf 7:6; 9:25; 10:20. **15b.** Job resolutely maintains his integrity before God. This is for him a ground of hope and the special glory of his tenacious faith. His faith and hope are that he will ultimately triumph and succeed with God's favour on his side. **18.** Language of the courts comes in here. **19.** '*make a case against me*' CV, cf Is 50:8. **20.** From here on, Job addresses God directly. **22.** Let God be plaintiff or defendant, as he wills. '*Call me*' CV, cf 9:16. Phrase is used of legal summons. **23.** There is no answer from God, so Job goes on to suggest that he is suffering beyond his deserts. Job, though 'perfect' (1:1) does not deny that he has sinned, but at the same time implies that God is punishing unjustly. **24.** 'Hide thy face'. Frequent biblical idiom, in good and bad connotations. Here in the sense of withdrawing his grace. Cf Ps 30 (31):8; Ps 13 (12):2; Ps 22 (21): 25. **25.** '*Will you harass a wind-driven leaf?*' CV, or put to **e** flight what scurries away of itself. This image is found in Assyro-Babylonian texts, cf Dhorme, *Choix de Textes Religieux Assyro-Babyloniens*, 363. Hymn to Ishtar, v 62. **26.** '*Bitter indictments*' CV or legal sentences. Not, as some have suggested, bitter-tasting medicines! 'faults of my youth' cf Ps 25 (24):7. **27.** Driver-Gray (ICC) and others discuss how one can be in the stocks *and* on a path . . . This is unreal exegesis. We simply have two juxtaposed figures to describe Job's harassed and circumscribed condition. Literally 'around the soles (roots) of my feet thou hast put a line', meaning simply 'take footprints'. **28.** Transposed by CV to after 14:2, which certainly is the better context and makes excellent sense. But there is no MS support, so retain in the usual place, with RSV. The person on whom all this attention has been lavished, is like a rotten thing and like a moth-eaten garment.

14:1—6 Elegy on man's frailty and brevity—Job **f** sees in his personal misfortune the lot of all humankind, cf 7:1. **1.** Even a patriarchal life, Gn 42:16, may be regarded as brief. Gn 47:9. **4.** Cf 4:17 and Ps 51 (50):5, 7. Usually interpreted as meaning man is sinful by nature, and so none can be free from sin. Therefore, argues Job, you cannot be so severe towards me. Job refers to man's basic uncleanness, as a palliative for his own case. The stress is on the physical (and so ritual) uncleanness from the moment of his conception cf Lv 15:19 and his birth Lv 12:2. But this uncleanness connotes a moral weakness, a propensity towards sin, and consequently traditional Christian exegesis has seen in this passage an allusion to original sin which is transmitted by generation cf Rm 5:12. For the knowledge of original sin in Judaism, cf Bonsirven, *Le Judaïsme Palestinien* . . . 2, 12—18.

6. As also vv 7 and 10, is a plea for a brief snatch **g** of relative happiness *before* death. The impossibility of enjoyment or bliss *after* death is a fundamental presupposition of the whole book of Job Cf 14:12—13. **7—9.** Is an allusion to the Palestinian practice of lopping off tops or other sections of trees that are old or decayed, and by so doing, fostering new shoots or growths. Cf Is 6:13. **7.** New life can spring from an old trunk: but man's sleep in death is fatal and final, knowing no awakening. **10.** Man is depicted, forcefully, as never rising out of death's everlasting grip. **13—16.** A vigorous flight of poetic fancy: if only God could send him to Sheol, just for a time, whilst his anger stalks abroad. If only it were certain that after a fixed period (13b) God would remember Job as he remembered Noah in the asylum of the Ark, cf Gn 8:1.

14. An all-important question forces itself upon (him) **h**

369h his mind or perhaps just hovers on the fringe of his mind—against all the known tenets of his contemporaries—so that anyway the *possibility* occurs to him '*were he to live again*' ... (CV). **15.** This sublime v suggests a loving dialogue between God and man. The greatness of Job lies in having thus transcended the limits of his own Jewish world, and outlined a reality whose full content can only be known in the New Israel of God. **16.** Job's momentary perception of a life after death now gives place to an obsessional sense of God dogging his every step. Read, as CV does '*and not keep watch for sin in me*' (following Kittel's note with the LXX). **18.** Even mountains collapse because of the elements or earthquakes. Much more so does man (v 19). **19.** Job is already far away from his momentary intuition, if such it was, of survival after death. **21.** (a) Usually explained in the sense that the 'self' of the dead person has no knowledge of what happens on earth yet is in some sense conscious of the pain and decay of the body in the grave as of the mournful existence of the soul in the underworld of Sheol. (b) Another interpretation has much in its favour. 'flesh' here means kith and kin as in Gn 37:27; Is 58:7. and '*nepeš*' or 'soul' is taken in the sense of serfs or servants, cf Gn 12:5; 14:21; 36:6; Ezek 27:13. (See note in Soncino Ed. p. 71). Then translate: '*Only his kin grieve after him only his servants mourn for him*'. Thus, Buttenweiser, who suggests that our author has ideas far in advance of his age.

15–21 THE SECOND CYCLE OF SPEECHES

370a The wholly inward drama of Job is carried a stage further. The contrast in character between Job and his three counsellors becomes more and more clearly marked. The 'friends' become more rigorous, less comprehending. Job's suffering is, if anything, intensified, but his faith and trust in God are yet more heightened. 'A large part of the spiritual splendour of this masterpiece is in the skilful psychological artistry that portrays the progress in thought of the stricken righteous man to a God who is 'Goel' or 'Vindicator' (cf V. Reichert in the Soncino Job, 72). We are not gainsaying those who hold that there is no action or movement in Job, and that therefore it is not a drama, but there is a wholly inward drama in the soul of Job whose faith and integrity were posited at the outset and come to be manifested as the poem proceeds.

b **15:1–35—The Second Speech of Eliphaz**—1–6, Job is reproved as being irreligious; 7–16, accused of presumption and irreverence; 17–35, the lot of the wicked is an evil conscience and then disaster. Eliphaz holds forth 'in the sonorous rhetoric and dignified tone of one advanced in years' (V. Reichert). Towards the end Eliphaz adopts a tone very noticeably different from that of his first speech. This is no doubt because he has grown convinced that Job's utterances really represent his settled mind and conviction. **2.** Job has referred to his own wisdom, boasted of it in 12:3 and 13:2. Eliphaz now makes fun of or disparages this 'wisdom', likening it to a 'Windy-science'. **4.** That 'fear of the Lord which is the beginning of wisdom'. '*you lessen devotion*' (CV); Job's way of taking could undermine religious belief in others. **5.** Cf Gn 3:1 of the serpent which was crafty, sly, astute. **7.** Fairly clear allusion to the text of Prv 8:22–31. It seems clear that Job is borrowing from Prv and not *vice-versa* (cf Dhorme, *Le Livre de Job*, 191). This is a small element towards the dating of the book of Job. **8.** 'have you listened in the council of God?' '*are you privy to the counsels of God*?' CV. The reference is to a court of God and attendant angels who form a 'council' or share in the more intimate secrets of revelation—this is the force of *sôd*. For God's court of angels cf 1 (3) Kgs 22:19; Jer 23:18, 22; Ps 89 (88):7. **10.** Eliphaz seemingly appeals to the resources of age and experience which would be greater than those of Job. Hebraic usage tended to assume that elders had more wisdom. **11.** Perhaps a reference to the mysterious message which Eliphaz claimed to have received from God in a 'still voice', cf 4:16. **12.** 'flash', i.e. with rage. **c** The word occurs only here and may be from the Aram. root *ramaz*—flash (with anger). **17.** Eliphaz now embarks on the positive part of his speech. He is giving ancient traditional lore and he also likes to argue from personal experience cf 4:8, 12; 5:3, etc. **19.** Our author puts in the mouth of Eliphaz a strictly and narrowly Israelite viewpoint. Job's opinions, he hints, are due to foreign, non-Hebrew influences. **20–35.** Eliphaz now expounds the theory of the ancients referred to. He favours the idea that man brings about his own misfortune by sinning. **22.** 'destined for the sword', feels that he is marked out a victim of the sword. Some have explained the 'sword' as a symbol of divine retribution, cf Is 31:8. **25–27.** The figure is that of a warrior making an assault against God. **29.** 'strike root in the earth'. Better, '*bend to the earth*'. The figure is that of corn heavily laden with grain or of fruit plants or trees whose boughs are borne down to earth by the weight of fruit. But one may read with Dhorme *salemô* for *minᵉlām*, and translate with CV: '*with no shadow to lengthen over the ground*'. **34–35.** Forms the conclusion to all that tradition has to say about the wicked or unbelievers. **35.** Is found almost verbatim in Is 59:4; Ps 7:14; a proverbial saying.

16:1–17:16 Job's Reply to Eliphaz—Mostly a **d** musing monologue; thus 16:6–17, 20–22, 17:1ff, 5–9, 11–17 are not obviously addressed either to his friends or to God; and in 16:18 it is the earth that is appealed to. Perhaps divide up thus: 16:1–5, Job could speak as his friends have done; 6–17, the horror of what he has suffered at God's hands; 18–17:5, his blood cries to heaven and God is his Vindicator; 6–16, again God's harsh treatment; Job is as good as dead in Sheol. **2.** 'miserable,' literally 'conforters of woe'. **4.** 'shake my head'. An insulting gesture, as we can see in Is 37:22; Ps 22 (21):7 and supremely in Mt 27:39; Mk 15:29. **10–17.** A horrifying picture of torture in body and mind, unrelieved by the Saviour's enduring love in Christian tradition. **12.** 'I was at ease'. A reference to the happy and prosperous life in 1:2 or better still as depicted nostalgically in 29:2. Then a new metaphor: God is conceived of as an archer shooting at a defenceless target. cf 7:20; Lam 3:12. **13.** 'his archers', better than '*arrows*' of CV, cf Jer 50:29. **18–19.** This very important passage furnishes the clue to some solution at 19:23–27. Job in the flash of a momentary prayer prays to be saved from the grave, or from having no time to call out before God his Witness and Advocate on his behalf who will testify to his utter uprightness. This Witness ('*ēd*) and Advocate (*sāhēd*) are one with the Goel of 19:25, and he is God who knows all and can testify to Job's innocence and see it vindicated. **20.** Not God, but *friends* it is who scorn me ... **21.** The sublime expression of Job's faith and confidence still in God. cf 9:32–33. There is no arbiter between God and Job; God's arbitration is only exercised between man and man. **22.** The settled conviction of Job, 'I shall go down where I shall not return' covers up the momentary flash of faith. God's sudden theophany in a storm supports the interpretation that Job never

0d wholly abandoned his belief in God who was to vindicate him.

e **17:3** 'give surety' literally *strike hands*. An idiom frequently used in Prv for the ratification of an agreement. The imagery is that of trade transactions. There is the same 'splitting' of God into two parties: God who persecutes Job and wrongs him, and God who would become surety for Job and undertake to see his cause righted with God, cf 16:21. **5.** Dhorme has '*One announces a parting of lots to his friends*' (while his children's eyes fail). This seems the most satisfactory rendering of the text without alteration. **9.** Job here contradicts Eliphaz's statement in 15:4 'you are doing away with the fear of God and hindering meditation before God'. Despite his sufferings and bewilderment Job holds on all the more strongly to his ideal of faithful innocence. 'This passage is the most surprising and lofty in the book' (Davidson). **10.** 'Come on again! return to the attack' says Job; 'you will no more prevail with arguments or assumed confidence'. **11—16.** The reflections of one near-despair yet not despairing. **13.** 'if I spread my couch in Sheol', cf Ps 139 (138):8. Note that Psalmist says: 'Thou art there . . .' **14.** *šaḥaṭ*—pit or grave, Koehler Baumgartner *Lexicon* ad voc. the worm, cf 21:26. **16.** This speech ends with the inevitability of Sheol as does 16:22. The 'bars of Sheol' does not occur elsewhere, but the 'gates of Sheol' is in Is 38:10. This hardly means more than Sheol simply; but later Christian tradition was to see a special significance in 'Gates of hell'.

f **18:1—21 Second speech of Bildad**—Bildad indignantly asks why are we treated as beasts (1—4); manifestly calamity and disorder overtake the wicked (5—21). Bildad's speech is replete with proverbial sayings and wise saws. The wicked man's downfall goes by stages: his light goes out (5—7), progress of the downfall (8—11), the final scenes (12—14), extinction of race and name (15—17), and men stand in awe and horror at his fate and memory (18—21) (Davidson). **5.** Light is not only an image of life, cf 3:20; 7:1; but also a symbol of happiness, 11:17. *šᵉḥîḇ*, aram. form for 'flame' cf Dn 3:22; 7:9; 'flame of fire' recurs in Sir 8:10; 45:19. The light burning in a tent or house symbolizes continued prosperity, cf 21.17, 1(3) Kgs 11:36; Prv 13:9; 24:20. **6.** Cf 29:3 where by contrast light was sign of prosperity. **7.** In prosperity and security he walked with firm, wide steps. Now he is constrained and cramped, cf Prv 4:12. **8.** Cf Prv 19:9. **9—10.** Hebrew is rich in words for a trap or snare. The wicked one is caught in them all! **9.** Seized by the heel, as in the story of the birth of Jacob, Gn 25:26. **15.** Weeds and growths will over-run his dwelling place, and strange beasts, too. Cf the picture of the desolation in Is 34:11. **16.** 'root and branch' originally meaning the entire family, has become proverbial for something *totally* done. Cf Am 2:9. **17.** No name upon the earth—perhaps the hardest fate of all. No children and nothing to be remembered by. **19.** The reversal of the blessings in Dt.

371a **19:1—29 Job replies to Bildad's second speech**—Divide up 2—6, 7—12, 13—19, 20—27, 28—29. The whole could be called a remonstrance of Job with his friends and God, and an appeal, despite the grave, to God and posterity. **2—6.** Job's plaint is still very noble; why outrage him since he is innocent? **3.** Ten times, i.e. repeatedly cf Gn 31:41. **4.** Exact force of this is not clear. Does it admit error or deny it? 'error' is a mild term, cf Ps 19 (18):13; for the wearing out of Job, cf 16:7—11. **6.** In other words, Job boldly states that his sufferings are due to the Will of God. Neither pest nor furies, nor human nor demoniac agencies are to be held responsible. Post-exilic Jewry hesitated: Who made you ill? devils or God?

Job seemingly does not hesitate. 'his net' for the *images* **371a** cf Lam 3:9; Hos 17:11. **7.** Cry 'violence' cf Jer 20:8; Hb 1:2. **12.** Images from siege-works and oncoming troops. **13—19.** All the society that normally surrounded and caused happiness to Job is now in revolt and embittered *against* him. cf Contrast of chh 29 and 30. It has been **b** pointed out that this whole scene supposes Job living at home and not on the village dunghill. However, we need not expect our poet to be meticulously consistent all through. Or it might be argued, his house had not been destroyed, though all else had. **19.** 'intimate friends', literally 'of my circle', (*sôḏ*), and perhaps we should imply confidential friends. **20b.** (a) '*I gnawed my skin with my teeth*' for this rendering cf Driver, 'Problems in the Hebrew Text of Job' VTS 3, *Wisdom in Israel and in the Ancient East*. (b) LXX offers a possible variant— 'my bones are gripped with spikes' or 'teeth'. 21 cf Lam 1:12. **23—24.** If Job's words could be preserved for future generations, *they would be proved true*. In other words he is asserting and emphasizing his conviction of faith. Inscribed leaden tablets and the inlaying of rock-cut inscriptions with lead were used in antiquity, cf Tac. *Annals* ii, 69; Pausanias, Pliny, etc. **25.** '*my vindicator*' **c** (CV) Redeemer RSV, with Vindicator in n. The 'Goel' in Heb. is primarily the next of kin who is bound by various obligations towards his kinsman, e.g. (i) to redeem him from bondage and debt, Lv 25:48—55. (ii) to avenge his death. Dt 19:6, 12. In Is 40—66 God is frequently called the Goel of Israel, cf 41:13; 43:14; 44:6; 47:4; 48:17; 49:7. For Isaiah it is a name of God. 'stand upon' literally *he will arise*. The word is used in a legal sense: to *come forward* as a witness or judge. 'at the last' is the rendering for '*aḥᵃrôn*; Koehler Baumgartner, *Lexicon* renders as *the last*. This seems to approach Kissane's suggestion that the word is in parallelism to *Gō'ᵃlî* ('redeemer'). Kissane goes further and renders 'The Eternal', appealing to Is 44:6 and 48:12. God, according to Job takes no notice of his misery now, but he will come *down to earth* and take notice. Perhaps a premonition of the Incarnation or condescension of God. **26.** 'without my flesh' or '*from* my flesh'. **d** The meaning of this is uncertain. CV places 26a after 27, and omits 26b as a duplicate. This may be justified. Certainly the text is difficult. The passage must be interpreted in the light of parallels in 16:19—22; 17:3; and 31:35—37, in which Job gives expression to his ever-growing conviction that in the end God himself will appear as his Vindicator and vouch for his innocence.

The many different interpretations are of two main types; Job expects an intervention of God either (a) *before*, or (b) *after*, his death. About (a) there is no theological difficulty, though the terms used do not seem to fit this interpretation so well. If we pursue (b), we could argue that Job will see God rise up in his defence when he is *in the state of disincarnation* ('without my flesh'). It was held that consciousness could function in some sense in Sheol. Popular beliefs clung to the idea that the shades haunted the tombs and could return momentarily upon earth, as in the story of Samuel's appearance to the witch of Endor, 1 Sm 28:3—20. Further light is thrown on these beliefs by Dt 1:8 which forbids calling on spirits, etc. For Job this momentary rise from Sheol would simply enable him to see the vindication of God's purposes, the punishment perhaps of certain individuals. If we interpret the text thus we can better understand the strong wording about seeing God contemplatively, '*eḥᵉ zeh 'elôah*, (26). The dead, being without eyes of flesh, only 'see' God in a special way (Samuel in 1 Sm 28:15 is compared to an Elohim). Thus

H

371d we explain how Job can momentarily rise to an exalted conviction and then plunge down again and continue to feel the anguish of his miserably human condition; for the course of his earthly existence is not one whit changed by this, cf 23:14.

No doubt Job's own mind is unclear, and we might have a fair presentation of his thought if we put 26 in the conditional: 'And were I, my skin being destroyed, to see him—if in my flesh I could see God—him whom I would see would be at my side; in my eyes he would no longer appear as my enemy'.

The exegesis of the Fathers of the Church, up to and including St Jerome, was largely based on the Gr. version or the Latin derived from it. The word '*anastēsai*' translates the Heb. word 'to stand up'; but this word also means 'resurrection' in Christian language. This caused this text to be associated with others when the doctrine of the resurrection was propounded. Thus Clement of Rome cites it alongside Ps 3:6; Origen with Is 52:10; Cyril of Jer and Amb relate it to Jb 14:7—10. Against these are Justin, Iren and Tert, none of whom associate this passage with the doctrine of the resurrection. Chrys several times urges that Job in this passage is not speaking of resurrection but of healing. Jer, however, formally affirms 'Job here prophesies the resurrection of the body in such a way that no one has written on this subject in so clear and certain a manner'. His exegesis, together with the Vg text, long dominated Christian interpretation. The puzzle remains: Jer. knew Heb. well, yet seems to side with the LXX on this. His interpretation of Vg remains as a witness to traditional belief in the resurrection, not as a witness to an older exegesis of the text.

e **27c.** 'My heart faints within me'! CV puts with v 26 and renders '*my inmost being is consumed with longing*; literally 'my reins fail'. The word used in 16:13, of the vital organs of the body pierced by God's arrows, cf Lam 3:13. (Lam 3:1—18 is a very Job-like plaint, with radiant hope in v 19). Then frequently, in a figurative sense of the seat of the emotions, cf Ps 16 (15):7; 73 (72):21; Jer 12:2; Prv 23:16. **29c.** 'judgement': correct both RSV and CV, reading *šaddai* (Kittel's second alternative in note ad loc). This represents *šdyn* in Ugaritic and *šadūya* or *šaduianu* in Akkadian; cf L. R. Fisher in VT 2, (1961) 342—43. Translate: '*They should fear the sword and the punishment of the sword as a result of rage. They should be mindful of these things in order that they might know the Almighty*'.

f **20:1—29 Zophar's Second Speech**—Zophar is irritated. The gulf between him and Job is widening (vv 2—3). He then goes on to describe, almost maliciously, the momentary triumph and catastrophic fall of the wicked. Their prosperity cannot endure; only disaster and death await the wicked (4:29). **2.** Zophar has waited long enough in exasperating silence, forced to hear words which have deeply wounded him. cf 19:2 and 19:29. **3.** He may be thinking especially of 19:29 or the dire warning which Job uttered against his friends. He claimed to speak from an understanding heart, not 'empty words', like Job in 11:2. **5.** The triumph of the wicked is short, as in Ps 37 (36):2. Job had asked for his words to be graven (for ever) upon a rock: Zophar, replies by pointing out the short-lived fate of the wicked, and is thinking perhaps of the taunt against the king of Babylon: 'how the oppressor has ceased . . .' (Is 14:4*a*). **6.** 'his height'. his pride (CV) is interpretative, cf 13:11. **7.** The crudity of Zophar's term is paralleled in 2 (4) Kgs 9:37. There is no need to disguise it in translation, as does CV '*like the fuel of his fire*'. **10—22.** Is a crude picture of gluttony,

of a type not unknown to Wisdom literature, cf Sir 37 31:12—17; 37:26—30. **11.** Though youthful vigour 'fills his bones', still it will be buried with him in the dust, i.e. he will die suddenly at the height of his vigour. **12ff.** Is a forceful description of the attractiveness of sin. **13.** Concealment of his hidden sins. **15.** Crude figure to convey the fact that a rich man must sooner or later give up his riches. The LXX translators, shocked at Zophar's expression have here substituted an 'angel' for 'God'. **16—17.** Asps . . . cf Dt 32:33. **17.** 'rivers' is perhaps 'quarters', 'division' (*peľaggôt*), 'honey and curd' symbolic of plenty. cf Ex 3:8. **20.** The insatiable anxiety and cravings of the greedy and avaricious. **22.** Passing from plenty to destitution in a trice, cf Ps 92 (91):8 for a sudden reversal of fortune. **23—29.** Terrors, earth, heavens, fire, darkness, all the weapons of God are turned against him, all the apocalyptic imagery, including the deluge (v 28).

21:1—34 Job's sixth reply, to Zophar—Job begins **37?** by demolishing the arguments of Zophar and the other friends. He maintains, from experience, that the wicked prosper, grow old, die in peace. 'Turn to me and be astonished' (2—6); 7—16, the wicked live in prosperity; 17—21, *de facto* misfortune rarely comes upon the wicked; 22—26, the mystery of Providence: 27—33, fate of the evil man; 34, final word of Job. **2.** Repeats, textually 13: 17. In 16:2 Job had noted that his friends were 'poor consolers'. **4.** Job senses more and more that he is 'up against God', 'my complaint'. cf 7:11; 9:27; 10:1; 23:2. **5.** 'hand upon mouth' is a natural gesture of those who would keep silence, cf 29:9; 40:4; Mi 7:16. In 2—6 Job invites their attention to the shocking truth which he is about to expound, viz: that the wicked (rather than the good) are prosperous. **7.** The theme of the whole ch is **b** stated in this couplet: it is the problem, unavoidable and generated by the facts of experience. Job's questions are strikingly like those of Jer 12:1—12. Jeremiah's language seems to have directly affected that of Job, cf Dhorme, *Livre de Job*, p. cxxxv, for a discussion of this point. 'reach old age', as opposed to Zophar's suggestion that they die young or suddenly, cf 20:5. **8.** Job boldly applies to the wicked the very terms traditional believers applied to the just! **10.** Fecundity of cattle is looked upon as a blessing of God. cf Ps 144 (143):14. **11.** Cf Zech 8:5, where the happiness of a city is expressed by boys and girls playing in its squares. **13.** Seemingly shocking blasphemy in the ears of the pious. **16.** 'the counsel of the wicked', as in Ps 1:1. Another allusion to this psalm is in v 18. **17.** 'lamp of the wicked' echoes 18:5*a* 'indeed the light of the wicked shall be put out'. (Bildad) Job seemingly maintains that it is rare for a wicked person to sink from affluence to abject poverty. **18.** 'how often' is understood again here. Job denies the contention of his friends that the wicked man vanishes completely. cf 15:30; 18:16ff, 20:7.

19. A further objection is thrust forward: he may **c** not suffer himself, but at least his children are punished. **20.** Let him experience it himself. **21.** In Sheol, the wicked have no knowledge of things of earth; and so they are not effected if their children suffer. cf 14:21—22. Eccl 9:5—6. **23—25.** One dies full of good things, another full of bitterness. They are alike in the dust and the same worm covers them, cf Eccl 2:14. This is Job's description of himself in 3:20 and 7:7. **27.** Job senses that his friends are hinting at his own former greatness, as pictured in 29. **32.** The wicked man has his place and memorial tomb, just like others, and indeed crowds file before it (33). **34.** In a word, Job concludes, facts are against your assertions.

22—31 THE THIRD CYCLE OF SPEECHES

The pattern of the colloquies is varied here. There is no need to assume, as so many do, that there was originally a regularity of pattern or structure which has got disturbed. Simply make 27:7—10 and 13—23 into Zophar's third speech. Ch 28 is a wisdom poem inserted at this point, a splendid composition. Chh 29—31 are Job's final summary of his cause, which might be called *apologia pro vita sua*. Without tampering with our received text we are able to observe with sufficient clarity the forward march of spiritual drama.

b **22:1—30 Third speech of Eliphaz**—This does not answer the points made by Job in Ch 21. Eliphaz is guided by cold a priori reasoning. God cannot be punishing Job for his piety, and God has nothing to gain from punishing him; therefore Job's great sins must be the cause of his sufferings and misfortunes. **4.** 'your piety' or 'your fear of God', as in 4:6 and 15:4, both passages from speeches of Eliphaz. **6.** Eliphaz starts listing a series of faults which would, he thinks, explain Job's present misfortune. Clothes, food, and drink are basic essentials and so the first objects of justice and charity, cf Mt 25:42—43. The faults listed by Eliphaz go directly against the prophets' precepts, cf eg Is 58:7; Ezek 18:7 **8.** As if the land belonged to the man of might ('*îš zerô'a* strong-fisted fellow or bully).

c Note here a genuine feeling for social justice and for the 'underdog' as elsewhere in Job **9.** Widows and orphans have a right to special treatment cf Ex 22:21; Dt 24:17; Is 1:7 **12.** Prepares for the words attributed to Job in 13—14. This v also recalls Is 40:24—27. Eliphaz purposes to suggest that in Job's mind is the idea of a God behind the clouds or too far away to occupy himself with human beings. Eliphaz attributes to Job the sentiments and language of the wicked in Ps 73 (72):11; 94 (93):7; Is 29:15; Ezek 8:12. In so doing Eliphaz is attacking a whole school of thought. **14.** Thick clouds veil God from mankind; therefore Eliphaz's point is reinforced. **15—16.** Refers to the period of the Flood. **19—20.** The just break out in cries of joy at the disappearance of the wicked ones. **21.** Eliphaz remains consistent to his viewpoint and ends with moral exhortation tinged with material utilitarianism. This is in part redeemed by the sublimity of the poetry.

For the translation 'agree with' (RSV) cf W. B. Bishai, 'Notes on HSKN in Job 22:21', JNES 20 (1961) 258—259; *hasken* in the text is explained by a Ugaritic root *skn*, meaning 'dwell' cf C. H. Gordon, *Ugaritic Manual* III. 1830. **22.** Cf Prv 4:10 from the mouth of God comes true teaching. 'Torah' is not specifically the Law, but teaching given by God cf Is 1:10.

26—30. Describes the joyous result of the rectification of all before God in characteristically Heb. terms.

d **23:1—24:25 Job's Seventh Reply**—**4.** Is a legal phrase meaning: 'set out my case in defence'. **8—9.** N, S, E, W. He is not there. This contrasts strongly with the more usual Heb. idea of God's omnipresence as eg in Ps 139 (138):7—12. **10.** Explains why God does not search for Job. It is because God, anyway, knows *all*, and so knows that Job is not guilty. So why insist upon a trial in order? Job would appear to have the quiet conviction of a serene conscience. This would come easily to the lips of an upright Hebrew; for the Christian there is always the fear of failing in humility. **10—12.** Forms a protestation of innocence. **14.** The unknowable future. **15—16.** Somehow Job's will has collapsed. Ch 23 deals rather with Job's personal problem, for Job cannot find marks of a righteous providence in God's dealings with himself. In Ch 24 the problem is seen in terms of the world in general.

24:1—12. Might be entitled 'God's indifference to **373e** injustice' **1.** '*times of judgement*' implies assize-times for sitting in judgement and dispensing rights among men. That God does appoint times for judgement is seen in Ps 75 (74):2—3.

2—8. A wonderful description of the wrongs which could be endured by a 'suffering proletariat'. A parallel passage, conceived and expressed in a very different tone is in 30:3—8.

All this throws light on the Hebrew society of a particular period, as on the author's mind. It witnesses to his solicitude for the 'submerged tenth' and a developed social sense. It might also be a mark of later Jewry, and contribute towards the difficult subject of the dating of Job, cf § 361 *l*. **8.** Drenched by the rain, as one can be **f** in the short Palestine winter, poor folk cling (*ḥābaq*) to rocks because they have no other shelter. **12—25.** After the wretchedness of the country, crimes in towns are vividly depicted. Vv 18—24 are particularly obscure. Dhorme maintains that they are no part of Job's speech, but should be inserted between vv 13 and 14 of Ch 27 in Zophar's speech.

Better to take 13—17 as 'evil-doers enumerated' and 18—25 as 'what is the fate of evil-doers?' RV margin inserts 'ye say' at beginning of v 18, suggesting that the ensuing vv represent the view of friends answering Job. Better understand as the answer of friends introduced with some irony by Job. Thus the sinner is borne away by the stream, the wicked man vanishes in Sheol, etc.

25:1—6. Third Speech of Bildad—A meditation on **374a** the lowliness of man alongside God Almighty. Bildad makes no attempt to answer Job, but simply dwells on the perfection of God.

3. God is likened to an army commander with limitless forces, 'troops' or hosts. Job had already spoken of such in 19:12 **4a.** Verbatim Job's words in 9:2. Bildad argues as Eliphaz in 4.17—19 and 15:14—16. The same thought comes in Eccl 7:20. **5.** Light is a symbol of purity and God is supreme Light. **6.** The same parallel of 'maggot' and 'worm' is found in Is 14:11. Hardly could the wretchedness of a human condition be better expressed, cf Ps 22 (21):7 'I am a worm and no man'. There is no need to *add* to the speech of Bildad. It remains simply, as it was meant to be, a short poem.

26:1—14. Job's Reply—**2.** Irony comes out forcefully **b** in Job's anguish. **3.** The words are particularly biting after Bildad's speech of only five vv. **5—14.** An exposition of the greatness of God. God's power and presence reach from Sheol to heaven above and *all* is his. **6.** Sheol is stripped, laid bare before him. Yet nothing is more mysterious than this kingdom of the shades: cf 10:21—22. The idea of this v is also found in Prv 15:11. Job had asked to be hid in Sheol to escape the eyes of God (14:13), but in vain. **7.** The 'N', *Ṣāpôn*, a celestial region in the 'N quarter' around which the stars appear to pivot. 'Empty space' *tōhû*, here, is not desert as in 6:18 and 12:24, but emptiness or vacuum as in Gn 1:2. **10.** Cf Prv 8:27. God, in creating, traces a circle over the face of the deep; *ḥāqaq* is to engrave, trace, mark out as in 14:5 and 19:23. Earth was conceived of as a mass surrounded by Ocean, analogous to the Apsu of the Babylonians. **12.** Rahab is the mythical sea-monster cf 9:13 and Ps 89 (88):11. **14.** 'The nervous brevity and sublimity of these words are unsurpassed' (Davidson, CBSC, ad loc). **14b.** Retain with RSV, Kittel, Dhorme, etc. There is no reason for suppressing this clause. This has the text taken up by St Thomas when proceeding to the sublimities of revealed truth of *Contra Gentiles* iv, i, Proemium.

27:1—6, 11—12 Job's speech continues—**2.** 'as God **c**

374c lives'. The phrase was used in oaths and adjurations. So too with the names Elohim and Yahweh in 1 Sm 14:39, 45; 2 Sm 2:27. Dhorme translates 'par Dieu', an old French oath formula. 'My right'. Because God will not hear his cause, Job is plunged into bitterness. He has already spoken of his bitterness of soul in 7:11; 10:1, and cf 3:20 and 21:25. 11—12. Form the closing words of Job's speech.

d 27: 7—10, 13—23 Zophar's Third Speech which is on the theme of Zophar's detestation of the wicked. 7. It is understood that he wishes ill to his enemy, and he can wish him nothing worse than being 'as the wicked'. 8. Tells of the God-abandoned state of the wicked. 9. Ṣārāh is 'distress', 'straits'. The wicked person has cut himself off from God's friendship. 13. Repeats almost verbatim Zophar's words in 20:29. 14. Is the reverse of what Job had previously maintained in 21:8. 15. 'buries'. Literally 'in death', but death here, as in Jer 15:2; 18:21 means death by pestilence. The wailing of women was omitted at funeral rites in times of pestilence. This one line occurs in Ps 78 (77):64b, from which it may be quoted. Contrast what Job had said about the burial of the wicked in 21:32. 16. For silver like dust cf Zech 9:3 19. All is a transient or evanescent dream. Riches vanish overnight. 20. As do the terrors of 22:10 22. The E wind or scorching Sirocco from the desert, cf 15:2. Used in Scripture to denote a destructive force. Vv 22 and 23 are omitted by CV, but they are to be retained with the MT, RSV, etc. 23. Clap and hiss in derisive mockery or contempt, cf Lam 2:15.

e 28:1—28 The Mystery of Wisdom which is inaccessible to man—Most critics have treated this ch as a separate poem, and a few have conceded that it might be by the same author as that of the rest of Job. It is possible to look upon it as a scene on its own, with a due place in the drama or poem as a whole, a sort of pause before Job's long monologue, 29—31. Another view is that of Tournay, RB 64 (1957), 321—39: this would place ch 28 after 24:25, and make one poem of 24:18—28:28. This arrangement would eliminate the abrupt start of ch 28; however we cannot assume (as too many do) that the original poem of Job was smoothly structured all through. If we read it as a wisdom poem on its own, then it has parallels in Prv 1—9; Wis 1:4—6; 6:12—9:18; Sir 1:1—10; 4:11—19; 14:20—15:10; 24:1—29. The poem is possibly incomplete, starts ex abrupt, and is irregular in metre.

f Structure and Content: 1—4 man untiringly digs for gold, silver, etc. 5—6, 9—11 the surface yields foods, the interior yields precious stones. 7—8, 12—14 the abode of Wisdom is inaccessible. 15—19 Wisdom cannot be purchased, cf Prv 3:14—8:10. 20—24 yet it is known to God who knows all. 25—28 God's creative plan for g man, who is to fear God. Note how vv 12 and 20 seem to serve as refrains, and lead up to a conclusion in v 28.

1—4. Breaking up quartz blocks and 'washing' for gold dust were known to antiquity. The copper mines of the Sinai peninsula are frequently referred to in Egyptian inscriptions. In the Bible the only other reference to mining and minerals is in Dt 8:9 where the glories of the promised land are listed, and among these: 'a land whose stones are iron, and out of whose hills you can dig copper'. 5. Overhead are the peaceful operations of agriculture, and the production of fruits, bread etc. cf Ps 104 (103):14. Contrasting with this is confusion and disorder underground. These are caused by fire and blasting, floods and the like. 6. 'sapphires' or lapis lazuli cf v 16. It plays a large part in the jewel-craft

of the Egyptians. 7. 'falcon' or kite. A keen-sighted 374 unclean bird is meant. But the identification is not certain. Dhorme translates it 'vautour' cf Lv 11:4, Dt 14:13. 12. The refrain. Note the parallelism of wisdom h and understanding as in Prv 9:10. 14. Deep or Ocean or Abyss—used as poetical and mythological terms cf Ps 107 (106):23. 16. Solomon got gold from Ophir; cf 1 (3) Kgs 9:28 and 10:11 17. glass in antiquity was sometimes looked upon as precious as gold cf Aristophanes, Acharnians 73. 18. Coral and crystal. cf Ezek 27:16; Prv 24:7. Once again there is uncertainty about the precious stone or gem meant. Yet the terms rā'môt and penînîm recur frequently in Prv 3:15; 8:11; 20:15; 31:10; Sir 7:19; 30:15. Coral is certainly abundant in the Red Sea region around Aqabah, and there are pearl fisheries. 25. God at the outset of creation 'weighed out the wind' or gave it weight so that it could part the waters. This was held by Rabbis as an example of God's providential care and forethought about all the universe and its purposeful workings. 27. (as already in v 23) we have a personification of wisdom. Wisdom is the plan of the universe in God's mind. God contemplates it, perfectly grasps its nature and essence. He alone is perfectly in possession of wisdom—or at least up to now the poet has insisted that wisdom is an exclusive possession of God. But now, suddenly with 28 a new idea is introduced, that of wisdom among men or something given to man and in which man can participate, cf Prv 8, especially vv 35—36. For the notion of wisdom accessible i and inaccessible to man, cf the sublime text of Bar 3: 9–4:4 (wisdom is inaccessible yet God reveals it to his favoured people Israel). Alongside this ch should go a careful reading of Prv 8 and 9; Sir 24; Wis 7:22—8:1.

The personification of wisdom is a literary device, as in Prv 14:1. It was developed after the Exile, the more so as polytheism was no longer a menace to the religion of the Jews. The markedly sapiential character of this ch shows that it is post-exilic, as indeed is the whole poem of Job.

29:1—31 40 Job's Monologue, a summing up—Job 375 surveys his life and once more protests his innocence. 29. Is a reverie on the days of old. It is a tableau of prosperity and of the enjoyment of success and esteem. These vv are very valuable to us as a picture of an ancient Hebrew ideal: 'prosperity is the blessing of the OT, adversity of the New' (Francis Bacon). Perhaps too, a momentary musing on the past was a relief from the miseries of the present which are set out finally in Ch 30. A solemn oath and protestation of innocence closes the monologue (31). 29:1. It is best perhaps to translate 'and Job continued b proverbwise and said:'. This keeps close to the MT. 2. The ground of all his happiness is God's guardianship, a great biblical idea, cf Nm 6:24, Ps 16 (15):1; 91 (90):11; 121 (120):7. Contrasting forcibly with this is Jb 13:27 'for you put bitter things on record against me, and send punishment on me for the sins of my early years'. 3. In the past the radiance of God had shone upon him cf Ps 18 (17):29 4. The Heb. suggests the time of fruits or autumn of his life 'when the fruits of God's favour and his piety were being gathered' (Driver-Gray). A very Jewish trait is perhaps shown here: seeing and feeling some result from piety prolonged. For besôd read besôk, cf Kittel's note, with the LXX 'when God screened my tent'. 5. At the height of his prosperity, and so, in Job's mind when God was with him. For 'children' read rather 'young men' (neʿārîm) and recall ch 1. 6. We have here not simply a poetic exaggeration, but also undoubtedly an allusion to rock-cut oil presses and vats with their channels. The remains of these are still visible in many

75c parts of Palestine where olive groves are found. **7.** Job's estate seems to have been near a large town, and in that large community he was held in the highest esteem, both in its affairs and in public gatherings. For the square or broad-place, cf Ez 10:9; Neh 8:1. **8—9.** What respect, esteem, and authority were his! Princes and the highest dignitaries showed respect for Job. **11.** Rather than arousing envy, Job's happiness was a source of blessing; he won the hearts of all by his good deeds. **12—17.** He was able to do good, and did good, and got a good name for so doing. **16.** Job interested himself in pleas for justice, **d** even of men who were strangers to him. **17.** MT literally 'jaw-teeth'; RSV 'fangs'. The wicked are likened to a wild-beast whose jaws are broken cf Ps 3:8 or Job 4:10 **18.** 'I shall die in my nest', i.e. surrounded by my children and grandchildren, a Hebrew ideal of old age and death. *Like the phoenix* (CV) is an old rabbinic tradition of strength, as in Gn 49:24 and Jer 49:35. **21—25.** Job returns to the thought of the deference and respect shown which had been his. This is what he most misses now: a very human trait in so many who have once tasted authority or adulation. **23.** The figure is that of refreshing rain, cf Dt 32:2. The *malqôš* or spring rain, which was and is very important for agriculture in Palestine, cf Prv 16:15. **25.** Describes an ideal position, king and chieftain and yet *a comforter of mourners*. So St Dominic, founder of an Order, champion of truth, and remembered as 'consoler of the brethren'.

e **30:1—31 Job's present misery**—Job contrasts his former happy state with his present misery. The change has been due, he would urge, not to his sins but to the action of God.

Divide up the ch as follows: 1—8, Those who mock at Job are outcasts of ill-repute. This constitutes a valuable piece of evidence for a study of Hebrew society and ideas of a post-exilic period, and perhaps even of a pre-exilic period, because it is difficult to gauge how far the poet is archaising or projecting back his ideas. 9—16, But *now* I am a byword; 16—23, A plaint of a sick and abandoned man: you do not answer me! 24—31, is a last despairing cry—yet not quite.

1. 'With the dogs of my flock': utter contempt is expressed. It could be argued that in the character of Job there are certain traces of a patrician pride or of a quasi—instinctive contempt for the 'proletariat'. 'Dog', or 'son of a dog' is a very strong insult in oriental language, and so too the phrase 'to rank or put with the **f** dogs'. **2.** Their vigour had perished by reason of under nourishment. We are reminded of the very great differences in well-being and physical capacities between the different classes and different nations— then as nowadays. **4.** 'mallow' represents the Heb. *mallûah* which are small thick sour-tasting leaves and which afford very little nourishment. The broom plant (*rōtem*) is the largest and most often seen shrub of the desert or steppe land. **5.** if these unfortunate ones draw near a civilized house, they are driven off. The Heb text has '*as* after a thief' (*kaggannāb*), so it is surprising to read 'these dregs of humanity could only exist by stealing', (V. E. Reichert, in Soncino *Job*, p. 151). **6.** They are ill-sheltered as well as ill-fed. **7.** 'nettles' is an uncertain rendering of *hārûl*, a plant which is characteristic of uncultivated regions of cf Jb 30:7; Prv 24:31. **8.** Irresponsible, *nameless men*. In such phrases is all the scorn and contempt of sedentarized people for the wandering folk of desert and steppe-land cf Gn 4:11. Vv 1—8 present a hideous picture of a heartless society, which allowed and accepted this 'submerged tenth'. **9.** 'song', in mockery cf Lam 3:14 **g** **11.** Most commentators take *yeter* as bow-string, but it

could also be tent-cord cf Jb 4:21. The meaning then is, **375g** demolish his tent and humble him. **14.** Continues the siege figure of v 12; this time we have the break-through. **15.** Nobility of rank is meant cf 16:12—14 and 19:12, where Job describes his misfortunes. **16.** For the idea of a soul poured out or ebbing away, cf Ps 42 (41):5. **19.** Job is become as the refuse upon which he sits, cf 2:8. **20.** The 'dark night of the soul' could hardly be better pictured. The situation is that of prayer unanswered and God looking us through and through. **21.** At this point Job reproaches God. **22.** Borne up and tossed about, as chaff before the wind. **23.** The house appointed for all the living, or the meeting-place of all the living is Sheol— which meant the end of all purposeful living for Job and his contemporaries. **24.** One of the most difficult vv in **h** the poem. It may not be possible to recover the original text. For *beî* read (cf Kittel's note) *beʿānî*; with the LXX read in the first person 'I have not . . . '; and in the second clause read (cf Dhorme in loc) *Yešawwēaʿ* and translate: 'Assuredly I have not extended a hand against the poor, if, in his misfortune, he cried towards me!' **25.** Note the tone of compassion or pity, which is not common either in Job or in the ancient world. **27.** 'Mine inwards' is the Hebrew way of referring to one's inner being which in this text 'boil and rest not'—a figurative expression for the tumult of emotions which rages within him cf Lam 2:11. **28.** *qōdēr* is generally used of the attire of a person in mourning. cf 2 Sm 19:25; Ps 38 (37):7. His darkened appearance is not caused by the sun, cf Song 1:6, but by his disease.

31:1—40 A Solemn Repudiation of Sin Job **i** now continues the apologia for his conduct which had begun in 29:14—17. We now have a solemn repudiation of all sin that might possibly have been imputed to him. This 'negative confession' is Job's way of countering the many accusations of sinfulness which have been heaped upon him all through the dialogues. Though this confession can be paralleled in Egyptian and Babylonian literature, still it remains valuable as a document showing something of the post-exilic Hebrew's conception of sin. The *form* of the negative confession is that of an imprecatory oath against oneself. This could be asked for in the trial of an accused person cf 1 (3) Kgs 8:31—32; Nm 5:20—22; Ex 22:10. Divide up **j** the ch as follows: 1—4, General considerations: Job's deliberate choice of virtue; 5—8, in matters of justice; 9—12, in those of chastity; 13—15, browbeating and extortion; 16—20, lack of kindness, 24—28, avarice, 29—40, vindictive wrath. The ch has been described as 'an amazing summary of the ethics of the Bible, a dramatic portrayal of the requirements of the good life as taught in the Torah and by the prophets of Israel'. (V. E. Reichert, in Soncino *Job* p. 157).

1. Job imposed a law upon himself of a NT vigour and **k** perfection, cf Mt 5:28. The Heb. phrase is, literally 'cut a covenant' because in fact the covenant victim was cut in two, and those who offered the sacrifice passed between the pieces cf Gn 15:10 and Jer 34:18. But perhaps Job is nearer the recommendations of Sir 9:5. **5.** 'falsehood' stands for insincerity, unreality, cf Ps 12 **l** (11):3; 26 (25):4; 41 (40):7. Both falsehood and deceit are personified. Job however has nothing to do with either. **7.** i.e. from the path of virtue cf 23:11. 'has gone after my eyes' means 'has yielded to the suggestions and temptations of these "windows of the soul"'. cf Nm 15:39. **8.** Is the imprecation following on the assertion of v 7, as with each section of this ch. **10.** The wife so accursed is to be both slave and concubine. **11.** A heinous crime, cf Hos 6:9. Adultery was to be punished by death,

375l cf Dt 22:22. **13—15.** Job's wealth and power could have been a source of pride and arrogance and of contempt for small folk. But no, Job has respected their personal dignity and the rights which are theirs. **18.** From his earliest days, care for the widow, the poor and fatherless has been instilled into him. It was part of his education. **22.** Failing to relieve those in want brings on this fearsome imprecation, and God is very close to his thoughts (23). **27.** Kissing the hand or wafting a kiss with the hand was, among Assyrians and Babylonians, a gesture

m of adoration and also a symbol of prayer. **28.** The real evil in indulging in pagan practices; they amount to a denial of the true God, Yahweh. **29.** Job's restraint and generosity towards enemies has been described as an example of the true Hebrew spirit; and cf Ex 23:4; Prv 24:17; 25:21. These texts, and this tradition of kindliness towards enemies in Israel needs to be set against the more usual OT picture of savagery and hate, cf Ps 109 (108) etc. **34.** Had he ever done wrong, the opinion of the mass of the people would have filled him with dread. A fear of the contempt of lowly folk would have kept him from sin. **35—37.** A plea to God to be heard. **35.** 'my signature', *tāwî*, or written mark in attestation. Legal phraseology, as in 19:24. **40.** 'The words of Job are ended'. This is seemingly an editorial of the kind found in Ps 72 (71):20. Job's connected discourses have come to an end, or at least some editor or annotator thought so.

376a   **32—37 THE SPEECHES OF ELIHU**

This section of the book of Job is often underestimated. Most critics look upon these chh as an addition which contributes nothing to the general run and argument of the book. The long debate between Job and his friends has reached its term. Job has summed up (29—31); *now* should come the intervention of Yahweh. In some such way argue the overwhelming majority of critics: yet there is much to be said for taking the text as we have it rather than reconstructing it. The argument from the language (best set out in Driver and Gray, ICC, Introd. §§ 22—29) is no more compelling for these chh than for the rest of the poem. There are passages of great beauty; sentences which cannot be forgotten, e.g. 33:4.

Also in the speeches of Elihu is developed the idea that **God's chastisements are for man's correction**; and ultimately we are not to think of senseless suffering, but suffering which can be corrective, remedial, even redemptive in the hands of an all-loving God, cf 33:19.

b So with Godet (*Studies in the OT* 215ff) we could say that 'far from being a mere by-play in the book, (these chh) are an indispensable feature of it'. This is perhaps the preferable viewpoint; but we can also reasonably hold that the Elihu speeches had been added by the author in a later redaction; this might explain the curious fact that Elihu is made to address Job by name and quotes the earlier chh *as if he had read them*. This would also explain why Elihu is not mentioned in the Prologue nor in the Epilogue. God's rebuke (in 42:7ff) is addressed only to the three friends. But it is not for us to demand that the author should always have been consistent with himself if and when he added pieces to his poem.

32. The ch may be divided as follows: 1—6a, prose prologue introducing Elihu's intervention; 6b—10, wisdom is not necessarily with the old; 11—14, Elihu has been disappointed by the reasons adduced. He expected more and better; 15—22, soliloquy revealing Elihu's state of mind.

1—6a The **prose introduction** to Elihu's speeches. **376** The intervention of Elihu is thoroughly adventitious and wholly unrelated to the general context: The author (or another?) who inserted the Elihu speeches must have sensed this when he constructed this prose prologue. There are other Elihus in Scripture, cf e.g., 1 Sm 1:1; I Chr 12:20; 26:7; 27:18. The name, literally, means 'My God is he'. **2.** 'son of Barachel the Buzite' and related to Abraham through his brother Nahor, cf Gn 22:21; cf also Jer 25:23 'Dedan, Thema, Buz, and all who cut the corners of their hair'. 'angry' for considering himself rather than God to be in the right. For the idea cf 40:8. **4.** Literally 'waited with words'. Elihu is depicted as younger than the friends. **5.** His wrath was kindled. Three times in five vv! **7.** Many years teach wisdom. A sapiential dictum. **8.** Shows a wonderful grasp of the inward dignity of man which stems from the spirit breathed into him by God. Elihu's theology is not superficial. **18.** 'within me'. Literally 'in my belly' cf Prv 18:8. **19.** Elihu's way of expressing the turmoil within himself. He is going to burst! All ch 32 serves to present this new and brash speaker.

33. Divisions—1—7, Elihu addresses Job; 8—11, **d** Elihu re-states Job's plea and claim to innocence; 12—28, God speaks to men variously; 29—30, the discipline of God is purposeful; 31—33, Job must listen (to what is coming in 34).

1. Elihu frequently addresses Job by name. This is peculiar to these Elihu chh. This has been said to indicate a certain familiarity, as between blood-relations. **2.** Rather pompous; yet in **3** he stresses his sincerity. **4.** Elihu has said something very great almost unconsciously: words which so well sum up the Heb. and the Church's attitude to creation. **5.** A sort of challenge: 'Set your words in order if you can'. **6.** 'I am toward God even as you'. Cf Augustine's *fecisti nos ad te*. We all have the same relationship to God. **8.** Elihu has listened to the dialogue of the friends. **9.** Job's protes- **e** tations of innocence have riled Elihu, cf 9:21; 10:7; 16:17; 23:10ff; 27:5 and 31. We could say that protestation of innocence is a major theme in Job. Elihu however is unfair. Job never claimed to be faultless, cf 7:21; 13:26, 'pure' I am innocent (a hapax legomenon). **10.** 'occasions', *tᵉnûʾôt*, cf Nm 14:34. **14.** God speaks one way, and in another. Man listens to neither. **15.** Recalls the experience of Eliphaz in 4:13. **16.** Opens the ears of men, cf Gn 20:3; 1 Sm 9:15. **19.** Another form of God's speaking is in the circumstances and disciplined chastening of illness. This is particularly applicable to Job's experience. **20.** 'his life', in the sense of appetite. **23.** 'if there be . . .', fitting in with Job's repeated appeal to a Vindicator of his cause. **24.** Note the *pit* (*šaḥat*), repeated in 24, 28, 30. Elihu is seemingly fascinated or obsessed by this. **30.** 'the light of life'. A phrase found in Ps 56 (55):13. A phrase beautiful in its suggestion of a life illumined by God's presence, and so contrasting with the darkness of the grave.

34. Divisions—2—9, Elihu summarizes Job's plea; **377** 10—15, the traditional thesis yet again stated: 'God never acts unfairly'; 16—20, it is unthinkable that the world's ruler is unjust! 21—30, God knows all when he condemns; 31—37, Job *in ignorance* criticizes God. **3.** 'for the ear tests words'. This is an echo of Job's own words in 12:11. The ear stands for the faculty of judgement, and the parallel is the palate which tastes and judges of food. **5.** Elihu is like an advancing the opponents' argument in a formal debate. **6.** '*in my wound the arrow rankles*' (CV) is a clever paraphrase. Heb. simply has 'my arrow' which is usually explained

77a as a metaphor for the wound inflicted by (God's) arrow. The 'arrows of God' are referred to in Job's speeches at 6:4 and 16:13. **10.** Cf Bildad's words in 8:3. Elihu echoes Bildad in vv 10–12. **12.** The very nature of God is incompatible with injustice. A great and classic tenet of Heb. as of Christian theology. God is he who can 'neither deceive nor be deceived'. **28.** The poor and lowly, who are ill-treated and oppressed, cry out—and are heard by God. **29–30.** God is not dependent on mens' actions; He is infinitely above and rules over all. **36.** '*let Job be tried to the limit*' CV, cf Job's own words in 7:18. **37.** Clapping of hands stands for an insulting gesture, cf 27:23. Job is said to 'clap his hands' in open mockery of God's truth, cf the striking text in Lam 2:15.

b **35.** 2–8, against Job's claim that righteousness is un-availing; 9–16, some explanation of why the innocent cry out. **2.** '*I am just rather than God*' (CV) is a very literal and good rendering. But there is also an idiom which makes *ṣidqî mēʾēl* = my justification before God. Hence RSV: Do you say, 'It is my right before God'. Elihu is in fact trying to tell Job that he has a false idea of what could justify him. **5.** Echoes the words of Eliphaz in 22:12. 5–7 God is infinitely above us and cannot be swayed by human conduct good or bad. **9.** Elihu may be suggesting that the innocent cry out by instinct and merely from feeling deeply, and that they are not really praying to God in their afflictions. **10.** 'who gives songs in the night' is correct, and better than 'visions' of CV which misses a beautiful idea. Elihu is referring to that joyous happiness of those who have been delivered by God, and whose joy keeps them singing through the night, as the Psalmist sometimes did, cf Ps 42 (41):8 and 92 (91):2.

c **Chh. 36–37**—On God's providential dealings with men, and of God as the true gauge of Job's sufferings.

36:2–21, God has a plan for human affliction; 22–33, a hymn to God's goodness and wisdom; 37:1–13, the effect of God's 'voice' in nature; 14–24, Job must learn the lesson of nature. **36:2–4.** Elihu is aware of his prolixity in speaking, and craves for patience in his listeners. **5–7.** A doxology calculated to show Elihu's theological equipment. **8–10.** Is said to be a reference to the story of the wicked Manasseh who was made prisoner and finally repented, according to 2 Chr 33:10–19. **12.** 'they perish by the sword'. Dhorme reads here 'they pass through the Canal' or the vertical shaft which leads down to Sheol. For this meaning of *šelaḥ* and a parallel passage cf 33:18, 'his life from passing through the Canal'. *Šelaḥ* in this instance is an equivalent of Akkadian Šalḥu or Šiliḥtu = a canal. **16–20.** Omitted, as being utterly corrupted, by CV, which gives the Vg version in a footnote. Read as in RSV, though there can be little certainty; e.g. 21 appears to follow on 18.

22–33. A hymn to God's goodness and wisdom. With Dhorme read 31 after 28, thus putting the benefits which flow from the rain after the rain. **22.** God is a Teacher, cf Ps 32 (31):8, 'I will teach you and instruct you in the way you shall go'; not 'master' nor 'ruler' here, cf *Môreh Ṣedeq* or Teacher of righteousness in DSS. **23.** There is very likely a reproach for Job in these words of Elihu. **25–26.** Stresses the transcendence of God. **27.** Cf Gn 2:6, '*ed*, mists or vapour.

d **37:1–4** The approaching storm causes Elihu's heart to bound. For thunder as the voice of God cf 28:26 and Pss 18 (17):13, 29 (28):3–4. **6.** Heavy drenching rain, of the kind well known in Palestinian winters, where all the rainfall comes in a few months—in quantity as much as in London over a year. **13.** The fury of the elements serves the purposes of God whether for the punishment of evildoers or for the showing forth of his **377d** mercy. **14–20.** Elihu rehearses before Job the wonderful deeds of the Creator. This preludes and anticipates God's own utterances in chh 38–41. **14.** Here again, as so often in the OT scriptures there is an insistence upon awareness of God and promptitude in listening to his every behest, cf B. van Iersel, *The Bible on the Living God*, 1965, p. 8. **18.** 'hard as a *brazen* mirror', the classic Heb. picture of the solid vault of heaven as in Gn 1:7. **21–24.** Elihu prolongs his description of a **e** storm. **22.** 'comes golden splendour'. Dhorme reads *zōhār* (shining) for *zāhāb* (golden), cf Ezek 8:2, Dn 12:3. God is girt about with dazzling light: man cannot face up to it. 'The springing of the light from the N is no reflection of meteorological fact or fancy but a poetical allusion to the ancient idea that the seat of the divinity was in that far unknown region'—Sutcliffe, CCHS (1) in loc. **24.** Therefore men revere him though none can see Him, however wise their hearts. Elihu ends here and is no more heard of.

38–42 THE LORD'S SPEECHES   378a

Introduction—In 31:40 we read 'the words of Job are ended', and those words in fact close the poetic dialogue which had lasted from ch 4. It ends with an appeal to the supreme tribunal:

O that I had one to hear my case,
that my accuser could write out his indictment!
surely I would wear it upon my shoulder
or put it upon me diadem-wise;
of all my steps I should give him an account;
like a prince I should present myself before him.
This is my final plea; let the Almighty answer me!
The words of Job are ended (31.35–37).

Job asks for judgement and does not fear it, and the judgement envisaged is that suggested in 19:25–29 ('I know that my Vindicator is alive', etc). Job not only calls upon God to judge, but has also already appealed to him as witness and umpire: 'Even now, see, my witness is in heaven' etc (16:19–21). N.B. the whole splendid passage. Previously he had refused the offices or inter- **b** vention of his friends (cf 13:3–12), and declared that he would refer to God alone (13:13–27), especially 18). God is to settle the debate. He alone knows Job's case. The friends have given all the explanations current in accepted and conventional morality. Job has shown, or at least felt, that these were insufficient.

Now the Lord God—Yahweh himself in his Supreme Being—intervenes and speaks in answer to Job. Yahweh deals trenchantly with Job's words in 38:2 and 40:2, and has no mercy on the 'friends' of Job, 42:7–8. (Elihu however goes unmentioned). The Epilogue links **c** up directly with Yahweh's speech, cf 42:7 'after the Lord had spoken these words to Job . . .'. The last contacts are between God and Job; but Job in fact only mutters a few words, cf 40:3–5 and 42:1–6. Yahweh's starting-point is that God's works are mysterious, unfathomable, even paradoxical. But rather than spin out colourless generalities, the author of Job makes God embark upon vivid and detailed descriptions of purposeful wonders. God is shown summoning Job and putting him through a set of questions (38:2–3): Where was Job at earth's foundation and building up? 4–7; Who sealed the sea, bound it in swaddling-clothes? 8–11; Who made the dawn, expelling night and crimes? 12–15; Who can reach depths of Abyss and Sheol? 16–18; light, dark, snow, seasons, all escape ken of man, 19–30. courses of stars and constellations are unknown 31–33,

378c clouds and rainstorms are heralded by the cock, 34—38.
d After these recurrent yet inexplicable phenomena Yahweh goes on to tell of *animals*, especially of those whose life and laws of reproduction escape us. Thus the lioness and the raven 39—41 goats and hinds 39:1—4 the wild-ass 39:5—8 the wild-ox, beyond all taming 9—12 the ostrich, not so stupid after all 13—18 the war-horse, fearsome in popular Hebrew imagination 19—25 and finally the hawk and vulture, lords of the air 26—30. Yahweh pauses. The long tirade overpowers Job who can only reply: Though I have spoken once, I will not do so again though twice, I will do so no more (40:5). Yahweh goes on relentlessly, and this time to
e tell of *extraordinary* beasts, the Behemoth (40:15) and Leviathan (41:1). These monstrous beings were in part suggested by the hippopotamus and the crocodile which the author would have seen in Egypt, but there is also in these pen-pictures an admixture of mythological themes and poetic verse. The genius of the author has gone to riotous limits in showing how Yahweh overwhelms Job, cf Steinmann, *Le Livre de Job*, 201.

With respect to the rest of the book the speeches of Yahweh stand on their own. They are monologues in which the author has excelled, perhaps because he has felt free of dialogue and its limitations. He paints unrestrainedly tableaux of the world's natural wonders. Then he closes with the description of two monstrous beings, which, as handled by the poet, defy classification. But, it could be argued, these two beasts stood rather apart in the fauna of the Nile valley and would easily be a source of wonderment to untravelled Palestinians.

379a **38:9—40:2 The first speech of Yahweh—38:1.** The common mode of many theophanies. God appears in a tempest and shows his power over the elements while revealing himself and communicating his message to men, cf Na 1:3; Ezek 1:4; Ex 19:16; Ps 18 (17):8—16; Ps 50 (49):3. **2.** 'who is this that obscures *divine plans* with words of ignorance?'—This is one of the challenging and hard words of the Lord God against Job whose pleading and speeches generate obscurity. There is in fact a double rebuke for Job (a) he has spoken ignorantly (b) he has obscured what should be plain, that the divine purpose underlines the constitution and maintenance of the world. **3.** 'Gird up your loins' . . . and prepare for the contest or challenge, cf Is. 5:27; Jer. 1:17. Job is going to be put through God's questioning.

Note the use of Yahweh, (the Lord) God's proper name, only here and 40:1, 3, 6; 42:1 throughout the Prologue and Epilogue, and nowhere else in the book.
b **4—11.** One of the finest passages in Heb. poetry. The earth is compared to an edifice the secret of whose structure belongs to God. The vast structure has a plan and foundations (6) and joyous onlookers. (7), of whom Job was not one (4). But there is no need to overstress the *building* ideas (*bases, cornerstone*, etc). Poetic speech should not be pressed too literally. The ordinary semitic world-picture—that of a firmament and bases of earth, etc—could be spoken of in the terms used here.

4. 'if you have understanding', literally *if you know understanding*, a Heb. idiom, as in Is. 29:24; Prv 4:1; 1 Chr 12:33. And understanding (*bînāh*) is often in parallelism with or a synonym for wisdom, cf 28:12; 39:17, and Dt 4:6; Is 29:14. **5.** 'the (measuring) line', cf Zech 1:16. The scale and measurements come first as they do in Ezekiel's building of the ideal
c temple, cf Ezek 40:3ff 43:17. **7.** The ceremony of laying the world's foundations called for joyous music, as did the foundation ceremonies of earthly buildings, cf Ez

3:10; Zech 4:7. The morning stars sing the hymn of **379** dedication at the rising of the sun; and these in turn are echoed by the 'Sons of God' or angels, cf 1:6 and 2:1 and as in all later Heb. thought, when all danger of polytheism had been eliminated. For the Phoenicians (e.g.) 'Sons of Elohim' were literally 'Sons of God'. Priestly tradition in Israel gradually introduced new nuances and modified documents, so that finally *benê'elōhîm* meant 'angels', as in Is 6:1—13; 1 (3) Kgs 22:19—22. The stars are thought of as existing before the world, in contrast to Gn 1:16. 'sang *in chorus*' (*rānan*), cf Is 12:6. The joyous singing of the heavens appears again in Is 49:13. **8—11.** Of the sea and its **d** bounds. We need to have in mind here the semitic world-picture and to recall the separation scene in Gn 1:10. The sea is conceived of as something 'born' (cf 8*b*), a sort of monster needing to be kept in restraint lest it should endanger God's building or the earth. From whom or how this monster is born is not said. Its origin, unlike that of earth, is not traced directly to God—at least in the ancient mythological background which the poet has drawn upon. But the poet makes it dependent on God (9) and God has supremacy over it (10—11); and this serves to illustrate the power, wisdom and unique character of God. The mythological background is blurred and countered by the fundamental monotheism of the author. As a poet he felt free to draw upon traits from polytheistic themes but rather by way of adornment (cf 7:12; 9:13; 26:12). We might perhaps compare the way in which Christian literary tradition, at the Renaissance, drew heavily upon pagan themes and mythology.

12—15. The constant return of morning light and all that ensues. All obeys God's order. The earth is imagined to be a great carpet or coverlet. During the night evil-doers pursue their wicked deeds under cover of darkness (24:15—16). Dawn shakes the great carpet and evil-doers vanish with the light. The idea is found in Aknaton's hymn, ANET 370—1. **14.** The meaning here is that the night deprives the earth of form and colour. But both are recovered at dawn, and earth as it were is stamped afresh, as clay is with a seal, so that all comes out in clear relief. The great joy of dawning light is that it gives ever-increasing clarity and relief to each and every object. **15.** The wicked lose their light; because the light of the wicked is darkness (cf Is 5:20); and the arm raised to commit a crime is shattered. **16—18.** The depths **e** and breadths of earth. More ironic questions are heaped upon Job: for Job's range is in fast limited in time and space. **16.** *The sources of the sea* are the hidden channels which were thought to connect the sea with the abyss under the world or 'waters beneath'. This 'abyss' is in parallelism with the sea (cf 28:14), and is the primaeval *tehôm* of Gn 1:2.

17. Death and Darkness are personified and in parallelism, cf Abaddon and Death in 28:22. The 'gates of death' are the gates of Sheol referred to in Is 38:10. The 'gates of death' occur in Ps 9:14 (15); 107 (106):18. We can compare here the narrative of the descent of Ishtar to the nether-world (ANET, 107). The gate-keeper, gates, bolts, door, etc, are all there. **19.** 'Light' is conceived of as an entity distinct from and independent of sun, moon and stars. The same notion obtains in Gn 1:3 and Sir 12:2. **21.** Note the withering irony of this couplet. Job was there then, when God was organizing his universe? cf the same thought in Eliphaz's speech 15:7. **22—30.** Snow, hail, etc, are grouped together **f** because they are all instruments of God's wrath, and God's weapons against his foes, cf Ex 9:2—16; Jos

10:11; Is 28:17. **23.** Cf Is 30:30; 1 Mc 13:22. **24.** *The* **79f** *parting of the winds* (CV), where the E wind is scattered cf Enoch 41:4. **25.** Is based on 28:26. Rain comes down in the way determined for it by God; so too does the lightning, however haphazard it may appear. 'cleft a channel' (*pālag*). The term is one used of irrigation. **26.** Rain comes down not only for man's benefit, but also over uninhabited country, for reasons known only to God. A wide aspect of God's providence is being inculcated here: in this way Job's considerations are made to look narrowly man-centred, cf Ps 104 (103):16—18, 20—22, 25. **28.** Rain and dewdrops have no human source or cause. **29.** Ice and hoar-frost are known in the hill country of Palestine—but rather rarely, so they are all the more wonderful. (For conditions of climate in Palestine cf Abel, *Géographie de la Palestine* I:127—129).

g **31—33.** Stars and constellations are next referred to because of associations with seasons and weather. **31.** Pleiades (*kîmāh*) and Orion (*kesîl*), as in 9:9. The fullest treatment of this constellation is in Dhorme, *Le Livre de Job* (1926) 118—119. **32.** 'Mazzaroth' is from a root nzr, hence *nēzer* diadem or crown; and it is to be distinguished from *mazzārîm*, cf 37:9. Dhorme makes *mazzārôt* to be the N Crown, a fine constellation on a level with the Great Bear. The heavenly constellations are linked together: and the laws governing them are in some sense responsible for the laws which govern us upon earth. For the 'laws of the heavens' cf Jer 31:35.

34—38. Atmospheric disturbances are beyond man's control. God alone holds sway there. First come the floods, brought about by rain, as in 22:11. Then the 'lightnings' obedient to the voice of God. **35.** 'Here we are' cf the famous text of Bar 3:33—35, perhaps **h** derived from Job. **36.** CV has *Who puts wisdom in the heart, and gives the cock its understanding?* The latter rendering is in part dependent on Dhorme, who for 'clouds' and 'mist' has *ibis* and *cock*. Ibis represents *tuhôt*, which stands for the Egyptians god Thoth, symbolized by the ibis. 'Cock' as a rendering of *Sekwî* is vouched for by the Targums and Vg. Both the ibis and the cock were reputed to have the faculty of prevision; thus the ibis foretold Nile floods, and the cock announced the dawn of day, and was credited with intelligence for doing so. Egyptian influences would thus be seen in this v.

i **39—41.** These vv introduce the animal world. Who feeds the wild beasts, the lioness, young lions or the raven?

A new section begins here, and ch 39 would better begin at this v (38:39). Brilliant pictures of the animal world serve to make God their Creator pass before the eyes and mind of Job. **40.** Would Job be concerned to provide food for them as God is? (cf Reickert in Soncino Job p. 203). **41.** God concerns himself not only with the king of beasts, but also with the much more lowly and perhaps despised raven. That God cares for the raven appears in Ps 147 (146):9.

j **39:1—4.** Mountain or wild goats, as in 1 Sm 24:2 and Ps 104 (103):18. There is something mysterious and unseen about their conceiving and bringing to birth. All these things, and much else, are in the hands of God. **5—8.** The wild-ass or 'supreme example of unrestrained freedom' (Kissane). Referred to frequently, especially in terms of intractability or fleetness of foot, cf 11:12; cf Gn 16:12; Hos 8:9; Is 32:14; Sir 13:19; Jer 14:6. **6.** 'the salt land' better 'the salt *flats*', denotes the desert in its most rigorous aspects as e.g. between Jericho and the Dead Sea, cf Jer 17:6. **7.** The wild ass shuns civilization; his domesticated brother is the patient drudge of man, as can be seen in any E town, trotting

through the noisy markets and shouted at all the while. **379j** **9—12.** Ass and ox are constantly associated as domestic animals, so our poet passes easily from the one wild counterpart to another. **9.** The *rêm* or wild-ox, **k** now commonly identified with the Assyrian *rimu*, the wild bulls hunted by Assyrian kings, and pictured on the great Ishtar gateway of Babylon. Tristram identified it with the aurochs, a species of bison, possibly the *urus* mentioned by Julius Caesar, *De Bel. Gal.* 6:28. The species, as so many others, is no longer extant in Palestine which has suffered a great diminution of fauna since antiquity, cf Abel, *Géographie de la Palestine* I, 219—34. These vv serve to show the complete contrast between the wild and tame species. God alone could bring about such a difference. **13—18.** The *renānîm* 'ostriches'. Vg rightly renders the word thus, but early versions did not recognize the term. The whole passage is notoriously difficult, and in LXX is all 'obelised' (i.e. reconstructed from other versions and added to the Gr. text, cf Rahlfs in loc). Yet the ostrich was a well-known desert-dweller, cf Lam 4:3; Is 13:21; 34:13.

13. Has been translated in twenty different ways! **14.** Refers to a popular belief that the ostrich leaves her eggs in the sand and abandons them. This has no foundation in fact, but we need not expect the author of Job to be a naturalist as well as a poet. **17.** The stupidity of the ostrich re-appears in arabic proverbs. **18.** But the ostrich outstrips any horse in speed. This brings us neatly to the subject of the war-horse. **19—25.** The war-horse. **l** In the Bible the horse is very often associated with war, cf Jg 5:22. Jos 11:4, 6, 9, 2 Sm 15:1; 1 (3) Kgs 5:6, 8; 2 (4) Kgs 3:7; 9:33; 10:2, etc. In poetic as in popular esteem the war-horse stood for something fierce and terrifying, especially for the Heb. who rarely had horses and never very many such weapons of war. These particular vv (19—25) have been cited as a model of Heb. poetry. **20.** The horse is compared to a bounding locust, but in Jl 2:4 the comparison is between the horse with its rider and the locust. **21—23** represents the war-horse in action, excited by the clash of arms and din of battle, cf Jer 8:6.

23. 'the flashing spear' more literally 'the flame of the spear', i.e. the iron-work gleams in the sun, cf Na 3:3. **26—30.** The hawk and eagle, two birds of prey. **26.** 'toward the S'. An allusion to the Southward migration of the hawk at the approach of winter. **27.** The eagle builds its nest in the most inaccessible rocks, as e.g. in the S region of Petra, cf Jer 49.16. **29.** The eagle can watch its prey from some high point. **30.** Eagles and other birds of prey gather round any carcass, cf the allusions of our Lord in Mt 24:28; Lk 17:37.

40:1—5. A short interchange between Job and the **380a** **Lord** making the end of the long speech of 38—39. Will Job now argue with God any longer? Job simply owns that he can make no reply. **2.** For the parallelism of 'Almighty' and 'God' cf 37:22—23. **4.** Job will keep his hand on his mouth, cf 21:5; 29:9.

40:6—41:26. The Second Speech of the Lord—In this we attain a summit of the poet's imagination and verve. The creatures so far depicted (we might say so far 'filmed') have been getting larger and larger. Now come two vast creatures, almost mythical in dimensions and characteristics. Job is to be crushed by the contemplation of some of nature's greater and more terrifying manifestations.

6—14. Job is ironically invited to equal God in power. **b** **6.** The usual formula for starting on a long speech, as in 28:1. **7.** Repeats the wording of 28:3. **8.** If Job is right, he is to quash God's ruling . . . . **10.** Ironically put 'Adorn yourself with grandeur and majesty'. Job is invited to imagine himself in control of the entire universe.

380b It is *God* who is crowned with honour and glory, as in Ps 104 (103):1. **11.** Another challenge to Job. It is in fact God's prerogative to humble the proud and punish wickedness. **13.** 'hide them all in the dust together' as in the story of Korah, Dathan and Abiram, cf Nm 16:31—34. 'the world below' i.e. Sheol from which no man returns. **15—24.** 'Behemoth' is a made-up name for the hippopotamus, cf RSV note. *Behēmāh* is the ordinary Heb. word for a beast; the plural form *behēmôt* is explained as a 'majestic plural'. Reference is made no doubt to the great brute hunted by Egyptians in the Nile-side thickets. Both the beasts described in this ch belong rather to the fauna of Egypt. The whole ch has a strongly Egyptian flavour and suggests that the author had travelled there and had seen much. The great strength of the hippopotamus is stressed in 17 and 18. Details of muscles, etc, appear here, possibly because the author had witnessed the cutting-up of a carcass after a successful hippo-hunt.

c **23.** The Jordan is selected as a type of a fast-flowing stream—which in fact it is. **24.** 'with hooks'. Heb. has *in his eyes*, and the reference is to the method of hunting the hippopotamus. Efforts were made to blind it, and then to pierce its nostrils with pointed stakes or spears. XLI RSV starts ch 41 here. Heb. and CV continue ch 40 to 32 (cf RSV footnote).

d **41:1—8 Leviathan.** The poet starts with a description of the crocodile which was at one time known in Palestine, notably at Nahr-ez-Zerka, N of Caesarea. cf Abel, *Géographie de la Palestine* I, 469—71; P E F Quarterly Statement, 1920. The poet however is carried away by his theme, and the crocodile comes near to being the dragon-like mythical creature of popular folk tales. The very name *Leviathan* suggests the great monster of chaos vanquished by God before the creation, cf 3:8. **2.** Refers to the treatment of prisoners captured by the Assyrians, cf the graphic description of Ezek 29:4 where the Pharaoh is compared to a great crocodile who is to be ensnared. **3.** *Tender* or 'soft words' seems to refer to a legend about crocodile's tears. **5—6.** Ironically put: will the crocodile become a little girl's plaything? a merchant's trading-piece? 'merchants', literally *Canaanites* who had considerable reputation as traders or merchants, cf Prv 31:24. 'divide him up'. The crocodile is altogether too powerful, too vast to be sold as ordinary fish. **7—8.** A warning note: don't engage in hand-to-hand fight with **e** crocodiles! **9.** The description now takes on more and more of a fanciful character. The crocodile is depicted in such exaggerated terms that something of the Leviathan of Phenician legend breaks through. **9—11.** The situation conjured up is that of combat with the beast. Hearts fail when face to face with it.

12—17. The beast's bodily frame. **14.** More literally, 'who can open the doors of his face'? **15—17.** Stresses the close-knit nature of the scales, cf Ex 26:3 of curtains which are close-joined or coupled to one another. **18.** The ancients had noticed that the crocodile sneezes at times in the sunlight, and exudes tear-like drops of water. 'eyes are like the eyelids of the dawn' cf 3:9. In Egyptian **f** hieroglyphs, crocodile eyes represented the dawn. **19—21.** Almost grotesque or playful writing here with at least poetic hyperbole. The author has touched up his picture with reminiscences of fire-breathing dragons. The mouth of the crocodile spits out fire and can set coals alight! For the picture and wording cf 2 Sm 22:9; Ps. 18 (17):9. **21.** *His breath*, literally 'his soul'. **22—24.** More emphasis on the beast's great strength. **25—29.** Weapons are futile and glance off this massive armour-plated foe. **30.** The image behind this v is that of a threshing-sledge, set with flints, of a type still used in Palestine. It is used to describe

the beast dragging itself through the mire. **31—34.** 'the **38** deep', as in Ps. 69 (68):3, 16, to represent the deep parts **g** of a river. The hyperbole is such that the artistic value of the latter part of the Lord's speech has been called in question. The Lord God, it has been said, brings out a zoological garden—to refute Job or crush him with wonderment at God's achievements. Moreover the display of beasts and birds is enhanced with that of two half-mythological creatures, Behemoth and Leviathan. Note how in Ps. 104 (103):26 Leviathan is created 'to sport with', as one of the 'games of God'. This may well be a facet of the thought of the poet of Job.

42:1—6 Job submits humbly with the words *I have* **h** *dealt with great things that I do not understand* (v 3). **5.** Is undoubtedly the key-v. In other words, traditional knowledge has now been replaced by a vision of the Divine Splendour. This might well be the lesson of the whole poem: Job has seen realized that hope which was formulated in 19:27: Whom I shall see and my eyes shall behold and not another. A certain stress in put on the difference between hearing or hearsay (yet faith comes from hearing . . .) and *sight* or a certain entirety of spiritual grasp and experience. Only is this sense can we talk of 'sight', for all Heb. tradition had it that no man can see God and live. **7—17. The Epilogue** **i** does not in fact constitute a pendant to the Prologue. There is no devil (Satan), no scene in heaven, no wife to urge Job to bless God who has vindicated him. The epilogue would, in the eyes of some, come better after 40:1—14, where Yahweh has brought the discussion to a close by showing that man cannot set himself up as judge of God's purposes.

7. Yahweh, the Lord, now turns upon Job's friends; Eliphaz alone is named, but all three are arraigned. They are reproached for not having spoken rightly about God. 'my servant Job' recalls the language of the Prologue, cf 1:8; 2:3. **8.** To avert God's wrath a complete sacrifice or holocaust is to be made of seven bulls and seven rams, as in the holocaust of Balak and Balaam, Nm 23:1—4. **9.** Job now becomes an *intercessor* on the level of Abraham (Gn 20:7), Moses (Nm 21:7) and Samuel (1 Sm 7:5; 12:19, 23). His friends, who had helped Job so little, were now to be spiritually enriched by him whom they had thought was a sinner.

Job's friends now disappear from the scene.

10—17. A last paragraph tells of the rich and generous **j** restoration to prosperity of Job. **11.** Many friends seemingly had abandoned Job in his calamities, Now they come crowding round. 'a piece of money' *qeŝitâ* (cf RSV note), as in Gn 33:19. The term is redolent of the patriarchal period. Thus a hundred *qeŝitah*, Jos 24:32. The value of the qeŝitah is debated. The versions, except Symmachus, translate it *lamb*, and the rabbis sometimes rendered it thus. Dhorme suggests that a lamb's worth was a unit of exchange. A *qeŝîtāh* would thus be the value of a lamb in silver or gold. The 'ring of gold' was for the nose or ear, cf Gn 24:47 and 35:4, and Is 53:21. **12—13.** Job's possessions are doubled, but the number of children remains as before. The names of the daughters are indicative of beauty, *Jemima* 'turtle-dove', cf the Arabic *jamameh*. *Cassia* is a precious perfume as in Ps 45 (44):9. **14.** *Keren-happûk* is literally 'horn of antimony'. Antimony is a black powder which was used by women to darken their eyes. In the ancient E world oil, unguents, and 'make-up' were often kept in a horn, cf 1 Sm 16:1, 13; 1 (3) Kgs 1:39. **15.** 'gave them inheritance'. According to Nm 27:8 daughters only inherited when there were no sons. Job's daughters were unusually privileged.

THE PSALMS

BY SEBASTIAN BULLOUGH O.P.

Editorial Note—The decision to base this Commentary on the original texts (see p. vii) raises special problems for a commentary on the Psalms. In the rest of the Bible the meaning of the original is adequately conveyed by the current English translations, with only occasional divergences of opinion; but for reasons explained below (§ 381b) translations of the Psalter differ so much that it is hardly possible for a commentator using the original text to give preference to one version over another.

The method of exposition used here, therefore, is as follows. First a heading is given for each psalm describing its general theme, followed by a short introduction. Then a translation of the Heb. text is given, a section at a time, in quotation marks. Parentheses ( ) are used for elucidatory insertions to complete the sense; square brackets [ ] for observations outside the actual meaning of the text. Outside 'quotes', a free précis is given to keep the thread of thought continuous. Verse numbers are those of the Heb. text, often one (sometimes two) more than those versions (such as RSV) which do not number the title often found as the first verse of the Heb. The method of transliterating Hebrew adopted in this article differs somewhat from that used in the rest of the Comm.

Difficult passages receive separate treatment. Various possible interpretations are numbered off (usually in order of their proximity to the MT), with reference to the versions which adopt these interpretations (though not necessarily in the exact words of these versions, since these often inevitably smooth over the problem). The versions referred to (with the abbreviations used throughout this commentary) are noted below, § 381c–d.

It is inevitable that in a relatively large number of passages it is not possible to say which is the correct meaning or interpretation of the text; if indeed one should speak of 'correct' in this context; poetry, especially that which has played such an important part in so many centuries of thought and devotion, is not so easily tied down to a single grammatical meaning. This commentary, at any rate, has not tried to make such a limitation; and this means that the reader using any current English version will be able to see the reason for and the value of the rendering he is following. It is of course always presumed that the reader has a text before him; the commentary is meant to be a supplement to personal reading of the text, not a substitute for it. Moreover, the reader should not be misled by the wide variety of possible meanings in certain passages. These do not usually affect seriously the general tenor of a psalm; and above all they form no bar to the appreciation of its religious sense. And this, finally, is the real value of the psalms. It is indeed for this very reason that the author of this commentary has not thought it necessary to give special emphasis to this in dealing with individual psalms. Attention is drawn to the most important section of the Introduction, § 381q–s, which expounds the spiritual themes which run through the whole of the psalter. But for the rest, he has tried to bring out the meaning of the text, and this meaning is a religious meaning.

Bibliography—Commentaries: A. F. Kirkpatrick, **381a** CBSC, 1902; C. A. Briggs, ICC, 1906–7; H. Gunkel, HKAT, 1926[4]; J. Calès, 1936; W. O. E. Oesterley, 1939; A. Cohen, *Soncino Bible*, 1945; E. J. Kissane, 1953–4; H. J. Kraus, BKAT, 1961; G. W. Anderson, PC(2), 1962; A. Weiser, ATD, 1959[5]; E.tr. OTL, 1962; M. Dahood, AB, (Pss 1–50), 1966; (Pss 51–100), 1968. **Studies:** H. Gunkel–J. Begrich, *Einleitung in die Psalmen*, 1933; T. Worden, *The Psalms are Christian Prayer*, 1963[2]; S. Mowinckel, *The Psalms in Israel's Worship*, 1962, E.tr. of Norwegian; H. Ringgren, *The Faith of the Psalmists*, 1963; P. Drijvers, *The Psalms, their Structure and Meaning*, 1965, E.tr. of Dutch. **Versions** are themselves a form of commentary, and the following annotated versions may be mentioned: *The Oxford Annotated (RSV) Bible*, 1962; *Les Psaumes* in BJ, 1955[2]; CV, vol. III, 1955; D. Winton Thomas, *The Text of the Revised Psalter*, 1963 (DWT).

For particular abbreviations used in this article, see § 381d below.

Of the above commentaries the best are Kirkpatrick, Briggs (both pre-Form-Critical); Gunkel, Weiser, Kraus (all Form-Critical or 'cultic' approach).

Introduction—1. The Psalter is a hymn-book, a col- **b** lection of sacred poems which became the hymn-book of Israel and subsequently of the Church. Like any collection of hymns ancient and modern, it contains some really good poems with true insight, genuine feeling, fine imagery, with graceful and powerful diction; while others are less good, sometimes jejune and run of the mill. The poems include many types, true hymns of praise, strongly personal religious lyrics, songs of joy and of sorrow, poems for particular occasions, epics and edifying meditations (see 7 below, 'categories'); they also touch a wide variety of religious ideas, from a bare belief in God, through a confidence in his friendship and forgiveness, to a proclamation of Israel's mission to bring all mankind to worship the true God: in fact the psalms represent the many facets of man's prayer, both in his community and in his own heart (see 11 below, 'themes'). But the Psalter is more precisely five separate hymn-books (see 3 below), with consequently a few duplicates. (It should be added that some authors regard these divisions as a late development.) Within each of the five 'books' are smaller 'Collections', labelled 'David', 'Qorah', 'Asaph', etc, which account for over 100 of the psalms (see 4 below). When these 'collections' or 'books' were formed is quite uncertain, but it was doubtless a process extending over many centuries, with much editing and re-editing (as with all hymn-collections) producing with a few exceptions a remarkable homogeneity of language in the

381b Psalter as we have it now (and have had it for nearly 2000 years) in the form of a temple hymn-book (see 6 below): some of the poems will have been written for this purpose, while others were evidently adapted for congregational worship. Still more uncertain is the subject of the composition of any given psalm, the circumstances, purpose and date of its original writing, and the extent of editorial work, and there are many diverse theories (see 8 below, 'origin'). Meanwhile the Psalter is there for us as a collection of prayers, as it was for Israel, for Christ himself, and for Jews and Christians throughout their history. It is perhaps the very fact of its constant use through so many centuries that has produced more textual difficulties than anywhere else in the Bible, since the Pss have been edited, copied, translated, excerpted, and variously used for so long that the **first task of the commentator is to establish as far as possible the meaning of the text itself.**

c **2.** The **text** of the Pss in Kittel's Bible (3rd ed.) is based on Codex L (Leningrad) written in A.D. 1008, collated by P. Kahle with two contemporary MSS, and so shows the Massoretic Text (MT) 'in its purest form' (B. J. Roberts, *OT Text and Versions*, 1951, 82). But the MT is itself artificially standardized (see § 25a—g) so that any evidence of the state of the Heb. text prior to the work of the Massoretes is important. Such evidence has now been provided by the Dead Sea Scrolls (11QPss, published in *Discoveries in the Judean Desert of Jordan*, IV, 1965). The text is very incomplete, but shows much of Pss 102—50. In general it corroborates MT; variants are noted in the commentary. It also contains a Ps 151, hitherto known only in the LXX.

The most ancient and venerable translation of the Heb. Pss is the Greek **Septuagint** (LXX). The Latin **Vulgate**, in the case of the Psalter alone, is a translation of this, slightly revised by Jerome, and for this combined witness we are writing LXX/V. Entirely distinct from these was **Jerome's** own translation from the Hebrew (Jer), c. 393, which was not included in the Vg but is often an important witness to the Heb. text at the time. The Aram. **Targum** (Targ) is a Rabbinic work of quite uncertain age, quite distinct (as are all Targumim) from those on other books, and probably a recension of various earlier texts made in the early centuries A.D. The Syriac **Peshitta** version (Syr.) is also of very uncertain origin, probably a Christian work of the 2—4 cent. A.D.

d Among **modern versions**, the following may be noted. The **Prayer Book Psalter** (PB) of Coverdale (1535), made under the influence of new versions of the time in Latin and German, as well as of the Vg, is perhaps the most graceful English translation of all, and was not displaced in Anglican worship by the **Authorized Version** (AV) or 'King James Version' of 1611, which is closer to the Heb. A revision of this was the **Revised Version** (RV) of 1884, with its marginal readings (RVm). The **Jewish American** text (JA) of 1915 follows RV or RVm, though occasionally it departs to get closer to MT or to Rabbinic traditions. Quite apart from the above tradition is the **New Latin Psalter** (NP) issued by the Vatican in 1945. Fr Lattey's **Westminster Version** (WV), also of 1945 but quite independent, also includes similar conclusions. The French **Bible de Jérusalem** (BJ) (Psalter 1950, revised 1955), an important critical (and literary) venture, represents an independent and frequently original critical opinion. An English version appeared in 1966. The American **Revised Standard Version** (RSV) of 1952 (Catholic edition 1966) sets out to be a revision of AV but is in reality a new text and incorporates the general conclusions of scholarship up to its time. Finally, the **Revised (Prayer Book) Psalter** (RPB) of 1963—4, while preserving the rhythm and diction of Coverdale. has corrected PB by the latest results of research and scholarship.

Among modern Catholic texts, some widely used in the liturgy today, the American **Confraternity Version** (CV) of 1955, though 'translated from the original' in fact usually follows the NP (but see e.g. 89:20; 104:8). So also do Fr **Frey's** pocket 'Psalm Book' (USA 1947), **Knox's** Psalms—with a completely original approach—first published 1947, and the **Fides** Psalms (Notre Dame, Indiana, 1955), together with other *ad hoc* translations in English liturgical books. The **Grail** Psalms are guided by BJ.

These versions provide evidence of nearly all current opinions on the meaning of the text. RV and especially RVm represents (rather conservatively) the critical position of the 1880s, as NP does of the 1940s (it generally synthesises the 'critical orthodoxy' of the time rather than presenting new features), and as RSV does of the 1950s; with BJ taking a more independent and original line, and RPB showing an opinion of the 1960s.

e One factual detail needs to be noticed in relationship to these versions—the numbering of the Pss is sometimes different. Occasionally two or more distinct poems have been joined together as one psalm (e.g. 19 and 22), and sometimes on the contrary a single psalm has been divided and counted as two (e.g. 42—43). The traditional division of the psalms is so ancient that in most cases all versions agree; but in certain places LXX has dealt with the matter differently, notably by counting Heb 9—10 as one; and consequently LXX (followed by Vg and by all versions dependent on them) is one behind the Heb numbering through most of the Psalter. The following table explains the situation:

Hebrew			LXX/V	
1 — 8	=			1 — 8
9 + 10	=			9
11 — 113	=			10 — 112
114 + 115	=			113
116	=			114 + 115
117 — 146	=			116 — 145
147	=			146 + 147
148 — 150	=			148 — 150

In this introduction and in the commentary the Hebrew numbering alone is followed. Thus the Breviary, Douay, New (1945) Latin Psalter, Confraternity, Frey, Fides and Grail, following LXX and Vulgate, are most of the time one behind (as in table above).

3. The five 'books' are divided as follows: **f**

I = Pss 1—41 (when God is usually addressed as Yahweh [Lord])
II = Pss 42—72 (usually addressed as Elohim [God])
III = Pss 73—89 (both addresses)
IV = Pss 90—106 (chiefly Yahweh)
V = Pss 107—50 (chiefly Yahweh)

The provenance of these 'books' cannot be deduced, and each contains examples of most types of psalm. Each book ends with a doxology, the most elaborate being at the end of Ps 72. Some regard this division into five 'books' as a late editorial device (e.g. Mowinckel II, 197), and Rabbinic and Patristic opinion often supposed the division to have been made on the analogy of the Pent. But evidence of the separate origin of the books (though

381f not necessarily in their present form) is shown in the fact of the **duplicates:** 14 (Book I) = 53 (Book II); 40 (Book I) = 70 (Book II); 108 (Book V) = part of 57 and part of 60 (Book II); while 135 and 144 are largely pastiches of other psalms.

g 4. Within each 'book' are **Collections**, older than the 'books' (for some collections contribute to several books). The biggest (counting 74 Pss including all the duplicates) appears in Books I, II, IV and V: the five 'David Collections' (Pss 3—41; 51—65 and 68—70; 101, 103; 108—10; 138—45; with a few single Pss labelled 'David': 86, 122, 124, 131, 133). The 'Sons of Qorah Collections' in Books II and III (42—49; 84—85, 87—89) are particularly good stuff. The 'Asaph Collection' (72—83) forms the bulk of Book III with 'Qorah II'. The 'Gradual Psalms' (or 'Songs of Ascents', see on Ps 120), form a popular collection in Book V (120—34). The 'Halleluyah Collection' comes at the end (146—50). The 'Hallel' (113—18) is today a collection in the Jewish liturgy (see on 113), which shows how (as in the Breviary) sets of psalms come to be placed together. The identification of these 'collections' depends mainly upon the titles in the Heb. text, where the formula e.g. lit. 'for David', is used. Some suppose this indicates the author, but it seems rather an idiom for the attachment of a label to indicate the collection: '(Belonging) to (the) David (Collection)', and this seems to be the main function of the titles (see 9 below).

h 5. As is the case with many liturgical texts, the **authorship** of the psalms remains entirely unknown. The traditional ascription of many (if not all) of the psalms to David, presumably deriving from these titles and their occasional expansion with a *mise-en-scène* from David's life, seems unlikely, in view of the diversity within the 'David' psalms and also their similarity to many in other collections. At the same time it cannot be excluded that the general pattern of the Heb. psalm may have had its origin with David, and indeed 'David' had become a recognized term for the Psalter already in the NT (Mt 22:43 with Mk 12:36, Lk 20:42; Ac 1 16 (and 20); 2:25,34; 4:25; Rm 4:6; 11:9; Heb 4:7) as in subsequent Jewish and Christian parlance. (A similar thing occurs with the use of the word 'Gregorian' to describe plain-song.) By the above NT passages Davidic authorship cannot be urged, though it cannot be demonstrably contradicted (cf Bib. Com. VII [1910], 1, 2, 6 [= EnchB 344, 348, 349]), and the problem becomes simpler when we consider the formula to refer to the 'collection' rather than to the author. The same thing applies to the 'labels' including the names of Qorah and Asaph. (Similarly the attribution of the older breviary hymns to e.g. St Ambrose is deduced often with difficulty through the examination of other writings of the author: a method which is not available for the Psalter, or is only used without much conviction.)

i 6. The **formation** of the Psalter doubtless took place over many centuries, for it includes ancient cosmic material allied to Babylonian, Canaanite and Egyptian religious poetry (e.g. 19 [first part], 29, 104); material from pre-monarchy (pre-11th cent.) tribal days of the settlement, when the gods of the nations are contrasted with Yahweh (e.g. 82); the 'Royal Psalms' which must have had at least their origin in monarchic days; songs of triumph of the divinely appointed king (e.g. 2, 110); as well as some patently post-exilic psalms (e.g. 137 *Super flumina Babylonis*); and the much more sophisticated material of the 'Wisdom' age (e.g. the alphabetical psalms as 111, 112), and the exaltation of the *Torah* (e.g. 19 [second part] and 119). It is probable that these didactic psalms were the latest additions to the **381i** heritage, deriving from the scribes of the post-exilic Temple. Nearly all types, of all ages, are found in nearly all the 'collections', and these were probably formed gradually from the time of the early monarchy and the Temple of Solomon, incorporating ancient popular material, together with current material of every age, constantly edited and refurbished into a fairly homogeneous whole. The 'collections' were then formed into 'books' and eventually into the one Psalter, to which a prose preface (Ps 1) was provided, certainly before, perhaps long before the 2nd cent. B.C. when the LXX translators knew the Psalter as we have it now. It should also be remembered that these successive editings resulted in the final Psalter being only a selection: there are similar poems elsewhere in the OT, e.g. Jon 2 and Hb 3, while Pss 18, 96, 105 also appear in 2 Sm 22 and 1 Chr 16. Among later Jewish compilations, there are e.g. the 'Psalms of Solomon' and several apocryphal psalms appear among the canonical in the Qumrân Psalter (11Q Ps^a).

j 7. Much in modern study of the Psalter has grown out of the investigation on Form Critical lines of the **categories** or literary genres of the psalms. In its detailed form this method was developed by H. Gunkel (d. 1932), especially in his posthumous work *Einleitung in die Psalmen* (ed. J. Begrich) of 1933. There are obviously many ways of 'categorizing' any collection of poems, thus in the Breviary *Exsultet caelum laudibus* (Apostles, Vespers) is plainly a hymn of praise, while *Audi benigne Conditor, nostras preces cum fletibus* (Lent, Vespers) is in penitential mood (a 'Community Lament'), and *Jesu dulcis memoria* is a personal prayer. The most famous 'categories' (*Gattungen*) of the psalms are those of Gunkel (usually numbered according to the chapters of his book): 2. Hymns, 3. Enthronement Psalms, 4. Community Laments, 5. Royal Psalms, 6. Individual Laments (no less than 40, and including the idea of trust), 7. Individual Thanks, 8. Smaller groups, including pilgrimage, community thanks, and legends, 9. Prophetic, including hymns of Sion, 10. 'Wisdom' or didactic psalms, 11. Liturgical types. (Many of these are obvious, but the category is often named in the commentary.) These categories are in the main followed by later authors, most notably by S. Mowinckel, *The Psalms in Israel's Worship*. An important modification is that many psalms in the large category of Individual Laments are to be treated as National Laments, which reduces the true Individual Laments (or 'Psalms of Sickness', e.g. Ps 6) to about 10. R. Tournay (in the introduction to the fascicule of the BJ 1950—5) reduces the main categories to four: 1. Hymns (including cosmic, historical, Sion and pilgrimage), 2. Prayers (collective and personal laments, confidence and thanksgiving), 3. Didactic Psalms, 4. Prophetic and Eschatological Psalms. T. Worden in *The Psalms are Christian Prayer*, 1961, analysing further the idea of prayer in the Psalter, reduces the basic types to two: lamentation and praise. Together with this literary study of the psalms goes the investigation of their origin upon their historical background.

k 8. With regard to the **origin** of the psalms, the opinion in Jewish and Christian antiquity was that David was the author of most, if not all, of the psalms, and this remained the traditional view until the 19th cent. although in the 16th—17th cent. some had proposed that Ezra was at least the editor of the Psalter. But with the advent of the 'Higher Criticism', especially with Ewald (1836), Delitzsch (1867), Wellhausen (1876),

381k Cheyne (1889) and Duhm (1900), it came to be generally accepted, on the basis of the identification of the historical background and the life of Israel reflected in the psalms, that most, if not all, of them were post-exilic, and that many references to 'enemies' or 'victories' referred to the Maccabean period; in other words, the Psalter became detached from the ancient history of Israel altogether. But with Kirkpatrick (1902) and Briggs (1906–7) we find a return, not indeed to David as author—too much had been learnt from the 'Higher Criticism'—but to ancient Israel, with the idea of a compilation extending from the days of the early monarchy (David) or before, into late post-exilic times in the manner outlined under 'formation' above. Much of the detailed theory of e.g. Kirkpatrick (pp. 1–lix) and Briggs (I, liv–xcii) remains
l viable today. But with Gunkel (1933) the application of the method of *Formgeschichte* to the study of the *Sitz im Leben* brought the first clear breakthrough of the notion that most, if not all, of the psalms have their **origin in the cult** or public religious ritual in Israel throughout its history, from primitive tribal cult to developed Temple liturgy after the exile. Anyone can see that hymns of praise and 'community laments' in the Psalter (as in the Breviary), together with the Songs of Sion (such as Pss 84, 87, 122), are 'cultic' in the sense of pertaining to community worship, and these 'obviously cultic' psalms number about 55. With regard to the others, the authors are divided. What of the 40 or so, usually classed as 'Individual Laments'? For Mowinckel (ch 7–8) the greater number of these are in fact 'national' and therefore 'cultic'; for Gunkel (ch 6) they are truly personal and represent an 'emancipation of religious piety from the cult'. The didactic or 'Wisdom' psalms are accepted by Mowinckel (ch 16) as 'non-cultic': such are 37, 49, 111, 112, 127, 128, 133, and the 'histories' of 78, 105, 106. Much emphasis is laid by all followers of the 'cultic' school upon the *Sitz im Kult* of certain psalms, as being liturgies to accompany certain special festivals. P. Drijvers, in *The Psalms, their Structure and Meaning*, 1965 (a translation and revision of the original Dutch of 1956), while in general following Mowinckel, has worked out (ch 9) for some psalms the complete course of a festival procession (see on Ps 118). With Gunkel special prominence is given to the 'Royal Psalms' as liturgies for the anointing and enthronement of the divinely appointed king; and for Mowinckel the course of a king's inauguration is seen in Pss 2, 101 with 72, and 110—other royal occasions being seen in 20, 21, 45,
m 132. This idea of the 'sacral kingship' leads to the notion of a festival of the 'Enthronement of Yahweh' as universal King, which for Gunkel is limited to psalms with the formula 'Yahweh is [or, has become] king', as 93, 96, 97, 98 (see on 93:2), but for Mowinckel extends to other 'processional psalms' as 47, 99. (These matters are discussed in the commentary on those Pss.) The supposition of such an annual festival in Israel, with a cultic enactment of the proclamation and enthronement of Yahweh as king, is replaced by A. Weiser (*The Psalms*, E.tr., 1962) by the supposition of an annual 'Covenant Festival' as the *Sitz im Kult* of the majority of the psalms, often including a cultic (dramatic) representation of the *Heilsgeschichte* (cf pp. 35, 42 and passim), and he absorbs into this pattern many psalms associated by Gunkel (and to a lesser degree by Mowinckel) with harvest and other primitive agricultural festivals, which (as indeed in all calendars) form an annual framework. H. J. Kraus (*Die Psalmen*, 1961), while following the general outline of Gunkel's work, rejects his former acceptance of the 'Enthronement Festival' in favour of a 'Liturgy before the Ark' as the central feature of the cult (p. xliii, and **38** excursus on Pss 24 and 132). One of the principal drawbacks of any 'cultic festival' theory, be it of the Enthronement, the Covenant, or the Ark, is that the existence of such a festival can be no more than a hypothesis to explain psalms where the further hypothesis of a liturgical structure is claimed. At the same time a 'cultic' explanation of many more psalms than the 'obvious' ones cannot since Gunkel's time be neglected.

9. Associated with the liturgical use of the psalms are **n** several words used in the **titles** (other than indications of 'collections'), which are probably musical terms or choral directions, the exact meaning of which now escapes us, so that many modern versions leave them in Heb. One need only think how mystifying the phrase 'To the Old Hundredth' would be, if we did not possess the key to its meaning and history.

(a) descriptive: *mizmôr* (= making music, LXX/V psalm; 57t); *šîr* (= song; 30t); *maskîl* (= ? understanding; 13t); *mikhtām* (= ?; 6t in 'David Collections', 16, 56–60); *šiggāyôn* (= ?; only Ps 7); *tephillāh* (= prayer; 5t, 17, 86, 90, 102, 142); *tehillāh* (= praise; only Ps 145).

(b) directive: *lammenasṣeah* (presumably = 'for the precentor') is prefixed to 55 Pss (including most of the 'David, Qorah and Asaph Psalms', usually preceding a presumed musical direction.

(c) musical: *neghînôth* (= strings; 4, 6, 54, 55, 67, 76, cf 62); *nehûlôth* (= ? wind; only Ps 5); *'alāmôth* (= girls = ? soprani; only Ps 46); *šemînith* (= ? octave = ? bassi; only Pss 6, 12); *gittîth* (= ?; 8, 81, 84); *Jedûthûn* (= ? name; 39, 62, 77): all quite uncertain.

(d) names indicating 'Collections' (see 4 above); and also some form of association with Heman and Ethan (88–89), Moses (90) and Solomon (72, 127).

(e) added to the name of David there is often a *mise-en-scène* of an event in David's life, when the sentiment of this psalm would be suitable upon his lips (3, 7, 18, 34, 51, 52, 56, 57, 59, 60, 63, 142, where see notes).

(f) enigmatic phrases in the titles of Pss 9, 22, 45, 53, 56, 57, 58, 59, 60, 69, 75, 80, 88 are probably references to tunes, which went by the name derived from the words of the song they were associated with (like *O salutaris*, or *Valet will ich dir geben*, as names of tunes in our hymn books).

(g) the titles of Pss 38, 70, 100 may indicate particular services, as evidently do those of Pss 92 ('Sabbath') and 30 ('Dedication').

(h) Though not in the titles, the word *selāh*, occasionally **o** appearing at the end of a stanza (but see on 67:2 and on 57:4), should be mentioned here, since it is likely that it is also some rubrical or musical direction. It occurs from 1 to 4 times in the course of 39 of the psalms (in all books except IV), and its meaning is quite uncertain. LXX translate *diápsalma* (= ? pause; so BJ), liturgical translations such as Vg PB RPB omit it. Most simply transliterate it. Etymologically it may derive from 'to throw up' (though the formation is unusual), so 'Raise (voices? hands? hearts? the note?)!'—but it is all very unconvincing. Jerome and Targum thought it meant 'For ever!': an exclamation like 'Amen'. It has been suggested it is a corruption of the Gr. *psalle* = 'strike up (an intermezzo)', or that it represents initials 's.l.h.' for some musical direction (like 'd.c.' in our scores). But the key to this puzzle seems irretrievably lost.

There are a number of variations in the titles (and Selah) in the LXX and Vg, and this shows some uncertainty in the tradition. Are these things part of the inspired text? The more general opinion is negative, since

31o they are the work of an editor and not of the author, and the Biblical Commission in 1910 did not insist on their 'genuineness' (at that time = part of the text), but only on their value as traditions (EB 346, 345), and this is probably their true value, with their indication also of the 'Collections'.

p **10.** All the psalms are written in verse (with the exception of the preface, Ps 1), that is, in the form of **Hebrew prosody** which depends for its metre upon the pattern of stresses (not syllables), 2, 3 or 4 to a line, with lines in couplets or triplets usually dominated by a parallelism of ideas or imagery, the couplets or triplets being then formed into stanzas of two or more members. Thus a stanza might be formed by two couplets of three-stress lines (3 + 3, 3 + 3), e.g. Ps 114. A very regular structure is rare, and one of the delights of Hebrew poetry is the frequent breaking of the rhythm, with sudden short lines, or longer stanzas. These things are often missed in the translations, but matters of metre and stanzaic construction of the Hebrew are often mentioned in the commentary. Eight psalms are built upon an **alphabetical acrostic**: Pss 9—10, 25, 34, 37, 111, 112, 119, 145.

q **11.** Lastly we should consider what is perhaps the most important element, namely the **spiritual themes and religious convictions** expressed in the psalms. The psalms are daily used by so many, that it is important to see in what ways they are expressions of prayer. We begin with the most basic and widest ideas and proceed to the narrowest and most specialized found in relatively few places.

There is the conviction—

(1) That our God, Yahweh the Lord, maker of heaven and earth, is the **one and only true God**. This unshakable belief pervades and is taken for granted throughout the Psalter, and is the centre of the faith of Israel and of Christendom. (Such a belief, as a continuous tradition, is unique to Israel in the ancient world.)

(2) That this one true God **cares about mankind**, and moreover has invited man to be his friend. This again is found everywhere, and is also unique in ancient literature. (See on Ps 5:8 and 117:2 for special phrases.)

(3) That it is therefore the most natural thing for man **to praise and thank him** (see on the particular word *hôdhū* in 67:4 and 106:1), since he is **King** of the world and **Lord** or creation. His kingship and our praise are usually closely linked (e.g. 96—99), and it is specially his own people of Israel that is called to praise and thanksgiving (e.g. 115, 118).

r **(4)** That nevertheless many people do not do this, and some even deliberately reject him: these are God's 'enemies', and so they are also my own (83:3; 139: 21—22). These are the 'wicked' and the 'fools' (see on 14:1; 38:6).

(5) That on the contrary it is for me to 'cleave to him' (e.g. 63:9; 73:28; 91:14) and to love him (e.g. 18:2) and to love his 'law' (*Tôrāh*) (all 119), and so be numbered among the 'just' and '**devout**' (*hāsidh*, see on 12:2) and his '**poor**' (*ānī*, see on 9:13).

(6) That God **judges** mankind, favourably the just, but with condemnation for the wicked, and it is for me to concur with God's judgement, and so to wish punishment upon the wicked—hence the 'imprecations' (see on 137:9 and esp. 109): a standpoint which Christianity would later qualify.

(7) That for me to reject God would be an offence against him: this is **sin**, which I acknowledge in myself (32 and esp. 38), but I know that God is ready to forgive (e.g. 32:1; 51:3, 11).

(8) That, further, I can **trust him** completely, for he is **381r** my 'rock', my 'refuge' (see on 18:3 for many of these figures), my shepherd (Ps 23): I should **call on him** and I know that **he will answer me**, 'true to his name' (23:3). These notions, forming the basis of the 'prayer of petition' in the psalms, are found everywhere and grow out of the preceding. They are surely applicable both to the prayer of the community (the 'cultic' aspect) and to the prayer of the worshipper in his own heart. The two last themes now following, are much more specialized, namely the convictions—

(9) That God has in some way **chosen Israel to be his s 'peculiar treasure'** (135:4), with a promise of special protection, and moreover **Sion** is his abode in the midst of his people (e.g. 74:2; 132:13), and his **Temple** there is the special object of my love and pilgrimage (74, 84, 122 and also 23:6). Furthermore **David's divinely-appointed kingship** is the symbol of this favour, and claims my loyalty (esp. 89, 132). This whole theme is eschatological in the widest sense of an awareness of God's presence (*parousía*) and indwelling here and now in my own life. For the Christian, Sion becomes the symbol of the Church of Christ, the son of David, the 'Israel of God' (Gal 6:16).

(10) That **Israel has a vocation** to bring all mankind eventually to worship the one true God, figuratively on Mount Sion: the 'universalist' theme growing out of the 'Sion' theme preceding, and presented most powerfully in Ps 87 (see on 87:4). The idea is based on the throne of David, whence the **Anointed King or Messiah**, prefigured in David the Anointed, shall rule all the world (esp. 72, 102:22—23; and cf 2 and 110). This is the Messianic Age, the fulfilment of which for the Christian has its beginning with the coming of Christ, and will continue to move towards its consummation at the end, towards which Israel is also looking as to the consummation of her vocation to mankind. Thus this Messianic theme is also eschatological in the narrower sense of looking towards the 'last days' when God shall deliver Sion (e.g. 69:36—37), where he will reign for ever (146:10).

BOOK I

1 A Prose Introduction to the Psalter—Not in **382a** metre, as is often (with difficulty) supposed, but in prose style: an edifying consideration of the happiness of the just and the fate of the wicked, with suitable echoes from the Pss and other parts of OT, as a preface to the hymn book.

1. 'O the happiness of the man [echo of Pss: 24t], who walks not in the counsel of the wicked [3t Jb], stands not in the road (as if starting a journey) with sinners, sits not in the company of scorners' [typical Prv word, 14t there]. **2.** But he 'meditates on the Torah . . .' [echo of Jos. 1:8], **3** is 'like a tree planted by brooks of water [echo of Jer 17:8], and all that he does shall prosper' [echo of Jos 1:8, though the actual phrase is of Joseph in Gn 39:3,23]. **4.** But the wicked are 'like chaff driven by the wind' [figure of uselessness 7t in OT, cf. Ps 35:5]. **5.** They shall not be able to stand up (to defend themselves as in a court of law) when the judgement comes, **6.** 'For the Lord knows (and is thus able to judge) the way (of life) of the just, but the way of the wicked shall perish (= end in condemnation).' RPB 'The LORD preserves . . .' = cares for (see DWT, as 31:8; 37:18; 144:3). Way = way of life elsewhere only in Prv (8t); cognate phrases in 112:10 and Prv 10:28.

2 The Victory of the Messianic King—The first of **b**

382b a number of Pss concerned with the sacred office of the king (2, 18, 20, 21, 45, 101, 110, 132), here specially shown as chosen by God. The king's anointing was a sacred act (1 Sm 10:1 'Has not the Lord anointed thee?'); thus the king was 'the Lord's Anointed' (*Mašīah* = Messiah), applied to both Saul and David. So the idea grew up of an ideal king who should rule over an ideal Israel, and eventually over all men, when all should worship the true God together with him. It is in this sense that we can best interpret the 'Anointed' (Messiah) in the Pss: here 2:8; 20:7; 28:8; 89:39—52, also 18:51 (David's successor), 45:8 and probably 84:10. The Gr. for Messiah is *Christos*, and the Christian sees the ideal king of the Pss as prefiguring Jesus Christ. The present Ps includes a wild imagery not unlike 110. For Mowinckel (I, 64) it is a cultic representation of the king's inaugural speech, and the idea of the king becoming God's son is not unfamiliar in the ancient world. The primitive imagery suggests the Ps is very ancient, and was doubtless adopted unchanged into the hymn book, like 110, partly because of its outstanding poetic quality.

1. 'Why have the nations raged . . . ?' **2.** The picture is of the kings taking up their stations against the LORD and his Anointed (Messiah): quoted in the prayer of the faithful in Ac 4:25—26. **3.** Their cry: 'Let us break their bonds . . . ropes' [LXX/V yoke so Handel n.41]. **4.** But God laughs them to scorn, **6.** Saying 'It is I have appointed my king, upon Sion my holy hill'. **7.** The words of the anointed king: 'I will proclaim the decree [lit. unto (? = concerning) the decree] . . . (the LORD) said unto me "Thou art my son . . . " ' The liturgy (midnight Mass), following Paul in Ac 13:33 takes *Ego hodie genui te* of Christ, as also Heb 1:5; 5:5. **8.** I will give thee the nations **9.** To break them [LXX repointing, 'shepherd them' = rule them] with a rod of iron—image taken up (from LXX) in Apoc 2:27; 12:5; 19:15, and so the phrase 'rule with . . .' **10.** The words now of the psalmist, or of

c the king: 'And now, o kings . . . **11.** Serve the LORD with fear, and quail (*gîlû*) with trembling . . .': this with the next phrase is one of the most difficult passages in the Pss: i. 'Quail with trembling': taking perhaps basic sense of *gîl* as 'be excited', hence 'quail', cf BDB; ii. 'Rejoice with trembling' :so most, taking usual sense of *gîl* 'exult', and the older commentators underlined the contrast in *exsultate ei cum tremore*; iii. 'Spend your lives in trembling': connecting with *gîl* = 'life stage' in Ps 43:4 (where see note), and with Ugaritic (Dahood, Bib 45 [1964] 399), whence 'spend life', and cf on Ps 139:16. iv. Eliminate *gîlû* in emendation under iv below.

12. The most enigmatic phrase follows: '*naššequ bar*, lest he be angry . . .': i. [supposing unlikely Aram. *bar* = son] 'kiss the son': Rabbis (Ibn Ezra here understands of the Messiah) PB AV RV ii. [reading? *še'ū mūsār*] 'grasp discipline': LXX/V RVm iii. [connect with *bar* = pure] 'kiss (= adore) purely (= sincerely)': Jer (*adorate pure*) Rabbis (Rashi here) iv. Bertholet (1908) emended, adding the letters of the uncertain *gîlū* to *bar*, to form *beraglāw* 'on his feet': ' . . . with trembling kiss (on) his feet (= do homage)'. Ingenious, but arbitrary and unparalleled, and 'kiss' is never followed by 'on'; but accepted by NP BJ RSV RPB v. Perhaps *bar* is no more than a dittography (of 'with trembling') and so can be omitted: ' . . . and quail, with trembling kiss [= do homage]': cf RPB.

d 3 A Prayer for deliverance from Oppressors—A Ps typical of its genre, called by Gunkel 'Individual Lament'; in notably regular metre. **Title:** Here begins the 'David Collection I' = 3—41 except 33 (no title): an occasion in David's life is then added, cf 2 Sm 15:44ff.

2. 'LORD, how they are increased, my oppressors . . . **382** **3.** Many are saying to my soul [perhaps = about me: NP RSV RPB] . . . **4.** But thou art a shield . . . my glory [= the one whom I glorify] . . . **5.** He answered me from his holy hill (Sion)': LXX/V 'heard me' Vg *exaudire*, to convey 'effective hearing' for God 'answering' prayer in Pss. *Exaudire* in Pss thus conveys more than 'graciously to hear'. **6—7.** I shall sleep without fear (cf 4:9 and perhaps 149:5). **8.** Here the rhythm quickens, expressive of the eventual hope: ' . . . struck my enemies on the jawbone' [cf. Jg 15:15, more drastic than 'cheek'; LXX/V without cause'] **9.** And final victory is the LORD's.

4 A Night Prayer—A favourite Ps full of calmness, in **e** spite of irregular metre, and regularly used at Compline. **Title:** 'For the Precentor, on strings (?) . . .'

2. 'When I call to thee, answer me [see on 3:5], God of my right [i.e. defender of my right as in a court of law], in the straits [lit. narrows, hence anguish, as Lat. *angustiae* is lit. narrows] thou hast made it wide [= easy] for me [cf 25:17; 118:5]. **3.** Sons of men, how long (is) my glory (to be) for disgrace, will you love emptiness . . . ?' i. so, variously, PB AV RV RSV RPB ii. [slight emend.] ' . . . how long (will you be) heavy of heart [= hard-hearted as Ex 7:14]? Why do you love . . . ?': LXX/V NP BJ, probably a better reading.

4. 'And know that the LORD has separated his holy one [*hāsīdh* see on 12:2] for himself' i. so PB AV RV RSV RPB ii. slight emend.] ' . . . that the LORD has made wonderful his holy one': LXX/V NP BJ iii. this reading inclines one to read as in 31:22 'The LORD has made wonderful his mercy to me (*hasdō lī*), and cf 17:7.

5. 'Tremble and sin not': 'tremble' not elsewhere in **f** Pss of a person: i. = tremble with anger: LXX/V RSV: so from LXX in Eph 4:26; ii. = stand in awe: PB AV RV NP BJ RPB. 'Commune with your hearts upon your beds, and be silent', i.e. calmly in the silence of the night, but the 'bed' may be rather (as perhaps in 149:5) a place of prostration in prayer. **6.** 'Sacrifices of righteousness' may mean ritually correct sacrifices (cf RSV RPB), or else 'just' or sincere sacrifices (cf CV). **7.** 'Lift up the light of thy countenance . . .': 'lift' is an unusual form: LXX/V 'is signed'. **8.** 'Thou hast set joy in my heart, more than the time their corn and their new wine increase', i.e. more than men have when . . . **9.** 'In peace together I will lie down and sleep' = both lie down and sleep (but unusual usage); NP BJ = 'as soon as I lie down, I sleep' (still more strange usage).

5 A Prayer begging for a Hearing—Another **g** 'Individual Lament', but for Mowinckel an example of one uttered in the name of the community. **Title:** *nehīlôth* only here = ? wind instruments.

2. 'Give ear to my words . . . my murmur, **3.** my king and my God [see on 44:5] . . . **4.** In the morning I present to thee (my prayer? my morning offering?)': unexpressed object uncertain, LXX/V take verb as 'stand by'. **5.** 'Not a God who delights in wickedness art thou': or 'a (false) god who delights . . . ' as RPB. **6—7.** 'The boastful' shall not come in, **8.** But I 'in the multitude of thy mercy' will enter: the famous word *hesedh*, usually *éleos*, *misericordia* in LXX/V whence 'mercy' in older versions. While mercy is included, the idea is more that of love and kindness (whence RV 'lovingkindness') especially in a superior for an inferior, and so of God, but also the loyalty between friends (whence RSV 'steadfast love'). Often linked with *'emeth*, which has the idea of 'true' as a 'true friend', whence LXX/V *alétheia*, *veritas*, but more exactly 'faithfulness', though a much warmer word is needed. The two are linked in e.g. Ps 117.

382g Perhaps 'friendship' covers both words most expressively, with 'love' or 'mercy' for *ḥesedh* and 'friendship' for *'emeth*. But consistent translation is not always possible. **10.** In the mouth of my enemy 'there is no firmness': BJ well 'rien n'est sûr'...'They flatter', as lit. 'making smooth', so LXX/V 'deceive', and so quoted Rom 3:13; but perhaps lit. 'dividing', so 'double-dealing'. **13.** But the just 'as (with) a shield thou shalt crown [or, surround] him'.

h **6 An Urgent Prayer for Relief**—An expression of misery, with striking hyperbole in vv 7—8; the first of the 'Seven Penitential Psalms' (6, 32, 38, 51, 102, 130, 143), rather a random collection of psalms of misery, but with a ray of hope at the end—22 and 88 are far more sad. For Mowinckel (II, 1) this and others (30, 32, 38, 39, 41, 88) have their origin in sickness. In the **title**, *ševmīnīth* may be connected with the word 'eight' and so mean 'an octave lower'(?), i.e. *bassi* (cf Intro. 9c).

2. 'O Lord, rebuke me not in thy anger': cf 38:2. **4.** 'my soul is shaken exceedingly, and thou, LORD, how long?' An aposeiopesis, completed by PB RPB 'wilt thou punish me?' **5.** 'Save me because of thy friendship [*ḥesedh*, see on 5:8], **6** for in death there is no remembrance of thee, in Sheol who shall praise thee?' [For 'praise' see on 67:4.] 'Sheol' is the abode of the dead, which the Hebrews, with the rest of the ancient world, saw as a place of reduced existence, of unspecified quality except as being so different from this world, that it is not even possible to pray. Although as Christians we have a new view of the after-life, the fact remains that we then shall not be able to sing God's praises in the same way as we do in this life. The LXX *Hades* and NP *Inferi* convey this vague idea, but Vg *Infernum* and Douay *Hell* have embarrassing overtones. RPB follows AV with 'the grave'. Other references to the impossibility of prayer in Sheol are at 88:11 and 115:17. **7—8.** Hyperbolic expressions of grief, which almost inevitably are adapted in translation: Heb. lit. 'I am weary with groaning, I make to swim [lit in Is 25:11, and nowhere else] every night my bed, with my tears I cause my couch to melt. **8.** my eye has become worn-out [as if moth-eaten] with grief, advanced (in years) amid my adversaries' [LXX/V 'I have grown old'] **9—11.** But now I order my enemies to leave me ('Depart from me...' is echoed in Mt 7:23, Lk 13:27), for the Lord is ready to help.

i **7 A Plea for Justice**—Title: *Šiggāyôn* (= ?) only here; the imagined circumstances are not easy to identify: perhaps Cush is a supporter of Saul (a Benjamite) in 1 Sm 22:8; Targ. takes as Saul himself, son of Qish. **2.** 'Lord my God, I have hoped in thee', **4.** I undertake to accept punishment if I have acted unjustly: **5.** 'If I have repaid with evil him who rendered to me (= my benefactor), and drew out my adversary without cause': these are pictured as two bad acts deserving punishment, and the difficulty is the meaning of 'drew out... without cause': i. = rescued my enemy, (who had attacked me) without cause, (when I should have fought him) = act of folly: PB AV RV NP BJ ii. = sent away my enemy empty-handed (lit meaning of 'without cause'): Jer iii. = plundered my enemy gratuitously (which is unjust): RSV iv. = plundered (him who) without cause (is) my enemy: RPB v. = LXX/V take with v 6: 'Then shall I deservedly fall down...' **7.** A call to God to rise in judgement **8** Amid the peoples, 'return on high' (to thy heavenly abode? or [emend.] 'be seated on high', i.e. for judgement: NP RSV RPB. **9.** 'The Lord judges the nations... **10.**... searches hearts and reins (kidneys)': for the Hebrews the heart is the seat of the intelligence, the kidneys (as particularly sensitive?) of the emotions (cf

also 16:7; 26:2; 139:13). **12.** 'God is a just judge', **382i** [gloss here in LXX/V and PB: 'strong and patient'], and he is always indignant at injustice. **13—14.** The difficulty **j** of these vv is to refer them to God or to man. LXX/V are ambiguous. By 15 it is clearly the wicked: i. '... (God) indignant every day, **13** unless he (God) turn, he will sharpen his sword, he has bent his bow... **14** and he has prepared for him(self) deadly darts... **15.** Behold he (the wicked man) gives birth to iniquity...: so? AV, (involving the least quick changes) ii. '... (God) indignant every day, **13** unless he (the wicked) turn, he (God) will sharpen his sword... **14**... prepared for him (the wicked) deadly darts... **15.** Behold he (the wicked)...: PB AV RV NP RSV RPB iii. '... (God) indignant every day, **13** unless he (the wicked) turn. Let him (the wicked) sharpen his sword. **14.**... prepared for him(self, or for the just) deadly darts... **15.** Behold he (the wicked)...: BJ **18.** The Psalmist thanks God for his just judgement.

8 A Song of Praise—a beloved Psalm, a true hymn. **k** Title: Gittith = ? a musical instrument from Gath; or LXX/V 'winepresses' = a tune?

2. 'Yahweh (Lord), our Lord (Adonai) [the first is God's proper name, the second a title]... thou who has set thy glory above the sky': 'hast set' *tenah*) is an awkward grammatical form: i. = *nāthattāh* = hast set: Jer PB AV RV NP ii. = *nittenah* = has been set: LXX/V iii. − *tunnāh* = has been repeated, − chanted (with very doubtful parallel in Jg 5:11): JA BJ RSV: BJ RSV connect with next verse (?) **3.** 'By the lips of babes and infants thou hast established strength...': i. = thou hast ordained strength = even the littlest ones have the strength to praise God and so confound his enemies: PB AV RV ii. = thou hast founded a bulwark against thy enemies: BJ RSV (having detached from the preceding 'lips of babes...') iii. = thou hast fashioned praise: LXX/V, i.e. praise in the sense of declaring God's power, or 'ascribing power' to him, cf 29:1; 68:35. LXX quoted in this sense in Mt 21:16, and here followed by NP iv. [emend.] 'Thou hast rebuked the strong' (cf idea of i): RPB (see DWT). To make an end of [lit bring **l** to rest] war and revenge. **4.** 'When I look at thy heavens' (far from earthly strife, I am moved to ask) **5.** 'what is man... the son of man (or, child of Adam)... [both terms underline mere mortal man] that thou visited him [verb as here basically 'to care for' and hence also of God's 'visitation']? **6.** Thou hast made him little less than *elohim*...' This is of course i. the proper word for 'God'; but ii. is also used for other (false) gods, e.g. Ex 20:3: in the Pss 82:1, 6; 86:8; 96:5; 97:7; 136:2 perhaps 138:1; and perhaps iii. for celestial beings in Jb 1:6; 2:1; 38:7, and cf *elim* in Ps 29:1; 89:7; iv. = 'officials of the community' only in Ex 21:6; 22:7, 8, 8, 27, and perhaps Jg 5:8, Ps 82:1, 6:138:1 and 58:2. According to these senses, there are various renderings here: i. the traditional rendering of LXX/V 'little less than angels' is thus quoted in Heb 2:7, and preserved in PB AV JA NP RPB ii. 'little less than God': Jer RV RSV iii. 'little less than a god' BJ. **7—9.** God's special favour to mankind is followed up: 'everything under his feet (= rule)' is quoted in 1 Cor 15:26 and Eph 1:22.

9—10 A Song of Thanksgiving and a Prayer for 383a Protection—This Ps is in LXX/V correctly given as one Ps, while the Heb. text divides into 9 and 10. A (slightly faltering) alphabetical acrostic runs through, and many ideas and phrases recur through 9 and 10. **Title:** 'Death for the son' is probably the name of a tune.

2—7. Thanks to God for his just judgement: my enemies are overthrown. **8—13.** The LORD's judgement from

383a Sion in the future: **10.** he is for me a 'refuge, or, stronghold', idea of safety out of reach (for a series of such metaphors see on 18:3). **13.** 'When he (God) seeks [= ? avenges] blood (shed), he remembers them: he forgets not the cry of the "poor"': 'seeks' = demands = exacts = avenges, is a usage peculiar to this Ps 9—10 (also in 10:4, 13, 15). The 'poor' or afflicted '*ānī* (30t in Ps) = the just man afflicted or reduced to poverty by the oppressors, often (13t) linked with '*ebhyôn*, more literally poor, became a technical term to represent the pious in Israel. The cognate word '*ānāw* (usually tr. 'meek') is used (11t) almost exclusively in this sense. **14—15.** A cry for help from God, who brings me 'from the gates of death' (cf 6:6). **15.** The supreme joy of living in Sion, God's abode (v 12). The phrase 'daughter of Sion', a poetical personification of the city, though used by the prophets, occurs only here in the Pss. **17.** *Higgaion* = 'meditation' (cf 19:15), or a musical instrument (in 92:4); but here (only here linked with *Selah*) probably a musical direction. **21.** 'Place fear upon them': 'Fear' is here mis-spelt, and was read by LXX/V as 'teacher'. 'Let them know that they are (but) men'.

b **10 (continues from 9)—1.** 'Why dost thou hide thyself at times (of distress) in trouble?': the phrase 'at times' = of distress, is only in this Ps (9:10 and here). **2.** 'In the pride of the wicked he burns [= ? hotly pursues, as in Gn 31:36] the "poor"': or, with LXX/V NP BJ 'the poor is burnt (with anger, incensed)'. **3—11.** The devices of the wicked, which are their own perdition, a very difficult section. **3.** 'The wicked man boasts of the (evil) desires of his soul, and the covetous blesses [euphemism = curses], despises the LORD': such substitution for an otherwise blasphemous phrase is found elsewhere, e.g. Jb 1:5: so RV NP RSV RPB; other versions arrange variously, LXX/V 'the covetous is blessed'. **4.** 'The wicked, according to the height of his anger [or, pride of his countenance], does not seek (God): (he says), "There is no God" (in) all his thoughts': so PB AV RSV RPB; others again variously, particularly RV NP taking as 'He (God) will not seek [= avenge]', if BJ. **5.** 'His ways are strong all the time'. = ? firm RV BJ; = ? prosperous NP RSV; = ? grievous PB AV; LXX/V = unclean. **6.** For ever '(I shall) not (be) in misfortune': an awkward line, but so most: it expresses imagined security. **7.** 'His mouth is full of curses': quoted Rm 3:14. **8.** 'He sits in an ambush of villages [or, courts, or (BJ emending) reeds], **9** like a lion, he seizes them, **10.** 'He is crushed, he bows (?)': i. 'The righteous [inserting *ṣaddiq* for the *ṣadhe* verse, missing in the acrostic] is crushed...'; RPB ii. 'the poor [from later in verse] is crushed...': RVm RSV iii. '(the wicked, like a lion) crouches [as if crushing himself] and lies low'; PB AV RV NP BJ. **12—15.** A call for God's help. **13.** The wicked say 'He (God) will not seek [= avenge, cf v 4 and 9:13]; but **14** thou hast seen (it)... **15**...thou shalt seek out his wickedness (and) find not [till there be no more to find]'. **16—18.** The Triumph of right: 'the LORD is king'.

c **11 A Declaration of Trust, in spite of my fear—1.** 'I trust in the LORD: how do you say to my soul, "Flee to your mountain, o bird"': but most emend with LXX/V 'Flee to the mountain like a bird'. There are those who would counsel flight from the wicked, but the Lord is here, and there is no need. **2.** 'They have fitted their arrow to the string [rather than 'in the quiver' LXX/V PB] to aim in the darkness at the upright of heart'. **3.** 'If the foundations be destroyed': 'foundations', a word only here, usually interpreted with Jerome ('*leges*') of established institutions; 'what has the righteous done?': but many read as 'what shall the righteous do?' **4.** But

we need have no fear, for the Lord is in his holy place, **383** and in heaven, and (CV well) 'his searching glance is on mankind'. **5.** The LORD searches the righteous and the wicked (alike), **6.** 'he rains upon the wicked snares, fire and brimstone': but many follow Symmachus, for 'snares' (unlikely) reading 'coals' (cf Is 54:16): so NP BJ RSV RPB. 'And storms shall be the portion of their cup': the idea of the 'cup' which I have to drink as my inexorable fate is not uncommon (see on 60:5 and 75:9), cf 'If this cup may not pass away' Mt 26:42, Mk 14:36, Lk 22:42; and see on Ps 16:5. **7.** '...His face shall look upon the upright': PB AV with LXX/V ('uprightness'); but others invert and emend slightly 'The upright shall look upon his face': RV BJ RSV RPB. Vv 5—7 are in a fine long metre, with a short line at the end.

12 A Psalm of Hope in Trouble—A variation on the **d** prayer in distress, and notable for its long metre, with stanzas clearly marked. The text is in places very unsure. The **title** includes *š⁰mīnīth*: cf on Ps 6.
2. 'Save, Lord, for the devout (man) has ceased (to exist), for the faithful have vanished from (among) the children of men': the 'devout', *ḥāsīdh*, is the one who has *ḥesedh* or friendship especially with God, and became a technical term for devout ('practising') Jews, the 'faithful', and particularly in Maccabean times denoted the opponents of hellenization, the 'Assideans', cf 1 Mc 2:42, 7:13, 2 Mc 14:6. It occurs 20t in the Ps, and was probably derived from the Pss; but because of its special force in Maccabean times it is thought by some to be a mark of a late Ps. **3—6** describes the wicked, 'with a smooth lip... in heart and heart' = with a double heart, cf 1 Chr 12:34, contrasting with 12:39 'a perfect heart'. **4.** 'A tongue speaking big (things)' = 'talking big': **e** Vg well '*linguam magniloquam*', **5.** 'Those who said, "To our tongue (we say), 'We will do mightily, our lips are with us...'"'. **6.** But because the 'poor' are ruined, the Lord will arise: 'I will place in safety (him who) blows for it': the last phrase is difficult: i. = 'him who gasps (= ? longs) for it (safety)': RVm NP BJ RSV RPB; ii. = '(safe) from him who blows at (= scorns, cf 10:5) him': PB AV RV (but Mowinckel, II, 60, thinks = gesture of witchcraft). **7.** But the words of the Lord are 'silver smelted in a crucible for the earth(?), purified seven times': the word 'crucible' occurs only here and follows the Targum: i. 'in a crucible on the ground [very doubtful]': AV RV RSV; ii. [emend. 'crucible'] 'separate from the earth', i.e. earth discarded in the smelting: Jer NP BJ (LXX/V same idea?); iii. [emend. 'for the earth'] 'silver smelted in a crucible, gold purified seven times': RPB (see DWT): *ḥārūṣ* = gold): by far the best solution. **8—9.** Protect us, Lord, for **9** the wicked surround us 'according to the height of vileness [? word only here] for [= ? among] the children of men':

13 A Prayer in Fear, followed by Hope—A good **f** poem, opening with a kind of hopelessness and ending with a song. The stanzaic construction is particularly good. The 1st stanza vv 2—3 is of long metre, with four beginnings 'How long...?'; a single couplet introduces the hope in v 4, and the 2nd stanza of trust is in shorter metre. For Mowinckel this is an example of a national lament, though in the person of one.
2. 'How long, o Lord, wilt thou forget me...? **3.** 'How long shall I have anguish in my soul...?' i. so RPB without emending: '*ēṣāh* related to Aramaic (see DWT); ii. others by emending: NP RSV; iii. 'place counsels (= anxieties) in...': LXX/V PB AV RV (BJ = of revolt). **4.** The single central couplet, expressing the fear 'lest I fall asleep (in) death': see on Sheol in 6:6, and **5** lest my enemies rejoice 'if I am moved (i.e. slip, lose my

33f foothold)'. **6.** 'But I have trusted in thy friendship': the word *hesedh*, see on 5:8. '. . . for he has dealt bountifully with me': the verb includes the idea of reward. LXX/V and PB add here (from the end of Ps 7) 'And I will chant to the name of the Lord most high'.

g 14 A Consideration of the 'Fool' and a Hope of Deliverance—This Ps alone (with its duplicate 53) has the 'fool' as its main preoccupation. (See also note at the end of 53 for the value of having this duplicate.) **1.** The 'fool' (*nābhāl*) is a character of Wisdom Literature, the opposite of the 'wise' (*ḥākhām*). The 'fool' is not merely witless, he is ethically reprehensible: he appears 5t in the Pss, here (and 53:1) saying 'There is no God', in 39:9 he insults the devout, and, worst of all, in 74:18, 22 he insults God. For a similar word *'ewīl* see on 38:6. '(Men) are become corrupt . . . there is none doing good': LXX/V PB, and retained (pleasantly) in RPB, add from v 3: 'no, not one'. **2.** God looks down from heaven to see if there be any that 'understand', the quality of the 'wise', absent in the 'fool'. The 'wise' therefore 'seeks God', but the 'fool' does not. **3.** 'The whole (of them) is turned aside [similar word in 53] . . . become corrupt': a word only here, Ps 53 and Jb 15:16, and related to an Arabic root meaning 'sour' (of milk), whence perhaps Jerome's *'conglutinati sunt'* and LXX/V 'become useless'. After v 3 LXX/V (followed by PB vv 5—7) have three verses not in the Hebrew. They come from Rm 3:13—18, which is a series of citations from Pss 5:10; 10:7; 36:1; 140:4 and Is 59:7f, after the quotation of our Ps 14·1—3 in Rm 3·10—12, and presumably entered Christian MSS of LXX from Romans.

h 4. 'Shall they not be punished, the doers of iniquity . . . ?' i. 'punished' = 2nd Heb. verb *yādha'* cognate with Arabic 'be quiet, submissive' = here 'be humiliated': so RPB (see DWT); ii. all others suppose the usual verb 'know', which is awkward with no object: = 'have no knowledge', or NP (CV well) = 'will they never learn?' **7.** 'Would that from Sion [i.e. from God's abode] should come the salvation of Israel': lit according to Heb. idiom 'Who shall give . . . ?' so lit LXX/V PB BJ. 'When the LORD brings back the captivity of his people': i. 'captivity' = captives from exile: LXX/V PB AV RV BJ (but to put an 'exilic' interpretation on this passage on the basis of this single phrase is questionable); ii. = 'restores the freedom of his people', i.e. bring back a state of freedom in contrast to 'captivity'; iii. = 'restores the prosperity of his people': NP RSV RPB, taking in the sense of a slightly different word in 126:1 (cf also KB Lexicon); similar phrases in 85:2; 126:1, 4, and cognate phrase in 68:19 where see note. In Jb 42:10 the word can only mean 'fortune' or 'prosperity', while Ezek 16:53 is ambiguous. The interpretation 'prosperity' here is by far the most likely.

i 15 Thoughts upon the 'Just Man'—Similar to 24:3—6, also in a context of entry into the Temple. Those who seek a liturgical origin for most, if not all, of the Psalms, see here a liturgy of admission to the Temple, and Mowinckel sees it as part of the liturgy of the festival of Yahweh. The lines are very regular. **1.** 'Lord, who shall sojourn [= be accepted as thy guest] in thy tent [= thy dwelling, thy home = the Temple] . . . on thy holy hill (Sion)?' **2.** The answer is, the blameless man, **3** who 'has no slander on his tongue'. **4.** 'Despised in his eyes (is) the reprobate': so most: but PB 'He is despised in his (own) eyes, rejected', cf Targum. 'But (in contrast) he honours those who fear the Lord'. 'He takes an oath to do evil, and does not change': i. = 'to do evil (to himself = to his own inconvenience), and keeps his oath': Jer PB AV RV NP BJ RPB [but not normal use of

'do evil']; ii. [emend. *lⁱre'ōh*] 'an oath to his neighbour, **383i** and keeps it' LXX/V cf PB which includes both renderings. This emendation is a better reading. **5.** He does not practise usury nor bribery.

16 Detestation of Idols, Adherence to God—A **j** poem of personal protestation. Title: *Mikhtām* of unknown meaning, only of a 'David' Ps, and only here in Book I, the others being 56—60 in Book II.

1. 'Preserve me, o God . . . **2.** I have said to the Lord, My master (*adonai*) art thou': so LXX and most, but Heb. 'Thou (fem.) hast said . . .' whence PB AV take as addressed to 'my soul (fem.)', so Ibn Ezra. 'My good (is) not upon thee (= ? apart from thee—perhaps emend to this?): i. = I have nothing good apart from thee: Jer RV NP RSV RPB; ii. LXX omits altogether, which makes the phrase suspect: BJ takes with next verse, emending iii. = of my goods thou hast no need: Vg cf PB AV. **3.** 'To the holy ones who are in the land, and the nobles of all my delight in them': an uncertain passage: i. = 'My delight is in the holy ones . . .' [emend. 'nobles']: Jer PB AV RPB; ii. ['nobles' emend. to 'made wonderful'] 'For the holy ones who are in the land, he made wonderful his will in them': LXX/V cf NP; iii. [slight emend.] 'As for the holy ones . . ., they are the nobles in whom I delight' RV RSV—the most satisfactory, though sense not clear. iv. [taking 'not upon thee' from v.2, and with drastic emendation] 'Belial [= worthless] are all the (so-called) holy ones . . .': BJ. **4.** In contrast to the 'holy ones' above, here are the idolaters—but the sense is uncertain: 'Their sorrows shall be multiplied, (when) they hasten after (false gods?)'. i. This general sense is adopted by most: PB AV RV NP RSV RPB, but much essential material has to be imagined, including the false gods. ii. LXX/V leave literal '. . . after(wards) they hastened' with no clear sense. iii. [slight emend. 'sorrows' to 'idols'] 'the idols are multiplied of those who run after them': Jer. The detestation of idols is now clear: 'I will not perform their libations of blood' [LXX/V for 'libations' read 'gatherings']. **5.** The Lord is my inheritance, my 'cup' (see on 11:6): my 'portion' or inheritance = all I have or care about, cf 73:26; 119:57; 142:6. **6.** 'Ropes (as for surveying property) have fallen for me (i.e. marked out my inheritance) in pleasant places: indeed (my) inheritance is beautiful [Aram. word, only here] for **k** me'. **7—11.** My thanks to God: '. . . at night my reins (kidneys = emotions, cf on 7:10) reprove me'. **8.** I have made myself always aware of God's presence, for he is 'at my right hand' as counsel for the defence cf 109:31; 142:5. **9.** 'Therefore my heart rejoiced, and my liver (= emotions, especially compassion, cf Lam 2:11) exulted': the word 'liver' as RPB is a repointing (see DWT) of 'glory' = perhaps 'soul', as explained by e.g. Ibn Ezra. Whether NP and RSV 'soul' follows this, or the repointing (with euphemism, as BJ) is uncertain. LXX/V have 'tongue'. For 'glory' = 'soul' see also on 30:13; 57:9; 108:2. **10.** 'For thou shalt not leave my soul in Sheol, nor suffer thy devout one [*hāsīdh* see on 12:2] to see corruption (or, the Pit)'. Once more the psalmist's trust that he will not be delivered to Sheol, or, death, (see on 6:6). There are three words in the Pss used to describe Sheol: (1) *šaḥath*, probably = 'the bottom', here 16:10; 30:10; 55:24; 103:4, (2) *bôr* = 'cistern' (Vg *lacus*), nearly always 'going down to . . .', 28:1; 30:4; 88:5, 7; 143:7, (3) *beēr* = 'well', 55:24; 69:16. *Šaḥath*, here, may be derived from *šūaḥ* 'go down', hence 'the Pit'; or from *šāḥath* 'destroy', whence 'corruption', and was thus read by LXX/V in this Ps and quoted from LXX in Ac 2:27 (Peter) and 13:35

383k (Paul) with reference to Christ's resurrection. Although Peter refers the Ps to Christ, this is rather an application of the passage, where the poet plainly refers to himself or to whoever uses the prayer. The translation 'corruption' appears in most versions since LXX (and Handel n. 32); 'the pit (of Sheol)' in RVm BJ RSV RPB. **11.** 'The path of life' is a phrase used only here in the Pss, but 3t in Pr (2:19; 5:6; 15:24, also opposed to Sheol and death); and although not occurring exactly in the NT (except the quotation of this passage in Ac 2:28), it has obvious NT associations, e.g. Jn 14:6, Mt 21:32, Lk 1:39, Ac 16:17.

384a 17 A Protestation of Faithfulness—Another personal protestation. **Title:** 'A prayer': the only one in Book I: of the others 86, 90, 102, 142, all but 90 are in 'David Collections'.

1—2. A plea to the 'just judge' for a hearing: and I shall be found innocent. **3—4.** Thou hast tested me . . . and thou shalt find . . . that 'at the word of thy lips I have kept the ways of the law': i. '. . . of the law': a word akin to the Akkadian and Arabic: so WV NP BJ (and Zorell's Lexicon)—distinct from the commoner word 'robber'. ii. [supposing usual word] 'I have kept (away from) the ways of a robber': PB AV RV RSV RPB—but it forces unwarrantably the use of 'to keep', and the natural 'keep the ways of a robber' cannot be right. iii. LXX/V 'I have kept (to) hard ways' = 'broken ways'? **5.** I have kept to thy 'tracks'—properly as 'traced' (by God), as a cart-track. **6—12.** A call for protection. **9.** For enemies surround me. **10.** 'their fat they have closed': a puzzling phrase, simply rendered thus by LXX/V: i. Many attempt to translate 'They are enclosed in their own fat': PB AV RV BJ. ii. Others adopt the easy emendation: 'The fat of their heart they have closed' = 'their gross [CV cruel] hearts . . .', cf 119:70 perhaps 73:7: so JA (cf RVm) NP RSV RPB. All express self-complacency. **11.** '(In) our footsteps now they surround me [or, us]': or, emending 'they come (at me), they surround me': Jer RPB (see DWT) cf RSV. **13.** '. . . Deliver my soul [= my life] from the wicked one (by?) thy sword [i.e.? the instrument of thy chastisement] **14** . . . by thy hand, from men, whose portion of life (is of this) world': a very uncertain passage: and LXXᴬ and LXXᴮ with Vg show further confusions in the Greek. 'And (with) thy hidden (treasure) thou fillest their belly: they have sufficiency of children [or, their children have enough], and they leave the rest of what they have to their babes': so literally—another very confused passage; but the general sense seems to convey the prosperity of my enemies. **15.** But by contrast 'I (if I live) in righteousness, shall see thy face; I shall be satisfied (i.e. find full happiness) to awake (and see) thy form': a very difficult passage [LXX/V 'satisfied when thy glory is seen']. The idea of 'seeing the form' of God is strange in the Pss, and to interpret this of awaking after death is so alien to the OT that it is unlikely.

c 18 Thanks for Victory—A hymn of thanksgiving for a king to utter, and placed on the lips of King David in 2 Sm 22, with a special mention of him at the end, probably added for this purpose, as is also the elaborate **title** indicating the moment in David's life. The fact that we have two recensions of this psalm (as with the duplicates), shows by their divergences the instability of the text, and leads us to expect instability elsewhere, when there is no other recension by which to check. The metre is mostly regular 3 + 3. **2.** 'I love thee, Lord, my strength . . .' **3.** Here is an almost complete list of the

various metaphors for strength and deliverance applied **38i** to God in the Pss: rock (as unscalable, unassailable), fastness (safe from pursuit), (deliverer—not a metaphor), rock (as firm and hard—see on 28:1), shield (as of a soldier), horn (as of a strong animal), refuge (as inaccessible). These are variously translated, but the sense is always similar. **4.** 'I call on the LORD (who is to be praised': i. so most: = worthy to be praised; ii. LXX/V [repointing]: 'praising, I call . . .'; iii. CV takes as 'Praised be the Lord, I exclaim'. **5—6.** His perils. 'The waves [as 2 Sm] of death encompassed me, the floods of Belial [perdition, a personification of devouring evil] overwhelmed me': Heb. here has 'cords of death', cf. 'cords of Sheol' in next v, i.e. cords enmeshing me, dragging me down to Sheol, probably mis-copied here: i. so RPB cf BJ CV (see DWT for 'Belial': 'waves' good parallelism here); ii. others keep 'cords' as in Heb.; iii. LXX/V 'pains of death' (exactly similar word). **7—16.** God answers, and a cosmic theophany is described: **d 8** the earth quaked. **9.** 'Smoke went up in his anger [or, in (= from) his nostrils—same word in Heb., as distended in anger?]' . . . **10.** 'He bowed the heavens and came down [cf 144:5], and a dark cloud (was) under his feet [the dark cloud of God's abode, cf e.g. Ex 20:21], **11.** He rode upon a cherub [image of a heavenly winged creature cf part of the furniture of the tabernacle Ex 25:18—22: similarly as king of the world in 99:1, but with a special sense in 80:2, where see note] and flew, and glided [rare word: of eagle Dt 28:49] on the wings of the wind'. **12—16.** further cosmic descriptions. **17—25.** Amid all this, the Lord rescued me. **30.** 'For in thee [= with thy help] I run (through) a troop [i.e. defeat my attackers]': an uncertain passage: i. so PB AV RV NP, supplying (awkwardly) 'through', and no parallel usage; ii. [repoint.] 'crush a troop': RSV; iii. [emend.] 'break through a hedge': RPB (good parallel with next line): the best reading; iv. LXX/V 'delivered from temptation' is of uncertain origin. Breaking down defences, leaping over a wall (of a city I am besieging): these are symbols of my victory in God's strength. **31—40.** Because God's way is perfect, and his word tried (as in the fire, cf 119:140), he gives me strength, **34.** 'he makes my feet (nimble, for safety in flight) as (the feet of) a hart' . . . **35.** He teaches me how 'to bend a bow of bronze'—a sign of great strength—**36.** his gentleness makes me great . . . **41—43.** The picture of victory in war, **44—46.** the submission of the nations: a suggestion of Israel's vocation to lead the world to God. **47—50.** All this is due to God's salvation. **50.** 'I will proclaim thee [hôdhāh see on 67:4] among the nations': quoted Rm 15:9 of the gentiles. **51.** places the Ps in the context of King David: God helps his 'anointed' (mašîaḥ see on 2:2).

19 A (1—7) **A Cosmic Hymn**—Ps 19 is in fact two **e** poems of quite different character, somehow combined in compilation. 19A stands alone in the Psalter: it seems to be a primitive song about the heavenly bodies praising God by their existence. It has been compared to Babylonian hymns to the sun, and even supposed to be such a hymn, adopted into the Jewish hymn-book. The only mention of God is in fact in the first line, under the primitive title of *El*, a title used by other nations in Canaan for their god, though here indeed represented as creator. It is also rare for a Ps to begin not with some invocation. The metre is remarkable for its long 4-beat lines. Ps 19B is a didactic poem of a much later age.

2—5a. 'The heavens (or, skies) recount the glory of God (*El*) . . . **3.** Day pours out [as a spring of water]

84e a word to day, and night shows knowledge to night'. **4.** But this is not in human speech, yet 'their sound is gone forth into all the earth ...' i. so LXX/V, followed by PB NP RSV [assuming emendation of *qawwām* to *qôlām*] ii. But RPB (see DWT) also has 'sound', taking *qawwām* = 'string' = 'musical note', as English 'chord', with no alteration of the text: but the usage has no parallel. iii. Heb. *qawwām* = 'their line', i.e. rope esp, for measuring, surveying (an inheritance?), so here = the limits of their influence: AV RV BJ— but the meaning is rather forced. The phrase ('sound' as in LXX) is taken up in Rm 10:18 of the apostles' preaching, and so often in the liturgy of the apostles (e.g. Offertory). **5b—7.** The song about the sun. Why is this here? Perhaps because the sun also joins in God's praise, though it is here only depicted as running its course. But the sun is a divine symbol, and for Christians 'the sun of justice, with healing in its wings' (Mal 3:20 [4:2 English]) is a symbol of Christ. 'For the sun he (God) has set an abode in them (the heavens)', and the sun is likened to **6** a bridegroom, and **7** an athlete about to run a race.

f **19 B** (8—15) **A Didactic Poem**—A quiet meditation on the delights of the Torah in very regular stanzas. It has much affinity with the great didactic Psalm: Ps 119. **8.** 'The Torah of the Lord is perfect': the famous word *Tôrāh*, translated in the LXX and the NT as 'law', more exactly means 'guidance, direction, teaching'. In addition to 24t in Ps 119, the word comes 9t in the Pss, either in a didactic context (Torah good for man) in 1:2, here, 37:31; 89:31; 94:12; or in an epic context (God gave the Torah) in 78:5, 10; 105:45; and once (78:1) = 'instruction' (of a teacher). **8—10.** Describes God's guidance of mankind, and each couplet begins with another of the great didactic words, almost synonyms of Torah: Torah itself, God's 'testimony' (or witness of justice), his 'precepts', his 'commandments', the 'fear of the Lord', his 'judgements': all words reappearing throughout Ps 119. **11—12.** The delights of the Torah, cf 119:72, 105, 127. **15.** 'O Lord, my rock [see on 18:3], my redeemer': 'redeemer' is *gō'el* = one who in law redeems a debt, or especially a matrimonial duty, and hence of God as the redeemer of Israel, especially in Is 41—63: not common in the Pss, and only here as an invocation.

g **20 A Prayer that God may answer a King's Requests**—This may have been originally a prayer before battle, later used in a 'cultic' way in commemoration of victory by re-enactment of the preparation. Those who see a liturgical pattern in this Ps, see vv 2—5 sung by a choir, with perhaps an anthem in v 6, with a soloist in v 7, a second choir in vv 8—9, and an anthem in v 10 with an *inclusio* in the word 'answer' echoing v 1. It is classed by Gunkel and Mowinckel as a 'Royal Psalm'.

2. 'May the Lord answer thee [cf on 3:5] ... may the name of the God of Jacob protect thee': phrases such as 'our help is in the name ...' are common, but the name itself as the agent is very unusual. **7.** 'Now I know that the LORD saves his anointed [= the king, cf v 10] ... **10.** 'O Lord, save the king: may he (God) answer us ...': but LXX/V, perhaps better, continue the imperative 'answer us ...' (so NP BJ RSV RPB); the massoretic punctuation, however, gives 'O Lord, save! May the king answer ...': so Jer PB AV RV; while PB ('the King of heaven') and RV ('the King') refer the title to God, but God is never referred to in the OT as simply 'the King'.

h **21 A Prayer for the King's Victory**—Another 'Royal Psalm', placed naturally after the preceding, 384h though not actually paired. One notices the regular metre. **2.** 'O Lord, in thy strength shall the king rejoice ...' 3—8 is an enumeration of the favours bestowed: many phrases from this section are applied to the saints in the Latin liturgies, e.g. *Desiderium cordis eius tribuisti ei* (v 3). 9—13 describes the victory. **13.** 'Be exalted, o Lord, in thy strength': an echo (*inclusio*) of the beginning ('strength').

22—This seems to be three separate psalms, somehow 385a joined together in the compilation: the first vv 2—22 is a poem of a man who cries to God in despair and dread; the second vv 23—27 is a calm call to the brethren to join in praise; the third vv 28—32 is a short poem looking forward to all men worshipping Yahweh. The themes are so different, the diction so without continuity, and the metrical patterns so distinct, that this conclusion seems unavoidable. Nevertheless Fr T. Worden, p. 64, shows this Ps as linking his two basic genres, lamentation and praise, in one at v 22.

22 A (2—22) **The Despairing Cry**—'The Hind of b the Dawn' in the **title** probably indicates a tune. **2.** 'My God (*Eli*), my God, why hast thou forsaken me?' [LXX/V and PB before 'why' insert 'Look upon me']. Obviously important for us is Our Lord's use of these words upon the Cross in Mt 27:46 (*Eli, Eli, lama š°bhakhtani*—the latter word being Aram., as in the Targum, for the Heb. here *'°zabhtānî*) and Mk 15:34 (*Eloi* ..., which may also be Aram., although the Targum has *Eli* as the Heb.; in some codices *Eloi* appears in Mt also). It would seem that when Christ used these words he was not saying that he was forsaken by God, but by quoting the opening words of this psalm he was in fact saying that he was experiencing what this psalm expresses, namely, the depth of human misery. **3.** 'My God (*Elohai* [cf *Eloi* in Mk?]), I call by day ... by night, and (there is) no rest [LXX/V 'not unto folly'] for me. **4.** But thou art dwelling in the holy place, o praises of Israel [= object of Israel's praise]': confidence that God is in the midst of Israel: i. so [repointing 'holy place'] LXX/V NP; ii. 'But thou remainest holy, o praises of Israel': PB; iii. [following massoretic punctuation] 'But thou (art) holy, sitting (enthroned) (on) the praises of Israel': AV RV BJ RSV RPB (a very strange figure). **5—6.** Our fathers trusted in c thee, **7—9** but my case now seems hopeless: 'I am a worm and no man ... **8.** They part their lips (gaping or laughing) ... they shake their heads (both gestures of scorn) [echoed Mt 27:39, Mk 15:29], (saying), **9.** "He turned [repointed with LXX/V and most] to the Lord, let him deliver him ..."': thus quoted in Mt 27:43. **10—12.** I owe thee everything: leave me not now, **13.** I feel as if I were surrounded by fierce bulls from Bashan (a great cattle-breeding area, Dt 32:14, Am 4:1), **14** by roaring lions ... **15—16.** I feel all the sensations of fear: weak as water, my bones falling apart, my heart melting, **16** my strength [some would emend to 'my palate': so NP BJ RPB] dried up, my tongue stuck fast: I am ready for the grave. **17.** Now it is as if hounds surrounded me: 'they are biting my hands and my feet', i.e. my extremities cf Targum: a problematic passage: i. Targum: 'they are biting [supposing a verb *kārû*, related to Assyrian *karu*, fell (trees): see BDB II *Kûr*] like a lion [= Heb. *ka'°ri*] my hands and my feet': it seems likely that Targum represents a word twice over: *kārû ka'°ri*; LXX kept the one, Heb. text the other; ii. Heb.: 'like a lion my hands and my feet' [no verb]: so RVm JA; iii. LXX/V 'They have dug at [=? pierced] my ...' [reading *kārû* from *kārāh*, dig]:

385c so PB AV RV NP RSV RPB, frequently seen with reference to the crucifixion [no 'lion']; iv. Jerome: 'they bound my . . .' [cf Symmachus: reading? *kārekû*, cf Aram. tie together]: so BJ. The merits of the readings 'they are biting [or, digging, or, tying]' of LXX &c., and the Christian interpretation, and 'like a lion' of the Hebrew, and 'biting like a lion' of the Targum, are not easy to assess: on the one hand the verb is very uncertain, and on the other hand *'arī* (lion) is not used in the Pss, but *'aryeh* 5t (2t in this Ps), and seems irrelevant here with the hounds. The metre would not easily admit of both traditions as in Targum. **18—19.** 'I (can) number all my bones' [LXX/V 'they have . . .], either because I am so wasted, like a living skeleton, or because they have stripped me naked; 'they are gazing, looking at me', in astonishment or derision, or at my nakedness; **19.** 'They divide my garments among them': quoted Mt 27:35, Mk 15:24, Lk 23:34, Jn 19:24. **20—21.** 'But thou, o Lord . . . rescue my soul [= my life] from the sword, my only one [= all I have = life itself: fem. because = my soul?—a phrase without exact parallel except for a similar passage in 35:17] from the grip [lit. hand] of the hound, **22** deliver me . . . my misery [so LXX/V NP BJ RSV RPB, emending Heb. 'thou hast answered me'] from the horns of the buffalo [rather than 'unicorn' as LXX/V PB AV]'.

d **22 B** (23—27) **An Invitation to Praise**—The reference to the 'assembly' places this short Ps in a 'cultic' context. **23.** 'I will tell of thy name . . . in the midst of the assembly (of Israel)': *qāhāl* of the people here and 107:32; of the devout in 89:6; 149:1, but also of the wicked in 26:5; cf similarly the *'ēdhāh* of Israel 74:2; 106:18, of the devout 1:5; 111:1, but also of the nations 7:8, of the wicked 86:14, of the (false) gods 82:1—though these words can have a sacred connotation, this is not always so. This v quoted in Heb 2:12. **26—27.** In the same assembly I will perform my vows [= my thank-offerings, or my promised gifts; cf 66:13—15; 116:14, 17, linking vow and sacrifice], and **27** the 'meek' (or, 'poor') will share in the meal (cf sharing in tithes Dt 14:29; 26:12 where 'eat and be filled' also occurs). Many monastic graces use this verse *Edent pauperes* . . . 'May their heart live for ever': 'their' LXX/V, i.e. the poor; Heb. 'your'.

e **22 C** (28—32) **All the World shall come to worship**— The 'universalist' theme of this short Ps was briefly suggested in 18:44, and has its greatest elaboration in Ps 87 (see esp. on 87:4). **28—29.** 'Let all the ends of the earth remember and turn to the Lord . . . **29** for he is the ruler among the nations. **30.** The text here is very unsure: i. 'They have eaten (*'ākelu*) and worshipped, all the fat ones [= prosperous] of the earth; they shall bow before him, all who go down to the dust [= unfortunate], and his own soul he does not [= no man can] keep alive': so apparently Heb. text, PB AV RV; ii. 'Indeed him (*'ak lô*) they shall worship, all the fat ones [= proud] . . .; . . . bow . . . who go down to the dust, and he who cannot keep himself alive': RSV; iii. 'Indeed him (*'ak lô*) they shall worship . . .; . . . down to the dust [= dead]; but my soul (in contrast) shall live for him [cf LXX/V]': BJ; iv. 'Indeed him (*'ak lô*) they shall worship, all who sleep [emended] in the ground [= dead]; . . . down to the dust [= dead]; but my soul . . .': NP; v. 'How shall they (*'ēk lô*) worship him, all who sleep [emended] in the ground [= dead]; . . . down to the dust [= dead]; but my soul shall live . . .': RPB: the advantage of this reading (unlike iii, iv above) is that it underlines the impossibility or worship in Sheol (see on 6:6): 'How shall they . . .?'—Of course

they cannot. **31—32.** 'A seed [= children: LXX /V my **385** seed] shall serve him . . . **32** and proclaim his righteousness to a people (to be) born, that he (the Lord—inserted by LXX/V) has done (all this).'

23 The Lord is my Shepherd—A favourite Psalm of **f** trust, recognized by most as a truly personal psalm (cf Mowinckel II, 17). Vv 1—4, in two stanzas of pleasantly irregular metre, have the figure of sheep properly led by the Good Shepherd; vv 5—6, in two stanzas of strict 3 + 2 metre, have a different picture: of the man well-provided for.

1—2. All that a sheep most desires is given him, when he trusts his shepherd: I am like that with God: green grass, 'water of restfulness' = that refresh me (cf LXX/V), so, legitimately, Knox 'cool water'. **3.** 'He restores my spirit' belongs metrically to the previous line. 'By tracks of rightness' = the right way, not the wrong way: he does not lead me astray. 'For his name's sake', i.e. he is true to his name: his name of 'shepherd' who does what a shepherd should do, i.e. (in the East) lead his flock. But there is also the idea of the name of Yahweh indicating his power, presence and help (cf 106:8): we 'know him by name' (e.g. 9:11; 91:14), 'love or praise his name' (5:12; 18:50), 'call on his name' (116:4), and so 'our help is in the name of the Lord [Yahweh]' (124:8), all frequent in the OT; and cf in the NT in the name of Jesus e.g. Ac 4:12. **4.** Even when I am walking 'through the darkest valley' (RPB, cf RVm NP BJ RSVm): almost certainly not to be translated 'the valley of the shadow of death', although this is probably indeed the literal meaning, with 'of death' as a way of expressing the superlative (see DWT), rather than, as older commentators supposed, a different word altogether (see also on 36:7). 'Thy rod [for hitting, or wielding—so also = 'sceptre'] and thy staff [for leaning on]': these are there for my defence, and so give a sense of security. **5.** Here the picture changes, and the rhythm also: the Lord provides all that is pleasant: a table of good food before me—in sight of (but out of reach of) my foes. This sentiment, common enough in the Pss, that my foes should be punished (here by not receiving the good things), needs to be understood in the sense of God's enemies being my enemies, and that I therefore concur in their punishment (with special clarity in 139:21—22). Anointing the head with oil is another pleasant thing: fragrant oil as a cleanser and means of refreshment needs to be thought of in terms of a world without modern soap etc (see on 133:2). 'My cup is well filled': so Knox well—yet another pleasant thing: not merely half-full. PB RPB 'full' is a little dull; LXX/V *inebrians* comes from the basic meaning 'sated', but is the wrong picture, as is a cup that 'runneth over' (AV RV BJ cf RSV), which is a tiresome thing. **6.** The Ps ends with the pleasantest thing of all: 'to dwell in the House of the Lord' for ever.

24 A Hymn about Sion, chosen place in God's g World—The theme of Sion, God's chosen abode. This may have been originally a liturgy, as Ps 15, and a 'cultic' representation of the solemn entry of the Lord to Sion (for Mowinckel, I 115, part of the procession at the 'Festival of Yahweh', cf also e.g. 68:25—28; 149:3). As a hymn it is expressive of the love of Sion.

1—2. The earth, and all things and people in it, belong to God, for he made it (quoted 1 Cor 10:26), **3—6.** But there is a special place, the hill of Sion, his abode, where **4** only the 'clean of heart' (cf Mt 5:8 from LXX) shall enter and **5** receive blessing, **6** '. . . seeking the face (of the God of) Jacob' [insertion of LXX/V followed by most; Heb. 'thy face, o Jacob'].

5g 7—10. The rhythm changes and the entry into Sion is imagined (or is liturgically enacted, with dialogue of pilgrims and priests): **7, 9** 'Lift up your heads, o ye gates!': i.e. gates closing a doorway in the wall: the gateway is apostrophized as if too small and low for the King of glory to enter: i. = 'raise your lintels, o ye gates': the most probable, although 'heads' = 'lintels' has no warrant; ii = 'hold your heads high [= be of good cheer], o ye gates', cf perhaps phrase in Jg 8:28; iii. LXX/V took 'heads' = 'princes' (for which there is ample warrant, esp. in Chr): 'lift up your gates, o ye princes' = 'leaders of the city, open the gates!': **h** but this reading is unlikely. The verse continues 'Lift up the eternal doors' [of God's abode]: LXX/V 'Be ye lifted up ...': and so most. **8, 10.** 'Who is this, the King of glory? ... Who is he, the King of glory?' This construction explains the variants of 'this' in the versions and *Messiah* n.33. **8, 9, 10.** He is the LORD, Yahweh, **10.** 'the Lord of hosts (= armies, $s^e bh\bar{a}'\hat{o}th$)': although $s\bar{a}bh\bar{a}$ is the ordinary word for 'army', this has become a title of God, first found with reference to Shiloh in 1 Sm 1:3, 11, and then on the lips of David (1 Sm 17:45 Goliath), to convey that Yahweh has the power of victory above human achievement; and first found in the prophets with Amos (9t, e.g. 3:13). The common form is 'LORD of hosts' as here; 'Lord God of hosts' in Am always, in Jer often, in Ps once (89:9), and cf the Latin liturgy; grammatically peculiar forms in Ps 59:6; 80:5; 20; 84:9, and 80:8, 15, found only in the Pss, suggest that the actual meaning of the phrase had become forgotten, as it has today.

i 25 An Alphabetical Meditation—This Ps (where each couplet begins with the next letter of the alphabet) is akin to the similar didactic Pss 34 and 111. Thoughts are brief and disjointed, probably to follow the exigencies of the alphabet. After v 2 the metre is notably regular, rather dully so.

1—3. 'Unto thee I will lift up my soul'. 'My God' in v 2 belongs to v 1, since the *Beth* verse should begin with $b^e kha$ 'In thee'. **4—5.** 'Teach me thy ways ...': reminiscent of v 119 and other didactic Pss. **14.** Part of the just man's reward is to share 'the Lord's secret counsel (*sôdh*)' [so RPB well (RSV 'friendship'?)], a notion not found elsewhere, except in Prv 3:32 [LXX/V read $y^e sôdhô$ 'his foundation', but this is the *Samekh* verse]. **16.** Again a cry for mercy, 'for I am an only child [= 'lonely', only here in this transferred sense, but cf 22:21 (note) and 35:17, where it = 'all I have left'] and "poor" [see on 9:13]'. **17.** 'The sorrows of my heart have become broad [LXX/V many]': but many read 'Ease the sorrows of my heart': so RVm NP BJ RSV RPB. **19.** 'Look at my foes ...' is a second *Resh* verse. **22.** Is an additional verse after the alphabet is finished: perhaps a pious addition, echoing the end of the *De Profundis* Ps 130.

6a 26 A Protestation of Innocence—In the manner of Pss 16—17. For Mowinckel uttered in the name of the people (I, 207), for others a personal poem. **1.** 'Judge me, o Lord,' for I know I am innocent: cf Ps 43. **2.** My reins (kidneys) and heart [= affections: see on 7:10] are open to thee, **3.** I am aware of thy friendship [the two words, see on 5:8], **5.** 'I hate the company [$q\bar{a}h\bar{a}l$ not in a sacred context, see on 22:23] of evildoers', **6—8.** '*Lavabo inter innocentes manus meas*, I will serve at [lit. go round] thine altar, **8.** I love the habitation (m^e'$\hat{o}n$) of thy house [LXX/V probably better: 'gracefulness of ...' (=? $n\hat{o}'\bar{a}m$), cf 27:4: Vg well '*dilexi decorem domus tuae*'] and the place of the dwelling of thy glory [= thy divine presence]'. This

stanza is used in the Roman Mass. **9—12.** Further **386a** protestations: **12.** 'My foot has stood on the level': again of a path in 27:11, and of flat country in 143:10; variously understood as a sure road (cf RPB 'standeth firm'), not devious as the wicked (LXX/V), or (morally) right (PB).

27 A (1—6) **Confidence, and Devotion to the b Temple**—This is almost certainly a distinct poem, in regular metre and textually straightforward, contrasting with the cry for help in vv 7—14, with its irregularity and textual difficulties, though the note of confidence in vv 13—14 may have brought them together.

1—3. 'The Lord is my light and my salvation ...' **4—5.** 'Only one thing I ask ... to live in the House of the Lord ... to gaze upon the loveliness of the Lord': this exact word 'loveliness' (so CV) is only here and 90:17 in the Pss, but see on a related word in 133:1. **27 B** (7—14) **A Cry for Help**—Probably a distinct c psalm with a typical psalm-opening. There are several obscure passages. **7.** 'Hear, o Lord, my voice (when) I cry ...' **8.** The exact meaning of this verse is uncertain: Heb. text: 'To thee my heart has said, "Seek ye my face [= my presence]"; "Thy face, o Lord, I will seek"', read variously: i. LXX: '... my heart has said, "I have sought thy face, thy face, o Lord, I will seek"': perhaps the best reading [emending persons]; ii. Vg: '... my heart has said, "My face has sought (thee), thy face ..."': so similarly Jerome, and NP [supplying object]; iii. AV RV RSV: '(When thou saidst,) "Seek my face"; my heart said to thee, "Thy face ..."' [adding phrase and changing order]; iv. PB cf BJ RPB: 'My heart hath talked of [or, with] thee, "Seek ye my face"; (and my answer is) "Thy face ..."'. **9—12.** 'Hide not thy face [attacked by RSV to preceding] ... **11** lead me by a level path [cf on 26:12] ...' **13.** 'Unless I had been confident of seeing the goodness of the Lord ...': 'Unless' in the massoretic text has the *puncta extraordinaria* (dots above the letters), the only example in the Pss (GK 5n), which perhaps make the word suspect: i. [omitting it] 'I am confident of ...': NP BJ RSV RPB; ii. [emending] 'O that I had been confident ...'; iii. LXX/V read as 'to itself' at end of previous v; iv. [inserting:] '(I had fainted) unless ...' PB AV RV **14** a word of courage at the end, similar to the end of Ps 31.

28 A Happy Song of Confidence—classed by Gunkel d as personal, by Mowinckel as national, by Tournay as thanksgiving. **1.** 'Unto thee, o Lord, I call, my Rock, **2.** I lift up my hands to thy holy sanctuary': 'sanctuary' a technical word for 'holy of holies' in Solomon's temple (1 (3) Kg 6:5 etc), only here in Pss. **8.** 'The Lord is strength for them. **9.** 'Save thy people ... be a shepherd to them ...': used in the *Te Deum*, with Vg '*rege eos*' as in the Vg of 23:1.

29 A Song to God as Lord of Nature—The religious e literature of the ancient world, not least of Babylon and Canaan (Ugarit), included hymns to the storm-god, and it is interesting to find that Israel has her own version of this theme, with Yahweh extolled as lord of nature. It would be unwise to insist that this Ps is a borrowing from a Canaanite source, even if verbal parallels are found with Ugarit and v 11 is recognized as purely Israelite, but it is easy to admit the plain parallel and ancient origin in early times in Canaan, making this one of the oldest in the Psalter.

1. 'Give [= ascribe RSV, RPB] to the Lord, o sons of God (or, gods), give to the Lord glory and power': 'sons of *ēlîm*': *ēl* is chiefly a word (as *elohim*) for the true God or false gods, but also apparently (as *elohim*, see on 8:6) for those of rank and dignity (and

386e cf perhaps 58:2): i. 'sons of God' = the faithful, cf Ex 4:22, Dt 14:1, Hos 11:1 where God calls Israel his son: RVm NP BJ (and LXX/V but cf v below); ii. = heavenly beings, or, angels (as Jb 1:6, perhaps Ps 89:7, cf 8:6): RSV RPB; iii. 'sons of gods' = other nations? or other gods?: RVm; iv. 'sons of the mighty' = mighty people: PB AV RV; v. 'give to the Lord rams (ēylūm)', i.e. for sacrifice: Jer (LXX/V and PB render twice). **2.** 'Bow before the Lord in adornment of holiness': i. = 'in his holy sanctuary' [cf Ugaritic]: LXX/V BJ; ii. = 'in sacred vestments': RVm NP RSV RPB (and cf Ps 96:9; 110:3); iii. = 'in beauty of holiness': AV RV; iv. = 'in holy worship': PB. **3—9a.** A magnificent series of declarations

f of God's power in nature: **3—5** water, thunder, cedars, = the Lebanon range, which he 'makes to skip like a calf, and 'Sirion [= Phoenician name of Mt Hermon, according to Dt 3:9] like young oxen' [rather than LXX/V 'the beloved like young unicorns'], **7—8** lightning, desert, **9a** birthpangs of hinds and goats, or, the fate of the forests: First phrase: i. 'makes hinds to be in travail': PB AV RV RSVm RPB (cf LXX/V); ii. [repoint.] 'makes oaks, or, terebinths, to quiver': NP RSV. The second phrase expects a parallel, but the older versions do not all recognize this: i. 'strips bare the forests': LXX/V PB AV RV NP BJ RSV; ii. 'makes goats to bring forth quickly': RPB (see DWT). The merits of NP RSV (trees) and RPB (animals) are the consistent pictures. **9b.** 'In his temple everyone cries (his) glory', for **10—11.** Yahweh who is king of nature is also the God of his own people Israel.

g 30 Thanksgiving for Delivery from Death—An 'Individual Lament'. **Title:** 'A song for the Dedication (ḥⁿnukkāh) of the House [= ? Temple]: Hanukkah is the name of the Jewish Feast of the Dedication, instituted by Judas Maccabaeus in 165 B.C. to commemorate his restoration of the Temple in that year (1 Mc 4:52, 2 Mc 10:1, cf Jn 10:22). The connexion between this Ps and feast is not too clear. For Mowinckel the Ps has its origin in sickness: see on Ps 6.

2—4. 'I will extol thee, o LORD, for thou hast brought me up (from Sheol) . . .' **5.** 'Sing to the LORD . . . 6** for momentarily (he is) in his anger, life is his desire [= what he seeks is to preserve life], for (one) evening weeping stays, and (then there is) joy in the morning'. **7.** I am confident, **8** . . . he has given strength 'to my hill' [= ? Sion, or, general security: = ? 'made me as a strong mountain': RSV]. **10.** 'For what advantage (can there be) in my blood [= either, my lifeblood, being alive, as 72:14; or, my bloodshed, i.e. death, as 50:16], when I go down to the Pit? Shall the dust of (the grave) praise thee, tell of thy friendship?' The familiar idea (cf on 6:6) that prayer as we know it ceases at death. **12.** 'Thou hast turned my mourning to dancing . . . 13** so that glory may sing thee': i. read as 'my glory' with LXX/V: so AV RV (meaning?); ii. = what is noblest in me = my soul (cf? 57:9; 108:2): so Rabbis (Ibn Ezra here) NP BJ RSV; iii. = 'every good man': PB; iv. [repoint kᵉbhēdhi] 'my liver' = emotions (see DWT on 16:9): so RPB by euphemism 'my heart'.

h 31. The three parts of this Ps are very clearly marked and there is little cohesion between them: it is probable that they are three separate poems: vv 2—9 a quiet prayer of confidence; vv 10—19 a passionate description of distress; vv 20—25 a proclamation of God's goodness with encouragement to love him. Each moreover has a proper phrase for the opening of a psalm.

31 A (2—9) **A Prayer of Confidence**—**2.** 'In thee, o LORD, I have trusted . . . 3** be to me a rock of refuge [see on 18:3] . . . 4** true to thy name [see on 23:3]

6. . . . Into thy hand I commend my spirit [quoted by **38** Jesus on the Cross, Lk 23:46 according to LXX 'thy hands'], thou hast redeemed me, my God of friendship' [see on 5:8]: these words (with *Deus veritatis*) are used almost daily at Compline. **7.** My trust is rewarded, **9** thou hast made my feet stand 'in a wide (place)' [opposite to 'straits' see on 4:2; 25:17].

31 B (10—19) **A Psalm of distress**—Similar in some **i** phrases to Pss 6 and 22A, this Ps has some singularly powerful descriptions. The opening phrase is as the opening of Pss 56 and 57, and the whole Ps has the authentic pattern of a complete psalm. **10.** 'Pity me, Lord, for I am in anguish [or, straits, see on 4:2]'; and there follow various pictures of distress, one of the most stinging being that **12** my acquaintances, whom I meet in the street, run away from me, afraid of encountering my misery [cf 38:12; 88:9]; **13.** I am forgotten as if I were dead, like an old utensil thrown away; **14.** I am frightened, when I hear them whispering about me. **15.** 'But I trust in thee, o LORD . . . 16** in thy hand are my times [= fortunes, a usage only here] . . . **17.** May thy countenance shine on thy servant [for this phrase, see on 67:2]'. **18—19.** A short imprecation upon the wicked, as often at the end.

31 C (20—25) **A Hymn of God's Goodness**—**20. j** 'How plentiful is thy goodness . . . for them that fear thee. **22.** Blessed in the Lord who has made wondrous his mercy to me [probably the clue to true reading of 4:4, where see note] in a besieged [or, strong] city': i. 'besieged', i.e. when help is needed (cf alarm in next line): RSV; ii. 'a strong, or, fortified city', i.e. safe: LXX/V PB AV RV NP BJ; iii. [emend.] 'in time of distress': RPB (see DWT). **23.** 'And I said in my trepidation I am cut off from before thine eyes'. **24.** 'Love the Lord': the only place in the Psalter where this simple advice is given.

32 An Acknowledgement of Sin—The second 'peniten- **k** tial psalm' (see on Ps 6). In the psalmist's mind his suffering is probably related to his sin, so that when the sin is removed, the pain will be removed also. But for the Christian reader the principal feature is the acknowledgement of sin in v 5. **Title** includes the description 'a *maskil*' (=? understanding: so LXX/V).

1. 'Blessed is he whose transgression is taken away [i.e. is forgiven], whose sin is covered (cf 85:3 same verbs] **2.** . . . to whom the Lord imputes no iniquity': quoted Rom 4:7—8. The idea of sin being 'covered' (not noticed, not imputed) is an image rather than a theological statement. Sin is also seen as 'blotted out' (especially 51:3, 11). **3.** 'As long as I was silent (regarding my sins) . . . 4.** . . . my life-sap [= vigour: uncertain word lᵉṣaddi only here and Nm 11:8 describing manna] was turned to the drought of summer [qayis]: i. so most, expressing pain or weakness; ii. LXX/V: 'I turned (= writhed) in my pain (šôdhi), when the thorn (qôṣ) was put in': a rather strange figure; iii. 'my heart (libbi) was turned to a field (sādhe) in the drought of summer': BJ. **5.** But I will acknowledge my sin, and indeed thou hast taken it away. An important element, only a few occasions stated in the Pss, e.g. 38:19; 51:5. **6.** 'Therefore every devout person [ḥāsīdh, see on 12:2] will pray unto thee'. The next phrase is certainly corrupt: 'At a time to find, surely . . .' i. = 'at a time (when thou mayest) be found, surely . . .': PB AV RV is very artificial and strains the syntax unduly; ii. LXX/V 'at a favourable time, except [or, but] . . .': is obscure; iii. [most emend] 'at a time of distress': so NP BJ RSV RPB. The text then continues easily: 'At the flooding . . .' **7.** Thou art my protection. **8.** The Lord's answer: 'I will instruct thee . . . 9.** Be **l** not like the horse and the mule, without understanding

86l with bit and bridle its adornment, to curb, (else it will) not come unto thee': 'adornment', though a usual word, is uncertain here: i. [emend.] '. . . with bit and bridle its jaws to curb': LXX/V PB AV; ii. '. . . its speed to curb': BJ reading a rare verb cf Jb 28:8, cf NP; iii. 'whose trappings (must be) bit and bridle, to curb . . .': RV; iv. [omit 'adornment, or, trappings' as a gloss] '. . . with bit and bridle to curb': RSV RPB. **10—11.** Describe the troubles of the wicked, the joys of the just, according to a familiar pattern. *Laetamini in Domino* . . . (v 11) frequent in the liturgy.

m **33 The Lord of Creation, the God of our People**— A true hymn in a remarkably plain and regular metre, with clearly marked stanzas. No title: the only one in 3—41 not labelled 'David'. **1—3.** 'Rejoice, ye righteous, in the LORD . . . **3.** Sing to him a new song . . .' [cf 40:4; 96:1; 144:9; 149:1]. **4—9.** All creation bears witness to his power and his justice. **7.** He gathers the sea 'as in a water-skin' [so LXX/V Jer NP BJ RPB cf RSV: reading *nôdh*, for *nēdh* 'heap' as in 78:13 of the Red Sea]. **12.** Blessed is the nation whose God is Yahweh, **16—17.** Human means will not bring victory: **18—22.** We trust in the Lord.

n **34 An Alphabet of Praise and Instruction**—A simple Ps in didactic form, regular metre, and alphabetical (without *Waw*—but an additional v at the end completes the 22 letters). In most of these features it resembles Ps 25: the thought is similarly somewhat disconnected. Admitted by Mowinckel (II, 111) as 'non cultic'. The **title** imagines a situation for David: that of 1 Sm 21.13ff, where, however, the king is called not Abimelech (or Vg Achimelech) but Achish.

2—5. 'I will bless the Lord at all times . . . **3.** The "meek" [see on 9:13] will hear (of this) and rejoice . . . **6.** They looked to him and were enlightened, and their faces will not be ashamed, [LXX/V, perhaps better, read 'Look to him, and be . . . and your faces . . .': so Jer NP RSV] **7.** Here is a "poor" (man)': the psalmist himself (see on 9:13). **8.** 'An angel of the Lord is encamped round about those who fear the LORD': the use of 'encamped' here is strange, and many, including LXX/V,

o paraphrase. **9.** 'Taste and see that the Lord is good [Vg *suavis*]' quoted 1 Peter 2:3. **10.** Thy holy people will lack nothing: **11.** '. . . infidels (*kephīrīm*) are indigent and hungry, but they who seek the LORD . . .': i. 'infidels' connected with Syr. and Arab. words of this meaning: so RPB (see DWT)—a distinct word from ii below; ii. 'young lions': the usual meaning of *kephīrīm*: PB AV RV BJ RSV—but it seems an extravagant contrast, and LXX causes doubt; iii. LXX/V 'the rich': an uncertain reading; perhaps a guess from context, cf NP. **12—15.** The didactic tone: 'Come, children, listen to me', followed by some rather elementary (but no less salutary) advice, including **15** the basic moral principle 'Avoid evil and do good, seek after peace and pursue it'. For **16** 'the (merciful) eyes of the Lord are upon the righteous . . . (but) **17** the (wrathful) countenance of the Lord is upon evildoers'. **18.** '(The righteous) cry out, and the Lord hears': most versions, with LXX/V, insert the subject. **19—23.** 'The Lord is close to the broken of heart . . . **20.** Many are the evils (that are the lot) of the righteous, but the LORD will save him, **21** watching over all his bones: not one of them shall be broken': quoted of Christ in Jn 19:36.

87a **35 A Cry for Help against my Persecutors**—An 'Individual Lament', with some notable textual obscurities. **1.** 'Plead (my case), o Lord, with them that plead against me [as in a court of law]', **2—6.** Take up weapons and put my foes to flight: in v 3 'spear and lance': **387a** the last (*seghôr*) having long been a puzzle: i. = lance, or, javelin, properly of the socket into which the blade fits, and so of the weapon itself: the Qumran *War Scroll* (IQM v, 7, 9) has provided this clue, using the exact word: so BJ RSV; ii. = battle-axe, cf Gr. *sagaris*, a Scythian or Egyptian word: RVm RPB (see DWT); iii. = a verb: 'close up (the road of attack)': LXX/V PB AV RV NP. **7.** Without cause they have laid snares to trap me, but **13** I put on sack-cloth and fast for them 'when they are sick' [LXX/V 'when they torment me'], 'and may my prayer return [or, returns] upon my bosom': a very obscure sentence, with no certain interpretation; merely given literally by LXX/V and older versions: i. = praying interiorly: NP cf Qimhi (cf Knox: 'hid itself in my bosom'); ii. = with my whole heart: RPB (see DWT); iii. = with my head bowed upon my bosom: RSV (cf v 14 'bowed'): perhaps the most favoured, but there is no warrant for such use of 'return' as here; iv. Ibn Ezra compares 79:12 'render sevenfold into their bosom', i.e. repay to them, so here = 'what I pray for, for them, may God repay also to me' (cf also Lattey in WV): perhaps the most convincing. **14.** My care for my **b** foes extends to mourning for them, as for friend, brother or mother [LXX/V omit 'mother'], 'bowed down darkly': cf 38:7; 42:10; 43:2. **15.** But 'they gather against me, they that smite me', doubtful word: i. [emend] 'they that smite me': RVm RPB (cf LXX/V 'scourges'); ii. [possible word, only here] 'smitten ones' = ? 'abject': PB AV RV (dubious); iii. [as above] 'smitten ones' = ? 'cripples': RSV (very dubious); iv. [another emend.] 'strangers': BJ (as in Kittel). **16.** A very uncertain passage describing those who mock at me: i. Heb. as it stands: 'Among the most profane of mockers of a cake (= ? feast), (they) gnash their teeth against me': AV RV cf PB: the cake (*mā'ōgh*) seems irrelevant, but some think of itinerant begging jesters: but this seems very far-fetched; ii [reading 'cake' as 'profane joke'—Rabbinic word] 'Among the most profane of mockeries of backbiting [or, joking] . . .'. JA, iii. [emend. 1] 'They tried me, sneering sneers at me, they gnashed . . .': LXX/V cf NP BJ RSV; iv. [emend. 2] 'When I was lamed, they mocked mockery at me . . .': RPB see DWT). **17.** 'LORD, how long wilt thou look on (and do nothing)? Bring back my soul [= my life] from their ravages, my only one [= all I have, see on 22:21] from the young lions [or, infidels, see on 34:11]. **18.** 'I will thank thee in the great assembly': cf 22:23. Here also the phrase marks a break, but here it seems the same psalm continuing. **19.** Let them not 'hate me without cause': quoted Jn 15:25. **21.** They gape at me (in laughter), saying Aha, aha! (see on 40:16) **22—28.** Again a plea for justice for me.

36. The two parts of Ps 36 are so clearly marked and **c** have so little in common, that it is most probable that they are two poems.

36 A (2—5) A Consideration of the Wicked—A strange psalm, with a difficult text. **Title:** 'For the servant of God, for David': only here and Ps 18 in a title. **2.** The first difficulty is the first word *ne'um* (utterance? utters?): only here and in Ps 110 does it stand as an opening phrase, otherwise (often in the prophets) always after a discourse, followed by the person uttering (usually 'saith the Lord'). Heb. lit: 'Utterance of transgression for the wicked in the midst of my heart: "There is no fear of God before his eyes"': last sentence quoted Rm 3:18. Variously approached: i. = 'A statement of the transgression of (?) the wicked (is) in the midst of my heart; there is no . . .': PB, unchanged in RPB ('my heart showeth me . . .'): perhaps the most satisfactory;

387c ii. = 'The transgression of the wicked utters within my heart: "There no . . ."': AV RV; iii. = '[as ii] . . . utters within his [emended: i.e. the wicked man's] heart . . .': Jerome; iv. = '(I think) in the midst of my heart: Transgression (i.e. the "evil inclination") says to the wicked: "There is no . . ."': Rashi, Qimhi, cf JA; v. = 'Transgression utters to the wicked deep in his [emended] heart: "There is no . . ."': NP RSV (sin personified—a doubtful solution); vi. = 'An oracle for the wicked (is) sin in the midst of his [emended] heart, there is no . . .': BJ (i.e. his guidance is not God, but sin); vii. LXX/V: 'The sinner spoke of sin in himself, there is no . . .' (reading?).

d 3. 'For he acts deceitfully to himself in his own eyes, to find iniquity to hate (it)': i. = 'he flatters himself that he cannot find in himself any hateful sin': suggested by LXX/V, followed by Jerome and BJ; ii. = 'he flatters himself, until his sin is discovered and hated': PB AV JA RPB; iii. = 'he flatters himself that his sin will not be discovered . . .': RV NP RSV. 4—5. Deceitful are his speech, thoughts and actions, and he will not reject evil. Whatever the exact interpretation of vv 2—3 the whole picture is plain enough. A strange psalm.

e **36 B** (6—13) **In praise of God's Goodness and Bounty**—A short and pleasant hymn, in three clearly marked stanzas. It is in marked contrast with the preceding. **6.** 'O Lord, thy mercy (*ḥesedh*) (reaches) to the sky [a more concrete image than 'heaven', but the word is the same in Heb.], thy friendship ('*emūnāh* [word related to '*emeth*: see on 5:8] to the clouds; **7** thy justice (is) like mighty mountains [lit. 'mountains of God (*ēl*)': a form of superlative: 'mountains—God! what mountains!', cf 68:16, of river 65:10, of trees 104:16, and of cedars 80:11; cf also on 23:4], thy judgements a vast ocean . . .' **8.** The lovely images continue in the second stanza: 'thy precious mercy' is **9** likened to richness (as of rich oil), to 'thy sweet streams', **10** to the 'fountain of life'; and 'in thy light we shall see light'. These figures of God's bounty are taken up, and only fully realized in the NT, especially Jn. **11.** The third stanza: 'Extend thy mercy to those that know [= recognize] thee . . .' **12.** Let not wickedness come near me, for **13** 'there [= far away from me] they have fallen down . . .': even in this gentle short psalm, the downfall of the wicked is not entirely excluded.

f **37 An Alphabetical Meditation on the Contrast between the Good and the Wicked**—Like most of the alphabetical psalms (as 25, 34), this psalm is disjointed and often repetitive; it is nearly all in a regular metre, with a new letter of the alphabet starting each stanza (comprising two couplets), unlike 25 and 34, where the new letter starts each couplet, or 111 and 112, where it starts each line. It has a very marked didactic manner.

1—2. 'Be not set on fire (with anger, or envy) because of the evildoers . . . **2** for they shall soon be withered away . . .' **3—4.** The *Beth* stanza: 'Trust in the LORD, and do good . . .': these represent the principal themes of the psalm. **11.** 'The "meek" [see on 9:13] shall inherit the land': quoted verbatim from LXX in Mt 5:5. **16.** 'Better is a little (that belongs) to the righteous than a great quantity of (riches—added by LXX/V) of the wicked': so LXX for Heb. 'than a quantity of many wicked'. **20.** 'The wicked shall perish . . . like the value of fields . . . like smoke . . .': the difficulty is *karim* 'pastures', and *karim* 'lambs', both being uncertain: i. = precious crops, or pastures that are burnt up: cf RV NP BJ RSV; ii. = best part of (sacrificial) lambs . . .: PB AV RVm JA (with Rashi); iii. LXX/V '(declared) precious and exalted (*kᵉrûm*): (meaning?); iv. [emend to *kūrim*] 'burnt in fiery furnaces': RPB (see DWT); v. Jerome:

'boast like a unicorn *kᵉrēm* = wild ox)'. **25.** The advice **38'** of an old man: 'I was a boy and now I am old, and I have not seen a just man forsaken . . . [cf 71:9, 18] **26** . . . he is gracious and lends': see on 112:5. **27.** 'Avoid evil and do good': some elementary, perhaps platitudinous, moral advice, cf 34:15. **28.** After '. . . preserved for ever' LXXᴬ and Vg add 'The wicked ('*awwālīm*) are pursued (Vg punished)', thus providing the missing initial *Ayin* for this stanza: so PB; while NP BJ RPB take this sentence as replacing 'preserved for ever'. **30.** '*Os iusti meditabitur sapientiam*' (a typical sentiment of this psalm) is often used in the liturgy, of a saint. **35.** '. . . the wicked in great power, like a green (tree) rising up [or, well-rooted, doubtful word '*ezrāh*]'; but LXX/V have 'like the cedars ('*arzē*) of Lebanon', which may be the right reading: so BJ RSV. **36.** But then 'I went by [with LXX/V: rather than Heb. = he went by, or, passed away], and, behold, he was no more'. **37.** 'Mark well the innocent (man)': so most, but 'mark' is an unusual usage (lit 'keep'), LXX/V PB 'keep innocence'.

38 By Distress is due to my sin—The third 'Penitential **h** Psalm' (see on Ps 6), with recognition of sin as in Ps 32. Title: 'To bring to mind', only here and Ps 70, may indicate liturgical use, for a memorial service (?).

2. 'Rebuke me not, Lord, in thy anger', cf Ps 6. **3—6.** I feel as if the Lord had shot arrows into me, my health were gone, and my wounds fester and stink—and all because of my sin and folly. 'Folly' occurs in the Pss only here and 69:6, and the corresponding 'fool' ('*ewīl*) only in 107:17; the 'fool' (esp. in Prv), like the similar *nābhāl* (see on 14:1), is seen as morally wrong and associated with the wicked: only here and in 69:6 does the writer see himself in that rôle. **7.** '. . . all day darkly [cf 35:14 of mourner] I wander . . . and **12** 'my friends stand away from my pain': as my acquaintances in 31:12; 88:9, 18 'I am ready to stumble, **19** but I am declaring my iniquity, I am anxious [Jerome '*sollicitus*'] about my sin': cf 32:5; 41:5. 51:5. **20—23.** The wicked are about me: forsake me not, Lord.

39 Man is but a Guest in this World—A personal **i** psalm with a fairly clear and pleasant stanzaic construction, including a quasi-refrain in vv 6 and 12 (with *Selah*). The **title** includes the name Jeduthun, as in 62 (where see note) and 77.

2. 'I said [= determined], I will watch my ways [= way of life: cf 'watch my step'], that I sin not with my tongue, . . . **3.** I am dumb with dumbness, I am speechless from good': so literally LXX/V, meaning?: i. = '(even) from (speaking) good (words)': PB AV RV RPB (so Ibn Ezra), cf CV? ii. = '(far) from good [= without comfort]': RVm JA NP; iii. = 'because of his [emended] (= the wicked man's) good (fortune)': BJ; iv. = 'to no avail': RSV (= ? ii above). **4.** '. . . in my meditation, fire is kindled': i.e. the more I think about my anxiety (what follows, v 5f), the more agitated I become. **5.** Tell me my span of life . . . 'let me know how I am ceasing (*ḥadhēl*) [= ? lacking]: i. = 'how much I lack = have yet to come of life': LXX/V PB; ii. = 'how frail I am [lit. ceasing = ? transient]': AV RV NP BJ RSV (dubious); iii. = 'how short my time is': RPB (see DWT); iv. [emend to *ḥeledh*, cf next v and 89:48] 'what duration there is for me'. **6.** My days are mere **j** handbreadths = a few inches long, **7** man walks about as a phantom [CV well, lit. 'image']. **9—12.** But thou, Lord, deliver me, make me not a reproach for the 'fool' (see on 14:1)... **12.** ... 'thou dost chasten a man, and consume [lit. cause to melt] his comeliness [lit. desirable things, LXX/V his soul] as a moth (consumes)' [rather than a 'spider' LXX/V, but Knox happily: 'his life

37j melts away like gossamer']. **13.** Hear me ... 'for I am but a guest with thee, a sojourner, as all my fathers were' (RPB): the Israelite always remembered that the land is God's and he is but a guest in it, e.g. Lv 25:23, Ps 119:19; indeed the whole world belongs to God (Ps 8:1) and we are all his guests in it (see further on 146:9). **14.** 'Spare me': Jer PB AV RV (cf LXX/V), but more literally 'Gaze away from me' (cf RSV) = 'turn thy gaze (of anger) from me'.

k **40 A** (2—11) **A Song of Deliverance**—A psalm of thanksgiving, almost certainly distinct from vv 12—18, which is a true 'lament'. **2—3.** 'I waited patiently for the LORD . . . 3 and he brought me up from the pit of mud': i. so RPB (Aram. word, see DWT, cf 69:15); ii. 'pit of noise' = 'horrible pit': PB AV RV; iii. 'pit of destruction': RVm cf BJ RSV; iv. 'pit of misery': LXX/V. **4.** He placed on my lips 'a new song' [cf 33:3; 96:1; 98:1; 144:9; 149:1], here 'new' in contrast to my thoughts in the 'pit', **5** 'blessed the man who trusts . . . turns not to the proud and to those who turn aside to falsehood [but RSV 'after false (gods)']'. **6.** Thou hast done many wonders, . . . 'there is none to compare with thee': lit. 'to set up unto thee', an unusual idiom only here, Ps 89:7 and Jb 28:17,19. **7.** It is not (burnt) sacrifice and (food) offering that thou desirest: 'ears [LXX: a body] thou hast fashioned [lit. pierced] for me (to hear thy commandments)'. **8—9.** '. . . In the scroll of a book it is written concerning me (as follows:) **9** to do thy will, o my God, has been my desire, and thy Law (tōrāh) is in the midst of my bowels [= affections]'. 'Scroll of a book' occurs also in Jer 36:2,4, Ezek 2:9 (of prophetic writing). LXX/V here: 'At the heading (kephalís) of a book . . .', but kephalís appears in Ez 2:9; 3:1, 2, 3 translating 'scroll'. What is the 'book' here? i. = the 'Law' (tōrāh) of Moses, although 'the Book' is only used once (perhaps) of the Scripture in Dn 9:2; ii. – God's 'book' where our deeds are written down (Ps 139:16 and cf 87:6 and 69:29). The section vv 7—9 is quoted (from LXX) in Hb 10:5—7. **10—11.** I have declared thy righteousness in the 'great assembly' (qāhāl), cf 22:23 and note there.

l **40 B** (12—18) **A Plea for Help**—A 'lament', almost certainly distinct from the foregoing, and having a true Ps invocation to begin. Moreover vv 14—18 reappear as Ps 70, but vv 12—13 here seem to be of one piece with vv 14—18. **12.** 'Thou, o LORD, withold not thy compassion from me . . . ' **13** for evils overwhelm me, 'my sins have overtaken me . . . **14** is more complete here than 70:2 where see note. **15.** May my persecutors be put to shame, **16** 'who say to me, He'āh he'āh!': a cry of triumph, hardly translatable with dignity, only here and 35:21, 25 in the Pss: PB RPB 'Fie!', AV RV RSV 'Aha!'. BJ Haha!'; LXX/V NP 'Euge!'—which rather misses the point, being a cry of encouragement (Douay "tis well!'); Grail and Fides (perhaps wisely) give it up, writing 'who jeer . . . **14—18** appear as a complete Ps at Ps 70, with small variations: see notes there.

m **41 A Prayer of one in Affliction or Sickness**—This is plainly a Ps having its origin in sickness (see on Ps 6), and shows how the Psalter provides for all fortunes of life. **2.** 'Blessed is he who has thought for the weak' **3.** 'The Lord shall preserve him and give him life . . .': a text often used when publicly praying for someone, esp. the Pope. **4.** 'The Lord shall support him upon (his) bed of sickness, all his bed thou hast turned [or, changed] in his illness' (so literally LXX/V): i. = 'thou makest his whole bed . . .': PB AV RV BJ = 'minister unto him' RPB; ii. = 'thou changest his lying down [= infirmity] in his illness [= thou healest him]':

NP RSV cf JA. **5.** 'Heal my soul, for I have sinned **387m** against thee': the supposed connexion in the mind of the psalmist between his sin and his punishment with sickness: see intro. to Ps 32. This verse is used in the ferial office at Terce. **6—9.** What my enemies say about me: 'When is he going to die? **9.** . . . A deadly thing [lit. thing of Belial] has come upon him, . . . he will not rise again'. **10.** But, what is much worse, 'even my friend [lit. my man of peace], whom I trusted, while eating my bread [= receiving my hospitality], has done much (to lift his) heel against me': the phrase is quoted by Christ in Jn 13:18 according to the Heb. rather than the LXX. **11—13.** But do thou, Lord, pity me . . . **14** is a doxology for the end of the first book, as at the ends of 72, 89, 106, with 'Amen and Amen' (one Amen in 106).

BOOK II

42—43 My Soul longs for thee, o God—A lovely **388a** poem, with real heartfelt poetic feeling, numbered in all texts as two, but forming a single psalm, as the refrain in 42:6, 12; 43:5 shows. Though intensely personal, it is seen by Mowinckel as uttered in the name of the community (I, 219, 227). **Title**: = 'the Qorah Collection I' (42—49), a remarkably good collection as is 'Qorah II' (84—89), all the items being genuine poems, and covering the main themes of the Psalter. One notices at once the typical Elohim of Book II, rather than Yahweh.

2. 'As a hart longs for brooks of water, so my soul longs for thee, o God.' **5.** 'These things (which follow) I remember and pour out before me my soul, how I would go through with the throng and lead them to God's House with the sound of praise and thanksgiving—a festive crowd.' The picture is that of a man remembering the pilgrimages he used to lead. **6.** The refrain reappearing **b** in v 12 and 43:5 'Why so downcast, my soul . . .?' We should read with LXX/V '. . . the salvation which I see and my God [from next v]', as in the other two refrains. **7.** '(But) my soul is (in fact) downcast before me: therefore I remember thee (and it encourages me to think of thy great power shown in our landscape) from the land of Jordan and the Hermons [i.e. the range in the north where the Jordan rises], from Mount Miṣ'ar [or, the Little Mountain (so LXX/V AVm RVm; PB = Little Mount Hermon), probably = Ṣa'orah in the Hermon range; though some see the Little Hill as = Sion, cf BJ]. **8.** (I think of thy power when) deep calls unto deep at the sound of thy cataracts [probably in the Upper Jordan—PB 'water-pipes' because the word also seems to mean 'conduit'], all thy breakers and waves (seem in my imagination to) have gone over me': this figure for being overwhelmed is also in the psalm of Jonah (Jon 2:4), and in Ps 18:5; 88:8. **9.** But 'the Lord commands his mercy . . . **10** my God, my Rock [see on 9:10; 18:3] . . . why must I wander so darkly [phrase only in 35:14; 38:7 and in this Ps, here and 43:2] . . .?' **12.** The second refrain.

43 continues without title: **1.** The theme of deliverance **c** continues: 'Give judgement for me, o God, and plead my case (as in a court of Law: cf 35:1)'. **2.** A pleasantly varied echo of 42:10. **3.** 'Send forth thy light and thy friendship ['emeth, see on 5:8]: they shall guide me and bring me to thy holy mountain (Sion) and to thy dwellings (in Sion, among men)'. Sion is my goal, as in the pilgrimage of my youth (42:5 above). **4.** 'And (there, once more) I will go unto the altar of God, to God the joy of my youth (gîlî)'. i. so LXX/V: gîl is a late Heb. word,

388c only otherwise in Dn 1:10 'youthful age': but it fits with the recollection of former pilgrimages, above, and accords with the Ugaritic 'life-stages', cf on 139:16, and see Dahood Bib 40 (1959), 168, and Zorell, *Lexicon* 150b. ii. = '... joy of my exultation': so most: the common word *gîl*, several times linked with 'joy': 'joy and exultation', but never 'joy of . . .'; this rendering also misses a treasured phrase, and the allusion above. This whole Ps 43 was used in the Roman Mass at the foot of the altar: this v 4 remains as an antiphon in some modern liturgies, in either the LXX/V or the other form. **5.** The refrain repeated a last time.

d 44 God's past Mercies and his present Abandonment of his People in spite of their Faithfulness— A psalm of special interest because of this unusual theme (see esp. vv 18—19). Classed as a 'National Lament', the psalm is supposed by Mowinckel to have been composed on the occasion of a national defeat. For Weiser this psalm is one of the most cogent examples of the *Heilsgeschichte* theme, with the dominance of the Covenant (v 18) in the 'cult-community' and as origin in the 'covenant festival'. **Title:** Qorah Collection.

2. 'O God, we have heard with our ears ... of thy deeds ... in the days of old.' **5.** 'Thou art my King': Yahweh as king of the world is frequent enough, but this personal expression of allegiance is rare: 'my king' addressed to God is found in 5:3; 68:25; 74:12; 84:4. **10—17.** 'But indeed thou hast now cast us off . . .' **18—19.** 'All this has come upon us though we did not forget thee, nor betray thy covenant.' The central theme of this psalm is here. **20.** 'Thou hast crushed us in a place of jackals [= desolate place], and covered us with deep darkness [rather than 'shadow of death': see on 23:4]'. **21.** But we did not 'spread out our hands to strange gods' [cf 81:10], yet **23** 'on thy account we are put to death all day': quoted Rm 8:36. **24.** '*Exsurge, quare obdormis, Domine*' [Ash Wednesday liturgy], **27** redeem us because of thy love.'

e 45 A Wedding Song—In its own right as a poem, this is one of the loveliest in the Psalter. But the question of its origin, and why it is in the Psalter at all, is much debated. **(1)** Those who would seek a 'cultic' purpose, see here a liturgy for a royal wedding, with the praise of the king as occupying the divinely appointed throne (v 8), at the centre of the cult (e.g. Mowinckel, I, 72ff), or else part of an annual festival of kingship. **(2)** Others reckon it to be a composition relating to a particular wedding (see below). **(3)** Or it may be a poem, written as if for an occasion: an unknown poet is imagined as composing his song on the occasion of a royal wedding and thrusting it into the hands of the couple at the ceremony. In such circumstances it becomes almost dull to try to identify the occasion: the most likely would be Ahab's wedding to Jezebel (who was from Tyre, v 13, cf 1 (3) Kg 16:31; and he had an ivory palace, v 9, cf 1 (3) 22:39), or of Jehoram (Joram) to Athaliah (whose mother was from Tyre, 2 (4) Kg 8:16, 26), or (traditionally) of Solomon to an Egyptian princess (1 (3) Kg 3:1). Whatever the original occasion, the poem entered into Israel's heritage, and the ideas of the king as the Lord's Anointed (v 8), of the permanence of his throne (v 7), and of the nations eventually coming to praise him (v 17), made **f** it applicable to the Throne of David. In this way it became 'messianic', i.e. looked forward to a time when Israel should lead all mankind to worship God. For us Christians the psalm looks forward to the messianic fulfilment begun with Christ, so that it came to be understood of the 'nuptials of the Lamb', when Christ weds his spouse the Church, the 'new Jerusalem' (Apoc 21:2, **38** 9). It is this messianic interpretation, Jewish or Christian, that has won this otherwise secular poem its place in the hymn-book of the Synagogue and the Church. And the 'canonization' of this P, together with the Canticle, has given a special place to human love in the sacred writings. The poem stands alone of its kind in the Psalter. Most of the body of the poem is in a long four-beat metre, which gives it a special solemnity. The **title** includes 'Upon Shoshannim [=? lilies]', only here, 69:1; 80:1 and cf 60:1, probably indicating a melody. It is described as 'a love song', and its quality is fully worthy of the 'Qorah Collection'.

2. 'My heart has poured out a goodly word, I will **g** speak my poem [lit. things made: DWT points out that this is the root meaning of the word 'poem': RSV 'verses'] to the king: my tongue is the pen of a swift scribe': i.e. eager, though some see it as 'professional' (cf Targum 'practised'), i.e. a court poet. **3—10** are addressed to the young man. **3.** 'Thou art fairer than sons of mankind . . . **4.** Gird on thy sword . . . **5.** Prosper thy glory—ride on! For the cause of truth and "meekness" (and) right! And thy right hand shall teach thee dread (deeds)': RSV for 'meakness' reads 'shall defend', while BJ emends more extensively to 'Stretch thy bowstring . . .' **6.** 'Thine arrows are sharp, peoples fall beneath thee, in the heart of the foes of the king': so lit. LXX/V, variously interpreted: i. = the arrows pierce the hearts of his foes: AV RV RSV RPB; ii. 'in the heart' = 'in the midst' of his enemies, peoples fall down: PB; iii. 'peoples (are) subject to thee [lit beneath thee], falls the heart [emended] of the foes . . .': cf NP BJ; iv. 'peoples fall . . ., fails every heart [supply *kālāh kol*] in the foes . . .'. **7—8.** 'Thy throne, God, (is) for **h** ever and ever . . . **8.** . . . therefore God, thy God, hath anointed thee': the great difficulty is 'God' after 'thy throne': LXX/V take it as an exclamation. But whose is the throne? God anoints the king immediately afterwards: i. = 'thy (God's) throne, o God, is for ever': PB AV RV BJ: and this is cut off from the anointing that follows; ii. = 'thy (king's) throne (is like) God's (throne, which is) for ever': RPB; iii. = 'thy (king's) throne (is) God's for ever': RVm: i.e. is a divine institution (the 'sacral kingship'); cf JA 'thy throne given of God' and RSV 'your divine throne' (see also on 110:1, noticing 1 Chr 29:23 of Solomon 'on Yahweh's throne'). But the above translation (iii) is not grammatically defensible; iv. = 'thy (king's) throne, o God (I call thee to witness), is for ever': though a little forced, links with the anointing to follow. The passage is quoted in Hb 1:8—9 with 'Thy throne, o God . . .' applied to Christ. **9.** A picture of pleasantness: the young king's scented robes, and 'from ivory halls the viols rejoice thee': so most since RV. **10.** 'Daughters of kings are among thy maids of honour, a queen stands at thy right hand in gold of Ophir [cf 1 (3) Kg 9:28, Solomon fetched gold from Ophir—in Arabia?]. Who is this 'queen' (*šēghal* = consort)? The bride, the queen-to-be, has not yet entered, but it may refer (proleptically) to her; some think of the queen-mother, others of the king's previous wives. **11—13** are addressed to the girl: 'Listen, o daughter . . . **12** the **i** king desires thy beauty: since he is thy lord [Vg here, incorrectly and confusingly, adds 'God', followed by PB], bow down to him, **13** and, o daughter of Tyre, with a gift the rich men of the people beg (to see) thy face' [for Tyre, see intro.]: i. 'o daughter . . .': so JA according to the Hebrew, and perhaps best; ii. 'and the daughter of Tyre (the bride) (comes) with a gift, the rich men . . .': PB AV RV RPB but slightly forced; cf BJ slightly emend-

38i ed; iii. 'and the daughters of Tyre (the bridesmaids?) . . .': LXX/V; iv. 'and the people '[= ? lit daughter] of Tyre (come) . . .': NP cf RSV. **14—16** describes the entry of the bride: 'The king's daughter, all glorious, (is) within (the hall), of woven gold is her dress': the word 'within' was rendered by Vg as 'inside', i.e. her glory within herself, with many allegorical applications. **15.** 'In coloured raiment she is led to the king . . .' **17—18** addressed to the young man. A most delightful poem.

j 46 World Cataclysm, but God stills men's Wars also—A short song, a genuine hymn, mostly in a fine long metre. **Title**: Qorah Collection; 'upon *ᵃlāmôth* perhaps means 'for soprani'(?). **2—4.** God is our hope, even in earthquake and flood. **5—7.** '(But there is) a river, whose streams rejoice the City of God': i.e. Sion is not to suffer in the world cataclysms, for **6** . . . 'God shall help her at the turn of the morning . . .' **8.** The refrain after the second stanza, 'The LORD of hosts is with us . . .' [see on 24:10], and note the rare 'Yahweh' in Book II]. **9—10.** God's power in nature shows that he also has power to make an end of men's wars. **11.** '(Therefore, o men,) cease (from your warfare)! [lit. relax, give it up] And know [= realize] that I am God (who has power over all things) . . .' **12.** The refrain again, after the third stanza.

k 47 A Hymn of Victory—Frequently classed as an 'Enthronement Psalm', for Mowinckel (I, 106) this is one of the most typical Pss for the 'Festival of the Enthronement of Yahweh' (cf also 93, 96—99, while for Weiser it is a liturgy for the Covenant Festival, and for Kraus for a procession with the Ark. One notices the short quick metre at the opening. **Title**: Qorah.

2—5. 'All ye peoples, clap your hands': lit. 'strike the palm', a gesture not of applause, but of joy (cognate phrase in 96:8); in Na 3:19 of derision; in Prv 3t of bargaining. **3.** 'For the Lord Most High is to be feared, a great King over all the earth. **4.** He shall subdue [rare word, see on 18:48] peoples under us . . . **6.** The most interesting and puzzling verse in this Psalm: 'God has gone up with a shout, the Lord with the sound of a trumpet (*šôphâr*)': those who see here an Enthronement at the Feast of Yahweh, or of the Covenant, see here the 'cultic' act of mounting the throne, for Weiser the 'consummation of the *Heilsgeschichte*'; for Kraus it would refer to a procession with the Ark up the Temple hill, (God's Presence is 'going up'), on a special feast day. Perhaps the reference is to a New Year's Day festival, when the shofar is blown (see on 81:4). Others again see the reference to God's eventual, **l** messianic 'exaltation' in the eyes of all mankind. The verse is aptly used in the liturgy on Ascension Day. **7.** 'Sing to God . . . to our King . . . **9.** God is King over the nations . . .': the phrase 'God is King' is much discussed: *mālakh* is a perfect tense expressing something that has happened (see further on 93:1): i. = 'is (and always has been) king': expressing something settled long ago; ii. = 'has (now) become king' or 'has now been declared . . .' is perhaps grammatically more satisfactory, expressing something has happened, and is insisted on by those who envisage an 'enthronement'; iii. the usual 'reigns' is non-committal, but seems not to look sufficiently into the past to convey the force of the perfect tense. **10.** 'The princes of the peoples are gathered with the God of Abraham': i. 'with' [repointing] follows LXX/V [= in the presence of]: so PB NP RPB; ii. 'are gathered (as) the people of the God of Abraham': represents the Hebrew pointing, but is awkward and stretches the sense: so AV RV RSV; iii. BJ assumes both words: 'gathered with

the people of . . .' 'For to God (belong) the mighty of the **388l** earth . . .': i. so NP RPB: for 'mighty' see DWT on an Arabic root (cf LXX 'rulers'?); ii. the common (and distinct) word is 'shields' [= ? protection]: so most, but the usage has no parallel; iii. Vg [with slight alteration] 'the mighty gods of the earth . . .'

48 The Love of Sion, Joy of all the World—A **389a** true hymn of pleasant quality, and in almost entirely regular metre, expressing a 'universalist' theme (v 5 the kings assembling in Sion). **Title**: Qorah. **2—3.** 'Great is the LORD, . . . in . . . his holy mountain, **3** Mount Sion, the recesses of the north, the city of a great king [LXX 'of the great king', thus quoted Mt 5:35, is followed by most]'. The phrase 'recesses of the north (*sāphôn*)' (cf NP BJ RSV RPB) presents a difficulty: it probably means 'a divine abode': the same phrase occurs in Is 14:13 of the heavenly throne 'in the recesses of the north' desired by the King of Babylon, and the remote mountain, like Olympus for the Greeks, as a divine abode was known in Eastern mythology, as in the Ras-Shamra texts, e.g. 'Who would drive Baal from the crags of the north [or? Saphon as a proper name]' (among *Baal Myths* in DOTT 130). The psalmist's use of the mythological phrase for the divine abode of the God of Israel is indeed daring; but perhaps no more so than the Latin hymn-writers' use of 'Olympus' for heaven, in e.g. the 5th cent. Lauds hymn for the Ascension. The older explanation, translating (unwarrantably) 'on the side (of Sion) to the north (is) city . . .' (cf LXX/V PB AV RV), is supposed to refer to the temple site in the north of Jerusalem. **4.** 'God in her citadels (is) . . . a refuge, **5** . . . kings have gathered (there) . . . **6** they saw . . . **8** (how) with an east wind [= a hot wind from the desert] thou dost dost shatter ships of Tarshish [= sea-going, not merely coastal vessels] . . . **9.** Lord of hosts [see on 24:10] . . .' **10.** God's love of Sion brings **11** his praise throughout the world. **13.** An encouragement to all to get to know the beloved city: 'Walk about Sion . . . number her towers, **14** learn to love [lit set your heart on] her ramparts, look closely at her citadels, so that you may tell of it to a later generation.

49 A Meditation on the Uselessness of Riches and b the Inevitability of Death—This Psalm represents the 'Wisdom genre' in the Qorah Collection. Textually it is one of the more difficult psalms, but the general theme is plain: the psalmist puts his puzzle to the world. Amid the uselessness of wealth, there may be in v 8 a reference to the need for a divine redeemer, but the exact meaning there is far from clear. **Title**: Qorah—the last of the 'Qorah Collection I'.

2—5. 'Listen to this, all ye peoples . . . **3.** All mankind [lit 'sons of Adam and also sons of man': some, as RSV, see here a distinction of 'low and high estate', see also on 62:10] . . . rich and poor alike . . . **5.** . . . I will open [= solve RSV] my riddle [= a thing hard to understand] on the harp [= in this song]'. **6—7.** Now here is my puzzle: 'Why am I afraid in the days of evil (when) iniquity at my heels surrounds me? **7.** (There are men) who trust in their own strength . . . and riches . . .' **8—10.** Is a very difficult passage: **8.** '(Yet) a brother (*'āh*) no man can indeed ransom, nor give the price of him to God': so AV RV (PB RPB take 'ransom' = 'deliver'); ii. [emend. 'brother'] 'Truly (*'akh*) no man can ransom (himself), nor give the price of him(self) to God': NP BJ RSV; iii. 'A brother cannot ransom; shall (any) man ransom? He cannot give the price of him(self) to God': LXX/V (printed Vg has no query). The context is really of the impotence of riches and the impossibility of bargaining with God; but if the emendation in ii. above is

389b correct, the idea of a redeemer is here expressed.
c 9. 'And the value of the ransom of their [read 'his'?] soul—and it will cease for ever, 10 that he may live yet to the end, and not see the Pit [see on 28:1]': the real difficulty is 'cease': i. = 'And the ransom of his soul is (too) costly; and it will never suffice [? lit 'cease for ever'] 10 that he may live . . .': NP RSV, and probably the best solution, though the rendering of 'cease' is doubtful. ii. = '. . . (too) costly—so he must let that alone [? lit 'cease'] for ever—10 that he may live . . .': PB RV RPB (RV takes v 9 as a parenthesis; RPB transposes v 9 to after v 10); also a doubtful rendering of 'cease': iii. = '. . . (too) costly; it is finished [? lit 'cease'] for ever. 10. Shall he yet live . . .?': BJ and cf AV? iv. LXX/V continues v 9 from v 8, and takes 'cease' = ? 'struggle'. The point seems to be the idea of man's impotence (from v 8) of himself to ransom himself (or his brother), or to live for ever, without God's aid. **11–12.** He (the helpless man, above) sees the wise and foolish die, and **12** 'their graves are their homes for ever': with LXX/V, so most, rather than Heb. 'their midst [= ? their inward thought is that] their houses (shall remain) for ever' (PB AV RV), which is very forced.
d 13. 'And man in honour shall not abide, he is likened to the beasts (which) perish': i. so PB AV RV NP RSV, but 'abide' really = 'pass the night'; ii. 'And man (when he is) in honour, shall not understand [emended cf v 21], he is likened to the beasts (and) resembles them [emended]: LXX/V, cf BJ; iii. 'And man (is) like an [emended] ox, (which) does not understand [as LXX], he is likened to the beasts (which) perish: RPB. **14.** 'This is their way [of life, or, their fate]: folly [or, foolish confidence] is theirs; and after them (other men) take pleasure in their sayings': i. 'after them . . .': so most; ii. [emend] '(this is) the end of them who take pleasure in their portion': NP RSV; iii. 'after them (other men) run [emend] at their command': BJ cf Jer. *Selah*
e after this v. 15. The text here seems very confused: 'They [impersonal] have appointed them (the fools of v 14) like sheep for Sheol; death is their shepherd [Vg 'depascet' = devours, cf PB AV, rather than expected 'pascet']; and the upright shall have dominion over them in the morning, and their form shall be for Sheol to consume from its habitation': i. [taking Heb. as it stands, a possible meaning] '. . . the upright shall have dominion [= ? shall not be condemned to Sheol]; in the morning [= ? overnight = quickly] their form shall be consumed by Sheol, so that they have no other habitation: RV NP BJ cf PB AV, but all very doubtful; ii. [emending] '. . . straight [for 'upright'] they go down [for 'dominate'] to the grave [for 'in the morning']; their beauty is consumed in Sheol, their only home': RPB cf RSV. The picture seems to be of Sheol inexorably claiming its victims when they trust in themselves. **16.** 'But (in contrast) God will ransom my soul . . .' **17–20.** We are then advised not to fear when the rich prosper, for the darkness of Sheol will be their eventual lot. **21.** 'A man (may be) in honour, but he will not understand: he is likened to the beasts (which) perish': i. so PB AV RV NP BJ, cf LXX/V; ii. 'a man (is) like an [emended] ox, (which) does not understand': RPB as for v 13; iii. 'a man in honour shall not abide [emended to = Heb. of v 13, which is questionable, see above]': RSV.
f **50 A Picture of God's Judgement on True Sacrifice**—God is pictured in a theophany, addressing the people on true sacrifice: prayer and praise, and not empty ritual. This is one of the few psalms, whose approach is that of the prophets of the OT, when God is portrayed as passing judgement on the people, and which Gunkel

classed as 'Prophetic Psalms' and Mowinckel as 'Oracles': **38** in such a category could be placed this one 50, with 75, 81 and 82. See also intro. to Ps 75. It is a good poem, of noble construction in three massive stanzas (vv 1–6, 7–15, 16–23). **Title**: '(Belonging) to (the) Asaph (Collection)', the only one in Book II.
1–6. The theophany: 'The God of gods, the Lord (Yahweh) has spoken . . . 3 he comes . . .', the theophanic fire before him. **4** to judge his people: **5** 'Gather to me my faithful [see on 12:2], who have made a covenant with me upon [= ? concerning] sacrifice' [so LXX/V, but most = 'with (an accompanying) sacrifice']; **6** and the heavens reply that he is judge. Note the opening phrase: 'God of gods' = El elohim, which is patient of **g** several translations: i. = 'True God among all (false) gods': LXX/V BJ; ii. = 'God, God' (the two different words applied to God): RV JA; iii. = 'The Mighty One, God': RSV; iv. = 'The most mighty God': PB AV RPB.
7–15. God addresses his people: **8** 'Not for thy sacrifices do I reprove thee . . . 9 (but) I will not take [= you need not offer me] bullocks . . . 10 for all the beasts of the forest are mine . . . 11 birds . . . wild beasts [*zîz*, see on 80:14, but LXX/V here 'beauty', cf perhaps Is 66:11]'. **12–13.** He continues in irony: 'If I were hungry, I would not tell thee . . . 14–15. (No.) offer . . . the sacrifice of thanksgiving [or, praise, see on 67:4]'. **16–23.** He then turns to the wicked: 'What (affair) of thine (is it) to declare my statutes . . . ? . . . 17. Thou hast hated correction . . . but now I rebuke you . . . 23 (but) he who offers sacrifice of thanksgiving [or, praise] . . . and orders his life aright, to him I will show the salvation of God'.
51 Miserere mei Deus—The most outstanding **h** expression of the conviction that man's sin can be 'blotted out' by God—the actual phrase is only here (vv 3, 11)—while in 32:1–2 we have the idea of sin being 'taken away', 'covered' or 'not thought-of' (see also on 65:4). More than any of the psalms, perhaps, it has an insight into spiritual values and the primacy of interior dispositions in worship. It is genrally taken (even by Mowinckel, II, 17) as a true personal prayer, but see note on vv 20–21 and it is counted as the third 'Penitential Psalm' (see on Ps 6). **Title** (vv 1–2 in Heb. text): '(Belonging) to (the) David (Collection II)'.
2. It is then ascribed to the moment of David's repentance after Nathan's visit (2 Sm 12:1ff). **3.** 'Pity me, o God, according to thy love; . . . blot out my transgressions': 'blot out' of sin, only here and v 11. **4.** 'Wash me . . . cleanse me': 'washing' of a person, in the moral sense, only here and v 9 (Jer 2:22; 4:14 of Jerusalem); 'cleansing' is used of ritual 'cleansing' (see v 9), but rarely in the moral sense. **5.** I recognize that I have sinned, and **6** that thou art 'blameless when thou judgest': LXX/V 'victorious [following Syr. use of the verb] when thou art judged [emended]', i.e. thou canst not be convicted by anyone: Rm 3:4 quotes from LXX (and cf PB here). **7.** I was conceived in sin = sin is part of my make-up; this passage cannot be claimed as demonstrating the doctrine of original sin, nor has it been so used by the Church, but it does show an attitude in accord with orthodox doctrine. **8.** The idea of inner faithfulness (see on 5:8) as distinct from external observance is important. **9.** 'Cleanse me with hyssop': lit. 'un-sin me', and the **i** reference is to the ceremony of ritual cleansing described in Nm 19:18, when, with a sprig of hyssop, water was sprinkled on the unclean person, his tent etc. Hence the Vg here 'Asperges me: sprinkle me', and the use of this verse when holy water is sprinkled on the people. **10.** Let me hear rejoicing, after feeling so crushed,

389i 13 ... take not from me thy holy spirit [probably = thy influence on my spirit, though PB and RSV write 'Spirit', perhaps reading too much into the text, but cf 139:7; the phrase 'holy spirit' occurs only here and Is 63:10, 11] ... 14. Strengthen me with a willing spirit [or, 'free, generous': connected with 'voluntariness', and hence applied to the 'prince', who cannot be compelled, whence **j** LXX/V 'princely', and see on 110:3] ...' 16. 'Deliver me from blood [plural, often = bloodshed, bloodstains or bloodguilt: many prefer the last, connecting with David] ...' 17. 'Master (*adonai*), may thou open my lips ...': the verse used at the beginning of the Divine Office. 18. The recurrent theme of this psalm: God's delight in true sacrifice: 20—21 'Look favourably upon Sion, may thou build up the walls of Jerusalem; then (and only then indeed) shalt thou delight in the "right" sacrifices [= liturgically correct] ...': i.e. only when Sion is built up by God himself will the official sacrifices have value. Thus the psalm ends with one of its principal themes. These verses have caused much comment, since they represent the only 'community' or 'cultic' sentiment in the psalm. (1) If the Ps is essentially personal, as is commonly supposed, then it may be that these vv. were added to adapt it for congregational use. (2) If, however, the Ps is in fact 'cultic', with the 'I' of the psalmist standing for the nation, then they would naturally form part of the whole. (3) Some suppose the addition to have been made with a particular rebuilding in view, e.g. Nehemiah. (4) But it seems most likely that the rebuilding of the walls is a symbolic expression of the Lord's care for Sion, my (or, the nation's) spiritual home; and the theme of genuine interior worship appears from v 8 onwards, applicable equally personally and 'cultically'.

k **52 An Apostrophe addressed to the Wicked, with a Warning to them**—A curious Ps which it is difficult to place: it has something of the prayer, of the curse, of the didactic manner, and there are some textual difficulties. The **Title** (David) ascribes it to the moment in 1 Sm 22:9 when David was betrayed to Saul. 3—4 'Why boastest thou of evil, o strong man?' God's mercy (*hesedh 'el*) (endures) all day; 4 destruction thy tongue devises, as a sharpened razor, thou worker of treachery': so the Heb. text as it stands: i. so Jer PB AV RV ii. '... o strong man unto iniquity (*'el hesedh*) [= shame, cf Lv 20:17])? All day 4 thy tongue devises injustice ...': LXX/V iii. '... [as above, NP well *'praepotens infamis'*, CV 'champion of shame'] all day 4 devising destruction; thy tongue is as a ...': NP BJ iv. 'Why ... showing thy strength against the devout (*'el hāsīdh*) all day; 4 destruction thy tongue devises ...': RPB cf RSV (cf Syriac).

5—6. 'Thou hast loved evil ... o tongue of treachery': these two stanzas form a balancing pair. 7. But God shall destroy thee, 8 and the righteous shall mock thee. 10—11. But I, because I trusted in God, shall be 'like a flourishing olive-tree ...': one of those apparently self-complacent expressions, understandable in terms of acceptance of God's reward and rejoicing at his judgement.

l **53 A Consideration of the 'Fool' and a Hope of Deliverance**—Duplicate of Ps 14 in 'David Collection I' in Book I, where see notes. Four times Yahweh of Book I appears as *Elohim* (God) as usual in Book II. The **Title** probably indicates a tune. The only important difference is in v **6** here: '... for God has scattered the bones of him that is encamped (against?) thee; thou hast put (them?) to shame, for God has rejected them' [the word 'encamped' is grammatically very doubtful, and LXX/V have 'man-pleasers', perhaps a better reading]; Ps 14:5 corresponding has: '... for God is with a righteous

generation; **6** you put to shame the counsels of the **389l** "poor", for the LORD is their hope', which shows a sounder text. The possession of this complete duplicate might throw light on the composition of the Psalter, apart from the Yahwist and Elohist editors. Was this 53 version adapted ('scattered the bones ...') to commemorate some victory? The unsoundness of 'encamped' in 53 discourages the idea, often proposed, of the end of a siege. But it would seem that the Psalm existed in two forms, and it is impossible to say which is the more original: only the sounder text of 14 speaks in its favour.

390a **54 A Confident Request for God's Help**—A short prayer in almost regular metre, in two stanzas. **Title** (David) refers to 1 Sm 23:19; 26:1, when David was betrayed. 3—5. 'O God, in (the power of) thy name deliver me ... 5 strangers have come up against me ... arrogant men ... *Selah*': for 'strangers' an almost exact parallel in 86:14 has 'insolent': so Targum and some MSS here, followed by NP BJ RSV RPB. 6—9. But God is helping me ... 8. 'In freedom [= willingly cf on 51:14; or, 'with a freewill offering' with RV RSV] I will sacrifice to thee', 9 and because thou hast rescued me, 'my eye has looked (down) upon my enemies': cf 92:12 with note, 112:8; 118:7.

b **55 A Cry of Pain, because of Treachery of a Friend**—The picture seems to be of one in a beleaguered city (v 10), who would fain escape (v 7 'wings of a dove'), for here even friends have become foes (v 13): it is a picture of the specially acute pain caused by this disillusionment, a typical 'lament', but with a special point, personal, but interpreted by some as national. Some would assign the psalm to a particular siege, but it may equally well be an imagination of this human situation. The **title** does not include a *mise-en-scène*.

2—6. An expression of fear. 'Give ear, o God, to my prayer ... 3 ... I am alarmed 4 by the voice of an enemy, before the shouting [so RPB see DWT; LXX/V 'oppression', so most] of the wicked ... 5. My heart is whirling within me, and deadly fears [so RPB, see DWT, rather than 'fears of death'] have fallen upon me. 7—9. The desire to escape: 'O for the wings of a dove ...'. 10. 'Destroy, o Master (*adonai*), divide [= ? confuse] their tongue [= speech] ...': i. so LXX/V PB AV RV NP; ii. 'Destroy their plans [word supplied], divide their tongues': Targum, so RSV RPB; iii. '... from the storm 10 which devours, o Lord, the [repointed] torrent of their tongue ...': BJ.

11—12. Wickedness and injustice are everywhere in the (beleaguered) city. 13—15. But it is not an enemy who has hurt me thus: I could have borne this ... but 14 'it is thou, a man of my own rank [so lit, and best, as BJ; others 'my equal', Vg 'homo unanimis'], my intimate, well-known to me; 15 we used to take sweet counsel together; in the **c** house of God we used to walk in agreement': the simple picture of a friendship, now turned to betrayal, has a very awkward phrase at the end: i. 'in agreement' (as above) = LXX/V: followed by PB RSV RPB; ii. Heb. text has 'in tumult' = ? the throng of pilgrims to the temple, cf the 'crowd' in 42:5?: AV RV NP: but doubtful; iii. transfer to next verse: '... house of God. Let them [emended] go in tumult, 16 let death come upon them ...': WV BJ. 16. The tone changes to an imprecation upon the traitors: 'Let death steal upon them ... 17. (But) I call upon God ... 19. He has redeemed me ... from the battle against me, for they are among (?) many (that fight) with me': doubtful grammar, so some would emend: 'For those that approach me [or, bowmen against me] are many': cf RPB 20 '(and) God shall hear (*yišma' 'el*) and humble them, and (he) dwells

390c of old' [strange usage]: i. so LXX/V PB AV RVm NP BJ RSV; ii. 'God shall hear and answer [= repay] them . . .': RV; iii. [connecting with preceding] 'even Ishmael (*yišmā'ēl* read as one word) and the [emended] tribes of the east': RPB. '(For they are men) who have no changes (of heart?) and have not feared God'. **21.** 'He (the friend of vv 14—15) put forth his hand against (those who were) at peace with him; he has violated his covenant; **22** smooth are the buttery (words) of his mouth, but battle is in his heart'; and the parallel continues with 'softer than oil' and 'drawn swords'. **23.** 'Cast upon the LORD thy care' [word only here: so LXX (quoted thus 1 Pt 5:7) Vg NP; lit. ? = 'what is given to thee' = ? 'thy burden': so PB AV RV BJ RSV RPB]. **24.** But my foes shall be brought to 'the pit of destruction': the two words together only here, see on 16:10.

d **56 A Prayer for Help amid Tears**—Another personal lament; textually very difficult. Title: 'Upon the dove of silence [or, a terebinth] of distance' is probably the name of a tune, and *mikhtām* a description, the keys to which have been lost. The incident in David's life is in 1 Sm 21:10—15.

2. Pity me, o God, for men have trodden me down . . . **3** . . . many fight against me (on) high': i. 'on high' = 'proudly': RV RSV (doubtful); ii. = 'o thou most high': PB AV NP; iii. [connect with next v] ' . . . against me. From the height of **4** the day . . .': Vg [LXX has the phrase earlier] (meaning?); iv. ' . . . against me. Raise me up [emended] **4** on the day . . .': BJ RPB. **4.** '(On the) day (when) I am afraid, I will trust in thee'. **5.** In this and the next v, the force of 'word' is open to several interpretations: 'In God I praise his word, in God I have trusted': i. = 'In God, whose word I praise, in God I trust': RSV RPB; ii. = 'In God, in whose promise I glory, . . .': NP; iii. = 'In God I praise my [emended] words . . .' = 'To God I direct my words of praise . . .': LXX/V. **6.** 'All day they injure my words, against me are all their devices': i. = ' . . . they mistake (PB), wrest (AV RV) my words . . .': so BJ; ii. = ' . . . they injure my cause . . .': RSV; iii. = ' . . . they molest me [omit 'words': CV 'my efforts']': NP; iv. [emend.] ' . . . they injure me (with) words . . .': Jer WV; v. [emend.] ' . . . they abominate my words . . .': LXX/V; vi. [emend. with Syr.] ' . . . they talk and take counsel together': **e** RPB (see DWT). **7.** 'They stir up trouble (? *yāgūrū*), they hide, they watch my heels [= footsteps], as if they waited for my soul [= life]': but most emend to 'they band together (like robbers) . . .': Jer PB AV RV NP BJ RSV RPB (see DWT). **8.** 'Because of iniquity, deliver them [or, deliverance for them], in (thine) anger bring down the peoples, o God': ['deliver' seems out of place here]: i. = 'Because of (their) iniquity, (shall there be) deliverance for them?': PB AV RV BJ; ii. = ' . . . iniquity, vomit them out [Aram. word, cf Jb 21:10]': BJm; iii. [emend. 'iniquity' to 'nothing'] 'For nothing [= ? 'On no account'] deliver them': LXX/V, cf Jer 'There is no deliverance . . .'; iv. [emend. 'deliverance' to 'weigh out = repay', cf 58:3] 'Because of iniquity repay to them': WV NP RSV RPB: the best solution. **9.** 'Thou hast taken account of my grief; place my tears in thy water-skin; is it not (all my sorrow, written down) in thy book? [cf on 69:29]'. The word *nôdh*, 'grief' (which could also mean 'wandering', so PB 'flittings', NP 'exile'), is assonant with *n'ôdh*, 'water-skin, or, leathern bottle', cf 119:83; and 'take account' is related with the word 'book'. These assonances make the images less startling in Hebrew. [LXX/V for 'water-skin' has 'sight'.] The psalmist is begging God to take account of his trials.

10. 'Then shall my enemies turn back . . . this I know **39** [= I am sure of], that (thou art) God to me': i. so LXX/V Jer NP [= thou art what God means to me]; ii. = 'that God is for me': so others (PB 'on my side'), cf on 118:6. **11—12.** The refrain from v 5 slightly expanded. **13.** 'Upon me, o God, are thy vows [= 'upon me (is the obligation to pay) the vows which I owe to thee'] . . .' **14.** 'For thou hast delivered my soul from death . . .': this appears almost verbatim in 116:8—9, but the text there is more straighforward and may be better preserved.

57 A Prayer of Confidence, even amid Lions—These **f** Pss 54—59 are all 'Individual Laments' amid various troubles, here amid persecutors pictured as lions. **Title:** David, with a *mise-en-scène* of hiding in a cave, referring to the episode at Adullam in 1 Sm 22:1, or at Engedi in 1 Sm 24:2—4. 'Do not destroy' is probably the name of a tune, used for Pss 57—59 and 75.

2. 'Pity me, o God, . . . **3** I call to God most high, to God who has care for me': the verb is *gāmar* = 'to complete': i. = 'does everything for me': AV RV BJ; ii. = 'fulfils his purpose for me': RSV RPB cf PB; iii. [reading *gāmal* = 'deal out to'] = 'benefits me': LXX/V NP, and perhaps a better reading: the use of *gāmar* as above is doubtful. **4.** 'He sends from heaven and delivers me, he has reproved him who treads me down (*Selah*) . . .' [Note the unusual Selah in the middle of the verse]: so LXX/V and most; others (PB AV RV) take as ' . . . delivers me (when he who) reproaches (me) treads . . .'; **5** 'My soul is in the midst of lions, (there) I lie: they devour the sons of men, their teeth (are like) spears and arrows . . .': the picture of the persecutors as lions appears (though with a different word) in 22:14. i. 'they devour': BJ RPB [cf Arabic root, see DWT]; ii. 'they devour' [supposing emendation to word only in Gn 25:30]: WV NP RSV; iii. 'they are on fire' [usual meaning of *lāhat*]: PB AV RV; iv. ' . . . I lie in anxiety [reading?]; sons of men, their teeth are . . .': LXX/V. **6.** 'Be exalted above the heavens [or, sky] . . .': a refrain **g** reappearing at v 12. **8—12** are reproduced with small variants in Book V (David Collection IV) in Ps 108:2—6. 'My heart is ready, o God . . . **9.** Awake, my glory, awake lute and harp . . .': i. literally, and together with lute and harp: = 'my singing of thy glory', as in 108:2, so LXX/V PB AV RV (also Ibn Ezra here): perhaps the most likely; ii. otherwise = 'awake, (for thou, o God art) my glory . . .' [i.e. he whom I glorify, cf 3:4; 106:20]; iii. 'my glory' = the noblest part of me = my soul: so NP BJ RSV, see on 30:13; iv. [repoint.] 'my liver' = emotions (see DWT on 16:9, and cf 30:13), so RPB by euphemism 'my soul'. 'I will awaken (the very) dawn': an active form: so RVm NP BJ RSV RPB, better than 'I will awake at dawn': LXX/V PB AV RV. **12.** The refrain cf v 6.

58 False Judges on Earth, but God judges truly— **h** This Psalm stands somewhat apart. The text is sometimes very unsound, but the general theme is plain. The Ps is specially notable for its highly coloured and imaginative pictures of the wicked: they are like snakes who do not even listen to the snake-charmers, like spilt water, like useless grass, like a miscarriage or abortion (perhaps like a disgusting snail), like thorn bushes fit only for burning. If the reading *'ēlīm* for *'elem* in v 2 is right, this Ps would take its place with Ps 82, where see intro. **Title:** see on 57.

2. 'Is it indeed true (*'elem?*) (that) you speak justice, judge (in) equity, o sons of men?': the problem is *'elem* a word only here, variously translated or emended: i. 'Is it truly indeed [reading *'ûlām*] . . .?': LXX/V Jer, and most likely; ii. 'Do you truly, o company [*'ēlem*], speak

0h justice . . . ?': Ibn Ezra (cf word for sheaves Gn 37:7, Ps 126:6, so = company?) PB AV; iii. 'Do you speak as a righteous company . . . ?' JA (referring to the judges); iv. 'Do you truly in silence [obvious meaning of *'elem*] speak justice . . . ?': RV, cf Targum, which suggests silence, i.e. refraining, when justice should be spoken: perhaps the most convincing without emendation; v. 'Is truly the justice you (should) speak (become) silence . . . ?': RVm[1]; vi. 'Do you truly, o gods [reading *'ēlīm*] (i.e. gods of the nations) speak justice . . . ?': RVm[2] BJ RSV (cf CV): contrasting with 'sons of men'; vii. 'Do you truly, o mighty ones [*'ēlīm* in this sense cf on 29:1 also **i** 8:6], speak justice . . . ?': RVm[3] NP RSVm RPB. **3.** The proscription of the unjust judges continues . . . **4.** 'The wicked are estranged from the womb . . . **5** their poison [elsewhere of snakes, dragons, arrows:] is like the poison of a snake, like that of the deaf adder stopping its ears [= refusing to hear], **6** which does not listen to the voice of charmers, of the skilful binder of spells': a colourful description of the wicked man, especially the judge who refuses to listen. **7—10** is an invitation to God to punish them: to 'break the jaws of the infidels [so RPB rather than 'lions', as most, see DWT on 34:11], **8** let them flow away like water, let them go, (as one who) tread• his arrows, so let them wither': the last piece is very uncertain. i. [The arrows appear in all the old versions, and 'to tread' is the usual word for bending the bow] so = '(When one) bends (the bow to shoot) his arrows . . . ': cf LXX/V PB AV RV NP, and cf similar ellipsis in 64:4, but very doubtful; ii. [The principal emendation is *hāṣīr* 'grass' for *hiṣṣaw* 'arrows] so = 'Let them wither like grass (that is) trodden': RPB cf WV BJ RSV, and most probable. **9.** 'As *šabbelûl* melts, let him (the wicked) go; (like) an abortion of a woman [already Jerome's rendering: LXX/V misread as 'fire falls'] they do not see the sunlight': the difficulty is *šabbelûl*, only here, apparently something slimy; and LXX/V 'wax', the Rabbis' 'snail' (the word remains in Rabbinic Hebrew), and Jerome's 'stinking worm' may be guesses: i. = 'as melting wax goes away . . . '. LXX/V; ii. = 'as a snail melts, let him go . . . ': PB AV RV NP BJ RSV cf Jer; iii. = 'as a miscarriage (that) melts away, like an abortion of a woman, they do not see . . . ': WV RPB (see DWT) **j** and the hideous picture is consistent. **10.** A famously difficult text: 'Before your cooking-pots [or, as LXX/V 'thorns', an exactly similar word] understand the bramble, the living and the heat alike he shall blow away': the fate of the wicked is to be like this: i. [The picture is of a camp-fire, blown away before the cooking starts] = 'before your cooking-pots feel (the heat of the burning) bramble, the green twigs [= living?] and the burning (twigs) alike he (God) shall sweep away': AV RV RSV, but very far-fetched; ii. [same picture] ' . . . the hot (wind) shall blow away the green twigs': NP; iii. [same picture] ' . . . thus anger [lit. heat] shall vex him, like (meat in the pot that is) raw [lit. living—?]': PB, very doubtful; iv. [same picture] 'Before your thorns understand the bramble, his (God's) anger shall take them away alive': LXX/V— not in itself intelligible, but it introduces the picture that follows; v. [The picture is of a bush that is destroyed before it is grown] = 'Before thorns grow [emended] into a bramble-bush, as if in anger they (the wicked) are stormed away alive': Jer; vi. [same picture] 'Before they grow [emended] into thorns like a bramble, green or burning, the (divine) anger sweeps them away' (i.e. thorns will merely serve to be either burnt or uprooted): BJ; vii. [same picture] 'before they grow, they are cut down like bramble, like thorns and weeds they are swept away': RPB (see DWT for the emendations): probably the best

solution, and the picture is simple; viii. 'Before they (the **390j** wicked) understand, like thorns, like weeds, (in his) anger he (God) sweeps them away': WV (less emendation): also good. **11.** 'The righteous shall rejoice when he sees the **k** vengeance; he shall wash his feet in the blood of the wicked': a hideous picture only really admissible in terms of joy at the divine justice, **12** for 'there is a God who judges (justly) on earth': 'who judges' is plural, after elohim, which could suggest 'there are (after all) judges (*elohim*) who judge . . . ', and cf the reading of v 2 above.

59 A Prayer for Deliverance, and Punishment of my l Enemies—A rather rough psalm in this series of 'personal laments'. Title: David, with tune as for 57, and assigned to the time of David's house-arrest by Saul in 1 Sm 19:11. **2—5a.** 'Deliver me from my enemies . . . **4** . . . strong men stir up trouble [or, emend to 'band together' as in 56:7] . . . **5** without iniquity (of mine) . . . ' **5b—6.** Invocation of God's help: 'Be aroused to meet me (= help me) . . . ' **7—8.** Description of the wicked: 'They run about [so PB RPB] in the evening, they howl [PB 'grin' = show teeth — snarl (the word is cognate with 'groan' see OED); LXX/V 'are hungry' perhaps because of v 16?] like a dog . . . **8** they pour forth [RSV 'bellow', RPB 'boast'] with their mouth, swords [so the old versions, = ? cruelties; but probably emend to 'taunts', cf WV NP RSV RPB] are on their lips, for (they say), Who hears? [i.e. Who will expose our misdeeds?]'. **9.** 'But thou, o LORD, shalt laugh at them . . . , **10** o my strength, I will sing to thee [as v 18, where **10—11a** comes as a refrain] . . . **12.** Slay not my enemies, lest my people forget . . . ': an unusual sentiment, with the idea of the humiliated enemy remaining as a living witness to God's judgement. **14** . . . that (men) may know that God rules . . . **15** = v 7 (the dogs), **16** 'they roam about . . . they growl [though RV 'tarry all night' is equally defensible]; **17** but I will sing thy strength . . . , **18** o my strength . . . [— v 10, but here textually sounder]'.

60 A Song when Defeat seems near—A true 'national **m** lament', whether related to an historical national calamity, or a general expression of confidence in God. Are the geographical names in vv 8—10 references to actual events, or a picture of an ideal kingdom? The oracular style suggests the latter. The possibility that this section is an independent utterance incorporated here is supported by the reappearance of vv 7—14 at Ps 108: 7—14. The long title includes **1** some unidentifiable musical terms, and **2** an elaborate reference to David's 'struggle' with Aram-naharaim (2 Sm 10:13—19), Aram-zobah (2 Sm 8:5—11) and Edom (2 Sm 8:13, but Heb. there has 'Aram'), with defeat at the Valley of Salt (2 Sm 8:14, but cf 1 Chr 18:12 with defeat of Edom at the Valley of Salt by Abishai not Joab). The details of the campaign, and Joab's part, are not exactly identifiable; moreover the Ps seems to refer to defeat, while the above episodes are victories. The title here seems to be a rather confused *mise-en-scène*.

3—5. 'O God, thou hast rejected us, broken us **n** down . . . **5** made thy people see hard (times) [but RPB 'drink bitterness', cf Syr. word, of wine, see DWT], made us drink the cup of reeling': for the idea of a cup that must be drunk = an inexorable fate, see on 11:6: here it is a cup whose wine reduces the drinker to reeling; the 'cup of reeling' is only here in the Pss, but is also in Is 51:17, 22. **6.** 'Thou hast given to those who fear thee a refuge [or, a banner] to flee to [or, display] before the bow [or, the truth]': the words 'refuge' and 'flee to' are from the same root, as are 'banner' and 'display'; the word 'bow' is an Aram. spelling, recognized by LXX/V Jerome and Syr.; 'truth' is an uncertain word

390n only otherwise in Prv 22:21. The exact 'picture' of this verse depends upon the meanings adopted for these words. It would seem to be in any case a metaphor, rather than the picture of an actual battlefield: i. [picture of a retreat in battle] '. . . a refuge, to flee before the bow': RPB, probably the best; ii. [similar, but a little forced] '. . . a banner, to display (to rally them) before the bow': RSV; iii. [perhaps ironical] '. . . a banner— (only then) to flee before the bow': LXX/V RVm WV NP BJ: with a Heb. play on words 'banner . . . flee'; iv. [picture of a spiritual rallying point] '. . . a banner to display because of the truth [= faithfulness]': cf Targum ('Abraham's faithfulness'), Ibn Ezra here: so PB AV RV

o JA. **7.** 'That thy beloved ones may be delivered . . .': i.e. saved through flight, or through rallying, according to interpretation of v 6. Though this verse links with the preceding, it appears also as introducing the following, in 108:7, marking the beginning of the section 8–14, which reappears in Ps 108. **8–10.** These vv are either in the manner of an ancient oracle, or else incorporate such a text: 'God has spoken in his sanctuary: I will exult [LXX of 108:8 has 'I will go up': so RPB here], I will divide up Shechem, measure the vale of Succoth . . .': God speaks as the owner, surveying his land: **Shechem** and **Succoth** [LXX/V translates the name as 'tents'] were early settlements of Jacob west and east of the Jordan respectively (Gn 33:17, 18), and Shechem was Abraham's first settlement (Gn 12:6) and became the capital of the Northern Kingdom (I (3) Kg 12:1, 25); **9.** Next **Gilead** and **Manasseh** represent areas of the land east of the Jordan, while **Ephraim** [the 'defence of my head' = helmet, as defence against invasion from the north] and **Judah** ['my lawgiver', hence sovereign: LXX/V here 'king', whence (cf Gn 49:10) probably = 'my sceptre' (as a *pendant* to 'helmet': so most] are central parts of the land west of the Jordan, and represent the twin kingdoms. All this is God's own land of Israel. Now come the surrounding lands, reduced to

p menial status: **10.** Moab is 'my wash-pot' = household utensil (*sîr*) as used also for boiling, cooking, etc; and 'over *Edom* I cast my sandal' = a gesture claiming possession, as in Ru 4:7. Both figures convey menial or subject status of those lands. i. The above is the most likely meaning; ii. Others connect the two: thinking of a basin for foot-washing (cf NP '*pelvis lotionis*') held by a servant [but the normal word for such a basin is *kiyyôr* as in e.g. Ex 30:18]; and of the sandal thrown to a servant to clean or carry (a menial task, cf Mt 3:11); iii. Others again think of the glorious helmet and sceptre on the hills of Judah, and the Dead Sea as a footbath down below by Moab, with Edom looking after my sandals. 'Over **Philistia** I shout in triumph' follows 108:10 with most [Heb. here has 'over me (= because of me?) shout, o Philistia']. LXX/V have 'pot of my hope' (reading?), and for Philistines (as always in LXX) 'strangers' and 'subject to me'. The general picture is of subjection of the neighbouring peoples. **11–14.** The argument of dependence on God is resumed from v 7: 'Who will lead me to capture a fortified city? [i.e. by myself I cannot undertake such a thing], who will bring me (for instance, among difficult places to attack, cf Obad 3) to Edom? **12.** (For, cf v 3) hast thou not abandoned us . . . ?' **13.** Help us therefore now, and **14** in God we shall succeed.

391a 61 A Prayer of the devout Man—including a prayer for the king: the author is loyal to God, to the Temple ('thy Tent'), to the King. **Title**: David Collection, on strings(?). **2.** 'Hear my cry . . . **3** from the end of the earth I call . . . [some see here the condition of an exile] . . . upon a rock (which is) too high for me (to get there by my

own strength) thou settest me [or, set me, with most] . . . **39** **5.** Let me dwell in thy tent [as often = abode, dwelling] for ever . . . **6** thou hast listened to my vows, thou hast given (to me) the heritage [or, with RPB 'the desire'] of those that fear thy name'. **7.** The prayer for long life for the king, **8** '. . . may thy love and friendship protect him [see on 5:8]': this (with Jerome and RPB) omits the Heb. word *man* (= ? 'appoint'; RSV 'bid thy love . . . '), syntactically embarrassing, which LXX/V saw as 'who . . . ?' **9.** 'Thus I will ever sing thy name . . . '

62 A Meditation on the Worthlessness of Man- b kind—A clear stanzaic pattern, with the opening couplets reappearing in vv 6–7 after *Selah*. The third stanza, from v 10 is in notably didactic style. **Title** includes the name Jeduthun (as Ps 39 and 77, and 39 has a similar theme), who was one of the temple musicians (1 Chr 16:41–42).

2–3. 'Surely unto God my soul (is) silence [= RSV 'waits in silence', but LXX/V 'is subject' and v 6 has 'be silent'] . . . **4.** How long will you (wicked men) set upon [uncertain verb, only here] a man, shatter him . . . like a leaning wall (that is easily pushed down) . . . ' **6–7.** = vv 2–3 with variations. **10.** Here is the point of the meditation: 'Indeed sons of mankind (Adam) are uselessness [or, vanity, or, a mere breath]; sons of a man are a lie in the balance to go up: together they **c** (are lighter) than uselessness [or, a breath]: i. = 'All mankind are worthless, when laid in the scales they go up, because a mere breath is heavier'; ii. [Some make a distinction, here and in 49:3 (where it is less cogent), between 'sons of mankind' = of low estate, and 'sons of a man' = of high estate; but this has no parallel in the OT, and though Phoenician parallels are mentioned, perhaps it should not be urged; here anyway they are not contrasted, but taken together] = 'Men of high degree and low degree are (equally) worthless: together in the scales they cannot outweigh a breath': so most; iii. = 'Mankind is worthless, sons of men are [collective] liars in (dealing with) scales, to [emended] deceive, they are altogether (formed) out of worthlessness': LXX cf Vg; PB follows LXX with ' . . . are deceitful upon the weights . . . '. **11–12.** Moral advice on ill-gotten gains, in the manner of Proverbs, and God is powerful, but **13** he is also a God of love, who 'rewards every man according to his work' (quoted in Rm 2:6).

63 A Poem of Longing for God—The psalm has **d** genuine poetic feeling, beginning with the picture of the man alone in the desert—the poet feels like that towards God. The reference to the 'king' in the last verse raises questions discussed there. **Title** refers to 1 Sm 23:24 or 2 Sm 16:2.

2. 'O God, thou art my God, at dawn I will seek thee [one word, derived from 'dawn'] . . . ': the psalmist pictures himself as thirsting and longing in a waterless and 'weary land' (RV RSV well). **4.** 'For thy friendship [see on 5:8] is a better thing than life itself (so nearly lost in the desert) . . . '. **6.** But now, my soul [= appetite, hunger] is satisfied as with delicacies [as fat and marrow are regarded], my lips, once thirsting, are now occupied with thy praise. **7–9.** If I think about it at night, I remember **8** that thou hast helped me . . . **9** '(and then) my soul clings to thee, thy right hand grasps me'. **10–11.** Even in this rather delicate psalm, the rightful punish- **e** ment of my persecutors is not forgotten: they shall go down to the depths (of Sheol, i.e. shall die), **11** 'they shall be handed over [corrected with LXX/V from 'they shall hand him over'] to the sword', and, when they are dead and unburied, to the jackals [rather than foxes as LXX/V PB AV RV]: a final indignity. This, like the other 'imprecations', is understood in terms of being at one with God in

1e the punishment of crime. **12.** 'The king shall rejoice in God, (and) everyone who has taken an oath to him [to God? to the king?], but the mouth of speakers of falsehood [i.e. those who have not taken such an oath] shall be stopped'. The sudden mention of the king (in the 3rd person) suggests various explanations: i. the reference is to the ideal order, when the king has his proper place, rejoices in God and leads his people in worship; ii. the reference is to the author himself, if he were King David; or was added with the title, to make the reference to David; iii. the reference points to a 'cultic festival' presided over by the king.

f 64 A Prayer for Deliverance and of Trust in God's Vengeance—A rather typical 'personal lament' of the David Collection, with several textual obscurities. **2–5.** 'Hear, o God, my voice . . . preserve my life'. **3.** Hide me from the wicked, **4** who whet their tongues like swords, bend [lit. tread] (their bows to shoot) their arrows [a curious ellipsis, cf 58:8, but the text is unsure there], (which are) a word of bitterness, **5** 'to shoot at the innocent in the hiding-places; suddenly they shoot and fear not': 'in the hiding places' is ambiguous in most versions, but may be: i. where the victim had hidden himself ('in . . .'); ii. the attacker's ambush: so NP RSV ('in' = 'from'); iii. = secretly — unexpectedly: so PB AV RPB; '. . . and fear not': Syr. has ' . . . and are not seen': so WV RPB, and better in the context. **6.** They make their evil plans, saying 'Who will see them [or, with Jerome **g** 'us']? **7.** They plan [or, search out] crimes: We have completed a plan (well) planned': i. so literally, cf RV; ii. [continuing from v 6] ' . . . who will see us, **7** search out (our) crimes? we have completed . . .': WV RSV; iii. [as i, but emending 'we have completed' to 'they have hidden'] 'they plan . . . they have hidden a plan . . .': NP RPB (see DWT); iv. [as ii, but emending 'we have completed' and linking with what follows] . . . search out our crimes? He (God) will search, he who searches . . .': BJ. 'And the inward parts of a man and a deep heart': regarded by most, as an exclamation or reflection on the preceding: 'For the inward part and the heart of man are deep'; but BJ attaches to the preceding '(God) searches the inward . . .'; and Vg (cf LXX) 'a man shall approach to a deep heart', linked with the following 'And God is exalted', has been variously used in mystical inter- **h** pretation. **8–9.** But God repays them in their own coin: he shoots an arrow at them, 'suddenly are their wounds, **9** so they make their own tongue a stumbling unto themselves . . .': so JA, cleverly following Heb.: i. = their bitter words are the cause of their own downfall: JA: Heb. as it stands is awkward, and AV RV RVm hardly translate it; ii. [emending] 'and he (God) causes them to stumble because of (?) their tongue': BJ RSV RPB. also apparently NP (*lingua* ablative missed by Fides); iii. LXX/V is very different and unhelpful, turning on the pointing of *pith'ôm* (suddenly) as *pᵉthāʾim* (babes): 'an arrow of babes became their wounds', with much complication of interpretation.

i 65 A (2–5) Praise of God in Sion—This seems to be a distinct composition from vv 6–14, linked perhaps by the idea of praise. In this short hymn there is the important idea of God's forgiveness to be found in Sion, with the acknowledgement (and perhaps even confession in RPB) of sins in v 4. **Title** with description as a 'psalm' and a 'song', as also in the next three Pss.

2. 'To thee praise is due . . . in Sion': repointing with LXX/V, probably better than Massoretic 'Praise (waits) in silence for thee' (cf AV RV), although cf 62:2: so most. **3.** ' . . . All flesh shall come to thee (in Sion) **4** (with) tales of wrongdoing [lit. (with) words of iniquity: RPB 'to

confess (their) sins']: our sins overcome us: thou wilt **391i** forgive them': i. ' . . . come to thee **4** to confess (their) sins': RPB, cf BJ; ii. ' . . . come to thee **4** on account of sins': NP RSV; iii. ' . . . come to thee; **4** iniquities prevail . . .': LXX/V PB AV RV. For forgiveness of sin see on 32:2; 51:3; 25:18.

65 B (6–14) A Hymn to the Lord of Nature—A fine **j** hymn in fairly regular metre, with good poetic imagery: each of the two stanzas ends with nature singing (vv 9, 14). **6.** 'By dread deeds in justice [RSV RPB 'with deliverance': LXX/V 'terrible in (thy) justice' attached to preceding v] thou dost answer us . . . hope of the distant sea ['isles' BJ RPB]'. **7.** Thy power shows itself in nature: in the mountains, **9** . . . and 'thou makest the doors of the dawn and the evening to sing'. **10.** The second stanza: every year's produce is part of God's work: 'a river of God' is probably a superlative, like 'mountains of God' in 36:7 (where see note), and cf 68:16; 80:11; 104:16, and = a very big river, as source of irrigation; but others see as meaning the rain. **12.** 'Thou crownest the year of [= with] thy goodness, thy cart-tracks are moist with sweetness [lit. 'fat']': i.e. 'sweet moisture is the mark of thy passage'; **13** even the desert is moist, . . . the hills and **14** pastures are clothed (with produce and livestock) and sing for joy.

66 A (1–7) A Call to Praise—A universal song of **k** simple construction in two stanzas, mostly of a long triple metre, distinct from the following. **Title:** here and 67 David's name does not appear, though they seem to belong to the collection 51–70.

1–4. 'Shout unto God, all the earth': so JA: the verb is used also of a battle-cry, and the corresponding nouns for a trumpet-call. **3.** Even God's enemies recognize his power: the verb here basically means 'to deceive': i. = 'thy enemies lie to thee' = 'are found liars (when they deny thee)': so LXX/V PB; ii. = 'flatter thee', i.e. are bound to praise thee, but with them it is insincere: NP BJ; iii. = ' . . . cringe to thee' (with a show of obedience): AVm RVm RSV cf RPB; iv. = ' . . . submit to thee', i.e. fail, collapse = disappoint = deceive: AV RV. **5–7.** An invitation to contemplate his works.

66 B (8–12) A Short Song of Israel—Probably a **l** separate psalm, linked by the theme of praise. A national song, with markedly regular shorter rhythm quite distinct from that of the preceding verses. **8–9.** An invitation to all peoples to bless our God, for he has preserved us. **10.** But he has also tried us like silver in the fire, and **11** has led us into a (hunter's or fisherman's) net (where we were trapped), but then **12** he 'brought us out to freedom': 'freedom' is an emendation suggested by LXX/V (so NP BJ RSV RPB) for Heb. 'abundance' (so JA, cf PB AV RV 'a wealthy place').

66 C (13–20) A Declaration of Devotion—This is **m** almost certainly a separate poem: a personal liturgical offering, in good fairly regular 3 + 2 metre, in three stanzas. **13–15.** 'I will come into thy house' = the Temple, to make my ceremonial offerings and fulfil my vows. **15.** I will offer fatlings, 'incense of rams' [= probably the smoke of the sacrifice, but the word usually = incense; cf 141:2]. **16.** An invitation to praise. **18.** Had I been wicked, 'my Lord (*adonai*) would not have listened', **19** but he did listen, and **20** . . . 'turned not away my prayer'.

67 An Invitation to all the World to Praise and 392a Thanksgiving—Plainly a community hymn; in three stanzas of fairly regular metre. **Title:** no mention of David, though there is in LXX/V. **2.** 'God be merciful to us and bless us' (RPB): the verb *ḥanan* conveys favour, and so, mercy, and is thus translated in the old versions

392a and RPB. The verb seems to convey doing something rather than feeling. 'And show us the light of his countenance' (RPB): the figure of God's countenance shining upon us is from the blessing in Nm 6:25 (almost verbatim here), and appears in the Pss at 4:7; 31:17; here, 80:4, 8, 20 (a refrain); 118:27 and 119:135. *Selah* at the end of v 2: nowhere else does it appear so early (after one verse: in Ps 82 after two verses). **3.** 'That (men) may know thy way . . . thy salvation'. **4.** A refrain, again in v 6: 'Let the peoples praise thee [or, 'give thanks to thee']': the context usually inclines us to one or the other translation: the force of *yôdhû* is rather that of proclaiming our relationship of indebtedness to God, whence Vg *confiteantur* here and consistently in the Pss; see further on 106:1, and excellently in T. Worden 60ff. The ideas of praise and thanksgiving are both included in the Heb. verb and what became its Latin equivalent. **5–8.** Let the nations rejoice in thy justice (refrain in v 6), and **7** thy blessings, including fruits of the earth. It is hardly necessary, because of this phrase, to suppose that this song belongs to a harvest festival.

b **68 A Song of Triumph**—Probably the most difficult and textually confused of the whole Psalter; but in spite of many obscurities the general theme of God's triumph is plain, considered in four distinct ways: vv 2–7 in heaven; vv 8–24 in conquering the land for Israel; vv 25–28 in the Temple; and vv 29–36 in all the world. The Psalm seems to be a unity (an image in v 5 reappears at v 34) and has some strong poetic imagery. The metre is an unusual 4 + 3, but often irregular. **Title:** '(Belonging) to (the) David (Collection II)'.

2–7 Triumph in Heaven—'Let God arise, let his enemies be scattered . . .' **5.** 'Sing to God . . . extol him who rides upon the clouds': the word 'extol' (*sālal*) = basically 'to throw up', esp. of a highway (*mesillāh*), as on an embankment: i. hence = (?) 'extol' [or, magnify]; although this sense is not found elsewhere, the parallels 'sing' encourage it: PB AV JA CV RPB; ii. [because of 'highway' and the following 'rider'] = 'cast up (a highway) for him': LXX/V Jer RV NP WV BJ [and cf the 'highway' of the Lord in Is 40:3, quoted in Mt 3:3, Mk 1:3, Lk 3:4]; iii. = (?) 'lift up (a song) for him'; this sense is not elsewhere, but again the parallels encourage it: RSV. ' . . . upon the clouds (*'arābhôth*)': the rendering is supported by the cognate Ugaritic phrase 'rider upon the clouds' used of Baal (see DWT and DOTT 125, 128), and v 34 'rider in the heavens': i. so PB AV JA BJ RSV RPB; ii. = 'through deserts' [the usual sense of the word]: Jer RV WV NP; iii. = 'upon the sunset': LXX/V, supposing a word related to 'evening'. 'In Yah [shorter form of Yahweh], (for this is) his name, and exult before him': the syntax is not clear: i. [connecting with preceding 'Sing to him'] ' . . . in his name Yah': PB AV; ii. [omitting 'in'] 'His name is Yah': LXX/V RV cf JA NP RSV; iii. [emending] 'Rejoice in Yah': BJ RPB. **6–7.**
c God consoles orphans, widows, **7** the lonely, prisoners; 'but the rebellious dwell in a parched land [rather than LXX/V 'tombs']': once more the fate of the just and of the wicked is contrasted. **8–24** is a continuous poetical description of God's **Triumph in the Conquest of the Land** for Israel. At the Exodus **9** 'the earth quaked, the heavens poured (rain) before God—this (is) Sinai': i. '—this (is) Sinai' [an explanation of the preceding]: so Jerome CV; ii. [omitted as a gloss]: BJ; iii. [connected with preceding] ' . . . earth quaked . . . (even) yon Sinai (also quaked)': PB AV RV WV RSV, but rather forced; iv. = 'the one of Sinai' = 'the Lord of Sinai' [connected with 'God'] RPB (see DWT); v. [emending] 'Sinai trembled': NP (see Kittel); vi. [omitting 'this' and

emending] 'before the God of Sinai': LXX/V. **10.** 'Thou **39** didst send generous rain . . . restore thy heritage . . . **11** thy animals [= ? thy flock = ? Israel: a quite unparalleled usage] lived there . . .' **12.** The beginning of a very difficult section: 'The Lord (*adonai*) gives the word (of command? for the conquest?); great (was) the company of the preachers' (cf PB and Handel, *Messiah* n. 37), i.e. probably those who announced the following cry of v 13 (RSV) or vv 13–15 (NP RPB). But the announcers are feminine: (lit.) 'The preachers (fem.) (were) a great army (*sābhā'*)': i. [fem., as often, = neuter] = 'the announcements are very many'; ii. [disregarding **d** the gender] = 'the preachers (of God's word) are a great army': PB AV; and Targum says = Moses and Aaron; iii. [disregarding gender, but introducing the message] 'the announcers (of the following) are . . . ': NP RSV RPB: perhaps RSV refers to the women in v 13? iv. [disregarding . . .] 'The Lord shall give the word to the preachers with great force': LXX/V; v. [insisting on gender] 'the women that publish the tidings are a great host': RV JA CV cf Jer; cf the maidens singing in v 26, the women at home in v 13, and a reminiscence of Deborah; vi. [inserting phrase from v 15] 'The Lord gives the (following) message to the (feminine) messengers: The Almighty has scattered [from v 15] a great army . . . ': so BJ; vii. It is possible that the 'great company of feminine preachers' is no more than a rubric directing a women's choir (cf title of Ps 46) to sing the following piece. The text then would read: 'The Lord gives the word [large choir of soprani] "The kings . . . flee . . . "'. **13.** 'Kings of armies (*sebhā'ôth*), they flee, they flee **e** [or, let them flee; not as LXX/V 'The king of powers (is) of the beloved, the beloved', a discernibly confused text]; she who dwells at home divides the spoil (echo of Jg 5.39?): this is either the proclamation of the 'preachers' (so NP RSV RPB), or a description of the conquest. **14–15.** Very enigmatic: continues the proclamation or the description: 'If you lie between the sheepfolds [doubtful word only here, cognate with doubtful word in Jg 5:16: LXX/V here *clerus*, portion, lot, so = ? enclosures; the word is dual, KB 'saddlebags', PB AV 'pots', BDB 'fireplaces'; most likely RV 'sheepfolds']; the wings of a dove covered with silver, and its pinions with paleness [colour of a young plant] of gold; **15** when the Almighty [*Shaddai*—only here and 91:1 in Pss] scatters kings in it, it snows on (Mount) Zalmon [only here and Jg 9:48, and not identified]': the main lines of possible interpretation are these: i. = 'Though you stay idle **f** among the sheepfolds (and do not fight [cf probable meaning of Reuben's unreadiness in Gn 49:14 and Jg 5:16]), yet Israel is as beautiful as a dove with the soft sheen on its feathers (i.e. even though you have not won the land yourselves, she is lovely); and when the Almighty scatters kings in it (the land), it (was as if it) snowed on Zalmon (i.e. the kings were as numerous as snowflakes)': cf RPB. [Ephraim is likened to a 'silly dove' in Hos 7:11, but as foolish, not as beautiful; and Israel perhaps to a turtle-dove in 74:19, but doubtful.] ii. [connect with preceding: the women are dividing the spoil] ' . . . while you (warriors) remain idle, (and among the spoils are objects of) silver and gold (as delicate as) dove's wings; when the Almighty scattered kings there [in the conquered land], it snowed on Zalmon [an otherwise unrecorded incident of the conquest?]': cf RSV; iii. [similarly, and taking 'the Almighty scatters' into v 13; . . . The women are dividing the spoil] ' . . . while you (warriors) remain idle, (they are decking themselves with) silver and gold (from the booty), (looking as lovely as) doves' plumage, or as snow on a dark mountain

92f [perhaps the meaning of Zalmon]': cf BJ; iv. = 'Why are you idle among the sheepfolds (like the picture of tranquillity that is) the sheen on a dove's wings . . . ?': cf RV. The fact remains that the interpretation of the **g** 'dove's wings' is quite uncertain. **16—17.** 'Mighty mountain [lit. 'mountain of God'——a form of superlative (so NP RSV RPB, see DWT), and cf on 36:7; 65:10], mountain of Bashan [east of the Jordan, and outside the Land]': either two vocatives, or (better) = 'a mighty mountain (is) the mountain . . .' with RPB, cf RV. LXX/V for Bashan read *dešen* 'fat', so Vg '*mons pinguis*'. 'A round-topped mountain (is) the mountain of Bashan' [or two vocatives, as before]: the word 'round-topped' is doubtful and only here and v 17: most connect with *gibbēn* 'hump-backed', others 'many-peaked' (RSV), 'high' (RPB), rigged (CV), or 'haughty' (BJ); LXX/V connected with *gebhīnāh* 'cheese', whence '*mons coagulatus*, curdled' (an uncertain picture). **17.** 'Why do you look down [? doubtful word, only here; = with envy(?); PB 'hop', cf AV RV], o round-topped mountains, (on) the mountain (Sion), where God delights to dwell . . . ?' The point of these difficult verses is that the hills of Bashan, however mighty, should not despise God's chosen hill of Sion. **18.** It is God who made the conquest for us . . . 'the Lord (*adonai*) came [emended] from Sinai into his holy place'. **19.** A famous verse, quoted in Eph 4:8, in the Ascension liturgy, and by Handel n. 36: 'Thou hast gone up on high [see on 47:6, similar phrase and possible origin], thou hast taken captive captivity': = proleptically 'the captives', so 'with captives in thy train' (so NP BJ RSV RPB); rather than 'taken captive [= defeated] captivity itself' with LXX/V and **h** the older versions, although this (the victory of Christ) is the point that Eph is making: i. = 'leading captives' is part of the picture of the conquest: God came from Sinai, conquers the land, and goes up to Sion in triumph; ii. = 'defeating captivity' is part of the theophany of Sinai, bringing in a new order. 'Thou hast taken [= received] gifts among men': but Eph has altered to 'given gifts to men': i. = ' . . . received gifts among men' so LXX/V and most [i.e. as conqueror]; ii. [taking *be* = 'from' as in Ugaritic] ' . . . gifts from men' i.e. as tribute: RPB (see DNT); iii. = ' . . . gifts in men' = 'men **i** as gifts', i.e. enslaved captives: NP BJ. **20.** A thanksgiving for the preceding: 'Blessed be the Lord, who daily carries for us': i. = 'bears our burdens': RV NP RPB; ii. = 'bears us up': Jer BJ RSV; iii. = 'loads us (with benefits)': LXX/V PB AV. **21.** 'To God the Lord (Yahweh Adonai) (belong) the issues of death' (so JA), i.e. he is master of life and death, rather than 'the escapes from death' (so most). **23.** He says 'I will bring (my people?) back from Bashan [RPB accepts the emendation 'from the fiery furnace' = Egypt] . . . from the depths of the (Red) Sea, **24** that thou mayest wash [so all, for Heb. 'break'] thy foot in blood (of thy enemies: cf 58:11), the tongue of thy dogs (to be) the portion [= fate] of it (the blood) from the enemies': the hideous picture of vengeance (cf 1 (3) Kg 21:19 etc).

j 25—28 The Solemn Worship in the Temple—'They (the people now in the Land) have seen thy solemn processions [so BJ RSV RPB], o God, into the sanctuary', **26.** Singers, musicians, maidens [*ʿalāmôth* cf 46:1] . . . (singing this anthem:) **27.** 'Bless God in the assemblies, the LORD from the fountain of Israel': i. [omit 'from'] = 'the LORD (who is) the fountain of Israel': RPB [the figure of the Lord as 'fountain of life' is found in Jer 2:13; 17:13, and perhaps Ps 36:10]; ii. = ' . . . the LORD, (o you who are) from Israel's fountain [= the source of the nation, cf NP *ex Israel nati*]': AV RV RSV cf NP

[cf Dt 33:28 Israel as 'the well of Jacob'; but not other- **392j** wise supported]. **28.** 'There is little Benjamin, leading them [an uncertain word]': i. = leading or managing the procession [lit. 'ruling']: NP BJ RSV RPB; ii. = lit. 'ruling', perhaps with reference to Saul being from this tribe?: PB AV RV; iii. = 'in ecstasy' [connected with word for 'deep sleep' Gn 2:21?]: LXX/V. 'The princes of Judah, their throng [so RSV: uncertain word only here: RPB 'follow after'; LXX/V 'leaders'] . . . of Zebulun . . . of Naphtali' [= two tribes of the north and south respectively, thus all representing the whole nation]. **29—36 God's Triumph in the World**—'Summon thy **k** might, o God; strengthen o God, that which thou hast done for us [= make it greater still (so LXX/V PB AV RV); or = show thy strength, o God, thou who hast wrought for us' (so RVm NP RSV RPB)]. **30.** From thy temple upon Jerusalem [i.e. whence thy strength comes to us; or, 'because of thy temple': this passage 29—30 is used (Vg *Confirma hoc Deus*) in the liturgy at Confirmation. 'To thee kings bring gifts': referring either to the temple above, or to subject peoples, below. **31.** 'Rebuke the beasts of the reeds [probably = Egypt, the traditional enemy, see v 32], the herd of bulls with the calves of the peoples [= their satellite nations]'; a very difficult passage follows, with several doubtful words and many suggestions: i. = '(Rebuke) . . . (those) trampling on those tried (by fire, as) silver [= rebuke those unjust to their victims]': RPB cf LXX/V; ii. = ' . . . Trample, (o God,) on those desiring [emended] silver [= money, as tribute]': cf RSV; iii. = '(the peoples) submit [lit. are down-trodden] with pieces of (?) silver [= bringing tribute]': PB AV RVm NP cf BJ; iv. = '(Rebuke) . . . trampling on the pieces (?) of silver [= cancelling the payment of tribute]': RV. 'Scatter the peoples (who) delight in wars': the general picture of v 31 seems to be a rebuke to the oppressor nations. **32.** Another difficult **l** verse, chiefly because of the otherwise unknown word *hašmannīm*, probably = 'bronze' (so KB), or perhaps = the title of some official; this shall come from Egypt: i. 'They shall bring tribute [lit. bronze] from Egypt': RPB (see DWT); ii. 'Let bronze be brought . . . ': RSV; iii. 'Ambassadors [or, nobles, or princes] shall come . . . ': LXX/V and most; iv. 'Let them bring (tribute) quickly [emended]': Jerome. 'Cush [= Ethiopia, figure of a distant nation] shall hold out its hands (in honourable greeting) to God (in Sion)': 'hold out' (cf ND BJ RPB) rather than the common verb 'to run', whence most 'hasten (to stretch out)'. The point here seems to be the submission of the nations, hostile Egypt and distant Cush, to the God of Israel—the 'universalist' theme, see on 18:44 and especially Ps 87. This theme now continues to the end: **33** 'Sing to God, o kingdoms of the earth . . . **34** to him who rides in the heavens of antiquity [= the highest and most ancient of the skies, see on 148:4; LXX/V translates 'antiquity' (defensibly) as 'east'; cf also v 5 above] . . . **35.** Give strength [= the praise due to his strength, whence LXX/V 'glory', see on 8:3] to God . . . **36.** Terrible (is) God in his sanctuary'.

69 A Poem about Alienation, and bearing it for 393a God's sake—A lament, not unlike Ps 22A, but with the special note in the prayer vv 6—22 of acceptance. Imprecations follow, vv 23—29; but the Ps ends with devotion to Sion. The plain meaning is personal, but the mention of the temple (v 10) and of Sion (v 36) may give it a congregational sense. The **Title** (David) includes probably the name of a tune, 'lilies'(?).

2. 'Save me, o God, for the waters have come up to my neck': so NP RSV RPB, which adopt the meaning 'neck' for *nepheš* (usually = 'soul'), with Akkad. and Ugar.

393a evidence (see DWT), cf also 105:18. The picture is of a man near drowning, **5** 'More numerous than the hairs of my head are those who hate me without cause [cf 35:19, quoted Jn 15:25]; . . . That which I stole not, (must) I now restore?': i.e. I am being accused of crimes which I did not commit: either an ironical question (JA NP RSV),
b or an exclamation (BJ RPB). **6—22. My Prayer:** 'O God, thou knowest my folly [a moral bad quality, attributed to the psalmist himself only here and 38:6 where see note] . . .' **8.** It is for thy sake that I suffer reproach and **9** loneliness (or, alienation): a notion not common in the Pss. **10—13.** 'Zeal for thy house has consumed me', i.e. devotion to the Temple, not shared even by my family. Quoted at the cleansing of the Temple ('the disciples remembered' the text) in Jn 2:17. Consequently 'insults . . . have fallen upon me': quoted of Christ in Rom 15:3. **11.** My acts of piety merely cause mockery . . . **13.** '(I became the subject of) songs of drinkers of strong drink': rather than 'drunkards'—just the men at the bar. **14.** But I pray to thee . . . **20** Thou knowest my troubles . . . **21** 'insults [PB "thy rebuke", cf Handel n. 29] have broken my heart, and I am in despair, I looked for pity, but there was none . . . **22** (Rather) they gave me gall in my food, and for my thirst they gave me vinegar to drink': partly quoted at the Crucifixion, Mt 27:34, 48, Mk 15:36, Jn 19:28—29, using the LXX words 'gall' and 'vinegar': the Gr. *cholē* denotes properly gall, but the Heb. word indicates a specific bitter herb, also 'poison' of a snake (whence RSV here).
c 23—29 The Imprecations: the tone changes to a desire that just punishment come upon my enemies (see on 109:6). 'May their table become a snare [probably = 'may they be betrayed by those who eat with them', i.e. their friends], and for their peace [plural, an uncertain word] a trap': i. = ? 'when they are at peace (at table), may the occasion trap them': so apparently MT, cf PB AV RV BJ; ii. = ?'. . . a snare, and [emended] a retribution and a trap': LXX/V Jerome and so quoted in Rm 11:9; iii. = ?'. . . a snare, [emended] for their friends a trap': NP; iv. = ?'their peace-offerings (RPB),
d or, sacrificial meals (RSV) a trap': so Targum. **24—26.** Further disasters are wished upon them, including **26** the ruin of their home (quoted Ac 1:20 with reference to Judas); **27** 'For they have persecuted him whom thou hast smitten [= me], and they add [emended] to the pain of thy wounded one [= me; emended]': so NP BJ RSV RPB cf LXX/V. **28—29.** Let their punishment continue **29** 'blotted out from the book of the living [so all, except RV (equally defensibly) "book of life"], and not be written with the just (therein)': the idea of God's 'book' appears in Pss 56:9; 139:16, and Mal 3:16, Dn 12:1; his 'writing' in Pss 87:6; 139:16, perhaps 149:9, and Is 4:3; but this phrase only here, clearly echoed in the NT ('book of life'): Phil 4:3, Apoc 3:5,
e 20:15. **30—37. Conclusion:** 'But I am (among the) "poor" [see on 9:13] . . . **31** and I will sing . . . in thanksgiving [*tôdhāh*, see on 67:4],' **32** and (this) will be 'good before the Lord more than sacrificed animals . . . **36—37.** 'For God shall deliver Sion, and build the cities of Judah', and they shall live there . . . This may be simply an expression of love of Sion, the ideal spiritual home, though some would see here a reference to an actual rebuilding of the city, and would suppose these verses to have been written or added at such a time, as with the last verses of Ps 51, where see note.
f 70 A Plea for Help—A duplicate of Ps 40:14—18 in the 'David Collection I', with small variations ('God' for 'the Lord (Yahweh)' and for *Adonai*). The opening word in 40:14 'Be pleased' is supplied here by RSV and RPB from

Ps 40, and in LXX/V, providing the familiar *Deus in* **393** *adiutorium meum intende* of the Divine Office. 70:4 'they turn back' is an easier reading than 40:16 'they are desolated'; and 70:6 'hasten to me' than 40:18 'think of me'. The version in Ps 40 has two more verses (40:12—13) at the beginning; it therefore seems to be a slightly longer version of the same poem; the absence of these verses in Ps 70 may account for the confused beginning in 70:2. Otherwise the readings of Ps 70 are more likely. For the **title** of Ps 70 see that of Ps 38. Ps 70 marks the end of the 'David Collection II' (42—70).
71 An Old Man's Prayer—A personal hymn of con- **g** fidence and thanksgiving for a lifetime of service: old age is mentioned in vv 9 and 18 (cf 37:25). There is no **title** in Hebrew. **1—3.** 'In thee, o Lord, I have hoped. **3.** Be to me a rock [see on 18:3 for these metaphors], a place (to which) to come always thou hast commanded (me), to save me': syntactically a little awkward, but the suggestion of God's welcome is most attractive: i. '. . . thou hast given commandment to save me': Jer PB AV RV; ii. [emending to = 31:3] '. . . a rock, a fortified place to save me': cf LXX/V BJ RSV RPB. **4—8.** Deliver me . . . **6** from my birth 'thou art my protector' [uncertain word only here: cf 22:10 where there is another uncertain word]: i.= 'protector': LXX/V Jer NP (see note, and Zorrell Lexicon), or read '*uzzī* = 'my strength'? = 'protection'; ii. = 'he that took me [lit.? 'severed me']': PB AV RV RSV RPB; iii. = 'my portion [as cut?]': BJ. **7.** 'I am like a (cause of) wonder to many [because of my troubles and thy rescue of me]'. **9—12.** 'Cast me not away in the time of old age . . .' **14.** 'But I will always hope and I will add (more and more) to all the praise of thee [i.e. praise thee more and more], . . . **15** . . . for I know the numbers (of thy mercies): the word 'numbers' only here, probably better thus than LXX[A]/V 'writing', or LXX[B] by error in the Gr. 'affairs'. **16.** 'I will walk in the strength of my Lord . . .': or 'I will enter' taken by RPB as = 'enter upon' = 'declare' (see DWT). **17—21.** 'From my youth thou hast taught me . . . **18.** And (now that I am come) to old age and gray hairs, o God, forsake me not . . . **22.** And I will praise thee always . . .'
72 The Messianic King—This last psalm of Book **h** II is in every way an interesting psalm: in the first place it is a real poem, glorifying the ideal king, with the messianic ideal of worldwide rule, expressing for the Jews the vocation of Israel, through the rule of God's 'Anointed' to bring all mankind to God, for the Christian the worldwide rule of Christ. It is a 'royal psalm' *par excellence*, which Mowinckel sees as the intercession of the people at a king's inauguration, depicting what a king ought to be and praying for the realization of this, and corresponding to Ps 101 where the king at the same ceremony produces his 'charter' or programme (I, 65—70). The description of the kingdom in vv 8—11 takes Solomon's empire as a symbol of the messianic kingdom, and thus gives rise to the simple **title**: 'Solomon'.
1—2. 'O God, endow the king with [so CV well: lit. 'give to . . .'] thy judgements [= thy ability to judge justly], and the king's son with thy justice': **2.** The first requirement of the ideal king is to rule justly. **3.** The very mountains and hills of his kingdom shall bring 'peace' and 'justice'; **5—7.** Delightful pictures from nature to describe his just rule: 'May he (live) as long as the sun [emending with LXX/V: so NP BJ RSV RPB] . . . and the moon . . . **6.** May he come down like rain upon mown **i** grass [the sweet smell of a fresh field], like showers watering the earth': the word here for 'grass', *gēz*, is from the root 'to shear' as of sheep, and is variously translated: i. 'mown grass' = aftermath, the short

93i grass after mowing: so AV RV NP (*gramen*), BJ (*regain*), RSV; ii. 'grass before it is cut': RPB; iii. 'a fleece', i.e. wool shorn off: LXX/V Jer PB (thinking of Jg 6:37?). This verse has been seen as a symbol of the Incarnation: e.g. *Descendit Dominus sicut pluvia in vellus* (in the old office of the III Sunday of Advent); and cf the office of the Annunciation (I Vespers) *Descendit in uterum Virginis sicut imber super gramen* (perhaps **j** more of an echo of Dt 32:2). **7.** The picture of the field continues: 'The just man [LXX/V 'justice', so, emending, also NP BJ RSV RPB] shall spring up (like a new plant), and abundance of peace, till the moon be no more [i.e. as long as the world lasts]'. **8—11.** The ideal king shall rule not only in his own perfect kingdom, but throughout the world, a symbol of God's worldwide rule. 'He shall rule from sea to sea': in view of the proper names following in v 10 we should probably see here a concrete picture of Solomon's empire, as a concrete symbol of the ideal kingdom, extending from the Red Sea to the Mediterranean, and 'from the River [often = the Euphrates] to the ends of the earth (where the known land ends)', cf the same phrases in Zc 9:10. **9.** 'His foes shall bow before him, and his enemies . . .': 'foes' represents an uncertain word: i. [emending, from context] 'foes': WV NP RSV RPB ii. [taking *Si'im* as a proper name] = ? 'Ethiopians': LXX/V Jer, and cf proper names in text line; iii. [connecting with the word 'drought'] = 'desert dwellers': PB AV RV with very doubtful parallels, e.g. Ps 74:14; iv. [cognate languages and some parallels suggest an animal] = ? 'the Beast' **k** (= foreign kingdoms): BJ. **10.** Tarshish [= the far west = ? Phoenician colony in Spain] and 'the Isles' [= remote coasts], Sheba [= ? Arabia, cf LXX/V] and Seba [= ? Cush or Ethiopia, cf Gn 10:7] shall bring gifts. Tarshish (1 (3) Kgs 10:22) and Sheba (the home of the queen, 1 (3) Kgs 10:1) both appear as places of Solomon's trade, and here contribute to the picture of his idealized reign. **11.** 'And all kings shall bow to him . . .' [for kings adoring cf 68:30; 102:16; 138:4. These verses are used in the Epiphany liturgy for the universal reign of Christ. **12—14** return to his just rule: he cares for the 'poor . . . **14** . . . their blood (not to be shed) [LXX/V 'their name'] is precious to him'. **15—17.** Finally blessings are invoked upon the king, and may he be prayed for—a sentiment rare in the Psalter (cf 122:8, **l** 9). **16** is the only really difficult v in this Ps: (the blessing on his land) 'May there be abundance [uncertain word] of corn in the land, on the tops of the hills may it grow thick [so RPB (cf? BJ), see DWT on Arabic root; rather than 'tremble' = RSV wave, NP rustle], like Lebanon may its fruit flourish, its grain [so BJ RPB emending; Heb. '(men of its) city', so LXX/V AV RV NP RSV cf PB] like the grass of the ground': various versions divide variously, but RPB's arrangement (as above) is best for both sense and metre. **17.** 'May his name (= memory) be for ever, together with [lit 'before'] the sun may his name endure [or, increase: uncertain word *yinnôn* only here], and may (men) bless themselves in him [cf Gn 22:18; 26:4, and similar in Gn 12:3, all of Abraham = 'regard themselves as blessed because of him'], all nations proclaim him blessed': LXX/V have 'may all nations bless . . . and all peoples proclaim . . .': so NP BJ RPB. A rabbinic tradition (Talm. San. 98b) regards the strange word *yinnôn* as a messianic name existing before creation, and translates this passage: 'before the sun, Yinnon is his name', connecting the name with increase or fruitfulness or offspring, perhaps associated with the word *nîn* in Ps 74:8, which LXX/V takes as 'kinsmen'. **18—19** form a doxology to conclude

Book II, the most elaborate of all—cf ends of Pss 41, **393l** 89, 106. '*Benedictus Dominus Deus Israel*' (Lk 1:68) is quoted from here. **20.** 'The prayers of David . . . are ended' is only found here.

BOOK III

Of the 17 Pss in this book, 11 form the 'Asaph Collection' **394a** 73—83, the rest forming the 'Qorah Collection II' (see on 84).

73 Why trouble to be good?—This Ps with genuine poetic feeling discusses the problem which presents itself some time to most religious people: but understanding only comes to us in the presence of God (v 17) and with realization of his care (v 23) and our response (v 25). The text is in some places very uncertain. The **Title** marks the beginning of the 'Asaph Collection' which is nearly all good stuff and includes nearly all the 'genres', beginning with a sort of 'Wisdom' type here, though the manner is much more primitive than the true 'Wisdom Pss' like 37, 49 or 111. Ps 50 is a single psalm of Asaph in Book II: see note on Ps 75.

1. 'Indeed God is good to Israel, to the clean of **b** heart': 'indeed' is no more than an assertive particle (BJ 'mais enfin'), though LXX/V NP take as an exclamation 'How good . . .!'; some emend the text for better parallel (but without warrant from the ancient versions): 'Indeed God (*'Ēl*) is good to the upright, God (is good) to the clean of heart': so NP RSV RPB. **2.** 'But (as for) me, (nevertheless) my feet had almost turned aside (from the right path), my steps had wellnigh been poured away [= slipped], **3** because I had become jealous of the arrogant, I would see the peace [= prosperity] of the wicked': i.e. I recognize that this feeling is a grave departure from the path of virtue, and I nearly fell into sin. **4—14** is an elaboration of this feeling: why trouble to be virtuous when sin seems so successful? 'For there are no pangs [? uncertain word] at their death, and stout is their body [uncertain word, only here]': the general sense seems clear; so JA, cf NP BJ RSV RPB (LXX/V uncertain reading). **5.** They do not have human troubles, **6** 'therefore they are loaded [or, garlanded, cf Dt 15:4] with pride and clothed with violence, **7** their eye(s) come out [= ? look out] from their fat (faces)': an expressive picture of too much prosperity, but uncertain: i. =? 'their eyes bulge out because of fatness': cf AV RV; ii. =? 'their eyes swell [=? have a proud look] because of their prosperity': PB RSV RPB; iii. [emend.] 'their iniquity comes from their prosperity': LXX/V; iv. [same emend.] '. . . from their gross (hearts)': NP BJ (see on 17:10). 'They have gone beyond the imaginings [very uncertain word] of (their) heart': **9.** 'they slander [RPB, cf Arabic root, see DWT, rather than 'place' (with) their mouths in the sky, on earth their (evil) tongue goes (abroad) [i.e., their evil words fill sky and earth]. **10.** Therefore his [LXX/V **c** 'my'] people return here': a puzzling phrase: i. so LXX/V AV RV [= the people return to evil ways]; ii. [reading *yaśībh*] in irony: 'he has brought his people to such a pass', CV; iii. [reading *lāhem* for *halôm*] 'the people turn to them' [= are persuaded to follow the wicked]: Jer PB NP BJ RPB; iv. [emending to *yehallelēm*] 'therefore the people turn and praise them': RSV. 'And the waters (*mē*) of fulness are drained [as from a cup, cf 75:9] for (= ? by) them': another doubtful phrase: i. so AV RV, cf PB BJ [= the people drink their full measure of the evil offered to them]; ii. [emended] 'And the days (*yemē*) of fulness are found for them': LXX/V (meaning?); iii. [emended] 'And who (*mī*) is found (that

394c is) full among them?': Jer (meaning?); iv. [emended] 'And no fault (*mûm*) is found [cf LXX] in them' [= the people turn to the wicked with approval]: RSV RPB (see DWT). **11—12.** They think that God does not see. **13—14.** What is then the use of having a clean heart and hands (cf 26:6)? **16.** I tried to understand by myself, but it was too hard, **17** until I came into thy presence: then I understood what will happen to them, **18—19** how they are destroyed in a moment, **20** 'like a dream when one wakes up, o Lord, on awakening [not LXX/V 'in the city'] thou despisest their phantoms': variously interpreted: i. 'on awakening, thou . . .' refers by anthropomorphism to God: so AV RV NP BJ; ii. 'thou' = the dreamer who wakes up, cf RSV (but such an impersonal usage is unexpected); 'o Lord' an exclamation; iii. [emend *Adonai* to *'enam*] 'on awakening they are no

d more': RSV RPB. **21—22.** 'Yet my heart is bitter, and (in) my kidneys [= emotions] I am pierced [or, 'changed' LXX/V]': i.e. I cannot escape from my old feelings; **22.** 'I am brutish [not LXX/V 'despised'] and ignorant like an animal [*behemoth* cf Jb 40:15 = ? hippopotamus (*chef-d'œuvre de lourdeur*: BJn)] before thee'. **23—24.** But I know thy care of me, **24** how '. . . after glory thou dost take me' (cf similar phrase, equally difficult, in Zech 2:12): i. = 'afterwards, thou shalt take me (into thy divine) glory': AV RV NP BJ [= into heaven, cf Gn 5:24 God 'took' Enoch, and 2 (4) Kgs 2:3 of Elijah; but 'glory' in this sense is very doubtful]; ii. = 'afterwards, thou dost receive me (with?) honour': Jer PB JA RSV [but this adverbial use of 'after' is doubtful]; iii. = 'thou dost receive me with (lit after?) honour': LXX/V iv. [emending] 'thou takest me on the path of honour' [i.e. part of God's care of me]: RPB (see DWT). **25—26.** Thou art my only desire . . . **26.** God is my 'rock' (see on 18:3) and my 'portion' (see on 16:5). **27.** The destruction of the wicked is not to be forgotten, of those who 'go a whoring' away from thee (AV RV, euphemisms in RSV RPB), a familiar figure in the prophets for the desertion of God by Israel, e.g. Jer 3:1, and in the Pss again in 106:39. **28.** 'And (as for) me, closeness to God [phrase only here and Is 58:2—Vg well *adhaerere Deo*] is good for me: I have set my hope upon the Lord God . . .'

e 74 A National Lament on the Destruction of the Temple—The Temple is in ruins: the poem either (1) refers to 586 (2 (4) Kgs 25:9) as to a contemporary event, or (2) to the desecration of 168 in Maccabean times (1 Mc 1:23), or (3) was re-used in the latter period, or (4) is an imaginary *mise-en-scène* of the destruction. The possible mention of 'synagogues' in v 8 might indicate a late date, but the meaning may be 'religious services' as in LXX/V. The text is at several places very insecure. **Title:** 'Asaph'.

1. 'Why hast thou cast us off . . . the sheep of thy pasture?': the figure of Israel as a flock is characteristic of the 'Asaph Collection' (here, 77:21; 78:52, 70—72; 79:13; 80:1). **2.** 'Remember thy congregation (faithful Israel), which thou didst acquire, . . . redeem (to be) the tribe of thine inheritance, Mount Sion where thou hast dwelt': here we have important theological elements: Israel is God's own 'congregation', his flock, his special possession (cf Ex 19:5, echoed in 1 Pt 2:9), redeemed, his own 'inheritance', where he dwelt (*šākhan*) on Mount Sion. The idea of God's 'indwelling' among men, called by the later Rabbis the *šᵉkhīnah*, with the (probably fortuitously) assonant Greek word *skēnē* (lit 'tent'), finds frequent expression in the Pss. **3—4.** The Psalmist invites God to look at the ruins of the Temple; **4** 'thine enemies have roared in the midst of thy (religious) meeting [or, meeting-place], they have set up their

banners as banners (of victory)': so RPB—for *'ôth* **394** (sign) = 'banner, standard', cf Nm 2:2. **5—6.** A description of the wrecking of the Temple: the text is uncertain: He (the wrecker) is known (=? seems) as one who lifts up axes in a thicket of trees [i.e. chops down the building as he might chop trees], **6** and now (they cut down) its carved work altogether with hatchet and adzes': i. so RV—and PB AV JA NP with slight **f** differences; ii. '. . . set up signs, **5** not knowing it was at the upper entrance. As in a thicket of trees with axes **6** they cut down its doors altogether, with hatchet and adze they broke it down': LXX/V; iii. 'they cut down [emended] at the upper entrance with axes the wooden trellis, **6** and now they break down its carving with hatchet and adze': RSV; iv. 'they cut down [emended], as one who lifts up axes in a thicket of trees, **6** so they break down its carving . . .': RPB; v. '. . . set up signs **5** one did not know [i.e. foreign] at the upper entrance; in the midst of the woodwork their axes, **6** they smash its doors with hatchet and adze': BJ. **7—8.** They set it on fire, desecrated it, **8** they said in their hearts, Let us destroy them [uncertain word: LXX/V "their kinsmen with them"], they burned all the meeting-places of God in the land [or, on the earth]': LXXᴮ/V show corruption in the Gr. text: 'Let us cause to rest [= cease] all the feast-days of God . . .': the word *mô'edh*, as in v 4, may refer to the place, or the occasion of (especially) a religious meeting, and if a place (AV RV 'synagogues'), the problem is raised of the origins of local worship in the Land. But it may refer to any feast, or place of worship, on earth. **9—10.** The psalmist now laments that 'our own banners' **g** are seen no more: 'banners' as in v 4, so RPB; but *'ôth* may mean 'sign' (in the sense of portents or miracles), linking with 'prophet' following (so most); 'there is no more prophet, and there is none with us who knows how long (this ruin will go on)'. **11.** 'Why dost thou hold back thy hand, and keep hidden (and inactive) thy right hand in thy bosom?': i. so RPB [slight emendation for 'keep hidden' for Heb. 'consume' see DWT]; cf RSV; ii. 'thy right hand (bring out) of thy bosom: consume (them)': cf RV; iii. 'thy right hand in thy bosom for ever [lit.? unto consummation]': LXX/V. **12—14.** But God has always been my king . . . **13** he divided the (Red) **h** Sea, destroyed the sea-serpents, **14** 'the heads of Leviathan', and 'gave him as food to a people, to wild creatures [uncertain word as in 72:9 where see note]': i. = 'to a people in the wilderness [i.e. to Israel]: PB AV RV (cf 72:9); ii. = 'to a people [=? race] of wild creatures [or omit 'people' as dittography]: BJ RSV; iii. [emending] 'to sea-monsters': NP RPB (sharks) (see DWT) [best in the context]; iv. [taking *Sīʾīm* as proper name] = 'people of the Ethiopians': LXX/V Jer. The passage refers to God's care of Israel at the Exodus, and the sea serpents and the mythical Leviathan may refer to Egypt and its destruction as perhaps in Is 27:1. But the Exodus theme is interwoven here with the mythology of creation and God's rule of nature in the next verses, and v 15 may refer to either, or to both. **15.** 'Thou hast opened up a spring (in the desert) . . . dried up permanent rivers [= ? Jordan] [LXX/V "rivers of Ethan"]': God's power over nature, as shown in the desert after the Exodus. **18.** Remember this now, o **i** Lord . . . **19** 'Give not the soul of thy turtle dove to a wild beast (*ḥayyath*), forget not the life (*ḥayyath*) of thy "poor" [see on 9:13]', with a play on words with *ḥayyath*: i. 'thy turtle dove' (*tûrᵉkhā*, usually a sacrificial animal) = Israel (cf dove in 68:14), but rather forced: PB AV RV NP ('dove to a [emended] vulture'), BJ RSV; ii. 'eruditam lege tua' (connected with *tôrāthᵉkhā*): Jer; iii. [emended

4i to *tôdhāthᵉkhā*] = 'of thy praise' = 'of those that praise thee': LXX/V RPB [probably the best solution]. **20.** 'Look upon the covenant [cf v 18], for the dark places of the earth are full of habitations of violence': i. so PB AV RV BJ RSV and cf LXX/V ('thy covenant'); ii. [repointed] 'Look upon (thy) creations, that they are full of darkness, the earth (is full of) violence': RPB (see DWT); iii. '... thy covenant, for the dark places of the earth and the plains [repointed] are full of violence': NP.

5a 75 God is the only Just Judge—In vv 3—6 it is God himself who speaks: this literary device of placing an extended speech on the lips of God (which Gunkel categorizes as 'Prophecy', §9, and Mowinckel as 'Oracle', II, 64) is rare in the Psalter and seems a speciality of the 'Asaph Collection': the only 'Asaph Ps' outside this series, Ps 50 in Book II, has a similar device, and it is found in this Collection here, Ps 81 and 82. **Title:** 'Asaph Collection' with a musical direction, for which see on Ps 57.

2. 'We give thanks to thee [see on 106:1], o God... and near is thy name, (they) recount thy wonders': i. so PB AV RV, but it seems unclear; ii. [emended] '... and those who call on thy name recount...': RPB; iii. [emended] '... and we call on thy name, we recount...': Vg Syr NP BJ RSV, cf LXX 'I recount'. **3—4.** The Lord now speaks: 'When I appoint the time [lit. 'take the appointment'—*mô'ēdh*, see on 74:8], I judge with equity (whatever men may do). 4 the earth may melt away... but I made firm its pillars (Selah)'. **5—6.** I reprove the wicked...: 'Lift not up your horn': a metaphor from an animal showing its strength, here in vv 6 and 11a in a bad, arrogant sense; elsewhere in the Pss in a good sense, v 11b, 89:25; 92:11, and of prosperity 112:9; 132:7; 148:14; and cf an echo of the good sense in the Benedictus, Lk 1:69, from 1 Sm 2:10.

b 6. '... nor speak with stiffnecked arrogance [lit. 'with an arrogant neck', a phrase not elsewhere]': i. so PB AV RV RSV and cf Jer and BJ; ii. LXX/V read as '... nor speak arrogance against the Rock (= God) [emended]: followed by NP RPB. **7—8.** Now the Psalmist speaks: 'For not from the east nor from the west, and not from the desert of the mountains (comes true judgement), **8** but (only) God is the (true) judge, he humbles the one and exalts the other': i. so Heb. text, and cf LXX/V; ii. [slight emend.] '... not from the desert [= south], nor from the mountains [= north]...': NP BJ RPB, with good parallelism, iii. [repoint.] '... not from the desert (comes) lifting up [cf 'exalts' at end of v 8]': PB AV RV RSV. **9.** The cup of judgement (see on 11:6 and 60:5) is in God's hand: a cup of 'wine fermented, (a cup) full of blended (wine); and he has poured out from it: down to its dregs all the wicked of the earth shall drink, shall drain': i.e. none shall escape the bitter cup of God's inexorable judgement.

c 76 God's Victory makes an end of War—A hymn of praise, and the only one in the Asaph Collection suggesting the 'Sion theme', i.e. God's universal rule from Sion, if vv 11—13 are to be so understood. It is a good hymn, with good imagery, and divided into four clear stanzas. **Title:** Asaph, with musical directions.

2—4. 'God is renowned in Judah..., in Israel... **3.** His dwelling is in Salem [= Jerusalem as in Gn 14:18; LXX/V 'in peace']... in Sion', **4** there he has put an end to war (Selah). **5.** (2nd stanza) 'Thou art... more glorious than the everlasting hills': 'hills of *tereph*', which usually means 'booty' or 'prey', but—i. it may here correspond to *'adh* = 'eternity' which perhaps in Gn 49:27 = 'booty', and strangely was substituted here for *'adh* in view of that passage (see DWT); ii. LXX/V may have

read *terem*: 'mountains of before [= antiquity]'; iii. **395c** Most emend to *'adh* = 'eternity': presumably NP RSV RPB; iv. '... more excellent than the mountains of prey [PB 'hills of the robbers']': PB AV (meaning?); v. '... glorious (in coming down) from the mountains of prey': JA, cf RV [i.e. returning from plundering the enemy in the hills]; vi. '... glorious. Mountains [= heaps (very unusual)] of booty **6** are plundered': BJ, but very forced. **6.** 'The strong [LXX/V 'foolish'] of heart were **d** despoiled, sank into sleep, all men of strength (in war) did not find their hands (to use weapons)': there is no other warrant for this idiom 'to find their hands': and LXX understood as 'find anything for their hands (to take)', and Vg as 'find anything in their hands', i.e. are emptyhanded. **7.** '... rider and horse fell asleep', i.e. war came to a halt. **8—10.** (3rd stanza) '... Who can stand before thee from the moment of thine anger?' **9—10.** The earth stood still at thy judgement (Selah). **11.** (4th stanza) 'For the anger of man (*'ādhām*) shall praise thee, the remnant of [=? those who escape from] angers (*hēmôth*) thou shalt gird on': cf Is 49:18, Jer 13:11, for God 'putting on' people: i. so RV BJ RSV (PB AV '... thou shalt restrain'), i.e. everything (including man's anger) shall turn to thy praise (PB); but this sense is very doubtful; ii. [emending] 'Men's thoughts shall praise thee, the rest of (his) thought will make festival to thee', LXX/V (at least showing the insecurity of the text), iii. [repointing] 'The anger of Edom shall praise thee, the remnant of Hamath shall make festival to thee [emend with LXX]': NP RPB (see DWT). The advantage of this last reading is that it shows the defeated enemies of Israel coming to praise God, and it leads on to the next verse most easily. Edom and Hamath lie to the south and north respectively; but some would read Aram (Syria) rather than Edom. All three names appear as David's enemies in 2 Sm 8:3—12, and are thus 'traditional' enemies. **12—13.** 'Pay vows to the LORD your God...': addressed to these nations (according to iii above), or to all mankind; for **13** 'he cuts off (= stifles) the breath [so BJ, others 'spirit'] of princes...'

77 A (2—16) **A Meditation on Hope in the Lord**—A **e** fairly regular form, with stanzas marked by Selah in vv 4, 10, 16, mostly of 3 + 3 couplets, almost certainly distinct from the short lyric of 77B. The **Title** includes the name Jeduthun, see on 62:1.

2—3. 'My voice (is raised) unto God and I cry out... and he will hear me, **3** in my day of distress [see on 3:2] I sought the Lord, my hand at night is spread out [lit. poured out] and tires not [lit. grows not numb], my soul refuses to be comforted': the phrase 'hand poured out' is unusual: i. = 'hands spread out' (cf 'raising hands' in gesture of prayer as in 28:2; 134:2): so most since Jerome; ii. = 'my sore ran and ceased not': PB AV following Rashi ['wound' as struck by the hand? cf Jb 23:2, but very uncertain]; iii. = 'with my hands (raised) before him [emended]': LXX/V; iv. [emended] 'my eye poured out (tears)' [cf Lam 3:49]: Targum JA; v. = 'my hand = my strength melts away': Ibn Ezra. **4.** 'I remember God and am troubled (Selah)'. **5.** 'Thou hast held the guards [word only here] of my eyes: I am stricken...': i. = 'held my eyelids (closed): I am stunned': RPB [eyelids: Targ, cf Jer]; ii. = 'held my eyelids (open, wakeful, watching): I am troubled': PB AV RV NP BJ RSV; iii. = 'my eyes kept [emended] the watches: I am troubled': Vg; iv. = 'my enemies [emended] kept watch (over me): I am troubled': LXX. **6—7.** I am **f** troubled when I meditate on God's dealings with Israel in the past. **8—10.** Has he cast us off, forgotten us?

395f (Selah.) **11.** 'And I said (in my meditation), "This is my weakening, the changing of the right hand of the Most High"': i. = 'This is what takes away my strength, namely that God's right hand is changed [i.e., used to do great things for Israel, but now no more]': cf PB AV RV NP BJ RSV; ii. [emend.] 'It (his right hand) is weakened, the right hand of the Most High is changed [= has lost its strength]': RPB (see DWT); iii. [emend.] 'Now I begin (to hope?), this is (the moment of) the changing (from punishment to mercy?) of . . .': LXX/V. **12–16.** I remember God's works. **16.** 'Thou hast redeemed . . . thy own people, the children of Jacob [= Israel] and Joseph' [named specially because, as Ibn Ezra explains, he saved Israel, and has the title of 'the Shepherd, the Rock of Israel' Gn 49:24]. Selah marks the end.

g **77 B** (17–21) **God is the Lord of Nature**—A short lyric in a pleasant 3 + 3 + 3 rhythm with colourful imagery and having associations with the 'psalm' in Habakkuk. It is the only true hymn of praise in the Asaph Collection.

17–19. Nature trembles before thee, **18** 'thy arrows' = lightning, cf Hab 3:11; **19** 'the sound of thy thunder in the wheel' most probably = the circle of heaven (AV); perhaps = whirlwind (RV NP RSV RPB)—but does thunder go with a whirlwind?—; BJ the 'roll' of thunder; 'lightnings lit up the world' as in Ps 97:4, cf Hb 3:11. **20.** 'Thy way is through the sea . . . but thy footprints cannot be recognized': God works invisibly. **21.** 'Thou hast led thy people as a flock . . .': this verse, with the typical Asaphite image of the sheep (see on 74:1), is almost certainly an addition here when 77B was attached to 77A, balancing v 16 with Moses and Aaron, for it turns the cosmic picture of vv 17–20 into a picture of the Red Sea. Yet, as it stands, the interpenetration of the two pictures is entirely admissible, see on 74:14.

h **78 A Didactic Epic of Israel**—This Ps, in a late 'wisdom' style, shows a strong 'party line' about worship in Jerusalem and devotion to the royal line of David, with rejection of the non-Davidic monarchy in the north. It traces the history from the Exodus to David. With Pss 105, 106, also 'Epics', it is classed by Mowinckel (II, 111) as 'non-cultic'. **Title:** Asaph.

1–4. 'Give ear, o my people, to my teaching [my *tôrāh*: only here in this sense outside Prov, see on 19:8] . . .' **2.** I will speak in a *māšal*—a tale with a moral (a 'parable'), and a *hîdhāh*—a puzzle, riddle that needs thinking out (a 'dark saying'), quoted Mt 13:35. **3–4.** We must pass on the stories to our children. **9–11.** A curious reference to the 'sons of Ephraim' who, though armed with bows, turned back on the day of battle; the first 'black mark' against the northern tribes: i. This refers to some episode of cowardice otherwise unknown; ii. It is a metaphor for not keeping the covenant and the law (v 10); iii. It forestalls the rejection of Ephraim (and Joseph) in v 67 for abandoning Jerusalem (Sion), **i** suggesting that they had been faithless throughout. **11** They forgot **12** God's wonders in the 'field of *Sô'an* = Tanis in Egypt, cf Nm 13:22. **13.** He divided the (Red) Sea and 'made the water stand up in a heap' [as in the song Ex 15:8: LXX/V repointing here 'as in a water-skin']. **14–22.** God led them through the desert, **23–25** gave them manna, **24** '. . . grain of heaven' [LXX/V 'bread from heaven' as in 105:40, taken up in Wis 16:20 (*panem de caelo praestitisti eis*), and by our Lord in Jn 6:31 of the Eucharist, and so in the Breviary for Corpus Christi]. **25.** 'So man did eat angels' food [or, bread]': the word 'angels' (LXX/V PB AV RSV RPB) is properly 'mighty' (RV BJ), and not the usual

word (messenger), and not used elsewhere of angels. **39** The traditional rendering 'angels' is also in the Jewish tradition: cf Targum and Rashi. **26–31.** And he sent them quails. **32–39.** Yet still they did not trust him (cf v 22), and **42** forgot what he had done for them. **44–51** rehearse the plagues in Egypt, with many parallels in 105:29–36. **51.** He smote . . . 'the firstfruits of their (Egypt's) strength': i. = young men (firstborn): NP BJ RSV RPB; ii. = chief ones = mighty: PB AV RV; iii. = firstfruits of their toil (= produce): LXX/V. **52–58. j** And he led them out 'as a flock' (see on 74:1), **54** and brought them to 'his holy mount' [*gebhûl* = mountain, cf Ugaritic, see Dahood, Bib 45 (1964), 396, and cf Arabic: so LXX/V; others have the usual sense of 'border'], **57** But they acted treacherously and 'turned round like a bow that cannot shoot': an uncertain phrase, also in Hos 7:16, and cf Zech 9:13: i. [from root 'deceive'] 'a deceitful bow' [which misses the mark]: AV RV NP BJ RSV; ii. [from root 'slack'] 'a bow whose string is loose': RPB (see DWT); iii. LXX/V 'a crooked bow' [=? deceitful, because it cannot shoot straight, so also perhaps PB 'a broken bow'?]. **58.** They provoked God with their 'high places' (of idolatrous worship). **59–64.** So he rejected Israel and **60** his dwelling at Shiloh (where the old sanctuary was, Jos 18:1; 1 Sm 1:3), and **61** he let 'his strength . . . his beauty' [= the ark, see on Ps 96:6 and cf Ps 132:8] be captured (1 Sm 4:11). **65.** 'But then the Lord awoke like one (who **k** had been) sleeping (to avenge the situation), like a strong man (who had been) overcome with wine'. The strong man was not now drunk with wine, anymore than the man who wakes up is still asleep: the picture is of one waking up to sudden action either from natural sleep, or from drunken stupor—in either case he is now wide awake. 'Overcome' (as LXX/V), a word only here, cf Arabic root (see BDB s.v. *rûn*), rather than 'exulting': i. = 'who (had been) overcome . . .' [as above, and with parallelism]: RPB; ii. = 'overcome with . . .' [rather missing the point]: NP BJ; iii. = 'suffering from the effects of . . . (*crapula*)' [also missing the point]: LXX/V; iv. = 'recovering from . . .': JA; v. = 'refreshed with . . .': PB (perhaps a euphemism?); vi. = 'shouting because of . . .': AV RV RSV (from the other root 'exulting', perhaps to avoid the drunken picture?). **66.** 'and he smote his enemies **l** behind', i.e. in the back because they were fleeing: the 'everlasting disgrace', so most; but some take as 'he drove them back', so RV RSV RPB. **67–68.** 'He rejected the tent of Joseph (or Ephraim) [i.e. Shiloh which was in Ephraim, cf Jer 7:12], **68** and chose the tribe of Judah . . .': the ark was eventually taken back to Jerusalem in Judah by David (1 Chr 13:5–14; 15:1, 25–29; cf 2 Sm 6:2–17; see on Ps 132), and **69** here he built his sanctuary: here is the climax of the theme of this Ps: **70–72** and he chose David from being a shepherd of sheep to be the shepherd of Israel—the Asaphite 'sheep' figure again. For us Christians, the line of David leads to Christ, the Good Shepherd.

79 A National Lament on the Destruction of 396 **Jerusalem**—A similar theme to that of Ps 74 (where see note on possible circumstances), but with an emphasis on a call for vengeance. The text here is sounder than that of Ps 74.

1–4. 'O God, the nations [*gōyim*, sometimes, and inconsistently, translated 'heathen', but the word has no necessary religious significance] are come into thine inheritance . . . they have made Jerusalem into heaps (of rubble)'. **5.** 'How long, o Lord, wilt thou be angry for ever?': **6–7** a first call for vengeance. **10.** Let God be known as a just avenger, **11** 'Let a prisoner's groan

6a come before thee ... leave over [=? 'preserve, spare'] those doomed to die [lit. 'sons of death', phrase only here and 102:21, but cf 2 Sm 12:5]': LXX/V an uncertain reading. **12.** A call for sevenfold repayment 'into their bosom', i.e. the wrap-across of the oriental tunic, where one carries things, = 'pay back into their pockets seven times what they have handed out to us': cf a similar sentiment in 137:8; and a difficult phrase in 35:13.

b **80 A National Lament over all Israel and a Hope of Restoration**—Ps 74 considers the Temple in ruins, Ps 79 Jerusalem, and here it is the whole land in terms of the whole of Israel, but with special reference to the northern territory, so that it has sometimes been thought that this Ps had its origin in the Northern Kingdom. Apart from the ark in v 2, there is no reference to the Temple or Sion. The stanzaic construction is marked with a refrain in vv 4, 8, 15, 18. The **Title** includes the words 'Lilies' (?) as in Pss 45 and 69, and 'Testimony' as in Ps 60: probably indications of a tune.

2. 'O Shepherd of Israel ... who leadest Joseph [see on 77:16] like a flock [the typical figure of the Asaph Collection, see on 74:1] ... sitting upon the Cherubim...': a reference to the carved winged creatures adorning the Ark (Ex 25:18—22), 'from between which' the Lord will speak (25:22), a symbol of God's dwelling with his people, and his care of them. (Other references to the Cherubim in the Pss, 18:11 and 99:1, are not **c** in this sense, but in a cosmic context.) 'Shine forth 3 before Ephraim, Benjamin and Manasseh': taken together with Joseph (Ephraim and Manasseh were sons of Joseph, and Ephraim often stands for the Northern Kingdom), these represent the tribes of the North. Benjamin was disputed territory: as the home of Saul (1 Sm 9:1—2; 10:20—21) it would be a traditional rival to the house of David. After the division in 1 (3) Kgs 12:20, 'only Judah' supported the house of David, but in 12:21 Rehoboam appeals to both Judah and Benjamin. It would seem that the early struggles between Judah and Israel were fought on Benjaminite territory. The present Psalm's interest in the northern territory, if not due to its origin, may be an envisaging of the whole area as an ideally united kingdom. **4.** 'Restore us, o God ...' (as a united kingdom?): the refrain. For God's countenance shining upon us, see on 67:2. **5.** 'Lord God of hosts': see on 24:10. 'How long dost thou set thy face against thy people's prayer?': so RPB (see DWT), supposing a verb akin to the Aram. root, used in the Syr. of Ex 4:21 ('harden heart'), though most take as '... dost **d** thou smoke [= be angry]' as LXX/V. **6.** 'Thou makest them eat the bread of tears, drink tears "by the gallon"': the same hyperbole as is used in English, *šālīš* being a third of an ephah, which is about 3 gallons. **8.** The refrain. **9—12.** Israel is likened to a vine: only here in the Pss, but cf Hos 10:1 and Ezek 17:6—10, and (with a different word) Is 5:2, Jer 2:21; transplanted from Egypt into the Land, **11** where it grew and overshadowed the 'mighty cedars' [so PB AV RVm JA RSV RPB: lit. 'cedars of God', a form of superlative, see on 36:7 and 68:16], **12** sending its branches as far as the Sea [Mediterranean, to the west] and the River [Euphrates, to the east]: again in terms of a united ideal Israel as in Solomon's time. **13—15.** But now thou hast broken down the walls of the vineyard, so that passers-by and **14** 'the boar from the forest and the solitary beast of the field' take its fruit: 'solitary beast' LXX/V: a similar word is used in Telugu, in India, for the fierce leader who goes alone ahead of a pack of wild boars (for this information I am indebted to a pupil, Mr Victor Peddi); others take as collective wild beasts, deriving perhaps from a root 'to

swarm, move'. So most also at 50:11, but LXX/V are **396d** different there. **15.** The refrain '... have regard for **e** this vine, **16** and maintain [uncertain word: so LXX/V RVm NP BJ; others take as a noun, 'the root' Jer (PB AV?) RSV RPB] (that) which thy right hand has planted, and (look down) upon the son [very uncertain] (which) thou hast strengthened for thyself': i. 'the son' = 'young plant': PB AV RV NP [but no parallel for this usage]; ii. 'the son' = Israel (cf Ex.4:22 'Israel is my son'), with the metaphor changed to men as in v 18: so (literally 'son') LXX/V Jer, cf Ibn Ezra; iii. Targum translates 'son' as 'anointed King'; iv. The whole phrase omitted as a mis-copy from v 18: BJ RSV RPB. **17.** But the vine has been burnt...: 'let them (who did this) perish'. **18.** The metaphor changes to Israel as God's 'right hand man', with the phrase 'the son of man (*adam*) thou hast made strong for thyself' probably mis-copied into v 16; for 'son of man' or 'child of Adam' = mere mortal, see on 8:5. **20.** The refrain.

81 A Festival Song in Praise of God's Goodness— **f** After a reminder of the ritual observance, the point of the festival is rehearsed in terms of a discourse of God, recounting his mercies to Israel. For this literary device see on Ps 75. There are several textual obscurities, and some regard vv 7—11 as a distinct composition, the nexus in v 6 being uncertain. The **Title** includes 'Gittith', see on Ps 8.

2 3. 'Sing ye merrily unto God our strength' (RPB): the verb conveys a loud cry with a note of joy; 'our strength' may indicate the Ark, cf. 78:61; 132:8. **3.** 'Raise a song, take up the drum, the sweet [see on 133:1] harp with the lute'. **4—5.** 'Sound the shofar [a trumpet made of a ram's horn] at the new moon, on the festival [*kēseh*, see below] for our feast day...': there are four problems here: (**1**) The Jewish (lunar) months begin at the new moon, and in Nm 10.10 a trumpet (of silver, Nm 10:2, *hⁱṣōṣᵉrāh* not *šōphār*) was to be sounded. But New Year's Day, the beginning of the seventh month, Tishri (Sept./Oct.) was (Lv 23:24, Nm 29:1), and is, among the Jews the special solemnity when the shofar is sounded, and this is very probably the 'new moon' here—Targum even inserts 'Tishri'. (**2**) The word **g** *kēseh* is uncertain, and the only occurrence, Prv 7:20 provides no contextual clue: i. = 'full moon': so Jer RV NP BJ RSV RPB, as also Vg in Prv 7:20, and the Syr. at 1 (3) Kgs 12:32 has *kes'a* for 'the 15th day of the month'; ii. LXX/V here have 'special day', cf PB AV, not limited to the full moon; iii. But Targum sees it as still referring to the new moon; so also Ibn Ezra, i.e. when the moon is 'covered' (*kāsāh*). This means that only one feast day is mentioned, and that is New Year's Day when the shofar is to be sounded. RPB has inserted 'and', to suggest that *kēseh* is a distinct feast day. (**3**) What is 'our feast day'? It is presumably identified with *kēseh*. i. If the 'full moon' is correct, it should be noted that on the 15th day (full moon) of Tishri is the Feast of *Sukkôth* (Booths or Tabernacles), a feast of thanksgiving and rejoicing for God's goodness to Israel in the desert (Lv 23:34, Nm 29:12), and many see this feast day here, as does the later Jewish tradition (e.g. Soncino Pss); though some in view of the mention of the Exodus in v 6 suppose that the reference is to the Passover, also kept at the full moon, but of the first month, Nisan (Mar./Apr.); ii. Targum and Rabbis continue the reference to the new moon of New Year's Day, as in iii above; iii. For Mowinckel (e.g. I, 122, 124), it is the festival of the Enthronement of Yahweh, for Weiser of the Covenant, and for Kraus the central festival of all Israel. (**4**) The blowing of the shofar on New Year's Day, or **h**

396h other feast day, is not commanded in the Pent, except for the Year of Jubilee (Lv 25:9) when the *ṭᵉrûʿāh* (loud noise = trumpeting) is commanded to be made on the shofar, so that the 'memorial-trumpeting' at the New Year (Lv 23:24; 29:1) may be associated with the shofar. But this Ps 81:4 may be a warrant for its use on New Year's Day. (The shofar appears in the Psalter elsewhere at 47:6; 98:6; 150:3, in the context of joyful music, with no ritual connotations.) **6.** 'He laid it (the ordinance) upon Joseph [= Israel, see on 77:16] as a witness [i.e. he commanded them to do this to bear witness to the event], when he (Joseph) came forth from the land of Egypt': i. so LXX/V Jer PB WV RPB (see DWT: 'al in Phoenician = 'from'); ii. 'when he went out over [usual sense of 'al] the land': RV RSV, cf AV; iii. 'when he (God) went out against the land of Egypt': RVm JA NP BJ; 'A tongue which I knew not, (that) I hear': i. = I (the psalmist) now hear a voice which I have not heard before, namely, the voice of God, which utters the following, v 7 to the end: i.e., an introduction to the divine utterance: NP BJ RSV; ii. = (When God went forth) I (Israel at the Exodus) heard the voice 'of one that I knew not', i.e. God's voice uttering what follows: RVm JA; iii. = (... Egypt, where) I (Israel) heard a language I understood not, i.e. the foreign language of the Egyptian taskmasters; or, after the Exodus, the voice of God from Sinai: AV RV; iv. [emending] (... where) he (Israel) heard a language he understood not, i.e. as above: LXX/V PB; v. RPB omits as 'a lectionary rubric which has crept into the i text' (DWT). **7.** The voice of God recounts his mercies to Israel: 'I relieved his [RSV emends to 'your', cf next v] shoulder from the burden, his [RSV 'your'] hands were freed from [lit. passed away from] (carrying) basket(s) (of building materials)': so LXX/V and most—the word means some receptacle, in 1 Sm 2:14 it seems to mean a 'pot', whence PB AV here 'potmaking'. **8.** 'In distress thou (o Israel) didst call me ... I answered thee out of the hidden thunder (on Sinai), I tested thee at the waters of Meribah': the place in the desert where the people 'contended' (*rîbh*) with Moses (Ex 17:2), and which was therefore called Meribah or 'Contention' (Ex 17:7, cf Ps 95:8; 106:32): LXX/V translate the name 'Contention', so also PB. 'Selah' marks the end of the first stanza of the discourse. **9—11.** God's discourse continues: **10** 'There shall be no strange god **11** for I am the LORD (Yahweh) thy God, who brought thee up ... : open thy mouth wide and I will fill it [a figure not found elsewhere]'. **12—16.** But '... Israel was not willing towards me [an unusual phrase] ...'. **14** Would that they would listen ... **16** those who hate the Lord 'would cringe to him (Israel, or, the Lord) [see on 66:3], and their time (of punishment) would be for ever. **17.** But (in contrast) I fed him (Israel) with the finest [lit. 'fat of'] wheat, and with honey from the rock I would satisfy him [emended with NP BJ RPB, Heb. 'thee': the persons are irregular here: others emend to make all 2nd person]'. The phrases are similar to those in the Song of Moses in Dt 32:13—14 and refer perhaps to the manna. The liturgy uses this verse for the Introit of Corpus Christi.

j 82 A Picture of the Court of Heaven—This Ps stands entirely alone, and is a picture of Yahweh judging the *Elohim*, who may be interpreted of the 'gods' condemned as mere mortals. The Jewish tradition, however, eschews an interpretation which recognizes, even in irony, existence of 'gods', and interprets of 'judges', which seems to be followed in Jn 10:34. The interpretation as of false gods is sometimes supposed to derive from an original polytheistic background (cf e.g. Weiser on Ps 82). But this Ps can be seen as no more than accepting the supposition of other gods of other nations, as frequently in the OT, e.g. Dt 4:7, and not excluding the mention of 'other gods', e.g. Ex 20:3, Dt 5:7; and on this background it seems to be a poet's fanciful picture of Yahweh, the supreme God, condemning the gods of the nations as non-entities. The Ps may be classed as 'prophetical' in so far as it includes a divine speech, a speciality of the 'Asaph Collection' (see on Ps 75). **Title:** Asaph.

1. 'God' (*ʿᵉlōhîm*) in this Book III is usually editorially **k** substituted for 'Yahweh (the LORD)', and here undoubtedly stands for the true God, pictured as standing up in the 'divine council' (RSV well) to give judgement. The 'divine council' is 'the council of *ʿĒl*', the most general word for a divinity: i. = 'the heavenly council' in a general sense: NP BJ RSV RPB; ii. = 'the assembly of the gods': LXX/V: i.e. all the gods invoked by mankind are imagined as assembled before Yahweh, and cf next phrase; iii. = 'the congregation of God', i.e. judges assembled by God: Jer RV JA; iv. = 'the congregation of the mighty': AV (PB 'princes')—for the use of el and elohim for less than divine beings, see on 8:6; v. = 'the assembly of the angels': Syr. 'In the midst of the gods (elohim) he holds **l** judgement': i. so Vg and most: the assembly of the false gods—the most likely in view of the ironical judgement in vv 6—7; ii. LXX (not Vg) and Jerome: 'In the midst, God holds judgement'; iii. = 'In the midst of the judges ...': JA with Targum and Rashi; i.e. God has assembled the judges of Israel and examines them: vv 2—4 is an indictment of false justice. This interpretation seems to be that of Jn 10:34 (see on v 6); for elohim = judges, see on 8:6; 58:2; iv. = 'in the midst of the angels' = the heavenly court: so Syr. and Ibn Ezra. **2—4.** The indictment by God, the supreme judge, against false execution of justice, especially with regard to the poor. This context supports iii above. **5.** But all these (false gods or unjust judges) have no understanding, and when God utters judgement nature itself is shaken (cf 76:9—10). **6—7.** 'I have said, "You are gods (elohim) ..." **7** never- **m** theless you shall die like men (adam, mortal man) ...': 'I have said' is taken by some as part of God's judgement resumed (so RPB); by others as introducing the psalmist's words (so NP BJ RSV)—the use of 'quotes' in these versions shows this. i. 'You are gods' is ironical: 'You, the false gods, call yourselves gods! But you shall die like mortals'; ii. 'You are divinely appointed judges, yet you are only mortal men'. The interpretation depends upon that of v 1. The passage is quoted by Christ in Jn 10:34. The context is as follows: v 30 Christ had said 'I and the Father are one'; the Jews said this blasphemy: 33 'Thou, being a man, makest thyself God'; 34 Jesus answered with the quotation: 'I said, You are gods', adding 35 'If it (the OT) calls them gods to whom the word of God came, ... 36 are you saying that it is blasphemy that he whom the Father ... sent ... should say, I am the son of God?' Here 'gods' = 'to whom the word of God came', i.e. God's representatives on earth, i.e. judges, as in the Targum. It is, however, to be expected that the Jewish interpretation would be followed by Christ in the Gospel. **8.** 'Arise, o God, judge the world ...': the psalmist's exclamation after witnessing the heavenly court.

83 A Denunciation of God's Enemies—God's **397a** enemies are Israel's enemies. The stanzas are clearly marked. The 2nd stanza enumerates the classical enemies of Israel, and the 3rd asks God to defeat his enemies as in the classical victories, especially under the Judges. There is no need to envisage an historical circumstance of such a confederation against Israel, nor to conclude

7a a date from the mention of Assyria. Anyone familiar with OT history recognizes the classical features and grasps the point of the identificaton of God's and Israel's enemies. The Ps is classed as a 'national lament'. **Title:** Asaph—in fact the last of this 'Collection'.

2–5. 'O God, keep not silent' [LXX/V by a confusion have '. . . who is like to thee?'] . . . **3** thine enemies . . . **4** are plotting against 'thy treasured ones'. **6–9. The**
b classical foes: they have conspired together: **7** Edom, Ishmaelites, Moab, are all well-known peoples on the borders of Israel to the south and east, also the Hagrites (1 Chr 5:10, 19—20), enemies of Saul, E of Gilead, **8** Gebal (= Arabic *Jibal*, S of Dead Sea, only mentioned here: not = Gebal in Phoenicia), Ammon and Amalek, still S and E, Philistia and Tyre, to the W and N, then **9** distant Assyria is pictured as helping 'the children of Lot' = Moab and Ammon (Gn 19:37—38). Selah. **10–**
13. The Classical victories: Do to them as thou didst to Midian (under Gideon, Jg 6—8), to Sisera the general, and to Jabin the king of the Canaanites (Jg 4—5) by the brook Kishon (Jg 5:21), **11** near En-dor (not named in Jg, but in Jos 17:11 named together with Taanach and Megiddo, which are named in Jg 5:19), **12** to Oreb and Zeeb, Zebah and Zalmunna (all Midianite leaders in Jg 7—8) . . . **14—16.** (4th stanza) 'Make them like thistledown [that is whirled about by the wind (so RPB, see DWT and KB); others have whirling dust, leaves, wind; LXX/V 'wheel'], like blown chaff . . .' **15.** Be to them like a forest fire. **17—19.** May they come to recognize that thou art the Most High.

c 84 A Song of Sion—This Ps expresses with special tenderness the love for Sion and imagines the bliss of pilgrimage there. We are all 'pilgrims at heart', to whatever shrine it is: and here it is the great pilgrimage to Jerusalem, the desire of so many hearts through so many centuries. Kindred Pss are 42—43 and especially 122. **Title:** 'Sons of Qorah' = 'Qorah Collection II' = 84—89. Like 'Qorah I' (42—49), this is a collection of good stuff, of value as poetry, and including in its short compass almost every genre, with the Sion theme recurring here and in 87. The title also includes 'Gittith', see on Ps 8.

2. 'Dearest of places thy dwellings, o Lord of hosts': the phrase 'LORD of hosts', as here, is the commonest form in the prophets, less common in the Pss, but 3t in this Ps, with once 'Lord God of hosts' in v 9: see note on 24:10. The word trs. 'dearest' above is a warm and
d affectionate word. **3.** I long for 'the courts of the Lord', a phrase for the Temple recurring in v 11, and in similar contexts in 65:5 and 116:19. **4—5.** The sparrows and swallows find a home there, a nest for their young—'thine altars, o Lord . . . 5 Blessed those who dwell in thy house, still they praise thee. (Selah)': the syntax of 'thine altars' is embarrassing: i. = an exclamation: 'Thine altars, o LORD!': so LXX/V and most, but such a use of an accusative is very doubtful; ii. = 'At thine altars': RSV (cf RPB), but such a use of the preposition is unwarranted, unless the very doubtful 1 Kgs 9:25 can be invoked; iii. RPB rearranges: 'At thine altars still they praise thee . . . Blessed are those . . . ': but this does not ease the difficulty. **6.** 'Blessed is the man whose strength is in thee—highways in their heart' = 'their heart is set on the highways (to Sion)': so RV RSV RPB explicitly; implicitly LXX/V JA NP BJ; but to speak of a thing desired being 'in the heart' has no parallel usage. Yet the idea of 'They are pilgrims at heart' is consistent with the
e theme of the psalm. **7.** 'Passing through the valley of the *bākā*': the difficulty is in this last word: i. = '. . . of the balsam-tree' [cf 2 Sm 5:23 = 1 Chr 14:14]: RVm WV, and cf other places named after trees in Heb. and most

languages (e.q. Oakham, Hazelton, Llangollen); ii. = **397e** 'the dry valley': NP RPB; iii. = 'Valley of Baca' [proper name, but cf i]: AV RSV; iv. = 'Valley of Weeping' [usual Heb. root]: LXX/V (Douay 'vale of tears', whence this phrase) PB RV; v. = '. . . of the Weeping Tree' [= *celtis australis*, whose sap is abundant, and the present Wadi-el-Meise—the Arabic name for this tree—is a valley near Jerusalem, near Rephaim (2 Sm 5:22), which would be a last stage on the pilgrimage: this would therefore be a particular valley named after this tree]: BJ with note. 'They made it a spring (of water)': i. = a **f** place where water is abundant: so most; ii. [emending] 'They drink from a well', i.e. 'find a well whereof to drink': RPB (see Kittel and DWT); iii. LXX/V 'In the place which he set' shows the way to a slight emendation: 'He made it a dwelling place' [i.e. habitable]. 'Also with pools [repointed] the early rain clothes (it: the valley)': i. so RSV RPB, and cf PB AV; ii. [retaining Massoretic pointing] '. . . with blessings the early rain . . .': RV NP BJ; iii. '. . . blessings the lawgiver [confusion with exactly similar word] provides': LXX/V, connecting with what follows, and suggesting God's encouragement to those who come to him, and providing a mystical interpretation. The 'picture' of this difficult verse is of the pilgrims tramping through that inhospitable valley, and their enthusiasm making it as if it were a well watered place. **8.** The picture of the pilgrims' march continues **g** 'from strength to strength' [perhaps the origin of this phrase], until they arrive at Jerusalem, where 'the God [repointed] of gods will appear (to them) in Sion': i. so LXX/V BJ RSV RPB, and cf PB; ii. [with Massoretic pointing] '(Each one) will appear before God in Sion: AV RV; iii. [emending] 'They will see the God of gods . . .': NP. **9.** Hear my prayer . . . (Selah). **10.** 'Our shield, see, o God': i. = 'O God, our shield [= defender], see': LXX/V PB AV RV NP BJ; ii. = 'O God, see our shield [= defender = the king (cf 89:19)]': Ibn Ezra RSV RPB. 'Look in the face thine anointed (*māsîah*, Messiah)': see on Ps 2: most see a reference to the king (RPB even has 'thine anointed king'), as to the symbolic leader of the ideal people of God, and for Christians the symbol of Christ; and Jerusalem was not only the holy city, but the royal city. Others, e.g. BDB and BJn, see a reference to the high priest who welcomes the pilgrims. **11.** 'Better is one day in thy courts than a thousand (elsewhere), I would rather stand at the threshold in the house of my God, than dwell in the tents of wickedness': the single word 'stand at the threshold' is found only here, some translate it 'be a doorkeeper' (PB AV RV RSV RPB), and it has been pointed out that the Qorahites are among the 'keepers of the threshold' in 1 Chr 9:19. It is not clear whether the idea is a place of humility (cf LXX/V *abiectus*); or a place of honour, since at any rate in the palace the office of doorkeeper was an honourable office (2 (4) Kgs 22:4; 25:8). **12.** 'For the LORD is sun and shade [lit. shield] **h** (to me) . . .': God is often spoken of as our 'shield' (cf v 10), but nowhere else is God called the 'sun' (the 'sun of justice' in Mal 3:20 [English 4:2] is not a direct reference to God), perhaps because of associations with sun-worship in the ancient world; the translation is therefore unsure: i. 'sun': AV RV NP RSV, cf PB; ii. = 'defence' [perhaps a different word altogether] as in Is 54:12, where LXX with Vg and most translate 'battlement', providing also a good parallel with 'shield': BJ RPB; iii. LXX/V omit the line, but substitute 'For the Lord loves mercy and faithfulness', a line perhaps lost in the Heb. **13.** '. . . Blessed the man who trusts in thee'.
85 The Perfect Land, where God's Glory dwells—A **i** description of the ideal Israel, where God dwells and all

397i is perfect and virtuous; a good hymn of pleasant construction in regular metre, with two stanzas. **Title:** Qorah.

2. 'LORD, thou hast been favourable to thy land, thou hast restored the prosperity [or, fortune, or, freedom, or, captivity: see on 14:7] of Jacob [= Israel]. **5.** 'Restore us again... break off [or emend to 'turn aside' with LXX/V] thine anger...': the verse (*converte nos...*) at the beginning of Compline. **7—8.** 'Wilt thou not bring us to life again...?': this couplet (*Deus tu conversus...*) is used in the Roman Mass. **9.** The 2nd stanza: 'Let me hear what God, the LORD, will speak, for he will speak peace with his people and unto his faithful, and let them **j** not return to folly': so the MT; the sense is uncertain: i. so Jer AV RV BJ (PB omits the word 'folly'); ii. [emending to *libbâm lôh*] 'and those who turn (their) heart to him': LXX, and similarly NP RSV; iii. Vg '... who turn to the heart' [= ? 'are converted'; but probably a textual confusion in the Vg]; iv. [further emend.] 'and to the upright in heart. Selah [for end of first couplet, cf v 3]': RPB (see Kittel and DWT). **10.** Salvation is at hand... 'that glory may dwell in our land', i.e. the glory (*kābhôdh*) of God's personal presence, as on Sinai e.g. Ex 16:10; 24:16, pictured only here as 'dwelling in our land', though the idea of God 'dwelling' in Sion is frequent (see on 74:2). In Ezekiel the 'glory' is seen as departing from Jerusalem in 10:18 and eventually returning in 43:5. This passage is therefore a prayer that God's personal presence may come to dwell in our land in the ideal messianic age: for Christians fulfilled in the Incarnation. **11—14.** 'Love and friendship meet [see on 5:8 for these words], righteousness and peace kiss one another' in the ideal kingdom, **12** 'friendship springs up out of the very ground, and justice looks down from the sky, **13** the Lord gives prosperity... **14** justice marches before him [cf 89:15], and peace [emended for 'and he shall place'] is the road where he walks [lit. 'of his footsteps']': so, emended, WV BJ RPB; others following MT take as 'And he shall place his footsteps as a way (for us)'. A remarkable feature of this section is the quasi-personification of the virtues in the messianic kingdom: nowhere else do the virtues meet, kiss, spring up, look down, march and form a pathway.

l 86 A Prayer of Confidence—This Ps, labelled in the title as of David, is very similar in many of its phrases to Pss in the 'David Collection I' in Book I, and though its pattern is familiar, it has delicacy of its own, and the 'universal theme' is forcefully stated in v 9. One notices the use of *Adonai* (Lord) 7t, more than in any other Ps. **Title:** 'David', the only one in Book III, and in the authentic manner of other 'David Psalms'; it is probably truly a part of the 'Qorah Collection II' which includes a variety of types and may well include also a 'David' in its series here.

1—7. 'Incline thine ear... for I am "poor and needy" [see on 9:13: the two words only here and 74:21 in Book III]'. **2.** I am one of the 'faithful' (*hāsîdh*: see on 12:2)... **3.** Have mercy, o *Adonai*, **4** 'for to thee do I lift up my soul' (in the sense of prayer, only here, 25:1 and 143:8), **5** 'for thou, o *Adonai*, art good [Vg *suavis*, cf 34:9] and forgiving...' **8—10.** 'There is none like thee among the **m** gods, o *Adonai*...' and therefore **9** all nations shall come and adore thee—the theme of Israel's mission to all men, as in 22:28 and especially Ps 87, here stated with particular clarity; part of the heavenly song in Apoc 15:4 is from this verse. **11.** 'Guide me, o Lord (Yahweh) in thy way: let me walk in thy friendship: unite my heart to fear thy name': the phrase 'unite (PB knit) my heart' is only found here: i. = 'make my heart one

thing': Jer PB AV RV JA BJ RSV; ii. [repointing] 'let my **39** heart rejoice': LXX/V RPB; iii. [emending?] 'direct my heart': NP. **12.** 'I thank thee [see on 67:4]...**13**... for thou hast delivered my soul...**14**... Arrogant men have risen against me': cf on 54:5, where this passage helps with the text. **15—17.** 'But thou, o *Adonai*, art a God compassionate...': almost verbatim from Ex 34:6. **17.** 'Show me a sign of thy favour [RSV well], so that those who hate me may see and be put to shame': BJ note: 'Les imprécations sont ici réduites au minimum'.

87 Sion, the City of God, where all shall be 39 **Citizens**—This is one of the most remarkable of the Psalms, with an astonishing expression of the theme of Israel's vocation to bring all men to God in Sion. The nations shall come, in the messianic age, to be counted by God as 'born citizens' of the City of God: see esp. v 4. The rhythm is irregular, spontaneous and quick, with recurrent phrases. Though the theme is plain, there are considerable textual difficulties. **Title:** Qorah (Collection II): there have already been two Qorahite songs of Sion, 48 and 84, but this is the greatest of them all.

1—2. 'On the holy mount stands the city he founded: **2** the Lord loves the gates of Sion more than all the dwelling-places of Jacob' (RSV well): lit. 'His (God's) founded (city) (is) upon the holy mountains: the LORD loves...' but others (with LXX/V) take as 'foundations' (in the ground), thus RPB 'loves the foundations he has laid'. **3.** 'He (God) is speaking [repointed] glorious (things [fem. pl.]) of thee, o City of God': introducing the oracle that follows after 'Selah': so WV BJ, but most with MT 'glorious (things) are (?) spoken of thee': though grammatically indefensible. The phrase *Civitas Dei* **b** comes from here and Ps 46:5. **4. God's oracle:** 'I will reckon Rahab and Babel as my friends [lit. 'who know me']': 'Rahab' (perhaps = 'proud') is usually taken as a nickname for Egypt, like 'La Superba' for Genoa: cf Is 30:7 'And Egypt,...I have called her Rahab' (though this text has its difficulties); but it is also apparently the name of a mythical sea-monster in Jb 9:13; 26:12; Is 51:9 and probably Ps 89:11. In any case Egypt provides the natural balance for Babylon. There is no connexion with Rahab, the lady of Jericho in Jos 2 and 6, who is spelt differently in Heb. After Egypt and Babylon, 'behold Philistia and Tyre with Cush [= Ethiopia]: this [= each] one was born here (in Sion)', i.e. counts as a born citizen with the fullest rights, more than an adopted or 'naturalized' citizen. Here we have the most extended statement, even to hyperbole, of the theme that all nations (not excluding our oldest enemies) shall become full citizens of Sion, the ideal City of God. For us Christians, the application of this theme to the universal mission of the Church is obvious. In the Pss the theme appears with progressive clarity in 18:44; 68:32; 22:28; 86:9 to here, and in 102:23, and in the prophets especially in Mi 4:1—8 and Is 2:2—4. **5.** 'And to Sion (it) shall be said: Each and each (of these **c** peoples) was born in her, and he, the Most High, shall establish her': 'each... each' is in Heb. idiom 'man... man' which explains the LXX and Vg repetitions of the word 'man'. But LXX[B] is notably different, and many follow this, emending variously the Heb. to introduce the word *'ēm* 'mother': i. Hebrew as above: so AV RV NP RSV, cf PB; ii. LXX[B]: 'Mother (*mētēr*) Sion says, "A man!" And a man was born in her'; iii. otherwise: 'A man says, "Mother Sion!" And a man...': so Brenton's LXX; iv. LXX[A] corrected: 'Is it not to (*mē tē*) Sion (that) one says, "A man!" And a man was born in her': so also Vg; v. 'And to Sion each one says,

98c "Mother!" For each one was born in her': BJ; vi. 'And Sion shall be called Mother, for each one was born in her': RPB. It would seem, however, slightly embarrassing to derive so startling a figure, of Sion as Mother, from an emendation based upon LXX^B, especially with the evidence of a divergent Greek reading. Parallels for a city as 'Mother' are in a woman's passing remark to Joab in 2 Sm 20:19, and in extended parables in Ezek 16:3, 45, and Hos 2.4, 7; 4:5, and a brief metaphor in Is 50:1, 1, but these hardly warrant the interpretation here, though the context of birth has its conviction. BJ and **d** Grail even caption this Ps as 'Sion, the Mother'! **6.** 'The Lord shall count [= mark off] as he writes up (the register of) the peoples (of the world): This one (placing a mark against each name) was born there (in Sion). Selah.' One of the most pleasantly fanciful pictures in the Psalter. **7.** 'And singing and dancing alike all of them [emended] (shall say), "My true home [lit. 'whole home'] (is) in thee" [emended with LXX/V and cf CV]': an uncertain passage: i. Heb. text: 'And singers like dancers (shall say), "All my springs [= wellsprings of joy etc] (are) in thee"': so Jer PB AV ('trumpeters' for 'dancers'), RV NP RSV; ii. = 'Whether they sing or dance, all my thoughts are in thee': JA; iii. LXX/V read. 'singers' as 'princes' and place after 'people' in the preceding verse, and they read 'springs' as 'abode', so the verse reads: 'As of merrymakers [i.e. dancers] all of them, (their) home is in thee': iv. [emending the unlikely 'springs' to 'singing'] 'And singing and dancing, all of them sing to thee': cf RPB (see DWT); v. [taking 'prices' and 'abode' as LXX] 'And princes (of all the peoples) among the dancers, all of them (find) their home in thee': BJ. In spite of the difficulties, this is a most delightful psalm.

e 88 Utter Sadness—This has been called 'the saddest psalm in the whole Psalter' (Kirkpatrick). It is the cry, full of pathos, of one who feels abandoned by God and by friends. In the other similar Pss such as 6, 22A, 31B, 38, there is always a ray of hope. But not here: the man is 'imprisoned' by his own misery (v 9) and cannot escape. Even death is utterly hopeless. All ends in loneliness and darkness. It is indeed the dark night of the soul, and as such has a real place in the Psalter, for this is part of human experience. For Mowinckel's view see on Ps 6. In the **Title**, after 'Qorah' are musical directions (cf Ps 53), and then an association with 'Heman the Ezrahite', who together with 'Ethan the Ezrahite' (title of next Ps) was among the four sages whose wisdom was surpassed by that of Solomon in 1 (3) Kgs 5:11 [LXX/V and English 4:31] (cf genealogy in 1 Chr 2:6), and about whom nothing more is known. The titles may be no more than ascriptions to classical sages.

2–3. 'Lord God of my salvation, by day I have cried, in the night before thee' (cf 22:3): or emending slightly: 'LORD, my God, I shouted by day, I cried..., **4–6** 'My soul is filled with sadness, my life is near to Sheol **f** [= death], **5**... like a man without help **6** free among the dead': this last is a puzzling phrase, accepted literally by LXX/V and Jer: in other contexts this word 'free' is always of slaves, once even in Jb 3:19 of a slave being free once he reaches Sheol, but 'free at least in Sheol' can hardly be the meaning here: i. = cast off, adrift, forsaken: RV RSV [but hardly within the meaning of word]; ii. = set apart, cut off from human company: JA BJ [cf cognate word for isolation of a leper in 2 (4) Kgs 15:5]; iii. [emended] 'I am become like to the dead': RPB (see DWT) [though good for context, the emendation is drastic]; iv. = 'my resting-place is among the dead': NP [connecting with a very doubtful word in Ezek 27:20]. 'Like the wounded [= slain] lying in the grave,

whom thou dost remember no more': the frequent idea of **398f** the finality of death, see on 6:6. **9.** 'Thou hast put my **g** acquaintances far from me, and hast made me an abomination to them': the deep distress of finding that my friends cannot bear to share my pain, cf 31:12; 38:12. 'I am imprisoned (in my misery) and I cannot get out.' **10.** I am almost blind with sorrow... I spread out my hands to thee. **11–13.** The hopelessness of the dead: there are no miracles for them, or 'shall the shades rise up to praise thee? (Of course not)'. [LXX/V, repointing, give a different turn: 'Shall the doctors raise them up to praise thee? (Of course not)'.] **12.** 'Is thy mercy spoken of in the grave... **13**... in the land of oblivion?': the last phrase is specially expressive of the attitude to Sheol. **16.** 'I have been suffering and (close to) dying from boyhood, I have borne thy terrors, I am numb': the last word is emended, the Heb. word being unknown elsewhere (KB suggests an Arabic root 'embarrassed'), and most translations convey some troubled state. **19.** 'Thou hast put far from me my loving ones and friends: my (only) companions (are) darkness': i. so NP BJ well, expressing the final loneliness and darkness; ii. = 'my companions (are in) darkness': RSV, cf AV RV; iii. [emend.] '... hast withdrawn my companions (from my sight)': Jer PB RPB; iv. [emend.] '(put far)... companions because of (my) misery': LXX/V.

89 A Poem of Hope and Disappointment—This Ps **h** is very logically constructed, with 'Selah' marking divisions after vv 5, 38, 46. Vv 2–5 outline the theme: 6–19 God's all embracing goodness, but also 20–38 his special love for Israel and his promises to David, the Anointed. But their fulfilment was conditional on Israel's faithfulness, and somehow 39–46 the promises have broken down and David is defeated on all sides. Finally 47–52 comes the question, How long will this continue? Perhaps it is best understood in terms of general human experience of frustration and disappointment, although it may have had its origin in some particular occasion of military defeat, and (Mowinckel, I, 225) become a 'cultic' prayer for similar occasions. **Title:** 'Ethan the Ezrahite', see on the title of Ps 88 with 'Heman': the two names are linked in the Book of Kings, and since 88 is labelled among the Qorahite Pss it is legitimate to suppose 89 to be in fact part of that collection too.

2–5. The preface: 'The mercies of the Lord I will sing for ever... **3** Thy love is built up [a unique usage]... thy friendship as firm as the sky': the first theme. **4.** The second theme (vv 20–38): God's covenant with David... **5.** 'I built up [same figure] thy throne'. **The First Theme: 6–9** The heavens praise thee... and **i** the 'congregation of the holy ones', i.e. either the liturgy on earth reflecting the praise of heaven, or, the heavenly assembly (cf v 8); **7** 'For who can compare with the LORD... among the sons of the gods?': variously interpreted: i. = 'the gods': PB RPB; ii. = 'sons of God' (LXX/V), or '... of gods' (BJ) = heavenly beings: RSV; iii. = 'sons of the mighty': AV RV [see on 8:6 and 82:1]. **8.** God is feared in 'the council of the holy ones', cf on v 6 above. **10–14.** Thou art ruler of the sea... **11** crushing Rahab [in this context apparently the sea monster, see on 87:4: LXX/V here 'the proud']... **12.** Thine are heaven and earth... **13** north and south [lit. 'right hand', which LXX/V read as 'sea']... Tabor and Hermon [the great mountains of the land]... **15–19.** 'Justice and (true) judgement are the foundation of thy throne, love and friendship [the two words, see on 5:8] go before thee [a rare picture, cf 85:14]'. **16.** Blessed are the people who know how to praise thee,

398i 17 'their horn is lifted up' [= are prosperous, see on 75:5], 19 'for our defence [lit. shield] (belongs) to the LORD, our king to the Holy One of Israel', i.e. our defence and leadership are in the Lord's hands (cf 84:10): i. so RV NP BJ RSV; ii. = 'The Lord is our shield, the Holy One . . . is our king': PB AV RPB; iii. = 'our help is of the Lord, of the Holy one . . . , our king': LXX/V. **The j Second Theme: 20.** 'Of old thou didst speak in a vision to thy faithful [to Nathan, 2 Sm 7:4–16, told as a 'vision' to David, 7:17] (with the promises that follow): I have set help ('*ēzer*) upon a mighty man, I have exalted one chosen (*bāḥûr*) from the people': i. so LXX/V PB AV RV [but 'I have set help' = 'I have helped' is not normal usage]; ii. [emend to *nēzer* cf v 40] 'I have set a crown . . .': NP BJ RSV RPB; iii. [another meaning of '*ēzer*] 'I have placed a youth above a mighty man [i.e. David above Saul], I have raised up a young man [*bāḥûr*] out of the people': cf BJn and CV; for this word 'youth' cf 1 Chr 12:1 and Ugaritic *ghzr* in the Legend of Aqhat (DOTT 125, 127n); 'young man' for *bāḥûr* is also better in this context. The best solution. **21–30.** David I anointed . . . **27** he shall call me 'Father': one of the rare OT references to God as 'Father'. **28.** I will make him . . . 'most high' ('*elyôn*, only here of a man) over the kings of the earth . . . **30** . . . 'and his throne as the days of heaven' = for ever: phrase only here and Dt 11:21 (also in a promise), but used of Pharaoh in the Aram. papyrus, the Saqqara Letter (DOTT 251, 253n). **31–33.** This is my promise to David, but if his children forsake my teaching (*tôrāh*), **33** I will punish them. **34–38.** 'Yet my love I will not break [or, emend to 'remove'] . . . ' **37.** 'His (David's) throne (shall be) like the sun . . . **38** like the moon for ever . . . and a faithful witness in the sky. Selah': the phrase 'a faithful witness in the sky' is not quite plain: i. = the moon stands witness as long as it endures, i.e. for ever; ii. = God himself in heaven is the witness; iii. [emending] 'As long as the sky endures': WV RSV RPB **k** (see Kittel, DWT). **The Third Theme: 39–46.** But nevertheless thou hast rejected thine Anointed . . . **40** renounced thy covenant . . . profaned his crown [cf on v 20] . . . **44** 'turned back [? blunted] the edge (*sûr*) of his sword': taking *sûr* from a root 'sharp', so most; but *sûr* usually = rock, or strength, so LXX/V Jer 'the strength of his sword', and BJ, emending, '. . . broken his sword on a rock'. **45.** 'thou hast removed the sceptre of his glory [emended]': i. so BJ RPB; cf.RSV ' . . . sceptre from his hand [emended]'; ii. Heb. 'removed (him) from his cleanness': so LXX/V Jer (meaning?); iii. = 'removed his glory [lit. brightness, cleanness]': PB AV RV NP [but very doubtfully possible]. **46.** 'Thou hast shortened the days of his youth, thou hast covered him with shame [RPB, for context, adopts the emendation 'grey hair']. **l** Selah.' **The Last Theme: 47–52.** 'How long . . . ? **48.** Remember (as for) me, what duration is' = 'how short human life is': the wording is awkward (though the sense is clear) and RSV emends to [lit.] 'Remember, Lord, what duration is', while RPB to [lit.] 'Remember how I am ceasing'. **51.** Remember our humiliations, 'how I (in the person of Israel) bear in my bosom the [emended] insults of many nations [for awkward Heb. " . . . in my bosom all many nations"]': so, emending as above, Jer PB RSV RPB, and NP BJ similarly; **52** Thy enemies 'insult the footsteps of thine Anointed'. **53.** A short doxology for the end of Book III, cf ends of 41, 72, 106.

BOOK IV

399a 90 A Reflection upon the Transience of Life—A poem whose measured dignity, combined perhaps with

the reference to sturdy old age, earned for it an association **399** with none less than Moses, and it is the only Ps bearing his name. Title: 'A Prayer of Moses, the man of God'. Few Pss in this book have titles, and the only reference to a 'Collection' is to David in Pss 101, 103.

1–6. 'Lord (*Adonai*) thou hast been a home for us **b** in every generation', i.e. thou alone art permanent, **4** for to thee 'a thousand years are but as yesterday . . . [cf 2 Pt 3:8]. **5.** Thou dost sweep them (the years, or mankind) away: they are like sleep [or, a dream] (which vanishes) in the morning; [here a new simile] as grass passes away . . .': the various versions divide this section differently, but the picture of transient human life is carried by all. **8.** 'Thou hast placed our sins before thee, our hidden (sins) [rather than the magnificent 'our world' of LXX/V, repointing] in the light of thy countenance; **9** all our days are turning (to their end) in thy wrath, we end our years like a whisper (whose sound fades quickly)': this last word 'whisper' (*hegeh*) comes from a root meaning 'to growl, mutter', hence 'to muse or meditate, as if talking to oneself', and is used, in various forms, of thunder, a lion, a dove, a mourner, a contemplative (Ps 19:15; 63:7; 71:24; 77:13; 143:5), a student (Ps 1:2; 37:30), a conspirator (Ps 2:1; 38:13), and a wizard. Hence the various translations here: i. **c** 'a sigh' (as fleeting): RVm NP BJ RSV RPB; ii. 'a tale that is told' (meditation that finishes?): PB AV RV; iii. LXX/V have a curious reading: 'our years have meditated [Brenton's LXX 'have spun out their tale'] like a spider'—Knox's Vulgate beautifully 'the work of a lifetime is only gossamer'. This interesting text renders *hegeh* twice: 1. 'meditate', 2. 'spider (from the Aram. *gᵉwāgay*). **10.** 'The days of our years, in them are seventy years . . . eighty years, and the more of them [emended with LXX/V] labour and sorrow . . .': for Heb. 'the pride (?) of them is . . .': RV cf PB AV (strength). 'For it passes quickly and we fly away': a doubtful passage, but so most (or similarly) since Jerome; LXX/V are quite different. **11.** 'Who knows the strength of thy anger? **12.** To count our days, so teach us [LXX/V is confused], that we may bring in a heart of wisdom': a very unusual and rather doubtful phrase. **13–15.** 'Return, o Lord . . . have pity . . . **14.** Give us mercy in the morning [cf. 143:8], and we shall rejoice all our days (in the evening of life) . . . **17.** May the loveliness of the Lord our God [see on 27:4 and 133:1] be upon us, and strengthen the work of our hands . . .': this whole piece was recited at the Office of *Pretiosa*, after Prime in the monastic office, as a blessing on the day's wok.

91 'Hid with the Highest thy Dwelling'—This **d** favourite psalm, frequently used at Compline, recounts the favours received by him who places himself with confidence under God's protection. The metre is fairly regular, the language and imagery are graceful, and the text for the most part is sound. Vv 1–13 are addressed (see on 1–3) to the faithful man, and vv 14–16 are the Lord's response to his faithfulness. There is no title.

1–3. 'Dwelling hidden by [lit. 'in the hidden place **e** of'] the Most High ('*elyôn*), thou shalt [emended] stay (as a guest) under the shadow of the Almighty [the traditional rendering of the ancient divine title *Šaddai*, in Pss only here and 68:15], **2** Saying [repointed] to the Lord "My refuge (art thou) . . . in whom I trust". **3.** For he will deliver thee . . .'. The changes of person in the Heb. ['Dwelling he shall stay . . . I say . . .'] are uneasy, and the uncertainty is reflected in LXX and Vg; it is easiest to emend or repoint as above, and then, like the rest of the Ps to v 13 inclusive, it is all addressed to the faithful man as 'thou'. Various versions

399e do this variously. **3—13.** A series of pictures showing how the man who trusts God is relieved of all fear, protected from 'the snare of the fowler', from 'the plague of destruction' [LXX/V read *debher* 'plague' as *dābhār* 'word': 'from the destructive word'], **4** under God's 'wings', with 'his friendship [see on 5:8] a shield and protection' [for 'friendship' RPB repoints 'forearm', the word for 'cubit', and cf Ugaritic for 'forearm', see Dahood, Bib 44 (1963), 295; and BJ transfers to after v 7, for the sake of metrical regularity]; **5** from (unseen) terror at night, from arrows (one can see) by day, **6** from 'a plague that walks in the darkness' [LXX/V again read *dābhār* 'word', which can also mean 'thing, matter discussed', whence the pleasant LXX *pragma*, Vg *negotium*, Douay 'business that walketh in the dark'], and from the 'scourge that destroys at noonday'. Again it seems mainly a contrast between darkness and daylight, but LXX/V for 'destroys' (*yāsûdh*) read *šēdh* (see on 106:37 'demon', whence Douay's well-known 'noonday devil', an expressive phrase in a hot climate, but unhappily apparently only a misreading of the text.

f 7. 'A thousand (presumably plagues, as above; or perhaps enemies, as next v) shall fall beside thee ...' **8.** Look and see the recompense of the wicked (who do not trust thee): cf Rm 6:23 'the wages of sin'; **9** 'But thou, o LORD, art my refuge ...' [cf v 2]: the sudden change to the man's exclamation is awkward, so that slight emendations have been proposed. i. 'But thou hast said, 'The Lord is my refuge': BJ RPB (the best way); ii. 'But thou—the Lord is thy refuge': WV; iii. 'But thou hast set the Lord as thy refuge': RSV. **10.** '(Therefore) no evil shall befall thee ... **11** for he shall summon his angels ... **12** on their hands they shall bear thee up, lest thou dash thy foot against a stone [quoted Mt 4:6, Lk 4:10—11]'. **13.** The final picture is of the man's defence against poisonous snakes: the lions and dragon of the older versions are now all thought to be various snakes: asp (as LXX/V), adder, viper (cf Aram. word, but 'young lion' is similar), and (more generically) serpent: so RPB (see DWT). **14—16.** The Lord speaks: The man 'cleaves to me in love' [so RSV well], so I will give him freedom, protection—for he has 'known my name', i.e. called on me by name, cf on 23:3.

g 92 A Song of Praise and Thanksgiving—This quiet and personal Ps is of regular construction in 4 plain stanzas. The note of the fate of enemies makes the briefest appearance in v 12. Title includes 'for the Sabbath Day' (only here), and it is said in the synagogue on Sabbath mornings.

2—5. 'It is good to give thanks [or, praise: see on 67:4] to the Lord ... **3** declare in the morning thy love, and thy faithfulness night after night' [lit. 'in the nights', cf 134:1]. **4** enumerates three (apparently stringed) instruments, uncertainly and variously identified. **6—10.** 'How great are thy works ... **7** the brutish [derived from 'animal', cf 73:22] ... the fool [see on 14:1] do not understand this, **11** 'thou hast raised up my horn [see **h** on 75:5] like (that of) wild oxen [rather than unicorns: LXX/V PB AV], and I am anointed with fresh oil': the word 'anointed' is uncertain: i. Lit., verb *bālal* of sacrificial mixing of flour with oil, e.g. Nm 7:13, hence? = 'I am anointed': PB AV RV [very doubtful]; ii. [same verb, emended] 'Thou hast anointed me': Targum Syr. BJ RSV RPB [but again the usage is uncertain]; iii. [from root *bālāh*] 'my wasting away [= my old age] (is soothed with) fresh oil': Jer—LXX/V include 'mercy'. For the pleasantness of oil, see on 23:5 and 133:2. **12.** 'My eye looks (down) upon my enemies ...': the translations usually add a note of vengeance or triumph here that is

implied, though not said, in the text. **13—16.** The just **399h** man is likened to a palm tree ... a cedar ... **14** planted in God's house ... : these verses are frequently used in the office of a Confessor.

93 The King of the World—God's kingship is as **i** immoveable and inexorable as the world itself and his control of it, and the holiness of his Temple should be equally immoveable. This Ps begins a cycle of Psalms of the 'Kingship of Yahweh' (95—100), and has much affinity with Ps 47. For Mowinckel's view see below on v 2. No title.

1—2. 'The LORD is King, robed in majesty ... girt with strength ...': 'Yahweh is King', the phrase is in 47:9, here, 96:10; 97:1; 99:1, and cf 146:10. The translation 'Yahweh has become king' is insisted upon by Mowinckel (I, 107; II, 222) and others, as referring to an instant of 'cultic' enthronement, while others again (with e.g. Kraus) maintain that 'Yahweh is king' must be taken with what follows, 'thy throne from of old ...' and so must signify 'is (and always has been) king'. Cf similar discussion on 47:9. The first stanza is composed of short quick lines in couplets (2 + 2), as at the opening of Pss 47 and 97. **3—5.** The rhythm lengthens into longer triplets (3 + 3 + 3), describing the powers of nature, and **4** above them all is God on high, **5** whose 'testimonies' [= decrees] are 'dependable'.

94 God's Justice shall prevail—A meditation on **j** present injustice, which has found a place among a series of Pss in praise of Yahweh as king. A didactic note enters at vv 8—11. No title. **1—7.** 'God of vengeance ... shine forth, **2** arise, o judge of the earth, render to the proud their deserts' ... Among their crimes is killing **5** the widow and the homeless (*gēr*) [see on 146:9], **8—11** 'Understand, o brutish ... o fools [see on 92:7] ...' **9.** The creator hears and sees, **10** chastises the nations, 'teaches mankind (*adam*) ...'—an exceptional notion, **11** 'he knows the thoughts of mankind ...' [quoted 1 Cor 3:20]. **12—15.** But on the contrary, 'blessed is he whom thou chastisest ... and teachest ...' **14.** God will not forsake his people [cf Rm 11:1], **15** 'for judgement shall (eventually) return to justice', i.e. judgement shall be governed by true justice [but RSV: '... return to the righteous']. **16—19.** 'Who will stand up for me (as in a court of law) against the evildoers? ... **20—21.** 'Shall the throne of destructions [= the unjust tribunals], which frames mischief by statute [cf RSV well], have any part with thee? **22—23.** But for me, 'the LORD has been ... my rock of hope'.

95 Venite Exsultemus Domino: the Invitatory—An **k** invitation to praise, used almost every day at the beginning of the office of Matins (as also in the Book of Common Prayer). The Breviary at the Invitatory uses a pre-Vulgate text, usually known as the 'Roman Psalter'. The 'kingship cycle' (93, 95—100) is resumed here ('king' in v 3). No title.

1—5. 'O come, let us sing to the Lord ... acclaim our Rock of salvation [on invoking God as 'Rock' see on 28:1, where as here and 144:1 LXX/V translate as 'God'; cf also on 18:3], **2** let us come to meet his face [= presence] with thanksgiving [or, praise, see on 67:4], **3** for the Lord is a great God, a great King above all gods': LXX[B] and Roman Psalter here add 'For the Lord will not reject his people'. **6.** 'O come, let us prostrate ... bow down ... kneel before the Lord our maker': various physical attitudes of worship. The first is usually translated 'adore' (*Venite adoremus*), since almost always it is used of bowing (usually to the ground) in honourable greeting to persons, or to God. Prostration is common; bowing (properly 'bending' used also of the knees) is

399k occasionally used of worship, in the Pss 22:30; 72:9 and here; 'kneeling' as an attitude of prayer only here and 2 Chr 6:13 (of Solomon), but 5 other times 'bending the knees' in prayer. **7—9.** 'For he is our God, and we are the people of his pasture, and the flock of his hand': a phrase without parallel, presumably = 'led by his strong hand'; RPB, however, rearranges 'his people and the flock of his pasture', see Kittel and DWT. 'Today if you **l** will hear his voice. **8.** Harden not your hearts . . .': the difficulty is whether to link 'harden not . . .' with the preceding, or with God's words 'Your fathers tested me . . .' of v 9: i. [with v 7] 'If you will hear his voice, harden not . . .': LXX/V PB AV RVm; ii. [rearranged] 'If you will hear his voice, you will know [inserted] his power [lit hand, transferred]. "Harden not . . .": RPB; iii. [with v 9] 'If (only) you would hear his voice! Harden not . . .': RV RSV; iv. [linked] 'If (only) you would hear his voice (saying), "Harden not . . .": NP BJ: probably the most satisfactory solution. '. . . as at Meribah . . . Massah in the wilderness': LXX/Roman Ps/V PB AV give the meaning of these two place names 'contention' (Roman 'exacerbation') and 'temptation, or, testing', names given to the place of the revolt, Ex 17:7, see on Ps 81:8 and cf 106:32. **10.** For forty years (in the desert) I loathed [Roman Ps: 'was close to'] (that) generation . . . **11** to whom I swore . . . , 'They shall not [Heb. idiom lit. 'if they shall'] enter into my resting-place [= the land where I make my abode]'. Vv 7b—11 are quoted in full in Hb 3:7b—11 (and phrases in 3:15, 18; 4:1, 3, 5). The text is used as an exhortation to holding to our hope and a warning against falling into disbelief.

m **96 A Hymn of Joy**—The kingship of Yahweh should be recognized by all peoples. This short and 'spirited psalm' (Kirkpatrick) is similar to 98, has echos in 29 and 93, and is almost entirely reproduced in 1 Chr 16:23—33 at the return of the ark under David. Mowinckel (I, 142ff) calls Pss 96—99 'Epiphany Psalms' for the Enthronement Festival. No title in Heb.: in LXX/V 'When the House was being built after the Captivity'.

1—3. 'Sing to the Lord a new song: sing to the Lord all the earth . . . **4—6** For the Lord is great . . . above all gods, **6** honour and glory (shall be) before him, strength and beauty in his sanctuary [1 Chr 16:27 his place]': 'strength and beauty' may mean the praise due to him for these, cf 8:3; 29:1; 68:35, or may be a reference to the ark, as plainly in 78:61, and cf 'the ark of thy strength' in 132:8. On the connexion between 'strength' and the ark, see G. Henton Davies in *Promise and Fulfilment* (Essays presented to S. H. Hooke), 1963. **7—9.** 'Give [RSV ascribe] to the Lord . . . glory and strength [see above] . . . **9** bow before the Lord in adornment of holiness [= 'sacred apparel', or other senses as in 29:2, see note there]. **10.** Say among the nations, "The Lord is king" [see on 93:2] . . .' **11—13.** Let all nature rejoice . . .

n **97 Joy before the King of the World**—Another short hymn in the 'kingship cycle'. The quick rhythm of the opening lines is noticeable as in the similar Pss 47 and 93. No title in Heb., but LXX, strangely, 'For David, when his land is established(?)', or, Vg '. . . restored'.

1—3. 'The Lord is king [see on 93:1—2], let the earth rejoice . . .'; **2** the divine majesty is pictured in terms of the theophany on Sinai (clouds and darkness Ex 20:21). **4.** 'His lightnings lit up the world' (as 77:19, cf Hab 3:11) . . . **7** 'All who serve idols shall be put to shame . . . all gods have bowed down to him': LXX/V have 'all his angels'—for meanings of *elohim*, other than God,

see on 8:6 and 82:1. Hb 1:6 quotes this passage ('angels') **399** from LXX. **8.** But Sion and her daughter(-cities) have heard thy judgements with joy . . . **10.** 'The Lord loves those who hate evil': so NP BJ RSV RPB emending from Heb. and LXX/V 'O lovers of the LORD, hate evil' . . . **11—22.** 'Light has dawned for the just . . .': so LXX/V (cf 112:4), followed by NP BJ RSV RPB, for the unlikely phrase in Heb. 'light has been sown', and so providing a fine line.

98 The World and Nature shall acclaim the King— o A short hymn similar to Ps 96. The only **title** is 'A Psalm'. **1—3.** 'Sing to the Lord a new song, for marvels he has done . . .' **2.** He has 'made known his salvation' . . . : here (and occasionally elsewhere) RSV and RPB have 'victory'. **4—6.** 'Acclaim the Lord . . .': **6.** Among musical instruments appear the trumpets (of metal) and the shofar (of horn), see on 81:4 for its ritual use. **7—9.** The acclaim of nature, the world (PB 'the round world'), its people, **8** the rivers shall 'clap their hands', a gesture of joy, not applause, cf similar phrase in Ps 47:2.

99 The Lord is King and he is holy—Another short **p** hymn in the series, but introducing the note of Sion. No title. **1—4.** 'The Lord is king [see on 93:1—2], the peoples shall tremble [with fear, not with rage as LXX/V, cf 4:5], he sits (enthroned) on the cherubim [probably in cosmic sense as 18:11, but perhaps, in view of Sion following, in the sense of the figures over the ark in the Temple as in 80:2: see notes] . . . **2.** The Lord is great in Sion . . . above all the peoples: **3** they shall praise thy name, great and awe-inspiring, for holy is it (the name) [or, 'is he' (God), with most since RV]. **5.** 'Exalt the Lord our God, and bow before his footstool (= Sion), (for) holy is he (God) [or, 'is it' (Sion), so LXX/V]. **6.** 'Moses, and Aaron among his priests [probably best thus punctuated: Moses was not a priest], and Samuel among those who call on his name . . . were calling unto the Lord and thou didst answer them . . . **9.** Exalt the Lord . . . bow to his holy mountain (Sion)'.

100 Jubilate Deo—A favourite psalm, the last of this **q** series (though not calling God 'king'), frequently used at Lauds in the Divine Office, and on weekdays in the synagogue. The famous metrical version of Sternhold and Hopkins (1560) 'All people that on earth do dwell . . .' has remained a favourite hymn, with its tune known as the 'Old Hundredth' since it belonged to this Ps in that edition. The ideas of serving the Lord, coming before him, and entering his gates; with gladness, singing and thanksgiving respectively, underline the basic notions of worship. It is classed by Gunkel as a true hymn (§ 2). The metre is pleasant. **Title:** 'A psalm for praise [or, thanksgiving: see on 67:4]'.

1—2. 'Acclaim the Lord [cf 98:4], all the earth, **2** serve the LORD with gladness, come before him with singing': the notion of 'serving' God, i.e. worshipping him, is not common in the Pss: only here and 2:11 as a call; and 22:31; 72:11; 102:23, referring to others who shall serve him. **3.** 'Know that he made us, and we are his . . .', or, 'and not we ourselves . . .': there are two traditions here: i. 'We are his . . .': the Rabbinic tradition shown in the Massoretic pointing and note (the Qre): so Targum Jer AVm RV JA NP BJ RSV RPB; ii. 'Not we ourselves': the consonantal text (the Ktib): so LXX/V PB AV RVm RSVm. **4.** 'Enter his gates with thanksgiving . . . **5** for his love is for ever . . .'

101 The Intentions of the Just Man—A curious **400** Ps that stands alone, being a meditation before God on the qualifications of the Just Man, within the last verse, perhaps the responsibilities of the Just Ruler.

00a The ascription to David, the ideal ruler, doubtless arises from this last v. For Mowinckel this is a particularly important Ps, as being part of a Coronation Festival, when with this Ps the king presents his 'charter' (I, 67); its counterpart being the people's intercession for him in Ps 72. But for Tournay the Ps is mainly didactic (BJ). The metre is regular throughout. **Title**: 'For David', see above; perhaps representing a small collection 'David Collection III' here (101–103) in Book IV.

1. 'I will sing of love (*ḥesedh*) and (true) judgement . . .': *ḥesedh* (see also on 5:8) connotes a love that is fulfilled in loving action, of which 'mercy' of the old versions from LXX is only an aspect without the breadth of meaning; RSV here exceptionally has 'loyalty' which is hardly loving enough; CV 'kindness' is not warm enough; NP '*gratia*' is too vague; and even '*amour*' of BJ **b** perhaps not active enough. **2.** 'I will apply myself to (following) a way (of life that is) blameless. O when wilt thou come to me?': the last sentence is variously understood (current editions of Vg omit the query and link with the preceding): i. Is this an echo of the mysterious words of David in 2 Sm 6:9 when bringing back the ark: 'How will the ark of the LORD come to me?'; ii. The usage of God 'coming' to someone is rare: the phrase appears in Nm 22:9, 20 'And God came to Balaam' of prophetic experience; iii. Perhaps it is a cry for the fulfilment of God's promise in Ex 20:24 'I will come unto thee and I will bless thee'. **3.** I will not set before my eyes (any) wicked thing. **5.** The slanderer . . . the proud . . . I will not endure [LXX/V, repointing, 'I will not eat with him']. **6.** My eyes are [= my favour is] upon the trustworthy . . . he shall be my servant': the responsibility of the master or employer. **8.** Every morning I will eliminate (by just judgement) . . . from the City of the LORD [= ? Jerusalem] all workers of iniquity: it is this last verse that suggests to many that this is the meditation of a king.

c **102** This Ps presents great problems, especially in the complete changes of thought and manner, so that it is most likely that either it represents three psalms put together, or at least that the central section vv 13–23 is a distinct fragment intruded into a single penitential psalm vv 2–12 continued in 13–28 or 29. We are taking them here as 102A, B and C, with the suggestion that A and C are one composition with B intruded.

d **102 A** (2–12) **A Penitential Psalm**—A true penitential, being a personal lament in distress with much affinity with 6, 38, 88, but with the briefest reference to persecution (in v 9). This piece 102A represents an attitude without hope, like 88, and taken alone would rival that Ps in unrelieved gloom; but if 102C is its proper conclusion, the ray of hope which characterizes the other penitentials is found here too. This (the whole Ps of course) is counted as the 5th Penitential Psalm (see on Ps 6). **Title**: 'A Prayer of one suffering [or, 'of a "poor" man'—see on 9:13] . . .'

e **2–3.** 'Lord, hear my prayer, and let my cry come unto thee': a verse frequently used in the Divine Office. **4–6.** 'My days are consumed like smoke, my bones are burnt as with fire. **5.** My heart is smitten and withered like grass, for I forgot to eat my bread [so most, but the Heb. grammar of 'forgot to' is questionable so the emendation is proposed 'I am wasted away for lack of eating . . .' (see Kittel, DWT), and adopted by RPB]'. **6.** 'My bones cleave to [i.e. can be seen under] my flesh (so wasted)'. **7.** 'I am become like a pelican [so most; RSV vulture; RPB owl] in the desert . . . like an owl [so most: LXX/V *nuktikorax* = ? night-heron (*nycticorax nycticorax*)] in the ruins': the exact creatures are uncertain, but the general picture is of desolation and loneliness. **8.** The **400e** 'solitary sparrow on the housetop' is another figure of loneliness. **9.** My enemies taunt me—the next two phrases are uncertain: i. 'They that are enraged [or, mad] against me': PB AV RV NP RPB; ii. 'They that deride me': RSV; iii. 'They that (previously) praised me': LXX/V BJ; Heb. lit. 'swore against [or, by] me': i. = 'have conspired against me': LXX/V PB AV RPB; ii. = 'use my name as a curse': RSV, cf RV NP BJ. **10–12.** My food is ashes, my drink is tears . . . **12.** 'my days incline like an (evening) shadow' [cf RSV well; i.e. pass quickly].

102 B (13–23) **A Song of Sion**—It is difficult to see **f** how this piece came to be annexed to the foregoing, unless by way of consolation. But it seems to be only a fragment of a song. Sion is seen in ruins (with a particularly touching picture in v 15), but only to rise as God's centre for all men in the new age (see on Ps 72 and esp. Ps 87). With this wide view of an ideal messianic future, it would cramp us to think only in terms of the historical exile of 587 and the subsequent rebuilding.

13–14. 'But thou, o Lord, dost remain [or, sit = enthroned] for ever . . .' **14** thou shalt have mercy on Sion . . . **15** for thy servants hold her stones dear, and have pity on her dust [RSV well]'. **16–18.** The nations and kings shall fear the Lord. **19–23.** 'This shall be written [or, recorded] for a later generation . . . **23** when the nations are gathered (in Sion) to serve the Lord'. The final verse (29) may belong to the end of this song and be read here (BJ places it after v 21).

102 C (24–28) **A Note of Hope in a Penitential g Mood**—It seems likely that this is the conclusion of 102A: the idea of shortened life is resumed, with the balancing thought of God's permanence; though this may be a separate fragment.

24–25. 'He has brought down my strength on the way, he has shortened my days; **25** I say, "O my God, take me not up at the half of my days" [cf Hezekiah's 'psalm' in Is 38:10]. **26–28.** The earth and sky shall perish, but thou shalt endure . . .: quoted in Hb 1:10–12. The last v **29** '(But) the children of thy servants shall remain . . .' may be the conclusion of 102B, but it also would form a conclusion to 102A–102C here.

103 A (1–18) **A Meditation on God's Love**—This Ps **h** is a real poem, with a grace of thought, imagery and diction, and marked especially in the stanza vv 13–14 by a tenderness that is outstanding. The metre is regular and the stanzaic structure is plain. Vv 19–22 are a hymn of praise that has become attached to the foregoing. **Title**: 'David', the last of this short 'David Collection III' (101–3).

1–5. 'Bless the Lord, o my soul . . . 3 He forgives thy iniquities . . . 5 satisfies (thee) with good things all thy life long [emended]': i. so RSV RPB (see DWT), cf RVm[1] NP BJ; ii. Heb. seems to mean 'thy adornment' (so Jer), = ? 'thy youthful grace', cf RVm[2] 'thy prime'; iii. [perhaps connecting with '*adh* = 'everlasting'?] 'thine old age': Targum JA; iv. LXX/V 'thy desire' (as object of 'satisfies')—reading? perhaps a guess? v. Ibn Ezra says = 'thy mouth' on the analogy of the equally difficult place in 32:9: so PB AV RV. 'Thy youth is **i** renewed as (that of) the eagle': cf Is 40:31 where Jerome's commentary says that it was commonly believed that eagles renewed their youth when moulting; the reference to Isaiah is more likely than a reference to the phoenix legend. **6–10.** The Lord is just . . . , **9** 'he will not contend with us (as in a court of law) for ever . . .' **11–12** 'For as the sky is high above the earth, so is his love strong upon [RPB emends to 'high above'] those who fear him; **12** and as far as the east is from the west, so far does he

400i remove our transgressions from us'. **13—14.** 'As a father has compassion on his children, so the Lord has compassion on those that fear him, **14** for he knows how we are made [lit our formation] . . .': the stanzas vv 11—14 are among the most tender in the Psalter.

j 103 B (19—22) A Hymn of Praise—The general tone, the thought and the metre (now lengthened, more regular and hymn-like) are different from the preceding, but this piece was probably attached here because of the idea of God's eternity in v 17 above, and the echo of v 1 in the last words here. Indeed it is possible that this section was deliberately added to the foregoing meditation, when it became included in the hymn-book, in order to give it a liturgical character. **19.** 'The Lord has established his throne in heaven, and his dominion [RSV well] rules over all'. **20—22.** A delightful call to all creation to 'bless the Lord'.

k 104 An Epic of Creation—A true hymn in fairly regular metre and stanzaic construction. Parallels are often quoted with the 14th cent. B.C. Egyptian Hymn to Aten. The imagery, esp. of the creation stanzas (vv 6—9) and of the occupations of daytime and nighttime (vv 19—23), is of particularly good poetic invention.

1—4. 'Bless the Lord, o my soul . . .' **2.** All creation is pictured as serving God: **3** 'He lays the beams of his upper room on the waters': the upper waters imagined, as in Gn 1:7, as above the 'firmament' or sky: God's abode is here; clouds are his chariot, 'he goes on the wings of the wind', cf 18:11; **4** the winds are his messengers, fire is his servant: quoted Hb 1:7. **5—9.** The psalmist now pictures vividly how things came into being at God's command: 'Thou didst set [repointing Heb. 'he set'] the earth on its foundations . . ., **6** didst cover it with the ocean as with a garment, (so that at first) the waters stood above (the level of) the mountains, **7** (until) at thy rebuke they (the waters) fled away . . . **8** (and now) the **l** mountains (seemed as if they) come up (revealed by the retreating waters), and the valleys (seemed as if they) go down, to the place thou didst appoint for them': the exact picture of v 8 is uncertain: i. 'The mountains come up . . .' (as above) is the most natural translation: so Vg Jer RVm WV RSV [but the subject in v 9 is again the waters]; ii. 'They (the waters) come up the mountains [= ? to the level of the mountains], go down the valleys . . .': PB AV RV BJ RPB with Targum 'go up from the ocean to the mountains' [but the grammar of 'come up' and 'go down' is embarrassing, as is the meaning after 'fled away']; iii. Ambiguous are LXX and NP ('mountains' and 'valleys' may be nom. or acc.) and translations of NP vary: Frey = i, Fides = ii; iv. To divide the subject is ingenious, if a little forced: 'As the mountains rose, they (the waters) went down the **m** valleys . . .': so CV. **9.** 'A boundary thou didst set (which) they (the waters) should not pass, nor return to cover the earth': this resumes the picture of v 7. **10—11.** The picture continues: 'Thou sendest forth springs in the valleys, between the mountains they (the waters—as in LXX/V) go; **11** they give drink to every beast of the field, (there) wild asses [but RPB 'zebras', see DWT and KB] quench their thirst. **12.** Upon them (the mountains) [or, by them (the streams)] the birds of the air dwell, between the foliage [uncertain word only here: LXX/V 'rocks', Jer 'groves', Targ 'branches'] they give 'song'. **13.** Thou waterest the mountains from above, **14** bringing up crops, 'bread from the earth', **15** wine, which 'rejoices the heart of man', oil which 'makes the face to shine'. **16.** The 'mighty trees' [lit. 'trees of Yahweh', see on 68:16] have sufficient . . . **17** where 'the birds make their nests, the stork [LXX/V 'heron'], her home (is) in the top of them

[emended, cf LXX/V]: i. so BJ RPB [reading 'head', as **40** often, = 'top', see Kittel, DWT]; ii. LXX/V [same reading] 'The heron's home is the leader of them': i.e. the tree with the heron's nest is the tallest of them; iii. Massoretic Text: 'The stork, cypresses [or 'firs', so most with Jerome] are her home': so PB AV RV NP RSV [but storks or herons do not nest in cypresses or firs]. **18.** Mountains are for the wild goats [LXX/V stags], **n** rocks for the badgers [so RSV RPB; LXX PB AV RV rabbits; NP BJ hyrax ('a small rabbit-like mammal, including Syrian rock-rabbit and S African rock-badger' OED)]. **19—23.** A pleasant description of night, when the animals come out, and day, when man goes to work. **24** '. . . The earth is full of thy creatures': so LXX RVm NP RSV RPB, cf Ugaritic (see DWT); Vg Jer PB AV RV 'riches' cf the usual sense of 'acquisition'. **25.** The sea . . . **26** with its ships, and 'Leviathan, whom thou madest to play with him': i. so BJ RPB: Leviathan, the mythical sea-monster is imagined as God's toy, cf Jb 40:29, and a rabbinic tradition about this is preserved in the Talmud, *Abodah Zarah* 3b (see DWT); ii. LXX/V see God as mocking Leviathan; iii. Others translate as '. . . to play in it (the sea)': so PB AV RV NP RSV. **27—30.** All these creatures depend upon **o** thee (cf 146: 15—16) . . . **29** '. . . Thou takest away their breath, they die . . . **30** thou sendest forth thy breath, they are created [or RPB 'become strong': another root, for context of preserving life rather than of creation], and thou renewest the face of the ground': the text is frequently adapted (taking 'breath' = 'spirit') for the liturgy of the Holy Ghost, RSV even writing 'Send forth thy Spirit' (with a capital). **31—35.** Glory to God . . . **35.** 'Let sinners be no more': a brief enough imprecation. 'Bless the Lord, o my soul', resuming v 1. *Hal*e*lū-yāh*: 'Praise ye Yah [= Yahweh]', the first of 23 occurrences of this phrase in the Psalter, always at the opening and/or the conclusion of a Ps (in 15 Pss—both opening and closing in 106, 135, 146—50).

105 An Epic of Israel—This epic has much affinity with **p** Ps 78, but not with its moralizing style. The text here is sounder and the order of events more coherent. The story here leads up to the Exodus and the desert, with a quick reference to Canaan in the last 9 vv. The next Ps begins with the Exodus, but has a different slant. 1 Chr 16:8—22 (when David brought back the ark) reproduces 105:1—15, as chanted by David and the sons of Asaph, together with 96:1—13 and part of Ps 106. There is no title.

1—6. 'Give thanks to the Lord' [see on 67:4 and 106:1] . . . **2.** Think upon [or, tell] his wonders . . . **4.** 'Seek the Lord and his strength [LXX/V repointing "become strong", RPB "find your refuge"] . . .' **7—11.** After this appeal to Israel, the story begins: 'He is Yahweh, our God' . . . **8.** He remembered his covenant **9** with Abraham, Isaac and **10** Israel, that he would give them Canaan, the 'lot' [lit 'rope', see on 16:6] of their inheritance. **12—15.** They were few, but **14** he protected them (saying), **15** 'Touch not my anointed ones . . . my prophets . . .': the only place where the patriarchs are called 'anointed', and only oncē was Abraham called a 'prophet' (Gn 20:7). **16—23.** Here follows the story of Joseph, when 'the staff of bread' was broken (Gn 37 and 39—50). **17.** He was sold as a slave, **18** 'they hurt his **q** feet with fetters, his neck went into an iron (collar)': i. so NP BJ RSV RPB ('they put . . .'): for *nepheš* (usually = 'soul') meaning 'neck' see on 69:2 and DWT there; ii. = 'his soul [= he] went into iron (chains)': Jer AV RV JA ('his person'—Ibn Ezra), and cf LXX; iii. The famous phrase 'The iron entered into his soul' of Vg and

00q PB, which has entered the language to convey embitterment, is unhappily a mistranslation, since 'soul' not 'iron' is the subject of the (feminine) Heb. verb. **22.** (The king also set Joseph) 'to instruct [emended with LXX/V and most: Heb. "blind"] his princes according to his will [lit "his soul": AV RV RSV "his pleasure"], and teach his senators wisdom [the pleasant rendering of PB: lit "his elders"]'. **23.** Eventually Israel came to 'the land of Ham' (Egypt), **25** and then Egypt turned against them, **26** but he sent Moses and Aaron **27** with signs: **28** darkness (the 9th plague) is mentioned first, 'and they did

r not rebel against his word': so the Massoretic text, and Jer AV RV, but the meaning is not clear: i. Ibn Ezra explains that after the darkness the Egyptians 'did not rebel' i.e. agreed to let them go (Ex 10:21–29) but afterwards refused; ii. Rashi explains that 'the plagues acted according to God's commands'; iii. Some suppose – 'Moses and Aaron did not refuse to perform their work'; iv. Vg 'And he (God) did not embitter his words': but this may be a partial correction of LXX; v. LXX 'And they (the Egyptians) were embittered at his words': no negative; vi. So, omitting negative: 'But they (the Egyptians) rebelled against his words': PB NP BJ RSV RPB. It should be noted that here, as in 78:8, 17, 40, 56; 106:7, 33, 43; 107:11, the LXX/V translate *marar*, for 'rebelled' from *mārāh*, but the meaning is not greatly changed. **29–36.** The plagues in Egypt, with many parallels in 78:42–51: see especially for 'firstfruits' in v 36 the note on 78:51. **37–41.** The Exodus and the desert. **42–45** he brought them out ... **44** to possess 'the labours of the peoples' = the fruits of other nations' toil. Hallelu-yah.

s **106 Another Epic of Israel: Israel the Unfaithful**— As Ps 105 relates God's care of Israel up to the Exodus, so Ps 106 depicts Israel's response, beginning from the Exodus, but showing the people's alternate faithfulness and faithlessness to the God who was ever ready with his mercy. Israel's frequent infidelity, together with her confidence in God's constancy, is a mirror of the human spirit, and this is surely the spiritual value of much historical material in the OT, here depicted in epic terms. Even when we are sinners, we know we can count on God's mercy. Thus the three epics, Pss 78, 105, 106, each look upon Israelite history from quite different angles, even though some phrases are common to all three, or all taken from the Pentateuch. The word 'Hallelu-yah' stands at the beginning and end of this Psalm.

t **1.** 'Give thanks to the Lord for his goodness [lit. 'for he is good']' is a phrase that recurs at the opening of Pss 107, 118 (also v 29), 136. The verb *hôdhū* (see also on 67:4) conveys our relationship of indebtedness to God—hence both praise and thanksgiving—and here with the following 'for his love is eternal' also the reason for our praise and thanksgiving, namely his love for us and his goodness to us. The Vg *confitemini* has almost acquired a special meaning in this context, both 'praise' and 'thanksgiving' being too narrow by themselves; NP *celebrate* hardly conveys the thanksgiving; 'give thanks' is also incomplete, but when *Hal^{e}lū-yāh* 'Praise ye Yah' is included, the idea is almost fulfilled. Vg *quoniam bonus* successfully suggests the reason for the *confitemini*, which is a little lost in the 'for he is good' of most translations. There is an echo of this verse on the lips of the Levites in the restored Temple in Ezr 3:11. **6– 11.** Now the main theme is tackled: Israel's sinfulness and God's mercy: **7** '... In Egypt ... they rebelled against the Most High [emended] at the Red Sea': Ex 14:11–12, the mutiny

against Moses: i. 'against the Most High' [reading **400t** '*elyôn*]: so WV NP BJ RSV RPB; ii. Massoretic Text ['*al yām*] = 'by the sea': PB AV RV, but with 'at the Red Sea' following, it is awkward; iii. LXX/V 'they became embittered [see on 105:28 last note] against those going up [= '*ōlîm*] at the Red Sea': this can hardly be the true reading, but it shows the text to be doubtful. **8.** But he saved them **12** And then they believed him ... **u** **13** but soon forgot ... **14** and 'had a wanton craving' [RSV well: phrase taken from Nm 11:4 of craving for food as in Egypt]... **16–18** Dathan and Abiram (Nm 16:1–35). **19–20.** The calf at Horeb [= Sinai] Ex 32:4) ... **20** 'and changed their glory into the image of an ox ...': loosely quoted from LXX in Rom 1:23. 'Their glory' is quoted as one of the *Tiqqune Sopherim*, or deliberate changes made by the rabbinic scribes to avoid irreverence. LXX^A showing perhaps the original text with 'his (God's) glory'. **21–33.** The further epic of the desert: **23** God thought to destroy them, but Moses 'stood in the breach' [the origin of this phrase?] and turned back his anger (Ex 32:32). **24.** But they despised 'the pleasant land' (refused to accept the spies' report on Canaan: Nm 14:10, 31), **28** and they 'yoked themselves to the Baal of Peor' (quoted from Nm 25:3), a god of Moab: a liaison punished with special severity, when they 'ate sacrifices of the dead': a strange phrase: Nm 25:3 says they 'ate' with the worshippers of Baal, i.e. took part in sacrificial meals, either = in honour of 'gods that have no life' (so NP RPB with Ibn Ezra), or – 'offered to the dead' (RSV—meaning?) **30** Phinehas (Nm 25:7–8). **32.** **v** Meribah—see on 81:8 and 95:8, where the reference is to Ex 17:7, while here rather to Nm 20:12–13. **34–39.** But when they entered the Land, they learned idolatry from the people, and **37** sacrificed their children to demons (*šēdh*: probably the Assyrian word *šēdu* = the colossal winged bulls of Assyrian temples: see also on 91:6 'the noonday devil'). **39** their conduct was that of a harlot (see on 73:27). **40–43.** So God punished them, **46** yet he 'gave them to compassion before all their captors' = 'caused their captors, to have compassion on them'. **47.** At the end a short prayer, 'Save us, o Lord ...', reproduced in 1 Chr 16:35–36 (cf on Ps 105). **48.** The Doxology for the end of Book IV, cf the ends of Pss 41, 72, 89.

BOOK V

107 A (1–32) The Hymn of the 'Redeemed'—A hymn **401a** in the grand style, of noble proportions, with a remarkable structure. The theme is thanksgiving by an ideal united Israel, gathered from the corners of the world (preamble vv 1–3) to thank Yahweh for their 'redemption' from various states pictured in each of the 4 stanzas: 1. out in the desert, 2. imprisoned in the dark, 3. in perils of sickness, 4. (a specially fine stanza) in perils of the sea. The second half of each stanza is a refrain 'They cried out to the LORD ...' followed by a balancing line applicable to the particular stanza, and 'Let them give thanks to the LORD ...' followed again by a balancing line. Nowhere else in the Pss is there a refrain pattern of comparable intricacy and regularity. The four pictures of tribulation are rather symbols of danger in human experience than identifiable phases of Israel's history (e.g. especially the sea). The messianic gathering has for the Christian an obvious symbolism, and for each one of us the poem has a message of hope. There is no title.

1. 'Give thanks to the LORD for his goodness [see **b** on 106:1]': as at the opening of Pss 106, 118, 136. **2.** The invitation to 'the redeemed of the LORD' to give

401b thanks to the Lord, who has **3** gathered them from the four points of the compass: for the last, the 'south', Heb. (with LXX/V and JA) has 'the sea' (*yām*) which as a compass-point usually means the 'west' (i.e. the Mediterranean), so that most read *yāmîn* 'the right hand' = (as often) 'the south' for one facing east. Some see here an allusion to the return from the Exile, but this would dull the picture

c of the ideal gathering. **4—5. (1st stanza)** Lost in the desert, hungry and thirsty; **6—9. Refrain**, with the balancing line (v 7) 'to come to an inhabited city' (see note on 107B). **10—12. (2nd stanza)** 'Sitting in darkness and gloom [or, 'deep shadow', see on 23:4], bound in fetters [so RPB (see DWT), rather than 'affliction' or 'want'] of iron, **12** ... they stumbled (under their burdens) and there was none to help'. **13—16. Refrain** with new balancing clauses. **17—18. (3rd stanza)** 'Sick [emended, see below] because of their sinful ways, afflicted ... **18** Their soul [= appetite] felt loathing for any kind of food, and they drew near to the gates of death': i. 'sick' (*ḥōlîm*) is a conjectural emendation, based on the context, changing one letter: so WV NP RSV; ii. Heb. has *'ewilîm* 'fools', which like *nābhāl* has a connotation of moral depravity (see on 14:1); it appears only here in the Pss, with 'folly' only twice (see on 38:6): so Targum Jer PB AV RV RPB [but folly seems irrelevant here]; iii. LXX/V 'He received them' at least shows the uncertainty

d of the text. **19—21. Refrain**, with God's healing in v 20. **22.** 'Let them offer sacrifices of thanksgiving': probably here = 'thank-offerings'. It seems unnecessary to insist that this v makes the Ps essentially liturgical or 'cultic'. In the Massoretic Text vv 21—26 and 40 are each preceded by an 'inverted nûn': the meaning of this is quite uncertain: it is often supposed that it indicates that these vv are somehow out of place, or in some other way notable. **23—27. (4th stanza)** 'Going down the sea in ships ...' **26—27** describes vividly sailing on a rough sea (almost uniquely in the OT): 'up to the sky, down to the depths; their spirit melted away ... **27** staggering [lit. 'behaving as at a feast (*ḥag*)'], reeling like a drunkard, and all their wisdom is swallowed up [PB AV RV RSV RPB have 'at their wits' end' for this expressive phrase]. **28—32. Refrain** with a longer balancing member in vv 29—30. The final balancing member, v 32, is of more general character: 'That they may exalt him in the assembly (*qāhāl*: see on 22:23) of the people ... in the session of the elders': this last word comes only 4t in the Pss (LXX *presbúteroi*): here = elders of Israel (cf Nm 11:16 etc); 105:22 = 'senators' of Egypt; 119:100 = older than myself; 148:12 = old men.

e **107 B** (33—43) **Praise of God's Power**—A fragment of a hymn (it has no true psalm-opening), attached to the end of the preceding, to which it makes a suitable conclusion, though it is plainly no part of that carefully constructed composition. The connexion may be the phrase 'inhabited city' in vv 4, 7 above, and here in v 36. **33—38.** He turns rivers into a desert, and conversely **35** a desert into 'pools of water' [cf 114:8] **36** where he lets the hungry dwell in an 'inhabited city'. **39—40.** But if they are brought low by misfortune (and are therefore open to attack from foreign princes), then **40** 'God pours contempt on (those) princes, and makes them wander in the trackless wastes': a quotation verbatim from Jb 12:21, 24. The quotation lies awkwardly (cf the long explanation required in v 39) and some would place it before v 39. It is possible that the 'inverted nûn' (see on v 22) indicates a dislocation here. **43** 'Who is wise (enough) to observe these things ... understand the Lord's love?'

f **108 A Psalm of Confidence**—Composed of extracts

from Pss 57 and 60 in Book II (where see notes), the idea **40** of God's praises among the nations providing the connexion. **Title:** 'David', the first of the small 'David Collection IV' (108—110): Pss 57 and 60 are both in 'David Collection II'.

2—6 = 57:8—12. **2.** The repeated 'my heart is ready' of 57:8 is absent here, and 'Even my glory' replaces 'Awake my glory' of 57:9, where see special note. In either case the text of 57 is sounder. **7—14** = 60:7—14, with the smallest verbal differences. **7.** In Ps 60 follows easily from what precedes, while here the nexus is less obvious, showing 60 to be the original. **10.** 'Over Philistia' here is a better reading than that of Ps 60.

109 On Persecution and Ingratitude (with the Great 402 Imprecation)—This is a psalm of the penitential type, and includes the Great Imprecation (or calling down of curses upon someone) in vv 6—20, the problems of which are discussed below (before v 6). It is possible that they are not the words of the psalmist at all, or are an intrusion here. But the violence of the imprecations remains, and they are best understood as unvarnished and unabashed statements of uninhibited feelings, as evidence of the violent injustices in human conduct that can provoke such feelings, and as a witness to the presence of anger confronting wickedness and ingratitude. C. S. Lewis, in his *Reflections on the Psalms*, discusses these things in ch 3 ('The Cursings') excellently, including the remark: '... the absence of anger, especially that sort of anger which we call *indignation*, can, in my opinion, be a most alarming sympton' (p. 30), suggesting 'a terrifying insensibility' and a 'total moral indifference'. These imprecations are at least far removed from that, and even if their literal terms are unacceptable in a civilized Christian society, the principle remains that the detestation of evil in human practice is right. **Title:** 'David'; and there is affinity with some 'David' psalms which include imprecations, as 35 and 69.

1. 'O God of my praise, be not silent': 'God of my b praise', a phrase not found elsewhere, = '(who is the object) of my praise', cf Dt 10:21 'he is thy praise'. **2—5.** For the tongues of evil men speak against me without cause, **4** 'in return for my love they accuse me [lit. 'become *śatan* to me'] ... **6—20 is the famous imprecation**, the bitterest and the longest of all, and peculiar in being directed against a single person: that of 69:23—29 being directed against persecutors, that of 83:10—19 against the enemies of Israel, and similarly the shorter passages as 35:26. There are three main interpretations: **(1)** It is uttered by the psalmist against the evil men of vv 2—5, taken collectively, though the sudden change to the singular is strange. **(2)** The imprecations are not 'my words' at all, but are the words of the evil men of vv 2—5 directed against me. On this interpretation vv 6—19 are in 'quotes', and v 20 means 'All the above is what my accusers would effect from the Lord' (cf JA, and see on v 20). Also v 28 'Let them curse ...' is seen as referring to those who utter the imprecations against me (see on v 28). **(3)** The imprecations in vv 6—20, or at least 6—19 or 6—15, are in fact a different composition, intruded into this Ps by an editor, as a suitable sequel to the ingratitude in v 5, without, however, the singular being altered. The plural is resumed at c least in v 27, and probably vv 21—31 would be part of the original psalm. Further, the 'little imprecation' of v 29, which might well be part of a psalm vv 1—5, 21—31, seems a little pale if it is part of a psalm including the fierce stuff of 6—20. Finally, there is the phrase about 'standing at the right hand' in v 6 and v 31 in quite different senses,

02c which would be surprising if they belonged to the same composition. On this supposition vv 6—20 are a strange fragment entirely occupied with imprecation. **6.** 'Set against [or, 'over'] him a wicked man': as an opponent in law, who will defeat him [cf NP BJ RSV), or [emending] 'Set against him one who shall declare him guilty' (RPB). 'Let an accuser (*śāṭān*, cf v 4) stand at his right hand', i.e. the proper place for the prosecutor, cf Zc 3:1. Here LXX takes *śāṭān* = *diábolos* = slander, but Vg transliterates *diabolus*, whence Douay 'the devil', PB AV 'Satan'. **7.** 'When he is judged, let him come out condemned, and let his prayer [= pleading for acquittal] be (regarded as a sign of) guilt': i. The whole picture is of a court of law, where it is hoped he will be condemned, and the word 'guilt', *ḥaṭā'āh*, usually translated 'sin' has a basic meaning 'to miss the mark' (as literally when slinging a stone, Jg 20:16), hence here = fail to get acquitted: cf BJm; ii. [emending 'prayer' to 'sentence'] 'Let his sentence be for guilt': RPB; iii. others: 'Let his prayer be (counted as) sin', i.e. may not even prayer **d** help him. **8.** 'May his days be few, his position let another take': the word *peḳuddāh* seems basically to mean what is appointed, attended to, but the exact meaning here is not clear: i. = his office or charge (which he is appointed to), hence LXX *episkopē* = charge, office of supervisor (hence also of bishop), hence Vg *episcopatus*, Douay 'bishopric'; the phrase is quoted in Ac 1:20 with LXX's word, giving 'bishopric' in Rheims and AV. This sense is followed by PB AV RV NP BJ (and Acts); ii. = his possessions (as appointed or belonging to him), cf *piqqādhôn*, 'store' Gn 41:36 (see Ibn Ezra), and perhaps Is 15:7; so RSV RPB; iii. Targum was plainly puzzled and has 'the number of his years', a simple parallel and perhaps = **e** 'appointed span'? **9—15.** May he leave a widow and orphans, and **10** his sons go begging 'and (reduced to) searching among their ruins': so Heb. Jer PB AV RV; or emend to 'be cast forth (even) from their ruins [= the miserable quarters they now inhabit]'. so NP BJ RSV NP, cf LXX/V. **11.** After his death, may his property be seized, **13** may he have no posterity, **14** and no remembrance. **16.** Because he persecuted the poor. **17—19.** He loved cursing: let it come upon him, cling to him. **20.** The **end of the imprecation:** 'Let this be [or, this is] what happens for my accusers from the LORD': 'what happens' can mean 'doing', or 'the reward for doing', and is variously rendered according to the interpretations indicated above (before v 6): i. (6—19) my words) 'Let this (the imprecation) be the reward for my accusers (sent upon them) from the LORD': Jer PB AV RV ('this is . . .'), NP BJ RSV RPB; ii. (6—19 my accusers' words) 'This is what shall happen [= what my accusers would like to effect] from the Lord (against me)': JA, cf LXX[B] *parà Kuríou*; iii. (same) 'This is the doing of my accusers before the Lord': LXX[Sin & A] *parà Kurío* **f** and Vg *apud Dominum*. **21—27.** Now the tone changes to a confident request for delivery: see note before v 6 for the supposition that the original Ps resumes here from v 5. **22.** 'I am "poor" [see on 9:13] . . . my heart is disquieted [so LXX/V repointing, also BJ RPB, for 'pierced', usually = 'slain'], **23** gone like an evening shadow [cf 102:12], shaken off like a locust [as an insect is brushed off], **24** my knees collapse from fasting, my flesh is wasted for lack of oil [= proper anointing, cf on 23:5; 133:2; or = fat PB AV RV so RSV 'body become gaunt'], **25** . . . (people) look at me and shake their heads (in scorn, or contempt, cf 22:8), **26** help me . . . **27** let them know . . . that thou hast done it'. **28.** 'Let them curse (as much as they will), but do thou bless!': on the supposition of the unity of the Ps, this passage

is seen by some to support the suggestion that the **402f** imprecations are 'their' curses on me, not mine on them (see note before v 6). **29.** The 'little imprecation', 'Let my accusers be clothed with dishonour . . .' of a fairly common type. Those who see 6—20 as an intrusion see here an expected feature of the original psalm vv 1—5, 21—31. Those who see the Ps as a unity, recognize a slight anticlimax here after the clothing metaphors of vv 18— 19. **30.** 'But I will praise the LORD in the midst of many [= in the assembly, cf on 22:23], **31** for he will stand at the right hand of the "needy" . . .': i.e. in support, as in 16:8; 142:5; not as prosecutor as in v 6 (cf end of note before v 6).

110 The Triumph of the Messianic Lord—One of the **403a** most exciting and mysterious of all the psalms, and of remarkable poetic quality. It describes the exaltation of the ideal King, in the ideal messianic age, seated at God's right hand, and exercising worldwide rule from Sion. The first stanza (vv 1—3) describes in a short, stirring, irregular metre the promise of God's gift of power. The 2nd stanza (v 4) shows the King invested with a priestly mission (an idea much developed in its application to Christ in the Epistle to the Hebrews). The final stanza (vv 5—7) expresses the world dominion of the King in a wild picture of death and destruction at his hands. This seems a far cry from the quiet seventh mode at Vespers on a Sunday afternoon, but these sometimes violent terms represent the central idea of God's dominion in the world. For Mowinckel (II, 64) the Ps is originally part of the liturgy of the anointing of the king (cf on Ps 2). There are several considerable textual difficulties, but almost every reading of the text provides magnificent poetic imagery. Title: 'David': the last of the 'David Collection IV'.

1. 'An utterance of the Lord (Yahweh) to my lord **b** (*adonai*)': the word 'utterance' (*ne'um*) is frequent in the prophets at the conclusion of an oracle delivered in God's name, and is usually translated 'Saith the LORD'. It is properly a noun, not a verb, linked with a name, nearly always of God. It is only here in the Pss together with the difficult Ps 36:2. And only here, as in 36:2, does it open a discourse. And here it is not so much a title or introduction, but forms part of the brilliant metrical pattern of the first stanza. A unique contrast is the linking of 'Yahweh' and 'my lord' referring presumably to a human lord, the king of Sion. Christ (Mt 22:41—45, Mk 12: 35—37, Lk 20:41—44) refers the passage directly to the Messiah, and the application of the Sion theme (see on 87.4) to Christ is nowhere so clear as it is here (cf Ps 2:7). 'Sit thou at my right hand' means a place of honour, e.g. for a queen Ps 45:10, a queen mother 1 (3)Kgs 2:19. Here it is an invitation to rule from that position: and cf 1 Chr 29:23 where Solomon sits 'on the throne of Yahweh', suggesting that the anointed king somehow shares the divine throne. The figure of 'the Son of Man at the right hand of God' is taken up by Christ (Mt 26:64, Mk 14:62, Lk 22:69) and elsewhere in the NT of the Risen Christ (Mk 16:19, Ac 1:34, 35; 7:55, 56, Rm 8:34, Eph 1:20, Col 3:1, 1 Pt 3:22 and 6t in Heb, 1:13 quoting directly, and cf 1 Cor 15:25). All these passages are probably echoes of our psalm. **2.** 'The sceptre (which is **c** a symbol) of thy strength, the Lord shall send forth from Sion . . .': the word 'sceptre' is a rod, used by a Shepherd (e.g. Ex 4:2), for punishment (e.g. Is 10:15), as a symbol of authority (Jer 48:17), and especially of Moses' 'rod of God' (e.g. Ex 4:20). So here = authority 'to rule in the midst of thy foes'. **3.** A very difficult verse: first regarding the pointing of the first word, and secondly the meaning of *nedhābhôth*, connected with the root 'free', and perhaps with *nādhibh* = 'prince' (i.e. a basically free man, under

403c obedience to no one): i. [*'amm^ekhā* as MT] 'Thy people (will be all) voluntariness' = 'come as free volunteers': Jer RV RSV; the phrase 'men of voluntariness (*ndbt*) of war' = 'volunteers for the war' occurs in the *Scroll of the War* at Qumrân (1 Q M vii, 5), giving support to this interpretation; ii. [same] 'Thy people (make to thee) freewill offerings [a frequent meaning, e.g. Ex 35:39]': PB AV [but the syntax is awkward]; iii. [*'imm^ekhā*] 'With thee (is) the principality [or, dominion]': LXX/V NP BJ; iv. [same] 'With thee (shall be a body of) princes': RPB. 'On the day of thy power (*ḥayil*)': i. = 'when thy power to triumph is shown forth': LXX/V Jer PB AV RV RPB; ii. [taking *ḥayil*, as often, = army] = 'on the day of thy warfare': JA, 'thy muster' WV, 'of (leading) thy army' RSV; iii. [repointing *ḥîl*] = 'on the day of thy birth [lit. travail]': NP, cf BJ, and cf end of the verse in

d LXX/V and NP. 'In ornaments (*hadh^erê*) of holiness': cf similar phrase in 29:2 (note), and 96:9: i. = 'in sacred apparel for the "holy war")': RVm[1] JA RPB; ii. = 'in the beauties of holiness': Targum AV RV NP [meaning?], cf LXX/V 'in the splendours of the saints'; iii. = 'in holy worship': PB, iv. [reading *har^arê*] 'upon the mountains of the holiness' = 'the holy mountains (of Sion?)': Jer RVm[2] BJ RSV [cf 'dew on the mountains of Sion' in

e Ps 133:3, and the next piece here]. 'From the womb of the morning to thee (comes) the dew of thy youth'—an outstandingly lovely line: cf AV RV RSV (all leaving 'youth' ambiguous): i. = 'thy youthful vigour comes upon thee, fresh as dew born that very morning': cf Jer; ii. = 'thy young warriors, vigorous as if newly born, are fresh as morning dew': cf RPB; iii. [omitting 'thee, the dew'; repointing 'youth'] 'From the womb, from [= before?] the morning, I have begotten thee': LXX/V with perhaps an echo of Ps 2:7; iv. [cf LXX] 'from the womb, from the dawn, is thy youth': BJ; v. [emend. 'womb' to 'before' and cf LXX] 'before the morning like dew I

f have begotten thee': NP. What is the 'picture' that emerges from these various interpretations of v 3? The messianic prince is seen as ruling from Sion: i. His people come to him freely on the great day, apparelled as for a holy war, and his youth is renewed like dew in the morning. ii. With him is the dominion on the great day, and upon the holy mountains his young men are gathered like dew in the morning. iii. With him are his princes on the great day, apparelled as for a holy war, and his young men are gathered like dew in the morning. Various translations adopt and combine variously the dif-

g ferent elements represented above. **4.** A short stanza stands alone: the Lord's unchanging oath: 'Thou art a priest for ever after the order of Melchizedek': most translations, since LXX, use this word 'order' (RVm 'manner'). The Hebrew word, based on the root for 'word', has hardly any parallel except in Jb 5:8 where it seems to mean 'a statement'. The messianic king is to have a priestly function, as David did: David's sons are even referred to as 'priests' in 2 Sm 8:18, and David himself, as king, wore the ephod and offered sacrifices in 2 Sm 6:14, 17; but this priesthood was not the official Aaronic priesthood, but one which belonged to the king as head of the people, and is transmitted to the ideal king of Sion, and so is likened to the pre-Aaronic priesthood of Melchizedek 'king of Salem' and 'priest of the Most High God' (Gn 14:18). The Christian tradition, beginning with the Epistle to the Hebrews (5:6 quotes this Ps and there are echoes in 7 further passages in ch 5—7) interprets this priesthood of that of Christ, the priest for ever. There are no other references to 'a priest' in the Pss, but only to priests among the people in 78:64; 99:6; 132:9,16. **5—6.** Here follows a violent picture (in a quick rhythm) of 'my lord'

at the right hand of Yahweh, exerting his 'rule' and **40** **6** his judgement among the nations, killing, 'filling (everywhere with) corpses (BJ well 'heaping up . . .'; Vg misunderstood LXX *ptōmata* as 'ruins') . . . over the wide world'. **7.** In the course of his mighty labours of destruction he pauses, and 'from a brook by the roadside he drinks', and 'therefore' refreshed, after bending to place his lips in the stream, he straightens himself up, ready to resume his task with new vigour.

111 An Alphabet of Wisdom—As in the other alpha- **h** betical didactic Pss, the ideas are a little inconsequent and repetitive, though less so than in 25 and 34. The climax is the declaration of wisdom in v 10 and is a real contribution (cf 34:12). Unlike 34 when each couplet begins the next letter, here each line (of 3 beats) starts with the next letter. The metre is entirely regular except for two slightly overweighted lines. A true 'Wisdom Psalm', it is admitted by Mowinckel (II, 111), with the next Ps, as 'non-cultic'. Only title: Halleluyah: see on 104:35.

1. 'I will give praise and thanks [one word: cf on 67:4 and 106:1] to the Lord . . . in the assembly: *'edhāh* 'assembly' = an appointed, or summoned company, and often, as *qāhāl*, = the assembly of Israel (cf on 22:23), but sometimes of the good, the wicked, etc. **2.** God's works are great, 'sought after for [= by] all (those who have) pleasure in them': awkward phrase, and LXX has 'sought out according to his will', Vg *exquisita*. **7** . . . 'his precepts are trustworthy, **8** firm for ever . . . having been made in faithfulness and uprightness [RSV 'to be performed in . . .']'. **10.** 'The first element of wisdom is fear of the Lord': cf Prv. 9:10: the attainment of true wisdom is the ideal of the developed OT philosophy in the later 'Wisdom' Literature.

112 An Alphabet of the Perfect Man—A 'Wisdom **40** Psalm' *par excellence*, and a kind of sequel to the previous Ps, and of similar pattern. It is in entirely regular metre and of rather undistinguished and platitudinous quality, except for its one long line in v 4. The perfect man is prosperous in this life and is well remembered afterwards. Ps 1 has its first and last words as echoes of this psalm. The only title is 'Hallelu-yah'; but Vg adds 'Of the return of Haggai and Zechariah', suggesting its use at the beginning of the new Temple.

1. 'Blessed is the man who fears the Lord . . .' taking up the thought of Ps 111:10 preceding. **2.** His offspring shall be mighty, **3** his home well-appointed . . . **4.** 'Light dawns in the darkness for the upright': the only long line and the only line of genuine poetry; 'he is kind, merciful and just': LXX[A], followed by RSV and implied by JA, has 'the Lord is kind . . .'. **5.** 'It is well with the man who is gracious and lends [RPB 'generous when he lendeth']': only here and 37:26 (with the same two words) is readiness to lend pointed out as a virtuous quality. 'And he orders his affairs [lit. 'words'] with (sound) judgement': more likely than RV 'maintains his cause in judgement', or Vg 'regulates his speech . . .'. **7** 'he will have no fear **b** of evil hearsay, his heart is fixed, trusting in the LORD': i. 'evil hearsay' about himself, i.e. gossip or slander, which he will not fear because of his innocence: LXX/V; ii. 'evil tidings', which will not disturb him: so Jer and most. **8.** '. . . He shall have no fear until [= for eventually] he will look (down) upon his enemies: i. = 'he does not care what they say': cf LXX and esp. Vg and BJ (*toisera*); ii. = 'he looks in triumph at his defeated enemies': so most, although this attitude does not seem part of the picture of the man; but see on 92:12, where it is consistent. **9.** He distributes bounty (quoted in 2 Cor 9:9), and his 'horn' is held high (in prosperity: see on 75:5

04b for this metaphor), **10** whereupon the wicked are furious with envy, but can do nothing about it: their hopes just 'perish', or come to nought.

c **113 A Family Hymn**—One of the most delightful of the hymns of praise, in a calm and even rhythm, with the happiest of pictures, both of God's exalted abode and his tender care of mankind. Pss 113—118 form the *Hallel* or Hymn of Praise of the Jewish liturgy, used on the greater feasts of Passover, Pentecost, Tabernacles, Hanukkah and New Moon. Only title: Hallelu-yah: see on 104:35.

1. 'Praise, o servants of the Lord, praise the name of the Lord': LXX/V here have *paîdes, pueri*, 'children' (with a slightly different construction: *Laudate pueri Dominum*). Only three times in the Pss do LXX have *pais* (Vg *puer*) for '*ebhedh* 'servant': 69:17; 86:16 and here (also in title of Ps 18): usually it is *doûlos, servus* (52t), though in the rest of the OT the translations seem almost interchangeable. Douay here 'children' has perhaps been encouraged by the last line and the

d delightful simplicity of the whole poem. **2—6.** 'Blessed be the name of the Lord ...' **3** from sunrise to sunset ... **4.** For he is high above the nations, and his 'glory' [= his presence] is above the sky, **5** where he lives so high up **6** that he has to 'bend his gaze downwards [lit. 'make himself low (so as) to look'] upon the sky (itself) and (this) earth': i. = the pleasant picture of God making an effort to look down even upon the sky—the upper surface, of course, of the sky, as when we look down from a jet plane on the upper surface of the clouds—cf NP BJ RSV; ii. = looking upon (the things that are in) heaven and earth: AV RV; iii. = he is so high, yet he looks ...: PB RPB; iv. [emending] 'looks down upon lowly things in heaven and earth': LXX/V. **7.** Nevertheless 'he raises up the poor from dust ..., **8** to make (them) sit with the princes, with the princes of his people': i.e. the 'poor' or devout (see on 9:13), whoever they are, within his people, become princes. V 7 is an echo from the Canticle of Hannah (1 Sm 2:8), which is also echoed in the Magnificat, e.g. Lk 1:52. **9.** But there is a still more wonderful mercy, when 'he gives to the childless a homestead, and children, and motherly joy' [lit. 'causes the barren to dwell in a home, joyful mother of children]. 'Hallelu-yah' at the end.

e **114 A Little Ballad of Israel**—One of the most charming, this psalm has the form and rhythm of a ballad, with four clear stanzas and an even rhythm. It describes with happy poetic invention Israel's entry into the Land, and the welcome that the Land gave them. LXX, Vg and Syr take the next Ps as one with this. No title.

1. 'When Israel went forth from Egypt, the house of Jacob from an alien people': the word 'alien' is probably related to the idea of speaking in an unintelligible or foreign way (cf AV RV RSV RPB). **2.** 'Judah became his (God's) sanctuary, Israel his domain': God is not named until the last stanza. Judah and Israel are here probably synonyms for the whole people, and the whole land belongs to God both spiritually and politically (cf Ex 19:5—6). **3—4.** A delightful picture in the 2nd stanza of the behaviour of the (Red) Sea at the Exodus, and of the Jordan at the entry of the people into the Land (Ex 14:21—29 and Jos 3:14—17), and **4** the joyful welcome of the Land. **5—6.** In the 3rd stanza the poet imagines himself watching all this, and cries out, 'What ails thee, o sea, that thou fleest? ... o Jordan ... **6** o hills ...?' These are graphic action-tenses, and some of the picture is spoilt when the questions are referred to the past as in LXX/V Jer PB AV RPB. **7—8.** But in the 4th stanza comes the answer: not only the hills of

the Land, but the whole earth trembles before its Master. **404e** The word 'Master' (*'ādhôn*) is only here in the Pss of God (twice of a human master, 12:5; 105:21). **8.** For he can do wonders in nature, as in Ex 17:6, Nm 20:11 and in the song Dt 32:13.

115—The divisions of the Pss in this area are very **f** uncertain, and the absence of titles adds to the uncertainty. **(1)** On literary grounds the units seem to be these (and we are following this here): Ps 114, Ps 115: 1—11 (cf Jewish liturgy), Ps 115:12—18, Ps 116:1—11 (or 9) (cf LXX/V), Ps 116:12 (or 10)—19, Ps 117. **(2)** LXX and Vg have been one behind since Ps 9 [= Heb. 9—10], and their units here are Ps 113 *In exitu* [= Heb. 114 and 115 taken as one], Ps 114 *Dilexi* [= Heb. 116: 1—9], Ps 115 *Credidi* [= Heb. 116:10—19], Ps 116 *Laudate* [= Heb. 117]: their division of Heb. Ps 116 is legitimate. **(3)** The Peshitta Syriac also takes Heb. 114 and 115 as one, and so from Syr. Ps 115 [= Heb. 116] they are also now one behind. **(4)** The Jewish liturgy reads Ps 115:1—11 and 115:12—18 separately, and similarly Ps 116:1—11 and 116:12—19, and these breaks can also be distinguished on literary grounds.

115 A (1—11) **Non nobis Domine**—A psalm chiefly **g** occupied with comparing the worthlessness of idols with the power of God, and having several echoes in Ps 135:15—20. LXX/V and Syr. attach it to the preceding, but it is quite certainly a distinct Ps. It is disputable whether a break should be made after v 11 (with the Jewish liturgy) or after v 13, since vv 12—13 seem to be a separate fragment, joined equally easily to the preceding or the following. No title.

1. 'Not to us, Lord ...': the first verse is a kind of antiphon with no regular metrical pattern. **2—7.** Here the argument begins in regular metre: 'How can [lit. 'Why do ...'] the nations say, Where is their God? **3.** For our God is in heaven ... **4.** But their idols are (mere) silver and gold ...' **5—7** They have a mouth ... eyes ... ears, (etc), but these are powerless. **8.** Let their makers, and all who trust in them, become (as powerless) as their products [or 'they are ...' with PB AV RSV RPB]. **9—11.** But, in contrast, Israel trusts in Yahweh ... **10** the House of Aaron (the priests) ... **11** indeed all God-fearing men ...

115 B (12—18) **A Short Benediction Formula**— **h** The first verses (12—13) may belong to the preceding, esp. as the theme of 'Israel ... Aaron ... God-fearing' reappears here; but on the other hand this may be the reason for the verses becoming attached to vv 10—11 above. Vv 14—18 are almost certainly a separate composition from 115:1—11.

12—13. 'God has remembered us, may he bless ... Israel ... Aaron ... **13** God-fearing men, the small with the great.' **14—18.** A short benediction in hymn-form, invoking God's blessing on 'you' (one notices the changes of person). **16.** 'The heavens (are) heavens (that belong) to the LORD' [cf 148:4], but the earth he gave to men. **17.** '(And while we are alive on this earth we should praise him, for) the dead in the silence (of Sheol) cannot do so so [see on Sheol 6:6], **18** so let us bless him now and for ever'. Some see in vv 14—15 the priests' answer to the prayer of the people in 115A.

116 A (1—11) **A Song of Love and Thanks for 405a Rescue**—The first part of this Ps includes many familiar themes on the danger of death, e.g. in Pss 6, 18, 102A, 118. The latter part of the Ps, at least from v 12 onwards, seem to be a distinct composition, but it is disputable whether the break should be made there, or before v 10, where LXX/V begin a new psalm *Credidi*. On balance it seems preferable to regard vv 10—11 as belonging to the

405a first part, and this has the support of the Jewish liturgical tradition, where vv 12—19 are read separately. This first part of Ps 116 = Ps 114 in LXX/V, so that for this moment the numbers are two apart. There is no title.

1—2. 'I have loved (the Lord), because the Lord hears my voice . . . **2** . . . and in my days I will call': so literally LXX/V: i. = 'as long as I live': PB AV RV JA RSV; ii. [emended with Syr] 'on the day when I call him': NP BJ; iii. [another emend.] 'when I call on his name':
b RPB. **3.** 'The cords of death have come round me (dragging me down), and the grip of Sheol has found me out . . .': cf similar phrases in 18:5—6 also expressing the final calamity of death (see also on 6:6); the word 'grip' here is a rare word (also in 118:5) conveying what is narrow, cramped (see on 4:2); the emendation 'snares' is accepted by NP BJ RPB. **4—6.** I called . . . 'Ah! LORD . . .': 'Ah!' an interjection only in the Pss here and v 16, and twice in 118:25, each time LXX/V have 'O Domine'—'O' is not otherwise used with the vocative in the Pss. The occurrence of 'Ah!' again in v 16 could argue for the unity of the Ps, or else explain the joining of the two sections. **7.** An address to my own soul (an infrequent device: cf 42:6 with refrains in 42:12; 43:5, 103:1—5). **8—9.** 'For thou (o God) hast rescued my soul
c from death . . . **10—11.** The tone and thought change somewhat, and LXX/V Ps 115 begins here. **10.** 'I have trusted . . .': a *pendant* to 'I have loved' in v 1 to conclude. 'For I speak, I am sore distressed' [quoted from LXX in 2 Cor 4:13]. **11.** 'I said in my trepidation [or, haste]: "All mankind is (but) a vain hope"'; 'All men are liars' does not quite translate: the root conveys that which disappoints, is illusory, e.g. a dry spring in Is 58:11, and in the quotation in Rm 3:4 the contrast is between man's fickleness and the sureness of God.
d **116 B** (12—19) **Quid retribuam Domino?**—There is not much doubt that this is a distinct Ps from the first part. Vv 10—11 above form a satisfactory conclusion to the first part, but LXX/V make these verses the opening of this part. The theme of these verses is, however, quite self-contained, and, although the theme of death reappears in v 15 here (with much difficulty of interpretation), the answer to the opening question in terms of liturgical vows occupies most of 116B and makes it a 'Temple psalm'.

12—14. 'What can I give back to the Lord . . .?' **13.** There is one thing I can do: I can grasp the 'cup of salvation', call upon his name, and **14** pay my vows (my liturgical thank-offerings, cf 22:26; 66:13—15) 'there indeed in front of all thy people'. The 'cup of salvation' is a phrase found only here: i. 'cup' as my portion, or lot, more often in the sense of inexorable fate as in 60:5 and 75:9, but also as a good sight in 16:5 and 23:5: here in one of these senses = 'I throw in my lot with God, and this means salvation for me'. Ibn Ezra takes in the sense of 16:5. ii. in view of the following reference to vows, and to sacrifices in v 17 (with the same phrase 'call on . . .'), it is often supposed to refer to a cup of liturgical libation (so Rashi), but there is no other OT reference to a cup in liturgical usage. These verses are used in the Latin Mass: '*Calicem salutaris accipiam . . .*'
e **15.** 'Precious in the sight of the Lord is the death of his saints [or, holy, or devout (*haṣīdhīm*) see on 12:2]': the interpretation of this verse in the context of the psalm is difficult: i. Such a one as pays his vows etc is a *ḥāsidh*, and the death of such a one, when he enters paradise, is a precious thing—this is the usual Christian interpretation, e.g. in the use of the verse in the old monastic office of *Pretiosa* that used to be recited after the reading of the Martyrology. But it is very difficult to imagine this thought entering the mind of the original writer. ii. 'precious' =

'costly', i.e. the death of the holy man would be too 'costly' **405** in the sight of God for him to let it happen, cf the difficult passage in 49:9—10—so Ibn Ezra. iii. similarly, as 72:14 'their blood is precious to him', i.e. is not to be shed, so here 'their death is precious', i.e. not to be brought about. The two latter are the more likely interpretations within OT thought, and this passage then links vv 12—14 with 'thou hast set me free (from death)' in v 16, i.e. from the final calamity. **16.** 'Ah! Lord . . .': see on 116:4 above. I am thy servant and my mother is thy handmaid, i.e. I am all thine, I am even born in thy household. Thou hast set me free. **17—19.** I will offer the 'sacrifice of praise', either liturgical, or perhaps spiritual sacrifice: see on 107:22.

117 In Praise of God's friendship—The shortest **f** and one of the loveliest of the Psalms. It shows a perfect pattern of rhythm and parallelism and brings out the qualities of God's friendship.

1. 'Praise ye the Lord, all nations, glorify him all peoples': the word 'glorify' here, common in Aram., is rare in Heb.: RV carefully uses the rarer word 'laud'. The word 'peoples', or tribes, is also rare, used only of foreign tribes in Gn 25:16; Nm 25:15 and here. **2.** 'For strong is his love towards us, and the Lord's friendship (remains) for ever'. Here we have the two great words of God's love *ḥesedh* and faithfulness *'emeth*, which, especially together convey his 'friendship' (see on 5:8). Moreover the idea includes his mercy, as in LXX/V and the older translations.

118 A Hymn of Praise and Hope, fulfilled in the **406** **Temple**—The last of the Hallel series (113—118), this Ps opens with a community hymn vv 1—4, followed by a long monologue vv 5—18 of a rather familiar pattern meditating on delivery from death and trust in God. From v 19 the solution is found in Sion and the crowded festivals in the Temple, ending with a refrain from the opening line. This Ps, with Ps 24, provides perhaps the most convincing evidence for a liturgical dialogue in a Ps, and it has been supposed to be an actual liturgy for the reception of pilgrims, or for a special feast, e.g. Tabernacles (if v 27 refers to branches?). The whole thing is seen as a procession, with a dialogue between the leader of the people, the priests, and the people from v 19. Mowinckel (I, 131, II, 28, 76) has several suggestions for the 'cultic' use of this Ps. P. Drijvers 86—88 has worked this out down to minute rubrical details, which will be indicated in the commentary, to show how far the 'cultic' hypothesis can be developed. Even if this is the origin of the psalm, in subsequent centuries it has become a single hymn, with the visit to the Temple seen as a symbol of all men coming as pilgrims to worship the true God. Indeed the psalm may have been originally conceived as a literary device, depicting such an ideal gathering.

1. 'Give thanks to the LORD for his goodness': for **b** this phrase see on 106:1. **2—4.** Israel . . . Aaron . . . God-fearing men are invited to make the same proclamation. These three titles are characteristic of these Pss, appearing also at Pss 115A:9—11 and 115B:12—13. **5—18.** The long monologue of personal lamentation and hope: 'From my anguish I called on Yah [= Yahweh, the Lord—this short form appearing 5t in this Ps, more than in any other]: Yah answered me with (the gift of) ease [lit. 'broadness, space': see on 4:2 and 25:17]. **6.** The LORD is for me': cf 124:1 = 'on my side' (PB AV RV RSV RPB) or other paraphrase as LXX/V 'is my helper' (thus quoted in Hb 13:6); the context is often warlike, e.g. Jos. 5:13, 2 Sm 20:11, 2 (4) Kgs 10:6. See also on 56:10. **7** '. . . and I shall look (down) upon those who hate me': cf 54:9 and see on 92:12; 112:8. **10—11.** 'All **c**

6c nations surround me: but in the name of the Lord I will repel them [an uncertain word] . . .': i. 'repel them': RPB [cf an Arabic root, see DWT]; ii. 'cut them off [or, down]': RV RSV, cf RVm ('down') BJ ('*je les sabre*') [but the verb otherwise only means 'to circumcise' and a different use is very unlikely]; iii. [repointing or emending] 'destroy them': PB AV [uncertain]; iv. [reading?] 'take vengeance on them': LXX/V. **12.** 'They surrounded me like bees, they blazed like fire among thorns': i. so [emending 'blazed' and 'among'] LXX/V RPB [the most likely]; ii. [emending 'blazed'] 'blazed like a fire of thorns': BJ RSV; iii. [same] 'burned as fire (burns) thorns': NP; iv. [following MT] 'were quenched like a fire of thorns', i.e. flared up quickly and came to nothing: AV

d RV, cf Jer PB. **13.** 'I was thrust aside (so that I was about) to fall, but the Lord helped me': so with LXX/V, NP BJ RSV RPB for Heb. 'Thou (my enemy) didst thrust me'. **14.** 'My strength and my song (is) Yah', i.e. 'the object of my song', verbatim from Ex 15:2, but RPB from an Arabic root (see DWT) has 'my defence'. **15–16.** Here the thought takes a new turn: 'O the sound of rejoicing . . .' **17–18.** I am saved from death. **19–21.** Now he prays imagining himself before the gates of God's house and **21** thanks God for this 'salvation' (or, if it is an actual liturgy, he asks admission, **20** the priests welcome him, **21** he thanks them). **22–24.** 'The stone which the builders rejected . . . **23** This is wonderful in our

e eyes . . . **24** This is the day (when we come to the Temple) which the LORD has made . . .' these verses in the Jewish liturgy of the Hallel stand apart and are repeated. The whole passage has several interpretations: i. As often in the Pss, Sion and its Temple are the centre of my longing, and here is the Temple before my eyes, and this is the day of fulfilment of my longing: cf the theme of Pss 84, 122. ii. The Temple and Sion, as often, are the symbol of the ideal messianic age, as the centre of worship for all men: cf the theme of Ps 87. iii. These are actual liturgical chants for an entry into the Temple, sung by the pilgrims ['our' in v 23]; the 'day' is the day of pilgrimage. iv. The 'stone . . . rejected' represents the Temple either ideally or actually restored: an interpretation that applies to all the above. v. The Christian tradition sees the 'stone' (as indeed the whole 'Sion theme') as a symbol of Christ. The text is quoted of Christ, by himself in Mt 21:42 with Mk 12:10, 11, Lk 20:17, and by Peter in Ac 4:11 and 1 Pt 2:7. vi. The Jewish tradition (cf, e.g. Ibn Ezra) sees the 'stone' as Israel, rejected but miraculously restored to fulfil her vocation of bringing the nations to God. vii. The Targum refers the 'stone' to David, translating this verse: 'The boy whom the architects abandoned was . . . the son of Jesse . . .' viii. The Easter liturgy makes special use of 'This is the day . . .' with reference to Christ's resur-

f rection. **25–27a.** A series of acclamations: 'Ah, Lord! Save (us)!': *Hôšĭ'āh-nnā*, whence the *Hosanna* of the NT (Mt 21:9, 15, Mk 11:9, 10, Jn 12:13—and one notices 'Hosanna to the son of David' in Mt, cf vii above) and our liturgies. 'Ah, Lord! Prosper (us)!' **26.** 'Blessed is he who comes . . .' quoted by the children in Mt 21:9 (cf 23:29), Mk 11:9, (cf Lk 19:38). 'We bless you . . .' (in a liturgical setting this would be the priests' answer to the pilgrims). **27b.** A very difficult passage: 'Bind a festival (*ḥag*) with '*abhôthîm*': the last word conveys something closely woven, usually a rope, perhaps foliage, perhaps a crowd. A special puzzle is the meaning of 'Bind a festival': i. = 'Bring together a festival with dense (crowds? foliage?)': LXX/V Jer (foliage); ii. = 'Form a procession with foliage': NP (branches carried), BJ (palms in their hands)—but nowhere does *ḥag* mean a

procession: it always refers to a day; iii. = 'Bind the **406f** sacrificial victim with ropes': PB AV RV RSV RPB [following Targum and Rabbis (Ibn Ezra)]—but nowhere does *ḥag* mean a sacrificial victim: a very doubtful rendering. 'Up to the horns [projecting corners, as **g** often] of the altar': i. = The crowds or foliage fill the Temple up to the altar; ii. = The procession marches right up to the altar; iii. = The victim is tied to the 'horns' of the altar. (If this is an actual liturgy, this would be ceremonial directions given by the priests.) Perhaps the most satisfactory picture of v 27*b* is that of the dense crowds filling the Temple at the festival. **28–29.** A final word of praise and thanks, including the repetition in v 29 of v 1.

119 An Alphabet of the Love of God's Law—In spite **h** of its obviously artificial framework, this Ps is an intensely personal protestation of its theme: 'How I love thy Law (*tôrāh*)', e.g. v 97, cf 127, 167. After the first 4 vv, the whole Ps expresses an 'I-Thou' relationship with God. The element of pain is present (with persecution by the 'arrogant') and mounts towards the end, esp. from v 153, and there is the suggestion in v 71 that it is 'good for me'; but the greatest expression of sorrow (v 136) is touchingly reserved for tears over those who do not keep the Law. The structure of the Ps involves much repetition, but there are many pictures of poetic insight not found elsewhere, such as joy in thy Law above worldly pleasures (see on v 14), 'running in the way of thy commandments' (v 32), 'they have smeared me with lies' (v 69), a 'wineskin in the frost (or smoke)' (v 83), God's word as a lamp to my path (vv 105, 130), 'breathing in' God's commandments (v 131), the lost sheep (v 176), and phrases such as 'Open my eyes to see' (v 18), 'Thy statutes have been like songs to me' (v 54), and 'I am thine' (v 94). The text is generally sound. The metre is nearly regular throughout.

The Ps is built upon an alphabetical plan, each **i** stanza of 8 vv has each verse beginning with the same letter of the alphabet, taking each letter in turn through 22 stanzas (22 × 8 vv = 176 vv). Moreover there are **8 key-words**, nearly synonyms of the 'Law', and each verse contains one of these (except vv 90, 122 and in fact 132). The 'perfect' stanzas use all 8 key-words, a different one for each verse: these are the stanzas beginning at vv 41, 57, 73 and 81; while the others repeat key-words and so do not include them all. The key-words do not stand in any particular order within the stanza, though there have been attempts (e.g. Briggs) to discern a pattern. The 8 key-words are the following (the order here being merely that of vv 1–11):

(1) *Tôrāh* 'the Law' (Vg NP *lex*), more properly 'guid- **j** ance or, direction', translated since LXX as 'law', the God-given norm of human moral conduct (see on 19:8). (A more specialized sense is of the Torah = the Pentateuch.) Occurs in every stanza but one (Beth).

(2) *'Êdôth* (here pointed *'edwôth*) 'testimonies' (Vg *testimonia*, NP *praescripta*, i.e. God's witnessing to, or manifesting, his will for man's conduct. In every stanza but three.

(3) *Piqqūdhîm* 'precepts' (Vg *mandata*, NP *praecepta*), in the sense of a duty imposed: a word proper to the Pss. In all but three stanzas.

(4) *Huqqîm* 'statutes' (Vg *iustificationes*, NP *statuta*), properly that which is engraved, i.e. solemnly declared as law. In every stanza but four.

(5) *Miṣwôth* 'commandments' (Vg NP *mandata*), what is commanded. In all but three stanzas.

(6) *Mišpāṭîm* 'judgements' (RSV 'ordinances', Vg *iudicia*, NP *decreta*), the duty imposed upon man by God's

406j judgement or decision. In every stanza but two (the word is used in a different sense in v 132). The above three terms are frequently used in Deuteronomy.

(7) *Dābhār* 'word' (Vg *sermo, verbum*, NP *verbum*), God's word by which he guides mankind. Absent in three stanzas, but probably to be restored in vv 3 and 37 by emendation. (8) *'Imrāh* 'saying' (RSV 'word, promise', RPB 'word', Vg NP *eloquium*), that which is uttered by God as his law. Absent in four stanzas.

In the (full) Massoretic note on v 122 mention is made of 10 key-words, as symbolic of the 10 Commandments, including also *Derekh* 'way' (but see on vv 3 and 37) and *Sedhekh* 'righteousness'.

k   **1—8.** (Aleph) 'Blessed are the blameless of life [lit. "way"], who walk in the Law of the Lord . . . 3 They have walked in his ways': since the 'way' comes only here and v 37 as a key-word (i.e. with no other key-word present), and in each case 'word' is absent from the stanza, it is likely that we should make the small emendation: '. . . walked according to his word': see further on v 37. **9—16.** (Beth) **14.** A special element in this Ps is my delight and joy in thy testimonies, above wordly pleasures of riches (here), money-making (v 36), gold and silver (v 72,127), treasure (v 162), thy Law is not a tiresome burden, but a joy. **17—24.** (Ghimel) **18.** 'Open my eyes that I may see the wonders of thy Law'. **19.** I am a wanderer on earth (*gêr* a 'sojourner', i.e. not in my own home): a sentiment rare in the Pss, see on 39:13. **21.** A brief reference at this stage to the 'arrogant' and **23** 'princes' who plot against me (cf v 161): it is unlikely that there is any reference to historical 'princes', they are probably no more than the leaders of the 'arrogant'. **25—32.** (Daleth) Nearly every line is a request to God to instruct me so that **32** 'I may run in the way of thy

l commandments'. **33—40.** (He) **37.** Here is the other occurrence of God's 'way' as an apparent key-word, when 'word' is again absent from the stanza, as in v 3; again we should probably read 'according to thy word' for 'in thy ways', esp. as the phrase 'enliven me according to thy word' [= 'give me a new kind of life, which is living according to thy word'] occurs in v 25. Moreover this suggestion is supported by the reading in the Qumrân Psalter (11Q Ps^a viii,1). (Unhappily the piece of the scroll including v 3 has been torn). The phrase 'enliven me' in this sense occurs no less than 9t in this Ps and nowhere else. **41—48** (Waw) A 'perfect' stanza with all 8 key-words. **49—56.** (Zain) **53.** 'Indigna-tion has seized me': so RV NP BJ RSV RPB: 'indigna-tion' is an uncertain word conveying some emotion. **54.** 'Thy statutes have been (like) songs to me': Vg pleasantly '*cantabiles mihi erant*'. **57—64.** (Heth) Another 'perfect' stanza with the 8 key-words. **57.** God is my 'portion', see on 16:5. **61.** For 'the cords of the wicked ensnare me', cf 140:6, and 18:5; 116:3 ('cords of death'), and 18:6 ('cords of Sheol'). **65—72.** (Teth) **66.** Almost lit. 'good taste and understanding [lit. 'goodness of taste', i.e. discernment] teach me'. **69.** 'The arrogant have smeared me with lies': LXX/V 'iniquity is multiplied'. **70.** 'Their heart is thickened like fat', cf 17:10; 73:7, of their insensitiveness. **71.** This psalm's unusual attitude to 'affliction': it is 'good for me, that I may thereby learn thy statutes, cf also v 75. **73—80.** (Yodh) A 'perfect'

m stanza. **81—88.** (Kaph) Another 'perfect' stanza. The theme is my longing for thy word, my spirit and my eyes pining, with the simile **83** 'I have become like a wineskin in [probably] the smoke': a 'skin' or 'leathern bottle' is used for wine in Jos. 9:4, 13, 1 Sm 16:20, for milk in Jg 4:19, and figuratively for tears in Ps 56:9. Here a worn-out state is expressed with the picture of the wineskin hung

up among the rafters (because disused) or perhaps in the **40** hearth (for maturing the wine), and anyway having a black and shrivelled appearance. The word for 'smoke' is found in Gn 19:28,28 (smoke from Sodom), and Ps 148:8, where the reference is to some weather phenome-non (LXX/V 'ice', see note there); LXX/V here have 'frost', which in view of 148:8 should be considered, and the picture of a worn-out leathern bottle thrown away outside and lying frozen is very abject. **85.** 'The arrogant have dug pitfalls for me': LXX/V '. . . have told frivolities to me . . .' **89—96.** (Lamedh) On the eternity of God's Law. **90.** No key-word in this verse, but perhaps *'emûnāh*, 'faithfulness', should be read as *'imrāh* which is absent in this stanza (though the Qumrân Psalter has the standard text). **94.** 'I am thine . . .' **96.** 'For all completeness I have seen an end: **n** very wide is thy command': one of the few uncertain passages in this Ps: i. = 'I have seen the end of all fulfilment [= of all things]': cf LXX/V PB; ii. = 'I have seen of all (things) the fulfilment [omitting 'end' as a gloss]' = 'that all things come to an end': RPB (see DWT), cf WV; iii. = 'I have seen (that there is) a limit [lit. 'end'] to all perfection': cf AV RV BJ RSV; iv. = 'I have seen an end to every purpose': JA. What-ever the translation, the 'breadth' or unlimitedness of God's command stands in contrast. **97—104.** (Mem) 'How I have loved thy Law': the central theme of the Ps. **105—12.** (Nun) 'Thy word is a lamp to my foot'. **107. o** The motif of affliction with the phrase **109** 'my soul (is) in my hand': an idiom also in Jg 12:3, 1 Sm 28:21, Jb 13:14, expressing the presence of danger. **112.** I have fol-lowed thy statutes 'for ever, always': i. so Targum PB AV RV RSV [*'ēqebh* commonly means 'always']; ii. [but basically it means 'what follows' = ? 'reward'] so LXX/V '. . . for ever, (because of the) reward'—explaining a curious passage in LXX/V; iii. so also 'for everlasting (is the) reward': BJ RPB, cf Ibn Ezra; iv. [connecting with a 'footprint', i.e. what follows] 'for ever (at every) step': JA, cf Rashi; NP similar (*ad amussim*). **113—20.** (Samekh) **117.** 'I look upon [or, 'delight in': RPB cf **p** Aram. root (see DWT)] thy statutes'. **119.** 'Thou hast counted as dross all the wicked': shows an emended text, reading *hāsabhtā* by changing one letter from *hišbattā*: i. so Jer NP RSV RPB, cf LXX/V 'I have counted . . .', a reading supported by the Qumrân Psalter (11Q Ps^a xi, 15); ii. [following the Massoretic Text] 'Thou hast caused to cease [= eliminated] as dross . . .': PB AV RV BJ; iii. 'I have counted as transgressors [*sārîm* for *sigîm*]': LXX/V **120.** The fear of God's judgements: a new element in this Ps. **121—8.** (Ain) **122** is the verse with no key-word at all, not even by emendation. **129—36.** (Pe) A 'perfect' stanza with the 8 key-words. **129.** For 'Wonderful are thy testimonies', Qumrân (entirely alone) has 'Streams of honey are . . .' **130.** 'The opening [word only here] of thy words giveth light': i. = 'unfold-ing': RSV well, cf 'declaration': LXX/V NP; ii. = 'going forth' [as from a door, a cognate word]: PB RPB; iii. = 'doorway': Jer, cf 'entrance': AV. **131.** The remark- **q** able picture of the man gasping for breath and breathing in God's commandments, which he longs for [lit. 'open mouth . . . breathe in . . . long for commandments']. **132** '. . . have mercy according to thy custom (*mišpāt*) . . .': where *mišpāt* is used, but not in the sense of the key-word (God's ordinances). **136.** The startling picture, the most violent of sorrow in this psalm, of streams of tears shed over those who do not keep thy Torah. **137—44.** (Sadhe) **140.** 'Thy word is tried (in the fire), i.e. trustworthy: rare of God's word, cf 18:31. **145—52.** (Qoph) **147.** 'I am early in the twilight' (of the

06q morning—uncommon, usually of evening) **148** before the 'watches' [LXX/V 'dawn'] I meditate on thy word: most take of 'night watches', but the picture is not clear, except to convey assiduous prayer. **153—60.** (Resh) Most of this stanza is taken up with the theme of my persecutors, but with the consolation at the end: **160.** 'The sum [lit. "head", whence LXX/V "beginning", cf PB AV JA] of thy word is truth'. **161—8.** (Shin) 'Princes have persecuted me without cause': see on v 23. **164.** 'Seven (times) in the day I have praised thee': while this may mean no more than 'frequently' as in 12:7 ('purified seven times'), it is invoked by St Benedict (*Rule* c.17) for the pattern of the Divine Office: Matins (and Lauds, see c. 13), Prime, Terce, Sext, None, Vespers, Compline. **169—76.** (Tau) **176.** 'I have gone astray like a lost sheep: seek thy servant': a touching picture nowhere else in the OT—the picture in Is 53:6 is different—but cf Mt 18:12 and Lk 15:4.

07a **120—134**—A favourite collection of 15 short psalms, each one entitled 'A Song of Ascents' or 'of Steps (AV Degrees)', cf LXX 'of Stairs' and Vg '*Graduum*' whence '**Gradual Psalms**' (cf Douay), which is sufficiently non-committal to be useful, since there is no satisfactory theory of the origin or exact meaning of this title. The flight of 15 steps in the Temple, mentioned in the Mishnah (*Middoth* 2:5) as 'corresponding to the 15 Songs of Ascents' and 'upon which the levites used to sing', offers no certain explanation, and the most general opinion is that it is a small collection used by pilgrims 'going up' to Jerusalem, even though only Ps 122 has any direct reference to pilgrimage, and less than half have reference to Sion (125, 126, 128, 129, 132, 133, 134). But it is a remarkably comprehensive collection, mostly of good poetic quality and including examples of most of the 'genres', personal, liturgical (133), 'wisdom' (127, 128), and even an imprecation (129), and is thus a kind of microcosm of the whole Psalter, even including one (132) with a character entirely its own. The 'Gradual Psalms' may well have been rightfully popular items, brought together with no particular connexion among themselves, perhaps used on pilgrimages and so eventually thus labelled.

b **120 The Song of one far from Home**—A short lyric, an example of the 'Individual Lament' in this series, with a pleasantly irregular metrical pattern. **1—2.** 'Unto the Lord I cried in my distress . . . **2** deliver me from the deceitful tongue . . .' **3 4.** In the 2nd stanza the 'deceitful tongue' is apostrophized (an unusual device): What shall be thy fate? **4.** To be showered with sharp arrows, and hot charcoal of broom (the roots of which bush make a specially hot fuel [LXX 'desert charcoal', Vg 'destructive']). **5—7.** 'Woe is me, for I am an exile in Meshek [Gn 10:2—a vaguely remote place] . . . in Kedar [among the nomadic Arabs, cf Gn 25:13 descendants of Ishmael], **6** . . . among (people who) hate peace: **7.** I (speak of) peace, but when I speak, they (are) for war.' [LXX/V took 'Meshek' as 'prolonged'.] The poet longs for peace and home: the names are probably no more than symbols of remoteness.

c **121 God's Watchfulness**—Four short stanzas in fairly regular metre. **1—2.** 'I lift up my eyes to the hills. Whence comes my help? [better than '. . . hills, whence comes . . .'] **2** My help is from the Lord . . .'. What is implied in the answer? i. Not from men's fortresses on the hill-tops, but from Yahweh. ii. Not from the hill-shrines of the false gods, but from Yahweh. iii. From the hills indeed, where Sion lies, the abode of Yahweh. **3—8.** The Guardian of Israel will not relax his watchfulness, and nothing shall ever harm thee.

122 The Joy of Pilgrimage—The Ps seems to express **407d** the joy of one who watches pilgrims going to Jerusalem, and then blesses the City from afar. One feels it is on the lips of an old man, who watches the pilgrims go. Others see it as on the lips of one approaching the City with a group of pilgrims, and blessing the City now in view. In spite of some textual obscurities, the theme of an overwhelming love of the Holy City is plain enough. 'David' is added to the **title**.

1. 'I rejoiced over those who say to me, We are going to the House of the LORD': i.e. I am made happy at hearing them say this. **2.** 'Our feet have been standing in thy gates, o Jerusalem': it is not clear who is speaking: versions which use 'quotes' (NP RSV RPB) close them after v 1: Syr. and the Qumrân Psalter (11Q Ps^a iii, 8) have 'my feet': i. The pilgrims have now arrived and say 'Our feet are standing . . .': disconnected from v 1; ii. Part of what they say to me (connected with v 1) = we have been there before; iii. = 'Our feet shall stand . . .' = part of the speech in v 1: so PB AV—the most natural, but the tense is embarrassing; iv. My answer to the pilgrims = we have been there ourselves before (and this is made easier with the Qumrân reading): perhaps the most satisfactory. **3.** An apostrophe to the beloved City: 'O Jerusalem, built like a city that is compacted together (in a unity)': the word 'compacted' is more generally used of unions or alliances among men, so perhaps 'whose houses stand close together within her walls' (RPB), or 'where men are of one mind together'. (The late Heb. form of the relative here and v 4 suggest a late date for this Ps.) **4.** 'Thither the tribes go up, **e** the tribes of Yah [= Yahweh], a testimony for Israel, to give thanks . . .': difficult but Qumrân gives an easier reading, see below iii: i. = 'the tribes go (to bear) witness for Israel': PB AV RV; ii. = 'the tribes go (according to the) testimony [= decree, cf often in Ps 119] (given) to Israel': NP BJ RSV RPB; iii. The Qumrân Psalter (11Q Ps^a iii,10) has '*ēdhath* 'assembly of' for '*edhûth* 'witness(for)', so one could read 'the tribes go, the assembly of Israel . . .': the easiest solution. [It should, however, be noted that there is apparently a lacuna immediately before.] **5.** 'For there have sat [= ? are set] the thrones for judgement, thrones for the House of David': Qumrân (iii, 11) has 'a throne for the House of David', which may be easier, but there is another lacuna before this. According to most, the meaning is that Jerusalem is the seat of justice, administered of old by the kings of the House of David. This is the sense of the translations that attempt to go beyond the literal words, which remain a little puzzling. **6—7.** A prayer for Jerusalem and those who love her. **7.** 'Peace within thy walls' [rather than LXX/V 'thy power', a similar word].

123 A Song of Trust—**1.** 'To thee I lift up my eyes, **f** o thou who art enthroned [so RSV RPB, lit. 'sittest, or, dwellest' as LXX/V PB AV RV] in heaven'. **2.** We watch for the least sign, as servants watch their master's hand: i. either the hand that supplies their needs—suggested by the end of v 2 'till he show us his favour'; ii. or the hand that can defend the servants from attack—linking with vv 3—4 (so Ibn Ezra); iii. or the hand that gives a sign of command—perhaps the most obvious sense, when the piece is taken alone. **3—4.** 'Show us mercy [or, favour] . . . in the contempt **4** we have received from those 'who are at ease' [word only here in the Pss: usually in a bad sense, esp. as opposed to the 'poor' (see on 9:13)] and from the 'proud' [an unusual form, pointed by the Massoretes as 'proud oppressors' (so JA)].

407g **124 The Lord is for us**—Some see in this Ps an expression of national thanksgiving (e.g. Gunkel § 8:4) after some national disaster had been averted (Weiser), and Mowinckel (I, 185ff) sees several of these Pss as belonging to the national Festival of Yahweh; though it may simply refer to the general history of the preservation of Israel, or in still more general terms to God's protection of all who trust in him. 'David' is added to the **title.**

1–5. 'If it were not that the LORD were for us' [see on 118:6, PB etc 'on our side'; LXX/V here, less well, 'in our midst']; followed by an invitation to all Israel to share the thought of this Ps; or this may be a liturgical direction = 'Let all the people repeat this . . .' **2** 'when men rose up against us, **4** the waters would have swept us away . . . **5** . . . the overbearing waters': the word 'overbearing', only here, is related to 'arrogant', of enemies, esp. in Ps 119: so AV RV 'proud waters'; but it may be related to 'to boil', whence 'raging waters' RSV RPB; LXX 'irresistible', Vg 'intolerable'. **6–8.** But the Lord has saved us, **8** 'Our help is in the name of the LORD': the frequent liturgical phrase is from here (and see on 23:3).

h **125 A Song of Confidence**—A pleasant lyric with excitingly varied metre. **1–2.** Those who trust in the Lord are likened to the symbol of all that is stable on earth: God's abode on Mount Sion. **2.** '(As) Jerusalem (has) mountains round about her (for her safety), (so) the LORD (is) round about his people . . .': LXX/V divide a little differently. **3.** 'The sceptre of wickedness shall not rest upon the lot [= portion of land received by lot] of the righteous, so that the righteous shall not (be tempted to) put forth their hands to wrongdoing'. **4.** May the Lord reward the good, and punish those 'bend their crooked (ways)'. 'Peace upon Israel!': a final exclamation (so RV BJ RSV well), independent of the metrical pattern.

i **126 Joy in what the Lord has done**—**1.** 'When the LORD restored the fortunes of Sion': so NP RSV RPB. But cf 14:7; 53:7; 85:2; apparently = 'restored the captivity' so LXX/V Jer PB AV RV BJ here. See fuller note on 14:7. 'We became as men restored to health [from *ḥālam* "to be healthy"]': the verb appears twice in the OT: Is 38:16 and Jb 39:4, but *ḥᵉlîmā* 'healthy' is common in Syr., and Targum here has 'like sick men who are healed'; furthermore the Qumrân Psalter here reads *ḥᵃlîmîm* 'healthy', as in Aram. or Syr. (*pace* the transcription in the Oxford ed. of 11Q Psᵃ iv, 10): i. so RPB 'like unto them that renew their strength' (and see DWT); ii. LXX/V 'as consoled': = above, or emended? But cf LXX of Is 38:16; iii. 'as in a dream': Jer PB AV RV NP BJ RSV: following the commoner verb *ḥālam*: lit. 'like dreamers'.

j **2–3.** Amid our laughter and joy, the nations recognize God's work. **4.** 'Restore our fortunes [cf on v 1], like the watercourses [or, wadys] in the Negev': the southern desert, where streams are dry in the summer and suddenly turn into torrents when the rain comes. **5–6.** A pleasant picture of restored fortunes: sowing the seed amid tears, but reaping the harvest with joy— a picture that has brought hope and consolation to many. **6.** To 'go' (one way) weeping, and to 'come' (the way back) rejoicing, is probably no more than the same picture of sowing and harvesting (cf 'bearing their sheaves'); but if the 'restored fortunes' are interpreted of a particular event, as the Exile, rather than of God's general care, then the 'going' and 'coming' would have a more literal significance.

k **127 All Things are received from God**—This is a true 'Wisdom Psalm', and is thus classified by most **40** (including Mowinckel, II, 111 'non-cultic'), and perhaps for this reason 'Solomon' appears in the title. A house, a city, daily bread, and perhaps even sleep, are God's gifts, and (vv 3–5) his loveliest gift is children. The sentence on sleep (v 2) is uncertain, and the nexus with vv 3–5 is unclear, so that many suppose that there are two short, unconnected 'Wisdom Psalms' here. Yet the inclusion of children among God's blessings makes an obvious sequel.

1. 'If the LORD build not the house . . . guard the city . . .' your work is in vain. **2.** 'It is in vain that you rise early, go late to rest [JA 'sit up late'], eat the bread of toil: thus he gives to his beloved sleep': the last word is unexpectedly spelt as in Aram., and the meaning is puzzling. The versions (except those named under iii and iv below) translate literally. The main **l** interpretations or solutions are as follows: i. In contrast to the labours of most men, the beloved will sleep peacefully, cf Eccl 5:11 of 'sweet sleep' as the reward of labour. ii. Most men are anxious and not conscious of God's care, but the beloved has no anxieties: his tranquil sleep is a special gift of God. iii. [Translating 'sleep' as an adverb—doubtfully legitimate] 'thus (i.e. all these things) he gives to his beloved during sleep': RVm JA NP BJ. iv. '. . . gives sleep' = the 'blessings of the bed' = plentiful offspring begotten: cf RPB (see DWT), leading on to vv 3–5. But this meaning is not elsewhere in Hebrew included in 'sleep', although Wis 7:2 links conception and sleep in the origin of man (cf WV note), and this interpretation does provide a nexus with the following. v. 'Sleep' is normally of natural sleep, but the context in Jer 51:39, 57, Jb 14:12 and (a verb) Ps 13:4 shows = sleep of death, though never as a gift or 'sweet sleep'. In view, however, of the 'inheritance' of children in v 3, it is just possible that when the beloved 'sleeps', his children continue his name. So T. E. Bird in CCHS¹ on this verse. vi. The simplest solution is to regard the word 'sleep' as a mis-copy perhaps of 'in vain' and to omit it, reading 'Thus he gives to his beloved': cf Kittel. It is unfortunate that in both the Qumrân texts of this psalm (11Q Psᵃ iv, and the fragment 1Q 11:2) so far published, this piece is missing. **3–5.** The blessing of children **m** (which some regard as a separate Ps because of the tenuous connexion above): **4.** Children begotten in youth are 'like arrows in a warrior's hand', i.e. a special blessing, because of their supposed natural vigour, and/or because they will be grown up in time to fight alongside their father and/or care for their parents' old age. **5.** 'He is a blessed man who can fill his quiver [LXX/V 'fulfil his desire'—?] with such (arrows)' [cf Is 49:2 for the figure of the quiver]; they will be able to stand up to their enemies in the gateway: i. If the picture of the warrior with his quiver is essentially warlike, this indicates repulsing attackers trying to force the city gates. ii. If the quiver is rather a symbol of plentiful power, the gates may indicate the place of justice, where the children will not be defeated by any oppression; or else the place of business, where they will prosper.

128 The Home of the God-fearing Man—Here we **n** have the material of a 'Wisdom Psalm' (cf the similar opening of Ps 112) turned into a genuine lyric, in three almost regular stanzas, with the pleasantest imagery and a reminder that the vision of Sion is the greatest blessing of all.

1–2. 'Blessed is every one who fears the LORD . . .' **3.** 'Thy wife is like a fruitful vine in the recesses [word used of recesses of cave, house, ship, remote land (cf 48:3)] of thy house': Knox well 'in the heart of thy

7n home'. LXX/V with PB AV 'on the sides [or, walls] of thy house' pictures a vine trained on the wall, while Heb. pictures the wife as the centre of the home. 'Thy children are like young stems of olive branches...': the word 'stems' suggests strong, fresh, cool and delicate plants, perhaps transplanted shoots: a rare picture in the OT of the delights of young children, here pictured as sitting round the family table. (Zech 8:5 pictures boys and girls playing.) **4.** The happy home is indeed God's blessing on the God-fearing man, but **5** there is an even still greater blessing: 'to look upon the goodness of Jerusalem' = either the beauty of Sion, or (with most) her prosperity; **6** and to see thy own grandchildren. 'Peace upon Israel!' an exclamation as at the end of Ps 125, but here it forms part of the metrical pattern.

o 129 A short Lament and Imprecation—Within the manner of the short lyrics of the 'Gradual Psalms', this lament is in the authentic style of the 'Penitentials', complete with an imprecation introducing a new and telling figure of desolation for the wicked in vv 6–8.

1–2. 'Often they have attacked me [so LXX/V well] from my youth'—with repeat as in 124:1–2—'yet they have not prevailed...' **3.** 'They cut, cutting into my back, they made long scars', or as most with Targum and Jerome 'The ploughers ploughed upon my back, they made long their furrows': the last word, only here and in an uncertain place 1 Sm 14:14, is inferred from the context as 'scars' or 'furrows'. LXX/V have 'Sinners [also Qumrân (11Q Ps^a v,5) for "cutting", or "ploughers"] devised [for "cut" or "ploughed": the verb is basically "engraved"] upon my back, they made long their iniquities [a similar word to "scars" or "furrows"]'. In any case the picture is of a tortured man, lying face down and being whipped; the reference may be Israel's 'youth' in Egypt, but may equally be a hyperbolic description (cf Ps 6) of humiliation and pain. If 'ploughing' is the right picture, there is a corresponding metaphor in English of a 'harrowing' experience. **4.** But the Lord is just and has 'cut the cords of the wicked', i.e. the cords by which a captive is bound [see also on 118:27b], or dragged [cf 'cords of Sheol' 18:6 and 116:3]. LXX/V read 'cut the throat [or, neck] of...' **5–8.** A short imprecation, or prayer that 'all who hate Sion' be put to shame, **6** be like the miserable withered blades of grass on a rooftop, **7** which no one harvests **8** and to which no passer-by says (as he says to a fine hayfield) 'God bless you'.

p 130 De Profundis—A Ps numbered among the 'Penitentials' (see on Ps 6), though it is not so much a lament over my fate (as are the others), but one of the clearest expressions of confidence in God's forgiveness of sin, cf esp. 32 and 51, and of the soul's longing for God, cf 42–43. For these reasons the psalm is regularly used as a prayer for souls in Purgatory. A special feature is the relation between God's mercy and man's 'fear' of him in v 4.

1. 'Out of the depths [sc. of my helplessness: in Pss the word is only here and 69:3, 15 in the figure of being stuck in the mud and overwhelmed by water] I have cried to thee, o Lord (Yahweh), **2** Master (Adonai) hear my voice... **3** If thou wilt mark [lit. keep, cf Vg observare] iniquities, Yah [= Yahweh]...': i. 'keep iniquities' = keep note of, watch for—an uncommon usage, but so most; ii. 'keep' = 'keep remembrance of' = not forget (and forgive): cf NP; iii. 'keep' = 'retain' in sense of Jn 20:23 'retain sins' = not take away, cover, put out of sight (cf Ps 32:1,2; 85:3); '... Master (Adonai), who shall stand? i. 'stand' = 'be able to remain (BJ subsistere)' in face of thy accusation; ii. 'stand' = 'stand up in a court of law' and plead

innocent; iii. 'stand' = 'resist' thy judgement: so LXX/ **407p** V, but the Gr. and Latin verbs usually have an object, so PB 'abide it', Douay 'stand it'—the Heb. verb is intransitive. **4.** But no, this is not the situation: 'for **q** with thee (there) is forgiveness'. The exact sense of the next phrase l^ema'an tiwwārē is obscure: i. 'because of (this) thou art feared' [a slightly forced syntax]: PB 'therefore shalt thou be...', BJ 'c'est alors que ...': = the proper 'fear' of God is the result of our recognition of his mercy; ii. 'because of (the fact that = since) thou art feared': Jer 'cum terribilis sis' = our 'fear' of God is the basis of our readiness to receive his mercy; iii. 'in order that thou be feared' [the most natural syntax]: cf AV RV NP RSV RPB = God's mercy instils into us a proper 'fear' of him—but it must be admitted that this is an unusual notion: 'fear' is usually inspired by his judgement, e.g. 119:120; iv. Vg reads tôrāh (Gk nómos): 'because of thy Law 5 I have waited...': the traditional Christian interpretation supposes this text; v. LXX^Sin A (LXX^B is lost here) by corruption read onoma: 'because of thy name'. **5–6.** There are difficulties also here: i. Heb.: **r** 'I have waited, o Lord, my soul has waited; and for his word I have hoped; **6** my soul (has hoped) for my Master (Adonai)...'; ii. LXX/V: 'I have waited for thee, o Lord; my soul has waited for thy [Vg his] word; **6** my soul has hoped for the Lord...'; iii. Qumrân (11Q Ps^a v,13, defective until:) '... LORD; my soul has waited for his word; I have hoped **6** (my soul) has hoped [an erasure here makes the ending uncertain]...'; iv. With the help of LXX/V and Qumrân therefore, the text could perhaps best be read: 'because of thy Law **5** I have waited o LORD; my soul has waited for his word; **6** my soul has hoped for my Master...' **6** '...hoped for my Master **s** more (eagerly) than they watch for the morning (who?) watch for the morning': i. = 'than they who watch [= watchmen]...watch...': perhaps the most natural—'watch' is a participle both times; ii. = 'than they [i.e. watchmen] watch for the morning, watch for the morning': a simple repetition to convey the weariness—perhaps the most graphic and attractive; iii. — 'than watchmen... (yea, more than) watchmen...': again a simple repetition: cf RV RSV RPB; iv. [re-dividing] 'my soul (has waited)...more (eagerly) than watchmen... (More eagerly than)watchmen... **7** shall Israel hope...' NP cf BJ; v. [repointing 'watching' to 'watches'] 'my soul (has waited)...from morning watch (to) morning watch [= always]': Jerome, cf LXX/V which somehow read '...until night'. And cf PB. However we translate this last phrase, the figure is clear enough as an expression of longing for the dawn, be it of the night watchman, the night worker, or the sleepless person: so my soul longs for God. **7–8.** Let Israel hope in the Lord, for with him there is mercy and redemption.

131 Humility and Trust—This little lyric is one of **408a** the shortest of the psalms (only 117 and 134 are shorter), but one of the most charming, with its graceful imagery of the babe with its mother. It is a protestation of trust that goes with the recognition that some things are beyond our understanding and skill. Its **title** includes the name of 'David', perhaps as befitting the character of the ideal king.

1. 'Lord, my heart is not high [= haughty], and my eyes are not raised [= proud], and I have not walked [= busied myself] with things greater and more wonderful than I (can understand). **2.** But indeed I have [lit according to Heb. idiom 'If I have not...', reflected in LXX/V] calmed and quieted my soul, (which has become) as a babe (lying quiet) upon (the breast of) its mother, as a babe is my soul': Heb. adds 'upon me',

408a which is probably a mis-copy of 'upon' preceding: i. so [omitting 'upon me'] 'as a babe (that is quiet) is my soul': cf PB AV RSV; ii. ['upon me' = ? 'within me'] '. . . is my soul within me': NP BJ RPB; iii. ['upon me' = ? 'with me'] '. . . is my soul with me (as with a mother)': Jer RV; iv. [for *gāmûl* 'babe', reading *gᵉmûl*] 'so is recompense in my soul': LXX/V; 3 'Let Israel hope in the LORD . . .': cf 130:7.

b 132 David's Vow and God's Promise—This Ps stands in a genre of its own: an entirely imaginary picture of an historical event, namely, when David fetched the ark into Jerusalem, and is pictured as having made a vow about this. The Ps is in regular metre and of clear stanzaic construction. It has been maintained (e.g. by Gunkel) that the Ps is a piece of dramatic liturgy to accompany a procession with the ark, or (Mowinckel I, 129) for the Enthronement Festival, or (Weiser) for the temple dedication.

1. 'Remember, o Lord, (with reference) to David, all his hardships [LXX/V meekness]': the construction 'Remember for David . . .' is not common, but is often used by Nehemiah (e.g. 5:19) and cf Ps 137:7: we might say 'Remember me for all my . . .' The older versions simply say 'Remember David and all . . .' **2.** Here David is pictured as making a vow to 'the Mighty One of Jacob [a phrase only here and v 5 in the Pss, and derived from Gn 49:24]'. **3—5.** The words of his (imaginary) vow, that he will not rest until he has found a place for the ark (quoted freely in Ac 7:46). ['I will not . . .' is in Heb. idiom 'If I shall . . .', cf on 131:2.] The fetching of the ark is in 1 Chr 13:5—14; 15:25—29, cf 2 Sm 6:2—19 (when David danced 6:14). **6.** David's men responded to his effort: 'Behold we have heard (of) it at Ephrathah, we have found it in the fields of *Ya'ar* [= 'forest'; RSV RPB 'Jaar'] = Kiriath Jearim ['town of forests'], whence the ark was brought 1 Chr 13:5—7, 2 Sm 6:3, and where for twenty years it had been 1 Sm

c 7:1—2. It is at first natural to suppose that the two names Ephrathah and Jaar (Kiriath Jearim) refer to one place; but they are not easily to be identified. Ephrathah is a name given to Bethlehem in Judah (5 m. S of Jerusalem) in Ru 1:2; 4:11, Mi 5:1 [English 2]; while K. Jearim is on the border of Benjamin and Dan (8m. W of Jerusalem): i. Some suppose that the name Ephrathah was also given to K. Jearim (it may mean 'fruitful place'), but there is no evidence; yet the name is apparently given to other places: Rachel's tomb (Gn 35:16) (in spite of the identification in 35:19) seems to be in a different place (1 Sm 10:2); and the Ephraimites are called Ephrathites in Jg 12:5 and 1 Sm 1:1 (though RSV has changed these to 'Ephraimites'). ii. A connexion between Ephrathah, Bethlehem and K. Jearim, may be found in the offspring of Caleb's wife Ephrath (1 Chr. 2:19; 2:50; 4:4, cf 2:50—51). These suggest association, if not identification. iii. But they can be taken here as separate places: 'We have so often heard of the ark being at Shiloh in Ephraim (= Ephrathah) in former times (e.g. Jos. 18:1, 1 Sm 1:3, cf Ps 78:60); and now we have found it at Kiriath Jearim'. iv. Or David may be pictured in his home town of Bethlehem (e.g. 1 Sm 17:12 [Ephrathite], etc) with his men (= at Ephrathah), when he receives the news: 'We heard the news about it at Bethlehem, and we went and found it at Kiriath Jearim'. Perhaps the most con-

d vincing solution to this problem. **7.** 'Let us go to his dwelling . . .': uttered either by the men who brought the news, or by David himself and his men. **8—10.** An apostrophe addressed by David to God asking him to take up his abode in the sanctuary prepared for 'the ark of

thy strength' (see on 96:6 and cf 78:61), where **9** the priests are 'vested with righteousness' or more likely = 'clothed in the (liturgically) correct (vestments)' and the devout populace [see on 12:2] are singing. The picture here is one of the Temple liturgy of a later age, imagined as functioning at the beginning under David, and it has more affinity with the account in 1 Chr 15 than with the quieter account in 2 Sm 6. **10.** And all this not to refuse David 'thine anointed'. These verses appear at the end of Solomon's prayer at the dedication of the Temple in 2 Chr 6:41—42. **11—12.** The theme of God's promise to David, cf 89:20—38, with the promise of his throne for his offspring (quoted in Ac 2:30), provided **12** they remain faithful. **13—16.** A further part of the promise is God's choice of Sion and **15** her prosperity ['I will bless her provisions' = LXX 'prey' (*thēra*), but LXX^Sin A mistakenly *chḗra*, whence Vg 'widow'] and **16** piety (echoing v 9). **17.** 'There I will cause to blossom a horn for David': for the figure of the 'horn' (of an animal) = prosperity, see on 75:5, but only here and Ez 29:21 is the horn pictured as growing out of the head and blossoming. **18.** Finally his enemies will be shamed, but his crown (cf 89:40, and perhaps 89:20) will 'flash' (cognate word of golden plate in Lv 8:5 etc, but usually = 'flowers' as Aaron's rod in Nm 17:23, whence LXX/V here).

133 In Praise of Brotherly Love—This pleasant psalm **e** praises the 'pleasantness' of unity. Whether or no the thought is based on the idea of blood brothers living together in peace (the same phrase being used of Abram and Lot, and of Jacob and Esau in Gn 13:6 and 36:7, and of a brother in the same house in Dt 25:4), the psalm has been loved for its evident wider applications, and the colourful comparisons in vv 2—3. It is usually classed as a 'Wisdom Psalm', but like the others among the 'Gradual Psalms' (127, 128) it has no lack of poetic invention. The **title** includes 'David'.

1. 'Behold how good and how pleasant (it is), brethren living together (in unity)!': the only place in the Pss where brotherly harmony as such is considered as an ideal. And it is a situation that is called *nā'îm* 'sweet' or 'pleasant' (cf the name Naomi), conveying, like the LXX *terpnós* here, all that is delightful in a pleasant experience. It is a word full of flavour, best felt by noticing the other things that are so described—apart from the context of the praise of God in Pss 135:3; 147:1 and the 'loveliness of the Lord' in 27:4; 90:17. There is friendship (Saul and Jonathan) 2 Sm 1:23, pleasant conversation Prv 23:8, wise teaching Prv 22:18, a well-furnished room Prv 24:4, pleasant property Ps 16:6,11, the physical beauty of the lover Song 1:16, and finally a musical instrument Ps 81:3 and David 'the sweet singer of Israel' 2 Sm 23:1. **2.** The 'pleasantness' is **f** then likened to two pleasant things, first 'good oil upon the head, going down upon the beard': a fragrant hair-oil, and one must remember (see on 23:5) the importance of anointing in the ancient world for freshening and sweetening the skin. But the text continues referring not only to oil that is pleasant, but to sacred oil that was poured upon the head of Aaron the high priest (Ex 29:7, Lv 8:12) and so upon his beard, 'which goes down upon the collar of his robes': the 'collar', lit. 'mouth', of the top opening of a tunic (cf e.g. Ex 28:32), not the 'skirt' of PB AV RV, nor the 'hem' of LXX/V: i. perhaps the most natural reading is 'the beard . . . which extends over the collar . . . [a priest's beard was not to be cut, Lv 21:5]': so JA with Rashi; but the fact that it is the same verb of the oil 'running down' and the beard 'extending' causes most to abandon this; ii. most with LXX/V (where

408f genders make it plain) take as '(the oil) . . . which goes down upon the collar . . .' Many consider the picture of the pleasant hair-oil to be confused by a later gloss 'the beard of Aaron . . .', giving a priestly and sacred turn which is really irrelevant to the argument. Thus e.g. Briggs and Kraus omit the phrase in their translations. **3.** The second 'pleasantness': the cool dew of the snow-capped Mount Hermon pictured as coming down upon the hot hills of Sion. 'For there (in Sion) has the LORD commanded the blessing: life for ever': dew is several times seen as a blessing and the gentleness of its coming is underlined, e.g. Dt 32:2 and cf the figures in Ps 72:6. The Qumrân Psalter (11Q Ps^a xxiii,10) omits 'life', giving a better reading '. . . blessing for ever', since 'Life for ever' is a most unlikely notion in the Pss, with no parallel. It also adds 'Peace upon Israel!' cf Ps 125, 128.

g 134 A Call to Praise, and a Blessing—The last of the 'Gradual Psalms'. Many see here a liturgical dialogue (see on v 3), and some even a formula for the 'changing of the guard' in the Temple. Otherwise it may convey the idea of God's blessing on each one who takes part in God's praises. The shortest Ps after 117.
1—2. 'Behold, bless ye the Lord, all ye servants of the LORD, who stand in the House of the Lord night after night [lit "in the nights"], **2** lift up your hands (towards) the holy (place) [so most; or "(in) the . . ." PB AV] . . .': LXX/V have an addition from 135:2 and divide different-ly. The call seems to be addressed to priests on duty in the Temple, and is therefore frequently used in monastic choirs at Compline. **3.** 'May the Lord bless thee [note the singular] from Sion . . .': the phrase is probably an echo from Nm 6:24 where the priests are to bless 'the children of Israel' with the form 'May the Lord bless thee . . .' in the singular, i.e. each one personally: i Thus the singular here may, with Nm 6:24, indicate a blessing on each one: ii. But some see the singular as the reply of the group addressed in vv 1—2 to the one who sum-moned them, the presiding priest.

h 135 A Hymn to God's Greatness—This Ps seems to be largely a pastiche of passages from Pss 115 and 136 and almost verbatim from elsewhere. The fact that the pieces lack cohesion here and are without metrical consistency suggests that they are not original here. The Ps was evidently constructed for liturgical use, which accounts for the introduction of the 'Levite' in v 20 and the Temple blessing at the end. Only title: Hallelu yah.
1—2. 'Praise the name of the Lord . . . [— 113.1],. . . (ye) who [a late Heb. form] stand in the House of the Lord [= 134:1 with the addition 'in the courts . . .' which appears there in LXX/V] . . . **3** Praise Yah [= Yah-weh] . . . sing to his name, for it (his name), is nā'îm [= 'lovely, pleasant' see on 133:1; Vg here *suave*]': i. so LXX/V (neuter, with 'name'), PB AV RV NP RPB BJ? (*il est aimable* = *son nom*?); ii. 'for it (to praise him) is a lovely thing': Jer (*decens*), cf 147:1; iii. 'for he (the Lord) is gracious': RSV cf Grail ('loving'?—missing BJ's i sense?) **4.** 'The LORD has chosen . . . Israel for his peculiar treasure [so AV RV well]': a special word here echoed from Ex 19:5 (also Dt 7:6; 14:2; 26:18), and again echoed in Eph 1:14, Tit 2:14 and esp. 1 Pet 2:9, often translated 'possession' (too colourless), and used especially of Israel's relation to God (though twice used of ordinary treasure in 1 Chr 29:3 and Eccl 2:8—late usage). **5—7.** The rhythm changes slightly: 'For I know that Yahweh [the LORD] is greater . . . than all other gods, **6** he does whatever his pleasure is [= 115:3] . . .' **7.** He is lord of nature [much = Jer 10:13 = 51:16] . . . **8—12.** He smote the firstborn of Egypt and led Israel

into the Land [all echoes of 136:17—21, where see **408i** notes]. **13—14.** 'Thy name, o LORD, is for ever . . . **14.** For the Lord shall sit in judgement on [RSV vindicate; PB RPB avenge] his people [quoted Hb 10:30], and have compassion . . .' [= Dt 32:36]. **15—18.** 'The idols of the nations . . .' almost verbatim from Ps 115:4—8, with a curious shortening in v 17 (= 115:6) where '*aph* 'nose' of 115 becomes '*aph* 'indeed'. **19—20.** But in contrast, 'Let the house of Israel bless the Lord . . . the house of Aaron, **20** the house of the Levite . . . those who fear the Lord . . .': cf 115:9—11 with the addition of the 'Levite', always translated 'Levi', but *Lēwī* has the article, so = 'Levite' (same meaning). The phrase 'house of the Levite' is only here (and 'House of Levi' only twice, in Ex 1:2, Zech 12:13), and neither Levite nor Levi are mentioned elsewhere in the Pss. The phrase was probably inserted here to emphasize the final liturgical blessing, which **21** includes both Sion and Jerusalem. Hallelu-yah at the end.
136 The Great Hallel—Often so called as distinct **j** from 'the Hallel' (or 'Song of Praise') which is Pss 113—118. It is most obviously noted for its refrain in every verse (as has the Qumrân text of Ps 145; Ps 118 has four such verses at the beginning). It is of notably regular metre, with the line of 3 beats, followed by the refrain of 2 beats throughout, with clear stanzas, vv 1—18 being 6 stanzas with 3 members, and vv 19—26 being 4 stanzas of 2 members.
1—3. 'Give thanks to the Lord for his goodness, for his love (is) for ever': see on 106:1 for a discussion of the exact words. **3.** '. . . to the Lord (*Adonai*) of lords . . .' **4—6.** Praise and thanks to the creator, who **6** 'spread [RSV well] the earth on the water': the picture is of the earth floating on the primeval waters, cf Gn 1:9—10. **7—9.** The luminaries: v 9 has an unusually long line. **10—12.** God's care of Israel; **12** 'with a strong hand and an outstretched arm': a phrase from Dt 4:34; 5:15; 26:8, with similar phrases elsewhere. **13—15.** The Exodus: **15** 'he shook off' Pharaoh (as in Ex 14:27), as one shakes off an insect in Ps 109:23. **16—18.** The desert and the **k** slaying of the kings. **19—20.** (2-verse stanzas now) The kings by name: Sihon of the Amorites (Nm 21.21—24) and Og of Bashan (Nm 21:33—35), linked in Dt 1:4; 3:1—11 (with Og's 'bed' 9 cubits long), Jos. 13:10—12 (only here and Ps 135:11 in the Pss), having become symbols of terrible enemies defeated, like Oreb and Zeeb etc in 83:12. **21—22.** God gave their lands to Israel, **23—24** having remembered us. **25—26.** The thought suddenly broadens to God's universal provision 'for all flesh', and concludes **26** with an invitation to praise 'the God ('*Ēl*) of heaven'; a phrase only found here (though 'the God ('*elōhê*) of . . .' comes in Gn 24:7, in the last v of the Hebrew Bible 2 Chr 36:23, and 5t in Ez-Neh). Vg adds a repetition of v 3 at the end (so also PB).
137 By the Rivers of Babylon—A Ps famous for its **l** expression of misery away from a homeland that is a holy place, but perhaps more so for the expression of vengeance at the end. The Ps is certainly exilic or post-exilic, but may well be a still later imagined *mis-en-scène* of the exile.
1. 'By the rivers of Babylon, there we sat down and wept . . . **2.** By the poplars in her (Babylon's) midst we hung up our harps [or other stringed instruments]'—having no more heart for music in our sorrows: the 'poplar' probably = *populus euphratica*, whose Arabic name is similar to the Hebrew here (see BDB); not = *salix babylonica* = weeping willow so misnamed because of LXX/V here 'willows'; the same tree, in Lv 23:40, Is 15:7, 44:4, Jb 40:22, is always associated with water, whence doubtless 'willow'. **3.** 'There our captors asked of us words of song, our plunderers [uncertain word only

J

408l here] (asked us) for (songs of) joy, saying, Sing to us (something) from a song of (your country) Sion'. 4. But 'how can we sing the LORD's song in a strange land?': this was their answer, for it would be a profanation to sing of Sion among her enemies. 5. At the same time, 'if I should forget thee, o Jerusalem, let my right hand wither!': i. 'wither', cf Ugaritic root (see DWT), forming a play on words with 'forget'—older authors reached this meaning by emendation, comparing 109:24 (see Kittel)· BJ RSV RPB; ii. 'forget [as in preceding phrase]': PB AV RV [all adding 'its cunning', i.e. ability to play music]; iii. [repointing] 'be forgotten' = as if no longer

m there: LXX/V NP. 6. Further curses on myself, should I forget Jerusalem. 7. In contrast to my love of Sion, 'remember, o Lord, (with reference to) Edom [cf idiom in 132:1] the "day" of Jerusalem, when they said, Strip, strip (her), to the foundations in her': the 'day' is of course the sacking of the city. The participation of Edom in the sacking is not mentioned in the historical accounts, but it is the point of Obadiah's prophecy, e.g. v 12 'on the day of thy brother', and of Ezek 35 e.g. v 5, and both Obad and Ezek speak of the doom upon Edom in punishment for this. 'Strip her (naked)' is either a metaphor of shame; or = 'laying bare' the city by tearing down her walls to the foundations (cf AV RV RSV PB RPB NP). 8–9. As doom was in store for Edom, may doom come upon thee, 'o daughter of Babylon, destroyed!': i. 'destroyed' = 'to be destroyed in punishment': AV RV; ii. 'destroyed' = 'wasted away, miserable': Jer PB RSVm, cf LXX/V; iii. [repointed] 'thou destroyer': NP BJ RSV RPB. 'Happy is he [= he does a good thing] who repays thee with the

n service thou hast served to us; 9 happy is he who shall seize thy babes and dash them upon the rocks!': this is the 'imprecation', or willing misfortune upon another, in its most virulent form, namely the praise of him who performs the act of violence upon the enemy, and moreover an act of particular hideousness. Even the great imprecation of Ps 109 does not involve such plain brutality as does this famous passage. It is small help to find the 'smashing of babies' (actually a different verb reserved for this) regarded as a hazard of invasion (though deplored) in 2 (4) Kgs 8:12, Ho 14:1 [English 13:16], Is 13:16. It is more useful to recognize (1) the possible existence of such cruel desires in the human make-up in situations of extreme stress, (2) the extreme suffering that can be caused to man by other men, to produce such violent feelings towards the oppressor (as lynching), and (3) the presence of indignation against injustice. For this problem see also the intro. to Ps 109, with a reference to C. S. Lewis's book, *Reflections on the Psalms*.

o 138 The Praise of God before all men—An 'everyday' kind of Psalm with no strongly marked features: a straightforward hymn 'for various occasions'. Yet the mention of 'all the kings of the earth' in v 4 is a gentle statement of the 'universalist' theme. **Title:** 'David', beginning the 'David Collection V' (138–45), nearly all of which have much affinity with 'David I and II' (3–41 and 51–70), especially in the familiar type of 'Individual Lament'.

1. 'I will give thee praise and thanks [one word, see on 67:4 and 106:1] . . . before *'elōhîm* I will sing thee': for discussion of the meaning of *elohim* for other than the true God, see further on 8:6 and 82:1 : i. = 'gods': Jer PB AV RV RSV RPB [but there is no context here of false gods, as e.g. in 82:1; 97:7]; ii. = 'angels' = court of heaven [as 'sons of *elohim*' Jb 1:6; 2:1]: LXX/V NP BJ (so Rashi); Syriac 'kings' is probably a mis-spelling of 'angels' under the influence of v 4; iii. = 'judges': Targum WV (so Ibn Ezra), and see on 82:1 and 58:2;

p iv. = 'mighty ones': JA, and cf the kings in v 4. 2. 'I will

bow towards thy holy temple . . . for thou hast made great **408** thy word above all thy name': an uncertain passage: i. so Jer AV RV NP, meaning? 'Thou hast made greater thy word [= promise] than thy name [=? renown]'—very doubtful; cf BJ [repointing] 'Thy promise is greater than thy renown'; ii. 'Thou hast exalted above everything [repointed] thy name (and) thy word': PB NP RSV RPB (following LXX/V for repointing); iii. '. . . above everything thy holy name': LXX/V [reading?]. 3. 'On the day I called . . . thou didst increase strength in my soul': following Vg (LXX similar), for uncertain Heb. word 'increase'. 4–5. The kings of the earth shall praise thee: cf 68:30; 72:11; 102:16. 6. 'For the Lord is high, but looks upon the lowly, and the haughty he humbles from afar': 'humbles' from a second Heb. root as in 14:4 (see DWT): so RPB; others with LXX/V 'he knows' =? 'he recognises for what they are'. 7. In my troubles thou givest me life . . . 8 . . . 'Forsake not [lit. 'let not go of': RPB well 'leave not unfinished'] the works of thy hands'.

139 God's Universal Knowledge and Care—The **409a** first two sections are a graceful recognition of God's knowledge and care of me (vv 1—13) and his creation of me (vv 14—18), followed by a short prayer against the wicked (vv 19—22) with the important notion (v 22) of God's enemies being my enemies. The numerous Aramaisms suggest a late date. The text is sometimes very uncertain. In the **title** 'For the precentor' occurs only in Ps 109, here, and Ps 140 in Books IV—V.

1. 'LORD, thou hast searched me and known me . . . 2 . . . understood my purpose . . . 3. My path [= my travels] and my lying down [= my staying at home (Aram. form)] thou hast sifted, thou art acquainted with all my ways': LXX/V divide differently, and read '. . . My path and my rope [properly of rushes, so? bed of rushes (so Brenton's LXX)] thou hast traced, thou hast foreseen . . .': the origin of these readings is unknown. 4. 'For there is not [= even before there is] a word [Aram.] on my tongue, thou hast known it . . .' 5. Thou hast beset me [as a besieged city—LXX/V PB 'fashioned me']. 7. 'Where can I go from thy spirit . . . flee from thy presence?' 8. 'If I go up [Aram.] to the sky [= the highest place] . . ., if I lie down [lit. 'spread out to lie down'] in Sheol [= lowest imaginable], thou art there;

b 9 if I take up the wings of the dawn, dwell in the furthermost [or westernmost] west [or sea] . . .': = wherever I go, up or down, east (dawn) or west (sea, i.e. Mediterranean, as often), thou art there. 11—12. 'And I said, Indeed darkness shall cover me [emended], and night (shall be) a girdle [emended with Qumrân] about me; 12 (but) also darkness shall not be dark from thee [meaning?], and night shall be light as the day: darkness (shall be) as light [Aram. words, but Qumrân has Heb. forms]': a difficult passage, the general sense of which seems to be: 'Even if I try to hide from thee under cover of darkness, the darkness will be illuminated by thee and thou shalt still find me': 'cover' is a generally accepted emendation of Heb. 'bruise', LXX/V 'trample'; 'girdle' (11Q Psª xx, 3) is read for Heb. 'light', providing a better parallel in v 11 than 'night (shall be) light about me', which belongs to the picture of v 12.; 'dark from thee' is difficult: i. =? 'dark with thee': NP RPB, or 'dark to thee': RSV, cf BJ [doubtful]; ii. = 'hides not itself [lit. is dark] from thee': RV [rather forced]; iii. = 'too dark for thee (to find me)': JA [probably the best]; iv. = 'darkened by thee': LXX/V [reading?]. 13. I cannot escape from thy watchfulness **c** (vv 7—12), for 'thine are my reins [kidneys = seat of emotions, cf on 7:10, or = vital organs], thou dost knit me together [RSV well] in the womb of my mother': 'thine are' = lit. 'thou hast possessed', which some take as

409c 'acquired' or 'made'. **14.** 'I will praise thee, for that I am fearfully (and) wonderfully made [so PB AV RV NP BJ; but some repoint 'thou art awesome . . .': so LXX/V RSV RPB] and my soul knows (that) right well [so LXX/V PB AV RV; others repoint 'And thou knowest . . .': so NP BJ RSV RPB]. **15.** My frame [lit. 'bone'; Qumrân reads 'my toil'] is not hidden from thee, when I was being made in secret, woven [RPB well] in the depths of the earth [= the hidden power of nature], **16** thine eyes beheld my imperfect form [so most since LXX/V, uncertain word *gôlem* only here =? as yet unborn; but perhaps read *gîlîm* 'my youthful lifestages', cf 43:4, and Ugaritic usage (see Dahood, Bib 40 [1959] 168) and cf on Ps 2:12], and in thy book [for God's 'book' see on 69:29] they (my lifestages) [or, my days, following] are all written; the days were (already) formed, [= although] not one (yet existed) among them. **17.** And to me how precious are thy purposes [as v 2], o God, how strong the sum [lit. 'head'] of them': LXX/V took 'purposes' for the similar word 'friends', and so in the liturgy *'Mihi autem . . .'* (Introit of Apostles), with the

d 'rule' of them. **18.** 'Would I count them (thy purposes), they were more than the sand; would I finish (counting them, if I could), I would still be with thee [i.e. thou art ever present]': an uncertain text: i. 'would I finish [from *qāsas*]': NP BJ JA RSVm RPB; ii. 'when I awake [from *qîṣ*]': LXX/V ('get up'), PB AV RV RSV—but the introduction of waking from sleep (having fallen asleep from weariness in counting?) is awkward, though Targum without embarrassment has 'awake in the world to come', and Ibn Ezra interprets of the apparent sleep of contemplation. The Easter Mass (*Resurrexi . . .*, Introit) quotes freely from here. **19.** In sharp contrast with the foregoing meditation on God's care, and even pursuit of me, and his wonderful creation of me, we have here a curious kind of prayer where the psalmist addresses God: 'If thou wouldst slay the wicked . . .': the rest is unsaid (it would be a good thing for everyone). An unusual

c kind of imprecation. Then 'men of blood would depart from me, **20** (they) who speak against thee [an uncertain phrase] for evil purpose, thy enemies [doubtful word: Aram.?] take up [?] in vain: i. 'enemies [so Targum] lift themselves up [repointed] in vain': NP; ii. 'enemies take (thy name) in vain: PB AV RV [but insertion unwarranted]; iii. 'they lift themselves up in vain against thee [emended from 'enemies')': RSV; iv. 'they take thy name [emended from 'enemies'] in vain'. RPB; v. 'they hold as of nought thy purposes [different emendation]': BJ; vi. 'they take in vain thy cities [exactly similar word to 'enemies']': LXX/V [the most natural reading, but the meaning is not clear]. **21–22.** 'Shall I not hate them that hate thee . . .? **22.** They have become enemies to me': the plainest statement of the principle underlying so many references to 'my enemies'. **23–24.** 'Search me and know my thoughts . . .': a return to the opening theme of the psalm.

f 140 A Prayer for Deliverance—A Ps akin to several in Books I and II, e.g. 54, 56, 59 and esp. 64, and including a colourful imprecation. **Title:** 'David', and includes for the last time 'the precentor'.

2–4. 'Deliver me, Lord, from the evil man . . . **4.** They have sharpened their tongue as a serpent, the venom of an asp is under their lips [quoted Rm 3:13] . . . **9.** Grant not the desires of the wicked man, further not his plot'. **10–11.** 'Those who surround me lift up [from v 9] (their) head . . . **11.** Let coals with fire be shaken out upon them, let them fall [repointed] into the mire [so RPB, uncertain word only here], let them not rise (out of it again)': so NP BJ RSV RPB; LXX/V and PB AV RV divide slightly

differently. **12.** 'Let not the slanderer [so JA RSV RPB, **409f** cf RV BJ, lit. 'man of tongue', LXX 'talkative man' (so Brenton)] be established . . .' **13–14.** '(But) I know that the LORD will do (right) judgement for the "poor" [see on 9:13] . . .'

141 A Prayer for Protection—A straightforward **g** prayer, which like 139–40 is similar in tone to many in Books I and II. Very difficult are vv 5 7, which is some sort of imprecation. **Title:** David.

1. 'Lord, I have called thee, make haste (to come) to me . . . **2.** Let my prayer be established (as) incense, the lifting up of my hands (in prayer) (as) an evening offering': the rendering 'as incense . . . as an offering' is that of LXX and all the versions, and in this form has entered the liturgy. **3–4.** Set a guard upon my mouth . . . **5–7** is one of the most obscure passages in the whole Psalter: 'Let a just man strike me [i.e. correct me] (in) kindness, and reprove me; oil of the head [or emend to 'the wicked' with LXX/V] let it not anoint [uncertain word] my head . . .': i. = 'Let a just man strike me (in) kindness, and reprove me; (but) let not the oil of the wicked [emended; = their honour or compliments, cf Prv. 27:6] anoint my head': LXX/V RPB cf RSV; ii. = 'Let a just man strike me—it is a kindness, and let him reprove me; but let not the oil of the wicked adorn . . .': BJ; iii. = 'Let a just man strike me—it is a kindness; and let him reprove me—it is as oil upon the head [a pleasant thing, cf 133:2]; let not my head refuse it': RV NP; iv. = '. . . let it not break [cf Nm 32:7 (Ibn Ezra) | my head': AV cf PB. 'For while yet (I live) my prayer is for their wickedness': i. = 'against their wickedness': PB BJ RSV RPB cf LXX/V 'purposes'; ii. = 'that evil may come upon them': AV (so Ibn Ezra); iii. = 'even when their wickedness torments me': cf RV NP. **6.** 'Cast **h** down by the sides [lit hands—'hand' = 'side' of road, river] of a rock are their judges, and (then) they shall hear [= understand] . . .': the picture of most interpretations is that of a precipice: i. so RV NP BJ: i.e. the wicked leaders of the people are rightly pushed over a precipice to their death, and then the people will understand; ii. 'Let their judges . . .': cf PB RPB; or 'When . . .': AV; iii. LXX text is confused: 'Their mighty ones (*krataioi* confused from *kritai*) near a rock were swallowed up . . .': Vg 'judges attached to a rock . . .' (a gruesome picture of judges tied to rocks and thrown over?); iv. [supposing 'rock' to have come here from the next v] '(When) they (the wicked) fall into the hands of [omit 'rock'] their judges (who will condemn them), then they will understand . . .': RSV. '(Then) they shall hear [= understand] that my words are sweet' [same root as in v 4 and Ps 133:1]: BJ understands 'my words' of what follows. **7.** 'Like one splitting and cleaving on the earth, **i** so our bones are scattered at the mouth of Sheol': the picture is not clear: i. 'Like a ploughman cleaving (furrows) upon the earth, so (like the scattered earth) are our [or, 'their'] bones . . .': cf Jer RV NP RPB; ii. 'As when one splits and cleaves (wood) upon the ground, so (like the abandoned chips of wood) are our bones . . .': PB AV; iii. 'As a rock [taken from v 6] (which) one splits and cleaves on the ground, so (like the scattered flakes of stone) are our [or, their] bones . . .': RSV (cf on v 6) [perhaps the best solution]; iv. 'Like a millstone [repointed] shattered on the ground, so are our bones . . .': BJ; v. 'Like a lump of earth [so Brenton] is broken upon the ground . . .': LXX cf Vg. 'Our bones' is part of the picture of calamity upon the wicked, while the reading 'their bones' refers to the judges of v 6. What is the whole picture of these mysterious verses? Perhaps: **4** I will have no part with the wicked, **5** I will not accept their praise,

409i **6** unjust judges will come to a bad end, and then people will understand, **7** but meanwhile we are scattered and die, **8** but I look to thee . . . The thing is very uncertain.

j 142 A Psalm of Distress—A typical 'Individual Lament' with protestation of innocence, comparable to others in the 'David Collections I and II'. The **Title:** '*Maskîl*' (a description of uncertain meaning) only here in Books IV–V; 'David (Collection V [138–45])'; 'when he was in the cave', as in Ps 57, an (imaginary) *mise-en-scène* in David's life (perhaps because of v.8), referring to Adullam in 1 Sm 22:1, or to Engedi 1 Sm 24:2–4—the only such ascription outside Books I–II, most of them being in 51–63; also the only Ps in Book V entitled 'A Prayer'.

2. '(With) my voice [= aloud, not only in my thoughts] I cry to the LORD . . .': BJ takes as an exclamation: '*A Yahvé mon cri! J'implore* . . .' **3–4.** I tell him of my troubles. **5.** The picture here is of a court of law, where I am on trial: 'Look to the right [or better with the Qumrân Psalter (11Q Ps^a XXV, 1) and LXX/V 'I look . . .': so PB AV RV (not JA) RSV RPB] and see, and there is none that recognizes me (as his client)': for my 'right hand', where my counsel for defence should be, see on 16:8 and 109:31. '. . . There is none that cares for my life [lit. 'seeks my soul': an uncommon usage]'. **6–8.** '. . . Thou art my hope, my portion [= all I have, see on 16:5] in the land of the living [i.e. my only hope for **k** survival] . . . **8.** Bring my soul [= me, my life] out of prison (that I may be able) to give thanks to thy name . . .': the significance of 'prison' [lit. 'enclosure', only here in Pss, and elsewhere only Is 24:22; 42:7 both metaphorical] is uncertain: i. = the prison to which I was condemned at the trial (v 5); ii. = general expression of misery, cf 88:9 (different word); iii. = danger of death (cf 'land of the living' in v 6, and 'prisoners . . . condemned to die' in Pss 79:11; 102:21), but not = Sheol itself—no parallel for this; iv. If this Ps really belonged to David, it might refer to the cave; v. It has been suggested that this Ps is the prayer of a prisoner. 'The righteous (who are my friends) shall (then) surround me (to congratulate me), when thou dost reward me (with liberty)': i. so most [but 'surround' is an uncommon verb, and is hostile in Ps 22:13]; ii. LXX/V Jer 'wait for me': Aram. sense of the verb; iii. [connecting with the word for a 'crown'] Targum: 'Because of me the righteous shall make a crown of glory for thee', whence 'put on crowns (of triumph) because of me', cf RVm JA (with Ibn Ezra).

l 143 A Prayer of Hope—The last of the traditional 'Seven Penitential Psalms' (6, 32, 38, 51, 102, 130, 143), akin to the preceding and in the penitential genre, with several phrases echoed from elsewhere (see on v 8). Spiritual ideas in v 10 are noteworthy. **Title:** 'A psalm (belonging) to (the) David (Collection V)'.

1. 'Lord, hear my prayer . . . in thy justice, **2** Enter not into judgement [= take up a case in law] with thy servant, for no living (man) is [= can be declared] righteous before thee': i.e. before God's judgement-seat we are all found to be sinners, none can be wholly acquitted. The context here is a court of law. LXX has *dikaiōthēsetai* 'justified', and this passage is echoed by St Paul in Rm 3:20, Gal 2:16, in the context of no justification through the old Law. **6.** I spread out my hands (in prayer), my soul is like a thirsty land (thirsting) for thee [cf 63:3 in 'David II']. **8.** 'Cause me to hear thy mercy in the morning', i.e. after the darkness of v 3, but 'mercy in the morning' is in a more natural context in 90:14, which suggests its **m** originality there and the echo here. **9.** 'Deliver me from my enemies . . . unto thee I have fled': i. 'I have fled':

emended with LXX/V, so BJ RSV RPB, for Heb. 'I have **409** covered'; ii. [repointing] 'I have been covered': Jer [but 'unto' is awkward]; iii. = 'I have covered myself': JA, cf PB AV RV 'to hide me' [but forced]; iv. [another emend.] 'I have hoped': NP [again 'unto' is awkward]. **10.** 'Teach me to do thy will': perhaps the only place where this simple prayer is uttered. '. . . May thy good spirit lead me': so LXX/V Jer PB JA BJ RPB; but the Massoretic punctuation indicates 'Thy spirit is good; lead me . . .': so AV RV NP RSV. The idea of God's spirit as an active power is rare: see on 139:7. '. . . into a flat land': i.e. without difficulties. **11.** 'May thou enliven me': a phrase similar to that 9t in Ps 119 (see on 119:37). **12.** 'Cut off my enemies' is a very brief imprecation.

144 A (1—11) A General Psalm—This is a curious **n** psalm, and is perhaps more than any other, a pastiche of ideas, pictures and phrases from other psalms. As a composition therefore it is unsatisfactory, the echoes being often very incomplete. Yet it has original features, as in v 1 'Who trains my hands . . .', v 2 'subdues the people . . .' and the Aram. word 'rescue' in vv 7, 10, 11. Vv 12—15 seem to be an independent composition (called 144B here), and vv 9—11 have their own problems of relationship to 144A or 144B. V 10 has a reference to kings, and to David in particular, which may link with an interpretation of v 2. Many regard this Ps as the prayer of a king, perhaps including 12—15 as a picture of the prosperity of his kingdom.

1. 'Blessed be the LORD, my Rock [LXX/V 'my God': see on 28:1], who trains my hands for war and my fingers for battle'. **2.** Here is a litany of words applied to God: 'my love [without exact parallel, but cf English phrase, and 'my strength' = 'he who gives me strength' in 28:7 together with 'my shield' as here: an attractive phrase, but RSV (and RPB?) emends], 'my fastness . . . refuge . . . deliverer . . . shield [see on 18:3], . . . who subdues my people under me': i. so LXX/V PB AV RV, with reference to a king governing his people, cf v 10; ii. [The Qumrân Psalter (11Q Ps^a xxiii, 14) has 'peoples', as also the close parallel 18:48 (2 Sm 22:48 closer): LXX of Ps 18 even has 'subdues' as LXX here] 'who subdues peoples under me': NP BJ RPB [slight emend.]; iii. [further emend.] 'who subdues peoples under him(self) [= God]': RSV. **3—4.** 'What is man that thou regardest him . . .?' [lit. **o** 'knowest', see DWT on 1:6; and cf 8:5 for the idea]. **5—6.** A short description of a theophany, with the pictures chiefly taken from the fuller description in 18:8—16. **7—8.** '. . . Rescue me [Aram. usage, only here vv 7, 10, 11] . . .': the rescue follows the theophany as in 18:17. **9—11.** 'O God, I will sing to thee a new song' [cf 33:3]. **9—10.** Seem to have little connexion with the preceding, and it is possible that there is here i. a fragment of a separate composition, echoing 33:2—3; ii. another piece of pastiche, brought into unity by the repetition in v 11; iii. in the event of 144 being a single Ps, the 'new song' introduces 12—15, which may in turn be an excerpt from a lost psalm.

144 B (12—15) The Blessing of Domestic Pros- p perity—Almost certainly a separate composition—no pastiche here, but a connected poem. If it is an independent Ps, the opening or invocation has disappeared in course of editing, unless it be 'I will sing a new song . . .' in v 9, and see iii above.

12. [The first word 'who, whose' or 'when, that' (thus in LXX/V and the older versions), is an editorial addition attempting a link with the preceding, and is omitted by NP RSV RPB] '(May) our sons (be) like (fresh) plants grown up in their youth [or with RSV '. . . our sons in their youth be . . .']; our daughters like corner-pieces [cf Aram.

409p word; only here and Zech 9:15 of an altar] cut (for) the structure of a palace [or temple]': an image of gracefulness even if the precise picture is uncertain: LXX/V '. . . adorned, decked out in the manner of a temple'. **13.** 'May our storehouses be full, overflowing with [so LXX/V Jer BJ; others 'furnishing', an uncertain word] every kind (of supplies). (May) our flocks bear thousands and ten thousands in our fields': LXX/V took as 'fertile and

q abundant'. **14.** '(May) our cattle [lit. domestic animals] be laden, with no breaking through and no coming forth, and no cry in our squares': there are different versions of this picture: i. = 'May our cows be laden (with young), with no miscarriage and no untimely birth, and no cry (of pain) . . .': RSV RPB [the most likely after the preceding]; ii. = 'May our oxen be laden [= have heavy loads of good things to pull], and there be no breaking through (the walls, by invaders), and no going out (through the breach, to surrender or exile), and no cry (of distress) . . .': Ibn Ezra, so PB AV RV NP iii. = 'May our cattle be fat, no ruined walls, no going through (the breach), no cry . . .': LXX/V BJ [general prosperity].

410a 145 An Alphabet of Praise of God my King—Unlike most of the alphabetical psalms, where the thought is disjointed and artificial (esp. 25, 37, 111, 112), this pleasant psalm has genuine religious and poetic feeling, with a tenderness of thought and grace of diction. It falls easily into stanzas, each verse starting with the next letter of the alphabet. The stanzas are marked off by changes of person. The text of the Qumrân Psalter is particularly interesting (11Q Psᵃ xvi–xvii): here there is a refrain 'Blessed be the LORD and blessed be his name for ever and ever' attached to each verse, the only similar arrangement being in Ps 136; and further, Qumrân includes the missing verse before v 14, which previously had been reconstructed from LXX and Vg. **Title:** 'David' = the last of the 'David Collection V' (138–45), and the word *Tᵉhillāh* ('Song of Praise') which though only here in a title, was adapted to become the Hebrew title for the whole Psalter.

1–3. 'I will extol thee, my God, (my) King [Vg neatly '*Deus meus rex*'] . . . [God addressed as 'thou', 2nd person] . . . **3** . . . of his greatness there is no

b searching [LXX/V 'end'] [3rd person here]'. **4–5.** Generations shall speak of thy wonders, **6–7** thy power . . . **7** thy goodness [Vg *suavitas* only here, but cf on v 9] . . . [2nd person]. **8–9.** 'The LORD is gracious . . . **9** good [Vg *suavis*, see on 34:9] to all . . .' [3rd p.]. **10–11.** 'May all thy works praise thee . . . **12–13** to instruct the children of mankind (*adam*) . . .' [2nd p.]. **14.** Before v 14 (the *samekh* verse), the verse for the letter *nûn* is missing in the Heb. text, but the lovely line (beginning with *nûn*) 'Faithful is God in his words, and merciful in all his deeds' is present in the Qumrân Psalter (11Q Psᵃ xvii, 2–3), which is close to what had been generally reconstructed from LXX/V and inserted in NP BJ RSV: the word here 'merciful' or 'holy' (*hasidh*) is frequently used of men as 'devout' (see on 12:2), but only here (Qumrân), and v 17 (usual text and Qumrân), and Jer 3:12 of God. This line, restored from Qumrân and LXX/V, makes up the stanza with v 14 (also a graceful line) 'The LORD upholds all who are falling, raises up all who are bowed down (with sadness)', cf 146:8 [3rd p.]. **15–16.** '*Oculi omnium in te sperant Domine* . . .': a verse often used in monastic graces [2nd p.]. **17–18.** The Lord is just . . . **18** close to those who call on him. **19–20.** 'He does the will of those who fear him': a bold statement, by hyperbole, for the fulfilment of the desire of those

united to God's will, but softened (and dulled to **410b** theological exactitude) in PB AV RV RSV RPB, and also in CV Frey and Grail, though it is literal in LXX/V NP Fides BJ. **21.** The *Tau* verse returns to the worshipper in the 1st person, as in vv 1–2; as it stands it is not a complete stanza, but an overweighted couplet to conclude.

146 A Hymn in Praise of God's Kindness—The first **c** of the set of 'Halleluyah Psalms' (146–50) with which the Psalter ends. It is a fine hymn in entirely regular metre (3 + 3), with clear stanzas. The diction is strong with economy of conjunctions (asyndeton), the sentences being joined sharply by parallelism or contrast. **Title:** Hallelu-yah: see on 104:35. LXX/V add 'Of Aggaeus and Zacharias', as in the next Ps 147 (LXX 146), the third part of 147 (LXX 147) and 148, and LXX only 138 (LXX 137). On what tradition this is based is unknown, but a connexion with the Second Temple is supposed, since these are plainly liturgical hymns.

1–2. 'Praise the Lord, o my soul. . . **3.** Trust not in princes, in the son of (mortal) man (*adam*), for whom there is no (true) victory [or, salvation]: **4** his (last) breath goes forth, he returns to his earth, on that day his thoughts [Aram. word only here] perish': one notices the strong asyndeton. **5–6.** 'Happy is he whose help is God . . . **6** maker of heaven and earth [quoted Ac 4:24, cf 14:14]'. LXX/V start the new stanza here (cf Kittel's Bible): 'He keeps his friendship ['*emeth*, see on 5:8] for ever, **7** he gives judgement for the oppressed . . .', he helps the hungry, the imprisoned, **8** the blind, 'those bowed down (with sadness) [same phrase 145.11], he loves the just, **9** he takes care of the homeless': this is *gêr* 'sojourner', i.e. one who lives not in his own home: it is not common in the Pss: in 39:13 we are 'God's guests', in 119:19 he is a wanderer, in 94:6, as here, an unfortunate. God cares for the fatherless and the widow—but not for the wicked: the smallest imprecation. **10.** 'The LORD will reign for ever . . . o Sion . . . Hallelu-yah'.

147 A Hymn of Praise in Three Parts—These **d** 'Halleluyah Psalms' are plainly designed for liturgical use, and this is a particularly fine one. Of special interest is the structure in three parts, each of which could serve as a short psalm alone; and this fact enabled the LXX, Vg, and Syr. Psalters to adjust their numbers by reckoning Part III as a distinct psalm. Yet the whole hymn is also a unity. Four themes appear in the same order in each part: Praise, Jerusalem, Nature, Concern with men. Each part is in 3 regular stanzas (4 in Part III), and in regular, singable 3 + 3 metre. The diction is good, and again the constant use of a sharp asyndeton gives a crispness to the lines.

Part I—1. '*Hallelu-yah* = Praise ye the LORD, for it **e** is good to sing to our God, for pleasant [see on 133:1], seemly (is) praise': the phrase '*Hallelu-yah*' is properly part of the title, but LXX/V after writing '*Alleluia*' as the title, rightly repeat it in the text, as above. The grammar of 'to sing' is uncertain, as are the divisions of the verse: i. 'Praise ye the LORD, for it is good to sing [infin.] to our God; for pleasant, seemly to praise': PB AV RV RPB; ii. '. . . for singing [noun, *psalmus*] is a good thing; to our God be pleasant, seemly praise': cf Vg—LXX BJ similar; iii. '. . . for it is good to sing [infin.] to our God; for he is gracious, seemly is (his) praise': RSV; iv. '. . . for he is good; sing [imperative] to our God, for he is sweet, seemly is (his) praise': NP. **2–3.** 'The LORD builds up Jerusalem, he gathers the outcasts [=? exiles, LXX *diasporá*, Vg 'scattered'], **3** heals the broken-hearted . . .'. **4–6.** But his power is

410e cosmic: he knows the number of the stars, 'he calls them by name . . .' **6.** He raises up the 'meek' [= the Lord's faithful, see on 9:13], he humbles the wicked: a likely peroration.

f Part II—**7** (a similar opening) 'Sing to the LORD with thanksgiving', with Temple music. **8.** He controls the clouds, the rain, 'makes grass to grow on the mountains [the parallel line is missing, but LXX/V supplies 'and crops for the use of man', from 104:14, and this line is included by PB NP BJ RPB], **9** gives their food to the animals. **10.** He delights not in [= has no need of] the strength of the horse (to ride), nor . . . in the legs of the man (to walk)': i.e. God has no need to travel either on horseback or on foot to command nature. **11.** But he does delight in those who fear him, and trust in his mercy: another likely peroration.

g Part III (Here begins Ps 147 in LXX, Vg and Syr.— see Intro. 2 and note before Ps 115)—**12.** 'Glorify the LORD, o Jerusalem . . .' **13—14** for he strengthens thy gates, blesses thy children. **15—18.** The cosmic theme is presented with a magnificent picture, extending over two stanzas: he commands nature, 'swiftly runs his word', **16** . . . 'snow like wool, hoar-frost [word only here in Pss, but in Ex 16:14 of manna, and cf another word in 148:8] like ashes . . . **17** . . . ice like breadcrumbs; who can stand before [= ? withstand] his cold?': so most following LXX/V, but the last phrase seems to be a kind of parenthesis, since the next line describes the melting, and an ingenious and small emendation gives the much more satisfactory reading 'the waters stand (frozen) before his cold' (see Kittel and DWT), and this is adopted by WV NP RPB. **18.** '(Then) he sends forth his word and melts them (the breadcrumbs = ice, or, the waters), he makes his (warm) wind blow, the waters flow (again)': a fine picture (helped by the above emendation) of frost and thaw. **19—20.** Finally the human theme: For all this cosmic power, God has care for the instruction of Israel, 'declaring his word to Jacob . . .', **20** a privilege not granted to any other nation.

h **148 Praise from All Creation**—A fine hymn of praise, in the first stanza (vv 1—6) from heaven, and in the second stanza (7—12) from earth, in regular couplets of 3 + 3 metre (except for the clumsy line in v 4), and a pleasant short couplet in v 12. Vv 13—14 form a Coda. Title: 'Hallelu-yah'.

1. 'Praise ye the LORD from the heavens (or, the sky)' = 'you heavenly creatures, utter praise from where you are'. The above paraphrase is more likely than PB 'Lord of heaven' or RPB 'Lord in heaven'. The phrase is balanced by the opening of the second stanza, v 7, 'from the earth'. **2.** Praise from his angels, his (heavenly) host [see on 24:10 for *ṣebhā'ôth*], **3**, sun, moon, 'stars of light' [LXX/V 'stars and the light'], **4** 'the sky of the sky': the sky is conceived as a cover over our heads: this is the cover over that, cf phrase in 68:34 and 115:16 and see an explanation of 113:6, cf 'the sky of the sky cannot contain thee' in Solomon's prayer in 1 (3) Kgs 8:27 = 2 Chr 6:18, and speech in 2 Chr 2:5 [English 4]. 'And the waters which are above the sky': a clumsy line as it stands, **i** but cf Gn 1:7 and Ps 104:3. **7—8.** The second stanza: Praise from the earth . . . sea . . . **8** fire, hail, snow, ice (*qîṭôr*, an uncertain word, see on 119:83, where perhaps = frost): i. = ice [from context?]: LXX/V Jer; ii. = ice [emended to *qerah*, see DWT]: RPB; iii. = frost [from context?]: RSV [and cf LXX/V of 119:83]; iv. = mist [since apparently = smoke in Gn 19:28, perhaps Ps 119:83, and related to word for 'incense']: PB AV RV NP BJ. **9—10.** Praise from the hills, trees, **10** animals, **11—12** from men:

rulers and peoples, **12** boys and girls, old and young— **410i** a delightful short couplet (2 + 2 metre) to conclude the stanza. **13—14.** The Coda: God's name is exalted, **14** 'and he has raised up the horn for his people [= made them to prosper, see on 75:5], praise for his faithful, for the children of Israel, the people near him [lit. 'people, his near one', used also of 'neighbour': but nowhere else is Israel called God's neighbour]': and the meaning is not clear: = praise for them (from others—part of their prosperity), or praise (of God) on their part.

149 Praise from Israel—Another hymn, essentially **j** liturgical (for the 'assembly of the devout'), in regular metre. Only here (v 3) and in 150:4 is 'dancing' introduced as an act of worship. The strange feature is the linking of worship and vengeance in vv 6—9. Title: 'Hallelu-yah'.

1. 'Sing to the Lord a new song [the opening also of Pss 96, 98 and cf 33:2; 144:9], his praise in the assembly [*qāhāl*, see on 22:23] of the devout. **2—3.** Let Israel rejoice in his maker . . . king, **3** . . . with dancing . . .'. **4.** He takes pleasure in his people . . . **5.** 'Let the devout exult in glory [= in glorifying him], rejoice upon their beds': i. = at night time, when thinking quietly, cf Ps 4:5; ii. = at night time as well as by day, i.e. always; iii. = in the solitude of the night as well as in the public assembly (so Ibn Ezra); iv. = able to sleep in security, because of their victory (vv 4, 7—9); [all the above, with most, take it as a bed to lie in;] v. [bed = a place to lie down on = a praying mat] so 'in the place of their prostrations': BJ; vi. Various emendations have been proposed: 'in their (liturgical) ranks', 'in their turns of guard [or, watches]' (see Kittel), 'in their abode [= the Temple]' (Briggs), 'according to their families' (Kraus), etc; none have any support of the ancient versions (Qumrân is missing here), but they suggest an uneasiness about the text. In the Vg form '*exsultabunt sancti . . . in cubilibus . . .*' the verse is often used of the saints in the liturgy. **6—8.** 'Let heights **k** (of praise) of God (be) in their throats, and a two-edged sword in their hands, **7** to wreak vengeance on the nations . . . **9** to execute on them the judgement written': a curious phrase, only here: i. = in God's 'book', see on 69:29; ii. = 'the appointed judgement': NP (cf CV 'the written sentence'); iii. some take of the writings of the prophets, but this would be very unusual. 'This is an honour for all his devout (*ḥᵃsîdhîm*)': the linking of the praise of God and vengeance as closely as this is most unusual. It is thought by some that the dance in v 3 refers to a war-dance, or a sword-dance, perhaps of a primitive kind, while othes think of a 'holy war', perhaps of Maccabean times (cf 2 Mc 15:27 'fighting with their hands, but praying with their hearts'). In any case the identification of 'my enemies' with 'God's enemies' (cf 139:21—22, and see on 23:5) needs to be borne in mind.

150 A Final Hymn of Praise in the Temple—This **l** fine hymn, with its regular swinging metre (3 + 3) in three clear stanzas of 2 vv each, concludes the hymn book with a flourish. The final couplet is in a pleasing short metre (2 + 2) in sudden contrast. Title: 'Hallelu-yah'.

1. 'Praise ye God ['*Ēl*: LXX/V 'The Lord' as in the others of this series] in his holy (place) [*qōdheš* = 'holiness']: i. = 'in his sanctuary': so Jerome and most; ii. = 'in his holiness': PB (parallel to 'his strength' following). 'Praise him in the firmament [*rāqîa*'] of his power': so most, literally, leaving unclear: i. = 'his mighty firmament' = the sky, his abode; ii. = 'the strength of his power': Jerome (*fortitudine potentiae*). One notices that Jerome deliberately rejects the translation '*firmamentum*' always elsewhere used in Vg, like

410l LXX *steréōma*: but both Gr. and Latin words only acquired the sense of 'firmament' = 'sky' through the Bible, the proper meaning being 'a solid support, or base'. The Heb. word means 'beaten out flat', hence perhaps here **m** 'the spread of his strength'. **2.** 'Praise him in his mightinesses [PB well 'his noble deeds'], praise him according to the multitude of his greatness'. AV RV RSV RPB in v 2 have 'Praise him for . . .', so perhaps also in v 1 'for his holiness . . . for his power . . .'? **3—5.** Now follows the Temple orchestra: the shofar (trumpet, see **410m** on 81:4), lute, lyre (or harp), **4** drum and dancing (i.e. dancing [cf 149:3] to a drum-beat), strings, and a wind instrument (of uncertain precise meaning), **5** cymbals 'of sound' (= noisy), cymbals 'of shouting' (= loud; but often connected with ritual, see on 81:4). **6.** Finally, not only the liturgical instruments, but 'everything that breathes' shall praise Yah (= Yahweh, the LORD). Hallelu-yah.

PROVERBS

BY R. A. DYSON S.J.

REVISED BY J. McSHANE

411a **Bibliography—Commentaries:** T. T. Perowne, CBSC 1899; C. H. Toy, ICC 1904; W. O. E. Oesterley, Westminster Comm. 1929; H. Renard, PCSB, 1943; J. J. Weber, 1949; J. H. Greenstone, 1951; J. van der Ploeg, 1952; C. T. Fritsch, IB, 1955; A. Guillaumont, BP, 1959; J. C. Rylaarsdam, PC (2), 1962; H. Ringgren, ATD, 1962; B. Gemser, HAT, 1963; A. Barucq, SBib 1964; R. B. Y. Scott, AB, 1965; H. Duesberg-P. Auvray, JB, 1957[2]. *Other literature:* D. W. Thomas, *Textual and philological notes on some passages of the Book of Proverbs,* VTS, 1955; M. Dahood, *Proverbs and Northwest semitic philology,* 1963.

b **Title**—In MT the title is *'Mishlē Shelōmoh'.* The word *'māšal'* seems originally to have signified 'likeness', 'resemblance' (e.g. 26:1f), then a short comparison (e.g. 25:25f), and eventually a sententious saying in general. But the word *'māšal'* in the bible also means 'to rule'. Hence a proverb is a moral injunction which should rule man's conduct (cf Nm 23:7. 18; 24:3, 15). Inspired though not divinely revealed, these proverbs skilfully fashioned over the centuries are 'profitable for teaching, for reproof, for correction, and for training in righteousness' (2 Tm 3:16). Their teaching is often enclosed in an expressed or hidden comparison which demands from the reader the effort of penetration necessary to grasp its meaning and import. LXX bears the title *paroimiai Salomōntos* which can mean either the 'Proverbs' or 'Parables' of Solomon. Vg has translated the word *'māšal'* by 'parable' in 1:1. The book was also known to the Fathers of the Church as the 'Wisdom of Solomon'.

c **Division and literary forms**—1:1–7—An introduction to Prv probably added by the final collector. (1) 1:8–9:18—A general invitation to acquire Wisdom. The style is that of intimate paternal exhortation, as is clear from the frequent reference to the father-son relationship, which incidentally seems to have been a criterion for the ch division. There is no regular strophic arrangement in this the most recently composed section of Prv, which has an affinity with Dt, Jer, and Deutero-Is. It is generally regarded as post-exilic though written before Sir. (2) 10:1–22:16—This section consists of a series of 375 proverbs attributed to Solomon and composed in couplets. There is no logical arrangement. Antithetical parallelism predominates in chh 10–15 and synonymous parallelism in the remainder of the section. The literary style is simpler than in the previous section consisting of simple comparisons without exhortation and frequent use of alliteration. This is generally regarded as the oldest part of the book. (3) 22:17–24:22—A collection of sayings attributed to the Sages, dealing with man's relations with his neighbour, and composed in quatrains of synonymous parallelism. The style differs from that of Section 2 for exhortation and motivation are introduced (e.g. 22:17f; 22f). There is moreover a clear relationship between 22:17–23:14 and the Wisdom of Amenemopet. (4) 24:23–34—An-

other small collection of sayings of the Sages warning against partiality and laziness. It is similar in style **411c** to the third section. (5) 25:1–29:27—This second collection of proverbs of Solomon is said to have been made by the men of Hezekiah (c 715–687). It falls naturally into two parts separated by 27:23–27 which is now out of context. The first part favours synonymous parallelism and is written in the hortatory style. It contains some quatrains in chh 25, 26 and 27. In the second part viz chh 28–29 which consists entirely of couplets (as does the first Solomonic collection of proverbs) antithetical parallelism predominates. On parallelism, see § 356e.
(6) 30:1–14—Composed of quatrains this little section is called 'The words of Agur' and may perhaps have been an appendix to Section 5. Its theme, man's insignificance in relation to God, is developed in Jb (40:4f; 42:2–6). (7) 30:15–33—It consists of numerical sayings based on observation of men and animals and resembles the style of Am 1. (8) 31:1–9—'Royal Wisdom': The words of Lemuel 'King of Massa' as spoken to his mother. (9) 31:10–31—An alphabetical poem on the ideal wife. Note: In the LXX the order of sections is as follows: 1, 2, 3, 6, 4, 7, 8, 5, 9.

Authorship—The text indicates that despite the general **d** title (1:1), Solomon is not the author of the complete work (cf 10:1; 22:17; 24:23; 25:1; 30:1; 31:1). Only the oldest sections (2 and 5) which form the heart of Prv are explicitly attributed to Solomon. This ascription to Solomon is in accord with Heb. tradition as witnessed by 1 (3) Kg 3:5ff and 4:29ff where Solomon is said to have spoken 3000 proverbs (as against 500 in sections 2 and 5 of Prv) relating to botany and zoology, whereas Prv deals mainly with right living. 'Curiously enough, the examples of this classification of observed natural phenomena are found in Prv chiefly in an appendix not attributed to Solomon.' (R. B. Y. Scott, AB, 18, 12). The historical value of the texts from Kgs is contested by the same author in VTS 1955, 262–79. **Solomon was regarded as patron of the Wisdom Movement in Israel.** To him were also ascribed Eccl, Song, and the 'Psalms of Solomon'. Despite the exaggerations of 1 (3) Kgs there can be no doubt that Solomon's reign was characterized by prodigious building achievements and commerce. It was also an age of great cultural development. His court with official secretaries and recorder was modelled on those of Egypt and Tyre where the Wisdom Movement was already flourishing. There are **proverbs** in the sections attributed to Solomon which may well **go back to Israel's golden age** e.g. 14:28–35; 16:10–15; 20:2, 8, 26, 28; 25:1–7. The proverbs of Section 5 were already ancient in Hezekiah's time (c. 700), since they are referred to in 25:1 as the 'proverbs of Solomon'. The remaining sections are later than 2 and 5; the final redactor was probably responsible for Section 1 which may have been written as an introduction to Prv in its present form, and for Section 9 which

411d forms its conclusion. **The book as it now stands is post-exilic**, possibly as late as the 3rd cent. B.C. 'The paradox of Israel's wisdom literature is that most of it was actually composed during the post-exilic period when there was no longer any court. This important fact helps to explain the peculiar stamp which the OT works assumed. Despite the royal and courtly origins of the movement, **the literature assumed a definitely religious orientation**. One can see this most clearly in the introduction which was composed (chh 1—9) for the collections in Prv.' (R. E. Murphy, *Concilium* 10, 69). The evidence of duplicates, the grouping of proverbs (e.g. according to antithetical or synonymous parallelism) and the order of the sections in LXX, help to establish the fact that Prv is a compilation of collections which were at one time independent.

e Purpose—The purpose of the book is to enable the reader, especially the young, **to live rightly**. For the attainment of this goal, it offers to the understanding wholesome teaching about **true wisdom** and to the will **powerful incentives for the ordering of life** according to the knowledge acquired. For the adequate management of life, however, there is required not only a knowledge of important philosophical and religious truths and a way of life in harmony therewith, but also the possession of a certain measure of **practical sagacity** in the conduct of everyday affairs. Hence its counsels are not restricted to fundamental beliefs and moral teachings but embrace all human activity. The book also aims at furthering piety. It would win the reader to the Wisdom contained in revealed religion and impress its principles upon every aspect of his life; so it presents them in a variety of forms and displays their excellence in a manner calculated to woo and inspire. It endeavours by earnest warning and by stressing the advantages of virtue, to shape the reader's life in accordance with its teaching.

f Doctrinal content—It seems impossible to draw up any satisfactory doctrinal synthesis of Prv for the book as it stands lacks orderly arrangement. It consists essentially of a collection of unrelated independent sayings belonging to different periods in Israel's history. Prv is concerned with **everyday human conduct**, with man in relation to God the creator, not specifically the God of the covenant, hence its neglect of the great events in OT salvation history. Though based on experience, the teaching of the Hebrew Sages is profoundly religious (e.g. 1:1—7). A Barucq, 26—30 traces points of contact between Prv on the one hand and Dt, the prophets, and Pss on the other, e.g. religion, morality, the problem of retribution.

g Retribution in Proverbs—Prv, like Tb and Sir, belongs to the 'optimistic' school. It resolves the problem of suffering along traditional lines, according to the Deuteronomist's thesis that **good is rewarded in this life and evil punished. Suffering and unhappiness are due to unfaithfulness to God; there is no reward or punishment beyond the grave**; the just live out their full life's span, the wicked die prematurely. (M. Dahood, p. 20, denies this, maintaining that 'there is in Prv solid evidence . . . for an advanced doctrine of life and punishment after death'. He examines Prv 10:16; 11:19:30; 12:28; 19:23; 23:18). The exceptions to the rule are merely ignored. This view was criticized by the 'pessimistic school', Jb and Eccl; the solution was to come with Wis.

h Sources of Proverbs—The Wisdom movement was international. 'Solomon's wisdom surpassed the wisdom of all the people of the east and all the wisdom of Egypt' (1 (3) Kgs 4:30). Sages were to be found not only in Egypt but also in Edom (Jer 49:7), in Phoenicia (Ezek

28:2, 6), in Babylon (Jer 50:35), and in Canaan **411h** (Jg 5:29). David's administration was modelled on the Egyptian court with its scribes and scribal schools. The scribe was a royal official (cf 2 Sm 8:17; 20:25; 1 Chr 18:16) in David's time as indeed in the reigns of subsequent monarchs. Doubtless it was in court circles especially under Solomon, who had **close ties with Egypt and Phoenicia**, that Israel's Wisdom movement began to flourish. The most striking point of contact between extra-biblical wisdom literature and Prv is to be found in a comparison of the Egyptian 'Instruction of Amenemopet' (inaccurately dated 1000—600 B.C.) with Prv 22:17—24:22. There are many other affinities with **Egyptian Wisdom literature** (cf Barucq, op cit, p. 34—37). Parallels have been noted with Accadian and even Sumerian texts; Canaanite sources are examined by W. F. Albright, VTS, 1955, p. 1—15, and more recently M. Dahood has published a monograph, see § 411a. The former writes: 'Prv may contain a very high proportion of matter originating outside Israel. But it is saturated with Israelite theism and morality', (Albright, op cit, p. 15). For an appraisal of the influence of this international Wisdom movement on Prv see § 357 and the commentary on the text.

Text and versions—Prv was originally written in Heb. **i** but the MT apart from the first section and the conclusion is not well preserved, hence the conjectural readings of D. W. Thomas, W. F. Albright, M. Dahood etc. The LXX has many variants and many additions compared to the MT and its material is differently arranged (*Cf note* § 411c, end). Omissions also are to be observed (e.g. 1:16; 4:7; 8:29, etc): cf Vaccari, *De Libris didacticis*, n. 57. Vg, translated from the Heb. about A.D. 398, was hastily done (cf *Praef. in libros Salomonis*, PL 28, 1307), but does not differ much from MT. In the course of time a number of additions from the LXX (Old Latin) were introduced into the text and of these about twenty remain in the Clementine Bible; this however does not exclude the study of other texts to determine their authenticity. Based on LXX are the Coptic version, the Hexaplar Syriac and the old Latin; other versions include the Peshitta Syriac, the Targum, and fragments of the later Gr. trans (Symm., Aq., Theod.).

Canonicity—The Jewish synagogue considered the book **j** canonical and ranked it among the 'Sacred Writings'. The Gr. translator of Sir appears to allude to it in Sir 47:17 (Vg 47.10), while Talmudic difficulties caused by certain inconsistencies in MT (e.g. 26:4—5) and by the realistic description of the adulterous woman (7:10—22) were settled by the Council of Jamnia, c. A.D. 100. The Christian Church has always acknowledged Prv as canonical. The NT has 14 citations from Prv and many allusions to it, cf Barucq op cit 287. Our Lord himself seems to have illustrated some of its maxims (e.g. Mt 7:24—27; Lk 14:7—11). The Fathers of the Church found in Prv abundant matter for the instruction and edification of the faithful, and today it holds an important place among the sapiential books in the lessons of the Greek and Latin liturgies. Passages from Prv are used as lessons in the Roman breviary, while in the Mass Prv 8:22—35 is applied to our Lady and the acrostic poem of Prv 31:10—31 is used in the Common of Holy Women.

1:1—7 Introduction—The title refers especially to **412a** 10:1—22:16 and 25:1—29:27 (cf § 411d) which form the greater part of the book. 2—6 state the purpose of Prv. (a) theoretical: to instruct the reader in true Wisdom; (b) practical: to have its principles accepted as the rule of life and basis of conduct. It is primarily intended for the

412a instruction of the young (4), but it will also enrich the store of those who are already wise (5). The motto (7) is the key-note of all the teaching that is to follow, and an epitome of its spirit.

b **2a.** Wisdom is the central theme of Prv and in the following verses its scope and functions are variously expressed. It is 'discipline' not only intellectual but also corrective. **3.** It instructs in wise and upright conduct. **4.** It matures the judgement, for it imparts 'shrewdness' (in a good sense) to the inexperienced. **5.** It makes 'wiser' those already wise, and gives skill and facility in the management of life. **6.** It enables one to understand a 'proverb' and whatever needs interpretation as well as the figurative language in which a proverb is often clothed: cf Perowne, 40. **7.** Religion—'fear of the Lord' or better 'reverence for the Lord'—is the first of the virtues and the foundation of right living. MT can also be rendered 'the chief part of Wisdom.

c **1:8–9:18 Section 1. A general invitation to acquire wisdom**—Note the threefold antithesis in this section. The evildoer invites to evil while wisdom invites to virtue: The adulteress seduces to evil but wisdom's appeal is to virtue. Folly offers the water and bread of death while wisdom prepares a banquet.

8–19 A warning against evil companions—**8a.** 'My son'. Throughout this section of Prv (chh 1–9) the sage addresses himself to the young with the affection and solicitude of a father. **11.** CV reading is preferable 'Let us lie in wait for the honest man' (reading *tām* for *dām*). **13–14** state the inducement that the robbers hold out to entice the recruit to join their ranks. **15–19.** The reason for avoiding such companions. **17.** If the bird sees the net, it takes alarm. In like manner, for youth to be forewarned is to be forearmed. **18.** Evil-doers really prepare destruction for themselves. **19.** Read with LXX *'aḥ^arît* (fate) for *'orhôt'* (ways). 'Such is the fate of every covetous man.' Those who plot against others dig their own graves.

d **20–33 The invitation of wisdom**—Objective Wisdom, i.e. the moral law which is an emanation of the essential holiness and justice of God, and which makes itself heard by the voice of conscience, the preaching of God's ministers, etc is here personified, and speaks and acts with divine authority. Wisdom puts on the mantle of the prophets (e.g. Jer. 5:1). The 'Scoffers' are defiant and cynical despisers of religion and morality: the 'fool' is 'one who is insensible to moral truth and acts without regard to it' (Toy). **23a.** Listen to my reproof (though Hebrew has imperfect, not imperative). This reproof is contained in the verses which follow. **26a.** Wisdom will justly rejoice that their obstinate perversity has been punished. **28.** Those who have deliberately rejected the counsels and appeals of Wisdom, will cry out to her in the day of distress, but solely to escape punishment; then, however, it will be too late; cf Jn 7:34; 8:21. **31.** As they sowed so they shall reap. Punishment is, in the just ordination of God, the natural 'fruit' of sin.

e **2:1–22 The Blessings of Wisdom. 1–4** form the protasis of which the rest of the chapter is the apodosis. Diligent application to the study of Wisdom will result in the fear and knowledge of God and divine protection (5–8); it will lead to right understanding and a good life. (9–11); it will save the young from evil men. (12–15) and evil women (16–19) in contrast with the fate of the wicked (22). **3.** Wisdom, prudence and understanding are different aspects of the same virtue. **5.** The fear of the Lord (cf 1:7) and the knowledge of God are the essence of true Wisdom. Only the virtuous can grasp and appreciate it. This and the following verses reveal

the deeply religious conception of Wisdom. **6.** As God is **412c** the author of Wisdom, he must also be the goal of every human search of it. **8a.** 'justice': or 'probity' **8b.** 'saints': God's devoted followers. The verse emphasizes the divine protection of searchers after true Wisdom. **9.** It is assumed that he who knows the good path will follow it. **11.** The transforming effect upon the character of the young of these companion gifts of wisdom is presented in a striking personification.

16. '**The Strange Woman**' is someone else's wife. **f** BJ comments, 'It is striking that in this the most recent section of Prv there should be so many warnings against the danger of adultery (cf vv 16–19; 5:2–23; 6:24–7:27)'. Prv 1–9 shows a dependence not only on Dt but also on the teaching of the prophets for whom adultery is not only a violation of the marriage bond between husband and wife, but infidelity to Yahweh, husband of Israel. Boström, *Proverbiastudien*, 1935, maintains that the woman in question is not simply an adulteress, but rather a non-Israelite woman seducing to idolatry as well as adultery (cf 7:14ff). The question remains open for there is no evidence that foreign fertility cults were very influential at this time. Since she is set in antithesis to Wisdom personified as a woman, some would take it as a reference to Folly, 'Dame Folly'; or to pagan wisdom personified as a **qedeshah**, a temple harlot, seducing the Israelite from true wisdom in the service of God. **17.** The woman who by her evil arts seeks to seduce the young, betrays not only her husband but also God, who was called to witness her fidelity to the marriage contract, which is of divine origin and sanction (cf Mal 2:14). **18.** The association with her leads to ruin and death. **19.** The harlot is like a whirlpool that engulfs its victims and from which there is no return. **20.** For an interesting comparison of Prv 2:20–7:3 and Dt 11:18–22 cf G. Buchanan, RB, 1965, 227–9. **22.** The happiness promised in the OT to the Chosen People consisted above all in the long and peaceful enjoyment of the Promised Land. Expulsion from it by exile or death was the principal sanction to the old economy: cf Ex 20:12; Dt 5:16; Ps 37(36):9, 22, 29. **22.** The unrighteous shall have no place in Israel. How this was to be effected is not stated here.

3:1–10. The Blessings of Obedience and Trust in g God—The sage in the deuteronomistic style exhorts the young man to heed his instructions; the reward will be a long and happy life, and the favour of God and man (1–4). He is to trust in God (5–6), fear him and avoid sin (7–8), and render him his due (9–10). **3a.** These two 'covenant' virtues are often recommended, 14:22; 20:28, etc. **8a.** MT has 'navel': The addition of a single letter gives the Heb. word for 'body' (*bāśār*). The practice of religion and morality will also promote bodily health. **9.** Offering of first fruits is the only cultic act recommended in Prv. **10.** With this promise of Dt 28:8. 'plenty': read with LXX *corn*, which suits the parallelism.

11–20 The Excellence of Wisdom—Even if you suffer **h** in the pursuit of Wisdom, do not be downcast (11–12); for it is well worth the cost (13–20). **12b.** The quatrain (11–12) anticipates an objection against the rich promise of the preceding vv; cf Jb 5:17f. Suffering is a corrective: it is the Lord's discipline and a sign of his love. **16.** Wisdom confers a long and honoured life upon those who are attached to her. **18.** The practice of Wisdom will result in advantages analogous to the beneficent effects of the tree of life, cf 11:30; 13:12; 15:4; Gn. 2:9; 3:24. **19–20.** Wisdom is a source of blessing because it has its origin in God who manifested it in the creation

412h of the world and still manifests it in the physical order of the universe.

i 21—26 The Security Given by Wisdom—It confers both strength and beauty (22); it preserves alike in action and repose (23—24); it is equal to any emergency (25—26). **22.** They will be as attractive on your person as a gracious ornament on a woman's neck. **26a.** Dahood (op cit p. 10) suggests 'For the Lord will be at your side'. **27—35.** A series of short, detached maxims enjoining kindness to one's neighbour, differing from the rest of chh 1—9 and more closely resembling the aphorisms of Solomon, especially 16:1—22. **32.** His intimate converse is with the upright.

413a 4:1—9 The Paternal Lesson—In a tender passage the sage repeats to his young disciple the lesson he himself had learned at the feet of his parents (cf Ex 20:12). It gives a charming picture of a pious Jewish household; cf Wordsworth's 'Wisdom doth live with children round her knees'. **3a.** 'tender': i.e. of youthful age. **6.** Both sense and grammar demand that 6 be placed after 7. **7a.** 'The beginning of wisdom (is) get wisdom'. A suggested emendation is: 'In the beginning of your strength, get wisdom'. **7b.** 'at all costs', cf 1:9.

b 10—19 The Two Ways—It is difficult to decide whether these are the words of the sage or of the father. The contrasted fortunes of the wicked and the just are presented as motives for right living. **12.** In a virtuous life there will be no narrow or difficult ways. **13.** 'instruction'; 'discipline', a virtue which demands a strict control of self. **16b.** The wicked are unable to sleep unless they have done some evil deed: cf Juvenal, Satire, 111, 281f. **17.** This v may mean either 'wickedness and violence are to them as meat and drink', or 'they get their living by fraud and violence'. **18—19** Wisdom is called 'light' since it helps us to walk through life in full daylight. Cf also Eccl 2:13 RSV and CV transpose 18 and 19.

c 20—27 Exhortation to Constancy—All man's faculties must co-operate in the moral life; this whole-hearted striving for virtue will also bring material blessings. **22b.** 'flesh': i.e. to 'their' whole being. **23b.** The heart is the inward source of spiritual life; to keep it pure, great diligence is needed. **25b.** The virtuous man fixes his eyelids (metaphorically for 'gaze') upon the goal and lets nothing turn them aside. **26b.** Take care that the way along which you wish to walk be the right way of virtue. **27.** One can deviate to the right by an excess of zeal or to the left by lack of it. *Virtus stat in mediis.* After 27, LXX, Vg insert two vv. It is difficult to decide whether these lines ever had any Heb. original or are the work of a scribe.

d 5:1—23 Warning against adultery—This is a continuation of 2:16ff. After the usual exhortation to give heed to Wisdom (1—2), the sage describes the deadly influence of the wanton woman (3—6), cautions the disciple to avoid her lest dishonour, destitution, physical deterioration and the pangs of remorse come upon him (7—14), urges him to conjugal fidelity (15—20), the motive presented being the fate of the wicked (21—23). **2b.** Text is corrupt. CV has conjectural reading 'And understanding may guard you'. **3.** cf 2:16. Mistress of cajolery (7:14—18), she invites to sin. **5.** To associate with her is to go the way that shortens life and leads to premature death. **6.** Text is corrupt. 'Life': in the moral as well as in the physical sense. She has no moral scruples. **7—14.** The folly of sexual licentiousness. **9b.** 'the merciless' refers apparently to the outraged husband; cf 6:34f. **10a.** The victim of lust is like the prodigal son who

'devoured (his father's) substance with harlots' (Lk 15:30) **413d** and was forced to become a hired servant. **11.** The physical results of sexual indulgence. **12—14.** The pangs of remorse and upbraidings of conscience form the terrible climax to the loss of honour and health and substance (Perowne). **14.** A difficult v which refers perhaps to condemnation to death by the judicial court according to the law against adulterers (Lv 20:10; Dt 22:22).

15—20 Eulogy of conjugal fidelity—The remedy is **e** to be found in the divinely ordained intercourse of marriage. In figurative and decorous language the disciple is exhorted to be content with his lawful wife and to give her all his affection. **15.** For the wife as a 'cistern' or spring, cf Song 4:15. **19.** The hind and the doe are, for the oriental poet, symbols of grace and feminine beauty; cf Song 2:7, 9, 17. CV inserts 6:22 after v 19, and suggests that 5:21—23 be read after 4:27. **21—23.** A final motive for conjugal fidelity. **23a.** He shall die for lack of the corrective influence of Wisdom. This is not just the death sentence which could be imposed but spiritual or moral death consequent on his foolishness.

6:1—19 Four recommendations of Wisdom—The **f** topics are strange in Prv 1—9: 6:20ff follow logically on 5:23. Three of these recommendations are written in the style of the 'Sayings of the wise men' (22:17—24:34): cf 6:6—11 and 24:30—34. They are followed by a numerical saying (16—19), resembling in form 30:15—33; then the subject of sexual immorality is continued from ch 5. The section 1—19 thus breaks the connexion and was probably inserted after the compilation of chh 1—9 as an exemplification of the principle announced in 5:23b.

1—5 The Danger of Suretyship—The practice of **g** being surety for a friend, and the folly entailed by that risk is a frequent subject of warning in Prv (11:15; 17:18; 20:16; 22:26; 27:13). Sir 29:14—20 advises caution in the matter of pledging security for others; Mt 5:42 and Lk 6:34—35 recommend suretyship as a work of charity. **1b.** 'If you have struck hands for your neighbour'. Striking hands was a way of sealing a bargain; cf 2 (4) Kgs 10:15. 'Neighbour' and 'stranger' ('another') are paralleled not contrasted. **3—5.** The endangered surety should take strong measures to force his friend either to meet his liabilities or to set him free from his bond. **5a.** 'from the hand': the addition of a consonant to the Heb. word for 'hand' (yād) gives 'hunter' (ṣayyād).

6—11 The Sluggard—The ant is often mentioned in **h** ancient folklore as an example of thrift and industry (cf 24:30—34). LXX adds a parallel passage on the bee, quoted in several patristic writings. e.g. Clem.Alex., *Strom* 1.6. **10.** These lines continue the remonstrance of the sage. **11a.** Want and poverty are dangerous assailants; they are like a highwayman who will make away with the sluggard's substance.

12—15 The Mischief Maker—**12a.** Literally 'a man of **i** Belial', a worthless, good-for-nothing person (cf its NT meaning in 2 Cor 6:15) **12b.** He deals in lying speech. **13—14.** Describe the underhand methods, the veiled suggestions of mischief makers.

16—19 Seven Things Hateful to God (cf 30:15— **j** 33)—A numerical device designed to arouse interest. (cf W. M. M. Roth's 'The numerical sequence X/X + 1 in the OT', VT 12 (1962) 300—11). There are 38 examples of this progression in the Heb. Bible, cf 'the words of Ahiqar' (ANET 428).

20—35 Warning against the Adulteress—This **414a** section is a continuation of ch 5, having the same general theme. Obedience to parental instruction is invoked against 'the sin which destroys purity and saps

414a foundations of family life' (24—35), Perowne, 69. **21.** Cf 3:3. **22—23.** Sense and syntax demand the inversion of these two vv Parental teaching will, like a lighthouse, guide the young man embarking on the sea of life (cf Dt 6:4—7). **24a.** 'Evil woman': a slight alteration of MT from *rā'* to *rēa'* gives the meaning 'wife of another'. **26.** MT is obscure. There is a contrast between the harlot and the adulteress; the latter is more dangerous: 'The married woman who is contrasted with the harlot makes a person of substance her quarry since he can keep him in comfort', D. Winton Thomas, VTS, 1955. **30.** '*Men despise not* the thief if he steals . . .' (CV), **31a.** sevenfold': according to Ex 22:1, fivefold was the legal limit of restitution; 'sevenfold' is here a general term meaning 'in full measure' (cf Mt 18:22). **33—35.** An allusion to the penalty and shame that both the law and public opinion inflict upon the adulterer. Nor can he escape the vengeance of an outraged husband.

b **7:1—27 The Adulteress**—After an earnest plea for obedience to his words (1—3), i.e. to Wisdom (4), that the pupil may avoid the adulteress (5), the sage describes her fatal wiles (6—23) and the fate of her victim (24—27). The ch has high dramatic merit. **2a.** The practice of Wisdom will ensure a happy life and save from premature death. **4b.** 'friend': 'one well known', here as in Ru 2:1, 'kinswoman'. The writer wishes to inculcate deep affection for, and familiarity with, virtue. **6.** The sage begins the description of a scene that he had more than once observed from behind an oriental window with its elaborate lattice work which forms an effective screen from the street, though permitting the watcher within to observe all that goes on without. BJ follows LXX, 'She looked out'. Barucq prefers the first p. sing. with RSV and CV. **8a.** The young man is pictured as taking the road where the house of the adulteress stood. **10—12.** Description of the Adulteress—**10b.** For the harlot's dress cf Gn 38:14. 'Wily of heart' MT is obscure; Vaccari renders 'with secret intent'. **13—20.** Her Invitation—She has promised a sacrifice of thanksgiving for a favour received. Such sacrifices ended in a sacred banquet to which friends were invited to consume the meats offered at the altar (Lv 3:16f; 7:15). **14b.** 'Today': the meat had to be eaten the same day or burnt. **15a.** 'So': since I am able to provide a banquet. **21—23.** The Youth yields—**22—23** must be taken together; they describe the brutelike stupidity with which the youth goes to his doom. **24—27.** Conclusion—The house of the adulteress is 'the way to Sheol' as is the house of Folly. (2:18f; 5:5; 7:23; 22:14).

c **8:1—36 The Appeal of Wisdom**—This ch forms the climax of the first section. Wisdom is personified as in 1:20—33, but with greater relief and richness. After an appeal to be heard attentively (1—11), she proclaims her salutary efficacy in human society (12—21), and her activity in the creation of the universe (22—31), concluding with yet another plea to seek blessedness in following her (32—36). 'Chh 8—9 are full of Canaanite words and expressions, and may go back to Phoenician sources more directly than any other material in Prv' (W. F. Albright, VTS, 1955).

1—11 The Call of Wisdom—'Listen to my appeal' (which follows in 12—31). 'Gates': cf 1:21, note. **5.** The simple fools are those who do not lead a 'wise' life: cf 1:22, note. Sagacity means true knowledge of the principles of life. **7a.** '*utters*': present tense. **8.** The Wisdom that speaks here neither is deceived nor wishes to deceive.

d **12—21 Wisdom's self-eulogy**—**13a.** is to be omitted as a gloss because of metre and context. **14—16.** An example of 'Royal' Wisdom (cf 28:16; 29:4, 14). Wisdom 414 alone can give these gifts to her friends. Here Wisdom attributes to herself qualities of which God is the source in Jb (12:13; she does not however identify herself with God. **15—16.** Rulers discharge their duties through the guidance of Wisdom. **16b.** Dahood, (iam cit p. 15), suggests 'By me princes rule and nobles—all legitimate rulers'. The sequence of verses in BJ is: 12, 14, 13, 17, 15, 16. **17—21.** The rewards of Wisdom. Those who seek her not only find her, but gain riches, honour, and blessings more valuable than gold. The idea is that of a patrimony built up for many years. **20—21.** Wisdom concludes her promises by affirming that she deals equitably with her friends.

22—31 Second part of Wisdom's self eulogy— e Wisdom in the Creation and Ordering of the Universe—Here the eulogy of Wisdom touches the sublime. Similar hymns are to be found in Wis 9:9—12; Eccl 24:5—27. 'In the prologue of his gospel, St. John has reproduced this movement of the hymns to Wisdom, transposing it and adapting it to the Word of God.' (M. E. Boismard, *St. John's Prologue*, p. 76) In this section Wisdom is described in relation to God from whom she takes her origin, not in relation to man and his destiny. Since she resides 'above' with God, she is made to take God's place. This does not mean that Wisdom is to be equated with God. Wisdom is most apparent in the orderly arrangement of the universe; hence she is presented at God's side presiding at the world's creation. She is anterior to the visible universe, the chief work of God's creation. 'The resemblance between this passage and the presentation of Christ as the "first born of all creation" is striking' (Barucq, op cit, p. 90f). **22b.** Wisdom was the 'forerunner of his prodigies of long ago' (CV). **23a.** The new critical edition of Jerome has 'ab aeterno ordita sum' replacing the Clementine 'ordinata sum'. **27—31.** Cf Gn 1:6—10. **27b.** 'When he marked out the vault over the face of the deep' (CV): the vault of the firmament whose rim seems to rest on the surface of the ocean. **30a.** 'Like a master workman' or perhaps 'like a beloved child' which would suit the context better. **32—36. Closing exhortation—32a.** 'Now therefore', because I give and am all this. **32b.** Omitted by CV.

9:1—18 The Choice between Wisdom and Folly— f The ch develops the antithesis, Wisdom (1—6) and Folly (13—18). Between them is inserted a section of general teaching (7—12).

1—6 The feast which Wisdom offers—Wisdom is here presented as the rich and virtuous mistress of a palace who invites her followers to a sumptuous feast. Her exquisite viands are life and insight. **1b.** 'seven pillars': 'the number invites mystical treatment (e.g. seven gifts of the Holy Spirit, seven Sacraments), but probably originally it signified completeness' (A. E. Morris in *A New Comm. on Holy Scripture*, 388). P. W. Skehan (CBQ 9 (1947), 190ff) suggests as result of detailed analysis that there are seven 'columns' rather than 'pillars'. Those are seven poems of uniform length which extend through chh 2—7 inclusive. Chh 1 and 8—9 are the framework 'within which these carefully wrought columns stand'. **3.** The maidens are sent out to invite Wisdom's guests. Cf 1:20. Mt. 22:2—10. Dahood (op cit p. 17), objects to this on the grounds that 'the semitic sense of propriety would preclude the sending out of female servants to invite male guests. This is avoided by taking *šāleḥâ* as 'She dismisses (her maidservants)'. This suggestion is rejected by Barucq (op cit p. 99). **4a.** 'Simple': in parallelism with the 'one without sense' of 4b. **6a.** The fruit of Wisdom is life in

414f the deepest sense of the word: cf 3:18; 4:13; Jn 17:3.

g 7–12. Contain short aphorisms drawn from some other source and introduced here by a later editor. **7–9** are in the style of 22:17–24, and deal with the opportuneness of correction, and 10–12 are isolated couplets. **10a.** Cf 1:7. **10b.** 'Holy': the parallel shows almost certainly that God is meant. The knowledge of God is the 'beginning' or 'chief part' of Wisdom, and the recognition of him in a practical way by the fulfilment of religious duties is true Wisdom. **12.** The individual both reaps the benefit of his wisdom and pays the penalty of his contempt for the moral law.

h 13–18 Portrait of Folly—This section is in sharp contrast to the picture of Wisdom given in 1–6. Folly, represented by a woman of vicious life, has, like Wisdom, her own house (14), where she spreads her feast (15), and then issues her invitation (16), couched, in part at least, in identical terms. This description has something in common with that of the wanton woman in 2:18 and 7:11–19. Here she represents vice in general, but in the mind of the sage impurity stands first among the vices. **13a.** 'Dame Folly is fickle'. **16.** cf 9:4. **17–18.** Her banquet is secret and fraudulent leading only to death. The emphasis is probably on sexual sins. The house of Folly is, so to speak, a grave that holds entombed all who enter: cf 7:27. Man is invited to both banquets. He must make his choice.

415a 10:1–22:16 Section 2: The First Collection of the Proverbs of Solomon—This is the central part of the book and the oldest portion: cf 411c. It consists of 375 proverbs, each of two lines formed strictly on the model of Heb. parallelism except for 19:7 where the text is corrupt. The parallelism from ch 10 to ch 15 is, as a rule, antithetical; from 16:1 to 22:16 synonymous or progressive. There is little attempt at subject grouping and no indication of the way in which the collection came to **b** be made. **10:1–10**—**2.** Cf 11:4. Only good works (here perhaps almsgiving, cf Sir 29:12) merit a long life; cf 11:19; 12:28. **3.** This v, like 2, is in harmony with the OT doctrine of temporal reward and punishment. **6b.** Does not fit here. It is also found in 11 where it is evidently in place. Perhaps the original half-verse was lost. CV transposes 6b and 13b. **7b.** 'Will rot' cf Sir 41:11. **9b.** A slight change in MT (*Yeroa'* for *Yiwwadea'*) gives '*shall suffer hurt*'. **10b.** Has come in by mistake from 8b. BJ and RSV prefer LXX reading, viz to close the eye to wrongdoing is mistaken kindness.

c 11–20 Proper Speech—**11.** The utterance of the just man is a source of wisdom and inspiration to others. **12b.** Love which forgives the transgressions of others; cf 17:9; 1 Cor 13:17; 1 Pt 4:8, Jas 5:20. **14a.** 'lay up knowledge': 'conceal their knowledge'. At times silence is golden; he who senselessly blurts out all he knows, only does mischief; cf 12:23. **15.** Wealth is a protection against the vicissitudes of life. **16.** For the good riches may lead to long life and happiness; for the wicked they only multiply sin. **19.** The wise man controls his tongue.

21–11:8 The Happiness of a Virtuous Life—**21.** The just man not only walks in the right way himself, but guides others along it. **22.** God's blessing is the chief reason for prosperity; human effort counts for little: cf Sir 11:23; Ps 128 (127). **23.** The man of sense practises virtue with the same ease that the fool commits evil. **24.** God will, in his own good time, mete out the requital that the wicked fear and the good desire; cf 1:26. **25b.** The tempest of divine retribution will sweep away the wicked (cf 1:27), but the just will stand like a house on the rock, unshaken by the storm; cf Mt 7:24–27. **26.** A

shiftless messenger gives more trouble than real service. **415c 27.** Cf 3:2; 4:10; Ex 20:12; Ps 55(54):24. A long peaceful life is normally the reward of piety. This belief was later challenged in Jb. **30.** Cf note to 2:21f. **31a.** J. Hoftijzer in VT 11 (1961) proposes 'La bouche juste prospère par la sagesse'. **11:1.** Cf Am 8:5. **2.** Pride ends in failure and disgrace; humility is a wise counsellor, bringing wisdom and honour. The words refer to any divine judgement. When God decides upon the chastisement of the wicked, riches are powerless to avert it. **5.** Cf 3:6. **7.** Is difficult. There is no satisfactory antithesis in the 2nd half of the verse in MT (Barucq's suggestion 'Hope based on riches comes to naught' is open to the same criticism). The LXX reading is preferable: 'When the righteous man dies, hope does not perish, but the boast of the wicked perishes'. This is not a reference to retribution after death. 'The (good and) the evil that men do lives after them.' **8.** The wicked fall into the peril in which they had plotted to involve the just, cf Mordecai and Haman, Daniel, Susanna. This concept is founded on the justice of God who governs the world.

9–16 The Public Good—**10b.** Upright citizens are **d** true promoters of the public good. **11a.** 'by the blessing of the upright' either by their prosperity as in 10, or the blessing conferred on a city by their presence and beneficent words (involving deeds). **12.** The discreet man, whatever he thinks, keeps his thoughts to himself. Cf 10:19; 17:27f. Amenemopet has 'Better is a man whose talk (remains) in his belly than he who speaks out injuriously' (ANET, p. 424). **14b.** 'An abundance of counsellors': cf 15:22; 20:18; 24:6. **15b.** Cf 6:1–5. **16b.** 'ruthless men'. The grace of true womanhood wins honour as surely as the ruthless acquire riches. This would be the only contrast in Prv between men and women. BJ keeps woman as subject (LXX); 'a woman who hates virtue is a throne of dishonour'.

17–23 Rewards and Punishments—The apparent **e** prosperity of the wicked is illusory. **19.** MT is uncertain: perhaps 'he who establishes righteousness' (Barucq). **21a.** 'Hand in hand': a Heb. expression meaning perhaps '**truly**' or '**rest assured**'. **22b.** Literally: 'is a fair woman lacking in taste'. The nose ring was a regular ornament of the oriental woman: cf Is 3:21. **23.** The desires of the just are satisfied, but the hopes of the wicked are doomed to disappointment.

11:24–12:12 Beneficence—**25b.** An agricultural **f** metaphor expressing the same thought as Lk 6:38. 'Give and it shall be given unto you.' **27.** The good seek (and find) God's favour; the wicked only bring upon themselves the evil they pursue. **28.** The man who trusts in riches without regard for virtue will wither and fall like a leaf without sap. **29.** He who manages his household stupidly will find his substance reduced to nothing and will become the slave of a more prudent man. **30.** The sense of 30b is uncertain in MT; following LXX we may read: 'The fruit of **virtue** is a tree of life, but violence destroys men's lives'. **31.** If the just will not escape the consequences of their faults 'on earth' how much less the wicked. (Dahood, op cit p. 25f claims that *bā'āreṣ* refers not to the earth but to Sheol. 'The biblical writer is evidently reacting against the traditional view that an equal lot in Sheol awaits all men. Even if all men were to be consigned to Sheol, the punishment of the vicious would be greater than that of the virtuous'.) **12:2.** Cf Wis 2:14–16; 4:16. **4.** 'A worthy wife is a crown to her husband, but a shameful one is (like) rot in his bones'. The Heb. phrase is 'a woman of power', i.e. the capable mother of a family who knows how to manage her household; cf 31:10ff. **6.** Slander, false testimony, etc, are like assassins

415f lying in wait for victims. **7.** Cf 10:25; 12:3; Mt 7:24f.

g **13—23 Use of the Tongue—13a.** 'By the sin of the lips the sinner falls into snares' (LXX), which the sincere and candid in speech escape. **14.** A man reaps what he sows. **18.** 'healing' viz by pouring the balm of kindly words into the wounds opened by ill-considered speech. **24—13:6 Labour—26.** Virtue gives its possessor an advantage over other men. The text, however, may be corrupt. **27a.** Appears to be a hunting metaphor. **28b.** Is a *crux interpretum*. For the view that this verse refers to the doctrine of afterlife cf **Bib** 41 (1960), 176—81. **13:1.** The addition of the letter h to the Heb. for 'father' gives: *'The wise son loves instruction'*. **2.** He whose counsels help others will share in the blessing he bestows; but the perverse seek only their own advantage in the harm they do their fellow-men. **6a.** 'whose way is upright': 'the man of integrity'. Goodness is the best guarantee of a proper life; cf 11:5.

h **7—12 Poverty and Riches—8b.** The wealthy can buy their way out of any peril. The last part of *b* seems to be an erroneous repetition of MT from the end of 1*b*. The thought is not characteristic of Prv and gives no contrast to *a*. The original reading has been lost. **9a.** 'rejoices': an emendation of the Heb. verb (*yiśmāḥ* to *yizrāḥ*) gives the preferable reading '*shines brightly*'. 'Light' and 'Lamp' are symbols of life and prosperity; cf 4:18; 24:20.

13—20 Docility—13. Observance of law, both human and divine, is recommended. Vg and DV add a couplet found in LXX after 9. **14b.** cf 10:11; 14:27. **15.** Gentle and considerate treatment of others wins their esteem. **17.** The contrast is between the mischief caused by an unreliable messenger and the success ensured by a competent envoy. **19.** The two lines appear to be unrelated. **20.** cf Sir 22:14 and 13:1.

416a **21—14:14 Rewards of the Just—21.** cf 10:24; 11:21, 27. **23.** The wide variety of renderings in the versions shows the obscurity of this verse. 'Fallow ground' may refer to land given its sabbatical rest, from which poor might eat (Ex 23:10f; Lv 25:1—7) or to marginal land left for use of poor; the point seems to be that 'man's injustice, thwarts bounty of nature'. (Rylaarsdam). **24.** cf 3:12. **25.** cf 10:3. **14:3a.** *'In the mouth of the fool there is a shoot of pride'*: 'The branch of pride springs from its stem in the fool's mouth' (Toy); cf Apoc 1:16. Some suggest 'the rod for his pride', i.e. his words will be a scourge to the fool himself. **6b.** Wisdom is readily found by the sincere seeker; cf 2:1—6. **8.** Foresight and a capacity to choose the proper course of action are characteristic of the prudent man. **9.** MT is obscure. By a change of one letter in the verb (ṣ to n), we may read: *'Among fools guilt abides, but among the just favour'*, i.e. of God. Fools always have a conscience burdened with guilt; only on the upright does God's favour rest. **11.** Cf 12:7. **13.** Cf Shelley's *Ode to a Skylark*: 'Our sincerest laughter with some pain is fraught, our sweetest songs are those that tell of saddest thoughts'.

15—25 Prudence—17b. 'but the prudent man endures much' (LXX). **19.** Moral goodness will triumph; the wicked will 'bow' as suppliants at the gates of the just.

b **26—35 Religion and the State—26.** *'In the fear of the Lord there is great security and for his children it shall be a refuge'*. Even the strong man must not rely on his strength, but on the practice of religion. **27b.** Religion gives strength to avoid sin which draws down divine chastisement; cf 13:14. **33b.** *'and even among fools it is made known.'* Wisdom also makes itself heard in the remorseful conscience of the wicked. CV, RSV, BJ follow LXX by

adding negative—'among fools it is not known'. Alter- **416b** natively, 'but will it be known in the heart of fools?' (Barucq).

15:1—12 Gentleness—2. The urbanity of the wise **c** makes knowledge pleasing and acceptable; cf 15:7. **3b.** Nothing escapes the eye of God; cf 5:21. **4.** A gentle tongue has the power to heal and lift up the spirit; cf 12:18. **7b.** The wise man knows how to communicate wisdom; the fool is himself too confused to be of assistance to others. **8.** External worship without interior holiness is not pleasing to God; cf 21:3, 7. This is one of the great prophetic themes. Cf Is 1:11—17; Jer 6:20; Am 5:21—25. **11.** Abaddon is a synonym for Sheol; cf 27:20. If the profound and mysterious abode of the dead lies open before God, how much more the thoughts and motives of men.

13—24 Happiness of Heart—15. True happiness is **d** found in contentment and joy of heart. **16—17.** Cf Amenemopet (ANET, p. 422) 'Better is poverty at the hand of God than riches in the storehouse. Better is bread with happy heart than riches with vexation'. **19.** cf Is 57:14. **22b.** Cf 11:14; 20:18. **24.** Virtue leads to life; sin leads to premature death.

25—33 Enemies and Friends of God—25b. 'widow': as typical of the poor and oppressed. God will not permit the removal of the boundary stone marking the limits of her land; cf Dt 19:14 and ANET, p. 422. **26b.** Perhaps the original reading was 'and gracious words are pleasing to him'. **27.** Inordinate desire of wealth leads to bribery and acts of injustice that eventually bring ruin; but the man of incorruptible honour will be rewarded with a happy life. **30a.** 'The light of the eyes': a radiant countenance. **30b.** A figure for physical well-being. **33a.** Religion is the basis of right living. Humble submission to God is the way to 'honour'; cf 18:12; 22:4.

16:1—9 Divine Providence—1. Man proposes but God **e** disposes. **2a.** 'pure (right) in his own eyes'; yet the final verdict comes from God. **4a.** MT permits the translation 'for his own end'. By making a thing to serve its own purpose, God makes it serve his purpose. **4b.** The wicked, by a deliberate choice of evil, fall under the divine law of chastisement and thereby manifest his justice. **6.** Kindness towards our neighbour can repay our debt to God; cf Lk 11:41. **9.** Cf 1.

10—15 The Ideal King—10a. The king's decisions are **f** divinely guided cf 2 Sm 14:18—20; 1(3) Kgs 3:4—28. **11b.** 'The bag', in which sellers kept their weights; cf 11:1; 20:10. **13b.** A ruler needs honest counsellors. **14.** It is perilous to antagonize a monarch; this was especially true of the Ancient East. 'In ugaritic mythology messengers are generally paired . . . (which) allows one to propose that *mal'akê* is dual rather than plural'. Hence 'The wrath of the king is Death's two messengers' (Dahood, op cit p.36). **15b.** 'like a spring rain-cloud', necessary for the ripening of the corn.

16—22 Wisdom and Humility—18b. Cf Lk 14:11. **g** **20a.** The 'word' refers to the divine admonitions contained in the Mosaic Law; cf 13:13. **21b.** A pleasant manner of imparting wisdom will make teaching more effective.

23—33 The Gift of Speech—23b. Cf 21. **25b.** A repetition of 14:12. **26.** Man is driven to work to provide himself with food; cf Gn 3:19 and 2 Thes 3:10—'If anyone will not work let him not eat'. **27—30.** Slander. **27b.** The tongue of the slanderer is like a devastating fire; cf Jas 3:5—6. **30.** The outward expression betrays the inner thought; cf 6:13. **31b.** The practice of virtue will lead to a venerable old age; cf 3:2; 4:10; 10:27. **32.** It is more glorious to control one's passions than to

416g win battles; cf Ovid (*Epist. ex Pont*. 11. 75): 'Fortior est qui se quam qui fortissima vincit moenia'. **33.** The favourable or unfavourable decision of the lot depends on God. In OT the use of the lot to decide public and private affairs, to resolve doubts, etc, was accepted; cf Ex 28:6; 1 Sm 2:28; 10:20ff; Jos 7:14; Lv 16:8; and in NT Ac 1:26.

417a **17:1–14 Kindness to Others—1.** Cf 15:16f. **2.** An intelligent servant may be raised to the position of son. **7.** A proposed correction of MT (*yeter* to *yōšer*) gives 'upright speech' (LXX). **8.** A difficult verse. The glitter of gold is a strong temptation and often the means of success in a dishonest undertaking. **9.** A true friend will overlook the faults of another; cf 1 Cor 13:7. **11b.** 'messenger' BJ suggests the destroying angel of Ex 12:23f. **14.** A small fissure in a dam may open the way to an overwhelming flood; so contention to a passionate outburst. 'The geometric progression of strife.'

b 15–26 Justice—17b. A friend is friendly at all times, but the specific function of a brother is for the hour when friendship is most severely tested. **18.** Cf 6:1–6; 11:15. **19.** Sin is the ordinary sequel to strife: ostentation, exemplified in the building of a pretentious house-door, can dissipate a fortune. **23a.** He receives a bribe from the fold of the garment in which it is concealed. **24a.** 'Wisdom is before the face of the wise', as the object of his contemplation and the norm of his conduct, whereas the fool is incapable of fixing his mind on anything. **26.** The v deprecates injustice in the law-courts.

27–18:5 Practical Wisdom—28. The value of silence. **18:4** The words of the wise are profound, beneficent and instructive. **5.** As in 17:26 the reference is to the perversion of justice in the law-courts.

c 6–15 Foolish Talk—6. The fool's thoughtless words involve him in disputes that call for punishment. **8.** Malicious gossip is eagerly welcomed and deeply affects men's thoughts and actions; cf 26:22. **9.** The slothful and the spendthrift make a well-matched pair. **10a.** 'The name of the Lord': all that which the ineffable name of Yahweh connotes. In true religion man finds a sure bulwark against the vicissitudes of life. **11.** The wealthy, by contrast, place their hopes in riches (which they think of as a high wall); cf 10:15. **12.** Cf 15:33; 16:18; Lk 14:11. **14.** When the spirit, which is the source of strength, is itself crushed, what hope is there? Cf 17:22.

d 16–23 Litigation—16. The reference is to the oriental custom of making presents to influential men to gain their favour and patronage; cf Gn 33:4–11. **17.** An admonition that both parties to a dispute must be heard. **18.** A doubtful case was settled by lot, thus preventing recourse to violence. **20.** Prudence is required in speech, for a man must accept the consequences of his words; cf 12:14; 13:2. **21.** Is a development of the preceding v. **22b.** Cf 12:4; 19:14; 31:10.

e 24–19:7 The True Friend—19:1b. The contrast and the parallel in 28:6 suggest the reading 'than a man who is perverse in speech *and rich*'. **2.** MT reads: 'Zeal, too, without reflection is not good' (cf Rm 10:2). A warning not to follow impetuously the blind impulse of passion. **3.** How often we blame God for our misfortune, though the fault is with ourselves. **4b.** Cf 14:20; 19:7. All proverbs in this first Solomonic section are in couplet form. The third line here (omitted by CV) is probably a fragment of another proverb.

f 8–15 The Man of Sense and the Fool—9. Cf 19:5. **11.** This maxim approaches the NT precept of the forgiveness of injuries, though the motive is good sense rather than love of God. **12.** A king's anger is a fearful

thing, but his favour is refreshing. **13b.** The incessant **417f** wrangling of a wife becomes as intolerable as the steady dripping of water from the roof. **14.** Cf 18:22; 31:10. 'True marriages are made in heaven.' **15a.** 'He who will not work reaches a state in which he cannot work' (Oesterley).

16–23 Respect for God—17. Cf Babylonian 'A pessim- **g** istic dialogue between master and servant', ANET, 438b. Cf also Mt 25:40. **18b.** Might be a warning against either excessive correction or over-indulgence, both of which may prove fatal. **22.** Another *crux interpretum*. Perhaps: 'A man's inactivity is his reproach, and better a poor man than one unreliable' (Dahood, op cit p. 42). **23.** Long life and prosperity are the normal rewards of the God-fearing; cf 14:27.

24–20:6 Correction and Laziness—24. 'buries his **h** hand in the dish' after the oriental fashion of eating. 'The mention of the sluggard always seems to evoke a humorous note' (IB). The chastisement of the irreligious will afford an object lesson to the merely ignorant. A simple admonition is sufficient for the man of sense. **27.** Perhaps ironical. **20:4.** The word rendered 'autumn' is a general one for the colder half of the year when ploughing is done. **5.** A clever man by shrewd inquiries can draw out of others their secret thoughts. **6a.** 'Fair promises are common, but faithful performance of them is rare' (Perowne).

20:7–15 Right Conduct—7a. The virtuous life of a **i** father also ensures the future for his children: cf 14:26. **8b.** 'winnows' i.e. dissipates; he quickly perceives evil and applies a remedy. **9.** Man cannot be absolutely certain that he is free from sin: cf 1 (3) Kgs 8:46; Jb 14:4; 15:14; Ps 19 (18): 13; Eccl 7:21; Sir 5:5; Rm 3:23; 1 Jn 1:8; cf also Amenemopet (ANET, p. 426). **10.** Cf 11:1; 16:11; 20:23. **11a.** Children show their character by their conduct; hence the training of the young must begin early. **12.** All man's faculties are the gift of God. The suggestion is that they must be used in obedience to him. **13.** Cf 6:9–11; 12:11; 19:15. **14a.** The buyer, in order to get an article cheaply, depreciates it, and then goes his way, boasting of his cleverness. 'The Sages saw much to provoke laughter. We are all bargain-hunters and we can visualize this scene' (J. Paterson, *The Wisdom of Israel*, 77).

16–25 Just and Unjust Acquisition—16. If a man **j** has been foolish enough to go surety for another, the creditor is to hold him to strict account. According to Ex 22:26; Dt 24:10–13, a man's garment could be taken as security. **20b.** 'his lamp': a figure for prosperity; cf 13:9. **21.** Cf the prodigal son, Lk 15:13. **24b.** 'how then (or, how little) can a man understand his way'. Man's intellect cannot comprehend the Providence which guides him. He must learn to trust God; then his life will be properly directed. **25.** By pronouncing the word 'Holy!' over an object it was removed from profane use (cf Mk 7:11ff) and reserved for God and sacred purposes. A warning against binding oneself by vow without due reflection.

26–21:5 King and Government—26. 'wheel', i.e. of **k** the threshing cart that separates the wheat from the chaff; cf Is 28:27. **27a.** 'The spirit of man', which is infused by God. Cf Gn 2:7 where the same Heb. word is employed to designate the vital principle or soul. Here, however, it rather means 'conscience'; cf 1 Cor 2:11. **30.** Chastisement effects moral improvement. **21:1.** The irrigator has full control over the water supply; so also God over his earthly representative. **2.** Cf 16:2. **3b.** The outer act without the observance of the moral precepts, is but an empty form; cf 15:8; 21:27; Am 5:22; Is 1:11.

417k **4.** The wicked place their happiness in self-exaltation and pride of place (cf 13:9 for the 'lamp' as a symbol of prosperity), but precisely in this consists their sin. **21:6—12 Malice—9b.** 'a house shared'. A transposition of the Heb. letters gives the reading 'roomy' (*rāḥāb*) (CV), cf 25:24. 'It is better to live in a corner-room on the roof, than with a brawling woman in a store-house' (W. F. Albright, *The archaeology of Palestine*, 234). **12.** God observes and punishes the actions of the wicked, cf Jb **l** 34:17. **13—29 Charity and Justice—14.** Cf 17:23; 18:16; 19:6. **16.** Cf 2:18; 5:5; 7:27. Most commentators understand the v to mean that evil men die prematurely. **18.** The chastisement of the wicked is, so to speak, the price paid for the immunity of the just. **20a.** The wise man is thrifty; the fool wasteful. **22b.** Knowledge and skill are superior to brute strength. **25—26.** He whose desires never materialize into action ruins himself, but the just man is ceaseless in his works of charity. **28.** A lying witness forfeits the right to be heard, but he who speaks only after careful consideration will always be heard. Neither the text nor sense is certain. Dahood suggests 'The false witness will be a wanderer, and the man who listens will forever be pursued' (op cit, p. 45). **29b.** 'makes firm his ways.' The comparison is between firmness of conduct and hardness of face.

m **30—22:16 Divine Sovereignty—30.** Cf 1 Cor 1:19; 3:19. **31.** Human effort is required but the final outcome of everything depends on God. **22:2.** 'The true remedy for social inequalities is to recognize who it is that has appointed them and the obligations of mutual consideration and respect which they involve' (Perowne); cf 29:13. **4.** Worship of God in true humility will win the divine blessing. **5.** Cf 16:17. **6.** The child is father to the man. **9.** Cf 14:21; 19:17. **11.** 'The Lord loves cleanness of heart: grace of lips pleases the king' (LXX). Purity of heart pleases God; graciousness in speech, earthly monarchs. **12.** God, who sees all, protects 'knowledge', i.e. the wise man, and brings to nought the subterfuges of the wicked. **13.** Humorous sarcasm to show how the indolent exaggerate difficulties; cf 26:13. **14.** The seductive mouth of the adulteress is like a deep pit dug by the hunter for his prey. **15a.** 'bound up': folly is part and parcel of his life. The discipline of the rod is the best remedy; cf 13:24; 19:18; 23:13; 29:15. **16.** Perhaps the best reading is: 'He who oppresses the poor only enriches him: he who gives to the rich only impoverishes him'. Evil done to the poor does not profit the oppressor, but rather, by the disposition of divine Providence, the poor themselves. 'The proverb means: either a law according to which difficulty stimulates effort and brings success, or confidence that God will reverse situations' (BJ).

418a **22:17—24:22 Section 3: The Sayings of the Wise—** This section is marked off from Part II by the introduction (17—21), by its hortatory tone, and by the strophic. arrangement (usually four lines to a strophe) instead of couplets. The first half of the quatrain generally contains a prohibition, for which the second half gives the reason. **b** **22:17—23:14.** Contains several striking similarities with the Egyptian instruction of Amenemopet. Barucq (op cit, 175—9) finds similarities to two passages of Amenemopet, in 22:17—21. He finds further points of contact in 22:22f, 24f, 28, 29; 23:1—3, 4—5, 6—8. For a list of comparisons cf also ANET p. 424. The Egyptian Wisdom writing cannot be acurately dated (c. 1000—600 B.C.). No conclusive argument has been produced for the dependence of Prv 22:17—23:14 on Amenemopet or of Amenemopet on Prv. The two collections of sayings may have a common source. **c** **17—21 Introduction**—The unknown author speaks to

the reader as to a son, after the fashion of chh 1—7, **418** exhorting him to study the maxims and to make them his spiritual possession. Through them he will acquire trust in God and an adequate answer for all who question him. MT is poorly preserved. **19b.** CV proposes the conjectural reading 'I make known to you the words of Amenemopet'. There are 30 sayings in this section. 'See thou these 30 chapters: They entertain, they instruct' (ANET, p. 424).

22—29. 22b. 'at the gate': at the city entrance, where **d** the court of law was held (Dt 21:19). **27b** The usual warning against suretyship; the creditors, in compensation, will seize even necessary furniture. **28a.** 'landmark' designating the limits of one's property. The land of the poor was often encroached upon by the powerful; cf 23:10; Dt 19:14; 27:17.

23:1—3 At Table—This saying inculcates respect and circumspection when dining with the great. **2a.** 'put a knife to your throat': probably a proverbial expression of self-restraint. **3a = 6b. 3b.** His hospitality may be only to cloak some ulterior purpose. **4—5 Against Anxiety for Wealth—5.** Riches can vanish in a moment. **6—8 The Niggardly Host—8b.** The feast will be a failure. The food will nauseate and agreeable conversation will be impossible. **9 The Fool 10—11 The Land of the Poor—10a.** Cf 22:28. **11a.** Literally 'redeemer', i.e. the next of kin who was bound by law to redeem his kinsman's land; cf Lv 25:25. Here it is God himself who will protect the widow and the orphan.

12—14 Training of Children—13b. Death here is the consequence of the sin, into which the pampered child will fall, rather than the effect of corporal punishment. This view is borne out by the next verse. (cf ANET, p. 428). **15—18 Reward of the God Fearing—16.** the heart **e** and the kidneys were regarded as the seats of intellectual and emotional life. **18.** cf 24:14. **19—21 Warning against Drunkenness and Gluttony. 22—25 Value of Parental Instruction. 26—28 Warning against the Harlot—26.** The sage identifies himself with Wisdom (cf chh 1—9). **27.** Cf 22:14. **28b.** She seduces men to betray the faith pledged to their consorts and to God; cf 2:17.

29—35 Against Intemperance—A graphic and humorous description of a drunkard. **30b.** Dahood, op cit, p. 49, suggests 'Who come to plumb the mixing bowl'. 'The text', he claims, 'is describing the bibbers who come to inspect the bottom of the wine-bowl'. **32b.** The species of snake meant is unknown; one common rendering is 'adder'. **33—34.** The physiological effects of drunkenness. **33b.** 'perverse': distorted. A reference to the distorted fancies and irresponsible speech of the drunkard. **34.** Is difficult. The ground will seem to rise and fall as though he were on board ship or at the mast-head in a rough sea. **35.** The half-stupid utterances of returning consciousness. The drunkard's first thought is to get back to his debauch.

24:1—22 Diverse Utterances—3—4. Practical utility **f** of Wisdom. The reference is to the actual building and furnishing of the home. **5—6.** Value of Wisdom in military strategy. **6.** Cf 11:14; 20:18. **7—10.** Contain couplets in the style of the 'Proverbs of Solomon'. **7a.** The line is obscure. 'Wisdom is a mountain (or corals) to a fool.' The meaning is much the same viz something beyond him, something he can't appreciate. **7b.** 'in the gate': in the place of public deliberation the fool will have no authority. **9a.** Sin is the aim and object of the fool's planning. **11—22 Duties towards One's Neighbour—11—12.**

18f Deal with the same subject. He who is able to prevent another's death and, on a weak pretext, fails to do so, will be held guilty by divine justice. **13–14.** Wisdom (virtue) is to the soul what honey is to the 'palate'. **15–16.** A warning against violence to the just. **16a.** 'seven' is a round number; cf Lk 17:4; Mt 18:21. The just man, no matter how often he is struck down by misfortune, will, with God's help, rise again, but the wicked succumb to calamity. **17–18.** To rejoice in the misfortune of enemies displeases God; perhaps his anger will turn from your neighbour to you. **19–20.** The wicked are not to be envied. **20a.** The prosperity of the wicked will not last. **20b.** Cf 13:9, note. **21–22.** The sage condemns rebellion against the king (cf Hos. 7: 3–7; 8:4). Note that LXX has five supplementary v after v 22.

g 24:23–34 Section 4: Further Sayings of the Wise Men—This small, independent collection of proverbs forms a second appendix to the first collection of the Proverbs of Solomon (10:1–22: 16). It has no fatherly advice to offer, but the portrait of the drunkard is replaced by that of the sluggard. **23b–25.** Partiality in judicial decisions invokes the curse of God and man; justice brings rich blessing; cf 17:15; 28:21. **26.** Straightforward speech is a mark of true friendship. **27.** An exhortation to get the land well in order and have a definite source of income before setting up a home and family, cf also 27:23–27; 31:10–31. **29.** This marks a big advance on Ex 21:23ff; cf Amenemopet (ANET, p. 422) and *Counsels of Wisdom* (ANET, p. 426). **33–34.** Cf 6:10–11.

419a 25:1–29:27 Section 5: Proverbs of Solomon: Second Series (cf § 411d)—The title informs us that, in addition to the proverbs of 10:1–22:16, other proverbs existed in oral or written form which were attributed to Solomon. At least they must have been ancient in the time of Hezekiah, King of Judah (c. 715–687), hence their ascription to Solomon (c. 961–922).

This section falls into two parts viz 25:2–27:22 and 28:1–29:27. (The intervening verses, 27:23–27, are out of context). In the first part synonymous parallelism predominates (as against antithetical in the second).

b 25:2–7 On Kings—**2b.** The inscrutability of God's designs in the government of the world (cf Rm 11:33f; 1 Tm 6:16) is both a proof and the glory of his transcendental Sovereignty over creation. Earthly rulers ought not to decide affairs without examination and discussion. **3a.** Dahood proposes 'netherworld' rather than 'earth' as translation of 'ereṣ (op cit p.52). **4–5.** Form a comparison. As silver must be freed from dross, so the ruler from evil counsellors. **6–7b.** Also form one quatrain. Cf Lk 14: 8–11.

7c–10 The Contentious Spirit—The forced withdrawal of a rash charge will only fill one with confusion. 'Do not talk about your neighbour's affairs lest you become known as a gossip.' **11–12**: a quatrain on the value of wise advice. **13c** is probably a gloss. **14.** The rising wind and gathering clouds unaccompanied by rain are an apt symbol of empty promises. **15b.** Forbearance and mildness overcome the greatest obstacles.

c 16–28 Moderation—**16a.** Self-control is recommended even in pleasant things. **19.** One cannot rely on a bad tooth or a tottering foot; nor can a disloyal friend be trusted in time of trouble. **21–22.** A quatrain on kindness to enemies. **22a.** 'coals of fire': the burning pangs of shame which may lead to repentance and charity; cf Rm 12:20. **24.** Cf 21:9. **25.** Cf 15:30. **26.** 'gives way' i.e. in the practice of virtue out of human respect. His weakness of character ruins his other good qualities. **27b.** MT reads 'and the investigation of their glory is glory'. Vaccari

suggests 'It is not good to eat much honey, and to search **419c** into majesty is no glory'; too much curiosity about the divine Majesty brings neither glory nor profit to man. CV is better 'nor to seek honour after honour'.

26:1–12 The Fool—**2.** A protest against the popular **d** superstition that gave magical power to a curse. Cf words of Ahikar (ANET, p. 429) **4–5.** Do not descend to the level of a fool unless it be to make him conscious of his folly. **6.** An incompetent envoy is harmful to the sender cf 13:17, 25:13. **7.** A fool can make no better use of a wise saying than a lame man of his limbs. **8.** In each case the act is absurd, for a sling is meant to discharge stones, not to hold them. In Vg the reference is to a casting of stones on the cairns sacred to Mercury and the comparison is with the folly of pagan superstitions. **9.** Obscure: 'Like a thornstick brandished by the hand of a drunkard' (CV). A wise saying may be misused. **10.** Is perhaps the most obscure and difficult in the book. CV, RSV and BJ have similar translations. Vaccari renders: 'The litigant sets everything in motion; he hires the foolish and the passer-by'. **11.** Cf 2 Pt 2:22. **12.** Presumption and self-conceit are worse than ignorance. **13–16 The Portrait of the Sluggard**—(corresponding **e** to the portrait of the drunkard in the first part of the section). Again the sluggard is humorously and ironically described. **13.** Cf 22:13. **14.** 'Movement, without progress'. **15.** Cf 19:24. **16.** Ignorance, the daughter of slothfulness, is the mother of presumption.

17 The Busybody—**18–19.** A condemnation of practical jokes in bad taste—**20–22.** Against malicious gossip.

23–28 The Hypocrite—**23.** A fair exterior hides the inner falseness of the flatterer. **25b.** 'seven'; cf 24:16, note. **26.** Though a man may with guile conceal his hatred for another, sooner or later it will be made public, perhaps in a judicial assembly. **27.** Mischief recoils on the perpetrator. **28a.** The text is corrupt. CV emendation is attractive 'The lying tongue is its owner's enemy'.

27:1–22 A Collection of Aphorisms on Various f Subjects—**1–2.** On boasting. **1.** Cf Jas 4:13f and Amenemopet, (ANET, p. 423). **3b.** Some suggest that 'provocation' is an addition; it is the fool himself who is a burden; cf Sir 22:18. **4.** It is the most tenacious and terrible of the passions: cf 6:34. **5–6.** Salutary rebuke. **5.** Love which fails to correct. **7.** Hunger is the best sauce. Cf Horace, *Sat* 11, 2, 38. **8.** There is no place like home. **9b.** Conjectural reading of BJ 'Sweetness of counsel consoles the soul'. 'But the sweetness of a friend, lo it is an aromatic forest' (Dahood, op cit p. 54). **10.** Hold fast to old friendships. In the day of trouble a tried friend of the family, if he be near at hand, is of more worth than a kinsman who dwells far off. **11.** The good conduct of the pupil will be the best proof of the character of the master's teaching. **12.** Cf 22:3. **13.** A repetition of 20:16. **14.** Excessive demonstrations of affection are suspect. **15–16.** A quatrain. Cf 19:13. **16.** MT is corrupt. It is as difficult to restrain a contentious woman as to restrain the winds or grasp oil. **17.** Social intercourse sharpens the wits. 'Conference maketh a ready man'. **18b.** 'honoured': Duty well done brings its own reward. **19.** As the face seen in water resembles the face of which it is a reflection, so do the hearts of men resemble one another in the essential features of their common nature. 'As water', however, is probably a mistaken translation of the Heb. kᵉmô = 'as'; hence the original text would read 'As face to face, so the heart of man to man'; as human countenances show differences, so too, there is diversity in the inner, moral being of men. **20a.** Abaddon: cf 15:11, note. The desires of men are as insatiable as

419f Sheol. **21.** Praise tests a man's virtue as fire tests metal. **22b.** 'Along with crushed grain' reads like a gloss and should be omitted. The proverb states graphically that the fool's folly is his nature.

g 23—27 Care of the Flock—This poem is out of context. It may have been a conclusion to some independent collection. The continual effort of the farmer is necessary against the day of want. **25.** 'the herbage of the mountains' (the upland pastures which are mown later) is gathered in. **26b.** The sale of flocks will purchase more land.

420a 28:1—29:27. The second part of this section— The courage of a good conscience; cf Hamlet: 'Conscience doth make cowards of us all'. **2.** The text is uncertain. Perhaps LXX is preferable—'*Through the fault of the wicked disputes arise, but a man of understanding settles them*'. **3.** 'A wicked man or "ruler" who oppresses the poor is a beating rain—and no bread' (LXX); he is like a rain which takes away man's food by flattening the grain and washing the seed out of the earth. CV reads 'a rich man who oppresses the poor', while RSV has 'a poor man . . . etc'! MT favours the latter, the context the former interpretation. **5.** Vice destroys the moral sense in man; but the sincerely religious man has a mind exquisitely attuned to the perception of all things, cf 1 Cor 2:14f. **8.** Money wrongfully acquired (cf Ex 22:25; Dt 23:19f) will finally fall into the hand of the charitable man; cf 13:22. **9.** Prayer made with an obstinate affection for sin is an insult to God. **11.** The ability to amass wealth is no sure sign of wisdom; a poor man who is discerning is able to see through the rich. **12.** When evil men are in power, the people suffer. **13.** Cf Ps 32 (31); 5f. **17.** Obscure. Perhaps it means that there is to be no sympathy for a murderer. **20.** A commendation of honest dealing. **21.** To pervert justice by showing partiality in the law-court is a grave sin; yet how many are tempted even by a small bribe! **24.** He who steals from his parents is ready for any crime. **25.** A man of grasping disposition rouses antagonism, but he who trusts in God and not in riches will prosper. **26.** 'He that trusteth in himself is entrusted to a great fool' (St Augustine).

b 29:2—14 Good Government—**3.** Cf the prodigal son (Lk 15:30). **6.** The path of the wicked seems enviable, but, in reality, it leads to disaster. 'Scoffers (at moral obligations) set a city on fire', by fanning the passions of men. Prudent men, on the other hand, bring calm. **9.** There is no coming to an understanding with a fool, either by severity or by banter. **13.** Although it takes all sorts to make up a world, it is God, who gives to all the 'light' of life and keeps them in existence; cf 22:2; Mt 5:45.

c 15—21 Education—**15.** Cf 10:1; 13:24; 17:21; 19:18; 22:15; 23:13. **18.** 'Vision' and 'law' refer to prophetic teaching, or to prophetic teaching plus the Pentateuch The salvation of a people and the individual stands in the observance of a divinely given law. **19.** The servant, like the son, must be corrected by the rod. **21.** MT is uncertain, the last word never occurring elsewhere. LXX has 'he who lives luxuriously from childhood will be a servant and finally will come to grief'. The Vg reading makes good sense.

d 22—27 Mildness and Humility—**23.** Cf 16:18. **24a.** 'is his own enemy', by incurring the guilt and penalty of a thief. **24b.** As a partner in crime he is like one who, having been put on oath in a law-court to reveal what he knows, conceals the perpetrator of a crime (Lv 5:1). The effect of the curse pronounced on his unknown partner falls on himself. **25a.** By yielding to human respect one may easily be led to do something wrong, or to refrain from doing what is right. **26.** It is the favour of God and

not of men that one must seek, for the destiny of men **420** depends on God alone.

30:1—14 Section 6: The Sayings of Agur—A short **e** collection of miscellaneous proverbs. The whole passage is reminiscent of Jb 40:4f; 42:2—6. **1.** Is enigmatic. **1a.** Constitutes a title. Agur, like Lemuel with whom he is to be ethnologically connected (31:1), came from Massa (if, as is probable, Maśśā' is a place name), a region in Transjordan originally inhabited by the Ishmaelites (Gn 25:14). In the course of time, however, Israelite families must have settled there, bringing with them their religion, for Agur is a worshipper of Yahweh (30:9) and both he and Lemuel have merited a place among the inspired writers. Maśśā', however, could also be read as a noun signifying 'oracle' (cf Is 13:1; Na 1:1). **1b.** Can only be conjectural. Are Ithiel and Ucal proper names (RSV, BJ) or not (CV)? Dahood translates 'The word of the man Leithiel, Leithiel and Ucal' (op cit, p. 57). **2—4.** The divine nature and its **f** attributes transcend human intelligence. A proof of this is to be found in the marvels of creation (cf Jb 38:4—11). **4c.** 'in a garment': i.e. in the clouds. **4e.** To know a man's name or his son's name, is to be well acquainted with him. The meaning of the v is that no man is responsible for the magnificence of the universe but the transcendent God, who is beyond the feebleness of human comprehension. **5.** The 'word of God' could refer to the law or the prophetic oracles. Here it probably means the teaching of the sages. Their doctrine is true and trustworthy like metal that has passed through the refining pot, cf Ps 12 (11):7; like a shield it wards off error. **6.** Do not give out your own thoughts as divine revelation; cf Dt 4:2; Apoc 22:18. **7—9.** A prayer to be kept from insincerity and from the evils of excessive wealth and poverty. Cf Solomon's prayer (1 (3) Kgs 3:8ff) **8.** Cf 'Give us this day our daily bread'. **11—14.** Four odious types: despisers of parents, self-righteous, proud, and extortionate. **13.** 'Men of haughty looks and supercilious bearing' (Toy).

30:15—33 Section 7: Numerical Sayings—The fact **g** that in LXX these vv stand after 24:34 indicates that they once formed a separate collection. MT is poorly preserved. This section is a good example of the use of numbers to attract attention. Cf 6:16—19; Am 1:3—13; (Mi) 5:4; Jb 5:19 etc. **15—16.** Four insatiable things. Sheol (cf 1:2; 2:18; 27:20), the barren womb, earth, and fire. **15a.** Is probably corrupt, and may be a gloss. In view of what follows, the original thought seems to have been that the leech is never sated with blood. **15b.** 'three . . . four': a rhetorical figure. **16a.** The reference is to the desire of a childless wife for children. **17.** Punishment of filial disobedience. **18—19.** Four wondrous things. **h** **19.** The soaring flight of a bird, the mysterious movement of a serpent, the path of a ship through the sea, the procreation and growth of a human being in the womb (cf Ps 139 (138):13—18; Jb 10:11)—or perhaps the birth in the heart of a youth of that affection by which he is drawn to a maid—all excite admiration. In the first explanation, '*almāh* means a young woman of marriageable age, presumably a virgin, who in lawful matrimony will realize the mysterious designs of Providence in the procreation of life. **20.** Is only loosely connected with 19 and is probably a gloss. Presumably it was thought to be an appropriate explanation of the last line of 19 where however there is no question of an immoral act; nor is the point of 19 their tracelessness but the wonder they excite.

21—23. Four things unbearable to society. **24—28.** Four things small but wise. **29—31.** Four majestic things. **31a.** 'cock': thus all the ancient versions, but some suggest 'the war-horse' accoutred for battle (cf Jb 39:19—25).

420h **32—33.** Learn to keep a modest silence. Self-glorification only rouses wrath that ends in strife.

i **31:1—9 Section 8: The Sayings of Lemuel**—This short collection consists of four quatrains containing counsels of moderation and generosity, given to the king by his mother. In terms of ardent affection (2), she warns him against impurity (3), inebriety (4—7), and urges him to befriend the helpless and judge with equity (8—9) MT is in a very poor state.

1. Superscription. 'Lemuel': cf 20:1. Massa was probably an Ishmaelite town in Northern Arabia cf Gn 25:14, **2.** 'What': thrice repeated, it expresses earnestness. 'of my vows': given as a result of vows; cf 1 Sm 1:11. **3b.** i.e. evil women, cf Sir 47:19—21. **6—7.** Two proper occasions for the use of wine, bodily suffering and mental distress; cf Ps 104 (103) 15; Mk 15:23. **8a.** 'dumb': defend those who have no one to plead for them.

j **31:10—31 Section 9: The Ideal Wife**—An anonymous, alphabetical poem, the 'ABC' of the ideal wife cf Pss 9—10, 25, 34, 37, 111—2, 119, 145; Lam 1—4; Na 1:2—8. The 'wisdom' of BJ is to be commended for its marginal insertion of the Heb. letters! Margaret Crook, JNES, 13 (1954), 137—40 suggests that the poem was originally a memorandum from an academic training school for girls about to marry men of substance or com-**k** munity leaders. **10a.** Lit. 'a woman of strength' or 'capacity'. The best English rendering is 'a worthy wife'. **11b.** 'and he will have no lack of gain', i.e. income. Her husband confides to her the management of the household, certain that all will go well. **13.** 'This may be the Hebrew counterpart of an Arabic proverb and should go as **420k** follows: "And wool is not lacking to her". In both the Arabic and Hebrew proverb, the capable woman (cf v, 10) is thought of as never idle: she is always at her wool' (D. Winton Thomas VTS, 1955, 290). **14.** From all quarters she provides maintenance for the household. **15c.** Is omitted by CV as a gloss. **16b.** 'with the fruit of her hands': with her earnings. **18a.** She perceives with relish that her commerce is profitable. **18b.** Either she works indefatigably, or, because the lamp is the symbol of prosperity (13:9; 24:20), her house is prosperous even in distressing times. **20.** Economy does not forbid charity. **24b.** Lit 'Canaanite': the word came to be synonymous with 'merchant' to whom she 'gives' the girdles she has woven in exchange for money, etc. The Canaanites or Phoenicians were the great mercantile people of the period. **25.** Her foresight has enabled her to face the future without anxiety. **27.** She keeps diligent watch over the conduct of her family and domestics. **28.** Peace and harmony reign in the household; she is appreciated and praised by husband and children. **29.** The encomium of her husband. **30—31.** Charm and beauty are prized in a woman, but they will pass away. Of how much more value is virtue founded on the 'fear of the Lord', i.e. on religion. 'Thus does Wisdom return in her last utterance to her first (1:7), and place once again the crown on the head of the godly' (Perowne). This picture of the ideal wife is a fitting conclusion to Prv corresponding as it does to the picture of Wisdom personified in the first section of the book.

ECCLESIASTES

BY F. BUCK S.J.

421a Bibliography—Commentaries: C. H. Wright, 1883; G. Gietmann, CSS, 1890; K. Siegfried, HKAT, 1898; G. A. Barton, ICC 1908; E. Podechard, EtBib 1912; A. L. Williams, CBSC, 1922; H. Odeberg, Uppsala, 1929; D. Buzy, PCSB, 1946; F. Nötscher, EchB 1948; A. Bea, 1950; O. S. Rankin, IB, 1956; E. Jones, Torch 1961; H. W. Hertzberg, KAT, 1962²; W. Zimmerli, ATD, 1962; K. Galling, HAT, 1963²; R. B. Y. Scott, AB 1965; *Other Literature*: H. L. Ginsberg, *Studies in Koheleth*, 1950; R. Gordis, *Koheleth, the Man and his World*, 1955²; O. Loretz, *Qoheleth, und der Alte Orient*, Freiburg, 1964; J. Muilenburg, 'A Qoheleth Scroll from Qumran', BASOR, 135 (1954) 20—27; R. E. Murphy, 'The Pensées of Qoheleth', CBQ 17 (1955) 304—14; M. J. Dahood, 'Canaanite-Phoenician Influences in Qoheleth', Bib 33 (1952) 30—52. For other works, see EOTInt.

b Name—The superscription (1:1) calls the book 'The words of Qohelet'. This Heb. word represents a participial fem. sing. derived either from the verb *qāhal* (assemble), otherwise unused in *Qal*, or from the noun *qāhāl* (assembly). The fem. form is explained by the fact that words denoting a function, an office or an activity, are often fem. (cf Ez 2:55 '*sōperet* = holder of the office of scribe'; Ez 2:57 '*pōkeret* = holder of the office of gazelle tender'). The Gr. trans., deriving Qohelet from *qāhal* (assembly), rendered the term as *Ecclesiastes* which entered into the Vg. *Ecclesiastes* means directly 'a member of the assembly' which is explained as one who convokes or addresses an assembly. Jer in his commentary (PL 23, 104) translated the term by *concionator*, i.e. a preacher. Others (cf Williams), insisting on the relation of the term with *qāhal* (assemble), like to interpret the name as meaning 'one who collects sayings of wisdom for the purpose of teaching'. E. Ullendorf, in a note on 'The Meaning of Koheleth' (VT 12 (1962) 215), refers to the Aram.-Syr. *qhl* (= litigious) and speaks of the 'one who argues'. In view of the fem. form, however, it might be more accurate to say that Qohelet signifies 'one who holds the office of speaker in the assembly'. This latter explanation would also permit us to regard the author not so much as a preacher, but as a teacher of wisdom.

c Composition and Structure—There are discrepancies in Eccl: he declares '*those now dead more fortunate than those who still live*' (4:2), but he states at the same time that '*a live dog is better off than a dead lion*' (9:4). Of the lazy fool, who folds his arms, Eccl says that '*he consumes his own flesh*' (4:5). In the same breath, however, he points out that '*better is one handful with tranquillity than two with toil and a chase after wind*' (4:6). There are also various passages (1:2; 7:27; 12:8) and especially the epilogue (12:9—14) which speak of Eccl in the third person. Whereas Eccl on the whole is written in prose, there are verse passages inserted which seem to modify the teaching of Eccl (cf 4:9—12; 4:17—5:6; 7:1—12, 18, 22; 10:1ff; 12:2—6). And some texts (3:17; 7:18*b*; 8:5; 12:12—14) are suspected, because they **421c** allegedly intend 'to render harmless certain heresies of the author'. These and other considerations have led scholars to detect various hands in the book of Eccl.

Siegfried distinguished eight authors who in the course of time influenced and altered the original text written by a philosopher of Greek leaning. Podechard affirms that only three-quarters of the book was written by Eccl; a disciple added the epilogue, a sage (*ḥākām*) several poetic verses, and a pious interpolater (*ḥāsîd*) made additions to counterbalance some of the shocking statements of the author. Buzy defends a similar position.

Without excluding every addition or alteration to the **d** text, more recently a reaction has set in against such a dissection of Eccl (cf Galling, Gordis, Zimmerli). It seems more difficult, at any rate, to deny the unity than to prove it. The work has been described as a series of reflections and jottings without much development and consistency, similar to the genre of 'Pascal's Pensées' (Murphy, Loretz). Although Eccl does not show a clear progression of thought, yet there is a thread of continuity and unity. 'All is vanity' (1:2) has been deliberately placed as the dominant idea in the beginning of the book. And with the same deliberateness it is said towards the end of the work: 'Rejoice, o young man, *while you are young*' (11:9). The first idea expresses the result at which the author arrives after every new investigation and reflection, whereas the second idea presents the same conclusion which the author draws over and over again. It is by no means impossible, therefore, to give a precise and definite outline of the book, whether we speak of thirty-seven sentences (Galling), of three considerations (Bea), or, as here, of six instructions.

The title (1:1) is followed by a statement of the theme (1:2—3). The first instruction (1:4—2:26) points out 'the purposelessness of human efforts'. A second instruction (3:1—22) shows how 'man is governed by the laws of life and death'. In the third instruction (4:1—5:6) Eccl discusses 'man's inhumanity to man and his lack of circumspection towards God'. The fourth instruction (5:7—7:12) deals with 'the deception of riches'. A fifth instruction (7:13—9:10) refers to 'the anomalies of the human situation', whereas a sixth instruction insists on 'the inconsistency of fortune' (9:11—12:8). An epilogue (12:9—14) contains 'a disciple's praise and warning'. **Author, Language, Date**—The superscription identi- **e** fies the author with king Solomon (cf also 1:12, 16; 2:7, 9). Though it may have been held up to the 19th cent. that Solomon was the author (cf Gietmann, 23ff), it is universally recognized to-day that this book cannot have been written by, or in the time of, Solomon. The anonymous author who identified himself with Solomon used this personation as a literary device to acquire the great king's dignity and authority for his work.

Language considerations, above all, make it impossible to accept the authorship of Solomon. Eccl is written in a late form of Heb. It may be assigned to the 3rd cent.

21e The lower limit is marked by Sir, composed about the year 180, since it makes use of Eccl's teaching (cf Sir 5:3 = Eccl 3:15; Sir 13:25 = Eccl 8:1; Sir 40:11 = Eccl 12:7). This lower limit is also indicated by fragments of Eccl found in Qumran. Muilenburg assigns the most ancient of those fragments (words of Eccl 5:13, 14; 6:3–8; 7:7–9) to the middle of the 2nd cent. The attempt, however, to fix the date of composition more exactly has not led to definite results. The presence of Aram. elements in the text of Eccl forms the main argument. Some scholars even suggested that Eccl had been translated from an original written in Aram. (Ginsberg). Dahood insists on a Phoenician-Canaanite influence. Although the linguistic argument may not be conclusive, the author's mental background, which shows the influence of Hellenism, excludes a date before Alexander. We may place its composition between 250 and 200 B.C. Since the writer is also said to display a certain acquaintance with Egyptian wisdom, it has been argued that he had come down from Palestine to Alexandria. Allusions, however, to Jerusalem, the temple, sacrifices, vows, the flora of Palestine, seem to indicate a Palestinian rather than an Egyptian setting.

f Doctrinal Contents—Eccl is not on the highest plane of OT revelation, still less that of the NT. It occupies a place all its own. 'Just as there was room and more than room for a St Thomas among the Apostles, so also there is a fitting place for this grave and austere thinker among the wise men of Israel' (W. Sanday, *The Early History and Origin of the Doctrine of Biblical Inspiration*, London, 1893).

Two attitudes of Eccl are conspicuous. First his absolute sincerity. He observes the world and gives his straightforward impression. It seems evident that the days in which the author lived were not exactly blessed by good fortune. And in his character there may have been a trend towards scepticism and melancholy. But he **honestly faces reality and paints it as he sees it.** His sincere encounter with reality enables him to find a hidden meaning in the darker sides of life. Thus his declaration: 'It is better to go to the house of mourning than to go to the house of feasting' (7:2) leads us to the understanding that a wise appreciation of life must rest on the fact that death ends all. Eccl was not a weak or superficial person; he wants to brace us for the storm.

A second striking attitude in Eccl is **his simple, but unshakable faith.** There may be misery in the world, chaos, unsolved enigmas, and the temptation may be great to deny the existence of God as well as his moral government over the world. But Eccl will never renounce his faith and will always insist on the simple practical duties of his religion.

g (i) The Doctrine of God—Eccl's belief in God is fundamental. He assumes the **existence of God.** In the 222 vv of his book Eccl mentions 41 times the name of God, employing the term *'elōhîm*. Explicitly God is addressed as the Creator (12:1) who created all that exists (11:5). God is omnipotent (cf 3:11; 6:10; 7:14; 8:17), he gives life (5:18; 8:15; 9:9) and takes it away (12:7). He grants prosperity (5:19; 6:2), enjoyment of life (2:24, 26; 3:13; 5:18), as well as the desire to search out everything (1:13; 3:11). God is the supreme ruler and his work is perfect, although beyond our comprehension (3:14; 5:1; 6:10; 7:13, 14; 8:17; 9:1). God is wise, for he knows the past (3:15) and the future (6:10), and does all things well (3:11, 14). He is holy and wishes that man may serve him in all sincerity (cf 4:17; 5:1, 3, 5–6; 7:18; 12:13). God bestows special care on the just and wise (9:1, 7) and blesses man's labour (2:24–

25; 3:13). He is also just: although he gave man a dif- **521g** ficult task (1:13; 3:10), yet he gives wisdom and happiness to the good (2:26; 8:12) and delivers them from evil (7:26). Quite differently does he deal with the wicked (2:26; 7:26; 8:13). Although he often delays his chastisement (8:11), yet he remains the judge of the good and the wicked (3:17) and will judge one day the works of all men (11:9; 12:14).

(ii) The Image of Man—Like every sapiential writing **h** Eccl deals mainly with **human life and its problems.** God has made man upright (7:29). In addition each man receives much from God (5:17, 18 etc). Now man was intended to revere God (3:14). Man, however, is sinful (7:20) and there are now 'just and wicked', 'good and bad', 'clean and unclean' in this world (9:2). It is, lastly, only the good who will also be wise (2:26).

As for the social order, there are kings and servants (10:16), oppressors and oppressed (4:1; 5:7), the rich and the working class (5:11). Wisdom, however, is not necessarily the patrimony of the rich (4:13; 9:15). Work (cf 10:18) and partnership (4:9–12) are important. And submission is at times the best attitude in face of despotic rulers (10:4–7). With regard to happiness there are some who are content with their lot (5:18), but many others remain unsatisfied (5:9), because their desires are too great (1:13; 2:1–3; 3:11; etc), so that a certain sense of frustration oppresses them (1:2, 14; 2:1, 11, 15, etc).

As for the end of man, **the universal law of death is stated** (3:19), the impossibility of taking one's earnings with one (5:15), and that each one will have to give account of his works (3:17).

(iii) The Idea of Wisdom—It is significant that Eccl uses the term *hokmâ* (wisdom) and *hākām* (wise) 44 times. God gives wisdom to the good (2:26; 7:25), but through application (1·17) and observation (8:16) man may perfect it (1;16). There is an **intimate relation between wisdom and happiness.** Wisdom illumines man's face (8:1), gives him vigour (7:12, 19; 9:16), shows the right way (10:2) and helps in dealing with others (9:17; 10:17). Lest the wise should become proud, Eccl tells him that wisdom does not answer all questions (8:17) nor protect against all evil (9:4) or death (2:15–16). But the wise man, because he is just and good at the same time (cf 2:26; 8:12–13), will always enjoy God's protection (9:1). How different is the case of the fool: he walks in darkness (2:14) and goes astray (10:2–3). The fool is dissipated (7:4, 6; 9:17), lazy (4:5), perverse (7:17), and God has no pleasure in him (5:3).

(iv) The Idea of Vanity—With the term *hebel* (vanity) **i** Eccl opens and closes his work (1:2; 12:8). Whereas the word 'vanity' occurs all in all some 70 times in the OT, it is found 36 times in Eccl. 'All things are vanity' (1:2). By this statement Eccl wishes to tell us that nothing here on earth or 'under the sun' may give man an unlimited happiness. 'Vanity', therefore, is not the expression of a pessimistic attitude, but rather a sobering realization of the limited character of all things.

Canonicity—The Jewish tradition, at least from the **422a** 1st cent. onward, considered Eccl as belonging to the collection of holy books. Jos.CAp (1, 8, 38–42) 98–97 B.C., 4 Esd (14:45–46) c. A.D. 100 and Bab Ba 14b, 15a, testify to the canonicity of Eccl. Further, the Mishna, *Yadaim* III, 5, 6f, records: 'I, Simeon ben Azzai, received as a tradition from the mouth of 72 elders on the day when they elected R. Eleazar ben Azariah to the presidency of the Assembly (at Jamnia or Jabneh in the years 90–100) that the Song of Songs and Qohelet defile the hands' (i.e. are sacred).

ECCLESIASTES

422a The Christian tradition does not appear to have ever had any doubt on the canonicity of Eccl. The only exception is Theodore of Mopsuestia (360—428) who, although he did not exclude Eccl from the Canon, assigned to it a lower degree of inspiration, for 'Solomon', he said, 'had not received the grace of prophecy, but only the grace of prudence'. His doctrine, however, was rejected by the Fifth General Council, held in Constantinople in 553 (Mansi, IX, 223).

b In LXX and Vg the book is placed among the Sapiential Books between Prv and Song. In the Heb. it is found among the *Ketubim*, between Song and Lam. It is the fourth book of the five *Megilloth* and by the end of the 11th cent. it was an established custom to read this scroll in the synagogue on the Feast of Tabernacles.

c Text and Versions—The Heb. text is well preserved in MT and its reliability has been considerably enhanced by the fragments of Eccl found in Cave 4 of Qumran. Those fragments, although they consist only of a few words pertaining to 5:13—17; 6:3—8; 7:1—2, 7—9, 19—20, are attributed by Muilenburg to mid-2nd cent. and do not show any variant readings of importance. It may be argued, therefore, that the quality of the few vv covered by the fragments of Qumran may be indicative of the whole text of Eccl.

The LXX follows MT closely and shows resemblance with Aquila's Gr. version. The *Peshitta* is very literal. As for the *Latin*, Jerome made a 1st trans. in 389—92 for his commentary. In the preface he tells us that he translated from Heb., following LXX when it did not differ too much; at times, he says, he consulted Aq, Symm and Theod (PL 23, 1011f). The *Vg* was Jerome's 2nd trans. made from the Heb. in 398. It was hastily done, for in three days he finished the translation of Prv, Eccl and Song (PL 28, 1241).

d Ecclesiastes and Revelation—Jeremiah (31:29—30) and Ezekiel (14:13—20; 18:1—32) rejected the teaching that the innocent would have to suffer because of the sins of their fathers, and insisted on individual responsibility and retribution: the righteous would enjoy prosperity and the wicked in turn would be afflicted. But reward and punishment were thought to take place in this world. This was still a long way from belief in eternal sanctions in the next world. The optimistic and oversimplified interpretation of this world's events had to be attacked. Calamity and affliction were not always and necessarily a punishment, neither was happiness in this world always the immediate reward of virtue. The book of Job contributed its share in creating dissatisfaction with the world. Eccl goes further in the same direction and shows that there is little real happiness in this world, only little joys like eating, drinking, marriage, and much emptiness and vanity. Thus Jb, and even more so Eccl prepare the way for a more realistic solution of the problem of good and evil, of reward and punishment. Wisdom takes up where Jb and Eccl left off, and pierces the mystery of retribution (Wis 2—5), leading on to the doctrine of blessed immortality or spiritual death for all eternity. In this context Eccl was necessary for the progress of revelation.

e 1:1 Title—Qoheleth (cf 1:2, 12; 7:27; 12:8, 9, 10), who 'holds the office of speaker in the assembly', is a teacher of wisdom. He is identified with king Solomon, the traditional patron of wisdom (1 (3) Kgs 3:12). This personification is a literary device (cf 1:12, 16).

2—3 Theme—All things (cf 3:19; 12:8): all the activities of life are meant, but the totality of the universe does not seem to be included. Vanity (*hebel*): 'breath', 'vapour', an exhalation which comes into existence and vanishes,

or more concretely 'the transitoriness and aimlessness **422e** of all that happens upon earth'. Vanity of vanities: expresses the superlative, i.e. utter and complete vanity. Gain: a commercial term, used 9 times in Eccl, in the sense of profit. Toil ('*āmāl*): the verb and noun of this root are used 35 times, sorrow and vexation, is meant. Under the sun: occurs 29 times (in Eccl only) and signifies every place where the sun gives light for life and work.

1:4—2:26 The purposelessness of Human Efforts— f 4—11. All creation is in a ceaseless motion, but man cannot discover any meaning in it. **4.** The earth, man's workshop, appears permanent, while man ever passes. This v was wrongly referred to in the erroneous condemnation of the Copernican system against Galileo in 1616. **5.** Continually the sun makes its wearisome round, without accomplishing anything. The sun hastens (lit pants): is eager to reach his goal. The earth is conceived as a stationary flat disc, resting on an abyss. At night the sun returns beneath the earth to the very same place whence it rises every morning. **6—7.** The movements of the winds (the same Heb. word is used 4 times to describe the winds' wearisome movements in circles), like those of the sun, are equally ceaseless and meaningless. And the streams with all their untiring flow accomplish nothing. **8.** All talking (*debārim*: lit the words), seeing, and hearing is useless toil, for curiosity will never be satisfied; man himself seems to be moving in meaningless rounds. Less probable Vg: all things are toiling to weariness, neither tongue, nor eye, nor ear can grasp and describe such toil. **9—11.** Monotonous repetition characterizes the happenings of nature as well as the doings of man. There is no progress. A thing is thought new, only because its previous existence is not remembered. Others (Gordis, Nötscher, CV) refer v 11 to persons only: man will soon be forgotten (cf 2:16). **12—18.** Man's wisdom cannot change the course of things. **12.** Eccl speaks in the name **g** of Solomon who had been rich in experience and wealth, full of wisdom and fit for the task of giving guidance with regard to life's problems. 'I was king': the past tense is peculiar, since Solomon continued to be king until his death. Similar careless statements concerning the history of Solomon are found in 1:16; 2:7, 9. They suggest that the author's identification with Solomon is but a literary device. **13—14.** That God gives existence to all things is simply taken for granted. To man God gave also the desire and the obligation to investigate all things. The wisdom that man has ought to be the guide. A chase after wind: Vg derived *reût* from *rā'a* 'to break' and translated 'afflictio spiritus' (vexation of the spirit). Bea refers it to *rā'â* 'to feed', 'to busy oneself'. The literal meaning of this phrase, used 7 times here, would be 'a feeding on the wind', i.e. to make a meal on food as unsubstantial as the wind. Koehler (*Lexicon*) explains it as 'desire, striving'. In either case it is said that all human activity is like desiring something illusory. **15.** Why? A proverb gives the answer: Human wisdom will never be able to change the course of things, since all things are ordained and cannot be different from what they are. **16.** Eccl, who so far has viewed the things of the world and human activity in the light of wisdom, considers his 'wisdom and knowledge' (probably synonymous terms to stress the amplitude of his wisdom) to be much greater than that of his predecessors. Solomon, of course, would not be able to speak of 'all who were over Jerusalem before me', since only David had preceded him. **17.** Eccl now seeks to gain greater insight by a study of wisdom's opposites—madness and folly. But this effort turns out to be just as frustrating as '*a chase after wind*'. **18.** Another proverb

514

22g sums it up: The greater the devotion to wisdom, the greater also the sense of frustration and defeat. He who does not care about wisdom, will be better off.

h 2:1—11, 12b Pleasure is no worth-while object of human effort—1—2. Even before enumerating his various experiences Eccl tells us the conclusion: pleasure, laughter, mirth are of no use. **3.** First he examines the worth of the sensual pleasures of the table, symbolized by wine. But he does not indulge in the use of wine without being concerned with wisdom: he wants to find out whether such a pleasure provides a satisfying purpose of life. With this end in view he goes to foolish excesses. **4—6.** From wine Eccl turns to other enjoyments: in a setting reminiscent of the splendours of Solomon's reign (cf 1 (3) Kgs 7:1, 2, 8; 9:15—19) he builds houses, plants vineyards, gardens, parks, fruit trees, and makes reservoirs of water (the so-called 'pools of Solomon' SE of Bethlehem cannot be regarded as referred to in this text, since they were built in the Roman period). **7.** The author, like Solomon (cf 1 (3) Kgs 4:22ff; 8:63; 9:20—21; 10:5), possesses slaves, some bought, and others born and reared in his own house; he has also flocks and herds. **8.** Still posing as the son of David (cf 1 (3) Kgs 4:7; 9:28; 10:14; 11:1—3) Eccl accumulates treasures and luxuries of sensual gratification. The Heb. conclusion of this v is obscure. Bea and CV omit it, as 'a corruption of the preceding words'. RSV, Rankin, Scott: 'Many concubines'. BJ: 'coffret par coffret'. **9.** As in wisdom (cf 1:16), so also in wealth Eccl surpasses all. But in spite of his pursuit of sensual delights he does not become their slave, since wisdom protects him. **10—11.** He recognizes that pleasure can be obtained and that toil is for man a source of joy. But when he weighs the gain against the effort, it all appears to him another 'chase after wind'. **12b.** Is better connected to v 11. Of what use will it be, if other men try to conduct the same experiments which the king has already conducted? Their conclusion would not be different.

i **12a. 13—17 Man's mortality deprives wisdom of her value—12a.** As in 1:17 Eccl ponders anew the opposites of wisdom, namely madness and folly, regarding them in their practical aspects. **13—14.** He perceives in wisdom an advantage over folly, since the wise man, enjoying the light of wisdom, is able to see, be it only the vanity of folly and the insufficiency of all things. But an old wisdom saying advises us to consider the end of all things (cf Prv 5:4, 11; 23:32; Sir 7:36). And the advantage of wisdom appears small indeed, since the same death overtakes all alike. **15—16.** With death comes also oblivion for both the wise and the fool. This is not what one would expect. **17.** This indifference on the part of fate and its neglect of human worth fills Eccl with aversion for life. **18—23 Human toil is equally valueless—18—19.** The obvious fact that the fruits of man's hard work will fall into the lap of another, and that this other may even be a fool, shows at once the worthlessness of toil. **20.** Whereas formerly Eccl loathed life (2:17), now despondency overcomes him. **21.** It does not seem just that a man who has worked hard should lose it all, and should lose it to another, a total stranger, who has never worked for it. **22—23.** Is it really worthwhile to worry and to toil? All restless days and sleepless nights seem to lead nowhere; indeed, rather seem to heighten anxiety and the sense of frustration. **24—26 Practical advice: Enjoy the ordinary God-given pleasures of life—24—25.** Eccl adjusts his mind to the realities of life and concludes that the best response man can give is to accept the circumstances of existence, to find joy in the ordinary pleasures of life, without forgetting to work. This statement is inspired by Eccl's belief that God himself

has it ordained and planned this way. **26.** This v has been **422i** held to be an addition made by a pious glossator, in defence of the traditional doctrine of retribution. The context, however, suggests another interpretation. As death does not distinguish between the fool and the wise (2:15), neither does life in the distribution of its gifts. 'Whatever man God sees fit' (lit: a man that is good in God's sight) is opposed to 'the sinner' which is here best understood as meaning 'the man with whom God is displeased' (cf Hertzberg, Galling). Some are more favoured by God, for wisdom and joy are given to them. But to others God allots the disappointing destiny—which in reality is 'a chase after wind'—of toiling and heaping up the fruits of his labours for the benefit of others.

3:1—22 Man is governed by the laws of life and **423a** **death—1—8.** God's appointed time for every human activity. The history of the world is a cycle of events, ordained by God. But man, although he is a participant in these events, can do nothing against them; he is governed by them. The antithetical enumeration of human activities stresses less their opposing aspects than the totality of all activities. **1—2.** Everything occurs when it must occur. Birth and death, the planting and harvesting have their determined hour. **3—4.** In the life of men and of buildings there is a fixed time for construction and destruction. Even man's emotions are products of universal necessity. **5.** 'To scatter' and 'to gather stones' has been taken to refer either to the pulling down of an old building and replacing it by a new one, or to ruining fields by scattering stones on them (cf 2 (4) Kgs 3:19, 25) and the gathering of stones to make fields fit for cultivation (cf Is 5:2). This v has also been interpreted (Midrash, Williams, Gordis, Rankin) as referring to marital intercourse or the abstention from it. The rest of the v would seem to support such an interpretation, since there may be a reference to passionate embraces (cf Prv 5:20; Song 2:6) and the abstention from them (cf Lv 15:23, 24). These embraces, however, can also be understood as salutations of friends (cf Gn 29:13; 33:4; 48:10). **6.** Eccl refers to the search after riches and honour: such possessions come and go. **7.** Probably a reference to the rending of garments as a sign of mourning (cf Gn 37:29; 44:13; 2 Sm 1:11; 3:31), and to the sewing together after the sadness is past. Similarly silence seems to indicate sorrow (cf 2 (4) Kgs 18:36; Jb 2:13; Ps 39 (38):2, 9), whereas joy expresses itself in words (cf Is 58:1; Ps 26 (25):7; 126 (125):2). **8.** These events affect not only the relationship between individuals, but also between nations. **9—15 Man is** **b** **unable to comprehend or change God's order—9.** Eccl returns to the crying question of 1:3. A negative reply is implied: no advantage accrues to man from all his toil. **10.** The activities, however, which Eccl enumerated in the preceding vv have the merit, or at least the effect, of keeping man occupied. **11.** According to Vg God has handed over 'the world' (Heb. '*ōlām*) to men, that is to say, the total of all events and of God's works has been placed in man's mind with the result that it is too great a task to grasp. It is possible (cf VDom 6 (1926) 357—9) and attractive to translate '*ōlām* by 'eternity'. So LXX. (cf RSV, Bea). In this case the meaning is that man's longing cannot be restricted and continues in unending tension. Some authors (cf Barton, Rankin) read '*elem* and explain it as 'ignorance, forgetfulness'. More recently '*ōlām* has been referred to a Ugaritic root *glm* with the meaning of 'becoming dark' (Gray, *The Legacy of Canaan*, VT Suppl. 5 (1957) 200). Although everything has been made good, beautiful, appropriate, man cannot grasp it, since God set darkness in his mind. This last view is most in keeping with Eccl's conception. **12.**

423b Since man, due to the inscrutability of God's purposes, cannot be satisfied, it is best for him to accept what comes his way and to enjoy life (lit 'to do good'). Ancient versions (LXX, Syr, Vg) and CV understand 'to do good' in a moral sense (cf 7:20). The meaning 'to enjoy life' is confirmed by other passages (3:22; 5:17; 8:15; 9:7; 11:9). **13.** Eccl cannot be accused of any materialistic or hedonistic view of life, since he considers the means of enjoyment and the ability to enjoy as God's gifts. **14.** And the thought of an unchanging world is not to be equated with a pessimistic outlook on life, but suggests God's permanence and is intended to lead man to humility and awe of God. **15.** Not only are all things determined by God, but all things are recurrent. God restores 'what has been driven away',

c i.e. that which is past. **16–22 The common fate of man and beast—16–17.** Corruption prevails at the very centre of the judicial administration, but Eccl believes in God's just judgement. The text, however, does not specify whether it is in this life or after death. **18.** This belief in God's eventual judgement, however, is not very consoling, for in a way men are similar to beasts. **19–20.** They are alike in the shortness of their life. Both have the same life-breath (*rûah*), but all, men and animals, return to dust (cf Gn 3:19). Eccl is not thinking here of Sheol, but simply of the common sepulchre. **21.** Breathing is the sign of life, but neither man nor animal have control over their life-breath which comes to them from elsewhere. Where does this life-breath go at the moment of death? The life-breath of man goes upward and that of the beast goes downward, some say. 'But who knows?' asks Eccl. Later (12:7) he affirms that the life-breath returns to its source. Here he wishes only to emphasize the common fate of man and animal: they end in death. **22.** The practical conclusion of Eccl's thought: Since man cannot return to life after he has died, let him enjoy to the full all the details of his present life—this is his privilege.

d **4:1–5:7 Man's inhumanity to man and his lack of circumspection towards God—4:1–3. Oppression characterizes all human activity—1.** Oppressions: tyranny and extortion rule. The oppressed are helpless and their woes pierce Eccl's very heart. **2–3.** Reacting to this scene of injustice and inhumanity Eccl declares the one alive less fortunate than the one dead and praises the lot of him who has never been. The author's gloomy mood contrasts with his later view (9:4). **4–6 The futility of rivalry—4.** Competition is the motive of every endeavour and toil. **5.** Although competition is a foolish motive, man is compelled to work, for idleness proves the ruin of one's welfare and health. **6.** Quiet steady work, although it may provide only 'one handful', would be better than competitive strenuous labour with its lack of rest and peace. **7–12 The foolishness of a self-centred life—7–8.** Eccl considers the folly of a lone and kinless miser who sacrifices all to accumulating wealth and never stops to ask himself for whom he is slaving. **9–10.** Proverbial wisdom is expressed here. A Jewish proverb from the Talmud declares: 'Either companionship or death' (*Taanith* 23a). A more modern version: United we stand, divided we fall. **11–12.** The reference is probably to two travellers who sleep together for mutual warmth and comfort, especially in the winter season. Bea applies the saying to the poor who have only one mantle which is also their only covering at night (cf Ex 22:26ff). In contrast with the short-comings and dangers of a self-centred life, Eccl praises the comfort and security of

e companionship. **13–16 The delusion of popular acclaim—**Various theories as to whom Eccl alludes, have been proposed. Joseph and Pharaoh, David and Saul,

and others have been suggested. More probably, however, **423e** Eccl speaks in general terms. **13–14.** An old king, obstinate and foolish, is contrasted with a poor, but wise youth. Whereas the old king, hardened in his opinions, no longer perceives the signs of the times, the youth overcomes the obstacles of youthfulness, poverty and imprisonment and rises to the throne. CV says in a note: 'that prison is probably his mother's womb, from which the king issues without possessions, cf 5:14'. **15.** Eccl describes hyperbolically the popular enthusiasm upon the young king's accession to the throne. **16.** This popularity is short-lived. Royal prestige is only a fleeting value, a delusion.

5:1–7 (MT 4:17–5:6) Advice on religious observance—1. Eccl exhorts to circumspection and right intention. 'To listen' carries in Heb. a meaning of hearing as well as of obedience. The emphasis may well be on 'obedience' (cf Vg and CV), for 'to obey is better than sacrifice' (2 Sm 15:22). The sacrifice of fools is here declared worthless, since they go through the motions of religious observance while rejecting interior submission to God's demands. **2.** The hasty recital of many prayers is condemned and the excess of words has to be avoided. Rash promises are perhaps included in this condemnation (cf CV), although promises and vows are discussed in vv 3–4. God's infinite greatness should inspire us with reverence. **3.** This proverbial saying praises the fewness of words: for many cares bring about sleepless nights of dreams and many words lead man into talking nonsense. **4–5.** Eccl refers with approval to Dt 23:21–23. Whosoever does not fulfil his vow, not only acts sinfully but foolishly (cf Ananias and Sapphira, Ac 5:4). **6.** This warning concerns hasty vows and irresponsible words (Lv 5:4). 'The messenger' may refer to God himself (LXX) or to God's representative (CV), an angel (BJ) or a priest (cf Mal 2:7). Probably God is meant; his anger, at any rate, will be incurred, if a sacred vow is treated as a matter of words only. **7.** MT (v 6) is corrupt, CV omits it as variant of v 2. Insert *be* before *debārîm: for as there is vanity in many dreams, so in many words also.* The idea seems to be that the more dreams one dreams, the less sense they make, and the more words one says, the less meaning they contain. Eccl exhorts to fear God, i.e. to observe his will, especially by being circumspect in one's prayers, promises, vows and general speech.

5:8–7:12 (RSV 5:8–20 = MT 5:7–19) The Decep- g tion of riches—8–9. The wrong occasioned by acquisitiveness. **8.** With realism Eccl describes the oppression of the poor and the violation of justice in his days: the realm seems to be an organization where each official strives to acquire wealth and where each from the top to the bottom oppresses the one below him. **9.** Heb. is obscure. *The profit of the land is for all; the king himself is served by the field* (Bea), that is to say, the country's product is shared by all officials, even by the king. This follows MT closely and seems preferable to CV which makes Eccl say something complimentary about the monarchy. **10–17.** Wealth does not give lasting satisfaction. **10–11.** The rapacity of the officials mentioned in vv 8–9 may have suggested these remarks. The increase of wealth does not bring greater satisfaction, but increases only the number of one's retainers. The rich man's only advantage is to look at his riches. **12.** The labourer, in order to make his living, works hard, grows tired and sleeps well. But the abundance of riches causes cares and anxieties which prevent slumber. **13–14.** At the expense of anxiety and sleeplessness wealth has to be protected. But an unfortunate speculation

23g or accident may ruin all for the rich man as well as for his heir. **15–16.** Eccl's words resemble Jb 1:21. When the rich man dies, he cannot take his wealth with him. But what is worse, he does not even know whether he will keep his wealth to the end of his life. **17.** *All his days he eats in darkness* (MT). The rich man is such a miser that he economizes on the cost of light. RSV, BJ, CV follow LXX and Vg: Though he had amassed riches, he did not enjoy them. **18–20.** Moderate enjoyment of the present life. **18.** It is possible for man to find a relative happiness in his work and in the enjoyment of food and drink. This moderate enjoyment of the present life is commanded by God. **19–20.** Riches are illusory as goals of human life. But if man accepts the material gifts which God offers and tries to be content, he will be truly happy. And he will not brood over his life's brevity, for the joys of life, though temporary, keep him from dwelling on the ills which afflict humanity (cf note

h in CV). **6:1–6.** Man is unable to enjoy riches and honour. **1–2.** Although riches and earthly possessions may offer limited satisfaction (cf 5:20), yet it happens unfortunately that a rich man may lack the ability to enjoy what life offers. He may not even have the satisfaction of leaving his possessions to children of his own. **3.** 'Hundred' is simply a round number. Numerous offspring and old age are considered great blessings (cf Gn 24:60; Ex 20:12). But if such a man cannot enjoy his possessions and does not receive honourable burial, his life becomes a tragedy. **4.** A still-born child (cf Jb 3:16; Ps 58 (57):8) without name and existence is more fortunate. **5.** A still-born child never experiences any sensation ('has not seen the sun') and never reaches consciousness ('has not known the sun'). Such a child escapes all trials and 'is at rest', i.e. is satisfied. **6.** The rich, although he may reach an extraordinary age, and the still-born child both have to descend to Sheol. The shorter and less agonizing way of the still-born foetus is preferable. **7–12.** The insatiability of desire. **7.** Man concentrates all his efforts on self-preservation and enjoyment without ever finding satisfaction. **8.** The desire of man, whether he be wise, foolish, rich or poor, is insatiable and destined never to be satisfied on earth. The poor man, therefore, although he may understand the right art of living, will not find satisfaction. **9.** This is the key to happiness: it is better to enjoy the good that is present than to yearn for the unattainable. **10–11.** 'To give a name' to something is equivalent to saying that 'it has already come into existence and has been determined in its being'. Applied to man it follows that his life in all its aspects has been foreknown and foreordained by God. And it is senseless for man to dispute with God—maybe Eccl alludes to Jb 32:12—for man's words are powerless. **12.** Another reason why expostulation with God is useless: man does not and cannot know what is beneficial for him, since he is absolutely ignorant as to the future.

i **7:1–12.** Certain things which are good. After having virtually asserted (6:12) that it is impossible to know what is 'good' in life, Eccl points out that there are certain things which may be pronounced 'better' than others. **1.** There is a play of words: *šēm* = name and *šemen* = ointment. Eccl considers a worthy reputation a greater good than opulence and beauty. The day of death is preferred, for it brings man's career to a close and a true estimate can be formed of the happiness of his life (cf 4:2; 7:8). When a man is born, on the other hand, no one can tell what manner of life will be his. **2.** A wise appreciation of life must rest upon the fact that death ends it all. Eccl does not contradict 2:24,

but he insists that any enjoyment of life must be coupled **423i** with fear of God. **3.** To suffer is to learn, for through the acceptance of suffering as a discipline man will be strengthened in his character and his understanding of life will be deepened. **4.** Experience confirms the statements of vv 2 and 3: the fool is only interested in pleasure, the wise man faces the serious aspects of life. **5.** From seeing, Eccl passes to hearing: the criticisms of a wise man are to be preferred to the compliments of a fool. **6.** In Heb. there is a play of words: *sîr* = pot and *sîrîm* = thorns. This verse, introduced by *kî* (= for, because), justifies the statement of v 5: 'the fool's laughter' (i.e. compliment) is noisy and short-lived like the crackling fire of thorns. **7.** This v, introduced by *kî* and therefore also related to v 5, declares that the wise man who stoops to 'oppression' (or extortion) and to bribes, becomes ultimately a fool. The meaning seems to be a further warning not to heed the 'song of fools'. **8.** This proverb stresses the sapiential teaching that it is the end of a matter or of an argument which really counts. The wise man, therefore, is 'patient' in hearing and examining and does not jump to conclusions, as 'the lofty spirit', the arrogant does. **9.** This general principle should guide the wise man: keep your anger down, for anger is the trade-mark of fools. **10.** Eccl warns not to make useless comparisons, not to escape into the past, but to make the best of life's circumstances as they are. **11–12.** Wisdom and inheritance (= possessions, riches) make a happy combination and hold out a prospect of happiness. Both wisdom and riches offer protection and defence against life's ills. It does not follow, however, that wisdom without an inheritance is of no value. Wisdom is superior to inheritance, for it assures the one who possesses it a long life (cf Prv 3:16).

7:13 0:10 The anomalies of the human situation— **424a** **13–24.** The world is an enigma. **13.** The activities of this world (= 'the work of God') are predestined by God and cannot be changed or improved (cf 1:15a; 3:15; 6:10). **14.** Also with regard to adversity and prosperity, man has nothing to say, but to accept whatever comes his way (cf Jb 2:10). He will never find out what the future may hold in store, (RSV); or, man cannot find fault, since God is the author of good and evil, (CV). **15.** Eccl now faces the problem which already agonized Job: the orthodox doctrine that the righteous live a long life and the wicked die quickly seems to have been inverted. **16–17.** Since apparently no strict relation exists between good and evil and reward and punishment, Eccl advocates moderation. He is speaking here not as a philosopher or theologian, but as a teacher of practical wisdom. Take the case of the overwise: he wants to be on the safe side and is just to excess; as a consequence he expects to receive his deserved reward. But, as it often happens, the reward will not be forthcoming, and the overwise will be appalled, disturbed (the root *šmm* in the Hithpael form means 'show oneself driven to astonishment, be appalled' and 'cause oneself ruin'; RSV BJ and CV adopt the latter meaning). Why should one risk such a disappointment? In other words: it does not make good sense to strive for extreme goodness on the assumption that happiness will certainly follow, for goodness cannot guarantee happiness. But extreme wickedness must also be avoided. Although a strict correspondence between wickedness and punishment seems to be lacking, yet extreme wickedness will reach the point where civil authority and society will exact penalties. By condemning extreme wickedness Eccl evidently does not endorse a certain moderation in

424a wickedness as allowed. Jer explains excessive justice in reference to the self-righteous who is never willing to forgive. Others see in it 'the excessive legalism of those early Pharisees' or 'punctiliousness and scrupul-**b** osity' (Williams). **18.** Eccl refers to the rules ('this' and 'that') stated in vv 16—17, namely to pursue with moderation the paths of righteousness and wisdom, and to avoid excesses. The God-fearing man will avoid the extremes and keep 'the golden mean'. **19.** Wisdom, i.e. knowledge and service of God, gives greater security to man than the power and influence of ten princes. 'Ten princes' may be a reference to the archons at Athens or simply be a round number. **20.** By this restriction Eccl does not intend to discredit wisdom, for wisdom evidently helps man to get the better of his mistakes. CV relates this v in a note to Rm 5:12 which speaks of original sin. **21—22.** Since man is far from being perfect, one must not expect too much. And the way in which others talk about one another must not surprise us, for often we have said much the same. **23—24.** In his endeavour to unravel the perplexities of life Eccl subjects his various experiences to a serious examination. But he has to confess that the world remains an enigma and that it is impossible to become actually wise. For in each single event there is much more than human wisdom can grasp. **25—29.** Woman is an enigma. **25.** Since practical wisdom is all that man can reach, Eccl applies his mind to seek for a reasoned judgement and finds that *'wickedness is foolish and folly is madness'.* **26.** Such a combination of wickedness and folly Eccl sees in the harlot or adulteress. Her heart and hands are her weapons with which she will ensnare the victims. Only he who is favoured and helped by God, can escape her, cf Prv 5 and 7. **27—28.** Eccl does not wish to be accused of making sweeping statements. He reiterates that he made a laborious and meticulous investigation into the whole problem of man-woman relationship. He mentions the proverbial statement which says that perfect men are rare, but perfect women non-existent. **29.** Eccl rejects this proverb (v 28) by declaring all men equally responsible. God cannot be blamed, since he made man upright (Gn 1:31). Men bring upon themselves perversity by their devious schemes **c** and actions. **8:1—9.** Wisdom and despotism. **1.** The wise man is best qualified to meet everyday situations and to gain insight into their meaning. Wisdom also is reflected in his radiant looks from which all harshness has disappeared. **2—4.** The author seems to have forgotten that he posed as Solomon. He exhorts that wisdom be put to proper use in one's relationship with the king. Maybe he refers to the oath of allegiance which was taken at the king's coronation (cf 1 Chr 11:3; 29:24). The king, at any rate, has to be obeyed for conscience's sake. Eccl also warns against any precipitate withdrawal of one's allegiance to the king and against any taking part in a conspiracy. For it is folly for any subject to oppose the king, especially since he possesses absolute power. **5—7.** The commandment alluded to is probably that of the king (cf Rm 13:1—5). Some commentators refer it to the law of God. The submissive subject shall not come to any harm. Such a submission is not difficult for the wise, since his practical wisdom enables him to know when to act ('times') and what to do ('judgements'). There follow four sentences in vv 6—7, each beginning with *kî* (= for, because); each is an additional argument why a wise man should obey the king: (a) there is a proper time for everything and a proper way how to go about (v 6a); (b) man has enough trouble without adding to it by open defiance of the king (v 6b); (c) nobody knows the future and only the present event

is in the reach of man (7a); (d) it is impossible to know **424** the future and one might as well use the present event in the best way (7b). **8.** All the various reasons which Eccl enumerates can be reduced to the obvious fact that the king is in power. And at present it is as impossible to dislodge the king as it is (a) to control the wind (CV: the breath of life); (b) to resist death; (c) to escape the consequences of war; (d) to expect that wickedness will bring deliverance. **9.** Eccl has carefully examined the various aspects of the king's power, outlined in vv 1—8. But although he preached submission, he cannot consider despotism a blessing for the subjects. **10—15.** There is no equal retribution in this life. **10.** MT with **d** only slight corrections suggested by LXX and the versions reads: *'Then I have seen the wicked brought to the grave and praised from the holy place and lauded in the city where they had acted thus. This also is vanity'* (cf Smith, RSV, Chicago Bible; Gordis; Jones). Eccl takes up the problem which also haunted Job (Jb 21:27—34) that retribution does not always quickly overtake evil-doers. **11—13.** The postponement and delay in punishment encourage the wicked and they add sin to sin. But Eccl states his firm belief in eventual retribution (cf 3:16f). The religious man has nothing to fear. The wicked man, however, runs the risk of disastrous retribution and will not live long, since his days quickly pass away like shadows. **14—15.** But there remains this anomaly: the belief in retribution and the reality of the human situation do not correspond. If the ultimate answer eludes man, there is this practical solution: to enjoy what life offers (cf 2:24; 5:19). Such an enjoyment is no escapism, but a duty imposed by God. **16—9:6.** Man's **e** lot after death is unknown. **16—17.** Eccl sought diligently to discover the meaning and purpose behind God's government, but he has to admit that God is always greater. He flatly declares that no intellectual effort or brilliance will succeed. **9:1a.** Although Eccl recognizes God's sovereignty and special interest in the righteous and their activities, he cannot understand God's ways. **1b—2.** Vg has *'nescit homo utrum amore an odio dignus sit'*; this text has frequently been quoted to prove that man cannot be sure whether or not he be in the state of grace. The text and context rather state that no man, not even the just, is able to tell whether he will get favour or affliction from the hand of God. There seems to be an absolute lack of discrimination (cf Jb 9:22f); the just and the wicked, regardless of their moral distinctions, seem to be reduced to the same level. **3.** The thought of a same fate for all has a degrading effect; it induces in men unbridled desires and madness, i.e. they deny, not so much in theory but in practice, the moral government of the world (cf 1:17; 2:12; 7:25; 10:13). **4.** Man, however, as long as he is alive, can hope for improvement. Life, though it may be miserable and meaningless, is better than death, just as a live dog, a most contemptible being (cf 1 Sm 17:43; 2 Sm 3:8; etc) is better off than the kingly lion (cf Is 31:4) that is dead. **5.** The living are superior to the dead, since they can contemplate death. For the dead all has come to an end and they are utterly forgotten. Eccl only speaks of retribution here on earth and says nothing about the future life. **6.** The strongest passions that are the mainspring of human activity are silenced in death. All relationship of the dead with the only world which Eccl knows is severed. **7—10.** Enjoy the good **f** things of life. **7.** RSV deserves preference. In spite of all the doubts and uncertainties which surround this life, one must live and enjoy the good things that God 'long ago' (*kebār*) has arranged and approved. **8.** White

24f garments, only mentioned here in the OT, were signs of rejoicing (cf Apoc 3:4, 5; 7:9). Fragrant oils were also used on such joyous occasions (Ps 23 (22):5; 45 (44):8; Prv 27:9; Is 61:3). **9.** Marriage is here mentioned as an element of happiness, likewise intended by God. Eccl's advice resembles Prv 5:18, 19; 18:22. **10.** Eccl underlines the limited time available and the necessity of work. He insists more on the urgency of work than on diligence, since the grave will cut short all activities.

25a 9:11–12:8 **The inconsistency of fortune**—11–17. The uncertainties of life. **11.** Closely related to the inscrutability of God's ways is the contingency and uncertainty of human activity: in sports, in battles, in work, in social relationships success does not always come to the deserving. Time and chance are important factors. **12.** Man does not know 'his time', either the time of death, or of a sudden disaster, or the right time for a particular undertaking. The illustrations, taken from the procedures for catching fish and bird, stress the suddenness and the decisiveness of the final swoop. **13–15.** This illustration may be understood in two ways: (a) a wise man could have delivered the city, but he was poor and nobody thought of asking him (Nötscher, Zimmerli); (b) the wise man saved the city, but he went unrewarded, since he was poor. The latter opinion seems preferable. But there is no need to seek any historical identification. **16.** For the superiority of wisdom over force cf 7:19; Prv 24:5. One would expect that the wise counsel of anybody, even of a poor man, would be heeded. That this is not the case, is one of the uncertainties and inconsistencies of fate.

b 17–10:3. Reflections on wisdom and folly. A series of proverbial sayings in a rather loose grouping. **17.** It is not the loudness of the argument that wins adherents, but its wisdom. The expression 'a ruler of fools' probably means 'an outstanding fool', 'an arch fool'. **18.** Read with RSV and BJ. CV omits this v. Wisdom is superior over brute force (cf v 16), but one sin, in a way, is more powerful, since it has disastrous consequences. This saying stresses the collective implications of wisdom and sin. **10:1.** In CV this verse is 9:18. This proverb illustrates the preceding utterance: insignificant causes produce great effects; this is all the more true with regard to the contagion of evil. 'A little folly' can deprive much wisdom of its effect, just as flies that got entangled in oil, die and decaying spoil the ointment's odour. **2.** Right and left symbolize good and bad. The wise man's mind is 'adroit' (Odeberg), disposed to do the right, whereas the mind of the fool is 'gauche', inclined to do the wrong. **4–7.** Meekness towards rulers. **4.** Eccl does not advocate compromise but counsels restraint. Such a cultivation of meekness in face of the capriciousness of a ruler is not weakness, but saves both parties from serious faults. **5–7.** Meekness is all the more necessary with regard to the exasperating and capricious behaviour of rulers. They blunder badly at times (although they may be well intentioned). The most inept are elevated to leading positions, whereas 'the rich', i.e. men of ancestral wealth and born leaders, are rejected. And social classes

c are forcibly reversed. **8–11.** Counsels concerning everyday actions. **8–9.** There is an element of contingency in all human activities. Each activity has its particular danger (e.g. the pit—fall into it; stones—be hurt by them) and there is the unforeseen, the accidental which is liable at every moment to interfere (e.g. break through a wall—the serpent). Eccl wishes to exhort to caution and prudence. **10.** With RSV and BJ. Wisdom

has a pragmatic value. What sharpness is to a tool, **425c** wisdom is to him who has it. He who is without it, will have to increase his efforts. **11.** The charmer is meant to make use of his skill before the serpent can bite. So also, wisdom is of little avail if made use of too late. **12–15.** Prudence in speech. **12.** Cf Prv 14:3; 18:7. **13.** The only progression in the speech of a fool is from folly to madness. Every word of his is foolish and even injurious (lit 'wicked madness'). **14.** The fool talks endlessly. But the foolishness of his loquacity can be seen in the fact that nobody knows what will happen next and certainly not what the outcome of life will be (cf 3:22; 6:12; 7:14). **15.** A fool does not know how to do the simplest thing; he cannot even follow a well-defined road leading to the city. It is not surprising that any work tires him beyond proportion. **16–20.** **d** Various counsels on the necessity of prudence. **16–17.** Eccl who maintained that kings and those in authority ought to be obeyed and respected, now turns his attention to another inconsistency of fortune: not all rulers are a blessing for their countries. Two kings are contrasted. One is a 'child' which can also mean a 'slave' or a man of 'low birth'. The emphasis is on his inexperience. In his company are frivolous princes who are rebuked, not because of eating and drinking, but because they engage in feasting at the wrong time, in the morning (cf Is 5:11). Better off is the land with a king of noble birth: such a well born king, with corresponding character and behaviour, will be a wise ruler. The princes of his entourage put their duties first; they eat with heartiness, but do not drink to excess. **10.** This and v 19 could be interpreted as independent sayings which warn against laziness and insist on the fact that money gained by work meets everything. In the context, however, these vv may refer to the rulers and their administration. Just as the roof of a house will collapse, the repairs of which have been neglected, so will the fabric of a kingdom fall into a ruinous condition, when the ruler and princes neglect their duties. **19.** The reason why king and princes can indulge in endless festivities is the money which makes it possible for them to obtain whatever they desire. **20.** Although the dissolute conduct of a ruler might suggest the idea of a rebellion, Eccl warns against even thinking evil of those in power. To justify his word Eccl does not refer to the law of God, but to the practical consideration of one's personal safety. The reference to 'the birds of the air' alludes to the mysterious paths by which secrets travel (cf the cranes of Ibycus). 11:1–6. Wisdom and **e** the spirit of adventure. **1.** Tradition understood this v and the following as an exhortation to the practice of benevolence towards others, a benevolence which does not stop at any precise limit, but helps seven, even eight, i.e. 'several', 'many'. It is good to act liberally in the days of prosperity, for man knows not when he may need the help of his fellow. A somewhat similar interpretation insists on generosity: help generously even those who are ungrateful, symbolized by 'the waters'. Because of the practical and realistic outlook of Eccl it is probable that here he speaks of commercial adventures, with an allusion even to maritime trade. The wise man must not invest all his resources in one venture, but spread his activities over a number of interests. By doing this he will face the inconsistency of fortune and reduce the element of uncertainty. Others (Nötscher) insist more on the spirit of adventure: Be daring, although your efforts may appear useless. Strange things happen. Throw your bread on the water, for it is possible that you will find it again. **2.** The interpretation of

425e this verse is related to that of v 1. With regard to almsgiving, 'generosity' is recommended. With reference to adventure in business, this verse counsels 'prudence'. **3–4.** Eccl reminds us that a certain tension between wisdom, the spirit of adventure and the inconsistency of fortune will remain. All things in nature happen according to laws, and certain causes (e.g. the cloud; the falling tree) produce their proper results. But man cannot get a complete knowledge of natural phenomena and their laws; he cannot be certain about wind or cloud. In spite of such a lack of knowledge man has to go ahead. He who wants to wait for absolutely favourable conditions, will lose his opportunity and accomplish nothing. Life, therefore, requires participation **f** and imposes fatal involvement. **5–6.** The supreme mystery is the question: How does life begin? (cf Ps 139 (138):13–16; Jb 10:10ff). Equally inscrutable are the acts of God who arranges all and yet cannot act arbitrarily. Man, therefore, is told to use every opportunity, for he never knows which effort will turn out well or whether all may do so. **7–12:8.** The moderate use of good things in life, especially in youth, with the remembrance of death and God's judgement. **7–8.** Life, circumscribed by 'light' and 'sun' (cf 7:11), is precious, meant for work as well as for enjoyment. 'The days of darkness' refer to death and Sheol (cf Jb 10:21; 17:13; 18:18; Ps 88 (87):13). 'All that is to come' signify the various events and opportunities of life. Others (Wright, Barton, Zimmerli) refer the expression to 'the days in Sheol'. The verse urges diligent use and enjoyment of the present time. **9.** It is typical of the teachers of wisdom to address their pupils as 'my son' (cf Prv 1:8, 10, 15; 2:1; 3:1, 21; 4:10; etc). On previous occasions Eccl has addressed his pupils directly (cf 5:1; 8:2f), but here for the first and only time he speaks to them as 'O young man'. This address, although it is less personal than 'my son', is very appropriate, since it is closely related with this final message. Life is to be lived and Eccl exhorts the young man to make the best of it. The Law had forbidden 'to follow after the desires of your hearts and eyes' (Nm 15:39). Eccl's recommendation seems to go against the direction of the Law. It is interesting to see that LXX (B) reads: 'walk *blameless* in the ways of your heart and *not* after the vision of your eyes'. It may also have been this kind of injunction which made some rabbis object to the inclusion of Eccl into the Heb. Canon. The opposition between Eccl and the Law, however, is only apparent. The young men are reminded that enjoyment of their youth does not extend to any excess or indulgence. Eventually they will have to give account and will be judged for the use of their **g** days. **10.** With RSV and BJ. Quickly passing away are 'youth and *šaḥ°rût*': this Heb. term is probably derived from *šāḥōr*, 'black', i.e. 'manhood', the time when the hair is black in contrast with the white hair of old age (cf Koehler, *Lexicon*). Eccl exhorts the young men, therefore, to avoid all that might injure mind and body and thereby cause resentment and grief later on. **12:1.** Eccl presses emphatically upon youth the importance of piety as their guide. 'Remember your Creator': this phrase, although not common, occurs elsewhere (cf Dt 8:18; Jg 8:34; 2 Sm 14:11; etc). The word 'Creator' is plural and should be understood as plural of excellence. This living faith in the Creator, to be founded in youth, will be a safeguard and solace in 'evil days', i.e. in the days of old age. **2–6.** This is an outstanding passage in Eccl. It is a figurative description of man's 'evil days', i.e. his old age. The expressions and images are unrivalled for poignancy and power. Although there is agreement on the

general outline and theme of this passage, yet there **425i** is divergence in the interpretation of details (cf Wright, 240–75; Barton, 186). But it must be noted that the metaphors are not always kept distinct and overlap each other at times. This passage may be compared with 'The instruction of Vizier Ptah-hotep' (ANET, 412). **2.** The description recalls the cloudy and rainy **h** sky of the Palestinian winter. Clouds darken the horizon. And when one storm ceases, soon another will come. The fading light depicts old age whose downward trend is as continuous as the succession of storms. **3.** 'The keepers': the hands and arms; 'the strong men': the feet; 'the grinders': the teeth; 'they who look through the window': the eyes. Others see a description of the impact of the storm upon the whole household or a picture of the gradual decay of a stately mansion. **4.** 'The doors': the ears; 'the sound of the mill': the voice; 'daughters of song': ability to sing. Deafness cuts the old man off from the world outside. And his voice becomes feeble, high-pitched, unmelodious. Some apply this verse to an old house in decay and closed for all festivities. **5.** The old are afraid to climb and they no longer like to be up and about. 'The almond tree blossoms' probably alludes to the white hair of old age. 'The sluggish grasshopper' suggest that the old have lost all their alertness of body and mind. '*The caper berry*' ('desire', RSV) can no longer stimulate the appetite of old persons. The old man is heading towards 'his lasting home', i.e. the grave (cf Tb 3:6). And the professional mourners are touting for custom. **6.** Two images are used to describe **i** the coming of death. The first one is a golden lamp held in its place by a silver cord. The cord snaps asunder, the lamp falls, the light is extinguished. The second image is a well over which a pulley is suspended for the purpose of drawing up water from the depths below. The pulley breaks down, and pitcher, rope, wheel and all, are precipitated into the well. Death will be as unexpected and final as the end of the lamp and the pitcher. **7.** As a result of death the two elements that constitute the living man will be separated. The dust returns to its kindred dust (cf Gn 2:7; 3:19). The life breath goes back to the source from which it came (cf Ps 104 (103):29; Jb 34:14–15). Thus man is back from where he started. And even God is back from where he began. Eccl affirms here his fundamental belief that life comes from God, but about man's state after death he remains silent. **8.** After all his experiences and reflections Eccl is back at his starting-point and repeats his initial verdict: 'All things are vanity'. Thomas a Kempis makes this verse thoroughly Christian when he writes: *Vanitas vanitatum et omnia vanitas, praeter amare Deum et illi soli servire* (Imitatio, I, 1, 11).

12:9–14 Epilogue: A disciple's praise and words of **j** **warning—9–11.** Are the work of one of Eccl's disciples who greatly admires and praises him. **12–14** are a still later addition, maybe from the hand of the final editor, and contain certain words of warning. **9.** Eccl's disciple adds the interesting statement that his master was not only a professional teacher of wisdom ('besides being wise'), but also sought to impart his knowledge to all ('taught the people'). In addition he examined, collected and published many proverbs. **10.** Eccl endeavoured to express his thoughts and sayings in the most attractive form, but he would never sacrifice truth for the sake of literary style. **11.** The words of the wise—this applies of course to Eccl's words—urge us forward: they are 'goads', i.e. stimulants to thought, and '*pegs*', centres around which to group correlated ideas. These sayings are lastly given by 'one shepherd' i.e. God, the fountainhead of

25j wisdom. **12.** Whereas the preceding verses praised the work and character of Eccl, these last verses (12—14) contain words of warning and advice for the reader. The reader is addressed as 'my son', a term commonly used throughout the sapiential literature (cf 11:9). 'Beyond these' refers probably to the wise sayings of Eccl mentioned in the preceding vv. Eccl's work deserves to be studied. But there is the danger that man in his search for wisdom may turn to other and less reliable books and grow weary, while forgetting that a real knowledge of a little is better than a superficial acquaintance of many branches of learning. **13.** What is the teaching of the whole book? The editor sums it up in the two following doctrines: 'Fear God and keep his commandments'. This, he declares, is the duty of every man. **14.** Why must we fear God? He will thoroughly judge everything that is done. The emphasis here is on 'every work' that will be judged. And since Eccl is not the author of this v, there is no need to examine whether a judgement in this life or after death is meant. **425j**

THE SONG OF SONGS

BY P. P. SAYDON
REVISED BY G. CASTELLINO S.D.B.

426a Bibliography—*Commentaries*: J. Fischer, EchB, 1950; A. Cohen, *The Five Megilloth*, 1952; A. Feuillet, *Lectio Divina*, 10. 1953; R. Gordis, 1954; T. J. Meek, IB, 1956; H. Schmökel, *Heilige Hochzeit und Hoheslied*, Wiesbaden, 1956, H. Ringgren, ATD, 1958; H. Schonfield, 1960; J. Winandy, *Le Cantique des Cantiques, poème d'amour mué en écrit de sagesse*, 1960; W. Rudolph, KAT, Gütersloh, 1962; A. Robert, R. Tournai, and A. Feuillet, EtBib., 1963; (this contains an almost complete bibliography down to its publication.)

b *Articles*: R. Gordis, 'A Wedding Song for Solomon', JBL 63 (1944), 263—70; R. E. Murphy, 'The Structure of the Canticle', CBQ (1949), 381—91; Id, 'Recent Literature on the Canticle of Canticles', CBQ 16 (1954), 1—11; Id, 'The Canticle of Canticles and the Virgin Mary', Carmelus 1 (1954), 18—28; F. Rivera, 'Sentido mariológico del Cantár de los Cantares', Ephemerides Mariologicae, 1 (1951), 437—68; 2 (1952), 25—42; H. H. Rowley, 'The Interpretation of the Song of Songs', in *The Servant of the Lord*, London, 1952, 189—234; A. Bentzen, 'Remarks on the Canonization of the Song of Solomon', S Or 1 (1953) 41—47; G. Bardy, 'Marie et le Cantique chez les Pères', BiViCh 7 (1954), 32—41; A. M. Dubarle, 'L'amour humain dans le Cantique des Cantiques', RB 61 (1954) 67—90; A. Neher, 'Le symbolisme conjugal, expression de l'histoire dans l 'AT', RHPR 34 (1954) 30—49; J.-P. Audet, 'Le sens du Cantique des Cantiques', RB 62 (1955), 197—221; Id, 'Love and Marriage in the OT' *Scr* 10 (1958), 65—83; M. Cambe, 'L'influence du Cantique des Cantiques sur le NT', RTh 62 (1962), 5—26; M. H. Segal, 'The Song of Songs', VT 12 (1962), 470—90; O. Loretz, 'Zum Problem des Eros im Hohenlied', BZ 8 (1964), 191—216.

c Title—The full Heb. title is 'The Song of Songs, which is Solomon's'. The first half is a periphrastic Heb. way of expressing the superlative, hence the meaning is 'the best of songs'; cf 'Holy of Holies' = most holy. It is indeed a beautiful poem, both for its lyrical inspiration and rich imagery as well as for the loftiness of its meaning. The second half of the title is generally considered by modern scholars as a literary device whereby the poem is attributed to Solomon in the same manner as the book of Wisdom is attributed to him, though written at a much later date.

d Canonicity and Place in the Canon—Its canonicity has always been recognized by the Church. Theodore of Mopsuestia (d. 428), who rejected its spiritual meaning and probably also its inspiration, had no followers (L. Dennefeld, *Der alttestamentliche Kanon der Antiochenischen Schule* Bib St 14 (1909), 47). His opinion was formally condemned by the Second Council of Constantinople, A.D. 553, as 'infanda christianorum auribus'; but according to others, there was no formal condemnation, and Theodore did not deny the inspiration of the Song. (cf A. -M. Brunet, 'Théodore de Mopsueste

et le Cantique des Cantiques'. Études et Recherches, **426c** 9, Ottawa, 1955, 155—70.) Among the Jews there were some doubts in the 1st cent. A.D., but these were dispelled in the Synod of Jabne (c. A.D. 100), chiefly by the authority of R. Aqiba who said, 'All the Hagiographa are holy, but the Canticle is most holy'. (cf *Mishna*, Yadayim 3, 5.) The first known list of canonical books to mention the Song is probably of the 1st cent. A.D., and is contained in the MS that contains also the Didache (cf J.-P Audet, JTS n.s. I (1950), 135ff).

In the Hebrew canon it forms part of the hagio- **e** grapha, the third division of the canonical books. In our printed editions of MT it is the first of the 5 Megilloth or 'Scrolls', i.e., Song, Ruth, Eccl, Lam, Est. The Alexandrine translators, however, arranged the books according to their literary character and so included song among the poetical books. In Vg too it is reckoned with the poetical books.

Contents and Analysis—The song is a love-song in **f** which two young shepherds praise each other's beauty and express their mutual love and desire for lasting union. The analysis is difficult because the sense of certain passages and the nexus between the several parts are not always apparent. Those who hold that it is a drama divide the poem into acts and scenes according to their way of representing the development of the action. On the contrary, those who reject the unity of the poem make of it a collection of songs varying in number according to their subjective criteria.

Some sections are easily distinguishable by the **g** recurrence of the refrain or by their opening words. On the grounds of these criteria we propose the following division:

1:1—2:7, the bride's yearning for the beloved; mutual praises; their meeting.

2:8—3:5, the bride is invited to the fields; in the evening they return to their homes; the bride is restless until she again finds her beloved.

3:6—5:1, the pomp of a royal pageant; the bridegroom is enraptured by his bride's graceful charm and beauty and rejoices in her company.

5:2—6:2, while the bride is on her bed, the bridegroom comes unexpectedly; when she rises to open he has vanished; she goes out in search of him; description of the bridegroom; the joy of their union.

6:3—8:4, the bridegroom's admiration of his bride's beauty; mutual praises; the bride declares her unswerving attachment to her lover.

8:5—7, the two lovers are inseparably united. 8:8—14, appendix.

Literary Form—Although it is universally admitted **h** that it is a love poem, there is no agreement as to the manner in which the subject is treated. This is a brief exposition of the different views:

(1) A collection of separate love-songs having no other link but the common subject, so J. G. Herder, *Lieder der Liebe, die ältesten und schönsten aus dem*

26h *Morgenlande*, Leipzig, 1778, 89—106; M. Jastrow, *The Song of Songs, being a collection of love lyrics of Ancient Palestine*, London, 1922; H. W. Robinson, *The Old Testament: its making and meaning*, London, 1937, 161f; H. H. Rowley, *The Interpretation of the Song of Songs*, JTS 38 (1937) 358.

(2) A collection of popular nuptial songs that were sung during the nuptial week, so J. B. Bossuet, A. Calmet. J. G. Wetzstein tried to find a support for this explanation in the marriage customs of Hauran in Syria. This theory was further developed by K. Budde.

(3) The Song is a drama. The dramatic theory has been proposed in two forms: (i) A shepherd girl is taken away from her home by Solomon and made his wife, so Frz Delitzsch (1875), F. Kaulen (1899). (ii) The shepherd girl is taken away by the king, but she remains faithful to her shepherd lover to whom she had pledged her heart, so J. F. Jacobi (1771), Ewald (1826), Harper (1902), Pouget-Guitton (1934), A. Geslin (1938).

(4) The Song is made up of lyrical dialogues alternating with monologues, with a slight dramatic movement, so the majority of Catholic interpreters.

(5) It consists of seven short poems running parallel to each other. There is no development of action, but only a progressive movement within the several poems. The general plan of each poem is: the yearning of one part for the other, mutual praises and the joy of their union. They are like seven penitential Psalms which, with a variety of literary devices, develop the same ideas of sin, repentance and pardon, D. Buzy in RB, 49 (1940) 161—94 and in his commentary PCSB 1946, 290.

i The first of these theories, in the form proposed by Herder, Jastrow and Robinson is certainly untenable. Throughout the whole poem there is unity of style and purpose, and this points to unity of authorship. But there is nothing against Rowley's explanation in so far as he admits unity of authorship and a certain development of the theme. (2) has no sufficient basis. Though love is considered in relation to marriage, there is nothing suggesting that we are assisting at a wedding. The dramatic theory is losing favour with critics. There is hardly any action, the dialogues and the change of scene are not enough to give it a dramatic movement. (4), though entirely acceptable, is rather vague and does not convey an adequate idea of the structure of the poem. The dialogue form is secondary. Even the development of the plot seems to be somewhat exaggerated. There is much to be said in favour of Buzy's theory, but the textual excisions and transpositions to which he has to resort have no justification except his own theory.

The Song is a collection of love-songs composed by one writer with one definite purpose. Love is represented with a view to marriage. The several songs are as many tableaux or episodes in the story of two lovers. A certain development corresponding to the development of their love may be admitted, but whether the poem describes all the stages of love from its inception to its culmination in marriage remains undecided. The dialogue, monologues and the part played by the daughters of Jerusalem are poetical devices meant to give life to the descriptions and to the sentiments of the two lovers.

j Systems of Interpretation—The most important problem of the book is its meaning and interpretation. Apparently Song is an erotic poem with or without a higher aim of describing love in its purest form or of extolling the excellence of monogamy and conjugal fidelity. This is the view prevailing among modern interpreters and we have no right to introduce any other sense unless we have solid reasons, and these reasons must be sought **426j** for not in the book itself but in other biblical books and in Tradition.

The Fathers of the Church were so strongly convinced of the spiritual meaning that they ignored the literal sense. The heterodox view of Theodore of Mopsuestia, who maintained that it celebrated Solomon's marriage with the Egyptian Princess, was condemned by the II Council of Constantinople (553); Mansi, *Sacrorum Conc. Coll.*, ix, 225—7. The allegorical interpretation is made very probable by the writings of the prophets who very often represent the relation between Yahweh and Israel as that of husband and wife. Yahweh chose Israel for his Spouse, arrayed her with gold and silver and rich garments and made her renowned among the nations for her beauty and splendour (Ezek 16:3—14; cf also Is 54:6ff; 62:4f; Jer 2:2 'the love of thy betrothal'; Hos 2:19f).

There existed therefore a tradition representing **k** Yahweh's relation to Israel as a marriage. This tradition is the strongest argument for admitting a higher and spiritual sense in Song. In order to give a clear idea of the manner in which this higher sense is expressed and should be understood, a few preliminary remarks are necessary.

An **allegory** is a sustained metaphor or series of **l** metaphors about the same subject, cf Is 5:1—6. All the details of the allegory have their own meaning. The **parable** is a fictitious but lifelike narrative composed to illustrate a fact or truth. The doctrine of the parable emerges from the narrative as a whole, not from its constituent parts, some of which may be mere embellishments without symbolical meaning. The essential difference between parable and allegory is that in the parable the two objects, the one illustrating and the other illustrated, are kept distinct and placed side by side, while in the allegory they are blended together and are represented as a single object. Sometimes parable and allegory run into each other and give rise to a mixed form, the parable mixed with allegoric elements. The *typical sense* differs widely from the allegorical. The latter is a sense understood and intended by the writer; the former is an additional sense intended by God and unknown to the writer except by revelation. The typical sense is always based upon the literal sense, proper or improper.

Of these, **the typical interpretation** does not seem **m** to have a sound basis. A type may be a historical fact or person or an ideal one. The historical type of the Song is generally considered to be Solomon's marriage with Pharaoh's daughter (1 (3) Kgs 3:1); so Honorius of Autun (*Expos. in Cant.* PL 172, 347—494), Bossuet, Calmet. But there is no evidence in Scripture or Tradition that a marriage of a polygamous king is a type of the essentially monogamous union of Yahweh with Israel or of Christ with the Church. The ideal type is the conjugal union in its ideal form, as instituted by God (Gn 2:24), represented in a concrete form but without any reference to historical persons (Miller, 6f). It is a fictitious marriage, described as a real one and representing God's union with man. A similar view has been propounded by Pouget-Guitton (146f), Geslin (38—105), Chaine (in A. Robert—A. Tricot, *Initiation biblique* [1948] 175), who maintain that the sacred writer intended only to describe conjugal love and to inculcate the sanctity of marriage as instituted by God. The Song is, therefore, a moral lesson on the sanctity and indissolubility of marriage, and conjugal fidelity. Nothing more than that was meant by the writer. But in the mind of God, the primary author of Scripture, the conjugal union

426m was to serve as a type of Christ's union with his Church and of his immense love for her. The Song represents in a parabolic form an ideal marriage foreshadowing Christ's union with the Church. This interpretation may be accepted, but it is doubtful whether the text provides solid ground for it. The writer indulges in his description of the two shepherds' love, their mutual yearning and admiration, but their union is passed over almost in silence. Although love is admittedly represented with a view to marriage, and the two lovers are certainly married, the writer concentrates upon their love rather than on their marriage. If this is true, we can hardly understand how marriage can be the main object of the book. But we can easily understand the writer's unwillingness to describe the happiness of married life if his object was really to symbolize God's love for man under the figure of human conjugal love.

n In **the parabolic interpretation** the Song describes, in its literal sense, the love between two imaginary shepherds with a view to illustrating God's love for man (Tobac, 110). Its meaning must be sought in the book as a whole, not in the several details, some of which serve only to render the picture more lifelike.

In its strictest form generally adopted by the Fathers, **the allegorical interpretation** applies the whole description of the marriage to Christ and the Church, and tries to find a meaning for all such details as the hair, eyes, lips, ect, of the bride. This system has led to the most varied, and sometimes fanciful, interpretations which are nothing else but pious accommodations. Some allegorical elements must, however, be recognized. The appellation of God as a shepherd is a familiar OT metaphor; cf Ps 23 (22); 80 (79):1; Jer 31:10; Ezek 34:11, 19; Zech 11:17. The designation of the shepherd lover as *dôdî* 'my beloved', which occurs thirty times in Song, recalls Is 5:1—6, an allegory in which the same word *dôdî* is used of Yahweh.

As neither the parabolic nor the purely allegorical interpretation fully satisfies the exegetical requirements of the text, modern interpreters mostly prefer the mixed or **parabolic-allegorical interpretation**. Song is essentially a parable placing side by side, as do the Gospel parables, two facts, an imaginary and a real one, and illustrating the one by the other. It follows, according to the hermeneutical rules of parables, that many details must be considered as mere literary embellishments having no historical reality corresponding to them. It must be remarked also that although the parabolic-allegorical interpretation has been preferred we do not deny that Song teaches, at least implicitly, a moral lesson on the sanctity of marriage which was later raised to the dignity of a sacrament by Christ.

o We pass now to define the object and the limits of this allegorical parable. Some interpreters as Nicholas of Lyra (d. 1340) and in recent times Joüon, following in the steps of Jewish interpreters, explain the book as an allegorical representation of Yahweh's dealings with Israel from the Exodus to the return from the Exile. Ricciotti, although rejecting the historical allegory of the Targum, propounds a form of parabolic allegory with historical traits (cf *Il Cantico dei Cantici*, 146—57, esp., 146f). In the same line also Robert-Tournay (cf *Introd.*, p. 14f, 23). Although a 'Judaic sense' must be admitted, the historico-allegorical interpretation has never been popular in Christian exegesis. In fact, it requires a great power of imagination to find a correspondence between the several literary features of the Song and Jewish history.

Other interpreters, from Hippolytus to modern times,

have applied the allegory to the union of Christ with the **426** Church. The basis for such an interpretation is provided by the NT which describes the foundation of the Church as a nuptial feast (Mt 22:1—14) and Christ as the Bridegroom (Mt 9:15; cf also Jn 3:29; 2 Cor 11:2; Eph 5:23—32; Apoc 21:9).

This interpretation, which is called 'the Christian interpretation', must be taken as a development of the Judaic sense in order to be fully acceptable. In the plan of divine providence the election of Israel was a preparation for the establishment of the Church by Christ. The foundation of the Israelitic theocracy and that of the Church were not two independent events, but two successive stages in God's work of redemption. God's love for Israel foreshadowed Christ's love for his Church. If Song, therefore, symbolizes Yahweh's love for Israel, it must necessarily symbolize also Christ's love for his Church. This is the fuller sense which, though not perceived by the Jewish reader, is certainly contained in it and intended by God. The two senses—Judaic and Christian—are two complementary senses forming together one sense and one interpretation which is that followed by the majority of Catholic exegetes.

The Judaic aspect of this interpretation, however, **p** requires to be defined more accurately. It is universally recognized that in the prophetic books Yahweh's relations to Israel are those of husband and wife. But in the earlier books Yahweh is represented as Israel's father and Israel as Yahweh's firstborn (Ex 4:22f). This image is further developed in Dt where Yahweh is described as a father carrying his son in his arms (1:31), educating him (8:5), and as the author of his existence (32:18); cf also Hos 11:1—4, etc. The marriage-figure originated with the prophets who, however, always represent Israel as a faithless wife divorced by her husband (Is 50:1; Jer 3:8; Ezek 16:1—58; Hos 2). There is not the slightest allusion to the first happy days of their marriage; Israel proved faithless from the very first day of her marriage (Ezek 16:15; Hos 9:10). There is no time from the Sinaitic alliance to the return from the Exile in which Israel could say of Yahweh 'He is mine and I am his'.

But Israel's infidelity and repudiation by Yahweh were not to last for ever. After having atoned for her misbehaviour she would be taken up again by Yahweh and reunited with him by an eternal bond of love. This reinstatement of Israel is clearly foretold by the prophets (Is 49:14f, 54:6ff; Ezek 16:59—63; Hos. 2:19f). It is this reconciliation or re-marriage of Yahweh to Israel which is the object of the Song. (Buzy, *Vivre et Penser*, III = RB 52 (1944), 77—90, followed by Robert.)

An extension of the allegorical interpretation is **q** the identification of the bridegroom with Christ and the bride with the faithful soul. This interpretation, first proposed by Origen, became common in the Middle Ages with St Bernard as its chief representative. Closely related to it is the Mariological interpretation. Not only is the Virgin Mary the holiest of all the members of the Church, but she also concurred in the accomplishment of the mystical union of the Son of God with humanity. Of mediaeval expositors Rupert of Deutz is one of the best. Although not common in the history of interpretation of the Song, it may not be out of place to say a word about the theory that sees in the Song an allegory about Wisdom. In the past it had already been suggested by E. Fr. Rosenmüller (*Scholia in VT*, 1830, IX, 2, 251ff). He considered the Song to contain the description of a 'marriage' between Solomon and Wisdom. In the first quarter of this century a Swiss pastor saw in Qohelet, Wisdom as destined to all men in general,

q and in the Shulamite of the Song a more intimate Wisdom reserved to a few (G. Kuhn, *Erklärung des Buches Kohelet*, Giessen, 1926; *Erklärung des Hohen Liedes*, Leipzig, 1926). Suffice here to say that the theory could find support in some passages of the Wisdom Books (cf Wis 8:2, 9, 16—18; Prv 7:4, 9:5; Sir 15.2 etc) as also in their language and style (cf Sir 24:17—27 and Song 1:3; Prv 9:5 and Song 5:1 etc).

r Author and Date—Tradition has always attributed the Song to Solomon. The authority of the title, however, is not decisive as it is either a later addition or a literary artifice. The language bears marks of a later origin. But the strongest argument against Solomonic authorship is the marriage allegory which originated with Hosea. The Song is therefore later than the 8th cent. B.C. If the subject of the Song is Israel's reconciliation with Yahweh, its date must be fixed at the end of the Exile or a little later. For Ricciotti it dates from the beginning of the 4th cent. (*Cantico dei Cantici*, 163); for Robert (*Le Cantique des Cantiques*, 10, 20) at the end of the 5th cent. There are no reasons for placing its composition as late as the Greek period.

7a 1:1 The Title—see § 426c.

1:2–2:7 First Song—2–4 Mutual yearning of the bride and her beloved—Although the suffix pronouns are masculine in MT, it seems advisable (with LXX and Vg) to interpret 2a and 3 as said by the lover in answer to the indirect opening invitation of the bride. Such an exchange of suffixes, masc. for fem., occurs again in 8:6—7, where the fem. is assumed by practically all commentators. Therefore we consider 2–4 as a kind of prologue (so also Robert) containing the presentation of the persons and the setting of the stage. **2a.** The bride yearns for the kisses of her beloved. **2b–3.** The beloved answers praising the bride with the same expressions that he will use again (4:10). Indeed, he values the embrace (LXX and Vg: *breasts*) of the bride more than wine. (Wine stands here for all possible pleasures, cf Eccl 2:3.) He feels himself attracted by her perfumes, that are of the choicest quality; her name, i.e. all her person, is like a bottle of scented ointment, which when poured out spreads its sweet fragrance abroad. Her charms are irresistible. **4.** The bride answers. She will follow him wherever he goes. 'Let us make haste'. Cf
b Jer 31:3. **4b.** Can be considered a statement of the bride that announces the conditions for the development of the action. The connexion with 4a and 4c is not immediately apparent and commentators have tried to lessen the difficulty by reading an imperative in 4b, and changing the suffix from 3rd person into 2nd: 'thy chambers'. However, difficulties are better met by taking 4b as an optative sentence in which the beloved is spoken of as 'the king', not an unusual term on the lips of the bride for the beloved, and a possible allusion to Yahweh, (Robert): *'Oh that the king were to lead me into his inner apartments!'* This would be in parallelism with the first sentence, and followed by an analogous answer of the beloved, 'We will be glad to rejoice in thee . . .'. (For the perfect used in optative sentences, see Joüon, 112k, p. 300). If, however, the term 'king' is taken literally as a different person from the lover, a good sense could be obtained by translating MT thus: 'If the king . . . it is *delightful* (or better: *rightful*) to love . . .'.

c 5–6 The bride's humble condition—**5.** The bride is presenting herself and asking 'the daughters of Jerusalem' not to mind the colour of her complexion. The Heb. for 'black' here means 'of a swarthy complexion, sunburnt'. But she was nonetheless fair. The 'daughters

of Jerusalem' occur again in 2:7, 3:5, 11; 5:8, 16; 8:4; **427c** Are they the bride's maids, or city ladies in contrast with the peasant bride, (Dussaud), or simply the inhabitants of Jerusalem (Robert)? The tents of Kedar were the goats-hair tents of the Kedarenes, a nomadic tribe dwelling in the N Arabian desert Gn 25:13. The curtains of Solomon are said to be the magnificent hangings of Solomon's temple (Joüon) or those of his palace (Siegfried, Budde). But according to the rules of Heb. poetry it is preferable to make 'Solomon's curtains' parallel to the 'tents of Kedar' and to read instead of Solomon the name of a place or tribe such as Salma, near Kedar (Miller, Ricciotti, Bea, Robert), or Salom (Pouget-Guitton), or Salem for Jerusalem (Buzy). **6.** She gives the cause of her dark complexion. She had to pass the long summer days guarding the vineyards, a hard task assigned to her by her malevolent brothers. The bride's vineyard has been identified either with the bride herself (Calmet, Miller, Guitton) or with her charms (Budde, Harper, Zapletal), or with Palestine itself and the true religion (Joüon), or simply Palestine (Robert). Why she abandoned her work is not stated. Perhaps she sought a better opportunity of meeting her lover; see 7f.

7–8 The bride in search of her lover—The bride **d** desires to meet her lover. For the beginning of the verse, cf Gn 37:16b. She is represented as a shepherdess tending her flock in the vicinity of her beloved without knowing precisely the place where he grazes his flock or where he rests and waters it at noon. The dialogue with the chorus, that tells her to keep near the place where the shepherds have raised their tents, because the lover is sure to come there at noon, expresses the intense passion of the shepherdess.

9–11 The bridegroom's praise of the bride—The **e** bride has found her lover who is fascinated by her beauty. **9.** The point of comparison is the splendour of the trappings of the royal mare, not the mare itself, (Joüon, Rosenmüller); or, allegorically, the promise to deliver the nation from her present low situation, as she was delivered from the bondage of Egypt (Robert). **10.** Her cheeks are beautiful with ear-rings, her neck with jewels. **11.** He promises to make her more beautiful with gold ear-rings and silver necklaces. Some interpreters believe that these are the words of a seducer trying to divert the guileless heart of the shepherdess from the simplicity of a pastoral life to the pomp and splendour of the court. But there is nothing in the text suggesting this sense. For the mention of the king, see 12.

12–14 The bride's praise of her bridegroom— **f** The bride very courteously returns her bridegroom's compliments. **12.** The scene is apparently the king's palace. But the king has no part in the dialogue nor is he addressed in the 2nd person or as 'my king'. We have here probably a tacit comparison. She will pour her perfumes upon the head of her beloved, thus showing her love for him, just as the king's attendants and courtiers pay homage to him, cf Lk 7:37f; Jn 12:3. **14.** He is also compared to a bunch of henna which grows in the plains of Engedi on the west shore of the Dead Sea. Henna was used by Arabs for tinting the nails with a red hue and for its smell.

15–2:3 Expressions of Mutual Love—The dialogue **g** reaches its climax. **15.** Her looks are full of candour. The dove symbolizes innocence and simplicity (Mt 10:16). **16.** Her reply almost repeats her lover's words but adds 'our couch is green'. Heb. '*eres* means 'bed' as in Ugaritic '*rš* and Babylonian *eršu*; if this meaning is kept it would indicate no doubt the

427g green grass on which they were lying. The context however suggests rather a shepherd's hut of green branches and leaves where the two had met. The 'bed' has also been identified with the hut of the Feast of Tabernacles (Ricciotti) or with the Tabernacle of the Desert (Joüon). **17.** Note the contrast between the bride's words (16) and the more elevated tone of the bridegroom's expressions of praise. She had said 'Our dwelling is a poor shepherd's hut'. He replies, 'Our habitation, adorned with our love, is like a king's palace with cedar beams and cypress ceiling'. In the mention of cedar and cypress as material of the house there may possibly be an allusion to the Temple, according to Is 60:13 and 35:2 (Delitzsch,
h Robert-Tournay). **2:1.** The bride with characteristic modesty describes herself as a *narcissus* which grows in the plains or more particularly in the plain of Sharon, and to a lily of the valley. In other words, she is as humble as a little meadow flower. Others see in the comparison of the bride with a *narcissus*, or the like, the identification of the bride with the spring vegetation and indirectly with the country of Palestine (Robert). **2.** The bridegroom turns this declaration of modesty into a flattering compliment. Your beauty among other maidens is that of a lily among thorns. **3.** Sensible of the compliment she replies in the same strain. You surpass all other men in beauty and goodness as much as an apple tree, (or fruit tree) surpasses all the trees of the forest. The image of the fruit-tree naturally evokes that of shade and fruit. She longs for, and sits down in, the shade of the tree enjoying its delicious fruit.
i **4—7 The union of the two lovers**—From the leafy hut we are taken to a banqueting hall to assist at the wedding of the two lovers. **4.** The bridegroom takes his bride into the banqueting hall or, as we should say, the reception hall. The Heb. 'house of wine' has received many different interpretations: cellar (Calmet, Ricciotti), 'Hut in the vineyard' (Harper), and 'Banqueting hall' (Joüon); allegorically, 'Palestine' (Robert). As the marriage ceremony consisted in the introduction of the bride into the bridegroom's home, we have here an allusion to the marriage feast. But the poet is more interested in their mutual love than in their wedding; he therefore omits all details to concentrate on their love. What follows, '*and (his) diglô upon me is love*', is obscure. From other passages where the root *dgl* occurs the meaning 'army, battle array' has been derived, sup-
j ported by the Qumran texts: '*he arrayed against me his army of love*' (so Joüon). But the context does not favour it. Others have interpreted *degel* as 'flag, banner'; and recently reference has been made to the Accadian *diglu* with the meaning 'gaze', which would simplify and clarify the situation. **5.** Vg-DV 'I languish' renders the idea better than R.S.V. 'sick', and we need not suppose she was ill as Heb. *hôlat* seems to suggest. **7.** These words are spoken by the bridegroom. The bride, over-whelmed by the power of love, has fallen asleep in his arms, and he entreats her friends not to disturb her rest. The gazelles are either a symbol of feminine grace or a mere poetical figure.
k **Allegorical interpretation.** Israel, reborn after the exile, desires to be reunited with Yahweh whose love she knows well. She will never let herself be led astray by the splendour of other religions. Yahweh will be her only God, her only happiness. Though few in number and unimpressive in their external appearance, the Israelites are beautiful in the sight of God as they are faithful to him. (Is. 54:6—8). Perhaps the end of the poem, by the mention of the love of the bride and her sleep,

intends to show that the restoration after the exile was **4** not so efficient and complete as the exaltation that followed the announcement of freedom had lead them to hope (Robert). The Church too rejoices in Christ, her Founder and the source of all her prosperity. 'Thy name' is the name of Jesus (cf St Bernard, Serm. 15 in Cant. PL 183, 846.) Though humble in her origin, the Church stands high in God's favour who loves and adorns her with supernatural gifts. The life of the just is a continual aspiration towards the mystical union with God.
8—3:5 Second Song—It develops the same theme on **l** the same lines, but with different descriptions. The bridegroom comes to meet the bride; they spend a happy day in the fields; during the night she becomes restless until she finds him again. **8—9 An unexpected visit from the Bridegroom—8.** She is still in her house when she suddenly hears her lover's footsteps approaching. He is poetically described as a gazelle or young hart running and leaping over the hills and mountains to arrive more quickly near his bride.
10—17 The Bridegroom's Invitation—10—13. He **m** invites her to come out; All nature has awakened to new life after the death-like sleep of winter. Instead of 'singing', with the ancient versions, many modern authors accept for *zāmîr* the meaning 'pruning', that could be the second one done in June—July (Dalman, Rowley). **14.** He repeats his invitation. We must not imagine the bride staying in her house and quietly listening to her friend's serenade before she rises to open. As remarked above, the dialogue form is a literary device to give life to the scene. **15.** Is considered by some to be a popular song sung by the bride in response to her lover's invitation. Buzy rejects 15—17 as a later addition. Joüon makes 15 **n** the beginning of another scene. But 15—17 may also be regarded as a dramatic description of the way the two lovers spent the day in the fields. Although it is not expressly stated that the bride accepted the invitation, this is at least implied in 17. **16.** Before parting she once more professes her unchangeable love. 'He pastures his flock among the lilies' denotes his ordinary work, hinting at the same time at a higher meaning, namely, his pre-dilection for fragrant flowers, the symbol of virtue. **17.** As night approaches they part. '*Before* the day breathes' (i.e. 'before the cool evening breeze begins to blow') and the shadows stretch out, he swiftly returns to the mount-ains. Thus 17 links up with 8 and cannot be regarded as a later addition. Others consider the scene taking place in the early morning, before the shadows of the night dis-appear. Symbolically it would be the hour of deliverance (Robert) 'rugged', Heb. '*Beter*' creates a difficulty. Many interpreters, on the ground of analogy (cf 4:6) take it as the name of an aromatic plant which they identify with the *malabathron*.
3:1—5 Seeking the Bridegroom—1. It was late in the **o** evening when the two lovers returned to their homes (2:17). Now with her heart and mind still full of the emotions of the day she imagines herself to be still with her beloved. There is nothing to suggest that she is relating a dream. **2f.** Unable to repress her emotions she hastens out in search of her beloved. Nothing is impossible to love, still less to a poet. **4.** Where and how she found him at that time of night, the words they exchanged, are matters that fall outside the poet's interest. **5.** The refrain, which recurs in 2:7 and 8:4, describes the quiet joy of the union of the two lovers.
Allegorical interpretation. In 2:8—14 it is the **p** bridegroom who seeks his bride; in 3:1—4 it is the bride who goes in search of her beloved. The two scenes re-

27p present their yearning for each other. Yahweh called Israel and Israel responded, and though for some time she turned her back on him, she returned once more to him, was received and made again the object of his love. The Fathers explain the bridegroom's leaping over the mountains as God's approach to man by way of the Virgin's womb, the manger, the Cross, the tomb and heaven (St Greg. the Great *In expos. Evang. hom.* 29, PL 79, 907). The description of spring means that God's appeal to man is made at a time when response is more likely to follow. Spring in fact is the time for love. But such details as the latticed window, winter, rain, figs, etc are mere parabolic elements.

28a **3: 6–5: 1 Third Song**—A contrast between the pomp of a royal marriage and the simple manifestations of love between the two shepherds. Buzy thinks 3:6–11 to be interpolated. Against Buzy, Robert maintains that the passage in question is not a description of a royal marriage feast, but rather a poetical description of the last return of the captives, and of the coming of the messianic kingdom. Solomon, who is the 'Messiah' is the actor and Sion is the scene (Robert, 191). If, however, the theory of the marriage is accepted, then the poet intended to emphasize the simple way of living of the countryfolk.

b **3:6–8 The Royal Procession**—**6.** The people are astonished at seeing a cloud of dust in the desert approaching the city and ask: 'What is this?' The point of comparison is not, as 7 might suggest, its fragrance but simply the rising cloud of smoke. **7f.** When the procession comes nearer, they can see Solomon's litter escorted by 60 of the most valiant men of Israel.

c **9–11 The Royal Pavilion**—**9.** When the procession arrives in the city, the king is seen on his 'palanquin'. Heb. *'appiryôn* is rendered 'pavilion' by Joüon, Buzy, or 'throne' (Miller, Robert), but the meaning 'litter' has been vindicated anew by Winandy (VT 15 (1965), 103–110). **11.** The mention of the king's mother is embarrassing. There is no evidence of the king being crowned by his mother. Moreover, if the king is Yahweh and his bride is Israel, who is the king's mother? If however the king is the Messiah and his marriage is the eschatological conclusion ('crowning') of the messianic kingdom after the last return from exile, then the 'mother' may be the nation (Robert), or with reference to Ps 87 (86), the mother might just be the city of Sion whose daughters are mentioned in v 11. But both the crown and the king's mother may be a mere literary development of the nuptial comparison.

d **4:1–6 The bride's beauty**—From Solomon's marriage feast we are taken back to the fields to admire once more the beauty of the bride. Or, in the ordinary development of the feast we would have, first, the arrival of Solomon (3:6–11), then the admiring description of the spouse (4:1–7) and finally the king's invitation to the spouse and union (4:8–5:1). (The invitation by the king to his friends and companions to enter with him and enjoy the fruits and the wine constitutes a difficulty in the materialist interpretation and even in the ordinary allegorical interpretation, but it would be quite in order if in the allegory we were to understand Wisdom personified, in **e** parallelism with Prv 9:5). **1.** Cf 1.15. **2.** Whiteness and symmetry of teeth are meant. **3.** Her mouth, or speech, is graceful. **4.** Her neck is stately as a tower. If the neck is a tower, the bucklers and the armour of the warriors are the necklaces and pendants. **5.** 'That feed among the lilies'; these words serve only to add gracefulness to the description; see 2:16. **6.** Is repeated with slight modification from 2:17 and is the conclusion of the

first part of the song, though perhaps loosely connected **428e** with the context.

7–9 The Bridegroom fascinated by his Bride's f beauty—**7.** Is similar to 4:1. 7b is applied by the Church in an accommodated sense to the Immaculate Conception: 'et macula originalis non est in te'. **8.** A slight change of MT gives: '*thou dost bring me back*, my spouse, from Lebanon . . .' following LXX, Syriac and Vg. This is preferred by some modern interpreters (Miller, Buzy, Robert etc); it is the bridegroom, not the bride, who is represented as coming from the mountains, cf 2:8, 17; 4:6; though this interpretation is grammatically difficult. 'Depart' is the bridegroom's invitation to the bride to come down from the mountains (Amana etc are peaks in the Antilebanon range) and to go with him to Jerusalem (Robert).

10–15 Other Praises of the Bride's Beauty—**10 g** recalls 1:2f. The bride's *caresses*, the expression of her love, are sweeter than wine, the symbol of joy and pleasure. **11.** Milk mixed with honey was, and still is, a favourite drink in the E (Power, VDom. 54f). Here it symbolizes sweetness of speech. **12.** MT reads: 'a garden enclosed . . . a spring shut up' some read 'a spring' twice, the two Heb. words *gan* and *gal* being easily interchangeable (Joüon, Buzy). Springs of water were sometimes enclosed by a wall with a locked entrance in order to make them inaccessible to intruders. **13.** The *conduits* conveying water from the enclosed spring irrigate an orchard of pomegranates and trees of exquisite fruits, henna and spikenard. The unusual plural *nerādîm* 'spikenards' and the repetition of the same word in the singular in 14 have led some interpreters to read *werādîm* 'roses', a word which occurs in Mishnaic Hebrew. **14.** A list of aromatic plants irrigated by the invisible spring. **15.** The poet reverts to the image of the spring. The bride is compared to a spring, which is not only inaccessible but also yields streams of water all the year round. Two qualities of the bride's love are here signified: it is unalterable and beneficent.

16–5:1 The Union—**16.** The garden is another meta- **h** phor for the bride. **5:1.** The lovers' meeting is represented as a marriage feast at which friends are necessarily present. But see above § 428d. Allegorical interpretation. The meaning of 3:6–11 must be considered in relation to the whole song. If this relation is one of contrast and if **i** 4:1–5:1 describes the pure love of two shepherds unaffected by the conventionalism of a more refined society, then 3:6–11 represent all that can defile or frustrate that love. But if there is no opposition between 3:6–11 and 4:1–5:1, the king's marriage may be taken to represent Christ's union with the Church, or his assumption of human nature in the Incarnation, or Yahweh's installation in the temple of Jerusalem.

The beautiful bride is Israel cleansed from her sins **j** and arrayed with her finest garments (Is 52:1), or the Church purified by the blood of Christ, 'cleansed by the laver of water in the word of life: . . . a glorious church not having spot or wrinkle . . . but holy and without blemish' (Eph 5:26f). The several parts of the body—eyes, hair, teeth, etc—are parabolic elements. God's love for man knows no obstacles. He so loved the world as to give his only-begotten Son (Jn 3:16); and this immense love is vividly described as drawing him near to mankind from distant and inaccessible places, i.e. from heaven. Man is beautiful in the sight of God because he is made in the divine image, but still more when he is adorned with sanctifying grace. The figure of the sealed fountain represents the inalienable love of the Church whose heart is shut to all affections but that for her divine Bridegroom.

428j The Fathers have applied the figure to the virginity of Mary.

k **5:2—6:3 Fourth Song**—Here too we have the usual theme: the bridegroom's yearning for his bride, the bride's description of her bridegroom's beauty, and the joy of their union. A new feature is the painful proof to which the bridegroom subjects his bride.

5:2—5 A Night Visit—**3.** Apparently she refuses to open for a trifling pretext (Calmet, Joüon, Ricciotti). But this is hardly compatible with the statement that even during sleep her mind is absorbed by her beloved. It is preferable to regard her words as a poetic device meant to account for the sudden disappearance of the bridegroom (Miller, Buzy). **4.** The bridegroom tries to open by passing his hand or finger through the keyhole and removing the bolt. On hearing the sound and perhaps on seeing his hand through the hole, she is seized by violent emotion.

l **6—8 In search of the Bridegroom**—**6.** Unable to open the door the bridegroom departs. The words 'my soul failed me when he spoke' are out of place, because as he had already gone, she could not hear him speaking. Some interpreters transpose these words after 4 (Miller, Buzy). But if we interpret *dbr* as 'to pass away, to depart', in accord with Arabic *dabara*, we obtain the sense: 'I fainted, etc'. No transposition is necessary. Immediately she hurries out looking for him and calling for him in vain. **7.** This ill-treatment is another poetical fiction meant to heighten her distress. **8.** As has been often remarked, the dialogue is sometimes intended to give a dramatic effect to the internal feelings of the actor. So we need not ask how the daughters of Jerusalem happened to be outdoors at that time of night.

m **9—16 Description of the Bridegroom**—**9.** The question of the maidens serves to introduce the following description.

n **6: 2f The Meeting**—**2.** The scene changes; the maidens have disappeared; it is daylight; the bride and the bridegroom are together in the garden. We are not told how the bride found her bridegroom. The poet depicts the amorous scenes by a few strokes and leaves it to the imagination to fill up the gaps. The bridegroom is in his garden planted with *balsam shrubs*, feeding his flock and gathering lilies. The two details of feeding the flock in the garden and gathering lilies, unlikely though they are, are two delicate touches which render the picture more attractive. **3.** The joy of their union is expressed with the same words as in 2:16.

o **Allegorical interpretation.** The salient traits of this song are: The bridegroom's unexpected visit, the bride's apparent indifference, the bridegroom's disappearance, the bride's night search and the description of the bridegroom, their union. Applied to the history of Israel these may refer to Israel's infidelity, punishment and conversion. The Church too sometimes seems to be deserted by her divine spouse. She is persecuted by her enemies who try to strip her of her bridal raiment, which is her sanctity. But she remains faithful to Christ, the most beautiful of the sons of man. In the Liturgy the description of the bridegroom is applied to Christ. Everlasting happiness is the reward for her fidelity. It has been observed that in the description of the bridegroom certain traits suggest a comparison with a building, (Robert and others). As, Solomon was represented before, appearing in his majesty, so here we have an allegory of the temple and perhaps, at the same time, of the 'palace' of Wisdom, for which see Prv 9:1ff; both of these are closely connected with Solomon. The song is particularly rich in ascetic applications. God knocks at the door of our heart in the quiet of the night, far **42** from the distractions of the world, in solitude (Hos 2:14); he comes unexpectedly, and we must be ever ready to respond. Those who are neglectful will miss the benefits of God's grace, and it is through penance that they may regain them. Sometimes God seems to abandon the faithful soul but it is only to test her attachment. The soul that comes out victorious is rewarded with more abundant graces and with the spiritual joy of a closer union with God.

6:4—8:4 Fifth Song—The analysis is difficult. The **42** beginning and end are in the style of the other songs, but the connexion and internal development of the ideas are not always clear.

4—9 Praises of the Bride—**4.** She is as beautiful as Tirzah, the old capital of the N kingdom (1 (3) Kgs 15:33). Tirzah, not Samaria, has been chosen as a term of comparison both for its connexion with the verb *rāṣah* 'to be pleased with', as well as for Samaria's association with heathen cult. Her beauty could conquer all hearts as a powerful army ready for the attack. **5a.** The words 'turn away your eyes from me' express the marvellous beauty of the bride's eyes. **5b—7.** See on 4:1b—3. **8—9.** A contrast between the polygamy of the oriental rulers and the monogamous union of the two shepherd-lovers. The mention of the maidens seems to overburden the rhythm in our passage, and therefore is omitted by critics like Dalman, Dussaud, Buzy, Robert. **10** may be considered as belonging to the description of the bride in v 4ff. And the words 'terrible as a powerful army' occurring in v 4c and 10 provide the limits within which the description of the bride occurs.

10—12 The bride's sudden appearance—**11.** The **b** subject is probably the bridegroom who alone is represented as going to his garden (4:16; 5:1; 6:1). But for others the subject is the bride. **12.** Going down to inspect the garden she, almost unawares, places herself on the chariots of '*ammî-nādîb*. The expression is difficult to explain. It is taken as proper noun by LXX and Vg, while modern interpreters generally translate 'noble people' (Joüon), 'prince of my people' (Pouget-Guitton), 'princely cortège' (Miller). As the word *nādîb* recurs in 7:1 in an analogous phrase 'noble daughter', it seems that we might retain the same meaning here and translate 'noble people', the final 'i' in '*ammî* being a paragogic 'i'. But the 'chariots of a noble people' hardly makes sense. Buzy's reference to the chariot carrying the Ark from Abinadab's house (2 Sm 6:3) is far fetched. Robert translates: 'I do not know . . . , my love has placed me on the chariots of my people, as a prince'. The resulting sense is not very clear. Perhaps it is preferable, with Pouget-Guitton, to translate '*ammî-nādîb*' by 'prince of my people'. Reference could be made to Nm 21:18 where a similar expression occurs, '*nedîbê hā'ām*', 'the princes of the people'. And if the subject is the bride, she, meeting the bridegroom's chariot, joins it (instinctively) by a sudden impulse and is invited to participate in the performance of the ritual dance of the marriage feast. In this way everything acquires a meaning.

13—7:5 Invitation to the bride—**13.** MT 7:1. The **c** beginning of the v, (*šûbî, šûbî*) is usually translated 'Return, return', said by the maidens (Robert) who wish to see the bride again. In the supposition that she is already there those words can be translated 'turn round' that we may see thee better during the dance (so also Vaccari). The expectation is enhanced by the rhetorical question: 'Why should you gaze upon the Shulammite, while she is performing the dance'. And indeed there follows the description of the dancing bride. She is called 'the

9c Shulammite', prob. = maiden of Sholem, Shunem 1 (3) Kgs 1:3 though hardly to be identified with Abishag. This appellation occurs here and in 7:1 only, and seems to be chosen for some literary motive rather than for historical reasons. 'two armies'. This has received many different interpretations. As *meḥōlaṭ hammaḥanāyim* is generally translated 'dance of two companies', the bride's words are taken either as a refusal of the maidens' invitation to dance (Vaccari), or as an acceptance (Miller, Ricciotti, Pouget-Guitton). Joüon, followed by Buzy and Robert, thinks that these words were spoken by the bridegroom, who modestly agrees that his bride should come before the maidens. *Meḥōlaṭ hammaḥanāyim* may also be rendered 'a chorus in two bands'. The bride is supposed to be advancing between two rows of girls singing alternately and accompanying their singing with a rhythmical movement of their bodies (Buzy). Robert interprets in the light of Jer 31 where the dance is also mentioned, and Gn 32 (for the mention of Mahanayim) as symbolizing the reunion of Israel with Judah.

d **7:1.** The praises of the bride are apparently sung by the two halves of the chorus alternately. **2a.** The literary taste of the oriental poet differs from ours. The image of the wine has been called forth by that of the goblet. **2b.** Palestinian farmers heap up the corn on the threshing floor and surround it with thorns to protect it from animals before carrying it their barns. But the image represents the heap of wheat surrounded with lilies, the symbol of purity. 3 is repeated from 4:5. **4a.** Her neck is compared to a tower for its erectness, and to ivory for its whiteness. **4b.** Heshbon was the ancient capital of the Amorites in Transjordan (Nm 21:25). Besides numerous cisterns excavated from the rock, it had a water reservoir, the remains of which are still visible on the left of the road from Amman to Madaba. Bath-Rabbim is an unknown locality, perhaps in the lands of the Ammonites, of Rabbath Ammon, the capital of the Ammonites (Jer 48: 3). But the geography of the author is more poetic than scientific. Joüon and Ricciotti think of Mt Hermon in connexion with the geographical names in these vv. Here again we have no right to impose our aesthetic rules on **e** the oriental poet. **5.** 'Your flowing locks are like purple'. In 4:1 they are black, but the poet has the right to vary the comparisons. The king is not Solomon, the supposed rival of the shepherd-lover, but the shepherd himself who is called king according to the nuptial language. The sense may be also: Thy tresses are so beautiful as to captivate even a king, cf 4:1; 6:5.

f **6—9 Other praises of the Bridegroom—6.** The exclamation 'How beautiful art thou!' which recurs in 1:15; 4:1, 7; and 6:4 suggest that it is the bridegroom who is speaking. **7.** The palm tree is a favourite figure in oriental poetry to describe the stateliness of a slender and graceful body. Tamar, (= palm tree) was also a frequent name for a woman. cf Gn 38:6; 2 Sm 13:1. **8.** The bridegroom is not content with admiring the bride's bodily perfections, he is also anxious to enjoy them.

g **10—8:4 The Joy of their Union—10.** The bride gives herself up entirely to her beloved. **12.** It is springtime, and she now invites him to the vineyards, where she will give him her love. **13.** The images are all expressive of love. The mandrakes are a fruit of the size and colour of a small apple. They ripen in May. Their flowers have a pleasant smell, and the fruit was believed to possess aphrodisiac properties (Gn 30:14), hence called also 'love-apples'.

8:1. She had already expressed her self-surrender to her bridegroom in the vineyard, far from the sight of men.

She now desires to show her love for him anywhere without **429g** shame or fear. **3f.** See on 2:6f.

Allegorical interpretation. In general it is identical **h** with that of the other songs, particularly the third which describes the incomparable beauty of the bride and her irresistible attractiveness. Points of special interest are: the uniqueness of the bride. As God has selected only one people in the OT, so Christ founded only one Church, whom he loved so much as to shed his blood for her (Eph 2:16). The heap of corn surrounded by lilies suggests the virginal fecundity of the Church. The image of the corn and the goblet of wine is, according to the Fathers, an allusion to the Eucharist. The bridegroom gathering the fruits of his palm-like bride is Christ rejoicing in the children of the Church and their virtues. The intimacy between Christ and his Church is as chaste as that existing between a brother and a sister. The Fathers agree in explaining 8:1 as the Synagogue's ardent desire for the Incarnation of the Son of God. Through his human nature Christ became like men (Phil 2:7; Heb 2:17) and their brother (Rm 8:29; Heb 2:11).

8:5—7 Sixth Song—The Triumph of Love. In this **430a** short song, which may be considered the conclusion of the preceding, the two lovers are represented in the fullness of their joy, united for ever with an indissoluble bond of love. 5a is considered by Robert to be the conclusion of the fifth song. If connected with what follows, then the poet is describing the nuptial cortège proceeding to the bridegroom's house. **5b.** These words were spoken by the bridegroom probably in the first days of their love. The beginning of their mutual affection is poetically associated with the apple tree and the maternal house, which are, in a different way, symbols of love. **6f.** A hymn of love. The masculine suffixes in 6 (as in 5) place the words in the mouth of the bride, but it is more likely that the bridegroom (identified with Yahweh) is here speaking to the bride (so Robert and others). He begs to remain inseparably united with her as a signet ring which is usually bound round the neck with a cord, or fastened to the arm. (Gn 38:18; Jer 22:24). His love is as strong as death which none can escape, and his passion is as inexorable as Sheol, which never gives back anyone who has come under its sway; like fire, which warms, burns, and consumes. Love is so strong and intense that it can neither be extinguished by flooding waters nor swept away by impetuous rivers; cf Rm 8:35ff.

Allegorical interpretation. Both Israel after the **b** exile and the Church declare their inseparable attachment to God. More particularly, Israel is described, according to some interpreters, returning from the exile accompanied by Yahweh (Is 52:12) who recalls to her memory her humble origin (Ricciotti). The Fathers generally refer the whole scene to Christ's marriage with the triumphant Church, Apoc 19:7f.

8:8—15 Appendix—After the magnificent apotheosis **c** of love in the preceding vv one inevitably regards 8—12 as an anticlimax. This section is therefore rejected as an interpolation by Meignan (545) and Buzy (360). Joüon with greater probability believes that it was added by the poet himself sometime after he had finished the poem. Robert sees in 8—12 two different epigrams (8—10; 11—12) with the same structure, written by a Pharisee, and both referring to the happiness under John Hyrcanus. Other interpreters, however, consider it to be the conclusion of the book.

8—10 The marriage bargain—8. We have a young **d** sister who is not yet of marriageable age, what shall we do when she is asked in marriage? The elder brothers, the

430d guardians of their younger sister, ask themselves what sum will they ask from the prospective suitor of their sister. In those times the prospective bridegroom had to pay a sum of money; cf Gn 24:53; 34:12; **9.** If she is comparable to a wall, i.e. a walled city, let us make it impregnable by constructing silver bulwarks; if she is a gate, or the city gate, we will bar it with cedar planks. In other words, the brothers are unwilling to give her away except for a very high price. **10.** The sister proudly claims that she is fully mature and that she has found peace since she has found the man of her heart.

e 11–12 Solomon's Vineyard—11. Baal-Hamon is an unknown place. It is not clear by whom these words are spoken. **12.** The bridegroom steps in. My vineyard, i.e. my bride, is here before me. I am ready to pay the sum you asked and an additional remuneration to you, the keepers of the vineyard. Solomon is the type of the wealthy man.

13–14 Conclusion—13. The price has been agreed upon and paid by the bridegroom who now addresses his bride: 'Let me hear in the presence of friends your consent to my demand'. **14.** She replies asking him to take her away with him wherever he pleases. According to Robert and others, these two vv identify Wisdom with the Shulammite. The bridegroom, after having been educated by Wisdom, asks her to instruct his friends also.

Allegorical interpretation. It depends on the literal **f** sense which is not clear. Supposing the appendix to be written by the same author, we can easily trace the main lines of interpretation. Bride and bridegroom are, in a particular way, the Church and Christ. The price which Christ had to pay for his bride was far in excess of what any man could offer: in fact, it was Christ's own blood (1 Pet. 1:19). The bride's brothers, trying to frustrate the marriage, are the heathen peoples and all the persecutors of the Church. The vineyard is a familiar metaphor for Israel (Is 5:1) and the Church (Mt 20:1f; 21:33ff). The bride's last words to the bridegroom express a desire for the consummation of their union in heaven.

WISDOM

BY W. WATSON C.R.L.

431a Bibliography—*Commentaries*; for a critical survey of these see J. A. Emerton, *Theology* 68 (1965) 376—80. W. J. Deane, Oxford 1881, sober but dated; J. Geyer, Torch, 1963; A. T. S. Goodrick, 1913, perhaps the best in English; J. A. F. Gregg, Cambridge, 1909, useful; C. Harris, in *A New Comm. on Holy Scripture*, 1928; K. Kohler, JE 12 (1907) 539ff; J. Reider, New York 1957, learned and helpful but uneven; also: C. L. W. Grimm, Leipzig, 1860, philological with many ref. to Gr. lit.; dated but still useful; P. Heinisch, Münster, 1912,
b best and most complete; J. Fischer, Würzburg, 1950; E. Osty, 1957²; J. J. Weber, PCSB. *Critical G^h Text*: J. Ziegler, ed. *Sapientia Salomonis*, Göttingen, 1962; *Sources*: T. Finan, Hellenistic Humanism in the Book of Wisdom', Ir TQ 27 (1960) 30—48; S. Lange, 'The Wisdom of Solomon and Plato', JBL 55 (1936) 293—302; P. W. Skehan, 'Isaias and the Teaching of the Book of Wisdom', CBQ 2 (1940) 289—99; id 'Borrowings from the Psalms in the Book of Wisdom', CBQ 10
c (1948) 384—97; *Theology*: F. C. Porter, 'The Pre-existence of the soul in the Book of Wisdom and in the rabbinnical writings', Amer Journ Theol 12 (1908) 53—115; F. R. Tennant, 'The Teaching of Ecclesiasticus and Wisdom on the introduction of Sin and Death', JTS 2 (1900—1) 207—23; J. P. Weisengoff, 'Death and Immortality in the Book of Wisdom, CBQ 3 (1941) 104—33; G. Ziener *Die theologische Begriffssprache im Buche der Weisheit*, Bonn, 1956.

432a Author and Canonicity—Although Gr. and Syr. give the title as 'Wisdom of Solomon', it is in fact generally accepted that the author wrote under a borrowed name. Such anonymity was customary among writers in the Ancient Near East. The author of Wis chose Solomon precisely on account of his world famous wisdom (cf 1 (3) Kg 5:9—14 etc); perhaps also because he felt a kinship with his intellectual father, as did the sages who produced Eccl or Song. The persuasion of corporate personality may have been strong enough even to cause such men to credit Solomon with their work. On the other hand, some commentators believe the editors and compilers of the bible ascribed Wis to Solomon. Certainly 'the Sage', as Chrys calls him, was a Jew well steeped in the OT and Jewish tradition and proficient enough in Gr. besides. Wis is placed between Jb and Sir in the LXX. It is one of the deuterocanonical books. On its place in the Canon, see §§ 14*gh*, 17*b*.
b Original Language—The original language of Wis is Gr. This is the opinion of most scholars. Wis contains many rare words, some not occurring in the LXX; others, like *teknophonos* (14:23) are *hapax totius graecitatis*; composite words are fairly frequent. However, Focke (*Die Entstehung der Weisheit Salomos*, 1913), Purinton (JBL 47 (1928) 276—304) and others consider that at least the first 10 chh were originally written in Heb. According to them, the language of this part of the book is 'translation Gr.'. This is seen in the awkwardness

resulting from a tendency to transfer words rather than **432b** ideas from the original into translation. Apart from the many hebraisms, this is apparent in 1:1, 5*c*, 14, 16; 2:5—6; 4:13—14; 5:16; 6:7; 8:4; 9:1, 3, 9, 11; 10:1, 8, 10. Peters (BZ 14 (1917) 1—14) even suggests that ch 9 was an acrostic psalm in Heb. (see commentary). These first chh also contain noticeably fewer particles and compounds; there are peculiarities in word-order and a more careful observance of the parallelism characteristic of Semitic poetry. Further, the content is Jewish and the audience evidently not intended to be Gr. Chh 11—19 in contrast are written in a less constrained style, with more rhetorical flourishes and frequent tautology. Use is made of pagan teachings and a different audience is aimed at. It is possible that the section apparently written in Heb. originated in Palestine; this was subsequently translated and used to preface the section composed in Alexandrian Gr. Cf E. A. Speiser, 'The Hebrew Origin of the First Part of the Book of Wisdom', JQR 14 (1924), 455—82; C. E. Purinton, 'Translation Greek in the Wisdom of Solomon', JBL 47 (1928), 276—304; F. Zimmermann, 'The Book of Wisdom: Its Language and Character', JQR 67 (1966), 101—35.

Although an Aram. fragment of Wis has been published by A. Marx in JBL 40 (1921), 57—69 there is no evidence that this was the original language, despite the opinion of Nahmanides (c. A.D. 1266) that it was 'written in difficult Aram.' and translated by the Christians. A fragment in Gr. was found at Khirbet Murd, but the Judean Desert has yielded none in Heb.
Date—The type of Jewish learning and the use of Gr. **c** and oriental literature exhibited by Wis are a mark of the 2nd and 1st cent. B.C. Characteristic of this classical period is Philo (c. 25 B.C. to A.D. 40). Certain indications help in determining the actual time when Wis was written. The author used LXX not HT; so the upper limit is c. 300 B.C. when translation of LXX was begun. He was also unacquainted with Philo, hence the lower limit is c. 40 B.C. This means that Wis must have been written for the consolation of the Jews during the persecutions under Ptolemy VII (145—17 B.C.) and Ptolemy VIII Physcon (or Euergetes II, 117—81 B.C.); cf 2 Mc 1. M. Hadas, in IDB 4, 862—3 suggests the Palestinian Heb. section was written during the reign of Alexander Janneus (103—76 B.C.), perhaps by a pietist group like the one at Qumran. This would explain the violent attack on Epicureanism 2:1.4—6. The Gr. section would then date to c. 30 B.C. when the Romans began to rule Egypt and deprived the Jews of their privileges. Dulière (see commentary on 14:12ff) maintains that at least the vv which seem to refer to Christ's passion (if not the whole book) were written after the death of Christ. It is significant that Wis is first mentioned in the Muratorian Canon (A.D. 180, see § 16*a*) among *Christian* writings. Also, no NT writer quotes Wis explicitly and the book was not accepted by the Jews. A further argument is the apparent reference to Hadrian's favourite, Antinous (died A.D. 130) in

531

432c 14:12ff. The vocabulary reflects that current in the 1st and 2nd cent. A.D. which explains why it seems out of place if Wis is dated earlier. However, though Dulière's reasoning is cogent, his views seem a little extravagant.

d Place of origin—Wis appears to have been written in Alexandria; even if chh 1–10 are admitted to be Palestinian, they were translated in this great sea-port on the NW coast of the Nile Delta. The evidence pointing to Alexandria is indirect, but strong. The largest number of diaspora Jews lived there, and it was at this great seat of learning, with its 'Museum' and its enormous library, that Jews were able to receive a classical Gr. education. Moreover, in Alexandria the LXX version was made (see § 26a). Finally, the author selected themes related to Egypt: the Exodus and idolatry (in Alexandria were sited the temple to Sarapis, and later one of the many statues to Antinous).

e Literary Form—Focke considered Wis to be a sustained 'syncrisis' or comparison. But most commentators identify the literary form as midrash, or a homily which includes midrash. Midrash is the reinterpretation of the past for contemporaries, a composition which glosses Scripture for instruction or edification. (see § 357h). Though classified among the five OT books of wisdom, Wis is different from them in form and temper. It does not consist of brief gnomic sayings (as e.g. in Prov), but is written in a flowing varied style. 4 Macc (see § 89k) is the work most like Wis: both are examples of late Gr. literature where Hellenic and Heb. elements have been combined; both use the form of a spoken discourse, though Wis interrupts with prayers, historical summaries and definitions. The style in these two books alternates between exposition and enthusiasm; the literary devices used are borrowed from the rhetoricians: alliteration, antithesis, assonance, definition, digression, recapitulation, sorites, syncrisis and synthesis. Unlike 4 Mc, which has throughout the form of a homily, Wis resembles the Cynic-Stoic diatribe. The motivation is exclusively religious, as in other apocrypha: any non-religious material is given a religious application. The audience was mixed consisting of Jews and Gentiles. For the Jews Wis offered consolation during their persecution; for the Gr. a cultured presentation of the Jewish religion in their own terms and language. Cf M. Hadas, loc cit 861.

f Unity and plan—According to Purinton the criterion for unity of authorship is the original language. But it is generally agreed that the book had only one author. This is true even if the first ten chh were once in Heb.: they were translated by the author and incorporated in his work. The style is consistent throughout and theme words are used to connect widely separated sections. A further indication of there only being one author is the wrong sense given to *metalleuein* in 4:12 and 16:25.

g There is no unanimity among scholars regarding the structure of Wis. Sixteen divisions are outlined by R. H. Pfeiffer, *History of NT Times*, 1949, 321f. The best way to gain an understanding of this book is to recover the plan envisioned by the author. This can be done not only by analysing the thought but also from a study of objective indications in the text itself. Thus the common division of Wis into 1–9 and 10–19 preserves the unity of the review of Israel's history in the last ten chh. However there is an abrupt change at 11:2; the subject is no longer wisdom but the Israelites ('they'), and a new theme is introduced (11:5) which continues till 19:5. This argues against 10–19 being a unit; the division is rather 1:1–11:1 and 11:2–19:22. This analysis is confirmed by the number of stichoi: there are

560 in each part (the last two of 19:22 form an inde- **433** pendent conclusion to the book). See A. G. Wright, 'The Structure of Wisdom 11–19', CBQ 27 (1965), 28–29. For the stichometric analysis see P. W. Skehan, 'The Text and Structure of the Book of Wisdom', *Traditio* 3 (1945), 1–12. These articles and the following: P. Beauchamp, 'Le salut corporel des justes et la conclusion du livre de la Sagesse', Bib 45 (1964), 491–526; J. W. Reese, 'Plan and Structure in the Book of Wisdom', CBQ 27 (1965), 391–9; form the basis for this plan:

Part I The Book of Eschatology 1:1–6:11, 17–21— **h** **A.** Exhortation to practise justice: 1:1–15; **B.** Statement of the wicked before being judged; denial of this view: 1:16–2:24; **C.** The triumph of just men stated and illustrated: 3:1–5:1 (Two digressions: 3:10–12; 4:10–14b); **B'.** Statement of the wicked after their judgement; refutation of this: 5:2–23; **A'.** Second exhortation to acquire wisdom and so reign for ever 6:1–11, 17–21.

Part II Description of Divine Wisdom 6:12–16, i 22–11:1—**A.** Wisdom is found by those who look for it: 6:12–16; **B.** Proposal to describe wisdom: 6:22–25; **C.** Solomon's example: 7:1–7; **D.** His honour of wisdom: 7:8–14; **E.** Prayer for guidance in describing wisdom: 7, 15–21; **F.** Wisdom described: 7:22–8:1; **G.** The fruits of wisdom: 8:2–8; **H.** Royal wisdom: 8:9–16; **I.** Resolve to pray for wisdom: 8:17–21; **J.** Prayer for wisdom: 9:1–18; **K.** Wisdom protected just men: 10:1–14; **L.** Wisdom protected a just people: 10:15–11:1.

Part III Midrash on Pericope from Exodus- j Account 11:2–19:4—**A.** Introductory narrative: 11:2–4; **B.** Observation on text: 11:5; **C.** First illustration of this: 11:6–14; **D.** Second illustration (a) 11:15–16; (digression: 11:17–12:22); (b) 12:23–27; (digression: idolatry: 13:1–15:17); (c) 15:18–16:4; (digression: 16:5–14); **E.** Third illustration 16:15–29; **F.** Fourth illustration 17:1–18:4; **G.** Fifth illustration 18:5–19; (digression: 18:20–25).

Part IV The New Creation 19:5–21—**A.** Title: 19:5; **k** **B.** New reformed creation to keep God's children safe: 19:6–12; **C.** Egyptians and Sodomites punished by blindness: 19:13–17; **D.** New relation between creatures: 19:18–21.

Conclusion: Doxology: 19:22.

Wis and Greek Culture—This book, written in Gr. **433** in one of the greatest of the hellenistic cities was evidently intended to be read by Greeks as well as by Jews. Not surprisingly Gr. influence is obvious throughout the work. But this must not be exaggerated. Some of the innovations turn out on closer examination to be the development of ideas deep-rooted in the OT (e.g. immortality, conscience). Also, the gulf between Semitic and Aegean cultures is not so wide: 'Greek and Hebrew civilizations are parallel structures built upon the same E Mediterranean foundation' (C. H. Gordon, *Before the Bible*, 1962, 9). However, Heb. thought is clothed in Gr. dress in Wis and both thought and style have benefited. The writer knew the teaching of Plato, the Stoics and possibly Pythagoras; he had read (or heard recited) works of Homer, the tragedians and perhaps Xenophon. S. Lange (loc cit 293) calls him *anima naturaliter platonica*, but the Sage was more likely an ordinary educated Jew. Being a Jew he used midrashic techniques and of course the OT. However, it is not accepted by all that he had only the LXX to work from; there are indications that he also consulted the HT.

Influence on NT—Of the NT writers, Paul and John **b** seem to have drawn on Wis the most. Paul uses or develops ideas first set out in Wis: God can be proved to

b exist from his creation (Wis 13:3—5; Rm 1:18—20), is forbearing (Wis 11:23 etc; Rm 2:4), all-powerful (Wis 12:12; Rm 9:20). Christ is the image (Wis 7:26; Col 1:15) and glory (Wis 7:26; Heb 1:3) of the Father and 'the wisdom of God' (1 Cor 1:24.30). The images of the potter (Wis 15:7) and armour (Wis 5:17—20) have been borrowed in Rm 9.21 and Eph 6:14—17. Similarly John's theology of the Word adapts passages such as Wis 8:3—4.6; 9:1.4.9; 11:24. The view of life and death in Wis is very like that in John: the basis of Life is communion with God (or Christ) and this true Life is not destroyed by death; Death entered the world because of the devil, but has only restricted sway over the earth. Man is free to choose between Life and Death and so become a child of God or the devil. Both present faith as an absolute trust in God's word, though they differ somewhat in terminology. Wis, one of the last books of the OT is a link between the Testaments. Much of it is used in the liturgy. Cf G. Ziener, 'Weisheitsbuch und Johannesevangelium', Bib 38 (1957), 396—418; 39 (1958), 37—60.

c Doctrine—Wis is outstanding in the OT for its depth of doctrine, yet the author is no theologian nor even a philosopher. His aim is to encourage his readers to seek wisdom and so gain eternal life. Man faces the dilemma of life or death: the stress is on individual responsibility. **God** for Wis is the traditional God of Israel, but with an insistence on certain of his attributes. He is infinitely wise (11:20) and a just judge who fits the punishment to the crime (10:15—18). God cannot be capricious or violent but is ordered and unostentatious in his acts. He loves all creation, and governs 'with great forbearance' (12:18), with pity for all, overlooking 'men's sins that they may repent' (11:23). He even tries to win sinners back, punishing them by a gradual process 'granting them time and opportunity to give up their wickedness' (12:20). Full punishment is reserved for the obstinate in sin. The author is acquainted with the **fall** (10.1—2, 2:24). But in spite of his fall, man retains his pre-eminence among creatures. He is destined to life eternal (2:23) which sets him apart from them and is the effect of his dignity as image of God. This incorruptibility is already possessed by man, and retained by observing the laws of wisdom (6:18). To accept wisdom's offer (6:16) is to win immortality close to God **d** (6:19—20). However there is no mention of bodily resurrection; the reward of the righteous is only vaguely described as immortality (3:4) and eternal life (5:15). In fact this eternal happiness is described as spiritual only: grace and familiarity with God, knowledge of truth and peace in God's kingdom. **Death** is the lot of the unjust (1:16), appearing almost as a personal power surrounded by his retinue. It is neither dissolution of the body, nor even sin (a deliberate act separating man and God), but the futile existence of the sinner. It is the result of lies (1:11), of idolatry (14:12) and in general of bad conduct (1:12). This punishment of the sinner begins in this life and is not reserved to the eschatological phase.

e The **personification of Wisdom** goes very far. Wisdom like God is intelligent, all-powerful and unchangeable (7:22—27). Capable of all God can do, Wisdom was his counsellor at creation (8:4), fashioning everything (7:22), able to do all things (7:27), to see (9:11), penetrate (7:24) and govern them (8:1). Wisdom also instructs (8:7; 9:11), guides (9:11; 10:10f), protects (9:11) and assists (9:10) men, living with them like a wife (7:28; 8:2.9). Wisdom however appears distinct from God 'for she is a breath of the power of God, and a pure emanation

of the power of the Almighty' (7:25), occupies a throne **433e** at his side (9:4) and enhances her noble birth by being as close to him as a bride (8:3). 8:3 shows that this description of wisdom is meant metaphorically; she is no consort goddess of God. Also elements of the description are contradictory if taken literally. How could wisdom, the bride of God, become wife to man as well? Wisdom has prudence to an eminent degree (8:6), but is not divine on that account. True, wisdom is personified more boldly than in Prv or Sir, and even identified with the divine spirit (1:4—6; 7:22—24; 9:17). However 'the holy spirit' is no more a real person than in earlier books of the OT. The author is writing to glorify wisdom and reveal to his readers the divine origin of the wisdom he professes (6:22). He is not speculating on the internal life of God: his aim is practical. In the context, as in other wisdom books, this presentation is mere personification. True, wisdom is of divine origin, because God's gift (7:7b; 8:21; 9:17). Divine wisdom appeared in the world God created and is communicated to wise men—so it is represented as detachable from God and capable of acting outside him. Ultimately, this is a literary device; wisdom is no hypostasis. For the contrary view see H. Ringgren, *Word and Wisdom*, Lund 1947.

Part I 1—6, 11, 17—21 The Book of Eschatology 434a The 5 sections of this part are arranged chiastically: A B C B' A', with 'C' as the central section (Reese). 1:14 also corresponds to 5:17.20 (Beauchamp). For Mariès (RB 5, 25—27) 1, 1—3.12; 3, 13—6, 11 and 6, 12—9, 17 are three poems with a structure like that in the Aeschylus. See also § 432h.

A 1:1—15 Exhortation to Practice Justice—This **b** may be an exordium to the book. **1.** 'righteousness' *dikaiosunē*: the rulers of the earth are addressed in their capacity as judges; see note on 6:21 for the connection between kingship and wisdom. Judges, to be righteous, must practice equity (9:3). The Egyptian goddess of wisdom, Isis (who replaced Thoth) is given the name 'Righteousness' in a contemporary inscription. 'simplicity of heart': sincerity, cf 5. **2.** To tempt God is to challenge him defiantly, to question his words and his ways (Nm 14:22; Ac 5, 9) and God himself forbade this (Dt 6, 16). The Lord will meet the needs of those who wait for him with patience (Lam 3, 25f; Phil 4, 19). See note on 2:24. **3.** 'his power': on the basis of 5:23 JB renders 'Omnipotence'. But the LXX and NT equivalent of Heb *šadday*, 'Almighty (God)' is *pantocratōr*, not *hē dunamis* as here. 'Power' is identified as God the Father in Mt 26:64; Mk 14:62; but as Christ in 1 Cor 1:24. 'convicts the foolish': the fool does not deny that God exists but that he is too aloof, ensconced in heaven on his holy throne (cf Ps 11 (10):4) to intervene in judgement of the wicked. See Ps 10 (9) and the wisdom psalm 14 (13):1. **4.** an indirect expression of the author's doctrine of individual responsibility. **6.** 'Wisdom' is here identified with God. 'his inmost feelings', lit 'kidneys', the seat of man's emotions as expressive of his moral life. In the OT 'kidneys' and 'heart' are associated as constituting the innermost sanctuary of man's personality; God is able to examine even these and know man's deepest secrets: Ps 7:9; 26 (25):2; Jer 11:20; 17:10; 20:12; cf Apoc 2:23. The phrase 'kidneys and heart' is ancient and perhaps of Canaanite origin as it occurs in a text from Ras Shamra. **8.** 'Justice' is personified, **c** an effect perhaps of Egyptian (cf note on 1:1) or Gr. influence. **10.** 'a jealous ear', an image of God's omniscience; cf 5:17; the OT teaching of God as zealously protective of his covenant-people is here somewhat weakened. Herodotus (*Histories* 3, 40) relates that

434c Amasis informed Polycrates that 'the Deity is jealous of success'. **13—15.** The sequence of ideas, as in 15:2—3 is (a) God's might in creation is affirmed; (b) the *Basileion* of Sheol (i.e. death) in the world is denied; (c) justice is affirmed to be immortal. '*Basileion*' is either 'diadem' (cf 5:16), 'dominion' or even 'palace'. The equation of Hades with a personified death in this context finds its rationale in the allusion to Is 28:15, 18 (LXX); cf P. Skehan, CBQ 24 (1962), 438. Wis never says that man is immortal (unless 'justice' is an abstract for the concrete 'just men'), but that he acquires immortality; see 3:4; 4:1; 8:13; 15:3. Immortality (cf on 2:24) is God's gift to men.

d **B 1:16—2:24 Statement of the Wicked before being judged; denial of this view—1:16.** 'But ungodly men by their words and deeds summoned death': for 'death' the Gr. has a pronoun which RSV considers as referring to an unexpressed *thanatos* ('death'). It is more logical and less hypothetical to refer the pronoun back to 'Hades' in 14*d*, especially as Hades is personified; but the sense is the same. 'a covenant' *suntheken*; Is 28:15 (LXX) reads 'We made a covenant (*diatheken*) with Hades (HT *māwet*) and pacts (*suntheken*) with Death (HT *še'ôl*)'. 'ungodly men' are either renegade Jews or possibly the Epicureans; cf A. Dupont-Sommer, 'Les "impies" du Livre de la Sagesse sont-ils des Épicuriens?', RHR 111 (1935), 90—109. **2:1.** Cf Jb 10:20; 14:1—2. 'to themselves' i.e. to each other (cf 6). 'life is short', a pessimistic view of life common to the OT (Gn 47:9; Ps 39 (38):5—7; Jb 7:1, 17, 21; Eccl 2:23) and Gr. literature (e.g. Sophocles). 'no one has been known to return from Hades': (cf v 5); the name for the Underworld (cf 1, 14) in Mesopotamia was 'the land of no return'. Others translate this v 'no one . . . can give release from Hades'. **2.** For 'smoke' as an image of the ephemeral see Ps 37 (36):20. 'More quickly than smoke shall they (the wicked) vanish'; 102 (101):3 'For my days are more transitory than smoke' (version of M. Dahood, AB vol. 16, 226 and 230). 'heart' considered the centre, the seat of intellectual activities by the Hebrews (over 200 times in OT) and the Gr. (Heraclitus, Aristotle, the Stoics and Epicureans). **3.** The traditional OT view was more complex: at death man resolved into his components, body (*bāsār*), vegetative soul (*nepeš*) and spiritual soul (*rûªh*). The vegetative soul remained near the corpse and had to be nourished; cf Gn 15, 2 '*I (Abram) am dying childless, and the libationer of my tomb is Eliezer of Damascus*' (version based on F. Vattioni, *Rivista degli Studi Orientali* 40 (1965), 9—12). **4.** 'shadow' used here in its Heb., not Gr., sense of transience; cf Jb 8:9; Ps 109 (108):23. **10.** Cf M. J. Suggs, 'Wisdom of Solomon 2, 10—5: A Homily based on the Fourth Servant Song', JBL 76 (1957), 26—33.

e **12—20 The just man tortured and condemned to death**—This is the first half of a diptych portraying the just man; for the other half see 5:1—7. M. Philonenko, TZ 14 (1958), 81—88 considers this a description of the Teacher of Righteousness, as known from the MSS of the Judean desert, especially the Hodayoth **12.** 'Let us . . . inconvenient to us' is borrowed from Is 3:10 (LXX); cf Ps 10 (9):8—9; IQpHab 1, 13: '(the righteous) is the Teacher of Righteousness'. In general, 'righteous man' labels a member of a religious or political party opposed to the ungodly party. **13a.** The Teacher was one 'to whom God made known all the mysteries of the words of his servants the prophets' (IQpHab 7, 4). A Revealer of Gnosis, he called himself 'a discerning interpreter of wonderful mysteries' (IQH 2, 13). **b.** 'child of the Lord' alludes to the Suffering Servant: cf 'Thou (God)

hast favoured me, thy servant, with a spirit of knowledge' (IQH 14, 23). **16.** 'he boasts that God is his father', as did the Teacher: 'Until I am old thou wilt care for me; for my father knew me not, and my mother abandoned me to thee, for thou art a father to all (the sons) of thy truth' (IQH 9, 35); cf Ps 27 (26):10. **17ff.** suggest the author actually knew 'the just man'. **19.** cf Is 50:6; 53:7. **20.** Cf Is 53:8 'he was cut off out of the land of the living'. 'a shameful death': scholars disagree whether the Teacher was crucified or not. 'he will be protected' lit. 'there will be his visitation'. Hope in divine visitation (Heb. *pqwdh*) is a common theme in the Qumran scrolls, but neither Wis nor the Hodayoth know vicarious suffering (cf Is 53:5). **23a.** is diametrically opposed to the **f** Mesopotamian belief as expressed in e.g. the Epic of Gilgamesh: 'O Gilgamesh, why wander so everywhere? You will never attain the life you are looking for; when the gods created man, they put mortality on mankind and kept immortality (balātam) for themselves' (Tablet M, col. 3, 2—5). **b.** 'in the image of his own *eternity*' according to the Syro-Hexaplar, possibly the original reading in the opinion of J.-M. Vosté, 'La Version Syro-Hexaplaire de la Sagesse', Bib 30 (1949), 213—7. LXX (A, B, S) has 'nature'. **24a.** 'but through the devil's envy death entered into the world'. The devil, in Heb. usually 'the Satan' (with the definite article), appears as an accuser in Zech 3:1—2 and was considered a member of the court of heaven, always roaming the earth, spying on men to accuse them to God. If his victims were innocent he would goad them to sin; e.g. 1 Chr 21, 1 'Satan stood up against Israel, and incited David to number Israel', and the prologue to Job. 'death' here is opposed to 'incorruptibility' and refers to the penalty incurred by Adam (Gn 2:7). It is not simply the decease of the body but death in an ethical sense, the "second death" of Apoc 2:11. Cf W. H. Learoyd, 'The Envy of the Devil in Wisdom 2:24', ET 51 (1939—40), 395—6. **24b.** There are two possible translations: (i) 'and those who belong to the former's (the devil's) faction tempt it (i.e. the world)', meaning that Satan and his angels tempted the first man, and continue to tempt all men. This depicts the master Spy and his agents roving through the world provoking the downfall of men, depriving them of salvation itself. For the meaning 'put to the test' of *peirazein*, see H. Cazelles, VT 9 (1959), 214. Cf A. M. Dubarle, 'La tentation diabolique dans le livre de la Sagesse (2, 24)', Me E. Tisserant, I, 1964. 187—95. (ii) 'and those who belong to his (Satan's) party experience it (i.e. death)'. This contrasts the punishment of wicked men who follow the devil with the reward of the just who 'are in the hand of God' (3:1) and 'at peace' (3:3). The Heb. verb *nāsāh*, which may lie behind the Gr., can signify either 'to have experience of' or 'to put to the test'. For Paul's use of this v in Rm 5, 12 see S. Lyonnet, 'Péché', DBS 7, 535ff.

C 3:1—5:1 The Triumph of just men stated and g illustrated—This central section has 100 stichs. The phrase 'unharmed just man' in both 3:1 and 5:1 forms the inclusion.

3:1—9 The Just Man—1. 'in the hand of God' is a **h** characteristic expression of the Egyptian sage Amenemopet; in the OT it signifies God's special protection: 5:16; Dt 33:3. The souls of the just will be near God, 4:10. **2.** 'foolish' see note on 1:3*b*. **4.** 'immortality' in the OT was considered as a return to life (a belief influenced by Canaanite religion) in expression of retribution and as a consequence of Yahweh extending his reign over the whole earth. Others viewed immortality as communion with Yahweh; see Ps 16 (15); 17 (18). Cf E. Jacob,

34h 'Immortality', IDB 2, 688—90. The nearest equivalent to *anthanasia* in HT is *'al-māwet*, 'immortality', already appearing in Prv 12:28 (cf M. Dahood, Bib 41 (1960), 176—81). Other, more positive terms denoting eternal life are *nᵉp̄āšōt 'aḥarit* and *ḥayyim*; see M. Dahood, AB I, xxxvi. 4.78.91.183.221ff.303. The idea of immortality is no new idea imported from 1st cent. Gr. philosophy; the borrowing may well have been in the opposite direction. **6.** 'like gold . . .' a common simile in the OT: Ps 26 (25):2; Prv 17:3; Jb 23:10 etc. **7.** 'the time of their visitation' i.e. of recompense in the other world (Jer 6:15) when Yahweh will judge and reward men. 'they will shine forth': this is a theme common to Jewish apocalyptic, e.g. '(Just men) will be seven times as brilliant as the sun' (II Henoch 66, 7); cf Dan 12:3. As it stands **7b** makes no sense. A Dupont-Sommer, 'De l'immortalité astrale dans la *Sagesse de Solomon* (III 7)', *Revue des Études Grecs* 62 (1949), 80—87 suggests that *kalamēi* ('stubble') is a corruption of an original *galaxīei* ('milky way'). This is supported by the parallelism between *7a* and *7b*, and the fact that *diatrechein*, here translated 'run', is a technical term for the coursing of stars. Cf 5:5; 7:28—29; Mt 13:43. The idea is neo-Pythagorean.

i 10—13a Digression anticipating talion of 11:5—10. On vv 1—10 see M. Delcor, 'L'immortalité de l'âme dans le livre de la Sagesse et dans les documents de Qumrân', NRT 77 (1955), 614—30. The MSS of Qumran acted as a 'catalyst' to the mystical trend of some psalms (cf on 3:4).

j 13b—19 1st Type: The Barren but unsoiled—This is the first of three types which illustrate the triumph of the just. **13bc.** 'the barren woman': barrenness for a woman was a dishonour, cf Gn 30:23. But there were exceptions e.g. Is 54:1 and the privileged *naditu*-women of Babylonia. **14.** 'the eunuch' i.e. the castrated (the primary meaning 'court-officer' is not intended here) who was excluded from the assembly of the Lord, Dt 23:1. But see Is 56:3—5; Mt 19:12. The sect of the Essenes practised celibacy.

k 4:1—6 2nd Type: The Childless but Virtuous—Specially relevant is 2 Sam 18:18 'Absalom in his lifetime had taken and set up for himself the pillar which is in the King's Valley, for he said, "I have no son to keep my name in remembrance"; he called the pillar after his own name, and it is called Absalom's Pillar to this day' (cf § 281d). **1.** The style is semi-proverbial. Cf Sir 16:3 and Plato, *Symposium* 209 A: 'For there are those . . . who are pregnant in soul . . . with those things that the soul should bear . . . wisdom and other virtues'. **2.** 'prizes that are undefiled': this acceptance of Gr. sports contrasts with the attitude in Palestine; cf 1 Mc 1:14—15. Paul also compares the struggle of Christians with the athlete competing in the games, 1 Cor 9:24—27 etc; cf Heb 12:1. The winner received a crown of olive, pine, laurel or parsley and was given a procession of honour by the citizens; cf 2 Tm 4:8; Jas 1:12; 1 Pt 5:4; Apoc 3:11.

l 7—9 3rd Type: The Just Man who dies young—For the first time in the OT a solution to this problem appears. **7.** 'at rest' cf 3:3. **8—9.** The association of wisdom and old age is attested in the texts from Ras Shamra: the god El, described as 'the father of years', is a basis for comparison in the Keret Legend: 'You are as wise as El'. In the Baal Epic the god is addressed thus: 'You are many years old, O El, and truly wise, the greyness of your beard has certainly instructed you'. But Job, like Wis, denies this: 'It is not the aged who are wise, nor the elders who understand what is right'

(32:9 as translated by M. Dahood, BibOr 17 (1965) **434l** 71).

10—14 Digression: Henoch—This historical example **m** anticipates the use of history in Part III. Henoch 'walked with God. Then he vanished because God took him' (Gn 5:24, JB) i.e. was assumed bodily into heaven. He is the exception in the P list of ten descendants of Cain who are said to have had extraordinarily long lives.

15—5:1 The Triumph of the Just—**15.** See Is 57:1. **n 17.** Again a reference to Henoch who came 7th in the list, corresponding to the 7th member of the Sumerian King List (considered the model for Gn 5) regarded as possessing special wisdom. **18.** 'The Lord will laugh them to scorn' for he sees their day of punishment coming; cf Ps 37 (36):13. 'dishonoured corpses' because unburied, the worst punishment possible: 1 (3) Kgs 13, 21—22; even an executed criminal had a distinguished grave: Jos 7, 26. **5:1.** Cf 2:12. On the last day 'the righteous man will stand' in front of his oppressors. IQH 4, 22 depicts a similar scene: 'I will stand, I will rise against those who despise me and my hand shall be turned against those who deride me'.

B' 5:2—23 Statement of the Wicked after their o Judgement—**2.** 'they will be amazed . . .' cf Is 52:14. **4.** 'byword' corresponding to the Heb. for 'taunt (-song)'; most examples in the OT are of anticipatory derision, but Tb 3:4 refers to the past: 'thou madest us a byword of reproach in all the nations', using *parabotēn oneidismou* (B, A) exactly as here. The vocabulary is further reminiscent of Is 53. Cf IQH 2, 23—24. 'They made me an object of shame and derision in the mouth of all the seekers of falsehood'. **5.** At Qumran the beatitude of the just is portrayed as an association with or an assimilation to the angels. This is clearly stated in IQS 11, 7—8: 'And those whom God has chosen, he has made an eternal possession, and has given them an inheritance in the lot of the holy ones and has joined their company to the sons of heaven in a community council and in a mysterious holy building, an eternal planting for all future ages'. Wis 5:5 is explained in 15—16 in terms of everlasting life and participation in God's kingdom; cf 3:14—15; 9:8—9, 16; 18:15—16, 24—25. 5:5 'explains the reward of the just after death in terms of an assimilation to the angelic life; and . . . this analogy, rather than the alternatives of the native immortality of the soul or a promised resurrection, is the formal element in his (the author's) inspired reflections on the subject': P. W. Skehan, CBQ 21 (1959), 527, cf 3:7. **6.** 'strayed', 'path' allude to Is 53:6. The **p** Teacher of Righteousness was called both the royal road leading to truth and the sun of Justice. See Nm 24:17; Mal 4:2; Testament of Juda 24, 1: 'a star will rise on you, and a man like the sun of justice will appear'. The sun-god was the god of justice, e.g. Shamash in Mesopotamia. **8—14.** Cf F. Romero, 'Como la sombra . . . (Sap 5, 8—14)', *Cultura Bíblica* 2 (1948), 248—52. **9a.** Cf 2:5; **9b—11.** Consecutive lines borrow from two consecutive lines of Jb (9:25—26). **14.** Cf Ps 35 (34):5—6. **16.** Cf 1:14. For 'crown' as a metaphor for glory see Jb 19:9; Is 28:5; Jer 13, 18; Prv 4:9. **18.** Cf Is 59:17; this imagery appears in Ps 7 and in St Paul. **22.** 'catapults' are described in 2 Chr 26, 15.

A' 6:1—11, 17—21 Second exhortation to acquire q wisdom—**1.** The theme 'wisdom' is only developed in the section 6:1—11 according to Dulière. 'listen', a call characteristic of wisdom literature; cf on 1:1. 'kings' forms an inclusion with 'you may reign' 6, 21. **3.** 'the Most High', in Heb. *'el 'elyôn*, the title of God as worshipped by Melchizedek, who called him 'maker of heaven

434q and earth' (Gn 14:19). The complete title appears to have been 'the Lord God Most High' (14:22 on the lips of Abram), here split up in the parallel stichoi (3*a*: 'the Lord'; 3*b*: 'the Most High'), a poetic device borrowed from OT poetry. Cf E. Z. Melamed, 'Breakup of Stereotype Phrases' in C. Rabin, ed., *Studies in the Bible*, 1961, 115–63. **4–5.** A similar idea comes in Ps 82 (81). **6.** 'pardoned in mercy': forgiveness by God is not indiscriminate and is only possible because he is a God of grace; cf Neh 9:17 'thou art a God ready to forgive, gracious and merciful'. **7.** God is impartial with his creatures: Dt 10:17; Prv 22:2; Acs 10:34–35. For **12–16** see below. **17–20.** An appendix to Part I. It is in the form of a sorites, a series of linked propositions making up a syllogism. **21.** For the concept of royal wisdom, i.e. a wisdom to govern and judge one's subjects with justice, see N. W. Porteous, 'Royal Wisdom', VTS 3 (1960), 247–61. The idea runs through Egyptian, Mesopotamian, Canaanite and Gr. literature.

435a Part II 6:12–16; 6:22–11:1 Description of Divine Wisdom—This part describes divine Wisdom, through which God communicates his reward to men. Only in these chh is wisdom personified.

b A 6:12–16 Wisdom is found by those who look for it—**14.** 'he who rises early' cf 2 Sm 15 and note on Wis 16:28. 'his gates' i.e. the gates of his city (Prv 1:21). The city gate was the place of commerce and law; the judge gave his decisions there. Most cities had more than one gate. **15.** Cf 7:11. **16.** Very similar is the dream of love in Song 3:1–5; cf 5:6–8 etc. But the borrowing may more likely be from Prv 1:20f; 8:2–3.

B 22–25 Proposal to describe wisdom—**22.** Jb 28:20–28 also describes Wisdom as inaccessible. **24.** Cf Prv 11:14: 'Where there is no guidance, a people falls; but in an abundance of counsellors there is safety'; and 15:22; 24:6.

c C 7:1–7 Solomon's example—**1.** This is like the egalitarian ideal insisted upon in 1QS (Hadas). Cf Sir 17:1. **2–3.** Cf 2 Esdras 4:20; 2 Mc 7:27; Jb 10:10–11. **4.** A reference perhaps to a work by Aeschylus. **7.** Ashurbanipal made a similar claim: the god Nabu gave him wisdom and he learned to read and write; cf R. B. Y. Scott, 'Solomon and the beginnings of wisdom in Israel', VTS 3 (1960), 262–79.

D 8–14 His honour of wisdom—**8.** 'sceptres', 'thrones' are grammatically plural, but logically in the singular. **14.** 'unfailing treasure', cf Lk 12:33.

d E 15–21 Prayer for guidance in describing wisdom—**15a.** Is variously translated 'May God grant me to speak as he would wish' (JB); 'according to the knowledge (that I have)' and 'as I desire it'. *d* or 'since he directs sages' (JB). **16.** Cf 3:1. **17.** 'elements'. *stoicheios* lit means 'standing in a row', 'an element in a series'; here the component parts of physical bodies. The Stoics called earth, water, air and fire the 'four elements'; the use of this term for the stars and planets however, is Christian and not earlier than A.D. 150. **20b.** An Assyrian medical text lists plants with the corresponding disease (which the plant cures) and the proper method of application and preparation in three parallel columns. In ancient times magic and medicine were not always separate disciplines, except in Israel, to a certain extent. For the respect due to a medical expert see Sir 38:1–15. **21.** An alternative reading for Dt 29:29 involves the omission of 'to the Lord your God'; this gives the early variant (of this v) 'The secret things, and the things that are revealed, belong to us and to our children forever'. The source is 4 Esdras 14, 26.45.46. (P. Skehan). 'fashioner (cf 8:6; 14:2) of all things' as God's guide

(8:4) and assistant (Prv 8:22–31; Wis 9:9). The assertion in 13:1 that God is the craftsman of all things shows the personification of wisdom here to be a literary device (see § 433e).

F 7:22–8:, 1 Wisdom described—22–24. The use **e** of 21 (a multiple of the perfect numbers 7 and 3) attributes to describe wisdom is influenced perhaps by *c*. fragment of the Stoic Cleanthes which gives God 26 epithets. Comparable also are the Jewish prayer Shema, with 16 attributes for the divine word, and the 50 names of Marduk in the Epic of Creation. The terms used here are evidently borrowed from Gr. philosophical language, but the thought remains pure monotheism. **22.** Alternatively 'she is within herself'. After this clause the adjectives come in groups of 3 to a line, the last three occupying each one line. **25.** Cf Ahiqar 94–95: 'to gods also she is dear. F[or all time] the kingdom is [hers]. In he[av]en is she established, for the Lord of holy ones has exalted her', cf ANET, 428c. **26.** 'a reflection of the eternal light', construing *apaugasma* as passive and so 'reflection, reflected image'; this would refer to the complete dependence of Wisdom on God. God's glory in the face of Jesus Christ is still to be seen and reflected in the Church (2 Cor 4:3–6). If active in meaning, then 'radiance' is a more suitable rendering, as in Heb. 1:3 and the patristic literature. See also Ps 50 (49):2 'Out of Sion, the perfection of beauty, God shines forth'. 'image': the change in meaning appears here already, as in the NT; it is no longer 'likeness' but 'perfect reflection of the prototype'.

G 8:2–8 The fruits of wisdom—2. Cf Sir 15:2b. **f** Ezek 28:12 is perhaps relevant '*You* (the king of Tyre) *married the Bride, full of wisdom and of flawless beauty*'; cf 28:27. **3.** The closeness of wisdom and God is symbolized much in the same way as that of Israel and her God by the prophets: Is 62:5; Jer 3:1ff. **7.** 'self-control and prudence, justice and courage' are the four Platonic cardinal virtues; the enumeration here is Stoic. 'virtue' *aretē*, is used in Homer of manly qualities. **8.** Propounding and solving 'riddles' was a valued form of diversion: Jdg 14:12; Ezek 17:2; 1 (3) Kgs 10:1. 'signs and wonders', events considered as the works of God, or as proof of his active presence among his people; this is especially true of the plagues in Egypt: Ex 4:28; Jl 2:30. 'time' (*chronos*) refers to the passing of time; 'season', (*kairos*) is a time of opportunity and decision, in Heb. *zemān*, a fixed, preordained time or period (Eccl 3:1; Dn 2:21). The expression 'seasons and times' is common to Gr. and Heb. idiom, though the latter reflects more the linear view of history, i.e. that times are appointed by God; cf Dt 11:4. Only God knows the outcome of history, Ac 1:7.

H 9–16 Royal wisdom—See note on 6:21. **10.** 'honour **g** in the presence of elders': the elders' way of showing respect is described in Jb 29:8 'the aged rose and stood'; the young men withdraw. Similarly, in the presence of the Suffering Servant 'kings shall see and arise, princes and they shall prostrate themselves' (Is 49:7). **11.** 'keen in judgement' as illustrated by 1 (3) Kgs 3:16–28. **12.** 'put their hands on their mouths' i.e. be silent in admiration; a Semitic gesture; cf Prv 30:32; Sir 5:12; Mi 7:16 etc. **13.** Cf Sir 39:9. **16.** Like the Chronicler the author here passes over Solomon's failings.

I 17–21 Resolve to pray for wisdom—19–20. These **h** vv are reminiscent of passages in the *Timaeus*. **20.** A correction of 19; the soul is more important than the body.

J 9:1–18 Prayer for wisdom—See N. Peters, 'Ein hebräischer alphabetischer Psalm in der Weisheit

5h Salomons Kap. 9', BZ 14 (1916), 1—14. Peters argues that this ch is a translation of an acrostic in Heb. As proof he adduces the following: the 'psalm' contains 23 vv, the number of letters in the Heb. alphabet; it is placed in Solomon's mouth; it fits loosely in the context; the practice of concluding a section with an alphabetic poem is followed in other wisdom books: Prv 31:10ff; Sir 51:13; and finally, this ch is more Heb. in character than the rest of the book. This prayer is based on Solomon's words in 1 (3) Kgs 3, 6—9 [see § 285b] and includes borrowings from the sapiential literature. It contains a theme common to three prayers of Qumran: the contrast between the All-powerful God and weak man. **1.** 'God of my fathers', lit 'God of the Fathers', an abbreviated form of the full title 'The Benefactor of Abraham, the Kinsman of Isaac and the Leader of Jacob'. **5.** 'a handmaid's son' in the Keret Epic is explained as equivalent to a slave or vassal; ANET, 143, n. 7; cf Pss 86 (85):16; 116 (114—15):16.

i K **10:1—14 Wisdom protected just men—1.** 'the first-formed (one)' derives from Gn 2:7; cf 1 Tm 2:13. This is also Philo's designation of Adam. 'father of the world' refers in Gr. literature to the Demiurge as creator (Plato, *Timaeus*) and God the Creator (Philo). Adam is presented as having produced all men. 'when he had been created alone', an echo of Gn 2:18 where 'alone' means 'without a wife' (i.e. Eve) Others interpret this as 'without a protector' (Grimm), but see v 11; or as indicating only Adam was directly created by God (à Lapide). 'delivered': the divine protection of a just man, vv 5, 12, or perhaps the 'nous' of Hermetic literature (9:11, 18). 'his transgression': original sin (cf 2:24); a better translation is 'a special transgression' as *idiou* lacks the article and follows the noun. On 1 Q 000 A. Dupont-Sommer, 'Adam "Père du Monde" dans la Sagesse de Salomon (10, 1—2)', RHR 119 (1939), 182—203. **3.** 'an unrighteous man'. Cain (Gn 4:8—13); 'he perished' see Gn 4:24. **4.** 'because of him' i.e. Cain and his descendants, notably Lamech. 'the righteous man', the same designation of Noah as in Gn 6:9. 'a paltry piece of wood': Noah's ark; cf 14:1—6. **5.** The Tower of Babel story, Gn 11:1—9. 'the righteous man' is Abraham, Gn 12:1—3. **6.** Lot; cf 2 Pt 2:7—8. Lot took refuge in Zoar which was spared, Gn 19:18—22. **10.** Jacob fled from Esau, Gn 27:41—45. **12.** 'his (Jacob's) enemies' were Esau again (Gn 32—33) and Laban (31:23ff). **13.** Joseph.

j L **10:15—11:1 Wisdom protected a just people 15.** According to P. Grelot, 'Sagesse 10, 21 et le Targum de l'Exode', Bib 42 (1961), 49—60, 10:15—19:21 is based on a synagogal commentary on the OT, from Alexandria or Palestine dating to the 1st cent. B.C. **16.** 'a servant of the Lord' i.e. Moses; cf Ex 3:12; 4:12; 7:1. **17.** 'holy men', the Israelites who despoiled the Egyptians of 'jewelry of silver and of gold, and clothing' (Ex 12:35—36) and gained their freedom in return for the years of forced labour. **20—21.** allude to Ex 15:1—21, but 21b seems to come from another source. **21a.** 'the dumb' does not in fact refer to Is 35:6 but is parallel to **21b.** 'babes', whose tongues God had loosened to praise him. The only source, then, of v 21 would be the Targum Yerushalmi (Grelot).

436a **Part III 11:2—19:4 Midrash on Pericope from Exodus-Account**

A 11:2—4 Introductory narrative—A digest of Ex 12:37—17:7 influenced by Ps 107 (106):4—6. According to Ziener the author of parts III—IV used a Passover Haggadah as material. **4.** 'they called upon thee', i.e. God, and no longer Wisdom. These vv, especially 4, form the text of the midrash, or rather homily, that follows.

B 5 Observation on text—'For through the very things **436a** by which their enemies were punished, they themselves received benefit in their need'. This theme is now illustrated by five antithetical diptychs. This v forms an inclusion with 19:4.

C 6—14 First illustration—The Egyptians suffer the **b** plague of the Nile, instead of which the Israelites drink water from a rock. **6.** *anti* 'instead of', occurs five times between 11:6 and 19:5. On first plague, Ex 7:14—25, see § 179d. **11.** 'absent or present', meant literally as in 14:17 where idolaters honour an absent monarch as though present, in statue.

D 11:15—16:14 Second illustration in three parts, **c** interspersed with digressions. (a) **11:15—16 The plague of little animals—15a.** Cf Rm 1:21. *b.* An anachronism: it was only in Graeco-Roman times that the Egyptians worshipped animals, notably the crocodile Sobek. Formerly such temple symbols as the sacred animal had been considered just one of a variety of means whereby a god could manifest himself. The author is referring to customs of his own time. 'irrational serpents' were venerated in Egypt, either because they were harmful or because they were good, like Buto (or Wazit) the ancient serpent-goddess of lower Egypt. Irrational as it might be, the serpent was fabled for its wisdom: Gn 3:1; Mt 10:16. *c.* A conflation of several 'plagues'. **16.** A secondary theme is here introduced, leading to a digression.

11:17—12:22 Digression—God punishes sinners by **d** stages, leaving them time to repent. **17.** Cf Gn 1—2. **18.** A description inspired by the fiery monsters and dragons of mythology; cf Jb 41:10—13. **20a.** 'at a single breath': of the god Marduk it was said 'when he moved his lips, fire blazed forth'. *d.* Cf E. des Places, 'Un emprunt de la "Sagesse" aux "lois" de Platon?', Bib 10 (1959), 1016—1017. 4 Esd and *The Testimony of the Twelve Patriarchs* both use this passage of Wis, and so indirectly a line from Plato's Laws (VI 757b 3—4). **22.** Cf in reverse order, Is 40:15 'Behold the nations are like a drop from a low-hanging cloud, and are accounted as the dust(?) on the scales'; the 'morning dew' of Wis corroborates M. Dahood's translation of *mdl* 'low-hanging cloud' (Me E. Tisserant I, 87). **12:3—22** is a supporting example for the digression: the Canaanites. See D. Gill, 'The Greek Sources of Wisdom XII 3—7', VT 15 (1965), 383—6. He finds in these vv a 'great number of words and phrases reminiscent of the language of Gr. tragedy. A closer analysis reveals further that the terms used here are especially common in those tragedies that deal with stories of child-murder and/or cannibalism: *Medea*, the *Bacchae*, *Heracles Furens*, and the House of Atreus cycle' (p. 384). **5.** 'A cannibal's feast of human flesh, and of blood from the midst (of an altar?). These merciless murderers of children' (Skehan). There is no evidence from other sources that the Canaanites practised cannibalism, but the many references in Babylonian and Assyrian texts show it was a customary last resort in time of famine. An historical inscription notes 'they ate the flesh of their children to ward off their starvation', and a literary work foretells 'there will be such a famine that mother will lock her door against her daughter'. The same motif occurs in a series of treaty-curses; cf D. J. Wiseman, *The Vassal-Treaties of Esarhaddon*, 1958, 61, lines 448—50; 69, lines 547—50. The OT uses a similar threat in Dt 28:53—57 (cf M. Weinfeld, Bib 46, 417ff). **8b.** 'wasp' (*Hymenoptera*: LXX Ex 23:28; Dt 7:20; Jos 24:12) or 'hornet' (*Vespa crabro*), a large colonial wasp with a very powerful, even dangerous, sting; they are common in Syria and

436d Iraq. These insects are only used in the OT in passages where God intervenes on Israel's behalf to drive out the inhabitants of Canaan. **10—11.** Because Ham, 'the father of Canaan', saw him naked when drunk, Noah cursed his grandson Canaan: Gn 9:22—27. **12.** For the idea of God as answerable to no one, see Jb 9:12; 2 Sm 16:10; Eccl 8:4; Dn 4:35. **13.** Monotheism was basic to Israel's faith. All other gods are dead idols, incapable of questioning God's actions. The idea of Yahweh's jealousy (1:10) eventually led to the doctrine of Israel's God as sovereign over all life, history and the universe. **15—18.** God's power is the source of his mercy. **16.** Cf Ps 62 (61):12f; Sir 18:1ff. **18.** Cf 11:20. **22.** 'thou scourgest our enemies ten thousand times more' jars as part of a context describing divine moderation. As in 6:11, 25 'chasten' here means 'to instruct'; but *muriotēti*, 'ten thousand times' is a *hapax totius graecitatis*; further, the formation of this word is strange. Kuhn suggested the original reading was *metriotēti*, 'by measure'. A. Vanhoye, 'Mesure ou Démesure en Sag. XII, 22?' RSR 50 (1962), 530—7 accepts this suggestion, adducing strong proof. He translates 'you give us a lesson when you punish our enemies with moderation'.

e (b) **23—27** continue 11:15f—24*b*. 'and came to regard the vilest, most contemptible animals' (JB). **26—27:** the second phase in God's punishment of enemies, when in cases of obstinacy he inflicts the supreme penalty; for the first stage cf 2, 10, 20. See also 2 Mc 6:12—16. 'experience' i.e. know by experience.

f **13:1—15:17 Digression: Idolatry—13:1.** 'foolish men' corresponds to the Heb. for 'men of idols'. **2.** Worship of sun, moon, stars etc was expressly forbidden the Israelites, Dt 4:19. Ps 19 (18):2—5 hymns the wonder of the heavens as pointing to their creator. 'wind or swift air': the OT states clearly that wind is God's breath (Is 40:7); he controls it (Prv 30:4) having created it (Am 4:13). **3.** Cf Eccl 3:11 'God has made everything beautiful'. **9.** Cf J. Smith, 'De interpretatione Sap xiii 9', VDom 27 (1949), 287—90. **10ff.** Using texts such as Dt 4:28 and Ps 115 (113):4—8 but chiefly the parable of Is 44:13—20 the author apostrophises idolatry. The theme appears in late Jewish writings (Bar 6 and the Sibylline Oracles) as well as in Gr. philosophy. **10.** 'a useless stone, the work of an ancient hand': naturally formed pillars were venerated as gods in Palestine, and in Athens the doorside herms (roughly carved phallic stones) lie at the origin of the cult of Hermes. Cf 'Hermes', E. M. Blaiklock, in *The New Bible Dictionary* (ed. J. D. Douglas), 1965, 520. The belief was that these sacred stones 'fell from the sky'

g (Ac 19:35) and so partook of the divine nature. Cf Hb 2:19. **12.** The idol-maker first satisfies his own hunger before turning the refuse to account; Is 44:16 adds the further detail that he warms himself as well. **14.** 'giving it a coat of red paint and colouring its surface red' or in JB 'smears it with ochre, paints its surface red'. *miltos* is either 'ochre' or 'red lead'; the practice of painting statues of men red and of women yellow favours the JB if the author had male and female deities in mind. Red is a sign of manliness: hirsute Esau was nicknamed Edom, 'The Red' (Gn 25:30; cf v 25) much as Adam was formed from the red earth (*'adamah*). Keret rouged himself in preparation for battle against Negeb. Cf C. H. Gordon, *Before the Bible*, 1962, 136, 168, 231. **15.** 'with iron' i.e. with a large iron nail (smaller ones were made of bronze); for this practice see Is 41:7; Jer 10:4. **18.** 'for health': interest in healing was a mark of Gr. religion. The god of healing was Asclepius, and Pausanias mentions temples dedicated to him at Athens, Epidaurus, North Africa etc. **43** These were the hospitals of the ancient world and attracted pilgrims. 'a prosperous journey' cf **14:1.** Only during the period of Solomon did Israel engage in sea-voyages. At the time of Wis the best sea-lanes were between Egypt and Rome, for grain-ships. **7.** Regarded by some as a Christian interpolation. The Fathers accommodate this passage to the Cross. **12—15.** **h** Athanasius quotes v 12 which he considers a prophecy of the cult of Antinous, instituted by Hadrian (A.D. 117—38). Antinous was Hadrian's 'favourite' in the worst sense (cf v 26) and considered by the Emperor as his son; he sacrificed himself voluntarily for Hadrian (in A.D. 130), who 'consumed with grief at an untimely bereavement, made an image of his *son*', v **15ab.** In fact he gave his dead favourite divine honours (15*c*) and instituted 'secret rites and initiations' (15*d*) under the title of Antinous at Antinoe (on the Nile), Athens, Eleusis and Arcadia. This licentious cult, 'the beginning of fornication' (12*a*), was widely diffused (Dio Cassius records its reaching Egypt) and statues of the deified Antinous erected by command of Hadrian (**16**). The whole passage is possibly a later interpolation, inserted when the cult was still the cause of great indignation; the reference was veiled, however, for fear of reprisals. Further fuel to this were Hadrian's violent suppression of Bar Kochba's revolt (A.D. 132—5) and his subsequent changing of Jerusalem to Aelia Capitolina. Cf W. L. Dulière, 'Antinoüs et le Livre de la Sagesse', *Zeitschrift für Religions-und Geistesgeschichte* 11 (1959), 201—27. **23—24.** Sexual disorders against nature are presented as the punishment of idolatry, and not the reverse; cf Rm 1:24f. **15:1.** asserts God's mercy. **2a.** Here the thought **i** is of simple power: God possesses us even if we sin; cf Jb 10:11—15 (LXX). *b.* true knowledge of God, i.e. commitment, is incompatible with sin. **3a.** From this follows that to know God is to be perfectly righteous (cf 1:15 'righteousness is immortal'). *b.* As a result, our immortality is made possible by our experience of God's power, a power that destroys death. (The same sequence of ideas occurs in 1:13—15.) There are two factors allowing Wis to conclude from God's power to our immortality: (i) the remote OT background which connects death (Sheol) and power; Death is the most powerful of enemies (Jer 9:20; Hos 13:14; Ps 49 (48):16; Dn 3:88) and Death's power is overcome by God's, as attested in the history of salvation. (ii) the context of the whole ch which is a polemic against idols. The idols are dead (see on 12:13) and so powerless; it is Yahweh alone who possesses might. On 1—3 see R. E. Murphy, ' "To Know Your Might is the Root of Immortality" (Wis 15, 3)', CBQ 25 (1963), 88—93. **4.** see on 13:14. **7.** For this satirical portrayal of the origin of clay idols see especially Jer 18:1—12; Rm 9:12. 'laboriously moulds each vessel': the earliest potter's wheel found dates to the 4th millennium B.C., but even after this larger pots were still made by hand. **8.** 'a futile god', see 13:1; 'man who was made of earth', cf Gn 2:7. **10.** repeats the LXX mistranslation of Is 44:20; HT has 'he feeds on ashes'.

(c) **15:18—16:4 The plague of animals and the j quails—15:18.** 'their lack of intelligence': *anoia* means 'folly', but Vg has *insensata* indicating an inanimate thing; cf C. Mohrmann, Vig Ch 6 (1952), 28ff. **16:2.** No mention is made here of the people murmuring (Ex 16:2—8) nor of God's anger (Nm 11:33f); cf Wis 19:12. **3.** 'those men': the Egyptians. 'odious creatures': the frogs of the second plague (cf 19:10), odious because unclean (Lv 11:10, 41), an estimation favoured by the

36j traditional association of the frog with the Egyptian goddess Heqt, who helped women in childbirth. **4.** Cf 11:8–10.

k 16:5–14 Digression—The Israelites in the desert had animals sent against them as a temporary warning. **5.** 'anger, wrath', seems here to have the meaning 'venom, poison' on the basis of the Semitic association of heat, anger and poison; cf LXX Dt 32:4; Ps 58 (57):5. 'Poisonous beasts' would then be parallel to 'writhing serpents' in the next line; cf Is 27:1. The episode here described is that of the fiery serpents, Nm 21:4–9. 'thy wrath did not continue to the end' due to Moses' intercession; nonetheless 'many people of Israel died' (Nm 21:6). **6–8.** The 'token of deliverance' was the bronze serpent (Nm 21:9). Wis carefully explains the symbolism of this action, **7.** 'of all', the same universalism as in 1:13f; 11:23–26; cf Jn 3:14–17. **9.** 'locusts and flies' refers to the eighth and sixth plagues (Ex 10:1–20; 9:8–12). The flies of the fourth plague (probably the Tabanid fly *Stomoxys calcitrans*) were the cause of the 'boils breaking out in sores', i.e. skin anthrax; this disease affects the hands and feet (9:11). 'locusts' attack man only indirectly by destroying his crops. Pliny (*Natural History* 8, 43) mentions that according to Varro a whole African tribe was put to flight by them. **11.** 'oracles': cf Ac 7:38; Heb. 5:12. 'unresponsive': *aperispastos* means 'not drawn hither and thither; not distracted (especially by business)'; cf 1 Cor 7:35. **12.** 'herbs' cf note on 7:20. 'poultice', usually a cake of pressed figs; cf 2 (4) Kgs 20.7. The Egyptian sorcerers were unable to treat the boils, Ex 9:11. **13b.** Illness was considered a slipping to the brink of Sheol. God was able to cure serious illness (e.g. Nm 12:1–15) but the context indicates more his power to bring the dead back to life (Dt 32:9; Ps 30 (29):9).

l F 15–20 Third illustration: From heaven the Egyptians receive plagues, the Israelites bread—16. The seventh plague (Ex 9:13–35) heavy hail with thunder, lightning and rain over Upper Egypt. The effect on the barley and flax crops is not mentioned here. **17.** The association of fire and water reflects medical as well as cosmological speculation; their union gives life. **20.** 'food of angels', the description of manna given by Ps 78 (77):25 (LXX); elsewhere it is termed 'bread of heaven' (Ex 16:4; Ps 105 (104):40). 'without their toil' or perhaps 'untiringly' (JB) i.e. unceasingly. **21.** 'thy sweetness': the sweetness of the manna ('the taste of it was like wafers made with honey', Ex 16:14) was symbolic of the same quality in God; cf Ps 34 (33):8; 119 (118):103. **28.** The most favourable time for prayer was at sun-up; cf Ps 5:4; Sir 39:5 etc. The Mishnah prescribes recitation of the morning prayer as soon as the first rays of the sun strike the mountains. See the Babylonian Hymn to Shamash, the sun-god, Tablet I, 14–15: 'You signal(?) the food-offerings to the Igigi; when you arise Shamash all mankind bows down (in prayer). cf ANET 387d **29.** 'will melt like wintry frost' as the hoarfrost-like manna did under the first rays of the sun.

m F 17:1–18:4 Fourth illustration: For Egypt darkness, for Israel a pillar of fire—17:1. 'hard to describe' cf Ps 92 (91):6–7; Rm 11:33–35. **2–3b.** 'darkness', 'long night' allude to the ninth plague (Ex 10:21–29) which lasted three days. The description of a khamsin dust-storm as a 'dark curtain' is apt; the fine dust of dry red earth whirled up by the storm made the air very thick and dark. On criminal activity at night see Jb 24:13f; Ps 10 (9):8–11. **3c–4.** cf Eliphaz' description of a nightmare, Jb 4:13–16. **7.** The greatest

magicians of Egypt were the chief lector-priests, **436m** graduates of the temple schools; there they studied the sacred writings, spells and rituals. Part of their task was the interpretation of dreams. 'All the magicians of Egypt and all its wise men' were called by the Pharaoh to do this 'but there was none who could' (Gn 41:8). **8.** Their failure is mentioned again during the plagues (Ex 9:11) despite temporary successes (7:11; 8:3); cf **n** Mi 3:7. **11.** 'conscience' occurs elsewhere in the LXX only in Eccl 10:20. 'Curse not the king in thy conscience' (HT: 'with thy friend'; cf Bib 46 (1965), 210ff). Denney, Dodd and Moffatt consider the term Stoic in origin, while Dupont and Pierce hold it originated from non-philosophical popular Gr. thought. Cf 'Conscience' by S. S. Smalley in *The New Bible Dictionary* 1965, 248–9. The idea is in germ in texts such as Gn 3:8; 1 Sm 24:5 ('afterwards David's heart smote him'); but the first clear use foreshadowing NT development is here. **12a.** It is the wicked who are terrified by fear: 'what the wicked dreads will come upon him' Prv 10:24; cf 1:26). The effect of God's sending his fear before the Heb when they entered the Promised Land is described in Ex 23:27f. **14.** For 'night' as a symbol of calamity see Mi 3:6. Late apocalyptic writings foretell the elimination of night: Zech 14:7; Apoc 21:25; II Enoch 65, 9. **18, 1.** 'thy holy ones': the Israelites who probably lived near W. Tumilat (in Goshen) and so missed the worst effects of the dust storm; cf Ex 10:23. **3.** 'flaming pillar of fire': the pillars of fire and of cloud are mentioned together in Ex 14:24; the pillar of fire alone appears in 13:21–22; Nm 14:14; Neh 9:12, 19. The fire, like the cloud, signified God's presence among his people. 'a harmless sun': because of the removal of its adverse natural effects such as sunstroke (2 (4) Kgs 4:18–20); cf Ps 121 (120):6. For its overpowering heat at midday, the sun was called the noonday devil (cf Ps 91 (90):6); this demon was also recognized in ancient Greece and identified with Artemis-Hecate or with Pan.

G 18:5–19:4 Fifth illustration: The 10th Plague and o the Exodus—5. 'they had resolved to kill the holy babes': Pharaoh's decree affected only male children, Ex 1:22. 'one child had been exposed and rescued', Moses (Ex 2). **6.** 'our fathers', the Patriarchs; cf Gn 15:13f; 46:3f. 'oaths' see note on v 22. **9a.** The celebration of the Paschal meal, when a yearling lamb (or goat) was roasted and eaten (Ex 12:1–13, 21–27, 43 10; Dt 16:1–8) 'in secret' meaning either 'at night' (Ex 12:6) or because the celebration then took place in private houses in contrast to the later practice of open and public sacrifice. **b.** 'they were singing the praises of the fathers' i.e. the Hallel (Pss 113–18 (112–17)). This Egyptian Hallel was not actually sung at the first Passover, but the author describes the rite as he knew it. **10–11.** Cf Ex 11:5–6; Wis inverts the order and omits any mention of beasts. **12.** This resembles Ishtar's threat at the gates of the Underworld: 'I will bring up the dead and they will devour (i.e. outnumber) the living'. Cf ANET, 107b 'their most valued children', their first-born sons. The eldest son had the right of succession, a claim on the family blessing and received preferential treatment within tribe and family. **13.** 'thy people . . . God's son' as in Hos 11:1; the expression in Ex 4:22 is stronger: 'Thus says the Lord, Israel is my first-born son'; cf Est 16:15. **14b.** i.e. at midnight as stated in Ex 11:4. **15–16.** 'a stern warrior': the destroying angel also had 'in his hand a drawn sword' when David made his unlawful census, 1 Chr 21:15–17, only against the Egyptians was there no staying his hand. God's angels are the '*mighty*

436o *warriors* who do his word, hearkening to the voice of his word', Ps 103 (102):20.

p **18:20—25 Digression: Death in the desert and Aaron's prayer—20b.** 'a plague came on the multitude in the desert': after two rebellions against Moses and Aaron, one by Dathan and Abiram when they refused to obey (Nm 16:1b, 2a, 12—15) and were punished by being swallowed by the earth (16:25—34); the other by Korah who claimed equal holiness with Moses and Aaron (16:3—7, 18—24) and he and his followers were consumed in fire (16:35). The people murmured saying 'You have killed the people of the Lord' (16:41) so the Lord in his anger caused a plague. **20c—25.** Aaron's intercession, recounted in Nm 16:46—50. **22.** 'appealing to the oaths and covenants given to our fathers': the Abrahamic Covenant was sanctioned by an oath on God's part (Gn 15:9—17); cf Ps 89 (88):19—37, 49; 110 (109):1—4. **23.** 'heaps': the dead numbered 14,700 according to Nm 16:49. **24.** 'his long robe': the vestments of Aaron, as prototype of the high priest, are listed in Ex 28:4 and described in vv 6—39; cf Sir 45:6—22. The high priest wore a turban of fine linen to which a diadem of pure gold was connected by a blue cord; also a coat, tunic and sash. 'the four rows of stones', three to a row, were set in the pectoral and symbolized the twelve tribes of Israel. 'the glories of the fathers were engraved': each stone bore the name of a tribe so that they would be 'like signets' (Ex 28:21).

437a **Part IV 19:5—21 The New Creation**
For this concluding section, which describes the new creation, see P. Beauchamp, 'Le salut corporel des justes et la conclusion du livre de la Sagesse', Bib 45 (1964), 491—526.

A 19:5 Title—Part IV is modelled on the creation account of Gn. This v is the equivalent of a title: for God's people 'an unexpected journey', for the Egyptians 'a strange death'.

b **B 6—12 New reformed creation to keep God's children safe—7a.** The 'overshadowing cloud' is connected to the creation account by 6a and 7b. This is the first episode of the new creation. **7b.** 'dry land (was seen) emerging' as in Gn 1:9; cf Ex 14:22. **7c.** 'and a grassy plain', cf Gn 1:11—13 for the same order: after the earth appeared, God commanded it to 'put forth vegetation' on the third day. **8—9.** Transitional vv; the events to be described (10ff) really happened before the events of **7** according to the scheme in Gn. 'leaped like lambs': the subject is 'the raging waves' (7); cf Ps 114 (113):3—6. 'praising thee O Lord' with the Canticle of Moses, Ex 15:1—22. **10—12.** The theme is the production of living things as in the heptameron, Gn 1:20—25, but in inverse order: animals, fish, birds instead of birds, fish, animals

(days 5 and 6). Wis uses LXX and HT. For the quails see **43**[?] 16:2.

C 13—17 The men of Egypt and Sodom punished by **c** **blindness**—The central part of the composition in Wis uses the central part of the heptameron, the separation of day and night (Gn 1:14—19); cf Ps 104 (103):19—23. **13.** 'prior signs in the violence of thunder': for this detail, not in Ex, see Ps 77 (76):18: 'The peal of your thunder came from the vault of heaven, your shafts of lightning lit up the world' (translation of M. Dahood, AB vol. 16, 109). Thunder is the usual herald of a theophany, cf Ex 9:13—35. **14.** 'Others', the inhabitants of Sodom (Gn 19), 'had refused to receive strangers when they came to them'. Although Lot (Abraham's nephew and not a native of Sodom) gave bed and board to his two angel guests, the men of the city were inhospitable from the moment they learned of the guests' arrival; however they were not treacherous. 'But these (the Egyptians) made slaves of guests (the Hebrews) who were their benefactors' and so were more to blame because guilty of treachery as well as inhospitality; cf Gn 45:17—20; Ex 1:8—14. **15—16.** Elaborates **14**. **17.** Describes the punishment meted out both to the men of Sodom 'at the door of the righteous man' (i.e. Lot:Gn 19:11) and to the Egyptians: blindness. Cf Dt 28:28—29.

D 18—21 New relation between creatures—This **d** section is a summary, connecting the foregoing comparisons, balancing 11:1—3 and recalling the main syncrisis 16:17—24. **19.** An illustration of **18**, inverting the order in the heptameron where each animal had its proper habitat. **21c.** 'nor did they (i.e. fire and flame) melt the crystalline, easily melted kind of heavenly food'. This is not an abrupt ending but corresponds to God's last act before the sabbath: the provision of food for man (Gn 1:29—30); cf Ps 104 (103):27f; 136 (135):25a. 'heavenly food', *ambrosia*, the food or drink of immortality in Greek mythology; cf Gn 2:9. The Gr. word is derived from *m(b)rotos*, 'mortal', with privative *a*; or from the Semitic for 'ambergris' to which were ascribed miraculous properties. Cf note on 16:20.

Conclusion 22—The conclusion to the book is a summing up of the theme of the whole composition and the aspect from which everything has been viewed: God's blessings on Israel. Here is the application of the midrash (Wright). Faith in God's continuous care for his chosen people is affirmed (Reese) to console the Alexandrian Jews in their persecution. The questions posed in chh 1—5 are here answered (Beauchamp). Marx (loc cit 67—68) quotes an alleged ending to Wis, recorded by J. Angelino (c. A.D. 1325) in an Aram. translation from Gr.; however this text is probably part of an unknown apocryphal work ascribed to Solomon.

ECCLESIASTICUS, OR THE WISDOM OF JESUS THE SON OF SIRACH

BY C. KEARNS O.P.

438a Bibliography—See lists in Di Lella, Bigot, Gelin, cited *infra*. *Introductions*: L. Bigot, DTC IV 2 (1911), 2028—54; A. Gelin, DTC *Tables générales*, 1090f; Eb. Nestle, HDB 4 (1902), 539—51; R. H. Pfeiffer, *Hist. of NT Times with an introd. to the Apocrypha*, 1963, 352—408; C. H. Toy, 'Ecclesiasticus' CBEB, 2, (1901), 1164—79; id 'Sirach', CBEB 4 (1903), 4645—51. *Commentaries*: G. H. Box and W. O. E. Oesterley, CAP 1 (1913); W. O. E. Oesterley, CBSC, 1912; C. Spicq, PCSB 6 (1951); V. Hamp, EchB 4 (1959, 569—717; N. Peters in EHAT (ed. Nikel), 1913; R. Smend, Berlin 1906 (outstanding); H. Duesberg and I. Fransen in SacB, 1966 (with penetrating doctrinal analysis); Perez Rodriguez in *Biblia Comentada* (ed. Profesores de Salamanca), IV, Madrid 1962, 1071—1305. *Text-critical studies* (for critical edd. of text and versions see § 441): A. A. Di Lella, *The HT of Sirach a text-critical and historical study*, The Hague 1966; M. H. Segal, 'The evolution of the HT of Ben Sira', JQR n.s. 1934/35, 91—149; A. Fuchs, *Textkritische Untersuchungen zum hebräischen Ekklesiastikus*, BibSt XII 5 (1907); on Gr. text J. Ziegler, J. H. A. Hart, as in § 441h; On Latin text, introd. to Benedictine ed. as *infra* § 441j; H. Herkenne, *De Veteris Latinae Ecclesiastici capp i—xliii*, Leipzig 1899; D. de Bruyne, RBen 40 (1928) 5—48; id ZAW 47 (1929), 257—63; P. Thielmann in *Archiv für lat. Lexicographie und Grammatik* 8 (1893) 511—61, and 9 (1894) 247—84. *Qumran connections*: J. Carmignac, 'Les rapports entre l'Ecclésiastique et Qumran', *Revue de Qumran* 3 (1961), 209—18; H. Germann, 'Jesus ben Siras Dankgebet und die Hodajoth', TZ 19 (1963) 81—87; M. R. Lehmann, 'Ben Sira and the Qumran Literature', *Revue de Qumran* 3 (1961) 103—16; id '"Yom Kippur" in Qumran', ibid 117—24; J. Trinquet, 'Les liens "sadocites" de l'écrit de Damas, des MSS de la mer morte et de l'Ecclésiastique', VT 1 (1951) 287—92; P. Kahle, *The Cairo Geniza*, Oxf. 1959², 13ff.

b Title—According to the evidence of the HT of ch 51 (colophon, emended), of the rabbinic citations and of Syr. the earliest title seems to have been *The Wisdombook of Ben Sira*: in Gr. *The Wisdom of Sirach* or *The Wisdom of Jesus the son of S(e)irach*. In English 'the author is usually called *Ben Sira* (in accordance with the Hebrew usage) or *Sirach* (according to the Greek); the mixture of the two (Ben Sirach) should be avoided' (Pfeiffer, p. 352). In Latin the title *Ecclesiasticus* is found already in Cyp. (*Testim.* II. 1, PL 4, 696 etc). Rufinus (who excluded Sir from the canon) explains this term as meaning 'of ecclesiastical authority' only, not canonical (*In Symb. Apost.* 38, PL 21, 374). It was an ecclesiastical or *church* book also in the sense that it was in use as a handbook for the moral training of catechumens (Ath. *Ep. fest.* 39, PG 26, 1177, 1437; Orig. *In Num. hom.* 27, PG 12, 780). In liturgical use it shares with Prv Eccl Song and Wis the generic title *Liber Sapientiae*.

Canonicity—As regards its acceptance by **the Jews 438c of Alexandria and in the Christian Church** Sir has the same history as the other deutero-canonical books of the OT, cf §§ 14f—15a. The question of its acceptance by **the Jews of Palestine** and the rabbinical tradition is complex. Divine inspiration, in some sense, is claimed for his book by Ben Sira himself (24:30—34; 39:6—11). His nephew in the Prologue sets him in that inspired tradition of 'the law and the prophets and the other books of our fathers' within which 'he himself in turn (*kai autos*) was led to write something pertaining to instruction and wisdom'. From early in the 1st cent. B.C. the successive recensions which Sir underwent in certain circles in Palestine testify to its acceptance, by some at any rate, as inspired. That view continued to manifest itself for centuries, down to the disappearance of the HT in later Christian times, through those scribes who in copying it arranged its verses in hemistichs in double columns as was the practice for canonical books. This practice is followed for the text of Sir in first cent. B.C. and A.D. MSS of Qumran and Masada and in the medieval Cairo MSS B and E (see *infra*). The inclusion of the massoretic points and accents in Cairo A and D and in a MS known to Rabbi Saadya of Bagdad (A.D. 920) is not without significance, since these signs are normally reserved for canonical books.

Across this tradition of canonicity cuts **rabbinical d tradition**, which however is not self-consistent. On the one hand Rabbi Akiba (died c. A.D. 132) numbers Sir with the 'outside' or extra-canonical books, the reading of which excludes from the World to Come (Smend, p. lii, and the *Tosefta* (c. A.D. 250) says 'the books of Ben Sira and all books written after the prophetic period do not defile the hands' i.e. are not canonical (*Yadaim* ii, 13 in CAP I, 271). On the other hand the Talmud and other rabbinical writings quote its sayings with approval more than eighty times, sometimes expressly under Ben Sira's name, and occasionally with the formula *it is written*, i.e. found in Scripture (Smend, xlvi—lvi; Cowley and Neubauer, *Original Hebrew of . . . Ecclesiasticus*, 1897, x, xix—xxx). The conflicting evidence seems to point to two **conclusions**: (1) The Pharisees, and their successors the Rabbis, excluded Sir from their canon; but they continued to quote it with approval—occasionally even as Scripture—because it is itself impregnated with the thoughts and wording of the proto-canonical books, especially the sapiential ones. (2) The Essenes, however, as long as they continued to exist, and subsequently in such times and places as their influence extended to, through MSS derived ultimately from their *scriptoria*, supported unwaveringly the tradition of the canonicity of Sir.

Authorship—Leaving aside the 'autobiographical' data **e** of ch 51 (whose authenticity is suspect) and confining ourselves to the indications of the Prologue and of the emended HT of 50:27 and of the colophon after 51:30, we find that the author's name was Joshua (Heb. *Yesua*',

438e Gr. *Iēsous* = Jesus), son of Eleazar, son of Sira (eliminating the name Simeon on critical grounds). In Hebrew idiom he is often called by his grandfather's name Ben Sira = Son of Sira. The data of the Prologue and of 50:27, some scattered autobiographical hints in other places (24:30—34; 33:16—18; 34:9—12; 39:12—16, 32—35), and the picture of himself which seems to underlie 39:1—11, when put together, show him as an inhabitant of Jerusalem, a member of the scribal class with the necessary wealth and leisure to devote himself to the study of the Scriptures which he loved; as one who in his maturity travelled abroad, mixed with upper-class society, found perhaps employment with some foreign potentate and on occasion ran the risk of death but each time providentially escaped; as one who, finally, in his later years, returned to Jerusalem and settled down to that life of reflection on the Scriptures and on God's dealings with men, of writing, and perhaps of school-mastering, which little by little, and almost without conscious planning on his part (24:23—34), produced as its fruit the Wisdom-book of Ben Sira.

f The **date at which he wrote** can be approximately fixed from the Prologue. This shows his grandson to have been of mature age 'in the thirty-eighth year of the reign of Euergetes'. This is best taken as meaning the thirty-eighth year of the reign of Physcon Euergetes II (Ptolemy VII), i.e. 132 B.C. The grandfather Ben Sira would have flourished 60 or 50 years previously, i.e. 190—180 B.C. This fits in with his reference in 50:1ff to 'Simon the son of Onias' in such a way as to show he had known him and that he was dead when this was written. The high-priest referred to was Simeon II, son of Jochanan II. He held office c. 219—196 B.C. This confirms 190—180 as the date of writing. For the historical background this date implies see § § 68c—e, 586c and cf on 35:18, 19.

439a Scope, Procedure and Contents—The author touches on his purpose and procedure in 24:30—34; 33:16—18; 39:12—16, 32—35; 50:27—29. Having been granted by the Lord a store of divine wisdom through study of the Law and the other Scriptures, personal experience, and reflection on life, he proposes to put it into writing, following at a distance—'like one who gleans after the grape-gatherers' (33:16)—the sages who have gone before. He calls on thoughtful men to ponder on his teaching and to put it into practice. The translator in the Prologue rightly emphasizes this practical scope of the work, with its insistence on the Law as the divine guide to human life. In **the first part of the book, chh 1—43**, this end is served by weaving together series of pithy sayings about life, couched in the form of the *māšāl* or verse-couplet after the model of Prv. Sir however differs from Prv in frequently grouping together in series couplets dealing with a single subject-matter, such as friendship, control of the tongue, wealth and poverty, family life etc. **Sub-divisions** of this first part are based on the occurrence at intervals of meditative passages of a theological character in which the notion of wisdom itself and its intimate relationships with God are expounded. Each such passage seems to serve as an introduction to the pragmatic considerations which follow on it, and possibly we have here an indication of the stages by which the book was gradually built up. For these sub-divisions see plan below.

In **the second part (chh 44—50)** the operation of divine wisdom is illustrated in another fashion, viz by considering it as it worked out the Lord's providential purposes for his people through the experiences of their Founders and Fathers from Enoch to the author's own

contemporary the high priest Simon son of Onias. This **439** section, strongly sacerdotal in outlook, constitutes one of the most complete and illuminating summaries of 'salvation history' in the OT. It is **easily subdivided** according to the successive personalities with which it deals. There follows ch 51 which is a kind of **Appendix** of prayer and reflexion only loosely connected with what precedes, and which raises problems of authenticity which are dealt with below.

Plan of the Book—Part One, 1:1—43:33: Wisdom **b** considered in its relationship to God and also in its ethical bearings on human life. Sub-divisions, on the basis explained above, are as follows:

a. 1:1—4:10	**d.** 14:20—16:23	**g.** 33:7—39:11
b. 4:11—6:17	**e.** 16:24—23:27	**h.** 39:12—42:14
c. 6:18—14:19	**f.** 24:1—33:6	**i.** 42:15—43:33

Part Two, 44:1—50:29, 'Praise of the Fathers of Old' (title in HT): Salvation history from Enoch to the high priest Simon II. Subdivided according to the periods and personalities successively dealt with.

Appendix, 51:1—30:—(a) A Prayer of thanksgiving for deliverance (1—12). (b) A Psalm of thanksgiving (found only in HT, between vv 12 and 13). (c) An Acrostic Poem: how wisdom is acquired and imparted (13—30). For more detailed sub-divisions of parts I and II see the commentators, e.g. the helpful tables in Oesterley, CBSC, xxix—xxxviii.

Authenticity of the Appendix ch 51—As just noted **c** ch 51 is made up of three parts. These, for convenience sake, are here called respectively the Prayer, the Psalm, and the Acrostic. The Prayer and the Acrostic are found in HT (Cairo B), in Gr. and in Syr. In Gr. the Prayer is headed 'A Prayer of Jesus son of Sirach'. After 51:30, as a subscription to the whole book, practically all Gr. MSS have some such formula as '(End of) the Wisdom of Jesus son of Sirach'; Syr. has 'Thus far the words of Yeshua the son of Simon who is called the son of Asira. The writing of the Wisdom of Bar Sira is ended'. That these ascriptions are based on Hebrew originals at this point is borne out by the colophon found in Cairo B: '. . . Thus far the Words of Simeon, the son of Yeshua, the son of Eleazar, the son of Sira . . .'.

On the other hand concluding formulae obviously intended to mark the close of the work of Ben Sira are found previously in 50:27—29, in both Gr. (as in RSV) and in HT as follows: 'Wise instruction and apt proverbs of Simeon the son of Yeshua, the son of Eleazar, the son of Sira . . .'. This raises the possibility that what comes after 50:29 is not necessarily part of the work of Ben Sira, but may have been added from other sources by a scribe who, for reasons of his own, attributed it to Ben Sira by boldly adding the second colophon after 51:30. This possibility is strengthened by the lack of internal cohesion between ch 51 and what immediately precedes, and amongst the two (or, in HT, three) component parts of the chapter itself. In actual fact most scholars today deny to Ben Sira the authorship of the Psalm; and since Sanders's publication in 1965 of the Qumran text of the Acrostic, expert opinion is turning sharply against Ben Sira's authorship of this also. As of 1967 the situation regarding the authorship of each of the three parts of ch 51 is as follows:

The Prayer—The Hebrew colophon after 51:30 having **d** been revealed as unreliable with regard to the Psalm and the Acrostic, Ben Sira's authorship of the Prayer also is left questionable. It has in its favour only the unsupported heading prefixed to 51:1 in Gr., and the fact that the passage is found in the HT, Gr. and Syr. MSS of Ben Sira's work. It is found in them, however, only

9d *after* the earlier concluding formula of 50:27—29. So far as external evidence is concerned, therefore, its authorship is uncertain.

e The **Psalm** is found, in Cairo B only, between vv 12 and 13. For trans. and commentary see § 450*f* From the time of its discovery its authenticity was maintained by its editor S. Schechter (1899) and, amongst earlier writers, by J. Touzard (1900), T. Nöldeke (1900), I. Knabenbauer (1902), R. Smend (1906); in recent years by M. H. Segal (1958), H. Duesberg and I. Fransen (1966). Its omission in Gr. and Syr., it is claimed, is due to the jubilant tone of the reference in v ix to the priesthood of the line of Zadok: 'Give thanks to him who has chosen the sons of Zadok for the priesthood, for his mercy endures for ever'. When Ben Sira wrote, the glory of the sons of Zadok had not yet been dimmed. Simon the high priest, eulogized in 50:1—21, was one of them. Later, however, in the time of Simon's son, Onias III, the tide of events set in against them. In 152 B.C. political pressure brought about the transfer of the high priesthood to the Hasmonaean line (cf § 70*b*), and the Zadokites never recovered it. Thus, it is argued, the Gr. trans. made in 132 B.C. (imitated subsequently by Syr.) omitted the reference to that divine choice of the house of Zadok which by that time the course of events had nullified.

As against this, however, it is clear that the suppression of the whole Psalm would have been a senselessly extreme measure when the elimination of the embarassing verse alone would have sufficed. The majority of commentators, therefore, impressed by the awkward manner in which the Psalm is inserted at the end of the Prayer which is already complete in itself, reject its authenticity. Many scholars, however, admit that it may well have been composed in the time of Ben Sira or shortly after, e.g. Fuchs, Box and Oesterley, Di Lella, and CV (Vol. III, 1066, p. 654). The tendency today is to attribute it to the sectaries of Qumran (so Di Lella, 103—5, J. Trinquet, P. Kahle).

f The **Acrostic**—On the strength of the facts that this poem is found not only in Gr. and Syr. but also in HT (Cairo B), and that its contents and tone fit in with the personality and method of Ben Sira as seen elsewhere in his book, it has until recently been attributed to him practically without question. However, since the publication by Sanders (see § 441*d*) of the recension of it found in 11QPs*a* (here called Q for convenience of reference), Ben Sira's authorship is seen to be highly questionable. Q is found in a Hebrew scroll which is assigned on palaeographical grounds to the first half of the 1st cent. A.D. This scroll contains a collection of psalm-pieces, both canonical and uncanonical, all of which, as a note in prose referring to 'David's Compositions' seems to show (col. 27), were taken to be the work of David (Sanders, p. 85). Owing to damage to the scroll only Sir 51:13—20 survives (col. 21) with a few words of v 30 (col. 22). This newly discovered HT gives a recension of the Acrostic notably different in textual detail, in tone and in imagery, though not in substance, from what is found in Gr., Latin, Syr., and Cairo B. Touching the question of its authorship in the light of this new text, Sanders's conclusions may be summarized as follows: (1) Of the various textual witnesses, (Q, Cairo, Gr., Lat, Syr), Q contains, if not the original text itself, at least the text closest to the original. (2) The Acrostic was originally an independent composition, written neither by David nor by Ben Sira. (3) Probably it was from the beginning what it still remains in its various recensions, 'a song composed by a Wisdom teacher as a plea to his students to gain wisdom

from him, and to espouse her as he had done in his youth' **439f** (op cit p. 85). This composition, however, was in Gr., Syr., and Cairo adapted to a place in Ben Sira's work 'only at great expense to the original poem' (ibid).

DOCTRINAL CONTENT

Excellent surveys of Ben Sira's doctrine are given by **110a** Oesterley in his commentaries in CBSC and (in collaboration with Box) in CAP I. Pfeiffer in his introduction gives a synthesis in which he skilfully presents at the same time a vivid portrait of the religious personality of the author. Duesberg and Fransen (in Italian) go deeply into the inner coherence of the rich and varied teaching of Ben Sira, eruditely drawing attention to its sources and parallels in the age-old wisdom-tradition of the ancient world. The present summary aims at an organic and comprehensive exposition, however brief, by taking as its basis the concept which dominates the entire book, **the concept of Divine Wisdom**. It is in fact the notion, one might almost say the Mystery, of Divine Wisdom, considered in its inner nature, its external manifestations and its multitudinous applications in nature, salvation history and the moral, social and religious life of the Israelite, that forms the basic fabric of Ben Sira's teaching. It was with the purpose of imparting *instruction, understanding, knowledge,* and above all of making *Wisdom* known, —'the wisdom of all the ancients' (39:1)—that he wrote his book (cf 24:30—34; 33: 16—18; 39:1—11; 50:27—29). It is under this heading, therefore, that we attempt in what follows to summarize the doctrinal content of the book, prefixing however a note on **The Messianic Hope** in Sir. Messianism in any **b** express and specific sense is found in Sir only in the hymn intercalated in HT after 51:12 (viii), and in the expanded text of Vg 24:34. In the sense, however, of a reliance on the promises made to Abraham and to David and his successors, and of an explicit recalling of the terms of these promises, allusions to the messianic hope are not lacking when called for by the context. See 36:12—16; 44:19—21; 45:25; 47:11, 22; 48:15.

Coming now to the concept of Wisdom, whilst it is **c** true that 'all wisdom comes forth from the Lord and is with him for ever' (1:1), nevertheless it must be externalized, it must come forth 'from the mouth of the Most High' (24:3) in the form of his creative and revealing word, before it can play its part in the universe and amongst mankind (39:17, 18, 31; 42:15; 43:5, 10, 13, 26). For Israel, that word and that wisdom are **embodied in the Law**. Wisdom in God is an unfathomable ocean, more abundant than the sea and deeper than the primeval Abyss (cf 24:28). But its waters overflow into the Book of the Law of Moses which in consequence bears within itself vitalizing forces comparable to the four rivers of Eden. Every moral precept and every ritual ordinance is a channel branching off from this mighty stream; and every faithful scribe is a husbandman who draws off its life-giving waters for the benefit of mankind (cf 1:26; 6:37; 15:1; especially 24:23—34).

Wisdom and the Temple Worship—When it is said **d** that 'to fear the Lord is the beginning of wisdom' (1:14), the fear spoken of is the religious fear fundamental in the OT. It is that reverential awe of the divinity which brings home to man that God is the one supreme and worshipful being, and which expresses this conviction both by rendering him the worship he requires (a worship which for the Israelite is that prescribed in the Law), and by doing his will in the sphere of moral conduct. This fear is the 'beginning' of wisdom in a twofold sense.

440d First, this religious attitude itself is the soil *in which wisdom takes root* and finds its nurture within the soul: 'to fear the Lord is the root of wisdom' (1:20). Secondly, the *choicest fruit* produced by wisdom, —its 'crown', 'full measure' and 'fulfilment' (1:18, 16; 21:11)—is to fear the Lord in the sense of offering him, from a full heart and with the proper moral dispositions, the prescribed **ritual worship of sacrifice and public prayer**. Ben Sira is unique amongst the wisdom-writers for the veneration and the enthusiasm with which he speaks of **the priesthood and the Temple services**. Witness his glowing eulogy of Aaron and the priesthood bestowed on him by God (45:6—22; cf 33:12); and the transport with which he describes Simon the high priest, (as he himself had often seen him), offering the sacrifice in full solemnity, 'with a garland of his brethren around him' in the presence of 'the whole congregation of Israel' (50:11—21; cf 47:8—10). The possession of this incomparable Service makes of Israel a priestly people, set apart among mankind for purposes of worship, like the oil of priestly consecration and the incense of the sanctuary (24:15). It is against this background that every Israelite is exhorted to 'fear' the Lord and reverence his priests, giving them their sacred dues (7:29—31).

e Wisdom and Moral Conduct—Fundamental though worship is, right conduct is more fundamental still. The Law is **essentially a moral law**. Ritual observances which are not accompanied in the worshipper by a virtuous life and fitting inward dispositions are roundly denounced (7:8—10; 34:18—35:12). From this root-principle stems that foliage of proverbial lore which bulks so large throughout the book. Its author enriches every area of the vast field of the moral commonplace in which 'the ancients', especially the compiler of Prv, had already so shrewdly toiled (24:30—34; 33:16—18; 39:1—3; for a lively summary of Ben Sira's contribution to this lore see Pfeiffer, 385—92).

f Wisdom and the Inner Life—Wise conduct in the broader fields of morality is within the reach of every prudent man, Israelite or not. But there is a choicer fruit of wisdom proper to the chosen people amongst whom wisdom dwells at home (24:8—12). This is **the special favour of God** bestowed on those who love him: the special intimacy with him which they enjoy, the special sensitivity to what he desires and the will to fulfil it, cost what it may of hardship, which they study to perfect (1:9, 10; 2:15, 16; 34:16, 17). This wisdom of the inner life is drawn first from the sacred Scriptures: the Law, the Wisdom Books and the Prophets (39:1—3). Nor is it only as a record of God's words that Holy Writ inspires and instructs, but also as a record of his dealings with the Fathers, and of their surrender of themselves to be moulded to his purposes—the thought that dominates chh 44—50.

g The profound **study of the Scriptures** which this implies demands to a great extent renunciation of other occupations (38:24). But there is a higher step than mere professional devotion to scholarship and reflection. Wisdom comes in the long run only by **the communion of mind with Mind**. The thinker must grow into the contemplative. The spirit of man must immerse itself in the Spirit of God and commune with him in the give and take of conversation, person to person. He must set his heart to rise early to seek the Lord who made him, and must make supplication before the Most High. Then, if the great Lord is willing, the seeker will be filled with the spirit of understanding and will direct his counsel and his knowledge aright (cf 39:5—8). 'Those who eat

me (says Wisdom) will hunger for more, and those who **44** drink me will thirst for more' (24:19—21).

This sweet familiarity, however, is not bestowed **h** until the seeker has been **purified by trial** in sense and in spirit. 'Wisdom at first will walk with him on tortuous paths, she will bring fear and cowardice upon him, and will torment him by her discipline until she trusts him, and she will test him with her ordinances. Then she will come straight back to him and gladden him, and will reveal her secrets to him' (4:17, 18; see 2:1—5; 6:18—31).

Wisdom and mankind at large—Wisdom, whilst **i** dwelling in Israel as in its proper home (24:8—12), was nevertheless, in a measure fixed by God, poured out from the beginning upon all mankind (1:9, 10; 24:6, 7). Man was created in the image of God, a spiritual being endowed with intellect and will, holding the supremacy among created things, and bearing in his conscience the moral law which God had given him to guide his conduct (17:1—12). The moral responsibility thus imposed was matched by the endowment of free will. The Lord 'created man in the beginning, and he left him in the power of his own inclination: If you will, you can keep the commandments, and to act faithfully is a matter of your own choice . . . Before a man are life and death, and whichever he chooses will be given to him' (15:14—17). The object here is to prove that God is not responsible for sin. Man is responsible, by abusing his free will. What then is responsible for man's abuse of this divine endowment? Ben Sira does not say it is the Fall of man. His paraphrase (17:1—12) of Gn 2 stops short of the Fall. In 25:24 he says 'From a woman sin had its beginning, and because of her we all die'. But *beginning* here is taken numerically: the first recorded sin is that of Eve. It is not said to have a *causal influence* on the sins of her posterity. As regards **the consequences of the Fall** Ben Sira does not go beyond the data of Gn 2:16—19. viz it results in the yoke of affliction which is laid upon the children of Adam, and results eventually in death (40:1—5*b*).

As to sin, Ben Sira traces it to a twofold root within **j** man himself. (1) The inherent defectibility of every man by the very fact of his creaturehood. 'All things cannot be in men . . . All men are dust and ashes' (17:30*a*, 32*b*; see 18:8—10). (2) But there is a more sinister element in man: an inherent propensity to moral evil. This is called by a Hebrew term variously translated as *inclination* (17:31 emended, not in RSV); *presumption* (18:10 Vg, not in RSV); *thoughts* (21:11); *imagination* (37:3). The underlying Hebrew is *yēṣer*, the word translated *inclination* in 15:14 (quoted above on free will). In the abstract, the *yēṣer* is free will, regarded as something ontologically good and morally indifferent. In the concrete, however, experience shows that man habitually misuses his free will; it shows itself in practice as impaired. This misuse of it so predominates that Rabbinism eventually came to use the term *yēṣer* exclusively in a pejorative sense, to describe that strong inclination to evil which Christians regard as one of the 'wounds' inflicted on human nature by Original Sin. (For rabbinical views on the *yēṣer* see G. F. Moore, *Judaism*, I, 479—81; III, 146, 147; S. Schechter, *Some Aspects of Rabbinic Theology*, chh 14, 15, 16; cp. R. E. Murphy, '*Yēṣer* in the Qumran Literature', Bib 39 (1958), 334—44). Ben Sira does not trace the origin of this evil propensity; he merely takes account of its existence. He is satisfied to explain sin as due, not to God, but to man's misuse of a good thing God has given him; and to explain that misuse itself as arising from a moral defectibility, and

40j still more from a moral disorder, in the sinner's own make-up. Why this is found in *every* man, he leaves unexplained. The lamentable fact remains: 'We all deserve punishment' (8:5, cf 21:2; 27:10). Every man is in fact a Satan to himself, and 'when the ungodly man curses his Adversary, he curses his own soul' (21:27). We must not blame the Lord for the sins of men, for he hates and abominates sin and has 'no use' for it (cf 15:11—13).

k Sin is evil. But **out of evil God draws good** in many ways. (1) The sinner's frailty is of itself a claim which excites God's compassion. (18:11—14). (2) In the Law he gives guidance and encouragement to avoid sin, and the practice of the Law gives moral stamina to keep sin's stirrings under control (21:12; 32:14—16; 32:23—33:3). (3) Consciousness of propensity to sin is an occasion of prayer, and prayer wins God's help to overcome sin or to avoid it (22:27—23:6), so that man can 'flee from sin as from a snake' (21:2). (4) Temptation overcome can thus be an occasion of merit (35:23*a*; cf 31:8—11). Finally, (5) even when sin has been yielded to, **repentance** for it draws men closer to God, and **amendment** cancels its effects: 'To keep from wickedness is pleasing to the Lord, and to forsake unrighteousness is atonement' (35:3; cf 17:24—29; 34:25, 26).

l But if evil is not repented of God will take note of it and punish it. He sees all man's thoughts and actions, good and evil, even the most secret, and 'judges a man according to his deeds', rewarding the good and punishing the wicked (16:11—14; see 17:15; 23:18, 19; 42:18—21). As to **the nature of divine retribution** Sir in its original form remains unshakably attached to the older views, unsatisfactory as these had already proved to the authors of Jb, Eccl and certain Ps, and close as he came in time to the theological turning-point when the new light would come breaking in. In this respect Sir is 'uncompromisingly conservative, and refuses to admit the possibility of the new views as to the future life. . . . A man's wickedness must receive its recompense either in his own person in this life, or, failing this, in the persons of his surviving children, since Sheol knows no retribution' (R. H. Charles, *Eschatology*, 1913[2], 167f; see also A. A. Di Lella, 'Conservative and progressive theology: Sirach and Wisdom', CBQ 28 (1966), 139—54). 'Do not envy the honours of a sinner, for you do not know what his end will be' (9:11, see also 12). After death the wrong-doer is punished only in the sense of leaving no children, or such as are to his discredit, so that his name is blotted out (23:24—27; 41:5—11). In the same way the just man will be rewarded by prosperity here below, even should he first have to undergo a period of purifying trial (1:13; see § 440*h* on the trials to be undergone before the fulness of wisdom is acquired). After his death, worthy children and a name long held in honour will carry on his reputation and be a permanent reward (30:4—6; 37:24—26; 41:11—13; 44:10—15). For the original Ben Sira, then, **Sheol remains the same vague shadow-world** which his OT predecessors had depicted, in which the shades of just and wicked mingle in one common lot of suspended existence. If it is referred to sometimes as a place of 'rest' (22:11; 38:23; 39:11), and even perhaps of 'eternal rest' (30:17, text uncertain), this is said in no positive sense, but only expresses the truism that with death the curtain comes down on the present life with its inevitable lot of 'anger, envy, trouble and unrest' (40:5, see vv 1—6; cp. Jb 3:11—19). Compared with this primitive next-world view the Expanded Text represents a remarkable doctrinal advance, § 442.

m

Wisdom in the Universe—Man is made in God's **440n** image, and has dominion over other living things (17:1—4). The larger world of nature has a meaning as a parable and an instrument of God's dealings with mankind (33:7—13; 39:22—31). But the world has a value apart from man (17:32). The sweep of God's power through the firmament, the penetration of his glance to the heart of the deep, the reflection of his beauty and the imprint of his skill in the innumerable armies of being that fill earth and sky and sea, the resistless energy with which he holds all these together and impels them forward to their goal—these are manifestations of the Lord which man in his littleness cannot convey nor even comprehend. It is fitting, therefore, that God should from the beginning pour out his wisdom upon *all* his works (1:9), so that wisdom can speak of itself as the medium of God's creating, sustaining and energizing power throughout the universe. After the manner of the Spirit of God when God began to create the heavens and the earth (Gn 1:1), Wisdom hung like a cloud above the earth, circled round the vault of heaven, walked in the depths of the primeval abyss, and marched upon the waves of the sea (cf 24:3—6). Ordered variety, purposive and unflagging energy, are the characteristics wisdom stamps upon the works of God (cf 16:26—30). To grasp something of what God's revelation of himself in nature meant to Israel's sages, **the Hymn to the Creator** (42:15—43:33) must be read and pondered, alive as it is with spiritual and aesthetic sensitivity, vibrant with awe and adoration and with a love that strives for utterance, groping for the Word as yet ungiven *Quantum potes tantum aude*: 'When you praise the Lord, exalt him as much as you can; for he will surpass even that . . . Who has seen him and can describe him? Or who can extol him as he is?' (43:30, 31).

Wisdom and God—'There is One who is wise' (1:8); **o** wise of his very nature. Wisdom is *with* him (1:1*b*), and when regarded as distinct from him, originates within him and comes forth from him (cf 1:1*a*; 24:5*a*). It was with him 'from eternity' (1:4*b*). Its eternity, however, is of that purely relative kind which the Hebrew '*ōlām* frequently expresses—pre-existence as compared with other things (1:4*a*; 24:9). For, in fact, wisdom was created (1:4, 9; 24:8*b*, 9*a*). But once created, it is to last for ever: 'From eternity, in the beginning, he created me, and for eternity I shall not cease to exist' (24:9). This creation of wisdom as something distinct from God was effected by his utterance of a word. The creative word which brought all other creatures into being, which first 'came forth from the mouth of the Most High' (24:3), was itself the externalizing of that wisdom which had hitherto been identical with God himself. Henceforth wisdom as distinct from God exists, and is the medium of his dealings with the world (42:15 and 43:26 as in comm. See 39:31).

Besides being just a 'word', the medium of God's **p** external operations, **is wisdom a person**? The texts show a gradation in this respect. In 6:24—31 wisdom is personified purely as a figure of speech, as the concluding phrases show. In 14:20—27 no advance on this is perceptible. The passage merges into 15:1—8 where, whilst 'her' personality takes on more concrete attributes, the note of metaphor is still predominant. It is an advance on this to present wisdom speaking of herself, as in 4:15—19 (HT). But it is of what happens in and to wisdom's votary that the passage speaks, not of wisdom's personality itself. The crucial passage is 24:1—22, where wisdom speaks in her own name, describing what she is and what she does. We have here a unity of concept, not merely of image. It is the concept of God's giving

440p of himself in and to the world which he has made. **Wisdom is presented as God's revelation of himself** in nature his handiwork, and in man his image. It is his revelation of himself also in the teaching which he gives in the sacred writings, and in the moral law which he implants in every heart. It is **his inward giving of himself**, too, to those he loves (4:10, 14; 45:1; 46:13): in the form of the light which makes them know him as a friend, and in the form of the impulse from on high which makes them respond in prayer to his advances (39:5, 6), rendering him their service and giving him the love of friendship in return (1:10; 2:15, 16; 34:16, 17). Wisdom is thus neither an abstraction nor just a single attribute of God. It is his many-sided self-bestowing, **personified** to make it comprehensible. But it is **not personalized.** It is not here presented as a hypostasis of God, coming to men to bring them the divine. Not yet. But in the growing light of revelation these inspired reflections on what God has begun to do for men, and on what he is calling them to, will soon be seen to adumbrate an ineffable fulfilment. One short step and the Sages of the OT will stand upon the threshold of the New. The Son of Sira will pass the pen to the Son of Thunder.

HEBREW TEXT AND ANCIENT VERSIONS

441a **The original Hebrew text** grew ever rarer once the Rabbis refused to Sir a place in their canon. Yet Jer. in the 4th cent. (*Praef. in lib. Salom*, PL 28 1307) and even Saadya in the 10th (§ 438c) were acquainted with Sir in Hebrew. Subsequently the HT disappeared and was not again available until the discovery of about two-thirds of it in one form or another amongst the great mass of the MSS of the Cairo Geniza in 1896 and following years (See Kahle, op cit 3—13). Four MSS of portions of Sir, called by editors A, B, C and D, were discovered. In the same Geniza material a fifth MS, E, was identified by J. Marcus in 1931; and further portions of B and C by J. Schirmann in 1958 and 1960. At Qumran, Cave 2 has yielded fragments of Sir 6, and Cave 11 part of Sir 51. Y. Yadin's excavation of Masada, the rock-fortress of Herod the Great near the Dead Sea, brought to light in 1964 a scroll containing a continuous text of almost 5 chapters of Sir.

b **Summary account of the Hebrew MSS**—(1) **The Geniza MSS:** A—six leaves, perh. 11th cent., containing 3:6—16:26. B—19 leaves, perh. 12th cent., containing 30:11—33:3; 35:11—38:27; 39:15—51:30, with many variant readings on the margin. C—four leaves, older than A and B, an anthology containing 4:23b, 30, 31; 5:4—8, 9—13; 6:18, 19, 28, 35; 7:1, 2, 4, 6, 17, 20, 21, 23—25; 18:30, 31; 19:1, 2; 20:4—6, 12(?); 25:7c, 8c, 8a, 12, 16—23; 26:1, 2; 36:16; 37:19, 22, 24, 26. D—a single leaf, 11th cent., containing 36:29—38:1. From the occurrence of marginal notes in Persian it was at one time concluded that texts A, B and D originated in Persia. In the light of the Qumran discoveries, however, Kahle concludes that the Persian glosses prove only that Karaites coming in the 9th cent. from Persia to Jerusalem had there participated in the copying out of Hebrew MSS of Sir already at that date derived from Qumran (Kahle, 26. For this episode see

c § 443g). A long battle has been waged over the authenticity of the Cairo MSS from the time of their discovery. From the beginning their genuineness as the *original* Hebrew of Sir was challenged by such scholars as D. S. Margoliouth and G. Bickell, who held them to represent

a late retroversion into Hebrew from the Syr. and/or Gr. **441** versions. I. Lévi (after some wavering) and E. Nestlé held the text to be partly original and partly a retroversion. With the original editors S. Schechter and C. Taylor, the majority of the experts of those days held for the authenticity, e.g. W. Bacher, T. Nöldeke, E. König, C. H. Toy, J. Touzard. The subsequent full-length commentaries of R. Smend (1906), W. O. E. Oesterley (1912), G. H. Box and Oesterley (1913), N. Peters (1913), accepted the substantial originality of the HT and the controversy seemed to die out. It has however been revived, and E. J. Goodspeed (1939), C. C. Torrey (1945), H. L. Ginsberg (1955), M. Hadas (1959) and some few others have again propounded the total retroversion hypothesis. A. A. Di Lella in his work on the HT of Sir (from which we have derived the above summary of the fluctuations of the controversy) incisively shows the feebleness of the case against authenticity. The Masada MS 'unmistakably confirms' this (Y. Yadin, p. 1 of his ed., noted *infra*), Di Lella's personal view is that some relatively few vv are best explained as retroversions from Syr. but that the great bulk of the text is the genuine HT of Ben Sira. *Critical edd.* of the first Geniza discoveries, MSS A B C D: H. L. Strack, with notes and vocab., Leipzig 1903; N. Peters, with vowel points and Latin trans. added, Freiburg i.B. 1905; R. Smend, with German trans., Berlin 1906; I. Lévi, with notes and glossary in German and English, Leiden 1904, reprinted 1951.

(2) **J. Marcus's MS**, also from the Geniza: E—a **d** single leaf containing 32:16—34:1. *Critical ed.*: J. Marcus, *The newly discovered original Hebrew of Ben Sira (Ecclesiasticus xxxii, 16—xxxiv, 1): The fifth manuscript and a prosodic version of Ben Sira (Ecclesiasticus xxii, 22—xxiii, 9)*, Philadelphia 1931.

(3) **J. Schirmann's further leaves of Geniza MSS**, namely: B—two leaves containing 10:19cd—11:10; 15:1—16:7. C—two leaves containing 3:14—18, 21, 22; 41:16; 4:21; 20:22, 23; 4:22, 23b; 26:2b, 3, 13, 15—17; 36:27—31. *Critical ed.*: A. A. Di Lella, 'The recently identified leaves of Sirach in Hebrew', Bib 45 (1964), pp. 153—167.

(4) **From Qumran Cave 2:** MS 2Q18—second half of 1st cent. B.C., contains fragments of 6:14, 15 (or possibly 1:19, 20) and of 6:20—31. *Critical ed.*: M. Baillet, DJD III, 1962, p. 75.

(5) **From Qumran Cave 11:** MS. 11QPsa—first half of 1st cent. A.D., contains 51:13—20, 30b. *Preliminary ed.*: J. A. Sanders, DJD IV, 1965, 79—85.

(6) **Yadin's Masada MS.**: Twenty-six leather fragments forming seven pages which date from first half of 1st cent. B.C., and contain 39:27—32; 40:10—19c; 40:26—44:17. *Preliminary ed.*: Y. Yadin, *The Ben Sira Scroll from Masada with introduction, emendations and commentary*, Jerusalem 1965.

So far, therefore, about two-thirds of the HT has **e** been recovered: 1100 distichs from the above MSS plus 8 more from rabbinical writings—a total of 1108 out of perhaps an original 1616 as represented by the Gr. uncial text.

The Greek Version made by Ben Sira's grandson c. **f** 132 B.C. is to be found above all in the great uncial codices of the LXX, A C S and especially B, as well as in the cursives which follow them. However, even in its primitive form as it left the grandson's hand this text was not an exact replica in Gr. of the grandfather's HT. The translator is conscious of this himself and apologises for it in the Prologue. Presumably he is referring to the circumlocutions and adaptations which he felt it necessary to introduce for the sake of his hellenistic readers. But

1f besides this he has in places misread his text or misinterpreted it, as the HT now shows. Moreover the HT which he had before him—and which, it is clear, was not the autograph of his grandfather but a not over-careful copy—was in poor textual condition. Furthermore, the grandson's Gr. text itself has in the course of its transmission suffered in an unusual degree from editorial alterations and from the scribal corruptions, omissions and misplacements to which all ancient texts are subject. (On the special question of the Expanded Text see § 442). In spite of such defects the Gr. uncial text of Sir has *de facto* held the position of 'primitive' text from the earliest Christian centuries, and has come down to us with a fulness of early MS evidence, ancient daughter versions and patristic citations which enable its original form to be in the main reconstituted with sufficient completeness, security and exactitude.

g One notable defect found in all Gr. MSS without exception is the **inversion of the true order of chh 30 to 36.** The correct order, found in HT, Latin, Syr. and some forms of the Armenian, can be restored in the Gr. after 30:24 by making the section 33:13*b* to 36:16*a* precede the section 30:25 to 33:13*a*. It would appear that the pairs of leaves on which these sections were written were accidentally transposed in the exemplar from which all the Gr. MSS are derived, but not in the exemplar from which the Latin trans. was made. Swete and Ziegler in their edd. of the LXX restore the correct order of the text but keep the old chapter and verse numeration, adding however in brackets the correct numeration as found in Latin. Rahlfs in his ed. (at 30:25) also restores the correct order and numbers the chh and vv accordingly, suppressing the old numeration.

h *Critical edd.*: H. B. Swete, *The OT in Greek*, II, Cambridge 1907³; A. Rahlfs, *Septuaginta*, Stuttgart 1952⁵; J. Ziegler, *Sapientia Jesu Filii Sirach*, Göttingen LXX, XII, 2, 1965. Ziegler's text and apparatus mark an immense advance on previous edd. His masterly introduction is indispensable for the study of text-critical problems. Basic for the study of the Expanded Text (§ 442), though now outdated in parts, is J. H. A. Hart, *Ecclesiasticus: the Greek text of codex 248 edited with a textual commentary and prolegomena*, Cambridge 1909.

i Syriac Versions—(a) The **Syrohexaplar** was made by Paul, Bishop of Tella, in 615–7. It is an important witness for the Expanded Text of Sir (§ 442*e*), reproducing as it does with great fidelity in Syriac the hexaplaric Gr. (cf § 28*b*). Edition: A. M. Ceriani, *Codex syro-hexaplaris Ambrosianus photolithographice editus*, Milan 1874. (b) The **Peshitta Syriac** (cf § 27*d*) of Sir was made c. A.D. 200, probably by a Christian. It was made from a type of text which in some particulars was superior to the exemplar of HT used by the grandson for his Gr. version, but which had already undergone some tendentious editorial alteration. Its basis seems to have been a Hebrew text of 'expanded' type. It preserves the correct order of the text after 30; 24, and is characterized by the large number of its omissions compared with the other versions. *Editions*: It was first edited by the Maronite Gabriel Sionita for the Paris Polyglot, Vol. VIII, 1635 (cf J. P. Arendzen in *Cath. Encyc.*, VI, 1909, p. 331), reprinted unchanged by Walton in the London Polyglot, IV, 1657; substantially the same text in P. A. de Lagarde, *Libri VT apocryphi syriace*, Leipzig-London 1861; A. M. Ceriani, *Translatio Syra Pescitto VT ex codice Ambrosiano sec. fere VI photolithographice edita*, 2, 4, Milan 1878.

j The Latin Version—now found in Vg is in reality a recension of VL. St Jerome did not regard Sir as canonical, **441j** and concerning it he says *calamo temperavi*: 'I restrained my pen' *(Praef. in lib. Salom.*, PL 29, 427). The present-day Benedictine editors of the critical text of Vg, combining their own findings with the earlier ones of Thielmann, Herkenne and especially De Bruyne, give an account of the Latin Sir which may be summarized as follows: This version was made, perhaps as early as the 2nd cent., from a Gr. exemplar which represented very fully the Expanded Text. The Latin which resulted lacked the Prologue *Multorum nobis*. It lacked also the *Laus Patrum* (chh 44–50) which in fact is unknown to any of the Latin Fathers previous to Isidore of Seville (d. 636). It contained, however, ch 51 in its entirety, and an intrusive ch 52, *Oratio Salomonis*, which in reality belongs to 2 Chr 6:13–22 and 1 (3) Kgs 8:22–31. In the 5th or 6th cent. this VL of Sir gained admission to the Vg. But in the meantime it had undergone notable alterations at the hands of scribes and editors. First, its expanded text was pruned and altered to reduce it to greater conformity with the unexpanded text of the Gr. uncials. Secondly, successive scribes set their hands to improving its latinity by inserting what they regarded as preferable alternative translations. Thirdly, the 'missing' prologue *Multorum nobis* was prefixed. Lastly, the *Laus Patrum* (chh 44–50) was inserted, possibly after Sir had already found its way into MSS of the Vg. In consequence of this complicated history the Latin Sir today offers a text more replete with doublets, variants and interpolations than any other book of the Latin Bible, but one which is at the same time of the greatest interest and importance for text-critical purposes, especially the question of the Expanded Text. *Critical ed.*: The text of Sir in the form in which it gained admission to MSS of the Vg has been brought out in an admirable critical edition by the Benedictines of the Abbey of San Girolamo, Rome: *Biblia sacra iuxta latinam vulgatam versionem ad codicum fidem*, Vol. XII, Rome 1964. A critical ed. of Sir in its pre-vulgate VL form is in preparation by the Benedictines of the Vetus Latina Institut of Beuron under the direction of Dom Bonifatius Fischer.

Other Versions made from the Gr. and occasionally **k** cited by text-critics are the Coptic, Ethiopic and Old Slavonic. The Arabic in Walton's Polyglot is from Syr.; R. M. Frank of the Catholic University of America has in preparation an ed. of MS Sinai 155 which is from the Gr. and follows the inverted order of chh 30–36 (A. A. Di Lella, op cit, 50, 154). On the Armenian versions the statements of experts are conflicting as to their number, nature, *editiones principes* and order of chh 30–36. Leaving aside Bishop Oskan's trans. from the Vg (1666), Ziegler makes use of Arm I (Zohrab), Arm II (Bagratuni), and Arm III. Both I and II have many omissions and lack chh 44–51. The recent findings of Leloir appear conclusive: Arm I and II normally follow Gr. but occasionally Syr. Both of them, however, have the correct order of chh after 30:24 (L. Leloir, DBS 6 (1960) 812f).

THE EXPANDED TEXT

NB. Special sigla used in this section (and in the com- **442a** mentary on Sir): HT I = the Hebrew text as it left the hand of Ben Sira. HT II = the Hebrew text as subsequently added to in one or more recensions. Gr. I = the grandson's Gr. version. Gr. II = the expanded Gr. version based on HT II. Sir II = the expanded recension(s) in a general sense, including HT II and Gr. II.

442a Plan of this section: (A) The textual witnesses. (B) Doctrinal content. (C) Essenian origin. (D) Qumran connections. (E) Divine inspiration.

(A) The textual witnesses—Besides the Gr. version of Sir which was made by Ben Sira's grandson and is contained in the uncials A B C S and their dependent cursives, scholars have long recognized the existence of another Gr. recension, nowadays called Gr. II. Its main witnesses are certain Gr. cursives and VL. The Peshitta Syr. and the surviving HT confirm that Gr. II is derived for the most part from a HT which differed appreciably from HT I, chiefly by its many additions. These consist of (a) short additions of a few words, or even single words, which often give a new shade of meaning to the whole phrase in which they occur; and (b) complete stichoi or verse-lines. These latter amount all-told in the Gr. witnesses to about 150. For textual corroboration of these by VL and Syr. see below § 442d, e.

b The Gr. MS evidence for these additions falls into two groups, the origenistic or hexaplaric (called by Ziegler the O-group), and the lucianic (called by Ziegler the L-group). (a) *The O-group*—On the hexapla in general see § 26k. On the O-recension of Sir see J. Ziegler, 'Die hexaplarische Bearbeitung des griech. Sirach', BZ n.f. 4 (1960), 174—85. Ziegler's researches have confirmed that a hexaplaric edition of Sir was compiled, probably not by Origen himself but by a follower. Its main differences from Gr. I were derived from then-existing Gr. MSS closely representative of Heb. originals. Its textual witnesses are: (1) Cursive MS 253 = Bibl. Vat. gr. 336, XI cent. (2) The syro-hexaplar (cf § 441i), (collated by Hart, op cit, 73—88). (3) Uncial MS V = codex Venetus, VIII cent., the only uncial to contain important readings of the O-recension. (4) The readings designated S[c] (in Swete S[ca]), i.e. corrections in a 7th cent. hand inserted in LXX(S). (5) Apart from VL the Armenian is the version most important for both O- and L-recensions. (b) *The L-group*—See J. Ziegler, 'Hat Lukian der griech. Sirach rezensiert?', Bib 40 (1959), 210—229. The connexion of the martyr Lucian of Antioch (d. A.D. 312) with the work of editing the Gr. Bible, both OT and NT, and the appropriateness of the term 'lucianic' to designate a certain recension of the Gr. OT, are much disputed. (For Lucian and 'his' recension see B. M. Metzger, 'Lucian and the Lucianic recension of the Greek Bible', NTS 8 (1962), 189—203; idem, *Chapters in the Hist. of NT Textual Criticism*, Leiden 1963, 1—41; rejecting the term 'lucianic' as a misnomer see D. Barthélemy, *Les devanciers d'Aquila* = VTS X, 1963, x and 126ff; see above § 26j). Here we take 'lucianic' merely as a conventional label for **c** this recension. Ziegler has established the existence of a 'lucianic' recension of Sir, and has also brought to light two important MS witnesses of it to add to the already well-known 248, viz 493 = Munich Staatsbibl., Gr. 551, XV cent., and 637 = Rome, Bibl. Casan. 241, XI cent. (Cf J. Ziegler, *Die münchener griech. Sirach-Hs. 493*, Munich 1962). It is now recognized that a great number of the additions found in the L-recension go back to a HT, not directly but through the hexapla and through certain Gr. translations which existed in the early Christian centuries, 'but whose names unfortunately we do not know' (J. Ziegler, Bib 1959, 219). VL and Syr. contain many readings of the L-recension, not in Sir alone but in other OT books as well, which readings, therefore, existed long before the time of Lucian. The principal Gr. patristic writers who witness to the O-text or the L-text of Sir are Clem. Alex., Chrys., and the comparatively late florilegists Antonius Melissa, Maximus Confessor, Antiochus Monachus (Cf Hart, op cit, 321—

70; Ziegler in BZ (1960) 185, mentions also Anastasius **44** Sinaita, John Climacus, John Damascene).

The importance of those additions of Gr. II which (in Gr. MSS) amount to a stichos or more is thrown into relief by Ziegler who in the Göttingen LXX prints them, not in the apparatus but in the text, in smaller characters. Most of these are given in English on RSV margin under the heading 'Other authorities add (or read)'.

The VL and the Expanded Text—The importance of **d** VL as a witness of the Expanded Text is clear from what has been said (§ § 441j, 442a; see also Smend, op cit, cxxix; Herkenne, op cit, 6). What is its relationship to Gr. II? Its correct order of chapters after 30:24 shows that its Gr. exemplar was older than the common exemplar of all known Gr. MSS (cf § 441g). VL's exemplar contained numerous additions of Gr. II type. The (incomplete) list in Smend (op cit ic—cxiii) notes 36 places in which VL supports passages of a stichos or more in Gr. II witnesses, and gives the VL text of 75 further stichoi proper to VL. That these additions, through the Gr. on which they are based, go back ultimately to an expanded HT is generally held today (cf Smend, op cit, xcviii, cxvii, cliii; Herkenne, op cit, 11f). As to the form of Gr. which immediately underlay the primitive VL, Smend holds that it was basically a MS of Gr. I, but one which retained far more traces of the influence of Gr. II than do any of the surviving MSS (op cit, xcviii, cxxiv). Herkenne substantially agrees (op cit, p. 11). Against this, De Bruyne holds that VL was based directly on a MS of Gr. II, but that many opposing readings of Gr. I entered it later. This would make VL the only known direct representative of Gr. II (RBen 1928, 41—43, 46; cf § 441j).

Syr. and the Expanded Text—See above § 441i. Syr. **e** was made direct from an exemplar of HT which represented a fusion of two Heb. recensions such as we have in the extant MSS of HT. In choosing between doublets in his HT, Syr. was often guided by the form which occurred in a Gr. exemplar which he had at hand—one which was not Gr. II but contained many of its readings. Thus, Syr. lacks the grandson's Prologue, as does Gr. II. It did not occur in HT and is relevant only to the grandson's translation. Of the approximately 150 additional stichoi of Gr. II, Syr. has 35, besides a number of shorter additions in common with Gr. II. It has also 37 stichoi, and many shorter variants, proper to itself. Not a few of these may well be of Christian origin, but many of them show the characteristic doctrinal trends of Gr. II and VL (see below § 442h).

The Hebrew MSS and the Expanded Text—The **f** Cairo MSS (cf § 441a—c) bear witness to the existence, at a very early date, of more than one recension of the HT. This conclusion had already been foreshadowed by the detection of Gr. II. It is supported by the text of many of the rabbinical citations of Ben Sira (cf Smend, op cit, xlvi—li). HT II differed from HT I chiefly by additions. Fuchs has shown (op cit 112—15) that the recension represented by Cairo MSS. A, B and C contains (apart from the psalm at 51:12) 90 passages, of the length of a stichos or more, added to HT I. Of these, 61 are merely alternative readings or wordings of the original. Almost all the rest, about 25 in all, are editorial additions of doctrinal significance, comparable to the characteristic additions of Gr. II. Examples are 11:15, 16; 15:14b; 15:15c; 16:15, 16; 31:6d; 51:1.

(B) Doctrinal content of the Expanded Text—A **g** number of the elements proper to Sir II are purely scribal: marginal glosses, explanatory expansions, alternative readings or renderings of one original text. Its truly

42g distinctive features, however, consist of *editorial* additions. A small number of these are admittedly Christian glosses, but on the whole they are supplements, pre-Christian in date, inserted in order to give expression to certain religious ideas not (sufficiently) represented in the original.

Thus Sir II stresses, on the part of God a more fatherly attitude towards mankind, and a more personal contact with individual men as such. He bestows his spiritual gifts on a man, making him acceptable to himself. He understands man's weakness and repeatedly forgives his sins; but if the sinner remains impenitent God hardens him in the moral darkness which hides from him the light of revealed truth necessary for his well-being. To this individual divine care man responds by the filial fear, by the trust, and especially by the love which join him to God, and also by the repentance which brings him back to God when that union has been broken by sin. God scrutinizes the actions of every man and 'visits' him with a retribution which apportions him a 'lot' of happiness or of misery. In this world, this brings honour and success to the well-doer, and shame and reproach to the evil-doer. In the next world it brings vengeance and sudden destruction to the sinner, salvation and life to the just man.

h The Eschatology of the Expanded Text is of outstanding importance as a clue to the origin of Sir II and requires a more particular exposition. Ben Sira himself was extremely conservative in his view of Sheol and of the lot of the individual after death (cf § 440 *1m*). It is significant that of the six passages in which the grandson (Gr. I), or his Heb. exemplar deliberately departs from the sense expressed by HT I, three have to do with eschatology, viz 7:17; 30:17; 48:11.

The Eschatology of Gr. II and VL—For typical expressions of the eschatology of Gr. II see its readings in 2:9c (not in RSV); 12:6c (RSVm); 16:22c (not in RSV); 19:18, 19 (RSVm); 23·4 (in Ziegler's apparatus crit., not in RSV). For typical passages of VL see the following, found in English in DV and KV (add. = a VL addition to the Gr. I text), 6:4 add.; 6:22 (23); 14:10 (20, 21); 15:5 add.; 15·8 add.; 17:23 (19) add.; 17:27, 28 (25—27); 18·22 add.; 21:10 (11) add.; 24:9 (14); 24:22 (31) add.; 24:32 (45); 24:33 (46) add.; 27:8 (9) add.; 34:13a (14a); 44:16 add.

To summarize: after death there is to be for each individual a day of judgement on which God will 'visit' him and make enquiry into all his actions. For the wicked it will be a day of wrath and vengeance. They will be consigned to 'the lower parts of the earth', there to undergo their 'lot' of darkness and pain. For the just it will mean entrance into the Future World, the Holy World, the 'lot' of truth. There they will enjoy eternal life, an everlasting reward which brings with it honour from God and a joy which never ends. An *intermediate state* between the time of death and the time of the final allotment of the everlasting reward is referred to in VL 24:32 (45), possibly also in the phrase 'into paradise' in 44:16 (Cf P. Grelot's art. on Lk 23:43, RB 74 (1967), especially 200—5).

i The Eschatology of Syr.—can be gathered from (a) an interpolation of 12 couplets, translated from a Heb. original, after 1:20, and (b) other passages scattered throughout, viz 1:12, 20; 3:1; 9:7; 17:20, 22, 23; 18:10; 26:28ef; 48:10. (All these passages except 26:28ef are available in E. tr. in the apparatus of Oesterley and Box in CAP I; the addition after 1:20 also in Hart op cit p. 91.) According to these passages there is to be a Day of the Lord on which he will reveal himself as judge. The subject-matter of his judgement will be both men's good deeds and their wicked ones, the latter having been record-

ed precisely with a view to their final recompense. The **442i** just, inscribed in the Book of Life, will enter the World of the Righteous to receive eternal life, to share an everlasting crown and eternal righteousness with the Holy Ones, the angels of God. In their company the just will rejoice for all eternity, telling forth the glory of God. Syr. thus introduces two ideas not found in Gr. II, viz the written record of man's bad deeds, and the just man's fellowship with the angels in the world of the righteous. Apart from that, Syr.'s eschatology is close to Gr. II's, covering (more cursorily) the same ground and sharing the same ideas.

(C) The Essenian origin of the expanded recen- **443a** **sion(s)**—In 1897 D. A. Schlatter published his monograph *Das neue gefundene hebräische Stück des Sirach.- Der Glossator des griechischen Sirach und seine Stellung in der Geschichte der jüdischen Theologie* (= *Beiträge zur Förderung christlicher Theologie*, I, 5—6, Gütersloh, 1897). His conclusion (arrived at when only 39:15—49:11 of the HT was available to him) was that the glosses were of hellenistic origin, coming from the hand of a certain Alexandrian Jew, Aristobulus (fl. 170—150 B.C.). When the remainder of the Geniza MSS were published this was seen to be untenable. J. H. A. Hart, in the Prolegomena of his ed. of MS 248, devotes a long chapter to the nature and origin of the glosses (op cit 272—320). His conclusion is that Sir II is a Pharisaic recension of the Wisdom of Ben Sira, and that the additions 'contain tentative Greek renderings of many of the technical terms and watchwords of the Sect' of the Pharisees (op cit 274). As their date of origin he favours the end of the 2nd cent. B.C. in the time of John Hyrcanus (op cit 287f). Though the hypothesis was welcomed by some scholars (e.g. Oesterley in CBSC, xcviiif; Box and Oesterley in CAP I, 282), the arguments brought forward for it are unconvincing. The group of writings with which the content of Sir II is compared (viz Philo and Josephus, with some reference to the Talmud and St Paul) is too late and too narrow to throw any significant light directly on the Pharisaism of the 2nd cent. B.C. It is also almost exclusively hellenistic. Considering that already in Hart's time it was held that many of the glosses were of Heb. or Aram origin, the passing over of the abundant contemporary Palestinian literature in these languages, much of it long previous in date to Philo and Josephus, left a fatal gap in his argumentation.

In 1951 the present writer submitted to the Pontifical **b** Biblical Commission in Rome a doctoral thesis entitled *The Expanded Text of Ecclesiasticus: its teaching on the Future Life as a clue to its origin*. This has remained unpublished, but for various reasons the writer feels encouraged to put forward here its main conclusions as containing what he believes to be the solution of the problem of the origin of the Expanded Text. These conclusions, arrived at on grounds of *content*, largely coincide with and support those established on purely textual and linguistic grounds in Segal's notable article of 1934 (cf Bibliography), dissenting however from his placing in the 2nd cent. A.D. the origin of the HT underlying Syr. The conclusions were arrived at independently of the Qumran material, not available at the time, but they are now seen to be remarkably confirmed by it. Within the last few years they have met with an encouraging measure of approval from a number of experts in the text-history of Sir (Cf J. Ziegler, with certain reservations, in BZ n.f. IV 1960, 183f; idem, Göttingen LXX, 73f; the Benedictine editors of the Vg, *Biblia Sacra* XII, Rome 1963, *Prolegomena*, xi; H. Duesberg and J. Fransen in SacB, 1966, 7—11 passim).

443b In the study referred to, the eschatological teaching of Sir II was compared in detail with the corresponding teaching of the works of Jewish Palestinian and hellenistic literature produced between 200 B.C. and A.D. 100. The main conclusions were as follows:

c (1) The HT of Sir II underlying Gr. II and VL, from the doctrinal and literary point of view depends to some extent on a group of Palestinian writings of the late 2nd cent. B.C., viz the *Book of Jubilees*, the *Testaments of the XII Patriarchs*, and especially the *Book of Enoch* A (= chh 1—36, following here and below Charles's analysis and dating of *Enoch* as in CAP II, 168—71).

(2) Its main sources, however, were *Enoch* B (chh 37—71) and *Enoch* E (chh 91—105, 108), which belong to the period 100—75 B.C.

(3) It shows dependence on one hellenistic work, the *Wisdom of Solomon*, with which it notably coincides in its reserved attitude regarding a General Judgement and the resurrection of the body. It coincides with it also in the use of certain terms and expressions.

(4) All this points to a date about the end of the reign of Alexander Jannaeus (103—76 B.C.), or perhaps slightly later, say around 60 B.C., as the date of origin of the form of HT II which underlies Gr. II and VL.

(5) Syr., by its paucity of eschatological passages, offers too narrow a field of comparison to arrive at a similar degree of probability regarding the HT which underlies it. The evidence points to the conclusions: (a) that the form of Sir II concerned was influenced in part by the *Book of Jubilees*; (b) that the said influence was checked by the overriding influence of *Enoch* B and *Enoch* E; (c) that consequently the HT of Sir II which underlies Syr. can be conjecturally dated to about the same time as the form which underlies Gr. II, roughly about 60 B.C.

d (6) *General conclusion.* The literature thus identified as basic to Sir II (*Book of Jubilees, Testaments of XII Patriarchs* and the specified sections of *Enoch*) was already at the time of the above investigation regarded as of Essenian origin (cf e.g. M. J. Lagrange, *Le Judaisme avant Jésus-Christ*, 1931³, 121ff, 130, 263—6, 329). This pointer was followed up. The glosses were studied with a view to their possible connection with the Essenes as these were known from the classical sources Pliny, Philo, Josephus and Hippolytus. Many converging lines of evidence were uncovered, all pointing to the conclusion that the additions as a whole were indeed the work of the Essenes. That was the position taken up and elaborated in the final pages of the study referred to.

e **(D) Qumran connections of the Expanded Text—** The thesis of the Essenian origin of the Expanded Text has been abundantly confirmed by the Qumran texts. These throw a flood of light on the religious background and textual history of Sir II, and point to Qumran itself as the place of its origin. To justify this statement would require a close comparison of the religious ideas, and especially of the eschatology, of Sir II with the corresponding elements of such Qumran literature as the Manual of Discipline (IQS), the Thanksgiving Hymns (IQH), the Commentary on Habakkuk (IQpHab) etc. Such a study is not possible here, but certain significant points may be noted. (1) The OT pseudepigrapha which give the clue to the Essenian origin of Sir II were much prized in Qumran. *Jubilees* is now known to be an early Qumranian work practically in its entirety. MSS of the nucleus, or earliest forms, of the *Testaments of the XII Patriarchs* (those of Levi and of Naphtali) have been discovered there. The relevant parts of *Enoch* (except, so far, *Enoch* B) are represented in no less than ten fragmentary MSS from Cave IV (Cf J. T. Milik, TYD, **443** 32—34). (2) Priests of the ousted Zadokite line were prominent at Qumran and the outlook of the sect was strongly sacerdotal. The Book of Ben Sira is likewise notable for its exaltation of the priestly order, and ends with a panegyric of the Zadokite line in the person of Simon son of Onias (50:1—24). In the nature of things it must have been highly prized by the sectaries. (3) Again, Ben Sira's express object was to present his contemporaries with a guide to moral life in which the pious Jew would find norms for right conduct in every circumstance—norms derived especially from God's revealed wisdom as crystallized in the Law. Now it was precisely a full and perfect living according to the Law that the sectaries aimed at. Their characteristic morality represented an attempt to reduce to practice not merely the express prescriptions of the Law, but its remote consequences in the sphere of practical virtue, piety and worship. For their initiates Ben Sira's work could well have served as a *vade mecum* of moral training. Its popularity at Qumran is in fact borne out by the discovery of remains of its HT both at Qumran itself and also at Masada (§ 441d), not improbably brought there from Qumran (Cf R. De Vaux, RB 73 (1966), 226).

On certain points, however, it would have been found f defective, progressively so as the religious ideas and practices of the sect evolved. Its personal religion was not sufficiently interior; its notions of repentance, personal acceptance and rejection by God, union with him by trust and love, were imperfect. Above all its eschatology was primitive, scanty and outmoded. In spite, then, of its initial popularity, such drawbacks would have led to its being set aside had not its admirers devised a method of bringing it into line on all those points, and of preserving it as an always living and actual text, reflecting their advancing views and adapted to their needs. That method was to 'gloss' it; to 're-read' it from time to time; in a word, to make precisely those successive re-interpretations or *recensions* of it whose traces we have been trying to distinguish, and whose end-product is the text of Sir II as we know it today. (For the practice of re-interpreting or 're-reading' OT texts, especially in the light of progressive eschatology, cf R. Tournay, 'Relectures bibliques concernant la vie future et l'angelologie', RB 69 (1962), 481ff; idem, RB 71 (1964), 506).

That those re-readings found their way through the g hexapla into surviving Gr. MSS may be due to an ancient 'pre-view' of the Qumran material enjoyed by Origen and his fellow-workers. In a passage brought to light by Mercati, Origen himself, speaking of the Psalter-text of his hexapla refers to a 'sixth edition *found together with other Hebrew and Greek books in a jar near Jericho* in the time of the reign of Antoninus (MS Antonius) the son of Severus', i.e. of Caracalla, who ruled A.D. 211—17. (G. Mercati, *Note di letteratura biblica e cristiana antica = Studi e testi* 5, Rome 1901, 28—60; cf H. B. Swete, *Introd. to the OT in Greek*, 1902, 53—55). The provenance of this jar and its MSS was quite possibly Qumran itself (Cf R. De Vaux, RB 56 (1949), 236f, 592; J. T. Milik Bib 31 (1950), 506). The Cairo Geniza MSS likewise may well be copies derived originally from a similar find of Hebrew biblical MSS made in a cave near Jericho about A.D. 790. The find (curiously similar in its details to the first find at Qumran in our own day) is described in a contemporary Syriac letter of Timotheus I, Patriarch of Seleucia (A.D. 726—819). For documentation and corroborative details see A. A. Di Lella, *Hebrew Text of Sirach*, 1966, 81—97.

(E) Divine Inspiration of Sir II—The comparatively h

3h few writers who have raised this question have concluded in one way or another in favour of the inspiration of the 'glosses'. (Cf D. De Bruyne, RBen 40 (1928), 47; F. Kaulen, *Einleitung in die heilige Schrift* II, (1913⁵), 196; J. Prado (Simon-Prado), *Praelect. Biblicae, Vetus Test*. II, (1954⁵), 441; C. Spicq, PCSB VI, 1951, p. 550).

The arguments advanced are persuasive, especially if understood particularly of that form which underlies VL. To them, however, the present writer would prefix this consideration: The Council of Trent, having listed the books of OT and NT accepted by the Church, defined as sacred and canonical 'the books themselves in their integrity with all their parts as they are customarily read in the Catholic Church and are found in the ancient vulgate latin edition' (DzS 1504). In the time of Trent it was in its VL form that Sir was found in the Vg and customarily read in the western Church. Not merely the book itself, therefore, but also those *parts* of it which belong to its integrity as it is found in the Vg, are canonical. The bulk of the additions of VL taken by and large have (as shown above) a doctrinal significance. To eliminate them to any notable extent would be to impair the doctrinal *integrity* of the book as it is found in the Vg and is customarily read in the Church. Sir II, then, as represented by VL, is a canonical text.

i Other considerations corroborate this in various degrees. (1) The liturgical usage of Sir II, particularly extensive in the western Church. (2) Acceptance of the Gr. II form as inspired Scripture by writers of the Gr. Church such as Clem. Alex., Chrys. etc (cf § 442c). (3) Acceptance of Sir in the Syriac-speaking Church in one of its Sir II forms.

On the problem of how the inspired character of the re-readings and successive recensions of OT books is to be theologically explained in the concrete, see § 42a–g.

j **Current English translations of Sir** arranged according to their basic text: A. *Of the Vulgate (VL)*: (1) DV, (See § 34c–d) and Challoner (see § 35c). The DV of Sir of course includes the readings of Gr. II as found in VL (2) KV, 1949, does likewise. In it some readings of VL not found in Gr. are placed in brackets. Its notes draw attention throughout to readings of Gr. and of HT. B. *Of the Greek text*: (3) AV, 1611. Sir in AV was made from the Gr. of the Complutensian Polyglot, which happened to be that of MS 248. AV therefore includes the intrusive Prologue as well as the genuine one (cf § 444a), and in its text many of the readings of Gr. II. (4) RV, 1894. In Sir this was based on the Gr. uncials and was at pains to exclude the Gr. II readings of AV. (5) E. J. Goodspeed, *Apocrypha*, 1938, 'an American translation'. For Sir it is based on Rahlfs's LXX, i.e. the uncial text, of which it gives a fluent and forceful translation. (6) RSV, 1957, also based on Rahlfs's LXX but with constant reference to the Cairo HT. On the margin it restores many of the passages of Gr. II deleted by RV (cf § 442c). (7) JB, 1966, based on BJ. In Sir, therefore, it is based on Gr. I, but readings of Gr. II are sometimes followed in the text and frequently cited in the footnotes, where also the variants of HT are noted. C. *Of the Hebrew text*: (8) In CAP II, 1913, C. H. Box and W. O. E. Oesterley give their own translation of Sir based on an eclectic text in which primacy of place is given to the Cairo HT. A valuable apparatus of variant readings of HT, Gr. I, Gr. II, VL and Syr. is included. (9) CV, Vol. III, 1955, includes Sir. 'The translation of Sirach, based on the original Hebrew as far as it is preserved, and corrected from the ancient versions, is nevertheless often interpreted in the light of the traditional

Gr. text' (*Preface*, p. v). The textual notes (pp. 692– **443j** 710), directed chiefly to the emendation of HT and the justification of the translation given, are presented with exemplary care.

NB. The English translation kept in view in the present commentary is RSV, which is based on Gr. 1, but takes account, in the text or on the margin, of variants of Gr. II, VL, HT and Syr. For following a similar method BJ is severely taken to task by L. F. Hartmann in an article ('Sirach in Hebrew and in Greek', CBQ 23 (1961), 443–51) in which he maintains that the only justifiable method for a modern translation of Sir is to follow, where it exists, the HT as corrected by means of the ancient versions, with the Gr. version employed as the primary source for the rest of the book (cf art cit, p. 443). To the present writer a distinction seems called for. The method described is certainly indicated where the object aimed at is primarily to establish a text or translation which will come as close as possible to the original as it left the hand of Ben Sira (cf art cit, p. 450). But other objects, too, are legitimate, and for them the rule laid down is too stringent. One such object is that of establishing the form, and explaining the meaning and the peculiarities, of the text of Sir as it has been read in the Christian Church from the beginning. (On the importance of the LXX in general from this point of view cf H. B. Swete, *Introd. to the OT in Greek*, 1902, 470–7). But from the beginning (apart from the Syriac-speaking Church which had its own translation direct from the HT) the whole of Christendom read the Book of Ben Sira, and felt its inspired impact, in its Gr. form alone, or in versions made from the Gr., such as VL, Coptic, Ethiopic and Armenian. This is one of the reasons which render not only justifiable but indispensable, *alongside* translations like those of Oesterley-Box and the CV, such versions also as those of Goodspeed, BJ, JB and RSV.

Prologue—To the genuine prologue some editions **444a** (e.g. AV) prefix a spurious one taken from MS 248 (Ziegler's ed., p. 127; Hart, op cit, xviii). This in turn borrowed it from a 6th cent. *Synopsis Scripturae Sacrae* falsely attributed to Ath. (PG 28, 376f; cf T. Zahn, *Geschichte des NTlichen Kanons*, Bd. II, (1890), 302–18). The other prologue, though not canonical, is genuinely by the grandson of Ben Sira. In RSV it is arranged in three paragraphs. (1) Israel has received a treasure in the Scriptures. Her scholars have a corresponding duty to spread the knowledge of them amongst 'outsiders', i.e. those unlearned in Scripture lore. With this in view 'Jesus' (Ben Sira) composed his work on a scriptural basis, treating of wisdom with the practical aim of helping his readers to live according to the law of Moses. (2) The translator asks his readers to remember the practical aim of the book, and to be indulgent to the imperfections which it, like any Gr. translation of a Heb. original, must exhibit. For the significance of the reference here in (1) and (2) to 'the law and the prophets and the others that followed them', and to 'the law, the prophecies and the rest of the books' cf § 14d. (3) Noting the date and place of origin of his version, (cf § 438f), the translator says his aim is to spread Ben Sira's doctrine amongst 'those living abroad', i.e. the Jews of the Dispersion, so that they too may be helped 'to live according to the law'.

1:1–4:10 Eulogy of Wisdom; man's duties to God, b his parents, his neighbour.

1:1–10 Wisdom's origin from God—(HT not available before 3:6). For the doctrine here cf § 440o. **2.** 'Who can count them?'—Only God, the one who

444b possesses wisdom in its fulness. See 8, 9. Heaven, earth, abyss: threefold division of the universe in Heb. cosmogony (Gn 1). **5** = Gr. II, RSVm. See § 440c. The fountainhead from which wisdom comes to men is the word by which God creates the world and reveals himself (cf 42:15; 43:26). The channels ('ways') through which wisdom flows out on men are the 'eternal commandments' of the law. See 24:23—27. To the question of **6** (and of **7** in Gr. II, RSVm), **8, 9** and **10** give the answer: the One who alone is wise of himself, by his creative word externalized ('created') his wisdom and apportioned it, in measured quantity to the universe ('all his works') and to mankind in general ('all flesh'), but 'supplied her' (unstintedly) to 'those who love him', i.e. to Israel.

1:11—2:18 Wisdom and the Fear of the Lord— Shows wisdom taking root in men (chiefly the People of God), and their response to it. For meaning of 'the fear of the Lord' cf § 440d. **13.** Refers to the happy life *on which he can look back*; happiness after death is not taught in the original work of Ben Sira. Cf § 440l. **14a** 'beginning': its root and choicest fruit. Cf § 440d. **14b** 'the faithful' i.e. Israel, whose patrimony wisdom is. **15.** Elaborates this; cp. 24:8—12. After 20 **Syr. interpolates** 12 vv of Hebrew origin (cf § 442i) describing the future reward of the just. It speaks of 'an eternal crown and eternal righteousness among the holy ones', 'life as an eternal heritage', inscription 'in the book of life'. **20—30.** To the refrain 'the fear of the Lord', anger, hypocrisy and self-exaltation are ruled out; meekness, patience and fidelity are inculcated. **2:1—5.** To serve the Lord brings trials (RSVm), which call for constancy. Cf § 440h. **6—11.** Persevering trust in the Lord wins his protection, mercy and forgiveness. VL (Vg. vv 6—10) mentions faith, trust and love: perhaps a Christian adaptation. **12—14.** A threefold 'woe' against fickleness and lack of trust. **15—18.** True fear and love of God do his will and trust his mercy. VL reads 18 (Vg 22) 'If we do not repent we shall fall etc', stressing an idea dear to Sir II.

c 3:1—4:10 Fear of God expressed in acts of virtue— **3:1—16** Filial piety. **6.** HT begins to be available. **14, 15.** Piety to parents wins forgiveness of sin. **17—24.** A humble sense of one's own limitations. **19** (Gr. II, RSVm). Meekness and humility will win the light that makes known the secrets of God's dealings: a characteristic teaching of Sir II. **26—29.** The stubborn man and the wise one: a contrast. **3:30—4:10. Kindness to the poor** and the unfortunate. **30.** On almsgiving see also 7:32— 35; 29:8—13. Cf Tb 4:7—11.

4:11—6:17 Description of Wisdom's Hardships and Rewards, followed by thoughts on conduct—**4:11— 19. Wisdom's Good Things** and her severe training— **13—16.** Wisdom and the inner life: it binds a man to the Lord, bringing life, joy, blessing and his love. **17—19.** How wisdom trains her clients. In HT wisdom speaks in the first person: for *her* read *my*, for *she* read *I*. For the doctrine see § 440h. **19.** A reference, perhaps, to Solomon's defection. See 47:19—21. **20—28. Sincerity in speech**—**22.** Against undue servility. **26.** The facts will sweep away our words if we deny that we are sinners. **27.** Repeats the thought of 22. **28.** All your life long ('even to death') let principle not favouritism be your guide. **29—31. Contrasts in conduct. 5:1—7 Against presuming on the Lord's forbearance**—**1.** 'I have enough' the false sense of security of the man who trusts in wealth. **5.** Do not go on sinning, presuming on eventual forgiveness by the Lord. Future 'atonement' is spoken of, not past. **6, 7.** Against presumptuous delay in turning to

the Lord. **5:8—6:4. Wise self-control in speech and 44..** **conduct. 9, 10.** Not expediency but truth should be your guide. **6:2—4.** Keep fleshly passion under control. 'Soul' in this passage renders Heb. *nepeš* which means the soul as the seat of *bodily* appetites. **6:5—17. Friendship, d false and true. 5—7.** Care in choosing friends. **8—13.** False friendship. **9b.** He will betray what you confided to him (see 6). **13.** Pseudo-friends are meant. **14—17.** True friendship, a gift of the Lord.

6:18—14:19 The Quest of Wisdom; cautions about social relationships follow. **18—37 Wisdom's Hardships and Rewards**—**20.** 'The uninstructed', Heb. 'the fool', i.e. (as usually in wisdom literature) the man culpably devoid of religious insight and moral feeling. **22.** VL here adds (Vg v 23b), from a Gr. II text which has not otherwise come down to us, 'but for those to whom it is known, (wisdom) abides even to the sight of God', *usque ad conspectum Dei*. This does not refer to the vision of God in heaven, but to God's *visitation* of the just, at death, to give them their reward. VL *conspectus* doubtless represents Gr. *episkopēs*, i.e. *visitation* in an eschatological sense. See VL *conspectus* in Sir 16:18; 18:20, and cf forms from *inspicere* and *respicere* in 2:21b (Vg): 15:8 (Vg); 23:24 (Vg v 34); Wis 2:20; 3:7 (Vg v 6b); 4:15; 1:19. **25.** Wisdom's discipline is a yoke. Cf 51:26. **28—31.** The seeker's toil is rewarded by the spiritual joy and security which wisdom gives, and the teacher's crown of honour. See 51:19—23. **32—37.** To grow in wisdom, frequent the company of the wise. **37.** Another source of wisdom: the Lord's 'statutes' and 'commandments', i.e. the law of Moses. See 24:23ff and § 440c. **7:1—9:16 Social relationships**—**1—10** On avoiding e ambition and presumption. **6, 7.** Admonition against the corrupt use of public power. **8, 9.** Against presuming on God's forgiveness without amendment of life. Cf 34:18f, and § 440e. **11—17.** Some social virtues. **14b.** Cf Mt 6:7. **15.** To till the soil is a work ordained by God. Cf Gn 2:5, 15; 3:17. **16, 17.** Act virtuously, for God will punish sin. **17b.** HT I reads, 'for the expectation of man is worms', a reference to the transitoriness of human life which ends in the corruption of the grave. This is one of the passages where the translator of HT I marks an advance on its eschatology, for he reads (Gr. I), 'the punishment of the ungodly is fire and worms'. He speaks not of the common lot of all mankind in the grave, but of the *punishment* of the *ungodly* man after death. The torment of the wicked in the next world by fire and worm became a stock notion in later Jewish eschatology. Cf Mk 9:48. Here it perhaps depends on Jdt 16:17 and (remotely) Is 66:24. The underlying HT of Gr. I here may well have already contained this reading (Cf Segal, JQR n.s. 25 (1934), p. 95). **18.** For 'gold of Ophir' cf 1 (3) Kgs 9:28; Jb 22:24; 28:16 and BDB s.v. **19—28.** Household and family virtues. **19.** Deprecates divorce; see 26; contrast 25:26. **20, 21.** Servants. Refers to Ex 21:2; Lv 25:39—43; Dt 15:12—15. **24, 25.** By oriental custom unmarried daughters are treated with strictness and their father chooses their husbands. **26.** See 21. **29—36.** Duties of religion. **29—31.** To reverence and support Levites and priests is an act of the fear and the love of God, and is commanded by the law. **31.** The sacrificial portions prescribed for their support. **32—36.** Works of mercy: to give alms, respect the dead, comfort mourners, visit the sick. **32.** See Dt 14:28f; 26:12—15. **33.** 'Kindness' was shown to the dead by mourning, by burying them fittingly (38:16), by solicitude for their dependents and their good name, and—as revelation progressed (see 2 Mc 12:42— 45)—by offering prayer and sacrifice on their behalf (see Tb 1:16ff; 12:12f). **8:1—19. On dealing with f**

44f **various classes of men. 9:1—9. Cautions about women. 9d.** 'in blood': adultery was punishable by death, Lv 20:10; Dt 22:22. **10—16. Various social relationships. 10.** Cf Lk 5:39.

9:17—11:6 Human Greatness, false and true—17, 18. Good government. **10:5.** For 'scribe' read 'lawgiver' (HT). **6—18.** Pride goes before a fall. **8.** Proud nations are humbled by the Lord: a prelude to 12ff. **11.** See comment on 7:17. **12—18.** The Lord's dealings with the proud peoples of salvation history; a commentary on 8, parallel to 16:6—10. **12, 13ab.** Preface to what follows: the sins for which those nations were destroyed were rooted in their pride. The 'beginning' of pride means the *first result* it produces, i.e. apostasy (12) and impenitence (13). **13c—17.** The fate of Sodom, Gomorrah and the Canaanites seems to be mainly in mind, but that of Assyria, Babylonia, Persia and Macedonia is not overlooked. **18.** The moral: pride ill befits man's lowly origin. **19—24.** The basis of true greatness is the 'fear' of the Lord, here taken in its broadest sense (see § 440d). **10:25—11:6.** True greatness and false. **26b, 27.** Boasting about what might have been is pointless when the facts proclaim its hollowness. **11:1.** See 39:4. **2—4b.** Judge not by appearances: whether looks (2), or size (3), (cf 1 Sm 16:7), or apparel (4b). **4c—6.** For the Lord can in an instant reverse the externals on which men's estimates are based. See Ps 105 (104):16—22; 1 Sm 9:21; 15:28.

45a **11:7—14:19 Miscellaneous Cautions**—discretion in conduct, the poor and the rich, the certainty of death. **7—9.** Meddlesomeness. **10—28.** Man's utter dependence on the Lord. One's lot in life does not ultimately depend on one's own efforts or ability, but on the overruling providence of God. He gives his lasting gifts only to the just. **15, 16.** Verses found not in Gr. I but in VL and Gr. II (RSVm), *and also in HT* (Cairo A)—an indication of Gr. II's dependence on an underlying HT in other places also. The contrast between the moral 'darkness' in which sinners walk and the 'love and upright ways' (HT) of the just is stressed in the Qumran literature. **18, 19.** A condensed parable. Lk 12:16—21 is closely parallel. **20—22.** A practical conclusion based on 17, viz **20** 'Be steadfast in your task' (HT), and **21** 'wonder not' that sinners prosper for a time, for (**22**) the Lord will redress the balance in the long run. **26—28.** The situation of a man at the end of his life will show whether, on the whole, his life has been pleasing to the Lord or not. His lot *after* death is not spoken of here **29—34.** Beware of plausible strangers.

12:1—7 Discretion in Almsgiving. 6c. The addition of Gr. II (RSVm), 'and he is keeping them for the mighty day of their punishment', represents an advance on the eschatology of HT I. In the light of parallels in *Enoch* (A) 10:12—14; *Jubilees* 5:10; 2 Pt 2:4, 9 etc, it means that God allows the malice of some sinners to accumulate until he inflicts an eternal judgement on them on 'the Mighty Day of their punishment'. **8—18.** False friendship. **18.** 'he will *wag* his head', a gesture of derisive triumph. Cf 13:7; Ps 22:7 (21:8); Mt 27:39. **13:1—24.** The poor and the rich: friendship between them is ill-advised, as likely to be unequal and insincere. The 'rich' spoken of are the worldly-minded rich. **7e.** 'wags his head': see on 12:19. **18.** There is a natural enmity between the shepherd's dog and the hyena that skulks about the flock, on the watch for a straying sheep. **24b.** 'And poverty is evil *which is due to impiety*' (HT). **25ff.** Sayings on joy **b** and sadness. **14:3—10. The miseries of the niggard. 11—19.** Death draws near, do good while yet you have time. **12b.** Translate: '*And that the covenant of Sheol*

has not been shown to you'. You have not come to terms **445b** with Sheol (the grave, death; see on 16b); it will inevitably claim you for its own. See 17b; contrast Is 28:15. **16b.** Translate: 'For in *Sheol there is no delight*'. Sheol is the underworld of OT eschatology. According to the older view here presented it was a place where all souls went after death, and remained in a state of suspended animation, unaffected by pleasure or pain (see § 440 1m). **14:20—16:23 The Pursuit of Wisdom**; principles of moral conduct—**14:20—27.** The eagerness and perseverance demanded of the seeker after wisdom, shown in a series of metaphors. **26.** Translate: '*He sets his nest in her foliage and lodges in her branches*' (HT). **15:1— 10.** The benefits which wisdom will bestow on her follower. **1.** Once again wisdom is identified with the law. **2b.** 'the wife of his youth': the expression is found in Prv 5:18; Is 54:6; Mal 2:14, 15, etc. It signifies the wife whom a man marries in early manhood and with whom mutual attachment grows stronger as life advances. Such is the attachment between wisdom and her devoted followers. The figure is graphically worked out in 51:13— 22, especially in the Qumran recension, cf § § 439f, 441d. **9, 10.** A 'footnote' on 5b. He to whom *wisdom* 'has not been sent from the Lord' cannot 'open *his* mouth in the midst of the assembly' to lead a hymn of praise. **15:11— 20 Free Will and Responsibility for Sin**—In vv **c** 7—9 it was stated that God withholds his gift of wisdom from the sinner. Does God himself therefore become responsible for sin? The answer is given here, but some of the relevant points are more fully indicated in 17:1—14 (man's spiritual nature and faculties, God's making known to him of the moral law with its sanctions). **11.** The blame for sin is not to be laid on the Lord, for he hates sin, and it would be a contradiction for him to 'do what he hates'. **12.** Nor is he as it were constrained to bring sin about for providential purposes: 'He has no need of a sinful man'. **13.** On the contrary, they who fear him can and do avoid sin, holding it in abomination as he does himself. HT brings out expressly his positive intervention to save them from sinning: 'The Lord hates evil and abomination, and does not let it happen to those who fear him.' **14.** Nor did God in the beginning create man with a nature already flawed, and thus incur responsibility for sin. When he created him 'he left him in the power of his own inclination'. 'Inclination' represents the Heb. *yēṣer*, on which see § 440ij. In the present context the *yēṣer* itself is neither a good 'inclination' nor a bad one, but has a 'neutral sense' (Oesterley and Box n.1.), which is very exactly rendered by 'free will'. **15 17.** Explain that this endowment places it in man's power to choose moral good or evil, with their consequences. Here lies the answer to the question posed.

15. God gave man helps to use his free will to choose the morally good: this 'good' he embodied in commandments which he made known to man. To these, man is faithful or unfaithful by his own choice. Cf 17:11—14. **16.** As further helps God added sanctions to his moral law, rewards for observing it, punishments for breaking it. 'Fire and water' are figures of reward and punishment. The doctrine is that of Dt chh 28—30, and the outlook is the older one of requital in this world and in the material order. 'Fire' here has no eschatological significance. **17.** 'Life and death' likewise are considered in their present-world aspects. Man chooses the one or the other, reward or punishment, according as he chooses moral good or evil. **18, 19.** The sanctions must inevitably follow, for the Lord is wise to see 'every deed of man' (**19**), and 'mighty in power' to requite (**18**). **20.** Conclusion: the sinner's indictment of God (11, 12) is

445c groundless. The Lord makes no one sin, commands none to sin, gives leave to none to sin.

d 16:1—5. The misfortune of having ungodly children. 6—23. The certainty of the punishment of sin. 6—10. Illustrated from biblical history. Cf 10:14—17. **6.** See Nm 11:1; 16:35. **7.** The Flood. See Gn 6:4; Wis 14:6. **8.** Sodom and Gomorrah. Cf Gn 19:24ff; Ezek 16:49 (their pride). **9.** Extirpation of the Canaanites. **10.** The murmurers during the Exodus, Nm 14. For the figure 600,000 see Ex 12:37; Nm 1:45f; 11:21:14:20—23; Sir 46:8. **11—14.** Individuals are likewise punished or rewarded. In a word 'every one will receive in accordance with his deeds' (**14**). **15, 16** are added on RSVm, once more a reading of Gr. II supported by HT II (Cairo A); see on 11:15, 16. For 16*b*, correcting RSVm, read '*his light and his darkness he apportioned to (the children of) Adam*'. Note once more the Sir II and Qumranic theme of moral light and darkness allotted by the Lord. Cf 11:15, 16; 17:17, 26 in Sir II. **17—23.** The folly of the sinner in thinking to elude judgement. Cf 23:18—20. **18, 19** are a parenthesis; **20—22** continue the reasoning of the fool (cf 23). **22.** Is clearer in HT: 'My good works who shall declare? What is there to look forward to? The sentence is far off', i.e. the sentence of requital is doubtful, or so far off as to be negligible. Gr. II and VL, as a kind of protest against this attitude, add 'The searching out of all is at the end': a characteristic assertion of a divine judgement to come.

e 16:24—23:27 On Creation and the Moral Nature of Man; miscellaneous admonitions and reflections— 16:24—17:24. Creation of the world, and of man as a moral being. (HT is missing from 16:27 to 30:10 except for occasional fragments). **24, 25.** Prefatory. What follows is based on Gn chh 1, 2. **26—28.** Creation of inanimate nature. **29, 30.** Creation of living things. **17:1—4.** Creation of man. **6.** Man's intellectual nature. Free will was probably mentioned in HT where VL has *consilium* 'counsel' (Vg 5*b*) and Gr. *diaboulion* ('inclination', RSVm), terms which translate *yēṣer* in 15:14, where see note. **7.** Man's moral nature. 'good and evil', referring to Gn 2:17. **8.** Man's power to know the Creator from his handiwork. **11—14.** The moral law imposed on man. **12.** Perhaps a reference to the promulgation of the law at Sinai; but it can well refer to Gn 2:17. **13.** The familiarity between God and man before the Fall (see Gn 2:16—22; 3:8). **14*a*.** The natural law which (as Gn 3:8 supposes) man was aware of from the beginning. **15—24.** Man's, and especially Israel's (17*b*) moral responsibility to God, enforced by God's scrutiny of his conduct. VL (Vg 24) adds here a reference to men being destined for 'the nether regions of the earth' and 'the lot of truth', two expressions of eschatological significance.

f 17:25—32 Exhortation to turn to God: the value of repentance and of humble prayer. **25, 26.** Repent, pray for pardon, and amend. Gr. II (RSVm) adds 'for he will lead you out of darkness to the light of health', voicing a favourite theme of Sir II: moral light and darkness allotted to men by God. See also 18, RSVm. **27, 28.** Sing the praises of the Most High while you are still alive. After death, in the dead world of Sheol ('Hades'), there is no praise of God. Against this older view (cf Ps 6:5; 30:9 (29:10); 88:10—12 (87:11—13); 115 (113):17; Is 38:18f; Bar 2:17 etc) an addition of VL (Vg 24—27) energetically protests. It calls that notion an 'error of the ungodly' (26), and insists that men 'live and give praise to God' in the future 'holy world' (*saeculum sanctum*) beyond the grave (25). For other references to that future 'holy world' in Sir II see 18:10 (Syr.), 'the

world of the righteous'; 24:9 (14, VL), *futurum saeculum*; **445** 24:33 (46, VL), *aevum sanctum*. **29—32.** God condescends to man in his frailty. **31***b* emended text (Oesterley): 'and how much more man who has the inclination of flesh and blood'. The 'inclination' is the *yēṣer* in its bad sense of propensity to evil. See on 15:14, and § 440*ij*.

18:1—14 The Creator, mighty and majestic, is g tender and merciful to man. 1*a*. VL, *Qui vivit in aeternum creavit omnia simul*, underlies the phrasing of the profession of faith of the 4th Lateran Council, repeated in Vatican I. *Creator omnium . . . sua omnipotenti virtute* simul *ab initio temporis utramque de nihilo condidit creaturam, spiritualem et corporalem* (DzS 800, 3002). Aug. took *simul* to mean *simultaneously* (*De Gen. ad. litt.*, 4:33, 34; 5:23; 6:3), but the Heb. underlying Gr. *koinēi* must be a formation of *yāḥaḍ* (to be united). The meaning then is 'unitedly', 'equally', 'all alike': God created all things without any exception (see Jn 1:3). **2***b*, **3.** A Gr. II addition (RSVm), emphasizing the universality of the Creator's power over all things, both sacred and profane. **4—7.** See 43:27—33. **8, 9, 10.** Man's insignificance and impermanence contrasted with the Eternal. Syr. adds: 'so a thousand years of this world are not even as one day in the world of the righteous'; see on 17:28 and cf § 442*i*. **11—14.** And yet the Lord regards man with tender compassion. In **12***a* VL has a better text: 'He sees the presumption of their heart that it is wicked'. 'Presumption' doubtless represents Heb. *yēṣer*; cf VL *praesumptio* in 37:3 (RSV imagination'), and see on 17:31; cf § 441*j*.

18:15—23:27 Advice on bridling the tongue and h other things—18:15—18 Graciousness in giving. **19—29.** On taking thought beforehand. **22***c*. An addition of VL voices the advanced eschatology of Sir II: 'for the reward of God (*merces Dei*) remains for ever'. Cf Wis 2:22; 5:15 (16). **28, 29.** Ben Sira's summary description of his own pursuit. **18:30—19:3.** Against prodigality and evil living. **19:1.** Is connected in HT (Cairo C) with 18:33: 'Do not be a squanderer and a drunkard, or there will be nothing in your purse. He who does this will not become rich; he who despises small things will be stripped completely', i.e. will beggar himself by his thriftless ways. **4—12.** Control of the tongue. **13—17.** Verify before you condemn. **18, 19.** An addition of Gr. II (RSVm). **18.** The notion of 'acceptance' (and 'rejection') by the Lord is characteristic of Sir II (cf RSVm 10:21; 23:28; and, not in RSVm, 17:17, 'he accepted Israel as a portion for himself'). **19.** Says 'those who do what is pleasing to him enjoy the fruit of the tree of immortality'. This voices the 'new' eschatology and is a figure of the eternal life of the just in the next world. The figure of 'the tree of immortality' is derived ultimately from Gn 2:9; 3:22—24, is applied to the spiritual life in Prv (3:18; 11:30; 13:12; 15:4), is found in descriptions of the next world in apocryphal literature (1 *Enoch*, 2 *Enoch*, *Test. Levi* 18:11, 4 *Esdras*), and signifies the happiness of heaven in Rev 22:2, 14, 19. **20—27.** Wisdom and craftiness contrasted. **20:1—27.** Use and abuse of the tongue. **28—31.** Miscellaneous proverbs (30f recur in 41:14*b*—15).

21:1—10 Thoughts on sin and sinners—2, 3. Three **446a** figures of the lethal danger of sin: a snake, a lion, a two-edged sword. In **2** sin is personified (cp. Rm chh 5—7). **3.** 'no healing', i.e. humanly speaking; but 1 shows that its effects can be undone by repentance, prayer and amendment. See § 440*jk*. **5.** See 35:13—17. **8.** To build up a fortune by dishonesty is to prepare one's own destruction. **9, 10.** Sinners may prosper for a time, but their end is ignominious—their bodies liable to burning as those of criminals, and the oblivion of

6a Sheol engulfing them. Sir II, however (VL 11c), after 'the pit of Sheol' adds 'and darkness and pains', referring to the punishment of sinners in the next world. (Eternal) darkness as an element in the torment of the wicked figures in Tb 14:10 (LXX, Sinaiticus) and in the apocryphal literature. Cf *Enoch* (A) 10:4—6; *Enoch* (E) 103:7, 8; *Jubilees* 7:29; *Pss of Solomon* 14:6—9; 15:10. According to the Qumran Manual of Discipline the followers of the spirit of falsehood will suffer 'eternal torment and endless disgrace together with shameful extinction in the fire of the dark regions ... in bitter misery and in calamities of darkness' (IQS, IV, 13, Penguin trans., G. Vermes, p. 77).

11—28 The wise man and the fool. (For 'fool' see on 6:20). **11.** For 'thoughts' read 'impulse' (Syr.) *yēṣer*, the evil tendency. See on 15:14. To keep the law is the way to control the impulse; more easily said than done, as St Paul will later testify (Rm 7). **13.** This was Ben Sira's own experience, see 24:30—34. **27.** Translate: 'when an ungodly man curses Satan (= the Adversary), it is his own self he curses', i.e. by yielding to his own evil impulse he is a Satan to himself.

22:1—6 Sluggards and discreditable children— 7—18. Thoughts on fools. **19—26.** Friends and how to treat them.

b 22:27—23:6. A prayer to the Lord for help against evil tendencies: (a) 22:27—23:1, against sins of the tongue; (b) 2, 3, against misguided thoughts and purposes; (c) 4—6, against pride and passion. **27.** The seal on the lips must not be the mechanical one of perpetual silence, but a control 'of prudence', knowing when to speak and when to be silent. **23:1.** The invocation 'Father' in 1 and 4 is unique in the OT as a direct personal invocation of God in prayer. J. Jeremias and others suspect it is an insertion of Gr. H1 is lacking here, but in the prosodic paraphrase in Heb published by J. Marcus (cf § 441*d*, (2)) the invocation is 'God of my father' (J. Jeremias, *The Central Message of the NT*, SCM, 1965, Ch. I; further literature in J. Dupont, *Le Discours de Milet*, Cerf, 1962, p. 357). Note, however, that in 51:10 the HT, as it stands, reads 'I cried "O Yahweh, you are my Father, for you are the mighty one who saves me"'. One of the Qumran Thanksgiving Hymns has the phrase 'For Thou art a father to all [the sons] of Thy truth, and as a woman who tenderly loves her babe, so dost thou rejoice in them' (IQH 9, 35f, Penguin trans., G. Vermes, p 182). **2.** Asks guidance for the higher faculties of thought and will ('mind', lit 'heart'), that they be checked and purified by the rod of God. 'Errors' are sins into which a man is betrayed without obstinate malice. Contrast Nm 15:22—29 with Nm 15:30f. **4.** 'Father', see on v. 1 and 51:10.

7—15. Control of the tongue. **16—27.** Three 'sorts' of sinners by impurity. They are the incestuous man (16cd); the fornicator (17); the adulterer (18—21) and the adulteress (22—27). **16.** 'Two sorts ... and a third'. Numerical proverbs on this model are a convention of wisdom literature. There is no sense of climax, as if the final item in the series outdoes the rest. Cp. 25:1, 2, 7—11; 26:5, 6, 28; 50:25. **16c.** Incest. 'with his near of kin', lit. (RSVm) 'in the body of his flesh'. The expression comes from Lv 18:6 which reads lit. 'None of you shall approach the flesh (or body) of his flesh etc'. In Heb. idiom near relatives are said to be of the same flesh. **18—20.** Cp. 16:17—23. **21.** See on 9:9. **28.** added by Gr. II (RSVm, Vg 38), refers once more to the privilege of being accepted ('received') by God. See on 19:18. **24:1—33:6 Wisdom coming forth from the Most High and imparted to man**; various practical counsels.

24:1—22 Wisdom praises Herself—1, 2. Wisdom, **446c** speaking from the midst of her own people (Israel), and in the presence of the angelic host—'the assembly of the Most High', (see Ps 82 (81):1; 1 (3) Kgs 22:19)—is about to proclaim the glory that is hers. On the personification of wisdom and on the doctrine of 1—22 see § 440*nop*. **3—6.** Wisdom's origin from the Most High and her presence throughout creation, a passage strongly influenced by Prv 8:22—31. **3a.** Originating in God, wisdom was externalized by his spoken word, i.e. by his creative command and revealed will. See on 1:5—8. 'Earth' here, and 'heaven', 'abyss' (5) and 'sea' (6a) catalogue the departments of the universe as conceived by the Hebrew mind. **3b.** The 'mist' to which wisdom is compared may be that of Gn 2:6 (meaning uncertain); but more probably wisdom is identified with the 'spirit of God' of Gn 1:2, hovering cloudlike over chaos. **4b.** Wisdom was enthroned alongside God himself, as in Wis 9:4, 10. 'In the high places', i.e. heaven, above the clouds, here pictured as the support of God's throne (see Ps 97 (96):2; 104 (103):3). **8.** 'vault', the 'firmament' of Gn 1:6—8. **6b.** Wisdom dominates the conscious creation also; see on 1:10.

7—12. At the command of the Creator wisdom settles **d** in Israel. **8b.** 'assigned a place for my tent', lit. 'made my tent to rest'. VL (12b) renders 'rested in my tent', opening the way to the mariological application; see below on 18 (RSVm). **9.** On wisdom's 'eternity' see § 440o. For VL's reference here (Vg 14) to 'the future world' see on 17:27f. **10—12.** Wisdom obeys the divine command to dwell in Israel, i.e. God entrusts his revelation of himself to Israel; see Rm 9:4. **10.** Wisdom's part in Israel's worship: an allusion to the 'pillar of cloud' (4b) in which wisdom was present (Wis 10:17), and which at the Exodus came down to mark the Lord's presence, first in the tabernacle (Ex 33:9, 10), and later in the Temple (1 (3) Kgs 8:10—13). 'Ministered': the Mosaic worship was the gift of God's revelation ('wisdom') to Israel. See on 15. **11b.** 'in Jerusalem was my dominion': besides the laws of worship, moral and civil laws were contained in the revelation for which 'wisdom' stands. The authority to interpret and apply them was in the hands of the priesthood 'in Jerusalem' with the king's cooperation. **13—14.** Wisdom's beneficent operation in and through Israel, described under the figure of flourishing and graceful trees. The 'cedar of Lebanon' was proverbial for its majestic growth, and the beauty and durability of its wood. The qualities of the 'cypress' parallel those of the cedar, as the Hermon range parallels the Lebanon. The 'rose plants' are the oleanders which are especially abundant about Jericho. These and the other trees mentioned figure the moral excellence which indwelling wisdom gives to Israel among the nations.

15. By imagery based on the description of the **e** sacred anointing oil and the incense (Ex 30:22—39) it is conveyed that wisdom, by revealing to Israel the acceptable way of worship (cf Rm 9:4), marks it out as a sacred and priestly nation. The key to this imagery is given by the reference at the end of 15 to (more exactly) *the frankincense smoke of the tabernacle*, the symbol of the People's liturgical prayer and adoration. **16, 17.** A figure of the spreading abroad of the religious and moral influence of Israel's possession of divine wisdom, and of the fruit it produced (especially, perhaps, by the Dispersion). **16.** The terebinth is 'a noble umbrageous tree, 20 to 40 feet or more in height ... spreading its boughs far and wide' (CBEB, 4976). **17.** For Israel as a fruitful vine see Ps 80:8—11 (79:9—12), and especially Ezek 17:5—15, where Judah, in her relations with the Nations

446e (Babylonia, Egypt), is figured as a 'spreading vine' which 'brought forth branches and put forth foliage'. Cf Sir 51:15. **18** (RSVm). An addition of Gr. II and VL, which describes wisdom as 'the mother of beautiful love, of fear, of knowledge, and of holy hope'. This passage, in conjunction with the VL translation of 8b (see above), helped to pave the way for the accomodation of 8—22 to our Lady in liturgical texts. (On the history and significance of this accomodated sense see E. Catta in *Maria* [ed. Du Manoir], VI [1961], 691—7, 813—31, bibliogr. 865). For wisdom as a mother see 15:2; Wis 7:12. The further addition of VL here (Vg 25) is apparently a Christian gloss based on Jn 14:6. **19—22.** Wisdom's invitation to gather her fruits and enjoy them. For wisdom's abundant banquet see Wis 9:1—6. **20.** 'Honey . . . the honeycomb': see, (referring to the law), Ps 19:10 (18:11); 119 (118):103. **21.** The appetite for wisdom grows by what it feeds on. Contrast Jn 6:35. **After 22** VL adds 'they who explain me shall have life everlasting'. The 'new' eschatology: a promise of eternal life in the next world to the 'wise', especially teachers, as in Dn 12:2, 3.

f 24:23—29 Wisdom in her plenitude is contained in the law. See § 440c. **23c.** 'congregations', Gr. *synagōgais*. The reference may well be to the reading of the law in the synagogue services, an institution already well-established in Ben Sira's time. **25—27.** To the four rivers of Eden (Gn 2:11—14), the Jordan and the Nile are added to fill in the picture of the law's abundance of wisdom. In 27a Gr. misread HT; for 'light' read 'the Nile'. **28.** The students of the law from the first to the last will never fathom the fullness of its doctrine.

24:30—34 The author spreads abroad the knowledge of wisdom like a channel branching off from a river. **30, 31a.** His first intention was to channel down the waters of the law to his own immediate disciples. **31b—34.** But as his work grew under his hand to unexpected proportions, he felt inspired to let his light shine 'afar off' to his countrymen everywhere, and to commit it to writing (like the prophets before him, 33a) for 'all future generations' (33b) cf 39:12.

g **Appended to 32** VL has a striking addition of eschatological significance, (Vg 45): 'I will penetrate to all the nether regions of the earth, and will visit all those that sleep, and will bring to the light all that hope in the Lord'. For VL these words are spoken by wisdom, for, (with MS 248), it prefixes to 30 (Vg 40) 'I, wisdom, . . .', thus putting in the mouth of wisdom the verses that follow. With Smend (Comm., p. cxviif), we take VL's addition to 32 to be, not a Christian gloss (as most commentators hold, cf Eph 4:9), but a Gr. II reading from a Heb. original. The eschatology connoted is at a stage of development found also in Wis, Dn and certain early apocryphal works. 'The nether regions of the earth' mean Sheol. 'All those that sleep' are the souls of the departed just, resting peacefully there as in an intermediate state. They 'hope in the Lord' because they look forward with confidence to the final happiness which he will assign to them on the day of judgement. On that day, by the ministry of divine wisdom, he will 'visit' them and, out of the darkness of Sheol, 'bring them to the light' of heaven. Compare the following passages (and further similar ones could be added) from other literature contemporary with Sir II: Wis 3:1—8; Dn 12:2, 3 (noting, however that our VL passage says nothing of the lot of the wicked nor of the resurrection of the body); *Enoch* (E), in three places: (a) speaking of the final judgement, 'In those days . . . the righteous shall arise from their sleep, and wisdom shall arise and be given to them' (91:10, CAP II, 262): (b) 'though the righteous sleep a long

sleep, they have nought to fear' (100:5, CAP II, p. 272); (c) 'Be hopeful; for aforetime ye were put to shame through ill and affliction; but now ye shall shine and ye shall be seen, and the portals of heaven shall be opened to you' (104:2, CAP II, 276); *Psalms of Solomon*: 'The destruction of the sinner is for ever and ever, and he shall not be remembered when [the Lord] shall visit the just . . . But they that fear the Lord shall rise to life eternal, and their life shall be in the light of the Lord, and shall come to an end no more' (3:13—16, CAP II, 635). **At the end of 33** also VL has an addition of eschatological significance (Vg 46): 'and I will not cease to instruct their offspring even to the holy age'. Cf VL addition to 9 (Vg 14), 'I will not cease until the future world', and see on 17:27, 28 (Vg 25). **34,** Repeated in 33:17.

25:1—11 Miscellaneous Counsels. **447**

25:13—26:18 On Women good and bad—24. The first recorded sin is that of Eve; the punishment that came upon our first parents meant that they and their posterity were shut off from access to the tree of life (Gn 3:22—24), therefore 'we all die'. See § 440i. **26.** Divorce her. Cf Dt 24:1—4. **26:17.** 'the holy lampstand', the seven-branched one of the Temple. Cf Ex 25:31—40. **19—27** (RSVm), an addition found in Gr. II (*L*-recension) and Syr., based on a HT II original (Smend). It continues the topic of good wives and bad.

26:28—28:12 Miscellaneous Counsels—27:16—21. Against disclosing secrets. **28:1—7.** Forgive and the Lord will forgive you. Cf Mt 6:14f; 18:21—35. **7.** Cf 7:36. **8—12.** Against quarrelsomeness. **13—26.** The mischief of a wicked tongue. Cf 51:2—6. **14.** 'slander', lit. 'a third tongue' (RSVm), i.e. the tongue of a third person, the other two persons being the one slandered and the listener. **15.** Calumny has been responsible for divorce. **21.** To be the victim of slander is a living death; better die outright and go down to the Underworld.

29:1—20 On lending, borrowing, giving, and going surety—9. 'the commandment', as in Dt 15:7—11. **11.** 'Lay up', translate 'Lay out', see v 9. **16—20.** Suretyship; a more indulgent view than that of Prv 6:1—5; 17:18. **19.** Refers to those who go surety for the sake of usury. **21—28.** A poor man can be happy, but a parasite not. **30:1—13 On bringing up children—7.** He frets over **b** every scratch the child suffers. **11.** HT (Cairo B, then E) is available until 34:1. **14—20. On health and sickness. 17.** 'eternal rest': the older view of the Underworld as a place of surcease. See § 440m. **18—20.** Good food is useless for the invalid who cannot take it. **21—25.** Sadness shortens life, cheerfulness prolongs it. **24.** Here begins the displacement in Gr. MSS which affects 30:24—36:16a. See § 441g. RSV keeps the correct order. **31:1—11 The right attitude towards wealth—4.** The antithesis of 3. **8—11.** How rare is the rich man who does not yield to the temptations of wealth. Cf Mt 19:23—26. **8b.** 'gold', Heb. *mamōn*, loan-word from Aramaic frequent in rabbinical Heb., but only here in biblical. Cf Mt 6:24; Lk 16:9—13. **31:12—31 Temperance in food and drink—22c.** 'be industrious', better 'show restraint'. **25—31.** Wine in moderation. **31.** HT: 'and quarrel not with him in company'. **32:1—13. Manners at a banquet—1, 2.** The one who presides. 'master of the feast', cf Jn 2:8f. **3—6.** Staid seniors to remember that music and song have their place there as well as words of wisdom. **7—13.** Youth to beware of illbred forwardness. **32:14—33:3 The Law a protection and a guide to life—32:18.** Gr. text in disorder. CV, emending HT: '*The thoughtful man will not neglect direction, the proud and insolent man is deterred by nothing.*' **33:1—3.** Keep the Law and it will keep you. **3b.** The Law is as sure a

447b guide as an answer direct from the oracle of God. On Urim and Thummim see Ex 28:30; 1 Sm 14:41f. **4—6.** Steadfastness of mind. **6.** As a mettlesome horse is eager to go, no matter who mounts him, so a shallow friend bestows his insincere ('mocking') friendship on all and sundry as suits him.

c 33:7—39:11 The Lord's Wisdom in governing the World: the writer's purpose in his study of it; followed by guidance on miscellaneous subjects— **33:7—15. Unity and diversity in creation. 7—9.** The calendar is ruled by one and the same sun, yet the Lord disposes that certain days and seasons excel the rest. **10.** All men are of the same clay, **(11)** yet the Lord has made their lots to differ. E.g. **12a,** the race of Israel he singularly 'blessed and exalted'; **12b,** and even within Israel certain groups are honoured above others. The priestly family he sanctified and 'brought near' to him, to exercise their ministry (Nm 16:5—10). **12c—d.** Other peoples he treated as aliens. The language here is that of Gn 9:25—27, where Canaan is made inferior to Shem. The contrast between *blessing* and *cursing* reflects semitic modes of thought and expression; predestination and reprobation in the theological sense are not involved. Israel is a chosen people, the others were *not specially chosen.* Cf Mal 1:2. **13—15.** As peoples, so individuals. All come equally from 'the hand of him who made them', but he shapes with sovereign mastery the life of each, as a potter his vessels. It is not a question of final requital but of the whole course of a man's life: the Lord is the 'ruler' of it all, as in 23:1. **14, 15.** The contrasting lots of the good and bad fortune of men, of the life and death of creatures, have their parts to play in the world as the Creator appoints. Even the sinner has his place in the plan as well as the godly. This is to be read in the light of 15:11—21, where account is taken of freewill.

d 16—18. Ben Sira's work is based on that of earlier sages, and is destined in turn for teachers who will succeed him. See § 439a. **17.** Repeats 24:34. **18.** 'leaders of the congregation': the instructors of the people in schools such as that referred to in 51:23, and those operated by the synagogues, already at that date existing in the Dispersion. See on 24:23 and 51:23—28. **19—31 Advice to the head of a house—19—23.** Not in his lifetime to make over to others property and independence. **24—29.** Strict treatment for a lazy slave. **30, 31.** Kind treatment for a good one. (N.B. HT is missing from 34:2 to 35:10.) **34:1—8.** The vanity of dreams and omens. **6.** Makes allowance for God-given dreams, of which Scripture records many. **9—17.** Experience is a good teacher, the fear of the Lord a better. **9.** 'travelled' (RSVm) rather than 'educated', cf vv 10, 11. **11.** The writer's own experience, enlarged by travel. See 39:4. **12.** The sagacity thus acquired enabled him on occasion to survive mortal dangers. **13—17.** Yet it is the fear of the Lord, more than cleverness, that wins divine protection. **16c.** Cf Is 25:4.

34:18—35:20 Worship of the Lord by (a) sacrifice and (b) prayer—(a) 34:18—35:12 Sacrifice: when displeasing to the Most High and when pleasing. The teaching is that stressed by the prophets from Amos onwards (Am 5:11—27; 8:4—10): ritual sacrifice pleases the Lord only when offered by one who is moved inwardly by the spirit of true religion and is faithful to the moral law. See § 440e. **18—26.** Unacceptable sacrifice. **35:1—12.** Acceptable sacrifice. (N.B. From 35:11 to the end of Sir HT is available in one MS or **e** another, with slight lacunae). **(b) 35:13—20 Efficacious prayer: that of the distressed, the just, the humble,**

and the People of the Lord. 13a. Oesterley's rendering **447e** of HT is preferable: 'He will not show partiality against the poor man', i.e. he will not favour the rich, as human judges may do. **16.** He that worships the Lord in the way that pleases him (see above) shall be accepted by him. **17.** Humility, the sense of dependence on the Most High, gives wings to prayer and makes it efficacious. **18—20.** Therefore the Lord will speedily hear the prayer 'of his People' (v 19) in their distress. The oppression of the Jews alluded to here and in the prayer which follows (36:1ff) refers to a general situation, not to a particular tyrant. Ptolemy IV Philopator of Egypt (221—205 B.C.) personally rode roughshod over Jewish susceptibilities, but Jews in his dominions were fairly treated. Antiochus III the Great, of Syria, ruler of Palestine (201—187) when Ben Sira wrote, was favourable to them (Jos.Ant. 12, 3, 3). Two things, nevertheless, made even the most tolerant Gentile rulers tyrants in Jewish eyes: (1) they *were* Gentiles, ruling only by right of force over the theocratic people; (2) the hellenistic and paganizing culture which prevailed wherever their rule extended. This latter factor, resented here by Ben Sira, was to kindle the Maccabean revolt twenty years later.

36:1—17 A Prayer for Israel—a well-knit composition, **f** its sections being vv 1—5, 6—10, 11—14, 15—16, 17. Some of its expressions are now found in the Eighteen Benedictions of the synagogue liturgy. See on 51:12 (1)—(15). The absence of express mention of messianic hopes is remarkable; they are implicit, however, in vv 8, 14b, 15b, 16. See § 440b.

1—5. Theme of the prayer: salvation for Israel fear of the Lord on the Nations. This 'fear' is not exclusively dread, but includes recognition of the truth about God leading to the worship of him. See § 440d. **3—5.** Enlightenment for the Gentiles through chastisement. **4.** As the Lord has shown the Gentiles how holy he is by his treatment of Israel—punishing their sins by subjecting them to his enemies—so now let him show Israel how holy he is by punishing the Gentiles in their turn for their sins and their tyranny. See Is 10:5—21. **5.** The happy result of the chastisement of the Gentiles, cf Ps 67 (66).

6—10. Renew the wonders wrought at Israel's deliverance from Egypt. **8.** 'the Day' is that of the Lord's judgement of his enemies: may he bring it quickly, with its fulfilment of Israel's hopes; see 15, 16. **11—14.** Gather together the scattered tribes of Israel that they may hold once more, as of old, their God-given inheritance: the Holy Land **(11)**, the Holy City **(13, 14a)**, the temple **(14b)**. **12b.** 'a first-born son': see Ex 4:22; Hos 11:1.

15—16. Glorify Jerusalem and the temple, ful- **g** filling the prophetic predictions in their regard. **14.** Alludes (like 49:12) to the messianic prophecy of Hag 2:7—9, which includes the conversion of the Gentiles. **15.** 'those whom thou didst create in the beginning', HT: 'the First of thy works', i.e. Israel, the First-born **(12)**. The sense is: vindicate Israel's prerogative as thy First-born and favoured son, by fulfilling the promise made to him. **16.** Reward the hopes of those who trust in the promise, by verifying it as the prophets foretold. **17. Conclusion of the prayer—17b.** The reference to Aaron in Gr. is due to a scribal error. Read, with HT and Göttingen LXX, 'according to thy goodwill towards thy people.' **17d.** 'the God of the ages': who can promise and foretell in one age, and fulfil in any later one at his own sovereign choice.

36:18—37:31 Need for discrimination and dis- 448a cretion in various circumstances of life—**18—20.** Discrimination in general. **21—26.** Discrimination in

448a choosing a wife. **24b**, 'a helper fit for him', see Gn 2:18, 20. **26.** Beware of the roving bachelor. **37:1—6.** Discrimination in the choice of friends. Cp. 6:5—17. **3.** 'evil imagination', i.e. the *yēṣer* or wicked propensity that turns friendship awry. See 15:14; 18:10; § 440*i*. **4, 5.** Gr. garbles sense of HT, which runs: 'A false friend has an eye to your table, but in time of trouble he stands aloof. A true friend will fight against your foe, and will raise a shield against your assailant'. **7—15.** Discrimination in choosing counsellors. **11.** Interested parties make poor counsellors. **12—15.** The best counsellors are god-fearing friends, your own heart, and the Most High himself entreated in prayer. **14.** 'watchmen': astrologers. **16—18.** Deliberation in plan, action and speech. **19—26.** False wisdom and true. **25, 26.** As long as Israel lasts, i.e. for ever, the name of its sages will be kept alive. See 44:10—15. **27—31.** Discretion in eating. The 'soul' is the bodily appetite, Heb. *nepeš*. Cf 31:19—22.

38:1—15 Physicians and medical care—1—3. The physician is to be treated with deference, even by kings, He is a minister of the Most High, 'created', (i.e. appointed) by him, for human needs. **4—8.** The healing power of medicines is also from the Lord. **5.** Reference to Ex 15:23—26. **7.** 'he' i.e. the physician (HT). **8.** The 'pharmacist' was by trade a perfumer (49:1; Ex 30:25; 37:29; 2 Chr 16:14) who also stocked salves and ointments. **8b.** Subject of the sentence is the Lord: pharmacist and physician are providential instruments for carrying on his healing work.

b **9—11.** In time of sickness turn first to the Lord by **9b** prayer, **10** repentance, and **11** sacrifice (of the type described in Lv 2:1—3). See 2 Chr 16:12, where Asa's fault is that he neglected this. **12—15.** The physician must also be consulted, as the Lord's appointed means of cure (see 1*b*). But he himself, too, depends on the Lord and must pray to him. **15.** For 'may he etc' HT reads: 'shall fall into the hands of a physician'. Sin can lead to sickness, either as a direct result or as a punishment sent by man's Maker. That all sickness results from personal sin is not stated.

16—23. Mourning for the dead—In itself it is a good work, and convention also demands it; but when unduly prolonged it is harmful to the living. **19.** A verse absent from HT and unclear in Gr. Editors conjecture: 'Persistent grief is worse than death; the heart abhors (lit 'curses') a life of affliction'. **21.** HT: 'Remember him not for *he has no hope*'. Gr. I (as in RSV) seems to represent a less hopeless view of the lot of the dead: 'Do not forget, *there is no coming back*'. See § 442*h* and comm. on 7:17. **22.** Death is the common lot; mourning will not change it. **23.** 'at rest' in the purely negative sense of the older eschatology. See comm. on 30:17, and § 440*m*.

c **38:24—39:11 Contrasting vocations of the manual worker and the sage—24.** Introductory: opportunity for study and reflection is necessary to acquire wisdom. **25—34.** The hand-workers' trades, demanding close concentration, preclude the study of wisdom. Examples follow. **25, 26.** The farmer. **27.** The engraver. **28.** The metal-worker. (N.B. HT is lacking till 39:15). **29, 30.** The potter. **30b.** 'with his feet', kneading the wet clay by trampling. See Is 41:25. **31—34b.** Although not fitted for public office, such workers are essential to the well-being of the state. **34b.** Read with Syr.: 'Their mind is on the practice of their craft'. Tied down to this, they cannot acquire the broader wisdom required to 'sit in the judge's seat' (33*c*).

38:34cd—39:11 The training, the function and the glory of the sage.38:34cd, 39:1. The basic subject of his study is the three orders of the Sacred Books: the Law, the Prophets, the Wisdom of the Ancients. **2.** Read **448c** 'discourses' in plural (Gr. II), i.e. the sayings or oral wisdom of the sages, passed on in the schools they founded. Cf 51:23—28. **4.** Another school of wisdom is service as counsellor in the court of some potentate, and the experience acquired by travel. Cf 34:9—12. **5—8.** Nevertheless the wisdom of the scribe is by definition religious and divine; its source is the Lord himself, and its surest channel is prayer, cf 51:13, 14, 19 (Gr.). **9—11.** The reward of the faithful scribe: honour in his lifetime, lasting fame after death. **11.** His name survives him and takes his place when he is dead, cf 44:14f.

39:12—43:33 Eulogy of the Lord in his governance d of the universe, and a hymn to God the Creator, with practical reflections interspersed. **13.** 'Like the moon at the full', he is filled with the reflected light of divine wisdom, (cf 24:30—34; 33:11—18), and calls on his fellow Israelites ('holy sons') to join in his hymn. **14.** Cf 24:14f. **16.** The theme of what is to follow: all the works of the Lord are good, and they all show forth his power and his providence. **17cd.** Refers to Gn 1:6—10; see Ps 33 (32):7. **19, 20.** The Creator's eye is all-seeing, his wisdom all-pervading. See 16:17—20; 17:15—20; 23:19f. **21.** Every created thing is good in relation to its purpose. **22—25.** The goodness of the Creator is manifested both by his benignity and by his severity. **22.** Gr. generalises where HT is concrete: 'His blessing overflows like the Nile, and like the River it inundates the earth.' The Nile and the River (i.e. the Euphrates), on which whole peoples and cultures depend, are figures of the Creator's bounty to the world and to mankind. **23.** His punishment of sinners is equally significant and effective. Example: Sodom and Gomorrah; see Ps 107 (106):34. **25.** As in Gn 1 and the OT view of salvation history in general, men, both good and evil, figure prominently in the Creator's plans from the beginning. **28—31.** An illustration of 25*b*, 'evil things created for sinners'. **32—35.** Conclusion of the reflective passage, echoing 14*b*—17*ab*.

40:1—10 The Hardships of Human Life: reflections on **e** Gn 3:17—19. Though all the Creator's works are good, man by his fall has brought suffering on himself. **1.** 'created', i.e. appointed: it is God's sentence on fallen man. 'the mother of all', mother earth from which man is formed, cf 16:29f; 33:10; Gn 3:19. **8—10.** An echo of 39:28—31. **10b.** 'on their account', see Gn 6:5—13.

11—17. What passes and what abides. 15b. 'unhealthy roots', fated to wither. **18—27.** A series of comparisons in patterned structure ending with a climax **(26, 27)** exalting the fear of the Lord. **28—30.** The wretchedness of a beggar's life. **30b.** Even the hardened practitioner must feel an inward torture. **41:1—42:8** A series of contrasts—**41:1—4.** Death unwelcome and welcome. **3, 4.** The older, naturalistic, view of death. cf 38:21—23. 'Hades', i.e. Sheol, the Underworld, is the end of all. See § 440*lm*. **5—13.** The memorials left by the wicked and the just: their children and their reputation after death. For the wicked, these decay; for the just, they prosper. **9.** HT: 'If you increase it will be for harm, if you have children it will be for sighing; if you stumble,— a lasting joy, if you die,—an execration.' **13.** See 37:25f; 39:9—11. **41:14—23.** Things to be ashamed of. **14b, 15.** Identical with 20:30f. **19.** HT: 'Of breaking an oath or a covenant; of stretching out the elbow at bread'. Cf 31:14—18. **23.** By being ashamed of the faults just listed 'you will show proper shame'. On the contrary **42:1—8. Lists actions one must not be ashamed of.** **9—14.** The care of daughters. **12.** Belongs to same topic **f** as HT shows: 'Let her not show her beauty to a man, nor tarry in converse among married women'—emphasi-

448f zing the seclusion of well-bred oriental young women. It is married women of disedifying life and conversation who are warned against, as the sequel shows. **13b.** Sense: 'And from one woman comes the wickedness of another'. **14a.** The wickedness of men, which the daughter will be warned against and shielded from, is not so insidious as the baneful friendship of the type of women spoken of. Thus 'does good' is taken ironically. **14b.** HT, possibly: 'And a shameful daughter is a source of reproach'.

g **42:15–43:33 Hymn to the Lord, Creator of the world—Concluding Part One of the book.** See § 440n. **42:15–23. The Lord's greatness in his works in general:** his unique glory, his omniscience, his omnipotence. **15c.** The creative power of the 'word' of the Lord. See § 440o; cf 1:5 (Gr. II, RSVm); 43:26b. **16.** As the sun gives light to all things, the Lord gives being, and all things reflect his glory. **17.** The 'holy ones' are the angels. Dt 33:2f; Jb 5:1; 15:15; Ps 89 (88):5–7, etc. Not even they can look upon the unveiled glory of the Lord, Jb 4:17f; 15:15f; Is 6:2. **18.** He fathoms the unfathomable in nature and in man. 'abyss', the 'deep' of Gn 1:2. **19.** Past and future to him are present. **21.** He is one, eternal, self-existing, self-sufficient. 'Counsellor', see Is 40:13f, cf Rm 11:33–36. **23.** All that he created is sustained and ruled by him. **24b.** 'nothing incomplete', HT: 'none of them without its purpose'. **25b.** For 'his glory' read with Syr. 'their beauty', i.e. the beauty of the things of God's creation.

h **43:1–26 The Lord's greatness in his works in particular. 1,** 'firmament': the visible vault of heaven, Gn 1:7; see Ex 24:10. **2–5.** The sun, Cf Ps 19 (18):4–6. **6–8.** The moon. The Hebrew 'orthodox' calendar, year, months, and festivals were ruled by the moon. **8c.** HT: 'banner of the hosts of the clouds on high'. **9, 10.** The stars. 'They stand as ordered', like sentinels at their posts, Cf Bar 3:34. **11, 12.** The rainbow. **13–17b.** The storm. **13.** HT: 'His power writes the lightning, and sets ablaze the flashes of his vengeance'. 'Vengeance' (RSV 'judgement'), see Jb 38:28–30. **14.** 'storehouses', see Dt 28.12, Jb 38.22, Jer 51:16. **17c–22.** Snow, frost, ice, fog and dew. **19b.** HT (after N. Peters): 'and makes its flowers to flash like sapphires'. **22.** For 'from the heat' render 'after the drought'. **26b.** HT: 'and by his word his will is accomplished'. See above on 42:15c. **27–33. Conclusion of the hymn: the Lord himself 'is greater than all his works'. 30ab.** Paraphrased by Aquin. *Quantum potes tantum aude quia maior omni laude.* **31b.** 'Who can extol him as he is?': the answer was yet future, Jn 1:18.

449a **44:1–50:29 Part Two of the Book: the Praises of the Ancients of Israel**—See § 439a. The 'fathers' are praised 'in their generations' i.e. in chronological order, beginning with Enoch (or more probably Noah, see on v 16) and ending with Simon the high-priest, the author's contemporary. The Lord's dealings with them and their response are hymned as examples of divine wisdom at work in salvation history.

44:1–15 Introduction—1. For 'famous men' read 'men of piety' (HT); see on v 10. The various types of men now to be mentioned 'were the glory of their times' (7b), i.e. *of their own day.* **3a–b.** Warriors and rulers like Joshua and David. **3c–d.** Counsellors and seers like Elijah and Isaiah. **5a.** Inspired psalmists. **5b.** 'Verses', HT 'proverbs'. See e.g. on Solomon, 1 (3) Kgs 4:32. **6.** For example the Patriarchs. **7.** Conclusion of the sentence begun in 3. **8.** Some men great in their own days left an honoured memory ever after, (9) others did not. **10.** Gives the reason of the difference. Those whose fame did not long survive were not men of *piety* ('mercy' RSV).

Cf 47:23–25; 48:16; 49:4–5. The Heb. *ḥesed* has many **449a** meanings, but in vv 1 and 10 it expresses *dutiful love* of God and *devotion to his service.* The great ones of the past who excelled in this will never be forgotten. Three things keep their memory alive: (1) **11–13,** their posterity flourishes, generation after generation; (2) **14a,** the honourable graves in which they were buried; (3), **14b, 15,** their reputation for 'wisdom' as well as piety, which shall last as long as Israel itself. See 37:26; 39:9–11.

16. Enoch is mentioned here in HT (Cairo B), Gr., **b** VL, but not Syr. Textual difficulties and the other reference to Enoch in 49:14 have puzzled commentators. Yadin, on the basis of his Masada MS (unfortunately imperfect here), argues for the transfer to 49:14 of the mention of Enoch here (See § 441ad; Y. Yadin, *The Ben Sira Scroll,* p. 38. See below on 49:14). **16a.** HT: (if we omit 'was found perfect', intruded from 17a): 'Enoch walked with Yahweh and was taken'. This refers to Gn 5:24, 'Enoch walked with God; and he was not, for God took him' (see also Wis 4:10–14; Heb 11:5). This is repeated in Sir 49:14b in HT: 'he also was taken within', or (emended), 'he also was taken from the face (of the earth)'; cf Gr. 'taken up from the earth'. For the older eschatology, with its limited view of life after death (see § 440l), the case of Enoch remained a perplexing exception, to be left in the vague terms of the primitive historian. The 'new' eschatology, however, with its advanced views of the state of the individual after death, made Enoch's mysterious lot the starting-point of an apocryphal Enoch-literature in which the secrets of the next world are laid open.

In this connection the reading of VL here is significant: **c** 'Enoch pleased God and was translated into Paradise'. The addition *into Paradise* represents in all probability a Gr. II version of an expanded HT, one which echoed the statements of such 2nd cent. B.C. apocrypha as the *Book of Jubilees* and the *Book of Enoch* that the destination to which Enoch was 'translated' was in fact 'the Garden' or 'the Garden of Eden', expressions which the LXX renders by *paradeisos.* See § 442h, § 443c. For the expressions referred to see *Jubilees,* 4, 23:CAP II, p. 19; *Enoch* (B) 60, 8:CAP II, p. 224; cf Slavonic *Book of Enoch,* text B, 8, 1:CAP II, p. 434f; 42, 2, ibid p. 456. **16b.** Read with HT, Armenian and certain Gr. and VL MSS, 'a portent of knowledge to all generations'. Enoch's passing was a prodigious and ever-memorable example of the benefits which accrue to those who possess knowledge (wisdom): he was exempted from the universal lot of death. Of his knowledge the *Book of Jubilees* says, 'He was the first among men that are born on earth who learnt writing and knowledge and wisdom' (*Jub* 4:17; CAP II, p. 19); and of his 'translation' Wis 4:10f says, 'While living among sinners he was taken up. He was caught up lest evil change his understanding or guile deceive his soul.' **17, 18. Noah. 17b.** 'was taken in exchange', HT: 'became a renewer', i.e. from him, after the Flood, humanity was renewed. **18.** See Gn 8:21; 9:9–17. **19–21. Abraham.** See Gn 17:4–6, 9–11, 24; 22:1–12, 15–18. **20c.** 'in his flesh', by circumcision. **21f.** 'the River': the Euphrates, as 39:22; see Gn 15:18; Ex 23:31; Dt 11:24. **22–23e. Isaac and Jacob. 22.** See Gn 26:3–5. **23fg.** Is printed by RSV at the beginning of ch 45. **45:1–5 Moses. 2a.** 'holy ones', i.e. angels, see on 42:17. **d** Gr. here takes *'elōhîm* of HT in this sense, with Ex 34:29–35 in mind; but the usual meaning 'God' is preferable. See Ex 4:16; 7:1. **3a.** HT 'By his words he made prodigies swiftly come to pass'; the plagues of Egypt. **3d.** 'part of his glory', see Ex 33:18–34:8. **4.** Nm 12:3–7.

449d **5b.** Ex 20:21; 24:18. **5c.** 'face to face', Ex 33:11; Dt 34:10. **6—26. Aaron.** See § 440d. **7a.** 'an everlasting covenant', Ex 29:9. **7c—12.** The priestly garments and ornaments, Ex 28. **10b.** 'Urim and Thummim', see on 33:3. **13—17.** To Aaron and his descendants alone was given the power to offer sacrifice, to bless the people in the Lord's name, to teach and apply the Law. See Lv 10:10f; Dt 17:8—13. **18, 19.** Rejection of rival claimants, Nm 16. **20—22.** Provision for priests' support, Nm 18. **23, 24.** The promise to Phinehas, Nm 25:10—13. **25cd.** Text uncertain; editors understand, 'the heritage of the king passes to one son alone, but the heritage of Aaron to all his descendants': a feature in which the Aaronic establishment surpasses the Davidic. **26.** An apostrophe to the living representatives of the Aaronic priesthood.

e **46:1—10. Joshua and Caleb. 1c.** 'in accordance with his name', which means 'the Lord saves'. **2—6.** Joshua's leadership in the conquest of Canaan; see Jos chh 6—11. **7—10.** The 'loyal deed' (Heb 'deed of piety', see on 44:10) of Joshua and Caleb; see Nm 14:6—38. **8.** 'six hundred thousand', see on 16:10. **9.** See Jos. 14:6—14. **11, 12. The Judges. 12.** Same expression in 49:10; not a reference to the resurrection of the body but, (as the remainder of this v shows), a prayer that the Judges and the Prophets (49:10), even though dead, may continue to flourish in their descendants, cf Is 58:11; 66:14. **13—20. Samuel. 13.** 'anointed rulers', Saul and David, 1 Sm 10:1; 16:13. **15.** See 1 Sm 3:19—20; 9:6—9. **16—18.** See 1 Sm 7:9—11. **19.** See 1 Sm 12:1—5. **20.** See 1 Sm 28:8—19.

f **47:1—11. David. 2.** 'the fat', not eaten, but reserved as holy to the Lord, Lv 3:3—5; so David was singled out as sacred to the Lord's purposes. **3—5.** See 1 Sm 17:31—54. **6.** See 1 Sm 18:6—8. **7.** See 2 Sm 8:1—14. **8.** Read, 'with all his heart he hymned and loved his Maker', emphasizing his love of God in the terms of Dt 6:4—5; see 22d. **12.** His organization of the temple liturgy, especially the music and chant; see 1 Chr 16:4—37; 25:1—8. **11.** See 2 Sm 12:13; 7:12—16. **12—22. Solomon. 13.** See 1 (3) Kgs 5:2—5. **14.** 'a river', HT 'the Nile'; see on 24:27 and 39:22. **15—17.** See 1 (3) Kgs 4:29—34; 10:1—13. **18a.** HT: 'And you were called by the glorious name by which Israel is called', i.e. 'Yahweh'; Solomon's name originally was Jedidiah, 'beloved of Yahweh', 2 Sm 12:25. **18b.** See 1 (3) Kgs 10:14—27. **19—21.** Solomon's defection. See 1 (3) Kgs 11:1—13, 31—36. **22.** An unwavering affirmation of the hope of a Davidic Messiah. 'a root of his stock', see Is 11:1, 10. **23—25. Reprobation of Rehoboam and Jeroboam.** See 1 (3) Kgs chh 12, 13; 2 (4) Kgs 17:19—23.

g **48:1—11 Elijah—1.** 'fire' and 'torch', explained in v 3. **2, 3.** For the drought see 1 (3) Kgs 17:1, 7; 18:1; for the bringing down of fire, 1 (3) Kgs 18:37f; 2 (4) Kgs 1:10, 12. **5.** See 1 (3) Kgs 17:21f. 'Hades', Sheol, the Underworld. **6.** Elijah's prophecies of doom: 1 (3) Kgs 21:21—24; 2 (4) Kgs 1:4; 2 Chr 21:12—18. **7.** See 1 (3) Kgs 19:15—17. **8.** See 1 (3) Kgs 19:15—17. **9.** See 2 (4) Kgs 2:1, 11; cf 1 Mc 2:58. **10.** See Mal 4:5f. **11.** Contains two verse-lines in HT. The first reads, 'Blessed is he who sees you and dies'. 'Sees' (a participle) probably refers to the future: Blessed will he be who, before he dies, will see you, i.e. when you come to inaugurate the messianic age (see v 10). The second verse-line, obliterated, is restored by Smend to read, 'And blessed are you yourself for you live on', i.e. happier than other mortal men you never died but still live on mysteriously 'in heaven' (v 9 HT). In Gr. 11a coincides with HT of first verse-line as above. In 11b, for the one verse-line **449g** of HT, Gr. has two. These run (reading with Smend *anapausei* = at rest, for *agapēsei* = in love), 'And who having fallen asleep are at rest. For we also shall surely live.' Gr. apparently adds tendentiously to HT in order to voice the 'new' eschatology. Merely to have seen Elijah before they died does not make the dead happy *now*. If they have 'fallen asleep' (LXX, ed. Ziegler) i.e. died the death of the just, they are now positively 'at rest'. Further, not Elijah (and Enoch) alone, as in the older eschatology, but all of the just, after death, 'shall surely live' in another world. For this advanced view even of Gr. I see § 442h and comm. on 7:17. **12—16 h Elisha and subsequent generations—12ab.** See 2 (4) Kgs 2:9—15. **12c—d.** Earthly power did not overawe him. See 2 (4) Kgs 3:13f; 6:14—16. **13b.** 'prophesied', i.e. exercised the miraculous powers with which prophets sometimes authenticated their mission. See 2 (4) Kgs 13: 21. **15a—d.** The destruction of the kingdom of Israel. **15e—16.** The survival of Judah for some time subsequently. Those in it who 'did what was pleasing to God' will be noted below. **15f.** 'rulers (HT 'a prince') from the house of David': the messianic promise to that house remained firm in spite of all. **17—25. Hezekiah and Isaiah. 17.** See 2 Chr 32:5, 30; 2 (4) Kgs 20:20. **18—21.** See 2 (4) Kgs 18:17—19:35; Is 36; 37. **23.** See 2 (4) Kgs 20:8—11; Is 38:7—8. **24, 25.** The message of Is 40—66. Ben Sira clearly attributes these chh to Isaiah. See Is 40:1—11; 41:21—29; 42:9; 46:9—12; 61:1—7.

49:1—7 Josiah and Jeremiah, with a reference to Judah's evil kings—**1.** As in 24:15 the figure of incense expresses zeal for the Mosaic cult. See 2 (4) Kgs 23:4—21; 2 Chr 35:1—19. 'Music at a banquet', cf 32:5f. **4a.** Kgs and Chr, besides the three named here praise also Asa, Jehoshaphat and Jehoash, but with reservations. See 1 (3) Kgs 15:11—15; 22:43—47; 2 (4) Kgs 12:2f; 2 Chr 19:2f; 20:37. **4b, 5.** The complement of 48:15f. See 2 (4) Kgs 23:26—27. **6.** See 2 (4) Kgs 25:1—21; Jer 36:27—32; 39:1—10. **7.** See Jer 1:5—10; 37:11—38:6.

8—16 Brief notices of some other famous men—8. i Ezekiel. See Ezek 1:4—28. **9. Job.** Read with HT: 'And he (Ezekiel) made mention of Job, who kept right ways.' See Ezek 14:14, 20. **10. The Twelve Minor Prophets.** See on 46:12. **11, 12. Zerubbabel and Jeshua.** See Hag 2:23; 1:12—15; Ez 3:2. 'prepared for everlasting glory' see Hag 2:6—9; see on 36:14. **13. Nehemiah.** See Neh 3—6. **14—16. Unfinished notes on the ancients before the Flood,** with Joseph added. They leave the impression that Ben Sira intended to fit in these pre-Noachic patriarchs too, had his work reached its final form. **14. Enoch.** See on 44:16. Yadin proposes to combine the data of HT of 44:16a with the present verse: 'Few like Enoch have been formed on earth (49:14), a sign of knowledge to all generations (44:16). And he walked with the Lord (44:16), and he also was taken within (49:14b).' **14.** 'No one', HT reads 'Few', leaving place for Elijah who shared Enoch's mysterious lot, see 48:9. **15. Joseph.** The intrusive line in Gr. (RSVm) belongs to 50:1. 'are cared for', read 'were cared for; see Gn 50:25; Ex 13:19; Jos 24:32. **16.** After Seth HT adds 'and Enosh'. 'Were honoured: **Shem's glory** was to be the ancestor of the chosen People after the Flood, Gn 10:21—31; **Seth's,** to be the ancestor of the virtuous part of humanity before it, Gn 4:25; **Enosh's,** that in his time 'men began to call upon the name of the Lord', Gn 4:26. **16b. Adam.** 'in the creation', understand perhaps 'by his creation'; his glory was, to be created directly by God.

450a **50:1—21 The High-Priest 'Simon son of Onias'.** This is Sim(e)on II, son of the high-priest Johanan II. He held office c. 219—196 B.C. being a contemporary of the author. See § 438*f*. Notwithstanding a contrary indication in Jos.Ant. xii, 43, he can be confidently identified with 'Simon the Just' of rabbinic tradition (see R. Marcus, *Josephus with an English Translation*, VII, 1957, pp. 732—6). **1c.** 'in his life': he was dead when this was written. **1c—3.** His repairs and improvements in the temple buildings; presumably the ones diplomatically encouraged by Antiochus the Great (Jos.Ant. xii, 3, 3, n. 141). **3b.** 'the sea', the magniloquent designation of the great laver of Solomon's temple, 1 (3) Kgs 7:23—26. **4.** He contrived to 'save his people from ruin' by his prayers when Antiochus IV threatened destruction in 217 B.C. (3 *Maccabees* 2); and by winning the friendship of Antiochus (see on 1*c*; see also Jos.Ant. xii, 3, 4, nn. 147—52). **5—21.** Simon as he offers the holocaust on the Day of Atonement. See 440*d*. The ceremonial is that of Lv 16:23—34, and of the *Mishnah*, *Yoma* 3ff, *Tamid* 7 (H. Danby's E.tr. pp. 164ff, 588f).

b **5.** Vested for the sacrifice, after the ritual bath (Lv 16:23f). **6—10.** Eleven comparisons to convey the sensation of awe and the ecstatic thrill of worship inspired by his appearance, cf the figures in 24:13—17. **11.** Cf 45:7—13. **12, 13.** Offering the sacrifice surrounded by the assistant priests. **13.** 'the whole congregation of Israel', also in v 20, traditional term for the People as an organized community, especially when assembled to worship the Lord or hear his word (see BDB s.v. *qāhāl*, 1.d., and 2). **14.** Completing the sacrifice by the libation of wine. See Nm 28:7—10. **16—19.** Fanfare of trumpets with choral song as the people prostrate in worship. See Nm 10:2, 10; 2 Chr 29:25—30. **20, 21.** Imparting the final blessing; formula in Nm 6:24—26. **20.** For 'and to glory in his name' HT reads 'And he glorified himself with the name of Yahweh'. The high-priest alone, on this one occasion in the year, had the privilege of pronouncing the name 'Yahweh'. *Mishnah*, *Yoma* 3, 8; 6, 2; *Tamid* 3, 8 (H. Danby's E.tr. pp. 166 with note 8, 169, 585; for conflicting evidence on date of cessation of this privilege see E. Kautzsch, CBEB, 3321, note 1). **22—24.** Prayer that God may continue to bless Simon and his priestly successors. **24.** HT: 'May his love abide upon Simon, may he keep in him his covenant with Phinehas; may it never fail unto him and his offspring while the heavens endure'. The recension underlying Gr., made after the high priesthood had passed away from Simeon's line (see § 439*e*), substitutes 'us' and 'our' for Simeon and his offspring.

c **25, 26 Reprobation of three bad neighbours of the Jews**—This seems to be a floating fragment, tacked on here at the end for safe keeping. **25.** On the form see on 23:16. For 'no nation' understand 'no people', i.e. no people *of God*. Cf Dt 32:21; Hos 1:9. Here, the Samaritans are said to be 'no people': they have apostatized. **26.** First, the Edomites or Idumaeans, implacable enemies of Israel both before and after the Exile. 'Mount Seir', S of the Dead Sea, was the centre of their power. Secondly, 'the Philistines', another enemy from old days. In Ben Sira's time their cities were strongholds of hellenistic paganism. Thirdly, the Samaritans, see on v 25. 'Shechem' in the centre of Samaria, the modern Nablus.

27—29 Subscription and final reflection—27b. HT: 'Of Simeon, son of Jeshua, son of Eleazar, son of Sira'. Editors agree, however, in eliminating for text-critical reasons the words 'of Simeon, son of'. The writer, therefore, is 'Jeshua, son of Eleazar, son of

Sira'. See § 438*e*. **28, 29.** A concluding reflection of **450c** sapiential stamp, similar to that of Hos 14:9.

51:1—30 Appendix to the Book—On its component **d** parts and disputed authenticity see § 439*c—f*. **(a) 1—12. Prayer of Thanksgiving for Deliverance.** In Gr. and VL it is headed 'A Prayer of Jesus the son of Sirach', probably a scribal addition. Those who accept its attribution to Ben Sira connect it with the autobiographical hints of 34:9—12; 39:4, taking it to refer to dangers undergone personally by himself. Others take it in a corporate sense as spoken in the name of the Heb. people, repeatedly threatened with destruction and unfailingly delivered by the Lord. So Rabanus Maurus (d. 856), Knabenbauer (1904), Smend (1906), the last arguing on the precarious basis that the interpolated psalm of HT after v 12 is authentic. Both individual and corporate factors are in fact involved. The prayer is a typical 'Psalm of Thanksgiving'. The liturgical setting of such compositions was a temple celebration on one of the great feasts in the presence of a group of worshippers. The psalmist sees in his own experience of distress and rescue not something purely personal but a demonstration in little of Yahweh's merciful dealings with the people as a whole. The by-standers for their part join whole-heartedly in the sentiments expressed, as being a testimony rendered to Yahweh's 'work from of old', his unfailing intervention at every crisis to 'save them from the hand of their enemies' (v 8). (See P. Drijvers, *The Psalms: their structure and meaning*, E.tr. 1965, pp. 97ff).

In its structure, too, this prayer follows the pattern **e** of psalms of its class (see Drijvers, op cit, pp. 86, 89—93). (1) 1, Declaration: his intention to praise and thank the Lord. (2) 2—7, narrative: the afflictions he endured. (3) 8—11*a*, his turning to the Lord when all human help had failed. (4) 11*b*—12*b*, his prayer was heard. (5) 12*cd* Conclusion: repetition of the 'declaration' of v 1. In the 'narrative' section quite a list of the calamities traditionally recounted in this type of psalm is presented: illness (2*b*), slander and scurrilous abuse from enemies (2*c*, 5*b*—6*a*), murderous plots and attempts on his life (3*c*—4, 6*b*—7*a*), desertion by friends (7*b*). **3c.** 'about to devour me': they treat him like an animal hunted or trapped for food. **4b.** 'which I did not kindle' is figurative. He was the innocent victim of aggression which he had done nothing to provoke. **5a**, 'the belly of Hades'; **6c**, 'near to Hades beneath'; **9b**, HT: 'and cried out from the gates of Sheol'; expressions common in the Psalms (for the 'belly' see Jon 2:2), meaning that under the onslaught of misfortune he was on the point of going to his grave, figuratively already standing upon or within the threshold of the Underworld. **10, 11.** He quotes verbatim the petitions and promises he made to the Lord in his distress, a feature of this class of psalm (Drijvers, op cit p. 92). **10ab.** HT: 'And I cried out, Yahweh, you are my father, for you are the mighty one of my salvation'. The epithet 'Father' predicated of the Lord in prayer, is very striking (see on 23:1). It is pointed out, however, that the expression here is 'a statement, and not a vocative' (J. Jeremias, *The Prayers of Jesus*, E.tr., 1967, p. 24).

(b) The Interpolated Psalm found between v 12 and **f** v 13 in HT (Cairo B). It is not canonical and its authorship by Ben Sira is more than doubtful. It may date, however, from about his time, and the tendency today is to seek its origin in the Qumran community. See § 439*e*. It consists of 15 vv, here numbered 12 (1)—(15). It is similar in pattern to Ps 136 (135), and has the same refrain. Many of its expressions closely

450f resemble, and may lie behind, those found in the *Shemoneh Esreh*, 'the Eighteen (Benedictions)', a Jewish daily prayer dating in its present arrangement from about A.D. 100. (Selections in C. K. Barrett, *The NT Background: selected documents*, 1961, pp. 162f). We reproduce it here in Taylor's translation as given in S. Schechter and C. Taylor, *The Wisdom of Ben Sira*, Cambridge, 1899, changing, however, the forms 'endureth' etc into 'endures' etc.

g **12.** (1) O Give thanks unto the Lord, for he is good; For his mercy endures for ever. (2) O give thanks unto the God of praises; For his mercy endures for ever. (3) O give thanks unto him that keeps Israel; For his mercy endures for ever. (4) O give thanks unto him that forms all; For his mercy endures for ever. (5) O give thanks unto him that redeems Israel; For his mercy endures for ever. (6) O give thanks unto him that gathers the outcasts of Israel; For his mercy endures for ever. (7) O give thanks unto him that builds his city and his sanctuary; For his mercy endures for ever. (8) O give thanks unto him that makes the horn of the house of David to bud; For his mercy endures for ever. (9) O give thanks unto him that chose the sons of Zadok to be priests; For his mercy endures for ever. (10) O give thanks unto the Shield of Abraham; For his mercy endures for ever. (11) O give thanks unto the Rock of Isaac; For his mercy endures for ever. (12) O give thanks unto the Mighty One of Jacob; For his mercy endures for ever. (13) O give thanks unto him that chose Zion; For his mercy endures for ever. (14) O give thanks unto the King of the kings of kings; For his mercy endures for ever. (15) And he will lift up the horn of his people: A praise for all his saints; Even for the children of Israel, a people near unto him. Praise ye the Lord.

h **(c) 13–30 Acrostic Poem**: a plea to young men to devote themselves to the single-hearted study of Wisdom—Originally the vv began with successive letters of the Heb. alphabet, an arrangement only partly represented by the defective HT which survives. For questions of text and authenticity see § 439*f*, § 441*d* (5). Sanders' conclusions (DJD, IV, p. 85) are accepted here. (1) The poem is of Palestinian origin and is the work, not of Ben Sira, but of an unknown wisdom-teacher (one of 'the celibates of Qumran' (?), op cit, p. 84). (2) The text of Q (11QPs^a) is the one closest to the original, if not indeed the original itself. It has been noted that the terms descriptive of wisdom as a bride, emphasized with oriental realism in the Q text, have been 'muted' (Sanders, p. 83) in the other recensions, Cairo B, Syr., and Gr. This last 'presents an interpretive recension of the canticle' (ibid); one, we would add, derived by Gr. from a Heb. recension other than B. Tempering the 'wisdom-spouse' imagery of Q, and with an eye to 39:5–8, it stresses the pursuit of wisdom rather as a religious and prayerful self-dedication (see vv 13*b*–14, 17*b*, 19*b*). It is Gr., therefore, that is kept in view here, representing as it does the form given to the canticle when it was adjusted to fit in as a conclusion to Ben Sira's book. **450h**

13–22. The master's own zeal in seeking wisdom from **i** his youth, and practising it when found. **1.** Gr. forges a link with 34:9–11 and 39:4. **13*b*, 14*a*.** See 39:5f. **17.** Gr. echoes 39:5f. **18, 19*a*.** He conformed his conduct to the wisdom which he found. **19*b*, 20.** Another echo of 39:5. **21, 22.** With wisdom the Lord has given him a gift of self-expression, both in prayer and in teaching. **23–30.** He invites young scholars to frequent his school. **23*b*.** 'school', HT (Cairo B; Q lacks vv 20ff): *bêt miḏrāš*, 'house of instruction'. This is the earliest occurrence of this technical term, and of a mention of the postexilic practice of masters giving lessons on the Scriptures in their own houses. **24*a*.** Read (Ziegler's ed.): 'Why are you yet lacking'. Why should their thirst for wisdom remain any longer unslaked when **(25)** there is a master at hand to dispense it gratis? It was a point of honour not to charge for Scripture lessons. **26.** The only price to be paid is that of diligent labour, the bearing of wisdom's 'yoke'. See 6:25–31. **27, 28.** As in his own case, the labour will be small in comparison with the fruit: 'much rest', i.e. peace of soul; and (figuratively) much 'silver' and 'gold', i.e. abundant spiritual riches, cf Prv 3:13–16; 8:10f, 18–21; Wis 7:8–11. **29.** HT speaks of the gratification shared in common by master and disciples: 'May my soul delight in my chair (of teaching), and you will not be ashamed to sing my praises.' 'Chair', Heb. *yᵉšîḇāh*, in sense of professor's chair, has derived meaning: (a) lecture-hall, and (b) the class which there assembled. **30.** A closing reference to the 'work' demanded by the study of wisdom, and the divine reward which it brings; see vv 26, 27. **Colophons** are subjoined in Gr., Syr. and Heb. MSS, on which see § 439*c*.

THE PROPHETICAL LITERATURE

BY L. JOHNSTON

451a **Bibliography**—M. Buber, *The Prophetic Faith*, 1949; D. Buzy, *Les symboles de l'AT*, 1923; O. Eissfeldt, 'The Prophetic Literature' in *The OT and Modern Study*, ed. H. H. Rowley, 1951, 115—61; A. Guillaume, *Prophecy and Divination among the Hebrews and other Semites*, 1938; A. Johnson, *The Cultic Prophet in Ancient Israel*, 1961[2]; J. Lindblom, *Prophecy in Ancient Israel*, 1962; S. Mowinckel, 'The "Spirit" and the "Word" in the Pre-exilic Reforming Prophets', JBL 53 (1934), 199—227; M. Noth, 'History and Word of God' in *The Laws of the Pentateuch and Other Essays*, 1966, 179—93; H. H. Rowley (ed), *Studies in OT Prophecy*, 1950; P. Synave and P. Benoit, *Prophet and Inspiration*, 1961; J. Skinner, *Prophecy and Religion*, 1922; B. Vawter, *The Conscience of Israel*, 1961.

b **Prophecy and Religion**—The very idea of a religion which is in any sense 'supernatural' involves the need for some means of communication with that which is beyond man's natural grasp. This can be done by various means—by omens or magic, for example; but one common way has been through persons endowed with special psychic gifts. The exercise of these gifts is often accompanied by an inhibition of normal powers of perception—by a state of ecstasy or trance; and this state can be induced by various means, by drugs or drink or the hypnotic effect of music or dancing. It may also, like hysteria, be contagious and give rise to the phenomenon of group ecstasy.

All of this is found in Israel (and it may be significant that it appears at a time when Israel was in close contact with a foreign civilization, that of Canaan; it is possible that from Canaan it passed into Israel. Thus 1 Sm 10:5—12 gives a clear example of 'group ecstasy' accompanied by music which affected Saul; the frenzied devotees of Baal (1 (3) Kgs 18:20—28) are described as prophets—a recognition of the similarity between these men and those who could be called prophets in Israel. 1 Sm 9:9 might suggest that prophecy is somehow connected with 'second sight'; Saul consults Samuel about his lost asses, in which capacity Samuel is called 'a seer', and the writer comments: 'he who is now called a prophet was formerly called a seer'.

c **The Prophetic Guilds (Sons of the prophets, 2 (4) Kgs 2:3)**—The mere fact that the psychological roots of this phenomenon were open to suspicion does not mean that it was necessarily valueless religiously. If God could make his will known through the casting of lots (cf for example 1 Sm 10:20ff) he could certainly use men like soothsayers. Indeed there was a certain appropriateness in this. There were two opposing but necessary elements in Israelite religion—the static and the dynamic, the institution and the spirit. As an organized religion it clearly had to have institutions (priest, king, law, ritual); but as a religion which depended from the beginning on the free action of God and on the concept of the divine supremacy, the institution

could never be allowed to stifle the divine initiative. There **451c** was therefore a certain appropriateness in 'the spirit of God' (1 Sm 10:6; 2 (4) Kgs 2:9) showing itself in this clearly non-institutional form, i.e. through **prophets**.

But although there is no doubt that these prophets **d** could really be moved by 'the spirit of God', it is true that their activity easily **lent itself to abuse.** The scene described in 1 (3) Kgs 22:5—12 shows clearly what could happen. In a nation like Israel—in any society where the supernatural is acknowledged and respected—the reputation of being a 'man of God' brought with it esteem and honour. Such men were sought after by the pious (like Elisha and the lady of Shunem, 2 (4) Kgs 4:8—10) and listened to respectfully by kings (like Nathan with David or Ahijah with Jeroboam, 1 (3) Kgs 11:29ff). But this honoured position would lead others not so gifted to seek to play a similar part—and the style was easily copied. So the pious confraternities of godly men who gathered round an Elijah could very easily become, as in the passage referred to, a coterie of courtiers prepared to say whatever the king wished to hear.

There is even in the same incident evidence of a still **e** more pernicious distortion. When the **king appeals to his prophets for a 'good word'** (and is reluctant to hear from the one prophet from whom he knows that no such word will come), it is not merely a question of foolish self-deception on the king's part and cynical time-serving on that of the prophets. The thought on both sides is that these men by their words and actions can actually produce the effect desired—that they could somehow control God's activity.

The Great Prophets—One can well understand, there- **452a** fore, that the time would come when men who claimed to speak for God would **dissociate themselves** strongly from what had become almost a profession: 'I am no prophet, nor a prophet's son' (Am 7:14). In such men, as the same text shows (Am 7:14f), what is of first importance is not the phenomena but the fact of being called, and of being **called to speak the word of God**. The Heb. word *nābî'*—normally translated 'prophet'—is connected with the Assyrian *nabu*, meaning 'to call'. It is uncertain whether the word is used in an active or a passive sense, 'one who is called by God' or 'one who calls, utters, **proclaims the word of God**'; but both together describe well the rôle of the prophet; he is called to speak the word of God, and he speaks the word of God not in virtue of his native genius or acquired skills nor even because of his own piety, but simply **in virtue of God's call.** The relationship between Moses and Aaron is described in terms of prophecy: 'See, I make you as God to Pharaoh, and Aaron your brother shall be your prophet' (Ex 7:1); which is further described: 'You shall speak to him and put the words in his mouth . . . He shall speak for you to the people, and he shall be a mouth for you and you shall be to him as God' (Ex 4:15f). This is the way that Israel understood the role of the prophet in relationship to God. It is for this reason that the accounts

452a of their calling figure so prominently in the prophetic writings—it is their authorization to speak in the name of God. 'Then the Lord put forth his hand and touched my mouth: and the Lord said to me, "Behold I have put my words in your mouth" ' (Jer 1:9), so that henceforth the prophet could say, 'Thus speaks the Lord'.

b The precise psychological reality underlying these descriptions—how, especially, the prophet is aware of the objectivity of his experience—inevitably escapes us; but it may have been analogous to the experience of the mystics, (Lindblom, chh 1—2). The analogy with mystical experience, as well as the prophetic accounts of their calling, make it clear that there was no question of 'possession' in which the prophet's faculties were used as a passive instrument. The call came to **men of a wide variety of gifts and character**, and they reacted to it in different ways according to their different temperaments, not as automata. The call of God was not destructive of the prophet's own personality; indeed it is significant that the one prophet who does speak of being 'constrained', Jeremiah (20:7), is the one whose writings are most strongly marked by the imprint of his personality.

c Cultic Prophets—What is the precise place of the prophets in Israel's religion as a whole? Partly in reaction against an earlier view that the prophets were rebels against the establishment, recent authors have gone to the opposite extreme in trying to show that they actually had an official place in Israel's religious institutions. It is certainly true that cultic prophets were known in Canaan, from which Israel drew so many of its ideas and practices (cf 1 (3) Kgs 18:20—28, quoted above § 451*b*). It is true also that the **association between the prophets and the place of worship** is striking. Samuel is called when ministering to the Lord in the sanctuary at Shiloh (1 Sm 3:1ff), builds an altar to the Lord at Ramah (1 Sm 7:17) and first meets Saul at a 'high place', (1 Sm 9:19). Jeremiah preaches about the temple at the gate of the Lord's house (Jer 7:1—15); Isaiah's inaugural vision takes place in the temple (Is 6); Ezekiel is a priest, pays great attention to the new temple envisaged for restored Israel (Ezek 41—47) and his teaching has obvious affinities with the book of Lv (cf § 523). We notice also that there are liturgical forms among the prophetic writings (see § 453*c* and EOTInt, 74). Mowinckel points out that the function of the **choir guilds** in post-exilic times was described as 'prophecy' (1 Chr 25:1, 2, 5), and suggests that these were descended from the prophetic guilds, the groups of men sometimes called 'the sons of the prophets' (e.g. 2 (4) Kgs 2:3) cf § 451*c—d*, and that the prophetic guilds too must therefore have played some part in the cult.

d The reaction is a sound one, and it is not merely a reaction but a swing of opinion. The prophetic attacks on abuses of worship cannot really be construed as an attack on worship as such, and their generally antagonistic **attitude to religious formalism does not imply a total rejection of all religious institutions.** But the evidence for the view that they were simply cultic officials does not seem to be convincing (cf de Vaux, AI, 384f). The work of the prophets can be understood in such a way as to take account of both the anti-cultic tenor of some of their preaching and the cultic environment of much of their activity.

e The Work of the Prophets—By the time of the great prophets of whom we are speaking, Israel was familiar with the idea of divine revelation, in the form of **divine intervention**. Indeed the existence of the nation was based on this idea and this fact. But by the 8th cent. **the great deeds of God belonged to the past**, and the concept was embodied in liturgical 'commemoration' in **452e** which those deeds were relived in such a way as to become a present reality. But a **liturgical commemoration** is, psychologically at least, very different from the actual event; and moreover Israel was exposed to other influences which threatened still more their attitude towards God who revealed himself in his deeds. They had come into contact with the Canaanite civilization, with its very different idea of divinity and of religion. In Canaan, the gods were to a large extent personifications of natural forces, especially that of fertility (Baal, one of the Canaanite epithets for god, means 'husband'); and religious practices were a matter of technique for influencing those forces. Something of this attitude affected Israel, so that, although the centre of their worship was not the cycle of nature as in other religions but the historical deeds of God, nevertheless the **liturgical commemoration of these deeds could become a ritual formula divorced from the appropriate internal attitude.**

At the same time sweeping **economic and social f changes**—from a pastoral, nomadic people to an agricultural, trading and urban state—had made Israel something very different from the brotherhood of desert days; and covenant law, and still more the spirit of the covenant, had failed to keep pace with the changes. The results were manifest—greed, injustice, a gulf between rich and poor with excessive luxury on the one hand and destitution on the other.

The time was clearly ripe for a **reaffirmation of the moral imperatives of the law of Sinai**; and this the prophets provided. Fearlessly and vigorously, by **warning, threat and tender appeal**, they proclaimed the word of God in the face of public opinion and the civil and religious authorities. But even more important than their moral teaching was the spirit which animated it. Behind the law of Sinai, they pointed to the God of Sinai. Each prophet had his own vision, but all alike were consumed with the reality of God, his majesty, his supremacy, his absolute transcendence. And yet this God was not impersonal Power, but a Person; a Person whose deeds were the expression of his personal will and who called for a **personal response from man**, the service of the heart, not the mechanical performance of prescribed activity.

This personal relationship was the real meaning of **g** the covenant: 'If you truly amend your ways, if you truly execute justice one with another . . . then I will be with you in this place' (Jer 7:5—7; RSV is slightly different). But God's concern was not restricted to the moral conduct of Israel; he is total Lord of all the world, and the prophetic **message extended also to the moral conduct of other nations** and to political and international relationships. The prophets differed in their conception of the relationship between Israel and other nations, from extreme nationalism in which others were made subject to Israel, to a real universalism in which they too were called along with Israel to the knowledge and service of the only God.

But it still remained true that Israel was **the Chosen h People**, called out of Egypt to be God's son (Hos 11:1); and it was with their destiny that the prophets were especially concerned. This future was generally painted in sombre colours; partly because of the need to counteract the triumphalism and complacency which so easily attached itself to the idea of being chosen by God. But it demands too ruthless a mutilation of the texts to restrict the prophetic message to these prophecies of 'Woe'. Beyond the judgement and cataclysm, they reach out to restoration in which a **'remnant'**, purged by disaster,

452h will survive to be a holy seed. The prophet's own character and circumstances contribute largely to the way in which he describes this future. It is often centred on a 'new David', **the Lord's anointed, a Messiah**. In days when the actual kings fell so far short of the ideal as to breed a mistrust of the monarchic system, this is to a certain extent natural, from another point of view surprising; but in either case, it is not merely a question of adapting contemporary ideology and language to an ideal future. It is a question of a penetrating assessment of the real meaning of the covenant and of the role of the king in relation to the covenant, as its embodiment. The same principle too should be applied to the prophetic hopes for the future. People sometimes speak of the prophets 'foreseeing' or 'foretelling' the future. But one difficulty about this way of putting it is that it means that in this case the prophet's words would be largely incomprehensible to his contemporaries, the people to whom they were in the first place addressed. It gives us a better understanding of the situation to realize that the prophetic preaching was based on a deep understanding of Israel's place in God's plan. They realized, for example, that the covenant meant that God's love for them was unshakeable, so that although the nation may have to pass through various calamities, 'it would come to pass after those days' that God would yet bless them. Again, they realized that the Davidic dynasty was the embodiment of the covenant and so in a certain sense the guarantee of God's presence with them; so that when king Ahaz feared defeat and dethronement Isaiah can reassure him with the words that 'a maiden would bear a child who would be called "Emmanuel"'.

In all such cases, no doubt it was the immediate situation which was uppermost in the prophet's mind. But of course his words apply also and often with even greater force to a future situation when God's plan would achieve its full realization. Authors sometimes speak in this connexion of 'a foreshortening of perspective' or of 'compenetration of images'. The latter phrase is slightly better; the former implies that the prophet actually saw an event of the distant future, only he saw it in the wrong perspective so that he thought it was nearer at hand than it actually was. But this is to reduce the prophets to something like soothsayers. They are much more than this. They are men of profound faith and spiritual insight. They do not give factual reports of a future clearly seen by miraculous vision. They speak from faith and the understanding born of faith.

i The prophets, therefore, though they deal with political events and social ills, are not simply enlightened political theorists nor social reformers. But neither is it even their theological and moral teaching which is most important. Indeed they have no clear-cut theological or moral system (though no doubt one can be constructed from their works). Their teaching is directed to the details of **the immediate situation**. They do not speak from the serenity of a timeless eternity, but from the **urgency of the here and now**. But it is this which is important and which gives the prophets, so to speak, an eternal contemporaneity. What they are is even more important than the facts of their message: 'I and the children whom the Lord has given me are signs and portents in Israel' (Is 8:18). Israel's existence depends on the belief that God has acted in the world. This action is God's self-revelation, **a personal communication**; but the aspect of 'event' inevitably tended to overshadow the aspect of communication; it tended to become impersonal. But it is precisely this personal element which was essential; and the experience of the prophets was a living demonstration and reassertion of the personal nature of God's intervention. God had indeed acted on them and in them, but his action was personal and the result was a 'word'. It was personal communication in which God seized the prophet in the deepest core of his being and with his whole being the prophet responded to the call. **The God who acts had acted in them, and the word-event became personal encounter in them.** Their work and their teaching is simply the reflex of this experience of theirs. No matter what individual and concrete situations their message envisages, it is always an affirmation that God is the living God and ever acting; and that his action is not confined to the great historical events of the past sedately commemorated in the liturgy, but must be a living reality within the experience of each individual here and now. It is, moreover, still the Almighty, the Holy Lord who acts. In his **historical intervention**, God's action was **j** an irruption from outside which cut through and across the ordered pattern of events: 'The sea looked back and fled, the mountains skipped like rams ... Tremble, O earth, at the presence of the Lord, who turns the rock into a pool of water' (Ps 114 (113):3—8). So it is too with the prophetic word: 'Behold, I am making my words in your mouth like fire' (Jer 5:14); 'Behold, I have put my words in your mouth ... to pluck up and to break down, to destroy and to overthrow, to build and to plant' (Jer 1:9—10). As in the deed, so in the word God's power is expressed; but it is not meant to be merely an objective event but a real personal communication, a personal encounter. God's word is like a fire, like a hammer which breaks rock (Jer 23:29), but it is in the hearts of men that it must work. 'Enter into the rock and hide in the dust from before the terror of the Lord and from the glory of his majesty. The haughty looks of man shall be brought low, and the pride of men shall be humbled; and the Lord alone will be exalted in that day' (Is 2:10—11).

Even more than the prophetic message, then, **the k prophetic experience is of permanent significance.** They are witnesses; they are witnesses to the reality of God, of God's word and God's spirit who convinces the world of sin and of righteousness and of judgement (Jn 16:8).

Christ is the fulfilment of prophecy not merely in the sense that many of their insights are realized in the events of his life, but in the sense that in him the personal nature of the divine intervention is complete; the word is made flesh; and in his death and resurrection (as in the prophetic threat and promise) judgement and redemption are proclaimed.

The Writings of the Prophets—The prophets were **453a** men of the spoken word rather than of the written; preachers rather than writers. The 'books' which compose the body of **prophetic literature** are the result of an **editorial process** to be considered later. There is a rich variety of forms in this literature, and an initial division of it would be into prose and poetry; but since this is purely extrinsic it seems better to divide it rather into narrative and pronouncement.

The **narrative portions of the books**, usually in prose, consist of **autobiography** or **biographical material** added by the prophet's disciples. In the first place comes the prophet's account of his call; then of his visions and dialogues with God; then of other incidents from his life. The account of his symbolic acts is particularly significant in the light of what has already been said about the importance of the prophets; these actions are not merely pedagogic, to drive home the message of the prophet; they are the word of God in operation, acted out in the life of these men who were in their whole persons bearers

453a of the word. To the prophet's disciples we owe the chronological notes attached to some of the teaching, and the 'legends' (stories of men or places with religious or devotional significance) such as the accounts of Jeremiah's sufferings.

b The **narrative portions of the books may contain teaching**—this is true of Hosea's account of his marriage, and the whole of Haggai is given in the context of a narrative about the building of the Temple—but the bulk of the teaching is given in the form of what may be called generally pronouncement. The core of the **prophetic pronouncement is the oracle**, originating in the prophet's ecstatic experience. Like the earlier Urim and Thummim oracle, this would probably be basically a brief, pregnant phrase; any word, and especially therefore the word of God, was a thing of power, an 'incantation'; and the whole shattering experience of the prophet's vision might remain summed up in his conscious mind in a single significant word or phrase, like Emmanuel (Is 7:14), or Ariel (Is 29:1) or *sheqed* (Jer 1:11). But the 'powerful word' which lies at the heart of the message may then be expanded in threat or promise for the future, or warning and exhortation for the present. The 'I am' which is the essence of a divine revelation is closely followed by 'Thou shalt', as in the Ten Words of Sinai, or as in the Code of Holiness: 'You shall be holy, for I the Lord your God am holy' (Lv 19:2). We must also bear in mind that the prophet is decidedly not a lifeless mouth-piece of God; even in the earlier seers, the oracle could be expanded into a more or less lengthy discourse (as with Balaam, Nm 23:7—24:24); this is even more to be expected of the prophets who were not merely ecstatic visionaries, but whose judgements were those of God (cf Jer 6:27—30).

c In this expansion, the greatest **variety of literary forms** was brought into play: taunt-songs, drinking-songs, dirge, lament, satire, diatribe, the form of the law-suit (cf J. Harvey, 'Le "Rîb-pattern" . . .', Bib 43 (1962) 172—96). Many forms were imitated or adapted from the liturgy: the blessings and curses; the lamentation ceremony (cf Jl 1:2ff); the *torah* or priestly instruction, including the question and answer form as in Mi 6:6—8: 'With what shall I come before the Lord? . . . He has showed you what is good: to do justice, and to love kindness, and to walk humbly with your God' (cf Ps 15 (14) on the conditions for entry into the Temple). And finally there is the sermon, possibly influenced by political and other speeches but connected too with the liturgy.

d Even thus developed, none of the prophetic pronouncements was very long; and a second stage comes when groups of pronouncements were gathered together in **small collections**. This may have been done under the guidance of the prophet himself; Is 8:16 suggests that the prophet had his rejected message written down for future reference: 'Bind up the testimony, seal the teaching among my disciples'; and Jer 36:2 (cf 30:2) explicitly refers to the writing of the prophet's words by Baruch. Mainly, however, the writing and collecting were the work of disciples; and the present arrangement of the texts shows that various such collections could exist independently; the new heading of Is 2:1 suggests that the collection chh 2—5 existed independently of ch 1 which has its own heading; Is chh 6—12 is again a separate collection of Emmanuel prophecies; and the collection of oracles concerning the nations in many of the prophets in surely the work of an editor rather than of the prophet himself.

e Moreover, the prophetic spirit was not restricted to the great figures whose names have come down to us. Among the followers of the prophets in particular, their message continued to be preached and pondered and enriched by others on whom the prophet's mantle had **453e** fallen; and on occasion the words of these other **anonymous figures** were incorporated into the work of the better known prophets. The best-known example of this is the addition of two collections from exilic and post-exilic times to the work of Isaiah (Is 40—55, 56—66); but the commentaries on the individual books will show that there are examples in nearly every book. The prophetic phenomenon is not so much due to the genius of certain outstanding individuals as testimony to the abiding presence of God's spirit in the covenant people; and prophetic literature, like the Law, was absorbed into the living tradition of Israel. The last stage in the formation of the prophetic **corpus** was the **gathering together of all the minor collections** into four 'books' under the headings of Isaiah, Jeremiah, Ezekiel and 'The Book of the Twelve'.

Apocalyptic—Despite their spiritual gifts and deep **454a** sense of the supernatural, the prophets were realists, and their world is a world we ourselves can recognize. Their realism, of course, depends on the reality of God and therefore includes a view of the destiny of the world and the purpose of God which leads them to speak of the future, even of the remote future, 'the last days'. But what in the great prophets was only one element in their thought, in later writers becomes so characteristic a trait as to form a specific type of literature—apocalyptic.

Apocalyptic literature flourished between the 2nd cent. B.C. and 2nd cent. A.D. Jeremiah had lamented that **the non-fulfilment of his predictions endangered the credibility of his message** (Jer 20:7ff); and as time went on this became an ever greater source of difficulty and scandal. The dark days of the Babylonian exile passed, and the high hopes of the return, and nothing had really changed. The promised salvation was not achieved; and worse still, Judah was once more subject to servitude and persecution (cf 2 Mc 3—7). It was a situation to test and break the faith of many.

It was in these conditions that apocalyptic literature **b** flourished. Its aim was basically the same as that of Second Isaiah and especially of Ezekiel—**to rouse the wavering faith of the Jews to renewed confidence** in the power and faithfulness of God. The aim was the same, much of the language and ideas was the same (and indeed was drawn directly from the prophets, especially those of the exile); but there was this difference, that the times had bred a certain impatience with history, so that these writers concentrate not on the present nor even the immediate future as in Second Isaiah, but on **the end of time**; they bring forcibly and visibly to the minds of their readers the final and definitive kingdom of God. Moreover, though these writers were heirs of the prophets, they have close affinities too with 'the sages', the men wise in the ways of the world and in the law who flourished in the post-exilic period. A first indication of this is in the very format of the books; whereas the prophetic literature is primarily the record of oral preaching with only a relatively small amount of narrative material, **apocalyptic** literature is generally almost entirely **in the form of narrative. It is teaching rather than preaching**. But the same influence can be seen also in the content of the books. They are really dealing with the problem which so exercised the didactic writers: 'Why do the wicked prosper?' And their answer is the same answer of faith: 'Yet a little while, and the wicked will be no more . . . Wait for the Lord, and keep to his way, and he will exalt you to possess the land; you

454b will look on the destruction of the wicked' (Ps 37 (36):10, 34).

c These circumstances account for the other elements in the form of apocalyptic literature. In despair of history, they appeal to the urgency of **the last days and the immediacy of the kingdom of God** at the end of time. But this means that they claim to know the secrets of the divine plan and the mysteries of providence (cf Eph 3:9)—'apocalyptic' means revelation, unveiling. But since they are not dealing merely with the future but **the future as the key to the present**, the solution to all history, they are thus led to present the future in a context of world-history—either a succession of empires as in Daniel or periods of history each marked by a specific characteristic as in the Book of Jubilees. This no doubt owes something to the 'learned' circles to which the apocalyptic writers were tributary, but it is basically no more than the appeal to history common to all the Bible (cf Is 40:21ff). This history is presented in the form of a prophecy of the future, though it is **vaticinium ex eventu—claiming to 'foretell' things that have actually happened**; but this is merely a way of saying: 'This too was foreseen by God'. The events spoken of are described in a highly figurative way; partly because in the circumstances of persecution this was a prudent way of avoiding the attentions of hostile authorities; but also because such figurative language is inevitable when dealing with the unknown future and appropriate when dealing with the unveiling of divine mysteries. The actual **d** figures used are drawn from various sources, but much of it is traditional biblical language, strange only in playing such a predominant part; this is certainly true of the language of natural cataclysm, and the animal figures probably go back mainly to Ezekiel, in whom they are the natural result of his environment (see § 510). Daniel was led to adopt similar language because of the similar situation in which his book was set, and after him they

become a literary convention. This device of *vaticinium* **454d** *ex eventu* leads in turn to the equally characteristic device of **pseudonymity**—again, not merely a way of evading the notice of the persecutors, but a necessity in a work which claims to be revealing mysteries—**the supposed author must be one who lived before the events 'prophesied'**. The same, finally, is true of the presence of angels which are so prominent in these books; again it is partly because of the Persian background to the first great apocalypse, Daniel—Hebrew angelology owes much to Persian influence—and partly because of the traditional Israelite idea of heavenly messengers, who would be particularly appropriate to convey heavenly mysteries.

It is difficult to say how far the 'visions' which the **e** apocalyptic writers claim to be reporting are merely a literary convention, and how far they represent some genuine spiritual experience. But certainly we would be wrong to think that their work is simply the delusions of a disordered imagination unbalanced by near-despair. It is true, and a fit subject for biblical witness, that God is the lord of history and that through all the apparently meaningless twists of history God is neither helpless nor unconcerned, so that no view of history can be accurate which does not include in its perspective the kingdom of God, the last kingdom, which shall not pass away (Dn 7:14). **This kingdom**, moreover, is absolutely supernatural; it is not of this world (Jn 18:36), not made by any human hand (Dn 2:45). But **though it does not belong to history, it is still worked out in history**. The actual chronology of the apocalyptic writers may be conditioned by their own times and their own minds; but their message is the same as that of the prophets, and the same as that of Christ—that it is in this world that the warfare between the powers of light and the powers of darkness is waged, from which the kingdom of God will emerge victorious (cf H. H. Rowley, *The Relevance of Apocalyptic*, 1963³, 166—93).

ISAIAH

BY A. PENNA

459a Bibliography—Commentaries: J. Fischer, BB, 1939; E. Kissane, Dublin, 1943; A. Bentzen, Copenhagen, 1943⁴; S. Mowinckel, Oslo, 1950; A. Penna, SacB, 1958 (chh 1–39); G. B. Gray, ICC, 1912; O. Procksch, KAT, 1930; J. Kröker, Giessen, 1961² (chh 40–66); C. C. Torrey, 1928; P. Volz, Leipzig, 1932; H. W. Hertzberg, Hamburg, 1939; H. Brandenburg, Giessen, 1961 (chh 40–55); S. Smith, 1944; C. R. North, 1952; L. G. Rignell, Lund, 1956 (chh 56–66).

b Special Subjects: F. Feldmann, *Die Bekehrung der Heiden* . . . Aachen 1919; R. Hala, 'The Universalism of Is', CBQ 12 (1950), 162–70; F. Dreyfus, 'La doctrine du reste chez le prophète Isaie', RSPT 39 (1955), 361–86; O. Loretz, *Das Reich Gottes nach dem Buche Isaias*, Innsbruck, 1960; St. Virgulin, *La 'Fede' nella Profezia d'Isaia*, Milan, 1961; J. Engnell, *The Call of Isaiah*, Uppsala, 1949; J. Coppens, 'La prophétie de la 'Almâh', ETL 28 (1952), 648–78; G. Fohrer, 'Zu Jes. 7:14 in Zusammenhang von Jes. 7:10–22', ZATW 68 (1956), 54–56; A. Alt, 'Jesaja 8:23–9:6. Befreiungsnacht und Krönungstag', *Fs A. Bertholet*, Tübingen, 1950, 29–49; J. Lindblom, *Die Jesaja-Apocalypse, Jes 24–27*, Lund, 1938; E. S. Mulder, *Die Teologie van die Jesaja-Apokalypse, Jesaja 24–27*, Groningen, 1954; W. Caspari, 'Jesafa 34–35', ZATW 49 (1931), 67–85; R. J. Tournay, 'Les chants du Serviteur. . . .' RB 59 (1952), 355–87; 481–512; C. R. North, *The Suffering Servant in Deutero-Isaiah. An Historical and Critical Study*, London, 1956²; A. Bentzen, *Messias-Moses redivivus-Menschensohn*, Zurich, 1948; H. Cazelles, 'Les poèmes du Serviteur . . .', RSR 43 (1955), 5–55; A. Bentzen, 'On the ideas of "the Old" and "the New" in Deutero-Isaiah', StudT 1 (1/2), Lund, 1948, 183–7; C. R. North, 'The "Former Things" and the "New Things" in Deutero-Isaiah', *Studies in OT Prophecy*, ed. H. H. Rowley, 1950; C. R. North, *The Second Isaiah*, Oxford, 1964; J. D. Smart, *History and theology in Second Isaiah*, 1967. For further bibliography see EOT Int, 303f, 330–2.

460a Contents—Older commentators had already noticed a clear distinction between chh 1–39 and 40–66, the latter being known as the 'Book of Consolation'. In this second section, a further distinction is now recognized: chh 40–55 and 56–66. The three sections are often called Isaiah, Second Isaiah and Third Isaiah.

b The first section was a **gradual compilation made up out of six smaller sections**, complete in themselves and distinct from each other. (a) ch 1, consists of reproaches, threats and promises; (b) 2:1–12:6: various **oracles on Judah and Jerusalem**, plus the account of the prophet's call in ch 6. The historical background is the period between c. 740–30 B.C. with frequent allusions to facts bearing on the Syro-Ephraimitic war and its consequences. In chh 7–11 the author foresees an invasion by Assyria but introduces the figure of 'Emmanuel'—a new David, endowed with exceptional

gifts of the Spirit of the Lord—who is somehow connected with the inglorious end of the invasion and the **460b** restoration of Israel. The section concludes with a short hymn of praise and thanksgiving. (c) 13:1–23:18: this groups together **oracles on the nations** in the following order: Babylon (13:1–14:23; cf 21:1–10); Assyria (14:24–27; cf 17:12–14); Philistia (14:28–32); Moab (15:1–16:14); Damascus and Israel (17:1–10); Ethiopia and Egypt (18:1–20:6); Edom (21:11, 12); Arabia (21:13–17) and Tyre (23:1–18). In ch 22 there are two oracles, one on Jerusalem (22:1–14) and the other on a specific individual, the steward Shebnah (22:15– **c** 25). (d) 24:1–27:13: often called the **Apocalypse of Isaiah** and interpreted as a prophecy of the end of the world. But in fact, despite its apocalyptic style, it depicts the end of some wicked city and the quite different destiny of Judah. It is not easy to give an exact interpretation of this section, but on the whole scholars at present agree that the historical background is the period just before the fall of Babylon (539 B.C.). (e) 28:1–33:34: this section is in many respects similar to the second. Generally speaking we can be sure of its unity, but there are parts of it, particularly ch 33, which are uncertain. The first vv (28:1–4) **foresee the imminent collapse of Samaria** (722 B.C.). In the following vv the prophet argues against an anti-Assyrian alliance which is being promoted by Egypt and the satellite states of Syria-Palestine. The prophet insists that faith, and moral renewal, are the only safeguard. Hezekiah, despite his piety, rejects the advice; there then follows the invasion described in detail in 29–31. The historical background is about 730–705. (f) 34:1–35:10: two contrasting and complementary pictures; first the **judgement of God upon the nations**, and secondly a lyrical **description of Israel's return from exile**. The historical background of the latter is the same as for 40–55, and since both chh 34 and 35 are closely linked, the same historical period is assigned to both. This first part of the book ends with an editorial appendix taken mainly from 2 (4) Kgs 18:13–20:19 dealing with the events of c. 705–701: the Assyrian invasion, Hezekiah's illness and the alliance with Merodach-Baladan.

The division of **Second Isaiah** is less clear. Here **d** we are not dealing with distinct sections, but with recurring themes. The historical background is fairly clear if the year 539 is taken as the *terminus ante quem*: **the fall of Babylon is portrayed as imminent**. Some of the oracles may well be a great deal older, but on the whole it is difficult to think of a period before about 560. One obvious unit in this book is the **four songs of the Servant of Yahweh** found in the following passages: 42:1–7; 49:1–6; 50:4–9; 52:13–53:12. Some of these are separated by a few vv (49:7–50:3; 50:11–52:12), which deal with the return from exile. One group of oracles is especially concerned with the fall of Babylon, coupled with a **polemic against idols**, and the contrast between the old and new prophecies (ch 48). These three

460d themes are also found elsewhere, viz 44:24—25, with the emphasis on the work of the Persian king, Cyrus; and 42:8—44:23, which stresses the promise of freedom and describes the return with great enthusiasm, every now and then breaking out into a polemic against idolatry (40:18—20; 41:6, 7; 44:6—20). Chh 54—55 describe the new Israel, with frequent contrasts between its present lowly state and brighter prospects for the future.

e Except for a few short passages, chh 40—55 are written in poetry. Generally speaking the style is good; but repetition, emphasis and other mannerisms tend to give these chh a rather precious quality, making them less original and not quite as fine as the first part. The same may be said of the **third part of the book**, apart from some passages such as ch 60 of high poetic quality; and it is equally difficult to give a precise division. The historical background is later, viz the **years immediately following the return from exile**, authorized by Cyrus in 538 B.C.

f Without going into detail, chh 56—66 may be divided as follows: **Israel's apostasy** (56:1—57:21); **true religion**, reproaches and promises (58:1—59:21); **the new Jerusalem**, salvation (60:1—63:6); collective prayers (63:7—64:12); **divine intervention**, promises and threats (65:1—66:24). Once more the themes of consolation and polemic against idolatry recur. The pessimism of these chh is not due to any lack of faith in the return from exile, but stems rather from the many set-backs which arose in the first years after the return. The prophet contrasts the future glory of Jerusalem with the existing state of wretchedness, never ceasing to recall his listeners to a more profound faith and more perfect justice, and energetically upbraiding those actions which helped to bring about moral and political distress.

461a Composition and Authorship of the Book—Isaiah speaks of a group of disciples to whom he entrusted particular 'revelations' (8.16). It is not possible to determine precisely the contribution his disciples made to the composition of the book, but it is certain that **the prophet did not publish a complete book**. The first vv of chh 1 and 2 are sufficient evidence of the existence of **smaller collections, which were compiled into one work**. The arrangement of the various sections shows that at least three of them could have existed in the time of the prophet, namely sections 1, 2 and 5 covering chh 1—12 and 28—33. They could have been compiled and published separately either by Isaiah or his disciples. It is less probable that they were written as a whole, since if this were so we might expect some continuity from chh 1—33.

b Instead, what we do find is two sections forming a unity in themselves inserted into the three mentioned above. The two insertions, chh 13—23 and 24—27, contain oracles with different historical backgrounds and with a different line of thought, and it is not easy to say how old they are. Some of the oracles on the nations could well come from Isaiah, whilst others, in particular the ones on Babylon (13:1—14:23) and on Tyre (ch 23), with a few additions from other prophecies, show some indication of belonging to a later period.

c On the whole, it would be difficult to think of a period prior to the exile for these two collections, even if a good deal of the material found in chh 13—23 is authentic, i.e. the work of the 8th cent. prophet. The oracles in chh 34—35 also originate from the time of the exile. The grouping together of all the chh from 1—39 came after the exile when it became possible to insert chh 36—39 from the book of Kgs.

d Chh 40—55 are pervaded by thoughts on the exile and its end. They must have originated between the years **461d** 586—539; but the two extreme dates are less probable, and in practice we can take it that these chh are **the work of a prophet who lived in Babylon towards the end of the exile**. Chh 56—66 have a Palestinian background (c. 538—520 B.C.); in themselves they might well be the work of second Isaiah, if we suppose his return to Judea with the first group of exiles; but this cannot be taken as proved or as the only possibility; they could also be the work of someone who was ideally suited to continue the work of the prophet of the exile, and indeed not necessarily the work of only one man. The collection of **e** chh 40—66 and their union with chh 1—39 could be placed at a time not much after the exile, that is to say when the various sections of chh 1—39 had received their final form. The final editor who brought together so many oracles with so varied a chronological background did in fact compose an excellent work. There is a variety of themes and different doctrinal interests, but certain ideas and expressions (such as the Holy One of Israel) and a profoundly religious sense of history give unity to the whole.

In short, we may say that the book of Isaiah has gone **f** through a fairly lengthy history not unlike that now recognized for other books of the OT such as Pent, Pss, Sm, Jer, etc.

The authenticity of Isaiah became a subject of lively debate on two counts. Liberal critics held that the book was a heterogeneous collection of different writings from different dates, especially from the last centuries of prechristian Judaism. This is now rejected by all.

Another theory held it inconceivable that so many **g** great oracles should be the work of an unknown writer, and thought it temerarious to contradict a tradition to which was attributed great value. The first of these reasons, viz the unlikelihood of an anonymous writer, is no longer of any consequence, but not so the second, even though this is not now so important as it was.

There is certainly no doubt about the existence of **h** such a tradition right up to the 18th cent., among both Christians and Jews; this has now further backing from direct documentation (Qumran MSS). But this only proves that the book already existed in its present form, as a single unity, some centuries before Christ. This is all that can be argued also from two facts which are important to a Christian, viz that the book is often quoted in the NT under the name of Isaiah, and that Sirach 48:20—25, (if we accept the more obvious interpretation) refers to Isaiah the prophet as the author of chh 40—66. The **i** decrees of the Biblical Commission of 1908 did not state directly that a Catholic must hold as a matter of doctrine that Isaiah wrote all 66 chh of the book commonly attributed to him, but nevertheless opposed the liberal tendencies dominant in critical circles at that time, EnchB 291—5. Today, both excessive splitting up into sections is condemned, and a system of dating which is too late; on the other hand, recognition is given to the existence of an Isaian 'school' which conserved the teaching of this great prophet, meditated on it and continued it.

Messianic Prophecy—The Songs of the Servant of j Yahweh—It would be impossible to sum up the 'doctrine' of the book of Isaiah in a few lines; it is renowned for its exalted notions of the holiness and omnipotence of God and his intervention into the world of human experience, as well as for its insistence on 'faith' for the individual and for society. But there is one theme that merits special attention; that which makes Isaiah loved by all Christian readers, that which makes his work as it were an anticipation of the Gospel itself. No other

461j prophetical writing contains such a wealth of **messianic prophecy**. Indeed the vision of freedom in chh 40—55, and of the new Jerusalem in chh 56—66, are remarkably significant both from a messianic and eschatological point of view, with a striking universalist and 'ecumenical' perspective.

k Concerning the person of the Messiah, there is no doubt at all that the predominant idea of chh 7—11 is that of a royal messianism, however the sign in 7:14 is interpreted. It is sufficient to read the first vv of chh 9 and 11. Here we have the development of Nathan's prophecy (2 Sam 7:11—16), similar to that found in some of the Psalms and in other prophetical writings. Such an aspect of messianism does not appear in chh 40—66, at least in any clear or noticeable fashion. Here, instead, there stands out the mysterious figure of the **'Servant of Yahweh'**.

l The Servant theme has a permanent fascination, but is also most difficult to define. In fact, there is disagreement amongst scholars concerning the number of texts about this mysterious person, about their origin, about the character of the person concerned (king or prophet?), about the nature of his mission, whether it is political or spiritual. There is also speculation with regard to the Servant's identity: is he an individual from OT history? Is he the Messiah? Does he represent a collective personality, the 'ideal' Israel, etc?

m For a detailed study which would answer these questions we must refer readers to individual monographs. All agree, more or less, in recognizing the outstanding religious significance of the word 'Servant'. There is also fairly wide agreement in recognizing this division of the four songs: 42:1—7; 49:1—6; 50:4—9; 52:13—53:12. As for the origin of these texts, we do not think that there are categoric reasons for denying that they were the work of the author of chh 40—55. Many, however, say that these texts—and perhaps others also—are passages from a single song, one which already existed or which was composed by Deutero-Isaiah himself, and which was sub-divided and inserted at various places by the editor.

n As regards the character of the Servant, certain passages (especially 49:5, 6) suggest political or kingly action on the part of the Servant. His sufferings, then, some would say, reflect the trials of the last kings of Judah (Jehoiachim and Zedekiah were deported to Babylon). On the whole, however, the prevailing features are those of a prophet who proclaims a new message, not only to the Israelites, but to all peoples. If there is some analogy between the figure of the Servant and David, and even more of Moses, it is also true that there is still more resemblance to Jeremiah whose life was a veritable vale of tears.

o On the question of **the identification of the Servant with the Messiah**, it would be superfluous to study afresh the Christian tradition, already made clear in the NT: the line of thought is clearly Servant = Messiah = Jesus Christ. The Heb. tradition presents more difficulty, but at least in the more ancient period the messianic interpretation seems to be well documented. And indeed, if the figure of the Servant refers to someone in the future through whom God will give salvation to all nations in the messianic era, then it seems clear that there can be no doubt as to his identification with the Messiah. For it is the Messiah who is charged with the same mission, according to the various texts which refer to him, even though there might be slight shades of difference in different traditions. It remains therefore that the novelty of the Servant songs consists above all in presenting an aspect of the Messiah which is not brought out elsewhere,

viz his sufferings and the value of the vicarious expiation **461o** attributed to those sufferings and to his death. This is the greatest contribution to the messianic idea. In addition, we must take into account the spirituality and the universality of the Messiah's mission, here expressed in a more marked fashion than anywhere else.

It would scarcely be possible to list the interpretations **p** of all who deny any similarity between the Servant of Yahweh and the Messiah. It is enough to say that the Servant's identification with other historical characters belonging to the time of Deutero-Isaiah, or even of a later period, is no longer debated. For a time, the collective interpretation, with reference to the people in exile, was popular with Jewish scholars in particular. This kind of interpretation is no longer prevalent, at least in that particular form. Many prefer what is called an historical-cultic, or liturgical-mythical interpretation—even allegorical—especially favoured by Lindblom. It is true to say, however, that the interpretations are far too many to be easily grouped under a common heading. But this uncertainty shows how difficult the question is; and, at least indirectly, suggests also that the most serious interpretation is still the traditional one.

Texts and Versions—On the whole, the Heb. text is **q** well preserved, with relatively few corruptions. These, along with some readings which are uncertain or suspect, demand particular examination in specific cases. In practice, the process of conjecture favoured by exegetes in the past is rarely used. There is now a pre-masoretic text preserved in two MSS (one mutilated) and various fragments from Qumran. Their evidence is valuable in so far as they confirm the integrity of the traditional text. In a few cases, the readings of the pre-masoretic text seem to be better than the MT, but even these are not immune from errors and omissions, etc. Amongst the ancient versions, the Gr. of the LXX must be respected, though the translation is far from perfect—it has recourse to paraphrase and adaptations which show that the sense of the Heb. was not always grasped.

The Vg is most useful; but as a help to textual **r** criticism it is of only relative value since it always presupposes the present MT. Also, Jerome could rarely resist making more obvious the oracles which were considered messianic.

But the problems and difficulties of text criticism need not be over emphasized, considering the far greater difficulties which face the exegete. Thus, the translation itself is often anything but easy, especially where the translator wishes to give an adequate rendering of the many beautiful passages of Heb. poetry.

Historical Background—Except for a few autobio- **462a** graphical details given in the text, anything said about Isaiah is usually legend of doubtful historical value. The description of the prophetic calling shows his strength of character (6:8); in chh 7 and 8 we learn a little about his family life (he was married and had at least two sons, 7:3; 8:3); and from 8:16 we gather that he enjoyed some success as a prophet. His poetic genius is evident from the style of the oracles, and their content portrays him as a reformer who firmly stated a precise policy for the kingdom of Judah.

Some of the historical allusions in the book can be **b** substantiated by the various data provided by other biblical writings and from the Assyrian texts of **Tiglath-Pileser III**, Sargon II and Sennacherib. The first of these kings tells of his **expedition** to eliminate the anti-Assyrian coalition and to protect his supporters, among whom was Ahaz of Judah (cf 7:1). Ahaz was being attacked by the Edomites and the Philistines (2 (4) Kgs 16:6;

462b 2 Chr 28:17—19), and also by the kings of Damascus and Israel, though this was not quite so urgent. Tiglath-Pileser (ANET 282—4) marched directly into Palestine against the Philistines and the Edomites, then returned to rout Damascus, which he did, incorporating its territory into Assyria. Then he turned on Israel and captured some of its territories around the lake of Gennesaret. Amongst the annals of his many conquests there is also a note of the **tribute paid by Ahaz**; this 'protection money' was a kind of vassallage. The statement of Ahaz' payment agrees perfectly with 2 (4) Kgs 16:7—9, and with 2 Chr 28:20, 21, and also with the hints given in the book of Isaiah. The baneful influence on religion of a policy based on subservience to a pagan nation is obvious from 2 (4) Kgs 16:16 and 2 Chr 28:22—25.

c   No more is said about Ahaz in the Assyrian inscriptions. On the other hand, they often mention Samaria and the various kings who succeeded amidst a series of revolts and intrigues. Is scarcely touches on this subject (17:3—6; 28:1—4), and it was clearly not his purpose to record all the facts. After Tiglath-Pileser had intervened in the affairs of Israel, his successor Shalmaneser V set about taming the hostile attitude of Hoshea, the last king to be set on the throne by Tiglath-Pileser, or at least approved by him. Shalmaneser besieged Samaria which put up a long fight and only capitulated to Sargon (722). Sargon, reputedly as distinguished as his predecessor, eliminated the kingdom of Israel, destroyed Samaria and other centres, and deported the most influential section of the population into Assyria, having first of all substituted others in their place (ANET 284; 2 (4) Kgs 17.1—6). Sargon also mentions other expeditions against the kings of Palestine and against Egypt, but never mentions Ahaz or his son, Hezekiah. Obviously, therefore, the kingdom of Judah continued its payment of tribute.

d   What we can glean from Is (30:1—7; 31:1—3) concerning the intense diplomatic activity against Assyria in the time of Hezekiah is amply confirmed from the inscriptions of Sennacherib, Sargon's successor. Both 2 (4) Kgs 18:2—7 and even more 2 Chr 29:2—31:21 speak enthusiastically about **Hezekiah as a religious reformer** (cf Sir 48:17—49:4) without revealing those aspects of him which are not quite so laudable (2 Chr 32:25, 31). Nor do we gather anything from these texts of the **rashness of his politics** (2 (4) Kgs 18:7; 20:13—15). Unlike the author of Kgs, Is makes no mention of the king's zeal for the worship of Yahweh, but he does emphasize his dangerous politics. But since Hezekiah was quite different from his sceptical father, Isaiah does not abandon him in the time of danger, but on the contrary even gives him a consoling oracle (37:2—7, 21—35; cf 38:1—8, 21).

e   Two accounts are given in the Bible of the consequences of Hezekiah's politics. One of them (2 (4) Kgs 18:13—16) shows him submitting to the king of Assyria and paying tribute; the other (2 (4) Kgs 18:13, 17—19:37; cf 2 Chr 32:1—23), describes a miracle obliging the remnant of the Assyrian army to leave Judah. This latter is more in agreement with the prophecies of Is which speak of **a triumphant march ending in tragedy** (10:27—34). But the two accounts are not actually contradictory, and indeed would fit the situation which is hinted at of Sennacherib's hasty withdrawal because of trouble at home (37:7) cf § 294b-h. There are at least four famous texts where Sennacherib celebrates his Palestinian expedition in 701, and if they are reduced to essentials, they all agree with the first biblical account: **the king exacted heavy tribute from Hezekiah and then returned with a rich booty**. Moreover, the longest of the four texts clearly states that Jerusalem was not attacked. The fact that

the Assyrian king makes no mention of the plague which **462e** spread through his soldiers—also put on record by Herodotus—is hardly surprising. For the rest, the annals of Sennacherib are fairly easily reconcilable with the biblical accounts, once we accept the different points of view. There is no need to suppose two campaigns, one in 701 and another some years later. The book of Is ends with the invasion of 701, which is in fact taken from Kgs. The prophetic oracles end with the prediction of this invasion and with a denunciation of those diplomatic intrigues which provoked it. The oracles cover a period of little less than 40 years: from 739 (the year of Uzziah's death, 6:1) to about 703. Within this time the kingdom of Israel disappeared and the Assyrian hegemony was established.

The historical background of **chh 40—66** is quite **f** different. The greater part of these chh refers to a period a little before 539, the year of the occupation of Babylon by Cyrus; 56—66 belong more to the years immediately following 539. The author of 40—55, if he is to be distinguished from the Isaiah of the 8th cent., gives no autobiographical details. Also, except for the mention of Cyrus (44:28; 45:1), and the emphasis put on the imminent fall of Babylon and the return of the Israelites, **no particular facts of the historical background are given** and none of the Babylonian kings is mentioned. This has given rise to two opposing theories. Torrey and **g** Simon, for example, say that in fact there is no mention of an exile in any real sense of the word, nor indeed of a return to the exiles' native land: all this must be accepted in the metaphorical-religious sense. On the other hand, S. Smith would see here a series of allusions to historical facts put forward by the anonymous prophet who is a kind of Fifth Column leader on the side of Cyrus. Few have been convinced by either of these arguments, which is not surprising. The book seems to suggest a renewed outburst of oppression by the Babylonians, though this may be simply oratorical hyperbole. This would agree with the sentiment expressed in Ps 137 (136), but it would be in contrast with the fact that not a few of the exiles were unwilling to take advantage of the authorization to return to Judah. There is in fact good evidence that many of the exiles actually achieved prosperity in their new home.

The historical facts indicated by **Second Isaiah** can **h** be limited to the period **between the accession of Cyrus of Anshan and his conquest of Babylon**: victory over the Medes in 550/49, and over Croesus of Sardis in 547/6. Nabonidus, according to recent documents the last king of Babylon, was opposed by many of his subjects, and with their support Cyrus was able to take Babylon in 539 without any difficulty. He immediately (538) authorized the return of the Israelites (2 Chr 36:22, 23; Ez 1:1—4), which took place in stages and on a small scale. Ez-Neh and the prophets Hag and Zech are the sources for information on the return and the many difficulties in Judah in the years that followed. The author or authors of chh 40—66 had in mind the consolation both of the exiles in Mesopotamia and of the community at Jerusalem about the years 538—520.

PART I DIVERSE ORACLES, 1—39.

1:1—31 Make yourselves clean!—The main idea of **463a** this ch is expressed in vv 16, 17. It is not the first oracle of Isaiah nor even an introduction to his book, but it does sum up quite well the essential point of his message, and contains several characteristic expressions which run through the book. After 1 (an editorial addition) the

463a sequence of ideas is as follows: a strong reproof of Israel's infidelity (2—9), condemnation of merely external cult (10—15), call to repentance with promise of divine pardon (16—20), lament over Jerusalem (21—26) and the vision of a changed future (27—31). The ch seems to be a unity; it is much more difficult to specify the historical background. The description of a calamity would perhaps place it at a time of war and confusion. If so, some think it might be the Syro-Ephraimite war (cf 7:1ff) or even the time of Sennacherib's invasion (cf chh 36—37). Certain expressions (6—8) support the latter.

The editor of v 1 delimits the term of Isaiah's activity, which began in the year of Uzziah's death (6:1) and ended under Hezekiah after 701. The four kings, all of them immediate successors of the same dynasty, present some chronological difficulties. The most probable dates seem to be: Uzziah or Azariah 767—739; Jotham 739—734/3; Ahaz 734/3—728/7; Hezekiah 728/7—699.

b **2—4.** In this description of the people's ingratitude, we can highlight a few of the more noteworthy theological ideas: divine fatherhood, holiness of God (the Holy One of Israel, a characteristic name in Is and rarely found elsewhere), seriousness of sin, defined above all else as abandoning God. **3,** together with the Gr. version of Hb 3:2, has given rise to the ox and ass in the manger.

c **5—9.** It is clear from 7—9 that it is the whole nation which suffers; the many wounds indicate misfortunes and general wretchedness due to an enemy invasion. If **8** describes Jerusalem being besieged, then the historical background most suited to this would be the Assyrian invasion (chh 36, 37). Survival will be solely on account of God's action in leaving a few survivors. This idea of a remnant, which pre-supposes severe chastisement but also the certainty of hope for the future, is one of the outstanding ideas of Isaiah (cf 6:13 and the name of his son in 7:3); this idea (cf Jer 3:14) is taken up by St Paul and applied to the problem of relationships between the Jews and Christians (Rm 9:29). For the healing efficacy of oil (**6**) cf Lk 10:34. Sodom and Gomorrha (**9**) are recalled as an example of divine chastisement (Gn 19:1—**d** 25) and as the symbol of serious vice. **10—15.** Condemnation of external worship. The expression 'to appear before me' (**12**) is due to the anxiety of the massoretes to wipe out all trace of anthropomorphism; more literally it would be 'to see my face'. This refers to the pilgrimages to the temple (cf Ex 23:17), the place consecrated by a special presence of God. In **11** two types of sacrifice are distinguished (holocaust and peace offerings) and the list of the most usual victims is given (cf Lv 1:3ff); in **13,** **14** some characteristic feasts are given (New moon and sabbath; cf Hos 2:11, Ex 23:12, 13) and then all the liturgical solemnities in general. This passage has some parallels in other prophetic books (cf Hos 6:6; Am 5:21—26; Mi 6:6—8; Jer 7:21—23): this does not in fact imply that external cult should be given up, but it is a plea that it should be the genuine expression of an interior holiness, and not an end in itself. The beautiful image of **15** (cf Ex 9:29; Jb 16:13) gives us some insight into the efficacy of prayer; it is not as though God feared that he might be constrained to restrain his justice (cf Jer 7:16; 11:14). The seriousness of guilt does not consist—as was often the case in pagan religions—in a ritual transgression, but in an act of violence against one's neighbour and **e** society ('hands full of blood'; cf 59:3). **16—20.** At first the language of ritual is used, but suddenly it becomes clear in what this purification consists which would be accepted in the eyes of God: to put aside every evil action and to lead a blameless life. The positive aspect, virtuous conduct, is described above all in terms of duty towards

one's neighbour, represented by the orphan and the **463e** widow, as often in the OT. The two comparisons ('like scarlet . . . crimson') in **18** are to be connected with the hands red with blood of v 15. If repentance is sincere (cf Jl 2:13; Lk 15:7), even the most serious sins will disappear and will be forgiven by God. In **19—20,** as happens quite often, truths of profound theological significance (relationship between sin and punishment, repentance and forgiveness) are followed by statements which seem to subordinate religion to material motives (obedience = prosperity; rebellion = punishment).

21—26. This passage, which is unexpected after the **f** proclamation of forgiveness, recalls vv 10—15. It is an examination of conscience carried out by the prophet. It proceeds in a series of antitheses, showing the contrast between their past state and the very different sinful present. The image of the harlot to show Israel's religious infidelity is quite common from Hosea onwards. In the list of vices and virtues (cf 17) we can see a reference to the decalogue (cf Jer 7:9), on the observance of which depends an individual's morality. For the idea of justice and its contrast with sin cf 5:7—10, 23. **22.** For the image of the dross cf Jer 6:29, 30; in the second part of the v there is an allusion to a mixture which will thin the wine. **25** is threatening, but also implies tender anxiety; chastisement aims at purifying the remnant of v 9 rather than its destruction. What stands out here is the possibility of a return to the practice of justice; for the symbolic names of Jerusalem cf Jer 33:16. **27—31.** These five vv are a **g** summary of the whole ch: severe threats of chastisement merited by a series of faults, impending distress (30, 31), but with a clear vision of ultimate salvation, the result of sincere repentance and a return to the practice of justice. In **29** there is an allusion to idolatrous practices, often connected with trees and sacred woods (Hos 4:13; Ezek 6:13; Jer 2:20 etc). It is not in fact certain that there is a reference to the gardens of Adonis. The *strong* of v **31** recalls the princes and the judges of the preceding vv (17, 23); *his work* is the social injustice so often stigmatized in the present oracle.

2:1—5:30 Threats and promises—The new title, **1,** **h** divides ch 2 from ch 1; it refers to the whole of the section chh 2—12, and is the work of the editor. Up to 4:1 the main subject is *the day of the Lord,* viz the realization of the prophesied chastisement of the kingdom of Judah, its capital in particular. The first (2:2—5) and the third (4:2—6) parts of this section seem to be out of context; they both have a messianic background, with universalist horizons.

2:2—5 Messianic peace in Sion—The temple of **i** Jerusalem rises symbolically to supreme heights to become the centre of the human race. All men hasten to it so that they can there worship the true God, reverence his law and hear his word. God will rule from Jerusalem with utmost justice, and he will rule over a world happy and utterly at peace. The prophetic vision looks to a distant and eschatological future ('in the latter days'). The image of the mountains rising high and of weapons being turned into instruments of peace is not unknown in classical literature (cf Virgil, *Georgics* I, 509; Ovid, *Fasti* I, 699). The ideas of ultimate justice and universal peace often recur in the descriptions of messianic times (cf 9:7; 11:5). The acceptance by mankind of Israel's faith is a frequent subject of Second Is. The passage recurs almost to the letter, but with an additional v, in Mi 4:1—4, and various hypotheses have been put forward to explain it. According to some, the original text is found in Isaiah and the text in Micah is derived: others think exactly the opposite; and yet others hold that there was a third source on which

463i both prophets depended. The passage is so lightly connected with the context here that it is hardly likely that Micah took it from Isaiah.

j **2:6—4:1 The day of the Lord**——The first part of this section forms a unified poem with refrains which enable it to be subdivided into smaller sections. Beginning with an accusation of idolatry and soothsaying, fostered by material prosperity (2:6—8), the poem proceeds in v 9 to indicate the theme of the following section: chastisement of human pride. Then there is a list of the various manifestations of such pride, with the refrains (11, 17 which is very like v 9, and vv 10, 19, 21) threatening humiliation and disaster which will drive men to seek for a refuge in inaccessible hiding places. This chastisement, which will fall on nobles, rich, everybody, seems to be connected with the state of general anarchy, resulting from disastrous warfare.

k **6—11.** This section begins (**6**) with a condemnation of the practice of divination, forbidden by the Law (Dt 18:9—14). The Heb. text is particularly difficult. The Gr., which many prefer, begins with the third person instead of an apostrophe in the second. The word 'soothsayers' justifies the preceding 'diviners', required by parallelism but lacking in the Heb. Similarly, the correction 'hands' instead of MT *sons* is now commonly accepted. In other places in the Bible (Nm 24:10; Lam 2:15 etc) 'to strike hands' is a gesture of derision, but obviously the context here demands rather admiration. Divination was practised among both Eastern peoples ('Chaldean' often means a sooth-sayer, astrologer, or interpreter of dreams; cf Dn 2:2—4) and Western (for divination amongst the Philistines cf 1 Sm 6:2; 2 (4) Kgs 1:2) and Israel was no doubt imitating such peoples, cf § 451*b*. The mention of material wealth (**7**) in the time of king Uzziah is confirmed in 2 Chr 26:6—10. The 'horses' and 'chariots' is an allusion to military strength (1 (3) Kgs 10:28, 29; 16:10; 2 (4) Kgs 13:7). The humiliation (**9**) already consists in the shame of bowing down before 'the works of their own hands'; and it will be evident in the surrender or submission after some general disaster. 'Forgive them not' is not found in DSS (1QIs*a*) which also omits the following v. At the end, emphasis is laid on the contrast between man's pride and the divine majesty. The Gr. inserts (cf 19, 21) also after v 10 some hint of the direct intervention of God, which will give rise to terror—so it seems—linked with some **l** fearful earthquake (cf Am 1:1). **12 10.** The two refrains of 17, 19 describe a disaster and its cause, and link it with the worship of idols (**8**); the humiliating failure of the idols is proof of their impotence (Is 44:9—20). This is preceded (**12—16**) by a description of the people and things affected by *the day of the Lord* (cf Am 5:18; Jl 1:15; Zeph 1:14). This day will especially aim at humbling the pride of men. At the end of v **12** the Heb. could be translated **low**, but also as 'and will strike him low' (= in order to strike him low, bring him down). In **13—16** emphasis is laid on the 'bringing low' of all which makes for the pride of man (the tower of Babel comes to mind). Mention of the mountain of Lebanon and of the plain of Bashan does not imply an upheaval of nature; their fertility is simply a metaphor to describe individual pride. It is possible that the allusion to fortifications and ships might be a reference to the might of king Uzziah or of Jotham (2 Chr 26:9; 27:3). Tarshish is usually located in Spain; the expression 'ships of Tarshish', without any geographical connotation, was used to indicate powerful ships suitable for long voyages, cf §§ 287*d*, 305*n*. **20—22.**

m The danger will convince all of the futility of idolatry. Idols can promise no salvation (cf Bar 6:34—38), and will be cast out as worthless wooden objects. The identification **463m** of the animals in **20** is not certain; they could be mice rather than 'moles'. **22.** Is not in the Gr., and many omit it as having little connection with the context. Nevertheless the recommendation it gives (cf Jer 17:5; Ps 146 (145):3, 4), with its somewhat pessimistic view of man's finiteness, may well be considered the logical sequence to the threatening oracle against pride and high-mindedness, and a preparation for the following vv which describe the helplessness of the powerful ones to prevent or impede the disaster. **3:1—5.** Now is specified in detail the effect **n** of God's intervention on 'the Day' with respect to Israel. It is general collapse. **1.** 'stay and staff', the pillars, moral or military, of the kingdom; these two terms were probably glossed by a reader as 'means of subsistence', and therefore as 'bread' and 'water'. **2.** Gives a list of guides and props of the State, political ('the mighty man and the soldier') and moral and religious ('the judge and the prophet . . . and the elder'). It is surprising to find the 'diviner' also mentioned (cf 2:6), but the word may be used without pagan connections (cf Prv 16:10). It may however be due to an interpolator, or it is even possible that, as for the 'skilful magician and the expert in charms' (**3**), the prophet includes in the general catastrophe the false supports of the state also, those who are often accorded respect amongst a superstitious people, without insisting on their illegality. The 'captain of fifty' was a subordinate military authority (2 (4) Kgs 1:9, 1 Mc 3:55). **4, 5** give the upheaval of the social order: power granted to the inept, lack of respect for persons who should have it. **6—8.** First of all (**6, 7**) the disastrous situation is **o** described—there is no one willing to assume responsibility for re-establishing social order or to govern; then the causes of the disaster are given-sins of word and deed (**8**). The necessary 'healer' of so many ills (cf 1:5, 6) cannot be found. The offer of leadership is designated by a 'mantle', that is to say, something which is utterly indispensable, and which, in normal times, not even the poorest person would be without (Ex 22:25; Dt 24:13). The translation, however, is still not absolutely certain.

9—15. It was the faults of the rulers especially which **p** brought about the disaster (12, 14, 15; cf vv 1—3); once they had disappeared, government passed into the hands of the incompetent ('children, women', 12; cf v 4), whom no one would accept as moral guides. In **9**, as well as sin, shameless justification or outright approval of shameful conduct are condemned. For the social injustices of 14, 15, cf 1:17, 23; Am 5:11; 8:4. These are the deeds that lay waste the symbolic vineyard of God (5:1—7). **10, 11.** Refer to divine retribution, but it would seem that this is not intended to be taken in any eschatological sense. The translation 'partiality' in 9 is uncertain; many would omit the comparison with Sodom (1:9). 'His people' in **13** is a reading from Gr. and Syr.; Heb. reads '*peoples*'. **16—24.** The chastisement will also strike the fashionable women of Jerusalem. The description of their trinkets and fashionable adornments cannot always be identified with certainty. The 'crescents' were ornaments in the shape of tiny moons; 'perfume boxes', according to the ordinary meaning of the Heb. (literally = 'houses of the soul') might be an allusion to magical objects; instead of 'armlets' and 'garments of gauze' others prefer respectively tiny foot-chains and mirrors. The last comparison ('instead of beauty, shame') is translated according to the MSS of Qumran (MT omits 'shame'); without correction it is possible to translate 'instead of beauty, burns'. **3:25—4:1.** After the shame **q** of the fashionable women comes the slaughter of the

463q men. The pronouns in **26** refer to Jerusalem; the 'your' of **25** would refer to the women. The lament is taken up near the gates, because they were the focal point of the city's life. **4:1.** Points to the extent of the massacre—six out of seven men killed. The text presumes polygamy—still common in Isaiah's time—and the idea that lack of children and descendants was regarded as a curse. The desperate situation is brought out by the fact that normally the man had to pay a sum of money to the girl's father, (Ex 21:10; I Sm 18:25) and that he was also responsible for the maintenance of the family. Now the fulfillment of these obligations is out of the question, and the initiative is left to the women who normally would have no say about their marriage arrangements: these were usually left to the parents.

r **2–6 God overshadows Sion**—The chronological indication ('in that day') does not refer to the preceding event but indicates a distant future. At that time, there will be a complete metamorphosis (for 4 cf 3:16, 24—26). The protagonists of this unprecedented change will be a minority (a few survivors, cf 1:9), who will be, however, a holy seed (**3**; cf 6:13) for the future. Because of certain passages which seem to be parallel (Jer 23:5; Zech 3:8; 6:12), the 'branch of the Lord' was often interpreted as being the Messiah; the law of parallelism (cf 'the fruit of the land') suggests rather an extraordinary fertility (= a gift from God) of the soil, in contrast with the situation as it was (3:7; 4:1). The imagery in **5, 6** portrays in vivid colours the idea of God's protection (cf Ex 13:21, 22; 40:34—38). The divine assistance will recall the miracles of the Exodus and a new 'creation' (**5**)—details also found elsewhere in the description of the messianic era (Jer 31:22). The 'filth' and the 'bloodstains' of **4** refer not only to the misery described in 3:24—26, but also, and above all, Israel's faults, including murder. The survival of the 'remnant' will come about through pardon (Jer 31:34) joined to some powerful purification through fire.

s **5:1–7 The vineyard of the Lord**—This brings to mind some of the Gospel parables (Mt 21:33—46; Mk 12:1—12; Lk 20:9—19). In the OT the image is highly developed in Ps 80 (79), but still not so completely as here. It is a parable with several allegorical elements. The labourers called into the vineyard (**2**) are often mentioned in the Bible; it is only here, in order to show God's intention to punish, that the labourer destroys his own work (**5, 6**). The application is given in **7**, but it is already made quite clear in **3–4** which are a summary of the relations between God and Israel. 'Briers and thorns' are terms which Is is particularly fond of (7:23—25; 9:17; 27:4). The four antithetical phrases at the end of **7** are sharply defined in the Heb. text, which gives two pairs of words whose assonance emphasizes the bitter contrast: *mišpāt -mišpāḥ, ṣᵉḏāqâ -ṣᵉᶜāqâ.*

t **8–30 Condemnation of sins**—Six terrible woes are uttered against specific categories of evil (**8–23**). These actions will incur chastisement (**24—25**), which will be **u** brought about by an enemy invasion (**26—30**). **8–23 Curses.** The first woe (**8—10**) is for the greedy who are never satisfied with their wealth. On their addiction to building fine houses cf Jer 22:13, 14; for the annexing of 'field to field', which was often unjust and violent, cf 1 (3) Kgs 21:1—16. According to Israelite law (Lv 25:13—16) property was almost inalienable. God swore to bring down luxurious palaces and to make the earth sterile. For the meaning of *bath, homer, ephah,* cf § 85 *a, e, f.* 'Ten acres' is the amount of land which could be ploughed in a day with ten pairs of oxen. What was produced was practically nil; in the second case it

was the tenth part of the seed. **11—12.** Drunkenness **463** (Am 4:1; 6:6) results from the indiscriminate use of wine and even stronger drink (given in Heb. as *šēkār*), and from the length of time spent in drinking, beginning in the morning, a time not suitable for drinking (Eccl 10:16, 17). Music during the feasting was very pleasant (24:8, 9); it is disapproved of here especially because of the religious indifference emphasized at the end of the vv. **15—16** are a fine definition of human transitoriness and of the holiness (6:3) of God. There is a great similarity between these vv and the refrain of 2:11, 17; perhaps they are an interpolation here. Threats of general disaster are given in **13, 14, 17.** Sheol, **v** depicted as insatiable (Prv 30:16; Hb 2:5), is the subterranean kingdom of the dead. 'Jerusalem' in 14 replaces, for the sake of clarity, the simple personal pronoun; in 17. 'Kids' is the reading of LXX (Heb. *dwellers*). **18—23.** The final woe recalls the second (11). First of all it condemns the perverters of the moral order (**20**), and the wicked whose evil conduct is made worse by a sceptical mocking attitude towards the judgement of the Holy One of Israel (1:4); and at the end partiality in judgement is condemned. **24—30. The Chastisement.** First of all a **w** threat is uttered in general terms. **24—25.** Much discussed, since 25 is very similar to the refrain in 9:7—10:4; here it is probably a gloss. Then more specifically in **26—30** it is shown that God will make use of a foreign people in his imminent intervention as judge; and from chh 7—10 we can see that Assyria is the nation in question. For the description of the powerful and invincible army cf Jer 4:5—6:26. God, in his omnipotence, can summon the most powerful army on earth with the least effort (a sign, even a whistle such as a shepherd might use). The army is compared to a sea which submerges everything, or to the spreading of a fearful darkness.

6:1—13 The prophetic call—This should come at the **464a** beginning of the book, as in the other prophets (Jer 1:4; Ezek 1:2—3:21). It is probably put here instead because the editor considered it a suitable introduction to chh 7—12 where the God King is presented. It is he who guides the earthly ruler, his actions which are contrasted with those of a king on earth (chh 7, 8). After the description of the vision (1—4) comes Isaiah's prompt acceptance (5—8); 9, 10 specify the nature of his mission, and 11—13 describe the final result, due not so much to the prophet's activity, as to divine intervention.

1—4. The chronological indication refers to 739 B.C. **b** The idea of God's greatness is expressed by the loftiness of his throne and by his train, perhaps made up of rays of light, which filled the temple. This is almost certainly the temple at Jerusalem, but the vision is in all probability perceived only intellectually, and is a vision above all of heaven. 'high' and 'lifted up' could refer either to the throne, or to the Lord. The seraphim constitute God's **c** court; they form two choirs rather than simply two in number. Elsewhere, the term signifies poisonous serpents (Nm 21:6), but here it is a question of spiritual beings. Their external form is somewhat like the cherubim of Ezek 1:5ff. Of the six wings, two signify readiness in the service of God ('with two he flew'), four serve to indicate the idea of profound respect: as creatures, the seraphim cannot look directly on God (that is why they cover their faces; the term 'feet' seems to be a euphemism, cf 7:20). In their song, the seraphim exalt the glory of God. The threefold repetition of 'holy' does not include *per se* a reference to the Trinity; it is just a normal way (Jer 7:4; 22:29; Ezek 21:32) of expressing a superlative.

The *trisagion* had a great influence on Jewish and **d** Christian liturgy. It is probably due to Is himself

464d rather than taken from an existing liturgical chant. In the Pent the adjective 'holy' is for the most part purely ritual in its meaning (holy as opposed to profane); elsewhere, however, it has clearly a moral significance. It is from this vision that Is obtains his idea of the omnipotence and the holiness of God so often proclaimed in his book (cf 1:4). The effects described in 5 are all part of the theophany. For the symbolism of smoke cf Ezek 10.4; Ex 14:19; 10:34; the smoke in no way hinders the vision, just as it is not impeded by the cloud in Mt 17:5.

e 5—8. Before this overwhelming majesty, the prophet's reaction is instinctive. His first words have been understood in different ways by the older translators, but *death* is the idea that best fits OT mentality (Ex 33:20; Jg 13:22). The unclean lips imply unworthiness to utter any efficacious prayer (1:15; Ps 17 (16):1). Purification is brought about by the symbolic gesture of one of the seraphim; purifying fire was taken from the altar of incense (Ex 30:1—10). All this was in an external vision. 8. 'Us' must be understood as a plural of majesty; or perhaps it refers to the seraphim. Isaiah's reply is indicative of his firmness and generosity, quite different from that of Moses, for example (Ex 4:10), or of Jeremiah (Jer 1:6). Moreover, this implies that the prophet has a choice, and that in theory at least, he can accept the call **f** or refuse it. 9—10. This text is well known since it is quoted so often in the NT (Mt 13:14, 15; Jn 12:39, 40; Ac 28:26, 27), and also because its content is so striking. Does God send Isaiah so that the people will become more culpable, and thus be cut off from salvation? The words seem to suggest this. But in order to avoid such a theological absurdity—sin which is directly willed by God—it is sufficient to remember that the Bible often attributes a thing directly to God, without specifying whether it is commanded or only permitted or tolerated. Here we are dealing with the second alternative. Before the prophet has preached to them, the people are free to accept his preaching or to reject it. Their perverse will, shown already on so many occasions, will be inclined to indifference or rejection. The natural consequence will be an increase of guilt and a greater obstacle to **g** the divine mercy. 11—13. The prophet is dispirited by the harsh words: will it be a question of complete destruction? God's response is unrelenting; destruction there will surely be. But surety for the future is expressed at the end. After the abandonment and the exile of the remnant (1:9) the new Israel will develop (cf Gal 6.16; Rm 11:15—32). This is the hope of a restoration and a reversal of fortune in the distant future.

465a 7:1—12:6 The Book of Emmanuel—In general, the background of these oracles is the period of the Syro-Ephraimite war, 735—732. It begins with a description of a meeting between the prophet and king Ahaz, on which occasion the prophet recommended a line of conduct based upon faith. The king's scepticism occasioned the prophecy of Emmanuel (7:1—17). The Assyrian invasion and its consequences are envisaged in 7:18—25, and in most of **b** chh 8 and 10. At the end, however, the failure of the Assyrians is clearly stated, a failure due to divine intervention. This intervention is linked with the coming of the messianic king, peace-loving, utterly just and full of the gifts of the Spirit of Yahweh. The section ends with a song of praise (ch 12). This is without doubt the most interesting part of Isaiah's message. Besides the fullness of the messianic vision which it gives, the prophet also shows a deep understanding of the religious sense of history and puts into proper perspective faith in God, as opposed to political intrigue and complex alliances. **c** 7:1—9 The policy of faith—This section corresponds

to 2 (4) Kgs 16:5—9 in its historical background, though **465c** the description of the meeting between Isaiah and Ahaz is found only here. The king of Damascus and the king of Israel were both intent on eliminating any obstacle to a grand alliance against Assyria. When the king of Judah opposed them they waged war in order to set up a more accommodating ruler in Jerusalem, the son of Tabeel (6). The name is probably to be connected with the district of Tabal, found in an Assyrian inscription. The meeting place of Ahaz and Isaiah is described exactly (3); its situation is doubtful; S. Smith identified 'the upper pool' with the inner pool of Siloam in the Tyropoean Valley, cf *Jerusalem*, 2, 127. The presence of Isaiah's son **d** is symbolic; his name expressed faith in a survival or at least in some future restoration (in Heb.: *šeʾār* = remnant, *yāšûb* = shall return; cf 1:9; 6:13). The words of the prophet are clear, even though the text leaves doubt on some particular details: the threat of the two kings will come to nothing. The situation will stay the same, both in Damascus as well as in Samaria and Jerusalem. The second part of 8 is difficult; the kingdom of Israel is forecast to last a further 65 years. Actually it came to an end much earlier. Unless something happened in 670 of which we are now ignorant, there is obviously some mistake. Such precise chronology, moreover, is hardly likely in a prophet and especially in Isaiah; on account of this many exegetes think that the text is a gloss. In any case, what is essential is the final pronouncement of the prophet, that the help of God and the realization of the prophecy must come through a sincere faith. In Heb., the connection between faith and survival is even more striking because of the assonance of the words: *taʾamînû* (= you will believe), *tēʾāmēnû* (= you shall be established). The policy of faith is the only way of salvation.

10—17 The Immanuel—If Ahaz has faith, God is ready **e** to guarantee the result by a sign, the choice of which is left to Ahaz. 'Sheol' (5:14), or the kingdom of the dead, is a correction; Heb. has *ask*, a mistake easy to make. The reply of Ahaz is a very religious one on the face of it (Dt 6:16; cf Mt 4:7); but in fact he does not want a sign since he does not believe in the policy of faith. He had already decided to ask for Assyrian help. It is this fact which explains Isaiah's protestation and his warning (13). However, the sign will still be given, but—and the whole context seems to imply this— it will now be a sign of destruction, and not some indication of favourable intervention; it will proclaim the certainty of the Assyrian invasion described below in 7:18—20.

The sign consists in the birth of a child who will be **f** given the symbolic name of Immanuel, i.e. 'God with us'. It should be noted that the sign is given to the Davidic dynasty more than to Ahaz alone (13). Hence it is above all the confirmation of the ancient oracle of Nathan (2 Sm 7:11—16). The name of the child is indicative of divine favour, though not necessarily with reference to immediate events; these will take a very different course from what the king hopes for (17). Apart from the name, two other details are given: the circumstances of his birth with respect to his mother, and the particular kind of food he shall eat in his first year. In 14, instead of '(she) shall call' a possible translation of the consonantal Heb. is 'you shall call'; this is supported by some MSS of LXX, and by Aq., Sym. and Theod. Generally, however, MT is preferred. 'young woman.' This **g** is a literal translation of the Heb. *ʿalmâ*. The word indicates a young woman of marriageable age. It is not used of married women but it refers to age rather than to a physiological state. The word occurs only eight

465g times in the Bible. The technical term for 'virgin' is b^etûlâ.

h The LXX translation of Isaiah, made before 150 B.C., renders 'almâ by parthenos, 'virgin'; and the Old Latin, following the LXX, has 'virgo'. Jerome adopted the same word in his version even though he was translating from the Heb. We may regard the LXX rendering as a witness to later Jewish tradition concerning the meaning of the prophecy. St Matthew's Gospel of course unequivocally states the virginal conception where this prophecy is quoted (Mt 1:23; cf Lk 1:35) using the word 'parthenos'. Over the centuries Providence had clarified the original foretelling as to the manner of the Saviour's coming, which was seen to be fulfilled in the Evangelist's des-**i** cription of it. Exegetes however are divided as to whether Is 7:14 refers in the first instance to a contemporary and normal birth (by Isaiah's wife, for example) which would itself prefigure the birth of the Messiah. The older and more traditional view applied the prophecy direct to the Messiah.

j Each of these interpretations has its difficulties. The traditional one finds it difficult to explain how there can be such a close connection between two events (the sign to Ahaz and the birth of Jesus) which are so far separated in time, and which seem to have no relationship to each other. Mt however, gives some weight to the messianic interpretation, and the chronological difficulty can be explained by the prophet's lack of perspective. Some modern Catholic exegetes favour a typical interpretation; the text describes the birth of some contemporary of Isaiah (probably Hezekiah), who is a type of the Messiah. Though not devoid of difficulties, this does facilitate the interpretation of **15**, **16**, which says that the Syro-Ephraimite invasion will end just before the child reaches the age of reason. Despite first impressions, the child's diet of 'curds and honey' would seem to indicate bad times (cf **21**, **22**), because it is a symbol of the Syrian invasion (**17**). This prophecy is complemented by the texts of 9:6, 7; 11:1–9.

k **18–25 Devastation**—At some undetermined future ('in that day', cf 4:2) the enemy will occupy Palestine. The invasion is not limited to the places mentioned in **19**, which are perhaps chosen under the influence of the preceding metaphor ('fly' and 'bee'). We need not necessarily think of a simultaneous invasion from the S (Egypt) and N (Assyria). There were invasions from Egypt, even after Isaiah's time (cf 2 (4) Kgs 23:19), but here the danger comes especially from Assyria; God himself will use this far-distant land as an instrument of chastisement. *Shaving the head* (**20**) is meant to imply spoliation, and includes also the idea of dishonour (2 Sm 10:4, 5). The word 'feet' is clearly a euphemism. The image of the whistle may not be universally approved on aesthetic grounds, but it certainly expresses well God's absolute dominion even over the pagan rulers. The two countries are mentioned because they are the traditional enemies of Israel; even when only one of them was actually concerned, they are still often mentioned together **l** (cf Hos 7:11; Jer 2:18; Lam 5:6). The final result will be spoliation on a grand scale, with the countryside abandoned to wandering cattle and wild vegetation. The same fate will overtake the cultivated lands also, particularly those which have been tended with care, like a precious vineyard (5:1–6). In hyperbolic terms it is said that every vine was worth a shekel—much more than normal price (Jer 32:9). The few who remain in the land (**21**) will have a great extent of territory at their disposal, but few possessions ('a young cow and two sheep'); they will be reduced to the pastoral life, but with the minimum of flocks. Consequently, their diet will also be **465l** a pastoral one; and therefore the food mentioned in **22** (cf **15**), contrasted with the feasts mentioned elsewhere (25:6), is a sign of misery, even though in other places milk and honey indicate times of plenty. The country has become like a deserted field full of 'briers and thorns', according to one of Isaiah's favourite expressions.

8:1–4 A son with a symbolic name—In v 18 Isaiah **m** draws attention to the significance of himself and of his two sons. The symbolism is attached especially to their names: Isaiah = Yahweh saves; Shearjashub = a remnant shall return (7:3); Maher-shalal-hash-baz = speed-booty-haste-spoil. This last name refers to the fate of the two kingdoms which are trying to bring ruin to the Davidic dynasty (**4**; cf 7:1); and this was brought about by the invasion of Tiglath-Pileser in 732, which destroyed the kingdom of Damascus and occupied part of the kingdom of Israel (9:1). What is narrated here was to happen in 735/4, before the birth of the child. The witness of authoritative persons would guarantee the truth of the prophecy, drawn up on a tablet in 'common characters', so called perhaps to distinguish it from 'sacred' writing written in a particularly elaborate style or in archaic characters.

5–15 God and the enemies of Israel—**8** recalls 7:2 **n** in its description of the terror roused by the Syro-Ephraimite invasion; this justifies the correction 'melt in fear' in **5** in place of the Heb. *rejoices in*. The guilt of the people is metaphorically described (cf Jer 2:13) as the abandonment of 'Shiloah', a pool not far from the spring of Gihon (2 (4) Kgs 20:20; 2 Chr 32:30); its tranquil water, in sharp contrast to the destructive flood of the enemy invasion, is a symbol of the loving action of God. In all probability the words 'the king of Assyria and all his glory' (**7**) are an explanatory gloss, but it is certain that the prophecy refers to **Sennacherib's invasion** (cf chh 36, 37). Even though the capital did not fall, this invasion spread throughout the territory of Judah, called here 'Immanuel's land'. This is not sufficient in itself to prove the divinity of the person named (7:14), but it is a fact that Palestine is nowhere else referred to as the country of a king or of an individual, since it is looked on as belonging to God (14:2, 25; Jer 2:7; Hos 9:3). The mention of Immanuel here supports the view that all this section centres round him, not simply 7:14. His presence, symbol of God's loving aid ('for God is with us', **10**), is a bulwark against all the powers of this world. The complete subjection of these powers to God's will is described in 9, 10, which are implicitly an oracle of consolation for Israel, linked with the idea that all these kingdoms are but instruments in the hands of God (10:5).

11–15. This autobiographical passage is inserted **o** for the sake of his disciples. God counsels him not to follow the mob in his judgement of events. For the politicians of Jerusalem, Isaiah's resistance to an Assyrian alliance (7:9) was 'conspiracy'. **12**. 'Fear and dread', cf 7:2; the true Israelite should fear God only. Many correct the text in order to bring it more into line with the preceding v; but it seems altogether preferable to retain the reference to God's holiness (6:3), which should engender deep respect and veneration. The Holy One of Israel can, however, in certain circumstances (Lk 2:84; 20:17, 18; Rm 9:32, 33 etc) also chastise and become a cause of ruin ('a stone of offence and a rock of stumbling'). Probably the word 'sanctuary' in **14** is a gloss. **16–20 The prophetic witness**—This section is of **p** biographical interest. Isaiah had a group of disciples to

465p whom he communicated revelations which were not always made public. Here, he calls their attention to the oracles on hope and trust symbolized by the names of the prophet and his two sons (cf v 3). Both the translation and interpretation of vv **19, 20** are fairly obscure. At the end, there is a forceful assertion of the truth of his witness (16) as opposed to the false soothsayers described in 19. The translation of the second part of **20** is uncertain, but the words do convey, without any doubt, a grave threat. Various forms of divination are emphasized in 19, including necromancy. Against such practices, cf Lv 19:31; 20:6; Dt 18:10, 11. But the text is also uncertain and obscure.

466a **8:21–9: 7 Darkness and light**—This is not the first time—and certainly not the only time—that this antithesis, so much used in Jn, expresses the contrast between evil and good, oppression and salvation. It is clearly expressed in 9:2, but is suggested at the end of ch 8 and the beginning of ch 9. The section describes the wretched and precarious state of the district around the lake of Gennesaret, which will be the area cut off from Israel's kingdom by Tiglath-Pileser. The future glory implies liberation (**9:1**). In the immediate context, the transformation is connected with the coming of the Messiah (9:2–7); in Mt 4:13–16 the text is quoted as the prelude to the Galilean ministry of the Messiah. Vv 21, 22 are obscure and probably out of context.

b **9:2–7 (MT 9:1–6)**—This section has a much more universal significance than the preceding one; the people (**2**) are not only the inhabitants of Galilee and a part of Transjordan (1). The succession from darkness to light coincides with a great joy, which is a gift of God. **3b** MT (v 2) **'thou hast not increased'** is usually corrected to fit the parallelism (reading *ha gîlâ*, 'rejoicing' in place of *ha-gôi*, 'the nation'). God has annihilated the oppressor, as he did the Midianites in Gideon's time (Jg 7:1; 8:21) There will be no wars in the future, therefore all military equipment can be destroyed without more ado (2:4). The cause of this great peace is given in **6**. Here is described the birth of a marvellous child, whom the context invites us to identify with the Immanuel (7:14; 8:8). The future king is given a long symbolic name which refers to his qualities of prudence and wisdom, power, goodness and peace. There is some analogy here with the names given to the Pharaohs at the moment of accession often intended to be kept secret; but there is no evidence

c for similar usage at the court of Jerusalem. Two facts seem to exclude any reference to Hezekiah or to another king: the solemnity with which the birth (not the enthronement) is described, and the significance of the name. It is certain that the name 'Wonderful Counsellor' (cf 25:1; 28:29; and 1QH 111, 10) is reserved for God and that never in the Bible do we find a king called *'el gibbôr*, 'Mighty God'. In exegetical tradition, the messianic interpretation occurs as early as Irenaeus (*Adv. Haer.* 3, 16, 3; PG 7, 922), and there are even **d** traces of it in rabbinic writings. Modern commentators take the child to be either Isaiah's son, or—more commonly—they interpret the text with reference to the ceremonial enthronement of Hezekiah or some other king. If the authenticity of the passage is accepted, however, it would be difficult to imagine that Isaiah would use such language of any contemporary king, even Hezekiah; cf 30:1–7; 31:1–3; 39:3–7. The context and the symbolic name, as well as the solemnity of the description, are all in favour of identifying the child with the Immanuel, i.e. some future person who is to embody Israel's hopes. The prophecy takes for granted all the traditional ideas concerning the kingship of the Messiah,

as they appear in 2 Sm 7:11–16 and in some Pss (cf esp. **466d** Ps 2 and Ps 110 (109)).

9:8–10:4 God's vengeance—The style (the refrain **e** will be noticed in vv 12, 17, 21; 10:4) and the content of this poem recall ch 5. It is an almost ruthless examination of conscience, interspersed with threats of chastisement and a reminder of past punishments.

The 'word' (**8**) is a decree of condemnation, especially against the inhabitants of the N kingdom, which disappeared finally in 722. A picturesque image of pride is given—the assurance which rebuilds even more elegantly than before (using stones and cedars instead of bricks and sycamores). In **11** Heb. favours the past tense (*raised*). As so often, two nations, one from the E ('Syrians' or Arameans') and one from the SW ('Philistines'), are used as symbols of an invasion coming from all sides. For some time, there will be many trials of strength against the Arameans (7:1ff) and the Philistines (1 (3) Kgs 15:27; 16:15). But God is still **f** not satisfied with their chastisement. The invasion has not brought about repentance; in fact, the people have increased their guilt, following the advice of unworthy leaders. For this reason God has punished them still more, and they are all guilty. The totality of guilt is expressed in the words 'head and tail, palm branch and reed'; but the identification of the tail as 'false prophets' **15** (MT 14) seems unlikely and is generally understood to be a gloss. **17.** The future chastisement is seen to be much more serious. God, who has so often defended the orphan and the widow, now has no compassion in their regard.

In **18–21**, (MT 17–20) anarchy and civil war are **g** depicted in the vivid imagery of fire. Such events could be identified with the frequent revolutions in the kingdom of Israel and with the warfare which is the background to these chh (7:1ff). 'His neighbour's' (**20**) rather than *his arm's* is a commonly accepted correction of the Heb. text. This striking phrase should not be interpreted in any cannibalistic sense (but cf Jer 19:9; Lam 2:20; 4:10). The internecine struggles are described under the names of 'Manasseh' and 'Ephraim', since these two tribes were the chief parties in the two kingdoms, and their founders were brothers (19; cf Gn 46:20). On the injustice of the judges (**10:1–4**), cf 5:23, where the image of v 4 is more fully developed. The Heb. text of the beginning of the v is very uncertain.

10:5–34 The end of Assyria—This long section is **h** somewhat complex. There are vv whose authenticity is doubtful, and some short passages which alternate from one theme to another. However, if we except 20–23 on the 'remnant' of Israel, the whole can be interpreted as referring to Assyria, accused of pride and therefore condemned to disaster (5–19, 24–27a). In lyrical accents, 27b–34 describe the irresistible onslaught of the Assyrian army against Jerusalem, only to meet reversal when the moment of victory appears inevitable. The invading army is eliminated. The whole of this section is a picture on the grand scale of **Assyrian might and the ensuing final disaster**; but it is also a valuable comment on the seriousness of sin and of the power of God's intervention in human history.

5–11. The idea of instrumentality is expressed by **i** the 'rod' or 'staff'; it is used, then thrown away. But here it is not just a question of casting it aside, but of chastisement because the instrument claimed credit for actions in which it was only the means. Success has led to overbearing pride and to an abuse of power in the execution of the chastisement willed by God. Other

466i city-states which suffered in these years of Tiglath-Pileser III are mentioned in **9**. Carchemish corresponds to later Jerablus, near the border of Turkey and Syria; Hamath (now Hama) and Arpad (now Tell Erfad) were in Syria, the first on the Orontes, and the second N of Aleppo. Calno has been identified with Kullankoy not far from Arpad. For 'Damascus' and 'Samaria' cf 7:8. The victory over these cities, and the hope for victory over Jerusalem, is seen as a victory of one's own gods over the gods of the conquered—a common idea; cf **j** 36:18, 19; 37:11—13. **12—19**. The prose style of the first v, with its change of speakers, explaining the divine intention of punishing Assyria's pride, perhaps indicates a gloss. Following upon this, and in striking imagery, (the nest and the eggs which are gathered at will) Assyria's boasting over her conquests and her spoils is described (**13—14**). The examples which stress the role of Assyria's instrumentality also indicate the absurdity of her pride; but she will be cut down in a chastisement whose awfulness is described as a relentless sickness and a devouring fire. God will be the direct force behind all this, he who is called 'the Holy One' and 'the light of Israel' (cf 2:3; 6:3; Ps 27 (26):1). In **19** there could be a reference to the survivors of the Assyrian army (37:36, 37); but the idea of a remnant, expressed in words similar to those in 6:13, would favour a reference to Israel. Perhaps the v originally belonged to another **k** context. **20—23**. These vv refer to the future of Israel seen in a vision with messianic undertones. Here recur ideas already expressed in 1:9 and 6:13—the justice of the divine chastisement, the need for sincere conversion and the abandonment of false hopes in diplomatic alliances (30:1; 31:1), the few who will be saved and, implicitly, the new life of the remnant in Jerusalem. At the beginning of **21** the Heb. uses exactly the two words which make up the name of Isaiah's son: šᵉʾār yāšûb **l** (7:3). **24—34**. The Assyrian oppression, which appears in v 5 under the images of 'rod' and 'staff', is compared with the Egyptian oppression in the time of Moses and before him; the end will be identical. **26** combines a reference to the crossing of the Red Sea (Ex 14:21—30) with a reference to the victory over the Midianites (9:4). The correction (RSV) at the end of **27** is very common. Rimmon is located about 11 miles NE of Jerusalem, and from there a swift march is described more or less in a straight line, without taking too much notice of the obstacles in certain places. The different localities, which cannot always be identified with certainty, were from Rimmon to Jerusalem (Nob is situated on Mt **m** Scopus). In the text there is often some assonance between the name of the locality and the recorded action: **30**. Hearken, O Laisha! Answer her, Anathoth! = haqšîbî ᵃyᵉšâ ᶜᵃniyyâ ᶜanātôt. But as they near Jerusalem and are on the point of taking it, suddenly the slaughter of the invader (37:36) is described, in imagery commonly used in the Bible (2:13; 6:13; 10:19; Ezek 31:3—9 etc). Many would substitute a word like 'axe' for *terrifying power* in **33** to maintain the parallelism. Despite these few uncertainties, the passage is one of extraordinary poetic beauty, and is a superb eulogy of the divine omnipotence.

n **11:1—16 The Messiah and his kingdom**—In contrast with the bustle and noise of the army on the march in ch 10, here is described the world-wide rule of a descendant of David, based not on arms but on perfect justice (1—5). This is a reign full of peace (6—9), with a new and glorious Sion as its centre (10—16). It is the complement of the prophecy which was begun in 7:14, and taken up in a special way in 9:2—7. Here the character of the king is described more fully, coming **466i** down from God with all the gifts of the Spirit of Yahweh, and justice and peace will be in his kingdom. **1—5 The Messiah**—The metaphors 'shoot' and **o** 'stump' denote at least a great weakening, if not a complete extinction of the dynasty. There will then arise a new David; and, to illustrate this thought, 'Jesse' is mentioned—David's father, rather than David himself. On the relationship between this v and Mt 2:23, cf comm. on Mt. The 'Spirit of the Lord' in the OT is used not in a Trinitarian sense but to express the action of God upon the world. Here he is mentioned as the one who distributes many gifts. In Heb. there is a list of six; in the Gr. and Lat., the number is seven. This latter is traditional in theological teaching and some would see it even in the Heb. text, either by regarding the Spirit of the Lord itself as a gift or by taking separately the terms 'fear' and 'piety'. But in fact the text does not intend to determine the number of the gifts of the Spirit.

Some of the terms used (*wisdom, understanding,* **p** *knowledge*) might seem to indicate intellectual qualities; but in Heb. they have rather a practical significance. All the gifts express the same idea, with slight nuances in the individual terms—the perfect knowledge of God's laws and the application of them. The effect of these internal dispositions is perfect justice, especially towards those who need it most. But to the impious, this same justice is a source of punishment. Many correct **4**, reading 'smite the violent one' rather than 'smite the earth' (Heb. ᶜārîṣ = violent one; ʾereṣ = earth). The Heb. could here refer to some kind of purifying gesture, since the earth itself is contaminated by murder (Gn 4:10). In 3—5 there is a development of 9:7. **6—11. Universal peace.** **q** This well-known passage is reminiscent of many classical texts (Virgil, *Georgics* IV, 22; V, 60, 61; Horace, *Odes* XVI, 32, 33). A strictly literal interpretation would reduce it to absurdity; it does not teach that the instincts of certain animals are actually to be changed. The meaning of the perfect harmony depicted here, between creatures normally hostile to each other, is apparent from **9**; harmony reigns amongst right-minded men; there will be no evil-doers among them, since all now acknowledge and follow the will of God (2:3, 4). It cannot be denied however that what is here envisaged is some sort of a return to the state in the Garden of Eden (there is a certain stress on the harmlessness of the serpent) or a picture like that of Rm 8:19—23. **10—16. The glory** **r** **of Sion.** The centre of this new world is 'the holy mountain' (9)—Jerusalem, and the Temple in particular (2:3). We are told who are to benefit from this peace and prosperity—not only the Israelites of the Diaspora, but also the nations, full of admiration and hope (49:22) at the sight of this wonderful Davidic king (the root of Jesse) who is an ensign to the peoples. The gathering together of the scattered Israelites is spoken of as being a 'second time', probably with reference to the liberation from Egypt. This future event is often represented as a new Exodus (49:22; Jer 16:14, 15; Bar 4:23, 24). This apparent reference to the return from Exile casts doubts on the Isaian authorship of the passage, but there is no need to see in the mention of Assyria an allusion to the Babylonian exile. Even in the time of Isaiah, Israelites were to be found for various reasons in Mesopotamia (in 'Assyria' and in 'Shinar'; cf Gn 11:2), and in the district bordering on the E (Elam), as also in Egypt (Pathros = Upper Egypt; Ethiopia or Kush = regions more to the S), and in Syria (Hamath, 10:9), and in the islands of the Mediterranean (= coastlands of the sea): here we have the four points of the compass.

466s In **13** we have the reverse side of the picture given in 9:20, 21. **16.** The new exodus will take place particularly in the N; here it is difficult to exclude the idea of the exile in Mesopotamia. Here, unlike the beginning of the ch, the return is the result of a tumultuous victory over the traditional enemies of Israel (Philistines from the W, Moabites, Ammonites and Eastern peoples from the E; Edomites from the S). 'The tongue of the sea of Egypt' (**15**) is the sea crossed in the time of Moses (Ex 14:22); the 'River' (7:20) is the Euphrates, divided to provide a crossing place at the new Exodus.

t 12:1–6 Praise of God—Two very short canticles (1–3 and 4–6). Both praise and thanksgiving are featured, as happens elsewhere in the book after the description of portentous events (25:1–5, 42:10 13; 44:23; 45:24; 61:10). Certainly the events portrayed in chh 7–11 call for such emphatic praise. The fount of salvation is a graceful and often repeated image (Ps 36 (35):10; Jer 2:13; 17:13; Jn 4:13, 14; 17:37–39, etc). The stress on salvation, the vision which reaches out to the ends of the earth, the reference to the Holy One of Israel, make this short ch a synthesis of some of the most beautiful and important ideas in the previous chh 1–11, and indeed in the whole book.

u 13:1–23:18. These eleven chh contain **the oracles on the pagan nations**, united into one section, as in Jer (chh 46 51), Ezek (chh 25–32) and Am (1:3–2:3). They are yet another testimony to the universal dominion of God, to whom even the people who do not acknowledge him must defer.

467a 13:1–14:32 The Destruction of Babylon—This is vividly described and attributed especially to the Medes. The city will be reduced to desert land, the favourite haunt of wild beasts. After a parenthesis (14:1–3) on the new Israel, the theme is once again taken up in lyrical terms (14:4–23, the inglorious end of the king of Babylon). The ch ends with a brief oracle on Assyria (24–27) and on Philistia (28–32). The two oracles on **b** Babylon have been the subject of much discussion. The view most commonly accepted today is that these oracles are the work of a disciple of Isaiah who lived long after him, perhaps the author of the second part of the book; the date given is about 550 B.C. The main reason for this opinion is that, in the time of Isaiah, Babylon was either insignificant or did not exist; therefore the theme of the two oracles in question would have no actuality, particularly when we remember that the great danger was Assyria. On the other hand, the content of the oracles is indeed the reflection of tragic incidents which happened after 587 B.C.

c 13:1–8—This might usefully be divided into three ideas which give alternate strophes: the order of the assault, given by God himself (2–3); the tremendous tumult of the assailants (4–5); the consternation of Babylon, powerless to reply (6–8). The 'signal' (5:26) or standard is placed somewhere where it would be seen by all. Those who are to execute the orders stemming from the divine anger are soldiers who are powerful and 'consecrated'—war in the OT often has a sacred character (Jer 6:4; 22:7; 51:27; Jl 4:9 etc). In v 17 the occupation of Babylon is attributed to the Medes; here it is a question of a coalition made up of different peoples from distant lands. In fact the army of Cyrus, conqueror of Babylon, was made up of several foreign elements. The coalition and the long march appear fairly commonly in similar descriptions (Jer 4:6; 6:22; 50:41; 51:27, 18) Jer 50:43 also records the lack of any serious **d** resistance by the Babylonians. **9–16.** A usual device in prophetical and apocalyptic writings is the participa-

tion of cosmic elements in a common destruction (65:17; **467d** Jer 4:23, 24; Ezek 32:8; Jl 2:10 etc). The elements are called upon to witness the tremendous *day of the Lord* (2:15). **12.** Which is to be understood of Israel according to some authors, implies some restriction of the cataclysm; some men, a very few, will survive. The 'gold of Ophir' was very precious and rare; on Ophir, see §§ 304c, 305n. **13.** Is based on ideas prevalent at the time: the earth supported upon enormous pillars, the heavens spread out like a huge curtain. **16.** Describes the terrible slaughter often meted out to the inhabitants of a conquered city (Ps 137 (136):9; Hos 10:14; 14:1, etc). In **14** the dismay of the foreigner is portrayed, perhaps because deportation is imminent; instinctively, salvation is sought through flight (Jer 50:16; 51:9). **17–22. e** Since only the Medes are mentioned, this is a fair argument for the supposition that the oracle preceded the unification of the Medes and Persians which came about in 550 B.C. For their character of merciless impartiality, cf Jer 4:30. The beginning of **18** is uncertain; literally the Heb. text reads: *and the bows of the young men shall be broken* (?), for the rest of the v cf Am 1:13; 2 (4) Kgs 8:12; 15:16. 'The Chaldeans' were called Babylonians at the time of the dynasty of Nebuchadnezzar (Jer 21:4); on the end of Sodom and Gomorrah cf 1:9. In vv **20–22** the place where Babylon used to be is colourfully described as a barren waste inhabited by beasts of the desert. 'Satyrs' (Heb.: 'hairy ones') are demoniacal beings belonging to popular folk lore. For similar descriptions cf 34:13 –15; Jer 50:39.

14:1–3 The Restoration of Israel. This section **f** might well be connected with 13:14; but its prosaic style and the content place it rather as the work of an editor who wanted to unite the two oracles on Babylon. The liberation from Babylon seen as a new election on God's part is worthy of note (41:8, 9; 43:10). Even more interesting is the idea of universality, even though the foreigner is not granted equality with the righteous. The idea is already broached in 2:1–4, but with similar imagery to 60:5–10. **4–23. The end of the king of g Babylon.** There is no need to identify the unnamed king; more than a single individual, what is presented here is the symbol of the hated tyrant. The section is beautifully presented in the form of a *māšāl*, which in this particular instance could be translated as a 'satire' or 'mocking song'. The taunting strains pervade the world of nature and even go down to the subterranean regions of the shades, for in some way the tyrant had done violence to this whole world, in order to gratify his avarice and love of pleasure. Now his treatment is worse than the most wretched of mortals. This outburst of joy at his plight must obviously not be judged in the light of NT charity; the lyrical quality of the passage, and its dramatic presentation, are none the less worthy of admiration. **4–11.** 'insolent fury' (4) so 1QIs[a]. Nature's **h** rejoicing in the enemy's downfall is merely a poetic image; it is a stylised allusion to the importation or exportation, as booty, of the precious cedar wood (2:13; 9:19; 37:24). This custom is well authenticated from Assyrian inscriptions. The Israelites believed that the dead continued to live a 'shadowy' life which was dreary and sad in a subterranean kingdom (Sheol). We are given here, in poetic language, the idea of an unaccustomed bustling (Ezek 31:17; 32:19) as the newcomer is welcomed in their midst. The concept is not devoid of irony. For v 11 cf 5:12; Jb 17:14. **12–15.** The mood might be described **i** as gleeful mockery. The identification of the star or constellation in **12** is uncertain. From the Latin translation—*Lucifer*—is derived the reference to Satan:

467i there are no grounds for such a derivation. In the soliloquy, full of exultation, there is also mention of the mount of assembly (**13**) (cf Ps 48(47):3; Ezek 38:6, 15; 39:2), an expression which is mythological in origin; it indicates a kind of Olympus, which is imagined to be in the far **j** distant and mysterious N. For v 14 cf Gn 3:5. **16—23.** The other 'shades' think especially of the contrast between past might and present wretchedness. The exile of the Hebrews is referred to in **17**; but the Babylonians had also deported other peoples. For the dishonour which was linked with lack of burial cf Jer 7:33; 8:2, etc. The comparison with an abortion is not certain, since the Heb. could be translated *like a despised branch*. At the end comes a curse, (though the text could also be taken as a simple future) against the descendants of the hated person. Concerning the fate of sons in similar circumstances cf 2 (4) Kgs 25:7. **22—23.** Are in prose; they gather up the two oracles on Babylon, repeating in part the thought of 13:21—22 (cf 34:11, Zeph 2:14).

k 24—27. The end of Assyria. This short oracle appears to be a summary of what has already been given in chh 9—10; even some of the phrases correspond (cf 9:17, 21; 10:4 for the image of the outstretched hand). A few authors prefer to place this section after ch 10, which would seem to be more suitable for the idea which is stressed here, of the destruction of the Assyrian army in Palestine, 'in my land and upon my mountains' (cf **l** 37:36; Ezek 36:1—15). **28—32. The fate of Philistia.** The idea is clearly stated that the lot of the oppressor becomes steadily worse, ending with the destruction of the Philistines, the traditional enemies of Israel. Also what is certain is that the danger comes from the N; there is more doubt about the date of the oracle (728/7, B.C.). A vexed point of discussion is the identification of 'the serpent', 'the adder' and 'the flying serpent'; they could be three individuals, or even two if, as is possible, the possessive pronoun 'its' refers to 'serpent' and not to 'adder'. During the period in question, at least three Assyrian kings attacked Philistia; Tiglath Pileser III, Sargon II and Sennacherib; so the creatures might indicate respectively all three or two of these kings. The 'poor' and the 'needy' of **30** are the survivors of the kingdom of Judah, the 'afflicted' of **32**, but the object of the divine protection. At the beginning of **32** there is perhaps a reference to a tentative alliance on the part of the Philistines with the kingdom of Judah. The flying serpent (27:1) belongs to popular folk-lore. It is not possible to be precise about the city mentioned in v 31. At least three cities, Gaza, Azotus and Accaron were in turn wiped out by Tiglath-Pileser, Sargon and Sennacherib.

m 15:1—16:14 The oracle on Moab—There is a contrast here between the almost frantic joy over Babylon's downfall, and the feeling of shame which is in part shared over the disgrace of Moab. Their vices are condemned, especially pride, but in general there prevails a sense of dismay about the catastrophe. This is more of an elegy than a satire. There are two oracles; the first extends to 16:12, whilst the second is practically contained within one v (16:14). The Isaian authenticity can be upheld, but gives rise to a certain amount of perplexity with regard to some of the stanzas which reproduce almost literally the oracle of Jeremiah (ch 48). Moreover the similarities seem to be restricted to certain sections; in Jeremiah's oracle we have only the ideas which are expressed in 15:2—6; 16:6—11, with a few things mentioned which do not occur in Isaiah. Cf § 500*f*. Moab was the name both of the district which lay to the E of the Dead Sea

and of its inhabitants. The Bible often speaks of **467m** the enmity between Moabites and Israelites, and there is also the witness of the stele of Mesha, the Moabite King, cf § 81*e*.

1—4. The invasion is briefly related with mention of **n** several place names. The section recalls 10:27—32. The many signs of grief are sharply emphasized—wailing, baldness, shorn beards, penitential garments, trembling. Not all the places mentioned have been identified. We shall only refer to those which are more certain: *Ar* = Rabbat to the S of the Arnon (wady Mogib): *Kir* = Kerak which stands on the hill overlooking the wady of the same name: *Dibon* = Diban where, in 1868, the stele of Mesha was discovered: *Nebo* = Kirbet el Mhaviet: *Heshbon* = Heshban which lies c. 35m. to the N of the Arnon: *Elealeh* = El -'al which is towards the N: *Medeba* **o** or Madeba still keeps the same name. The order which is followed in this list would presume that the invasion came from the S, and in fact could well be an invasion of the Edomites who dwelt in the S and the SW. But other factors, including the direction of the flight hinted at in 15:7, would suggest rather an invasion from the N. It must be remembered that in almost all these oracles concerning this district, the invader is the Assyrian army. The mention of the S cities emphasizes the large extent of the territory which was invaded. Also it must be borne in mind that in these vv, as in the ones which follow, the Heb. text rarely appears to be correct; but in general the versions, the MSS of Qumran, and comparison with Jer allow for corrections which give a fair degree of certainty.

5—7. The dreadful destruction rouses pity in the p onlooker—a pity which is expressed in hyperbolic language but which is not intended to be taken ironically. 'Zoar' was on the S edge of the Dead Sea (Gn 13:10); for the scattered fugitives to have this point as the goal of their flight scarcely seems to favour the theory of an Edomite invasion. The other places mentioned were also apparently in the S, except 'Luhith' which was perhaps not far from Madeba. The Brook of the Willows has been identified with the wady el-Hesa S of the Dead Sea. **8—9.** The description of general mourning is followed by a hint of something even more terrifying in the future; perhaps the action of the *lion* is to be identified with what is to happen according to 16:14. Nearly everyone agrees that the 'Dimon' in 9 should be changed to Dibon (2). The other two places have not been identified with any certainty.

16:1—5. This is one of the most disputed sections both **q** in regard to translation and to interpretation. In **3** the fugitives from Moab speak, beseeching protection and sanctuary. If it is admitted that their plea is continued to **4**, then there can be no doubt: those who are addressed are the inhabitants of the kingdom of Judah. This would justify the allusion to the future messianic kingdom, described in terms which recall 9:6, 7; 11:3—5. **2.** Describes the sad column of refugees, expressively describing those who would naturally arouse most pity (the daughters of Moab). Sela in v 1 is better known under its Greco-Latin name of Petra, capital of the kingdom of Nabataea. The text also refers to the request for booty, for which cf 2 (4) Kgs 3:4. **6—12. r** This is the section which has most in common with the text of Jer. Some of the ideas have already been noted (general mourning, including the prophet's own grief, consternation, destruction). Also some of the place names have already been encountered. What is new here is the accusation of a pride which has no limits, and is the chief reason for the disaster. Kir hareseth is

467r very probably to be identified with Kir-heres (11): Sibmah was not far from Heshbon (Jer 48:32); the 'sea' is the Dead Sea. The 'raisin cakes' are mentioned elsewhere (2 Sm 6:19; Song 2:5), but the mention of them here is strange. At the conclusion of the section (12) there is reference to propitiatory prayers; this is intended to be understood ironically with regard to the useless **s** pagan practices (47:13); 1 (3) Kgs 18:26—29). **13—14.** Despite some difficulties the oracle may be taken as authentic. It corroborates the first oracle, but with something new added—the application of the idea of the 'remnant' (1:9; 6:13) even to Moab. 'The years of a hireling' is probably meant simply to stress the fact that this is the maximum limit, 'not more than three years'; a hired labourer would be most reluctant to work longer than he has to. The event here predicted is identified with the Assyrian invasion, but we can only guess at the particular expedition of Sennacherib or any other king.

t 17:1—14 The oracle on Damascus—This is the editor's title. In fact, part of the ch (vv 12—14) is concerned with Assyria, threatened in an aside; the remainder (1—11) is much more concerned with Samaria or with the kingdom of Israel than with Damascus. The events described in ch 7 justify treating these two together. The oracle, whose authenticity is generally admitted, is before 732, when Damascus was occupied, and can be dated almost certainly to 735/4. It was at that time that the anti-Assyrian league was organized. The first strophe is devoted to Damascus (1—3); in the second (4—6) and third (7—9) Israel's future is spoken of; and in the fourth (10—11) the idolatry of the Israelites is condemned. The threatened chastisement of Damascus occurred in 732 with Tiglath-Pileser's occupation. Israel's fate, on the other hand, came to its tragic conclusion in 722, whilst the oracle on Assyria was fulfilled with the expedition of Sennacherib in 701 (chh 36, 37).

u 1—3 The chastisement of Damascus—The destruction of the kingdom is predicted here as elsewhere (Am 1:3—5; Jer 49:23—37). The image is a common one; Assyria will become like a desert, useful for pasturing sheep but not much else. 'Her cities . . . for ever', cf LXX. (Heb. reads *the cities of Aroer*), is commonly accepted. The fate of Damascus will be similar to that of Israel. The Aramean kingdom is styled 'fortress' of the N kingdom, Ephraim, since it served as a bulwark between **v** it and Assyria. **4—11 The end of Samaria.** The ruin of Samaria is predicted in some indeterminate future ('in that day'; cf 2:12), under the metaphor of the fat man who becomes lean (10:16); the prophet insists, in two comparisons, on the survival of a small 'remnant'. As when corn is reaped or olives gathered, so here, something will escape the destruction. The Valley of Rephaim, near Bethlehem (Jos. 15:8) was famous for its fertility (2 Sm 27:13). In **7, 8** the conversion of the survivors is predicted against a messianic background. This is described as a return to the *Holy One of Israel* (1:4), with an accompanying repudiation of idolatry, an evil which was always active amongst the people of Israel. In addition to a general reference to idols, specific reference is made to 'Asherim' and 'altars of incense' (RSV rendering of Heb. *hammānîm*). The Asherim were groves or just simply wooden poles in honour of a female divinity; the altars of incense were braziers which were used in the worship of idols, but exegetes are not in agreement over the translation of the difficult word *hammānîm*. **9.** Recalls 2; but 2 is usually corrected, and reads in the Heb. *their fortresses will be abandoned like a forest or a*

tree-top (?). LXX gives 'Hevites' and 'Amorites'. For **467v** these two pre-Israelite peoples of Palestine, cf Ex 3:8; 13:5 etc. **10** and **11.** Describe Israel's faults when, abandoned by God, they followed their own course which, despite seeming success in the beginning, was doomed to failure. The idea is expressed by the image of the farmer who cultivates a sterile plant. RSV 'slips of an alien god' (the last word 'god' is not in MT) implies an interpretation which would identify such swiftly growing plantations with the 'gardens of Adonis' (cf 1:29); such an identification, however, seems scarcely probable. **12—14. Woe to Assyria.** The initial image fixes the **w** attention on the number of the assailants, rather than the actual noise they make. But God's intervention is sufficient, since such a great commotion will be reduced to a mere nothing ('like chaff', cf 29:5; Ps 83 (82):14). For the remainder see 10: 27—34; 37:36.

18:1—7 Oracle on Ethiopia—This concerns the **x** district to the S of Egypt, which is called in Heb. *Kush*, and translated by the ancients and many moderns as *Ethiopia*. The great destruction (**3—6**), despite its seemingly cosmic character, refers to a particular event, not specified but identifiable from the context (10:16—19, 33; 14:25; 17:13, 14; 37:36) as the end of the Assyrian invasion in 701. This section brings out very sharply the omnipotent action of God. These events are followed by homage to Yahweh from a people who are strong, and who dwell in a land of flowing rivers (**7**); that is to say, the Ethiopians (cf Ac 8:27). This passage is probably a later addition (cf 19:16—25); the same description of the people can be read in v 2. Even though the text is rather obscure, it would seem that this people had sent messengers to Jerusalem with proposals which were not accepted—almost certainly an attempted diplomatic venture against Assyria (30:1; 31:1). God does not want such a political move; he himself will devastate the Assyrian army. It must be noted that at this time prior to 701, Egypt was governed by a Kushite or Ethiopian dynasty, which was inaugurated by Shabaka; this explains the contact between Jerusalem and the people of Kush. The 'vessels of papyrus' are mentioned also by Pliny (*Nat. History XII, 72*). At the beginning of the section the imitative quality of the words (*silsal kenafayim*). The 'rivers' can be identified with the Atbara, the Blue Nile and the White Nile.

19:1—25 The Oracles on Egypt—The editor of the **468a** text puts a singular title here, but there are really two oracles: the first (1—15), in elegant poetry, forecasts the ruin of the country, and blames above all the heads of state, and derides the so-called wisdom of the 'wise men' of Egypt. The Isaian authenticity can be admitted without difficulty. The second oracle (16—25), written in rather mediocre prose, develops the line of thought already found in 18:7, and predicts the conversion of Egypt and its unification with Assyria and Israel in a purely religious sense. There are many who deny the Isaian authenticity of this passage. Various indications, amongst which are the similarities to ideas in the book of Jonah, suggest a later era than Isaiah. Perhaps we can say that this oracle, like the similar prophecies in 18:7 and 23:15—18 belongs to the editor who made this collection of oracles on the nations.

1—4. This describes the conquest of Egypt by a 'hard **b** master', (4) assisted by internal struggles. The whole is presented as willed and brought about by God who is here described in the style proper to the theophanies ('riding on a swift cloud', cf Dt 33:26; Ezek 1:4; Hb 3:12); the images used are often similar to those

468b found in Ugaritic texts. The first king to invade Egypt was Esarhaddon (680—669), but Sargon II and Sennacherib had already defeated the Egyptians (2 (4) Kgs 17:4; 19:9). Here, the fierce king (4) could be one of these two; the preference lies with Sargon II who was the conqueror at Rafia in 720. From Egyptian history we know that there was a period of anarchy and revolt during the effete 23rd and 24th dynasties, until the

c establishment of the Kushite dynasty c. 715. **5—10.** A great drought brings an end to a period of prosperity; the description is probably metaphorical, at least in part. All the nations feel the effects of it, but in a special way those whose existence is intimately connected with irrigation. The description might be compared with a similar one found in Jer 14:2—6. The translation 'white

d cotton' (9) is not certain. **11—15.** Amongst 'the wise men' we must include probably the sorcerers. It is well known that there existed in Egypt a long tradition of 'sages', who delivered themselves of *counsels* or what we might call salutary maxims. There is here a satire on the very origin of their tradition. So many of the wise men, in so far as they acted as the moral guides of the people, did not know how to forecast or even suggest remedies for the present disasters. God's action in sending a 'spirit of confusion' (29:10; 1 (3) Kgs 22:23) must be understood in the sense brought out by 6:9, 10. For the final metaphor ('head and tail'), cf 9:13. Perhaps this is also an addition to the text. Zoan, in Gr. *Tanis*, was close to an eastern tributary of the Nile in the place where the present San el-Hagar stands. Memphis, which was for a long time the capital of the kingdom, was about

e 28 m. S of what is now Cairo. **16—22.** The repetition of 'in that day' stresses the messianic—eschatological character of the oracle. The first part (16—17) speaks of the Egyptians' reverential fear of the Lord, and also of his people. This is a practical application of the vision in 2:2—4, to which the phrase 'purpose of the Lord' seems to refer. For the image of men changed into fearful women cf Jer 50:37; 51:30; Herodotus VIII, 88, 3. The second section (18—22) speaks of the conversion of the Egyptians; the Lord will prove to be their protector. But there is also a hint of a chastisement to come, which will end in a return to God

f and his renewed assistance (**22**). Amongst the signs of conversion will be the adoption of the Heb. language, here alone styled 'language of Canaan' from the ancient name for Palestine. A further sign will also be the custom of swearing by the name of the Lord. Rather unexpectedly this conversion seems to be limited to 'five cities'; perhaps this definite number is an allusion to Jos. 10:3—27, where the Heb. occupation of Palestine is given as the effect of the conquest of five cities. But practically speaking it indicates the totality, and not just a small section of the Egyptian cities.

g One of these cities is specifically mentioned, the City of the Sun. This translation is most probable, but there are several textual variations. The city is often identified with Leontopolis, where, in the Hellenistic period, the Heb. of the diaspora erected a temple; if this is so, it gives a much later dating to the oracle. Others have thought of *Heliopolis* (city of the Sun god). The most probable hypothesis is that it is either a messianic reference (The Messiah sun of Justice, Mal 3:20); or that it is a reference to *Beth Shemesh* (house of the Sun), which was, at least for a short time the resting place of the Ark (1 Sm 6:9—21). This Egyptian city would be the dwelling place of God, the ideal

h Jerusalem of the messianic era. The 'altar' (**19**) is also an indication of conversion, in that it does not belong naturally to the 'midst of Egypt's land'. The **468i** 'pillar' must be taken in the sense of territorial limit or boundary, and therefore, of ownership (cf Jos. 22:26—29). The 'sign' and the 'witness' are the terms of a kind of contract which even in some way binds God to be favourable to the Egyptians. **23—25.** The idea which **i** is expressed here marks a real **climax** in revelation, surmounting the limitations of nationalism. Two nations which had been inveterate enemies now became friends— and even more astonishing—friends too with a third people which had more than once suffered at their hands (7:18). The 'highway' has a symbolic value. Israel has a privileged position, but all three peoples share in the gift of election and the promises. Bearing in mind the symbolic meaning often attached to the words 'Egypt' and 'Assyria', one cannot consider the fulfilment of a prophecy such as this without taking into account the version given in 2:2—4 and other similar texts.

20:1–6 Oracle on Egypt and Ethiopia—The theme **j** is connected with 18:1—6 and 19:1—5, and predicts the ruin of these two peoples. A fact which is unique in Isaiah, though frequent in Jer and Ezek, is that here the message is confirmed by the symbolic action of the prophet. For three years the prophet will go 'naked and barefoot', a symbol of the future imprisonment of the Egyptians and the Ethiopians. At the end is described the dismay of those who had placed their hope in a people who could not even defend themselves (30:3, 4; 31:3). This disillusionment will strike all who had relied on an anti-Assyrian alliance, among whom were the Hebrews, and particularly the Philistines ('the inhabitants of this coastland'). Undoubtedly Isaiah must have walked through the streets wearing strange garments (Jer 28:10); that he should have gone completely naked, and for such a long time, is improbable. For the verification of the prophecy cf note to 19:1—4. Amongst other things, we know that Pharaoh acquiesced in the demand of Sargon II concerning the extradition of Jamani, the Philistine king of Azotus (ANET 285—7). The oracle should be dated with reference to the destruction of this city, 711 B.C.

21:1–10 Oracle on Babylon—In 21:1 to 22:14 there **469** are four oracles with strange titles, and the difficulties are not restricted to the translation or interpretation of the title. The first of these oracles concerns 'the wilderness of the sea'. The vital part of this section is the exultation over the fall of Babylon (9). First of all the prophet describes a battle, the outcome of which fills him with anguish and sorrow, though he seems to feel for the assailants. **10.** Addresses the Israelites— the oracle is directed to them. The passage begins with a terrible vision described in poetic but obscure style. The title has been interpreted as the equivalent of *mât* **b** *tâmti* (*land of the sea*), and according to Accadian inscriptions this would indicate the district around the Persian Gulf. Here the whole district is destined to be reduced to a desert. The enemy invasion is described as a whirlwind in the desert (the Negeb) S of Judea. In his vision the prophet contemplates the scene with consternation and even with incredulity (3—4). In so far as this implies dismay, it can hardly apply to the prophet's attitude to the fall of Babylon, and in fact, some have seen here rather a reference to the assault upon Jerusalem. But a thing may be incredible because nothing has pointed the way to its verification, even though it might be longed for. On **Elam**, which might stand for Persia, and on Media **c** cf 11:11; 13:17. A contrast is drawn in v 5 between the preparation for battle which should have been

469c made and the universal and stupid indifference. For the circumstances which prevailed in Babylon at the time of the tragedy cf Jer 51:39; Dn 5:1; Herodotus 1, 191. With great dramatic skill, the prophet in **6—9** calls upon an individual to stand as sentinel and receive the news, then go and tell it in all haste to his fellows. Cyrus did not destroy the statues of the gods; here it is said that they were destroyed; but the prophet is not writing a chronicle, he is simply basing himself on what normally happened in similar circumstances. But the rest of the passage does present the idea of the uselessness and discomfiture of the false gods (cf 46:1—7). For the image of the 'threshed and winnowed one' (10), cf 41:15; Am 1:3; Jer 51:33.

d **11—12 Oracle on Edom**—Instead of Edom the text has *Dumah*, which could be translated as *Silence* or *Silently*; but there is no doubt that we are concerned here with the district S of Judea. 'Seir' is often used for Edom. Night and morning are doubtless used in an allegorical sense. The idea is that a time of sorrow will be followed by a brief respite (morning), and this in turn will give way to an indefinite period of anxiety. The final line is intended to convey the sense of a moral rather than of a material return. The comparative mildness of the punishment announced is explained by the fact that the Assyrians were not much interested in a district which was poor and semi-desert. But Sennacherib (ANET 287) speaks of the acknowledgement of his supremacy on the part of Kammusunabdi, king of Edom. Perhaps the brief oracle of Isaiah is proper to this period.

e **13—17 Oracle on the Arabian tribes**—The title could be translated 'Desert' instead of 'Arabia', but it certainly refers in general to this country. At the end we are given a picture of devastation, but it is not complete; what was said about Moab is repeated here (16:13, 14). The object of this oracle are the inhabitants of Kedar, an Ishmaelite tribe which lived a more or less semi-nomadic life (Gn 25:13; 1 Chr 1:29) to the E of Palestine (60:7). First of all the oracle speaks of the inhabitants of two oases; those of the first—the Temanites—are invited to give help to the others—the Dedanites—who have fled in terror. The text, however, could be translated also in the sense that the two peoples should give help to others unnamed. If this section refers to events known to us, it should be reckoned one of the more ancient prophecies of Isaiah. The Assyrian inscriptions (ANET 284—6) mention expeditions in Arabia in 732 (Tiglath Pileser III) and in 715 (Sargon II).

470a **22:1—14 Oracle on the Valley of Vision**—The title comes from v 5 which is a reference to Jerusalem, but in a symbolic rather than a topographical sense, despite the fact that in the city and in the district round about, valleys are to be found. The prophet is moved by the slaughter he sees in his vision and even more by the general indifference. He then contrasts the multiple precautions taken to ensure material defence (**8—11**) with the lack of attention to the only effective means of protection, moral revival. The section could refer to Sennacherib's invasion (10:27—34); but a reference to some previous occasion is not excluded; that it refers to the occupation by Nebuchadnezzar is much less probable.

b **1—4.** It is not possible to ascertain whether this noisy exultation is connected with some particular episode or is just a sign of the indifference of a people bent upon pleasure. The mention of flight and lack of resistance would seem to point to the events described in 2 (4) Kgs 25:4—6; but similar incidents occurred also in the time of Sennacherib, at least in some of the places occupied by

him. In fact, the text does not demand that we see here **470b** the fall of the capital. For v 4 cf 21:3, 4, 10; the periphrasis 'daughter of my people' to indicate the citizens themselves occurs only here in Isaiah, but is found in other prophets. **5—11.** 'tumult and trampling and confusion' **c** corresponds in Heb. to a series of assonances (*mᵉhûmâ umᵉbûsâ umᵉbûkâ*). Elam and Kir (11:11; Am 1:5; 9:7) are named perhaps because they are distant countries towards the E. In the Assyrian army there were often mercenaries or allies from other countries. *The protection of Judah* is not necessarily Jerusalem; the text ('has taken away the covering') could indicate the disappearance of hope and the collapse of almost all the kingdom, as did happen in the time of Sennacherib. For the defence works (**8—11**) cf 2 (4) Kgs 20:20; 2 Chr 32:3—6; Sir 48:17; for 'House of the forest' cf 1 (3) Kgs 7:2—6; 10:17. The 'old pool' is the 'upper pool' of 7:3; the lower one has been identified with Birket-el-Hamra; the 'reservoir between the two walls' could be the pool of Shiloah (8:6). For the divine chastisement cf 5:26. **12—14.** Repentance **d** is described in terms of the common signs of sorrow (15:2, 3: 32: 11, 12, Jl 2:12—17). Instead of this repentance there reigns a real hedonistic spirit (Eccl 9:9, 10). **14** is meant to accentuate the seriousness of the fault, but is not intended to affirm the impossibility of God's pardon.

15—25 Oracle on Shebna—This is the only individual **e** prophecy in Isaiah. He is sent to reprove a high dignitary of the Court, prophesying his degradation. He speaks of Shebna's successor, hinting at a similar fate for him also. It is most probable that this last detail is a later addition. Shebna was the steward of the palace with wide powers over various subordinates; his office is mentioned already at the time of Solomon (1 (3) Kgs 4:6).

The accusation is concerned with the pride and arrogance displayed in the building of a magnificent tomb. His fall is described with a wealth of expressive imagery. The identity of Shebna is not known; a seal found at Lachish bears this name but of course it could never be proved that it is the same person. In 36:2 he appears again, this time holding an inferior position. In this text (36:3) there appears also the name of Eliakim; nothing more is known about him, except for the position promised to him here. The *peg* image appears to be somewhat prosaic, but perhaps it is used here because it aptly prepares for the idea of the fall (25) as well as for the shameless nepotism which prevailed (24). The *key* metaphor is much more elegant, and is used in the same sense in the NT (Mt 16:19; Apoc 3:7).

23:1—18 Oracle on Tyre—This is divided into two **f** parts. The first describes the end of Tyre (written in superb poetry) and the consequences, particularly economic (1—14). The second part, in prose, is a pronouncement on the restoration of Tyre and its conversion (15—18). Very few would defend the Isaian authorship of 15, 18, which are perhaps additions influenced by Jer 25:11, 12; 29, 10.

The authenticity of the first prophecy depends on its interpretation. If it refers to the total occupation of the island on which Tyre stood, this in fact did occur in Alexander's conquests 333/32; and then it is difficult to uphold the Isaian origin. But the text could refer to one of the many occasions when the Assyrians or Babylonians overran the Tyrian dependencies on the mainland in which case Isaian authenticity would be quite possible. There are some who sweep aside these difficulties by stating that the original prophecy referred to Sidon, occupied more than once during these years. The oracle may be compared with that of Ezek (26:1—28:29). A corrupt text gives rise to certain difficulties of translation.

470g **1–5.** In dramatic fashion, the destruction is already seen as past history; the news of it spreads terror and confusion, and particularly for the people who travel across the main commercial traffic ways which, as Ezek constantly reminds his readers all converge upon Tyre. The great merchant fleets (ships of Tarshish; 2:16) were informed of the disaster by the Cypriots, or, (as the text may be read) as they were on the point of weighing anchor from the *country of the Kittim* to make for the Phoenician coast. The name is derived from *Kition*, a Phoenician colony in Cyprus, and in the Bible stands for the Aegean islands, Greece, and even the islands and the coast of the Mediterranean (Gn 10:4; Jer 2:10 Dn 11:30; 1 Mc 1:1). LXX substituted the name of Carthage, another Phoenician colony. It refers in particular to the traffic with Egypt, which is well documented from ancient narrative **h** and pictorial records . **3.** Shihor (Jer 2:18) is a synonym for the Nile or the name of one of the Delta tributaries. The 'merchants of Sidon' are not only those from the famous city N of Tyre; Sidon often stands for the whole of Phoenicia. The words in v 4 (referring to the grief felt by all ancient peoples at the idea of dying without leaving descendants behind) presume a massacre: the city is like a sterile woman. The speaker appears to be the city of Tyre, 'the stronghold of the sea', addressing the whole **i** of Phoenicia under the name of Sidon. **6–14.** Some of the foregoing images are repeated here in part; as elsewhere, there is some insistence on the fact that God is the remote cause of what has happened. The survivors from the city and from Phoenicia in general ('virgin daughter of Sidon', **12**; cf 37:22; 47:1) are invited to go over to the colonies in Spain (Tarshish) and in Cyprus (in Heb., Kittim). Canaan (**11**) stands for Phoenicia (cf Jos. 5:1 in LXX). In **10** there is an invitation to the various colonies, represented by Tarshish, to consider themselves as being henceforth free; but the text is obscure. There is much more discussion about **13**, which is probably an interpolation in whole or in part. The name Tyre does not appear in the Heb., and the whole v is of very uncertain construction. If it is intended to convey that Tyre was besieged and destroyed by the Chaldeans (13:19) and not by Assyria, then this must refer to Nebuchadnezzar, who according to Josephus (Ant, X, 228) besieged Tyre for thirteen years, after he had conquered its mainland possessions. **j** **15–18.** The song of the harlot, sung in satirical strain, does not imply directly any reference to a life of debauchery; the image is often used when it is a question of trade or commerce. Wealth will return at some future date, but it will be used above all for the maintenance of the cult in Jerusalem (60: 5–7). This section recalls 18:7; moreover it is an adaptation of Jeremiah's prophecy with its mention of 70 years. The fate of Tyre is in some sense equated with that of Jerusalem.

471a **24–27 The Apocalypse of Isaiah**—These 4 chh form a whole with their own particular characteristics: they are notoriously difficult. The name *Apocalypse* is commonly given to them, but the title is only correct in a special sense. We do not have here a style which is strictly 'apocalyptic', nor a theme which is 'apocalyptic' in the sense of 'eschatological'. The section, as with other prophetical texts, contains a diversity of literary forms. The 4 chh are full of veiled allusions, vivid descriptions of cosmic events, and an eschatological background; but there are other elements which prevent us from saying that we have here a straightforward apocalyptic vision.

b There are two further questions which are much discussed: who is the author of the chh and what is their meaning? Both questions are interrelated. In general, the Isaian authorship is denied; authors point out the lack of any precise historical background, the fact that there **471I** are ideas here which are not found elsewhere in Isaiah, the enigmatic thought, the grandiose style with purely rhetorical emphasis etc.

There is no doubt that chh 24–27 seem to be much **c** more similar, at least in their form, to chh 40–55 than to the first part of Isaiah. The hypothesis that these chh might belong to the same period as 40–55, perhaps even from the pen of the same author or from writers of the same mind as he, is quite feasible. But the interpretation of the text must necessarily influence one's view on this. One of the fundamental themes is the destruction or occupation of a great city, described here under many different titles but never explicitly named. The identification of this city and its misfortunes would provide the answer to many problems. The name of Babylon is the one most commonly suggested by exegetes, but it is not the only one (some speak of Carthage or of Rome). There is much less agreement concerning the conquest which is described: is it that by Cyrus in 539, or Xerxes in 485 or Alexander the Great in 331? The first seems most probable.

All these questions, which are, so to speak, on the **d** periphery, should not deter us from enjoying the beauty of some of these sections, and the wealth of theological meaning within them—the emphatic assertion of the omnipotence of God, his divine intervention in this world and much else. The chh begin with the description of a catastrophe which is seemingly universal, but which is actually confined to a famous city (24:1–23); there is then a hymn of thanksgiving (25:1–5), linked with the picture of a divine banquet and the picture of Moab's fate (25:6–12). The main theme of 26:1–19 is one of praise and thanksgiving, whilst in 26:20–27 the anger of the Lord is uppermost. Ch 27 is mainly concerned with the fate of Israel.

24:1–6 General Catastrophe—The various antithe- **e** tical terms in **2** indicate mankind in general; and before this heaven and earth are included in the general cataclysm. It is easy to conclude that what is here being described is the end of the world and the universal judgement. But v **6** speaks of survivors; and parallels found elsewhere enable us to see that the extent of the chastisement is relative. The grounds for the chastisement are given in **5**, expressed in terms characteristic of the relations which existed between God and the Hebrew people (law, covenant). This however does not necessarily mean that there is a reference here to the pact made on Sinai. The Bible recognizes also a covenant with all mankind (Gn 9:16) and it is not surprising that similar events should be described in similar terms. In this passage, the guilty ones are apparently all men; but in actual fact, they are the inhabitants of the city mentioned in v 10.

7–16a The city of chaos—From a world conflagra- **f** tion a transition is made to a more specific disaster: all signs of joy disappear ('wine, strong drink', cf 5:11). The result is a picture similar to the one given in Jl 1:10–12. For the comparisons of v **13**, which indicate the paucity of the 'remnant', cf 17:6. The 'remnant' is composed of those who escaped from slaughter, who are left 'in the midst of the earth', (cf 2:2, 19:24; Mi 4:1). The unnamed city is described by one of the two words (*tōhû*) used in Gn 1:2 to describe primordial chaos. Here it could be used to convey the meaning of 'city reduced to chaos' by destruction; but it has more probably a moral significance (41: 29; 1 Sm 12:21), 'a city most corrupt' through the immorality of its customs. It could even be because it was the centre for something regarded as the ultimate in evil, as idolatry was for the Hebrew. There are many possibilities regarding the identification of the city; but

471f certainly according to the Bible (from Gn 11:9 to Apoc 18:21) no city other than Babylon would be more apt to personify this idea of sin and evil. A hymn of praise on the occasion of the fall of the hated city (14—16) is composed by the survivors (13), calling on neighbouring peoples to give glory to God.

g 16b—23 The Judgement of God—The theme of 1—6 is repeated but in somewhat different language. Here the stress is more on the idea of God's judgement. The prophet begins by expressing sorrow and indignation at the guilt of mankind. The imagery of 17—18, dealing with the difficulties encountered in attempted escape, is also used in Jer 48:43, 44; the three words used in Hebrew are alliterative (*pahaḏ wāpahaṯ wāpaḥ*). Then a cosmic catastrophe is described in language which recalls the Flood story (Gn 7:11) and based partly also on contemporary ideas of cosmology (cf 13:13)—but the description is not merely hyperbolic. The final conclusion is an acknowledgement of God's rule in the same sort of perspective as **h** that seen in 2:2—4. Amongst those who are punished are included 'the host of heaven'—hardly to be identified with the powers of evil in the NT (Rm 8:38; Col 1:13, etc); here it simply means the heavenly bodies (34:4; 40:26; 45:12), though there is no need to consider them as living beings. What we have here is quite simply, as elsewhere, nature sharing man's fate. In **22**, Sheol (14:9, 15) is described. The term set for the chastisement (for many days) must not be understood according to Christian eschatological ideas.

i 25:1—5 Canticle of thanksgiving—The purpose of the canticle links it with 24:7: the fall of the city of chaos. The passage is not brilliantly original, but it does stand out for the beauty of the poetry and the contrast drawn between the protection of the wretched and the chastisement of the proud. These elements give the passage a messianic background. Many would substitute *proud* (Heb., *zēḏîm*) for 'aliens' (Heb. *zārîm*) in v 2. In **3** the translation could be in the singular with reference to the future people of God. The thought expressed in **4** is very common in the Bible; the poor man who is protected, in general (but not always) indicates the Israelites. Even in **5** there are many who would change 'aliens' to *proud*.

j 6—12. First of all a banquet is described, the symbol of the blessings which will be a part of God's kingdom. With a sense of universality quite unexpected, this is extended to all people (cf Mt 22:2—70). All of this is intended to convey the sense of great friendship with God, but suddenly the prophet mentions an obstacle or something which is unbecoming (veil) and which will be removed. Those who interpret this passage along the lines of 2 Cor 3:15 are too close to NT thought; perhaps here it is a question of a symbol of sadness or strife. Amongst the things which will be removed there is also *death*; this could mean the cessation of a massacre, but in fact the context is not opposed to the idea which St Paul sees in it (1 Cor 15:54), perhaps in the sense of a return to the first **k** condition of man before sin (Gn 2:19, 20). The concept of universal peace and harmony is all the more emphasized by what happens to Moab (15:1—16:14), shown here as the proud one who will be brought down with no possibility of deliverance. A few commentators would correct the text, eliminating the reference to Moab, which is here perhaps out of context but is certainly most likely because of ancient enmity. On the other hand, others see Moab as the central point of the whole section, and make it refer to the Nabatean invasion about 270 B.C. The text can be maintained if we see it as a symbol of the 'ruthless' of vv 4, 5 rather than a reference to a specific people.

26:1—19 Canticle of Praise—There is some analogy **471l** here with 25:1—5, but this canticle is much longer and richer in themes. The *strong city* is Jerusalem, described as in 60:18—22. This is the prelude to the idea of a symbolic Jerusalem, the heavenly city, which is contrasted with the city which will be destroyed (5; cf 24:10). The insistence upon the wretched or poor of the Lord (6; cf 25:4) puts this text in line with the post-exilic texts which often deal with this theme. From v 13 there are alternating thoughts which are characteristic of the sapiential literature with its yearnings for a genuine piety, nourished by the covenant (Ps 22(21):2; 39(38):4; 55(54):5 etc). In v 12 not only does *peace* appear as a gift from God, but also, (and this expressed in a most original way), every action of man which is worthy of praise is referred to God. In **14** there is an emphatic denial of the possibility of returning to the former deplorable conditions—the oppressors are scattered and destroyed: they will not return. **15.** The national revival under David is referred to. **16.** Is corrupt. It is probably better to read the verbs in the 1st person. **17—18.** Yahweh is the author of Israel's prolonged suffering. **19.** Yet he who lets fall the life-giving dew and can bring back the dead to life will also restore his chosen people, Israel. Some commentators see in this v an explicit affirmation of a future resurrection at least of the just, and consequently regard the v as of post-exilic origin. On the other hand it is possible to view it as a metaphorical and poetic allusion to suffering and misfortune in terms of death and Sheol, the land of shades, cf Ezek. 37:1—14 (the vision of dry bones). It should moreover be taken in conjunction with v 15 where the issue is one of national rather than personal survival.

26:20—27:1 The Anger of the Lord—Unless we **m** transpose the order here, these vv return to the theme of God's dealings with the nations who are guilty. They will be punished because of their injustices. Whilst this is being done, the just are invited to hide themselves so that they will not be included in the disaster. **27:1.** This (always in the indeterminate future, 'in that day'), is described in the imagery of God's victories over the primaeval monsters (cf Ps 74(73):13, 14; Ps 104(103):26; Ps 148:7 etc). As elsewhere, mythological language is used to describe concrete events. A text which is very similar to the one under consideration, using the same rather horrific imagery, is to be found in a Ugaritic fragment, (cf C. H. Gordon, *Ugaritic Manual*, Rome, 1955, 148).

27:2—13 Israel's destiny—Expressive of the peaceful **n** future of Israel, the image of the vineyard stands out (2—5). The picture it gives, with a few uncertainties arising out of the translation, presents a surprising contrast with 5:1—7; in this latter, everything is brought to an end in scorn and rejection, whilst here everything is expressive of love and anxious care. There is some stress on the undesirable elements (*thorns and briers*: **5, 6**), but even they are given the choice between destruction and insertion into the chosen people. This is **o** followed by the metaphor of the root which grows until it becomes immense (16:8; Ps 80(79):11, 12). God treats Israel in a very special way: he punishes her, even with exile; but all works to a purpose; it is an act of mercy, ending with her revival. This latter theme is expressed through the elimination of the symbols of idolatry—cf 17:8. There will be a re-unification of those who were scattered throughout the peoples (**12, 13**; cf 11:12; 49, 22), whilst for the city of chaos (24:10) there will be not the slightest hope (**10,11**). The *Brook of Egypt* is the modern el-Arish on the borders of Palestine. On the sound of the trumpet cf Jl 2:1; Zeph 1:16; Mt 24:31; 1 Cor 15:52.

471p **28—33 Oracles on the kingdom of Judah**—This section has a marked unity, similar to chh 1—12 but without the book of Emmanuel. Apart from reproving many vices and defects, the prophet opposes—as he did in the time of Ahaz—the political alliances accepted by Hezekiah. The section can be defined as the *Woes* (28:1; 29:1, 15; 30:31; 31:1; 33:1; cf 5:8,11 etc.) Ch 28 begins with a prophecy on Samaria (1—6), followed by a list of threats to various persons (7—22); it ends with two beautiful parables taken from agricultural life (23—29).

472a **28:1—6 Woe to Samaria**—With the repeated imagery of the 'fading flower' is described the imminent end of the kingdom of Israel or Ephraim, which came about in 722 through the Assyrians ('one who is mighty and strong'). For the vice of drunkeness cf Am 6:4—6; Hos 7: 5—7. Samaria is named periphrastically, but with a geographical precision—standing on a hill surrounded by valleys and plains (*crown of the rich valley*). For the **b** image of the first ripe fig cf Na 3:12. Probably **5** and **6** are out of place; but they do not contradict the contrast drawn between the end of the guilty and the future of the 'remnant' (1:9), which will have as a crown and a diadem not a city, but God himself; and it will be God himself who will give aid to the judges and to the fighting men. This supposes the possibility of enemy assault, but comes rather unexpectedly in the context.

c **7—22 Vice in Judah**—The fate of Samaria should serve as an example to the inhabitants of Judah, because in the S kingdom also there was evidence of depravity: drunkeness and orgy. Isaiah here upbraids above all two categories of people: the priests and the prophets (7:13), who should have been, but were not, impartial judges (Dt 19: 17) and attested messengers of God. On strong drink cf 5:11. The prophets reply to the threat with ridicule (**9—10**), saying that it is ill-deserved, and repeating a series of words, probably without any precise meaning but in such a way as to imitate the stammerings of an infant or someone wishing to teach them their business. In Heb. v 10 sounds as follows: ṣaw lāṣāw ṣaw lāṣāw, qaw lāqāw qaw lāqāw, zᵉᶜēr šām zᵉᶜēr šām. The prophet (**11—13**) takes up the ridiculous phrase and uses it to state once more the inevitable invasion of the enemy, when there will be heard in Judah a tongue unknown. To them and to all the others who have responsibility he pronounces **d** chastisement (**14—22**); it will mean ruin. Ironically the prophet reveals that their confidence is based upon an illusion (*covenant with death, agreement with Sheol*, cf *5:14*), and they will become aware of this at the moment of the chastisement (**18**). It is a skein of *lies* and *falsehood*. The beginning of **17** speaks of an ideal justice, such as is described for the messianic times (9:7; 11:5). An even clearer messianic reference is seen in **16** (cf Mt 21: 42—44; Rm 9:33; Eph 2:20; 1 Pt 2:4—6). The two comparisons in **20** emphasize the seriousness of the calamity (Assyrian invasion) and the difficulty in overcoming it. In **21** there is an allusion to two battles in the time of David (2 Sm 5:20, 25; 1 Chr 14:11, 16).

e **23—29 God is just and consistent**—To forestall any possible accusation of levity in God's action, which now protects, now punishes, the prophet turns to two small 'sketches': the plough and the threshing sledge. These two instruments are used alternately—diverse means are used according to circumstances. Not all the plants mentioned can be identified with certainty; in **27**, **28**, various methods are described for threshing. The final sentences neatly express the tendencies of the OT to refer everything directly to God, but they by no means intend to convey that farmers learn their trade solely by revelation.

29:1—8 Woe to Jerusalem—There is a parallel **472** between ch 28 and this ch. Here also the ch begins with a *Woe* to a city (1—8) and ends with a series of reproaches and predictions (24). The threat, not motivated by any precise reproach, is limited to **1—4**, where a terrible siege is described. But with a multiplicity of metaphors there is a continual stress on the fact that the end will be very different from what is foreseen. God frees his people. The section says, basically, what is said in 10:27—34, although in a different way. For the 'voice of a ghost' etc, cf 8:19. This section is before 701, but it is impossible to deduce a precise date from the generic expression in v 1. There is not the slightest doubt that it is Jerusalem the prophet is speaking of. The name **g** *Ariel* does not appear elsewhere, at least in this sense. Particularly because of the contrast with v 2 there is a symbolical meaning attached to this name here. If we take into account the reading of 1QIsᵃ Uriel, then it is possible that there is similarity between Jerusalem (in accadian Urusalim) and Ariel with a change of the divine name, (not *Shalem* = a canaanite divinity, but *El* = God). If then we accept the meaning of 'sign' for the first part of the name Uru,—this has a good philological foundation—then we would have the idea of a 'sign of God'. Because she is so terribly chastised, Jerusalem will become an eloquent sign of warning. Others see it as meaning 'brazier or altar of God' (cf 31:9; Ezek 43:15).

9—24 Reproaches and predictions—The apostrophe **h** in v **9** is probably the prophet's reply to the scornful reception of his audience (28:9—14). The drunkenness and 'staggering' indicate moral blindness; these things are attributed directly to God as in 6:10. With an image which is not infrequently found (cf 19:14; 1 (3) Kgs 22:23), the sending of a profound sleep is attributed directly to God (in Heb. the same terms as in Gn 2:21), and this has produced moral insensitivity. It is probable that the words prophets and seers are explanatory glosses. The inability to understand the prophetic teaching (= the vision) is described twice over with the image of the sealed book (Apoc 5:1ff) and with the image of the illiterate. The reproaches start with the lack of true piety (**13**: cf Mt 15:7—9; Jn 4:23). For the second part of **14** cf 1 Cor 1:19. Amongst those actions which they try to keep hidden from God, there are perhaps included certain diplomatic overtures (28:15; 30:1—3; 31:1—3). This attempt is ridiculous just as it is ridiculous to want to judge God's actions: the distance between God and man is so great. The contrast, potter-clay, (to be taken **i** in a relative sense to safeguard human liberty) is quite frequently used (Jer 18:6—10; Rm 9:20—23). In **17—24** the prophet describes a radical change for the better, one which does not seem to be limited to freedom from the Assyrian invasion. The *Lebanon* (**17**) was the symbol of abundant vegetation (2:13); in this case it states that in the future it will produce more fruitful crops. Compared to a normal field, it will be like a dense forest because of the abundance of its produce. In **18**, which could be **j** joined to 24, there are echoes of 9 (cf 35:5). The joy of the *Holy One of Israel* (1:14) is caused because of the disappearance of the vices which are so often mentioned throughout the book (5:23; 10:12; 28:14; 22). False testimony is mentioned in the beginning of **21**. Israel's state of inferiority will disappear, and even the pagans will be converted, when they see the favours which God bestows upon his people (2:2—5; 11:10; 26:9).

30:1—7 Embassy to Egypt—In this ch also there is a **473** notable alternation of themes: embassy to Egypt (1—7); chastisement of the people because of their hostility (8—17); conversion and repentance (18—22); the happy

473a future of Sion (23—26); judgement of God on his people (27—33). The initial event, whose date we cannot determine precisely (all that is certain is that it occurs before 701), contains several similarities with 7:3ff. The prophet condemns the political schemings since they imply a lack of trust in the divine assistance. Even though he was much more pious than this father, Hezekiah gave his consent to an alliance with Egypt. The prophet reveals what will be the actual effect of such a move (36:6). The true Israelite would seek protection under the wings of God (Ps 17 (16):8; 36 (35):8; 57 (56):2; 91 (90):1) or at the most under the shadow of his king (Lam 4:20).

b In **4** *Zoan* (19:11) and *Hanes* were perhaps temporary seats of the Pharaohs and of some of their plenipotentiaries; the second mentioned (= Henassijeh el-Medineh) was much more to the S, in the centre of Egypt. In the description of the fauna of the Negeb (21:1), there is a mixture of hyperbole and fantasy ('flying serpent', 14:29; 27:1). 'Rahab', the name of a primaeval monster (51:9; Jb 9:13; Ps 89 (88):11), is also at other times the symbolic name for Egypt (Ps 87 (86):4); despite its power, great or small, Egypt will stay inactive. In fact, the only help from her will be a derisory one (37:9).

c **8—17 The hostility of the people**—This section recalls 28:7—16, but here the opposition to the prophetic teaching is from everyone, and not just from certain classes of people. Therefore the threatened chastisement is a general one. For what is described in v 8 cf 8:1; here, we are not told what should be written: perhaps it is the symbolic name in v 7 with what follows. Instead of 'book' we could translate 'bronze' (Jb 19:20). The words *seers* and *prophets* correspond to *rō'îm* and *hōz'îm*; cf 1 Sm 9:9. For the defiant protest cf Am 7:16, 17. It will be observed with what insistence the name of the 'Holy One of Israel' (1:4) occurs. The ideal line of conduct is suggested in **15**, a conduct which is not followed, the peaceful policy of trust (7:9). For the sarcastic mention of horses, it will be remembered that it is a question of the arms which were hoped for from Egypt (31:1; 36:6). At the end, the idea of the remnant (1:9) is expressed in a metaphor found only **d** here. **18—26 Conversion and restoration**—The defeat and drastic decimation of the nation does not correspond to the real desire of God; these things are merely the consequences of guilt (**18**). A sincere conversion would suffice (cf v 15) to change the course of events. Normally, such an ideal state of friendship would be verified in the future 'remnant'. To indicate the incomparable blessing of such a state the prophet speaks of a delightful food of a rare kind, which even the cattle will feed upon. A complete devastation of the Assyrian army is foreseen in **25 e** (37:36), but the authenticity of this is suspect. The reference to the heavenly bodies is common to this kind of writing (24:4; 65:17; 2 Pt 3:13; Apoc 21:1). Also the word *sevenfold* is frequently found as an indication of an outstanding but indefinite number (Gn 4:15; Ps 12 (11): 7; 79:12).

f **27—33 The end of Assyria**—A theophany in traditional imagery speaks of *'the Name of the Lord'*—a fairly common circumlocution for the divine majesty. The various anthropomorphisms are chosen to accentuate the idea of punishment. For the metaphor of the *sieve* cf Mt 3:12; for the 'bridle' cf 29:10; both really say the same thing. In contrast we have the description of the happiness of the Israelites, in liturgical language (**29**). The dramatic end of the Assyrian army (**31—33**) can be compared with 10:27—34. The timbrels and the lyres are supposedly in the hands of the Israelites who rejoice at the destruction **g** of their enemies. A burning place corresponds to the word Tophet (Jer 7:31), and indicates the pyre—or the place where it was lit—in the valley of Ben Hinnom (= **473g** Gehenna), S of Jerusalem; this was a place of idolatrous or at least unlawful worship. In particular there were sacrifices to *Moloch*, and there are some who see a reference here to this god in the word *Melek* translated as *king*. But here the ritual language appears to be of secondary consideration; all the prophet is trying to convey is the idea of slaughter, and he uses the image of some enormous place of execution or burning.

31:1—9 More about the alliance with Egypt—This **474a** theme goes as far as v 5; afterwards comes the description of return or conversion. The content of the thought of 1—3 runs parallel to 30:1—7, 15, 16 (cf also 22:11). Here again there is the contrast, developed by St Paul, between 'flesh' and 'spirit'. Israel will only be saved by having recourse to God whose protection is described under the image of the maternal wing of a bird (Dt 32:11; Mt 23:37) and of a lion that does not fear the shepherds; in the last example, the shepherds are taken to be the symbol of the invading enemy. The turning back to God (**6, 7**) is shown by the repudiation of idolatry (30:22). Amongst the many descriptions of the end of the invasion, this is the most clear (**8**, *sword, not of a man*) cf 37:36. Even though the words used are different, at the end there is a reference to 30:33 and perhaps to the name *Ariel* (29:1).

32:1—8 A reign of justice—This is written in a sapien- **b** tial style, without any reference to the alliance with Egypt or to the invasion from Assyria. Nevertheless it can be considered as a continuation of ch 31 in so far as it describes the justice to be inaugurated after the Assyrian enemy has disappeared. The justice of the reign which is described is based above all on the uprightness of the heads of state, (for the opposite, cf 1:23; 3:14, 15; 10:1 etc) but also on the willingness of the people. For the imagery used in **2** cf 30:2; Lam 4:20; and for that of **3, 4** cf 30:9—11; 35:3, 4. The 'tongue of the stammerers' **c** (**4**) probably relates to the activity of the judges, no longer unjust or fearful, but firm teachers of right conduct. The sapiential tone of **5—8** is evident; everyone will have the place and the consideration he deserves in the future kingdom, without going into the specific position of particular individuals. Here we have the opposite picture from 5: 20, 21. The coupling of faults against God and against one's neighbour stands out: both are considered at the same level.

9—14 Feckless women—A similar picture to the one **d** given in 3:16—26. The chastisement includes all, not only the women. The text appears to speak of complete destruction (13:20—22); but if we take into account the hyperbole and the lack of any precise reference to the occupation of Jerusalem, then what we are given here could also apply to the Assyrian invasion. In that case, and especially because of the first words of **10**, the prophecy must be dated a little before 701. The fields were devastated and many of the fortifications were razed to the ground. For the various signs of strife and consternation, cf Jer 4:8; 16:6; 41:5. The *palace* is not necessarily the royal dwelling; it is intended to denote elegant houses in general. The translation 'hill' and 'watchtower' is preferable to the simple transcription ('Ophel' and 'Bahan'), since there is no question here of the famous E hill of Jerusalem (2 Chr 27:3; 33:14) nor of any other topographical position in the city (*Bahan* does not occur elsewhere). It is a question of 'rocks' and 'towers' of defence in general.

15—20 The Restoration—This is the opposite of the **e** picture just given. Security and justice are here accompanied by abundant harvests and blessings of every kind. This is that messianic—eschatological vision which

474e recurs throughout the book. Here, everything is attributed to the creative 'spirit' of God (44:3; Ps 33 (32):6; 104 (103):30 etc). For the transformation into a 'fruitful field' and 'forest' cf 29:17. **19,** corrected from the Heb., is probably a gloss. This could be read hypothetically (*even if the forest . . .*) and without any specific meaning for the words 'forest' and 'city'. Others see here a reference to Assyria and her fate. The final phrase accentuates the fruitfulness of the soil providing pasture where the animals safely roam (cf 30:23—25).

f 33:1—24 Messianic future—The title is relative, but it is difficult to find another without using a multiplicity of phrases. The initial theme is stated in v 1. The rest can be considered as a prayer (2—6) followed by divine intervention (7—16) and the vision of a bright future (17—24). The authenticity of the ch is disputed, but it can be upheld. The suggestion that the passage is a 'liturgy' is worth considering, but it has not been proved. The ch, in which several of the vv are almost identical with vv of chh 28—32, is not outstanding for its originality; there are also serious difficulties for the exegete in some of the allusions.

g **1—6.** The threat of **1** can be referred to Assyria; this becomes clear if the second verb is translated, as is possible, by 'plunder' rather than 'deal treacherously'. The 'thunderous noise', which often accompanies a theophany, is the voice of God (Ps 29 (28); 3—9; Am 1:2; Jer 25:30). On the power of the 'arm' of the Lord, which is here mentioned as an efficacious defence, cf 51:9. The interpretation of **6** is most uncertain; the theme is rather like that of the sapiential poetry and suggests at the outset a reference to the 'precepts'. Every blessing ('salvation', 'justice', 'wisdom', etc) comes from the most **h** high God. **7—16.** The description in **9** of a disaster or chastisement is clear (24:4). Those parts of the land which are most luxuriant in vegetation (for 'Lebanon' and 'Bashan' cf 2:13; 'Sharon' is the plain surrounding Tel Aviv, 'Carmel' is the hill above Haifa) become like a desert. The translation of **7f,** and therefore its interpretation, is doubtful. The reference to 'covenants' (**8**) and to 'witnesses' is most enigmatic (in Heb. the verbs are in the active and it is 'covenant', used as the object of the verb, and not 'covenants'). Perhaps it is a reference to the frequent transgression of the Sinaitic pact and the repudiation of the prophets (= witnesses?); but this could only be so if the text were to be corrected simply on the basis of speculation or it may perhaps be an allusion to some action of Sennacherib (not mentioned in the historical books) which was faithless and insulting (cf 1 Mc 6:62); this has the advantage of being more faithful to the context; for in fact, the threats in **10—12** seem to refer to those who were responsible for so many calamities, that is, the Assyrians. The contrast between 'sinners' and the just is most frequent, with or without the prospects which are in store for them; the best comparisons are with Ps 15 (14):2—5; 24 (23):3—5. It will be remarked how the recompense of the just is limited to worldly prospects: Isaiah has no special contribution to **i** make on this theme. **17—24.** For the future, what is most important is the liberation from an invader (**18, 19**: for the 'obscure speech' cf 28:11; 36:11) and consequently a life of contentment in Jerusalem. In **17** there appears the messianic king, or perhaps Hezekiah after the Assyrian danger had passed. But the first interpretation is not convincing, and the second one is not satisfactory. The 'king in his beauty', to take it anthropomorphically, could be God, as in **21, 22,** where he is a most strong protector, superior to any kind of human defence, *the* ruler and *the* saviour in every sense. Concerning the

influence of royal ideology on these visions, cf the last **474i** chh of the book where the imagery is even stronger than in v 20 but without the notion of 'the kingship of God'. **24** and the end of **23** can easily be fitted into the general context (cf 35:5—8). The first section of 23 can be joined to 21, thus continuing the idea that even a big ship should be cared for, so that it would not in fact be a cause of harm.

34:1—35:10 Judgement on the nations,—liberation j of Israel—There is a close connection between these two chh, while they differ in content from the preceding ones. On the other hand, the similarities and analogies with chh 40—55 are many, and between ch 34 and the prophecy on Babylon (13:1 etc). The composition of these chh must be dated about the middle of the 6th cent. B.C. The words of ch 34 about Edom are reminiscent of the prophecy of Obad.

34:1—7. As in 30:27—31, the prophet speaks first of **k** all of a judgement affecting all the nations, and then goes on to deal with one people in particular, namely Edom which was S and SE of Judaea. The disaster assumes cosmic dimensions (4). 'Doomed' (**2**) translates a verb which means to destine something to extermination since it was consecrated to God (Jos. 6:17—21; 1 Sm 15:3—23). To have no burial (**3**) was the depth of shame or dishonour (Jer 7:33; 8:2). On the sword *sated* with blood cf Jer 46:10. The mention of sacrifice (**6**) suggests that the list of victims is intended in an allegorical sense; it is a question of human slaughter. *Bozrah* has been identified with Buseirah, some 28 m. to the SE of the Dead Sea. **8—17.** The two expressions (61:2; 63:4) 'day of ven- **l** geance' and 'year of recompense' are used here of the adversaries of the Israelites. The metaphor of some terrible fire in **9, 10,** and the images from wild life in **11** (cf 13:21, 22; 14:23) are not mutually exclusive; they are analogous images used to describe the transformation of the land into a wasteland or a desert. It is the end of any kind of social life. A 'night hag' (**14**), in the MT, corresponds to Lilith, a feminine demon in Babylonian mythology. Doubtless there will be a kind of weird animal life in this wasteland, and the prophet refers the reader to 'the book of the Lord' (**16**). This might be (as some authors say) the actual text we are dealing with; but the reference seems to be to something already in existence, perhaps the similar passage in 13:9—22. The terms of v **17** are those used when dealing with the division of an inheritance or of property. **35:1—10.** The **m** weird vision in ch 34 is followed by the contrasting picture of the liberation or redemption of Israel. **1, 2** correspond to 34: 9—11. For the three geographical terms, cf 33:9; the whole country is deemed worthy of a great theophany. Men also should prepare for the solemn moment of vengeance and recompense (34:8). **5—7,** written in a style which often recurs in chh 40—55, should be taken in a symbolic sense, although in Mt 11:5 the text is quoted in a literal sense. It is inconceivable that in such a time of joy and well-being there should be any who are sick (33:24), or even that nature should be unfavourable. The sacred character of Jerusalem is represented by a street which is free from every kind of contamination (**8**). The allusion to the return from the exile is clear in the last v; the authenticity of it in this place is doubtful. It recurs in 51:11, and there is a parallel in other texts for each term in the expression.

36:1—39:8 Historical Appendix—The account is **475a** taken from 2 (4) Kgs 18:13—20:19; see the commentary on this passage, § 294. The differences are very slight; only in ch 38 (= 2 (4) Kgs 20:1—11) does there appear to be any notable difference; the chief one is the omission

5a of 38:9—20 in Kgs. In Isaiah there is no account of the important information given in 2 (4) Kgs 18:13—16. The brief section 38:9—20 contains the canticle of Hezekiah, a lamentation of great antiquity adapted to express the similar sentiments of this pious king. Probably this brief addition was the work of the editor.

b **38:9—20 The Canticle of Hezekiah**—The text here is corrupt. The translation is often based on conjecture and is not always the only possible interpretation. As in some of the Psalms, a historical title is given: (cf Ps 18 (17); 34 (33); 56 (55) etc). 'A writing' is a good translation of the Heb. *miktāb*, but this is generally considered to be a corruption of *miktām* (Ps 16 (15):1; 56 (55):1; 58 (57):1 etc), the meaning of which is much more doubtful.

c **10—15.** This section has the characteristics of a lamentation. Some years before 701, when his illness probably occurred, Hezekiah would be less than 40 years of age; according to Ps 90 (89):10 he was in middle age. If he died, then he would have had to spend the other half of his life in Sheol, a place of sadness (5:14). 'See the Lord' (**11**) i.e. to share in the liturgical life of the Temple (1:12). The metaphor of the tent which is removed is much clearer than the piece of cloth, but the application is clear. The contrast between the two images is a beautiful one (the Lord = Lion; Hezekiah = a bird which laments). **15.** 'My sleep has fled' is a common translation but the RSV footnote gives a more literal rendering of the Heb. 'I will walk

d slowly all my years'. **16—20.** The main idea is thanksgiving for the miracle, but the text is practically incomprehensible, especially at the beginning. If in **16** we adopt a correction which is not too bold we might translate: '*Lord, my heart hopes in Thee, my spirit revives*', etc, which appears to be more suitable as a transition from lamentation to thanksgiving. Following out a line of thought which is fairly frequent (Ps 6·6; 30 (29):10; 88 (87):5, 12; 115 (113):17), the Canticle states that by snatching Hezekiah from death, God has assured for himself a worship that a dead man would not have been able to give him. The end of **18** contains the proposal so often expressed in Psalms of a similar nature (Ps 22 (21):31, 32; 48 (47):13—15; 68 (67):4, etc). **20.** Seems to be a liturgical addition, since the canticle would be of more practical use for collective prayer.

PART 2 THE BOOK OF CONSOLATION, 40—55

See introduction, 460*d*, 461*d*, 462*f*.

76a **40:1—41:29 Promises of liberation**—These alternate with the exaltation of the greatness of God (40:12—26), condemnation of idolatry (41:21—24), a description of the works of Cyrus (41:1—5, 25—29) and other less prominent themes. They are addressed to the exiles in Mesopotamia.

b **40:1—11. The joyful announcement.** The usual sense of the word translated 'warfare' is, in Heb., *army*; in fact, rather than a state of warfare, the allusion is to a state of anguish and suffering (Jb 7:1; 10:17; 17:14), a consequence of 'iniquity' (for the connection between the two thoughts cf 38:17; Jn 9:2). The chastisement is called 'double', by hyperbole. The order is given (**3—5**) by an angel of the heavenly court (Zech 1:9—14). He calls for an ideal road instead of the fearsome desert which separates Mesopotamia from Palestine. In the gospel the v is used in a moral sense (Mt 3:3; Jn 1:23). The return

c is like a new exodus; the 'glory of the Lord' will accompany the exiles (Ex 13:21, 22; 14:19, 20). After the dialogue

between the angel and the prophet (cf 6:8), there comes a **476c** statement which is aimed at removing the scepticism caused by the power of the Babylonians: no one can put any obstacle in the way of a divine decree, since man's power is limited ('grass that withers', 'flowers that fade'). Probably v 7 is a gloss (it is lacking in the LXX; cf 1 Pt 1:24—25). The scene now changes with a delightful flight of poetic fancy. The joyful tidings are given in Jerusalem by a woman—that would be the more natural translation; others think of some official spokesman. The caravan of exiles is guided by God, described, as so often in other places, as an attentive shepherd. (Jer 23:3; Ezek 34: 11—22; Jn 10:1—16). The 'reward' or the 'recompense' are these same returning exiles, who are always God's property (Ex 19:6) but are now booty snatched from the Babylonians and therefore they belong to the successful warrior (**10**). **12—26. Greatness of God.** The hymn **d** begins with a description of creation. God, like a workman, manipulates with the greatest of ease the various parts of the universe. Instead of 'measure' (**12**) the text has *third of a measure*, but without specifying the unit of measurement. For **13** cf Rm 11:34; 1 Cor 2:16. In addition to God's omnipotence, his omniscience is brought out too. In **15—17, 21—23**, which are obviously hyperbole, the various images (2:13) quite happily convey the idea of the immense distance between God and creatures. Even more extraordinary is the comparison with the nothingness of idols (**19, 20**) which here—as elsewhere—are regarded simply as fetishes, having no value at all, and even materially useless, (rotten wood). The 'circle of the **e** earth' (**22**) is the highest section of the heavens, or the firmament; this is an expression similar to the one in Jb 22:14. The title 'the Holy One' is also characteristic of this part of the book. The emphasis on the minor role of the stars (servants ready to execute every command, **26**; cf Bar 3:33—35) is a polemic against the astral religion of the Babylonians. **27—31. Trust in God.** The sense of **f** abandonment and pessimism of the exiles is taken seriously (41:10—16; 43:1—8). They believed that they had been abandoned by God; consolation is held out to them in an urgent reminder of God's omnipotence and goodness; their doubts and fears are shown to be groundless—strength comes from trust in God. In **31** there is reference to a popular legend of the powers of the eagle to renew its own strength. He who believes and hopes in God will not succumb to spiritual weariness. **41:1—5. Cyrus. g** The person the text deals with is never named. Some have identified him with Abraham, but the text undoubtedly suggests a reference to the Persian king who had already annexed Media and perhaps had already defeated (in 546) Croesus of Sardis. By a literary artifice frequently used in these chh, the 'coastlands' (the islands and the coastal regions of the Mediterranean) are called to attend a legal hearing. Cyrus had already begun his victorious march from the E (Persia). He acts, unwittingly, as a 'servant' (45:3, 4; Jer 27:6) or instrument of God (10:5). **4.** Affirms the eternity of God; this phrase, or one like it (43:10; 44:6; 48:12) is frequently used; it is the equivalent of 'I am the Alpha and the Omega' found in Apoc. In **6, 7** (certainly at least in 7) there is the sarcastic description of the making of an idol; the vv are out of context and should be read after 40:19. **8—20. Israel h and the pagan nations. 8—10.** Are connected with 40: 27—31. To strengthen their trust, the prophet puts them in mind of the main favours which God had given them, their choice as a people, his friendship with their founder, continual protection. There is a hint here of Abraham's migration (Gn 12:1ff); the name 'servant' is equivalent to *chosen, friend*. But all this has not saved

476h Israel from becoming weak and despised as a *worm* (14). Now, in her favour, God intervenes, he who succours the needy (17); he comes as the 'redeemer' (Heb: *gō'ēl* = a close kinsman to whom belongs the right and duty of revenge and ransom). God himself will rout their adversaries, and Israel will become like a steam roller or a 'threshing sledge'; cf 28:27. In **17—20** appears a theme which is quite frequent: the Syro-Arabian desert will become a region easy to cross and a place most pleasant (abundant waters, cool shade, 30:25; 55:13). So many signs of protection cannot leave the pagans indifferent. The identification of the trees (**19**) is not certain. **21—29.**

i God, idols and Cyrus. The uncompromising denial (**21—24**) of any kind of power to idols (40:18—20) is linked with a reference to the prophetic charism. This is a theme which will often recur, particularly in ch 48. God had predicted events which had already been realized (the 'former things'); this is a guarantee for the recent predictions of the future (the 'things to come'); these latter include Israel's restoration which was still in doubt; and among the former is the coming of Cyrus (**26**), about which the idols had said nothing. We do not know the prophet who had prophesied similar events in Jerusalem (**27**). The advance from the N (**25**), in no way contradicts v 2; whoever came from Persia-Media would reach Palestine always from the N, to avoid crossing the desert.

j 42:1—7 The Servant of Yahweh—This is the first of the four sections (49:1—6; 50:4—9; 52:1—53:12). It is not easy, (but neither is it necessary), to find a connection here with the context; perhaps this passage was inserted to contrast the two quite different 'servants' (41:8). There are certainly traces in the Targum of a messianic interpretation of this passage; in Christian tradition, it already appears in Mt 12:17—21. God's pleasure in the 'servant' is clearly an indication that the title is in no way degrading. On the possession of the **k** spirit of Yahweh cf 11:2. 'Justice' here corresponds in practice to 'truth' or even to 'true religion'. In **2** the Servant is shown to possess those characteristics which belong to the prophets; he is guileless but firm, patient with that forbearance which seeks the best in human nature (he knows how to obtain results even from 'the bruised reed' and 'the dimly burning wick'). His mission involves difficulties and sorrows (**4**); it will succeed because it corresponds to the innermost desire of God and he steers its course. The purpose of this mission is a liberation, which could be identified with that which put an end to the exile (**7**; cf Ps 137 (136):3), but which could also have a purely moral character (cf 5:30; 9:2; 45:7; 58:8 etc). The second interpretation agrees much better with the title 'light to the nations'. This, like the title 'covenant to the people', seems to suggest a more general meaning; if it refers to an individual, he will be the instrument whereby new relationships are set up between God and man.

l 8—12 The idols and the Almighty—The theme of 41:29 is continued in vv **8, 9**, with the appeal to prophecy (cf 41:22). The call to a hymn of praise in **10—12** can be taken as the conclusion of a section; cf 44:23; 49:13; 55:12, 13. The 'new song' (Ps 33 (32):3; 40 (39):4; Apoc 14:3) emphasizes the extraordinary quality of the event, that is, the liberation from exile. All should participate in this praise, even nature (the sea and the desert). Since the desert had to be crossed, then its inhabitants, who were more or less nomads, must also share in the thanksgiving. For 'Sela' cf 16:1; for 'Kedar' cf 21:16.

477a 42:13—44:23 The Return—This is not a historical account of the event. It is represented as imminent and even as already having happened (43:1—8; 44:1—5). At **47** the same time the divine omnipotence is exalted, calling to mind the various attributes and blessings of God or making the usual polemic against the idolaters (42:13—17; 43:9—13; 44:6—20); there is also the story of the relationships between God and Israel (42:18—25; 43:14—28; 44:21—23).

13—17 The intervention of God—A series of anthro- **b** pomorphisms and vigorous images contrasts the imminent action of the powerful warrior (52:10; 59:16,17; 63:1—6) with his apparent indifference in the past (57:11). The theophany is described with the usual references to the inanimate world; once more there is a repetition of the theme of 41:18, 19. The idolaters will know their shame. The blind are mentioned, **16**, perhaps just to symbolize Israel's inability to bring about the return solely through her own power; there is not necessarily a reference here to moral blindness. The contrast between darkness and light refers to the miracle of the pillar of fire (Ex 13:21). **18—25. The blind and the deaf.** There is no doubt **c** that this section is dealing with moral blindness. The fact that the nation is a 'servant' (41:8) increases its responsibility. It is a very serious matter for a 'messenger' (= apostle) among the gentiles to be deaf. This is the only place where such characteristics are attributed to Israel. With a small correction we could translate '*deaf as he to whom I send messengers*'; in other words, and as happens not infrequently, there is a reproof here directed towards those who treat the prophets shamefully. Even the translation 'my dedicated one' is doubtful because of the uncertainty of the Heb. The 'law', **21**, has a generic meaning here; it is the whole of revelation as seen in the light of the covenant on Sinai. The present condition of Israel is not a denial of the very special relationship this latter involves, but rather the consequences of the people's guilt. Their slavery is not so much the effect of the power of Babylon as the result of the divine abhorrence of their deeds. The prophet puts himself on the same level as the others: 'we have sinned'; but the verb is usually taken in the third person.

43:1—8. The Return of Israel. In **8** the transgressions **d** of the people are brought to mind, and some commentators would link this v with what follows; but the whole section is the exaltation of God who has fulfilled, or is about to fulfil (return of the Diaspora, **5, 6**) his designs for those who belong to him (**7**). Some of the many attributes of God appear also elsewhere (1:4); but it would be difficult to find a more emphatic statement of God's love for Israel than we have here. He is Israel's creator, redeemer and saviour (all these terms recur in these chh). The substitution of other people for Israel in captivity is proof of God's absolute dominion over all peoples. For Egypt and Ethiopia cf 18:1; Seba (Gn 10:7) must be in the present Sudan. If the references to these places are to be taken literally, then the prophecy would have been realized at the time of Cambyses (in 525) and not Cyrus. **9—13. e God and idols.** The style here is that of a judicial debate (41:1, 21); God's omnipotence is contrasted with the impotence of the idols. In so far as the Israelites are the guardians of the prophecies (41, 26) they are God's 'witnesses'. The insistence on the concept of 'salvation' is most noticeable, and is a leit-motif of the second part of the book. In the first place this indicates the liberation and the return to Jerusalem, or a liberation which has already taken place; often, however, it includes a reference which is messianic and eschatological. **14—28. f God and Israel.** This is a story of love and ingratitude. To the various attributes which have already been encountered, there is now added the notion of the 'King'

477f of Israel (33:22). On behalf of his people, God has brought low Babylon and the Chaldeans (13:19). The translation of **14** is conjectural; literally it would read: '. . . and I will bring down the fugitives, all of them, and the Chaldeans in the ships of their joy'. The memory of the passage through the Red Sea (Ex 14:21, 22) will be overshadowed (Jer 23:7, 8) by the forthcoming miraculous events. The
g transformation of the desert (40:3; 41:18, 19) will be beneficial even to the wild beasts who inhabit this region (13:21, 22). All of this is due to the divine initiative, since Israel's conduct was unworthy; even in her liturgical life (1:11—15) Israel has not been punctilious. Her sin, generously pardoned, is long-standing and far reaching (**27**): its consequences were slaughter and the shame of exile. The 'first father' is Jacob (Gn 27:36) rather than Abraham; the mediators are the prophets, and perhaps not always those who were false (Nm 20:12).

h **44:1—5 The future of Israel.** God does not repudiate the choice of his servant (41:8). He means to repeat the miracle wrought in the time of the patriarchs, by increasing to an extraordinary degree the number of his people both by natural means ('my blessing on your offspring') and through the conversion of the pagans (**5**). This must be the meaning of the transformation and fertility of the desert **3f**; there is no suggestion in the context of a material return from exile. In v **2** Jeshurun (= 'upright just', perhaps in contrast to *Jacob* = 'supplanter' Gn 25:26) is the name for Israel as in Dt 32:15; 33:5, 26. The writing upon the hand, **5**, is a reference to tatooing or the property-
i mark on a slave (Gal 6:17). **6—20. God and the idols.** This is the longest section of anti idol polemic in the book (40:18—20; 41:6, 7; 43:9—13). As in other places, the argument is not a reasoned piece of philosophic or theological writing; it is a fierce satire, which sees the idols as fetishes, and uses an argument *ad hominem* which no doubt had some factual foundation but is primarily intended to persuade. The aim of the polemic is not proselytism, but is an attempt to dissuade the deported Israelites from being dazzled by the exotic religion of the Babylonians.

The beginning of the section repeats the themes which have already occurred (41:4, 27; 43:10, 15). For the metaphor of the 'Rock' cf 17:10; 26:4. The idolaters, for the very reason that they have nothing to witness about, are called in 'witness' (**9**) to contrast them with the
j 'witness' given by the works of the true God. The description of the individual actions (**12—14**), from the felling of the trees to the erection of the statue, is aimed above all at emphasizing the useless labours of the skilled artisan, who therefore stands condemned of foolishness (**15—17**). All he does, in fact, is to put on the same level the cooking of a meal and a religious act (the wood he uses is the same material for both). An even more telling sarcasm is seen in Wis 13:1 where the material for the idols is a cast-off piece from the workman's shed (cf v **19**). At the end of the section however, idolatry is said to be the consequence of intellectual perversion (Rm 1:25). For the image of the
k 'ashes' cf Prv 15:14. **21—23.** Israel is addressed with a reminder of the divine protection, vastly different from that which the useless idols can give. 'These things' (unless this small section comes from another context) refer to vv 9—20; there must have been no lack of apostasy in Mesopotamia due to material motives or through excessive esteem of the religion of their masters. The pardon they have received (1:18) is insisted upon as a major proof of divine love. In return for his divine initiative God wishes from them an act of good will (return to me; cf Lam 5:21). Compare v 23 with 42:10—12.
l **44:24—45:25 The mission of Cyrus**—The Persian

king is spoken of especially in 44:24—45:8, but even in **477l** the other vv his action is always to some degree envisaged; as indeed in every ch up to 48.

44:24—45:8. Cyrus. God reveals himself as creator, **m** and he also reveals himself through the prophets. The idols can give us insight into the future; but here it is also stated, with reference to the historical events, that God can quite easily bring to nought the false claims of those who practice divination, so widespread in Babylon. But if God has revealed something it is certain to happen, even were it to demand a miracle on the grand scale (the drying up of all the rivers). Thus, Jerusalem will rise through the action of Cyrus, because Yahweh has so decreed it. In actual fact, the Persian king through his decree (2 Chr 36:23), at least indirectly, laid the foundations for the restoration of the city and of Israel. The title of 'Shepherd', besides applying to God, is often applied to the Messiah and to the leaders of Israel (Ezek 34:2ff). Amongst the pagans, only Cyrus receives this title; in Jer 27:6 God calls Nebuchadnezzar 'my servant'. If these chh are dated c. 540, it is not strange to find the name *Cyrus*; but it *would* be curious to find it, if the text were composed two centuries before this. Cyrus' advance is guided and facilitated by God; its outcome, on which the fate of Israel depended, would in the long-run result in a proof of God's almighty power (**45:1—7**). For the contrast between light and darkness cf 5:20, 30; 9:2; 42:16. In **8** there is a poetic expression of the 'salvation' that was on the way for Israel. It is easy to discern here a messianic content in the future 'righteousness' (9:7; 11:5), without having to substitute concrete terms for an abstract notion as the Vg does in this context. **9—25. God, Israel, the nations. n 9—13.** Presuppose not only doubt and scepticism in Israel, but also a negative reaction to the revelation that the restoration would be particularly attributed to the work of a pagan, and not a co-religionist. In the parable of the potter, and the relationships between father and son, God condemns such an attitude as presumptuous; there is an implicit affirmation of the divine paternity (1:2, 4; 63:16). The metaphor of **o** the potter must be understood within the limitations of its context (cf 29:16). God in his omnipotence is free in what he does; if he has chosen to effect something through Cyrus, then he will do so. The Israelites, as was prescribed for Heb. slaves (Ex 21:2—6, Dt 15:1, 12), will be freed without any ransom. This is not in contradiction to 43:3; for it was indeed true that the Israelites did not have to hand over those countries to the Persians as a price for their freedom. These same peoples are shown as being the 'property' of Israel in the future (**14**). What we are dealing with here is an illustrative example; the context presumes the unification, and not necessarily by force, of Israel with all the nations. It is the vision of 2:2—4 expressed in other terms (cf 49:7; 60:14; 61:5). In **p 15** the prophet himself speaks; he recognizes the inscrutable mystery of God's designs (Rm 11:33). It is monotheism which distinguishes Israel from the other nations, and because of this, her condition is the very opposite of the idolaters. In **18—22** the ideas which have already been put forward are now grouped together: God is creator, redeemer (saviour), the author of prophecies which are true, the one God as opposed to the nothingness of the idols. The words 'Seek me in chaos' recall 15 and 18; Israel did not have to grope her way blindly in an uncharted land (in Heb., in both cases the word is *tōhû*; cf Gn 1:2).

477p On the other hand, the fact that God can be easily found in no way contradicts his inaccessibility as 15 reveals it. In **23—25** we have one of the finest statements of the universality of the future religion. St Paul quotes it twice, using the essential of its message (Rm 14:11; Phil 2:10, 11). On the efficacy of the word of God cf 55:11.

478a **46:1—48:22 The fall of Babylon: old and new prophecies**—The first theme occupies the whole of ch 47, but is also referred to in chh 46 and 48; the second theme prevails in ch 48. Other themes, treated more or less fully, are those of idolatry, Cyrus' victories, the unworthiness of Israel.

b **46:1—7.** There is no comparison between the idols, which are a heavy load for the beasts of burden, and God who has carried the Israelites from the time of the Patriarchs onwards like a loving father who bears his child on his shoulders. There is a further distinction: God saves Israel, the idols are only saved thanks to the beasts. 'Bel' stands for Baal-Marduk or simply Marduk, the national god of the Babylonians; 'Nebo' (Accadian *Nabu*), worshipped in particular by the people of Borsippa, was the god of writing and the divine interpreter. Here is described what normally happens when a city is wiped out; there is no contradiction of the historical event, according to which Cyrus appears very respectful of the Babylonian religion. For **6, 7** cf 40:18—20; 44:9—20. It is ridiculous to hope for **c** salvation from the idols. **8—13.** The apostrophe is particularly aimed at the apostates among the Israelites. They are reminded of the fundamental truths: the unique character of their God, the author of prophecies which were infallibly fulfilled (42:9; 44:7). The 'bird of prey' is Cyrus (45:1); the metaphor emphasizes the swiftness of Cyrus' action and the wealth of the conquered countries (45:3). On the twofold notion deliverance-salvation cf 45:8; the Heb. text has the same term (*justice*). This salvation is imminent even though they are 'far from *justice*' (**12**, cf v 8).

d **47:1—15 The end of Babylon.** Both by its theme and by the lyrical quality of the writing this ch puts us in mind of the similar prophecy in chh 13 and 14. The great city where the Chaldean dynasty then flourished (13:19) is portrayed as an elegant queen who would be clothed like a slave and have to do manual labour ('take the millstones and grind'), strip off her robe in order to cross the rivers or canals (the beginning of **3** is a gloss). The expression 'virgin daughter' refers to the people (23:12; 37:22), but it is chosen here because it is poetically more powerful; it evokes sympathy or disdain, according to the feelings of the hearer. Her fate is decreed by 'the Holy One of Israel' (1:4). The idea of slavery is expressed all the more strongly by contrast with the descriptions of her past, 'tender and delicate, **e** mistress of kingdoms'. The relationships between God, Israel and Babylon are similar to those forecast more than a century before between the two first and Assyria (10:5ff). Now will come the reckoning because of the cruel abuse of power and because of a pride that knew no bounds. The pitiable condition of the sterile woman or the widow is often emphasized in the OT. On magic arts and divination cf 44:25; the treatment here is ironical (**12, 15**). For the futility of the counsels, cf 19:11—13. In **13** astrology, which was widespread, comes in for its share of irony, but not astronomy which had made considerable progress in Babylon. The fire (**14**) does not necessarily indicate a conflagration; it is the symbol of a complete destruction which for Babylon would only be verified much later, but could be said to have started with Cyrus' occupation. In **15** a quite small **478** correction would give the better translation *your sorcerers* instead of 'who have trafficked with you'.

48:1—11. Israel's unworthiness. A series of **f** comparisons brings out the favours Israel has received and her own unworthiness. To be called Israelites, to swear by the name of Yahweh, to worship the true God—such are the signs of special favour (Rm 9:4, 5); but on the peoples' side, there is nothing but unfaithfulness and injustice. 'Judah' is the founder of the tribe which was to have the major role (Gn 49:8—12), at least after the dispersion of the N kingdom. *Waters* (= 'loins' in the translation, **1**) is used euphemistically. Pride and false confidence in Jerusalem (**2**) are also portrayed in Jer 7:4, but even more strongly than here. For the metaphor 'iron sinew', 'brass' cf Ex 32:9; Dt 9:6; Ezek 3:7—9; Jer 3:3; Ac 7:5. Israel is accused of disloyalty (1:21—23) from the outset. The author shares the opinion of Ezek 16:4—19; 20:5—13 with regard to Israel's religious sense in the old days—unlike Jer 2:2. If God pardons Israel and bestows fresh favour upon her, then it will be through his mercy, and also to put a stop to any false conclusions the pagans might draw about his power (**11**; 52:5; Jer 14:21). The ancient and recent prophecies (41:22, 23) emphasize God's omniscience. No doubt they refer to precise happenings, but it is **g** only possible to indicate these conjecturally; whilst the ancient prophecies could include all previous revelation, particularly those things which referred to the end of the two kingdoms, the more recent prophecies would undoubtedly take in Cyrus' coming, the fall of Babylon and the return of the exiles. **12—22. Cyrus h and the liberation of the Israelites.** In this new appeal, God, wishing to inspire confidence, does not speak to the stiff-necked people, but rather to those who were given his promises, his chosen ones (41:9; 43:1). For **12, 13** cf 41:4; 44:6; 45:12. The occupation of Babylon will come about through the action of Cyrus (44:28; 45:1ff), object of the divine predilection. Many would read *my beloved* instead of 'the Lord loves him'. The envoy who appears together with 'his Spirit' is probably the Servant of Yahweh (42:1); perhaps this **v** is taken from another context. Others, correcting the text or giving a particular sense to *rûah* (= spirit), would say that this refers to Cyrus. A few of the Fathers, making use of an exegesis now no longer followed, see in this text an allusion to the revelation of the Trinity (the envoy = the one 'sent', = the Son of God). **17.** To the titles which have already appeared (41:14) is added that of 'master' or 'guide' (30:20, 21). The conditional **i** promises given in **18, 19** are expressed in language taken from the accounts of the patriarchs (Gn 22:17; 32:13). The capture of Babylon is presumed to have happened already in **20, 21.** The transformation of the desert (41:18; 43:19, 20) follows upon the order to depart (52:11, 12; 55:12, 13). Many continue the description of the return, reading here the section 49:9*b*—13. **22.** Comes from 57:21; it was perhaps inserted here to mark a threefold division (9 × 3): 40—48; 49—57; 58—66.

49:1—53:12 The Servant of Yahweh: The Liber- 479a ation—The first theme appears in 49:1—6; 50:4—9; 52:13—53:12. The second occurs much more often, and can have various shades of meaning. Sometimes it is referring to the condition of the exiles (49:24—26; 50:1—3, 10—11; 51:1—16; 52:3—12), sometimes it looks forward to life in the new Jerusalem (49:7—23; 51:17—23; 52:1—2).

49:1—6 The Servant of Yahweh—This is the second **b**

79b (42:1—7) of the four songs. Here the Servant is depicted with stress on the divine predilection, which makes his prophetic or missionary task efficacious (his tongue is 'a sharp sword, a polished arrow'). It is a task which will encounter obstacles and suffering (4). But a political mission can be inferred from the song (that of organizing the restoration of Israel), and also the identification of the Servant with the people ('my Servant, Israel' 3). Many would reject the latter inference, taking 'Israel' to be a gloss. It is much better to interpret 'Israel' here in the limited sense of the 'remnant', the ideal Israel—a limitation imposed by 5.

c In 5, 6 it is possible to read a reference to the return from exile, and therefore to the action of Cyrus; or to compare Cyrus with the Servant; but a moral return is also feasible, a conversion of Israel to God. In this latter hypothesis, the Servant would be proclaiming a message on the necessity of conversion, such as often appears in Jer; he would resemble Jeremiah in the difficulties he encounters, as well. Some spiritual mission of this kind to Israel seems to be required by the fact that this same *Servant* is also 'a light to the **d** nations' (42:6). **7—13. Israel in her native land.** It is still disputed whether or not 7—9a are to be reckoned as part of the song. If they are, the political side of the Servant's activity is being stressed; if (as we think) they are not, then the passage refers to Cyrus: he sets free a despised and apparently rejected people who will become an object of great wonder (7; cf 45:14, 15; 49:23). For the beginning of 8 cf 61:2. The distich 'I have kept.... to the people' is probably taken from 42:6. In 9b—12 the return is pictured, in images which we have seen before (40:3, 4; 41:18; 43:19, 20); but the emphasis leads us to a glimpse of a distant messianic—eschatological future. Indeed, v 12 includes a return from all the diaspora, and not merely from **e** Babylonia. *Syene* = Assuan, near the first cataract of the Nile; the Heb. *sinim* was often taken to mean *Chinese*, with 'missionary' implications. For 13 cf **f** 42:10; 44:23. **14—21.** The pessimism of the exiles (40:27) was shared by those who stayed behind in Jerusalem (14). We see God reassuring them in two very beautiful images: mother-love (Hos 11:1; Jer 31:9), and that of memory kept alive through a written symbol (44:5; Ex 13:9; Gal 6:17; Apoc 7:3, 4; 13:16, 17). Restoration, therefore, is so certain that it is quite legitimate to think of the re-building as having taken place already (17). The returned exiles are compared to a precious ornament (3:16—24; 11:5; Jer 2:32). It will not be a mere restoration, but something quite new, far better than the past; it is the vision of 60:1ff. For the idea of barrenness cf 47:9; its application to the exile is possibly due to a gloss ('exiled and put away' is **g** omitted in LXX). **22—26.** At a signal from God (5:26; 11:12; 13:2; 18:3) the nations will compete in supporting the return with the greatest honours (45:14; 60:4, 14; 66:12). Through a series of hyperboles he foretells a complete transformation for Jerusalem, the converse of what is in store for Babylon (47:1—5). Babylon was still very powerful; few believed that rescue was possible (24). But God the Saviour (43:3) can and will do it. The hyperboles 'eating their own flesh' and 'being drunk with their own blood' (cf 9:20, 21; 19:2, 3) probably refer to intestine struggles; the ease with which Cyrus occupied Babylonia certainly revealed an absence of harmony and a spreading anarchy.

h 50:1—3 Israel has not been rejected—God bitterly observes that pessimism still persists; this was the attitude with which they listened to the proclamation of

rescue (2). God, wishing to guarantee the event, appeals **479h** to his own omnipotence. The drying-up of the sea (42:15) and perhaps the darkened sky, hark back to the exodus (Ex 14:21, 24). The opening image is full of meaning: the wife put away and the children sold, in accordance with Heb. Law (Dt 24:1—4; Ex 21:2—7). There has been a separation, but God has had no part in it. He has not drawn up a 'bill of divorce' or handed his own children over to a creditor. Nevertheless, the Exile did involve the breaking of a contract, not by God's choice, but because of the people's faults, which they must expiate; the liberation will restore the earlier state of affairs. It is one of the most beautiful passages on the love of God for his people (49:15; 54:5—10); for an even more tender expression cf Jer 2:2.

4—9 The Servant of Yahweh—This has affinities **480a** with the second song (49:1—6): it is the Servant who is speaking, of his preaching mission and its difficulties, which here include personal violence (Mt 26:67; 27:30; Jn 18:22). All is overcome by meekness, and by a deep faith in God, his protector. This prepares us for the fourth song (52:13—53:12), which is far more dramatic. The mission will be conducted especially among the wretched ('him that is weary'; cf 42:3). He then has recourse to a hypothetical argument in forensic language (41:1). For the last phrase, pointing to the failure of his opponents, cf 51:6; Jb 4:19; 13:28.

10—11. These vv do not form part of the song, but **b** are a kind of comment, inviting the oppressed to listen to the Servant's voice, and threatening the opponents with the torments they deserve. On these latter will fall the evil they themselves have devised (Ps 7:16; 57 (56):7). The *fire* does not imply the fire of Hell; like 'brands', it means something harmful, such as insult or persecution.

51:1—16 God will bring about salvation—The **c** apostrophe is addressed to the sounder part of the people, to the authentic descendants of Abraham (Rm 4:12) who is metaphorically called 'rock' (*Sara* = 'quarry'). St Paul, too, insists on the uniqueness of the chosen pair (Rm 4:19). The 'garden of the Lord' and 'Eden' (cf Ezek 28:13; 31:8) are a new element in descriptions of the return; elsewhere a transformation of nature is referred to, but with no reference to Gn 2:8—15. 'Law' and 'justice' (4) indicate true religion (42:6; **d** 49:6). In 5 the meaning of 'deliverance' (Heb. *justice*) and of 'salvation' depends on the context: if the apostrophe is addressed to everyone, the two words have an eschatological sense; otherwise, they have the sense of liberation from exile. For 6—8, cf Mt 24:35; for v 8 cf also 50:9. **9—11.** This vigorous **e** apostrophe is repeated almost word for word in v 17 and in 52:1. The prophet looks for the intervention of God's omnipotence (his 'arm'—a common anthropomorphism). The miracle recounted in Ex 14:21, 22 will have to be repeated, though in different circumstances. Another reference, probably, to the Red Sea crossing is the victory over 'Rahab' (30:7) and the 'Dragon' (27:1): mythological names which, taken by themselves, would tend to remind us of the beginnings of the world. **11.** Is a gloss taken from 35:9, occasioned by the word 'the redeemed'. **12—16.** Again the note of pessimism and **f** lack of trust. With emphasis (48:12, 15) God is presented as the Consoler (40:1) and as omnipotent (42:5; 44:24). Fear is no longer justified, because to all intents and purposes the Babylonians are already conquered. The **g** Pit (14) is the realm of the dead (5:14). After such a strong emphasis, the simple assurance that the prisoner will not die or starve comes as a surprise. Perhaps the

480g text has suffered alterations. The beginning of **16** takes for granted that the people as a whole is carrying out a prophetic mission (Jer 1:9); the following phrase recalls 49:2; and finally he speaks of the creation, and of a fresh election of Israel. Unless we are dealing with an amalgam of glosses from a variety of texts, the future mission of Israel among the nations (45:6) is connected with a new creation (65:17; 66:22), thus underlining the exceptional nature of the event.

h **51:17—52:2 The new Jerusalem**—The passage proceeds by way of contrasts. It describes the past and present humiliations with realism; they are inflicted by the divine wrath (29:10; Jer 25:15—26), in order to make the future glory more splendid. The image of widowhood (49:20, 21) is fully developed, with phrases which occur frequently in Lam (1:2, 5, 9; 2:11, 19—21, etc). The other side of the picture is drawn, briefly in the opening apostrophe, and then in the complete change of situation——the woman who was once oppressed now has her glory restored, and rejoices in the humiliation of her oppressors. For **23** cf 49:26; Jos 10:24; 1 (3) Kgs 5:3 (17); Ps 110 (109):1 etc. The transformation is described in **52:1—2** (it is the antithesis of 47:1—5). In the holy city (48:2) there will be no room for anything in any way evil or impure (35:8; Apoc 21:2); in particular there will be no place for the foreign oppressor, the 'uncircumcised and unclean' (Lam 1:10).

i **52:3—12 The liberation**—This will be accomplished free of charge (45:13) to the purchasers (50:1), who have become such by the will of God, and not by the usual means of acquiring rights over something. This does not mean that it was without good reason that Israel had been a 'slave' in Egypt and Mesopotamia: her faults had merited it. **7—10.** Repeat ideas expressed before (40:1, 3, 6; 44:23; 49:13; 51:9 etc). In this glorious return note the insistence upon peace and salvation as well as 'redemption'; these are themes which look upon the release from exile with a much deeper awareness of the 'history of salvation'. On **11, 12,** cf 48:20. It is the new exodus, under the guidance of God (40:11).

481a **52:13—53:12 The Servant of Yahweh**—This is the longest of the four songs (42:1—7); it is the most universal, richest in its teaching (the original idea of vicarious expiation stands out in this respect), but also the most difficult.

b **13—15.** It begins like the first song (42:1). Although it stresses sufferings more than the others (14; 53:2 etc) the song begins with a clear affirmation of triumph and exaltation; it explains later that such glory is only the result of suffering and violent death. In v 15 the LXX rendering 'they will be astonished at him' is generally preferred to the Heb., which is uncertain (= 'he will sprinkle'?). On the obsequious gesture ('shall shut their mouths') cf Jb 5:16; 21:5; this reaction is provoked by what is said in v 14 (Jb 2:7; 19:13—20) but also by the Servant's exaltation.

c **53:1—3.** The Servant's life is proof of God's omnipotence ('arm'; 51:9). The speakers ('we') are probably the kings and the nations of 52:15. **2.** Harks back to 11:1; 52:14. In spite of his seemingly total failure, he grows up under the complacent eye of God ('before him'). Mankind repudiates him as something contemptible; in his presence they make the symbolic gesture of screening

d their faces (Jb 30:1, 9—19; Ps 31 (30):11). **4—6.** The sin-suffering relationship, so often repeated in Jb, is taken for granted. Both sin and suffering are vividly presented (**6**), but equally emphatic is the stress on the diversity of persons it affects. This is where the

song's originality lies: the Servant suffers intensely, **481** but it is to expiate the sins of other men; his pain brings health and salvation to sinners. For the meaning attributed to **4** in Mt 8:17 cf comm. in loc. For the use made of **5** in the development of the concept of redemption, cf Rm 4:25; 2 Cor 5:21; Heb 9:28; 1 Pt 2:24; 3:18. **7—9.** The sufferings culminate in violent death. **7.** Is **e** an echo of Jer 11:19; many hold that the life of Jeremiah served as a model for this song; but the Servant's patient submission, and his loving acceptance of suffering, distinguish him from both Jeremiah and Job, who frequently break forth into lamentations and sometimes curses. **8.** Is particularly difficult. The opening can be *without* or *from* (instead of 'by'); the idea of unjust judgement makes better sense, however. Many substitute *fate* for 'generation', to bring out the general indifference, and adopt the Gr. reading (*stricken to death*) in place of the simple 'stricken'. In any case, **9** makes it obvious that death is involved. Dishonour is even attached to this burial (with the 'wicked', often identified with 'the rich man' in the OT). **10—12.** Such **f** apparently inexplicable sufferings were carrying out a divine plan: the death will constitute a sacrifice of expiation for sinners, and will be the beginning of an unprecedented glorification. It is hard to see the precise idea of resurrection in **10**: what is certainly there is the idea of success after death. **11.** Could yield the doctrine of resurrection: the two Qumran MSS confirm the LXX: *he shall see the light* (in place of the simple 'he shall see'). The blessings stemming from his expiatory death will become 'justification' in the theological sense: of many— that is, of all (Rm 5:15, 19). For the end of the song, cf Lk 23:34. The text does not equate the Servant with the great ones of this world; the Heb. can be translated: *Therefore will I assign him the many for his portion, and numberless shall be his spoil*—i.e. he shall have a universal authority, the nature of which is only to be understood in the light of later clarification (Mt 28:18; Eph 3:8; Col 2:15). It is the triumph of the 'redeemer' in the moral sense rather than in the sense of 41:14.

It would be ingenuous to underestimate the difficulties **g** raised by these **four songs**: see § 461*l—p*. But there is no doubt at all about the **theological importance of their message.** The Servant is chosen by God for the mission of establishing justice on earth, not only for Israel but for the world. He performs this task with humility and gentleness, but in spite of this he meets with neglect and opposition which develops into persecution. This is a situation familiar throughout Israel's history, in the experience of the prophets particularly. But the final song provides a dramatic and unexpected climax: the result of the Servant's sufferings is not failure but success, and **success not in spite of but precisely through his sufferings.** This is a brilliant break-through on the problem of undeserved suffering which had painfully preoccupied Israel for so many years. In arriving at his insight the author was no doubt influenced by reflection on the experience of the prophets, Jeremiah in particular, and of the nation itself. Jeremiah too suffered undeservedly in his task of interceding with God on behalf of the nation (Jer 15:11); and the sons of Abraham who were supposed to be a source of blessing for the world (Gn 12:3, 22:18) found themselves condemned to shameful exile. The genius of the author lies in combining the two horns of the dilemma this posed: it is *through* his sufferings that the Servant fulfils his task to mankind. **Suffering** therefore is not necessarily to be seen a a sign of the sinfulness of the sufferer; it **can be the**

81g burden of the sin of others, and the suffering itself be not a punishment but an atonement: 'he was bruised for our iniquities; upon him was the chastisement that made us whole'. Reflection on these passages was an important element in the early Church's understanding of the role of our Lord, and of his death as a vicarious expiation.

82a **54:1—55:13 The Future of Jerusalem**—This is the theme of ch 54, taken up again from a slightly different point of view in ch 55 as an exhortation to the returning exiles. Ch 54 has several points of similarity with ch 60 and other texts scattered here and there in chh 40—66. The vision of 2:2—4 is here realized. Passages like these could give rise to an intensely nationalistic interpretation but in fact they contain expressions which support a universalist, supra-national sense. The vision of a messianic eschatological era is put before us, following the re-birth of the chosen people. The description of this future age together with that of the last chh of Ezek, paved the way for the vision of the heavenly Jerusalem so dear to the Apoc and to the Fathers.

b **54:1—17.** The exile spelt a rupture between the people and God (50:1). The nation became like a childless woman or a widow (Bar 4:16). When the exile ended, the mother recovered not only her children of former days, but many more. Thus it was by God's gracious favour that the city was obliged to extend its area, as is implied in the image of the tent (2). The cities which had been destroyed will rise again and will expand to the four corners of the world (3). In practice, the future epoch will entail a return of the power of David; the ruler of the city will be, as it were, a new David (11:1). God pledges all his power to realize this prophecy ('God of hosts . . . of the whole earth'); he pledges himself also because of the ties which bind him to Israel (Maker, Holy One, Redeemer; 1:4; 41:14; 43:1), but specially as a 'husband' (50:1), a metaphor commonly used from the time of Hosea. On his

c abandonment of the people, cf 50:1; 60:15. Here there is a particularly delicate trait in the mention of the 'wife of youth' (Jer 2:2; 31:3). The future stability of this love and of the covenant is assured by the reference to a covenant which had never been revoked (that of Noah; Gn 9:9—16), and to the unchanging laws of nature. There is no explicit mention of the need for a new covenant, but this is pre-supposed; from the context it is evident that many of the elements present in the parallel prophecy of Jer 31:31—37 are present here also. Prosperity is explicitly promised (13) by the poetic description of a city built of precious stones (33:20; 52:1, 2; Apoc 21:14—21), which is to be understood as a symbol of the supreme good, and above all of a spiritual good ('taught by the Lord'). God will never again be angry with his people; though others will attack it in the future, they will do so in vain (15—17). God will protect his people jealously, because they are his 'servants'—a term which should probably be understood as 'descendants' (cf *heritage* of

d the *Servant of the Lord*, 53:10). **55:1—12. An exhortation.** Here, as so often in the prophetical writings, the vision of an ideal city, in which everything is presented as a gift from God, is followed by an insistent plea for the effort of man. It is a simple solution of the problem which arises from the irresistible power of God and human freedom. The ch begins with an invitation to take part in a symbolic, messianic banquet, which is prepared for those who hunger and thirst after righteousness (Mt 5:6;

e 26:26—28). Not only water, 1, (cf 35:6; Ps 36 (35):10; Jer 2:13), but also bread, wine and milk figure in similar symbolic descriptions (Gn 49:11, 12; Song 4:10). According to Jer, the early Church adopted, on the

basis of these texts, a custom of giving a little wine and **482e** milk in the rite of baptism. **3.** The future covenant is, as it were, the definitive realization of the covenant with David (Ps 89 (88):29—38). Then the entire people will enjoy the blessing promised to David (5), and will become a guide and a source of light to the pagan nations (4, cf 42:6; 49:6). **6—12.** The tasks involved are now en- **f** umerated: to forsake unrighteousness, to seek God, not to criticize the sometimes inscrutable ways of God (8, 9; Rm 11:33), not to place obstacles in the path of the irresistible divine Word (10, 11; Heb 4:12). The power of this word will soon be made manifest: it will bring about without delay the return, which is described with the usual images (12, 13; 41:18, 19; 43:19, 20; 44:23).

PART 3. CONSOLATION FOR THE SUFFERING ONES OF ZION, 56—66.

Its content is often similar to that of chh 40—55, but it **g** has several particular characteristics of its own. The return is already accomplished, for the geographical background is no longer Mesopotamia, but Palestine, and in particular Jerusalem. Among the messages of consolation there are exhortations to eradicate vices, but there are still more numerous promises of a future which will compare favourably with the present. After a pericope about foreigners and eunuchs (56:1—8), we come to extended passages in which the thought is coherent and developed: the apostasy of Israel (56:9—57:21), reproaches and promises (58:1—59:21), the new Jerusalem (60:1—63:6), a prayer of the community (63:7—64:12), and finally the intervention of God with promises and threats (65:1—66:24).

56:1—8 Foreigners and eunuchs—vv 1—2, which **483a** refer to the whole community, proclaim the proximity of 'salvation', and the happiness of the righteous man. It is an invitation to a real 'conversion', with the assurance of divine intervention (55:6, 7). The observance of the sabbath, on which there is such insistence in late texts, was dear to the heart of the earlier prophets also (1:13; Am 8:5; Hos 2:11).

The Jewish law distinguished between foreigners who **b** lived among the Israelites (*gērîm*) and others (*nokrîm*). The former had certain limited rights; an assimilation of the latter was foreseen only after some generations, and only for certain races (Dt 23:4—9). Here foreigners are without any distinction set on a par with Israelites, provided that certain basic duties are performed. Eunuchs were excluded from the community (Dt 23:2); they were despised (3 'dry tree'; cf Lk 23:31); here all such distinctions are eliminated (Wis 3:14).

The monument (5) is understood in a symbolic sense. **c** In 7, the foreigners share in liturgical life (1:11—15), and there is also a beautiful definition of the temple (Jer 7:11; Mt 21:13). **8.** Foretells a return of the Diaspora but presupposes that the return from Mesopotamia has already taken place: hence the passage refers to a date after 539, perhaps to the years immediately following.

56:9—57:2 The wicked shepherds—56:9—57:21 is **d** divided into reproaches (56:9—57:13) and promises (57:14—21). The former are addressed to the religious leaders (56:9—57:2) and then to all the people (57:3—13). The unusual apostrophe at the beginning foretells punishment, but perhaps it is not so much an invitation to an invading enemy (= 'beasts of the field') as a sad statement of fact: the people are unworthy, their shepherds still more; so that anyone could attack it, and with justice, granted the general sinfulness.

The metaphor of dogs (11) is suggested by the fact **e** that they are used to assist shepherds (Jb 30:1); there

483e is probably a reference to the failings of these dogs (their ineptitude, laziness, and greediness), and also to the contempt with which the ancient Israelites regarded these animals (Ps 22 (21):17; 59 (58):7; 1 Sm 17:43; 2 Sm 9:8; 16:9). For **12**, cf 5:11; Wis 2:6—9; it seems to be a fragment of a drinking song (cf 23:16). Amid so much negligence on the part of the shepherds, disorder reigns in the country, so much so that death is considered a happy release (**57:1, 2**). Here there is a glimpse of a new attitude to death and the after-life (cf Wis 3:1—13; 4:7, 11—20).

f 57:3—13 Apostasy—From the leaders, the prophet passes to all the people, presenting his accusations in the form of a trial (41:1). The stern apostrophe implies the condemnation of magic (2:6) and idolatrous practices: adultery and prostitution are understood in a religious sense. The irreverent gestures in **4** (cf Ps 35(34):21) are signs of haughtiness and arrogance (5:19; 28:9—15). On the idolatrous rites practised near sacred trees and groves cf 1:29; Hos 4:13; Jer 2:20; 3:6 etc. On child-sacrifice, cf Jer 2:23; 7:31; it was practised particularly in the Valley of Ben Hinnom or Gehenna (30:33). There seems to be a reference to a valley of this kind in the obscure **6**; men found their *portion* in such rites, while for a true Israelite his *portion* was God (Jer 10:16). **7.** Is a reproach against idolatrous cults on the high places, to which there are frequent references in the historical and prophetical books. Behind the door and on the jambs, passages of the Law were to be hung (Dt 6:6—8); Israel had placed there an idolatrous symbol. If we press the metaphor which is developed here, and accept the probably meaning of the last word of the v. (in Heb. *yād* = hand; but sometimes in a euphemistic sense), it is possible **g** to argue that it was a phallic symbol. Israel is described by hyperbole as practising its idolatry as low as Sheol, the underground home of the dead (unless the reference is to necromancy; 8:19; 19:3). There is no doubt whatever that **10** refers to the frequenting of idolatrous foreign sanctuaries (Jer 2:23—25); but it is uncertain whether **9** refers to the Ammonite deity *Molech* or to a king (Heb. *Melech*; cf 30:33). God has been patient and long-suffering; Israel has abused his patience and denied him reverence and honour; although it would have profited much by doing so (end of **13**). Instead, Israel has worn itself out in venerating idols, which certainly will not be able to help it now; the irony is biting, especially because the probable meaning of the term rendered as 'collection of idols' is *profits*.

h 14—21 Promises to the faithful—The resemblance between **14** and 40:3 is only partial; here the road starts from Jerusalem and is meant to make the return of the diaspora easy. In **15** attributes of God's majesty (6:1, 3; 40:26 etc) are combined with an equal insistence on the divine mercy and protection. The oppressed and the suffering (Mt 5:3, 10) are promised a new life (46:13; 52:1, 2; 61:2—11; Ezek 11:19; 18:31). The motive for the reconciliation (**16**) should be noticed; it is not so much that 'the spirit proceeds' from God, as that God desires to prevent the total destruction of the '*spirit*' or **i** '*breath of life*' (Gn 2:7). The chastisement may be only temporary; then there will follow the time of consolation, especially for the afflicted. **18.** There is some controversy over the translation and interpretation of the phrase 'fruit of the lips'; it can be understood in the sense that the great blessings of God will stimulate praise and thanksgiving, but others prefer to correct the text or to construe it differently. **19** and **21.** (cf 48:22) Are mutually complementary: the word peace has in Heb. a wider connotation than it has in our languages;

its antithesis is expressed in **20**, which underlines not **483** only the interior anguish, but the total misery of the people.
58:1—59:21—The section may be divided into four **j** parts: on true religion (58:1—14), the corruption of the people (59:1—8), a confession of sins (59:9—15*a*), the intervention of God (59:15*b*—21).
58:1—14 On true religion—The prophet had to stress **k** the faults of the people. His list of faults indicates that the people were given to grumbling, accusing God of hard-heartedness because he did not fulfil the requests of people who thought they were doing all that was required of them (**2**). In particular, they stressed their observance of the fasting laws (Zech 7:5; 8:19). But God despises the kind of penance which is limited to apparently outward attitudes (**5**; cf Mt 6:16); he does not condemn the practice in itself, but the anti-social vices (oppression of the poor, contempt for socially inferior classes etc) which accompanied it. In pointing to the acts which are pleasing to God in practice, the prophet lists the works of mercy (Jas 1:17), emphasizing that such acts of charity are far more valuable than fasting which is unaccompanied by a genuine religious sense. If the community would only alter its ways, then it would find prosperity (= light; 9:1; 60:1, 3), salvation and security (this is the meaning of 'righteousness', cf Dn 9:24), and generous assistance from God (glory of the Lord; 52:12; cf Ex 13:21, 22; 14:19, 20). There would then be a tender relationship of friendship between God and the people, but the people must give up its exploitation of the weak. On 'the pointing of **l** the finger' (**9**) cf Prv 6:13; but the context (59:3, 7) seems to indicate that what is meant is not a mere vulgar gesture, but an act of violence against one's neighbour, either in his person or in his property (cf Jb, 'the clenched fist'). **11.** The new upsurge of life is compared to a garden rich in water (Jer 17:8; Ps 1:3) and in plants (cf 51:3); the city will at the same time be rebuilt. Elsewhere we find symbolic names (1:26), but they are particularly frequent in these chh (12; 60:14, 18; 61:3, 6; 62:2 etc). On **13**, cf 56:1—8. **14.** As the final consequence of a true religious attitude we find the pleasure of being a friend of God, and the peaceful possession of the blessings promised to the patriarchs; Israel will be like a strong warrior who takes possession of a vast territory, passing from mountain to mountain.
59:1—8 The corruption of the people—The fact that **m** the present situation is far different from this is not due to God, as if he had lost his power, but to the sins of the people (50:1), who force God to hide his face (64:6) in disgust at their ways. Here too the list of faults concerns above all relationships with one's neighbour: murder (1:15), oppression, lies, calumny, fraud and dishonesty in the courts (1:17, 23). Self-deception and trickery are the order of the day. On the end of v **4** cf 33:11; Jb 15:35; Ps 7:15. Two strikingly original symbols (breaking an egg to eat it, weaving cloth to make clothes) bring out not only the wickedness of a particular kind of conduct (the eggs are 'adder's eggs', and the weft a 'spider's web'; 11:8; 14:29; 30:6) but also its futility (and indirectly, the harm that ensues to the men who do such things). The authenticity of v **7** is suspect, cf Prv 1:16. The irreligious know no peace (57:20, 21), and are incapable of finding it (**8**: cf Rm 3:17).
9—15*a* A confession of sin on behalf of the com- n munity—Without any introduction, the text breaks into a humble acknowledgement of sin. The writer, with perfect sincerity, recognizes that the sad conditions following the return from exile have been fully merited. These years have proved a delusion, 'darkness' instead

33n of 'light' (58:10), and instead of 'justice' and 'salvation' the people have found life insupportable. 'Noon' (16:3) is a symbol of security, 'twilight' (21:4) a symbol of uncertainty and malaise. **11.** On the symbolic reference to 'doves' cf 38:14; the comparison with 'bears' is found only here (elsewhere the idea is expressed by a reference to lions: Ps 38 (37):9). Even those who pray acknowledge that sins against one's neighbour are the gravest of all **(13, 14)**; 'revolt' must carry the meaning it has in Dt 19:16, 'to outrage, to injure the rights of another'. The outcome is a total subversion of moral values.

o **15b–21 The intervention of God**—In response to this humble prayer, God intervenes as a warrior, with weapons whose significance is explained. Similar texts are found in Wis 5:17–20; 1 Thes 5:8; Eph 6:14–17. On the arm of the Lord cf 51:5, 9. God thus settles accounts with the wicked, with the oppressors of the poeple **(18)**. His vengeance is compared to a 'rushing stream', which the powerful breath of God brings from the four points of the compass. The 'redeemer', God, will redeem Jerusalem; St Paul (Rm 11:26) adapted this v to indicate that redemption came from this city. **21.** (in prose) Is perhaps an addition; it speaks of a new covenant and of the un-interrupted guidance given by God, which is described in terms of a prophetical call (51:16; Jer 1:9).

p **60:1–63:6**—This is a **hymn to Jerusalem glorified**, mingled with promises and reassurances of salvation. It may be divided thus: the new Jerusalem (60:1–22); the envoy of God (61:1–3); the new order (61:4–9); the happiness of the new order (61:10–11); the new Sion (62:1–9); the saviour (62:10–12); the treading of the winepress (63:1–6). This last section is very like 59: 16–20 and seems to be its logical conclusion. This leads some scholars to transpose the passage to follow ch 59; but it can also be regarded as a suitable development of 62:8, 9.

The section is a closely connected whole. The historical background is the sad period at the beginning of the restoration. The prophet's message is intended to instil hope and confidence in these difficult days; but his escha-tological vision, as he does so, is important in the develop-ment of the idea of a universal religion.

484a **60:1–22 The new Jerusalem**—First the glory of the city is described (1–9), then its re-building (10–18), and finally the light which surrounds it (19–22). The lyrical tone of the song is evident, especially at the beginning, and its literary beauty has often been remarked on.

b **1–9.** Stands in sharp contrast to 47:1–15, but the glory of Jerusalem exceeds that of any queen. Such great 'light' and 'the glory of the Lord' (6:3) symbolize complete salvation. There is no place for shadow or 'darkness', which covers pagan nations and is a symbol of ignorance (9:2), of lack of direction and of unhappiness. The peoples of the earth will enjoy the light only if they make their way to the chosen city and humbly accept its spiritual leadership (2:2–4). Their offerings (18:7; 19:21) denote their acceptance of the monotheistic religion of Jerusalem.

c On v 4 cf 49:22; 66:20. The 'abundance of the sea' **(5)** is the wealth of maritime nations. The offerings of nomadic or semi-nomadic peoples are carried to Jerusalem on animals of the desert. **6.** Midian, Ephah and Shebah are names of peoples living on the coasts of the Gulf of Elam (Gn 10:7; 25:4), the country of perfumes and spices. **7.** The tribes of 'Kedar' (21:16) and of 'Nebaioth' (Gn 25:13) were of Ishmaelite origin, and were mainly shep-herds. The mention of an 'altar' is not necessarily a proof that this passage was written after the rebuilding of the temple (completed in 515), because an altar was erected

immediately after the return in 538 (Ez 3:3). Some of the **484c** exiles are repatriated from western lands (4). Their homecoming is visualized in the striking image of the 'ships of Tarshish' (2:16) which when first sighted by the watchmen on the shore seem like a flight of 'doves'. **10–18.** Exiled Israelites, offerings from foreign peoples, **d** and the pagans themselves flock into Jerusalem to trans-form the city into a blaze of beauty, a beacon beckoning the whole earth (49:23). The walls have yet to be built; this excludes a date later than that of Nehemiah (cf Neh 3:1–32). In this symbolic description of the city the walls are not for defence: peace will be so secure that the city gates will stay open even during the night **(11)**. The sole purpose of the gates is to permit the entry of humble pilgrims and offerings (Zech 14:14). In a context of this kind, the threat (Jer 27:8; Zech 14:18, 19) mentioned in **12** is astonishing, and is probably a gloss inserted later. On **13**, where the exact identification of the various trees is uncertain, cf 41:19. The circumlocution 'place of my **e** feet' is usually reserved for the Ark (Ps 99 (98):5; 132 (131):7), though it is also applied to the earth as a whole (66:1; Mt 5:35). Here it denotes the temple, though one cannot deduce from so strongly symbolic a text that the temple was already rebuilt: the context of chh 60–62 shows that in fact it was not. **14.** On the submissive attitude of the nations, cf 45:14; 49:23 etc; their sub-mission is voluntary, and their motives are hinted at in the two symbolic names (1:4, 26; 58:12). The humiliations of former days (54:6) are mentioned only to stress the glory of the present time. After the metaphor in which Jerusalem is described as a babe at the breast, the prophet proclaims the purpose of all these great blessings, namely, to ensure that those attributes of God which are most marked in chh 40ff shall be recognized everywhere: on 'the mighty One of Jacob', cf 1:24; 49:26. The last phrases of **17** (peace, righteousness; 32:16, 17) and **18** show the meaning to be attached to the more material symbols used earlier (9:9): bronze, gold etc. **19–22.** The apostrophe began (1, 2) **f** with the theme of light, and it closes with the same symbol (Apoc 21:23; 22:5). This light is no passing radiance, but a vast undying blaze, because it is derived not from creatures such as the sun or stars, but from God himself. This is obviously allegorical: it is sufficient to note what is said about the sun in **19** and **20**, and to call attention to the end of v 20 (the disappearance of all sorrow). On **21** cf 54:13; 57:13; 58:14; Mt 5:5; on 'the shoot of my planting' cf 5:2; 11:1; 27:2–4. In the new Jerusalem there will be a quite unusual growth of population (49:19–21; 54:1–3); promises like those made in the age of the patriarchs (Gn 17:6; 18:18; 24:60) will be fulfilled again, in a spiritual sense. Did this prophecy have, originally, only a messianic and eschatological significance? Since it was pronounced in a particular historical period, it must have had also an immediate relevance at the time; one must admit some historical foundation for it, even if only on a very small scale (and, of course, one must not forget the Heb. tendency to emphasize everything).

61:1–3 The envoy of God—The language has the same **g** characteristics as that used in the songs of the Servant of Yahweh (42:1–7), and therefore some exegetes have claimed that this text too refers to the Servant (some even appeal to Lk 4:17–21 in support of this view). Their case is by no means proved. The reference here is to a person (who may be called a type or symbol of the Messiah) charged with a specific task, namely, comforting the afflicted in Sion during the period immediately after the exile. On the 'spirit of the Lord', cf 11:2. 'Anointing' denotes in this text, a special election for a definite **h** mission (cf Jer 1:5); in Ac 10:38 the word is used of Jesus

484h Christ. On the announcing of 'good tidings' cf 41:27; 52:7; on the 'year of favour' and the 'day of vengeance' (**2**) cf 34:8; 49:8. 'Captives' and 'prisoners' are in practice synonyms for 'brokenhearted' and 'afflicted' (58:6, 7). On **3**, where the text is not quite certain, cf 3:24, in which the contrary process is described (cf also 60:21).

i **4—9 The new order**—Facts already described in ch 60 are again proclaimed in a less elevated style. The rebuilding (44:26; 49:8; 58:12) refers to Jerusalem and to all the places which still bore traces of the many enemy invasions. This work, like the work connected with agriculture and sheep-rearing, will be carried out by aliens (60:10), in contrast with that earlier period when all the Israelites who remained at home had been shepherds and vine-dressers (according to 2 (4) Kgs 25:12). **6.** Re-echoes Ex 19:6 (cf 1 Pt 2:9; Apoc 5:10). The mentality, already evident in 2:2—5, according to which the universality of one religion in the future in no way detracts from the supremacy of Israel, is also evident here. The pagans form the new laity, and the Israelites the new priesthood, because they are closer and more pleasing to God. On the second half of v 6 cf 60:5, 11; 66:12. On **7** cf 40:2; 50:6, but note that here the exile is presumed to be over. On the attributes of God in **8** cf Ps 37 (36):28; for the remainder cf 59:18, 21; **9** echoes 19:25.

j **10—11 The fullness of joy**—The community expresses its joy and gratitude for all the gifts of God. The images of the bride and bridegroom (Jer 7:34; 16:9) are combined to stress the complete happiness of the people at the two blessings so highly praised in chh 40:66: 'salvation' and 'righteousness'. They are presented as the ornaments of a bride (49:18), and as the 'garland' of a bridegroom (**3**; cf 3:20; Ezek 24:17). In **11** the prophet assures men that God will one day make the magnificent picture a reality. This indicates that the whole description of 60:1—22 refers to the future. On the metaphor of 'bringing forth shoots' cf 45:8; Jer 23:5; Zech 3:8.

485a **62:1—12 The new Zion and the Saviour**—In 61: 10 the prophet was speaking in the name of the community; here he emphasizes his determination to continue proclaiming a message of consolation. Note the difference between the role assigned to 'light' here, and to its role in 60:1; the symbolism is identical, but the point of view is different, for in ch 60 a longed-for future is considered as already present. On **2** cf 60:3; 61:11. The new symbolic name is not specified (65: 15); it could be that mentioned in v 4. The imagery of **3** is superior to that of 49:16 as an expression of God's pleasure: the 'crown' brings to memory 28:1—5, even though the context is very different. There follows a metaphorical reference to marriage (61:10), expounded **b** both in negative (divorce 54:6) and positive terms. The double geographical reference (to the city and the land) is dictated by the need for a parallelism, but the reference is to the Israelites in general, as always. At least some of the symbolic names in the Bible were names of women: for example 'Forsaken' = '*azûbâh* (cf 1 (3) Kgs 22:42), 'My delight is in her' = *Ḥepsî-bâh* (cf 2 (4) Kgs 21:1). In **5** the marriage is still to take place; in reality, it is rather a reconciliation which is called for (50:1; 54:8—11). To avoid a double reference (*bridegroom* used both of the inhabitants of Jerusalem and of God), it is preferable to read *thy architect* (Heb. *bōnēḵ*) rather than *your sons* (Heb. *bānāyiḵ*) **c** and to read the verb in the singular. **6.** The watchmen (21:6—9; 52:8) are given an unusual task: not to stand watch, but to implore God by constant prayer to fulfil

his promises, beginning with the material restoration **485** of the country, which is still far off. In **8, 9** there is a promise that there will be no more invasions (51: 6—8; cf Jer 5:17), that there will be fertility of the soil, and peace; note that here the Israelites themselves work the land (61:5). There is no contradiction in this, for the various metaphors referring to a spiritual world stand, in practice, for one and the same reality. **11.** On God's swearing an oath cf 45:23; 51:9. The saviour is presented as in 40:9, 10; he comes along a road (**10**) which is only superficially identical with that described in 40:3—its meaning recalls rather 57:14. On the symbolic names of **12** cf 61:6; 35:10; 62:4.

63:1—6 The Winepresser—This lovely passage con- **d** nects up with the end of ch 59, but we would scarcely be justified in transposing the text, since similar themes recur so often in these chh. We are not told who the mysterious warrior is: he is the symbol of God's vengeance on the nations. His identification with the Messiah, though often asserted, has not been proved; certainly the 'Winepresser' has nothing in common with the Servant of Yahweh. On 'Edom' and 'Bozra' cf 34:5, 6, but here the **e** Edomites are mentioned as a symbol of the nations hostile to Israel; there is no need to seek an allusion to a precise historical fact. Many, indeed, omit the two geographical names, and replace them with similar Heb. words meaning 'stained with red' and 'more than an avenger', which fit well into the context; the bespattering signifies the slaughter which has taken place (**2, 3**). For v 4 cf 61:2. The punishment of the adversaries is accomplished by God alone (**6**); the identity of the warrior is here made evident.

63:7—64:12 Collective Prayer—The resounding **f** victory above ought to be followed by a hymn of thanksgiving or of praise. Instead we have here a lamentation, rich in feeling and full of trust in God. Though it does not answer all the difficulties, the best historical context would seem to be that of the sad years 536—520 B.C. First of all the divine favours are extolled (63:7—14); then the community makes its sorrowful appeal (63:15— 64:12). **7—14.** The prophet expresses the feelings of **g** the community. The motive of his praise is God's constant assistance to Israel; this is the theme of much of the Psalms. The first event in which God appears as saviour is the liberation from Egypt. For the fine expressions of love and concern cf 46:3, 4; Dt 7:8; Hos 11:1; Jer 31:9 etc. The rest of Israelite history is summed up in the contrast between v **10** and the following vv. Disobedience and rebellion call down God's vengeance, but his love and the memory of his association with Israel cause him to pardon them as soon as ever there is a sign of repentance among the people. The power of God (his 'arm') was manifested gloriously in the crossing of the Red Sea (Ex 14:16—22). The mention of the 'holy Spirit' (10, **h** 11, 14) does not imply the revelation of the mystery of the Trinity; such personification is not uncommon to describe the action of God in the world (Ps 51 (50):13; Wis 1:5; 9:17). God acts directly, when he could make use of the 'angel of his presence' (cf Ex 33:2; Zech 1:11, 13; Mal 3:1). The 'valley' (**14**) is Palestine; the action of the 'Spirit of the Lord' produces an effect in men analogous to that of instinct in animals (flocks which instinctively descend to the lowlands, cf Jer 8:7).

15—19. The prayer contains an appeal to the power of **i** God and his mercy, for it seeks a miracle of divine love. To the title of 'Redeemer' (41:14) is joined the more emotional one of 'Father', as is indicated also by the reference to the two patriarchs, founders of families. The word is used in a collective sense; only in the NT

485i does the idea of the divine fatherhood in respect of individuals appear. According to the Hebrew mentality (6:9) the moral aberration is attributed to God as its 'cause'. The 'servants' of God are all faithful Israelites; for the concept of 'heritage' or possession cf Ex 19:5. **18**, **19**. Recall Lam 2:7; Is 33:22; 51:19—21. The final distich (which begins ch 64 in the Vg) foresees the theophany which will bring divine assistance and the discomfiture of the adversary.

j **64:(1) 2—7.** The appeal for a divine intervention against the enemy begins with a simile difficult to interpret because of a corrupt text. The simile is based on the destructive force of fire. For v **4** cf 1 Cor 2:9. **5**—the end of the v is very uncertain—proclaims the generosity of God towards the weak and the justice of his wrath against sin. The confession of guilt is accompanied by powerful similes (**6**; cf Lv 12:2; Lam 1:8; Is 1:30). God's anger is just; for the image of the hidden face cf 8:17; 54:8; **57:17**. Destruction is the natural result of guilt. **8—12.**

k The plea is renewed (63:16), insisting on human weakness (man is mere clay), on the relations between God and his people, and on the ruinous state of the place where the temple stood and of the whole region. Before such a catastrophe God cannot remain unmoved.

l **65:1—66:24 Intervention of God; Promises and Threats**—The two chh seem to be a unity, with the exception of 66:10b—24 the work of the editor, perhaps—and indicate a common background, namely the years 538—520 B.C. between the return and the rebuilding of the Temple. One can detect in them, besides the usual pessimism, internal divisions in the community.

486a **65:1—25 The Fate of Israel—punishment and reward**—This title is chosen to avoid excessive subdivisions: against idolaters (1—7), the 'Remnant' of Israel (8—10), the apostates (11—16), new heavens and a new

b earth (17—25) **1—7.** In a plaintive tone God reveals his desire to assist (for a free application of the text cf Rm 10:20, 21) and the indifference of the people, rebellious and provocative, which followed the 'devices' of its heart (Jer 3:17; 7:24; 9:13 etc). Among the abuses cited are the use of impure foods (3—4), including swine's flesh (Lv 11:7, 8; Dt 14:8), and contact with tombs (Mt 23: 27), connected perhaps with the practice of necromancy (8:19; 29:4) and possibly with sacred prostitution ('in secret places'); the sacrifices in 'gardens' indicate idolatrous or illicit worship in sacred groves (1:29; 57:5), while the offering of incense 'upon bricks' possibly alludes to altars illicit because not made of stone (Ex 20:25). The words of **5** suggest initiates of secret rites who consider outsiders impure. The punishment (**6, 7**) is described in terms of collective responsibility, and is provoked especially by the acts of idolatry (57:7; Hos

c 4:13; Jer 2:20 etc). **8—10.** But this corruption is not universal; a handful will be saved. This is the concept of the 'Remnant' from which the new Israel will emerge (6:13). The number is small, like a few bunches of grapes in a vineyard (17:6), but sufficient, since God confers upon them the promises (**9;** cf 57:13; 60:21). Their future prosperity is symbolized by an improvement in the fertility of the soil: the barren 'Valley of Achor' (Jos. 7:24—26), not far from the Dead Sea, will be able to feed flocks; the 'Valley of Sharon' (33:9) will not lose its rich fertility, as the text might seem to imply, but flocks will be able to graze there because its fertility will be such that it can sustain even their depredations (cf 30:23, 24;

d 32:10). **11—16.** The people are divided into two classes, with corresponding fates: the servants of the Lord (41:8), and the apostates. The former will enjoy a sort of messianic banquet (55:12); the latter will be excluded from this and

will suffer a fearful affliction or will be slaughtered. Their **486d** crime is described as an act of worship to two Canaanite divinities, called in Heb. *Gad* (= 'Fortune', the *Tyche* of the Greeks) and *Menî* (= 'Destiny' = the goddess Manât of Arabic mythology?). Among the new Israel descended from the 'Remnant' there will be no place for idolatry (**16**) nor for sorrow. For the formula of blessing and swearing cf Jer 24:9; 29:22. **17—25.** This new life **e** is symbolized by a new creation, to be taken in a hyperbolical and metaphorical sense to indicate a complete break with the past. There will be no more tears, no more premature death; then death at the age of 100 years will be considered the result of a curse, since a normal life-span will be longer (**20, 22**). For v **21** cf 62:8. God will be close at hand to anticipate every least desire (**24**; cf 20:19; 58:9). **25.** Recalls clearly 11:6—9, while the mention of the serpent, which alone will continue in its misery, refers to Gn 3:14.

66:1—24 Sorrow and Glory in Jerusalem—The title **f** is only approximate, to avoid too many sub-divisions. These might be: the true worship (1—4), salvation and punishment (5—18*a*), the glory of the Lord amidst the nations (18*b*—19), return of the diaspora (20—22), new worship and punishment of the rebels (23, 24).

1—4. God in his majesty (6:1; 60:13) has no need of **g** a material temple, preferring his adoration in spirit and truth (Jn 4:21—24; cf 1:11—15; 29:13). Most pleasing to him are the humble and the contrite in spirit (57:15). The people, however, show indifference, and prefer idols to God ('abominations'). **3.** Can be translated by contrasting the two members of each pair (one sacrifices oxen, but also kills men, etc), thus highlighting the inconsistency of a piety which coexists with immoral actions (murder, idolatry) or illegal actions (offering unclean animals like dogs or pigs). Others prefer to unite the two members into a single proposition, understanding a comparative particle (*he who slaughters an ox is like him who* etc); in this case there would be a strong condemnation of sacrificial rites. But a comparison with analogous texts (1:11—15) always makes necessary a distinction between rites good in themselves and their ineffectivness if accompanied by unworthy conduct. The consequence is just punishment (57:6—13; 65:12).

5—18*a*. God apostrophises the pious and condemns the **h** indifferent or sceptical (5:11; 28:9—12). For the latter the punishment decreed in the theophany of v **6** is now described; the mention of the temple in such descriptions does not in fact necessarily involve its material existance. The symbolic birth of **7—9** is meant to give assurance of the miraculous development of those who fear God (5) or the 'Remnant' of Israel (48:19; 54:1—3; 60:4, 9 etc). For **10, 11** cf 65:18; 60:16; 57:18; 61:2; for **12—14** cf 60:5; 61:6; 49:15; 58:11. The return mentioned in **12** concerns the Israelites of the diaspora in general, not necessarily those deported to Mesopotamia (already returned, at least in part). The theophany of the punish- **i** ment is similar to many others (15, 16; cf 19:1; 27:1; 29:6; 30:27). God declares that he knows the crimes of these villains (**18*a***) and of all who do the actions described in **17**, where there is mention of unclean foods ('swine's flesh . . . mice', cf 65:4; Lv 11:29) and of a rite in 'the gardens'—certainly pagan, or at least unlawful.

18*b*—19. Here and in 20, 21 the text is in prose; its **j** authenticity, together with that of 22—24, is disputed. But even if this is a case of an interpolation, there is no reason to doubt its inspiration. The expression 'all nations and tongues' is characteristic of late texts (Zech 8:23; Dn 3:4, 7). **19.** On the sign cf 7:14; here, however, it

486j should probably be understood as *standard* (5:26; 11:10; 13:2 etc). The purpose of the mission of the 'survivors' (= members of the remnant?) is to spread the knowledge of the true God, with the corresponding admiration of **k** his power and majesty. Of the peoples mentioned, 'Tarshish' has been referred to often (2:16; 60:9), as also the 'coastlands' (11:11; 40:15 etc); 'Put' and 'Lud' lay along the African coast of the Red Sea (Gn 10:6); 'Javan' (Gn 10:2) is to be identified with Ionia, 'Tubal' was on the coast of the Black Sea. Many see here two other peoples of the regions beside the Black Sea, namely *Meshech* and *Rosh* (Ezek 38:2; 39:1), names which have been altered to give the present phrase 'who draw the bow'. In practice the reference is to a mission to distant **l** lands in four directions. **20—22.** The return of the diaspora is described with the usual images, which appear here with a special emphasis (49:22; 60:9). The reverence and respect which accompany a sacred rite are displayed.

The priests and levites are Israelites of the diaspora who **486** have returned to Jerusalem, or perhaps pagans who have accompanied these. The context does not in fact exclude this latter hypothesis, which would indicate an advance beyond a narrowly racial outlook (56:3, 7). For v 22 cf 60:20; 65:17—23.

22—24. The reference is to a monthly and weekly **m** pilgrimage (1:12); naturally a symbolic and not a real action is meant. In Zech 14:16 the pilgrimage is annual. More important is the fact that all men take part in it (2:2—4). Near Jerusalem (Jer 7:32:33) the macabre vision of **24** will confront the pilgrims. The 'worm' and the 'fire' are means and symbols of corruption; the first is natural for bodies; what is extraordinary is that the punishment is eternal, and there is no rapid destruction. But the text does not speak of the fire of hell, though it is possible to see in it a symbol or type of this (cf Mt 9:47, 48).

JEREMIAH

BY M. McNAMARA M.S.C.

487a **Bibliography—Commentaries:** J. Knabenbauer, 1899; B. Duhm, Tübingen and Leipzig, 1901; C. H. Cornill, Leipzig, 1905; F. Giesebrecht, HKAT, 1907²; A. W. Streane. CBSC, 1913; G. Ricciotti, Turin, 1923; F. Nötscher, BB, 1934; id, EchB, 1947; A. Condamin, EtB, 1936³; L. Dennefeld, PCSB, 1946; A. Penna, SacB, 1952; J. P. Hyatt—S. R. Hopper, IB, 1956; W. Rudolph, HAT, 1958²; A. Gelin, BJ, 1959²; A. Weiser, ATD, 1960⁴; J. Bright, AB, 1965; P. Volz, KAT, 1928². **Studies:** S. Mowinckel, *Zur Komposition des Buches Jer*, Kristiania, 1914; J. Skinner, *Prophecy and Religion: Studies in the Life of Jeremiah*, 1922 (reprint 1955; paperback 1961); D. J. Wiseman, *Chronicles of the Chaldaean Kings (625—556 B.C.) in the British Museum*, 1956. For further literature see EOTInt, 346—65.

b Historical and Religious Background—In 18:1—12 Yahweh tells Jeremiah that he controls the destinies of nations as a potter does clay. In the prophet's own time this was illustrated in a remarkable manner: empire was replacing empire. From c. 650 onwards Assyria was tottering to her grave. By 632 Josiah (640 609) availed himself of the situation to begin to purge Judah of Assyrian gods and syncretistic practices. He extended the reform, and with it, doubtless, political control, to the former Assyrian province of Samaria (2 Chr 34:8—13). Availing itself of the enemy's weakness, Babylon revolted and in 626 the Aramaean Nabupolassar proclaimed himself king and declared war on Assyria. In Judah Josiah proceeded with his reform which he sealed in 622 by destroying all the local shrines and making the Temple the sole place of worship. This was done under the influence of a Law-book found in the Temple, called the 'Book of the Covenant', probably part of our present book of Dt. A solemn Passover was celebrated to solemnize Judah's renewal of the Covenant with Yahweh (2 [4] Kgs 22:1—23:27).

In the meantime the struggle between Assyria and Babylon continued. The fate of the former was really sealed by the destruction of Nineveh in 612. In 609 Pharaoh's armies marched to the Euphrates to aid Assyria. Josiah of Judah hoping for Assyria's destruction attempted to block the Egyptian advance at the pass of Megiddo. He lost his life in the endeavour (2 [4] Kgs 23:29f). The nobles elected Jehoahaz (also called Shallum) to succeed him but after three months the Pharaoh Neco had him exiled to Egypt where he died (22:10—12). Neco now placed Jehoiakim on the throne of Judah and levied a heavy tax (2 [4] Kgs 23:31—35). Judah was now a vassal of Egypt, but not for long. In 605 the Babylonian armies under the command of the crown-prince Nebuchadnezzar, smashed the Egyptian armies at Carchemish on the Euphrates (46:2ff) and swept south through Palestine. In August of that same year Nabupolassar died and Nebuchadnezzar hurried back to Babylon to occupy the throne. In 604/3 his

armies were again in Palestine and soon Jehoiakim **487b** submitted to him. In Dec. 604 Babylon crushed a rising in the Philistine city of Ashkelon. In 601 Nebuchadnezzar marched against Egypt but suffered serious losses in a conflict at the Egyptian frontier. He returned home to reform his armies. Jehoiakim rebelled and his country was harassed by marauders from the neighbouring states (2 [4] Kgs 24:2), presumably at Nebuchadnezzar's behest. Nebuchadnezzar marched against Judah in 598 but Jehoiakim had died before he laid siege to Jerusalem. He was succeeded by Jehoiachin who surrendered the city on March 16, 597. The king, queen-mother, nobles and craftsmen were deported to Babylon and the weakling Zedekiah placed on the throne. In 594/3 the new king steered clear of a new anti-Babylonian league but, due to the machinations and power of the pro-Egyptian party in Judah, by 589 the country was again in open revolt. Nebuchadnezzar acted rapidly. In Jan. 588 Jerusalem was blockaded. Soon only Lachish and Azekah of the cities of Judah remained unconquered. Eventually these fell and finally in July 587 Jerusalem also. Zedekiah was captured while trying to escape, sent to Nebuchadnezzar's headquarters in Syria, blinded and exiled to Babylon where he died. Deportation from Judah was then systematically carried out and Gedaliah put in charge of the country, now reduced to a Babylonian province. After a short period of governorship Gedaliah was assassinated and a further deportation followed.

Jeremiah's Prophetic Ministry—It is against this **c** background that the prophet carried on his mission to Judah. He was born at Anathoth (1:1 q.v.) at the beginning of Josiah's reign (640, B.C.). When called to prophesy in 626 (1:2) Josiah had already begun his reform work in Judah and Israel. His early prophecies (1—6, portions of 30 31) may have been directed to the N Kingdom, and inspired by a hope of the return of those exiled in 721; cf §§ 488b, 497b. His oracles on the 'Foe from the North' are also from this early period; cf § 490i. When the Book of the Covenant was found in 622 (2 [4] Kgs 22) he was probably still at Anathoth and unknown in Jerusalem. It was the prophetess Huldah who was consulted by Josiah. He would have favoured Josiah's reform and may even have preached fidelity to the covenant made by Josiah (11:2—8), a king he admired (22:10). Of his oracles between 622 and 609 we know little. He laments the exile of *Shallum* (Jehoahaz) in 609 (22:10—12) and in the same year opens his real public career by a sermon in the Temple (chh 26—7). Only the favour of princes loyal to Josiah's reform saves his life (26:16—24). *Jehoiakim's* neglect of the reform (see **d** on 7:18f) and unjust rule draws down the prophet's censures (21:11—22:9, q.v.). The victory of Carchemish (46:2—12) in 605 proves his oracles on the foe from the N to be correct. Barred from access to the Temple, in the same year he dictates his earlier oracles against Judah and Jerusalem to Baruch who writes them in a scroll which is read publicly the following year. Jehoiakim

487d has the scroll destroyed and tries to kill the prophet and his scribe. They are protected and a new scroll is written (ch 36). Towards 600—598 he has words of praise for the Rechabites (ch 35). Popular sentiment expected the return of *Jehoiachin* from exile,. Jeremiah preaches against this in season and out of season (see on 22:20—30). During the years 594—3 he combats false prophets in Babylon and Jerusalem (chh 27—29), and forecasts Babylon's downfall after seventy years of supremacy (51:59—64; 29:10f). Ch 24 comes from the same period. *During the final revolt* (589—587) he urges capitulation to Babylon (chh 37:39; 21:1—10; 34:1—7) and the certainty of Babylonian victory, despite the lifting of the blockade on Jerusalem (34:8—32). He purchases family property and declares this a divine pledge of the future reconstitution of the nation. (chh 32f). While attempting to go to Anathoth, he is arrested, accused of desertion to the Babylonians and of demoralizing the garrison and populace by his preaching. Cast into a dungeon, he is finally removed to custody in the quarter of the guards where he remains until Jerusalem falls (37:11—38:28). He then becomes an associate of Gedaliah after whose assassination he is forced by refugee Jews to go with them to Egypt, where he utters his last-recorded oracles (ch 39—44).

e **The Babylonian Chronicle**, published by Wiseman, gives the history of the Babylonian Empire and the background to Jer from 626—594/3 and 557/6 B.C. It is essential for a proper understanding of the biblical history of the period. For a summary and study of it see D. N. Freedman, BA 19 (1956), 50—60. An Aramaic letter from Palestine to the Pharaoh from the end of the 7th cent. (probably 604) is also important; cf J. Bright, BA 12 (1949), 46—52; J. Fitzmyer, Bib 46 (1965), 41—55.

The Lachish Letters—The letters (ANET, 321f) were written by members of the Jewish garrison just before Lachish fell to the Babylonians, therefore about 589/8 B.C. They shed a good deal of light on the history of the last days of Judah. Reference is made to a prophet in letter III, while in VI we find a passage strikingly similar to Jer 38:4, q.v. It was once thought by some that the prophet mentioned was Jeremiah and that VI could be brought into connection with his political activity. This is denied by D. Winton Thomas (*The Prophet in the Lachish Ostraca*, 1946.). O. Eissfeldt (*The OT and Modern Study*, 153) thinks the evidence is insufficient for a definite answer.

f **Text and Versions**—The oldest MSS of the HT come from Qumran though in fragments (late 3rd cent. B.C.—1st cent. A.D.). Some have already been published (Jer 42—49 in DJD 3 [1962], 62—60). The fragments published agree basically with the MT, which was already known as having a well-conserved Hebrew text. The LXX was made in the 3/2 cent. B.C. and differs in a remarkable manner from the MT. It is c. one-eighth (2,700 words) shorter than MT and has an inverted order for the oracles against the Gentiles (which LXX inserts in a different position to that of MT. cf 500*a*, and for some other passages (e.g. 10:1—16). Its omissions are mainly, though not solely, of repetitions found in the MT. A Hebrew MS from Qumrân (4Q Jer[b]) with 10:1—6 shows that the peculiar LXX text is a translation from a Heb. original, different from the text of the MT tradition. We cannot yet explain how the two-fold form of the text of this book arose.

g **History of Composition**—Even a cursory reading will show that the present text of our book is in glorious disarray, with little literary, logical or chronological order. Ricciotti (p. 39) has aptly styled it a *zibaldone*, **487** a scrap-book. Since Mowinckel's study (*Zur Komposition . . .*) it is usual to distinguish three types of material in the book: A: Poetry, mainly oracular; B: biographical prose narrative (presumably from Baruch); C: Prose discourses in deuteronomic style. Though some (e.g. Duhm; H. G. May JBL 61 [1942], 139—55) believe the C sections are later (See § 492 *m*) compositions bearing little or no relation with Jer's real preaching, very probably we have in it sermons and oracles of the prophet as transmitted by the deuteronomic school (cf 7:1ff; 26). The three types of material were transmitted independently before being combined to form our present book. The history of the book's composition is a complicated one, almost impossible to trace. We know little of the content of the first and second scrolls of 605/4 (ch 36, though it probably now stands somewhere in chh 1—25, and may even form the framework of these chh). Since it was read thrice in one day it must have been rather brief. Hyatt 787 would restrict it to the bulk of chh 1—6 and possibly including 8:4—9:1 (cf 8:18—9:1 with 36:5—9). Whereas Mowinckel and Rudolph think it comprised A material, T. H. Robinson (ZAW 42 [1924], 209—21) and EOT Int, 351f) prefer to find it in C. The first scroll of 604 was probably handed down and expanded in various ways as the diverging texts of MT and LXX testify. Our present text is the outcome of this complicated process. Certain rules guided the editors in their work and we can, for convenience sake, divide the entire book in the following manner:

Book I   1:1—25:14 Prophecies of Doom against Judah and Jerusalem.

Book II   Chh 26—35 Prophecies of Weal.

Book III   Chh 36—45 The Sufferings of Jeremiah.

Book IV   Ch 25:15—38: Chh 46—51.

Historical Appendix Ch 52.

The Message of Jeremiah—The prophets were God's **h** messengers to the chosen people and to humanity. Their prophetic charism fitted them to understand God's revelation as given to Israel, to interpret this anew, for contemporaries and for future generations.

Yahweh is Sole God, Lord of Creation and Master of History—Yahweh created and controls the world and natural order (27:5; 5:22; 8:7; cf 10:12f; 31:35f). There is no other God beside him; idols are 'no gods' (2:11), 'worthlessness' (2:5). Yahweh is a living God, the source of life (2:13); idols cannot help (2:13—28). God is in heaven but active on earth, near to all men (23:23). He alone knows man's thoughts (11:20; 17:10). Yahweh is *master of history*, controlling the destinies of Israel and pagan nations, as a potter controls his clay (18:1—12). He summons Nebuchadnezzar, 'his servant' (27:6) to punish Judah but will punish Judah and all nations alike for their sins (25:15ff; chh 46ff). He plants and uproots nations as he wills (18:7ff; etc).

Yahweh and Israel—God has freely chosen Israel and **i** made of it a people apart. Israel is the first fruits of God's harvest (2:3), and thereby consecrated to him; his own heritage (12:7—9), his vineyard (12—10) and his flock (13:17). He has bound her to himself by a special covenant (7:23; 11:4; 24:7; 31:33); he is thereby her spouse (3:1ff) and she his beloved (11:15; 12:7). He requires of her that she act in accord with her dignity and his love for her (2:2ff; 6:16 etc). *Yahweh is a God of love*. This teaching is clear from the images already referred to and is central to Jer's preaching. Yahweh calls on Israel to remember this; to recall and return to the love of her youth which he himself has not forgotten (2:2; 3:19). He is a merciful (*ḥāsîd*) God, 'loyal-in-love'

487i (3:12). Her ingratitude pains him (2:5—31f etc). If he must punish Israel it is merely to make her realize salvation stands in him alone (3:21—25 etc). His plans for Israel are plans for welfare and not for evil, to give her a future and a hope (29:11). He repeatedly invites Israel to return, assuring her that she will be lovingly accepted back (29:12ff etc etc).

j **The Individual**—The individual's relation to God is given special prominence in Jer's teaching, principally because of his own sensitive nature and his personal relation with God. We see this in his 'Confessions' (cf § 493a.) The New Covenant with God's people will entail a very personal relation of each to God (31:33—34). *True religion* consists in a personal relation to God, which makes each attentive to his voice (7:22f q.v. etc). *Sin* is a violation of covenant Law. *Its real roots* lie in the stubbornness of *man's heart* (7:24:13:10; 23:17), in 'incircumcision of heart' (13:10; 18:12; 23:17), which prevents him from hearing God's voice, from 'knowing him'. But man's heart is weak, tortuous (17:9). *Repentance* consists in recognizing this and in turning to God. It implies change or circumcision of heart (4:3f).

The New Covenant—God has plans for healing man's malice and weakness. In the new Israel the root cause of these will be removed. **A New Covenant will be made** which, unlike the Mosaic, will be written on men's hearts and the power given him to know God. He will be given a new heart and his sins will be forgiven. cf 31:31—34, q.v.; 24:6f; 32:36—41. This prophecy of the New Covenant in 31.31—34 is the culmination of Jeremiah's teaching on God's relation to man. Cf further § 498a, b.

k **The Messiah**—The Royal House of David had ill-served the true good of Israel. Its kings were shepherds who misled and scattered—in exile—the flock of Yahweh's pasture. In 21:1—23:3 we have a series of oracles directed against the last kings of Judah. The ingathering of the exiles would undo the work of these kings. Over God's new flock there will reign a righteous shoot, or a genuine scion, of David. His rule will be a just and wise one, one of salvation for Judah (23:3—6, q.v.). **This is the sole text** in which Jeremiah speaks of an **individual personal Messiah**. The reason for this lies probably in a general disappointment with the last of the Davidic kings. **His messianism, like that of Ezekiel, is mainly impersonal.** Jeremiah's role was to emphasize the internal character of the religion of the new people of God. His one oracle, nonetheless, plays its part in the development of messianic doctrine and inspires Zech 3:8; 6:12, the 'Righteous Branch' later becoming a messianic title: (cf Lk 1:78). See further Skinner 310—19.

l **Jeremiah and Prophecy**—The **real importance of Jer**, however, does not lie in such specific points of doctrine, most of which are found in some form in other parts of the Bible. It lies in **his own personality** and in his own **personal relationship with God**.

This does not, of course, distort his role as prophet. He is aware that he was called by God and acted under his influence; personal does not mean purely human; on occasion he refused to give an oracle until God had spoken to him (cf 42:4). But others too claimed to be prophets, could introduce their oracles as the word of Yahweh (cf 28:2, 13), and use symbolic actions (cf 27:2ff; 28:10—11). Such men curried favour with the people by prophesying weal instead of insisting on the observance of God's law; they deceived themselves, and others, by their nationalist fervour and a one-sided view of the Covenant doctrine. But it was not always easy to distinguish such men from true prophets. Jer gives two criteria (28:8—9; cf Dt 18:21f): conformity with the **487l** prophetic tradition, and the fulfilment of prophecy. (On the question of cult prophets and Jer's relation to the cult, see O. Eissfeldt in *The OT and Modern Study*, ed. H. H. Rowley, 1956, 116—26; 134—45; and also § 452c.

But over and above this, Jer was conscious of a personal relationship with God which guaranteed his mission. He never confused his own thoughts and desires with the voice of God. What made him speak as he did was an almost irresistible divine power (20:9), but one with which he had to cooperate—he accepted his mission freely but reluctantly (1:4—8) and could have lost it through infidelity (15:18—19). And above all in those passages known as the 'Confessions' the personal voice of Jer comes to us, his 'spiritual biography'.

This personal note running through the book is not **m** an intrusion into the prophetic message, an infringement of the pure word of God. On the contrary, it is precisely this which **makes the book of Jer a high-water mark** in the history of prophecy, in Israel's religious development, in mankind's religious education. The prophet is not a mechanical, mindless, impersonal soothsayer; he is one whose mind and heart have been seized by the word of God; the word of God does not merely come through his lips—it is in him first before it comes through him to others. And this plays its part in making evident that religion too is not merely a matter of impersonal law on the one hand and mechanical observance on the other. Religion too is a matter of personal relationship between man and God. The covenant is the formulation of this personal relationship, and the covenant law is its expression. It is love which led God to take the first step in this relationship; and that love is such that he will not be satisfied with anything less in return. Personal relationship involves personal responsibility.

Jeremiah found, and movingly displays to us, that sometimes this personal relationship is a burden almost too great for human strength. **The message of woe** which he was bidden to give to his friends and fellow-countrymen **was torture to his sensitive nature**; it brought on his head the dislike of many; and he did not even have the mixed pleasure of seeing his words verified (20:7—10). All of this meant that the word of God which he received so generously became bitterness to him (15:16). But it is in this suffering that his vocation finds fulfilment (15:19); the word of God does indeed 'destroy and overthrow' but also 'plants and builds' (1:10). Jer's own personal experience here is itself a message for the people; because for them too God's choice and God's love does not mean blessing regardless of their deeds; it may, and indeed will, mean suffering—but suffering in order that they may finally find the Lord with their hearts. And all of this is a foreshadowing of the way in which personal union with God is finally achieved, when the Lord is 'led like a gentle lamb to the slaughter' (11:19), and by his suffering makes many righteous (cf Is 52:13—53:12).

The Influence of Jeremiah—The influence of the **n** teaching and example of Jeremiah **on future generations was immense**. It can be seen in Ezek (16:62; 34:25; 36:25—28), on Second Isaiah (49:1—8; 51:7; 53:7f 59:21) on later Psalms, etc (cf P. Bonnard, *Le Psautier selon Jérémie* [Lectio Divina], Paris 1960), Dn 9, Baruch, etc. From Jer 31:31—34 the Qumrân community styled itself 'the New Covenant'. In the NT, his influence on Paul is especially noticeable. This new son of Benjamin (Rm 11:1), set aside from his mother's womb to be the apostle to the Gentiles (Gal 1:15; Jer 1:5) preached the fulfilment of many of Jer's prophecies, e.g.

487n the New Covenant (2 Cor 3:6ff), true circumcision (Rm 2:29 etc), interior religion etc. And probably he was inspired by Jeremiah in his entire treatment of the Law, grace and liberty. For Jeremiah's teaching in general cf Skinner, passim, and Hyatt, 784—7.

488a 1:1—25:14. BOOK 1 ORACLES AGAINST JERUSALEM AND JUDAH

In this first major collection we can distinguish two parts: A. 1:1—6:30:Oracles mainly from the time of Josiah (626—609 B.C.); B. 7:7—25:14: Oracles and other material, mainly from the period subsequent to Josiah. While treating chiefly the reign of Jehoiakim (609—598) it has material also from the reigns of Jehoahaz (= Shallum; 609—608), Jehoiachin (598—597) and Zedekiah (597—587). There is also some material of a later date. The material in Book I is mainly of type A (cf §. 487 *g*). While most of the C material of the entire book is found in chh 1—25 (7:1—8:3; 11:1—14; 16:1—13; 17: 19—27; 18:1—12; 21:1—10; 22:1—5; 1—14) these chapters carry little B material (cf 19:1—20:6). This first book is, then, a compilation of originally distinct sources, though the composition may well have the scroll Jeremiah himself dictated in 605/4 B.C. as its groundwork.

b 1:1—6:30 The Call of Jeremiah and Oracles from the Reign of Josiah—On Josiah's reign see § 487*b*; on the relation of Jeremiah to Josiah's reform, § 487*c*. This first part may be divided as follows: 1) Prophetic call (ch 1); 2) Oracles on the national apostasy (ch 2); 3) the Return of the northern tribes and of Judah (3:1—4:4); 4); oracles on an invasion from the N (4:5—6:30). In these earlier poems, in ch 2 in particular, Jeremiah shows marked dependence on his predecessors, on Hosea in particular (cf Skinner, 21f; 64f; K. Gross, *Die literarische Verwandschaft Jeremias mit Hosea.* Berlin 1930; id, 'Hoseas Einfluss auf Jeremias Anschauungen', *Neue Kirchliche Zeitschrift* 42 (1931), 241—56; 327—43).

c 1. Call. 1—2 were probably prefixed by Baruch to the scrolls of 605/4 (cf 36:2f) and were intended to introduce Jer to the audience and to show that he was a true prophet, sent by God (cf 26:15). Anathoth, place-name, perhaps from the goddess 'Anat (cf 'Ashtaroth), corresponds in name to the modern Arab village 'Anata c. 3 m. NW of Jerusalem. Since there is no evidence of pre-Roman occupation here, Anathoth of Jer's day was probably located at present-day Rās el-Harrūbe, near 'Anata (cf BASOR 62 [1936], 17—26). Anathoth was a priestly city (Jos 21:17f) where the priests would naturally serve at the local high place or sanctuary. Jer may have been descended from the priest Abiathar (1 [3] Kgs 2:26) but this is uncertain. The high place of Anathoth would have been destroyed with the others by Josiah (cf 2 [4] Kgs 23:8*a*). The 13th year of Josiah (639/8—609 B.C.) was 627/6, and refers to Jer's prophetic call, not to his birth as Hyatt (p. 798) believes.

1—2 introduce that part of Jeremiah's prophetic activity; a later redactor added 3 to make the introd. cover the greater part of the remainder of the prophet's career. The 'fifth month' is July/August 587 when the Temple was set on fire (cf 52:12f). Jer was active and prophesied for some time afterwards (cf 42:7ff; 43:8ff; 44:1ff). The Heb. *dābar* can mean both 'word' and 'action'. In 1 it probably connotes both; in 2 it means 'divine oracle'.

d 4—10 The Call of Jeremiah—The narrative or the prophet's call and the divine character of his mission would naturally stand at the beginning of the scrolls of 605/4

B.C. Like Jer, Isaiah (ch 6) and Ezekhiel (chh 1—3), **488** have also left us accounts of their prophetic vocation. **4.** The 'word of the Lord' as in 1, means a divine oracle. This 'word', as in **1**, probably came in 627 B.C. **5.** Before his birth, Jeremiah was 'consecrated', i.e. set aside by God for a special mission (cf Is 49:5; Gal 1:15 dependent on this text of Jer); purification from original sin in the womb is not meant. Being 'known by God' means 'predetermined, set aside'. Jer's mission was that of a prophet to the nations, Israel included, to utter oracles of weal and woe against them (cf 10; 5:14; 18:7—9), not, as in Paul's case (Gal 1:15f; Ac 9:15), to convert the Gentiles. **6.** Like Moses (Ex 4:10) and unlike Isaiah (6:5) Jeremiah's shy and sensitive nature shrank from the difficult mission. He was then a 'youth', (Heb. *na'ar*), anything from 15—25 years. **7.** God would not take no for an answer, and reminded the diffident youth of the power of the divine presence that would accompany him in his mission. This power would bring Jer to prophesy (20:9) and bring the prophecies themselves to fulfilment (3f). Jer's weakness and diffidence were really a boon, helping him to distinguish between his own inclinations and the divine message (cf § 487*l*). **9—11.** The better to impress the **e** import of his word on Jer's mind Yahweh uses a symbolic action. This was in line with the Semitic mentality and that of the OT and NT prophets. By touching his prophet's lips, Yahweh made known that Jer was his accredited mouthpiece; oracles given through Jer would come to pass; to Jer, then, was given power over nations and kingdoms, decreeing, by divine command, their destruction or their prosperity. For the nature of such oracles cf 18:7—9. 'To destroy and overthrow' (cf 24:6; 31:28) are probably a gloss. God's words aptly describe Jer's entire prophetic career. He was the herald of God's chastisement and mercy to Israel and the nations; cf e.g. 18:7—9; 25:15ff; chh 46—51; chh 2ff; 30—31 etc etc. **11f. The Almond Rod**—The vision probably came at a slightly later date as Jer was contemplating a 'stick' cut from an almond tree he was holding in his hand. Playing on the word 'almond' (*šāqēd*) Yahweh reminds Jer that he himself was watching (*šōqēd*) over the oracles he gave to his prophet and would bring them to fulfilment. The almond tree probably got its name from the fact that it is among the earliest to bloom in Palestine ('watching, waking' out of winter sleep).

13—19 Vision of the Boiling Pot—Some time later, **f** while looking at a typical Palestinian pot of the period, with broad mouth and rounded base (example in ANEP, p. 44, no. 147, 3rd from left; p. 45 top right), and probably placed badly on the fire and tilting southward, Jer was reminded that this was a symbol of the punishment in store for Judah. God's burning anger would boil over and bring punishment on Judah in the form of an invasion from the N, (then the usual route of entry for the Mesopotamian armies to Palestine). The enemy ('all the kingdoms of the N' 15) is not here named. Rather than a reference to the Scythian invasion of c. 626 B.C. this is a prophecy of a general nature on the punishment of Judah. Such an invasion would appear unlikely in 627/6 but was a menacing reality in 605, after the battle of Carchemish, when these words were read to Jerusalem. See further § 490*i*—*k*. **17—19.** Jer was comforted. He had God's word within him (9f) and by divine aid, would withstand the onslaught launched against him by his own people.

2:1—37 Divine Indictment on the Nation's Apos- 489a **tasy**—This ch entirely in verse, is a classic example of the prophet's attack on the sins of the chosen people. It

489a is, apparently, the earliest preaching of Jeremiah and comes from the period before Josiah's reform of 622, i.e. 627/6–622. The effects of Manasseh's reign (cf 21:5–17; 2 [4] Kgs) were then still visible. The date indicated by the moral situation depicted agrees with 18 in which Assyria (finally destroyed in 609) appears as a world power. As yet there is no threat of punishment; this enters only in 3:4ff. In these early oracles Jeremiah's dependence on his predecessor Hosea is evident; cf Hos 12:18; 3:1 (marriage bond); 2:16f; 9:10; 11:1 (history).

b Hosea preached against the N kingdom and it may well be that these first words of Jer were also directed to the remnant left behind in Israel after the final destruction in 722. They may even be a meditation on the fate of the N kingdom. Whatever their original occasion or purpose they were read to Judah and Jerusalem from the scroll of 605/4 (2:1; cf ch 36), and, as they now stand, are directed against Israel's S sister. Anything said against Israel could be applied to Judah (cf Is 28:1–4; 7ff). Ch 2 is a combination of short sermons which Jer gave on various occasions. Authors are not agreed on the division of this ch. Bright (17), e.g., unites 2–3 with 14–19, separating them from 4–13, while Rudolph (11f) takes 2–13 as a unit.

c 1–2a Introduction—The divine command may well have come in 605, before he was commanded to write down his oracles (ch 36).

2b–3 Former Fidelity—The prophet recalls Israel's devotion to God during the desert sojourn; with the settlement in Canaan and the passage of years her love has now grown cold. The imagery of Israel's union with Yahweh as that of bride (wife) to husband was already used by Hos 2:21f. 2b is the only place where *hesed* ('devotion') is used of human love. Elsewhere it refers to God's love for Israel (*hesed we'emet*). The unsavoury side of Israel's desert history (idolatry, golden calf, murmurings etc), though doubtless known to Jer (cf 7:24f), is passed over in silence.

d 4–13 Unparalleled Forgetfulness of divine Favours—The introduction (4) indicates that this is a new oracle. It is still from Jer's early preaching and was apparently addressed originally to the N kingdom, Israel. **5–7.** The ideal situation, described in 2b–3, was of short duration. When Israel came into possession of Palestine, God's loving care for them during the terrors of the awful desert journey (cf Dt 32:10; 1:19; 8:15) was soon forgotten. Though given Palestine as a land to be sanctified by the observance of God's law (cf Ps 105 (104):44f; Dt 12:1) and the abolition of idolatry, they **e** succumbed to the immoral practices of Canaan. **8.** The ruling classes are chiefly to blame; the priests by infidelity to revealed teaching (cf Hos 4:4–10 etc), the rulers (lit. 'shepherds'), i.e. kings, princes etc, and finally the prophets, the cult prophets who made light of God's Law by their general attitude and favoured the Canaanite religion of Baal by neglecting to condemn it. Jer directs his attacks principally against these three classes (2:26; 4:9; etc etc). **9–13.** God invites his people to consider how unnatural their apostasy really is (cf Is 1:18; Mi 6:1–8) Cyprus, lit. 'Kittim'; Kedar, see on 49:28f). **13.** Cf Ps 36 (35):8; Jn 4:10ff, 7:38.

f 14–19 The Dire Consequence of Apostasy—14. When Israel was sacred to God her enemies were punished (3f). Her later history indicated that she was treated as a slave. By Israelite law the slave who was purchased or captured was to be set free after seven years (34:14; Ex 21:2) but one born to an Israelite (i.e. a homeborn servant), could not (Ex 21:4). 'Israel' may here have originally meant the N kingdom, destroyed and exiled

since 722 B.C. The entire passage would then be a **489f** meditation on Israel's past history which would serve as a reminder for Judah. **16** may have been added by Jer himself when he consigned the oracle to writing against Judah in 605, cf § 487d. Memphis (in Heb. 'Noph', cf 44:1; 46:14) the ancient capital of Egypt, was near Cairo; Tahpanhes (44:1; 46:14), modern Daphne, was a frontier fortress commanding the road from Egypt to Palestine. **17f.** 'To drink the waters of . . .' means 'to seek aid from . . .'. Israel had forsaken the source of living water, of genuine help. Assyria, destroyed for all intents with the loss of Nineveh in 612, and finally in 605, is still seen as a major world power. **19.** The true source of Israel's plight is given.

20–28 Her Sin is proved—God now gives three **g** examples to show his people how they have forsaken him. **20–22.** Past history. Violation of God's law ('yoke', 'bonds') began as soon as the chosen people settled in Palestine. The Canaanites worshipped on 'high places' with trees, and so did Israel and Judah until Josiah's reform in 622 (cf 2 [4] Kgs 22:4–8). Cult prostitution was practised at these Canaanite sanctuaries. In 20, however, the harlotry referred to probably means idolatry, unfaithfulness to Yahweh, her spouse. For the imagery of the vine cf Is 5:1–7. For 22 cf Is. 1:18. **23–25.** Examples of idolatry. **23bc.** In the 'valley' of Hinnom, a site of Moloch worship outside Jerusalem (cf 7:31, 19:2–6). **23d–25.** Her lust for idolatry and immorality is compared to that of a wild ass. **26–28.** Israel will be humiliated. The 'trees' or 'pieces of wood' and 'stones' were the *'ašerôt* and *maṣṣēbôt*, or steles used as objects of worship in the high places (cf Hos 10:1f). **28.** CV with LXX adds properly to MT 'and as many as the streets of Jerusalem are the altars you have set up for Baal'.

29–32 Yahweh's Lament—God's past punishment **h** was merely corrective, but was in vain. The present generation is asked to be more responsive to the divine appeal; not to abandon God as something worthless, someone to be shunned. Again, reference is made to Israel as God's bride (cf 1; for the adornment, cf Is 49:18; 61:10).

33–37 Israel's unrepentant arrogance—The image **i** of 23f is taken up. As the wild ass does not keep to any path so Israel abandons the true way pointed out by God's law (33, 36). **34.** A somewhat obscure verse referring to the murder of the innocent (CV, with LXX, omits 'poor'). If a man were caught in the act of theft it would be permissible to kill him (Ex 22:2). **36f.** Is directed against some Hebrew party planning an Egyptian alliance, but further we cannot say. Such parties were in evidence in Judah before Jeremiah's day (cf Is 30:1ff etc). The oracle could come from Josiah's reign and from Jer's early preaching. Some authors, however, (e.g. Rudolph, 20) take 26f as an addition from the time of Jehoiakim. Jer, as earlier Is, preaches trust in God alone. 'Hands upon the head' (37) was a sign of mourning (2 Sm 13:19; ANEP, no. 459).

3:1–4:4 The Return of the N and S Kingdoms— j Two parts: (1) 3:1–5; 3:19–4:4, almost entirely in verse, go together and are closely connected with ch 2. Like ch 2, the vv probably belong to Jer's earliest preaching (626–622) and were possibly intended originally for the N kingdom; contrary view in Rudolph 23. (2) 3:6–18, mainly in prose, though largely from Jer's early preaching (cf 6) is partly exilic.

3:1–5; 3:19–4:4. Return of the N Kingdom— **k** **1a** '. . . saying' (RSV note), with which the MT opens, (omitted in LXX, RSV, CV), is probably the sole

489k remaining word of some longer introduction, such as 'The word of the Lord came to me saying' (cf 1:4; BJ); This new title, introducing 3:1—5; 3:19—4:4, indicates that these vv once formed an independent collection cf 51:59—64.

l **3:1—5 Israel's return excluded by Law**—**1.** According to divine law (Dt 24:1—4) a divorced and re-married wife could never be remarried to her first husband. Such a 'wife' (thus LXX, Vg, CV, for 'land' of MT, RSV, BJ) is considered unclean. **2.** Cf 2:20ff; cf Dt 24:4. **3.** The 'latter' (MT) rain fell in March—April, hence 'spring' of RSV, CV. There probably was a drought shortly before (5:21ff; 14:1ff); droughts were considered as punishment of infidelity to God's law (Dt 11:17; 28:24). In **4f** a note of repentance appears, and God invites his people to return in 3:19—4:4, the continuation of 1—5.

m **6—18 The Return of the N and S Kingdoms**—This composite passage breaks the continuity of 3:1—5; 3:19—4:4. **6—11a.** The new introduction (**6a**) indicates a new passage. **8.** The exile of 722 meant Israel's divorce. Yahweh cast the unfaithful spouse out of his house (cf 11:15), an indication that 1—5 were first intended for the N kingdom. 6—12a from the reign of Josiah (**6**), refer to the moral situation in Judah before 622. **12—14.** An invitation to the N kingdom, at home and in exile, to repent and have God bring them back as part of true Israel with Jerusalem as its centre. This passage, too, is probably from Jer's first years when Josiah had plans for re-uniting Israel to Jerusalem (14); cf 2 Chr 24:6f. The passage parallels 31:2—6; 15—22. **15—18.** A later exilic passage, inserted here through the catchword 'return'. The ark probably perished with the temple in 587, if not earlier (cf M. Haran, IEJ 13 [1963] 46—58). The exile of 587 is presupposed. The vv may, however, be from Jer.

n **3:19—4:4 Return possible through repentance**—3:1—5, of which this is a direct continuation, showed that the Law barred the return of the divorced, i.e. exiled, spouse. But God's love is according to the requirements of law and 3:19ff indicates how he awaits the return of the prodigal spouse. **19.** Cf Is 1:2f. **20.** This image is replaced by the more familiar biblical one of husband/spouse. **21.** Yahweh picks up the first signs of repentance; cf 5. **22—25.** God's renewed invitation and

o Israel's reply. **4:1—2.** Yahweh's reply to Israel's repentance, recalling that if this is to be true and acceptable it must be proved by deeds. Then the promises made to the patriarchs (Gn 12:3; 18:18; 22:18; 26:4) will be fulfilled and the nations will desire to be prosperous like her (cf Is 65:15). With BJ in 2cd read 'in you' for 'in him' of MT, RSV, CV. **3f.** Good deeds are mere external signs; real conversion lies in the heart which is to be purified of vices ('thorns'). The same idea is expressed in 4 as 'circumcision of the heart', an expression probably introduced by Jer and found in the later portions of Dt (10:16; 30:6; cf Ezek 44:7; Ac 7:51; Rm 2:25—29).

490a **4:5—6:30 Invasion from the North**—These chh centre round an invasion of Palestine by an unnamed enemy from the N, already announced in 1:15. **4:5—31.** Describes the advance of this enemy from Dan. Ch 5 gives the reason for the invasion, i.e. God's wrath against his people, while ch 6 takes up 4:31 and describes the enemy's attack on Jerusalem. It is not easy to determine when Jer composed these poems. They could come from the reign of Josiah—the invasion would then be seen in prophetic-poetic vision. They could likewise date from any later period, even from the final invasion of

587 B.C. They are inserted in their present position **490** because of their connection with 4:4cd.

4:5—31 Peril from the North—5—8. Raise the alarm! **b** 'The prophet's mind is the seismograph of providence, vibrating to the first faint tremors that herald the coming earthquake' (Skinner 38). Jer is now shown in greater detail how the threat made in 1:14ff will be fulfilled. **6.** 'Standards' are to show the roads to Jerusalem where safety may be sought. **7.** The invading king is compared to a ravaging lion. **11f.** The gathering storm. The storm is the storm-wind of Yahweh; his visitation to punish his people (cf 23:16—20; Hos 13:15). **11f.** However, are critically uncertain. **13—18.** The invasion **c** advances. **13.** A description of the invader. **15—18.** Word of the invasion is passed on by sentinels in Dan, on the northernmost border of Israel; then, further S, from Ephraim, the former centre of the N kingdom; cf Is 10:27b—32. **19—22.** An expression of grief by the patriot poet. **23—28.** Devastation on every side. **29—31.** General panic as the invasion advances to the gates of Jerusalem. **30.** Cf Is 61:10; 3:18—24; 2(4) Kgs 9:30; her lovers despise her cf 30:14; Lam 1:19; Ezek 23:22. The theme is taken up in ch 6.

5:1—31 Universal Corruption, the Cause of this d Punishment—This ch, in the form of an interlude, gives the reason for the invasion. Judah's sin has caught us up with her. **1—5** describes the universality of the corruption in Jerusalem. **6.** The three beasts (cf Dn 7) symbolize the devastation yet to come, a recurring theme in Jer (2:19; 14:20f; 30:15 etc). **7—9.** Stress the same idea. **10f.** The Lord commands the enemy to destroy the unfruitful vineyard, no longer his (cf 2:21; Is 5:1ff; Ps 80 (79):7—16). Omit 'not' after 'make'; cf 6:3 and see to 18. **12f.** Denial of God's activity in history and of the divine mission and veracity of the true prophets. **14.** Cf 1:9—12; 1 Sm 10:17. God's Word will act on the **e** sinful nation like fire on dry wood (cf Obad 18; Zech 12:6). **15—17.** The invasion will prove God's words true. The poetic description in 15 is rather general and cannot be pressed in determining the particular nation intended. **18f.** While the doctrine of 18, in prose, is perfectly Jeremianic (cf 3:14ff; 4:1ff etc) the v is clearly out of context. It is probably an exilic addition, intended to tone down the sombre picture just painted and remind Judah that a remnant will always remain. Such combinations of prophecies of weal with predictions of woe are common in Isaiah (8:8—10; 10:27b—33f; etc). No preacher would spoil the effect of his language in this way. 'Not' in 4:27 and after 'make' in 10 are similar additions. **19.** Too, in deuteronomic prose, is probably an exilic addition. **20—24.** A comparison with nature's obedience to God highlights 'this people's' (a pejorative expression; cf 5:14; 6:21 etc Is 29:13 etc) malice. **25—31.** A further description of the nation's corruption, particularly of its leaders.

6:1—30 The Enemy at the Gate. Jeremiah an f Assayer of the Nation's Moral Depravity—Ch 4 ended with the enemy before Jerusalem. This ch takes up the theme and the invader is invited by God to launch the attack on the faithless city.

1—8 The Inhabitants of Jerusalem invited to flee the Doomed City and the Enemy invited to attack—**1.** 'The people of Benjamin' here are the inhabitants of Jerusalem which was on the borders of Benjamin and Judah, the greater part of it being in Benjamin's territory (Jos 18:10; Jg 1:21). Jer himself was from this tribe (1:1). 'Tekoa', modern Hirbat Tequ, was c. 10m. S; 'Bethhaccherem', not certainly identified, probably near Bethlehem, c. 5 m. S. **3.**

490f A traditional manner of describing a ruined city (33:12; Is 13:20; cf 34:11). **4a.** The invading army speaks; **4b.** The cry of despair from the besieged. **6–8.** A divine command to the besieging army. Sin must be punished. **8.** Shows the entire passage is merely a threat: disaster can be averted by repentance; cf 18:5–11; Lk 19:41–44; Mt 23:37).

g 9–15 The Coming Destruction Due solely to Judah's Sin—9f. 8 contained an invitation to repentance. General moral depravity make this impossible and so the enemy is told to wipe out what remains of Israel. The 'remnant' here means 'what remains', i.e. leave nothing. It has not the technical sense found in Is (1:3; 6:13 etc). For 'they shall glean' of MT and LXX read with RSV, CV BJ, 'glean' (imperative). Some (e.g. Rudolph, Gelin in BJ) take 9 as addressed to Jer commanding him to seek further (cf 5:4f) whether any good could be found in Judah that could avert God's anger. **10.** Uncertain whether it is God or the prophet who speaks. **11.** Jer's oracles effect what they express (see to 1:9f); oracles of doom effect destruction. **13–15.** Universal corruption once again. Instead of preaching the inevitable punishment, the prophets said all was well ('peace' in Hcb. sense) and would remain so.

h 16–27 An Invitation to Repentance—God gave two major gifts to his people in the Law (16) and the prophets (17). The former showed them the true way to peace and happiness, while the prophets were as watchmen (cf Hos 9:8; Is 21:11; 56:10; Hb 2:1) who foresaw the disaster stemming from defiance of God's law and warned them to pay heed. **16f.** Is cited and given a further meaning by our Lord (Mt 11:29). **20.** See on 7:21–23. The 'sweet cane from a distant land' (cf Is 43:24; song 4:14; Ezek 29:19) is the well-known aromatic plant (*acorus calamus*) from India (cf Pliny, *Natural History*, 12, 48; 13, 20ff) **22–26.** A final description of the invasion and of its results **27–30.** The prophet has been given the mission of testing and assaying Judah's metal. When put in the refining furnace nothing remained, i.e. all was base metal (29).

i Excursus. The Enemy from the North chh 1–6—At his call in 627/6 B.C. Jer was told that Yahweh would call 'all the tribes of the kingdoms of the N' against Judah (1:13–15). This is the invasion described in chh 4–6 (cf 4:6; 6:1.22). The invading enemy comes from afar (5.15), from the farthest parts of the earth (6:22); an ancient nation (5.15). Its armies are equipped with horses and chariots, bows and spears (4:13.29; 6:23). It speaks a language unknown in Judah (5:15). The earlier view, still defended by some (Condamin, Penna, Hyatt) held that the enemy envisaged is the Neo-Babylonian empire. This power, however, was only beginning in Babylon in 626 and did not really make itself felt in Palestine until the battle of Carchemish in 605 B.C. In actual fulfilment, of course, the foe from the N *were* the Babylonians and at a later period Jer (13:20; 25:9; cf 46:24) refers to them as such. This does not mean Jer knew in his earlier visions that this foe would be the Chaldeans. Recall that Hyatt (p. 779) believes these 'early' oracles of Jer on this foe are from the reign of Jehoiakim.

j Another view, originating with Venema in 1765 and still widely held, maintains that it refers to the invasion of Palestine by the Scythians in 630–625 B.C. mentioned by Herodotus (I, 103–6). A defence of this view and an exposition and critique of the objections brought against it can be seen in H. H. Rowley, 'The Early Prophecies of Jeremiah in their Setting', BJRL 45

(1962–3), 198–234 = *Men of God*, 1963, 133–68, **490j** esp. 140–8 (with exhaustive bibliography). Cf also H. Cazelles, RB 74 (1967) 24–44. The Scythian invasion of Palestine, unattested by archaeology or other sources outside Herodotus is subject to serious difficulties and has been abandoned by a number of scholars after F. Wilke (*Beiträge zur Wissenschaft von Alten Testament*, 13 [1913], 222ff).

A. C. Welch (*Jeremiah*, 1928, 97ff) believed these **k** early prophecies were vague eschatological predictions (cf Zeph ch 1), referring to no individual concrete foe. This appears improbable in view of the insistence on punishment by war. Rudolph (45), Gelin (BJ) and others take it that in these early visions Jer was shown that an enemy would come from the N to punish Israel but was not told the identity of this foe. Hence, the enemy remains unnamed. Such an invasion, highly improbable in 626–620, when the prophecies were made, may have occasioned the reproach suffered by the prophet for unfulfilled predictions and Jer's lament (cf 20:8f). When Jer was commanded to write down his earlier prophecies in 605/4, after Carchemish, there was no doubt in anyone's mind as to the true identity of the enemy from the N. Jer may then have touched up his earlier prophecies in the light of their fulfilment. Further bibliography in Rudolph 43 and esp. Rowley op cit, 141ff.

7:1–20:18 Mainly from the time of Jehoiakim— **491a** This section, like others in Jer, is composed from earlier and smaller collections and contains all three classes of material, A, B and C. (cf 487g) It is idle to attempt to determine the criteria according to which it received its present form. The section contains the following minor divisions: 1) chh 7–10; 2) chh 11–13; 3) chh 14–17; 4) chh 18–20 (cf Rudolph). Chh 7–10 are taken to be a collection in themselves as the next introd. is found in 11:1. Within this collection we have oracles and episodes from various periods, mainly in oracular poetry (class A), occasionally (7.1–8:3) in deuteronomic prose (C). 9:11–15, in deuteronomic prose, is probably a later addition.

7:1–15 The Temple Sermon—This passage is in **b** deuteronomic prose (C). A shorter form of it and its sequel in the biographical prose of Baruch (B) can be seen in ch 26. The earlier original form of the sermon is probably that of B. 7:1–15, would then be an expansion of Jer's preaching or a recasting of it in deuteronomic style. Some authorities, however, believe the C style is original and that used by Jer, believing even that 7:1ff formed part of the original scroll (cf EOT Int 351f). The substance of this sermon is that the Temple is no guarantee of divine protection; this can be found only in genuine conversion. The passage is, then, well placed after chh 1–6.

1. From 26:1 we know the command came at the begin- **c** ning of the reign of Jehoiakim, i.e. Sept 609–April 608 B.C. **2.** We cannot say which gate is intended. 26:1 says 'court'. **3–6.** God will remain with Israel only if they are holy (cf Ex 33:5), i.e. only if they fulfil his Law, living in proper relations with their neighbour, avoiding idolatry and remaining aloof from pagan customs. Some false teachers, presumably priests or prophets, if not both, were teaching that, irrespective of moral conduct, the very existence of Yahweh's temple was sufficient guarantee of the safety of the city and nation. This basis of the super- **d** stitious hope apparently originated in the belief that, by permitting the destruction of his shrine, Yahweh would show himself weaker than the gods of the invading armies. The superstition on the Temple's inviolability, while probably originating in 701 (cf Is 37:10ff, 22ff etc), would have been greatly strengthened by the centralization of

491d cult in Jerusalem by Josiah in 622 B.C. (cf § 487*b*). **7—11.** So far had the superstition gone in 609/8 that the people came to the Temple, considering themselves safe in its shelter, despite their intention of continuing an immoral life. **11.** With Is 56:7, is cited by our Lord in Mt 21:13. The crimes listed in 9 are violations of the commandments.

e 12—15. Shiloh, the first sanctuary of the Ark, cf 1 Sm 1—4. Its destruction, not attested elsewhere in the Bible (except, perhaps, Ps 78 (77):60), about 1050 B.C., is verified by excavation. cf Eissfeldt, VTS 4 (1957), 138—47. In Jer 7 and 26 we have the beginning of the theology of the spiritual Temple. God is not bound within any material building. Such externals are intended to lead man to his creator and when they prove an obstacle rather than an aid God will remove them. Service of God without a Temple during the exile further purified Jewish belief (Ezek 10:4ff; 11:22). A new temple and its glory became a theme with later prophets (Ezek chh 40—48 esp. 47:1—12; cf Zech 14:8f; Is 4:18; Ps 46 (45):5; in the NT, cf Jn 2:18—22; 4:13; 7:37—39; Apoc 22:1f; see Y. Congar *The Mystery of the Temple*, 1962). In Jer's day his teaching was novel, revolutionary and not acceptable. His sermon almost cost him his life (cf 26:7ff).

f 7:16—8:3 Against Abuses in Worship—This passage, still in deuteronomic style, appears as part of Jer's Temple sermon. Yet this can hardly be the case, as we know from 26:16ff that a riot followed on Jer's threat against the Temple. What we have here is other doctrine of Jer from the deuteronomic school as a development of 7:1—15. The passage shows the futility of exterior works without a genuine attitude of obedience to God's will as expressed by earlier and contemporary organs of revelation. This pericope is to be interpreted in the light of other deuteronomic passages of our book. **16—20.** Jer was, apparently, wont to intercede for his people. It may have been a regular function of the prophets (cf Am 7:22f) and Jer may have thus been connected with the cult (cf 11:18—23; 12:1—3, 5f; 14:1—15:4, 10f, 15—21; 20:7—13; see EOT Int 117, 356). In his intercessory role Jer is like Samuel (I Sm 7:9; Jer 15:1) and Moses (Ex 32:11ff etc; Jer 15:1); see also Gn 18:23ff (Abraham) and 2 Sm 14:17 (David). Now, and again in 11:12ff; 14:11f (cf 15:1), he is commanded to discontinue this **g** practice. God's wrath will not be averted from an impenitent people. **18f.** The 'queen of heaven' is probably the Assyrian-Babylonian goddess Ishthar, i.e. the planet Venus. She bears the same name (*šarrat šamē*) in Akkadian. Her cult, probably introduced during the reign of Manasseh and suppressed after Josiah's reform, appears to have revived during the reign of Jehoiakim (cf 44:15ff). The entire family took part in her worship (44: 19). The cakes were in the form of an eight-pointed star, goddess' emblem (49:19; cf ANEP no. 529 and p. 313). The libations were poured out in her honour.

h 21—23 Merely External Sacrifice Rejected—In holocausts the entire victim was consumed by fire (Ex 29:18; Lv 1:3ff); in other sacrifices part was left for the priests and for a sacred banquet. Here God ironically tells the offerers to consume the entire sacrifice themselves. He will have none of it. It represents nothing God desires, (i.e. their good will) and is entirely theirs. **22f.** Is the main text on which many older, and some contemporary writers (N. Snaith, ET 58 [1946—47] 152f; C. J. Cadoux, ibid 43—46), base the view that for the prophets all sacrifice was to **i** be rejected. To interpret the passage justly we must take into consideration the parallel of 6:20, but particularly the deuteronomic pericopes 11:12ff; 14:11ff; 15:1ff. In 6:20 holocausts and sacrifices are rejected, not because they are evil in themselves but owing to the offerers' evil

dispositions (6:19). In 11:3 Yahweh declares cursed those **491** who do not observe the terms of the covenant and in 11:12 says he will not listen to their prayers (cp. 7:16), i.e. because of their evil dispositions. In 14:11f he tells Jer not to intercede for them. Their fasts, supplications and sacrifices he will not accept, again, (understood) because of their sinful intentions. In 15:1 we read that even the intercession of Moses and Samuel before God in favour of the sinful people would prove useless. The idea and sequence of these passages are the same as in I Sm 15: 11—22, which text may have inspired them (cf Samuel's intercession in Jer 15:1). In I Sm 15:11 Samuel intercedes before God in Saul's favour, but in vain. Saul is rejected because he did not obey the voice of the Lord (19) because the Lord delights in obedience to his word rather than in burnt offerings and sacrifice (22). This, too, is the idea of Jer 7:16—23 and other passages (Is 1:10—17; Hos 6: 6; Am 5:21—7 etc) where sacrifice is rejected by God; **j** cf further, H. H. Rowley, 'The Meaning of Sacrifice in the OT", BJRL 33 (1950), 89—93; *The Unity of the Bible*, 1957, 38—62; ET 59 (1946—7), 305—7, B. Vawter, *Concilium* vol 10, no. 1 (Dec. 1965). 61f. God's command during the desert period was to obey his word, i.e. to carry out his Law (cf Ex 19:5; Dt 5:29). His religion consists in a general attitude of soul towards him rather than in individual external acts. 'I did not command them concerning holocaust and sacrifice', therefore means: 'My command to Israel was in obedience of soul rather than in the letter of these precepts'. Sacrifice was part of Semitic religion from pre-historic times and was certainly prescribed by Israelite custom and law during the desert wanderings. Prescriptions on the matter are found in the oldest portions of the Pent. (Ex 20:24; 23:18; cf Dt 12:6ff) and must have been known to Jer (cf Rudolph, 53), and accepted by him as of divine origin.

24—28 Further Emphasis on the Same Theme— k Note that the desert period no longer appears in the idealized fashion of 2:2f; 6:16. Defection began already during the wanderings.

7:29—8:3. Sinful Rites in the Valley of Hinnom— 29. An elegy on Judah personified. For the custom of cutting the hair during mourning see Mi 1:16; Jb 1:20. **30.** Despite Josiah's reform (2 [4] Kgs 23:4) conditions in the Temple were now as in the time of Manasseh (cf 2 [4] Kgs 21:4.7). This sad state of things continued up to 587; cf Ezek 8. **31.** Topheth was an artificial high-place (cf 2:23) in the valley of Gehenna, running E and S of the city. Such child-offerings, typical of Moloch-worship (32:35) and condemned in Lv 18:21 (cf Gn 22), were here offered to Yahweh. **32—34.** The punishment at the city's **l** destruction would correspond to the crime. Lack of proper burial was considered a terrible punishment among the Jews (cf 22:19). **8:1—3.** All four classes, so often mentioned in our book, were to be desecrated in like manner. Note the irony in 2. 'This is a terrifying description of the suffering Jerusalem is to meet with; but it is more terrible still that all so came to pass' (Rudolph, 55).

8:4—9:25. Verses on Various Occasions—With the **492a** exception of 9:1—15 (probably a later addition) and 9: 24f this passage is entirely in verse, composed by the prophet on various occasions and brought together by himself (for the scroll of 605/4?) or by a later editor.

8:4—7 The People's Conduct Incomprehensible— They keep charging towards wickedness like a war horse (6; cf Jb 39:19—25) whereas such migratory birds as the stork, turtledove, swallow and crane (RSV; 'thrush' CV; exact equivalent of Heb. word uncertain) return in due season (7). What we call instinct the Hebrews saw as God's command (cf Jb 38:39—41). **8—12. Against Scribes, b**

92b Prophets and Priests—8f., (probably a new pericope, independent of the preceding), is directed against 'scribes'—the first mention of this class in the Bible. The 'Law of the Lord' is probably divine revelation. Possession of this as in inert letter or tradition is of no avail; it must be properly interpreted and made the norm of everyday behaviour. True wisdom consists in doing God's will. The context is not sufficiently explicit to permit us to determine who the scribes were or how they changed the Law into falsehood. **10—12.** Against prophets and priests who give a sense of false security. It parallels 6:12—15, and, except for 10, is omitted by LXX.

c 13—17 Judah a Rejected Fruit-tree—13. God speaks. **14—16.** Judah's answer on seeing the imminent disaster. **17.** God speaks. The particular kind of serpent (RSV 'adder') intended in MT is uncertain.

18—23 Jeremiah's Grief over his People's Sufferings—Here the prophet shows himself a true brother of his people: their sufferings rend his heart (cf 14:17 etc). The situation described presupposes some invasion and was probably composed about 597 after the country had been ravaged by Arabs (cf 35:11; 2 [4] Kgs 24:2). **19.** Has Yahweh, Israel's King, abandoned his Temple; (contrast 7:11—15). **20.** This v leads some to believe the poem was composed on the occasion of a drought (cf 14:1—10) but this conclusion is unnecessary. **22f.** Gilead was noted for its balm, used by physicians (46:11; cf Gn 37:25). But the wound inflicted on Israel by devastation is too deep and does not heal; cf Is 1:5f. The LXX, Vg and RSV number 8:23 of MT and CV as 9:1 and give 26 vv to ch 9.

d 9:2—9 (MT 1—8) The Corruption of the People—The similarity of 1 with the preceding v explains its insertion here. The passage is parallel to 6:27—30.

10—22 Dirge over the Ravaged Land—10. Cf 4:25 and see Skinner, 22f. **12—16.** In prose, appear to be a later deuteronomic insertion intended to explain why the devastation just described came about (cf 22:8f). **17—22.** This is the only explicit mention of professional keeners in Israel (cf however, Sir 38:16ff; Mi 5:38; cf Am 5:16; 2 Chr 35:25). The practice was still current in Jerome's day (*in loc.* PL 24, 744). The dirge itself is found in **21** where Death (*māwet, môt*) is personified, as in Is 28:15, 18. The passage may reflect Canaanite (Ugaritic) tradition where Mot, the god of death succeeds in killing his enemy Aliyan-Baal.

e 23f (MT: 22f) True Glory—The text is referred to by another descendant of Benjamin in I Cor 1:31; 2 Cor 10:17. See also on 8:8f.

25f (MT: 24f) Circumcision is Worthless—25, 'circumcised, but yet uncircumcised'; lit. 'circumcised in the foreskin'. They lack true circumcision, that of the heart, i.e. obedience to God. See on 4:4. **26 (25).** For circumcision among Egyptians (some classes, at least) see Herod. II, 37.104; for 'Phoenicians and Syrians of Palestine', ibid 104; for Arabs, Gn 16 and Jos. Ant 1,214. Circumcision in Ammon, Edom and Moab, not mentioned elsewhere, is implied by the opprobrious term 'uncircumcised' being levelled only against the Philistines (Jg 14:3; I Sm 14:6 etc). If we take 'all the (RSV 'these') nations are uncircumcised' of MT (and RSV) as original the reference is to circumcision of heart. The Heb. word *'arēlîm* is, however, probably a corruption of *hā'elleh*, 'these' (CV, BJ). The threat in this v is spelt out in the oracles against the nations (25:15—38; chh 46—49). 'In the days to come' Paul will develop the theme of true circumcision (Rm 2:25—29 etc).

f 10:1—16 The Folly of Idolatry—The pagan gods are mere nothingness, creatures of human craftsmanship—hence not to be feared (**1—10**). The God of Israel, on the contrary, is a living God, master of the universe and the **492f** elements. He has chosen Israel for himself (**12—16**). The passage is clearly alien to its present context which is directed against the immorality and syncretism of Judah. It is now generally held that it is not from Jer. It was probably composed for the Jews in exile, hence, very likely, before 539, though it may be later. It appears to be dependent on second Isaiah (cf Is 40:19—22; 41:7—29; 44:9—20; 46:6f. Cf also Ps 115 (113):2—8; 135 (134): 15—18; Wis 13:2ff) and inspired the Letter of Jeremiah, i.e. Bar ch 6. Vv 12—16 are found again in 51:15—19.

17—22 Deportation is Near—19f. Jerusalem com- **g** pares herself to a tent; cf 4:20; cf Is 54:2. **21f.** A reflection of Jerusalem, or more probably, of the prophet. The 'shepherds' here are the kings and princes (cf 2:8; 6:14; 8:9). **22.** A dramatic conclusion. The enemy advances from the N; cf 1:15 etc. The pericope was probably composed shortly before Nebuchadnezzar's advance on Jerusalem in 598.

23f Prayer of Jeremiah— Most probably from Jer **h** himself despite 7:16; 11:12ff; 14:11f. **25.** Not in harmony with the context or Jer's teaching (cf 9:9; 15f) is generally taken as a later gloss; cf Ps 79 (78):6f.

11:1—14 Plea for Fidelity to the Covenant—Heavily **i** deuteronomic in style, language and teaching; compare v 3 with Dt 27:26; 4 with Dt 4:20; 5 with Dt 7:12f; 6:3; 11:9 ('Milk and honey'); 'as this day'; Dt 2:30; 4:20, 38; 6:24; 8:18; 10:15; 29:27 and also with Jer 25:18; 32:20; 44:6.22f; 'Amen', cf Dt 27:15—26; v 8 with Dt 29:18 (but also with Jer 3:17; 9:13; 13.10, 16.12; 18:12; 23:17. 1—14 is clearly from the deuteronomic source (cf § 487g) but probably represents, nonetheless, the genuine teaching of Jer, despite the contrary view (Duhm; Cornill) denying any connection with Jer's career. The passage is the principal text in the discussion on Jer's relation to Dt and Josiah's reform of 622, cf § 492o—p. **1.** A typical C introduction; cf 7:1; 18:1, 21:1; **j** 35:1; cf 25:1; 34:1. Like 7:1; 18:1; and unlike the other C texts, no chronological indication is given. **2.** Omit 'hear (ye) . . . this covenant' of MT, LXX, Vg and RSV as an interpolation from 6 (so CV, BJ, Penna, Rudolph) and for 'say ye' (pl.) of MT read 'say' (sing.) with LXX. **3.** 'Cursed etc', found also in relation to 'this law' in Dt 27:26. What pact 'this covenant' refers to is not stated. Rudolph, 71f, says the only possible one is that of 4f, i.e., the Sinai Covenant (Ex 24; cf 7:21—23), so also Weiser 95, Hyatt 905f and JBL 59 (1940), 512, already König, Volz etc. Weiser 95, Bright 89, and Volz would take the passage as referring to the reign of Jehoiakin. Others **k** take 'this covenant' (cf 2 [4] Kgs 23:3) unspecified here, to refer to that contracted by Josiah in 621, (2 [4] Kgs 23), shortly before Jer's sermon of 11:1ff, according to this view (Skinner 100, 102; Rowley, *Studies in OT Prophecy*, 1950, 157ff; *Men of God*, 159—67; Eissfeldt, *The OT and Modern Study*, 153; cf Bright 89). This opinion, despite difficulties, is probable. On the view that takes the vv as a later tendentious fabrication, see Excursus. **4f.** Only the essential element of the covenant is given. By genuine, internal obedience to his Law is Israel God's true people. **6—8.** If 'this covenant' is that of **l** Dt, contracted anew by Josiah, Jer is here commanded to preach its observance. 'Cities of Judah and streets of Jerusalem' (6), a stereotyped expression is not to be pressed; cf 10:12; 33:10; 44:6, 17, 21. If Jer preached Josiah's reform he certainly insisted on its internal, rather than its external aspects. 7f appear to be exilic. **9—12.** The prevailing syncretism is considered a conspiracy against the Sinai Covenant. **13.** In v, and out of

492l context, it is probably a gloss from 2:28*b*. **14.** See on 7:16.

15—17 Exile not averted by Sacrifice—Though 15f are textually uncertain the general sense is clear. Sinful Israel has no right to present itself at the Temple (or 'remain in Palestine'? cf 3:1, 8). God's good pleasure is not won by mere external cult. Disaster is sure to come.

m **Excursus. Jeremiah's Relation to Deuteronomy and to Josiah's Reform**—Here we must distinguish between the relation of the Books of Jer and Dt as they now stand and the prophets' relation to the original Book of Dt that inspired Josiah's reform in 622. As we have seen our present book of Jer has some deuteronomic sections, coming, apparently, from an exilic redaction. These may be said to depend on Dt, in its original or exilic edition. These later sections of the Book of Dt may, in turn, be dependent on the genuine teaching of Jer.

n The question at issue is whether Jer's preaching shows dependence on the early edition of Dt and what were Jer's relations, if any, with Josiah's reform and centralization of cult in 622. That the prophet must have known the Book of Dt that led to Josiah's reform is clear. Some hold that the (C) sections of Jer which favour the covenant and cult (11:1ff etc) as expounded in Dt are exilic inventions of the deuteronomic editors, in an attempt to show that their views had the support of the prophet of Anathoth (Bentzen, *Introd.*, 118f; Hyatt 906). These believe that Jer's teaching on the cult (cf 7:16—8:3 etc) and the Law-Book (8:8) exclude any support by the prophet for Dt Josiah's reform. This position is highly improbable. An intentional inventor, claiming Jer's support for Dt and the reform, would express himself less obscurely

o than does the author of 11:1ff. Other authors (Skinner, 100—7; Rowley: 'The Prophet Jeremiah and the Book of Deuteronomy', *Studies in OT Prophecy*, 157—74; *Men of God*, 159—67; Eissfeldt, *The OT and Modern Study*, 153) hold that Jer at first welcomed Josiah's reform instigated by the book of Dt, even advocating its acceptance throughout Judah (11:1ff) but later changed his attitude because his hopes in it were not realized (18:8).

p Though the evidence does not warrant a definite answer, the nature of things and the prophet's teaching indicate that Jeremiah would have welcomed any method tending to reduce syncretism. He may have at first advocated the destruction of the local shrines. With the external means of reform he would not, however, go very far. His divine message made him see that the evil lay deeper, within men's hearts. Without a genuine return to the essence of religion, i.e. internal obedience to God, all external means and actions were useless. This, too, of course, is the teaching of Dt, which, being a law-book, prescribes for the external forms of cult as well. Between Jer and Dt, then, when properly understood, there is no contradiction and the prophet may well have been inspired by it. Cf further, Condamin 103—6; Rudolph, 73f.

493a **11:18—12:6 Jeremiah's Confessions 1; Danger of Death at Anathoth**—This is the first of a group of passages known as the 'Confessions of Jeremiah'. The other texts are: (2) 15:10—21; (3) 17:12—18; (4) 18:18—23; (5) 20:7—18. In these the prophet lays bare his innermost soul, his trials and his colloquies with God. They reveal to us his sensitive nature and help us trace his spiritual itinerary. These confessions probably are short compositions Jer wrote down for his own personal use on different occasions during his life of trial. Their insertion into the book of Jer is due to Baruch or some other editor. Cf G. M. Behler, O.P. *Les Confessions de*

b *Jérémie*, Tournai, 1959; Skinner, 201—30. This first of the confessions speaks of a plot by Jer's relatives

(12:6) and by the men of Anathoth (11:23) on his life, **493** in which the unsuspecting prophet was almost caught unawares (11:19). The date and occasion of the plot are uncertain but it could well be the destruction by Josiah's men of the local high-place at Anathoth (c. 622) at which Jer's priestly family may have functioned (cf 1:1). It would then be a suitable sequence to 11:1—17. But a date **c** from any period of Jer's life is also possible. To obtain a more logical order some authors rearrange the verse-sequence. Cornill and Köberle put 12:1—6 before 11:18—23; Rudolph has the following sequence: 11:19; 12:6; 11:19; 12:3; 11:20—23; 12:1f, df. 7—12; BJ puts 12:6 between 11:18 and 19; CV has 12:1—6 between 11:18 and 19. If the original order has been disturbed reconstruction according to our logic is hazardous. It is better to interpret the passage as it stands. **18f.** Jer **d** considered his discovery of the plot as coming from God. The plan was to kill the celibate Jer (cf 16:2) whose memory would then not be perpetuated in his children. For 'with its fruits', read, preferably, 'in its vigour', correcting MT's *belahmô* to *belēhô*, or, with Arabic *lahm*, understanding the MT word as 'sap'. The Vg, DV rendering ('let us *put* wood in his bread') follows the LXX and Targum reading *nasîtāh* ('let us put') for *nashîtāh* ('let us cut down') of the MT. Jerome's Vg rendering is messianic. Is 53:7, describing the Suffering Servant, depends on 19*a* and Jer is thus a type of Christ. **20.** A true representative **e** of OT morality Jer prays to be avenged; cf Mt 5:38; cf Lk 23:34; 1 Pt 2:23. **12:1—5.** The problem of the success of the wicked. If the vv are in their right context the problem arose for Jer out of his own plight. This, in any case, is the oldest datable OT text where this problem is raised. It is raised again in the Pss (e.g. 38 (37); 50 (49) and 74 (73) etc) and in Job. The posing of the question naturally was due to the emerging individualism of the time and, in particular, to the sensitive nature of Jeremiah; contrast Ex 20:5. Jer is told to strengthen himself and prepare for greater trials yet to come. The thickets of the Jordan were noted for undergrowth and lions; cf 8; v 4 is a gloss or stray v; cf ch 14.

7—13 Yahweh's Lament over Fallen Israel—The **f** people he loves has turned against him and he has now handed her over to her enemies for chastisement. Many take 13 as a gloss or as a misplaced v.

14—17 The Exile; Repatriation and Conversion of Israel's Neighbours—As elsewhere (see to 5:18f), an oracle of doom against Judah is followed by one against her plunderers. Jer was, in fact, sent to prophesy against all nations (25:15ff). On their deportation see 48:7, 46f (Moab); 49:20 (Edom). Since the idea of pagan nations becoming proselytes is a favourite exilic and post-exilic one (Is 14:1; 18:7; 19:16ff; 44:5; Zech 3:10; 8:20—23; cf Jer 48:47; 49:6) this prose passage is, probably of the same period, though Weiser (107) considers it Jeremianic.

13:1—11 The Useless Loin Cloth—Three questions **g** arise from this passage: (1) Did Jer perform the action in reality or in vision? (2) If in reality, did he go to the Euphrates? (3) What is the significance of the action? On the first two questions opinion is divided. Jerome (Prol. in Os; PL 25, 818) thinks Jer 12:1—11 (cf 25:15—17) recounts a vision and so do Condamin, 115f; Penna, 126; Rudolph 85; Weiser, 110f. Their reason is that two return journeys to the Euphrates (some 625 m. from Jerusalem) cannot be supposed. A single journey took Ezra 100 days (Ez 7:9) Aquin, Dennefeld, Buzy (*Les symboles de* **h** *l'A.T.*, 1923, 120—6), Gelin (in BJ) and others believe the actions took place in reality. These take *perat* of the MT to mean not the Euphrates but the modern Wadi Fara' (cf Parah, city of Benjamin, Jos 18:23), 3½ m. NE of

93h Anathoth. Aquila, too, they note, renders *perat* of 4 as *Phara(n)*. Note CV rendering 'Pharat'. The difficulty with this view is that the symbolism requires that the river in question be the Euphrates, not a river in Palestine. And it is in no way certain that the modern Wadi Fara' was

i called the *Perat* in Jer's day. The symbolism of the passage is, in the main, clear. The loincloth (in 1f, 11) stands for Yahweh's people, his renown, praise, beauty (11): Jer symbolizes Yahweh. This much is certain; what follows less so. The decay of the loincloth near the waters of the *Perat* seems to signify that Israel became corrupt when she went to the waters of the Euphrates (cf 2:18), i.e. when she sought help from Mesopotamia and became affected by her religion. Before that she was intact. Now God will not wear the loincloth any longer, i.e. Israel is rejected. The date of the vision or action is uncertain; nor do we know if Jer preached this parable in public.

j **12–14 The symbol of the Wine Jars**—In prose. The passage is scarcely a sermon. The remark was possibly addressed to topers and may have been a current proverb. Their reply to Jer's banal question is prompt: 'We know that!' The prophet applies the imagery to Judah. The entire population will be made drunk by Yahweh's anger, i.e. rendered incapable of action (cf 25:25–27; 48:26; 51:7.57) and destroyed. The passage is a threat of pending disaster and may come from the reign of Jehoiakim or Zedekiah.

k **15–27 Various Oracles 15–17.** An admonition to walk straight again while there is light (cf Jn 12:35), fittingly inserted after 12–14. **18f.** An oracle against Jehoiachin and the Queen Mother Nehushta. The king was only 18 when he came to the throne in 598 (2 [4] Kgs 24:8) and the Queen Mother most probably enjoyed great prestige during his short reign of three months. He was deported in 16/16 March 597, on this king cf further 22:24–30. **19.** No mention of such destruction or exile is known for 597. The oracle was, however, verified in 588/7 B.C. **20–27.** The prophet speaks to Jerusalem to whom immoral conduct is now second nature. (23). Her sins will be punished by deportation and 22, 26 describe realistically how women were treated by the victorious invader. The passage may date from Jerusalem's last days, though, owing to its similarity with chh 1–6 some attribute it to the prophet's early preaching.

494a **14:1–17:27.** The introductions in 14:1 and 18:1 indicate that chh 14–17 is a section composed of heterogeneous material assembled by an editor.

14:1–15:4 The Great Drought—Mainly in verse. 2–6 Description of the drought; 7–9 Communal lament; 10–12 Yahweh's reply; 13–16 Jeremiah appeals in vain for the people; 17f Description of the ravages wrought on Judah by war and hunger; 19–22 New communal lament because of the drought; 15:1–4 Another divine reply. Many (e.g. Rudolph 91; EOTInt 356) consider the entire passage a unity; some (Weiser 121; Bright 103f) as composed of originally independent pericopes; Weiser believes we have here two distinct pericopes referring to droughts; 2–6 and 14:17–15:4; hence the plural '(con-

b cerning the) droughts' in the MT title. The entire passage can be compared with Jl 1–2. Some think that here we have a 'prophetic liturgy' in which Jer may have played the role of intercessor for the people (cf Weiser, 122; Eissfeldt, *OT and Modern Study*, 145–7; *OTInt*, 118, 356). Since droughts were common, this passage cannot be dated with certainty (cf 3:3a; 5:21–25; 8:18ff), though Rudolph 91 ascribes it to Jer's early years.

c **1.** An editorial introduction to 14:1–15:4 in the usual style, but here inexact as it is not Yahweh who speaks in 2ff. 'Drought'. MT's plural, unless we accept Weiser's

view, is probably a plural of intensity (GK, § 124e). **494c 7–9.** A communal lament; a common form of Temple service. The prophet may here be citing a traditional hymn (Skinner 130f) or composing one on traditional lines. It consists of (a) general confession of guilt (cf Dt 9:4ff; Ps 51 (50):6 etc) (b) plea and reason for divine mercy. **10–12.** Yahweh considers the repentance expressed as insincere and transitory (cf Hos 9:9) and does not accept it. **11f.** In prose but from Jer; cf 7:16; 11:14; 15:1). **17–22.** Into this new communal lament the perspective of war (18) enters. **15:1–4** On the intercession of Moses see Ex 32:11ff; 31ff; Nm 14:13–20; cf Ex 17:11ff; on that of Samuel, 1 Sm 7:9; 12:19. See also above to 7:16.

15:5–9 Jeremiah's Lament on Jerusalem—Though **d** this pericope is connected in the MT and Vg with the preceding passage ('then', cf BJ, absent from LXX and Syriac), it is an independent oracle on the destruction in store for Jerusalem and the cities of Judah (7). Since partial exile is implied in 7 ('winnowed' = scattered) the oracle was probably occasioned by the first siege of Jerusalem (597 B.C.), cf 13:18f, or by the invasions that preceded it; cf 2 (4) Kgs; I Sm 2:5; 24:2ff **9.** 'Mother of seven', i.e., a large number (1 Sm 2:5 Ru 4:15; Is 4:1); 'her sun', i.e. her hope, her children (cf Mi 3:6; Am 8:9). Her future is dim.

10–21 Jeremiah's Confessions 2; Failure and e Repentance. Cf note to 11:18. This has no connection with the preceding pericope but is inserted here through the catch-word 'mother' in 9 and 10. In this passage Jer tells us of a spiritual crisis that almost led him to despair and blaspheme. (18) **10** Like Job (Jb 3;3) Jer curses the day of his birth (cf 20: 14–18). His mission has brought him nothing but contradiction and contempt. **11.** He even interceded for his enemies before God, surely a peak in OT spirituality (cf Mt 5:43). On Jer's intercessory prayer see to 7:16. His role as intercessor was apparently exercised in public and known to all. **12–14** (omitted in CV) **f** are probably stray vv, wrongly inserted here 13f occur again in MT 17:3b–4 where LXX omits them. **15.** Cf 12:3. **16f.** For 17 see 16:8f which the verse presupposes. **18.** Jer almost blasphemously accuses Yahweh of playing **g** him false (cf 20:7), becoming a 'deceitful brook': a wadi that allures the weary traveller but has no water (cf Jb 6:15–20; Mi 1:14; Is 58:11). How far from the days when he preached that God was the source of living waters! (2:13). **19–21.** The divine reply and the second call of **h** Jeremiah. Yahweh does not excuse his prophet's backsliding. No man, not even the prophets, can question the rectitude of God's ways (cf 12:1a). Despite the power of the prophetic word within him (20:7, 9) he remains a free agent and must ever perfect himself further. As God's mouthpiece he must speak what God wants; not what nature may prompt. **20.** Jer's initial call (1:17–19) is reinforced by God. As on other occasions, so also here Jer has to experience in his own soul the significance of the oracles he preaches to others. Although this section of the Confessions is often assigned to a later date in Jer's life, e.g. the reign of Jehoiakim (cf Skinner 209, Penna 144; Rudolph 100; Weiser 131 . . .), an earlier date, even one shortly after his vocation or c. 621, is also possible (cf Rowley, *Men of God* 155f).

16:1–13 Jeremiah's Mode of Life—A warning i to Israel—This passage brings together three commands of God to Jeremiah on how he is to regulate his life so that it will be a sign to Israel, a constant reminder of truths they are ignoring, i.e. the doom shortly to come on them. He is to remain celibate during his life not merely at Anathoth as M. D. Goldman thinks (Austral. Bible Rev 2 [1952], 43–47); and is not to visit any house of

494i mourning (5—7) or merrymaking (8f). This uncommon mode of behaviour would make people reflect and seek its significance, particularly in Israel where prophetical symbolic actions were well known (Is ch 20; Hos chh 1 and 3; cf Is 7:3; 8:1—3 etc). The Church, too, reminds us that certain of her institutions, such as religious life and observance of the evangelical counsels are signs, pointers to other truths and portents of life in the eternal kingdom. See chh 5—6 of the Constitution on the Church and the Decree on Renewal of Religious Life of Vatican II. Jer's unusual way of life was directly contrary to his nature and earned for him the hatred of his fellow-countrymen;

j see 15:10—18. **10—13.** He must also explain why they are to be punished. It is because they have abandoned God's law and covenant. We find the idea repeated in 22:8f and it is found in Assyrian texts shortly before Jer's day. Cf ANET 300*a* and see to 22:8f. The command to celibacy must have come in his youth; the others could be from any period in his life. This autobiographical prose passage may have been originally in verse. **14f. Repatriation**—Practically identical with 23:7f (q.v.) and inserted here by an editor to offset the grim picture just painted; see to 5:18ff.

k 16—18 Double Punishment for Judah—The fishermen and hunters are the Babylonians. They were renowned in both crafts as we know from biblical texts (Hb 1:15—17—contemporary with Jer; Gn 10:9) and from the monuments (ANEP Nos. 114; 184—6). The idols are lifeless, corpses. The 'abominations' (cf Dn 9:27; 12:11) are these idols, or the immoral practices of paganism, or perhaps both.

19—21 Conversion of the Heathen—Like 3:17; 12:14—17 (q.v.), this passage is probably an exilic or post-exilic composition, though some authors believe part (Cornill, Nötscher) or all (Condamin 147; Weiser 141) is from Jer.

l 17:1—4 Guilt that cannot be erased—An iron stylus with diamond point was used for engraving on hard material such as stone (cf Pliny, *Natural History* 37, 15; Jb 19:24). Israel's heart is of stone (Ezek 11:19; cf Jer 24:7), and her sin is so deep-rooted as to be indelibly engraved (cf 13).

2—3*a*. Apparently a gloss (cf CV, BJ). Their sin is also inscribed on the horns of the altars (cf ANEP 575) etc reminding God not to accept their prayers. **3*b*—4.** Exile is the punishment.

m 5—13 Various Wisdom Sayings—These vv probably from Jer, apparently once circulated as independent units, and were inserted here since the first one may refer to Zedekiah and the exile. **5—8.** In the parched Orient a tree cannot prosper away from a spring or river, cf Ps 1:3. Neither can a man who forsakes God, the source of living water (cf 2:13; Ps 119 (118):8 etc), for human help (cf Is 8:5ff; 28:14—18; 30:1—5 etc). A comparison with Ezek 7:3—21 led Cornill to surmise that the vv were directed against Zedekiah. **11.** The words may have been directed against Jehoiakim (cf 22:13—19). For the idea

n see Ps 49 (48):17; Prv 13:22 etc. **12f.** Yahweh in his Temple is the true hope of Israel (cf 14:8). 'Our *holy place*' (MT, CV, BJ) is the Temple or sanctuary (RSV) where Yahweh is enthroned above the Cherubim. This praise of the Temple is in no way incompatible with 7:13—15; cf Mt 23:37f. 'shall be written (Heb. *yikkātēbû* in the earth' (MT, RSV), i.e., not indelibly as on stone etc (cf 1); their names will be blotted out from the Book of Life. For 'earth' (Heb *'āres*) in sense of 'dust', see Ex 10:5; Nm 22:5; Jb 14:8; cf Rudolph 107. Following Ugaritic where *'ars* can mean 'underworld' M. Dahood renders: 'shall be enrolled in Hell', i.e. enlisted for death,

(Bib 40 [1959], 164); cf Rudolph 106. Some (e.g. BJ, **49c** C V) emend *yktbû* to *yklmû*, 'ashamed'. For 13*d* cf 2:13.

14—18 Jeremiah's Confessions 3 (see on 11:18). **o Prayer for Vengeance—14** 'Heal me . . . be healed' is common in prayers of supplication (cf Ps 6:3; 41 (40):5 etc) and does not necessarily refer to bodily health. **15f.** His trials now are the mocking taunts of his enemies on his unfulfilled prophecies of doom. This suggests a date prior to the victory of Babylon at Carchemish (605 B.C.). Jer never took pleasure in prophesying evil; cf 28:6—9. **17f.** A prayer for divine help for himself and for his enemies' destruction; cf 15:15.

19—27 Observance of the Sabbath—The reference **p** to kings (25) and to the gates of Jerusalem still intact (25, 27) bring the pre-exilic period to mind. Still, the entire tenor of the admonition and its reference to material observance alone is alien to the spirit and teaching of Jer. That sabbath observance was well established before Jer's day (Ex 20:8—11; Hos 2:11; Am 8:5 etc), and that he would preach against its profanation is clear; but he would scarcely do so in the language here used, which is very similar to Neh 13:15—22, from which period the passage probably comes. It may, however, rest on genuine words of Jer; cf 7:3; 11:3; 22:4f.

18:1—20:18 Potter's Vessels. Confessions of q Jeremiah—Another editorial section, composed from oracles, biographical prose and autobiographical verse. It really comprises two more or less parallel parts: 1. Jeremiah at the potter's workshop, followed by a verse section (18:1—17); Jeremiah's Confession 4 (18—23); 2. Symbol of the potter's flask and Jer's suffering (19:1—20:6); Jeremiah's Confession 5 (20:7—18).

18:1—12 A Revelation at the Potter's Workshop—1. Editorial in the 3rd person to an autobiographical section. **2.** It is possible that there is no direct revelation but that Jer considers an ordinary experience in the light of revealed principles. **3f.** The potter's house, in the lower city, was probably near a spring to the S of Jerusalem. 'Wheel', lit. 'the two stones'. 'The apparatus consisted of two stone wheels on a vertical axle, the lower of which was spun by the feet, while the upper carried the clay which the potter shaped as the wheel revolved', Bright 124; cf Sir 38:29f. The potter fashioned what he desired, though not necessarily at the first attempt. If dissatisfied he broke down his handiwork and began all over again.

7—10. Show that the fulfilment of divine threats and **r** promises, even when expressed unconditionally, is subject to the human response. They are all for man's welfare and an element of divine pedagogy is present; for an example of such threats see Is 38:1—5; cf Jer 26:3; 36:3; 2 Pt 3:9. It is this element that makes the interpretation of prophecies none too easy. For a really unconditional promise see 2 Sm 7:13ff; Ps 89 (88):19ff. For the image of God as a potter see Gn 2:7f; Am 7:1; Is 29:16; 45:9; Rm 9:20—23; **11f.** Judah's hardness of heart (cf 17.1) does not make any change in the divine plan likely. An invitation to penance is given nonetheless. The entire passage comes from some indeterminable period before 597.

13—17 Judah's Apostasy Unnatural—14 is a textually difficult verse, MT being corrupt. The idea expressed, however, is that genuine sources of water do not run dry. Though Yahweh is such a source (2:13), Israel has abandoned him for idols. See also Albright HUCA 23 (1950/1), 23f; M. Dahood ZAW 74 (1962), 207—9.

18—23 Jeremiah's Confessions 4 (see on 11:18f). **s Another Prayer for Vengeance—18** tells of yet another plot against the prophet's life (cf 11:18ff). What

494s occasioned this one, or when it was hatched, we cannot say, but the plan was to find in his discourses ground for his condemnation. His enemies may have been from among the priests, the wise (counsellors?) and prophets, and their plan may well have been to show that his teaching about these classes was deserving of death. **19f.** Cf 17:16; 7:16; etc. **21—23.** The prayer for vengeance is stronger than that of 12:3; 15:15; 17:18. 'Forgive not their iniquity' means the same as 'blot out not their sin from thy sight', i.e. let it ever be before you; do not fail to punish it. The theological question of justification is not touched on. These vv are excised by Duhm, Cornill, Streane etc as unworthy of the prophet. Yet he was a man of his time. Christ's new command (Mt 5:21ff) had not yet come.

t 19:1—15 Symbol of the Broken Flask—It has for long been recognized that ch 19 is composite. In it we have an earlier portion narrating a symbolic action performed by Jer which has later been expanded. The original narrative comprised merely 1—2a (omitting 'the valley of the son of Hinnom at'); 10—11a (as far as 'never be mended') and 14f. This describes how Jer, at God's command, bought an earthen vessel, went with elders and priests to the Potsherd Gate and broke it there, cf 1:9f. Then Jer went ('Potsherd Gate' may have originally stood for 'Topheth' in 14) to the Temple and preached the same message to all (**14f**). The expansion, dependent on 7:31—34, is intended to show how the disaster is due to the human sacrifices offered in Topheth. For further details cf the larger commentaries e.g. Bright, 127ff.

u 20:1 6 Jeremiah in the Stocks—**1**, This Pashhur, distinct from the person mentioned in 21:1, and Ez 2:38; 10:22 etc, was a priest (1), false prophet (6) and chief of the Temple police. His duty was to maintain order within the sacred precincts (cf 29:26). **2.** The stocks (cf 29:26; 1 Chr 16:10) were probably similar to the Roman *nervus* or *lignum* (cf Ac 16.22ff). The feet and hands were inserted into grips and the body kept bent. The upper Benjamin Gate must have been near the Temple (cf 37: 13). **3.** Pashhur's doom would prove the truth of Jer's message. We are not told (unlike 28:16f) of the fate of Pashhur. He was probably exiled in 597. 'Terror on every side' was a favourite expression of Jer (6:25; 46:5; 49:29) and much to his chagrin, he was so nicknamed by the Jerusalem populace! (20:10).

v 7—18 Jeremiah's Confessions 5 (cf on 11:18ff). **His Interior Crisis**—It falls into three parts: 7—9 Jer's lament over the difficulties of his vocation; 10—13 The persecution he undergoes and his trust in God; 14—18 He curses the day of his birth. It is debated whether we have here one, two or three originally distinct passages. The despondency of 14—18, in particular, sounds strange after the trust of 11—13. But in such spiritual crises sudden changes of mind are understandable and the entire passage can be interpreted as a unit. Its insertion in the present context is due to 'Terror on every side' of 3 and

w 10. **7.** (cf 15:18) **8.** (cf 15:18). **10—13.** (cf on 3). Even his friends turn against him; cf 18:18; Ps 35 (34):4—8, 15f etc. He recalls Yahweh's earlier promises (1:17—19; 15:19—21) and regains peace of soul. In 13a he uses a liturgical versicle of praise; cf Ps 6:9; 22 (21) 22 **14—18.** Cf 15:10a. Jb 3 is closely related to these vv and probably dependent on them. The strong language is due, in part at least, to oriental hyperbole. For somewhat similar language by a modern Syrian farmer against his recalcitrant horse (!) see Condamin 145. No precise date can be determined for 7—18, but they are probably from the end of Josiah's, or the beginning of Jehoiakim's, reign.

495a 22—24:10 Against Kings and Prophets—The editor has compiled this part from two existing collections (21:

11—22:8; 22:9—40) to which he prefixed (21:1—10) and **495a** appended (ch 24) other material. The first collection (21: 11—22:8) is on the kings—given in chronological order—from Josiah to Zedekiah (included) and concludes with a description of the ideal messianic king. To this closed unit the editor prefixed a prose section on Zedekiah, which connects ch 20 (Pashhur) with 21:11ff (Zedekiah). Why ch 24, from the beginning of Zedekiah's reign, was given its present position in the book we cannot say. **21:1—10 Fate of Zedekiah and Jerusalem**—The **b** passage falls into two parts: A reply from God to a query of Zedekiah (1—7) and a message for the people (8—10). In 37:3—10, we find a very similar episode to that of 7—10, with some differences of detail. 8—10 are found again in 38:2—4. Despite the similarities of 1—7 and 37:3—10 a number of modern expositors believe the passages refer to two distinct episodes (Condamin, 179; Penna, 171; Weiser, 177, n. 7; Bright, 217) whereas some earlier ones held they were merely different accounts of the same incident. Seeing that the entire section (1—10) is from source C, it appears that what we have here is a deuteronomic composition based on 37:3—10 (Mowinckel Rudolph, 124, Hyatt, 977) and other parts of Jer (Vogt, 19f). **1.** Pashhur son of Malchiah (mentioned again in **c** 38:1) is to be distinguished from Pashhur son of Immer of 20:1. For Zephaniah cf 37:3. **2.** Zedekiah hopes for a repetition of the miracle of 701 B.C. (cf 2 [4] Kgs 19:35; Is 37:36f). **3—7.** Cf 34:2—7; 38:17. In the former, as here, the threat is unconditional; in 38:17 it is made dependent on Zedekiah's behaviour. **8—10.** For a justification of Jer's action, see Skinner 261ff.

21:11—23:8 Oracles Regarding Kings—**11.** Omit **d** 'and' with LXX, and also 'say'. This is a title to the collection of oracles in 21:11—23:8; cf 23:9. **21:11—22:9.** Though it may have been originally directed against a particular king, probably Jehoiakim, this passage is here intended as a general exposition of the role of the king of Judah in God's plan. That role is to uphold the Sinaitic Covenant by promoting social justice (cf Ex 22:20—23 [21—24]). The oracle is given in verse (A) in 21:11b—14; 22:6f and repeated in deuteronomic prose (C), 22:1—5. 8f. **21:13f.** Most probably against the royal palace (cf 22:13—15). **22:1—5.** Cf 7:1—7 and 17:19—27. The exact parallel to **8f** (C!), found in a text of Ashurbanipal (668—633 B.C.) should be noted. It reads: 'Whenever the inhabitants of Arabia asked each other: 'On account of what have these calamities befallen Arabia?' (they answered themselves.) 'Because we did not keep the solemn oaths (sworn by) Ashur, because we offended the friendliness of Ashurbanipal, the king, beloved by Enlil' (ANET, 300a). **10—12.** On Shallum, i.e. Jehoahaz cf 2 [4] Kgs **e** 23:31—34). He was made king after Josiah's death in 609 and after three months was led captive to Egypt. **11f.** In prose, explain 10. **13—19.** On Jehoiakim (609—598); cf 18. He replaced Jehoahaz and ruled an already oppressed people harshly, taxing them to live luxuriously himself in a better palace (13—15; cf 2 [4] Kgs 23:37). For his attitude to Jeremiah see 26:1ff; 36:1ff. **18f.** 'Ah my brother, etc'. The usual form of lamentation (34:5; 1 [3] Kgs 13:30). He died and was buried just before the siege of Jerusalem in 598, but the tomb was probably later violated. See also P. Joüon RSR 27 (1937), 335f. **20—30.** **f** On Coniah, (28) i.e. King Jehoiachin (598—597). He succeeded his father Jehoiakim at the age of 18 but reigned only three months, being deported to Babylon by Nebuchadnezzar in March 15/16 597. He was a bad king (2 [4] Kgs 24:9) but popular with the masses, many of whom considered him legitimate king of Judah even when in exile and looked forward to his repatriation (27:16ff;

495f 28:1—4; ch 29); cf W. A. Albright, 'King Jehoiachin in Exile', BA 5 [1942], 49—55). From cuneiform sources we know he was well treated in Babylon. He was grandfather of Zerubbabel, who governed Judah after the exil. The queen-mother Nehushta, who probably played an important role during his reign (26; 13:18), was exiled with him (2 [4] Kgs 24:15). **24.** Contrast Hag 2:23 (on Zerubbabel). The current belief in Jehoiachin's repatriation explains Jer's emphasis on his rejection by God.

g 23:1—8 The Messianic King—1—4. Probably directed against the vacillating Zedekiah (cf 6) and his advisers. For the theme of Yahweh the Good Shepherd cf 31:10; 50:6; Ezek 34; 37:24. **5f.** 'A Righteous Branch'; The Heb. (ṣemaḥ ṣaddîq) may also be rendered as 'legitimate heir'; cf J. Swetnam Bib 46 [1965], 29—40. In either case the text is speaking of a future king ('in the days to come', **5**) whose name Yahweh Ṣidqênû, 'the Lord is our righteousness' (**6**), describes his reign. Possibly the new name has an intentional reference to the weak Zedekiah. This is the only place where Jer speaks of a personal Messiah; see also 30:9; 33:14ff; cf 30:21. The passage however with others helped to keep messianic hope alive and inspired Zech 3:8; 6:12. See further § 487k and Skinner 310—19. **7f.** Absent from LXX, almost verbally as 16:14f, q.v.

h 23:9—40 Against False Prophets—Here we have a collection of oracles against false prophets who by their teaching and example led the people astray. They formed a special group and are often mentioned together with the priests. They were in some way connected with the Temple and cult, though what their precise function was we cannot say with certainty; cf O. Eissfeldt in *The OT and Modern Study*, 119—26; 128—34. On the problem they present see E. Siegman, *The False Prophets of the OT*, Washington 1939; cf also chh 27—29.

i 24:1—10 The Two Baskets of Figs—This dates from the deportation of 597 B.C. and is directed against those left behind who considered themselves just and the deportees rejected by God. Jer tells them that the contrary is the case. The true Israel of God will be created in exile.

j 25:1—14 Seventy Years of Exile. Conclusion to the First Book of Prophecies—The pericope serves as a conclusion to the First Bk of Prophecies (Chh 1—24) at the basis of which book there probably lies the scroll of 605/4 B.C., i.e. from the 4th year of Jehoiakim (36:1ff). The present passages tells of a sermon Jer delivered in that same year. By the first year of Nebuchadnezzar (25:1) the author may mean his accession year Aug. 605/Apr. 604. (For synchronisms from 459—c. 440 see ANET, 222cd). With the victory of Carchemish in the spring or summer of 605 Babylon was sole master of W Asia. Jer's prophecies on the foe from the N (cf § 490i) were proved true. He here foretells that Judah and the surrounding nations will be subject to Babylon for 70 years, after which Babylon will be destroyed (9:11ff). The passage, however, is from the deuteronomistic source and is best considered as an elaboration of Jer's original sermon.

k The MT is longer than LXX which omits 1b, the reference to Nebuchadnezzar, and to Babylon and the land of the Chaldeans in 9 and 11f. It also omits 13b, 14 and ends with 'everything written in this book'. The sermon, then, would originally have referrred only to Judah and Jerusalem. The MT expansion intends to extend the threat to embrace Jer's oracles on the pagan nations as well. It is better to take 25:1—15 as the compiler's ending of Bk 1 (Rudolph, 149; Hyatt, 999) than as Jer's (Baruch's) introduction (cf Volz) or conclusion (Skinner, 240, Weiser, 217) to the original scroll of 605/4. **11.** Actually, reckoning from 605, the duration was 67/66 years. But

70 is a round number (Is 23:15.17; Akkadian parallel **495l** in E. Vogt, Bib 38 [1957], 236), for a lifetime (Ps 90 (89):10). The same prophecy occurs in 29:10, from c. 597 B.C. cf also 27:7.

15—38 Against the Nations—To be taken with 46—51, § 500. cf § 487g.

26—35. BOOK II: PROPHECIES OF WELL-BEING.

We may consider chh 26—35 together as containing, in **496a** one way or another, prophecies of weal. The central section is the 'Book of Consolation', chh 30—31. To this there was naturally attached chh 32—33 on the Restoration of Jerusalem and Judah. Ch 35 contains a divine promise to the Rechabites. 34 may have become attached to 35 before becoming inserted in its present position, though it, too, carries a conditional promise to Zedekiah (34:1—7). Chh 26—29 recount Jer's conflicts with the religious leaders and may have become united before insertion into our book. Chh 27—29 (q.v.) against the prophets, certainly did form a separate booklet at one stage. They finally became inserted where they now stand, probably because of the prophecies of well-being in 27:22; 29:10—14. Ch 26 may have been prefixed as an introduction, and intends to show Jer's divine right to speak against false prophets (Rudolph 154).

26 The Temple Sermon. Jeremiah's Arrest. Fate of b Uriah—This ch may have originally stood before ch 36, relating the writing of the first scrolls of Jeremiah. The entire ch 26 is from Baruch (B source).

1—6 The Sermon—1. 'In the beginning of the reign', i.e. in the accession year (see on 49:34) i.e. Summer-Autumn 609–Apr. 608, cf § 125c. For commentary see on C's account in ch 7:1—15.

7—19 Arrest and trial of Jeremiah—7—9. For belief c in the indestructibility of the Temple see on 7:3—6, 12—15. **10.** The priests and prophets were in the Temple enclosure; the princes in the palace adjoining the Temple court. **11.** The religious leaders wanted the death sentence; cf 18:18; 20:10f. **12—15.** Note the dignity and modesty of Jer's reply. It was prudent, humble and firm (Jerome); he was conscious that he spoke not in his own name but in that of him who sent him. He reminded his judges how God avenges the blood of the innocent (cf Gn 4:10; 1 [3] Kgs 21:19; 2 [4] Kgs 9:36; 2 Sm 21:1ff). **d 16f.** The beginning of Jehoiakim's reign; the princes are, probably, the religious and just counsellors Josiah had gathered about him. Ahikam (**24**) was a minister of Josiah (2 [4] Kgs 22:12) and father of Gedaliah (39:14), who later befriended the prophet. The princes, already connected with Josiah's reform, would have looked favourably on Jer's preaching and were not on the best of terms with Jehoiakim (cf 2 [4] Kgs 23:30). They assisted Jer again when he had his oracles put in writing some five years later (ch 36). Those of them who remained alive were probably deported in 597 (2 [4] Kgs 24:14), leaving Zedekiah without wise counsel, and Jer without influential friends during the last days of Jerusalem. **18f.** Micah, the minor prophet. He lived a hundred years earlier. The citation in 18 is found in Mi 3:12, and gives us an indication of how highly the prophet's words were treasured and how faithfully they could be transmitted. The repentance of Hezekiah is probably that referred to in Is 36:22—37:4 = 2 [4] Kgs 18:37ff, during the siege of Jerusalem by Assyria in 701.

20—23 The Fate of Uriah—The incident is related by e Baruch to let us know how fortunate Jer really was. There must have been an extradition agreement between

496e Jehoiakim and Egypt. We know nothing further of this true prophet Uriah. He is scarcely the one referred to in Lachish Letter III (ANET 322; cf Rudolph 157). On Elnathan see ch 36:12, 25 where he is friendly towards Jer. Whether the incident of Uriah took place before or after this sermon we cannot say; most probably after. It shows us that Jer was not absolutely alone in his preaching at that time.

f **27–29 A Pamphlet against False Prophets**—These chh once circulated as a unit before they were inserted into the book as it now stands. This we can see from certain peculiarities found in these chapters, and not elsewhere in Jer 1) The spelling of Nebuchadnezzar; elsewhere in Jer (MT) written as Nebuchadrezzar; 2) Theophoric personal name-endings are written as -yāh (e.g. Yirmᵉyah); elsewhere in the book as -yahū (e.g. Yirmᵉyāhû). The exceptions in 27:1, 4; 29:21, 22, 24, 27, 29f (mainly for Jer's own name) are due to scribal errors. While the distinctions in 1) are retained in RSV those of 2) are not. 3) Jer is constantly referred to as 'the prophet', as is also the false prophet Hananiah. The three chh, in turn, come from different sources; 27 is in the first person while 28 and 29 are in the third person and come probably from Baruch (B). All have the same theme: Jer's conflict in word and deed with the false prophets who filled the Jews in Palestine and Babylon with vain political hopes of success against Nebu-

g chadnezzar. The booklet, or ch 29 at any rate, may have been used in propaganda against these prophets. Chh 27 and 28 relate incidents from the same year, as probably does ch 29, i.e. 594/3. We have seen how 51:59–64a refers to the same date. The year was one of unrest in Palestine and in the kingdoms E of the Jordan. Earlier scholars connected this with the advent of Psammetichus II to the throne of Egypt. The Babylonian Chronicle, published by Wiseman, gives us the true background. From this we learn that in 595/4 Nebuchadnezzar had to quell a local rebellion in Babylon. News of the monarch's difficulties must have soon reached the W and promoted kinglets to plan an alliance against their overlord (cf D. N. Freedman, BA 19 [1956], 58).

h **27 Judah and her Pagan Neighbours must serve Babylon or Perish**—1. For 'Zedekiah', the MT (cf CV), except in 3 MSS reads 'Jehoiakim'. The v, absent from LXX, is a gloss from 26:1. The year was neither 609 nor 597 (cf 3 etc), but most probably that of ch 28, i.e. Zedekiah's 4th year (ct 28:1), 594/3. 2f. The purpose of the embassy of these kings (for the omission of Philistia see VT 1 [1950] 143) was, presumably, to have Zedekiah and Judah enter an anti-Babylonian league. 4–7. The term of Babylon's supremacy applies to pagan nations as much as it does to Judah (cf 29:10; 25:11); in fact Jer's prophecy of 70 years refers rather to the duration of Babylon's power than to the length of Judah's exile. 8–12. Even pagan nations had their court prophets and their message is the same as most of their Jewish

i counterparts. 13–15. Subjection to Babylon, which had a divinely appointed role, was Jer's constant theme. He knew that in this alone stood Judah's hope of survival. It was elementary political wisdom, but this was not the basis of Jer's preaching. The other prophets in Judah were only too prone to take any difficulty, or rumour of trouble, in Babylon as a sign of that power's imminent destruction and as an incentive to revolt. Babylon, like Assyria (cf Is 18:3–6), will be destroyed only when God sees fit. 16–22. The sacred vessels, carried to Babylon in 597 (cf 2 [4] Kgs 24:13 Dn 1:5) were palpable evidence of Judah's humiliation and a reminder of the reality of Jer's prophecy on the Temple (7:1ff; 26:1ff).

These vessels were returned by Cyrus (cf Ez 1:7ff). **18. 496i** Intercession is again mentioned. Apparently, it was a normal function of genuine prophets (cf § 491f). Zedekiah must have followed the prophet's advice and the embassy sent to Babylon (52:59–64a) was, apparently, to assure Nebuchadnezzar of Judah's allegiance. **28 Jeremiah and Hananiah. True Prophet against j False**—1. LXX has simply 'in the fourth year of Zedekiah, king of Judah in the fifth month', i.e. Tebet (Dec.–Jan.) 594/3. MT's 'the beginning of' is a gloss from 26:1; 27:1. For Gibeon in Benjamin, see Jos. 10:2 etc. 2f. Hananiah introduces his 'oracle' in the same manner as the true prophets were wont to: 'Thus says the Lord'. Like them, too, he uses symbolic actions. MT in 1a rightly connects this episode with the preceding. It probably occurred very soon afterwards and in 2f Hananiah refers to Jer's oracle of 27:16–22. 4. Recall that many then recognized the exiled Jeconiah (Jehoiachin) and not Zedekiah, as the true king of Judah, and ardently awaited his return; see to 22:20–30. 24–30. Hananiah pandered to popular desire. Jeconiah was then honourably treated in Babylon and free to move about in 594. The same was true in 592 as we know from Babylonian sources (ANET 308bc; Albright, BA 5 [1942], 49–55. 5f. Jer had no reply from God for his adversary **k** (cf 42:2–7). He only expressed his own personal desire. We see again how clearly he could distinguish between his deepest desires and God's inspired word. 7–9. He recognized Hananiah as a prophet but did not know yet that he had really been sent by God. The audience must have been equally perplexed. Jer's reply recalls (1) that Hananiah's preaching was at variance with that of earlier prophets. He was thinking principally, no doubt, of Isaiah and Micah (cf 26:18) from Judah, and of Hosea and Amos in Israel (cf also 1 [3] Kgs 22:8ff). And Israel had fallen as these predicted. In times of crisis their theme was repentance or punishment. Jer would have known they uttered oracles of weal on other occasions; (2) that genuine prophecies of weal are known as such on their fulfilment; cf Dt 18:20–22. 10–12. Jer was still carrying his yoke of wood (cf 27:2). Hananiah was probably acting sincerely. His death two months later, prophesied by Jeremiah, would let the people see which of the two was truly sent by God.

29 Letters to the Exiles in Babylonia—In this ch **l** we have a letter of Jeremiah to the exiles in Babylonia (1–15, 21–23; 16–20 are a later addition), an indication of the repercussions of this letter, and the terms of a letter in response to these which Jer dictated for transmission to Babylon (24–32). The atmosphere and the date are the same as in chh 27 and 28, i.e. 594/3 B.C. But here we get a glimpse of the situation among the exiles of 597 in Babylonia.

1–15, 21–23 The Letter of Jeremiah—1–2. The **m** exiles were from the upper classes and were awaiting a sudden change of fortune to bring them back to their homeland. The nationalistically minded prophets were as busy there as in Jerusalem. 3. The embassy of Zedekiah was probably to assure Nebuchadnezzar of Judah's allegiance. This in itself was proof to the exiles of the influence of Jeremiah in royal circles. The oracle of 51:59–64a was most probably sent on the same occasion and the passage may have originally stood after ch 29 (cf Bright, 207ff; EOTInt 354; Rudolph, 295). Elasah was probably a brother of Ahikam (26:24, q.v.). Gemariah, not mentioned elsewhere, was hardly Jer's brother (cf 1:1). Contact between the exiles and the homeland was being already maintained by letters. 5–9. **n** The nobility and craftsmen, under the influence of the

496n false prophets' preaching, would not wish to settle down to normal life; cf 1 Thes 4:11f; 2 Thes 3:10ff. **7.** The idea of praying for one's enemies (though done by Jer himself, 18:20) and for an impure pagan land (Am 7:17; Hos 9:1ff) was then revolutionary and a foreshadowing of Christ's teaching. **10—14.** The exile is merely intended to purify Israel. God's plans are for her welfare. **15, 21—23.** The two false prophets were probably put to death as an example to others. The manner of punishment was rare in Babylon. They were also of immoral character (cf 23:14), but were, doubtless, executed for political activity. **16—20.** Break the continuity and are probably an addition by an editor or reader under the influence of ch 24.

o 24—32 Repercussions of the Letter—This passage is loosely put together from a second letter of Jer written some time after the first. When Jer's letter was read in Babylon, Shemaiah, one of the prophets there, took it on himself to write to Jerusalem directing the priests and the chief-priest Zephaniah (a successor of Pashhur; cf 20:2) how to deal with what they considered excited, mad, prophets such as Jeremiah (25—27). The exiles apparently considered themselves the true Israel. **29—32.** Zephaniah must have been friendly towards Jeremiah and Babylon. He read the letter, perhaps as a warning, and unlike Pashhur (20:1f), did not molest the prophet.

497a 30—31 The Booklet of Consolation—These two chh form a literary unity and, in the introduction provided by a deuteronomic redactor (Rudolph) or by Baruch (Weiser 265), are described as a 'book' (of comfort) which Jer compiled at God's command (2). Whereas Stade and Smend (1893) thought none of the material came from Jeremiah, later scholars pass a more favourable judgement. Volz and Rudolph consider authentic practically all the v section (save 31:35—37) and of the prose section, 31:31—34; EOTInt 361 takes 31:2—22 as certainly, and 30:5—21 as probably genuine. Hyatt (1023), on the contrary, would restrict the authentic oracles to 30:5—7, 12—15; 31:2—6; 15—22. Bright (285) prefers to speak of certain earlier and later oracles of Jer, expanded and supplemented in certain **b** cases in exilic times. Another question arising from these chh is when, and for whom, were these genuine oracles composed. In view of the numerous references to the N kingdom, many scholars believe that, like 3:1—4:4, they were originally addressed to the N tribes, not to Judah. The references to Judah would then have been added later. In this view the oracles, again as 3:1—4:4, are generally attributed to Jer's earliest preaching (626—616). Thus EOTInt 361f; Rudolph, 172f; Weiser, 265f. Some would even connect them with Josiah's expansionist policies (2 [4] Kgs 23:15—20). Other authors however, object to this treatment of the text and hold that the oracles were composed at various periods (Bright, 285) or after the destruction of Jerusalem in 587 (Hyatt, 1022f). Jer's association with Gedaliah at Mizpah is seen by some as sufficient reason for the reference to the N Kingdom or N tribes (Skinner, 298—309). There is no reason why some of the genuine oracles could not have originally been directed to the exiled N tribes and later applied to Judah by Jeremiah himself; see ch 2, § 489b. The view held on their origin does not generally affect the exegesis. As the oracles now stand they refer to repatriation of the exiles and the reconstitution of God's people.

c 30:1—24 The Restoration of Israel and Judah—**1—2.** Whatever their original intent the oracles as introduced here refer to both Israel and Judah. **5—7.** As they now stand the vv tell Jacob (i.e. Israel) that before being redeemed they must undergo purification by trial. It

is the Day of the Lord (Am 5:18—20; Zeph 1:14—18 etc). **497c 8f.** This liberation will introduce the messianic reign. Probably an inspired exilic prose interpretation of 5—7, (cf 34:23f; 37:24f; Hos 3:5). The Messiah does not figure prominently in Jer's teaching; cf § 487k. **10f.** Absent from LXX, are repeated in 46:27f q.v. Their Jeremianic authenticity is denied by some because of similarity with 7, Is 41:8—10; 43:5; 44:2f. **12—17.** Unless we omit 'it **d** is Sion' (Heb. *siyyôn*) of 17 (MT, RSV) as a gloss (thus CV), or with the LXX read instead 'she is our quarry' (Heb. *sêdēnû*), 12—17 refer to Judah, not to Israel. **18f.** The restoration of the fortunes of Jacob. 'City and palace', i.e. Jerusalem or Samaria, with the royal palace; better, as collective 'cities and palaces'. The cities will be rebuilt on their mounds, lit. 'tells'. A 'tell' is an artificial mound formed from the accumulated debris of ruined cities, cf Jos 11:13. **19—22.** The nation will be rebuilt spiritually as well as materially. There shall now be native rulers over them, no longer Assyrian or foreign governors. **23f.** Practically identical with 23:19f whence the editor has borrowed them, to end, as he began (5—7), with the theme of judgement of Israel's or Judah's foes.

31:1—40 The New Israel of God—The general theme **e** of the passage is reconciliation of Israel with her God, her repatriation and the reconstitution of the true Israel from all the twelve tribes. The central theme is introduced in the very opening v, then developed in various ways and, finally, by a form of the Semitic literary device called 'inclusion' repeated at greater length at the close (31—34). The unity of theme is, doubtless, due to an editor working on originally distinct oracles on the New Israel. Some of these appear to come from Jer's earliest preaching (2—6; 15—22) and were probably addressed originally to the N kingdom only. It is to be compared with 3:1—4:4. **7—14**, as they now stand, may well be from exilic times, and 23—30 may also be later adaptations of Jer's words. The editor worked these various oracles, as best he could, round the central theme of the New Israel. **1 Introduction**—This v is better understood as a **f** thematic introduction to the collection than as the conclusion of the preceding section (MT 30:23f by 'inclusion' seems to be complete, repeating in substance 5b, 7), or as an independent v standing outside both sections.

2—6 God Reconciled to Israel in the Land of Exile—**2f.** The words are apparently addressed to the N Kingdom only; but see introd. to chh 30f. Yahweh wants Israel to return to the love of her youth by genuine conversion (3:12ff, 22ff). God intends to allure her into the wilderness, there to begin her training in true love of him over again (Hos 2:14f). As a faithless wife she was divorced by exile (3:1) but only that the process of reconciliation with Yahweh may recommence among the exiled ('the people who survived the sword') while they await repatriation to Palestine, i.e. Israel's resting place (Dt 20:9). We have here the basis of the theme of the New Exodus which Second-Isaiah was to develop. **4—6.** In the new Israel there will be no syncretistic cults; the sole centre will by Yahweh's Temple in Jerusalem. **6.** Shows that Jer could not have been opposed to Josiah's centralization of worship in Jerusalem; cf § 492o—p.

7—14 Jubilant Return Journey—Israel was exiled to **g** the N and to Media (8; cf 2 [4] Kgs 17:6). God is now represented as the Good Shepherd gathering his scattered flock together (cf 23:1ff). The vv are very similar to Second-Isaiah (Is 40:3—5; 41:18—20; 43:1—7; etc etc) and some (e.g. Bright, 286) consider them an exilic adaptation of genuine oracles of Jer; others (e.g. Hyatt,

497g 1029) believe all, save 9c, are post-exilic. Volz, Rudolph and Weiser take them as genuine, but the first two reject 14 as a priestly addition. These take the similarities with Second-Isaiah as due to the resemblances in the situation, not to literary dependence.

h **15—22 End of Rachel's Mourning—15.** The deportees were put in a concentration camp at Ramah (modern er-Ram, c. 7 m. N of Jerusalem) before deportation in 587 (cf 40:1). Rachel, the mother of the N tribes through Joseph and Benjamin, died near Ramah (Gn 35:19, q.v.; 1 Sm 10:2). Those who take the vv as addressed to Judah, or to all the chosen people, believe that Rachel's mourning at Ramah refers to the deportation of 587. It is more probable, however, that here Jer is thinking only of the N tribes and represents their mother as rising from her tomb at Ramah to wail over the fate of her children, deported in 721 B.C. **16f.** Cf 29:11. **18f.** Show how this is possible through the repentance of Ephraim, i.e., the

i N Kingdom (cf 3:22—25). **21.** Contains a new summons by Yahweh to Israel to return to Palestine from exile. **22a.** Is a further remark addressed to Israel and creates no difficulty. **22b.** On the contrary, is the most mysterious and difficult text of the entire book. 'The Lord has created a new thing on the earth; a woman protects (Heb. $t^e s \hat{o} b \bar{e} b$) a man' (RSV). The Heb. word rendered 'protects' in RSV is literally 'surrounds' (Vg.); 'encompasses' (CV; cf AV, 'shall compass'), but can also mean, 'defend, protect' as in RSV (cf Dt. 32.10; Ps. 32 (31):10).

The new thing created is, doubtless, this new relation of woman to man which will be a characteristic of the New Age or of the New Exodus. What the relation consists in is most uncertain. Jerome's view, referring it to the virgin birth of Christ ('a man') in Mary's ('woman') womb ('shall surround'), has had little following. For a view referring the text to Mary's protection of Christians see G. B. Olasson, V Dom 16 (1926), 295, 304. On the supposed Messianism of the text cf A. Condamin RB 6 (1897),

j 396—404. The half-verse is now variously understood. Some take it to mean that in the new age situations will be such that women will not need protection. On the contrary, they will protect man. This view is unlikely. Others take it to refer to the homeward journey through the desert, when, against ordinary procedure, women will surround the caravan instead of remaining in the security of its centre (cf E. Nácar, EstBib 1 (1942), 405—36). Some take it to refer to the woman courting the man she wishes to wed (cf CV), a new thing in Israel. The woman may be Israel herself, seeking Yahweh, her former husband (cf 3:1). Bright (282) thinks it may be a proverbial saying, indicating something surprising or difficult to believe. Duhm takes it as a witty and slightly sceptical remark of some reader who also added 26. He emends $t^e s \hat{o} b \bar{e} b$ to $tiss \hat{o} b$ ('becomes'). The text would then mean 'Note the change of gender: the woman has been turned into a man'! Condamin emends the last two words to $t \bar{a} \check{s} \hat{u} b$ $l^e geber$, 'the woman returns to the man', i.e. Israel to Yahweh (cf 3:1). See further L. Reincke, Beitz. z. Erklär. des AT, Vol. 3, Münster 1854; F. Ceuppens, *De prophetiis Messianicis in V.T.*, Rome 1935, 428—33. With 22, the verse section ends. The following are prose sections, some of them based on, or reproducing, genuine oracles of Jeremiah.

k **23—26 The Rebuilding of Jerusalem**—The passage presupposes the exile of 587 and is probably later than Jer's day. 26 is now generally regarded as a gloss; see to 22b, end.

27—30 Individual responsibility—This passage, too, refers to the New Israel and seems to presuppose the

exile. It is probably based on genuine words of Jer. **497k** Though **29f** are found in Ezek 18.2, the words must represent a current proverb of Jer's day when the problem of individual responsibility was being more keenly felt; cf 12:1f.

31—34 The New Covenant—This passage was denied **498a** to Jer by Duhm, because he considered it unworthy of the prophet (Duhm understood 33 to speak of learning the Law by heart!) While some still doubt their Jeremianic origin, the verses are, in general, now attributed to him, although not necessarily as his *ipsissima verba*. 'As regards its authenticity, one can only say that it ought never to have been questioned' (Bright, 287). The vv are, in fact, the synthesis and culmination of the prophet's teaching. The passage is 'one of the mountain peaks of the Old Testament', (Hyatt 1037). Jer realized the weakness and waywardness of the human heart (17:9f) which was really known only to God (17:10; 20:12). The root of Israel's sin was in her heart; she refused to listen to the voice of God. Her heart was rebellious (5:23), stubborn (13:10; 23:17), uncircumcized (9:26; 4:4). He prophesied that the deportees of 597 would be brought back to the homeland. They were the good figs, the seed of the New Israel. God would *give them a new* **b** *heart* to understand that he was the Lord. They would return to him *with their whole heart*; they would be his people and he their God (24:6f). Just before the destruction of the city in 587 he prophesied that the exiles would return and become again his true people. One heart and one way would God give them, and he would make with them an eternal covenant (32:36—41). In view of this, our present passage (31—34) is best dated towards the destruction of the city in 587 or shortly afterwards. It was probably addressed originally to all the Jews, not merely to the N Kingdom, as those who attribute its composition to the early days of Jer generally maintain. 'The house of Judah' (31) would, in that case, be a later gloss. **31.** The prophecy will be fulfilled 'in the days to " come', i.e. at some unspecified future date. In 27 this expression, refers to the reconstruction of Israel and Judah and in 38 to the rebuilding of Jerusalem. In view of 24:7; 32:36—41 Jer may have thought this prophecy of the New Covenant would be fulfilled at the repatriation after the 70 years of exile. The New Covenant, like the Old, will be with the nation, God's new people. **32.** The old Covenant is that of Sinai, written on tablets of stone (Ex 24; 31.18; 34:27f; Dt 5:22). It was a bilateral contract according to which prosperity or punishment followed on Israel's fidelity or infidelity to it. Its violation by Israel is the theme of the historical and earlier prophetic writings; cf Jer chh 3—4 etc. 'I was their husband' or 'master' (MT $b \hat{o}' alt \hat{i}$) i.e., they should have observed the (marriage) contract. The Heb. word occurs again in 3:14 and the thought is that of 3:1—4:4 etc. The LXX, the Peshitta and OL read $g \bar{a}' alt \hat{i}$, 'I exiled (rejected) them', and so also some modern authors (cf CV), but the MT can **d** be retained. **33f.** God's remedy is radical. The root of the trouble lay in the heart which was not responsive to God's law expressed externally. The New Covenant, or Law, will be given in their very hearts. As the contemporary prophet Ezek put it, God will replace their stony heart by one of flesh (Ezek 11:19; cf Jer 24:6f) and God's grace would incline this heart to seek its Maker. The principle of the New Covenant is interior: man is directed to God from within and there will be no need to devise new means to turn men to the knowledge of God. This true knowledge of God is both theoretical and practical—knowing Him as Israel's Covenant-Spouse and acting accordingly. It was often stressed by Amos (2:20; 4:1,

498d 6; 5:4; 6:6) and Jeremiah (2:8; 4:22; 9:3, 6, 24; 22:16 etc). Josiah lived according to it (22:15f). The passage does not exclude external forms of worship; it merely stresses the pre-eminence of the internal. Since there can be no union between God and a sinful nation, the new happy state presupposes the complete pardon of Israel's sins.

e Ezek made similar prophecies for the exiles of 597 (Ezek 11:18—20) and 587 (Ezek 36:25—27; cf Is 55:3; 59:21; 59:21; 61:8; Bar 2:35; Ps 51(50). Both prophets, in accord with general prophetic perspective, probably believed this would be fulfilled in the New Israel to arise at the repatriation of 538. The vision of both was likewise restricted to the new nation of the Jews; no mention is made of the Gentiles. But God's plans were not such. This New Israel did not materialize with the repatriation of 538. The Qumran community which considered itself 'the New Covenant' was in no sense the fulfilment of Jer 31:31—34. This New Covenant was established by Christ's Death (Mt 26:28; par.), and was promulgated and explained by NT preaching and teaching, particularly by St Paul who showed how Christianity solves the problems of Law and grace, sensed so acutely by his fellow Benjamite (2 Cor 3:6; Rm 11:27 etc; Heb 8:6—13 (citing Jer 31:31—34); 9:15f; 1 Jn 5:20). See further Skinner 320—34; Coppens, CBQ 25 (1963), 12—21; B. Kipper, *De Restitutione Populi Israel apud Prophetam Jeremiam*, Rio Grande do Sul, 1957.

f **35—37 The Certainty of God's Promise**—Though similar to genuine oracles of Jer (cf 33:20—26; 5:22; 8:7; 18:14) this passage may be a later development (cf Is 40:12; 51:15 etc) and intended to emphasize the truth of promises just made; cf Am 11:1f, 29.

38—40 The Dimensions of the New Jerusalem—The city shall be completely rebuilt and shall be entirely holy, the valley of Hinnom (7:31f; 19:2, 6; 32:35; 2 [4] Kgs 23:10) not excepted. The 'Tower of Hananel' (cf Zech 14:10; Neh 3:1; 12:39) was at the NE corner; the 'Corner Gate' (2 [4] Kgs 14:10) was probably at the NW of the city. The location of Goah (Zech 14:5) and Mt Gareb are unknown. These vv, composed after 587, prepare the symbolism of Ezek 40—48.

g **32 Purchase of Land as a Pledge of Restoration**— This ch tells us how, when during the final Babylonian assault in 588/7 all seemed lost for Judah, Jer was commanded by Yahweh to acquire possession of some family land in Anathoth. This symbolic action was an earnest of Yahweh's promise that normal life and commerce would again return to Judah. For a parallel from Roman history during Hannibal's siege of Rome see Livy, 26, 11, 6. Ch 32 also tells us how a Law of Lv (ch 25) from P was applied in Jer's day. The promise of restoration (15) explains the present position of this episode. Probably before being inserted in its present position its
h original account was elaborated. The original nucleus is, apparently, found in 6—17a, 24—29a, 42—44, which is autobiographical. 17b—23, 28—41 are expansions of Jer's prayer (16—17a, 24f) and Yahweh's answer (28a, 42—44) while 1—5 are editorial, explaining the occasion of the passage. Some authors reduce the original nucleus further still, taking 16—44 as editorial. The entire ch gives a good idea of the fortunes of Jer's words within Jewish tradition—genuine oracles, later inspired elaboration, editorial additions.

1—5 Editorial Introduction—Jer's arrest and imprisonment is narrated in chh 37f, q.v. The date was 588—587, probably summer, 587. He was under 'house arrest', like Paul in Rome (Ac 28:16, 30f). For his prophecies here recalled see 27:6; 34:2—5; but esp.

37:17; 38:3. Humanly speaking all seemed lost for Judah. **498h**
6—44 The Purchase and its Significance—6—8. We **i** know nothing further of Hanamel, Jer's cousin. The right and obligation of pre-emption came to Jer from Lv 25:25ff (P); cf Ru 3:9—13; 4:1—12. His cousin may have availed himself of the lull in the fighting (37:11f) to enter the city, although he could, conceivably, have entered it during the siege (cf Jos.Ant. 5, §§ 499—509). **9—15.** Jer paid the full value of the land. 10—15 give us a good idea of how contracts were then made. Money was then weighed; coined money came in only after the exile. The deed was probably written in duplicate on a single sheet of papyrus; one text was then rolled up and sealed, the other left open for consultation. For the procedure cf L. Fischer, ZAW 30 (1910), 136—42; for examples from the Judaean desert Y. Yadin, IEJ 12 (1962), 236—38. For Judaean seal of Jer's time see R. de Vaux, RB 45 (1936), 96f. It was probably common then to put such deeds in earthenware jars for safe keeping. We find the same practice later in Elephantine and Qumrân. **15.** Shows how hope of a joyful future is part of Jer's message. Taken in conjunction with his repeated prophecies of deportation it implies repatriation (cf 29:10f etc).

33 Rebuilding of Jerusalem and the Permanence of j the Davidic Dynasty—Two complexes of promises, which follow naturally on ch 32 and with which the first one, at least, is connected in **33:1**. The first group **(2—13)** develop the theme of 32:15. It is hard to say how much comes from Jer and what is later development. The other complex (14—26) is absent from LXX and is probably an addition of oracles from a later writer. **14—18.** Depends on 23:5f, but speaks of the permanence of the Davidic dynasty where 23:5 spoke of an individual Davidic king. It also applies the name of the Davidic king ('*Yahweh-sidqênû*') of 23:6 to the New Jerusalem. **19—22; 23—26.** Depends on and develops 31:35—37, applying it to the Levitical priesthood.

34 The Fate of Zedekiah. The Pact broken—The **k** present ch comprises two distinct messages of Jer, both from the last months of Judah's independence. The first **(1—7)** contains a promise to Zedekiah on condition that he follows a divine command (4f). This explains why the ch is inserted in its present context. The other pericope **(8—22)** tells of the punishment that awaits violation of God's law.

1—7 Fate of Zedekiah—From 7 we know the message is to be dated 589/8 when Nebuchadnezzar was fighting against the remaining Judaean cities before launching the final onslaught in Jerusalem. The tense atmosphere of this period is well illustrated by the contemporary Lachish Letters (ANET 321f). In letter v (ANET 322c) we read that the Jewish garrison 'are watching for the signals of Lachish' . . . and that they 'cannot see Azekah'. It had possibly just fallen to the Babylonian forces. For these letters see W. F. Albright, BASOR 61 (1936), 15f; 73 (1939), 16. Jer was still free and preached (32:3—5; 37:8—10,17; 38:17—23) that Jerusalem would fall. The promise of 4f is conditional and was not fulfilled (cf 39:7; 52:8—11). On 5 see to 22:18.

8—22 The Pledge to Released Slaves Broken— l Refers to an incident that took place during the siege of Jerusalem which began in January 588 B.C. (52:4). Intending to win God's favour, and probably for military reasons (defence, provisions etc) slave owners agreed to abide by Covenant Law (Ex 21:2ff) and sealed their solemn pact by a religious rite (18f). According to the Law, Hebrew masters were obliged to set free their Hebrew (not their pagan) slaves at the end of six years. Their

498l present action (10f) was really a general amnesty, no time reckoning being considered. After this pact was made, Pharaoh's army advanced on Jerusalem and the Babylonians had to lift the siege to advance against them (37:5, 11). It was during this period that the pact of freedom was broken and Jer spoke against the immoral

m behaviour (21). The incident shows how shallow was Judah's repentance (cf 5:2 etc). **18f.** For the rite of cutting the animal in two and passing between the parts see Gn 15:9—17. While doing so, the contracting parties apparently invoked on themselves the fate of the divided animal if they failed to observe the terms of the covenant. For an exact 8th cent. parallel cf J. Fitzmyer JAOS 81 (1961) 181, 201. **19.** 'The people of the land, (RSV) 'the common people' (CV) Heb. *'am hā-'āres*. It is better to render with Bright (220 etc) as 'the landed gentry' (cf 2 [4] Kgs 23:30 etc). The Heb. expression had taken on a pejorative meaning by NT times.

n 35 The Faithful Rechabites—This ch narrates an incident from the reign of Jehoiakim (7), i.e., 609—598. From 11 we gather it must be at the very end of this period, i.e., 599/8, when Nebuchadnezzar had the surrounding nations plunder Judah after her revolt, and his own defeat by the Egyptians in 601; cf 2 (4) Kgs 24:2. The Rechabites were a clan that traced its descent from the 9th cent. Jonadab ben Rechab (6) who physically aided Jehu in his purge of the dynasty of Ahab and in the slaughter of the prophets of Baal (2 [4] Kgs 10:15—17, 23f). The way of life he is said to have introduced (6f) was probably a conscious reversion to that of the desert wanderings and a reaction against the immorality introduced by material progress in the N Kingdom. It also recalls the manner of life of the later nomadic Nabataeans

o (cf Diodorus Siculus, 19, 94). This desert ideal, similar in certain aspects to that of the Nasirites (Nm 6; cf Jg 13:4—7; 1 Sm 1:11), had ancient roots in Israel, and the Rechabites may be in some way connected with the Kenite clan (cf 1 Chr 2:55) which, in turn, appear to have some relation with Moses (cf Jg 1:16). Jer did not follow the Rechabite way of life but admired their fidelity to the founder's rules. **2.** 'House of the Rechabites'; better: 'clan or community of the Rechabites'. **3f.** These individuals mentioned are otherwise unknown; for Maaseiah however, cf 21:1; 29:25; 37:3. **18f.** The promise made to the Rechabites. We know nothing certain of their subsequent history (but cf Neh 3:14). Their ideal of asceticism and their witness to the supremacy of the spiritual were kept alive in Jewish communities such as Qumrân and in Christianity, e.g. in religious life.

36–45 BOOK 3: JEREMIAH'S SUFFERINGS

499a Episodes from the life of Jeremiah. The greater part of the material, if not all of it, comes from Baruch, the prophet's faithful scribe and companion. Ch 36 tells us how the first scrolls with Jer's prophecies of doom were written in the 4th year of Jehoiakim (605/4). The remaining chh tell of the last days of Jerusalem and the sequel to the city's destruction. The tragic figure of Jeremiah stands throughout in the centre of the picture. From the final siege onwards, then, we have here a continuous biography of the prophet. It is possible that at one stage of the formation of the book much more biographical (B) material was to be found together with chh 36—45, but was later transposed to other places. Rudolph (211), in fact, thinks all the Baruch (B) material was together at one time, forming a separate book. He gives its original order as: chh 26; 19:1—20:6; 36; 28f; 51:59ff; 34:2—7; 37ff. The **499a** original order is of course, hard to determine and of small importance for exegesis. While we here group chh 36—45 together as Book 3 and title it 'Jeremiah's sufferings' we realize that ch 36 is but loosely connected with what follows and has not as central theme the sufferings of the prophet. The narrative of chh 36—45 is, to a large extent, self-explanatory and can here be treated summarily.

36 Baruch writes the Prophecies of Jeremiah— b This narrative is unique in that it tells us in detail of the writing of an OT book and describes for us how books were written in 7th cent. Judah. For more information see J. P. Hyatt, 'The Writing of an OT Book', BA 6 (1943), 71—80.

1–8 The Writing of the First Scroll—The 4th year of Jehoiakim was 605/4 (April to April). This, we may recall, was the year of Nebuchadnezzar's victory at Carchemish (46:1ff) which proved how true Jer's prophecies on the foe from the N were. The threat was more real than Judah would have been to believe in 609 (cf 26:1ff; 7:1ff). **2f.** Only the oracles of doom against Judah and the surrounding nations were consigned to writing and the work was intended to bring Judah to a better frame of mind. The material used for writing was probably papyrus. On the relation of this scroll to our present book cf § 487g. **4.** It was then customary to use scribes for such purposes. Baruch was of noble lineage (ch 45; cf 51:59; 32:12). **5.** We do not know why **c** Jer though not in prison (cf g), was barred from the Temple. Access to it may have been forbidden after the Temple sermon of 609 (cf 26:1ff; 7:1ff). **6f.** Fixed fast days were then few in Israel, but one could be proclaimed for some national calamity, such as drought (cf ch 14) and threat of enemy invasion. One may already have been announced, or, more likely, Jer was certain one soon would be. His message was to be read to the common people who would come in great numbers on such an occasion. The impending peril should make them better disposed to heed God's words. **8.** The scroll was read only in the following year (9), which reading **8** (unless a gloss from 10a) announces proleptically.

9–26 Reading and Burning of the Scroll—9. The **d** 9th month of Jehoiakim's 5th year was December 604. The fast proclaimed in this month was probably due to the threat of Babylonian invasion. From the Babylonian Chronicle we know that in this same month the Babylonian armies captured and sacked the Philistine city of Ashkelon (cf 47:1—7). The danger to Judah, still nominally an Egyptian vassal-state, was real (cf Hb 1:5—11; Jer 5:15—17; 6:22—26). It was probably only some time later that Jehoiakim submitted to Nebuchadnezzar (cf [2] 4 Kgs 24:1). **10.** Shaphan was Josiah's secretary of state (2 [4] Kgs 22:3 etc). Gemariah, his son, was probably brother of Ahikam (26:24), and also, perhaps of Elasah (29:3). They were all friendly to Jer (cf 25). These chambers about the Temple were used among other purposes for meetings (cf 35:2). **11—19.** Gemariah probably grew anxious about **e** what was read in his father's chambers and went to his father who was with others in the palace. Of these only Elnathan (who fetched Uriah from Egypt, 26:20—23) is otherwise known to us. Here Elnathan and the other princes (25) befriend Jer. Apparently they still stood for Josiah's reform and political measures. **22.** It can be cold in Jerusalem in December ('the ninth month') cf Jn. 10:23. **26.** Had not Divine providence protected Jer and his scribe they would have suffered the fate of Uriah (26:20—23) at Jehoiakim's hand.

499f 27—32 A Second Scroll is written—29—31. For the prophet's judgement on Jehoiakim see 21:11—22; 22:13—19. No son of Jehoiakim ever really reigned as king of Judah. His son Jehoiachin (22:24—30) was monarch for a mere three months and was exiled before his first regnal year began. Zedekiah, who succeeded him, was Jehoiakim's brother. **32.** What 'the many similar words' added to the original scroll were, we cannot say. Neither do we know how this second scroll fared in history.

g 37—38 Incidents During the Siege of Jerusalem— The deportation of 597 robbed Judah of the most balanced of her nobility and placed on the throne the weakling, Zedekiah. The struggle between the pro-Egyptian and pro-Babylonian parties still went on. About 594/3 Zedekiah succeeded in steering clear of an anti-Babylonian alliance, promoted possibly by Egyptian intervention (see on ch 27f.). The anti-Babylonian party finally gained the upper hand and by 589 Judah was in revolt. Though we cannot determine the genesis of this, we may surmise it was connected with the accession of Hophra (589—570; cf 46:14—30) to the Egyptian throne. Only Tyre and Ammon of the Palestinian statelets took part (cf Jer 40:13—41:15; Ezek 21:18—32). Zedekiah himself appears to have wavered between peace and war (21: 1—7; 37:3—10; 38:14—23) but was the creature of the anti-Babylonian military leaders of Judah. By autumn 589 the Babylonian armies were in Judah and in January 588 Jerusalem was blockaded (52:4; 2(4) Kgs 25:1). Nebuchadnezzar himself remained at Riblah (52:10) in Syria. While Jerusalem was blockaded operations were carried on against the cities of Judah, the plan apparently being to reduce these before launching the final assault on the capital. Finally, of these only Lachish and Azekah held out (34:6f; the Lachish **h** Letters, ANET 322). Sometime during the campaign, probably summer 588, an advance of the Egyptian forces made the Babylonian army lift the siege of Jerusalem (37:5). This helped the morale of the defenders (34:8—11; 37:3—10) but it was short-lived. The Egyptians were repelled and the assault on Jerusalem now began in earnest. Zedekiah would have surrendered, in accord with Jeremiah's constant advice, had the military leaders permitted (38:14—23). Finally in July 587 (52:5f) Jerusalem fell. Zedekiah was arrested while attempting escape (52:7ff), and was sent to Nebuchadnezzar who had him blinded and exiled. A month later, on Nebuchadnezzar's orders, the city was set ablaze and deportation systematically carried out.

37:1—10. Babylonian Withdrawal does not mean security—1f are editorial, showing what the neglect of Jeremiah's words, written in the scroll of 605/4 (cf ch 36) meant for Judah. **3—10.** Jeremiah is certain God's plan will be brought to completion. Jerusalem is doomed. The vv are most probably from the eye-witness Baruch. For the relation to 21:1—10 cf § 495b.

i 37:11—38:28 Arrest and Imprisonment of Jeremiah: Two Accounts—37:11—21 and ch 38 each tell how Jer was arrested and taken to the princes (37:11—14; 38:1—6), thrown into an underground prison where he was left for some time (37:15f; 38:6—13) and was removed to the quarters of the guards (37:21; 38:13) where he remained until the fall of Jerusalem (37:21 with 52:6; 38:13 with 39:14f). During his imprisonment Zedekiah consulted the prophet who told him he would be handed over to the king of Babylon (37:17—20; 38: 14—26). The two accounts differ on the reason for Jer's arrest (cf 37:17—21; 38:1—3), possibly on the first

place of imprisonment (cf 37:15f; 38:6), on the reason **499** for the change of place of confinement (cf 37:17—21; 38:7—13), and on details of the audience with Zedekiah. In 37, e.g., this is at the first place of confinement (37: 17—20) whereas in 38:14—27 it appears to have taken place after the prophet was removed from this. It is **j** possible, of course, that we have two different series of events from the last troubled days of Jerusalem. Most modern scholars, in fact, favour this view. The numerous similarities, none the less, favour the view of those, such as Skinner, 258f, and Bright, 233, who see here in 37f a double account of the same episodes, accounts that are complementary rather than contradictory. Thus, the dry cistern of 38:6 may well be the dungeon of Jonathan's house of 37:16 (not mentioned in ch 38). Another argument in favour of this view is that in 38: 28b—40:6 we find a twofold account of Jer's release. These two accounts, combined in the passage, may originally have been continuations of a twofold parallel narrative of his arrest found in 37:11—38; 23.

37:11—15. Attempted Journey to Anathoth and k Arrest—The attempted journey may have some connexion with the purchase recorded in ch 32. The Benjamin Gate was apparently at the N side of the city, leading to the land of Benjamin (cf 20:2; 38:7; Zech 14:10). The main enemy offensive would be launched from this side, which was the most vulnerable. **16—21.** Secret interview with Zedekiah, showing the weak character of the king (inwardly wishing to follow Jeremiah's directions [38:16. 19] but afraid to do so) and the firm reply of the prophet. **38:1—6.** The prophet put into a miry cistern. **4.** 'Weakening the hands of . . .' (MT, RSV), i.e., demoralizing (CV). The same Heb. expression is used in the contemporary Lachish letter 6 (ANET 322) of the (pro-Babylonian) princes of Jerusalem. **7—13.** Jer rescued through the intervention of an Ethiopian eunuch. The prophet's oracle concerning this person (39:15—18) may have originally stood after v 13. **14—23.** Final interview with Zedekiah. **24—28.** Seem out of place. Holz, Rudolph and Hyatt prefer to put them after 37:17—21.

39:1—40:6 After the Fall of Jerusalem. Jeremiah l is released—Compiled from a number of sources which must be delimited if we are to understand the text correctly. Firstly, 39:15—18 really belongs after 38:7—13, q.v. and is inserted in its present position to remind us that the oracle must have been fulfilled. Next, 38:28b is continued, not in the following v (i.e., 39:1), but in 39:3 (cf RSV, note to this v). Then, 39:3 is not continued in 39:4 but in 39:14. 38:28b. 39:3, 14, then, go together and give us a summary account (perhaps from Baruch, Hyatt, 1079) of how Jer was released from custody and remained in Judah. The sequence is clearer if we omit 4—13, absent from LXX, as a later insertion. But it is probable that the LXX omits them by homoeoteleuton. A second account **m** of Jer's release is found in 11f. (+13a?) and 40:1—6 which originally went together. 39:13, or at least 13b, is a later addition to harmonize the two accounts. 39:15—18 originally stood after 38:7—13. The two accounts are probably variants of a single incident and may have continued the twofold narrative of the prophet's arrest (37:11—21; 38:1—28a), but two distinct incidents are not impossible in view of the turmoil following the catastrophe. In **39:3** it is uncertain which of the obscure Akkadian words are personal names, place-names or mere titles; hence the difference of the number of persons found in the versions: Vg 8; LXX 5; Syriac 3

99m or 2; RSV 4; CV, Bright 2. The 'middle gate' was somewhere within the city. **39:4.** According to Vincent the 'gate between the walls' was to the S, at the lower end of the Tyropoeon Valley.

n 40:7–41:18 Governership and Assassination of Gedaliah—Here we have a historical narrative (found more briefly in 2(4) Kgs 25:22–26) of Gedaliah's frustrated attempt to restore peace to Judah and commence the work of reconstructing a nation from the ruins. Since no mention is made of Jer, the passage is scarcely from Baruch. Gedaliah, son of Ahikam (40:5), was of the nobility of Judah. His father, Ahikam, was a court official to Josiah and Jehoiakim and a protector of the prophet (26:24; 2[4] Kgs 22:12.14). His grandfather Shaphan may have been the official of Josiah mentioned in 2[4] Kgs 22:3ff. From 39:14; 40:6 we know that Jer stood beside Gedaliah during his period as governor of Judah. Some believe that the oracles of the Book of Consolation (chh 30–31) date from this period (cf § 497b). We cannot say how long Gedaliah held office: it could be anything from one to four years (cf 41:1).

40:7–12 The Fugitives gather about Gedaliah— 7. Mizpah, N of Jerusalem, either modern Tell en-Nasbeh or Nebi Samwêl (cf Bright, 255), recalled former glory (cf Jg 20:1–3; 21:1; Sam 7:5ff; 10:17) and was chosen as the provincial capital.

o 40:13–41:18 Assassination 40:13–16. Gedaliah's goodwill left him unsuspecting. We do not know why the king of Ammon plotted his assassination. This king, already involved in the anti-Babylonian plot of 594/3 (cf 27:3), may have favoured or aided the revolt of 589/7 (cf Ezek 21:18–32; MT 23–37) and may have resented Gedaliah's pro-Babylonian policies. **41:1.** Gedaliah was killed in the October of some unspecified year, but scarcely in 587 (cf 40:7–12). The tragic event was later commemorated by a fast (cf Zech 7:5; 8:19). **4–10.** The cities from which the pilgrims came once formed part of the N Kingdom, but were probably annexed by Josiah (cf 2 (4) Kgs 23: 15, 19f) to Judah, accepting the Temple as the true centre of worship (cf 31:6 etc). The signs of mourning (**5**) show that they came to lament over the ruins of the Temple, which still remained a sacred place. They could also have come on the occasion of the Feast of Tabernacles (in the 7th month) or for the civil New Year (a little later). We do not know why Ishmael induced them to enter Mizpah. **9.** For these defences of Asa (911–870 B.C.) cf 1 (3) Kgs 15:22. **10.** Jeremiah, though not mentioned, was probably among the captives; cf 42:2. **11–18.** Rescue of the captives. **12.** It is probably the pool referred to in 2 Sm 2:13. (cf J. B. Pritchard, BA 19 [1956], 66–75; 23 [1960], 1).

p 42:1–44:30 Jeremiah in Egypt—From 42:1 to the end of 44 Jer once more occupies the centre of the picture. The basic narrative is probably from Baruch (cf 43:3) but it has received the imprint of the deuteronomic editor at certain points, notably in 42:9–22 and 44:1–14.

42:1–43:7 The Flight into Egypt—42:1–6. As earlier (28:6–9, 12–14), so now, Jer will not answer in God's name until God speaks to him. **7.** He must wait ten days for God's answer. **8–22.** Yahweh replies. God's plans are to build up a true Israel (**10**; cf 29:11 etc) but this he will do only if they cooperate by remaining in Palestine.

q 43:8–44:30 Jeremiah in Egypt—The biography of Jer has ended and in this section we have his final words. These were, doubtless, spoken at various times between his arrival in Egypt (c. 582) and the death of the Pharaoh **499q** Hophra (44:30) in 570. Of the prophet's activity in Egypt, where he probably died, we know nothing. **43:8–13.** Employing a symbolic action (cf 51:59–64a; 13:1–11; chh 27f). Jer forewarns the refugees that they will find no safety from Nebuchadnezzar in Egypt. That land too is doomed. Nebuchadnezzar invaded Egypt in 568/7 (ANET 308d) but did not conquer it. Tahpanhes (cf 2:16) was in the E part of the Delta, towards Palestine. **13.** 'Heliopolis', Heb.: 'the House of the Sun (god)'; cf CV. Each of the obelisks that stood before the temple (erected by Thutmose III, 1502–1448 B.C.) was called 'Cleopatra's Needle'. One of these is now in London; another in New York. **44:1–30.** The deuter- **r** onomic diction is particularly noticeable in 1–14. In 1–30 we find prophetic discourses to the Jews of Egypt in general, or to special groups of them. There were probably large groups of Jews in various parts of Egypt before the fall of Jerusalem in 587; cf E. G. Kraeling, BA 15 (1952), 50–67. **1–14.** Jer rebukes the Jews. **1.** Migdol, site unknown, was near Tahpanhes; Memphis (2:16), modern Mît Rahneh, near Cairo; Pathros was upper, i.e., S Egypt. The Jewish colony of Elephantine in these parts, though prominent only some time later, may have already existed in Jer's day; cf Kraeling, loc. cit. These names show the extent of the Jewish colonies. **15–19.** The Jews defend their cult of the Queen of Heaven against Jer. For this cult see on 7:18. **20–28.** A further rebuke of the Jews. **29f.** A sign concerning the Pharaoh Hophra (589–570 B.C.). This king's accession to the throne may have occasioned the final tragic revolt of Judah against Babylon cf § 499g. He sent aid to Zedekiah during it (37:5). He was finally dethroned and executed by Amasis who succeeded him (570–526 B.C.). Jer gives this future event as a sign of what awaits his rebellious audience. For the sign cf Is 7:11–17; 37:30; 38:7; Ex 3:12, etc.

45 A Message to Baruch—Jer's faithful scribe and **s** lifelong companion has been content to narrate his master's activity with little or no mention of his own person. Only when necessary does he refer to himself; in ch 36, passim, on the writing of the first scrolls in 605/4; in 32:12f, 16 as witness to his master's act of purchase during the first siege of Jerusalem and finally in 43:3, 6 where he refers to suspicions harboured against him after the Fall of Jerusalem. Yet, in his youth in 605/4 he was a man of some ambition (45:5). Perhaps he had dreamed of entering on a diplomatic career. His birth and education would have made this easy and his brother later distinguished himself in this field (51–59). His association with Jer in 605 put an end to this, bringing the royal anger on his head (cf 36:19, 26). Those same years 605/4 brought their share of suffering to scribe and master alike. In the present ch we learn of his ambitions (5) and mental anguish (3). Unfortunately, we cannot identify precisely the object of the one or the cause of the other. God's reply, through Jer (4f), **t** must have brought little consolation. In an imminent national catastrophe, in which the Almighty himself would have to undo his own work, Baruch should not be preoccupied with his personal ambitions. As a reward for his service his life will be spared him while the nation is ruined. 'As prize of war' (5; 38:2; 39:18), i.e. as a booty (CV), may be an expression of military origin (Bright, 184f), and means that this much will be taken from the fray. By placing the oracle at the end of the narrative, Baruch, or an editor, tells us how it was fulfilled (cf 39:15–18). At some earlier stage it probably stood after ch 36 or at the end of the scrolls of 605/4.

L

499t There is no need to doubt the trustworthiness of 45:1 and assign the oracle to a later date. This candid confession of Baruch shows his sincerity and sets a seal on his record of the events of Jer's life. How Baruch ended his days we cannot say. He may have edited the work of Jer in Egypt or in Babylon, where he finally migrated according to tradition. His role of faithful scribe was not forgotten in Israel and two pseudonymous writings, one of them canonical, the other apocryphal (2 Baruch) bear his name.

25:15−38; 46−51. BOOK IV; ORACLES AGAINST THE NATIONS.

500a In LXX this section comes in 2nd place, see Introd. § 487f. Oracles against pagan nations were a feature of the preaching of some of the prophets. Such oracles were doubtless given on various occasions and were gradually made into collections which were later inserted into the prophetic books. We have such collections in Is 13−23 and Ezek 25−32; cf also Am 1:3−23; Na 1:1f; Zeph 2; Zech 9:1ff. It is natural that in the process of transmission some oracles were expanded, non-genuine ones added and that a certain amount of contamination between the various collections took place. That the collection of oracles against the nations of Jer also circulated independently before being inserted into the book is indicated by the different arrangement in LXX and MT. The original title of the collection was probably that of LXX: '*What Jeremiah prophesied against the nations*'. 25:15ff was added to 25:13 before LXX inserted this collection. This it did between 25:13 and 15 (14 being absent from LXX). They were first apparently inserted in the same position in the MT but were later transferred to their present position, i.e. after ch 45. For possible reasons of this change cf EOTInt, 364. The original title was left behind, however, to become the ending of MT 25:13, with which cf 46:1.

b **25:15−38 The Cup of Judgement on the Nations**— This is an expanded form of words of Jer, the 'prophet to the nations' (1:5). It is hard to say what is original and what expansion. EOTInt, 364, limits the original core to 15−17; 27−29. Some list of nations may, however, have well been included. The section was added as a conclusion to 1−13 (14). It gives the theological reason underlying the oracles, i.e. the universality of divine justice. The figure of the 'cup of God's wrath' first appears in Jer's day (cf 13:12−14; Hb 2:16; Lam 4:21). **25.** Zimri is unknown. F. Perles corrects to Zamki, which he takes as a gloss (in alphabetic code) for Elam. **26.** Sheshach (RSV footnote) is a cipher-writing of Babel (Babylon). **30−32; 34−38.** The punishment is viewed as a manifestation of the Day of the Lord; cf Is 2:6−22; 3:1−15; 34:1−4; 5−17; Zeph 1:14ff.

c **46−51; Oracles Against the Nations**—We have in this collection oracles against nine pagan nations. We follow here the order of MT, noting for each, in brackets, the position of the oracle in the widely divergent LXX list.

46:2−28 Oracle Against Egypt 1 (2)—605 B.C. Probably composed just before the battle c. May-June 605. Nebuchadnezzar was in sole command of the Babylonian army at Carchemish, but became king only in Aug. 605. **3f.** The Egyptian officers (or Jer in vision?) urge their armies to battle. **5f.** The Egyptians are routed. The Babylonian Chronicle describes their defeat in a similar manner; cf BA 19 (1956). **7−10.** For Egypt, the tide of conquest is now stemmed. **11f.** Her wound is incurable. She has become a laughing stock;

cf 8:22; 30:13. **13−26.** An oracle on Nebuchadnezzar's **500c** invasion of Egypt (13), telling of the country's terror at his advance. Though Nebuchadnezzar never conquered Egypt (this was effected only in 525), he invaded it in 568/7 (ANET, 308d). Although, like 43:8−13, it was fulfilled only later, the oracle may date from the monarch's march against the Philistine plain in 604 (cf 36:9−32), threatening Egypt, or from 601 or 587. **14.** Migdol (44:1; **d** cf Ezek 29:10), on the NE border of Egypt, probably modern Tell el-Heir; for Memphis and Tahpanhes see to 2:16. **15.** Apis, the bull-god of Memphis, considered an incarnation of the god Ptah, is powerless against Yahweh's anger. **17.** The Heb. for 'lets go by' is *he'ebîr* and may contain a reference to the Pharaoh Hophra (588−569), in Egyptian *Ha'abre'*. Cf also Is 30:7. **25f.** Amon of Thebes, i.e. the chief-god of the capital city of upper Egypt; present-day Luxor. **27f.** The passage is found also in 30:10f and is probably out of place here.

47:1−7 Oracle against the Philistines 2 (4)—Cf **e** 25:20. **1.** If 'before Pharaoh smote Gaza' (absent from LXX) is original, it may refer to the Pharaoh Neco's sack of Gadytis (generally identified with Gaza) after the battle of Megiddo (i.e. from the N, cf 2) in 609, mentioned by Herodotus (II, 15g). It could also be an attack on Nebuchadnezzar's forces there in 601, mentioned in the Wiseman Chronicle. But the chronological indication of MT may not be original and the reference is probably to the Babylonian invasion of Philistia in 604 known from the Babylonian Chronicle (Wiseman 68). Malamat (IEJ 1 [1950−51], 154−59) favours a Scythian invasion in c. 609. **4.** The Philistines were believed to have come from Caphtor (Am 9:7), i.e. probably Crete. **5.** 'Anakim', cf Jos 11:21f. The Heb. is *Emqām*, 'their valley' (Vg), which Heb. radicals are probably to be understood through Ugaritic as 'their strength' (CV). For gashing as a sign of mourning cf 16:6; 41:5. The Babylonian campaign of 604 was probably against Ashkelon. An Aramaic letter from this period from a Palestinian king begging Egyptian help against Babylon may well be from the ruler of Ashkelon (cf J. Bright, BA 12 [1949], 46−52; J. A. Fitzmyer, Bib 46 [1965], 41−55). Philistia was probably in league with Tyre and Sidon against Babylon (4). For other oracles against the Philistines cf Am 1:6−8; Is 14:28−31; Ezek 25:15−17; Zeph 2:4−7.

48:1−47 Oracle against Moab 3 (9)—An oracle **f** against Moab is to be expected from Jer; cf 25:21. She was a traditional enemy of Israel (Gn 10:30−38; Nm 22−24; 2 [4] Kgs 13:20 etc). She made *razzias* into Judah, presumably at the request of Babylon, in 600−598 (2 [4] Kgs 24:2) and rejoiced at the destruction of Jerusalem in 587 (Ezek 25:8−11; Zeph 2:8−10). Moab as a people appears to have passed from history soon after 587, as archaeology informs us that sedentary life disappears there. The country was apparently overrun by Arabs c. 550. The present oracle is peculiar for its length, the abundance of place-names and its close relation to Is 15−16. In fact, the prophetical section of Is (i.e. 15:2−6; 16:6−11) is almost entirely in Jer 48:1−47. Albright (JBL 61 [1942] 119) thinks both oracles refer **g** to an invasion of Arabs c. 650. In this case, the oracle, if from Jeremiah, is employing earlier material. The occasion of the oracle on Jer's part may have been the Moabite raids on Jewish territory c. 600−598 (2 [4] Kgs 24:2) or the projected anti-Babylonian alliance of 594/3 (27:1−11) in which Moab participated. The present long oracle is composed of shorter units. It is hard to say how much is genuinely from Jer. **7.** Chemosh

00g was the national god of Moab (cf v 46; Nm 21:29; 1 [3] Kgs 11:7 etc). **13.** The parallelism with Chemosh suggests that here 'Bethel' is a divine name, referring probably to the syncretistic cult of Yahweh practised at Bethel in the N Kingdom (cf J. P. Hyatt, JAOR 59 [1939], 81—98). For identifications of the place names cf Rudolph 263—5 and A. Kuschke in Fs Rudolph, Tübingen, 1961, 181—96. On Moabite culture cf A. H. van Zyl, *The Moabites*, Leiden, 1960, with R. de Vaux's review in RB 69 (1962), 471—3.

h **49:1—6 Oracle against Ammon 4 (6)**—The kingdom of the Ammonites lay due N of Moab, which was constantly encroaching on its S border, the town of Heshbon repeatedly changing hands (cf 49:3 with 48:2). The Ammonites, in turn, pressed northwards, annexing the territories of Gad and Reuben after these tribes were deported in 732 (2 [4] Kgs 15:29). For earlier opposition between Ammon and Israel cf Jg 3:13; 10:6—11; 1 Sm 11:1—11; 2 Sm 10:1—14. Her later history is parallel to that of Moab and Edom q.v. She rejoiced at the destruction of Jerusalem (Ezek 25:3—7) and was implicated in the assassination of Gedaliah (40:13—41:15). **1.** Milcom was the national god of Ammon. **4.** For 'valleys' read 'strength' as in 47:5, q.v. **5.** Cf 20:3; **6.** Cf 48:27.

i **49:7—22 Oracle against Edom 5 (5)**—The reciprocal hatred between Edom and Israel was much more deep-seated than that between Moab and Ammon, perhaps because of the presumed blood relationship: The Edomites were descendants of Esau, (Gn 25:29f; etc). For earlier conflicts cf Nm 20:14—21; 2 Sm 8:13f; 2 [4] Kgs 14:7. Edom actually helped the Babylonians at the final revolt of Judah in 589/7. The memory of Edom's behaviour on the fall of Jerusalem was not lost (Ezek 25:12—14; Mal 1:2—4; Is 34:5—17; 63:1ff; Ps 137 (136):7). An oracle from Jer against her was to be expected (cf 25:21). The present oracle in prose and verse is probably composed of genuine words of Jer and from earlier and later prophetic utterances. Much of it is found in Obadiah. Thus 14—16 = Obad 1—4; 7 = Obad 3f; 9b = Obad 5ac; cf 19f with 50:44—46 etc. Unlike the doom oracles against Moab (48:47), Ammon (49:6) and Elam (49:39), here no ray of hope is held out for Edom. She is to become the symbol of evil itself (Is 34:5f; 61:1f). **7.** Teman, a district in Edom, here as elsewhere, stands for the country itself. **13.** Bozrah, modern el-Buseirah, was the chief city of Edom.

j **49:23—27 Oracle against Damascus, Hamath and Arpad 6 (8)**—The three Aramaean cities figure prominently in the history of the 9/8th cent. and were made part of the Assyrian Empire by Tiglath-pileser III (738—732 B.C.); cf 2 [4] Kgs 16:9; Is 9:10; 36:19; 37:13; 2 [4] Kgs 18:34; 19:13. After a revolt, subdued in 720 (ANET 284bc; 285bc), nothing further is heard of Hamath and Arpad and none of the three figures in the history of Jer's day. As no mention of them is found in 25:15ff the prophecy may be earlier than Jer (Rudolph 721). It could also very well be an earlier one applied by Jer to Damascus on some occasion now unknown to us (cf Bright, 337).

k **49:28—33 Oracle against Arab Tribes 7 (7)**—Kedar was a well-known Arab tribe of the Syrian desert, between Palestine and Babylon (Gn 25:13; 1 Chr 1:29; Ps 120 (119):5; Song 1:5; Jer 2:10; Ezek 27:21). We find oracles against them also in Is 21:16f; 42:11; 60:7). Hazor, of course, is not the famed city of Palestine (Jos 11:1 etc). Here it is a region in the Syrian desert, unless we are to take it as an aggregation of unwalled villages in Heb. *hªṣērîm*, pl. of *hāṣôr*). The 'kingdoms of Hazor' would then be the chieftains of these villages.

Kedar, led by its king, made a serious invasion of Trans- **500k** jordan Syria c. 650. For Ashurbanipal's campaign against them see ANET 290—301. Nebuchadnezzar, too, marched against them in 699/8. Jer's oracle may date from this campaign (so Wiseman 31f). The oracle may be an earlier one from c. 650 (see to 48:1—47) adapted to this later situation (cf Bright, 338). **28.** 'The people of the east', Heb. *Bªnê Qedem*, a well-known tribe of the Syrian desert (Gn 29:1; Jg 6:3.33; Jb 1:3). **29.** Cf 6:25; 20:3f, 10. See further R. Gofnah, *Yediôt*, 27 (1963), 173—9; A. Malamat, '"Haserim" in the Bible and Mari', ibid, 180—4; both in Heb. with Eng. summaries.

49:34—39 Oracle Against Elam 8 (1)—Elam, E of **l** Babylon, was an ancient civilization. It aided Merodach-baladan (cf Is 39:1—8) against Assyria in his abortive revolts of 721—710; 704—702, and thereby, doubtless, aroused false hope in Judah. Nebuchadnezzar seems to have marched against it in 596/5 (cf Wiseman 36, 72f) and later bids for independence were likely. The present oracle was made 'at the beginning of the reign of Zedekiah' (34), which in Heb. is a technical expression for the accession year, i.e. the period between the assumption of power and the following first of Nisan; in this case a mere month 15/16 March—Apr. 597 B.C. Elam, and the prowess of her archers (**35;** cf Is 22:6; Pliny, *Natural History* 37, 27) may have aroused hopes of Babylon's destruction.

50:1—51:64 Oracle on the Destruction of Babylon m 9 (3)—That Jer prophesied the downfall of Babylon we know from 52:59—64; cf also 25:26. The same is implicit in his prophecy of the Seventy Years (29:10; 25:11f), or the term of the lives of Nebuchadnezzar (605—562), his son (562—560) and grandson (560—556), as MT 27:7 puts it. As the years of their exile passed by the Jews read the course of political events in the light of Jer's prophecies. They looked forward joyfully to the downfall of Babylon and their return to the homeland. What we have in Jer 50:1—51:58 (as also in Is 13:1—22; ch. 40ff, and perhaps in Is 21:1—10) are a series of separate poems from the exilic period on the keenly-awaited destruction of their Babylonian master, which had now come to be considered an oppressor. The perspective is so entirely exilic that the author can be presumed to be living in Babylon. This author can hardly be Jer, who was taken **n** to Egypt (43:8ff) where he probably died. For Jer, Nebuchadnezzar was Yahweh's servant (25:9; 27:6; 43:10 etc), punishing Judah by divine command. In 50:17; 51:34 he is viewed as an oppressor. For Jer the destruction of Judah and Jerusalem was decreed by God; for 50:33ff these are seen as evils for which Babylon will be destroyed. For these and other reasons the poems are now generally taken as having been composed after Jer's time. Since the fall of Babylon is considered imminent (51:13, 33 etc), the poems seem to have been composed at a rather advanced date in the exile, but before the Persians under Cyrus appeared on the horizon. The destruction of the city is expected to be the work of the Medes (51:11; cf 51:27) and no mention is made of the Persians. Most of the poems are, then, probably earlier than Second Isaiah and may date from c. 556 B.C. towards the death of Neriglissar, the grandson of Nebuchadnezzar (cf MT 27:7). They are songs of hope, expressing the assurance of faith, founded on Jer's prophecies. There is no need to date any of them later than the exile. In fact, seeing that the destruction of Babylon and ensuing slaughter as described in them are so much at variance with the peaceful capitulation of

500n the city in 539, none of them could well be post-exilic.

o **50:1** Superscription to chh 50—51 or to 51:59—64. The latter half of the verse, i.e. 'concerning the land of the Chaldeans, by Jeremiah the prophet', absent from the LXX (27:1), is repetitious and probably not original.

51:59—64a Genuine Oracle of Jeremiah against Babylon—This section, although it follows on 50:1—51:8 in the LXX (21:1—28:58), must have once occupied a different position in the HT where the oracles against the nations appear to have finished with 51:58 + 51:64b, 'and they shall weary themselves. Thus far the words of Jeremiah'. At a later period 51:59—64a was placed in its present position and the editor then took 'thus far the words of Jeremiah' from 58 to have them end the book. In doing so, however, he took the Heb. word that preceded them, i.e. weyā'epû, 'and they shall weary themselves' (cf CV, RSV note), which now in 64b become meaningless. It is a sign of the complicated history of the text of Jer.

p Seraiah was a brother of Baruch, Jer's scribe (cf 32:12; Bar 1:1). The MT (RSV) says Zedekiah went to Babylon, whereas according to the LXX (CV, BJ) only a delegation was sent. In either case, a quarter-master was required to arrange lodgings etc. The 4th **500q** year of Zedekiah, i.e. 594/3, was that of the projected anti-Babylonian league in Jerusalem (cf 28:1; 27:3) when Jer prophesied a period of supremacy of 70 years for Babylon, followed by her downfall (27:7 etc). The purpose of the mission was, doubtless, to assure Nebuchadnezzar of Judah's allegiance. There is, then, no reason to doubt the historicity of the episode. The 'book' referred to (**60**) was probably only a single page. **61.** The words were probably said secretly to the chosen few. **63f.** The symbolic action would, by God's power (1:10), effect what it signified; cf 13:1—7; 17:2; 19:1, 10; 32:9; 43:9. The writing was now 'in the water' for the doomed city.

52 Historical Appendix—51:64 clearly indicates that **q** this ch is a later addition to our book, just as Is 36—39 are to Is 1—35. It was probably added to show, or recall, how Jer's prophecies were fulfilled. The ch is practically indentical with 2 (4) Kgs 24:18—25:30 but omits the assassination of Gedaliah (2 [4] Kgs 25:22—26, found in Jer 40:13ff) and adds (28—30) a precise list of the number of Jews deported to Babylon. This list was probably compiled from Babylonian sources.

LAMENTATIONS

BY M. LEAHY, REVISED BY T. HANLON.

501a Bibliography—*Commentaries*: A. W. Streane, CBSC, 1913; A. S. Peake, CBi[1], 1911; G. M. Ricciotti, 1924; S. Goldman, in *The Five Megilloth*, 1946; L. Dennefeld, PCSB, 1947; G. Rinaldi, 1953; F. Nötscher, EchB, 1947; M. Haller, HAT, 1940; T. Meek, IB, 1956. *Other literature*: N. K. Gottwald, *Studies in the Book of Lamentations*, 1954; B. Albrektson, *Studies in the Text and Theology of Lamentations*, 1963.

b Title and Place in the Canon—In MT the Book is entitled *Ēḵāh* ('How') which is the initial word of the first, second, and fourth chh. The Rabbis (and Jerome in the *Prologus Galeatus*) referred to it as *Qînôt* (Elegies or Laments) and an equivalent title was adopted by LXX (*thrēnoi*) and by Vg (*Lamentationes*). It is one of the five Rolls or *Megilloth* which form part of the third division of the Heb. Bible known as the Writings, see §§ 13e 14e. In LXX, Syr. and Vg, however, the Book comes after Jer, among the 'Prophets'.

c Literary Form—Each of the five chh which comprise the book contains 22 divisions, which is the number of consonants in the Heb. alphabet. The first three chh are arranged in strophes of three and ch 4 in strophes of 2vv. Chh 1, 2 and 4 are acrostic poems, i.e. the opening word of each strophe begins with its respective letter of the alphabet, but in the third ch the same letter begins each verse of a strophe. The fifth poem is not alphabetical but it does have 22 vv. This acrostic form, found in other sections of the Bible (Pss, Prv), was an aid to memory. Here it also serves to emphasize the completeness of misery and grief. Since it is artificial one can hardly expect the logical development of a theme. Unlike other similar acrostic passages, however, Lam does not become monotonous. Originally the poems were independent but were later joined since their subject matter was identical. All the Lamentations with the exception of ch 5 are written in a 'limping' rhythm, known as *Qînāh* because of its use in this book; in *Qînāh* rhythm each verse has two parts with, as a rule, three significant words in the first and two in the second, cf 356g.

d Subject-matter—The book contains laments over the destruction of Jerusalem by the Neo-Babylonians in 586 B.C. and the sufferings endured by the people (and by the poet himself, cf ch 3) before, during and after the siege. But it is no barren lamentation—it has a lesson to teach. The unbelievable had happened. The holy city, Yahweh's sanctuary, had been destroyed and all Judah's leaders dispersed or killed. The land itself was being occupied by foreigners. Was Yahweh unfaithful to his promises or powerless to save his people? If this was so, then those who made terms with and sacrificed to the deities of the conquerors, had sense and right on their side. But there were those who realized that God's promises were conditional on the conduct of his people. They remembered the repeated warnings of Jeremiah. They saw in these disasters the punishment of their repeated transgressions and the fulfilment of

the prophet's words. Though as yet no 'future' was **501d** visible yet they must continue to trust their God and to hope in a deliverance, which would be his answer to their repentance and the ultimate fulfilment of his promises.

Authorship—Jewish tradition attributes the book to **e** Jeremiah. The LXX has this preface: 'And it came to pass after Israel was taken captive and Jerusalem laid waste, that Jeremiah sat weeping, and lamented with this lamentation over Jerusalem, and said'. (Cf a similar text in Vg). The Talmud (BabBa 15a) also states that Jer was the author, and the Gr. and Latin Fathers take it for granted. However, neither its title nor its position in the Heb. Bible (where it is placed among the 'Writings' and not next to Jer) suggests any such authorship. Moreover, recent criticism has clearly shown that not all the poems are by the same author and few commentators today would maintain the Jeremian authorship of any of the poems.

The following are the principal difficulties in the **f** way of any ascription to Jer: (i) In the first poem, the order of the Heb. consonants is the normal one, whereas in the next three chh *Pe* comes before '*Ayin*. This variation would tend to show that the second, third and fourth are not by the author of the first. (It may well be, however, that the Heb. poets enjoyed a certain liberty in the arrangement of the consonants of the alphabet). (ii) The complaint in 2:9 that the prophets of Jerusalem 'obtain no vision from the Lord' would seem to imply that the author of the second Lam is not Jer since he, at least, was a prophet. (Perhaps, however, the words mean that the prophets have received no vision of encouragement from Yahweh.) (iii) Vv 17 and 20 are quoted against the Jeremian authorship of ch 4. In 17 the poet includes himself (note the 1st pers. plur.) with those who expected Egyptian aid whereas Jer never did, but showed himself hostile to alliance with Egypt (cf Jer 37:5—10); and in 20 he speaks of King Zedekiah with reverence whereas Jer spoke of him in disparaging terms, Jer 24:8—10. (iv) The phraseology of Lam varies from that found in Jer; moreover here we have poetry whereas Jer is mainly prose. (v) After the destruction of Jerusalem Jer remained only a few weeks before being taken to Egypt, and his reactions then were different from the reactions in Lam (cf Jer 39—43). (vi) Lam is not attributed to Jer in the Heb. The LXX may reflect a later tradition. Had Jeremiah been the author, these poems would have been included in Jer.

Most critics today uphold a plurality of authors because of the differences in the poems. Their liturgical use would explain why they were joined to form one book.

Doctrine—The author emphasizes the power of Yahweh; **g** the destruction of Jerusalem is his work for it was he who brought the Neo-Babylonians to be his agents in effecting the destruction, 1:14; 2:17; 4:11. He lays stress upon the justice of Yahweh, 1:18; 3:42, but

501g reminds his readers that, although just, Yahweh is also infinitely merciful, 3:22f. He frequently states that it is because of their sins and those of their religious leaders that the people are suffering, 1:5, 8 etc. When composing the Office of Tenebrae the Church searched the Bible for words to express our sorrow for Christ in his sufferings; she could find nothing more apt than these Lamentations.

502a **1:1—22 The First Lamentation—1—11 The Desolation of Jerusalem—1.** The city, normally crowded since it was the political and religious centre of the kingdom, now sits solitary, emptied by the exile of many of its inhabitants; she that was once great among the nations is now become as a widow and a vassal. **2.** She is not consoled by 'her lovers and friends', i.e. by her political allies, the surrounding nations who sided with her against Babylon; they have all turned against her, she is alone. **3.** The inhabitants who remained behind after the destruction of the city chose voluntary exile in Egypt because they found the Babylonian yoke intolerable (cf Jer chh 42f); Judah, which personifies the nation, dwells among the heathen, without, however, finding rest; all her persecutors overtook her in her distress. **4.** The city-gates, the recognized places of assembly in Eastern towns, are destroyed; the priests sigh because the temple-ritual has ceased; virgins are sorrowful because they can no longer take their appointed part in the joyous religious processions (cf Ps 68 (67):25). **6.** The daughter (of) Sion (i.e. Sion; we have here the genit. of definition) has lost all her majesty; her princes, weakened by hunger, were an easy prey for the Babylonians. The poet has in mind the flight and capture of King Zedekiah and his princes, Jer 39:

b 4f. **7.** The clause 'all the precious things . . . of old' should be omitted as a gloss; there is a line too many and without this clause the strophe gives better sense. **9.** Her filthiness is in her skirts, i.e. her sins are exposed for all to see. The last clause interrupts the description and is a cry to Yahweh for compassion, because the enemy has triumphed. **10.** The Babylonians stole her treasures.

c **12—22 An Appeal for Compassion—**In this section, except in 17, Sion is the speaker. **13.** Is a graphic description of the calamities which befell the city. The figures used are those of a fire, a net, sickness; **14.** HT is corrupt but the more probable reading indicates that the crimes of Jerusalem are the yoke which the Lord made and laid it on her neck; the sufferings of Jerusalem are but the due punishment of her crimes. The last line but one means that the Lord abandoned her to the fate of sinners (cf Jb 8:4). **15.** In two images, that of a solemn feast at which the victims offered are the flower of Sion's army, and that of a winepress in which the blood of the people of Judah is trodden out, the destruction is presented as the work of the Lord as

d the first cause. **17.** The poet interrupts the wailing of Sion to affirm that although Sion spreads forth her hands in a gesture of entreaty, no one is found to console her. **20.** Sion, betrayed by men, turns to Yahweh and speaks as though still under siege. **21.** The last clause is an appeal for retribution on her exulting foes. **22.** Sion continues her prayer for retribution, pleading that her foes are guilty as well as she.

e **2:1—22 The Second Lamentation—1—17 The Desolation of Jerusalem and Judah the Result of Yahweh's Anger—**In this lamentation and in the fourth the poet describes the horrors of the siege and the ruin of Jerusalem. **1.** For the expression 'the daughter

of Sion' cf 1:6. The Lord has brought misery upon the **502** city; he has cast down from its proud pre-eminence the city of Jerusalem (lit 'the glory of Israel'); he has not remembered his footstool, i.e. the temple with the Ark of the Covenant (1 Chr 28:2). **2.** Jacob is here a synonym of Judah. By delivering them up to the heathen he has deprived the kingdom of its sacred character as his elect (cf Ex 19:6), and the princes of their sacred character as consecrated rulers in the theocratic kingdom. **4.** He has ranged himself against his people; his right hand—the hand which shoots the arrows—he has brought into position. MT *niṣṣāb* ('standing') is to be corrected to *hiṣṣîb* ('he had fixed') which was read by LXX and Vg. **6a.** And he has broken his temple-enclosure as a garden is stripped when its fruit is gathered. **8.** Yahweh is depicted as using a measuring **f** line, for precision in his work of demolition. The rampart and wall are left in such a dilapidated state that they are said to mourn. **13.** The poet addresses himself to Jerusalem. It would be some comfort for her to know that her disaster is not unparalleled, but the poet can find no example of a like calamity. **14.** The false prophets bear a heavy responsibility for Jerusalem's unhappy state. Had they candidly unveiled her iniquity and foretold its consequences they might have averted the catastrophe which has now befallen her, cf Jer 14:13; 23:17. **17.** The poet repeats that it is Yahweh who has destroyed Jerusalem; in the days of old he had decreed chastisement for disobedience (cf Lv 26:14ff; Dt 28:15ff).

18—22 An Exhortation to supplicate Yahweh— g 19. Contains a line too many and the last member is to be deleted as a gloss. The night was divided into three watches of four hours each; the four-fold division (cf Mt 14:25) is of Roman origin. Jerusalem is exhorted to pray for her children in whom the future lies. **20.** Sion, accepting the invitation, supplicates Yahweh to remember that the sufferers are his chosen people, and asks whether he is indifferent to the atrocities which occurred during the siege, (cf 2 (4) Kgs 6:26—30). **22.** Yahweh summoned the terrors of war, plague and famine (lit 'terrors on every side', Jeremiah's favourite saying) as at other times he summoned the multitude of his worshippers.

3:1—66 The Third Lamentation—1—24 A Lament 503a of Personal Woe—Besides being the centre of the book this Lamentation is also the most artistic; not only does each verse begin with a separate letter of the alphabet but also each member. In it the poet uses 'I' and 'we' and therefore must be considered as representing the nation. Because of the similarities, (particularly in 1—24 and 48—66) to the situation of Jeremiah, this more than other sections is invoked in favour of his authorship. **12f.** The Lord is here likened to a hunter shooting arrows (lit 'daughters of the quiver') into the poet's body. **17f.** His life is one of unrelieved desolation and he has lost hope. **19.** Immediately overcoming his despair, he appeals to Yahweh to be no longer unmindful of his affliction. **21.** This (what is related in 22—23) I call to my mind, 'therefore may I hope'. **22f.** His hope is inspired by remembrance of Yahweh's unfailing mercies despite the sins of men. They are ever fresh (23a).

25—39 Resignation to the Will of Yahweh—This **b** section teaches that man in the midst of suffering should submit himself to Yahweh and patiently await his help. **27.** A man must accustom himself from youth, when character is being formed, to bear with courage and confidence the trials of life. **29.** 'To put the mouth

03b in the dust' is an expression of humble and silent submission—the mouth filled with dust cannot speak. **31—33.** Contain an inducement to resignation to the Lord's will because the suffering will not last for ever, and Yahweh in his mercy will soon grant relief (31f); he, like a true father, does not cause pain capriciously (lit 'not from his heart'). **34—39.** Contain a further inducement. Injustices are not committed unknown to God; it is he who permits the wrongs wrought by man, in particular those wrought against his people by their conquerors. No one has the right to complain, least of all those who have merited punishment for their sins. The writer here assumes that a sinful man deserves death, yet the Lord, although he is inflicting suffering, allows him to live.

c **40—47 The Application to Israel of the above-mentioned Counsels—40f.** The poet, speaking in the 1st pers. plur., invites his compatriots to examine their consciences and earnestly seek pardon through repentance.

d **44.** 'cloud' i.e. of his anger. **48—66 Another Lament of Personal Suffering—48—51.** He suffers especially because of the Hebrew women who are completely at the mercy of their captors (51), having lost their husbands and sons. Or 'maidens of my city' may refer to the smaller towns and villages which were dependent on Jerusalem. The precise meaning of 51a is obscure; it may mean that constant weeping has made him physically ill. **52—54.** The poet, looking back over the past, describes in language which in part at least is figurative (54) the sufferings which he endured at the hands of his enemies (cf Jer

e 38:6—13). **60—63.** His enemies are meanly hostile, they are plotting against him and in all their movements (lit 'when they sit down and when they rise up') he is the subject of their taunting songs. **65.** 'You will give them hardness of heart, thy curse upon them!' The poet's desire must not be judged by Christian standards of morality. Cf Ps 28 (27):4.

f **4:1—22 The Fourth Lamentation—1—12.** A vivid portrayal of the horrors of the siege which affected everyone irrespective of social status—**1.** The citizens of Sion once comparable to fine gold and precious and hallowed stones are now esteemed worthless. **3.** 'ostriches', who by nesting on sand and not in inaccessible places expose the chicks to danger (cf Jb 39:13—16). **6.** Sodom was not attacked by the soldiers of an invading army and thus escaped the atrocities frequently perpetrated by them. **9.** Cf Jer 6:25; 11:22; 14:18. **10.** Starving mothers boiled and ate their children (cf 2 (4) Kgs 6:26ff). **11—13.** The destruction of Jerusalem is the work of the divine anger, although it was widely thought that Yahweh would not permit an enemy to enter the city where his temple stood.

g **14—16 Insurrection against the Guilty Leaders— 14.** After the fall of the city, the religious leaders, fearing the wrath of those whom they had deceived, wandered blindly through the streets, not knowing where to seek refuge; they were polluted with innocent blood so that people could not touch their garments (14b) lest they contract ceremonial defilement, and hence they were treated like lepers.

h **17—20 Futility of the Hope of Help from Egypt—**

18a the Babylonians 'dogged our steps', i.e. those who **503h** came into the open spaces had to seek shelter because the besiegers from their siege-towers began shooting arrows and hurling stones at them. **20.** 'The breath of our nostrils', i.e. King Zedekiah, was taken near Jericho (Jer 52:8f). He was so called because under him the Jews had hoped to maintain their national life.

21f An Imprecation against Edom—The Jews were **i** bitterly hostile towards the Edomites (cf Ps 137 (136):7; Obad 10ff); Edom stood by the Babylonians, and, as a reward, when Judah was conquered, they gave over to her the rural districts. **21.** Is a sarcastic invitation to Edom to rejoice while it can, for its glee will be short-lived; it will soon be chastised. The cup is here a metaphor for divine punishment of sin.

5:1—22 The Fifth Lamentation—This, which is not **j** acrostic (cf § 501c), is not strictly a lament but rather a prayer (Vg entitles it 'Oratio Jeremiae prophetae') for the Jews—the exiles and those left behind in Judah—whose unhappy state is recounted (2—18) in order to secure Yahweh's mercy. **4.** With the loss of independence have come heavy taxes even on the necessities of life. **5a.** MT reads: 'upon our neck we are pursued', but the consonants of the word rendered 'upon' are identical with those for 'yoke' and perhaps the text had both words originally. The restored text would read, (RSV) '(with) a yoke upon', etc. **6.** They were engaged to serve the Egyptians and the Assyrians (i.e. the Babylonians who acquired the former Assyrian Empire) to procure sustenance, for the exiles had no land to cultivate. **7.** Here we have a common complaint but from 16 it is clear that he does not place all the blame on their parents for there he states that the people who were suffering had also sinned. The latter, therefore, merited their own punishment, but on account of the iniquities of their parents they were more severely punished, 'not more severely than they deserved, but more severely than they would have been, had their parents not sinned . . . on account of our solidarity the growing guilt of a sinful race may finally draw down on it a punishment that the hand of God had previously withheld' (E. Sutcliffe, *The OT and the Future Life*, 1947², 87). **8.** Instead of having a Davidic king they are now **k** governed by pagans. The 'slaves' who 'rule' were Babylonians who rose to official positions. **9.** The remnant in Judah bring in what little food they can collect in peril of raids by desert nomads who take advantage of the unsettled conditions. **16.** They have lost their national prestige. The crown was a symbol of independence (Ps 21 (20):4; Jer 13:18) and also of joy (Tb 19:9; 31:36; Prv 4:9). **17f.** They are full of grief for this, namely, for the devastation of the hill of Sion which is such that jackals wander about on it. **19.** Sion, Yahweh's earthly throne, is destroyed but Yahweh reigns forever, and thus (**20**) there is hope that he will some day restore Judah, his special kingdom. **22.** The poet is convinced that the rejection can be but a temporary one; definitive rejection is inconceivable. God's goodness and his fidelity will prevail over his anger: Pss 89 (88):2—3; 103 (102):8—11; Is 57: 15—18; Jer 3:12.

BARUCH

BY P. P. SAYDON

REVISED BY T. HANLON

504a Bibliography—J. Knabenbauer, CSS, 1907²; E. Kalt, BB, 1932; L. Dennefeld, PCSB, 1947, tome vii; H. St J. Thackeray, *The Septuagint and Jewish Worship*, 1923², 80—111; W. O. E. Oesterley, *An Introduction to the Books of the Apocrypha*, 1935, 256—71; O. C. Whitehouse and C. J. Ball in CAP, I, 569—611; A. Penna, SacB 1953; V. Hamp, EchB 1950; A. Gelin, BJ, 1959².

b Baruch—Baruch, Heb. *bārûk* 'blessed', the son of Neriah, the son of Mahseiah Jer 32:12, belonged to a noble family, his brother Seraiah being a high official in the court of king Zedekiah, Jer 51:59. He is first introduced to us as Jeremiah's secretary in 604 B.C., Jer 36:4. Later, he assisted Jeremiah in the purchase of a field in Anathoth, Jer 32:12f. After the fall of Jerusalem and the murder of Gedaliah he was carried away with Jeremiah to Egypt, Jer 43:2—6. Nothing is known from Jer of his later years. We have no evidence that he ever went to Babylon. Baruch was a man of strong character, Jer 43:3, but, apparently, less strong than his master in his resignation to the impending ruin of Jerusalem, Jer 45:3.

c Contents and Structure of the Book—Bar, as in Vg, consists of two parts of different origin, chh 1—5 being attributed to Baruch and ch 6 to Jeremiah. In LXX the two parts are separated. For the sake of clarity they will be treated here separately.

The Book proper falls into three parts: (1) 1:15—3:8—a confession of sins (1:15—2:10) and a prayer for mercy and deliverance (2:11—3:8). This is preceded by an introduction 1:1—14. (ii) 3:9—4:4—a panegyric on Wisdom (i.e. the Law) which has been abandoned by Israel and this has brought about the present suffering. (iii) 4:5—5:9—a message of comfort and encouragement in their captivity.

d Although the three parts are linked together by a common historical background, their literary features are so different that they can hardly be considered as parts of the same theme. The three parts seem to be separate compositions originating from the same historical conditions rather than parts of the same original work. This is to a certain extent borne out by the fact that the Gr. text of Part I closely resembles that of the latter part of Jeremiah.

e The Epistle or Letter of Jeremiah, Bar 6, is a rambling denunciation of idolatry and a warning to those in the Diaspora lest they should be impressed by the gorgeous manifestations of idolatrous worship. After the introduction (1—7) the letter has ten points which reiterate the lifeless and useless nature of idols. The conclusion to each section forms a refrain. The arguments used are all borrowed from the Pss and Prophets.

f Place in the Canon—In most MSS of LXX Baruch comes immediately after Jer and followed by Lam and the Epistle. In Vg the Epistle forms ch 6 of Baruch and both follow Lam.

Original Language—Baruch and the Epistle have **504g** been preserved in Gr. Jerome knew of no Heb. text (*Praef. comm. in Jer*. PL 24, 680; *Praef. in vers. Jer*. PL 29, 848). But the majority of modern critics maintain that they were both originally written in Heb., see EOT Int 592—4. Thus Bar 1:15—3:8 closely resembles Daniel's prayer in Dn 9:4—19 and may be based on it; it that case it certainly goes back to a Heb. original. Eissfeldt is also of the opinion that the poems in 3:9 to 5:9 were originally composed in Heb. Again, the directive of 1:14 indicates liturgical use and argues to a Heb. original. The Gr. translation too would indicate dependence on the Gr. version of Jer and Dn. Theodotion's version made from Heb. includes Bar.

Authorship—In the past, in favour of Baruch as **h** author, it was pointed out that the City and the Temple are presumed destroyed (2:26; 4:31), that the people are in exile (3:8, 10; 4:26) and that the Babylonians are the cause of their misfortunes (2:21—22; 4:15—16). This, it was claimed, indicated an exilic author whose purpose was to exhort and console the exiles.

However, very few today would uphold any relationship between this Book and Baruch, the secretary of Jeremiah. The book is a much later composition, addressed to another generation whose sufferings were in many respects comparable to the Exile; and by a well-known literary device the book was attributed to Baruch. This necessitated his going to Babylon rather than Egypt, cf Jer 43:6, because the book required an exilic situation, e.g. Bar 3:8.

Parts of Bar appear to be dependent on Dn, see above, § 504g, which would indicate a date in the 2nd cent. at the earliest, but more probably the 1st cent. B.C. The poems in 3:9—4:4 with the speculation on Wisdom would appear to be dependent on Jb and to reflect the Maccabean era. And lastly 4:5—5:9 suggests dependence on Jb and Dan. On the other hand the 11th Ps of Solomon is dependent on this section. (Pss Sol 11:3, 6—8 and Bar 4:37; 5:1—8).

Critics are not agreed on a precise date, but generally place the composition in the Maccabean era or soon after. Generally three authors are proposed for the three sections mentioned above. Later these were joined together because of their similar themes. A few critics put the composition after A.D. 70, making 4:5—5:9 dependent on Pss of Solomon whose composition they also retard. However, the Roman invasion would have left a greater mark on the book.

Letter of Jeremiah—The writer displays a knowledge **i** of Babylonian idolatry which suggests that he is a Jew living in Babylonia, contrasting their worship unfavourably with his own. Moreover, the style is by far inferior to that of Jeremiah. It lacks the impassioned outbursts, the elegiac tone, the emotional effects, characteristic of Jeremiah's style. Compare the Letter with Jer 10:2—16 which is parallel to it. Had it really been written by the prophet Jeremiah a later editor would

504i have united it to Jer rather than to Bar. The author is much later than Jeremiah and was dependent on his letter to the exiles (Jer 29). It is difficult to assign a date for composition but since the Hellenistic era (after 300 B.C.) was a particularly dangerous one, the author's warnings against idolatry and apostasy would have been opportune then, especially for those in the Diaspora. The author is obviously inspired too by the denunciations and satire on idols in Is 44:9—20. The peculiarities of the language indicate a Heb. original.

j Canonicity—Baruch and the Letter are excluded from the Jewish canon. There is evidence, however, that Bar was accepted by the Jews, though later rejected. Theodotion's version includes it. Moreover, Bar and the Epistle occur in ancient lists which rigorously exclude the non-canonical books, under the title 'Jeremiah with Baruch, Lamentations and the Epistle' (Swete, Intr. 203—10). There is also evidence that Bar was read in Jewish synagogues on certain festivals during the early centuries of the Christian era (Thackeray, 107—11).

k Doctrinal Content—The doctrinal element of Bar is common to other biblical books, especially the prophetical writings. The confession, with its threefold element of proclamation of God's justice and power, confession of the people's sins and prayer for forgiveness, is cast in the usual form of confessional prayers, cf Ez 9:5—15; Neh 9:6—37; Dn 9.4—19. Wisdom, which is identified with the moral law or the Sinaitic covenant, is the source of life and happiness. It is a gift of God, and man cannot acquire it nor find it with all his wealth and labour. Idols are vain things and their worship is degrading.

The Messianic doctrine in 2:35 is that of Jer 32:40. 5:1—4 predicts in a fuller sense the spiritual restoration of Jerusalem in Messianic times. The literal Messianic interpretation of 3:38 is based on Vg.

505a 1:1—2 The Title probably refers to 1:3—3:8 only. The fifth verse must be reckoned from 587—6 when Jerusalem was captured and the Temple destroyed. Insert fifth' before 'month' in accordance with ? (4) Kgs 25,8. The reference to Babylon in connexion with Baruch is required by the nature of the narrative which presupposes an exilic situation.

b 3—14. The Reading of the Book and Sending of an Offering to Jerusalem—Eissfeldt considers this passage 'a later insertion for it not only separates 1:15 from 1:2 to which it was intended to be the direct sequel, but it also presupposes a quite different situation from that in 1:1—2 and the rest of the book with this title. It does not, like the latter, presuppose the period after the disaster of 587 (1:2), but (1:7, 10) the time after Jehoiachin's deportation (598) when the Temple was in existence and the sacrificial cultus was still in being (v 10)', EOTInt 594. The argument however does not appear to be conclusive. If the silver vessels were the replacements in the Temple after the spoliation of 598 how did they get to Babylon (v 8) before 586? Perhaps as a further tribute in kind? Kgs has no mention of silver vessels to replace the gold ones taken by Nebuchadnezzar, but one might reasonably assume that they would replace the loss with vessels in as precious a metal as they could afford. Ez 1:7—11 speaks of a return of sacred vessels under Cyrus on the return from exile. There is no mention of anything earlier. Eissfeldt refers to Bar 1:7, 10, 14, as an indication that the historical situation is that prior to 587 when the Temple was in existence and sacrifice still practised. It is well to point out here however that in Jer 41:5, i.e. after the fall of Jerusalem, there is also reference

to 'cereal offerings and incense to present at the Temple **505b** of the Lord' thus indicating that an altar had survived or been reconstructed and that in some sense the Temple, even if only a blackened shell, was still in use. Again, before 586 the high priest Seraiah was still in Jerusalem but after its capture he was put to death (2 (4) Kgs 25:18) and his son Jehozadak carried off into exile (1 Chr 6:15 RSV). Thus the 'high priest' (RSV) of verse **c** 7 (LXX 'priest') was not in fact the official high priest since this was impossible while Jehozadak lived. He may have been a relative whose genealogy like that of Jehozadak was traced back to Shallum through Hilkiah, 1 Chr 6:14. Interpretation of the narrative is of course made more difficult by the evident freedom with which historical detail is treated.

10—14 A Message to the Inhabitants of d Jerusalem—10. It is supposed that Baruch carried a message to those left in Jerusalem. Although the temple had been burnt and the altar destroyed, a provisional altar may have been set up on which the priests could perform the liturgical service; cf Jer 41:5. **11f.** The exhortation to pray for Nebuchadnezzar is an echo of Jeremiah's recommendation, Jer 29:7. Here the author is dependent on Dn (5:2, 11, 13, 18) where Belshazzar is also, erroneously, introduced as the son of Nebuchadnezzar when in fact he was the son of Nabonidus. The expression 'many days', **12**, corresponds to the 70 years of Jer 25:12; 29:10. **13.** They acknowledge that their punishment is deserved. **14.** The book, i.e. the confession contained in 1:15—3:8, was to be read in the temple, in its empty shell or on its ruins, on a certain unspecified feast-day, probably the Feast of Booths, (RSV, with A, has 'feasts') and on other days of meeting. Thackeray identifies the feast with New Year's Day, and the days of meeting with the Sabbaths intervening between the anniversary of the capture of Jerusalem and the anniversary of its burning, 9:1—4.

15—2:10 The Confession—It has striking similarities **e** to Daniel's prayer in Dn 9:4—19. **15.** Cf Dn 9:7. God is just and punishment is fully deserved. **10 10.** Cf Dn 9:8, 10. All classes have sinned. The same enumeration occurs in Neh 9:32. Jer 32:32. **20—22.** The calamities are the fulfilment of the threats announced by God through Moses, Lv 26:14—39; Dt 28:15—68, and later prophets, Jer 11:7f; 6:10—13; etc. **2:1f.** Cf Dn 9:12. The writer develops the thought expressed in 20—22. God has made good the word which he had spoken against their rulers and all the people by bringing upon them plagues unparalleled in man's history. **3.** That they would eat the flesh of their own children was predicted in Lv 26:29; Dt 28:53 and Jer 19:9; cf also Lam 2:20; 4:10 and Jos Bell. Jud. 6, 3, 3—4. **4f.** Another punishment: subjection to foreign powers and oppression. 4a agrees with Ez 9:7a; 4b with Jer 42:9b; 5 with Dt 28:13. **6—10.** God is just in inflicting such a severe punishment, because he had forewarned the people.

2:11—18 The Prayer—After the confession they make **f** an appeal for deliverance from captivity. **11.** Cf Dn 9:15; Jer 32:21. God, who, in the past, has delivered them from their enemies, can deliver them now too. **12.** Cf 1 (3) Kgs 8:47; Dn 9:15. **13.** Cf Jer 42:2. **16f.** If they are left to perish, there will be none to worship God, because the dead in *Sheol* cannot praise him, Ps 6:5; 88 (87):11; 115 (113):17. The expression 'Look down from thy holy habitation' may be paralleled by Is 63:15 where 'dwelling' (LXX house) means 'heaven'. **18.** A difficult verse. The sense seems to be: that those who are alive (unlike those in v 17) and who have those

505f sentiments, honour God. The expressions 'greatly distressed', 'to go bent over', 'failing eyes', 'hungry soul' denote sorrow, humility and repentance; cf Dt 28:32, 65; Prv 27:7, Ps 42 (41):9, 11, Sir 12:11.

g **19—26 God's Past Threats and the People's Obstinacy—19.** Cf Dn 9:18b. **21—23.** Jeremiah had always advocated a policy of peaceful submission to Babylon, because he knew only too well that resistance meant only destruction and devastation; cf Jer 27:6—11, 12—15. **24f.** For particulars cf Jer 8:1—2; 21:7—9; 24:10; 27:8—13; 32:36; 36:30. In the narrative of the siege of Jerusalem nowhere do we read of the desecration of tombs, but there is evidence of such profanations in the Assyro-Babylonian inscriptions. Those who were still living died a terrible death: Lam 2:12; 20f; 4:9.

h **27—35 God's Kindness towards his People— 28—30a.** Cf Lv 26:14:39; Dt 28:62. **30b—33.** Predictions of the people's conversion, Lv 26:40—45; Dt 30:1—10. **34f.** The writer passes on from the national post-exilic restoration to the Messianic restoration which is described here with words and ideas borrowed from Jer 31:31—34.

i **3:1—8 A Last Appeal to God's Mercy**—They have repented; may God now forgive them and bring them back to their country. 'A soul in anguish' and 'a wearied spirit' are expressions denoting sorrow for sin; cf Ps 51:17; Is 57:15. **2.** The words *'for thou art a merciful God'* are read in Vg, a few Gr. MSS and the Old Latin. **3.** The interrogative form is supported by the parallel passage in Lam 5:19f. Can God really reign in heaven and let his people be destroyed, as if he were unable to save them? The contrasting of human weakness and mortality with the divine eternity and omnipotence is adduced as a motive for mercy: cf Ps 90 (89); 102 (101):23—28. **4.** They are on the brink of the grave on account of their fathers' sins. The correction of 'dead' to 'men' is unnecessary, because a desperate condition is sometimes compared to death, cf Is 26:19. **5—6.** If God takes their sins into account, he will punish them accordingly, but this would impair his honour because the heathens will think that he is unable to save them. They have now repented, may he fulfil his promise completely.

j **9—4:4 Wisdom leads to Life**—Israel was a privileged people because they had a law given by God, such as no other people had. But they have transgressed the law and have consequently sunk into the depths of misery. All the evils which have befallen Israel are due to the transgression of the Law which is here identified with Wisdom, the source of life, as elsewhere in the Sapiential literature.

k **9—14 The Transgression of the Law is the Source of their Calamities—9—10.** An invitation to listen to the teaching of Wisdom, i.e. to keep the commandments of the Law which is a source of life and happiness, Dt 30:15—20. Israel neglected it and was punished. **14.** Since God's law is the source of peace, Israel must strive after it with all her power. The Law enlightens the mind, strengthens the will in the performance of what is right, and grants length of life, happiness and peace to those who keep it.

l **15—31 Wisdom is beyond Man's Reach—15.** Man must seek Wisdom; but where does she dwell? Where are the treasures which she bestows on those who seek her? Cf Jb 28:12. The answer is given further on. **16—21.** Wisdom lies beyond man's reach. Mighty princes, powerful hunters: all these passed away; and generation after generation strayed away from the right path.

22f. The peoples most renowned for their skill, the 505k Canaanites or Phoenicians, Ezek 28:4f, the Themanites, who dwelt in S Edom, Jer 49:7, the Hagarenes or Ishmaelites, Gn 25:12f, who sought after earthly wisdom, the merchants of Merran and Teman; all these failed to find Wisdom. **24—28.** The immeasurable universe, God's dwelling, does not possess Wisdom, nor did the giants, the renowned men of old, Gn 6:4. This prepares the way for 32ff where the divine origin of Wisdom is declared. **29—31.** Develop the same thought; cf Dt 30:12f.

32—37 Wisdom dwells with God—32—36. God m alone, an all-knowing and almighty God, knows Wisdom, Jb 28:23. **36.** He has communicated it to the Israelites in the Mosaic Law. The Law was given to Israel out of God's love. It could not be acquired by human means. No other people had a Law like it. But Israel transgressed the Law and, as a punishment, they were given up into the hands of their enemies. **37.** In Vg and VL the subject of 'appeared' and 'lived' is 'he', i.e. God. Hence Gr. and Latin Fathers have applied this verse to the Incarnation. But the context requires 'Wisdom' as subject of the two verbs. After being communicated to Israel Wisdom remained on earth making her abode amongst men. The personification of Wisdom and the idea of her dwelling among men occur also in Sir 24:12—16. The NT takes up this theme and applies it to Christ, through whom revelation has been brought to perfection.

4:1—4 Exhortation and Conclusion—1. This n Wisdom is the Law which subsists for ever. **2—3.** A last exhortation. Israel, hold fast to the Law and walk in its light, lest God should take away from you the advantages of the Law and bestow them upon another people.

5—5:9 God's Promises of Restoration will be 506a fulfilled—The situation envisaged is that of the Exile, and from 4:9—29 Jerusalem, personified as mother of the nation, addresses the neighbouring towns and her own children who are scattered abroad.

5—9a The People punished for their Sins—5. The exiles, despite their condition, are still called by the name of Israel, a name which recalls a glorious past. **6.** God's punishments are corrective not vindictive. **7.** Idolatry was the inveterate and most heinous sin of Israel. Idols are called demons in Dt 32:17. **8.** The figure of God nursing his people is vividly described in Hos 11:3f: cf also Dt 1:31; 32:10; Is 63:10; for the figure of Jerusalem-mother cf Is 51:18.

9b—16 Jerusalem's Lamentations—14—16. Jeru- b salem again entreats the neighbouring cities to have compassion on her. **15f.** Are reminiscences of Dt 28:49f; Jer 5:15ff.

17—29 Jerusalem's Message of Comfort to her c **Children—17f.** Jerusalem can afford no help. **21—24.** She exhorts them to pray to God and feels confident that he will soon deliver them.

30—5:9 A Message of Comfort to Jerusalem—This d is the answer to Jerusalem's lament—**30.** Jerusalem must not despair. God who has chosen her for himself and given her his name as Yahweh's dwelling-place, will comfort her. **31f.** The destruction of the enemies of Israel, especially Babylon, had long before been predicted by the prophets; cf Is 13; 47; Jer 25; 50. **33—35.** The devastation of Babylon is described here with features borrowed from the prophets: thus 33 = Is 51:22f; Jer 50:11—13; 34 = Is 47:9; 35a = Jer 51:58; 35b = Is 13:21; Jer 50:39. The word *daimonia* 'devils', which occurs also in the parallel passage Is 13:21, probably stands for a word meaning 'wild animals' as those enumerated in Is 13:21 and Jer 50:39. **36f.** Words

06d and ideas reflect Is 43:5; 49:18; 60:4. The description has its full application in the Messianic restoration. **5:1–3.** Jerusalem will be reinstated in her former glory. The outlook is Messianic. Cf Is 52:1; 60; 61:3. **4.** She will be the seat of a righteous power, and all her citizens will enjoy peace. **5.** A repetition with slight variations of 36f. **7–9.** The ideas and phraseology recall Is 40:4; 49:9f; 52:12; 55:12.

e 6 The Letter of Jeremiah—The prophet addresses the Jewish captives warning them against idolatry; see above § 504*i*. **1.** The Title does not form part of the Letter but has been added after Jer 29:1. RSV verse numbering is followed here.

2–7 Introduction—**2.** Cf Jer 25:8f. **3.** This seems to be inconsistent with Jer 25:12; 29:10. But 'seven' may be a symbolical number having no mathematical value (cf Dt 28:7; Dn 3:19) and 'generation' may be taken in the sense of an indefinite period of time. Cf the analogous expression 'a thousand generations', Dt 7:9; 1 Chr 16:15; Ps 105 (104):8. The expression 'seven generations' is therefore parallel to 'many years' and 'a long time', not their equivalent. **7.** God himself speaks directly. My angel (cf Ex 23:20–22; 32:34), is looking after you, or (according to others) he, or I, will not leave your sin unpunished.

f 8–15 Idols are Powerless—**8f.** The priests did not hesitate to appropriate the gold and silver ornaments of their gods, and even make gifts of them to the hierodules in the temple precincts.

g 17–23 Idols are Useless and Insensible Images—**23.** The refrain; cf 16.

24–29 Idols are Helpless and Unconscious of Offences—**23.** In 7, 50, 56, 70 it is said that idols were only overlaid with gold; but among the many idols there may have been some made of solid gold. **28.** The priests make any use of the sacrificial offerings, but nothing is given to the poor and to the sick. Priests had a share of the sacrificial victims. They were also the treasurers of the temple revenue, and sometimes embezzled their gods' property. **29.** Contrary to the prescriptions of the Jewish Law (Lv 12:4; 15:19f) women in a state of ceremonial uncleanness could partake of the sacred meals. If idols were true gods, they would never tolerate such profanation.

h 30–40 Further Illustration of the Idols' Impotence—**30.** Jewish legislation debarred women from the altar service. **31f.** The superiority of the Israelites' **506h** God is further emphasized. All such signs of mourning (32) were strictly forbidden to Israelite priests, Lv 21:5. **33.** This must have been shocking to a pious Jew to whom anything that came near the presence of God became holy. **34–38.** A series of implicit contrasts between the One God of the Israelites and the Babylonian gods. Unlike them God is a just judge rewarding good and punishing evil, Dt 32:35; 1 Sm 26:23; he sets up kings and deposes them, 1 Sm 2:8; he gives riches, 1 Sm 2:7; he requires vows to be performed promptly, Dt 23:21; he can save from death, 1 Sm 2:6; he gives a blind man his sight, Ps 146 (145):8, delivers a man from distress, Is 25:4, helps the widows and the orphans, Dt 10:18; Ps 146 (145):9; Is 1:17.

41–44 The Gods dishonoured by their Wor- i **shippers**—**41.** The Babylonians dishonour their gods by asking of them what they cannot do. **43.** They dishonour their gods also by the immoral Ishtar cult. Women with a cord round their waists, sat in the streets, probably near the temples, burning bran, the smoke of which was believed to possess aphrodisiac properties, and expecting to be accosted by a male worshipper. After having performed her shameful religious duty she reproached her less fortunate neighbour for not having had the same favour. Cf Herodotus I, 199.

45–52 Idols are the Work of Men's Hands—**45.** Cf j Jer 10; 3f; and esp. Is 44:12–30. Man is mortal; how can he produce a god that is immortal and eternal? Idols therefore are a lie and an object of shame bequeathed by artisans to posterity.

53–56 Total Helplessness of Idols—Unlike the God of the Israelites, Dt 17:14f; 28:12, 14, the Babylonian gods can neither set up kings nor give rain. **53.** This is, perhaps, a popular saying meaning: They can plead as much as a crow.

57–65 Idols are utterly Worthless—**65.** The refrain k again.

66–69 The Idols' Powerlessness is further emphasized—Beasts, which are able to move, are better than they. **69.** Once more the refrain.

73 Conclusion—A righteous man having no idols is better than a worshipper of idols. The second term of comparison is implied, and we need not suppose that some words have fallen out. For similar construction, cf Gn 37:27; Nm 14:3, etc.

EZEKIEL

BY E. POWER S.J. AND E. MAY O.F.M. CAP

507a Bibliography—*Commentaries*: J. Knabenbauer, CSS, 1907; G. A. Cooke, ICC, 1936; J. Ziegler, EchB, 1948; J. Bewer, 1953; A. van den Born, Roermond Maaseik, 1954; W. Zimmerli, BKAT, 1956f; H. G. May, IB, 1956; P. Auvray, BJ, 1957²; W. Eichrodt, ATD, 1959f; F. Spadafora, SacB, 1960; G. Fohrer, HAT, 1955.

Other literature: G. Hoelscher, *Hesekiel der Dichter und das Buch*, Giessen, 1924; W. Grankowski, *Le messianisme d'Ezéchiel*, Paris, 1931; J. B. Harford, *Studies in the Book of Ezekiel*, London, 1935; C. Howie, IDB, 1962; W. Irwin, 'Ezekiel Research since 1943', VT 3 (1953) 54—66; N. Arbuckle, *De Renovatione interiore exulum prout ab Ezechiele depingitur*, Rome, 1962; H. H. Rowley, 'The Book of Ezekiel in Modern Study' BJRL, 36 (1953) 146—90; J. Harvey, 'Collectivisme et individualisme, Ezek. 18:1—32 et Jer 31:28', ScE 10 (1958) 167—202; G. Rinaldi, 'Termini di "colpevolezza" e "non-colpevolezza"', BibOr 1 (1959), 50ff; C. Howie *The Date and Composition of Ezekiel*, 1950; J. Steinmann, *Le prophète Ezéchiel et les débuts de l'exil*, 1953.

b Historical Background—See also §§65*f*—*k*, 296, 487*b*. Ezek is chiefly concerned with the period between the death of Josiah, 609 and the fall of Jerusalem, 587. During this time Babylon replaced Assyria as the dominant world power. Long before this however outlying provinces of the Assyrian empire had gradually been gaining their independence. In 622 Josiah instituted a great religious reform and even extended his boundaries someway to the N. His reform was however seriously jeopardized by his rash attempt to stop Neco of Egypt linking up with the declining Assyrian armies against **c** Babylon. For the moment Judah was a vassal of Egypt. In 606 however, Nebuchadnezzar crossed the Euphrates and defeated Neco at Carchemish. In the following months Nebuchadnezzar invaded and annexed Palestine. Some years later, the inhabitants of Judah revolted, thus bringing upon themselves another invasion by the Babylonian king. This time he exiled the king of Judah, Jehoiachin, plundered the palace and Temple, carried off the sacred vessels and deported many thousands of the nobility, craftsmen and troops to Babylon, 598/7.
d Jehoiachin's uncle, Mattaniah was made king instead and his name changed to Zedekiah. Discovered by Nebuchadnezzar to be intriguing with the Egyptians, Zedekiah's land was once more invaded with the disastrous results recorded elsewhere. After the capture of Jerusalem, the ravaged land was not made a Babylonian province but abandoned to the depredations of its neighbours. Zedekiah was blinded by order of Nebuchadnezzar and deported to Babylon.

The **religious condition** of Judah during this period was similar to that of nearly a century earlier and was due to the same causes. A great religious revival was followed by a corresponding idolatrous reaction. Pious kings were replaced by impious successors, Hezekiah by Manasseh and Amon, Josiah by Jehoiakim and Zedekiah.

Foreign alliance or dependence introduced foreign wor-**507** ship, and old Canaanite religious practices flourished in both periods. The deportation of the best elements of the population in 597 must have aggravated the existing evils. Thus there is no reason to think that Jeremiah and Ezek exaggerate in their descriptions of the moral and religious depravity which made chastisement inevitable and sealed the fate of Jerusalem and Judah.

Contents—The book is divided into three main parts: **e** threats of punishment against Jerusalem and Judah, chh 1—24, prophecies against Gentile neighbours, chh 25—32, and promises of a restoration of the exiles, chh 33—48. The threats are varied by denunciations of the crimes committed, practical instructions and rare gleams of hope of a better future. In view of recent theories on the composition of the book, a detailed synopsis of its contents is necessary to give the reader a clear idea of its logical structure.

In the introduction to the first part, chh 1—3, Ezek **f** receives his prophetic mission with appropriate instructions from Yahweh who appears to him in Babylonia enthroned on his heavenly chariot. The first cycle of threats, chh 4—11, begins with a prediction by means of symbolic actions of the siege and fall of Jerusalem and the death and dispersal of its citizens, chh 4—5. The country too, from the Egyptian desert to Riblah on the Orontes, will be devastated for the sins of its inhabitants, chh 6—7. Transported in a vision from Babylonia to Jerusalem, Ezek beholds the idolatrous worship which defiles the sanctuary, the execution of the guilty citizens and the destruction of the city by fire. Yahweh abandons his sanctuary and city, but through his prophet sends a message of hope to the exiles to whom he promises a new heart and a new spirit, chh 8—11. The second cycle of threats, chh 12—19, begins with another symbolical prediction of the fall of Jerusalem and the exile, with special reference to the fate of Zedekiah. There is an emphatic proclamation of the fulfilment of prophecy, and a denunciation of false prophets, chh 12—13. The exiles now ask Ezekiel to consult Yahweh on their behalf. He refuses; but he exhorts them to a true repentance and assures them that Yahweh spares the innocent when he punishes a nation for their sins, ch 14. There is no hope for Israel, Yahweh's unfruitful vineyard, for the wood of the unproductive vine is useless except as firewood, ch 15. A long historical retrospect of the sins of Israel shows that her punishment is just and inevitable. The lesson is enforced by the examples of Sodom and Samaria, already punished though less guilty, ch 16. Zedekiah, a perjurer, doomed to deportation, suggests a picture of the Messiah by contrast, ch 17. The prophet again informs the exiles that they will not be punished except for their own sins, reminds them of God's mercy, and urges them to repentance, ch 18. A poetical elegy on three exiled princes, Jehoahaz, Jehoiakim and Zedekiah, aptly concludes the cycle, ch 19. The third **g** cycle opens with another request from the exiles to consult Yahweh on their behalf. Once more Ezekiel refuses; he

07g denounces the sins of their fathers and their own, but finally predicts future conversion and restoration, ch 20. Nebuchadnezzar, the sword of Yahweh, is next depicted as entering the land to exterminate its inhabitants, ch 21. Another denunciation of the sins of Judah follows, and all classes of her citizens are shown to be guilty, ch 22. A further historical retrospect of the sins of the N and S kingdoms, Oholah and Oholibah, shows that Judah's chastisement is just and inevitable, ch 23. The last ch announces the beginning of the siege of Jerusalem and the death of Ezek's wife the same day, whom he is forbidden to mourn as a sign to the exiles not to mourn the fall of Jerusalem. The news of that event brought to the exiles by a fugitive will detach Ezek's tongue from his palate and give him free use of his prophetic gift.

h The second part of the book starts off with a prophecy of the destruction of Ammon, Moab, Edom and Philistia, ch 25. Next come three prophecies against Tyre, ending with brief indications of the fall of Sidon and the restoration of Israel, chh 26—28. Finally seven prophecies predict the fall of Egypt, and one also her subsequent restoration though not to her former greatness, chh 29—32.

The promises of restoration begin with the arrival of the fugitive announcing Jerusalem's fall. Here Ezek expands his teaching on personal responsibility. Not the remnant left in Palestine and doomed to destruction but the exiles shall possess the land, ch 33. Former shepherds of Israel are denounced. There is a promise of the reign of a new David and the abiding presence of Yahweh, ch 34. The ruin of Edom, Judah's implacable enemy and chief occupier of her territory, is again foretold, ch 35. The prophet predicts the restoration of Israel, the rebuilding of her cities, multiplication of her seed and the bestowal of a new heart and a new spirit, all this not through her own merits but for the glorification of Yahweh's name among the Gentiles, ch 36. The vision of dry bones restored to life and the symbolical action of joining together two rods prefigure the revival of the nation by the return of the exiles, and the reunion of the sceptres of Judah and Israel, ch 37. The destruction of Gog and his army represents Yahweh's final victory over the pagan world, chh 38—39. Finally there is a lengthy description of the new temple, the new cult and the new holy land, chh 40—48.

508a Ezekiel and his Mission—Ezek (*Yehezqē'l* 'God is strong or 'God strengthens') son of Buzi, was a priest, undoubtedly of the line of Zadok. He must have been of a certain age and standing to be included among the influential citizens of Jerusalem deported with their king Jehoiachin by Nebuchadnezzar in 597. His residence in Babylonia was at Tel-abib, apparently the chief settlement of the exiles. Tel-abib was on the 'river Chebar' which is generally identified with the Nār Kabari or Grand Canal S of Babylon in the vicinity of Nippur. Ezek was married but his wife died on the first day of the siege of Jerusalem, Jan. 588. His custom of dating his prophecies and his adoption of the Babylonian calendar are naturally attributed to the milieu in which he lived and prophesied. He received his prophetical vocation in June 593. The last dated prophecy belongs to the year 571. All our knowledge of Ezek is derived from his own writings, and the dates of his birth and death remain unknown. He must have witnessed the religious revival of Josiah and the subsequent idolatrous reaction, and he must have died in exile.

b While the mission of Jeremiah was to the Israelites in Palestine, that of Ezek was to the exiles in Babylon. He had to maintain Yahweh worship among them and pre-pare them for the restoration. It was a difficult task. The **508b** exiles were a rebellious people inclined to idolatry. They were isolated from their own temple and cult and accessible to the seductions of Babylonian ritual and pagan environment. The chief obstacles to their conversion were presumption on the one hand, despair on the other. At first they were convinced that the exile would be speedily terminated and that Yahweh, who had miraculously preserved Jerusalem from the Assyrians, would not now allow the Chaldeans to destroy his city and sanctuary. They also believed that they were being punished unjustly for the sins of their ancestors; that they were the innocent victims of national responsibility. Such an audience was little disposed to heed prophetic discourses which assured them of the proximate and certain ruin of the nation, and of the need of their conversion so as to obtain a hearing from Yahweh and escape a similar fate. Only when the prophet's authority was firmly established and the exiles' disbelief dissipated by the fall of Jerusalem could his preaching bear fruit. We can understand therefore why Ezek was inhibited in the use of his prophetic gift during a long period and why supernatural manifestations, symbolic actions, parables and popular sayings were particularly necessary to excite interest and secure a minimum of attention from an unprepared and incredulous audience. The many predictions of the fall of Jerusalem **c** and of the destruction and dispersal of the inhabitants of Judah were directed against the presumption of the exiles. The repeated lessons on personal responsibility and divine mercy counteracted their despair. Far from being involved in the ruin of the nation, they were to be the nation resuscitated. The many descriptions of the sins of Israel in all its history and in all classes of its population were intended to convince the exiles that her chastisement was just and inevitable. The mass of Israelites in Palestine was guilty and doomed to destruction. Since Ezek had no mission to preach to them he made no effort to convert them. His solicitude was for the exiles on whom all his hopes were centred. More fortunate than Jeremiah, he knew that his labours though at first unfruitful would be recompensed by a measure of success in the not too distant future.

It has been suggested (Van den Born, Auvray, **d** Steinmann, Herntrich, Harford, Bertholet) that Ezek ministered first in Jerusalem until its destruction in 587, and thereafter in Babylon among the exiles. In this view the prophet's threats of punishment, like those of Jeremiah, were addressed to the Israelites in Palestine. For Babylonian exiles were reserved the announcement of future salvation and the magnificent plan of reorganized temple worship. This hypothesis however is not easily reconciled with the text of the prophecy and seems based on a misunderstanding of the prophet's mission and character. The address to Jerusalem from Tel-abib near Babylon is couched in the style of Isaiah and Jeremiah. In it Ezekiel clearly distinguishes between the exiles whom he addresses in the second person, and those in Jerusalem whom he threatens in the third person. Had he ministered in the Holy City we would expect from him an emphatic message of repentance, as in Jeremiah. Instead, we find him trying to convert the exiles on whom all hopes of a restoration were based, and who had to be disabused of their errors and convinced of God's justice and holiness before they could become the objects of his mercy and the recipients of his favours. That we learn more of the actual conditions of the exiles from Jeremiah than from Ezek is explained by their different characters. Ezekiel, with total concentration on his main object, gives

508d little information about himself and his surroundings. He is not discursive and self-revelatory like Jeremiah. Finally, the hypothesis of a Jerusalem ministry for Ezek would necessitate numerous textual alterations which in the present state of our knowledge would not seem warranted.

e Some commentators continue to depict Ezek as the victim of hallucinations; as afflicted with the physical maladies of aphasia and catalepsy. Such errors are due partly to a rationalistic interpretation of supernatural manifestations, partly to a misunderstanding of the texts. The prophet's frequent visions and symbolical actions were intended to secure the attention of incredulous hearers and prepare them for the day when the fulfilment of his oft-repeated prophecies would make them acknowledge his authority and follow his guidance. The visions also taught the necessary lesson that the dominion of Yahweh extended beyond the land of his own people to all parts of the world. Since Ezek's tongue was 'attached to his palate' from the beginning of his prophetic ministry to the fall of Jerusalem, it was not from aphasia that he suffered while prophetically active, but from certain restrictions in the use of his prophetic gift. The binding with cords is another figurative indication of the moral obligation of seclusion imposed on him by Yahweh. Not catalepsy but Yahweh's command made him lie on his right and on his left side during long periods. He was likewise ordered to prepare his own food in the sight of the people during these periods, which he could not have done had he been deprived of all power of movement by catalepsy.

f Theology—Ezek has been accused of originating the exaggerated cult of the Law which characterizes later Judaism. The accusation is based on the theory of Wellhausen that the ritual laws of the Mosaic code are a development of the code of Ezek. Our increased knowledge of the Ancient E has shown, however, that an extensive ritual developed early in all E religions. The prophet's code is ideal and selective. He ignores important legal institutions of earlier date and adopts those which suit his purpose. His exclusion of Levi from a tribal portion of the land shows that he regards the whole tribe of Levi as dedicated to the service of the sanctuary. It is most unlikely that later Judaism, while ignoring his descriptions of the temple and holy land, adopted and developed his legal code.

g Nonetheless Ezek was certainly influenced by the Priestly tradition. This is evident in his *concept of God* as the Holy One, remote, transcendant, who demands corresponding holiness in his people through obedience to covenant laws and liturgy. In fact, the motive given for the restoration is vindication of God's Holy Name. For Ezek, Yahweh has not the intimate, personal relationship evident in Jer or Is (cf the inaugural visions: Ezek 1; Jer 1; Is 6). Furthermore, there are close resemblances between Ezek and the Code of Holiness in Lv 17—26 (e.g. Ezek 18:6—9; 44:20—31; cf parallels in Van den Born, which led him to consider Ezek a pseudepigraph). Especially is this true in the matter of renewed, reformed cultic observance. Along with this, however, Ezek is an eloquent exponent of the need of interior religion. He insists on a sincere conversion to Yahweh, on a new heart and a new spirit. In these respects, he is a bridge between Israel before the Exile, and Judaism of the restoration.

h One of Ezekiel's greatest contributions is his emphasis on *personal responsibility for sin*. Though this concept shows up in Jer 31:29, and would be taken up again in the wisdom literature, it is Ezek of all the prophets who shows most clearly that Yahweh is not unjust in **508** punishing rebellious Israel, and that reward and punishment is something essentially individual. Each man will be punished for his own sins, not those of his father, not those of another generation (chh 18 and 33). This concept in turn leads to the thought of an interior, spiritual regeneration which will effect the union of man with God in the restoration (36:26ff). It is perhaps along these lines, as well as in his messianic outlook, that the prophet speaks most urgently to the hearts of men today.

Messianism—As a religious teacher Ezek is simple and **509** earnest and usually enforces his lesson by frequent, even tedious repetitions. Only his messianic prophecies require some explanation. They present a striking example of the lack of perspective which at times characterizes prophetic visions of future events. Ezek sees on the same plane two distinct future events, the proximate national restoration and the remote re-establishment of the messianic kingdom. He combines these visions in his descriptions of a messianic restoration. That is why his messianism is so distinctively national and material, and why a literal fulfilment of many of his prophecies cannot be expected in that the messianic kingdom was not national but universal, not materially but spiritually peaceful and prosperous. The Messiah is a sprout of the dried-up trunk of the Davidic tree which becomes a magnificent cedar. He is a good shepherd contrasted with the many bad shepherds of Israel. He is above all a new David. His kingdom is depicted as material and national, the promised land enlarged by David's conquests. His subjects are the twelve Jewish tribes with an admixture of alien residents. The peace **b** of this kingdom is secured by weakening or destroying hostile neighbours, Philistia, Edom, Moab, Ammon, Tyre and Egypt. The defeat and destruction of Gog and his army after the establishment of the kingdom is an assurance of Yahweh's permanent protection. Fertility and fecundity of sterile regions indicates material prosperity. The new temple, in the main, is a reproduction of Solomon's temple. The new laws are Mosaic and national. Conditions of entry into the kingdom are a sincere conversion, a new heart and a new spirit. This picture of a Jewish messianic kingdom which was never realized may have little appeal for modern readers, but was undoubtedly helpful to Ezekiel's contemporaries who needed encouragement amid the trials of the exile to prepare themselves for the coming restoration. There is an economy in divine revelation. The expiatory sufferings of the Messiah and the exclusion from his kingdom of the Jews who rejected him did not form part of Ezekiel's message.

Composition and Authorship—Fifty or sixty years **c** ago few doubted that the book was composed by the prophet Ezek in the Babylonian Captivity, e.g. Smend, Cornill, Bertholet. More recent decades have witnessed, along with this traditional view, a bewildering array of opinions. Thus Kraetschmar, aware of the patchwork character of the book, supposed two recensions, one in the first person and the other in the third, later combined by Ezekiel, the latter recension depending on the first. Other authors, e.g. Hermann (1908) thought it a series of groups of prophecies put together by Ezek and/or a later editor. Others again would more drastically limit the work of the prophet (Hölscher, to the poetical sections = 170 out of the 1,273 vv in the book; Irwin, 251 vv; H. May, about 40% of the book), and make a later author responsible for the prose sections or remainder. Still others (Torrey, Burrows, Van den Born)

09c suggest that the entire book is pseudepigraphical, having been written by some post-exilic author and then attributed to a real or fictitious exilic prophet. Most arguments against unity of authorship are based on linguistic data, or a supposed literary dependence of Ezek on the Priestly Code (Lv) and especially the Code of Holiness (Lv 17—26). More recent writers, however, without ignoring the difficulties of the text, have returned to a more conservative position. Thus, Cooke, Howie, Fohrer, Zimmerli and Eichrodt regard the substance of the book as consisting of the preachings of Ezek in exile from 593 onwards. The issue today is not so much whether one should ascribe the prophecies to Ezek as rather whether he was responsible for the composition of the book and if so to what extent. In the view of Eissfeldt the old opinion that Ezek compiled the book as we now have it cannot be sustained. 'On the other hand however the book clearly contains a framework of passages deriving from the prophet himself, namely those which are couched in the first-person form', EOTInt 373. The hand of redactors may be seen in this as in other prophetical books though such men might well be disciples and their work reflect the prophet's teaching.

d The text at times is considerably disordered, as in chh 4, 10 and 24. Messianic prophecies in the first part of the book are generally considered later additions (16:57—63 and 20:33—44 more probably, 11:14—21 and 17:22—24 less probably). Other subsequent insertions are 3:16b—21; 27:9b—25a; 28:20—26; 39:17—20; 40.10 18. For reasons suggested by the context we may well attribute the present position of such passages to a redactor without, however, denying their authenticity. Moreover the present text contains a number of minor errors, omissions, amplifications and glosses. Most of these can be explained by the fact that Ezek often repeats himself so as to drive home a point to his audience—something quite natural in a teacher. Some of the repetitions are probably later additions.

e Text and Versions —The Heb. text of Ezek is less well preserved than that of any other OT book. Our chief help in re-establishing it is the LXX based on a Heb. text older than MT. Here as elsewhere deeper corruptions are common to MT and LXX. Frequently, however, the Gr. reveals a gloss or omission in MT and supplies a correction of a corrupt reading. Sometimes the context, sometimes the metre in poetical passages will establish the superiority of the LXX readings. The qînāh metre more commonly used by Ezek is well known; superfluous additions in MT which are omitted by LXX can be detected. At other times however the Gr. translator misunderstands the Heb., or evades a difficulty by an omission or an approximate rendering. No general rule can be given, but an intelligible LXX variant is usually preferred to an unintelligible MT reading. Our knowledge of the Gr. text of Ezek has been increased by the publication of the Chester Beatty (Ezek 11—17 with lacunae) and the Scheide (Ezek 19—39 with lacunae) papyri dated in the early 3rd cent. before Origen's Hexapla. The fact that the new text has some MT readings not found in our oldest and best Gr. MS (B) does not in any way diminish the value of the LXX variants mentioned above. Scholars previously believed that three Gr. translators each rendered a different part of the book. This conclusion, based on the different renderings of the divine names in the MSS has been upset by the evidence of the Scheide papyri. Now it is more probable and natural to ascribe the whole book to a single translator. The Syr. version occasionally supports corrections derived from LXX. Vg almost invariably follows MT.

1—24 Threats: Chastisement of Jerusalem and Judah. **510a**

1—3 Introduction: First Vision and Call.

1:1—28 The Theophany—This fantastic vision is perceived like a dream by the inner not outer senses. There is an atmosphere of mystery and awe. The imagery used, Cherubim, anatomical description, the four faces, and the atmospheric accompaniments may be traced back both to OT sources and to the influence of other nations, Babylonian, and Canaanite.

1—3. Time and place. **1.** The 'thirtieth year' is **b** enigmatic. Suggested reckonings from the birth of Ezek and from the reform of Josiah are unparalleled. Most probably 'thirtieth' is a corruption of the regnal year (12th or 13th) of Nebuchadnezzar. **2—3.** The second indication, June 593 B.C., which is not in the first but in the third person, brings the date into conformity with the other dates in the book, all reckoned from the captivity of Jehoiachin in the first year of Zedekiah, 597 B.C., Nisan (March—April) being the first month of the year. The place is Nār Kabari (Grand Canal) flowing SE from the Euphrates in the latitude of Babylon and re-entering it at Nippur. Tel-abib, situated on this canal, was the chief settlement of the Jewish exiles deported with Jehoiachin. **4.** The storm-wind, dark cloud and fire or lightning are the usual accompaniments of a theophany; cf Ex 19:16. The vision as the harbinger of evil comes from the N, the region of darkness and calamity. *'from the midst of the fire something gleamed like electrum'* (CV). like an amalgam of gold and silver; **5—14.** On the Cherubim cf Ex 25:18; 1 (3) Kgs 6:23. **c** They are called ḥayyôt, 'living creatures' here, and 'cherubim' in 9:3 and ch 10. The Babylonian karūbu was an inferior deity who guarded the gates of temples and palaces and might also be an idol-bearer. Cf ANEP, 332, 609, 614, 644, 646—50. This monster had the head of a man, the body of a lion or an ox, and the wings of an eagle A few commentators interpret faces as 'aspects'; but the wings the eagle aspect are distinguished from the faces in the description. Face-forward-movement in all four directions without turning requires four faces. The figure of the cherub is based on that of the karūbu but is not a reproduction of it. **7.** The jointless legs and rounded soles exclude bending and turning. **8.** Omit 'on their four sides'. CV rearranges the text: vv 7, 10, 9, 12, 8, 11. **10.** The faces, respectively, express the intelligence, strength, majesty and swiftness of the cherubim. Omit 14 (LXX). It was the fire which flashed and moved. **15.** MT 'of their faces' is unintelligible. Read: **d** 'one (wheel) beside each of the four living creatures' (CV). **16.** 'chrysolite': topaz, a bright yellow stone. The eyes were probably ornamental, as in a peacock's tail. **22—28.** The platform resting on the heads of the **e** cherubim is likened to the firmament, God's footstool; cf Ex 24:20. Its firmness and colour are indicated by the comparisons. **23.** MT gives the cherubim three pairs of wings by a dittography, rendered loosely in Vg 'straight', properly in LXX 'outstretched'. The meaning seems to be that the platform extends as far as the outstretched wings. Perhaps omit **25.** The voice seems premature and the letting down of the wings a repetition. **26.** Words like 'likeness' and 'appearance' are used to safeguard the spirituality of God. **27.** 'electrum' or 'bronze', cf 1:4.

The theophany in Babylonia gave an important lesson to the exiles. They shared to some extent the pagan belief that the power and presence of a god were restricted to a particular region. By his majestic appearance in a

510e foreign land Yahweh manifested his omnipotence and omnipresence.

f 2:1–3:15 Call to the Prophetic Ministry—God informs Ezek of his mission, makes him his interpreter and finally sends him to preach to his fellow-captives at Tel-abib.

2:1–7 The Task—Ezek prostrates himself in fear and reverence before the glory of God. A voice bids him rise and he obeys, strengthened by the spirit. The expression *son of man* is equivalent to man, simply. It occurs ninety times in this book and stresses the littleness of man compared with the greatness of God. Elsewhere, Dn 7:13, it becomes a messianic title; cf Mt 8:20. **3.** The Israelites are characterized as a rebellious nation (not 'nations' as in MT). **6a.** The exact metaphor is uncertain in Heb. To 'sit upon scorpions' (RSV) seems to refer to a dwelling among unruly and dangerous men. **7c.** 'they are a rebellious house'; house is accidentally omitted in MT.

g 2:8–3:3 The Message—God presents Ezek with a written scroll containing lamentation and mourning and woe, and orders him to eat it. We learn from this that God is the real author of what Ezek preaches, and that the divine communications are threats of punishment. The eating of the scroll is not real but symbolical, since the vision affects only the internal senses. On the scroll form, cf Jer 36. **9.** The prophet says 'a hand' indeterminately, to avoid anthropomorphism. **3:1.** The book is sweet as a gift from the God of all consolations; cf 2 Cor 1:3–5.

3:4–11 The Sending—Ezek is now sent to the exiles, the recipients of his instructions. God warns him that his rebellious and hard-hearted hearers will not heed his words (cf Is 6:9–10; Jer 5:21), and strengthens the prophet to persevere against all opposition. **6b.** Cf Christ's words on Capernaum and Bethsaida (Mt 11:21; 12:41).

12–15 The Vision disappears; Ezekiel goes to Tel-abib—14. Ezek was not transported to Tel-abib; a supernatural force uplifted him spiritually and impelled him thither. His commotion of soul was due to reaction and a realization of the difficulties of his task. **15.** Exhausted by his experiences, he remained overwhelmed for seven days at Tel-abib until a fresh revelation restored him to his senses.

h 16–21 The Prophet's Responsibility—Ezek is remarkable for his teaching on personal responsibility, which is a departure from the widespread earlier concept of corporate responsibility of the Israelites as a collective entity. Here the subject is discussed from the prophet's point of view. He is compared to a watchman. (A fuller treatment is given subsequently: 14:12–23; 18:1–32; 33:1–20). Both prophet and sinful hearer are responsible if no warning is given. Only the sinner is responsible if a warning is given but left unheeded. The punishment contemplated is death. Prolongation of life is the reward of the prophet's fidelity and of the sinner's conversion. The passage considers first the habitual sinner, then the virtuous man who falls into sin. Conversion is equally necessary and salutary in both cases.

i 22–27 Silence and Seclusion—These vv may belong to the introd. or to the first cycle of prophecies. God orders Ezek to remain in his house and refrain from preaching. The binding with cords and attachment of the tongue to the palate are figurative indications of the seclusion and silence imposed upon him for seven and a half years, ending only with the fall of Jerusalem (cf 24:25–27; 33:21–22). **25.** Yahweh is the author of both mutism and binding. There is no reason to

suppose that the binders were exiles who thought Ezek **510** demented, still less to attribute his silence and seclusion to physical maladies like aphasia and catelepsy. The motive for the precept was the unworthiness and unpreparedness of the exiles: cf v 27.

4–12 First Cycle of Threats against Jerusalem 51 and Judah.

4:1–5:17 Symbolical Announcement of the Siege of Jerusalem and the Exile—A more orderly arrangement of the text would be as follows: siege of Jerusalem, 1–3, 7. Famine during the siege, 10–11, 16–17. Length of the exile, 4–6, 8. Unclean foods during the exile, 9–12, 15. Annihilation of the citizens, 5:1–4. Explanation of the symbols, 5:5–17. The determination of the periods represented by days during which Ezek lies on his left and on his right side is disputed, but the following solution seems the most tenable. Since the days represent years they cannot refer to the siege of Jerusalem. Nor can they refer to the iniquity of Judah and Israel during the divided monarchy, since Judah's iniquity cannot be reduced to forty years and Ezek represents the chastisement of sin, not its commission. As periods of symbolical expiation they can only refer to the exile. Israel's exile, 721–538, lasted 183 years. Judah's, 587–538, lasted 49 years. The figures 190 and 40 years preserved by LXX are round numbers in close agreement with these periods of exile. The MT reading of 390 probably represents an attempt to equate the combined periods, 430 years (390 + 40) with the length of the Egyptian Captivity. The use of 'Israel' as a designation of the N kingdom after Samaria's fall is admittedly exceptional, although not without parallel; cf Is 11:12. Since the prophet was ordered to prepare, cook and eat his food in the sight of the exiles, we cannot suppose that he was literally bound or paralyzed. Yahweh's command confined him to his house, and when the prophet lay down he had to lie on his left side during the first period, on his right during the second. **4:1–3, 7 Siege of Jerusalem**—Yahweh orders Ezek to **b** take a clay brick or tablet (used in Babylonia for diagrams or writing) and on it to portray Jerusalem in a state of siege. The siege wall, which may have been a circle of forts, the mound built up against the city wall, the camps of the besiegers and their battering rams are all depicted. It is possible that the various terms refer to one huge machine or siege tower; cf Bib 35 (1954) 147–8. The iron wall encircling and isolating the besieged is represented by the iron griddle (normally used for baking bread) which Ezek erects between himself and the city. Then the prophet who represents the Babylonians besieges the city, menaces it with bared arm and prophesies against it. This diagram predicts a future event, as did the inscription in Is 8:1. **10–11, 16–17 Famine during the Siege**—The **c** rationing is symbolic of the famine. Ezek is restricted to a daily ration of 20 shekels of bread (about 8 oz.) and a sixth of a hin of water (about 2 pints). Water rationing would be felt particularly in the hot climate of Babylonia. **16.** The phrase 'breaking the staff of bread in Jerusalem' considers bread as the sustenance of life; it will be entirely removed, 'broken'. Cf Lv 26:16. **4–6, 8 Length of the Exile**—As the Oriental faces the E in determining directions, the left side indicates the N, the right side the S kingdom. The expiation is not vicarious but symbolical. **8.** '*distress*', not 'siege'. **9, 12–15 Unclean Foods during the Exile**—The **d** mixture of wheat and barley, beans and lentils, millet and spelt, was unlawful just as sowing two kinds of corn in one field or using two kinds of cloth for one garment,

11d Lv 19:19; Dt 22:9—11. The prescribed fuel for baking was also unclean and revolting. Ezekiel's prayer obtained a mitigation of this uncleanness. Dried dung of animals is still frequently used as fuel. Bread is sometimes baked by making a fire over flat stones, spreading the dough on the heated stones and covering it with embers (Vg: '*subcinericios panes*'). Following LXX, the period mentioned is 190 (MT 390) days, to which 40 must be added as suggested above. Food eaten in exile was unclean because sacrifices and offerings of first fruits by which it was sanctified were impossible.

e **5:1—4 Annihilation of the Citizens**—The last of the symbols refers to siege and exile combined. Shaving Judah with a razor indicated the completeness of its devastation, Is 7:20. Here the order given to Ezek symbolizes annihilation of the inhabitants of Jerusalem. Some perish within the city by famine and pestilence, others outside the city by the sword. Still others are deported but shall not escape the sword. A few are spared from the massacre but not even all of these shall survive. The fact that this remnant is ignored when the symbol is explained would not seem to justify excluding vv 3—4 as a later addition. **4b.** (After 'in the fire'): '*and you shall say to the whole house of Israel*' (LXX).

f **5—17 Explanation of the Symbols**—The symbols indicate the punishment of the inhabitants of Jerusalem for their iniquities. Jerusalem was the religious centre of the world. The Jews were God's chosen people united with him by a special covenant. Instead of being an example to the Gentiles, they surpassed them in wickedness. Hence their punishment will be without parallel. **10.** Cf 2 (4) Kgs 6:24—29; Jer 19:9; Lam 4:10. **12.** Deportation will not end the punishment; the sword still threatens the exiles. **13b.** When the evils predicted come to pass the sufferers will recognize the prophetic character of Ezekiel's words, which were intended for them as well as for his fellow-exiles. Communications were maintained between the exiles and the Palestinian Jews. '*till I am appeased*' (CV) expresses anthropomorphically Yahweh's satisfaction at the completion of his task. **16—17.** Are regarded by some as a later addition. Repetitions, however, are common in this book. Blood is elsewhere coupled with pestilence. As distinguished here from blood shed by the sword in battle, it may refer to homicides, fatal accidents, judicial executions.

12a **6:1—14 Announcement of the Punishment of Judah**—The previous threats of chastisement were directed against Jerusalem and its citizens in particular. The high places on the hills were conspicuous centres of idolatrous worship. The instruments of punishment are sword, famine and pestilence. **3.** The places personified represent their inhabitants. Omit **5a** as being a repetition of **4b.** The shrines of the idols are profaned by the bones of their worshippers. **8.** 'I will leave some of you alive' is omitted in LXX; already indicated in 5:3. **9.** A remnant will be converted after the deportation. The comparison of idolatry with marital infidelity is common in prophetic literature. **11.** Clapping of hands and stamping of feet denote exultation (cf 25:6), not at the abominations but at their punishment. **13a.** Ezek distinguishes between his fellow-exiles 'you shall know' and the Palestinians ('their slain'). **14.** Riblah, on the Orontes River at the N extremity of David's kingdom identified by Ezek with the promised land.

b **7:1—27 Second Announcement of the Punishment of Judah and Jerusalem**—The subject matter of this prophecy is the same as for the preceding. It emphasizes the imminence of the catastrophe, its inevitability, and

its enormity. It belongs apparently to the first year **512b** of Ezekiel's ministry. **1—9.** The judgement is imminent. The time, the day, the evil, the end has arrived. **2.** The four corners of the land indicate the whole of Palestine. LXX places **2—3** after **8—9. 7.** Hebrew uncertain; '*the climax has come*' (CV). **10—19.** The **c** punishment is inevitable. **10—11.** MT uncertain. **12.** The buyer rejoiced in satisfying his desire, the seller regretted the surrender of his possessions. They are now equal. **13.** The principle is illustrated by the sale of land which returned automatically to its original owner in the jubilee year (Lv 25:28). Hence, irreparable destruction. The verse, though, may be a gloss. **20—27.** The enormity of the calamity appears from the profanation of Yahweh's sanctuary and his complete abandonment of his people. **23.** '*Make the chain*' (MT) (RSV; 'desolation') might refer to a binding of captives. **27.** Omit 'the king mourns', found in MT but not in LXX. Ezek never calls Zedekiah 'king'.

8—11 Idolatrous Worship in Jerusalem and its d Punishment—In this vision dated a year and two months (LXX 'one month') after the first, Aug. 592 B.C., Ezek is transported in spirit to Jerusalem and beholds there: (1) various forms of idolatry practised by the citizens, (2) the slaughter of all the idolatrous worshippers by avenging angels; (3) the destruction of the city itself by fire; (4) Yahweh's abandonment of his city and sanctuary. The vision concludes with a prediction of restoration. The detailed description of the heavenly chariot, mostly borrowed from ch 1, seems to be an editorial addition. CV presumes a major dislocation of text in these chh and reads: 8:3, 5—18; 9:1—11; 11:24—25; 8:1—2, 4; 10:20—22, 14—15, 9—13, 16—17, 1—8, 18—19; 11:22—23, 1—21.

8:1—18 Idolatrous Worship in Jerusalem—Mention **e** is made of four species of idolatry: Idol worship, Animal worship, Tammuz worship and Sun worship. The first was Canaanitic in origin, the second Egyptian, the third Babylonian. Sun worship was common.

1—6. 3. The 'image of jealousy' set up as Yahweh's rival, which provokes his jealousy by receiving the cult due to Yahweh alone. This idol was probably Asherah, Baal's consort, originally set up by Manasseh, 2 (4) Kgs 21:7, removed by Josiah, ibid 23:6, and reinstalled by a later king. Josiah's reform, like that of Hezekiah, was followed by an idolatrous reaction. **5.** Omit 'in the entrance' (LXX). **7—12.** Egyptian divinities were common- **f** ly represented as animals. The 70 elders were offering incense, behind closed doors, to various Egyptian gods. **8.** The digging or enlarging of the hole presents no difficulties when one remembers that it took place in a vision. **11.** 'Jaazaniah son of Shaphan' must have been an important person, though he is not mentioned elsewhere. **12.** 'every man in his room of pictures', i.e. idol room (Versions). 'the Lord has forsaken the land': Since Yahweh seemed to have abandoned them when he permitted Josiah's death, the Babylonian depredations, the exile of influential citizens, they would now seek relief from propitiation of other gods. **13—15.** Tammuz (the Adonis of the Phoenicians) was a fertility god who was supposed to die in the heat of summer and return to life in the spring. The women lament his departure to the underworld, cf § 261f. **16—18.** Ezek, led back to the inner **g** court, sees in the space between temple and altar 25 men with their backs to the temple, facing the E and adoring the sun. **17c.** 'they put the branch to their nose'. Perhaps emend: 'they present their *stench* to *my* nostrils'. Others (CV) see here a putting of the branch to Yahweh's nose and suggest an analogy with the Egyptian sun god Re,

512g who is pictured with a vine branch at his nose to signify the transfer of creative power, divine breath, to living things.

h 9:1—10 Punishment of the Idolaters in Jerusalem—Ezek now beholds six angels of destruction who, by Yahweh's order, slay all the idolatrous citizens but spare the innocent who have had their foreheads marked with a sign. **2.** The upper gate: the N gate of the inner court. Solomon's bronze altar had been removed to the N side of the temple by Ahaz, who replaced it with a stone altar, 2 (4) Kgs 16:14. 'put a mark (MT: *tau*) upon the foreheads'. *Tau* means mark. It also indicates the last letter of the Hebrew alphabet, shaped like a cross. The text does not refer to the letter, nor does it indicate the nature of the mark. Innocent Israelites are spared by means of this sign as were their forebears long ago in Egypt by means of blood smeared on their doorposts (Ex 12:21—23). Here Ezek once more emphasizes personal responsibility. Only the guilty are punished. **8.** Manifestations of pity and intercession are unusual in Ezek. Here they intensify the dramatic effect.

i 10:1—22 Destruction of the City by Fire—The account is incomplete. It has been suggested that the second part was missing or illegible, and that a redactor filled the lacuna with a second description of the chariot. The only novelties in this description are the name *Cherubim* for 'living creatures' and *galgal* for 'wheel', and the attribution to the cherubim of the eyes which adorned the wheels (MT). Yahweh also abandons his temple. **1—7. 1** Is probably interpolated. It repeats 1:26 and interrupts the text. **8—17.** The Cherubim and the Wheels. The spirituality of the cherubim is less apparent here than in ch 1. **14.** The first face was that of 'the cherub' **j** i.e. an ox. **18—22.** Yahweh returns to the chariot which then leaves the temple by passing through the E gate. **11:1—25.** This announces the punishment of the wicked counsellors in Jerusalem and the conversion and restoration of the exiles in Babylonia. The two episodes are similarly introduced by proverbial sayings which express the false security of the wicked citizens of Jerusalem and their contempt for the exiles. Thus there is a literary connexion between them. The objection that the wicked counsellors were already slain in ch 9 ignores the fact that the visions of the citizens' slaughter and the burning of the city are prophecies of future events. The visions of the evil counsellors and idolatrous worship do not refer to the future. The terrible punishment naturally follows its primary cause, idolatrous worship. The traditional order of the text should be retained.

k 1—13. Ezek sees 25 of the chief men devising evil counsel at the E gates of the city. They declare themselves protected from destruction by the city wall as meat in a caldron is protected from consumption, or from the fire. The prophet announces to them that the corpses of those for whose death they are responsible shall remain within the wall like meat in a caldron, but that they themselves shall be deported from the city and slain by the sword, (cf Jer 52:24—27; 2 (4) Kgs 25:18—21).

l 1. Jaazaniah and Pelatiah, as princes of the people, would be well known to the exiles. **3.** '*Is not the time near to build houses?*' (MT). The phrase seems to refer to repairs made necessary by Nebuchadnezzar's visit in 597, and would then reflect the citizens' confidence in the face of prophetic threats. The figure of the caldron and the meat is used in 24:1—14 in a different sense. **10.** 'the border of Israel': Riblah, scene of Nebuchadnezzar's executions. LXX omits **11—12**, possibly as superfluous.

14—21 Who shall possess the Land of Yahweh?— 512 The inhabitants of Jerusalem say to the exiles: *You are far from Yahweh; the land is given in possession to us.* But the prophet announces that they themselves will be removed far from Palestine, while the despised exiles shall return to it, purify it, and possess it as Yahweh's people. **19.** 'one heart': '*a new heart*'; cf 18:31; 36:26. Ezek predicts a thorough renovation of both nation and individual.

22—25 Conclusion of the Vision; Yahweh abandons Jerusalem—The heavenly chariot appears last on Mt Olivet, whence Christ was to ascend into heaven.

12—19 Second Cycle of Threats against Jerusalem 513 **and Judah.**

12:1—20 Exile and Devastation—By means of symbolic actions Ezekiel foretells: (1) the exile in general and the fate of Zedekiah in particular; (2) the devastation of the land. He makes public preparation for a departure in the daytime by collecting his belongings and putting them outside his dwelling. While the people look on he departs by night, passing through a hole he has made in the wall of the city and with his hand covering his face, possibly a simulation of blindness. This would be a forewarning of what would happen to Zedekiah, who fled Jerusalem through a SE gate but was captured and blinded before he was led into exile. The second symbolic action, eating and drinking publicly with obvious anxiety, depicts fear of starvation caused by the coming siege.

1—16 Exile and Fate of Zedekiah—2. The prophet's **b** unusual actions would serve to arouse the curiosity of the unbelieving exiles. **3.** The preparation was by day, the departure by night. This verse predicts the exile in general. The necessities would be few: food, waterskin, staff, clothes. **5—6.** These verses refer to Zedekiah in particular. The covering of the face would seem to symbolize the blinding of the king before his deportation. **10.** MT somewhat obscure.

12:21—14:11 Prophecy and Prophets—Ezek first **c** refutes popular sayings about prophecy. Then he inveighs against false prophets and prophetesses. Finally he sets down the conditions for obtaining answers from Yahweh through a prophet.

21—28 Sayings about Prophecy—22. The first proverb scoffs at prophets for unfulfilled predictions. Time passes, but their words do not come to pass. Yahweh answers that Ezekiel's prophetical threats will be fulfilled immediately, thus giving the lie to the proverb. **23c.** 'the fulfilment': MT 'word': **27—28.** The second proverb has particular reference to the destruction of Judah and Jerusalem. This prophecy will be filled without delay, not 'after many days and in times afar off'.

13:1—16 The False Prophets—CV sees a considerable **d** disarrangement of text within ch 13 and gives the following verse order: 1—2, 5, 7—8, 10—16, 3—4, 6, 9, 17, 22—23, 18—21. False prophets are defined as 'those who prophesy out of their own minds', announcing to the people as the words of Yahweh their own thoughts and wishes, but 'have seen nothing', i.e. lacked supernatural vision. They are like foxes in ruins, undermining instead of building up; like whitewashers of a wall, hiding instead of repairing weaknesses. Their punishment will be exclusion from the people and the land of Israel. **9.** 'council': '*community*'. Not to be recorded in the register of the house of Israel means rejection. **10—13.** If special meaning is to be given to individual terms in the figure of speech, the wall may be the false belief that Yahweh would protect Jerusalem unconditionally, and by the storm may be understood the Babylonian invasion.

13e **17—23.** The false prophetesses not only attributed to Yahweh their own inventions when prophesying in his name, but adopted Babylonian magical practices. They made bands for the joints of the hand and veils for the head to be used as amulets to avert evil influences. Superstitious belief in the efficacy of these amulets gave the power of life and death to their dispensers. **18.** The prophetesses preyed upon souls, promising length of life to the sinners who bought their charms and threatened with death the just who refused them. They profaned Yahweh by prophesying falsely in his name. **22.** Justice, not amulets, gives length of life.

f **14:1—11 Worshippers of Idols consult Ezekiel—** He is ordered to threaten them with extermination unless they renounce idolatry, and not to answer their queries under penalty of sharing their fate. **3.** 'taken their idols into their hearts': their idol worship is both internal and external. **5.** Yahweh's purpose is their salvation through repentance. **7.** The strangers would be pagan slaves who accompanied their masters into exile. **9.** The prophet who is seduced and answers the demands of idolaters will be exterminated with them. 'I, the Lord, have deceived that prophet'. For the ancient Israelites, who by-passed secondary causality, every action good or bad was attributed to Yahweh. We would speak today of the deception occurring through the permissive will of God.

g **14:12—16:63 Total Corruption of Judah and Jerusalem—**Ezek first describes the justice of Yahweh in punishing sinful nations, and then the sinfulness of Israel, unfruitful vine and unfaithful spouse. Her punishment, severe and inevitable, will be followed by a restoration, cf § § 508h, 514i.

12—23 Justice of Yahweh's Punishment—When Yahweh chastises a nation, he spares the just but not their sons and daughters. In the punishment of Jerusalem, however, some will escape into exile to reveal by their manner of life the justice of Yahweh's judgement. Thus the general law of personal responsibility admits exceptions. Just as some of the guilty are spared here, so some of the just will perish with the wicked, 21:3. **14.** Three examples of just men. Noah lived amid widespread corruption; Job remained just in a pagan milieu. As for Daniel (MT: Danel), it is improbable that the prophet of that name is meant here. There was an ancient Phoenician sage named Danel as we know from the Ras-Shamra tablets, cf § 525b. We may assume that Danel was an ancient historical figure introduced into Phoenician mythology as Job was introduced into Hebrew wisdom literature. **22—23.** The conduct and actions of the fugitives must have been evil to convince the earlier exiles of the justice of the punishment.

514a **15:1—8 Jerusalem, the Unfruitful Vine—**Elsewhere, Israel is compared to a cultivated vine or vineyard (Is 5:1—7; Jer 2:21) which fails to respond to the care of the cultivator and produce fruit. Here they are compared to the wild vine of the forest which is good for nothing but to be used as fuel for the fire. **4.** Both ends of the vine, Israel and Judah, have been burnt, i.e. destroyed. There remains only the charred centre, namely Jerusalem, in which any sap of life survives. But Yahweh will complete the destruction.

b **16:1—63 Jerusalem, the Ungrateful Spouse—1—7** Yahweh's care for Jerusalem as a Child. This vivid allegory has a traditional theme. Israel's idolatry is compared to harlotry. The prophet depicts Israel as a foundling. The previous possessors of the land are her parents in the sense that Israel learnt their wicked ways. The Amorites are the Semitic immigrants who invaded Canaan in the 19th cent. B.C. and possibly to be **514b** identified with the Canaanites, cf *Encyclopedic Dictionary of the Bible*, 1963, 72—73. The 'Hittites' are the non-Semitic people to the N who invaded the land later on. These people were the pre-Israelitic inhabitants of Canaan. Cf art on *Gentile neighbours*. From them Israel absorbed not only some of their racial strains but some of their pagan ritual and customs. **4.** Newborn children are still washed, rubbed with salt and swaddled by Palestinian Arabs. **7.** 'full maidenhood': 'ornament of ornaments' (MT): *'age of puberty'* (CV).

8—34 Jerusalem, Unfaithful Spouse—8. A covering **c** with the extremity of the garment meant betrothal; Ru 3:9. The covenant was espousal. **16.** The last part of the verse is dubious in MT, and omitted in most modern versions. **20—21.** Sacrificing Yahweh's children to placate false gods was the height of iniquity. Infants were first slain and then burned as holocausts to Moloch at Jerusalem, 2 (4) Kgs 16:3; 17:17; Jer 7:31. **26.** In describing the sins of Judah Ezek here mentions foreign worship introduced by foreign alliance. The first alliance with Egypt was that of Hezekiah, made with the Kushite Pharaoh and then punished by Sennacherib's invasion. Many cities were detached from Judah and incorporated into the Assyrian province of Ashdod. **30.** 'How lovesick is your heart' (RSV); Hebrew uncertain; *'how wild your lust!'* (CV). Others: *'I am filled with anger against you'*; CBQ 23 (1961) 460 2. **32—34.** Judah differed from ordinary harlots in that she sought for and paid her lovers instead of being sought for and paid by them.

35—43 The Chastisement of Jerusalem—She shall **d** be handed over defenceless to her paramours who will strip her of everything, and as Yahweh's appropriate agents will execute on her the sentence pronounced on adulteresses and shedders of blood. **30.** The shedding of the children's blood means human sacrifice. **37.** *'whether you loved them or loved them not'* (CV): probable reference to Judah's fickleness in adopting and abandoning false gods. **40.** *'an assembly against you'*, a kind of tribunal of the nations. The adulteress is stoned, the murderess has her own blood shed. **41.** 'Women' here means nations, and particularly Judah's neighbours who rejoiced in her humiliation.

44—58 Jerusalem compared with Samaria and e Sodom—A comparison confirms the justice of the sentence passed on Jerusalem. She had sinned more than Samaria and Sodom. Since they had been punished, she too must be punished. **45.** She imitated her heathen Hittite mother; cf v 3. The husbands are national as distinguished from foreign deities. The sisters adopted Canaanite gods and offered them human sacrifices. **46.** Jerusalem lay between Samaria and the 'daughter' cities to the N (larger territory, *'elder sister'*) and Sodom with its dependent 'daughter' cities to the S (smaller area, *'younger sister'*). Both had suffered much for their crimes, Sodom through the cataclysm which overthrew it Gn 19:23—25 and Samaria through the Assyrian Exile. **50.** MT 'as I have seen': *'as you have seen'* (some MSS, versions). Possibly an allusion to the still visible ruins of Sodom and the rest of the Pentapolis. **53.** Not only will Sodom and Samaria be restored, but, unexpectedly, Jerusalem as well 'that you may be ashamed'. **56—57.** The name Sodom came to be used proverbially of great perversity, Is 1:9ff; cf Mt 10:15; 11:23—24. The same would now be true of Jerusalem.

59—63 Re-establishment of Jerusalem; a New f Covenant— Israel had broken her oath, violated the covenant of Mt Sinai. After she has expiated her crimes Yahweh will establish a new covenant with her out of his

514f sheer benevolence. The new covenant will be far greater than the old. It will be eternal, as in Hos 2:19—24; Jer 31:33. It will embrace all nations, here symbolized by Samaria and Sodom; cf Ps 87 (86); Is 2:3; 60:3ff; 66: 8ff; etc. The new pact would be fully realized in the Church of the New Dispensation; cf Rom 9:1—8; Gal 4: 26ff. This promise of re-establishment is surprising in this context and may be a later addition.

g 17:1—24 Fall of Zedekiah; Advent of Messiah— By means of a parable or allegory Ezekiel announces the enthronement of Zedekiah, his alliance with Egypt and revolt from Babylon, his deposition and deportation. He then contrasts the perjured and fallen monarch with the messianic king and his universal reign.

1—10 The Parable—Parables, like symbols, arouse interest. **3.** The eagle is Nebuchadnezzar who deposed Jehoiachin and enthroned Zedekiah. **4.** Deportation of Jehoiachin to Babylon. **5.** Zedekiah is compared to a well-watered willow shoot, i.e. comfortably enthroned in Jerusalem. His rule was weak, so he is further compared to the lowly vine. **7.** The second eagle is Pharaoh Hophra, *pace* Greenberg, JBL 76 (1957) 304—9, who attempts an identification with Pharaoh Psammeticus II. **8.** Consequences of Zedekiah's ignoble alliance with Egypt.

h 11—21 The Interpretation—The parable narrates the sin and punishment of Zedekiah. By violating his solemn oath of allegiance he offended Yahweh in whose name he had taken the vassal oath and broke faith with Nebuchadnezzar. **16.** Zedekiah did die in Babylon. **18—19.** In the ancient Near East oaths were considered inviolable. Yet vassal oaths were often broken, seemingly without qualms, even when taken in the name of local gods. The kings of Israel and Judah were no exception. Among the prophets it is Ezek who is most severe against the breaking of vassal oaths taken in Yahweh's name; cf also 21:23—29. **22—24 The Messianic King**—He is a sprout of the Davidic tree; cf Is 11:1. Unlike Zedekiah the lowly vine, he becomes a magnificent cedar planted on the heights of Sion; cf Is 2:2ff. His kingdom is universal; all nations find shelter therein. Cf Mt 13:31—32. All kings recognize its divine origin. This promise is appropriate to, and even suggested by the context.

i 18:1—32 Personal Responsibility—Ezek corrects the mistaken notion that children are punished for the sins of their parents. Each individual, he points out, is responsible only for his own sins. And if the just man sin or the sinner be converted, neither the former's good deeds nor the latter's evil deeds will be remembered. Then the prophet invites all to a true repentance. He assures them of the mercy of Yahweh, who is more ready to pardon than to punish. Such teaching on personal responsibility and divine mercy was particularly necessary when over-emphasis on national responsibility and divine justice led to despair. Ezek was not unaware of the implications of communal responsibility (he himself was suffering an unjust exile at the time). But of all the prophets, it is he who stresses most the concept of every man having to answer for his own faults.

1—4. The proverb. The speakers claim self-righteously that they are being punished for the sins of their forebears. By implication, Yahweh is unjust, they are innocent. Cf Jer 31:29. Ezek goes on to establish his thesis.

5—9. The just man. The precepts mentioned summarize important obligations: purity of worship, sexual purity, social justice and charity. Whoever observes them is just and will not die prematurely. **6.** The mountains are the idolatrous high places. **8.** 'increase': profit. Interest could be exacted from a foreigner but not from **j** an Israelite; Ex 22:24; Lv 25:36. **10—13.** The wicked

son of a just father. **10—11.** Following LXX: *'But if he* **514** *begets a son who is a thief, a murderer, or who does any of these things (though the father does none of them), a son who eats . . .'* (CV, BJ). The unjust son dies for his sins and is not saved by his father's justice. **14—20.** The just son of a wicked father. This is the case envisioned in the proverb. **17—20.** Life for the just son and retribution for the wicked father refute the proverb. **21—29.** The convert and the pervert. God's mercy to the repentant sinner and the need of perseverance in the practice of justice complete the teaching. God is more pleased to pardon than to punish, but repentance is necessary for pardon and no sinner is safe from chastisement. **30—32.** Ezek extends a heartfelt invitation to repentance, as John the Baptist was to do later on. **32.** Because of v 23 some would read *'death of the sinner'* instead of 'death of anyone who dies'.

19:1—14 Elegy on the Princes of Judah—This **k** lamentation aptly concludes the second cycle of prophecies. It is a poetical composition in *qînāh* or of elegiac metre, found again in 26:17—18; 27:3—9, 25—26; cf § 356*g*. Each verse has five beats, three in the first member and two in the second. The elegy here is also a parable. Two princes are represented as young lions, sons of a lioness, and a third as a vine-branch. Though the exact meaning is something of a problem, what follows is offered as a probable solution. Zedekiah is the vine-branch, as above in ch 17. The lions, appointed by the lioness, are Jehoahaz who was deported to Egypt and Jehoiachin who was exiled to Babylon. Jehoiakim is not mentioned because he died in Jerusalem 2 (4) Kgs 24:5. The view that the second lion symbolizes Zedekiah is based on an assumption that the lioness is Hamutal, wife of Josiah and mother of Jehoahaz and Zedekiah. But the lioness in the midst of lions seems to refer not to the queen-mother but to Judah in the midst of foreign nations. The lioness moreover appoints the second king, whereas Zedekiah was appointed by Nebuchadnezzar. Finally, the second monarch is deposed before the third is mentioned.

1—4 Jehoahaz—1. 'princes' (MT): 'prince' (LXX). **l** The phrase 'your mother' in vv 2, 10 indicates that the whole poem is addressed to Zedekiah. **3.** *'she exalted* [favoured?] one of her whelps'; G. Driver, Bib 35 (1954) 154. The detailed description, as frequently in a parable, pertains to the lion rather than to the prince symbolized. **4.** Jehoahaz, after a three-month's reign, was deported by Neco to Egypt where he died. The figure of the lion probably derives from Gn 49:9: the symbolism of David's house.

5—9 Jehoiachin—Like Jehoahaz, Jehoiachin the son of Jehoiakim was appointed without foreign influence. He ruled three months before his exile to Babylon. Tablets referring to his allotted rations in captivity have been discovered in the royal palace there. **8.** 'The nations' refer to Babylon's vassals.

10—14 Zedekiah—10. Probably: *'like a fruitful vine'*. To disregard the MT phrase 'in your blood' altogether would disturb metre and parallelism. The figure of the lion is abandoned because Israel is now a vassal state, Zedekiah, a creature of Nebuchadnezzar. **12—13.** Prediction of the deposition of Zedekiah and the exile. Nebuchadnezzar is the 'east wind'. **14.** Zedekiah is made responsible for the fire. Without shoots, he can have no successor.

20—24 Third Cycle of Threats against Jerusalem 515 **and Judah.**

20:1—44 Israel's Past and Present Sins, and Future Restoration—In August 591 B.C. the elders of Tel-

15a abib again request Ezekiel to consult Yahweh for them. Once more the prophet assures them that Yahweh will neither listen to them nor reply to them. He recalls instead the sins of Israel and the need for conversion.
1–4. The date is about eleven months after the last given, ch 8. **4.** 'judge them' means 'accuse them'. **5–9. Sins in Egypt. 6.** 'a land flowing with milk and honey' was a classical phrase indicating fertility, in OT as in the Rās Shamra tablets. **7–9.** The Covenant of Sinai was based on monotheism. Idol worship merited extirpation. Yahweh spared the Israelites that his name as an omnipotent protector might be honoured by the Gentiles. **10–17 Sins of the first generation in the desert. 11.** Observance of the law was recompensed by length of life; non-observance was punished by death. **12.** Sabbath observance was particularly important in the exilic period when sacrifices and other ritual observances were impossible.

b 18–26 Sins of the second generation in the desert. They sinned in spite of warnings. Yahweh did not exterminate them, for his name's sake. **25.** The statutes and ordinances which were not good for Israel and death-dealing may possibly refer to laws which they failed to observe through their own fault. The phrase may also refer to Canaanite observances, like the sacrifice of firstborn to Moloch, into which Yahweh permitted them to fall. In a sense, Yahweh's gift to them of Canaan exposed them to the possible seductions of pagan worship. Cf on 14:9, Yahweh's holiness guaranteed that any law he imposed must be objectively good. **26.** God's purpose was to terrify them by the enormity of their crime. St Paul teaches similarly that God allowed sin to abound that man might realize his own weakness and seek divine aid; cf Rm 5–6.

c 27–29 Sins in Canaan. 28. Worship on the high places was more usually associated with Canaanite divinities and included licentious practices. **29.** The word bāmāh 'high place' is here popularly derived from the Heb. verb ba' 'go in', used of conjugal relations and suggesting in the context an infidelity to Yahweh. The philological derivation is unknown. **30–32. Sins in exile.** Worship of idols made the exiles unworthy of a hearing from Yahweh. **31.** Though human sacrifices were not unknown in Babylonia, the reference to Moloch offerings here is surprising and may be an interpolation. **33–44 The Restoration.** Yahweh will reassemble his people from the nations among whom they are dispersed as in a second exodus, and will judge them. The wicked shall perish and the good shall return to Palestine. **37.** 'I will make you pass under the rod', the shepherd's rod under which his sheep pass as they enter the fold at night. Yahweh will count the number of those permitted to return (LXX). **40.** This promise, coming as it does between the sins and their chastisement, seems out of place and may be a later addition.—N.B. Some versions follow a different verse enumeration in the following. Their 20:45–49; 21:1–32 is equivalent to MT 21:1–37. We follow RSV, with MT in brackets.

d 20:45–21:32 (21:1–37) The Sword of Yahweh against Jerusalem and Ammon—Ezekiel sees a fire consuming all the trees of Judah, a symbol of the sword of Yahweh massacring all the inhabitants. Then, in verse, he describes the sword and its word of destruction. In the third scene Nebuchadnezzar (the sword) consults his oracles at the cross-roads to determine whether he should first assail Jerusalem or Rabbah of the Ammonites. The oracles say: Jerusalem. Next, Ammon's subsequent punishment is predicted. This final invasion of Judah began in winter, 589 B.C.

20:45–21:7 (21:1–12) The Fire and the Sword— 515d The S kingdom of Judah is like a forest about to be burned. Just as a forest fire spares no tree, so Nebuchadnezzar will not spare any person, just or unjust. This prophecy of indiscriminate slaughter by a human agent does not contradict the prophet's teaching on man's individual responsibility before God. Ezekiel's symbolic act of groaning foretells the sapping of men's faculties and strength in the face of such great punishment.

8–17 (13–22) The Song of the Sword—The text is **e** uncertain at times. **10.** 'You have despised the rod, my son, with everything of wood'. The meaning seems to be that Zedekiah despised all authority, even that of Nebuchadnezzar. **12.** 'slap your thigh', an expression of grief; cf Jer 31:19. **14.** 'clap your hands', an indication of approval, exultation.

18–27 (23–32) Nebuchadnezzar at the Cross-roads—God orders Ezekiel to make a graphic representation of the two possible roads open to the Babylonian invader. The roads branch off from Riblah on the Orontes, one SW to Jerusalem, the other SE to Rabbah of the Ammonites. Ezek pictures Nebuchadnezzar at Riblah as he decides, through divination, to march on Jerusalem. **21.** Conventional means of divining are used: teraphim or household gods, the liver of slain animals, and the shaking of marked arrows in a quiver in order to select one blindly. **22.** The lot falls on Jerusalem. It marks the guilt of that city for having violated the oath of allegiance to Nebuchadnezzar. **26–27.** 'until he comes **f** whose right it is': the saying reminds one of the oracle in Gn 49:10. If this be a messianic context, 'It' may refer to Jerusalem or, more probably, the Davidic dynasty. Others understand the vv in a non-messianic sense as referring to the coming of Nebuchadnezzar, destined by God to execute his judgement on both city and king; cf W. Moran S.J., Bib 39 (1958) 405–25.

28–32 (33–37) Chastisement of Ammon—Having smitten Jerusalem, the sword will turn against Ammon. The punishment is assured, but deferred. According to Jos.Ant. 10, 9, 7 Ammon was devastated five years after Jerusalem's fall. The ominous oracle turns up here rather than in ch 25, as a complement to the warning against Jerusalem.

22:1–31 The Crimes of Jerusalem—There is first an **g** enumeration of various crimes of the citizens. Jerusalem, filled with fugitives during the siege, is then compared to a melting-pot used for base metals. Finally the sins of various classes are recorded: princes, priests, high officials, prophets and common people, to show that all are guilty.

1–16 The City of Blood—Ezek mentions idolatry and bloodshed, the major crimes of Jerusalem, along with many others. **4.** The sense is: you have hastened the day of punishment and lessened the years of your life. **10.** 'they humble women who are unclean in their impurity': 'who coerce women in their menstrual period' (CV). **13.** 'I strike my hands together', a gesture here meant to disclaim responsibility; cf Nm 24:10.

17–22 The Melting-Pot—The figure would seem to **h** refer to a destruction rather than testing or refining. Israel had become dross, worthless metal, to Yahweh. **19.** Those gathered into the midst of Jerusalem apparently are the country people seeking shelter in the capital.

23–31 The Universal Corruption—All classes of people have sinned grievously. There is no one to save the nation from destruction. **24.** A land 'not purified or moistened by rain' is a land that is arid, unfruitful, unblessed by Yahweh. **25.** 'prophets' (MT): 'princes' (LXX), i.e. the lions of ch 19. **27.** Nobles or high officials

515h are meant here. **28.** False prophets have covered over weaknesses with unauthorized prophecies of security. **29.** The people of the land are ordinary citizens. **30.** There was no saviour, perhaps like Moses, to avert God's wrath.

i 23:1—49 Infidelity and Punishment of Samaria and Jerusalem—Ezek uses bold imagery to develop the comparison begun in ch 16. Samaria and Jerusalem are two sisters espoused to Yahweh but unfaithful to him. The elder sister Samaria has already suffered for her infidelity at the hands of her paramour Assyria. How inevitable then is the destruction of the far more unfaithful sister Jerusalem, by Babylon her lover! Samaria represents the larger N kingdom of Israel; Jerusalem, the smaller S kingdom of Judah.

1—4 Infidelity in Egypt—The sisters are accused of idol worship in Egypt. **4.** The names are symbolical. Oholah (Samaria) is usually interpreted: 'her own tent', while Oholibah (Jerusalem) means 'my tent in her'. It would appear that the former refers to the schismatic temple and worship in Samaria, as contrasted with the legitimate temple and cult in Jerusalem. For another symbolic name for Jerusalem cf Is 62:4. The 'sons and daughters' are the Israelites.

j 5—10 Infidelity and Destruction of Samaria—She allied herself with Assyria under Jehu in 841, and more permanently under Menahem in 738. Foreign alliance introduced foreign worship. Her revolt from Assyria and alliance with Egypt led to her destruction in 721.

11—21 Infidelity of Jerusalem—Instead of learning from her sister's fate, Jerusalem acted even more shamefully with the Assyrians, Babylonians and Egyptians. Ahaz introduced the alliance with Assyria, Hezekiah with Egypt. Alliances with Egypt and Babylonia followed each other after Josiah's death.

22—35 Chastisement of Jerusalem—The paramour Babylon, formerly loved but now despised, will be Yahweh's instrument in inflicting a most terrible and merciless punishment. **23.** 'Pekod', the *Puqudu* of cuneiform inscriptions (cf Jer 50:21), an Aramaic tribe on Elam's border; 'Shoa', the Assyrian *Shutu*, a name which appears also on the El-Amarna tablets; 'Koa', the *Qutu* in Assyro-Babylonian literature. The names refer to peoples E of the Tigris who were subject to Babylonia. **24.** The lovers will come against Jerusalem *'from the north'* (LXX). **25.** 'cut off your nose and your ears': in Egypt, mutilation of the nose was the punishment for adultery. **32—33.** Hebrew text is disordered.

k 36—49 Recapitulation of the Sin and Punishment of the Sisters—Additional sins, particularly human sacrifices, are mentioned. **38.** Omit 'on the same day' (LXX). **40.** The strangers from afar to whom messengers were sent are the Egyptians, Assyrians and Chaldeans with whom the Israelites sought alliances. **42.** Text and sense uncertain. There is apparent reference to the reception of the foreigners. **43.** *'Oh! the woman jaded with adulteries! Now they will commit whoredom with her and she . . .!'* An aposiopesis, or incomplete sentence. The completion would be: 'she will enjoy it!' The author dare not reveal the depth of the woman's degradation. Cf G. R. Driver, Bib 35 (1954) 155. **45.** *'But just men will judge them'*. The Chaldeans are considered just in so far as they are instruments of divine justice. **46.** *'summon an assembly'*, a judicial trial. **48.** 'Women': nations.

l 24:1—27 Announcement of the Siege and Capture of Jerusalem—Two symbolic actions indicate the siege. The caldron previously mentioned (11:3) is filled with choice meats to be cooked by fire. The choice meats represent the principal citizens. Fire is then applied to the empty caldron to remove the rust which defiles **515i** it—an indication of complete destruction. Ezekiel's wife dies suddenly on the day the siege begins. His omission of usual mourning rites symbolizes the attitude recommended to the exiles on learning of the city's fall.

1—8 The Full Caldron—The date of the beginning of the siege must have been revealed to Ezekiel. It was the 10th of Tebet (Dec.—Jan.) in the 9th year of Zedekiah, 589—588. Later the Jews marked the anniversary by a solemn fast, Zech 8:19. **5.** Wood, not bones (MT) was piled beneath the caldron. **6.** Not the rust but the meat and bones are to be cast out without discrimination since all are for destruction. **7.** The uncovered blood of the innocent slain in Jerusalem clamors for vengeance, as did the blood of Abel (Gn 4:10; cf Jb 16:18). Since all blood was sacred to Yahweh, even that of animals slain in the hunt had to be covered over with dirt, Lv 17:13.

9—14 The Empty Caldron—The caldron of the city **m** (Jerusalem) defies all attempts to purify it, and must be entirely destroyed. The Heb. text is in some disorder. RSV and CV translate adequately, with some conjectures. **15—27 Unlamented Death of Ezekiel's Wife**—By his unusual attitude towards the death of his wife the prophet becomes a sign to the exiles. He is forbidden to mourn her death publicly; they are forbidden to lament the destruction of Jerusalem. **17.** The public rites of mourning were baring the head and the feet, veiling the lower part of the face or beard, and partaking of a special mourning meal. For the latter, cf Jer 16:7; Tb 4:18. **18.** 'So I spoke to the people in the morning'. Transpose, perhaps, to 19*b* (CV). **22—23.** The text is in disorder. Ezekiel's words in these vv interrupt the speech of Yahweh in vv 21 and 24. **26—27.** The restrictions imposed on Ezekiel's prophetic ministry shall cease when a fugitive from Jerusalem reports that the city has fallen; cf 33:21ff.

25—32 Prophecies Against Gentile Nations. 516
25:1—17 Prophecies against Ammon, Moab, Edom and Philistia—Like Isaiah and Jeremiah, Ezekiel too predicts God's judgement on the Gentile nations: Ammonites, Moabites, Edomites, Philistines, Phoenicians and Egyptians. He does not denounce their idol worship but their malevolent attitude towards Yahweh's sanctuary and people, because their hostility is the chief obstacle to a messianic restoration.

1—7 Ammon—The Ammonites will disappear and Ammon will be a camping-ground for desert dwellers, her E neighbours. **3.** *'Because you said "Good!"' at the desecration of my sanctuary'*. Ammon's sin was hostility to the temple, land and people of Yahweh. **7.** 'I will destroy you'; cf 21:33—37.

8—11 Moab—The Moabites will share the same fate as **b** the Ammonites. **9.** The text is corrupt but the sense is clear. All of Moab will be exposed to invasion. The shoulder is the mountain side to the N, protecting Moab and its important cities: Beth-Jeshimoth (Suwēme at NE end of Dead Sea), Baal-meon (Ma'in, S of Suwēme) and Kiriathaim (Kureiyāt, S of Baal-meon). **12—14 Edom**—The judgement on Edom, descendants of Esau, will be executed by the Jews themselves (Edom was made vassal during the Maccabean period). Edom had long been hostile to the Israelites, and even participated actively in the overthrow of Jerusalem, Obad 11—14. **13.** 'from Teman to Dedan'. Teman (lit 'the south') is possibly modern Tāwīlan, a village near Petra. Dedan is identified with El-'Olah, an Arabic village S of Edom. **15—17 Philistia**—God himself will punish the Philis- **c** tines by ravaging their whole seacoast. **16.** The Cherethites seem to have formed a separate group within the

16c Philistine nation; their name reflects their Cretan origin.

26:1—21 First Prophecy against Tyre: its Sin, its Punishment—Tyre was the richest and most powerful of the Phoenician cities. Built on an island a half mile or more off the N coast of Palestine, it was impregnable so long as the Tyrians retained command of the sea. It had dependent cities and considerable territory on the mainland, together with colonies and trading-posts in the islands and on the coasts of the Mediterranean. Its general policy, dictated by commercial interests, was submission and payment of tribute to the great powers who invaded Palestine, and the maintenance of friendly relations with its neighbours. Though the Tyrians sided with Zedekiah in his revolt against Nebuchadnezzar they nevertheless rejoiced at the fall of Jerusalem, their commercial rival, whose trade they hoped to inherit. The ruin of Tyre is attributed to Yahweh without mention of human agents; in point of fact it was a gradual process. Nebuchadnezzar struck the first blow, besieging the city for 13 years c. 586—574 B.C. (29:18; cf Jos. C. Ap 1, 21), but he does not seem to have destroyed it. It was captured by Alexander the Great in 332 B.C. Final ruin came at the hands of the Saracens in A.D. 1291. In the case of Nebuchadnezzar the description of his siege given in Ezek is largely conventional. The prophet magnifies the part played by horses and chariots but makes no mention of special measures needed for the capture of an island city. A similar use of conventional language in eschatological prophecies is generally recognized.

d 1—6 Sin and Chastisement 1. The date is spring 586. MT does not specify the month. **2.** '*Good! the gateway of the peoples is broken*'. Tyre rejoices over Jerusalem's downfall, envisioning commercial benefit at her expense. **4.** 'a bare rock'. In Phoenician (*sûr*) and Heb. (*sôr*) the name Tyre means 'rock'. **5.** The daughters are the dependent cities on the mainland.

7—14 Nebuchadnezzar's Siege of Tyre—The long 13 year siege is the initial stage of Tyre's punishment. **8.** The cities on the mainland are first reduced. Siege wall, mound or ramp, shields, are all ordinary features of a siege.

15—18 Effect on Tyre's Neighbours—15. They will tremble at the news of Tyre's fall. **16.** They will manifest the usual signs of mourning. The princes of the sea are the rulers of the islands and coastal colonies in league with Tyre. **17. The lament:** if this could happen to so powerful a city as Tyre . . .!

19—21 Oracle on Tyre—20. 'the Pit': the abode of all the dead in the netherworld, usually called Sheol, here conceived as a hole or cave of darkness.

e 27:1—36 Second Prophecy against Tyre: Lament for Tyre—The city is likened to a magnificent ship whose construction and destruction are described in elegiac verse. The detailed prose description (10—25) which occurs between the two verse sections is probably a later addition.

1—9a The Building of the Ship—5. 'Senir': either a peak of the Antilebanon range, like Mt Hermon (Song 4:8), or Mt Hermon itself (Dt 3:9). **6.** Bashan is N Transjordan, famous for its forests and cattle. *Chetthim* refers to part of, or to the whole of Cyprus and its inhabitants. The red pine of Cyprus was much used in ship-building. **7.** 'serving as your ensign': probably to be omitted as disturbing the metre. Elishah is usually identified with Cyprus. **8—9.** 'inhabitants': '*princes*' (LXX). The four Phoenician cities which put their skilled men at Tyre's disposal were Arvad and Zemer (or Samar, a conjectural emendation of MT 'Tyre') on the coast N of Lebanon, Sidon on the coast further S near

Tyre, and Gebal (Byblos) in a central position on the **516e** coast.

10—25a Commerce of Tyre—10. Mention is first made **f** of nations which gave Tyre military aid. Lud, which elsewhere in OT refers to a region in W Asia Minor, here seems to refer to a region and people of NE Africa. Put seemingly refers to an African region W of the Nile Delta, possibly part of Libya. **11.** 'men of Gamad', probably the Egyptian *Kamadu* and the *Kumidi* of the El-Amarna tablets, an area near Hermon. **12—24.** This list of peoples is mainly geographical: Tarshish in the far west—Javan (Ionia), Tubal, Meshech in Asia Minor—Beth-Togarmah in Armenia—Rhodes (MT: Dedan) in the Greek Archipelago—Edom, Judah, Israel, Damascus, Helbon (near Damascus)—Uzal, Dedan, Kedar, Sheba, Raamah in Arabia—Haran, Canneh, Eden (Bit-Adini), Asshur, Chilmad in Mesopotamia. **13.** Javan, Tubal and Meshech gave slaves and bronze vessels. **14.** Beth-togarmah sent draught horses, war horses and mules. **19.** 'cassia and calamus': sweet-smelling ingredients used in making incense and the sacred anointing oil; cf Ex 30:23. **24.** Strong and well-twisted cords were part of the Mesopotamian wares.

25b—36 Wreck of the Ship—27. The entire cargo and **g** crew go down with the ship. **29—32.** Other crews leave their ships in mourning, and intone a lament for Tyre. **35—36.** The Mediterranean peoples are stupefied, their kings terrified. But rival trading nations hiss at Tyre in derision, and rejoice at its misfortune.

28:1—26 Third Prophecy against Tyre: Sin and 517a Punishment of the Prince of Tyre—The prince is here regarded less as an individual than as an embodiment of the state; cf Is 14:4—23. The first part of the elegy, vv 1—10, is more realistic and better preserved textually than the second, vv 11—19, in which the metre is scarcely recognizable. A short oracle on Sidon, vv 20—23 and a prediction of the restoration of Judah, vv 24—26, complete the chapter.

1—10 Pride and Humiliation of Tyre's Prince—2. In his pride he thought himself a god, and his island capital the throne of a god. **3.** 'wiser than Daniel': cf 14:14. **8.** 'into the Pit': cf 26:20. **9.** The prince's death will show that he is but a man, not a god. **10.** 'uncircumcised': godless. Death without funeral rites was considered a great calamity.

11—19 Elegy on the Prince—In this fanciful attribu- **b** tion to the prince of more than human prerogatives many authors have seen the influence of pagan mythology. More recently it has been suggested that this section has more points of contact with the Paradise story of Gn 2—3 than with any other biblical passage or known mythology pattern; that therefore it is a piece of native Hebrew tradition; cf J. L. McKenzie S.J., JBL 75 (1956) 322—27. **12.** 'signet of perfection': a perfect seal-ring on God's hand, exercising divine authority. **13.** Description of the prince as Adam in Eden before the fall, although the list of precious stones, reminiscent of Ex 28:17—20 seems scarcely authentic. **14—15.** The Heb. is uncertain. The general sense seems to be that Tyre's fall from perfection will be like the fall in Paradise; the prince was blameless until he sinned. 'the holy mountain of God': God's residence somewhere in the N; cf v 2, also Is 14: 13. The 'stones of fire' may be a reference to the precious stones. **16—18.** The prince's sin was wrongful trade. Great trade brought beauty, beauty produced pride, and pride the loss of wisdom, the folly of sin.

20—26. The prophet predicts briefly the punishment **c** of Sidon, mother city of the Phoenicians, through pestilence and the sword. The removal of Israel's enemies is the

517c prelude to the Restoration. God will manifest his sanctity to the Gentiles by restoring Israel.

d 29:1–16 First Prophecy against Egypt: Ruin and Restoration—The prophecy is dated the 12th of Tebet (Dec.–Jan.) 588–587 B.C. The pride of the Pharaoh, who is compared to a mighty crocodile, shall be humbled. Egypt, which proved to be an unreliable support for Israel, shall first be devastated and then restored, but not to her former greatness.

1–5 Egypt, the Crocodile—Cf Is 27:1. Pharaoh is described as a great crocodile wallowing complacently in the security and richness of the Nile and its streams. He will be humbled. Caught by a fisherman's hook, he and his satellites will be removed from their natural element and cast into the desert, unburied, a prey for birds and beasts.

e 6–12 Egypt, the Weak Staff—Denunciation of Egypt as a weak and unstable ally of Israel. She was like a reed staff which suddenly breaks, piercing the hand of its user or harming him through a fall. In point of fact, Egypt had sent only token help to Judah; cf Jer 37:5–7. **10.** 'from Migdol to Syene', the length of Egypt, from the fortress Migdol on the NE boundary to Syene, modern Assuan, to the S.

13–16 Restoration of Egypt—Egypt will be restored but not to its former greatness. As a minor power confined to Pathros in Upper (S) Egypt, this people will no longer deceive Israel by an alliance, but will serve to remind Israel of her own iniquity. Historically, the Persian Cambyses (529–522 B.C.) overcame Egypt and incorporated it into the Persian Empire.

f 17–21 Second Prophecy against Egypt: Conquest of Nebuchadnezzar—This is the latest of Ezek's dated prophecies, March 571. Nebuchadnezzar, servant of Yahweh, is to be given the land of Egypt as payment for his unrequited labours in the long and arduous siege of Tyre. The riches of Tyre which had been exhausted will be compensated by the riches of Egypt. **21.** '*I will make a horn sprout*'. The horn is a symbol of strength and appears frequently in messianic contexts. In any case, the Babylonian conquest of Egypt in 568 B.C. made Ezekiel's co-exiles more ready to accept his teaching.

g 30:1–19 Third Prophecy against Egypt: the Day of Yahweh—This undated prophecy portrays the fate of Egypt on the day of judgement for all nations; cf Is 13. **4.** The foundations are the neighbouring nations who fought in Egypt's armies. **5.** On Put and Lud, cf 27:10. 'Cub' (MT): '*Libya*' (versions). **6.** 'from Migdol to Syene'; cf 29:10. **14.** Pathros is Upper (S) Egypt. Zoan (Tanis) is in the Delta and Thebes in Upper Egypt. **15.** Pelusium was on the NE boundary, Memphis (LXX) was S of Cairo. **16.** '*Syene* (LXX) shall be in great agony. Thebes shall be breached'. The text that follows must be reconstructed. **17.** 'On' is Heliopolis, N of Memphis; Pi-beseth is Bubastis, N of Cairo. **18.** Tehaphnehes, or Taphnes, a port city in the NE Delta.

h 20–26 Fourth Prophecy against Egypt: Breaking of Pharaoh's Arm—The prophecy is dated 7th Nisan 587. The might of Egypt will diminish, that of Babylon increase, symbolized by broken and strengthened arms respectively. **24.** Pharaoh shall groan before Nebuchadnezzar like a man mortally wounded.

31:1–18 Fifth Prophecy against Egypt: the Cedar is felled—The prophecy in poetic form is dated May 587. Using images which occur elsewhere in the OT, Ezek compares Egypt to a magnificent cedar which is now laid low. Tree symbolism is frequent also in the mythology of the Middle E.

i 1–9 The Cedar's Beauty—**3–4.** The ancients thought

that springs came from the waters beneath the earth. **517** The trees are symbolical of the neighbouring nations. **8–9.** Even the trees in the garden of Eden could not rival this cedar. There is an element of hyperbole here, in that Babylonia and Assyria (at an earlier date) were more powerful than Egypt.

10–14 Felling of the Cedar—Ezek now employs the 'taunt-song' made famous by Is 13–14. **10.** The punishment of pride. **13–14.** The felling of Pharaoh brings ruin to the nations who depended on him, and who perish with him. **15–18 Effect of the Fall**—Nature mourns and men tremble. While the peoples on earth quake at his fall, those already in Sheol, the Pit, are consoled to know that now the high and mighty Pharaoh has sunk to their level; cf Is 14:8–15. **18.** Pharaoh's association with those slain by the sword implies privation of burial rites.

32:1–16 Sixth Prophecy against Egypt: Lament 518 for Pharaoh—The date is uncertain, probably spring of 586. Pharaoh, who represents all Egypt, is likened to a crocodile.

1–10 Destruction of the Crocodile—**1.** The date varies in MT (11th month, 586) and LXX (12th month, 585). **2.** The sense seems to be that while Pharaoh considered himself a roaring lion among the nations, in reality he was but a crocodile (RSV, 'dragon') limited to its own environment. **4.** As above, 29:1–5. When removed from its natural element the crocodile becomes the prey of birds and beasts. **5.** Ezek passes easily from the symbol, the crocodile, to the reality, the Egyptians. **7.** The cosmic disturbances associated with the day of judgement emphasize the greatness of the catastrophe.

11–16 Completeness of Egypt's Destruction—The utter desolation of the land causes consternation in other nations. Some mourn, some shiver in anticipation of like punishment at Babylon's hands.

17–32 Seventh Prophecy against Egypt: Pharaoh b in Sheol—We may date this last prophecy against Egypt six weeks after the preceding one; LXX adds *in the first month*. It describes Pharaoh's descent to the netherworld and his condition there. Noteworthy is the distinction of two classes in Sheol, the Pit. The heroes of old have a privileged position in the upper part of the underworld; cf Ps 49 [48]:15. The uncircumcised and those slain in battle occupy a lower level in the Pit. With these latter are associated the Egyptians and other war-like nations, oppressors of weaker peoples. There is no mention of Israel here.

17–21 Pharaoh descends to Sheol—**19.** There is a c dislocation of text here. The phrase 'Whom do you surpass in beauty...?' (19) should follow v 21, as in LXX. It represents the words of the most powerful of the heroes in Sheol. BJ relocates after v 21*a*, CV after v 21*b*.

22–32 Pharaoh's Associates in the Pit—**22–23.** Assyria, first of the powerful but proud nations, is in disgrace at the bottom of the Pit. **24–25.** The once mighty Elam which had extended from the Persian Gulf to Assyria, suffers the same fate. **26–27.** Meshech and Tubal, always associated in OT (cf 27:13), represent N war-like and barbarous peoples. **29.** Pharaoh is the addressee. **29–30.** The selected list of those in Sheol is completed with mention of Edom, the princes of the N (Syrians?), and the Sidonians. **31.** Pharaoh will find some measure of comfort in finding that these other oppressors share his disgrace.

33–48 Promises: Purification and Restoration of d Israel.

33:1–33 Conditions of Salvation—Ch 33 introduces the third part of the book. It repeats and develops four instructions already given. The first and second treat of

18d the prophet's functions and personal responsibility. The third and fourth are admonitions addressed respectively to the Israelites in Palestine who were not deported, and to Ezekiel's companions in exile. The occasion of the prophecy was the arrival of a fugitive with news of Jerusalem's capture, narrated in the third section.

e **1—9 The Prophet's Functions**—A prophet is like a watchman who is obliged to be on the alert and to give warning of an enemy's approach; cf 3:16—21; 14:9—11. **3—5.** If the prophet gives due warning, the sinner alone is responsible for what happens. **6.** If the prophet fails to warn, he too is responsible. **8—9.** Repetition of the consequences of a Prophet's warning or failure to warn. **10—20 Personal Responsibility**—Punishment of the nation for sins in which the exiles participated causes the latter to despair of pardon. Ezek reminds them of Yahweh's justice and mercy. He will not blame them for the sins of others and is always ready to pardon repentant sinners; cf 14:1—8; 18:1—32. **13—16.** The just man must persevere in justice; the sinner must repent and repair the wrong he has done. **17—20.** God's ways are just, and forbid despair. Repentance of evil and perseverance in good will bring salvation.

f **21—29 Admonition to the Israelites who were not Deported**—Ezek is informed of the fall of Jerusalem, and at the same time receives full liberty of speech in preaching to the people. He rejects the claims of those not exiled to the possession of Palestine. **21.** It would seem better to correct 'twelfth' (MT) to *eleventh* year. The news reached the exiles about six months after the city's fall. **22.** Ezek was in ecstasy from the evening to the following morning when the fugitive visited him, as already announced, 24:26. **23—29.** The survivors in Judah argue that the land belongs to them. Abraham as an individual possessed the land; they, his descendants, more numerous and able to populate and utilize the land, have a stronger claim to it. Ezek tells them that as sinners they are doomed to destruction. And indeed, many of them must have suffered in the subsequent deportation, 589 B.C., mentioned in Jer 52:30. **30—33.** Yahweh reproaches Ezekiel's fellow-exiles for their duplicity in listening to the prophet but not heeding his words or carrying out his instructions. **32a.** '*lo, you are to them like a love song, pleasantly sung with musical accompaniment*' (BJ). **33.** Their eyes will be opened in the day of their chastisement.

19a **34:1—31 The Bad Shepherds replaced by a New David**—In this prophecy Yahweh compares Israel to a flock of sheep, neglected, preyed on and dispersed by bad shepherds. He intends to purify them, to restore them to their old pasturage where they shall find abundant nourishment and where a single shepherd, called David and the Servant of Yahweh, shall rule them in peace and holiness; cf Jer 23:1—8.
1—10 The Bad Shepherds—**3.** The unworthy shepherds: kings, priests, prophets, took full remuneration for duties which they did not perform. **4.** They did not assist the weak, the sick, the wounded and strayed who needed their ministrations. Instead they ruled the flock harshly. **8.** The wild beasts were foreign nations. **10.** The unworthy shepherds or leaders will be called to account and deprived of their office.

b **11—16 Yahweh, Shepherd of his Flock**—Prediction of the restoration. Yahweh himself will shepherd the flock; cf Is 40:11; Ps 23 [22]. **12.** As a shepherd reunites his scattered sheep, so shall Yahweh reunite his scattered people. **16.** Yahweh will do all that the evil shepherds failed to do. Omit 'the fat and the strong I will destroy' as a probable interpolation.

17—22 Judgement and Purification—**17.** The Heb. **519b** word for flock includes goats as well as sheep. Rams and he-goats in particular indicate the ruling classes inclined to selfishness. The stronger animals, having satisfied themselves, trample the pasture and foul the waters. The judgement implies removal of disturbers from the flock. **20.** The fat are the oppressors, the lean the oppressed. **23—31 The Messiah and his Reign**—The messianic **c** kingdom is often represented as a revival of David's kingdom. The Messiah is a new David, servant of Yahweh. His reign will be prosperous and peaceful. The new covenant is a covenant of peace. That in the same context Yahweh himself and the new David (Messiah) are said to shepherd Israel apparently did not have any fuller significance for Ezek. Later, Jesus was to apply the prophecy to himself: Jn 10:11—16. **26.** '*I will place them about my hill*' (LXX). A reference to Mt Sion; cf Is 2:2—4.

35:1—15 Devastation of Edom—The prophets depict **d** the messianic restoration as the re-establishment of Israel in all her ancient territory. After the fall of Jerusalem Edom had occupied a considerable part of Judah and aspired to possession of all Israel. The punishment of unbrotherly Edom, already predicted in 25: 12—14, is again announced here as an integral part of the programme of the restoration. **2.** Seir refers to the mountainous region of Edom, and at times is identified with Edom. **5.** Edom's sin is perpetual enmity towards Judah, manifested particularly in the recent calamity either by their slaying of Israelite fugitives or by handing them over to the Chaldeans, Obad 14. **6.** '*you have been guilty of blood and blood, I swear, shall pursue you*' (CV). There is a play on words: Edom and *dām* 'blood'. **10.** The Edomites wanted possession of Judah and Israel which belonged to Yahweh. **11.** Application of the *lex talionis* to Edom. **12.** 'given us to devour': given for our sustenance. **14.** MT is corrupt. It is Edom who rejoices, not the whole earth. The thought appears more clearly in v 15.

36:1—38 Re-establishment of Israel: Preparation e of the Land and Purification of the People—The Gentiles attributed Israel's degradation to the weakness of Yahweh, her protector. Hence Israel must be re-established so that Yahweh's name be no longer blasphemed. The devastated land will increase in fertility and the sinful people will be spiritually regenerated. The prophecy is conditional and depends for its literal fulfilment on the cooperation of Israel with the designs of Yahweh. It was spiritually fulfilled in the spiritual Israel, the Church founded by Christ.
1—15 The Mountains of Israel shall be Blessed—**1.** The mountains refer to the mountainous land of Judah, in contrast with that of Edom. **8.** The restoration is imminent. **13—14.** '*you rob your people of their children*', possibly a reference to natural calamities like famine due to the soil's aridity, but more probably a reference to the nation's past dismal political history.
16—38 Israel shall be re-established and spiritual- f ly regenerated—**16—23.** First, the motive for the messianic renewal is explained. It is not for Israel's sake nor due to her merits; it is because Yahweh's holy name should no longer be blasphemed by the Gentiles who considered him unable to protect his people. **24.** The exiles will return to Palestine. **25—29a.** Prediction of the people's spiritual regeneration. Washing with water and the infusion of God's spirit suggest a baptismal regeneration; cf Jn 3:5. **31—32.** The necessity for repentance for past infidelities. **36.** Neighbouring nations will recognize the hand of the Lord and no longer ridicule his holy name. **37—38.** Yahweh will multiply his people. The comparison with

519f sheep suggests the numerous flocks assembled at the solemn feasts in Jerusalem.

g 37:1—14 The Vision of the Dry Bones restored to Life—This vision refers to the revival of the defunct nation of Israel, hopelessly scattered in exile. It does not teach the resurrection of the body, as often interpreted, but may be said to prepare providentially for later revelation on the resurrection of the dead. The scene of the vision was a plain near Tel-abib already mentioned in 3:22. **11—14 Interpretation of the Vision**—The dry bones represent the House of Israel as politically non-existent, and not the dead on the last day. The graves were the places where dispersed Israelites lived as strangers in foreign lands. Re-establishment of the exiles in their own land was the revival of the nation.

h 15—28 Reunion of the Separated Kingdoms—The symbolic action of joining together two sticks or rods signifies the reunion of the divided kingdoms of Judah and Israel by God's will. They shall form a single nation under a single ruler, the new David, in their ancestral territory. Yahweh will make an eternal alliance with them and establish his sanctuary within them. The prophecy is messianic, spiritually fulfilled in the one true Church.

15—20 The Symbolic Action—Judah and Joseph whose names are written on the sticks were the tribal ancestors whose descendants played the leading roles in the kingdoms of Judah and Israel. The division which had separated Israelite from Israelite shall be no more.

i 21—28 The New Israel—**21—23.** The exiles shall return and form a new kingdom. **24—25.** The new David (Messiah) shall rule over them forever. **26—27.** Yahweh will make an eternal alliance with them. **28.** From his sanctuary in their midst he shall become known to the Gentiles.

520a 38—39 Final Victory of Yahweh over the Pagan World—While Israel enjoys peace and prosperity in her native territory after the restoration, Gog, ruler of the N nations, leads a mighty army against her. Yahweh protects his people by annihilating the hostile forces when they reach Palestine. There is a description of the burning of weapons, the burial of the slain, the feasting of predatory birds and beasts. Ezek's main object is to assure his hearers of Yahweh's permanent protection. The genre used is apocalyptic, shot through with symbolism. The meaning may be literally historical, messianic, or eschatological. Those who understand the prophecy in a literal historical sense attempt to identify Gog with some specific foreign invader, e.g. the Seleucids. Others, who interpret in the messianic sense, see in Gog and his army the forces of evil seeking vainly to destroy the Church founded by Christ. Other authors take the prophecy in an eschatological sense, as the struggle between the forces of good and evil which will precede the last judgement. There is no good reason to suppose that Ezek is not the author of these chapters, though they do interrupt the sequence from the national restoration (chh 33—37) to the building of the Temple (chh 40—48) and mythological elements are included.

b 38:1—23 Gog's Invasion of Israel—There is a description of Gog's army, his designs against Israel, and finally his defeat by Yahweh. The nations mentioned represent all the might of paganism, drawn from the far reaches of the earth. These kingdoms of the world rise against the kingdom of God, symbolized in restored Israel, but their attack is doomed to failure. CV arranges the text of ch 38 to read: vv 1—13, 17—23, 14—16.

c 1—9 Army of Gog—**2.** '*Gog and the land of Magog*' (LXX). MT has: '*Gog, land of Magog*'. We are not certain as to the meaning or derivation of the names Gog and Magog. The name Gog has been linked with Agag (1 Sm 15:8—33), with Gyges the king of Lydia, and with various historical personages. In the messianic and eschatological understanding of the passage, Gog is a fictitious name symbolizing all the forces of evil ranged against God's people, a sort of Antichrist. Magog would likewise be a fictional name, though in Gn 10:2 a Magog appears with Meshech and Tubal among the sons of Japhet. In Apoc 20:8ff. Magog is an independent figure at the side of Gog; both are kings summoned by evil spirits at the end of the millennium to fight against God's people. They are destroyed by fire from heaven. The Gog passages in Ezek profoundly influenced later apocalyptic literature (Hen 56, 4—8; 4 Ez 13; Sib Or 3, 319, 512). **3—6.** Meshech and Tubal as well as Gomer and Beth-togarmah (vv 3 and 6) were countries far to the N by the Black Sea. It was from the N that invasion of Israel was traditionally expected. The addition of Persia, Cush (Ethiopia) and Put (W of Nile Delta) to the line-up of armies emphasizes the ferocity and power aligned against God's People. **7.** Yahweh decrees the enemy expedition. **8.** 'After many days . . . in the latter years'. In a prophetical context the phrase 'in the latter days' indicates the future, simply (Nm 24:14; Jer 48:47). In a messianic context it signifies the end of the OT era and the beginning of the messianic age.

d 10—17 Gog's Designs—He plans to plunder a peaceful and naturally unprotected people. 'who dwell at the centre [navel] of the earth', i.e. Israel. It was not unknown for ancient peoples to refer to their own homeland as the navel or centre of the earth. **13.** The enquiries of the trading nations are explained by the fact that traders attended armies to purchase the plunder, including slaves; cf 1 Mc 3:41; 2 Mc 8:10. **17.** Former prophecies of the destruction of Israel's oppressors are meant here.

e 18—23 Destruction of Gog and his Army—Yahweh himself annihilates the enemy. The description of the theophany is conventional. Earth trembles, birds and fishes, men and animals are terrified, mountains are overturned, rocks are rent and walls collapse. The enemies slay their own men as in Jg 7:32; 2 Chr 20:23, perish by pestilence, 2 (4) Kgs 19:35, by hailstones, Jos 10:11, and by lightning, Gn 19:24. Brimstone is associated with lightning owing to the sulphurous odour accompanying the electrical discharge, Iliad VIII, 135; XIV, 415.

f 39:1—24 Sequel to the Victory—A recapitulation of the preceding prophecy stresses the destruction of the invaders from the N. This is followed by a description of the burning of weapons, the drawn-out task of burying the slain, and the feasting of the birds and the beasts. **1—8 Recapitulation**—**3.** The striking of the bow from the hand of the attacker is a new feature. **6.** Gog's own land will suffer, as well as the 'coastlands' of his allies.

9—16 Burning of Weapons and Burial of Slain—Uninterrupted peace following the victory makes weapons useless, and indicates that this would be the last attempt to war against Israel. **11.** '*Valley of Abarim*', i.e. of Travellers, referring to the heights E of the Dead Sea; 'Valley of Hamon-gog', i.e. of the multitude of Gog, so named for the great numbers of invaders who were to die there in battle. It would take seven months to bury all the remains and so purify the land. **16a.** The reference to a city called Hamonah is probably a gloss.

g 17—24 The Feast of the Birds and Beasts—The slain are likened to a sacrificial feast prepared by Yahweh. The corpses are so numerous that before they can be buried many will serve as food for carrion birds and

20g animals. **21—24.** The causes of the exile and restoration.
Fulfilment of the Prophecy against Gog—As with
most apocalyptic literature the meaning here is not self-
evident. Many widely-differing viewpoints have been
suggested. Some see a fulfilment of the prophecy before
the end of the OT era, and suggest a connexion with
the Seleucid oppression. Others interpret in a messianic
sense, which would seem preferable since Ezek contemplates a messianic restoration; cf Apoc 20:7. The
judgement of the Gentile neighbours, chh 25—32, was the
necessary prelude to the establishment of the peaceful
messianic kingdom. Gog comes from afar to plunder that
kingdom already established. In this view he and his
army represent the forces of evil seeking vainly to destroy
the Church founded by Christ. As with Antichrist, so with
Gog, there have been any number of attempts to identify
him with individual persecutors in the course of history.
Not the least fanciful suggestion has been the identification of Gomer with Germany, Meshech with Moscow,
etc.

h 25—28 Final Prediction of the Restoration—This
oracle is a summary conclusion of the restoration prophecies. **27—29.** The return of the exiles, their spiritual
regeneration, and Yahweh's abiding presence among
them, all sanctify his name.

21a 40—48—Some modern scholars have questioned whether
Ezek wrote these chh, or whether they may not represent
the work of some later author. Without going so far, we
may admit that some additions or changes have been made
by a later redactor.

In this last section of the book Ezek concludes his
prophecies on the Restoration with a detailed and magnificent (if at times tedious) description of the New
Temple, the New Cult and the New Holy Land. Catholic
tradition has usually regarded this picture as a figurative
adumbration in Jewish colouring of the Messianic King
dom, the Church of Christ. Some modern exegetes suggest
a more realistic interpretation. It is difficult to suppose
that a practical programme for the expected historical
realization is here presented to the exiles. The rebuilders
of the temple, guided by prophets, made no attempt to
realize the plan of Ezek. His legislation, which ignored
the high priest and was sometimes at variance with the
b Mosaic code, was never accepted as authoritative. In his
description of the New Holy Land there are several
features, especially the temple river, which defy a realistic
interpretation. An ideal Messianic Restoration on the lines
of Isaiah's picture of the New Jerusalem seems less open to
objection. The prince, however, scarcely suggests the
Messiah. His liberty is restricted and possible abuse of
his authority is forestalled by legislation. On the other
hand Ezek, unlike Isaiah, never depicts the Messiah
except as a New David. It seems better, therefore, while
recognizing the difficulty of the problem, to accept the
traditional interpretation. In all his prophecies of the restoration Ezek appears to visualize the messianic period.

c 40—42 The New Temple—(1) The Outer Court and its
Gates. (2) The Inner Court and its Gates. (3) The
Temple Buildings. (4) The Buildings of the Inner Court.
(5) The Dimensions of the Sanctuary. The text of these
chh is often corrupt and unintelligible. In the limited space
at our disposal we have confined ourselves to a description
of the New Temple. A few of the details are necessarily
conjectural.

d 40:1—27 The Outer Court and its Gates—1—4.
Ezekiel is transported in spirit to Jerusalem and ordered to
communicate to the house of Israel what is there revealed
to him. The date is the 10th Nisan (Mar.—Apr.) 573
B.C. From an undetermined high mountain the prophet

sees the temple; cf Apoc 21:10. A resplendent angel **521d**
in human form guides Ezek and takes the various
measures with a reed or measuring rod and a cord or tape
for longer measures. **5. The measurements** are in cubits;
see § 86a—b; Ezek's cubit equalled the ordinary cubit
plus a handbreadth, or c. 21 inches. **The wall** enclosing
the sacred area was a reed or 6 cubits (about 10 ft 4 in)
in thickness and in height. **6—16. The E gate** is described
as being the most important, though similar to the
N and S gates (vv 20—27). It was an unroofed
passageway with walls or buildings on either side. A flight
of 7 steps led up to the outer threshold which was 6 cubits
long, 10 cubits wide. This gave admission to a corridor 13
cubits wide, flanked on either side by 3 lodges or rooms 6
cubits square. Two pillars each occupied a space of 5
cubits between the rooms. An inner threshold similar
to the outer led into a porch which communicated with the
court. The porch was 8 cubits long and 20 wide. The entire
structure was thus a rectangle 50 cubits long and 25 wide,
and fitted with slitted windows looking onto the court. Two
pillars in the porch were adorned with palm trees. **17—
19 The Outer Court** had 30 chambers fronted with
pillars (42:6). They probably adjoined the outer wall and
corresponded to the porticos in Herod's temple. There was
also a paved space all around, extending as far inwards as
the gates. The distance from these gates to the corresponding gates of the inner court was 100 cubits, so the
outer court was 150 cubits wide on all sides.

40:28—47 The Inner Court and its Gates—28—37. e
The inner gates differed from the corresponding outer
gates only in being reached by a flight of 8 steps instead
of 7, and in having their porches not at the inner but at the
outer end. **38—43.** Ezek, led to the E gate, sees the **tables**
for preparing the sacrificial victims; and those for laying
out the instruments used in the sacrifices. **44—47.** Ezek
enters the **Inner Court.** He sees a room beside the N gate
facing S and another beside the S gate facing N. They are
for the priests, the sons of Zadok, charged with the
service of temple and altar. The inner court is said to be
100 cubits long and wide; an obscure measure, probably
incorrect. Other indications show that the inner court,
including the temple, was 200 cubits long. The altar of
holocausts was E, in front of the temple.

40:48—41:26 The Temple Buildings—Ezekiel's **f**
temple, like Solomon's, had four parts: Vestibule, Holy
Place (Hekal), Holy of Holies (Debir) and Lateral
Building. An ascent of 10 steps led to the **Vestibule.**
From there the angel leads him to the **Holy Place** (RSV
'nave') but when they come to the **Holy of Holies** (RSV
'the Most Holy Place') the angel enters alone. This
entering by himself may be compared to that of the high
priest on the Day of Atonement, Lv 16. It is interesting
to note that the entrances to each part of the Temple,
the Vestibule, the Holy Place and the Holy of Holies, are
progressively smaller as one reaches a precinct of greater
holiness.

41:5—11 The side chambers or lateral building, g
enclosing the Temple on three sides, N, S and W, had
three stories, each with 30 rooms in which most probably
were stored the sacred vessels and Temple treasure. Two
doors in the outer wall on the N and S gave access to the
lateral building, which was bordered by a paved space of 5
and a free space of 20 cubits. **12—20.** A building due W of **h**
the sacred edifice probably served as a **store room** for
wood and a shelter for cattle. **15.** All the walls of the
vestibule, holy place and holy of holies were panelled, and
the **panelling** itself decorated with alternating palm
trees and cherubim. Two faces of the cherubim, the human
and the lion, were represented in profile. **21—26.** The holy

521h place and the holy of holies had double folding-doors, rectangular in shape. The door of the vestibule was apparently a wooden screen. Before the holy of holies stood a wooden altar, 2 cubits square and 3 in height, provided

i with corners or horns. Probably it was the Altar of Incense. One may recall the Canaanite sanctuary at Beth-Shean (Level VI; time of Ramesses III) in the sanctuary of which there stood an altar of brick. Beyond this was a flight of seven steps leading to an upper chamber (flanked by store rooms) in which was a second altar, see G. M. Fitzgerald, 'Beth-Shean' in *Archaeology and OT Study* ed. D. W. Thomas, 1967, 191–2.

j **42:1–14. The Buildings of the Inner Court**—There were two large buildings parallel to the temple on its N and S sides and separated from it by the free space outside the lateral building. The entry from the outer court was at the E end. The rooms in these buildings were used by the priests for dining and vesting, since the priests were forbidden to eat sacred meals or wear priestly garments outside the inner court.

k **15–20 Dimensions of the Sanctuary**—The entire square space enclosed by the outer wall measured 500 cubits (LXX) on all sides. MT has 500 reeds, or 3,000 cubits. To justify the MT reading some commentators suppose a vast unoccupied space surrounding the temple precincts to safeguard their sanctity (v 20). But the free space surrounding the outer wall is elsewhere estimated at only 50 cubits; cf 45:2.

522a **43–46 The New Cult**—Yahweh now enters his temple and prescribes how he is to be worshipped there. (1) The Theophany. (2) The Altar of Holocausts. (3) Prince, Levites and Priests. (4) Offerings. (5) Feasts and Sacrifices. (6) Inalienability of the Prince's Domain. (7) Kitchens.

43:1–12 The Theophany—**1–2.** In a vision Ezek sees Yahweh enter his new temple by the E gate. **3–9.** Conducted into the inner court, the prophet beholds the glory of the Lord and hears his voice. Yahweh will dwell forever among his people. They shall no more profane his holy name by their infidelities, i.e. by burying the corpses of their kings in the S part of the temple hill and even at times in the palace garden, and by having the palaces of their kings separated by only a wall from the sacred edifice. Solomon's temple had no outer court; only the single wall of the inner court separated it from his palace. **10–12.** Yahweh orders Ezek to promulgate the plan and measurements of the New Temple together with the laws regulating temple service now being revealed to him.

b **13–27 The Altar of Holocausts and its Consecration**—**13–17.** The altar is assumed to have been of stone. It was of massive proportions. The altar proper consisted of three square blocks placed one on top of the other. The lowest was 16 cubits square and 2 high; the middle, 14 cubits square and 4 high; the topmost—the altar surface—12 cubits square and 4 high. The altar had horns or projections at all four corners. At the base of all three blocks was a border or rim half a cubit high. These rims probably formed channels for receiving the blood of the sacrificial victims. The ascent to the altar

c was by steps on the E side. **18–27. The consecration of the altar** lasted 7 days. The consecrators were the priests instructed by Ezek, not the prophet himself. The salting of the holocausts (v 24) is noteworthy. Lv 2:13 prescribes salting of cereal offerings but not of animal sacrifices. On the latter, cf Mk 9:48.

523a **44:1–31 Prince, Levites and Priests**—The prince is the vicegerent of Yahweh who is king of the new theocratic state. Among his privileges is a special place

for sacrificial meals at the E gate of the outer court. This **523** is the **Closed Gate**, one that may never be opened because Yahweh had entered by it. The king therefore had to enter the court by another gate and thus attain entry to the E gate. It is generally assumed that we have here an allusion to a certain gate of Marduk's great temple in Babylon which was opened only twice a year. By homiletic accommodation not a few of the Fathers see in this gate, through which God alone has passed, a figure of Our Lady's perpetual virginity. **4–14.** The Israelites are re- **b** proached for having permitted foreigners and uncircumcised persons, whom they employed in an inferior capacity as temple servants, to enter and profane Yahweh's sanctuary. These inferior temple servants of foreign origin must be replaced by a particular class of Levites: those who at one time exercised sacerdotal functions but who had been degraded by their idol worship and infidelity to Yahweh. To these are committed the guardianship of the gates, slaughter of the victims, and menial offices in general. They are not to discharge the functions or enjoy the emoluments of the priesthood. **15–31.** The priests **c** are no longer all the male descendants of Aaron in general, but the descendants of Zadok in particular. Aaron left two sons, Eleazar and Ithamar. Abiathar, the high priest in David's time, was descended from Ithamar. His disloyalty led to a transfer of the sacerdotal dignity to the loyal Zadok, a descendant of Eleazar, 1 (3) Kgs 1:26, 35. The fidelity of Zadok and his descendants in the service of Yahweh at a time of general apostasy motivates their choice as priests in the New Temple. Most of the obligations of the priests will be found in the Pent; sometimes they are imposed exclusively on the high priest whom Ezek ignores entirely. **29.** *'whatever is under the ban* **d** *in Israel shall be theirs'*, i.e. all that has been withdrawn from profane use and dedicated to the Lord. **30.** The *terûmāh* or tribute was a special offering levied on all fruits and amounting in rabbinic times to a fiftieth of the harvest. **31.** This food prohibition applied also to the people.

45:1–17 Allotment of Land to the Priests and to the **e** **Prince; Weights and Measures; Offerings**—**1–8.** **The sacred tract**—The land assigned to priests, Levites, city and prince is specified. A portion of land 25,000 cubits long and 20,000 cubits broad is measured out. Half of this, enclosing the sanctuary and a vacant space of 50 cubits all around it, is for the priests. The other half is for the Levites. S of this is a space 25,000 cubits long and 5,000 wide for the city. E and W of the entire space already measured is the portion of the prince, 25,000 cubits square. It extends to the Mediterranean on the W and to the Dead Sea on the E. This ample provision for the prince is designed to correct the ancient abuse by which monarchs arbitrarily appropriated tribal territory.

9–12 Weights and Measures—The prince must not **f** oppress his subjects. He must exercise a special control over weights and measures. Along with the land monopoly fostered by royal greed and collusion with the wealthy (Mi 2:2; Is 3:12–15; 5:8–10), dishonesty in business had been a grave social evil of pre-exilic Israel and constantly condemned by the prophets, cf Hos 12:8; Am 8:5. The *ephah* was a dry measure, the *bath* a liquid measure, both here standardized according to the *homer*, a dry measure of about 10 bushels, or 80 gallons. cf § 86e–h.

13–17 Offerings—The people offer their prince a 60th part of their wheat and barley, a 100th part of their oil, and a 200th part of their flocks. In return he must provide all public offerings and sacrifices.

23g **45—46 Feasts and Sacrifices 45:18—20**—Two feasts of expiation, on the first of the 1st and 7th months, (LXX), replace Yom Kippur. Sacrifices are offered. **21—25.** The feasts of Passover and Tabernacles are celebrated on the dates assigned by the law but the sacrifices are different, and are accompanied by offerings of an ephah of meal and a hin of oil. There is no mention of the paschal lamb (surprisingly enough), of barley first-fruits and booths, nor is the feast of Pentecost mentioned. **46:1—8.** Next are considered the Sabbath and New Moon feasts. On such occasions the E gate of the inner court is left open and the prince has the privilege of assisting at the sacrifices on the threshold, without being seen by the

h people in the outer court. **9—12.** The rule that those who enter the outer court by the N gate would leave by the S gate is meant to maintain order, and binds both prince and people. Six lambs and a ram are the sacrifices for such feasts; on New Moon feasts, also a bullock. The usual accompaniment of an ephah of meal and a hin of oil is prescribed except in the lamb offerings, when the amount is left to the liberality of the prince. When the prince makes a voluntary offering he may assist at the sacrifice in the porch of the E gate. **13—15.** Every morning a lamb must be offered as a holocaust together with the 6th of an ephah of meal and a 3rd of a hin of oil. The law also prescribed a similar evening sacrifice, but exacted a lesser quota of meal and oil.

i **46:16—18 Inalienability of the Prince's Domain**—Only to his sons can the prince make a permanent gift of part of his domain. Such a gift to any one else is but a loan, and reverts to the prince automatically in the *'year of liberty'*, the next sabbatic year when Hebrew slaves were freed from bondage.

19—24 The Temple Kitchens—The kitchens for cooking sacrificial meats, sin-offerings and guilt-offerings eaten by the priests in the inner court, were naturally attached to the dining-rooms already described, at the W extremity of these buildings. Only the N kitchens are mentioned, but we may assume that there were others on the S side. The kitchens for the laity were in four enclosures, occupying the four angles of the outer court. Here the flesh of peace-offerings was cooked and eaten.

24a **47—48 The New Holy Land**—The prophet first describes the Temple River, then the boundaries of the land, and lastly the distribution of the land. The Presence of God in his Temple, indicated by the river which flows therefrom, may be compared with the glory of the Lord in ch 9:3. There the Almighty passed judgement on a wicked generation; here in the new age he dispenses benefits to a chastised and repentant people. They are envisaged as dwelling in peace within their restored borders in a prosperous and fertile land. Nature itself will partake of God's favour.

44:1—12 The River—Water, especially in the dry countries of the E is a familiar symbol of abundance, whether of earthly or spiritual benefits, cf Jn 4:14; 7:38. Sometimes it may also indicate punishment, Is 8:5. The symbol is not confined to Israelite tradition. Apart from the utility of water, its movement suggests life: 'Of all inanimate things that which has the best

marked supernatural associations among the Semites is **524a** flowing (or, as the Hebrews say, "living") water', W. Robertson Smith, *The Religion of the Semites*, 1907, 135. So potent are the life-giving waters of the river issuing from the Temple that they even transform the Dead Sea into a fresh-water lake teeming with fish. A descriptive detail is that of the fishermen drying their nets by the Dead Sea. But there will still be salt in the marshes and swamps of that area—no doubt because the Dead Sea region was a highly useful source of that commodity as indeed it still is today.

13—23 The Boundaries—All the tribes will be W of **b** the Jordan. The N boundary is to be from the Mediterranean Sea to the Entrance of Hamath. Evidently it is the limits of David's kingdom under consideration, cf 2 Sm 8:3—12; 2 Kgs 14:25, see Map 6B. The line would be roughly from the present Tripoli to somewhere near Kadesh on Orontes, S through the region of Damascus to a point where it would meet the Jordan W of Gilead. Hauran (Ezek 47:18) is probably a district like Hamath and Damascus, the Assyrian province of Haurina, which had to be included in the messianic kingdom because it contained Aramaean territory subject to David. The **c** E boundary would of course be mainly formed by the Jordan since all the tribes are now envisaged as being settled on the W side. The S boundary is to run through Meribath-kadesh ('Ain Qudeis), probably Kadesh Barnea, to the Brook of Egypt (Wadi el-'Arish) and the Mediterranean Sea. The W limit would be the Mediterranean Sea up as far as a point roughly W of the Entrance of Hamath. This would include most of Phoenicia.

48:1—35 The Distribution of the Land—Ezek begins **d** by giving foreigners in the Holy Land a share in its territory. The distinction between Jew and Gentile tends to disappear in the messianic kingdom. He then assigns a strip of land to each of the twelve tribes, seven to the N and five to the S of the previously reserved territory. The order from N to S is: Dan, Asher, Naphtali, Manasseh, Ephraim, Reuben, Judah, the reserved territory, Benjamin, Simeon, Issachar, Zebulun, Gad. Each tribe divides its land by lot among its families and alien residents. Judah and Benjamin have privileged positions next to the sanctuary. The tribes of servile origin on the mother's side, Dan, Asher, Naphtali and Gad are furthest removed from the sanctuary. Levi has no portion among the tribes. Therefore the Levites in the reserved territory are a tribal unit, not merely degraded priests. Ezek's distribution is mathematical. He takes no account of tribes that have disappeared anciently like Reuben and Simeon, or recently like those of the N Kingdom, nor of the variety in the population of the tribes and the fertility of the land. The recon- **e** stitution which he contemplates is not practical; it is ideal, or messianic. A recapitulation of the description of the reserved territory gives new information about the city. It will be peopled by members of all twelve tribes. It will have twelve gates named after the twelve sons of Jacob, not the twelve tribes, because Joseph and Levi replace Ephraim and Manasseh. Lastly, the name of the city will be **Yahweh is there** (RSV 'The Lord').

DANIEL

BY M. McNAMARA M.S.C.

525a Bibliography—*General:* W. Baumgartner, 'Ein Viertel-jahrhundert Danielforschung', TRu 11 (1939), 59ff, 125ff, 201ff; 1962[4], EOT Int., 1965, 512—29, 588—90. *Commentaries*: S. R. Driver, CBSC, 1922; J. A. Montgomery, ICC, 1927; J. Göttsberger, BB, 1928; R. H. Charles, Oxford, 1929; id, CAP, I, 625—64; A. Bentzen, HAT, 1952[2]; J. Linder, CSS, 1939 (a revised version of Knabenbauer's work in the same series); A. Jeffrey, IB, 1956; P. J. de Menasce BJ, 1958[2]; N. W. Porteous, ATD, 1963, text cited; E. tr. *Daniel: a Commentary*, 1965; P. G. Rinaldi, SacB, 1962[4], 29—34.
Special Studies: H. Junker, *Untersuchungen über litera-rische und exegetische Probleme des Buches Daniel*, Bonn, 1932; H. L. Ginsberg, *Studies in Daniel*, (Texts and Studies of the Jewish Seminary of America), New York, 1948; H. H. Rowley, *Darius the Mede and the Four World Empires in the Book of Daniel*, Cardiff, 1935; Werner Dommershauser, *Nabonid im Buch Daniel*, Mainz, 1964; C. Kuhl, 'Die drei Männer im Feuer (Daniel Kapitel 3 und seine Zusätze)', BZAW, 55, 1930; F. Zimmermann, 'The Story of Susanna and its Original Language', JQR 48 (1957—58), 236—41; R. A. F. MacKenzie, 'The Meaning of the Susanna Story', Cana-dian JTh 3 (1957), 211—18; F. Zimmermann, 'Bel and the Dragon', VT 8 (1958), 438—40; M. Noth, 'Noah, Daniel und Hiob in Ez xvi', VT 1 (1951), 251—60.

b The Person of the Prophet—Our information about Daniel is derived solely from the book that bears his name. The name Daniel (Heb. (1:6) *Dny'l*, vocalized *Daniyyē'l*, = 'God judges' or 'God rules') occurs in the name lists of the post-exilic period (Ez 8:2; Neh 10:6) and was probably also borne by a son of David (cf 1 Chr 3:1 but cf 2 Sm 3:3). It corresponds to the Akkadian *Danilu* which is attested as a proper name from c. 2000 B.C. (cf De Fraine VDom. 25 [1947], 127). The Daniel (Heb. *Dn'l*, vocalized *Dani'ēl* by the later Massoretes) mentioned in Ezek 14:14—20; 28:3 and given as a pattern of wisdom and righteousness is no contemporary of the exilic prophet Ezekiel. His connection with Noah and Job (14:14) shows that he is a character of hoary antiquity. The radicals of the Hebrew names (*Dny'l* and *Dn'l*) also differ, cf § 513g. A legendary figure mentioned in Ugaritic litera-ture bears the same name (*Dn'l*, vocalized Dan'il, or Dan'el) as the person in Ezek; both may refer to the same person or be based on similar traditions; cf P. Joüon, Bib 19 (1938), 283—5; B. Mariani, *Danel, 'il patriarca sapiente'* . . . Rome 1945.

c From the book of Daniel we learn that the protagonist was led captive to Babylon by Nebuchadnezzar in the 3rd year of Jehoiakim, king of Judah (605 B.C.). According to Jos. (Ant. 10, 10, 1), dependent seemingly on Dn 1:2; 2 (4) Kgs 24:14—17; cf 2 Chr 36:6f, Daniel belonged to the royal family of Zedekiah, the last king of Judah. Together with other Jewish youths Daniel was educated at the royal court of Babylon, where, however, they all

kept to their religious practices. Daniel's extraordinary **525** skill in the interpretation of dreams raised him to a position of the highest rank in the Babylonian empire. After the fall of the Neo-Babylonian kingdom Daniel remained in power during the reign of Darius, who con-templated making him chief minister over his whole realm. Daniel fared well also during the reign of King Cyrus, remaining in exile at least until the 3rd years of this king (10:1) i.e. until 536—535 B.C.

Contents and Analysis—The general theme of the **d** book is the uniqueness of the God of the Israelites and his superiority over all heathen gods. This is demonstrated by the experiences of Daniel and of his companions (chh 1—6 and ch 14) and by the prediction of a universal and lasting reign of peace and justice (chh 7—12). This theme makes the p.c. section of the book fall naturally into two parts, chh 1—6 and chh 7—12. In part 1, which may be called 'the stories section' some of the experiences of Daniel and his companions in the court of Babylon are narrated in order to show the uniqueness of the God of the Jews. In part 2, or 'the visions section', Daniel relates his visions and their interpretation.

The two parts differ from one another both in literary form and in historical outlook. In part I the writer is mainly concerned with the Neo-Babylonian empire and hardly displays any interest in the Persian and Greek age. His interest is, moreover, centred on three kings and the four Jewish youths, particularly Daniel. No mention is made of the general situation of the Jewish exiles. In part 2 the writer's attention is concentrated on the age of Antiochus IV (175—164 B.C.) and he is horrified at the sight of the persecuted Israelites. His sorrow is assuaged not by the remembrance of a glorious past, but by the hope of a brighter future. The Babylonian age has no part in his visions, but he describes the Seleucid domination with a richness of detail unusual in prophecy.

The Apocalyptic Character of the Book—Dn belongs **e** to that class of Jewish literature called Apocalyptic, in vogue from the 2nd cent. B.C. until the 2nd cent. A.D. For a description of the genre, see § 454a. The apocalyptic writers derived their influence from their firm belief in God's promises of a better age and from their unshakeable conviction in his universal providence which they express-ed in a literary form that was the product of the time. In this way they helped to strengthen the faith of their contemporaries and keep them united together as one soul inseparably attached to God amidst all persecutions. This literary form of apocalyptic was especially useful during the persecutions of Antiochus when the sacred books of Judaism were sought out and burned (1 Mc 1:56f) and the royal inspectors went through Judah enforcing the edict of persecution (1Mc 1:51). The divine message conveyed under the form of visions would more easily pass unnoticed then it would if written in a directly didactic or historical style.

Position in the Canon—In LXX, Theodotion and Vg **f** Dn ranks fourth among the major prophets, while in MT it

650

25f is classed among the Hagiographa. The difference may by explained by assuming that the book became recognized as inspired, and was added to the canon, when the collection of prophetic writings had already been closed, see § 14*e*. The Jews of Alexandria arranged the books of the OT according to criteria of apparent date and literary form, and so Dn found itself among the prophets. It was received as canonical in Judaism most probably in the 2nd cent. B.C. as 1 Mc 2:59f (written c. 100 B.C.) cites examples from the book as well as from other works of the canon. It is not certain that Daniel was accepted as canonical in Qumran; cf DJD 1 (1955), 150; 3 (1963), 114—16.

g The Deuterocanonical Additions—The Gr. and Vg versions of Dn have some sections which are not in the Heb.—Aram. text. They are: the prayer of Azariah (3: 24—45); the Song of the three children preceded by a prose interlude (3:46—90); the story of Susanna (ch 13 in LXX and Vg) and the story of Bel and the Dragon (ch 14 in LXX and Vg). None of these sections appears to have formed part of the original work. The Qumran text of Dn 3:22—28 (1QDan, 50—1 B.C.) is identical with the MT and shows no indication that anything has been omitted. Chh 13 and 14 were probably composed in Heb. or Aram. in the 2nd cent. B.C. and belong to the rich Danielic literature that apparently then existed (cf § 454*d*). The hymns of ch 3 were probably inspired compositions that once circulated independently and were conveniently inserted into their present contexts. Dn 3:24—45 was probably composed in the 2nd cent. B.C. (cf § 529*e*). The canonicity of all these passages, (cf § 16*e*), is recognized by the Church.

h The Language Problem—In the Heb. Bible Dn is written in two languages. 1:1—2:4*a* and chh 8—12 are in Heb.; while 2:4*b*—7:28 are in Aram. The languages of the Qumran fragments are the same as those of MT, the text of 1QDan 2:2—6 changing from Heb. to Aram. at 2:4 as in the MT. The d.c. sections are preserved only in Gr. Various views have been put forward to explain the bilingual character of the p.c. work (see Eissfeldt, p. 516). Many believe the language of the entire work was either Heb. or Aram., parts of which were later translated. Others consider both languages as original and attribute the bilingual phenomenon to the sources used or to the fact that the work was first published in parts and later combined in book form. The bilingual character of the work is probably original and is in some way connected with the composition of the book. The problem, however, still remains as uncertain as the pre-history and composition of the book itself.

i Text and Versions—Our oldest texts of Dn are from Qumran Cave 1 (published in DJD 1 [1955], 150—2) with Dn 1:10—17; 2:2—6; 3:22—28; 3:27—30 and Cave 6 (published in DJD 3 [1962], 114—16) with Dn 8:20—21 (?); 10;8—16; 11:33—36 and 11:38. These texts date from c. 50—1 B.C. and c. A.D. 50 respectively. All the Qumran texts are identical with our present MT, some minor differences, mostly orthographical, apart. This seems to indicate that Dn had a fixed text already in the 1st cent. B.C., some hundred years after its composition. The Qumran texts are, however, fragmentary, and our MT presents no difficulties in these passages. In other sections of MT the Heb.—Aram. original seems to have been badly preserved and shows many discrepancies from the early versions, which, in some cases, make better sense. This does not necessarily prove that these versions were made from an original differing from the present MT: the discrepancies from MT may be due to interpretative renderings or to traditions not conserved in MT.

The obscurities of MT are understandable when we con- **525i** sider that the author who gave us our present book seems to have re-worked earlier traditions and that this work which was composed c. 166 B.C. may have later been glossed and altered before our present definitive MT was established. Despite its obscurities and seemingly corrupt readings the MT of Dn represents, on the whole, the substance of the original.

The earliest versions are LXX and Theodotion. The **j** former was probably made in the 2nd cent. B.C. and when compared with the latter it looks more like a paraphrase than a translation (A. Bludau, 'Die alexandrinische Übersetzung des Buches Daniel und ihr Verhältniss zum massoretischen Text, Bib St, 2 [2/3, 1897], 206). On account of its divergences from the MT it was never received in the Church (Jer PL 25, 514) and is now extant only in a single MS (*Codex Chisianus*, 11th cent.) and in a fragmentary form (3:72—6:18; 7:1 —8:27) in some Chester Beatty papyri from the first half of the 3rd cent. The Syro-Hexaplaric version is made from LXX. The LXX of Dn was, from a very early date, superseded by the version of Theodotion c. A.D. 180. This is probably a revised edition of an older version made from the MT and independent of the LXX (H. B. Swete, *Introd. to the OT in Greek*, 48).

The Vg is made from the Heb.—Aram. text current in Jerome's time, a text that was very closely related to, if not identical with, our present MT. Occasionally Jer follows Theodotion in the p.c. section. He translated the d.c. sections from Theodotion.

Date and Authorship—The traditional view of both **526a** Jews and Christians has been that the author of the book was the 6th cent. Daniel, episodes from whose life are recounted in chh 1—6. The first to propound a contrary view was the pagan Neo-Platonic philosopher Porphyry (died c. A.D. 304) who attributed the work to an anonymous writer living in the time of Antiochus Epiphanes, 175—164 B.C. (Jer. PL 25, 491). This view, which soon fell into oblivion, was revived in the 17th cent. and became common from the 19th cent. onwards. It is the theory which, in one form or another, is generally held today.

The arguments for this later dating of the book are **b** many and convergent. The *Hebrew* of the work resembles that of writings subsequent to Neh, rather than that of the exilic prophet Ezek. The *Aram.*, too, represents a more recent form of the language than that of the 5th cent. papyri and of Ez (G. R. Driver JBL 45 [1926], 118). The presence of at least 15 Persian loan words and 2 Gr. words argues a date from the late Persian or early Gr. period as the earliest possible time of composition. The *religious phraseology* is that of the later post-exilic period and not that of the exilic age. God, for instance, is never called 'Yahweh' except in a citation in 9:2 and in a liturgical passage of the same ch. Instead, he is referred to by the metonym 'heaven'.

The **historical inaccuracies** of the book indicate **c** that the author could not have lived or written in the 6th cent. B.C. The siege of Jerusalem and deportation in Jehoiakim's 3rd year (605 B.C.) recounted in 1:1f is unknown to oriental history. In ch 5 Belshazzar is called son of Nebuchadnezzar and made last king of Babylon. We know that the last king of Babylon was Nabonidus, whose son, Belshazzar, was never really king and had no blood relation with Nebuchadnezzar.

Again, the person, work and prophecies of Daniel seem to have been entirely unknown before the Maccabean period (1 Mc 2:59f). Ben Sira (c. 185 B.C.) does not include Daniel in his praises of the great men of Israel from Enoch to Simon, son of Onias (d. 196 B.C.) though the

526c three major and four minor prophets receive mention (48: 29—49:10).

d The visions of Daniel with their mass of historical detail such as the marriage of a royal daughter (11:17) and unsuccessful political alliances (11:8) are completely different from the style of the earlier prophets. It is improbable that such minor details would be the objects of a divine revelation. The literary form of the book is nearer to the apocalyptic, current in the 2nd cent. B.C., than to the prophetic. The very doctrine of the book points to the same age. What it has to say on the angels, their office and names as well as on the resurrection and final retribution represent the teaching and phraseology of the later post-exilic period rather than the exilic age as we know this from Ezek and Deutero—Isaiah.

For these reasons, it is generally accepted today that the book as it now stands was composed c. 166 B.C. There are those who wish to connect the visions in some way with an exilic prophet of the name Daniel. Kruse, for instance, (VDom. 37 [1959], 147—61; 193—211) considers the book to be an exilic writing that was re-edited in c. 300 B.C. and c. 164 B.C. The exilic basis is quite uncertain though there are certainly older traditions in chh 1—6 and possibly in 7—12. The fact remains, however, that our present book is from Maccabean times and it is as such that the exegete must interpret.

e The Maccabean date of chh 8—12 is now generally admitted. Some expositors detach ch 7 (written in Aram.) from 8—12 (written in Heb.) and consider it pre-Maccabean. The pre-Maccabean character of chh 1—6, and thus the unity of our book, is also debated. Most commentators take these chh to be earlier than 7—12 and place their composition c. 300 B.C. H. H. Rowley defends the unity of the entire work and a Maccabean date for chh 1—6 (HUCA 23 [1950—51], 233—73; VT 5 [1955], 272—6) though he admits that the Maccabean author of our book used earlier sources in the composition of chh 1—6. There are arguments for both views. On the one hand chh 1—6 differ from 7—12 in the occurrence of Persian words and Babylonian setting of these chh. Neither Nebuchadnezzar nor Darius can in any way be taken as types of the impious persecutor Antiochus, cf however § 531c. On the other hand the same phraseology and fictitious chronology, with the Median kingdom before the Persian, appears in both parts cf §528a—c; 531h.

f The time seems ripe for a reconsideration of the pre-history of Dn 1—6, or at least chh 2—5, in the light of non-biblical material recently published and of other relevant texts that have for long been known. We give a summary of this evidence below, proceeding from the better to the less known. We shall return to it later as we believe it throws some light on the pre-history of Dn 2—5 and consequently on the composition of the work and on the question of its unity.

g (1) Ch 4. It was perceived by F. Hommel. (Theol. Literaturblatt 23 [1902], 145ff; 204ff) and E. Dhorme (RB 9 [1912], 37ff) that the account of Nebuchadnezzar's madness and banishment from his kingdom in ch 4 is based on Nabonidus' withdrawal from Babylon to the oasis of Taima. 'Nebuchadnezzar' of this ch is then the Nabonidus of history. That such is the case is now made clear by a Qumran text (4QOrNab, published provisionally by J. T. Milik in RB 63 [1956], 407—11; E.tr. in G. Vermes The DSS in English, 1962, 229) from c. 50—1 B.C. The Qumran text parallels, but is not identical with, Dn 4 and recounts the cure of Nabunai, i.e. Nabonidus, king of Babylon who was afflicted by a grievous ulcer for 7 years in Taima. He was cured, however, not by Daniel but by an anonymous Jewish exorcist (cf § 530i). The Harran

inscriptions of Nabonidus, published and studied by **526** C. J. Gadd (Anatolian Studies 8 [1958], 35—92) tell us of this sojourn in Taima and in the surrounding Arabian desert. The inscriptions, which have certain similarities with Dn 4, inform us that the withdrawal from his capital was occasioned by the opposition of the Marduk clergy and the people of Akkad towards the religion of the moon-god Sin which he wished to introduce. The sojourn lasted for the period of 10 years predetermined by his god Sin (cf Dn 4:13f). At the appointed time he returned to his capital and was well received by his people (cf Dn 4:36). During the desert sojourn it appears that he had communities of Jews in his company. This seems to indicate that Dn 4 is based on historical events of the reign of Nabonidus (556—539 B.C.) Later Jewish tradition, or the editor of Dn, has worked over this material, replacing the name Nabonidus with the better-known Nebuchadnezzar and possibly giving the name Daniel to the anonymous Jewish protagonist of the earlier account.

(2) Ch 5 in which Belshazzar, the son of Nabonidus, **h** is called the son of Nebuchadnezzar corroborates this view of ch 4. Before A.D. 1887 when it was deciphered in cuneiform texts, the name Belshazzar was unknown outside Dn and Bar 1:11 and texts dependent on them. The fidelity with which Dn has preserved the name shows the book retains certain clear links with exilic times. In ch 5, however, the father of Belshazzar has taken on certain traits of Nebuchadnezzar (cf 5:3, 13). Again, the episode is probably a rewriting of earlier material that may go back to exilic times; cf § 531bc.

(3) Chh 2 and 3 may also be connected with traditions **i** originally associated with Nabonidus. His own inscriptions and the censorious remarks of the Marduk clergy bear witness to this king's preoccupation with dreams and their interpretation cf § 527f. Nabonidus considered himself called by Sin to restore the moon-god's temple at Harran, reintroduce there the god's statue and restore Sin's cult to its rightful place in his kingdom. Nabonidus speaks of his dreams disturbing him in a manner reminiscent of Dn 2:1; 4:1. A dream-vision of Sin during his accession year bade him restore that god's temple. This he apparently did in his 3rd year. 'Nebuchadnezzar's' first dream in his problematical 2nd year (see on 2:1) may then be based on a vision of Nabonidus just before the rededicaton of the Harran temple during his third year and the solemn transfer there from Babylon of the statue of Sin. The statue set up by 'Nebuchadnezzar' (ch 3) would then be the statue of Sin which Nabonidus made at Babylon and which enraged the Marduk clergy see § 527f. These chh, then, are probably based on traditions connected with Nabonidus. As they stand in Dn, however, they represent a later adaptation of earlier sources, an adaptation due in part, if not entirely, to the Maccabean editor; cf e.g. 2:43.

(4) Ch 6 appears to be an episode from the reign of **j** Darius I (522—486 B.C.) inserted in its present position as a result of the chronology adopted by the editor of the present book, a chronology that makes a Median kingdom under Darius succeed the reign of Belshazzar 5:30f; cf § 528a—c. The exile deported in 605 was then too old (c. 100 years!) for the responsibility conferred on the hero of this chapter. The episode may have originally referred to some anonymous Jew who was later given the name Daniel; cf ch 4 and Qumran text.

There are good indications, then, that Dn 2—6 are **k** based on old traditions that go back in good part to exilic times and principally to the reign of Nabonidus. The traditions of these chh most probably took shape among the Jewish communities of Babylonia who retained

26k memories of their relations with Nabonidus and his kingdom. This origin will explain the strong Babylonian colouring of chh 2—6. These traditions may have been taken to Palestine at a later date. W. F. Albright has surmised that the 2nd cent. B.C. saw a return of Jews from Babylon to Jerusalem (cf BASOR 140 [1955], 30, n. 14), who may have taken the traditions of Dn 2—6 with them (cf Freedman BASOR 145 [1957], 31). These earlier traditions were taken up by a later editor, preferably by the author of Dn 7—12, who worked them into a certain unity by replacing the name Nabonidus—unmentioned in biblical records—by the better-known Nebuchadnezzar and by making Daniel the Jewish protagonist of the greater portion of the narratives. It is apparently the Maccabean author of chh 7—12 that is responsible for the chronological framework within which chh 1—6 and the entire book are placed. This same person may have added certain concepts and phraseology of his own in his re-editing of the earlier narratives of chh 1—6.

l We may thus give our view on the origin of the book of Dn: chh 7—12 (i.e. the Visions) are from Maccabean times (c. 166 B.C.). The author of this part prefaced his visions by traditions that originated in Babylon, some of which show a close relation with the events of the reign of Nabonidus. He worked over this earlier material and imprinted a certain unity on it without, however, removing all traces of its earlier and independent origin. He placed the entire work within a fictitious chronology, for some reason unknown to us. We believe that this view is well-founded on the evidence of the book of Dn itself and has the support of extra-biblical material. What the real historical content of chh 2—6 is we cannot now say. It is quite possible that future discoveries will throw more light on this aspect of the question.

m **The Purpose and Doctrine of the Book** These critical questions on the book's pre-history are secondary from the point of view of the inspired author's message. The purpose of the Maccabean writer who gave us the work as it now lies before us was to strengthen his loyal coreligionists during Antiochus' campaign to stamp out Judaism. The practices of the true religion were then forbidden under pain of torture and death (1 Mc 1:60—64; 2 Mc 6—9). The sacred books of the Law were sought out and destroyed (1 Mc 1:56f). Even before the actual persecution broke out the faith of many in Israel had grown weak (cf 1 Mc 1:11); the savage persecution must have made many others doubt the reality of divine providence. In order to give comfort and strength to the confessors of the true religion the author of Dn put before them the examples of earlier Jews who remined loyal to their religion and who were saved and rewarded by God for their fidelity, winning respect for their faith among the Gentiles. This was the teaching of Dt 4:6 etc. Throughout these chh (1—6) the author insists on the reality of God's dominion over the affairs of men and on his special providence towards Israel. He recalls how God punished those who acted sacrilegiously towards the sacred vessels of the temple (5:2, 23), a reminder of the fate that awaited Antiochus (cf 1 Mc 1:21—23; 6:12f). In the second part (7—12) he shows how the entire course of their sad history was foreseen by God and assures them that this same God will destroy their oppressors and bestow eternal glory on those who remain loyal to him.

n The **doctrine of the book** revolves about the central theme of **God** as **the eternal Master of History**. This teaching the author had from the earlier prophets. Is 17:3—6 depicts God enthroned peacefully above the world, ready to intervene in its affairs when he sees fitting. Man's feeble efforts will not alter his plans. From Jeremiah Israel learned that God controls the destinies **526n** of Israel and her pagan neighbours alike, as a potter his clay (Jer 18:1—12). He plants and uproots nations at will (18:7ff; etc), punishing all indiscrimately for their sins (Jer 25:15ff). The author of Dn takes this doctrine and, by the aid of popular narrative and apocalyptic vision, brings it anew before the mind of his hard-pressed contemporaries. **God's Kingdom is not merely something of the future. It is ever active in the affairs of men.** He is a living God (6:27), the King of Kings and Lord of heaven and earth (cf 2:47). He makes kings and unmakes them (2:21). His kingdom is an everlasting kingdom and his dominion endures through all generations (3:100; MT 3:33). Human rulers are expected to acknowledge this dominion and God ordains events to show them how he can bring low their pride when they refuse to do so. 'Nebuchadnezzar' acknowledged it and had his kingdom restored to him (4:31—34), while the blasphemous behaviour of his son Belshazzar spelled the end of the dynasty (ch 5). God is sole master of human affairs and has not left humanity without divine guidance as to his will. This can be found, not by pagan diviners, but by revelation made to members of his chosen people. Pagan magicians prove helpless when there is question of the divine significance of events (2:7—10, 19ff; 4:4ff; 5:8, 11ff) God rules over the kingdom of men and gives it to whom he wills (4:22, 29). His providence towards the faithful confessors of Israel in the past (chh 1—6) is guarantee of this people's final supremacy. The author, however, sees humanity as progressively deteriorating and growing ever stronger in its opposition to God. To illustrate this point he chooses a succession of four kingdoms (chh 2 and 7). He has here in all probability, the Babylonian, 'Median', Persian and Greek empires in mind, but is more interested in these as symbols of human kingdoms in general than as a mere historical succession of four powers. Human malice and arrogance reaches its zenith with Antiochus Epiphanes of the Greek empire. This tyrant acts as if he were God himself, setting aside the cult of the true God for his own and even changing the times and seasons (cp 7:25 with 2:21). In the apocalyptic section we are shown how this was all foreseen by God. Finally, when human rule has become so perverted as to constitute opposition to everything divine, God intervenes in history. In the magnificent vision of 7:9—14 (cp 2:44f) we see judgement passed on the earthly kingdoms and the introduction of the Kingdom of God, symbolized by 'one like a son of man', i.e., like a human being. The kingship over human events that is God's by right (3:100; MT 3:33) now becomes a reality on earth in the saints of the Most High, i.e., in God's chosen people. This kingdom is a universal and everlasting one in which all dominions will serve and obey God (7:14, 27).

Messianism—This universal and everlasting rule of God **o** on earth is, of course, the messianic kingdom. It will be introduced by God himself without human aid (2:34, 44f). One may be surprised that no mention is made of the person of the Messiah. Some authors have, indeed, thought that by 'one like a son of man' (7:13f) the Messiah is intended. As will be seen at greater length in the exegesis of this passage and in excursuses, (cf §§ 527m, 528e, 534c), the 'one like a son of man' is no more that a symbol for God's Kingdom, the Saints of the Most High or the pious Israelites. All, for our book, mean one and the same thing. The messianism of the entire book is, then, impersonal. The author concentrates his attention on the introduction of the Kingdom itself and makes no mention of the Son of David who will rule this kingdom. In this he is in line with the general messianic teaching of the late

526o exilic, Persian and early Greek period. The glorious future God has prepared for his people was always more central to Jewish teaching than the person of the Messiah. Even such a classical messianic prophet as Isaiah could speak of this without mentioning the new Davidic King (cf Is 2:2—4; 1:25—28; cp 32:1ff). The disillusionment brought about by the behaviour of historical kings of the House of David led such prophets as Jer and Ezek to concentrate on the new reign of Yahweh. The same is true of Deutero—Isaiah and some post-exilic prophets. It was only after the age in which Dn was written that Jewish attention reverted to the role of a personal Messiah in God's New Kingdom on earth. Belief in this role was well established by NT times, as we know from Jewish writings and the NT itself. The messianic teaching of Dn is none the less important for this. In fact, we can say that in our book this teaching reaches a peak by laying stress on the supernatural character of this kingdom, its heavenly origin, its universal and everlasting character. And when the prophecies were realized the kingdom was introduced by a personal Messiah, calling himself the Son of Man, who, besides being Son of David, was also truly Son of God.

p **The Future Life**—In the author's vision God's kingdom is ushered in after the destruction of Antiochus Epiphanes (7:11—14; 25—27; 8:25f; 9:26f). Strangely enough, he fails to mention the introduction of this kingdom after his description of the death of Epiphanes in 11:40—45. Instead, he goes on to speak of a new period of unsurpassed distress for God's people. The just, destined for eternal life, will be spared during this new crisis (12:1). These, and other just of former generations to be raised from the dead, will then enjoy eternal life and shine like stars in the firmament, while the wicked are destined for eternal opprobrium (12:3f, 13). We have here the first clear teaching among the Jews of the bodily resurrection of the individual Israelite. It is the main contribution of the work to the deposit of faith. This belief sustained the martyrs during the persecution of Epiphanes (cf 2 Mc 7) and may have been known in Israel before the time of the author of Daniel (cf Is 26:19). The doctrine of the resurrection as found in Dn 12:1—3, 13 lacks that clarity later teaching will give it. Firstly, the text does not state clearly whether this new life will be lived in heaven or on earth. Then again, our author mentions the resurrection of only some of the Israelites. The resurrection of the Gentiles does not interest him. It is also probable that he speaks of the resurrection of the just only (see to 12:1—3). This, apparently, is also how *Ps. Sal.* 3, 13—16 (c. 50 B.C.) understood the text. Later revelation will fill in these outlines and show how the resurrection is universal, for Jew and Gentile, just and damned.

q **Determination of the Time and the Hour**—One could get the impression from Dn that the Kingdom of God was to follow immediately on the time-reckonings given to him (7:25—27; 9:24—27; 12:6f, 11f). Yet, the divine reply to a question of his on the matter was that the book was sealed (12:9). While the apocalyptic seer may have expected the fulfilment of his prophecies to coincide with the downfall of Antiochus, the exact time of fulfilment was not revealed to him. This lack of perspective is common in prophecy. The exact hour of fulfilment is never revealed and the reason, apparently, is that in most, if not all, of God's prophecies there is an element of divine pedagogy. Prophecies are part of God's plan for man's salvation and man's response is taken into account in the time of their fulfilment (see to Jer 18:1—12). A hundred years is to God as one day (2 Pt 3:9). He reveals to none either the day nor the hour of their fulfilment (Mk 13:32; Mt 24:36; Ac 1:7).

The Angels are often mentioned by Daniel. Myriads **526r** of them surround God's throne, ever ready to minister to him (3:25; 7:10) and to execute his decrees (4:13, 17). Gabriel bears God's message to Daniel (9:21f; cf 10:4ff etc) and explains to him the significance of his visions (8:6; 9:21). Angels save the youths in the fiery furnace (3:28) and Dn in the lions' den (6:22). Michael is the patron angel of Israel (10:13, 21; 12:1). Even pagan nations have guardian angels to defend their cause before God (10:13, 20).

The principles enunciated in the book are as relevant **s** now as they were in the time of Antiochus, and the message of the work is as lasting as that of the Apocalypse, its NT counterpart. Above historical events God sits enthroned, governing human affairs, overcoming evil and ever leading his people towards their final destiny. For us, as for Dn, the final denouement of this drama remains a mystery. The consummation will come 'at the appointed time'. We, like him, must await the fulfilment.

1:1—21 Deportation and Education of Daniel and **527a** **his Companions**—The account as it stands serves as an introduction to the narrative (chh 2—6) and vision sections (chh 7—12) of the book, though it may once have circulated as an independent unit; cf 1:21.

1:1f Daniel's Deportation—The Bible knows nothing of a deportation at this date though it gives detailed information for the period (cf Jer 25:1ff with 46:2; 36: 1—29). The Babylonian Chronicle of the period (cf E. Vogt, Bib 37 [1956] 389—97) agrees with 2 (4) Kgs and mentions no siege or deportation before those of 598. It appears that Dn 1:1f depends on a tradition that confuses Jehoiachin and Jehoiakim, and places the siege of 598 in the latter's reign: cf 2 (4) Kgs 24:10—16 with 2 Chr 36:6—10. Cf however E. Vogt, Bib 37 (1956), 395f. This is but one of the anachronisms of our didactic book: (cf § 526c ff). The sacrilegious use of the temple vessels will bring a divine punishment on Belshazzar (5:2f, 23f)—as a similar crime will later do for Antiochus Epiphanes; 1 Mc 1:21—24; 6:12f. Shinar is an archaic appellation for Babylon connoting its idolatry (Gn 11:1ff) and iniquity (Zech 5:5—11). 'And he placed the vessels in the treasury of his god' is probably a gloss. The chief deity of the Babylonians was Marduk, also called Bel, (4:1—22) whose temple Esagila was renowned. Nebuchadnezzar is an alternative form of the more usual Nebuchadrezzar, which corresponds to the Akkadian *Nabukudurri-uṣur.* 'Nabu (= Nebo), protect the boundary.'

3—7 The Education of Daniel and his Com- **b** **panions—3f.** At the siege of 598 Nebuchadnezzar deported princes and craftsmen together with king Jehoiachin (2 (4) Kgs 4:10—17). Education in Babylonia had begun some millennia before Daniel's time. The Sumerians passed on to later generations the custom of initiating young scribes into the difficult art of writing cuneiform. It was also in the interest of the unity of the Assyrian and Babylonian Empires to have foreign nobility well versed in the language and literature of Babylon, as their loyalty on repatriation would be thus better assured. It is uncertain, however, what 'the letters and language of the Chaldeans' means here. It may be the cuneiform or Aramaic language and the general culture of the Chaldeans or Neo-Babylonian empire. On the Chaldeans see § 65e—k. After the fall of Babylon 'Chaldeans' came to mean a class of professional wise men (Herodotus I, 181, 183); in Strabo the term means a class of Babylonian wise men devoted to astronomy, while in Diodorus Siculus (II, 29—31; cf Pliny, *Natural History* 6, 30) it means a caste of priestly magicians. In Dn 2:2, 4f, 10; 4:7 (Mt 4:4); 5:7—11 and perhaps in 3:8 'Chaldeans' mean this

527b learned class. In term is a general one including wise
c men; magicians, enchanters and sorcerers; cf 2:2,
4. Magic was forbidden by the Mosaic Law (Lv 20:27;
Dt 18:10—12) but it is nowhere said that Daniel
or his companions ever practised this art. It is also
possible that in 4 'the letters of the Chaldeans' denotes the Babylonian culture in general, and not necessarily astrology; cf 17 **5f.** Among the many students,
our book is interested only in the four Jews who figure
in the following chh. The change of name signified their
subjection to a new power (cf Gn 41:45; 2 [4] Kgs 23:34;
24:10, 17). Daniel's new name Belteshazzar probably
represents the Akkadian *balâtsu-uṣur* or *balât-šar-uṣur*
'protect his life' or 'protect the life of the king'. In its
Heb. form, Belteshazzar, it recalled Bel i.e. Marduk,
the God of Babylon (4:5). Abednego, the new name of
Azariah (= 'Yahweh is helper') may represent the
Babylonian *Abdi-Nabu* 'Servant of (the god) Nebo'.
Shadrach, given to Mananiah (= 'Yahweh is gracious')
may be a graphic change of Marduk, the radicals of both
names being similar in the square Heb. script. The
meaning of Meshach given to Mishael ('= who is what
God is') is uncertain, possibly 'who is like (the God)
Aku; in Akkadian *Mi-šu-Aku*, Aku being another name for
the moon-god Sin.

**d 8—16 The Loyalty of the Youths to their Religion—
8.** Among the humiliations of exile for a Jew stood the
sojourn in an impure land (Am 7:17) and the necessity
of eating unclean food (Hos 9:3). Certain foods were
prohibited to the Jews (Lv 11), and in pagan countries
the wine and meat may have been offered to the gods
before being served at table. It was forbidden to partake
of such food because of the danger of idolatry (Dt 32:38;
Ac 15:29; cf 1 Cor 10:21). Daniel and his friends determine to abide by the Jewish ritual law (ct 16 1:10—13)
requesting the chief eunuch Ashpenaz (3) to be permitted
to live on other food. **9f.** Though favourably inclined
towards the request, his position did not permit him to
run risks. **11—13.** The request for the ten-day trial on
pure food is addressed to the steward (Heb. *ha-melṣur*,
taken as a proper name by early versions), a subordinate
official under Ashpenaz, who had the immediate charge
of the youths. **14—16.** The effects being less serious for
him, the request is granted. The results are excellent and
the diet is continued for the entire period of their
eduction.

**e 17—20 Daniel and his Companions introduced to
the King—17.** God rewarded the youths' loyalty to their
religion by extraordinary wisdom. This consisted chiefly in
the knowledge of those moral and practical principles that
were necessary for the high positions which they were
later to occupy. God's special gift to Daniel was the
power of interpreting visions and dreams. Chaldean
priests claimed to be able to interpret dreams and
visions after a course of study; Dn (2:11; 4:3f; 5:8)
will show the futility of their science. Daniel will insist
on the divine origin of his charism when he employs it
(2:27f, 47; 4:6). Dreams were considered in the ancient
East as possibly containing divine messages: hence the
importance attached to their interpretation. For the Bible
see e.g. Gn 37:5—10; 40—41; Nm 12:6; Jb 7:14; Mt
27:19 etc. **18—20.** The king finds the youths wiser
than any of his own state magicians: this superiority
will be brought out in chh. 2, 4 and 5. All four youths
entered the king's service. **21.** The first year of Cyrus
is 539, when he became king of the Neo-Babylonian
empire. The chronology of the v differs from that of 6:1
and 9:1 where the reign of Darius the Mede is said to have
succeeded the Neo-Babylonian. Daniel was in the court

and service of Cyrus after the king's first year according **527e**
to 6:29 and 10:1. This is a further instance of the lack
of a precise chronology in the book (cf 1:1f) and suggests
that ch 1 once circulated independently of the others.
Introduction to 2 and 3—Believing that chh 2 and 3, **f**
like ch 4, are based on traditions connected with Nabonidus and his cult of the moon-god, Sin, we think it fit
to treat here of some aspects of this king and his reign
that appear to throw light on episodes narrated in
these chh. Nabonidus and his mother were devotees of
the moon-god Sin whose temple, Ehulhul, at Harran
lay in ruins since 610—while the statue of Sin was
taken to Babylon. Nabonidus believed he had a divine
vocation to rebuild Ehulhul and reinstate the statue of
Sin. Both he and his mother believed their deity conveyed
his commands to them in dream-visions.

In his accession year (556 B.C.) Sin in a dream
commanded him to rebuild Ehulhul quickly (Gadd,
Anatolian Studies, 8 (1958), 57; E. Vogt, Bib 40 [1959],
97). This he could not do immediately as the Medes were
in possession of Harran. He appears to have rebuilt the
temple and reinstated the statue in his third year. (E.
Vogt, Bib 40 [1959], 57). He describes the event as
follows: 'Such was the word of the great Lord Marduk
and of Sin . . . I was afraid at their high command, I
was seized with anxiety and my countenance was troubled.
I caused my wide-flung troops to advance from Gaza on
the border of Egypt, from the Upper Sea beyond the
Euphrates to the Lower Sea. The kings, the princes, the
governors and my far-flung troops . . . came to restore
Ehulhul, the temple of Sin that is in Harran' (S.
Smith, *Babylonian Historical Texts*, 1924, 44). This
rededication, as we saw, included the transfer of the
statue of Sin from Babylon to Harran (cf Gadd, 65;
Vogt, 95). This statue appears to have been made before
the rebuilding of Ehulhul (ANET, 313a), and must have
differed from the usual ones. The Marduk-clergy say of
it '[He made the image of a deity] which nobody had
(ever) seen in (this) country . . . he called it by the
name of Nanna (i.e. Sin)' (ANET, 313a). Nabonidus
speaks more than once of his dreams which at times disturbed him (cf Gadd, loc cit 62; Vogt, art cit 94) and had
dream interpreters who gave favourable interpretations
(cf ANET, 309f n. 5). The Marduk-clergy mock his
pretensions of receiving divine revelations in dreams:
'(It was) he who stood up in the assembly to praise
hi[mself], (saying) "I am wise, . . . I have seen what
is hid[den] . . . I have seen se[cret things], the god
Ilte'ri (i.e. Sin) has made me see a vision . . ."' (ANET
314b).

2 Nebuchadnezzar's First Dream—The ch shows **g**
how God's will can be seen in dreams only if the interpreter
is specially enlightened from heaven. Daniel interprets
the king's dream as showing how earthly kingdoms will
pass away and how upon their ruins God will set up a
universal and everlasting kingdom. This dream parallels
the vision of ch 7—and as it stands in Dn is probably a
re-elaboration of earlier traditions. It is similar to the
story of Pharaoh and Joseph in Gn 41.

**1—13 The Magicians unable to interpret the King's h
Dream—1.** The date is inconsistent with 1:5, 18. In the
second year of Nebuchadnezzar Daniel and his companions had not yet completed their course of education,
and could not therefore be involved in the edict issued
against the wise men (13). The difficulty is not solved
by the assumption of a double way of reckoning which
would make Nebuchadnezzar's second year coincide with
the third year of Daniel's education (Goettsberger, 19,
Driver, 17). Other interpreters introduce textual changes

527h and read sixth (Montgomery, 141) or twelfth (Linder, 133) instead of second. The date probably refers to the second year of Nabonidus, and to his dream concerning his statue of Sin, or to the temple Ehulhul which he most probably built during his third year. The effects of the dream on the king recall Nabonidus' own words: 'In the night season a dream was very disturbing . . .' (Gadd op cit 63). **4.** With the reply of the Chaldeans the text changes abruptly from Heb. to Aram., a fact noted in the MT and versions; 'Aramaic', of the MT is, however, probably a gloss. 'O king, live forever' = 'Long live your majesty'. **5f.** The king will not be satisfied with a mere interpretation: they must first give him the contents of the dream itself. This will assure him of the veracity and genuineness of their interpretation (9). 'The word from me is sure, i.e. I proclaim an irrevocable sentence. The king's threat, though severe, was in accord with the custom of the times. Nabonidus is accused of dealing very harshly with his enemies (cf ANET, 312d) and he himself describes as treason the opposition of the priests and people of Babylon to his religious plans (Gadd, 57–59; Vogt, 93). The magnitude of the threat and of the promises indicates the importance the king attached to the dream. **7–9.** Nabonidus and his strained relations with the Marduk-clergy (= Chaldeans) of Babylon are a good background to this passage.

i **14–23 Daniel promises to interpret the Dream— 14f.** Seeing the danger in which the wise men are placed Daniel prudently (cf 1:20) went to Arioch, the royal officer who had already set about giving effect to the edict of extermination. The fact that Daniel had not been consulted, though he had been found ten times wiser than all the magicians of Babylon (1:20), is a further indication that the various episodes of the book had once a separate existence. The royal decree affected him as it did all the other wise men (13). **16** raises a difficulty. Daniel could not enter the king's presence without being introduced, as is expressly noted in 24f. The difficulty is removed by deleting with Theodotion the words 'went in and' (cf CV, BJ). Other commentators see a combination of two sources in the passage and some take 17–24a as a later insertion. **17f.** The designation 'God of Heaven' is found in the post-exilic books of Dn, Tb, Jdt, Ez and Neh, and in the Elephantine Aramaic papyri (5th cent. B.C.) 'Mystery' (Aram. *raz*) is a word of Iranian origin and originally means 'secret'. The term is common in the Qumran writings and in the NT. The secrets of God's mind can be known only through revelation: hence Daniel's request for prayer.

j **24–28a Daniel introduced before the King—26– 28a.** The king puts the same question to Daniel as he did to the diviners (5, 9). The contrast between Daniel and the magicians, and between Judaism and pagan divination, is highlighted. There is a God in heaven who communicates with earth, revealing mysteries to men (cf 11). God had actually done so in the king's dream which referred to events of 'the latter days' (cf Is 2:2; Mi 4:1 etc), i.e. to events beyond the age of Nebuchadnezzar and to the final kingdom which God is to introduce on earth.

k **28b–35 The King's Dream**—Daniel replies clearly and decidedly to the king's wish, giving first the dream (29–35) and then its interpretation (36–45). His interpretation is as certain as his exposition of the dream is clear (45; cf 9). **31.** Compare this description of the terrifying colossal statue with what the 'Verse Account' of the Marduk-clergy has to say on the statue, presumably of Sin, made by Nabonidus: '[When he worshipped it] its appearance became [like that of a . . . demon crowned with] a tiara' (ANET 313b). This important text is, unfortunately, very badly preserved. **32–35.** The statue, presumably of some god, was composed of four metals of decreasing value: gold, silver, bronze and iron. The feet on which the entire colossus rested were of a mixture of iron and tile. This rendered the whole statue extremely weak and it crumbled when a stone cut from a mountain without human agency struck it on the feet. The destruction of the statue was then, due to the weakness of this mixture. The rock, on the contrary, grew to become a great mountain and to fill the entire earth.

36–45 The Interpretation of the Dream—36. The **l** plural 'we' may refer to Daniel and his companions; cf, however, 2 Cor 1:4–14. **37f.** The gold, the most noble of the metals, signified Nebuchadnezzar himself, or rather the Neo-Babylonian kingdom, of whose kings he was the most illustrious. That the kingdom rather than an individual king is intended is indicated by the other metals which signify kingdoms, not kings. The title 'king of kings' was common in the Persian age but was unusual earlier (cf Ez 7:12). Jer 27:6; 28:14 (cf Dn 4:17–19) speaks of God giving the birds of the air into Nebuchadnezzar's hands. His empire stretched from Mesopotamia to the Nile and could be thus considered world wide. We may note the author's interest in universal empires, which will all be destroyed and superseded by God's kingdom. **39.** The other metals signify three other empires that will successively arise after that of Nebuchadnezzar. Little is said of the second and third, except that the second will be inferior to that of Nebuchadnezzar and the third will be universal; cf the third beast of 7:6 and cf 8:4. **40.** Special attention is paid to **m** the fourth kingdom which will be strong and destructive like the iron that symbolizes it; cf 7:7ff; 8:5ff. **41f.** The composite character of the feet indicates that the fourth kingdom will finally be divided into two parts of unequal power. **43.** An attempt will be made by inter-marriages to give a greater stability to the two rival kingdom, but the attempted union will be as unsuccessful as that of iron with tile. These intermarriages are noted in 11:6, 17. **44f.** 'In the days of those kings' i.e. the kings of the entire series of kingdoms that has been mentioned (cf 45). The fifth kingdom, symbolized by the rock hewn from the mountains without human agency (34), will be introduced by God alone. The book will return to this doctrine later (7:13f, 18, 26f; cf 11:34). This final kingdom is said to destroy all the preceding ones, as if the four still existed at its inauguration. This is a detail required by the nature of the image and not by its meaning. In 39ff the kingdoms are said to arise successively.

46–49 Acknowledgement of God's Superiority and n Elevation of Daniel and his Companions—46. The writer's intention is to show how impressed the king was. It is idle to inquire how such a strict monotheist as Daniel could accept divine honours as sacrifice and incense, or whether he accepted them at all. **47.** The titles 'God of gods' and 'Lord of kings' are to be taken in a polytheistic sense (cf 3:29). Nabonidus calls his moon-god Sin 'king of gods', 'lord of lords' (Gadd, 59 etc; cf ANET, 311ff) and boasted that Ilte'ri (= Sin) revealed hidden things to him in a vision (ANET, 314b). 'Lord of kings' was also a title given to earthly rulers; cf Ezek 26:7; Ez 7:12; cf Dt 10:17. **48f.** The king kept his promise (6). The references to the high offices conferred on Daniel and his companions found at the end of chh 1, 2, 3 and 5 (cf 6:28 [29]) suggest that

27n the various episodes of these chh were first recounted as independent narratives.

28a Appendix 1. The Four Kingdoms symbolized by the Statue—It is now generally admitted that the four metals, as interpreted by Dn 2:37–44, symbolize four historical kingdoms. There is agreement about the identification. In determining which kingdoms are referred to in ch 2 we must take ch 7 into consideration as it is generally admitted that the four kingdoms in both chh are the same. Ch 8 must also be considered, since the second beast of this ch appears to correspond to the fourth of ch 7. Finally, we must bear in mind the general **b** chronology of the book. Daniel identified the first kingdom, symbolized by the head of gold, as the Neo-Babylonian (2:38). The fourth empire of ch 2, symbolized by iron, corresponds to the fourth of ch 7 where only the Greek empire can be intended. This is clear from the identification of the fourth beast of ch 7 with the he-goat of ch 8 which symbolizes the Greek empire (8:21). Both beasts are characterized by a small horn growing greater and stronger and making war on the Israelites. This is Antiochus IV. The harsh character of the fourth kingdom is noted in both ch 2 and ch 7: cf 2:40; 7:7, 19. The intermarriages occurring during the fourth kingdom according to 2:43 are those of the Gr. empire mentioned in 11:6, 17. This Gr. kingdom must be taken as that of Alexander and his successors. The Jews (cf 1 Mc 1:1–10) did not distinguish Alexander's reign from that of his successors. For the Jews there was but one Gr. empire, represented mainly by Antiochus IV. This is also the view of Dn The he-goat of ch 8 is the Gr. empire and embraces all the kings down to the time of Antiochus; cf also § 534*a*. The Gr. empire was preceded by that of Persia whose universal dominion is noted in 2:39 and 7:6; cf 8:4 The ram of ch 8 crushed by the he-goat (i.e. Greece) is identified, partially if not entirely, with Persia (8:20; see on 8:3).

c Between the Neo-Babylonian and Persian empires, Dn places a second, insignificant empire. There is no place for this in real history; and this has led some scholars to interpret the four kingdoms as (i) the Neo-Babylonian, (ii) the Medo-Persian, (iii) Alexander's, (iv) that of Alexander's successors. Thus Lagrange, RB 13 (1904) 503ff; D. Buzy, *Les symboles de l'AT, 1923,* 266–80 = RB 27 (1918) 403–26; L. Dennefeld, *Le Messianisme,* 1929, 173. But this division of the Gr. empire is not usual in the Bible, and we have seen that according to Dn an empire of the Medes under Darius is placed between the Neo-Babylonian and the Persian empire. This is probably the second kingdom here and in ch 7. On all these theories see the exhaustive study of H. H. Rowley, *Darius the Mede and the Four World Empires,* 61–173.

d There was a widespread view in early times of a world history growing increasingly worse. In Hesiod (*Works and Days,* 109–201) four ages of such history are spoken of and are symbolized by the metals gold, silver, brass and iron; the same metals as we have in Dn 2. The sequence of kingdoms known in sources of the 2nd cent. B.C. was Assyria, Media, Persia and Greece. It is possible that Dn merely replaced Assyria of this sequence by Babylonia, a kingdom of greater topical interest. On both these points see J. S. Swain in *Classical Philology* 35 (1940), 1–21. This would be in keeping with the general character of the work; cf Nabonidus–Nebuchadnezzar and cf § 526*k*. The actual historical sequence was of less interest to Daniel as these four kingdoms in his work appear to have a symbolic value, representing the course of history before the inauguration of the kingdom of God.

Some authors e.g. Eerdmans, *The Religion of Israel,* Leiden, 1947, 222–7 Löwinger (cf Bib 30 [1949],

126f; Kruse (VDom. 37 [1959], 156f), believe the **528d** dream of ch 2 is older than the Maccabean interpretation (2:36–45). These take the metals to symbolize 4 kings or kingdoms of the early or exilic period. This theory really refers to the pre-history of the book rather than to the present book.

Appendix 2. The Messianic Kingdom—The fifth **e** kingdom of the series is that of God. The inauguration of this kingdom is stressed in chh 2 and 7. In ch 2 this kingdom is symbolized by a stone that becomes a mountain and fills the entire earth (cf Is 11:9); in ch 7 it is represented by 'one like a son of man' i.e. like a human being (7:13f; cf § 534*c*). It will be introduced by God alone without any human aid (2; 34f, 44f; 7:13f, 27). Unlike the kingdoms that precede it, this one will be of heavenly origin (7:13f; cf 7:2) and can be justly called the kingdom of heaven. Once introduced, it will become universal (2:35, 44) and continue to be the possession of God's elect for ever (7:14, 27). In the perspective of our book it would not be quite exact to call this kingdom Messianic, as the person of the Messiah, son of David, is not mentioned in Dn. Messianic this kingdom was, however, both in divine intent and historic realization. Dn 2 and 7 are, in fact, the most precise of the Messianic prophecies, having nothing of the poetic descriptions of the Messianic age that we find in the earlier sacred writings. Although the coming of this kingdom is closely **f** associated with the collapse of the fourth empire, which with most authors we have identified with the Gr. kingdom, we must not take it that the chronological succession was intended by the sacred writer as immediate. The exact time of the inauguration of the kingdom of God was as much a secret to Dn (cf 12:7–9) as it was in the NT period (Ac 1:7; Mt 24:36) and as the date of the Parousia is to us. In fact, these prophecies of Dn are, in part, still in the process of fulfilment and will be fully realized only at the Parousia (cf 1 Cor 15:24–28).

3 Nebuchadnezzar's Statue and the Fiery Fur- **529a** **nace**—We have seen (§ 526*i*) how this ch is probably based on traditions connected with Nabonidus' statue of Sin which the Marduk clergy considered an innovation and with the king's cult of Sin which they resisted. C. J. Gadd thinks it probable that Nabonidus had worship rendered to his own person (art cit 41f). Irrespective of its pre-history, the object here is: (i) to illustrate the uniqueness and supremacy of the God of the Israelites; (ii) to lay down a rule of religious conduct, namely, the faithful must choose martyrdom before apostasy. For later references to the story see 1 Mc 2:59; Heb 11:34.

1–7 The Erection and Dedication of the Golden **b** **Idol**—**1.** The ch is probably to be connected with the preceding, as Hippolytus noted (2, 2). The erection of the statue would then have followed soon after the king's dream. The MT bears no date to ch 3. The 18th year of Nebuchadnezzar to which the LXX and Theod date the incident is probably an insertion intended to connect the erection of the idol with Nebuchadnezzar's destruction of Jerusalem in his 19th year (2 [4] Kgs 25:8; Jer 52:12), which, in another reckoning would be his 18th. The statue was probably an idol whose veneration was of special importance to the king, as that of Sin was to Nabonidus. The dimensions of the colossus are given in the Babylonian sexagesimal system and equal c. ninety feet by nine feet. The height includes both the statue and its pedestal. Colossi such as this were well known in antiquity: that of Rhodes was c. 100 feet high. Dura, in Akkadian = 'circuit' or 'fortress', was

529b common in Babylonian place-names. The exact site of this particular one is unknown. Nabonidus had his military camp at Dur-Kurashu, near Sippar, and summoned thither 'the people of Babylon and Borsippa, [with the people] dwelling in far regions, [kings, princes and] governors, from the borders of Egypt on the Lower Sea to the Upper Sea' so as to mourn his mother (Gadd,

c 53: Vogt, 92). **2f.** It was required of high-ranking officials to assist at certain functions in Babylon as we know from various texts. The Jewish administrators (2:49; 3:12) would also have to attend. **4—7.** The Aram. words rendered 'harp' (CV 'psaltery') and 'bagpipe' in 5 are loan-words from Gr. Aram. had borrowed Gr. words before the reign of Alexander cf J. J. Rabbinowitz, Bib 39 (1958), 77—82. The furnace, unless it was specially designed for execution, was probably a kiln for baking bricks. Death by burning was known in the east in early (cf Code of Hammurabi, 25, 110; ANET 167*b*, 170*c*), exilic (cf Jer 29:22), Persian and later times. The furnace was like a lime kiln. It had an opening at the side (48, 93 [26]) for stoking and removing ashes and another at the top (21).

8—12 The Accusation against the Jews—'Chaldaeans' here denotes the inhabitants of Babylon rather than the magicians (cf 1:4; 2:2). The omission of any reference to Daniel, a more important official than any of the three Jews (2:49), indicates that these episodes once circulated independently. Ch 6 gives a parallel story in which Daniel alone figures.

d **13—18 The Jews' Courage and Faith**—The king's rage is explained by the importance he attributed to the adoration of the idol he had erected. The climax of the story is here reached; Judaism comes face to face with idolatry which a pagan king wishes to impose on it. The defiant words 'who is the god that will deliver you out of my hands?' (15) echo those of Sennacherib, 2 Kgs 18:33—35, and suggest some claim to divine prerogatives. They also introduce the following vv which show how such a God exists. **16—18.** The general sense of these vv is clear though their exact syntactical construction is less so. The sense is that the youths do not feel obliged to answer the defiant words of the king; they trust in God and are ready to face death rather than adore the idol. The context excludes any doubt of God's power on their part. A probable rendering of MT, in keeping with the context, is: **16.** 'it is not for *us* to answer you on this point' i.e. the king has defied God, and God himself will prove him wrong by rescuing his servants. **17.** 'If the God whom we serve can save us from the white hot furnace and from your hand, O king, he will save us'. Uncertainty of deliverance, and not doubt of God's power, is expressed (cf 95 [28]f) **18.** 'But even if he will not (save us), know, O king, that we will not serve your god . . .'. Others understand as: 17 'if our God is able to save us (as we believe) . . . 18 or not (as you believe) . . .'

e **19—23 The Three Jews in the Burning Furnace**—The youths were thrown into the furnace through the opening in the top. Special attention is paid to the youths being bound and clad as these details help to highlight the miracle (92 [25], 94 [27]). The exact rendering of the Aram. terms for the headgear and other pieces of apparel is uncertain.

24—90 The Miraculous Deliverance of the Three Youths—This section is not found in the MT and is absent from the Qumran fragment cf § 525*i*. The section consists of three parts; the prayer of Azariah (25—45); a historical interlude (46—50) and a song of

thanksgiving (51—90). None of the passages appears to have ever formed part of the Aramaic-Hebrew text. They **529** were probably inserted here by the versions because the MT 25 (92) appears to indicate that something is missing between 23—24 (91). On their canonical character, see § 525*g*. We adopt LXX numbering of vv. The hymn of Azariah is especially suited to its context.

24—45 The Prayer of Azariah—This is a confession of **f** the sins of Israel and of God's justice (24—33) ending in a prayer for deliverance (34—45). It is similar to 9:4—19 and Bar 1:15—3:8; cf also Neh 9:16ff. The prayer was composed in Heb. or Aram. during some persecution, most probably that of Antiochus IV, the 'unjust king, the most wicked in all the world' (32). 38 and 40 suit the Maccabean age well. Though attributed to Azariah the hymn is really a communal lamentation. It is all Israel that speaks in it, and it is to all Israel, not to the three youths, that it refers. It is appropriately inserted in its present context, the Jews in the furnace being a symbol of Israel in the crucible of suffering. **24f.** show that the prayer is a later insertion. The flames were rendered harmless only later (50). **26—33.** Contain a fundamental belief of revealed religion. God is just in all his doings and Israel's tribulations are due to her sins against the covenant which God made with her fathers; cf Dn 9:3ff 2 Mc 6:12—17; 7:18; Dt 28:15ff etc. The unjust king can scarcely be Nebuchadnezzar, the head of gold of 2:38. Nebuchadnezzar's wickedness is not stressed by the earlier prophets and in chh 2—5 he receives honourable mention. The unjust king is probably Antiochus, the arrogant, sacrilegious and blasphemous persecutor of chh 7—11 and of the books of Maccabees. **34—36.** Is a prayer to God to remember his covenant with **g** their fathers in which he promised to deliver Israel from their tribulations (cf Gn 15; 13ff; 22:17f) and make them a great and strong nation (Gn 12:2f: 15:5). **37f.** The pitiful plight of the few faithful Jews contrasted sadly with these promises; cf Is 51:2. The general religious situation described in these verses is that of the early Maccabean age, without prophet (1 Mc 4: 46; 14:41; cf Dn 9:7; Ezek 7:26; Ps 74 [73]:9 or temple service etc. **39f.** The youths, or rather Israel, beg God to accept the sufferings of his persecuted servants instead of the temple sacrifices that can no longer be offered; cf 2 Mc 7:37f. 40 is used in the Offertory prayer of the Mass. **41—45.** A promise of amendment and a final prayer to God to remember his covenant, deliver Israel and confound her enemies; cf 2 Mc 7:37f.

46—50 Historical Interlude—**46—48** are a duplicate **h** account of 22f derived from another source. **49f.** Or some similar account, may have once stood between 23f of the Aram.-Heb. text though the Qumran fragment is here identical with the MT; cf on 91 (25).

51—90 The Song of the Three Youths—This is a litany psalm, as Ps 136 (135), made up of two parts, distinguished from one another both by their contents and the form of their responsory. The responsories are probably liturgical additions. The date of composition of both parts of the hymn is quite uncertain. **51—56.** The first hymn extols the God of Israel who resides in his holy temple i.e. heaven (cf Ps 29 [28]) and who views all things from his lofty throne. **57—90.** Or the *Benedicite* **i** is an invitation to all creatures to praise God: to all heavenly creatures (57—63); natural phenomena (64—66, 69—73); (67f are omitted by the Vatican MS of Theodotion and are very probably to be deleted as repetitions); terrestrial beings (74—81) and, finally, to man and to the three youths in particular (82—88). In 88*a*

529i the youths are addressed in the second person, and then in 88*b* are referred to in the first person. 88*b* may be due to the editors who inserted the hymn in its present context and applied it to the three youths, saved from impending death in the midst of the flames. **89.** Is a well known liturgical versicle; cf 2 Chr 7:3; 6.

j MT 24–30—The King's Recognition of the True God—24f. Here we return to the MT. The king must have been seated opposite the side-opening of the furnace watching the execution of the sentence. He manifests his surprise in seeing four men, unfettered and unhurt, in the furnace whereas only three were bound and cast into it. The fourth 'like a son of God' is the angel mentioned in 49f and 95 (28). **26.** 'The Most High God' is a designation of the God of Israel in the Psalms. Elsewhere in the Bible the expression is used only by non-Jews (Gn 14:18; Nm 24:16; Is 14:14; 2 Mc 3:31). **27–30.** The extraordinary character of the miracle is noted by the dignitaries present. The king is particularly impressed by the fact that the God of the three youths had intervened to deliver his loyal servants. He had believed there was no God who could save them from his hands (15) and now acknowledges that there is but one such God, the God of Israel (cf 16–18). A royal decree (96 [29]) severely prohibits blasphemy against this God and the youths receive promotion. With the loyal decree cf 2:46; 6:26f; 2 Mc 3:36.

530a RSV 4:1–18 (MT 3:31–4:15) Nebuchadnezzar's Second Dream—This is the fourth and final episode from the reign of Nebuchadnezzar narrated in the book. It tells how, in accord with a dream interpreted by Daniel, the king was deprived of reason and banished from society for a period of seven years. After humbling himself before God he was restored to reason and welcomed back to his kingdom. We have seen (§ 526*i*) how the ch was long since seen to be based on traditions connected with Nabonidus' withdrawal from Babylon and his sojourn in Taima. He himself tells us that he abandoned Babylon **b** for Taima because of the attitude of the people and Marduk clergy to his cult of the moon-god Sin (Gadd, 57ff Vogt, 93) and remained in the Arabian desert for 10 years, the period pre-determined by Sin. During his desert sojourn the kingdom of Babylon remained loyal to him. He returned to Babylon some time before his kingdom and capital were conquered by Cyrus in 539. The Qumran text (4 QOrNab) shows that 'Nebuchadnezzar' of Dn 4 is really the Nabonidus of history. This text reads: 'The words of the prayer which Nabunai, king . . . of Babylon, prayed . . . [when he was afflicted] by a grievous ulcer in Taiman by decree of the [Most High God]: "I was afflicted [by a grievous ulcer] for seven years . . . and an exorcist pardoned my sins, and he was a Jew . . . [and he said]: 'Recount this in writing so as to give glory and [exaltation] to the name of the [Most High God'. And I wrote thus]: 'I was afflicted etc'. (cf RB **c** 63 [1956], 408; G. Vermes *The Dead Sea Scrolls in English*, 1962, 229). Dn 4 then, is a reworking of old Jewish traditions about Nabonidus' sojourn in Taima. As it now stands it is intended to illustrate God's supreme dominion over pagan powers and his mercy to those who humble themselves before him. The episode in Dn is narrated in the form of a royal circular addressed by the king to all his subjects. The narrative begins in the first person (4:1–18), then changes abruptly to the third person (4:19–33) and then back again to the first (4:34–37). A similar abrupt change from the first to the third person is found in Nabonidus' inscription that narrates his desert sojourn

(Gadd, 91ff); cf Tb 1:3–3:6 (1st pers.); 3:7ff (3rd **530c** pers.).

4:1–3—The opening lines of the proclamation **d** contain a summary of its contents. The body of the edict is made up of two couplets after the manner of the Hebrew Psalms (cf Ps 145 [144]:13) which indicates its Jewish origin; cf however 31f.

4:4–9—The LXX, under the influence of its rendering of 3:1, dates the dream to the king's third year. The king at this time was in his palace, prosperous, lit. 'flourishing', like the tree of the dream which terrified him. **6f.** Unlike ch 2, the king here narrates the contents of his dream to the official dream-interpreters. Their inability to help prepares the entrance of Daniel, **8f** who, as usual, is introduced only after the magicians have failed in their task (cf 2:27; 5:10ff). His court name Belteshazzar is recalled and is linked up with Bel i.e. Marduk, the chief deity of Babylon. 'The spirit of the Holy God' (cf Jos 24:19) or less likely 'of the holy gods' (cf 5:11, 14; 13:45) is considered as a source of inward illumination; cf 2:22f, 47; cf Gn 41:38.

10–18 The King relates his dream—The king in his **e** dream saw a huge tree, planted on the centre of the world, reaching to the heavens, visible to all and providing shelter to bird and beast; cf 2:37f. An inscription of Nebuchadnezzar compares Babylon to such a tree: for similar biblical comparisons cf Ezek 17:22f; 19:10–14; 31:3–9; Is 10:33f. **13.** 'Watcher' or 'sentinel' is a late Jewish name for an angel. Dn 4:13, 17 and 23 are the only biblical occurrences of this term, which is also found in extra-biblical literature. In 1 Enoch the angels are called 'holy watchers' (15:9) and 'watchers of heaven' (12:4; 13:10). The same terminology is found in the Damascus Document (3, 4 CAP II, 805) and in the Genesis Apocryphon (2, 1) from Qumran (IQApoc). The Angel with a loud voice ordered the tree to be cut down, but the stump was to be left encircled with a metal clamp. The last figure marks, most likely, a transition from **f** allegory to reality. As the cutting down of the tree symbolizes the calamity that was to befall the king, the metal band must certainly refer to the restraint imposed upon him, or to the iron bands with which he had to be bound during his madness. The king, not the symbolic tree, will eat, among wild beasts, the grass of the earth etc. The most humiliating of all is that his heart, which according to the Heb. and ancient psychology is the seat of the intellect, will be made like that of a beast. The state will last seven times i.e. seven years (LXX, 4QOrNab), a round number for the period required for his humiliation. This period is irrevocably fixed by God (24) and promulgated by the watchers who aid him in governing the world (cf 1 [3] Kgs 22:19ff; Jb 1–2; cf Col 2:15). Through Nebuchadnezzar God will show to all that he alone is master of the destiny of kings and empires. This is the central theme of the book (cf § 526*n*) and repeated elsewhere in the Bible 1 Sm 2:7ff; Ezek 17:24; Ps 113 [112]: 7f; Jb 5:11ff; Lk 1:52; etc etc.

19–27 The Interpretation of the Dream—19. The **g** narrative changes abruptly from the first to the third person (cf § 530*d*). **26.** Antiochus Epiphanes (2 Mc 9:11f) is forced to recognize the divine origin of all human powers, as Nebuchadnezzar here; but too late. God punishes humans, Israelites (2 Mc 6:12–17) and even non-Israelites (Wis 11:22–26; 12:20–22) with a view to their correction. 'Heaven' is a metonym for God in later Judaism cf 1 Mc 3:18 etc and the 'kingdom of heaven' in Mt. **27.** The king can avert the impending evil by effective repentance i.e. by good deeds and almsgiving cf Wis 12:20. The theological doctrine of the meritoriousness of

530g good works is clearly implied; cf Tb 4:11; 12:9; Sir 29:12.

h **28–33. The Fulfilment of the Dream—28–30.** The twelve-month period indicates the respite granted for repentance. The actual execution of the sentence was on the occasion of a further sin of pride on the king's part. Nebuchadnezzar embellished Babylon, making its splendour and that of his royal palace proverbial. **30** is reminiscent of his praises of Babylon recorded in inscriptions: 'My dear Babylon, the city which I love'; 'the palace, the wonder of the people, the seat of royalty, the abode of happiness'. But it fits also Nabonidus who rebuilt Taima: 'He made the town beautiful, (and) built (there) [his palace], like the palace in Babylon' (ANET, 313d). **31f.** Such a mysterious voice, called a *Bath Qôl* ('echo'), is often mentioned in rabbinic literature as a mode of divine communication; cf Mt 3:17; 17:5; Jn 12:28. **33.** The form of insanity with which the king was affected is scientifically known as 'lycanthrophy' or 'insania zoanthropica' in which the patient imagines himself to be a beast and behaves like one. The king's external appearance became, to a certain extent, similar to that of a beast. The humiliation befitted his pride.

i **34f.** The ideas expressed in his praises of God occur in other biblical books: e.g. 34b in Ps 145 (144):13, 35a in Is 40:17, 35b in Is 24:21, 35c in Is 43:13; 45:9; Jb 9:12. They are also, however, reminiscent of Nabonidus' praises of his moon-god Sin: 'Sin, lord of the gods . . . in whose hands all of every function of heaven is held, king of kings, lord of lords . . . with the fear of whose great godhead heaven and earth are filled . . . without them, who does anything?' (Gadd, 61; Vogt, 94). **36f.** At the end of his Taima sojourn Nabonidus was welcomed back to his kingdom (Gadd, 63). His reign was shortlived and inglorious, his kingdom falling to Cyrus in 539. No mention is made of Nabonidus' insanity in Babylonian inscriptions.

531a **5 Belshazzar and the Fall of Babylon**—Ch 4 has shown how the throne was restored to 'Nebuchadnezzar' when he humbled himself and acknowledged the sovereignty of the true God. The present ch tells how his son, Belshazzar, lost the throne after his sacrilegious use of the sacred vessels of the temple of Jerusalem. Belshazzar is presented as the son of Nebuchadnezzar (cf also Bar 1:11f), the king who brought Daniel (13) and the temple vessels (2f) from Jerusalem; who made Daniel chief of the magicians (11f), who was humiliated by God and restored to his kingdom (18–22): in other words the monarch described in chh 1–4. In chh 5, 7 and 8 Belshazzar is called king and in ch 5 his father seems to have passed from the scene. Ch 5 recounts an episode from the last night of the monarch while 7:1 mentions his first, and 8:1 his third year. We know from historical records that Belshazzar was the son of Nabonidus and it seems that he had no blood relationship with Nebuchadnezzar. It is likewise clear from these same records that the last king of the Neo-Babylonian empire was Nabonidus and that his son Belshazzar was never really king of Babylon. This indicates that ch 5 is of the same character as ch 4, and perhaps chh 2 and 3 as well, i.e. a popular narrative in which the name Nabonidus has been replaced by that of Nebuchadnezzar.

b Like chh 2–4, ch 5 is best considered as a late composition, though very probably based on earlier traditions on the fall of Babylon. The very name 'Belshazzar' shows that it retains some true historical reminiscences. This name was unknown outside the Bible (Dn and Bar 1:11f) and sources dependent on it, until it appeared in cuneiform tablets not deciphered until 1887. It is possible that Dn 5 relates historical fact in

a popular fashion. Although historical sources make it **531** clear that he was not king of Babylon, he may have been considered king by the populace because of his father's long sojourn in Taima. In fact the 'Verse Account' says his father 'let everything go', 'entrusted the kingship' to Belshazzar on his withdrawal to the Arabian desert (ANET 313cd), and during this sojourn Belshazzar was in charge of the army and of the affairs of the homeland (cf ANET loc cit and 306ab). We do not know how Belshazzar ended his days. The Nabonidus Chronicle (ANET 306bd) informs us that Babylon opened its gates joyfully to the Persian forces; there was no fighting and Cyrus was acclaimed as liberator when he later entered the capital. Nabonidus was not in the city when it yielded. **c** He was taken captive when he later returned there and appears to have been honourably treated by Cyrus. The Gr. historians knew another tradition. Herodotus (1, 191) and Xenophon (*Cyropaedia* 7, 5, 15f) say the city was carousing when the Persian troops entered it unawares. The latter notes that Cyrus, guided by his officers Godatas and Gobryas (= Gobaru of the Nabonidus Chronicle, ANET, 306), made his way to the palace where the king awaited them with drawn sword but was overpowered and killed. This is similar to the tradition preserved in Dn 5 and it is possible that both are based on historical fact, the 'king' in question being Belshazzar who feasted as his father, Nabonidus, fled before the Persian troops.

In its present form, ch 5 intends to show how God punishes kings for the sacrilegious use they make of sacred vessels of the temple. As such it served as a reminder to the Jews of the fate that awaited a later Belshazzar, Antiochus IV (cf 1 Mc 1:21–23; 6:12f. On the question of the historicity of this chapter cf H. H. Rowley JTS 32 (1930–31), 12–31.

1–4 Belshazzar's Feast—1. No indication is given **d** for the occasion or date of the feast. The date may be determined from 30f, i.e. the last night of the Chaldean dynasty which we now know to have been the 15th of the month Tishri (= 11th Oct.) 539 B.C. The name of the king, *Belšassar*, which corresponds to the Babylonian *Bel-šar-uṣur*, 'Bel protect the king', must be distinguished from Belteshazzar, the Babylonian name of Daniel (see on 1:7 and cf 5:12). In the Gr. versions, Vg, DV and KV the single name 'Baltassar' represents the two different Babylonian names. The number of guests was not extraordinary for an oriental feast. **2–4.** When he had tasted the wine, i.e. when he was already under its influence, the king sacrilegiously ordered the sacred vessels of the temple of Jerusalem (1:2) to be brought into the banquethall. During Persian rule, concubines, i.e. wives of inferior rank, were permitted to these banquets. We are ill-informed on the presence of true wives at feasts during Babylonian and Persian times. Insult was added to profanation when the sacred vessels were used for libations to the Babylonian gods amidst the songs and chants of the revellers.

5–6 The Writing on the Wall—The sacrilegious use of the temple vessels brought immediate condemnation from God. For similar descriptions of fear cf Is 21:3; Ps 69 [68]:23; Na 2:10.

7–9 The Magicians unable to read the Writing— **e** As the magicians appear to be introduced twice to the king, some think the order of these vv is disarranged. W. Baumgartner, in Kittel's *Biblia Hebraica* 3rd ed., transposes 8a between 7a and 7b. The existing order is quite understandable in a popular narrative and can be retained. The king requests the reading of the writing and its meaning and promises rich rewards. Purple

31e and the golden necklace were worn by persons of high rank (cf Est 8:15; Xenophon, *Anab.* 1, 5, 8). The meaning of the title 'third' (Aram. *taltî*, 29 *taltâ*) is not quite clear. Some take it as the third in rank after the king and queen-mother; others as third after Belshazzar and Nabonidus, the king's father. This is most improbable, as the king's father plays no part in this ch. The ordinary word for 'third' in Aram. is *telîtay*, not *taltî* or *taltâ*. *Taltî* probably represents the Heb. *šālîš*, which is, in turn, a loan-word from Hittite and denotes a high-official in close attendance on the king; cf A. Cowley in JTS 2 (1919—20), 326f; Montgomery, 256. As usual, the magicians are unable to help the king and Daniel has to be introduced.

f 10—28 Daniel Interprets the Writing—25. The writing on the wall, according to MT, was: *menê'*, *menê'*, *teqêl ûparsîn*. The repetition of the first word and the plural ending of the last are not attested by Theod., Vg or Jos. (Ant. 10, 11, 3); and Jerome (PL 25, 521) expressly says that there were only three words written on the wall i.e. Mane, Thecel and Phares. Only these three words *menê'*, *teqêl* and *perês* are interpreted by Daniel in 26—28. For these reasons many take these three words to be the original reading in 25 and correct the MT accordingly. The MT in 25 may well be original, however, as 26—28 interpret the writing merely through word-play. It is easier to explain the omission of the other words in the versions than to give a reason for their introduction into MT. **26—28.** *Menê'*, *teqêl* and *perês* and their Gr. and Lat. transcriptions are the Aram. names of the three weights known in Heb. as the mina, the shekel and the *peras*, or half-mina. These three weights may have been written in current symbols or in cuneiform. This may explain the magicians' inability to read the writing. Daniel interprets the special meaning attached to these three words through the root-meaning of the consonants that compose them, and these he understands as verbal, not as nominal, forms. Thus; *Menê'*: God has numbered (Aram. *menāh*) your kingdom and put an end to it'; *teqêl*: 'you have been weighed on the scales (*teqiltâ*) and found wanting'; *perês* is interpreted through a double word-play: 'your kingdom is divided (*perîsat*) and given to Media **g** and Persia (*Pârâs*). It is possible that, in some earlier form of the material in this ch, the writing on the wall may have had some other meaning than that given it in 26—28. Various views on what this earlier meaning may have been are put forward. A common one, relying on MT 25, is: 'Numbered (*menê'* can mean either numbered or a mina): a mina, a shekel and (two) half minas'. The proportion of the weights is: 60, 1, 30 + 30. The mina represents the flourishing kingdom of Nebuchadnezzar; the shekel is Belshazzar; the two half minas are the Medes and the Persians considered as one kingdom. So Riessler, Goettsberger, Linder, Bentzen. Others take the weights to represent the kings Nebuchadnezzar, Evil-Merodach and Belshazzar or the Neo-Babylonian, 'Median' and Persian kingdoms. The writing may have been some proverb current at the time (a later example is found in the Mishnah tractate *Ta'anith* 21b). These theories appear to refer to the pre-history of the text.

h Appendix—Darius the Mede. Darius the Mede is represented in 5:31 (6:1) as the immediate successor of the last king of the Neo-Babylonian empire. The same is true of 9:1 (q.v.) where he is called 'Darius, son of Xerxes, of the seed of the Medes'. In 6:28 Darius is mentioned before Cyrus and the succession in chh 7—10 is Belshazzar (7:1; 8:1), Darius (9:1), Cyrus and the Persian kings (10:1ff). From 5:31 and 9:1 it appears clear that the author has placed a Median

kingdom, under Darius, between the Neo-Babylonian **531h** and Persian empires. This same view of a Median empire also appears implicit in the four world empires of chh 2 and 7 (cf § 528a–c). This view of a Median king ruling between the downfall of the Neo-Babylonian empire and Cyrus is a misconception of the history of the period as known both from the Bible (cf 2 Chr 36:22f; Ez 1:1ff; Is ch 41) and profane sources. There is indisputable evidence that Cyrus was the first king of Babylon after the collapse of the Neo-Babylonian dynasty. The Persian troops entered Babylon on the 16th of Tishri (= 12th October) 539 B.C.; Cyrus entered Babylon on the 3rd Marchesvan (= 28th October), and in the contract tablets, the earliest of which is dated 24th Marchesvan (= 19th November) Cyrus is already called 'king of Babylon'. There is therefore no room for an interregnum following the fall of Babylon.

The suggestion that the designation 'the Mede' is **i** a textual corruption or later addition and that the real name of the king is Darius Hystaspes (M.-J. Lagrange, RB 13 [1904], 501f; E. J. Kissane, IrTQ 14 [1919], 43—57; J. Goettsberger, 49) has not met with general acceptance; the name recurs in 9:1 (cf also 11:1) and seems presupposed in 6:29. Other commentators argue that Darius was not an independent sovereign, as the Aram. text of 5:31 says simply that he *received* the kingdom, i.e. the power, but not that he *succeeded* (Vg) to the throne of Belshazzar. His position therefore was that of a governor or an associate king or subordinate king. Consequently he is identified with Gobryas, the general who led the Persian army into Babylon (E. Vigouroux, DBV 2 [1910], 1297—99); with Cambyses, the son of Cyrus whose name is sometimes associated with that of his father in the contract tablets, and is called 'king of Babylon' while his father is called 'king of lands' (Boutflower, 142—67); with Astyages, the last king of Media, captured by Cyrus, who however spared his life and appointed him governor and viceroy of Babylon; cf 14:1 (B. Alfrink, 'Darius Medus' Bib 9 [1928], 316—40; Linder, 279—81); with Cyaxares, the son of Astyages according to Xenophon, *Cyr* 1, 5, 2 etc. On all these theories and the difficulties they encounter, see Rowley, *Darius the Mede ... 7—53*.

None of the theories just listed solves all the **j** difficulties regarding Darius the Mede, and it seems best to accept that Dn has introduced a Median kingdom between the Neo-Babylonian and that of Persia. In the story of Bel and the Dragon, 14:1 (13:65)—part of the Daniel cycle of traditions though not part of the original Aram.-Heb. text—the correct historical order is given, Cyrus succeeding Astyages, the last king of the Medes. We cannot yet say, therefore, why the author here makes Darius the Mede king of a Median empire between the Neo-Babylonian and the Persian. Like Nebuchadnezzar in chh 4—5, he seems to be a composite figure, part-Median, part-Persian. Future discoveries and study may throw further light on this as earlier ones have on Belshazzar: cf P. de Menasce, BJ, 13f.

6 Daniel in the Lions' Den—The story is parallel **532a** to that of the youths in the furnace of ch 3. Both stories stress the supremacy of Daniel's God and the duty of observing the religion of this One True God even in the midst of persecutions. But while ch 3 dwells on the negative duties of religion, ch 6 deals with its positive duties. Both stories were known in Maccabean times; cf 1 Mc 2:59f.

With 6:2ff we have passed from the Neo-Babylonian

532a empire to the reign of Darius. But he governs according to 'the laws of the Medes and Persians' (8—12), a designation for the Persian empire; cf 1 Mc 1:1; Est 1:19 etc; and the empire is now divided into satrapies. This suggests the Persian Darius I (522—486 B.C.). Darius I is also one of the Persian kings referred to in Dn 11:2. The probabilities, then, are that our narrative refers to some pious Jew during the reign of Darius I. This king professed the religion of Zarathustra (cf § 310*h*) and was favourably inclined towards the Jews (cf Ez 6). It is probable that our narrative once circulated independently; it has certain peculiarities of style not found in the other chh; e.g. Daniel is called 'this Daniel' (3, 6, 29). The chronology of Dn, which supposes a kingdom of the Medes under Darius, may have led the final redactor of the work to include this episode in its present position. The narrative, if historical, scarcely refers to the Jew exiled in 605 B.C. (1, 1f) for Daniel would then be c. 100 years old when Darius intended to entrust the control of the empire to him (4)!

b 1—9 The Ministers' Plot against Daniel—1. Darius I Hystaspes (522—486 B.C.) according to Herodotus (III, 89), divided his vast empire into 20 satrapies, Syria-Palestine being the 5th in number. The number of satrapies was not stable. Darius' own inscriptions speak of 21, 23 and 29 satrapies. In later times the word 'satrapy' was used of minor administrative divisions and Appian (Syr. 62) speaks of 74 of them. Est 1:1 mentions 127 provinces i.e. satrapies (cf Est 3:12) of the Persian Empire under Xerxes (486—465 B.C.) Both Dn and Est reflect this later use of the word. **2f.** The three presidents or supervisors to whom the satraps were responsible are nowhere else mentioned. Ez 7:14 speaks of seven counsellors of king Artaxerxes (I? 465—423; II? 404—358 B.C.). **3—5.** Daniel soon distinguished himself, and the king's proposal to promote the Jewish exile above all others in the kingdom aroused the jealousy of the satraps and the two supervisors. Since his conduct as a statesman was above suspicion, they devised a plan to bring his religious conduct into conflict with the law of the king. **6—9.**

c Consequently the supervisors and other state functionaries came thronging (CV) or by agreement (RSV: the exact rendering of the Heb. is uncertain) to the king to have him unwittingly sign a decree that would bring about Daniel's death. Their plan was that the king issue an apparently innocent decree which, by virtue of the character of Medo-Persian law, would be irrevocable. The unchangeable character of Medo-Persian law is noted by Est 1:19; 8:8. Diodorus Siculus (3, 17, 30) narrates how this led Darius III (336—330 B.C.) to permit a death sentence to be carried out though he was informed, and admitted, before its execution that the sentence was unjust. It is not clear from **7** whether prayers were to be directed to the king as a god. This seems implied but the point is not stressed. There are no clear indications that Persian kings considered themselves gods; for Antiochus Epiphanes cf 11:30. The author of Dn 6:8 does not explain how the 120 satraps came in concert to the royal palace to plot against Daniel. LXX attributes this plot to the two supervisors alone but its reading is hardly the original one.

d 10—13 Daniel Faithful to his God—10. Knowledge of the decree and its purpose did not make Daniel alter his religious practices. In a quiet upper-room of his house (cf Ac 1:13; 9:37, 39 etc) he prayed thrice daily towards Jerusalem, the dwelling-place of the God of the Israelites. In later times the three hours of prayer were: (i) in the morning, at the hour of the morning sacrifice;

(ii) in the afternoon, about three o'clock, at the **532** time of the evening sacrifice; (iii) in the evening at sunset (E. Schürer, *A History of the Jewish People in the Time of Jesus Christ*, 2, I p. 290, n. 248; cf G. F. Moore, *Judaism* II, 219f). This custom was probably an ancient one; cf Ps 55 (54):17. Jews prayed both kneeling (1 [3] Kgs 8:54; Ez 9:5; Mt 26:39 etc) and upright. **11f.** His enemies knew of his hours of prayer and could easily observe him through the open window.

14—23 Daniel Delivered—Notwithstanding the king's efforts, Daniel was thrown to the lions. But in spite of all precautions, which made it clear that all human aid was impossible (**17**) God delivered him.

24 (25) Daniel's Accusers Condemned—The punish- **e** ment meted out to the false accusers was according to the principle of retaliation. But the slaughter of their families, though in conformity with primitive conceptions of justice (cf 2 Sm 21:5—9) and Persian practice during the reign of Darius I (Herod III, 119) was against the personal responsibility inculcated in Dt 24:16; Jer 31:29f Ezek 18. The accusers of Daniel, according to the HT, were the two supervisors and satraps and perhaps a host of minor officials (7f); according to LXX only the two supervisors. In a popular account like that of the present ch the HT generalization creates no difficulty.

25—27 (26—28) The King acknowledges the God of f Israel—The narrative ends, as does that of ch 3, by a royal proclamation of faith in the power and everlasting kingship of the living God of Daniel. The phraseology of the edict is very similar to that of Nebuchadnezzar in 3:98—100 (31—33) and 4:31—34.

28 (29) Conclusion—We meet once again the chronology that is peculiar to Dn; the reign of Darius placed before that of Cyrus. This ending may be from the final editor; cf § 526*j*. and 1:21.

With its doctrine of the power and everlasting kingship of God and of his intervention on behalf of his faithful servants, ch 6 forms a fitting ending to the narrative portion of the book and prepares for the second part where these themes are central.

7—12 The Visions—This section contains four visions. **533a** These run chronologically parallel with the episodes narrated in chh 5 and 6. Daniel saw his first and second vision during the 1st and 3rd years of Belshazzar, respectively (7:1; 8:1); his third in the 1st year of Darius the Mede (9:1) and his fourth and final one during the 3rd year of Cyrus (10:1). In these visions the history of the chosen people is narrated in the form of prophecies received by Daniel. The seer's message develops at length a theme that was already foreshadowed in Nebuchadnezzar's first dream, namely the destruction of all hostile powers and the establishment of a universal and abiding kingdom. The writer is not merely a historian recalling Israel's past history, nor a theologian teaching the basic doctrine of the uniqueness and supremacy of the God of Israel. He is also, and above all, a prophet predicting the triumph of God, the establishment of a spiritual kingdom upon earth, and its glorious consummation in heaven. Though this section develops themes already touched on in the first part it is clearly marked off from it by a change in the literary form and the historical outlook of the writer. It is possible that in sections of the second part (in ch 7 in particular) as in ch 2—6, earlier sources have been used.

7 The Vision of the Four World Empires—As in **b** Nebuchadnezzar's first dream (Ch 2), four successive empires are represented by symbols given in the descending order of value, and in both, the four

33b empires are replaced by a fifth established directly by God. In ch 7, however, the author dwells at length on the persecution of the people of God by a king of the fourth empire and on the special punishment that awaits this king.

c 1—8 The Vision—1. On Belshazzar, king of Babylon see § 531a. The ascription of the vision to his first year may be intended to indicate the beginning of the reign of the last Chaldean king. 'Dream and visions': dream, like Nebuchadnezzar's in 2:4; but Daniel himself (7:2ff, 8ff) speaks of 'visions'. There is scarcely any difference between the two in this text. **2.** The 'Great Sea' is not the Mediterranean as in Jos 9:1 but the abyss which in Babylonian mythology was considered as being inimical to the gods. The same idea is used symbolically or poetically in the Bible: cf Is 27:1; 51:9; Pss 74 (73): 11—14; 89 (88):9—11; Jb 7:12; 9:13. In the new **d** creation there will be no 'sea' (Apoc 21:1). **4.** The first beast was like a lion with eagle's wings: a composite symbol combining the king of the animal and bird kingdom. Representations or winged lions are common in Assyrian and Babylonian art. This animal, like the head of gold of ch 2, symbolized the Neo-Babylonian empire. The removal of its wings removed its character as a monstrous hybrid. It is then made human by being made to stand erect and by receiving a human heart i.e. a human intellect. The last detail is a clear reference to Nebuchadnezzar (4:13, 31) and the entire description may refer to his recognition of the true God. In this manner he regained true human dignity. It is not certain, however, that the author intended this last point. **5.** The second beast was like a bear, second in ferocity only to the lion (Prv 28:15; cf Is 11:6f). It was raised up on one side i.e. in a semi-couchant position, ready to pounce on its prey (Driver, 82; Montgomery, 288) or, erect on its hind legs in an aggressive posture (Junker, 41).

e The symbolism of the 'three ribs' between the bear's teeth has been a source of difficulty for interpreters. Some have taken it to denote that which remained of the prey the bear had devoured: cf Am 3:13 (see Rinaldi, 103). Others have seen in it a symbol of the kingdoms of Lydia and Babylonia conquered by Cyrus, and Egypt subdued by Cambyses (Linder, 301, taking the bear to represent the Medo-Persian empire). R. M. Frank (CBQ 21 [1959], 505—7) has shown that the Aram. word *'il'in* is to be understood here through Arabic as meaning 'tusks', not 'ribs'; cf CV. The three tusks between the bear's teeth indicate the beast's ferocity. The bear, like the silver of ch 2, symbolizes the Median empire; the command to devour refers to the destructiveness of the Medes (cf Is 13:17f). **6.** The third beast was like a leopard, an animal noted for its swiftness (Hb 1:8). The four wings on its side or back probably indicate its speed. The beast, like the bronze of ch 2, symbolizes the Persian kingdom. For the speed of Cyrus' conquests cf Is 41:2ff. The dominion of this kingdom is noted here and in 2:39; it may also be symbolized by the four heads of the beast (cf 8:4). Other expositors take the four heads to typify the four Persian kings of 11:2 (Goettsberger, 54; Charles, 178) or the four divisions of Alexander's empire (Linder, 301).

f 7f. The seer pays special attention to the emergence of the fourth beast. It is so monstrous that he finds nothing in the animal world with which to compare it. Its cruel and destructive nature is symbolized by its iron teeth. The monster symbolizes the Greek empire, the fourth kingdom, strong as iron, of 2:40. It is the last and most universal-minded of all four. What

'the little horn' typifies will be explained in detail **533f** in 24f. The representation of historical realities by animals was a common feature of apocalyptic symbolism. The 'Vision Section' of the Book of Enoch (chh 83—90) roughly contemporary with Daniel, writes the entire history of Israel in this manner.

9—14 The Divine Judgement—The first act of this **g** drama has shown the series of world powers, enemies of God and aiming at universal empire, arising out of the abyss (2) i.e. they are of earthly origin (17). The second act describes God's judgement on these human pretensions and the inauguration of his own kingdom, and appropriately opens in heaven. **9f.** Before describing the actual judgement the seer tells us of the solemn preparations made for it. First of all the thrones for the divine judge and his unnamed assessors are set up. Then the judge, the Godhead himself, takes his seat. He is appositely called 'The Ancient of Days' an aged, venerable person, with hair as white as wool. Having seen the entire course of history, he will pass just judgement on the arrogant presumptions of the four kingdoms about to be arraigned before him (cf Jerome PL, 25, 531). The fire surrounding (cf Ezek 1:4, 27) and issuing from the throne may indicate that the sentence would be given immediate effect. Myriads of angels stand by ready to execute his orders. The court sits and the indictment is read to the accused, i.e. all the misdeeds of the four symbolical beasts are recalled as if read in a book. **11f.** The construction is cumbersome but the **h** sense is clear. While the seer's attention is concentrated on that majestic sight of the divine court, the fourth beast is condemned to be burnt on account of the arrogant and blasphemous words which the little horn was uttering. The seer is concerned only with the little horn which he identifies with the beast itself and is uninterested in the other horns. The fate of the little horn, i.e. Antiochus, was the point that most of all interested his readers. He assures them that divine judgement had been passed on him. The other beasts, i.e. the earlier empires, survive for an unspecified time after the power has been taken from them. The expression 'a time and a season' denotes a fixed, but unspecified period of time; cf P. P. Saydon Bib 36 (1955), 48f. **13f.** After the destruction of **i** the hostile powers, symbolized by the monsters from the abyss, the visionary sees the heavenly kingdom being introduced. One 'like a son of man' comes in the clouds of heaven, i.e. from heaven. He is thus, in origin, unlike the monsters that arose from the abyss. The expression 'son of man' which is rare in Aram. but common in Heb., especially Ezek, simply means an individual, a member of the human race; cf Nm 23:19; Ps 80 (79):17; Is 51:12; cf Dn 10:16. As the monsters from the abyss were *like* beasts, so is this heavenly being *like* a 'son of man' i.e. like a human being. He is a symbol of the fifth kingdom, the heavenly kingdom of God comprised of humans. From the Ancient of Days he receives universal dominion. Unlike the beasts which have been deprived of their power, his will be an everlasting, untransferable and imperishable sovereignty. See Appendix 2, § 534c.

15—27 The Interpretation of the Vision—15f. **j** Angels explain the later visions to Daniel also and appear as interpreters of visions in Zech 1—6; Ezek 40—48. **17f.** The angel's reply is a summary of the entire vision: the four beasts stand for four kings, or rather for four kingdoms represented by them (cf 23) and the 'holy ones of the Most High' shall receive an everlasting kingship when these kingdoms are destroyed (cf 26f) The expression 'Holy Ones of the Most High' occurs only in Dn (7:18, 22, 25, 27) and, in Heb, in the DSS CD

533j 20, 8. The designation 'holy ones' occurs more frequently in the Bible. Ordinarily it refers to the angels; only rarely does it denote the pious on earth, (Ps 34 [33]:10; Dn 7:21; 22b; 8:24). In 25a 'holy one of the Most High' certainly means the pious Jews persecuted by Antiochus, and this appears to be the sense in 18 also. The perfect parallelism between 14 and 18 make this clear. **19f.** Daniel once again shows special interest in the fourth beast, in its ten horns and in the little horn that displaced three others and acted arrogantly. **21f.** Are an amplification of 8 or 11. The author repeats the essential points of the vision the better to impress the divine message on his readers' minds. In his description of the little horn the author passes insensibly from the figure to reality.

k **23f.** The fourth kingdom is that of Alexander and his successors. The last horn, different from all the others, is certainly Antiochus IV, the little horn of 8 and 8:9. The three kings whom he laid low were very probably the two sons of Seleucus IV, the legitimate heirs to the throne, and his own son Antiochus who was co-regent with his father from 175 to 170 B.C. (cf Bib 36 [1955], 262; (J. Starcky Les livres des Maccabées, BJ, p. 248 n. a to 2 Mc 4:38). The ten kings of 24a may include the three of 24b; Antiochus IV was the eighth Seleucid king. **25.** The arrogance of Antiochus and his persecution of the Jews will be given in greater detail in 8:9—14, 23—26; 9:26f; 11:21—45. The (sacred) 'times' are the liturgical services of the temple, the feast days (cf 1 Mc 1:39, 45; 2:34) etc; 'the Law' is the Jewish **l** religion in general; cf 1 Mc 2:20f, 27 etc. The persecution will last 'a time, two times and half (lit 'a division of') a time', generally understood to be three and a half years (cf 4:13, 20). Therefore the saints or pious Israelites will be delivered into the hands of the persecutor for $3\frac{1}{2}$ years. This was approximately the length of the duration of the period of persecution. The altar was desecrated on the 15th of the month Chislev, i.e. Dec. 6th, 167 B.C. and was re-dedicated on the 25th Chislev three years later (1 Mc 1:54; 4:52). The edict of persecution was published some months before the actual desecration of the altar (1 Mc 1:41—53; 2 Mc 6—7). Antiochus died in the autumn of 164 B.C. (cf Bib 36 [1955], 262; 423—5), a short while before the rededication (cf 2 Mc 9—10:8). C. Schedl (BZ n.s. 8 [1964], 102f) takes the time indication of 25 to mean ($3\frac{1}{4}$) lunar years or 1150 days (= 2300 evenings and mornings of 8:14) and refers it to the period between 15th Chislev (6th Dec.) 167 and 31st Jan. 163 B.C., the latter date being that when Judas would have fortified mount Sion (cf 1 Mc 4:60). He takes this time reference, as those of 8:12—14 and 12:11, 13, to be Maccabean additions showing how the prophecies were fulfilled. While probable for the other texts the view is hardly required here; cf on 9:27.

m **28 Conclusion**—The concluding remark prepares for the visions of the following chh in which the same problem is treated.

534a **Appendix 1—The Fourth Empire.** The identification of the little horn with Antiochus IV is supported by the parallel vision of ch 8 where the little horn of 8:9 is interpreted in 23ff as a king of the Greek empire (cf 8:21f) The arrogance, blasphemy and persecution of the little horn of chh 7 and 8 are what 11:21—49 and the books of Maccabees ascribe to the Greek king, Antiochus IV. The Sibylline Oracles 3, 281—400 (CAP 2, 385f), composed c 150 B.C., consider the little horn to be **b** Antiochus. St Ephraem, Bar-Hebraeus and some other early interpreters considered the fourth kingdom to be

the Hellenistic empire (cf Rowley, Darius the Mede, **534** 184f). The fourth kingdom was identified with Rome in the apocryphal 2 Esdras 12:10ff (1st cent. A.D.) and this identification became the commonly accepted one among Christian writers (cf Rowley, op cit 70ff). The little horn of ch 7 was then considered to be the Antichrist who is to arise at the end of time. Although this cannot be accepted as the original sense of ch 7 it has a solid foundation in Dn. Antiochus' attack on the chosen people is a true type of the permanent, and of the final, on-slaught of the forces of evil on the religion and worshippers of the True God. Even Daniel himself, in 11:40ff (q.v.) appears to pass naturally from the persecution of Antiochus to pure eschatology. Apoc 13 applies the imagery of ch 7 to Rome's persecution of the early Christians. St Paul can draw on Dn in his description of the Antichrist in 2 Thes 2, 3—10 etc (cf B. Orchard Bib 20 [1939], 172—9). The doctrine of Dn is sufficiently universal and its imagery plastic enough to apply to all times. While our author is working with the succession of empires, Babylon, Media, Persia and Greece, these are more important to him as symbols of world powers than as historical realities.

Appendix 2—The Son of Man. cf § 652b. In the com- **c** mentary we have understood 'a son of man' (13f) in its ordinary Heb. sense of 'a human being' and taken it as a symbol for the people of God. This is the interpretation that the context itself suggests. First, it appears that 'a son of man' is merely a symbol. As the monsters like beasts, arising from the abyss, symbolize four kingdoms (17) so will 'one like a son of man coming on the clouds of heaven' be a symbol of something, most probably of a divine kingdom. 18 and 27 tell us what is symbolized: it is the holy ones of the Most High, i.e. God's people. The dominion given to the holy ones of the Most High in 18, 27 is the very same as that conferred on one like a son of man in 14. This collective sense of the expression is now adopted by a number of authors, e.g. Riessler, 70; Buzy, Les symboles . . ., 291; Goettsberger, 56; Rinaldi, 109. Neither the immediate context nor the general doctrine of the book require us to see any other sense in the expression. Daniel, as we have noted (§ 526o), nowhere speaks of a personal Messiah.

Judaism also awaited a personal Messiah, the son **d** of David who would be king of God's people in the new Israel; cf Gn 49:10; Is 9:6 (MT 9:5)f; 11:1—5; Pss 2, 110 (109) etc. Since the kingdom promised to the faithful of Israel in Dn 7 is, de facto, Messianic, it is but natural that the chapter came to be interpreted later in the light of these other texts and that 'one like a son of man' of 13f was considered as the Messiah; all the more so as the Messianic prerogatives of many earlier texts (e.g. Gn 49:10; Is 9:6) correspond to those granted to the 'Son of Man' in Dn 7:13f. This genuine develop-ment of doctrine will explain how Christ calls himself 'the Son of Man' in the Gospels (Mk 14:62 etc. cf § 652c—d). 'The Son of Man' seems to be used by Christ as the equivalent of 'Messiah' (cf Mt 9:6; 17:21, etc). It is **e** quite uncertain whether pre-Christian Judaism had already come to consider the Son of Man of Dn as the Messiah and whether the 'Son of Man' had become a title for the Messiah. The Parable section of 1 Enoch (chh 37—71) has numerous references to the 'Son of Man' who, apparently, is understood to be the Messiah; but this section of the work is, unfortunately, not found in Qumran and may well be a Christian production. In the apocryphal work 2 Esdras (13, 3) from c. A.D. 65—100 the Messiah is called 'the Man' (i.e., 'the Son of Man') and is seeing rising from the sea and flying with

534e the clouds of heaven; a clear reference to Dn 7:13. It does not follow that the author considered the passage of Dn as messianic; he may merely have transferred features derived from the Son of Man of Dn to the Messiah; cf S. Mowinckel, *He That Cometh*, Oxford, 1956, 357. And even if he had considered the Son of Man as the Messiah it would not indicate that the identification was current in Our Lord's day, even in apocalyptic Judaism. Within rabbinic Judaism, R. Joshua ben Levi (A.D. 200—50) calls the Messiah ben David by the name '*Anani*, i.e. the Cloud-Man, with reference to Dn 7:13. Neither does this text tell us anything of the general situation in NT times within Rabbinic Judaism. Neither, in fact, does the view of R. Akiba (+ A.D. 135) who, apparently, took Dn 7:13 as messianic; cf G. F. Moore, *Judaism II*, Cambridge (U.S.A.), 1929, 336. The origin and exact signification of the title 'Son of Man' in the Gospels present well-known problems. Many strands of tradition have led up to the title and its signification; see C. H. Dodd, *According to the Scriptures*, 1952, 117f; E. W. Eaton, *The Book of Daniel*, London, 1956, 93ff; 182—85; E. J. Bowman, ET 59 (1947—48), 238—88, etc.

f Some commentators prefer to combine the individual and collective interpretation, considering the Son of Man to represent both king and subjects together to form one indivisible whole, one empire. Thus in 7:13 the Son of Man is an individual receiving the power to rule over the holy people, while in 18 and 27 the people, on account of their intimate association with their king, are represented as reigning with him; cf Apoc 20:4, 6. Thus Lagrange, RB 13 (1904), 506; idem, *Le Messianisme*, 228; de Menasce, BJ, 67, n.b.

It is true that there is a close relationship between ruler and empire in ancient thought—this is indeed why in 17 'kings' are mentioned. But it is still true that the author is primarily thinking of 'kingdoms' rather than of individual kings (cf 8:20; 2:37). The ancient versions (LXX, Theod, Vg) and some moderns (e g CV) render the word as 'kingdoms'; and one MT MS has in fact 'kingdoms' instead of 'kings' in 17. It is moreover clear from 23f that this is the sense—the fourth kingdom is referred to, whence ten kings are to arise.

g And even if the author were thinking of an individual king in 17 it would not follow that he must necessarily have thought of an individual Messiah for the messianic kingdom. Unlike all other ancient kingdoms Israel could conceive of itself without a human king. The true king of Israel was the Lord (cf 1 Sm 12:12, etc); and in fact it was historically longer without a human king than with one. Cf Rinaldi, 107. In view therefore of the non-personal messianism common during the Persian and early Gr. periods, the non-personal messianism of the book as a whole, and the weakness of the evidence for a personal Messiah in the present context, it seems improbable that the 'one like a Son of Man' refers to a personal Messiah.

Other authors hold that the text of Dn 7:13f is older than the Maccabean interpretation of it given in 21—27 (Gressmann, *Messias*, 401; Mowinckel, *He That Cometh*, Oxford, 1956, 348—53; Kruse, VDom. 37 (1959), 155—7; 192—211); and that the earlier text refers to the Son of Man as a heavenly person, whereas the Maccabean interpretation took it as a symbol of the pious Jews. According to Mowinckel, 1 Enoch, 2 Esdras and the NT depend on this earlier tradition and not directly on the present book of Dn. If this view were shown to be true we would have two strata of revelation and two views of the Son of Man in Dn. As yet, however, one

can only say that the interpretation is possible. **534g** Bibliography in Rinaldi, 33 and Vögt, LTK 7 (1962), 300.

8 The Vision of the Ram and the He-Goat— 535a With ch 8 the language changes back to Heb. In imagery, language, literary form and, to a certain extent, in doctrinal content, this ch is closely connected with the preceding. In both, we have a vision of empires under the symbolism of animals, and an interpretation given by an angel. Both dwell on the persecution of 'the holy ones' by 'the little horn'. There are, nevertheless, differences between the chh. Whereas in ch 7 the persecution is followed by the establishment of a new kingdom, in ch 8 the seer has scarcely a word of hope for his oppressed people. The reader has to wait for the final ch before this reappears (12:1ff), though a glimpse of it is given in 8:25 and 9:24. Ch 8, then, cannot be regarded as a doublet of ch 7 (Montgomery, 324), nor as an explanation of the second and third kingdoms of the first vision (Linder, 329). It is an independent vision, consistent with the first in general significance, but having its proper scope and outlook.

1f Introduction—The chronological introduction in **b** the first person, unlike 7:1, is probably from the same hand as the body of the ch. The visionary takes us back in spirit to Neo-Babylonian times. By the 3rd year of Belshazzar, which he apparently contrasts with his 1st year, the writer may mean the last year of the king and of the Neo-Babylonian empire. The Chaldean kingdom, though mentioned here in its king, has no further role in this or the remaining visions. Daniel is transported in spirit (cf Ezek 8:3; 11:24 etc) to 'Susa the *citadel*' in the province of Elam. 'Susa the citadel' appears to have been a current designation (cf Est 9:12 etc) for this chief city of the ancient civilization of Elam. The city was sacked in 645 B.C. but was rebuilt and surrounded by strong walls (whence, probably the name 'Susa the citadel') by Darius I c. 521 B.C. and became one of the residences of the Persian kings (cf Neh 1:1; Est 1:2 etc). From nearby Anshan came Cyrus. The Achemenid dynasty to which he belonged had conquered that part of the Median empire and occupied Susa by 596 B.C. After his conquest of the city of Babylon Alexander marched on Susa, emptied the treasury and left the family of Darius III in the city to study Greek. The stream Ulai, the Eulaeus of classical writers, flowing close to Susa (Pliny, *Natural History*, 6, 27) was an ideal setting for the vision of this ch and may have been chosen intentionally by the author.

3—12 The Vision—3. Daniel standing on the eastern **c** side (cf 4f) of the stream sees on the opposite side a ram with two horns of unequal size, the larger one appearing later than the other. The ram symbolized the kings of the Medes and Persians (20). It is uncertain whether Daniel here views the Medes and Persians as a single empire or as two distinct ones. As he notes that the higher horn i.e. the Persians (cf 2:39; 7:6), came up later than the Medes, it seems that here, as elsewhere, (cf §§ 528a—e, 531h) he distinguishes the two kingdoms, even though they are represented by a single beast. On the other hand, the two-horned ram is attacked by the he-goat i.e. Alexander, and *both* its horns are broken by it (7). The discrepancies may be explained by assuming that the author has here re-edited earlier material: cf also § 533a. **4.** The ram butting to the W, N and S represents principally, if not solely, the conquests of the Persian empire, in particular those of Cyrus 'whom victory met at every step' Is 41:2. The E from which the Persians hailed

535c (cf Is 41:2) is not mentioned, though it was known to the Jews (Est 1:1). Cambyses (529—522 B.C.) conquered Egypt (the S) and Darius (522—486) marched against Scythia (the N) in 516 and against Greece (the W) in 492—490 B.C. In 480 Xerxes sacked Athens (cf 11:2), a dishonour that Alexander the Great later **d** avenged. **5—7.** The he-goat is the Greek empire (21). The single horn on its forehead is its first king, Alexander the Great, who is represented as advancing furiously and with lightning speed eastwards to attack the ram, i.e. the Persian kingdom. The expression 'without touching the ground' vividly describes the speed of Alexander's march in his war against Persia. He defeated the Persian forces at Granicus (334 B.C.), Issus (333) and finally, in a decisive manner, at Arbela in 331 B.C. Before his army the Persian forces proved powerless; cf 1 Mc 1:1—7. The Indian campaign of Alexander does not interest Dn. **8.** At the height of his power and pride (cf 1 Mc 1:4ff) Alexander fell ill and died at Babylon in 323 B.C. at the age of thirty-two years. The great horn was broken. On his death his empire was divided between four of his generals: Cassander getting Macedonia and Greece; Lysimachus, Asia Minor; Seleucus, Babylonia and Syria and Ptolemy, Egypt. These are the four horns, facing **e** the four winds of heaven (cf 11:4). The first two had no part in the history of the Jews. **9—12.** The history of the Seleucid dynasty is passed over, and mention is made of one king only, Antiochus IV (175—164 B.C.), the little horn which made war against the S (Egypt); (cf 11:25—30; 1 Mc 1:16—20; 2 Mc 5:1—14; the E (Persia and Parthia; cf 1 Mc 3:27—37; 6:1—17; 2 Mc 9:1—4; Dn 11:44) and the glorious land (lit 'the glory'; Heb. *ṣebî*) i.e. Palestine. Palestine is again called 'the glorious land' in 11:16, 41; cf also Jer 3:19; Ezek 20:6, 15; Zech 7:14. In 8:9 Theodotion and Jer read *ṣābā* 'host' instead of 'glory': the meaning is still the same: Antiochus marched against 'the host' i.e. the pious Jews; cf 10—12. **10.** The host of heaven means the stars which here symbolize the pious Jews (cf 12:3). The little horn growing greater and greater until it reached the host of heaven represents the arrogance of Antiochus and his insolent attack on the religion of the Jews, many of whom fell victims of his arrogance like stars hurled down from heaven (cf Apoc 12). **11.** Antiochus now proceeds to wage war on God himself (cf 11:36—39), the Prince of the host of pious Israelites, whose daily sacrifice he abolished and whose sanctuary he cast down. The daily sacrifice (Heb. *tāmîd*, 'continual sacrifice') was offered twice daily in the evening and morning (cf to 6:11). On this sacrifice see Ex 29:38ff; Nm 28:3ff; on the abolition of divine worship by Antiochus see 1 Mc 1:45ff; Dn 9:27; 11:32; on his profanation of the temple cf 1 Mc 1:21—24, 47, **f** 54; 4:36—59. **12a.** Is obscure and possibly corrupt. The sense of the Vg is that the suspension of sacrifices was in punishment of the people's sins; cf 3:37; 2 Mc 6:12—17 and Dn 8:23. Various emendations have been put forward. Many omit 'host' or take it as the continuation of v 11 (CV, BJ). Linder, 337 and P. P. Saydon (CCHS [1]) emend *saba'* 'host, army' to *ṣebî* 'beauty' and take it with v 11 giving the sense: Antiochus treated irreverently not only the temple but also all Palestine, the land of beauty (cf 9) by erecting 'altars throughout all the cities of Juda' (1 Mc 1:47). Then 12 is made to read thus: 'and iniquity was set upon the place of the daily sacrifice', the allusion being to the abominable idol or pagan altar (see on 9:26f) erected on the altar of sacrifice, 1 Mc 1:54. Retaining MT, Driver, 117 and Goettsberger, 62 interpret as follows: An armed garrison was wickedly placed by Antiochus in the **535f** neighbourhood of the temple for the purpose of supressing more effectively the divine woship. B. N. Wambacq (*Jahvé Seba'ôt*, 1947, 126f) understands the MT as follows: A host (i.e. the stars representing the pious Israelites; cf 10, 13) has been given over (i.e. to the power of the enemy) together with the daily sacrifice through violence, or to be violently treated. This appears the best understanding of the text; cf 24. Antiochus will also try to stamp out the true religion by destroying the books of the Law which embodied the true religious and moral principles (1 Mc 1:60). Success will crown this iconoclastic campaign.

13f Duration of the Desecration of the Sanctuary— g 'Unto evening and morning 2,300'. This peculiar time expression can denote either 2,300 days or 2,300 evenings and mornings i.e. 1,150 days. The first sense is adopted by LXX, Theod, Vg and by many ancient and some less recent commentators. This period is then generally taken to refer to the time between Antiochus' campaign in Egypt in March 169 B.C., followed by his attack on Jerusalem (1 Mc 1:18ff), and the peace terms offered by Lysias to the Jews in July—August 163 B.C. (1 Mc 6:58—61), an interval of six years four months or c. 2,300 days (Linder, 342ff). A more natural, and now the more common, explanation is to see in the figure 2,300 the number of daily sacrifices (offered evening and morning) that were omitted because of Antiochus' profanation of the temple, i.e. 1,150 evenings and 1,150 mornings, or 1,150 days. This corresponds roughly to three and a half years and is generally identified with the time, the times and half-time of 7:25. The sanctuary was rededicated on nearly the same day on which it had been desecrated three years before (1 Mc 1:54 (57); 4:52) but the edict of persecution, and the persecution itself, began some time earlier (1 Mc 1:29ff, 41ff). C. Schedl (BZ n.s. 8 [1964], 102f) believes that the 1,150 days refers to the period between the desecration of the altar on 15 Chislev (6th Dec.) 167 B.C. and the fortification of mount Sion (cf 1 Mc 4:60) on 15 Shebath (31st Jan.) 163 B.C. He takes this time indication of 8:14 to be a Maccabean addition designed to show how the prophecy was fulfilled; see on 7:25.

15—27 The Interpretation of the Dream—15f. cf **h** 7:16ff. In the HT there is a play on the word *gāber* 'man' and Gabriel 'man of God' or 'God is strong'. Gabriel, God's messenger, is mentioned again 9:21 and in Lk 1:19, 26. **17.** 'Son of man', as in Ezek, denoted the weakness or inferiority of human nature in relation to God and the angels. 'The end time' in which the events of the vision will occur simply means 'the appointed time' (19), 'the time of God's wrath' (19), i.e. the persecution of Antiochus. The expression 'end time' occurs again in 11:35, 40; 12:4, and can also refer to the end of the world to which the doctrine and imagery of these visions may by typically referred. **18.** The contents of the vision and the presence of the angels stunned Daniel. **19.** There will be an end for this period of wrath and tribulation. All the calamities that befell Israel were considered as the manifestations of God's wrath and as punishments for their sins; cf 3:37f; 9:4—19; 1 Mc 1:64 (67); 2:49; 3:8; 2 Mc 6:12—17; Is 10:25 etc. **20—22.** Cf on 5—8. **23—25. 23.** 'When sinners (or 'sins') have reached their **i** measure'. It is not clear whether the sins are those of Israel or of the pagan empires. If the sins of apostasy etc of Israel are intended, the persecution of Antiochus is considered as a just punishment for them; cf 1 Mc

535i 1:11—16; 2 Mc 6:14. The other sense is more probable; the iniquity of all pagan empires reaches its culmination in the arrogant, sacrilegious and blasphemous behaviour of Antiochus, a bold-faced king, skilled in the art of dissimulation and duplicity; cf 1 Mc 1:30f. **24f.** The words 'not by his own force' omitted in RSV, CV, are probably interpolated from 22. If genuine, they imply that Antiochus will become powerful by intrigues or by divine permission. 24d—25ab appear corrupt. By slight textual emendations in part based on LXX, we get the following sense: **24d.** 'he shall destroy the mighty ones; **25ab** his cunning shall be against the holy ones, his treacherous conduct shall succeed.' (cf CV). RSV renders MT which has essentially the same sense. 25 notes how Antiochus will be destroyed by God alone
j without human agency; cf 2:45; 11:34. **26.** The truth of the vision 'of the evenings and mornings', i.e. the duration of the persecution, is confirmed. The truth of the entire vision is also implied. As in 10:1; 11:2 (cf Apoc 19:9; 21:5; 22:6) the angel asserts that the vision is not for the exilic period in which Daniel is presumed to have received it. The contents of the writing will be revealed when the crisis comes, 441 years later in Daniel's chronology (9:25—27), 375 years later in ours. The seer of Apoc 22:10, unlike Daniel, is told not to seal his book of prophecies as the time of their fulfilment is near.

536a 9 The Prophecy of the Seventy Weeks—The visions of chh 7 and 8 had shown Daniel the sad plight that awaited his people and their religion under Antiochus. The lamentable position in which the faithful servants of God were placed during the long nightmare of Antiochus' rule (171—164 B.C.), particularly during the latter half of it (167—164), was in ironic contrast with some of the earlier prophecies made to Israel. Through Jer 29:10f the Lord had promised that after Babylon had been permitted to punish her for the space of seventy years God would take her back to Palestine because his plans for Israel were 'plans for welfare and not for evil, to give them a future and a hope'. This promise must have sounded empty to some during the years 167—164 B.C. Even before the persecution had broken out many Jews had gone over to Hellenism, finding only a source of misery in God's law (1 Mc 1:11—15); the actual persecution led others to apostatize (cf 1 Mc 1:52; 2:16; Dn 7:27; 11:30; 12:4, 10). It is this problem of a seemingly unfulfilled prophecy that the apocalyptic seer solves in the present ch. The ch is composed of two parts: the general background and a prayer of Daniel, 1—23; the prophecy of the seventy weeks, 24—27.
b 1—2 Introduction—The prophecy is dated in the first year of Darius the Mede, therefore a short time after the fall of Babylon (5:31). In **1** Darius is called the son of Xerxes. In reality Xerxes I (486—465 B.C.) was son of Darius I (522—486 B.C.) and grandfather of Darius II (423—404 B.C.). The first year of Darius is explicitly noted, as with it the Neo-Babylonian empire had ended and the prophecies of Jeremiah on Israel's return to Palestine for a better life should have been fulfilled. On two occasions Jeremiah spoke of seventy years during which Judah and the surrounding nations would serve the king of Babylon. The first occasion was in 605 B.C. (25:11) the second after the first siege of Jerusalem in 598 B.C. (29:19). At the end of this period God would visit Babylon and restore his people to their homeland. Babylon did actually rule Syria—Palestine for seventy years or so, from 609 or 605 to 539 B.C. The seventy years of Jeremiah are, however,

to be taken rather as a round number signifying a long **536b** period of time. The prophecies of Jer were fulfilled in the permission to return given by Cyrus in 538 B.C. (cf 2 Chr 36:20—22; Ez 1:1ff; cf Is 40:2); but this fulfilment of the prophecies was very imperfect and God's promise through Jer was again recalled and considered unfulfilled in 520 B.C. as Jerusalem still lay in ruins (Zech 1:12). **2.** The prophecies of Jer already formed part of the collection of canonical books; cf Sir, prologue and § 14d.
3—19 Daniel's Prayer—In his endeavour to under- **c** stand the meaning of Jeremiah's words Daniel turns to God in prayer. His prayer is modelled after a type that seems to have been common in times of national calamity, characterized by the following features: confession of sin; acknowledgement of God's justice; appeal to his mercy and a prayer for forgiveness. Examples of such public prayers are to be found in Ez 9:6—15; Dn 3:26—45 (q.v.) and finally Bar 1:15—3:8 which may depend on Dn 9:3—19; cf B. N. Wambacq. Bib 40 (1959), 463—75. In its phraseology the prayer draws heavily on earlier books of the Bible. It may also depend on liturgical texts as only in this part of Daniel (9, 13, 20) does the divine name Yahweh occur. This prayer intro- duces the vision of 24—27 as it gives the theological reason why Israel is punished, and why the period of tribulation spoken of by Jeremiah has now been prolonged sevenfold. It is not, then, an interpolation as has been suggested by some (Marti, 64; Charles, 226f; Goetts- berger, 69; Bentzen, 41f). The central theme of **d** **4—14** is that all Israel's sufferings are due to her abandonment of the covenant. God is just in all that he has done (**14**). Moses (Lv 26; Dt 38 etc) had taught them that infidelity to the covenant would bring tribulation and exile; God would chastize them sevenfold (Lv 26:27 etc) for their sins. The evils that had now befallen Israel and Jerusalem merely show that God has 'carried out the threats he spoke against them' (**12**), having watched over his words to fulfill them (**14**; cf Jer 1:12; 31:28) The greatest calamity that has ever occurred under heaven' is the profanation of the sanctuary in Antiochus' attempt to exterminate the one true religion. As regards the phraseology, 4b agrees almost verbally with Neh 1:5 and Dt 7:9; 5f with 1 (3) Kgs 8:47; Dt 17:20; Jer 44:4, 21; Neh 9:34.
20—23 The Apparition of the Angel—20 gives a **e** summary of the preceding prayer of confession and petition on behalf of God's holy mountain, i.e. Jerusalem (16). **21.** The angel Gabriel whom Daniel had seen on a previous occasion (8:16) is sent from heaven. In swift flight (so Vg and the ancient versions) he comes to Daniel at the time of the now-forbidden evening sacrifice (cf 8:11, 13f; 7:25), offered at c. 3 p.m. (cf on 6:10 [11]). **22f.** The moment Daniel began his prayer of petition, and manifested his desire to understand the prophecy of Jeremiah on the period Jerusalem should lie desolate (2) a divine revelation was made in heaven (cf 10:12). The angel had come to instruct him on the meaning of this prophecy.
24—27 The Prophecy of the Seventy Weeks—It is **f** well to state first some principles that appear useful, and perhaps necessary, for a true understanding of the passage: (i) The vv are to be interpreted in the light of the plan and doctrine of the entire book. The events referred to by the author are to be determined, where possible, from parallel passages of his work. (ii) The seventy weeks of years correspond to the seventy years of the prophecy of Jeremiah multiplied sevenfold. The sum total of the subdivisions 7 + 62 + 1 must then

536f amount to 70, i.e. the subdivisions must be taken as running consecutively and, neither in whole nor in part, concurrently. (iii) The chronology according to which the author put 490 years between the first and last event recorded need not necessarily correspond to the time reckoning we now use, one that was worked out after the date of composition of Dn. (iv) The early versions are affected by their theological view of the prophecy and can be used in textual criticism only with reserve. (v) No use whatever is made of the prophecy in the NT. (vi) The prophecy is a reply to Daniel's desire to understand God's mind on the ruins of Jerusalem (22f; cf 2) and to his prayer for the holy city (7, 12, 16—19). This invites us to interpret it primarily of the city and the sanctuary.

The point of Jeremiah's prophecy that chiefly interested the seer was the 70 years duration of the *ruins* of Jerusalem (2). In the prayer, too, he refers almost solely to the sad plight of Jerusalem, God's own city (12, 16, 18f) and to the desolate sanctuary (17), the holy mountain (20). 24—27 is God's answer to this prayer on behalf of the holy mountain (20), i.e. the temple. 26—27 is clearly Maccabean in its perspective and narrates the fate of the temple in the same manner as 7:25; 8:11—14;

g 11:31. **24.** It is universally admitted that the 70 weeks are 70 seven-year periods (cf Lv 25:8) or 490 years. This period is divided in 25—27 into three unequal parts 7 + 62 + 1, of which the last part is further subdivided into two halves (27b). The end of each period, and the beginning of the first, is marked off by some special event, a fact which tends to show that the parts are intended to run consecutively. 'Seventy weeks are decreed (i.e. decided by God) . . . to finish the transgression etc', i.e. it has been decided by God, that only at the close of the period will three things offensive to God be removed and three benefits be bestowed. The negative elements to be removed are transgression, sin and iniquity. These are the three classical terms in the OT for sins against God; cf S. Lyonnet *De Peccato et Redemptione*, Rome

h 1957, I 38—40 = VDom. 35 (1957), 74—76. At the end of the period (i) transgression will stop, i.e. will be definitely checked; (ii) sins (Kethib) or rather 'sin' (Qere) will end (lit 'be sealed up'); sin will be sealed up and thus prevented from doing any more harm; (iii) iniquity will be atoned. This is the only passage where this expression 'to atone iniquity' occurs in the OT, though of course the idea occurs more often there. Atonement is used here in the sense of appeasing God, offended by sin. We are not told whether the iniquity that will be atoned for is that of Antiochus, the apostasy of the Jews, or whether it is sin in general. To this threefold negative element corresponds a threefold positive element consisting in (i) the bringing in of everlasting righteousness, i.e. a state of friendship between God and man in which God's supreme rights and man's obligations deriving therefrom will be recognized; (ii) 'the sealing of vision and prophet' i.e. the visions and prophecies of Dn 7—9 etc, or of Jer 25:11; 29:9 etc will be authenticated, shown true, in their fulfilment (cf Jn 3:33; 6:27). The metaphor is taken from the sealing of documents to attest their genuineness (cf 1 [3] Kgs 21:8; Jer 32:10, 11, 44); (iii) the anointing of a most holy place (lit 'a holy of holies'). 'A holy of holies' is used in the OT to denote the temple, the sanctuary, the altar. In 1 Chr 23:13 alone does it refer to a person. Here 'the anointing of a holy of holies' most probably refers to the rededication of the temple and of the altar of sacrifices in 164 B.C. (1 Mc 4:36—40; 2 Mc 10:1—8).

i The only element of this v that appears to be clearly connected with the immediate end of the persecution **536i** of Antiochus is the 'anointing of a holy of holies'. The 'bringing in of everlasting righteousness', and perhaps the other elements as well, show us another aspect of the kingdom of God to be given to 'the holy ones of the Most High' after the destruction of Antiochus (7:13f, 18, 26f). Independently whether the angel intended or Daniel understood 24 to refer to the fifth kingdom, the prophecy had to await the advent of Christ for its complete fulfilment. He took away the sin of the world (Jn 1:29) and made expiation for iniquity by his death. By his grace he introduced a reign of righteousness and is, in his Body, (cf Jn 2:21; 4:13f; 7:37—39; Apoc 21:22) the New Temple of which the prophets spoke (cf Ezek 47:1ff; Zech 14:8ff; Jl 1 [4]:18). 24, then, appears to be Messianic in the same sense as the prophecies of chh 2 and 7 i.e. it refers to the kingdom of God that will be introduced after the destruction of the persecutor of the Jewish religion. Only in Christ, however, is the prophecy fully realized.

25—27. The vv tell us what will take place before **j** the prophecy of 24 is fulfilled and, by a re-interpretation of Jeremiah's 70 years, take us from the beginning of the exile to the punishment of Antiochus. As elsewhere in the book, details are given only for the reign of Antiochus (26f) **25a.** The first week (c. 587—538 B.C.) and the entire period commences with the 'going forth of the word' i.e. the utterance of the divine decree or divine communication through Jeremiah (25:11; 29:10; cf 2) on the return from exile and the rebuilding of Jerusalem. This date is probably to be reckoned, not from 605 (Jer 25:11) nor from 598 (Jer 29:10), but from the destruction of Jerusalem in 587 B.C. when the decree began to take effect (cf Is 55:11). If we do assume 605 or 598 B.C. or some other date as the *terminus a quo* for the period, then we must take Dn's first 7 weeks, as Jer's 70 years, as merely a round number to cover a period whose exact duration may have been unknown to him. The end of this week is, in any case, the end of the exile; and the advent of 'one who was anointed and a prince' marks the beginning of the next period, during which Jerusalem will be rebuilt. This 'anointed one and prince' is probably Cyrus, Yahweh's anointed, Is 45:1, who by his decree of 538 B.C. permitted the Jews to return to their homeland and rebuild the temple (Ez 1:1ff; 6:3—5; 2 Chr 36:23). It could also be Joshua or Zerubbabel, leaders of the people during the restoration that followed the repatriation (Ez 2:2; etc; Hag 1:1; Zech 3:1). The view that makes the first week begin with Cyrus' edict of 538 B.C. is not probable; the starting-point in Daniel's re-interpretation must be the same as that of the prophecies of Jeremiah. **25b The Sixty-two Weeks or 434 Years (538—170 k B.C.)**—The MT in its accentuation divides the first period of 1 week from the succeeding 62. The sense, as we have seen, requires the same. The 62 weeks during which Jerusalem will be rebuilt is, then, the period between 538 B.C. when Cyrus gave permission to the Jews to return and the 'cutting down of an anointed one' i.e. the murder of the High Priest Onias III in 170 B.C. During this period Jerusalem will be rebuilt and fortified 'with square and moat' i.e. provided with broad spaces and ditches round about it. But times will be hard; cf Ez 4. Neh 4:6. An evident difficulty immediately presents itself. Between 538 and 170 B.C. we have only 368 years: Daniel's 434 years is 66 too many. This difficulty is more apparent than real. Due to the lack of documents, the chronology of the period between the beginning of the exile and the advent of the Gr.

36k empire (312 B.C.) was most uncertain for the Jews. In general they considered it to have been longer than it really was and the error naturally affected their general chronology even after the beginning of the Gr. period. The chronology adopted by the Egyptian Jew Demetrius (c. 200 B.C. and roughly a contemporary of our book's author) errs 70 years by excess, almost the same as Daniel's 66. Even the chronology of Josephus is c. 33 (BJ 6, 4, 8), 50 (Ant. 12, 11, 1) or 60 (Ant. 20, 10, 2) years too long. Daniel's period of '62 weeks' is then practically the same as that of Demetrius and Josephus in Ant. 20, 10. It may have been a current one in Daniel's day, or may merely be a round number to bridge the years between the return under Cyrus and 170 B.C.

l 26f The Final Week 171–164 B.C.—The end of the 62 weeks and the beginning of the final week is marked by the 'cutting down of an anointed one' who is to be distinguished from the 'anointed one and prince' mentioned at the end of the first week (25a), 434 years earlier. This 'anointed one' is Onias III, the pious High Priest lured from sanctuary at Daphne, near Antioch, and assassinated by Andronicus, the minister of Antiochus, in 170 B.C.; cf 2 Mc 4:30–35; on his virtues see 2 Mc 3:1ff; 4:1ff. He is 'the prince of the covenant, of 11:22. In 170 B.C. Antiochus had his own son and nephew assassinated. **26b.** 'and he shall have nothing' (RSV) renders rather literally a two-word elliptical and obscure Heb. phrase which is variously paraphrased; 'he shall have no help' (Junker, 75; Rinaldi, 129); 'he shall have committed no crime' (Theod). The Vg renders 'Non erit eius populus qui eum negaturus est'; if genuine (cf VDom. 19 [1939], 146) this is a Messianic paraphrase. With some Heb. MSS we may suppress the word 'and', join 'the city' with the preceding, and read: 'he shall be cut down while he does not possess (i.e. is away from) the city'. We must then read 'sanctuary' instead of 'city and sanctuary' in the following passage; cf CV. 'The people of the prince who is to come' are the mercenaries of Antiochus who pillaged Jerusalem and the sanctuary without destroying them; cf 1 Mc 1:20–24. 'And his (or 'its') end will be like a torrent' probably refers to the last stages of the sacrilege and persecution. If they refer to Antiochus they mean that he will be swept away by a divine judgement as by an overwhelming flood; cf 1 Mc 6:8–16. Until the end of the persecution, at the time determined by God, there will be war and desolation. The various phases of this entire **m** period are described in 27. **27.** The strong covenant which the leader (mentioned in 26) will make with the many (cf 11:30–32) is an allusion to the co-operation Antiochus received from many apostate Jews who abandoned the true covenant with God; cf 1 Mc 1:11–15. For half a week i.e. for three years and a half (or 'in the middle of the week') Antiochus will cause all sacrifices in the temple to cease. This we know Antiochus did on 15th Chislev (i.e. 6th Dec.) 167 B.C.; cf 8:11ff; 7:25; 11:30f. In their stead there will be 'on the wing, *the horrible abomination*' (*šiqqûṣ mešōmēm*), traditionally rendered 'the abomination of desolation'. This expression occurs four times in Dn (9:27; 11:31; 12:11; 8:13 'the sin of desolation' or 'the desolating sin') and has a general meaning, denoting any abominable idolatrous object causing horror to the faithful. The author of 1 Mc referred it to the altar Antiochus set up over the altar of holocausts (1 Mc 1:54, 59), which was probably dedicated to Zeus Olympius as the temple was (2 Mc 6:2). This god (cf 11:38) was probably identified with the Syrian god Baal Samem, of which Daniel's *šiqqûṣ mešōmēm* is seemingly

an intentional distortion. The 'wing' on which the abomi- **536m** nation was set up according to Dn is generally taken to be the pinnacle of the temple. More probably it is the ramp that led up to the altar of holocausts; on this ramp see Jos BJ 5, 5, 6. After a specified period the divine wrath will be poured out, completely destroying the abomination. The beginning of a new age, to which 24 refers, is tacitly implied.

Appendix—The Messianic Interpretation of the n Prophecy of the 70 Weeks. (For the various interpretations see F. Fraidl, *Die Exegese der Siebzig Wochen Daniels in der alten und mittleren Zeit*, Graz 1883.) The various interpretations of this prophecy may be grouped under two headings: the historical interpretation and the Messianic interpretation. In the commentary the historical interpretation has been propounded, as this is the one indicated by the text of 9:25–27 and by the position of the verses in the general context of the visions. It is the view now generally followed by commentators.

From the 2nd cent. onwards vv 25–27 have been **o** taken by Christian writers as a direct prediction of the coming (25) and death (27) of Christ and of the abolition of levitical sacrifice by his death on the Cross (26). This view has been put forward in various forms: cf Fraidl op cit and Driver, 143–50. The direct Messianic interpretation of the text has been more recently advocated by G. Closen in VDom. 18 (1938), 47–56, 115–25. In this interpretation 'an anointed one and prince' of 25 is identified with 'an anointed one' of 26 and the divisions of 7 and 62 weeks are taken together as a single period of time between 'the going forth of the word' and the 'cutting down of an anointed one'. The 'word' of 25 is further taken to be a decree on the return or rebuilding of Jerusalem, and is generally assumed to be that of Artaxerxes I in 458 (Ez 7:12 26), 69 weeks, i.e. 483 years, from this will bring us to A.D. 25–33 for the end of the 70 week period and connects the prophecy directly with the activity and death of Christ. The difficulty with this view **p** of 25–27 is that it is based only on certain elements of the prophecy and ignores their general context. Its treatment of the biblical text seems forced; 'the word' is in our view the divine one to Jeremiah rather than a much later edict. The 7 weeks and 62 weeks appear to be two distinct periods, not one as this view is obliged to consider them. In other words, the Messianic interpretation does violence to the biblical text, in order to see in it a chronology that refers to Christ's death c. A.D. 30. The theory, too, seems unreal as the proponents of the Messianic interpretation appear to be working on a chronology that was probably unknown to the people of Daniel's or of our Lord's day. A more serious difficulty against this Messianic interpretation is that no use whatever is made of Dn 9:25–27 by Christ or the Apostles, a fact that seems to indicate that it was not considered by them to be a Messianic prophecy.

It is then better to take 25–27 as referring directly **q** to the persecution of Antiochus IV. Verse 24, on the contrary, speaks of the age following on the destruction of the persecutor and is Messianic in the same sense as the prophecies of chh 2 and 7, i.e. it shows us an aspect of the new kingdom to be introduced by God **which was inaugurated by Christ and will be perfected** at the Parousia. 24 can then be considered Messianic and eschatological in the direct sense. If certain phrases cf 25–27 are also Messianic and eschatological, it is in a typical, not in the direct sense.

537a **10—12 Revelation of History from the Beginning of Persian Rule to the End of Time**—This revelation is a brief survey of the history of the Persian and Seleucid reigns and of the diplomatic relations between the Seleucids and the Ptolemies. It is carried down to the time of Antiochus, whose end is also mentioned. The prediction of the triumph of the righteous at the end of the world closes the revelation. Unlike the other visions where historical events are revealed by the use of symbols, this is a direct communication of historical events by an angel to Daniel. It consists of a long introduction (10:1—11:1), a brief history of the Persian empire (11:2f) and a detailed one of the Seleucid kingdoms (11:3—45) ending with a revelation of the resurrection (12:1ff).

b **10:1—11:1 Introduction. The Apparition of the Angel—1.** This vision, like the first (ch 7), is introduced by a chronological indication in the third person, whereas the vision itself is narrated in the first. For 'the third year of Cyrus' (536 B.C.) LXX reads 'the first year', probably an emendation; cf 1:21. 'King of Persia': before the conquest of Babylon Cyrus is called 'king of Anshan' (ANET, 315*cd*) and 'king of Persia' (ANET, 306*b*). He appears to have abandoned these titles at the fall of Babylon and calls himself instead 'king of kings', 'the great king' and particularly 'king of Babel'. Only once do we find him called: 'king of Persia'. Xerxes abandoned the title 'king of Babylon' styling himself instead 'king of the Persians and the Medes' (cf R. Ghirshman, *Iran*, 1954, 191). The title 'king of Persia' became a common designation of the Persian kings only in the late Persian or early Greek period. It is common in Ezra but the older documents in the book have 'king of Babel' e.g. 5:24; cf also S. R. Driver, *Introd. to the Literature of the OT*, 1913[9], 546. 1*b* gives the contents of the word—the wars and tribulations that awaited Daniel's people.

c **2—3.** Daniel's three-weeks mourning was probably due to a presentiment of the trials of his people about to be revealed to him (cf 14). He desired to know the future destiny of the people (12). **4.** 'The great river' elsewhere in the Bible means the Euphrates. Many take 'the Tigris' as a gloss, though it is better retained. The vision of 8:2 was on the Ulai. The 'first month' is Nisan. **5f.** Daniel saw what he thought was a man, (lit 'a son of man'). The description is reminiscent of Ezek 1:13. The superhuman being was probably an angel and perhaps Gabriel who had appeared to him before: 8:16; 9:21. He can hardly be taken as the Son of Man of 7:13f as H. Kruse believes (VDom. 37 [1959], 201ff), cf Apoc 1:13—15; 2:18. **7—9.** The cause of the terror was not the vision, which Daniel's companions did not see, but perhaps a flash of lightning and a thundering noise which preceded the vision; cf Ac 9:7; 22:9. **12.** An example of the efficacy of prayer accompanied **d** by fasting; cf Tb 12:8. **13.** Though the angel set out at once (12) as in 9:21, he was impeded on his journey and held back for 21 days by 'the prince of Persia', i.e. its tutelary angel who tried to intercept the message which might contain unfavourable decrees against the people entrusted to his care. All peoples had their tutelary angels (cf Dt 32:8 LXX and Qumran Heb fragment) who defended the cause of the nations confided to their charge before God; hence the struggle of the angel of Persia with the divine messenger bearing the decree. Finally Michael, an angel of higher rank or an archangel (Jude 9), came to his aid. The messenger left Michael to continue the struggle with the angel of Persia and continued on his journey to Daniel. This sense is given by reading *hôdartîw*, 'I left him' (with **537** LXX and Theod.) instead of *nôdartî*, 'I was left' of the MT. Apocalyptic writers represent the events of history as decided between the heavenly powers before they are enacted on earth (cf Apoc 12). Dn 10:13ff is then probably no more than a dramatic representation of the nations' opposition to the people of God and of God's absolute control of all nations. **15—19.** Daniel faints **e** but is restored by the heavenly visitor. **20—11:1.** These verses are probably disarranged. Charles (p. 265) and Montgomery (p. 416), followed by BJ, rearrange them thus: 20*a*, 21*a*, 20*b*, 21*b*, 11:1. Another possibility is that in 20—11:1, as in the whole ch, we have a redactional combination of two slightly different forms of the same narrative (Junker, 99). The angel calls Daniel's attention by a rhetorical interrogation (20*a*); he then declares that he will announce to him what is written in the book of truth (21*a*), the destinies of mankind being, as it were, written by God in a book and therefore unalterable. The object of this announcement is the continuation of the struggle with the angel of the Persians and after this is over, the beginning of a further struggle with the angel of Greece, against whose nation severe things have been said in the revelation borne to Daniel. The struggle with the angels will end with victory for the revealing angel as he is aided by Michael, the great patron angel of the Jews (**20***b*, **21***b*). The sense of the passage is not quite clear, however. Neither is that of **11:1** where Gabriel appears as the helper of Michael from the first year of Darius the Mede. This is hardly consistent with the context, which represents Michael as the helper. It is preferable to remove 11:1*a* as a gloss (Montgomery, 416; Junker, 99; Bentzen, 44; CV; BJ) and to read: 'standing as a helper and as a defence for me' as a continuation of 21*b*.

11:2 The Persian Age—The history of the Persian **f** kings concerns only four; Cyrus, during whose reign the seer had this vision (10:1), and three others. 'The fourth' is doubtless the fourth of this series and not the fourth to arise after Cyrus. The three kings intended are probably the first three of Cyrus' successors: Cambyses (529—522), Darius I (522—486) and Xerxes (486—465). On the wealth of Xerxes and his military expedition against Greece in the year 480 B.C. cf Herod 7, 20—99. It cannot be inferred that the prophet knew of only four Persian kings, of whom Xerxes was the last. As he was not particularly interested in the history of them all, he chose to mention four on account of the relation of the fourth king with Greece, whose intervention in Palestine he intended to narrate at greater length.

3f Alexander the Great (336—323 B.C.)—3. A **g** powerful king ruling over an immense empire and crushing all resistance is a very appropriate description of Alexander the Great; cf 8:5—8; 7:23. **4.** The suddenness of the end of Alexander's short-lived empire is vividly depicted, (cf 8:8 'the great horn was broken'). None of his generals who succeeded him had any blood relation with Alexander or enjoyed his power. Likewise none of their successors were of Alexander's kith and kin. His illegitimate son Heracles and his posthumous son Alexander were both murdered in 309 and 311 respectively.

5—20 The Conflicts of the Seleucids and the h Ptolemies—Coele-Syria was for many years the bone of contention and the scene of many wars between the kings of Syria and of Egypt. **5.** The king of the south is Ptolemy I, son of Lagus, who, after Alexander's death, secured Egypt for himself and ruled it first as satrap (323—305) and then as king (305—285).

537h Seleucus I Nicator, another of Alexander's generals, was one of Ptolemy's princes or captains. At the convention of Treparadisus in 321 he received the satrapy of Babylon; in 316 he fled to Egypt, where he became Ptolemy's general; in 312 he recovered his satrapy and extended his dominion over all Asia Minor. He made Antioch his capital. Seleucus' empire was thus more extensive than that of Ptolemy. **6.** After some years, hostilities broke out between Ptolemy II Philadelphus (285–247) and Antiochus II Theos (261–246), grandson of Seleucus I, over the possession of Palestine. In order to bring about a peaceful settlement Ptolemy II gave his daughter Berenice in marriage to Antiochus II, who had divorced his wife Laodice. After her father's death Berenice was divorced by Antiochus, and later murdered with her child by Antiochus' first wife (Jerome ad loc); cf 2:43.

i 7–9. Ptolemy III Euergetes (247–222) and Seleucus II Callinicus (246–226). *'After some time'* (these words are to be transposed from the end of 6 to the beginning of 7) Ptolemy III, brother of Berenice, and therefore 'a branch from her roots', arose in the place of Ptolemy II, and with a view to avenging his sister's murder marched into Syria, reached its outer defences, entered into Seleucia and Antioch, the stronghold of the king of Syria, and returned to Egypt with a rich booty. He had to desist from attacking the king of Syria on account, very probably, of an insurrection in Egypt. After two years Seleucus II made a reprisal attack against Egypt, but was defeated and had to retreat.

j 10–19 Antiochus III the Great (223–187)—10f. Seleucus III Ceraunos (226–223), the son and successor of Seleucus II, was killed during a campaign in Asia Minor, and was succeeded by his brother Antiochus III, who resumed the war with Egypt, and conquered the Egyptian possessions in Syria (219). Antiochus then (217) moved in the direction of Egypt and met the forces of Ptolemy IV at Raphia, on the borders of Egypt and Palestine. Each army had c. 70,000 men. Antiochus was defeated (Polybius 5, 8) leaving c. 17,000 dead. **12.** Despite his decisive victory the weak-willed voluptuary Ptolemy IV did not follow it up. **13f.** From the outset of his career Antiochus had as his ideal to restore the single empire of Alexander. After his defeat at Raphia he restored his army, reconquered Asia Minor and in 204 entered into an alliance with Philip V of Macedon. c. 203 Ptolemy IV and his queen died in mysterious circumstances and were succeeded by their infant son Ptolemy V (204–180). The 'many who shall rise against the king' of Egypt (14) are Antiochus III, Philip of Macedon his ally, and the many insurgents in Egypt who were dissatisfied with the rule of Agathocles, the prime minister of the **k** infant king Ptolemy. It is not clear who are the 'men of violence' from among the Jews that are to rise up in fulfilment of vision (14) during the reign of Antiochus. They are probably the Tobiads, an influential family of the reign of the Ammonites, part of which changed its allegiance from the Ptolemies to the Seleucids about this time; cf Jos.Ant. 12; 4, 6 and Ricciotti, *History of Israel* II, 220–223. This new pro-Seleucid policy on the part of the Tobiads and other Jews prepared the way for the introduction of the Hellenistic and pagan customs which lay at the root of the apostasy and persecution that were soon to come under Antiochus IV. We do not know what prophecy they fulfilled in so acting; probably that contained in Dn itself.

l 15f. After the parenthesis of 14 *b* Daniel reverts to the campaigns of Antiochus. After his alliance with Philip of Macedon Antiochus invaded Coele-Syria in 202 and reached Gaza, the 'well-fortified city'. He then returned to Asia Minor and the Egyptian army, under **537l** Scopas, marched to invade his Syrian territories. Antiochus advanced against him and utterly routed the Egyptian forces at the battle of Panion later Caesarea Philippi, (Mt 16:13). After this victory Antiochus took possession of Palestine, 'the glorious land' (cf 8:9).

17. Antiochus never invaded Egypt. Though he had **m** intended to acquire all the kingdom of Ptolemy, he preferred to come to equitable terms with him owing to the interference of Rome. So he made an alliance with him, giving him his daughter Cleopatra in marriage, which was celebrated at Raphia in 192. The unusual expression 'a daughter of women' probably denotes Cleopatra's excellent character and administrative qualities. By this political marriage Antiochus intended to simulate friendship with Ptolemy hoping to get a peaceful footing in Egypt without irritating the Romans. The marriage alliance proved as unfruitful as did that of Berenice with Antiochus II (6ff). The plans of Antiochus III were foiled, for Ptolemy's generals, distrustful of Antiochus' show of friendliness, were constantly on their guard, and Cleopatra was on the side of her husband rather than on that of her father. Antiochus never got possession of Egypt. **18f.** In further- **n** ance of his grandiose plans for re-establishing the single kingdom of Alexander the Great, Antiochus marched into Asia Minor and Greece after Cleopatra's marriage. In 191 he was defeated by the Romans at Thermopylae and again at Magnesia in 190 by the Roman general Lucius Cornelius Scipio, the commander who not only checked Antiochus' insolence but made him submit to humiliating terms of peace. He was obliged to send hostages to Rome and pay a war indemnity of 12,000 talents within twelve years (Livy, 37, 45); cf 1 Mc 8:6f. One of the hostages sent to Rome in 189 was Antiochus, the younger son of Antiochus III. He was the future notorious Antiochus IV referred to in 21ff. The meaning of the last phrase of 19 is uncertain. Antiochus met an ignominious end in 187 in Elymais in Persia, where he was killed as he attempted to plunder the temple of Bel to help him pay his war indemnity. The cuneiform chronicle (B.M. 35603) gives the exact date as 3/4 July 187 B.C.; cf Bib 36 (1955), 262. **20.** Antiochus III was succeeded by his son Seleucus IV Philopator (187–175), 'who sent a *tax collector* through the glorious kingdom'. The allusion is to the mission of Heliodorus, the prime minister of Seleucus, to plunder the temple of Jerusalem (2 Mc 3:1–40). After twelve years of an inglorious reign Seleucus was murdered by Heliodorus.

21–45 Antiochus IV Epiphanes, the Great Per- 538a secutor of the Jews (175–164)—For the fourth and last time the writer informs his readers of the reign and persecution of Antiochus. His interest in the age and person of the persecutor is evinced by the abundance of details with which his story is retold. Antiochus was the brother of Seleucus IV, and was a hostage in Rome for 14 years. At Seleucus' request the Romans released Antiochus and took Demetrius, a son of Seleucus, in his place (cf 1 Mc 7:1). While Demetrius was on his way to Syria, Seleucus was killed and Antiochus hastened to seize the throne which legitimately belonged to Demetrius, Seleucus' son. On Antiochus' relations with the Jews see 1 Mc 1:11–6:16; 2 Mc 4:7–10:9. For an appreciation of his character see F. M. Abel, 'Antiochus Epiphane' *Vivre et Penser* (= RB) 1re série (1941), 231–54.

21 Antiochus' Accession—To the Jews Antiochus was not a *theos epiphanēs*, 'a manifest god', as he boastfully called himself, but a despicable man. He had no right to the throne: the normal successor of Seleucus would have been his elder son Demetrius, hostage of Rome.

538a Next in line of succession would be another son of Seleucus who seemingly enjoyed the favour of the people of Antioch. Antiochus arrived at Antioch unsuspected and usurped the throne by intrigue.

b 22—24 His Rise to Power—22. The army he completely destroyed was probably that of Heliodorus, who, after having murdered Seleucus IV, attempted to oppose Antiochus and to seize the throne. The prince of the covenant is probably the High Priest Onias III, murdered by Andronicus in 170 (2 Mc 4:34; see on 9:25f). In this same year (170 B.C.) Antiochus had his nephew and his own son Antiochus done to death (cf Bib 36 [1955], 262 and J. Starcky in *Les livres des Maccabées*, BJ, 248, n. *a* to 4:38) by the agency of this same Andronicus. As Antiochus himself does not appear to have been implicated in the murder of Onias, other commentators believe the 'prince of the covenant' was the young son of Seleucus IV, also murdered at the order of Antiochus in 170 B.C.; cf H. H. Rowley ET 55 (1943—44), 24—27. **23.** Probably describes Antiochus' duplicity, cf 8:24 and 1 Mc 1:30. **24.** He was a senseless spendthrift, a fact well attested by ancient historians (cf Livy, 41, 20; Polyb. 26, 10; 1 Mc 3:30). Unlike any king that preceded him, he would visit the richest provinces not to collect taxes but to lavish gifts apparently to secure their allegiance in preparation for his coming invasion of Egypt. Other interpreters take this verse to refer to Antiochus' plunder of the provinces to fill his empty coffers (cf Montgomery, 452; Rinaldi, 145).

c 25—28 Antiochus' First Egyptian Campaign, 170—169 B.C.—Cf 1 Mc 1:17—20. The war was provoked by Ptolemy VI Philometor acting on the insensate advice of his ministers, probably his guardians, Eulaeus and Lenaeus. Antiochus defeated the young king between Pelusium on the borders of Egypt and Mt Casius, captured the fortress of Pelusium, and went on to occupy the whole of Egypt. Ptolemy, while attempting to escape, fell into the hands of Antiochus. In order to achieve the complete subjugation of Egypt, Antiochus cunningly simulated friendship with his royal prisoner Ptolemy, whom he lavishly entertained at table and maliciously pretended that he only intended to restore him to his throne. But Alexandria held out and Ptolemy Physcon (Euergetes II), brother of Ptolemy, was proclaimed king. When Antiochus departed from Egypt Philometor and Euergetes were reconciled, and Antiochus' plans for a complete and permanent occupation of Egypt were foiled. On his way back to Syria Antiochus made a detour to Jerusalem and plundered the sanctuary (1 Mc 1:21—24).

d 29—30a Antiochus' Second Egyptian Campaign, 168 B.C.—When the brothers Ptolemy VI and Euergetes II had been reconciled, Antiochus marched once more towards Egypt, but the issue was quite different from that of the preceding campaign. The Roman Senate, to whom the brothers had appealed, sent the legate Popilius who, on his arrival at Alexandria, ordered Antiochus to withdraw immediately from Egyptian soil (Livy, 45, 12). 'The ships of the Kittim' of MT 30 are 'the Roman galleys' (Vg, DV, KV). Kittim primarily denotes the island of Cyprus (from Mt Kition on the south side of the island); cf Gn 10; 4; 1 Chr 1:7; Is 23:1; later the word came to refer to the islands and coasts of the Mediterranean Sea (Jer 2:10; Ezek 27:6) and later still, to the western maritime peoples (1 Mc 1:1; 8:5) e.g. the Macedonians. Here, as in some Qumran texts, it denotes the Romans; cf Nm 24:24.

e 30b—39 Antiochus persecutes the Jewish Religion—30b. After being unceremoniously turned out of Egypt, Antiochus 'withdrew his army into Syria in high dudgeon indeed and groaning in spirit' (Polyb. 29, 27;

Livy 45, 12). The Jews were to become the victims of **538e** Antiochus' humiliating experiences. On his return journey through Palestine he decided to hellenize the Jewish nation as part of his plan to unite culturally and religiously what remained of his empire. A pro-hellenistic party had already arisen among the Jews (1 Mc 1:46—57; cf § 595c); Antiochus now singled out those potential allies, but massacred other Jews, on the pretext that popular support was given to a revolt against Menelaus, the High Priest he had appointed in Jerusalem; cf 2 Mc 5:1—14, covering this period. **31—32.** Having avenged himself on his enemies in Jerusalem, Antiochus returned to Antioch. Then early in 167 he sent Apollonius with an army 22,000 strong and orders to put the men to death and sell the women and children as slaves (1 Mc 1:29—32; 2 Mc 5:24—26). On the same occasion Antiochus had a citadel, the Akra, built near the temple as a fortress for his soldiers and as a shelter for renegade Jews (1 Mc 1:33—35). In the autumn of the same year came the edict of Antiochus proscribing the practice of Judaism (1Mc 1:41ff; 2 Mc 6—7) and the abolition of sacrifice (cf chh 7, 8 and 9). On the 15th Chislev 167 the horrible abomination was set up in the temple. The impious Jews who had abandoned the covenant were then made apostates by means of deceitful promises; cf 1 Mc 2:16. 'The temple and fortress' (31) probably refers to the temple, built like a fortress (1 Chr 29:1, 19) and serving as the bulwark of the Jewish faith. **32b.** Though there were many apostates (cf 1 Mc 2:16), the faithful Jews were strong enough to challenge their persecutors; cf the stories of Eleazar (2 Mc 6:18—21) and that of the mother and her seven children (2 Mc 7). **33—35.** 'The nation's **f** wise men' are the Hasideans or Hassidim mention of whom is first made in 1 Mc 2:42 when they join forces with Mattathias in his revolt against Hellenism (167 B.C.). It appears that this group of pious Jews, entirely devoted to the Law (1 Mc 2:42) arose as a reaction to Hellenism when Jerusalem was proclaimed a Gr. city in 174 B.C. By their knowledge of the Law of Moses and the Prophets they were able to teach others the right course. These Hasideans were apparently the forerunners of the Pharisees. During the persecution of Antiochus many of them perished but the group was eventually saved from extermination by the assistance of the Maccabees. Daniel calls this Maccabean aid 'a little help'; for him the victory of the confessors and the introduction of God's kingdom is the work of God alone; cf 2:34f, 45; chh 3, 6 and 7. Many joined the ranks of the Maccabees insincerely, fearing the drastic punishment of Judas (1 Mc 3:8; 6:21—27; 7:5—7) and became traitors to their people when opportunity arose.

36—39 'Antiochus, God Manifest'—These vv describe **g** Antiochus' self-deification and self-identification with Zeus Olympios or Jupiter Capitolinus, and his self-exaltation over the gods of his fathers and the God of the Jews. The description of Antiochus' anti-Jewish campaign corresponds perfectly to that of the little horn in chh 7 and 8; thus: he will do what he likes, 8:25; he will exalt himself, 8:10, 11, 25; he will speak haughtily, 7:8, 25; he will have a short-lived success, 7:25; 8:12, 24f during the reign of God's wrath with his people, 8:12. This is further evidence for the identification of the little horn of chh 7 and 8 with Antiochus. Antiochus assumed the title *theos epiphanès*, 'the Manifest God', in 169 after his victorious campaign in Egypt. From 169 to 166 he is represented on coins with the emblems of divinity, and the inscription is *Antiochos Theos Epiphanès*. But from 166 onwards his figure is that of Zeus Olympios and the inscription is 'King Antiochus, God manifest, Victory-bearer' (F. M. Abel, loc cit, 245f).

438g A comparative study of the coinage of the era has shown that only on coins destined for the Seleucid empire proper is the king called 'God'; coins destined for use outside Syria bear the king's name without the appellation 'God'. This tends to show that Antiochus intended his claim to divinity to be taken seriously within his realm; cf O. Mørk Holm, *Studies in the Coinage of Antiochus IV of Syria*, Kopenhagen, 1963, 71f. See also 2 Mc 9:12.

h Antiochus made Jupiter Capitolinus or Zeus Olympios the chief deity of all his empire. Consequently the local Syrian deities, especially Apollo, the tutelary god of Syria ('the god of his fathers' 37) and Tammuz (Adonis), the beloved of women—a Phoenician deity so-called because its annual festival was celebrated especially by women—fell gradually into discredit. **38.** Instead of the god of his forebears Antiochus worshipped 'the god of fortresses' very probably Jupiter Capitolinus, who appealed so strongly to his imagination during his prolonged sojourn in Rome, and to whom he built a temple near Antioch (Livy, 41, 20; 42, 6). **39a.** MT appears to be badly vocalized. A very slight change in the vocalization gives the following sense: 'to defend the strongholds he shall station a people of a foreign god' (CV, BJ), the reference being to the foreign soldiers who garrisoned the fortresses of Jerusalem and Judah; cf 1 Mc 1:33; 3:36, 45. The king's favourites were greatly honoured by him, and to them he distributed the land in return for services and, possibly, as a bribe, cf 2 Mc 4.8—10.24.

i **40—45 The End of Antiochus**—These vv appear to narrate another—this time, successful—expedition of Antiochus against Egypt after that of 168. **40.** This war was provoked by Egypt invading Syrian territory. 'At the time of the end', or 'the appointed time'; the time decreed by God; as usual, the seer insists on God's control of human affairs. **41.** During his march on Egypt Antiochus shall pass through Palestine 'the glorious land' (see 28) and massacre many Jews. For some unexplained reason he shall bypass Edom, Moab and the greater part of Ammon. **45.** On his journey northwards he shall pitch his royal pavilion ('*appadnô* in Heb.; a loan-word from the Old Persian *appadana*) between the sea, i.e. the Mediterranean, and the glorious holy mountain i.e. Mt Sion, but shall die with none to help him. The last phrase appears to assume that the persecutor shall die in Palestine, though this is not explicitly stated.

j These vv do not in the least harmonize with the evidence of the historical sources at our disposal. We know of no third campaign of Antiochus against Egypt, nor is one likely in view of his expulsion by the Romans in 168. We are well informed on the death of Antiochus. He marched against Parthia to subdue a revolt and died at Gabae (Polyb. 31, 11), near Aspadana (the modern Ispahan) in Persia (cf 1 Mc 3:31—37; 6:1—16; 2 Mc 9:1—28. For a study of the varying accounts of his death, see M. Zerwick VDom 19 (1939), 308—14). The cuneiform chronicle of the Seleucid kings, BM 35, 603 (published in *Iraq* 16 [1954], 202—12 and in *Bib* 36 [1955], 261f), which follows the Babylonian chronology, says that news of Antiochus IV's death reached Babylon in the 9th month (i.e. Chislev = 19th Nov.—19th Dec.) of the 148th year (of the Seleucids) i.e. 164 B.C. His death can then be placed c. 1st Nov. 164 B.C., a month or more before the rededication of the temple of Jerusalem on the 25th Chislev (= 16th Dec.) 164; cf 2 Mc 9; 10:1—8. The year 149 (of the Seleucids) given by 1 Mc 6:16 as the year of Antiochus' death follows the Syrian chronology. For events of a civil or political nature 1 Mc follows this Syrian chronology, whereas it dates religious events according to the temple chronology which was the same as the Babylonian. Thus the rededication of the altar **438j** is ascribed to the 148 year of the Greeks (1 Mc 4:52), i.e. 164 B.C., though we know that news of the persecutor's death had reached Jerusalem before the rededication (2 Mc 1:13). For the chronology of the books of Maccabees, see J. Schaumberger Bib 36 (1955), 423—35 and F. M. Abel—J. Starcky in BJ, pp. 35—49.

Porphyry (Jerome PL 25, 598), followed by Goetts- **k** berger (p. 87), accepts the reference to a third expedition of Antiochus against Egypt. This is highly improbable. Linder (p. 474) and others regard the verses as a recapitulation of the chief events of Antiochus' reign from 171 to his death. This too seems improbable as the entire ch narrates events in precise chronological order. Neither do the vv give the impression of being a duplicate and shorter account of Antiochus' campaigns added by a later editor. Such an editor would have been conversant with the accounts of the death of Antiochus as we find them in Mc. Some earlier and many modern commentators believe that the author has passed from history to eschatology in 40—45. The vv then speak of a final attack of unrighteousness (cf 40 'at the end-time') under a leader of whom Antiochus was a type. In making the persecutor perish in Palestine Dn may be dependent on Ezek 38—39 (cf Is 10; 36—37). This is not certain, however, as the attack on God's people is not dwelt on in 40—45, as it is in Ezek.

12:1—3 The Final Triumph of the Righteous—In 539a whatever sense we take 40—45, the passage speaks of the death of Antiochus. This implies the end of the era of persecution. The time has come for the fulfilment of the predictions of 7:13f, 18, 26f and of 9:24. Dn, however, makes no mention of the introduction of God's kingdom on earth spoken of in those prophecies. Instead, he speaks of a last and final persecution which will be followed by the resurrection of the dead and the eternal felicity of the just. 1-3 is, then, purely eschatological. The time referred to in **1** is not that immediately following the death of Antiochus, but some remote period determined by God and preceding the Resurrection. It will be a time of unprecedented distress, greater even than that of the persecution of Antiochus. During the period of trial Michael, the patron angel of the Jews (10:13, 31; cf Apoc 12) will take up the cause of the faithful ones among his people. Only those will be saved whose names are enrolled in the book i.e. the book of life (cf Ex 32:32; Ps 69 [68]:29; Is 4:3) or those who are predestined for eternal life. The sense seems to be that they shall escape death; the others, i.e. the impious Jews, shall lose their lives. **2a.** Certainly speaks of the bodily resurrection of a certain group. The extent of this resurrection, and the identification of the group in question, are less certain. The general view of scholars is that the text refers solely to the Israelites, though some commentators include non-Jews as well. Most interpreters take 'many' in its normal partitive **b** sense of 'not all'. **2a.** Would then refer only to the resurrection of a portion of the just and unjust, e.g. to the righteous and arch-sinners of Israel, or of humanity in general; or, preferably, to the persecutors and persecuted of the final trial of 1. Others (e.g. E. F. Sutcliffe *The OT and the Future Life*, 1946, 138—40; cf B. J. Alfrink Bib 40 [1959], 359f) think that the text requires a reference to the resurrection of the Israelites in general. B. J. Alfrink has shown that the text can be understood in another way. First of all, he notes that 'the many who sleep in the dust' and 'are to arise' are not those of the final persecution of 1; the just of this trial are to be 'saved', i.e. they shall not die. 'The many' of 2a are, then, from among the Israelites who had died before this

539b final tribulation. 'Those who shall live forever' of **2b** refers to those two groups of pious Israelites, i.e. those who escaped death at the final trial and those who had died before it, but are raised from the 'dust of the earth'. The text then speaks only of the resurrection of the righteous of Israel. The others ('some', lit 'those') who rise to shame may be a gloss, denoting the remainder whose resurrection is not mentioned, cf Is 66:24. This understanding of the text is in conformity with 2 Mc (7:9, 14, 23:36; 14:36) which speaks only of the resurrection of the just. The resurrection of the wicked **c** was of less interest to Judaism. The NT, too, speaks principally of the resurrection in general or of that of the just. Jn 5:28f and Ac 24:25 (cf Apoc 20:5—15) are the sole NT texts that refer to the resurrection of the wicked. That they too will arise bodily has been clearly taught and defined by the Church. Dn (12:2) is certainly the first clear testimony to the bodily resurrection of the just. It is possible that it was derived from earlier revelation (cf Pss 16 [15]:9—11; 49 [48]: 16; Is 26:19). The book, however, made the doctrine clear and certain and the belief was a source of strength and consolation during the persecutions of Antiochus, as the episode of the mother and her seven sons in 2 Mc 7 shows. The book of Wisdom brought out the spiritual aspect of the resurrection (ch 3) and the NT perfected God's revelation on the after life. **3.** 'The wise' (cf 11:33, 35) and 'those who turn many to righteousness' form, according to the law of parallelism, one class which comprises those who have a practical knowledge of God, obey his Law and show others how to follow it. During the persecution of Antiochus the Hasideans were such (cf 1 Mc 2:42).

d 4 The Sealing of the Vision—On the sealing up of the book cf 8:26; Is 8:16; 29:11. The visions are to be made known only at 'the end-time', i.e. during the actual persecution of Antiochus. Many shall go about seeking knowledge, or go through the unsealed book, and find there the required doctrine on divine providence and the fate that awaits those who persecute God's people, as well as the rewards that are in store for those who remain faithful to revealed religion. This appears the best meaning of the MT. Some commentators explain through Am 8:12: 'many shall seek the word of God in vain': others correct to 'many shall fall away and evil shall increase' (CV, BJ; cf LXX).

e 5—13 Conclusion—5—7. After the command to seal the book Daniel takes part in a conversation between two angels and the man, i.e. angel, already mentioned (10:5f, etc), who had carried the divine revelation to him. Daniel's question recalls 8:13f, but seems to refer to the end of the extraordinary things of the preceding three chh. **7.** Cf Dt 19:15. The answer is that of 7:25: Three years (lit 'times') and a half. A further time indication is added, which however is very vague. The shattering of the power of the holy people (MT, RSV) refers, if the text is sound, either to the persecutions of Antiochus or to the persecutions of the last days. Persecution will cease only when the holy people appear to be annihilated. By emending the text, the following sense may be obtained: 'When the power of the oppressor comes to an end' (CV, BJ), i.e. when Antiochus is dead, persecution will cease, Antiochus being the last oppressor. The text is perhaps intentionally ambiguous: the precise time of the final consummation **f** is a mystery not to be revealed (cf 9). **11f.** These vv break the sequence of ideas and appear to be later additions intending to show how the prophecies were fulfilled in various events after the rededication of the altar (cf Rinaldi, 153). This will explain the differences between these two time indications and those already

given. C. Schedl (BZ n.s. 8 [1964], 104) takes 1,290 **539l** days to be the period between the 15th Chislev (= 6th Dec.) 167 and the 6th Sivan (= 19th June) 163 B.C., i.e. from the erection of the pagan altar (1 Mc 1:54) to the Feast of Weeks (Pentecost) which was celebrated in 163; cf 1 Mc 5:54; 2 Mc 12:31. 164 B.C. was a leap year of 384 days; the other years are reckoned as lunar years of 354 days each. Schedl believes that 1,335 days runs from 7 Ab (= 31st July) 164 to the 13th Adar (= 27th March) 160, i.e. from the date Judas marched to Sion after his victory at Beth-zur (cf 1 Mc 4:36ff) to the defeat of Nicanor (cf 1 Mc 7:39—49; 2 Mc 15:1—36). These chronological indications, as that of 8:14 (q.v.), he takes to be Maccabean additions showing how the prophecies were fulfilled. **13.** Daniel has fulfilled his mission. It is not for him to 'know the day or the hour' of the fulfilment of his prophecies. He can now die in peace and await the resurrection of the body. This doctrine, with which he comforted others, can now serve as a consolation for himself.

13, 14 The Deuterocanonical Appendices—The **540a** stories of Susanna and of Bel and the Dragon were collected by the Greek translators from a cycle of Daniel traditions and incorporated into Dn as an appendix. They never formed part of the original book. They differ in style and character from the episodes of chh 1—6, having solely the hero of the various narratives in common. It appears that there existed in Palestine a rather large literature on Daniel; J. T. Milik has published some further traditions from this cycle from among the DSS (cf RB 63 [1956], 407—15). The stories of chh 13 and 14, as they are read in LXX, and Theod (Vg), differ from each other in their position in the book and in certain details, the differences being probably due to the fact that chh 13 and 14 once circulated as independent narratives and that LXX has a varying form of the tradition behind it. Jer notes that ch 12 is the end of the Heb. Dn, and that the following stories are translated from Theod.

13 The Story of Susanna—In LXX and Vg it follows **b** ch 12, whereas in Theod it is placed at the beginning of the book, perhaps because in 37 Daniel is called a young man. Theodotion's choice, in any case, indicates that ch 13 once existed independently of ch 14. The ch is reckoned as one of the finest literary passages of the OT. It is quite different in character and style from chh 1—6 and can scarcely have originated in the same milieu. The exilic setting seems artificial and the narrative probably originated in Palestine. The author's purpose is uncertain. It may have been merely to narrate an example of how a pious woman was unjustly condemned by wicked judges and saved by God. The narrative, however, insists on the fact that the witnesses who had condemned Susanna were not duly cross-examined. From this some have concluded that the story was composed as an attack on lax judicial procedure and advocates a more rigid examination of witnesses when there was suspicion of collusion. We know that the Pharisees, under Simon ben Shetach (c. 100 B.C.), accused the Sadducees of such laxity and advocated the examination stressed by Dn 13: 48f, 52—59; cf Mishnah tr. *Aboth* 1, 10. In this view the composition of ch 13 is placed c. 95—80 B.C. (cf CAP I, 644). The point is not certain and others date the ch to the 3rd cent. B.C.; cf A. Lefèvre in RF, 781. The original language, despite the puns in 55, 59 (q.v.), was probably Heb. or Aram. For a comparison of the differences between Theod and LXX see J. T. Marshall, 'Susanna' in HDB 4 (1902), 631.

1—4 Susanna's Virtue and Social Condition—1f. c

540c Unlike chh 1—6, no time indication is given. The name Susanna (= lily), does not occur elsewhere in the OT. Joakim (= Jehoiakim, cf 1:1) and Hilkiah are common Hebrew names. **4.** The situation described suits exilic times. Jer 29:4—10 had urged the exiles, deported in 598 B.C., to build houses and plant gardens during their exile and to seek the welfare of Babylon as their exile would be a long one. Many Jews did so and grew rich in Babylonia, refusing later to return to impoverished Palestine; cf § 462g.

5—14 The Two Lustful Elders—5. During the exile the Jews appear to have been allowed to live according to their own laws and institutions. Ezek 8:1; 20:1, 3 mentions the presence and activity of the Jewish elders in the exilic community. 'That year' either refers to a date that has not been preserved or has a general meaning: 'in a certain year'. We do not know the identity of these two elders. Jewish tradition has taken them to be the two false prophets mentioned in Jer 29:21—23. The quotation is either an unwritten prophetic saying or an allusion to some passage such as Jer 29:23.

d 15—27 Attempted Seduction—This part of the narrative is condensed by LXX into the vv 19*b*, 22*b*, 23. The story implicitly contrasts the modesty of Susanna with the lust of the elders. From the Law of Moses, which her parents had taught her (3), Susanna knew that the unfaithful wife was punished by death (Lv 20:10; Dt 22:22; cf Jn 8:5).

28—43 Susanna falsely Accused and Condemned to Death—30. The entire household knew that Susanna would be accused publicly by the elders (cf 27) and accompanied her before the assembly. **31.** To satisfy their lust the elders invoked Nm 5:18 and had the suspected adulteress unveiled. Later Jewish Law (Mishnah, tr. *Sota* 1, 5) legislated against such immodest behaviour, and forbade the unveiling of especially handsome women. **34.** The judges here act the part of witnesses and, in accord with Lv 24:14, laid their hands upon the head of the accused. The community accepted the accusation of the two elders and, without any examination of the witnesses, condemned Susanna to death.

e 44—64 Susanna Acquitted—A herald called on the bystanders to bring forward any evidence of the person's innocence known to them (Mishnah, tr. *Sanhedrin* 6, 1f). 'The elders' are the larger group from among whom the perjured judges were chosen. **51.** Daniel's cross-examination was simple, i.e. the identity of the tree under which the adultery was committed. The perjured judges would be expected to recall whether it was the mastic (or lentisk) evergreen plant or the large evergreen oak. In Greek there is a play on the words 'mastic tree' (*schinos*), and 'cut in two' (*schisei*) and between 'evergreen oak' (*prinos*) and 'saw' (*prisei*). This is no proof of a Gr. original for this ch as the phenomenon could be also in the Aram. or Heb. original (cf HDB a.c. p. 632), or freely introduced by the Gr. translator. For cases of paronomasia in Heb cf Jg 7:25; 10:4 etc; cf also P. P. Saydon in Bib 36 (1955), 36—50; 287—304. On this chapter, cf M. Wurmbrand, 'A Falasha Variant of the Story of Susanna', Bib 44 (1963) 29—45. **540e**

14:1—42 The Stories of Bel and the Dragon— 541a These two stories, connected with each other in time and place but wholly unrelated to the story of Susanna, form a single narrative closing the book of Dn. In Theod they follow immediately after ch 12 and are preceded by the title 'Vision 12'. In LXX they follow 'Susanna' and bear the title 'From the prophecy of Habakkuk, the son of Jesus, from the tribe of Levi'. The LXX also calls the Daniel of these stories a priest, i.e. from the tribe of Levi whereas in 1:1, 3, 6 he appears to be rather from the tribe of Judah. Like chh 1—6 these stories show the superiority of the God of Israel to pagan deities. They are entirely different from chh 1—6, however, as in ch 14 the author ridicules idols and their foolish worshippers whereas in chh 1—6 the superiority of the God of Israel is shown by direct divine intervention in human affairs. In its polemic against idols ch 14 is in the spirit of later wisdom writings (cf Wis chh 13—14 and Bar 6). The stories belong to the Daniel cycle of traditions and were probably composed in Heb. or Aram. in Palestine. The date of their composition is quite uncertain: in the 3rd cent. B.C. according to Lefèvre, RF, 781; during the persecution of Antiochus VII (139—128 B.C.) according to W. Davies (CAP I, 65). The stories are self-explanatory; the burlesque nature of the narratives explains the presence of such elements as the ingenuousness of Cyrus and the journey of Habakkuk from Judah.

14:1—21 The Story of Bel 14:1. The last v of ch **b** 13 in Vg is not the conclusion of the Susanna story but the introduction to the following narrative and modern versions number 13:65 as 14:1. Astyages was the last king of Media; he was defeated and made prisoner by Cyrus, who then annexed his kingdom. This chronology is then a true one and shows that the ch is not from the same author as those who wrote, or edited, chh 1—12. The verse also shows that a different time reckoning from that of the p.c. book was known in the Daniel cycle of traditions. This may indicate that the chronology found in chh 1—12 is fictitious, rather than the result of a confused historical tradition (cf § § 526*kl*, 528*d*). **3.** Bel is here another name of Marduk (cf 4:5); his temple in Babylon was called Esagila. The 'artaba' (3) (RSV 'bushel') was a Persian measure (Herod I, 192) whose value varied in time and place. In Syria and Egypt 12 artabas would equal c. 4.7 hecto-litres or c. 13 bushels. On these measures see § 86*e—h*. On the food offered to the gods in Babylon see G. C. Gadd 'Babylon Myth and Ritual' in *Myth and Ritual*, 1933, 42.

23—42 The Story of the Dragon—The word 'Dragon' **c** denotes here, like Gr. *drakōn*, a large serpent. There is no evidence that dragons were worshipped as gods in Babylon; cf S. Landersdorfer 'Der Drache von Babylon' in BZ 11 (1913), 1—4. Habakkuk (33ff) is called a prophet only in Theod. **36** is probably inspired by Ezek 8:3. **41f.** are similar to 6:20; and 33—42 are another form of the tradition found in ch 6.

HOSEA

BY D. RYAN

542a Bibliography—*Commentaries*: Jer.PL 25 815–946; W. R. Harper, ICC 1905; G. Rinaldi SacB 1959; E. Osty BJ 1960[2]; A. Deissler, PCSB, 1961; H. W. Wolff, BKAT, Neukirchen, 1968[2]; with complete bibliography; J. A. Ward, *Hosea, a theological commentary*; 1966; *Other Literature*: N. H. Snaith, *Mercy and Sacrifice; a study of the book of Hosea*, 1953; A. Gelin, 'Osee' in DBS 6 (1960) 926–940.

b Name and Life of the Prophet—The prophet's name means '(Yahweh or God) has saved'; the divine name has fallen out, but the full form, Hoshaiah, is found in Neh 12:32. The last king of Israel bore the same name as the prophet. The names Joshua, Isaiah and Jesus are derived from the same root meaning 'to save'. Of his place of origin and social position, and other circumstances of his life nothing is known beyond what can be gleaned from his book. He is described as the son of Beeri, 1:1. His interest in the N Kingdom, his intimate knowledge of its political and religious conditions and the absence of any mention of Jerusalem suggest that he was of Israelite rather than of Judean origin. As most of the metaphors and images in the book are taken from agricultural life (cf 4:16; 6:3; 8:7; 9:2, 10, 16; 10:1, 11–13; 13:3; 14:6–8), it has been inferred that the prophet was a farmer. The inference, however, does not seem to be sufficiently warranted, as the prophet's peculiar imagery may be due to his profound love of nature. He married Gomer, the daughter of Diblaim, from whom he had three children.

c   The story of **the prophet's marriage** has, since the days of St Jerome, been a subject of controversy. It has been repeatedly asked whether the prophet in the first three chapters is relating history, vision, or allegory. Long lists of names may be drawn up in support of the several interpretations which may be grouped in two classes: the literal and the non-literal. In favour of the non-literal interpretation it is urged: (*a*) that it is inconceivable that a prophet of Yahweh should dishonour himself by such a shameful marriage or that God himself should command a union so repugnant to the moral sense; (*b*) that the domestic events narrated in 1:3–9 took too much time to serve as the basis of a moral lesson to the people; (*c*) that the prophets were sometimes commanded by God to perform actions which it was impossible to perform except in a vision, cf Ezek 4:9–17; (*d*) that the close connexion between the act itself and its symbolic meaning, 1:2, clearly suggests that the prophet's main concern is the religious state of his people, not the story of his domestic life.

d   To these arguments the supporters of the literal interpretation reply: (*a*) what is in itself repugnant to the moral sense remains so even if it is the object of a vision or an allegory; (*b*) the moral lesson is based not so much on the symbolic names of Hosea's children as on his marriage. In any event, Is 8:1ff, 7:1 and 10:20–21 show that the children's symbolic names kept the father's message before the people over a period of **542d** years. (*c*) from the fact that certain actions commanded by God could not be performed except in a vision it cannot be inferred that all actions commanded by God to his prophets were performed in a vision, cf 22:11, etc.; (*d*) this is true, but does not show that the prophet's marriage was not real.

All are agreed that the prophet's marriage has a **e** symbolic meaning. A distinguishing feature of a symbolic action is its unusual and extravagant character. Thus Ahijah rends his new garment in 12 pieces, (3) Kg 11:30; cf also Is 20:2; Jer 19:10. The symbolic action is really a dramatic representation of an abnormal moral or religious situation intended to make the people realize the situation more vividly. Such actions, which no man under normal conditions will do, may be performed either actually or in a vision. They are considered to be performed in a vision when the moral lesson is intended for the prophet alone. But when the lesson is intended for the people, the symbolic action must be considered as really performed.

The application of these considerations to Hosea's **f** marriage shows that it was real. No one will deny that marriage with a woman of evil character is out of the common run. All will likewise agree that the moral lesson inherent in Hosea's marriage was intended for the people not for the prophet who needed no proof of the people's wickedness. The prophet's experience, of course, would have given him a unique insight into Yahweh's love for Israel and lent passionate conviction to his preaching. The people must have been shocked on seeing the prophet bringing home a dishonoured wife and, it is reasonable to suppose, manifested their disapproval, thus providing him with an opportunity to insist on the hideousness of their faithlessness to Yahweh despite Yahweh's immense love for them. It was manifested in the first instance by his love for Israel when she was an object of contempt (cf the symbolism of Hosea's marriage to a harlot and Ezek 16), and was revealed in all its power when he pardoned her adultery and took her back (Hos *passim*).

The literal interpretation has, however, been given **g** another form. Gomer was, at the time of her marriage, of an irreproachable character. She is called 'a wife of harlotry' (or: 'of fornications') on account of her later misbehaviour. When she had borne three children to Hosea, she gave her love to another and abandoned her husband. But Hosea still loved his erring wife and after some time brought her back. Hosea's action in taking back his adulterous wife is just as effective for teaching the generosity of Yahweh's love as marriage to a woman of evil repute. The most serious objection to this view is that the phrase 'wife of harlotry' is intended to be an accurate designation of the woman at the time of her marriage to Hosea. Yet another view has been put forward in more recent times by Wolff 12ff. He starts from the use of the term harlotry in 4:12 and 5:4 where the ir-

42g religious spirit which draws Israel away from Yahweh is **h** described as 'a spirit of harlotry'. In fact, Israel had given herself to the worship of Baal, and any young Israelite woman who was imbued with the spirit of the age would be a worshipper of the fertility god The specifically sexual aspect of the term would derive from the practice by which young women consecrated their virginity to Baal by offering themselves—perhaps only once—for sexual intercourse to worshippers at the shrine of the fertility god. The phrase 'children of harlotry' describes the children born of a sexual life which was, in the first instance, consecrated to the pagan fertility god; it does not imply that they were illegitimate or that they had been conceived before marriage. Hosea's wife would then be an average Israelite woman who was governed by the spirit of the age in which she lived. This view resolves satisfactorily a number of difficulties but leaves some doubt about the effectiveness of the prophet's action. In the circumstances described by Wolff, would the prophet's marriage be sufficiently dramatic to teach an effective lesson? And was this rite of sexual initiation so general that Hosea was left with no option but to marry such a woman? (Cf H. H. Rowley, 'The Marriage of Hosea', BJRL 39 (1956) 200—233).

i Date—All are agreed that Hosea was called to the prophetic ministry during the reign of Jeroboam II (783—743 B.C.). Since the prophecy of the fall of Jehu's dynasty made at the beginning of Hosea's ministry (1:4) was fulfilled in 743 with the murder of Zechariah, Jeroboam's son and successor, the prophet must have begun to preach some time before 743 B.C. It could have been as much as five years before, if all the events of ch 1 occurred in the reign of Jeroboam II. If 13:10 and 16 are concerned with the capture of king Hoshea and the beginning of the siege of Samaria, the ministry of Hosea continued down to 724, but there is no evidence that he was active after the fall of Samaria in 721. Some scholars give an early date for the accession of Hezekiah (Noth 729 B.C.; Wolff 725 B.C.) and in their chronology Hos 1:1 could be accurate. If, however, Hezekiah's reign began in 716 B.C. (so many, including BJ), it is unlikely that Hosea was active at such a late date.

j The best explanation of 1:1 is that it originally contained the title of 1:2—9 and referred only to the 'days of Jeroboam'. 'in the days of Uzziah, etc, kings of Judah' was added by a Judean redactor. BJ limits the prophet's activity to the years 750—730, and assumes that the Judean redactor filled out 1:1 with the names of the kings of Judah after the pattern of Is 1:1. For the history of this period, see § 65a—c.

k The **religious situation** may be described as a confused medley of a perverted Yahweh-worship and an idolatrous Baal-worship due to a misconception of the true character of Yahweh. The calf-worship was the official cult. Though not originally an idolatrous worship, the calf being intended only as a representation of Yahweh, it was certainly against the prescriptions of Ex 20:4 and led most naturally to idolatry. When, later, king Ahab, who had married a Phoenician wife, introduced Baal-worship into his kingdom, 1 (3) Kgs 16:30, not only was a new form of religion, characterized by its licentious cult, set up in the kingdom of Israel, but the Yahweh cult itself became evermore contaminated by idolatrous influences. As in the days of Elijah 1(3)Kgs 18:21, the people worshipped Yahweh as well as the Canaanite deities. They still kept the Sabbath and held their annual festivals, 2:11, offered sacrifices to Yahweh, 5:6, 8:13, and swore by Yahweh, 4:15. They worshipped Yahweh at Bethel, 4:15, and burnt incense and gave

themselves up to debauchery on hill-tops, 4:13f; they **542k** made idols of silver and gold, 8:4; 13:2. Yahweh, their God, was conceived as one among other gods. He demanded sacrifices which they offered punctiliously, but he had no regard, they thought, to their moral conduct and internal dispositions. Hence religion came to be considered as the performance of acts of worship rather than a system of religious truths and moral precepts. Hosea's preaching was directed against both the calf-worship and the Baal-worship. Both were breaches of the ritual law of the covenant and were accompanied by misconceptions of the nature of the covenant God as well as a complete neglect of his moral demands.

Contents and Analysis—It is difficult to give a logical **l** division of the whole book. Chh 1—3 are easily distinguishable from the rest. The prophet's affection for his unfaithful wife represents in a dramatic manner Yahweh's love for his ungrateful and unfaithful people. The remaining chapters contain, in an abridged form, some of the prophet's discourses loosely connected with one another, but all subordinated to the central theme—God's love and the people's ingratitude. Chh 4—8 form one group of discourses in which the prevailing thought is Israel's guilt with occasional references to punishment. The prophet denounces the depravity of the people which he traces back to their ignorance of God and to the bad example of the priests, ch 4. He then arraigns in a special manner the kings and the priests, the leaders of the nation, who are held responsible for the general degradation of public life, 5:1 14. If Israel will repent sincerely, God will forgive them, but at present their sins appear to be beyond remedy, 5:15—6:11a. Revolutions, anarchy, and decay of national strength are the disastrous consequences of their having forsaken God, the only source of their strength, and turned for assistance to foreign powers, 6:11b—7:7 and 7:8—16. The prophet denounces once more Israel's most grievous sins; idolatry, an unlawful dynasty and foreign policy, and announces imminent punishment, ch 8. In chh 9—13:16 the leading idea is this imminent punishment with frequent references to Israel's sins.

The Teaching of Hosea—Hosea's teaching about **God 543a** and Israel's service** of him is firmly rooted in history, and it is particularly with the events leading up to the establishment of the covenant that this history begins. On one occasion, Hosea reaches back into patriarchal times, but it was to discover a source of Israel's wickedness and not the beginning of her blessings (12:2ff; 12). Yahweh is above all the God of Israel (i.e. of the twelve tribes cf 3:5; 4:6 etc), who rescued his people from Egypt (2:15; 11:1; 13:4) and cared for them lovingly and tenderly in the desert (9:10; 13:5; cf 2:14). It is there that he binds them to himself in a covenant love (cf 1:9; 6:7; 8:1). He is their only God (13:4), who is in sole control of the elements and the cycle of the seasons (2:8—9, 21—23), and is therefore the only source of their welfare and salvation (2:8, 21f; 13:4); all other gods are nothing but the work of man (8:4—6; 13:2).

Besides this familiarity with the monotheism of the **b** first great commandment (cf 12:9; 13:4), Hosea is aware of the **moral obligations of the covenant**. The list of crimes in 4:2 recall the fifth, sixth, seventh and eighth commandments of the decalogue (cf Ex 20:2ff).

The **cult law of the covenant** was also known to Hosea; he refers to various feasts, including the Sabbath, in 2:11. It has often been claimed that Hosea and the other prophets rejected Israel's sacrificial system. It is hard to see how they could reject such a substantial portion of the covenant law, and continue to remain

543b faithful to the covenant God. Closer consideration of the texts and of the nature of the prophets' mission show that the prophets were not innovators. They condemned hypocrisy in the forms of worship prescribed by the law, and outlawed aberrations in the cult which tended to identify Yahweh with pagan fertility gods; they did not attack the sacrificial system as such, but only its abuses (cf note on 6:6). The real test of a man's sincerity in the use of the cult forms of the covenant was his fidelity to the moral norms which were given by Yahweh as the standards of his covenant people (cf 4:1—2; Mt 5:23; Jn 14:15; Jn 4:7—21).

c   Although Hosea is familiar with the legal terms and forms of the **covenant**, he sees the relationship not just as a matter of law, of rules and regulations. It is a living, personal relationship founded on the intimate knowledge of each other shared by the parties to the covenant. Yahweh first knew Israel and loved her; Israel learned to know Yahweh through his saving acts—or, at least, she should have done. This relationship was governed by the covenant virtues, especially *'emet*, constancy or fidelity; *hesed*, loving kindness, mercy or, simply, love; and *da'at*, knowledge (cf also *sedeq* (righteousness) in 2:19; 10:12*a* rendered 'salvation' by RSV in 10:12*b*; *mišpāṭ* (justice) in 2:19, rendered 'judgement' in 6:5, and *raḥªmîm* (mercy or compassionate love) in 2:19). The inconstancy of Israel contrasted with the fidelity of Yahweh to his promises. *hesed* expresses the idea of a kind, devoted and merciful love. The knowledge implied by the covenant was not a merely intellectual experience; the term describes the intimate communication in love between two persons, and this meaning of the word finds a characteristic application when it is used for marital intercourse (cf Gn 4:1; Lk 1:34, lit. 'for I know not man'). It is the absence of these covenant virtues in the covenant people, which highlights the failure of Israel to respond to absolute fidelity in love on the part of Yahweh, and manifests her monstrous ingratitude.

d   **Hosea's own experience** of the covenant God and his passionate identification of himself with Yahweh's wishes for Israel encouraged him to express himself freely in describing **the God of Israel**. He sees him as a lion or a leopard lurking in the shadows waiting to pounce on its prey (13:7), or as a she-bear enraged by the loss of her cubs (13:8). At other times, he is like dry-rot in Ephraim and Judah (5:12). To describe his beneficent action on Israel, Hosea compares him to dew (14:6) and to an evergreen tree (14:9). But it is in describing Yahweh as the loving husband of a woman who is a harlot and adulterous (chh 1—3) that Hosea is most startling. Yet it was Yahweh himself who invited him to learn this lesson in the school of marital infidelity and estrangement. He learned it well and transmitted it with a depth of feeling which derived from his personal trials. With this audacious figure, he hoped to draw Israel away from Baal, her chosen partner, from whom she expected fertility and wealth, and lead her to an understanding of Yahweh as the sole source of her gifts (2:8—9) and her faithful lover (3:1). It was a dramatic correction of the faith of Israel in terms of her current errors.

e   It is particularly in this emphasis on the bond of love uniting Yahweh and Israel that many scholars see a link between **Hosea and Dt**. The frequent use of *'āheb* = to love in both Hos and Dt excites attention. There are, however, many other points of contact between the two books, whether in terminology, theological attitudes or points of law (cf the list of references to Dt in the Scripture index of Wolff). This fact raises the question of the dependence of Dt on Hos. Wolff thinks of Hosea as

belonging to, or being associated with, a prophetico- **543** levitical group, centred especially on Shechem, which was closely concerned with the formation of the book of Dt. Obviously they drew on earlier traditions. Was the use of the word 'love' (*'āheb*) in the covenant context one of them? Moran (CBQ 25 (1963), 77—87) has established quite clearly that *'āheb* belonged to covenant terminology long before its appearance in Hosea (cf Ex 20:6; Jg 5:31), and its use can be paralleled in treaties as early as the 18th cent. B.C. There are also differences in the use of the term in Dt and Hos. Hosea, however, **f** brought to this word a new experience and his influence may have contributed to the warmth of religious fervour which pervades the book of Dt in its present form, and contrasts with the earlier use of *'āheb* as a legal term in the field of politics, national and international. Jer, (2:1—7; 3:20; 31:22; 51:5), Ezek (16:23) and Deutero-Isaiah (50:1; 54: 5—8, 10; 62:4—5, 12) profited by the emphases of Hosea, while Song develops his principal theme. He himself had carried the process of revelation a stage further than the covenant law. Dt 21:18ff imposed the penalty of death by stoning on the stubborn and rebellious son, but Yahweh's heart recoils from such a punishment (Hos 11:8). Dt 24:1ff prescribes that a woman divorced for adultery may not be taken back by her husband when she has given herself to another; but Yahweh ordered Hosea to take back Gomer as a sign of his abiding love for Israel and his eagerness for a reconciliation. As a later prophet was to say: 'My thoughts are not your thoughts, nor your ways my ways' (Is 55:8).

Within the framework of the covenant, as seen by **g** Hosea, **God's anger** is only a passing phase; it can never be a permanent feature of his relationship with Israel: its function is medicinal and instructional: it wounds only to heal (cf Is 54:8). Although some of the most violent expressions of God's anger are found in the book of Hosea, his love triumphs in the end. It is with this impression of a loving God that the book leaves the reader, and he can only wonder that already in the 8th cent. B.C. God had revealed his nature so clearly. It remained for the Incarnation and the insight of St John to have him described quite simply as the God who is love (cf 1 Jn 4:8).

The Messianic Age—As far as the future is concerned, **h** Hosea looks forward to a perfect reconciliation in love which has been initiated in the Incarnation, and moves towards its consummation (Apoc 19). Like Jer (31:31—34), Hosea expects a new covenant 'in righteousness and justice, in steadfast love and in mercy' (2:19), a new and united Israel as numerous as the sands of the sea (1:10—11), and a Judean editor of the book saw this happening under the leadership of a Davidic king (3:5). Cf E. H. Maly, 'Messianism in Osee, CBQ 19 (1957) 213—225.

Text—The Heb. text of the book of Hosea has been **i** badly preserved and this to a certain extent accounts for its obscurity. Some passages may be confidently emended with the help of LXX, but others are corrupt beyond emendation, and critical conjecture is the only means to make the text yield a reasonable sense. Vg is of little help for the restoration of the original text.

A. 1—3 Hosea's Marriage and its symbolic sense— 544a 1:1 Superscription—see § 542*i—j*. **2—3** Hosea's marriage—see § 542*g—h*. The children share their mother's disgrace, although 'children of harlotry' does not **necessarily mean that they were born in adultery. The** prophet's children, representing as they do a people untrue to God, are called adulterine in the same sense as their

544a mother, the nation of Israel, is called adulterous because of her unfaithfulness to God. 'Gomer, Diblaim': there is no symbolism in these names.

b **4–9 His Children**—The first son was called Jezreel. This symbolical name refers to the events narrated in 2 (4) Kgs 9:21–26, 30–37; 10:7–11. The sanguinary deeds there recorded were to be avenged by the downfall of Jehu's dynasty and the extinction of the kingdom of Israel. Two points deserve consideration. First, the birth of Hosea's firstborn fell in the last years of Jeroboam or in the six months of the reign of his son Zechariah, the last of Jehu's royal descendants. Consequently Hosea began to prophesy during the last years of Jeroboam II. Secondly, the prophet considered the overthrow of Jehu's dynasty as the beginning of a period of political decadence to culminate in the extinction of the N Kingdom. It cannot, therefore, be inferred that he expected the end of the kingdom of Israel to come with the downfall of Jehu's dynasty, especially as he lived under other kings after the fall of Jehu's house. The place of the collapse of the Israelite forces will have been the Vale of Jezreel which stretches from the town of Jezreel, the modern Zerin, in a SE direction down to the Jordan. Jezreel, not Samaria, is mentioned here on account of the massacre perpetrated by Jehu and of its assonance with Israel.

c **6.** The prophet's second child was a daughter, whom he calls 'Not pitied'. The verb used here (*r ḥ m*) implies love and pity and might be translated 'to show compassionate love'. Both the verb and the noun derived from it are used to describe the covenant relationship between Yahweh and Israel (cf Hos 2:4, 19, 23, Ex 34.0, Dt 10.10 etc). The name of the child symbolizes the rejection of this covenant relationship.

7. God will, however, have mercy on the house of Judah. This parenthetical remark interrupts the narrative of the prophet's domestic story and is generally considered to be an interpolation made in the S Kingdom. It may reflect the deliverance of Jerusalem from the Assyrians in 701 B.C., but the prophetic vision extends beyond the current situation. **8f.** 'Not my people': this also involved the renunciation of the covenant which was frequently formulated in the words: 'I shall be your God and you shall be my people' (cf Lv 26:12; Dt 27:9 etc).

d **10–2:1 Promise of a Brighter Future** —**10.** Quite suddenly, the prophet's outlook becomes brighter, and the rejection is represented as a temporary punishment which will be followed by a magnificent restoration. Israel will increase to extraordinary numbers (cf Gn 22:17; 32:13) and will be taken up again by God as his sons, the sons of a living God who can restore them to life (cf 6:2) and protect them from all evil. **11.** The kingdoms of Judah and Israel will be reunited under one leader and will come up to Jerusalem from their land of captivity, because the day of Jezreel, a day of humiliation for the old Israel, will be a day of triumph for the new Israel. Although the prophet has clearly in view the return from captivity, his words find more dramatic fulfilment in the Messianic age, when the children of Israel, the 'Israel of God' (Gal 6:16) or the Christians, will be the object of the divine favour and will become numerous as the sand of the sea (Rm 9:25f; 1 Pt 2:10), forming one kingdom under one king, the Messiah. These vv (1:10–2:1) are transferred by some commentators (and BJ) to follow either 2:23 or 3:5. They may have been placed in their present position to balance the sombre tones of vv 2–9. **2:1** symbolizes the reversal of the misfortune implied in 1:6 and 9.

e **2:2–13 Israel on Trial for Infidelity**—This section resembles the judicial hearing of a divorce case. Yahweh speaks throughout and is cast in the varying roles of **544e** convener of the court, witness, judge and the one who administers punishment and the one who arranges a settlement. Hosea's own experience (ch 3) lends pathos to the message he transmits. **2.** Those who have remained faithful to Yahweh are called on to join in accusing the nation as a whole. 'Plead'—i.e. in a law court. Israel's desertion of her God is described in the legal formula of divorce and implies a finality in her act of abandonment. Undaunted by her blatant misconduct, Yahweh pleads hopefully for her conversion and return. 'Harlotry' and 'adultery' may refer to emblems or marks associated with the worship of Baal. The removal of them would involve the rejection of the pagan god and the abandonment of lewd forms of worship. **3.** Yahweh threatens Israel with exspoliation and death, the penalties for adultery (cf Ezek 16:37; Lv 21:9; Dt 22:23). He will render her helpless as in the day of her birth (cf Ezek 16:4–8), and leave her to die of thirst. The image of the dry and barren land appropriately describes the punishment of one who sought to guarantee an abundance of rain and lush fertility by worshipping a pagan fertility god. **4–5a.** Yahweh will no longer show any mercy to his people. Both individually and collectively (mother and children) they have forsaken their God. It is not the prophet who threatens to suppress all natural affection towards his innocent children; it is Yahweh who is about to withdraw his favour from an unfaithful people.

5b–8. In the Canaanite fertility myths, the fertility **f** of the land was guaranteed by a marriage between the land and the divinity (Baal). This marriage was reproduced symbolically in cult prostitution at the shrine of the fertility god. Israel adopted these beliefs and practices of the indigenous Canaanite tribes to guarantee an abundant supply of her principal needs in food and clothing. Even as she makes use of this ritual, she must be taught its ineffectiveness. The land becomes a wilderness of briers and stones, but still she persists in the pursuit of her lovers. She is no weakling they have led astray, but a woman stubborn in adultery who flouts her husband's love and wilfully goes her way. She can only learn where it leads by painful humiliation. She did not know it was Yahweh who fed and clothed her. She would only learn by wandering through a wilderness, hungry, thirsty and naked, calling to lovers who could not help her. **9–13.** 'Therefore' **g** (*lāḵēn*) in prophetical literature indicates the transition from accusation to the threat of punishment. Here the punishment is aimed at Israel's conversion, not her destruction. Because it is Yahweh who controls the seasons, he can impede the growth of crops to highlight the helplessness of Baal and the futility of Israel's pursuit. She will be exposed in the presence of her lovers as they stand by unable to help (cf Ezek 16:37). In time of famine, there is no place for joy, and when the harvest fails, there is no festival. Israel's ancient feasts had become occasions for honouring Baal; they will lapse into the silence of a disillusioned hope. Vine and fig tree spell peace and prosperity for Israel; they will become savage forest, a shelter for wild beasts to threaten her security. In **13**, Israel's lovers are clearly identified as the Baals. Disillusioned by their failure to help, Israel will return to her God. Cf the parable of the prodigal son, Lk 15: 11–32.

14–23. A New Beginning and a New Covenant— **h** When Israel has paid the penalty of her infidelity, Yahweh will come to her rescue once more. The love which once united them will be renewed and, on the basis of a new covenant, Israel will enjoy the blessings which are the

544h reward of fidelity in the service of Yahweh. 14—15 describe the renewal of love in the wilderness, while 16—23 outline its consequences. 16—23 can be sub-divided on the basis of the recurring phrase 'on that day' in 16, 18 and 21.

14. The wilderness is the setting for the tender exchanges which rekindle the fire of Israel's love. It provides the solitude in which, alone with Yahweh, Israel suffered no distractions from her erstwhile lovers. For 'speak tenderly' cf Jg 19:3. It was from there, too, that she had first moved into the land of abundance, the Promised Land. She quickly forgot where its blessings came from and re-learned through the pain of desertion. **15.** The gifts of Yahweh are now restored to her and her entry into them gives better promise than her former entry into Palestine. The first passage through the Valley of Achor was accompanied by a disaster (Jos 7:25ff) which will not be repeated. Her love for Yahweh will be marked by the freshness of youth which will recall the days of their first espousals when 'she came out of the land of Egypt'. She is given the opportunity of making a fresh start with the
i guarantee of a better future. **16f.** 'In that day'—an expression used to introduce promises for a new era of salvation which opens with the day of Yahweh. The prophets may have expected a more immediate fulfilment, but many of these promises are fully realized only in the Messianic age. Israel will no longer call Yahweh 'Baali', i.e. my Baal, but '*îsî* 'my husband'. Baal (lit. master or owner) has sometimes the meaning of 'husband' cf Gn 20:3, Lv 21:4, etc, and is therefore a synonym of '*îs* 'man, husband'. But Baal is also used to denote the Canaanite deities and its use is condemned on account of its heathen associations. Cf the NT conception of the Church as the Bride of Christ, Eph 5:32. In Hosea's time, Yahweh was worshipped under the name and by the cult of Baal, but the future relation of Israel to Yahweh will be that of a faithful spouse, and all memory of the Baal-worship will be wiped out. Note that in 17—23, it is Yahweh who takes the initiative in healing the breach with Israel and in showering gifts on a once ungrateful bride.
j **18.** The relations between Yahweh and the new Israel are described as a new covenant; cf also Is 55:3; Jer 31: 31—34; 32:40; Ezek 16:60; 34:25; 37:26. One feature of this covenant is peace and security; cf Is 11:9; Ezek 34:25; Mi 5:9ff. **19f.** 'Betroth': The Heb. verb describes the concluding act in the legal process of marriage and involves the payment of the marriage price to the father of the bride. The man and woman are then husband and wife. It only remains for the husband to take his wife home and to consummate the marriage. The covenant is therefore represented as a permanent union sealed by bridal gifts of righteousness and justice, of love, mercy and fidelity. Life in terms of this relationship will deepen Israel's awareness and knowledge of Yahweh her God. Cf Is 11:9; Jer 31:33 for the fuller knowledge of God which will be characteristic of the New Covenant. **21f.** Jezreel refers to the fertile plain SE of Mt Carmel which was taken from Israel by Assyria in 733 B.C. In the restoration, this fruitful land will be Israel's again, with a guarantee from Yahweh of abundant yields. Its crops will no longer be seen as gifts of Baal, and its name will spell blessing ('God sows') instead of disaster (cf 1:4—5).

23. Exile will end and Israel will be sown again in the land of promise. Under a new covenant, she will once more be the object of compassionate love. Yahweh will call her 'my people', and she will respond 'my God' (cf Ex 20:2; Lv 26:12). The general sense is clear, but translation is difficult because of inconsistency in the use of pronouns. Cf the use of this text in Rm 9:25 and 1 Pt 2:10.

3:1—5 Gomer's Reconciliation with her Husband— **544k** This ch carries on the story of Hosea's love for Gomer. She had deserted him for another man (2:2), but in his love he found strength to accept the humiliation of buying back his own wife. Yahweh's love for an Israel more unfaithful than Gomer gave point to his command, and encouraged Hosea to be more generous than the letter of the law (cf Dt 24:4). It is unlikely that there is question here of a second marriage. The meaning of the text does not demand it, and the lesson of Yahweh's love for a fickle Israel is better taught if Hosea is here concerned with the same woman as in ch 1.

1. This verse is dominated by the word *love*. Its l fourfold repetition contrasts most effectively the generous fidelity of Yahweh and Hosea with the selfish prodigality of Israel and Gomer who lavish their affection on unworthy partners. 'love cakes of raisins': The raisins were reckoned to be a gift of Baal and were eaten during the cult by his worshippers. **2.** Assuming that the *ordinary* price of barley was about one third of a shekel per seah (or measure, cf 2 (4) Kgs 7:18), 'a homer and a lethech' would be worth about 15 shekels (a lethech = $\frac{1}{2}$ homer; 1 homer = 30 seah). The price paid by Hosea would then be the value set on a slave (Ex 21:32). The reference to 'paramour' in v 1 suggests a liaison with one person and makes it unlikely that Gomer had become a cult prostitute. Presumably the price was paid to her lover.

3. The last words in the Heb. text of this v are m altered by most commentators to give: 'and for my part, I shall not go unto you'. This implies that Gomer is not fully reinstated for some time after her return. Through the withholding of conjugal rights (cf Am 2:7) she must learn to need Hosea's love. This would find a ready application in Yahweh's treatment of Israel as outlined in v 4. The suggested change finds little support in the versions with the exception of the rather free rendering in Vg. RSV translates the last words of the v as they stand. Even in this translation, however, there are indications that Gomer was not fully reinstated on her return. 'Many days' means for a long time; it does not mean 'always'. 'You must dwell as mine' can then scarcely be an exhortation to fidelity. Fidelity is for always. In this view, the phrase 'you must dwell as mine' should be rendered: 'You must wait for me'. We are not told how long she must wait. The phrase 'many days' seems to have in view the application of this incident to Yahweh and Israel (cf v 4) and do not necessarily imply long years of marital restraint on the part of Hosea and Gomer. If the verse is taken to contain a thrice repeated invitation—or command?—to Gomer to be faithful and a concluding protestation of fidelity on the part of Hosea, then 4—5 would give the symbolic meaning of 1—3 and not merely of 4. **4f.** The people of Israel will not be restored to their former rights as soon as they repent. They must still live without those institutions of society and cult which they regarded as essential, whether for the worship of Yahweh or of false gods is not entirely clear.

Although the cultic items mentioned here were used in n earlier times in the worship of Yahweh (cf e.g. Gn 28:18, 22; Jg 17:5) their importance decreased, and, in some cases, they later merited condemnation. Pillars which had a commemorative function in the cult and recalled the presence of the divinity were roundly condemned in Dt 16:22, probably because they represented the male divinity in the fertility cult. The teraphim were images which were sometimes used for divination (cf Ezek 21:26). The ephod was either an image or some part of the priest's adornment used in giving oracles or drawing lots (1 Sm 23:6; cf § 191*b*, *c*). The loss of these objects

544n deprived Israel of the means for learning the wishes of her God, means she had abused in forbidden forms of worship. Hosea's judgement on the monarchy in the N Kingdom is generally unfavourable. In v 4 he implies that Israel was punished for her misuse of these institutions and must now live without them before being reunited to Yahweh in lawful worship under a Davidic king. Their fear of Yahweh is turned to joy when they share in his 'goods' (cf 2:8–9)—more accurate perhaps than 'goodness'. It is likely that the words 'and David their king' (cf Jer 30:9; Ezek 37:22) and 'in the latter days' (cf Is 2:2; Jer 23:20) were added by a Judaean redactor to give a Judaean flavour to the eschatology of Hosea.

545a **4:1–11:11 Comminatory Oracles—This section of the** book contains oracles of accusation and reproof of varying length, which seem to have been put together in rather arbitrary fashion. They may follow roughly a chronological order.

b **4:1–3 The People on Trial for their Crimes—1f.** 'Controversy': implies a legal process. The same root is found in 'contention' (v 4) and 'plead' (2:2). God's accusation is based on the terms of the covenant. Israel has failed in the covenant virtues of faithfulness, kindness (*hesed* elsewhere 'steadfast love' in RSV) and knowledge of God (cf 2:19–20; 4:6). The people ignore the commandments in their dealings with one another. **3.** 'Therefore' introduces the punishment imposed 'mourns', more accurately, 'dries up'. The link between cosmic disorder and moral disorder is a common feature in OT salvation history (Gn 3:17; Jer 12:4; Is 24:3–6 etc) and finds its echo in Rm 8:19–22.

c **4–10. The Priests on Trial for their Failure to Teach and to Lead—4.** The conduct of the priests is now the subject of judicial investigation. Legal terms predominate (cf 4 and the 'eye for an eye' principle in 6), and, when the accusations have been made, the penalty is imposed (6, 9–10). 1–3 had outlined the moral decadence of the people, but 4 goes on to assign the responsibility for it to the priests. The translation of 4 is difficult, but most commentators accept the conjecture of RSV. The first part of the verse might be rendered more clearly, if more literally:

> Yet it is not just anyone that one should accuse;
> it is not just anyone that one should chastise.
> But it is against you, O priest, that I enter my case.

The priest addressed is representative of his class. He is not necessarily the chief priest of a sanctuary who is personally held responsible for the state of the people (cf the plural in 8–10). **5.** 'Stumble', i.e. under the chastising hand of God (5:5; 14:1) which otherwise sustains and guides the just man in the way. 'The prophet also . . .': these words are probably a gloss (cf Mi 3:11; Jer 2:8 etc). Hosea is not critical of the prophets and 'the prophet' mentioned here does not re-appear subsequently. 'Your mother': either the whole nation (cf 2:2; Is 50:1), or, literally, the priest's own mother. The members of his family are punished with him (cf 6; Am 7:17; Jer 22:26).

d **6.** The crimes with which the priests are charged are specified. Like the people, they have rejected knowledge (i.e. of God, cf v 1), and have forgotten the law (cf 2), but theirs is the greater guilt because of their failure in leadership (cf Ezek 34). 'Knowledge of God' involved knowledge of the events of salvation history and the nature of the God who revealed himself through them (cf 11:1; 9:10; 13:5f; 2:10; 8:1; 6:7). It included a knowledge of his will expressed in his law (cf 2). It was not merely intellectual knowledge, but a knowledge which

involved submission to God's will as expressed in the terms **545d** of the covenant in cultic and moral law. It was knowledge which was deepened by experience of life in terms of the covenant love which linked Israel with Yahweh. Ignorant of the covenant law and lacking in experience of intimacy with Yahweh, the priests of Israel had nothing to give to their people. They had failed in their duty to instruct (Dt 33:10; Mal 2:7; Ezek 44:23); for this they must suffer with the nation. 'Children': literally 'sons'. The priesthood was hereditary and future generations would suffer for the neglect of their fathers (cf Am 7:17). **7.** Their sins increased in proportion to their number—a reference to the multiplication of places of worship (cf 8:11; 10:1). **8.** The priests encouraged idolatrous worship. It was a way of increasing their income, since they lived from their share of the offerings. They were not providing a service for the people, but sought only the satisfaction of their greed.

9–10. The punishment they will share with the people **e** will leave them hungry. The acts of ritual prostitution by which they seek to ensure fertility and increase their numbers will remain unproductive. It is Yahweh, not Baal, who can give the increase (cf 1:10).

11–14. Debauchery and drunkenness played havoc among the religious institutions of the Israelites. The people, led astray by a spirit of apostasy from God, turn to wooden images for advice and consult their divination rods. They worship their gods on hilltops with all the immoral ritual of the Canaanites. But the young, inexperienced women will be punished with less severity, all responsibility resting with their elders, whose example they follow, and with the priests, who encourage and participate in (read v 14 *they themselves* instead of 'the men themselves') the licentious cult of the Canaanites. A people having no knowledge of God's law will perish (**14c**).

15–19. As translated in RSV, this section is **a warn-** **f** **ing to Judah** not to follow in the steps of Israel (cf 15 and 17). Some commentators (e.g. Wolff and Deissler) regard 'Judah' (15) as a gloss, and take the passage to refer to Israel alone. **15.** 'Gilgal': almost certainly the Gilgal near Jericho of Jos 4–5 (cf also 1 Sm 11:13–15). Formerly a shrine associated with sacred traditions of Israel, its cult had now been debased (cf 9:15; 12:11). Beth-aven ('house of iniquity' cf Am 5:5) is an ironic designation of Bethel ('house of God') which had a long history as a sanctuary in Israel (cf Gn 28). After the Schism it became with Dan one of the principal sanctuaries of the N Kingdom (cf 1 (3) Kgs 12:29). Its form of worship became increasingly corrupt. Swearing by Yahweh was not sinful, was even commanded (cf Dt 6:13; Jer 4:2), but many Israelites were invoking Baal with the name of Yahweh in the centres of idolatrous worship. **16.** The obstinate Israelites have become like an unmanageable heifer; is it now possible that Yahweh will lead them like a lamb to spacious pastures? For the interrogative sense see GK § 150a. **17.** Ephraim (the N Kingdom) has forsaken Yahweh to cling to idols. The prophet invites Judah to let Ephraim meet his inevitable fate alone. Scholars who take the whole passage to refer to Israel (cf above) emend and translate the obscure text of 17b–18 in a variety of ways. **18.** cf 11–12 and 7. **19.** Calamity will fall on them like a storm-wind which will carry them far away from their country and there they will have to acknowledge the uselessness of their idolatrous worship.

5:1–7 The Crimes of Israel and its Leaders bring **546a** **Inevitable Disaster—1.** The prophet arraigns the priests, the leaders (= 'house of Israel') and the royal family for their failure to guarantee the dominance of 'judgement' (Yahweh's will in the broadest sense) in the life of Israel. They had failed in their responsibility to

546a 'judgement'. Others understand **1d**: 'for the judgement (which follows) pertains to you'. Mispah: either on the border between the N and S Kingdoms about 8 miles N of Jerusalem, or Mizpah in Gilead (Jg 11:29). Numerous statuettes of Astarte from the 8th cent. B.C. have been found on the former site and show an active fertility cult in the town at the time of Hosea. (Mt) Tabor: rises above the NE corner of the plain of Jezreel. Was no doubt 'a high place'. **2.** Shittim: cf Nm 25:1ff. In Transjordania opposite Jericho; scene of Israel's first veneration of Baal. **3f.** Although the people have been thus ensnared, their internal dispositions are not hidden from God. They are hardened sinners: the spirit of apostasy has so overwhelmed them that they are unable to appreciate the holiness and justice of Yahweh and to return sincerely to him. **5.** The arrogance of Israel is here personified and speaks as an accusing witness against the nation on trial. The reference to Judah derives from a glossator who applied the lesson of Israel to his native province at a later date. **6f.** Sacrifices without the internal dispositions of repentance and obedience are useless; cf 6:6; 1 Sm 15:22. Yahweh has left them because they have treacherously broken the pact with him as a woman breaking the marriage bond; cf Jer 3:20. The fruits of this religious infidelity are illegitimate ('alien'). The new moon with its feast should ensure fertility; instead it brings disaster.

b **8—15.** The background to this section is provided by the Syro-Ephraimite war (735 B.C. cf § 64*j—k*). **8.** The three towns are in Benjamin and lie along the route going N from Jerusalem. The order (from S to N) suggests an attack on Israel by Judah. The Syro-Ephraimite forces probably withdrew from Jerusalem at news of the arrival of the king of Assyria, Tiglath-pileser III, on their N boundaries. The king of Judah profited by the occasion to annex some territory (cf v 10). **9.** 'the tribes of Israel': i.e. the twelve tribes. Hosea is thinking in terms of a united people, and goes on to condemn, **10**, the action of the king of Judah in taking over territory belonging to his fellow-Israelite (cf Dt 19:14; 27:17; Prv 22:28 for the law condemning such conduct between Israelites). **11—12.** Ephraim had begun to experience oppression in the execution of God's judgement on it through Assyria. According to the terms of the covenant (cf Dt 27—28), Yahweh had no option but to punish Ephraim for its idolatry. He allows the structure of society to disintegrate; like a house consumed by rot, it is ready to fall. 'moth': **c** many now prefer the translation *'rottenness'*. **13.** The gaping wounds of war at least made Judah and Ephraim aware of their condition (cf Is 1:5ff), but, in spite of the guidance of Isaiah and Micah in the S and Hosea and Amos in the N, they misread the cause of it. They treated it as a political ailment which could be healed by strong alliances and payment of tribute (cf 2 (4) Kgs 15:19ff; 16:7; 17:1ff), but the cause ran deeper, and the untreated disease must take its course. The great nations ('the great king' was a title of the king of Assyria cf Is 36:4) had power only as the instruments of Yahweh, the sole Lord of history (cf Is 10:12ff). **14—15.** Under the figure of an irresistible lion, he carries out his threat to punish Ephraim and Judah in spite of their calls for rescue to their erstwhile allies. The aim of the chastisement is to convert. Yahweh leaves them in helpless desolation, returns to his place (probably heaven, cf Mi 1:3), and awaits—almost anxiously—their repentance and return. RSV, following LXX, reads 'saying' and makes v 15 an introduction to 6:1. It seems better to omit the word.

d **6:1—11a The Insufficiency of Israel's Repentance; her Sins**—1—3 are cast in the form of a penitential chant

(cf § 356 *g*). It is as if the people were responding to **546** the expectation of Yahweh (5:15), and were repenting of their sins. Their very words, however, show an inadequate understanding of God's wishes and a list of crimes from the past and present (vv 6—11a) shows an unflagging pursuit of wickedness.

6:1—3 Israel's Repentance—1. It is characteristic of **e** penitential chants in the Psalter, as here, that more emphasis is placed on reasons for confidence in God than on actual confession of, and sorrow for, sins. These vv reproduce characteristic words of Hosea (return: 2:9; 3:5; 5:4; torn = rend in 5:14; heal: 5:13; 6:1; 11:3; 14:5; 'know': 4:1, 6) and imply that the people's return was a response to his preaching. For the idea of Yahweh as healer cf Ex 15:26; Is 30:26 etc. **2.** 'two days . . . third day': i.e. in a very short time. 1—2 refer to wounding and not death; there is no question here of resurrection from the dead. 'revive': either restore us to full health, or preserve us in life. 'raise us up', i.e. from the sick bed. 'live before him': this expression derives from a belief that death separated a person from Yahweh (cf Ps 6:6; 30 (29):9; 88(87):11ff). From the time of Tert, this passage has been applied to the Resurrection of Christ from the dead and is read in the liturgy of Good Friday with obvious reference to the Resurrection on Easter Sunday. Although the text of Hosea is not directly concerned with the Resurrection of Christ, there is some justification for its use in the Liturgy of Holy Week. It draws attention to God as the Master of life and death and to the blessedness of life in his presence, themes which recur most dramatically in the Resurrection of Christ. **3.** 'know': the people show eagerness for knowledge of Yahweh, lack of which had brought them disaster. 'dawn . . . showers . . . spring rains . . . water . . . earth': these terms reflect the modes of thought which still dominated Israel's thinking. The fertility cult, a nature cult, was concerned precisely with those benefits which Baal had failed to grant. In thinking of a return, Israel is more concerned with the material advantages (cf Jer 5:24) which should counteract Baal's failure than with the real implications of 'knowledge of God' (4:1—2).

4—6 God's Hesitation—4. The people's return is based **f** on a superficial grasp of its implications and Yahweh has little hope of re-establishing lasting covenant virtues ('love' = *ḥesed*). **5.** But if God punishes them, it can never be said that he does so without warning. The efforts of Hosea were preceded by the activities of Elijah, Micaiah, the son of Imlah (1 (3) Kgs 17ff) and Amos, but Israel remained inconstant. Her fickleness contrasts with the strength and constancy of Yahweh's 'judgement'—a term which describes the pattern of life in a covenant relationship. It involves not merely the correct administration of justice, but the perfect attitude towards one's covenant partner. **6.** The people sought salvation in the **g** multiplicity of their sacrifices (cf 5:6). Sacrifice for them had become a salvation technique; the more frequently it was used, the more efficient it became. As part of the ritual prescribed by covenant law, sacrifice had given vivid expression to a union in 'steadfast love' and intimate 'knowledge', a union of God with Israel, and Israelite with Israelite (4:1—6). Divorced from these virtues, it became an act of hypocrisy and was the object of Yahweh's loathing (cf Is 1:11—15; Am 5:21—24; Mi 6:6; Mt 5:23; 9:13; 12:7 etc). To regard the statement as a rejection of all sacrifice is to misunderstand the force of such absolute (negative) statements in the Bible cf § 543*b*.

7—11a Israel's Persistence in Sin—7. RSV takes **h** Adam to refer to the place of that name in Transjordania

546h cf Jos 3:16. We have no evidence concerning Israel's sin at Adam ('there' in 7b implies a reference to a place in 7a). The improbable Heb. reading 'like Adam' suggests that Israel's infidelity can be compared to Adam's breaking faith with God, and may even be an extension of his inconstancy. **8.** 'Gilead': the name suggests some city in Transjordania where the territory called Gilead lay N and S of the Jabbok; exact identification unknown. The nature of the 'evil' done is not specified. Attempts to link 'blood' with the sacrificial offering of children must fail for lack of evidence. **9.** The text is corrupt and the sense obscure. Shechem was an ancient sanctuary (cf Gn 12:7; Dt 27:11; Jos 24), a levitical city (Jos 21:22) and a city of refuge (Jos 20:7). Wolff has suggested in explanation of this v that Shechem was a centre of orthodox worship of Yahweh which was hated by the official priesthood of the N Kingdom; they even lay in wait for worshippers who made their way to it. It is noticeable that Hosea never condemns Shechem as he does Bethel, Gilgal, Mizpah, Tabor and Samaria. **10.** Many read 'Bethel' instead of 'house of Israel' (cf 'there' in 10b). 'house of Israel' may mean 'the territory of land of Israel'. (cf 8:1; 9:15) If the latter meaning is accepted, the v is a summing up of what precedes. Otherwise it recalls the sin of Bethel, already condemned (cf 4:15). 'a horrible thing': cf Jer 5:30; 18:13; 23:14. The exact reference here is uncertain. **11a.** This sentence is a later addition. Jer 51:33 shows that 'harvest' can describe an act of God's judgement and condemnation. Judah is here reminded of the fate that awaits her for her evil deeds—unless she learns the lesson of Ephraim.

i **11b–7:2 Hopelessness of Repentance—11b.** God's efforts to bring the people back to him, **7:1**, and to heal the disease of Israel served only to lay bare the wickedness of the people who persisted obstinately in their evil course practising falsehood, house-breaking, and highway robbery. **2.** They did not even consider that God took their sins into account, and yet all their misdeeds stood around them and were committed in his presence.

j **7:3 7 Conspiracies—3f.** The prophet passes from the consideration of social disorders to political disorders. The people, or their political leaders, deal treacherously with their king. While they rejoice the king by an outward show of devotion, they are inwardly *raging* like a burning oven and plotting against his life. 'adulterers' may mean infidelity in general. When their plans are mature, the conspirators wait for an opportunity to carry them out, just as a baker ceases to kindle and to stir the fire from the kneading of the dough until its leavening. **5.** On a certain day, perhaps the king's birthday, the princes, i.e. the ringleaders, while banqueting with the king, went mad with wine and joined hands with *assassins*. **6f.** Their hearts were really *burning* (LXX), as an oven, with intrigue. At one time their violent passion seemed to have *abated*, but all of a sudden it burst out like a blazing furnace devouring their rulers. **3–7.** Are an allusion to the eventful times which followed the death of Jeroboam II. Four kings had fallen victims of conspiracies, and yet none of them had turned to Yahweh for assistance.

k **8–16 The Foreign Policy of Israel and its Result— 8.** Israel in her utter helplessness wanders farther from Yahweh seeking for aid from foreign nations. But instead of being relieved, she plunges deeper into difficulties. Ephraim has become entirely imbued with a pagan spirit and now she is like a cake which is not turned while it is being baked and is therefore half-scorched and half-raw, consequently unfit for any use. **9.** The moral strength and the temporal prosperity of Israel have been absorbed by those very nations with which it came into contact, and **546k** now it is powerless like an old man whose hair begins to turn grey. Yet they do not understand that their own perversity has reduced them to this wretched state. **10.** Their arrogance is manifest on their faces, and they refuse to return to Yahweh. **11.** Their foreign policy is one of indecision. Like a dove heedless of danger they turn now to Egypt and now to Assyria. **12.** But no human help will avail them. As they wander away, God spreads his net over them and brings them down like birds and punishes them as their wickedness deserves. 'Chastise' *yāsar*, implies here as in 5:2 that Yahweh's purpose is to instruct not to destroy Israel.

13. Destruction now awaits the ungrateful people. **l** Though Yahweh has delivered them many times, and is still prepared to rescue them, they speak to him lying words of repentance and attribute to Baal what they have got from him (cf 2:7, 10; 11:3b). **14.** Their cries to Yahweh are never sincere, and their prayer follows the pattern of Canaanite worship. In cult prostitution, they cry out to their gods, and implore fertility with forbidden rites (cf 1 (3) Kgs 18:28; forbidden in mourning ritual Dt 14:1 etc). **15.** Though Yahweh gave them strength to win their victories, they plan to eliminate him from their lives (cf 8:12). His person and wishes are not to be considered. **16.** The folly of their confidence in other gods and foreign nations is further emphasized. They are like a bow which makes the arrow swerve from the target. Yahweh can no longer use them to achieve his aims. A disastrous end awaits them, prepared by the leaders who should have saved them. 'Derision in Egypt': Egypt had probably backed the anti-Assyrian forces of Syria and Israel in the Syro-Ephraimite war (735 B.C. cf § 293e–f). Pekah was then king, but he was murdered and supplanted by Hosea (2 (4) Kgs 15:29 31), who pursued a pro-Assyrian policy, at least initially. The prophet sees Egypt, the rejected ally, mocking the folly of Israel as she falls prey to the Assyrian army.

8:1–4 Israel's Sins and the Coming Doom— 547a A general indictment of Israel. The main charges are violation of the covenant, unlawful government, calf-worship, the foreign policy and idolatrous worship.

1. The prophet is commanded to sound the alarm because the Assyrians, like a vulture, are about to swoop down on the land of Israel. For 'house of Yahweh' = land of Israel cf also 9:15; Jer 12:7. **2f.** First charge: They have broken the covenant and ignored the law which is at the heart of the covenant. 'Law' (torah) implies more than rules and regulations. Basically, the word means 'teaching' and includes God's revelation of himself with what this implies for man in his relations with his covenant God and his fellow men. **4a.** Second charge: Their kings were chosen without reference to Yahweh and were installed by methods which violated God's law (cf 7:3–7). Cf 1 (3) Kgs 11:29ff and 2 (4) Kgs 9:1ff for the part played by Yahweh through his prophets in designating kings. Dt 17:14ff outlines the place of the king within the covenant. **4b–6.** Third **b** charge: The calf-worship was introduced by Jeroboam I (1 (3) Kgs 12) and remained the official cult till the downfall of the kingdom. The calf was set up in Bethel and Dan and served either as a throne for Yahweh or as a symbol of his fruitful strength. Although Yahweh continued to be venerated at these shrines, the use of such figures opened the way to infection by idolatrous forms of worship. There is no evidence that such a calf was set up at Samaria. It was, however, the capital of the N Kingdom and the symbol of the official cult could easily

547b be said to belong to it (cf 10:5). This accusation is based on the law against images Ex 20:4; Dt 4:23.

c **7—10.** Fourth charge. Israel's foreign policy is as senseless as the sowing of wind, but the result will be as disastrous as the reaping of a whirlwind. A poor harvest will punish them. Whatever grain is saved will go to 'aliens'—either taken by Assyria as spoils of war, or given by Israel to buy an alliance. **8.** Her wealth is dissipated in useless alliances and her territory dismembered. Already in 733 B.C., the Assyrians had taken Galilee and Gilead. Israel had become a useless vessel, fit only for the rubbish dump (cf Jer 22:28; 48:38). **9.** 'a wild ass': either Assyria which spurns the company of Israel and is yet pursued by her with gifts, or, more likely, a stubborn and wilful Ephraim who goes her way alone (cf Jb 39:5—8). **10.** 'gather them up': i.e. for judgement cf Zeph 3:8. LXX in 10*b* followed by RSV, implies that the Kingdom and its ambitions are moving to an end. The Heb. text might be translated: *Soon they will wilt under the burden of the king of princes,* i.e. they will shortly experience the burden imposed on prisoners and subject peoples by the king of Assyria.

d **11—14.** Fifth charge: Idolatrous worship. **11.** Altars should be symbols of devoted service, but the altars built in Israel were an occasion of sin. The cult which was centred on them was a mixture (syncretism) of elements from the worship of Yahweh and of Baal. The more often it was practised, the more frequently did Israel sin. **12.** This text presupposes that some elements of the law (*tôrāh,* cf § 547*a*) but not the whole Pent (later called *tôrāh*), were already committed to writing. **13.** The Israelites were more interested in the meal which followed the sacrifice than in the religious significance of the whole rite (cf Jer 7:21). 'return to Egypt' can be understood either literally or metaphorically. Literally it would imply captivity or exile in Egypt. The threat of captivity in Egypt does not fit into the political and military pattern of the time of Hosea, but exile was a real possibility, since many Israelites would seek refuge there from the Assyrian army. Metaphorically, 'return to Egypt' could describe any captivity or exile which would recall the earlier sufferings of Israel in Egypt, and would aptly describe the Assyrian captivity which followed the Assyrian invasion. **14.** 'Maker': this description of Yahweh occurs elsewhere only in post-exilic texts: Is 27:11; 44:2; 51:13. There are also echoes of Am 1:4, 7, 10; 2:2, 5. Hosea is critical of splendid palaces which suggest forgetfulness of God and fortifications which imply excessive confidence in human strength. The prosperity of the long reigns of Uzziah (Azariah) in Judah and Jeroboam II in Israel made it possible to build on such a scale.

e **9:1—9 Exile puts an end to Festal Joys—1.** While the people celebrate their harvest festivals and express their gratitude to the gods from whom, they believe, all their material blessings come, the prophet severely condemns these heathen rejoicings and announces their coming end. **3.** 'return to Egypt': cf 8:13 and comment. The people will either flee to Egypt or be taken captive to Assyria. Both Egypt and Assyria are unclean, because, unlike Israel which is 'Yahweh's land', they belong to pagan gods. The produce of these lands is therefore unclean (cf Ezek 4:13). **4.** Far from Yahweh's land, they will be unable to offer him sacrifices. Their bread will be like bread eaten in a house of mourning and therefore unclean (cf Nm 19:14ff). The last section of this v ('for their bread . . . house of the Lord') is probably a later Judaean interpolation which was inserted with Temple regulations **f** in mind (cf Dt 23:18; Ex 23:19). **5.** Their festivals will

no longer be celebrated. **6.** RSV changes MT which how- **547f** ever gives good sense: *'they depart from destruction'*, i.e. they flee before the scourge of Assyria. Memphis: near the apex of the Nile delta. Famous for its pyramid tombs which were already two thousand years old in the time of Hosea. As they lie dead in the Egyptian city of tombs, their dwellings and treasures in the land of Israel are left to nettles and thorns.

7—9. The text of 7 and 8 creates some difficulty and is **g** generally emended. RSV incorporates one (unnoted) emendation in its translation, reading 'the people of my God' for 'with my God' (MT) in v 8. Israel will learn by bitter experience that the days of punishment foretold by the prophet have come. She has regarded him as a fool and a madman because sin had blinded her to the divine origin of his message. In fact, the prophet is sent as the watchman to warn God's people of approaching danger (Jer 6:17; Ezek 3:17 etc). Instead of helping they hinder him, and hate him for his accusing words. This rejection of God's own watchman recalls the shameful act of Gibeah (Jg 19—21) which so brutally received the wandering Levite. Their sin, like Gibeah's, will be severely punished by God. Some commentators (e.g. Wolff; Deissler; BJ) take the words 'The prophet is a fool, the man of the spirit is mad' to be direct speech and understand them as comment from the crowd who listen to Hosea.

10—17 Israel's Early Corruption—Israel has been **h** ungrateful to God ever since the early days; conversion has become hopeless. **10.** God found Israel (i.e. the twelve tribes) in the wilderness with that joyful satisfaction with which one finds a bunch of grapes or a first ripe fig when they are not expected. The episode of Baal-peor (Nm 25:1—3) was the beginning of a long series of backslidings. Man is like the things he loves and so Israel became detestable like its gods. **11.** The unrepentant Ephraim will now lose his glory with the swiftness of a fleeing bird. The glory of Ephraim is that signified by his name which is similar in sound to *pārah* 'to increase' hence fruitfulness (Gn 48:19). In other words no more will there be birth, pregnancy or conception in Ephraim. **12.** And the children whom they may now be bringing up will be taken away. **13.** The text is corrupt. As emended and translated in RSV it develops the idea of 12*a*. **14.** The prophet realizes that punishment is inevitable since the people have given no grounds for pardon. Their hostility to him personally (cf 9:7) would justify his joining with Yahweh in their condemnation. It is, however, difficult to say whether this v is an endorsement of Yahweh's determination to destroy Israel (as in vv 11—13) or a plea for a reduction of sentence. If there were fewer children in existence, the punishment would be to some degree diminished. For this idea cf Lk 23:29. **15.** Gilgal: The incidents referred to may have occurred at the time of entry into the Promised Land (cf Baal-peor in v 11 and Mi 6:5), or there may be question of the introduction of monarchy into Israel and the rejection of Saul which were centred on Gilgal (cf 1 Sm 11:15; 15:12, 21ff). In any event, Gilgal became a centre of unlawful worship (cf 4:15; 12:11; Am 5:5). 'drive . . . out': cf Gn 3:24. 'my house', i.e. my land. For 'hate' and 'love', cf N. Lohfink, CBQ 25 (1963) 417. **16—17.** Like a tree which is stricken **i** by disease, or shrivelled from lack of moisture, Ephraim shall bear no fruit. If perchance children are born, they will not survive, and those remaining in Ephraim will be scattered among the nations. Note the irony in the punishment mentioned in 11—12, 14, and 16. The women of Israel sought fertility by consorting with Baal; only barrenness can teach them the folly of their ways.

547j **10:1—8 Israel's Prosperity, Idolatry, and Ruin—** The theme of this discourse is that treated before: God's tender love for his people, the people's unresponsive attitude, and the impending disaster.

1. Israel has been prosperous like a luxuriant and fruitful vine; but the more prosperous she became, the more altars she built. **2.** Men's hearts are divided between Yahweh and Baal (contrast Dt 6:5), or, as in RSV, are 'false, deceitful'. They will be punished by the destruction of those altars and pillars to the use of which they attributed their prosperity. **3.** Is a confession which the people will make ('now they shall say') when punishment overtakes them. Then they will acknowledge that it was the helplessness of their kings and their lack of fear of Yahweh that have brought about the national crisis. **4.** The court diplomacy consists in words without truth, false oaths, and alliances with foreign nations; but punishment will spring forth like poisonous weeds in the furrows of a field.

k **5f.** Their powerless gods will be carried to a foreign land. The inhabitants of Samaria will be seized by terror on account of the calf of Bethaven (cf 4:15), they will mourn over it, and its priestlings will wail because both their god and its precious ornaments will be carried to Assyria and given as a present to the Great King (cf 5:13).

7f. Samaria is inexorably doomed; the king, like a chip on the waters continually tossed by the waves, is unable to withstand the Assyrian flood which is about to sweep through the land cf Is 8:7f. 'High places': the places in which illicit worship was carried out; either located on hills or artificially raised above the surrounding terrain. 'Aven' = Beth-aven as in v 5. '*āwen* to mean 'wickedness'. The people will be so terrified at the approach of the Assyrian army that they will prefer to be buried under the crumbling mountains than to fall into the hands of their enemies.

l **9—16 Punishment is Certain; an Appeal for Repentance; Misplaced Trust brings War**—Both the division of this section and its interpretation are difficult. It is variously emended by commentators. The interpretation given here follows RSV. Israel's persistence in sin makes punishment inevitable, but the way of repentance can bring her relief. She stubbornly rejects the guidance of her God and relies on physical force. She must bear the consequences of her folly. **9—10.** These vv take up the theme referred to in 9:9 (cf Jg 19) Israel's sinful conduct at this place, begun so long ago, continues. In the first instance, their sin brought the chastisement of war; their current behaviour must similarly be punished. Their punishment was earlier administered by the other tribes of Israel; now nations are gathered against them (cf Is 7:18) to afflict them for their 'double iniquity', i.e. of then and now.

m **11—12.** Ephraim is compared to a heifer to which was assigned the easier work of threshing (cf Dt 25:4). But the heifer has become unmanageable and Yahweh must lay on her the heavier joke of ploughing and harrowing. Though this harder work may humiliate her, she can profit by it. She must sow the right seed and plough it in, if she is to reap the harvest of steadfast love. It is only by living according to the terms of the covenant that she can hope to share in its benefits. The practice of righteousness is the sure test of Israel's repentance and the necessary condition for Yahweh's saving intervention. 'Rain salvation': a suitable metaphor for a people immersed in fertility worship (cf Is 45:8). Another interpretation turns on the words rendered by RSV 'I spare her fair neck'. Wolff takes them to mean: 'I became aware of the goodness (lit) of her neck,' i.e. for work. 11—12 then describe **547m** Israel's call to service and 13*a* the disappointing fruits of her labours. Similarly CV. Deissler regards 12 as a gloss which interrupts the connection between 11 and 13*a*. He reads for 'spared' of RSV: 'I put a yoke on her strong (lit perfect) neck'.

13—15. Israel disregarded the counsel of her God and **n** failed to sow what might be called 'covenant seed'. She will reap the fruits of her failure. Chariots and warriors will not save her (cf Is 31:1—3). 'Shalman . . . Beth-arbel': presumably a reference to some recent battle of striking ferocity and cruelty. Vg identifies Shalman with Shalman of Jg 8:5, but it is much more likely to be the Moabite king, Salamanu, who is mentioned as a tribute king in the lists of Tiglath-pileser III (745—727 B.C.). We can only assume that he attacked Beth-arbel and massacred the inhabitants, since extant records do not mention such an event. Beth-arbel is generally, though not certainly, identified with Irbid in Gilead. In any event, it was some town in Israelite territory bordering on Moab. 'house of Israel': if Bethel of MT is retained, it is representative of the cult which brought disaster to the nation. 'storm': i.e. of war. The Heb. 'dawn' is variously interpreted. The moment when light appears is full of hope and the promise of life (Is 8:20; 58:8); it is the time when Yahweh's help is most effectively sought (cf e.g. Ps 63 (62):2). The abandonment of the king at dawn implies his total rejection by God (Deissler). 'Dawn' may also refer to the dawn, i.e. beginning, of the conflict. In fact, King Hosea was taken captive in 725 B.C. before the siege of Samaria began.

11:1—11 God's Anger yields to his Tender Love— **548a** From the beginning, Israel was the object of Yahweh's compassionate and tender love. Her cool, deliberate and stubborn rejection of this love provokes him to anger, an anger which moves him to punish, even tempts him to destroy, his son (9:11ff; 10:6ff). In the conflict between anger and love, it is Yahweh's love which prevails (cf v 8). Anger is only an interlude; it is Yahweh's love which will control the history of his people and give them a fresh start in the Promised Land. For chh 11—13, cf J. L. McKenzie, CBQ 17 (1955) 287—99.

1. In chh 1—3, the love of Yahweh for Israel was **b** expressed in terms of marital love (cf 3:1, where the same verb is used as here). Here Yahweh is compared to a loving father who cares for his son and lavishes affection on him, only to have it spurned. The figure of the 'child' emphasizes that Yahweh loved Israel from the beginning, at a time when he was helpless (cf Ezek 16:4ff). His love for Israel moved Yahweh to help, to care for, to educate his son. It is on this long and demanding process of upbringing and education that stress is laid rather than on any idea of generation (cf also Is 1:2ff; 30:9; Jer 3:14, 19 etc). In the context of Baal worship, however, Hosea may be emphasizing that Israel is more truly the son of Yahweh than of Baal and the mother goddess. This text **c** is applied in Mt 2:15 to the return of Christ from Egypt. Christ is identified with Israel, and Israel with Christ. He sums up its hopes and aspirations, and in him will her destiny be fulfilled. Christ is now the chosen instrument of God, is more truly his Son, than Israel. God will work through him to bring salvation to his people who have, as it were, gone into bondage in Egypt (cf Hos 9:3, 6; 11:5). In calling Christ from Egypt, God inaugurates a new era of salvation which begins with a new Exodus and aims at life in a new Promised Land (cf Hos 10:11). All this is the gratuitous gift of a loving, merciful and forgiving God (cf Hos 11:8—9). It is easy to see how these ideas reflect the thought of ch 11 of Hosea.

548d 2–3: 'more I called': i.e. through the prophets. The text might also mean: '*No sooner had I called them than they went from me*' (Wolff). Israel's first fall came shortly after the Exodus (cf 9:10). Although Israel devoted his attention to Baals and idols, it was really Yahweh who taught him to walk, like a father leading his child by the hand, and took him into his arms when he tired or stumbled (cf Is 40:11; Dt 1:31). He healed him when he hurt himself. There may be an implicit reference to the Exodus in the use of the verb 'healed' (cf Ex 15:26), but it may also have a more general significance (cf Hos 6:1; 7:1).

e 4. Difficult. RSV introduces the idea of an animal drawn by cords which are better suited to men than to animals. Yahweh eases the yoke so that the animal may eat, and he actually feeds it. While Israel must give devoted service, it should be a labour of love which has its compensations in the loving attention of Yahweh. It is, however, more likely that the figure of the young child is still before us. God loved it with an intensely human love ('cords of man' (MT)) and became like one 'who raises an infant (reading '*ûl* instead of '*ōl*) to his cheeks' (CV), and bends down to feed it (CV, BJ, Wolff, Deissler). 5. Israel's deliberate rejection of Yahweh must be punished by exile. Experience of life outside Yahweh's land is the only way they can learn what life without him is really like. 'shall be': this is emphatic in the Heb. The idea may be: 'Assyria *shall be* their king in spite of their present efforts to jettison him'; cf king Hosea's efforts to escape from Assyrian dominion, presumably on the death of Tiglath-pileser III (727 B.C.) (2 (4) Kgs 17:4ff). 6. The effects of the Assyrian invasion. Others '*consume their prattlers and devour them for their (evil) counsel*' (Wolff; Deissler).

f 7. The difficulty of this v is illustrated by the variety of translations of emended texts, e.g. CV: 'His people are in suspense about returning to him, and God, though in unison they cry to him, shall not raise them up'. Wolff renders 7*a* as in RSV, but for 7*bc* he reads: 'They call on Baal, but he does not raise them up'. RSV gives good sense and states Yahweh's firm intention to punish Israel. 8. But will it be to the point of destruction? Yahweh cannot face the prospect of destroying the child on whom he has lavished such care. He could never blot out Israel as he had done to the 'cities of the valley' (Gn 19:29), Admah and Zeboim (cf Gn 14:2, 8; Dt 29:23). Sodom and Gomorrah are usually mentioned in this connexion, but it is suggested that A and Z were the names which stood out in the Deuteronomic—and therefore N—tradition about the destruction of these cities. 9. In the struggle

g between his anger and his love, Yahweh's love prevails, He will punish but not destroy because he is a merciful God and not a revengeful man (cf Is 55:6–9). 'again': this does not imply that Yahweh had destroyed Israel on a previous occasion. Rather, he has no intention of allowing Israel to return to the state he was in before his call. Note that Yahweh's compassionate treatment of Israel goes beyond what is human because of his holiness. 10. The introduction of Yahweh in the third person, and the ideas, suggest that this verse may be an insertion which reflects post-exilic thinking (cf 1:10; 3:5). 'those returning from the west' is improbable in Hosea who only spoke of exile in Egypt and Assyria (cf vv 5 and 11 and Is 11:11; 43:5–6; 49:12). 'roar': not a call to judgement as in Am 1:2, but an unmistakeable call of deliverance. 11. 'birds . . . doves': indicating perhaps the speed and ease of their return (cf Ps 55 (54):6; Is 60:8). 'trembling': the verb *ḥārad* indicates fear rather than excitement.

h With their awareness of sin sharpened by exile, the people are not hopeful of favourable treatment, and are apprehen- **548i** sive of this new intervention of Yahweh. Something unforeseen might also frustrate them, when they are on the point of being rescued and restored. 'to their homes': to the Promised Land, Yahweh's land, for a fresh start. 'says the Lord': *neʾum yhwh*. This formula has not occurred in the section 4:1–11:11, and here provides an editorial conclusion to these chapters. Coming at the end of v 11, it affirms that the promise of deliverance really is the word of Yahweh.

11:12–14:8. (MT 12:1–14:9)—A series of accusations **549** against Israel is dominated by the certainty of her punishment, but the concluding discourse (14:1–8) gives hope of a fruitful repentance.

11:12–12:14 (MT 12:1–15) Israel's Deceit since the days of Jacob: her Punishment—Although not entirely homogeneous, a certain unity is conferred on this section by the insistence on the theme of deceit (11:12; 12:1, 7f) and the references to Jacob (12:2–4, 12). 11:12–12:1 brand Israel's religious and political life as deceit and lies. In 12:2–6, Israel's deceit is traced back to the trickery of his patriarchal ancestor Jacob. 7–9: Israel's wealth, acquired by treacherous means, can only bring about a return to the spartan conditions of nomadic life. 10–14: Yahweh's efforts at helping Israel through the prophets contrast with Israel's insolent reliance on self chosen allies and other gods.

12a. 'me': either Yahweh or the prophet. **12b.** The **b** translation is uncertain, and the text is often emended (cf RSV), although MT might stand. Judah's fidelity is contrasted with the failure of Ephraim. Some regard 12*b* as a gloss (Hosea's estimate of Judah was generally unfavourable, cf 5:10; 6:4, 11; 8:14); but it is intelligible on the lips of Hosea at a time when the N Kingdom was crumbling. **12:1.** The futility of Israel's alliances. 'east wind': the burning sirocco which brings drought and blight (cf 13:15; Gn 41:6). Israel only harms herself by such alliances. 'bargain': lit covenant, alliance. For the use of oil in covenant ritual, cf D. J. McCarthy, VT 14 (1964) 215–21; it is not merely a gift. **2.** 'indictment': Heb. *rîb*, translated 'controversy' in 4:1; = lit 'a law-suit'. 'Judah': the parallelism and the context indicate that one should read 'Israel'. The accusation of Israel was directed against Judah by a later Judean hand. **3.** Mention of **c** Jacob in v 2 evokes unfavourable memories of Israel's ancestor (cf Gn 32:28 for the change of Jacob's name to Israel). For 3*a* cf Gn 25:26. The grasping of Esau's heel and the later deceit by which Jacob acquired the birthright (Gn 25:29ff; 27) are linked through the name Jacob. 'he takes by the heel' or 'he supplants' (RSV note on Gn 25:26). 'manhood' or 'wealth' (cf Gn 32:24–28). 'strove': implying 'dared to strive', i.e. a manifestation of presumption and pride. **4.** Very difficult. Why 'angel' (not as in RSV: 'the angel')? Gn 32:24ff speaks of 'a man' and 'God'. Why did Jacob weep if he prevailed? The text may mean that Jacob deceitfully altered his tactics to get what he wanted. Gn 32:24–28 makes no reference to the weeping of Jacob, but the story may have come to Hosea in a different form, as is supposed by Wolff who suggests that 'angel' is a gloss to avoid the statement that Jacob wrestled with God. The text can then be translated: 'But God ('ēl) showed himself master and prevailed; he (i.e. Jacob) wept and sought his favour. God met him at Bethel and spoke with him there.' Israel should now imitate the weeping and prayer of Jacob so that Bethel may become a place to meet God and receive a blessing (cf Gn 28). It is certainly more accurate to have Yahweh as subject of the verbs 'met' and 'spoke' (cf Gn 28:13; 35:1, 10). Cf P. R. Ackroyd, VT 13 (1963) 245–59.

549c 5. A doxological insertion. For similar passages, cf Am 4:13; 9:5—6. 6. 'return': may refer implicitly to Jacob's return with the help of his God (Gn 28:15, 21). 'love and justice': for these terms cf 2:19; 6:4—5. Yahweh recalls Israel to her covenant obligations. For 'waiting on God',

d cf Pss 25 (24):5; 37 (36):34. 7—8. Cf Am 8:5. RSV: Israel's ill-gotten gains can never pay for his sins. Others: 'With all my riches, no guilt can be found in me which is sin'. 9. Yahweh enters as judge but his judgement is salvation. He is the same Yahweh who brought Israel out of Egypt, and must now teach Israel her sin and failure through the hardships of nomadic life (cf 2:3, 14). 'appointed feast': better: 'appointed meeting', i.e. in the desert. 10. Cf 6:5. God warned his people through the prophets. 11. 'Gilead': cf 6:8; 'Gilgal': cf 4:15; 9:15; 12:12. 'naught': the nothingness of idols and idol worship (cf Ps 24 (23):4; 31 (30):6).

e 12—14: This further incident from the story of Jacob (cf Gn 27:41ff; 28:2; 29—30) is introduced as a contrast to 13. It was no glorious interlude in the history of Israel. Jacob was forced to leave the land of promise as a consequence of his deceit (cf Gn 27:41ff), and was further humiliated in toiling for his wife. In contrast (add: 'But' at the beginning of v 13), Yahweh delivered Israel from servitude in Egypt under Moses, the prophet, and through his leadership 'preserved' (the same verb as 'herded' in v 12) him. Jacob toiled in his own interest, but Yahweh's intervention was a gift to Israel. It was little appreciated by an ungrateful Ephraim, which pursuing its own interests, 'exasperated' (CV) its God. For Moses as prophet, cf Dt 18:15f. Blood-guilt: cf Lv 20:9ff.

550a 13:1—16 Utter Destruction the Fate of Israel—The cause of Israel's decline is re-affirmed in the references to her sins (vv 1—2, 6, 10), but this passage is distinguished by the figures used to emphasize the certainty, the appalling effectiveness and the definitive nature (3, 7—8, 13—16) of the punishment which has already begun to afflict Ephraim (cf v 10).

b 1. For the position of Ephraim among the twelve tribes cf Gn 48; Jos. 24 and the importance of Shechem as the central shrine; 1 (3) Kgs 11:26ff; 12. 'Baal and died': 'died' in Heb. is part of the verb *mût* or *môt*. In Ugaritic literature, the protagonists in the cult epic of the dying and rising god are Baal and Mot (i.e. Death). Mot overcame Baal in the autumn and was in turn relegated to the underworld in the spring. By associating with Baal, Israel sought to guarantee life and fertility, but found himself subject to Mot instead: 'and died' (cf 4:10; 9:11ff; 16f). The reference may be to the Assyrian threat in 733 B.C. (cf 5:11; 8:8). 2. 'kiss calves': cf 1 (3) Kgs 19:18. 3. Cf 6:4*b*. Also Is 17:13. The figures used imply total extermination.

c 4. Cf the opening words of the Decalogue, Ex 20:2; Dt 5:6. Yahweh recalls once more who he is and what he has done in order to highlight the ingratitude of Israel (v 6). Note the verb 'to know' (also in v 5) to describe the relationship between Yahweh and Israel (cf 4:1; 6:3; 8:2). 5. 'knew': the reading of LXX ('I fed' or 'I shepherded') is preferred by many (e.g. CV), because of v 6. Yahweh's saving activity included rescue from Egypt, and protection and support in the desert. 6. 'fed to the full': these words provide a transition from the desert to the settled prosperity of the Promised Land. Israel was fed in the desert and was ungrateful (Ex 16; Nm 11); she was sated with the abundance of the Promised Land and was equally forgetful of her Benefactor (Dt 31:20; 32:12—18).

d 7—8. Cf Am 3:12; 2 Sm 17:8. 9. Yahweh is lord of history; even those that Israel calls her allies are subject to his control cf 12:1; Is. 10:12ff. 10—11. There were

always those in Israel who felt that the monarchy **550d** derogated from the supreme position of God among the people, and accepted it with reluctance. Their attitude is reflected in the account of the institution of the monarchy in 1 Sm 8:4—22; 10:17—27; 12 (as opposed to the account in 1 Sm 9; 10:1—16). The prophet Hosea seems to belong to this stream of tradition since his view of the monarchy is unfavourable (cf 3:4; 7:3f; 8:4). 10 implies that king Hosea, the last of the N kings, has been taken captive together with his court, and suggests 724 B.C. as the date for this prophetic discourse. 'save': probably an ironic reference to the king's name—Hosea, meaning '(Yahweh) has saved'.

12. 'bound up': as a legal document is carefully bound **e** up and sealed to ensure its continuing effectiveness (cf Is 8:16). 'kept in store': hidden away like a treasure. Israel may have forgotten her past sins, but the debt of punishment incurred is stored up against her and must be paid in the hour of judgement. 13. Israel's suffering is compared to birth pangs (cf Jer 6:24; 22:23; Is 26:17 etc), but like a child who is unnaturally unwise, he does not know the hour of his birth and present himself for entry into a new life. Israel is equally foolish in failing to understand that through sufferings he can pass to a new life by repentance. In this figure, Ephraim is compared both to the mother—as the one who suffers, and to the child—in failing to understand what the time requires, in spite of repeated instruction. 14. The rhetorical questions imply **f** an unspoken objection: Yahweh, who has power over life and death, should have helped with the birth, so that the child should not die in its mother's womb (cf for the mother's womb as the grave, cf Jer 20:17; Jb 3:10). But Israel has been warned and there can be no remission of her sentence on compassionate grounds. God therefore calls on Death and Sheol to destroy them. Other commentators see here a solemn affirmation on the part of God that he will redeem and ransom his people Israel from the power of Death. The first two questions in RSV must then be read as statements; the second two, as a mocking challenge of Death and Sheol. The last phrase, a threat, must then be limited to Ephraim. Part of this v according to LXX is used rather freely by St Paul to mock Death which has been rendered powerless by the resurrection of Jesus Christ (1 Cor 15:54—57). 15. 'reed plant': probably an Egyptian word which may carry an implicit reference to Israel's ally (cf 12:1). 'east wind': cf note on 12:1; it not only destroys vegetation; it dries up the wells. Once again the punishment fits the crime. Israel is punished in her fertility for her misplaced faith in fertility gods. 'shall strip' etc: the prophet passes from the figure of the E wind to the reality of the Assyrian army which will strip Ephraim of her treasures. 16. The specific mention of Samaria, the capital of the N Kingdom suggests that she is now being called on to bear the full weight of punishment (cf also v 10). The siege began in 724 B.C. For the savage treatment of women and children cf Ps 137 (136):9; 2 (4) Kgs 15:16.

14:1—8 (MT 14:2—9) Repentance, Forgiveness and **g** Renewal of Fruitful Love—This last section opens with an invitation to conversion (1—2*a*) followed by a prayer of repentance (2*b*—3), and culminates in a solemn promise of forgiveness which will restore to Ephraim the security and prosperity of life with Yahweh. It is he who will give to her the fruit she had sought from idols.

1. 'have stumbled': the past tense here contrasts with **h** the future in 5:5; Israel has already begun to experience the consequences of her wickedness. 2. 'words': i.e. sincere words of repentance and commitment, a more acceptable offering to Yahweh than the hypocritical repetition of

550h ritual sacrifices (cf 6:6; 8:13). 'take away all iniquity': a request for pardon of the sin and remission of the consequent punishment. 'fruit of our lips': a source of good (cf Prv 12:14; 13:2). **3.** Israel abandons her former ways of reliance on human help and idol worship. 'horses': may refer to Egyptian help, cf Is 30:16; 31:3. The verbs could be read as present ('*do not save*', '*do not ride*', '*we say no more*') to describe the current situation. Bereft of the support of Assyria, of Egypt, and of the gods she worshipped, the orphan Israel turns to Yahweh *because* (Heb.) he alone has compassionate love for an orphan. Israel's experience has taught her where to look for real support.

i **4.** Israel's sincere repentance opens the way for Yahweh's healing action (in contrast to 7:1). 'love': the characteristic word of 3:1 and 11:1 re-appears with renewed emphasis on the supreme freedom of God's love for Israel. **5–8.** The effects of Yahweh's love are described in terms which recall the language of Song (cf Song 2:2, 3, 13; 4:11; 5:1; 6:11). They are also a reminder to

Israel that it is Yahweh who can grant the gifts that she **550i** sought from the fertility gods (cf 2:8). **5.** 'dew': outside the very brief rainy seasons, dew is the only source of moisture for the land and the crops which cannot ripen without it. It became a symbol of life and prosperity (cf Dt 33:28; Is 26:19; 2 Sm 1:21 etc). **7.** 'shadow': cf Ezek 17:23; Ps 36 (35):7; 91 (90):1 etc. Life-saving protection from the deadly rays of the burning sun. **8.** Yahweh has nothing to do with idols; he alone cares for Ephraim and unfailingly (cf 'evergreen') provides for them. 'fruit', in Heb. *peri*, suggests the name Ephraim (cf Gn 41:52). At long last, Yahweh will make Ephraim live up to her name.

Epilogue—9. The vocabulary and form of this v derive **j** from Wisdom circles (cf §§ 356—9) in which the prophetical writings were transmitted. Similar passages in Jer 9:11 and Ps 107 (106):43 suggest an exilic or even a post-exilic date for the v. The addition of these words some hundreds of years after Hosea had ceased to preach bear witness to the eternal relevance of his message.

JOEL

BY M.N.L. COUVE DE MURVILLE

551a Bibliography—*Commentaries:* J. Knabenbauer, CSS 1924²; A. van Hoonacker, EtB 1908; S. R. Driver, CBSC 1915; J. T. Carson *New Bible Comm.* 1953; M. Delcor, PCSB 1961; J. Trinquet, BJ 1953. *Other Literature:* A. S. Kapelrud, *Joel Studies*, Uppsala, 1948; R. Pautrel, 'Joel', DBS 4 (1949) 1098—104; J. A. Thompson, 'Joel's Locusts in the light of Near Eastern Parallels', JNES 14 (1955) 52—55; J. Bourke, 'Le Jour de Yahvé dans Joel', RB 66 (1959) 5—31, 191—212.

b The Prophet and his Date—Joel (= 'Yahweh is God') son of Pethuel, from his frequent and exclusive references to Judah and Jerusalem, Sion and the Temple and the priestly ministrations, seems to have prophesied in Judah, probably in Jerusalem itself. No explicit indication is given of the period in which he lived. Older commentators assigned him to the 9th or 8th cent. B.C. Recently Kapelrud has argued for a date c. 600 B.C. Most modern critics prefer a date following the reforms of Nehemiah and Ezra. Arguments in favour of this are: the absence of any reference to a king or to the N Kingdom, the fact that Assyrians and Babylonians do not appear as the actual enemies of the people, the assumption that the people know no God but Yahweh and no worship but the Temple worship. On the other hand the absence of definite reference to the Greeks indicates a period before the Greek conquest of 333. The anti-Gentile tone, the concern for the cult and the impression given of a community led by the ancients and the priests would harmonize best with the period after the work of Nehemiah, i.e. between 400—350 B.C.

c Contents—MT divides the book into four chh. LXX, Vg, RSV make Heb. ch 3 into 2:28—32 so that Heb. ch 4 becomes their ch 3.

d The **unity of the work** has been much discussed, Vernes (1872), Duhm (1911) and Bewer (1912) postulated different authors and different periods for the two parts of the book; Trinquet accepts this. Kapelrud, Pautrel, Bourke, Delcor maintain a single author. **The careful construction of the book is an argument in favour of the single author.** The prophecy falls into two parts; the first part comprises chh 1 and 2 in which Jl describes a terrible locust plague and exhorts priests and people to penance. 2:19—27 contains the oracle which is Yahweh's favourable reply to his people. The Fathers and ancient commentators saw in the locust swarms of chh 1—2 a figure of future enemy invasions. But the text is better understood as the description of an actual locust plague and drought. In several non-Biblical texts armies are compared to locusts, and locusts to armies, but locusts are never the symbols of armies (cf J. A. Thompson). Later on in the Biblical tradition, apocalyptic writings borrow the theme of locusts from Jl and give them symbolic significance cf Apoc 9:3—11. In the second part, 2:28—3:21, Jl envisages the era of God's definitive intervention in history; the nations advancing against Jerusalem will be judged by God but Sion will be a safe refuge

for his people who will be renewed by God's spirit; Yahweh **551d** dwells in Sion and he inaugurates the perfect age, which is described in terms of paradisiac abundance.

Bourke has shown that both sections are carefully **e** composed according to a chiastic (Gr. chiasmos, a diagonal arrangement) pattern, i.e. a b c X c b a, where X stands for the central theme of the composition surrounded by 'layers' in reverse order; this is a complex example of the Semitic literary device known as 'inclusio' (cf § 794d). A further refinement appears to be the occasional inversion of two layers. The first part of the book can be analysed as follows: (a) agricultural desolation, 1:2—12. (b) proclamation of a solemn assembly, sound of the trumpet, priests' lamentation, 1:13—2:1a. (c) the Day of Yahweh, 2:1b—2. (X) the army of locusts, 2:3—9. (c) the Day of Yahweh, 2:10—11. (b) call to penance, sound of the trumpet, proclamation of a solemn assembly, 2:12—20. (a) agricultural abundance, 2:21—27. The structure of the second part is as follows: (a) prophecy of the sending of the spirit, 2:28—29. (b) the Day of Yahweh, 2:30—31. (c) Sion as refuge, 2:32. (d) judgement on the nations, 3:1—8. (X) the army of the nations, 3:9—11. (d) judgement on the nations, 3:12—14a. (b) the Day of Yahweh, 3:14b—16a. (c) Sion as refuge, 3:16b—17. (a) prophecy of paradisiac abundance, 3:18—21. The 'kernel' of both parts of the book is thus a hostile army, but in the first case it is the instrument of God's wrath and leads to penance and forgiveness; in the second case the army of nations is judged with finality. The ironic question of the peoples 2:17 is answered by the dwelling of Yahweh in Sion 3:17, and the abundance which follows the locust plague 2:21—26 is only a foreshadowing of the abundance of the messianic age 3:18—21.

Doctrinal Value—*The Day of Yahweh.* Jl's thought is **f** dominated by the idea of the Day of Yahweh, cf on 1:15; and further, a prophet is one who announces the judgement of God on contemporary events; so for Jl a plague of locusts and the agricultural disasters of his community are a manifestation of the Holy God of Sinai intervening in history to punish man, as in Dt 28:15ff. Jl, following Ezek, combines the requirements for moral conversion with the sacerdotal view of the efficaciousness of communal penance led by the priests. The passages from 1:13f and 2:17ff are still used in the Lenten liturgy of the Roman rite.

Eschatology. The Day which his contemporaries have **g** experienced is for Jl only a microcosm of the Final Day which will be a complete manifestation of God's holiness and power. It will inaugurate a new era. The God of Israel who has in the past used natural events and foreign invaders to chastise his people will now manifest himself in Sion so that Israel's transcendant relation to him will be vindicated. The nations, on the other hand, whose prosperity is only part of the process of history, pass away and that passing is a judgement on their wrongdoing.

The Outpouring of the Spirit. Jl foresees a charismatic **h** outpouring of God's spirit which will extend to all members

551h of the restored community, giving them life and strength in contrast to the essential weakness of man. St Peter in his Pentecostal sermon, Ac 2:14—36, quotes Jl 2:28—32 as fulfilled in the miraculous gift of tongues. He substitutes 'in the last days' for 'after that' of MT, LXX but this accords with the sense, (cf § 553a) since the gift of tongues in the Church is the manifest inauguration of the Messianic age, according to the NT anticipated eschatology (cf The Kerugma § § 667b, 668ac). It is fitting that the little book of Jl, which is so powerful a mediation on history, steeped in the past tradition of Israel's writings, should have the distinction of supplying the text for the first apostolic sermon on the day of Pentecost.

552a **1:1—2:27 A Locust Plague seen as the Day of Yahweh; Public Penance and God's Answer.**
1:1 Title—'The word of Yahweh that came to' is an old formula employed in the title of Hos, Mi, Zeph. Pethuel is not found elsewhere in OT; LXX Bathouel is probably a correction according to Gn 22:23 etc.

b **2—12 Agricultural Desolation**—The prophet describes the unprecedented destruction wrought by locusts and its effect on all classes of society. **2.** 'The land' is Judah with which alone Jl is concerned. **3.** For the command to transmit a tradition to future generations cf Dt 4:9; 6:20. **4.** Four words designate the locusts, *gāzām* (the root in Arabic and New Heb. means to cut off); *'arbeh* the word commonly used for locust (perhaps derived from *rābāh* to multiply); *yeleq* (derivation doubtful); *ḥāsîl* (root meaning to finish off, consume). The words may indicate stages in the locusts' development since these are readily distinguishable. When a locust swarm settles the females bury their numerous eggs; these hatch as small hopping locusts which immediately begin to devour the vegetation. When they have grown larger they progress by walking and finally when their wings have developed they are ready to fly away on the wind to start the process again. As however other terms are found for locusts in the OT and these may refer to different kinds of locusts, it seems more likely that Jl uses several names in rhetorical amplification to underline the destructive effect of successive locust swarms. **5.** 'Drinkers of wine', the object of prophetic reproof in the past, cf Is 5:11—12, are the first affected by the catastrophe. 'Sweet wine', the partly fermented juice of the grape **c** which was the first wine ready for drinking. **6.** 'A nation' is applied to the locusts whose immense numbers are often alluded to, Ps 105 (104):34, Jg 6:5; 7:12, Jer 46:23; 51:14. 'The fangs *of a lioness*' probably one of the several words for lion; LXX 'lion's whelp'. **7.** Explains the emphasis on the teeth of the insect. The locust, which is only $3\frac{1}{2}$—4 inches long, can gnaw off the bark of trees and small branches break under the weight of the clustered insects. **8.** 'Lament' fem. sing. imperative of *'ālāh*, hapax; meaning supplied by similar root in Aram. The community is addressed and some term like 'Oh daughter of my people' understood cf Jer 6:26. **9.** Cereal and drink offerings were made daily and accompanied the morning and evening burnt-offering of a lamb, cf Ex 29:38—42, Nm 28:3—8. These offerings were the token of God's presence and favour and their cessation was a national calamity. 'The house of Yahweh', the Temple. **10.** Grain, wine, oil are the three usual terms of agricultural blessing, cf Dt 7:13, Hos 2:8. 'Wine', here *tîrôs* which is must, the unfermented juice of the grape. 'Oil' *yiṣhār*, the freshly pressed juice of the olive in its first state. 'The wine *fails*'; the hiph'il *hôbîs* can be derived from *yābēs* to be dry, withered, or from *bôs* to be ashamed, confounded. There is probably a play on words which alludes to both meanings here and in 1:11; 12 (twice);

17. **12.** Pomegranate, palm and apple are trees highly **552** prized in Palestine. The apple tree or apple *tappûah* is mentioned rarely in the Bible, Prv 25:11, Song 2:3, 5; 7:9; 8:5. Jl here alludes to a drought cf 1:18—20, 2:3, which often accompanies the arrival of locusts cf Am 7:1—6. Since locusts are not strong in flight they are mainly borne along by the wind and in Palestine are brought by the scorching wind from parts of the Syrian or Arabian desert.

13—20 A Call to Public Penance—Priests and **d** ancients are to summon the people to penance, for the Day of Yahweh is near as a day of destruction; description of the terrible drought. **13.** 'Gird yourselves' here used absolutely, but implying the complement 'sackcloth' supplied by RSV, cf 1:8. The wearing of sackcloth was originally a sign of mourning, cf 2 Sm 3:31 which became an act of penance, required here because the daily sacrifices, sign of the normal relations between Yahweh and Israel, have ceased. **14.** 'Sanctify' is used for convoke, cf 2:15, either because of the holiness of the object in view or of the religious rites which accompanied it. Fasting, consisting in the temporary abstention from ordinary and innocent bodily enjoyment, can be an expression of sympathy with human affliction cf 2 Sm 1:12. More often in the Bible it is a religious act, expression self-abasement and sorrow for sin and seeking to obtain God's favour. Cf Ez 8:21 for the proclamation of a general fast. 'Gather, elders, all the inhabitants of the land'; the elders are the leaders of the people cf 1 (3) Kgs 21:8. **15—20.** Probably contain the tenor of the supplications which the community are to address to Yahweh. **15.** The same as Ezek 30:2, 3 for the first half, and Is 13:6 for the second. The Day of Yahweh was originally a popular expression, expressing the expectation of a victorious manifestation of God's power. The prophets warned that it would be a judgement on Israel, cf Am 5:18, and political catastrophes were seen as the warning of the approaching 'Day'; here Jl sees agricultural disasters in this light. 'As *šōd* (destruction) from *Šadday*', a play upon words which Driver tries to render 'as an overpowering from the Over-powerer'. *Šadday*, an ancient name for God which P represents as being the name known to the patriarchs cf Ex 6:3. Etymology uncertain, could be connected with the Akkadian *sadû* mountain; it is used with an archaic effect in a group of post-exilic writings, e.g. Jb. **16.** **e** Joy, especially that which accompanies the religious festivities cf Dt 16:11. **19.** For the comparison of drought to fire cf Am 7:4. **20.** 'The wild beasts' lit 'beasts of the field, land'; usually of domestic animals but 1 Sm 17:44 must be 'wild beasts' which gives a better progression to the sense here. 'Cry to thee', the verb *'ārag* is only found here and in Ps 42. LXX, Vg 'look up to'; translate 'long after thee'.

2:1—11 The Day of Yahweh has come; the Army of f Locusts—Jl describes the onslaught of locusts in epic language which echoes the language of theophanies. He sees the locust plague as the Day of Yahweh, an intervention of God in the normal course of events which occurs to fulfil a providential purpose. **1.** 'Trumpet' the curved horn of cow or ram used principally for battle. Its sound is connected with the manifestation of Yahweh on Sinai cf Ex 19:16, 19, and it accompanies the Day in Zeph 1:16. 'For the Day of Yahweh *has* come for it *was* near' i.e. the Day announced in 1:5. **2a.** The same as Zeph 1:15c, cf Ex 19:16, Am 5:18, Ezek 30:3. The dark clouds which accompany Yahweh's intervention are especially suitable in this description of locusts which can obscure the sun by their compact numbers; cf for this and other traits in the succeeding vv the texts collected by Driver,

552f pp. 87—91. 'Like blackness' reading *kišeḥôr* for MT *kešaḥar* 'like dawn'. This alteration respects the consonants of MT but it is a facilitating reading. Dawn which comes quickly in the E could well be an image of the rapidity with which the locust swarm deploys and the extent of its spread. The difficulty felt in the sudden passage from terms of darkness to an image of light is lessened if it is remembered that Jl is using in 2*a* elements borrowed from another prophet; the transition to his own composition brings the juxtaposition of opposing metaphors. Lit 'until the years from generation to generation' i.e. for ever. **3.** Travellers have commented on the blackened appearance of the countryside after the passage of locusts as if ravaged by fire, and also on the absolute disappearance of every green thing. **4.** For the opposite comparison of war horses to locusts cf Jer 51:27, Jb 39:20. **5.** The comparison with chariots is suggested by the noise of a locust flight heard from afar, the crackling sound by the noise of their eating. **6b.** Expression borrowed from Na 2:10, the exact meaning of which is uncertain; lit 'all faces gather in beauty' perhaps 'lose colour and freshness'. **8.** Cf Prv 30:27 for a similar observation on the orderly progress of locusts. 'Weapons' *šelaḥ*, sg. for collective pl.; a word only occurring in late writings. 'They are not halted' lit 'they do not break off (their course)'. **9.** In the E, windows consist merely of an opening with lattice work. **10.** Cosmic disturbances are the traditional accompaniment of a theophany, which is the visible intervention of Yahweh in the world; the giving of the Law on Mt Sinai is their prototype. Here Jl borrows his images and his terms from Am 8:8—9, Is 13:10, 13, Ezek 32:7. **11.** Thunder is the voice of Yahweh cf Ex 19:19. As on Sinai Yahweh spoke to Moses, so here there can be a dialogue between God and his people; contrast 4:16 where the voice of Yahweh spells destruction for the nations. 'His army' i.e. the locusts, cf v 25.

g **2:12—20 The Public Penance and God's Answer**— A divine oracle calls for sincere repentance; the prophet summons priest and people to penance and prayer. The divine judgement is averted and in a second oracle Yahweh promises the end of the locust plague and a return of abundance. **12.** 'Return', *šûb* to turn back is frequently used in OT for a turning away from evil and a turning to God. It thus implies repentance and conversion. The heart was for the Hebrews the seat of the mind, the symbol of the thoughts and decisions of a man. **13.** 'Rend your hearts', true sorrow must accompany the outward observance, cf the parallel idea in the expression 'circumcision of the heart' Dt 10:16, Jer 4:4. 'For he is gracious .....' expression borrowed from Ex 34:6. 'Steadfast love', *ḥesed*, the relation of faithful preference which binds the parties of a covenant. **14a.** 'Who knows . . .' same expression as Jon 3:9. 'A blessing', agricultural prosperity as a blessing from God is frequent in Dt, cf 7:13, 16:20 etc. Here God's own gift serves to re-establish the sacrifices designed to ensure his good will. **15.** Jl takes up again and expands the call to penance of the second section. **16.** All conditions of men are to be called to the assembly, even bride and bridegroom who might consider themselves excused. 'Congregation', *qāhāl*, trs. by LXX *ekklēsia*; esp. used in post-Exilic literature to designate the cultic assembly of Israel. **17.** 'The vestibule', in the Salomonic temple the room at the entrance of the covered part of the temple: the altar was in the open air in the court outside, cf 1 (3) Kgs 6:3, 8:64. The priests would address their prayers towards the sanctuary i.e. Westwards, in contrast to the idolaters of Ezek 8:16 who stood in the same place but faced

E. The prayer of the priests is a collective lamentation, cf **552g** Ps 79 (78). 'A byword among nations'; LXX, Vg translate 'that the nations should rule over them', which is possible grammatically but less likely since foreign domination is not in question. **18.** 'Jealous' of his good name among the heathen nations, cf Ezek 36:5. **19—20.** **h** Yahweh's second oracle promises the end of the locust plague and the return of prosperity. It assumes that the first oracle (vv 12—13) has been obeyed and that penance has taken place. 'The Northerner', the only example of this adjective from *ṣāpôn*, N. The enemy from the N who executes Yahweh's judgements had become a classic theme of prophetic literature; cf Jer 1:13, Ezek 26:7. The epithet could therefore be applied to the locusts by analogy, though a NE wind could historically have brought locusts from the Syrian Desert. It would then have driven them into the desert of S Judah (*a parched and desolate land*) and finally into the Dead Sea (*the eastern sea*) and the Mediterranean (*the western sea*). 'Rear' *sôp* an Aram. word, occurring only in late Heb. (Chr; Eccl). 'He has made great his doing', used of man and, by analogy, of the locusts, in a pejorative sense, implying overweening action; used of God in v 21 in a good sense.

21—27 Agricultural Abundance—The description of **i** the restored fertility of the country answers symmetrically the description of desolation in 1:2—12. It begins as a hymn of thanksgiving spoken by the prophet and ends as the word of Yahweh. **22.** Pasture returns, cf 1:18, 19; the fruit trees flourish, cf 1:12. **23.** The end of the drought is the cause of this renewed abundance. 'The early rain for your vindication,' *hammôreh lisedāqāh*. *Môreh* is a rare word, synonym of *yôreh*, which is the reading of some MSS in 23*c*. Its obvious meaning here is the early rain of autumn, which falls in Palestine between Oct.—Nov. and marks the beginning of the wet season. In 23*c* the word occurs again between two others which undoubtedly refer to rain. *Sedaqah*, usually translated 'righteousness', implies the right ordering of the relations between God and man, i.e. bountiful generosity on God's part according to the disposition of his covenant, and on man's side a faithful observance of the terms of the covenant resulting in his prosperity. Cf Dt 11:13—17 for the connection between the rains and the covenant. So rich a notion can only be partially translated, but one can suggest as the primary meaning: 'for he has given for you the early rain for prosperity'. On the other hand *môreh* can also be read as a participle meaning 'teacher'. So the Targum, Symmachus, Vg have translated 'the teacher of justice', a Messianic interpretation from which the Qumran sect took the title of its chief figure. One cannot exclude a play on words and a possible secondary allusion here, especially in view of Semitic ideology which links the life-giving rain to a royal, messianic figure, cf 2 Sm 23:4 and esp. Is 30:20, 23 where both *môreh* and the promise of rain are found together. 'Abundant rain', esp. of the heavy winter rains, cf Song 2:11. 'The latter rain', the spring rain at the close of the wet season, between March and April. **24.** In contrast to 1:10. **25.** In contrast to 1:4. The plural 'years' may imply that there have been several locust invasions. **27.** The climax of the first part of Jl. It re-affirms the special relation of Israel to Yahweh and a presence of God in his people.

2:28—3:21. Eschatological Vision of a New Order **553a** **Inaugurated by a Second Day.** **2:28—29 (MT 3:1—2) The Outpouring of the Spirit**—**28.** 'Afterward' lit 'thus at the end'; for this expression cf 'at the end of days' used to introduce the

553a final perspective of history e.g. Is 2:2. Spirit; the spirit of God in the OT is the power which creates and gives life, in contrast to flesh which is inherently feeble. God's spirit can become in man the principle of extraordinary and supernatural acts, esp. prophetic power cf I Sm 10:6. The abundant outpouring of the spirit is a feature of Messianic times, cf Is 32:15; 44:3; 59:21, Ezek 36:27; 39:29. Jl foresees the fulfilment of Moses' wish, 'Would that all Yahweh's people were prophets', Nm 11:29. 'All flesh' can mean all mankind, but here Israel is meant and Jl emphasizes that all ages and conditions are included so as to constitute a sacred community. Dreams and vision marked out a prophet cf Nm 12:6.

b **30—32 (MT 3:3—5) The Day of Yahweh and Sion as Refuge**—A description of the Day with apocalyptic symbols which imply that it will be a second Exodus for Israel. **30.** 'Portents', the word used to describe the signs and wonders wrought by God during the Exodus, cf Ps 78 (77):43; 105 (104):5, 7; 135 (134):9. **31.** Darkness, fire, columns of smoke are portents which accompanied the Exodus; blood, as in the First Plague, Ex 7:19, but here on a cosmic scale. **32.** Salvation is for Israel, which is in a special relation to Yahweh by knowing his name; but the expression is general, 'all who call', and is so used by St Paul, Rom 10:13. 'On Mt Sion there shall be those who escape', explicit quotation of Obad 17.

c **3:1—8 (MT 4:1—8) The Case against the Nations**—An oracle of Yahweh who is seen as accusing the nations as if in a trial. **1.** 'When I restore the fortunes of' can also be translated 'when I bring back the captive of'. **2.** 'The Valley of *Yehôšāpāt*', 'Yahweh has judged'; The name here and in v 12 is chosen for its symbolism and is followed by the same verb, to judge. In v 14 it is 'the Valley of Decision'. Since the 4th cent. A.D. the Valley of Jehoshaphat has been identified with part of the Kidron Valley, E of Jerusalem. The belief that this will be the scene of the Last Judgement is found in popular Jewish and Moslem as well as Christian eschatology. Jl however says nothing of a universal judgement but speaks only of the judgement on the heathen enemies of Israel. **3.** 'For wine' i.e. cheaply, for a passing sensual gratification. **4.** Ironical question, since the treatment of Israel has been unprovoked. **6.** For the slave-traffic of the Phoenicians cf Ezek 27:13, I Mc 3:41, 2 Mc 8:11. The Greeks, lit 'the sons of the *Yewānîm*', (Iawan = Ionia). Syrian slaves, among whom Jews would be reckoned, were much sought after in Greece. **8.** The Sabeans, a people of SW Arabia with whom the Jews had trade relations, cf Jer 6:20.

d **9—11 The Army of the Nations**—The Prophet speaks; the heathen are invited to arm and come up for a great contest with Yahweh. **9.** 'Let them come up' against Israel as the army of locusts in 1:6. **10.** A conscious reversal of Mi 4:3, Is 2:4 with their perspectives of infinite peace. **11.** 'Hasten' *'ûšû*, hapax, meaning uncertain. 'There', i.e. at Jerusalem. 'Thy warriors', *gibbôr*, mighty one; used of angels in Ps 103 (102):20, (cf Ps 78 (77):25).

e **12—14a The Judgement on the Nations**—Oracle of

Yahweh putting into effect the punishment of the **553c** nations. **12.** Yahweh now sits as judge and pronounces his judgement. **13.** Spoken by God to his warriors, cf Is 63:2—3 for the same image of the destruction of foes. For the later association of angels and the harvest image of judgement cf Mt 13:41, Apoc 14:17—20. **14a.** Valley of Decision, or 'of Threshing'; another symbolic name for the place of judgement.

14b—17 The Day of Yahweh and Sion as Refuge— **f** The prophet speaks and returns to the theme of the Day and the special rôle of Sion, cf vv 3—5. **14b.** The Day is near, cf 1:15; 2:1. **15.** The same imagery as 2:10, but whereas the first day was a judgement on Israel here it is to be destruction for the nations. **16—17.** Are made up of elements borrowed from elsewhere, **16a** = Am 1:2. **16b.** Cf 2:10. **16c.** Refuge, stronghold, frequently used of God in the Pss, cf 62 (61):2. **17a,b** = 2:27, cf Is 8:18. **17c.** Cf Is 52:1. The voice of Yahweh, which is likened to the thunder or to the lion's roar, is unintelligible to the nations, but gives an oracle which expresses his special relation to Sion. The city will no longer be profaned by strangers, who have no share in the life and faith of Israel but have been the instrument of God's judgement on his people cf Ezek 11:9.

18—21 The Glorification of Israel—The last section **g** of Jl's prophecy affirms, with themes borrowed from previous prophetic tradition, that a time of perfect harmony between God and his people will come. **18.** 'In that day', imprecise cf Am 9:13, in the ideal period which will follow the judgement on the nations. For the poetic description of overflowing abundance as a token of God's favour, cf Am 9:13. The fountain issuing from the Temple, prob. suggested by the Spring of Gihon, is a symbol of the divine blessing which comes from Sion, cf Ezek 47:1—22, where the symbolic waters flow Eastward. 'The Valley of Shittim', *naḥal haššiṭṭîm*, The Wady of the Acacias. *Naḥal* is a rocky water-course, dry except in the rainy season; it could hardly be the meadow of the Acacias in the plains of Moab (Nm 33:39). Many identify it with the Wady es-Sant, which corresponds in name and flows Westward from Bethlehem; this would explain Zech 14:8 as combining two traditions when he makes the waters flow partly into the Dead Sea and partly into the Mediterranean. **19.** In contrast the land of Israel's foes, of which Egypt and Edom are typical examples, will become a desolate waste. 'In their land', if this means Egypt and Edom it would refer to a massacre of Jewish refugees or settlers, not otherwise known from the Bible. **20.** Jerusalem has a permanent place in God's plan, in contrast to powerful states whose decay is part of the process of history, cf for the expression Is 13:20, also the oracles against the nations Jer 46—51. **21.** 'I will avenge their blood and I will not clear (the guilty)'. So LXX; but MT gives good sense: 'I will hold innocent their blood (which) I have not held innocent' i.e. Yahweh will no longer permit the oppression of his people which he suffered in the past. The book ends with the affirmation of God's abiding presence to his people which is the principle of its glorification and of its transcendance.

AMOS

BY D. RYAN

554a Bibliography—*Commentaries*: M. Delcor, PCSB, 1961; S. R. Driver, CBSC; W. R. Harper, ICC, 1905; J. Knabenbauer, CSS, 1886; E. Osty, BJ, 1960½; G. Rinaldi, SacB, 1963; J. Touzard, Paris, 1909; A. van Hoonacker, EtB, 1908; H. W. Wolff, BKAT, Einleitung, 1:1–2:16; 1967. *Other Literature*: J. L. Crenshaw. 'The Influence of the Wise on Amos' ZATW 79 (1967) 42–51; V. Maag, *Text, Wortschatz und Begriffswelt des Buches Amos*; Leiden 1951; A. Neher, *Amos, contribution à l'étude du prophétisme*, 1950; H. H. Rowley, 'Was Amos a Nabi?' in *Eissfeldt-Festschrift*, Halle, 1947; 191–8; H. W. Wolff, *Amos' geistige Heimat*, Neukirchen 1964.

b Date of the Prophet's Activity—The title (1:1) informs us that Amos delivered his oracles sometime during the period when Jeroboam II (783–743 B.C.) of Israel was contemporaneous with Uzziah of Judah (781–740 B.C.), which means, in effect, from c. 780–740 B.C. On the historical background, see § 64j. Although the earthquake (1:1) was a memorable one (Zech 14:5), it does not help, since the exact date is not known. It is a chronological detail which would have helped the very earliest readers of Amos. Internal evidence points to the latter part of Jeroboam's reign. It was a period of great wealth, luxury and confident security (4:1–3; 6:1–7 etc), when Jeroboam's battles had already been fought and won (cf 6:13). Some statements of the prophet (5:27; 6:14) suggest an awareness of the Assyrian menace which became a reality only with the accession of Tiglath Pileser III (745–727 B.C.).

c The Life of Amos—(a) **Private Life**. Amos was not a man of noble rank, nor was he extremely poor. In 1:1, he is called a *nôqēd*, a word which is applied to Mesha, king of Moab, in 2 (4) Kgs 3:4 (where RSV has 'sheep breeder'). In Arabic, the cognate word describes one who raises a special breed of sheep valued for their excellent wool. In 7:14, Amos declares that he is a *bôqēr* (cattle-tender). In view of the reference to flocks in 7:15, many read *nôqēd* in 7:14, but Amos may have tended both flocks and cattle. His shepherd life was centred on Tekoa (1:1), the modern *Tequ'a*, lying on a Judean hill six miles S of Bethlehem. From 7:14 it further appears that the future prophet was employed in dressing sycamore trees (a kind of wild fig). The dressing probably consisted in nipping (LXX *knizōn* Vg *vellicans*) the fruit to release an injurious insect which impeded ripening. Since these trees grew, not in Tekoa which was about 3,000 feet above sea level, but on the lower slopes of the Judean hills to E and W, Amos must have moved widely over a landscape which ranged from semi-desert to fertile field. His writing is rich in imagery drawn from experience in his daily tasks (cf 2:13; 3:4, 5, 12; 5:19, 24; 6:13; 8:1). Wolff has recently drawn attention to the links between the writings of the prophet and the simple wisdom of the family or tribe. This wisdom is one of the most important sources for the prophet's thinking and it is there that

we should look for an understanding of his message and **554c** not to the more sophisticated circles of the cult prophets, among whom Amos is sometimes given a place by commentators.

(b) **Public Life**—Amos himself tells us that he was **d** 'following the flock' when Yahweh called him: 'Go, prophesy to my people Israel' (7:15). In obedience to the divine call (3:8), Amos, though a Judean, set out for the N Kingdom to prophesy against the social and religious vices of the nation. It seems that the royal sanctuary at Bethel was most frequently favoured with his words so much so that professional jealousy provoked the local priest, Amaziah, into opposition (7:10ff). The latter denounced Amos to Jeroboam who apparently took no notice. Amaziah then addressed Amos contemptuously as a visionary, ordered him to leave at once for his native Judah and earn his living there. Amos made it clear that he was no professional prophet; he did not pretend to trained skill in prophesying, nor derive his commission from any society of men. Nor did he depend on prophecy for a living; he had another source of livelihood. He immediately demonstrated his independence by daringly predicting enemy invasion, barbarous treatment of Amaziah's own wife by invading soldiers, the massacre of his children, the confiscation of his land, and his death outside the borders of Palestine. No one would ever pay such a prophet for such a message, but he spoke the word of God. Nothing certain is known of the duration of Amos' mission; he may well have resumed his former profession after a relatively short period of activity.

The Social and Religious Conditions censured by 555a Amos—(a) **Social Conditions**. There was a marked contrast between the two main classes, the rich who were few and the poor who were many. The former lived in houses of hewn stone panelled with wood and ivory inlay; they partook of sumptuous banquets and looked with disdain on those at the other end of the social scale. The poor were in dire distress and, as inequality in the distribution of wealth increased, their lot became more wretched still. They were oppressed and exploited by the rich. Over a period of years the agricultural population had suffered losses not only from the Syrian armies which overran the land (2 (4) Kgs 12; 13:24–25), but also from the drought, the blasting and the blight which affected the crops (cf 4:7–9). Some were therefore compelled to borrow money at a high rate of interest and to mortgage their holdings of land. Failure to meet the money-lender's demands resulted in foreclosure. Although the laws of Israel (Lv 25:25ff) decreed that the former owner could at anytime redeem the land for money and that at the year of jubilee it was to be returned free, the administration of those laws in the days of Amos was in the hands of a corrupt executive which readily accepted bribes from the wealthy. When the borrower had no land, he was compelled to mortgage his person, and failure to pay resulted in slavery. The wealth derived from

555a slave labour, from excessive interest on loans, from exorbitant rents and from commercial deceit went to provide further luxuries for the rich and their well-pampered women folk. It is against this social structure that Amos reacted so violently (cf 3:13—15; 4:1—3; 5:7, 10—15, 24; 6:1—7; 8:4—8).

b (b) **Religious Conditions**—The people of the N Kingdom worshipped at the shrines of Bethel (3:14; 4:4; 5:5; 7:10), Gilgal (4:4; 5:5), Dan (8:14), and Beersheba (5:5; 8:14). In spite of the origin of the shrines at Bethel and Dan (cf 1(3) Kgs 12:26ff), Amos does not condemn them in the terms of the editor of Kings (1 (3) Kgs 12:30; 13:33f etc), who was concerned about Jerusalem's position as the central sanctuary (cf Dt 12:10ff). Like Elijah before him, Amos accepted that the use of these sanctuaries was not necessarily incompatible with sincere worship of Yahweh. He did, however, inveigh against a splendid ritual with its multiplicity of sacrifices, elaborate processions to the accompaniment of music, and frequent pilgrimages of little spiritual worth. The noisy and convivial cult generated a false sense of religious well-being which made the worshippers oblivious to their obligations in justice, and unconscious of the hypocrisy of their acts of worship.

Shortly after the time of Amos, Hosea was pre-occupied with the worst corruptions of the cult of Baal which had infected the worship of Yahweh (cf Hos 2; 4); cult prostitution was common practice at the shrines of Israel (Hos 4:10ff). Only in Amos 2:7 is there reference to similar abuses. 4:5 and 8:14 suggest that more than one divinity was worshipped at the Israelite shrines, unless one thinks of forbidden forms of the worship of Yahweh. Against all these errors, Amos opposed the sincere worship of Yahweh, the God of Israel; the touch-stone of sincerity was the practice of justice and care for the needs of one's fellow men.

c **Doctrine**—The teaching of Amos is particularly important because he is the first of the writing prophets. (a) **Yahweh the Creator and Controller of the Universe**—The doxologies (4:13; 5:8f; 9:5f), which may well be later than Amos, present Yahweh as the God who formed the mountains and created the winds, who made constellations, and regulates the movements of the seas and the succession of day and night. In a passage which can with greater certainty be attributed to Amos, Yahweh's control is manifest in his use of nature's powers to chastise his people (4:7—11).

d (b) **Yahweh is God of all Nations**—The universalism of Amos is startling at a time when Israel was self-consciously nationalistic (6:1, 13). Yahweh determines the destinies of nations, whether Philistines, Syrians or Ethiopians (9:7). The nation called to punish Israel will only be an instrument in his hand (6:14). Yahweh will judge all nations and arraign them as their God; he will condemn them for their acts of inhumanity which are breaches of the laws of universal morality (1:3—2:3). In practice, therefore, Yahweh is the only God.

e (c) **Yahweh the God of Israel**—The unique relationship between Yahweh and Israel is clearly stated: 'You only have I known of all the families of the earth' (3:2 and note). Although Amos never uses the word covenant (except in another context, 1:9), nor refers to the covenant virtues of love (ḥeseḏ) and fidelity ('emeṯ), the covenant relationship is implied in the use of the verb 'know' and the form of address 'my people' (7:8, 15; 8:2; cf Lv 26: 12). He shows familiarity with covenant laws (2:8, 11), and attributes the choice of Israel to the time of Moses (2:10; 3:1—2). Yahweh's choice of Israel was free and reversible; it carried with it no immunity from judgement.

In fact, his judgement of Israel will be more rigorous **555** because, having received more, more is expected of them. (d) **Yahweh's Justice**—While Hosea regarded Israel's **f** sin especially as an outrage on divine love, Amos thought of it as a provocation of divine justice. Yahweh being himself pre-eminently just will not tolerate injustice in the world over which he rules. He judges all nations, including Israel, impartially; he asks that Israel should do likewise, giving to each his due. Her injustices, however, cry to heaven for vengeance, and contrast with her elaborate liturgy, a situation which evokes the wish of Yahweh: 'Let justice roll down like waters' (5:24). Because Israel does not heed his wish, **the day of Yahweh** will be for her, not a day of light and success, but a day of darkness and destruction (5:20).

Yahweh is not a vindictive God, consumed by a passion for vengeance (5:4) is the invitation of one who awaits with loving heart the return of his erring children, and the prayers of the prophet easily move his mercy to put a restraining hand on his punishing justice (7:3, 6).

The Composition of the Book—From a literary point **g** of view, the material in the book might be classified as follows: (a) **oracles** against the nations including Israel and Judah (1:3—2:16); (b) groups of **prophetic sayings** condemning current abuses and pronouncing the judgement which will inevitably follow unless repentance and reform intervene (3:9—4:12; 5:1—6 (1—3 is cast in the form of a lament); 5:7—6:14 (with the exception of 5:8—9); 8:4—14; 9:7—10); (c) **biographical material** (7:10—17); (d) **autobiography** in the form of visions (7:1—9; 8:1—3; 9:1—4). 3:3—8 might also be classified under this heading in so far as it describes Amos' experience of the prophetic call and justifies his prophetic activity; (e) **doxologies** (4:13; 5:8—9; 9:5—6); (f) **isolated sayings**: 1:2 and 3:1—2. 1:2 comes at the beginning of the book and may have been chosen to set the tone of the whole book, or in another view, of the oracles against the nations; (g) an **editorial inscription** (1:1); (h) an **epilogue** containing an oracle which speaks of the **messianic prospects** for Israel and the house of David.

While most of this material is taken to be authentic, justifiable doubts have been cast on the authenticity of the oracles against Edom (1:11—12) and Judah (2:4—5), the doxologies (4:13; 5:8—9; 9:5—6) and the epilogue (9:11—15).

The book offers little evidence for discovering the process of selection and compilation by which this material was brought together. There is no clear line of development from beginning to end and the work of the compiler(s) has disturbed the patterns of composition in several places (e.g. 7:10—17 interrupts the series of visions; 5:8—9 disturbs the sequence of vv 7 and 10). The nature and full extent of the records containing the prophet's teaching, as well as of the biographical and autobiographical material from which the book was compiled, must remain matters for speculation.

1:1 Title—'words . . . saw'. This phrase does not **556a** imply that the prophet beheld the words written and copied them down, but refers to the complementary elements of vision (cf 7:1—3, 4—6, 7—9; 8:1—3; 9:1—4) and teaching (often described 'the *word* that the Lord has spoken', cf 3:1; or simply 'this word', cf 4:1; 5:1) in the prophet's message (cf also Is 1:1; Hos 1:1; Mic 1:1 etc). See 554b for further comment on this v.

2 The Tone of the Prophet's Message—2a is **b** variously interpreted. The verbs ('roars . . . utters his voice') may both refer either to awe-inspiring peals of

56b thunder (cf Jb 37:2—4), or to a marauding lion as he pounces on his prey (cf 3:4, 8 and Hos 13:7f). Some take the first verb to be the roaring of a lion, and the second, the sound of thunder (cf Ps 18 (17):13). Yahweh comes in judgement from Sion, his earthly abode (cf Pss 46 (45); 84 (83); 87 (86) etc). The severity of his judgement is implied in the failure of the pastures ('*burned up*' better than 'mourns') and the withering of vegetation even in the fertile garden land of Carmel (cf 9:4; Song 7:6). Drought will bring famine, disease and death to man and beast (cf 4:7).

c **3—2:5 The Crimes of the Nations and the Inevitable Punishment**—For oracles against the nations, cf also Is 13—23; Jer 46—51; Ez 25—32. All nations must come before the bar of Yahweh's justice; he is not merely the God of Israel. Note the fixed pattern of each oracle. 'Three . . . four': expresses an uncertain number which, in any event, is excessive. In each case, a specific transgression is mentioned as characteristic. 'Fire': an unavoidable consequence of war (e.g. Jos 8:19). Damascus (v 5) and Ammon (v 15) are also punished by exile. The oracle against Judah may well be a later insertion. The series of oracles moves towards the climax of Israel's judgement: she has no reason to be complacent as she witnesses the plight of the nations.

d **3—5 Judgement on Damascus—3.** Damascus was capital of Aram (Syria) which was often in conflict with Israel (cf § 64e. 'Threshing sledges of iron' were made of heavy planks which were studded underneath with basalt or iron teeth. They were pulled—usually by oxen—over the heaped up corn on the threshing floor; the corn was thereby shelled and the straw cut to pieces. In view of vv 6, 9, 11 and 13, some commentators understand the charge in the literal sense; it is much more likely to be a metaphor describing the cruel treatment meted out to the inhabitants of Gilead. **4f.** In punishment Yahweh will send the flame of war (cf Jg 9:20) into the palaces of Hazael and Benhadad III, the two recent kings who caused such suffering to Israel (cf 2 (4) Kgs 8:7—15, 28—29; 10:32—33; 13:3ff, 24). **5.** 'bar', i.e. of the city gates, a vital element in city fortifications (cf 1 (3) Kgs 4:13 etc). 'Valley of Aven' (MT: *biqʿaṯ ʾawen*; LXX: On): identified variously with Baalbek in the plain between Lebanon and Antilebanon, or with the plain of Damascus. 'Beth-eden', either an unknown city near Damascus, or the Aramaean kingdom of Bît-Adini on the Euphrates. BJ suggests that both names in the text may be symbolic names for Damascus. 'Kir', uncertain, but most likely remote from Damascus cf Am 9:7. Is 22:6 links Kir with Elam to the E of the Tigris (cf also 2 (4) Kgs 16:9).

e **6—8 Judgement on Philistia**—Four of the five Philistine city-states are mentioned, Gath being omitted. The sin with which Philistia and particularly Gaza is taxed is the carrying off of a whole people to be sold as slaves to Edom. For Philistia and the slave trade cf Jl 3 (4):6—8. The city-states of Philistia will be devastated and what remains of the Philistines thereafter, will subsequently perish. Contrast the fate of Joseph (5:15) and Jacob (9:8).

f **9—10 Judgement on Tyre**—Tyre's sin of slave-trading (cf Jl 3 (4):6) is aggravated by the crime of perfidy. 'covenant of brotherhood': 1 (3) Kgs 5:12 (26); 9:13 support the view that the prophet has in mind the covenant or treaty concluded between Solomon and Hiram, king of Tyre, which established a relationship of brotherhood between the people of the two kingdoms. Otherwise one must pre-suppose Tyrian treachery towards other Phoenician cities.

11—12 Judgement on Edom—11. Edom, with here- **556g** ditary and unchecked hatred, persecuted Israel, its blood relation (i.e. 'his brother', cf Gn 25:22ff; 27:40—41; Nm 20:14—21 and the references in RSV). The conflict continued during the period of the kings (cf e.g. 2 Sm 8:13; 2 (4) Kgs 14:7) and bitter feelings were aggravated by the conduct of Edom at the fall of Jerusalem in 587 B.C. (cf 137 (136):7) **12.** Teman, variously described by commentators as a district, city or tribe of Edom (Jer 49:7, 20 etc). Bozrah, an important Edomite city, present-day el-Busaireh, 20 m. SE of the Dead Sea.

13—15 Judgement on Ammon—13. Greed for land **h** drove Ammonites to acts of the grossest brutality, which are not without parallel in ancient times, even in the history of Israel (cf 2 (4) Kgs 8:12; Hos 14:1; and 2 (4) Kgs 15:16). **14.** Rabbah, principal city of Ammon, nowadays called Amman. **15.** As in vv 5, 8; 2:3, the rulers are mentioned specifically in the account of the punishment. Their responsibility, and therefore their guilt, was greater; it was they who took the decisions which issued in such inhuman conduct.

2:1—3 Judgement on Moab—1. The Moabites **i** desecrated a royal corpse, that of the king of Edom, by cremation. Nothing further is known of this act. Among the Semites, the fate of the soul was in some way linked with the treatment of the body, and undisturbed burial was essential for its peace (cf Is 14:18ff). Moab is not accused of a crime against Israel, but against an enemy of Israel (cf § 556g). This may well be a sign of the absolute value which Amos set on certain norms of morality; Yahweh's justice for him was universally applicable. This attitude, however, was not shared by all his contemporaries or their descendants (cf 2 (4) Kgs 23:16—18). The campaign conducted by Israel, Judah and Edom against Moab (cf 2 (4) Kgs 3:4ff) would provide an historical basis for a friendly interest in Edom. **2.** 'Kerioth': possibly Kir Moab, nowadays Kerak. 'Trumpet': is often mentioned as an accompaniment of battle cf 3:6; Zeph 1:16.

4—5 Judgement on Judah—4. Judah's sin is the **j** rejection of Yahweh's law. The phrases 'the law of Yahweh', 'his statutes' and 'walk after' recall the Deuteronomic literature (cf e.g. Dt 4). This oracle against Judah may have been inserted by a later writer to point Amos' message more specifically at Judah. For Amos, the term Israel embraced the whole of the Chosen People (cf 3:1). 'lies': i.e. idols which fail them in the hour of need (cf Wis 13:10ff).

6—16 The Crimes of Israel and the Sentence—The **557a** prophet, whose mission was to Israel, works through the oracles against the neighbouring states towards a climax. The Israelites complacently deplore the sins of their neighbours and approve the threatened punishment. Having thus gained the attention and good-will of his audience (cf the speech of Stephen in Acts 7 for a similar technique), Amos unexpectedly points to their own transgressions. Their guilt is aggravated by failure to use the helps which Yahweh provided and ingratitude for his generous interest. Israel's sins are listed in greater detail than those of the nations. **6b.** 'sell the righteous for silver': the reference here is either to heartless money lenders or to corrupt judges. To recover their money the former would sell into slavery an honest man who was forced by circumstances to borrow, and could not meet his obligations when the debt fell due; they would do this even for a trifling debt ('a pair of shoes' cf 8:6). The corrupt judges when bribed, would give judgement against the man who had right on his side (this is probably the meaning of 'righteous' here). In

557a the context of law courts, legal contracts and decisions, the 'sandals' had a symbolic value, and their exchange or theft might involve the transfer of considerable properties (Ru 4:7; Ps 60 (59):8; 1 Sm 12:3 Gr.; Sir 46:

b 19). **7a.** The rich ground down the poor (Is 3:15); the lowly found their modest purposes thwarted, particularly in the law courts (cf 5:12; Is 10:3). **7b.** 'same maiden': 'same' is not in MT, although the noun has the definite article. It is not easy to identify her. Those who translate 'the same maiden' may see the sin in the abuse of a servant girl by both her master and his son. It is much more likely that the woman in question is a cult prostitute, even though the usual technical term (*qᵉdēšāh*) is not used. The consequence of the action is described in cultic terms ('my holy name is profaned'), and v 8 develops the accusation of immoral worship of a false god, or gods, or it may be even of Yahweh. In the last case, the immorality would arise from the form of worship and the general neglect of justice and charity (cf Hos 6:6). Intercourse with a cult prostitute was the symbolic enactment of the union between the fertility god and earth and was believed to effect the fertility symbolized, not so much by itself as through the patronage of the fertility god. This practice was characteristic of the worship of the fertility god, Baal, and sometimes infected the worship of Yahweh, the God who really exercised the functions attributed to Baal (on this topic cf Hos *passim* and commentary).

c **8.** Cf Ex 22:26f and Dt 24:12f for the covenant law governing garments of the poor taken in pledge. 'lay themselves down': either for sacrificial banquets, cult prostitution, or incubation rites. The use of these garments in worship could not relieve the worshippers of their obligations in justice and brotherly love. 'fined': probably unjustly. 'in the house of their God': (a) i.e. Yahweh, whose worship should, of course, take such a different form; or (b) their God, i.e. their conception of Yahweh which has nothing in common with Yahweh as he really is; or (c) their god, i.e. Baal or some such pagan god.

d **9—12 Yahweh's Care for his People—9.** The people's guilt is increased by their ingratitude for the abundant gifts of Yahweh. 'Amorite' is a general designation of the pre-Israelite population of Canaan on both sides of the Jordan (cf Jos. 24:18); it is a characteristic term of the Elohist tradition. Hyperbole is used in the description of the height and strength of the Amorites, and even in the picture of their destruction; in fact, many of them lived on in Palestine with the Israelites (cf Ex 23:29, 32). **11f.** The presence of prophets and Nazirites in Israel was a gift of Yahweh (cf Hos 12:10). They were his intermediaries who communicated his will to the people by word and example. Nazirites were ascetics whose lives were consecrated to God (cf Nm 6:1—21; Jg 13:4—5, 7; cf Jer 35). The Israelites debauched the Nazirites by forcing them—against their vow—to drink wine, and commanded the prophets to be silent when they would speak a message from Yahweh (cf 5:10; 7:16).

e **13—16 Judgement on Israel—13.** As they move to escape, the weight of God's judgement will impede them; they will be cumbersome as a laden cart. **14—16.** Those who place their confidence in speed of foot, in physical strength, in skill with the bow (cf Ps 44 (43):6), or in a fleet-footed horse (cf Ps 20 (19):7—8), instead of in Yahweh, will be left defenceless (cf 9:1). Even courage will desert the courageous when confronted by the terrors of Yahweh's judgement day.

558a **3:1—6:14 Amos' preaching to Israel**—The second section of the book contains a selection of accusations, threats, exhortations and prayers spoken for the benefit **558** of Israel.

3:1—2. An Invitation and a Threat—1. Yahweh has a right to a hearing, but he hopes for a hearing which is a willing response to the love he showed Israel when he delivered her from Egypt. 'Israel' here seems to include the S as well as the N tribes since all were delivered from Egypt. **2.** 'known': not: intellectually aware of, but: with you alone of all races have I established the intimate relationship of covenant love. Cf the use of 'to know' for marital relations, e.g. Gn 4:1; Lk 1:34, literally: 'I know not man', etc. Yahweh's love is not unconditional and in giving more to Israel than to any other people he expected more in return. 'therefore': a surprising conclusion for Israel. She expected only favours from her national God once the cult was performed as required. It was Amos' mission to remind Israel of her moral obligations; if her cult was to have meaning and an adequate response was to be made to the love of a generous God, her conduct towards others must reflect his love, justice and mercy. Coming as fulfilment of prophecy, Yahweh's punishment should direct men's minds to the prophet's message.

3—8 Origin and Authority of the Prophet's Mes- b sage—Amos' threatening message to Israel made him an unwelcome messenger. His right to prophesy was queried (cf 7:12ff). In these vv (3—8), he argues that the prophetic call is irresistible; it comes from Yahweh whose message the prophet is obliged to communicate. The sequence of the argument is aimed at forcing an unavoidable response to the final question: 'who can but prophesy'? Each example is an illustration of causality; 3—5, 6b establish—on the basis of common experience—that there is no effect without a cause, and 6a and 8, no cause without an effect. The conclusion is drawn in two directions: (i) if the prophet speaks, it is because the Lord has inspired him; (ii) if the Lord inspires his prophet, the prophet has no option but to speak. Neither the message nor the authority is his. The passage is sometimes compared to the inaugural vision in Is 6; Jer 1; Ezek 1ff. Some elements of the prophet's message are reflected in his choice of figures. **3.** 'two': an implied reference, perhaps, to Yahweh and Israel, cf Ex 25:22; 30:36 where RSV 'meet' is the same Heb. verb as 'made an appointment' here. **4.** 'lion': cf 1:2; and 3:8; Israel has become the prey of Yahweh who is about to pounce. **5.** Cf Is 8:14; Yahweh has set a trap for Israel, which she cannot now escape. **6.** 'trumpet': the air raid siren of antiquity, cf 2:2; Jl 2:1; Hos 5:8; Jer 6:1; Ezek 33:3. 'has done': the Israelites did not distinguish between what God permits and what he directly causes. Neither did they differentiate primary and secondary causes; everything that happened was in some way attributed to Yahweh; cf Is 45:7; 1 Sm 16:14. **7.** 'servants the prophets': so frequently in Jer e.g. 7:25. This v may be a gloss. **8.** The point of the piece. He is not a prophet of his own choice, but he demands a hearing for the word of Yahweh cf 7:14—15; Jer 20: 7—9.

9—15 The Doom of Samaria—9—10. Enemies of **c** Israel are called to witness in Samaria the chaos and confusion (i.e. 'tumults' cf 2 Chr 15:5, where the same Heb. word is rendered 'disturbances' in RSV) which arises when a society no longer knows 'how to do right'. No one is sure of his rights, least of all the poor. Wrong doing has become second nature (cf Is 5:20) to those who store up in their mansions (cf v 15) the wealth they have amassed by robbery and violence. **11.** Such conduct will not go unpunished. The 'adversary' is not named;

58c in the time of Amos, Assyria constituted the greatest threat, and although called to witness the disorder in Samaria, she is not explicitly invited to inflict the punishment (cf Is 5:26ff). The strongest physical defences are easily overthrown where confusion reigns among the defenders. 'Tumults' in v 9 is the same Heb. word as RSV 'confusion' in Dt 7:23 and 'panic' in 1 Sm 5:9. Internal strife absorbs the resources which should
d be devoted to defence. **12.** A comparison between the bits of the sheep rescued by the shepherd from the lion and the scraps of their expensive furniture saved by the voluptuous Israelites from the catastrophe which will overtake them. Although responsible for every sheep, if the shepherd could produce any fragment of the carcase with the mark of the lion's teeth, he was absolved from restitution (cf Ex 22:13). Others translate: *So shall be rescued the people of Israel who are settled in Samaria on the corner of a couch and a cushioned bed*: i.e. only a few of those who live in luxury (cf 6:4ff) will be rescued. This is scarcely the doctrine of the 'remnant' (cf Is 10: 20ff; 7:3) since the tone of the oracle is pessimistic (but cf 5:15; 9:8). **13—14.** The invitation may be addressed to Egypt and Assyria (cf v 9). 'house of Jacob': although in 9:8—9 it refers to the twelve tribes, here it seems to be limited to the N tribes. 'God of hosts', armies, battles; cf Is 6:3. 'Bethel': To prevent the people of the newly created N Kingdom from going up to worship in Jerusalem, Jeroboam I gave new life to the patriarchal (Gn 12:8; 35:7) shrine of Bethel. He set up there a golden calf (1 (3) Kgs 12:26ff, and commentary) either as a symbol of, or better, as a throne of Yahweh. Although Amos has no hesitation in passing judgement on the insincerity of Israel's cult (cf 4:4—5; 5:21ff; 8:4—6), he nowhere attacks it as idolatrous (but see note on 8: 13—14; cf de Vaux, AI 333ff). The 'horns' of the altar were horn-shaped projections from the four corners (Ex 27:2). The blood of victims was rubbed on them (Ex 29: 12; Lv 4:7 etc), and asylum was claimed by grasping them (1 (3) Kgs 1:50; 2:28). Their destruction meant an end to the sacred power of the altar and symbolized the failure of every escape route and refuge from the wrath of God. **15.** The finds in the excavations at Samaria, where these houses were probably located, suggest that they were adorned by panelling and furniture with ivory inlay (cf 1 (3) Kgs 22:29; Ps 45 (44):8).

e 4:1—3 Amos censures the Women of Samaria—1. He likens these pampered and wanton upper class women to the 'cows of Bashan'. Bashan, a district beyond the Jordan, was noted for its well nourished flocks and herds (Dt 32:14; Ps 22 (21):12; Ezek 39:18). Those lazy women fatten on the poor; they urge their husbands to provide them with luxuries by fair means or foul. They drink to excess (cf Is 5:11—15; particularly in Samaria Is 28:1ff, 7—8). **2.** 'by his holiness': Yahweh must swear by himself, since there was none more holy whose name he could invoke. 'hooks': evokes the picture either of fish being hauled from their native habitat, or of prisoners being dragged along by hooks in their noses—an Assyrian practice (Is 27:29). **3.** 'breaches': i.e. in the city walls. 'Harmon': unknown. BJ and others change the text to read: 'towards Hermon', which lay to the N of Bashan on the way to Assyria. For Isaiah's strictures on the women of Jerusalem cf Is 3:16—4:1; 32:11.

f 4—13 Formalism in Worship—4—5. In sarcastic tones, the prophet marks the contrast between their zeal for accurate and regular observance of the laws of cult and their neglect of justice and brotherly love. They believed that Yahweh would overlook their evil ways provided they did not fail in ritual. The transgression lies in the

insincerity of the worship, not in the making of incorrect **558f** offerings. 'Bethel': cf note on 3:14. 'Gilgal': cf note on Hos 4:15. The offerings mentioned were all prescribed by the law: morning sacrifices, Nm 28:23; tithes are required every three years (a rendering which could stand in this v) in Dt 26:12. 'three days' here may be part of Amos' sarcasm about the frequency of their ritual acts. BJ translates 'on the third day'. **5.** 'thanksgiving', Lv 7:12ff, 'freewill offerings', Lv 7:16. 'leavened': the law forbidding the use of leaven (Lv 2:11; Ex 23: 18) may not have been in existence in the time of Amos; Lv 7:13; 23:17 require the use of leaven. In any event, Amos was not concerned with the violation of a ritual prescription, but with the formalistic hypocrisy of the act. 'proclaim ... publish': Dt 12:18 required that members of the offerer's household and the local Levites should be invited to partake of the sacrificial banquet which followed on the free will offering. The prophet seems to hint at unnecessary ostentation and greater interest in the festivities which followed the sacrifice than in the spiritual requirements for sincerity in offering it. What had been instituted for the service of God became an instrument of selfish pleasure.

6—13 Punishment but no Repentance—Commenta- **g** tors count seven scourges in the five strophes marked off by the refrain in vv 6, 8, 9, 10, 11; 6, famine; 7, drought; 9, blight/mildew, and locusts; 10, war and plague; 11, earthquake. They refer to past occasions when by chastisement Yahweh tried to teach repentance. The pathetic repetition of the refrain reflects the disappointment of a loving God whose justice has so far been tempered by his love. Every time he intervened, he suffered a rebuff. Israel's failure to respond by repentance (cf Mk 1:15) drives Yahweh to confront them with the full power of his divinity as Creator and Lord (cf 12c, 13). **6.** 'cleanness of teeth': from lack of food. Famine was relatively frequent in Palestine (cf Gn 12:10; 41: 54; 1 Sm 21:1; and nearer to the time of Amos 1 (3) Kgs 17:12; 2 (4) Kgs 4:38; 8:1). **7ab.** The winter **h** rains sometimes fell as late as February. If they failed and were not supplemented by later spring rain, then the harvest in May was in jeopardy. **7bc—8.** The drought was not universal. It is not necessary to imagine fields and cities so close to one another as to require miraculous distribution of the rainfall. Cities with water in their cisterns could not spare enough for those who, weakened by thirst, *staggered* (better than 'wandered') from neighbouring towns to find water. For similar cases of drought, cf Jer 14:1—6; Jl 1:19—20. **9.** 'blight': literally, the 'scorching' produced by the sirocco. Locusts devour everything in their path (cf 7:1; Jl 1:4). **10.** 'after the manner of Egypt': a particularly virulent form of pestilence which could not easily be cured (cf Dt 28:27). The scourge of war swept away the young men and the horses on which Israel relied for security. The air was filled with the stench of unburied corpses. **11.** The destruction of Sodom and Gomorrah had become proverbial and is introduced to describe a tremendous upheaval (not necessarily an earthquake), from which Israel was rescued at the last moment, when it seemed as if she must be totally destroyed. The brand snatched from the fire may symbolize an Israel deformed and spent (cf Zech 3:2ff).

12f. As is usual in such oracles, the word 'therefore' **i** marks the transition from reproof to punishment. Since Israel has failed to learn and to mend her ways, a worse fate awaits her. The nature of this disaster is not stated, and Israel anxiously awaits a meeting with her offended God, who is both omnipotent and omniscient. **13.** This

558i is the first of three doxologies given in Amos; the other two are found in 5:8f and 9:5f. In each case, the doxology follows on a threat of punishment and adds force to the threat by exalting the power of him who comes in judgement. Few scholars would attribute these doxologies to Amos, since they differ from the rest of the book in style and content. These are, however, determined to some extent by the literary form which is chosen, viz a hymn. Literary affinities belong to the later literature of Second Isaiah, Job 38, and some Psalms. Whatever is held about their authorship, their meaning in the book is clear. 'makes the morning darkness': by causing clouds to appear. LXX reads: 'morning and darkness'. The MT is best rendered: *'makes dawn of darkness'* (cf 5:8*b*).

559a **5:1–6, 8, 9 The Prophet laments the Destruction of Israel—1.** The prophet calls on the people to hear his lament for Israel; he mourns for her as if she had already fallen. For the use of this literary form in the prophets cf Jer 9:17–22; Ezek 19; 27. **2.** 'no more to rise': he foresees the end of the N Kingdom 'virgin Israel': cf also Jer 18:13; 31:4, 21. A similar phrase, 'virgin daughter of Sion, Babylon', etc, is found in contexts which suggest that the emphasis is on the tenderness and delicacy of the virgin on whom violent punishment falls all the more harshly (e.g. Is 47:1; Jer 14:17) or whose conduct is all the more surprising (e.g. Is 27:22; Jer 18:13). The pathos of Israel's plight is deepened in that she dies before marriage (cf Jg 11:38). Is there a suggestion here that she dies without experiencing the joys of intimacy with Yahweh (cf Hos *passim*)? **3.** Ninety per cent of Israel's forces will be destroyed. The survival of a tenth suggests that, although Israel as a nation may finish, the race may yet survive. **4–5.** 'seek me and live': the moral implications of 'seek' are clearly stated in Hos 10:12; they must enquire what is the will of Yahweh and find life in conformity to it (cf Mt 6:33). There is no **b** other way to escape disaster. For 'Bethel' and 'Gilgal', cf 3:14; 4:4. 'Beersheba': another patriarchal shrine (cf Gn 21:33; 26:23–33). No comment is made on the fate of Beersheba, scarcely a sufficient reason for believing that the text is not authentic (cf 8:14). In 4: 4–5, the prophet condemned the formalism of Israel's worship. Vv 4–5 here, when taken in conjunction with 8:14, give grounds for suspecting idolatrous elements in the cult of those places. Bethel is the name of a god in Jer 48:13. **6.** The prophet repeats his appeal of v 4. 'house of Joseph': the N Kingdom. LXX reads: 'for the house of Israel' instead of: 'for Bethel'. **8–9.** This doxological insertion breaks the connexion between 7 and 10. The doxology proper may be limited to 8 (cf the formula at the end of 4:13 and v 8 here), to which 9 was later added. 'Pleiades and Orion': two particularly brilliant constellations also mentioned together in Jb 9:9; 38:31f.

c **7, 10–17 The Brief Prosperity of Injustice; Inevitable Punishment**—This section is composed of snippets of Amos' teaching in which he condemns the thwarting of justice in the law courts (7, 10), forecasts the failure of ill-gotten gains (11–13), appeals for a reversal of moral standards (14–15), and, when his appeal is ignored, proclaims inevitable disaster (16–17). **7.** RSV takes this v in the 2nd pers. pl. In the MT, it is 3rd pl., and many commentators insert *hôy* (Woe to . . . as in 5:18; 6:1) at the beginning of the v, giving the meaning: 'Woe to those who turn' etc. 10 follows easily on 7 in this interpretation (= BJ). 'wormwood': a bitter herb, a symbol of bitterness among men (cf Dt 29:18 and Am 6:12). The bitterness of their justice con-

trasts with the sweetness of the law of Yahweh (cf Ps **559** 19 (18):10; Mt 11:28). **10.** 'gate': the open space at the city gate was the setting for law courts and the transaction of public business (cf Prv 31:23; Dt 21:19; Am 5:12, 15). The 'poor' were probably tenants of greedy landlords who forced an extortionate share of the produce from the helpless tenants, and bribed the judges to back them in the law courts. Their enjoyment of the profits will be short-lived. 'not drink': cf Zeph 1:13; Dt 28:30. **13.** This attitude is scarcely in keeping with the tone of Amos' preaching, and many treat the v as a later insertion by a writer of the wisdom tradition. It is held to be authentic by others who regard it as a statement of a melancholy fact. **14–15.** Accepted moral standards had **d** been reversed by the people of Israel (cf Is 5:20; 1:16ff); Amos appeals for conversion. 'Yahweh . . . with you': a sure guarantee of success and survival (cf Jos. 1:17; Nm 14:43; 23:21 etc). 'remnant': what will be left after judgement. cf Is 4:3; 10:20 etc. **16–17.** 'therefore': this particle usually introduces the punishment which follows on condemnation (cf 3:11; 4:12 etc). The previous vv here contain an exhortation and originally may not have preceded v 16. It is likely that between 15 and 16, the prophet was made aware of the rejection of his appeal. 'skilled': cf Jer 9:17; 2 Chr 35:25. 'vineyards': normally the setting for joy (cf Is 16:10). 'I will pass through': cf Ex 12:12. The nations chosen to chastise Israel are only the instruments of Yahweh (cf Is 10:12ff).

18–20 The Day of Yahweh—Ideally, the day of **e** Yahweh was for Israel the day on which Yahweh would intervene to destroy the enemies of Israel and establish his universal dominion, with Israel as the chosen instrument and chief beneficiary of his rule. This tradition seems to be well established in the time of Amos who sets out to correct the notion that, irrespective of her conduct, Israel will share in the triumph of Yahweh. cf Jl 1:15; 2:1f; Zeph 1:15 etc. Jl 4:1 predicts a favourable outcome for Israel on this day, and in post-exilic literature it became the occasion for the final triumph of the just over the wicked e.g. Mal 3:19–23; Is 26: 20–27:1. In the NT, it is the day of definitive judgement (cf 2 Cor 1:14 etc) and of the ultimate triumph of Christ over all his enemies. cf on Mt 25:31ff. **19–20.** None can escape the chastisement of Yahweh.

21–27 Hypocrisy in Worship—21–24. Amos has **f** already touched on this theme in 4:4–5; 5:4–5, and it recurs in the other prophetical books (e.g. Is 1:10–16; Hos 6:6; Mi 6:5–8 etc). Their sacrifices, festivals, sacred chant and music stand condemned; they are an insult to the covenant God whose outstanding attributes are absolute justice, unfailing fidelity, and generous and forgiving love. These virtues were conspicuously absent from the lives of those who made use of the cult; it should have involved a public declaration that they were one in mind and heart, in word and in action, with the covenant God. In fact they used it as if it were a ritual technique to satisfy the whim of a self-centred God. Once he was placated, they could go their wicked way with impunity. Blinded by selfishness they misunderstood the nature of the covenant God, and made a mockery of his ritual by the injustice of their lives (cf 24). **25–27.** The answer **g** expected to 25 is: 'No', but it is a 'No' which must be understood in its context. 21–23 referred to the sacrifices as then offered by the Israelites; the insincerity that accompanied them meant that they could never be acceptable. The meaning of the question in 25 is clear if one adds: 'of such a kind' after 'offerings'. For a similar absolute statement concerning sacrifice, cf Jer 7:22. The

559g prophets spoke in the name of the covenant God and constantly invoked the covenant law, of which the sacrificial system was an integral part. Total rejection of it would involve infidelity to the covenant, the very attitude the prophets condemned. On this topic, cf H. H. Rowley, *The Unity of the Bible*, 30—61; de Vaux, *AI*, 428, 454. For similar absolute statements in the NT, cf Lk 14:26; Mt 5:29f. 'Sakkuth . . . Kaiwan': names of one or two Assyrian deities associated with Saturn. Already in the time of Amos, Assyrian elements were to be found in Israel's worship, and are evidence for increasing Assyrian influence which would culminate in the fall of Samaria in 721 B.C. (cf 2 (4) Kgs 15ff). The Israelites will carry into exile the images of the gods to whom they had turned for help, cf Jer 48:7; 49:3; Is 46:1—2; Hos 10:6; they have become booty for the conquerors. 'beyond Damascus': almost certainly implies exile in Assyria, which had already embarked on an expansionist policy.

h 6:1—7 The Luxury and Conceit of the Leaders will be Punished—This section consists of two 'Woes' (1, 4) followed by a 'therefore' (7) introducing the punishment. **1.** 'Sion': Amos is primarily concerned with Israel, and the incidental reference to Jerusalem is surprising. It seems to be confirmed by the reference to 'these kingdoms' in 2. Isaiah's preoccupation with Judah and Jerusalem did not prevent his speaking about Samaria (Is 28). 'Samaria': the capital of the N Kingdom since the days of Omri (cf 1 (3) Kgs 16:23f). 'first of the nations': ironical. 'come': as to their leaders and judges. **2.** Cities are mentioned which had experienced, or would experience a disastrous change in fortune (cf Is 10:9). 'Calneh', probably Kullankög in N Syria, fell to the Assyrians in 738; Hamath, on the Orontes, in 720 and Gath in 711. Since these events come after the time of Amos, commentators tend to regard the v as a later addition. Others see a reference to earlier misfortunes of these cities in the time of Shalmaneser III (859—824 B.C.), or on the occasions mentioned in 2 (4) Kgs 12:18; 14:28; 2 Chr 26:6. 'these kingdoms': i.e. Israel and Judah, which in spite of their conceit, will share a similar fate. **3.** They refuse to believe that the nation will perish, while by luxurious living and neglect of leadership, they hasten the evil day. 'seat of violence': or '*settling of violence*', i.e. enemy occupation. **4—6.** The luxurious life of the leaders. 'ivory': cf 3:15 note. 'ruin of Joseph': the break-up of the N Kingdom. **7.** As a punishment for their failure to lead, they shall lead the people into exile.

i 8—14 Rejection and Punishment—Yahweh's decision to reject Israel is confirmed by an oath (8), and is followed by the horrors of war (9—10, 11). Israel's crime and false confidence are recalled once again (12—13) and punishment re-affirmed (14). **8.** 'by himself': cf 4:2 note. 'city': MT without the article. Probably Samaria. **9—10.** Difficult. 'burns': i.e. to dispose of the body in time of plague. Although the Israelites did not usually practise cremation, there may have been exceptions (cf de Vaux, AI, 57). RSV note: 'make a burning', i.e. of incense and perfumes (cf Jer 34:5 etc). The text may be corrupt. 'not mention': for fear of adding to the disasters which have come in the name and power of Yahweh. **12.** Israel had deformed justice in an unnatural way. **13—14.** 'Lodebar' and 'Karnaim', probably two Transjordanian towns of no great significance which were recently taken by the Israelites. Such puny efforts will achieve nothing against the nation that Yahweh will send. They will oppress the whole country from Hamath on the Orontes in the N to the region of the Dead Sea (cf 2 (4) Kgs 14:25).

560a 7:1—9:4 The Visions—This section contains a series of five visions (7:1—3, 4—6, 7—9; 8:1—3; 9:1—4), **560a** interrupted by a biographical section in 7:10—17 and a group of short oracles in 8:4—8, 9—10, 11—12, 13—14. It concludes with a doxology in 9:5—6, followed by a further oracle on the fate of Israel (9:7—10).

7:1—3 The Vision of Locusts—In Israel's view, a plague of locusts was entirely suitable for punishing the Egyptians (Ex 10:12ff): it was a shock to discover that Yahweh would afflict his own people with such a disaster (cf 4:9—10; Jl 1). **1.** 'latter growth . . . king's mowings': the royal levy (cf 1 (3) Kgs 4:7ff, 26ff) was taken on the earlier growth which was sown before mid-January. The 'latter growth' was sown between mid-Jan and the end of Feb. A locust attack at the time 'of the shooting up of the latter growth' would be even more disastrous than usual, since they would destroy both crops at different stages of development, the latter growth which had just begun to appear, and the earlier growth which was not yet ready for cutting (so E. Power, Bib 8 (1927) 87—92). For others, 'the latter growth' was the second crop on which the people depended, since the first crop had gone to the king. The obscurity of the passage arises from a lack of accurate knowledge of the terms used. **2.** 'grass': here a general term, 'vegetation'. The prophet intercedes for his people as did Moses (Ex 32:11 etc), Jer (15:1; cf 2 Mc 15:14), Ezek (9:8) and Dn (9:15—19). 'small': Amos had a more realistic view of Israel than her leaders (cf 6:1—7, 13, 14). **3.** Yahweh shows himself a merciful God.

4—6 The Vision of Devouring Fire—'fire': either **b** drought (cf 1:2; 4:7—8), or fire from heaven (Gn 19:24ff). This scourge was of such violence and power that Amos saw it drying up the primeval deep (Gn 1:2), which receded to let dry land appear. The pillars of the earth were set in this deep (Ps 75 (74):4; Jb 38:6); its waters fed the springs from below the earth and the rain clouds from above the firmament.

7—9 Vision of the Plumb Line and the Bulging c Wall—**7.** A plumb line would normally be used in the building of a wall, but similar instruments are referred to in descriptions of coming destruction (cf 2 (4) Kgs 21:13; Is 34:11). Is 30:13 describes the parlous state of Jerusalem in terms of a bulging wall. As is clear from vv 8—9, preparations are being made for the destruction of Israel, who is untrue to the standards of Yahweh's covenant law. 'pass by': i.e. pardon (cf 8:2; Mi 7:18; Prv 19:11). **9.** 'high places . . . sanctuaries': primarily, but not exclusively, Bethel and Dan (cf 1 (3) Kgs 12:26—33). For a description of these 'high places', cf § 104, and de Vaux, AI 284ff. 'the house of Jeroboam' came to an end with the murder of Zechariah, Jeroboam II's son and successor (2 (4) Kgs 15:8ff), in 743 B.C.

10—17 Amos and Amaziah Clash—This biographical **d** interlude is inserted on the basis of the reference to the end of the house of Jeroboam in v 9. **10.** Amos was charged by his religious opponents with a political crime, as was later to happen to Christ (Lk 23:2). This incident illustrates the danger of close association of priesthood and political power. In such circumstances, there is a constant temptation to confuse political and religious issues. **11.** A misquotation of the prophet, since Amos had not said that Jeroboam himself would die by the sword—nor did he (cf 2 (4) Kgs 14:29). **12.** 'seer': there may be a mocking reference to his visions (a visionary). The term 'seer' had a respectable history (cf 1 Sm 9:9). 'eat bread': i.e. earn your living. It was precisely this point which Amos denied. He was not a professional prophet; he did not depend on royal favour for bread and board; nor was his message tempered to the whim of a royal patron (cf 1 (3)

560d Kgs 22). Amaziah also feared that Amos would appropriate a share of the offerings which were customary on visits to the sanctuary (cf 1 Sm 9:7) or prophet (cf 1 (3) Kgs 14:3). **14.** 'no prophet': not a professional prophet (cf 13 note). 'a prophet's son': nor a prophet by birth. RSV note: 'sons of the prophets': a member of a group of prophets, cf 1 Sm 10:5ff; 2 (4) Kgs 2. 'herdsman and a dresser', cf § 554c—d. **15.** He was directly commissioned by God to bear his message to Israel, and he does so without fear or favour. **16—17.** The priest's rejection of the word of God means that he will share Israel's fate. cf Hos 4:5—6 for a similar chastisement of the delinquent priest's family. This is the first of many such incidents in the long history of conflict between prophets and priests in Israel (e.g. Hos 4:5—10; Is 28:7—13; Jer 19:14—20:6 etc).

e **8:1—3 The Vision of a Basket of Summer Fruit—** **1—2.** The summer fruit is a symbol of Israel ripe in its sins and ready to be devoured. There is a play on the Heb words *qayiṣ* (summer fruit) and *qēṣ* (end) which are of similar sound. Amos sees *qayiṣ*, but this brings to mind *qēṣ*, the end which is to come on Israel. **3.** 'in silence', 'be silent!' or: '*Hush!*' The Heb. word is an interjection, cf 6:10.

f **4—8 Fraud and Exploitation will be Punished—5.** Rich merchants resent the recurrence of the Sabbath and other feasts which force them to suspend their dishonest trading (cf Hos 12:7f; Mi 6:10ff). For 'ephah' and 'shekel', cf § 86e. **6.** Cf 2:6 note. **7.** 'the pride of Jacob': the meaning of this phrase is uncertain. Comparison with 4:2 and 6:8a suggests that it is an epithet of Yahweh himself, which draws attention to the proper object of Jacob's (Israel's) pride. It is unlikely that Yahweh would swear even ironically by the unchanging conceit of Jacob (cf 6:8). **8.** The land itself trembles at such injustice and an earthquake adds to the afflictions of the people. The movements of the earth are compared to the ruffled surface of the Nile. The changes of level involved in the annual inundation of the Nile occurred too slowly to be a suitable figure for the dramatic shock of an earthquake, although it may be the dramatic contrast in level which the prophet had in mind. Cosmic upheaval involving earthquakes, darkening of the sun and moon (v 9) are, received prophetic imagery to depict Yahweh's coming in judgement (cf e.g. Is 13:10; 24:18—20 etc). Such forebodings belong to the poetry of prophecy and do not require a literal fulfilment. In fact no words could adequately describe the fate which awaited Israel.

g **9—10 The Terrors of Yahweh's Judgement Day—9.** The failure of the sun will turn the day of Yahweh into a day of darkness (cf 5:20). This figure is so common in prophetic literature (e.g. Is 13:10; Jl 3:4; 4:15 etc) that it is scarcely necessary to link it with an eclipse of the sun within the lifetime of Amos. **10.** 'sackcloth': the penitential garb of prophets (Is 20:2; Zech 13:4) and of mourners (Is 15:3). 'baldness': here the voluntary baldness of mourners (Mi 1:16; Jb 1:20 etc).

11—12 Hunger and Thirst for the Word of God— Having ignored the word of God in times of prosperity, they experience the lack of it in time of crisis. They frantically look for a message of hope, a sustaining word, an assurance that their troubles will soon be at an end; they are met on every side by unanswering darkness. 'sea to sea' either: from the Mediterranean (W) to the Dead Sea (S), or, more generally, from one end of the earth to the other.

h **13—14 Idolatry Punished—13.** The nation's hope was in its young people. **14.** 'Ashimah': cf 2 (4) Kgs 17:30, a foreign divinity introduced to Samaria. Ashambethel is mentioned among the divinities venerated by the Jewish colony in Elephantine in the 5th cent. B.C. MT reads *'ašmat*, i.e. sin of Samaria; a pun on the god's name is probably intended. Dan was the most northerly sanctuary, and Beersheba, the most southerly. LXX read 'your god' for 'way'. MT can easily be altered to read 'your beloved', a reading accepted by many. In each case, the phrases are not entirely clear, but there is an implication that although Yahweh was worshipped in these three shrines, other divinities were also accommodated. Their worshippers will perish.

9:1—6 Vision of the Collapse of a Crowded **i** **Sanctuary**—The people are assembled for worship in a sanctuary. The prophet sees, not a symbol, but Yahweh himself standing beside the altar and commanding that the building be thrown down on those assembled (1a). Those who escape death in the building have no hope of eluding the divine anger (1b—4). **1.** 'altar': the scene is probably set in the sanctuary of Bethel. 'smite': the order was not given to the prophet, but to some member of the heavenly court, cf 2 Sm 24:16; Jb 1—2, or perhaps the nation called to punish Israel (cf 6:14). **2.** 'Sheol . . . heaven': often used to mark the limits of the universe (cf Jb 11:8; Ps 139 (138):8). Sheol, the underground abode of the dead, where all who died were believed to lead a shadowy existence without distinction of place for the wicked and virtuous (Is 14:9ff; Ps 6:5 etc). **3.** 'Carmel': the reference is not only to the height of the mountain, but also to its numerous caves which might be chosen as a place of refuge. 'serpent': the sea-monster Leviathan which was thought to dwell in the sea (cf Is 27:1). **4.** Yahweh makes it clear that his power is not limited to the territory of Israel. 'set my eyes upon them': usually a sign of divine favour (Jer 39:12 etc). **5—6** **Doxology.** This is the third of the doxologies (4:13; 5:8) which celebrate the universal power of Yahweh, who comes as a searching and rigorous judge. **5.** 'touches': possibly, with lightning; otherwise, to produce an earthquake. 'Nile': cf 8:8. **6.** 'upper chambers': God dwells in the heavens (cf Ps 14 (13):2 etc). 'vault': the sky conceived by the ancients as an arch resting at its extremities on the earth.

7—10 Israel not Immune from Punishment— **j** Various elements are brought together here. 7—8ab reiterate the sentiments of 8:2, but a saving clause is added in 8c. 9 and 10 may originally have been separate; taken together, they emphasize the complete control of Yahweh over the fate of good and bad among his people. None will escape his judgement. **7.** Several times Yahweh had affirmed the privileged position of Israel (2:10, 11; 3:2; 2:15; 8:2). They took refuge in this position, and sought thereby to escape condemnation and punishment. They readily accepted that Yahweh should punish nations which had not shared in the election of Israel implied in the rescue from Egypt. Yahweh declares that he had already intervened in the history of these nations, but this did not exempt them from punishment. Nor would Israel's deliverance from Egypt shelter them from the just anger of their God. 'Ethiopia' or Cush: cf Nm 12:1; one of the sons of Ham, Gn 10:6. Jer 13:23 suggests: Israel can no more change her attitude than the Ethiopian can change the colour of his skin. There was an ancient and well-founded tradition that the Philistines came from Crete (Caphtor; cf Jer 47:4f). They were long in conflict with Israel (cf Jg 13ff; 1—2 Sm). 'Syria': also an enemy of Israel (2 (4) Kgs 8:12; 10:32). 'Kir': cf 1:5. **8.** 'sinful kingdom': Israel. 8c—10 imply that the good will not share the fate of the sinners, and involve the survival of a virtuous remnant. This teaching was hinted at in 5:3,

560k

560j 15. **9.** The figure of the sieve is not easy to understand. Does the pebble retained in the sieve represent the sinner reserved for punishment, or the good man preserved from disaster? Certainty is not possible, but the former seems more likely (cf Sir 27:4). **10.** Other texts spoke of the complacency of the wicked (6:1—6; cf Is 28:15; Mi 3:11).

k **11—14 Epilogue: Restoration**—This epilogue (11—14, or, as some would hold, 8c—14) concludes the book on an optimistic note. It must be regarded as a later addition, and assigned to the exilic or post-exilic period. It presupposes the collapse of the Davidic dynasty in 587 B.C.; the reference to the Edomites (12), and the phraseology of the passage are paralleled in the exilic and post-exilic literature. **11.** 'booth': Heb.: *sukkāh* (cf *sukkôth* = the feast of Tabernacles, Neh 8:15—17); a makeshift and impermanent structure. It is probably used instead of 'house' to symbolize the depressed state of the dynasty after the fall of Jerusalem in 587 B.C. 'days of old': in Solomon's time. **12.** 'Edom': traditionally an enemy of

Israel; they incurred particular displeasure for their **560k** part in the disaster of 587 B.C. (Is 63:1—6; Jer 49:7—22; Ps 137 (136): 7—9; Jl 4:19). 'called by my name': literally, 'upon whom my name is invoked'. The phrase implies possession (cf 2 Sm 12:28; Is 63:19; Jer 7:10). **13.** Besides the restoration of the Davidic dynasty, and **l** perhaps as a consequence of it, the afflicted countryside will be extraordinarily fertile. Corn and grape crops will be so abundant that they cannot be harvested in time for the ploughing and sowing which must follow. **14.** 'restore the fortunes': a phrase which is characteristic of the exilic literature (Jer 32:14; Ezek 16:53 etc), and is sometimes translated: 'bring back the captives (i.e. the exiles) of my people Israel'. Cities will be rebuilt and Israel will live in security and prosperity in their native land, from which they shall never again be forcibly removed. This prospect of messianic blessing awaits fulfilment in the eschatological kingdom (cf Jn 14:3; 16:22; and Ac 15:16f where Am 9:11—12 is quoted according to LXX).

OBADIAH

BY S. BULLOUGH O.P.

561a **Bibliography**—St Jerome, PL 25, 1097–118; E. B. Pusey, *Minor Prophets*, 1860; Knabenbauer, CSS, 1924[2]; Condamin, S.J., *L'Unité d'Abdias*, RB 9 (1900) 261ff; Van Hoonacker, EtB, 1908. J. Bewer, ICC, 1912; H. C. O. Lanchester, CBSC, 1918; L. H. Brockington PC (2), 1962; A. Weiser, ATD, 1956.

b This is the shortest book in the OT, consisting of a single ch, but St Jerome wrote (on v 1) that 'quanto brevius est, tanto difficilius'. The considerable **difficulty of the Book** arises from its brevity, from the references to historical events not easily identifiable, from the absence of any date or autobiographical material, from the problems raised by parallels elsewhere, and lastly from several grave textual obscurities.

c About **the Prophet himself** Jer reports a Jewish tradition that he is the same as the steward of King Ahab, who bore the same name, who sheltered the hundred prophets, 1 (3) Kgs 18:3–16, and whose tomb was shown at Samaria together with those of Elisha and John the Baptist. The prophet's name in MT is *'Obadyāh* (that of the man in 1 (3) Kgs is, with a negligible variant *'Obadyāhû*), and it appears in AV as Obadiah. The name means 'Servant of Yahweh'. There are in all 12 characters in OT (chiefly in the lists in Chr) bearing this name or its variant. The tradition about the pronunciation seems to be quite unstable, various forms of Abdias or Obadiah being current: LXX, according to codices and in the different texts, provides many variants of both patterns, and for the 12 persons Vg has 4 times Abdias, thrice Obdia, twice Obedia, once Obadia, once Obdias and once the acc. Obdiam. It is impossible seriously to identify the prophet with any of the other 11, and it must be admitted that beyond the prophecy itself nothing is known of the author.

d **The Theme of the Book** is the pride of Edom (the neighbouring kingdom to the S, and akin to Judah being descended from Esau), 2–4, and their destruction, 5–9, on account of their unbrotherly attitude to Judah at the time of the latter's calamity, 10–14, which will bring on them God's wrath, 15–16, and retribution from Judah, who will triumph over all nations, 17–21. This last section envisages the restoration of all Israel and concludes with a Messianic sentence on Yahweh's universal kingship.

e **The Jeremiah Parallels**—Jer 49:7–22 is also a prophecy against Edom, wherein are some sections which are almost verbal parallels with Obad; not, however in the same order. The parallels are these (3 b and part of 5 have no parallel);

Obad	1 b	2	3a	4	5a	5b	6
Jer	49:14	15	16a	16b	9b	9a	10

Some literary dependence must be supposed, either of one on the other, or of both on an older source. The supposition will depend on the date assigned to Obad. There are some isolated phrases with parallels in Joel:

in Obad 11 and Jl 3:3, Obad 15a and Jl 1:15, Obad **561e** 15b and Jl 3 (4):4 and Obad 17 and Jl 2:32 (3:5).

The Problem of the Date—The only fair treatment is **f** to place before the reader the principal evidence in Obad on which he may base a conjecture. A date must be sought when the following circumstances may be verified: (1) Edom feels secure, but ruin is coming upon her at the hands of her former allies, 1–9. (2) Jerusalem has been invaded by foreigners, and men flee from the city, 11–14. (3) Edom meanwhile stands aloof and even joins the invaders, 10–14. (4) Both Israel and Judah are in captivity, 20. The inheritance of Palestine and the punishment of Edom by the returned exiles is seen in the future, 15–16, 17–21.

There are three main groups of opinions: (1) *A pre-* **g** *exilic date*, emphasizing the hostility of Edom (e.g. Knabenbauer). Edom began (and continued) a state of revolt against King Joram of Judah c. 847 B.C.; 2 (4) Kgs 8:20–22; 2 Chr 21:8–10. About the same time the Philistines and Arabs invaded Judah and Jerusalem itself, 2 Chr 21:17, and since Edom was still in revolt it may be supposed that they joined the invaders. Amos' prophecies against Edom (esp. 1:11 on their hostility), dating from about 760 B.C., look back to these events, and similarly Joel's remarks about deportations by Tyrians, Sidonians and Philistines, Jl 3 (4):2–7, refer to this period, so that Joel, Amos and Obadiah form a more or less contemporary group in the 8th cent. B.C. The position assigned by tradition to Obadiah among the XII is also adduced in support of this date. On this theory Jeremiah was of course long posterior to Obadiah. Calamity upon Edom is to be taken as a threat, not as a past event.

(2) *An exilic date* (held by St Jerome and many **h** since), emphasizing the invasion of Jerusalem, which is identified most easily with the catastrophe of 586. Edom's hostility is not indicated in the historical account of 586, but it is clearly suggested in contemporary exilic documents such as Lam 4:21–22: Ezek 35 (the whole ch has the same theme as Obad, esp. v 5); and Ps 137 (136):7, which at any rate in its present form is plainly exilic. The calamity that overtook Edom is supposed to be at the hands of the Babylonians (whom they had supported in 586) after the fall of Jerusalem when they penetrated into Egypt, overrunning Moab and Ammon *en route*, Jos.Ant. 10, 9, 7, and therefore probably Edom also. On this theory the parallels are contemporary, and both may depend on older sources reflecting the earlier troubles with Edom in the time of, e.g., Amos. The identification of place-names of the Babylonian exile in Abd 20 is connected with an exilic date for Obadiah (6th cent.).

(3) *A post-exilic date*, emphasizing the chastisement of **i** Edom (e.g. Wellhausen and many moderns, incl. Van Hoonacker). Here the captivity of Jerusalem is regarded as past, and the chastisement of Edom by her former allies is beginning. A connexion is made with Mal 1:2–4, written c. 480 B.C., where Edom is described as already

61i devastated, and although Petra, one of the principal cities of Edom, was not occupied by the Arabs until 312, as Diodorus Siculus relates, 19, 94, it is easy to suppose Arab invasions of their territory long before this, especially as already c. 444 we find an Arab element of some importance in Palestine offering resistance to the work of Nehemiah at Jerusalem, Neh 2:19ff. The Edomites may well at first have made common cause against Judah with the Arabs in Palestine, only as the Arabs grew stronger to be abandoned by them and eventually defeated. On these suppositions Obad is dated a little before Malachi, c. 500 B.C., and the texts in Jeremiah are of course older, though it is unlikely that they are source of those of Obad.

A few authors (e.g. Hitzig) place the book as late as the ruin of Petra in 312 and claim that the deportation of the Jews refers to that by the Egyptians about this date, recorded by Josephus in Ant. 12, 1, 1.

j **The Unity of the Book**, small as it is, has been questioned, chiefly on the grounds of chronological incoherence, it becoming thus possible to assign each section to the most convincing date. P. Condamin, RB 9 (1900), 261ff, demonstrated the unity of the book on a metrical basis, and although one might admit the incorporation of older material, esp. in the opening vv, it seems unnecessary to postulate a multiplicity of authors.

k The **style** is regular classical Hebrew without obvious signs of either archaic or late post-exilic diction, if one excepts the word *qetel* in 9, which occurs only here. Its root is unknown in the earlier books and is found only in Jb 13:15; 24:14 and Ps 139 (138):19. The metre is in some places regular but in others inconsistent, while certain sections appear to be in prose. The text of some verses is uncertain.

62a **1 Introduction**—The 'vision', i.e. prophecy; cf § 452*i*. '*A report we have heard from Yahweh, and an ambassador among the nations has been sent*'; The LXX and the Jer parallel have 'I have heard'. After 'Thus says . . .' we expect a divine utterance, which this section appears not to be. Van Hoonacker (henceforth written Van H.) takes the section, together with the substance of the report, 'Rise up' as an 'aside', introducing Yahweh's words in 2. Others take the three sentences 'Thus says . . . We have heard . . . and a messenger . . .' as a triple introduction to the divine utterance (thus Schegg, and Knox's translation suggests this). Knabenbauer, following LXX 'I have heard . . .', takes the speech as beginning at that point, and as the utterance at once of God and the prophet.

b **2–4 Edom's Pride**—**2.** Jer 49:15 for 'utterly' has 'among men'. *deceived* **3** 'Rock' (singular), *Sela* has no article in Obad (though it has in Jer 49:16*a*), and is perhaps a proper name (cf RVm) as in Jg 1:36; 2 (4) Kgs 14:7 and Is 16:1, where Vg translates 'Petra' (with capital). The identification with the present Petra in Transjordan, an Edomite stronghold (cf **i** supra), is doubtful since there were several such rock-hewn cities in that area, as Jerome (on 4) already observed. 'Why *is saying*, Who will . . .' is not in Jer.

c **5–9 Edom's Fate**—Difficult. In **5** the Jer parallel (49:9) has the thieves and grape-gatherers in inverse order, and their activities are not a question but a statement: the grape-gatherers will not leave a remnant, the thieves damage till they have had enough. This yields a more reasonable sense. Furthermore the awkward 'How you have been destroyed' does not appear at all, and the Vg mistranslation here perhaps makes it suspect— Van H. transfers the sentence to the beginning of 6. Jer seems here to have preserved a better reading, and in view of this and the next v here, the meaning seems to be not that something will be left, but that Edom will lose all at the hands of invaders under the figures of thieves and grape-gatherers. I would therefore reconstruct as follows: *If thieves come to thee, if raiders of the night, shall they not steal their fill? If grape-gatherers come to thee, shall they leave a remnant?* **6:** the last Jer parallel (49:10), and no longer verbal in Heb. Knox, translating Vg, sees a contrast to the preceding: 5 'at least they had been content to carry off what needed them . . .', 6 'But now, see how Esau is ransacked . . .', which offers an explanation of Vg. **7.** In HT this v begins with 'Even **d** to the border', which enables some (incl. Van H.) to attach the words to the end of 6. Jerome noted but rejected this possibility. Yet it simplifies translation: '*sought out his hidden things even to the border*'. If, however, the phrase really belongs to 7, the question arises, whose border is indicated? The abandonment of Edom by her allies is described. If it is the allies' border, then the sense is that Edom's delegates (or refugees) are turned out of those lands; if it is Edom's own border, the probable meaning is that the Edomites are turned out of their own land, at least as far as their own border, or else that Edomite conquerors are driven back within their own borders (cf Knox); but in any case the rendering is forced and requires much supposition. 'Your trusted friends': MT has simply *lahmᵉkā*, 'thy bread', which might conceivably be attached to 'men of': 'men of thy peace, thy bread', but this is unsatisfactory and various emendations have been proposed. Van H. attempts to derive a word from a cognate root (found in Syriac and Arabic) and translates '*tes associés*'. Since, however, LXX ignores the word, I prefer to omit it as a dittography of the preceding word. 'There is no understanding of it' is considered by some to form part of the rhetorical question 8. **9.** 'Teman': the **e** 'South', represents Edomite territory (cf Am 1:12, where linked with Bosra), and their dismay will itself be the cause of their own failure. 'By slaughter'. LXX and Vg rightly include in 10. Obad has a slight peculiarity of style according to which such brusque juxtapositions of nouns and verbs are not unusual, e.g. 5: 'If thieves, . . . if plunderers . . .', 7 has no conjunctions and 12 'over the day of your brother, in the day of his misfortune', so that here 'By slaughter, for the violence', is not surprising.

10–14 The Reason of the Calamity is Edom's f unbrotherly conduct towards Judah—**12.** 'misfortune', Heb. *nōker*, 'estrangement' only here, but cf the cognate *neker* only in Job 31:3 where it is parallel to '*êd*, 'misfortune', which occurs in 13 here. The word therefore does not necessarily refer to an exile (cf Knox). 'You should not have rejoiced'. lit '*Enlarged your mouth*', perhaps in laughter, though 'mouth' may merely mean 'words' (as in Dt 17:6), and so the phrase may mean 'talking big', 'be not arrogant, or taunting' **13.** 'You should not have looted his goods' probably: '*Lay not a hand upon his glacis*'. In MT the active verb 'stretch out' has a fem. ending, for which read *yād*, 'a hand'. The word *hêl*, 'glacis' or 'rampart' occurs with 'wall' in Lam 2:8. Vg ('exercitim') and RSV ('good') read *hayil* in Obad 13.

15–16 The Day of the Lord, a frequent notion in the **g** prophets, sometimes considerably developed from the day of triumph of Judah to the eschatological notion of the everlasting Day of the Lord at the end of time, cf §§ 551*f*, 581*a*. The meaning here seems to be chiefly the first, though 'all nations' in 15 and the last words of 21 suggest a more universal application. The wider horizon from this v to the end has suggested to some that this section is a later composition. Yet the theme of the condemnation of Edom continues: as Edom has done, so shall it be done to

562h her, she shall share the fate of the nations. **16.** 'As you have drunk', probably the cup of bitterness (a common figure, cf Jer 25:16; Mt 20:22). 'You' most probably refers to Judah, and then the nations in their turn shall drink the same cup, and become nonentities, when Judah triumphs (Van H., Knox, others). Some, however (e.g. Knabenbauer) understand the phrase of Edom having joined the drunken orgies of the invaders of Jerusalem, and of the nations then holding similar orgies in Edom (though Knabenbauer himself in the second member sees the cup of bitterness). 'stagger'; RSV emending an uncertain text. Some would read *bale'û* 'swallow down', cf Kittel.

i **17—21 The Triumph of Judah—18.** Jacob stands for Judah, and Joseph for the N Kingdom, as does Ephraim in 19. It is important to note that 17—19 envisage a restored Israel without 'partition', who will inherit once more the whole of Palestine including its outlying districts. Israel's vengeance upon Edom is pictured also in Ezek 25:14. **19.** A geographical description of the triumph of the united Israel: southwards they shall possess Edom (Esau), westwards Philistia (on the coast), northwards *'Ephraim shall possess the country of Samaria'* (this reading involves the rejection of the accusative 'the land of' before 'Ephraim', which certainly looks like a confusion), and eastwards Benjamin (the area N of Jerusalem) shall

j possess Gilead (which is across the Jordan). **20.** The extension N and S is further described together with the return of the exiles. A very difficult v. Many emendations have been proposed. The most convincing for *hahēl hazzeh*

is Bewer's reading *ba Hᵃlah*, 'in Halah', which is the place **562** in Assyria whither Israel had been deported, 2 (4) Kgs 17:6; 18:11; 1 Chr 5:26. This provides the balance of another place-name, and supports an exilic date for the book. These emendations underlie the conjectural translation in RSV and bring out the parallelism there:

> 'The exiles in Halah who are of the people of Israel shall possess Phoenicia as far as Zarephath' (far N of Palestine);
> 'and the exiles of Jerusalem who are in Sepharad shall possess the cities of the Negeb' (the S of Palestine).

There remains the problem of Sepharad: the name comes only here in the OT, and in later Heb. it indicates 'Spain' (so that Spanish Jews are still called Sephardim, as opposed to the Ashkenazim or Jews of Central and Eastern Europe). Jerome said that the Jew who taught him told him it meant the Bosphorus, whither (he said) Hadrian had deported the Jews. Jerome himself, however, adds that the obvious meaning is somewhere in Babylonia. Modern commentators have suggested Saparda in Mesopotamia (mentioned in Sargon's inscriptions). Upholders of a date in the Persian period prefer to identify with Sparda (= ? Sardis) in Asia Minor (mentioned in the Behistun inscriptions).

21. 'Saviours', the title applied to the heroes of **k** old, Jg 3:9, 15, who delivered the people, though LXX reads the passive, 'those who are saved'. The book ends on a Messianic note, 'And the kingdom shall be the Lord's'.

JONAH

BY N. ARBUCKLE O.F.M.

563a Bibliography—*Commentaries*: J. A. Bewer, ICC, 1912; L. H. Brockington PC (2), 1963; A. Feuillet, BJ, 1951; F. Nötscher, EchB, 1948; T. H. Robinson, F. Hurst, HAT, 1964³; J. D. Smart, IB; A. Weiser, ATD, 1956². *Other literature*: G. C. Aalders, 'The Problem of the Book of Jonah' 1948; B. S. Childs, 'Jonah, a study in OT Hermeneutics', Scot JT 11 (1958) 53—61; A. Feuillet, 'Les Sources du livre de Jonas', and 'Le Sens du livre de Jonas', RB 54 (1947), 161—86, 340—61; 'Jonas' in DBS 4 (1949) 1104—31; E. Haller, 'Die Erzählung von dem propheten Jona', *Theologische Existenz Heute* 65 (1958); O. Loretz. 'Herkunft und Sinn der Jona-Erzählung', BZ 5 (1961), 18—21; J. Schildenberger, 'Das Buch Jonas', *Bibel und Kirche*, 17 (1962), 4—21; W. Vycichl, 'Jonas und das Walfisch', Mus 69 (1956), 183—6.

b Literary character—Jon is different from the books of the other Minor Prophets among which it is found. For, whereas the others record for us the oracles and preaching of the prophets with very little biographical detail, Jonah tells us more about what the prophet did than about what he said. The problem of the prophet's literary character which vexed exegetes in the past has largely been resolved in the light of a better understanding of the relationship between inspiration and literary genre. Most exegetes now hold that Jonah is **didactic fiction, a sermon in the form of a story**, and, as such, manifests many of the characteristics of that type of literature.

c There is a **disregard for historical detail**. At the time about which the book purports to tell (v 1 identifies the protagonist of the story with the Jonah mentioned in 2 (4) Kgs 14:25—i.e. in the reign of Jeroboam II, 783—743 B.C.), the residence of the Assyrian king was Asshur and not Nineveh which only became capital in the time of Sennacherib (704—680). The edict of the king (3:7ff) which is Persian rather than Assyrian in character, and the legendary size of Nineveh both serve the didactic purpose of the author although they are historically unfounded. Other historical facts which one would expect to find in an historical account are of no interest to the author of Jonah—who was the king of Nineveh? From what were the men of Nineveh converted? What became of Jonah and the Ninevites afterwards?

d Similarly the author of such literature need not worry too much about the **improbability** of his story. That a prophet should be sent to preach repentance to the Gentiles is a thing unheard of in Jewish history. Not even Elisha (2 (4) Kgs 8:7—15), who foretold the death of the king of Damascus, nor Jeremiah, who was commissioned as the 'prophet to the nations' (Jer 1:5), are said to have preached thus. There is an obvious **disproportion** between the simple proclamation of destruction pronounced by a complete stranger from a politically insignificant kingdom and the total and complete conversion in one day of all the citizens of a (for that time) impossibly large city, the supposed capital of one of the greatest kingdoms of the biblical E. Sober history never **563d** accredited such a conversion to the Chosen People, notwithstanding the incessant preaching of the prophets. Cf Ezek 3:5—7. **Miracles** are multiplied with abandon. Unlike the miracles found in Israel's history which had a lasting effect on the economy of man's salvation, the proportionately large number of miracles narrated in the brief story of Jonah produces no lasting effect whatsoever.

Many scholars in the past hesitated to accept Jonah as **e** unhistorical because of **difficulties** they felt in reconciling this conclusion with the comparisons drawn by Our Lord between the sojourn of Jonah in the whale and his own Resurrection. Moreover the fictional character of the book is not consonant with the opinion of many of the Fathers (e.g. Aug, PL 33, 382; Jer, PL 25, 1132; Cyril Jer, PG 33, 848). However in Mt 12:39—42; 16:4 and Lk 11:29—32 our Lord is referring his listeners to three incidents, all of which are known from the Scriptures: Jonah's sojourn in the whale, the conversion of the men of Nineveh, and the visit of the Queen of the South to King Solomon. There is no call for our Lord to establish the historicity of these events. Jonah and the Ninevites evoke a situation—an example for the Jews—just as much as the queen of the S, since all are well attested in Scripture. All have the one source; the literary character of the accounts is immaterial. It is for this same reason that the Church can use both Mary Magdalen and the Prodigal Son as examples of penitents. Likewise the witness of the Fathers in the realm of literary criticism testifies without doubt that in their time the book of Jonah was deemed to come within the literary category of history. Corresponding conclusions with regard to the historicity and, therefore, the possibility of the miracles narrated in the book were made. To-day, with a greater knowledge of ancient literature than was available to the Fathers, exegetes have good reasons for placing Jonah in this category of didactic fiction.

From a very early date (cf e.g. Cyr.Alex. PG 71, 615) **f** there has been speculation regarding the **sources** from which our author drew his material. Attempts have been made to relate the story of Jonah and the fish to extrabiblical mythology: to Perseus and Andromeda, Hercules and Hesion, or to the Semitic god-fish Dagon also venerated under the name of Oannes, but there is no positive evidence to establish such dependence on any of the tales suggested. More important are the **biblical sources** out of which the author may have composed his book. Feuillet convincingly traces much of Jonah back to Jer and Ezek. He recognizes a dependence of Jon 3:10*b* on Jer 18:7—8; connexions of a textual nature between Jon 3:8 and Jer 25:5; 26:3, 36:3, 7. A thematic likeness exists between Jon 3:3 and Jer 36; verbal similarities between Jon 3:8—9 and Jer 26:2—3. The vocabulary of the storm scene in Jon 1 is reminiscent of Ezek 26—28. Finally, Jon 4 bears many similarities to the story of Elijah in 1 (3) Kgs 19:4ff. Because of this dependence on

563f earlier biblical literature, Feuillet (BJ 18) concludes that the book belongs to the category of didactic midrash.

g Date—The book appears to have been composed sometime after the Exile when Jewish attitudes had grown narrowly nationalist (cf *infra*). The language shows strong Aram. influence similar to that found in the later books of the OT, e.g. Ez, Neh and Dn. Some of the expressions, such as 'the God of heaven' (1:9), are of late usage among the Jews, cf Ez 1:2; 2:11; etc, Neh 1:4, 5; 2:4, etc, Dn 2:18, 37, etc. The literary characteristics suggest that the book was written at a time when OT authors were inclined to present lessons under the guise of history, cf narrative sections of Jb, Jud, Est and Dn.

564a Doctrine—The precise doctrinal interpretation of Jonah depends on whether it is taken to be an allegory or a parable. For those who favour an **allegorical interpretation, Jonah**, whose name means 'dove', **symbolizes the Chosen People; Nineveh** stands **for the whole pagan world** which does not know Yahweh but which is still an object of his mercy. Jonah (Israel) refuses to fulfil his mission to spread knowledge of Yahweh and of the true monotheistic religion to the Gentiles. He is subjected by Yahweh to adversity (the storm); is led into exile (the sea-monster) and delivered therefrom. Even after the exile Israel has the same mission to fulfil towards the Gentile nations, yet still remains obstinate against the divine command. It is true that Israel is sometimes symbolized by a dove, cf Hos 7:11; 11:11; Ps 68(67):13; Song 2:14; 4:1, etc; that the king of Babylon at the time of the exile is likened to a 'monster' (Jer 51:34; 50:17; Is 27:1) which swallows and regurgitates Israel, cf Jer 51:44. It is also true that Israel should have been a witness to Yahweh before the other nations. There are, however, reasons against such an allegorical interpretation. The fish is not an instrument of punishment for Jonah but one of salvation; the message of Jonah is one not of monotheism but of inevitable doom.

b Most interpreters prefer the **parabolical interpretation. The mercy of God extends to all nations and is not restricted to the Chosen People.** Consequently, threats directed against the Gentiles by the prophets of Israel are not irrevocable. The Israelites cherished the belief that Yahweh would not carry out his threats against themselves if they would repent of their evil ways. To his vigorous description of the day of Yahweh the prophet Joel adds: ' "Yet even now", says the Lord, "return to me with all your heart, with fasting, with weeping and with mourning; and rend your hearts and not your garments". Return to the Lord, your God, for he is gracious and merciful, slow to anger, and abounding in steadfast love, and repents of evil. Who knows whether he will not turn and repent and leave a blessing behind him . . .?' (Jl 2: 12ff), cf also Neh 9:31; Ps 103(102):8—12. In Jonah the Gentile king expresses this same hope, using the exact words of Joel: '*Who knows whether God will not turn and repent . . .?*' (Jon 3:9); and Jonah, albeit grudgingly, extends Yahweh's forbearance to the Gentiles: 'for I knew that thou art a gracious God and merciful, slow to anger, and abounding in steadfast love, and repentest of evil' (4:2). In other words, that which was considered a prerogative of the Chosen People, namely, Yahweh's mercy, is here extended to the Gentile nations. The principle enunciated by Jeremiah that 'if that nation, concerning which I have spoken, turns from its evil, I will repent of the evil that I intended to do it' (18:8) is illustrated and extended to the Gentiles by the author of Jonah.

c The corollary to this first lesson is that the threats against the nations, no matter how irrevocable they may seem when made, are in fact conditional. This presented a difficulty to the Jews, since the proof that a prophet spoke **564c** in the name of Yahweh was the fulfilment of his oracles, cf Dt 18:21f. If Yahweh was not, after all, to detroy the Gentiles, what was to be made of the prophets who foretold not only this destruction but the future glory of Israel? The author faces up to this problem. He uses the first half of the book to show beyond doubt that Jonah, even against his will, is a prophet of Yahweh. The other half of the book is devoted to Jonah's mission: 'Yet forty days and Nineveh shall be overthrown' (3:4). No more absolute message could be delivered. Yet even this threat is conditional; and God repents of the evil which he had said he would do to them (3:10).

Although not the direct lesson of the book, other doctrinal points underlie the parable. Yahweh is the God of the Gentiles and he has a providential interest in their well-being; he listens to their prayers (1:14), accepts their sacrifices (1:16) and their repentance (3:10). He is the Lord of all nature; he commands the winds and the seas (1:4, 15); he is the God of heaven who made the sea and the dry land (1:9); he is master of the beasts (1:17), of plants (4:6), of the smaller creatures (4:7), of the sultry wind (4:7)—all of which serve his purpose.

Jonah plays an important part in the development of **d** the notion of **universalism**. This was of two kinds, one **centred round the temple** and the Davidic dynasty, the other **disengaged from any nationalistic element.** The prophet Amos preached a negative sort of universalism: the guilt of all men before Yahweh. Isaiah professed a more positive but more centralized universalism, one with Jerusalem as its spiritual and dynastic centre, cf Is 2:2—5. Jeremiah marks a step forward by his insistence on interior conversion rather than exterior conformity. This opens the way to a less nationalistic universalism. In chh 40—55 of Second-Isaiah the notion of universalism is further freed from its connexions with Jerusalem. However, with the restoration of the temple after the exile there was a renewed stress on the importance of Jerusalem, cf Is 56—66. The decentralized universalism again comes to the fore with Malachi, due, perhaps, to the decline in the religious fervour of the people, cf Mal 1:11. The book of Jonah reflects this stage. One can be a citizen of Nineveh or a Gentile sailor and still adore Yahweh and be pardoned by him without coming to Jerusalem. This is the nearest that the OT reaches towards a true universalism divorced from Jerusalem. With the advent of Hellenism and the danger of syncretism the stress is once more on Jerusalem and the temple as the centre of true worship. Universalism is only complete in the NT with the preaching of the Good News to both Jew and Gentile, Greek and Barbarian.

1—2 Jonah the Prophet of Yahweh—The author sets **e** out to show that Jonah is certainly sent by Yahweh. **1—2.** The accent is on 'the word of the Lord'. Circumstantial details as to where and when are irrelevant to the author's purpose. The city of Nineveh is discussed elsewhere (under 3:3—4); 'cry' with religious meaning or, as we find in the earlier prophets, 'prophesy'; 'their wickedness . . .' cf Gn 6:13 for a similar instance: the pagans are also responsible to Yahweh for their actions. **3.** Jonah wishes to escape and (4:1) to avoid co-operating in the spiritual good of the despised and hated Ninevites. He takes ship in the opposite direction to Nineveh and makes for Tarshish (perhaps Tartessus in Spain) the furthest inhabited land, cf Is 60:9; 66:19; Ps 72 (71):10. 'From the presence of the Lord' means to avoid serving God, cf Jer 15:1, 19; 17:16, although, as here, it can also involve physical separation from the place of one's vocation. **5.** For similar sea-faring language cf Ezek

54e 27; Ps 107 (106):23—30; Ac 27:19. 'And was asleep'. the true prophet should be the one who watches and gives warning, cf Ezek 3:17ff; 33:1ff. Here the pagan sailors do the praying while the prophet sleeps unconcerned. **7.** 'Come, let us cast lots', cf Prv 16:33. Divine Providence concurs with superstitious practice to indicate the cause

f of the storm. **8.** 'On whose account . . . upon us' is not found in the LXX and some modern versions omit, e.g. BJ and CV. **9.** 'I am a Hebrew', this is the name by which the Jews were known to others; among themselves they were 'Israelites'. 'I fear', that is, I believe in, and act accordingly; 'the God of heaven', cf § 563*g*. **10.** The question is one of amazement rather than enquiry. **11—12.** By making Jonah suggest the action to be taken the author exculpates these good pagans for their future action. It is vain to analyse Jonah's intentions or the morality of his action. The author's purpose in introducing this situation is obvious from 1:17. **13.** Contrast the willingness of the pagans to save the Israelite with the Israelite's chagrin at the salvation of the pagans, 4:1ff. **14.** The sailors recognize Yahweh's will in what has happened and what must now happen, and pray that they may be exonerated. **15—16.** The calm shows that it is all Yahweh's doing; and the sailors offer sacrifice and make vows to Yahweh. Their 'fear' should probably be taken to mean the same as Jonah's fear in 1:9.

g **1:17—2:10 Jonah and the great fish—17.** This is equivalent to 2:1 in MT. It is the key verse to the first part of the narrative explaining the drama that has gone before and providing a way out for Jonah while maintaining the tension of the story. 'The Lord appointed a great fish', as in 1:1 the stress is on 'the Lord'; this is Yahweh's doing, cf also 4:6, 7, 8. The author intends to recount a prodigious act of God; he does not attempt to identify the 'great fish', and neither should we. Attempts to lessen the wonder by finding a fish, be it whale, shark, or any other with a gullet wide enough to swallow a man and a stomach capacity to house him, are foreign to the author's intentions and the character of the story. The same, too, must be said for attempts to interpret the 'great fish' as being some sort of ship.

h **2:1—9 The Psalm—**Most exegetes to-day consider this psalm to be the work of an author different from that of the rest of the book. Some regard it as an earlier composition which the author of Jonah has used here, others as a later addition to the book. It is also suggested that the psalm would fit better after 2:10. Too much insistence, however, should not be put on the images evoked by this psalm of thanksgiving. As in other hymns of thanksgiving, common figurative expressions are used to describe the danger from which the psalmist has been delivered. Moreover, from the author's point of view Jonah has been saved from the perils of the sea and the psalm can justifiably come before 2:10. **10.** Again Yahweh is responsible. The author does not specify the landing place: possibly the **564h** place from which he had set out?

3—4 The Conversion of Nineveh: Jonah's anger i reproved—3:1—2. Jonah is again commissioned to go to Nineveh and preach Yahweh's message there. This time Jonah complies. **3—4.** 'Nineveh': it is not necessary to try and justify these measurements by interpreting them as referring either to the city's circumference or to the city and its surrounding districts. In fact Nineveh measured about three miles across and about eight in circumference. The author is using hyperbole; the larger the city, the more wondrous its conversion. 'Yet forty days . . .', a straightforward unconditional proclamation of doom. LXX reads 'three days'; forty days, however, is the traditional period of penance. Some scholars think that 4:5 should follow 3:4. After preaching, Jonah waits to see what will happen. Where 4:5 now stands, Jonah already knows the result, cf 3:10. **5—6.** The Ninevites listen to Jonah and do penance. **7—9.** 'By the decree of the king and his nobles' is terminology more common to the Persian period than to the Assyrian. The practice of including the beasts in penitential acts, although not unknown in Assyrian times, was more common among the Persians. The title 'king of Nineveh' is, likewise, an anachronism for the Jonah mentioned in 2 (4) Kgs 14:25. **10.** 'God repented', in this anthropomorphic way the author reveals the conditional nature of Yahweh's message. This is the climactic point of the whole story, prepared for by what has gone before and justified by what follows.

4:1—11 Jonah reproved—Jonah is angry at the j outcome, especially as he had foreseen such a result and had tried not to have part in it. **2.** 'Thou art a gracious God', cf § 564*b*. **4.** 'Do you do well to be angry?', or 'Have you reason to be angry?' (CV). God is not expecting an answer from his disconsolate prophet; he now shows Jonah that there is no justification at all for his anger. **5.** Cf 3:4. **6—8.** God works a compound miracle for Jonah's instruction. 'And the Lord appointed', it is all Yahweh's doing. After the momentary joy that the plant affords him, Jonah is again disconsolate enough to wish to die rather than live. A similar story is told of Elijah, 1 (3) Kgs 19:4ff. Jonah's annoyance is aroused not only by the plant episode but by his entire situation. He cannot avoid the force of Yahweh's argument. **9—11.** 'Who do not know . . .', children and, perhaps, others who are sinners rather through ignorance than malice. The cattle, involved in the penance, are included in the pardon: Yahweh is the Lord of all life. There the author leaves Jonah and Nineveh. He has made his point clear: the mercy of God extends to all people. There is no room for the narrow nationalistic attitude of certain Israelites who wished Yahweh's mercy only for themselves and his anger for all others.

MICAH

BY D. RYAN

565a Bibliography—*Commentaries*: A. Deissler, PCSB, 1964; A. George, BJ, 1958[2]; A. Weiser, ATD, 1963[2]; J. A. Bewer, 1949; R. E. Wolfe, IB, 1956; J. M. P. Smith, ICC, 1911. *Other literature*: A. George, 'Michée', DBS 5 (1957), 1252ff; B. Renaud, 'Structures et Attaches littéraires de Michée', 4—5, 1964; W. Beyerlin, *Die Kulturtraditionen Israels in der Verkündigung des Propheten Micha*, Göttingen, 1959; A. Cannawurf, 'The Authenticity of Micah 4:1—4', VT 13 (1963) 26—33.

b The Prophet—Micah is the sixth of the Minor Prophets in MT and Vg. In LXX it follows Hosea and Amos; this is chronologically better, for the prophet was a younger contemporary of Hosea. His long ministry covered nearly the same years as that of Isaiah (c. 740—695 B.C.). Cf note on 3:12. The prophet's name 'Who is like Yahweh?' (cf 7:18) is not uncommon. It was the name of a 9th cent. prophet (1 (3) Kgs 22) from whom he is distinguished by the epithet 'the Morashthite' ('of Moresheth' in RSV 1:1; Jer 26:18), after his birth-place, *Môreśet-Gat*, a village about 30 miles SW of Jerusalem.

c The Unity of the Book—There is near unanimity in attributing chh 1—3 (with the exception of 2:12—13) to the 8th cent. prophet. For the rest, opinion varies. The most radical scholars would see the end of Micah's preaching in 3:12, and attribute the subsequent chh to later writers. Here the view is taken that in chh 4—7, 4:11; 5:1—6, 10—14 and 6:1—7:7 belong to Micah. The remaining sections derive from writers of the exilic or Persian periods and reflect the circumstances of those times.

d The Message of the Book—The social, religious and political background to Micah is much the same as for Amos, Hosea and Isaiah (cf §§ 554b, 542i and 462a). Although the prophet is more immediately concerned with Jerusalem and Judah, his statements concerning Samaria (1:5—6) show his interest in the city which is shortly to fall. The fate of Samaria gave cause for reflection on the future of Jerusalem in which so many of the sins of Samaria could be seen. For these Micah upbraided Jerusalem and re-echoed the message of Isaiah, his more distinguished contemporary. His charge sheet listed: their arrogance which made them rely on their own resources and not on Yahweh (1:10—16; 5:5—6); the greed of the wealthy and powerful clique which ruled—or rather, misruled—the city, and heartlessly displaced the poor in their violent acquisition of property (2:1—2, 9; 3:1ff; 6:12); the corruption of justice in the law courts (3:11; 7:3); dishonesty and lying in business (6:10—12); deceit and venality in the teaching of prophets and priests (3:5, 11); the worship of idols (5:10—14), cult prostitution (specifically in Samaria, 1:7), the superstitious abuse of sacrifice (6:6—7)—an accumulation of evil conduct which results in the breakdown of ordinary human relationships (7:5—6).

e A just God cannot allow such crimes to go unpunished,

and the prophet foretells afflictions which are certain **565** and drastic (1:6—16; 2:3ff; 3:6—7, 12; 5:10—14; 6:13ff). In this judgement the nations themselves are involved (1:2 and cf 5:15), if they do not obey the God of Israel.

Micah himself was conscious that his message of almost unrelieved gloom would not find ready acceptance (2:11), but it was a necessary consequence of the moral condition of the people. In one or two passages, a measure of hope can be discerned: in 5:1—4, when he foresees the emergence of a messianic ruler of Davidic stock, who will bring peace and security to a people purified by suffering; and in 6:1—8, the gentle pleading of a merciful God can be felt through the tension of a formal trial. In 6:8, the prophet sums up the teaching of Amos, Hosea, and Isaiah in an immortal statement of Yahweh's requirements of his covenant people. He can make these demands because Israel's history is but the story of God's fidelity in covenant love (6:3—5).

These elements of hope for the future—the messianic **f** king inaugurating an era of messianic peace based on covenant-love—were enshrined by later writers in the return of the exiles from Babylon and the subsequent glory of a reconstituted Sion (2:12—13; 4:6—8, 9—13; 7:8—10). With Yahweh reigning on his holy mount, the nations of the earth come streaming to Sion to learn from him the art of peace and to forget the techniques of war (4:1—5; 7:11—12). All this will be possible for Yahweh 'does not retain his anger forever, because he delights in steadfast love' (7:18).

1:1 Superscription—The work of an editor; cf Is 1:1; **566** Hos 1:1 and Am 1:1; and notes. 'word': the book as a whole is presented as the 'word of Yahweh'. 'saw': cf note on Am 1:1. Although visions of Micah are not clearly and specifically recorded as in Am and Is, there are elements of vision in his prophecies, e.g. 1:3—4, 6; cf also § 533b.

1:2—3:12 Israel on Trial; Accusations, Condem- b nation and Punishment—In the opening vv (1:2—4), the scene is set for the trial of Israel at which Yahweh is an accusing witness (2), the judge who condemns Israel's conduct as sinful (5) and the one who administers punishment (6f). There follows a series of texts which mingle accusations and punishments and follow neither logical nor chronological order. The law suit of Yahweh with Israel is taken up again in 6:1ff cf Hos 4:1ff.

1:2—7 Samaria's Doom—2. 'against you': although **c** Yahweh's judgement is here primarily concerned with Samaria, the nations also stand condemned and can learn from the fate of Samaria. Others translate 'among you' and picture Yahweh joining the nations as they witness the condemnation and punishment of Israel (cf Am 3:9, 13). **3.** 'his place': i.e. the heavens (cf Ps 14 (13):2 etc). **4.** For similar imagery and to describe Yahweh's coming in judgement cf Am 9:5; Is 24:19 etc. **5.** The concentration of sin in the capital cities brings disaster. Although Judah and Jerusalem are also culpable, the

66c prophet speaks only of the fate of Samaria in 6—7. **6.** 'heap'—of ruins. 'pour down': Samaria was set on a steep hill which dominated the surrounding countryside. **7.** Her sin was licentious worship of idols. 'hire of a harlot': a reference to cult prostitution (cf Am 2:7—8: Hos 4:14 and notes). Samaria, called to be the faithful spouse of Yahweh, prostituted herself with idols. This was the source of her wealth which, in the hands of her captors, would again become a harlot's hire.

d 8—16 Invasion—The prophet's lament for the towns of the SW (10—15) is introduced by the explanatory vv 8—9, and concluded by an invitation to share in mourning rites (16). The prophet is deeply grieved at the fate of his native district. He plays on the meaning of each town's name to make it an omen of disaster. The pun, however, is not clear in every case. The text probably refers to the invasion of Sennacherib in 701 B.C. **10.** 'Tell . . .' cf 2 Sm 1:20. 'Beth-le-aphrah': i.e. House of Dust. 'Roll . . . dust': a mourning rite (cf Jer 6:26 etc). **11.** 'Shaphir': i.e. 'Beautiful Place' is subjected to 'nakedness and shame'. There is a play on the sound of *Saʿᵃnān* and 'come forth'; *yāṣᵉʾāh*. **12.** 'Maroth': i.e. 'Bitter Things'. **13.** 'the beginning of sin': the reason for this statement is not clear. **14.** Juda must give up Moresheth-gath. Moresheth suggests the Heb. word for 'fiancée' and explains the reference to 'parting gifts' which were given by a father to his daughter on the occasion of marriage. 'deceitful thing' in Heb., *ʾakzāb*, cf Achzib. **15.** God will bring a conqueror, literally, 'one who dispossesses' on Mareshah, a name which suggests 'possession'. 'the glory of Israel', probably a reference to the monarchy. Once more the king will be homeless and hunted like David in the caves of Adullam, cf 1 Sm 22:1; 2 Sm 23:13. **16.** Mourning rites cf Am 8:10; Jer 7:29.

e 2:1—5 Unjust Wealth of the Powerful; their Fate— 1. They plot evil with full deliberation and with unholy zeal they hasten to execute their plans. **2.** They evict the poor from their houses and holdings to make way for great estates, cf Is 5:8 and § 555a. **3.** God also has his plans. **4.** The text of this v is uncertain. The taunt song mockingly re-echoes the grief of the wealthy as they are taken captive and witness the distribution of their property. **5.** All the people suffer the consequences of their masters' evil actions. No one of the Chosen People will be left to cast a measuring line on a plot of the Promised Land.

f 6—11 The Prophet is Challenged; his Reply 6. Like other prophets (Am 5:10; Is 28:9ff; Jer 28), Micah was challenged. **7.** It is better perhaps to close the quotation after '. . . his doings?' in 7c, not as in RSV. The prophet's adversaries find re-assurance in the thought that Yahweh is patient, and disaster for his people is not his doing. In 7d, the prophet sets out to show that his ominous words are justified, but their message is grasped only by the just. **8—9.** The violence of those Israelites who disregard the covenant (note the repetition of 'my people' in 8 and 9 and cf Hos 2:23) casts them in the rôle of enemies. **10.** The Promised Land has been defiled by sin; it cannot be a place of rest (cf Dt 12:9). Other interpreters (BJ) put the words 'Arise . . . rest' on the lips of the wicked cf v 9, and translate 10b: You demand a crushing pledge for a thing of no consequence. **11.** Micah outlines the only message acceptable to this drunken people: encouragement to go on imbibing and, in an artificial sense of security, to ignore the present dangers (cf Is 5:11, 22; 28:7; 30:10; Jer 28:1ff).

g 12—13 Release and Restoration—The style, thought and vocabulary of these vv suggest that they derive from the same source as 4:6—7. They may have been inserted **566g** here as a corrective to 8—11 in the light of Ezek 34; 37:15—28; Is 40:1f; 52:12 etc. The historical reference is to the fall of Babylon with the consequent release and return of the exiles. **12.** Cf Ezek 34:11ff. **13.** 'He': i.e. Yahweh, who will lead his people from the cities in which they had been held captive. In contrast to their experience of human monarchs, they can feel secure in the leadership of Yahweh, their king.

3:1—4 The Crimes of the Leaders—1—3. The leaders **h** whose duty it was to uphold justice have only plundered the people (cf 2:2, 8—9; 3:11; Am 5:10—15 etc). Their savagery is compared to the butchering of cattle for food. 2a draws attention to the complete reversal of ordinary moral standards (cf Is 5:20). **4.** When the time of reckoning comes, they will cry in vain to Yahweh, as the poor cried in vain to them.

5—8 The Failure of the Prophets—'Professional' **i** prophets were often associated with the principal sanctuaries. They were God's spokesmen and their function was to instruct and warn, to communicate the divine will to king and people. Since they were, in a sense, dependent on the king for bread and board, it was not easy for them to criticize royal policy and forecast national disaster as its outcome, cf §§ 451c, 452c and l (3) Kgs 22:1—28. The prophets were also consulted by people in difficulties who sought a divine answer to their problems. On such occasions, it was customary to bring an offering to the prophet (cf 1 Sm 9:7) and there was an ever present risk that a generous offering would guarantee a re-assuring response (cf Mi 3:5, 11). Truth can be a bitter medicine which the sick are unwilling to take and the half-hearted physician is unwilling to prescribe. The failure of these 'professional' prophets to prescribe the truth for the nation's ills merited the condemnation of those prophets who were specially called by God to make known his will without fear or favour, even at the risk of their lives (cf Am 7:12ff; Is 28:7; Jer 23:9ff etc). **5.** As long as they can eat their fill, they answer 'All is well'. But if anyone refuses them gifts, they denounce and threaten him. 'Peace': cf Jer 6:13f; 23:16f. **6.** 'night': the time when divine messages were often received (Nm 12:6; Dn 2:19 etc). What had been the time for communicating with God is now become a time of terror (cf Am 5:18—20). **7.** 'cover their lips'; as was required of lepers (Lv 13:45) and mourners (Ezek 24:17, 22). **8.** Micah's approach contrasts with the weakness of the 'professional' prophets. Equipped by the spirit of God with unflinching courage and a strong sense of justice, he preaches the unpalatable truth of Israel's sins. BJ and others treat 'with the spirit of Yahweh' as a gloss (cf Is 11:2ff). Its omission scarcely alters the sense, since the prophet's strength and justice come from Yahweh.

9—12 The Destruction of Jerusalem—The crimes of **j** the leaders and prophets have been noted (2—3, 5—7); they are now called on to hear their sentence. Their conduct brings disaster not merely to themselves but also to the Holy City and the Temple. This was blasphemy to the ears of those who, by their twisted logic, found security for their wrongdoing in the presence of Yahweh on Sion. It was as if he had become a morally indifferent, but nationally committed divinity, who would rejoice, **10**, at the growth of his city and ignore its being built with blood (3:2—3). **11.** The priests and 'professional' prophets were closely associated with the rulers, too closely to pass judgement on their conduct (cf Is 3:2). They accepted their warped ideals, perverting justice and truth for gain. 'is not . . .': It was a delusion to

566j rely on God the essentially holy, in order to sin with impunity. This same delusion blinded the leaders in the time of Jeremiah, cf Jer 5:12; 7; also Ezek 10 and 11:22—23 for the abandonment of the city by Yahweh. **12.** Failure in leadership would bring down the city and temple in ruins.

For a similar threat to the Temple, about 100 years later, priests and prophets demanded the death of Jeremiah (Jer 26). He was saved by the intervention of some elders who recalled the prophecy of Micah 3:12 (Jer 26:18), without however referring to the glorious future of Sion as described in 4:1—4. This is obviously relevant to a discussion of the origin of 4:1—4.

567a **4—5 Future Glories of Sion**—The text passes rapidly from the prospect of Sion's destruction to the picture of her future glory. Commentators take the view that this transition is not the work of the 8th cent. prophet but of writers in the exilic or early post-exilic periods, to whom they attribute most of the material in chh 4—5. Micah's prophecy of the destruction of Jerusalem in 3:12 invited the insertion of the corrective text, 4:1—5, surely one of the most beautiful passages in the OT, which opened the way for the addition of further texts predicting a better future. All are now agreed that 4:1—5 is a late text, but there is great difference of opinion as to how much of 4:6—5:15 belongs to Micah. Eissfeldt (*Introd. OT* 411) gives him only 5:10—14; BJ, 4:6—8, 9—10, 11—13; 5:1—5, 10—14; Deissler, 4:11; 5:1—5*a*, 6*b*, 10—14, while for Renaud, all the texts in chh 4—5 are late. Here Deissler's view is followed, except in regard to 5:5—6.

b **4:1—5 Yahweh Enthroned on Sion; the Nations of the Earth come to him**—The final vv of ch 3 forecast the destruction of Jerusalem and imply its abandonment by Yahweh. Vv 1—4 see Yahweh enthroned in a restored and more glorious Sion, dispensing knowledge and justice to the nations of a world· at peace who now worship the God of Israel on Sion. 1—4 are also found in Is 2:2—4, but they are not the work of either Micah or Isaiah. The setting of Sion on a lofty mountain (cf Ezek 40:2; Zech 14:10; Ps 48(47):2), the pilgrimage of the nations to Sion (Is 60; Zech 8:20ff; 14:16), the teaching of the nations by Yahweh (Is 51:4; 45:22) and the picture of idyllic peace (Zech 3:10; Jer 30:10; Ezek 34:28) are features of the post-exilic messianic outlook for which Sion became the centre and source of universal salvation. The development of such ideas at a time when Sion was in a lamentable state is a tribute to the faith of the people in Yahweh. Christians still await the fulfilment of this prophecy in the heavenly Jerusalem (cf Apoc 21:2, 10ff), where Christ has already been established as king (Apoc 14:1 etc). **1.** 'in the latter days': a stock phrase to describe the eschatological era, or end-time; it runs from the foundation of the Church to the end of the world. 'established'; implies permanence. **2.** Non-Jewish peoples will turn to Israel's God for guidance in ordering their lives. For Yahweh in the role of teacher, cf Ex 24:12; Ps 27 (26):11 etc. 'ways': the moral principles underlying God's decisions; effectively, for man, the ten commandments (cf Ex 24:12). 'the law'; the article is not in MT, and the word might more accurately be rendered 'instruction' (CV) or *teaching* (cf Ps 94 (93):12). **3—4.** Yahweh is the source of just decisions which will give peace among nations. **5.** A liturgical addition to 1—4 (cf Is 2:5). It relates 1—4 to the current experience of the worshipping community and gives them an opportunity of expressing their determination to be faithful to Yahweh, no matter what the nations may do.

6—8 Yahweh Re-assembles his Scattered Flock and **567** **Reigns in Sion**—The Babylonian captivity provides the setting for this text which gives promise of restoration to the scattered exiles (cf 2:12—13, a text which is inserted here by some commentators). The terms 'gather' (e.g. Jer 31:8), 'driven away' (e.g. Jer 23:3), 'afflicted' (e.g. Jer 31:28), 'lame' (Zeph 3:19), belong to the literature of the Exile. 'Remnant' is used to describe the restored, regenerated and active remnant, as e.g. in Zeph 2:7, 9, not the remnant of Is and Am, where the emphasis is on the fact of rescue and survival. The passage is dominated by the thought of Yahweh as Shepherd-Ruler of his people (cf Ezek 34). **6.** 'In that day': the day of divine decision, in this case, to restore his people. The exiles must wait on its coming, which is certain, but they cannot hasten it. **7.** When a worthy people is re-assembled, Yahweh will again be king in Sion. This relationship between the kingship of Yahweh and the restoration is also featured in Is 52:7 and, in an eschatological context, in Is 24:23. The link with the 'Yahweh reigns' Psalms (93 (92):1, 96 (95):10; 99 (98):1) should also be noted. cf § 381*m*. **8.** 'Tower of the flock': a symbolic name for Jerusalem; it conveys the security which derives from the presence of Yahweh, watching over his flock (Zech 10:3). 'former dominion': the royal power and dignity of the Davidic ruler will be restored to the city now bereft of a king.

9—10 The Exile, a Painful Birth; a Happy Out- **d** **come**—The reference to Babylon in v 10 links these vv with the Exile, and 'woman in travail' recalls Jeremiah's frequent use of this theme to describe the anguish of Jerusalem (Jer 4:31; 6:24 etc). The events of 597 B.C. or 587 B.C. may well provide the background to this text. Some commentators, however, regard the mention of Babylon as a later addition, and relate the text to the Assyrian threat of the last years of the 8th cent. B.C. **9.** 'no king . . . counsellor': the question implies an answer to the effect that there is a king and counsellor, but the situation is so critical that the king is helpless. This view of the situation is confirmed in v 10. **10.** Exile is to be the immediate outcome of this crisis, but it is not the end. Israel must suffer and be humbled before she is raised up. God's covenant love and mercy will prevail over the demands of his justice. The positive value of suffering underlies this message of hope.

11—13 The Illusory Triumph of the Nations—v 11 **e** could well describe the siege of Jerusalem in 701 B.C. (cf Is 29:1ff), and 12 reflects the thinking of Mi 2:3 and Is 10:5—15, but the language of 12—13, and the content of 13 belong to a later time, and have a distinctly eschatological tone. The strong nationalism of v 13 is characteristic of later apocalyptic literature. **11.** 'gaze upon': i.e. with malicious joy at her misfortune (cf Obad 13). **12.** 'thoughts of the Lord': a common phrase in Jer, cf 49:20; 50:45. For the thought, cf Is 55:8. **13.** 'Arise'; an invitation to Jerusalem to rise from the inactivity and helplessness of the Exile (cf Is 51:17; 52:2; 60:1). 'iron . . . bronze' cf Dn 7:19 etc. Is 41:15 uses a similar figure to describe Israel's crushing victory. 'gain . . . wealth': booty was frequently consecrated to Yahweh, cf Jos. 6:24; Lv 27:28. This v, however, is most closely related to Hag 2:7ff. 'Lord of the whole earth': a post-exilic title of Yahweh (cf Zech 4:14; 6:5). **5:1—4 (MT 14—5:3) The Ruler from Bethlehem** **f** **Brings Peace**—Although 1*a* is obscure, the whole v leaves no doubt that a time of crisis has found Israel helpless; she is forced to accept insults offered to her king. But the situation is not without hope and Micah foretells

67f the rise of a ruler whose features resemble those of the messianic king drawn by Isaiah, his contemporary. At a time when their leaders had failed them, each refers to the dawn of a new era which will open with the birth of a son of David's clan (cf Is 9:6—7); in each, the royal mother is mentioned (cf Is 7:14); in each, the work of the promised ruler involves the restoration of his people (cf Is 7:3; 9:1—7 RSV), and culminates in universal peace (cf Is 9:6—7). The foreshortening involved in the prophetic vision of messianic times precludes any clear indication of when this ruler will appear.

g **1.** 'siege': of Jerusalem by Sennacherib in 701 B.C. 'strike . . . cheek': cf Jb 16:10. The Assyrian leaders treated the king and his advisers with contempt (Is 36). 'ruler': literally, 'judge'. The word refers to the king and may have been chosen only for its assonance in Heb. with 'road' (*šôpēt—šēbet*). In view of 3:11, however, there may be a measure of condemnation in the choice of the word. The insult was more or less deserved (2 Sm 7:14) and confirmed the need for a new ruler whose judgements would reflect the justice of Yahweh (cf 4:3). **2.** 'Ephrathah': Ephrath, originally the name of a clan in Bethlehem to which Jesse the father of David belonged (1 Sm 17:12), was sometimes used as the name for Bethlehem (Gn 35:19; 48:7). Bethlehem may have been added here as an explanatory gloss on the name Ephrathah (cf Gn 35:19), which is clearly the antecedent to 'who' (cf 'among the clans') The insignificance of the clan Ephrathah and the limitations of Bethlehem contrast with the power and splendour of Jerusalem. Yet the capital city would fall and peace would come from the shepherd background of David's native town (cf 1 Sm 16:11 and Mi 5:4; 1 Cor 1:27; 2 Cor 12:9). 'ruler': Jer 30:21 also uses this word, not 'king', in a messianic context. 'King' may have been discredited by recent experience of the monarchy. 'from of old': a reference to the origin of the Davidic dynasty 300 years earlier (cf 1 Sm 16). The evangelists (Mt 2:6; Jn 7:42) found in this v a clear statement concerning the birthplace of the Messiah.

h **3.** Those who assign this passage to the exilic period or later (e.g. Renaud) understand this v in terms of 4:9—10 (see note); the Jewish community (4:10: 'daughter of Sion') would, in some sense, give birth to the Messiah through the pangs of oppression (cf Is 66:7—9). This view would open the way for a consideration of Mary, the eschatological daughter of Sion, as Mother of the Messiah and Mother of the Church (cf R. Laurentin, *Structure littéraire et théologique de Luc I—II*, 1957, 152—62). The majority of commentators, however, see a reference to Is 7:14 and the mother of Immanuel. Through the birth of her child she brings to an end a period of distress, and by giving birth to the Prince of Peace (Is 9:6; Mi 5:4), she is most intimately associated with his work. 'them': the Israelites destined for punishment. 'rest . . . return': either: the survivors, the 'remnant' (Is 7:3), will return from exile to form the nucleus of the messianic people under the messianic king, or: the breach between the N and S Kingdoms will be healed in messianic times (cf Ezek 47:13ff). **4.** The ruler takes his stand to guard his kingdom as a shepherd guards and feeds his flock. It is because he is equipped with the strength of God that his reign brings security and success (cf Is 9:6; 11:1ff; 1 Sm 2:10).

i **5—6 (MT 4—5) The Self-Assurance of Judah**—As it stands in the RSV, this text expresses the confidence of the people of Judah and Jerusalem in their own ability to deal with the Assyrian threat. It contrasts with 5:4, where the success of the messianic king derives from God. BJ, Deissler and others re-arrange the text in the order:

4, 5a, 6b, 5b, 6a to give: '. . . to the ends of the earth. **567i** And he shall be peace, and he shall deliver us from Assyria when he comes into our land and treads within our border. When the Assyrian etc . . . drawn sword'. In this arrangement, 5a and 6b are linked with 1—4, while 5b and 6a belong to the present section. **5.** 'raise': the raising up of princes was usually an action of Yahweh (cf Jer 23:4; Ezek 34:23). 'seven . . . eight': an indefinite but adequate number (Eccl 11:2). **6.** Such success will accompany their efforts that they will carry the offensive into enemy territory.

7—9 (MT 6—8) The Remnant among the Nations— **j** Under Yahweh's guidance, the remnant will achieve a position of supremacy among the nations. **7.** 'in the midst of many peoples': Although this phrase made its appearance at the time of the Exile, when Israel was literally scattered among the nations, its use in Ezek 5:5—and here—is intended to set Israel at the centre of the world (cf Ezek 38:12). It is to this centre that the nations of the earth shall turn (cf 4:1ff). 'Tarry not . . . nor wait': dew and rain are not subject to man's control, but God's (cf Jer 14:22; Jb 38:28). The survival and subsequent development of the remnant is the work of God. **8.** Israel is promised victory over her enemies (for 'lion': cf Nm 23:24; 24:8). The figure of the lion is linked with the 'dew' of 7 through 2 Sm 17:12 where a silent, sudden and devastating attack is compared to the falling dew. For the 'Lion of Judah', cf Apoc 5:5. **9.** 'Your': singular. The change of person and number suggests that this is an addition to vv 7—8.

10—15 (MT 9—14) Israel and the Nations Must Rely k on Yahweh—The message for Israel is implicit in vv 10—14 in which Yahweh rejects the aids and supports on which Israel so often relied instead of on Yahweh. There is no reason why these vv should not be attributed to Micah. v 15, a later addition, applies the message explicitly to the nations. **10.** Cf Is 2:7; 33:1f; Hos 1:7 etc. **11.** Cf Jer 5:17. **12.** Although sorcery (Ex 22:18) and soothsaying (Lv 19:26) were forbidden, they seem to have flourished in Israel (cf Is 47:9; Jer 27:9; Is 2:6 etc). **13.** 'pillars': emblems of male fertility gods. **14.** 'Asherim': either stakes of some kind or trees which were symbols of the female fertility divinities. **15.** The theme of divine vengeance is common among the prophets (e.g. Na 1:2; Jer 46:10) and is given great prominence in later apocalyptic writing (Zech 14:17—19; Apoc 14:10; 16:19).

6:1—7:7 Israel on Trial: Accusations and Condem- l nation—As in the opening chh, the prophet casts his message in the form of a trial (cf 1:2ff). 1—2 set the scene; 3—5 draw attention to Yahweh's favours and, by implication, deplore Israel's response. 6—7: sensing the condemnation which must follow, the people ask through a spokesman how God may be placated and are reminded of their covenant duties (8). In 9—16, specific accusations are made (10—12; 16a) and are immediately followed by condemnation and punishment (13—15; 16b). In 7:1—7, the prophet testifies in the form of a lament (1—6) and re-affirms his faith and hope in Yahweh (7).

1—2. 'mountains': they can be witnesses of the **m** proceedings for all time, cf Gn 49:26. Similarly 'enduring foundations', and 'heavens and earth' in Is 1:2. 'controversy': cf Hos 4:1; 12:3, 'contend': in Heb., the same word as 'reason' in Is 1:18; it may imply the possibility of a hopeful outcome.

3—5. God has never burdened the people with costly **n** sacrifices; on the contrary, he has poured untold blessings on them. **3.** The questions could be completed with the words: 'that you treat me so'. This v is put on the lips

567n of the Crucified Christ in the liturgy of Good Friday; it is the gentle protest, made without resentment, of the unrequited love of an infinitely loving God (cf Is 5:4; Jer 2:31f). 'my people': implies the covenant relationship; cf Hos 2:23; Ex 20:2; Lv 26:12. **4.** As in Amos (2:9f; 3:1) and Hosea (2:17; 11:1; 12:14), the deliverance from Egypt and the covenant rank first among the favours of Yahweh. This is the only passage in the prophets to mention Aaron and Miriam. **5.** Balaam's curse was turned to a blessing (Nm 22—24). 'Shittim to Gilgal': covers the events in Jos. 3—5. 'saving acts': lit, 'justices'.

o **6—8.** These vv are cast in the form of a torah liturgy, cf Pss 15(14); 24(23):3ff and commentary. **6—7.** Ask whether God can be placated by gifts and sacrifices of the most extravagant kind, which Israel, it seems, was prepared to offer. 'first born': shows how far Israel was ready to go in this direction of ritual satisfaction (for human sacrifice cf Gn 22; Dt 12:31; 1 (3) Kgs 16:34). **8.** But something quite different was required: the practice of justice, brotherly love and humility. It was on these virtues that man's relationship with God must be based, not merely on the performance of ritual (cf Am 5:21—24; Hos 6:6; Is 1:12ff; Ps 50 (49):7ff and Mt 5:23—24).

p **9—16 Yahweh testifies and condemns—10—11.** For similar acts of fraud, cf Am 8:14 and Dt 25:13—14. **12.** BJ and Deissler retain the Heb. text (cf note in RSV) and read this v after v 9. Violence, fraud and deceit will be punished by deprivation and famine as described in 13—16. **16.** For the sins and deceits of Omri and Ahab cf 1 (3) Kgs 16ff. Although significant politically, these kings were disastrous for Yahwism.

q **7:1—7 The Prophet testifies**—The prophet bears witness in a lament for the moral decadence of his people. He too gives warning of approaching chastisement (4b). **1.** No fruit of good works is to be found in spite of the prophet's preaching (cf Jer 8:13). **2a.** Cf Lk 18:8. **2b—3.** Characteristic accusations of the prophets, cf Mi 3:2, 9—11; Hos 4:2; Is 1:15 etc. **4a.** Cf 2 Sm 23:6—7, a text which draws attention to the 'prickly' character of the wicked as well as to their ultimate end. **4b.** 'watchmen': the prophets, cf v 7 ('look to' is the same Heb. verb), and Hb 2:1. **5—6.** Describe the breakdwon of civil and family life, cf Mt 10:36. **7.** In spite of the personal sorrow involved in fruitless preaching (v 1), Micah retains his faith in Yahweh from whom he hopes for better things.

r **7:8—20**—This section is marked by features which are characteristic of psalm literature. It may reflect the different phases of a liturgy in which vv 8—10 give expression to confidence in ultimate deliverance. 11—13 **567** could be an oracle spoken by the prophet or priest in answer to the prayer of the personified community. 14—17 are a prayer of petition for victory over the nations. 18—20 concludes the psalm with praise of Yahweh and motives for unfaltering trust. Cf § 381j. If vv 8—20 are treated as a literary unit, it can scarcely be earlier than the fall of Jerusalem (cf v 11), and belongs most probably to the Persian period (cf also v 8). Not all commentators, however, regard this section as a literary unit. Eissfeldt (*Introd. OT* 411—12) is almost alone in admitting the possibility of Micah's authorship for these vv, although he does point out the links with Jer 30—31.

8—10 Sion's Confidence in Yahweh—8. 'enemy': either Edom (Is 34:5; Obad 10ff; Ps 137 (136):7) or Babylon (Ps 137 (136):1ff); if this is an 8th cent. piece, the enemy is Assyria. 'I': Sion, which is here representative of the people as a whole. **9.** Cf Ps 41 (40):4; 51 (50):4. **10.** The dramatic change in Sion's position will give the lie to the unbelievers' mocking question and their roles will be reversed (cf v 8).

11—13 Oracle: Restoration of Sion—11. For the re- **s** building of the walls of Jerusalem after the Exile, cf Neh 2—4; Ps 102 (101):13ff; 147 (146):2. Since the eschatological Sion will act as host to the nations (cf v 12; 4:1ff), the city boundaries must be extended. **12.** 'they': not merely the returning exiles, but Jews and convert Gentiles who will come in pilgrimage to Sion (cf Zech 8:20ff; 14:16ff; Is 60:1ff). **13.** Cf 5:15.

14—17 Petition for Victory—14. For Yahweh as **t** shepherd, cf 2:12; Ezek 34; Ps 23 (22). 'alone': although they dwell in a land of luxuriant vegetation, they do not share in its fruits,—a figurative description of the poverty of the returned exiles. 'Bashan and Gilead': in Transjordan, renowned for their abundant pastures and consequently for their cattle (cf Jer 50:19 etc). 'days of old': Bashan and Gilead were among the districts first captured by the Israelites, cf Dt 3:10, 13 etc. **15.** 'I will show them': read: '*show us*' (BJ and others). **16.** 'lay etc': a gesture of astonishment, cf Prv 30:32; Jb 21:5. 'deaf': either: from Yahweh's thunder (cf Jb 26:14), or: stunned by the course of events. **17.** 'lick the dust': cf Gn 3:14.

18—20 Praise and Grounds for Trust—For the theme **u** of the mercy of God towards sinners, cf Ex 34:6—7; Ps 86 (85):5, 15 etc. God 's mercy derives from the love he has pledged in the covenant to which he is eternally faithful, a re-assuring note on which to end a book which had much to say about the sins of Israel.

NAHUM

BY S. BULLOUGH O.P.

568a Bibliography—St Jerome, Pl 25, 1231—72; Van Hoonacker, EtB, 1908, A. Halden, *Studies in the Book of Nahum*, 1947; S. M. Lehrman, in *The Twelve Prophets*, ed. A. Cohen, 1961; J. P. Hyatt in PC 1962².

b The Prophet—All we know is that he was an 'Elkoshite'. The place is unknown in OT, but there are three main theories of the identification of Nahum's home.

(1) *Alqush*, about 24 m. N of Nineveh, where Nahum's tomb is still shown, and is a place of pilgrimage for Christians, Mohammedans and Jews. There is, however, no evidence of this tradition before the 16th cent., and although a birthplace near Nineveh might seem to be supported by Nahum's apparently accurate topography of that city, 2:6 (7), and his graphic account of its calamity, it is more probable that this identification was made later on account of his prophecy. (2) *Elcesi*, a village in Galilee, was proposed by Jer (prologue). He writes of 'usque hodie in Galilaea viculus, parvus quidem et vix ruinis veterum aedificiorum indicans vestigia; sed tamen Judaeis, et mihi quoque a circumducente monstratus'. Perhaps = modern el-Kause near Ramah in Galilee (WV, xxiv). Although Carmel and Lebanon are named in 1:4, a Galilean village is unlikely at the time of Nahum, whose interest furthermore centres on Judah, 1:15 (2:1) and 2.2 (3). (3) *Elqush* 'beyond Bêth-gabrê of the tribe of Simeon' is the solution given in *The Lives of the Prophets* attributed (doubtfully) to Epiphanius, a native of Judea (403) (PG 43, 409 reconstructed text). Bêth-gabrê probably = the modern Beit-Jibrin (Eleutheropolis), 20 m. SW of Jerusalem; about 6 m. E of this village there is a well called Bir-el-Qaus (Driver). This is the most likely identification. The prophet's name *Nahûm* means 'comfort', an expanded form being 'Nehemiah'.

c The Date of the Prophecy—The mention of the fall of Thebes (No-Amon; in Egypt) as a past example, in 3:8—10, gives us 663 B.C. as a *terminus a quo*, while the fall of Nineveh in 612, described as impending, gives us a *terminus ad quem*. But the period may be further narrowed by the consideration that Nahum alone among the prophets has no word of vituperation for the Jews, which may indicate the period after 622 when Josiah's reforms were in full vigour: his only word to Judah, 1:15 (2:1), is an exhortation to the observance of festivals; cf 2 (4) Kgs 23:21. Nahum's prophecy may have been occasioned by the beginning of Assyria's collapse with the fall of Asshur, 50 m. S of Nineveh, to the Medes under Kyaxares in 614. A date in this period would make Na little later than Zeph, contemporary with Jer and a little earlier than Hb.

d The Problem of the Acrostic Poem—Several of the Pss, Lam and Prv 31:10—31 are constructed as an alphabetical acrostic, each v or section beginning with a new letter. It has been observed that Na 1 contains traces of a similar construction, and since Bickell in 1880 various attempts have been made to reconstruct the text on the basis of the whole alphabet. As it stands,

the Heb. text from 1:2 to 1:9 provides an acrostic (with **568d** certain lacunae) of the first half of the alphabet. After 1:9 the provision of an acrostic requires considerable alteration of the text and shuffling of lines. On these suppositions the opening poem reaches to 2:2 (3), excluding 2:1 (2). (Note that in LXX, Vg and English Bibles 1:15 = HT 2:1, with consequent different verse-numbers in ch 2; Heb. vv are placed in brackets in this commentary.) An example of a complete acrostic reconstruction is to be found in Van H. Authors are, however, divided, and the difficulty is that the acrostic in 1:2—9 is so convincing that it is hard to ignore it, while the evidence after this is so vague that it is hard to admit it. It is generally supposed that the section 1:2—2:2 (3) represents either a complete acrostic poem, or else part of one followed by another non-acrostic fragment, the whole being prefixed to the prophecy on Nineveh by way of introduction. Authors are also divided about whether the introductory poem or poems are by Nahum himself, or by another, but there is no direct evidence against his authorship, and it seems most likely that he himself made use of relevant sections of other poems of his own to serve as an introduction to his main prophecy. Indeed Nahum's vivid style seems to run through the whole book.

Theme and Analysis of the Book—On the above basis **e** 1:2—15 with 2:2 (1:2—14 with 2:1, 3) are the introductory poem or poems, the theme of which is the power of God and consolation of Judah. The main prophecy begins at 2:1 (2), excludes the misplaced 2:2 (3), and continues to the end of the book. The theme is the fate of Nineveh, the oppressor.

The Style is highly coloured and poetical, representing **f** some of the most vigorous poetry in Heb. literature, making use not so much of rare words as of unexpected forms, especially of verbs. The metre is often excited and irregular, and the ring of the words, to which we call attention occasionally in the commentary, is by no means entirely obscured in translation.

1:1 The Title Elkosh: cf 568*b* **569a**

2—15, 2:2 (2—14, 2:1, 3) The Introductory Poem(s): b a description of God's power.

2—6 The Lord is mighty—2. This v begins with *aleph* ('*Ēl*), starting the acrostic. 'Jealous', a word which with its by-form is used only of God: Knox well translates 'a jealous lover'. *The Bible in Basic English* (1949) has 'who takes care of his honour'. **5.** 'The earth is laid waste', MT *tiśśā* 'is lifted up', so RV 'upheaved'. **6.** 'are broken asunder', reading *nisṣᵉtù*.

7. The Lord is good to those that trust him, '*a refuge*' **c** in the day of trouble.

8—11 The Lord is Severe—8. 'his adversaries', MT **d** 'her place'; LXX 'rebels' suggests Heb. *bᵉqâmâw*, therefore 'those who rise up against him' cf Ps 18 (17):49. **9.** 'You'—God's enemies in general: the poem has no particular application. 'Not take vengeance twice': once is enough to annihilate them. **10.** From the Vg reading 'like (*kᵉ*) thorns', and *kôh*, 'so', we can reconstruct, '*For as tangled thorns* [which burn easily], *so at their drink* [*kôh*

569d $b^e sob'\bar{a}m$] the drunk have been consumed'. **11.** 'and counselled villainy': HT 'Counsellor of Belial (= worthlessness)'; cf 1:15.

e **12–15, 2:2** (12–14, 2:1, 3) **The Second Introductory Poem (or second part of the one): the Consolation of Judah**—The analysis is difficult and the text uncertain: 13, 14, 15 (2:1), 2:1 (2), 2 (3) seem to be addressed alternately to Judah and to the oppressor. 2:1 (2) (to the oppressor) begins the main prophecy, and it is usually supposed that 2:2 (3) (to Judah) should follow upon 1:13, or 1:15 (2:1). The following is an analysis fairly generally held (Van H.): 1:12–13 and 2:2 (3), the consolation of Judah through her deliverance from the oppressor. 1:14, oracle against the oppressor. 1:15 (2:1), the promise to Judah of peace. It may be that 14 and 15 are fragments of another poem altogether, used by Nahum to conclude his introduction on a hopeful note. **12.** Difficult: LXX is very **f** different and the whole passage is doubtful. **14.** WV alters to the 3rd person, 'concerning him' (the oppressor), which eases the transition from the previous v, if this v is **g** indeed part of the same poem. **15** (2:1). An Isaian figure (52:7), with the exhortation to Judah that suggest the period of reform. 'wicked' 'Belial', usu. an abstract noun 'worthlessness' as in 11, and very rarely, as here, applied to a particular person (cf 2 Sm 23:6 and perhaps Jb 34:18); Basic OT, well, 'the good-for-nothing man'. The reference is of course to the detested officials of the Assyrian army of occupation, who now will no more be seen in the land.

h **2–3 The Main Prophecy.**
2:1–6 (2–7) **The Attack on Nineveh—1** (2). 'The shatterer', lit 'the scatterer' in MT and Vg. To revocalize as $mapp\bar{e}s$, 'shatterer' (cf Jer 51:20, and the verb nine times in 51:21–23) is perhaps more expressive. 'Man the ramparts' etc: a series of ironic commands to the now hapless oppressor. **3.** (4). 'The shield . . . is red'—either by the sun (WV, cf 1 Mc 6:39), or being of copper, or painted. 'Scarlet', the colour of the military cloak (cf Mt 27:28 and Xenophon, *Cyrop.* 6, 4, 1) and of more recent soldiers' uniforms. 'flame': $lapp\bar{\imath}d\hat{o}t$, 'torches', though admittedly the word occurs in the next v. 'Chargers' reading $p\bar{a}r\bar{a}s\hat{\imath}m$ for MT $b^e r\hat{o}s\hat{\imath}m$, 'fir trees = (?) 'spears' (RV), 'prance', lit 'reel' as of a drunken man, and so '*act wildly*'. **4** (5). A typical Nahum v with its colourful verb-forms. **5** (6). 'are summoned': the v refers either to the desperate defenders, whose confusion makes them 'stumble', who man the walls and prepare a 'mantelet' (a word found only here, presumably part of the fortifications); or else to the Babylonian attackers, who 'disappear among the embankments', attack the walls and prepare the 'mantelet' or shelter for those who work the battering-ram. **6** (7). 'The river gates' = MT lit, indicate either (1) 'river sluices' (WV), letting in the water—and cf references to the flooding of Nineveh at its fall in Ctesias and Diodorus Siculus (see Van H.), or (2) 'moat-sluices', emptying them—and remains of dams and sluices are still visible, or (3) gates where the river Khusur or the canal passed through the city—vulnerable points, or (4) 'bridge-gates'. Probably the reference to flooding is the most likely, esp. in connexion with the figure in 8 (9).
i **7–10** (8–11) **The Sack of the City—9** (10). 'Plunder' etc: the cries of the invaders are imagined. 'precious', MT $k\bar{a}b\hat{o}d$, is not represented in Vg and may be a corrupt copy of the preceding or following word. This v finds a striking parallel in line 45 of the Babylonian tablet, now in the British Museum, commemorating the fall of Nineveh (publ. 1923 by C. J. Gadd).
j **10** (11). Again typical of Nahum's vigorous Hebrew.
k **11–13** (12–14), **3:1 The Lions' Den is destroyed—13**

(14). 'Your chariots': we expect the lion figure to **569l** continue and could read with Davidson and Driver $sib^e k\bar{e}k$ or $subb^e k\bar{e}k$, '*thy thicket*', used in Jer 4:7 of the abode of a lion. 'Your messengers', once more the occupying power. **3:1.** The wicked city is still seen as a lions' den, full of 'plunder'—the same word as 'prey' in 12 (13) above.

3:2–7 The Disgrace of the Harlot—The fate of the **l** city is now described under a new figure. **2–3.** Are particularly colourful examples of Nahum's excited style.
8–10 The Warning of the Fate of No-Amon—8. This **m** was the city in Egypt, near the modern Karnak, known to the Greeks as Thebes. Amon was the god in whose honour its great temple was built. No = Egyptian *net*, 'city', so sometimes merely called 'No' as in Jer 46:25; Ezek 30:14ff. In Ezek 30:15 occurs the famous pun on the god's name, $h^a m\hat{o}n N\hat{o}$, 'the *multitude* of No', which gave rise in rabbinic tradition to the identification here of Amon and 'multitude', whence Vg 'populorum' and AV 'populous No'. Jerome, writing 'Alexandria', is conscious of the anachronism and explains that he is merely giving the modern name—though the identification happens to be wrong. 'The Nile' lit 'the rivers', the proper word for the Nile (on which Thebes is situated), and referring to the many branches and canals. 'Sea', the vastness of the Nile. 'Water her wall', reading *mayim*, which is better than MT *miyyām*, 'from the sea is its wall'. **9.** Ethiopia (Cush, S of Egypt), Egypt itself . . . Put (Africa) and the Libyans. Put is always translated 'Libya' in the versions, except here, where the Libyans (*Lûbîm*) are also named. **10.** We cannot but remark once more on Nahum's sturdy-sounding verb-form here. No-Amon (Thebes) was captured by the Assyrian Ashurbanipa in 663, and this completed for the time the subjugation of Egypt begun about ten years previously by his father Esarhaddon. The disaster, though some 40 years before Nahum's prophecy, was evidently still fresh in men's memories.
11–19 Final Apostrophe to Assyria—11. 'Be dazed', **n** a word usually meaning 'hidden' and of doubtful meaning here. **13.** 'The gates', i.e. the mountain passes forming entrances to the land, cf e.g. the 'Cilician Gate'. **14.** Ironic commands to fortify the city; cf 2:1(2). Clay was kneaded with the feet. Excavations, e.g. those near Nineveh itself in 1935, show the use of sun-dried mud-bricks, as well as of fired clay-bricks (see Bévenot in WV).

15–16. But the fortifications will be of no avail, for **o** 'There will the fire devour you, . . . *young locust devour you*'—this last reading involves the omission of *kaph* before the locust, and a masc. verb. The young locust (*yeleq* 'bruchus'), before it can fly, is the most destructive; ravaging the land it becomes a mature insect (*'arbeh*), strips off its wing-sheaths and flies away. So far the locust is the scourge of Nineveh. Now, with sarcastic imperatives, it is symbol of what Nineveh might be: now if you will, 'Multiply yourselves like the locust' etc. All thy mercantile glory is of a sudden disappeared, as a swarm of locusts that has taken to flight. **17.** 'princes', 'scribes', two Assyrian **p** titles of uncertain meaning, probably connected with Assyrian roots of these meanings. The second is found only here and in a by-form in Jer 51:27 (Vg Taphsar), but has nothing to do with *tap* 'children' as Vg here. All will be lost like a swarm of locusts: merchants soldiery, scholars. 'Clouds of locusts', lit 'locusts of locusts', the same word spelt differently in Heb., the second form being found besides only in Am 7:1, and being probably no more than a correction of the first, not found elsewhere. **19.** Lit '*There is no dimming of* your hurt', an unusual phrase, the noun occurring here only, though from a root of established meaning.

HABAKKUK

BY S. BULLOUGH O.P.

570a Bibliography—Jerome, PL 25, 1273—338; Van Hoonacker, EtB, 1908; Millar Burrows, *The Dead Sea Scrolls of St Mark's Monastery*, vol 1, New Haven, 1951; Theodore H. Gaster, *The Scriptures of the Dead Sea Sect*, 1957; S. M. Lehrman, in *The Twelve Minor Prophets*, ed. A. Cohen, 1961; J. P. Hyatt, PC (2) 1962.

b About the **Prophet himself** we know nothing. He may, or may not, be identified with the prophet Habakkuk in Judah who in Dn 14:32—38 was miraculously transported to the lions' den in Babylon. Chronologically it is possible, though the king in Dn is unnamed and so the story undated. Pseudo-Epiphanius' *Lives of the Prophets* puts Habakkuk's birthplace at Bethzocher, which may be the same as Bethzacharam in 1 Mc 6:32f, the modern Beit-Sakariyeh not far from Bethlehem and the traditional 'Hill of Habakkuk' (cf on 2:1). The Prophet's name in Heb. *Ḥᵃbaqqûq*, is of peculiar form and uncertain meaning.

c The **Divisions** of the book are clearly marked. The first part, 1.2—2:4, is cast in dramatic form, being a dialogue between the prophet and God. There follow the 'Woes of the Wicked', 2:5—20, and lastly the Canticle, ch 3.

d The **Theme and Manner** of Hb are quite his own. He is deeply preoccupied with the age-old problem of injustice on earth and God's apparent inactivity. A definite rhythm of thought runs through the whole book. At first there is the dialogue in which the problem is stated, and on the answer coming from God that he will indeed intervene, the problem is pushed a stage further with the consideration of the wickedness of him whom God sends to punish the evil. Habakkuk has a manner of soliloquizing—in 1:14—17 he broods over the iniquities of the coming invader, and in 2:1 he speaks to himself. The argument culminates in God's reassurance that, come what may, it is the faithfulness of the just man that will count in the end, 2:4; this is the passage that is quoted three times by St Paul. In the next section, the 'Woes', the prophet once more turns to reflect upon men's wickedness, and he formally stigmatizes certain sins. Finally, in the Canticle we find Habakkuk's thought still running to the same rhythm, though here presented in lyric form: the prophet again asks God to come, 3:2, and then describes the might of his power, 3:3—11; he considers his terrible judgement, 3:12—15, and confesses his own terror, 3:16—17, but in the end, as before, he feels reassured that trust in God, come what may, will bring consolation.

e The **Date of the Prophecy**—Habakkuk's argument is so perennial that it fits every age, not least our own. The reference, however, to the Chaldaeans (Babylonians) places it at a time of their ascendancy, but evidently before their invasion of Palestine. It was the victory of the Babylonians at Carchemish, under Nebuchadnezzar in 605 that made them masters of Western Asia. It was not long, before Nebuchadnezzar invaded Palestine and King Jehoiakim 'became his servant three years', 2 (4) Kgs 24:1, which cannot have been later than 602—599 (the

latter's death). We can therefore suppose Habakkuk to **570e** have prophesied between the years 605 and 602. This is further borne out by the fact that since Josiah's death in 609 his religious reforms had been set aside and his successors Jehoahaz and Jehoiakim both 'did evil in the sight of the Lord', 2 (4) Kgs 23:32, 37, and Habakkuk's words in 1:2—4 and 2:5—19 certainly reflect the unhealthy moral condition of those reigns.

Suggestions, however, have not been wanting, which place the prophecy later, during the exile (the prophet's name is claimed as a Babylonian type), or even as late as the time of Alexander, though the moral reflexions are by most regarded as early. The Canticle is frequently held to be late, especially by those writers who regard the psalms to be mostly of late post-exilic composition.

The **Qumrân Scroll** (1QpHab) is a commentary woven **f** round the text of Hb, showing a few interesting variants. The 'psalm' of Hb (ch 3) is not included, but we cannot infer from this that it was not known to Qumrân. It had only not the same relevance for their purpose. For Qumrân, Hb's theme of the *Torah*, the 'law', becoming 'numb' (1:4), and of the growth of injustice in the world (1:2—4), is applicable to those who betray the *Torah* by opposing the 'rightful teacher' (of their own party) and in particular to the wicked priests' (of Jerusalem, ix, 4) (e.g. i, 11—13; ii, 1—8; vii, 4, viii, 8 etc), and because of this the Chaldeans, who are idolaters (1:16), will come and destroy; and these are identified with the 'Kittiim' (=? the Romans).

1:1 The Title—'The prophet': only Hb, Hag and Zech **571a** receive this formal title in the heading.

1:2—2:4 The Dialogue. **b**

2—4 The Prophet speaks, uttering his complaint that there is strife and injustice in the world, while God remains silent. **3.** Vg and, still more, LXX have a better disposition of the phrases than MT. 'Arise', from *nāśā'*, must be read in the Niph'al—the Qal is never intransitive.

5—11 God's Answer—He will intervene, eventually. **c** His intervention came with the Babylonian invasions. **5.** 'Look among the nations' appears in LXX as 'Look, you despisers', with the same word as in v 13 for Heb. *bôḡᵉdîm* ('faithless men') Qumrân in their commentary (ii, 1) imply this reading here: 'Look, you faithless men'. This v is quoted from LXX in Ac 13:41 with reference to Christ. **6.** Chaldeans, *Kaśdîm*, or Babylonians. **8.** 'press on': the word *pāśû*, of doubtful meaning, should be omitted as a doublet of *pārāśāw*, 'his horsemen'. The repetition of this word is probably also a doublet, so that we proceed at one 'They come from afar . . .' (cf the neat rendering of Basic OT). **9.** 'Terror of them **d** goes before them' is doubtful: for 'before them' Vg has 'a hot wind': so Qumrân 'an east wind'. **11.** 'Guilty men' (*wᵉʾāśēm*) is doubtful: Qumrân reads (iv, 9) 'And he sets (*wᵉyāśem*) this, his strength, as his god' (Gaster reads as 'devastates'); and Bévenot in WV had already suggested 'And sets up his altar to his god',

571d which is the most satisfactory, esp. now in view of Qumrân.

e **12–13 The Prophet speaks again**, explaining further his concern: indeed the Lord will intervene, but what of the injustice of the appointed scourge itself? **12a**. 'We shall not die' = MT and all older versions, but this is one of the 18 *Tiqqûnê Sôp̱erîm* or Corrections of the Scribes, included in the Massoretic notes, where the text was deliberately altered to avoid an apparent irreverence. The supposed original here was '*Thou shalt not die*', altered to avoid the suggestion of such a possibility. This is probably the true reading, and is followed by WV, Basic and many moderns. **12b**. 'And thou, o Rock, hast established him for chastisement' supposes God addressed as 'Rock' (as often); but the syntax is strained, and it is more likely to refer to the appointed scourge: 'as a rock is his chastiser . . .': so Qumrân, and cf BJ. **13**. The clumsy last word in MT is omitted by LXX, probably rightly, reading 'when the wicked swallows up *the just*' (WV).

f **14–17 The Prophet's Reflections** on the ruthlessness of the coming scourge. **14**. '*He will* make men like the fishes': 'he' is the wicked of 13, and is surely to be read here (with WV and Basic), since the fishing figure continues in 15–17 in the 3rd person. The words for the fishing tackle are all rare, but their meaning is obvious from the context. **16**. He deifies his weapons (cf 11 if the text is there right); Driver notices that according to Herodotus 4, 62 (rather than 59–60) the Scythians were wont to offer sacrifice to a scimitar as a symbol of Ares.

g **2:1 The Prophet's Soliloquy**—'Watch' from root 'to guard'; and 'tower' either = fortified place or = watch-tower from another root 'to guard'. Bévenot says that the traditional 'Hill of Habakkuk', about 3 m. S of Jerusalem, not far from Bethlehem, is a magnificent vantage-point, WV, xxv and 33. '*what answer he (yās̆îb̲ for 'as̆îb̲) will return to my argument*' is given by the Syr., and is followed by Van H., WV, and BJ, and is preferable to MT, LXX and Vg.

h **2–4 God's Answer**—**2**. The prophet is to write the message plainly, 'that he may run who reads it', that it may be read quickly and easily. Hence the well-known saying. **3**. It is not certain what 'vision' is referred to. It may be (1) the oracle of 4 (the most likely), or (2) the theophany of ch 3, or (3) the fulfilment of the threats in 1:5–11, or (4) the Messianic triumph at the end of time. 'Apparebit in finem, et non mentietur: si moram fecerit, expecta eum, quia veniens veniet' is used of the coming of Christ in the Advent liturgy, and similarly 'Qui venturus est veniet, et non tardabit'. The latter passage is quoted in Heb 10:37, also according to LXX, introducing the important quotation of 4. St Jerome here deliberately wrote 'visus' rather than the feminine 'visio', because of the application

i to Christ. **4**. 'shall fail' reading lit 'is covered', which corresponds to LXX. 'Faithfulness' rather than 'faith', though, as Bévenot observes, 'faith' = belief in the divine mysteries, is a NT conception legitimately developed from the OT idea of faithfulness to the divine precepts. Basic has 'good faith'. St Paul quotes this passage in Rm 1:17, Gal 3:11, Heb 10:38. In Rm and Gal 'his' is not included, but LXX here has 'my faith' and Heb. transfers the possessive to 'my just one'.

j **5–19 Woes pronounced against the Wicked**—Five Woes are here uttered against different types of evil-doers, cf Is 5:8–30 where six are given though some think there were originally seven, cf Mt 23. The 'Woe' constitutes a distinct literary form. **5**. 'Wine is treacherous': so MT but awkward. LXX for *yayin* (wine) reads '*yôneh* 'arrogant' showing the uncertainty of the text. Another suggestion was *hoy* 'woe to . . .'. But

Qumrân (viii, 3) shows us the best reading with **57** *hôn yib̲gôḏ*: 'Wealth betrays an arrogant man and he shall not abide', cf BJ.

6b–8 (i) Woe to the Usurer—**6b**. 'Pledges': MT *ᵉab̲tît̲*, **k** 'usury' (only here, but cf '*ab̲ôt̲* in Dt 24: 10–13). The Chaldeans seem in particular to be the cruel usurers here, who will, however, come to a bad end.

9–11 (ii) Woe to the Embezzler—**11**. 'The stones will **l** cry out', Lk 19:40, on the lips of Christ, takes up the figure from here. 'The beam', a rare word found only here, MT continues '*from the wood (work)*', but Jerome follows Symmachus and Theodotion (v his comm.).

12–14 (iii) Woe to the Extortioner—cf Mi 3:10 of **m** Jerusalem. **13**. cf Jer 51:58 of the useless labour of Babylon, which will so shortly be destroyed. **14**. Cf Is 11:9.

15–17 (iv) Woe to the Debauched—**15**. 'From the cup **n** of his wrath' is a widely accepted emendation. For 'on their shame' (nakedness), Qumrân read 'meetings', with applications to the 'wicked priest'. **16**. 'And stagger' is the reading of Qumrân (xi, 9), important as an example of the confirmation of an emendation based on LXX. For the 'cup of reeling' cf Is 51:17, 22; Zc 12:2. In the context of drinking, the familiar figure comes easily of the 'cup of the Lord' (cf 'calix in manu Domini,' Ps 75 (74):9). 17b is a repetition of 8b.

19, 18, 20 (v) Woe to the Idolater—**18**. Evidently fits **o** after 19, which begins this Woe.

3 The Canticle of Habakkuk is a lyric psalm of great **p** poetical power, somewhat loosely attached to the rest of the book, though the dominant ideas reoccur. The text in MT is frequently uncertain, but Vg generally preserves a surer reading; it will not be possible, however, here to explain fully all the details of reconstruction of MT that are involved. In general pattern and in several characteristics the canticle resembles the Psalms, especially in the presence of presumed musical directions at the beginning and end, and the indication *selāh* in 3, 9 and 13. Hence some suppose that it is a liturgical fragment appended to this book (cf § 570f). The Canticle may be summarized thus: The poet contemplates God's power and asks for his mercy, **2**, he pictures his coming in majesty, **3–4**, and the terrible effects upon nature, **5–11**, the punishment of the wicked, **12–14**, and his final triumph, **15**. Finally the prophet expresses his fear, **16–17**, but immediately also his trust in God's mercy, **18–19**.

1 The Title—'Shigionoth', *Sigyônôt̲* cf in the title of **q** Ps 7 *S̆iggāyôn* (Vg 'Psalmus'). Probably a musical term, of uncertain meaning. Some connect with the root *s̆āgāh* or *s̆agag*, wander', hence 'in a wandering (free) rhythm' (Driver); or with an Assyrian root 'mournful' (WV). Many leave untranslated.

2 Introduction—For 'in the midst of the years renew it' **r** LXX has the peculiar reading 'in medio duorum animalium', a text preserved in the Dominican Breviary (5th Resp. at Christmas Matins), though not in the Roman, which does, however, retain 'ut animalia viderent Christum natum'. This text or Is 1:3 is probably the origin of the traditional ox and ass at Bethlehem. 'In the midst of the years' means either (1) in the course of history, or (2) in a few years time, or (3) now—between past and future. 'Thy work', to be revived, is God's work of mercy.

3–4 The Theophany—**3**. 'Teman': a proper name? N of **s** Edom? or = 'the south'? 'Paran': towards Sinai, the site of the original theophany. **4**. 'Rays', cf Moses' countenance after the vision, Ex 34:29f, 35.

5–11 The Effects on Nature—**5**. 'Pestilence', *res̆ep̲*, 'a **t** flame': Jerome tells us that the Jews claimed this as the name of a prince of devils (like Beelzebub) and the one who tempted Eve. **7**. 'Cushan (= Cush, only here) in affliction':

71t lit 'under . . .', a phrase otherwise unknown: the ingenious emendation should be noted: 'Ôn (Heliopolis) trembled, **u** the tents of Cushan feared . . .' (Nowack and Marti). **9b.** Difficult. MT lit 'oaths ($\check{s}^e bu\acute{\,}\hat{o}t$); tribes, or, rods; a saying': whence Jewish American 'Sworn are the rods of the word', meaning unsure 'Rods' = 'arrows' (RSV), though unwarranted (cf v 14) has aided many attempted renderings. **10.** 'The raging waters swept on': the picture of sudden floods in the dry wadys after a storm causing terror to the desert tribes. But the translation is doubtful and the reading of the Murabba'at Scroll of the Twelve Prophets (xix, 12) should be noticed, coinciding with Ps 77 (76):18 'The clouds poured forth water'. **11.** In the brilliance of God's storm the sun and the moon have no further function. For God's arrows cf Pss 7:14; 38 (37):3.

v 12–14 The Effects on the Wicked—13a. 'thy anointed' may refer (cf the parallel) to the people or to the king or to his Messianic successor. **13b.** The house of the wicked is imagined as a man, whose head is struck off, laying bare the neck; though many for 'neck', $saww\bar{a}'r$, read $\d{s}\hat{u}r$

'rock' (of the foundations). **14.** RV, WV and many under-**571v** stand the shafts, staves or sceptres as belonging to the victim, though New Psalter, RSV and others emend to 'thy staves'. *Matteh*, 'staff', is not, however, used as a spear-like weapon, any more than of an arrow (cf 9b), but only for support in walking, and (occasionally, figuratively) for beating.

15 God's Triumph—'Surging' from root $\d{h}\bar{a}mar$ as in **w** Ps 46 (45):4.

16–17 The Prophet's Fear—16b. 'my steps', reading **x** $^a\check{s}urai$ with Wellhausen and others. **16c.** 'who invade us. LXX is more probable 'the people *around me*'— perhaps *negdî*. **17.** The picture of the desolation that will follow God's scourge.

18–19 The Prophet's Consolation—18. He who trusts **y** will rejoice in God who saves him. Jerome ('et exultabo in Deo *Jesu* meo'), interpreting directly of Christ, leaves the word untranslated to show the connexion between the Holy Name and its meaning. **19.** 'Choirmaster' and 'stringed instruments', as in e.g. Ps 4.

ZEPHANIAH

BY N. ARBUCKLE O.F.M.

572a Bibliography—*Commentaries: A. B. Davidson*—H. C. O. Lanchester, *CBSC, 1920; A. George, BJ, 1952; J. M. P. Smith, ICC, 1912; G. W. Stonehouse*—*G. W. Wade, Westminster Comm.* 1929; C. L. Taylor, *IB*, 1956. *Other Literature*: G. Gerleman, *Zephanja, textkritisch und literarisch untersucht*, Lund, 1942; J. P. Hyatt, 'The Date and Background of Zephaniah', *JNES* 7 (1948), 25—29; J. Paterson, 'Zephaniah' *HDB* (2), 1963; L. P. Smith—E. R. Lacheman, 'The Authorship of the Book of Zephaniah', *JNES* 9 (1950) 137—42; D. L. Williams, 'The Date of Zephaniah', *JBL* 82 (1963), 77—88.

b The Name and Person of the Prophet—Zephaniah means 'the Lord treasured' or 'the Lord protected'. No record of this prophet is found elsewhere, though the name occurs again: Jer 21:1; 29:25, 29; 37:3; 2 (4) Kgs 25:18ff; Zech 6:10ff; 1 Chr 6:36 (MT 21). It is by no means certain that the Hezekiah mentioned in the prophet's genealogy was the king of that name (721—695) and that Zephaniah was, therefore, of royal blood. That Hezekiah was the king of that name has been alleged by some to account for the unusual length of the prophet's genealogy compared to that of other prophets. Others explain this latter fact as an attempt to show that Zephaniah, although his father's name was Cushi, which means 'Ethiopian', was, nevertheless, of true Jewish stock.

c The Date is given in the title as 'in the days of Josiah, . . . king of Judah', (640—609, 2 (4) Kgs 22:1). It was in the 18th year (622) that king Josiah introduced his religious reform, 2 (4) Kgs 22:3—23:25. Zephaniah's reference to idolatry (1:4ff), his opposition to Assyrian influence (1:8; 2:13—15), and his appeal to the people to return to the worship of the true God (e.g., 2:3) are indications of a date preceding the reform of 622. It has sometimes been thought that the reference to 'the king's sons', 1:8, demanded a later date in the reign of Josiah— he was only 26 in 622—when his children would have been of mature age. But 'the king's sons' could refer to the members of the royal family in general. Likewise the term 'the remnant of Baal', 1:4, means 'every trace of Baal worship' and does not necessarily postulate a date after 622 when only a remnant of Baal worship remained to be 'cut off'. Zephaniah was, then, a contemporary of Jeremiah, who began his work in the 13th year of Josiah's reign, 627 B.C. (Jer 1:2), and of Nahum.

d The Theme of the Book is a call to the people to repentance, and an assurance of God's love for them, esp. 3:15—17, but the approach is through the direst threat of calamity. God's judgement is presented in 1:7—18 in terms of the 'Day of the Lord' ('Dies irae dies illa'), a figure frequently used by the prophets, especially previously by Jl, Am and Is (whence Zephaniah may have got the idea), and later by Jer (only his later work, 46:10), Lam, Obad, Ezek, Zeck and Mal. There is danger in the air: Assyria, the mighty power, has already devastated Palestine just 100 years before, and her own catastrophe will come with that of all the nations. Judah, if she remain faithless, will share their fate (as in fact she did

some 36 years later) but the Lord will remember the **572** faithful remnant, and will restore them to glory, and indeed all the nations will come to adore him in the end. It is here, just for an instant, that the book of Zephaniah opens out a wider eschatological view, 3:9—10.

The Religious Value of Zeph lies in the fact that **e** while he condemns the particular external faults of his day—worship of false gods, 1:4—5; the adoption of foreign customs, 1:8; violence and fraud, 1:11; faults against ritual, 3:4; false prophecy, 3:4;—he also recognizes and condemns the deeper, interior causes of these sins: pride, 1:16; 2:10, 15; 3:11; rebellion, 3:1; lack of confidence in Yahweh, 1:12; 3:2. Sin is a personal affront to Yahweh and not merely the transgression of an external order. This is a negative proclamation of an interior, spiritual religion. True religion is to 'seek **Yahweh, seek righteousness, seek humility', 2:3. These** are the religious qualities which will be found in the Remnant. They will be humble, lowly, seeking refuge in the name of Yahweh, doing no wrong and fearing no evil, since Yahweh their God and Champion is in their midst, 3:12—18a.

Influence—The claim that one OT author has been influenced by another is always precarious. It is possible, however, that Jer inherited some of his expressions and ideas from Zeph (fright before the ruined city, the appeal to be open to instruction, Yahweh's anxiety to warn his people: Zeph 2:15; 3:2, 5). Perhaps, too, Ezek 22:24—28 takes its inspiration from Zeph 3:1—4; while Joel 2:2 undoubtedly borrows from Zeph 1:15. There are no explicit references to Zeph in the NT, perhaps because Zephaniah has no recognizable Messianism. But see on 3:12.

The Division of the Book is best made according to **f** its general themes. It has four parts: (a). 1:1—2:3. The Day of Yahweh against Judah, with a prologue (1:1—3) and epilogue (1:18b) which extend the horizon to a cosmic judgement. The section fittingly closes with a call to conversion (2:1—3). (b).2:4—15. A central piece, as in Ezek and Jer (LXX), occupied with threats against the nations, following the four points of the compass, W, E, S, N. (c). 3:1—8. Further threats against Jerusalem. (d). 3:9—20 Promises fill the last place, as in Am, Mic, Jer (LXX), Ezek, Obed and Jl. The book ends with two short psalms, 3:14—15, 16—18a, followed by a promise of restoration probably dating from a later age, 3:18b—20.

The Unity of the Book—Arguments once brought against the authenticity of sections of Zeph from an historical point of view (e.g. 2:3, 7, 8—11), or because of their cosmic character (1:2—3, 18b), do not find favour with most exegetes today. However, reservations are made with regard to the genuineness of 2:11 and 3:9—10. The conversion of the nations here represented seems to depend on the 'book of consolation' (Is 40—55) and does not fit well with its present context. The two psalms, 3:18a—19 and 3:20, seem to presuppose the exile of 587 and look forward to the glorification of Judah, besides conforming little with Zeph 2:3; 3:11—13. Most critics today regard them as not original to the book. Introductory

72f formulae ('On that day . . .' etc), explanatory glosses and variations have been added without substantially changing the meaning of the text.

The Text—The Hebrew Text is good, needing only slight alteration. A probable restoration of the few difficult texts that are to be found (e.g. 2:1—2, 6, 14; 3:17—18) is rendered possible by modern critical methods and by reference to LXX.

73a **1:1—2:3 The Day of Yahweh against Judah—1:1**. For a discussion of the title cf 572*b*.

2—6 The Threat against Judah and Jerusalem—Zeph foresees a judgement in which both man and beast will be wiped out. Perhaps the practice of representing false gods in animal form explains the inclusion of the beasts, cf Ezek 8:10. For sin through the animal world, cf Gn 3. **4.** 'Idolatrous priests', i.e. of Baal. MT has the word reserved for pagan priests, cf Hos 10:5. Confer the contemporary account of their elimination, 2 (4) Kgs 23:5. MT adds 'with the priests', as in DV, a gloss to explain the more difficult word used for priests. **5.** 'On the roofs' as the obvious place for the worship of the heavenly bodies, cf Jer 19:13; 32:29. 'Swear by Milcom': omit 'swear' the first time: 'Who bow down to the Lord and yet swear by Milcom'. Milcom was the god of the Ammonites, cf 1 (3) Kgs 11:5, 33; 2 (4) Kgs 23:13, one of the Semitic deities (as Moloch) whose name derives from *melek*, 'king'. **6.** 'Or enquire of him' adds nothing and is possibly an addition to the MT.

b **7—9 The Day of the Lord**—The threat is addressed to the worshippers of Baal. Calamity will come on that day, the victims of the sacrifice being Judah and the guests her foes, although these, too, might be included in the sacrifice, cf 2 (4) Kgs 10:18—28 where Jehu invites and sacrifices the priests of Baal. The guests are generally held to be the Assyrian armies, although the Scythians have been suggested (Davidson—Lanchester). **8.** 'The king's sons': LXX: 'the king's house'. This latter is the more likely interpretation, taking into account the age of Josiah at the time. One notices that the young king himself does not come under the condemnation. 'Foreign attire' i.e. alien idolatrous customs. **9.** 'Who leaps over the threshold': this refers either to (i) a pagan superstition, cf 1 Sm 5:5 (Driver), (ii) to rapacious courtiers hastening to cross the threshold of the king's palace (Van Hoonacker), (iii) to those who are nearest the king's throne ('dais' rather than 'threshold') and who are condemned for the injustice of their administration (George), or (iv) to those who make arrogant entry into the temple (*the* Lord's house) (St Jerome). 'Their master's house' probably refers to the king's palace and supports either (ii) or (iii) above.

c **10—11 The Threat against the merchants of Jerusalem**—Leaving the royal courtiers, the prophet now turns to the 'rich'. In Biblical thought this term included the idea of 'persecutors of the poor and defenceless' as well as that of material wealth. **10.** The Fishgate, mentioned in Neh 3:3; 12:39; 2 Chr 33:14, was in the N wall not far from the NW corner of the city. 'The Second Quarter', also named in 2 (4) Kgs 22:14, was probably a new section added to the city, perhaps that enclosed by the new outer wall of Manasseh, 2 Chr 33:14, which included the Fishgate. 'From the hills': on which Jerusalem was built. **11.** 'The Mortar': this expression is only found here, in Prv 27:22 (a mortar for grinding), and in Jg 15:19 (a cavity in a jawbone?). Although the appellation is uncertain, it presumably refers to the valley occupied by the Second Quarter, the commercial centre of the city. 'Weigh out silver', the medium of exchange before the use of coins, cf Jer 32:9f; Zech 11:12.

12—13 Against those who tempt Yahweh—i.e., those **573c** who trust in their riches. 'Thickening upon their lees': an image of imperturbable complacency drawn from the vocabulary of wine-making, cf Jer 48:11. Their blasphemous assurance is voiced in the second part of v 12.

14—18 The Day of Yahweh is near—For the pre-exilic **d** Israelite the Day of Yahweh (sometimes just '*that day*') indicated some future intervention of Yahweh in human affairs, usually depicted in vague terms embracing both politico—historical vicissitudes and cosmic catastrophes, cf Am 8:9; Jl 2:31ff (MT 3:4ff); Zech 14:1ff. The best description is that of Am 5:18ff. The Day of Yahweh had two aspects, the destruction of the Gentiles and the triumph of Israel. From the time of Amos, however, the prophets envisaged the destruction of the Chosen People as well, a remnant only being left. The notion of future happiness of Israel persisted nevertheless, cf Am 9:11. This happiness is described in several ways: as the destruction of Israel's enemies, Zech 12:4ff (a necessary condition to Israel's peace); as the purification of the race, Zech 13:1; Mal 3:2; as a bestowal of the Spirit of Yahweh, Zech 12:10; and finally as the giving of an abundance of life-giving water, Jl 3:18 (MT 4:18); Zech 14:8. For Zephaniah it forebodes a day of destruction for all men. Some critics wish to attribute the extension of the Day of Yahweh to the whole earth (v 18*b*) to a later author; but there does not seem sufficient justification for this.

2:1—2 A Fragmentary Oracle—Not easily connected **e** with the preceding nor with the following. The precise meaning is also unknown. BJ does not attempt to translate v 1*a* 'Come together' and 'hold assembly' translate a Heb. word usually connected with gathering straw and generally has this meaning. The sense, perhaps, is that the shameless nation should gather together to be destroyed as chaff, cf Ps 83 (82):14; Jl 2:5. 'Before you are driven away', with the help of LXX, is the common rendering of an uncertain passage.

3 Call to Conversion—The preceding fragment concerned the 'shameless nation'. 3 is directed, in contrast, to the 'poor of the land'. While the rich merchants are threatened with destruction (1:10—13, 18), the 'poor of the land' are exhorted to conversion. In the OT the 'poor' or 'humble', because of their material condition, were considered to rely on Yahweh and on his providence, in contrast to the 'rich' who were proud and the enemies of Yahweh and of his poor. In this way the term 'poor' took on a religious meaning, although the social meaning of the term was not altogether superseded, cf Is 26:6; Ps 18 (17).27, 37(36).14. When the Messiah comes he will be 'poor' or 'humble', cf Zech 9:9 (Mt 21:4—5; Jn 12:14—15; also Zeph 3:12).

4—15 Oracles against the Nations—These oracles, **f** found in other prophets also, are not occasioned by sheer vindictiveness for humiliations and defeats received in the past (although this is not absent), but by a desire for the final triumph of Yahweh. The nations who opposed Yahweh's Chosen People opposed Yahweh himself.

4—7 The Nations to the West—**4.** Four Philistine cities are named, but not the 5th Gath, which had apparently ceased to exist after the 8th cent. 'At noon': in broad daylight, with no difficulty whatsoever, cf Jer 6:4; 15:8; or 'by noon', in no time at all. **5.** 'You nation of the Cherethites' (or Cretans, cf LXX) probably Cretan emigrants in Philistia, cf Am 9:7; Dt 2:23. Jerome rejected the reading 'Cretans', saying that 'Chorethim' means 'perditorum', following Aquila, Theodotion and Symmachus. Hence DV: 'O nation of reprobates'. **6.** 'Sea coast' is omitted by LXX and may have been added to MT. The land of the Philistines is still the subject. For

573f the practice of making pasture land out of conquered cities cf Is 34:13f; Mi 3:12 **7.** After punishment Judah shall be restored. This is a traditional theme among the prophets (cf Is 4:3; 7:3; 10:20—22; 14:1f; Am 3:12; 5:15) and does not necessarily presuppose the exile. There is therefore no reason to deny this theme, nor the theme of the remnant, to Zeph, as some wish to do. Zeph says only that she will return to her primitive state of happiness. A condition of this restoration will be the ownership of the land of the Philistines.

g 8—11 The Nations to the East—Moab will be punished for its hostility to Judah. **8.** 'Made boasts against their territory': lit: 'magnified themselves', perhaps meaning that Ammon and Moab had encroached on their territory, cf Am 1:13; Jer 49:1; also Jer 48:26, 42. **9.** RSV gives us the probable meaning of a v which has several rare words. 'Sodom and Gomorrah' are proverbial examples of destruction, cf Is 1:9; Jer 49:18; also Gn 19. Moab and Ammon were the hereditary rivals of Israel from the time of the Exodus, Nm 22—25; Dt 23:4—7; Jg 10—11. Here they are to be punished for their 'pride', manifested in their ridicule of Yahweh's people, cf also Is 10:5—15. It should not be presumed that these vv refer to the Babylonian exile (cf Ezek 25:3f, 8f), and, therefore, belong to a later period. We do not know enough about the history of these peoples to exclude other possible historical instances. **11.** Yahweh's triumph over the false gods: 'he will famish them' (probable meaning of a rare word); CV 'when he makes the gods of the earth to fade away', for want of the offerings, which will be brought to Yahweh instead (3:10). Many consider this verse to be a later addition. **12 The Nations to the South**—Only a fragment of this oracle is preserved. Ethiopia might well include Egypt as these two are often associated: Is 43:3; Na 3:9. 'My sword': the theme of Egypt's punishment by the sword of Yahweh is found in several places in the OT: Ezek 30:4—25; 32:20.

h 13—15 The Nations to the North—Assyria is the enemy *par excellence* and is left to the last. Geographically it lies as much E as N of Jerusalem; but an invader coming from that direction would come round the N edge of the desert and so approach Jerusalem from the N. **14.** There is a certain amount of doubt about the identification of the animals and birds of this v. The main point is that they are wild creatures associated with empty places and ruined buildings, cf Ps 102 (101):6f. **15.** 'I am and there is none else', cf Is 47:8, 10 where Babylon pronounces these same words. Cf also Sir 36:10. Hissing for the ancients expressed horror, especially in face of disaster, cf Jer 18:16; 19:8; 25:9, 18, etc. The hand-waving would seem to imply something similar. In fact this destruction of Nineveh took place in 612 B.C.

i 3:1—8 The Denunciation of Jerusalem—1. There are two roots possible for the verb *niḡ'ălâ* from *gā'al* = 'to redeem' or 'to defile'; and *hayyonâ* can be either 'the dove' or from *yānâ* 'to oppress'. RSV and most versions have the more obvious meanings in the context: 'defiled' and 'oppressing'. Jerusalem is being upbraided for the obduracy and injustice of her inhabitants. **3—4.** Judgement is passed on the princes, priests and prophets. The judges are 'evening wolves that leave nothing for the morning'. The image of roaring lions and of wolves evokes the idea of greed. The verb 'leave' occurs only here and is of doubtful meaning; this is the usual translation. **5.** Despite the crimes of Jerusalem's leaders, Yahweh remains constant in his justice. The last member of this v is also uncertain and is rendered variously: BJ 'he (Yahweh) knows no iniquity' (and the phrase is regarded as a gloss), CV omits it entirely: LXX 'he knows not

injustice in (his) demand, nor injustice in strife'. **6—7. 573** The example made of the nations as a warning to Jerusalem was in vain; her sins increase. 'They were eager to make . . . corrupt' for the literal phrase 'they rose early and corrupted . . .'. **8.** 'I arise as witness': Yahweh as a witness for or against men is a familiar notion, especially with the judgement that follows.

3:9—20 The Promises—9—10 Conversion of the j Nations—These vv promise conversion to the nations. 'To change to a pure speech' means to worship Yahweh. 'With one accord' interprets the literal phrase 'with one shoulder' which in the OT is usually used in a context of bearing a burden. Nevertheless, the RSV gives the most probable rendering. The RSV of v 10, however, hardly suits this context, which seems to deal with pagan nations rather than dispersed Jews. Further, LXX 'among my dispersed ones' leads us to suspect the text. Various attempts have been made to reconstruct this v: (1) 'Beyond the rivers of Cush they shall offer me incense, the daughters of *Put* shall bring me an offering', where *Pût* is read for *pûṣai* (Put and Cush are often paralleled: Na 3:9; Jer 46:9; Ezek 30:5; 38:5; cf Gn 10:6), and 'my suppliants' gives way to 'offer me ˌincense' (Ewald, Davidson). (2) 'From beyond the rivers of Cush, from Put they will bring my offering', where 'my suppliants' is considered a corrupted doublet of '*ēber* 'beyond' (Bullough, CCHS (1)). (3) CV accepts Procksch's suggested reconstruction by Kittel: 'From beyond the rivers of Ethiopia and as far as the recesses of the N, they shall bring me offerings'. BJ, Van Hoonacker and others who accept MT, reject the reference to the dispersal as a gloss. Finally, that 9—10 formed part of the original Zeph is questioned by many, cf 572f.

11—13 A Remnant, chastened and repentant, shall remain—A familiar theme in the post-exilic writings, 'a people humble and lowly' (12). The idea foreshadows the more explicit teaching of the NT, Mt 5:3, 5; 11:5; Lk 1:52—53; 4:18; 6:20.

14—18a Psalms of Consolation—Jerusalem can **k** rejoice in her security because Yahweh her king and protector lives in her midst and no one can harm her further, cf also Ezek 48:35; Apoc 21:22ff; 22:3. **16.** 'Let not your hands grow weak' means 'be not discouraged' (CV), cf Is 13:7; Jer 6:24, etc. **17.** MT 'he will be silent in his love'. The OT notion of Yahweh's love is dynamic and not easily reconciled with Yahweh's silence. Yahweh is 'silent' when he fails to come to the aid of his faithful (Ps 35 (34):22), or when he does not punish the sinner (Ps 50 (49):21). RSV, CV and modern versions generally accept a corrected reading of MT: 'he will renew you in his love'. **18a.** 'as on the day of festival' is found in LXX and is joined to the preceding v. This arrangement is accepted by most modern versions (RSV, CV, BJ). A similar construction is found in Hos 12:9(10). **18b—20 Return of the Dispersed—18b.** 'I will remove disaster from you, so that you will not bear reproach for it' follows an amended reading of MT (*hawwâ miśśe'ēt 'ālêkā*). Another possible reconstruction is suggested by Gerleman: 'I have removed from thee the day in which reproach was brought against you': *hayyôm* (mem omitted in MT through haplography) *maś'ēt* (*śe'ēt* from *nāśā'* with olf semitic relative *ma*) *'ālêkā herpâ*. *nāśā' herpâ*,' to inflict reproach', cf Ps 15 (14):3. **19.** 'I will change their shame . . .': the word translated here 'shame' (*boštām*) and made the object of the sentence is interpreted differently in other modern versions. CV and BJ treat it as an abbreviation of the phrase (v 20) 'when I restore your fortunes'. Regarding the authenticity of these last vv, see 572f.

HAGGAI

BY A. MARSH O.C.S.O.

574a **Bibliography**—*Commentaries*: St Jerome, PL 25, 1387ff; S. R. Driver CBi 1906; A. van Hoonacker, EtB, 1908; H. G. Mitchell, ICC, 1912; W. E. Barnes, CBSC, 1917; S. Bullough, WV, 1953; K. Elliger, ATD, 1956[3]; D. Winton Thomas, IB, 1956; A. Gelin, 1960[3]; D. R. Jones, Torch, 1962; P. R. Ackroyd, PC (2). *Other Literature*: P. R. Ackroyd, 'Studies in the Book of Haggai', in *Journal of Jewish Studies*, 2 (1951) 163ff; Th. Chary, *Les Prophètes et le Culte à partir de l'Exil*, 1955, 118—38; R. T. Siebeneck, 'The Messianism of Aggeus and Proto-Zacharias', CBQ, 19 (1957), 321f.

b **The Prophet**—Haggai (*hag*, a feast) is the first of the post-exilic prophets. Apart from references to his preaching activity in Ez 5:1; 6:14, our only source of information concerning him is his book. The two short chh (38 vv) of his book however provide almost no biographical data. 2:3 may indicate that Haggai was an old man at this period of his prophetic ministry, and 2:10—14 (Haggai consults the priests) may imply that he was not himself a priest—but these inferences are of doubtful value. Perhaps Haggai's great concern for the Temple points to him being a cult prophet. In any case, the rôle he played in the Temple's restoration shows him as a forceful character who spurred on the people of Judah and their leaders in a time of religious crisis.

c **The Historical Background**—The prophecies of Haggai reflect a crucial moment in Israel's history after the return from exile. The edict of Cyrus (538) had allowed the restoration of the Jewish community and cult in Palestine and as a result a pioneer group of exiles under Sheshbazzar had returned to Jerusalem almost at once. Work on the ruined Temple commenced (Ez 5:16), but in the years that followed little progress was made owing to fewness of numbers, lack of resources and hostility of neighbours. Meanwhile, Sheshbazzar was succeeded as *pehah* ('governor') of Judah by his nephew Zerubbabel, son of Shealtiel (Ez 3:2, 8 etc) and grandson of Jehoiachin, the king of Judah who had been deported to Babylon (2 Kgs 24:12). Zerubbabel seems to have arrived in Jerusalem at the head of a further group of returning exiles (which included the high-priest Joshua) some time before the second year of the Persian Darius I (Hag 1:1). By this date (520) 18 years had passed since the return of the first exiles but the work of rebuilding the Temple had still not progressed beyond the foundation-stage. It was now that Haggai came forward (soon to be followed by his contemporary Zechariah) to rebuke his countrymen for their long neglect of Yahweh's sanctuary and to urge them on to resume its reconstruction. These exhortations had their effect, work recommenced, and the Temple was restored within five years (515).

d **The immediate occasion** of Haggai's oracles was probably the revolts which broke out in the provinces of the Persian Empire at the accession of Darius I in 522. Although Darius eventually succeeded in quelling them it was not perhaps until the end of 520 that his position was secure. To Haggai these upheavals may have seemed **574d** a prelude to a final world upheaval (2:6—9, 21—22) which would usher in the Kingdom of God in which doubtless Zerubbabel, being of David's line, would have a messianic role (2:23). The time therefore appeared opportune for hurrying on the rebuilding of the Temple so that Yahweh might return to it (Ezek 43:4—5).

e **The Book**—The prophecies of Haggai, all delivered within the space of four months (Aug.—Dec. 520), may be conveniently divided: (1) An exhortation to rebuild the Temple (1:1—11). An appendix records that this appeal produced its effect (1:12—15*a*). (2) The future glory of the Temple (1:15*b*—2:9). (3) The unworthiness of the people (2:10—14). (4) A promise of blessing (2:15—19). (5) A promise to Zerubbabel (2:20—23).

The careful dating of each oracle, the habitual reference to Haggai in the third person, the chronicling of results (1:12—14), and some signs of disorder in the text (cf commentary)—all this renders it unlikely that Haggai himself edited these prophecies. The final editing may be the work of a disciple not long after the close of Haggai's ministry (but cf Ackroyd for a later date).

f **The Message**—It was Haggai who saw the danger to the religious life of the Jewish community arising from the prolonged neglect of the ruined Temple, for in preexilic days the Temple had been the centre of Yahwistic faith and worship. Hence the Temple and its reconstruction is Haggai's supreme interest and all his oracles are connected with this theme. For the prophet, current economic difficulties due to poor harvests, inflation etc are a consequence of the people's neglect of its duty to rebuild Yahweh's house (1:2—11), but once the work of 'setting stone on stone' is undertaken Yahweh's blessing is assured (2:15—19).

g The Temple is moreover, as in Ezek, the object of messianic promises—despite its present modest appearance the future glory of the Temple is to surpass the splendour it possessed in the former days of the kingdom (2:6—9). With this messianic Temple-theme Haggai has linked several other traditional messianic motifs—the eschatological upheaval (v 6, cf Is 13:13; 51:6; 64:1; 66:22), the 'conversion' and tribute of the nations (v 7, cf Is 44:5; 45:14; 51:4—5; 56:3—8; 60:4—9), the glory filling the Temple (v 7, cf Ezek 43:4—5), peace (v 9, cf Is 2:2—4; 9:5; 11:1—9 etc). 'This prophecy is probably most fully realized in the "Temple" of Christ's own glorified body (Jn 2:19—21) together with Christ's members who are so many stones in the Mystical Temple (Eph 2:20—22) in and through which they find the peace and glory that Ag promised' (Siebeneck, 316). Another promise of messianic significance is that made to the civil head of the community, Zerubbabel (2:20—23)—he is assured of a special role as Yahweh's chosen servant and representative ('signet ring') in the new age which the Temple's rebuilding presages. In this way the community's messianic expectations crystallize around

574g the Temple being restored and its restorer, David's descendant, Zerubbabel—royal messianism and the Temple are thus linked together as in the original promise to David (2 Sm 7:1—17:—it is not David who will build a house i.e. Temple, for Yahweh, but Yahweh who will build a house, i.e. dynasty, for David).

575a **1:1—11 Exhortation to rebuild the Temple**—An appeal to people and leaders to resume the reconstruction of the Temple. It is to the neglect of this duty that present distress is to be attributed. The sequence of thought seems rather disjointed and it is possible that we have here either (a) a connected series of five brief sayings 2, 4, 5—6, 7—8, 9—11, gathered together because of their related subject-matter (Ackroyd) or (b) a combination of two sections, 1—6 + 8 and 7 + 9—11 (Gelin following Eissfeldt).

1—4 The Temple still in ruins—1. The date is August 520, eighteen years after the first return of exiles under Sheshbazzar. 'Governor' (*pehah*) is a vague term signifying merely a royal Commissioner who, possessed of temporary and limited powers, was in charge of some specific project. **2.** 'This people' (the designation is depreciatory cf Is 8:6) consider the moment inopportune for restarting building operations. **4.** The state of Yahweh's house is compared with the people's living conditions—they at least have roofs over their heads ('panelled' may simply signify 'roofed') while the Temple remains roofless.

b **5—8 Let the People reflect on their conduct**, on the paths they have been following (so the sense of CV, BJ rather than 'consider how you have fared'—RSV). **6.** The viewpoint is that of deuteronomic theology—blessings or curses follow upon the observance or non-observance of the covenant stipulations (cf Dt 28). Let the people mend their ways (**7**) and set to work. **8.** Since only timber is called for perhaps some of the ruined Temple's stonework still stands—a roof and interior woodwork are the chief requirements. **9—11.** These vv closely parallel the thought of 4—6 (doublets?)—the state of Yahweh's house is compared with the people's houses, recent misfortunes are enumerated and attributed (but more explicitly this time) to Yahweh as their cause. **9.** 'I blew it away'—perhaps an image of the speed with which the scanty harvest was used up, but others translate, 'When you brought it (the offering) into the House (i.e. Temple) I blew it away (i.e. despised and rejected it)'—so Barnes, Ackroyd.

c **12—15a The Effect of the Prophecy**—People and leaders obey the summons and set to work encouraged by Haggai's assurance of Yahweh's assistance. **12.** 'Remnant of the people' does not refer exclusively in Hag and Zech to the returned exiles, but to the whole community (including resident Jews left in Judah after 587) living in and around Jerusalem. **13.** 'I am with you'—a promise of God's efficacious help in accomplishing the task (cf Ex 3:12; Jer 1:8 etc). This brief oracle (possibly the summary of a longer address) is echoed in 2:4. The title 'messenger of Yahweh' (*mal'ak-Yahweh*) is unusual for a prophet but cf Is 42:26; 2 Chr 36:15. **15a** (CV 14b). This date is only loosely linked with the preceding v (the Heb. Bible has a paragraph mark after 14) and is generally considered to be the remnant of an introductory phrase to which should be attached 2:15—19 with its promise of material blessing (cf commentary *infra*).

d **15b—2:5 The People are Encouraged**—The date is October 520. After the initial labours of a few weeks the builders apparently lose heart at the magnitude

of the task confronting them—they despair of restoring **57?** the Temple to its former splendour. But Haggai encourages them: Yahweh is with them (cf 1:13)—his assistance guarantees the ultimate success of the enterprise. **3.** It seems unlikely that Haggai himself or any of his audience had in fact seen the first Temple, destroyed nearly seventy years previously. **4—5.** The triple exhortation to courage and the promise of help ('I am with you') which accompany Yahweh's command are likewise found in Yahweh's charge to Moses' successor Joshua to cross the Jordan and take possession of the land (Jos. 1:2—9). In both cases the success of the task enjoined is assured because of Yahweh's assistance. **5a.** With its reference to the covenant (cf CV, BJ) interrupts the parallel phrases 'I am with you/My spirit is in your midst' and is usually considered a gloss.

6—9 The Future Glory of the Temple (cf § 574g)— **e** The thought of the preceding vv is carried a step forward—the former 'glory' of Yahweh's house will be surpassed by its future 'glory' (splendour, wealth). **6.** Cosmic upheaval accompanies Yahweh's eschatological intervention when he establishes the messianic age. LXX reads here 'Yet once will I shake' which is quoted in Heb 12:26 where it is taken as messianic, stressing the 'only once more' of Christ's Second Coming. Previously the people ignored God's warnings and were punished; 'much less will we escape if we reject him', Heb 12:25. **7—8.** Among the nations political upheaval will result in their 'treasures' flowing into Jerusalem as tribute (or into the Temple as offerings) and thus Yahweh will fill his house with 'glory'. The obvious reference is to the new splendour of the Temple enriched by the silver and gold of the nations (**8**); elsewhere 'the glory filling the Temple (or Tabernacle)' denotes Yahweh's presence in the sanctuary, e.g. Ex 40:34—35; 1 Kgs 8:11; Ezek 43:5; 44:4).

10—14 Consultation with the Priests—The date is **f** December 520. The oracle in 14 applies a priestly decision on a matter of levitical practice. **12—13.** Uncleanness is more contagious than holiness, for while holy flesh does not communicate its holiness, legal uncleanness (from contact with a corpse) can be communicated (Lv 21:11; 22:4). **14.** The lesson of the Torah is applied to the people but only the principle laid down in 13 is expressly invoked: the people are unclean and consequently their sacrificial offerings also. This may refer to the people's previous neglect of the Temple which has tainted their service and rendered their offerings unacceptable. The severity of the rebuke however contrasts strangely with the glowing promises of 2:6—9. Hence many consider the rebuke as aimed at the Samaritan rather than the Jewish community and connect it with the incident recounted in Ez 4:1—5 where Samaritan offers of cooperation in the Temple's reconstruction are rejected. Since Samaritan cult of Yahweh was combined with that of other deities (cf 2 Kgs 17:24f) the prophet may be reacting rather against the participation of these syncretists ('unclean') in the community's worship, or even against the religious syncretists within the Judaean community itself (cf Bright, *History of Israel*, 1960, 350, 352).

15—19 Promise of Future Blessings—In the context **g** these vv do not seem well placed (but cf Jones, p. 50) and many would transpose them after 1:15a owing to the affinity of ideas which they show with ch 1. Previous crop failure was due to culpable neglect of Temple (ch 1), but now that rebuilding is under way Haggai promises Yahweh's blessing on the harvest. **15—17.** The people must reflect on the misfortunes they suffered

575g before they responded to Haggai's appeal. 'How did you fare'—so LXX followed by RSV, CV, BJ for the meaningless Heb. *mihyôṭām* which is perhaps a miscopy of *min-hayyôm* ('from this day') in the line above (Bullough). 'Yet you did not return to me' (17)—again LXX followed by RSV, CV, BJ—is borrowed from Am 4:9 (to which the rest of this v is parallel) to replace the awkward Heb. phrase in Hag. **18–19.** Should probably read (cf emended text in BJ) omitting 18*b* as a gloss: '*Consider from this day forward: will grain still be lacking in the barn? Will the vine, the fig tree, the pomegranate and the olive tree still yield nothing? From this day forward I will bless*' namely, the harvest.

h **20–23 Promise to Zerubbabel** (cf § 574*g*)—This oracle (dated the same day as 2:10–14) is addressed exclusively to the civil governor Zerubbabel with whose future messianic role it is concerned (cf Zech 6:9–15). 'The whole passage is in fact typically messianic' (Chary, 133). **21–22.** Cosmic and political upheavals again accompany Yahweh's intervention (cf 2:6–9). **23.** 'On that day'—the eschatological day of Yahweh. 'I will take you'—expresses a divine choice for an important mission in the history of salvation as in the case of Abraham (Jos 24:3) and David (2 Sm 7:8). Like these Zerubbabel too is called 'my servant' by Yahweh (Gn 26:24; 1 Kgs (3) 11:13; Ezek 34:24) who has 'chosen' him (cf 1 (3) Kgs 11:34; Is 43:10; 44:1) and who will make him like a 'signet ring'. The signet ring, used for signing letters (1 Kgs 21:8), bore its owner's personal mark and represented him and his authority (cf Gn 41:42; Est 3:10; 8:2). As Jer 22:24 shows, Yahweh's previous rejection of King Jehoiachin is now reversed in favour of his grandson, Zerubbabel, in whom God's messianic promises to David's house now rest and from whom the eventual Messiah, Christ, will in fact descend (Mt 1:13; Lk 3:27).

ZECHARIAH

BY D. RYAN

576a Bibliography—A. van Hoonacker, EtB, 1908; H. G. Mitchell, ICC, 1912; J. Knabenbauer-M. Hagen, CSS, 1924²; A. Gelin, BJ, 1948; F. Horst, HAT, 1963³; D. Winton Thomas, Zech 1—8, IB 6 (1956), 1053—88, and R. C. Dentan, Zech 9—14, IB 6 (1956) 1089—1114; M. Delcor, PCSB, 1964; K. Elliger, ATD, 1964⁵ (with bibliographical material up to 1964); EOTInt, 429—40, 762; P. Lamarche, *Zacharie 9—14, Structure littéraire et Messianisme*, 1961; in EtB. The Bibliography covers the period from Knabenbauer's comm. in 1922 to 1958; F. F. Bruce, 'The Book of Zechariah and the Passion Narrative', BJRL 43 (1961) 336—53.

ZECHARIAH 1—8

b **The Prophet Zechariah**—Zechariah, (Heb. Z*ekaryāh* = 'Yahweh remembers', or 'Yahweh has remembered'), was a contemporary of the prophet Haggai as we learn from Ez 5:1; 6:14. Hag 2:3 suggests that Haggai was one of the old men who had seen the Temple before the fall of Jerusalem sixty six years earlier. Since Ezra (5:1; 6:14) mentions Zech in the second place, he may imply that he was younger than Haggai. In 1:1, 7 Zechariah is described as the 'son of Berechiah, son of Iddo', whereas Ez 5:1; 6:14 state that he was 'the son of Iddo'. In accordance with biblical usage, the two statements are not incompatible; 'son of' can express the relationship between grandson and grandfather (e.g. 2 (4) Kgs 9:14 and 20). Neh 12:4 numbers an Iddo among those priests who returned with Zerubbabel, and 12:16 assigns a Zechariah to the priestly house of Iddo. This may be the prophet who in fact shows an interest in ceremonial matters (cf chh 3, 4, 6) and in the Temple (*passim*). It is not clear whether 'son of Iddo' expresses a relationship of blood or membership of a priestly class.

c Another view of the phrase 'Zechariah, son of Berechiah, son of Iddo' recalls that Is 8:2 gives 'Zechariah son of Jeberechiah' as the name of one of Isaiah's witnesses and suggests that Zechariah 9—14 (a separate work) was originally attributed to Zechariah son of Jeberechiah, the prophet of the 8th cent. B.C. even though it was written in the late 4th cent. B.C. (cf § 579a—c). When the two parts of the present book were brought together, they were united under the name of Zech, and the fathers of each Zech were included in such a way as to suggest that the three were related as father, son and grandson. For an understanding of this view it is essential to appreciate that Berechiah and Jeberechiah could be variants of the same name, and that in the 4th cent. B.C. it was not unusual to attribute one's literary efforts to outstanding personalities of Israel's antiquity.

Although it is not certain that Zech was a priest, the priestly interests of the prophet liken him to Ezek who was priest and prophet. Both give prominence to angels and emphasize the divine transcendence. Like Ezek, Zech describes the purification of the Holy Land (cf

5:3, 8—11). As frequent cross-references will show, **576c** he was steeped in Israel's prophetic traditions and refers specifically to the 'former prophets' (1:4; 7:7). His writings also manifest some of the characteristics of apocalyptic literature which became increasingly popular in the post-exilic period (cf § 454). Some of the ancient versions (LXX, VL, Syr) attribute some psalms to this prophet.

The prophet began to preach in the month between **d** the second and third prophecies of Hag, i.e. in the 8th month (Oct.—Nov.) of the 2nd year of Darius (520 B.C.). Cf Hag 1:1; 2:1, 10; Zech 1:1. The latest of his dated prophecies belongs to 518 B.C. (7:1), whereas Haggai's activity is limited to 520 B.C.

The problem of identifying the author of Zech 9—14 will be discussed in § 579.

Historical Background—The same as for Hag, cf § 574c. The historical background to chh 9—14 is considered in § 579.

Division of the Book—Few commentators would now **e** attribute chh 9—14 to the Zech of the 6th cent. B.C., the author of chh 1—8. Although some themes are common to both parts of the book, the differences are such as to make secure the conclusion that they come from different hands. This matter is discussed more fully in the introduction to chh 9—14, § 579. Chh 1—8 consist of a series of eight visions (1:7—17; 1:18—21 (MT 2:1—4); 2:1—5 (MT 2:5—9); 3:1—10; 4:1—6a, 10c—14; 5:1—4: 5:5—11; 6:1—8), preceded by an introduction (1:1—6), and interspersed with various oracles (2:10—7; 4:6b—10b; 6:9—14). Chh 7—8 include a question on fasting (7:1—3), the prophet's reflections on the question (4—14) and his answer (8:18—19), as well as a series of oracles concerning the future of Judah and Jerusalem (8:1—17, 20—23).

The Visions—The eight visions in Zech 1—6 bring **f** together in a distinctive, if stereotyped way elements which are found in earlier prophetic writings: (a) an introduction: 'I saw' or 'he showed me' (cf 1 (3) Kgs 22:17; Am 7:1); (b) a heavenly scene involving either a theophany or the participation of heavenly beings (cf Is 6:1; 1 (3) Kgs 22:19ff); (c) a conversation between the prophet and Yahweh (e.g. Is 6:7—8; Jer 1:6—7) or, in the case of Zech, between the prophet and one of the heavenly beings; (d) the meaning of the vision, sometimes in the form of a message from Yahweh (e.g. Am 7:8; Jer 4:5). It is sometimes unjustifiably assumed that all the visions occurred during the one night, since only one date is provided in chh 1—6, i.e. in 1:7, and reference is made to the awakening of the prophet in 4:1. It seems better to suppose that these visions represent the prophetic experience on a number of occasions.

Absolutely speaking, these visions could be regarded simply as a literary form through which the prophet expressed his message, but there seems no reason to doubt their reality in the case of Zech.

The dominant role of visions in Zech reflects a

76f gradual transition from earlier prophetic literature with its emphasis on the word of God which the prophet hears as opposed to the divine communication which the writer sees, a feature which is characteristic of apocalyptic literature.

g The Message of Zechariah—The short book of Hag the contemporary of Zech is almost totally taken up with the rebuilding of the Temple. Zech, however, shows a wider range of theological and religious interest. Although he begins with the **anger** of Yahweh (1:2) and returns to it from time to time (1:15; 18—21, against the nations; 5:1—4; 7:11—14), the book is not dominated by the brooding figure of an angry God. On the contrary, the message of Yahweh is described as 'gracious and comforting' (1:13) and, at the very beginning of the book (1:3), an invitation to repentance is presented to the people by a God who is eager to have his people return to him so that again he might be generous in their regard. The generosity of his **mercy** and **forgiveness** can be seen in the passages which speak of the restoration and glorious future of Jerusalem (2:1—5 (5—9), 10 (14), 11—12 (15—16); 8:1—13, 20—23).

The first important step towards this glorious future is the rebuilding of the Temple and while the human effort of Zerubbabel and his friends is important (4:6ff; 6:9—14), they can achieve nothing without **Yahweh's Spirit** (4:6). Yahweh also helps with the restoration of the cult by purifying priest and people from their accumulated guilt (3:1ff). The omniscient **providence** of God will care for his people (4:1ff) and, coupled with his **omnipotence**, will protect them from the nations (1:15; 2:8 (12)).

h Such favours are not conferred on the city and people after the manner of an indulgent parent. Yahweh is presented as a **transcendent** God, who is accessible to man through the ministry of angels (cf 1:9, 19 and 1—6 *passim*), and whose demands in the matter of right and wrong are absolute. The opening verses of the book (1:2—6) leave no doubt about the cause of Yahweh's anger; it is the people's failure to keep his commandments (1:6) and to obey the warnings of the prophets (1:4). The specific elements of prophetic teaching which were neglected are pinpointed by quotation (cf 7:9—10) and Zech returns frequently to the **moral demands** which must be met if progress is to be made, whether in the rebuilding of the Temple (6:15), in the effectiveness of the priesthood (3:7), or in the renewal of the city (8:14—17). If Israel has sinned, there follows the inevitable cycle demanded by God's justice and love, of punishment, repentance and return (1:2—6; 5:1—4; 8:2 etc). The **holiness** of Yahweh in Zech is clearly not a ritual holiness, a balancing factor in the religious outlook of a man who, while he campaigned for the restoration of the Temple, was also willing to abandon fasting rites which had lost their point (7:1—3; 8:18—19).

i The so-called **messianic texts** (3:8; 6:12) seem to use the messianic terminology particularly of Jer (23:5; 33:15) in the context of the return from Babylon when the hopes of restoration of the Davidic dynasty (Ezek 45:7) were focused on the person of Zerubbabel. Zech looks rather at the immediate future than at distant messianic horizons. While the dominant theme of his book could be described as the coming of Yahweh to his people, he attaches this coming to the restoration of the Temple. Yahweh will renew his choice of Jerusalem (1:17; 3:2) and will dwell again in the midst of his people (2:10 (14)), who are once more attached to him in the covenant relationship (2:11 (16)) with all the richness of life that this implied (1:17; 2:4—5 (8—9);

8:3—13). Dt-Zech is also concerned with the coming of **576i** Yahweh but he will give eschatological depth to the thinking of his predecessor, a process which is perhaps foreshadowed in 8:20—23, which is often taken to be an addition to Zech and more closely related in thought to Dt-Zech.

1:1—6 Introduction—1. The day of the month may **577a** have dropped out of the text (cf 1:7; 7:1). Syr has 'the first of the month'. 'eighth': according to the Babylonian reckoning cf § 87g. The date was Oct.—Nov., 520 B.C. For Darius I, cf § 67c. For Zechariah, cf § 576b. **2.** Although the anger of God with his people is a recurring feature in prophetic literature, it is never a permanent factor in the covenant relationship. Like Yahweh's jealousy, it springs from love and an eagerness to preserve his ties with his covenant people (cf Am 3:2; Is 47:6; 57:16 etc). 'fathers': the pre-exilic generation, on whom the accumulated wrath of God had fallen in the destruction of city and temple and the exile (cf Neh 9:16 where 'fathers' are distinguished from the Mosaic generation; also Neh 9:32). **3.** 'them': the context makes it clear that the reference is to the contemporaries of the prophet, not to the 'fathers' of v 2. For a similarly vague 'them', cf Jer 1:8. On the title 'Yahweh of hosts': **b** cf § 109c. 'Return': frequently in the prophets with the implication of moral reform and true conversion of heart (e.g. Am 4:6, 8, 9; Hos 6:1; 7:10). 'I will return': when used of Yahweh, the verb describes a revival of interest in his people and renewed support (cf Is 63:17; Ps 80 (79):14). Jer 31:18 suggests that without Yahweh's help, Israel is unable to return (cf Zech 12:10). **4.** 'former prophets': those who had preached to earlier generations of Israel, and especially Jer (cf 25:5). The phrase was later applied in a technical sense to the books of the Heb. Bible between the Pentateuch (Torah) and the Latter Prophets, which began with Is. **5—6.** The everlasting effectiveness of the word of God is contrasted with the passing nature of mortal man (cf Is 40:6—8; 55:11). The prophets themselves will perish, though their words will survive because they are the words of Yahweh. The fact that their words came true was the ultimate proof that they spoke the word of Yahweh (Dt 18:21—22). 'repented': the act of repentance which took place when the fathers found themselves in exile; it illustrates how the returned exiles should respond to the prophet's preaching. 'purposed': the Heb. verb implies great deliberation (cf Zech 8:14, 15; Jer 4:28; 51:12 etc).

7—17 1st Vision: The Angel and the Horses—7. The **c** date given is mid-February 519 B.C. **8.** 'man': a superhuman being identified in v 11 as 'the angel of Yahweh' (cf Dn 8:15; 12:5). 'riding . . . horse': these words create a dilemma; they are not repeated in vv 10—11. Then there is the inconsistency between 'riding' and 'standing' in this v, and the surprising duplication of red horses. In such groupings in apocalyptic literature, colours tend not to be repeated (e.g. Apoc 6:1—8). A scribe may have inserted the words because he felt it inappropriate that the angel of Yahweh was standing on the ground while the other persons were mounted on horses. If this phrase is omitted, there would be only three horses, whereas in the LXX there would still be four. Cf 1:18; 2:6, and particularly 6:1—7 for the use of four in similar pieces. 'myrtle': a common feature in the Palestinian landscape (cf Neh 8:15). Its significance here is obscure. Perhaps there is an implicit reference to Is 41:19; 55:13 with the suggestion that the work of Israel's restoration has already begun. 'glen': unidentified. 'sorrel': i.e. reddish-brown. The relation of the horses' colours to the role of their riders is not

577c clear (cf 6:1ff and Apoc 6:1—8). **9.** The usual exchange between the prophet and the angel (cf also 1:19; 2:2 etc). Is, Jer and Ezek spoke directly to Yahweh, although in Ezek the interpreting angel does appear (cf 8:2ff; 40:3ff). He becomes more frequent in later literature (cf Dn 7:16; 8:15 etc). In Zech, he acts more generally as intermediary between the prophet and the divinity, bearing messages in both directions (cf vv 12—14). He is here distinct from 'the man among the myrtle trees'.

d 10. 'patrol': has overtones of supervision and control. The Heb. phrase conveys the idea of moving to and fro. The immediate function of these messengers was to survey the situation throughout the earth—in fact, the Persian Empire (cf 'world' in Lk 2:1). **11.** An interval has elapsed since v 10. 'remains at rest': the disturbances which followed the accession of Darius had subsided. **12.** The angel speaks as representative of Jerusalem and Judah. 'seventy years': cf Jer 25:12; 29:10 and commentary. **13.** 'comforting words': cf Is 40:1; 57:18 and context. **14.** 'the angel': not the angel of vv 8, 11. 'jealous': Yahweh guards jealously his special relationship with Israel, but the outcome is more frequently chastisement (Dt 5:9f; Ezek 5:13 etc) than rescue (here, 8:2; Is 9:7 (6) and 37:32 where RSV 'zeal' translates the same Heb. word as here). **15.** For the thought, cf Is 47:6 and Is 10:12—19. 'at ease': a moral fault in Am 6:1; Ps 123 (122):4; Is 32:9—11. **16.** Takes up the theme of v 3. Cf Ezek 8—11 for Yahweh's abandonment of the temple before the fall of Jerusalem. 'house . . . built': a slow process. Permission to re-build was granted in 538 B.C. (Ez 1:2); work was limited to the altar of holocausts (Ez 3) until the 2nd year of Darius (Hag); the building was completed in 515 B.C. (Ez 6:15). In 519 B.C., the work was resumed (cf Hag 1:15). 'measuring line'; here, 2:1 (2:5) and Jer 31:39 implies reconstruction; in Is 34:11, destruction. **17.** Cf Ps 126 (125). 'choose': cf Dt 12:14; Ps 132 (131):13ff.

e 18—21 (MT 2:1—4) 2nd Vision: The Four Horns and Smiths—18—19. 'horns': a symbol of belligerent strength (cf Dt 23:17; 1 (3) Kgs 22:11; Dn 7 and 8), here representing Babylon and her allies. 'four'; denotes totality. 'Israel' is not repeated in v 21 and is probably a gloss; she had already fallen to the Assyrians in 721 B.C. **20—21.** 'smiths': representing Yahweh's agents of destruction (Ezek 21:31).

f 2:1—5 (MT 2:5—9) 3rd Vision: The Man with the Measuring Line—1—2. 'man': not necessarily an angelic figure. He may represent those who were taking practical steps to re-build the walls of the city. Hag and Zech would give the temple priority. 'measuring line': cf 1:16 note and Ezek 40:3. 'came forward': literally, 'came out'; i.e. from the presence of the divinity. **4.** 'villages without walls': in time of war, villagers often took refuge within the walls of a nearby city. 'multitude': Jerusalem will spread beyond its former limits. For the growth of its population after the exile, cf Is 49:19ff; 54:1ff; it is to be swelled by the advent of Gentile nations (Ps 87 (86)). **5.** This promise contrasts with the preoccupation of the post-exilic community with the re-building of the walls (cf at a later time, Neh 2:17ff). 'fire . . . glory': the inhabitants are assured of the abiding protective presence of Yahweh which Israel experienced during the Exodus (cf Ex 13:21; 40:34) and subsequently (1 (3) Kgs 8:10—11; cf Ezek 43:1—5).

g 6—13 (MT 2:10—17) An Appeal to the Exiles—This section interrupts the sequence of the visions. It is addressed to the exiles in Babylon, whereas the visions are directed to the returned exiles in Jerusalem. At first sight it would seem to be appropriate to the situation

immediately before or after the fall of Babylon in **577** 539 B.C. (cf Is 48:20). But not all the exiles returned on that occasion and Zech may well be renewing the call of Dt-Is. Improved circumstances and enhanced prospects warrant such a call (1:11, 16, 21; 2:4—5). **6.** 'land of the north'; i.e. Babylon (cf v 7 and Jer 1:13ff). 'spread you abroad': LXX has: 'I will gather you from the four winds', a reading preferred by many commentators. Others treat 'for I . . . heavens' as a gloss. **7.** 'daughter of Babylon': a poetic personification of the city which may imply the helplessness of the city before its divinely ordained fate (cf Is 47). **8.** 'after his glory sent' can hardly be right. 'his glory' is never found as subject of a verb in the OT. The usual sequence would also put the message of Yahweh after: 'Thus said the Lord of hosts.' The text is corrupt but it broadly reflects the thought of 1:14—16, 18—21. 'me': more likely the prophet than the angel. **9.** 'Behold . . . served them': spoken by Yahweh and introduced by 'Thus said . . .' in v 8. 'Then you . . . sent me': referring to the prophet (cf also 4:9; 6:15 and Dt 18:21—22). 'shake my hand': a menacing gesture (cf Is 11:15; 19:16 and 2 (4) Kgs 5:11 where the same word occurs in MT). For the reversal of the exiles' role cf Ezek 39:10; Ex 12:35—36. 'you will know': cf Dt 18:21ff; Ezek 2:5. **10.** Cf 1:16; 2:10; **h** 9:9; Zeph 3:14—15. A further stage in the work of restoration after the exile. Yahweh had abandoned the temple before the city fell (Ezek 8—11); he is now about to return. This prophecy is intended to promote the work of rebuilding the temple which must be completed before Yahweh can 'dwell in the midst of you'. **11.** Takes up the theme of Is 56:6ff. Both in Is ('my covenant') and here ('my people'), it is accepted that the Gentiles will share with Israel her covenant relationship (cf 8:20—23). This was a logical development from the teaching of Dt-Is on monotheism (41:4; 42:5ff; 45:9ff), but the returned exiles neglected to implement it by an effective missionary effort. **12.** Yahweh is rarely found as subject of the verb 'inherit'; but cf Ex 34:9; Dt 32:9; Ps 82 (81):8 Heb). 'holy land': first occurrence of this phrase in the OT (again in 2 Mc 1:7). The land is consecrated by the presence of Yahweh in the temple of Jerusalem (Ps 114 (113):2). **13.** Strikes a note of care in preparation for the return of Yahweh (cf Heb 2:20; Zeph 1:7 and Ezek 43:1—9). 'roused': the same verb as 'wakened' in 4:1. Yahweh has remained inactive and seemingly indifferent to Israel's fate until she should learn the meaning of her sufferings (cf Is 42:14). Elliger holds that 13 is a liturgical formula used to conclude a reading from the prophet in the temple. The v would then refer—not to the return of Yahweh to the temple after the exile—but to the coming of Yahweh through his word.

3:1—10 4th Vision: Rehabilitation of Priests and i People—1. 'Joshua': the high priest and spiritual head of the returned exiles (cf Hag 1:1; Ez 3:2). His father was among those sons of Levi who went into exile (1 Chr 6:15) and he himself was probably born in Babylon. 'Satan': here an agent of God rather than the adversary he was later to become (cf 1 (3) Kgs 22:21; Jb 1:7; 2:2; 1 Chr 21:1). 'accuse': the verb śāṭan implies more than accusation. The attentions of Satan could result in physical humiliation and harm. Satan seems to act as Yahweh's agent in the punishment of Judah and Jerusalem. **2.** Yahweh intervenes to restrain him. 'brand . . . fire': cf Am 4:11. Joshua represents those who have returned from captivity. **3—4.** 'filthy garments': while clean garments are a sign of joy (Eccl 9:8) and torn garments a sign of mourning (Lev 21:10), the 'filthy

577i garments' here represent the sins of the people which brought the afflictions of exile (cf vv 4 and 9). Much of Israel's guilt still remained to be expiated, but Yahweh's generous mercy intervenes to blot it out. There is no need to look for some personal sin of Joshua.

j 5. Apparently Joshua had been bareheaded, another accompaniment of sorrow and mourning (cf Ezek 24:17). For the turban of the high priest, cf Ex 39:28, 30. 'clean': the term used can also mean 'ritually pure'. Through the mercy of Yahweh, both he and the people are now in a position to exercise their priestly roles (Ex 19:5; 28:1ff). This is another important step in the restoration of the post-exilic community. 7. 'walk in my ways': a Dt formula (e.g. Dt 8:6). Moral integrity is the first foundation of a fruitful priesthood. 'charge': probably refers to the obligations of his office. 'rule ... charge': in the absence of a king, the high priest is given wider control of the sanctuary than in pre-exilic times (cf 1 (3) Kgs 2:27; 2 (4) Kgs 16:10ff; 2 (4) Kgs 22:24; also Ezek 45 *passim*). 'right of access': the translation is not certain, but the context suggests that Joshua will be associated with the angels (= 'those standing here'), not through resurrection, but by sharing in their intimacy with God and by participating in their

k role as intermediaries between God and man. 8. 'your friends': his associates in the priesthood. 'good omen': the better future involves forgiveness of sin (vv 4, 9) and peace (v 10). 'Branch': the abrupt reference to the Branch creates difficulty; the text would run more smoothly and is intelligible without it. Some commentators treat it as a gloss which was added when expectations of the Davidic line seemed to be on the point of realization in the person of Zerubbabel. Taken as part of the original text, the sentence implies that the restoration of the priesthood will be a good omen for the revival of the Davidic dynasty or for the coming of the Messiah. Cf Jer 23:5; 33:15 for the term 'Branch' to describe the Davidic Messiah. 9. 'stone with seven facets': some commentators identify the stone with the 'top stone' in 4:7, or the foundation/cornerstone in Is 28:16, but it was probably a precious stone (cf 'seven facets') adorning the breast of the priest or his diadem. The inscription may well have been *qōdes lᵉyāhû* which has seven consonants cf Ex 28:36; 39:30; Zech 14:20. If this understanding of the 'stone' is correct, it confirms the view that the reference to the Branch in v 8 is an insertion. 10. The peace and blessing of messianic times (cf Mi 4:4 and Zech 8:11ff).

l 4:1–6a, 10c–14 5th Vision: The Lampstand and the Two Olive Trees—The account of this vision is interrupted by the passage inserted in vv 6b–10b and (probably) by the insertion of v 12. Without those interruptions the text runs smoothly. 1. The sleep into which the prophet had fallen suggests that some time had elapsed since the previous vision. 2. The repetition of 'seven' recalls the seven branched candlestick, but the 'lampstand' here is more elaborate. The multiplicity of lights is intended to represent the omniscient providence of God (cf 10c). 'olive trees': representing persons cf Ps 52(51):8; Jer 11:16; Hos 14:7. 6a. 'Then ... me': these words are the introduction to: 'These seven are ...' in 10c. For vv 6b–19b, cf next paragraph. 10c. The explanation is not intended to suggest that Yahweh had seven eyes; the number seven emphasizes rather the way in which the providence of God is present throughout the *whole* earth (cf 1 (3) Kgs 8:29; Dt 11:12; Ps 33(32):18; 34(33):16). The phrase 'range ... earth' is found also in 2 Chron 16:9

(where RSV has 'run to and fro'). The ranging eyes of **577l** Yahweh are closely linked with divine activity (cf Prov 15:3; 2 Chron 16:9). Some commentators suspect **m** that the 'seven lamps' derive from the seven planets of Babylonian astrology with which Israel became familiar during the Exile. This influence is, however, not certain, since the number seven was associated already with the seven branched candlestick. 12. A gloss? The 'pipes' were not mentioned in vv 2–3. It may have been inserted by a scribe who, failing to understand the reference to the 'two sons of oil' (Heb. for 'anointed' in the RSV v 14), thought the two olive trees were simply supplying the oil to the lampstand. If the v is genuine it may describe the role of the two anointed in maintaining the symbol of Yahweh's active interest in things terrestrial through their princely and priestly activities. The vision would then represent not only the intimate association of the high priest and the prince with Yahweh (cf 'stand by the Lord' in v 14 and cf 'access' in 3:7), but also the way in which he would require their co-operation in the future. 14. 'two anointed': in the pre-exilic period kings were anointed; it is in accordance with this practice that Zerubbabel, the Davidic prince, should have been anointed. It is not clear whether in fact, at the time of the vision, he had been already anointed. In the post-exilic period, the royal anointing was appropriated by the high priest (cf on this question De Vaux, AI, 399–400). Zerubbabel and Joshua are here portrayed as the two messiahs (anointed; messiah of David and messiah of Aaron) of the post-exilic period.

4:6b–10b Zerubbabel and the Reconstruction of n the Temple—6b. This section begins with the phrase 'This is the word of Yahweh', a typical formula for introducing a prophetic message. It distinguishes this section from the visions. 'not by ...': a principle frequently invoked by the prophets (cf Is 31:1–3; Ps 20(19):7; 44(43):6). 7. 'great mountain': may represent the political and military power obstructing Zerubbabel (cf Jer 51:25 and Is 40:4). More concretely, it could refer to the heaped up ruins of Jerusalem and its temple. 'top stone': to Zerubbabel will be given the privilege of placing the crowning stone on the building. This prophecy is intended to encourage Zerubbabel in the work he had begun (cf Hag 1:15). 'grace, grace': may have the same force as Italian: *'com'è bello!'*, 'how lovely!'. 10. 'small things'. the modest beginnings of the post-exilic community (cf Hag 2:3). 'plummet': a conjectural translation of an obscure word. It is here associated with the reconstruction; elsewhere, in a context of destruction (cf Am 7:7; Is 30:13).

5:1–4 6th Vision: A Flying Scroll—1. 'flying': **578a** winging its way to the limits of the land (cf v 3). 2. The scroll measured about 30 ft × 15 ft, and was presumably open as it passed the prophet. Scrolls thirty feet long have been found, but the breadth is rarely more than 12 inches. The prophet may have wished to emphasize that the curse was written large so that it could be read as it passed (Hb 2:2). 3. Cf Ezek 2:10. The curse follows on the breaking of the covenant law (Dt 27:15ff). For fear of a curse, cf e.g. Nm 5:16ff. 'land': i.e. Israel, or, more specifically, Judah, because the sins being punished are breaches of the covenant between Yahweh and Israel. 'steals ... swears falsely': cf Ex 20:15, 7. Two sins are mentioned, one representative of those who injure their fellow men, while the other characterizes those who have little reverence for God. These sins, may, however, have been rampant among some sections

578b of the people in Judea (cf note on next v). **4.** Some refer this v (and vision) to the past as if it recalled the punishment already endured by the people of Israel (van Hoonacker). Sellin (followed by Elliger) identifies the thieves and the perjurers with the inhabitants of Judea who had not gone into exile and now defrauded the returned exiles. It seems best, however, to understand the vision—with the other visions—in the context of restoration. With the restoration of the priesthood and the rebuilding of the temple, the renewal of the covenant could take place. It would involve the reading of the curses (cf Dt 27:15ff and Neh 10:29), which would serve as a warning to the people not to fall into their earlier sins. There is no escaping the judgement of God (Am 5:18—19). The attack on the house of the sinner focuses attention on the responsibility of each one for his own sins (cf Ezek 18).

c 5—11 7th Vision: The Woman in the Measure—5. 'goes forth': i.e. from the heavenly regions. **6.** 'ephah': cf § 86e. 'And he said: ... land': a gloss anticipating v 8. **7—8.** 'leaden': an unusually heavy cover for what was probably an earthenware jar. It probably represents the measure of control which Yahweh has over wickedness. 'Wickedness' in Heb. is a feminine noun. This may explain why the figure in the ephah is a woman. In Heb. tradition, however, woman can symbolize what is seductive (cf Prv 5; 6:24ff; 7:10ff). Zech's symbol may represent not so much sin or wickedness in general, as idolatry (cf 'house' in v 11, and note). If so, his choice of symbol may involve an implicit condemnation of cult prostitution (cf Is 57:3—9). Ezek foretold that Israel would be cleansed from idolatry after the exile (33:22ff; 37:21ff). **9.** 'stork': the comparison suggests that they were capable of rapid and prolonged flight. The 'two women' are presumably divine agents who by the way they apply themselves to their task reflect Yahweh's eagerness to purify the land. **11.** 'Shinar': i.e. Babylon (cf Dn 1:2). 'house': perhaps a temple or sanctuary for the idol representing the personified figure of Wickedness. The word 'base' (in Heb., $m^e k\hat{u}n\bar{a}h$) is quoted in support of this view, as it is used in a cultic context in Ez 3:3 ('base of the altar') and 1 (3) Kgs 7:27, and is here taken to mean the pedestal on which the idol is set. Cf Apoc 14:8 for Babylon as the source of wickedness among the nations.

d 6:1—8 8th Vision: The Four Chariots—1. 'chariots': not so much symbols of war (e.g. Is 22:6f; Zech 9:10) as an efficient means of transport. It is not clear that this vision is concerned with war (cf v 8). In his reference to the 'two mountains', Zech may be drawing on Babylonian imagery which pictured Shamash, the sun god, emerging from between the two great columns of the earth. The chariots may then resemble the chariot of the sun, and the two mountains would guard the approach to the divinity. **2—3.** While many suspect that the colours of the horses are related to their destinations at the four points of the compass, it is difficult to see how this is in fact realized. **5.** 'four winds': i.e. the four points of the compass. 'presenting': cf Jb 1:6; 2:1. 'Lord of all the earth': implies the universal dominion which Yahweh exercises over the whole earth (cf 4:14); he can execute punishment or lavish blessing as he will. **6.** The destination of the red horses is not mentioned. They may have remained at the entrance to the divine dwelling which by implication would be the eastern point of the compass. The text may be defective. **7.** 'patrol': cf note on 1:10. **8.** If 'Spirit' refers to the divine anger (cf Jb 4:9 etc), then 'set ... at rest' would mean something like 'assuage my anger' (so ICC;

cf Ezek 5:12; 16:42) by an act of judgement on Babylon **578i** (= 'the north country', cf 2:6). The gift of the Spirit is also a source of consecration to the service of Yahweh (cf Is 11:1ff; Nm 11:25). If the text is here rendered: 'have made my Spirit rest on', it could imply the conversion of Babylon from the worship of Wickedness (cf 5:11) to faith in the God of Israel. Delcor and Elliger think of the Spirit resting on the exiles who were still in Babylon and inspiring them with courage to return.

9—14 A Symbolic Crown—9. This introductory **e** formula suggests that what follows is not a vision (cf 7:4; 8:1). van Hoonacker notes the close parallel to 3:8—10 and doubts whether the action described ever took place in reality. **10.** Some word like 'gifts' or 'offerings' may have been lost after 'take'. The persons named are not otherwise known to us, although Zephaniah, the father of Josiah, may be the 'second priest' who was put to death by Nebuchadnezzar (Jer 52:24—27). **11—13.** As the text stands, Joshua, the high priest is crowned. Most commentators take the view that his name has been substituted for Zerubbabel, the Davidic prince (cf 1 Chr 3:19; Hag 1:1 etc), for the following reasons: (a) the Heb. word for 'crown' ('$^a teret$) is used in a number of passages for the royal crown (2 Sm 12:30; Ezek 21:26 (31); Ps 21 (20):3); no passage speaks of the high-priest wearing an '$^a teret$. (b) 'Branch' in v 12 is an echo of Jer 23:5; 33:15, where it represents the Davidic leader of the post-exilic period. (c) The statement that 'he shall build the **f** temple' identifies the Branch with Zerubbabel (cf 4:9). (d) The terms in which the Branch is described in v 14 and his relationship with the priest make it impossible to identify him with Joshua (cf also 4:14). The change of name would have been made when Zerubbabel faded from the scene without successors, and supreme control was exercised by the high priest. We know nothing of Zerubbabel's fate, but it is clear that the hopes which centred on him as the person to restore the Davidic dynasty were not realized. 'grow up in his place': or, substituting 'Shoot' for 'Branch': the Shoot ($\dot{s}emah$) for upward shall he shoot' ($yi\dot{s}mah$). For dramatic growth **g** from humble beginnings in a messianic context, cf Is 11:1ff; Ezek 17:22ff; Dn 2:34—35. 'royal honour': clearly used of a king in Ps 45 (44):4. 'peaceful understanding': peaceful relations between church and state were not always characteristic of Israel's history (cf 1 Sm 15:10ff; 1 (3) Kgs 22; Is 7). In the pre-exilic period, the king ultimately controlled the temple and the officiating priests (cf 2 (4) Kgs 16:10; 21:5; 23:4 etc). **14.** 're-minder': this word is elsewhere rendered: 'memorial' (e.g. Nm 31:54). It is a form of offering which is intended to remind Yahweh of certain needs of Israel, e.g. of their need of forgiveness, and thereby to win forgiveness (cf Ex 30:16; Nm 10:9—10). In view of the association of the crown with the Branch, the first object of Yahweh's concern should be the welfare of his royal representative. Through him, the returned exiles who made the offering, and all the returned exiles, would benefit ('reminder for (the benefit of)' rather than 'to', cf Nm 31:54). The continuing presence of the crown in the temple would serve as a permanent reminder to Yahweh of Zerubbabel's need of his support (cf Ex 28:29 'continual remembrance'; 28:12; 13:9). **15.** Commentators hesitate to take this v with vv 9—14. Delcor puts it after 6:8; ICC joins it to 4:8—10a, 6a—7. It might however stand here as a conclusion to the section 1:7—6:14 which the editor has put under the one date (1:7; Elliger). 'those who are far off': the Jews still in exile, or perhaps, the Gentiles (cf 2:11; Hag 2:7). 'you shall know ...': cf 2:9. 'And this ...': from Dt 28:1a. Either the prophet,

78g or an editor, makes future progress depend on the keeping of the commandments.

h 7:1–3 A Question on Fasting—1. The date: Nov. 518 B.C. **2.** 'the people of Bethel': MT reads simply 'Bethel'. Alternative renderings of the text are: 'Bethelsharezer, his chief official, and his men sent to ...' or 'Bethel sent Sharezer, the royal official, and his men to ...' There is then some doubt as to whether the question came from the people of Bethel or from some prominent members of the Jerusalem community. **3.** 'house': i.e. the Jerusalem temple. 'prophets': the cultic (or professional, as opposed to charismatic) prophets who were permanently associated with the sanctuary and exercized a teaching role there. 'I': the use of the first pers. sing. pronoun may confirm that v 2 contains the name of an individual, unless one is to think of a personification of Bethel. 'fifth month': the month in 587 B.C. when the temple at Jerusalem was destroyed (2 (4) Kgs 25:8ff). It is not clear whether the question was directed to Zech or not, Elliger supposes that he witnessed it and took the occasion to speak to the people *about* the question rather than in reply to it. The reply is found in 8:18–19.

i 4–14 True Religion; Consequences of its Neglect— 5. 'seventh': recalling the murder of Gedaliah (2 (4) Kgs 25:25; Jer 41:1ff). 'for me': fasting was a common feature of mourning (2 Sm 1:12; 1 Sm 31:13 etc) and penitential (Neh 9:1–2) rites. Since 587 B.C., the Jews by fasting mourned their loss and acknowledged that sin had produced the disaster. Thus the people, not Yahweh would benefit by their fast. **6.** 'eat ... drink': if these words refer to sacrificial meals, the prophet is accusing the people of allowing self-interest to dominate their use of fasts and feasts (cf vv 7–12). Alternatively: since their eating and drinking are for themselves and cannot benefit Yahweh (cf Ps 50 (49):7–15), so also their fasts. For Delcor, this v implies that with the restoration, fasting and mourning should cease. One eats to satisfy hunger and one mourns only when there are grounds for sorrow (cf Neh 8:9ff). **7.** 'When Jerusalem': i.e. under the monarchy in the pre-exilic period. 'these the words': as the text stands this phrase seems to refer to the summary of prophetic teaching in vv 8–10 which make explicit the implications **j** of vv 5–6. **8.** The mention of Zech by name suggests the secondary character of vv 8–10 (cf 7:4; 8:1 etc 'to me'); v 11 could follow quite easily on v 7. **9–10.** For parallels to this summary of prophetic teaching, cf Am 5:14; Mi 6:8; Is 1:11ff; Jer 5:28; Is 58:1–12 and Zech 8:16f. **11.** 'stubborn shoulder': a metaphor derived from animals which refuse to accept the yoke. **12.** 'law': better: 'teaching'. **13–14.** The effects of their misconduct. 'no one': not to be taken literally, although after the fall of Jerusalem the population was much reduced (cf 2 (4) Kgs 25:11–12; Jer 40ff).

k 8:1–8 The Restoration of Jerusalem; Renewal of the Covenant—This chapter contains a series of oracles introduced by: 'Thus says the Lord of Hosts.' They need not have been spoken on the same occasion. **2.** 'jealous': cf 1:14f. **3.** For the return of Yahweh to Sion, cf 1:16; 2:10 note. 'faithful': cf Is 1:21–26. 'holy mountain': cf Is 11:9; Jer 31:23. **4–5.** Zech foresees the fulfilment of the prophecies in Jer 30: 19–20; 31:4–5, 13; Is 65:19ff. **6.** An invitation to faith in the power of Yahweh. **7.** The return of the exiles. 'east country': Babylon. 'west country': probably Egypt; may also include Asia Minor, Greece and some of the Greek islands cf Is 11:11. **8.** The renewal of the covenant (cf Jer 31:31ff). 'my people ... their

God': the covenant formula (Lv 26:12; cf Hos **578k** 2:19–20).

9–17 The Past and Present Contrasted—9. 'be **l** strong': an invitation to courage (cf Jg 7:11; 2 Sm 2:7) rather than to hard work, though the latter is not excluded (cf Hag 2:4). 'prophets': Hag, Zech and perhaps others. **10.** For the hazards of the early days cf Hag 1:6, 9; 2:16–19. In addition to internal strife, the Jews were harrassed by the neighbouring peoples (Ez 4–5; and at a later date, Neh 4:7 (1); 4:1 (3:33)). **11.** Cf Hag 2:18–19. **12.** Cf Hag 2:9. The peace and prosperity will follow on fidelity to the covenant (cf Hos 2:22; 14:8; Am 9:13). **13.** 'byword of cursing': 2 (4) Kgs 22:19. Jer 22:19 shows that the curse was used by invoking the fate of Israel on others: 'may God make you like Israel'. 'blessing': cf Gn 12:2; Hag 2:19. 'fear not': a typical formula of re-assurance at a turning point in the development of Yahweh's plan for Israel (e.g. Gn 15:1; Ex 14:13; Jos 1:6–7, 9). **14.** Cf Lam 2:17. **16–17.** Yahweh's change of attitude is not purely arbitrary; if he is to bestow covenant blessings on the restored community, they must respond by fulfilling their covenant obligations. Cf 7:9 note.

18–19 Answer to the Question on Fasting—Cf **m** 7:3. **18.** 'fourth ... tenth': these two fasts were not mentioned in the original question; the former recalls the breaching of the walls of Jerusalem (cf 2 (4) Kgs 25:3; Jer 39:2), while the latter lamented the arrival of the Babylonian troops to begin the siege (2 (4) Kgs 25:1). 'love ... peace': in the context of ritual and temple worship the prophet keeps insisting on right relations with their fellow men as the test of real sincerity in worship.

20–23 The Nations to Share in Israel's Worship and Blessings—These vv are apparently intended to round off the section which began in 7:1 (cf 'entreat the favour' in 7:2 and 8:21). Elliger attributes them to an editor, or editors, if v 23 is taken on its own. **20–22.** The fulfilment of the expectations of Is 45:14ff; 60:1–22; 2:2–3. The outlook here, however, is less nationalistic. Progress in the rebuilding of the temple may have warranted the prophet's optimistic view of the future. **23.** More nationalistic than 20–22, and probably from a different hand (cf Is 45:14). It does however use 'God' ('*elôhîm*) which would have a wider appeal than Yahweh, the name of Israel's God. 'Jew': literally, 'a Judean man'.

ZECHARIAH 9–14

Author and Date—The majority of commentators now- **579a** adays separate chh 9–14 from chh 1–8 and use the term Deutero-Zechariah (referred to as Dt-Zech) for the last six chh in much the same way as Deutero-Isaiah is applied to Is 40–55. The grounds for thinking that chh 9–14 are not the work of Zechariah, the contemporary of Hag, may be summarized as follows: (a) Zech was vitally concerned with the re-building of the Temple (2:16; 4:9; 6:13) and the restoration of the priesthood (3:1ff) in the years 520–518 B.C. This concern is entirely absent from Dt-Zech; the Temple is simply taken for granted (14:16) and two priestly families are mentioned without comment (12:13). (b) Zech considers at some length the relationship between the high-priest and the Davidic prince. There is no evidence that such a question was of interest to Dt-Zech. (c) Commentators find it easier to understand certain passages in Dt-Zech against the background of the early Greek period. 9:1–6 is thought to reflect the pattern **b** of Alexander's invasion of Palestine in 332 B.C. 14:1–2 may be inspired by the recent capture of Jerusalem by

579b Ptolemy I Soter in 312 B.C., while 11:14; 14:10, 21 suggests that the Samaritan schism was a live issue at the time of writing (see commentary). This break with Jerusalem probably occurred in the latter part of the 4th century B.C. (d) In Zech, a large part of his message is cast in the form of visions (cf cc 1—6), a form which is absent from Dt-Zech. Zech frequently speaks in the first person, whereas only one instance of this practice occurs in Dt-Zech (11:7ff). Neither does Dt-Zech date his oracles as happened with the utterances of Zech (1:1, 7; 7:1). (e) Differences in word usage and choice of phrase are also clear. For example, different Heb. words are used for 'remnant' in 8:6, 11 (*še'ērît*) and 14:2 (*yeter*); for 'dwell' in 2:14—15; 8:3, 8 and in 9:6; 14:11 etc. The phrase 'On that day' which is found 18 times in 9—14, occurs only 3 times in 1—8. Formulae which are used with great frequency in presenting the words of Yahweh in 1—8 (cf e.g. 1:3, 4, 16; 3:7 etc, and 1:7; 4:8 etc) are scarcely to be found in 9—14 (only 11:4). (f) Zech is more specific and exact in his handling of texts from Scripture (e.g. 7:9—10), whereas Dt-Zech is more allusive in his method. On this point, cf Delcor, RB 59 (1952) 385—411. (g) Zech has a whole series of texts (1:3—6; 3:7; 5:3—4; 6:15; 7:9—13; 8:16—17) recalling specific moral obligations and including references to 'words' (1:6; 7:12), 'statutes' (1:6) and 'law' (or teaching, *tôrāh*; 7:12); these texts have no counterpart in Dt-Zech.

c These reasons seem adequate to justify the separation of chh 1—8 and 9—14. Some commentators would go further and claim that the differences between chh 9—11 and 12—14 are such as to require diversity of authorship. Chh 12—14 have their own introductory title, are written almost throughout in prose, and are much less historical and more eschatological than chh 9—11. A difference in the attitude to the Samaritans is also noticeable in 9:10, 13; 10:7 on the one hand and 11:14; 14:10, 21 on the other.

The view which reads chh 9—14 against the background of the last decades of the 4th cent. B.C. is followed here. It is unlikely that any section refers to the Maccabean period since Sir 49:10, written about 180 B.C., seems to suppose that the canonical book of the Minor Prophets was already complete at that time.

d The Message of Deutero-Zechariah—The variety of opinion on the unity of Dt-Zech (cf § 579c) makes it questionable whether one should attempt to summarize the teaching of chh 9—14 under one title. Some would prefer to see separate titles for chh 9—11, and 12—14 (or even: for chh 9—11, 12—13 and for 14). Since, however, the outlook in 9—14 is generally apocalyptic, there are sufficient grounds for presenting their teaching in a unified way (Lamarche has recently made an elaborate defence of the unity of authorship of chh 9—14).

e Dt-Zech is dominated by the thought of the **final conflict** (cf 9:1—8, 11—15; 10:3—7; 11:1—3; 12:1—9; 13:7—9; 14:1—5, 12—15) between Yahweh (with his people) and the nations, who represent the forces opposed to Yahweh's plans for his people and his kingdom (cf Ps 2; 46(45)). Traditional enemies of Israel will crumble under the weight of Yahweh's might (9:1—6; 10:11*b*—11:3; 12:3; 14:12—15). His people will fight with more than human effectiveness (9:13; 10:6—7; 12:5—8); they acknowledge the source of their strength (12:5) which comes to them through God's fidelity to the covenant (9:11). He is the good shepherd (9:16) whose care for his sheep contrasts with the neglect of his human counterparts (10:3ff; 11:4—17). He is the true source of blessings (10:1—2), not the idols which have led his people astray (10:2; 13:2).

Victory will only be achieved by passing through **579**f the agonies of the end time. Jerusalem will succumb for a while (10:6; 13:7—9; 14:2); she must **suffer** for her sins (12:10; 13:2; 14:1—2) and learn to **repent** (12:10—13:1). **Purification** will follow (13:1—6) as a preliminary to any **covenant renewal** (13:9; cf 9:11ff).

Victory will prepare the way for the inauguration of the **messianic king**, whose universal rule will be characterized by justice, humility and peace (9:9—10). His reign is the forerunner of **Yahweh's universal kingship** (14:9) which will be acknowledged by the nations coming in pilgrimage to Jerusalem (14:16—19). His reign will be marked by the abundance of paradise (9:17), continual warmth, unfailing light (14:6—7) and unending streams of life-giving waters (14:8).

Dt-Zech and the New Testament—Although no **f** certain quotation from Zech can be found in the NT (Mk 13:27 par., cf Zech 2:10; Mk 10:27 par., cf Zech 8:6 must be regarded as doubtful examples), Dt-Zech figures prominently, particularly in the Passion narratives: Zech 9:9 in Mt 21:5 and Jn 12:15; 11:12—13 in Mt 26:15 and 27:9; 12:10 in Jer 19:37 (cf Apoc 1:7); 13:7 in Mt 26:31 and Mk 14:27. This is perhaps not surprising in view of Dt-Zech's pre-occupation with the agonies of the end time and the establishment of God's universal dominion. What is, however, curious is the fact that Dt-Zech is used more frequently than Dt-Is in the Passion story. Lamarche therefore asks 'if the Evangelists regarded these chapters as the culmination of messianic prophecy, as an image of Christ which is both more profound and more precise than the figure of the Suffering Servant' (p. 8).

Lamarche believes that literal exegesis leads one **g** to see in the King-Shepherd of Dt-Zech (he takes 9:9—10; 11:4—17; 12:10—13:1; 13:7—9 to refer to the same individual, a view not shared by all) both a contemporary of the prophet and the Messiah. This picture of a Messiah who is rejected and put to death is one of the outstanding features of these chapters which are clearly influenced by the Servant Songs of Dt-Is. 'The figure of the Messiah who suffers for us (Is 53) is completed by the figure of the Shepherd who leads his flock into purifying trials (Zech 13:7—9). The image of the Messiah who saves us by his sufferings and death is completed by the image of the Shepherd who is pierced and who by his death leaves the repentant people in the position that they must look for everything from the generous mercy of God. No wonder that both Christ and the Evangelists used both Dt-Is and Dt-Zech to give a complete picture of the mission and Passion of the Messiah' (p. 146, n. 1).

While commentators would agree on what one might **h** call the messianic drift of several passages in Dt-Zech, they would differ in the measure of accommodation they would see in the NT use of those passages. The texts could have been brought to mind by the similarity of situations in the NT and Dt-Zech, since it can scarcely be established that current messianic expectation was based on a messianic understanding of these texts. This raises the question of the 'fuller sense' of Scripture and the understanding of messianic prophecies, which is discussed elsewhere (§ 51), and makes intelligible the remark of Delcor: 'It is unnecessary to remark that the meaning given by NT authors to one or other passage of Dt-Zech will not necessarily enlighten us on the literal meaning in Dt-Zech' (p. 555).

9:1—8 Judgement on Syria, Phoenicia, and Phili- i stia—**1.** 'Oracle': this word is not found in Zech 1—8. 'word': the word of God's judgement is directed against cities of Syria, Phoenicia and Philistia which, at one time

579i or another, have been enemies of Israel. The progress of this judgement seems to follow the path of the invasion of Syria and Palestine by Alexander the Great in 332 B.C. (For details, cf Elliger, ZAW 62 (1949/50) 63ff; Delcor, VT 2 (1951), 110ff), although certain features would fit quite easily into the pattern of Assyrian conquest in the 8th cent. B.C. (cf Is 10:5—11). 'Hadrach': the capital city of an independent N Syrian kingdom; it lay about 330 km NE of 'Damascus', the capital of Syria. 'rest upon': the Heb. might also be rendered: 'Damascus is its camping place'. 'For to the Lord belong . . . Israel': he can therefore exercise judgement over them. If the principle of v 7 ('it too shall be a remnant . . .') applies here, then the process of divine judgement is aimed at incorporating these peoples and territories into the people and the land of Yahweh—in a state of subjection, however, rather than on terms of equality. Dahood CBQ 25 (1963) 123—4 takes the MT to mean: 'the surface of the earth' and does not accept the RSV conjecture 'the cities of Aram'.

j 2. 'Hamath': about 200 km N of Damascus. Its kingdom extended southwards at least as far as Riblah (cf 2 (4) Kgs 23:33; 25:21). The ideal northern limit of Israel in some traditions was Dan (Jg 20:1; 1 Sm 3:20 etc); in others, it was the Euphrates (Gn 15:18; Dt 1:7 etc); in still others, 'the entrance to Hamath'. This latter phrase in some cases refers to the southern end of the great valley of the Lebanon (Ezek 47:15ff; Nm 13:21); in others, to the northern end (Jos 13:15; Jg 3:3). 'Tyre': seems superfluous here in view of v 3. The Heb. verb reads: 'Though she is very wise', implying the mention of one city only. The wisdom of Tyre and Sidon were traditional (cf Ezek 27—28), but here a note of mockery underlies the reference (as in Ezek 28:2—10); the trials of the Phoenician cities arise from excessive reliance on human wisdom and too little attention to the will of Yahweh. 3—4. The shrewdness of Tyre has enabled her to amass wealth and to build strong fortifications (Jos 19:29; 2 Sm 24:7), but they will provide no defence against Yahweh, who acts through his agent (in this case, Alexander; cf Is 10:5 for Assyria in a similar role). Tyre fell to Alexander in 332 B.C. after a seven months'

k siege. 5—7. The enmity of the Philistines, already manifest in the time of the Judges (Jg 13—16), persisted right down to the time of the Maccabees (1 Mc 10:86, 89; 11:60; 12:33). Their resistance to the rebuilding of the walls of Jerusalem (Neh 4:7 (MT v 1)) would not have endeared them to the returned exiles. Now the Jews look forward with relish to the humiliation of their traditional enemies, but not to their total destruction. A remnant will join the Jews in the worship of Yahweh (v 7). Ashkelon's fear at the fate of Tyre was conditioned by the close political and economic ties which linked the two cities in the 4th cent. B.C. 'a mongrel people': cf the fate of Samaria after it had fallen to the Assyrians in 721 B.C. (cf 2 (4) Kgs 17:24ff). 'its blood': MT 'its bloods'. The Philistines will be called on to adopt the Hebrew practice of draining blood from slaughtered beasts (Dt 12:16, 23f) so as not to eat meat with blood (cf Ezek 33:25). 'abominations': a term often applied to idols (cf Jer 4:1; Dt 29:17 etc). Lv 11:10—12 and Is 66:17 use it for forbidden foods. Is there perhaps a reference to foods offered to idols (cf 1 Cor 10:14ff)? 'Jebusites': the original inhabitants of Jerusalem. According to Jos 15:63; Jg 1:21, they continued to live in Jerusalem together with members of the tribes of Judah and Benjamin (cf Jg 3:5f). They were eventually absorbed by the Israelites. 8. 'encamp': here with defensive intent; aggressively in Is 29:3. 'house': Jerusalem with its temple, or, more probably here, the (newly extended)

territory of Yahweh's land. For this meaning of 'house', **579k** cf Hos 8:1; 9:15.

9—10 The Messianic King—9. 'Rejoice': this word is **l** often used in a general sense in the OT, but it recurs with noticeable frequency in passages which refer to the kingship of Yahweh (e.g. Ps 97 (96):1; 149:2, 1 Chr 16: 31) and to his saving intervention (Is 34:1—4). Two passages link it with the birth (Is 9:3ff) and the enthronement of the messianic king (Ps 2:11 MT; RSV and many commentators correct the text). 'shout aloud': particularly in the context of battle, a cry of victory (Ps 41 (40):11; Is 44:23), or a battle cry (1 Sm 4:5; 17:20). More significantly for the present passage, it describes the way in which the people acknowledged Saul as their king (1 Sm 10:24) and celebrated the kingship of Yahweh (Nm 23:21; Ps 81 (80):2; 95 (94): 1—2). A number of passages in exilic (Is 52:7—8; Zeph 3:14,17) an post-exilic (Zech 2:10 (14); Jl 2:21,23ff) literature invite Sion to rejoice in a similar way at the approach of Yahweh who comes to save, but the picture of the king 'riding on an ass' here excludes a direct reference to Yahweh-King. Alexander's triumphal progress (9:1—8) may have evoked the prospect of Israel's deliverance through the human representative of Yahweh's kingship, the Davidic Messiah. 'triumphant' (Heb. *ṣaddîq*): usually and perhaps better, rendered 'just' (or 'righteous'), which could stand here since justice is a feature of other messianic texts (e.g. Is 11:4—5). It is through the exercise of this justice that the Messiah **m** will establish peace (Is 11:6ff; 9:6—7 (5—6); Jer 23:5—6; 33:15—16; 2 Sm 23:3 and here v 10). 'victorious': literally, 'saved' (the passive participle of the verb found in Jer 23:6; 33:16; cf also Dt 33:29). The passive form makes it clear that the king's safety and success derive from Yahweh. 'humble': the same term is used of the messianic people of Israel in Zeph 3:12. Delcor emphasizes the religious aspects of this term in Zeph and suggests that it is equivalent to: just, pious, believing (cf Ps 10 (9):2, 9, 12, 17; 12 (11):5 where RSV has 'poor' or 'meek'). Attempts have been made to identify this humble and devout king with the Suffering Servant on the basis of Is 53:11 ('righteous' = *ṣaddîq*, as here for 'triumphant') and 53:7 ('afflicted' = *na'aneh*, probably from the same root as *'ānî* = 'humble' here; but *na'aneh* means 'humiliated' rather than 'humble'). In Zech, however, there is no question of a suffering Messiah. Links with the other Servant songs are even more tenuous. 'riding on an ass': contrasts with the horses and chariots of v 10. It is scarcely intended as a humiliation; more probably it recalls the ancient usage of Gn 49:11; Jg 5:11; 10:4, where the possession of an ass is a mark of distinction (cf also 1 (3) Kgs 1:33, 38 for David and Solomon riding on a mule). 'colt . . . ass': parallel to 'ass'; therefore only one animal is intended. 10. 'cut off': **n** usually describes punitive action taken by Yahweh against Israel on the nations. Here it states dramatically that universal peace will be established without the help of arms on which Ephraim and Jerusalem relied too often in the past (cf Hos 1:7; Is 31:1—3). That Yahweh himself will intervene to destroy the weapons of his own people is new in prophetic literature (cf Is 9:3—4; Ps 46 (45): 9ff for his destruction of enemy weapons). 'Command peace': 'command' is too strong; 'speak peace' is perhaps sufficient (cf Ps 122 (121):8). The Messiah's aim will be to build up universal peace with justice as its foundation (cf Is 9:5—6; 11:1—9; Ezek 34:25; Ps 72 (71):7). 'sea to sea': from the Dead Sea (or perhaps the Red Sea, cf 1 (3) Kgs 9:26) to the Mediterranean Sea. 'River': Euphrates. 'ends of the earth': although messianic peace

579n will originate among the Jews within the limits of the Holy Land ('sea to sea', 'River') it is intended that all nations shall share in it (cf Is 52:10; and Ps 72 (71):8 and 1 (3) Kgs 5:4; 1 Chr 22:9 for the kingdom of Solomon).

o The lively faith in a Davidic Messiah reflected in this passage is remarkably independent of the current ineffectiveness of the Davidic dynasty. Judah had now been without a Davidic king for almost three hundred years, but it still pinned its hopes on one of his descendants. Similar preoccupations motivated the author of Chronicles when writing at a slightly later date (cf § 297e). The material and political failure of David's line was never allowed to obscure the divine origin of this hope. It rested on the word of God (2 Sm 7) and was guaranteed by God's fidelity to his promises. When the Davidic Messiah appeared, God's power would be at work to accomplish what lay beyond the reach of human endeavour. This faith and hope were still active in the time of Christ (Mt 21:4—9 and parr.).

p **11—17 Return of Exiles and Restoration of Sion—** **11.** 'you': fem. sing. referring to Sion. 'blood of my covenant with you': Heb. literally: '*blood of your covenant*' (cf Ezek 16:60—61). A reference to Ex 24:4—8. The mingling of the blood in the bowls and the sprinkling on the altar and on the people probably symbolizes the establishment of a blood relationship between the divinity (represented by the altar) and the people. As father of his people, Yahweh will show a father's mercy to his wayward children. Israel's consciousness of the paternal role of Yahweh was reflected in the numerous proper names containing the element *ab* (e.g. Abijah: 'Yahweh is (my) father'). 'captives': either those taken by Alexander during the invasion of 332 B.C. or by Ptolemy I Soter who captured Jerusalem in 312 B.C. 'waterless pit': cf Gn 37:20:24; Jer 38:6—13. **12.** 'stronghold': Jerusalem. 'prisoners of hope': i.e. those who kept hoping for rescue. 'double': the background to this idea is provided by Is 40:2; 61:7; Zech 1:14—15. **13.** In former times Assyria (Is 10:5), Egypt (Jer 47:6) and the Greeks (Zech 9:1—8) have been the instruments of Yahweh's anger. In the last great conflict of the end time, a re-united Israel will be his instrument of victory over the nations. The re-union of North and South is a familiar expectation of the post-exilic period (cf Jer 33:7ff; Is 49:5—6). 'over your sons, O Greece': regarded by many commentators and BJ as a gloss on metrical grounds. One might add that although the Greeks were responsible for the current distress the text suggests a broader sweep to include the defeat of **q** all the enemies of Yahweh and Israel. **14.** 'lightning . . . trumpet . . . south': echoes of Sinai (cf Ex 19:16—19; Dt 33:2; and above 9:11). This picture of Yahweh, the warrior chief, equipped with the weapons of the storm may owe something to the Canaanite representations of the storm god Baal Hadad. He is usually depicted with a club (= thunderbolt) in one hand and a stylized lightning flash (sometimes in the form of a spear) in the other (cf also Ps 18 (17):13—14). **15.** In terms which recall Ezek 39:17—20 (in an eschatological context) and Jer 46:10, the prophet describes the crushing victory of Israel with Yahweh at their head. He draws on the cult for his metaphors ('blood . . . bowl . . . corners of the altar'). **16.** When the tumult of battle is past, an era of peace and prosperity will begin. 'flock': cf Ps 95 (94):7; Ezek 34. 'crown': although the Hebrew terminology is different, Is 62:3 also likens Israel to a 'crown' and 'diadem'. **17.** 'it': in this rendering, the reference is to the land or the people. The MT seems to have Yahweh in mind, but the Heb. word for 'fair' is never used elsewhere of Yahweh.

The rest of the v is awkward in Heb.; there is a suspicion **579q** that 'young men' and 'maidens' were added to interpret the text in terms of the expected growth in Israel's population in messianic times (cf 10:8—10). The original may have read: '*it (the land) will make grain and new wine flourish*'. Cf Jer 31:12; Zech 8:12 for similar conditions of paradise.

10:1—2 Yahweh, the True Source of Blessings— **r** The reference to abundant grain and new wine in the previous verse may have suggested the introduction of this passage at this point. **1.** For Yahweh's control over the rains, cf Ps 135 (134):7; 147 (146):8; Jl 2:23 etc. 'spring rain': important for the final ripening of the grain crops. It fell during Mar.—Apr. **2.** 'teraphim': domestic gods in Gn 31:19; in Ezek 21:21(26) are consulted in divination. Josiah sought to eliminate them (2 (4) Kgs 23:24; in 1 Sm 15:23 RSV is rendered 'idolatry'). Here there may be an implicit reference to the false gods of the Greeks. A similar misjudgement on the part of Israel concerning the origin of rain and fertility is recorded in Hos 2:5—13 (7—15). 'shepherd': their choice of counsellor means that, in effect, they are without guidance (cf Ezek 34: Jer 27:9; 29:8). The leaders, too, may have turned from Yahweh to the Greek gods. 'wander': perhaps into exile. The verb may describe the errant ways of Israel which are a prelude to exile.

3—12 Rescue and Restoration—In this section, direct **s** speech of Yahweh alternates with passages which speak of him in the third person. **3.** 'shepherds': the occurrence of this word in v 2 may have influenced the editorial decision to put this section here. In view of what follows, however, it is unlikely that 'shepherds' refers to the leaders of Israel; Yahweh's anger is directed against the foreign rulers (the Seleucids and/or Ptolemys) who dominate his people, 3a is taken to be a gloss by Elliger and as the conclusion of 1—2 by Ackroyd (PC (2)). 'he-goats' (note RSV): cf Is 14:9 where 'he-goats' is also rendered 'leaders' in RSV. 'steed': contrast 9:13; cf Jb 39:19ff for a splendid description of the war horse. **4.** A series of meta- **t** phors to describe (a) good ruler(s). 'cornerstone': cf Is 28:16; Ps 118 (117):22. 'tent peg': Is 22:23. 'battle bow': ancient oriental kings were often depicted with a bow in their hands. Here it is a symbol for effective royal leadership in battle (cf Jer 49:35 and ANEP 184, 390). 'shall come': the same verb is used in Is 11:1; Mi 5:1; Jer 30:21 to describe the origin of the Messiah. It is not surprising that this verse of Zech concerning a ruler(s) of Judah (no doubt a Davidic king) was later presented in messianic terms by the Targum (cf 9:9—10). **5.** 'the foe': although this word does not occur in the Heb. text, there is little doubt about the meaning (cf Mi 7:10). 'Yahweh is with them': without Yahweh's help they could accomplish nothing; with his help, their success will exceed all natural expectation. **6.** 'house of Joseph': northern Israel. 'have compassion': the verb used here (*rāham*) recalls the name of one of Hosea's children which appears in the RSV as 'Not Pitied' (Hos 1:6; cf also Hos 2:23 (21)). 'I am . . . God': a re-affirmation of the covenant relationship (cf 9:11). **7.** 'Ephraim': cf 9:10, 13 for a similar **u** interest in the N kingdom of Ephraim (also Ezek 37: 15—19; Hos 1:11 may be post-exilic). **8.** 'signal': lit 'whistle'. In Is 5:26; 7:18, Yahweh whistles to call the nations to chastise his people. Here the reverse is the case. 'many as of old': war had reduced their numbers. For this aspect of restoration, cf Is 54:1—3; 60:1ff; Zech 2:5 (9). **9.** 'remember': implies an element of repentance and perhaps a turning to Yahweh in prayer (cf 'answer' in v 6; Dt 30:1—3). 'live': LXX read: 'they will bring up their children'. **10.** 'Egypt . . . Assyria': the recent

579u invasion of Ptolemy I Soter saw many Jews taken captive to Egypt. Assyria, however, had ceased to be effective on the international scene since the fall of Nineveh in 612 B.C. Some evidence can be adduced in favour of its here referring to the Seleucid kings, but it is more likely that, taken in conjunction with Egypt, it is a traditional, comprehensive description of the enemies of Israel and

v Judah (cf Is 27:13; Jer 2:18; Is 11:11, 16). 'Gilead': was originally occupied by Israel (cf Jos 22:9 etc). It is mentioned in a similar context in Mi 7:14; Jer 50:19. 'Lebanon': was never occupied by Israel. On this and metrical grounds, it is often taken to be a gloss. Elliger reads: 'and Lebanon will not be enough for them'. Lebanon figures in other passages which depict the restoration of Israel (e.g. Hos 14:7−8; Is 35:2; 60:13 etc), but not in a territorial sense. 'no room': cf v 8 and note. **11.** The restoration is presented in terms of a new Exodus. This theme was also used in describing the return from Babylon (cf Is 40; 51:9−11). **12.** Generally taken to be a gloss because of the occurrence of Yahweh in the third person. 'them': the restored Israelites. A slight change would give: 'Their strength shall be in the Lord'; a reading preferred by several commentators and BJ.

580a **11:1−3 Proud Nations shall be Humbled—1.** 'Lebanon': Is 10:33f and Ezek 31:3, 8 suggest that this section is concerned with Israel's powerful enemies, their kings and allies, and that it serves as a conclusion to 10:3−11, with 12 as a gloss. In the present context, Lebanon with its cedars could be a symbol for the Seleucid dynasty which ruled over Lebanon as well as over Judah. A less likely view would link vv 1−3 with what follows, in which case the cedars, cypress and oaks would represent the disastrous leaders of Israel (cf v 5). 'fire': the all consuming anger of God (cf Is 9:19 (18); 10:17). **2.** 'cypress . . . oaks': smaller kingdoms more or less dependent on the kingdom or ruler represented by the cedar. **3.** 'shepherds . . . lions': the rulers of the enemy nations (Jer 35:36; Ezek 32:2). 'glory': probably their pastures (cf Jer 25:36), i.e. their kingdoms. 'lions . . . jungle': cf Jer 49:19; 50:44. The choice of metaphor with its reference to the Jordan in the territory of Judah does not necessitate the identification of the lions with leaders of the Jewish community. The text is merely stating that the natural habitat of the lions (i.e. the territories of the kings in question) will be devastated.

b **4−17 The Allegory of the Shepherds**—Ezek 34 and 37:15ff provide the literary antecedents of this passage. **4.** The present shepherds are so little concerned with the welfare of the people that Yahweh calls on the prophet to give them leadership in accordance with the terms of the covenant (cf v 10) by which they became *his* people in the first instance. The prophet is to be the visible representative of Yahweh; his words are the words of Yahweh (cf v 11). At times it is difficult to decide whether it is he or Yahweh who speaks (cf vv 8*a*, 10*b*). 'doomed': while the use of this term implies that disaster will inevitably follow an unchanged pattern of conduct, it does not exclude the hope of a change. The sending of the prophet is in the nature of a last, despairing effort (cf Is 6:8−13). **5.** The blessing which invoked the name of Yahweh shows

c that the persons concerned were Jews. For an illustration of what was involved, cf Neh 5:1−11. 'go unpunished': better: '*are not aware of their guilt*' (cf Jer 50:7). Not only do they not feel guilty, but they see in their ill-gotten gains a sign of divine favour and in their activities a form of religion. This blindness is unpardonable in the leaders of Yahweh's people, particularly if they happened to be priests. This may well have been the case, since the high-priest was the leader in the Jewish community of the post-

exilic period. **6.** Often taken to be a gloss by commentators **580c** (e.g. Elliger) who would have v 7 follow immediately on v 5. 6 can, however, be understood as the unfolding of the implications of 'doomed' in v 4 (see note). 'men . . . shepherd . . . king': this statement may reflect the internal struggles for power (cf v 9) as various factions among the Jewish leaders (priesthood?) sought to win the favour of the alien (Seleucid?) king when they should have been caring for the people. Their efforts will only make them victims of those whom they have courted, and the way will be open to them 'to crush the *land*' (not: 'earth' as in RSV). 'none': not in the MT, which has: 'I will not deliver from their hand'. The statement may be confined to those who were involved in intrigue, since a more merciful outcome is foretold in 13:8. **7.** Attention has been drawn to d the practice of Palestinian shepherds who carry two staffs (cf Ps 23 (22):4 and E. Power, Bib (1928) 434−42), but the dependence of this passage on Ezek 37:15ff may be more relevant here. 'Grace': for this term, cf Ps 27 (26):4 (RSV: 'beauty of the Lord'); Ps 90 (89):17. It seems to imply the gracious and effective help which Yahweh dispensed from his sanctuary (where this message may have been communicated) to the members of the covenant community. 'Union': generally taken to be a *hapax legomenon* in the OT and, when derived from a root meaning 'to bind' understood as an abstract term in the light of v 14. Delcor, however, derives it from another root and translates: 'those who take in pledge'. He then understands 'Grace' to represent the flock, while 'those who take in pledge' are the priests in Jerusalem allied to the Samaritans (cf v 14). **8.** 'month': either: e a brief period, or the span of time when grace was offered (and refused (so BJ)). 'I destroyed': more likely the words of Yahweh than of the prophet. 'three shepherds': since Delcor remarks that at least forty views have been offered concerning their identity, the most that can be said is that they were probably leaders of three important factions in the Jewish community (cf notes on vv 6 and 9). **9.** The scant attention paid to the prophet results in his withdrawal. He no longer tries to impede the forces which will destroy the Jewish community not even those operating from within (cf 'devour the flesh of one another'). For the thought, cf Jer 15:1−2. **10.** A symbolic action which was understood by the observers for whom it was intended (cf 11). 'I had made': the prophet speaks in the name of Yahweh. 'all the peoples': as the text stands, it could be understood in the light of Ezek 34:25ff. The 'peoples' would be the neighbouring countries with whom Yahweh had, as it were, made a pact, so that his own people might dwell in peace. Many, however, prefer to read 'all the people', i.e. Israel, N and S. The breaking of the staff would then relieve Yahweh of his covenant obligations to his people. **11.** 'watching': cf 'detested' in v 8. **12.** If the scene is set in the temple (cf v 13), the prophet could be addressing the priests. His words indicate that the animosity of the leaders was such that a refusal would not have surprised him. They seem to have paid quite promptly, perhaps in the hope of being rid of him. 'thirty': an expression of contempt? It was the value set on a slave (Ex 21:32). **13.** 'treasury': Torrey (JBL 55 (1936) f 247−60) has insisted that the MT can be retained (as against, e.g. RSV) and translated either: 'founder' (i.e. of metals), or: 'foundry' (as in LXX). Eissfeldt later showed (Forschungen und Fortschritte 13 (1937) 163f; also Delcor, VT 3 (1953) 73−7) that there was a foundry in the first Temple for the smelting of precious metals offered in the sanctuary. 'lordly': irony. 'cast them etc': this gesture may have served to emphasize that the money really belonged to Yahweh, the true shepherd of Israel,

580f and that in paying the price of a slave, the Jewish leaders were, in effect, showing contempt for their God. As a consequence, the prophet, **14**, proceeds to break the second staff, an action which almost certainly reflects the final rupture between the Samaritans and the Jews. This came about early in the Gr. period and was given permanence by the building of a temple on Mount Gerizim (cf § 67f). **15.** Another symbolic action to illustrate Yahweh's intention to replace the good shepherd who has been rejected with a wicked shepherd. **16.** He is heir to the worst traditions of evil rulers already condemned in Ezek 34:3−5. **17.** 'worthless shepherd': his identity is not known. 'deserts': cf Jo 10:13. Elliger treats v 17 as a separate unit which was added to give hope to the people now experiencing the hardships of the worthless shepherd's rule.

g **12:1 Title**—This v serves as a title to chh 12−14 which are distinctive in style and approach. The text of these chapters is for the most part in prose and is divided into a number of small units with the frequent repetition of the formula 'On that day'. Reference is made to Jerusalem, Judah, and the land, no longer to Israel (with the exception of the title) as in chh 9−11. The outlook is eschatologico-apocalyptic, particularly in ch 14. 'Israel': the texts which follow are concerned with Jerusalem and Judah; Israel must then be understood in the most general religious sense in so far as Jerusalem and Judah are representative of the chosen people. 'stretched' etc: cf the doxologies in Am 4:13; 5:8−9; 9:5−6; and Is 42:5.

2−9 Yahweh the Strength of Jerusalem; Victory over the Nations—**2.** 'a cup of reeling': the chastisement of the Exile is described in similar terms in Is 51:17, 22 while Jer 25:17 speaks of the cup of God's anger against the nations. Here the term is used to state that Jerusalem will be Yahweh's instrument for the chastisement of the nations. 'the peoples round about': the phrase might seem to refer to the neighbouring peoples, but v 3 suggests that it embraces all non-Israelite nations. 'it (?) . . . against Judah . . . Jerusalem': the MT is scarcely intelligible, and is probably a gloss. Elliger believes it comes from the same hand as 3b ('and all the nations . . . against it'), 4bα ('But upon the house of Judah I will open my eyes'), 6a ('On that day . . . round about'), and 7−8, which are intended to emphasize that Judah as well as Jerusalem will participate in the great battle and in the ultimate victory. V 7 certainly creates the impression that there was rivalry between the people of Judah and Jerusalem. A slight emendation would give: 'And Judah also will be in a state of siege' (cf *Biblia Hebraica*, **h** ed. 3, Kittel note). **3.** 'on that day': also in vv 4, 6, 8, 9, and 11. Of itself, it does not have an eschatological significance; it can, however, acquire it from the context, as happens here. For 'the day of Yahweh', or 'the day of the Lord', cf § 553a. 'Heavy stone': This metaphor is usually illustrated by reference to Jerome who recalled a game which he saw young people playing in Palestine and which is said to date from the Hellenistic period (cf ICC). The children competed with one another to see who could lift heavy stones to the greatest height in spite of the danger of serious injury in the handling of these stones. The Heb. verb for 'hurt' suggests tearing and laceration rather than the crushing effect of a heavy stone falling on someone. 'all the nations of the earth': this phrase makes it clear that there is question, not of an historical siege, but of the eschatological assault on the city of God. This is a common theme in apocalyptic literature (cf Ezek 38:14−16; Jl 3 (4):11). **4.** Cf Ezek 38:4, 15 for horses in the apocalyptic battle. Yahweh himself will intervene (cf 2 (4) Kgs 6:18ff). 'open my eyes': look with favour

on. **5.** The sight of the besieging forces and Yahweh's **580h** dramatic intervention produce a generous recognition of the source of Jerusalem's strength. Does 'their God' carry an implicit reference to rivalry between rural Judah and Jerusalem? Cf vv 6−17. **6.** The similes are chosen **i** to convey the speed and thoroughness with which the clans of Judah will dispose of their enemies. Cf note on v 2. **7−8.** These two vv are distinguished not only by their content (cf note on v 2), but also by the use of Yahweh in the third person, as opposed to the first in the rest of the passage. 'tents of Judah': an archaizing phrase to describe the inhabitants of Judah apart from the city of Jerusalem. 'glory': either their vanity, or the object of their pride, perhaps the Temple. 'glory of the house of David' would seem to imply effective reconstitution of the Davidic dynasty in the end time, since, at the time of writing, (end 4th cent. B.C.), its influence was almost nil. 'that of': these words are not found in, nor are they necessarily implied by the MT. While the writer of 7−8 **j** is willing to concede the pre-eminence of Jerusalem and the Davidic line, he is more than eager to ensure that the rest of Judah shall not be forgotten. Insufficient evidence makes it impossible to decide whether there was widespread discontent in rural Judah and sharp rivalry with Jerusalem, or whether the writer is recording his personal irritation at the airs of the capital city! 'put a shield': the same Heb. verb is rendered 'protect' in Is 31:5, which would be more accurate here. 'like David': for David's strength cf I Sm 17:34ff. 'like God': or, 'like divine beings'. 'like the (an) angel of Yahweh': a gloss inserted by a scribe who understood the text to mean 'like God' and fought shy of the direct comparison between God and a human being. **9.** There is some doubt as to whether this v concludes the previous section (so RSV) or opens the next (so JB). 'seek': there is no suggestion that failure is possible; in fact, v 10 presupposes success. 'purpose' (Ackroyd) is better.

12:10−13:1 Repentance and Regeneration—**10. k** Victory in the eschatological conflict is followed by an outpouring of the spirit, a concept inspired by such texts as Ezek 39:29; 36:25−27; Is 44:3. What spirit? Proceeding as it does from Yahweh, it is in one sense, his spirit. It is more narrowly defined by 'compassion' and 'supplication'. The Heb. word for 'compassion' is rendered 'favour' in the frequently recurring phrase: 'to find favour in the sight of'. In general, it is that which makes a person pleasing to God. 'grace' would be better than 'compassion'. 'supplication': Dn 9:3, 17, 23 is perhaps the best illustration of what this term implies here. Daniel's supplications (9:4−19) include an admission of guilt, expressions of sorrow and petitions for deliverance from the just anger of God. Dn 9:3 also links the prayer with fasting and penitential garb. Yahweh's gift of the spirit results in a changed attitude; the people of Jerusalem now share Yahweh's own reaction to their former conduct, and mourn particularly for one who suffered from their misdeeds. 'look on him': so Theodotion and Jn 19:37. MT reads 'on me': in view of the difficulty in assuming that 'me' refers to Yahweh, those who accept this reading (e.g. Lamarche) think of the one who suffers as Yahweh's representative (cf 10:8, 10); his sufferings are also Yahweh's. Others avoid the difficulty by retaining a direct reference to Yahweh and attributing a metaphorical meaning to the verb *dāqar* (here and in 13:3, RSV has 'pierce'), e.g. to insult (cf Delcor, RB 58 (1951) 189−99 who stresses the dependence of this passage on Ezek 36:16−32). This is **l** scarcely adequate since the mourning which follows is for someone who has died. Who then is 'pierced'? It is clear that he was a person of importance since a national

801 lamentation is called for. His work was in some sense the work of Yahweh which provoked opposition, since the lament for his death coincided with a return to Yahweh's way of thinking. Even after his death, one is left with the impression that people looked on him expectantly, hoping to receive some benefit (cf especially the use of the verb *nābaṭ* (RSV 'look at') in Nm 21:9; Ps 34 (33):5; 119 (118):6; and the noun *mabbāt* (RSV 'hopes') from the same root in Zech 9:5. For belief in the power of a deceased prophet to intercede for his people, cf 2 Mc 15:14ff. These features lead one to think of the Servant in Is 52:13—53:12. While there are points of similarity, it must be admitted that the notion of redemptive death and vicarious satisfaction for sin are scarcely present in Zech.

m In this passage, the death of the person in question is set in an eschatological context and is to that extent symbolic or typical. At the same time, the way in which his role is depicted may owe much to contemporary or recent experience. Is it possible that a charismatic prophet had recently suffered violent death at the hands of the cult (or: professional) prophets in league with the royal house, the priests and people (12:10, 12, 13; and cf 13:7—9 note)? It is clear from 13:2ff that these were associated with the idolatry and the unclean spirit which filled the land. They were responsible for misleading the people. A charismatic prophet would necessarily be opposed to them and it may be that their hatred of him (cf 10:8, 11) drove them to kill him (cf Jer 6:13—15; 23:9ff etc for the opposition between Jeremiah and the Temple prophets

n who ultimately attack him physically (Jer 26:8)). Through the merciful outpouring of Yahweh's spirit, the people have come to understand what had happened and even the parents of professional prophets are tempted to treat them as they had treated Yahweh's representative (cf 'pierce' in 12:10 and 13:3), if they should attempt to practise their profession again. In the eschatological context, this prophet becomes the symbol of Yahweh's care to make known his will and man's violent rejection of proffered salvation. Humiliation and suffering followed by repentance become the only means of rescue. 'only child': cf Jer 6:26 and Am 8:10 where a public lament is compared to the mourning for an only son. Delcor makes use of these passages to support his view that the lamentation in v 10 is not for someone who has died, but for the way in which

o Yahweh has been offended (not: 'pierced'). Mourning for those killed in war may, however, contribute substantially to the laments in Jer and Am. **11.** 'Hadad-Rimmon': the name combines the name of Hadad, the western Semitic storm god, with Rimmon, an Aramaean weather god known to have been venerated in Damascus (2 (4) Kgs 5:18; the name goes back to *rammānu*, a Babylonian weather god). Ugaritic texts have made it clear that Hadad was sometimes identified with *baal shāmēm*, the Baal of the heavens. As a result, the laments for the death of Baal (in the autumn; cf ANET 139) were associated with Hadad, at least in the west. 'plain of Megiddo': there may have been an annual mourning festival for Hadad Rimmon on the plain where the fertile land was to be found. Syr.'s rendering of the passage recalls the death of Josiah and 2 Chr 35:25 gives some grounds for believing that the lament for his death was repeated subsequently. Since the lament apparently took place in Jerusalem, it

p is unlikely to be relevant here. **12—14.** A list of those who are to participate in the lament. The royal line is represented (for Nathan, a son of David, cf 2 Sm 5:14; 1 Chr 3:5 and Mt 1:7 as compared with Lk 3:31) and also the priestly line (for Shimei, cf Ex 6:17; Nm 3:18). The prophetic group is not mentioned perhaps because

it was not an hereditary office or perhaps because, as sug- **580p** gested above, it was the group immediately responsible for the death of the person being mourned. In v 14, the less important families are included in general terms. The separation of men and women is still characteristic of Jewish worship. **13, 1.** Purification follows on repentance (cf Ezek 36:25) and is the dominant idea here. The abundant waters which are a feature of other texts describing eschatological blessings (e.g. Ezek 47:1ff; Is 44:3, cf Jn 7:38f; 19:34) may also be in mind.

13:2—6 The End of Idols and False Prophets—The **581a** purification of the land involved particularly the elimination of idolatry and of those prophets who misled the people either by failing to warn them against idolatry or by allowing—even fostering—confusion between the worship of Yahweh and the worship of idols (cf Dt 13:2, 6; Jer 23:9—15; Ezek 13). **2.** 'names . . . remembered no more': not only must the idols disappear but their very names must be forgotten. The Heb. 'remembered' might also be rendered 'invoked'; what was essential was that the name should no longer be remembered *and* used as if it were an effective religious invocation (cf Ex 23:13). 'prophets': although unqualified, the term clearly refers to false prophets (similarly, Jer 23:9). 'unclean': cf Ezek 36:25 where this term is again linked with idolatry (cf also Ezek 22:15; 24:11 etc). **3.** The hatred is such that the false prophet will be deprived of the protection he might normally expect from his own family. For the law governing the punishment of false prophets, cf Dt 13: 1—11 (2—12). 'pierce': see note on 12:10. **4.** 'hairy mantle': the traditional garb of the prophet, cf 2 (4) Kgs 1:8; Mk 1:6. **5.** Like Amos before him (Am 7:14—15), but for a different reason, the prophet insists (without foundation?) that he has never been a professional prophet; he always made his living on the land. **6.** His accuser **b** persists and points to the wounds on his body (Heb. 'between your hands' = on your back? or breast?) which suspiciously resembled marks which were self-inflicted in the worship of fertility gods (1 (3) Kgs 18:28). The prophet's answer to the accusing question is obscure. The Heb. word *mᵉahᵃbay* (here RSV 'friends'; lit = lovers) is used in Hos 2:7; Jer 22:20; and Ezek 16:33 etc for Israel's lovers, i.e. the false gods to whom she turned. In each case, Israel is spoken of in the feminine and the word for lovers is masculine (as here). This at least sows a doubt about equating 'lovers' with 'false gods' here in Zech. In view of his attitude in v 6, it is unlikely that the prophet would want to admit that he got these wounds in the sanctuary of his friends, i.e. the fertility gods (Lamarche). Instead he asserts that he was wounded in a 'brawl with his companions' (BJ). This assertion is also likely to be untrue; after all he was a false prophet who was trying to save his life; he had often lied before for less!

7—9 A Shepherdless People Punished and Purified c for the Renewal of the Covenant—Some commentators (e.g. ICC; Delcor) put this section after 11:1—17 and are then confronted with the choice of identifying the shepherd in v 7 with either the good shepherd of 11:4ff or the bad shepherd of 11:15—17. The terms used in 13:7 ('my shepherd'; 'the man who stands next to me', BJ 'my companion') lend support to the view that it is the good shepherd (cf also Mt 26:31), but Delcor argues strongly in favour of the bad shepherd on the following basis: (a) 13:7—9 completed 11:4—17 in so far as 11:4—14 speaks of the past, 15—17 of the present and 13:7—9 of the future (not a very strong argument since 11:15—17 are also concerned with the future, without, admittedly, the happy outcome of 13:9); (b) the reference to the sword

581c in 11:17 and 13:7; (c) the sequence 11:16—17— 13:7 is to be explained by reference to Ezek 34:4—5 on which Dt-Zech depends. (d) the term '*my* shepherd' and '*my* companion' do not create an obstacle to this view, since all kings of Judah, good and bad, were, in a sense, 'sons of Yahweh' (cf 2 Sm 7:14; Ps 2:7) and might reasonably be called his shepherds and companions. Then Cyrus, a pagan king, is called 'my shepherd' in Is 44:28.

d Elliger and others prefer to treat 13:7—9 as an independent piece which in its development runs parallel to 12:1—13:1 and is therefore eschatological rather than historical in its outlook. He sees in the shepherd a messianic figure whose sufferings reflect the birth pangs of the messianic age (cf 12:10—13:1; Is 52:13—53:12; Jn 16:21; Apoc 12:2). In the absence of specific evidence, either view is tenable, with the present position of the passage favouring the second interpretation. There is no textual evidence that it was ever elsewhere. **7.** 'sword': cf Is 34:5—6; Jer 47:6; Ezek 21:15—23. 'the man . . . to me': this phrase is obscure. In Heb.: 'a man of my family or company', or: 'a man, my companion'. '*āmît* the Heb. word for 'companion' (or: 'family, company') is found in several passages in Lv (e.g. 19:17; 24:19 etc). It is rendered 'neighbour' by the RSV (and BJ) and is the equivalent of brother, member of the people, fellow-Israelite (cf Lv 19:17—18). In Lv, it describes a status which is the basis for certain rights including the expectation of just treatment. Yahweh's command to the sword seems all the more paradoxical when his relationship with the person in question seems to demand protection and rescue **e** rather than death. The paradox of the Servant is, however, no greater (cf Is 53:6, 8—10; Mk 14:27). 'scattered': while in Ezek 34:15 scattering refers to the Exile, exile is not necessarily implied here (cf 1 (3) Kgs 22:17). 'little ones': the weak and insignificant members of the people (cf Jer 30:19). Koehler, however, translates 'shepherd boys' which would represent leaders of inferior rank. **8.** 'third': cf Ezek 5:2ff. **9.** The surviving third must undergo further purification (cf Is 6:13). It is only then that they can call on Yahweh (Is 58:9; 65:24) and be joined to him in the covenant. For the remnant, cf Is 1:8—9; 7:3; 10:21; Ezek 5:3f; 22:18—22 etc. In the 8th cent. prophets, it describes those who will survive the Assyrian invasion; Jer and Ezek think in terms of the exiles who will return, while the post-exilic prophets identify the remnant with a small group who had returned (cf Hag 1:12). Here the idea serves to emphasize the degree of purification required before union with Yahweh is possible. 'refine': cf Is 1:25; Jer 6:29. 'my people . . . my God': the covenant formula: cf Lv 26:12; Dt 26:17—18. For the renewal of the covenant in the prophets, cf Hos 2:23 (25): Jer 7:23; 11:4; 24:7; 30:22; 31:31; Ezek 11:20; 14:11; 16:60; 36:28; 37:23—26.

f 14:1—21 The Final Assault; Victory for Jerusalem; Yahweh Reigns as Universal King; Homage of the Nations—This chapter embraces a wide variety of material and although the sequence of ideas may not be entirely logical (e.g. vv 6—8 and 12), it is possible to understand the chapter as it stands within the framework of 'the great eschatological conflict which culminates in the establishment of the universal kingship of Yahweh. Elliger distinguishes three phases in the composition of the chapter. To the first would belong vv 1—3, parts of 4 and 5 (i.e. 'On that day his feet shall stand on the Mount of Olives and the Mount of Olives will be split in two. Then the Lord your God will come and all the holy ones with him', 6—9, 11*b* (i.e. 'for there shall no more be curse, Jerusalem shall dwell in security'), 13—14, 16—17, 19. He attributes the rest of the text to a second

phase with the exception of glosses, which he considers **581** certain in vv 5 ('and you shall flee . . . Judah') and 7 ('it is known to the Lord'), and probable in 2 ('but the rest . . . from the city'), 10 ('to the place of the former gate'), and 14 ('even Judah will fight against Jerusalem'). This analysis must serve as an illustration of one way among many by which commentators account for the variety of material in the chapter.

1. 'day of the Lord': see note on 12:3. **2.** The final **g** assault of the nations on Jerusalem achieves initial success with the capture of Jerusalem. 'half': cf 'two thirds' in 13:8. Such fractions need not be understood exactly; they give some idea of the disastrous consequences of the war. **3.** Yahweh himself intervenes in the role of warrior God (cf Is 10:26; 51:9—11 etc). 'go forth': from heaven (cf Mi 1:3). **4.** 'Mount of Olives': Yahweh approaches from the east, the point of the rising sun and therefore the source of life and salvation (cf also 6:1). There may also be an echo of Ezek 11:23; 43:2, where, however, the name of the mountain is not given. From a military point of view, Yahweh's approach from the east is unconventional, since most successful sieges gained entry to Jerusalem from the N (cf however, David in 2 Sm 5:6—10). The power which carves up mountains and levels valleys makes light of conventional defences. For earthquakes as an accompaniment of theophanies, cf Jg 5:4—5; Mi 1:4; Ps 18 (17):7 etc. **5.** This v is corrupt; cf BJ for an alternative rendering. RSV may have Is 40:4 in mind; the re-arrangement of the hills and valleys provides easy access on the E side of the city which was normally protected by the steep Kidron valley. 'earthquake . . . Uzziah': cf Am 1:1. 'holy ones': Yahweh's heavenly assistants, cf Dt 33:3; Ps 89 (88):5; Jb 15:15. The description of the conflict is interrupted at this point as if it had already been brought to a successful conclusion. Cf vv 12—15 for further details of the battle.

6—11: a series of texts (vv 6—7; 8; 9; 10—11) **h** describing the blessings of the end time. **6.** RSV's reading of the obscure MT presents an optimistic view as in v 7 (so Elliger). Delcor reads: 'On that day there will no longer be (sun) light, but cold and frost' and understands the text to say that the day of Yahweh must go through a period of darkness (cf Am 5:18) before emerging into a triumphant and perpetual light (v 7). **7.** Cf Is 60:19—20; Apoc 21:23ff. The transition from darkness to light is characteristic of the saving acts of Yahweh e.g. Mi 7:8—9; Is 9:1—2 (8:23—9:1) etc. **8.** 'living waters': a development of Ezek 47:1 where the waters flowed only to the E. Delcor believes that the writer here combines Ezek 47:1 and Jl 3(4):18 (he accepts the identification of the valley of Shittim with the Wadi es Sant to the W of Bethlehem, and therefore to the W of Jerusalem). 'eastern sea': the Dead Sea. 'western sea': the Mediterranean. Jerusalem's water supply was limited to one spring, Gihon, so that the abundance of 'living waters' implies a stupendous transformation (cf Ps 46 (45):4; Is 33:21). **9.** The whole operation moves towards the establishment of Yahweh's dominion over the whole earth and the universal acknowledgement of his kingship (cf also v 17 and note). 'will be one': cf Dt 6:4. 'his name': also a feature of Dt theology (cf § 225 *a—c*). **10.** The prominence of Jerusalem will be heightened (cf **i** Is 2:2) by the levelling of the surrounding hills. The boundaries of this process are set at Geba and Rimmon, the N (cf 2 (4) Kgs 23:8; 1 (3) Kgs 15:22) and S limits of ancient Judah. Geba was 9 km NE of Jerusalem (cf Jos 21:17) and Rimmon in the Negeb, 17 km NE of Beersheba (cf Jos 15:32). A more restricted view is taken of 'the whole land' here than

581i in chh 9—11 (cf e.g. 9:10; 10:6—7). This could reflect diversity of authorship and/or a change in the historical setting. The fixing of the N limit in such a position as to exclude the territory of the former N Kingdom may indicate that the Samaritan schism has already taken place (cf 11:14). 'Gate of Benjamin': since Benjamin lay to the N, this gate was in the N wall probably towards the E. 'former gate': BJ 'First Gate'; location uncertain, although it is sometimes taken to be an alternative title for the 'Corner Gate', which was probably at the NW corner of the city. These points of reference on a line running E—W would indicate the E—W boundaries of the city. The N—S limits run from the Tower of Hananel (cf Neh 7:2; 12:39), roughly in the middle of the N wall, to the king's wine presses, which are presumed to be S of the city. For this v, cf Jer 31:38, which was written after 586 B.C. **11.** 'curse': cf RSV note. For the earlier use of this word, cf RSV 'devoted things' in Jos 6:18—24; (and de Vaux, AI, 260—2). Delcor rightly asks if the term may not have come to mean '(total) destruction' in post-exilic literature.

j **12—15.** Return to the description of the battle (cf v 5). **12.** Describes the plague which will afflict the nations. **13.** 'a great panic': the same term is used in Dt 7:23; 1 Sm 5:9. 'each . . . fellow': cf Jg 7:22. **14.** 'even Judah . . . Jerusalem': a gloss? Does this mean that Judah will join in the battle to recapture Jerusalem which has been taken (cf v 2)? Or is it an expression of resentment (cf 12:7)? The MT might also be translated 'in' Jerusalem (Elliger; Delcor). The losses from plundering (cf v 2) are made up by the wealth of the nations (cf Is 60; Ezek 60.10). **10—19.** Are concerned with the pilgrimage of the remnant of the nations to Jerusalem to pay homage to King Yahweh on the feast of Booths (§ 105 h). For the connexion between the feast of Booths and the kingship of Yahweh, see commentary on the *Yahweh mālak* psalms (93 (92); 97 (96); 99 (98)). de Vaux (AI, 506) emphatically rejects any possibility of an enthronement

feast of Yahweh on the occasion of Booths. This feast **581j** was always an agricultural feast and the mention of Yahweh-King in the context of this feast is more or less accidental. 'The entire passage is devoted to the eschatological triumph, to that "Day" when Yahweh will be king over the whole earth (v 9), and the feast of Tents is mentioned only because it was the main feast for pilgrimage to Jerusalem.' **17.** 'rain': the ceremonial of the feast included libations of water which were accompanied by prayers for rain. For Yahweh's role in bringing rain, (cf Jer 14:22; Hos 2:8 (10) etc). **18—19.** Egypt gets special mention for two reasons: (i) she was, at the time of writing, the principal enemy of the Jews (cf siege of Jerusalem by Ptolemy I Soter in 312 B.C.); (ii) a special form of punishment was required, since she would not be affected by lack of rain, depending as she did on the Nile.

20—21. Are concerned with the ritual holiness and the **k** appropriate consecration of the animals and utensils involved in this massive pilgrimage. Horses do not get a good press from the prophets; they are symbols of secular power (cf Is 31:1—3; Zech 10:5; 12:4). Since the nations would inevitably use them when coming on pilgrimage, they must become 'holy to Yahweh' in the eschatological age. 'holy to Yahweh' was formerly reserved for the high-priest's crown (Ex 28:36). Lest the immense crowds should create a shortage of sacred vessels, the writer foresees an upgrading of 'pots' (used for inferior purposes) to the rank of 'bowls' (used particularly for sprinkling blood on the altar), and of all the ordinary pots to the rank of temple 'pots' for boiling the flesh of the sacrifices. 'trader': or 'Canaanite'. It is hard to see how the increased activity at the sanctuary could be maintained without the help of traders. This leads commentators to prefer the rendering 'Canaanite', which seems preferable. In the context, it is unlikely to refer to the Gentiles, but may describe the Samaritans who have already been excluded from participation in the eschatological blessings (cf v 10 and note).

MALACHI

BY A. MARSH O.C.S.O.

582a **Bibliography**—*Commentaries*: J. M. Powis Smith, ICC, 1912; C. Lattey, WV, 1934; R. C. Dentan, IB, 1956; L. H. Brockington, PC (2); and see Bibliography for Haggai, 574*a*, for Driver, van Hoonacker, Barnes, Chary Elliger, Gelin, Jones etc. *Other Literature*: R. Pautrel, 'Malachie' DBS 5 (1957) 739—46; G. Rinaldi, *La Profezia di Mal 1:11 e la S. Messa*, in *Eucharistia*, ed A. Piolanti, Rome, 1957; M. Rehm, *Das Opfer der Völker nach Mal 1:11*; in '*Lex tua Veritas*', Festschrift für H. Junker, ed. H. Gross-F. Mussner 1961, 193—208.

b **The Prophet**—It seems unlikely that Malachi is his personal name. Jerome in the Prologue to Mal mentions, and himself adopts, the opinion of the Jews that the author was Ezra, (PL 25, 1541f). The Aram. paraphrase (Targum) of Pseudo-Jonathan inserts the name of Ezra in the first v, and LXX in place of Malachi has 'of his messenger'. It thus appears that early Jewish tradition retained no memory of a prophet named Malachi, a strange fact if a prophet of that name exercised his ministry during the post-exilic period. The most probable view therefore regards the author of these prophecies as anonymous, the name Malachi ('my messenger') in 1:1 having been borrowed by an editor from 3:1 to designate the unknown prophet. This appears the more plausible since the identical superscription 'An oracle of the word of the Lord' likewise introduces Zech 9—11; 12—14, two anonymous collections of prophecies which immediately precede Mal at the end of the prophetic Canon: Mal would then form a third such anonymous collection.

c **Date of the Book**—The convergence of evidence suggests that Malachi (traditionally the last of the prophets) be dated somewhere in the first half of the 5th cent. B.C. The people have returned from exile for they are under the rule of a *pehah* or governor (1:8)—a title which agrees with the usage of the Persian period. The Temple has been rebuilt (1:10), a task which was not completed until the 6th year of Darius I, 516/515 B.C. (Ez 6:15). Some time indeed must have elapsed since that date, for the neglect of divine worship and the contempt of the altar rebuked by Malachi (1:7) would not have been possible for some years after the dedication of the Temple, which had been celebrated with enthusiasm (Ez 6:16). Moreover, the similarity and in part the identity of the abuses which Malachi on the one hand and Ezra and Nehemiah on the other strove to correct, point to the prophet having laboured about the same period as they. Thus, the withholding of tithes 3:8, 10—14; Neh 10:32—39; 13:10—13); the practice of mixed marriages (2:10—16; Neh 10:28—30; 13:23—31), the laxity of the priesthood (1:6—8), and social oppression (3:5; Neh 5:1—13) are common characteristics of the age in which **d** both prophet and reformer were active. Since Malachi gives no hint of any official action having been taken against the abuses which he is attacking, his ministry may be seen as paving the way for the reforming action of Nehemiah. Nehemiah himself arrived in Jerusalem in **582d** the 20th year of Artaxerxes I, 445 B.C. (Neh 3:1; 8:2 cf § 311*b*), returned to the Persian court in the 32nd year of the same king (Neh 13:6), but some time later came back again to Jerusalem (Neh 13:7). Since it was only during his second term of office that Nehemiah dealt with the abuse of mixed marriages some would place Mal between the two missions of Nehemiah i.e. c. 430 B.C., but this seems to exceed the evidence. Another factor in determining Malachi's date is his dependence on the deuteronomic legislation which identifies priest and levite, whereas the later priestly code distinguishes the sons of Aaron (priests) from those of Levi (ministers). Malachi would seem then to antedate Ezra the scribe with whom the promulgation of the priestly code is usually associated (Neh 8). The precise date of Ezra's arrival in Jerusalem however is disputed by scholars (458? 428? 398?); cf § 311.

Plan of the Book—The book falls naturally into six **e** sections, each built on the same dialogue pattern. Yahweh or his prophet makes a statement, the audience voices its objections, the prophet replies by developing his theme in a short discourse. This dialogue structure, though owing something perhaps to literary artifice, seems to reflect the thrust and parry of genuine controversy in which the prophet engaged with his contemporaries.

(1) 1:2—5. Yahweh loves Jacob-Israel. But Israel is dissatisfied and questions his love for them, which, however, is manifest by the favour shown to them in comparison with the hard lot of the descendants of Esau, the brother of their own progenitor Jacob. (2) 1:6—2:9. Yahweh is prevented from showering his favours on the chosen people for they do not render him the honour and reverence that are his due. The priests despise his name by offering polluted sacrifices. It would be better for the Temple to be closed and an end put to these useless offerings, for in the whole Gentile world a pure offering is made to his name which is honoured throughout the world. (3) 2:10—16. The men of Judah are condemned for their marriages with pagans, and the divorce of their legitimate wives. (4) 2:17—3:5. Yahweh is accused of seeming to favour the wicked, and the existence of a just providence governing the world has been questioned: 'Where is the God of justice?' The answer is given: after his messenger God will come himself to the Temple as a refining fire. When he has purified the priesthood, they will again offer worthy sacrifice. He will swiftly give **f** judgement against sorcerers, adulterers, perjurers, and oppressors of the weak. (5) 3:6—12. Yahweh has been constantly faithful to Israel, while Israel has been constantly unfaithful to Yahweh. Nonetheless, if they will repent God will again turn to them. They must pay their dues to tithes and offerings—this will bring its reward from God in renewed prosperity. (6) 3:13—21. Again are mentioned complaints of Yahweh's seeming injustice. But true worshippers are written in a book of remembrance before Yahweh and they shall be his special

82f possession on the great day of his judgement. God will spare them. On that day men will again recognize the different lot of those who do, or do not, serve God, for that day will consume the wicked like stubble while the sun of justice will shine on the good who will triumph over the wicked.

The prophecies conclude with two *appendices* whose authenticity is disputed: an exhortation to remember the Law of Moses (3:22), and a prediction that Elijah will be sent before the great and terrible Day of Yahweh to work harmony of spirit between fathers and sons lest Yahweh at his coming strike the land with a curse (3:23—24).

83a Doctrinal Content—Malachi, like every prophet, addresses himself primarily to his contemporaries, and his message is therefore dictated by the needs of his times. The Israelites were in a relatively miserable condition. Subject to foreign rule, they enjoyed no prosperity and the glowing predictions of second Isaiah and Haggai had so far failed to materialize. Many questioned Yahweh's fidelity (1:2f) and/or his justice (2:17; 3:14), while a decline in religious fervour among both priests and people showed itself by abuses in cult and morals.

These conditions explain the emphasis of Malachi's opening theme on **Yahweh's faithfulness** to his choice of Jacob-Israel whom he loves (1:2—5). Yahweh does not change (3:6), and his original preference of Jacob to Esau still holds good for their descendants. Israel however has proved unfaithful to Yahweh by failing to worship him with due reverence—hence the prophet's insistence on **cult** and the proper performance of the Temple ritual.

b The *priests* are condemned for their negligent service of the altar, the unworthy victims they offer are rejected (1:6f)—for such a casual attitude to the externals of worship expresses an interior contempt for Yahweh (1:6b—7, 12), denies him the honour and reverence due to a father and master (1:6a), and refuses to a great king (1:14b) the marks of respect they would not fail to pay to a merely human ruler (1:8). Malachi's view of priestly obligations is not limited to cult-duties, however, as is clear from the portrait he sketches in 2:4—8 of the ideal priest as exemplified in Levi of old: the priest is a teacher, well versed in the Law, observing it himself, and instructing others in it. But here too the priest's fidelity to his teaching office is understood by Malachi as an expression of that 'fear and awe' (2:5) which the Levite owes to Yahweh.

The cult obligations of the *layman* too are not overlooked and Yahweh's rights are asserted: to offer a less valuable sacrifice than was vowed is to cheat Yahweh (1:14), just as to withhold Temple dues is to rob him (3:6—10).

c Malachi's denunciation of Israel's unfaithfulness extends beyond cult deficiencies to the question of **mixed marriages** and **divorce** (2:10—16). Marriage between Jews, worshippers of Yahweh, and pagan women, the daughters of foreign gods, is an act of unfaithfulness—it is treachery against the nation, a violation of the ancestral covenant, and a profanation of the Temple, Yahweh's dwelling place: a Jew guilty of such a marriage deserves to be deprived of both civil and religious rights. These mixed marriages frequently involved as a condition the repudiation and divorce by the Hebrew husband of his Israelite wife whom he had married in early manhood—this too Malachi condemns in vigorous terms as hateful to Yahweh (2:16), an act of injustice, and a violation of the marriage covenant-contract to which Yahweh himself had been witness (2:14). Yahweh shows his disapproval of such conduct by refusing to accept the people's offerings or be placated by their tears of entreaty **583c** (2:13). In his attitude towards divorce Malachi goes beyond the deuteronomic legislation which expressly allowed for divorce-cases (Dt 24:1—4), and harks back to the primitive ideal of the indissolubility of marriage (Gn 2:23—24), thereby preparing the way for the unequivocal doctrine of Christ (cf Mt 19:3—12).

Defending Yahweh against complaints of injustice **d** Malachi has recourse to the traditional prophetic theme of the **Day of Yahweh** when God will intervene in judgement. On that day all 'will again see a distinction between the just and the wicked' (3:18) for remembrance is kept of the just and as God's special possession they shall be spared the fate of evildoers whom that Day will consume as stubble by fire (3:16—21). This Day is envisaged as inaugurating an era of true worship and justice—the Lord will come to the Temple to purify the priests that they may offer acceptable sacrifice, and there will be speedy judgement against those guilty of social injustice and other crimes (3:1—5). Of special interest is Malachi's reference to a *precursor* ('my messenger') sent to prepare the way before Yahweh (3:1), who is identified with the great prophet Elijah (3:23). The NT sees the fulfilment of this prediction in the precursor of Jesus, John the Baptist, whose role was 'in the spirit and power of Elijah' (Lk 1:17; cf Mt 17:10—17). (N.B. In interpreting prophetical eschatology allowance must be made for lack of chronological perspective; cf § 452h.

In describing the Day of Yahweh our prophet makes no mention of the nations outside Judah—is his eschatological perspective exclusively nationalistic? This depends on the interpretation given to his announcement of a **pure oblation** offered to Yahweh in every place **e** (1:11). The Temple priests were offering defective victims as sacrifice to Yahweh contrary to the express prescriptions of the Law (cf Dt 15:21). Such unacceptable sacrifices Yahweh rejects (1:10) for 'from the rising of the sun, even to its setting, my name is great among the nations: and in every place incense is offered to my name, and a pure offering' (1:11). Does this refer to Malachi's own time or to some future age? Three opinions may be listed which relate the affirmation to the prophet's own time. (1) The reference is to the sacrifices offered by the Jews of the Diaspora, scattered throughout the pagan world. But Malachi seems to speak of sacrifices offered not only on Gentile soil but by Gentile peoples. Besides we know of only two such Jewish Temples—at Elephantine and Heliopolis—which hardly does justice to the universal tone of 1:11. Nor would the cult of Elephantine have been considered pure by Malachi as the Jews there worshipped other gods besides Yaho (Yahweh): cf A. Vincent, *La Religion des Judéo-Araméens d'Éléphantine* (1937) 562, 622ff, 654ff. (2) The reference is to the sacrifices of praise and prayer offered by Gentile proselytes of the Jewish faith. But the text speaks of real not metaphorical sacrifice, while the fewness of such proselytes in Malachi's day again fails to do justice to the prophet's picture of a universal offering. (3) The reference is to the worship paid by the pagan nations each to its own supreme deity—or more especially, by the Persians to Ahura Mazda ('God of Heaven'—a title applied to Yahweh in Neh 1:4f; 2:4, 20; Ez 1:2; 5:11f; 6:9f, etc)—inasmuch as all genuine worship of the gods is in reality worship of the one God, Yahweh. Pautrel asks whether such an open-minded attitude towards pagan worship is conceivable on the part of a prophet whose starting point is the election of Israel (1:2—5). Certainly Malachi's condemnation of marriage with 'the daughter

583e of a foreign god' (2:11) would suggest his rejection of pagan cult also.

f Catholic exegetes generally agree in referring 1:11 to future, messianic times, because: (1) as we have seen, it does not apparently refer to any sacrifice of Malachi's own time. (2) The conversion of the nations with the universal recognition and worship of Yahweh is a constant feature in the prophetic description of the messianic era (cf Mi 4:1–11; Zeph 3:9; Hag 2:7; Zech 8:20f). (3) The pure oblation in every place implies the abolition or modification of the Mosaic Law (which restricted legitimate sacrifice to the Temple at Jerusalem) and so points to a new or messianic age. In this interpretation therefore our prophet looks forward to a future epoch when the Gentile nations, converted to Yahweh, will offer him acceptable worship and sacrifice.

This prediction of a pure oblation offered by the nations in messianic times has been understood as referring to the Sacrifice of the Mass by patristic tradition (e.g. Justin, *Dial. cum Tryphone* 117) and the Council of Trent (Sess. 22, cap. 1–Dz 939). While the ultimate fulfilment of this prophecy is to be sought, in the light of NT revelation, in the Eucharistic Sacrifice, the views of Malachi himself are less precise and he must not be credited with visualizing the actual mode in which his prediction was realized.

g What did Malachi visualize? According to Chary (p. 181f), Malachi, aware of and impressed by the purity of the cult offered to Ahura-Mazda the 'god of heaven' (a cult widespread in the Persian Empire), and comparing it with the decadent Temple worship of his fellow Israelites, foresaw (in virtue of the prophetic charism) that the worship of Yahweh in messianic times would embody the perfection (as to purity and universality) of this contemporary pagan cult. According to Pautrel (743f), Malachi, confronted by the actual degenerate state of Israelite cult which was unworthy of Yahweh, envisages the ideal cult i.e. the worship really due to God, demanded by the honour of his name, and commensurate with the divine rights. This ideal worship is conceived as the reverse of present conditions—a pure sacrifice for defective sacrifice, a world-wide cult for one restricted to Jerusalem. Such an ideal is independent of considerations of space and time, and could only be actually realized in a new or messianic age since it presupposes, as previously noted, the abrogation or modification of the Mosaic Torah. (c) Our text is thought by some to express also a rejection of Jewish sacrifice as such and the substitution of the new Gentile sacrifice in its place. But Malachi in his view of the future age seems to allow for the continuance of the Temple as the centre of Yahweh-cult and of a purified levitical priesthood who will offer sacrifice pleasing to Yahweh, 3:3–4 (cf Rehm, 205f).

In conclusion it may be noted that among Catholic authors A. Gelin (RF, 1959², 1, 573) holds that only the typological sense of 1:11 refers to the messianic sacrifice (of the Mass) while its literal sense refers to the pagan worship of Malachi's day.

584a **1:1 The Title**—'The oracle of the word of the Lord', occurs elsewhere only in Zech 9:1; 12:1, introducing two anonymous collections of prophecies. The name Israel, which had been used politically of the N Kingdom, is now employed theologically (as in Dt) to designate the people of God, the Jewish community as a whole.

2–5 God's Special Love for Israel—First Section. These few vv introduce the prophet's denunciation of the sins of priests and people by providing the historico-theological basis of Israel's obligations towards Yahweh— the divine predilection. Yahweh's special love for Jacob-Israel was the fundamental article of Heb. faith (cf Hos **584** 11:1; Dt 7:7f; Ezek 16) but their present plight leads the Israelites to question it. But Yahweh's faithfulness to his choice of Israel is shown by the fate of Edom which Israel has been spared though they are brother-nations. **3.** 'Love' and 'hate' express concretely election and rejection. It was probably by recent incursions of the Nabateans that Edom's mountain home had been made a wilderness. **4.** God's choice is irrevocable, his rejection of Edom is 'forever'. It will be the 'wicked country' in contrast to the land of Israel 'over' which Yahweh will reign, **5**—this sense fits the context better than a reference to Yahweh's universal dominion 'beyond' the confines of Israel (RSV, BJ, CV).

6–9 Israel's Sinful Sacrifices—Second Section. b The priests are rebuked—they do not show Yahweh the honour and respect due to a God who is a father and a master, but rather despise his name, **6.** Contempt of God's name is contempt of God himself for whose person the 'name' often stands practically as a synonym. This contempt is shown not so much by their words as by their actions in offering polluted food and defective victims as sacrifice (forbidden by the Law, cf Dt 15:21; 17:1), though they would not dare to offer such sorry animals to the Governor in fulfilment of civil obligations, **7–8.** So long as they act thus they cannot expect God to be favourable to them, **9.**

10–11 The Universal and Pure Oblation—Far better to close down the Temple than to make such unworthy offerings which Yahweh entirely rejects, **10.** 'He will rather be pleased with the offerings of the Gentile nations throughout the world . . . which anticipate the pure offering to be sacrificed in messianic times, the universal sacrifice of the Mass' (CV footnote)—cf supra. 'From the rising of the sun even to its setting' is a geographical expression signifying universality (i.e. from E to W). All agree in amending MT in 11b: LXX translates probably correctly (reading *miqṭār* for *muqṭar*) 'In every place incense is offered to my name and a pure oblation' (cf RSV, BJ). Heb., *muggaš*, is a passive participle and may be understood in either a present or a future sense. 'Oblation' (*minḥāh*) can apply to animal sacrifice as well as to cereal offerings (cf 13)—there is no implication therefore that the messianic sacrifice will be an unbloody one.

12–14 Further on Sinful Sacrifices—The thought of **c** 6b–8 is repeated in **12–13.** The priests' casual attitude to the offerings and victims they accept for the altar betrays their lack of reverence for God. Their duties are a burden to them and they insult Yahweh ('sneer at me') by accepting from the laity for sacrifice animals which are 'torn' (WV), lame or sick—do they expect Yahweh to accept these? (cf 9). Worse still is the case specified in **14** where the duty of offering sacrifice springs not from obligation but from a voluntary promise: to substitute a blemished victim for the one freely vowed incurs God's curse, for it is an affront to a great King.

2:1–3 Threats against the Priests—The priests are **d** given a commandment—probably that implicit in the passage, namely, to amend their ways and give honour to God by the right performance of their duties. If they will not heed, God 'will curse their blessings' (2), which may be understood of poverty in contrast to the levitical revenues or privileges they had hitherto enjoyed. In a more general sense it may refer to the blessings and curses attached to the observance or non-observance of the covenant stipulations (cf especially Dt 28) since the covenant (with Levi) is mentioned in the following verses. **3.** The priests are threatened with the most ignominious

584d treatment which their irreverent conduct towards Yahweh deserves, but the details of this treatment have been understood in different ways. CV takes it that the shoulder of the victim allotted to the priests by Law (Dt 18:3) is to be withheld from them, while the dung (stomach contents) of the victims will be cast on their faces. Other suggestions are that God threatens to break the arm raised in blessing (BJ), or to cut off seed and posterity (RSV), or to prevent the seed in the soil from yielding its crop. According to Jones (p. 190), 'rebuking the seed' means cutting off the posterity of Levi i.e. the present generation of priests.

e **4—9 The Ideal of the Priesthood now Debased—** God gives this commandment (in 1) either that his covenant may abide with Levi (RSV) or because his covenant was with Levi (CV)—the latter sense implies the former as its consequence. On the covenant with Levi i.e. the priestly caste, cf Nm 25:12f; Dt 10:8—9; 33:8—10 (cf Chary, 166—70). Malachi's terminology is deuteronomic and does not distinguish Levite from priest. **5.** Both parties to the covenant were faithful to their undertaking—Yahweh bestowing life and peace and Levi serving Yahweh with due reverence. **6.** The prophet draws a (somewhat idealized) portrait of the priests of former days: three characteristics are specified—their priestly decisions (*tôrôt*) were just, their lives were holy, their instruction preserved others from evil. (The priest has a duty to instruct others for he is the messenger of Yahweh, **7.**) In contrast stand the priests of Malachi's day who fail on all three points—instead of guiding, they themselves go astray and lead others astray by their instruction, **8**, and their priestly decisions (*tôrôt*) are vitiated by respect of persons, **9.**

585a **10—12 Marriages with Pagans—** In this **third section**, the prophet turns from priest to people and condemns the marriages of Jews to pagan wives. **10.** Yahweh was the common father of all Israelites (cf Ex 4:22) and the 'Creator of Israel' (Is 43:15)—hence all Israelites were brothers. These relationships of fatherhood and brotherhood were founded on the ancestral covenant between Yahweh and the nation (Ex 19:5f) which bound them into one social and religious unit under Yahweh. Any violation of the covenant—in this case by marriage to a non-Israelite—was to break faith with one's fellow Israelites. It was also to break faith with Yahweh, **11**, for by marrying pagan women who worshipped foreign gods, Judah bound itself to gods other than Yahweh, Israel's 'one Father' and 'one God' (10*ab*), and so (indirectly) profaned Yahweh's dwelling place, the Temple (cf Ezek 45:18—20). Marriage with the pagan inhabitants of Canaan was forbidden because of the danger of perversion to idolatry (Ex 34:11 16; Dt 7:1—4). **12.** An Israelite guilty of such a marriage deserves to be deprived of both civil and religious rights. Such seems to be the sense of this v (cf PC (2)). The 'awaker and answerer' of HT is usually emended ('*ēd* for '*ēr*) to 'witness and advocate' (RSV, CV). Jones (p.195) suggests emending to read the proper names 'Er and Onan' i.e. the sons of Judah by a Canaanite women, both killed by Yahweh (Gn 38:2, 7, 10)—these would be types of the offspring born of mixed marriages.

b **13—16 The Evil of Divorce—** The thought moves on from mixed marriages to divorce since in practice the two evils were connected. **13—14.** Yahweh refuses to accept the sacrificial offerings of the people, despite outward signs of penitence and tears of entreaty, because of the unfaithfulness of Jewish husbands in divorcing their legitimate Hebrew wives in order to marry pagan wives. To the violation of Yahweh's covenant (10) they add the

violation of the marriage covenant to which Yahweh had **585b** been witness. **15.** The Jewish husband is exhorted to be faithful to the wife of his youth, for the purpose of marriage is to rear 'godly offspring' i.e. children who will be faithful to Yahweh, a purpose which is defeated if wives and mothers are the 'daughters of foreign gods' (cf Dentan). Such appears to be the general meaning, but the v is very obscure and various interpretations have been suggested (for a representative list of which cf E. Zolli in *Antonianum* 31 (1956) p. 305f). The CV translation 'Did he not make one being, with flesh and spirit' (cf also BJ) supposes a reference to the union of man and wife in one flesh (Gn 2:7, 22—24) with the consequent indissolubility of the marriage bond. **16.** Let the husband then not break faith with his spouse, for divorce is unjust to the wife and hateful to Yahweh.

2:17—3:5 The Day of Yahweh—fourth section. 17. **c** Convinced that the just man is rewarded by temporal prosperity and disheartened by present difficult circumstances, some of the people complain that Yahweh favours the wicked rather than the just. The complaint does not necessarily come from those who have grown sceptical or tepid—it was rather for the pious Israelite that the prosperity of the wicked constituted a scandal (Jb 21:7—8). Perhaps underlying the question 'Where is the God of justice?' is disappointment at Yahweh's delay in intervening to inaugurate the messianic age, which had been considered imminent (cf Hag 2:6). **3:1.** Malachi replies that the Day of Yahweh's intervention-judgement (cf Am 5:18 etc) is close at hand, but Yahweh is first sending a messenger to prepare the way (cf Is 40:3). After the messenger there will come to the Temple 'the Lord whom you seek' (cf 2:17*c*) and the messenger of the covenant. This latter messenger is distinct from the messenger-precursor previously mentioned, for his arrival in the Temple is simultaneous with that of Yahweh whom in fact the title rather obscurely designates (cf Gn 16:7; Ex 3:2; 23:20). **2—4.** Yahweh will come as a refining fire to purify the priests that they may offer acceptable sacrifices to Yahweh 'as in the days of old' i.e. the days of Levi the ideal priest (cf 2:3—6). Our Lord's action in cleansing the Temple (Mk 11:15—19) is in the spirit of this text—symbolically ending a worship which had become corrupt and preparing the way for the new. The judgement of the people follows, **5.** 'Adulterers' probably means those who had contracted marriage with pagan women after divorcing their Israelite wives.

6—12 Tithes and Retribution— The thematic repeti- **d** tion of Yahweh's faithfulness to Israel links this **fifth section** with the first (1:2—5). **6.** Yahweh does not change, but remains faithful to his choice of Israel—hence, Israel still survives (in contrast to Edom, 1:3?): so, RSV. The possible translation of 6*b* 'nor do you cease to be the sons of Jacob' (CV) contrasts Yahweh's constant faithfulness with Israel's constant unfaithfulness (they are true descendants of 'Jacob' i.e. the supplanter, deceiver, cf Gn 27:36). The people are called upon to amend their ways, **7**, specifically in the matter of tithes, **8**, for by withholding the payment of Temple dues (cf Dt 14:22f) they are robbing God. According to Lv 27:30f; Nm 18:21—31 (both P texts) the tithe was a tax levied for the maintenance of the clergy at the central sanctuary. For robbing God the people are cursed, **9**, by failure of the crops as the sequel shows (cf Dt 28:15f). If they will be faithful in paying tithes God will be faithful in providing the fertilizing rain (from the 'floodgates of heaven'—cf Gn 7:11) so necessary for the crops of Palestine, **10.** Not only will the soil be fruitful, but its produce will be protected from the locust and other destructive agencies, **11.** (Note technique

585d of emphasizing exclusively the point at issue while prescinding from other aspects of the question: obviously other duties besides tithes must be fulfilled to gain the promised blessings).

e **13–4:3** (Heb. 13–21) **Triumph of the Just on the Day of Yahweh**—This **sixth** and last **section** returns at greater length to the complaints of God's justice mentioned in 2:17f. While the just man draws no profit from serving God, **14**, the evildoer prospers, **15**. These vv clearly express the painful doubts of pious Israelites disturbed by the prosperity of the wicked if, with the LXX, BJ and WV, we translate **16a** '*Thus* they who feared the Lord spoke with one another'. By reading '*then*' for '*thus*' the HT (followed by RSV, CV) understands 14–15 as reporting the talk of sceptical Israelites with which 16a contrasts the conversation of faithful worshippers of Yahweh—but then it is surprising that the conversation of these latter is not recorded in detail. **16b.** The names of those who fear Yahweh are kept in a special book of remembrance (cf Ex 32:32; Is 4:3; Dn 7:10; 12:1): they will be Yahweh's *segullāh* or special possession (cf the covenant promise in Ex 19:5) in the Day of Yahweh's judgement, **17**, and will be spared the fate of the wicked, **18**, who will be consumed as stubble by fire, **4:1**. The punishment of the wicked is portrayed in strong metaphorical language which, if taken literally, would suggest their total annihilation leaving them 'neither root nor branch'. For the fire-imagery employed in depicting the Day of Yahweh cf Is 5:24; 10:16f; 30:27; **585e** Zeph 1:18; 3:8; Jer 21:14. For the just that Day will usher in an era of prosperity and peace, **2** as they bask in the 'healing rays' (lit *wings*) of the 'sun of justice': cf representation of sun-god as a winged solar disk in Egypt, Persia etc. 'Sun of justice' is an epexegetical genitive—the sun which is justice (with 'justice' here connoting victory as in the Second Isaiah e.g. 41:2; 45:8; 46:13; 51:5, 6, 8 etc). This victory over the wicked is expressed very concretely in the imagery of **3** (cf Mi 4:13): the wicked trampled underfoot by the just.

4:4 (Heb. 3:22) **Exhortation to obey the Law of** **f** **Moses**—This v may be an editorial appendix briefly summing up the prophet's message or it may form the conclusion of the preceding section. The deuteronomic character of the v (e.g. Horeb to designate the mountain called Sinai in the JP traditions) is consonant with Malachi's own terminology.

5–6 (Heb 3:23–24) **The Coming of Elijah**—These vv form an epilogue added (probably) by an editor. They identify the anonymous messenger-precursor of Yahweh in 3:1 with the prophet Elijah. The great prophet Elijah had been carried up into heaven in a fiery chariot (2 Kgs 2:11) and it is now announced that he will come again before the day of Yahweh to restore peace and harmony. The Gospels understand this prediction of John the Baptist who by the greatness of his mission embodied anew the spirit and power of Elijah (Mt 17:12; Lk 1:17).

1 AND 2 MACCABEES

BY T. CORBISHLEY S.J.

586a **Bibliography**—*Commentaries*: J. Knabenbauer, CSS, 1907; H. Bévenot, BB, 1931; F.-M. Abel, EtB 1949², BJ 1961³; J. W. Hunkin, in *A New Comm. on H. S.*, 1928; A. Penna, SacB, 1953; D. Schötz, EchB, 1948; J. Dancy, (1 Mc) 1954. *Other Literature*: F.-M. Abel, *Topographie des Campagnes Machabéennes*, RB 32–5 (1923–6); D. de Bruyne, *Le Texte grec* . . . RB 31 (1922) 31–54; W. O. E. Oesterley (1 Mc) and J. Moffat (2 Mc) in CAP; E. Schürer, *The Jewish People in the Time of Christ*, 1908²; M.-J. Lagrange, *Le Judaisme avant J. C.*, 1931; E. Bikermann, *Die Makkabäer*, Berlin, 1935; R. H. Pfeiffer, *History of NT Times*; 1949; A. Mittwoch, 'Tribute and Land Tax in Seleucid Judaea', Bib 36 (1955) 352–61.

b **General Introduction**—In many ways the Books of Maccabees are amongst the most easily intelligible of the OT. The story they have to tell—the account of the successful resistance of the Jewish people to a foreign tyranny—is one which is characteristic of human history in all ages, with this important difference that in Mc great stress is laid upon the religious nature of the uprising and upon the assistance received by the Jews from God. There are few difficulties of interpretation, and very few passages of great theological importance. Such difficulties as occur are mostly of minor historical detail, though there are a number of perplexities raised by the fact that the two books often treat of the same incidents from slightly different points of view.

The title Maccabeus, strictly appropriated to Judas, the third son of Mattathias, is thought to be derived from the Heb *maqqābāh*, meaning a 'hammer'. It was afterwards used of the whole family of Mattathias, and eventually came to be applied by the Fathers to the seven sons and the mother whose story is told in 2 Mc 7.

c **Historical Background**—The general situation has been described elsewhere (§ 68c–e), but a somewhat more detailed account of contemporary history is necessary for an adequate understanding of the Books. After the death of Alexander the Great in 323 B.C., his vast **586c** empire split up. The wars of his successors, lasting for some forty years, eventually resulted in that pattern of E Mediterranean states which was to endure until Rome absorbed them all. Apart from Macedonia, mistress of most of the Greek mainland, the two great powers in the Middle E were Syria, with its capital at Antioch, ruled by the Seleucid dynasty (so called from its founder Seleucus), and Egypt, with its capital at Alexandria, ruled by the Ptolemies. Between these two lay Palestine, at first belonging to Egypt, but shortly after 200 B.C. falling to Syria, as the result of the vigorous policy of Antiochus III, who, no less than his successor Seleucus IV, respected the Jewish religion. But Antiochus IV (Epiphanes = the Illustrious) began a policy designed to secure political unity by the imposition on his heterogeneous kingdom of religious and social uniformity. This involved requiring of the Jews certain practices which were an abomination to the devout. Unfortunately, within the Jewish people there were always to be found many who were prepared to sacrifice the Law of God for their own ambitious ends, and a 'Hellenizing party', prepared to admit the requirements of Antiochus, sprang up and split the unity of the nation.

The theme of Mc is the history of how a single family, **d** rallying the forces of resistance, managed to prevail over the 'collaborationists', backed by the might of Syria. This success was due to several factors: first and foremost was the genuine religious fervour of the faithful party; second, the leadership and military skill of Judas and his brothers; and third, the chronic civil strife within the kingdom of Syria itself. It is necessary to give some account of this if we are to follow the story at all clearly.

The table below will make it clear that when Antiochus IV ascended the throne he was usurping the power that should have descended to his nephew. This nephew subsequently challenged the claim of the son of Antiochus IV and became Demetrius I. This was the beginning of a

e

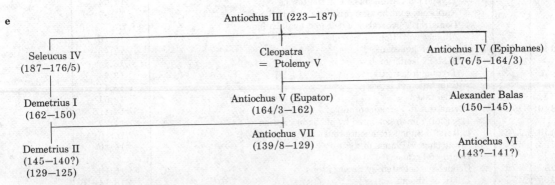

	Antiochus III (223–187)	
Seleucus IV (187–176/5)	Cleopatra = Ptolemy V	Antiochus IV (Epiphanes) (176/5–164/3)
Demetrius I (162–150)	Antiochus V (Eupator) (164/3–162)	Alexander Balas (150–145)
Demetrius II (145–140?) (129–125)	Antiochus VII (139/8–129)	Antiochus VI (143?–141?)

B.C.	Seleucid Era		I Mc	2 Mc
323		Death of Alexander the Great	1:7	
175	137	Antiochus Epiphanes succeeds	1:10	4:7
174	138	(Hellenization begins)	(1:11ff)	(4:8ff)
172	140	'First' expedition against Egypt by Antiochus Epiphanes:		4:21f
		Epiphanes in Jerusalem		4:21
171	141	Menelaus becomes high-priest		4:24
169	143	Epiphanes' 'second' expedition against Egypt	1:21	5:1
168	144	Temple plundered	1:21	5:15ff
167	145	Apollonius in Jerusalem	1:29	5:24
		'the desolating sacrilege'	1:54	6:2
166	146	Revolt of Mattathias	2:24	
		Death of Mattathias	2:70	
		JUDAS MACCABEUS leader	3:1	8:1
165	147	Victories over Apollonius	3:11	
		(at Bethhoron) over Seron	3:23	
		(at Emmaus) over Nicanor and Gorgias	4:3ff	8:9ff
		(Antiochus Epiphanes in Persia)	3:37	
164	148	Lysias defeated	4:28—34?	11:1—12
		TEMPLE PURIFIED	4:52	10:1—8
163	149	Successes in Idumaea, Gilead, etc	5:1ff	8:30ff
				12:18—25
				10:24—38
				12:26—31
		Death of Antiochus Epiphanes:	6:16	9:28
		Antiochus V (Eupator) succeeds	6:17	(11:22, 3)
162	150	Judas attacks the citadel	6:20	
	(149)	Eupator in Judaea: takes Bethzur	6:31ff	13:1
161	151	Demetrius I lands in Syria	7:1	14:1
	(150)	First attempt to impose Alcimus (Bacchides)	7:1—25	14:4
		Second attempt (Nicanor)	7:27ff	14:14ff
		Defeat of Nicanor (13 Adar)	7:43ff	15:28
160	152	Third attempt to restore Alcimus (Bacchides)	9:1	
		Death of Judas	9:18	
		JONATHAN leader	9:31	
		Expedition across Jordan	9:39ff	
159	153	Alcimus orders destruction of the Soreg:	9:54	
		his death	9:56	
158	154	'Two years' peace'	9:57	
157	155	Bacchides fails at Bethbasi:	9:68	
		peace	9:70	
152	160	Alexander Balas lands at Ptolemais	10:1	
		Jonathan high-priest	10:21	
151	161	War between Demetrius I and Alexander	10:48ff	
		Death of Demetrius	10:50	
150	162	League between Ptolemy and Alexander	10:57	
		Demetrius II lands in Syria	10:67	
147	165	Apollonius in Judaea: defeated by Jonathan	10:69ff	
146	166	Breach between Ptolemy and Alexander	11:1ff	
		Death of Alexander Balas	11:18	
145	167	Demetrius II succeeds	11:19	
144	168	Jonathan at Ptolemais	11:24	
143	169	Trypho rebels against Demetrius	11:39	
		Jonathan supports Demetrius	11:44	
		Trypho puts Antiochus VI on the throne	11:54	
		Antiochus confirms the privileges of Jonathan	11:57	
		Demetrius's generals are defeated by Jonathan	11:73; 12:30	
		Alliance with Rome renewed	12:1ff	
142	170	Capture of Jonathan	12:48	
		SIMON leader of Jews	13:8	
		Trypho driven off:	13:24	
		'Liberation of Israel'	13:41	
141	171	Citadel taken	13:51	
140	172	(Demetrius in Persia:capture)	14:1, 3	
		(18 Elul) Simon honoured by public inscription	14:27	
139	173	Letters to Simon from Antiochus	15:1ff	
138	174	Anthiochus VII lands in Syria	15:10	
		Death of Trypho		
137	175	Cendebeus defeated by Simon's sons	16:10	
135	177	Death of Simon:	16:14—16	
		JOHN HYRCANUS succeeds	16:23	

series of dynastic quarrels which considerably helped the Jewish revolt and eventually led to the downfall of the power of Syria. A further factor that must be noted is the enmity between Syria and Egypt. The latter country was never reconciled to the loss of Palestine and open war broke out on more than one occasion.

(For 586e see p 743)

f   Meanwhile, in the background, the threat of Rome was a constant reality. Although not yet prepared to assume direct responsibility for any Asiatic territories, the Roman Senate was concerned to secure her interests in the Levant by playing off one power against another. Thus, when Syria seemed likely to prevail against Egypt, it was Rome's envoy, Popillius Laenas, who stayed her advance. The defeat of Antiochus the Great at Magnesia in 190 B.C. had been so absolute that it secured the prestige of Rome in the E for nearly a cent. Incidentally, too, it saddled the Syrian kingdom with a debt which seriously hampered the warlike preparations of the Seleucids. We may well believe that Rome would welcome any *rapprochement* with the Jews, so long as it did not involve active intervention in the revolt.

g   A few words may be added concerning the politico-religious situation in Judaea itself. After the annexation of the country by Antiochus the Great, there remained a fairly strong pro-Egyptian party, represented amongst others by the high-priest and the 'traditionalists' generally. Against these stood the 'progressive' Hellenizing party, with the wealthy Tobiad family at its head. It seems to have been the policy of Antiochus III and Seleucus IV to try to conciliate the former by showing deference to the religious susceptibilities of the Jews and by financial support of the temple. This policy was reversed by Antiochus IV, possibly owing very largely to the intrigues and suggestions of the Tobiad family and their supporters.

h   **Chronology**—The problem of Maccabean chronology has been discussed by different scholars, with different results. The Seleucid era is taken as the basis of dating in both books, but there is some uncertainty about the precise determination of this era, cf § 124c. It seems most probable that the author of 1 Mc reckons his years from Nisan to Nisan, and that the first year of the Seleucid era (*sc.* the era dating from the reign of Seleucus I) runs from Nisan 312–Nisan 311 B.C., whilst for the author of 2 Mc the reckoning is from Tishri to Tishri (Nisan = March/April; Tishri = Sept./Oct.). Thus any event falling between Nisan I and Tishri I in any given Julian year would be attributed to different years by the different books. This will account for a number of apparent discrepancies as that in 2 Mc 13:1 and 14:4 events appear to be dated a year earlier than in the corresponding passages of 1 Mc. (Knabenbauer has a good short treatment with references to the standard authorities; Bévenot is slightly fuller but agrees on the whole with Knabenbauer. The most recent discussion by J. Schaumberger (Bib) 36 (1955) in the light of a recently published Babylonian MS comes to substantially the same conclusions).

(For 586i see p. 744)

THE FIRST BOOK OF MACCABEES

587a   **Composition**—The original language was almost certainly Hebrew, as is inferred from the number of Hebraisms in the existing Greek version. A few of these are indicated in the commentary. The author, clearly a devout and believing Jew, with a first-hand knowledge of Palestine, seeks to tell in a straightforward manner the story of his people's deliverance from the danger of perversion. The 587a author concentrates on the operation of natural causes—the tenacity and skill of Judas and his brethren, the dissipation of the Syrian forces, the moral support of Rome—but he is above all alive to the importance of the religious spirit with which the Jewish leaders imbued their followers and the role of their struggle in the plans of God. It is religious history, in the manner of the ancient religious history, and subject to the same conventions, cf § 144a.

The date of composition cannot be determined with b any precision, but there is no need to suppose that it was much later than the reign of John Hyrcanus, who died in 103 B.C. The Book must certainly have been completed before Rome became hostile to the Jews, in view of the attitude of the writer to the Romans, which would have been unthinkable after Pompey's entry into the temple in 63 B.C.

Contents—After a brief introduction (1:1–9), giving c the broad historical setting of the events to be narrated, the author first describes the causes leading up to the revolt headed by Mattathias, with a brief account of his achievements and death (1:10–2:70). He then (3:1–9:22) narrates in some detail the activities of Judas, first of all under Antiochus Epiphanes (3:1–6:17) and then under Antiochus Eupator and Demetrius I, concluding with an account of the death of Judas. The next section is devoted to the deeds of Jonathan (9:23–12:53), and the last section is concerned with the work of Simon, closing with his death and the succession of John (13:1 16:24). The narrative covers a period of about 40 years.

1:1–9 Prologue: Alexander's Empire divided at d his Death—The account of the rise of the Syrian kingdom naturally begins with the pivotal fact of Alexander's conquests. These started in 332 when he began his march from Greece ('the land of Kittim', used in the OT of the Greek-speaking lands; cf 8:5. Gn 10:4, Jer 2:10), and included the whole of SW Asia as far as the Punjab, as well as Egypt. They are impressively indicated in 2–4. He had previously become king of Greece, i.e. of that Hellenistic kingdom which was constituted by his conquests, and of which Syria seems to have been regarded as the legatee. The evidence that Alexander formally divided his empire before his death is not convincing, and 6 must be understood to refer to the arrangements which he made in his lifetime for the administration of the different satrapies; the actual division into the constituent kingdoms of Macedonia, Syria and Egypt was the result of the wars of the Diadochi. Alexander's generals and their successors, which began soon after his death and produced misery and devastation for forty years (9).

10–15 Antiochus Epiphanes: Attempted Helleniza- e tion of Palestine—Antiochus the Illustrious (Epiphanes) seized the throne of Syria in 175 B.C., and a party in Judaea lent themselves to his design to Hellenize the Jews. The internal situation amongst the latter is more fully developed in 2 Mc; cf § 586 c–g. The desire of the Hellenizing party to co-operate with Antiochus doubtless represents an attempt to curry favour, but must also be understood as the latest manifestation of the chronic tendency amongst the Jews to assimilate themselves as much as possible to the religious and social conditions of their neighbours. The institution of the (characteristically Gr.) gymnasium led to a desire to conceal the traces of circumcision, a desire with obvious religious implications (14f). The practices hinted at in the words 'sold themselves to do evil' (*sc.* were prostituted) remind us of one of the great moral dangers of the new tendencies. The Greeks were notoriously given to unnatural vice.

587f **16—40 Antiochus invades Egypt: He pillages the Temple and Jerusalem is sacked**—This attempt of Antiochus to aggrandize himself at the expense of the young king of Egypt was checked by Rome, 168 B.C. 2 Mc 5:5 makes it clear that it was the behaviour of some of the Jews during his absence which provoked the king's anger. **21.** For the 'golden altar' and other objects cf 1 Kgs 7:48, 50. They had been removed by Nebuchadnezzar (2 Chr 36:7) and restored by Cyrus (Ez 1:7; 5:14). **24— 28, 36—40.** Afford a very good example of the way in which the author of I Mc rises from the plain prose of his narrative passages to a style which is reminiscent of the more poetical portions of the OT. It is interesting to compare Ps 79, which may have been composed at this time.

The 'chief collector of tribute' (**29**) is apparently the Apollonius of 2 Mc 5:24, where he is styled *Musarchēs*; cf *ad loc.* It seems probable that we should read *captain of the Mysians* here too, the presumed original Heb. *śar hammussîm* having been misread as *śar hammissîm*.

In **33** is described the fortification known as the castle or citadel (*akra*). It is referred to frequently in accounts of the later campaigns. Its precise situation is uncertain, but the more common opinion is that it was situated close to the temple (cf 4:41), near its S or possibly SW end. (The 'city of David' is often identified with the region of Mount Sion, but 7:32f suggests that the author distinguished them, RB 35; 518ff).

g 41—64 Hellenization enforced by Antiochus—The policy indicated here (and more fully described in 2 Mc 6 and 7) was meant to produce a uniform religious and social system as an important factor in the unification of the very heterogeneous Syrian kingdom; cf Roman Emperor-worship propaganda. In making their heroic stand the Jewish victims of the persecution anticipate the later Christian martyrs and all Confessors who maintain the rights of God as against those of Caesar. **43.** Many adopted his religion, *sc.* the form of worship prescribed by the king, possibly though not necessarily including worship of himself as a manifestation of Zeus. According to Josephus (*Ant.* 12, 5, 5) the Samaritans actually addressed Antiochus as 'God made manifest'. **44—50.** Describe the attack made upon all forms of Jewish worship of the true God, and the legal observances which were its safeguard. Circumcision, the sign of the individual's belonging to Yahweh, was naturally a practice ruthlessly forbidden by the Syrian authorities. **49.** The Vg reading *justificationes Dei* is represented in the Gr. by *dikaiōmata* = *prescriptions, ordinances* (of the Law). This is one of a number of passages in which the name of God is found in Vg though not in LXX. The author of I Mc seems to have been most scrupulous in his avoidance **h** of the sacred Name. **54.** Note the way in which the date of this infamous act is perpetuated. The equivalent date is between 10 and 17 Dec., 167 B.C. The *desolating sacrilege* was, according to Josephus, an idol-altar actually built upon the altar of sacrifice in the temple. 2 Mc 6:2 suggest that the altar was consecrated to Zeus Olympios. It is not clear why Vg renders *abominandum idolum desolationis.* For the expression cf Dn 9:27; 11:31; 12:11; Mt 24:15, etc. **59.** Bears out Josephus—'the altar which was upon the altar.' In addition to the altar in the temple, the Syrians set up statues (Hermae?) and shrines in the streets of Jerusalem and other cities of Judaea. (**55**; cf Jos. Ant. 12, 5, 4).

i 2:1—14 Mattathias and his Sons—So far we have been told of the cruelties of the Syrians, and the emphasis has been laid on the defection of the Hellenizers rather than on the resistance of the faithful. **1.** Now we come to **587i** the account of active opposition, initiated by one family from Modein, some 15 m. NW of Jerusalem. Doubtless there were many such centres of resistance, but it is the incident described in 23—25 which marks the beginning of organized rebellion, resulting in the liberation of Judaea. Joarib, from whom Mattathias was descended, is mentioned in 1 Chr 24:7 as receiving by lot the first of the 24 courses of the priesthood. Simeon is called by Jos. (Ant. 12, 6, 1) the son of Asmonaeus, but it is thought that Asmonaeus (*hasmōnay*) is a collateral form of Simeon: hence the family is frequently called Hasmonean. **2—5.** Gaddi = Lucky; Thassi = Zealous; Maccabeus (cf § 586*b*) = Hammer; Avaran = Beast—sticker (cf 6:43ff); Apphus = Cunning. In **7—13** we have another example of the poetical side of I Mc.

15—26 Modein: the Incident of the Apostate Jew— As a member of the priestly family, Mattathias was naturally invited to set an example to the rest by offering sacrifice at the bidding of the king. His refusal is in marked contrast to the conduct of Menelaus, the high-priest, (2 Mc 5:15). **24.** Phinehas, cf Nm 25:7, 11. **27—48 Beginnings of Revolt**—'The hills' (**28**) and 'the **j** wilderness' (**29**) are probably to be located E and S of Hebron. The incident recorded in 32—38, the slaughter of the Jews who refused to resist on the Sabbath, stamps the movement as essentially religious, and reminds us that we are here dealing with a holy war and with no mere nationalistic uprising. **38.** 'So they attacked them on the Sabbath' = the Syrians attacked the unresting Jews. **40.** After that gesture it was no contradiction that the Jews should come to see that the service of God demanded that they should be prepared to fight even on the Sabbath.

42. The 'company of Hasideans' (*Hªsîdîm* = the Pious) who now join Mattathias are the forerunners of the later Pharisees, a sect of specially devout Jews, cf Lagrange, 56, 272. The 'sinners' and 'lawless men' of **44** are the Hellenizing Jews; while the 'arrogant men' of **47** (literally, 'sons of pride', a common Hebraism) are the Syrians and others who oppose God's law. 'Gain the upper hand': literally, 'Yield the horn'; another Hebraism, one of the numerous indications of an underlying Heb. original.

49—70 Death of Mattathias—The moving exhortation **k** of the dying Mattathias is worthy to rank with many noble passages in the Bible. The OT examples referred to in **52—60** are recorded in Gn 22:2; 41:40; Nm 25:13; Jos 1:2; Nm 14:16; 2 Sm 7:13; 2 (4) Kgs 2:1; Dn 3:50; 6:22. **52.** Is of particular interest with reference to Gn 15:6 and Rom 4:3.

3:1—26 Judas Maccabeus succeeds his Father: his **588a Early Successes**—The eulogy of Judas in **1—9** has been reconstructed in Heb. by C. F. Burney to produce an acrostic poem with the initial letters JHUDH HMKBY (JTS (1919—20) 319ff). The reconstruction involves some manipulation of the existing text.

10. It was Apollonius who was responsible for the sack of Jerusalem (1:29; 2 Mc 5:24). According to Jos (Ant. 12, 7, 1) he was governor of Samaria. But this may be a mere inference from the present passage. **13.** Seron (= Hiram) is described by Josephus as governor of Coele-Syria. The mention of Bethhoron (**16**) suggests that he came by the regular route from the coastal plain to Jerusalem. The town itself, consisting of an upper and a lower half, lies some 10 or 12 m. NW of Jerusalem. It was on the line of Joshua's famous pursuit of the Amorites (Jos 10:10), and by it the Philistines marched against Saul (1 Sm 13:18). The weakness of the army of Judas and the fact that Jerusalem itself was strongly

588a garrisoned by the Syrians (1:35) suggest that the march was no more than a surprise raid, which succeeded because of its very boldness. The time for regular campaigns of reconquest had not yet come. **18.** 'Heaven': in accordance with the practice mentioned in § 587g of avoiding the use of the Name.

b **27—41 Counter-measures of the Syrians**—Lysias, commissioned by Antiochus to take the necessary steps, sends into Judaea an army under Ptolemy, Gorgias and Nicanor. Hitherto, against the scattered resistance of isolated bodies of Jews, Antiochus had been able to enforce his will without any great military power. The realization that a more organized form of resistance, under a leader of obvious capacity, had to be broken, leads to more elaborate measures. The parallel passage (2 Mc 8:8ff) informs us that Ptolemy was governor of Coele-Syria, having presumably replaced Seron after his failure.

c The Persian expedition referred to in 31, 37 ('the upper provinces' = *the original regions*) was intended not merely to recoup the king, whose exchequer had been drained by the large indemnity imposed on Syria by the Romans after Magnesia (190 B.C.), but also to repress the rising power of Mithridates I, who had succeeded to the Parthian throne in 171 B.C. and was becoming too powerful for a mere vassal of the Seleucid kingdom. 'It is probable that to Antiochus the Jewish trouble seemed a small enough affair compared with the Parthian menace in the E. Some modern scholars speak sarcastically of the Jewish books which represent the events in Judaea as the things of central importance in the world and pretend that Antiochus' chief preoccupation was the ill success of the local government forces in dealing with the Jewish bands. No doubt from the point of view of Antiochus the Jewish books greatly exaggerate the importance of events in Judaea, just as from the point of view of the Persian king, we may believe, the Greek books greatly exaggerated the importance of the battle of Marathon. In regard to the influence destined to be exerted on the subsequent history of mankind, the Gr. books and the Jewish books were right. Of all that was happening in the kingdom of Antiochus, the events in Judaea were by far the most important in their consequences for the mind of man in the ages to come.' (CAH[1] 8, 513f).

41. The Gr. reads 'slaves', but the Syriac reading suggests that the original text had 'fetters' which suits the context better. For 'Syria' read *Edom*, the error being due to the confusion of *rosh* and *daloth* in the Hob. original. The Edomites were traditional enemies of Israel; and for Edomite activity in the slave-trade see § 556f. 'Philistines', lit 'strangers', thus regularly referred to in LXX; cf 4:22, 30; 5:66.

d **42—60 The Mustering of the Jews**—In face of the threat from the NW (Emmaus, 40, the site of the Syrian camp, is some 15 m. WNW of Jerusalem, according to the identification with the modern 'Amwas; others would place it at El-Qubeibe, some 8 m. NW of the capital, which would agree with the 60 furlongs of Lk 24:13) Judas drew out his forces as far as Mizpah, a sacred site associated with Samuel (1 Sm 7:5f) and probably to be identified with Nebi Samwil, some 6 m. NW of Jerusalem. There they besought the help of God. There is some difficulty in **48.** Wellhausen, followed by Bévenot, suggests that the Jews opened their sacred books in order to find some reassuring message, even as the Gentiles were accustomed to consult oracles. (2 Mc 8:23 would bear out his interpretation). In **'49** stirred up' = *summoned*. The exemptions in 56 are in accordance with the prescriptions of Dt 20:5ff.

4:1—25 Defeat of Gorgias (and Nicanor) at **588e** **Emmaus**—The parallel passage (2 Mc 8:24ff) makes it clear that Gorgias was here acting in concert with Nicanor, and that Judas scored a double victory, apparently over the force led by Nicanor, at Emmaus, and then over the force led by Gorgias, which had attacked the Jewish camp, S of Emmaus; cf 17. If Gorgias had already been appointed to the command in Idumaea, the attack would be from the S concerted with Nicanor's advance from the N. But it is possible that Nicanor and Gorgias advanced together from the coast as far as Emmaus, and that Gorgias there attempted a turning movement. In any case Judas scored a brilliant victory in compelling the Syrian army, greatly superior in numbers, to withdraw from Judaea. **6—16.** Describe the victory over Nicanor's force, which is pursued as far as Gazara (Tell Jezer), a distance of 5 m. The plain of Idumaea is used apparently of the region W of Judaea; Idumaea normally refers to the district to the S of Judaea, but cf 1 Mc 5:59 where Gorgias, 'commander of the strongholds in Idumaea', is found in command in the neighbourhood of Jamnia. For the attack on Nicanor Judas apparently divided his force, taking with him 3,000 lightly armed men (**6**) out of the 6,000 he had in all (2 Mc 8:16, LXX). The remainder were doubtless left to protect his rear against the attack by Gorgias, which did not develop when Gorgias realized that Nicanor was in flight. Gorgias fled and Judas plundered his camp at leisure.

26—35 Defeat of Lysias at Bethzur—Lysias with a **f** still larger army now advances from the region SW of Jerusalem. Bethzur, *i.e.* Beit Sur, N of Hebron and some 22 m. SSW of Jerusalem (cf 2 Mc 11:1 16), though the fortress for the possession of which this battle seems to have been situated a little farther to the W.

36—59 Entry into Jerusalem: Purification of the **g** **Temple: Encaenia**—Stationing a force to prevent interference on the part of the garrison in the citadel (41; cf 1:35), Judas carefully purifies the temple. He destroys the idol-altar ('the stones that had been defiled'), dismantles the altar of sacrifice, and stores away the constituent stones until the time when some prophet should arise who could be consulted as to their further disposal. A new altar is built and everything renewed for the temple-worship. The Feast of Dedication is celebrated on 25 Chislev, three years since the setting up of the desolating sacrilege (1:54). This encaenia—the renewal of the altar—became an annual feast; cf Jn 10:22. (Jos.Ant. 12, 7, 7 calls it the Feast of Lights.) For the parallel passage cf 2 Mc 10:1—8.

60—5:8 Fortification of Sion and Bethzur: Cam- **589a** **paigns against Idumaeans, etc**—The temple mount is fortified against the citadel-garrison; Bethzur (cf 4:29) is occupied and strengthened, presumably as a preliminary to the campaign described at the beginning of ch 5.

Having secured the Holy City, Judas now proceeds to extend the area of his conquests. He is encouraged to do this by the persecution of the Jews settled amongst the heathen peoples of Idumaea and elsewhere: the *sons of Esau, sc.* the Edomites living in Akrabatene, a ridge SW of the Dead Sea; *the sons of Baean* (cf Nm 32:3), living in Baal Meon, E of the Dead Sea; the Ammonites, NE of the Dead Sea, led by Timothy. This campaign against the Ammonites is more fully described in 2 Mc 10:24—38. (Bévenot does not accept the identification of Jazer here with Gazara in 2 Mc 10:32, but it seems simpler to do so. In Nm 32:3 it occurs in close connexion with Heshbon and Beon [Baian], and is probably situated some 23 m. ENE of Jericho).

589b **5:9–54 Campaigns in Galilee and Gilead**—Dividing his forces into three parts, Judas plans campaigns to deliver the faithful Jews in Galilee and in Gilead, the district E of Jordan. Simon is given the task of rescuing those in Galilee, and this he successfully achieves (21–23); Joseph is left with a garrison to protect the base in Judaea, but with strict orders not to undertake any offensive action—his disobedience in this respect being punished (55–62); Judas himself marches into the regions E and NE of Jordan and wages a highly successful campaign.

c The details of the campaign are difficult to follow. In **9** we are apparently informed that all the Jews who had escaped massacre had taken refuge in Dathema. In **26, 27** we learn that many of them were shut up in Bozrah . . . 'and in the other cities of Gilead'. Wellhausen suggests cutting the knot by emendation, reading *were gathered together from* in place of 'were shut up in' (26, 27), whilst in **27** he would read *this city* or *stronghold* (viz Dathema). The latter suggestion is probably necessary; but there does not seem to be any need for the other changes suggested. The situation seems to be as follows. Many Jews had been massacred; but the earliest reports (**13**) were exaggerated. It appeared later that, in addition to those besieged in Dathema, there were others imprisoned in different cities in Gilead, doubtless awaiting execution (**26**). Judas set out first of all to relieve Dathema; but on receiving news from the Nabateans (**25**) (the famous nomad tribe, later to become predominant in Transjordania: cf 2 Cor 11:32), he turned aside to attack Bozrah first. Since Judas took Bozrah (**28**) it is clear that it must have been in possession of the people of Gilead, and therefore there must be some corruption in **27** which suggests that they were attacking their own cities. Therefore it seems necessary to accept some emendation of that verse on the lines of Wellhausen's suggestion, or at least to understand 'strongholds' in 27*b* of Dathema alone.

d As to the location of the places mentioned, the following seem to be the most acceptable suggestions. Dathema = ? Charax *sc.* El-Kerak, some 45 m. E of the Sea of Galilee, cf 2 Mc 12:17, or perhaps T. Hamad. Bozrah, presumably the most southerly of the places referred to, since Judas, coming up from the S attacked it first, may be identified with Bostra (Busra eski-Sham), some 50 m. ESE of the Sea of Galilee and about 12 m. from Dathema (= El-Kerak), the stronghold of **29**, a night's march away. Carnaim is probably Sheikh Sa'ad, some 23 m. E of the Sea of Galilee, whilst Raphon (**37**) seems to be El-Rafe, some 17 m. NE of Carnaim. Ephron (**46**) which Judas attacked on his return march, seems to be situated a few miles E of the upper Jordan, since Bethshan (**52**), the modern Beisan, is the same as the ancient Scythopolis, and is apparently not far from Ephron. The other places mentioned have not yet been satisfactorily identified.

13. The land of Tob (cf Tobiani 2 Mc 12:17) was apparently the region immediately to the E of the Sea of Galilee.

Of Simon's brilliant campaign in Galilee, we are given tantalizingly little information. Even the locality of Arbatta (**23**) is uncertain; but presumably it lay somewhere in N Samaria. Possibly it is Narbata, 10m. NE of Caesarea.

e **55–68 Joseph suffers Defeat: Judas restores the Situation**—On his return to Jerusalem Judas found it necessary to undertake a campaign in the coastal plain to restore the situation which had been weakened by the defeat suffered by Joseph in consequence of his rash and disobedient sortie against Jamnia. According to 2 Mc 12: **589e** 8, Judas had undertaken an expedition against Jamnia not long before his march into Gilead, and possibly Joseph and his associate thought that it would be an easy matter to imitate that sortie. But not only were they not of the Hasmonaean house, they were acting contrary to orders, and their attempt met with disaster. Judas marched S, took Hebron, some 20 m. S of Jerusalem, and then turned W towards Marisa (cf 2 Mc 12:35). Having displayed his power as far as the coast at Azotus, he returned to Jerusalem.

6:1–17 Death of Antiochus Epiphanes—In 2 Mc **590a** this event is recorded before the purification of the temple, but there is no doubt that it actually occurred after it. (For the reconciliation cf 2 Mc 9:1ff). It seems probable that this attempt on the temple of the goddess took place early in the king's absence, since one of his motives for going to 'Persia' was to raise money (3:31), so the reports of the disaster to Lysias (**6**; cf 4:26ff) and of the purification of the temple (**7**; cf 4:36ff) and of the capture of Bethzur (ibid; cf 4:61) are rightly described as having reached him later. It is probable, then, that some considerable interval elapsed between the attack on the Persian temple and the king's death, though it is interesting to note that, in his account of the death of Antiochus, Polybius (31:11) speaks of him as having been 'driven mad, as some say, by certain manifestations of divine anger . . .'.

The circumstances of the usurpation of the Seleucid throne by Antiochus Epiphanes made it necessary for him to take steps to secure the succession to his son, since the lawful heir, Demetrius, was now of an age to claim his rights, as he subsequently did (ch 7). Antiochus had left his son, of the same name, in the care of Lysias (3:33). Now, for some reason, he entrusts his affairs to Philip (**14**). This was to give rise to a struggle between Lysias and Philip, from which the Jews were to benefit (63).

18–47 Eupator in person invades Judaea—Judas, **b** having fortified the temple mount (4:60), now proceeds to reduce the citadel, held by a Syrian garrison and a number of apostate Jews. On an appeal from the garrison, the king, who has just succeeded to the throne, raises an exceptionally large army and marches to its relief. Once again the line of march is from the S, and the key-fortress of Bethzur (cf 4:61) is invested. Its actual surrender is not mentioned until 49, but the fact that the battle between Judas and the king's forces was fought at Bethzechariah (**32**ff), which is N of Bethzur, shows that the position must have been at least neutralized. Notice the fascination exercised upon the mind of the writer by the elephants, stimulated to battle by the sight of 'blood', even if it is only the juice of grapes and mulberries. **43.** Eleazar, son of Saura, is, according to the Gr. reading, *ho Auaran*, the Eleazar Avaran, 2:5, meaning probably 'beast-sticker', a name presumably given to him posthumously because of this exploit. He was therefore the brother of Judas.

48–63 Siege of Jerusalem: Peace—After the reduc- **c** tion of Bethzur and the victory of Bethzechariah, the king made his way without difficulty to the Holy City. Fortunately for the Jews the siege he began had to be broken off because of the approach of Philip (cf 14), who resolved to enforce his claim to the title of regent conferred upon him by the late king, against Lysias, the acting regent. The possibility of an attempt by Demetrius to claim the throne (7:1) was an added reason for coming to some arrangement with the Jews. After concluding an armistice the king treacherously orders the destruction of the fortifications of the temple mount.

7:1–25 Demetrius: Intrigues of Alcimus, etc— **d**

90d Demetrius' landing at Tripolis (so 2 Mc 14:1) 'with a few men' (Polybius says there were 16 in all) is made the occasion of a difficulty, since 2 Mc 14:1 speaks of a great power and a navy. Either 2 Mc is using rhetorical exaggeration or more probably Demetrius would have an army waiting for him. Marching upon Antioch (2: 'the royal palace of his fathers'; cf Dn 4:30, where a similar expression in Gr. is used of the capital Babylon), he is welcomed by the army who put to death Antiochus Eupator and Lysias. Approached by a deputation from the Hellenizing party of the Jews, headed by the high-priest Alcimus, he appoints Bacchides, governor of Coele-Syria, 'the province beyond the river' (Euphrates) *sc.* from the point of view of Persia, to undertake the task of suppressing Judas.

e 19. Crampon suggests that 'from' is a mistake for *to* Jerusalem. According to him the Hebrew *min*, used here (as in Gn 11:12; 13:11; Is 22:3, etc) of motion towards has been mistranslated as meaning away from. The correction will enable us to understand Bethzaith as a suburb of Jerusalem (cf Jos. Ant. 12, 10, 2—Berzetho, perhaps the same as the later Bezetha: JosBJ 5, 4, 2). 24. 'he prevented those in the city from going out into the country', *sc.* to vex the faithful; or possibly, by means of some exemplary punishment, he prevailed on those who were seeking to desert from his army to stay and fight.

f 26–50 Defeat and Death of Nicanor: 'Nicanor's Day'—In response to a further appeal from Alcimus, Demetrius sends a fresh force under Nicanor. According to 2 Mc 13:19ff, Nicanor is at first friendly and only resorts to violence under pressure from the king. (This Nicanor is apparently to be distinguished from the Nicanor of 3:38, etc, since the latter was fighting in Judaea at a time when, according to Josephus, the other was with Demetrius in Rome.) It is not known where Capharsalama (31) was, but some identify it with the Khirbet Deir Sellam, some 5 m. N of Jerusalem. We do not know in what direction Judas had withdrawn on the dismantling of the temple fortifications by Eupator (6:62). After this first defeat, and in spite of the assurances of the priests of their loyalty to the king, shown by their offering sacrifices for him (33: cf Ez 6:10), Nicanor seeks to suppress the Jews by force. In a final battle at Bethhoron (cf 3:16) or Adasa (40: according to Jos.Ant. 12, 10, 5, this is some 4 m. from Bethhoron), Nicanor is killed, 'first in the battle'. This need not mean that Nicanor was the first casualty in the whole engagement, especially as Josephus says that he fell 'at length', but merely that, in the closing stages of the fight, as soon as Nicanor fell, the rest fled. It is possible that the Gr. text means *Nicanor the general was slain*. The pursuit to Gazara (45; cf 4:15) covered a distance of some 20 m. Then they sounded *the solemn trumpets* (cf 4:40; Nm 31:6).

This great victory over Nicanor was celebrated with a special thanksgiving service, which became an annual festival, held on the anniversary (13 Adar) even in the time of Josephus (Ant. 12, 10, 5). It lapsed later possibly because of the immediate proximity of Purim (14 Adar).

g 8:1–32 Alliance with Rome—It was entirely in accordance with Rome's foreign policy in the E Mediterranean at this time that she should have encouraged the Jews in their revolt against the Syrian power. Whilst reluctant to assume any responsibilities which would require warlike action on her part, she was glad to foster any tendencies which would weaken the stronger powers. The treaty negotiated between Judas and the Senate is precisely what we might have expected. 'Doubts have been thrown on its existence on the ground that to recognize the Jewish state as an independent power would

have been a *casus belli* between Rome and Demetrius, **590g** and that, as a matter of fact, the Romans let the Hasmonaeans down before Demetrius without giving them any help. These objections have no force in view of the fact that Rome behaved in just the same way with regard to the rebel Timarchus ... The Senate had indeed no intention of intervening by armed force in Syria; it desired only to embarrass Demetrius by giving countenance to his enemies' (CAH (1) 8:519).

The general impression of Rome's power, prestige and **h** moral qualities recorded in 1–16 is not vouched for by the sacred writer as necessarily accurate in all its details, but simply as what Judas heard (1), as he doubtless did. 2. 'among the Gauls' may, as Mommsen held, refer to the subjugation of Cisalpine Gaul by Rome in 190 B.C., but there seems no reason to refuse the more natural identification with Galatia in Asia Minor, which would be of greater interest to the Jews. We know of a campaign in that district conducted by Manlius Volso in 189 B.C. 'Large sums, sometimes amounting to 200 talents, were extorted from numerous cities' (CAH (1) 8:228f). 3. Spain was annexed in 201 B.C. but only partially pacified at the time. 4. 'The kings from the ends of the earth' are presumably the Carthaginian leaders, Hannibal and Hasdrubal, coming from Spain. 5. The king of the Macedonians (lit Kittim) (cf 1:19) refers first to Philip V defeated at Cynoscephalae in 197 B.C. and then to Perseus defeated at Pydna in 167 B.C. 7. Antiochus the Great was defeated at Magnesia in 190 B.C., but was not actually taken alive. 8. 'India and Media' must be corrupt. Risberg suggests Pisidians and Milyans; Crampon, with greater probability, Ionians and Mysians. 9–10. Refer to the Aetolian War of 191–188, the general being M. Fulvius Nobilior. The details of 15–16 are not entirely accurate. The Senate did not meet daily, and there were of course two consuls. But in the absence of his colleague, either of them might be described, as in effect he would appear to the eyes of a visiting foreigner, as supreme head of the state.

17. Eupolemus may be the Palestinian Jew who wrote **i** on OT subjects at this time (cf Schürer, 3, 474–477; 2 Mc 4:11). Akkos or Akkhos: a name in a priestly family. If Eleazar is the hero of 6:43ff, this Jason will be a nephew of Judas. Meyer suggests the martyr of 2 Mc 6.

For the treaty, cf Bévenot *ad loc.*, who gives an interesting comparison with a treaty concluded between Rome and Astypalaea in 105 B.C. (Text in Hicks: *Man. Gr. Hist Inscrr.*, 347–9). 28. 'they shall keep these obligations and do so without deceit' is the counterpart of the obscure phrase in 26: 'they shall keep their obligations without receiving any return'. Knabenbauer is perhaps right in seeing in these passages indications that there was no strict equality envisaged. In both cases, it was Rome who would decide the nature of the obligations incumbent both upon herself and on her partner; nor were the Jews to hope for any return for their assistance.

9:1–22 Death of Judas—It seems not unlikely that the **j** speed with which Demetrius acted after the disaster to the army of Nicanor caught Judas unawares. Nicanor had fallen on 13 Adar and in the first month of the following year, *sc.* Nisan, a fresh Syrian army was already in Jerusalem (3). Even allowing for an intercalary month, this gives only a few weeks for the news of the defeat to reach Antioch, for the raising of a new army and for the march S through Galilee. 2. 'Gilgal' is most probably a corruption of *Galilee* (cf Jos.Ant. 12, 11, 1; in Jos 12:33, the reverse corruption has occurred, Gilgal in the Heb. having become Galilee in LXX). Arbela is the modern Khirbet Irbid or Arbed, not far from the W shore of the

590j Sea of Galilee and near the Horns of Hattin, site of the great Christian defeat by Saladin in A.D. 1187. Mesaloth (Heb. m^esillôt) is the steep descent from the caves in this region; cf JosBJ 1, 16. **4.** Berea, perhaps El-Bireh, 10 m. N of Jerusalem, is not far from (5) Elasa (El-'Ashshy). **15.** 'mount Azotus', is an attempt to smooth out the difficulty of Gr. 'the mountain of Azotus', that city lying in the maritime plain. The error probably arose in the Heb. original, 'aṣdōḏ (Azotus) being confused with 'aṣēḏôṯ 'he pursued them even to the *mountain-slopes*'.

It seems clear that Judas had some premonition that this was to be his last battle. There is a lack of his customary confidence in the words he addresses to his few followers, and though there is no lack of courage in his day-long resistance, it is surprising to find him deceived by the old trap of the retreating right wing and the encircling left. For the sepulchre at Modein, cf 13:25ff.

591a 23–31 Election of Jonathan—The death of Judas was a great blow to the cause. 'The lawless' and 'the doers of injustice' (the Hellenizing Jews) took heart, and the prevailing scarcity (**24**) was apparently used by Bacchides as an opportunity to bribe those in need to come over to his side; cf Jos.Ant. 13, 1, 1. There seems to be a striking personification in **24**: '*the very land itself went over to the side of Bacchides*' (cf Hos 9:2 *vinum mentietur eis*; Hb 3:17 *mentietur opus olivae*, etc). **25.** Suggests the appointment of quislings as local officials. The reference to the absence of a prophet (**27**) recalls 4:46 and the anticipations, not necessarily of the Messiah, but at least of some spiritual leader. The sad plight of the Jews was made more obvious by the lack of any leader. Hence the election of Jonathan (**30**), who took upon him the leadership. It seems strange that there was no automatic succession.

32–57 Jonathan Leader: Bacchides and Alcimus again in Judaea: Death of Alcimus: Bacchides withdraws—Jonathan seems to have succeeded to the leadership of Judaea in circumstances not unlike those which prevailed when Judas was chosen. It is true that the temple was freed from its pollution, but the Jewish army was forced to take to the desert (**33:** Tekoa is some 5 m. S of Bethlehem, Asphar 3 m. further S), whilst Jonathan sent his brother John with a caravan, including, as Bévenot suggests, their wives and children, as well as their treasures, to seek safety with the Nabataeans, who had shown themselves friendly on a previous occasion; cf 5:26. However, one tribe or party amongst them, *the sons of Jambri* (the name Ya'amru is conjectured on a Nabataean inscription), sallied out of their stronghold at Madaba, some 12 m. E of the N end of the Dead Sea, and captured the whole party. Jonathan undertook a punitive expedition against them (**37**ff), and on his return was intercepted by Bacchides who had crossed the Jordan.

b (**34** has apparently crept into the text by an erroneous copying of **43**: it has no connexion with what has preceded.) Bacchides contrived to force the Jews into a position between his army and the marshy lands on the E bank of the Jordan near its mouth. In the ensuing engagement Jonathan personally attacked Bacchides. After the Syrian force had been driven back some distance the Jews succeeded in crossing the Jordan back to their own country. But Bacchides proceeded to hold the whole region down by a series of forts (**50, 52**), stretching from Dok, the fortress of Jericho, and including Emmaus (cf 3:40), Bethhoron (3:16), Bethel (which is Beitin, some 10 m. N of Jerusalem, watching the old road from Jericho), Timnath (Tell Tibneh, some 12 m. NW of Bethel) and Pharathon, (cf Jg 12:15; being the modern Far'ata, W of Sichem); Tephon is unidentified. For Bethzur and Gazara cf 4:29; 4:15.

The action of Alcimus referred to in **54** is thought to **591c** be the destruction of the Soreg, the low wall separating the Court of the Gentiles from the inner Court to which the Jews alone were allowed access. Such an action would symbolize his desire to Hellenize the temple, and, though not as drastic as the setting up of the altar to Zeus by Antiochus Epiphanes, would be most repugnant to devout Jews. His paralysis and death put an end to the project. The departure of Bacchides is not explained, but presumably he felt that the military occupation of the land had been adequately secured, whilst the death of the high-priest may have relieved him of any necessity to persevere with a religious policy for which he had no inclination. At any rate Judaea was untroubled for two years (**57**).

58–73 Return of Bacchides: Treaty—However, the **d** intrigues of the Hellenizers against Jonathan went on and eventually they prevailed upon Bacchides to return with an army. Again Jonathan was forced to take refuge in the desert, after eluding an attempt to capture him. In **61** 'they seized' may refer either to the party of Bacchides— as Josephus interprets it—or, more probably, (RSV), to the faithful Jews; the 'leaders in the treachery' being the Hellenizers. Bethbasi (**62**) is Khirbet Beit Bassa, some 3 m. ESE of Bethlehem. Bacchides besieged the Jews here, being apparently supplied by the local Bedouin. Jonathan divided his forces, leaving Simon to hold the fortress whilst he himself attacked the allies of Bacchides, under their leader Odomera, and thus cut off the supplies on which the Syrians depended. The success of this attack, coupled with a victorious sortie by Simon, forced Bacchides to raise the siege. **69.** Rather implies that Bacchides had entered upon the expedition with some reluctance (cf 57, 59), and Jonathan found little difficulty in arranging a favourable peace. With his final withdrawal, Jonathan was able to establish a semi-independent principality with its military centre at Michmash (Mukhmas, about $7\frac{1}{2}$ m. SE of Bethel), and to set about reducing the power of the Hellenizers. But the citadel of Jerusalem was still held for Demetrius, and 10:6, 7 implies that Jonathan was not authorized to raise troops and was required to give hostages for good conduct.

10:1–47 Demetrius and Alexander Balas bid for e the Support of Jonathan—Demetrius, already surrounded by hostile powers in Pergamum, Cappadocia and Egypt, now finds himself threatened with civil rebellion, when a young man, claiming to be the son of Antiochus Epiphanes and backed by the king of Pergamum, makes a bid for the Seleucid throne. Deciding to conciliate Jonathan, he formally recognizes what was a *fait accompli*, the independence of Jonathan, by withdrawing the garrisons from Judaea, with the exception of Bethzur and the citadel, and the Jewish leader soon establishes himself in the Holy City, rebuilding the fortifications of the temple mount. Alexander, on his side, goes even further, appointing Jonathan to the high-priesthood, which has apparently been vacant since the death of Alcimus, and giving him the title of king's friend, presumably with something of the status of client-king of the Roman Empire. Demetrius goes further still by remitting the tribute due to him. The three districts of Samaria-and-Galilee (**30**) are named in 11:34—Aphairema, Lydda and Rathamin. We get a clue in **36** to this astonishing liberality on the part of Demetrius—shortage of manpower. Ptolemais (**39**) was hardly in the king's gift, being then occupied by the supporters of Balas (**1**), and it seems likely that the king was thus hoping to embroil the Jews with his rival. The sums mentioned in **40** and **42** (£3,200 and £1,067 respectively) together with the different amounts of tribute referred to in **29** and **30**

91e give some indication of the material value to the king of the Judaean dependency.

f 48—66 Jonathan's Relations with Alexander and Ptolemy—Jonathan's decision to support Alexander may have been dictated not merely by doubts as to the sincerity of Demetrius (46), but also by the realization that, with the support of Egypt, the former was more likely to prevail, as indeed happened. But in spite of his victory over Demetrius (48—50), 'it was a sign of the subordination to Egypt which marked the new state of things in Syria that Alexander seems to have resided more in Ptolemais than in Antioch' (CAH¹ 8, 324). The scene described in **59—62** indicates that Alexander still felt the need to cultivate the friendship of Jonathan, possibly foreseeing the coming breach with Ptolemy. In addition to other marks of honour, Jonathan receives the titles of First Friend, General and Ethnarch **(65)**, i.e. he receives formal confirmation of his position as leader of the military forces in Judaea and as civil governor in that area.

g 67—89 Jonathan defeats Apollonius, General of Demetrius II—With the attempt of Demetrius II to regain his father's throne, the position of Jonathan is once more threatened. Apollonius, governor of Coele-Syria, tries to suppress the Jewish high-priest, but not only does the latter with the help of his brother Simon force Apollonius out of Joppa, but he also succeeds in reducing several Philistine towns. **77.** Is obscure and no satisfactory explanation can be suggested. It may mean that Apollonius travelled to Azotus with a small escort, like a simple traveller, though when he got there he did not stay but joined his large force of cavalry in the plain outside the city. The purpose of this is not clear. Josephus helps us to understand what happened next (Ant. 13, 4, 4). Apollonius 'secretly' **(79)** posted 1,000 of his cavalry in a wady. Jonathan drew up his army in a hollow square, with orders to remain on the defensive **(80, 81)**, until the enemy cavalry were exhausted and much of the ammunition used up. Then he attacked the infantry, unprotected by the cavalry and routed them. As a result of this success Jonathan was honoured with the title of Kinsman, receiving the appropriate insignia. Ekron, 12 m. NE of Azotus was given to him as a private estate **(89)**.

92a 11:1—19 Alexander and Ptolemy at War: Death of Both—It is not certain what precise policy Ptolemy had formulated when he invaded Syria. According to Diodorus and Josephus he originally intended to help his son-in-law Alexander against Demetrius. Probably he was merely hoping to turn the situation to his own advantage, and to that end was prepared if it should prove more profitable, to sacrifice his son-in-law. Jonathan prudently supported the invader, escorting him as far as the river Eleutherus, the boundary between Phoenicia and Syria proper **(7)**. Having got possession of Antioch and formed a league with Demetrius, Ptolemy joined battle with Alexander, who was defeated and fled into Arabia (? in the neighbourhood of Palmyra; there is a Palmyrene inscription of 155 B.C. bearing the name Zabdiel; **17)**, where he met his end. However, Ptolemy himself died a few days later, of wounds received in the engagement, and the way was clear for Demetrius to assume the crown. **18.** The Egyptian garrisons in the coast towns (cf 3) were destroyed by the inhabitants of those towns.

b 20—37 Jonathan is reconciled to Demetrius II— Apparently Demetrius did not feel himself strong enough to break with Jonathan, who played his cards skilfully and persuaded the king to renew the concessions made by his father, numbering him amongst *his chief friends* **(27)**, and remitting the tribute from Judaea and the three Samaritan districts (10:30; 11:34) on payment of 300

talents (approx £97,500). The king ratified his decision **592b** in letters addressed to Jonathan himself and to Lasthenes (the Cretan who had been responsible for the operations leading to his restoration), who is styled, after the oriental fashion 'kinsman' (31) and 'father' (32). The districts mentioned in 34 are Aphairema (Ephraim: 2 Sm 13:23; 2 Chr 13:19; Jn 11:54), some 6 or 7 m. N of Bethel, Lydda (Ludd) NE of Jamnia and Ekron, and Rathamin (probably the Arimathea of Mk 15:54, etc = Beit-Rima, between Lydda and Shechem, or possibly Rentis, a little further W).

38—53 Jonathan supports Demetrius against c Trypho—The Cretan mercenaries who had put Demetrius on the throne became a source of odium to the Syrians, especially to the army **(38)**, who felt themselves disgraced by their presence; Diodotus 'the Rake' (Trypho), who had been a governor at Antioch under Alexander, took this opportunity to set up a rival to Demetrius. He concerted a plot with an Arabian Imalkue (conceivably an associate of the Zabdiel with whom Alexander had taken refuge, possibly having his son with him), to proclaim Alexander's son king as Antiochus VI. Jonathan at first continued his support of Demetrius, but later changed his allegiance, perhaps because the latter, who had undertaken to withdraw his garrisons from the strongholds of Judaea (41, 42: cf 10:12) and from the citadel of Jerusalem, failed to implement his promise. Moreover Antiochus showed a readiness to confirm and to extend the privileges enjoyed by the surviving Hasmonaeans (57ff).

54—74 Jonathan supports Antiochus VI against d Demetrius: Victory in Galilee against the latter's Generals—Antiochus conferred a marked honour upon the Jews by appointing Simon governor of the whole coastal region from below Tyre to the frontiers of Egypt. 60. 'beyond the river' i.e. through Coele—Syria, the province W of the Euphrates, cf 7:8. These operations were directed against Demetrius and his partisans, ostensibly on behalf of Antiochus, though of course the Jews would benefit directly from this extension of the power of their arms.

Meanwhile the generals of Demetrius invaded Galilee **e** and Jonathan marched against them, to the region of Kadesh, some 15 m. N of Genesar (67—the first mention in Scripture of the Lake of Gennesaret). Hazor is some 3 m. SW of Kadesh. Absalom **(70)** is perhaps the man referred to in 2 Mc 11:17. Chalphi = Alphaeus (Mt 10:3).

12:1—23 Embassy to Rome and Sparta—3. The **f** ambassadors chosen were to go to Rome first and to Sparta on their return journey, which was performed under a safe-conduct given by the Romans (4). The letters were sent in the name of Jonathan the high-priest and 'the senate of the nation'—the *gerousia* mentioned by Jos (Ant. 12, 3, 3:? cf 2 Chr 19:8), later the Sanhedrin, a name which is first found in Jos. (Ant. 14, 9, 4) under Hyrcanus II—the priests and the people as a whole. The Onias of 7 is Onias I, a contemporary of Arius I of Sparta (309—265). Jos. (Ant. 12, 4, 10) misplaces this document hopelessly. In **9** the Jews make it plain that the kinship alleged by the Spartans to exist between the two nations does not alter the fact that they themselves possess the revelation of God, which is their chief hope and comfort, though they are not unwilling to accept the friendship of Sparta. The statement that the Jews had prayed for the Spartans in an interesting and valuable sidelight on the spirit of genuine Jewish piety, which was by no means so exclusive as is sometimes suggested by its more Pharisaical aspects; cf Bar 1:11. **15.** Is a more

592f explicit expression of the confidence the Jews had in the aid of God, as being of incomparably greater value than any human alliance. At the same time, they do not reject any natural assistance that is compatible with their supreme allegiance. The statement in the letter of Arius to Onias (**21**) that the Spartans were descended from Abraham need not be taken too seriously. It is little more than a conventional opening, like the term *kinsman* (**11**:31); the passage often referred to in Jos. (Ant. 14, 10, 22), in which the Pergamenes speak of friendship existing between their ancestors and the Jews in the days of Abraham is another such empty compliment.

g 24–32 New Campaign against the Generals of Demetrius—The fact that Jonathan was able to intercept the invading army in the land of Hamath (**25**), on the middle Orontes, is a striking indication of the reality of Jewish might at this time. True, the Syrian army made its escape by means of a stratagem (by leaving fires burning in their camp to create the impression that they were still there even after they had retreated), but the general effect was a real victory for the Jews. The success of Jonathan against the Zabadeans, somewhere to the NW of Damascus, is also a measure of his power.

h 33–54 Simon's Successes in the South and in Judaea: Jonathan is betrayed to Trypho—Simon (**11**:59) had been made governor of the coastal regions S from Tyre, and in this capacity he prevents an incipient defection of Joppa to the party of Demetrius. Chaphenatha (**37**) is obscure, and no certain interpretation can be given. One suggestion is that it means *hunger-wall* and may have formed a part of the blockading works. Adida is 3 m. E of Lydda, dominating the Shephelah or low hills between the coastal plain and the central range of Judaea. Vespasian had a fortified camp here during the siege of Jerusalem (JosBJ 4, 11, 1). **50.** In spite of the first report Jonathan is not killed immediately (cf 13:23).

593a 13:1–11 Simon succeeds Jonathan—After being chosen to succeed his brother as leader (? and high priest, cf 13:36; 14; 35), Simon first completes the fortification of Jerusalem and then garrisons Joppa with fresh troops, possibly because the former garrison was likely to support Trypho. **11.** Absalom: cf 11:70.

b 12–30 Trypho invades Judaea, puts Jonathan to death and usurps the Kingdom of Syria—Simon, hearing that Trypho was preparing an expedition against him, occupied the position fortified by his brother on a previous occasion, Adida, 12:38, and after Trypho's treacherous offer to release Jonathan in exchange for a ransom and on surrender of hostages, convicted him of deceit. When the invasion took place by the road from the coast (Adora = Dura, 5 m. WSW of Hebron), Simon, moving on interior lines, managed to keep between Trypho and the capital (**20**), to prevent the relief of the citadel-garrison. Eventually Trypho was compelled to withdraw beyond the Jordan. There he killed Jonathan, and having buried him at Baskama (= ? Tell-Bazuk, NE of the Sea of Galilee) returned to Antioch.

25. Jonathan's remains were rescued by Simon and buried at Modein, his native place (2:1), in a sepulchre which, (according to Jos.Ant. 13, 6, 6), still stood in his day. Traces of it are to be found in modern times (DBV IV 1186f). The monument carried trophies to symbolize Jonathan's might by land and sea.

c 31–53 Simon seeks the Favour of Demetrius II; his Successes—The usurpation of the Syrian crown by Trypho led Simon to restore his support to Demetrius. The latter granted complete autonomy to the Jews— 'the yoke of the Gentiles was removed from Israel'

(**41**)—and the event was noted by being taken as the **593c** starting point for a new chronological era, as is testified by some extant copper coins of Simon. All that remained was to expel the garrison from the citadel and from Gazara (4:15). Macalister (*The Excavation of Gezer*, I, 209) discovered there the remains of a Maccabean palace, bearing a Greek imprecation, calling down fire 'upon the palace of Simon', presumably the sentiment of some prisoner-of-war condemned to work on the edifice. The seal was set on the work of the Hasmonaeans by the final reduction of the citadel of Jerusalem (**50**), for so long a thorn in the side of the faithful Jews (1:35, etc). The feast which was instituted on this occasion is no longer kept. Simon then proceeded to fortify the mount *opposite* the citadel (**52**). John, famous in history as John Hyrcanus, succeeded his father as governor of the coastal district and commander-in-chief of the Jewish army.

14:1–15 Judaea under Simon—The defeat of **d** Demetrius by the Parthian king, Mithridates I (Arsaces (**2**) being a name assumed by all the Parthian kings, after the founder of the dynasty) still further strengthens the position of Simon. The occupation of Joppa (**5**) gives a valuable outlet to the sea, a fact presumably underlying the nautical features of the family sepulchre at Modein (13:29). The possession of Gazara, Bethzur and the citadel (**7**) gives him the keys of Judaea. The different strongholds are provisioned and fortified (**10**), and although the language of **4** is to be explained as rhetorical exaggeration, since the peace was broken towards the end of his reign (15:39), this time is undoubtedly one of great peace and prosperity. Above all, of course, it is a time when the Law is carefully observed and offenders *destroyed* (**14**).

16–24 Renewal of Alliances with Rome and e Sparta—It seems desirable, as Bévenot suggests, to read **24** before **16**; there is no evidence to suggest that Simon sent two embassies at this time, whereas 16 follows naturally on **24**. The order of events then is: Embassy to Rome; renewal of Roman allianc (**24**, **16–19**); on their return the ambassadors visit Sparta (**21**), and the Spartans send a letter renewing the pact made with Jonathan (12:23). Apparently the same ambassadors were employed as on the previous occasion (**22**; 12:16).

25–49 Inscription in Honour of Simon—There are **f** a number of perplexities in the passage, due to some extent to the fact that the inscription may have been a Heb. translation of a Gr. original, and the Heb. finds some difficulty in expressing the long sustained syntax of the proclamation; there are also several slips on the part of copyists. The general sense is however clear enough. The document gives a brief summary of the services rendered by the Hasmonaean family in general (**29–31**) and of Simon in particular (**32–35**); it then describes the honours already conferred upon him (**35**), his further services (**36–37**), and the confirmation of his office by Demetrius II (**38**). 'For he had heard' (**40**) is based on the authority of the better Gr. MSS, which read *ēkouse*, but there can be little doubt that the other reading *ēkousthē* (= *it has been heard by the Jews*) is correct since (*a*) Demetrius was a prisoner in Parthia at this time (**3**), and even if he had heard of the embassy to Rome, he could have done nothing about it; (*b*) he had already confirmed the appointment of Simon as high-priest (13:36). (Bévenot suggests that *Spartans* should be read in **40** in place of 'Romans', since the latter had not called the Jews 'brethren'. Perhaps *Romans and Spartans* should be read.)

28. 'Asaramel' seems to imply an original Heb. form **g** *śar 'am 'ēl* = 'Leader of the people of God', as a title

93g conferred on Simon. Read therefore, 'Simon the high-priest *and leader of the people of God*'. This will, it is true, introduce into I Mc the only explicit mention of the Name of God, but in such a case as this it is probably no more difficult than say, in the parallel Israel. **34.** Gazara is actually some 17 m. from Azotus, but their territories may have been adjacent.

48. 'Temple Treasury'—the very word of the Gr. is preserved in Jn 8:20 'in gazophylacio'—which presumably included archives as well as actual treasures. The copy was put in safe keeping, as the possession of Simon and his descendants.

h 15:1–14 Antiochus VII seeks the Support of Simon against Trypho—Antiochus, brother of the captive Demetrius, was a man of energy for all his extreme youth (he was only 20 at the beginning of his reign), and soon took in hand the defence of his kingdom against the usurping Trypho. His letter to Simon before his landing is an explicit and formal recognition of all existing privileges (including one not previously mentioned, that of coining money; though we know that Simon had been striking coins at least a year before this). Landing in Syria he drove Trypho before him as far as Dor (Tanturah, 9 m. N of Caesaraea), where he blockaded him **(10–14).**

i 15–24 Various Letters from Rome in Support of the Jews—The authenticity of the first letter (**16–21**) is upheld by a curious mistake of Josephus, who puts a similar document, bearing the names of Lucius Valerius as consul, and of Numenius and Alexander as ambassadors, into the reign of Hyrcanus II (*Ant.* 14, 8, 5). The Lucius of **16** is presumably L. Calpurnius Piso, consul in 139 B.C. Ptolemy is Euergetes II, king of Egypt 145–116. For the allusions in **17, 18**, cf 14:24. Demetrius was, of course, by now a prisoner, but the news of his capture could not have reached Rome before the embassy left. Attalus II, king of Pergamum, 160/159–139/138 B.C.; Ariarathes V of Cappadocia, 163–c. 130 B.C.; Arsaces (cf 14:2) = Mithridates I king of Parthia, 171–138; Sampsames a town on the Black Sea coast, E of Sinope: Delos, Samos and Cos are islands in the Aegean, Rhodes the chief island of the Dodecanese group; Sicyon, neighbour of Corinth, had naturally become much more important since the destruction of the latter place in 146 B.C.; Myndos, Cnidus and Halicarnassus are all situated in (the last-named being the capital of) Caria, in the SW corner of Asia Minor; Phaselis is a seaport in Lycia, E of Caria; E of Lycia is Pamphylia, with Side an important harbour; Aradus is an island, containing a town of the same name, off the Phoenician coast; Gortyna is on the island of Crete; Cyrene is the capital of Libya in N Africa. As will be seen the names are are arranged in no recognizable order, and it would be interesting to know what were the relationships existing between Rome and these scattered communities, most of them outside the limits of the Roman Empire, though well within her sphere of influence.

j 25–16:10 Antiochus VII breaks with Simon: his General, Cendebeus, is defeated by the Sons of the High-Priest—Once Antiochus had pinned Trypho down (15:14), he apparently felt strong enough to demand reparations for the extra-Judaean annexations (28: cf 12:33; 13:43), and even for the citadel of Jerusalem, which he claimed as part of his kingdom. Simon's answer is entirely justified, though we have no means of judging how far 100 talents (£32,500) would provide an adequate compensation for the loss of Gazara and Joppa. The seaport at any rate represented a serious loss to the Syrian king, but the Jews were entitled to recoup

themselves for the extensive damage that had been **593j** inflicted on their country under the Syrian domination. The issue could be decided only by force, and whilst Antiochus pursued Trypho (who first escaped to Orthosia, N of Tripolis, but was captured and compelled to commit suicide; cf Strabo 14:668), he left the management of the Jewish affair to Cendebeus, (**38**), whom he made supreme commander (*epistratēgos*) of the coastal plain, presumably the position which Simon, with a slightly different title (*stratēgos*) had formerly held (11:59). Having occupied Jamnia, he proceeded to construct a strong base at Kedron, $7\frac{1}{2}$ m. NE of Azotus to command the route into Judaea. John, who had been appointed commander-in-chief of the Jewish forces, with his headquarters at Gazara, (cf 13:14), then came to consult his father, Simon who left the conduct of military affairs in the hands of his two sons, Judas and John. For the first time we hear of cavalry employed by the Jews (**4, 7**). The victory, which occurred in the plain between Modein and Kedron, was followed by pursuit as far as Azotus. The towers into which some of the Syrian army fled are similar to those mentioned in 2 Kg 17:9; 18:8.

16:11–24 Death of Simon: John succeeds—Pto- **k** lemy, the son of Abubus, was possibly an Idumaean (Bévenot), but the treachery of this attack on Simon is a melancholy conclusion to the noble story of the efforts of the Maccabees on behalf of their country. Fortunately the attempt of Ptolemy to betray his people into the hands of Antiochus as the price of his own elevation to the high-priesthood was foiled by the energy of John, who established himself in Jerusalem in succession to his father. It is true that Antiochus was able to impose tribute on the Jews for a time, in return for their continued occupation of the disputed strongholds of Joppa, Gazara and the rest (cf 15:30), but the strength of Syria was waning and John's reign marks the beginning of a period of independence which was not finally ended until the coming of Rome, cf **15** Dok is a fortress on a height a little to the NW of Jericho. **19.** Ptolemy apparently sought to bribe some of the officers in John's army to desert. **24.** Nothing is known of 'the chronicles' of his priesthood, which was presumably some sort of official journal.

THE SECOND BOOK OF MACCABEES

Introduction—The author of the Second Book ex- **594a** plicitly states that he is merely summarizing the five books of Jason of Cyrene, and there is no reason to doubt that these would be composed in Greek, so that the original language of the epitome would almost certainly be Gr. This is borne out by certain expressions almost of the nature of puns: e.g. *agein agona* 4:18. The author's aim is quite clearly to glorify Judas Maccabeus as the instrument of Divine Providence, the other members of his family receiving scarcely a mention. The story closes at the period of Judas's triumph.

The literary character of the book is different from **b** that of the First. Where the author of the First Book is content to tell a straightforward story—though this does not imply that there are not passages of real elevation in his work—the author of the Second is far more sententious and much more prone to stress the supernatural elements in the events narrated. His style is more florid and even turgid; where the former writer is careful to use reverential paraphrase for the Name of God, the latter uses the term freely; where the former acknowledges frankly the need for Sabbath warfare, the latter adopts a more conservative attitude. In sum, the difference might be expressed by saying that the author of the Second Book is bent on 'edification', whereas the author of the First

594b prefers to let the facts speak for themselves, though he is nonetheless deeply conscious of the divinity shaping the ends of man. The author of 2 Mc is thus a preacher rather than a historian. The relationship of 2 Mc to 1 Mc may be compared with that of Chr to Kgs.

c **Contents**—Prefixed to the actual narrative portion are two or three letters (**1:1—2:18**), and a brief foreword by the epitomist (**2:19—32**). In **3:1—7:42** he outlines the events leading up to the outbreak of the revolt. The rest of the book is taken up with the account of the exploits of Judas Maccabeus, the first part (**8:1—10:9**) dealing with events in the reign of Antiochus Epiphanes, the second (**10:10—15:36**) with those under Eupator and Demetrius I. (Though cf on 9:1, where it is shown that the events of part at least of ch 10 relate to the previous reign.) The last three vv of the Book form the epitomist's own epilogue. (15:37—39). The Book covers about 15 years.

d **Date of Composition**—The evidence for the date of composition is inconclusive, but, in spite of Willrich's theory which would make Jason a contemporary of Philo, it is most natural to suppose that the Book (or at least Jason's history) was composed whilst the effects of the Maccabean liberation were still felt and before the conquest by Rome. It is possible that the author of the 'five books' is the Jason of 1 Mc 8:17 (? nephew of Judas), who was sent on the embassy to Rome. Some even suggest that the work was composed by Jason on that occasion to support the case of the Jews at Rome. This, of course, is a speculation without proof or possibility of refutation, but it is at least as well based as any other. If we press the words in 15:37—'from that time the city has been in the possession of the Hebrews'—it will be necessary to conclude that the history was written before the death of Judas and the ensuing 'great tribulation in Israel' (1 Mc 9:27).

To the epitome of Jason's work are prefixed certain letters (1:1—2:18) of a later date (see the commentary). The date of the latest of them (possibly 125 B.C.: cf on 1:10) naturally makes the date of composition of the Book as we have it at least as late as that. But it is not necessary to suppose that the Second Book is any later than, if indeed it is as late as, the First.

e **1:1—2:18 Introductory Letters**—It is not clear whether there are two or three letters prefixed to this Second Book, but the best division seems to be that of Meyer, and others: (i) 1—7: a greeting from the Jews of Jerusalem to those at Alexandria. This letter concludes: (Given) 'in the reign of Demetrius in the one hundred and sixty-ninth year'. (ii) 7b—9: 'We Jews wrote to you . . .' This is a letter urging the Alexandrian Jews to observe the Feast of Dedication, 25 Chislev (cf 1 Mc 4:59), to celebrate the purification of the temple by Judas. The letter concludes (9): 'In the 188th year'. (So almost all the MSS: many modern scholars would emend to 148, as in two inferior MSS; this would mean that the letter was written about the time of the actual purification of the temple (cf 1 Mc 4:52), which would give more point to the letter. We do not know why such a letter should have been written forty years later.) (iii) 1:10—2:18, an account of the death of Antiochus and a record of the Nehemiah fire-miracle.

The second letter marks the defection of Jason (cf 4:7ff) as the occasion of the beginning of the trouble. **8a** is a summary statement of the sufferings of the Jews: 'they burnt the gate' (1 Mc 4:38; 2 Mc 8:33) and 'shed innocent blood' (1 Mc 1:39) and in general of the persecution. There is no mention of the battles fought by Judas. The whole emphasis is on the answer to prayer.

8b. Obviously refers to the purification of the temple **594e** (cf 1 Mc 4:50—1).

The third letter is undated and the only chronological indication (apart from the events narrated in 12—17) is the address to Aristobulus (**10**), who is known (from Clem. Alex., *Strom.* I 22, PG 8, 893; Euseb. *Praep. Evang.* 9, 6; etc) to have been a Peripatetic philosopher and to have dedicated an allegorical interpretation of the Pent to Ptolemy Philometer (180—146 B.C.), which would seem to imply a date for the letter earlier than the year 146 B.C.

Who is 'the king' (**11**), 'Antiochus' (**14**)? The obvious **f** answer is Epiphanes, since he was certainly the chief oppressor of the Jews. The only difficulty is that the account of his death (**15—16**) does not seem to agree with that given in 9:1—16. For this reason some would find here an account of the death of Antiochus the Great; but all the evidence goes to show that he treated the Jews well. Moreover, a reading of this passage and of 9:2 strongly suggests that the same incident is being referred to in both places. Bévenot suggests that, for motives of prudence, the writer of the letter thought it unwise to refer to recent incidents, and elected to repeat the well-known facts about the death of Antiochus the Great, leaving it to the recipients of the letter to read between the lines, seeing in the death of the former king a premonitory example of the way in which God punishes all impiety. This seems more satisfactory than to say, with Knabenbauer, that in the letter we have an account, based on an early and exaggerated report, of what had happened to Epiphanes in Elam.

There are a number of textual difficulties in the letter. **g** **10.** Bévenot follows Torrey in suggesting that the original reading was *'the Senate of the Jews'* (not 'the Senate and Judas'), as in some Syriac MSS.

The second part of the letter (1:18—2:18) deals with **h** two main themes—the 'fire-miracle' of Nehemiah and the concern of Jeremiah for the safety of the Ark of the Covenant. The relevance of these incidents (not elsewhere recorded in OT) is obvious; they must have been the theme of much speculation at the time of the dedication of the temple, so similar in many ways to the dedication which had taken place on the return from the Babylonian Captivity. For the general circumstances of this return cf Ezek and Neh. This particular incident is presumably derived from the (lost) memoirs and commentaries of Nehemiah (2:13). **20.** There can be little doubt that the 'thick liquid' is to be explained in conjunction with the 'Nephthar' (**36**) as being some kind of inflammable substance akin to naphtha, which is found in Persia. The continuity between the temple fire and the new fire kindled at the time of the return is to be understood as meaning that the materials which had produced the former fire had been preserved and served for this first kindling of the sacrificial flame. The actual kindling, it is implied, was miraculous (cf 1 Kg 18:38). The author apparently connects the name 'Nephthar' with the root *ptr*, meaning 'to separate'. **23.** Jonathan is apparently the Johanan of Neh 12:22. The Jonathan mentioned in Neh 12:11 belongs to a later generation.

There is nothing in the extant writings attributed **i** to Jeremiah to bear out the statements in 2:1—12 except for the Epistle of Jeremiah in Bar 6. The connexion of 1—7 with what precedes and what follows is presumably that the story of Jeremiah's hiding the Ark, etc leads up to the passage in 7, which is appropriate to the circumstances of the letter, as are the references to Moses and Solomon (cf Lv 40:32 1 Kg 8:11; Lv 9:24; 2 Chr 7:1; Lv 10:16f).

94j **2:19–32 Author's Prologue**—With **19** we come to the actual words of the epitomist. The central theme of the letters quoted has been the purification and dedication of the temple, and the author now proceeds to show how this is the climax of the life-work of Judas, related at great length in the five books of Jason of Cyrene, and here summarized for the benefit of those who might not have either the time or the inclination for a reading of such a lengthy history.

95a **3:1–40 Peace under Onias III and Seleucus IV broken: Frustration of the Attempt to rob the Temple**—The politico-religious situation here implied was roughly as follows. After the annexation of Judaea by Antiochus III (c. 200 B.C.), both he and his immediate successor Seleucus IV sought to conciliate the traditionalist pro-Egyptian party, headed by the family of Onias, the high-priest, whilst the Tobiad party, representing the 'progressive' Hellenistic idea, was making its way to power by a close *rapprochement* with the Syrian authorities. This involved, as we shall see, the betrayal of the religious faith and traditions of the Jews. Thus Simon (**4**), whether he was or was not of the Tobiad family, was certainly of that party, and set out to ingratiate himself with the governor of Coele-Syria, Apollonius of Tarsus, by informing him of the wealth of the temple. (The Syrian kings were acutely embarrassed financially as a result of the indemnity imposed on them by the Romans in 188 B.C.; cf 1 Mc 3:29; 8:7; 2 Mc 8:10) The king, informed by Apollonius, entrusts the affair to Heliodorus, who is mentioned in inscriptions as the king's vizier. The amount of money in the temple was equivalent to something like £855,000 of our money (£130,000 + 725,000), part of it forming a sort of benevolent fund, whilst the rest had been deposited there, presumably for safety, by a member of the Tobiad family. This suggests that Simon was prepared to betray his associates as well as the deserving poor. Hyrcanus is mentioned in Jos.*Ant.* 12, 4, 2–11. **11.** 'Son of' may mean no more than *descended from*. The vivid description of Heliodorus's sacrilegious attempt and its frustration is a characteristic passage (11–20).

b **4:1–22 Onias denounces Simon: Jason usurps the High-Priesthood: Introduction of Hellenizing Practices**—**4.** 'Apollonius, the son of Menestheus': the reading of most of the Gr. MSS, *mainesthai* is now universally given up in favour of *menestheos*; cf 21.

c The death of Seleucus was, as we know, brought about by this Heliodorus, who sought to make himself king (Appian, *Syr.* 45). But (**7**) Antiochus IV, with the help of neighbouring kings, succeeded in expelling him and ascended the throne. Jason (a Gr. name adopted by him, presumably as resembling his original name Joshua) shows his Hellenizing tendencies. The attempt to obtain the high-priesthood held by his own brother and his attempt to bribe the king by means of the temple funds show the depths to which the official leaders of the Jews had sunk, and set in an even stronger light the fidelity and self-sacrifice of the Maccabees. **8.** 360 talents = £117,000; 80 talents = £26,000—this sum apparently to be paid annually: 150 talents = £49,000. **9.** 'citizens of Antioch', either because enjoying certain special privileges associated with their Syrian citizenship or as a mere empty title. **11.** Supports the statement of 3:2 about the exemptions allowed to the Jews by previous Seleucid kings; cf Jos.Ant. 12, 3, 3f. We know nothing of John, but the reference to Eupolemus is interesting as being connected with an incident, the embassy to Rome (1 Mc 8:17ff), which is later than the victory of Nicanor with which 2 Mc concludes. If Jason of Cyrene were the Jason of that embassy he would have personal acquaintance with this **595c** Eupolemus.

12. The Gr. is *hupo petason* ('in a *petasos*') and the **d** *petasos*, the characteristic Greek hat, is probably to be understood as a symbol of Gr. ways in general. 'The citadel' is not the Syrian-occupied *akra* of 1 Mc 1:35 etc, but probably the site of the later Antonia. **15.** Means that they ceased to care for their traditional glories and thought only of winning a name for excellence in Greek pursuits. **19.** 'Hercules' = the Tyrian Melkart. **20.** Since 300 didrachmas = £16, 'construction of triremes' must be understood rather as contributing to the equipping of them.

23–50 Jason is replaced as High-Priest by Mene- e laus—Menelaus: Josephus says he was also called Onias and was a brother of Jason: this is clearly a confusion. Jason had replaced his brother Onias (cf 4:7, 10). Menelaus is thought to be a member of the Tobiad family, which is borne out by the fact that when he flees, he goes to the 'land of Ammon' (**26**), where the Tobiads are known to have had a stronghold. **28.** Sostratus was the Syrian governor of Jerusalem. **30.** Tarsus and Mallus are both in Cilicia. Onias had gone to Antioch some time before (**5**). **33.** Daphne is a suburb of Antioch, with a sacred precinct, some 5 m. SW of the capital. The pillaging of the temple by Menelaus (**32**) and Lysimachus (**39**) enrages the people and goads them to an outburst against their leaders.

5:1–27 Beginnings of Persecution—The preceding **596a** ch gives a very good idea of the disorders caused by the unscrupulous conduct of the Hellenizers at Jerusalem, and it is hardly surprising that Antiochus should have decided to intervene in person, on his return from his Egyptian expedition. The invasion referred to in **1** is the second only in the sense that the contemplated expedition, mentioned in 4:21f, counts as the first; cf 1 Mc 1:20; Dn 11:28. For the portents of **2, 3** cf:

> Fierce fiery warriors fight upon the clouds
> In ranks and squadrons and right form of war . . .
> The noise of battle hurtled in the air,
> Horses did neigh and dying men did groan.
> (Shakespeare: *Julius Caesar*, II 2).

5. Jason had fled into the country of the Ammonites (4:26) when Menelaus had been awarded the high-priesthood by Antiochus. Now, hearing that the latter was dead, he attempts to regain his position, but unsuccessfully. **8.** Aretas, King of the Arabians; cf 1 Mc 5.25. **9.** 'kinship'—an allusion to the letter of 1 Mc 12:21, in which the Spartans claimed kinship with the Jews.

Antiochus not unnaturally interprets the revolt of **b** Jason against Menelaus as an attack upon his own authority, and after his reverse in Egypt he is in no mind to brook insubordination in Palestine. This first persecution therefore had as much a political as a religious motive, though the two were closely connected. He also desired to get into his possession the treasures he had heard of (3:7), some of which he had been promised, but had not received (4:8ff, 27). For the attempt of Heliodorus, cf 3:14ff. **21.** 1,800 talents = £585,000. **22.** Philip, who now replaces Sostratus (or Crates, 4:29) as governor of Jerusalem, is mentioned as persecuting the Jews savagely (6:11). **23.** The Samaritans, too, are oppressed. Gerizim; cf Jn 4:20. **24.** Finally, Antiochus sends Apollonius (two years later; cf 1 Mc 1:30) to stamp out all opposition to the new religious policy. '*Musarchēn*', i.e. *commander of the Mysians*; cf on 1 Mc 1:30. We know from Polybius that there was a corps of Mysians in the Seleucid army

596b (Polybius 31:3, where he describes a procession at Antioch, which took place a few years after these events, in which 5,000 Mysians took part). **27.** Judas Maccabeus now appears, with a small group of nine companions (presumably including his father and brothers; cf 1 Mc 2:1). 'The defilement' referred to is of course the contamination of heathen practices; cf 14:3.

c 6:1–31 Measures by Antiochus to introduce Hellenism: Martyrdom of Eleazar—The general features of the situation have been discussed in 1 Mc 1:43ff; cf in particular 1 Mc 1:54 for the 'desolating sacrilege', the altar to Jupiter Olympius (2) **5.** Diodorus (34:1) describes how a sow was slain on the altar and the Jews forced to partake of it. **8.** 'at the suggestion of Ptolemy' (4:45), who appears to have been in charge of religious propaganda. **10.** Apparently refers to the incident described in 1 Mc 1:60ff.

18–31. The martyrdom of Eleazar. 19. 'The *instrument of torture*' (*tumpanon*); either a rack, perhaps cruciform (Wilcken), or a bastinado; cf 30. The verb formed from the Gr. word is used in Heb. 11:35, which seems to be a reminiscence of this passage.

d 7:1–42 The Seven Brothers—This passage is closely linked with the story of Eleazar and the same spirit breathes through both. The faith and constancy of the brothers and of their mother speak for themselves, as also does their certainty of immortality. The style of this account—the detailed description of the tortures, the presence of the king, whom the young boys address with such boldness—is a feature of this type of 'edifying history', see 593*b*. The barbarous nature of the punishment need hardly surprise us: for roasting, cf Jer 29:22; for scalping, cf Herodotus 4:64; for cutting off of hands, feet, etc, cf Xen. *Anab.* 1:9:13. Antiochus III had thus treated his own cousin (Polybius 8:23).

11. Is, of course, most important as evidence for Jewish faith in the resurrection of the body; whilst **13** does not imply that there would be no resurrection for the wicked, but only that there would not be a resurrection to the life of happiness but to eternal death.

597a 8:1–7 Early Successes of Judas—What has preceded is largely introductory to the main purpose of the book, which is to recite the achievements of Judas Maccabeus. The latter at first necessarily confines himself to local action against isolated positions. This would involve some splitting of his forces, and may explain why, although 6,000 is given as the number of men raised (1), in 1 Mc 4:6 Judas has only 3,000 men in a later engagement against Gorgias; cf ad loc.

b 8–23 Measures and Counter-measures of Apollonius and Judas—**8.** Philip: the governor of Jerusalem (5:22; 6:11), apparently appointed to bring about the religious changes desired by Antiochus. For Ptolemy, cf 1 Mc 3:38; 2 Mc 4:45; 6:8. **9.** Nicanor and Gorgias, 1 Mc 3:38, etc. For the whole passage, cf 1 Mc 3:27–60. **10.** The tribute: cf 1 Mc 8:7; 2 Mc 3:7. According to Polybius 21:17, the period of payment was 12 years (from 188 B.C., the date of the treaty of Apamea), but we know from Livy (42:6) that in 173 B.C. Apollonius was at Rome apologizing for the delay in paying, and although the report of his speech on that occasion seems to imply that he was bringing the final instalment ('*omne advexisse*'), it may be that the Romans had granted a moratorium and that he was bringing the payments up to date. **11.** One motive for this expedition against the Jews is then to raise money by taking and selling slaves. For the slave-dealers accompanying the expedition, cf 1 Mc 3:41. **13.** Not all the Jews who left the forces of Judas were cowards or deserters; cf 1 Mc 3:56. **19.** Sennacherib:

cf 2 (4) Kgs 19:35. **20.** Of the battle against the **597** Galatians we have no other mention, but presumably it occurred during a campaign fought by Antiochus III in Media against a rebel satrap, Molon, in 220 B.C. Molon is known to have had a force of Galatians in his army (Polybius 5:40–43). The Jews would presumably constitute a part of the mercenary army under Antiochus; there is much evidence to show that the Jews often served as mercenaries under the Hellenistic kings.

There is some corruption at the beginning of **23.** LXX says: *Eleazar also*, which looks like a clumsy attempt to introduce a fourth captain (22) to make up the total of 6,000 men; but it may be authentic. **22.** 'Joseph' should almost certainly be *John*. Judas had no brother Joseph; cf 1 Mc 2:2.

24–29 Victory over Nicanor (and Gorgias)—This **c** victory is described at greater length in 1 Mc 4:1–25. The two accounts are derived from different sources, since I Mc says practically nothing about Nicanor, whilst Gorgias and Lysias, not mentioned in 2 Mc, there play a more prominent role; cf 1 Mc 3:38, etc.

30–36 Defeat of Timotheus and Bacchides—30–33 appear to be wrongly inserted here. 34–36 clearly refer to the events immediately following on the defeat of Nicanor. Moreover, the reference to Jerusalem, etc in 31–33 should be connected with ch 10. In 1 Mc 5:6–8 there is a reference to a campaign against the Ammonites, under Timothy, apparently shortly after the temple purification, and this may be part of the same campaign.

9:1–29 Death of Antiochus Epiphanes—The inser- **d** tion here of the account of the death of Epiphanes should not be taken to imply that the author regarded it as preceding the temple purification; cf 10:9. It certainly did not do so, as is clear from 1 Mc 6:1–17. Possibly Jason, or his epitomist, did not wish to break the story of the successes of Judas, and therefore anticipated the interpolation of the fortunes of Antiochus. Moreover, there is evidence to suggest that Jason was not very careful about chronological sequence; and in any case he may have inserted here a complete account of the adventures of Antiochus in the E, which had begun some time before and would naturally close with the account of his death, which the epitomist has extracted.

2. Since the city where the temple was is said to have **e** been in Elam (Elymais 1 Mc 6:1; cf Polybius 31:11), the name Persepolis must be understood to mean not the well-known capital of Persia, but simply a Persian city, i.e. a city of the Persian Empire (= Persia). **3.** According to Polybius, Antiochus died at Tabae (? = Gabae, near Aspadana, which ought perhaps to be read here for 'Ecbatana'). If, as suggested above, the campaign against Timothy took place after the temple purification, then Antiochus must have heard the news of this too, but the author suppresses this fact since he had not yet dealt with the incident.

8–17. The somewhat rhetorical nature of the des- **f** cription of the king's sufferings and remorse is characteristic of 2 Mc. **19–27.** The terms in which this letter is couched suggest that it was intended as an appeal to the different countries composing the king's realm, and we may well believe that where 'Jews' stands in this version (19), other copies would insert Syrians, Phoenicians, and the like. Antiochus at times condescended to a style of conduct which seemed to express a desire to show his 'democratic' spirit; cf Polybius 31:4. **29.** Has caused some perplexity. According to 1 Mc 6:14, 55–56, 63, Philip was made regent and succeeded in occupying Antioch, but was driven out again by Lysias. According to Jos.Ant. (12, 9, 7) he was captured and killed by

597f Antiochus V (Eupator). Possibly he went to Egypt before his attempt to seize power, with the object of concerting measures with Ptolemy.

10:1—8 (9) Purification of the Temple: Encaenia—For the events of this passage cf 1 Mc 4:36—59, where they are treated at greater length. The 'two years' of **3** is not to be taken literally, since the actual interval was three years precisely; cf our own expression 'a couple of years'. **9.** Bears out what was said in 597*d* about the death of Antiochus following the temple purification.

598a 10—23 Victories over the Idumaeans, etc— 11. The 'appointment' of Lysias was merely the formal ratification of an existing situation, though it is significant as reversing the decision of Antiochus Epiphanes (1 Mc 6:14) to replace Lysias by Philip. It was of course Lysias who took the initiative in all this (1 Mc 6:17). **12.** Ptolemy is governor of Coele-Syria (cf 8:8), but is probably not Ptolemy son of Dorymenes (1 Mc 3:38, etc). **14.** Gorgias is now governor of Idumaea; cf 588*c*. The 'mercenaries' are the Philistines. **16—19.** For Judas's exploits cf 1 Mc 5:3—5.

b The incident of **18—23** is in keeping with the general purpose of 2 Mc, the contrast between the virtue and wisdom of Judas and the weakness and corruption of those about him. Doubtless there were such traitors; but it would be wrong to suppose that Simon was one of them. Certainly he was not put to death with the traitors (22), and the part he plays in 1 Mc is sufficient testimony to his uprightness and general worth. **10.** 'Joseph and Zacchaeus' may be a corruption of Joseph son of Zechariah; cf 1 Mc 5:56, where he is concerned in a dangerous act of insubordination. **20.** The 70,000 *drachmas* possibly represent the ransom of 700 men at the normal rate of a mina a head. The total is something less than £4,000.

c 24—38 Defeat and Death of Timothy, Leader of the Ammonites—It was suggested in § 597*c* that the account of the campaign there mentioned against Timothy had been displaced, and should occur after the purification of the temple (i.e. after the early vv of this ch), possibly forming part of this campaign. (It ought to be stated that not all interpreters accept the identification of the Timothy of 8:30 with the Timothy of this ch.) At any rate, the capture of Gazara (1 Mc 5:8 = Jazer) seems to be the incident described in 32—37.

d 11:1—38 Defeat of Lysias: Treaty—It seems probable that this campaign of Lysias is the one described in 1 Mc 4:26—35, i.e. before the death of Antiochus Epiphanes and the purification of the temple. (Its dislocation is another example of the confusion of the source employed by the epitomist (cf 8:30; 9:1—29). The writer is giving the story of what happened, but is not particularly concerned with problems of chronology.) It seems clear the Lysias is here acting, not in conjunction with the king, who is not mentioned, but on his own responsibility. (In ch 13 the young king is mentioned, although there Lysias must still have been largely responsible for the operations.) Moreover, Bethzur (**5**) is almost certainly the place mentioned in 1 Mc 4:29. Further, the first of the letters (**16—21**) reads as though it were sent off in the absence of the king; cf **18** 'everything that needed to be brought before him'; there is some MS authority for reading '*I have agreed to*', etc. The date of this letter (**21**) is towards the end of a month Dioscorinthius, which is thought to be a novel form of (or a mistake for) Dystros (= Adar). The second letter (**22—26**) must have been written shortly after the receipt of the news of the death of Antiochus Epiphanes, since it reads like a proclamation at the beginning of a new reign. Eupator and still more Lysias **598d** would be aware of the danger threatening from Egypt and from Philip (9:1—29) and would be anxious to conciliate the Jews. This second letter is addressed to Lysias, but obviously with the intention that it should be communicated to the Jews, as a sort of covering letter for the following one. The letter (**27—33**) to the Jews from the king, dated 15 Xanthikos (= Nisan) is intended to provide a safe-conduct for those Jews desiring to travel between Jerusalem and Antioch, presumably on their return from the Passover celebrations. Menelaus will be the high-priest of 4:23; 5:5, etc.

The last letter (**34—38**) from the Roman ambassadors **e** bears the same date, possibly by a mere coincidence, though it may be an error in copying. Quintus Memmius is otherwise unknown. Titus Manius is probably T. Manlius Torquatus, known to have been an ambassador in Egypt about 164 B.C.; he may have received some commission in connexion with Syrian affairs.

12:1—31 Fresh Outbreaks: Punishment of Jamnia 599a and Joppa: Defeat of Timothy—This is a very confused ch and bears all the signs of being a mere collection of disconnected material concerning campaigns with no sort of interrelation. The events of **10—31** are certainly those recorded in 1 Mc 5:24—53, whilst the events of **3—9**, which have no connexion with the generals mentioned in **2** and, as we shall see, do not lead naturally to 10, are entirely without a firm chronological reference. Further, the mention of Timothy, mysterious as are his appearances and disappearances (2, 10, 18, 24), strongly suggests that this passage should be read before 10:24—37, a passage which ends with an account of his death. Some would cut the knot by supposing that this is a different Timothy, which is possible, but (a) the fact that he is operating in the same vicinity and (b) the statement in 10:24 that he had already been overcome by the Jews are reasonable grounds for maintaining the identifications. (However cf Bévenot, Introduction, § 9).

Of the generals mentioned in 2, nothing more is heard **b** of any except Timothy. Nicanor is probably different from the Nicanor of ch 14. The hostility of the coast towns to the Jews was of course nothing new, but there is no evidence as to what occasioned this fresh outburst. But in that world of intrigue (Egypt-Syria, Philip-Lysias, Antiochus-Demetrius) there would be many occasions for minor party incidents.

The outline of events dealt with in 10—31 is more **c** clearly indicated in 1 Mc 5:24—53 and it will suffice here to resolve one or two minor problems. **10.** The nine furlongs cannot, of course, be reckoned from Jamnia or even from Jerusalem (8, 9), as the fighting next described occurred in Transjordania. Something has clearly been omitted, either by the epitomist or by a copyist; cf 17. **13.** Caspin is probably the Chaspho of 1 Mc 5:26, which may be the modern Khisfin, some 10 m. E of the Sea of Galilee. **17.** The ninety-five (750 furlongs) can hardly be reckoned from Khisfin, and it seems likely that 17 should come between 9 and 10, so that the 750 furlongs will be reckoned from the neighbourhood of Jerusalem, which would bring them within striking distance of the Tubianites; cf Tob 1 Mc 5:13. Charax cf 1 Mc 5:9, etc. **20.** For 120,000 the Old Latin reads 12,000, almost certainly correct. **27.** Ephron, cf 1 Mc 5:46. **29.** Scythopolis is called Bethshan in 1 Mc 5:46. **31.** The Feast of Weeks = Pentecost (32).

32—46 Defeat of Gorgias—This is apparently paral- **d** leled by 1 Mc 5:65ff, although Gorgias is not there mentioned (but cf 1 Mc 5:59). We know that he was in command in Idumaea ('the land to the South', 1 Mc 5:65),

599d whilst Marisa (35) is some 12 m. ENE of Hebron. Esdris (36) is probably another form of the name Azariah (cf 1 Mc 5:60), whilst the incident of the idol-amulets (40), seems to be connected with the reproof of 1 Mc 5:62.

e **43–46.** Is of course one of the best-known passages in Mc. Its dogmatic importance is considerable, testifying as it does to a clear-cut and confident belief in **personal immortality** and in the value of **intercessory prayer for the dead.** The force of the words is strengthened rather than weakened by the objection that 'such an idea is unparalleled in Jewish Literature'. Here is no vague echo of a conventional platitude but a definite statement of the writer's personal conviction, the witness of one consciously taking sides in a debate about the fact of survival. As is well known the Sadducees rejected the doctrine of the resurrection of the body (Mt 22:23), and it may well be that it was during this period of struggle between the orthodox party, represented especially by the Hasideans (1 Mc 2:42), later to become the Pharisees, and the Hellenizing party within the priesthood, constituted by the sceptical Sadducees, that the doctrine of personal immortality began to assume a sharper definition. To that definition such a passage as the present may well have contributed. The gesture of Judas would of course become widely known, and would serve to deepen and strengthen the faith that it yet presupposed.

43. 2,000 drachmas. It is interesting to contrast with the 300 drachmas which was all that could be raised for the Tyrian festival (2 Mc 4:19).

For Pharisees and Sadducees cf Lagrange, 56, 304ff, 353ff.

600a **13:1–26 Eupator in Person fails: Peace**—According to the parallel passage (1 Mc 6:18ff), the occasion of this expedition was an appeal from the garrison in the citadel at Jerusalem, which Judas was attempting to reduce. The presence of Menelaus with the army (comparable to that of Alcinus with Bacchides, 1 Mc 7:9, 12) suggests that he knew that he could not hope to hold the position of high-priest by any personal merit and that the Hellenizing party in Jerusalem was not strong enough to support him: he could come only as the nominee of a foreign power. The 'deceitfulness' (3) consisted in the fact that he pretended to be inspired with patriotic motives but was a mere self-seeker. He was put to death at Beroea (Aleppo)—but probably, as the account in Josephus implies, at the end of the campaign, when (23) Antiochus was seeking to conciliate the Jews; Ant. 12, 6, 7; cf 1 Mc 6:59. The account of the death of Menelaus is not clear, but suggests that he was killed by being buried alive in (? smouldering) ashes.

b In **22, 23** Jason, or his epitomist, glosses over what would have been a serious reverse for the Jews but for the rebellion of Philip. But it is true that this fact, coupled with the prolonged resistance of Bethzur and the military skill of Judas, prevented the king from reaping the fruits of his victory and turned what might have been a disaster to the Jewish cause into a reason for thanksgiving. The king did withdraw, having been weakened (23, 24; 1 Mc 6:60).

Was Judas appointed governor of the coastal districts, **600c** as Simon was afterwards (1 Mc 11:59)? There is no mention of it in 1 Mc, and the Gr. Text says that Antiochus appointed Hegemonides governor. Some emend 'Hegemonides' to *hegemona*. On the whole, it seems safer to conclude against the view that he was actually appointed. **24.** 'He' is apparently Antiochus.

14:1–14 Intrigues of Alcimus—For Demetrius **d** cf 1 Mc 7:1 and 586*e*; for Alcimus (3) cf 1 Mc 7:5. 'In the times of separation' *sc.* in the early days of the persecution when the Jews who desired to remain faithful shunned all dealings with the heathen; cf 38; 1 Mc 1:53; 2:33; 2 Mc 5:27.

There were apparently three attempts to restore Alcimus, two by Bacchides (1 Mc 7:8ff; 9:32ff) and this attempt by Nicanor (after the failure of the first attempt by Bacchides (1 Mc 7:25ff), but before his second attempt, which was successful).

15–36 Relations between Judas and Nicanor— **e** The account here given of the attitude of Nicanor to Judas is much fuller than that in 1 Mc 7:26ff. The preliminary skirmishing round Dessau (an unknown locality: does the reading Lessau, found in some MSS, suggest the truth, *sc.* Laisa, near Bethhoron: cf 1 Mc 9:5?) is not mentioned in 1 Mc, which also suggests that Nicanor was hostile to Judas from the beginning and that his friendship (**24**; cf 1 Mc 7:27) was hypocritical. But 1 Mc has compressed, omitting the earlier phases. Thus 1 Mc 7:26*b*ff will correspond with 30 here. **26.** 'Successor': more probably *deputy*; cf 4:29.

37–46 Death of Razis—This passage has perplexed **f** the moralists, and has been cited by heretics either as a defence of suicide (so the Donatists: cf Augustine, *Contra Gaudentium* 1:26–31) or as proving that 2 Mc is not inspired. But whilst we must condemn the act of Razis as objectively wrong, we may, with the author, praise the determination to die rather than to risk apostasy. That he was in good faith is clear from **46.**

38. The Gr. means: '*Formerly, at the time when the* **g** *Jews were not consorting with the heathen (cf 3), he had made the choice of Judaism*' (Bévenot: 'he had aimed at maintaining the purity of the Jewish religion').

15:1–37 Defeat and Death of Nicanor—Judas, **h** who had withdrawn from Jerusalem in a NW direction *towards* Samaria, had taken up a position at Adasa (1 Mc 7:40), due N of Jerusalem, having eluded Nicanor's army at Bethhoron. The parallel passage (7:26ff) deals more at length with the military operations, 2 Mc as usaul being interested in the more 'edifying' details—Judas's dream and prayer (11–16; 21–24). Cf 1 Mc 7:49. **37.** The Jews did not retain possession of Jerusalem for long (1 Mc 9:23ff), but there was no return to the former desecration of the temple precincts and in comparison with that the mere military occupation of the capital was a relatively tolerable matter. (If we press the meaning we must suppose that the Book was completed before the death of Judas.)

37–39. Form a delightful and entirely characteristic **i** Epilogue: cf the epitomist's Prologue (2:20–33).

THE TEXT OF THE NEW TESTAMENT

BY J. M. T. BARTON

601a Bibliography—H. Höpfl, O.S.B. *Introd. Gen. in S. Scripturam, Tractatus de Inspiratione, Canone, Historia Textus, Hermeneutica*. Ed. 6a (ed. I. Leloir, O.S.B.), 1958. M. J. Lagrange, O.P. *Introd. à l'étude du NT. Deuxième Partie: Critique textuelle, II. La critique rationnelle*, EtB, 1935; H. J. Vogels, *Handbuch der neutestamentichen Textkritik* 1923; L. Vaganay, *An Introd. to the Textual Criticism of the NT.*, E. tr, 1937. F. Kenyon, *Handbook to the Textual Criticism of the NT.*, 1912[2]; *Recent Developments in the Textual Criticism of the Greek Bible*, 1933. *Our Bible and the Ancient Manuscripts*, 1958[5]; *The Text of the Greek Bible*, rev. ed., 1949. E. Lake and S. New, *The Text of the NT*, rev ed., 1928. K. W. Clark, 'The effect of recent textual criticism on New Testament Studies' in *The Background of the New Testament and its Eschatology*, ed. W. Davies and D. Daube, 1956. G. Milligan, *The NT Documents: Their Origin and Early History*, 1913; R. M. Grant, *A Historical Introduction to the NT*, 1964; Bruce M. Metzger, *The Text of the NT, Its Transmission, Corruption and Restoration*, Oxford, 1964; Duplacy, 'Histoire des manuscrits et histoire du texte du NT', NTS, 1966, 124–39; V. Taylor, *The Text of the NT*: a short introduction, 1961; A. T. Robertson, *An introduction to the Textual Criticism of the NT* (1925); A. Souter, *The Text and Canon of the NT* 1912: 2nd ed. 1954; B. M. Metzger, *Annotated bibliography of the textual criticism of the NT*, Copenhagen, 1955. id 'Recent discoveries and investigations of the NT Mss' JBL, 78 (1959); J. Duplacy, *Où en est la critique textuelle du NT*; 1959, 13–20. H. J. Vogels, 'Critique textuelle du NT' DBS II (1934) 256–74. B. Botte, 'Mss grecs du NT' DBS V (1954), 819–55. A. F. J. Klijn, *An Introduction to the NT*, Leiden, 1967.

b Origin of the NT Text—The text is made up of the 27 books that collectively form the NT. According to the traditional reckoning, which takes no account of scribes or assistants, the books were the work of not less than eight authors, were written at various dates, and at times differ markedly in sundry particulars. In terms of the order of their arrangement in the modern printed texts there are four narratives known as Gospels, an historical work referred to as the Acts of the Apostles, 21 Epistles (14 by St Paul, three by St John, two by St Peter and one each by St James and St Jude). There is, lastly, the book known as the Apocalypse of St John. Many of these works cannot be dated with exactness, but traditionally they all came into existence in the period between the ascension and A.D. 100. These 27 books occupy no less than 657 pages of text in Nestle's *Novum Testamentum graece* (25th ed, 1963).

c Disappearance of the original autographs—It is commonly accepted by the world of scholarship that the original manuscripts as they first came forth from their inspired authors, are no longer in existence or have completely disappeared, probably for all time. These autographs, and their first copies, have perished, in ways that would include (a) destruction by Christians in times of persecution to prevent the manuscripts from falling into the hands of heathens, (b) destruction by the persecutors themselves; and, doubtless in great measure, (c) ordinary wear-and-tear, by the daily use made of the precious writings in the Christian communities to which they were addressed. It will be contended, a little later, that all these works were written on material that would easily wear out or be destroyed by bad conditions of storage, and it has, indeed, been argued that all the originals had perished by the middle of the 2nd cent. (Cornely-Merk, p. 126). Though all the books originated in the apostolic body or under its direction, it is not necessary to assume that all were actually written by the hands of the apostles themselves; hence it is possible that not all the manuscripts were regarded as equally sacred. Tertullian's reference in *De Praescriptione Haereticorum*, c. 36, to 'the very apostolic letters' is usually discounted as rhetorical. The reputed autograph copies of Matthew's Gospel found in the grave of Barnabas in Cyprus and the alleged autograph of Mark are not accepted as evidence of the originals' survival. It is, in fact, noteworthy that orthodox writers of the 2nd cent., in their disputes with Marcion, the Gnostics and other early heretics about the exact reading of a text, made no effort to appeal to the witness of the originals, this in itself being a fair indication that the autographs were no longer available. We may conclude, then, that the 2nd cent. writers were essentially in the same position as all later students of the NT, in so far as they were forced to depend upon more or less accurate copies.

d Circulation of the NT Text—This subject is fully treated by Milligan, 171–99. Here it need only be said that many of the writings 'notwithstanding their often limited address and occasional character, possessed an undoubted vitality and power of growth' (op cit, 173). We may well believe that the autographs of St Paul's Epistles, having been diligently read in the Churches to which they were sent, would be kept in storage for reference, and would be from time to time copied for the benefit of other communities. Apart from such congregational use it is not unlikely that even private persons would be allowed to make copies in part or in whole. In course of time more and more copies would be made, so that, by the middle of the 2nd cent., many of the Churches in the Roman Empire would have possessed copies of the four Gospels, and, in some instances, of other writings. The relative ease with which such works could be circulated is made clear in an article by Sir W. M. Ramsay: 'It is the simple truth', he writes, 'that travelling, whether for business or for pleasure, was contemplated and performed under the Empire with an indifference, confidence, and, above all, certainty, which were unknown in after centuries until the introduction of steamers and the consequent increase in ease and sureness of communication'. ('Roads and Travel (in NT)' in *HDB*, Extra volume, 396). A merchant in Hierapolis in Phrygia made,

601d according to the inscription on his tomb, the journey from Asia to Rome 72 times. (CIG, 3929).

e **Imperfections of copies**—Unfortunately the copies of NT documents that have come down to us are always, in some degree, imperfect ones, since 'owing to the frailties of the human hand and eye and brain, it is impossible to copy large quantities of matter without making mistakes.', F. Kenyon, *Text of the Greek Bible*, 9. Among various causes that have led to erroneous copying one may mention confusion between letters (e.g. the Gr. capitals Θ and *O*), dittography (i.e. accidental repetition of one or more letters), transposition of letters, and homoioteleuton (i.e. the omission of a line owing to the use of several words or clauses successively with repetitions or similar endings). There are also many instances where deliberate alterations have been made by the copyist in the interest, real or supposed, of accuracy, elegance, sound doctrine, and so forth; cf Lagrange, 32—40; also RB (41) 1933, 481—98.

f **External Form of the Greek Codices**—Throughout the first two centuries of Christianity the NT writings were, doubtless, circulated on rolls or sheets of papyrus, a word probably derived from the Egyptian *pa-p-yer*, meaning 'the (product) of the river' or 'the river plant'. It had been in use as a writing material for many centuries, the earliest papyrus writing-material being one found at Saqqara in Lower Egypt in 1693, which contains accounts dating back to the third millennium B.C. The preparation of the plant for use as a writing material was described by the elder Pliny. First, the pith (*byblos*) of the stem was cut into long strips. These, laid first vertically and then horizontally, were gummed together into a single sheet, which, after drying and rubbing down with ivory or a shell, was ready for use. The horizontal strips were those mostly used for writing, as the lines were better marked and the sheets could be more easily rolled inward on that side (known as the *recto*, the back being styled the *verso*). Occasionally, however, when space for further writing was wanted, the *verso* was used. It is possible that there is a reference to this practice in Apoc. 5:1 to 'a book written within and on the back', as though the woes were too numerous to be contained on the *recto* alone. (Cf A. Deissmann, *Light from the Ancient*

g *East*, E.tr. 1927 ed 35). The customary size of a sheet of papyrus was 9—11 inches by 5—3½. Thus a short letter (e.g. 2 Jn) could be written on a single sheet, or, where more space was needed, two or more sheets could be fastened together to make a roll. The following lengths in feet have been calculated for NT documents: Rom 11½; Mk 19; Jn 23½; Mt 30; Lk and Ac 31—2. By way of comparison a book of Thucydides would occupy a roll of 30—35; a book of Plato's *Republic* a little more than half of this. Whereas at one time it was commonly supposed that the NT documents would have been written originally on papyrus-sheets fastened together to make a roll, it is now becoming increasingly evident that the use of sheets will have dated back to the 2nd cent., and, very probably, to the first. In Egypt, more especially, the papyrus form of codex dates back early for Christian literature, whereas the roll continued to be used more usually in the case of pagan writings. Dr. C. H. Roberts in his monograph *The Codex* (*Proceedings of the British Academy*, xl, 1954, 169—204) has drawn attention to the conclusion that 'when the Christian Bible (to use a slightly anachronistic term) first makes its appearance in history, the books of which it is composed are always written on papyrus and always in codex form . . . and the contrast is even more remarkable when we recall that the country where early texts were found was where the roll originated,

and in which parchment (with which the codex began) was **601** scarce'.

So much for the use of papyrus for Christian literature **h** in the first centuries. By the end of the period of the persecutions vellum or parchment began to be used for the better type of book, but it is not to be supposed that its use originated in the copying of Biblical manuscripts. It had been known for many centuries in the form of skins, and its improved form may be traced back to the reign of Euemenes II of Pergamum (197—158, B.C.). From its place of origin came its Gr. name of *pergamene*, whereas the word for vellum (*vitulina*) was formerly reserved for parchment made from the skins of very young calves (*vitelli*). It had one great advantage over papyrus, in that it could be manufactured in any place and not merely in a restricted area, and it far surpassed papyrus in flexibility and lasting quality. On the other hand, it was much dearer than papyrus, though even the latter was beyond the means of the poorer folk, who were obliged to use old documents, on which the earlier writing had been either washed out or erased.

The ink (*to melan*, 'the black stuff' cf 3 Jn 13) was **i** made of soot mixed with gum and diluted with water. It lasted well, but as it did not penetrate the papyrus-fibres it could be washed out readily, a fact that illustrates the terms used in Col 2:14, wherein Christ is described as 'wiping out the hand writing of (the) decree that was against us' (*Rheims Version of 1582*).

The custom of using a scribe to take down letters at dictation was widespread. For some evidence of Paul's habits cf 2 Thes 3:17; 1 Cor 16:21; Col 4:18. Gal 6:11 may indicate that he wrote this epistle with his own hand.

Meaning and Necessity of Textual Criticism—The **602** faultiness of the copies made from the original autographs has already been emphasized. A special discipline has developed over the centuries with a view to recovering the text of the original documents. Textual criticism, also called lower criticism, is that which deals with the establishment of the best available text of a work that has (at least in many instances) been handed down in manuscript form and copied by many hands. (Higher criticism, cf § 91*b*, studies the literary content of the text as established by textual criticism.) It has as its secondary purpose to account for the variant readings that are to be detected on comparing one copy with another, and, so far as may be, to trace these readings to their respective archetypes. In the absence of the original documents the work of the textual critic is principally concentrated on the large number of Gr. and Lat. codices of various dates that form our most important source for the re-discovery of the original writings.

The principal division of the codices, according **b** to the manner of their writing, is into **uncials** (literally 'inch-long' letters) or majuscules, in which the script employed is made up of separated capital letters, often very elegantly inscribed, and into minuscules, also styled **cursives**, which are written in a running hand, with ligaturing of the letters. It would be a mistake to regard MSS written in uncials as being invariably older than those in cursive script. In fact, cursive writing was already in existence at an early date, but was mainly used for private letters, and not for literary composition. In the 9th cent., Theodore the Studite (759—826, cf Dtc 15, 287—98) or some other worker in the Studium monastery at Constantinople, invented an especially beautiful cursive hand that became dominant in the Byzantine empire. Unfortunately it was all so much alike that it is often difficult to tell one MS from another on the score of writing only. It is not to be inferred that an uncial is necessarily more

602b important than a cursive, since it has been frequently established that many uncials are witnesses to a late text, whereas many cursives have derived from very early ones. Among NT cursives of special importance may be mentioned 33 (9th–10th cent., considered by Eichhorn and Hort as the best in this script) and those of the family 1 (associated with the name of Kirsopp Lake) and family 13 or the Ferrar group (named after W. H. Ferrar of Trinity College, Dublin, who in 1868 discovered that the minuscule MS 13 forms a single group with 69, 124 and 340). 'In short', wrote Professor Lake (1872–1946), 'it is neither the date nor the script of a MS which determines its value for the critic, but the textual history of its ancestors' (op cit, 12).

c   It should be added that the minuscules vastly outnumber the uncials. Gregory's list published in 1908 and cited here simply for the sake of comparison with later lists of figures, claimed that, at that time, there were some 4,000 NT codices comprising 161 uncials, more than 2,000 minuscules, 1,556 lectionaries (i.e. service books containing a large amount of Scripture, though not continuously in the order found in NT documents), and 14 papyri. These figures have been greatly increased in the course of the intervening half-century since 1908, and this as a result of more recent discoveries and assignments, so that, for example, the latest list includes 2,533 minuscules and 1,838 lectionaries, cf Kenyon, *Our Bible . . . 1958*, 164; also for an earlier estimate, F. M. Braun, O.P., *La Sainte Bible*, 10 (1946), 485–7.

d The Division of the NT Text—Ancient divisions into *stichoi* or 'sense-lines' and per cola et commata (that is, respectively, by clauses in a sentence and minor divisions) may be ignored. Only two methods of division are important for our purpose, i.e. those into chh and vv. The ch division is attributable to Stephen Langton (d. 1228), at that time a doctor in the University of Paris, and later Cardinal-Archbishop of Canterbury, 'perhaps the greatest of our medieval archbishops'. His division was first made for the Vg, but it later passed into use in the Heb. and Gr. texts. The Complutensian (or Alcala) polyglot Bible (published in 1522) has ch-divisions. The v divisions were first attempted by Santes Pagnini, O.P. (d. 1541), in a new rendering of the Bible, published at Lyons in 1527. Later the Parisian printer, Robert Estienne, (Stephanus), published in 1557 at Geneva a Gr. NT in which the v divisions were the work of Stephanus himself. In 1555 he published a complete Latin Bible, in which he used Pagnini's v-divisions for OT protocanonical books, while employing a modified form of this for the NT and the OT *deuterocanonica*. Previously his third (folio) edition of the NT in 1550 was the first Gr. Testament to contain a critical apparatus, based upon fifteen relatively late MSS. It is generally admitted that the present ch-and-v divisions are critically valueless, frequently spoil the sense, and would, in many instances, be better away. They are, however, indispensable for reference purposes.

e The MS Codices of the NT—In the absence of the original autographs and of their first copies we are thrown back upon MS codices of a later date that give a more or less faithful copy of the text. Some of these are of early date (the most ancient, more or less complete, ones being of the 4th cent.), whereas, as is well-known, the MS codices of the Latin and Gr. classics are of much later date. But there are not a few portions of MSS that are older than the 4th cent., the oldest so far discovered being the Ryland papyrus 457 (Jn 18:31–33, 37, 38) which on palaeographical grounds may be dated to the first half of the 2nd cent., not more than fifty years

after the gospel's composition. There are also 14 chh of **602e** St John's Gospel written on an Egyptian papyrus dating from about the year 200. (Cf V. Martin, *Papyrus Bodmer II*, 1956.) From the 3rd cent. come many more MSS, the most famous of these being the Chester Beatty codices, which included portions of various books of the Gr. Bible, dating from 2nd to 4th cent. Perhaps the most remarkable group among these was a collection of 86 pages taken from the Pauline epistles, the original corpus having been one of 104 pages. (Cf G. Zuntz, *The Text of the* **f** *Epistles*, 1953.) In the 4th cent. there are a number of papyri, and also the great codices, notably the Vaticanus (B) and the Sinaiticus (Aleph) written upon vellum. On account of their great value to textual critics something must be said in detail of these two MSS. **Codex Vaticanus** is in the Vatican Library in Rome, dates from the early fourth century, and contains both the Old and the New Testament books, but in the latter all is lacking after Heb 9:14, and the missing books include the Pastoral Epistles and the Apocalypse. In its present form it is made up of 734 leaves, whereas the original codex in its complete form had about 820 leaves. Its place of origin is disputed. Hort considered it might have been copied in Rome, whereas other scholars were in favour of S Italy or Caesarea. Various arguments, notably the association of its text with the Coptic versions and with Origen leads Kenyon to think rather of Egypt and Alexandria (Cf *Text of the Greek Bible*, 86.) **Codex Sinai-** **g** **ticus**, *Aleph*, was, as is well known, discovered by the German scholar Constantin Tischendorf in the monastery of St Catherine on Mount Sinai between the years 1844, when he saw some leaves of the OT, and 1859, when he succeeded in inspecting the NT, in addition to many more leaves of the OT. The greater part of the find went to the Imperial Library at St Petersburg, and from Russia it was bought in 1933 and is now housed, for the most part, in the British Museum. In its present state it is made up of 393 leaves, of which 43 are at Leipzig, 3 fragments at Leningrad, and 347 in the British Museum. As in the case of the Vaticanus there are many opinions on its place of origin, but 'the preponderance of opinion is in favour of Egypt' (Kenyon, *Text*, 81). Out of the many NT codices known, few contain the whole of NT. Most of them contain only a part, e.g. the Gospels or the Acts, or the Catholic epistles, or the Pauline corpus or the Apocalypse. Many are no more than lectionaries that contain such portions of the Gospels and apostolic writings as were customarily read in the Church's liturgy.

Codices are divided according to their contents into **h** pure and mixed. Pure codices give only the original Gr., whereas mixed codices, in addition to the original text, provide commentaries or *Scholia* or versions (these last including bilingual codices such as Gr. and Lat., or Gr. and Syr.). There are also codices known as *palimpsests* (from the Gr. *palin* = 'again' and *psao* = 'to scrape'), or rescripts, i.e. documents in which the original MS has been scraped out and new writing superimposed. Perhaps the best known example of a palimpsest is the famous Codex C (**Codex Ephraemi rescriptus**), a 5th cent. MS, originally of the whole Bible, which in the 12th cent. was used again as writing material for some works of S. Ephraem the great Syrian doctor (d. A.D. 373). Fortunately it has been found possible to recover the older (that is, usually the more valuable) text by means of chemicals or ultra-violet ray photography.

Some of the codices have names pointing to their past or present place of storage (e.g. Vaticanus, Alexandrinus, Sinaiticus, Claromontanus) or their former owners (e.g.

602h Coislinianus from Coislin, a former Bishop of Metz) or Laudianus (after Archbishop Laud of Canterbury).

i **Systems of Reference to the Codices**—The manner of referring to the various codices has varied, and there are, at the present time, several systems of reference. Since the time of Dr John Mill (d. 1707) and, in particular, since Wettstein's great edition of 1752ff, it has become customary to use letters of the Latin alphabet to designate uncials and Arabic numerals for the cursives. The system was improved by Tischendorf and Scrivener, who added the Gr. letters Gamma to Omega and the Heb. letters from Aleph to Daleth. So A = Codex Alexandrinus, B = Codex Vaticanus, C = Codex Ephraemi rescriptus D = Codex Bezae or Cantabrigiensis (presented to the Cambridge University library in 1581 by Theodore Beza, the Reformation scholar), and *Aleph* = Codex Sinaiticus.

j Gregory, whose enumeration of MSS has already been cited, in his book *Die griechischen Handschriften des NT* (Leipzig, 1908) retains the old capitals (Aleph, A—Z, Gamma—Omega) for the 45 oldest uncials or uses numbers 01—045; for the remaining uncials available at that date (58 years ago) he uses the numbers 046—0161. Minuscules are designated by the numbers 1—2292 (note again that this latter figure has been considerably increased by the passage of more than half a century) with the addition of the letters e (= *evangelium*), a (= *apostolicum*) or p (= *paulinum*) to indicate the part or parts of NT contained in a particular codex. Lectionaries are shown by Arabic numerals preceded by 1. Papyri are noted by the letter P followed by Arabic numerals from 1—76. (Cf List in Metzger *Text of NT* 247—56.)

k More recently still, Freiherr Hermann von Soden (1852—1914) distinguished three classes of codices by the Gr. letters *delta* (= *diathêkê* = covenant) for the whole NT; *epsilon* (= *evangelion*) for the Gospels and *alpha* (= *apostolos*) for the remainder of NT. He also designed an ingenious but unduly complicated system for showing at a glance the absolute or relative dating of a codex. Thus numbers 1—99 stand for codices dating from the 4th to the 9th cent.; 50—99 stand for subsequent codices. In the later codices the first number indicates the century. Thus *delta* 1 = Codex B (Vaticanus) of the 4th cent.; *delta* 2 = Codex Sinaiticus, also of the 4th; *delta* 3 = Codex Ephraemi of the 5th cent.; *delta* 121 = a codex written in the 11th cent.

For ordinary use the oldest method is perhaps the most important, but either of the two later systems has something to recommend it. On the whole the balance of approval among textual critics inclines towards Gregory's relatively simple and easily memorized system.

l **The chief MS Codices**—For a list of these codices reference may be permitted to the late Sir Frederic Kenyon's work, *The Text of the Greek Bible*, which has in ch 3 a sufficiently full account of the MSS of the NT. For a short list of Gospel MSS, cf F. M. Braun, op cit, 486, in which the MSS are divided into four groups, after the manner of Père M. J. Lagrange's 'Projet de critique textuelle rationelle du NT", RB 41 (1933), 481—98. These are (1) The B group, a moderate and generally faithful revision of the now unavailable originals) = les bons (i.e. codices B, Aleph, C, T, Z, L, and Daleth (for Mk). (2) The A group (a thoroughgoing revision in the interests of stylistic excellence (the prototype of the famous *textus receptus* of the Renaissance humanists) = *les antiochiens* (i.e. A, E[e], Omega, Daleth (non-Marcan), H[e], V, G[e]). (3) The D group (a thorough revision with an eye to harmonization and simplified readings) = *divers* i.e. D[e] and W (Mk 1—5:30). (4) The C group (occupying a position intermediate between B and D) = *césarien*

(i.e. W, N, Theta, Pi, K[e]). These groups will be more **602l** fully explained in the following section on the families of Gr. codices.

The highly important Codex *Aleph*, or Sinaiticus, **m** acquired by the British Museum from the Soviet authorities in 1933, is well described in the pamphlet *The Mount Sinai Manuscript of the Bible*. The most sensational discovery of recent times is that of the **Chester Beatty papyri**, to which attention has already been drawn, first publicly announced in *The Times* (19 Nov. 1931) and fully discussed in Kenyon's *Recent Developments in the Textual Criticism of the Greek Bible* (1933). The discovery is valuable in three ways. It carries the Gr. Bible text back for some decades and provides a substantial portion of 3rd-cent. NT MSS; it shows a text free from all trace of Byzantine revision, and not manifesting the prominent W variants; and it confirms the early use of the codex form of book by the Christian community.

The Families of Greek Codices—It is common knowledge that there is a considerable variety of readings between the numerous NT codices, but it was not until the time of **Albert Bengel** (1687—1752) that the problem was simplified by dividing the MSS into families. The term is clearly explained by Kenyon in his *Text of the Greek Bible* 11: 'If in a given Manuscript of any work some words are wrongly transcribed or a passage omitted, every manuscript copied from it, or from copies of it, will have the same mistake or the same omission; and if among the extant manuscripts we find that several have the same important mistake or omission, it is legitimate to argue that they are all descended from the manuscript in which that mistake or omission was first made.' That is, we may assign the various MSS to different families or groups with characteristic types of readings, much as Shakespearean scholars distinguish in the text of Hamlet in the pirated First Quarto of 1603 from that of the Second Quarto of 1604, and both of these from the readings of the First Folio of 1623. Bengel divided the MSS known to him into Asiatic and African, an arrangement that roughly corresponds to Westcott and Hort's later division into Syrian and Alexandrian. **J. J.** **b** **Griesbach** (1745—1812) is specially remembered for having produced an edition of the Gr. NT in two volumes in which, for the first time, the *textus receptus* of the earlier editors was abandoned in favour of a more critical text. It was he too who developed the 'family' hypothesis on lines that are still recognized as sound. He classified **three groups of** MSS i.e. (1) **The Alexandrian** or Origenian, so called because the type appears principally in Origen's quotations, in codices A, B, C and L, and in **the Egyptian (Bohairic and Sahidic) versions.** (2) **The Western**, so styled because its characteristic readings are found in the Latin Fathers and in Codex D (Bezae). (3) **The Constantinopolitan**, which is the text found in the great majority of Gr. MSS. He judged the last to be less valuable than the other two, but his principle was that, in default of any exclusion on grounds of internal criticism, a majority verdict of two to one among the groups was to be accepted. **K. Lachmann** (1793—1851) made further progress by excluding a great mass of the extant MSS as containing a text that was palpably late. His aim was to arrive at an edition of the text not in the form in which it was first produced by the sacred writers, but in the form in which it had circulation in the 4th cent. So, for practical purposes, he divided the MSS texts between two great families, the E (A, B, C, etc and Origen) and The W (D, D[2], D[3], the Old Latin, the Vulgate, etc.). The editions of Tischendorf and Tregelles depend mainly upon the principles accepted

3b by Lachmann. At the same time, one must needs detect a vice of method in Lachmann's textual study, since he was too ready to count, rather than to weigh, his authorities, and was overimpressed by the virtue of a majority verdict.

c The Cambridge scholars **Brooke Foss Westcott** 1825—1902) and **Fenton John Anthony Hort** (1829—91) were responsible for the most important edition of modern times. It was first projected in 1853 but was not finally published until 1881. It was accompanied by a long introduction by Hort on the critical principles that had guided the selection of MSS. Neither scholar was, however, a specialist in palaeography or comparative philology. They did, in the event, succeed in arranging and explaining the textual significance or the quantities of codices amassed by Tischendorf. Their text is excellent, but there is no adequate critical apparatus. The notes on selected readings are a poor substitute for a full justification of the readings they adopted.

d By applying a number of tests, such as the evidence for conflation (i.e. the fusing together of two variant readings into a single unit) in the Patristic use of the NT, and of internal criticism, they were able to distinguish four types of text. These were, first, the **Syrian** (not to be confused with Syriac), which is that of the vast majority of MSS, and which, in their view, was an eclectic text (i.e. one borrowed freely from various sources), following now one earlier text, now another, and frequently combining two texts into one. A familiar example of this is Lk 24:53, where one set of early authorities (*Aleph*, B, C, L, with the Coptic versions and the Sinaitic and Palestinian Syrian) read 'blessing God', Codex D and the Old Latin versions have 'praising God', and the majority of MSS (i.e. the Syrian group, including Codex A, twelve other uncials, all the cursives, the Vg, and some other versions) have 'praising and blessing God'. Westcott and Hort further distinguish three pre-Syrian types of text i.e. **the Alexandrian, the Western, and the Neutral.** Of these the first is the least important, since it depends almost certainly upon the Neutral tradition, and the changes made in it are very slight. The other two, however, are very early and go back as far as we have knowledge of distinctive texts. On Westcott and Hort's showing there was a time, earlier than the 4th and probably earlier than the middle of the 3rd cent., when the NT was transmitted in two great traditions—the Western and the Neutral. Then a group of copyists or editors probably in Syria and possibly in Syrian Antioch, produced an eclectic text that sometimes followed the W, sometimes the Neutral, and sometimes, as in the example given from Lk 24:53 and others of the same kind, combined the two texts by conflation.

e Of the two earlier and supremely important texts they regard the W as a very early and very corrupt source, a product of free interpolation and paraphrase, at a time when the need for scrupulous preservation of the original text was, as yet, imperfectly appreciated. Hort in his judicious summing-up of the merits and defects of the W text remarks upon the far attempts that have been made to 'set up an exclusively or even predominently W Gr. text as the purest reproduction of what the apostles wrote'. (Intr. 120) True, the 'eccentric Whiston' took pains to translate 'the Gospels and Acts from the Codex Bezae' and 'the Pauline Epistles from the Codex Claromontanus', but was almost alone in his preference. (*Introduction*). But he argues that a confrontation of the W text with the Neutral would induce most scholars to pronounce the W not merely to be the less pure text, but also to owe its differences in a great measure to a perilous confusion between transcription and reproduction, and even bet-

ween the preservation of a record and its supposed **603e** improvements and the distrust thus generated is only increased by further acquaintance (op cit, 121).

For Westcott and Hort the Neutral text (as found in **f** the great uncials *Aleph* and B, and in some other MSS) is the most reliable text. One exception, however, they make, for they lay stress upon the W text's omissions or *non*-interpolation, on the ground that a text that is so prone to interpolate and expand would not be likely to omit except for some critically excellent reason. In the interval since 1881 the methods and results of these two great scholars have been so often attacked that it is important to realize that in certain vital respects, their work remains unshaken, though seventy years have elapsed since the definitive edition of their text and introduction appeared in 1896.

In the first place, it is not open to doubt that **the g vast majority of extant** MSS **represent a later text.** Kenyon (*Text of the Greek Bible*, 203) prefers to style it the **Byzantine recension** (or revision), because this title 'makes no assertion as to its origin, but merely records the unquestioned fact that it is the text which dominated the whole Church of the Byzantine Empire'. Secondly, it is all but certain that the **Neutral** tradition represents an exceedingly **pure and early stage** of the text, and that it has in its favour the oldest vellum MSS of any size, i.e. Codices *Aleph* and B. Later criticism, however, tends to regard Westcott and Hort's contention regarding the quasi-innate superiority of the Neutral family not as one that is unfounded, but as one that, up to the present time at least, is insufficiently proved.

The Neutral text is, indeed, one that comes, as regards **h** its main representatives, from only one corner of the Christian world, and that is thoroughly attested by one version only i.e. the Bohairic or N Egyptian Coptic version, since the earlier Egyptian version (i.e. the Sahidic) does not give it such definite support. The three chief Fathers who bear witness to it (Clement, Origen, and St Cyril of Alexandria) are all Alexandrians, and of these Clement has been shown, since the time of Westcott and Hort, to have an unexpectedly large W element in his text. So far as can be ascertained all the MSS giving this type of text were written or copied at Alexandria. In spite of Hort's surmise that 'B and Aleph were both written in the W, probably at Rome' (op cit 267), it can hardly be doubted that B was written at Alexandria, and that, though Aleph was probably written at Caesarea, it is based upon the Alexandrian text brought to Caesarea by Origen when he left Alexandria in A.D. 231.

There is, in fact, ample evidence to support the view **i** that the Neutral family may represent the revised, as compared with the unrevised text. True, as Kenyon writes (*Recent Developments*, 85) 'If it is the result of editorial handling, the editor was one who was seeking an original text. It is not harmonistic, it does not cultivate smoothness of phrase, it does not seek additions. It may be described as an austere text.' In any event, it is a local, not a universal text, and is to be controlled with the help of other texts. Of these the most notable is the **large Western group** principally found in the Gr. uncials D (Gospels and Acts), E² (Acts) and Dᵖ (Pauline epistles) together with a number of old Latin MSS, and, as regards a considerable proportion of their readings, by the old Syr. versions (i.e. the Sinaitic and Curetonian). Of these the old Latin and the Old Syriac are by no means in complete agreement. Many of the readings of the oldest Syr. versions are aligned with B rather than with the Old Latin group. Yet the evidence of the versions supporting

603i it does at least go to show that the W text, in one form or another, has a greater claim to be heard than Hort ever suspected, and this not only in its omissions, but in its additions. At times, in fact, it seems to give a purer and less revised reading than the so-called Neutral texts. The value of von Soden's text has been candidly assessed by Metzger (*Text of NT*, 142–3). Despite the final judgement that the edition 'remains a monument of broad research and immense industry [which] must be taken into account by every serious textual critic,' the work suffers (a) From the effect of accepting a two to one majority in the three main texts as fairly decisive, whereas one of them (the Koine type) is largely secondary and derivative; (b) From the inclusion in his I-text of 'such heterogeneous elements as the W witnesses, the Caesarean text, the Old Latin, and the Old Syriac, as well as witnesses which are mixed with the Koine text'. (c) From an overemphasis of the contaminating influence on the texts of Marcion and Tatian, and (d) from the very high proportion of errors found in his text as printed, when tests have been applied to it. Another leading authority Professor E. C. Colwell in his essay 'Religion in Life' (in *The New English Bible Reviewed* (1965) 37) refers to von Soden's edition as 'a text now universally repudiated by scholars' which appears to be a distinct overstatement.

j In recent years as a result of work by Kirsopp Lake, Robert Blake, B. H. Streeter and others, a new group has been identified—**the Caesarean family**, made up of the so called Koridethi MS (Theta), the Washington MS (W), two groups of minuscules known as families 1 and 13, certain other minuscules (e.g. 28, 566 and 700), and the Chester Beatty papyrus No. 45. Textually this group holds a position intermediate between the W and the Neutral families, though in its major variants it usually sides with B. It derives its importance from its association with Origen, Eusebius and the school of Caesarea. Since its influence was felt as far away as Armenia and Georgia there is evidence for its not being a merely local text. Yet it seems that B. H. Streeter's hope to establish it as an independent authority with right of place beside the Alexandrian and the W groups has not, so far, been realized. Even now, after a good many years of recognition as an important factor in textual criticism, it may be felt that more study is required before any definitive verdict can be registered.

604a It does not follow from all these data that **the NT text** is an uncertain one. **It is better attested than any other work of ancient literature**, and the difficulties arise rather from an excess than from a deficiency of evidence. Most of the variants are quite trivial in character and have no important bearing on doctrine. Hort's familiar dictum has been often quoted for the estimate that the amount of significant variation can hardly form more than a thousandth part of the entire text (op cit, 2.) This statement has been criticized quite recently by Professor E. W. Clark in PC (2), 1962, 670. He considers the estimate far too low, since a thousandth part of the NT text would amount to no more than twenty lines of Nestle's text. And he rightly maintains that a mere count does not help very much. There are, as examples he gives can show, passages in the NT where a very small change does have some influence upon the doctrine taught in the text. He instances Rm 8:28, where the Rheims version reads: 'To them that love God all things cooperate together unto good', but where the RSV reads, in the light of a better MS tradition: 'In everything God works for good with those who love him', in which 'God' is rightly established as the subject of the sentence. Other examples could be cited where the **60** mistakes made in earlier editions of the NT have been corrected by the advent of more recently discovered and better texts.

On the whole, the conclusion must be, in the present **b** state of our knowledge, that, whereas the W and Byzantine texts show abundant traces of free editorial revision, this is less evident in the MSS and versions that make up the Neutral and the Caesarean groups. Their revision was the work of scholarly editors who desired an authentic text rather than an easy one. These texts have neither the substantial additions of the W group nor the harmonizing and stylistic alterations of the Byzantine. We can regard them as the best available for the recovery of the authentic (or earliest obtainable) text of the NT, while relying, as opportunity offers, on such sporadic readings in other MSS as can be shown to be of early date.

The upshot of much of the discussion about these **c** groups may have tended to produce the impression that the Byzantine text, based as it is on later and generally inferior MSS, may be safely disregarded as unimportant. This is far from being the true state of affairs, and Professor K. W. Clark has pointed out (in 'The Effect of recent textual criticism upon New Testament studies' (*Background of NT*, 43.)) this text 'has recently attained importance in its own right'. It is not that there has been any reversal on Westcott and Hort's verdict about the Byzantine text's secondary character. It is now realized that these MSS 'may bear additional witness to the early text and also to later forms employed in the Church'. 'Next to knowing how the New Testament originally read, it is important to learn how later generations of believers made it read.' In another paper, Professor Clark has emphasized the fact that 'variants in the NT text are often laden with theological significance, and may well have theological motivation'. ('Textual Criticism and Doctrine' in *Studia Paulina*, Haarlem, 1953). Hence, at the present time, the study of the Byzantine text is by no means the least important work of textual criticism.

In the task of reconstructing the text, we rely not **d** only on texts and versions, but on **patristic quotations**. So Iren. quotes the NT about 1800 times (on which cf W. Sanday and C. H. Turner, *Novum Testamentum Sancti Irenaei*, Oxford, 1923), Clem. Alex. 2,400 times, Orig. some 18,000 times. The shorter quotations are sometimes an unreliable guide to the text, because the Fathers frequently quote from memory, and, as so often happens, do not quote accurately. It is related that Jeremy Taylor quoted Jn 3:2, a very easy text, nine times in all, yet only twice in the same form of words, and never accurately! The once famous Anglican Dean F. W. Farrar used to claim that he could reconstruct *Paradise Lost* by heart, if it should happen to perish, to which a colleague replied that he had often heard Farrar quote Milton's poem, but had never heard him quote it correctly! The longer quotations, however, when there is agreement among witnesses from an early date, are a valuable guide to the primitive text as it first came from the pens of its inspired writers.

Printed Editions of the Greek NT—The *editio* **e** *princeps* of the Greek NT (i.e. the first printed edition of the book) is Vol. V of the **Complutensian Polyglot** (Alcalá), finished in 1514, published in 1522, and later re-edited in the Antwerp Polyglot of 1571 and by Gratz at Tübingen in 1821.

Almost simultaneously (1516) **Erasmus** produced a **f** Gr. text with a Latin version and notes. His claim to have used the oldest and best codices is unsubstantiated, and the last six vv of the Apoc (wanting in his MS) were

04f supplied by translating the Vulgate Latin into Gr.! The famous 'Three Witnesses' text (1 Jn 5:7—8) was inserted in the third (1522) edition on the authority of a solitary Gr. MS, the Codex Montfortianus or Britannicus (61; 15th or 16th cent.) which is preserved at Trinity College, Dublin, and is there open for inspection. A little later, the Aldine edition (Feb., 1518/19) was published by Aldus Manutius at Venice, and the Paris edition (1534) by Simon Colibaeus.

g Robertus Stephanus, already mentioned, printed four editions. The third (1550) is the *editio regia*, dedicated to King Henri II, and in the fourth (1551) the division into vv first occurs. For the text he mostly used Erasmus, revised according to the Alcalá Bible. Theodore Beza (d. 1605) produced many editions of the NT (e.g. those of 1565, 1585, 1588, and 1598), based mainly on Stephanus, but with some use of MSS and Fathers.

In 1623 Bonaventure and Abraham Elzevir printed at Leyden a mixed text based on Stephanus and Beza. In the preface to the second (1633) edition occur the celebrated words: 'Textum ergo habes nunc ab omnibus receptum: in quo nihil immutatum aut corruptum damus'. This **textus receptus** as it was styled thereafter was, until comparatively recent times, much esteemed and frequently reprinted.

h The first really critical edition appears to have been that of **John Mill** (1645—1707) who in the year of his death issued the third (regia) edition of Stephanus with an apparatus containing some 30,000 variants, drawn from 78 MSS. The great **Richard Bentley** (1661—1742) never carried out his project for a new critical edition. The work was later undertaken with varying degrees of success by **Wettstein** who (as has been noted above), first established the system for referring to MSS by letters and numbers), **Bengel** and **Lachmann**. The last-named scholar set aside the evidence of the printed texts, in particular that of the *textus receptus*, and sought to recover the text in existence in the 4th cent. His first edition came out in 1831; his second, with notes on the readings added by the great philologist **Philip Buttman**, of *Lexilogus* fame, appeared in 1842 (Vol. I) and 1850 (Vol. II).

i Of later editors one may specially mention **Tischendorf**, whose eighth edition (1864—78) has yet to be surpassed by the new Oxford text of which the first volume (Mark) and the second volume (Matthew) appeared respectively in 1935 and 1939. It met with severe criticism, and it seems unlikely that such a work can be continued by a single editor (cf the late T. W. Manson JTS 1942 (vol. 43, 83—92). Since 1948 a plan has emerged for an international Gr. NT, which will be preceded by eight volumes of materials to be consulted. It is planned to make use of the textus receptus (whereas the Oxford text made use of Westcott and Hort) because that text contains most of the material, often in the form of conflated readings, and the critical notes will thus be much reduced in number (cf M. Black, NTS, IV (1958), 344f).

j T. W. Manson argues forcibly for the use, as a medium of collation, of the *textus receptus*, which fulfils the twofold criterion of being old enough to avoid any danger of becoming out-of-date, and of making fairly certain that such corrections as would appear in the apparatus would be genuinely significant.

Of recent non-Catholic editions one need only mention **604j** Nestle's 'resultant' based on the majority verdicts (in case of disputed readings) of the three editions of Tischendorf, Westcott and Hort, and Bernhard Weiss. Professor Clark in his essay already cited on 'The effect of recent textual criticism on New Testament studies' has made a careful examination of Nestle's text of Mk's Gospel and has established that this text stands closer to Westcott and Hort than other critical texts of the present day. In the whole Marcan Gospel, one-twelfth of the NT, there are only 89 changes from Westcott and Hort, and, of these, not more than 34 are significant, and hardly any affect the meaning. As often with 'resultant' and eclectic editions the best that can be said is that they may prepare the way for something better and more adventurous.

Nestle was first issued in 1890, and the 25th edition, **k** by Erwin Nestle and Kurt Aland, came out in 1963. For this edition Aland had planned a completely new work, to be set up in new type with new text-divisions, and many changes in the apparatus, based on a study, by a team of trained assistants, of all the variants available in facsimile, microfilm or photostat. (Fr K. Aland in NTS 6 (1960), pp. 179—84). A fore-taste of this, for the Gospels, is now available in Aland's *Synopsis quattuor Evangeliorum*, 2nd (unaltered) ed., 1965. The changes made in the 25th ed. are to be found (in German only) at p. 31*. In 1966, Aland and others issued a Gr. NT for the use of translators published by the United Bible Societies.

Early printed editions of the Gr. NT prepared by **l** Catholics were those of the Complutensian Polyglot (1514, pub. 1522, cf supra), Erasmus (1516, dedicated to Pope Leo X), Aldus (Venice, 1518) and the Antwerp Polyglot (1571). Thereafter, apart from text-critical studies on the Gr. NT such as those of R. Simon (1689, 1690), K. Alter (in his NT Graecum, 2 vols, Vienna, 1786—7), and J. L. Hug (1808), Catholics took little part in preparing critical editions until J. M. A. Scholz published his *NT graece* (Vol. I, 1830; Vol. II, 1836). He examined and collated nearly 1,000 MSS. Authorities differ about his care and competence as a collator. Gregory says that his collations are very good (*Canon and Text of NT*, 1907, 452).

Among recent scholars who have prepared editions of **m** the Gr. NT, mention should be made of the editors of the three latest and best Catholic editions, which are those of the celebrated Bonn professor, H. J. Vogels, published in Düsseldorf (1920ff), that of the late P. Augustin Merk, S.J., first issued in Rome in 1933, as *Novum Testamentum graece et latine* (and frequently revised and reprinted) and the work of a Spanish scholar, Padre J. M. Bover, S.J., *Novi Testamenti Biblia Graeca et Latina* (printed in a very beautiful Gr. type, 1943, revised ed. in 1950 and 1952, 4th ed. 1959). Of these Vogels is far closer than the others to the rather antiquated edition of A. Souter (1910, rev. ed. 1947) and to the *textus receptus*. By way of contrast (to quote Professor K. W. Clark's phrase, art cit, 33): 'Westcott-Hort, Nestle, Bover and Merk form a tight critical group with comparatively little difference among them'. None of these editions is completely satisfying.

THE JEWISH WORLD IN NEW TESTAMENT TIMES

BY J. L. McKENZIE S.J.

605a Bibliography—*General*: J. Bonsirven, *Le Judaisme palestinien au Temps de J.-C*, 1934[2]; Werner-Förster, *Palestinian Judaism in NT Times*, 1964; F. C. Grant, *Ancient Judaism and the NT*, 1960; M.-J. Lagrange, *Le Judaisme avant J.-C*; 1931[3]; G. F. Moore, *Judaism in the first centuries of the Christian Era*, 1927–30; D. S. Russell, *Between the Testaments*, 1960; E. Schürer, 'Diaspora', HDB, extra vol. 91–109; J. Vandervorst, 'Diaspora'. DBS 2 432–45. *Qumran*: M. Burrows, *The Dead Sea Scrolls*, 1955; id *More Light on the Dead Sea Scrolls*, 1958; M. Black, *The Scrolls and Christian Origins*, 1961; T. H. Gaster, *The Dead Sea Scriptures*, 1956; F. M. Cross, *The Ancient Library of Qumran and Modern Biblical Studies*, 1958; P. Benoit 'Qumran et le NT', NTS 7 (1961), 276–96; H. H. Rowley, *The Dead Sea Scrolls and the NT*, 1961; G. Vermes, *The Dead Sea Scrolls in English*, 1962; J. T. Milik, *Ten Years of Discovery in the Wilderness of Judaea*, E. tr. 1959. D. S. Russell, *The Jews from Alexander to Herod*, Oxford, 1967.

b Introduction—At the beginning of the Christian era Jerusalem and Judaea were the centre of the Jewish world. Outside of Palestine, Jewish settlements were found in most of the large cities of the eastern Roman Empire, and in Babylonia. The largest and most influential communities were in Babylonia and Egypt. While the Jews living abroad were somewhat assimilated to the Gentile population of the cities in which they dwelt, the powerful influence of Palestinian Jewry imposed on Jews everywhere a unity of religious belief and practice which gave Judaism a distinctive character, and prevented its absorption by Greco-Roman culture.

c Sources—The principal contemporary sources for the history of Judaism are:

A. Flavius Josephus (b. A.D. 38), the Jewish historian; fought in the rebellion of A.D. 66–70; was taken and pardoned by the Romans, and became a client of the Flavian house. In the *Jewish Antiquities* and the *Jewish War* Josephus has preserved much information about pre-Christian Judaism not found elsewhere; but he is uncritical in his use of sources.

B. Rabbinical Writings: (a) The *Mishnah*, a collection of the oral traditions of the Rabbis by which the Law was interpreted, amplified, and applied to particular situations. These traditions are *Halakhic* (legal) or *Haggadic* (doctrinal). Since the collection was not made until the close of the second cent. A.D., it must be employed with caution to determine Jewish ideas of the NT period. (b) *Midrashim*, or interpretations of the Scriptures.

C. Apocalyptic Literature. A great number of works appeared during the period 200 B.C.–A.D. 100 which, under the pseudonym of ancient figures (such as Henoch or Esdras), pretended to be predictions of the downfall of the great heathen powers and the establishment of the Jewish kingdom of God. It is uncertain how far these works represent the prevailing sentiments of Judaism of the time.

D. The Qumran texts, produced by an apocalyptic **60** sect during the 1st cent. B.C. and 1st cent. A.D.

E. The New Testament, especially the Gospels.

F. Profane historians. Tacitus (*Historiae* V) gives a brief sketch of Judaism. Other Roman historians (Suetonius), and satirists (Horace, Juvenal) allude to Jewish beliefs and practices. These works, which exhibit a profound anti-Jewish prejudice, are biased and inaccurate; but they indicate a common attitude towards Judaism among the Gentiles.

I PALESTINIAN JUDAISM

Up to the fall of the monarchy in 586 B.C., the Hebrew **d** religion and the Hebrew nation had been identified. The restoration of the Jewish commonwealth under the Persians in 538 B.C. did not restore the original conditions. In NT times many more Jews lived dispersed in Gentile lands than in Palestine itself. The language of Palestinian Jews was no longer Heb., but Aram. (another Semitic language closely akin to Heb.) which was spoken throughout most of the Near E. Palestine was now, instead of an independent state, a province of a world empire, with a much smaller area than that ruled by the Heb. monarchies. The territory in which Jews formed a majority of the population was limited to Judaea, Galilee and Peraea. This territory was an island in a sea of Gentile populations which surrounded it on N, E and S. Most of the Palestinian Jewish population belonged to the humbler peasant and tradesmen's classes. The loss of political independence meant that Judaism became a religion; the kingdom of God, the theocracy, existed only as an ideal to be realized in some distant future. But the consciousness of the identity of religion and nation survived in Judaism to express itself in two different directions: the political nationalism of the Hasmonaean period (165–163 B.C.) and of the Zealots who rebelled against Rome in A.D. 66, and the religious nationalism of the Pharisees.

It was in these four centuries, and in Palestine, that **e** Judaism developed those distinctive traits which made it unique in the ancient world. Several factors contributed to this: the successful effort of the Jews in Babylon to resist assimilation; the feud with the Samaritans, in which the Jewish community closed itself against any foreign admixture; the promulgation of the Law by Ezra, by which Jewish life was based upon the strict observance of the Law; and the Maccabean wars, in which the threat of Hellenization was successfully resisted by violence, and a short-lived Jewish state was established.

The effort of the Jews to retain their distinct identity and to preserve themselves against foreign influence resulted in a characteristic exclusivism. Palestinian Judaism refused any contact with Gentiles beyond that of bare necessity—a theory which was never abandoned, although it was impossible to reduce it to practice. The Jew was required by law to do business with his own, to marry his own, to enjoy social relations with his own. Any contact with a Gentile caused ritual impurity.

605e Gentiles defiled land, houses and food. The obligations of justice and charity were not as strict towards Gentiles as they were between Jews. Just those features of Jewish law and ritual which emphasized the separation of the Jew from the Gentile were most insisted upon. The Gentiles usually, and not always without reason, thought the Jews were haughty.

f Social and Economic Conditions in Palestine—The social and economic conditions of Palestine in NT times were generally similar to those which were found throughout the eastern Roman Empire, especially to those of the neighbouring regions of Syria and Egypt. It is the opinion of some writers that Palestine was one of the most prosperous countries of the empire; but it is difficult to be certain about this. Palestine was an agricultural country. Its principal crops were wheat and barley, of which there was normally an annual surplus for export. Besides the grains, Palestine produced fruit in abundance: olives, figs, grapes, dates. In NT times the forests of Palestine had not yet been destroyed; and, while it is a question how rich this resource of Palestine was, we can be certain that timber was abundant in comparison with modern times. The pasturing of sheep and goats, mentioned so frequently in the OT, was still carried on, but it no longer had the economic importance which it possessed under the Heb. monarchy. Palestinian Jews in NT times were not engaged in trade and commerce on a large scale. Outside of Jerusalem, there was no Jewish city of any importance; and Jerusalem itself was not a great market. Trade and commerce were centred in the cities of the coast and in the Decapolis, which were the ports of entry for foreign goods and the agents of export for Palestinian products. These cities were entirely or predominantly Greek. The cities on the shore of the Lake of Galilee were also important trading centres for the region; but here again there was a large Gr. population. In Jerusalem itself there were a few wealthy Jewish merchants and bankers; but they were a small minority. Their economic importance, of course, was out of all proportion to their numbers.

g Palestine at the time of Jesus had probably reached the peak of its population in ancient times. Exact figures are not available; two million (including Transjordan) would be a conservative estimate. The country had enjoyed peace since the Roman conquest by Pompey in 63 B.C., and had not yet suffered the horrors of the revolt of A.D. 66–70, which left the country ravaged and depopulated. In spite of the emigration of Jews to foreign countries, conditions were favourable to a rapid growth of population.

The population of Palestine was not racially homogeneous; indeed, it had never been. Of the three divisions of the country, Judaea, Samaria and Galilee, Judaea was the most Jewish both in population and in ideas and practice. Samaria was regarded by the Jews themselves as an alien enclave—a judgement which was hardly accurate; the mixed origins of the Samaritans were more Heb. than anything else, and the religion of the Samaritans was a schismatic Judaism. Galilee was so mixed as to be cosmopolitan. Its cities were mostly Gr, its rural areas mostly Jewish; but there was a free interchange between city and country. This was reflected in the language of the three regions; it is probable that Judaea spoke mostly Aram., while Gr. was probably as important in Galilee as Aram. Some scholars think Jesus and his Apostles, like most of the Galileans, were bilingual. Among themselves, however, Jews employed Aram.

h The prosperity of the three regions was proportionate to their Gentile population. Galilee, blessed with a more fertile soil and with better communications to the outside **605h** world, was the richest part of the country. The great trade route which connected Egypt with Damascus, Syria and Mesopotamia passed up the coast without touching Judaea and Samaria directly; it then turned north-east and went through the heart of Galilee. The route from Damascus to Arabia was easily reached from Galilee, while the route from Arabia to Gaza ignored Judaea altogether. Hence Judaea retained its Jewish insularity, and looked with some suspicion on the Galileans as half heathen.

There was a certain tension between Jerusalem and **i** the Judaean countryside, and still more between Judaea and Galilee. Jerusalem was the residence of the priestly aristocracy and the wealthy merchants and landlords, whose wealth was built upon the labourers and the peasants. It was also the centre of Jewish learning, where the most distinguished rabbis were found. Their legal decisions were binding on the poor workers, for whom the Pharisaic interpretation of the Law was often impossible. Jerusalem had the typical urban contempt of the countryman. In one feature Galilee excelled Jerusalem, and that was Jewish nationalism. It was in Galilee that the revolt broke out in A.D. 66. The ruling classes of Jerusalem, whose position depended on political and economic stability, were of necessity linked with the government, whether it was the government of Herod or of a Roman procurator. The Gospels contrast the enthusiasm of the Galileans for the Messianic kingdom with the coldness of the men of Jerusalem.

It is difficult to speak of social classes among Palest- **j** inian Jews; for even in NT times the Jews had begun to manifest that social solidarity which has been so characteristic of them throughout their subsequent history. Theoretically, the Jews were a democratic society; at the time of Jesus the Hasmonaean aristocracy was practically extinct, and the Herodian aristocracy was never accepted by the Jews. The Jewish aristocracy was composed of a few priestly families, who were also the wealthy families. This does not mean that all the priestly families were wealthy; they were not. Pride in Jewish blood was so great that any Jew who could vindicate his ancestry regarded himself as socially the equal of any other. Practically, of course, things did not work out this way. The Jewish aristocracy was an aristocracy of wealth rather than of blood. At the same time there was the aristocracy of the masters of the Law, which was not coterminous with the aristocracy of wealth. Jewish social classes were fluid and hard to define; but there were divisions and a certain social unrest beneath the superficial unity of Palestinian Judaism.

It was quite otherwise with the economic classes, which **k** had reached a fixed stratification in NT times. There were no middle classes between the wealthy and the poor; and both wealth and poverty were extreme. Wealth came from commerce and ownership of land; since these remained in the same families, fortunes grew through successive generations. Dives of the parable, Lk 11:19ff., was an extreme example, but the wealthy could recognize themselves in his portrait. Whether they were, as a class, as insensitive to the needs of the poor as Dives of the parable is open to question. Almsgiving was much recommended by the rabbis; but we can be certain that whatever almsgiving was practised did nothing to remove the horrible social blight of poverty.

The employments of the poor were agriculture, the crafts, and unskilled labour. The Lake of Galilee gave employment to a large number of fishermen, whose product was consumed throughout Palestine; this class is of

605k interest to the reader of the Gospels because the first disciples of Jesus were chosen from it. Jesus himself was a craftsman, and not on the lowest rung of the economic ladder; the craftsmen were better off than others. In a village like Nazareth Jesus may have been the only man to practise his trade; in Jerusalem he would have had his shop in one of the bazaars in which it was customary for merchants of the same wares and workers of the same craft to congregate. Some writers speak of whole villages devoted to a single craft.

l Beneath the craftsmen we find the peasant. The peasant tilled the soil of a wealthy landowner who probably resided in Jerusalem. The peasant himself resided in a village with other peasants, each of whom had his strip of land in the neighbourhood. The yield, of course, was not to be compared with that of modern agriculture. The peasant had to meet the rent, the taxes and the tithes. We do not know what the rent may have been; the taxes paid to Rome were 25 per cent of the yield. The tithes for the Temple came to 22 per cent of the remainder. The peasant was expected to pay a second tithe for the poor; it is thought that this was rarely paid. Nor is it likely that the full Temple tithe was always paid. If the rents corresponded to these obligations—as they probably did—it is not hard to calculate how much was left for the peasant.

Rents, taxes and tithes were paid in kind. Taxes were not collected by the Roman officials themselves. The estimated revenue was based on a census; we read of such a census in the year of the birth of Jesus. The taxes were then farmed out to speculators, the 'publicans' of the Gospel, and the contract was awarded to the highest bidder. The tax-farmer was then free to collect as much revenue as he could; his profit, of course, was what he collected above the price he paid for the contract. He could appeal to the Roman military to enforce his requisitions. Cf § 622a.

m Beneath the peasant was the unskilled labourer, the 'hireling' of the Gospel. Slavery in Palestine was comparatively rare; Jewish sentiment was opposed to the enslavement of one Jew by another, and the country was not wealthy enough to import large numbers of slaves from abroad. But the very existence of slavery depressed the unskilled labourers. They hired themselves out for whatever work was available, usually by the day. There was always a large number of unemployed; and competition depressed the income of the labourer still more. But it is not likely that the difference between this proletariat and the skilled worker was really great. The poverty of the mass of the population of Palestine probably did not differ much from that of the average population of the Empire, but it was appalling. On the other hand, we must not judge the attitude of these people towards their poverty by our modern ideas. They were born to it, and economic stratification prevented any higher ambitions. A drought, a war, an insect plague inevitably meant slavery or starvation; but the poor were accustomed to face such dangers as a normal part of life.

Furthermore, the dignity of manual labour was much praised by the rabbis. The fact that a man earned his living by manual labour was not a social stigma. Not only Jesus and Paul, but many of the great rabbis practised a trade; and they were accepted in the homes of the great because of their knowledge of the Law. The poor, if we may judge from some Gospel passages, had very free access to the homes of the rich.

n Below the unskilled labourers were the social outcasts. Like the Samaritans, a Jew of mixed origin, or a Jew who took on Greek ways, was an object of disdain. A tax-farmer like Matthew or Zachaeus was a moral leper. The sick, the crippled, the aged and the orphans who had no families to support them were at the mercy of an unfeeling world. Beggars were common. There were always men who were discontented with Roman rule, or who had fallen under the suspicion of the authorities, who fled to the desert and a life of banditry, preying impartially on Jew and Gentile alike. There was often a strong bond of sympathy between such bandits and the poor and the extreme nationalists. **605m**

Debt was an additional curse on the poor. Since their margin was so small, any emergency threw them into the hands of the moneylenders; and we have no reason to believe that the Scribes could not circumvent the law prohibiting interest between Jews. The interest rates were probably exorbitant, although we cannot give exact figures; we know that the honourable Brutus charged 50 per cent in Rome. While this did not always result in personal enslavement, it did mean economic enthralment for the peasant, who lived at subsistence level, or less, when he fell into debt. There is no historical evidence that the law of jubilee, with its universal remission of debt, was ever observed.

One effect of the general poverty was (surprisingly) that early marriages were the rule. A boy or girl of twelve years was regarded as grown enough to leave the home; the family wished to be rid of them as soon as possible. If the boy could not find a trade from his father or his relatives, he was cast into the great reservoir of the unemployed. Early marriage and childbirth were followed in the natural course by premature senescence, which meant that more helpless persons were thrown upon society.

The food of the poor was very simple. Only the few **o** wealthy could afford the luxury articles of diet imported from abroad. The staples of the poor were wheat or barley bread and dried fish. Meat was a rare treat. Vegetables—leeks, lentils, beans—and dried fruit were Palestinian products. Wine was produced in Palestine and was in common use, although the best wine was exported. The poor man would scarcely have more than one set of garments: the tunic, which was his ordinary dress, and a cloak for inclement weather and for sleeping. The houses of the poor were of stone, one or two storeys, usually shared by several families; the very poor might share a room among several families. The houses, even in the villages, were built very close together; only narrow alleys were left for passage and for the disposal of refuse. The site of the village was determined by the availability of water; it would be an unusually favoured site if there were more than one well. The water supply was supplemented by cisterns.

It is important to understand this background of the Gospels and the early expansion of Christianity. Christianity was the only movement of any kind in ancient times which arose in the masses. Jesus himself, like his first followers, belonged to the poor, and he spoke to them in the first place. They listened to him, because he was one of themselves. When Christianity spread into the great cities of the Roman Empire its appeal was to the poor; and it reached the upper classes from below.

The Temple and the Priesthood—The Temple of **606a** Jerusalem, as the one place where sacrifice could be legitimately offered, was the official centre of Jewish worship. It was the desire of every pious Jew, whether in Palestine or abroad, to visit the Temple at one of the great annual feasts; and we are told that many travelled long distances to gratify this desire. The second Temple, dedicated in 516 B.C., stood until the erection of the

06a Temple of Herod at the beginning of the Christian era. This great structure, planned on a truly magnificent scale, was completed shortly before it was razed to the ground by the Romans in A.D. 70 (cf comm. on Jn 2:20).

b The priesthood enjoyed a position of great importance, certainly greater than it had under the monarchy. The priesthood was a distinct hereditary order. Priests might marry women of non-priestly families; but they must be undefiled virgins or widows of pure Israelite extraction. The high-priest might marry only an undefiled Israelite virgin. Contact with death was prohibited, since this caused ritual uncleanness. The priests had to be free of any physical defect which marred their appearance or disqualified them to perform priestly functions. They were inducted into the sacerdotal office by a rite of consecration called 'filling of the hands', in which they received in their hands portions of the sacred flesh of the sacrificial victim. Since the number of priests was far in excess of that necessary for the Temple service, they were divided into twenty-four courses, each of which served in turn. Within the courses there were further divisions into specialized offices, which involved a difference in rank. The Levites, like the priests, were a hereditary order. They were entrusted with subordinate duties (singers, janitors, servants of the priests).

The priests and the Temple services were maintained by revenues from the people. To the priests belonged first-fruits and the first born of animals, and the money paid for the redemption of first-born sons; portions of sacrificial victims; tithes on all produce or profits; voluntary and votive offerings; and a half-shekel annual tax on every male Israelite over twenty years of age. The Jerusalem Temple, like many pagan temples, was used as a place of safe deposit for money and valuables. The Temple had its own police force, the jurisdiction of which was not limited to the Temple.

c The power of the high-priest was much increased during the post-exilic period. Under the imperial governments of Persia, Syria and Rome, the high-priest was the supreme native magistrate under the provincial authorities. The Maccabees were a priestly family; and in Simon (140 B.C.) the offices of high-priest and head of the independent Jewish state were united. This double dignity was retained by the succeeding members of the Hasmonaean dynasty (except Alexandra) until its fall before Pompey (63 B.C.). This overweening power of the high-priest met with an actively hostile reaction from the Pharisees, and it created a deep cleft between the sacerdotal aristocracy and the mass of the people. This cleft was widened by the Hellenistic inclinations of priestly families, both before and after the Maccabean wars. After the Roman conquest the high-priests were appointed by the Roman authorities. By political manoeuvering the members of a few priestly families kept the appointment for themselves. The influence of high-priests after their term of office (such as Annas) was very great.

d The worship of the Temple was conducted in a sumptuous manner, and the contributions of the people to its support were heavy. The chief daily services of the Temple were the burnt-offering on behalf of the people each morning and evening, and the offering of incense daily at the same time. The Levites accompanied these offerings with vocal and instrumental music. There was always a large attendance of the public at these daily services. On the Sabbath and the major festivals more numerous victims were offered. It is characteristic of post-exilic Judaism that the expiatory and propitiatory purpose of sacrifice was emphasized rather than the joyous and grateful sentiment of many pre-exilic offerings. The

attitude of the pious Jew towards the ritual of the Temple **606d** is expressed in Sir 50:1ff.

The Scriptures—It is impossible to determine exactly **e** when the first collection of sacred books was made. The Jews, under the leadership of Ezra, bound themselves to the observance of the Torah, or Law of Moses, Neh 8—10. The date of this event is uncertain (cf § 311*a*–*d*). It is clear from the prologue of Sir that a collection which included 'the Law, the Prophets and the Writings' was in existence in 130 B.C. We do not know by what authority it was determined which books should be included in the collection. The sacred books should have been in the custody of the priesthood, and it is to them that the first collection should in all probability be attributed. But we find that the Scribes subsequently asserted their authority to exclude books from the collection. The vagueness of this determination is seen in the existence of two collections of sacred books: those circulating in Palestine, represented by the OT in Heb., and those in use in Alexandria represented by the OT in Gr. which contained more books than the Palestinian collection. cf § 15*a*.

The influence of the sacred books on Judaism cannot **f** be overestimated. The Law was the entire basis of Jewish life and piety. Both the Law and the Prophets formed the material of the synagogue lessons. The use of the Psalms in the Temple liturgy and in the worship of the synagogue coloured the language and the attitude of Jewish prayer. The ordinary Jew was familiar with the text of the sacred books. Mohammed called Judaism 'the religion of the book'. To the Jew his books comprised all wisdom and learning, and a complete code of right conduct.

The Law—The five books of Moses, called the *Tôrah*, **g** were the most highly venerated of the sacred books. *Tôrah* actually means 'instruction' or 'doctrine' rather than 'law'; and from the narrative portions as well as from the legal portions were deduced conclusions about God, his Providence, and human conduct. 'Law', however, expresses accurately the attitude of Judaism towards these books. The basis of legal observance was faith in the covenant of God with Israel and in divine retribution. The minute regulations of the Law extended to almost every detail of life; and what the Law did not explicitly touch was covered by applications, sometimes quite far-fetched, of general precepts. As a matter of fact, the laws of the Mosaic code were never intended to be such a universal and detailed guide of conduct. The extension of legal obligation into every detail of private and public life could not but result in an externalizing of religion to some degree. By some Jews mere external observances were esteemed as grave as duties of piety, justice and charity. From the fact that the greater number of precepts is prohibitive it follows that there was a certain negative character about Jewish observance.

Special emphasis was placed on those observances **h** which were distinctive of Judaism: circumcision, the Sabbath, the legal cleanliness. Circumcision was not, in its origins, a peculiarly Jewish practice; but in pre-Christian centuries it had become such a mark of Judaism that Jews who wished to adopt the Gr. way of life and Gr. manners resorted to a painful surgical operation in order to rid themselves of the sign of their religion. The Sabbath observance was understood to mean a complete rest from all activity. Even food should be prepared on the preceding day. The distance which one might walk was restricted to 2,000 cubits (about 3,000 feet); by leaving a bundle of food, however, one was considered to establish a temporary domicile which enlarged the scope of travel. A whole block of houses, or a quarter of a city, might be considered as a single residence. There were 39 kinds of work

606h classified as violations of the Sabbath rest. The weight which one could lift without violating the Sabbath was determined. It is not surprising that the Roman authorities found it simpler to exempt the Jews from military service than to adjust military discipline to the Jewish Sabbath.

607a The obligation of legal cleanliness was, if observed strictly, an almost impossible burden. The obligation of cleanliness was originally intended for the priests actually officiating in the sanctuary. Its extension to all Jews of any state or occupation meant either constant ablutions or constant uncleanness, which rendered one unfit for religious exercises. There were various degrees of uncleanness according to the nature of the object touched, and six kinds of water were distinguished for purification from these various degrees. Contact with Gentiles, or with the dead, or with certain diseases, or with a person who had contracted uncleanness, or any sexual process were all defilements. Food had to be protected against uncleanness, in addition to the dietary regulations, which meant in practice that it could not be handled by Gentiles. Generally, the laws of cleanliness were simply not observed, especially where Jews and Gentiles dwelt together.

b From the Law was deduced the obligation of wearing *ṣîṣît*, fringes at the corners of the outer garment; *tᵉpillîn* (*phylacteries* in the NT), boxes containing small scrolls on which were written Ex 13:1–10, 11–16; Dt 6:4–9, 11:13–21, attached to the head and the arm by straps; and of placing at the door-post *mᵉzûzôt*, small boxes containing scrolls on which were written Dt 6:4–9, 11:13–21. The devout Jew was obliged to recite the *Shema*, Dt 6:4–9, 11:13–21; Nm 15:37–41, the Jewish profession of faith, each morning and evening. Fasting was characteristic of Jewish legal piety as a token of repentance and as an expression of petition in difficult times. Some annual fasts were of general obligation, but most fasting was done out of private devotion. The Law imposed the celebration of the three annual 'pilgrim-feasts' (at which pilgrimages were made to the Temple): Passover, in remembrance of the Exodus of the Hebrews from Egypt; Pentecost, in remembrance of the giving of the Law; and Tabernacles, in remembrance of the sojourn of the Hebrews in the desert. The original agricultural character of these feasts disappeared completely. Besides these there were the New Year, and what became the greatest Jewish feast, the Day of Atonement (*Yôm Kippûr*), when expiation was made for the sins of the whole people.

c The Law, however, was more than a series of minute regulations of external conduct. It was possible for Hillel to sum it up in the rule, 'Do not to another what you would not have him do to you', and for the Saviour to point out as its greatest and first commandment, 'Thou shalt love the Lord thy God with thy whole heart', and as the second, 'Thou shalt love thy neighbour as thyself'. But the vast number of precepts—they were reckoned at 613—certainly helped to create a characteristic feature of Judaism, a deep sense of sin and guilt. This sense of sin undoubtedly can be traced back to the Exile itself, and to the teaching of Jeremiah and Ezekiel, who insisted on the truth that the national disaster was due to the sins of the people. The prayers of Judaism are filled with confessions of sin and cries of repentance. Contrary to pre-exilic practice, sacrifice was viewed chiefly as an atonement for sin. The Law furnished a definite measuring-rod of righteousness. Hence, if the prescriptions of the Law were observed, it was possible for the Jew to develop a feeling of self-righteousness; and we find this sentiment marching side by side with the sense of sin.

The Scribes—The study and interpretation of the Law **607** was in the hands of those who are called in the Gospels Scribes and doctors of the law. Originally the interpretation of the Torah was the function of the priests; but the Scribes as such were not priests, although priests were included in their number. Once the Law was accepted as the basis of Jewish life, it was necessary to determine its meaning, and to apply it, as far as possible, to any situation that might arise. Hence came the Scribes. The name is first given to Ezra, 'a ready scribe in the law of Moses'. The Scribes had no official position; and their opinions had no authority except that of personal influence and public opinion. But this authority was enough. They were legislators, teachers and judges. They sat 'in the chair of Moses', and were addressed by the title of *Rabbi* (master). The study of the Law was, in the eyes of the devout Jew, the highest occupation of man (cf Sir 39:1–11). It was not remunerative; many of the Scribes, who did not enjoy an independent income, were quite poor and supported themselves by a trade. Their function was 'to build a fence around the Law': to protect the perfect observance of the Law by additional regulations. These regulations were formed by deducing them from the text of the written Law. There were two kinds of interpretation: the *Halakhah*, an interpretation, **e** application, or extension of the precepts of the Law into a rule of conduct; and the *Haggadah*, an amplification of the narrative and doctrinal portions of the Law by the addition of legend, speculation or sheer imagination. The Haggadah was especially concerned with the future and the heavenly world, about which it pretended to give much information. The Halakhah was always based, at least in appearance, on an inference or a deduction from the written Law, however far-fetched these conclusions might be. Thus conclusions were formulated from single words or letters, or even from punctuation or the order of the words. By adding the numerical values of the single letters, and by redividing the sum, new words or sentences could be formed (*gematria*), from which a precept could be deduced. The same end could be reached by inverting the letters according to the alphabetical order in reverse, and forming new words. The regulations thus formulated grew into a second legal system, the oral law, which was proposed as of equal authority with the Law of Moses; indeed, the beginning of oral tradition was attributed to Moses himself.

The oral law was the object of tradition. A dis- **f** tinguished scribe would gather around himself a group of disciples who preserved his teaching, and in their own generation amplified it. Until after the beginning of the Christian era there was no written basis for the teaching of the Scribes. Memory was all-important. The schools of the Scribes were by no means uniform in their interpretation of the Law. Difference of opinion was a constant cause of quarrels; a quarrel between the schools of Hillel and Shammai is said to have issued in fatal violence on one occasion. These two schools were, according to the Jewish sources, the principal schools of the last century B.C. The school of Hillel was mild in its interpretations; that of Shammai was inexorably rigorous. These two tendencies were active, whether these two men were their creators or not.

Much of the casuistry of the Scribes is judged **g** unfavourably by moderns. There are many allusions in the Gospels to the over-emphasis they placed on external observances (tithing mint, anise and cummin, and neglecting mercy, justice and faith), the devices by which they evaded obligations of the Law (e.g. the evasion of the obligation of supporting one's parents

607g by consecrating one's goods to the sanctuary), and the hypocrisy which masked their refusal to live by their own precepts (binding intolerable burdens on men, while refusing to lift a finger). They treated those who were ignorant of the Law, or who did not observe it, with a lofty contempt. But among their number were found some who were 'not far from the Kingdom of God'. It is thought that the first Jewish Christians must have included a not inconsiderable number of men who, like St Paul, had devoted their lives to the earnest study of the Word of God, and who attempted to live by this Word as they understood it.

608a **The Sanhedrin**—The Aram. word *sanhedrin* is identical with the Gr. *synedrion*, assembly or council. When this institution arose cannot be definitely determined. From earliest times local government had been conducted by a council of the 'elders', men whose age, rank and wealth gave weight to their decisions. It was probably not before the Greek period (after 330 B.C.) that the Jerusalem council, called the Sanhedrin, came to wield legislative and judicial authority for all Judaea, and to claim the same authority not only for Palestinian Judaism, but also, so far as the dispersed Jews consented, for Judaism of the Diaspora as well. The presidency of the Sanhedrin was vested in the high-priest, who was the supreme native magistrate under the imperial governments. The original composition of the Sanhedrin was exclusively aristocratic: members of the high-priestly families, and the 'elders' of the lay aristocracy. It was probably during the Hasmonaean period that scribes also were admitted. These classes are the 'chief priests, elders and scribes' of the Gospels. In NT times the party of the Pharisees was in the ascendancy in the Sanhedrin. The number of its members was seventy-one. Members were admitted either by co-option or by appointment of the imperial government; the method is not certainly known.

b The competence of the Sanhedrin was originally very broad, including all religious questions, and all civil and criminal cases which the imperial government did not reserve to its own officers. Before the Roman period (63 B.C.) these reservations were very few; and the Romans limited the civil authority of the Sanhedrin to Judaea proper. But even the Hasmonaean rulers quarrelled with the Sanhedrin, and these quarrels, on occasion, broke out into armed strife; and Herod and the Roman government restricted the jurisdiction of the Sanhedrin very considerably. Capital crimes (except trespassing in the Temple area) were removed from its competence. It was the supreme authority in determining the interpretation of the Law, both oral and written; these decisions were valid for the Diaspora. It had its own police force.

The procedure of the Sanhedrin favoured the accused. In capital cases, the arguments of the defence were heard first, and favourable testimony was irreversible. Unfavourable testimony could be reversed. A delay of one day should intervene between the trial and a sentence of condemnation. A majority of one sufficed for acquittal; a majority of two was required for condemnation.

c **The Hasidim**—In the Maccabean period there appears a party among the Jews known as the Hasiddeans (Heb. *ḥāsîd*, 'pious'). They were a group devoted to the perfect observance of the Law; and, while they took active part in the Maccabean revolt, they refused to fight on the Sabbath, even in self-defence. Under the Hasmonaean rulers they appear again as hostile to the pretensions of the priestly rulers. They represent the sentiments of the lower classes as opposed to the aristocracy. It was from this group that there evolved **608c** the far more famous Jewish sect, the Pharisees.

The Pharisees—The name (Heb. *perûšîm*, 'separated') **d** was probably given to the sect by their enemies as a term of opprobrium. It became, however, the accepted designation of the group. They were called 'separate' because of their exact observance of all the prescriptions of the Law, which set them apart not only from the Gentiles, but also from less observant Jews.

Distinctive Pharisaic tenets are reported by the ancient sources as follows. *Firstly*, the acceptance of the oral law, 'the traditions of the ancients', as of equal validity with the written law. This meant in practice that most of the Scribes were Pharisees. Pharisaic interpretation was generally more rigorous and imposed all the precepts of the Law as equally grave. *Secondly*, belief in human freedom under the control of divine Providence. This problem was attacked by the Pharisees, if we may trust Josephus, by affirming both terms of the antinomy: human freedom, and effective control by divine Providence. *Thirdly*, belief in the resurrection of the body. *Fourthly*, belief in the existence of the angels. It is doubtful whether these last two points should be called peculiarly Pharisaic doctrine.

Pharisaism was a religious, not a political, movement. **e** But the struggles of the Pharisees with the Hasmonaean dynasty made them prefer a friendly and liberal foreign government to an enlargement of sacerdotal power; and they lived peaceably under Herod and the Romans as long as the imperial government did not interfere with perfect observance. The kingdom of God they believed, would be established by divine intervention, not by human efforts. Government by foreign powers was divine punishment for the sins of the nation, and as such should be accepted submissively; but, on the other hand, it was a profanation of the Holy Land and of the Chosen People, and an obstacle to the establishment of the kingdom of God. As such, it should be overturned by rebellion. Since there was no such thing as a Pharisaic political policy, Pharisees were active in all the wars and rebellions of the Jews from the Maccabees to the insurrection of Bar Kochba in A.D. 135.

It was Pharisaism which imposed its permanent **f** stamp upon Judaism. The great catastrophe of A.D. 70, in which the city and the Temple were destroyed by the Romans, wiped out all other parties in Palestinian Judaism. But even before that date the Pharisees dominated Judaism. Their perfect observance of the Law won them the admiration, if not the affection, of the mass of the people; and their opposition to the sacerdotal aristocracy, which was often dishonest and rapacious, put them on the side of the common people. Their emphasis on the study and the observance of the Law, and on exercises of piety which were independent of the Temple, made it possible for Judaism to survive as a religion after the disappearance of the priesthood and the Temple liturgy. They were not democratic, and did not intend to be; but their aristocracy was spiritual, as they understood it. Unfortunately their spiritual aristocracy too often degenerated into mere pride. The haughtiness of the Jew towards the Gentile was found sevenfold in the Pharisee. Their withdrawal from profane contact meant, in practice, withdrawal from the human race. The Gospels show them in an unfavourable light. The Pharisees, nevertheless, represent what had once been the highest and purest form of Judaism.

The Sadducees—The origin and meaning of the name **609a** are uncertain. The Sadducees were the party of the priestly aristocracy, which claimed descent from Zadok.

609a The party seems to have arisen from community of interests. The wealth of the priestly families made common cause for them with other wealthy and conservative circles. They were concerned with preserving the high state of the priesthood. The Pharisees were not anti-sacerdotal nor anti-ritual; their strict interpretation of the Law allotted ample revenues to the priests. But they opposed the political activity of the priesthood, and set up a standard of legal observance which the priests wee unwilling to follow. Hence the Sadducees rejected the oral tradition, and admitted only the written law as valid; they had, however, their own traditions, and included Scribes in their party. The difference was not in the theory of interpretation, but in the binding force of tradition. In penal laws and in some Levitical laws the Sadducees were more rigorous than the Pharisees. Their religious beliefs were more conservative, clinging to older forms of Jewish doctrine. This was not based on any theological principle; it was a consequence of their worldliness, and of their lack of any real interest in religious questions. Of all parties and classes of Judaism, the Sadducees were the most favourable to Hellenistic culture. According to Mt 22:23, Ac 23:8, and Josephus, the Sadducees denied divine Providence, the resurrection of the body and the existence of angels.

b Like the Pharisees, the Sadducees had no political policy; priests appear both in rebellion against the imperial government and working in collusion with it. But they were politically active; their politics, however, had no principle except the advancement of their party and the preservation of sacerdotal wealth and power.

The Sadducees had little influence on the common people, nor, apparently, did they seek it; they were more concerned with dealing dexterously with the imperial government. They had no lasting influence on Judaism; with the destruction of the Temple in 70 A.D. the priestly party disappeared altogether from history.

c Other Groups—Josephus describes the Pharisees, Sadducees and Essenes (see below) as 'philosophical sects', in an attempt to explain them to his Roman readers. Along with them he names 'a fourth philosophical sect', the **Zealots** (Ant 18, 23–25). There were a group of fanatical nationalists in the tradition of the Maccabees, who asserted their zeal for the kingdom of God by violent means. The movement seems to have begun with a revolt against the census of Quirinius. Judas, the leader of this revolt, was a Galilean, son of Eleazar who was executed by Herod; and his son Menahem was the leader of the last stand of the Jews at Masada in A.D. 66. Because of their violence and the practice of assassination, they were also called **Sicarii** (from the Latin *sica*, a dagger). But it must be borne in mind that these names denote not so much a party (still less a 'philosophical sect') as a movement; (cf § 605*n*). The **Herodians** were probably a political party, though not much is known about them. They were probably supporters of the house of Herod and the Roman rule which backed this house, perhaps hoping that the Romans would restore authority over

d Palestine to Herod's family. Finally, there were the **People of the Land**. This designation was originally applied to the inhabitants of the rural districts of Palestine, often of mixed Jewish and Gentile extraction, who were affected only slightly, or not at all, by the religious reforms of Ezra and still less by the Pharisaic movement and the oral law of the Scribes. In NT times the designation was extended, in a contemptuous sense, to all of any class or position who were ignorant of the Law or careless of its perfect observance. To the Pharisees, 'this multitude that knows not the Law is accursed'. The

people of the land were the 'publicans and sinners' with **609** whom the Saviour mingled freely, unlike the Pharisees; they were the 'little ones' to whom the Father revealed what he had hidden from the wise. The mass of the people, sustaining itself in poverty by hard labour, was unable to listen to the instruction of the Scribes, or to execute the precepts of the Law. The people of the land were habitually unclean. It was in them, nevertheless, that the essence of Judaism was found: life according to the moral principles of the Law, the simple piety of daily prayer, Sabbath observance, synagogue worship, and occasional visits to the Temple, and the hope in the kingdom of God to come. It was to such that Jesus addressed himself, and by whom he was at first so cordially received. Unlike the Pharisees, he associated freely with them and taught them; it was a feature of his ministry worth notice that 'the poor had the Gospel preached to them'. For he was himself a member of their class, and from them came his apostles.

II THE QUMRAN SECT AND THE ESSENES

Our knowledge of Palestinian Judaism has been trans- **610** formed by the discovery of the documents known as the **Dead Sea Scrolls**. In the spring of 1947 two Bedu shepherds discovered by accident some scrolls in jars in a cave of the cliffs near the Wadi Qumran on the western side of the Dead Sea. By devious paths four scrolls came into the possession of the Syrian metropolitan of Jerusalem, Mar Athanasius Yeshue Samuel, and three scrolls were purchased by E. L. Sukenik for the Hebrew University of Jerusalem. Scholars of the American School of Oriental Research identified the four scrolls of the patriarch as ancient, in February 1948, and Professor Sukenik reached the same conclusion independently for his scrolls. The unsettled political conditions of Palestine at the time moved the patriarch to bring his scrolls to the United States. Three scrolls were published by the American Schools of Oriental Research, but the fourth was not opened for fear of damage. These four scrolls were purchased by the State of Israel in 1954 and the original seven are now all on display in Jerusalem. The fourth scroll was opened and published in Israel. The value of the scrolls impelled the bedu to **further ex-** **b** **ploration** of the caves near the Dead Sea and when fragments began to appear in antique dealers' shops in Jerusalem the Department of Antiquities of the Hashemite Kingdom of Jordan undertook a systematic exploration of the caves from 1951 to 1956, in co-operation with the Dominican École Biblique et Archéologique Francaise and the American School of Jerusalem. The explorers discovered **thousands of fragments**. The search was extended to the Wadi Murabba'at, south of the Wadi Qumran and to Khirbet Mird, the site of a ruined Byzantine monastery and of the Hasmonean fortress, Hyrcanium. At the Wadi Murabba'at, documents dating from the second Jewish rebellion (A.D. 132–5), a papyrus of the 7th cent. B.C. and a scroll of the Minor Prophets from the 2nd cent. A.D. were discovered. At Khirbet Mird, were found documents from the end of the Byzantine period and the beginning of the Arab era in Greek, Christian-Palestinian Aramaic and Arabic.

Archaeology of the Site—A group of ruined buildings **c** on a natural platform at the foot of the cliffs on the west shore of the Dead Sea had been known for centuries; explorers had taken it for granted that it was a Roman fort. A cemetery certainly not Moslem is adjacent to the ruins. The site was excavated by G. Lankester Harding, Director of the Department of Antiquities of Jordan,

10c and Roland de Vaux of the École Biblique. Five campaigns of excavation disclosed an extensive building complex which had been inhabited during three periods. The buildings were erected upon the foundations of an Israelite fortress abandoned in the sixth cent. B.C.

d Two phases were distinguished in Period I. Period I*a* consisted of temporary structures in use before the construction of the central buildings. Most of the remains of these structures were incorporated into the buildings of I*b*. The exact date of the central buildings could not be determined. Coins began in the reign of John Hyrcanus (134—104 B.C.) and continued to the end of the Hasmonean period (37 B.C.), and were most numerous from the reign of Alexander Jannaeus (103—76 B.C.). Period I ends with destruction by earthquake in the reign of Herod the Great (after 37 B.C.). This must be the great earthquake of 31 B.C. There is no sign of reoccupation before the reign of Archelaus (4 B.C.—A.D. 6). Period II extends from the reign of Archelaus to A.D. 68 and ended in violent destruction. The evidence indicates that the site was a point of resistance during the Jewish rebellion and fell to a Roman attack. During Period II it was occupied by a Roman garrison to near the end of the first cent. A.D. It was then permanently abandoned.

e Some of the caves, it appears, were occupied by hermits, at least at times, but were not used regularly for the storage of manuscripts; the manuscripts were probably stored there during the emergency at the end of Period II, and the group never returned. Some of the manuscripts were stored in jars probably made for the purpose.

f The area of the ruins is roughly square, about 250 feet on a side, and the central building complex, also square, is about 125 feet on a side. A large room belonging to Period II contained long plaster tables and wooden benches. This furniture and some inkwells make it all but certain that this room was the scriptorium. The great hall with plastered floor and plastered pillars was identified as the hall of assembly; a round stone pavement was assumed to represent the podium of the reader or the presiding officer. That the hall was also the dining room was suggested by the discovery of over 1000 pieces of pottery, almost a complete table service, in an adjoining room. Other rooms had facilities for food storage, baking, the manufacture of pottery, and metal working. The group probably was housed in caves and tents.

An extensive water system secured water from the W. Qumran, a seasonal stream. The wadi was dammed and the water distributed through aqueducts and canals into storage basins; the excavators found seven large cisterns and at least six small pools. One large cistern had a wide flight of steps; it is not certain that this was a bathing pool, since steps to make it possible to secure water when the level is low are found elsewhere and do not demonstrate bathing, still less ritual bathing. Bathing was more probable in the smaller pools.

The cemetery contained about 1,100 graves, too many for the estimated population of the site at any one time; and it has been suggested that extern members or associates who lived elsewhere were buried at Qumran. Some of the skeletons were female. In contrast with contemporary Jewish practice no objects were buried with the bodies.

g **The Scrolls**——Those found in Cave 1 include the seven scrolls of the first discovery. (1) The Isaiah MS published by the American Schools of Oriental Research, containing the complete text. (2) Another scroll of Isaiah, fragmentary, published by Sukenik and Avigad. (3) A commentary on Habakkuk 1—2. (4) 'The Rule of the Community' ('The Manual of Discipline'), containing regulations for the

government of the group, admission of candidates, conduct, **610g** punishments, and some ritual prescriptions. (5) A collection of thanksgiving hymns. (6) The War of the Children of Light and the Children of Darkness, containing regulations for the conduct of an apocalyptic war between the sect and the enemies of the Jews. (7) A Genesis apocryphon written in Aramaic, the last of the scrolls to be opened, an imaginative expanded account of Gn 5:28—29; 12:10—15:2.

Eleven of the hundreds of caves explored contained **h** thousands of fragments. Fragments of every canonical book except Esther have been discovered, including parts of Tobit and Sirach of the deuterocanonical books. Fragments of the apocryphal books include the Book of Jubilees, the book of Enoch, and the Testaments of the Twelve Patriarchs. The Damascus Document, hitherto known only in a MS discovered in the genizah of the synagogue of Old Cairo and published by S. Schechter in 1910, was found in several copies at Qumran. 'The Rule of the Congregation' is a fragment which parallels and supplements 'The Manual of Discipline' and probably represents a different period of the community. There are fragments of commentaries on Isaiah, Hosea, Micah, Nahum, Zephaniah and the Psalms. Other fragments contained liturgical formulae and wisdom texts.

Date of the Documents and Identification of the 611a Community. The date of the first cent. B.C. and the first cent. A.D. suggested by W. F. Albright and others on palaeographical evidence has now been confirmed by the archaeology of the site. S. Zeitlin and a few others maintain that the scrolls are medieval forgeries. This hypothesis is unlikely both because of the archaeological data and because of a Carbon 14 test made on the linen wrappings of the scrolls, which indicated a median date of A.D. 33. For these reasons a connexion has been proposed between the Qumran group and **the Essenes**, mentioned by Philo Judaeus (first cent. A.D., *Quod omnis probus liber sit*, 12—13, 75—91), Jos (BJ 2. 119—61) and Pliny the Elder (*Naturalis Historia*, V, 17, 73).

Pliny located the Essenes on the W shore of the **b** Dead Sea in a place which must be Qumran or very near it. Josephus called the Essenes one of the three philosophical sects of the Jews (distinguished from the Pharisees and Sadducees). They are recognized as holy men, abstain from marriage, but adopt children. They own goods in common and new members renounce their property. They worship at sunrise and spend the day in manual crafts. After bathing they partake of a common meal. They wear white when they are not working. They speak only in their proper turn. Their officers have absolute power. A candidate is admitted after three years of probation, and must take a solemn oath to observe the rules of the community and to keep its secrets. Offences against the rule are punished by privation of food or by expulsion. Admission, expulsion and punishment are decided by a community vote. They observe the Sabbath more rigidly than the Pharisees. They are divided into four grades. They believe in the immortality of the soul. They have sacred books and believe they have the power of prophecy. They had a lay order which observed the other rules but permitted marriage. They study and discuss the Law in groups. They emphasize the divine supremacy and believe in predestination. The picture given by Philo is not substantially different.

There are both parallels and divergences between **c** Josephus and the Qumran texts. The period of probation is two years in Qumran. There are not four divisions or grades. The divine supremacy and predestination appear in the scrolls, but whether the immortality of

611c the soul does, is disputed; cf G. Vermes, p. 6. Josephus and Philo say nothing of priests, but the priests are prominent in the Qumran scrolls. Celibacy is not evident in the Qumran sources. The parallels, in the opinion of most scholars, are more weighty than the divergences. Both the geographical area and the general identity of tone and spirit have convinced most scholars that the Qumran community was Essene. Differences can be explained by the hypothesis that the scrolls and the ancient writers represent different stages of development, or by the omission of peculiarly Jewish details in Philo and Josephus, who wrote for Gentile readers.

d **The Damascus Document** (or **The Zadokite Fragment**) is now recognized to have such remarkable affinities with the **Qumran texts** that a common origin is to be accepted. This document describes a group which migrates to Damascus and enters into a new covenant. The covenant theme is prominent in the Qumran texts. Damascus is possibly an allegorical name signifying Qumran itself or merely the departure of the sect from orthodox Judaism. The doctrine and the rules of the Damascus Document are in harmony with the Qumran; again, the two sources probably represent different stages of development.

e The **Qumran documents contain no clear historical allusions** except to a Greek king Demetrius and the lion of wrath who crucified his enemies (the fragmentary commentary of Nahum). This most probably refers to the crucifixion of eight hundred Pharisees by Alexander Jannaeus (103—76 B.C.) after the Seleucid king Demetrius III Eukairos had retired from his invasion of Palestine. Allusions elsewhere employ fictitious or cryptic names. 'The Teacher of Righteousness' encountered 'The Wicked Priest' on the Day of Atonement. The Wicked Priest later fell into the hands of his enemies. It is not clear that the Teacher of Righteousness suffered death at the hands of the Wicked Priest. The Wicked Priest is identified with Simon (142—135 B.C.) by F. M. Cross, with Jonathan, Simon's predecessor (160—142 B.C.), by J. T. Milik, with Aristobulus II (67—63 B.C.) by A. Dupont-Sommer, and with Menelaus, who purchased the office of high priest during the reign of Antiochus IV (175—164 B.C.) by H. H. Rowley. A people called the Kittim are described as powerful and cruel conquerors; they must be either the Seleucids (H. H. Rowley) or the Romans (the majority of scholars).

f There is wide agreement among scholars that the **origins of the Qumran sect lie in the Maccabean period**. The sect is quite possibly an offshoot from the Hasidim, who at first supported the Maccabees in their struggle for independence but rejected the Hasmonean dynasty when its rulers assumed the office of high priest. (cf § 608c)

g **Organization and Discipline.** The sect included priests and laymen. The priests are called the sons of Aaron or the sons of Zadok, probably a reference to the priestly line of Zadok appointed by David. The sons of Aaron had legislative and judicial power. An assembly of 'The Many' seems to be the members in full standing. The group was governed by a council of twelve laymen and three priests. The Damascus Document mentions a priest inspector of The Many and a superintendent of the camps. **The Manual of Discipline** mentions an inspector who presides over the Many and a superintendent of The Many. The assembly of The Many voted on the admission of candidates, the infliction of punishment, and the readmission of expelled members who had repented and atoned. Members were admitted after two years of probation. The oath was taken at the beginning of the

probation. After one year the candidate was admitted to **61** some of the community functions. Property was held in common. The rules emphasize the virtues of community **h** life and punish severely anti-social defects. Only full members were admitted to **the common meal.** No ceremony is mentioned in connexion with the meal except the blessing of the bread and wine by the priest. It is probable that this meal represented **the eschatological banquet** which in Jewish belief would be celebrated in the Day of the Lord (Is 25:6). In the assembly members were seated according to rank—priests, elders, the rest of the people—and they were to speak only in turn. Where ten were assembled, one should be a priest, and there should be one engaged in **the study of the Law day and night.** During a third of each night the members kept a vigil in reading, the study of the law, and the common recitation of the blessings. During the day they engaged in manual labor. **The calendar of the Qumran group differed** from the calendar used in contemporary Judaism, and the sect attached great importance to their calendar.

Doctrines. The sect thought of itself as **the true i Israel** which would survive the eschatological tribulations. Membership in the true Israel was not by birth alone but by **a free personal decision.** Their covenant was **the new covenant** of Jer 31:31—34 and Ezek 36:22—28. The predestination mentioned by Josephus is reflected in the doctrine of **the two spirits,** the spirit of light or good and the spirit of darkness or evil, called Belial. Man is subject to the influence of these two spirits. He is sinful, but is saved only through the forgiving mercy of God.

The sect believed in **two Messiahs,** the Messiah of **j** Aaron and the Messiah of Israel. This reflects the importance of the priesthood in Qumran beliefs. The Messiah of Aaron takes precedence over the Messiah of Israel, who must be the Messiah of the house of David. It is not clear whether the sect expected the appearance of the Messiah in the present age. That the teacher of Righteousness was a messianic figure is extremely doubtful. **The Teacher of Righteousness** was apparently **k** the founder of the sect, venerated second only to Moses, and perhaps the author of some of the thanksgiving hymns; but he is not clearly an eschatological saviour. A Teacher of Righteousness was expected to appear in the last days, but this figure is not necessarily identified with The Teacher of Righteousness who founded the sect. Nor is he clearly identified with the Messiah of Aaron.

The sect belonged to apocalyptic Judaism; cf **l** § 454a—e. The group was highly conscious of **the end of days.** The final period would involve an eschatological conflict in heaven and on earth. The battle of the spirits of light and the spirits of darkness in heaven would be paralleled by the battle of the sons of light and the sons of darkness on earth. This battle is described in the war scroll. Neither the resurrection of the dead nor the punishment of the wicked after death is mentioned clearly. In the final salvation the righteous are admitted to eternal bliss, there is a new heaven and a new earth and a new Jerusalem, and the redeemed become morally perfect. They will be purified from error and sin, they will have everlasting joy in eternal life, and they will receive a crown of glory and a garment of light.

Relations with the New Testament. Before the **6** Qumran scrolls were discovered apocalyptic Judaism was known only from Daniel and certain apocryphal books. The Qumran sect was one of the apocalyptic groups. The apocalyptic themes do not appear in the Judaism of the Pharisees or of the Sadducees. Certain apocalyptic

612a doctrines and images appear in the apocalyptic books, the Qumran scrolls, and the NT. **Some contact between the Qumran group and primitive Christianity** seems to be established; but the origin and the significance of the points of contact cannot as yet be defined precisely.

b The Johannine writings manifestly exhibit more points of contact with Qumran than any other NT books. F. M. Cross has pointed out the following phrases in John 'the spirit of truth and of deceit' (1 Jn 4:6), 'the light of life' (Jn 8:12), 'to do the truth' (Jn 3:21), 'sons of light' (Jn 12:36), 'life eternal' (Jn 3:15 and elsewhere). Cross observes that the idea of knowledge as 'a revealed eschatological knowledge' appears in the scrolls and in Matthew, John and Paul. The opposition of flesh and spirit is emphasized in the Qumran scrolls and in the NT. Cross points out the common features between the spirit of truth and the spirit of wickedness and the conflict of the sons of light and the sons of darkness and 1 Jn 3:7—10; 4:1—6. The type of spiritual interpretation found in the Qumran commentaries has no parallels in rabbinic interpretation but does resemble some NT uses of the OT.

c The organization of the Qumran sect has **some resemblances to the organization of the primitive Christian community; but there are also notable differences.** The importance of the priestly order at Qumran has no counterpart in the Christian community. The designation of 'The Many' for the assembly appears in Ac 6:2, 5; 15:12. The Inspector of the Qumran community is not dissimilar in power and functions to the *episkopos* (bishop) of the NT.

d The ceremonial meal of the group has features which suggest a liturgical anticipation of the messianic banquet (see above). This feature appears in Mk 14:25 and Lk 22:14—19. The anticipation of the Second Coming appears in 1 Cor 11:26. But there is no true parallel to the Lord's Supper as a commemoration and a re-enactment of the sacrificial offering of himself by Jesus Christ. Community of possessions appears at Qumran and in the primitive Christian church (Ac 4:32ff). There is no parallel in the Qumran texts to the counsels of Jesus that his disciples bestow their goods on the poor (Mt 19:21; Mk 10:21; Lk 18:22). The practice of celibacy at Qumran is controverted; but the counsels of Jesus (Mt 19:10—12), repeated by Paul (1 Cor 7:7—8) have no correspondence with Qumran.

Kurt Schubert has pointed out other resemblances. Both in Qumran and in the NT poverty is proposed as a virtue. There is a resemblance between the **Qumran texts and the Gospel passage concerning persecution for the sake of righteousness** (Mt 5:11). The directions given for the correction of a delinquent brother in the Manual of Discipline are remarkably close to the directions given in Mt 18:15—17; the offender should be rebuked in the presence of witnesses before any charge is presented to the general assembly.

e The essential and **decisive difference** between the Qumran sect and the primitive Christian church **is the central position of Jesus Christ in Christianity.** Nothing in Qumran remotely approaches the Christian fact. In addition E. Stauffer has pointed out eight substantial differences: (1) Clericalism; the importance of the priestly class at Qumran; (2) Ritualism; the ceremonial regulations of Qumran are far more complex than anything in the NT; (3) The direction to love the children of light and hate the children of darkness, contradicted by the command of Jesus to love one's enemies (Mt 5:43ff; Lk 6:27ff); (4) Militarism (the war of the sons of light and the sons of darkness); Jesus explicitly rejected violence in the promotion of his **612e** teaching (Mt 26:52); (5) The interest of the Qumran group in the calendar; (6) The esoteric character of the Qumran sect and its teaching, while Jesus expressly denied any teaching which was not public (Jn 18:20); (7) The two Messiahs of Aaron and David at Qumran; (8) The repudiation of the temple cult and priesthood by the Qumran sect, while Jesus celebrated Jewish feasts and participated in the temple worship, as the primitive Christian community did (Lk 24:52; Ac 3:1). In addition, Stauffer notes that Jesus proposed himself as superior to the Law, which the Qumran sect venerated at least as much as the Pharisees. The Sabbath observance of the Qumran group was rigid, but Jesus proposed a liberalism concerning the Sabbath which was frequently a point of controversy (Mk 2:32ff; Jn 5:8ff; 9:1ff). These and other points render impossible any hypothesis that primitive Christianity was a derivation from the Qumran group, though, as has been pointed out there was certainly some contact, the precise nature and significance of which is still being investigated.

III. THE DIASPORA

Judaism of the Diaspora—The name Diaspora (Gr. **613a** 'dispersion') was given to those Jewish communities which were settled outside Palestine. The dispersion of the Israelites abroad began with the deportations of the conquered by the Assyrian and Babylonian rulers in the eighth, seventh and sixth cent. B.C. Many of the early exiles lost their racial identity and were absorbed by the population of the area where they dwelt. The Babylonian exiles, however, in large measure retained their distinctive character, adhered to Jewish religious beliefs and practices, married their own and dwelt in Jewish communities. During the Gr. period there was a great migration of Jews to foreign countries for trade. By the last century B.C. large Jewish communities had been established in Syria, Egypt, Asia Minor, Mesopotamia, Babylonia, Persia, Greece and Italy. The number of Jews of the Diaspora is estimated in millions. Their language was Gr.; it is thought that most of them were ignorant of Heb. or Aram. The largest communities were found in the great cities, such as Antioch, Alexandria and Rome. The most important Jewish centre outside Palestine was in Alexandria; it was notable not only for its numbers and wealth, but also for its intellectual activity.

Most of the Jews of the Diaspora were engaged **b** in trade. They dwelt in separate quarters of the large cities, and were granted privileges of self-government under their own ethnarch by imperial and municipal authorities. This was an extension of the policy of the Hellenistic states and the Roman Empire of granting freedom to private religious associations. The Jews were really separate independent municipalities, and had the power of arrest for offences against the Law. While they did not always possess citizenship, their importance in commerce brought them so many privileges that they were often in a better position than the citizens themselves. Under Julius Caesar (d. 44 B.C.) the Romans initiated the policy of conferring Roman citizenship throughout the empire; and many Jews, like St Paul, possessed this right in addition to their Jewish privileges. This world-wide network of Jewish communities, most of which were wealthy and influential, looked to Palestine for religious leadership, and to Jerusalem as its spiritual capital. Without the contributions of the Diaspora to the support

613b of the Temple the priesthood could scarcely have maintained itself.

c The privileges of the Jews and their commercial success were not without accompanying troubles. They aroused the envy of the native population, which was further inflamed by Jewish exclusivism. In more than one instance this ill-feeling erupted into rioting, as at Antioch, Alexandria and Caesarea, and in charges laid against the Jews before municipal and imperial authorities. At Alexandria there was an almost perpetual feud between Jews and Gentiles; the great Jewish philosopher Philo once led a delegation to appeal to the Emperor Caligula (A.D. 37—41). The Jews were expelled from Rome more than once, and elsewhere had their privileges revoked. Up to A.D. 70, however, these troubles were only temporary; and the Jews always regained what they had lost.

d **The Synagogue**—This characteristically Jewish institution (Gr. *synagōgē*, meeting-place) was the centre of religious life in the Jewish communities of the Diaspora. Synagogues existed in Palestine also; every village of any size had its synagogue, and larger cities and towns had more than one. When and where the synagogue arose is not known; it may have been in the time of Ezra (the 5th or 4th cent. B.C.), and it probably had its roots in the meetings for prayer and discourse conducted by the Jews in Babylonia during the Exile. The purpose of the synagogue was reading and instruction in the Law; it presupposed that those present were unable to attend the worship in the Temple. Elementary schools for children seem to have been a normal complement of the synagogue; the Law was the only subject of study. The meetings were held on the Sabbath and on feast days; in later Judaism week-day meetings were added. The synagogue was governed by the elders of the synagogue; in strictly or predominantly Jewish communities these may have been identical with the civil authorities. The management of the synagogue and the maintenance of order in the services was in charge of the 'ruler of the synagogue'. None of the officials were priests; the synagogue was a lay organization. There were no officers appointed to conduct the synagogue services; members of the congregation were called upon to read the Law, to

e explain it, to lead the prayers. Originally the services were conducted in private dwellings; in NT times communities of any size possessed a synagogue building. Many of these were large and built in a grand style. The principal articles of furniture were: the ark or chest in which the scrolls of the Law were kept, the tribune on which speakers and readers stood, lamps, horns and trumpets for ceremonial purposes. Men and women sat in separate groups. The service began with the *Shema*, the Jewish profession of faith (Dt 6:4). There followed a prayer, the reading of the Torah in Heb., a translation or paráphrase of the passage in the vernacular, and an explanatory discourse. (On the Gr. translation of the Scriptures, see § 26a—j) The Law was so divided that the whole was read in the course of three years (or in one year according to the system of the Babylonian rabbis).

f **Jews and Gentiles**—The exclusivism of the Jews and their resistance to Gentile culture was not and could not have been entirely successful. That Judaism was affected by ideas from foreign sources is certain; the extent of this influence cannot be determined exactly.

Hellenistic culture is the name given to the diffusion of the Gr. language, learning, arts and customs throughout the E and the Mediterranean littoral following the conquests of Alexander (d. 323 B.C.). The culture of Greece, thus presented to a world-wide audience and adopted by

it, shook off its peculiarly Gr. traits and became universal. 613 The kingdoms of Syria and Egypt, one or the other of which ruled Palestine from the death of Alexander to the Maccabean wars, were both Hellenistic.

The impact of Hellenistic culture on the Jews had g different effects in Palestine and in the Diaspora. Palestinian Judaism, which had erected itself into a tightly homogeneous community, was better able to resist it than the Jewish communities which supported themselves by commerce in the large hellenistic cities. Again, we must distinguish between the externals of Hellenistic culture and the religious and philosophical ideas of Hellenism. Judaism both at home and abroad was at first swamped under the externals of Hellenistic culture. The common articles of trade and of daily use, food, clothing, furniture were Gr. in name and in style. A great number of Gr. personal names appear among the Jews in the Hellenistic period (Andrew, Philip, Alexander), many of them altered from a Heb. name of similar sound (Joshua and Jason). Even such definitely Jewish buildings as synagogues were erected in the Hellenistic architectural style. Because of the severe restrictions of the Law on the use of images, the Jews seem to have been touched very lightly by the plastic arts of Greece; but there was much study of Gr. literature and philosophy, even in Palestine. Civil h government in Jewish communities adopted many features of Hellenistic cities. Even in Palestine many Jews enthusiastically adopted Gr. costume and such Gr. practices as athletic contests, baths and theatres. The members of the sacerdotal aristocracy were the leaders in this movement of hellenization; it was they, also, who abetted Antiochus Epiphanes in his efforts to impose hellenistic worship, which led to the Maccabean rebellion. As a result of the wars of the Maccabees, Palestinian Judaism cast off many of the externals of Hellenism; the Pharisees professed to reject it entirely, the Sadducees were still sympathetic, and the people of the land were more or less hellenized according to their environment. But Palestinian Judaism admitted no real infiltration of Hellenistic thought, and very little even of hellenistic literary forms. The Scribes and Pharisees refused to learn anything from the Greeks.

The same cannot be said of Judaism of the Diaspora. i The principal literary works of the Diaspora which have survived are the Book of Wisdom (written 150—50 B.C.) and the writings of Philo of Alexandria (b. about 30 B.C.). For the question of Gr. influence on Wisdom cf § § 431e, 433a. That Philo was a student of Gr. philosophy, and that he looked on it with favour, is evident from his works. His aim was to show that the Law, the sum of all wisdom for the Heb., was a philosophy like Platonism or Stoicism. In details his thought shows the effects of Gr. philosophy. If Philo is a true example of Alexandrine Judaism, then the assimilation of Gr. thought had gone far. But Philo remains a Jew; and the amazing conglomeration of peculiarly Heb. and Gr. ideas in his works issues in strange confusions—which may aptly illustrate the confusion of many a Jew in the presence of the wisdom of the Greeks.

Other foreign influences on Judaism are less certain. j From Babylonia the Jews acquired a number of ancient superstitious practices, some of which have survived into modern times; but it cannot be said that Babylonia contributed anything to Jewish religious beliefs. The influence of Persia has been seriously discussed. These resemblances have been noted between Judaism and the religion of Zarathushtra: belief in a world destiny, a final conflagration, an evil spirit, a final judgement of good and wicked, the ultimate triumph of good over evil, and the

613j resurrection. A closer study of these resemblances shows that many of them are specious; that no connexion can be found through which Persia could have influenced Judaism; and that the roots of these doctrines are found in the Scriptures and the traditions of Judaism. The whole question is fully treated by Lagrange, *Judaïsme*, 388–409.

14a Proselytism—Judaism of the NT period was moved by two opposing tendencies: the nationalist, particularist, exclusivist tendency by which Judaism formed a tight front against the Hellenistic world, and the intrinsic universalism of the doctrines of Judaism. The Jews had only to read their sacred books to realize that their God was the one true God of all mankind, and that all men should know him, all races and tongues should serve him; from Zion proceeded revelation for the whole world. At the beginning of the Christian era particularism, represented by the Pharisees, had triumphed there was no sect or movement within Judaism which stood for universalism. But the inherent tendency towards universalism could not be suppressed; and it found an outlet in proselytism, the admission of Gentiles to the practice of the Jewish religion.

b There were several obstacles to proselytism. Besides the particularist spirit of official Judaism, there was the obstacle of anti-Jewish prejudice. Jewish exclusivism was the one force which opposed the Hellenistic amalgamation of many nations, cultures, languages and religions into one universal, supranational culture; Gentiles recognized this, and resented it. Even before the Christian era, and more frequently afterwards, Greek and Latin literature show not only numerous anti-Jewish allusions, but formally anti-Jewish compositions, which the Jews felt themselves obliged to answer. There is a striking similarity between the anti-Jewish prejudice of the ancient world and modern anti Semitism, which is not an effect, nor even a by-product of Christianity. But there were also favourable factors. Gentile prejudice moved many of the Jews of the Diaspora to present Judaism in the manner best calculated to attract Gentiles, by suppressing any emphasis on Jewish external practices, such as circumcision and the Sabbath, and expounding the real essence of Jewish doctrine; the pure concept of the one supreme God, and lofty standards of Jewish morality. Such a presentation was sympathetically **c** received by many Gentiles. Among educated Hellenistic circles the old Gr. polytheism had been done to death by the criticisms of the philosophers; Platonism and Aristotelianism conceived of God in an abstract and impersonal fashion, but freed of the debasing traits of the ancient gods of the Greeks; and Gr. philosophers, from Socrates to the Stoics, had worked out a system of morality which was not unworthy of comparison with Jewish morality. But philosophy alone left a religious hunger; and the Hellenistic world was very receptive to oriental religious cults, even to such fantastic rites as those of Mithras or of the Great Mother. Furthermore, the breakdown of nationalism in the hellenistic world separated religion from the nation. All religions appealed to a wider audience, and there was a tendency to identify all gods. Judaism, then, came before the Gentiles with the aura of mysticism which the Greeks attributed to the Orientals.

d There were two classes of proselytes: 'fearers of God', and true proselytes. The fearers of God accepted the Jewish doctrine of God and the Scriptures, attended the synagogue, and observed the Sabbath and the dietary laws; but they were not required to submit to circumcision nor to undertake the complete observance of the Law. **614d** These were probably far more numerous than the true proselytes. The true proselytes, by adopting Judaism in its entirety, actually became Jews; they included one oriental royal family.

Proselytism was not limited to the Diaspora; in spite of Pharisaism there were proselytes in Palestinian Judaism as well. Here Pharisaism was somewhat inconsistent with itself; the Gospels credit it with proselytizing zeal, in spite of its narrow religious nationalism. No more striking example of proselytism can be found than that of John Hyrcanus (135–104 B.C.), who forced the Edomites to submit to the full yoke of Judaism.

Proselytism did not solve the tension between universalism and particularism. Judaism did not assimilate the Gentiles. The true proselyte, by becoming a Jew, not only adopted Jewish beliefs and practices, but had to abandon his Hellenism and enter the Jewish community. Judaism was still a nation as well as a religion, and one could accept it on no other terms. Once the missionary activity of Christianity reached the Greco-Roman world, and especially after the Jewish rebellion of A.D. 66–70, we hear little of proselytism among the Jews.

IV BELIEFS AND MORALITY

It is impossible within the limits of this sketch to present **615a** a complete summary of the doctrines of Judaism, as they are complicated by wide variations between different periods and different centres. The doctrines discussed below are characteristic of the NT period. They are treated under four heads: God, angels and demons, Messianism, and eschatology.

A. God—The Jewish conception of God is based, first and foremost, on the OT; and the OT is filled with an overpowering sense of the divine presence and the divine activity in the world. God is the supreme lord of nature and of history. He is personal, with a personal interest in his creatures which the OT often describes in language which is altogether human. He is the supreme reality, as real to the ancient Hebrew as himself. But in the NT period the simple faith of the ancient Hebrew had been somewhat modified; and the influences which operated upon Jewish belief in God are not always easy to trace.

The existence of God was not, for the Hebrews, a **b** speculative question. In all Heb. literature there is no effort to demonstrate the existence of God. Herein Judaism was a true child of the ancient faith of the Hebrews, with its sense of the divine reality; and it was unacquainted with the curiosity of Gr. philosophy, which, once it had destroyed the gods of the ancient polytheism, was under the necessity of constructing a supreme being from its own intellectual processes. When the fool said, 'There is no God', Ps 14 (13):1, he denied not the existence of God, but his effective government of the world. The author of the Wisdom of Solomon, who was certainly acquainted with Gr. philosophy, calls 'ignorance of God' folly, Wis 13:1; but he means ignorance of the true nature of God, not of his existence.

The Divine Names—The proper personal name of the **c** God of the Hebrews was *Yahweh*; cf § 165*a, b*. In NT times this name was never uttered except by the priests in a few liturgical functions. It is uncertain when its use was abandoned; it seems to have occurred between the 5th and 3rd cent. B.C. Nor is it easy to assign a reason for this avoidance of the traditional name. The opinion that it was due to an exaggerated fear or reverence is not accepted by many modern scholars.

615c Some believe it was to protect the name from profanation by use in magical formulae; others, that it was abandoned from a monotheistic scruple. The deities of heathendom were distinguished from one another by their personal names (Zeus, Apollo, Aphrodite, etc); in order that the God of the Hebrews might not be esteemed one of many, his distinctive personal name was suppressed for the more universal 'God' or 'Lord'. Yet even these designations were used with restrictions. 'God' (*elōhîm*) is not used outside the Bible. 'Lord' (*ad̠onāi*, Gk *kyrios*) is used only in the Bible and in prayer. In extra-biblical Jewish literature and, we may suppose, in Jewish conversation, God was usually designated by circumlocution: the Name, the Place, the *Shekinah* (dwelling), the Power, the Heavens, the Most High, the Holy One (this last usually followed by the doxology 'Blessed be He'). Such modes of speaking certainly suggest a great advance in reverence, not to say timorousness, over the bold addresses of many of the Psalms (which, however, were used liturgically during this period), and an increasing reserve in converse with God. They suggest also a more remote sense of the divine personality and presence.

d Monotheism—The belief in one only God as the basis of religion distinguished Judaism both from Gentile religions and from Gr. philosophy. There was no ancient religion which did not admit and worship a plurality of gods. Many schools of Gr. philosophy professed belief in the existence of one supreme being. This conviction, however, was the fruit of philosophical speculation; Judaism based its belief on the revelation of the one God whom it worshipped. This fundamental doctrine is expressed in the *Shema*, which the devout Jew recited twice daily: 'Hear, O Israel, the Lord our God is one Lord'.

e As the Jews came more closely into contact with the great Gentile cultures of the ancient world, their rigorous monotheism responded to these cultures, which, from every point of view except that of religion and morality, were superior to their own, by a vigorous polemic against polytheism. The Jews thus protected themselves against the powerful attraction which these cultures exercised, and asserted their own superiority. Examples of such polemic already appear in the OT, and are found with more frequency in the extra-biblical Jewish literature of the last centuries B.C. Nor does it seem unfounded to see in monotheism the basis of the harsh judgement which Judaism passed against heathendom, and of the Jewish tendency to condemn Gentile culture root and branch as essentially sinful. Certainly the religious beliefs and the moral principles of Judaism were far superior to the religion and morality of the other ancient nations; but the Jews were austerely intolerant of Gentile culture as a whole, and blind to any elements of good which it might contain, because it was based on the folly of polytheism.

f The Divine Attributes—Extra-biblical Jewish literature lays particular emphasis on three divine attributes: majesty, spirituality and holiness. The OT speaks with sublime eloquence of the majesty of God; extra-biblical Jewish literature echoes the OT, but with a difference. In the OT Yahweh, while majestic, is not remote; transcending the world, he is not an abstraction. The God of Judaism is more remote from human affairs, less personal and more abstract. This does not mean that Judaism made no effort to penetrate the majesty of God; a favourite subject of Haggadic speculation was the heavens and the divine glory, which are more than once described in some detail. There were seven levels of the heavens; the seventh was the abode of God himself. These speculations were regarded as the most difficult and advanced, to which the student must not be admitted until he has **615** been well prepared.

It is difficult to analyse the Jewish conception of **g** the spirituality of God. The OT, like the Hebrews who were its authors, is material-minded; it exhibits no concept of purely intellectual activity such as was developed by Greek philosophers. Yet the OT and Judaism were always aware that God is a spirit, no matter how often they may speak of God's eye, or ear, or hand, or mouth. But we find that Judaism hesitates to employ such metaphors of God. Many of the vivid anthropomorphisms of the OT are suppressed by abstraction and circumlocution in LXX. What was lacking in Judaism was a positive concept of spiritual reality. The Hebrew concept of life was animal; they had no philosophy by which they might formulate an idea of rational or intellectual life. Hence the denial of material composition in God left only an abstraction; and this was another step towards making the divine reality more remote and less personal.

The holiness of God is a peculiarly Hebrew idea, for **h** which English has no adequate word. Holiness is not so much a divine attribute as divinity itself; it is everything which distinguishes God as such from his creatures. In modern language, it is the divine transcendence. It is more than moral goodness, although this element is not excluded; it is the physical and moral superiority of God over his creatures. In Judaism the moral aspect of holiness received greater emphasis. One of the titles of God used most frequently in the rabbinical literature is 'the Holy One'.

The doctrine of **Providence** in Judaism was, in **i** many ways, well developed. No truth is proposed in the OT with more emphasis, both by discourse and by narrative, than the truth of the intervention of God in human affairs. The dominant thought of Jewish belief in Providence was that whatever happens is the work of God. This doctrine, however, was applied principally to events on a national or world-wide scale: the history of the Jews, in particular, and of the great world-empires of ancient times. The idea of the action of God on the individual soul was much less well developed. In this, as in other doctrinal questions, the Jewish mind was more interested in the external. The question of the relation of the doctrine of Providence to human liberty and responsibility was not solved in Judaism, or, rather, not raised. Josephus says that the Pharisees occupied a middle position between the Essenes, who denied human liberty, and the Sadducees, who denied Providence; but most scholars think that Josephus has over-simplified the teachings of these parties. In Judaism, as we know it from the extant literature, human liberty and responsibility are asserted together with the truth that all that happens is the work of God; the apparent antinomy is ignored. A consequence of Jewish faith in divine intervention was a ready belief in stories of the marvellous and miraculous. Exaggerated credulity appears on almost every page of rabbinical and apocalyptic literature, which abound in anecdotes of the marvellous which are not only grotesque, but, often enough, indecorous, yet all calmly attributed to God.

The doctrine of Providence implies divine omni- **j** science and foreknowledge of human events, and this Judaism affirms; and from the doctrine of the divine foreknowledge flows the doctrine of predestination. Here Judaism advanced far beyond the doctrinal basis of the OT, especially the apocalyptic literature, which reveals future events as antecedently decreed and determined. The election of Israel as the Chosen People implied the reprobation of the Gentiles, who are, consequently,

615j regarded as hopelessly beyond the pale of salvation.

A counterweight to the depersonalization of God is found in the emphasis laid by Judaism on the divine goodness and mercy. Jewish prayer is full of expressions of thanksgiving for the divine benefits. And while Judaism is highly conscious of sin, it also has deep faith in divine mercy to the repentant sinner. But the divine mercy was not thought to reach all sinners. Judaism divided all mankind into two classes: the good, whose occasional falls were quickly repented and easily forgiven, and the wicked, who were impenitent and obdurate. For these God neither had nor could have any mercy. Among the obdurate sinners were included all Gentiles and the Hellenizing Jews; for the Pharisees, all who did not observe the Law were accursed. These harsh views of the official circles of Judaism had little or no effect on the piety of the ordinary Jew.

k Another effect of the abstract and transcendental concept of God was the personification of certain divine attributes. This has a basis in the OT: the spirit of God brooded over the surface of the waters (Gn 1:2), the Lord sends forth his word to do his work (Is 55:11), the widsom of God is his helper in the work of creation (Prv 8:22ff); and many other texts could be cited. In the OT these personifications are not really distinct from God himself; they are poetic and imaginative locutions about the divine attributes as manifested in creation. In Judaism such personifications are used very frequently, especially the spirit, the word (*Memra*), the wisdom, the *Shekinah* (dwelling, i.e. presence). The spirit is the creative force; by the *Shekinah* God is present everywhere. With one exception there is, in the thought of Judaism, no real difference between these personifications and God himself. They are used as substitutes for the divine name, and they permitted the Jews to speak of the external works of God without attributing these to him directly. The exception is Philo of Alexandria, who seems to have treated the personified attributes as beings intermediate between God and the angels, with a distinct reality of their own.

16a B. Angels and Demons—Angels are mentioned frequently in all the books of the OT, both early and late. They appear as bearers of the divine revelation, as executioners of the divine judgements, and as the heavenly retinue of God. Judaism expanded the doctrine of the angels far beyond the basis of the OT. The angels were conceived as spiritual beings, at least in the sense that they were not composed of gross terrestrial matter; but here again the Jews lacked a positive concept of spirituality, and did not elaborate the idea beyond that of the mere negation of body. The speculations of the Haggadah abound in descriptions of the material form of angels, which was certainly thought to be invisible to the mortal eye; they are described as gigantic winged human forms. In the rabbinical writings the angels are given a fiery nature, based on a misunderstanding of Ps 104(103):4. The theory of angelic choirs already appears in the Books of Enoch; seven choirs are mentioned in 1 Enoch, nine in 2 Enoch. The names of seven archangels are given: Uriel, Raphael, Raguel, Michael, Sarakiel, Gabriel and Jeremiel. Michael is the guardian spirit of Israel (cf Dn 10:21).

b The interest of Judaism in the angels corresponds to its feeling that God was remote. In the OT, where the sense of God's present reality is so pervasive, the angels play a relatively small part. In Judaism there was a need to multiply intermediaries. Many operations which the OT ascribes to God directly are attributed to angels in Judaism. This appears in LXX, **616b** where the angel of the Lord sometimes replaces the divine name of the original Hebrew, and in some uncertain passages of the MT, where the divine name and the angel of the Lord have become inextricably confused. In the speculations of the Haggadah the functions of the angels have been notably expanded beyond the doctrine of the OT. Judaism also describes them as the divine retinue; but the imaginative expansion of detailed description lacks nothing for fullness. The angels preside over the elements of the material universe, and over the celestial bodies—a quaint view which survived into the Middle Ages, when, fused with the Aristotelian theory of separate intelligences, it resulted in the theory that the movements of the celestial spheres were governed by angels. They presided over nations, each of which has its guardian spirit—a deduction from Dn 10:20f. They intervene actively in history and are the agents of the miraculous. But their most important function was that of intermediaries of the divine revelation. In the older prophetic books the prophet speaks the word of the Lord which he himself has heard. In Zech and Dn, however, an 'interpreting angel' appears, who communicates the word of the Lord, or explains the meaning of the visions of the seer. In the apocalyptic literature the interpreting angel is the usual medium by which the seer is informed of heavenly things.

It may almost be said that the OT contains no **c** demonology, so rare and so obscure are the allusions to a world of evil spirits. The demonology of Judaism was more indebted to foreign sources than to the OT. Here again the Haggadic speculations supplied what was missing in authentic sources. Like the angels, the demons were known by name; the chief of the evil spirits was Satan (mentioned in Jb 1 and 2, and Zech 3, but not certainly as an evil spirit); the Heb. word means 'adversary', 'accuser'. Satan appears to be identical with the Mastema mentioned occasionally in extra-biblical Jewish literature. Another evil spirit frequently mentioned is Beliar or Belial. The Heb. word *bᵉliya'al* probably means 'useless'; in the OT a 'son of belial' is a good-for-nothing, i.e. wicked person. The origin of the evil spirits was a subject of great interest in the Haggadah. Obviously they could not have been created evil, so their wickedness was attributed to some sin. The most commonly accepted belief was that they were the 'sons of God' of Gn 6:1—4, who sinned with the 'daughters of men'.

Ordinary Jewish belief was disfigured by a great deal of superstition, which was probably of Babylonian origin. Babylonian demonology was very highly developed. Almost every conceivable evil, mishap, or inconvenience was attributed to demonic malevolence; and the innumerable demons which threatened human welfare could be warded off only by incantations and magical rites. Such incantations and magic were practised among the Jews; the wearing of amulets against demons was very common.

C. Messianism—The Messianic conception of the Jews **617a** may be defined with Bonsirven as 'the conviction that the chosen people of God cannot disappear, that it will attain its peak and reach the fullness of the ideal predestined for it by God only in a future more or less remote, at "the end of days"' (*Judaisme* I, 341). The stream of the Messianic hope runs all through the OT. Its fullest development in extra-biblical literature is found in the apocalyptic books. There are many allusions in the NT to the Messianic expectation; and it is clear

617a from these allusions that the form which it took in NT times was material, temporal and national, rather than spiritual, eternal and universal. This conception we may trace in the literature, especially in the apocalyptic writings and the Qumran texts.

b The Messianic future was called the 'days of the Messiah', or 'the end of days', although two different conceptions lay beneath these two designations. The days of the Messiah looked principally to the national restoration of the Jews; the end of days looked rather to the universal consummation of the world. In both of these the accomplishment of the Messianic future was the effect of a direct divine intervention, a cosmic manifestation of God in his majesty and power; this divine intervention, rather than the work of the Messiah himself, was the cause of salvation. The Messianic era was to be initiated by the precursor of the Messiah, who was Elijah, the angel of the covenant (based on Mal 3:1, 4:5; cf 583d). The coming of the Messiah was preceded (or accompanied) by the Messianic tribulations. This was based on the apocalyptic predictions in the prophetic books of the OT (such as Is 24—27); this period was of indefinite duration, and was filled with temporal and spiritual calamities, convulsions of nature, the triumph of the wicked, etc. The coming of the Messiah coincided (in a general way) with the end of the world; and the belief that this was near seems to have been widely accepted in NT times. Jewish speculation was much interested in trying to determine when the consummation would come, and several calculations are found. The most popular seems to have been that which reckoned the duration of the world at seven periods of one thousand years each (after the seven days of creation); the last period, the millennium, was initiated by the coming of the Messiah, and the establishment of a kingdom of material and sensible joy on earth. After this period, the just were to be translated to 'the world to come'. This belief in a thousand years of earthly joy was accepted by some of the Fathers of the Church and by many Christians during the earlier centuries of our era.

c The Messianic kingdom is, in every conception, identified with the kingdom of Israel restored to Palestine from the dispersion; but extra-biblical Jewish literature exhibits great confusion in its descriptions of the Messianic kingdom. With Bonsirven, these conceptions may be classified, although it is impossible to eliminate some overlapping (*Judaïsme* I, 418ff.).

Conceptions of the Messianic Kingdom—A. Messianism of two periods: 'the days of the Messiah', in which the kingdom of Israel is restored and the Gentile nations destroyed, occur on earth. 'The world to come' is realized in a supraterrestrial universe, where the just are rewarded with all joys.

B. Transcendental Messianism: in this conception there is no messianic kingdom upon earth. The scene of salvation is heaven or paradise.

d C. Eschatological Messianism: this is a contamination of A by B. In this form, which exhibits several variations, the resurrection and the judgement are transferred from 'the world to come' to the messianic times upon earth; or, the days of the Messiah are prolonged into infinity, with no sharp division between the days of the Messiah and the world to come; or, the present world is transfigured into the transcendental world to come, with no change of scene from earth to heaven.

Eschatological Messianism was the most common belief among the Jews in NT times. The other conceptions are found in two of the most important apocalyptic works, besides other writings: Messianism of the two periods is found in the Apocalypse of Esdras, and the **617** Books of Enoch (which are not a literary unity) contain both transcendental and eschatological messianism. In the apocalyptic writings the fate of the heathen nations is treated with some uncertainty. At one time they are destroyed in the war which the Messiah (without any human aid or earthly power, but by the miraculous intervention of God) wages against them; at another, they are preserved through the messianic times, during which they war against the Messiah and the kingdom of God upon earth, to meet final judgement and destruction in the world-catastrophe of 'the end of days'. As a matter of fact the apocalyptic writers were much less interested in the fate of the nations than in the restoration of the kingdom of Israel.

The centre of the national hope was the messianic **e** kingdom, the 'kingdom of God'. In the OT Yahweh himself is king of Israel (cf Pss 93(92); 95(94)—100(99). The kingdom of God is identical with the Jewish kingdom, whether it be located on earth or in heaven. In Messianism of two periods and eschatological messianism the kingdom of God on earth is established in Palestine. The centre of the Messianic kingdom is Jerusalem, expanded in size and rebuilt with becoming magnificence. The whole face of the country is to be transformed in the messianic times. A semi-arid country, it will abound with streams of water and will be prodigiously fertile. Material felicity and the satisfaction of all sensible desires will prevail, and, with all the Gentile nations destroyed, universal peace will reign. But the kingdom is not exclusively of this material and national character. The establishment of the kingdom presupposes a moral renovation of the people; the wicked have no place in the kingdom. The worship of God will be carried out in the Temple with all solemnity, and the wealth of nations will be laid under contribution to serve his cult.

The Messiah—The Heb. word *māšîaḥ* (Gr. *christos*) **f** means 'anointed one'. This title is not applied to the expected deliverer in the OT (some exegetes think the word is applied to him in Dn 9:25). In the OT it is used of kings and priests, the sacredness of whose office was indicated by a rite of consecration in which anointing was used. In the books of Enoch and Esdras the Messiah is pre-existent in heaven before his appearance on earth; he is superhuman, occupying a position between God and man, but not identified with either; and he is endowed with transcendental properties. In the books of Enoch (where he is also called the Elect One) he appears suddenly and supernaturally in the glory of his triumph; but this view was not generally accepted in Judaism. The more traditional conception represented the Messiah as coming to war against the enemies of Israel, and to establish the kingdom of God on earth. In the Psalms of Solomon, which belong to the 1st cent. B.C., he is represented as a human king, a great warrior, who reigns over the restored kingdom of Israel in Palestine. There is an element of vagueness in the conception of the Messiah as king, in spite of the fact that the coming of the Messiah king is characteristic of the messianic hope in the OT, and is mentioned very often in the prayers of Judaism. He will reside in Jerusalem, govern his people, and give judgement in legal cases. But his work as an agent either of spiritual or of material blessings remains undefined. Bonsirven points out that he is not represented in extra-biblical Jewish literature as a miracle-worker. In rabbinical literature, unlike apocalyptic, the transcendental and superhuman qualities of the Messiah are suppressed, and his pure humanity is emphasized.

7g The idea of a suffering Messiah escaped Judaism entirely. It is not found in apocalyptic literature, and only a few allusions appear in the rabbinical writings. It is quite probable that the idea was suppressed as much as possible after the preaching of Christianity. The few allusions which exist are based on Is 53. But the reconciliation of the suffering servant of the Lord there described with the Messianic king was too difficult; and so we find the sufferings attributed to another Messiah, the son of Joseph. The Messianic king is the Messiah, the son of David, although he is once said to be the son of Levi, hence a priestly king. This idea probably arose as a consequence of the union of royal and sacerdotal dignity in the Hasmonaean dynasty.

This brief summary can do no more than indicate the wavering and uncertainty of Jewish ideas about the Messiah, who was sometimes human, sometimes superhuman, sometimes earthly and national, sometimes transcendental and universal. This vagueness in the mind of Judaism itself shows why the Messianism of the Gospels was proposed with such caution and reserve.

h **D. Eschatology**—Belief in retribution of divine justice for good and evil is basic in Jewish doctrine; and nothing did more to sustain the religion of Judaism through the centuries during which the national life was extinct and the Jews submitted to Gentile empires both at home and abroad. The concept of God exhibited in the OT and in Jewish belief was that of one who is not indifferent to right and wrong, but imposes his moral law on all men, who rewards its observance and punishes sin. But divine justice certainly is not manifest in this life; hence there must be a continuation of life beyond the grave, in which the good receive their reward and the wicked pay the penalty of their misdeeds. One of the most remarkable features of the OT is the almost complete absence of this doctrine in the pre-exilic books. Yet the few sketchy allusions to a future life which we find there do not permit us to conclude that the religion of the OT lacked any idea of eschatological retribution. When the doctrine reached a fuller development, it was based on that firm faith in divine justice which pervades the entire OT. It can be said with certainty that Judaism is not indebted to any foreign religion for its doctrine of retribution and the future life. Of all the ancient peoples, the conception of the after life was most completely developed by the Egyptians; but there is no trace in the OT, or in the literature of Judaism, of any Egyptian influence in this field of belief, although the Hebrews throughout their history were in contact with Egypt; cf Sutcliffe, *The OT and the Future Life*, London, 1947².

i It is difficult to disengage Jewish eschatological beliefs from the Messianic hope, since the establishment of the Messianic kingdom was the ultimate act of divine retributive justice; hence the present division is somewhat artificial. It may be justified, however, as a consideration of the individual destiny of the good and the wicked, while the Messianic faith is more concerned with the national destiny.

As indicated above, the 'days of the Messiah' follow the establishment of the Messianic kingdom on earth; they are, therefore, a transition between 'this world' and 'the world to come'. It is in the world to come that the just receive their full reward; the Rabbis say of certain sinners that they have no part in the world to come. But just as there is confusion concerning the earthly and the heavenly kingdom of God, so likewise there is uncertainty whether the recompense of the righteous begins with death or the resurrection. Where the earthly Messianic kingdom is emphasized it is obvious that the resurrection **617i** must precede any reward of the just.

The Judgement—The retribution is preceded by a **j** judgement of good and evil. The judgement on all mankind precedes the establishment of the Messianic kingdom. More generally God, and not the Messiah, is the judge. This conception of a general judgement is based on the 'Day of the Lord' in the prophetic books of the OT (e.g. Am 5:18ff). It is the principal act in all the Messianic-apocalyptic schemes, by which God defeats his enemies and vindicates his people; but there is no agreement on its precise place in the end-process. While it is a universal judgement, the apocalyptic literature treats it as a judgement of the wicked alone. The record of the righteous deeds of the good is kept in the book of life. The judgement, as already indicated, deals with nations as well as individuals; hence there is a confusion of national and ethical elements in the idea of the judgement. Judaism never arrived at the idea that men were weighed in the judgement purely on their ethical merits.

Life after Death—The ancient Heb. conception of the **k** nature of life after death was extremely vague at best. Hence, when the question was asked concerning the state of the just between death and the resurrection, which was to come at 'the end of days', it is not surprising that there was no certain answer. More generally, the just were thought to remain in a state of suspended animation. An exception to this is the Book of Wisdom (cf Wis 3:1ff). Outside of this book the ancient concept of Sheol survived in Judaism, at least as far as the intermediate state was concerned. Sheol was the receptacle of all the dead; it was a place of neither joy nor pain, but simply the negation of human life as it is known by experience. For the just, it is true, Judaism conceived it as a state of quiet repose; but the wicked were not really punished in Sheol, since their pains were reserved for the period following the general judgement. In the Books of Enoch we find four compartments in Sheol: for the just who died as martyrs, for the other just, for the sinners who were not punished on earth for their sins, and for the sinners who were punished on earth for their sins; these last do not rise. The Fourth Book of Esdras describes seven joys of the just and seven tortures of the wicked until judgement. The doctrine of the rabbinical writings was the most refined. Here the judgement takes place at death, and the just are rewarded immediately in heaven, or in Eden, the location of which is undefined.

The Resurrection of the Righteous—It is impossible **l** to state when belief in the resurrection of the dead arose in Judaism. Not all the apocalyptic writings contain this belief; and even in the NT period it was not universally accepted. Judaism never arrived at a consistent position on the universality of the resurrection. The righteous arise to share in the joys of the intermediate terrestrial kingdom; the place of their ultimate reward is uncertain. It is located in heaven, or in a supraterrestrial Paradise or Eden, or on the renovated earth, or in a terrestrial Eden. The eschatological Paradise is depicted after the manner of the primitive Paradise of Gn 2, with the tree of life and the waters of life. The reward of the just consists in eternal life, understood in the minimal sense: continuation of life in the body. This eternal life is free from pain; it is a life of quiet repose in the satisfaction of all sensible desires. According to some Rabbis, the bodies of the just will be endowed with colossal size in the resurrection. The risen just will be free from sin and perfect in all virtue. According to the

617l Rabbis, their chief joy will be the study of the Law. A hint of higher things is seen in the belief that the ultimate happiness of the just lies in communion with God. Some Rabbis distinguished seven degrees of the just (accommodated to the seven heavens); only the seventh and highest degree 'see God'. This conception is not that of the beatific vision in Christian theology.

m Punishment of Sinners—There is equal or greater divergence about the punishment of the wicked. Judaism wavers between annihilation or eternal punishment after the judgement, or limits eternal punishment to notorious sinners, such as apostate Jews or Gentile persecutors; or the wicked are believed to remain in Sheol. For those whose wickedness is less than supreme, there may be temporary punishment, followed by release or annihilation. The place of the punishment of the wicked is Gehenna (or Tophet). The former name (Heb. Gê-hin-nōm) belonged originally to the ravine SW of Jerusalem, which was regarded as accursed and defiled by the human sacrifice which had been offered there under the Hebrew monarchy. It was used, consequently, as a place to cast unclean refuse. There is much Haggadic speculation on the location and the dimensions of Gehenna. The chief torment of the wicked was fire; and Haggadic speculation never wearied of conceiving new tortures for the damned.

These details should not obscure the fact that there was in the ancient world no other belief which had the moral force of Jewish belief in divine retribution.

618a Jewish Morality—Jewish morality was erected on the firm basis of faith in the moral character and the retributive justice of God. There was no other religion of the ancient world which proposed a true religious basis for ethics. The religious motive of ethics in Judaism was based not only on reverential fear, but on the love of God, 'the first and greatest commandment of the Law'. The Law itself was the complete rule of conduct. The Law was imposed upon Israel as a part of the covenant; in return for the election of Israel as the people of God, the people undertook the obligations laid upon them in the Law. The emphasis which Judaism placed upon the Law as a rule of conduct induced a change in the conception of sin. In the prophetic literature sin is a personal offence against God, rebellion, adultery against the divine love; in Judaism sin is a legal transgression. These two conceptions are not mutually exclusive; it is a question of emphasis. The obstacle to right conduct was called in the rabbinical literature the yēṣer hā rā', the 'evil inclination'. By the Law this inclination was brought under control, which was at best imperfect.

Here, as elsewhere, only some of the more characteristic features of Jewish morality can be noticed.

b Social Relations—The Law commands the Jew to love his neighbour as himself. But the question of the scribe, Lk 10:29, 'Who is my neighbour?' was never answered by Judaism. Generally, the neighbour meant a fellow-Jew; Gentiles were not included in the obligations of justice and charity. Harsh as this statement may seem, it summarizes Jewish theory on social relations, as far as the theory was formulated; but the practice of Jews, especially in Gentile communities, did not correspond with the theory. To admit that Gentiles deserved the same consideration as Jews would have seemed to be a denial of the very covenant of election. Hence the rule of conduct was to abstain from social relations with Gentiles; friendships should be formed only within the Jewish community. The obligations of justice and charity were relaxed towards Gentiles, to a degree which was never determined exactly. One could take advantage of the error of a Gentile in a business transaction, or,

according to some authorities, deceive him. Lost articles, **61** or even stolen goods, need not be returned to their Gentile owners. Usury might be exacted from Gentiles. There was no obligation to protect them from death or injury, and no prohibition against taking vengeance upon them. No gift was to be made to them; and, in theory, salutations were not to be extended to them. The danger of 'profaning the name' (i.e. of bringing trouble against the Jewish community) was admitted as a reason for giving Gentiles equal treatment with Jews. These and similar determinations were largely—but not entirely—theoretical; in many instances Jews and Gentiles lived together in harmony.

An effect of the legal distinction between Jews and **c** Gentiles was a solidarity within the Jewish community which, apart from its exclusiveness, is one of the most pleasing features of Jewish morality. The Jew in need could count on the help of his Jewish neighbour, even at the cost of great inconvenience. Almsgiving was a sacred duty, much inculcated in the oral Law, and it was regarded as a highly meritorious means of expiating sin. The Jew was supposed to share in the joys and sorrows of his neighbours: to attend their family festivals, to grieve with them in a disaster or a bereavement, to visit the sick, to assist the imprisoned.

The treatment of slaves, both according to the Law and in practice, was far more humane than in any Gentile code. Ancient slavery was pure chattel slavery, and the owner was responsible to no one for the life of his slave. While the Law made a distinction between Jewish and Gentile slaves, the Jewish owner did not enjoy, even over his Gentile slaves, the right of life and death. The owner was forbidden to inflict any permanent injury, and such an injury would give the slave the right of freedom; but no punishment was enjoined if a slave died, through oversight, from severe treatment.

Family Morality—To the Jew marriage was the ful- **d** fillment of the concept, 'Increase and multiply', Gn 1:28. Children, as many as possible, were God's blessing upon a marriage; and it was a duty to procreate a large family. Consanguinity, impotence and difference of religion were impediments which prohibited marriage. Polygamy was permitted under the Law; but it seems that it was practised rarely in NT times, for economic reasons, if for no other; only the wealthy could afford a harem. And there are indications that monogamy was regarded as a higher ideal.

The position of the Jewish wife was, in general, **e** higher than that of the wife in Greco-Roman culture. The misogyny of the Talmud is so profound as to be amusing; but it is an indirect testimony to the freedom of women. In theory the wife was, under Jewish law, the property of her husband; but the prevailing practice of monogamy was a protection of her position, although she was in every respect absolutely dependent upon her husband. In theory, also, Jewish law was ruled by the double standard; unlawful intercourse was not regarded as adultery unless the woman was married. Divorce was permissible under the Law; but the scribes were divided on the meaning of the 'shameful thing' which is assigned in Dt 24:1 as a reason for divorce. The school of Shammai permitted divorce for adultery only; the school of Hillel is credited with the opinion that divorce was permissible if a wife cooked badly, or if the husband found another woman who pleased him more. Divorce was a privilege of the husband alone.

Children were bound very strictly to revere and **f** obey their parents, and to support them in their old

618f age. The power of the father was not unlimited, as in Roman law, which conferred on the father the dominion over life and death; but, according to the Law, rebellion or grave irreverence was a capital crime, to be decided by a court of law. Exposure of infants, especially female, which was so common in Hellenistic communities, did not occur among the Jews. The father controlled the marriage of his children through the law of the purchase of the bride.

Both in law and in practice Jewish family morality was immeasurably superior to the family morality of Hellenism. It kept the Jewish family together as a stable and tightly knit unit, in which the members supported one another, and the substantial obligations of parents and children were observed. The family was also a religious unit, in which common prayers were recited and the festivals celebrated. The family solidarity of the Jews must be reckoned among the reasons for the sturdy resistance of Judaism to assimilation.

g **Individual Morality**—Among the distinctive features of Jewish individual morality we may notice Jewish esteem of chastity, and Jewish esteem of wealth. It is fairly safe to say that chastity was nowhere esteemed in the Hellenistic world except among the Jews. With them an unmarried girl was supposed to be a virgin, and her seducer could be legally compelled to marry her or to pay the purchase price. A betrothed virgin or a wife was punished by death, according to the Law, for un chastity; and, while it is not certain that this penalty was usually inflicted, Judaism did esteem chastity as the crowning virtue of woman. The death penalty was laid upon the male accomplice also, if the woman were a betrothed virgin or a wife. A woman was either an unmarried virgin, and protected by the property rights of her father, or a wife, and subject to the property rights of her husband. Prostitution was strictly forbidden. The unnatural vice which so disfigured Hellenistic

h culture was forbidden by Jewish law. On the other side we have the esteem of wealth, which was regarded as a sign of God's blessing, poverty was a curse, and a probable sign of sin. In this connexion it is fair to notice that the average Palestinian Jew was extremely poor. In most employments he competed with slave labour; he had, as Canon Deane puts it, no margin, and was separated by not much more than one day's wages from

618h destitution; a minor disaster could reduce him and his family to slavery. In such circumstances, it is easy to understand that Judaism was somewhat loose in its standards of honesty, especially where Gentiles were concerned, and why it tolerated almost any way to turn a penny which was less than actual theft. One will scarcely find in extra-biblical Jewish literature a forthright condemnation of avarice. The wealthy aristocracy lived in opulence, and were envied and hated at the same time. The poor man could console himself with dreams of the Messianic kingdom, in which every man would be rich.

In summary, Judaism did impose upon its followers a standard of morality which was far above anything in the world of its times. The average Jew was by all known standards a good man and a religious man.

Jewish Piety—The sources for the religion of Judaism **i** do not offer us much information about the personal religion of the average Jew, 'the people of the land'. Yet the Law, the cult, and the doctrines of the rabbinical and apocalyptic writings do not tell the whole story. Jewish piety appears at its best in the prayers which have been preserved. From these it is evident that the Jew lived in close personal communion with God. God is addressed not only as creator and king, but also as father. He is solicitous for his creatures. Jewish prayer never omits the elements of adoration, praise, and thanksgiving for past mercies, and offers its petitions with full confidence that they will be heard. Judaism, as is evident from its Messianic aspect, is a religion of hope and confidence. Prayer occupied a very large part in the life of the Jew; the *Shema* and the *Shemōneh 'Esrê* (the 'eighteen benedictions') were to be recited daily; prayer was offered at meals and at the beginning of important activities. The Jew was not ashamed to pray in public, although the Pharisees carried external devotion to the point of mere display. The consciousness of sin and professions of repentance are never lacking; and there is firm confidence in the goodness and mercy of God. There is a strong sentiment of resignation to the will of God; the evils which come upon the people are the just punishment for their sins, and repentance will hasten the coming of the Messianic kingdom. Judaism is a religion of external observance; but it also fostered a genuine interior piety unique in its time.

Note. For a Bibliography of the Qumran documents the reader may consult C. Burchard, *Bibliographie zu den Handschriften vom Toten Meer*, BZAW, n. 76, 57–65, n. 89, 1–359 (to end of 1962).

THE PAGAN WORLD IN NEW TESTAMENT TIMES

BY W. REES

619a Bibliography—General: J. P. V. D. Balsdon, 'The Roman Empire in the First Century', PC(2); C. N. Cochrane, *Christianity and Classical Culture*, 1944; J. Felten, *Ntliche Zeitgeschichte, oder Judentum und Heidentum zur Zeit Christi und der Apostel*, 2 vol., Regensburg, 1910; A. J. Festugière and P. Fabre, *Le monde gréco-romain au temps de Notre-Seigneur*, t. I, *Le cadre temporel*, t. II, *Le milieu spirituel*, 1935; T. R. Glover, *The Ancient World* 1935; R. Livingstone, *The Legacy of Greece* 1922; R. H. Pfeiffer, *History of NT Times* 1949; M. Rostovtzeff, *Social and Economic History of the Roman Empire* 1957[2]; E. T. Salmon, *A History of the Roman World from 30 B.C. to A.D. 138*, 1937[3]; J. E. Sandys, *A Companion to Latin Studies* 1935[3]; A. N. Sherwin-White, *Roman Society and Roman Law in the NT*, Oxford 1963; L. Whibley, *A Companion to Greek Studies* 1931[4]; **Government:** CAH vol. x, 1934, vol. xi, 1936; H. Grose Hodge, *Roman Panorama*, 1944; G. H. Stevenson, *Roman Provincial Administration* 1939; **Religion:** L. R. Farnell, *An Outline History of Greek Religion* 1921; A. J. Festugière, *Personal Religion among the Greeks* 1954; A. J. Festugière and P. Fabre, as above, t. II; W. Warde Fowler, *The Religious Experience of the Roman People* 1911; see also §§ 628–32; **Morality:** P. Benoit, 'Sénèque et S. Paul', *Exégèse et Théologie*, t. II 1961; E. R. Bevan, *Stoics and Sceptics* 1913; Epictetus's *Discourses* (various E.trs *e.g.* Carter in Everyman's Lib.); **Habits and Customs:** Friedländer, *Roman Life and Manners* (4 vols., 1908–13); J. Carcopino, *Daily Life in Ancient Rome*, E.tr. 1956; Merrill C. Tenney, *NT Times*, 1965.

INTRODUCTION

b The Hellenization of the East—We must first recall some facts of history. Civilization appeared in the East some time before 3000 B.C., but it was not till after 1000 B.C. that the first whole nation of Europeans, the *Greeks*, became civilized. They had learnt much from the East, but they soon surpassed their teachers and made some important innovations (widespread education, democratic government, etc) which the East had never known. Soon after 500 B.C. the *Persians* marshalled all the strength of the East to conquer Europe. The small Greek states, inspired by Athens, utterly defeated them. From that time onwards the E nations in deed though not always in words recognized the Greeks as the foremost nation in the world. Europe had overtaken and outstripped the East. In the next cent. the Greeks under *Alexander the Great* conquered the Persians and founded an empire stretching from Egypt to India. It soon broke up into several portions, but Greek kings maintained themselves in Egypt, Syria and Asia Minor, and proceeded to plant their European culture among the ancient nations of these lands. A Greek ruling class established itself all round the E Mediterranean. New Greek cities arose, and the Greek language, Greek manners and ideas, went on spreading for centuries till all the educated class **619** was Greek in culture, though no longer, for the most part, of Greek blood.

Roman Intervention—But the Greek states proved **c** unequal to the task they had undertaken, the Europeanization of the Near East. They decayed and their work was in danger of perishing, when a stronger power came to the rescue. This was Rome. The Romans were the second nation in Europe to become civilized. It was to Greece, to Athens especially, that they owed their civilization. They adopted the Greek culture in all its fullness in the 2nd cent. B.C., and in the next century they undertook the direct government of the E Mediterranean lands. As soldiers, statesmen and lawyers they had valuable gifts denied to the Greeks, and under their patient supervision Greek civilization was at last solidly established in these lands. The process was more than half completed in the times of the NT. A similar process is at present taking place in these countries, but today the work is only beginning: in our Lord's time it was far advanced. These countries, including Palestine, were far more European then than they are now. Only the Jewish religion had not been submerged by the flood from the west.

The Strata of Society—There are therefore three things **d** to be distinguished in these countries: first, the national characteristics of the native races (Phrygians, Syrians, Egyptians, etc); secondly, the Greek culture and language which were being overlaid on these; thirdly, the Roman government which was using its influence to promote the Greek penetration. Society was therefore complicated and changing: the old and Asiatic was everywhere losing ground before the new and European. In country districts the lower classes—small farmers, labourers and slaves—lived much as their ancestors had lived a thousand years before, spoke the Egyptian or Lydian or other language, kept up many old customs and worships, and no doubt resented both Greek fashions and Roman rule. Their gentry and middle class had adopted Greek ways and the Greek language, and regarded themselves as Greeks. They were estranged from their own uneducated countrymen, whom they looked down upon as practically a different and inferior nation, and though they did not welcome Roman rule they felt nearer to the Romans than to the mass of their own backward countrymen. In all towns of any size Greek was the official language and all the townspeople had at least a smattering of it. At the top of the social scale stood the Romans—that is, the Italian or half-Italian officials, officers, merchants and visitors. Their status as members of the ruling race caused them to be treated with a special respect, and they themselves, though men of very varying merits and culture, were apt to assume an air of superiority over even the choicest spirits among the subject races.

The E Mediterranean world was therefore a complex world: a foundation of many races, some decadent and some backward, a civilization derived from Greece,

9d and a Roman political framework into which all was being fitted.

GOVERNMENT

20a **Roman National Tradition and its Expansion**—The national character of the Romans was narrower and duller than that of the Greeks, but surpassed it in some valuable qualities, the so-called civic virtues, the qualities that make a good citizen—industry, shrewdness and dexterity, thrift, everyday honesty, fidelity to promises, attachment to home and country and courage to defend them, obedience to law and authority, dislike of change and novelties, respect for the rights and possessions of others, and firmness in vindicating one's own. Such a character is not showy, but it wears well and can endure storms. The faults to which it is liable are narrowness, rigorism, arrogance, callousness, avarice, coarseness and intemperance—faults which are all too common in Roman history. Yet this was the character which had made the Roman state the strongest that the world had yet seen.

b This national character or tradition did not spring from the blood but was hammered out slowly under the pressure of circumstances, or rather, of Providence. It was already formed by 300 B.C. within the small Roman state. It became in a century or two the character of an Italian nation, a compound of many races among which the Romans were only one. By the Christian era the descendants of the original Romans were degenerate, but the tradition was still vigorous and still expanding. Its chief representatives were now the people of the Italian country towns. In the 1st cent. A.D., it took hold of the leading men in the adjacent lands, especially France and Spain. Few of them had a drop of Roman or Italian blood, but henceforth when we speak of Romans we mean chiefly these men. They had a right to the name for they carried on the great tradition of civic virtues and public service.

c **Autocracy and Emperor-worship**—The Roman Empire, the mighty state established by the Romans, now encircled the Mediterranean and had lately been advanced northwards to the Rhine and Danube. Shortly before the birth of Christ, its government had become an autocracy. It was the form of government which both Greeks and Romans of an earlier age, when they lived in small democratic or aristocratic states, had hated with a fanatical hatred. But autocracy was considered the only practicable government for a large state—it was reserved for the English to solve that problem by means of representative assemblies. So first the Greeks, and now the Romans also, had to submit to despotism. Hatred of it continued long among the educated of both peoples, kept alive by their earlier literature, especially the oratory, which was the chief study of young men of the wealthier classes. To soothe them, the despots kept much of the language and forms of republican days; the Roman monarch was not called King, but only First Citizen and Commander-in-chief. The mass of the population, however, both in Italy and elsewhere, felt little discontent. They were not sufficiently educated to make painful comparisons between the present and the past, and they enjoyed more material comfort than they had in republican times.

d The power of the Roman emperors (as we now call them) depended on their control of the armed forces, not on hereditary title or on election. The army alone could oppose or dethrone the emperor, and with its support he could defy the opinions and wishes of civilians. Over them his power remained absolute, and neither custom nor **620d** law ever placed any effective limit on it. The reigns of the bad emperors present a hideous picture of tyranny and servility. The ancient senate or council of nobles still remained. It was not hereditary, but consisted of those who had held the chief offices of state. To be a senator was the highest ambition of a public man, but the senate seldom dared to disagree with the emperor.

In the E provinces of the empire it had long been **e** the custom to treat kings as gods, to offer sacrifices and incense to their statues, and to build temples to them. These E countries now paid the same honours to the emperors. The earlier emperors repudiated any claim to divinity and forbade such worship in the west (Suetonius, *Aug.* 52, Tac. *Ann.* 4, 37), but they tolerated it in the E, and in time it inevitably spread and came to be regarded as a political necessity. To refuse to worship the emperor was considered disrespectful, disloyal, and therefore treasonable. It became a capital crime.

The Central Government and the Provinces—Italy **f** and to a lesser degree Egypt (on which Italy depended for corn) came directly under the emperor's control, and so did a great deal of the finances and military supervision throughout the empire. These many calls upon him led to the growth of an enormous bureaucracy. It consisted of men who owed everything to the emperor, his own slaves and freedmen (i.e. liberated slaves) or men of humble origin whom he had advanced and enriched. Under some weak or suspicious emperors freedmen became millionaires and in effect prime ministers of the empire. The empire, apart from Italy, was divided into thirty or forty provinces. Each province had its governor who was appointed by the emperor or through his influence, and usually held his post for a period of one to three years. The bigger provinces were governed by senators, the smaller ones, like Judaea, by men of the next highest class, the 'Roman knights' In this way men who had lived in the servile atmosphere of Roman society and scarcely knew what freedom meant, found themselves for a short time raised to the position of despots. Not a few, as we should expect, succumbed to the temptations of power, and ruled as tyrants. While they were in office, there was no remedy except rebellion. After their departure their subjects could accuse them to the emperor. Under a just or a jealous emperor we may believe that provincial government was tolerable, but even under Augustus there were some scandalous cases (Velleius II, 117, Seneca, *De Ira* II, 5).

The Mission of Rome and the Growth of Roman **621a** **Law**—The establishment of Roman autocracy came after a miserable sixty years of misgovernment and civil war. Autocracy brought the blessings of peace, order, and security, blessings which hardly anybody then living had experienced before. We cannot wonder that many Romans were more inclined to welcome these blessings than to repine at the loss of the old constitutional government. They found consolation in the thought that Fate had given supreme power to Rome not for the sake of the Romans only, but also of the many nations that Rome now governed. This glorious destiny seemed both to justify and compensate for the sacrifice of liberty. Rome had been divinely chosen to give peace, unity, and order to the world. The truth of this belief is beyond any doubt and appears much more clearly to us than to the Romans of Christ's time: Rome was God's instrument first for the civilization of Europe, then for its Christianization, as the breaking down of frontiers all round the Mediterranean made the spread of the Gospel immensely easier. 'Thou hast given a single home

621a and country to the separated nations of the earth. What was once a world, thou hast made into a city'. So a later poet described it. We must not on that account shut our eyes to Rome's faults: Assyria and Babylonia were also God's instruments, as we are expressly told by the very prophets who denounce their sins and foretell their punishment.

b The deep desire of the world for peace and the lofty conviction of the mission of Rome were most finely expressed by the Roman poet Virgil who died about fifteen years before our Lord's birth. Other nations, he says, could outshine the Romans as artists and men of science, but Rome is divinely called and specially endowed to rule the world and to maintain peace and just government in it. It was a noble hope, a glorious ideal, only imperfectly realized, but the very proclamation of the ideal by Virgil and others no doubt inspired many a Roman and many a Roman-minded Spaniard or Greek to labour for its fulfilment.

c The Roman mind was conservative yet progressive, that type of mind which almost refuses to admit that anything ought ever to be changed, yet does in fact carry out revolutions which are the most radical and permanent, because they are the most gradual, careful, and detailed. Thus the Roman lawyers professed to remain faithful to their ancient code drawn up in the 5th cent. B.C., and declared their dislike of all abstract moral or political principles such as those of the Greek philosophers. But by a gradual process they embodied in their own law a more complete application of these very principles (especially those of the Stoic philosophy) than any Greek state had ever done. It was the Roman who could grasp at once the broad principle and the mass of prosaic and tedious detail, and who combined an endless patience and willingness to compromise with a tenacity of purpose which persisted from cent. to cent. However, it was not until A.D. 212 that Roman Law became the law applicable to all the free population of the empire, who then all became Roman citizens.

d **Distinction between Roman Citizens and Provincials**—We know that the Roman citizens numbered about five millions in the time of Christ (*Res Gestae D. Aug.*, 8) while the whole population of the empire may have been anything from fifty to a hundred millions or even more, about equally divided between slaves and free men. Throughout the provinces there was a sharp distinction drawn between citizens and non-citizens or 'provincials' as they are usually called. Roman citizens were privileged both by custom and by law. Firstly, whether they were Italians or not, they shared in the respect, influence and social importance which naturally go to members of a ruling class. Secondly, they alone were within the sphere of Roman civil law, while the provincials were allowed on the whole to keep the laws or customs which they had before the Roman conquest. But in their relations with the provincials the Roman governors still retained not a little of their original character of military commanders of conquered territory. They had a summary jurisdiction of such a wide kind over both their property and their lives as almost to justify us in saying that the provincials lived under perpetual martial law. Any action which was construed as being directed against the government could be punished with extreme penalties (crucifixion, enslavement, exile, confiscation, flogging, etc) at the governor's

e discretion and without appeal. It was this power, the so-called *coercitio*, that was used in the case of many Christian martyrs. Every government must be armed with some such power in time of grave emergency, but its mere retention (even if infrequently used) through 62 long periods of peace and security seems utterly contrary to the best traditions of European states, ancient or modern; and we have no proof that its use by Roman governors was very infrequent. From this dangerous power the Roman citizen was largely protected: he must be dealt with according to much more detailed and well-defined laws, and on a capital charge he could appeal to the emperor's court. The Roman franchise was rarely bestowed on whole districts, but it was often given to individuals for some public service or eminent merit, to the original citizens of the Coloniae (see § 622g) and to every soldier enrolled in the legions (i.e. heavy infantry).

Roman Taxes—Various taxes were paid to the Roman 62: government. *Tributum* was the general name for direct taxes, which were paid in one form or another by all provincials over the age of fourteen, but not by Roman citizens. In some cases it took the form of income-tax (about 10%), in others it was a property-tax (about 10% of the annual value), and in Egypt it was a poll-tax of apparently moderate amount. The chief indirect taxes, paid both by citizens and provincials, were: (1) Customs duties, usually from 2% to 5% of the value of goods, levied not only on the empire frontiers but also on the boundaries of the eight or nine large customs-areas into which the empire was divided. (2) An excise of 1% on goods sold by auction and of 4% on the sale of slaves. (3) A legacy duty of 5%, not paid by near relatives or on small legacies. (4) A tax of 5% on the value of a slave emancipated by his owner. For the purpose of assessing the *tributum* a census of all the provinces was taken every fourteen years.

These taxes are light in comparison with those we b pay. If they ever did become burdensome under the empire, as they had sometimes been under the republic, it was due to abuse of the method of collecting, or to some local causes. For the *tributum* each district was assessed at a certain sum, and the local authorities were left to collect this in their own way and by means of their own servants. The indirect taxes in each area were leased out to a firm or firms of (generally Italian) financiers, who undertook to pay a certain sum into the treasury and collected the taxes through their employees or slaves. These **tax-farmers** were the *publicani* in the proper sense, but the word came to be loosely applied to the actual collectors employed by them or by others. These indirect methods of collection no doubt saved trouble to the government, but they placed temptations in the way of both municipalities and tax-farmers. The central government probably kept a sharp eye on the intermediaries, for we hear little about rapacious taxation. We hear more complaints about the governor's right of requisition, i.e. compulsory purchase or hire of anything (including labour) needed for the administrative staff or the forces.

The Roman Army—The empire had a standing army of c at least 250,000 men. About three-quarters of these were stationed on the most vital frontiers, the Rhine, the Danube, and Syria. The forces were everywhere divided about equally into legions and auxiliaries. A legion consisted of about 5,000 men, who were all Roman citizens. They were infantry carrying considerable armour (helmet, breastplate, greaves, and shield) and furnished with a short sword and two six-foot spears (*pila*), used mainly for throwing. They served for twenty years and were provided with a livelihood afterwards. The auxiliaries consisted of cavalry, archers, slingers, etc, divided into units of 500 or 1,000 men. They were not Roman citizens as a rule. Lastly, there were the emperor's

22c guards, 10,000 or more in number, housed in barracks in the suburbs of Rome.

d The Roman army had once been a citizen-army raised by general conscription. It was now a professional army, and the majority of its men were no longer of Italian blood. The power of conscription was always retained, but in ordinary times it was never enforced in Italy, and probably very seldom in the provinces, for enough volunteers seem to have been forthcoming to fill the ranks. No doubt most of the officers were still of Italian origin, and Roman discipline and training were maintained in all their sternness and efficiency. But the ordinary soldier's chief loyalty was not to Rome but to the person of the emperor, or to his own legion or commander. A short period of military service was still essential for every man who wished to hold high office at Rome, but the vast majority of men had no experience of it. Peace and security had made it possible for a great state to free the bulk of its population from military service—probably for the first time in the history of the world.

e The Romans had now no maritime enemies, but some naval squadrons were kept up, mainly as a protection against pirates. They were based on about six ports, including Alexandria, and Seleucia, the port of Antioch.

f Municipal Government and Coloniae—Municipal government was a shadow of the bygone city state. But owing to Roman influence the democratic elements in the city constitution had vanished, even in Greek lands. The civic officials were chosen not by popular vote but by the city council, of which they then became members for life. The officials were not only unpaid but were required and often compelled, by express promises in advance, to contribute substantially to various public expenses, the construction or repair of public buildings, the cost of festivals and amusements, etc. Half the money which nowadays would be raised by rates came out of the pockets of the city officials. Only the wealthy therefore could hold such offices, and each municipality was in fact a plutocracy. The poorer citizens took the comforts provided for them and were apparently contented, or at least resigned.

g Scattered throughout the provinces were towns called *coloniae*—towns founded fairly recently by the Roman government, many as homes for soldiers discharged after the wars of the cent. before Christ. In theory they were small fragments of Italy: the original settlers were all Roman citizens, only Roman law was valid, the official language was Latin, and the town was to some extent outside the sphere of the provincial governor. Later on we find the descendants of the first citizens forming a privileged class amidst a mixed population of non-citizens, and clinging proudly to Latin tradition or sentiment. St Paul visited several of these towns: Pisidian Antioch, Philippi and Corinth were among them.

h Merits and Demerits of the Roman Empire—The Romans gave several centuries of unprecedented peace to all the countries round the Mediterranean; they found south-western Europe a semi-barbarous land and raised it to civilization; they were the first imperial race who made any attempt to consider the welfare of their subjects, and they ultimately raised these subjects to the same level as the rulers; they worked out an unsurpassed code of civilized law; and they unconsciously smoothed the way for the spread of Christianity. On the opposite side of the account we have to admit that there were five centuries of autocratic government, alien to the earlier traditions of civilized Europeans; that methods of government were brutal and inhuman as compared with the previous usages

of both Romans and Greeks; that the evils of a plutocratic **622h** society were present—extreme contrasts of riches and poverty, and the steady vulgarization of the higher classes.

RELIGION

Ancient paganism was not one in teaching and organ- **623a** ization, as Catholicism is, nor was it made up of exclusive and independent sects, as was earlier Protestantism. It was a great jumble of many worships and doctrines, base and noble, crude and refined, competing yet seldom persecuting, continually borrowing from one another yet distinguishable. Modern Hinduism is just such another jumble. We must first look at the chief ingredients which went into the mixture. There were six of these: the four chief national religions of the Mediterranean world (those of Egypt, Syria, Greece and Rome), the Mysteries, and lastly Greek philosophy.

Egyptian Religion—The religion of Egypt was the most **b** ancient of the pagan religions. At its highest level it had taught the immortality of the soul and a judgement after death, and it had exalted one supreme god (the sun-god Ra) so greatly as to approach to monotheism. But these wholesome elements were embedded in a mass of gross or trivial superstition—animal worship, endless magical formulae, etc. Under Greek influence some attempt was made to detach them, and two divinities, Isis and Serapis, became well known as far west as Italy. Their worship encouraged the expectation of a future life and included some ascetical and perhaps moral preparation for that life.

Syrian Religion—The religion of the Syrians and **c** Phoenicians, the paganism against which the Jewish prophets had fought, was the lowest of the great national religions. But it still survived in Syrian villages, and colonists had carried it to Cyprus, Tunisia and Sicily. It was a religion which exploited human fear, lust, and ferocity, and it is hard to discover any good side to it. In the past at least it had encouraged human sacrifices, and perhaps infants were still sometimes burnt in honour of Moloch. It still continued to promote and consecrate the foulest immorality, and its temples still had their sacred prostitutes.

The primitive religions of Asia Minor are little **d** known to us. They seem to have resembled that of Syria in many respects. The chief divinity was a goddess worshipped under many names. In Egypt, Syria and Asia Minor the most famous temples had in the course of ages acquired immense riches—vast estates and thousands of slaves. Guarded by popular veneration, these great possessions had survived and even increased amidst all the political changes. By the time of Christ the head-priests who governed them had come to rank as great noblemen in Egypt and as semi-independent princes in Syria and Asia Minor.

Greek Religion—The Aryan tribes who conquered **e** Greece and Italy in the Bronze Age introduced their ancestral religion into both countries and gave it the most honourable position there. It was a religion of many gods or spirits, who seem to have been associated with some natural object or with some portion of man's life (birth, marriage, harvest, war, etc). Above them all was the supreme god, the sky-god Deus or Dius. This 'Aryan religion' had a very different history in the two countries. In Italy it was added to rather than changed, but in Greece changes came rapidly. Various gods and religious practices which the Gr. invaders found in the country were accepted

623e into the religion of the conquerors, and the result was complete polytheism: the sky-god, Zeus, still retained a nominal presidency, but seven or eight other divinities held a position almost of equality, and we may believe that for each district its own chief local god quite overshadowed Zeus. There was a general belief in a life after death, but it was imagined as a vague shadow of this life. There was a rough moral code, for the gods rewarded courage, honesty

f and hard work. But while the intellect and the moral sense had as yet made no progress among these early Greeks, their imagination was awake and soon reached an astonishing degree of poetical refinement. Countless stories were made up, in which the gods appear as essentially human figures, more powerful, dignified or graceful than the common run of men, but neither better nor wiser. Imagination often proved stronger than

g reverence. This stage of Gr. religion would very likely have been outgrown and forgotten in time if a supreme poet, *Homer*, had not embodied a multitude of these stories in his two great epic poems, some time between 950 and 750 B.C., and by so doing made them immortal. He had no idea of being a religious teacher, but in fact he became the most compelling religious teacher that the Greeks ever had. The fascination of his poetry bound them fast to his earth-born gods for a thousand years and frustrated all the efforts of religious reformers. The whole notion of the Divine was lowered, and the vital distinction between the Divine and the human, so easy even to the ignorant among us, remained blurred to

h the majority of Greeks. Homer often tells of gods disguised as men, and often of semi-divine beings ('*heroes*'), the offspring of a divine and a human parent. Many families claimed to have a god among their ancestors. There were many cases too in Gr. history of distinguished men who after their death were worshipped as gods or demi-gods. *Alexander the Great* was persuaded by his courtiers that none but a god could have begotten him, and he claimed and received divine worship during his lifetime. It soon became the custom in Asia and Egypt to treat kings and even governors as gods. In consequence of all this, all kinds of ideas about a fusion or union of the divine and human, about incarnate gods and deified men, were trite and commonplace to the Greek mind. It was only to the Jew, with his much loftier and truer notion of the Divine, that such an idea was a startling novelty.

Later movements shook, though they could not overturn, the Homeric theology. There are two of these which need special description, the Mysteries and Greek philosophy.

The Mysteries—On these, see §§ 628–32.

i Greek Philosophy—In the 6th cent. B.C. a new kind of wisdom was heard of among the Greeks, a genuine invention of their own, and a startling one. Certain Greeks of Asia Minor put forward theories which attempted to explain the origin of the world in terms of mere matter without reference to any divine power whatsoever. They were materialists and practically atheists. This was the unpromising beginning of Greek philosophy and this materialism continued for centuries as *one* of the strands in it. But other theories, idealistic and even mystical, soon appeared. Here we can only mention Pythagoras (about 530 B.C.). He was influenced by the Mysteries, but introduced some doctrines apparently new to Greece, especially the notion that the soul was destined to inhabit a succession of bodies, some human and some animal. This was bound up with the view (derived perhaps from India) that matter was essentially evil and that the union of soul and body was a calamity

or punishment. Pythagoras organized his disciples into **623i** semi-monastic societies, which lasted for a century or two.

A new chapter begins about 430 B.C. with the **j** appearance of Socrates the Athenian. He wrote nothing and some branches of his teaching are uncertain, but he was the greatest personality in the whole story of ancient philosophy. An unwearied searcher for truth and a devastating critic, deeply religious, immensely interested in the practical implications of philosophy, possessing at once the zeal of a lonely prophet and the exquisite sympathy, urbanity and humour of a perfect man of the world, he made an indelible impression on the ancient world both by his life and by his death—he was executed on the charge of impiety. He and his great pupil Plato were much impressed by the Mysteries and by the teaching of Pythagoras, and helped by these they reached a belief in one God and in a perfect spiritual world, and worked out a higher moral code than the Greek world had yet known. They did not reject the old Greek religion, but had hopes of purifying and reforming it. They failed: their arguments and their eloquence could not induce the masses to give up the Homeric theology. Few other thinkers even attempted such a reform. When we come to the next great philosopher, Aristotle, who lived during the middle of the 4th cent. B.C., we can see that philosophy and religion are parting company: he attempted, independently of religion, to erect a theology and morality on sound rational foundations, and produced the firmest system of pure philosophy which the ancient world knew, the system which the great Catholic thinkers of the Middle Ages were able to adapt to Christian truth. Two other philosophies arose which had the widest influence of all in Roman times—Stoicism and Epicureanism (see § 625c–f).

Thenceforth philosophy and religion went their **k** separate ways without an open quarrel. Men who desired an intellectual basis for their beliefs and a more enlightened morality lost interest in religion. They paid outward respect to it, they regarded it as good and necessary for the ignorant and unintellectual, but they themselves drew all their inspiration from some philosophy. In the 2nd cent. B.C. it seemed that before long even the ignorant would cease to care for religion and that it would disappear altogether. Two or three generations however before the birth of Christ the tide began to turn. Educated society, especially in Italy, was frightened at the prospect of a godless populace and a general dissolution of all religious scruples. A revival of paganism, based more on policy than on conviction, had definitely begun when our Lord was born, and continued steadily for two or three centuries, gathering more and more sincerity as it went on. The Roman government did all in its power to promote it. But the cleavage between religion and morality still remained serious at the time of the Apostles.

Roman Religion—The 'Aryan religion' which the Italic **l** race had brought into Italy (see § 623e) had received considerable additions at an early date from Etruscan sources and the mixture which resulted formed the early Roman religion—a polytheism like the Homeric religion, but the Italians had not the vivid imagination which created the Greek mythology. If there ever were any Italian stories about Jupiter, Juno or Vesta, they disappeared without leaving a trace. There was an elaborate ceremonial, and a special veneration for many very primitive divinities such as Saturnus the patron spirit of sowing, Ceres who presided over harvest, Vesta the protectress of the hearth, and for a multitude of others, and the ancient

231 sky-god of the Aryans still remained at the head of the pantheon under the name of Jupiter. With a few additions from Greece and elsewhere, this religion remained the official religion of the Roman state, respected even by non-Romans for its close connexions with Roman public life, and with the mighty power of Rome.

m There was the same rough moral code that we find in early Greek religion. Long before Christ the Romans had identified each of the greater Greek gods with some Roman god and in this way had grafted on their own religion the whole Homeric mythology with all its imaginative appeal and also all its disadvantages. Its connexion with the state kept the Roman religion alive in Italy and gave it an honourable position in the Latin provinces of the W, but Greek, Egyptian and Asiatic cults were now competing with it in Italy and ultimately all gained a firm foothold there. For emperor-worship see § 620e.

24a **The Resulting Confusion. Moral Standards**—Such were the chief materials which were joined together to form the patchwork of 'pagan religion'. Every conceivable mixture of them was to be found in the same family or even in the same mind. One member of a family might frequent the ancient temples of Jupiter or Poseidon, another might put all his hopes in one of the Mysteries, a third might care only for Isis, and a fourth might be a Stoic and look with tolerant superiority on all the rest. Or again the same person might successively, or even simultaneously, try to drink from all these fountains. There was no definite moral standard associated with religion in general or with any one religion. The most diverse moral levels could claim to be equally pious and devout. We find pagans who attain to a serene and refined piety which might almost remind us of a Victorian parsonage, and we find others who can still call themselves devout though sunk in superstition or lust. There is a similar contrast in Hinduism between the austere mystical Brahmin and his grosser co-religionists.

b There were other grave weaknesses: there was no controlling authority either in teaching or government, no organization, hardly what can be called a clergy, and no theology.

c **Authority, Theology**—In Egypt and in Rome some sort of central authority had once existed, but had long ceased to operate. The religious authority of the emperor as head of the Roman state-religion was exercised occasionally, but only to protect Italy from un-Roman devotions. As a rule every temple was independent and secure from all interference except when the civil power intervened to repress disorder. No pagan denied the right of the state to interfere in religion, and the worship of the emperor also implied an acknowledgement of such a right. Yet if we call the emperor the head of the pagan religion, he was a head that rarely governed.

d In Egypt, Syria and Asia Minor we find a large body of professional clergy—priests whose priestly office was the main business of their lives. Even in Egypt they seem to have counted for little as a spiritual force, and elsewhere for even less. Among the Greeks and the Romans the majority of the priests were not professional: they had secular work to do, more urgent and exacting than their sacred duties. Their priesthood was a side-occupation, which might add dignity to a public career or provide a graceful occupation for old age. In such circumstances little special training or knowledge would be necessary or possible. With such a clergy and with the severance between religion and philosophy, it is natural that no body of pagan theology ever grew up. The appeal of religion was to the senses, imagination and emotions: it provided hardly anything to satisfy the intellect or win the heart of a thinking man, hardly any rational foundation for faith and devotion, or incentive to holiness. There was an intellectual and spiritual 624d mediocrity about the pagan religion. In its whole history e it did not produce one great spiritual book comparable to the best which Mohammedanism or Hinduism have to show. Those which come nearest (the works of Plato, Epictetus, Marcus Aurelius, Plotinus) are essentially philosophical works pathetically trying to catch the spirit of religion. We cannot therefore class ancient paganism among the great non-Christian religions of the world.

Let us glance at some of the externals of paganism: f **Temples**—By far the commonest type throughout the empire was that evolved by the Greeks of the 5th cent. B.C.—the oblong building of white marble or light-coloured stone, with low-pitched roof supported on every side by pillars. Its wide prevalence even in alien lands far away from Greece is a remarkable proof of the power of Greek artistic tradition, for it embodied the most characteristic qualities of this tradition—an infinitely delicate sense of proportion and harmony, and an extraordinary self-restraint. Other peoples have perhaps had as deep a feeling for beauty, and have expressed it as finely in their architecture, but in *this* style the Greeks have had no equals. A Gothic cathedral would no doubt have shocked them as something florid and riotous. In the same way if we, nursed in our very different traditions, were to come upon a well-preserved temple in the midst of a Greek city (not a picturesque and famous ruin in the wilderness) our first feeling might well be that the building was tame and plain. Time and effort would be needed to appreciate its beauty.

The temple was regarded as a house for the god, not g for his worshippers, and therefore the interior (usually one chamber, the *cella*) was not on the same scale as that of our churches. One of the very largest interiors, that of the temple of Artemis at Ephesus, was 145 feet by 65. In the *cella* stood the chief statue of the god. It was frequently of a large or even colossal size—that of Athena in the Parthenon at Athens is said to have been forty feet high including its pedestal. In some of the bigger temples the *cella* seems to have been wholly or partly open to the sky—in other cases the light must have come mainly from the open door. The *cella* was often adorned with other sculpture, with votive offerings or with paintings. The altar stood in the open air before the entrance. It was on the open space before the temple, not inside it, that crowds gathered at festivals.

Statues of the Gods—Greek tradition aimed at depict- h ing the gods as beautiful or noble *human* figures, and the great sculptors had carved some of their masterpieces to be erected in temples. But some lewd or bestial forms remained even among the Greeks, and many nightmare shapes continued to inhabit the temples of Egypt and Asia. What degree of idolatry was there—how far did the pagan believe that the statue was the god? We i may be sure that hardly any educated man held such a belief. The making of divine images was carried on quite openly, and every god had many images. An educated man could not believe that Apollo, for example, was identical with some one statue, or that he somehow inhabited or animated a thousand statues. But no doubt some such beliefs did survive among the uneducated masses, especially in the more backward countries. Against these latter pagans the denunciations of the OT writers were still valid.

Sacrifices—Sacrifice was a constant part of pagan j

789

624j worship. Animals of various kinds, cakes, meal, fruit, wine, milk, honey and flowers were among the things offered to the gods. Some gods did not receive animal sacrifices. Many of the things offered were either destroyed in the ceremony (the wine poured out, etc) or became the property of the temple authorities and were consumed or sold by them. But an animal, after a portion had been burnt on the altar, was usually eaten by the worshipper and his friends at the temple or near it, and so a sacrifice would normally lead to a dinner. In the same way great public sacrifices often involved public dinners. These public sacrifices were often accompanied by elaborate ritual, with rich vestments, incense, chants and musical instruments. Greek sacred choral music had once reached a high artistic level, but it is doubtful whether these masterpieces were often heard now. Greek tradition scarcely regarded any religious festival as complete without a series of athletic contests, but this association of religion and athletics never became popular in the W. The Greeks also were very fond of religious processions which often walked surprising distances.

k **Prophecy and Oracles**—Some temples had a reputation for curing diseases, and drew many pilgrims on that account. But many more pilgrims travelled to the numerous shrines which claimed prophetic inspiration, i.e. an oracle of some sort. Oracles were found in abundance both in E and W. Delphi was the most celebrated in Greek lands; one of the most frequented in the W was the great temple of Fortuna at Praeneste close to Rome. Many methods were used: trance-talk, dreams, lots, interpretation of sounds animate or inanimate, etc. Some oracles seem to have regularly used fraud or equivocation, but as a rule there was nothing worse than ignorance and superstition.

l Prophecies and omens meet us everywhere in ancient paganism. Whenever an animal was sacrificed, its internal organs were examined for omens, and even the sober Roman religion used an elaborate system of divination from the flight of birds. The higher religions have generally tried to repress man's foolish belief that he can peer into the future. The blind guides of ancient paganism shared this belief, no doubt. They certainly encouraged and exploited it. (See Dill: *Roman Society from Nero to Marcus Aurelius*, 451—73.)

MORALITY

625a **Moral Ideals in the Time of Christ**—I have said that the highest moral ideals were founded on philosophy, not religion. The two noblest efforts of philosophy had been those of Plato and Aristotle (§ 623*jk*), but at the time of Christ both these philosophies were in eclipse. Another system, that of the Stoics, had come to dominate the world. Next to Stoicism the widest appeal was probably made by the philosophy of Epicurus, who taught just before 300 B.C. He had given a new shape to the materialism and atheism which we noticed in early Greek thinking (§ 623*i*).

b **Epicurus** taught that atoms, falling aimlessly through space, had combined by pure accident to form this present world, which was bound in the course of ages to break up again by the separation of the atoms. Man therefore must not labour to please any god or to prepare for any future for himself or for his race. He had only his own single earthly life to think of. The highest proper motive for his action was pleasure. In the catalogue of pleasures Epicurus gave the foremost place to those of the intellect and imagination, but such a philosophy would, even at its best, encourage a refined individualism, and at its worst might serve as excuse for almost any

degree of sensuality. Its most eloquent exponent was **62** a Roman, the poet Lucretius, who, fifty years before the birth of Christ, attacked all religion as the greatest curse of human society, and pleaded against it with a fervour worthy of an evangelist. In the century before Christ many eminent Romans had been Epicureans, but there were not so many in the following century.

Stoicism: Its Teaching and Influence—The Stoic **c** philosophy had been built up by three men of whom none was a thinker of the first rank. The world, according to the Stoics, was a single living being, whose soul was God—indeed the world could rightly be called God. Every part of it, man included, was a part of him, and was in itself as incomplete and worthless as a finger severed from the body. Each man therefore existed purely for the sake of the world and had no claim to any individual happiness here or hereafter: the hope of immortality was foolish. Moreover, as man had no true individuality, there was no such thing as free will. All his actions were determined by the motion of the Whole to which he belonged. But once a man recognized his insignificance and heartily acquiesced in it, he came into his true greatness, for though a fragment, he was a fragment of God. Nothing could thwart him as long as he subordinated himself utterly to the Whole. By acknowledging himself to be nothing he became omnipotent. He had within himself all that he needed for a perfect life. He was not only invincible against temptation and suffering, he was insensible and inaccessible to them. Pleasure and pain, health and sickness, riches and poverty, were all alike to him. They were 'indifferent' to him. This doctrine **d** of the self-sufficiency of the soul and the indifference of its environment was the core of Stoic morality. Thus the false idea that God is one with the world led to the two opposite results of unnatural self-effacement and unnatural self-exaltation. Moreover the Stoic outlook was limited to this present life almost as much as that of the Epicureans: perfect happiness must be found here and now if it is to be found at all.

This erroneous and sombre philosophy had gained **e** immense influence among educated and half-educated pagans when our Lord was born, and it continued to dominate men's minds for another two centuries. It pervaded the atmosphere of the time and reached countless persons who were not formal adherents of any philosophy. A class of philosophical missionaries had come into existence, men who preached moral philosophy in popular language, not to students but to all who cared to listen. Their teaching, though somewhat mixed, was more Stoic than anything else, and through them the Stoic catchwords and the outlines of Stoic morality reached many of the uneducated. Thousands became half-Stoic without realizing it. Stoicism appealed to the Romans more strongly than any other form of Greek philosophy. Its stern maxims found an echo in their national character. In short no other moral code exercised such a wide influence in antiquity, and this influence was nearly at its height in the time of Christ.

With all its faults Stoicism must have done immense **f** good. It overrode racial differences and taught a brotherhood of men. It encouraged justice, public spirit, courage and self-control. It supported society when ancient sanctions of morality were weakening. It must have saved many a prosperous man from sensuality or arrogance, and many an unfortunate one from servility or despair. But the ordinary man must always have been repelled by its uncompromising doctrine of self-sufficiency and by its cheerless outlook on the future: it made such enormous demands on men and offered so little in return. It was

625f more suited to strong self-centred characters than to the diffident and sociable, who are more numerous. For these or other reasons Stoicism failed to win the masses, and ultimately declined and disappeared.

I have described the outstanding moral ideal. Turning now from theory to practice, I will content myself with sketching a few aspects of pagan society which bring out the moral differences between it and ours.

g Comparison of Ancient and Modern Moral Conditions—In some details the Roman world compares favourably with ours. National rivalries and hatreds within the empire, though not dead, were hardly ever carried to the point of bloodshed. Religious persecution had hitherto been a rare thing. Drunkenness never seems to have become the curse which it has been in N Europe. Gambling was moderate compared to its present-day scale. Duelling, which has been till lately a serious evil, was almost unheard of among the civilized nations of antiquity.

On the other side, there were evils which are unknown or less known among us:

h Despotism—To what I have said already (§ 620c) I need only add that the sight of irresponsible power wielded on a vast scale, when there was not in the world a single state governed constitutionally or democratically, must have been a corrupting influence, aggravated by the lapse of generations. The political ideals of Greek statesmen and thinkers (one of the most valuable things that Greece had given to the world) seemed lost for ever, and the loss was a great *moral* loss.

i Slavery—Slaves formed a large proportion, a third or even more, of the population of the more civilized provinces. There were slaves in every household except the poorest, and there were often hundreds working for a rich man. Great gangs of slaves tilled the large farms of Italy and Africa, and laboured in mines and factories, where they were often trained to a machine-like efficiency which would be impossible with free workmen. These industrial slaves seem in many cases to have been treated little better than animals, and naturally became brutalised and savage beings. Household slaves received a more humane treatment; some were highly educated or trained in medicine or the arts. But even in this milder form slavery offered terrible temptations to cruelty and lust. Both law and custom had sought to limit the owner's power, but in practice such restrictions seem for some reason to have been of little use. At any rate we still find cases where slaves are brutally maltreated or killed with impunity. Slaves who had done good service were often liberated, and such freedmen were now accepted nearly everywhere as equals by freeborn citizens. Some public offices however were closed to them. The supply of slaves had always to be maintained by importation. Barbarian chiefs outside the empire sold their captives or subjects to dealers who resold them at the great slave-markets. Rebels within the empire were sometimes reduced to slavery as a punishment.

j Infanticide—Pagans were still permitted by their laws to allow a newly-born child to die if its father did not wish to bring it up. Several indisputable cases occur in or near the time of Christ, but it is impossible to say how common the horrible practice was. If we may judge by the indifferent tone in which it is referred to, it would seem to have been not rare.

k The Amphitheatre—The inhuman sports of the amphitheatre were one of the worst blots on the Roman world. It was the Etruscans who first amused themselves by making slaves or prisoners of war fight one another to the death. The practice was copied by the Romans, and became one of their national sports. The Greeks in **625k** general looked upon it with aversion, and many cultured Romans came to loathe it, but they reluctantly gave the populace what it enjoyed. The amphitheatre was invented for the murderous pastime and numerous ruins justly perpetuate the memory of Roman brutality. The sport spread to all parts of the empire except Greece. Its victims were of several classes: slaves bought for the purpose, criminals who were not Roman citizens, subdued rebels, prisoners taken in wars with the frontier tribes, etc, and sometimes volunteers from among the free citizens. Some of the slaves (called 'gladiators') were carefully trained for the exhibition, but many of the performers received no special training. After every victory, whether over foreign tribes or rebels, it became the custom to set large numbers of prisoners to kill one another in the amphitheatres. There were also fights between men and animals and the slaughter of unarmed men by animals. High Roman officials were compelled by custom to provide such entertainments and to preside at them in person. In Italy and the W provinces not only men but women also, even the Vestal Virgins themselves, could and did witness these massacres. Great multitudes were enabled frequently, without personal risk, to gloat over the agonies of others; it was a perfect training in cruelty and cowardice, and a plentiful crop of both appeared in due time.

Relations of the Sexes—In the Asiatic provinces long **626a** ages of polygamy had inevitably robbed women of the honour and respect which are their natural right. European influence had now restored monogamy, but had not yet restored women to their rightful position. They were a depressed class even among the upper, or Greek, portion of society. They were unequal partners in their own homes, and counted for very little outside them. A wife had her own rooms in the house and did not meet her husband's guests or eat with them. Roman tradition however, which prevailed in the W provinces, gave much greater freedom and importance to women. Unmarried daughters could not indeed choose their husbands, but after marriage women lived on something like an equal footing with men. The influence of women in Roman history is considerable.

Roman law allowed either husband or wife to dissolve **b** the marriage at will, by merely making a short statement before witnesses. In the E provinces the husband alone could use this easy method, while the wife could only obtain divorce by legal process. The richer classes both in E and W made extensive use of these powers, and marriages were freely made and unmade. Children usually remained in their father's care and endured, as best they could, a succession of stepmothers. There were laws imposing severe penalties on adultery in which a married woman was involved, but they seem to have been seldom enforced. With this exception, unchastity in a man, married or single, was regarded as a small fault or none. We should have expected the Stoics to teach a higher standard of male morality, but they did not: a great Stoic moralist like Epictetus contents himself with advising moderation in immorality. Greek opinion on the subject of certain incestuous unions and on homosexual vice had sunk into a state of disgraceful laxity, little better than that of the Asiatics. The Romans still looked on such things with a severer eye, but they never used their power to attempt any reform in the E provinces, and moreover their own standard was now declining. Finally there was the consecrated unchastity surrounding many temples in Syria and Asia Minor: the Romans did

626b not interfere, but they successfully resisted any W spread of these abominations.

HABITS AND CUSTOMS

c Education—Schools throughout ancient times seem to have been practically always private schools, not those of the medieval and modern type controlled by some sort of corporation. Although we hear, especially in the E provinces, of municipal grants of money towards schools, the master seems to have depended largely on the fees of his pupils. The average slave seems to have received very little education, and for free men education was entirely voluntary. The proportion of illiterate persons seems to have been much bigger than in W Europe today. We know little about the education of women, but many Roman women of the richer class were certainly well-**d** educated. Education was in three stages as with us. After elementary education up to twelve, a boy spent about four years at a secondary school, where the chief study was the works of the poets, Greek poets in the E, and both Greek and Latin poets in the W, where the Greek language was a regular part of a liberal education. Other subjects (history, geography, mythology, astronomy, etc) were included incidentally in the reading of the poets. Greek boys seldom learnt Latin, but received considerable training in athletics and music, subjects which the Roman schools neglected. The next stage, for those who wanted it, was a period devoted to the study of rhetoric—a survival from democratic days. The students wrote speeches for imaginary occasions and delivered them with the prescribed intonation and gestures. Bad models were often followed and sophistry or a florid style was the frequent result. The training explains why it was as natural for the average Greek or Roman to declaim or to quibble as it is for the average modern to sentimentalize or over-analyse. In Greek lands philosophy might be substituted for rhetoric. Endowed professorships of both subjects existed in various places, and some Greek cities, especially Athens, Alexandria, Tarsus and Marseilles, had a reputation for learning and drew crowds of students, though there was not the organization of a modern university.

e Occupations—Both Greeks and Romans held manual work in greater contempt than we do (Aristotle, *Politics* 3, 5. Cicero, *De Officiis* 1, 42). The Romans indeed regarded all work done for a salary or a fee as somewhat dishonourable. They had less scruple about profits gained by trade, and it was the Roman middle class who carried industry and finance to a pitch of efficiency never reached before. They used many of the devices of modern finance—bills of exchange, banking, insurance, and joint-stock companies. Mines, factories and large-scale farming were conducted with skill and rigid economy. Slave-labour was employed, ruthlessly trained and disciplined. Its efficiency and cheapness enabled many articles to be produced almost as economically as in the modern world with all its machinery, and gave big industry much the same advantage over the small man. There is no doubt that the free workmen, especially the semi-skilled or unskilled, were in a bad position. Such men were seldom employed in large enterprises or as household servants. They worked singly or in small groups. They had therefore little chance of forming the associations by which modern workers have improved their condition, and moreover the government forbade all such association except for worship or mutual insurance. In special distress the workman had nowhere to turn except to private charity. Public hospitals and poor relief did not exist. Free corn and occasional free meals could be obtained in some large **626e** cities, but that was all.

Cities—The first century of the empire was one of the **f** great building ages of the world. Many new cities were founded and old ones were adorned with modern buildings. The majority of the great new buildings were intended for utility, comfort or luxury. There were theatres, amphitheatres, baths, town-halls, law-courts, market-buildings, and in some cultured cities public libraries. Every town of any size had its public baths (with halls and shady walks often attached) for frequent bathing was now the fashion everywhere. Immense sums were spent on water-supply and drainage. But we do not find great schools or colleges or hospitals. Except in frontier areas, city-walls and fortresses were non-existent or neglected. Antioch was a mighty stronghold, but Corinth was an open city. A modern visitor to the cities of this time would at once be struck by the number of colonnades or pillared walks. They formed some part or adjunct of most large buildings, and they lined the principal squares and streets, roofing in what we should call the pavement. Old cities like Rome and Jerusalem had many crooked narrow streets, but the newer ones (Antioch, Ephesus, Troas, Thessalonica, Philippi, Caesarea, etc) were better planned, with straight and broader streets. Big cities had many pleasure-grounds, public and private, in their outskirts, with groves, grottoes, ornamental waters, and of course colonnades. Antioch is said to have been the only city with street-lighting and perhaps only Rome had a well-organized fire-service. Rome had over a million inhabitants, Antioch and Alexandria at least half a million each, Jerusalem perhaps a hundred and fifty thousand.

Houses—The sharp contrast between riches and poverty **g** is very evident here. In the towns the poor lived in buildings of wood or sun-baked brick, and the villages in many parts of the empire were clusters of miserable huts, round or square. The houses of the wealthy were as big and as luxurious as those of 18th cent. Europe, but in an inferior style. Beauty and even grandeur were sacrificed to piece-meal display and tasteless comfort. There was a want of order and dignity. Every moderate-sized town-house was built round a small courtyard: the big houses enclosed several, and larger, courtyards. The best rooms were on the first floor, which was often the highest. The facade towards the street was plain. Country houses had even less unity, and were rambling collections of fine and luxurious parts. The Romans loved the country much more than the Greeks, and a wealthy Roman often had five or six houses in the country or by the sea. In big cities, especially Rome, the poorer middle class lived in huge tenement-houses of six or seven storeys. Everywhere the furniture would appear scanty to us, except in well-to-do dining-rooms where a number of huge couches, holding three reclining persons each, would fill most of the room.

Daily Routine, Meals, etc—Very early rising was **h** the rule, in order to have the coolest hours for work. This was compensated for by a sleep after lunch. There were usually three meals. Breakfast was a very light meal, there was a substantial lunch about noon, but the largest meal was eaten some time between four and seven o'clock, generally after a bath. It was eaten in a leisurely manner and then people seem usually to have retired for the night. Greek tradition favoured simplicity and moderation in food and drink, but the Romans were less abstemious and coarser in their taste. Both Greeks and Romans regularly mixed their wine with two or three times it volume of water, usually hot water. Beer was drunk in several countries, but distilled liquors were

6h unknown. The custom of reclining at the evening meal was now universal among men, both rich and poor. The diner lay on his left side, his feet pointing away from the table, and handled his food with his right hand, using the fingers or a spoon. Couches were used in the richer houses, cushions or rugs in the poor ones. Women and children, if they were present, sat on the edge of couches or on some kind of low seat.

i Dress—Dress throughout the empire, both male and female, consisted essentially of two garments: (1) A shirt-like garment, reaching to the knees for men, to the ankles for women (*chiton, tunica*), made usually of white or light-coloured cloth. Women wore a belt with it, men often did. (2) A large piece of woollen cloth, irregular oblong in shape and longer than a blanket (*himation, pallium*). This was wrapped round the body over the *chiton*, rather like a shawl but in one prescribed way. Women drew it over both shoulders, men over the left shoulder only, as a rule. It was usually coloured, more brightly for women than for men, but Roman citizens on ceremonial occasions wore a voluminous white *himation* called a *toga*. Men engaged in active work wore the *chiton* only, so as to have the arms free. Women out-of-doors drew the *himation* over the head to form a sort of hood. Men went bare-headed or wore a cap or a flat broad-brimmed hat. Greek custom favoured sandals but shoes or boots were common in the W. Clean-shaving had been the fashion for centuries, and was still rigidly maintained by the Romans, but beards were no longer rare in the E. Short hair was the universal rule for men.

Travelling—Roman roads, the first metalled roads **627a** ever made, but rough and narrow compared with ours, were spreading all over the empire. Harbours were being built or improved. Highwaymen and pirates were fast disappearing. Travel was becoming easier and safer, but even the Romans could not make land-travel nearly as fast as it was in our stage-coach days. Sea-travel was quicker and therefore cheaper. There were plenty of ships which carried both passengers and cargo. They were sailing-ships—only warships were propelled by oars. But navigation was still so backward that it was necessary to suspend all sailing between November and March. During that time Rome was almost cut off from the provinces. Yet travelling was easier than ever before. The removal of national frontiers helped towards the same result. More people travelled for pleasure, and among the richer Romans we now hear of a class whom we may call tourists; they travelled chiefly in Italy, Greece and W Asia Minor. In these areas comfortable hotels came into existence. Elsewhere only rough accommodation was to be found, and travellers endeavoured to stay in private houses whenever possible. The Romans had not the Greek passion for exploring. They never troubled to trace the European coast-line beyond Denmark, and though their armies often marched through the Alpine passes, no Roman attempted or desired, as far as we know, to scale the peaks. (Cf W. M. Ramsay, 'Roads and Travel in NT', HDB extra vol., 375—403; R. M. Blomfield, 'Ships and Boats', ibid, 365—8.)

PAGAN RELIGIOUS MOVEMENTS AND THE NEW TESTAMENT

BY HENRY WANSBROUGH O.S.B.

628a Bibliography—C. K. Barrett, *New Testament Background: selected documents* 1957; R. Bultmann, *Primitive Christianity in its contemporary setting* 1949, E.tr. 1956; L. Cerfaux, 'Gnose' DBS 3 (1938): 659–701; L. Cerfaux, and J. Tondrieu, *Le culte des souverains dans la civilisation gréco-romaine* 1957; F. Cumont, *Oriental religions in Roman paganism* 1907, E.tr. 1911; A. J. Festugière, *L'idéal réligieux grec et l'évangile* 1932; id, *Personal religion among the Greeks* 1954; id and J. Fabre, *Le monde gréco-romain au temps de Notre Seigneur, 2: le milieu spirituel* 1935; F. C. Grant, *Roman Hellenism* 1962; id ed. *Hellenistic religions* n.d.; R. M. Grant, *Gnosticism and early Christianity* 1959; M. P. Nilsson, *Geschichte der griechischen Religion, 2* 1950; A. D. Nock, *Conversion* 1933; id *Early Gentile Christianity and its Hellenistic background* 1964. reprinting essays published 1928, 1952; K. Prümm, 'Mystères' DBS 6 (1960): 10–225; id, *Religionsgeschichtiches Handbuch für den Raum der altchristlichen Umwelt* 1943; H. Rahner, *Greek myths and Christian mystery* 1957, E.tr. 1963.
N.B. Works referred to incidentally in the course of the article are fully cited there, and are not included here.

b Introduction—Rationalist thinkers of the last cent., and especially the beginning of this, claimed to explain much of Christian rite and even doctrine as derived from those of the pagan world which surrounded the nascent Church. Scholars seized upon any superficial similarity between the NT or early Christian practice and contemporary pagan religious movements, claiming that Christianity was indebted for such elements to paganism, without stopping to examine thoroughly either the outward manifestation or the inner logic of these elements. Most of these scholars approached the subject from classical studies—and it cannot be denied that classical studies had advanced to a far more rigorous standard of science than biblical studies at that time—and were only too ready to find again the subject of their classical and humanistic studies in other fields also. Biblical scholars were slow to reply with the answer that the elements of Christianity claimed to have found their way into the NT from paganism can in fact also, and more plausibly, be accounted for as coming from Christianity's Jewish heritage and from theological reflection on the final revelation in Jesus Christ.

c The forerunner of this attempt to explain away Christianity was the Calvinist Isaac Casaubon, who in 1655 published his *Exercitationes de Rebus Sacris*, in which he ridicules Catholic sacraments as being the direct product of pagan mystery cults. Among the more influential initiators of this way of thought in modern times were the following: R. Reitzenstein, who claimed that the Christian doctrine of baptismal rebirth is derived from the pagan rites of Iran (1910), or—as he later claimed—from the Mandaean sect (1921); W. Bousset, whose monograph *Kyrios Christos* (1921²)

derived the Christian concept of death and rebirth to **628** immortality from the myths of the dying and rising gods of the mystery cults of the hellenistic world; A. Loisy, who tried to prove in *Les mystères paiens et le mystère chrétien* (1930) that Paul drew the whole idea of redemption from paganism and applied it to the tragic crucifixion of Jesus, thus transforming it into a source of cosmic redemption.

In more recent times R. Bultmann ('Gnosis', TWNT **d** 1 (1933)) considers the gnostic way of thought to have had a formative influence on Paul, an opinion still maintained in his *Primitive Christianity . .* (1949). According to C. H. Dodd in his *Interpretation of the Fourth Gospel* (1953) 'similarities of expression' between gnostic and Johannine writings 'suggest a common background of religious thought' (p. 36); but in ten years Professor Dodd—and indeed the whole current of learned opinion—has swung considerably, largely due perhaps to the impetus given by the discoveries at Qumran, until in his *Historical tradition in the Fourth Gospel* (1963) he does no more than indicate gnostic parallels to a couple of passages (pp. 320–1, 342, 361–3).

Among **Catholic theologians** the influential works of **e** Dom Odo Casel and the Maria Laach school in the late 1920s and 1930s gave currency to the belief that at least the rites of early Christianity had been influenced in minor respects by pagan mystery rites, and that the Christian concepts of mystery, of representation of Christ's sacrifice in the Eucharist, and of union to Christ's death and resurrection in baptism could be fully understood only with reference to the pagan cults which formed the background religious atmosphere during the period of their formation.

In recent years, however, it has become clearer that, **f** while in later cent. reciprocal influence between Christianity and pagan cults is undeniable (though the influence on Christianity remained always quite superficial—cf H. Rahner, *Greek myths . . .*), during the formative period of Christianity neither mystery cults nor gnosticism, still less Mandaeism (for which see J. Schmitt, 'Mandéisme', DBS 5 (1957)), exerted any great influence on it. Owing to the discoveries at Qumran and to a better understanding of the Jewish background to the NT, many elements which were formerly thought to have been assimilated from pagan or heterodox Jewish sources can now be seen to be part of the orthodox Jewish world in which the Church is born.

Pagan borrowing unlikely—It is *a priori* more than **g** unlikely that the Church of the Apostles borrowed from paganism, at least consciously—and rites can hardly be borrowed unconsciously though of course both doctrines and ways of thought may be unconsciously adopted. The NT writers were acutely aware of two things: their continuity with Jewish tradition, and their separation from the pagan world. The one indeed implies the other, for the history of Israel is a continuous struggle of trying to avoid assimilation to other nations. At the time of

328g Christ their separatism was a by-word, evoking among their gentile neighbours indignation or more usually contempt. Cicero (*pro Flacc.* 67) calls Judaism a *barbara superstitio* (i.e. they refused to adopt any part of the only civilization worthy of the name). Tacitus mentions their *adversus omnes alios hostile odium* (Hist. 5:5:6). Paul continues the tradition of this separatism (2 Cor 6:14—17); he opposes the wisdom of the Greeks to true

h Christian wisdom (1 Cor 1:17—31). It is of the promises to the Jews that Christ is the accomplishment (Rm 1: 1—4), of their revelation that he is the fullness (Heb 1:1). Only after much heavenly and earthly persuasion are the gentiles admitted to the ranks of the Christians (Ac 10—11:18), and then only on certain conditions (Ac 15, etc). This was not the attitude of a nascent Church which would set out to enrich its wavering message from all sides, or elaborate its impoverished theology with the aid of pagan theories. But could elements have slipped in unnoticed from the pagan milieu in which the early Christian communities grew up, so that Paul thought he was preaching Christ crucified while all the time he was viewing the crucifixion through spectacles borrowed from devotees of the mystery cults?

i In order to answer this question we shall sketch briefly some of the chief religious movements of the 1st cent. A.D., and see how much each one has been claimed to have given to Christianity and with what justice. It must be stressed that it is impossible to give here an adequate account of these movements in themselves. Enough can be presented only to attempt an answer to our question, perhaps incidentally providing a glimpse of the religious world in which the nascent Church found itself. But first some general remarks on the religious language of the NT may be apposite.

629a Evidence of language—Linguistic studies, many long published, suggest that Paul and John betray much less close contact with the pagan philosophical and religious world than many have claimed. To some extent, of course, they reflect by their language the general intellectual climate which pervaded the pagan world of the time, whose terminology was partly formed of concepts originally derived from religious or philosophical circles. But use of such terms no more indicates adherence to the system from which they were originally drawn than does the use of 'essential' denote adherence to Aristotelo-scholastic philosophy, or of 'atomic' any profound borrowing from nuclear physics. On the contrary, a specific connexion with some definite intellectual system is made the harder to establish by the tendency of the Greeks to avoid any sort of technical jargon (on this see the admirable article by A. D. Nock in JBL (52) 1953:

b 131ff). So the evangelist Luke's medical knowledge is reflected, not in any special medical terminology, for none existed (cf H. J. Cadbury, *Style and Literary Method of Luke* I (1919):39—72), but in a more precise and telling use of ordinary language. Similarly the terms which NT writers are said to have borrowed from the technical language of the mystery and other pagan cults are in fact terms of common parlance as well. E.g. *epoptēs* (2 Pt 1:16) is not necessarily used in the sense of a vision received at the height of a ceremony of initiation into a mystery cult, since it also has a well-attested profane use (W. Michaelis, in TWNT 5 (1954): 374—5). Similarly *embateuōn* (Col 2:18) is translated by Dibelius 'at the initiation ceremony'; but—quite apart from the fact that the inscriptions to which he refers do not justify this translation—it has a purely neutral use in 2 Mc 2:30 and Philo: *Plant.* 80 which fits here

c far better: 'investigate thoroughly'. The case for borrow-

ing of expressions used in the cult of the emperor is some- **629c** what stronger. Clearly *epiphaneia* and *parousia* are used in the Pauline epistles with the connotations which they had long had in relation to the adulatory welcome, with semi-divine honours, accorded by cities of the Near East at the reception of conquering monarchs (see below). The Christian writers adopt them, not because they are indebted to such scenes for their ideas, but because they can find no words better to convey the pomp and glory of Christ's final coming. It is however absurd to go on from this modest discovery to claim that the use of the terms *kurios sōtēr* and *evangelion* is similarly derived from the cult of the emperor, and that the conception of Christ as Lord and Saviour, whose coming into the world is the Good News, is made possible only because of the use of such language on adulatory inscriptions about the emperor (Ehrenberg and Jones, *Documents illustrating the Reigns of Augustus and Tiberius*, no. 98). Such terms are in fact already widely used in the LXX of God, in the sense in which they are adopted by the NT.

Rather is it true, as Nock points out (art cit), that **d** when we compare the NT with other contemporary religious literature, we find a positive lack of common religious terms, almost as though they were being deliberately avoided. Thus the common stoic term *daimōn* occurs only once, and in its place is used *daimonion*; the religious terms *katharsia, katharmos* etc are avoided, while *katharismos* occurs in seven different passages of the NT, but only once outside the Bible (Lucian, *Asin.* 22), *Prophēteia* occurs a score of times in the NT, but in profane literature not before the 2nd cent. A.D. (Kraemer in TWNT 6 (1959):784), while the common word in profane literature *manteuesthai* is used only once, and then of a non-Christian prophetess (Ac 16:16). It has often been claimed that Paul's use of *teleios* reflects mystery cults; but in fact it is used by Paul in a normal and neutral sense, while far more remarkable is the total absence of the stock religious terminology from this root: *teletē, atelestos* etc. *Palingenesia* and *anagennasthai* are indeed used in stoic terminology, as in the NT. But whereas in the NT they have the sense of 'resurrection' in Stoic literature they are used in connexion with the Stoic theory of different world-periods (cf F. Buchsel in TWNT 1 (1933) 685—8 and G. Dey, *Palingenesia . . .* 1937. The word *musterion* itself in its NT usage is totally independent of the mystery cults (G. Bornkamm, in TWNT 4 (1942) 831). Since Bornkamm wrote, it has become possible to see more clearly the line of development from its employment in Dn through the Qumran texts.

Examples could be multiplied indefinitely, but enough **e** has been said to indicate that from the point of view of language the NT shows remarkably little influence from the surrounding pagan religious milieu. One need only contrast the language of Philo or Josephus, and their wide adoption of Gr. religious language from their sophisticated environment, in their efforts to make their hellenistic audiences understand and sympathize with Jewish ideals, to realize that the NT is written from within a closed circle, deeply imbued with the language of the LXX, and directed to a closed circle which can understand only if it is familiar with this terminology.

The Pastoral Epistles and the Epistles of Peter show **f** some measure of accommodation to the surrounding pagan world, a slight lowering of the linguistic barrier, and Heb speaks largely the language of Philo and Alexandrian hellenized Judaism. This it shares with Wis, which goes a long way in using current, originally Stoic, terminology. But of the dozen terms listed by J.

629f Weber (PSCB 6:391) as reflecting Stoic language, not one occurs in the NT. The NT holds itself more aloof than Wis from the world of thought which surrounds it.

g From a linguistic point of view, then, we are struck primarily by the lack of contrast between the NT and its surrounding religious milieu. It shows less, not more, connexion with its surroundings than might be expected from a movement which developed in a society which it wished to convert. If, far from their language being influenced by their hellenistic environment, the authors of the NT did not even accommodate their language in order that hellenized hearers might more easily understand the Christian message, it is *a fortiori* improbable that they were sufficiently close to pagan religious movements to assimilate their rites and doctrines.

h **Imperial cult**—One of the religious phenomena which is most clear to see from the monuments which have come down to us is the cult of the emperor. It is also one which has left clear traces in the NT. Alexander the Great himself claimed to be a god, and was followed in this by his Seleucid successors. In Egypt the tendency goes back to the early dynasties. Among the Seleucids the best-known example is Antiochus IV, whose claim to be god is still visible on his coinage. Towards the end of his life his coins bear the eternally youthful face with the horns of divinity, beneath the inscription *Theos epiphanēs* (god made manifest). Among the sober and matter-of-fact Romans the oriental custom of divinizing rulers took a long time to establish itself; in the reigns of Augustus and Tiberius laudatory inscriptions ascribing divine honours to the emperor are found exclusively in the E. Claudius and Vespasian continued this moderation, but not so Caligula, Nero and Domitian, who compelled all the members of their empire to participate in this cult. Refusal to comply with this order was the occasion of the bloody persecutions reflected in Rev. The logion 'Render to Caesar the things that are Caesar's and to God the things that are God's' (Mk 12:17), may also reflect the cult of the emperor. It is addressed to the party of the Herodians, and we know that Herod the Great centred his city of Sebaste on a temple of Augustus. Our Lord may be reproving this infidelity.

i Divinization was not confined to the supreme ruler. Divine honours were offered both to Marcus Cicero and to his brother Quintus after their terms as governor in the E. The brothers congratulate themselves on their moderation in refusing (Cicero, *ad Att.* 5:21:7; *ad Q. frat.* 1:1:9). Similarly the scene described in Ac 12:21–2 is clearly staged as an apotheosis, in which Herod Agrippa elicits divine honours, and is speedily punished by a painful and humiliating death. On his first missionary journey even Paul is hailed by the Lycaonians as a god (Ac 14:11), and hastily disclaims any such pretensions.

j **Significance**—The question arises of the significance of these divinizations, and of the degree of honour which they were intended to express. The juncture of the title 'god' to those of 'saviour' or 'benefactor', in contexts in which we would find the last two quite adequate, is so frequent in our sources that it is hard to believe that it implied much more than a compliment to one who had saved the city from some grave political danger, or had become in some other way its signal benefactor. It is granted too easily to have any far-reaching significance. It was used largely as a political measure. From the time of Alexander ruler-cult had been employed as the great unifying force between disparate elements of a vast empire, united only by allegiance to its ruler. This allegiance was expressed in, and fostered by, the cult. More moderate rulers would content themselves with

a cult of the emperor's *genius*—we would say his lucky **629j** star—and this was Augustus' solution at Rome itself. But the undisguised cult of the emperor himself, and the attribution of the title of 'god' did not mean much more.

It is, then, merely superficial to pretend that in **k** calling Jesus 'son of God' or 'God' the first Christians meant no more than the pagans who addressed their rulers as *divi filius* or *divus*. The same nomenclature conceals a world of difference. The Christian concept of Jesus' divinity is given a content entirely different from this pagan usage by the whole tenor of NT christology (cf § 653*a–d*).

The Gods and Mysteries—The gentile religious scene **630a** in the 1st cent. A.D. may be analysed into three main elements: the old traditional cults, new largely oriental cults, and initiation rites; these last cannot be wholly separated from the oriental cults in general because they build upon them; it will nevertheless be convenient to consider them separately.

The **traditional cults** were inherited from the old city states of classical Greece and of Italy, in which the classic Olympian deities (Zeus, Athena, Apollo etc, to whom the Latin Jupiter, Minerva etc were early assimilated) received a cult laid down by law and conducted largely by the magistrates of the state, who were ipso facto ministers of the state religion. Long before our period this form of religion had begun to lose its hold; already in 47 B.C. Varro was fearing that the old gods would perish from sheer neglect (*Antiq.*, 141). The all-too-human conduct which the myths ascribe to the gods had largely discredited them in the eyes of the educated classes; the best attempt to save them which could be made was to reinterpret them as personifications of virtues, or in terms of archetypal images. Yet this never **b** wholly succeeded, and the state cults became largely a matter of empty form, sustained only by the fear of national disaster if the wrath of the gods were brought down by some deliberate or inadvertent fault or infringement of taboo. An amusing picture of the lengths to which this could go is provided by Theophrastus' caricature of the Superstitious Man (*Characters*, 17). At Rome particularly—and Rome, being political if not cultural mistress of the world, set standards far and wide—the state cult was riddled with superstition, dominated by omens drawn from astrology, dreams or consultation of sacrificial victims' entrails. The cult of the gods was wholly divorced from any ideals of moral conduct; these were provided by the wide dissemination of a popular form of Stoicism. Religion devoid of theology and divorced from morals had little attraction. Augustus did indeed attempt a revival of traditional Roman piety—more out of nationalism and concern at the rapid decline in standards of morality than out of any concern for the worship of the gods—but all the efforts of Horace and Virgil do not seem to have had great effect. The evidence **c** of numismatics shows that the state cult became increasingly the prerogative of a few old aristocratic families. In Greece too the same process of gradual atrophy is apparent; inscriptions in honour of the city gods become increasingly rare in the Roman period, and are dedicated by a far smaller range of families, who often vaunt their long ancestry. Often children are mentioned as priests, showing that heredity rather than merit was the qualification for office. The state cult had, then, become a manifestation less of religious devotion than of family pride. Nevertheless it was this form of cult, together with the private cult of household and agrarian deities, which withstood Christianity longest. Temples

630c were constantly rebuilt in the first centuries of the Christian era; although the funds were provided by conquerors or a few rich families, there must have been some worshippers to use these vast edifices. However the decline in the state of religious buildings at Athens after the withdrawal of Hadrian's financial support is dramatic; if fervour is to be judged by the collection-plate, fervour at Athens was low. But it was the ancient gods which must bear the full brunt of the polemic of the early Church Fathers, whom we cannot suppose to have been beating the air.

d One major factor in the decline of the traditional state cults was the political turmoil of the Mediterranean world. One of the chief functions of the gods of the city was to protect their clients in war and against invasion. But from the time of Alexander onwards conqueror succeeded conqueror, sweeping all before him. To what good, then, the cult of the gods who were powerless to stave off such calamities? Rather than abandon the whole system men turned to other gods. Perhaps they—particularly the gods of the conqueror—might be more
e effective protectors. Hence a plethora of state cults arose, till in the early 2nd cent. Athens recognized 14 ancient cults and 14 new ones to the extent of permitting their clergy official seats in the theatre. At so small a town as Lindos of Rhodes the clergy of eleven cults are mentioned on an inscription of A.D. 45. (Whether there was much popular interest in these cults or not, it was these which provided the low-priced meat which had been sacrificed to idols, and which posed such problems for early Christian consciences [Ac 15:20; 1 Cor 8]).

f As awareness of the oneness of the hellenistic world became more explicit, so did the realization that cults basically local in origin, and still basically betraying their local attachments, could not suffice. A god to claim the worship of the new-found brotherhood of men must be, if not unique, then at least universal. This awareness expresses itself in two different ways. Among educated men we find an increasing turning towards a god of reason, the quintessence of some philosophical quality, a universal quality to which all men must bow. Thus Marcus Aurelius addresses Nature: 'You are the source of all, contain all things, and are the goal of all' (*Sol.* 4, 23)—a commonplace of Stoic thought which has a close parallel in Rm 11:36. In its turn the homage paid to the gods of reason had its effect in generating a regard for reasonableness in the sphere of conduct, so that a sort of natural ethic was developed, founded upon the Stoic doctrines of the equality of men before god and the love of man for man (cf Bonhoeffer, *Die Ethik des Stoikers Epiktet*, 1894). This formed the moral climate in which the NT was formed, and finds many echoes in the NT, especially Jas and the other moralizing passages of the Catholic Epistles. Paul's attitude to slavery, for example, is very close to that of Seneca (*De benef.* 3, 38).

Among those for whom philosophy had less appeal it led to the adoption of new universal cults, whose popular nature gave more satisfaction to the religious feelings than did the sedate and formalistic traditional cults.

g **The oriental cults**—Most of these new universal cults originated in the enthusiastic atmosphere of the E: Syria (cult of Adonis), Asia Minor (Cybele), Phrygia (Attis), or Thrace (Dionysus); the Egyptian cult of Osiris, and the artificial, composite cult of Serapis, evolved by the Ptolemaic kings of Egypt, also enjoyed great popularity. It is neither possible nor to our purpose to describe here all the varieties of these cults; they share a common origin and a common pattern. All are **630g** based on the cycle of nature; vegetation and foliage die in the autumn and are reborn in the spring. The cult-ritual is intended to assist this rebirth, and to promote, by a sort of sympathetic magic, the fertility of crops and harvest (vide, for Attis, Pausanias, *Descriptio Graec.* 7:17). It included therefore wild and ecstatic, dervish-like processions, in which symbols of fertility were carried (cf Lucian, *De salt*: 79), among them the phallus, sometimes symbolized by a pine tree. At the climax of **h** these processions came the most blatant representations of sexual fertility, either a *hieros gamos* (Livy: 39: 14—18) or the unveiling of the phallus (Villa dei misteri, Pompeii). The vine being an essential element of Mediterranean agriculture, religious enthusiasm was supplemented by liberal quantities of wine, resulting in the wildest of manifestations, such as the tearing and eating of raw flesh (as in the rites of Dionysus, cf Euripides' *Bacchae*). It has been suggested that indiscriminate ecstatic 'speaking with tongues', which Paul deprecates at Corinth (1 Cor 12—14), is a legacy brought by these recent converts from the religious services of their pagan past. It certainly was a feature of manifestations of religious fervour in the hellenistic world.

To these basically nature cults accrued at an early **i** stage **myths concerning a nature-hero** or god, who personified the spirit of vegetation, and underwent the same process as the annual cycle of vegetation. The sacred drama of the rite would include the enactment of his funeral procession, accompanied by laments and mourning (Theocritus, id 15), and the return to life of the vegetation. The myth of Isis and Osiris, for example, included the scattering of the dead hero's (Osiris') body, which corresponds to the autumn sowing of next year's crop. Then Isis, representing the female element, or mother nature, goes to search for the dead hero, and so brings the vegetation to life; whether the hero himself is brought back to life will be discussed later. One ex- **j** ample of these myths may serve to give a typical outline of them all, that of the popular Eleusinian mysteries, celebrated at Eleusis near Athens. Persephone, the daughter of Demeter, was, while gathering flowers, carried off to the underworld by the god Hades. Demeter, the mother goddess, or nature goddess, searches inconsolably for her daughter, while all vegetation dies. Eventually Hades is persuaded to restore Persephone to the earth for nine months of each year, and vegetation returns to the earth for that period. Here, however, untypically the male element is lacking, with the result that the sexual union which usually produces fertility is worked into the story somewhat artificially. But it must be stressed that the myth is always secondary to the nature ritual, both in genesis and in importance.

The **diffusion** of these originally oriental forms of **k** worship to other parts of the hellenistic world occurred chiefly by means of traders and slaves (cf S. Dill, *Roman Society from Nero to Marcus Aurelius*, 1904, 560—9). At Delos, the centre of the E slave-trade, we early find a medley of these cults. The cult of Egyptian Serapis came to Greece through the great commercial port of the Piraeus; the Roman port of Ostia abounds in temples to Isis, Serapis and Attis. They seem to have reached Rome at the beginning of the 2nd cent. B.C. (Cybele was installed on the Palatine hill in 204, and we find the Dionysiac cult in 189 B.C.), although it was only two centuries later, after repeated attempts by the senate to suppress them on account of their licentious character, that the majority of oriental cults began to be granted the recognition of a place within the sacred *poemerium*.

630l But by the end of the 1st cent. A.D. Juvenal is complaining that the Syrian Orontes (signifying Syrian cults) has long been flowing into the Tiber (*Sat.* 3,62). The appeal of these cults lay in their dramatic character, and in their concern with the basic forces of nature, life and death. According to the historian Zosimus (4:3:3), the Greeks considered life not worth living without them. As Cumont points out (*Oriental religions*, ch2), they do represent a higher and more satisfying form of religion than the cold ritual of the state cults with its clutter of superstition and taboo.

631a Initiation rites—It is to these oriental cults that are attached the initiation rites which figured so largely in the attempts to explain Christianity as the product of syncretism. The secrecy which was an essential part of these rites has caught the imagination of historians, but at the same time left us inevitably ill-informed about them. We cannot be sure at what period they became generally diffused; there is no doubt that the great period of their diffusion began only in the 2nd cent., but there are sure traces of them in the W already in the 1st cent. B.C. and A.D. *villa dei misteri* at Pompeii, and the underground basilica of the Porta Maggiore at Rome). Initiation into the Eleusinian mysteries remained possible only at Eleusis, but Cicero speaks of it, and the emperors Augustus and Tiberius had themselves initiated; the sanctuary is full of statues from many lands, dedicated during the Roman **b** period. Nor can we know how general was the initiation. It has been calculated that the Mithraea so far discovered could hold only a minute portion of the immense throngs which popular imagination has admitted to these most popular of all mysteries. As regards Mithraism, however, it should be noted that the spread of this cult begins only at the end of the 1st cent. A.D. Cumont, in his exhaustive *Textes et monuments figurés rélatifs aux mystères de Mithras* (1896—99) concludes: 'Speaking generally one can say that Mithraism was always excluded from the Hellenistic world' (II, p. 241). In all Greece and W Asia Minor, the cradle of Christianity, the cult is attested only at the Piraeus, and by one terra cotta plaque from Tarsus of uncertain date. Mithraism has, therefore, little direct connexion with the NT.

c Doubtless initiation was expensive enough to daunt many (Apuleius, *Metamorph.* 11:28). At a later period, however, these rites were both widespread and very popular. Pausanias, on his tour of Greece in the late 2nd cent., finds the country full of them. From inscriptions we know of mysteries of Hecate on Aegina, of Antinous in Mantinea, of Demeter on Lerna, as well as many others. One pious lady, Fabia Aconia Paulina, boasts that she was initiated at Eleusis, into three separate mysteries on Lerna, and again at Aegina, besides undergoing the initiation to Isis and the *taurobolium* (vide infra). The Fathers of the Church still direct the full strength of their polemic against them, selecting for comment the most debased elements. All this tells us, however, little for the period which concerns us; the assumption so often made, that the wide diffusion attested for later centuries existed already in the 1st cent., is simply unfounded.

d The essence of **initiation** was admission by some mysterious and testing rite into a secret society and the privileges of some sort of intimacy with the god or hero of the cult. Apuleius describes as much of the initiation ceremony of his hero, Lucius, as he dares (*Metamorph.* 11,23—24). The ceremony itself was preceded by a bath of purification. Then the priest imparts some secret

knowledge (some of these watchwords have been pre- **631d** served for us, e.g. by Clement of Alexandria, *Protrept.* ch 2), and enjoins a preparation of ten days' abstinence from meat and wine, at the end of which comes the nocturnal initiation itself. The mysteries of this ceremony Apuleius may not divulge; the priest has beforehand amply stressed that the trials to be undergone are so terrifying that no one would subject himself to them without the express command of the goddess. The author merely hints darkly at a descent into the realm of the dead, and a vision of the sun and of the celestial court at midnight. In the morning the new initiate is arrayed in rich vestments and led out so that the people may celebrate his new birth. Some time later Lucius has scruples that this initiation into the mysteries of Isis may be insufficient, the knowledge imparted may not be sufficiently accurate and full. So he has himself initiated— **e** notwithstanding the expense and inconvenience—into the mysteries of Osiris and the order of the Pastophores as well (ibid 29—30). Livy also relates the ten days' preparatory abstinence, followed in this case (the initiation is into the mysteries of Bacchus) by a banquet and a bath of purification, still before the initiation proper (39,9); but he obviously has no access to the inner secrets of the rite. The Mithraic rite was centred upon the *taurobolium*: the high priest descends into a pit at the climax of the ceremony; above him a bull is slaughtered, so that he is drenched in the blood, and even drinks it; he then comes out and is 'adored' (Prudentius, *Peristeph.* 10,5,1006) by the onlookers.

There are here, clearly, a number of points which have **f** at least a superficial **parallel with Christian rites**: a bath of purification, a banquet of the confederates, the idea that the rite constitutes some sort of rebirth, and that the initiate (in the Mithraic rite) receives some sort of divine property from partaking of the blood of the bull (representing the god). The accompanying myth has always some idea of life out of death. Are we to equate these points with baptism, the Christian bath of regeneration, by which we rise from death with Christ to a new life by the power of his blood, and with the eucharist? Some of the points can be summarily dismissed. The bath of purification is not, as it is in the case of baptism, a part of the rite of initiation; it is a preparatory purification which can be separated—as it is in Apuleius' account—by an interval of ten days from the initiation itself. It fulfils, moreover, a natural human instinct to cleanse oneself before contact with the divinity, which is to be found in many religions. It **g** is this instinct which baptism utilizes, without any borrowing from specific rites, unless it be Jewish rites of purification; but in any case the significance attached to the bath is wholly different. Similarly the banquet of the confederates corresponds to the natural tendency of associates to express their companionship by eating together; we find no further sacramental symbolism than this in the banquet of the mystery cults; there is no question here of commemorating the covenant with the divinity by the actual meal; Livy shows that it may even precede the initiation.

More difficult to fathom is the overall meaning of the **h** rite. What is this rebirth? Does it grant immortality, and, if so, of what kind? Cumont asserts again and again in various works (*Oriental religions; Astrology and religion among the Greeks and Romans; Afterlife in Roman paganism*) that initiation granted some sort of immortality, relying on one text which contains the word *apathanatismos* (immortalization). But Nilsson (*Geschichte . . . p.* 659) has shown that in its context

1h the word means only a temporary elevation to a divine state in order to receive a mystical experience, after which the priest concerned returns to his normal mortal condition. Initiates into the rites of Isis are indeed said to be *quodam modo renati* (Apuleius, *Metamorph.* 11,21) after a kind of voluntary death. But there is no hint that this death in any way obviates death in the normal human way of things; it seems merely to make the rest of life in some way a higher kind of life. A text of Cicero which has often been used in the sense of immortality (*De legibus* 2,36), may be equally well interpreted in the same sense. He says that from the Eleusinian initiation *neque solum cum laetitia vivendi rationem* **i** *accipimus, sed etiam cum spe meliore moriendi.* It is not easy to give a positive content to this higher kind of life; for Apuleius it involves some almost mystical intimacy with the divinity. Juvenal shows that it could bind to various annual purifications and other hardships, which he mocks (*Sat.* 6,522ff). Only very rarely is the observance of a moral code implied, as on an inscription to Atargatis in Syria. Other texts are late and unreliable, being suspect of the influence of Christian ideas. Thus Frazer, in *The Golden Bough* (Part 4, Adonis, Attis, Osiris, Vol. 1, p. 224) claims that Adonis is raised from the dead; but, apart from a general reference to Theocritus, id 17, he adduces as evidence only the Christian interpretations of Origen and Jerome. The Christian apologist Firmicus Maternus (*De err. prof. relig.* 22) tells us that at a certain point in the mysteries of Osiris the priest cries: 'Take courage! As the god is saved, so you also shall be delivered from your miseries'; which is inexplicit enough. The pseudo-Homeric Hymn to Demeter (5. 480—3) concludes: 'Happy the man who has seen these holy (Eleusinian) rites; those who have not witnessed them will not have the same lot in the damp darkness of the underworld'. Many other classical texts (cited by Allen and Halliday, *The Homeric hymns* (1936) ad loc) betray a similar vagueness in their hope. There is no hint of a resurrection here. A Mithraic inscription of the 4th cent. (CIL 6:510) claims that its subject is *in aeternum renatus*; but this may well be an exaggeration, for the Mithraic initiation rites could be repeated every twenty years, and other texts claim only that the subject is *viginti mundus in annos*, cleansed for twenty years.

j Can the negative result obtained from the ritual texts be supplemented by the myths which were an integral accompaniment of the mystery rites? If the rite identifies the worshipper with his god and the god was originally a vegetation god who rises again, then surely the initiate himself rises again? The school of historians of religion would claim that both the idea of Christ's resurrection in the first place, and the transfer of his risen state to those baptized in his name, have their origin here. But **k** neither of the two premises is solidly based. The claim that the worshipper is identified with the god in the mystery rites is usually supported by Apuleius' description referred to above. When the initiate issues forth after his initiation, clothed in fine array, he is not, as is usually asserted, worshipped as the incarnation of the god. In fact this is the signal not for an act of worship but for a roistering celebration of his new birth by the onlookers. The Mithraic text in which the high priest is 'adored' seems more promising. But firstly, this refers not to the initiation of a new member but to a ceremony in which the person concerned has already the honour of the high priesthood; secondly, we are relying on a hostile Christian interpretation of the ceremony; thirdly, *adorare* can denote merely the reverence paid to an important

person. As Nilsson points out (*Geschichte* . . . p. 660), **631k** the expression 'son of god' is never used of initiates in the pagan sources, as it is used of those who have become partakers of the divine nature by Christian baptism. God of course is called their father, but in a way employed in religious language centuries before the spread of the mystery rites, which certainly denotes no such special relationship as does the Christian use.

The claim that there is some connotation of resurrec- **l** tion in these rites may give us pause. At first sight it would seem that, since the vegetation is reborn, the god who personifies that vegetation must also return again to life. Therefore whatever the degree of association with the god achieved by the rite (identification is not necessary), it would be intended to secure a similar resurrection. But curiously the god does not rise again according to the myths. This is explained by the ancient biology according to which the grain must die before a new ear springs from it. It was from Osiris' dead body that the corn grew; only later did Isis gather together his members and enable him, not to rise again, but to reign in the underworld. Pausanias (1,4; 7,17) at least is clear that Attis does not rise again (Nock, *Early Gentile Christianity* . . . p. 105—6, accepted a different view in 1928; but cf Nilsson, *Geschichte* . . . p. 657). The climax of the Eleusinian mysteries was no resurrection of the deity, but the showing of an ear of new corn. Admittedly Plutarch concluded after seeing the mysteries at Delphi that the 'obvious interpretation' of the sacred drama was as bringing back Semele, the corn-goddess, from the underworld (*Quest. Graec.* 293 C); this is, however, only his interpretation of a particular rite. This is slender evidence to support the theory that Christian belief in the resurrection of Christ is drawn from pagan nature-myths.

But certainly part of the attraction of the mystery **m** cults lay in the promise of some sort of comfort after death, although this was less important as well as less definite than has been claimed. The frequent representation in funerary art of Dionysiac banquets suggests that the devotees of Dionysus looked forward to this form of existence after death. In spite of the scepticism of educated men, many still believed in some sort of shadowy existence in the underworld after death. Initiation into the mysteries was hoped to make this in some measure happier (cf K. Pruemm, 'Mystères', DBS 6 (1960), 171). This is a far cry from the Christian hope in the resurrection of the body.

In short, the Christianity of the NT is worlds apart **n** from these cults. Instead of a vague and ill-defined body of myths concerning shadowy semi-divine figures, the Christians claimed a personal God who guided all history and sent into the world his Son, the very details of whose life were known. Instead of a demi-god vainly killed and now confined to the half-life of the underworld, the Christians vaunted a divine Saviour who offered himself to death of his own will, and rose to a glorious new life. Instead of magical and licentious rites, which wrested dubious advantages from a host of deities, the Christians pledged themselves in their sacrament to the love and service of the one God, who rewarded them with the joy of union to himself. The pagan rites involved no personal commitment, neither to a single god, nor to a body of belief, nor to a moral code; the Christian bound himself to all these. Pruemm (*Handbuch*, p. 308) gives no quarter: 'Future generations will be simply nonplussed by the seriousness with which profound connexion was claimed between the mysteries and Christianity on so many important doctrines!'

631o At best then the pagan mystery rites prepared the seed-bed where Christianity was to be planted (Pruemm hesitates to say even so much, art cit, col. 168). They manifested and fostered a readiness for Christianity, a desire for the values which it was to offer, for a personal relation to God, for assurance of happiness beyond the grave, and for a ritual of sacraments. But of borrowing by NT Christianity from these rites there can be no question.

632a Gnosticism—R. Bultmann is particularly insistent on the part played by Gnosticism in shaping Christianity: 'Gnosticism and Christianity have affected each other in a number of different directions from the earliest days of the Christian movement', he claims (*Primitive Christianity* . . . p. 193), or 'ideas originating from the gnostic redemption myth are used to describe the person and work of Jesus Christ and the nature of the Church' (p. 211). He asserts that the 'dualism of the two realms of light and darkness, truth and falsehood, above and below' is gnostic in origin; but since he wrote these words in 1949 it has become abundantly clear that the Fourth Gospel could have derived this dualism from circles such as the sect of Qumran.

b What then is this gnosticism which so influenced Christianity? In its widest sense gnosticism is more an attitude than a system of beliefs, centred on the conviction that salvation comes by knowledge. There have been Christian gnostics, Jewish gnostics, and gnostics who were neither Jew nor Christian. Thus some have been able to claim that gnosticism was a Christian heresy, while others assert that Christianity is only a branch of the wider phenomenon of gnosticism. The writings of gnosticism as a system are found in the Corpus Hermeticum; its first treatise (Poimandares) may have been written before A.D. 100, although the majority date from the 2nd cent. From these writings we may gather an idea of the central **doctrines** of the hellenistic system **of gnosticism**: salvation is by knowledge of God, of oneself, and of the Way. God is supreme and absolute; since the world is basically evil God can have had no contact with it, but created it by an intermediary, the demiurge, and rules it through powers or emanations from himself, the 30 aeons. Man is composed of three elements, body, soul, and *nous* (the word literally means 'mind'). This highest element in man has descended from the upper heavens, falling through all the spheres, and successively putting on the evil of each, until it is finally buried in the evil

c elements of a material body and soul. The Way which must be known for salvation is the return to the upper heavens. The *nous* is to rise again, shedding successively the layers of evil in which it is clothed: the material body, the irrational soul, the 7 vices of the planets, and finally the pneumatic body, before it is laid bare and is ready to be united to the divine powers. For this salvation are necessary a saviour and a revelation. The saviour is the heavenly Man who leads fallen man into the fullness of the heavenly Man. He first became incarnate, but escaped being imprisoned in the usual layers of evil, for he disguised himself and eluded the rulers of the heavenly spheres who were waiting to entrap him; hence he can lead

d other men back to the divine powers. The revelation required is some experimental knowledge of that divinization of the soul which will be revealed after death; at this moment, the moment of rebirth, there occurs a complete change of form in man; his 7 vices are expelled and replaced by the 10 powers of God. Although his appearance is unchanged, his inner *nous* is now saved, and nothing that may happen thereafter to his exterior body has any importance. One immediately asks in what

this experimental knowledge consists; but the answer **63** varies from a high mystical experience to the product of gross magic (cf A. J. Festugière, 'Cadre de la mystique hellénistique' in *Me. offerts à M. Goguel*, 74—85).

This gnosticism of the Corpus Hermeticum seems to **e** be a nightmare parody of Christian belief, devoid of sobriety or realism, and mingled with fantastic myths and monsters. Parts of it are indeed found among Christian heretics of the 2nd cent. We should not, however, be misled by the similarity of the gnostic myth to Christian doctrine about the saviour into overstressing the similarity between the two systems in their entirety. It is the myth alone which shows this resemblance. The attitude towards knowledge, for example, is wholly different. For Paul and John, with their semitic heritage, knowledge is no mere intellectual assent but an inner adherence transforming the whole person and his activity (cf Hos 2:22; Jer 24:7; Jn 1:10—11). The gnostics are Platonic; saving knowledge is confined to the *nous*, and has no effect on the way of life. Gnosticism is, further, shot through with the conviction that matter is fundamentally evil, a conception which has no place in Christianity.

The primary question for us is that of the **date of f origin** of these beliefs. The early Church Fathers considered Simon Magus to have been the founder of gnosticism, because he was given the title 'great power of God' by the Samaritans (Ac 8:10). R. M. Grant, in his *Gnosticism* . . . , maintains that it grew out of the ruins of Jewish hope of a restoration of Israel, when the fall of Jerusalem in A.D. 70 made it imperative to reinterpret their apocalyptic hopes on a less material level. Bultmann asserts that gnosticism is now known to be pre-Christian (*Primitive Christianity* . . . 193—4), but fails to substantiate his assertion. The problem is basically one of sources; we see speculations about intermediaries, the distinction between God's essence and his powers, between the intelligible, the heavenly and the sublunary worlds, theories about a universal and heavenly Man—all elements in the gnostic system—already in Philo and the Jewish apocalyptic literature dated to the first half of the 1st cent. A.D.; fifty years later, at the very end of the NT period, begins the Corpus Hermeticum with its full development of gnosticism. Between the two points comes **g** Paul, in whose writings can be found some expressions which could be said to reflect gnosticism if they had been written in the 2nd cent. Of individual expressions it is almost impossible to be sure that they have gnostic connotations. Bultmann, for instance, claims that the elements of this world (*stoicheia*) of Gal 4:3, 9, etc, are allusions to the evil powers which rule the various spheres in the gnostic myth (op cit p. 225). But Paul could derive his expression equally well from the usual profane meaning of the word (G. Delling in TWNT 6 (1959) 685—6). In this case he would, admittedly, be making use of an expression derived originally from stoic philosophy. But by this time the stoic world-picture had become such a commonplace that its terms could hardly be avoided. Similarly the rulers of this world (*archontes*) in 1 Cor 2:8 need not be a gnostic expression; it could refer to the late Jewish view that each nation had its own protecting and guiding spirit.

Perhaps the most forceful and influential attempt to **h** show that Paul consistently used the language and ideas of the gnostic myth at least in Eph, has been made by H. Schlier in *Christus und die Kirche im Epheserbrief* (1930). He pieces together texts from the epistle to show that Paul has constantly in mind the myth of the saviour which we find later in gnostic writings. He does not merely refer to this myth; he uses its ideas to

632h express his own message. We can agree that Paul has been brought face to face with theories which will later develop into 2nd cent. gnosticism; to some extent he also uses their terminology to drive home his basic theme that Christ's victory has subdued and eliminated any intermediaries which stand between us and God (as, according to Judaism, the angels who mediated the Law stood). But Schlier further claims that Paul's concept of Christ's cosmic lordship, and of the Church as the body of which Christ is the head, are drawn from the gnostic myth. He claims that they cannot be a development from Paul's previous use of these figures in Rm and 1 Cor, since there the body is Christ, while here Christ is the head, set over against the body. P. Benoit, however, (in RB 46 (1937), 346–61, 506–25, reprinted in *Exégèse et Théologie*, 2) explains the development as due to a new psychological horizon brought about by the gnostic crisis at Colossae. In Rm and 1 Cor Paul was considering primarily Christ's working in the individual Christian and the Church on earth. The gnostic claims have forced him to lift his eyes to the heavenly scene; in this connexion he is forced to use slightly different images. Thus, since he is considering Christ in his exaltation, but the Church still on earth and not yet grown to its full perfection, he must use an image which expresses indeed the union of Christ and his Church, yet allows for some degree of opposition. Hence he arrives at the figure of the head and members of the same body, and of Christ united with but distinguished from his spouse the Church. Schlier himself, in *Der Brief an die Epheser* (1957) 90ff, though seemingly unaware of Benoit's criticisms, reaches roughly the same

conclusions: ideas already in the background in Rm and **632j** 1 Cor come into the foreground after the crisis at Colossae, and enable Paul to express his answer in terms familiar both to the Christian communities and to his opponents.

The development of Paul's theology, then, which we see in Eph, can be said to be caused by contact with gnostic or pre-gnostic ways of thought, in so far as this directed Paul's attention to problems which he had not previously treated. Fresh from his strife with gnosticism he expresses his conclusions partly in language which has gnostic echoes, but without any dependence of thought; rather can his thought be seen to continue and develop in a direct line from the earlier epistles.

Conclusion—The attempts to explain away Christianity **k** as a syncretistic phenomenon were built upon the unexamined consideration of superficial similarities. Probing has shown that these similarities, where they do exist, are incidental, provide no indication of borrowing, and are incorporated in systems so radically different that the inner logic of these seeming similarities shows them to be highly diverse. The only point of real contact is in the sphere of ethics; the widely-diffused Stoic ethic was largely acceptable to Christianity, so that similar maxims and moral teaching are often found in the NT and in the works of pagan moralists. The judgement on Paul's relations to the hellenistic world made by E. Schwartz (*Goettingischer gelehrter Anzeiger*, 173 (1911). 667) may be applied to the NT as a whole: 'His is an untamed, creative, lordly nature. It forms and shapes afresh, for new life is in ferment within him and bursts the old wineskins'.

THE CRITICAL STUDY OF THE NEW TESTAMENT

HISTORY AND RESULTS

BY W. J. HARRINGTON O.P.

633a Bibliography—J. Levie, S.J., *The Bible, Word of God in Words of Men*, 1961; W. D. Davies, *Invitation to the NT*, 1967; E. Gutwenger, S. J., 'The Gospels and Non-Catholic Higher Criticism', CCHS (1), 1953, 604*a*–609*a*; W. J. Harrington, O. P., *Record of the Fulfilment: The NT*, London 1968; V. Taylor, *The Formation of the Gospel Tradition*, 1935[2] E. Dinkler, 'Form Criticism of the NT', PC (2), 1962, 596*a*–597*d*; J. L. McKenzie, S. J., *Dictionary of the Bible*, 1965; R. Marlé, *Bultmann et l'Interprétation du NT*, Aubier 1966[2]; R. E. Brown, 'After Bultmann, What?—An Introduction to the Post Bultmannians', CBQ 26 (1964), 1–30; P. J. Cahill, 'Rudolf Bultmann and Post-Bultmann Tendencies', CBQ 26 (1964), 153–78; J. M. Robinson, *A New Quest of the Historical Jesus*, 1959; C. H. Dodd, *Historical Truth in the Fourth Gospel*, 1963; A. Cardinal Bea, *The Study of the Synoptic Gospels*, 1965; B. Vawter, 'The Historical Theology of the Gospels', *Homiletic and Pastoral Review*, 62 (1962), 681–91; W. Harrington, O.P. and L. Walsh, O.P., *Vatican II on Revelation*, Dublin 1967; J. Dupont, O.S.B., *The Sources of Acts*, 1964; B. Rigaux, O.F.M., *Saint Paul et ses Lettres*, 1962; S. Neill, *The Interpretation of the NT*, 1861–1961 Oxford 1966; R. M. Grant, *The Interpretation of The Bible*, 1965; C. H. Dodd, *History and the Gospel*, 1964[2].

b It would be an impossible task, within the compass of a single article, to give a comprehensive summary of the history and achievements of modern critical study of the NT. We have been content to sketch the rise of the 'critical approach', while treating more fully of the schools and methods predominant at the present day. Special attention has been paid to the Catholic reaction to and evaluation of these methods. While Gospel Criticism must claim the lion's share in this brief survey, the history of the critical study of the other NT writings has not been neglected. On the whole, we have thought it more profitable to stress the positive contributions of critical scholarship. On higher criticism in general see § 91*d*.

I PROTESTANT CRITICAL STUDY OF THE GOSPELS.

c **The Rise of Modern Critical Study of the NT.** We may find in the German Aufklärung (Enlightenment) of the 18th cent. the manifestation of a notable characteristic of modern study and of biblical exegesis as a whole, namely the denial of the supernatural; the denial of everything beyond human reason. The mysteries of the faith were first declared to be all explainable by reason and thus not really mysteries at all; from that position it was a short step to conclude that no special divine revelation was necessary and God was adequately manifested in nature. Thus the distinctive character of and need for the Jewish and Christian revelation were reduced if not entirely removed. Miracles were held to

be impossible because the physical laws of the Universe **633c** were but the expression of the immutable will of God. What of the Gospel miracle stories? In the view of some critics, they were consciously fictitious narratives composed by the writers of the Gospels, in some cases built up out of purely natural events, in other with no historical basis at all.

These and many similar ideas were of course made **d** public at a much earlier date in the writings of the English Deists. By the middle of the 18th cent. however, their day was over, as far as England was concerned and the ideas were transplanted to Germany, cf § 93*a*–*c*. The first significant German representative of the move- **e** ment in the biblical field was H. S. Reimarus (1694–1768), from whose work G. E. Lessing published a number of fragments after the author's death, cf § 93*b*. The last of these was also the one which caused the greatest sensation, viz *The Aims of Jesus and his Disciples*, which appeared in 1778. Jesus, the author insisted, was to be stripped of all supernatural qualities and regarded in the light of the Jewish messianic expectation of his time: as a Messiah who would deliver his people from the Roman yoke and establish an earthly kingdom. The miraculous events of the Gospel were ordinary cures, later magnified and heralded as supernatural occurrences, or were simply invented. It was the disciples of Jesus who changed his conventional idea of messiahship into a spiritual one; and to do this successfully they resorted to deception on a grand scale.

Later writers, like H. E. G. Paulus (1761–1851), react- **f** ed against the assertion of gross fraud, but their approach was no less radical. Jesus was a moral preacher of great persuasiveness, while his disciples were not knaves but simple-minded, ingenuous folk. The miracles of Jesus could be explained away on natural grounds. On the whole, Paulus thought it was enough to distinguish between the objective fact, purely natural and the subjective 'fact' supplied by impressionable witnesses. It soon became clear to many German critics that Paulus's line of argument could not be sustained. Granted that he had rejected the accusation of fraud as unrealistic and recognized the tendency of primitive peoples to magnify ordinary events; there remained a fatal flaw—his failure to realize that the narrative before him was his only source of information. Hence the 'natural explanation' was in reality little more than a rather ingenious conjecture. Moreover the net result of such a line of thought was to produce a narrative so artificial in character as to make it impossible to accept as a record of what actually occurred. Another solution—that of myth—was discovered. Adopting C. G. Heyne's analysis **g** of myth in classical literature, J. G. Eichhorn had applied it to the OT and argued that it was not permissible to separate the external envelope—the narrative of a wonderful event—from the natural event, if any, underneath, for which one had no evidence at all. The narrative must be taken as a whole; and the whole was

3g presented as a wonderful and supernatural occurrence. It could not of course be accepted as a record of what actually took place and the only alternative was to regard it as myth. In this way Eichhorn and his pupil and successor Gabler, interpreted many parts of the OT. Heyne—the classical scholar and senior colleague of Eichhorn—had distinguished (1) the **philosophical myth**, in which a story was evolved to explain some fact of human experience, such as the sense of guilt and sin; (2) the **historical myth**, in which some eponymous hero gradually accumulated stories about him as the centuries passed.

h For a long time critics hesitated to apply myth to the NT, partly because its historical character appeared to be so inseparably connected with Christian faith, partly because the time between the events described and the traditional dates of the records was not enough to allow myth to develop. D. F. Strauss, in his *Life of Jesus* (1835), got over the latter difficulty, both by arguing that the records were based on ancient OT episodes later applied to the Messiah, and by postponing the dates of the Gospel writing to the middle of the 2nd cent. A.D. What Strauss failed to do, however, was to make any adequate inquiry into the actual circumstances of the composition of the NT literature and study its character in the light of the historical period in which it took its rise.

i This task was taken up by F. C. Baur (1792—1860), founder of the new school of Tübingen; and in evolving his interpretation, Baur made full use, not only of Hegel's philosophy of religion, as indeed Strauss had done, but also of his philosophy of history. In particular, he vigorously applied the hegelian process of thesis—antithesis—synthesis to the history of apostolic Christianity. The thesis was represented by the Petrine faction with its Jewish—Christian particularistic and legalistic outlook. Hellenistic Christians of universalistic tendency, the Pauline party, represented the antithesis. The resultant synthesis, fruit of mutual concessions, gave rise in the 2nd cent. to Catholicism. Each NT writing reflected one or another of these tendencies and might be dated accordingly, Baur maintained.

j During the second half of the 19th cent. the late dating of the Gospels, demanded by the systems of Strauss and Baur, was steadily abandoned. Mk was now taken to be the earliest Gospel, written before A.D. 70, while Mt and Lk were held to have been written between A.D. 70 and 90. These were the positions adopted by the historic-critical school of **Liberal Protestantism**. Already, at the beginning of the century, F. Schleiermacher (1768—1834), influenced by Kantian philosophy, had accepted the banishment of religion from the sphere of theoretical knowledge and had made it a function of sentiment. Later, A. Ritschl (1822—1834), founder of liberal Protestantism, maintained that religious judgements are independent 'judgements of value' based exclusively on the feelings of approbation or disapprobation elicited by religious conceptions seen in relation to the highest good. Those conceptions which arouse the feeling of approbation are of religious value and worthy of becoming objects of faith; the question of their objective reality is neither important nor capable of solution. This is the doctrinal basis of the liberal Protestant distinction between the Jesus of history and the Christ of faith: if from the standpoint of historical research Christ may be reduced to insignificant proportions, his importance remains nevertheless untouched from the standpoint of religious value. Hence, the

liberal Protestants could treat the gospels and the **633j** Jesus of history very freely, even recklessly; in their opinion, no harm could be done to religion, since it was not based on history. A. von Harnack (1851—1930) became the most prominent representative of the liberal school.

In his book, *The Messianic Secret in the Gospels* **634a** (1901), W. Wrede maintained that not until after the resurrection was the messianic dignity of Jesus affirmed and that, in consequence, the many injunctions (in Mk) to observe secrecy are a literary device to account for the silence of the earliest traditions. In other words, a dogmatic Christ has been superimposed on the historical Jesus. J. Weiss (1863—1914) demonstrated the dogmatist, *a priori* values in liberal Protestantism but, on the other hand, exaggerated the eschatological element in the gospel: the kingdom of God is wholly future and transcendental. A. Schweitzer, in his famous work *The Quest of the Historical Jesus* (1906), went beyong Weiss with his extreme doctrine of 'thoroughgoing eschatology'. Jesus preached the eschatological kingdom of God which he at first thought would be realized during his life-time. Then, the conviction dawned on him that he must suffer for others in order that the kingdom might come. The ethics preached by Jesus formed a provisional code for the short interval which separated the world from its destruction—'interim ethics'.

The movements and schools which we have outlined, though they differ widely among themselves, are all marked by one basic factor: a philosophical prejudice against the supernatural previous to the examination of the facts. In contrast to other theologians, these rationalistic critics would like to consider themselves 'independent'; in fact, they were rigidly bound by their philosophical presuppositions. At the same time, we should emphasize that there were not wanting great scholars who, all this while, defended the historical basis of Christianity—men such as Theodor Zahn, J. B. Lightfoot, and H. B. Swete.

The year 1918, the end of the First World War, marks, **b** in some respects at least, a turning-point in Protestant biblical research in Germany. We have noted that, in the earlier period, Protestant exegesis, on the whole, was characterized by radical hypercriticism and extreme scepticism. But, after 1918, emphasis was placed more firmly on constructive theological synthesis and the enduring religious aspects of the problems at stake. The classic work begun by G. Kittel in 1932, *Theological Dictionary of the NT*, is a significant illustration of the trends of the period. Cardinal Bea could describe it as one of the most important and reliable works of Protestant biblical research. When we take into account that the long list of collaborators makes it truly representative, we are assured that the climate has really changed.

With regard to the exegesis of the NT, this more **c** recent period has been marked by a more thorough study of Jewish life and thought in the time of Christ and in the apostolic period. This study was given a quite unexpected emphasis by the discovery of the Qumran and kindred documents in 1947 and later years. Side by side with this interest, the study of the Hellenistic religious background in which early Christianity developed and expressed itself has been pursued with equal intensity. A third, more technical aspect of research, since 1918, is the *Formgeschichtliche Methode*, applied chiefly to the gospels.

Form Criticism of the Synoptic Gospels. Im- **d** mediately after the First World War, in the years between

634d 1919 and 1922, a new approach to the synoptic gospels developed in Germany. The explanation of the relations between the gospels in terms of common literary sources had led to the Two-Source theory: Mk is the earlist of our gospels and the other two are dependent on Mk and on a collection of sayings of the Lord, designated by Q. But these two sources were relatively late and represented a developed stage of the tradition. Attempts to break them down into earlier written sources met with no real success. The course of the gospel tradition between its beginnings and its well-nigh final form in Mk and Q remained shrouded in darkness. Literary criticism alone seemed powerless to pierce the gloom. The only hope lay in going back behind the written sources and studying the oral tradition. The name given to the new approach, *Formgeschichtliche Methode*, indicates a method which concentrates on the form or structure of the primitive gospel tradition. In English, it has become known as Form Criticism. The method is not entirely new: it had already been applied to parts of the OT, notably Gn and Ps, by H. Gunkel; but it is within the field of synoptic criticism that it has grown and developed.

e The two most influential exponents of the method, in its application to the synoptic gospels, have been Martin Dibelius and Rudolf Bultmann, though the first step had been taken by K. L. Schmidt (*The Setting of the Story of Jesus*, 1919). Bultmann (*The Form Criticism of the Gospel*, 1919) and Dibelius (*The History of the Synoptic Tradition*, 1921) differ notably in their approach; yet they presuppose a number of common principles: (1). The synoptic gospels are not literary units but mosaics of varied fragments. Consequently, the evangelists are not so much authors as compilers who have grouped isolated and disparate elements into a framework of their own devising. The synoptic gospels are not literature in a true sense, but belong to the category of popular literature; or they might be described as 'infra-literary'. (2). The gospels are not biographies; none of them gives an historical and consistent picture of the life of Jesus. The gospels, in fact, are not concerned with the Jesus of history; rather they are testimonials to the faith of the Christian community in the Saviour of the world. (3). The constituent elements of the gospel tradition are the product of the first-generation Christian communities. The faith of the first-century Christians was coloured and shaped by the *Christus-Mythos*—the 'myth of Christ'. In the light of this faith the community created the gospel. The demands of preaching, apologetics, and the cult gave birth, in the primitive communities, to popular narratives developed around sayings or actions (real or invented) of Jesus, or formed under the influence of motifs borrowed from Jewish and hellenistic milieux. This combination of creative faith and practical demands leaves little room for anything of real historical value in the gospels.

f A cardinal postulate of Form Criticism is the creative power of the community; this postulate leaves little room for eye-witnesses. Here the form critics are subject to a philosophical presupposition. For the creative role of the community is a concept ultimately founded on hegelian philosophy: the idea immanent in humanity is expressed especially in a collective fashion. Hence, the primacy is accorded to the community to the detriment of individual witnesses. For these critics, too, there is no question of distinguishing the Jesus of history from the Christ of faith: since the transformation of Jesus began as far back as our traditions go, Jesus is forever lost to sight behind the primitive community.

Since Bultmann and Dibelius viewed the gospels as **63** compilations of varied fragments, they set about analysing the gospels and classifying their component parts. It is a basic assumption of Form Criticism that originally the traditions circulated in separate oral units which may be classified according to their forms. The gospel material as a whole falls into two main groups: logia (sayings of Jesus) and narrative material (stories about Jesus). Although both critics accept this general division, they do not quite agree in subsequent classification. In his classification of the logia, Bultmann distinguishes six groups: proverbs, prophetic and apocalyptic sayings, community rules, personal proclamations ('I' sayings), parables, apophthegms. Dibelius classifies the logia under the general denomination of parenesis ('persuasion', 'exhortation')—because, in his view, they were collected for instructive and hortatory purposes—and does not treat them in detail. Analysis of the narrative material has proved more difficult, and here the two critics differ widely. Bultmann is satisfied with these three headings: miracle-stories, anecdotes and legends (edifying and unhistorical passages), and the Passion-narrative. Dibelius has five groups: paradigms, *Novellen* (miracle stories), legends (edifying narratives), myths (e.g. baptism, temptation, transfiguration), and Passion-narrative. To the apophthegms = paradigms, the British scholar, Vincent Taylor, has given the simpler and more descriptive name of Pronouncement Stories: a narrative leads up to and is concerned solely with a saying or pronouncement of Jesus (e.g. Mk 12:13—17). It is important to observe that, after this painstaking analysis, the critics admit that the forms rarely occur in a pure state and that for the most part we have to do with *Mischformen*, with 'mixed types'.

The classification of the traditional material is only **63** a first step. It is far more important to trace the origin and development of the literary forms. For that purpose, we must see them against the background of the primitive community, and we must establish the needs that gave rise to them and the tendencies they represent. In a word, their *Sitz im Leben*, the life-situation out of which they have grown, must be determined. Dibelius starts with the offices or functions of the primitive community, especially with the fundamental office of preaching. 'In the beginning was the sermon' is his foundation thesis. This preaching naturally demanded examples; thus, the paradigms were born. As time went on, details were added, and the *Novellen* appeared—the work of later anonymous storytellers. He is vague about the legends and myths and does not attribute them to a community office; but they are later than the other forms and quite unhistorical. Bultmann starts with the gospel text and, by a close analysis of it, eliminates additions and retouches. These modifications are due to motifs and points of view that may be identified as we study the tradition which evolves as it passes from one gospel to another—especially as it passes from the canonical to the apocryphal gospels. When we have determined the laws of this evolution, in their light we can fix the initial phase of the tradition and rediscover its primitive form, or, at least we may discover the 'motif' that has given rise to the tradition. The *Sitz im Leben* of the elements is to be sought in 'debates' within communities: in these 'debates', the tradition was shaped under the influence of apologetic, polemical, and dogmatic needs. Bultmann believes that, for the most part, the process took place in the Palestinian communities, but that the miracle-stories and legends took shape in Hellenistic circles. Some of the discourse tradition is also traced to the hellenistic world.

A serious methodological error is the critics' leap **b**

635b from literary criticism to historical criticism. Dibelius not only attributes his paradigms to 'preachers' and his *Novellen* to 'storytellers', but asserts that the *Novellen* are a later form and thus less likely to be historical. It is not easy to see why the minister of the word could not use both pronouncement-story and miracle-story, and it is reasonable to feel that both forms go back to the earliest tradition; at least we may not date them on the basis of *form* alone. Bultmann, too, is guilty of the same error. The 'motifs' he invokes are doctrinal and are concerned with substance rather than with form. Thus, he affirms that a word of Jesus justifies a practice of the primitive Church (e.g. Mk 2:20 and the question of fasting); that a discussion of Jesus with the Pharisees throws light on a living issue between Jews and Christians (e.g. 2:27 and the sabbath observance); that an action of Jesus establishes a matter of faith or cult (e.g. 2:10 and the forgiveness of sins; 14:22—25 and the eucharist). These observations are indeed enlightening, but Bultmann takes a fatal step: the words of Jesus have not been recalled in view of such circumstances; they have been *invented*. This conclusion takes him well beyond the limits of literary criticism.

c Nonetheless, the positive contribution of Form Criticism is great. We are well aware now of literary units within the synoptic gospels and of the frequent loose linking of these units. We no longer seek to trace a strictly logical sequence of thought throughout a gospel or throughout a long passage of it; rather, we recognize that at times—frequently, in fact—we need to study a pericope sentence by sentence, for isolated sayings may be joined by a system of catchwords, or simply juxtaposed. It is no longer open to question that many smaller literary compositions stand behind our written gospels. While we cannot accept the 'storyteller' of Dibelius and while we recognize that the 'preacher' as conceived by him is an artificial figure, we admit that the first christian preachers did help to shape the tradition. We also realize that there was a development of the tradition, a process which, partially at least, is still visible in the gospels. It is not only legitimate, but illuminating, to seek the *Sitz im Leben* of the units of the tradition. The 'motifs' of the critics are arbitrary, but there are other, genuine factors which did govern the selection of the sayings of our Lord and the stories about him. In particular, we have been made aware of some of the interests of the early Church, the milieux in which elements of the tradition were shaped; cult, mission preaching, and catechetics—the activities of a living community. There were, of course, other concerns; but all of them sprang from the impact of the new faith on men who had accepted Jesus as Lord. We can well be thankful to Form Criticism for making us conscious of these factors, for now we are more keenly aware that our gospels have taken rise within the Church of Christ.

d When it has been relieved of the impossible load it had been asked to carry, the method of Form Criticism shows us the real influence of the early Church on the formation of the gospel tradition. It did not create that tradition, as Bultmann would have it, but it did mould forms of it and it did interpret the tradition in the light of experience. We owe to Form Criticism our awareness of these facts, and, to some extent, the explanation of them, and we owe to it the identification of many of the literary units of the tradition. How valuable the contribution has been may be judged from the work of such outstanding scholars as Vincent Taylor, C. H. Dodd, and Joachim Jeremias. In fact, all serious students of the NT today (including Catholic scholars, **635d** of course) are to some extent Form Critics.

Demythologising the Gospel—We have noted that **636a** D. F. Strauss, in a systematic manner, applied the concept of myth to the interpretation of the gospel. W. de Wette (1780—1848) saw that there was no question of simply eliminating myth in the hope of attaining a religious or scientific truth which can exist independently of it; it was a question, rather, of discovering the positive element which can be precisely expressed only in mythic terms. In his turn, R. Bultmann held that not merely particular narratives or incidents embody mythological elements, but that the whole of the gospel story is based on a mythical conception of the universe (for instance, the three-storied universe of heaven, earth, and hell, the incarnation and the resurrection, the eschatology of the NT, and the miracles). In all his works (notably in *The NT and Mythology*, 1941), Bultmann refers to myth as to a reality sufficiently known and not in need of explanation. Mythic thought is purely and simply opposed to scientific thought and, as such, is unacceptable to modern man. In point of fact, his notion of myth did not take cognizance of recent studies which have tended to show that myth, as symbolic expression, is an essential part of the pattern of human thought and discourse, and that it can never be entirely replaced by logical discourse. For Bultmann, the 'mythological' language of the NT has to be translated into the language of modern man—in practice, into the categories of existentialist philosophy. A principal task of theology is *Entmythologisierung*, the 'demythologising' of the NT message.

b The term suggests a negative approach, whereas Bultmann was profoundly concerned to bring the religious value of the NT home to modern man. Criticism of the biblical writings does not consist in the elimination of mythical expressions, but in their interpretation. Demythologisation is a method of hermeneutics, an existentialist interpretation which seeks to manifest the intention of the myth. And, despite its mythological language, the NT does answer the question about the meaning of human existence. This meaning is found in the proclamation of the decisive eschatological act of God in Christ; the life and death of Christ have made existence meaningful and have shown its fulfilment. In Christ, man encounters God, for the proclamation is a personal encounter which demands a personal response. Knowledge of the historical Jesus, however, is not essential to Christian faith. In order 'to believe' it is not necessary to know about Jesus, but rather to meet him in our experience as he comes to us in a living, present challenge. It is impossible, and unnecessary, to go behind the *kerygma*, the proclamation.

The Post-Bultmannians—Many of Bultmann's stu- **c** dents and disciples have become so radically independent of their master's positions that they form a trend of their own; we can speak of the post-Bultmannians. The most prominent of them are E. Käsemann, E. Fuchs, G. Bornkamm, H. Conzelmann, and G. Ebeling. A notable characteristic of the latest school is a new interest in the historical Jesus. The kerygma presents Jesus as the Lord, as God's means of bringing redemption to men, and as marking the inauguration of the eschatological era. It is important to show that the kerygmatic portrait is a faithful representation of the historical Jesus. This, in fact, is a new 'quest of the historical Jesus' (J. M. Robinson). About the turn of the century, NT scholarship was largely concerned with the 'quest of the historical Jesus'—that is, the search to discover what really happened in the life of Jesus of Nazareth. Because

636c it is the faith of Christians, and not facts about Jesus, which confronts us in the gospels, Bultmann had considered the quest futile. The form critics of the post-Bultmannian school, while they do not consider that a full life of Jesus is possible, do recognize that the Jesus of history is essential to the preaching of the NT. However, they are not intent on showing that the kerygma is true (because it lies in the realm of faith and so, beyond proof), but that the kerygma is faithful to Jesus. Bultmann's interpretation of the NT had its roots in Heidegger's existentialism, cf *Time and Being* (1927); the post-Bultmannians are more concerned with the *later* philosophical thought of Heidegger. But whatever the undoubted contributions of the Bultmannian and post-Bultmannian movements, they need to be measured against the impersonal, non-existentialist exegesis of scholars like J. Jeremias, O. Cullmann, and V. Taylor. The remark of R. E. Brown is apposite: 'Catholic biblical scholars who have had to learn to read Scripture without scholastic glasses are going to be somewhat dubious about substituting another pair of spectacles made in Germany.'

d Redaction Criticism—There has also been a reaction against the earlier form critics in another way. Where Form Criticism has helped to make us aware of the importance of pre-Gospel tradition (often at the expense of the evangelists' role), *Redaktionsgeschichte* ('redaction-history')—Redaction Criticism—has drawn our attention to the contribution of the evangelists. They were not entirely free because they were working with traditional material, and they often wished to respect pre-existing literary units. But we are aware at last that they worked with more freedom than we had been wont to believe. The evangelists are authors and the gospels are personal works, each having its own definite stamp and character. Three scholars in particular have contributed to our understanding of this factor: G. Bornkamm, W. Marxsen, and H. Conzelmann, (though, again, all present-day NT scholars are, to some extent, redaction critics).

e The Fourth Gospel—At the end of the last century and in the early years of this century, scholarship went through a period of extreme scepticism about the Fourth Gospel. Since it was taken to be a product of the hellenistic world, it was thought to be almost entirely devoid of historical value and to have little relation to the Palestine of Jesus. The synoptic gospels had served as a basis for the author's investigation and account for any grains of fact in his work. Since the end of the Second World War the situation has changed. Now the dependence of John on a postulated, early oriental Gnosticism (such as Bultmann's proto-Mandean gnostic source) seems more unlikely than ever. It is recognized that OT speculation on personified wisdom, as well as the thought patterns of sectarian Judaism (Qumran), can effectively account for elements that had seemed to argue for some Gnostic affinity. Again, whereas it had been thought that John had been influenced by Philo, the evidence now points towards a common background shared by Philo and John. At the same time, any influence of the *Hermetica* is being discounted. In short, a majority of scholars are coming to agree that the principal background of Johannine thought is the Palestinian Judaism of Jesus' time. Here, links with Qumran literature are of special interest. Both John and the Qumran sectarians were influenced by currents of thought prevalent in certain circles of Judaism at the time. In the Fourth Gospel a form of dualism is expressed in contrasts: light-darkness, truth-falsehood, life-death. The meaning of these expressions is very close to that of similar ones in the Qumran

texts. The Johannine, like the Qumran, dualism is **636e** monotheistic, ethical, and eschatological (expecting the victory of light) and hence differs from Gnostic dualism.

A particularly significant tendency of recent scholarship **f** is a re-evaluation of the historical standing of the Fourth Gospel. In his *Historical Criticism in the Fourth Gospel* (1963), C. H. Dodd comes to the conclusion that, despite the manifest theological development of the gospel material by John, the evangelist, to an extent hitherto not sufficiently recognized, followed a tradition parallel to, but largely independent of, the synoptic tradition. At the same time there is a special relationship between Jn and Lk. Although it may be that some of the many contacts can be explained by the influence of Lk on the final form of Jn, the greater number are so distinctively Johannine that the influence must lie in the other direction. Lk's research turned up Johannine traditions and these he built into his work. This would point to the early formation of a Johannine tradition, long before the final edition of the Fourth Gospel.

II CATHOLIC CRITICAL STUDY OF THE GOSPELS

The Rise of Catholic Critical Study of the Bible— **637a** Catholic biblical scholarship, which until about 1890 had continued in a severely traditional climate since the condemnation of Simon's work (cf § 92*a*), had produced little in the field of literary or historical criticism. The destructive nature of so much of that criticism only served to perpetuate this attitude within the Catholic Church. At most, Catholic reaction to rationalism took the form of defensive apologetics, and the apologetic attitude encouraged extreme conservatism. In their attacks on rationalism, scholars were too often blind to the valid scientific conclusions which had been reached by Protestants. A more unhappy result was that this same attitude drew suspicion on Catholic authors who were alive to the positive achievements of Protestant scholarship and who realized that scientific study of Scripture was an imperative task; cf § 96*e*.

However, in the later pontificate of Leo XIII, things **b** began to improve. The year 1890, mentioned above, was not chosen at random: it is the date of the foundation of the *École Biblique* in Jerusalem by M.-J. Lagrange, O.P. Looking back over the distance of more than threequarters of a century, it is more evident than ever that he was the dominant figure in the rise of modern Catholic biblical scholarship. Lagrange launched the *Revue Biblique* in 1892 and in 1900 projected the series of *Études bibliques*—rigidly scientific commentaries on the books of the Bible. The work of Lagrange and men of similar outlook, like F. von Hummelauer, S.J., already exposed to sustained and often bitter criticism (by fellow Catholics), was seriously threatened by the Modernist crisis. In the field of exegesis, the chief representative of Modernism was A. Loisy. His works, together with his entire intellectual orientation, did immense harm to the progress of Catholic exegesis; in many minds, and among certain ecclesiastical authorities, mistrust was engendered against progressive tendencies in exegesis. Yet, significantly, in the immediate wake of the crisis, Lagrange published his commentary on Mk (1911). It was an epoch-making event in the history of Catholic NT exegesis: the first truly scientific commentary on a gospel.

The reaction of the Church to the situation of **c** Catholic biblical studies in the period before 1914 took two forms, the exercise of a restrictive discipline and

37c the encouragement of scientific study and training; cf § 96*f*, *g*.

d It was the period of the Modernist crisis. There was real and deep uneasiness among Catholic exegetes. The cloud of suspicion which, for a time, had fallen on such a scholar as Lagrange, still hovered on the Roman horizon. An action like that of the then Holy Office, which in 1923 placed on the Index several editions of Brassac's *Manuel biblique*, was not calculated to set fears at rest. Exegetes were tempted to specialize in one of the auxiliary biblical subjects, matters less likely to be controversial. But all this was to change—right in the middle of the Second World War. And yet, it is true to say that the instrument of change, the encyclical *Divino afflante Spiritu* (1943) of Pius XII, rightly regarded as the 'Magna Charta' of Catholic biblical studies, would have been impossible without the dedicated work of enlightened scholars from the turn of the century onwards. This encyclical, in its repercussions, is surely one of the most important papal documents in the history of the Church. It is remarkable for the broadness and serenity of its views, and for the absolute confidence it places in the goodwill and competence of Catholic biblical scholars. Happily, it can be said that this confidence was not misplaced, for the present reawakening of the Church to an awareness of the role of the Bible in her life is due in great measure to the dedicated men praised by Pius XII and to their successors. A remarkable reflection of this was the consistently scriptural orientation and flavour of the documents of the Second Vatican Council. The teaching authority of the Church has thus acknowledged its indebtedness to Scripture scholars and other theologians who are fully alive to the revival of biblical studies.

38a Critical Study of the Gospels—The new freedom enjoyed since 1943 has made for a truly amazing advance in the quality and range of Catholic biblical scholarship. One of the first results was a readiness to assimilate all that was best in the work of Protestant scholars; it was to be expected that Form Criticism would make a notable impact. In truth, the biblical scholar rapidly drew far ahead not only of the Catholic public, but of the theologians trained in a different school. Hence, a certain reactionary current persisted. It came to the surface in a rather unpleasant attack on the Pontifical Biblical Institute a year or so before the Council. The *Instruction on the Historical Truth of the Gospels* issued by the Biblical Commission in 1964 is, in part, a reply, and a devastating one, to this attack. But it is not only a defence. An essential feature of the document, whose main purpose is to underline the truth of the deeds and words recorded in the gospels, is its acknowledgement of the need for genuine intellectual freedom in the pursuit of biblical studies. So, it passes quickly to its chief concern—a recommendation of the scientific study of the gospels as the only way to understand them properly. The Catholic exegete does not have to plough a lone furrow; he can draw on the resources of the past. But, as a man of the twentieth century, he must make use of the specific contributions of modern research. So, while observing the rules of literary and historical criticism which guide the interpreter of ancient documents or literature ('rational hermeneutics'), and those other norms which take into account the inspiration of the Bible ('Catholic hermeneutics'), he will pay special attention to the 'historical method' in its widest sense. It is explained that the historical method means, in practice, the study of sources, built on a solid foundation of textual criticism, literary criticism, and linguistic studies. Follow-

ing *Divino afflante Spiritu*, special attention is drawn **638a** to a study of the literary forms used by the sacred writer; obviously, the principle must be extended to the gospels. In short, the exegete cannot afford to neglect any means that may give him a better understanding of the nature and background of the gospel testimony.

Predictably, the document contains a significant state- **b** ment on the use of Form Criticism in the study of the gospels. It is acknowledged that the sound elements of the method will help the exegete to gain a fuller understanding of the gospels. At the same time it is asserted that inadmissible philosophical and theological principles, have tended to vitiate the method and its conclusions. The distinction between the literary method and its prejudicial principles of a philosophical or theological nature is of paramount importance, but it is not new. It has, for some time, been accepted and followed in practice by many scholars—not all of them Catholic by any means. We have given above an adequate indication of the positive contribution of Form Criticism. Our study has concentrated on the synoptic gospels; we may certainly take it that the Catholic approach to the Fourth Gospel is no less scientific. It is enough to mention recent commentaries on John, those of R. Schnackenburg and R. E. Brown—both massive studies of outstanding quality.

III HISTORICITY OF THE GOSPELS

The dogmatic constitution *Dei Verbum* of the Second **c** Vatican Council reasserts the Catholic affirmation of the historical value of the gospels. It declares that the Church 'has firmly and with absolute constancy maintained and continues to maintain that the four gospels, whose historicity she unhesitatingly affirms, faithfully hand on what Jesus, the Son of God, while he lived among men, really did and taught for their eternal salvation, until the day when he was taken up (cf Ac 1:1f) (Art. 19). Its explanation of this historicity explicitly refers to the fuller treatment of this subject by the Biblical Commission's *Instruction*. The Church has always affirmed the historical value of the testimony of the evangelists. To appreciate the reasonableness of this contention, we need to take account of a number of factors; in the first place the fact that the apostles, companions of Jesus during his public ministry, witnesses of his death and of his glorification, had, after those events, understood more clearly—had seen in a new light—what their Master had said and done. Now that he had entered into his glory and that they had been enlightened by the Spirit of God, they at last grasped who and what he was; it is their witness and their preaching which come to us through the written gospels.

Modern scholarship has made clearer **how the gospels d have grown:** from the oral tradition through partial written accounts, to the gospels as we know them. Drawing on this rich treasure of oral tradition and written narrative, the evangelists, each in his own way, have set before us the story of Jesus. Now it is impossible to tell a story without at the same time in some way bringing out its meaning; only so can a selection be made from among the myriad details and facets of what happened. It is considered the duty of a modern historian to present not only his interpretation of events but also a full enough, 'neutral', account of the events for the reader to evaluate his interpretation. The evangelist makes no attempt to do this: he presents only the events as he—and, behind him, his community— see them with the eye of faith. And this is an authoritative view, since the inspiration of the scriptures means that

638d their view is guided by the Spirit. Hence in order fully to seize the message of our Lord's words we must read them in the arrangement and with the emphasis indicated by the evangelist. Ordering and selection are two means by which the evangelist brings out this message. Similarly with our Lord's actions; we must attempt, not so much to push behind the evangelist's account of the 'brute' facts, as to penetrate to and absorb the meaning which the evangelist, under the guidance of the Spirit, saw in the event. The theology of the evangelists is no private interpretation but the interpretation presented to us by the first generation of Christians under the inspiration of the Spirit.

e Our task of seeing events with the eye of the evangelists is made no easier by the gap in centuries and in culture which separates us from them. The most fundamental difference is that they were steeped in biblical imagery. The English language too has been widely influenced by biblical language, but to the early Christians—especially those sprung, like Mt's community, from Judaism—a biblical phrase would suffice to conjure up a whole context which could immediately teach the significance of an event, the fulfilment of a promise or the associations of an action. Thus what may seem to us to be pointless or merely lively details, or even wild predictions of calamity, are in fact instances of allusive language whose meaning would be immediately clear to the first audiences of the gospel, but requires on our part laborious reconstruction. Two prime examples of descriptions of happenings where such allusive language is employed as to enable the initiated reader to appreciate the full significance of the event, while leaving to the uninitiate the impression that he is reading a commonplace account of the event, are those of the Feeding of the Five Thousand and of the Messianic Entry into Jerusalem. Similarly the eschatological discourse of Mt 24, far from being a prediction, literal fulfilment of whose terms is to be expected in the minutest detail, is intended as an assessment, couched in terms of the imagery of the prophetic writings, of the theological significance of the event (cf § 715*c*). A reader innocent of this OT imagery can only presume that the account purports to present him with history; as soon as this imagery is perceived and evaluated the chapter is seen to contain rather a theology of history. It is the task of the exegete to penetrate the evangelist's form of expression, superficially misleading to us as it may often be, to uncover the message which he wished to express.

f The evangelists wrote for an audience of believers. The meaning and not the historicity of Jesus' words and actions were their primary concern; their historicity might be assumed. Hence penetration to the 'actual events' will assist our understanding of the gospel message only in so far as it enables us to see more clearly the light in which these 'actual events' were viewed. It is of less interest to the believer to know what the centurion meant when he acknowledged that the crucified Jesus was 'Son of God' (Mt 27:54) than to know the meaning of this title to the inspired evangelist. It is immaterial how many men actually accompanied Jesus on his entry into Jerusalem; the evangelist is more concerned to tell us that this entry was the accomplishment of the prophecies that the Messiah would come to his city (cf § 732*de*), and in function of this intention accounts them a 'very great crowd' (21:8). He is writing in the light of the full appreciation of the significance of the actions and the person of Jesus which came only in the course of time, and after the out-pouring of the Spirit at Pentecost. This does not mean that the events described did not occur;

it means only that the intention which rules the description **638** of them is not a determination to prove that they occurred, but a desire to show their significance to the Christian.

Nor does this imply that the historical events are **g** not important. Indeed 'the denial of the importance of historical facts would carry with it a denial of what is of the essence of the Gospel, namely, that the historical order—that order within which we must live and work—has received a specific character from the entrance into it of the eternal Word of God' (C. H. Dodd). The one basic fact upon which the gospel reposes is the fact of Jesus—for, in the NT, the self-revelation of God is centred in the life, teaching, death, resurrection and exaltation of Jesus Christ, the Son of God—and the picture of Jesus which emerges from the different texts is a remarkably consistent one. However, we need to go beyond the evangelists because, although they have given us a fourfold account of the Good News, they themselves are not the authors of the Good News. They have put the story of the Lord in writing, but that story had existed long before they wrote. Between Christ and the evangelists come the apostles and the first preachers. Thus, we return, ultimately, to the early Church, for it was the Church that shaped the basic gospel which was afterwards passed on to us, according to the viewpoint of each, by the evangelists. We have, then, three stages: Jesus Christ, the apostolic Church, and the evangelists. It is only when we have taken all three into account that we can really understand the gospels. This discernment of the 'three stages of tradition by which the teaching and the life of Jesus have come down to us' (*Instruction* § 6) shows an appreciation of the development of the gospel material that we owe, in large measure, to Form Criticism.

It is evident, however, that, as we have seen, we may **h** not undervalue the contribution of **Redaction Criticism.** True enough, the evangelist is the spokesman of a living Church and his work is kerygmatic: to herald Jesus Christ, his saving deeds and words. The person of Jesus, seen and interpreted in the light of the resurrection, is the centre of salvation history; and the presentation of his person and teaching, seen in that light, is necessarily theological. As one who selects, synthesizes and interprets the apostolic tradition the evangelist, to a greater or lesser degree, is a theologian. Though he does not intend to write a detailed biography of Jesus he has indeed a care for the historical and a certain biographical interest; but his intention remains, fundamentally, kerygmatic and theological. Each of the evangelists wrote with a specific purpose in view and not only selected and arranged the material, but could on occasion adapt it, to suit that purpose; we must keep in mind the distinctive individuals and their viewpoints.

Hence it is clear that in any assessment of their **i** historicity, the **theological dimension of the basic gospel facts** should not be lost to sight. This is so true that we might say of Luke that this evangelist was an historian because he was a theologian. His view of the *pragmata*, the 'events' (1:1), was coloured by his reflections on the relevance of the traditional *logoi*, 'teaching' (1:4) for his own time. If this teaching, the sayings of Jesus about the importance of human relationships, about the virtues of patience, perseverance, poverty of spirit, about the necessity of persistence in prayer, did have a far-reaching importance for all time, then it meant that the period after the resurrection and ascension had a value peculiar to itself as circumstantially influential for salvation, and not merely as a short interval before the Second Coming. This idea moulded Lk's interpretation of

638i the tradition, but immediately raised the question of the relationship between Lk's contemporary situation and the life of Christ. For Lk, salvation had come with Christ; after the ascension, men would be saved through him and because of what he had accomplished. The events of the life of Christ were decisive for the world, constituting the beginning of the last days. For Lk, too, Christ was the fulfilment of all the promises, in spite of the outward circumstances of his life which blinded the eyes of the Jews to the reality before them. This implied that all that went before Christ was merely preparatory. Yet, preparation, fulfilment in Christ, and eventual universal salvation through him in these last days, though constituting quite distinct epochs, nonetheless together form one divine plan for the salvation of the world, a plan progressively realized through history (cf § 766e–h). In his very discernment of a divine plan, Lk the theologian has drawn attention to a real dimension of this history.

j Again, in this context, we may consider **the resurrection of Jesus.** Obviously, the resurrection is of paramount importance in the NT; but how are we to understand it? Jesus had reserved the post-resurrection manifestation of himself to witnesses whom he had chosen (Ac 2:32; 10:41; 13:21; 1 Cor 15:8). From Pentecost onwards, the resurrection became the centre of apostolic preaching because it revealed the fundamental object of Christian faith (Ac 2:22–35). This gospel of Easter is first and foremost testimony to a fact: Jesus was crucified and had risen. This is the message of Peter to the Jews (Ac 3:14f) and his confession before the Sanhedrin (4:10); it is the teaching of Philip (8:35); it is the argument of Paul (13:33; 17:3) and his profession of faith (23:6). Always it is the same Easter experience; and it is consistently presented as a fulfilment of Scripture. Yet, we need to bear in mind that the apostolic preaching had developed a theological interpretation of the fact of the resurrection. It is the Father's glorification of the Son (Ac 2:22f; Rm 8:11) and thus sets the seal of God's approval on the redemptive act. By it, Jesus is constituted 'Son of God in power' (Rm 1:4), 'Christ and Lord' (Ac 2:36), 'chief and saviour' (Ac 5:31), 'judge and Lord of living and dead' (Ac 10:42; Rm 14:9; 2 Tim 4:1). Returned to the Father, he can now send the Spirit (Jn 20:17–22). Now at last the full meaning of his earthly life appears: he was the manifestation of God here below, of God's love and of his grace (2 Tim 1:10; Ti 2:11; 3:4). It is inevitable that the words and works of Christ, seen now in the full light of Easter faith, should present a new dimension to those who had formerly heard and seen without fully understanding. And the resurrection itself, even in the gospels, is something much more than 'resuscitation', a mere raising from the dead. The historical fact is at the same time a theological fact. **638j**

In short, when we stress the historical nature of **k** Christianity and the substantial historicity of the Gospel, we would do well to recall the declaration of *Dei Verbum*: 'This economy of Revelation is realized by deeds and words, which are intrinsically bound up with each other. As a result the works performed by God in the history of salvation show forth and bear out the doctrine and realities signified by the words; the words, for their part, proclaim the works and bring to light the mystery they contain' (art. 2). Here we are reminded that revelation is an 'economy', that is, a divine providence directing men and their history towards salvation. The direction is given by an interplay of word and action, in such a way that neither words alone nor actions alone provide Revelation. The doctrine taught by God and the mysterious divine realities he communicates to men are made concrete, visible and credible by the things he does in the course of sacred history. The events, on the other hand, get significance, become revelation, when their meaning is expressed in words (L. Walsh). The evangelists have brought out the *meaning* of the Christ-event: Christ, who is God and Man, not alone brought us the ultimate, inner truth about God and man's salvation but is himself, in his own person, the fullness of Revelation. They have not written to gratify a purely historical curiosity about past events, but to bear witness to the revelation of God—a revelation rooted in history.

THE FORMS OF NEW TESTAMENT LITERATURE

BY G. GRAYSTONE S.M.

641a Bibliography—W. G. Kümmel, *Introd. to the NT*, NTL E.tr. 1966; A. Tricot, 'Genres littéraires du NT', RT, 1954[3], 314–55; E.tr. *Guide to the Bible*, 1960[2], 514–63; C. H. Dodd, *The Apostolic Preaching and its Developments*, 1963[3]; A. M. Hunter, *Introducing the NT*, 1957[2]; C. F. D. Moule, *The Birth of the NT*, 1966[2]; R. Bultmann, *The History of the Synoptic Tradition*, E.tr. 1963; F. C. Grant, *The Gospels, their Origin and Growth*, 1957; K. Koch, *Was ist Formgeschichte*, Neukirchen, 1964; L. Alonso Schökel, *The Inspired Word*, 1965; R. Wellek and A. Warren, *Theory of Literature*, 1963[3]; J. Moffatt, *Introd. to the Literature of the NT*, 1911; J. N. Sanders, 'The Literature and Canon of the NT', PC (2), 1963; A. Robert, 'Littéraires (Genres)', DBS 5 (1957), 405–21; L. Venard, 'Historique (Genre) dans le NT', ibid, 4 (1949), 23–32; A. Feuillet and P. Grelot, 'La Critique littéraire du NT', RF 1 (1959[2]), 142–51; L. Cerfaux, *The Four Gospels*, E.tr. 1960; X. Leon-Dufour, *Les Evangiles et l'Histoire de Jésus*, 1963; O. Cullmann, *The Earliest Christian Confessions*, E. tr. 1953[2]; S. Neill, *The Interpretation of the NT*, 1966, and see also Bibliography, § 633a.

b Introduction—In determining the forms of NT literature, scholars have used a **twofold approach**, **comparative** and **analytic**. The first seeks comparisons with apposite ancient writings, e.g. OT, Jewish literature (OT apocrypha, DSS, Hellenistic and rabbinical writings), Greek and Roman literature, and the papyri. The analytic approach involves careful study and inter-comparison of the NT books themselves, their antecedents, circumstances of composition, structure, purpose and teaching.

c With certain qualifications to be mentioned later, NT literature may be broadly classed as **Historical Narrative** (Gospels, Acts), **Epistles** (Pauline, Catholic) and **Apocalypse**.

I. Historical Narrative (Gospels, Acts)—The Gospels according to Mt, Mk, Lk and Jn contain the story of Christ and his teaching. This story is completed by Ac, which deals with the spread of the Christian faith in Palestine and the Greco-Roman world. The first three gospels resemble one another in many respects. They are called Synoptic, because it is often possible to arrange their texts in parallel columns, so as to embrace them, as it were, by a single glance (*sunopsis*). They may rightly be taken together, then compared with Jn, markedly different in character.

d 1. The Gospels (a) The Synoptics—in spite of first impressions, are not 'lives' of Christ; the information they contain is too meagre, the sequence of events too vague—above all, their purpose was not biographical. Their literary form is best approached by examining their common title, *euangelion*, 'good news' (English 'gospel' has the same etymological sense). The expression is found with various connotations in classical and *koinè* usage, but the literary form is specifically Christian, with no exact parallels in other religious literature. It must be studied in the light of the Christian oral preaching **641d** which preceded and begot it. In NT times, and until the second century, *euangelion* did not signify a book, but an oral message, viz the good news of Messianic salvation, preached first by Jesus (cf Mk 1:15), then by the apostles after him—foretold by the prophets (notably Second Isaiah, apparently the immediate source of the term, cf Is 52:7–10), and now realized by Jesus Christ.

The Oral Gospel (cf also § 634d)—For two or three **e** decades after the Ascension, the 'good news' was preached and taught by the Church before being written down. This oral gospel comprised *kerygma*, preaching to unbelievers, and *didachè*, instruction of believers. The primitive apostolic kerygma (cf Peter's sermons in Ac 2:14ff, 3:12ff etc; 1 Cor 15:3ff) consisted in the public proclamation by witnesses in the name of God, of the Passion and Resurrection of Jesus, as fulfilling the Messianic prophecies of salvation, and concluding with an exhortation to conversion. To this basic message were soon attached, besides a fuller account of the Passion, some details of Christ's public ministry. A choice of episodes was made and set in a simple framework of chronology and geography (cf Ac 10:36–43). These brief accounts were preached, first in Palestine, then elsewhere, by the apostles and disciples, by the Hellenist missionaries (Ac 8:4ff) and by Paul, assisted by those charismatic preachers called 'evangelists' (Ac 21:8; Eph 4:11; 2 Tm 4:5). Meanwhile, the gospel was adapted as *didachè* for the instruction of Christians; this involved a further choice of material (cf D. Stanley, 'Didachè as a constitutive element of Gospel Form', CBQ 17 (1955), 336–48).

In its twin elements of *kerygma* and *didachè* the oral gospel was developed. Though tenacious oriental memory and the use of mnemonic devices (rhythm, alliteration, balance, repetition etc) made for substantial accuracy in transmission, rigorous material exactitude was not sought. Episodes tended to lose their position in place and time, and, according to the ordinary laws of human testimony and oral transmission, while essentials remained unchanged, there was variation in accidentals. Secondly, through repetition, the units of oral catechesis tended to become reduced to essentials, schematized in a particular 'form'. Thirdly, the gospel material was interpreted and adapted to meet the needs both of external preaching and apologetic, and of catechesis, liturgy, law etc within the Christian communities. This adaptation, carried out under the control of apostles and other eyewitnesses, was not perversion or falsification, but rather a deeper penetration into the meaning of the gospel message, by the light of the Holy Spirit whom Christ had promised (Jn 14:26). Finally, as time went on and the first witnesses were passing away, some of this oral material was put into writing (cf Lk 1:1ff), probably by way of small vade-mecums for the use of preachers and teachers. From these emerged the major Synoptic sources (cf § 645b–d) and finally the canonical gospels.

42a The Written Gospels—From the above analysis it is clear, as the form-critics claim, that the Synoptics are to some extent compilations. Hence it is possible and legitimate to isolate the units of which they are composed and to investigate their literary forms, e.g. miracle-stories, 'pronouncement stories', parables and allegories, wisdom and prophetic sayings etc (cf § 634d). Yet it would be wrong to regard the Synoptics as mere collections of anecdotes and sayings, strung together in a loose literary framework of no historical value. For one thing, the essential framework (Ac 10:36–43), not to speak of a good deal of grouping, was itself derived from primitive oral tradition. Moreover, the evangelists were truly authors, cf § 636d. Each had his own style and manner of narrating, his purpose and special interests, which guided him in selecting material or omitting, in transposing or grouping, discreetly emphasizing, modifying, interpreting. Thus, guided by the same Spirit as their oral predecessors, they continued and completed the shaping and presentation of the 'good news'.

b **Mk**, the faithful echo of Peter's catechesis (Papias, in Eus. HE 3, 39:15), is closest in structure to the primitive *schema* of Ac 10:36–43. It is a good example of the type of popular instruction used to introduce men to Christianity. Details of chronology and geography are few, the manner is simple and direct, the style popular and somewhat rugged, narrative—vivid and colourful—predominates, discourse is kept to a minimum. It would be a mistake, however, to minimize Mark's individuality. The structure of his gospel forms the basis of Lk and Mt, and he has a well-defined theme that dominates his work, viz 'the good news of Jesus Christ, the Son of God' (1:1; cf 15:39). This is developed not by arguments but by episodes vividly described; so that, reading Mk, we encounter the person of Jesus the Messiah, Son of God yet Son of Man, rejected by men but triumphing by the Cross.

c **Mt**, the Judeo-Christian gospel, is more complex. It has the appearance, firstly, of a kind of manual of Christian instruction. The author, writing more as a teacher than a historian, is much concerned with the orderly presentation and marshalling of his material. He skilfully groups the teaching of Jesus into five great discourse-programmes that divide up the gospel, each prefaced by a narrative section, each concluding with a similar formula. Stereotyped phrases, rhythmic sequences and numerical arrangement assist his presentation. However, his purpose is also dogmatic and apologetic—to present Jesus as Messiah, who, though rejected by the Jewish leaders, fulfilled the OT expectations and realized on earth God's kingdom and presence among men. The 'fulfilment' *motif* is underlined by a distinctive use of OT prophecy, which has been compared both with rabbinical exegesis and with the DSS biblical commentaries. The theme of the coming of God's kingdom is developed in quasi-dramatic fashion, beginning with prelude (chh 1–2) and skilful *mise-en-scène* (chh 3–4), continued in seven 'acts' till the climax of the kingdom's establishment in suffering and triumph. Mt's narratives, in contrast with Mk, are concise and summary, stripped of concrete detail.

d **Lk**, with preface and dedication after the manner of classical authors (1:1–4), is a more literary production. After careful enquiry and according to the tradition of eye-witnesses, the author proposes to write *kathexēs*, i.e. in sequence. He clearly intends an historical work, more exact and complete than his predecessors, and takes care to link his gospel with profane history (2:1; 3:1–2). For all that, his chronology is no more exact than that of Mk, whose order he follows. In other words, Lk is still

a 'gospel', based on the apostolic *catechesis*, not classical **642d** annals, history or biography. Yet it is a gospel with a distinctive theology of its own, that determines the considerable modifications and additions made to the Marcan tradition. Lk's theme, developed with great art and psychological insight, concerns the joyful good news of a Saviour, Christ the Lord (cf 2:11), who inaugurates a new era of salvation for all, especially the poor, the sinner, the pagan. The gospel begins and ends in Jerusalem; thither the life and teaching of Jesus is orientated (cf the 'Journey Narratives', 9:51–18:14), for the Holy City is the place where salvation is accomplished. Thence the gospel will be preached to the pagan world, as Luke narrates in his second volume (Acts).

Conclusion—The first three gospels bear within them- **e** selves abundant marks of the historical—respect for their sources, notably the oral tradition which preceded them, simplicity in presentation and archaism in tone, restraint in theological elaboration. Yet their primary purpose was not historical; the evangelists were not professional historians or biographers, still less stenographers, reproducing the words and deeds of Christ with rigorous exactitude. They wrote the 'good news', even as the apostles and witnesses had taught it by word of mouth, to inculcate faith, nourish and defend it. The literary form of the Synoptics is historico-doctrinal, i.e. history clarified in the light of Christ's resurrection and the descent of the Holy Spirit, history interpreted and applied, under the guidance of the Church, to the needs of a living faith.

On the origin and literary form of the gospels, cf the excellent summary in the Instruction of the Pontifical Biblical Commission, 'The Historical Truth of the Gospels, § 2' (April 21st 1964): 'Unless the exegete, then, pays attention to all those factors which have a bearing on the origin and the composition of the gospels, and makes due use of the acceptable findings of modern research, he will fail in his duty of ascertaining what the intentions of the sacred writers were, and what it is that they have actually said'.

(b) The Fourth Gospel The Fourth Gospel is a true **f** *euangelion*, reproducing the basic lines of the primitive *kerygma*. Yet it differs notably from the Synoptics, in material, presentation, style and vocabulary, and theology. As Clem.Alex. well expressed it, after the other gospels had stated the material facts (*ta sōmatika*), John composed a spiritual (*pneumatikon*) gospel (*apud* Eus. HE VI, 14, 7). His purpose is manifestly doctrinal. The gospel opens with a profoundly theological passage, the 'prologue' (1:1–18), which sets the tone for, in fact synthesizes, the whole gospel. Likewise, Jn's purpose is briefly stated at the end of the gospel (20:30–31). He writes, not to convert, but to perfect the faith of Christians in Jesus as Messiah and Son of God, so that believing they may have life through him. For this purpose he selects a certain number of events, called 'signs', chiefly miracles, seven in number, which also have a deeper, spiritual meaning. These are carefully spaced over the first part of the book (chh 1–12) so that, accompanied by a discourse of Jesus which explains their meaning, they progressively reveal the glory of the Word made flesh till the time of full revelation at the 'hour' of Jesus (chh 13ff). The Jewish liturgical feasts provide setting and framework for Jesus' public ministry, and, by a literary device known as 'inclusio' cf § 794d, the gospel begins and ends with a 'week' carefully marked. Symbolism, often sacramental in character, is found in numbers, things, words and events, and is frequently underlined by a characteristic play on the double meaning

642f of words. More than Mt, Jn exhibits certain features of the drama: prologue and epilogue, and a series of scenes in which vivid dialogue and skilful character-portrayal bring to life the gospel episodes. Beneath the surface facts of increasing antagonism between Jesus and the Jews lies a drama much deeper—the conflict between Light and Darkness, Jesus and Satan; and the dramatic tension is maintained and developed till the final *dénouement*, when the 'Prince of this world is cast forth' (12:31).

Jn is thus theological in purpose, without, however, excluding secondary polemical aims (e.g. against the Jews or the Gnostic Cerinthus). Nonetheless it is no mere collection of meditations or series of fictitious symbols and allegories. The author solemnly asserts that he is a witness of what he has seen and heard (cf 1:14; 19:35), and his disciples in a postscript declare the same (21:24)—for his doctrinal purpose depends for its attainment on witness that is true. Accurate portrayal of the Jewish scene before A.D. 70, and links in thought and expression with the world of the DSS, point to an authentic and independent tradition, possibly preached or taught before being written down. In Jn, then, the spiritual and symbolical is not opposed to, but rather superimposed upon, the historical. Mature meditation by the light of the promised Spirit has revealed deep divine truths hidden in the material facts, has shown how historical words and deeds are symbolic of the transcendent working of Jesus and his Church in men's souls. More, then, than the Synoptics is Jn a mixed *genre*. We might call it 'historico-mystical'—or perhaps rest content with Clement's pregnant phrase, a 'spiritual gospel'.

g 2. Acts of the Apostles—Ac is intimately linked with Lk in style and vocabulary. It is dedicated to the same Theophilus, refers back to Lk as the 'first book' (1:1) and takes up the story where Lk left off. It is, then, a sequel to the third gospel, the second part of his 'history of Christian Origins'. It is a literary work, composed with art and method, and belongs to the historical *genre*—for, as in Lk, the author is at pains to be well informed; he respects his sources, and external evidence confirms his historical probity. His methods suggest comparisons with classical history. Firstly, there are the speeches inserted at each stage of the narrative—these are summaries, no doubt, but not free and artificial compositions; certainly they perfectly suit the situation of time, place and person. Secondly, the author incorporates a 'travel diary' into the second part of Ac (the 'we-sections', 16:10–17; 20:5–21:18; 27:1–28:16). Here, however, besides the classical writers, the author had biblical models before him: Ez, Neh, Tb and 2 Mc. Thirdly, the title later given to the book, *praxeis*, i.e. acts, deeds (of apostles), was applied by the Greeks to writings recording the exploits of famous men like Hannibal or Alexander.

At the same time Ac cannot be reckoned as chronicles, annals or personal memoirs, nor is it a history of the twelve apostles, nor yet a biography of Peter and Paul—the narrative is too fragmentary and there are significant omissions. The author's primary purpose was religious, to give religious instruction by means of history, to show how, by the power of the Holy Spirit, the gospel spread—beginning 'in Jerusalem and all Judea and Samaria', then turning to the pagan world, 'even to the end of the earth' (1:8). This religious purpose determines the plan of the book and its omissions; stages of development are marked by the insertion of 'summaries' (2:42–47; 4:32–35; 5:12–16; 6:7; 9:31; 12:24); events of vital importance are narrated three times (the conversions of Saul and Cornelius, the Apostolic Decree of the 'Council

of Jerusalem'). Hence Ac is not primarily a work of polemic, **642** nor an apology or piece of special pleading—though we may admit that, granted his central purpose, the author did wish at the same time to be the apologist of the Christian faith before the pagan world, or to show how Paul's apostolate was a continuation of that of the Twelve.

II. The Epistles—The NT epistles, fourteen in the **643** Pauline corpus and seven Catholic Epistles, are not a homogeneous group. Some are true letters, others are letters only in outward appearance.

Letters or Epistles?—In ancient literature one can distinguish (a) the private letter, destined for specific recipients, and usually familiar in style (cf the letters of Cicero and esp. the Egyptian papyri). (b) In contrast to this was the letter addressed to public officials, groups or the public generally, and this was usually written in a more formal style, often dealt with a particular subject and was composed according to established literary norms, (cf those of Seneca and Aristotle). We may for convenience refer to the former as 'letters' and the latter as 'epistles'. A. Deissmann, (*Licht vom Osten*, 1923[3], 116–213) held that all Pauline epistles except Heb, together with 1 and 2 Jn, are true letters. Certainly Paul's epistles for the most part were written to meet the needs of specific recipients in a given situation; they were often conversational in style, meant to take the place of a personal visit. Undoubtedly, they must not be regarded as systematic expositions of Christian doctrine, to be interpreted in the abstract. On the other hand, Paul also clearly intended his letters as a means to complete his teaching and diffuse it beyond the circle of his immediate readers. His epistles contain theological and moral teaching of a general character, in passages composed with studied care (e.g. 1 Cor chh 12–15; 1 Thes 4:13–5:11; Rm 1:18–11:36). He wished his letters to be publicly read in the communities (1 Thes 5:27) and interchanged between communities (Col 4:16); he foresaw that they would circulate widely, and warned against forgeries (2 Thes 2:2; 3:17). It might be preferable, then, to speak of an intermediate *genre*, viz letters with some epistolary features. Heb, 1 Jn, 1 and 2 Pt, Jas and Jude (some add Rm, Eph, Pastorals) are undoubtedly epistles, but not uniform in type.

General Structure—Ancient letters consisted of three parts: the superscription, giving the names of sender and recipient, with a greeting (*chairein*, Lat. *salus*); the body of the letter; lastly, in place of a signature, the concluding salutation (*erröso*, Lat. *vale*, *salve*); cf Ac 15:23–29; 23:26–30. The NT epistles follow in general this structure, with certain exceptions. In the superscription, the name of a fellow-sender is often included, following Jewish and Near-Eastern usage. The greeting assumes a Christian form, e.g. 'grace and peace', usually followed by thanksgiving and prayer, or doctrinal expansion and doxology. The body of the epistle may be divided methodically (e.g. Gal, Rm), or developed without apparent connexion (1 and 2 Cor, Phil); sometimes dogmatic and moral sections are distinguished (Rm, Eph, Col). The final salutation becomes the Christian blessing, e.g. 'the grace of Our Lord Jesus Christ be with you' (1 Cor 16:23), greetings are sent to and from particular individuals (as in the papyri), often with a greeting in the writer's own hand, or with a doxology (2 Pt, Jude, Rm).

1. The Pauline Corpus—Rm exhibits here and there **b** the form of a letter, but habitually that of an epistle (cf Lagrange, *Romains*, xxxi f). Paul had no direct acquaintance with his readers, though he wrote to prepare for his intended visit (1:10–15; 15:14–33). He used the op-

643b portunity to present a systematic exposition of the main points of his 'gospel' regarding the relations of Christianity and the Mosaic Law. It is a literary work, the most carefully composed of his epistles, with thesis stated at the beginning (1:16—17) and systematically developed. Dogmatic and moral sections are distinct, and the major divisions conclude with doxologies (8:31—39; 11:33—36; 16:25—27). Rm provides good examples of the argumentative devices used by Paul, some familiar to the Rabbis (e.g. antitheses and comparisons, strings of proof texts, reasoning from the greater to the less and vice-versa), others popular with Cynic and Stoic philosophers (e.g. the diatribe, a series of short questions and answers, often introducing a fictitious interlocutor, cf 3:1ff; 4:1ff etc). Skilful use of diatribe and personification gives to certain sections (e.g. chh 5—8) almost a dramatic character.

c 1 and 2 Cor, on the contrary, are more properly letters, 'occasional writings'. 1 Cor treats without logical sequence of the most varied topics, whether in answer to questions, or to correct errors and abuses reported to the apostle. 2 Cor, whatever be said about its unity (one letter or a combination of several?), is a genuine letter, perhaps the most typically 'Pauline' of all. Gal, too, is a letter, written in the heat of combat, like a torrent of burning lava, charged with the deepest emotion and indignation— a marked contrast to the serene and methodical exposition of the same subject in Rm.

d Eph, Phil, Col and Phm are known as **Captivity Epistles** from their allusions to Paul's bonds. It is, however, disputed whether Phil was written on the same occasion as the other three; certainly in style and doctrine it approximates more closely to Rm, Cor and Gal; cf § 909a. It is a true letter, an outpouring of the heart, with no visible order or sequence. Col, written to a community Paul had not founded or visited, is somewhat formal in tone, though still a letter. The bearer, Tychicus, was accompanied on his journey by Onesimus, a runaway slave from Colossae, whom Paul was sending back with a letter of reconciliation, viz **Phm**. This tiny letter, written in familiar style in Paul's own hand, compares favourably with two letters sent by Pliny the Younger to a friend, one to ask pardon for a fugitive freedman, the other to thank him for the favour granted (*Letters*, 9:21, 24). **Eph**, which reproduces about half of Col and resembles it in many ways, is impersonal in character, less a letter than an epistle, perhaps a kind of encyclical to the churches of the Lycus valley.

e 1 and 2 Thes, written in lieu of a personal visit, are true letters, full of affection, with instruction on specific points, completing the teaching given orally. The so-called **Pastoral Epistles** (1 and 2 Tm, Ti) deal with the same subjects and errors, and stem from the same milieu. They are not as personal as the earlier letters, from which they differ in style and vocabulary. Though addressed to individual pastors, they contain instruction for all pastors, and for the communities themselves. They are not so much letters as instructions in epistolary form, the beginnings of Canon Law, yet rich also in doctrinal teaching.

f **Heb** stands in a class apart. Without address or preamble, the author plunges at once into his thesis, the pre-eminence of Christianity, with its one mediator, over the old dispensation. Well-developed doctrine alternates with pressing moral exhortation, the style is rich and oratorical, the form elegant. Heb, however, is not a theological treatise, but a 'word (discourse) of exhortation' (13:22), a kind of sermon or homily, mainly general in tone, but intended to encourage and instruct a particular

community exposed to trials; hence the epistolary con- **643f** clusion, expressing the hope of an early visit (13:18—25). There are analogies with the edifying synagogue address among the Hellenist Jews; cf the apocryphal 4 Maccabees and Ac 13:15.

2. The Catholic Epistles—Jas, 1 and 2 Pt, 1, 2 and 3 **644a** Jn and Jude are commonly called 'Catholic Epistles', as if destined for all Christians, like encyclicals. The title does not, however, suit 2 and 3 Jn.

Jas, apart from introductory greeting, has none of **b** the other features of a letter; it is addressed to all—or at least all Jewish—Christians (1:1). It belongs to the *genre* of *paraenesis*, a series of moral exhortations or instructions in loose sequence. Abundant liturgical allusions suggest that it was meant to be read in the course of public worship. In form it reflects the sapiential literature of the OT, read in the light of Christ's moral teaching, especially the Sermon on the Mount. Basically Semitic in style, Jas shows evidence of the use of Gr. rhetorical devices, e.g. the diatribe.

1 Pt, with its broad destination to the faithful of Asia, **c** its good Gr. style and absence of personal allusion (apart from the brief final salutation, 5:12—14), is more an epistle than a letter. Basically it consists of exhortations and moral instructions designed in part to uphold Christians in persecution. It might be called a pastoral homily. Some hold that, for the most part (at least till 4:11), it is a baptismal sermon, even a baptismal liturgy, with its hymns, instructions and homilies; cf E. Boismard in RB 63 (1956), 182—208; 64 (1957), 161—83; id, *Quatre Hymnes Baptismales, Lectio Divina* 30, Paris 1961. **2 Pt** is even less a letter than 1 Pt. The address is more general (1:1), a doxology takes the place of the final greeting (3:18). It is a kind of edifying homily designed to put the faithful on their guard against false teachers. Its somewhat composite structure, with marked dependence on Jude in ch 2, is offset by unity of style, strongly hellenistic in colouring. **Jude** resembles 2 Pt in many ways (also ending with a doxology, 24—25). It is an epistle or homily of general destination.

1 Jn scarcely affects the form of a letter, with its **d** absence of address, opening and closing greetings, and personal allusions. Yet it does presuppose a concrete situation, unrest caused by false teachers to a definite group of readers, who are addressed familiarly as 'little children' and 'dearly beloved'. 1 Jn, which closely resembles the Fourth Gospel in language, style and ideas, develops in simple and rhythmic fashion the parallel themes of light, justice, love and truth. It might be called a paternal homily. **2 and 3 Jn** are genuine brief letters, personal and familiar in tone, the one addressed to a particular church ('The Elect Lady', 2 Jn 1), the other to an individual, Gaius (3 Jn 1).

III. Apocalypse—On the apocalyptic genre, see **e** § 454a—e. Apoc is introduced as an apocalypse, a witness, a prophecy. It is a revelation (*apocalupsis*) from Jesus Christ of things soon to happen, to his servant John; he bears witness to what he sees, and his witness is that of Christ himself (1:1—3; 22:6—21). His revelation, then, is authentic, his visions real, no mere literary convention. It is a prophecy (1:3; 22:7, 9, 18—19), its author a prophet, called by Christ (1:9ff); he speaks with the authority of the ancient prophets to the seven churches of Asia (chh 2—3), though beyond them he addresses all Christians. As with all apocalyptic, his purpose is practical—to reanimate Christian faith and hope during the Roman persecution of the late first century. Allusions to this persecution, notably the patent symbolism of chh 13 and 17 with regard to the worship of Caesar and Rome,

o

644e give Apoc the character also of an anti-Roman and anti-Imperial manifesto.

The body of the book (4:1—22:5) contains prophetic revelation. Though the general plan is a matter of dispute, the *ensemble* has real literary unity. Apoc unfolds like a grand drama, liturgical in character, the scene continually changing, the action developing on two planes, earth and heaven. Unity is assured by the first vision of God, the heavenly court and the Lamb triumphant (chh 4—5), which constitutes, as it were, a permanent stage setting; also by constant communication between earth and heaven, through the comings and goings of angels. Dramatic emotion is maintained and developed till the final *dénouement* of 19:11—22:5, the triumph of good over evil, of God and Christ over their enemies, and the establishment of the heavenly Jerusalem. Throughout, after the manner of apocalyptic, the seer translates his visions into the conventional language of symbols, be they living creatures (e.g. the Lamb denoting Christ; the Beast, the Roman Empire), place-names (e.g. Babylon for Rome, Jerusalem for the Church), or numbers (7, 12 and multiples denoting plenitude and universality, half of seven denoting something precarious or disturbing, etc). In this use of symbolism, the seer displays great powers of assimilation. He borrows from the OT, especially the prophets, to such an extent that Apoc is almost an epitome of OT imagery, a Christian re-reading of the OT. He also uses Jewish apocrypha, NT eschatological passages (e.g. Mt chh 24—25 and passages in 1 Thes and 1—2 Cor), oriental folklore and hellenistic imagery. Yet his work remains personal.

Obviously the apocalyptic *genre* will govern the interpretation of the book; the seer's conventional symbols **644e** must be re-translated into the ideas he sought to express. Thus Apoc is not a history of the world or of the Church by epochs, nor is it merely eschatological, describing the end of the world. The author writes in the first place for Christians of the late 1st cent., in fact he takes his literary stand some decades previously—after the manner of apocalyptic—and so describes events up to his own time as in the future. Yet his foundation canvas (chh 4—5) is universal in character, and the consummation (19:11—22:5) is truly eschatological, though already foreshadowed in contemporary events. Thus, behind the historical struggle of Church and Roman State, the prophet sees a decisive conflict between God and Satan, ending in final victory for God and the annihilation of his enemies. Apoc thus becomes a message of Christian hope, a theology of history that is universal and timeless in value.

Conclusion—NT literature was not the work of professional writers. In this sense it may be termed 'popular'. **f** Yet, compared with contemporary literature, the NT books are profoundly original in character. In origin, formation and development, they were conditioned by the needs of Christian propaganda; all present the 'gospel', either under the form of apostolic catechesis, or as an extension of it. Though not immediately dependent one on the other—apart from the Synoptics among themselves, Col and Eph, 2 Pt and Jude—they exhibit a real organic unity. They were all born of the same faith, and all had the same essential purpose—to make known the person and work of Christ, principle and author of salvation.

THE SYNOPTIC PROBLEM

BY B. C. BUTLER O.S.B.

45a **Bibliography—History** with survey of proposed solutions—X. Léon-Dufour in RF, 2 (1959), 143–334; A. G. Da Fonseca, *Quaestio Synoptica*, 1953³; convenient modern review of the history of the two-Document Hypothesis: W. R. Farmer, *A Skeleton in the Closet of Gospel Research*, 1961, more fully id, *The Synoptic Problem*, 1964; **General**—J. Hawkins, *Horae Synopticae*, 1909²; F. P. Badham, *S. Mark's Indebtedness to S. Matthew*, 1897; R. Bultmann, *The History of the Synoptic Tradition*, E.tr. 1963; W. G. Kümmel, *Introd. to the NT*, NTL, 1966, 33–60. F. C. Burkitt, *The Gospel History and its Transmission*, 1906; W. Sanday (ed.), *Oxford Studies in the Synoptic Problem*, 1911; E. W. Lummis, *How Luke was Written*, 1915; H. G. Jameson, *The Origin of the Synoptic Gospels*, 1922; B. H. Streeter, *The Four Gospels, a Study of Origins*, 1930⁴; H. J. Chapman, *Matthew, Mark and Luke*, 1937; B. C. Butler, *The Originality of St Matthew*, 1951; Pierson Parker, *The Gospel before Mark*, 1953; L. Vaganay, *Le Problème Synoptique*, 1954; P Benoit, *L'Évangile selon S. Matthieu*, BJ, 1961³, 12–29; Lagrange's Introductions to his commentaries on Mk, 1929⁵, Mt, 1927⁴, Lk, 1927⁴; an important early study was Lachmann's *De Ordine Narrationum in Evangeliis Synopticis in Studien und Kritiken*, 1835; **Synopses— Greek**: Kurt Aland, Würtemberg, 1964, of outstanding utility; Lagrange, Barcelona, 1926; Huck Lietzmann, Tübingen 1936⁹; **English**: *Gospel Parallels*, Nelson 1949 (RSV, Huck Lietzmann's arrangement); A. T. Robertson, 1922 (RV); J. M. T. Barton, *A Catholic Harmony of the Four Gospels*, 1930 (DV, Lagrange's arrangement); L. Johnston and A. Pickering, 1962 (KV); S. J. Hartdegen, *Chronol. Harmony*, 1942, (CV, Lagrange's arrangement).

b **The Synoptic Problem** is posed by the similarities and differences between the first three (or 'Synoptic') Gospels. These are the data which lead us to ask whether there are any direct dependencies between two or more of these Gospels, and whether two or more of them share one or more common sources (literary or oral). The data may be summarized as follows:

A Through a total of about 200 vv, mainly comprising discourse material and scattered about in various parts of the Gospels (often in different contexts), there runs a strong similarity, or even virtual identity, between Mt and Lk in content, presentation and language; but there are no parallels for most of these vv in Mk. They constitute what we shall here call the 'Q' material or the 'Q' passages (*Quelle*, 'source' (German)). The detailed temptations of Christ after his baptism are a good example of 'Q' material. The temptations are not specified in Mk, but are given in almost identical detail in Mt and Lk; yet the order of the temptations is different, and there are a few differences in wording.

B (1) Mk contains 673 vv. The substance of over 600 of these is found also in Mt, and of about 350 out of the 673 the substance is found in Lk.

(2) Where a section of Mk has parallels in both Mt and **645b** Lk, the majority of Mk's actual Gr. words is usually found in both Mt and Lk; or at least in one of them. When a section of Mk has a parallel in only one of the other two, there is again a marked similarity in wording and phraseology between Mk and the parallel passage. This parallelism of content and wording is combined with a similarity of approach to the incidents recorded that emerges very clearly if contrasted with the highly individual approach of Jn in the few passages (few, that is, till the Passion narrative is reached) where he relates an incident also recorded in one or more of the Synoptics.

(3) The order of Mk's sections or incidents is generally found also in Mt or Lk or in both; and Mt and Lk hardly ever agree in their order of incidents *against* the order of Mk.

(4) Where all three are parallel, the frequent agreements in detail of all three, and the frequent agreements of Mk with one of the others against the third, stand in marked contrast with the relative paucity of agreements of Mt with Lk *against* Mk.

(For the above summary I am indebted to B. H. Streeter, op cit).

The full force of these data is only appreciated when **c** the Gr. text of the three Gospels is carefully studied and compared. This is best done with the help of a Gr. Synopsis The extent of similarity is too great to be explained by similarity of purpose coupled with coincidence. Some theory of connexion is required. Such connexion may be direct or indirect. (Thus, if documents X and Y are connected, the reason may be that (a) the author of X used Y as his source; or *vice versa*; or (b) that the two authors used some third document (or oral tradition) as their common source; or (c) that some third author or oral teacher used X or Y as his source, and in turn became a source for Y or X—this third author or teacher would then have provided a 'missing link' between X and Y. The Synoptic Problem is a specimen of a type of literary problem that frequently occurs when some historical event or tradition is recorded in two different authorities).

In seeking a solution of a problem of this type, it is a good working hypothesis that simpler solutions are to be preferred, other things being equal, to more complicated ones; and that conjectural, or non-extant, sources are not to be supposed unless the data of the problem require them.

Oral sources or written? A theory which sought to **d** explain the data of our problem purely by the common use of the same oral traditions would hardly, in the judgement of most scholars, do justice to the extent and character of the parallels and similarities. And it would have to suppose a *Greek* oral tradition more rigidly fixed than we have the right to assume. Moreover, it is equivalent, critically speaking, to the hypothesis that all three Gospels are derived, in their 'Markan' sections, from a Proto-Evangelium, a conjectural (non-extant) original Gospel. This was **Lachmann's presupposition**, and he showed conclusively, on the basis of the existing agreements,

645d *coupled with the relative absence of agreements* (in these sections) *of Mt and Lk against Mk*, that the Proto-Evangelium must have been something very similar to Mk: in fact, we may say, a (lost) *first* edition of Mk, a Proto-Mark. If this solution was to be accepted, it became desirable to determine the extent of the differences between Mk and Proto-Mark, and this must be done by examining the agreements of Mt and Lk against Mk in the relevant passages. Their total determinable extent was however found to be exiguous, and at length, in the early years of the present century, the followers of this trail gave up the theory of a Proto-Mark, and substituted the simpler theory that Mk itself was used as a source by the authors of Mt and Lk. They failed to notice that, by taking this step, and thereby admitting that there is *direct* dependence (between Mt and Mk on the one hand, and Mk and Lk on the other), they had not only thrown overboard the presupposition of Lachmann's arguments, but had in consequence destroyed the basis of his logic. *If* the explanation of the similarities and differences between Mt, Mk, and Lk in their 'Marcan' sections is *not* due to direct utilization of one Gospel by another but to common use of a source other than any of them, then the source must have been remarkably like Mk. But *if* the possibility of direct utilization is entertained, then we have three alternative solutions, all equally probable on the evidence so far discussed: (a) Mt may have been the source of Mk, and Mk the source of Lk; or (b) Mk may have been the source of Mt on the one hand and Lk on the other; or (c) Lk may have been the source of Mk, and Mk the source of Mt. (W. R. Farmer, in *The Synoptic Problem*, suggests that the evidence can be met by supposing that Mt was the source of Lk, while the author of Mk 'conflated' Mt and Lk. See below, § 646h.) It seems to be correct procedure to suppose, at least provisionally, that we have to search for a *written* source (or written sources) as the solution of our problem. But in view of what we know, or can reasonably assume, about the primitive Church, we should allow for the possibility of considerable interference from oral tradition.

646a **Alternative solutions**—In patristic times the existence of this problem was hardly noticed. It is, however, worthy of remark that St Augustine held that the author of Mk was a 'foot-follower and abbreviator' of Mt (*De Consensu Evang.*, 1, 2, 4. (PL 34, 1044)). Among the numerous solutions put forward in more recent times the following may be singled out for mention here:

(1) **The Two-Document Hypothesis: original form**—as propounded by C. H. Weisse, (*Die evangelische Geschichte*, 1838; his arguments were perfected by H. J. Holtzmann, *Die Synoptische Evangelien*, 1863). On this hypothesis, the data listed under B above were to be explained by a conjectural *first* edition of Mk (or Proto-Mark), which would have been utilized as a source by the authors of Mt, Mk and Lk. The data described under A above were similarly explained by a conjectural Discourse Source (later named, for convenience, 'Q'), utilized as a source by Mt and Lk.

(2) **The Two-Document Hypothesis: modern form.** This solution eliminates Proto-Mark, and makes Mk itself a source used by Mt and Lk. It retains 'Q', though it is prepared to understand by that symbol not a single document but a number of small written collections of sayings of Jesus. This solution has recently been re-argued by S. McLoughlin, *The Synoptic Theory of Xavier Léon-Dufour*, 1965, (unpublished).

b (3) **The Four-Document Hypothesis**—an elaboration of (2) by Streeter, which takes account of the fact that, besides their 'Q' material and the material which

they share with Mk, Mt and Lk have each also material **646** which is peculiar (i.e. without parallel in another Gospel). (a) The 'four documents' are thus Mk, Q, M (the source of Mt's peculiar material), and L (the source of Lk's peculiar material). N. B. Streeter held that Mt's Infancy Narrative probably came from oral sources, and Lk's from a document which may have been composed in Heb. (b) Streeter also suggested that Lk's Q material and L may have been combined, before Lk was composed, to form what we may call a Proto-Luke; this the author of Lk will have combined with his borrowings from Mk to produce Lk.

(4) **Lagrange's Modified Two-Document Hypo-** **c** **thesis.** In 1911 and 1912 the Pontifical Biblical Commission published a series of Replies concerning the Gospels of Mt, Mk and Lk and their mutual relations (Dz 3561—78). The effect of these, so far as concerns our Problem, was to discountenance the Two-Document Hypothesis as put forward at that time, and to give weight to the argument that tradition points to the priority of Mt. In the years that followed, solutions based on varying degrees of literary dependence and oral tradition found favour with many Catholic scholars anxious to reconcile the priority of Mt with the Two-Document Hypothesis. The one worked out by Lagrange in his commentaries on Mk, Lk and Mt was widely accepted in Catholic manuals, introductions and commentaries between 1911 and 1950, and even today is only slowly yielding ground to other views, notably that of Vaganay and Benoit (see below). Lagrange's detailed survey and analysis of the basic data of the Problem remain a classic of Catholic scholarship, eminently worthy of the attention of a serious student. A simple outline of his position in non-technical language will be found in his *Gospel of Jesus Christ*, 1, 2–6. He held that Mk (through Peter's preaching) and Aram. Mt depended on the oral apostolic catechesis; that (Gr.) Mt reproduced and freely edited, with additions, the substance of Aram. Mt, depending also on Mk; that Lk depended on Mk and (partially, i.e. especially as regards Discourses) on Mt; further, that the authors of Mt and Lk each used some smaller proper sources for material peculiar to them individually.

(5) **The Priority of Mt.** H. J. Chapman revolted **d** against the Two-Document Hypothesis. He argued that Mt is the first of our extant Gospels and was a source for Mk (he thought that Mt could have been used by some early Christian teacher—St Peter?—as a basis for oral teaching, and that Mk is a written record of such oral teaching; thus Mt is not the immediate, but the ultimate, source of Mk). He agreed however that the author of Lk used Mk as a source. As regards Lk's 'Q' material, he held that this derives directly from Mt; Q itself is thus eliminated.

(6) **Pierson Parker** agreed with Chapman that Mk shows abundant evidence of dependence on a source, and that Mt shows us the sort of source that this will have been. But he held that Mt is not itself Mk's source, but that both Mt and Mk depend on a source, named by him K, which was a sort of Proto-Matthew. He also accepted the dependence of Lk on Mk. He disagreed with Chapman on the subject of Q, arguing on grounds of vocabulary that Mt's 'Q' material stands out from the rest of Mt as derived from a special source. He therefore held that Mt and Lk depend on Q.

(7) **A Post-Lagrange Hypothesis**: Vaganay, Benoit. **e** Vaganay's *Le Problème Synoptique* attempts to push beyond Lagrange's hypothesis and to find concrete and specific answers to points which it had left in shadow. e.g. Is Mk really independent of all written sources?

646e Through what stages, in Aram. and in Gr., did Aram. Mt pass before its substance was incorporated in Mt? As for Lk: what specifically is meant by saying that it shows 'partial' dependence on Mt, i.e. for the Discourses? and what is the literary origin of the 'great interpolation' Lk 9:51–18:14, much of the contents of which is found dispersed in Mt, especially in Mt's Discourses? In face of such questions, Vaganay and, in substantial agreement with him, Benoit have evolved a somewhat complex hypothesis, postulating not a few conjectural and non-extant documents. As this hypothesis is gaining ground just now, we here expound it in less summary fashion than the others, making free use of the account given of it by A. Jones in CCHS (1) (pp. 853f), and using also Vaganay and Benoit, opp cit.

f Like Lagrange, these authors identify the source Q with the Apostle Matthew's alleged original Aram. gospel. This represented the Jerusalem apostolic catechesis (Baptism to Resurrection) which Peter preached. Of Aram. Mt many Gr. translations were very soon made (Papias). These translations were used by our three evangelists each of whom adjusted his source to his purpose. Thus Mk, for example, omitted many sayings of our Lord, notably the opening discourse, and arranged the narrative-matter in his own way. In this Lk has followed him fairly closely but filled in many of his omissions of discourse. The Gr. Mt completely re-organizes the narrative-sequence and, to some extent, the discourses—though apparently his arrangement of the five great discourses is due to his source, the Aram. Mt.' Mk therefore does not depend exclusively on an oral source (Peter), but probably also on a Gr. form of Aram. Mt.

g Besides Aram. Mt and supplementary to it, it is conjectured that there soon grew up, also in Aram., an autonomous Sayings Collection, R(= Recueil), a kind of miniature or supplementary Q, considerably smaller than Aram. Mt. Of this, too, many Gr. translations were made. Our canonical Mt is based on Mk, on a Gr. form of Aram. Mt, and on R. The author of Mt in fact undertook to present the content of the oral catechesis (and so of Aram. Mt) 'more fully than Mk, his predecessor, of whose work however he made considerable use . . . From the original gospel of Mt he took over the discourses in their entirety, even adding to them with the help of other traditions', i.e. in particular the sayings of R, which he 'quarries for the structure of his great discourses'. Lk is based on Mk, on one of the Gr. translations of Aram. Mt, and on R which he incorporates into 9:51–18:14. Thus Lk and (Gr.) Mt are independent of each other; there is no direct dependence of Mk on Mt; but there is direct dependence of Lk on Mk and of Mt on Mk. (As in other hypotheses, Mt and Lk have each their own sources for what is proper to them respectively, such as their Infancy Narratives).

h The present writer, while admiring the industry that has gone into the construction of the Vaganay—Benoit solution, and welcoming the considerable inroads that it has made on the supposed 'priority of Mk', may be allowed to offer two comments. (1) The complexity of the hypothesis makes its truth doubtful. Methodologically, and other things being equal, a theory is to be recommended for its simplicity; and a theory involving five non-extant sources and ten lines of dependence, even if true, could hardly be *shown* to be true. (2) As usual, the hypothesis needs to be tested in comparative analysis of actual passages in the Gospels. Vaganay has offered specimens of such work in illustration of his hypothesis. Reference may be made to B. C. Butler, 'The Synoptic Problem

Again', (DowR vol. 73, 1954–5) and *M. Vaganay and* **646h** *the 'Community Discourse'*, NTS 1 (1955), where one such specimen is subjected to detailed examination and doubts are cast on the validity of Vaganay's analysis.

(8) *Mk a conflation.* As indicated above, Farmer has recently declared his adherence to a solution of the Problem which is substantially that offered by Griesbach in 1783: Mt, he suggests, is a source for Lk; Mk is the latest of the three Gospels, and results from a conflation of Mt and Lk. The reaction of the critical world to this *revenant* among solutions remains to be seen. Here it may be said that, while it deals with most of the data, it supposes an extraordinary and persevering virtuosity on the part of the author of Mk which some will find hard to believe.

Critique of The Two-Document Hypothesis. In its **647a** modern form this has held such a central place in NT studies, that a critique of it may serve to open up the whole subject in a useful way. This is now offered, in brief compass.

I. THE SO-CALLED 'Q' PASSAGES.

(1) 'Q' is a conjectural, non-extant, document. The onus of proof lies on anyone who appeals to a conjectural document. The interpretation of Papias's reference to a work which he calls the 'dominical Logia' is too uncertain to afford a firm basis for 'Q'.

(2) If Q existed, its extent, and to some degree its nature, are uncertain. (a) It need not have included *all* the material shared by Mt and Lk but missing from Mk. Where a saying is preserved in Mt and Lk in widely divergent forms, it may have been transmitted to them along different channels. It almost certainly must have been so transmitted if, in any instance, Mt and Lk appear to give divergent translations of a single Aram. saying (it is here assumed that Christ usually spoke in Aram.); for Q, if it existed, must have been a *Gr.* document by the time at which it was utilized by the authors of Mt and Lk; and the closeness of their actual Gr. wording in very many Q passages shows that they were using the *same* Gr. translation of the original Aram. sayings.

(b) Q could have included a great deal that is *not* **b** *shared* by Mt and Lk; there is no guarantee that either author included in his Gospel the *whole* of any of his sources — and we know that (if they both used Mk) neither of them included the whole of Mk. This consideration may be of great importance. If, for instance, it can be shown that the Q material regularly coheres organically with its **contexts in Mt, while it is only loosely and artificially** inserted into its contexts in Lk, there will be a strong argument for reckoning to the supposed Q document a good deal of the Matthaean contexts of the Q material; Q will thus tend to swell to something like the proportions, and to approximate to the character, of Mt. Taken by itself, however, the so-called 'Q' material adds up to a rather shapeless mass of unconnected sayings, with one or two possible indications of narrative settings.

(3) There are five passages in which all three Synoptic Gospels are connected, but in which the agreements between Mt and Lk against Mk are too numerous to be coincidences: (a) Mt 13:31–32, cf Mk 4:30–32 and Lk 13:18–19; (b) Mt 18:6, 7, cf Mk 9:42 and Lk:17:1*b*, 2; (c) Mt 12:25–32, cf Mk 3:23–30 and Lk 11:17–23, 12:10; (d) Mt 10:9–14, cf Mk 6:8–11 and Lk 10:4–11; (e) Mt 22:34–40, cf Mk 12:28–34 and Lk 10:25–28.

In these passages we have: agreements between all **c** three Gospels; agreements between Mt and Lk against

817

647c Mk; agreements between Mt and Mk against Lk; relative *absence* of agreements between Mk and Lk against Mt; and the fact that the Lk passages are not in the same contexts as their parallels in Mk—but where Mk and Lk are *directly* connected they nearly always follow the same order of narration (i.e. agree as regards contexts). The natural interpretation of these data is that, in these passages *Mt is the connecting link* between Mk and Lk; or in other words (since Lk can hardly be the direct source of Mt and an indirect source of Mk) that in these passages Lk is dependent on Mt (unless we suppose the dependence of both Lk and Mt on a conjectural Proto-Matthew). If, however, Lk is dependent on Mt (or a Proto-Matthew) in these five passages, it becomes probable that the same explanation is applicable on a far wider scale. Thus the data which have given rise to the Q Hypothesis (which is a constituent part of the Two-Document Hypothesis) would be explained by Lk's direct dependence on Mt (or Proto-Matthew).

d These five passages are an embarrassment to the supporters of the Two-Document Hypothesis. Streeter suggested that they indicate 'overlapping' between Mk and Q, i.e. these incidents or sayings were recorded independently by the authors of Mk and Q. He then argued that, in these passages, Lk used Q (and did not use Mk), whereas Mt 'conflated' Q and Mk, i.e. built up his own version by combining elements from his two sources. This explanation does not arise naturally from the data, but is dictated by the exigencies of the Two-Document Hypothesis. Perhaps no solution of the problem can avoid supposing a certain amount of conflation of sources, but Mt's alleged behaviour in (a) and (d) above seems very irrational. On (a), Streeter himself comments: the differences between the Q and Mk versions of the parable 'are entirely unimportant . . . no one antecedently would have expected that Mt would take the trouble to combine the two versions'. And in reference to (d) he points out 'the almost meticulous care with which Mt conflates Mk and Q—the only real additions he has to make are the words "gold" and "Gomorrha"'.

It will be observed that we have left the door open for the possibility that the link between Mt and Lk in these passages (and therefore, presumably, in other Q passages) was a conjectural Proto-Matthew. It is important to bear in mind that, if this solution is accepted, it rules out the dependence of Mt on Mk in these passages; Mk must, in this hypothesis, depend either on Mt or on Proto-Matthew.

e (4) If Q existed, it presumably contained a sermon, the source of Mt's Sermon on the Mount and Lk's Sermon on the Plain. Lk's sermon is far shorter than Mt's; and, apart from the 'Woes' and about three longish vv, it contains hardly anything not found also in Mt's sermon. There are parts of Mt's sermon which are found not in Lk's sermon but elsewhere in Lk. Lk's sermon is almost destitute of special Jewish colouring and relevance; it is practically a colourless discourse on love of neighbour. Admitting that Mt's sermon may have been enlarged by insertion into it of material not originally belonging to this context, we must still ask: Was the supposed Q sermon unrelated to the Palestinian situation of our Lord's preaching; and has it been 'Judaized' by the author of Mt? Is it not more probable that the original sermon was strongly Palestinian in colouring and relevance, and that Lk has 'edited this colouring out' in order to make the sermon suitable for Gentile readers? And why should not Lk have exercised this editing process on Mt itself? Why suppose Q?

At the end of the Sermon on the Plain, Lk has: 'After he had ended all his sayings in the hearing of the people . . .'

(7:1). This corresponds to the transitional clause at the **647e** end of Mt's Sermon on the Mount: 'Afterwards, when Jesus had finished these sayings . . .' (7:28). But this clause in Mt is a typical 'Matthaean formula', repeated in substance at 11:1, 13:53, 19:1, and 26:1. In each case, as in 7:28, it occurs at the end of one of Mt's five great blocks of discourse, and is thus part of this Gospel's structural plan. If Lk is not dependent on Mt, his reproduction (in his own language) of the formula at Lk 7:1 suggests that Q must have contained the five discourses *and* the narrative matter to which the formula is, in each case, the transition and introduction.

f (5) Another Mt formula ('there men will weep and gnash their teeth'; six occurrences in Mt) is found in Lk 13:28f, which is parallel to Mt 8:11f, the first occurrence of the formula in Mt. Again, Lk 9:57—10:24 seems to show Lk's editing of material borrowed from Mt 8:19—22; 11:21—23, 25—27; 13:16f.

(6) Lk's verbal divergences from Mt in his Q passages are nearly always towards typically Lucan *style*, or in some other way give the impression that they are less primitive than the Mt versions. The criterion of poetical form led C. F. Burney (*The Poetry of our Lord*, p. 7) to conclude that in most Q cases ('though not in all') Mt preserves the more original form of our Lord's sayings.

(7) Frequently, a Q passage which fits organically into its context in Mt seems to have only an artificial *editorial* link with its context in Lk. This suggests that Lk is borrowing from a source which, if not Mt itself, is utilized more extensively by Mt. Q begins to expand in Mt into the contextual field of the certain Q passages in that Gospel; it begins to approximate to a Proto-Matthew, if not to Mt itself.

g An argument urged against Lk's dependence on Mt is that Q passages in Lk hardly ever have the same contexts as the corresponding passages in Mt; why should an author regularly put his borrowed material into new contexts? (It should however be noticed that, if Mt and Lk are both borrowing from Q, at least one of them has, on nearly every occasion, altered the Q context of his loan—unless Q was simply a hotch-potch of *disjecta membra*). The answer is probably to be sought in Luke's editorial problems. (a) For whatever reason, Lk hardly ever interferes with what he borrows from Mk, except to alter its style; he will not insert new material inside a Marcan paragraph (he did in fact try to conflate Mk with another source—Q, Mt, or Proto-Matthew—at 3:1ff, where synoptic parallelism first begins in his Gospel; he soon gave it up, perhaps because it proved too difficult—conflation undoubtedly is a very difficult literary procedure). But the Q material in Mt is often embedded in Marcan contexts, from which, therefore, Lk had to extract it if he was to be faithful to his rule: do not interfere with Marcan material. (b) On a generous estimate, the Q material constitutes less than a quarter of the whole of Lk. He had also, among his sources, Mk and his special sources (e.g. for the Infancy Narrative). If it was at a rather late stage of composition that he decided to utilize Mt, the easiest way would have been to *mark*, in his copy of Mt, the passages which he intended to use, and then fit them in wherever he could (cf H. G. Jameson, op cit).

The important result of the arguments listed above is, that there seems little reason to believe in a 'Q' consisting of a mere haphazard collection of sayings. The Q material, when it came into Luke's hands, was probably part of a larger whole, in fact of a kind of Gospel—whether Mt or Proto-Matthew (should good reason be found for conjecturing a Proto-Matthew). Note that Lk's

47g source for the main body of his Q passages must have been in Gr. On the style of 'Q', see below.

II. MK'S PRIORITY, OR MT'S?

48a The relative paucity of agreements between Mt and Lk against Mk in passages (except the five listed above) where all three Gospels have parallels is commonly taken to mean that Mk is, in these passages, the 'connecting link' or 'middle term' between Mt and Lk. (Farmer, however, regards the agreements of Mt and Lk against Mk in these passages as extensive enough to constitute a stubborn surd on the hypothesis of the 'Two Documents'. His own theory—that Lk used Mt and that Mk conflated Mt and Lk—resolves this surd). There are three ways in which Mk could have been such a connecting link: either (a) Mt was written first, and was used as a source by Mk, which in turn became a source for Lk; or (b) Mk has the priority and was used as a source by the authors of Mt on the one hand and Lk on the other; or (c) Lk has the priority and was used as a source for Mk, which in turn became a source for Mt.

b These alternatives are exhaustive (if we exclude Farmer's theory of an all-pervading conflation), unless we take into consideration the possibility of a Proto-Evangelium as a source for two, or all three, of our Gospels. If such a Proto-Evangelium was the source of all three Gospels, then, as Lachmann rightly argued, it must be envisaged as a Proto-Mark. If it was the source only of Mk and *one* of the other two Gospels, then it could have been either a Proto-Mark or a Proto-Matthew or Proto-Luke, and Mk itself must have been the remaining Gospel's source for the common material. Proto-Mark is under a cloud (and in the opinion of the present writer is to be rejected); and no-one, so far as he knows, wishes to make Lk or a Proto-Luke the source of the common material in both Mk and (indirectly, via Mk) Mt. It therefore seems reasonable to ask whether any of the three other hypotheses will meet the facts: priority of Mk, priority of Mt, or priority of a Proto-Matthew as the source of both Mt and Mk. In each case, we should be forced to infer the dependence of Lk on Mk (and this is in fact commonly conceded).

As, however, Proto-Matthew, if it ever existed, is not extant, it will be convenient to compare Mk directly with Mt, while bearing in mind that evidence which appears to point to Mk's dependence on Mt may, at least in some cases, be equally well explained by the dependence of both Mt and Mk on Proto-Matthew. We shall only accept the Proto-Matthew hypothesis if driven to do so, since it supposes a non-extant document, and two lines of dependence (Proto-Matthew source of Mt; Proto-Matthew source of Mk) instead of one (Mt source of Mk).

c (1) A. E. J. Rawlinson (in *The Gospel according to St Mark*), a convinced adherent of the Two-Document Hypothesis, suggested that at various points Mk 'perhaps' or 'probably' or 'no doubt' depends on (a Roman edition of) Q. Cf his remarks on Mk 1:2; 1:12f; 3:22—30; 4:21—25; 6:7—13; 8:15; 8:34—9:1; 9:33—37 (a 'catena of Sayings' probably derived from Q); 10:30; 10:35—40. Mk 10:38 (the reference to baptism, omitted by Mt in the parallel passage, may be an editorial addition); 12:38—40 (Mk appears to be summarizing from memory the anti-Pharisaic discourse which apparently stood in Q, and which Mt reproduces 'at fuller length') 13:9—13 (probably stood in Q). We may add that Rawlinson thought that in ch 4 Mk was probably drawing upon some existing collection of parables; this could have been 'Q', though Rawlinson does not suggest it.

Thus Rawlinson finds signs of dependence on a **648c** previous source (usually Q) in passages scattered through nine of the first 13 chh of Mk, although Q is supposed to be mainly discourse, and Mk has little discourse. V. Taylor (*The Gospel according to St Mark*) prefers dependence not on Q but on 'the Lesson Book of the Roman community'—a document at least as conjectural as Q. We have already suggested doubts about the reality of Q, and in each of the above-mentioned cases it is Mt which guides us to the probable version contained in Mk's source (except for the 'collection of parables', not further determined). Here then is evidence, provided by an ardent believer in the Two-Document Hypothesis, that Mk utilized a source or sources; and it is clear that this source could have been Mt or Proto-Matthew. But if Mk is prior to Mt and was Mt's usual source, we have the awkward result that, time and time again, Mt must have turned from a passage in Mk which we now recognize to show traces of editing, and restored the more original form of Mk's source. No impartial critic could fail to recognize the gravity of these facts for the supporters of the Two-Document Hypothesis. Note that, in his contribution to *Oxford Studies in the Synoptic Problem* (1911), Streeter himself had held that it was 'beyond reasonable doubt' that Mark was familiar with Q; in *The Four Gospels: a Study of Origins*, he withdrew from this position, in the year before the publication of Rawlinson's commentary on Mark.

(2) C. F. Burney, who accepted the Q Hypothesis, **d** examined the poetic forms of the sayings of Christ in *The Poetry of Our Lord*. He says that there are passages in Mk's versions of sayings where 'a characteristically clearcut form of antithesis' preserved in the other Gospels 'has been to some extent lost in Mark . . . The inference is that the other Synoptists cannot, in these passages, have been drawing from Mark, but that both they and Mark were dependent upon a common source (Q)'. But if we reject the notion of Q, we can explain Burney's data either by Mk's dependence on Mt or by the dependence of both Mt and Mk on Proto-Matthew.

(3) There is thus good reason to pursue a paragraph-by-paragraph comparison of Mt and Mk, in order to determine (a) when Mk would seem to be the source which explains what we find in Mt; (b) when Mk itself seems to be based on a source; (c) when Mt shows us the sort of thing which Mk's source would have contained—whether because Mt was actually Mk's source, or because Mt and Mk are both dependent on Proto-Matthew. Such a complete examination cannot, of course, find place here (cf Chapman and Butler, op cit), but a few examples can be given.

(a) Mk 13:33—37; cf Mt 24:37—25:46. Mk 13 **e** contains the longest discourse given by Mk. Up to v 32 inclusive it is closely paralleled in Mt, though Mt 24:9—14, which is contextually parallel to Mk 13:9—13, seems to come from a different source (Mt's real parallel to Mk 13:9—13 is Mt 10:17—22). But the relations between Mt and Mk 13:33—37 are odd. These vv bring Mk's discourse (already long, compared with others in Mk) to a conclusion. In place of them, we find in Mt 61 vv of continuing discourse. These 61 vv of Mt include practically everything contained in Mk's five vv, but these contents are *scattered* among Mt's 61 vv, always in appropriate contexts (note that the *faithful servant* of Mt 24:45 would, for the evangelist, suggest, e.g., Peter, the *key-bearer* of the Kingdom, for whom cf the *door-keeper* (also provided with keys) of Mk 13:34*b*). The Matthaean parallels to these items in Mk 13:33—37 cannot be accidental; this must be

648e excluded by reason of the identity of general context. But it is hardly possible that the author of Mt could have broken up Mk 13:33—37 into small pieces and fitted these pieces, one by one, into a number of new contexts derived from some other source, and could have done it so well that each item seems to belong organically to the context in which it occurs in Mt. The only reasonable view is that these vv of Mk are a 'telescoping' of what we find in Mt's 61 vv (or of such paragraphs among them as contain the items found also in these vv of Mk).

This view is raised almost to a certainty, when we remark that Mk's *absent master*, who may (very unreasonably) come back 'suddenly' and at night, and will yet expect to find his servants on the watch for him (though presumably they had also been hard at work during the daylight), is really a combination or 'conflation' of the *master* of the Talents parable (Mt 25:14—30), who keeps normal and expected hours, with the *thief in the night* (Mt 24:43f (v 42 should be appended to Mt's previous paragraph)). By 'telescoping' these two figures Mk has produced an incongruity.

This example, then, suggests that Mk was not the source of Mt, but that either Mt was the source of Mk, or both of them depended on Proto-Matthew.

f (b) As mentioned above, Mk 13:9—13 has the same *context* as Mt 24:9—14; but its real *parallel* is Mt 10:17—22. Burney states that this passage of Mk is distinguished from the rest of the discourse in which it is placed in Mk by its rhythm. He further points out that the discourse as a whole is 'eschatological' in content, but this is not true of these vv (Mk 13:9—13). But Mt 24:9—14, like its context in Mt, *is* markedly eschatological; whereas Mt 10:17—22 (= Mk 13:9—13, though in different context) is, as it should be, in a non-eschatological context in Mt.

Burney therefore, accepting the Two-Document Hypothesis, suggests that these vv were borrowed by Mk from Q, whence also the author of Mt would have borrowed them at Mt 10:17—22. We should then have to assume that Mt, copying Mk up to this point, recognized that he had already utilized the Q extract (Mk 13:9—13) in his own ch 10; he therefore omitted it here (though he does not normally mind having doublets), and substituted for it Mt 24:9—14. But whence did he obtain these substituted, and contextually far superior, vv? Did he 'make them up'? Is it not far more probable that Mt 24:9—14 belonged originally to their present context, and that it is Mk who has departed from his source (whether Mt or Proto-Matthew) by substituting for these vv those which Mt 10:17—22 gives in their proper context? (The author of Mk may have thought that the references to Christian degeneration in Mt 24:9—14 were too strong meat for his readers.) It will be observed that if Mk is here the source of Mt, we have to suppose a dislocation of source material by *both* authors: first, Mk deserts his current context and inserts a piece of Q; then Mt deserts his Marcan source and inserts a passage of unknown provenance. But if Mt (or Proto-Matthew) is the source of Mk, only one dislocation has occurred, namely that in Mk.

g Once again, a subsidiary point serves to confirm the verdict against Mk's priority. Burney not only separated Mk 13:9—13 from its context on rhythmical grounds; he further pin-pointed Mk 13:10 (within this little group of vv) as a rhythmical intruder. He subsequently noticed that the Mt parallel (Mt 10:17—22) *lacked this intrusive gloss*. However, the 'gloss' does occur in Mt—at 24:14, rounding off Mt's alleged *substituted* passage. There is no critical evidence that

Mk 13:10 is unauthentic (unless its omission by Lk **648g** be taken as such). If it is authentic, then it is a nail in the coffin of Mk's priority. We cannot believe that Mt not only excised the major rhythmical intrusion from Mk and was able to fill the gap by invisible mending with a fragment of tradition whose origin is quite unknown, but also (a) purified the vv thus taken from Mk of the 'sub-intrusion' (and used them, thus purified, in his ch 10), and (b) used this sub-intrusion to complete the 'invisible' patch which he inserted in his ch 24 to replace the major excision from Mk. We conclude that, unless Mk depends on Mt, both depend on a common source which contained, in different places, both Mt 10:17—22 and Mt 24:9—14. If this source is to be called 'Q', then Q swells beyond any proportions which Lk justifies us in assigning to it. The source would more truly be a Proto-Matthew.

(c) It will be observed that the results of our examination in (a) and (b) are convergent. The conclusions separately reached are immensely strengthened thereby. Similarly, the total case against the priority of Mk is largely built up by an accumulation of such convergent evidence. This evidence is scattered *passim* in the first 13 chh of Mk, compared with parallel passages in Mt, (as for Mk 1:2, the data here are so awkward for the Two-Document Hypothesis that supporters of it have suggested, without any basis in the manuscript tradition, that this v in Mk is unauthentic).

We are driven to the conclusion that either Mk used Mt as a source, or both Mt and Mk used Proto-Matthew as their source. In either case, unless we accept Dr Farmer's revival of the Griesbach solution and regard Mk as a conflation of Mt and Lk, Mk will have been used as a source by Lk.

The Proto-Matthew hypothesis appeals to a non- **h** extant conjectural document, and the burden of proof therefore rests on those who support it. One argument often proposed is that Mt's version of the common material is more polished, reverent, and refined than Mk's; this might suggest that while Mk has copied Proto-Matthew rather closely, Mt has 'improved' his source. Mt, it is said, is a literary composition, while Mk reads 'like a shorthand account of a story by an impromptu speaker'. Mt lacks picturesque details which are found in Mk, and often lacks Mk's redundancies. Again, on six occasions when Mk puts *Aramaic* words on Christ's lips, Mt lacks them (cf Streeter, op cit, pp. 162—4). The argument is a strong one, though it might possibly be turned by appeal to 'oral interference': if an oral teacher had used Mt as a basis for his teaching, and if Mk were the written record of such oral teaching, then Mk's informality and crudity would have a natural explanation. (As regards Mk's Aram. words, F. P. Badham, *St Mark's Indebtedness to St Matthew*, p. 48f, says: 'It is a thing to be felt, not argued about, that it was a later generation that required . . . the actual wonder-words'. Evidence is abundant in Mk that this Gospel caters for the interests of 'a later generation', and does not cater for the Jewish-Palestinian interests of the readers of Mt. Defenders of the Two-Document Hypothesis who appeal to Mk's Aramaicisms should note that the linguistic substratum of Mt is profoundly Semitic, and that this substratum is considerably blurred or diminished in Mk).

Vaganay holds that there are traces in Mk of a special *Petrine* oral teaching, and he further argues that such Petrine elements in Mk have left their print, here and there, on Mt. If that is so, we are practically bound to concede that Mt had access to Mk, and therefore that Mk's source could not have been Mt; the case for Proto-Matthew would thus be established. We may

648h be permitted to think that the case is still *sub judice*.

i Meanwhile, we can perhaps make some progress towards determining more closely the contents and structure of Mk's source, leaving the option between Mt and Proto-Matthew momentarily open. Mt, as all admit, is a carefully edited composition. Cf e.g. the five great discourses. One of Mt's editorial devices is his use of the recurrent formula, as in the phrase 'And it came to pass, when he had finished . . .' which succeeds each of the great discourses. Another is a system of 'referring back' from one context to another by a procedure which produces what have come to be called 'doublets'. Now whereas a formula coheres with its context on each occasion of its use, *one* member of a doublet will cohere with its context, the other member may be only loosely attached to its context; in such a case, the function of the loosely attached member is to 'refer' to the other member and its context. Thus, Mt 5:32 and 19:9 constitute a doublet. The former member of this pair, 5:32, is required by its context, with which it inseparably coheres. But the latter member, 19:9, is unnecessary to its context; indeed, it has been appended to a paragraph already completed in the previous v (8). In other words, Mt (or his source) has added the saying in ch 19 in order to remind his readers of what was said on the subject of divorce in ch 5. (In a modern book, a footnote reference could serve the same purpose).

One would suppose that such an editorial device as this would come at a late stage of Gospel-building. When, therefore, we find that, in this and other instances, Mk has the doublet saying or v in the context in which, in Mt, it constitutes a 'reference back', it may be felt that we have an argument in favour of Mk's dependence on Mt itself, not on some earlier Proto-Matthew.

Similarly, of the 25 examples of Matthaean formulas listed by Hawkins, 12 are found to have one or two occurrences in Mk. Such use of formulas by Mt again suggests a relatively late stage in the crystallization of our Gospels, and Mk's dependence on them again militates against the view that his link with Mt is by way of their common use of Proto-Matthew. In any case, we seem justified in thinking that, if Proto-Matthew had a real existence and was Mk's source, Mt must be a not very greatly altered 'second edition' of it. It should however be noted that Proto-Matthew could have lacked Mt's opening genealogy of Christ and his Infancy Narrative (though I think Lk's 'Matthaean' source probably had both these).

649a **External Evidence.** (a) When passages elsewhere in the NT raise the suspicion that they may have a connexion with the material contained in the Synoptic Gospels, they nearly always seem to reflect the influence of the Matthaean form of this material. Thus 1 and 2 Thes present an eschatological teaching which (with the exception of 1 Thes 5:3 which suggests Lk 21:34–36, but here it is probably Lk that is dependent on 1 Thes, not vice versa) is totally explicable—where not distinctively Pauline—only by reference to the eschatological material in Mt (cf J. B. Orchard, 'Thessalonians and the Synoptic Gospels', Bib, 1938). Again, Gal 2:7f seems to show a knowledge of what is found in Mt's version of Peter's confession at Caesarea (Mt 16). C. H. Dodd (ET 1947, 293ff) pointed out various elements in St Paul which he shares with Mt and not with the other Synoptic Gospels. Jas has numerous links, especially with the Sermon on the Mount, though occasionally the similarity

seems to be to Lk rather than to Mt (J. Chaine, *L'Épître* **649a** *de S. Jacques*, lxiv ff, referred to in B.C. Butler 'St Paul's Knowledge and Use of St Matthew', DowR, LXVI (Oct. 1948) 367ff).

(b) In the sub-Apostolic age allusions to the Synoptic **b** tradition nearly always approximate to Mt more than to Lk or Mk. The witness of these allusions is sometimes minimized by the suggestion that often they may relay oral tradition rather than any of our written Gospels. Even so, it would be significant that the common oral tradition of the churches, judging by this evidence, agreed rather with Mt than with Mk or Lk. Reference may be made particularly to the Didache, which depends, for most of its evangelical allusions, on Mt or on a Matthaean form of the tradition (B. C. Butler, 'The Literary Relations of Didache, ch 6,' JTS, 1960, 265ff, 'The "Two Ways" in the Didache', JTS 1961, 27ff. Note however that Didache ch 16 shows clear dependence on Lk or 'Proto-Luke'). This would be extremely important if we could accept Audet's dating of the Didache (A.D. 50–70, more or less); but this dating is doubtful (J. P. Audet, *La Didachè*, 1958).

Early patristic statements throw little clear and direct light on our problem. The meaning of Papias's statement that Matthew 'composed the dominical Logia in the Heb. language' is disputed (cf M. Jouvyon, 'Papias', DBS VI (1960), 1104–1109). His other statement, on the authority of 'the Elder', that Mark wrote down the oral teaching of Peter, probably refers to Mk; it cannot however be pressed so far as to exclude all use of documentary sources by the author of Mk and in any case would be consistent with Peter's dependence on Mt or Proto-Matthew.

Conclusion. The Synoptic Gospels are probably inter- **c** related by literary, not merely oral, links. If all conjectural sources are to be excluded, the evidence requires that Mk depends on Mt; and that Lk depends on Mt (for his Q material) and on Mk (unless, as Farmer holds, Mk is a conflation of Mt and Lk). If conjectural sources are not excluded, it is possible that Mt and Mk on the one hand, and Mt and Lk on the other, are connected by the common use of a lost Gospel which could be best described as a Proto-Matthew, a document of which our Mt is a fairly faithful 'second edition'—but it would still remain possible that both Mk and Lk depend on Mt. (Pierson Parker sought to establish the reality of Q by statistics of style; the present writer has criticized his findings in 'The Synoptic Problem Again', DowR 1954–5, 26ff). If Proto-Matthew is admitted, then it would be possible to argue that Mt itself is lightly indebted to Mk.

Further progress may be expected along the lines of Form Criticism; an example is to hand in Dupont, *Les Béatitudes*, 1954[1]. Such study may enable us to say with confidence whether or not a conjectural Proto-Matthew is required. Unless it is required, it should be excluded: *entia non sunt multiplicanda praeter necessitatem*. For the sake of clarity, it must be emphasized that the Proto-Matthew which may prove to be required must have been in the Gr. language (i.e. our problem would not be solved by an 'Aramaic Matthew'). It is indeed possible that some of Lk's so-called Q material is derived, independently of Mt, from Aram. sources. But much of Lk's Q material, like Mk in general, is too similar in its Gr. to the Gr. of the corresponding passages in Mt to be explained as resulting from independent translations of Aram. originals.

JESUS CHRIST IN HISTORY AND KERYGMA

BY P. GRECH O.S.A.

650a **Bibliography**—G. Bornkamm, *Jesus of Nazareth*, E.tr., 1960; C. Braaten-R. Harrisville, *The Historical Jesus and the Kerygmatic Christ: Essays on the New Quest of the Historical Jesus*, 1964; id *Kerygma and History*, 1962 (quoted as B-H); R. Bultmann, *History of the Synoptic Tradition*, Oxford, E.tr. 1963; id *Jesus Christ and Mythology*, 1958; id *Das Verhältnis der urchristlichen Botschaft zum historischen Jesus*, 1960; H. Conzelmann, *Grundriss der Theologie des NT*, 1967; J. R. Geiselmann, *Jesus der Christus, I, Die Frage nach dem historischen Jesus*, 1965; J. Jeremias, *Das Problem des historischen Jesus*, 1960; E. Käsemann, *Essays on NT Themes*, E.tr. 1965[2], X. Léon-Dufour, *Les évangiles et l'histoire de Jésus*, 1963; F. Mussner, *The Historical Jesus in the Gospel of St. John*, 1966; S. Neill, *The Interpretation of the NT (1861–1961)*, 1964; N. Perrin, *Rediscovering the Teaching of Jesus*, 1967; H. Ristow-K. Matthiae ed. *Der historische Jesus und der kerygmatische Christus*, 1960, quoted as R-M, contains numerous essays by authors of all denominations; J. M. Robinson, *A New Quest of the Historical Jesus*, 1959; J. M. Robinson-J. B.-Cobb, *The New Hermeneutic*, 1964; K. Schubert, *Der historische Jesus und der Christus unseres Glaubens*, 1962 (Essays by various Catholic authors); W. Trilling, *Fragen zur geschichtlichkeit Jesu*, 1967.

I. THE DISCUSSION ON THE HISTORICAL JESUS

b The discussion regarding the relationship of the historical Jesus to the kerygmatic Christ immediately evokes certain connotations which are now inextricably associated with the theology of Rudolf Bultmann: form-criticism, myth, demythologizing, meeting Christ in the word of God, etc. But these concepts, or their forebears, were already very much alive in the research of the last century, and we cannot fully understand Bultmann's position or the presuppositions of the post-Bultmannian controversy without at least a notion of what went on from Reimarus to Kähler, cf § 633*e*–*j*.

c From Reimarus to Kähler—Until the end of the 18th cent. the Gospels were almost unanimously accepted at their face value as a description, written by eye-witnesses or their associates, of the person, life and teaching of Jesus of Nazareth. In 1774–78 G. E. Lessing published posthumous selections from the manuscript of a colossal work by **H. S. Reimarus**, who had died a few years previously. In this treatise Reimarus championed a natural, philosophical religion and did not have any scruple about removing the historical foundation of the Gospels, destroying the supernatural element in them and explaining it away as a product of the inventiveness of the disciples. Both Jesus, the self-styled Messiah, and the disciples avail themselves of current Jewish eschatological expectations to support their newly founded religion. The publication of the work caused a commotion in Germany, and it was never accepted seriously, but it aired certain problems which were being developed in a more scholarly

way by other authors. The first of these ideas, discussed **650c** also by Semler, was the dissociation of religion from historical events. In fact, Lessing himself, the editor of the *Fragments*, stressed the principle, since become almost a dogma for many authors, that 'the contingent truths of history can never become the proofs of necessary rational truths'. Reimarus also roused prejudice against the supernatural in the Gospels, and took account not only of the eschatology of Jesus and his environment, but also of the transposition of the ideas of the disciples into the Gospel narrative, cf § 633*e*. Later writers explained the miraculous element not as due to fraud, but to imaginative description by credulous and primitive people of events which were purely natural. H. E. G. Paulus was the great exponent of this view.

That this was too facile a solution was perceived by **d** **David Friedrich Strauss**, who, in 1835, published the second of two volumes of *The Life of Jesus*. Strauss was a pupil of F. C. Baur, who had explained the rise of the Christian Church in a Hegelian way, as the result of action and reaction (thesis, antithesis, synthesis) in the two main forces at work in the 1st cent.: Jewish Christianity and Hellenistic faith. According to Strauss, during the period of formation of this synthesis, the figure of Jesus became clothed in 'myth'. This does not mean that the stories about him are inventions of a mere imaginary nature. They are stories which portray a philosophy, or better, a theology in narrative garb just as the *Fioretti* about St Francis are a true to life picture of the personality of the saint but are not meant to be taken historically. The mythical element is derived from the Old Testament, Judaism, Hellenism and Christian experience, and was blended into a deliberate pattern by the evangelists late in the 2nd cent. cf above, § 633*e*–*i*.

Such a theory can be pushed too far, and in actual **e** fact **Bruno Bauer** (d. 1882) stated that it was not the myth that was the product of the community but the community that was produced by the myth, as was Jesus himself, who never existed. On the other hand, there was also a Catholic reaction to Strauss. In 1838 **J-E. Kuhn** published a 'scientific' account of the life of Jesus in which he conceded to Strauss that the Gospels were not meant as a purely historical account of the life of the Lord, that is, if history is conceived as consisting of a complete narrative of facts linked up as cause and effect. The Gospels are kerygma; they are *sacred* history; they do not have the intention of presenting an impersonal account of what happened but of proving that Jesus was the Messiah and the Son of God; they insist on those facts which prove the fulfilment of prophecy. As such they are not historical but trans-historical (*übergeschichtlich*). Hence what is contained in their lesson is not myth but theology; they were not a chance production of an impersonal community but were intentionally written by the disciples to prove a point. The selection of the material contained in them and its disposition was determined by the theological end in view.

50f At the turn of the century we witness a completely different reaction to the line of thought initiated by Strauss. The liberal *Leben-Jesu-Forschung*, culminating in **H. Weinel, A. Harnack** and **E. Renan**, possessed unlimited faith in the possibility of using the synoptic Gospels as sources for the reconstruction of the life and personality of Jesus, and maintained that our present faith should have as its foundation not the faith of the primitive Church that wrote the Gospels but the teaching of Jesus himself. This teaching was principally moral, as Jesus' eschatological expectations were unreliable. Renan's Jesus is a source of romantic idealism. Anything supernatural, especially the miracles, was explained away, or given a natural interpretation. Harnack made the message of Jesus consist of the idea of the brotherhood of man under the fatherhood of God, from which Christ derived his idea of Sonship.

g The liberal neglect of eschatology was soon to produce another reaction in its favour. **Johannes Weiss** stated that Jesus was not a moral preacher or a Protestant pastor but an eschatological herald who made use of the apocalyptic 'Son of Man' expectations of contemporary Judaism. He did not inaugurate the Kingdom of God but only preached its imminence. He knew that he would be killed by the Jews but foretold that he would come back to judge the world as the Danielic Son of Man. He also preached ethics, but only an interim ethics, valid in the face of the imminent catastrophe. According to **Albert Schweitzer** even Weiss was not consequent enough in his thought. Jesus not only preached the kingdom, he acted it as well, for when he saw that his message was not being received he went up to Jerusalem, revealed himself as the Messiah before the High Priest, and forced his own death, through which, he believed, the Kingdom would come.

h If we want to complete the picture of the line of thought leading to Bultmann we cannot neglect a small book published in 1892 by **Martin Kähler**, *The So-Called Historical Jesus and the Historic, Biblical Christ*, (E.tr). It was hardly noticed at the time, but was later to play an important role in the development of the form-critical school. Kähler is anti liberal. He maintains that the gospels are not concerned mainly with the historical Jesus (*der historische Jesus*), i.e. Jesus as he really lived in Palestine, but with the historic Christ (*der geschichtliche Christus*), the Christ of faith. It must be underlined that he did not deny the historicity of the Gospels, but was only pointing out the futility of the liberal research on the life of Jesus. The liberals were mistaken about the whole purpose of the Gospels. The Christ of faith also comes out, but in completely different form, in the research of the *Religionsgeschichtliche Schule* to which Bultmann partly belongs. This school (of the 'history of religions') did not study the NT in isolation but considered it as a product of various religious ideas current in the world of the 1st cent. **W. Bousset** and **R. Reitzenstein** made a thorough study of the mystery religions in Hellenism and explained how Pauline theology, much of which was later projected on to the Gospels, arose out of the contact with Greek theosophy. The title 'Lord' with which the Church honoured Jesus has parallels, and therefore sources, in the dying and rising vegetation deities of the mysteries. The kerygmatic Christ is not wholly Palestinian in origin.

i When Bultmann came on the scene, therefore, the stage had already been prepared to receive his theories. Several problems were still being discussed while various conclusions had been reached among Protestant NT scholars. A heated controversy was raging between those who maintained that the Jesus of history was not **650i** recoverable from the Synoptic accounts of his life, and the liberals who affirmed that it was; the concept of myth in the Gospels was generally accepted; the eschatological school had come to the fore with Schweitzer; the historical Jesus had been separated from the Kerygmatic Christ; there already existed the distinction between *historisch* and *geschichtlich*; the creative power of the primitive community was being accepted; the supernatural was diligently expunged from the Gospel narratives; the importance of history as a basis of faith was being devalued; Hellenism was being studied with reference to the formation of the kerygma; and the philosophical ideas of the age were being applied to the study of the Bible.

Rudolf Bultmann—Immediately after the end of the **651a** first World War, K. L. Schmidt, M. Dibelius and R. Bultmann applied to the synoptic tradition the method of *form-criticism* which H. Gunkel had so successfully applied to the OT. This theory postulates a period of oral transmission of the material contained in the Synoptic Gospels before it reached its written stage in Mk and Q. The oral traditions connected with Jesus assumed various literary genres or 'forms' each of which has its own history and its own *Sitz im Leben* in the situation of the Primitive Church, whether in Palestine or in the Diaspora. The primitive community did not merely transmit the sayings of Jesus or his deeds; it adapted them to its own situations and created new ones. Hence the Gospels are not accounts of what happened, but kerygmatic documents projected back into the life of Jesus. Their interest is merely kerygmatic and they tell us little, if anything, about the biography or personality of the historical Jesus; cf § 634*e*.

The name of Bultmann, however, is more directly **b** connected with the theory of **de-mythologization** (*Entmythologisierung*). As this is intimately related to the subsequent discussions on the relationship between the historical Jesus and the kerygmatic Christ we must examine it in some detail. In the latest German edition of *Jesus Christus und die Mythologie*, (1964), originally written in English, Bultmann achieves the final form of his theory. We shall follow this book in our exposition. Bultmann maintains that the primitive Church conceived the Christian kerygma in the patterns of thought of the world-picture of the 1st cent., in which transcendental gods, angels and devils break into the natural concatenation of events producing supernatural happenings which are quite unacceptable to the thought patterns of 20th cent. man. The NT presents the saving events, from the Incarnation, Death, Resurrection, Pentecost and sacramental life, to the deification of the Person of Christ in the Hellenistic world, in a mythological language. Now mythology is not pure invention. It conveys certain philosophical ideas clothed in a literary garb borrowed from Jewish apocalyptic, Gnostic redemptive theories and OT forms. Once this mythological garb is dropped the central message can be picked up by 20th cent. man and re-translated into a philosophy which he can understand, but which, at the same time, is akin to the central message of Christ. This is the process of de-mythologization. It differs from the method of denial of the supernatural used by the Liberals in so far as these denied the supernatural outright and retained nothing of the message of Christianity except a few moral norms which corresponded to the philosophy of the Romantic Age. De-mythologization, on the contrary, does not deny but re-interprets. The central core of the message is retained as is the 'scandal' which intrinsically belongs to it.

651c The contemporary philosophy which is best suited to tune in to the message of the NT is **existentialism**, especially as it is presented by Heidegger, who distinguishes between mere being and existence in man. Mere being (*Vorhandensein*) is existence on the level of every common object, not as a responsible human being. It is unauthentic existence, a slavery to anxiety as regards the future. Authentic existence (*Dasein*) is brought about by a decision to exist on the human level. Now the bible message is existentialist in nature. It is not a collection of truths to be believed but a summons to me to take a decision as regards the I-Thou relationship with God. Everything which does not have an existentialistic bearing on this decision is myth. Building on this philosophy Bultmann lays down the principles of de-mythologization. It will consider only those elements in the kerygma which are related to my own existence and to my I-Thou relationship with God; it will clarify the agreement of the faith with existence and will make use of Heidegger's philosophy, not in the sense that it reduces the faith to a philosophy but merely to pave the way for an existentialistic understanding of the Word of God. After all every theology presupposes a philosophy.

d The parallel to *Vorhandensein* and *Dasein* is found in the Christian myth of humanity's 'fallen state' (*Verfallenheit*) and existence in faith. In our fallen state we are slaves of anxiety, *merimna*, which we try to overcome through our feeble human efforts, and consequently fall into the greater sin of *kauchesthai* or self-exaltation, glorying in our power, which worsens the situation. Man can only pass from *Verfallenheit* to *Dasein* by means of *Faith*, through which he renounces the search for security by means of his own strength and makes a leap to God. By doing so he gains true liberty and lives 'in the Spirit'. To make this act of faith man must accept God's judgement in Jesus Christ, which is both a duty and a gift, *charis*. Hence Bultmann retains the scandal of Christ and the act of God. This can be interpreted as something objective, happening outside me, or something immanent, through which God changes my mind. But if the scandal is retained why de-mythologize at all? Bultmann bases his theory on 1 Cor 1:18ff where this 'scandal' is emphasized. What he really renounces is any manifest, objectively verifiable action of God. The act of faith must be made in the dark, in my own soul, with no verifiable foundation in history, although the word of God is historical in so far as it is occurring in history and comes to me through history.

e In *Neues Testament und Mythologie* (1941) Bultmann defined his position with regard to the life of Christ. This is represented mythologically in the Gospels. Christ is represented as a pre-existent being, born of a virgin and working miracles to signify that God has something to say to me in Jesus. The Cross of Christ is explained in terms of the distinction between *historisch*, an objectively verifiable happening in the past, established through research, and *geschichtlich*, the meaning of the event which transcends time and can only be accepted through faith. The cross is 'historic' in so far as it actually happened but its significance is *geschichtlich* ('historical'): 'In the cross of Jesus God wanted to make clear to me that he has spoken his liberating judgement on me as a sinner. I have only to admit my sinful state and my powerlessness, and to believe that God has passed over all to win my authentic existence'. The cross is re-enacted every time the Kerygma is preached and my response to the saving event is Faith: the confession of powerlessness which has been condoned by God. The Resurrection, on the other hand, is neither historic nor historical. It is not an event, because essentially mythological, but God produced this persuasion **651** in the apostles to signify to them that victory over death which can be ours in the Cross. As the condemnation is symbolized in the Cross so our deliverance is signified by the Resurrection. This redemption is not eschatological in the sense that it is temporally in the future. It happens now in my present faith, obedience and love. That is why the resurrection is an integral part of the Kerygma. The saving act of God regarding me happens in the proclamation of his Word. This word is preached today in the Church hence salvation happens within the context of the Church, and remains an historical event.

Against the background of this theology we must now **f** examine Bultmann's position as regards the problem of the relationship of the historical Jesus with the Christ of Faith. This is best brought out in the publication of a lecture by Bultmann (*Sitzungsberichte der Heidelberger Akademie der Wissenschaften*, 1960, 3), in which the author poses himself two problems: that of the historical continuity of the Proclaimer Jesus and the Proclaimed Christ, and the related question of the objective theological relationship between both. The first of these two problems is easily answered in so far as the Primitive Community simply presupposes the identity of the Risen Christ with the Jesus of history. He is the Messianic Son of Man and the exalted Lord. Jesus, however, was not a Christian—a Christian is one who believes in the Risen Christ—he belongs to Judaism. So does the problem of relationship limit itself to the mere existence of Christ or does it have to take into account his significance and his message? According to Bultmann, Paul and John completely disregard the 'how' and 'what' of Jesus and are content merely with presupposing his 'thatness', at most, his crucifixion. The author himself, in consequence of his form-critical theories, does not think that we can know very much of what actually happened in Jesus' life and of his words. He argues that those who **g** require the continuity of the 'how' and 'what' of Jesus with the kerygma usually do so in two ways: either by requiring the significance and the message of Jesus as the historical foundation and legitimization of the kerygma, or by saying that the kerygma is already implicitly contained in the life and preaching of Jesus. Bultmann does not accept the first possibility because he maintains that the kerygma has been projected backwards into the life of Jesus instead of being used as its legitimization. He accepts the second alternative in the sense that it merely reaffirms historical continuity, but if it goes on to claim that the message of Jesus itself is kerygmatic in so far as it places us in front of a decision, then he rejects the explanation because it makes the kerygma unnecessary. His own position is that the kerygma cannot preach a mere historical figure of the past. It must represent Christ as ever present, and he is present—in the sense in which Bultmann understands the Resurrection—in the word of the Church. To refer to historical events, especially if they are 'supernatural', to legitimize one's faith, destroys the essence of faith which is a leap in the dark and not 'sight' by means of verifiable miracles.

Bultmann's system, which takes into account the con- **h** tinuity between the historical Jesus and the Kerygma, seemed illogical to philosophers such as **Karl Jaspers**. The transition from unauthentic to authentic existence was brought about by an objective fact of history. Jesus could, at the most, have provided an example, but a decision is a purely subjective matter which can be taken for other reasons. The same objection is made by **S. Ogden**, who maintains that the existential transition can be made even outside the Christian Church, but when

651h it does take place, it is *ipso facto* Christian in so far as it is contained in the message of Jesus. On the other hand, orthodox Protestant theologians like **E. Stauffer**, **W. Künneth** and **Joachim Jeremias** maintain that Bultmann goes too far on the liberal side. Stauffer wrote a life of Jesus in which he buttressed the historical reliability of the Gospels by means of extra-canonical material. Künneth maintains that 'there can be no compromise or peaceful agreement between the truth of the NT message of Christ and the pseudo-Kerygma of Bultmann' (B-H, p. 119), if only for the reason that even Bultmann's idea of myth is historically and philosophically incorrect. But the scholar who has done most to restrain German research from going too far is

i **Jeremias.** Apart from his excellent work on the parables and on the Eucharistic words of Jesus, by means of which he set the example of how the form-critical method can be used constructively, his pamphlet *Das Problem des historischen Jesus* (1960) has become the programme of the 'right-wing' theologians in this discussion. Jeremias credits the new theology with recognizing the 'out-of-grace-alone' character of salvation, but says that it is in danger of voiding the Christian message of the Incarnation formula 'The Word became flesh', of substituting Paul for Jesus, of devaluating the act of God in the man Jesus, and of returning to docetism. The beginning of our faith does not lie in the kerygma but in the historical fact of the life of Jesus. It is not understandable why so much emphasis is placed on the presence of kerygmatic theology in the Gospels, as, actually, so little Pauline theology is found in them; indeed, they give us quite a faithful

j picture of the pre-Easter situation. The return to the historical Jesus is not recommended to us by the fidelity of the sources alone. The kerygma itself preaches that God reconciled the world to himself through a fact in history. The meaning of the death of Christ is not an interpretation of the Church, it is the explanation of Jesus himself. Paul is not understandable without Jesus. Hence we are under obligation to continue research into the life of Jesus by every means at our disposal: source and form-criticism, background studies, Aramaic philological inquiry and eschatological historical investigations. If it is objected that in this manner our faith rests on subjective research, Jeremias answers that this activity is only our 'Yes' to the Incarnation at a definite point in history. We therefore cannot separate history from kerygma without falling into the extremes of either Ebionitism or docetism. History and Kerygma are related to one another as call to response. This response is directed towards God in the way of thanksgiving and towards man as witness. The Church's preaching is not revelation; it leads to revelation, as Jesus is not merely one presupposition out of many, but the one call which requires an answer.

652a **The Post-Bultmannians**—It is among those scholars who take their inspiration from Bultmann, however, that the discussion about the value of historical research on the life of Jesus is carried on most animatedly. During the period between the publication of Käsemann's programmatic lecture in 1954 and the present day, which is still dominated by J. M. Robinson's *New Quest*, an immense literature has appeared on the subject. Here we can only study some representative writings which lead up to the latest synthesis by Norman Perrin. The problem under discussion can be formulated as follows: It is now agreed that we cannot go back to the liberal quest of the life of Jesus, which discarded the kerygma and sought to find a moral message (usually the fatherhood of God) in Jesus' consciousness. After Strauss and Bultmann

this is impossible both methodologically and theologically. **652a** If, therefore, we now consider Christianity to consist in faith in the Christ of the Kerygma, is it possible, and does it make sense, to rediscover the life and teaching of Jesus?

Ernst Käsemann opened the debate in a lecture which **b** is now published in English in *Essays on NT Themes* (SCM 1964). It is the declared intention of the author to steer a middle course between rationalism, which makes Jesus into a figure like ourselves, and supernaturalism, which, by admitting the miraculous element in Jesus, turns him into a *theios anēr* for the acknowledgement of whom an unacceptable *sacrificium intellectus* is required. Miracles are not a sound basis for faith, and Jesus was no mere wonder-worker, but the Kyrios. The life of the earthly Jesus, however, has its relevance for faith, as the Early Church was not minded to let myth take the place of history or a heavenly being that of the man of Nazareth. Nevertheless it is the Cross and Resurrection of Jesus which is of most import to our discussion. Among the evangelists themselves, Mt, Mk and Jn absorb history into kerygma, thus stressing the continuity of Jesus with the Christ and saving the historical side of Jesus from becoming mere abstraction. Lk's Jesus in 'historical', for Lk turns eschatology into *Heilsgeschichte*. Revelation cannot be brought within a causal nexus. It **c** stands out in so far as it invades history and takes place within it. It can be accepted or rejected, while historical facts can be overlooked but not rejected. Even the Fourth Gospel, with its emphasis on anti-Docetism, cannot but stress that Jesus Christ 'came in the flesh', but to cling firmly to history as the Synoptics do is to express the *extra nos* of salvation. The life of Jesus is constitutive of faith because the earthly and the exalted Lord is one. The Easter faith is the foundation of the Easter kerygma, but not the first or only source of its content. Rather, it was the Easter faith that took cognizance of the fact that God acted before we became believers and witnessed to this fact by assimilating the life of Jesus into its proclamation. Hence, research into the life of Jesus is theologically legitimate; it is also possible, within the limits of strict radical criticism, because many historical elements are still preserved in the Gospels. The Synoptic Jesus, even though he may not have claimed to be the Messiah or the Son of Man, spoke in such a way that the transition from his implications to the Church's proclamation is a logical one: the implicit becoming explicit, the 'once' of Jesus becoming the 'once-for-all' of Christ.

Three years after Käsemann's lecture, **G. Bornkamm d** published his *Jesus of Nazareth*, in which Käsemann's programme found a practical application. But whereas Käsemann and Bultmann gave more importance to Jesus' words Bornkamm considers Jesus' action and what may be called his personality: the impact he made on his immediate entourage. The Church continued Jesus' eschatological message in terms of Christology. Bornkamm goes so far as to pronounce Bultmann's demythologizing insufficient in so far as it is a theology of *significat*, not *est*. The immediate concern of theology is not with finding a new self-consciousness for man but with finding his 'new being in God' (B-H 172—197). An analogous position is taken up by **H. Conzelmann** in his *Grundriss der Theologie des NT* (1967): The tension between future and present, between suddenness and continuation in Jesus' teaching on the coming of the Kingdom, is resolved by means of the imperative of taking an existential decision, here and now, whether to accept the Kingdom, God's gift of 'life', or to reject it. The Church translates this message into a decision regarding the acceptance of Christ. The theologian **H. Diem** comes to the same

652d conclusion as Käsemann by examining the problem from a Reformed point of view. He rejects both the liberal and the 'supernaturalist' solutions and refers to Strauss for a middle way out, which he finds in the fact that the Church stressed the continuity of the Christ with Jesus by putting into Jesus' mouth the Son-of-Man sayings.

e The post-Bultmann group, therefore, came to a kind of consensus on three main points: the rejection of the liberal quest; the acceptance of continuity between the historical Jesus and the Christ of faith, hence the legitimacy of enquiring into the pre-Easter history of Jesus; and the acceptance of demythologizing with reference to an existential message for the present generation. This leads us logically to the **'New Quest' movement** represented by **J. M. Robinson**. The New Quest is to be studied in conjunction with the 'New Hermeneutic' of **E. Fuchs** and **G. Ebeling** (cf *The New Hermeneutic*, ed. Robinson-Cobb 1964).

f Whereas Bultmann finds his existential message in the theology of Paul and John, and relegates Jesus to the pre-Christian era, **Fuchs** and **Ebeling** reverse the position. Their main theme is the 'word-event' (*Wortgeschehen, Wortereignis*), the attitude or decision which surfaces in language. This happens in the language and actions of the historical Jesus, in so far as he can be known through direct research. His essential attitude is one of *faith*. In fact, he identifies himself so completely with the will of God that he acts in the place of God. The existential decision of faith constitutes Christianity. It is not primarily belief in Christ but an echo of the very faith which animated Jesus. This position is termed 'neo-Liberalism' by Robinson, but is typically Protestant on account of its insistence on the written word as the source of faith. Hence every explanation is merely the hermeneutic of this word. The historical Jesus and the Christ of faith are identical in so far as the existential faith we draw from both word-events is identical. It may be objected that we can also appeal to the 'Righteous Teacher' of the Qumran scrolls for a similar decision. **H. Braun** (R-M 142) answers that one need only compare Christ's idea of righteousness with that of Qumran——the unbounded generosity of God to which corresponds the unbounded moral generosity of man, as compared with the juridical and mathematical righteousness of the Righteous Teacher——to be able to confess Jesus as The Christ. One does so not by following historical connexions but by echoing the 'So God acts' of Jesus, by presenting oneself with empty hands to God. Braun maintains that Paul and John developed this message though they added to it mythical ideas from Hellenism, which, anyway, do not belong to the essential confession of Christianity.

g **J. M. Robinson** (*A New Quest of the Historical Jesus*, 1959; new German revised edition 1967) begins by arguing that the liberal quest is both methodologically impossible and theologically illegitimate. If a new quest is possible, it is not because new sources have been found or because we have new ideas about the Gospels, but because we have a new notion of history and existence. History is not the arrangement of facts in categories of cause and effect: 'Today history is increasingly understood as essentially the unique and creative, whose reality would not *be* apart from the event in which it becomes, and whose truth could not be *known* by Platonic recollection and inference from a rational principle, but only through historical encounter. History is the act of intention, the commitment, the meaning for the participant, behind the external occurrence. In such intention and commitment the self of the participant actualizes itself, and in this act of self-actuation the

self is revealed' (p. 68). Into this notion of history **652h** the idea of de-mythologizing is introduced. Once myth is removed we are not left with a symbol objectifying a human personality for authentic existence but with the meaning of Jesus of Nazareth 'as the act of God in which transcendance is made a possibility of human existence' (p. 84). The kerygma is not the objectifying of a new principle but a historical encounter with God. The New Quest, therefore, essentially consists in an encounter with the historical Jesus (which is not the same thing as the 'earthly Jesus', but the Jesus who is known from 'history'). In Robinson's own words: 'The purpose of a new quest must derive from the factors whish have made such a quest possible and necessary, a generation after the original purposes had lost their driving force and the original quest had therefore come to an end. A new quest must be undertaken because the kerygma claims to mediate an existential encounter with the historical person, Jesus, who can also be encountered through the mediation of modern historiography. A new quest cannot verify the truth of **i** the kerygma, that this person actually lived out of transcendence and actually makes transcendence available to me in my historical existence. But it can test whether this kerygmatic understanding of Jesus' existence corresponds to the understanding of existence implicit in Jesus' history, as encountered through modern historiography. If the kerygma's identification of *its* understanding of existence with *Jesus'* existence is valid, then this kerygmatic understanding of existence should become apparent as the result of modern historical research upon Jesus. For such research has a legitimate goal: the clarification of an understanding of existence occurring in history, as a possible understanding of my existence. Hence the purpose of a new quest of the historical Jesus could be to test the validity of the kerygma's identification of *its* understanding of existence with Jesus' existence' (p. 94). 'In the case of a new quest, this focal problem would consist in using the available source material and current historical method in such a way as to arrive at an understanding of Jesus' historical action and existential selfhood, in terms which can be compared with the kerygma' (ibid). In fact, in the latter part of his book, especially in the German edition, the author attempts to provide some examples of rapprochement between historiography and kerygma as two channels which lead to the same understanding.

As a result of this theorizing from Käsemann to **j** Robinson, **Norman Perrin** recently published a book with the title *Rediscovering the Teaching of Jesus* (SCM, 1967). No such attempt had been made since T. W. Manson's *The Sayings of Jesus* (1949), but Perrin is much more radical. His selection of Jesus' authentic sayings is based on a strict application of the criterion of dissimilarity, the criterion of coherence and the criterion of multiple attestation, but when in doubt he discards. His stand on the problem of the historical Jesus, which is partially influenced by Robinson, is summarized by the author himself as follows: 'We are prepared to maintain (1) that the NT as a whole implies that Christian faith is necessarily faith in the Christ of the Church's proclamation, in which proclamation historical knowledge today may play a part, but as proclamation, not as historical knowledge. As proclamation it helps to build the faith-image, to provide the content for a faith which "believes in Jesus". Then (2) in face of the varieties of Christian proclamation and in view of the claim inherent in the nature of the Synoptic Gospel material (Earthly Jesus = Risen Lord), we may and we must use such historical knowledge of Jesus as we possess to test the validity of

52j the claim of any given form of the Church's proclamation to be *Christian* proclamation. Then (3) in view of the further claim inherent in the nature of the Synoptic Gospel material (situation in earthly ministry of Jesus = situation in early Church's experience) we may apply historical knowledge of the teaching of Jesus directly to the situation of the believer in any age, always providing, of course, that we can solve the practical problems involved in crossing the barrier of two millennia and radically different *Weltanschauung* necessary to do this' (p. 247).

k Bultmann's reaction to Robinson's thesis is rather negative. He objects that an independent research into the life of the historical Jesus would make the Kerygma superfluous. Why did the Church not simply repeat the kerygma of Jesus instead of turning the Proclaimer into the Proclaimed? Even as regards the theses of Käsemann, Conzelmann, Fuchs, Ebeling and Braun, Bultmann is sceptical whether from the Synoptic proclamation of the Messiahship of Christ we can conclude to anything more than the 'thatness' of Jesus, but little, if at all, of the modality and significance of his prophetical message.

From this summary examination we can see that the wheel has turned full cycle from the initial 19th cent. quest to the modern views of Robinson. The circular movement, however, is rather a spiral one, as many positions have been abandoned and new dogmas introduced. Among the followers of Bultmann today the teachings of form-criticism are undisputed; de-mythologizing assumes different shades but is universally admitted in so far as it requires an existential interpretation; the supernatural is not even given a chance to restate its case; the doctrines of Strauss and Kähler have become basic to every theory; and widespread scepticism reigns as regards the possibility of reconstructing the picture of the earthly Jesus. On the other hand there is a tendency to return to the historical Jesus at least through an existential interpretation of history and to state that there is a continuity between the message of Jesus and the Kerygma: what is implicit in one is explicit in the other.

53a **Contemporary Catholic Thought**—It is now pertinent to ask how Catholic scholars have reacted to Bultmannian theology and post-Bultmannian theories. It can be said that on the whole, **the reaction is not one of rejection but of selection**. Although they see eye to eye more with O. Cullmann than with Bultmann—and prefer speaking of *Heilsgeschichte* rather than do mythologizing—some scholars make more concessions to the latter than the former is prepared to concede. The way indicated by J. Jeremias and N. A. Dahl seems to be acceptable to the majority. R. Schnackenburg, F. Mussner, A. Wikenhauser, K. H. Schelkle, X. Léon-Dufour, R. Marle, J. De Fraine and H. Schürmann examine the problem from different angles and come to the conclusion that Form-Criticism is right in saying that the Gospels had a long life in oral tradition before being written down; that they do not permit us to write a continuous 'biography' of Jesus in the modern sense of the word; that they reflect the faith of the Easter Church in Christ; that they want to demonstrate Jesus as the Christ; and that the transmitted sayings are given back after a post-Resurrection understanding. It is also admitted that there are different 'forms' or 'literary genres' in both oral transmission and writing. Catholic scholars distinguish three layers of theology in the Synoptic Gospels: the theology of the evangelists, that of the early Community, and the theology of Jesus himself. What Catholic exegetes do not admit is that the early Community *created* sayings of the Lord and *invented* stories about his life. It is also denied that

the stratum of Community theology is so thick that it is **653a** impossible ever to work through it to the sayings of Jesus himself. These views are officially recognized in the **b** Decree on Revelation in Vatican II. 'Literary forms' are acknowledged, and so is the process of oral transmission (n. 12). About the historicity of the Gospels the Council states: 'Holy Mother Church has firmly and with absolute consistency held, and continues to hold, that **the four Gospels** just named, whose historical character the Church unhesitatingly asserts, **faithfully hand on what Jesus Christ**, while living among men, **really did and taught** for their eternal salvation until the day he was taken up into heaven (see Acts 1:1f). Indeed, after the ascension of the Lord the Apostles handed on to their hearers what he had said and done. This they did with that clear understanding which they enjoyed after they had been instructed by the events of Christ's risen life and taught by the light of the Spirit of truth. The sacred **c** authors wrote the four Gospels, selecting some things from the many which had been handed on by word of mouth or in writing, reducing some of them to a synthesis, explaining some things in view of the situation of their Churches, and preserving the form of proclamation but always in such fashion that they told us the honest truth about Jesus. For their intention in writing was that either from their own memory and recollections, or from the witness of those who themselves "from the beginning were eyewitnesses and ministers of the word" we might know "the truth" concerning those matters about which we have been instructed (cf Lk 1:2—4)' (n. 19).

The Decree, therefore, concedes everything to form criticism both as theory and as method with the exception of the legitimacy of doubt as to the basic historicity of the facts and sayings narrated in the Gospels. We must go deeper into the reasons for this exception as at present it is being subjected to numerous attacks by the left-wing critics.

The **objections against the Catholic thesis** have **d** been summarized, lately, by Norman Perrin in his book *Rediscovering the Teaching of Jesus* (1967). As regards the sayings of Jesus he lays down the principle that 'the nature of the synoptic tradition is such that the burden of proof will be upon the claim to authenticity' (p. 39). Perrin reminds us that the ancient world did not have the same appreciation of factual accuracy as we moderns do; he also reminds us of the fact that the early Church so completely identified the Risen Lord with the Jesus of history that it was a matter of indifference to her by which of these certain logia were spoken, as long as they were Christ's. Against the Catholic insistence that the **e** 'Community' is too hazy a concept to be endowed with creative power he objects that modern scholars have studied diverse groups within the 'community', such as prophets, scripture interpreters and evangelists. Even the 'eyewitness' argument does not impress him because the NT notion of 'eyewitness' is so different from ours; according to Luke, for example, Paul was an eyewitness! Lastly, he holds that in spite of all the good will of the evangelists to be as 'historical' as possible and rely on eyewitnesses, evangelists like Luke have no difficulty in changing facts and words to suit their editorial theology. As regards the sayings, only those can be accepted which (1) belong to the oldest stratum in the Early Church; (2) bear a dissimilarity to traditional emphases in Judaism and in the Early Church; (3) have foreign material which logically coheres with that established as authentic through Criterion n. 2; (4) are attested by all or the majority of the sources behind the Gospels. Perrin does not think much of the Scandinavian

653e attempt to compare the transmission of the sayings of Jesus to that of contemporary rabbis. About this we shall speak further on.

f **In answer to Perrin**, we may agree that he is quite right in saying that for the Early Church the historical Jesus was identical with the Risen Lord, he was one and the same person. From this, however, we cannot infer that any word spoken by the 'Lord the Spirit' was transferred to the past historical figure. There is no evidence for this in the NT. When, in 1 Cor 11, Paul speaks of receiving the Eucharistic words 'from the Lord' the terminology he uses: 'receiving' and 'transmitting', is rabbinic terminology then in common use for the transmission of rabbinical sayings. Indeed, all the evidence we have points to the contrary. We would expect, when reading the Apocalypse, so full of sayings of the Risen Lord, that we would find these sayings in the mouth of the historical Jesus, at least in John's Gospel, which comes from the same school. But we do not. The form of the post-Resurrection sayings is easily discernible, it speaks to the Churches in the present tense. All that John himself claims is that when the Spirit comes the Church will receive a deeper understanding of the words of the Earthly Jesus. (Jn 14:26; 16:13). And it is this re-interpreted word which John gives us back in his Gospel.

g The argument applies *a fortiori* to the Synoptics. This is not to say that these latter hand on the *ipsissima vox Jesu* in every case. Perrin is also right when he points out that especially Luke the historian handles his tradition to make it fit into his theological pattern. This only means, however, that he hands it on together with his own interpretation, not that he creates it *ex novo*. The true meaning of 'eyewitness' can only be perceived if we take seriously the attempt of the Scandinavian school

h to shed light upon this intricate problem. In his lecture at the Oxford Congress on the Four Gospels in 1957, **H. Riesenfeld** (*The Gospel Tradition and its Beginnings*) advances a thesis which was later expanded by B. Gerhardsson in *Memory and Manuscript* (Lund, 1961). These two authors make a minute study of the milieu in which the sayings of Jesus were transmitted. As Perrin says, the ancient world did not think of the relating of actual facts as the modern world does. But this argument cuts both ways. In the Hellenistic world, speeches served to bring out the author's philosophy, and perhaps the speeches in Acts follow this pattern. But in the Jewish rabbinical world sayings were handed down literally, repeated from memory, word for word, at the most synthesized or surrounded by a *midrash*, but never betraying the mind of the original speaker. This thesis was heavily criticized. Morton Smith denied that such was the practice before the year A.D. 70. W. D. Davies accepts the main tenet of the theory but remarks that the Early Church did not treat Jesus as a rabbi but as the New Moses himself. Whatever the defects of Riesenfeld's and Gerhardsson's argument, it had the great merit of recalling scholars to study the milieu of

i the transmission of the Logia. Recently Thorleif **Boman** approached the argument from another angle, that of the transmission of folklore (*Die Jesusüberlieferung im Lichte der neueren Volkskunde*, Göttingen 1967). After summing up the results of research on folk-transmission to date, Boman applies them to the tradition of the life and words of Jesus. He is not so rigid as his Scandinavian predecessors and freely takes into account the findings of Form-Criticism and *Traditionsgeschichte* as well as *Redaktionsgeschichte*; he even allows for some additions to the words of Jesus, but on the whole he agrees with T. W. Manson who asserts that the problem of the primitive

Church was not to create new sayings but to select **653** some from the already numerous ones for its own purposes (p. 30). This new light from unexpected quarters does much to shed serious doubt on the form-critical dogma of free creations by the Community.

We said above that the words of Jesus could very well **j** have been handed down to us together with a midrash: an exegetical explanation which charismatic interpreters in the Primitive Church gave concerning both the words and deeds of the Lord. Is it at all possible to discover the limits within which such a paraphrase could move? W. D. Davies' critique of Gerhardsson, viz that the Church regarded Jesus as the New Moses and not as a simple rabbi, gives us good reason to state that the early community could take the same liberties with the words of Jesus which it used to allow itself with the sacrosanct words of Moses. The Pentateuch has not only come down to us in its original text but also in an Aram. paraphrase. The Targums can provide us with a means of comparison and indicate to us the extent to which midrash can permit itself to go. In his excellent study on *Scripture and Tradition in Judaism* (Leiden 1961), G. Vermés summarizes with approval Renée Bloch's conclusions in her article on midrash in DBS: 'Its point of departure is Scripture; it is a reflection or meditation on the Bible. It is homiletical, and largely originates from the liturgical reading of the Torah. The Palestinian Targum probably reflects the synagogal homilies which followed the reading of the Bible. It makes a punctilious analysis of the text, with the object of illuminating any obscurities found there. Every effort is made to explain the Bible by the Bible, as a rule not arbitrarily, but by exploiting a theme. The biblical message is adapted to suit contemporary needs. According to the nature of the biblical text, the midrash either tries to discover the basic principles inherent in the legal sections, with the aim of solving problems not dealt with in Scripture (*Halakhah*), or it sets out to find the true significance of events mentioned in the narrative sections of the Pentateuch (*Haggadah*)' (p. 7). Another point of comparison is **k** provided by the alterations to the Synoptic sayings in the Gospel of Thomas. Very often such alterations, where they exist, consist of the addition of a few words here and there which give the saying a Gnostic slant. This teaches us that alterations of the words of Jesus by the Church could range from leaving them as they stood, through minute alterations of a theological character, to more substantial midrashic additions as in the case of John. The rejection of Thomas by the Church also teaches us how careful the orthodox community was not to accept unauthentic sayings or interpretations of sayings which were not in accordance with the mind of the Spirit of the Risen Lord. Whatever we may think about such accretions one thing is certain: sayings were not created, but only explained. It could happen that an explanation became detached from the main sayings and was transmitted on its own, but in our analysis of the Synoptic tradition *the burden of proof will be upon the claim to lack of authenticity*. Whatever the form of a saying it can never be a betrayal of the mind of the speaker.

We must now examine more closely **the criteria of 654 authenticity which Perrin uses** in his analysis. These are the criteria of dissimilarity, of coherence and of multiple attestation. The second can be reduced to the first, and the third does not prove that a saying attested by a single source is doubtful for that very reason, if it can be proved that the source is reliable in other instances. The **criterion of dissimilarity** leads us into a vicious circle. It is asserted that Jesus could not have spoken any 'com-

54a munity-sayings' or made rabbinical pronouncements, and that any sayings in those forms cannot be ascribed to Jesus. Such a tautology is based on frequently unproved dogmas of the form-critical school, which limits its research to the post-Easter community. **Heinz Schürmann** has recently proved that form-critical analysis can also be extended to the pre-Easter community. Although the results of his enquiry have not yet had a broad application, and are liable to be modified by further research, his thesis is there to stay and the older form-critics cannot but revise their theories in the light of more recent studies.

b Schürmann (*Die vorösterlichen Anfänge der Logientradition*, in R-M, 342—370) asserts that we should not look for a *Sitz im Leben* for the words of Jesus solely in the community of the Risen Christ. If we take into account what we know of the circumstances in which Jesus lived with his disciples many logia fall naturally into their proper place. The author distinguishes between an internal and an external setting. The foundation of the internal setting is the continuum of faith in Jesus' person among the disciples before and after Easter. Jesus must have made it plain to them in some way or other that he was not a simple rabbi or prophet, but one who has come to introduce the end of days. Their response belongs to this situation as well. Though we may not know exactly how this dialogue took place many of the sayings and episodes that have been preserved in the Synoptics belong to such

c a setting. More important still is the setting in the external life of the disciples. Jesus gathered men around himself and sent them out to preach even in his lifetime. He endowed them with some special authority and taught them in such a way that they would be able to repeat his message easily and understandably. They were to preach the coming of the Kingdom (about which we hear so little in the post-Easter Kerygma) as in Mt 10:7; 13:44, and the call to repentance (Mk 4:25; 13:35). Moreover, Jesus and his disciples formed some sort of community, even though loosely. Hence such sayings as the call to discipleship in Lk 9:58.62, or exhortations to the disciples as in Mt 6: 34 find a natural setting. Lastly, they must have possessed some community regulations which explain Mk 9:50 and similar passages.

d Schürmann's theory needs much perfecting and testing, but it certainly cannot be denied outright. It will need years of scholarly study to be able to apply it to the single sayings and episodes, but when this work is done the work of the older form-critics will have to be revised drastically.

From this summary examination we can conclude that although the 'life' of Jesus is framed in kerygma and covered with a layer of interpretative faith, it is nevertheless not impossible to penetrate down to it by means of critical research and bring out the selection of facts and logia which the primitive Church deemed worthy to preserve for us. These do not constitute a biography in so far as they cannot always be arranged in a chronological or logical order, nor can we be sure that we have the *ipsissima vox* or a filmed account of the works of Jesus. But that the Gospel narrative reproduces the essence of the preaching and activity of the Earthly Jesus, thanks to the fidelity of Jewish ways of transmission, can hardly be seriously doubted. However, once we have acquired some knowledge of the historical Jesus, will it be of any relevance to our faith today in the Risen Christ?

II. THE HISTORICAL JESUS AND THE CHRIST OF FAITH

655a The answer to this question depends on how the continuity between the historical Jesus and the Risen Christ is conceived. In Bultmann it appears to be a conceptual continuity. Christ is risen in the Kerygma **655a** and is alive in the preaching of the Church. Käsemann's continuity is, to say the least, logical or theological, Robinson's existentialist. The Primitive Church believed in a *personal* continuity, and that is why certain Catholic scholars like Léon-Dufour refuse to consider the problem. If we accept a personal resurrection the problem does not exist in the Bultmannian sense. In a Catholic sense, however, it is not meaningless to ask what part the historical Jesus played in the preaching of the Church about the Risen Christ. How does he fit into the Kerygma? The dichotomy between the historian and the man of faith was ruled out in Pius X's encyclical against the Modernists (*Pascendi* DzS 3485, 3496) in 1907, and Catholic scholars have always perceived the danger of such a dichotomy.

Had the NT only consisted of the Pauline Corpus it would have been rather difficult to answer this question, for Paul rarely appeals to the Jesus of history to confirm his preaching. The ultimate authority is the OT. Whenever he does appeal to a word of Jesus (1 Cor 7:10; 9:14; 11:23) it is final, and much more authoritative than his own ruling. It is certain that in Paul's time there already existed collections of sayings and miracles of the Lord, but as a tradition parallel to his *didachē*. With Mark we can already see the process of their absorption into the Church's preaching taking place, and this reaches its zenith in John. John not only does not put the words of the Risen Lord into the mouth of Jesus; he puts the words of Jesus into the mouth of the Risen Lord. John's Kerygma is formulated in the substance of the words of Jesus. It is Luke, however, who provides the key to the solution of this problem. In his time, some concise form of the life of Jesus had already entered the Kerygma in its technical sense of a sermon announcing Christ to unbelievers (Acts 10:37ff). And in the prologue to the Gospel Luke **b** tells Theophilus that the purpose of his book (or books) is to persuade him of the *asphaleia* (reliability, trustworthiness) of the *didachē* he has received. Theophilus already believed in the Risen Christ. The story of Jesus was meant to strengthen his faith in the preaching of those who had witnessed everything from the beginning (Lk 1:4). The essence of faith consisted in the belief that salvation had come to us through the death and resurrection of Jesus, who is now honoured as the Lord. This is an act of God in history, and Theophilus has already believed in this act of God. Luke now wants to inform him about the historical period in which God entered history, about the worldly dimension of faith (Lk 1:1). The author expects Theophilus to conclude, after reading the story of Jesus and of the Apostles, that Jesus is really the Christ and that he has brought us the promised eschatological gifts of salvation. The same purpose can be attributed to Mark, who, in an incisive sentence at the very beginning of his Gospel expects the believer to conclude that Jesus is the Son of God (1:1); and the same purpose is explicitly mentioned by John who asks the reader to believe that 'Jesus' is the Christ, the Son of God. John leaves us in no doubt concerning the oneness of Jesus and the Christ. In the opening paragraph of his first epistle John combats the incipient gnostic docetism of his day by insisting that the word he was preaching was no kerygma disconnected from history, but that 'which we have heard, which we have seen with our eyes, which we have looked upon and touched with our hands' (1 Jn 1:1). To minimize the Jesus of history, therefore, is to destroy the Christ of faith, at least in the opinion of the evangelists.

655c It is evident that the evangelists who look back at the life of Jesus do so with the eyes of faith, and impress the seal of faith on their narrative. But does this mean that their report is to be considered as a document of faith but not of history? If this were so we would expect to find the message of Jesus expressed in the terminology of the Primitive Church. Instead, certain key concepts which we find in the preaching of Jesus, such as Son of Man and Kingdom of God, are hardly ever used in the same sense in the epistles and Acts. The preaching of Jesus was purposely incomplete. It left many loose ends, especially as regards Christology and eschatology. These loose ends were tied up in the Resurrection. After the Resurrection, therefore, the Church could not preach its message simply using the words of Jesus, because its understanding of his person and of eschatological times had progressed and reached a new level. On the other hand, the faithful had to be certain that the Kerygma was a legitimate interpretation of the person and work of Jesus: that it was a logical development. Hence the necessity of composing the Gospels and teaching believers about the words and deeds of the historical Jesus. These were only a part of the full faith in the Risen Christ,

d however. **The words and deeds of Jesus had to be completed by the interpretative function of the Scriptures and explained in the light of the Spirit of the Risen One. What is given back in the Gospels, though a faithful rendering of the historical Jesus, is already complete in its interpretation.** An analogous case, however imperfect, is that of certain biographies of canonized saints. The writer certainly bases his study on sound documents but he writes already with the conviction that he is writing about a saint, and reads virtue in every word and action of his hero. Such biographies cannot be called unhistorical. They serve the purpose of providing a foundation for and increasing a devotion which already exists for other motives.

e But in the case of faith, **can contingent facts of history provide a sure basis for absolute faith?** The negative answer to this question has become a dogma for many modern scholars and provides them with a reason for denying the relevance of the historical Jesus. Any outright denial, however, has too much of the sweeping statement about it to be useful for scholarly research. Bultmann underlines his negation by stating that faith that is based on a historical argument is not faith at all, as it is based on reason. It is the faith of the older liberals. On the other hand faith does not ask for a *sacrificium intellectus*, hence the supernatural cannot be accepted without being first demythologized. Catholic theology has always maintained that before asserting that 'Jesus Christ is the Son of God' rather than that 'Buddha is the Son of God' I must have some reason for committing my faith to one and not to the other. An *act* of faith cannot be blind if it is to be human; it

f must be founded on reason. **History, therefore, will provide the springboard for my act of faith.** The *contents* of faith, on the other hand, are not intelligible to me, otherwise they will not constitute faith at all, but only a philosophical premise. They demand of me a *sacrificium intellectus* in so far as I have to renounce any understanding of their intrinsic evidence; but having placed my faith on reliable authority, I know that there cannot be any intrinsic contradiction, even though I cannot prove it directly. St Paul calls this '*the folly of the* Cross' (1 Cor 1:18), and to demythologize it in such a way as to render it understandable is to reduce faith to a philosophy of words (1 Cor 1–2). With Paul again, however,

I assert: 'I *know* in whom I have placed my trust . . .' (2 Tim 1:12), which makes my act of faith humanly acceptable. This knowledge, in a revelation which has taken place in the historical figure of Jesus of Nazareth, is provided by history.

g But are not the historical dogmas of today the discarded hypotheses of the future? It all depends upon the evidence of course. That Caesar conquered Gaul, that Raphael was a painter, that Napoleon was defeated at Waterloo, and that a naval battle was fought at Jutland can never become discarded hypotheses. I can be as certain of this as I can be of anything upon which I base my actions. If the evidence is not clear I am not dealing with a historian's dogma but with a hypothesis. Of course there is always new evidence turning up that will shake the results of present day research, but there are certain facts which have been established beyond doubt. Is the story of Jesus one of them? Bultmann maintains that beyond the existence and violent death of Jesus we cannot go. What is important is the '*das*', not the

h '*wie*' (the 'thatness' not the modality of Jesus). This is all derived from the *a priori* denial of the supernatural. When it is assumed as a dogma that miracles cannot happen, the evidence of history has to be twisted round to make it fit into a definite pattern. Is it not more reasonable to discuss objectively the evidence we possess for the supernatural in the life of Jesus and then adapt our philosophical views accordingly? Bultmann states that 'miracles' do not enter into our modern *Weltanschauung*. Today we think in terms of science, he argues, and we know that the chain of cause and effect is not broken by supernatural irruptions. Apart from the fact that this is a very Newtonian way of looking at things— modern scientists are much more wary—certain very extraordinary happenings do take place today, at Lourdes, for example, and elsewhere, especially in the E. Would it not be more prudent to take cognizance of such happenings before denying outright the Gospel evidence for the supernatural? The deeds of Jesus were preached to friends and foes alike by people who had lived with him, to people who had known him. They had nothing to gain but everything to lose by speaking as they did. When it is a case of multiple contemporary evidence it is very difficult for a historical fact to become a discarded hypothesis in the future.

i **What, however, is the theological relevance of the 'supernatural' in Jesus' life**, and why is there so much insistence upon it? It is there to call our attention to God's intervention in history. The disturbance of the chain of cause and effect, of itself, proves nothing. It only calls attention and causes wonderment. The presence of God's revelation is witnessed to by the appeal of the explanatory words to the light of inner truth and by the witness of the Spirit (1 Jn 5:7 and passim in Jn's Gospel). The daily sequence of cause and effect leads the mind to God's 'ordinary' presence in the world. The breaking of this chain is indicative of the '*ephapax*' of the extraordinary irruption of God into human history for a special revelation. As Käsemann rightly remarks, the fact that revelation takes place in a historically verifiable Person and not only within the mind is the expression of the *extra nos* of salvation. We can add to this that the presence of the 'supernatural' expresses further its *sine nobis*. If God decided to enter into the cycle of history, historical research becomes a search for God.

j Here a distinction made by N. Perrin may come in useful. The Germans distinguish between *historisch* and *geschichtlich*. Perrin clarifies and extends this distinction in terms intelligible in English. He dis-

655j tinguishes between *historical, historic,* and *faith-knowledge* of Christ. 'First there is the essentially descriptive historical knowledge of Jesus of Nazareth ... Then, secondly there are those aspects of this knowledge, which, like aspects of any knowledge of any figure from the past, can become significant to us in our present in various ways. Thirdly, there is knowledge of Jesus of Nazareth which is significant only in the context of specifically Christian faith, i.e. knowledge of him of a kind dependent upon the acknowledgement of him as Lord and Christ' (op cit p. 234). The combinations of possible concessions of these three kinds of knowledge and their interdependence are an important criterion for pinpointing the positions of the various theologians who have taken part in the discussion on the historical Jesus. At one extreme we have the old liberal school which concedes full historical knowledge that gives birth to a moral historic knowledge of Jesus, faith knowledge is reduced to a minimum. At the other end Bultmann discounts historical knowledge and underlines faith-knowledge. For Robinson it is the historic knowledge of Jesus which forms the essence of the New Quest and moves parallel with faith-knowledge. The New Hermeneutic, as Perrin remarks, has a tendency 'to blur the distinction between statements possible on the basis of academic historical research and statements possible only on the basis of faith' (p. 241). Perrin's own position has been outlined above (§ 652*j*), and, with certain modifications, it would be as acceptable as the position of Käsemann if both of these authors did not cast a thick mantle of scepticism over the possibility of having a clearer knowledge of the historical Jesus.

k As a conclusion of this section we would like to outline our views on the possibility of and interdependence between the above-mentioned kinds of knowledge. We have already stated that in spite of our acknowledgement of the claims of form-criticism we believe that **the Gospel account of Jesus is basically historical, including the miraculous element.** The picture of Jesus which emerges from an independent historical study of the Synoptics has certainly a 'historic' value in so far as it addresses our generation and spurs us on to an existential decision. But we cannot limit the influence of Jesus to that alone, otherwise Jesus would not differ from Socrates or any other personage of history. The knowledge of the historical Jesus is a springboard from which we make the leap of faith in Jesus the Christ, and it serves as a means of testing the claims of the kerygma. **The decision which we must make after reading the life of Jesus is not merely moral or existential; it is eschatological, in the sense of submitting to an Act of God in history.** Once this Act of God has been acknowledged we can then reread history with the eyes of faith and substitute 'Christ the Lord' for Jesus'. Moreover, our faith in the action of God in history will vouch for the objective truth of the essential facts of salvation history (always within the limits of literary genre, though this may be 'myth') as presented in the inspired books of Scripture.

As regards Jesus and the Church, I do not merely believe the Church presenting Jesus as the Christ. I also accept Jesus' presentation of himself and of the Church, as well as the interpretation of his own actions. The Church completes this interpretation not independently of the historical Jesus but as a prolongation in history of the *ephapax* of the Person of Christ.

In the third section we shall now pass on to consider the deeds and words of Jesus as a presentation of himself upon the stage of history.

III. THE PERSON AND TEACHING OF JESUS

In the article *Theology and Tradition in Apostolic* **656a** *Times* (§ 665), we examine the Gospel data about the life and teaching of Jesus in the context of the Kerygma, and place both logia and narratives in the *Sitz im Leben* of primitive Christianity. Moreover, in the discussion in Section II of the present article we said that between the Historical Jesus and the Risen Christ we must admit not only a logical but also a personal continuity. On the other hand, we admitted that the logia and narrative traditions underwent an evolution between the time of their collection and the final process of being written down in the Synoptic Gospels. In the present section we shall try to pick out those traditions which have a major claim to authenticity and collocate them in the original *Sitz im Leben* of Jesus' ministry, in so far as this is possible. It is only in this way that we can test whether the Primitive Church's conviction that its faith in the Risen Lord as a natural consequence of its experience of the historical Jesus is valid or not.

The Kingdom of God: Under the heading 'The Last **b** Days' in the above cited article, we collect the Kingdom sayings of Jesus as they are delivered to us in the Synoptic Gospels and group them under different headings according to the various interests of the collectors or the Evangelists. We also make a general claim that they are in substance authentic and that the interpretation of the Kingdom which we find in St Luke is a logical interpretation in history of the prophetical message of Jesus. In this section, for apologetical reasons, we shall have to take a more radical approach and limit our examination to those sayings whose authenticity is generally accepted. For further claims we shall have to offer proofs. As a basis for discussion Perrin's very radical listing of Jesus' sayings in his book *Rediscovering the Teaching of Jesus* (SCM 1967) has been chosen. We shall, however, offer our own interpretation.

Jesus never defines clearly what he means by the **c** Kingdom of God; he takes its knowledge for granted. His sayings and parables clarify and correct already existing notions, and add some touches to the OT hope. At the end of Jesus' ministry, a careful disciple well versed in the Scriptures would have understood how Jesus differed from the Pharisees and the Apocalyptists and how he developed OT thought, but he would only have been able to tie up loose ends after the Resurrection and the descent of the Spirit.

The contemporary ideas about the '*ôlām habbā*', **d** the **Age to Come,** a phrase which corresponds most loosely to Jesus' Kingdom of God, have already been outlined in the article *Tradition and Theology.* Here it suffices to make a few summary statements, necessarily sweeping, to provide a background against which Jesus' doctrine can be studied. The scriptures recognize God as King. He created the world, guided Israel and rules over history. In effect, however, his kingship is not recognized: either by Israel, whose history has been one of recurring infidelity, or by the nations, who do not even know his Name. The Prophets therefore envisage a future time in which God will rule actively. Israel will be moved by the Spirit to observe a New Covenant (Jer 31:31; Ez 37) and the nations will all come in pilgrimage to the mountain of Yahweh. The Pharisees of Jesus' time, as far as their doctrine can be reconstructed from rabbinic sources, interpreted this teaching spiritually enough, but they insisted on the universal rule of the

656d Torah, which will be widely known and followed in Messianic times. This necessarily excluded the ignorant riffraff and sinners, the *'am-haāres*, whom they despised. The primarily religious concept of the universality of God's rule could be interpreted as meaning the dominion of Israel over all nations, and in that connection had some bearing on that of the Essene communities (especially Damascus and Qumran). These have been described as half-way enthusiasts between the Maccabees and the Zealots. Their hope was nationalistic, and they desired nothing more ardently than to see the Romans driven out of Palestine by the Coming Leader. The Apocalyptists awaited a spectacular arrival of the Son of Man accompanied by cosmic signs. He would judge sinners and establish a kingdom of justice and peace.

e Jesus makes it clear that the Kingdom of God has 'come upon' Israel (Lk 11:20). God has inaugurated his active and dynamic rulership to fulfil his promise to his people. This rulership, symbolized in Jesus' exorcisms, represents God's triumph over demonic powers. The Kingdom has therefore entered quietly, without ostentation. The astrological observations of the apocalyptists are of no avail. The coming of the Kingdom is devoid of all drama. Jesus states that in his preaching the Kingdom is already among the expectant Jews (Lk 17:20). But its march is not going to be at all an unambiguously victorious one, as the exorcisms may lead one to believe, for it will be plundered by men of violence. John's imprisonment had already proved that it is a sign of contradiction. Nevertheless, from John onwards it is here to stay (Mt 11:12). The presence of Jesus should be a cause of joy. It recalls the Messianic wedding feast from which all signs of mourning should be removed (Mk 2:19f).

f In spite of the presence of the Kingdom, the full realization of God's rulership is still a future fact. The disciples have to pray, as the Jews did in the *Shemoneh 'Esreh* that his Name may be hallowed and his Kingdom come (Lk 11:2—4), and they must persevere in this kind of prayer to survive the violence which surrounds the Kingdom (Lk 11:5—8). They are God's elect, and their sufferings will be vindicated (Lk 18:1—8). The preaching of Jesus, therefore, is only the sowing of a seed, the insertion of a mass of leaven (Lk 4:31f; Mt 13:33) which possesses an internal power to grow, silently but steadily. This did not coincide with any of the popular expectations of the 'Age to Come', but whoever had eyes to see could read the signs of the times (Mk 13:28f) and humble himself to 'receive' God's gift with simplicity (Mk 10:15). The signs could only be understood by those who penetrated deeply into the meaning of scripture and recognized in the preaching of Jesus the absolving hand of God. The parables of the prodigal son (Lk 15:11ff), the good shepherd (Mt 18:12) and the lost coin (Lk 15:8f) reveal God's loving initiative and are directed against those who, blinded by their own self-righteousness, could not rise to the occasion when God began to manifest his love for sinners.

g The inability to recognize the signs of the times would keep the self-classed *élite* out of the Kingdom, whose doors would be flung open to the pariah and to the gentile (Mt 8:11f). God calls the whole nation, but owing to the scarce response only a few qualify for approval (Mt 22:14). And even the outcasts themselves, who have been received into table-fellowship with the Lord, must be careful to preserve the new righteousness of the Kingdom to qualify for final election (Mt 22:11—13). However, it is these who are the main guests of the Kingdom (Mt 22:1—11): sinners, prostitutes and taxgatherers (Mt 21:28—32). And even if they have been called at the eleventh hour their recompense is equal to that of those who have toiled longer, for everything proceeds from the goodness of God (Mt 20:1—8). If there is anything that excludes from the Kingdom, it is precisely self-righteousness. It is much better to present oneself empty-handed before God and be willing to receive his gift than to force his hand by vain boastfulness before him (Lk 18:9ff). The Pharisees must therefore understand that the first shall be last, and the last first (Mk 10:31). One must behave like a child to qualify for election (Mk 10:15). **656g**

Jesus' preaching is therefore primarily directed **h** against the blindness and bad will of the Pharisees (Mt 11:18f). They are the apathetic generation that do not respond to God's call (Mt 11:16f), who are so attached to their old institutions that they are unable to hold the new wine of God's grace (Mk 2:2f). This applies also to the priests and the scribes, and to all those who are so engrossed in the letter of the law that their eyes are blinded by the brilliance of the Spirit when it appears.

To those who acknowledge the presence of the Kingdom Jesus has a stern and clear message. The value of the Kingdom is absolute. All the rest must be abandoned for its sake (Mt 13:44ff). Its recognition calls for a quick eschatological decision and existential resolution as in the face of an imminent crisis (Lk 16:1—8). Anything less decisive will scarcely bear fruit, or will bear it in a lesser degree. The love of this world suffocates the workings of God's grace (Mk 4:3—9). The intrinsic power of Jesus' preaching is itself a sign which should produce immediate penitential effects as Jonah's word did among the Ninevites (Lk 11:29f). Hence, before committing oneself to receive the Kingdom the believer must carefully weigh all the sacrifices it entails lest his conversion be only half-hearted (Lk 14:28—32). This applies particularly to attachment to riches, which makes the entrance to the Kingdom a narrow one indeed (Mk 10:24f; Mt 7:13f). One must also have the courage to confess Jesus before men (Lk 12:8f), because it is the strength of faith which makes the believer participate in the victory over Satan (Mt 17:19f).

Faith in the initiative of God's loving forgiveness **i** should evoke an ethical response from the believer. The announcing of the Kingdom reveals two things: the fatherhood of God (cf J. Jeremias' insistence on the original meaning of the word *Abba* in the Lord's prayer, which he translates 'dear Father', an appellation hitherto unknown), and the brotherhood of man. We should therefore deal with our neighbour as God has dealt with us, making no distinction of caste or race (Lk 10:29ff) and forgiving as we have been forgiven (Mt 18:23—30). The standard of ethical perfection is the perfection of God himself. His initiative of reconciliation should spur us to reconcile adversaries (Mt 5:38—41) and to surrender our most beloved possessions for the sake of peace. (Mt 5:43—48). What defiles a man, therefore, is not impure food but unethical feelings and actions (Mk 7:14—16).

Conspicuously absent from this outline of Jesus' **j** teaching are those elements which, according to the theories of radical form-critics, originated in the primitive community, such as those sayings which apply to communal living, the sending of the Apostles to preach, Jesus' presentation of his own Person, the prediction of his passion and resurrection and the apocalyptic Son of Man logia. On the other hand, the experienced reader can easily observe that the doctrine of the Kingdom as exposed above coincides in all but word with Paul's doctrine of justification by faith; therefore, if the conclusions of

56j Form-Criticism had to be pushed to the furthest extremes, even the doctrine of the Kingdom would be denied to Jesus. How much more simple is it to state that it is the primitive Church that evolved the doctrine of Jesus rather than putting its own doctrine into his mouth. Moreover, according to Schürmann's latest studies, the community-sayings and the mission-logia could very well have their *Sitz im Leben* in the primitive circle of disciples around Jesus. We shall now proceed to examine Jesus' presentation of himself as Messiah.

57a   Jesus' Self-designation: Jesus preached the Kingdom in prophetic style. He did not preach the 'Social Gospel' of Gladden, Rauschenbusch and Matthews at the turn of the century. Jesus was an eschatological prophet. The fact that he did not preach a merely future Kingdom but announced it as already present makes him *the* Eschatological Prophet. He speaks with authority. There remains a gap, however, between the Eschatological Prophet and the Christ of the post-Easter Church. Did Jesus himself fill that gap? Did he present himself as the Messiah? We develop elsewhere the meaning of the Christological titles as used by the primitive Church (in §§ 676–8). Here we shall limit ourselves to examining whether Jesus actually applied to himself the titles 'Christ', 'Son of God' and 'Son of Man' as a first reading of the Gospels seems to imply. The question is an old one, but Form Criticism has compelled the post-Bultmannians to renew the discussion in a

b modern key. Let us begin with the title '**Christ**'. In H. Conzelmann's latest book: *Grundriss der Theologie des NT* (1967), the title Christ is not only denied Jesus but it is affirmed that he actually repudiated it. The author holds that the title is missing in Q. In Mark it is only to be found in the trial of Jesus, which is editorial theology and not historical reportage, and in Peter's confession at *Caesarea Philippi* (Mk 8:29f). Conzelmann (p. 150) and R. H. Fuller (*The Foundations of NT Christology*, 1965, p. 109 which reverses the conclusions of his earlier work *The Mission and Achievement of Jesus*) follow F. Hahn's interpretation of this passage (*Christologische Hoheitstitel*, 1966³, p. 225) which explains away vv 30–32 as editorial, and leaves Peter's confession 'Thou art the Christ' with Jesus' answer 'Get behind me Satan, for you are not on the side of God, but of men'. Fuller finds no need for explicit Christological declarations as he believes in the 'post-Bultmannian' implicit Christology, implicit, i.e. in Jesus' authoritative preaching and deeds. He therefore explains all Christological titles in the Synoptics as products of the Church. His exegesis of Mk 8:28–33 is far-fetched. It presupposes too lightly that the 'Messianic Secret' and the passion prediction are editorial interpolations. Jesus would certainly not be enthusiastic to proclaim himself as the Messiah, when he knows that this title recalls innumerable undesirable connotations in a Jewish audience. But he welcomes the confession of the disciples who demonstrated that they at least have understood the signs of the times. He immediately goes on, however, to interpret the title in the light of the Servant hymns, and this is what gives scandal. If Jesus really disclaimed the title of Christ it cannot be understood how he ever came to be called 'Jesus Christ'.

c   The Messianic claim at the trial is so inextricably linked with the titles '*Son of God*' and '*Son of Man*' that they have to be studied in the same context. Recent monographs on the trial of Jesus are legion, and the form-critical studies on the answers of Jesus before the Sanhedrin are tending to cast serious doubts about their historicity (cf Eduard Lohse, *Die Geschichte des Leidens*

und Sterbens Jesu Christi, 1964, and, on the Catholic **657c** side A. Feuillet, *Le triomphe du Fils de l'Homme*, in *La venue du Messie*, 1962). The arguments against historicity are (1) The disciples could have had no eye-witnesses at the trial; (2) Jesus' answer in Mk 14:62 is made up of two OT quotations (Ps 110, 1 + Dan 7, 13) which are easily attributable to the Church; (3) The *Sitz im Leben* of this logion is anti-Jewish accusations in the primitive Church: the Jews killed their Messiah; (4) The real reason of Jesus' condemnation was his table-fellowship with 'Jews who had made themselves like gentiles' (Perrin), or some other reason, but not an open Messianic claim. These arguments are partly true, but they do not put out of court the evangelical accounts. Even if the disciples themselves were not present at the trial, nothing is more natural than that they should have informed themselves of the proceedings from people who were present (cf Jn 18:15). It is not impossible that the two quotations substitute the actual words of Jesus at the trial, although it is not evident why Jesus could not have quoted them himself: in the Synoptics he usually answers insidious questions by means of biblical citations, which would have been the most prudent way of acting. Moreover, even if the *Sitz im Leben* of the narrative as it now stands is an anti-Jewish accusation does it necessarily imply that it is not founded on facts? Nothing would have been easier for the Jews to refute than such an assumption.

On the positive side, it is beyond doubt that Jesus was **d** crucified, which means that he was condemned by the Romans. The inscription on the cross, also an undoubted fact, read 'King of the Jews', which means that Jesus was delivered to Pilate as a Messianic pretender. The real reason why the scribes and priests wanted to remove Jesus out of the way was his constant attack on their hypocrisy and self-righteous attitude, but they had to present the nation with a more solid basis for condemnation. The fact that anyone claimed to be the Messiah did not automatically render him worthy of the death penalty; Bar-Cochba was not condemned to death by the Jews. His claim was in line with their nationalistic expectations. Jesus must have claimed Messiahship in a blasphemous way, and nothing is more consistent with this supposition than that he claimed for himself divine prerogatives. His answer in Mk 14:62, therefore, whether reproduced to the letter or not, essentially represents the admission he made before the High Priest. And if his accusers **e** pressed him into making a claim for divine authority it could only have been because he had been heard making some statement to that effect in his preaching. In fact, the question of Jesus' authority and provenance was not new. The Pharisees had already discussed his extraordinary wisdom and could not account for it through heredity or education. Hence the famous 'Johannine' logion Mt 11:27 is at home in such a setting as Mt 13:54–56 or Mk 11:28. Similarly, the 'Son's' ignorance of the Parousia (Mk 13, 32) would be a rather cumbersome saying for the Church to invent when it was endeavouring to exalt the Son above everything. Moreover, these two logia are consistent with Jesus' use of 'Abba' and with the parable of the unfaithful labourers (Mk 12:1–9). The Sanhedrin, therefore, had good reason to defy Jesus to interpret his Messiahship in terms of Sonship and accuse him of blasphemy when he did so.

As to the title '*Son of Man*', we give later some **f** reasons for its authenticity (cf § 666k). Since that article was written Morna Hooker has published her excellent book *The Son of Man in Mark* (1967) in which she argues against A. B. J. Higgins, H. E. Tödt, and others that Jesus did use the expression. She adduces

657f the classical argument that the Church hardly used this title any longer and therefore could not have put it into Jesus' mouth; and also that Jesus used it to denote himself. We shall treat further about this subject later on. From a purely exegetical point of view, the meaning of the Christological titles in the Early Church is far more developed than their use in the Synoptics. In this sense we can speak of 'implicit Christology', not, however, in the sense that Jesus never claimed any Messianic powers and that he was only acknowledged as Messiah after his resurrection.

g As a confirmation of the above we must add that Jesus requires faith not only in his message but also in his person. The saying in Lk 12:8 is considered authentic by Perrin, who gives as its original 'Every one who acknowledges me before men, the Son of Man will acknowledge before the angels of God'. The antithetical second part about the denial of Jesus may well be secondary, as Perrin states; but, assuming the identity of Jesus with the Son of Man, if the acknowledgement of Jesus' person is necessary for salvation it is clear that Jesus does not present himself as a simple prophet with a message unconnected with his own person. So Peter's confession in Mk 8:28 need not be out of place in the ministry of Jesus. The acknowledgement which Jesus asks for is the confession of his Messiahship.

h We have established that Jesus came to preach the presence of the eschatological Kingdom, and that he preached it not as something apart from himself. It is now logical to ask: What is Jesus' own role in these eschatological happenings? He has not come only to announce. Did Jesus give an interpretation of his own mission, especially of his own death? Did he claim a place in the final judgement alongside God as judge? These questions are hotly debated but demand an answer.

658a Jesus and the Future—Most modern authors agree that the Passion predictions (Mk 8:31; 9:31) are basically authentic. It only needed a little natural insight to foresee that with his constant attacks on the Pharisees and priests Jesus was heading towards destruction. This had been the way of the prophets before him, and Jesus felt that his too would be a violent death. The two sayings quoted above, however, contain also a prophecy about the resurrection, and Mk 10:45 gives an interpretation of Jesus' death in eschatological terms. Is this to be judged later theology which has been ascribed to Jesus or does it have a ring of authenticity? Many contemporary form-critics explain Mk 10:45 as a Hellenistic dogmatical development of Lk 22:27, coming from the Pauline school. Apart from the Aramaisms *tēn psychēn autou, anti pollōn* and the non-Pauline *lytron*, which give it a Palestinian background the saying is confirmed by the words of Institution. So it is better to begin our investigation with the Eucharistic words of Jesus whose authenticity

b can hardly be doubted. It is immaterial whether we accept the Markan account as the older, as Jeremias and W. D. Davies do, or whether we think that the Lukan-Pauline account brings us nearer to the Antioch-Palestinian source, as Schürmann opines. We are always within less than a decade from the death of Jesus, and Jeremias' judgement on the problem is still valid: 'That in the remaining space of at most a decade after the death of Jesus the Eucharistic rite should have been freely created, and the account of the Lord's Supper invented as an aetiological legend, is as much incapable of proof as it is improbable. It is even improbable that in the first decade after the death of Jesus the tradition should be in any essentials obscured; against that we have to set the complete unanimity in content of the

mutually independent reports of Mark and Paul which **658** came from different sections of the Church. Since the tradition of Mark, besides its material indications of a very early age, possesses a further guarantee of trustworthiness in its Palestinian origin (Semitisms), we have every reason to conclude that it gives us absolutely authentic information' (*The Eucharistic Words of* **c** *Jesus* 1955 p. 132). E. J. Kilmartin (*The Eucharist in the Primitive Church* 1965 p. 35) concludes, after a critical comparison of the Markan and Pauline versions of the words of institution, that the original words must have been: 'This is my body which is given for many: do this in remembrance of me . . . This cup is the new covenant in my blood'. Jesus, therefore, interpreted his death as an atoning death. The Kingdom of God is not a continuation of the old dispensation but is the New Covenant of Jer 31:31. His own death is a sacrificial death inaugurating this covenant. His death is also the death of the Suffering Servant of Isaiah. In the light of this text Mk 10:45 remains no longer strange. Indeed, it is Bultmann's insistence that these words are a later Hellenistic interpretation that now seems so antiquated. It is evident that the theology of the Church regarding the person and death of Christ is much more developed than the words of Jesus himself, but we do not think that it can be maintained with any degree of seriousness that this theology was either created *ex nihilo* or had as foundation merely the implicit claim to Messiahship contained in the expurgated version of the Kingdom sayings.

We must now move a step further and enquire into the **d** eschatological-apocalyptic position of the Son of Man, and ask **whether the identification of Jesus with the eschatological Son of Man goes back to Jesus himself** or was made later by the Church. It cannot be doubted that the evangelists equated Christ with the Son of Man and that in their editorial theology the identification is normal. The question whether this identification goes back to Jesus is more complicated. The title occurs in three groups of sayings: the 'earthly', the 'suffering' and the 'apocalyptic' group. A complete enumeration according to sources is given by R. H. Fuller on pp. 96f of *The Mission and Achievement of Jesus* (1954). The earthly and apocalyptic sayings occur in both Mk and Q, and suffering logia only in Mk, and never in combination with the future sayings. Bultmann draws certain conclusions from this grouping which are summed up by Fuller as follows: '(1) Only the "present" and "future" usages belong to the earlier strata of the tradition. (2) The "suffering" usage is an invention of Mark, and its secondary character shown by the fact that it is not fused with the "future" usage. (3) The "present" usage Bultmann recognizes as authentic, but not as Messianic: it is simply the Aram. periphrasis for "man" or "I". (4) The "future" usage is probably authentic to Jesus, and Messianic. But Jesus does not identify himself with the Son of Man: he merely announces his coming as one distinct from himself' (p. 97). In his later book Fuller denies the authenticity of the present sayings and develops the opinion of H. E. Tödt as regards the future logia by admitting not only a soteriological continuity between Jesus and the coming Son of Man but also a Christological one though it be not personal. Salvation now through Jesus leads to final salvation through the Son of Man. The personal continuity, which was then projected backwards on the present and suffering sayings, is due to the Church. This theory is very radical and needs careful examination.

The critical problem of the Son of Man is related to **e**

658e the meaning of the term, which, in its turn, is connected with its provenance. Scholars agree today that the expression is not of Hellenistic but of Palestinian origin. There can only be three sources: it can derive from Daniel 7 (or Henoch), from Ezek, or it could be an expression currently denoting a personal pronoun. The Ezek hypothesis has again been revived by E. Schweizer in his commentary on Mk (NTD) in 1967, but modern British scholars rightly pay little attention to it as Jesus hardly ever connects himself with Ezek. Moreover, there is nothing to witness that 'son of man' was used instead of 'I' at the time of Christ. Its context is usually Danielic. Now if the Church identifies Christ with Jesus' Son of Man it could only do so in an apocalyptic context, so there is no reason why it should project the saying back to the lips of Jesus in his earthly capacity. The saying does not appear in the framework of the Gospels but only in logia, and it does signify 'I'. The 'Present' sayings, therefore, have no explanation either from contemporary Judaism or from early Church theology. This makes them pass the test of the criterion of dissimilarity and that of multiple attestation. They must be authentic. Now if the 'present' sayings are authentic, and Son of Man is equivalent to 'I' in the mouth of Jesus, then the 'future' sayings must refer to Jesus as well and Mk 8:38 can only be analysed as a *parallelismus membrorum* where Jesus affirms that he himself will come as judge with the angels of heaven.

f But if the equivalence of 'son of man' and 'I' was unknown in Judaism how did Jesus come to use it? It can only be explained by the fact that **the Messianic secret** is not merely Markan editorial theology, it **goes back to Jesus himself**. Jesus could not make apocalyptic claims for himself without first introducing his own person in terms of biblical connotation. He knew himself to be the Prophet of the eschatological age and read his own fate, which he accepted as the will of God, in the scriptures, especially in Is 52 and 53, in Wis 2.4.5, where the righteous is said to judge his persecutors, and in Jeremiah. Having foreseen his own death he was certain of his glorification as vindication, and his return as judge could find no better explanation than in the book of Daniel. If the Church could read this connexion in the Scriptures it is hard to see why Jesus should be denied this insight as well, especially when there are form-critically authentic sayings to confirm it. As has been explained elsewhere (§ 676) Jesus merely presented his own person in terms of biblical connotations and left it to the Church to draw out a full Christology from his utterances. The 'implicit Christology' of the post-Bultmannians which persistently destroys all Christological logia falls between two stools. We can only either attribute the whole story of Jesus to the pious meditation of the Church or admit once for all that Jesus was fully conscious of being the Messiah.

g Jesus preached the presence of the Kingdom of God, the arrival of eschatological times. He connected this advent with his own person. His witness did not consist only in words, it was borne simultaneously by 'signs and wonders': by the **miracles** of the Lord. In the historical sketch in the first part of this essay we saw how the supernatural in Jesus' life was either explained away as an invention, or given a natural explanation, or interpreted allegorically. Radical critics today, although still maintaining the old scepticism regarding the supernatural, admit that Jesus did perform actions which in the eyes of his contemporaries were 'miracles'. It is usual to quote Bultmann in this context, who, in his book *Jesus* (Siebenstern edition p. 119) affirms that it cannot be doubted that Jesus did perform healings and exorcisms. **658g** N. Perrin writes (*Rediscovering the Teaching of Jesus* p. 136) 'Another factor entering into the discussion at this point is the increasing willingness of critical scholars to accept the premise that Jesus did, in fact, "cast out demons" in a way considered remarkable by his contemporaries. The evidence for this is strong. We have the testimony of the Jewish sources; the fact that such stories occur in all strata of the tradition, including the two earliest, Mark and Q (criterion of multiple attestation), and the authentic Kingdom-sayings related to exorcisms, especially Matt. 12:28 par. Today the pupils of the original form-critics are prepared to accept elements of the tradition their teachers rejected'. Even if one insists on being thoroughly radical and does not give credence to the Gospel accounts, it is impossible to deny the contemporary evidence of the Epistles. When Paul writes to the Corinthians that he performed miracles among them (2 Cor 12:12) or that there were many in their midst who had the gift of healing or of tongues (1 Cor 12:4ff) he was stating hard facts; and if the Apostles performed miracles why could Jesus not have done likewise?

When we come to study the literary composition of **h** the miracle stories in the Gospels and Acts it becomes evident that we cannot always interpret them at their face-value (cf the encyclopaedic work of H. van der Loos: *The Miracles of Jesus*, Leiden 1965). Rabbinic miracle-stories as well as those of Philostratus and Lucian have taught us much regarding the form of these narratives. Again, the editorial intertwining of OT reminiscences and the overlay of kerygmatic interpretation sometimes make it quite difficult for the historian to perceive what 'actually happened' in particular cases, but render the accounts theologically richer, which is the explicit intention of the Evangelist. We have already examined the editorial theology of the miracle stories elsewhere. Here we must limit ourselves to examining the meaning of Jesus' miracles in the context of the preaching of the Kingdom.

There is a difference, however, between the Gospel **i** miracles and the Hellenistic and rabbinical wonders or exorcisms. The former are not only wonders, they are *signs*, and eschatological signs which require *faith*. The Kingdom of God is the 'power of God unto salvation' (Rom 1·16). The revelation of this power takes place through two channels, the word of God and visible signs. Both are laden with power and *plērophoria*, persuasiveness, and both bear witness to the salvific will of God. This witness is complementary. Jesus preaches as 'one endowed with authority', not like the rabbis (Mk 1:22). At the same time power flows out of him and heals the sick (Lk 6:19). Hence miracles have a kind of 'sacramental' function. They are visible signs of the spiritual salvation which accompanies the arrival of eschatological times. They are not mere symbols, however, for they already contain the incohate power of the kingdom. The exorcisms are a sign that the Kingdom of God is present and that Satan has been vanquished (Mt 12:28). The healing of the sick is a visible sign of the *sōtēria* of the Kingdom; the raising of the dead is a sign of the new life. Hence the miracles are what the Germans call *Tatverkündigung*, kerygmatic actions. They are there to call attention and to speak to those who have ears to hear. They do not only call attention to the Kingdom but also to the bringer of the Kingdom. John says that at Cana Jesus revealed himself to his disciples, (Jn 2, 11) and the controversy which arose around the man born blind (Jn 9) was a Christological controversy around

658i a miracle. It demonstrated that Jesus was endowed with salvific power which not only required the response of faith (Mk 5:34; 10:52; Lk 7:50; 17:19) but called for a decision (Lk 10:13).

j **Miracles elicit faith but they do not force it.** Of itself a miracle proves nothing. The bible itself admits that the magicians of Pharaoh worked wonders and that the Antichrist will seduce many by means of his miracles. The Pharisees interpreted badly the miracles of the Lord. Hence they are not a metaphysical 'proof' which makes of the contents of faith the conclusion of a syllogism, or reduce faith to vision. They are signs in whose presence the only reasonable response is faith: in the case of the Gospel miracles, faith that God had inaugurated eschatological salvation and that Jesus was its bringer. Hence, the function of miracles is fully described by the word used in their regard in the Epistle to the Hebrews (2:4): *synepimartyreō*, 'to testify at the same time', or mutual witness of kerygma and signs. Both proceed from the Spirit and both address themselves to that interior light in the spirit of man which, itself aided by the Spirit of God, distinguishes truth from falsehood.

659a We have hitherto tried to establish a doctrinal, Christological and soteriological continuity between Jesus and the Risen Christ. **Is there also a personal continuity?** This depends on whether we accept the **Resurrection as a historical fact** or not. Although the main current of Christian theology has always maintained that the Resurrection actually happened, it is also certain that we are not dealing here with an observable phenomenon verifiable through the usual channels of historical research. This does not mean that we are justified in denying or doubting its factualness, or in reducing it to a purely subjective persuasion, because there are means of reaching moral certitude other than those provided by the positive sciences. Bultmann maintains that the actual fact of the Resurrection is not important. The empty sepulchre and the apparitions are of a secondary nature. What is really essential is that Christ is risen *for me*, that he lives in the kerygma and sheds light on the meaning of the Cross. This interpretation is equivocal. The spiritualizing subjective interpretation was already known and combated by John in his first epistle and in the Gospel. If John resisted the Hellenistic tendency to demythologize in his time it is not evident how we can be faithful to his message by succumbing to the same temptation in ours.

b Although the Resurrection is not 'historical' in the same sense as the crucifixion, because it is not fully verifiable, this does not mean that historical research cannot contribute to establishing the fact of Christ's rising from the dead. Modern traditio-historical criticism has traced the development of the Easter narrations from the very primitive Kerygma through 1 Cor 15 up to their final written stage in the Gospels. The Resurrection narratives lived in confessions of faith, in the *Didache*, and in controversy against both Jews who denied the facts and gnostics who spiritualized them. The Gospel narratives are derived from various traditions, which, at times, are a little difficult to combine together, but the main facts they insist upon are to be found in all

c accounts. These are **the empty tomb and the apparitions.** The fact that Jesus' tomb was found empty proves nothing in a positive way. It can be interpreted in so many ways. But it certainly has a negative value inasmuch as if the body had been found in the tomb there could not have been any faith in the Resurrection. The apparitions cannot be denied historically. There were hundreds of Christians who testified that they had seen **659c** the Risen Christ and suffered persecution for their conviction. Does this *prove* the Resurrection however? Our developing knowledge of psychic phenomena today can provide us with various other explanations. But this narrows the range of possibilities provided by the empty tomb and does not prove that Christ did not rise again. An outright denial can only be based on philosophical prejudice. As Rengstorf rightly remarks (*Die Auferstehung Jesu* 1960[4], p. 114), ultimately, faith in the Resurrection is faith in God the Creator. If the possibility of the former is denied it cannot be understood why the latter should be maintained at all. **The witness d of the apparitions**, therefore, though credible and able to dispose the mind to believe, **is not the ultimate criterion of our faith in the Resurrection.** It is only the material substratum of our faith. The formal reason why we believe is **the witness of the Spirit** who 'witnesses simultaneously' (Heb. 2) by means of miracles, charismata and interior testimony that what the Apostles saw corresponded to the reality worked by God. Paul's ultimate appeal to prove his doctrines was to the Spirit (Gal 3:2). God confirms the witness of the Apostles and excludes the possibility of misinterpretation by means of his added testimony.

As we said above, the historicity of the manifestations **e** of the Spirit in Apostolic times cannot be doubted. Today the Spirit renders testimony to Jesus through the Sacraments (1 Jn 5:7). It is He who shows us the pattern of Revelation into which the numerous pieces provided by history can be fitted. Historical research, therefore, does not prove the truth of revelation but contributes to its credibility so that faith becomes the product of God's gift together with the collaboration of man.

In the preceding enquiry we made use exclusively of **f** Synoptic material. This does not mean, however, that we agree with Bultmann when he asserts that John could very well do without the historical Jesus to build up his theology. We intend to prove exactly the contrary.

Recent research on **the Johannine question**, as exemplified by R. Brown's excellent commentary on the Fourth Gospel (AB 1966), has more or less come to the conclusion that John did not write his Gospel to supplement the Synoptics, as was formerly thought. Nor did he make extensive use of the first three Gospels. It seems that he drew on his own tradition which was contemporary with and parallel to the pre-Markan tradition. The final redaction of his Gospel bears some marks of cross-influence from the emerging Lukan tradition and perhaps a slight dependence on Mark himself. His own tradition is independent, and should be judged with the same criteria as the pre-Markan tradition with regard to historicity. It can be said in general that at times the Synoptic tradition is historically more reliable, while at others the Gospel of John preserves narratives and sayings which are more exact. Each case must be examined on its own merits.

To say that John drew on a reliable tradition is not **g** the same as saying that the Fourth Gospel can be used without further ado for an exact reconstruction of the life of Jesus. Even less than the Synoptists did John mean to write a biography of Jesus. He wanted to compose **a witness to the Sonship of Christ for the Church of his own time** (A.D. 90—100) with a view to combating Jewish and Gnostic-docetic tendencies and confirming the sub-Apostolic community in the teaching of the Apostles. Hence his historical material underwent extensive theological elaboration before it reached its final stage:

859g 'And so, although we think that the Fourth Gospel reflects historical memories of Jesus, the greater extent of the theological reshaping of those memories makes Johannine material much harder to use in the quest of the historical Jesus than most Synoptic material' (R. Brown, p. 49).

h A most valuable contribution to this problem has recently been made by the Catholic Franz Mussner in his booklet *The Historical Jesus in the Gospel of St John* (1966). Beginning with the observation that the Johannine Jesus speaks John's language he argues that the Gospel answers questions raised at the time of its composition, particularly with regard to Christology. The time-interval between the facts described and the time of writing gives us a perspective which is of hermeneutical importance for the Johannine interpretation of the history of Jesus. This Johannine act of vision can be analysed by means of the gnoseological terminology he employs, e.g. 'to see', 'hear', 'come to know', 'know', 'to testify' and, especially, 'to remember'. This remembrance or *anamnesis*, in the biblical sense of representing, is bringing the past to life once more **659h** in the union of generations separated by time but united by the Apostolic 'We' gathered around the Christ. The historical knowledge attained by this act of vision is transported into the service of the Kerygma, not by means of a personal subjective meditation of the Gnostic type, but through the authentic interpretation of the Spirit of the Risen Christ, supported by the tradition of the Early Church.

The conclusion is evident. John not only cannot dispense with the historical Jesus but proclaims his kerygma as a paraphrase of the words and deeds of the Jesus of history, making them relive in his own community and putting them at the disposal of the Risen Christ, who is one with the historical Jesus. Therefore, although, as historians, we must be careful how we use the Fourth Gospel for the reconstruction of the life of Jesus, as theologians we can assert that the Jesus of history is as indispensable to the Christ of faith as the historical tradition about Jesus is indispensable to John the Theologian.

THE MOTHER OF JESUS
IN THE SCRIPTURES

BY G. GRAYSTONE S.M.

660a Bibliography—H. C. Graef, *Mary: a history of doctrine and devotion*, 2 vols, London, 1963—5; P. Gaechter, *Maria im Erdenleben*, Innsbruck 1953; F. M. Braun, *La Mère des Fidèles*, 1952; 1954[2]; R. Laurentin, *Queen of Heaven*, E.tr., Dublin 1956; id *Structure et Théologie de Luc 1–2*, 1957; J. Patsch, *Our Lady in the Gospels*, E.tr. 1958; P. G. Duncker, 'Our Lady in the OT', in *Mother of the Redeemer* (ed. K. McNamara), Dublin 1959, 1—29; C. Kearns, 'Our Lady in the NT', ibid, 30—41; R. Feuillet, 'La Vierge Marie dans le NT', in *Maria, Études sur la Sainte Vierge* (ed. H. Du Manoir) VI, 1961, 15—69 (with ample bibliography); S. Garofalo, *Mary in the Bible* E.tr. Milwaukee 1961; A. George, 'Marie', in VTB, 1962; M. Thurian, *Mary, Mother of the Lord, Figure of the Church*, E.tr., London 1963; E. C. Messenger 'Our Lady in the Scriptures', CCHS (1), with bibliography to 1950; H. Daniel-Rops, *The Book of Mary*, E.tr. 1960; G. Graystone, *Virgin of all Virgins*, Rome 1968.

b Introduction—Study of Mary in the Scriptures has made considerable progress in the last few decades— 'Protestants have been rediscovering Mary *through* Scripture; Catholics are rediscovering her *in* Scripture' (Laurentin, *Queen of Heaven*, 37). The method used may be theological; examining NT texts within the framework of a dogmatic treatise, or grouping biblical data under the appropriate heads of biblical theology. It may also be chronological, following either the sequence of Mary's earthly life, or else the order of the NT texts and traditions. It is this last method we shall follow, for it respects the special character of each stage of tradition and also illustrates the organic development of Marian doctrine. We shall insist on the literal sense and interconnexion of texts, together with their relation to the oracles and great religious themes of the OT.

c I. Earliest Allusions—The primitive Christian kerygma (§ 665*b*) centred exclusively on the good news of Jesus Christ. Subsequently a few indirect allusions to his Mother are found in Paul and Mark. The earliest is Gal 4:4—5: 'But when the time had fully come, God sent forth his Son, born (literally, 'made, come to be', Gr. *genomenon*) of woman, born (*genomenon*) under the Law, to redeem those who were under the Law, so that we might receive adoption as sons'. The centre of interest here is God's Son, pre-existing, made man for our salvation. The allusion to his Mother is incidental; she is not named, there is no mention of her privileges. If the expression 'woman' does not preclude virginal birth, neither does the term *genomenon* necessarily imply it—it is chosen to mark the passage of the pre-existing Son to a new mode of existence, viz human and under the Law. Nonetheless, Mary's rôle at the dawn of salvation is insinuated. She is, as it were, the point of insertion of the Saviour into the human race at the determined time; thereby he is enabled to share our condition so as to redeem us. He

was born of a woman so that we might become sons of **66** God.

The first explicit mention of Mary in the gospel **d** tradition is found in Mk 3:31—35. When Jesus was told that his mother and brethren were outside seeking him, 'he replied, "Who are my mother and my brethren?", and looking around on those who sat about him, he said, "Here are my mother and my brethren. Whoever does the will of God is my brother and sister and mother"'. This is a first instance of what Braun (62) calls the 'law **e** of separation'—during his public ministry Jesus proclaimed his independence of all human ties, even those of son and mother; he took his stand at the side of God, knew no law but his Father's will. Moreover, he sought continually to raise men's minds from the material to the spiritual; the closest relationship to him meant nothing if spiritual kinship were wanting (cf Lk 11:27—28: 'Blessed is the womb that bore you . . . blessed rather are those who hear the word of God and keep it'). This is not to deny Mary's prerogatives, but to forewarn us that, when later her motherhood is exalted, it is not merely physical maternity that is meant, but also the faith and loving cooperation that went with it.

On Mk 6:3 and the brethren of Christ, see § 663. **f**
II. The Testimony of Matthew—Mt's Infancy Gospel (chh 1—2) is independent of Lk's, from which it differs in literary form, explicit emphasis on OT fulfilment, and more sombre tone. Prominence is given to Joseph, Jesus' legal father, through whom he enters the royal and messianic line of David (1:21). Hence the allusions to Mary are all the more significant. Mt emphasizes the virginal conception of Jesus by the power of the Holy Spirit. His genealogy, following the male line of descent, concludes significantly, 'Jacob was the father of Joseph, the husband of Mary, *of whom Jesus was born*'. (1:16); each time Jesus is named, he is linked with Mary his mother (1:18; 2:11, 13, 14, 20, 21). Mt's teaching is stated formally in 1:18—23; in spite of disagreement on details of interpretation, the emphasis on Mary's virginal and supernatural conception is beyond dispute. She was found to be with child 'of the Holy Spirit'; the angel tells Joseph, 'that which is conceived in her is of the Holy Spirit'. Mt adds that all this happened to fulfil Isaiah's prophecy, **g** 'Behold a virgin shall conceive and bear a son, and his name shall be called Emmanuel (which means, God with us)', and concludes, '(Joseph) knew her not until she had borne a son,' (thereby excluding marriage relations during the period with which he is specially concerned, without implying that they took place subsequently).

That Isaiah 7:14 (cf Mi 5:3) refers to the extraordinary conception and birth of the Messiah by God's special intervention is not universally accepted, though it can be strongly argued (Duncker, 13—29). What is certain is that Mt, following LXX, so understands and applies it, and by his studied interpretation of the symbolic name 'Immanuel' suggests—what the rest of his gospel makes

60g clear—that the Messiah born of Mary was more than human.

h **III. The Testimony of Luke**—Lk also emphasizes Jesus' Davidic descent and virginal conception by the power of the Spirit. Yet his Infancy Gospel (chh 1—2) is quite independent. It is universalist in tone, suffused with Messianic joy, and artfully arranged in the form of a diptych, featuring on the one side the Baptist, Zechariah and Elizabeth (summing up what was best in OT tradition), and on the other, Jesus and Mary. If the figure of the Saviour is central, Mary is close to that centre. The reader, in his turn, is brought closer to the Mother of Jesus. He learns of her inmost feelings (1:29; 2:33, 48), of her failure to understand (2:50), and how she kept in mind the events of Jesus' infancy, continually pondering them in her heart (2:19, 51). From her the nucleus of Lk's narratives derives in large part— and the evangelist continued her work of meditation, presenting his narratives in quasi-anthological form, borrowing (without express citation) style, sentences and expressions from appropriate OT passages, which now find their 'fulfilment' with the dawn of the Messianic era.

i **(a) The Annunciation**—The Annunciation to Mary (1:26—28) closely parallels that to Zechariah, with some remarkable contrasts. In the striking introduction (26) Mary is presented as a 'virgin'—a word applied to no other NT woman as a title—and as a 'virgin betrothed'. This note of paradox is accentuated by Mary's subsequent question, '*How shall this be, because I know not man?*' (34), a v much discussed of recent years. To the present writer, the traditional explanation—that Mary had already resolved (possibly vowed) perpetual virginity— still seems the most natural, both in the immediate context and in the wider literary and theological setting of Lk 1—2. Just as Abraham was called to sacrifice his only son, bearer of the promises, so was Mary called to sacrifice her hope of motherhood; yet, as Abraham received back his son as if from the dead (cf Heb 11:19), so by God's power,

j Mary became Mother of the Saviour. Thus she stands as the climax of that series of OT women, naturally childless, made fruitful by the power of God bringing life out of death, so that they became mothers of predestined children (cf Sarah, Rebekah, Samson's mother, Hannah). In Mary was fulfilled both the desire of motherhood, and the desire to belong wholly to God as his handmaid by the consecration of virginity, in response to that call for exclusive love of God found in Dt 6:5, Hosea, the Prophets and Psalms.

661a The Angel greets Mary with a salutation never before heard in Scripture. 'Hail' (Gr. *chaire*) is better rendered '*rejoice*', the etymological meaning. In the light of what follows, it alludes to the prophetic oracles addressed to the Daughter of Zion (Israel personified), bidding her rejoice and fear not, because the Lord, her king, is in the midst of her as Saviour (Zeph 3:14—16; Zech 2:10— 12; 9:9; Jl 2:21—27 etc). 'Daughter of Zion' is now no longer a symbol, but a living reality, Mary sums up in herself the expectations of her people, receives in their name the announcement of salvation, makes its realization

b possible. The child to be born of her is Lord, King and Saviour. 'Full of grace', Latin: *gratia plena* Gr. *kecharitōmenē*, according to the several senses of *charis* from which it derives, may be rendered 'highly favoured' or 'favoured one'; 'full (filled) with grace' or 'gracious,

c pleasing'. It should be noted that *kecharitōmenē* (perfect participle passive of *charitoō*) denotes a lasting and permanent effect, and that it takes the place of a proper name; cf the significance of the name, as denoting nature

or function, in the Bible, and the importance of divine **661c** imposition or change of name in such cases as Abraham, Sarah, Jacob and Peter. Already, like the Bride of Canticles (Song 4:7; 6:4) Mary is *par excellence* God's Favourite, permanent object of his predilection, full of grace, cf Comm. on Lk, in loc.

The Child to be born is announced in terms of the **d** messianic oracles as Saviour, King and Son of David (31—33). Mary's question (34) neither implies doubt nor imposes any condition—she simply asks, in view of her dedicated virginity, how the angel's words will be realized. Gabriel replies that the child will have no father but God, and so will be holy and 'Son of God' (35)—though the expression does not certainly indicate the divinity of the child, yet the OT allusions carry the thought further. 'The Holy Spirit will come upon you, and the power of the Most High will overshadow you': the 'power of the Most High' alludes to the cloud of divine glory and presence, which overshadowed the Tabernacle and **e** filled the Dwelling (Ex 40:34—38), just as later it filled the Temple (1 Kgs 8:10—11). Mary, then, is the new tabernacle or dwelling-place of God, a sanctuary enshrining the divine presence, whence is born one who is eminently holy, the Son of God himself. In this way— according to many—Mary's divine motherhood is insinuated in the obscure language of OT type and foreshadowing.

Mary, unlike Zechariah, was required to give consent, **f** and freely did so. 'Behold I am the handmaid (Gr. *doulē*, female slave) of the Lord'—Mary's chosen self-designation (cf 1:48), which expresses not merely humility (cf 1 Sm 25:24), but also the fact that she enters willingly into the divine plan of salvation; cf Hannah (1 Sm 1:11, 18), and the title 'Servant of Yahweh' applied to the instruments of salvation in the OT, and to Jesus in the NT, fulfilling Is 53. 'Let it be to me according to your word' (*Fiat mihi . . .*) Mary's 'Yes' to the Angel's message, prototype of the Christian's *fiat* in the Lord's Prayer (Mt 6:10), prelude of her Son's *fiat* in Gethsemane (Lk 22.42). They are words of humble obedience (antithesis of Eve's disobedience), of loving acceptance of **g** her rôle as virgin-mother of the Saviour, above all, words of faith, counterpart of the faith of Abraham her father. OT history begins with Abraham's act of faith in the promises, NT history begins with Mary's act of faith in their fulfilment. Yet Mary did not appreciate everything clearly from the first; though worthy of all praise, her faith, like that of every Christian, was characterized by obscurity and limitations. Did she realize at the Annunciation that she was to be Mother of God? If she did—as tradition from the 2nd cent. has asserted—it was not through any blinding flash of light, but in a vague and obscure manner, expressed in terms of those OT oracles and types alluded **h** to above. We may say of her as of Abraham, that she went forth in faith, not knowing whither God was leading her (Heb 11:8). Fuller realization would come only gradually, in the light of further revelation unfolded in subsequent events, coupled with her own reflective and prayerful response to God's advances (2:19, 51).

(b) The Visitation—The narrative of the Visitation (Lk **i** 1:39—56) is suffused with the Lucan theme of Messianic joy—at the sound of Mary's greeting, the infant in Elizabeth's womb 'leaps for joy' (44), joy at the presence of the Messiah (cf the same expression in the OT oracles, e.g. Ezek 36:26—27; Jl 3:1; Mal 3:20). Jesus acts through his mother, the doctrine of her mediation (developed by John) is already suggested. Filled with the Spirit, Elizabeth declares Mary blessed beyond all women, and salutes her with the first 'beatitude' of

661i the gospels—'Blessed is she who believed' (1:45; contrast Zech, 1:20). She effaces herself before Mary, as **j** John her son will later do before Jesus, 'Why is this granted me, that the mother of my Lord should come to me?' (43). The allusion is certainly to the mother of the Messiah (cf Ps 110 (109):1) in terms that recall the 'queen-mother' of OT times (cf 1 (3) Kgs 2:19; Dn 5:10—12). Because of the numerous and striking similarities between the Visitation narrative and that of the transfer by David of the Ark to Jerusalem (2 Sm 6:1ff), many see here a further allusion to Mary as the Abode or Throne of God, and interpret 'mother of my Lord' to mean Mother of God.

k Stimulated by the realization that Elizabeth, through divine light, knows what has taken place, Mary breaks her silence, and emotions long pent-up find expression in a spontaneous outburst of praise and gratitude to him who has done great things for her (the *Magnificat*). Her thoughts find natural expression in the words of the OT Scriptures. It is not of course necessary to suppose that Mary uttered the canticle in precisely the same form in which it has come down to us or that it perfectly fits its present context, but it well reflects Mary's humility, self-**l** effacement and habit of tranquil reflection. Moreover, as 'Daughter of Zion' she voices the sentiments of the people of God. The supernatural conception of Jesus is the apogee of the joyful and miraculous births of the OT; hence the *Magnificat* borrows from the Canticle of Hannah (1 Sm 2: **m** 1—10). Still more, as the humble virgin, does she personify the 'Poor of Yahweh', whose 'lowliness the Lord has regarded' (48; cf Ps 31 (30):7), echoing the phrases of Psalms, Prophets, Wisdom Books and Pentateuch. In the name of Abraham's race, she gives thanks that the promises are fulfilled, that the Messiah is here (50—53). Thus the *Magnificat* is the model of the prayer of the people of God, the Church; and, as the personification of God's messianic people (cf Mal 3:12), like the Spouse of Canticles (6:9), Mary exclaims, 'Behold from henceforth all generations shall call me blessed'—because she is Mother of the Saviour. Here the cultus of Mary, archetype of the Church, is foreshadowed.

n (c) **Nativity, Presentation, Finding in the Temple**— In the rest of Lk's Infancy Narrative, the figure of Christ is more to the fore. In the story of the Nativity (2:1—20), Mary's action of swaddling the child and laying him in the manger (2:7) is the 'sign' whereby the shepherds find and recognize the Messiah, inseparably linked with his mother **o** (2:12, 16). Again, Mary's mediation is hinted at. Similarly, at the Presentation, Jesus, as the new Samuel (cf 1 Sm 1:24—28) and the Lord who comes to his Temple (Mal 3:1), presents himself to his Father through his faithful mother. Their destinies are linked. She submits to purification after child-birth, as he submits to the ceremony of redemption of the first-born. Simeon, addressing Mary alone, associates her in his prophetic oracle with the contradictions Jesus will meet in the course of his redemptive mission: 'a sword will pierce your soul'. **p** Though the precise background of these last words is disputed, their general sense is clear. They are certainly a foreshadowing of Calvary (cf Jn 19:37). Jesus is the Suffering Servant of Is 53, Mary is his Mother.

With the incident of the Finding in the Temple (2:41—52), Simeon's prophecy begins to be realized, prefiguring Calvary. The narrative, which has many links with the Johannine tradition, reaches its climax in Jesus' words, **q** 'How is it that you sought me? Did you not know that I must be in my Father's house (*or* about my Father's business)?' And Lk adds: 'They did not understand the saying which he spoke to them'. Mary had been living with

Jesus at Nazareth in circumstances undistinguished by **661e** anything extraordinary. Suddenly, without transition, she is called to ascend to the hidden and mysterious plane of the divine. She had spoken to Jesus of the sorrow of 'thy father', i.e. Joseph, Jesus replied to her of the affairs of 'my Father', i.e. God (cf a similar procedure in Christ's discourses in the Fourth Gospel, e.g. Jn 2:19—21; 4:10—15, 31—34; 6 passim). His words were not a rebuke but **r** an invitation to reflect, to ascend higher, an appeal to her faith; and so the story closes significantly with a last glimpse into Mary's soul—she was carefully keeping all these things in her heart, entering daily more and more into the mystery of her Son.

(d) **Mary at Pentecost**—There are remarkable parallels between the story of the Infancy of Christ and that of the infancy of the Church (Ac 1—5). In particular, the descent of the Holy Spirit on Mary at the Annunciation, whereby she was made the type and instrument of definitive salvation, preludes his descent at Pentecost (cf Lk 1:35 and Ac 1:8). By her *fiat* Mary prepared for the birth of the Church, the opening of the era of grace. It is fitting, then, that she should be found in the upper **s** room, mentioned apart from the other holy women (Ac 1:14), by her prayers preparing for the descent of the Spirit, the birth of the Church. Here Lk suggests what Jn later made explicit, Mary's maternal rôle as the new Zion, engendering the messianic people of God.

IV. The Johannine Tradition—The Fourth Gospel, **t** though historical, is intensely personal in style and language, deeply theological and replete with symbolism— long reflection by the light of the promised Spirit has revealed deep meanings underlying apparently simple words and events. All Jn's narratives are related to the gospel as a whole, must not be taken in isolation; around the central doctrine of the manifesting of the glory of the Word Incarnate, all else, mariology included, finds place. There are two Marian scenes, which frame the public ministry of Jesus: Cana (2:1—12) at the beginning, Calvary (19:25—27), at the consummation. In vocabulary, structure and teaching, the two texts offer many parallels; comparison with each other and with the third Johannine text on Mary (Apoc 12) will help to clarify their meaning.

(a) **Cana**—The Cana narrative develops on two planes. **662a** The first is the **historical** plane, in the immediate context. To this belongs Mary's thoughtful and discreet request to Jesus for material wine, followed by his much-discussed answer (4)—to all appearances a refusal, underlining the 'law of separation' between himself and his mother by the use of the terms 'woman' (unusual for a son to his mother) and '*what to me and to thee*' ('what have we in common', 'let me be'). Yet Mary does not take his **b** words as an absolute refusal, in fact she immediately instructs the servants in a manner that suggests that she expects something extraordinary ('*Whatsoever* he shall say to you, do you'). Her confidence was not misplaced. Jesus, even though his time had not yet come, turns the water into wine, works a miracle. Thus the first miracle of Jesus' public ministry, with, as its fruit, the faith of the apostles, was worked at Mary's intervention.

Secondly, there is the **theological** plane, in the **c** context of the whole gospel. The narrative is essentially Christ-centred, it concerns the first of seven 'signs' wrought by Jesus, i.e. miraculous events with a deeper, spiritual meaning. The Cana 'sign' is the climax of the opening week of the public ministry, centrepiece of Jn 1—4, where Jesus progressively reveals himself as the Messiah, introducing a new economy of salvation, fulfilling and surpassing the types and expectations of the old. Thus the Cana scene, where Jesus changes the water

2c of the old Jewish purifications (6) into the best wine (10), is a symbol of the supplanting of the old rites by the new ones of the Messianic age. At his 'hour' (*infra*), Jesus will grant a new wine, which will be revealed then as the Eucharist.

d With all this Jesus' mother is closely concerned, as the pointed introduction shows: 'the mother of Jesus was there'. She is the 'Woman', allusion (cf Jn 19:26; Apoc 12:1) to Gn 3:15 and second Isaiah, designating Mary as the new Eve, new Zion, mother of the messianic people (*infra*). Yet her role as the 'Woman' is not yet **e** fully realized, for Jesus' 'hour has not yet come'. In Johannine usage, Jesus' 'hour' is the time when he fulfils his personal destiny and his glory is fully revealed, viz his Passion and Exaltation (cf 7:30; 8:20; 12:23, 27; 13:1; 17:1). Then messianic gifts—the Spirit, the sacraments, especially the Eucharist—will be fully revealed and imparted, and the sense of Jesus' words made clear. It will also be the hour of the Church (21:15—17), **f** the hour of Mary, the 'Woman' (19:25—27). At Cana, that hour is not yet, Mary is still under the 'law of separation', but that separation is already fruitful; the 'sign' of Cana, wrought through Mary's intercession, foreshadows full union with her Son in the inauguration of the new alliance, the outpouring of the messianic wine in the Church.

(b) Calvary—The second Marian scene, at Jesus' 'hour' (19:25—27), introduces Mary in similar fashion—'*there stood by the cross of Jesus his mother*',—and again Jesus addresses her as 'Woman'. What Jesus did was certainly a last act of filial piety, entrusting his bereaved mother to John, who took her to his home. Yet it is evident that the evangelist intends something further, not simply a private gesture, but an act of public and messianic significance. **g** Note the solemnity of the context—beginning with the affirmation of Jesus' kingship, continuing with words and incidents fulfilling the messianic oracles; cf especially v 28, 'Jesus knowing that all was now finished . . .'. Moreover, it is not John that is addressed first (as one might expect were it merely a gesture of filial piety), but Mary, as if to impose on her the duty of motherhood ('Woman, behold your son'). John is referred to, not by name, but as 'the disciple whom Jesus loved'—as in other instances in Jn (cf Nicodemus, the man born blind, the Samaritan **h** woman), his representative character is insinuated. The other disciples having fled, he remains the type, the optimum representative of those who, by keeping Jesus' commandments, are loved by him and by his Father (14:15, 21, 23; 15:13—15), true disciples who keep his word and become his spiritual kinsmen (cf Mk 3:31—35; 10:29—30).

If John's position is official and representative, so is Mary's. For she is addressed as 'Woman', allusion, as in **i** Apoc 12 (*infra*) to Gn 3:15, 20. Mary is the new Eve, mother of all the living, type of the Church. Others see in the 'Woman', as with Apoc 12, the personification of the Messianic Zion of Isaiah, once barren, then in labour, and finally bearing children, the new people of God (Is 26:17—20; 49:21; 54:1; 66:7—9: cf Jn 16:19—23). In fine, at his 'hour', Jesus as King (19:14—15, 19—22)— just as he gives the gifts of the Spirit, the Church and the sacraments—gives us his Father as our Father (cf 20:17), his mother as our mother. 'From that hour the disciple took her to his own home'—to receive Jesus is to receive his mother (cf 1:11—12).

j **(c) The Woman Clothed with the Sun (Apoc 12)**— Like all the figures of Apoc, the 'woman clothed with the sun' is a symbol, symbol first of all of the Church of the Old Law and the New, with her twelve tribes and twelve apostles, the Zion of second Isaiah, resplendent as God's **662j** Bride (Is 60:1ff). In the pangs of childbirth (Is 26:17ff) she gives birth to a male child, the Messiah, who is assumed into heaven. The Dragon attacks the Woman, she flees to the desert where God prepares for her a place of refuge, and the Dragon attacks the rest of her '*seed*'— allusions to the earthly pilgrimage of Israel old and new, and the persecution of her faithful, cf §§ 968*b*—9*b*.

There are obvious difficulties in the way of applying the **k** passage to Mary, e.g. the birthpangs seem to exclude the joyous and virginal birth of Bethlehem, and the Woman has other children. Yet the birthpangs are metaphorical, alluding to the sorrows of messianic times (especially Calvary, cf Jn 16:19ff), and Mary is spiritual mother of Christ's brethren (Jn 19:25—27). On the positive side some allusion to Mary seems incontestable. There are, **l** first, the clear allusions to Gn 3:15 (the **Protoevangelium**)—the woman, attacked by the serpent, with the rest of her 'seed'. Though the interpretation of Gn 3:15 is still a matter of dispute (Duncker, 1—12), recent study of the oracle in the light of the Yahwist tradition to which it belongs has indicated, first, that the 'seed' of the woman is eschatological and individual (i.e. the Messiah), secondly, that the 'woman' is not merely individual but also representative. Eve, in fact, is but a point of departure, she appears only in view of posterity, of the Messiah's mother who will share his victory. So now, Mary, the new Eve, united with her Son, shares his victory over Satan and death (cf B. Rigaux, RB 61 (1954), 330—48).

There are also the allusions to Sion's childbearing. **m** It is hard to imagine that the seer did not have in mind Mary suffering on Calvary, sorrowful mother both of the Messiah and of the new people of God, who, in a mysterious way, retains even in glory the pangs of Calvary, as her Son keeps the marks of his sacrifice (5:6). Through Mary's compassion at the foot of the cross, the people of God realized their vocation, begot and gave to the world both the Saviour and the messianic people. Thus the 'Woman' of Apoc 12, the new Eve both individual and representative, refers in one total literal sense both to Mary (as type) and to the Church (as antitype). The **n** mystery of the Church, Mother Sion, Virgin Spouse (cf Eph 5.25—27, Apoc 21.12ff), is viewed in Mary as in a type; she is the perfect image, personification of the Church, glorious in heaven, yet mysteriously retaining the sorrows of Calvary, which persist in the Church on earth till the consummation (Apoc 21.2ff).

Conclusion—The NT texts assign to Mary an unobtrusive place, not for her own sake, but wholly in relation to her Son and his redemptive work. Therein lies her **o** importance. She thus appears at the basic moments of NT history: at the beginning of Christ's life (Mt, Lk), at the opening and close of his ministry (Jn), at the birth of the Church (Ac) and at the consummation (Apoc).

Like so many links in a chain, these texts show a remarkable development of teaching. Paul says little of Jesus' earthly life and so is not specially concerned with his mother; he yet insinuates in passing (what his disciple Luke will develop) that she is the link between the two testaments. The earliest gospel tradition—while emphasizing the unique position of Jesus as Saviour—calls Mary the 'Mother of Jesus', a name which is found to define her whole function in the work of salvation. In the **p** later Infancy Gospels, Mt, whose interest centres more on Joseph, yet constantly sets Jesus, Messiah and Emmanuel, in relation with his mother, emphasizing her virginal conception. Lk brings us much closer to Jesus' Mother. He sets forth the voluntary character both of her virginity and of her response to her vocation as Mother of

662q the Saviour. He presents her as the Virgin *par excellence*, Daughter of Zion, crowning achievement and personification of the true Israel, as God's Privileged One, Full of Grace, the new Tabernacle and Throne of his Presence. Her true moral greatness is based on her faith, nourished by ever-deeper pondering on the mystery of Jesus. She is the First Believer, Handmaid of the Lord in humble self-effacement and loving response. Her cultus is foreshadowed, her position as Mother of the Suffering Servant sketched, her rôle of mediator is suggested and her

r relation to Christ's 'brothers'. Finally, Jn defines more accurately Mary's rôle with regard to men; she is the Woman, the new Eve side by side with the new Adam, the new Zion, spiritual mother of the redeemed. This rôle, already prepared during Jesus' public ministry, becomes effective at his 'hour'. Lastly, she appears as archetype, personification, eschatological image of the Church in glory.

THE 'BROTHERS OF THE LORD'
BY DOM R. RUSSELL

663a These form a group (Mt 12:46ff; Mk 3:31ff; Lk 8:19ff; Jn 7:3ff; Ac 1:14; 1 Cor 9:5) of whom James, Joses (Joseph), Simon and Jude are expressly named, Mt 13:55; Mk 6:3. 'Brothers' and 'sisters', which are the words used, can mean strictly sons and daughters of the same parent, or (as Heb. and Aram. had no word for 'cousin'), stand for varying degrees of blood relationship, e.g. Gn 13:8; 29:12; Lv 10:4; 1 Chr 23:22f (followed by LXX). The term, once coined, would pass into NT Gr. It is not therefore necessary to hold that they were sons and daughters of Mary the mother of Jesus, and they are

b never said to be so. 'First-born', used of Jesus, Lk 2:7, is a technical term for the male who opened the womb and was specially consecrated to God, Ex 13:2; Lk 2:23. (An inscription from probably just before Christ records the death of a woman bearing her 'first-born'. Bib 11 (1930), 373—90). Mt 1:25 is only interested to establish Mary's virginity at the time of Jesus's birth and 'until' is not concerned with what follows, cf Dt 34:6; 2 Sm (2 Kgs) 6:23; 1 Mc 5:54 'not one of them *was slain till they had returned in peace*'.

c The Gospel indications (cf Lagrange, *Marc*, 79—95) are that Jesus was Mary's only son: The account of the finding in the Temple reads naturally of an only child, Lk 2:41—52. In Mk 6:3 Jesus is called 'the son of Mary', a description fitting the only son of a widow. The attitude of the 'brothers of the Lord' who show disapproval or give advice on Jesus's mission, is, given Jewish respect for the first-born, that of elder kinsmen, cf Mk 3:21; Jn 7:3ff. On the cross, Jesus entrusts his mother to John, which would have been unnatural if she had other sons, Jn 19:25ff.

d Thus on deeper study Mary's **perpetual virginity is suggested, though not demonstrated by Scripture.** But what is basic to the belief is the **Church tradition of the first four centuries.** From the beginning, she was always given the name 'Virgin', (Epiphanius, *Adv. Haer.*, 78, 6, (PG 42, 705)). Jer., in his *De Perpetua Virginitate B. Mariae* (PL 23, 193—216), written c. A.D. 383 against Helvidius, is able to show that the latter is innovating, and he appeals to the testimony of 'the whole series of Ancient Writers, Ignatius, Polycarp, Irenaeus, Justin Martyr and many other learned men going back to

e apostolic times'—Tertullian being the only exception. Cf also, as illustrating the universality of the tradition, Ephraem, PG 3, 545; Did. Alex., PG 39, 832; Aug., PL 38, 999. 'It is difficult to understand how the doctrine

of the Virginity of Mary could have grown up early in the **66** second century if her four acknowledged sons were prominent Christians, and one of them bishop of Jerusalem' (Bernard, *Jn*, i, 85). Mary's perpetual virginity, best **f** understood as consecration to her Son and his redemptive work, is for Catholics a doctrine of faith, defined by the Council of the Lateran, A.D. 649, Dz 256; cf 91.

But the subsidiary question of the **exact relationship of the 'brothers' to Jesus** is not easy, cf J. B. Lightfoot, *Gal*, 252—91; H. J. Chapman, JTS 7 (1906), 412—33; A. G. Murray, CR 23 (1943) 351—6; E. F. Sutcliffe, ibid, 494—8; V. Taylor, *Mk*, 247—9, followed by PC (2) on Mk 6:3. The view of Epiphanius, that they were **g** the sons of Joseph by a former marriage was frequent in antiquity and provided a convenient answer to objections against the perpetual virginity of Mary. But the apocryphal accounts from which it derives do not bear the marks of a true tradition, nor accord with the Gospel narrative of the Infancy; they also run counter to the Church's sense of the virginity of St Joseph.

Let us examine the crucifixion accounts. Mt 27:55; **66** Mk 15:40 say that 'many' women looked on from afar and mention Mary Magdalen, Salome (Mk, apparently the same as 'the mother of the sons of Zebedee', Mt) and 'Mary the mother of James (the Younger or the Little, Mk) and Joses'. Mk goes on to mention 'Mary (the mother) of Joses (v 47) and 'Mary (the mother) of James' (16:1), probably referring to the same Mary, though in v 40 some MSS read 'Mary the mother of James and the mother of Joses'. This is the Mary whom **b** Helvidius identified with the mother of Jesus, but it is inconceivable that the Lord's mother should have been so described, and the natural supposition is that this Mary is the mother of the 'brothers of the Lord' already mentioned by Mt, Mk. Jn (19:25) says that Jesus's mother stood by the cross 'and his mother's sister, Mary (the wife) of Clopas and Mary Magdalene ...'. If he means four women, 'his mother's sister' could be Salome; and her sons, James and John, would then be Jesus's cousins. This might go with their mother's request (Mt 20:20—28; Mk 10:35—45) but seems counter to the general feel of the Gospels, e.g. Jn 1:35ff; and if it is **c** like Jn's reticence to omit his mother's name, it is still more so to omit all mention of her. Again, the fourth woman could be Mary the mother of James and Joses, but different from the wife of Clopas. On the other hand, if, as Jerome thinks, Jn mentions *three* women only, then 'his mother's sister' (which may stand for cousin or sister-in-law) is Mary (the wife) of Clopas, and she is the mother of James the Less and Joses. Finally the 2nd cent. writer Hegesippus says (EusHE 3, 11; 3, 32; 4, 22) that Clopas, St Joseph's brother, Jesus's paternal uncle, was father of Simon who, like James, was Jesus's cousin; he also seems to imply that Jude was Simon's brother, Lagrange, 89—90.

Jer. further holds that Clopas is the same as Alphaeus, **d** given as father of the second James in the list of the Apostles; and later writers seek to prove that Clopas and Alphaeus are renderings of the same Aram. name, that 'Judas of James' in Lk's list is the Apostle Jude, and that Simon the Lord's brother is Simon the Apostle, Mt 10:3; Mk 3:18; Lk 6:16; Jude 1:1. It is argued that there must be more than coincidence in the occurrence of these names, and suggested that Joses, not chosen as Apostle, may be the again unsuccessful candidate of Ac 1:23. Thus 'the brothers' would be distinguished not so much *from* as *among* the Apostles, cf 1 Cor 9:5. However this **e** further, attractive theory is open to serious criticisms (V. Taylor, 248): the identification of Clopas and

664e Alphaeus and of James of Alphaeus and James the Less is problematic. In the Gospels the 'brothers' seem unconverted (Mk 3:31; Jn 7:5) until after the Resurrection, when the Lord appears to James (1 Cor 15:7); they are distinguished from the Apostles in Ac 1:14; they are never associated with Mary of Clopas but with Mary the mother of Jesus and St Joseph; (did Clopas die early and Joseph and Mary give a home to the family?).

f It remains uncertain whether Jn mentions three or four women at the cross. What is certain is that Mary, the mother of James and Joses, was there and Jesus' mother's sister was there, but are they the same and the same **664f** as Mary, the wife of Clopas? One would suppose so, but then Mary the mother of James and Joses is never called mother of Simon and Jude, whose father, according to Hegesippus, was Clopas. Thus, there may be two pairs of cousins.

James, 'the brother of the Lord', a quasi-royal title with contemporary overtones, is later found at the head of the church of Jerusalem, Ac 15:12, 21:18ff; 1 Cor 15:7; Gal 1:19; 2:9, 12, cf Recueil L. Cerfaux, I (1954) 50—53, reproducing RSPT 12 (1923) 140—3.

TRADITION AND THEOLOGY
IN APOSTOLIC TIMES

BY PROSPER GRECH O.S.A.

665a Bibliography—General: J. Barr, *Old and New in Interpretation*, 1966; J. Bonsirven, *Theology of the NT*, E.tr. 1963; R. Bultmann, *Theology of the NT*, E.tr. 1959; O. Cullmann, *Heil als Geschichte. Heilsgeschichtliche Existenz in NT*, Tübingen 1965; W. D. Davies, *Invitation to the NT*, 1967; C. H. Dodd, *The Apostolic Preaching and its Developments*, 1944²; *According to the Scriptures*, 1952; A. M. Hunter, *Introducing NT Theology*, 1963; L. Lemonnier—L. Cerfaux, *Théologie du NT*, 1963; B. Lindars, *New Testament Apologetic*, 1961; J. L. McKenzie, *The Power and the Wisdom: An Interpretation of the NT*, 1965; *Myths and Realities: Studies in Biblical Theology*, 1963; M. Meinertz, *Théologie des NT*, Bonn 1950; F. Nötscher, *Zur theologischen Terminologie der Qumran Texten, Bonn 1956; Q. Quesnell, This Good News*, 1964; A. Richardson, *An Introduction to the Theology of the NT*, 1961²; R. Schnackenburg, *New Testament Theology Today*, E.tr., 1963; E. Stauffer, *New Testament Theology*, 1963; G. Wright—R. H. Fuller, *The Book of the Acts of God*, 1960; H. Conzelmann *Grundriss der Theologie des NT*, 1967.

Judaism and Hellenism: J. Bonsirven, *Palestinian Judaism in the Time of Jesus Christ*, E.tr. 1965; W. D. Davies, *Paul and Rabbinic Judaism*, 1948; G. F. Moore, *Judaism in the First Centuries of the Christian Era*, Harvard 1927; S. Monwinckel, *He that Cometh*, E.tr., 1959; K. Prümm, Art *Mystère* in DBS; *Religionsgeschichtliches Handbuch*, Rome, 1954; D. S. Russell, *The Method and Message of Jewish Apocalyptic*, 1964.

Dictionaries: J. J. von Allmen, *Vocabulary of the Bible*, E.tr., 1965; J. Bauer, *Bibeltheologisches Wörterbuch*, Graz 1967³; G. Kittel, *Theologisches Wörterbuch zum NT* Stuttgart 1933ff, now being translated into English; X. Léon-Dufour, *Vocabulaire de Théologie Biblique*, 1962; J. L. McKenzie, *Dictionary of the Bible*, 1965.

The Gospels: R. Bultmann, *History of the Synoptic Tradition*, E.tr., Oxon. 1963; J. Jeremias, *The Parables of Jesus*, E.tr., 1963; T. W. Manson, *The Teaching of Jesus*, Cambridge, 1935²; *The Sayings of Jesus*, 1949; N. Perrin, *The Kingdom of God in the Teaching of Jesus*; 1963; *Rediscovering the Teaching of Jesus*, 1967; R. Schnackenburg, *God's Rule and Kingdom*, E.tr., 1963; V. Taylor, *The Formation of the Gospel Tradition*, 1935².

St Paul: A. M. Hunter, *Paul and his Predecessors*, 1951; F. Prat, *The Theology of St Paul*, E.tr., 1942; H-J. Schoeps, *Paul: The Theology of the Apostle in the Light of Jewish Religious History*, E.tr. 1961; D. E. H. Whiteley, *The Theology of St Paul*, 1964.

St John: J. Crehan, *The Theology of St John*, 1965; E. K. Lee, *The Religious Thought of St John*, 1950; E. M. Sidebottom, *The Christ of the Fourth Gospel*, 1963.

Christology and Original Sin: L. Cerfaux, *Christ in the Theology of St Paul*, E.tr., Freiburg, 1963; O. Cullmann, *Christology of the NT*, E.tr., 1963²; A. M. Dubarle, *The Biblical Doctrine of Original Sin*, E.tr., 1964; F. X. Durrwell, *The Resurrection. A Biblical Study*, 1964; R. H. Fuller, *The Foundations of NT Christology*,

1965; S. H. Hooke, *The Resurrection of Christ as History and Experience*, 1967; M. D. Hooker, *The Son of Man in Mark*, 1967; B. van Iersel, *'Der Sohn' in den synoptischen Jesusworten*, Leiden 1964; S. Lyonnet, Art. *Péché* in DBS; L. Sabourin, *Rédemption Sacrificielle*, 1961; *Les Noms et les Titres de Jésus*, 1961; V. Taylor, *Jesus and His Sacrifice*, 1937; *The Person of Christ in NT Teaching*, 1958; *The Atonement in NT Teaching*, 1945²; A. Wainwright, *The Trinity in the NT*, 1962.

Church and Sacraments: L. Cerfaux, *The Church in the Theology of St Paul*, E.tr., N.Y., 1963; O. Cullmann, *Peter. Apostle, Disciple, Martyr*, E.tr., 1953²; J. Jeremias, *Jesus' Promise to the Nations*, E.tr., 1958; *The Eucharistic Words of Jesus*, E.tr., 1966; E. J. Kilmartin, *The Eucharist in the Primitive Church*, 1965; R. Schnackenburg, *The Church in the NT*, E.tr., 1965; *Baptism in the Thought of St Paul*, E.tr., 1964; Th. Worden, *The Sacraments in Scripture*, 1966.

Salvation: L. Cerfaux, *Le Chrétien dans la Théologie Paulinienne*, 1962; W. D. Davies—D. Daube, *The Background of the NT and its Eschatology: Studies in Honour of C. H. Dodd*, Cambridge, 1954; S. Lyonnet, *La storia della salvezza nella Lettera ai Romani*, Naples 1966; R. Schnackenburg, *The Moral Teaching of the NT*, E.tr., 1965; V. Taylor, *Forgiveness and Reconciliation*, 1941.

PLAN

1 Kerygma
2 The Holy Spirit
3 The Last Days
4 Jesus of Nazareth
5 The Christ
6 The Cross
7 The New Israel
8 Salvation
9 Conclusion

Methods of Biblical Theology—The last quarter of a **b** century has witnessed an immense step forward in the study of NT Theology. It began with the publication of the first volume of Kittel's *Theologisches Wörterbuch zum NT* in 1933. Since then much original research has been carried on which has led to a number of conclusions now commonly accepted by scholars of various denominations. But although it is now possible to write a biblical theology of the NT which will not be unsatisfactory, every new monograph that appears reveals unsuspected horizons and reminds us of how much work has still to be done.

There is still no common agreement about the method to be followed. That adapted by F. Ceuppens in his *Theologia Biblica* (1938ff), a mere exegesis of proof-texts adduced by theologians in their various treatises, is certainly useful for assessing the importance of these texts, but can hardly be called biblical theology, for

65b it only deals with a few aspects which coincide with the divisions of systematic theology but do not represent the essential facets of biblical thought.

c Hence those biblical theologians who take the NT rather than text-books of dogmatic theology as their starting point are definitely on the right track. But the question arises how to deal with a book which, though having one Divine Author, is also the product of a plurality of human authors. Should the various 'theologies' of the NT be treated separately, as Meinertz and Bultmann do, or should the NT be considered from the point of view of inspiration and treated in a homogeneous manner? Stauffer and Richardson follow this latter method. There is something to be said in favour of either of these systems, but each suffers from one great disadvantage: the NT is treated statically, as if all the ideas contained in its various parts had reached their final form where they stand. There is evolution in the thought of the NT in so far as new truths are continually being revealed, old truths understood more deeply, and fresh ideas deduced from earlier ones. This evolution must be taken account of, described when possible, and reconstructed when the links are not obvious. The 'vocabulaire' method (Kittel, Vigouroux, *Vocabulaire Biblique*, *Vocabulaire de Théologie Biblique*, *Bibellexikon*, etc) goes a long way towards solving this problem in so far as the evolution of certain key concepts in the NT is traced, and it is undeniable that these wordbooks are of inestimable value to students and scholars alike, but it hardly needs demonstrating that lack of cohesion and systematization obscures the relationship which each entry has to the whole and renders any assesment of the relative importance of each single concept most difficult.

Karl Prümm, some years ago, published an exhaustive theological commentary on 2 Cor. This work opened the eyes of many a scholar to the importance—hitherto often neglected—of what we may call the 'between-the-lines theology' of the Apostle, in the presuppositions at the back of his mind at the time of writing. A complete theology of the NT will only be possible when such research has been extended to all the writings of the NT.

d Another method which, till now, has received very scant attention, but which begins to be advocated by various scholars, is **the historical method**. The theology of the NT is treated as the outcome of **the preaching of the Apostles** which began with the bare Kerygma but later **developed into the rich theology** contained in the writings **of Paul and John** under the influence of diverse causes, incorporating the life and teaching of Jesus into the living faith of the Church. Such a theology would endeavour to describe this development, indicate its causes and various ramifications, and point out **how certain concepts of the NT evolved organically and logically to the theology of the Fathers of the Church**. In the present article an effort will be made to adopt this method as the most suitable for the purpose of the Commentary. But the reader must constantly keep its limitations in mind. First of all, the development of doctrine described is more logical than chronological, ideal rather than real. This is necessarily so for lack of sufficient documents. The writings of the NT are occasional scripts which have been given by Providence not to satisfy the curiosity of historians but to instruct the faithful; any reconstruction of their development of thought, therefore, must fill in the gaps by means of suppositions. Secondly, it must be kept in mind that during the Apostolic and sub-Apostolic period there was a real development of dogma in the strict sense of the word, i.e. new truths were continually being revealed, and therefore the deposit of truth received additions; this ceased **665d** after the last book of the NT had been composed. The later development inside the Church did not come about by means of the addition of new truths but followed from a deeper understanding of the deposit of faith.

Evolution of dogma is partly an historical process, **c** and as such has *certain causes which can be observed* and studied. Even new revelations do not occur at random. God often makes use of certain events in time as occasions on which to speak his word. Is it possible to identify these causes or occasions of the evolution of theology in NT times? The fashion at the turn of the century was to explain almost everything in terms of contact with hellenistic thought and religion. Jesus expected an early coming of the Kingdom and was little more than an apocalyptic prophet. Paul rationalized this hope in terms of hellenistic mystery religions, Christianity being born semi fortuitously from a synthesis of Petrine-Jewish preaching and Pauline Hellenism. The chief exponent of this view was Adolf Harnack.

In 1941 Martin Werner made an attempt at explaining this evolution through internal causes. In his book *Die Entstehung des christlichen Dogmas* he argued that the mainspring of the development of Christian dogma was the delay of the Parousia. This was a step forward in so far as the causes of theological progress were sought inside Christianity itself. Werner's theory cannot be maintained today, however, because it is too exclusive and founded on mistaken suppositions.

Present-day scholars are more wary. Various studies **f** published in the last twenty years have shed much light on this problem, even if not always directly. We here give a tentative enumeration of **the historical causes**, which under the revealing and inspiring action of the Holy Spirit, helped the primitive kerygma to develop into the theology of the NT: (1) A deeper understanding of the OT in the light of recent events and new interpretations; (2) Controversy with the Jews; (3) Missionary problems among Jews and Gentiles; (4) Community problems; (5) The developing liturgy; (6) Alexandrine theology and the general hellenistic mentality; (7) The adaptation to the belief that the Parousia would not come as soon as many people expected; (8) Rabbinic theological methods and principles; (9) The particular psychology and background of the individual authors of the NT.

The Doctrinal Background (a) The OT—We must **g** now pass on to study the Kerygma more closely, observe its reactions on Jews and Gentiles, and see how it developed. But before we do this it is useful to take a quick glance at the background of ideas which the average frequenter of the synagogue or agora possessed more or less explicitly.

The believing Jew accepted the teaching of Moses **h** and the Prophets that there is one God, who is the lord and sovereign of all, the only living and true God, not like the idols of the Gentiles: Yahweh. This God made the world and all the inhabitants thereof, over whom he rules with justice and kindness, but who have no right to argue with God. He chose Israel from all nations out of pure loving kindness that through it his blessing might flow to all peoples. This choice was sealed by means of a covenant according to which Israel pledged itself to acknowledge no other God but Yahweh, and to serve him alone according to the Law which he revealed to Moses. The history of Israel bears witness to God's special care of his people; punishment and forgiveness alternate accordingly as the Jews violate or turn back to the Covenant. Thus Yahweh is Lord of History, who acts with a purpose. The right attitude to adopt towards him is one

665h of unconditional obedience to his commandments and of unlimited faith in his initiatives. The main sins, in fact, are idolatry, unbelief, and social injustice. These, however, receive forgiveness if repentance sets in. The present imperfect order both in political as well as in individual spheres is due to sin, but a day will come when God will send a King who will reestablish the ideal order which prevailed before sin entered the world, will restore Israel to its original destiny, and bring judgement upon nations and individuals who have been disobedient. The sign and means of the coming of this Kingdom are a generous outpouring of the Spirit of God upon Israel.

i (b) **Rabbinism**—The Pharisees, whose widespread influence was out of all proportion to the size of their sect, retained the essence of this doctrine, but while they developed various points that distorted others through over- or under-emphasis. Monotheism was never questioned, but excessive pride in being God's chosen race endangered the absolute gratuitousness of Israel's election. Even in the case of the individual, too much insistence on the minute observance of the Law spread the feeling that there existed a mathematical relationship between our good works and God's recompense, which was conceived as strictly due to the just man. Many even held that it was sufficient to belong to the pure race of Abraham to be saved when the day of the glorification of Israel arrived; in fact, one of the missions of Elijah, who would precede the end, would be to purify the chaff from the grain so that only Israelites of pure blood remained. The end would include the absolute glorification of the Law, which is immutable and eternal, and which will then reign on all nations, because for this end—the universal observance of the Torah—God created the world. Eschatological times would be preceded by the advent of Elijah. It is not clear whether the Jews expected a Messianic reign on earth or whether they believed that the Danielic Son of Man would bring about apocalyptic events without a preliminary terrestrial reign. In any case, in 'the End' all nations would be judged, Israel gathered together, 'yetzer' (the power of sin inclining to evil) and death would lose their power, and all would adore Yahweh forever.

j (c) **Paganism**—The average Gentile in the hellenistic world was far removed from the ideas which we have just described. It is true that he observed the ritual of temple or shrine worship just to keep on the right side of the gods, but his typical attitude was one of anxiety and scepticism, as his religion offered him no stabilizing or reassuring background of thought in a world which chance and fate rendered senseless. The age-old legends of the gods which had been ridiculed by some philosophers, de-mythologized by others, were hardly taken seriously except as a justification for human frailty. Many of those who sought to penetrate more deeply into their religious feelings found some consolation in the syncretistic cults imported from the E, especially in the form of 'Mystery Religions'. These, at least, promised a personal relationship with the god together with some sort of salvation. The common man tried to combat chance through belief in magic and superstition, especially astrology. The philosophers were mainly concerned with ethics. The Stoics insisted on a world-order or general pattern to which the individual should conform to remain on the right path. This system, which claimed a numerous following, was the one which could best be reconciled with Judaism, and consequently with Christianity. There were Gnostic tendencies in the first century which paved the way for the later doctrine with its complicated rationalizing philosophy.

1. KERYGMA

The Kerygma to the Jews—From this summary des- **66** cription of the religious background of the world in which the Apostles preached the Gospel, it should be clear that the enunciation of the main Christian truths could not be presented to Jews and Gentiles in an identical manner. There are specimens of both methods in Ac. The Kerygma to the Jews can be reconstructed from the speeches of Peter in the first chh. Even if these discourses were not actually pronounced by Peter or Paul as they stand, there seems to be general agreement nowadays that they reflect **the Kerygma of the Early Church.** The specifically Christian enunciation of the New Message presupposed everything that the Jews believed in so far as it had not been distorted by rabbinic teaching, but it added some new facts anchored in history and experience which called for a re-interpretation of the Bible and a re-shaping of ideas.

The passages from which the Kerygma can be re- **b** constructed, according to Dodd's enumeration, are: Ac 2:14—39; 3:13—26; 4:10—12; 5:30—32; 10:36—43; 13:17—41; which are reflected in Gal 1:3f; 3:1ff; 4:6; 1 Thess 1:10; 1 Cor 15:1—7; Rm 1:1—4; 2:16; 8:34; 10:8f. To these must be added Heb. 6:1. **The message of salvation** itself can be summed up in the following points: (1) You are now witnessing or experiencing the workings of the Holy Spirit; (2) If the Spirit has been poured upon Israel in such abundance it is a sign that the 'latter days' foretold by the Prophets have arrived; (3) This has come about through the birth, life, and miracles of Jesus of Nazareth whom the Jews killed, but whom God raised from the dead as we ourselves bear witness; (4) This Jesus God has constituted Lord and Messiah by taking him up to heaven and placing him at his right hand; (5) All this took place according to the Scriptures. It is part of God's saving plan 'for our sins', and fits in with the faith of our fathers; (6) The risen Jesus is the New Moses who will come to lead the Eschatological Israel to final redemption as the Son of Man on the clouds of heaven; (7) If you believe the word that is being preached to you, repent and be baptized, you will be saved.

The Testimonies—Such assertions naturally sounded **c** heretical to Jewish ears. A crucified Messiah was inconceivable. Even though the *Book of Enoch* (38, 2; 46, 4; 47, 1.4; 53, 6; 62, 5f) interpreted Is 53 messianically the understanding was that the Messiah would be persecuted because he was The Just One; but few, if any, went so far as to push it further than that. The sonship of Christ, if understood literally, was blasphemous (Mk 14:63f). The rejection of Israel with the admission of the Gentiles, and especially the setting aside of Moses and the Law shook the very foundations of the faith of the Chosen People.

It was therefore necessary for the preachers of the new **d** doctrine, who maintained the redemptio-historical continuity of the events which they announced with those in Israel's history, to demonstrate that these things had already been foreseen and foretold by Moses and the Prophets, and that they constituted but a logical development of Israel's *Heilsgeschichte*. St Luke insists (Lk 24: 27, 45) that Jesus himself provided a key to the interpretation of the Torah, especially after his resurrection. It is also probable that he indicated the passages which spoke of him and which had spoken to him to guide him in his mission (18:31—34). The Apostles, therefore, possessed a collection of '**proof-texts**' at hand through which they could demonstrate the continuity of God's plan of salvation. These texts were primarily and originally **e**

6e apologetic in purpose but later on they served as a quarry from which the material for the construction of Christian theology could be drawn, each text having a history of its own. Recent studies by Rendel Harris, Dodd, and Lindars have all converged to shew that the Primitive Church possessed a collection of 'testimonies', either written or oral, which were commonly used in controversy, preaching, and teaching. Dodd gives the following list of testimonies: Gn 12:3; 22:18; Dt 18·15—19; 2 Sam 7:13—16; Ps 2; 8; 22; 31; 34; 38; 41; 42; 43; 49; 80; 88; 110; 118; 132; Is 6:3—10; 9:1—7; 28:16; 29:9—14; 40:1—11; 40—42; 49—53; 61:1—10; Jer 31:10—34; Dn 7:9—22; 9:27; 12; Hos Passim; Jl 3f; Am 9:11f; Hb 2:3f; Zech 9:14; Mal 3:1—6; Tb 7:7; Wis 2:21.

The reader will have observed that some quite long passages are included in this list. In fact, Dodd has demonstrated that the Christians did not cite these texts without any reference to their context. It was not single vv, but often whole passages that were referred to, a method not unknown in rabbinical exegesis. It must be remarked, however, that the above listed passages are not the only messianic scriptures quoted in the NT, but they seem to be the most current among Christians. They can be grouped under four headings, Messianic Scriptures, Apocalyptical and Eschatological texts, Passion texts, and the Scriptures of the New Israel. We shall have occasion to examine their influence on NT theology later.

f It is evident that **the Kerygma to the Gentiles** had to take a form different from that in which it was presented to the Jews. The Apostles had little in common with the Hellenistic religious world. And as it was impossible to present Christ to people who did not even believe in the One God, the kerygma had to begin with the apologetics of monotheism. The two discourses in Ac 14:15—18 and 17:22—31 are certainly reminiscent of the Gentile kerygma and can help us to reconstruct it.

The preacher started with the only thing that was shared in common, the sentiment of piety towards god. The Gentiles have laudable intentions in practising their religion, but err in the object and manner of their cult because they adore images of stone and metal representing all kinds of living forms instead of the Living and Unseen God. Although invisible, God is not unknowable, for he can be discovered and known through his works (Rm 1:18) and through the traces of his goodness and mercy towards us scattered around us. He it was who created heaven and earth, and guided the history of mankind through his providence, so that men may know him as their father. The Gentiles, however, misrepresented God, thinking they were doing the Deity a favour by taking part in the cult at the shrines. God is the Giver, our duty is merely to render thanks. These times of ignorance have now been overlooked by God, and in his mercy he has brought about a time for repentance, but he has also appointed a day on which to judge the world. This he will do through Jesus, whom he appointed judge and saviour by raising him from the dead.

The specifically Christian note at the end should be kept in mind as it includes all the elements of the Jewish kerygma in Gentile dress: Forgiveness, Fullness of times and *Heilsgeschichte*, the Messiahship of Jesus through his resurrection, and the Parousia.

g Once having believed, **the neophytes were instructed** in the new faith. A fundamental element in this instruction was the teaching about the deeds and sayings of Jesus which tended to strengthen the faith of the believers in his Messiahship and Sonship and to instruct them in the new spiritual interpretation of the Law which

Jesus had taught. These sermons constituted the primitive 666g nucleus which later developed into our Synoptic Gospels. Moreover, the interpretation of Scripture according to its Christian meaning, the significance of the new liturgical rites, and the import of the Resurrection of the Lord formed part of the *paradosis* or *didache* which was the catechism of the Primitive Church. The initiation into the new mysteries was graded according to the spiritual understanding of the neophytes (1 Cor 3:1), so that those who had advanced further received the 'wisdom of God in mystery' (1 Cor 2:6f).

In time, cases of conscience and practical problems h cropped up which necessitated a doctrinal as well as a practical solution and compelled the Teachers of the Church to delve deeper into the Scriptures, think out new solutions, and beg for new revelations. These problems were connected with the missionary work of the Apostles, the organization of new communities, the relationship of the new Faith with traditional Jewish practices, and problems regarding the new precepts given by Jesus. The necessity to defend the faith against the objections of Jews and Gentiles also led to deeper reflection and study, and the outcome of all was that the bare facts of the Kerygma and primitive *paradosis* developed into **a theology** which, though far from being systematic, possessed an internal logic of its own. Various points were stressed and developed according as circumstances demanded, so that the general picture of this theology is far from homogeneous.

We shall now pass on to examine this theology under the various headings of the Kerygma.

2. THE HOLY SPIRIT

The Holy Spirit in the Kerygma—The argument in 667a Peter's **Pentecost** sermon runs as follows: You have witnessed signs and wonders, these have been produced by the Holy Spirit. If the Spirit has actually been poured forth in such abundance, it is a sign that the Last Days have arrived, for the Prophets of old foretold that the days of the Messiah would be marked by an extraordinary activity of the Spirit (Ac 2:14—36).

The main premise of the argument is not of a philosophical nature; it is a hard fact of experience produced by the power of God 'that your faith might not rest in the wisdom of men but in the power of God' (1 Cor 2:5). Luke makes it clear that in the beginning, as in his own days, signs and wonders were performed by the Spirit, as they had been performed by Jesus during his lifetime, with the purpose of drawing men of good will to believe. The summary in Ac 2:43, following immediately on the Pentecost recital, covers the main episodes of Ac. Now the faith which the preachers of the Gospel wanted of their hearers was faith in the Lordship of the Risen Christ. Hence the belief that **the Spirit 'vindicates' Christ by bearing witness to his messiahship** is primitive in the Church, as the old hymn cited in 1 Tm 3:16 proves and Heb. 2:4 and 1 Pt 1:12 expressly state.

It was with this intention in mind that Luke depicted b the events of the Pentecostal outpouring so vividly and dramatically. John relates that Jesus gave the Spirit to his apostles immediately after his resurrection (Jn 20:22, cf Dnz. 434), but **Luke emphasizes the Pentecost episode** because his purpose differed from that of John. In John the reception of the Spirit is the logical outcome of the glorification of Jesus, and the whole Gospel converges on that point (Jn 16:7). The author of Ac wanted to set into relief the essential part which the Spirit played in the spreading of the Gospel together with the fact that

667b the Spirit which had only been given to the guiding personalities of the history of Israel now becomes the possession of all those who believe, as Joel had foretold would happen in the last days. The believer in Jesus, therefore, is not excluded from the communion of Israel, but rather becomes a member of the eschatological Israel that had been announced in the Law. That is why Ac had to begin with Pentecost.

c From Pentecost onwards the special intervention of the Spirit runs through the whole of Ac like a silver thread. On certain occasions the descent of the Spirit is accompanied by external manifestations, usually the gift of tongues (2:4—33; 10:44ff; 19:5f) and fire (2:2); occasionally the earth trembles (4:31; 8:17f) and various miracles are performed (6:8; 7:55; 8:5). That these charismata had an apologetic value is evident from 1 Cor 14:21—25. The gift of tongues which the Corinthian Community possessed in abundance, consisting essentially in praying or praising God in a foreign language, understandable to anyone whose native language it might be, but not always to the community or even to the one who spoke it, was substantially identical with the pentecostal miracle described in Ac 2. On that occasion it proved to be an object of scorn to some but a sign of divine intervention to others. By quoting Is 28:11f Paul hints that this charism is not necessarily a sign of faithfulness in the people who receive it. Prophecy, on the other hand, penetrates the profoundest secrets of the heart and has an immense apologetical value which could lead to a sincere conversion (v 25).

d The public witness of the Spirit to Christ is summed up beautifully in Heb. 2:4 'God also bore witness by signs and wonders and various miracles and by gifts of the Holy Spirit distributed according to his own will'. But even these charismata do not prove anything unless the utterances which they provoke are in line with the teaching of the Apostles. No one can say 'Jesus be cursed' in the Spirit (1 Cor, 12:1ff), for 'every spirit that does not confess Jesus is not of God' (1 Jn 4:1ff).

e The experience of the Spirit is the believer's firmest anchor in moments of doubt. In his controversy with the Galatian Judaizers Paul appeals to this experience to persuade his readers not to go back to circumcision and the Law: 'Let me ask you only this: did you receive the Spirit by works of the law, or by hearing with faith?' (Gal 3:2). This evidently refers to the external manifestations of the Spirit, but the Holy Ghost accompanies these visible signs with an internal witness, perceived only by the receiver.

f The classical text illustrating internal witness is Rm 8:15f (= Gal 4:6): 'When we cry "Abba! Father!" it is the Spirit himself bearing witness with our spirit that we are children of God'. This charismatic utterance is a good example of how 'I will pray with the Spirit, and I will pray with the mind also' (1 Cor 14:15). Thus the testimony of the Spirit has a persuasive influence on the individual which is best described in the words of Paul's prayer in Eph 1:16—23 that God may give the recipients of the Epistle 'a spirit of wisdom and of revelation in the knowledge of him, having the eyes of your hearts enlightened that you may know what is the hope to which he called you, what are the riches of his glorious inheritance in the saints . . .'.

g The same doctrine is repeated in the Johannine writings. Jesus promises the disciples that they will receive the Spirit, and St John comments: 'by this we know that he abides in us, by the Spirit which he has given us' (1 Jn 3:24 = 4:13). It is also the Spirit that teaches us that Jesus is the Son of God who came by water and blood, so that spirit, water, and blood (the Glorification of Christ as participated in Baptism and the Eucharist) bear witness together, 'and the Spirit is the witness, because the Spirit is the truth' (1 Jn 5:6—8). **667**

We thus have a complete doctrine running through **h** the whole of the NT according to which our faith in Christ does not rest on worldly wisdom but on the witness of the Spirit, borne by means of signs and wonders in Christ's name, and through an internal persuasion in line with the teaching of the Apostles.

The Spirit in the age to come—At this point it is **i** prudent to ask whether the NT doctrine of the witness of the Spirit rested solely on the Joel text, or whether there were also other texts which could allow of a further development of this theology of the Spirit. **What does the OT teach about the Spirit?**

'In the OT, "Spirit of God" is one of the ways in which God's action may be mentioned without actually making the anthropomorphic statement that God did this or that. Thus "Spirit of God", like the Word and the Wisdom of God, becomes a periphrastic description of God's initiative and action in the creation, providential ordering, redemption and eschatological deliverance of the world as a whole and of Israel in particular. God's Spirit is a reverential way of speaking of his presence . . . or of his *dynamis* in action' (A. Richardson, *An Introduction to the Theology of the NT*, 1958, 103).

With this in mind we can group the OT passages in **j** which the Spirit is mentioned under five different headings. First of all there is the cosmic activity of the Spirit of God (e.g. Gn 1:2; Job 33:4; Ps 104:30). But by far the most conspicuous activity of the Spirit is the 'heilsgeschichtlich', implying God's guidance of the history of Israel to the end envisaged by him. This is most evident in the period of the Judges, when Israel's theocracy reached its zenith (cf Jg 3:10; 6:34; 11:29; 13:25; 14:6, 19; 15:14). Even during the kingdom the Spirit's activity is placed in relief (1 Sm 11:6; 16:13, 23; 1 Kgs 22:19—24; 1 Chr 12:18; 2 Chr 15:1; 18:18—22), and is stressed by the Prophets, especially in Isaiah (Is 34:16; 48:16; 63:10, 11, 14; Ezek 18:31; Zech 4:6; 7:12; 12:10). The Spirit guides Israel by raising leaders at the opportune moment, advising them on their course of action, prohibiting undesirable resolutions from being carried out, punishing transgression, and allowing rebellious leaders to be deceived by false spirits. The third activity of the Spirit, his witness through the Prophets, is but another aspect of his historico-redemptive action. Ezekiel is the most explicit as regards this experience (cf 2:2; 3:12, 14, 24, and passim). Moreover, even God's beneficent presence is attributed to the Spirit (e.g. Ps 51:11f; 139:7; Wis 9:17).

If God's closeness to his people and his guidance of **k** their historical past were attributed to the Spirit, we should expect the Spirit to play a still more important part in the ideal future when God sends final salvation to Israel and to the nations. This eschatological activity is, in fact, predicted in various passages: Is 11:2; 42:1; and 61:1 say quite clearly that the Spirit will rest on the coming Messianic King; Is 32:15; 44:3; and Joel 3:1ff speak about the Spirit resting on the People of God in the last days; and such texts as Is 59:21; Jer 31:31; Ez 11:19; 18:31; 36:26f; 37:7—14; 39:29 make the New Covenant with Israel consist in this, that God will put his Spirit into the hearts of his people so as to turn them from stone to flesh, and render them capable of doing his will.

We can therefore sum up the OT evidence as follows: **l** Through his Spirit God made the world; he raised Israel

671 and guided his people along their path through history with a view to establishing his Kingdom. He spoke to them through the prophets, finding scarce response; nevertheless he remained faithful to his promises and predicted a future order in which the Spirit will rest in all its fulness upon the Messianic King of Davidic descent, so that he may establish in Israel an ideal kingdom. Everyone will possess the Spirit as the prophets did of old, and in this way, with the law written in their hearts, and driven by the Spirit, they will be loyal and obedient to God, and fulfil the purpose of their election.

m It is only to be expected, therefore, that this doctrine should be taken up by **the Primitive Church** and applied to itself as the New People of God in the light of its pentecostal experience. Even where these texts are not cited explicitly, they are referred to implicitly in so far as the Eschatological Community considered itself the rightful heir of God's promises to Israel which would be instrumental in bringing the history of salvation to its final end. Once the Christians were persuaded of this, it was only a question of time until the above cited texts would be exploited more fully.

668a **Christ and the Spirit**—The idea of **the Holy Spirit as the gift of messianic times** runs through the whole of the NT. In the OT the giving of the Spirit and the Messiah had never been related to one another. Isaiah had predicted that the future King would possess the Spirit, and Ezekiel had asserted that the Spirit would be given to the People of God, but the connexion between both was not clear. This is not to be wondered at considering the lack of clarity with regard to the relationship between the Messiah and eschatological times prevalent at the time of Jesus. A well known text in the *Testament of Levi* does, however, connect the two, and this text acquires a much greater value as it seems to refer to the Heavenly Messiah:

> In his priesthood shall sin come to an end,
> And the lawless shall cease to do evil. . . .
> And he shall open the gates of paradise,
> And shall remove the threatening sword against Adam.
> And he shall give to the saints to eat from the tree of life,
> And the spirit of holiness shall be on them (Levi, 18).

b In the NT, the connexion between the glorification of the Lord and the giving of the Spirit is established beyond doubt, and it can be affirmed that the Messianic gift *par excellence* is the Holy Spirit. John the Baptist announced from the very beginning (Mk 1:8; Jn 1:33) that Jesus would baptize with the Holy Spirit. Jesus did receive the Spirit at his baptism, but Luke asserts that he received it again after his ascension (Ac 2:33), this time to give to those who believed in him: 'Being therefore exalted at the right hand of God, and having received from the Father the promise of the Holy Spirit, he has poured out this which you see and hear'.

c This doctrine is not only Lucan, it is Pauline as well. Rm 1:4; Eph 1:3; and Ti 3:5 repeat Peter's statement in Ac, so that the saying that God poured out the Holy Spirit upon the believers through Jesus Christ our Saviour (cf 1 Cor 15:45) becomes a fixed formula in the Church. It is in John, however, that this doctrine receives its fullest development. Jesus repeats so often that unless he is glorified his disciples will not receive the Spirit that even if we allow for some Johannine paraphrase, it is practically impossible that such a universally accepted doctrine did not have as its source the words of the

Master himself (Jn 7:37ff; 14:15ff, 26; 16:7; 16:12— **668c** 15).

The redemptio-historical activity of the Spirit on the d New Israel—already appears in the Gospels, especially where they speak of the descent of the Holy Ghost upon Jesus. The word 'redemptio-historical' (heilsgeschichtlich) in this context implies that the Spirit is God's agent in leading historical events to their destined end, which, in God's mind, is the salvation of mankind to the eternal glory of God. As Luke builds an entire theological doctrine about the Holy Spirit in relation to Jesus and the Primitive Church, it will be useful to cast a glance at his line of thought.

e The first two chh of Lk, which offer an excellent example of Lucan composition and theology, emphasize from the very beginning that the birth of Christ was prepared by the Spirit like that of the prophets of old. Even his predecessor, John the Baptist, was filled with the Spirit from his mother's womb (1:15, 42). The miraculous birth of Jesus was the work of the Spirit (1:35), and the canticles which comment his birth are also inspired by the Holy Ghost (1:67; 2:26).

f The solemn anointing of Jesus as the Prophet and King foretold by Isaiah is described by Luke in 3:1f. The *bat qôl* 'Thou art my Son, my Beloved, with thee I am well pleased' recalls Is 42:1 'Behold my servant, whom I uphold, my chosen, in whom my soul delights, I have put my spirit upon him' thus designating Jesus as the Servant-Messiah. Later, Luke 4:1 sets the scene for the guidance of the Spirit throughout Jesus' ministry, and the Lord himself solemnly confirms his anointing with the Spirit by applying to himself in the synagogue of Nazareth the words of Isaiah (6:1f) 'The Spirit of the Lord is upon me, because he has anointed me to preach good news to the poor . . .' (4:16–19). Without abounding in repetition, Luke makes it clear that the Spirit accompanied Jesus during all his life, and the author of Heb. affirms even that Jesus' very death on the cross became an atoning sacrifice which purifies our 'conscience from dead works to serve the living God' through the 'eternal Spirit' (9:14).

g The doctrine of the anointing of Jesus with the Spirit was so fundamental in the primitive Church that it formed part of the original Kerygma (Ac 10:38). It is not imprudent to ask why it is stressed so much and what theological significance it bears. It was common doctrine among the Jews of Jesus' time that there were no more prophets in Israel who possessed the Spirit like the great prophets of old, but that the history of Israel would make a fresh start in messianic times precisely through the abundance of the Spirit. It is therefore understandable how the Evangelists stressed the messiahship of Jesus and the introduction of a new aeon, as also the fact that God was speaking to Israel through Jesus by stressing the activity of the Spirit. But they also had an apologetical purpose in view, namely to indicate that Jesus' death was part of God's plan of salvation and should not be a cause of scandal. If the Spirit led Jesus throughout his life and anointed his death, the Cross must have some higher significance.

The Holy Spirit in the Church—Once the Holy Spirit **669a** had passed on from Jesus to his disciples, the Gospel message which he had preached in the power of the Spirit continued to be preached in the same power by the Church. It is the Spirit that intervened at crucial moments in the history of Israel, and it is the Spirit who intervenes at crucial moments in the history of the Church, taking upon himself all major decisions. When Luke wrote Ac enough had already occurred to enable him to perceive a certain pattern or redemptive history, and the very way

669a in which he stresses apparently insignificant episodes demonstrates that he meant to emphasize this pattern. One of his principal purposes, in fact, was to illustrate the transition of the offer of salvation from Israel to the gentiles. It is understandable that this is an event of unsurpassed importance in the religious history of the Jewish people. Luke therefore actually takes pains to stress that it was the Holy Spirit who worked out all the details of this transition. In the episode of the Ethiopian minister who had contacts with the Gentiles the Spirit it twice represented as operative: He commands Philip to join the eunuch and removes him as soon as his mission is completed (Ac 8:29, 39). The Spirit increases the number of believers (9:31). The climax is reached in ch 10 with the conversion of Cornelius. Against the witness of the Spirit even the Jerusalem diehards are powerless. Later, Paul and Barnabas, the two protagonists of the Gentile mission are set aside by the call of the Spirit (13:2ff) who guides their mission in such detail by way of command or prohibition that the Gospel reaches Europe (16:6f; cf Rm 15:19). The crowning event is reached in the council at Jerusalem; when the great decision is taken Peter does not hesitate to proclaim that 'it has seemed good to the Holy Spirit and to us . . .' (15:28). Therefore, the Spirit that raised Samson and Saul, directed the wars of the Israelites, spoke through the Prophets, and freely gave of his power to direct the history of salvation, is now at the height of his activity at the time when history has entered its eleventh hour.

b **The Spirit: The Word of God**—But to direct the missionary activities of the Apostles is not enough if penetrative power is not granted to their preaching. In fact, just as Spirit and Word of God are almost synonymous in the OT, the Gospel derives its persuasive power from the Spirit in the New, becoming the 'Sword of the Spirit' (Eph 6:17) 'piercing to the division of soul and spirit . . .' (Heb. 4:12f). The Spirit produces conviction in speaker and hearer (1 Thes 1:5); it is no mere philosophy which rests on rational arguments alone (1 Cor 2:4), but it carves itself upon the hearts of men (2 Cor 3:3; cf Ac 4:8, 31; 5:32). Thus, to use a military metaphor, the Spirit is not only the general who directs operations, it is also the 'dynamite' that blasts the way for the advance and the organizer that consolidates gained ground.

c This last aspect, **the work of the Spirit inside the Church**, can be studied at its best **in the theology of St Paul**. The Apostle addresses the Church of Corinth as the 'Temple of the Holy Spirit' (1 Cor 3:16), in which the Spirit is appropriated by means of baptism: 'for by one Spirit we were all baptized into one body—Jews or Greeks, slaves or free— and all were made to drink of one Spirit' (1 Cor 12:13). In fact it is the reception of the Spirit which differentiates the baptism of John from that of Christ, the former being a mere symbol of moral conversion in preparation for the great gift of Messianic times.

d By receiving the Spirit the believer received an earnest of his eschatological deliverance. It is only in the '*ôlām habbā*' (the Age to Come) that he is totally and irrevocably saved, but in this provisional aeon he receives the Spirit as a 'first instalment' of the complete gift to be received later—this is the real meaning of the word *arrabōn* in 2 Cor 1:22 and Eph 1:13f: a partial participation of the blessings of the world to come. Although supernatural and redemptive, the spiritual blessings which we receive here, even justification itself, are only provisional, for 'through the Spirit, by faith, we wait for the hope of righteousness' (Gal 5:5). This hope is maintained alive by the Spirit

himself, who directs our gaze towards the Resurrection **669** and seals us apart for the day of Redemption (Rm 8:11, 23; 15:13; Eph 4:30).

What are the gifts which we receive from the Spirit **e** during this interim period? Once the experience of the Holy Spirit had been linked with the prophecy of Joel, and was interpreted as a sign of the arrival of the 'last days', it was only logical to apply to the life in the Spirit the New Covenant texts of the OT, Jer 31:31f; Is 59:21; Ez 11:19; 18:31; 36:26f; 37:7–14; 39:29. These texts insist on the promise that the Spirit will transform the hearts of stone in Israel to hearts of flesh. Although there are only two explicit quotations from these texts in St Paul (2 Cor 3:3; 1 Thes 4:8), and his terminology changes stone-flesh to flesh-spirit, there can be little doubt that these testimonies stood at the back of his mind when he wrote Rm 8. Ch 7 had spoken of the 'law of sin' which commands without helping to perform, ch 8 is all about the 'law of the Spirit of life in Jesus Christ' which sets us free from 'sin and death' (8:2).

When the Risen Christ gives us his Spirit we are **f** considered to be 'in Christ', sons of God, heirs and co-heirs of Christ (8:16f). Our bodies become temples of the Holy Ghost (1 Cor 6:19) and will be raised up together with Christ. We are pleasing to God and live in his friendship (Rm 8:6). Once the *dynamis* of the Spirit is operative within us we are able to overcome 'sin' and the 'flesh', the *yēṣer harā'* which is the power of sin in us driving us to evil. If we follow the promptings of the Spirit we shall also enjoy the fruits of the Spirit: 'love, joy, peace, longsuffering, kindness, goodness, faithfulness, meekness, self-control' (Gal 5:22), especially love of God (Rm 5:5) and hope (15:13; Gal 5:5). It is therefore imperative that we should not grieve the Spirit (Eph 4:30), nor quench it (1 Thes 5:19), for the more we surrender ourselves to the Spirit the better can we penetrate into the mysteries of God (1 Cor 14:2).

The Spirit guides the Church—The power of the Holy **g** Spirit as experienced by the individual is merely a participation of that same power operative within the Eschatological Community. The **prayer of the Church is guided by him** 'for we do not know how to pray as we ought, but the Spirit himself intercedes for us with sighs too deep for words. And he who searches the hearts of men knows what is the mind of the Spirit, because the Spirit intercedes for the saints according to the will of God' (Rm 8:26f), 'for we are the true circumcision who worship God in the Spirit' (Phil 3:3), words which recall those of Jesus to the Samaritan woman in Jn 4:23.

The Holy Spirit is also the principle of unity in **h** the Church, as 'he who is united to the Lord becomes one spirit with him (1 Cor 6:17), and through baptism also becomes one body with him 'for all were made to drink of one Spirit' (1 Cor 12:13), which also recalls Jesus' dialogue with the sinner of Samaria. Thus fellowship is attributed to the Spirit just as love is attributed to God and grace to Christ (2 Cor 13:14). This is explainable in so far as it is the Spirit who pours God's love into our hearts (Rm 5:5). Eph 4:4 crowns this thought with the lovely hymn to Unity, 'There is one body and one Spirit, just as you were called to the one hope that belongs to your call, one Lord, one faith, one baptism, one God and Father of all, who is above all, and through all, and in all'.

In the actual order of things the Holy Spirit gives **i** unity through those 'whom the Holy Spirit has made guardians, to feed the church of the Lord' (Ac 20:28), and who have the duty to watch over the charismatics lest they contradict the Kerygma (1 Cor 12:13). Thus, while the

69i Spirit produces the wonderful diversity of charismata which are so often enumerated in St Paul, and about which more shall be said, he also maintains the organic unity of the living body of Christ (12:8ff, 28ff; Rm 12:6ff; Eph 4:11).

j St John is more preoccupied with the witness which the Spirit renders within the Church to truth. He is 'The Spirit of truth whom the world cannot receive' (14:17), who enables the Church to achieve a deeper understanding of the words of Christ (14:26) and of the things that are to come (16:13).

k **Continually fertilized by the Spirit, the Early Church** formed a body of doctrine and a form of prayer which **tended to become stable**. But the NT also enables us to study the transition of this Early Church to the Later Church which followed the death of the Apostles. The primitive charismatic word is already being written down or transmitted orally in a stable form—hence the rise of the canon of the NT and of tradition. There is a growing preoccupation with 'right doctrine' in the face of rising heresies (Jud 4; 2 Pt 2:1, 21; 1 Tm 1:10; 4:1, 6, 13; 6:3, 20; 2 Tm 2:2; 3:10; 4:3; Ti 1:9, 14; 2; 1; 3:9). The Apostles have created a deposit of faith which must be handed down to the *episkopoi* and by these to their successors. The accent therefore shifts from the charismatic to the elder or bishop in the later Church. 'Canon law' begins to appear (cf 1 Tm 3:1—13) as injunctions are more detailed and juridical than earlier. There is also a de-eschatologizing tendency which appears at its best in John, the master of realized eschatology. All this does not mean that there were no spiritual gifts in the later Church, or that there had been no laws in the earlier communities, or even that the Parousia was forgotten. Nothing can be further from the truth. We only notice a change of emphasis from miraculous charismata to the ordinary charismata of every-day government, from the 'utterance in the Spirit' to the written or transmitted word. But the Spirit has not ceased to operate. Whereas earlier his activity was more creative it is now predominantly preservative. His role in the inspiration of Scripture is stressed (2 Pt 1:12), and so is his help in the preservation of the deposit of tradition: 'Guard the truth that had been entrusted to you by the Holy Spirit who dwells within us' (2 Tm 1:14). The historical church has followed the direction traced by the later writings of the NT. It did not break with the NT, just as the sub-apostolic Church did not break with the Pauline Church. The Spirit is as operative today as it was then, though its activities may be less spectacular.

l **The Spirit within the Trinity**—The theologically minded reader will have observed that the NT is more concerned with what the Holy Spirit does than with what He is. This should cause no surprise as revealed truths have the primary purpose of serving our salvation not our curiosity. However, the desire to know more about the Spirit is only natural, and during the ante-Nicene period the discussions which arose about divinity and personality in Christ were applied to pneumatology. That the Spirit is divine cannot be doubted from the foregoing. But is the Spirit a mere personification of the Power of God, as it was in the OT, or a distinct person like the Son? **The trinitarian formulas**, which are as old as the oldest writings in the NT are rightly referred to in this connexion (1 Cor 12:4ff; 2 Cor 13:13; Ti 3:5; Jud 20f; 1 Pt 1:12; Mt 28:19). If the Spirit is placed on a par with the Father and the Son, and there is no definite order in which the Three Persons are mentioned, especially in St Paul, it is only logical to apply the speculations about the divinity and personality of Christ to the Spirit and

affirm that He is a Person distinct from the Father and **669l** the Son but One God with them. Paul goes very far in 1 Cor 2:11 when he says that 'the things of God no one knows save the Spirit of God'. This is no mere personification, nor is the injunction that we are not to grieve the Holy Spirit of God in Eph 4:30.

There is nothing explicit in the NT about the 'procession' of the Spirit from the Son as there is about His procession from the Father (Jn 15:26), Later theology deduced the procession from the Son from the fact of the sending of the Spirit by the Risen Christ, which brings us back to the phenomenon of Pentecost.

3. THE LAST DAYS

A Question of Method—The Pentecostal outpouring of **670a** the Spirit led the primitive Christians to the conclusion that the last days foretold by the prophet Joel had arrived. Believers were already enjoying the eschatological blessings promised to Israel.

If we wish to trace the evolution of **the eschatological consciousness of Christians** living during the NT period it is not advisable, and not possible either, to limit our investigation to Ac. Although Luke has certainly preserved archaic elements in Peter's speeches in the first chh, his editing belongs to a later period when de-eschatologizing was already on its way. The Apostles' question in Ac 1:6, however, is immensely revealing and can very well serve as a starting point for our enquiry: 'Lord, will you at this time restore the kingdom to Israel?' It seems as if Jesus had preached in vain. His words were certainly at the back of the Apostles' mind when they asked this question, but the Spirit had not yet sorted them out into the doctrinal synthesis presented in Syn. The first question to ask, therefore, is what Jesus had thought about **the Kingdom of God**, see § 656*b*-*k*. Radical critics will answer that it is impossible to answer this question because the Syn. already present an interpretation of the words of Jesus. But even Bultmann, the master of form-criticism believes that he can reconstruct the teaching of Jesus from Syn., in fact he begins his *Theologie des NT* with the ch on Jesus' teaching concerning the Kingdom. We can only remark that even if the presentation of the first three Gospels includes an interpretation, we can rely on what we have already learned about the Spirit and rest assured that this interpretation is authentic.

The Kingdom of God—It must be admitted, however, **b** that out of a multitude of sayings of the Lord the primitive Church was especially concerned with those that contained a message related to the situation in which it found itself at the period in which the sayings were collected. We know from other sources that the first Christians were under constant persecution from Jews and Gentiles alike; that they survived only through their firm faith in the Messiahship of Jesus and the hope of deliverance when the Lord comes again. They looked forward to an early parousia, but their preachers exhorted them to patience and long-suffering, insisting that the day of the parousia was unknown, that the Gospel had to spread and grow, and that certain signs would precede the end—even though this would come like a thief in the night.

1. The sayings of Jesus about the Kingdom, **c** therefore, can be grouped under different headings which reveal to us both the doctrine of the Lord and the preoccupations of the Primitive Church. The first group confirms the conviction of the Church that the fullness of times has been reached and that these were the last days. Hence John the Baptist had been the Elijah who was to

670c have come (Mk 9:13; Mt 11:9) and Jesus was 'He that cometh' as his signs had proved him to be (Mt 11:2ff). The old aeon had therefore ceased with John and now was the age of the Spirit (Lk 16:16), in fact, the Kingdom of God (*basileia* can also be translated 'sovereignty' or 'kingship' of God as denoting God's victory over evil and Israel's enemies promised in the OT) was present among (or in) the hearers as Beelzebub had been overpowered (Lk 11:20). The Christians were witnessing what kings and prophets had desired to see and had not seen (Mt 13:17). 'Today' is therefore the time of salvation (Lk 19:9). It was only those who were blind to the signs of the times that did not recognize the blessings of the Messianic age (Lk 12:56). To such people the words and parables of Jesus were meaningless (Mk 4:11f), for while they were expecting spectacular signs and portents to herald the arrival of eschatological times, the Kingdom of God had crept in unostentatiously and was already there (Lk 17:21). The history of salvation had reached its eleventh hour (Mt 20:10ff).

d 2. 'The time is fulfilled, and the kingdom of God is at hand; repent and believe in the gospel' (Mk 1:15). This was the main theme of the preaching of Jesus as enunciated by Mark; it also constituted the core of the message of the Apostles (Lk 10:9). According to the internal disposition of the hearers these words are an invitation (Mt 22:2) or a threat (Lk 10:11). To those who believe the Kingdom is something to be desired and prayed for: 'Thy kingdom come' (Mt 6:10). But the whole accent lies on the urgency of the message; even the duty to bury one's own father is no excuse for delaying to answer the invitation to follow Christ (Lk 9:60).

e 3. The third group of sayings collected by the Primitive Church can be labelled 'apocalyptic'. The Son of Man—a title chosen by Jesus with specific reference to the Messianically interpreted Danielic figure—will come in power upon the clouds of heaven to judge the world (Dn 7; Mk 13:26f; 14:62), and will sit upon his judgement seat with the angels round him (Mt 25:31). Those especially who did not believe in him (Lk 10:12) or who did not follow up their faith with works of mercy (Mt 25:41ff) will bear the brunt of the judgement. The Son of Man's judgement, however, is only a culmination of another judgement which has been going on through history ever since Jesus preached the gospel of the Kingdom. This is the fire of judgement and purification which the Lord was sent to enkindle (Lk 12:49)—a theme later developed by John. But when will Jesus come again? Certain apocalyptic signs will precede his coming (Mk 13:24f), but the coming of the Kingdom was announced as so near that those who walked with Jesus would see it come (Mk 9:1; cf Mt 16:28). Jesus' own generation would behold it (Mk 13:30) and the Apostles would not even finish their mission in Israel till the Son of Man came. On the other hand, no one knew the day or the hour except the Father (Mk 13:32) for the end would come like a flash of lightning (Mt 24:27).

f 4. The Christians who collected these texts looked forward to an early coming of the Lord, but as the parousia did not come, they recalled other words of Jesus which, understood in the light of events and under the guidance of the Spirit, consoled them in times of trouble and exhorted them to longsuffering. Jesus had foretold that a time would come when they would have to pray, watch and wait for his return. He had compared himself to a nobleman who departed to a distant land to be crowned king and return (Lk 19:12); what are his subjects to do in the meantime? They should be similar to virgins awaiting the arrival of the bridegroom, with lamps lighted (Mt 25:1) and to men ready for a journey, with their loins **670** girt (Lk 12:35); they should pray and be on guard inside the house of their lord (Mk 13:33ff) for if they betrayed their trust and behaved reprehensibly they would be punished on his return (Mt 24:48—51). As the hour of his coming was absolutely unknown there was always the danger that they would fall asleep (Mk 13:35f). They should therefore have the prudence of a man who knows that a thief will enter his house during the night. He would be foolish if he dozed off (Lk 12:39f), as people did in the days of Noah and were consequently drowned by the flood (Lk 17:26). On the other hand, they should be on their guard not to be led astray by false alarms. Wars and crises of war, earthquakes and famines are not the end, they are only signs of the approaching end (Mk 13:7f).

5. The days of waiting would be a period of suffering **g** and persecution. It would be no time of rejoicing, as when the bridegroom was among his friends, but a time of fasting (Mk 2:19f) for the Christians would drink of that same chalice of which Jesus himself had drunk (Mk 10:39). They would be dragged before councils and synagogues, flogged and put to death because they bore witness to the Gospel (Mk 13:9f). In all this oppression they would yearn to see one of the days of glory of the Son of Man, but this will be denied them till the time arrived (Lk 17:22). Out of love for his elect, however, God would not permit that these days of tribulation should go on for ever without intervening (Mk 13:20). But woe to him who tries to save himself from persecution by denying Jesus, it is much better to lose one's life for the sake of the Gospel and find it again in eternal life (Mk 8:35). Men being what they are, however, it is inevitable that many should succumb and charity grow cold (Mt 24:12). But those who suffered in patience and remained faithful would be avenged on the day of the Lord's coming (Lk 18:6ff), their retribution would be great, and the little flock would receive the kingdom (Lk 6:23; 12:32).

6. Impatience avails nothing, because the Kingdom— **h** the Gospel—must grow before it bears fruit. It is only the seed that has been sown, and it takes time to develop (Mk 4:26f), but when it does it will spread over all nations, and all will take shelter in its shade (Mt 13:32). This is the period of fermentation of the word of God (Mt 13:33), and no one should expect a perfect community of believers. Wheat and weeds grow together (Mt 13:24f) just as good and bad fishes are hauled together into one net (Mt 13:47f). The judgement will separate them, and the supreme test will be perseverance in faith and the faithful practice of the Lord's teaching especially as contained in the Sermon on the Mount. The wicked will be cast into eternal fire away from God (Mt 25:41).

7. Full retribution will come collectively at the general **i** resurrection; but what will happen to those who die before the resurrection? Although it was more in line with Jewish thought to think of eternal life as the resurrection of the whole man, in fact as the resurrection of 'man', i.e. collectively, or, even more biblically, of the resurrection of Israel, it cannot be denied that in Jesus' time it was not uncommon among the Jews to assert that the souls of the dead entered the 'coming aeon' (ha '*ôlām habbā*') immediately after death. This was a result of hellenistic influence, which emphasized the distinction between a mortal body and an immortal soul in man, but it is well attested in the apocrypha and in Rabbinic writings (cf SB 4; 2,799—976), and Jesus accepted the doctrine when he affirmed that God was the God of the living and not of the dead (Mk 12:27). In fact he made full use of

70i it in the parable of the rich man and Lazarus in Lk 16:22f, thus laying the foundation of the development which this point of view was to receive in later NT writings and in Christian theology. In times of persecution, therefore, the Christians had to remember that it was much more prudent to fear God than a human judge, who could only kill the body, not the soul (Mt 10:28).

j   8. The believer must therefore have only one end in view, that of entering into the Kingdom at whatever price: family, friends, and possessions must be renounced, and even things as dear to a man as his own eye or foot should be cast away if they obstruct his entry into the Kingdom (Mk 9:45—48). His justness must be more profound than that of the sanctimonious scribes and pharisees (Mt 5:20): he must become like a child, and learn to receive everything from God's hands (Mk 10:15). The keys of the Kingdom are in Peter's hands, it is for him to admit or cast out (Mt 16:19). The Pharisees, on the other hand only keep people out without themselves entering (Mt 23:13), so that they will be preceded by sinners and harlots who will enjoy the fellowship of Abraham, Isaac, and Jacob (Mt 21:31; Lk 13:28). Among those who enter, the least one is greater than the greatest of the prophets of the old dispensation, John the Baptist (Lk 7:28); how much greater will he be then, whoever takes seriously, preaches, and practises the little injunctions of Jesus about the ethics of the Kingdom (Mt 5:19)? Blessed is he who shall eat bread in God's Kingdom (Lk 14:15); if anyone remains faithful to Christ in the midst of temptation this beatitude is fully his (Lk 22; 28ff).

671a **The Kingdom-Logia of Jesus**—Once we perceive how well this collection of sayings fits into the situation of the Primitive Church it is only natural to ask whether it can be explained by saying that out of a multitude of sayings the Church mainly chose those which spoke to her in the situation in which she found herself, or whether the Christians created sayings which suited the situation and placed them in the mouth of Jesus. Certainly, men like Paul were tremendously scrupulous about distinguishing their own sayings from those of the Lord (1 Cor 7:10, 12). Furthermore, it was highly dangerous to invent sayings which would expose the believers to the derision of those very Jews who had heard Jesus preach but a few years earlier, and it was so much easier to suppress embarrassing sayings than create new ones. The Christians did neither. They retained sayings which were in seeming contradiction and incorporated them into their doctrine. Lastly, the creation of new sayings would have betrayed a lack of faith in the apostles which is hardly justifiable from what we know of them from other writings of the NT.

b   It is conceivable, however, that certain sayings were retouched to render an interpretation possible—as the differences in the Synoptic traditions make us suspect—or expanded by an explanatory paraphrase, especially where words of the Risen Christ through the Spirit clarified the original logia—as in John (Cf Jn 16:12ff). But to suppose that Jesus' logia were created *ex nihilo* is as unscholarly as it is arbitrary.

c   It is permissible to ask, nevertheless, what Jesus' own interpretation of the Kingdom of God might have been. Such a question is not easy to answer. Apart from the fact that we do not possess all the logia of the Lord, among those that have been transmitted to us we find some that present the Kingdom as still coming or near at hand, others saying that it is here already and that it must grow, still other texts warn us that the hour of the coming of the Kingdom is unknown but that it will come

during the lifetime of Jesus' own generation. Was Jesus **671c** mistaken, as the liberal theologians affirm? Or is there an interpretation which coordinates these logia into one rational doctrine? This problem is not only ours. When the evangelists recorded the sayings of Jesus in their Gospels they were well aware that the *parousia* had not come, and would not come as soon as many had believed. They also had more sayings of Jesus at their disposal than we possess. It is not to be wondered at, therefore, that the composition of their writings affords at the same time an interpretation of the collection of logia concerning the Kingdom of God which had much more right to be credited as reflecting the mind of Jesus than that of any modern exegete. As St Luke posed himself this question explicitly let us examine it briefly:

Luke's Interpretation of the Kingdom—We have **d** already observed that the word 'basileia' can be translated as both kingdom and kingship or sovereignty. In Lk it is equated with 'Gospel' and 'Eternal Life', a concept later developed by John. Lk 18:17 is an interesting starting-point 'Whoever does not receive the kingdom of God like a child shall not enter it', which means that whoever shall not accept the Gospel shall not enter into eternal life, and in the next v the 'ruler' asks Jesus 'What shall I do to inherit eternal life?' and Jesus answers (v 24): 'How hard it is for those who have riches to enter the kingdom of God'. St Luke also equates the Kingdom with *sotēria*, 'Salvation'. Together with *sotērion* the word occurs five times in the first two chh where the preaching on the Kingdom is introduced and which provide a theological commentary on what is narrated in the later chh.

Lk 21:24-33 considered in the context of Lucan **e** theology provides a key to the interpretation of the Kingdom concept. In v 24 Jesus affirms that after the destruction of Jerusalem there will be a 'time of the Gentiles'. When this has been fulfilled apocalyptic signs in the heavens will follow and then the Son of Man will come. When these signs 'begin' to occur our redemption is near. 'Truly, I say to you, this generation will not pass away till all has taken place' (v 32). What does this saying mean?

We must rule out the possibility of its meaning that **f** the final parousia will take place within this generation. For supposing that Luke wrote during the lifetime of the second or third generation, 'this generation' had already passed and the parousia had not yet come. Moreover, he warns us quite often that we must not expect an early parousia (cf especially 19:11). Our positive explanation, therefore, is that **the Kingdom was ushered in at Jesus' glorification: Passion-Resurrection-Pentecost.** Its continuation in time is only secondary, for men appear before the Son of Man even before the parousia. The end will come at the Parousia, and with it final and full salvation, but no one knows when. Calvary-Jerusalem is THE END, or Eschaton, in so far as it closes a period of promise and forms one theological whole with the absolute end, or fulfilment. We therefore have the following parallelism: Calvary = Redemption—Judgement—Glorification—Kingdom; Parousia = The Plenitude of Redemption—Judgement—Glorification—Kingdom. These four realities actually happened and were inaugurated on Calvary but will be consummated and brought to their fullness at the Parousia. Both Jesus and Luke, therefore, considered **Calvary-Parousia as one event,** theologically speaking. Jesus preached salvation in prophetic language and stressed the theological reality. Luke repeated Jesus' message but was more explicit by subjecting it to a historical analysis in the light of events. Our proofs are the

671f following: (1) On Calvary we have the 'signs' mentioned in the apocalyptic discourse, thus giving it an apocalyptic flavour: the sun is obscured, the earth trembles, the veil of the temple is rent in twain; Jesus' words to the women of Jerusalem: 'Blessed are the barren . . . for if they do this when the wood is green what will happen when the wood is dry?' mean that judgement has come now upon Jesus, what will happen when the time of their children arrives? (2) 21:28 has *archomenōn de, toutōn ginesthai*. On Calvary these events only *began* to happen (The sense of *archomenōn* here is pregnant, cf TWNT 1, 477, even though *archomai* is usually a simple auxiliary). This was a sign that our *apolytrōsis* is near (v 28). The word is Pauline and carries with it the same meaning as *lytrōsis = sōtēria* in Lk 1:69; 2:38 thus applying to our whole mystery of salvation not merely to the Parousia.

The only disturbing v in this section is 27, 'And then they will see the Son of Man coming on a cloud

g with much power and glory'. Did Luke have the Parousia in mind when he related these words? No, because immediately after come the words 'When these things begin to happen . . .' But when the Son of Man comes at the Parousia he does so in a flash and things end there. So this v most probably refers to the glorification of Jesus; in fact, Jesus declares before the Sanhedrin '*From now on* the Son of Man will be sitting at the right hand of the Father' (Lk 22:69, a clearer version than Mk 14:62. Luke interprets Dn 7 through Ps 110). Stephen too sees 'the heavens open and the Son of Man sitting at the right hand of God' (Ac 7:56). Luke therefore interprets Jesus' reference to the Danielic Son of Man in a sense not necessarily apocalyptic though fully eschatological.

h One of the most convincing arguments for this interpretation of the Kingdom of God is the good thief's petition for mercy 'when you come into your kingdom'. Jesus answers 'Today you will be with me in paradise' (Lk 23:24f) which means that Jesus entered his kingdom at his *analēmpsis* (elevation) and that the Kingdom can also be equated with 'Paradise' if looked at from this point of view.

i From what we have said we can conclude that in Luke's view, the ESCHATON, or, as Jesus calls it, the Kingdom of God, is one theological reality including Death-Resurrection-Parousia. This *eschaton* is a supra-temporal reality not analysable in terms of time. It was preached by Jesus as one event with a strong emphasis, in prophetic fashion, on its theological unity rather than on its duration, although even this aspect is not neglected. It began to be understood in terms of history after the Resurrection and Pentecost, when the Spirit clarified the understanding of the Church that the *eschaton*, though the end of *Heilsgeschichte* (Salvation History), is not necessarily the end of history. The *eschaton* touches history at two points: at the Incarnation and at the Parousia; between them the Kingdom is operative in history through the earnest of the Spirit. Luke's variations, therefore, provide us with an interpretation of the words of Christ which is far from being a misunderstanding. The whole point lies in understanding that a prophet is not a historian of the future. His is a call for repentance, especially in the face of a calamity which is so certain and is of such magnitude that it is felt as imminent. Jesus looked forward. Luke looked forward, backward, and around him. His was the task of translating a prophetic message into theological language.

j **Contemporary Rabbinical Views**—Our interpretation of the meaning of *Basileia* (Kingdom) finds confirmation in the fact that Jesus' teaching concerning the Kingdom coincided in great part with contemporary **671** Jewish teachings and theories about the *ha 'ōlām habbā'*, the world to come. In the now classical article in SB cited above, the meaning of 'the future aeon' varies between the world into which just souls enter after death, or the future supernatural world of absolute salvation, and the ideal state in this world introduced by the Messiah and the resurrection from the dead. The idea of the Kingdom overlaps more or less that of *'ōlām habbā'* in so far as it denotes the supernatural kingdom at the end of times, the Kingdom Christ entered at his Resurrection, and the blessings of the Messianic age, all aspects of the manifestation of the Sovereignty of God in judgement and salvation.

St Paul—Resurrection and Parousia—The apostle **672** is an excellent theological interpreter of Christ's prophetic message. His letters are usually occasional writings composed in response to concrete situations. When they deal with the problem of eschatology, therefore, they do so to answer certain queries posed by the communities. The average Christian had learned in the *paradosis* (tradition) that **the last days** foretold by the Prophets **had arrived**, that Jesus was the Messiah who was to come, and that the Risen Christ would return to judge the world and save those that believed in him. But dangerous speculations soon arose through impatience, lack of faith, or over-confidence. In Thessalonica and Corinth some people had doubts about the fate of the dead before the Parousia (1 Thes 4:13ff; 1 Cor 15:12ff). Others considered the parousia so imminent that they refused to work to earn a living (2 Thes 3:6ff). Still others manifested a sort of scepticism regarding this doctrine and asked too many questions about the manner of the resurrection (1 Cor 15:32f, 35). At a later period, when 'realized eschatology' was gaining ground, some Christians went to the opposite extreme denying any resurrection at all and affirming that it had already occurred (2 Tim 2:18). All these questions, together with others which arose spontaneously in the Apostle's mind, posed a challenge to his theological dynamism. He reasserted the traditional doctrine, but deepened it immensely through reflection on the Torah and contemporary theories.

Dn 7 and 12 provided enough material for meditation, **b** especially as they had been explicitly referred to by Jesus himself. But contemporary Jewish theology, both rabbinic and 'apocalyptic', was far advanced as far as eschatology was concerned. Paul did not accept any of the Jewish theories as they stood; for none of them took into account a Messiah who had been crucified and rose again, but from the currents of thought represented in the *Apocalypse of Baruch, 4 Esra*, and in the rabbinic traditions he could well accept many elements which he incorporated into the kerygma.

Paul shared the faith of the Primitive Church that **c** the Christians were living in the last days, in eschatological times, and therefore had the right to appropriate for themselves all that was written in the Torah 'for our instruction, upon whom the end of the ages has come' (1 Cor 10:11). It was the world's last chance: 'Now is the acceptable time . . . now is the time of salvation' (2 Cor 6:2). The coming of the Son of God meant that the times had reached their fullness (Gal 4:4) and that the hour which had long been in the mind of God for uniting things in heaven and things on earth had arrived (Eph 1:9). God was now clearly showing that he was faithful to his promises (Rm 3:26). Even in the sphere of revelation the Christians were privileged in so far as the mystery of the reception of the Gentiles into the fellowship

72c of Israel has only been revealed to them in the fulness of time (Eph 3:4f; Col 1:26f).

d So far, Paul had merely developed the doctrine which he himself had received. His own contribution, as far as we can conclude, is the **insertion of the Resurrection of Jesus into the pattern of the doctrine of the Last Days**. With the Resurrection, our resurrection has begun. It is a spiritual resurrection, but it is also the foundation of the true resurrection at the Parousia (1 Thes 4:14; 1 Cor 15:20; 2 Tm 2:18).

e The dominant theme of this last period of redemptive history is the return of Christ on the last day. Although Jesus, who took the form of servant, has been declared 'Son of God' at his Resurrection, it is at his **Parousia** that he will be triumphantly revealed as the only Sovereign, King of kings, and Lord of lords (1 Cor 1:7; 1 Tm 6:15). The Parousia—a word in common use to denote the state visit of an emperor—will also be the signal for the resurrection and glorification of those who have already 'risen with Jesus' (1 Cor 15:23), but it will also entail judgement. The judgement theme, not only in Paul but in the whole of the NT, is one of encouragement (2 Thes 1:6ff; 2 Tm 4:8) as well as of warning and exhortation (Rm 2:5, 15f; 14:10; Eph 6:8). Thus the life of the believer is one of hope and expectation.

f The Parousia was looked forward to, desired, and prayed for rather than feared. It was a stable dogma in primitive Christianity, and its certainty rested on that of the Resurrection of Jesus (1 Cor 15). Paul saw himself standing between two great events: backed from behind by his faith in the Risen Christ he walked forward towards the parousia, waiting 'for his Son from heaven, whom he raised from the dead, Jesus who delivers us from the wrath to come' (1 Thes 1:10). If the believer dies with Jesus, he will be raised again with him (Phil 3:10f; Col 3:3f; 2 Cor 13:4). Hence a doubt about the possibility of the resurrection was fatal to the hope of the Christian for it removed the foundation of his whole existence as believer. This is the reason why Paul expands the argument at such length in 1 Cor 15. In the later Paulines this hope is rendered more explicit: 'I know whom I have believed, and I am sure that he is able to guard until that Day what has been entrusted to me' (2 Tm 1:12; Ti 1:2). The Christian's whole psychological and spiritual existence, therefore, can be summed up in the words to Titus (2:13f) 'Awaiting our blessed hope, the appearing of the glory of our great God and Saviour Jesus Christ, who gave himself for us'; for in spite of the fact that we have already been 'justified, sanctified, redeemed, and vivified' our redemption and justification are still an object of hope, and in their entirety will only be received on that Day. What we now possess is only an earnest of the Spirit (2 Cor 5:5; Rm 8:23; Eph 4:30). The parousia will bring us the justness for which we now hope (Gal 5:5), the redemption of our bodies and adoption as sons of God (Rm 8:23), the richness of glory and inheritance (Eph 1:18; Col 3:24), salvation (Rm 8:24), and life eternal (1 Thes

g 5:10; 1 Tm 4:8; Ti 3:7). The greatest event, however, will be our glorification together with Jesus, which has already begun with his Resurrection (1 Cor 15:23) and that whether we be found awake or asleep (1 Thes 4:16; 1 Cor 15:51f; Phil 3:20f), although Paul and his generation hoped to be found alive at the Parousia. This hope was so vivid that they sensed the parousia as imminent (2 Cor 5:1–5), breaking out in such exclamations as 'Maranatha', 'The Lord is near!' (Phil 4:5). These expressions, however, must be understood as the product of desire rather than as dogmatic assertions, for

although Paul's thought was dominated by the idea of **672g** the coming of Jesus, which could happen at any moment, in his cooler moments the Apostle was as perplexed as the Pauline exegete as regards 'the times and moments'. He retained the teaching of Jesus and the Church that the Parousia will come 'like a thief in the night' (1 Thes 5:2–4). Even in his earliest letters he warns the Christians about false alarms 'as if the day of the Lord were imminent' (2 Thes 2:2), because the present period between the resurrections was one of tribulation and ingathering. Primitive preaching had asserted that the parousia would come when the Jews repented (Ac 3:19). Paul had a broader view of the history of salvation and included the Gentiles as well. The Parousia would come when the Gentiles came in and the Jews removed the veil which covered their eyes (Rm 11:25f). All this takes time. Moreover, the Jewish idea of 'tribulation in the days of the Messiah' was translated into christological terms by the Church and by Paul as the idea of Antichrist who would bring about the culmination of the days of tribulation foretold by Jesus (2 Thes 2:3–10). This dispelled any idea of immature imminence.

On the other hand, Paul's vivid faith in the two great **h** events of Resurrection and parousia dwarfed the period in between so that he could assert that the time is *synestalmenos* (1 Cor 7:29), an expression which we can paraphrase by 'telescoped', thus underlining the motifs of urgency and contingency. In the face of such urgency the world appears as fleeting (1 Cor 7:31), and riches, possessions, family, tribulations even liberty itself possess only a relative value (1 Cor 7:26, 30). Loss of time is a great sin with regard to the parousia (Rm 13:11) and the believer's duty is to 'redeem' the time by means of works of mercy and charity (Col 4:5). Eph 5:16; 2 Cor 8:14 and Gal 6:10 speak in the same terms. This approach had the advantage of underlining the fact that theologically speaking the Resurrection of Christ and the Parousia were one theological reality which touched time at two places so that the intervening time is only accidental; its only reason for existing is the unpreparedness of the Jews at the time of Jesus' first coming and it is therefore a prolongation of God's long-suffering.

In spite of his parousia-mindedness Paul did not **i** lay aside the contemporary Jewish idea that the souls of the righteous entered the future aeon at the point of death. He baptized it by placing Christ in the *'ōlām habbā'* so that when the body is laid aside the believer enters into life 'together with the Lord' (2 Cor 5:8f; Phil 1:23f), an idea which is carried forward in Heb. 9:27.

Post-Pauline Problems—Paul was a man of faith. The **j** parousia was so vivid in his mind that he already experienced it as present and envisaged himself as sharing it with the last generation. But there were people in the Church whose faith was not so strong. These grew impatient at the delay of the Lord's coming and sought an explanation from the preachers of the Gospel. **The later writers of the NT** do not minimize the parousia, in fact, Rev dramatizes it to such an extent as to provide an overwhelming assurance of its coming to the persecuted communities. On the other hand, certain themes which are hinted at in the Gospels and in Paul are developed further so as to provide the grumblers with a rational answer. The three most important ideas which fall into this category are (1) the 'telescoping' of the times (2) the salvation of the individual after death (3) realized eschatology.

2 Pt 3 deals explicitly with the problem against **k** those scoffers who asked sarcastically: 'Where is the

672k promise of his coming? For ever since the fathers fell asleep all things have continued as they were from the beginning of creation' (v 4). The author of the epistle has his answers ready: The world has already been destroyed once by water, it will be destroyed again by fire (vv 5ff); the delay of the parousia is merely a time of grace for repentance (vv 3, 9, 15). In fact **the Day of the Lord can be hastened by godliness** (v 12), an idea already present in Ac 3:19 and Rm 11, which may lead to the assumption that had the world been prepared to receive Christ and his message, his glorification and the Parousia would presumably have coincided in time.

l 2 Pt 3 restates Jesus' doctrine that the parousia will come like a thief in the night (v 10). But the most interesting reflection in this ch is 'that with the Lord one day is as a thousand years, and a thousand years as one day' (v 8). This is history looked at *sub luce aeternitatis* and adds something to 1 Cor 7:29. Real duration does not count for much. Compared with eternity all time is contingent, and contingence is presented in the guise of imminence.

m The second idea, that of **life after death**, is developed in Rev. In 6:9—11 and 20:4 it is affirmed that the souls of those who have suffered for Christ are alive in heaven. These 'souls', in the Gr. sense of spirit as distinct from body (a sense unusual to the Bible, where 'soul' usually refers to the whole living person), are preserved 'under the altar' until the day their fellow-sufferers join them. In 20:4 it is said that they participate in the 'first resurrection' and reign with Christ for a thousand years. This is metaphorical language. The Jews could not conceive of life after death if not as 'resurrection'; and transcendence is presented as futurity. The long yet limited unknown period between the 'first' and 'second' resurrection is therefore a form of realized eschatology in so far as those who lost their life for Christ in this world have already found it in the next: the coming Kingdom.

n But it is **St John** who is the master of **realized eschatology**. This takes place in history rather than in a transcendent kingdom. With the glorification of Christ, as with his second coming, judgement has come upon the world so that unbelievers are already condemned (Jn 3:18). The hour is coming—in the parousia—but has 'now' come: when God will be adored in truth (viz his sovereignty recognized according to his will, hence the coming of his Kingdom) (Jn 4:23); when the dead will hear the voice of the Son of God and live (Jn 5:25); when the ruler of this world, the devil, will be cast out (Jn 12:31). These themes of judgement, resurrection, sovereignty of God, victory over Satan and glorification are all eschatological themes and are looked forward to in the parousia by the other authors of the NT, but in John they are fully transported into the present, without any denial of their futurity.

o In spite of these explanations **the Early Church remained forward-looking**. Its great expectation was the parousia. The thought of the coming of Jesus dominated the life of the believers, and the whole of the Christian existence was looked at from this point of view. It was as if history had received a great push at the Resurrection and was still travelling under that momentum towards its goal which is final redemption at the Parousia. Hence everything received a quality of transitoriness and contingency. Even the blessings of the Resurrection, the gifts of the Spirit themselves, had an interim quality about them. They are merely provisional. The great deliverance and redemption is about to come on 'that Day'.

Further Theological Development—With the passing **672** of time, when the Parousia assumed the proportions of a relatively tiny speck in the future, and with Gr. philosophy gaining in importance, theologians turned to the immortality of the soul and immediate judgement, punishment and glorification after death to feed the hope of Christians. The Redemption achieved by Christ in his first coming gained in magnitude as the final redemption at the parousia lost in proportion, and theology became predominantly backward-looking. Catholic theology added nothing to what the NT had thought as the dogmas it sought to develop were already present in the Primitive Church. It only changed the emphasis for pastoral purposes. However, modern theology will render a great service to contemporary biblical spirituality if it can re-establish the psychological dominance of the Day of Redemption and become forward-looking once more. It need not give up what it has gained through the ages, but can re-order these data to recapture the same perspective that Paul and the early Christians had, which constituted the motive power of their dynamic existence as Christians.

4. JESUS OF NAZARETH

The Historical Jesus—'You know the word which he **673a** sent to Israel, preaching good news of peace by Jesus Christ (he is Lord of all), the word which was proclaimed throughout all Judea, beginning from Galilee after the baptism which John preached: how God anointed Jesus of Nazareth with the Holy Spirit and with power; how he went about doing good and healing all that were oppressed by the devil, for God was with him. And we are witnesses to all that he did both in the country of the Jews and in Jerusalem. They put him to death by hanging him on a tree' (Ac 10:36—39).

According to this and other speeches in Ac which help us to reconstruct **the primitive kerygma**, it was the custom of the Apostles to include the good works, signs and wonders of Jesus of Nazareth in their kerygmatic discourses to Jews and Gentiles. The Christ they preached was the Risen Christ, the coming Son of Man, but the *Kyrios* was identical with the Jesus whom Pilate had crucified in Jerusalem but a few years earlier. The fact that this man had been crucified was repugnant to the hearers, and needed justifying. Of course the Christians had nothing to hide. All that was needed was an objective exposition of the treacherous trial and condemnation of the Master. After all, the sufferings of Jesus coincided in such detail with so many predictions in Scripture that they should be considered as part of God's plan and need surprise nobody. Jesus was a just man. He had done nothing but good during his lifetime as many of the hearers could testify. If he was a man approved by God the Cross was not a scandal but a mystery.

The Formation of the Gospel Tradition—To **b** substantiate these claims the Christians began to elaborate **a detailed support to their Kerygma**. The Passion narrative was perhaps the first to reach a more or less stable form, which is due to repetition of and attention to significant detail. It is probable that some of these passion-stories were even put down in writing.

At the same time, the Apostles and those who **c** had followed Jesus during his lifetime began to collect narratives about the good deeds and miracles of the Lord. These were of use in apologetic sermons, and very soon a number of such stories grouped together and formed cycles of narratives even during the period of oral transmission.

73c As Jesus had preached longer in Galilee than in Judaea, and as the greater number of disciples seems to have been Galileans, it is no wonder that the majority of miracle stories have Galilee as their setting.

d When **Mark** wrote his Gospel, therefore, he did not start from scratch. He already possessed a vast amount of written and oral material to draw upon. But why did he write a Gospel? Was it merely to satisfy the curiosity of the readers, or their devotion, by presenting a 'life of Jesus'? The Gospel of Mk can hardly satisfy the pre-requisites of a biography, even in the Gr. sense of the word, nor is it apt to satisfy the piety of the faithful as the 'lives of the Saints' are, for it mainly consists of arid miracle stories with some sayings of the Lord in between. Mk had no other purpose in recording these facts and sayings in writing than that which their very collection had. But in putting together these traditions Mk impressed upon the whole collection his own theology, as was also the case with the other three Gospels. We must therefore distinguish two theologies in the Gospels: that of the material itself, and that of the Evangelist. This latter can be reconstructed from the choice of the material, its ordering in relation to the whole, the framework and occasional editorial remarks, and the changes introduced.

As research in this field is still in its infancy, we shall limit our survey to a few salient points in the life of Jesus and try to examine the theological development of some of the narratives about Jesus especially in Syn. This section has the same end as the whole article, namely that of arousing the curiosity of the reader to take up further research on his own.

e The Formation of the Passion-narrative—As we have it now in the Gospels it is not a pious story which can serve as a background for the 'stations of the Cross', although it does serve that purpose as well. Its end is apologetical. The earliest oral stage that we can imagine is the simple narrative in bare outline, with an accent on the unjust condemnation of Jesus; this sufficed to demonstrate his innocence. When Mk records the narrative, it has already reached a second stage. The trial scene is worked out in detail. The rest of the story is there either because it belongs to its essence, or because it recalls some prophecy in Scripture. The editorial comment in Mk 14:49 prepares the reader for this scriptural parallelism. The Passion-psalm Ps 22 provides most of the detail: the parting of the garments (v 9 = Mk 15:24); the mocking of Jesus (v 8 = Mk 15:29); 'Eloi Eloi' (v 2 = Mk 15:34); and the vinegar (Ps 69:22 = Mk 15:36).

f St Matthew carries the scriptural proof further. It is evident that the Evangelists are all out to bring their gospels 'up-to-date' with the latest ideas in the Church (Marxen). This tendency is clear in the whole of Mt, but the First Evangelist is especially keen on proving that Jesus' death took place 'according to the Scriptures', hence, according to a pre-established plan of God. Apart from Mt 26:56 (= Mk 14:49) this idea is stressed right at the beginning of the Passion story in Mt 26:54. Mt also inserts the whole story about Judas (27:3—10) which recalls Zech 11:12f; Jer 39:6—15; 18:2f. Mt 27:24—26 (= Mk 15:15) is also formulated in such a way as to recall Dt 21:6ff. Another sign of Mt's pre-occupation is Mt 27:43 (Ps 22:9) which is added to the preceding v (= Mk 15:12) to stress the scriptural evidence.

g As **St Luke** probably did not follow Mk's account of the passion it is difficult to make comparisons. But the section 23:2—16 which is much longer than its parallel in the other synoptics is obviously in harmony with the **673g** general tendency of the author of Ac (as in Paul's trials) who is at pains to demonstrate that the Roman state cannot find anything to condemn in Christian teaching or way of life; in fact it takes it upon itself to defend the Christians against the Jews (Ac 16:36; 18:12ff; 19:35ff; 23:26ff; etc). The three Gospels agree on one point: they reach their climax in the declaration of Jesus that he is the Son of God, the Christ. The argument is therefore focussed: If Jesus is innocent, if his death was even foretold by the Spirit, then his claim to be the Christ, the Son of God must be valid.

St **John's** account of the Passion agrees in essentials **h** and in purpose with that of Syn., but it contains much more anti-Jewish controversy, a tendency which is in line with that of the fourth Gospel at large. It is also more theological in character. God's foreknowledge is expressed in a different manner in Jn. In 18:4 it is said that Jesus knows everything that is to befall him. Being the Word made flesh he has the power to annihilate his adversaries, as one single word from his mouth reveals (18:7); but he submits willingly, and even forbids his disciples to resist (v 21). To justify his doctrine Jesus refers to the witness of 'those who heard me', those self-same disciples who were preaching the word and themselves suffering persecution. In fact, the famous dilemma in 18:23 has them in mind as well. But resistance is of no avail because those who are not of the truth cannot understand the truth about Jesus' Kingship (18:33—38). Even Jn stresses that Jesus' condemnation was unjust (18:31f, 39). But the Jews had the Torah, and 'by that torah he ought to die' (19:7, which is Jn's version of 'secundum scripturas'), the reason being that he declared himself to be the Son of God (Jn 19:7 = Mt 26:63f = Mk 14:61f = Lk 22:70). The Jews have therefore refused their King and chosen Caesar in his stead; but by the irony of fate the crucifixion of their King is at the same time his glorification (Jn 19:11, 15, 19), thus fulfilling the Scriptures (v 30). The blood and water that issue from Jesus' side are precisely the sacraments that vivify and bear witness (19:34, cf 1 Jn 5:6ff). The sparing of Jesus' bones (19:36) is not merely a fulfilment quotation as in Mt but points out Jesus as the true Paschal Lamb (Ex 12:46; Zech 12:10). This is an excellent example of how Jn handles the stuff he receives from tradition, treating it as a skeleton around which to build his own theology.

Formation of the Miracle Narratives, cf § 658 g—j **674a** The man whom the Jews had delivered into the hands of the gentiles to be crucified was no evil-doer. He had spent his life doing good. Indeed, God himself had borne witness that he was 'he that cometh'. The many Galileans among the Christians recalled many episodes which referred to the ministry of Jesus among them. These were collected and recited in both Kerygma and paradosis to justify Jesus in the eyes of the hearers as well as to persuade them that he was the Messiah. The echoes of the primitive Kerygma in Ac provide us with the key to the theological interpretation of the Galilean ministry and of the plentiful miracles worked there: 'Jesus of Nazareth, a man attested to you by God with mighty works and wonders and signs which God did through him in your midst, as you yourselves know . . .' (Ac 2:22); 'The God of our fathers glorified his servant Jesus . . . the Holy and Righteous One' (3:13f). These two texts, together with the longer one from ch 10 quoted at the beginning of this section shew that the primitive Christians looked upon the miracles of Jesus as signs that 'God was in Christ' bearing witness.

674b However, even in the pre-Markan oral stage of transmission, the miracles of the Lord had acquired a much deeper significance than that. The miracles were *sēmeia*, the signs of the times (Mt 16:3). They were effective as an integral part of the gospel to the poor, but it was only those people who had 'eyes to see' who could read such signs and find in them the marks of the ideal kingdom predicted by Isaiah. The Pharisees and Sadducees were not spiritually mature enough to read the signs of the times, and were therefore irritated (Mt 16:1—4).

c The wonders which Jesus worked can be divided into three groups (we accept Richardson's division, op cit, p. 97): The Messianic miracles, exorcisms, and nature miracles. Hints at the interpretation of such miracles are to be found in the preaching of Jesus himself. The Church accepted and developed these principles of interpretation—especially references to Scripture—in such a way that when the miracles came to be recorded the simple narrative was interlaced with interpretative allusions to the OT so that the narration came to acquire a theological value besides its historical one. (Cf Richardson's note reading the word *mogilàlos* in Mk 7:32 = LXX Is 35:6).

d To John's question 'Are you he who is to come?' (Mt 11:3) Jesus answers: 'Go and tell John what you hear and see: the blind receive their sight and the lame walk, lepers are cleansed and the deaf hear, and the dead are raised up, and the poor have good news preached to them' (vv 4ff). This is a conflated quotation of Is 35:5f and 61:1f. The latter Isaianic text, in fact, receives full treatment in the Nazareth sermon in Lk 4:16—30, and dominates the whole of the Lucan Galilean ministry, so that the 'gospel to the poor' combines both preaching and healing, the clearest *sēmeion* that the days predicted by the prophets had arrived and that Jesus' contemporaries were witnessing Messianic times. The fact that Jesus was the 'light of the blind' both physically and morally gave rise to the additional explanation of the miracles as symbols or moral values—an interpretation which reached its zenith in the Fourth Gospel. The 'pronouncement-stories' (Taylor's terminology; = Bultmann's 'Apophthegmata' and Dibelius' 'Paradigmen', e.g. Mk 2:3ff; 3:1ff), besides having the same value as the other miracles are couched in such a way as to reach their climax in a famous saying of Jesus which thus remains better impressed in the hearers' memory as a sort of dogma.

e **The exorcisms**, too, belong to the oldest strata of theological interpretation. They were not mere signs of Jesus' benevolence and power; they showed clearly that 'the prince of this world' had lost his power and hence the Kingdom of God was present (Lk 11:20). This victory is dramatized in the story of the temptations of Jesus (Mt 4:1ff; Lk 4:2ff). Thus the exorcisms not only bear witness to the presence of Messianic times but even to the divine sonship of Jesus (Mk 3:11). The age of darkness under the dominion of the devil ceased and the age of light had dawned. As St John puts it: 'Now shall the ruler of this world be cast out' (12:31), 'the ruler of the world is judged' (16:11; cf SB II, 552).

f The miracles belonging to the third group, **the natural miracles**, are those which are richest in scriptural connotation, and as a consequence receive a more elaborate theological interpretation. The theme of God's dominion over the elements and over life, which he himself created, is a constant one in the OT. The elaboration of this theme takes place in the way of catch-phrases which link up the episode to a similar one in the history of Israel, thus presenting Jesus as Elijah or Moses redivivus,

with the comparison all in his favour. When Jesus revives **674** the dead young man of Nain, for example, Luke's remark that he handed the boy back to his mother (7:15) recalls Elijah's miracle in 1 (3) Kgs 17:23. But Elijah prays, Jesus does it with a simple command. Certain details provided by Mk in the raising of Jairus' daughter (5:21—24, 35—43) such as the closing of the door, the admittance of parents only, etc, recall 2 (4) Kgs 4:32—37. Jesus is therefore the New Elijah-Elisha, only much greater.

That the multiplication of loaves was interpreted **g** in the Church as a sign of the New Moses is evident from Jn's treatment of it (Jn 6:28—34). The third nature miracle narrated by Mk is the stilling of the sea and Jesus' walking over the waters (4:35—41; 6:45—52). A comparison with Pss 65:7; 89:9; 93; 107:23—30 will immediately reveal the connotation. Jesus, like Yahweh, is Lord of the elements. The amazement of the onlookers: 'Who is this . . .?' and Jesus' words 'It is I' (*'ani hû*, as God revealed himself in the OT, cf Jn 8:24, 28) were clear signs for those who had eyes to see and ears to hear.

The assertion that the miracles described in the **h** Gospels have a theological purpose does not necessarily lead to the conclusion that they lacked historical truth. The Apostles were addressing people who had known Jesus and lived with him, and who could very easily have contested the truth of many a statement had the narratives lacked foundation. The Church transmitted these episodes in a way which made it easier for the hearers to understand them with reference to Messianic prophecies.

Editorial Interpretations of the Miracles—While **i** Mk has a seemingly haphazard arrangement in his Gospel, Mt is more systematic. The way in which he sandwiches five layers of discourses between as many strata of narrative material is understood by many scholars to derive its inspiration from the pentateuch so that the Gospel assumes the significance of a New Torah of the New Moses, in spite of the fact that the connexion between the narrative layer and the consequent discourses is often logically slender. But Jn brings this technique to perfection. Immediately after the miracle of the multiplication of loaves Jesus declares 'I am the bread of life' (6:11, 25) and continues with the Eucharistic sermon. In 9:5 he gives the explanation of the healing of the man born blind: 'I am the light of the world'. Before the resurrection of Lazarus Jesus explains 'I am the Resurrection and the Life' (11:25). These examples make it clear the Jn wished the miracles to be understood not merely as apologetic arguments (as the blind man himself does), but also as signs and symbols which reveal the presence of the Messianic Blessings and lead to absolute faith in the divinity of Jesus: 'Before Abraham was, I am' (8:58).

With **the Transfiguration**, the apex of the Galilean **j** ministry is reached in the Syn., cf Mk 9:2—8 and parallels. The evidence of 2 Pt 1:16ff proves that the episode was well known in the Church and already formed an integral part of the *didaché*. The account in Mk has already reached a theological stage of interpretation and aims at presenting Jesus as the New Moses-Elijah, the Prophet who is to come. The parallels of the Markan narrative with Ex 24 and 34 are too close to be passed over lightly. The 'holy mount' of 2 Pt and the 'high mountain' of Syns. are clearly figures of Sinai. Mk's 'after six days' (after what? Lk has 'about eight days'!) and the cloud recall the six days during which the cloud covered Sinai; 'on the seventh day he called to Moses out of the cloud' (Ex 24:16). Moses' shining face and the

874j terror of the Israelites on his return is signified in Lk 9:29 and Mt 9:15. These are merely external parallels, but the injunction of the *bat qôl* 'Hear ye him' links up with the direct prophecy of the New Moses in Dt 18:15: 'The Lord your God will raise up for you a prophet like me from among you, from your brethren—him shall you heed.' The first part of the voice from heaven, on the contrary, refers, as in Jesus' baptism, to the Suffering Servant in Is 42:1. That Moses and Elijah were more or less identified as eschatological figures appears from Mal 3:21—24. Moreover, Peter's suggestion to construct tabernacles for Jesus, Moses, and Elijah harps on the eschatological theme of God's tabernacling among the Israelites in Ezek 37:27; 43:7; Zech 2:10f; 8:3. Lk, moreover, renders the idea of the New Moses explicit by noting that the three spoke about the *exodos* which Jesus was about to accomplish in Jerusalem (9:31). As in 9:51 Lk speaks about Jesus' *analēmpsis* (cf 'Assumptio Moysis'!); the parallelism is complete.

875a The two narratives of the Passion and the activity in Galilee did not remain without any connexion even in primitive preaching. In his speech to the Jews at Antioch, Paul gives relevance to **the journey of Jesus from Galilee to Jerusalem:** 'and for many days he appeared to those who came up with him from Galilee to Jerusalem, who are now his witnesses to the people' (Ac 13:31). This is not merely a Lucan remark. All three Syns. give prominence to this journey, but it is Lk who based a whole theological construction upon this passage in the kerygma.

b Lk found the material for his construction in the teaching of the prophets concerning **Jerusalem** and in the distinction current in his time between the 'present Jerusalem' and the 'celestial city' (cf Gal 4:25f; Rev 3:12; 21:2, 10). His thesis is that, ironically enough, God chose precisely that city which rejected his revelation as the stage upon which the main events in the history of salvation were to be acted. In spite of the city's ultimate effort at rejection, all will take place there according to divine counsel. The city itself will be destroyed as a sign of its counter-rejection by God, but another heavenly Jerusalem will replace it that God's promises may stand. It is therefore part of God's plan that Jesus should suffer and be glorified in Jerusalem. Lk dramatizes the episode, turning the journey from a geographical one into a theological comment on God's redemptive-historical plans. The thesis is carried forward in Ac, for a parallelism is created between Jesus' itinerary and that of the Church. Just as Jesus journeyed to Jerusalem, preaching his gospel on the way, then suffered and was glorified in that City, so also the Apostles (Paul especially) preached the gospel on their way to suffering and final glorification in Jerusalem, the celestial city.

c Already in 9:31 Lk connects Galilee with Jerusalem, for the Exodos of the New Moses is to take place there. It is in this earthly Jerusalem that he must lead forth his people into the heavenly Jerusalem, for he must be 'taken up' to heaven there (Marxen assumes that according to Mk the Parousia will take place in Galilee, but this opinion is based on a very doubtful exegesis of Mk 16:7).

d Jesus knows that Jerusalem is the city 'that kills the prophets', on the other hand, it is necessary that a true prophet should not die outside Jerusalem (13:33f). God had chosen that city that his Name might dwell there and be a light to the Gentiles (Is 2:3; 2 (4) Kgs 21:4). But its constant lack of response had brought about its material ruin more than once (Jer 9:11; Ezek 5:5ff; Lk 21:24; 23:28). Nevertheless, Jerusalem will be the centre of the Kingdom of God in Messianic and

eschatological times (Is 52:1ff; 60; 61:1ff; 65:17ff; **675d** 66:10ff; Rev 3:12; 21:2, 10). The salient point in Luke's account is therefore the Entry into Jerusalem, which is Jesus' *Thronbesteigungsfest*. He is come to bring Isaianic peace to the humble and lowly who are ready to receive him (Lk 19:38), but the scorn of the Pharisees will bring about the city's downfall (19:41—44). Jesus dies, rises again, ascends into heaven, and sends down the Spirit in Jerusalem. What God had decreed for it has been fulfilled. But the city continues in its rebellion. As it treated Jesus it will also treat his Church and his disciples: Stephen, Peter, and Paul. Its final destruction is only a sign that the Old Israel has been rejected, and must cede its place to the New People of God in the New Jerusalem.

The Passion-narrative and the Galilean ministry, **e** linked together with the journey to Jerusalem, already form a Gospel in themselves. In fact, Mk has little more. But Mt and Lk add on **the Infancy narratives.** Their purpose in so doing is not the satisfaction of the reader's curiosity. The infancy stories are deeply theological and apologetical in character.

The kerygma had proved the messiahship of Jesus **f** primarily from his resurrection, but the Jews had numerous objections against Jesus' claim, one of them being that he came from Nazareth, while he should have been a descendant of David, hence from Bethlehem (Jn 7:41). Faced with this and similar difficulties, the Primitive Church began to collect information about the birth of the Lord and His infancy, delving more deeply into the Scriptures to collect those details which would explain the facts as they stood.

Mt goes bluntly to the point. His Gospel begins with **g** the genealogy of Jesus which proves that he was Davidic, then goes on to group some narratives around five texts of Scripture (Mt 1:2—17 = Lk 3:23—38; while Mt leads the line up to David, Lk goes as far back as Adam, in accordance with his universalistic tendencies). Although Mt's source of the infancy stories seems to have been different from Lk's, the tradition of the Virgin Birth is constant. The LXX interpretation of Is 7:14 (*parthenos* for *ha 'almah*) is confirmed by facts and therefore adopted as it stands, thus anticipating objections similar to those raised by Celsus a century later.

Theologically speaking, **the Magi narrative** has two **h** great merits: It incorporates the proof text Mic 5:2 (with minor adaptations pointing out Jesus as the Messiah of Judah, and glorifying Bethlehem), and demonstrates how materially the Jews understood Scripture, without being able to read the 'sign', which cannot be said of the Gentiles. The flight into Egypt connects the Messiah with redemptive history, making him the proper representative of his people through the text of Hos 11:1. As Israel was brought out of Egypt, 'baptized' in the Red Sea, tempted in the desert and witnessed God's glory, so the sequence Egypt-baptism-temptation-transfiguration shows Jesus to be the Epitome of Israel. That the massacre of the innocents was invented to justify Jer 31:15 is not credible, first of all because the text in itself is not clear, and contains adaptations to the story, and because the episode is too much in keeping with what we know of Herod. It is only after the Herodian persecution that Jesus returns to Nazareth, thus becoming a 'Nazarene' in fulfilment of what the 'Prophets' had foretold (Is 11:1 or 49:6?).

Luke's first two chapters, in spite of their apparent **i** lucidity, are a composition of the most sophisticated nature. The annunciation-birth-narratives about John and Jesus form a diptych in LXX style which immediately

675i transports the reader into the remote past when judges and prophets were born. The time sequence in Lk, however, is not fixed according to Jewish dynasties alone, it is incorporated into general world history to signify its universal value (Lk 1:5; 2:1; 3:1f). The narrative has a double purpose: that of introducing the reader to the narratives which follow, and the more important one of providing a commentary on that great moment which proved to be such a turning point in history. The theological thought in these two chapters runs parallel with Gal 4:4 and can be summarized thus: A joyful moment has arrived in history (1:5, 13). The salvation and redemption which God had provided for the whole world and his special promises to Israel are now finding their fulfilment, through God's faithfulness in sending his Son Jesus, born of Mary the Virgin, the Daughter of Sion, into the world. That Jesus is the Messiah is testified by John and by the Spirit, who moves all these events and presses world history into the service of redemptive history (2:1). The days foretold by the prophets are here; Jew and Gentile alike—the poor especially—are called to believe in the Christ and render thanks to God for the salvation he has provided.

j **Historicity of the Gospels**—It should be clear from the foregoing that **the Gospels** are not simple biographies in the modern sense of the word, but highly complex **theological compositions** making use of historical material for specific purposes. This material is often pressed into OT patterns or Jewish categories thus acquiring something of the shape of the mould, but it is never disfigured beyond recognition. The primitive readers of the Gospels were used to such literary forms, and would never have accused a writer of untruth merely because he followed accepted custom and fitted traditions into a pattern. One thing is certain. The Apostles and Disciples regarded themselves as '**witnesses** to the people' of all that Jesus did and said 'from Galilee to Jerusalem'. Had they falsified their testimony in any way, they would have completely betrayed their mission.

5. THE CHRIST

676a **The Christological Kerygma**—'Let all the house of Israel therefore know assuredly that God has made him both Lord and Christ, this Jesus whom you crucified' (Ac 2:36). According to the Lucan narrative the Apostles made this astounding Christological statement but a few days after they had shown their total incomprehension of Christ's mission in Lk 24:19f 'Concerning Jesus of Nazareth, who was a prophet mighty in deed and word before God . . . but we had hoped that he was the one to redeem Israel'.

How did this change take place? Luke outlines the answer: the Apostles' belief in the Resurrection, the reshuffling of their concepts on scriptural sayings about the Christ (Lk 24:45) and the events of Pentecost had completely altered their vision. St John adds another reason: the deeper understanding of Jesus' own words (Jn 14:25). These few hints suffice to help us understand the development of **the Apostles' re-interpretation** of the person and the work of Christ. In spite of such confessions as the one at Caesarea Philippi their idea of the Messiah had not yet gone very far beyond contemporary Jewish expectations.

b **In the light of the Resurrection**, however, things looked very different. God had raised Jesus from the dead, and therefore there was still time for the fulfilment of their hopes. But in what way was Israel to be redeemed? Obviously not in any political sense: hence the need arose

for the Apostles to re-think their Christology all over again. **676** Their raw material consisted of the sayings and deeds of the Master himself together with the words of Scripture concerning the Christ. Their interest was not philosophical but redemptive-historical. Their main problem was: **Who, in reality, is Jesus?** What does Scripture say about him? What is his mission and how is it being fulfilled? The various books of the NT represent various stages in the attempt to answer all these questions.

Messianic Expectations—Had Jesus, during his life- **c** time, wanted to say openly that he was **the Messiah** in the Christian sense of the word, he could hardly have said: 'I am the Christ', for the simple reason that *Masîah* had not yet become the *terminus technicus* to denote 'him that cometh', although it was fast becoming universally accepted as such by contemporary Jews. Such a statement made openly to the Jews, moreover, would have aroused in their minds a hundred and one connotations which Jesus would hardly have liked to endorse.

We have already referred to Jewish eschatological **d** expectations at the time of Jesus, and said that the *eschaton* was expected with or without a personal Messiah. In those circles where 'The Son of David' or 'The Prophet' was expected, he was to play a predominantly political role. It is true that the Messianic age was thought to be connected with numerous spiritual blessings, such as the resurrection of the dead (Sot. 48*b*), the cessation of physical evil (Ex.R. 23:11), the perfect observance of the Torah (Eccl.R. 11:8, 1), the congregation of Israel and the destruction of the evil *yēṣer*, etc. The accent, however, lay on the political supremacy of Israel over the Gentiles (Num.R. 2:13; Eccl.R. 2:8, 1; Sifr.Lev. 6, 111*a*; 13, 111*b*; 41, 112*b*; Hag. 5*b*; Mekh Ex., 7).

Jesus' Self revelation—It is for this reason that we **e** never read in Syn. that Jesus makes an unambiguous and open claim to be the Messiah. He answers John's disciples with a reference to Scripture (Mt 11:2ff); he forbids his disciples to tell anyone that he is the Christ (Mt 16:20); even the devils who confess his messiahship are reprimanded. The *locus classicus*, which is so disputed however, is Jesus' confession before the High Priest (Mt 26:63; Mk 14:61; Lk 22:67). Mt's '*su eipas*' is not an unconditioned affirmation, so that both Mk and Lk are right in their seemingly contradictory interpretations. Christ's answer to Caiaphas as to whether he was the Messiah, the Son of the Most High, can be paraphrased in everyday language thus: 'Well, that's one way of putting it, but I tell you . . .' and Jesus passes on to say what he himself meant by Messiah.

If Jesus was reluctant to accept the title of Messiah **f** so as to prevent false interpretations of his mission, he nevertheless spent all the time of his public ministry indoctrinating both his disciples and the Jews as to the real nature of his mission and the identity of his person. This he achieved through the technique of **scriptural connotation**. He selected a few passages of Scripture referring to 'him that cometh' and moulded the different aspects into one idea. He did not complete the picture himself but left it to his disciples to draw the ultimate conclusions from these texts in the light of the Resurrection, so that 'fulfilment of Scripture' in Jesus is not the mere verification of predicted facts but the re-thinking of OT sayings in the light of contemporary events in such a way as to discover their redemptive-historical significance in the mind of God.

Jesus and the OT—The first set of prophecies we would **g** expect any messiah to refer to would be, of course, the grand passages in Is: 7:13f; 8:8ff; 8:23—9, 6; 11:1—16; 19:18—25; 32:1—17; 35:4—10; together with Am

76g 9:11—15 and Hos 1—3. These texts speak clearly about the future Davidic King who would re-establish an ideal kingdom in Israel; they were the self same passages which provided the rabbis with material for their speculations, and it was a too literal interpretation of them that led into the error of expecting a political King-Messiah. It should cause no wonder therefore, that Jesus, who avoided calling himself Messiah in the open, never referred to these passages directly. Those who had eyes to see could read the fulfilment of these prophecies in his actions, as Jesus himself pointed out in his cryptic answer to John's disciples in Lk 7:22 = Mt 11:5 which is a reference to Is 35:5f, and in which he only points to his works and miracles. His choice of Is 60:1ff as applied to himself in the synagogue at Nazareth and his repeated reference to the same passage in the beatitudes calls attention to the social and spiritual nature of his mission excluding any political ends. The Church later took up these prophecies and applied them to Jesus in their fullest sense, as the evangelists themselves bear witness in their editorial applications in Mt 1:23; 4:13ff; Lk 1:3, 32f, 79; 3:3, etc, but only when everyone had understood that 'My kingship is not of this world' (Jn 18:36).

h If Is was left out of the picture because his description of the Messianic King might have caused misunderstanding, Jesus made full use of Dn 7. His portrayal of the Messiah was primarily eschatological and apocalyptic. He always refers to himself as the 'Son of Man' (29 times in the Syn. sayings). This Aramaic expression *bar nasha* means merely 'man', 'person', and is used in Ezek, in Pss, and in Dn. That Jesus has Dn in mind appears from his explicit application of the prophecy to himself in Mt 24:30; 26:64 and parallels.

i Before we go on to examine what Jesus meant by this appellation it is useful to examine two critical questions upon which our exegesis will depend. Firstly, did Jesus himself use the expression '**Son of Man**' or was it placed in his mouth by the Primitive Church, as Lietzmann and his followers maintain? Even if we do allow for some cases when 'Son of Man' was put into Jesus' mouth by the evangelist, there can be little doubt that the expression was personally used by the Lord. Outside the Syn and Johannine logia we only find 'Son of Man' used once, in Ac 7 (Stephen's speech). This shows that the expression was not a commonplace in the Primitive Church. It is therefore difficult to understand, to say the least, why the Church should place an appellation in Jesus' mouth which she herself did not use.

j Secondly, conceding that Jesus did use the expression 'Son of Man', is it certain that he referred it to himself or did he think of someone distinct from his own person? To answer that the identification of Jesus with the Son of Man was brought about by the Church is rather far fetched; and Jesus' answer to the High Priest's question would be unintelligible. Mt 26:64 was interpreted by Caiaphas as blasphemous because it referred to the speaker himself.

k The Son of Man—In Dn 7 we have theology of history just as in Rev. God's people are menaced by four different empires, and Antiochus IV blasphemes the Name of God. But the Almighty will execute judgement, and this he will do through 'One like a son of man' (v 13) who comes to the Ancient of Days with the clouds of heaven, is presented before him, and receives 'dominion and glory and kingdom, that all peoples, nations, and languages should serve him; his dominion is an everlasting dominion, which shall not pass away, and his kingdom one that shall not be destroyed' (v 14). The seer is then given an explanation of the vision: the four great beasts are four kings, 'but the saints of the Most High shall receive the kingdom, and possess the kingdom, for ever and ever' (vv 18, 22, 27). **676k** The faithful remnant of Israel is represented by one 'man'. The metaphor oscillates between the individual and the collective.

However later Jewish interpretation was decidedly **l** in favour of the individual. There can be no doubt that 4 Esdras 13:3ff refers back to Dn 7 or the tradition which lies behind it, and identifies the Son of Man who comes out of the sea with a redeeming Messiah (v 25) whom God calls 'My Son' (or Servant). Henoch 46 carries on with the notion that the Son of Man will destroy nations. Moreover, he is pre-existent in so far as he has been chosen and put aside by God before the creation of the world (48:6). The Isaianic spirit of wisdom, spirit of understanding, etc rests upon him (49:3), and he is explicitly called God's Anointed (Messiah) in 52:4. The Son of Man on his throne of glory is not only superior to kings (62:5) but also to angels (69:27). His messianic meal will be shared by all his elect (62:14).

It is now easier to understand **why Jesus chose** pre- **m** cisely **this appellation** to reveal his identity. Although its essential connotation is the theme of judgement upon the nations that blaspheme God, it lacks the political ring of the Isaianic messianic passages. It is essentially eschatological and spiritual, and is capable of extension in so many ways: especially as regards pre-existence, the Kingdom of God, the Messiah's glorification, his divine sonship, and his collective-representative character. All these side-lines were in actual fact developed in all directions and beautifully linked up with the other titles selected by Jesus. Let us now examine the limits within which Jesus himself used it.

R. H. Fuller divides the texts in which Jesus calls **n** himself 'Son of Man' into three groups: those that refer to his earthly mission (8 texts); those that refer to the 'suffering' Son of Man (9); and the eschatological group (16) (*The Mission and Achievement of Jesus*, 1954, p. 9f). The relative superiority of the third group emphasizes the eschatological connotation of the title. Dn 7:13 lies in the background of all these sayings, which is understandable. The Danielic text speaks of the kingdom, and, as we have seen, the Kingdom preached by Jesus is primarily eschatological. The bringer of the Kingdom, then, must also be an eschatological figure. This eschatological figure, however, is alive now, at the time of talking to the Jews, and is one and the same person as Jesus of Nazareth. He is therefore 'Son of Man' even during his earthly life. But even the 'earthly' texts represent Jesus as superhuman, as one who has 'come' on earth (Mt 11:19; Lk 19:10; Jn 3:13); who can forgive sins—a thing only God can do (Mt 9:6); who is lord of the Sabbath (12:8); lord of angels (18:41); and can be blasphemed against like God (12:32). These are hints at pre-existence which are later developed. The humiliation-glorification motif in Phil 2 is also present in texts like Mt 20:28; Mk 10:45 and Mt 19:28. John is most explicit on this matter (3:13f; 6:62; 12:23; 13:31).

The Suffering Servant—In hinting at the pre-existence, **o** foretelling the glorification, and stressing the eschatological judgement of the Son of Man Jesus did not go beyond the limits of Dn 7. What is not found in the prophet is the **'humiliation' motive**. In fact, Jesus himself provides a logical sequence by linking up the Danielic texts with the Servant of Yahweh poems in second-Isaiah. In Lk 22:37 he explicitly applies Is 53 to himself; and Mk 10:45 together with the Eucharistic words of the Lord at the Last Supper (Mt 26:28; Mk 14:24; Lk 22:20) have clear allusions to the same passage. The bridge is established through the word '*paradidonai*' which occurs

676o in Is 53:6, 12 (LXX), and is so often repeated in the Son of Man sayings (Mk 9:12; 10:33; 14:21; 14:41; Lk 22:22; 24:7; Mt 26:2) that it decidedly precludes mere coincidence. Once Jesus had provided his disciples with the key to the interpretation of his passion, it was merely a matter of logical development to eviscerate the theology of Is 53 and construct the doctrine of the Atonement, as we shall see in the next ch.

p Therefore, although Jesus' words are not as explicit as the hymn in Phil 2, they provide the Apostolic Church with all the material for producing the sequence: pre-existence—humiliation—death—glorification—judgement, by identifying Christ with the Danielic Son of Man and the Isaianic Servant of Yahweh.

677a Son of God—This is another Christological title which became very common in the Primitive Church, but which creates problems as regards its use by Jesus himself. In the OT the King and the People of Israel are often called 'Son of God', and both the apocrypha and the rabbis extend the title to the pious of Israel and to the Messiah (cf SB 3, 15—22). This never caused any scandal however, as it was understood metaphorically. But the Primitive Church applied the title to the Risen Christ in much more than a metaphorical manner (Ac 13:13; Rm 1:3). How did she arrive at such an understanding of the glorified Lord? Various theories have been put forward: Bousset maintained that 'Son of God' was a Hellenistic title applied to Jesus. Bultmann corrects this statement saying that the title originated in Palestine as a synonym for Messiah, but later acquired a Hellenistic significance in the mission field. J. Jeremias tries to derive *hyios* from *pais*.

b Before we discuss the influence of Ps 2:7 and 2 Sm 7:14 on the mind of the Church we must first enquire, as we did in the case of the 'Son of Man', whether Jesus himself used this title as referring to himself. Two serious works appeared in recent years in addition to Cullmann's *Christology*, which allow us to answer the question in the affirmative: B. van Iersel *'Der Sohn' in den synoptischen Jesuworten* (Leiden 1961), and Th. De Kruiff *'Der Sohn des Lebendigen Gottes': ein Beitrag zur Christologie des Mattäusevangeliums* (Rome, 1962).

c All four Gospels agree that Jesus was put to death because he claimed to be the Son of God (Mt 26:63; Mk 14:61; Lk 22:70; Jn 19:17). That this accusation was not interpreted as intended by the Jews to refer to a mere claim of messiahship is evident from Luke's pains to separate the two accusations, and John's exclusive insistence on Sonship. But it is to be asked further *when* Jesus had put forward such a claim: in the Syn. we only find prudent allusions but never a clear claim 'I am the Son of God'. This fits in with the messianic secret as described above. The congregation that heard Jesus speak, however, could not mistake his intentions.

d Firstly, Jesus' distinction between *ho pater mou* (my Father) and *ho pater hȳmōn*, (your Father) never *ho pater hēmon* (our Father) in a univocal sense is certainly meaningful. Then comes the *baṯ qôl* in Mk 1:11; 9:7 which may have Is 42:1ff as its background, but reinforces the idea of sonship by replacing *pais* with *hyios*. The evil spirits converge in their testimony (Mk 5:7; 3:11; Mt 4:3; 8:29; Lk 4:3, 9, 41; 8:28). In spite of all this, the confessions of the Apostles in Mt 14:33; 16:16; 27:54 could not have merely the above mentioned witnesses to their faith. An explicit declaration of Jesus himself must lie at the bottom of their persuasion. In fact, four texts in Mt together with their parallels are declared authentic beyond doubt by van Iersel. These are Mt 11:27; 21:33ff; 24:36; and 28:19.

In Mt 24:36 (Mk 13:32) Jesus reveals the Son as **677** higher than the angels through the climax reached in the sentence, while the parable of the vineyard in Mt 21:33—41 stresses the superiority of the Son above the prophets. He is 'the heir' while the others are mere servants. But the text which speaks so clearly that it is commonly styled 'Johannine' is Mt 11:27 (Lk 10:22). Van Iersel surmises that the *Sitz im Leben* of this logion is provided by such situations as Mt 13:54ff; Jn 6:42; 7:27, or the confession of Peter. The Lucan version is perhaps nearer the original. The words of Jesus oppose his divine sonship to sonship from Joseph. They cannot be explained in any adoptionist sense therefore, and they also imply a certain consciousness of pre-existence.

We may conclude with van Iersel (p. 183)—and these **f** conclusions apply to the title of 'Messiah' as well—that Jesus never styled himself directly 'Son of God', but the way he refers to God as 'his' Father and to himself as 'Son' shows that he considered the father-son relationship between God and himself as particular. During his lifetime this particular relationship was not realized fully by his disciples, but after the Resurrection the words of the Lord were brought together with Ps 2 and 2 Sam 7 and their idea of Jesus' Sonship thus came nearer the mark. Sonship has at first a functional sense referring to Jesus' mission. It is later applied to his Person and being; in Rm 1:3 this stage has already been reached. So *ho hyios tou Theou* (the Son of God) becomes a fixed title similar to the *hyioi* (sons) in Hellenism but with a particular meaning. The full realization of the meaning of Jesus' Sonship leads to the elaboration of his pre-existence, which had already been implied by him. The last step is reached in such passages as Phil 2:6—11 and in Jn where the emphasis on pre-existence is as great as that on the Resurrection and 'Son of God' assumes the personal static sense of equality with God.

Th. De Kruiff, who examines Matthew's editorial **g** theology in addition to Jesus' own words comes to the same conclusion (146—9). If Mt interprets Christ's words he does so in the right direction. Jesus is no mere man, nor a mere New Moses or prophet. He is superhuman (12:6) and pre-existent, as the *elthon*-texts and Mt 22:41—46 show. In the baptismal formula (28:19) Jesus is placed on the same level as the Father and the Spirit, which is an assertion of Jesus' divinity, for Matthew being a good Jew was aware that there was only one God who transcended beyond measure even the highest creature. The baptismal formula, however, is not primarily static and metaphysical but soteriological: it stresses the part Father, Son and Spirit play in the history of salvation and in sanctification. The accent lies on the one hand upon the love of the Father and the *exousia* (authority) he gave the Son, on the other on the perfect obedience of the Son. The step from *exousia* to *ousia* (being) however, is but a short one and was bound to be taken immediately.

The Risen Christ in the Light of the OT—The second **h** stage in the apostles' understanding of Christ was reached when the words of Jesus were explained **in the light of the Resurrection and of the scriptural texts** bequeathed as a key to the Church by the Risen Lord himself (Lk 24; 44ff). The fact that God had glorified Jesus and exalted him to Heaven required deeper answers to the question 'Who is Jesus?' than those given by the disciples during the earthly ministry. The Danielic designation 'Son of Man' which Jesus himself had chosen now assumed a new significance. Jesus, in his glorified state, is the Heavenly Man who is to come with the clouds of heaven to judge the world. The application of the Servant scriptures to Christ also became natural. But why had Jesus not executed

77h judgement immediately? What was his state in the period between Resurrection and Parousia? The answer came from Scripture. The texts quoted in the NT are legion. Dodd has sifted out those which seem to be primitive and fundamental and were probably used as '**testimonia**' by the whole Church (*According to the Scriptures*, 114—23).

i Ps 2 was a favourite quarry in early times. Culminating in v 7 'Thou are my Son, this day have I begotten thee' which was applied to the Resurrection of the Lord, it is to be looked upon as the foundation of statements like that of Paul in Rm 1:3f 'the gospel concerning his Son . . . who was designated Son of God in power according to the Spirit of holiness by his resurrection from the dead, Jesus Christ our Lord . . .'. Apart from the 'Sonship'-sayings of Jesus himself, this psalm too played a decisive part in forming and stabilizing the title '*Hyios tou Theou*' ('Son of God'), just as Ps 110 is responsible for the title *Kyrios* ('Lord') (cf the possessive *our* Lord in the archaic *marana tha*) rather than any hellenistic appellation. This latter psalm was cited as an apologetic text by Jesus himself in Mt 22:42; it should not be wondered at, therefore, that the Church made such an extensive use of it that the expression 'sits at the right hand of God' was even incorporated into the Creed. Likewise, Ps 8:4ff attracted attention both because of the expression 'son of man' and also because it refers to glorification. Ps 118, quoted by the Lord himself, attracted even greater attention as a messianic psalm. And lastly we have the Suffering Servant texts which give rise to the title of *pais*, viz Is 42; 43; 44; 49; 50; 51; 52; especially 53, together with Pss 22 and 34. Gn 12:3 and Dt 18:15, 19 also played a part in shaping the christology of the early Church.

j The majority of these texts speak about someone who has been glorified by God after having been humiliated. They therefore fit in perfectly with the fact of the resurrection and the passion of the Lord. Moreover, they contain appellations which were used by the Lord himself, or which were applied to him: Christ, Son of God, Son of Man, Lord, and Servant. Consequently, the Church deepened the exegesis of these passages to describe the Messianic function of the Risen Christ. Of course it was at the Parousia that the Kingdom would be finally and fully established, but even at present the Lord is blessing all nations as had been foretold to Abraham (Ac 3:26).

678a Kyrios—When the Apostles felt the need to find a word which would describe the present position of the Risen Christ, the title 'Kyrios' presented itself as the obvious choice. It had been hinted at by Jesus himself (Mt 22:43ff quoting Ps 110), and, although it could simply mean 'Sir' in everyday usage it had acquired a very technical sense in religious usage: both Jewish and Greek. For the Greeks and Romans the various divinities of the mystery-cults were *kyrioi*, so was the deified Emperor. Among the diasporated Jews Kyrios was the LXX word which served to translate the Tetragram, so that in both cultures it implied divinity. The fact that Paul refers OT passages about God (Kyrios) to Jesus without even giving any explanation goes to show that the equivalence is not accidental but intended.

b The kerygma stressed the fact that Jesus became Lord at his glorification (Ac 2:24—36) and as such became the object of liturgical cult. This dogma was so fundamental that it became the most primitive confession of faith: the first creed was 'Jesus is Lord' (Rm 10:9; 1 Cor 12:3; Col 2:6). Such a confession had the advantage of confirming the believer's faith in the Resurrection as a fundamental historical fact, of clarifying the present status of Jesus, and of placing him over and against the pagan divinities and principalities according to whether **678b** the accent was laid on Jesus or on Lord. Although in Ac 2:36 *Kyrios* is almost synonymous with *Christos* it does say something more, and points to a different aspect. The Christ is a giver, the Kyrios is a receiver, he is an object of cult. Moreover, as the primitive Christian hymn in Phil 2:5ff shows, the early Christians believed that Jesus' Lordship was not only limited to the post-Resurrection period; He had always been Lord from the very beginning. The earthly ministry merely suspended temporarily the show of it, but the Resurrection immediately restored to him his pre-existent privileges.

A Christian is one 'who calls upon the name of Jesus' **c** (Ac 2:21; 9:14; Rm 10:13; 1 Cor 1:2), which probably refers to the confession of Jesus' name at the baptismal ceremony. We sometimes even find prayers addressed to him: Stephen prays Jesus to receive his spirit (Ac 7:59), and Paul to be delivered from 'the thorn in the flesh' (2 Cor 12:8). These are prayers of individuals; the community prayed 'Come, Lord Jesus' (Rev 22:20). G. Delling in his book *Der Gottesdienst im NT* (Göttingen, 1952) sums up 'The resulting facts do not seem to lack importance to enable us to judge the position of Jesus in the early Christian cult. Christ constituted its real content. Faith in him played a decisive part; the hymns praised the salvation which we have had through him; the burning expectation of the community looked forward to him. Through him the old man was overcome; in him the new existence was present; "in him" was the community reciprocally founded. He was present in the Eucharistic Meal, his Spirit manifested the life of the liturgy, "in his name" God was prayed to and thanked'. (p. 112). It remains a fact, however, that in the vast majority of cases it is God (the Father) who is the object of prayer and thanksgiving.

The Christ—If 'Jesus is Lord' became a confession of **d** faith and an integral part of the liturgy of the Early Church, **Jesus the Christ**, or simply Jesus Christ became such a common expression that the two names are interchangeable. Now that Jesus had died and risen again, the title of Messiah which he had accepted with reluctance during his lifetime because of possible erroneous interpretations, and which he filled with its proper meaning by referring back to genuine OT teaching, could be applied to the Risen Lord without any fear, and even acquired a fuller significance. 'Christ' becomes so much of a proper name that had it not been for parallel titles and for some texts which provide a special context it would have been next to impossible for us to surmise what the Primitive Church meant exactly by it. The classical text is Ac 2:36 which has already been quoted in connexion with the title 'Lord'. God made Jesus 'Christ', that is, he gave him full Messianic power, dignity, and mission by raising him from the dead (Ac 10:38) as he also constituted him 'Son of God' (Rm 1:3f). An even more interesting passage, however, is Ac 3:19—26: 'Repent therefore, and turn again, that your sins may be blotted out, that times of refreshing may come from the presence of the Lord, and that he may send the Christ appointed for you, Jesus, whom heaven must receive until the time for establishing all that God spoke by the mouth of his holy prophets from of old . . . God, having raised up his servant, sent him to you first, to bless you in turning every one of you from your wickedness'. From this text we understand that the coming of 'the Christ' is a grace which the Jews must prepare for through their repentance. 'Messiah' now becomes an eschatological expression which looks forward to the coming of the Risen Jesus, with the Danielic Son of Man as a background. The Christ will

678d exert his full messianic powers at the Parousia. Till the appointed time, he is in heaven blessing his people as a new Abraham and a new Moses.

e Ps 2, in which the titles **Son and Christ** stand in parallelism, is to be cosidered as the foundation of this doctrine, as it also explains the content of the word 'Son'. Jesus had applied the word to himself, but the psalm provided a theological explanation: the sentence 'this day have I begotten thee' was applied to the Resurrection, when Jesus was 'declared Son of God' (Rm 1:3f). His Sonship is again functionaal and is part of *Heilsgeschichte*.

f Divine Sonship in St Paul—The idea of Sonship as understood and elaborated by St Paul is concisely presented by Richardson: 'The Gospel concerns God's Son (Rm 1:3f, 9), and this is what Paul had preached (2 Cor 1:19); God had sent forth his Son, born of a Jewish woman, that we might become God's adopted sons (Gal 4:4f); though he was the object of his love (Col 1:13), God had not spared him (Rm 8:32), in order that we might be reconciled through him (5:10) and be conformed to his image (8:29), until we attain to the unity of the faith through the knowledge of his Son (Eph 4:13). In the fellowship of God's Son (1 Cor 1:9) we await his parousia (1 Thess 1:10) and the day when all things have been subjected to the Son and the Son himself is subjected, that God may be all in all (1 Cor 15:28). Here is the *kerygma* of apostolic Christianity presented with the help of a term which, though familiar to Gentiles in the context of popular Hellenistic religious beliefs, has been made to serve as an instrument of missionary instruction' (A. Richardson, *An Introduction to the Theology of the NT*, 1958, 151). Heb. goes even further: The Son is higher than the angels (1:8) for he is set over God's house (3:6). Moreover, he was Son even during his lifetime (5:8).

g If God has 'sent' his Son, it means that even before the fullness of times **the Son pre-existed** (Gal 4:4; Rm 8:3); this has already been said of the Son of Man. In fact, it is 'Christ' who guides the history of Israel (1 Cor 10:4). Once pre-existence has been so firmly established, the step towards absolute divinity is but logical. If we assume that the hymn in Phil 2 is pre-Pauline it means that this stage was reached very early in the Church as the epistle is more or less contemporary with Mark's Gospel. Christ is in the 'form of God', he is 'God blessed forever' (Rm 9:5; 2 Thess 1:2; Ti 2:13). This permits Paul to apply to Jesus OT sayings referring to Yahweh (1 Cor 1:31; 2:16; Rm 10:9—13; Eph 4:8; 2 Thes 1:8ff etc).

A Step forward in Christology—Once these conclusions were asserted with firmness many problems arose which transcended the usual categories of the Torah and the Prophets. The main problem was: What is **the relationship between the pre-existent Christ and God?** The later sapiential books, Rabbinic speculations and hellenistic theories were called in to provide an answer. Their ideas were not accepted bodily by primitive Christianity, but they served to spark off certain notions which, with the aid of the Spirit, fermented Christological thought and led to Nicaea and Chalcedon. We shall review very briefly these **Jewish-Hellenistic speculatins** so as to be able to understand better their Christian application.

h We find the first attempt to speculate on the relationship between Christ and God in the Pauline hymn in Col 1:15ff, where Christ is described as the *eikon* (image) of the invisible God, in whom was created all that was made, for he was the firstborn of creation. This is strongly reminiscent of the attribute of Wisdom in Prv **678** 8:22—31. Especially in the later books of the OT Wisdom is so strongly personified that it readily suggests itself to an NT author looking for a parallel to the pre-existent Son of God. Christ's creative activity and the revelation of the wisdom and power of God in him also link up with God's creative word, through which he not only made the world but also governed the destinies of Israel (Cf God's *dābār* is Pss 33:69; 107:20; 147:15; Is 55:10ff; Wis 18:15).

At the time of Jesus, the OT sayings about God's **i** Wisdom and Logos had crystallized into three sets of theories: the rabbinic 'memra Yahweh', *Torah* and the Philonic 'Logos'.

In the Targumim we often come across the expression **j** 'memra di Yahweh'. SB, who made an extensive study of this expression (2, pp. 302—333) come to the conclusion—to which both Moore (1, 417ff) and Bonsirven (1, 145, 217) subscribe—that *Memra* is not identical with the OT *dōbār*. It is not a hypostasis nor an intermediary, but merely another designation for the Tetragram which it was unholy to pronounce. The sayings about the pre-existence of Wisdom, however, gave rise to the rabbinic speculations on *Torah* which was also created from the beginning and for whom everything was made which was made.

Philo develops the concept of Wisdom by applying **k** to it the concepts of Greek philosophy, turning it to Logos. His Logos is not identical with the Stoic 'anima mundi' it is a personification of the Platonic archetypes, being the ideal or plan on which the creation was modelled and through which it is governed. The Logos is the medium of intercourse between God and the world (Dodd, *The Interpretation of the Fourth Gospel*, p. 68). Man himself has a heavenly archetype according to which he was created and which is immanent in him in the form of *nous*, enabling him to rise again to the *Logos* and to God. There is therefore a heavenly ideal man and a created earthly man. This leads us back to Henoch's speculations about the Son of Man who is the Ideal Man who should come back at the end of days.

In the hellenistic world, on the other hand, we often hear of a 'divinity' and of *hyioi tou theou*, 'sons of God' especially with regard to the heavenly man in Gnosticism. In our opinion, although the familiarity of such names might have helped the apostles in their mission, the concepts connected with them had no bearing on their doctrine, which soon became obvious to the neophytes, although these might have recognized certain resemblances especially to the mystery cults. The same applies to the title *sōtēr* which we have sufficient evidence to derive from the OT without having to recur to the titles of hellenistic kings and deities.

Although **the Christology of the NT** cannot be said **l** to be derived from rabbinic, Philonic, or Hellenistic sources, it remains true that material for constructing a coherent Christology was borrowed from them. This material was used in much the same way as Greco-Roman architectural designs and proportions contributed to the creation of a completely different third style in the Renaissance. Brunelleschi's churches would never have existed had he not studied classical architecture, but no one would ever dream of calling Santo Spirito in Florence a Greco-Roman temple.

Christ the Image of God—Let us now go back to **m** Col, the Pauline monument to Christology. What Paul said in Col 1:15—17 Prv 8 had said about Wisdom, Philo about the Logos, and the rabbis about the Torah. But whereas these latter merely personified an abstract

78m concept, whether it be wisdom, or God's plan or God's Law, Paul was speaking of a concrete and historical person, Jesus of Nazareth who died and rose again. The word *eikōn* used by Paul is reminiscent of Adam being God's *eikōn* in Gn 1:26f. This is not surprising, for Christ, as we shall see subsequently, is the New Adam. But Paul is speaking here of the pre-existent Christ. In 1 Cor 1:24 he had already called Christ 'the wisdom of God' and 'the power of God' in so far as he reveals God's counsel and his redemptive initiative. In Col Christ is represented as playing a part both in the creation (1:15–17) and in the redemption (vv 18f). He is both the first-born of creatures as well as the firstborn from the dead, the image of God, i.e. the revelation of the invisible God, in Whom dwells the fullness of the Godhead 'corporally'. As in him all things were created and hold together so also in his Resurrection all things come to a new birth and the members of the Church hold together (1:16, 18, 20) as the members of a body are kept in unity by the head. All these attributes coincide in all but word with the assertions about the Johannine Christ-Logos; and although both Paul and John are primarily interested in salvation rather than in creation they both lay a solid foundation for the later Nicaean definition. Heb. adds the weight of its evidence that God created the world through Christ (1:2) who reflects the glory of God and bears the very stamp of his nature, being above all angels (1:3).

n The 'pastoral' consequence of this doctrine, which is at the same time its explanation, is provided by Jn 14:9–11 'He who has seen me has seen the Father, how can you say, "Show us the Father"?' ... The words that I speak to you I do not speak on my own authority; but the Father who dwells in me does his works. Believe me that I am in the Father and the Father in me.'

679a The New Adam—When St Paul and St John speak in this manner they implicitly refer to the Jewish persuasion, found in apocalyptic and rabbinic sources, that **the Messianic age can be compared to a new creation.** Paul continues this thesis representing **Christ as a second Adam** in 1 Cor 15:45–49, Rm 5:14ff, and Phil 2:5–11. The idea is pre-Pauline, as the temptation narratives show, and presupposes some rabbinic speculations which came to be woven around the Genesis account. Adam was conceived of as reaching to the skies in stature—only after his fall was he reduced to a mere 300 feet in height; the dust for his formation was gathered from the four quarters of the earth; his sin introduced physical death and lost us the glory of God (*Apoc. Moses* xxi, 6).

b In 1 Cor 15 Paul presses the contrast between Adam and Christ. Adam precedes in time but not in dignity (v 46); he is a mere living being but transmits no life which can inherit the Kingdom (vv 45, 50); we merely bear his image being flesh and blood (v 49). The Risen Christ, on the contrary, is a life-giving Spirit, he is 'heavenly' as are also those who are in him through faith and baptism, for as Christ is God's *eikōn* so those who believe in him become spiritual and heavenly (Col 1:14).

c The contrast is even more pronounced in Rm 5:12–19. Adam brought sin, and consequently death, into the world through his disobedience; hence we are subject to judgement and condemnation. Christ's obedience, on the contrary, calls down God's free and abundant grace unto justification and life, for he did not think that equality with God was something to be held to with avidity (Phil 2:6). Unlike Adam, who, though but man, willed to become like God, Christ was really God but became man. For this reason he was exalted by the Father so that men and angels should pay him homage and praise his Name:

the exact opposite of what happened to Adam (Phil 2:9). **679c** Whereas this latter dragged down his descendants with him to death, Christ's Resurrection draws all believers to life eternal (1 Cor 15:20–22).

The High Priest—It should be clear that Christology **d** had moved forward from the simple kerygmatic pronouncement of Peter in Ac 3 where Jesus is represented as the New Moses and New Abraham who blesses his people from heaven (Ac 3:26). It is this very idea, however, which, taken up by the author of Heb. and enriched by the later Pauline doctrine, becomes the corner-stone of the doctrine of **Jesus the High Priest**. The epistle weaves together two primitive testimonies, Ps 2 and Ps 110 with the Philonic doctrine of heavenly patterns (5:5). Ps 110 at an earlier level of interpretation had already given rise to the title of *Kyrios*; the whole psalm being Messianic, the verse which speaks about Christ 'Priest forever after the order of Melchisedek' is now developed. Jesus himself had used sacrificial language when speaking about his death; consequently Heb, like Phil, affirms that Christ offered the sacrifice of obedience to God's will (5:8; 10:7), for which he entered the heavenly tent once for all to sit at the right hand of God (8:1) and be the mediator of the New Covenant. The sacrifices offered daily by the priests of the Old Covenant were only shadows of a deeper reality, of a pattern in heaven (5). Now we are experiencing this reality and the New Covenant is in vigour, the essence of which is the writing of God's laws on the minds and hearts of those who believe (10) so that they need no exhortation to 'know the Lord' (11). Their sins are forgiven and remembered no longer (12) for Christ stands 'in the presence of God on our behalf' (9:24) until he comes again, not to deal with sin, for sin has been abolished once for all, but to 'save those who are eagerly waiting for him' (28).

Cur Deus Homo?—Even in Heb, therefore, the **e** glorified Lord is declared to be High Priest and Christ with an eschatological, or rather an apocalyptic end in view. It is in the last day that Jesus will exercise his Messiahship to its fullest and lead his people to final redemption. As the Old Covenant is the shadow of the New, this age is the shadow of the next. But it is also in Heb. that we find an attempt to answer the question *why* Jesus became man like ourselves, and why he was raised up to heaven. The answer to the first query is pastoral, not philosophical: by being man, and in every respect tempted like all of us but without sin, he can sympathize with us when we approach him in his heavenly glory (4:15). On the other hand it was necessary that he should be raised to a state of immortality that his priesthood might last forever (7:26–28). He is a Priest 'after the order of Melchisedek' because this latter 'became a priest not according to legal requirement concerning bodily descent but by the power of an indestructible life' (16). Like the Risen Christ, he was without beginning, without end, without genealogy (3). For a close rabbinic parallel cf Gen. R. 43, 6 and SB 3, 693.

The Word of God: God—The **Christology** of the **f** NT reaches a new peak, certainly the highest, **in St John**. Whereas in earlier NT writers the centre of interest had been the Risen Christ, in St John the accent shifts to the pre-existent Word. This stage is arrived at under the influence of the Wisdom speculations and presupposes inside the Church the doctrine we already found in Col and Heb. We also find, however, an incipient strain of dualistic thought, strictly monotheistic and Christian, which at the time of Jesus can be clearly observed in the Qumran literature. The concepts of 'light',

679f 'life', 'knowledge', and 'revelation' with their opposites are as prominent in Qumran as they are in Jn. Certain notions borrowed from Hellenistic religions and thought had seeped through Palestinian Judaism, and even if they were transformed in the process they are still recognizable. In St John they served to produce a clearer picture of Christ.

g John's interest in the pre-existence of Jesus, moreover, has no metaphysical motivations. It is merely required by his way of presenting the place of the Incarnation in redemptive history. The elements of the Johannine theory are not unknown to Syn, but it is only in the Fourth Gospel that they form a coherent whole. Even the words of Christ which John accepted from the Church, and which, as we have noticed when speaking on the Synoptic logia, already pointed to an admission by Jesus to divine Sonship, are sometimes paraphrased in such a manner as to render a meaning which the Church, under the influence of the Spirit, had already imposed upon them. Thus, what is implicit in Syn is explicit in Jn, just as what remained implicit in Jn became explicit at Chalcedon. We shall now attempt to give **a summary of John's teaching about Christ.**

h Because of sin 'the world' sat in darkness and in the shadow of death (1:5; 5:24; 1 Jn 3:14; 5:24). Its main fault was that it did not 'know God' in the biblical sense of acknowledgement with thanks (cf Rm 1:18ff). God's love takes the initiative (3:16). He had already shown his mercy in times past by giving the Torah through Moses, but now he gives grace and truth through his Son (1:17). Christ being the perfect revelation of the Father, whoever knows him knows also the Father (14:7 and passim) because he is in the Father and the Father in him (14:10 and passim). Christ is God's **Logos**.

i It is easy to be deceived by the identity of the name with the stoic and philonic 'logos' and interpret the Johannine expression in terms of these philosophies. The resonance of Prv 8 in the prologue warns us to be cautious. In fact, when we consider the influence of the Wisdom-sayings on Colossians we find a precedent in the Church which cannot be ignored. The question remains, however, how the transition from *sophia* to *eikōn* and later to *logos* occurred. God's wisdom, like *logos*, has a double function: a cosmic one and a redemptive-historical one. It existed before the creation of the world and assisted God in its creation (Prv 8; Job 28). Wisdom came out of the mouth of God like a pure word (Sir 24:3) and is 'the breath of the power of God', 'a pure emanation of the glory of the Almighty' (Wis 7:25). It is the 'brightness of everlasting light', 'an unspotted mirror of the power of God' and the 'image (*eikon*) of his goodness' (Wis 7:26). The Lord himself loved her and she is privy to the mysteries of the knowledge of God (8:3f).

j Jn makes precisely the same claims for Christ, but seems to avoid the word *sophia* because of its connotation of the worldly wisdom of the Greeks (cf 1 Cor 1—2). Logos, on the other hand, expresses very well the concept of that wisdom which came out of God's mouth, but has a richer connotation because it recalls the saving power of the *dᵉbar Yahweh*. In fact, *logos* is found in parallelism with *sophia* in Wis 9:1ff and it replaces Wisdom in its redemptive and punitive functions in Wis 16:12; 18:15f. Sir 24:8ff, 23ff equates it with *torah* and makes it dwell in Sion. Through his Logos, therefore, God creates, reveals, saves, and judges. The Logos was with God, he was God. Through him was created all that was created; he shone on the world through the prophets, but the world understood him not. Now he has become flesh and pitched his tent among us. Jn does not say that the Logos came to dwell in Jesus, but that it became Jesus so that Jesus himself could say *ego eimi, 'anî hû* (I am), the exclusive prerogative of God (Jn 8:24—28; 8:59f; 10:33ff). Christ the 'Only Begotten', being one with God who sent him (10:30), is the revelation of God on earth, so that whosoever honours him honours God (5:23), whosoever believes in him believes in the Father, whoever hears or sees him hears or sees the Father (12:44—50). Thus when we hear Jesus saying that he is in the Father and the Father in Him (14:10), or that he does the will of the Father (6:38), or even that the Father is greater than him (14:28), such sayings are not to be understood as metaphysical pronouncements but as redemptive-historical logia. The Son has come to lead everything to the Father, and in this sense the Father is greater. But if we recall the Son is God and that there is but one God we cannot say that the Nicean translation into philosophic terms is incorrect. The Logos-Son doctrine in Jn teaches us in what sense the Synoptics' claim of the Son is to be understood.

679 **k** **The presence of Christ in the world is the judgement of the world.** Whoever rejects him is already judged (3:36 and passim) though this does not preclude the eschatological judgement of the Son of Man (5:27). John knows perfectly that Christ is a cause of scandal, as Simeon had already declared. He became *sarx*, weak humanity, and as such is not distinguishable from other men. But his works and words are 'signs' which 'his sheep' understand. Those who are not scandalized, and by means of their faith penetrate the veil of the flesh to perceive the Logos in him, 'behold his glory, glory as of the only Son from the Father' (1:14). This realized eschatology must not lead us to suppose that Johannine theology forgot about Jesus' coming on the last day. The fact that Rev calls Jesus 'the Logos of God who alone knows the Name' (19:12f) points to the same school of thought, and it needs no proof that Rev is wholly concerned with the glorified Christ and the final redemption which will be wrath through him on the last day.

l All these sayings about Christ are retained by **the post-Apostolic Church.** Many primitive titles dissolved, but the halo of connotation around them remained and merged into its neighbour, creating a solid body of doctrine and corollaries that were felt rather than expressed. Soon, however, as had already happened at the time of John and Paul, assertions were heard that offended the sensitivity of the Church. The reaction which set in brought with it the need to clarify concepts and sharpen terminology. This was done with the help of contemporary Gr. philosophical word usage. But too much emphasis on disputed problems drove much of the NT doctrine into the shadow, as too much stress on the static study of the person of Christ brought about some oblivion of his mission. The Councils of Nicaea, Ephesus and Chalcedon gave added splendour to the theology of the person of Christ, and this light has illuminated Catholic theology ever since. While remaining loyal to the truths expressed by the Great Councils the modern theologian will do well to revive the rest of the teaching of the NT on the Christ and reset it in its redemptive-historical context.

6. THE CROSS

680a **The Kerygma of the Death of Christ**—Although Ac were certainly written after 1 Cor, Luke's account of the kerygma in chh 2, 3, 4, 5, 10 and 13 seems to have preserved a more archaic form of the preaching of the Cross than the Pauline formula in 1 Cor 15:3.

80a The immediate end of the mention of the death of Jesus in the apostolic sermons in Ac is merely to show that having been foretold by the Scriptures it had been foreknown by God. That the cross was a triumph, not a tragedy, is to be understood from the fact that God raised Jesus from the dead, constituting him Messiah and Son of God in power. Through him we now receive remission of sins (Ac 2:14 19; 3:13–26; 4:10–12; 5:30–32; 10:36–43; 13:17–41). In St Paul the kerygmatic formulation has already suffered an increase and assumed its final crystallized form: 'I delivered to you as of first importance what I received, that Christ died for our sins in accordance with the Scriptures, that he was buried, that he was raised on the third day in accordance with the Scriptures . . .' (1 Cor 15:3). Christ therefore 'died for our sins'. Is the new accretion a development of the older form or was it born in the initial stage of the Kerygma, but in different environments?

b We have already seen how the controversy against Israel had determined the form of transmission of the passion-narrative. The Jews objected strongly to a crucified Messiah, as they have done ever since. The first Christian answer was, therefore, to find passages in Scripture which could be interpreted as foretelling the passion and death of the Lord, thus relating the sufferings of Christ to the purpose of God. What was this purpose? Could God not have prevented the death of his Anointed? Was it really necessary that the Messiah should suffer, and if so, why? Such questions come to the mind spontaneously, and were actually asked by both Jews and believers. The answer had to be sought in two primary sources: Scripture and the words of Jesus.

c **The Passion Sayings—Had Jesus himself foreseen his own death?** And if he had, did he interpret it as the necessary outcome of circumstances or **as connected with the purpose of the Father?** We must try to work out the answer from the Passion-sayings in Mk 2:19f; 8:31; 10:12, 31; 10:33, 38, 46; 12:1–12; 14:8, 17–25. 34–48; Lk 12:49f; 13:32f; 17:25, and the sayings during the Last Supper and the Passion. But first we must ask the question whether these are genuine logia or merely creations of the community placed in Jesus' mouth for apologetic purposes. This could have been the case had the Apostles not been convinced of the fact of the Resurrection, which was their greatest proof of the Messiahship of Jesus. The suffering servant passages in Isaiah were sufficient as an explanation of the death of the Messiah, so why have recourse to what is tantamount to false witness without any necessity at all? It is certainly possible that Jesus' predictions of his own passion acquired an added colouring from the events themselves, as synoptic comparison gives us good reason to suspect, but we cannot see any valid reason for doubting that Jesus substantially foretold that he was about to suffer at the hands of the Jews, be put to death and rise again. The guards at the sepulchre are our best witnesses. Many of the synoptic predictions are mere prophecies of an event, but some others, which must be examined in detail, provide an interpretation as well.

d **The first hint at the redemptio-historical significance of the passion** is to be found in the logion in Mk 8:31: 'And he began to teach them that the Son of Man must (*dei*) suffer many things.' In biblical language, *dei* does not express fatalistic submission but indicates the will of God which leads nations and individuals towards a salvific end. Jesus accepted the will of God from the Scriptures which spoke to him of the Christ: 'The Son of Man goes as it is written of him' (Mk 14:21, 49); and in other places he cites certain texts

which later became the fundamental testimonies of the **680d** primitive Church. Besides the references to the Ebed-Yahweh texts (explicitly quoted in Lk 22:37) he cites Ps 118:22f (Mk 12:10f), Zech 13:7 (Mk 14:27) and Ps 22:1 (Mk 15:34). In a sense, Jesus actually looks forward to his passion. He calls it 'his hour' (Mk 14:41), a word which acquires deep theological connotation in Johannine theology. His resignation to God's will is not merely passive, for he recognizes a soteriological purpose in the Father's will which forms an essential part of his mission. We cannot therefore speak of mere resignation; his is positive obedience. Is it possible to learn God's purpose from the passion-sayings?

In the Markan text quoted above **the Danielic passage** **e** **on the Son of Man and the Servant songs of Isaiah converge on Jesus,** who affirms that it is written of the Son of Man that he must suffer (Mk 14:21, 49). However, there are no traces of a suffering Son of Man either in the OT or in Judaism. In 1 Henoch 46:4–9 the Servant terminology is only faintly reflected in sayings about the Son of Man, hence we can only presume that the convergence had only started in late Judaism but was brought to completion by Jesus. It is also useful to bear in mind that in the Prophets both the Suffering Servant and the Son of Man at times denote an individual, at times stand for the whole of Israel. In the NT they are referred to the historical person of Jesus but the collective idea is constantly in the background, so that especially in St Paul, the transition from 'Christ' as individual to 'Christ' as collectivity becomes not only natural but also traditional.

We now come to **the classical logion in Mk 10:45:** **f** '. . . whoever would be first among you must be slave of all. For the Son of Man also came not to be served but to serve, and to give his life as a ransom for many' (*lutron anti pollon*). Is this saying genuine, or is it merely later doctrine distilled from Is 53 and attributed to Jesus? The word *lutron* is a *hapax* in the NT; the Church used *apolutrōsis* or *lutrōsis* to express the same thought. It would have been more logical to find the common terminology in Jesus' mouth had the saying been attributed to him from later theology. The very use of the word, therefore, is a sign of genuineness. But what does it mean, especially with the preposition *anti*? *Lutron* was the price paid to ransom or redeem anything from slave to a pawned bracelet. The act of redemption itself was called *lutrōsis*. While the secular meaning of ransom or price of ransom remained but tended to fade into the background in the OT, the group *lutron lutrōsis* became more and more connected with *gō'ēl* (redeemer). The *gō'ēl* can be the next of kin redeeming a relative from bankruptcy, but it was usually referred to God who redeemed Israel from Egyptian bondage and from Babylonian captivity (cf Is 41:14; 43:1; 44:6; Dt 7:8). In Mk 10:45 the basic significance of a price paid for deliverance is certainly present (Cf 1 Pt 1:18f), but the context calls for an interpretation in terms of the '*ebed Yahweh* song in Is 53. The logion, in fact, speaks of (1) serving (obedience); (2) of giving one's life; (3) ransom; (4) vicarious payment (*anti*); (5) of the multitude which enjoys the benefits of this ransom. All these elements are present in the Isaianic text. The Servant was 'crushed on account of our sins', 'the chastisement of our peace was upon him' (v 5); 'The Lord gave him up (*paredōken*) for our sins' (v 6); he was humbled (v 8) and led to death (ibid), bearing the sins of many (*pollōn*) for whose iniquities he was delivered (*paredothē*, v 12).

This theme is rendered more explicit in **the logion pro-** **g** **nounced at the Last Supper.** Jesus speaks of his blood

680g which is 'poured out for many (*hyper pollōn*)' (Mk 14:24) and of his body 'which is given (*didomenon*) for you' (Lk 22:19). The blood of the Covenant in Mk immediately recalls to mind the sprinkling of blood on the occasion of the ratification of the covenant in Ex 24:4—8 as well as the promise of the new covenant in Jer 31:31. Jesus calls his death his 'baptism' (Mk 10:38; Lk 12:49f), a metaphor which Paul later developed into the doctrine of baptism into the death of Christ (Rm 6:3).

h **The Testimonies**—From this summary examination of **Jesus' own interpretation of his coming death** we come to the conclusion that the nascent Church was in possession of a set of soteriological ideas which she could refer back to her founder: **The will and purpose of God, ransom, vicarious suffering, the new covenant and the supreme hour of redemptive history. The theme of sacrifice is present in all but word** for Christ's sayings abound with sacrificial terminology. **The Church now goes back to the Scriptures indicated by Jesus, looks up new texts** pointed out by the Spirit, and develops these leitmotifs into a more complete and comprehensive doctrine.

i **The OT passages** most frequently used by the Church for apologetical purposes are Pss 22; 24; 31; 34; 41; 69; 109; 118; Is 42: 43; 49; 50; 52; 53. Some of these texts, as we have seen, had been referred to by Jesus himself, others were chosen by analogy. The exegetical schools at work within the Christian community interpreted in targumic fashion not only the vv which were of the greatest relevance but whole *pesher* passages which provided the context, thus creating a rudimental theory of the atonement on which later more profound thought could be founded. Such passages as Is 52:13 which says that the Servant 'will be raised and glorified' (*hypsōthē setai kai doxasthēsetai*) became the pillar of Johannine theology; the connexion between Christ's sufferings and deliverance from 'sin' and sins is established through Is 53:5 (1 Pt 2:25); 53:10 (Rm 8:3); 53:11 (1 Pt 2:24); 53:12 (Rm 4:25; Heb. 9:28); the element of obedience alluded to by Jesus in Mk 10:45 is strengthened by Is 53:7f, 12. (Cf Ac 8:32f; Phil 2:7ff); the notion of *diathēkē*, Covenant in Jesus' blood recalls Zech 9:11 (*en haimati diathēkēs*); the theme of intercession in Heb. Rm 8, 34 is provided by the MT of Is 53:12 (cf Ps 22: 22ff) while the whole of Is 53 (especially v 10) harps on the theme of sacrifice. The word 'redemption' recurs frequently in the Pss; in Ps 34:22 (a passion psalm, cf v 20) we find the word '*lutron*' with reference to 'the souls (lives) or his servants'.

From these texts alone the Church was already able to form a connected statement that Jesus was obedient to God's will unto death. This death was an offering for sin, through it we are redeemed and receive forgiveness of sins. Thus the New Covenant foretold by Jeremiah is established in Christ's blood. God exalted and glorified his Servant who now makes intercession for us.

j **The Notion of Sacrifice**—The part of this train of thought which needed most clarification was that about **the sacrificial aspect of Christ's death. How was it developed by the Church**? As usual, the first source of reference was the OT, but we shall also see that rabbinic theology too left its mark on NT teaching.

k **In the pagan world** around Israel, sacrifice played an essential part in almost every cult. It was considered as a gift to the deity or semi-deity to render him propitious. There was little, if any, correspondence between the act of propitiation and the internal ethical disposition of the offerer (Cf K. Prümm, *Religionsgeschichtliches Handbuch*, 490—504). **The OT** is much more logical

about sacrifice, both as regards the act itself and as **680** regards the disposition of the offerer. Whatever may have been the primitive pre-biblical meaning of animal sacrifice, the Priestly Code gave a theological explanation which held its own even in NT times. Lv 17:11 prohibits the eating of blood 'for the life (*nepeš*) of the flesh is in the blood; and I have given it for you upon the altar to make atonement for your souls; for it is the blood that makes atonement, by reason of the life'. We can call this the priestly view. It has its foundation in the Israelite dogma that God is Lord of life (Nm 27:16; Job 12:10; 34:14; Ps 104:29f) which he takes back because of sin (Gn 3). Although the word for life used in Hebrew is *nepeš* it still retains the connotation of physical life as symbolical of transcendental life. Hence the philosophy of sacrifice is the recognition that God is the sole master of life, and that our lives are strictly due to him because of our sins; in sacrifice man dies a symbolical death that he may receive back his life in God's friendship.

It is evident that such a rational explanation in the **l** OT appears late, and was a product of reflection on the part of both priest and offerer. And we must not be surprised to find popular piety degenerating into formalism that recalls magic. It is against such degeneration of cultic piety that the prophets thundered. They did not forbid sacrifice, but they stressed the uselessness of the material act of offering slaughtered animals unaccompanied by internal acts of repentance and obedience. The classical texts are Is 1:10—20; 66:1, 4; Ps 50:8ff; Jer 6:20ff; 7:21ff; Hos 6:6; 8:11ff; Am 4:4; 5:22 etc. In all these passages the emphasis lies on obedience to the law and a contrite heart.

The heritage of the prophets passed on to **the rabbis**. **m** They too did not disapprove of sacrifice as such, in fact Yoma 5a has the same saying as Heb. 9:22: 'There is no atonement except by blood', and Yoma 8, 8 in the Mishnah affirms that sin-offering and unconditional guilt-offering effect atonement (both these texts were written after the destruction of the temple and the cessation of sacrifice), but 'death and the Day of Atonement effect reconciliation if there is repentance'. The typical outlook of the rabbis was the 'prophetic view' which laid more stress on internal disposition, especially repentance and observance of the Torah, than on the cultic rites themselves. While the temple was still standing the Pharisees respected the institution, while proclaiming loudly that it was the disposition of the heart that counted; but after the destruction of Jerusalem with the cessation of sacrifices, repentance and good works remained the only means of expiation. Of course the disappearance of the institution was deeply felt, but it was not considered as indispensable. Rabbi Johannan ben Zakkai's attitude can be considered as typical: 'Do not grieve, my son (at the destruction of the temple), for we have an atonement which is just as good, namely, deeds of mercy' (Abot d. R. Nathan 4, 5; cf Moore, *Judaism*, 1, 503).

This rabbinic solution led to the development of another **n** set of ideas which provided a background to Pauline doctrine on the atonement: **the treasury of merits** and the doctrine of **vicarious atonement**. The calculation of a man's merits in proportion to his good works was almost mathematical in Judaism. Marks gained for good works made up for those lost through sin, and a superabundance of merits in one saint, especially the Patriarchs, could be distributed among the whole of Israel (R. Stewart, *Rabbinic Theology*, 1961, 127—32). This way of thinking was repugnant to Paul in so far as it was applied to man, but it was constantly in his mind when speaking about the work of Christ in favour of mankind. Another Jewish

80n theory which Paul and the Church possibly took into consideration was the *aqedat Isaac*, the sacrifice of Isaac. This was regarded as a sacrificial act in consequence of a divine command, which, though never consummated, had expiatory effects with regard to Israel's sins: 'Reckon to our account the *aqedath Isaac* who was bound on an altar before Thee' (Targ. on Mic 7:20).

81a St Paul: the Sacrificial Texts—From the foregoing considerations we can now understand how the NT authors who wanted to penetrate deeper into the meaning of the sacrifice of Christ had two ways open to them: They could either stress the value of the death of Jesus as a **bloody sacrifice** or stress the aspect of **obedience**. These two views are **not mutually exclusive**. We are only speaking of emphasis on one aspect or the other— the Levitical or the Prophetic. In actual fact our supposition is verified by the soteriology of Heb., which takes a predominantly Levitical standpoint, and that of Paul, who follows the prophetic-rabbinical tradition.

b St Paul accepts the Church's interpretation of the death of Christ as a sacrifice and speaks about death, blood and the cross as instruments of atonement; but he rarely, if ever, tries to answer the question as to the manner in which the physical death of Christ is a sacrifice, or why it was necessary at all. He brings in and develops the covenant idea, but the force of his argument lies in Christ's obedience unto death. Sacrifice, covenant and obedience are therefore the three main stays of Pauline soteriology, but in the construction he also interweaves developed notions of propitiation, ransom, redemption, reconciliation, etc.

c The main sacrificial texts in Paul are Rm 3:25; 1 Cor 5:7; 2 Cor 5:21; Gal 3:13 and Eph 5:2. Although the Levitical idea of sacrifice certainly lies at the back of all these texts, the Apostle's soteriology receives its primary inspiration from the figure of the Suffering Servant in Isaiah. In Rm 3:21—26 Paul affirms that since Jews and Gentiles have sinned and need the glory of God, they are justified not by any good works they might have done, but by God's merciful initiative. Faithful to his promises, God provided an expiatory sacrifice (*hilastērion*) in Christ's death. The *hilastērion* was technically the cover of the ark of the covenant which stood between the cherubs, and was sprinkled with blood on the Day of Atonement. We are therefore right in the middle of traditional sacrificial concepts with all their richness of connotation: the sprinkling of Christ's blood, the covenant, atonement, the High Priest, the Holy of Holies, forgiveness and death. These themes are later developed by Heb., but they are also present in Paul.

d In Eph 5:2 Christ's death is said to be a 'fragrant offering and sacrifice to God'. These words are a quotation from Ex 29:18 (cf Ezek 20:41) and bear out the thought later explicitly stated in Heb. that the sacrifices of the OT were a shadow of the true sacrifice of Christ. We are also led back to Exodus by the description of Christ as the paschal lamb in 1 Cor 5:7. John made much of this comparison. The underlying thought seems to be that it will be the blood of Jesus which will save the People of God in the eschatological exodus.

e Two Pauline texts on which so much has been written, but which still remain a crux, are Gal 3:13 and 2 Cor 5:21. Paul tells the Galatians that Christ became 'a curse' for us, as the Law puts under a curse every man who hangs from a gibbet. Is this merely a piece of rabbinical sophistry or does it express a theological truth in mythological garb? As Prat points out, the passage cannot be interpreted in isolation. According to Jewish principles of solidarity it is a member of the family, tribe or race that can make

atonement for the sins of his group; hence Jesus had to **681e** be 'flesh' (human) to redeem his brethren (cf Heb. 2:10—14). As all flesh was subject to the power of sin—which Paul simply calls 'sin'—it incurred the curse of God. Christ therefore wilfully took upon himself the flesh of sin—barring personal fault—and died the death of the cursed to redeem his brethren from the curse under which the Law had placed them. By becoming 'like us in all things' Christ was entitled to represent us before God, so that the blessing which he merited could then pass on to us as well. The word *hamartia* (sin) in 2 Cor 5:21, however, also recalls the Suffering Servant who 'made himself an *asham*, an offering for sin' (Is 53:10). Christ's death too, therefore, was an offering for sin. The same Isaianic passage underlies Rm 4:24f; 8:4; 1 Cor 11:23ff; 15:3; Eph 5:2 and especially Phil 2;6—9.

After a close study of the Pauline account of the words **f** of institution of the Eucharist W. D. Davies (*Paul and Rabbinic Judaism*, 1948, 253) comes to the conclusion that the Markan version of the Last Supper saying is closer to the original than the Pauline. The latter, although substantially faithful, bears a rabbinic colouring and possesses an interpretative element that shifts the emphasis from the idea of death to that of covenant (1 Cor 11:25). The blood of the Lord is a means of instituting the new covenant which consists in the forgiveness of former transgressions and the putting of God's law into the hearts of the people so that obedience becomes an internal urge not an external yoke (Jer 31:31; Is 27:9). In the believer this takes place through the gift of the Spirit (Rm 7:18; 11:27; 2 Cor 3:6). We have already noted that the interpretation of Christ's death as the striking of a new covenant goes back to Jesus himself. Paul develops the idea which will be developed even further in Heb. The Redemption is a second exodus.

St Paul: Obedience unto Death—Had anyone asked **g** Paul, however, in what specific way the sacrifice of Christ became efficacious he would undoubtedly have answered in typical rabbinic fashion: **through Jesus' obedience and submission to God's will**. The two passages which speak about this obedience, Rm 5:12—21 and Phil 2:6—8, are so clear as hardly to need any comment. Death accepts its value from obedience. It is perfect submission carried to its furthest conclusion, death (*mechri thanatou*). According to rabbinic doctrine, an obedient man can also atone for the faults of others and make up by his merits for their demerits if he forms one group with them. This lies at the back of Rm 5:19: 'by one man's obedience many will be made righteous'. Death is therefore the chalice in which the libation of obedience is offered to God for man's disobedience.

Propitiation and Reconciliation—A question which **h** arises naturally is whether Christ's sacrifice had any effect on God. Did it 'placate' his wrath, as the word 'propitiation' seems to imply? The English translation is misleading. It is true that *hilaskomai* does have this primary sense in classical Gr., but in biblical Gr. such a meaning finds no support. It is its secondary meaning 'to make expiation for sin' which comes out in the four passages which contain the word: Rm 3:25; Heb. 2:17; 1 Jn 2:2; 4:10. In neither Paul nor John is there any hint of an angry God being placated, but rather of a loving God who himself takes the initiative of providing man with a means of salvation: 'God shows his love for us in that while we were yet sinners Christ died for us' (Rm 5:8); 'In this is love, not that we loved God but that he loved us and sent his Son to be an expiation for our sins' (1 Jn 4:10). As we have already seen, the word used in Rm 3:25 has the added connotation of the Hebrew liturgical term *kappôreth*,

681h the cover of the ark of the covenant on which the glory of God rested, and which was sprinkled with blood on the Day of Atonement. We were all sinners in the sight of God and unworthy of his 'Glory', and as the sacrifices of the Old Law were not really effective, God provided **an expiatory sacrifice** for us in the blood of Christ and gave us a raft of salvation to which we may cling through faith.

i The effect of expiation is not the placation of God's wrath. *Orgē* in Paul, as in rabbinic theology, denotes eschatological judgement and punishment for sin (even in Rm 5:9) it is true. But this does not mean that God's sentiment changed from wrath to love through the Cross. Love and loyalty to his promise were present before the Cross. It was love that prompted the Cross and made re-admission possible (*katallagē*). Rm 5:10f and 2 Cor 5:18—20 make this clear: 'God was in Christ, reconciling the world to himself, not counting their trespasses against them . . . We beseech you . . . be reconciled to God' (2 Cor 5:19f). Through the Cross we therefore obtain *eirēne* (peace) with one another (Jews and Gentiles) and with God (Eph 2:12—17). **Reconciliation** takes place on a cosmic scale, including the heavenly powers (Col 1:20).

682a Christ and Adam's Transgression—In spite of God's love and condescension it is impossible to overlook the fact of **sin**. Paul's classical assertion, which summarizes numerous parallel sayings and reveals the background of Is 53:10—12 is to be found in Rm 4:25: Christ 'was put to death for our transgressions and raised for our justific-ation'. But the Apostle's most original contribution to the bearing of **the Atonement** on sin is his doctrine of **the expiation of Adam's fault through Christ's obedience**. The *locus classicus* is, of course, Rm 5:12—21, but the passage cannot be understood in isolation. It is an integral part of both Rm and of Pauline theology in general, and must be studied in this context.

b Paul's letter to the Romans is a panegyric of God's loving-kindness and of the necessity of faith in the work of Christ. The writer emphasizes the sinful-ness of both Jews and Gentiles to exalt the efficacy of the atoning death of Jesus and the necessity of faith. If sin had brought so much harm to humanity God's grace through Jesus Christ made up for it superabundantly. One man effected our reconciliation with God, as it had also been one man who had caused our ruin. The influence of the former, however, surpasses by far that of the latter (Rm 5:15).

c The Apostle argues from **the fact of death**. He means primarily physical death, but in the OT and in the Pauline epistles death has a strong moral connotation. It is the effect of sin, which in itself is moral death (Rm 7:13, 24) and leads inevitably to eschatological death. Its presence is therefore a sign of God's displeasure, in fact it was through sin that it came into the world, and one sin in particular: Adam's (Rm 5:12). Once Adam had com-mitted transgression he fell under the power of sin, the *yēser ha rā'* of rabbinic theology. The chain reaction of this evil inclination and transgression made 'sinners' out of the whole of mankind so that Paul can assert that 'all have sinned and are deprived of the glory of God' (Rm 3:23). The fact of being deprived of the glory of God is not merely the effect of personal transgressions, for even when a culpable transgression was not yet possible, before the giving of the Law, there was death in the world, indicating God's displeasure with mankind. The state of separation from God and man's deprivation of the divine splendour are therefore attributed to Adam's sin. This was a common doctrine in Paul's time. In the *Apocalypse of Moses* (20:1f), Eve reprimands Adam whom she had just seduced to sin: 'I know that I am bare of the righteous-ness with which I had been clothed, and I wept and said to him (Adam): "Why hast thou done this to me in that thou hast deprived me of the glory with which I was clothed?"' (Note the parallelism between 'glory' and 'righteousness'). The rabbis translated this into their own terminology affirming that through Adam's sin the *shekinah* (God's glory and presence) receded to the first heaven, and it receded higher up in consequence of other personal sins (Num R. Naso 13, 2). Consequently, every man who is born into Adam's family falls under the curse which weighs on it. Such a background of corporate guilt is a commonplace in the OT (cf Jos. 7:16—26; Ex 20:5). The tribe or family were corporately bound up with the common ancestor whose blood runs in their veins. Paul can therefore assert that 'we were by nature sons of wrath' (Eph 2:3). Moreover, as 'glory' in its fullest biblical meaning includes the power of God, his presence and guidance, it comes as no surprise to us that, when man is deprived of it, he lacks the strength to fulfil the purpose for which he was created (cf Rm 7).

With this in mind we can now understand vv 18—21 **d** more easily: 'Then as one man's trespass led to condemn-ation for all men, so one man's act of righteousness leads to acquittal and life for all men. For as by one man's dis-obedience many were made sinners, so by one man's obedience many will be made righteous. Law came in, to increase the trespass; but where sin increased, grace abounded all the more, so that, as sin reigned in death, grace also might reign through righteousness to eternal life through Jesus Christ our Lord'.

Christ, therefore, **through his Resurrection e especially, is head of a new progeny, a new Adam** 'for as in Adam all die, so also in Christ shall all be made alive' (1 Cor 15:22). If Christ's 'inclusive humanity' and 'inclusive Israel' have been glorified, it means that the whole of Israel and of mankind is potentially glorified if it is united to him through faith and baptism. Christ's resurrection is the foundation of our resurrection and the main argument of Christian hope. (1 Cor 15: 21f, 42—49).

From what we have said we can conclude that **Christ f saved us by way of satisfaction**. Sacrifice is the supreme act of adoration, the offering of life itself in obedience to God. The purpose of creation, especially of the creation of man, had been the acknowledgement of the sovereignty of God, which led to life. The disobedience of the first representative man destroyed the purpose of creation. The supreme obedience unto death of the Second Adam re-established it. (Cf J. de Fraine, *Adam et son Lignage*, Bruges, 1959, 202ff.).

Redemption—Paul would have added that Christ's **g** sacrifice saved us by way of 'redemption'. The group of words *lutrōsis, lutrousthai, apolutrōsis, antilutron*, developed exclusively by the Pauline school, possesses diverse meanings according to connotation. In the OT the *gôêl* is usually the next-of-kin who brings a relative out of debt, therefore, from bondage. Hence the *gôêl kat 'exochēn* is God who redeemed Israel out of Egyptian bondage and out of Babylon (Dt 7:8; Is 41: 14; 43:1; 44:6; 47:4; 51:11; 52:3f, 12). He did not redeem Jacob by paying a price, so the parallelism is not to be taken too literally. In consequence of all the vicissitudes of history the word came to acquire an eschatological meaning (Lk 1:68; 2:38). In Gr. circles the word was strongly reminiscent of the manumission of slaves (*lutrōsis*) with the accompanying ceremony of payment to a god. Paul uses the term in its full richness of meaning. He connects it with expiation (Rm 3:24), sanctification (1 Cor 1:30), the blood of Christ (Eph

682g 1:7), sin (Col 1:14) and lawlessness (Ti 2:14). The blood of Christ is the 'price' with which we were bought back to freedom (1 Cor 6:20; 7:23). In fact Christ is the *antilutron* for (*huper*) all, an expression which is strongly reminiscent of *lutron anti pollōn* in Mk 10:45. Paul leaves the metaphor undeveloped, without asking to whom the price has been paid. To ask further questions as some of the Fathers did would carry the comparison beyond the intention of the Apostle.

h The *heilsgeschichtlich* sense of 'redemption', however, receives further development. In the same way that God led 'his people' out of Egypt and Babylon in times past, so now he redeemed 'a people of his own' (Ti 2:14) into the promised land of eschatological expectation. Definite redemption is a thing of the future and as such an object of hope which will be fully realized at the Parousia (Lk 21:28; Rm 8:23; Eph 4:30). Moreover, as the disorder caused by sin was cosmic as well as spiritual, the whole of creation 'groans in travail' until it receives redemption form the violence to which sin has subjected it (Rm 8:22f).

i Hebrews: The Aspect of Obedience—From the foregoing summary examination of Paul's soteriological doctrine we can state that the Apostle develops the teaching of Jesus taking into consideration the aspect of death, covenant and obedience. His main stress lies on obedience. He initially develops the covenant idea but lays no specific emphasis on the fact of the death of the Lord. On the contrary, **Heb., the greatest soteriological epistle in the NT, penetrates into the deepest significance of the blood of Jesus.** At the same time it takes the obedience aspect of Jesus' sacrifice into consideration no less than Paul, and the covenant idea recurs constantly throughout the latter.

j We have already examined the Christological doctrine of Heb. against the background of Philo's theory of heavenly patterns. Christology and soteriology are inseparable in this epistle, the former being the foundation of the latter.

The first two chh speak about **Christ as the eschatological revealer**, higher than the prophets, and higher even than the angels through whose mediation the Law was given. He is God and Lord (1:9f) but at the same time shares our nature in the flesh. Being a brother he became a perfect high priest on our behalf when he entered heaven after his resurrection (2:14—18). In spite of his dignity he was obedient unto death. Heb. translates this Pauline expression into its own terminology: 'Although he was a Son, he learned obedience through what he suffered; and being made perfect (at his resurrection) he became the source of eternal salvation to all who obey him, being designated by God a high priest after the order of Melchisedech' (5:7—10). It is Christ's obedience which rendered his sacrifice acceptable for God does not delight in offerings (10:5) but in acts of submission 'Lo I have come to do thy will' (10:7, 9).

k The Blood of the Covenant—The covenant theme is present in a full-length citation of Jer 31:31—34 which Heb. interprets in the light of the eschatological *ephapax* (the 'once-for-allness' of God's saving initiative) of 9:26. The new covenant consists in the forgiveness of sins and in the definite fixing of God's law in the hearts of his people so that the continual backsliding of the people of Israel will not occur any more (8:6—13; 10:15ff). With the death of Jesus the old covenant became obsolete and the new bond was established once for all.

l But the greatest contribution of this epistle is the illustration of **the sacrificial aspect of the blood of Christ.** The author has Lv 17:11 constantly at the back of his mind. He also makes full use of the Philonic heavenly **682l** patterns and of ritual worship in the temple of Jerusalem. His purpose is a practical one, aiming at confirming the faithful in their steadfastness, lest they be tempted to deny their faith. But he argues his point theologically on the basis of the new covenant given by God in place of the old one, which, being a mere shadow of eschatological reality, was necessarily imperfect. A new covenant also required a new ministry, which would be as much above the old ministry as the new covenant surpassed the old in dignity (8:1—8). The pattern of Jewish cult had been a mere symbol, a copy of the true original which would become real in the age to come. Thus the outer tent of the temple where priests entered to offer sacrifice was merely a symbol of the present age, the age of time. As long as 'the present age' is still in vigour a sacrifice is a mere symbol of forgiveness. So much for the priests, the outer tent, and sacrifice; but the holy of holies, into which the high priest entered once a year carrying the blood of atonement, represented heaven, the blessings of the Messianic age, which now become our inheritance (9:1—10). As the high priest entered the holy of holies carrying the blood of ritual cleansing, Christ the God-Man entered heaven, bringing with him his own blood. And as he was without blemish he could not offer sacrifice on his own behalf but on behalf of his brethren in the flesh. As he is the Son of God his sacrifice is not finite and repeatable. It is offered through the Eternal Spirit, who had led Christ in his ministry of obedience; it is therefore certainly acceptable 22). The author gives no reason for this general principle, is also eternal, purifying the conscience of the people of God and rendering them worthy of serving the Living Lord in the New Covenant cult (9:11—14).

Obedience was not the only constitutive element in the **m** sacrifice of Calvary. Death and blood were necessary because a will becomes valid through death. God had therefore bound the blessings of the messianic age to 'death'. Even the old covenant was ratified by means of blood without which there can be no forgiveness (9:15—22). The author gives no reason for this general principle, contenting himself to establish it *a posteriori* from the fact of the necessity of sacrifice in the old law. But at the back of his mind is the saying in Lv 17:11 according to which blood belongs to God because in it is life. God is the giver and sole master of life, which he takes back as a punishment for sin. The constant recurrence of death in nature and in ritual reminded man of his debt to God (10:3). The death of the Son of God on behalf of his brethren in the flesh was a perfect sacrifice which occurred once at the end of the old age obtaining forgiveness and releasing eschatological life. It is this 'once-for-allness' that marks the superiority of the NT. The death of the old age through the death of the Son of God rendered valid God's *diathēkē* ('will' or 'covenant') and gave us the inheritance of his promises (9:23—28).

Even in Heb., however, **final redemption** will be **n** achieved when the New Israel will be gathered together with the High Priest in the Holy of Holies, the Tabernacle not made by hands, the eternal Sabbatical Rest, the abode of the Heavenly Patterns. All this will take place **at the Parousia.** At present we look forward to the day when Christ will come 'to save those who are eagerly waiting for him' (9:28).

The Soteriological Value of the Resurrection—The **683a** bridge that spans the period between the death of Jesus and his Second Coming is **the Resurrection**. The annunciation of **the fact of the Resurrection** belongs to the most primitive strata of the Kerygma. Samples of such preaching are to be found in Ac 2:14—36; 3:12—26;

683a 4:8—12; 5:29—32; 10:34—43; 1 Cor 15:1—9; Mk 16:9—15 and in the well polished Resurrection narratives in the Gospels. In a form-critical study of the Resurrection Kerygma, Dodd discovered a pattern which includes five elements: (1) The missing Lord; (2) The appearance of Jesus; (3) Greetings formula; (4) Joy of the apostles at recognizing Jesus; (5) A word of command. The accompanying post-Resurrection stories in the Gospels are usually of an apologetical or didactic nature (C. H. Dodd 'Essay in the Form-Criticism of the Gospels' in *Studies in the Gospels*, ed. D. E. Nineham, 9—35). When we speak of the Resurrection as having an apologetical function, this is not to be understood in the same sense as when we speak of Passion-apologetics. The apostles were really apologetic about the Passion, and sought to persuade the Jews that it did not constitute any objection to the Messiahship of Jesus as it had been foreknown by God. But they used the Resurrection as a first class proof of Jesus' messianic dignity. They themselves had been witnesses of the appearances of the Lord, and Jesus himself had foretold his resurrection (Mk 8:31; 9:9f, 31; 10:34; 14:28). The Scriptures had also foreseen the victory and glorification of the Righteous Sufferer as well as the enthronement of the Messianic King at the right hand of God (Pss 110:1f; 22:19—31; 16:8—11; 118:22; Is 53:10—12). It is more difficult for us to understand why the announcers of the gospel insisted that it was not merely the Resurrection that took place in accordance with the Scriptures but also the fact that Jesus rose again on the third day. Ex 19:10f; Hos 6:2 and Jn 1:17 may seem rather far-fetched as testimonies but, as Richardson (p. 192) rightly remarks, what refers to Israel is understood to refer to the Messianic King as well, in whom the nation finds its fullest representative. The sequence election-witness-suffering-glorification as referring to Israel is the pattern on which the Gospels are based and repeats itself in Ac with reference to the Church

b The Church, therefore, made use of the Resurrection to prove that Jesus is the Christ. It was also affirmed from the very beginning that **faith in the Risen Christ brings salvation**. But it was only later that **the soteriological significance** of this event was more deeply understood. Echoes of the primitive phrase 'the power of the Resurrection', which refers to the soteriological power with which Christ was endowed at his glorification, and which made itself manifest at Pentecost, are to be found in Rm 1:3f; Phil 3:10; Eph 1:19f; 1 Pt 1:3; 3:21. The classical saying is Rm 4:25: Jesus 'was put to death for our trespasses and raised for our justification'. **The efficacy of the Resurrection** is placed at a par with that of Jesus' death with reference to the mystery of reconciliation. It is thus the foundation of our faith and hope, not only because it provides us with a solid argument for the Messiahship of Jesus, but also, and mainly, because it is through the Risen Christ that the eschatological blessings which God had prepared for mankind, and which became ours at the sacrificial death of Jesus, were actually communicated to us. It is the **Risen Christ who sends down the Spirit** received at his enthronement (Ac 2:33). As with the death of Jesus all those who enter into relationship with him through Baptism underwent symbolical and representative death as an atonement for their sins (Rm 6:3—7), so through his resurrection we too have risen again with Christ. If the Second Adam is in Heaven the whole of mankind is potentially there too, and the believer lives in the hope of his actual resurrection. Such is the Pauline argument in 1 Cor 15:12—28 (cf Rm 6:5—9; Col 2:12; 3:1).

c **The Victory of the Risen Christ**—The authority and

power with which the pre-existent Son of God had been **683c** endowed before his Incarnation, and which had been hidden during his earthly life, were received back at the resurrection. **The whole of creation is given to Christ** that he may exercise his saving power on man, spirit, and matter (Mt 28:18; Mk 16:19; Ac 2:33; Rm 8:34; 1 Cor 15:25; Eph 1:20; Heb. 1:3; 1 Pt 3:22; Rev 3:21). This doctrine is solidly founded on the scriptural testimony of Pss 2 and 110.

The Risen Christ has been proclaimed High Priest; **d** he also plays the part of **the New Moses** who will lead the New Israel to the eschatological Exodus (Ac 3:17—26; Heb. 3:12—4, 13). In the OT it is God who is the *Sōtēr* (Saviour) of Israel. In the NT it is still God who takes the initiative of saving (Lk 1:47; 1 Tm 1:1; Ti 1:3; 2:10; 3:4), but Christ becomes *Sōtēr* par excellence through his resurrection. This title was freely given to gods, heroes and emperors in the Hellenistic world, but the context of the *sōtēr*-sayings in the NT is so biblical that there is little danger of misinterpretation (cf Jn 4:42; Ac 13:23; Phil 3:20; Eph 5:23). In fact it is the NT itself which points out to us the way in which Christ became **our Saviour**. He set us free from sin, death, the world, the elements, the power of evil, and from Satan.

Christ's main victory is that over sin, the *Yeser* **e** *ha-rā'* within us which makes use of our weak nature (the 'flesh') and the ineffective Law to lead us to actual transgression and death (Rm 7:7—12). Jesus now gives us his own Law, the Law of the Spirit. The power of the Holy Ghost is stronger than that of 'sin' in our flesh. Hence the ideals formerly pointed out by the Law of Moses but unattainable because the Law was powerless, can now be actually lived through the power of the Spirit (Rm 8:2—5). It is true that physical **death** continues to reap believer and unbeliever alike, but even this last enemy will be conquered by Christ before he submits his Kingdom to the Father (1 Cor 15:26).

The sphere of action of sin is '**the world**'. Once 'sin' **f** is conquered, even the world will be overcome. Although this is a doctrine which belongs to the Pauline school (cf Ti 2:12) it is **John** who makes it his favourite theme. Jesus is the Light and Power who rescues the world from the darkness and destitution in which it lay before the Incarnation (Jn 1:9; 3:19; 8:12; 12:46f; 16:33; 1 Jn 4:17; 5:4f). The Johannine Christ has therefore full right to be called 'The Saviour of the world' (1 Jn 4:14).

As it is not against flesh and blood alone that man has **g** to combat, but also against **the powers** that lord it over this world (Eph 6:12), even these spirits must be brought into subjection if Christ's victory is to be complete. Through the Cross they have been actually reduced to impotence and their defeat will be complete at the final Redemption (1 Cor 2:6ff; 15:24). At present however: 'I am sure that neither death, nor life, nor angels, nor principalities, nor things present, nor things to come . . . will be able to separate us from the love of God in Christ Jesus our Lord' (Rm 8:38f). The same victory is described in military terms in Col 2:15 and Eph 6:12. Both Paul and Rev draw upon OT imagery to describe Christ's victory over the powers of evil. Pss 74:12—14; 89:8—10; Job 9:13; 26:12f even make use of mythological figures such as the allegory of Yahweh's conflict with the dragon. The NT authors feel authorized to adopt this imagery applying it to Jesus against a background of contemporary theology based on later writings of the OT, the Apocrypha, and the words of the Master Himself (Rev 2:7, 11, 17, 26; 3:5, 12, 21; 21:7).

The commander-in-chief of the enemy forces is Satan, **h** who will be vanquished by Christ in single combat. Jesus

83h referred to Satan during his ministry (Mk 3:22–27; Lk 10:18; Mt 8:29). But the victory is really eschatological (Rev 12:7–17; 19:20f; 20:1–3). In the present age Satan is rendered innocuous (Rm 16:20).

i Angels and men on earth and in Hades acknowledge **the victory of the Lord** (Phil 2:10), which also **extends backwards in time**. However 1 Pt 3:19 may be understood, the essence of its theological concept is that Jesus' death profited those who died before Christ. Rm 10:7 and Eph 4:8–10 point in the same direction (cf Schelkle, *Petrusbriefe*, TKNT, 104ff).

j **St John**—The doctrine of redemption through the death of Christ was so developed by Paul and his school that later authors had very little, if anything, to add, even if soteriology retained its central position in their writings. **John** himself, who made such an enormous contribution to Christology, has little original material in his soteriology. In his latest book, *The Cross of Christ*, Vincent Taylor, who has spent his life researching the biblical doctrine of the Atonement, concludes that John translated into his own terminology the common doctrine of the Church and of earlier writers. Taylor considers as distinctive of John the doctrine on 'glorification', 'exaltation' and 'judgement' which we have already considered in the preceding chapter.

k **Theories of the Atonement**—It is not the work of the biblical theologian to construct a 'theory' of the Atonement. Certain extremist theories like the penal theory of Calvin which holds that Christ redeemed us by suffering in our stead the penalty due to our sin, even damnation itself, and the moral influence theory which goes to the other extreme and affirms that Christ redeemed us by setting an example of obedience are not to be rejected for what they affirm, which in part, at least, is true, but because they are very incomplete and do not satisfy the requirements of biblical data. Even J. A. Wilson's 'theory of mystical redemption' based on Johannine christology fails to satisfy the tenets of Pauline soteriology. St Anselm's theory in its original form is too juridical for our modern outlook but the doctrine of vicarious satisfaction to which it gave rise is the one which fits best into the Pauline pattern. The NT authors quite understandably make use of contemporary theological words such as 'sacrifice' and 'blood' which today offend the sentiments of various theologians, who therefore try to 'demythologize' soteriology, making it fit into our philosophical categories. If demythologization merely implies re-interpretation in terminology understandable to the modern mind then little can be objected against it. But if it means removing the scandal of the Cross, which was as repugnant to the Jews of Paul's time as it is to the modern liberal school, the believing theologian can only console himself with Paul's sharp reply 'The word of the cross is folly to those who are perishing, but to us who are being saved it is the power of God' (1 Cor 1:18).

7. THE NEW ISRAEL

684a **The Self-knowledge of the Primitive Community**—The ecclesiological doctrine of the primitive Christian community did not grow out of some original kerygmatic enunciation, as was the case with the various themes already examined. It sprang from the self-awareness of a *de facto* existing community which possessed sufficient distinguishing characteristics to enable it to emerge from the community of Israel.

b When 1 Thes, possibly the earliest extant writing in the NT, came to be written, the Church had already been in existence for over two decades and had reached a stage of self-awareness which is reflected in the epistle. 684b The only author who purports to lead us back to the very beginnings of the Church is Luke. But, although Ac preserves for us some priceless traditions from the pre-epistolary period, they themselves stand in the service of an ecclesiological thesis which was only reaching maturity at the time of composition. This thesis lends its colour to the events related. It does not follow, however, that Luke's second book is unreliable as a historical source. The first part especially contains archaic traditions; but Luke's purpose in choosing and moulding his material differs from ours when we study the evolution of the self-awareness of the Church.

It is nevertheless possible to argue back even from c later writings to the primitive institutions and to the reflections to which they gave rise. Many of the ideas contained in the Pauline epistles especially are traditional in character and reveal an early stratum of thought. We must admit, however, that it is difficult, if not impossible, to discover a continuous line of evolution. Our only possibility of remaining on scholarly ground is to distinguish **three periods in the history of the NT Church** which correspond to three stages of self-awareness. The first is the period of **gradual detachment from Israel** ending with the persecution of Christians on a large scale and the consequent mission to the Gentiles (Ac 8:11). **The acceptance of the Gentiles** into the Church carried the process of reflection a stage further. The third period is that of **the 'later Church'** towards the last decade or two of the century, when the Apostles were dying out and the Church was preparing itself to face history. It is commonly called *Frühkatholizismus* in German schools, and already presents most of the characteristics of the Church of the Fathers.

The Church of Jerusalem—The Lukan passage Ac d 2:37–47 has nothing about it which excludes it from being archaic. It mentions certain practices which had already fallen out of use at the time of writing, and others which existed from the very beginning. Repentance and baptism in the name of Jesus, including confession of him as Lord (2:36, 38), were essential conditions for receiving the Holy Spirit (38), thus revealing that the promises to the fathers were being fulfilled among the 'people of the last days' (17). Moreover, as de-eschatologization is one of the main characteristics in Ac, we cannot but see in 2:39 an expression which recalls the eschatological community that awaits the coming of the Lord. The distinguishing marks of this group of Jews are devotion to the Apostles' teaching concerning the resurrection and messiahship of Jesus, fellowship, 'the breaking of bread' in addition to temple worship, and community of goods (42–45). Their daily lives continue to be totally Jewish except for the modifications just mentioned. In appearance they were merely another sect alongside the Essenes or the Qumran community. But their new beliefs were so fundamental that in the long run they were bound to lead to a final break with Judaism.

We can therefore describe **the nascent Church** as a e community of Jews who believed in the messiahship of Jesus and expected his return from Heaven to establish definitively the Kingdom of God, yet who, in the meantime, entered through baptism into fellowship with the Risen Lord, with the Apostles and with one another. This fellowship gained strength by means of the Eucharist. The driving power of the community was the Holy Spirit, the gift of eschatological times.

The Community—It is clear from the evidence of Ac f that the Church never thought of itself as a merely spiritual entity existing solely within people's souls. From

684f the very beginning it was **a tangible group** which could be counted (2:41; 4:4) and included certain less saintly personalities such as Ananias, Sapphira and Simon. But it is not easy to define its relationship with the Jewish people. It was neither a number of individuals with a definite faith like the Sadducees, nor a separate community living apart from Judaism like the inhabitants of Qumran. While continuing to share the full life of the ordinary Jew, the Christians organized themselves into **a community** with a definite programme of ends and means. The fact that they shared their possessions indicates that they took the Essenes as representing the fullness of Jewish spirituality, but they did not identify themselves with any of the 'monastic' sects because their faith was entirely different. The best word they could find to describe their own group was *ekklēsia*.

g Ekklesia. How did this word originate?—Is it a translation of an Aramaic original or did it arise in hellenistic circles? Had it been used by Jesus or was it placed in his mouth by the later Church? Is *ekklesia* the equivalent of our word 'Church'? All these questions require an answer before we can proceed further.

h Modern scholarship is of the opinion that the word was actually used by Jesus, although it is to be found only in Mt 16:18 and 18:17 (cf Cullmann 6, 108 TWNT). It forms an integral part of the logion 16:18, which enjoys textual security and is certainly of Palestinian origin. There is no reason why the primitive Community should have accepted this logion so universally if, as is alleged by those who deny its authenticity, it arose in Petrine circles in opposition to Pauline claims. The word used by Jesus was probably *qāhāl*, which is the usual expression behind the LXX *ekklēsia*. The Aram. *Kenishta* occurs too late in rabbinic literature (about A.D. 250) to be considered a serious rival, and the word *'ēdāh* is never associated with *ekklēsia* in the LXX. The question has its importance when we ask what the word *ekklēsia* means in this context. *Qāhāl* means an assembly, a congregation, and in the OT is strongly reminiscent of the Jewish assembly at the foot of Mt Sinai while the covenant is being enacted (Dt 31:30, cf Ac 7:38). The word is also translated *synagōgē* in LXX, but the acceptance of this name by a Church which wanted to distinguish itself from the Synagogue would have caused confusion. In fact the Church is only called 'synagogue' once, at Jas 2:2.

i What, therefore, **did Jesus mean** when he said 'I shall build my *qāhāl*'? We have seen that Jesus' main concern was with the Kingdom of God, which, though eschatological in nature, has also an earthly aspect valid between the Resurrection and the Parousia. The new wine of Jesus' preaching could not be contained in old wineskins, nor could the institutions of the Old Israel contain the spiritual dynamism of the Gospel. Jesus therefore felt the need to reorganize Israel and its institutions in such a way as to render them capable of becoming a vehicle of the Kingdom. This would be *His* qahal, the assembly of the New Covenant in opposition to the old assembly at the foot of Sinai, which had betrayed its vocation through unbelief (Cf Mt 26:28). The Messianic community would never betray its calling, because the gates of death—the dominion of Satan—would never prevail against it. This would be the community which would receive the promises made to the eschatological Israel. Twelve disciples were chosen to represent the twelve tribes, but allowance was made for the Gentiles to share the messianic blessings within the New Israel.

j It had been Jesus' intention, originally, that the whole of the Jewish nation should become his *qāhāl*. But the

disobedience of the Jews made it clear that the New Israel **68** would be limited to the faithful remnant of Israel.

When the need arose to translate Jesus' sayings into **k** Gr., the work *ekklēsia* had already been chosen by Gr. speaking Christians to identify their own community both because it rendered the idea of the New Israel and because it stood in opposition to *synagōgē*. By translating Jesus' word *qāhāl* (or whatever might have been the Aram. original) by *ekklēsia* the Church identified itself as it already existed with the community which Jesus had had the intention of founding, thus giving us the first authentic interpretation of the word of Jesus in Mt 16:18. *Ekklēsia* therefore **stood contemporaneously for the liturgical gathering of Christians, the group of believers in local centres, and the body of believers in all regions**.

The group-consciousness of the primitive Christians **l** must have existed from the very beginning and received continual strength at **the liturgical meetings**. They had a special corner of the temple where they gathered together (Ac 5:12); they 'broke bread' in private houses; they shared their possessions in common; but the incident that raised their group-consciousness most was the persecution which completed the break with Israel (Ac 8:1). **Faith and Repentance—The first condition for 685 admittance** into the New Israel is **faith**. The disciples are simply called 'believers', viz those who believe in the Lordship of Jesus: 'Let all the house of Israel therefore know assuredly that God has made him both Lord and Christ, this Jesus whom you crucified' (Ac 2:36). Lordship includes the Resurrection, glorification and Messiahship of Christ, as well as the Parousia. We shall speak at greater length of the nature of this faith; at this point it is sufficient to say that 'faith' is not merely a theoretical assent but something eminently practical. It is operative in charity (Gal 5:6; 1 Tm 5:8) and binds to obedience (Rm 1:5; 16:26). Thus it is the corporate Christ that atones from Adam's disobedience. Faith is the supreme act of trust in God's saving mercy as well as a grateful submission to his loving initiative. It is itself a gift and a gratuitous call (Rm 8:28ff; 12:3). Unbelief is therefore the greatest of sins (9:32), and loss of faith is practically irremediable (Heb. 10:26–31).

This strict requirement of the Primitive Church is **founded on the practice of Jesus** during his earthly ministry. **Belief in the Gospel** was, according to Mk 1:14, the chief imperative of the Lord (cf Mk 16:16; Mt 17:20). The motivation of this belief was the recognition of the 'signs of the times' (Mt 16:1–4). Jesus refused to produce spectacular signs from heaven, but merely referred to the fulfilment of prophetic visions through his evangelization of the poor (Lk 4:16–27), and only the poor in spirit could understand his message. In fact, righteousness and poverty were required as necessary dispositions that the word of God may take root in the heart (Lk 8:4–15 and parr.). Once the Gospel was gladly received the believer was able to rise to faith in Jesus himself as Messiah and Son of God (Mt 16:16).

The same practice was adopted by the Church im- **c** mediately after the Ascension. *Metanoia*, in the sense of a moral return to the spirit of the Torah and the prophets, was considered to be an absolute necessity for salvation. Faith in Jesus now became **faith in the Risen Lord**. The Fourth Gospel is very explicit about this doctrine (cf Jn 3:18; 4:48; 8:24; 11:8, 27).

Baptism was the third requisite for admittance into **d** the Messianic Community, beside repentance and faith. This rite appears as an essential element in the early traditions of Ac, and the Pauline epistles leave us in no

685d doubt that it was the ceremony of incorporation into the eschatological community. It is not difficult to explain the adoption of such a rite by the primitive Church in view of the current practices in contemporary Judaism. But it is not at all evident why baptism should have occupied such a central position. Jesus himself never baptized, though according to John 4:2 his disciples did. The apostles also left baptism to their collaborators, seldom baptizing in person (Ac 10:47; 1 Cor 1:14ff). We witness the growth of theological interpretation of the rite until it develops into the richest of biblical symbolisms. How did all this happen? In spite of its sacramental singularity Christian baptism did not spring from nowhere. It had its precedents as well as numerous factors which explain its development.

e **Purification with water** after certain contacts is attested all through the OT. The rite rendered the penitent suitable to participate in cultic actions (Lv 7:19f). The Essenes and the Qumran sectaries had baths built into their settlements, and seem to have used them for purification purposes. What interests us most in Judaism, however, is **the baptism of proselytes**. The rite of *tebelah* was required of godfearers who asked to become Jews, together with circumcision and a sacrificial offering. Unlike ritual purification it was administered only once and possessed a definite significance.

f Opinions differ as to how far back into the first cent. A.D. the practice of baptizing proselytes can be traced. But, as by the turn of the century we read of discussions among rabbis whether baptism or circumcision constituted the essential rite of admittance into Judaism (cf W Davies, *Paul and Rabbinic Judaism*, London 1948, p. 121), it is extremely probable that the practice is much older and that certain speculations found in rabbinic writings already existed in 1st cent. Judaism, as we shall see later on.

g **John the Baptist** practised a similar rite, which gave him his name. This, too, was no mere ritual purification, for it took place only once and incorporated the repentant Israelite into the Remnant of Israel, which in a spirit of contrition and humility expected the coming of the Kingdom of God and the Last Days. It was therefore an eschatological rite.

h We do not know whence John received the idea of baptizing. Now, with such precedents as proselyte baptism, Qumran, John's practices, and the baptizing activity of the disciples in Jesus' lifetime it is not difficult to understand why the Apostles adopted this rite immediately after receiving the Spirit. There was a difference, however, between **the baptism of the Apostles** and all that preceded it. The Risen Christ had received from the Father the blessings of the messianic age to be distributed to all who believed; so the Risen Lord's solemn command to the apostles in Mt 28:19 to go and baptize all nations describes a rite which was no longer a symbolic preparation for but a sacramental fulfilment of the promises of the messianic age. **The outpouring of the Spirit** on those who were baptized bore witness to this fact.

i The connexion between the 'spirit of purification' and water was already known in Qumran (1QS IV, 20ff), but the early Christians went further, understanding by 'Spirit' the eschatological gift promised by Joel. The early traditions insist on the external manifestation of the Spirit at baptism because it bore witness to the presence of the 'last days' and hence to the messiahship of Jesus. In later theology the argument becomes even more explicit (Jn 19:34; 1 Jn 5:6ff). In Ac 10:47f the Spirit descends *before* baptism to show the way to hesitating Peter. At other times the coming of the Holy Ghost follows the **685i** 'laying on of hands' by one of the apostles (Ac 8:17; 19:5). Luke is mainly concerned with external charismatic manifestations with an apologetic purpose. Paul, on the other hand, looks on the Spirit as an internal sanctifier. Baptism 'seals' the believer with the Holy Ghost (Rm 4:11; 2 Cor 1:21f; Eph 1:13f).

By becoming a member of the eschatological remnant, **j** of which the Messiah was the epitome, the believer also acquired **a special relationship to Christ**. He was baptized 'into' (*eis*) or 'in the name of' (*leshem*) Christ (Gal 3:27; Rm 6:3) just as people were baptized 'into' John the Baptist (Ac 19:5) and 'into' Moses (1 Cor 10:1), thus becoming members of the group that followed them. The relationship with Christ acquired in baptism, however, is not exhausted by the idea of discipleship or **group-belonging**. In Gal 3 Paul argues that God's promises were made to and received by Abraham's 'seed', who is Christ. The play on words is not merely formal. The faithful descendants of Abraham are represented by and included in the Messiah. They '**put on Christ**' at Baptism (Gal 3:27) and are 'established with him' (2 Cor 1:21f). **They participate in his death and burial** by stepping symbolically into the baptismal bath, and rise again with him when they emerge (Rm 6:3; Col 2:12f). Thus Christ's atoning death is not something performed above the head of the community. His obedience unto death becomes theirs through faith and baptism. Jews and Gentiles are incorporated into Christ's corporate personality as the epitome of the New Israel and of the whole of mankind (Rm 5:12ff; 1 Cor 15:20, 45). They become the new Corporate High Priest that offers sacrifices acceptable to God through Jesus Christ (1 Pt 2:5).

The entrance of the Gentiles into the Church **686a** contributed to as great an evolution in the concept of Baptism as it did to the idea of the Church itself. The circumcision and baptism of Gentile proselytes in the synagogues had been a common practice in Judaism, and the rabbis had made frequent reflections on such rites. Most of their affirmations about proselyte baptism could now be applied with the necessary alterations to the reception of Gentiles into the Church. The baptismal rite itself seems to have been similar. It was preceded by an interrogation of the convert to ascertain whether he was fully conscious of what he was about to do and of the consequences of his action. Then a summary instruction was given (Montefiore-Loewe, *A Rabbinic Anthology*, 1938, 578). We seem to have reflections of these practices in Ac 8:35 and Jn 9:35-38.

According to **rabbinic doctrine** Israel became God's **b** elect through circumcision, baptism in the Red Sea and sacrifice. Similarly the proselyte becomes a true Israelite through baptism, circumcision and sacrifice (G. F. Moore, *Judaism*, 1, 1927, 331ff). He thus became a 'newly-born child' (*Yeb* 62a; *Berakoth* 47c) and a co-heir of Israel (*Rabb. Anthol.* 560); his sins were forgiven him (ibid p. 210) and he could now walk under the protection of the Shekinah (ibid p. 569ff) having become a son of Abraham (ibid pp. 276; 564; 574). The similarity of this doctrine to that of Paul hardly needs pointing out. The Apostle connects the crossing of the Red Sea with the *Shekinah* in Baptism (1 Cor 10:1ff); the Gentiles become co-heirs of Christ (Eph 3:6); their sins are forgiven them (1 Cor 6:11); and they become the seed of Abraham (Gal 3:7). The theme of the newly born child is taken up later (Ti 3:5; 1 Pt 2:2; Jn 3:5-8).

The fusion of Jews and Gentiles into one Church, **c** **the True Israel,** takes place **through Baptism**. Ac 2:38-41 already makes it clear that membership of the

686c Church is acquired through this sacrament. The Gentile passes through the 'Exodus' stage in the baptismal font (1 Cor 10:1) and is 'sealed' with a spiritual identification mark as the Jews were on the eve of their departure from Egypt (2 Cor 1:21f). They therefore become one body with the believing Israelites in the same Church (1 Cor 12:12f; Eph 4: 1—16). They are the new circumcision (Col 2:12ff; Eph 1:13f) and the true seed of Abraham (Gal 3:27). The baptismal waters give rise to the similitude of the Church as **Bride of Christ**, bathed before her wedding (Eph 5:26f) and also recall the deluge, in which only those who went into the ark were saved (1 Pt 3:20ff). The ecclesiological and baptismal theology of the Fathers of the Church is based on these metaphors, especially the later Pauline ones. The fact that some of them are rabbinic in origin does not mean that Christian Baptism was treated on the same level as proselyte baptism. The former had an entirely new significance. It was an eschatological sacrament that gave the Holy Spirit, not a mere sign of conversion. If rabbinic metaphors were applied to the new rite this was only by analogy for the essence was entirely different.

d **Baptism was not magical** in its effects. It required faith in the Lordship of Christ and a change of heart and *Weltanschauung* which was commonly called '*metanoia*' (Ac 8:12—17; 16:14f, 31f; 18:8; 19:5; and especially 2:38—41). The cleansing of the heart (Heb. 10:22f) and regeneration are bestowed by God only on those who embrace the new faith in all earnestness.

The Eschatological Community—We saw earlier that the Church considered itself as the community of the end of days. We also examined the eschatological expectations of the early Christians and their continuous state of tension. But there was another community in Israel at the time that also thought of itself as the eschatological community. Was there much **difference between the Christian converts and the Qumran sectaries**?

The Essenes, if such they were, regarded themselves as living in the end of days between two great events, the death of the Teacher of Righteousness and the coming of the Messiahs (of the houses of David and Aaron); The last days would be preceded by a period of tribulation and suffering. They too interpreted the Scriptures as referring to details in their own history. They compared their final salvation to a second exodus, which was expected to take place forty years (later interpreted symbolically) after the death of the Teacher of Righteousness.

e The exegetical technique of **interpreting OT sayings as referring to the Messianic Community** was therefore not new. The primitive Church probably had a school of exegetes who put into circulation of collection of 'testimonies' from the Torah and the Prophets interpreted from a Christian angle (cf K. Stendahl, *The School of St Matthew and its use of the OT*, 1954); these testimonies could have been either oral or written. The state of eschatological tension was also common to both communities. Anyone who reads the Habakkuk commentary however, cannot fail to note the arbitrariness of the sect's interpretation of Scripture which compares so unfavourably with that of Paul and the Evangelists. The strength of Christian exegesis lay in the persuasion that Christ had really risen from the dead, and was reinforced by the tangible experience of the Holy Spirit. Viewed in the light of these two events Christian exegesis, though stretched at times, is never artificial, stiff, or arbitrary.

f **'In Christ Jesus'**—Another factor which distinguishes the Church from the sectarians is the persuasion that the Eschatological Community already partakes of the blessings of the Age to come for through Baptism the Christian has entered into **fellowship with the risen** **686f** **Christ**. This thought finds its clearest expression in a phrase which must have arisen quite early in the Church, but which received its fullest development from St Paul: **'In Christ Jesus'**, or, alternatively, **'Christ in us'**. 'In Christ' is used 164 times in Paul alone. Very often it simply means 'Christian' or 'in a Christian manner' (e.g. Gal 1:22; 1 Cor 3:1), its opposite being 'in Judaism' or 'in the Law'. At other times it means 'through Jesus Christ'. Thus the Apostle can boast, have confidence or rejoice 'in Christ Jesus' (2 Thes 1:4; Phil 3:3f; Col 1:24). But in a number of cases it refers to the special relationship which the believer has acquired with Christ. We have already stressed that 'Christ' does not refer to the individual person of Jesus alone but to his corporate Person in the same way as Adam and Abraham denote the human and Jewish races respectively. We are Abraham's seed (note the singular in Gal 3:16) as well as the New Adam. Christ inherited God's promises, the Spirit especially, for those who through faith and Baptism have become one person 'in him'. **The concept of corporate personality** does not exhaust itself in mere representation, as a nation is corporately present in an ambassador, nor in family inclusion, as the offspring is present in the father's person as regards fortune and status. Christ is the inclusive Son of God who, through his Spirit, transforms the body of believers into heirs of the Promise. In many instances **'in Christ' and 'in the Spirit'** are interchangeable. They are applied to faith (1 Cor 12:9/Gal 3:26), love (Col 1:8/Rm 8:39), peace (Rm 14:17/Phil 4:7) etc. To be in the Spirit is to be in Christ for the corporate Christ is the Spirit's sphere of operation (Rm 8:9; 1 Cor 1:30). Hence we are sealed in Christ or in the Spirit (Eph 4:30; 1:13) and sanctified in either (Rm 15:16; 1 Cor 1:2).

Like all synonyms the two expressions have a nuance of **g** difference of meaning. The interchange becomes impossible when 'in Christ' refers to our election by God (Rm 8:39; 2 Cor 5:19) or to Christ as the second Adam (Rm 3:24; 5:12ff; 1 Cor 15:22; Eph 2:13), i.e. when Christ is represented as Messiah and as mediator between God and man (cf F. Prat, *The Theology of St Paul*, 1926, 2, 391ff).

The same force is possessed by the expression 'Christ **h** in us'. Christ inhabits our bodies through his Holy Spirit, as the parallelism 'Christ in you' and 'The Spirit of Christ in you' proves (Rm 8:9—11). He lives in the community as well as in the individual (2 Cor 2:5); He grows in stature in the same measure as the believer grows in faith (Gal 4:19). He even comes to replace our earthly nature, the old man in us, with a new personality (Gal 2:19f).

We can therefore conclude that **'in Christ' all that** **i** **happened to Jesus**: death, resurrection, glorification, gift of the Spirit, also **happens to those who become one with him** through baptism. Whatever Christ has done or has received, is likewise done or received by the Church. The best illustration of this parallelism is the Church's suffering with Christ. Ac present the martyrdom of the Church as a parallel to that of Jesus (cf for example, the Passion echoes in the martyrdom of Stephen, and Paul's culmination of judgement in Jerusalem). Paul is explicit about this identity in 2 Cor 1:5—7; Phil 3:10 (cf 1 Pt 4:13), especially in Col 1:24, where the Church is said to fill up the sufferings of Christ in his members.

We have already studied the activity of the Spirit **j** in the Church and need not repeat anything here. The Spirit is the essence of the New Law predicted by Jer

686j (31:31) which gives life to the New Covenant that comes into force at the death of Christ.

k *Koinōnia*—This participation in the messianic blessings of the Spirit in Christ is referred to as '**fellowship**' (*koinōnia*). In the NT the word occurs with various epithets: the believer has fellowship with Christ (1 Cor 1:9), with the Spirit (2 Cor 13:13), with God (1 Jn 1:3), with fellow-believers (1 Jn 1:7), with the Church (Gal 2:9), in the Gospel (Phil 1:5), in the sufferings of Jesus (Phil 3:10), in the faith (Phm 6) and with the Apostles (1 Jn 1:3). All these expressions tend to show that 'fellowship' was the current word that denoted the fraternal sharing of eschatological blessings poured down by God with the Holy Spirit after Christ's resurrection and distributed to believers by the apostles by means of word and sacrament.

l In Ac 2:42 *koinōnia* stands alone without any qualifying epithet. It almost certainly refers to the community of goods which is described in the subsequent verses and in Ac 4:32−37. The primitive Church based itself on the model of the Jewish ideal as lived in Qumran, Damascus, the Essene communities, and by Christ and the Apostles. When the number of believers became too numerous, *koinōnia* ceded its place to *diakonia*. The apostles were entrusted to collect contributions from Gentile communities for the sustenance of the 'saints' in Jerusalem (Rm 15:26; 2 Cor 8:4). This financial fellowship formed the substratum of an ideal spiritual fellowship in the universal Church.

687a **The Apostles and Peter**—**The Apostles** provided the foundation for this fellowship. Outside their common wealth there could be no *koinōnia* with Christ. They were the official witnesses of the Resurrection and possessed an explicit mission with full powers from Christ. In the OT, vocation and mission were necessary for the making of a true prophet (cf Ezek 13:1−7). In the NT it is either Christ or the Spirit who 'sends' (cf Mt 28:18f; Ac 13:3). 1 Cor 9:1 proves that the vision of the Risen Lord was an essential element. The Apostles received authority (Lk 10:16) and possessed the power to bind and loose (Mt 18:18). Of all these powers they actually made full use: they taught (Ac 15:23−29), reprimanded (Gal 1 and 2 Cor) and confuted erroneous ideas (Gal 1:8). The Pastorals reveal that their immediate successors were endowed with the same power and authority, as we shall see.

b If communion with and subordination to the Apostles were necessary to maintain communion with Christ, fellowship with and obedience to **Peter** were no less necessary. He was their head and representative, as his fellow-apostles bear witness. After his conversion, Paul feels the necessity of going to pay a visit to the Rock (Gal 1:18; 2:2) who was the primary witness of the Resurrection (1 Cor 15:5). Matthew and Luke as editors of the words of Jesus each in his own way arrange these logia so as to emphasize the interpretation with reference to Peter's leadership. The way in which Matthew annexes other genuine sayings of Jesus to Mk 8:29 provides a wonderful sequence which brings out Jesus' intention most clearly (Mt 16:16−18). Luke too, by making Peter put a pertinent question in 12:41; interprets the parable that follows in such a way that Cephas becomes 'the faithful and wise steward whom his master set over his household'. Ac bear witness to Peter's prominence as representative of the Twelve. He is the chief speaker immediately after Pentecost; it is he who takes the decision to admit Cornelius into the Church and who leads the momentous discussion at the Council of Jerusalem.

c Such a consensus cannot be explained without reference to a commission by the Lord himself. John **687c** attributes this commission to the Risen Christ (21:15−18). It is Peter's duty to feed Jesus' flock with the word and power of the Spirit. But even before his death Jesus spoke unambiguously about the primacy of Peter. The classical text is Mt 16:16−18 (cf commentaries) in which Peter is personally nominated foundation-rock of Jesus' own *qāhāl*. This foundation will be so firm that 'the gates of *Sheol*'—the resting place of unredeemed mankind, still subject to sin—will not prevail against it. The new foundation possesses the power of the life-giving Spirit who will ultimately triumph over sin and death among those who believe in Jesus. Peter holds the keys of the Kingdom. He is the major-domo who administers the blessings of the messianic age. Together with and at the head of his fellow-Apostles Peter has the power of re-ordering the New Israel in such a way as to render it an apt receptacle of the Kingdom of Heaven. This includes all those provisions which any head of any community is bound to make for the good of his society. The measures taken by Peter are immediately ratified in heaven. The orders he gives with reference to the necessities of the new *ekklēsia* have the same binding value as if they issued from God himself.

The logion in Lk 22:31f is no less strong than the **d** Matthean saying. Satan was about to provoke the loss of faith of the Apostles. Jesus obtained through his prayer that Peter should pull himself together again and in his newly found confidence confirm the faith of his brethren.

The Gospels contain no word about Peter's successors, **e** but they do not exclude them either. In fact the words of Jesus are rendered richer and acquire more lasting value if they are not restricted to the immediate contingencies of the period but projected into the Church's future and rendered valid for all times. As long as the Messianic blessings are to be administered inside the Church, and as long as adaptational measures must be taken in Christ's society there is need for Peter. Actually, the powers conferred by Jesus on Peter were much broader than those we see him exercising in the Primitive Church, thus leaving room for expansion to those who, in the *ekklēsia*, thought of themselves as 'Peter', and were recognized as such by the successors of the Apostles.

The Eucharistic *Koinōnia*—We have seen that the **f** Church is the home of the Kingdom, where believers are one in Christ and in the Spirit. They enjoy fellowship with Christ, with the Apostles, and with one another. The bond of *koinōnia* is the **Eucharist**, through which God's family can perpetuate its gratitude for the ever-present Cross of Jesus.

It is not easy to trace the development of **eucharistic g doctrine** in the NT. Except for the institution narratives in the Gospels further texts come incidentally. The Gospel narratives themselves are most probably crystallized liturgical formulas taken bodily from the altar and inserted into the story of the Last Supper. It is through the study of these liturgical sayings, however, that it is possible to go back to Jesus' own institution, for even though his words might have suffered some alteration his intention was preserved with the utmost fidelity by the Church in prayer. (Cf J. Delorme and others, *The Eucharist in the NT* 1964).

The four institution narratives in Mt 26:20−29; **h** Mk 14:17−25; Lk 22:14−25 and 1 Cor 11:23−25 fall into two groups Mk/Mt and Lk/Paul which differ in form but only slightly in content. Apart from critical questions which are discussed in the commentaries, we assume that the Supper took place in a Paschal context, with the Exodus narrative as historical background. The words of Jesus

687h interpret his death in terms of the Jewish liturgical action, which is an epitome of God's saving initiative in the history of Israel.

The figure of the Suffering Servant, delivered for the sins of many, lies constantly in the background (*to huper humōn didomenon* in Lk 22:19, cf 1 Cor 11:24). The sacrificial language of this passage has already been examined in the preceding section on the Atonement. The death of the Messiah is a real sacrifice. The shedding of his blood inaugurates the New Covenant foretold by Jeremiah (31:31; 1 Cor 11:25). The very word *eucharistēsas*, from which the Christian liturgical practice took its name, denotes thanksgiving for a free gift of God to mankind. The waters of eternal life that issued from the side of the dying Jesus reach the Church through the Eucharist.

i **The words of institution** contain an explanation of the rite itself. Jesus envisaged it as the Paschal celebration of the New Israel with references both backward and forward on the line of redemptive history. 1 Cor 11:26 makes it clear that the Eucharist 'proclaims the Lord's death'. It is an *anamnēsis* or remembrance of the death of Jesus. In biblical language the past is not remembered merely psychologically. Especially when it is remembered by God it becomes operative in the present (cf 1 (3) Kgs 17:18), bearing witness to what has happened. The Eucharist, therefore, is not only the supreme profession of faith in the death of Jesus; it also reproduces its power in the actual present. The death that took place only once (*ephapax* in Heb. 7:27; 9:12; 10:10) breaks in again during the rite and releases once more the saving power of the Atonement for the salvation of believers. It thus drives forward towards the ideal eschatological meal in the Kingdom of Heaven and to the final apocalyptic Exodus (Mt 26:29; Mk 14:25). Moreover, the identity of bread and body, wine and blood, provides the believer with food and drink that issue directly from the Cross. It offers communion with the Sacrifice of Christ.

j St Paul and St John, each in his own way, elaborate the themes indicated by Jesus. **Paul conceives of the Eucharist** as the new manna of the New Israel. The rabbis had believed that in the last days the miracle of the miraculous bread from heaven would be renewed (SB 2, 481). As the Atonement was considered by Christians as the New Exodus, it was logical to interpret the Eucharist as the New Manna (1 Cor 10:1–6). Paul also stresses the sacrificial aspect of the Eucharist. It is an altar on its own right, just as the Jewish and heathen sacrifices were an altar. And, as participation of heathen sacrifices led into communion with the heathen demon, so also participation of the body and blood of Jesus led into communion with the sacrifice of the Lord (1 Cor 10:16). The Eucharistic loaf is broken into small pieces and distributed to the faithful. They therefore partake of one loaf and of one Body of Christ. This participation keeps them united in one Body, Christ's corporate person. In this manner the 'Breaking of the Bread' becomes both symbol and cause of fellowship with Christ and with the Church (1 Cor 10:17).

To become efficacious the Eucharist must be received with the selfsame faith as is demanded by the Cross of Jesus. This faith should be operative through charity (Gal 5:6). Lack of charity profanes the Body of Christ, because it treats the sacred meal on the same level as common food. This brings about an unworthy reception of the Sacrament, and consequently God's judgement on the whole community (1 Cor 11:18f, 27, 29).

k To summarize: Paul's original contribution to Eucharistic doctrine is his clear affirmation that the Breaking of the Bread is **a real sacrifice**; that **the identity of** **687l** **bread and Body, wine and Blood** is to be taken literally; that participation in the sacrificial meal implies participation in the sacrificial death of Christ; that **the Eucharist unites the participants into the one Body of Christ**; and that the eschatological manna keeps the People of God alive 'until the Lord comes'.

St John makes no reference to the institution of **l** the Holy Eucharist in the narrative of the Last Supper, because he includes all his Eucharistic doctrine in ch 6. Jesus' sermon took place in the synagogue at Capernaum on the Wis (16:20) theme *'Thou didst feed thine own people with angels' food, and send them from heaven bread prepared without their labour, able to content every man's delight and agreeing to every taste'*. It therefore takes up the motif of the eschatological manna in messianic times. In fact, the setting on the Galilean mountain side and the grumbling against Moses/Christ recall the murmuring of the Israelites in the desert. This eschatological manna, of which the multiplication of loaves in a 'sign', can be interpreted as referring to the revelation brought by Jesus (6:35–50) as well as to the Eucharist (6:51–59). Jesus' words scandalized Jews and disciples in the same way as Jews and docetists were scandalized by the doctrine of 'God in the flesh' in John's own time. Hence the evangelist, in typical Johannine fashion, paraphrases in a targumic manner the Eucharistic words of Jesus to score a point against Jews and heretics in his own circle. His doctrine does not differ much from Paul's, but whereas Paul thinks of the Eucharist in a soteriological context John places it against the background of the Incarnation.

Being the food of the True Israel the new manna is the 'true food' (6:55) because it is neither symbolical as the old manna was nor does it belong to this world. Those who ate manna died (58) but whoever eats the flesh of Jesus has eternal life and is a candidate for the resurrection of the just (53f; note the realism of the verb *trōgein* 'munch' in v 54). Communion gives fellowship and inserts the believer into that same life which Christ receives from the Father (56f) and communicates through his Spirit (63); cf on Jn 6.

John's specific contribution is his crude realism in **m** interpreting 'This is my body'. Whatever mystical interpretations may be woven around the words of Jesus, no one who doubts about the Real Presence can found his denial on John.

The Gentiles enter the Church—The first turning **688** **point in NT ecclesiology** came about with the definitive admittance of the Gentiles into the Church. The fulcrum of Ac is ch 15, containing the description of the Council of Jerusalem. This ch stresses the doctrinal consequences of the persecution of Stephen and the conversion of Cornelius. These two episodes were vivid memories in tradition; they are reported so incisively by Luke because they mark the final break with Judaism and the turning of the Church to the Gentiles. Let us see how the author of Ac treats them.

The central point of the Centurion story in ch 12 is **b** that God has made the uncircumcised Gentiles heirs to the promise to Israel. The sign of the promise is the Holy Spirit, and **Cornelius** and his household receive it without either being circumcised or baptized, but only through faith in Jesus. In the Centurion's house a Gentile Pentecost takes place. The Jews had rejected the new religion, as their stoning of Stephen had demonstrated (Ac 8:1–3). The subsequent persecution stresses the caesura. Hence God's gifts pass on to the uncircumcised who thus become co-heirs of the Kingdom.

This reasoning, of course, is fruit of later theological **c**

688c reflection. At the time of happening, the significance of the events was by no means clear. In fact, **the council of the Apostles** met to discuss the signs of the times, their meaning, and possible consequences. The outcome of the discussion was that the Gentiles were accepted as full members of the Church without any obligation of receiving circumcision. Peter's main argument is the experience of the outpouring of the Spirit. The testimony is corroborated by quotations from the Prophets (Amos 9:11f; Jer 12:15; Is 45:21). The Spirit was proof enough, but the Church was not content with that. It had to defend its position against the Jews. As usual it turned to the Scriptures and to the intentions of Jesus; so also around this theme a group of **testimonies** was collected.

d Jesus and The Gentiles—The principal texts were, according to Dodd, (*According to the Scriptures*, p. 74ff) Dt 29:4; Is 1:9; 6:9f; 8:18; 10:22f; 29:10; Hos 1:10, 2:23; Hb 2:3f. They mainly emphasize the hardening of the Jews and their subsequent rejection, the survival of the faithful remnant of Israel and the incorporation of 'Not-my-people' into the seed of Abraham. But certain Christians might have objected that it had not been Jesus' intention that the Gentiles should be admitted to full fellowship with the circumcised. The Risen Christ had left the Church in no doubt whatsoever regarding his will: 'Go therefore and make disciples of all nations . . .' (Mt 28:19; Ac 1:8). Nevertheless the objection may be pressed with reference to **the sayings of the earthly Jesus**, and the evangelists had this objection in mind when they composed their Gospels.

e In an excellent study on this subject Jeremias, (*Jesu Verheissung für die Völker*, Stuttgart 1956) comes to the following conclusion: The whole question should be studied against the background of contemporary Jewish ideas regarding the Gentiles and of the missionary zeal of the diaspora Jews. The rabbis commonly regarded the Gentiles as lost; only through incorporation into Israel by means of circumcision could they have any hope of reconciling themselves with God, even though they could never rise to the status of full blooded sons of Abraham. Consequently every effort was made to bring Gentiles into the Jewish commonwealth, make them accept circumcision, offer sacrifice and be baptized so that they would observe the Torah. There were many, however, who accepted monotheism but did not receive circumcision. These were the 'God-fearers' from among whom most of the Gentile converts to Christianity came.

f Jesus had nothing in principle against the Gentile mission. His 'Woe' in Mt 23:15 is directed against the hypocrisy of the Pharisees who loaded the new converts with unbearable human traditions without themselves observing the spirit of the Torah. As regards Jesus' view of the Gentiles themselves, it coincided with the traditional scriptural idea about those who were outside the commonwealth of Israel, but it never degenerated into narrow nationalistic spite. Jesus remained neutral towards the Samaritans without surrendering the common Jewish claims. His background of thought was not political or anti-Roman, nor was he interested in avenging Israel politically. Rather, his rejection by the Jews (Lk 4:16ff; 13:1ff; Mt 23:37) brought him much nearer to the despised Gentiles than any of his contemporaries.

g Jesus goes further still. He positively promised the Gentiles a share in salvation; the Ninevites and the Queen of Sheba (Mt 12:41f), Tyre and Sidon (11:22) and Sodom and Gomorrah, who were denied resurrection by the Jews (10:15), are explicitly mentioned and opposed to renegade Israel. In the judgement *all* nations will stand at the throne of God, and will only obtain acquittal if they have believed in Jesus (8:10) and submitted to the **688g** Wisdom of God (12:42), if they showed mercy to the suffering (25:31—46) and repented at the prophetic message (12:41). These will be seated together with the Patriarchs in the Kingdom of Heaven (8:11) while their true carnal descendants can lay no claim on God's glory (3:9). God is not tied down to Israel in his deeds of mercy as Scripture shows and Jesus' miracles confirm (Lk 4:25ff). People will therefore come from E and W, N and S and recline at table in the Kingdom while the children of the Kingdom will be cast out (Mt 8:11).

Christ's redemptive activity includes the h Gentiles. The OT figures with which he identifies himself, the Davidic King, the Danielic Son of Man and the Servant of Yahweh, all announce the good news of deliverance to the nations. The saying in Mt 8:11 (Lk 13:28) refers to the eschatological pilgrimage of the Gentiles to the Mountain of God, a concept that condenses the OT doctrine regarding the manifestation of Yahweh to the Gentile world and the acceptance of his Glory (cf Is 2:3; 19:23; 40:5; 45:20ff; 55:5; 62:10; 66:18; Jer 3:17; Zech 2:11; 8:21ff; Ps 47:9f).

If such a doctrine was so clear in the Torah and **i** the Prophets **why was the Church so hesitant** when the moment came to accept the Gentiles? The answer is that the Gentiles were expected to accept circumcision and become Jews. The fact that the Spirit came down on uncircumcised people caused a revolution of thought which was not at all easy to accept by minds which had been trained to look upon all non-Jews as unclean and reprobate. It needed the direct intervention of the Spirit to make the words of Jesus understandable in their true meaning and shed light on the true interpretation of the Prophets.

The Testimonies regarding the Gentiles—The **j** solution of one problem raised innumerable others. What, now, would be the Church's relationship with the Old Israel? How would the new converts fit into the new structure? The answer to these two questions was sought out with reference to **the prophetic doctrine of the eschatological People of God**. We have frequently seen that the Church thought of Jesus as the New Moses who inaugurated the New Covenant. The Christians went back with their thought to the exodus from Egypt, the scene of the election and formation of the People of God. Ex 6:6; 19:5; Lv 26:9—12; Dt 7:6; 14:2; 26:18 are classical texts that make clear that God chose the Israelites as his own people delivering them from bondage not because they were greater or better than the rest but merely out of love, and out of loyalty to his promises to the Fathers. The essence of the covenant on Sinai was that the Israelites should recognize Yahweh as their only God and he would dwell among them to protect and bless them. When the Jews repeatedly broke the covenant, and wandered away from the ideal which God had in mind, the Prophets envisaged another people in the future, faithful to God, founded on a new covenant and ruled by the Spirit (cf Jer 31:31—34; 32:38ff; Ezek 11:20; 14:11; 37:27; Hos 2:3, 25; Zech 8:8; 13:9). The Prophets beheld the Gentiles, who are 'not-God's-people' as forming part of 'God's people'. The vision projected itself into eschatological times, so the Apostles were at liberty to apply these prophecies to the times in which they were living and extensively develop the theme in Rm 9:25f; 15:7—12; 2 Cor 6:16; Ti 2:14; Heb 8:10; 1 Pt 2:9ff and Rev 21:3. According to this development of thought the New People become the Temple of God, who lives in their midst (2 Cor 6:16; Rev 21:3/Lv 26:12; Ezek 37:27); 'Not-my-people' become 'My-people' (Rm

688j 9:25/Hos 2:23); they are redeemed from iniquity (Ti 2:14); a new covenant is formed (Heb. 8:10/Jer 31:31—34) the essence of which is the indwelling of the Spirit who teaches a new law; their mission is to announce the mercies of God who called us to Light (1 Pt 2:9f/Is 43:20f). The New People is God's own creation which is neither circumcision nor uncircumcision (Gal 6:15) but exists in Christ through faith (2 Cor 5:17).

k **What, then, of the Old Israel?**—What of the promises to the Fathers? These questions were the object of profound meditation by Paul, who gives an exhaustive answer in chh 9—11 of Rm.

Paul admits that the Jews have all the redemptio-historical privileges, summed up in the Person of Jesus Christ himself, who was a Jew (9:4). Moreover, the promises God made to the Fathers still stand; He has not changed his way of dealing with Israel, for he still acts according to the same principles. Paul's major premise is that the title of 'descendant of Abraham' does not refer to his carnal descendants, for Hagar's son and Esau both descended from the Patriarch and yet they are not the bearers of God's promise (7—13). God's election depends solely on loving-kindness, not on moral or ethnic factors (14—21). Now as God chose Israel freely he can extend his free elective purposes to the Gentiles in the present time (22—26) and incorporate them into the faithful remnant of Israel so that they will form the eschatological people of God foreseen by the Prophets (27—29), founded not on hereditary considerations but merely on God's promise and free election, so that no one can boast. The call of the Gentiles also serves as a punishment to the unfaithful Jews. Now it is no longer blood which decides whether one is an Israelite or not, but merely the one great quality which was present in Abraham: Faith (10:12).

l In spite of everything, however, **God has not rejected His people**. The Jewish remnant still exists and is incorporated into the true Israel: Christ. The rest are blinded only for a time (11:3—6, 7—10). They will see the light once more when all the Gentiles have come into the Church (11). At present, they are jealous as well as stubborn. Now if this stubbornness is proving so fruitful to the rest of the world, we can conclude that when they submit themselves to Christ the blessing on the world will be much greater, in fact it will mean the final salvation of the nations (12).

m **As to the Gentiles** they should remain humble, remembering that they have been grafted into the old olive tree and are alive only because they receive the blessings promised to Jews (17—24). Once the newly grafted branches flourish the broken ones will relive again (25f) because the gift of God and his promises are irrevocable (28ff). This chapter in the history of salvation has been written by God to show us that no one can boastfully lay any claim on God's favours, for it is from him that everything comes with only love as its source (32).

n **The Body of the Christ**—It could be asked, however, and it probably was very much discussed, whether the Gentiles stood on the same footing within the Church as the convert Jews. Or were they to be despised as people 'afar off', as the Gentiles were usually considered by the Israelites? Even admitting that they were 'near' (Eph 2:12ff) should they be treated as 'strangers', like the sympathetic Gentiles living in Israel, or as 'sojourners', like the ancient Canaanites who remained in Palestine? After all, these convert Gentiles were uncircumcised and not Israelites of pure blood. Elijah would discard them if it came to picking out the true Jews in the Age to Come.

Paul's answer is scattered all over his letters. We can **688m** see various trends of thought already taking shape in Rm and 1 Cor. But it is in Eph that his theories come to maturity and are exposed systematically.

The vocation of the Gentiles with no good works to **o** boast of and yet accepted as full members of the commonwealth of Israel forms the very core and essence of the 'mystērion', God's great mystery which had been concealed from the ages but is now revealed to his apostles. **Jews and Gentiles now form one 'body' in Christ**. We have already examined how Paul summarizes his idea of Christ's 'corporate personality' in the expression 'in Christ'. But to those who were not familiar with Jewish concepts—and this was something which was felt rather than expressed—the expression could mean little. So Paul uses a metaphor which was common in both Hellenism and Diaspora Judaism, and which came very near to the idea of corporate personality as applied to Christ: as individual person and as Church (cf e.g. Rm 12:4). This was the word 'sōma', body. It is used by Philo, Josephus, and by various Hellenistic authors in the sense of a society, and by Roman authors in the sense of a professional corporation (cf J. Meuzelaar, *Der Leib des Messias*, Assen 1961, 66 and 149ff). The word as used by Paul was more heavily charged with meaning than it was in hellenistic usage because it did not merely denote a society, but referred directly to the glorified body of the Messiah as well as to his Eucharistic body (1 Cor 10:17; Rm 4:27). At the same time, a parallel idea begins to develop in Paul's mind, that of Christ as Head (1 Cor 11:3f). At first the two concepts develop independently on parallel lines, but they are brilliantly knit together in Col and Eph.

Eph begins with a hymn to God's grace as revealed in **689a** Jesus Christ, bearer of the eschatological promises, who reconciles in himself creation and God (1:3—10). The final reconciliation is a thing of the future, but already in the present Jews and Gentiles ('we' and 'you') have been sealed with the Holy Spirit as a guarantee of our final inheritance (11—14). The Church, as the field of soteriological activity of the Risen Christ, is called his '*plerōma*', a Gnostic term not used in a Gnostic sense. It therefore 'completes' Christ by surrounding him with his corporate personality, the receptacle of his eschatological blessings, and at the same time itself is 'completed' by Christ in so far as his heavenly gifts perfect it continually (21f).

If the Church surrounds Christ as his extended personality it follows that whatever happens to him also happens to her. Thus, as Christ lives, has been raised up and ascended to Heaven, so also we ourselves who are included in him are made alive, have been raised up and sit with him in his heavenly glory. We have been created anew in him for good works in the same way as we had been created in Adam with sin as a consequence (2:5).

2:12—19 provides the core of the argument. Before **b** their conversion the Gentiles were alienated from the commonwealth of Israel, strangers to God's promises, living without hope in this world. They were separated by a high wall from the Chosen People (a metaphor taken from the Temple edifice), this wall being the Law. Now that Christ has died for our sins and delivered us from the curse of the Law, there is no longer any dividing barrier. As a New Adam, he has created in himself one new man, the corporate person of the Living Christ, in whom Jews and Gentiles are reconciled with one another to God. Those, therefore, who were afar off are now near: not through their own merit, lest they should boast, but through the pure mercy of God. The Gentiles are not 'half-Israelites' like the proselytes, but fellow

689b citizens of the saints (the primitive community of Jews in Jerusalem) and full members of God's household (19).

This 'house' is built up of Jews forming one wall and Gentiles forming another with Christ as cornerstone. It is founded on the Prophets and the Apostles and is a temple to God, inhabited by his Holy Spirit (20f).

c Paul claims that it is his privilege to preach this mystery. If Jews and Gentiles accept it with humility and gratitude they will both receive the fullness of the promises of God (3:17—19). They do not form two co-existing groups loosely linked together, but they are knit close to each other with one Spirit, one bond of peace, one hope, one Lord, one faith, one baptism, one God and Father of both (4:1—7). The Risen Christ pours down his charismata on both, providing his body with joints so that all members may operate properly (in love and unity) and the whole body grow to the stature of its Head (9, 15f). This is the practical purpose of the epistle. The doctrine of the 'Mystical Body' has its *Sitz im Leben* in the friction between Jews and Gentiles. Paul uses it as a theological preamble to any exhortation to love and respect one another.

d Christ and the Church—The Apostle further compares the relationship between husband and wife with that which exists between Christ and the Church. Christ is head of the Church in the same manner as the husband is head of the wife. This relationship is not merely juridical. Christ loves the Church, he nourishes her with his fullness, washes and purifies her from her sins and gives himself up for her salvation (5:25—29). And as husband and wife become one in matrimonial union (Gn 2:24) so Jews and Gentiles become one body, which is that of Christ the Head (Eph 5:31; for this interpretation cf 2:15). The two complementary concepts of Christ as Head and the Church as Body have now been united into a new metaphor.

e Once the reader has mastered the Pauline thesis as expressed in Eph the texts in earlier epistles become clear. Rm 12:4f, 27 adds little to what we have already said, but 1 Cor 10:17 is interesting. Paul applies the doctrine of the Corporate Body of the Risen Christ to Eucharistic theology, implying that **the Eucharistic Body of the Lord is the symbol and cause of union** between Jews and Gentiles, poor and rich, slaves and free citizens, who are all 'members' of Christ and in Christ.

f The metaphors of head, body and *plerōma* used by Paul might not have been new. They were current in contemporary Judaism and Hellenism, but their application to the recently revealed '*mystērion*' was entirely original and was the greatest Pauline contribution to NT theology.

g Paul's ecclesiology was not an isolated phenomenon. It developed together with other conceptions of the Church. We have already seen how Ac reflects the theology of its author. **Matthew** holds similar ideas (cf W. Trilling, *Das Wahre Israel*, Leipzig 1962; R. Schnackenburg, *Die Kirche im NT*, Freiburg 1961). He stresses the rejection of the Old Israel and the formation of the True Israel which brings fruit worthy of the Kingdom (Mt 21:43) through faith and good works. The good works, however, follow the Spirit rather than the letter of the Torah (5—7). The True Israel is not limited to one people but is open to all. The word of the Risen Christ in 28:19 is not an isolated logion but the climax of an entire theology. The structure of Christ's new institution is designed to contain the eschatological gifts of God's promise. All those who are called by God can enter and find salvation of which the intermediaries and dispensers

are the Apostles, Peter especially. Like the *Shekinah* of **689g** old, Christ himself is eternally present in the community to quicken it till the end of time. It is clear that Paul went much further, but this brief reference to Mt reveals that the Apostle's theology was firmly anchored in fundamental ideas which were held universally.

The Later Church—Excepting the brief paragraph on **h** Mt, the theology of the Church which we have been studying is based on earlier writings of the NT. The Church is aware that she is the eschatological community foretold by the Prophets. Her self-awareness is 'mystical' in so far as it emphasizes her relationship to God and to the Risen Lord. Later writings, **the Pastoral Epistles** particularly, reveal another facet. When we read these letters we are surprised to find an almost completely de-eschatologized organization which looks forward to a long life in history before the final end comes. Whereas the Church of the great Epistles, like Raphael's Plato, pointed upwards, the Church of the Pastorals is Aristotelian and points downwards. The climax of the Spirit's activity now lies behind. He is still active, it is true, but his main concern is to preserve rather than to create, to correct misunderstandings and defend the revealed truth rather than discover new horizons.

The Church is still 'the household of God' but i it is also the 'pillar and bulwark of the truth' (1 Tm 3:15). 'The truth' is the true doctrine transmitted by the Apostles, with an accent on the moral aspect; for with the disappearance of the Apostles the danger of anarchy and individualism set in. Speculations about 'the Law' and scriptural interpretation contrary to the teaching of the Twelve were being made (1 Tm 1:3—7; 6:3; 2 Pt 1:20; 2 Jn 9—11; Rev 2:15 et passim). This caused confusion of thought, life and order, and necessitated strong action on the part of those who best knew the Apostles' minds. The reaction was threefold: an insistence on the unaltered retention of the deposit of faith entrusted to the Elders by the Apostles (1 Tm 6:20; 2 Tm 1:13f; 2:2), an exhortation to the practice of virtue (passim in Pastorals, especially 2 Tm 3:1—9; 4:1—5), and a greater emphasis on Church order and authority.

The Deposit of Faith—Thus Hymeneus and Alexander **j** are 'delivered to Satan' (1 Tm 1:20), as the evildoer in Corinth had been by Paul (1 Cor 5:3—5) for having taught that the resurrection of the body had already taken place (2 Tm 2:17f). Others who held a form of Gnostic doctrine regarding prohibition of marriage, abstinence from certain foods and speculations about angels and genealogies (1 Tm 1:3—7; 4:1—5) were argued against with an appeal to Scripture as interpreted within the Church and by the Church (2 Tm 5:16; 2 Pt 1:10; 3:15) and to the living tradition of the teaching of the Apostles. Insistence on Scripture and tradition was typically rabbinic, but there was a difference in the authority with which the tradition was transmitted. The master rabbi, duly delegated by means of imposition of hands, taught with scholarly authority. The **'elder'** (*presbyteros*) or **'overseer'** (*episkopos*), also ordained with the laying of hands of the Apostle and the presbytery (1 Tm 4:14; 2 Tm 1:6; Ac 13:3) **taught with apostolic authority** (1 Tm 4:11) for his election was referred to the Spirit (Ac 13:2; 1 Tm 4:14) and the Truth was entrusted to him by the Holy Ghost (2 Tm 1:14).

The Hierarchy—In spite of the charismatic character **k** of the office of 'elder', appointment to it begins to be subject to 'canon law'. 1 Tm 3:1ff explains the essential qualities candidates to that office and to the office of deacon should have. It must not be believed, however, that

689k the existence of elders or overseers and deacons was new in the Church. Phil 1:1 presupposes their existence, and the author of Ac is certain that their origin goes back to the Jerusalem Church (6:1—6; 14:23; 20:17, 28). The problem arises when we ask what their distinctive function was and how they originated.

l In a matter of such notorious obscurity we had better start from the clearest period. **Ignatius of Antioch** who died about 110—17 leaves us without any doubt that every church, at least in Asia Minor, had an *episkopos* at its head, a body of *presbyteroi*, and deacons as three distinct and subordinate groups (Eph 5:1f; Mg 7:1; Trall 2:2; 7:2; Phil 4:5; 7:2). The bishop has supreme authority and represents Jesus Christ.

m The letter of **Clement of Rome**, written about A.D. 95, does not distinguish the elders from the overseers in name. We are informed that they offer (Eucharistic) sacrifice and gifts (1 Clem 44:4), but Clement also makes the comparison between the Christian officers and the High Priest, priests, and Levites in Judaism. This means that he knows the Ignatian hierarchy too, although he has not yet found a name for the 'High Priest' (1 Clem 40). Even in *Didache* the terminology is still interchangeable though we are informed that the *episkopoi* have taken over much of the work of the 'prophets and teachers'. In the NT *episkopos* and *presbyteros* refer to the same office (Ac 20:17 = 20:28; Ti 1:5 = 1:7). Their authority differed from that of an Apostle because it was not derived directly from Christ, as the Apostle's was, but through the instrumentality of an Apostle. It can hardly be doubted that in every city they presided over the liturgical services. One of them must have presided over the rest, on the model of the Sanhedrin where the High Priest presided over the chief priests and elders. In fact we find the Jerusalem Church in Ac 15 acting according to this pattern with James at its head. As long as the original disciples, who later received the exclusive name of Apostles or The Twelve, were living, it was they who presided over the body of elders. But when they started dying out and the congregations became too numerous, they chose one of their collaborators from the body of elders and gave him the power to preside and ordain other elders (Ti 1:5); he had the duty to watch over the congregation (1 Tm 3:1—7; 1 Pt 5:1—5). At a later date the presiding elder appointed by the Apostle or by another presiding elder received the exclusive name of *episkopos*, while the others were simply called *presbyteroi*.

n The eschatological community of **Qumran** had a parallel organization, also based on the model of the Sanhedrin. The Great Rule mentions the body of elders (6:8). A priest and overseer (*mekabber*) presided over the community (6:12—20; Damascus Rule 9:17—22). Levites are just taken for granted. We therefore have the *mekabber*, priests, and Levites as a parallel to bishop, priests and deacons.

o **The Two-fold Character of the Church**—Does **the juridical aspect** of the Church appear suddenly as a consequence of de-eschatologization? Is this a radical change in the nature of the Eschatological Community? If we suppose with Schweitzer that Jesus had had no intention of founding a Church, and if we hold that the Church was only an outcome of disappointment at the absence of the Parousia, then such an opinion would be rational. But we have already had various occasions to see that the delay of the Parousia was only responsible for a change of emphasis and not for a change of ideals. Jesus had the intention of re-ordering the New Israel to hold the new wine of the Kingdom of God. But in substance it was to be a continuation of the Old Israel, hence the **689e** parallelism of organization was not alien to the intention of Jesus, and the Apostles did nothing else but interpret his mind and obey the commands of the Risen Christ. This they did from the very beginning. Law, order, and sanction are to be found in 1 Cor. In the early epistles, however, as other themes of greater importance were treated, the aspect of Church Order receded into the background and only came to the fore when the need was felt to emphasize faithfulness in transmitting the deposit of faith. **The Spirit entrusted this tradition to an organized society.** The Church of the Pastorals is not a break with the Church of Paul. It is the development of a second theme which had been built up as a kind of counterpoint to the first main theme. The interwining and balancing of these two themes, the 'mystical' and the 'juridical', have always constituted the sonata-like beauty of the Church. A denial of either would ruin its loveliness.

8. SALVATION

The Kerygmatic Theme—All the archaic kerygmatic **690a** discourses in **Ac**, whether original or imitation, call for repentance, Baptism and faith in Christ, promising remission of sins and salvation in return.

'Repent, and be baptized in the name of the Lord Jesus Christ for the forgiveness of your sins' (Ac 2:38); 'Repent, therefore, and turn again, that your sins may be blotted out, that times of refreshing may come from the presence of the Lord' (3:19); 'There is salvation in no one else, for there is no other name under heaven given among men by which we must be saved' (4:12); 'To give repentance to Israel and remission of sins' (5;31); 'To him all the prophets bear witness that every one who believes in him receives forgiveness of sins through his name' (10:43).

The Pauline version, according to Luke, is: 'Through this man forgiveness of sins is proclaimed to you, and by him everyone that believes is freed from everything from which you could not be freed by the law of Moses' (13:38f; AV has 'justified'); But in Rm 10:9 Paul repeats the traditional formula: 'If you confess with your lips that Jesus is Lord and believe in your heart that God raised him from the dead, you will be saved'. Cf C. H. Dodd, *The Apostolic Preaching.*

The Rabbinical Doctrine of Salvation—What could **b** these words have meant to the average Jew who heard them? What did the Apostles themselves mean by them? To answer these questions we must first examine **the doctrine of salvation prevalent in the Synagogue in the first cent.** The man-in-the-street usually received his religious ideas from the sabbath meetings in the synagogue where the Pharisees were most influential. It would not be wrong to say therefore, that in spite of other sects in Judaism the prevalent mentality was that of the scribes and rabbis of the Pharisaic school. In our exposition we shall follow SB's excellent synthesis (3, 38ff; 4, 3ff).

The rabbis believed that the giving of the Law to **c** Israel was an act of love on God's part. It was, however, not entirely gratuitous for the Law had been offered to all nations, and whereas the rest preferred to follow their evil inclinations, Israel alone accepted it. Abraham himself had been called because he had come to know God of his own initiative. Hence he merited his vocation (Jos. Ant., 1, 7, 1; Jubilee 12:1). The world itself was created for Abraham, Israel, Moses and the Law. This last was given to Israel '*post praevisa merita*' that the Jew might

690c earn for himself even more merits. It should be studied in every detail for from its thorough knowledge obedience could not but follow almost automatically. In spite of the *yēṣer hārā'* which created difficulties, it lay completely in man's power to observe the precepts of the Torah. Even Adam's sin did not stand in the way of perfect obedience, for after all evil inclination was balanced by the good inclination or *yēṣer haṭṭôḇ* and by the light which the Law itself offered.

d Every Israelite, even the most humble like the *ammê ha'āreṣ*, overflowed with merits earned through his constant obedience. Every single good action was registered in God's account book, while every fault was written down on the debit sheet. Merits and demerits were weighed against each other at the judgement, and intrinsic meriting value, and God owed a reward to the tipped. We have already had occasion when speaking of eschatology to examine the Jewish notion of life after death, resurrection, etc. The individual who was saved entered the garden of Eden, and lived a life of bliss contemplating the Torah for eternity.

e The Gentiles had no hope of retribution at the resurrection; only *gehinnom* awaited them. Even the 'proselytes of the gate' were excluded as only circumcision made people candidates for salvation (R. Stewart, *Rabbinic Theology*, 1961, 147). It was commonly held that every Jew would be saved, if not through his personal merits, at least through the merits of the Fathers. Salvation, therefore, was based on man's righteousness (*sedāqāh* = justice, charity, almsgiving), and little if anything was left to God's mercy. There was no place for grace in rabbinic soteriology. Good works possessed an intrinsic meriting value, and God owed a reward to the upright Jew as well as to righteous Israel.

An individual's faults could be deleted totally or in part by means of personal atonement, including almsgiving and prayer on man's part and the provision of the sacrifice on the Day of Atonement on God's.

f Although this was the prevalent doctrine in Jesus' time it was by no means shared by everybody. Apart from the Sadducees who professed a rather liberal view, the 'poor of Israel' understood the spirit of the Torah much more profoundly than the Pharisees understood the letter and made reliance on God's saving mercy their characteristic attitude. The beautiful hymn to Grace at the end of the Qumran Rule was certainly much nearer to the OT than to the rabbis in spirit.

g **The Biblical Doctrine of Salvation** —We must now examine what **the genuine doctrine of the Torah** is regarding man's salvation. God chose Israel out of love: 'But not because of your righteousness or the uprightness of your heart are you going in to possess their land; but because of the wickedness of these nations the Lord your God is driving them out from before you, and that he may confirm the word which the Lord swore to your fathers, to Abraham, to Isaac, and to Jacob' (Dt 9:5). Israel's election, therefore, was founded on a promise, a free gift of God, not on any merits on the part of the Fathers. The only motive of God's action was love. Abraham's grateful acceptance of the promise was a supreme act of faith which was reckoned to him as righteousness (Gn 15:6). The Covenant, too, was a gift received with acknowledgement; every Israelite made an act of faith by reciting the lovely primitive Credo in Dt 24:5—10 previous to making an offering. God remained loyal to Israel as long as Israel retained her loyalty towards him, but in actual fact, Israel's repeated backsliding in history compelled God to punish his chosen race over and over again, without, however, abrogating

his promises to the fathers (2 (4) Kgs 21:12ff). **690g** Israel was therefore continually in debt before God. It was for mercy she pleaded not for just judgement, as the penitential psalms recited in the temple liturgy prove. If the first covenant had been rendered void through Israel's infidelity, God himself remained faithful to his promise, and again promised a new Covenant which, this time, would never be annulled (Jer 31:31; Ezek 37:26ff).

The piety of the nation reflects itself in that of the **h** individual: 'Enter not into judgement with thy servant, for no man living is righteous before thee' prays the pious Israelite (Ps 143:2). His relations with God are not based on the rights of the just but on faith: 'In thee I put my trust' (8); and if he walks in uprightness it is God who leads the way: 'Teach me to do thy will, for thou art my God' (10). Hence 'for thy name's sake O Lord' not for any rights on man's part 'preserve my life' (11). Ps 19:10ff and Mich 7:9 also attribute man's righteousness to God's action, but it is the Book of Job that presents the best model of man's relations with God. The pious sufferer is accused by his friends that he is being punished for his sins. Job protests that he is a just man (ch 29) and actually questions his fate, affirming that he is not being treated according to his works. God's answer out of the whirlwind makes no appeal to logic or mathematics but only to the divine sovereignty and wisdom. Obedience to God's will is merely a duty for which man cannot claim a salary; he can only bow his head before God and adore his divine Will and Wisdom, as Job does in his final surrender in 42:1–6.

The NT authors cited Gn 15:6 and Hb 2:2—4 to prove **i** the necessity of faith in man's dealing with God. He is the giver, never the receiver, for man stands continually in debt. The pious individual feeds his thought with meditation on God's saving actions in history and prostrates himself in thanksgiving.

The two pictures we have drawn of pharisaic and **j** biblical spirituality are diametrically opposed to each another. It must be kept in mind, however, that they are both caricatures. The Bible insists as much on good works as the Pharisees do, and among the Pharisees there were not a few who were outstanding for their piety. It remains true, however, that the general trend of pharisaism had deviated from the true spirit of the Torah. It failed to distinguish piety from faultlessness and identified righteousness with mathematical rules of mechanical observance or precepts. In the Torah disobedience is severely reprimanded, and no one who is disobedient can be saved. But obedience of itself does not constitute righteousness. It is only part of justness, whose essential constitutive is piety towards the Godhead, of which faith is the epitome.

After this summary examination of the biblical and **k** pharisaic ideals of salvation it becomes comprehensible why **the word of the Gospel always found a split judgement in the audience**. The letter-minded, those brought up in the traditions of men took scandal at the Cross, which 'is folly to those who are perishing' (1 Cor 1:18). The self-satisfied had no room for a redeemer (Gal 2:21); they redeemed themselves through their good works; they felt no need of *metanoia* because they thought that their merits outweighed their demerits. The Crucified Christ is considered an insult to the Law: 'for being ignorant of the righteousness that comes from God, and seeking to establish their own, they did not submit to God's righteousness. For Christ is the end of the Law' (Rm 10:3f). 'Their minds were hardened; for to this day, when they read the Old Covenant, that same veil remains unlifted' (2 Cor 3:14).

690l The pious, on the contrary, accept the coming of Christ as yet another mighty and merciful deed of God which completes the history of salvation. Their humility makes them acknowledge the necessity of repentance. Faith is already their habitual attitude. In contrast with 'those who are perishing' 'those who are being saved' (Ac 3:47) 'receive the word with eagerness, examining the scriptures daily to see if these things are so' (cf 17:11). In the last resort, it is the spirit of Scripture that renders witness to the Apostles' preaching; even miracles only persuade if Moses is listened to with humility (Lk 16:29—31).

m *Sōtēria*—Although the Kerygma was in line with the spirit and letter of the Scripture, believers perceived that there was something entirely new in the message which had been preached to them. The word **salvation** (*sōtēria*) and the different concepts associated with it took on a new meaning. Salvation nearly always implies deliverance, personal or national, from an impending evil: illness, death, invasion, oppression or bondage. In a national context it usually refers to deliverance from Egyptian bondage, Babylonian captivity or danger of invasion. Salvation in God's action in response to faith in him (Hos 6; Is 31:1—5; Ps 33:16—22). It is projected into the future in an eschatological garb until its very meaning acquires an absolute quality (Is 11:1—10; Jer 31:31ff; Ez 37:21—28). In certain passages it is an apocalyptic concept (Is 65:17; Dan 7 and 12). In some cases it refers to the spiritual situation of an individual (Ps 51:14).

n **In apostolic preaching** (Ac 4:12; 13:26; Rm 1:16; 10:1; 2 Cor 1:6; 7:10; Phil 1:28, Heb. 1:14 etc) the word is used in an absolute sense, which reveals that it had already acquired a fixed significance in Christian usage. It had been used by **Jesus Himself** in connexion with his miracles, which were also 'signs' of the salvation promised by the Prophets (Mt 8:25; 14:30; 27:40, 42, 49). This salvation is of a spiritual nature (Lk 7:50; 17:19) and is Christ's answer to faith (Mk 5:34; Lk 8:48). As a consequence, the Christian community logically associated salvation with the Kingdom of God inaugurated by Jesus. 'Salvation' in an absolute sense, therefore, came to mean **the mighty act of God in Jesus Christ on behalf of mankind**. It represents the climax of a series of salvific acts which calls for absolute completion at the Parousia, for as the Kingdom is primarily eschatological so is salvation. It is a thing of the future, an object of hope. The phrase 'will be saved' (cf Mt 10:22; Jn 10:9; Ac 2:21; Rm 10:9) is so frequent that it is taken for granted as needing no explanation; and had it not been for Rm 5:9—11 we would have scarcely been able to detect its meaning at all. The argument in Paul runs as follows: We should have faith and confidence in the love of God as regards our future eschatological salvation. Our hope has experience as its foundation, for if when we were still in our sins and could lay no claim to God's mercy, the Father took the initiative and justified us, reconciling us to himself, how much more now, that we are his friends and heirs of the promise will he do all he can to save us on judgement day? This makes it clear that in its comprehensive sense, salvation is **eschatological**. We are now only on the way to final salvation. At the Parousia we shall be saved from judgement (cf 1 Cor 3:15) and saved

o for the Kingdom (2 Tm 4:18). Nevertheless, *sōtēria* has also **an earthly aspect**, valid between the two mighty salvific acts of God, the Resurrection and the Parousia. But its description is negative rather than positive, i.e. we can make a list of the 'evils' from which we have been already saved and regard salvation as the absence of these evils.

Deliverance from sin in forgiveness is the first and **691a** primary effect of salvation in the interim period. Jesus had already restored the notion of **sin** to its biblical purity. He placed it entirely on a moral basis and freed it from the legalistic interpretations which had grown round it (Mt 15:2f). He taught the necessity of confessing it humbly rather than boasting of our good deeds (Lk 18:13f). A person who is afflicted with some physical evil is not necessarily a sinner (13:2). Sin is an estrangement from God as the parable of the Prodigal Son teaches; Christ has come to seek out the lost sheep, the lost drachma. Once they are found they are forgiven (Mt 1:21; Lk 1:77; 7:37ff; Mk 2:5—10, 17). All sins will be forgiven, except the sin against the Holy Ghost, the wilful rejection of the light of the Spirit.

Paul delves deeper into the metaphysic of sin in chh **b** 5—7 of Rm. 'Sin' is conceived of as a tyrannical power which lords it over men, rendering them slaves (6:17). It does give them a wage, but in the long run this wage is death (23). Sin first deceives then kills (7:11). It has its seat in the 'flesh' (human nature considered under the aspect of weakness), where it lies dormant until it is woken up by the Law (18, 24). The divine precepts indicate that a certain action is wrong, but they give no help against the tyranny of sin (6:20; 7:7—12); hence man is helpless (5:6), he does not do what he considers to be right but what he knows to be wrong (7:15—20) for sin drives him to do it. He is free enough to be able to merit punishment, but not strong enough to be able to resist effectively. As a consequence, man becomes a 'sinner', i.e. he loses God's friendship and favour (5:10) because he disobeys (19). Sin still remains in the baptized Christian who has, however, 'died to sin' (6:2) in so far as it still tempts him, and if consented to can still dominate the 'mortal body'; but God's grace through Jesus Christ makes it possible to resist this evil inclination and achieve victory (14; 7:25). The origin of 'sin' was Adam's transgression (5:12ff) but the New Adam more than made up for Adam's offence, thus bringing down God's justification and forgiveness (18).

The Law and Death—The wage of sin is **death**, but **c** from this too, the man who is saved has been delivered. Death means usually physical death, having spiritual death as its cause and eschatological death as its consequence (cf Prv 7:2; 23:13; Rm 7:10; 8:6; 2 Cor 7:10). Rev (2:11; 20:6; 21:8) calls eternal damnation the 'second death'.

The Law of Moses is good and holy, but helpless **d** against sin (Rm 7:7—12) as it only indicates what is wrong but does nothing to provide help. The Christian is 'saved from the Law' in so far as he receives the Holy Spirit, the Spirit of power, who not only teaches us what is to be done but helps us in its achievement (Rm 8). The Law and sin have the 'flesh' as their kingdom. As long as man relies on himself alone he will remain helpless (Gal 4:13). From this too we are delivered by the power of God if we place our trust in him, and consequently we are delivered from all those evils that have their seat in the flesh: concupiscence (Rm 7:7), anxiety (1 Cor 7:32), pride and vain glory (1:19; Rm 2:17), and fear (8:15; Gal 3:3). It is the 'old man', Adam, who is made of flesh. This old man is now buried and has risen to a new life, no longer animal but spirit, with Jesus Christ (Rm 6:6).

Forgiveness (*aphesis*) would have been quite a **e** straightforward concept had Luther not insisted that the sins of the justified are forgiven only in so far as they are not imputed by God (cf *Konkordienformel* 3, 23), as justification only consists of a change of judgement on God's part who treats the sinner as if he were no longer

691e so. It is true that the past can never be cancelled, but the consequences of an action can. Sin has guilt, estrangement from God, and punishment as consequences. All these are cancelled in Baptism (Ac 2:38; 3:19; 5:31; 1 Cor 6: 11). An internal renovation and cleansing takes place in the newly baptized (1 Cor 6:11). This is however not yet reconciliation. Forgiveness only removes the obstacles to reconciliation and justification; a sinless man still has no right to the free gifts of justification and salvation which are given gratis through Jesus Christ.

f Within the Christian Community itself, the Apostles receive the power from the Risen Christ to remit sins committed after Baptism (Jn 20:23). This was done presumably by means of the laying on of hands (1 Tm 5:22; cf Dz. 1692).

g The next step after forgiveness is **reconciliation** (*katallagē*). Popular theology often pictures Christ pleading before an angry God and trying to placate his anger against man. The biblical picture is very far removed from such a distortion of the notion of reconciliation. Sin does bring about an estrangement of man from God; a state of enmity exists which will reach its climax on the 'Day of Wrath' (Rm 2:5). But it was God himself who from pure love and faithfulness took the initiative of reconciling man to himself (not vice-versa) (5:10), and not only man, but the whole of creation which was straining under sin (Col 1:19f). The Apostles received the commission to preach the good news that the way to reconciliation was now open to all, and to exhort Jews and Gentiles to be reconciled to God through Jesus Christ his Son (2 Cor 5:18ff).

h **Justification and Sanctification**—A more intricate concept is that of **Justification**. It is around this doctrine that the whole of the Reformation controversy revolves. Paul's teaching of justification by faith will be considered in a later context, here we shall limit ourselves to examine the meaning of justification as such. For the sake of clarity we shall refer to *dikaiosune* as righteousness and to *dikaioō*, *dikaiōsis* as justify, justification. Sometimes Paul speaks of the righteousness of God as one of his attributes. Here we are concerned with the righteousness of man. We have already examined the doctrine of the rabbis and of the OT. Paul is in strict opposition to the former and accentuates the latter, rendering it fully Christian. Much of the theological controversy centres round the real meaning of the word *dikaioō* which is a forensic term signifying 'to acquit', 'declare just' (LXX), or 'condemn' (mainly classical Gr). The theological content of a word, however, cannot be deduced merely from philological premises. It must be established from the context and the background of thought.

i In St Paul the word-group is almost always used in the general comprehensive sense of 'salvation'. This equivalence is already to be found in the OT where God's *righteousness* (as an attribute) and his salvific initiative are interchangeable (cf Pss 64:5f; 68:28f; 70:15f; 97:2f in the LXX; Is 46:12f; 5:15f; 59:17; 61:10f). Pauline justification however, only includes the earthly aspect of the eschatological gift received through Christ, not its final apocalyptic aspect (Rm 8:28—31; but cf Gal 5:5). It is something which has already happened at the moment of believing and gathers in itself all the interim effects of the Redemption, including 'justification' in its philogical sense, as can be seen from Rom 5:1—11. The fruits of justification are peace with God and reconciliation (1, 10), access to the grace in which we stand (2), hope of glory (2), the outpouring of love in our hearts through the Holy Spirit (5), deliverance from the eschatological wrath of God (9), reigning in life (17, 21), acquittal (the

specific LXX meaning of justification (18; 8:33) as **691i** opposed to 'condemnation').

Rm 6 presents righteousness as fruit of the dynamic **j** power of the Spirit (6:13f) which delivers us from the contrary power of sin (2, 7 passim). The new law of the Spirit is not a dead letter powerless to help, it fulfils the just requirements of the law within us (8:2, 4), making us sons and heirs of God, fellow heirs of Christ (15f). The unmistakable sign that one has received God's justification is the manifestation of the Spirit in him through the charismata (Gal 3:1—5).

The fact that God called us while we were yet sinners **k** does not imply that the new righteousness is compatible with unrighteous living. Moral uprighteousness or 'sanctification' is part of justification in so far as it is produced by the Spirit. It is precisely on the basis of good works that God will judge and acquit or condemn us on the last day (1 Cor 6:9 11; also Rm 14:10ff; 1 Cor 9:23—27; 2 Cor 5:10).

What the primitive Christians called salvation and Paul **l** called justification **John calls Eternal Life**. The metaphor of life is frequent in the OT as in all the NT authors, but John makes it a pivotal idea of his Gospel. The Synoptic Christ preaches the Kingdom of God; John's Christ comes that 'they may have life' (10:10). The adjective 'eternal' which often qualifies 'life' does not merely refer to infinite duration but has also a qualitative sense. In Jewish usage (cf 4 Ezra 7:12f; 8:52, 54) 'eternal life' or 'life of the Age to come' stands in contrast with life in time or life in This Age. In Jn it refers primarily to the eschatological life following the Resurrection of the Dead (5:28f), but it also refers to present salvation, the aspect which Paul calls justification. The believer is 'alive' in a pregnant sense (5:25f; 9:25). Future eternal life is only a consequence of present eternal life, God's gift at Baptism (3:5). This doctrine is epitomized in the Lazarus story. As Dodd remarks (*The Interpretation of the Fourth Gospel*, 148), resurrection is a symbol of transition to that life which is life indeed because it is proof against bodily death. 'Eternal', therefore, as applied to the present interim period, means belonging to the non-temporal world in the Platonic sense. Translated into theological terminology it means eschatological or supernatural.

The Gentiles and Justness—This notion of salvation, **692a** primarily based on the OT, was acceptable to the convert Jews who were the first to belong to the New Israel. **New problems** arose, however, as soon as the Spirit signified that it was time for the **Gentiles** to enter the Church. The Divine Spirit had come down on Cornelius, an experience which was interpreted as meaning that even the Gentiles were called to participate in the eschatological gifts and in salvation. Till then the Jews had continued to receive circumcision and observe the law of Moses in all its detail. But when the Spirit came down on the uncircumcised, it was asked whether the Gentiles too should take upon themselves the full burden of the Law and be circumcised. Was their faith in Christ, expressed through Baptism, sufficient to make them participate in the Blessings of the Age to come? The question arose before the writing of Rm and Gal; is it possible to reconstruct its history from the account in Ac?

Luke considers **the Council of the Apostles** in 15:1— **b** 35 as the turning point of the history of the Early Church. Its importance is theological as well as historical. It marks the full and final break with Judaism. It is not only the temple that has been abandoned but the Law as well. The Council brings to their logical conclusion the lessons learnt from the Cornelius episode. The doctrine of

692b **salvation through faith** without the Law receives the official sanction of the Church.

c Ch 15 contains a great deal of Lucan editorial theology. The author makes a 'big scene' out of it, perhaps combining various happenings together into a theological whole. The speeches, fully Lucan in their present form, go back to the tradition that Peter consented to freedom from the Law while James advocated the four provisos, still prevalent in some communities at the time of writing. As the speeches stand in their present form they have the function of presenting the traditional theological, moral, and scriptural reasons for the abolition of the Law. They also possess an apologetical value against certain Judaisers in Luke's circles. The narrative is told from only one point of view. Another viewpoint is that in Gal.

d In **Peter's discourse** at the Council, the first argument (15:6—12) is that from tradition: 'A long time ago' God had chosen him from among the Jerusalem community to preach the word to the Gentiles. These believed God, who knows the heart of man; he therefore rendered witness to their faith by sending the Spirit exactly as he had done at Pentecost, signifying that there was no distinction between Jew and Gentile. God treats both alike, purifying their hearts through faith. Consequently, the imposition of the Law upon the Gentile converts would be superfluous as they had already been cleansed and had even received the eschatological gift. Indeed, such an imposition would be tempting God as it implied a doubt in his witness. The Law is unbearable anyway, and if the Jews themselves could not bear it how can it be expected of the Gentiles that they should observe it? Therefore 'we believe that we shall be saved through the grace of the Lord Jesus Christ, just as they will'. This conclusion is surprising: we would have expected: 'they will be saved through grace just as ourselves'. But the argument is there to persuade Jews rather than Gentiles. If the Gentiles received the Spirit without circumcision it means that the Jews too have been saved through their faith apart from Law and circumcision. The same appeal to the experience of the Spirit is made by Paul in Gal 3:2—5.

e James agrees in principle (Ac 15:13—21) but advocates a practical compromise. The four restrictions in 15:20 are taken from Lv 17 and 18. Even in the OT they were enforced upon the Gentiles living in Israel. In the NT period they have psychological rather than moral value, functioning as shock-absorbers to prevent an abrupt transition. This is confirmed by 15:21: 'Moses has been read in the synagogues from the days of old' i.e. the Gentile converts, who usually came from among the 'God-fearers', the quasi-proselytes, who frequented Jewish services, were already familiar with them and perhaps already practised them.

f Justification through Faith—St Paul goes to the root of the question in Rm and Gal. He founds his doctrine, as the Church had done before him, on the OT, understood according to the Spirit and on the words of Jesus. We have already seen what the biblical concept of salvation was. Jesus not only opposes his idea of righteousness to that of the Pharisees but even purifies some of the OT precepts themselves. In Mt 6 he stresses that the justness of the Kingdom is higher than that of the Pharisees, opposing his own interpretation to theirs in the seven antitheses. Righteousness is a gift of God to those who thirst after it (Mt 5:6). God cannot be expected to come and thank man for observing the commandments. We are merely unworthy servants who can only do our duty without being able to boast that we have given anything to God (Lk 17:7—10). The parable of the publican and the Pharisee in 18:9—14 is the best illustration of this doctrine.

Paul builds on this teaching. We have already seen **692g** that his notion of justification is a comprehensive one, making it almost synonymous with the older term 'salvation', which comprehends all the eschatological gifts given by the Spirit. Justification however, includes the notion of *dikaioō* in its forensic sense of acquitting, declaring just. Does this imply that justification is essentially a mere change of attitude on God's part without any corresponding change in man?

The answer to this question depends upon the inter- **h** pretation we choose to give to the phrase '**justification by faith**'. Before we begin our summary discussion we must make a very important observation. It must be constantly borne in mind when reading Rm and Gal that Paul is not thinking predominantly in terms of single persons but in terms of groups: Jews and Gentiles. His language is redemptive-historical (*heilsgeschichtlich*) rather than pastoral. He is concerned with God's action in history not only in Rm 9—11 but in the whole of the doctrinal part of Rm, even in ch 7 where the personal 'I' stands for the un-redeemed Jew. If we bear this in mind many apparent contradictions in Paul's doctrine resolve themselves quite naturally. The reader will understand this better if he compares the analogous case of the doctrine of predestination in Rm 9:6—22. Some theologians have tried to base their theories of predestination to glory on a passage which speaks of the predestination of two peoples to faith, creating immense confusion of thought and distorting the meaning of the passage.

Paul's main preoccupation is to vindicate the absolute **i** righteousness, fidelity, and transcendence of God. Man is entirely at the receiving end; he cannot give anything to God which is not already due to him, nor can he claim anything in return: 'Who has given a gift to him that he may be repaid? For from him and through him and to him are all things. To him be glory forever. Amen' (Rm 11: 35f). There can therefore be no boasting before God by people who are but useless servants: 'What becomes of our boasting? It is excluded' (3:27). **God's loving initiative** in sending Jesus for our sins is so inconceivably great that nothing should be allowed to minimize its significance. If we assert that we are able to save ourselves through the Law the death of Christ loses its value: 'I do not nullify the grace of God; for if justification were through the law, then Christ died to no purpose' (Gal 2: 21).

We are justified apart from the Law. God justified **j** us, i.e. he sent Christ to save us and called us to faith, while we were yet sinners. This should be understood in the sense that God saved us when we had nothing to recommend us, being sinners. It does not mean that we are sinners after justification or that justification is an excuse for sin, as the sequence in Rm 5:8f makes clear. 1 Cor 6:9—11 also speaks to the same purpose: we cannot inherit the Kingdom of God (final salvation, although we are already justified) if we are thieves, adulterers, etc, as some of us were before justification. A change of life is necessary.

Paul does not limit the use of the word 'Law' to the **k** ceremonial aspect; he extends its meaning to the moral precepts too (Rm 2:21ff). The pharisaic idea of meriting God's favourable judgement through human endeavour is therefore excluded. The Pharisee would say that God will only justify you if you are righteous. Paul asserts the exact contrary: **God justifies the sinner.** Once justified, however, **moral righteousness is made possible** and actually given through the indwelling of

92k the Holy Spirit; the Law of the Spirit frees us from the power of sin (8:2). What the Law justly required, but through weakness could not be fulfilled, can now be observed by the Law of the Spirit (4). A return to sin will cause loss of justification, we return to 'death' (6:1–4:8, 9). This is not impossible even for believers. Hence after justification moral righteousness forms an integral part of 'the grace in which we stand', but it is no longer an excuse for boasting, first of all because our good works are only made possible through the help of God's Spirit (without it we were helpless: 6:14) and secondly because our good works are accepted and even repaid by God as an act of sheer grace, without any obligation on his part, not because of their intrinsic value (21–23).

l The truth that **man is at the receiving end of things** and cannot claim anything back from God had been understood neither by Jews nor by Gentiles. Each in his own way had endeavoured to exalt himself above God's grace; the Gentiles striving after wisdom succeeded in knowing God but did not pay him due honour nor render thanks (1:18ff). As they did not 'know' (in the sense of acknowledge) God through wisdom Divine Wisdom let them fall into the most heinous perversities (1 Cor 1:21; Rm 2) that they might acknowledge their bankruptcy and turn to God in pure faith (1:24ff; 11:32; 1 Cor 1:21f). The Jews, on the other hand, strove to please God the wrong way. Instead of acknowledging their indebtedness to God, they made him their debtor. In place of thanking Yahweh for having chosen Abraham, they boasted that they were the only people who did God the great honour of accepting his Law. This attitude did not correspond to that which the OT calls 'Faith'. It was therefore logical that in their haughtiness the Jews should find no place for Christ (Rm 10:2–4). The Law, with its unreachable ideals, had been given to them as an eye-opener, to let them perceive how powerless they were to do good. Instead of acknowledging in all humility that the nation as a whole fell far short of its mark they despised the Gentiles as far below them and considered themselves as the light of the blind (2:17–24).

m When the Gospel was preached, those who admitted their moral bankruptcy and grasped at the Cross for salvation fitted into the design of God (3:23f) while those who persisted in their anthropocentric striving implicitly rejected God's saving mercy and signed their own condemnation 3:9–20). The Jews were acting as they had always done in their history, rejecting the grace of God offered them in preference of others. They should therefore not despise the Gentiles, for both are accountable to God; their only hope of salvation is the grateful reception of the Grace of God in Jesus Christ.

n Paul insistently affirms that the Jews stand in need of the justification of God because they did not succeed in observing the Law. This is an assertion that regards the nation as such, but what if an individual did actually observe the Law, would God justify him? And if he does, could not that individual claim that he has been justified because of his righteousness? Paul answers the question with reference to himself. He was a Pharisee, 'as to the righteousness under the law blameless. But whatever gain I had I counted a loss for the sake of Christ . . . in order that I may gain Christ and be found in him, not having a righteousness of my own, based on the Law, but that which is through faith in Christ, the righteousness from God' (Phil 3:7–9). Paul is far from asserting, however, that he can relax his efforts and rely passively on faith: 'I pommel my body and subdue it, lest after preaching to others I myself should be disqualified' (1 Cor 9:27).

o It follows that the righteousness of God is necessary

not only for those who have sinned, but also for those who **692o** have kept the law irreprehensibly. Men who rely on their own righteousness are '**in the flesh**', those justified by God are '**spirit**'. The change does not come about by a mere change of outlook on God's part, but through the infusion of the Holy Spirit who operates a real transformation, putting to death the deeds of the body and bearing witness to our divine sonship, helping us to behave as sons. The Spirit inserts us into Christ Jesus. 'In Christ', as part of his corporate personality, we shine before God through the *doxa* (glory) which the glorified Christ extends to those who are in him (Rm 8:9–16, 30). The foundation of this transformation is **faith**.

The Gift of Faith—What is this *pistis* (faith) that is **693a** so potent before God? It is not a virtue which merits reward Pauline faith is an attitude in which man admits his bankruptcy in relation to his Maker. He realizes that even when he has given everything, and if he is sincere he must admit that he has not done so, there is still no proportion between what he can offer and the salvation for which he thirsts. He therefore accepts the witness of the Apostles that God sent Christ to bridge this gap and accepts salvation as a gift from God not as his own conquest. Once justified he submits mind and heart to the guidance of the Spirit living in an attitude of obedience to God and Christ (3:21–27). Faith is a confession of God's righteousness, his fidelity to his promises, his mercy and goodness It places man in his allotted position at the receiving end. It is no mere intellectual assent, though this element is essential to it (1 Cor 1:21); it is the submission of the whole personality which finds expression in obedience and good works (Gal 5:6). It is therefore pointless to ask whether a justified Christian should have faith or works. He remains righteous if he has 'faith working through charity' (ibid). This description of Pauline faith is based on Paul's own beautiful confession of faith in Phil 3:4–11.

Faith is 'reckoned as righteousness' by God **b** (*elogisthē autō eis dikaiosunēn* (Rm 4:3). To reckon is to place on man's account. The sinner has nothing to offer except his faith. Even this makes no strict demand on God. The believer only hollows out the cavity and trusts in God to fill it up. God in his turn is satisfied with this attitude and as an act of grace treats the repentant sinner as if he possessed sufficient righteousness to receive justification. This he does, not to reward man's merits which are non-existent but as an act of grace in loyalty to himself and to his promises (4:1–8). After justification man's actions do receive merit, not because intrinsically meritorious, for they remain human and disproportionate to the eschatological gift of God, but because through grace God reckons them to our account and condescends to repay us for them with eternal life (2 Tm 4:6–8, Rm 8:12f).

Other Aspects of Faith—The Pauline doctrine of **c** justification was written in the heat of controversy and refers predominantly to the initial act of God that makes man just. As time went on and the controversy died down the Church focussed its attention upon the spiritual needs of the believers, and faith came to receive **other shades of meaning.** In Heb. the accent lies on trust in God: 'Faith is the assurance of things hoped for, the conviction of things not seen' (Heb. 11:1; the whole ch is an illustration of this definition). It therefore corresponds to the attitude of the Christian described in Rm 5:9f, which we would describe as **hope** of eternal salvation.

We have already examined the emphasis of the Pas- **d** torals on the acceptance of the right doctrine taught by the Apostles and transmitted by the Church. Faith, therefore, corresponds to this demand and is an intellectual

693d reception of these truths and obedience of their practical implications. This **change of terminoloy** must have caused some confusion in the minds of some Christians who, remembering the trite Pauline formula 'salvation through faith apart from works', applied it *in sensu composito* to their own situation (as Luther did later). They emphasized the intellectual element and the element of trust denying the value of good works. **James** felt the need to correct this misunderstanding. He does not go to the root of the matter, explaining the difference between the traditional Pauline formula and faith as it had come to be understood owing to the changed pastoral situation, but goes about his business in a practical way affirming bluntly that faith as mere intellectual adherence to doctrine without accompanying good works is dead, and does not lead to salvation (Jas 2:14—26).

e It is often said that James did not understand Paul. This statement is too sweeping. He was concerned only with giving a blunt practical solution without any exegetical frills. His reference to Abraham's justification through works and not through faith alone is a confutation to those who wanted to prove the contrary citing the traditional testimony, Gn 15:6, often used by Paul. James was concerned with faith and works *after* justification and stressed the fact that Abraham, once justified, kept friendship with God through his good deeds (Jas 2:23).

f Lastly, the fact that **St Matthew** makes so much of the Sermon on the Mount, representing Jesus as the New Moses who delivers the New Law to the New People of God shows that **the Church never** for a moment **minimized the value of good works.** The Pauline controversy was a clarification not a denial.

g The Call to Faith—We must return to the question of **the initial moment of justification.** It is pertinent to ask whether man can claim for himself at least the merit of believing, or, if faith is a gift, why it is given to some and not to others. This same question was asked by the primitive Christians themselves, and we receive tentative answers from Paul, Luke, and John.

h Paul insists that the preachers of the Gospel are not philosophers (1 Cor 2:1—5) but mere witnesses who faithfully transmit a message (4:2). Their word is charged with the power of the Holy Spirit (Rm 15:19) who produces conviction (*plērophoria*, 1 Thess 1:5) in both speaker and hearer. The acceptance of the Gospel, therefore, is not a matter of opinion but of obedience (Rm 11:30ff). It is both a gift, for **'election'** has only love as its motive (8:29f), and a duty. The believers who place themselves on the way to salvation (*sōzomenoi*) have no reason to boast for it is God who 'begins the good work' (Phil 1:6). Unbelievers, on the contrary, have only themselves to blame if they are on the way to perdition (*apolloumenoi*) as the 'aroma of Christ' has been offered to them as well (2 Cor 2:15f). But what is the ultimate reason why one man accepts the Gospel while another rejects it? Is the Spirit not at work in both? Paul gives no answer to this question but leaves the word to Luke.

i Even Luke stresses God's grace in election to faith; only those believe 'who were ordained to eternal life' (Ac 13:48). It is the Lord who opens the heart enabling the hearer to give heed to the word of the Apostle (16:14). But **a certain disposition is presupposed.** Jews of the nobler kind, like those of Beroea (17:4) receive the word with joy, and delve into the Scripture to confirm their faith. Others are disobedient and blaspheme the way (18:8ff). Felix and Drusilla, who are not a model of chastity, find the Gospel too hard for their lax ways (24:24ff). This does not mean that the righteous receive the word while the unrighteous reject it, for even those who believe were once sinners and need repentance (2:38), but a certain thirst after righteousness is necessary, otherwise the seed of the Gospel will not bear fruit (Lk 8:5—15). Can this disposition, at least provide a cause for boasting? Paul answers: 'What have you that you have not received? If then you received it, why do you boast as if it were not a gift?' (1 Cor 4:7).

The same principles of election and moral disposition **j** are upheld by **John**. It is Christ who chooses the believer, not the believer who chooses him (Jn 15:16). God is at liberty to choose sheep even from outside the fold of Israel (10:16), and the chosen ones bear the world's hatred (15:19). John thinks of all those who are about to believe as God's children scattered all over the world; they will immediately recognize the voice of their Shepherd as soon as they hear it (10:26f; 15:52). The elect have been prepared by the Father who gave them to the Son (6:37). Hence faith in Christ is God's gift (44, 65). To hear the voice of Jesus one must walk in the light, and at least strive after righteousness (3:18—21). Consequently those who do not perform the works of God do not believe in Jesus (8:47). This refers to the Jews who take offence at the words of the Master (6:41; 7; 8; 11:50. etc).

Paul, Luke, and John agree therefore that God's **k** Wisdom prepared both Jews and Gentiles for the coming of Christ. The righteousness they would have arrived at was not sufficient to press any claim on God for justification. Both fell short of their mark. But those who took their preparation seriously and thirsted after true righteousness were found well disposed when the call actually came; those who either discarded striving after righteousness altogether or were too proud to submit to God's justification did not rise to the occasion when the call came, and disbelieved.

9. CONCLUSION

It has been our endeavour in this article to follow **the l growth of NT theology** from *kerygma* to *paradosis*. It should be apparent that the supreme law which guides this development is **the necessity of adaptation:** apologetical, pastoral, and circumstantial. Not all that the Apostles taught is written down in the NT. Much of the great fresco that once covered the walls of the Church has faded away. What remains in the NT and what can be reconstructed through Tradition is only a precious glimpse of the whole. It should be sufficient however to lead us on the way of salvation and guide our feet along in the surrounding darkness until the great Light of the Parousia reveals to us the ineffable glory of God's Wisdom.

The evolution of doctrine in the life of the Church **m** also followed the same rule or adaptation. The statement that it is heretics who make theology may be paradoxical, but the constant need of the Church to defend itself against error has rendered it true. From a certain point of view this is very fortunate, for we would never have had the beautiful Christological synthesis of Chalcedon had it not been for Arius, Theodorus and Nestorius. Nor would Augustine have delved so deeply into St Paul to give us his doctrine of Grace had it not been for Pelagius. The Lutheran controversy too contributed its part to theology and spirituality. And today our theology is no less controversial than that of our fathers.

This **emphasis on controversy**, however, **has its n drawbacks**. The truths opposed to the great heresies are not always the most fruitful pastorally, but they occupy the foremost part in our theological text-books, having been studied beyond proportion. **Biblical theology will**

help us to restore the balance if it is studied on its own. But if it is considered as a mere handmaid of scholastic theology it can render very little. An exegete can spend much time but gather little fruit by trying to prove that there was one Person but two wills in Jesus, if by doing so he neglects the specific teaching of the NT, on which the rich spiritual lives of the primitive Christians were based. Biblical theology and historical theology intersect at several points but do not overlap. Like a road and railway track that intertwine they lead to the same end but enjoy different panoramas. Till now biblical theology has been studied too much at the points of intersection with little reference to its own path. In this essay we have tried to clarify these points of intersection, but we paid more attention to keep the same proportions among the various problems discussed that prevailed in the Apostolic and sub-Apostolic Church. If modern theology also tries to restore these proportions and apply them to pastoral needs the Church of today will be all the richer for the effort.

THE LIFE OF ST PAUL

BY D. J. O'HERLIHY

701a Bibliography—John Chrysostom, *De Laudibus S. Pauli*, PG, 50, 471—514; E-B Allo, *Paul, Apôtre de Jésus Christ*, 1942; G. Brillet, *Un Chef d'Eglise, St Paul*, 1956; L. Cerfaux & J. Cambier, 'Paul' DBS, VII, fasc 36, 1961; A. P. Davies, *The First Christian*, N. Y., 1957; A. Deissmann, *Paul: A Study in Social and Religious history*, E.tr. 1957; P. Feine, *Der Apostel Paulus*, Gütersloh, 1927; C. Fouard, *Saint Paul and his Missions*, E.tr. 1894; J. A. Grassi, *A World to win; the Missionary Methods of Paul the Apostle*, N. Y., 1965; J. Holzner, *Paul of Tarsus*, E.tr. St Louis, 1944; J. Klausner, *From Jesus to Paul*, 1944; W. L. Knox, *St Paul*, 1932; L. Murillo, *Paulus et Pauli Scripta*, Rome, 1926; A. D. Nock, *St Paul*, 1938; A. Penna, *St Paul, the Apostle*, E.tr. 1960; K. Pieper, *Paulus, seine missionarische Persönlichkeit und Wirksamkeit*, Münster, 1926; F. Prat, *St Paul*, E.tr. New York, 1929; W. M. Ramsay, *St Paul, the Traveller and Roman Citizen*, 1895; G. Ricciotti, *Paul, the Apostle*, E.tr. Milwaukee, 1953; B. Rigaux, *St Paul et ses lettres*, Paris-Bruges, 1962; B. W. Robinson, *The Life of Paul*, Chicago, 1956; H. J. Schonfield, *The Jew of Tarsus*, 1946; A. Tricot, *St Paul, Apôtre des Gentils*, 1928; A. N. Williams, *Paul, the World's First Missionary*, New York, 1954.

Editor's Note—This article fits into its place in the series of general articles of the NT as a synthetic study of St Paul: his career, ministry, methods and personality. Its object is to present as a meaningful unity the sum of all those significant items about Paul which are found scattered, according to the demands of subject-matter, throughout other articles of the Commentary, especially those on Ac and the Epistles. In those articles the problems are stated, the data analyzed, and the findings proposed. In this one, the questions are not thrashed out again, nor are new ones proposed; rather, results elsewhere arrived at are accepted; and on disputed matters—such, for example, as various points of Pauline chronology, and the precise value of the biographical data implied in the Pastoral Epistles—the author opts for the views which he finds most acceptable, integrates them in his synthesis, and moves on. The aim is to give a rapid and balanced summary, not a series of detailed discussions. For these the reader is referred to the relevant articles of the Commentary with their respective bibliographies. He may be further referred to such recent studies as J. Dupont, *Études sur les Actes des Apôtres, Lectio Divina*, 45 (1967) especially 'Problèmes de Chronologie: les visites de Paul à Jérusalem', 163—241; and P. Benoit, 'La deuxième visite de S. Paul à Jérusalem', Bib 40 (1959), 778—92. On the place in which Paul received his schooling from his earliest boyhood (infra § 701b), it should be noted that Van Unnik, by a new interpretation of Ac 22:3 and 26:4, makes a strong case for Jerusalem rather than Tarsus. Cf W. C. Van Unnik, *Tarsus or Jerusalem: the city of St Paul's youth*, E.tr. by G. Ogg, 1962 (Dutch original, 1952).

Birth and Education—St Paul was born in the city of **701** Tarsus at the dawn of the Christian era. Tarsus was the capital of Cilicia, Greek in language and Roman through the favour of Caesar. Distinguished for commercial advantages no less than for literary attainments, the town on whose coins civic pride had stamped the boast 'First and Fairest and Best' was 'no mean city'. Like most trading centres in the Greco-Roman world, it had a Jewish colony into which the future Apostle was born. It appears that the boy was given two names at birth: Saul, an honoured name in the tribe of Benjamin to which he belonged, and Paul, in token of the Roman citizenship which he inherited. For a provincial such citizenship implied a special privilege, conferred for service and goodwill to the Roman cause or purchased for a substantial figure. Saul's early formation was on traditional lines, and it is not likely that he attended the public schools of Tarsus. But he could not altogether escape the influence of a pagan and prosperous city. Temples and theatres abounded outside the quarter inhabited by his race; popular quotations occur in his writings; and the imagery of trade, athletics and war may partly be based on the memories of childhood. Together with two names, he had two languages from his youth—Aramaic' being the home language of the strict Jew in Asiatic lands, and Greek, the language of the synagogue in the Mediterranean world. He would shortly become acquainted with Hebrew.

For the purpose of graduating as a master of the Law **c** he was sent to Jerusalem to complete his studies. Possibly some members of the family resided in the Holy City, where at a later stage his sister's son saved his life. The Schools of Hillel and Shammai—two rabbis of the Herodian period—were then in the ascendant, and Saul joined the former under the direction of Gamaliel I. He was fortunate in having as teacher one whom the Mishnah eulogizes and of whose repute St Luke preserves an echo, Ac 5:34. While more attention was paid in the schools to the utterances of men than to the word of God, yet Saul acquired, at the feet of Gamaliel, an incomparable knowledge of Heb. lore and made his own the peculiarly Jewish methods of argument which he was later to employ in presenting the Christian message to his compatriots. And apart from progress in knowledge, he was to preserve from the home of Pharisaism a burning zeal for the integrity of doctrine and tradition and for rigorous observance of the Mosaic legislation, 'as to righteousness under the law blameless' (Phil 3:6b). It appears that he left Jerusalem some time before the Baptist inaugurated the movement which Jesus took over and dominated. The years of Pilate's procuratorate are obscure in the life-story of Saul. From scattered notices in his writings it is legitimate to conclude that he devoted his adolescence to acquiring a fuller knowledge of the Law and to advancing more and more along the path marked out for him by his teacher in Jerusalem. His zeal will have found an outlet in the school attached to the local synagogue and he may have been consulted as an expert by the Tarsus

701c sanhedrin, of which he was not a member on account of his age.

d Conformable to the Talmud recommendation, 'He that hath a trade in his hand, to what is he like? He is like a vineyard that is fenced', Saul had been initiated into the occupation of his father, the local craft of making tents and cloaks out of Cilician cloth, and he remained a manual labourer to the end. He supported himself in this way, even when he was actively engaged in preaching the Gospel (1 Cor 9:12b), and may have wished to emphasize in his person the dignity of manual labour against the tendency of Roman society to relegate handwork to slaves. He never married (1 Cor 7:7). We have no knowledge of his personal appearance apart from the description in the apocryphal *Acts of Paul and Thecla*: 'a man of little stature, thin-haired upon the head, crooked in the legs, of good state of body, with eyebrows joining the nose somewhat hooked; full of grace, for sometimes he appeared like a man, and sometimes he had the face of an angel'. Many writers think that they find, in St Paul's writings and in St Luke's account of him, evidence that he suffered from shortness of sight or from some affliction of the eyes. The 'thorn in the flesh' of 2 Cor 12:7 connotes, according to many, a form of physical illness, about which it is difficult to be precise (cf § 894d). The Latin Fathers suggested headaches while modern writers are divided between epilepsy and malaria. But whatever the malady was, it is interesting to reflect that the volume of his achievement was accomplished, not in the strength of a healthy body, but in spite of a disability that cost him much distress.

702a Conversion and Mission—While Saul tarried in Tarsus, epoch-making events took place in Palestine. The long-awaited Messiah came, preached for the appointed time and was rejected by his own. His disciples, dispirited by the death of their master, were conforted by his reappearance and transformed by the effusion of the Holy Spirit. In the knowledge that the Jews had made a tragic mistake in rejecting the Messiah, they set themselves to the task of repairing the error and of converting Israel to its Lord and Saviour. But the leaders of the Jews were not disposed to follow the advice of Galilean fishermen and, moreover, were disturbed at the success of the new Gospel. The preaching of a young deacon set a seal on their opposition to its progress. Among the Jews represented as disputing with Stephen were some from the synagogue of the Cilicians, and Saul may have been among them and may have lent himself to the campaign which culminated in the trial before the council. For **b** Stephen's speech and execution cf. §§ 828e−829d. On that occasion Saul kept the garments of those who stoned Stephen and 'was consenting to his death' (Ac 8:1). The pogrom saw him emerge in the role of chief inquisitor, raiding the synagogues and invading the sanctuaries of domestic life in a grim determination to extirpate the new religion. Nor was he satisfied with a local extirpation: he would reach as far as Damascus whither, it was thought, some Christians had fled to escape the fury which raged in Jerusalem. Armed with letters of credence from the high-priest and an escort, he hastened northwards and was struck down by a miracle in the midst of his frenzy and converted to the faith he persecuted. That St Luke regarded this event as of capital importance in the life-story of St Paul is evidenced by the circumstance that he tells it three times, once in his own words (Ac 9:1−19) and twice in those of St Paul (Ac 22:3−21) and (Ac 26:9−19). On the different ways in which Lk uses his sources, see § 821b.

c The supernatural character of the conversion is placed beyond all reasonable doubt by the various historical **702c** details and statements of Ac as well as by the testimony of St Paul and the tradition of the Church. Rationalist critics are compelled to find an explanation for the episode in harmony with their preconceived opinions, and many adopt the view made popular by Renan, to wit, that Paul merely recognized that Jesus was the Son of God. Others contend that Saul imagined, under the stress of emotion, that he saw him who, the Christians believed, had risen from the dead. Neither St Paul, however, nor his biographer retain any vestige of this alleged emotional urgency. Saul had acted 'ignorantly in unbelief' (1 Tm 1:13) and was firmly convinced that he had to do many things against Jesus (Ac 26:9). Ananias openly claims that Jesus had appeared to Saul on the way (Ac 9:17) and Barnabas tells the Apostles how Saul saw the Lord and how the Lord spoke to him (Ac 9:27). Saul himself is certain of having seen Christ, arguing thence to his status as an Apostle (1 Cor 9:1) and to equal rank with Peter, James and the Twelve (1 Cor 15:8). If Christ did not really appear to Saul on the way to Damascus, then Saul who says that he saw Jesus either wished to deceive his hearers or was himself deceived. No one suggests that he was a deliberate liar, and the case for self-deception is excluded by the factual statements of Ac as well as by the strength and consistency of his post-conversion career. It would be strange indeed if illusion could have created or conserved the life of the Apostle of the Gentiles. Much has been written about the psychological preparation of the Apostle, as if he had long been impressed by the beauty of Christianity and recently moved by the heroism of Stephen. But whatever the influence of Stephen's prayers—'Si Stephanus non orasset Ecclesia Paulum non habuisset'—it is difficult to attach any great importance to this 'psychological preparation' in view of the concordant testimony of Acts and Epistles which represents the conversion as something sudden, startling and unforeseen.

In the city of Damascus whither he was led by his **d** companions Saul received a commission: he was set apart to carry the name of Jesus 'before the Gentiles and kings and the son of Israel' (Ac 9:15). At this early stage he perceived that the name of Jesus was the only saving name. The jealous champion of the Law saw in a flash its utter helplessness as an instrument of salvation and became convinced that men could not be saved except through faith in Jesus Christ who had been crucified in the name of the law. It is interesting, too, to notice that the words which he heard on the road to Damascus— 'I am Jesus whom you are persecuting' (Ac 26:15)— enshrine the doctrine which he made peculiarly his own, that the faithful make up one body of which Jesus is the head, continuing through time the work of redemption.

When he had recovered from the ordeal in the house **e** of Judas and had been baptized by Ananias, he withdrew for a time to Arabia (Gal 1:17). Returning to Damascus he preached the divine sonship and messianic character of Jesus in the synagogues. But the Jews were unwilling to be taught by a renegade and in an effort to kill him sought help from the soldiery of the Ethnarch of Aretas. It was then that the disciples took him and let him down in a basket from a window in the wall. He went to Jerusalem to see Peter and had difficulty in overcoming the suspicion in which he was held by some Christians. But Joseph Barnabas, 'a good man', vouched for him to the Apostles, and a fifteen-day association with their leader clearly demonstrated that Saul also was among the prophets. A vision accorded to him in the temple enlightened him further in respect of his future career

702e and he left for Tarsus. The length of time that was allowed to pass between his conversion and his official summoning to the work of heralding forth the Gospel gave him an extended insight into the way of providence on the one hand, and on the other hand into the workings of grace in the human heart, thus constituting a suitable preparation for the office of preaching to a world which ignored Providence and had become insensible to divine inspirations.

f The beginnings of the apostolate to the heathen world are curiously interesting. St Peter, appropriately, had taken the first steps in this direction, receiving Cornelius the centurion into the Church, but that he had done what Jewish Christians found hard to bear is proved by the circumstance that he had to justify his action on his return to Jerusalem. At Antioch on the Orontes, one of the chief cities of the Greco-Roman world, refugee Christians, unauthorized, proceeded to address themselves to the heathen, and with a fair measure of success. Barnabas was sent from the Mother-Church to foster the beginnings of the predominantly Gentile community, and on being satisfied that there was a wide field of apostolate, he secured the services of Saul whom he had befriended a few years before and of whose destiny he was not unaware. By their united efforts the word of the Lord increased and the disciples became numerous enough to attract the attention of the public. It was here that they were first called 'Christians'. Perhaps it was at this time that Saul, during an errand of mercy in Jerusalem, became the recipient of the visions and revelations to which he refers in 2 Cor 12:1–4. But Antioch was to be his base and thence, set apart by order of the Holy Ghost, he sailed on the first missionary journey.

703a First Missionary Journey—The itinerary was through Cyprus (the home-island of Barnabas), Perga in Pamphylia, and the Galatian towns of Antioch, Iconium, Lystra and Derbe. It ought to be noted that in the course of the expedition the leadership of the party, hitherto directed by Barnabas, passed to Paul, the name which his biographer uses from this point onwards. St Jerome reckoned that the change of name commemorated the victory over Sergius Paulus, in much the same way as Scipio was called Africanus from the conquest of Africa. The failure of the Jews to accept the Gospel was borne in on Paul at this early stage of his missionary endeavour: 'It was necessary that the word of God should be spoken first to you. Since you thrust it from you, and judge yourselves unworthy of eternal life, behold, we turn to the Gentiles' (Ac 13:46). Despite opposition, the work of the missionaries was not without fruit for God stood by them and rendered witness by miracles to the words that proclaimed his grace. They revisited the communities which they had established and consolidated the work by appointing priests ('elders', Ac 14:23, RSV) in every Church.

b Circumcision and Mosaic Observances—The applause which greeted the return of the delegates to Antioch was short-lived, for 'some men came down from Judea and were teaching the brethren, "Unless you are circumcised according to the custom of Moses, you cannot be saved."' (Ac 15:1). It is difficult to state in precise terms the facets of the problem which now embarrassed St Paul and continued for a decade (but see comm. on Gal., §§ 895*eh*, 897*e*) to disturb his churches. He had founded communities in Southern Asia Minor on the basis of the absolute equality of Jew and Gentile: to become a full member of the Christian Church faith and baptism alone were necessary. Others—the name 'Judaizers' has been coined to indicate them—held that such

membership was not complete and that circumcision was **703** necessary as well as baptism for the full possession of the privileges of the Christian state. The point of view might easily be current in Palestine: The Palestinian Gospel— that according to St Matthew—represents Jesus as perfecting, not abrogating, the Law (5:17). Jesus himself was circumcised: and the Church of Jerusalem, under the guidance of the pious James, had not ceased, in spite of persecution, to hope to win the Jews to Christianity on the sole basis of accepting Jesus as the Messiah. 'It was one thing to let a small group of Gentiles be received into the Church without circumcision in consequence of a manifest divine intervention, but quite another to have multitudes entering the Church upon the simple condition of faith all over the world' (Lattey, WV 2, 218).

For Paul the question was one of policy as well as of **c** principle. To accept the Judaistic claim was to make nugatory his whole mission to the Gentile world, and to renounce the hope of gaining that world for Christ. But above all, the thesis of the Judaizers struck at the nerve-centre of the Gospel, denying by implication the intrinsic merit of the Cross. To set up national or racial prerogatives within the Christian Church was an outrage to his conviction that Christ died for all without distinction and, in the light of his intimate experience, both before and after his conversion, he was satisfied that a religion, whose motive-power was Law, would never bring men to God.

To remove the occasion for disquiet, it was deemed expedient to go to Jerusalem and consult the Mother-Church. Paul and Barnabas represented the Antioch community that stood for freedom from the Law (cf Comm. on Gal for discussion of mutual relation of the visits mentioned in Ac 11 and 15, and Gal 2, § 897*c*). In the Holy City the Apostles recognized Paul's title to apostolic rank and approved the method employed by him in preaching to the Gentiles.

At an official assembly Peter took the initiative and **d** spoke in favour of gentile freedom, 'Now therefore why do you make trial of God by putting a yoke upon the neck of the disciples which neither our fathers nor we have been able to bear?' (Ac 15:10). He was supported by James, the alleged patron of the Judaizing party, who sought confirmation of the ruling in the OT. Yet James thought it wise to add certain prohibitions with a view to respecting the feelings of Jews in mixed communities. On these lines, as the rescript sent to the churches shows, agreement was reached and the commendation of Paul and Barnabas together with the repudiation of their opponents made it clear that the victory was theirs. The choice of Judas and Silas to be bearers of the apostolic decree may have confirmed all this, for in Silas Paul found such a kindred spirit that he chose him, in place of Barnabas, as his chief companion on the second missionary journey.

Second Missionary Journey—They traversed Syria **e** and Cilicia and the Galatian towns evangelized on the first journey. Forbidden to preach in Proconsular Asia, they struck north to the frontier of Bithynia. This district they were not allowed even to enter, so they turned west again, skirting Mysia and reaching the coast at Troas, where a heavenly vision called them to Macedonia. At this point in the narrative of Acts occurs the first 'we-section', indicating that St Luke was already in the party. Timothy had been taken on at Lystra. They reached Europe at Neapolis, the terminus of the well-known Egnatian highway, and hurried to Philippi which was the foremost town in that part of Macedonia. The ministry there had three phases: 1, the preaching at the river bank with the conversion of Lydia; 2, the expulsion from a

'03e slave girl of a divining spirit followed by the flogging and imprisonment of the preachers; 3, the conversion of their jailer. The Philippi ministry is significant in that it was here, in a Roman colony, that Paul first insisted so strongly on his Roman citizenship. The converts mentioned specifically by Luke differ in social rank and religious education and serve to illustrate the Pauline maxim that in Christ there is neither Jew nor Greek, bond nor free, male nor female. And the sequence of their conversion is symbolical of the progress of the Gospel outside Palestine—through the ghettos of the dispersion on to the Greek world and to Rome, the centre of civilization. Paul and Silas moved west along the main road to Thessalonica, the Macedonian capital, and here they preached for a short time and with some success among the heathens. But the hostility of the Jews forced them to flee to Beroea, and we find Paul for a brief moment at Athens—sorrowful and alone—before making Corinth, on the maritime route between Rome and the E, the real centre of missionary endeavour at this time. The exordium of a discourse to the Athenian philosophers survives to show that he could use the language of the higher culture when occasion required, but the anxiety to be of service to all was checked, in his relations with paganism, by an innate repugnance for anything to do with the worship of idols. He spent eighteen months at Corinth, plying with Aquila and Prisca the trade of tent-maker, by which means he avoided becoming a burden to the converts and running the risk of being equated in their minds with a social or political adventurer. On meeting with opposition from the synagogue, he changed, under divine inspiration, a Jewish mission for a predominantly Gentile and fruitful one: 'And the Lord said to Paul one night in a vision, Do not be afraid, but speak and do not be silent; for I am with you, and no man shall attack you to harm you; for I have many people in this city.' (Ac 18:9—10). It was from the capital of Achaia that he wrote 1 and 2 Thess.

'04a **Third Missionary Journey**—After his return to his base on the Orontes, the third journey was undertaken almost immediately. He passed through 'the region of Galatia and Phrygia' and sought out Ephesus, where he held disputations in the synagogue for three months and later in the house of a certain Tyrannus for upwards of two years. The circle of believers slowly widened and the Gospel, thanks to the new converts, was carried into the valley of the Lycus with the formation of Christian groups in the cities of Colossae, Laodicea and Hierapolis. To this period are assigned the major Epistles—Galatians to the beginning, unless it be assigned to a date before the Council of Jerusalem (cf § 895c.), Romans to the close, and the Corinthian letters in between. All are occasional writings with the exception of Romans, which is a treatise setting forth with clearness and distinction the fruit of his meditation on the central problem of the time—the relations between the Church and the Synagogue. At the end of the Ephesian ministry, Paul 'resolved in the Spirit to pass through Macedonia and Achaia and go to Jerusalem, saying, 'After I have been there, I must also see Rome' (Ac 19:21). The work of setting up the **b** Church in the E had been completed. From Jerusalem to Illyricum (Rm 15:19) he had fully carried out the preaching of the Gospel in the eastern world, and now he was determined, when he had handed over in Jerusalem the money contributed by the Gentile Churches to the poor of the Mother-Church, to seek a field of preaching in the extreme west where Christ had not been known. Paul obviously attached much importance to this subsidy for the benefit of the poor of Jerusalem, no doubt as a con-

crete proof of the loyalty of Gentile Christians to their **704b** fellow believers in Judaea. He little guessed that his visit to Rome would be delayed for some years, and that ultimately he would arrive thither, as a prisoner, on appeal to Caesar. Yet the future was casting its shadows before. At Ephesus a notable disturbance almost cost him his life (Ac 19:23—31); at Corinth a change of plan was rendered necessary by the knowledge that the Jews were plotting against him (Ac 20:3); and in the course of the return journey from the Aegean the Holy Spirit, in city after city, testified that bondage and affliction awaited him (Ac 20:23).

Arrest and Imprisonment—He arrived in Jerusalem **c** in time for the feast of Pentecost and, as he was completing with others a ritual purification, undertaken on the advice of James, Asiatic Jews stirred up the multitude and 'laid hands on him, crying out, Men of Israel, help! This is the man who is teaching men everywhere against the people and the law and this place; moreover he also brought Greeks into the temple, and he has defiled this holy place' (Ac 21:27—28). And they would have beaten him to death but for the timely intervention of the Roman Tribune. From the steps of the fortress of Antonia Paul addressed the mob in the vernacular, recalling his education at the feet of Gamaliel, his zeal for the Law of Moses, how he had persecuted the Christians, and how he had been converted. His subsequent reference to the divine commission to preach the Gospel among the Gentiles, though he himself pleaded to be allowed to preach in Jerusalem, roused the Jews to fury, whereupon the Tribune gave orders to bring him into the fort and to examine him under the scourge. This was a contravention of the 'Lex Porcia', and the Tribune, on being made aware of the circumstance, found himself in an embarrassing situation, not unlike that of another Roman in the presence of a greater than Paul. To escape from it he presented the prisoner to the sanhedrin, without result, and Paul, for his part, was comforted by a voice from heaven: 'Take courage, for as you have testified about me at Jerusalem, so you must bear witness also at Rome' (Ac 23:11). At this point a plot to kill the Apostle was discovered, whereat the Tribune had Paul spirited away by night to Caesarea, the residence of the Roman Governor.

Palestine had been re-attached to the Province of **d** Syria at the death of Herod Agrippa I in 44, and it was unfortunate that at this time the Governor should have been a wicked man and a time-server. Tacitus notes with cruel precision the character of Felix before whom Paul now stood: 'Antonius Felix, per omnem saevitiam et libidinem, ius regium servili ingenio exercuit' (Hist, 5, 9). After some days the high-priest arrived in Caesarea with a pleader, Tertullus, who led the prosecution and urged that Paul was a disturber of the peace which Felix had been at pains to establish in Palestine. Paul denied having caused any disturbance in Jerusalem and, while admitting that he served God 'according to the Way, which they call a sect' (Ac 24:14), affirmed his belief in the Law and the Prophets, and the general resurrection, and stressed his endeavour at all times to have a conscience void of offence in regard to God and man. The Governor, though he had no doubt about the prisoner's innocence, adjourned the case, giving orders that Paul be kept in bonds but treated with indulgence. He would later come to appreciate the wisdom and independence of the prisoner, but in the hope that a ransom would be paid for the freedom of one so influential he kept the Apostle in chains. On his removal from office two years later, things began to happen under the determined and energetic rule of his successor. Flavius

704d Josephus contrasts Festus favourably with his predecessor (BJ 2, 14), and his prompt handling of the present case compares to advantage with his predecessor's dilatory tactics. The NT portrait of his character reveals that curious combination of contempt and fear which Roman officials usually exhibited in their relations with the Jews. To the Jews of Jerusalem Festus replied that the prisoner was in custody at Caesarea and that there he would remain. Yet, when the accusations broke down in Caesarea, he showed himself willing and even anxious to oblige them. But Paul sensing a danger to his life, of which Festus must have been unaware, appealed to Caesar, thus overriding the jurisdiction of the Governor's court. Soon after this the prisoner had an opportunity of which he gladly availed himself to state his case and his mission before a distinguished audience, King Herod Agrippa II and Bernice. Cf Ac 26 for Paul's apologia, which is a model of moderation and prudence, remarkable for the respect shown to his hearers and to the Law which he venerated but whose domination was now at an end. At its conclusion 'Agrippa said to Paul, In a short time you think to make me a Christian! And Paul said, Whether short or long, I would to God that not only you but also all who hear me this day might become such as I am—except for these chains' (Ac 26:28—29).

e He was taken away by sea, bound for Italy, and Luke who accompanied him has left a detailed report of the long and dramatic journey. For some obscure reason—none better has been put forward than the traditional one, that, having brought the matter up to the moment of writing, there was nothing more to say—Luke's narrative breaks off with the master in Rome, where 'he remained two whole years in his own hired lodging'. His imprisonment was no bar to the progress of the Gospel. The 'word' spread among the jailers and even into the imperial residence, and the prisoner became well-known throughout the whole Praetorian camp. It was a period, too, of literary activity, four Epistles named from the imprisonment having survived. To the Philippians, a dear and docile congregation, he writes out of the fullness of his heart of the peace and spiritual joy which he wishes his children to share. In Ephesians he celebrates the Trinity of Eternal Love coming forth for man's salvation, and hymns the primacy of Christ and the grace-plenitude that flows from him to the Church. Colossians is a less objective exposition of Christ's pre-eminence, for in the Lycus valley philosophy had made an effort to draw the Christian Faith within its own sphere and to absorb it as it had done with so many pagan mythologies—hence the frequent warning against the danger of being cheated by plausible speech or deprived of their rights by philosophy and vain deceit. Alone among his extant writings, the letter to Philemon is addressed to a private individual on a personal matter. It bespeaks from him a kindly welcome for an unprofitable slave. While an extraordinary freshness and charm make it, in the literary order, a pure gem, it has an enduring value in that it gives an insight into Paul's approach to social and political evil.

f Release and later Journeyings—According to age-old tradition, he was released at the end of two years and Spain may have had the benefit of his preaching, if only for a brief space. A visit to the extreme west is recorded in the first-century Letter of Clement (5:5—7) and St John Chrysostom echoes the tradition in *Epist. ad Hebr. Praef.* From scattered references in the Pastoral Letters some indication is given of the stopping places in Paul's last missionary tour eastward. At Crete he left Titus behind to set in order what was still defective; Ephesus

was to have the benefit of Timothy's kindly rule. From **704** Macedonia he wrote to these delegates counselling them to be good ministers of Christ Jesus, able to exhort with sound doctrine and to rebuke the gainsayers. He wintered in Nicopolis, sending thence Titus to Dalmatia after his successful work in Crete. On the return, he touched at Troas, remaining some time with Carpus; at Miletus where Trophimus had to be put ashore on account of illness; and at Corinth where Erastus remained. During the journey to Rome or on arrival there he was rearrested, and the honourable custody of a few years before gave way to imprisonment in one of the city's dungeons where it was none too easy to locate him. The temper of the times had changed so much in Rome that Christians were in mind and spirit like people besieged; in the press of contemporary events faith alone sustained them.

In the second letter to Timothy-whom he besought to come to him with all speed—Paul gives us to understand that he is awaiting the end, without that expectation of release which we find in the Epistles of the captivity, but with the quiet assurance that 'there is laid up for me the crown of righteousness, which the Lord, the righteous judge, will award to me on that Day' (2 Tm 4:8).

Martyrdom—Tradition has it that he was beheaded at Aquae Salviae, a few miles outside the walls of Rome, and that friends had him buried in a cemetery half-way back to the city. Over the *cella memoriae* erected by an early Pope a Roman Emperor built a vast basilica in the fourth century, and we still possess Constantine's laconic epitaph: PAULO APOSTOLO MART. . . .

Paul's Relations with the Twelve—At the same time **g** and in the same city, though by a different method, St Peter suffered martyrdom, and throughout the centuries Rome combines the cult of the two and jealously guards their tombs. It is sometimes alleged that this posthumous association is not justified by their relations during life, and that the Antioch 'incident' (Gal 2:11—14) is only one of many which might have been recorded. But the 'incident' creates no difficulty if properly understood. More serious is the charge that Paul, being cast in a different mould, never became quite one with the other Apostles and that, being a Hellenist, he was obviously tempted to introduce pagan conceptions into a Christianity that was still unformed and defenceless. Such a theory is not in accord with the facts. Paul was a Jew by race, 'circumcised on the eighth day, of the people of Israel, of the tribe of Benjamin, a Hebrew born of Hebrews' (Phil 3:5) and despite the straying of Israel and the misfeasance of her leaders he cherished to the end a strong and tender love for his kinsmen according to the flesh (Rom 9:1—5). And if it is unfair to cut him off from his race and his upbringing, it is wrong to suggest that he was independent of Christianity in its earliest form. Paul did not differ from the other Apostles in his appreciation and preaching of the Gospel: 'Whether then it was I or they, so we preach and so you believed.' (1 Cor 15:11); 'I went up by revelation; and I laid before them (but privately before those who were of repute) the gospel which I preach among the Gentiles, lest somehow I should be running or had run in vain' (Gal 2:2). It would make this section too long to outline the arguments for the view that 1 Thes echoes the rhythms of the primitive catechesis which was a source of the Gospels. The connexion of baptism with the death and resurrection of Christ is taken by many to indicate a 'Hellenizing' tendency, but the proof that the viewpoint is not exclusively Paul's is that he takes for granted that the symbolism is familiar to the Romans and

04g Colossians, who were not his converts. The evidence of the Epistle to the Romans is decisive, for that Epistle implies the possession by the Romans of the full tradition of Christian teaching, even in regard to abstruse points. This highly didactic document closes with a warning against false teachers who arouse dissensions and set up obstacles 'in opposition to the doctrine which you have been taught' (Rm 16:17). If, on occasion, as in Gal 2:6—7, Paul uses language which appears to be uncomplimentary to his predecessors in the apostolic office, it behoves us to inquire if this was not occasioned by the employment of their names by Judaizers in the interests of party propaganda and as a drag on the wheels of progress.

h Missionary Methods—Paul had an advantage over his fellow Apostles in that he had an early and reliable biographer. Not that Acts is a biography in the strict sense: it is rather an apologia defending St Paul from the criticisms of his detractors. Its summary character is made clear by a perusal of the Epistles to Corinth, where the author recalls the true circumstances of the apostolic life and wherein the word overflows from the fullness of love and contemplation: 'For I think that God has exhibited us apostles as last of all, like men sentenced to death; because we have become a spectacle to the world, to angels and to men. We are fools for Christ's sake, but you are wise in Christ. We are weak, but you are strong. You are held in honour, but we in disrepute. To the present hour we hunger and thirst, we are ill-clad and buffeted and homeless, and we labour, working with our own hands. When reviled, we bless; when persecuted, we endure; when slandered, we try to conciliate; we have become, and are now, as the refuse of the world, the offscouring of all things' (1 Cor 4:9—13). 'Five times I have received at the hands of the Jews the forty lashes less one. Three times I have been beaten with rods; once I was stoned. Three times I have been shipwrecked; a night and a day I have been adrift at sea;' (2 Cor 11:24—25). Of these humiliating experiences, Luke recalls only a few (Ac 14:18; 16:22—23) and of other obstructive influences, he barely preserves an echo. Yet, thanks to him, we are made familiar with the method of evangelization conceived by the master, and catch a glimpse of the genius displayed in its execution. It was Paul's policy to concentrate, after the manner of a general, on strategic points, organize them thoroughly, and make them a base for further operations. He was in the habit of revisiting the scenes of his former labours and when prevented from doing so, kept in touch by letter or by chosen delegates.

05a The dispersion of Israel has been looked on in the light of a providential preparation for the Gospel. The synagogues of the Hellenistic world gave Paul a platform whence he could reach not alone his kinsmen according to the flesh, but also that fringe of the Gentile world which had been attracted to the religion of Yahweh. It is possible to trace in Ac the story of the failure of the Jews to believe, in view of which failure they ought not to have complained when the missionaries turned to the Gentiles: 'It was necessary that the word of God should be spoken first to you. Since you thrust it from you, and judge yourselves unworthy of eternal life, behold, we turn to the Gentiles' (Ac 13:46; cf 17:5—9; 18:6; 19:9; 28:24—29). While he announced the revelation of the Son of God to all, his message took on different aspects with different audiences. To the Jews, he spoke of the history of salvation, how Israel had been chosen to be the carrier of the Messianic Hope, and how that Hope had been fulfilled in Jesus of Nazareth (Ac 13:16—41). To the Gentiles, he dwelt on the eclipse of religious truth,

pointing out the folly of idolatry and its attendant vice, **705a** and the necessity of turning in worship to the One True God who in those days had called men to their primal obligations through an accredited representative, his Son Jesus Christ (Ac 14:14—16; 17:22—31). The teaching is found in more developed form in the Epistles that carry his name and that are sometimes called 'the foundation documents of Christianity'. While these Epistles were written for a definite purpose and to meet particular needs, it is obvious that they presuppose general instruction. They follow on what he and others had already orally taught, assuming a knowledge of much of which they themselves say little, and in that assumption creating difficulty for commentators. It is essential, therefore, to place them against a background of Church life and in a setting of Christian tradition which was in existence before they were written. A direct appeal to that tradition is made twice in 1 Cor, the first, 11:23, being of peculiar interest, because it shows that the Mass was being said and Holy Communion received for some twenty-five years before the abuses in Corinth provoked this written account of the institution of the Eucharist. We **b** should resist the tendency to regard these letters as systematic formulations of Christian belief, for most of them were occasional, in the sense that they were promoted by, and written with reference to, a particular situation. It is a tribute to the genius of their author that writings so produced should constitute a heritage of perennial value. Concerning his status as a writer it ought to be observed that ancient classic literature offers no precise parallel to the Pauline letters, either in structure or in tone. There is a freedom and variety in them that have no ancient analogy except in the letters which the discovery of Egyptian papyri has recently disclosed. Though the style has not been universally admired, owing to its anacolutha and parenthetic interruptions, it carries an impression of power and sincerity that a more polished diction would not secure. An attentive reading of the Pauline 'corpus' compels the conclusion that the author, while remaining a stranger to the figures and forms of the rhetoricians, was fully alive to the possibilities of the plastic speech of Hellenism. His was a talent remarkable for lyrical utterance combined with an ability, sometimes displayed, to match the graceful order of ideas with a formal beauty of expression.

Fellow-workers—Paul was careful in the choice of **c** collaborators. It seems, indeed, that loyalty to him and use of his methods were demanded of all those in close association. Many-sided men, like Barnabas, did not feel at home with one whom nature had fashioned for the first place. Talented speakers, like Apollo, must have thought it strange to see eloquence set aside in order that the Christian Thing might stand forth for what it was, a 'demonstration of the Spirit and power' (1 Cor 2:4). Among those of whose services he constantly availed himself were: the timid and affectionate Timothy, his 'truly-beloved son; Titus, a stronger character, highly valued because ready for every kind of work; Silas, of whom we know little beyond the circumstance that he shared with his leader the double privilege of Jewish blood and Roman citizenship; and Luke, the 'beloved physician', who shielded the master from criticism. These men, whatever their natural talents, became under inspiring leadership lieutenants of very high quality. Trained under his eye and profiting by his example, they were able to extend his work and, if need be, to take his place. It is interesting to notice in connexion with these fellow-workers that some of them, if not all, were the

705c converts of other men, and this confirms Paul's strong unity with those who went before.

d Character and Genius——However much we admire the impetus given to early Christianity by the missionary labours of St Paul, it would be unjust to allow the greatness of the work to obscure for us the character of the worker. St John Chrysostom, having commented on the Pauline writings with a mastery and an eloquence that have never been surpassed and seldom equalled, composed seven panegyrics on the Apostle. No writer in English has written more beautifully about him that J. H. Newman. Under the caption 'St Paul's characteristic gift', he says: 'To him specially was it given to preach to the world, who knew the world: he subdued the heart, who understood the heart. It was his sympathy that was his means of influence: it was his affectionateness which was his title and instrument of empire'. In virtue of this gift of sympathy the Apostle was able to spread about his person an aura of fragrance and to exercise on his fellows a kind of magnetic attraction: 'For though I am free from all men, I have made myself a slave to all, that I might win the more. To the Jews I became as a Jew, in order to win Jews; to those under the law I became as one under the law——though not being myself under the law——that I might win those under the law. To those outside the law I became as one outside the law——not being without law toward God but under the law of Christ——that I might win those outside the law. To the weak I became weak, that I might win the weak. I have become all things to all men, that I might by all means save some'. (1 Cor 9:19—22). Human nature, even in its unregenerate state, was an open book to him. Though he had never been a heathen and was no longer a Jew, yet he was a heathen in imagination and a Jew in the history of the past. Scattered throughout his writings there are specimens of the tender affection which his great heart had for all his kind. What a mixture of admiring love and plaintive denunciation did the thought of his own race inflict upon him! (Rm 9: 1—5).

e The consciousness of exalted office——dealing in priestly fashion with the Gospel of God——was to him a personal humiliation, for he realized that he himself was weak and one of the sinful race for whom Christ died: 'But we have this treasure in earthen vessels, to show that the transcendent power belongs to God and not to us' (2 Cor 4:7). As a consequence he used his awful apostolic power only at the call of duty, rejoicing to exhibit himself on that footing of human weakness which he shared with his hearers and converts. That is why he found himself in a position to conceive such great love of the brethren. After the pattern of Almighty God and in imitation of Jesus Christ he cherished to a high degree the virtue of compassion, and a character which was impetuous and unyielding by nature became gentle and affectionate under the influence of grace. The affection in which he held his own converts was as tender as it was strong. With the unselfish love of a mother he brought forth the image of Christ in the souls of Galatians (Gal 4:19); with the devoted sympathy of a nurse he cherished the Thessalonians and recaptured the language of infancy in order the better to be understood (1 Thes 2:7); with the strong solicitude of a father he exhorted and adjured all to walk worthily of the God who called them to his kingdom (Eph 4:1). How he rejoiced at the orderly array of the Colossians and grieved at the thought of their being **f** cheated and led astray! (Col 2:4—5). 'His mind', says Newman, 'was like some instrument of music, harp or viol, the strings of which vibrate, though untouched, by

the notes which other instruments give forth'. How he **705i** deplored divisions and abhorred enmities in the Christian body! (1 Cor 1:10—12). These he conceived as an offence against nature and above all as injurious to the Saviour who died to restore the unity of mankind. Fraternal charity was always in his thoughts, and no man hymned it as well or practised it so assiduously: 'If I speak in the tongues of men and of angels, but have not love, I am a noisy gong or a clanging cymbal. And if I have prophetic powers, and understand all mysteries and all knowledge, and if I have all faith, so as to remove mountains, but have not love, I am nothing. . . . Love is patient and kind . . . . (1 Cor 13). Christian altruism owes its noblest expression to him: 'Count others better than yourselves. Let each of you look not only to his own interests, but also to the interests of others' (Phil 2:3—4); and Christian humanism its motto: 'Finally, brethren, whatever is true, whatever is honourable, whatever is just, whatever is pure, whatever is lovely, whatever is gracious, if there is any excellence, if there is anything worthy of praise, think about these things' (Phil 4:8).

Such high and noble sentiments flowed spontaneously **g** from St Paul's appreciation of the Christian Mystery. His mind worked by intuition, and he saw more clearly than others the universal efficacy of the redemption. If salvation is for all men, and if in Christ there is neither Jew nor Gentile, it is because the power that works salvation is not the Law of Moses but faith in him who 'was put to death for our trespasses and raised for our justification.' (Rm 4:25). The Law of Moses was holy and just and good, but it was powerless to save. And how unequal to the struggle with sin were those who had nothing but that law to help them. Paul explained by a vivid description of the conflict between the higher and the lower self occasioned by the commands of God's positive legislation (Rm 7:14—25). In further setting aside the claims of Jewish propaganda he stressed the primacy of the life of grace over external observance, and showed himself more deeply acquainted with the spirit of the Gospel than many of his contemporaries. Christians, therefore, though freed from the Mosaic Law, were not free from all law, for they were subject to the law of the Spirit and had to keep their minds fixed on the things of the Spirit.

Another intuition that appears constantly in his **h** writings is the freedom of the sons of God. The death of Christ set men free from the tyranny of sin and the grave, and the Christian lives a new life in union with the risen Christ. In virtue of that union the Christian gives glad and willing service, inspired and borne along by the Holy Spirit. The 'slaves of Christ' are the only men who are truly free, for 'where the Spirit of the Lord is, there is freedom' (2 Cor 3:17).

'Slave of Jesus Christ' was the title which he himself loved beyond all others. From the time that his eyes were opened after his experience on the road to Damascus he dedicated himself completely to the Master. Henceforth faith in Jesus Christ was the power that charged his energies, the star that shaped his course, the wings that gave him flight. In a striking passage in Col 1:13—20 he recalls the primacy of Christ with the object of confirming the teaching given to that Church by Epaphras. Existing before the world of men and of angels, present to his followers from the beginning of this life and their goal in the next, Jesus Christ was the object of Paul's heartfelt praise and undying love: 'Who shall separate us from the love of Christ? Shall tribulation, or distress, or persecution, or famine, or nakedness, or peril, or sword?' (Rm 8:35). 'For to me to live is Christ, and to die is

05h gain' (Phil 1:21). 'I have been crucified with Christ; it is no longer I who live, but Christ who lives in me' (Gal 2:20*a*).

i To think of Jesus crucified as the power of God and the wisdom of God, to be urged on by an enthusiasm and a personal love for him that still burns and inflames across the centuries: all this was granted to Paul—and to such a degree that the expression 'in Christ Jesus' occurs as a refrain in his writings and recapitulates all his thoughts. Old age did not wither nor custom stale the beautiful relationship. From the darkness of a Roman prison he spoke of the light that the Saviour brought, shedding rays of life and immortality through the gospel which he had been appointed to herald (2 Tm 1:10). And though he felt that the end was at hand, he was not put to the blush, because Jesus, to whom he had given his confidence, had the means to keep his pledge safe.

The imagination is busy with the picture of the old man Paul in prison. Did the memories of thirty years of toil in the service of the Lord crowd in upon him? Some of those memories were painful, appeals unheeded, invitations spurned and grace rejected. Others were consoling: so many of the same mind, cherishing the same bond of charity, and the peace of God watching over their minds and hearts in Christ Jesus. One thing is certain: he had fought the good fight, had finished the race, and had kept the faith. He could look forward to the future with calm and serenity: 'The Lord will rescue me from every evil and save me for his heavenly kingdom. To him be the glory for ever and ever. Amen' (2 Tm 4:18).

THE CHRONOLOGY OF
NEW TESTAMENT TIMES

BY T. CORBISHLEY S.J.

706a See Table on next page.

b Bibliography—U. Holzmeister, *Chronologia Vitae Christi*, Rome, 1933 is a complete handbook to the whole problem of Gospel chronology and has an exhaustive bibliography. A more recent discussion is L. Girard, *Cadre chronologique du ministère de Jésus*, 1953; Ogg, *Chronology of the Public Ministry*, Cambridge, 1940, is the most accessible to English readers; E. Stauffer, *Die Dauer des Census Augusti*, *Texte und Untersuchungen* 77(1961); C. H. Turner, 'Chronology' HDB; 'Chronologie' DBS; 'Natale', *Encic. Cattol.* 8 (1952), 1667f. Most other modern treatment is in periodical literature. E. Power, 'Jn 2:20 and the Date of the Crucifixion', Bib 1928, 257; P. Benoit, *La deuxième visite de Paul a Jerusalem*, Bib 40, 1959, 778–92; J. Jeremias, ZNW, 1928, 98–103; T. Corbishley, 'The Chronology of the Reign of Herod the Great', JTS 36 (1935) 22ff; id 'Quirinius and the Census', Klio 27 (1934) 122–48; CBQ 1945, 223–30; 1946, 298–305. See also G. Ogg, *The Chronology of the life of St Paul*, London, 1968.

c Note—The whole problem of NT chronology has been raised by the false calculation of the beginning of the Christian era by Dionysius Exiguus (c. A.D. 520). He seems to have been misled by taking Lk 3:23 to mean 'Jesus was about beginning his thirtieth year'. Working back from 'the fifteenth year of Tiberius' (= A.U.C. 781) he apparently calculated that Christ was born A.U.C. 753, which he called 1 B.C., assuming that Christ was born at the *end* of that year. But, since we know that Herod died three years before that date, Dionysius' system is at least that much in error. To establish the correct dating is difficult, but a probable scheme can be produced. The procedure followed in this article will be to establish such dates in secular history as are relevant to NT history. The results of the investigation are given in the table overleaf.

A. Pivotal dates from secular history

d 1. The death of Herod the Great—This took place (Jos.Ant. 17,191; *BJ* 1,565) 34 years from the death of Antigonus (A.U.C. 717) and 37 years from the time when his claim to the throne was recognized by the Triumvirs in Rome (A.U.C. 714): other chronological indications show that he had not completed his 34/37 years, and the date of his death is almost certainly just before the Passover of the year A.U.C. 750 (= 4 B.C.).

e 2. The governorship of Pilate—this lasted ten years and came to an end not long before March A.U.C. 790 (= A.D. 37) (cf Jos.Ant. 18,89).

f 3. 'The fifteenth year of Tiberius'—Scholars have now given up the attempt to argue that Tiberius' regnal years may have been dated from the time (? A.D. 12) when Augustus associated Tiberius with himself in the government of the Empire. There is absolutely no evidence to support such a suggestion. Indeed Tiberius' accession was by no means automatic (cf Tacitus *Ann.* 1,11). As Fotheringham puts it: 'All our evidence points

to one conclusion, that the regnal years of Tiberius **706i** throughout the whole Empire were reckoned from his succession to full imperial authority. ⌈Sept 17, A.D. 14⌉', (JTS 35, (1934), 150). Cf also CBQ 7 (1945), 223–30; 8 (1946), 298–305. Tacitus (*Ann.* 4,1) *C. Asinio, C. Antistio consulibus nonus Tiberio annus erat* indicates the normal Roman method of reckoning. We know that Asinius and Antistius were consuls in A.D. 23. On this reckoning the 15th year of Tiberius would be A.D. 29, though it is possible to hold that it ran from Sept 28– Sept 29 (cf Girard, *Cadre chronologique*, 43–54, for an overwhelmingly convincing marshalling of the evidence). The argument accepted by some that Lk may have been working according to an old method of dating the reigns of Syrian kings, by which the 'first year' is that fraction between Sept 17 and the beginning of the civil year on Oct 1, has little to commend it. There is no evidence to suggest that there was anything but one generally accepted scheme of dating throughout the whole Empire.

4. The death of Herod Agrippa I—The indications **g** given in Jos.Ant. 343, 350, 351 taken together seem to suggest that this occurred at the beginning of A.D. 44, though it might have been late in 43.

5. The famine under Claudius—Cassius Dio (60, **h** 10–11) tells us that there was a serious famine at Rome in A.D. 42. Josephus refers to a famine at Jerusalem at some period in the procuratorship of Fadus and/or that of Alexander. Niese reads *epi toutou* which would make the famine occur under Alexander who succeeded Fadus, probably in 46. But the MSS read *epi toutois*, which seems to have been the reading known to Eusebius and Cassiodorus. Niese, presumably on grammatical grounds, prefers the reading of the 10th cent. Epitome. If we restore *epi toutois* we may suppose the famine to have begun under Fadus who became procurator on the death of Herod Agrippa I in 44.

6. The Proconsulship of Gallio—An inscription **i** found at Delphi makes it certain that there was a Gallio governing Achaea in A.D. 52. It is impossible to discuss it briefly, but a full account is to be found in *The Beginnings of Christianity* by F. Jackson and K. Lake, V, xxxiv.) The more probable conclusion is that he entered on his term of office in the autumn of 51, the normal term of office being a year.

B. The chronological indications given in the NT 707 documents.

1. The birth of Christ—We know that this occurred before the death of Herod the Great, i.e., before A.U.C. 750 (= 4 B.C.). A more precise dating depends on the much discussed passage in Lk 2:2 '*This census was first made when Cyrinus (= Quirinius) was governor of Syria*'. (The translation suggested by Lagrange: 'this census took place before Q was governor of Syria' is just possible grammatically, but is generally found unacceptable.) A difficulty arises from the fact that whilst Josephus speaks of a census under Quirinius in A.D.6 (Jos. Ant. 18,1ff—cf Ac 5:37), he makes no mention of an

CHRONOLOGY OF NEW TESTAMENT TIMES

706 a	Events of Secular History		Events of Sacred History
A.U.C.		B.C.	
714	Herod the Great recognized at Rome by the Triumvirs	40	
717	(Oct.) Herod takes Jerusalem	37	
742	P. Sulpicius Quirinius consul	12	
744	P. Sulpicius Quirinius, governor of Syria	10	
746	Sentius Saturninus, governor of Syria	8	Nativity of Jesus Christ
748	P. Quinctilius Varus, governor of Syria	6	Flight into Egypt
750	Death of Herod the Great: Archelaus succeeds him in Judaea: Herod Antipas becomes tetrarch of Galilee	4	Return from Egypt
		A.D.	
759	Archelaus deposed: Judaea becomes a Roman province under procurators. Quirinius, as governor of Syria a second time, holds census of Judaea	6	Christ, at the age of 12, goes up to Jerusalem with his parents
767	(Sept.) Tiberius succeeds Augustus	14	
780	Pontius Pilate, procurator of Judaea	27	
781		28	(or early 29) St John Baptist begins his mission
782	Coss. C. Fufius Geminus, L. Rubellius Geminus	29	Christ is baptized
783		30	First Passover of Public Life
784		31	Second Passover of Public Life
785		32	Third Passover of Public Life
786		33	(3 April) Crucifixion
787	Herod the tetrarch at war with Aretas IV of Nabataea	34	Martyrdom of Stephen: Conversion of Paul
788		35	Paul in Arabia
789		36	Paul returns to Damascus
790	End of Pilate's term of office: Tiberius dies: Herod Agrippa I becomes king of Trachonitis, etc.	37	Escapes from Damascus: First visit to Jerusalem
791		38	
792	Deposition of Herod the tetrarch	39	
793		40	? Conversion of Cornelius
794	Claudius emperor: Herod Agrippa I, king of Judaea	41	
795	Famine at Rome	42	Paul brought from Tarsus to Antioch
796	Death of Herod Agrippa I	43	Peter in prison
797	Fadus, procurator of Judaea	44	Paul's 'Famine Relief visit' to Jerusalem (?)
798	Famine in Judaea	45	
799	Alexander, procurator of Judaea	46	
800		47	
801	Cumanus, procurator of Judaea	48	
802		49	Council of Jerusalem: Paul's third visit
803		50	(spring) Paul arrives in Corinth
804	Gallio, proconsul of Achaea	51	(autumn) Paul before Gallio
805	Felix, procurator of Judaea	52	
806		53	
807	Nero succeeds Claudius	54	
808		55	
809		56	
810		57	Paul's first captivity—Jerusalem and Caesarea
811		58	
812	Festus, procurator of Judaea	59	Voyage to Rome begun: winter in Malta
813		60	Paul arrives in Rome
814		61	
815	Albinus, procurator of Judaea.	62	Paul released
816		63	
817	Gessius Florus, procurator of Judaea: Great Fire at Rome	64	Christians persecuted at Rome
818		65	
819	Jewish War begins	66	
820		67	Martyrdom of SS Peter and Paul (?)
821	Death of Nero	68	
822		69	
823	Jerusalem captured by Titus	70	

707a earlier census or of an earlier governorship of Q. Mommsen held that, whilst there was evidence for an earlier governorship, this could not have been during the reign of Herod. But cf JTS 26 (1936), *A note on the Syrian governorship of M. Titius*; Klio 27 (1934), 122—48: *Quirinius and the Census*, (both by T. Corbishley); and it is possible that Q was in fact governor of Syria from A.U.C. 743—6 (cf also W. M. Ramsay JTS 7 (1917) 229ff). There remains the odd fact that Tertullian (*Adv. Marcionem* 4:19) connects the census with the name of Sentius Saturninus, who governed Syria from A.U.C. 746—8. The most natural interpretation of all the evidence seems to be that Q instituted the census, which was completed by Saturninus, who could have taken over from Q in A.U.C. 746 (= 8 B.C.), which becomes the most probable date for the Nativity.

b **2. 'About thirty years old' (Lk 3:23)**—This is probably the crucial text in all this discussion. As we have seen (**706c**) it was a misunderstanding of this phrase by Dionysius which has falsified the existing scheme of B.C./A.D. dating. On any acceptable dating of the Nativity and the First Passover, Christ is *at least* 32 or 33 when he begins the public ministry. Girard (*Cadre chronologique*; 63—66) makes these further points. 30 was the required age (both amongst Jews and Greeks and Romans) for exercising public responsibility. (He quotes Num 4:2s.; Dion Halic., *Ant. Rom.* 4,6). Further, the Jewish fondness for round numbers seems to be especially shown in referring to ages. ('not yet 50' Jn 8:57; 'more than forty' Ac 4:22; to which could be added Gen 11:14, 18, 22 and, interestingly, 41:46 'Joseph was thirty years old when he entered the service of Pharaoh'). Girard also refers to 2 Sm 23:8—39, where 'the Thirty' turn out to be thirty-seven.

Since, then, Lk qualifies Christ's age by saying he was 'about (*hōsei*) thirty', it hardly seems unreasonable to translate this as 'in his thirties'. If we are prepared to accept this, all difficulties disappear. It is because scholars have been obsessed with the need for a minimal interpretation of Christ's age, that they have been reduced to forcing the evidence at some point. The earliest tradition, quoted by Iren. (*Adv. Haer*, 2,22,46 (PG 7,783—6)) insists that Christ had reached his fortieth year. He refers not only to Jn 8:57 ('thou art not yet fifty') but also to the universal witness of the *seniores* who had known John in Asia, some of whom had seen the other apostles. As E. Power says: 'Considering that it is the only apostolic tradition outside the Gospels that has come down to us about the age of Our Lord, and that it possesses the strongest claims to authenticity, we should be loth to reject an interpretation of it which may, after all, be that intended by Irenaeus' (Bib 9:281).

c **3. The date of the Crucifixion**—According to J. K. Fotheringham in an article which has won general acceptance (JTS 12 (1911—12) 120ff) the only two years, during the ten years of Pilate's governorship, in which the Crucifixion can have taken place are A.D. 30 and 33. (The argument is based on astronomical considerations, concerning the dating of the Passover. We know that Jesus Christ died on a Friday (Jn 19:31) and it is generally held that that Friday was the 14th Nisan, the day of the Paschal full moon. It is a question therefore of calculating in which years Nisan 14 fell on a Friday. However, not all commentators hold that Jesus died on the 14th. 'Jn 19:31 has been misinterpreted by many exegetes', writes J. E. Belser, 'Correctly understood this text proves that the 15th Nisan was the day of Christ's death' (*The History of the Passion*, E. tr. 1929, 182). No certainly therefore can be attained by this method of calculation.

As between 30 and 33 the following points should **707d** be taken into account.

(a) The earliest date at which John the Baptist can have begun his preaching, on the normal interpretation of 'the fifteenth year of T', is the autumn of 28, which would mean that the first Passover of the Public Life would be that of 29. If we accept 30 as the date of the Crucifixion, this would mean returning to the generally discredited view of a one-year ministry. Hence it seems preferable to suppose that by the 'fifteenth year', Lk really meant 29, with the first Passover in 30. This will imply a three-year Ministry and Crucifixion in 33. But cf §§ 641c—642c.

(b) *Geminis consulibus*: there is an early tradition **e** that the Crucifixion took place 'Geminis coss,' sc. when C. Fufius Geminus and L. Rubellius Geminus were consuls. This we know to have been A.D. 29 (cf Tert. *Adv Jud* 8 (PL 2, 616 B) '*Huius* [*sc Tiberii*] *quintodecimo anno imperii passus est Christus, annos habens quasi XXX cum pateretur . . . Coss. Rubellio Gemino et Rufio Gemino*'; Lactantius, *Inst Div* 4:10:18 PL 6, 474 *cuius* [*sc Tib*] *anno quinto decimo i.e. duobus Geminis consulibus . . .*). At first sight, of course, the linking of the year 29 with the death of Christ seems to be an argument against regarding 33 as the date of the Crucifixion. But the tradition really supports what I have called the natural interpretation of the 'fifteenth year'. As this was the one clear date given by Lk and as, from the *Fasti Consulares*, the corresponding consular names could easily be known, the names of the Gemini would be early associated with Lk 3:1. If the 'fifteenth year' had been thought of as referring to any other date, the corresponding consular names would certainly have got themselves attached to the story of the Public Life—'the acceptable year of the Lord' (cf. Clem.Alex., *Strom.*, I, 21, 145 (PG 8:885)). Whether this year was to be thought of as a strict calendar year would seem to most people unimportant. Thus the *Geminis coss* tradition strengthens the case for regarding the 15th year as coinciding at least in the major part, with A.D. 29.

(c) *Jn 2:20*—'*this temple was built 46 years ago*' **f** (which seems the more correct rendering: cf Power: Bib 9:268ff) would be useful if we could establish the date of Herod's Temple. Power (loc cit) and the present writer (JTS 36 (1935) 22ff) have come to the same conclusion (though on different grounds) that the passage points to A.D. 30 as the year of this Passover, Jn 2:13. But it is far from certain that it occurs here in its chronological order. The Synoptics record a cleansing of the Temple at the end of the Public Ministry, Mk 11:15—18; Mt 21:12—17; Lk 19:45ff, and this too is connected with a Passover. It is probable that there was only one cleansing (see comm. in loc) and that Jn's order is theological rather than chronological.

(d) The same caution applies to a passage in Jos.Ant **g** (18:113ff) in which we are told of an unsuccessful campaign fought by Herod against Aretas IV, the father of Herod's repudiated wife. One reason which precipitated hostilities was precisely this repudiation, in favour of Herodias. The date of the campaign is certainly not earlier than 34 and may be as late as 36. If Christ died in 30 and John, therefore, in 29, we have at least five years between the repudiation and the outbreak of hostilities, which seems unlikely at best. Not admittedly a strong argument but, again, a piece of evidence that suits a later rather than an earlier date.

On the whole then, whilst 30 cannot be altogether ruled out, it can be justified only by forcing the evidence at some point, just as a date later than 8 B.C. for the

'07g Nativity can be maintained only by disregarding some item in such evidence as we have.

708a **3. The date of St Paul's Conversion**—Attempts have been made to establish this from the presence of the 'ethnarch' of Aretas at Damascus. Some would argue that that official could not have existed before A.D. 37, when Caligula put Damascus under the jurisdiction of the Nabataean king. But the status of Damascus and the extent of the power of the Nabataeans at this period are far from clear. I would myself put the conversion in 34. The events of Ac 1—8 may not have occupied more than a year. If 3,000 were converted at Pentecost, it would surely not be long before the numbers rose to 5,000 (Ac 4:4) and the material needs of the community would be felt fairly soon. (Ac 6: appointment of deacons); nor need we suppose that a long interval elapsed between Stephen's selection and his death. Paul's escape from Damascus 'after three years' (Gal 1:18) will thus have occurred in 36 or 37. It may be possible to associate the precautions of the ethnarch of Aretas with the war then raging between the king and Herod (cf § 707g). We know that the Nabataeans controlled the trade-routes to Damascus from the S at this time (cf A.H.M. Jones, *The Cities of the Roman Provinces*, p. 292), and the growth of their power was sufficient to call for a full-scale campaign by the governor of Syria (Jos.Ant. 18,124). (NT references: Ac 9; Gal 1:15; Ac 11:25—30; 2 Cor 11:32; Ac 15.)

b The passage in Gal 1:15 has been the subject of much debate. The famous visit to Jerusalem 'after fourteen years' (? from conversion or from the first visit) must presumably be either the 'famine relief visit' of Ac 11 or the 'Council of Jerusalem visit' of Ac 15. Dom Bernard Orchard has collected the authorities for the view that the relief visit occurred in 46/47 (cf BJRL 28 (1944) 174; to which add Benoit, Bib, 1959; and cf § 895d). I have argued above (706h) for the view that the famine must have been felt earlier than 46, and the visit of Paul to Jerusalem recorded in Ac 11 seems so closely connected with the death of Herod Agrippa (certainly not later than the very beginning of 44) that it seems difficult to separate the two events by two years or more. However, given the uncertainty as to the date of Paul's conversion and the vagueness of the reference to 'fourteen years', it is impossible to have any kind of certainty in this particular matter.

c **4. The Council of Jerusalem**—The Gallio inscription (§ 706i) makes it probable that Paul came to Corinth in A.D. 50 (spring), staying there for eighteen months until he was brought before Gallio (Ac 18:12 seems to hint that Gallio had only recently arrived). This makes the date of the Council probably the previous year, 49.

The rest of the dating of Ac depends largely on the **708c** dates of the procurators of Judaea. Josephus is vague, but the years given in the table may be taken as probable.

The Gospels an uncertain basis for chronology— **d** From what has been said above and elsewhere in the comm. (e.g. § 642) it should be clear that no sure chronology can be constructed on the basis of the Gospel data or order. Apart from a Passion narrative, which itself is not without chronological difficulties, the rest of the Gospel story is made up of a great diversity of anecdotes and sayings put together to bring out in the best way the particular aim which the Evangelist had in mind in writing the Gospel. It is possible to distinguish certain 'collections' of material within the Gospel framework, but the order of the material within such a 'collection' is again by no means necessarily chronological. For the rest one finds a great many essentially disconnected stories. Thus the Gospel of St Mark in many places seems to consist of 'a number of unrelated paragraphs set down one after another with very little organic connexion, almost like a series of snapshots placed side by side in a photograph album. These paragraphs are sometimes externally related to one another by a short phrase at the beginning or end, but essentially each one is an independent unit, complete in itself, undatable except by its contents and usually devoid of any allusion to place. . . The older view that the Gospels were attempted biographies of Jesus, as adequate as the education of the Evangelists and the circumstances of the time would allow, has given place to the recognition that each of them was produced to meet some specific, practical and religious needs in the church of its origin and that it is those needs which have very largely controlled each Evangelist's choice, arrangement and presentation of material and distribution of emphasis', Nineham, *St Mark*, 27—29. Thus while it may be said that the Gospels present the life of Jesus in the sense that they proceed from his birth (Mt, Lk) to his public ministry and end with the Passion and Resurrection, the order of events in detail may not be assumed to be of itself chronological. It is Luke who is most conscious of the need 'to write an orderly account', Lk 1:3, and it is his Gospel in which one finds the largest number of chronological indications linking his narrative to secular history.

When we come to the **Acts of the Apostles** also by Lk (cf § 822e) this attention to chronological order is seen to be even more pronounced; at least in the second half of the Book. It must be admitted that in the first part such indications of chronology are largely missing, no doubt because Lk did not find them in his sources. Later in the work however he was able to supply them from his own experience and investigation.

ST MATTHEW

BY HENRY WANSBROUGH O.S.B.

709a Bibliography—Commentaries: P. Benoit, BJ, 1961[3]; S. C. Johnson, IB, 1951; M.-J. Lagrange, EtB, 1927[4]. J. Schmid, RNT, 1959[4]; J. Schniewind, NTD, 1950[5]; J. C. Fenton, Pelican Gospels 1963. **Other works:** P. *Benoit, Exégèse et Théologie,* 1961; M. Black, *An Aramaic Approach to the Gospels and Acts,* 1967[3]; G. Bornkamm, G. Barth, H. J. Held, *Tradition and Interpretation in Mt,* E.tr. 1963; R. Bultmann, *History of the Synoptic Tradition,* E.tr. 1963; B. C. Butler, *The Originality of St Matthew,* 1961; D. Daube, *NT and Rabbinic Judaism,* 1956; C. H. Dodd, *The Parables of the Kingdom,* 1935; J. Dupont, *Les Béatitudes,* 1958[2]; R. H. Fuller, *Interpreting the Miracles,* 1963; B. Gerhardsson, *Memory and Manuscript,* Lund, 1961; J. Gnilka, *Die Verstockung Israels,* Munich, 1961; J. Jeremias, *Eucharistic Words of Jesus,* E.tr. 1965; id, *Parables of Jesus,* E.tr. 1963; G. D. Kilpatrick, *Origins of the Gospel according to St Matthew,* 1946; K. Stendahl, *The School of St Matthew,* Lund, 1954; G. Strecker, *Der Weg der Gerechtigkeit,* Göttingen, 1966; W. Trilling, *Das Wahre Israel,* Leipzig, 1959.

b 1 Authority and Authorship of the First Gospel— 1. Allusions in the Earliest Church Fathers may be used to show existence of a gospel before their time of writing. But the force of such allusions is not easy to assess, for (1) The gospels themselves use traditional elements as sources. Long before the gospels were written down the sayings of Christ were in circulation in the Church; the Fathers may therefore be drawing on pre-gospel tradition rather than the gospels themselves. (2) As a rule the Fathers give rather allusions than exact quotations which can be attached to a particular passage of our written gospels. Thus the seeming allusions to Mt in Clement of Rome (13,2; 46,8) (c. A.D. 95) could derive from oral tradition of the sayings of Jesus. Similarly the clear similarity to Mt 6:2–13 of the *Didache* (8,2; 15,4) (c. 120) could be due to an anterior document, since Mt is here himself using a source (cf § 716*b*) which could have been used, independently of Mt, by the author of the *Didache.* The first indisputable references to Mt are therefore in the Epistle of Barnabas 4:14 (A.D. 100–30), where Mt 20:16 = 22:14 is quoted explicitly as written scripture, and Ignatius, *Ad Smyrn.* 1:1, (A.D. 107) who quotes a phrase from Mt 3:15 which reflects Mt's own theology (cf § 714*h*), and so cannot derive from previous tradition.

c 2. Tradition of Matthean Authorship—The earliest source to attest that Matthew wrote is **Papias,** bishop of Hierapolis c. A.D. 110–30 (dates given by M. Jourjon, DBS 6 (1960) 1108, though some scholars would put him twenty years earlier). His testimony is reported by Eusebius of Caesarea (HE 3,19), but almost no firm conclusion may be drawn from it. Eusebius has no high opinion of his intelligence, and blames him for misunderstanding the apostolic teaching on eschatology, and for credulity; nevertheless he reports his words 'for the information of scholars'. Papias is himself reporting **709** the words of John the Presbyter, who he says knew the Apostles. These words may be translated 'Matthew arranged in order the sayings in the Hebrew dialect, but each translated them as best he could'. Every important **d** word in this sentence has been so disputed that, even if Papias be accepted as a trustworthy witness on this point, the content of his evidence is too doubtful to serve as a solid basis of argument. 'Sayings' could indicate Jesus' own sayings, or sayings (stories etc) about him; the work could therefore have been either a mere collection of sayings (such as was Q; cf § 709*f*) or the gospel as we know it. 'The Hebrew dialect' could mean either the Aram. language (known at this time by the name 'Hebrew'; the Heb. language was probably then known only to scholars, the language of Palestine being predominantly Aram., or the Heb. way of debate and exposition (so J. Kürzinger 'Das Papiaszeugnis und die Erstgestalt des Matthäusevangeliums', BZ 4 (1960) 19–38). 'Each' could refer to readers of Matthew's work, or to Mk and Mt themselves, working on the 'sayings'. 'Translated' might mean translation from one language into another or—following the more common usage in contemporary rhetorical treatises—exposition and exegesis. The dictum of Papias has been taken as proof that Mt wrote a gospel in Aram., a gospel which has been supposed by many Catholic scholars to underlie all three canonical synoptic gospels (Lagrange, Chapman, Vaganay, Benoit). But in fact Papias' remarks are so polyvalent that scholars interpret and manipulate them to accord with the conclusions which they draw from other evidence. **The remainder of the tradition** may well be dependent on Papias, since at least some of his phraseology often reappears, e.g. in Irenaeus (in Eus. HE 5,8) c. A.D. 180. One witness which may well be independent is that of the title of the gospel '*Kata Matthaion*' which dates from the mid-second cent. Origen (in Eus. HE 6,25) in c. 233 is the first to add that the author was the erstwhile tax-collector.

3. Internal Evidence—The gospel contains two **e** passages where special attention is paid to Matthew. In 9:9 the tax-collector, called Levi by Mk and Lk, is named Matthew. In 10:3, correspondingly, the Apostle Matthew is described as 'the tax-collector', a description absent from Mk and Lk. This trifling attention to Matthew is hardly sufficient to have generated the tradition that this Apostle was author of the gospel; on the contrary it is just sufficient to add a minute *confirmatur* to this tradition which must have had other foundations. But the practice of pseudonymously attributing a work to a well-known figure—by a literary fiction, more or less transparent, putting it under his patronage—was so widespread in Jewish and early Christian circles that it cannot *a priori* be excluded that the attribution to the apostle also is a literary fiction (so Kilpatrick, 138–9).

2 Sources of Mt—The interrelationships between the **f**

09f first three gospels is a notorious problem; see § 645*b*. It will be sufficient to state here that this commentary is based on the theory that Mt used as his sources primarily Mk and the collection of sayings of the Lord known as Q. In addition he also had his own sources, not available to the other evangelists, some written and some oral; these latter can be distinguished because the vocabulary is in part distinctively Matthean and in part sharply divergent from his usage, e.g. 1–2; 14:28–31; 27:3–10, 24–25 (cf Kilpatrick p. 37–58). Kilpatrick (p. 14–36) suggests that all the written material was drawn from one written source, which he calls M; the existence of this single document is, however, far from proved. B. C. Butler has pointed out (DowR 66 (1948) 367–83) that Mt's proper material frequently shows striking similarity with Pauline teaching, and even expression, concluding that 'it is therefore an attractive hypothesis that at least large masses of Matthean material existed in written form (and in the Greek language) before St Paul's epistles were written' (p. 382).

g **3 Date**—Since there is no dispute that Mt, at least in anything approaching its present form, is posterior to Mk, it must be dated some years after Mk (cf § 746*d*). The inclusion of the passage about the temple-tax indicates a date not much later than 97, since it would have little interest at least after the abolition of the *fiscus Judaicus* in that year (cf § 728*j*). The rift between Jews and Christians evident in Mt also fits this period. This rift is definitely complete (cf 10:17; 23:34), unlike Mk, Mt carefully speaks of '*their* synagogues' (cf § 721*i*). The lack of interest in any Jewish group other than the Pharisees (Kilpatrick 120–21) suggests a date after 70, since only this group survived the destruction of Jerusalem in any organized form. No argument for the chronological relations between Mt and the sack of Jerusalem can be drawn from Mt 24, for the destruction is described in purely theological rather than historical terms (cf § 736*e*); nor from 22:7 (cf § 733*i*). It has been argued that an early date fits better the retention of Jewish practices (observance of the sabbath: 12:1–14; respect even for alimentary prescriptions of the Law: § 726*d,f*); but as late as the Council of Laodicea (c. 360) it was necessary to forbid Christians to observe the Jewish sabbath, and some alimentary prescriptions of the Law remained in force among Christians till at least the end of the second cent. It would, therefore, be rash to give a date for Mt more precise than the last third of the first cent.

10a **4 Character of the Gospel—1.** Far more than the other gospels Mt has a profoundly Jewish atmosphere. Not only does he constantly suppose in his readers familiarity with things Jewish: Heb. writing (5:19), the three principal good works of almsgiving, prayer and fasting (6:1–8, 16–18), the temple-duties of priests (12:5), temple-tax (17:24–27), phylacteries, tithes and purifications (23:5, 23, 27), washing the hands in token of innocence of blood-guilt (27:24). In addition, his own method of teaching frequently recalls that of the rabbinic schools; some elements he shares with Mk e.g. a rabbinic form of dialogue (§ 757*a*), a rabbinic grouping of controversies (§ 734*a*); others are typical of Mt alone, e.g. teaching arranged on the model of Jewish methods of exegesis (§ 717*b*), casuistry (10:13; 18:15–18; 23:8–10, 16–28), groupings according to the perfect number or seven (7 parables in ch 13, 7 charges in ch 23). These elements would fit admirably the translation proposed for Papias' words 'in the Hebrew way of exposition' cf § 709*d*. Perhaps most striking of all are three major preoccupations proper to Mt:

1. The fate of Israel: Mt insists that Christ's mission **710b** was primarily to them (10:5; 15:24); he is the Son of David promised to them by the scriptures as Saviour (§ 734*i*). Yet at every step he is baulked by the official representatives of the Jews (§ 724*e*), until he is compelled to turn to the gentiles and create a new Israel (§§ 733*e*, 743*g*).

2. The problem of the Law: Mt's terminology is full of legal expressions: lawlessness, just, justice, worthy, and the cognate theme of judgement (§ 738*f*). A table of frequency is instructive:

'just'	Mt 18 times	Mk 2 times	Lk 11 times
'justice'	7	0	1
'lawlessness'	4	0	0
'worthy'	9	0	8
'judgement'	12	0	4
'gehenna'	7	3	1

The sabbath and other precepts of the Law are still accepted as having binding force. Mt is not willing simply to jettison them. He only insists that the Law must be interpreted not in the materialistic way of the scribes and Pharisees, but according to the principle of the higher law of love (cf 5:17–19; 7:12; 8:4; 12:1–14; 15:1–20; 22:34–40; 23:3 and notes, especially § § 717*j*, 734*g*, 738*h*).

3. The fulfilment of scripture: An invariable element **c** in the early Christian preaching was reference to the scriptures to explain the happenings in 'these last times' (e.g. Ac 2:14–36); especially true was this of the narratives of the Passion, which are to a great extent shaped by the scriptural quotations whose fulfilment they show (cf § 739*a*). Mt applied this process throughout Jesus' life. Fulfilment of the prophecies is the keynote of his infancy narratives, the scripture quotations which they fulfil forming the climax of each incident reported (cf § 712*j*). Seven times (2:23; 4:14; 8:17; 12:17; 13:35; 21:4; 26:56) Jesus is shown, at critical stages of his life, as acting thus precisely in order to fulfil the scriptures; in this way is each phase explained and justified. In two cases especially the way in which allusions to scripture are somewhat artificially engineered is reminiscent of contemporary rabbinic exegesis (2:23; 27:3–10). The former case is compared by Stendahl (p. 191–9) to the methods of exegesis now known at Qumran, especially in 1 Qp Hab. This concentration on the literal fulfilment of scriptural phrases, which were originally certainly not meant by their human author as prophecies of details in Christ's life, can throw a modern reader off balance. Jesus, as the Messiah, is indeed the fulfilment of the whole of scripture, of the promises of God and the hopes of his people. But he is this fulfilment by his whole person and by his life's work rather than because little details of his life happened to correspond to phrases in the OT, often only when removed from their contexts. But Mt was a 1st cent. Jew, affected by the rabbinic method of using scripture, and expresses the important truth that Jesus fulfils the OT by pointing out a wealth of correspondences which to us seem less central. Cf Fenton, pp. 17–19.

2. Striking after Clarity is a marked characteristic of **d** Mt. We have already seen this motive at work in the rearrangement of Mk's order, so as to bring into the same place teaching on the same subject (§ 710*a*). Similarly within a passage Mt will often leave out many of the lively 'human' touches given by Mk, in order to throw the main lesson into relief, thus the miracle stories in Mt 8–9

710d are considerably shorter than their models in Mk. He can make minute adjustments in a narrative for the sake of clarity (8:6; 12:4). He emphasizes his lesson by several members of identical construction (the seven antitheses in 5:21–48; the three good works to be done secretly in 6:1–8, 16–18; the true and false disciple in 7:24–27), or by the process of 'bracketing' (giving a key-word or phrase at beginning and end of the lesson: 6:19, 21 'treasure'; 18:1, 4 'greatest in the kingdom of heaven'; 12:39, 45 'evil generation'). This type of bracketing is often expanded into the elaborate antithetical pattern of chiasmus which is often found in the OT (12:46–50; 15:3–6; 18:10–14; 23:16–22; cf P. Gaechter *Literarische Kunst im Matthäusevangelium*, 1966; J. C. Fenton, TU 73 (1959) 174–9. It is for these reasons that many have suggested that the sketch of a Christian scribe in 13:52 is a portrait of Mt's ideal. Kilpatrick and Stendahl rather regard the gospel as the product of a liturgical and catechetical milieu where the scriptures and the message of Christ were intensively studied and meditated, and of which the author of Mt is no more than the—'deliberately pseudonymous' (Kilpatrick p. 139)—mouthpiece. On **Mt's attitude to history** see § 638*c–k*.

711a **5 Theology**—Mt has been described as the Gospel of the Kingdom; the theme of the kingdom of heaven can indeed be taken as the central core round which the gospel is built. Not only does he use the expression 'the kingdom' far more often, but the great discourses of Mt can, with some degree of verisimilitude, be regarded as built round the theme: chh 5–7 as describing the conditions of entry to the kingdom, 10 messengers heralding the kingdom, 13 the nature of the kingdom, 18 mutual relationships within the kingdom, 24–25 the final manifestation of the kingdom. On Mt's concept of the kingdom see § 715*f*. The other themes of Mt may be seen in subordination to this.

b **1. Christology**—Christ is the Lord of this kingdom. Mt is not concerned to give us an intensely 'human' image of Jesus, but presents a somewhat hieratic picture of a Jesus whose divine power constantly shines through. It is as though Mt constantly has in the back of his mind the great figure of the final judge in which the presentation of Christ reaches its finest climax (cf § 738*g*). Already during his earthly life those who acknowledge Christ address him invariably as 'Lord'—used in the other gospels only occasionally and without the pregnant sense it has in Mt—while it is only those who refuse to recognize or follow him who call him 'master' or 'rabbi' (9:11; 12:38; 19:16; 22:24; 26:49). Mt uses freely the title 'Son of God' (cf § 714*j*), which at least hints at, though it does not necessarily demand on the part of the speaker, recognition of his divinity. He also employs the title 'Son of Man' with much more freedom than Mk, to show Jesus' exalted position even on earth (cf § 719*k*).

c But, even more than in his use of titles, it is by subtle editorial touches that Mt presents the portrait of Christ: he passes over mentions in Mk of emotion in Jesus whether of anger or tenderness (cf §§ 723*d*, 729*b*, 730*j*, 731*c*, 739*k*), seeming thus to raise him above them; he stresses Jesus' supernatural knowledge (11:27; 12:15, 25; 22:18; 26:10) control of his destiny (§ 739*d*), and the supernatural awe which he inspires (§ 726*a*, 743*h*). In the miracle stories there are no longer the gay and turbulent crowd scenes of Mk; instead the onlookers fall into the background, leaving the suppliant face to face with the awful majesty of Christ. Yet, at the same time, Jesus maintains his simplicity in Mt; there is nothing pretentious **d** about him; he is rather the **humble king**, ruling his kingdom in gentleness, whose sympathy is with the

humble, the oppressed and down-trodden (8:17; 9:10– **711** 13; 11:1–6), and whose kingdom is open only to such (5:4–12; 18:1–5 and notes). By Mt, steeped in the OT, this aspect of Jesus is developed largely in function of the fulfilment of the prophecies of the OT. He twice adds quotations from the prophecy of the servant of the Lord in Is (8:17; 12:18–21). This prophecy is clearly alluded to already by Jesus himself (20:22–23, 28; 26:28); he must himself have meditated his future sufferings in terms of it, cf § 727*i*. The earliest preaching (1 Cor 15:3) and the passion-narratives themselves show clear traces of it (cf §§ 739*b*, 761*u*, 762*f*). But for Mt this was a datum of tradition which played no special part in his theology. Mt's own two citations of the servant-prophecies are in the context of his healing activity; in the first case (8:17) it is Jesus' lowliness in caring for the disabled which fulfils the prophecy; in the second (12:18–21) his quiet humility in refusing to allow his miracles to be published abroad. Above all, Jesus' gentleness and approachability are seen in his great appeal to those who are overburdened (11:28–30), and in the way in which he chooses to make his solemn messianic and royal entry into Jerusalem, riding on a donkey (20:1–9), where again Mt is careful to point out the fulfilment of the prophecy.

In this most Jewish of the synoptic gospels the **e** significance of Jesus is shown especially by his **fulfilment of OT figures**. In the infancy narratives he is seen to be at once the new Abraham, Israel and Moses (§ 713*bc*). It has been suggested that the structure of the gospel is based on the five books of Moses, the Pent, since, if the infancy and passion narratives are regarded as prologue and epilogue respectively, the remainder falls into five great sections; this is, however, somewhat artificial. But a number of other hints are to be found that Jesus is a new Moses e.g. in the forty days and the high mountain of the temptations (4:2, 8 § 715*d*), the promulgation, also from a mountain, of the perfection of Moses' law (5:1–2), the feeding of the multitude with bread in the desert as Moses fed them with manna (14:13–21). But the theme of the accomplishment of OT figures shows most strongly in Mt's reiterated use of the title 'son of David' (cf § 734*i*); Jesus fulfils the promise to David, which becomes ever more prominent in biblical and post-biblical literature, that God would send to Israel a deliverer who would sit on the throne of David for ever. Under the Roman occupation this deliverer was conceived in almost purely political terms, cf § 715*f*. Jesus, by his allusions to Ps 110 (109), intimates that their expectations of an earthly son of David were insufficient (22:42–45; 26:64); this may be why the title retained prominence only in the gospel where the Jewish heritage of Christianity is most to the fore.

2. Ecclesiology—It is to be expected that in the 'gospel **f** of the kingdom' (cf § 711*a*) teaching on the Church should play a special part. At the centre of this teaching stands the proclamation that **Christ is present in his Church**. This is the message of the first of the many scriptural texts adduced by Mt, in which Jesus' name and so his mission are given as Emmanuel, God with us (1:23). It is the burden also of Christ's final promise, given in the fulness of his power (28:20). Between these two brackets to Mt's gospel stand recurrent references to Christ's presence in the assembly (18:20), in his missionaries (10:40), in any who are received in his name (18:5), in all those in need (25:35–45). When the disciples are persecuted it is because they represent Christ (10:17–25; 24:9), imitating also his sufferings (cf § 721*h*). They may rely for their protection on the Spirit of the Father (10:20), that same Spirit which

11f came upon Jesus at his baptism (3:16; 12:18). It may be that, when Jesus comes to the rescue of the disciples on the sea, Mt intends an allegory in which the ship represents the Church (14:22—33—so Tertullian).

g Mt catechetic and moralistic interests are reflected in his increased **concentration** on the disciples rather than on the apostles. Of Mk's ten mentions of the apostles Mt's omits nearly half. In Mt the disciples clearly represent all followers of Christ, i.e. all later members of the Church: what is taught to them applies also to all Christians. From various touches Mt's portrait of a disciple may be built up. He insists that all are called by Christ (those, and only those, who take it upon themselves to attempt to follow Christ are not accepted, 8:19 and note; 19:16—22); he underlines the need for immediate obedience to the call and total renunciation (4:18—22 and note; 8:21; 9:9; 19:21). This is brought out still more by the invariable and schematic nature of the accounts; Mt has filed them down to a minimum to spotlight their essential lesson. All the followers of Christ equally are called to perfection (5:48, § 730h, 731a), a perfection which is repeatedly described only in terms of total generosity and of love shown to any who are in need. It is in this that the 'will of the Father' consists (cf 7:21; 12:50; 6:10).

h Yet sometimes Mt has also in mind a certain group of the disciples who will form the **hierarchy in the Church**. Out of respect for them he minimizes their faults whenever possible (§ 724e). In the section on the formation of the disciples, common to all the synoptics (13:53—17:27), Mt especially underlines Jesus' special care for their instruction, and already suggests that they, by their co-operation with him in his work now, will carry it on as his representatives after his departure (cf § 725k). The special instructions which set the tone for their conduct towards those in their charge are given in 18:1—35.

i Among all the disciples, and more clearly than in any other gospel, **Peter** has a special position. Mt alone adds to the list of the Twelve that Peter was the first (10:2). It is Peter who walks on the water in 14.33, see § 720b. At Caesarea Philippi he is clearly the leader. Mt's attitude to Peter is shown by the part he gives him as spokesman (15:15—in Mk's parallel it is simply 'the disciples' who speak; 17:24; 18:21—in Lk's parallel the speaker is not given), though in this he only continues the common synoptic tradition of Peter's leadership (17:4; 10:27; 26:33). It is Mt who gives the most explicit account of Peter's commission as foundation-rock of the Church (16:17—19).

j **6 Structure of the Gospel**—Mt's didactic care and skill shows no less in the arrangement of the whole than in the construction of each unit. The gospel falls clearly into seven sections, of which the central five are each subdivided into a narrative part and a discourse:

1. Prologue:	Infancy Narratives (1—2)
2. The Kingdom Appears:	The Preliminary Manifestation (3—4) Sermon on the Mount (5—7)
3. Jesus' Saving Mission:	Ten Miracles (8—9) Missionary Discourse (10)
4. The Hidden Kingdom:	Opposition and Division (11—12) Parables of the Kingdom (13)
5. The Kingdom Develops:	Formation of the Disciples (14—17) Community Discourse (18)
6. Towards the Passion:	Mounting Opposition of Judaism (19—22) Judgement Pronounced (23—25)
7. Passion and Resurrection (26—28)	

711j

Chh 1—2 Birth and Infancy of Jesus—The earliest **712a** preaching of the Church, as seen in Paul and Ac, took its starting-point from the Baptism of Jesus and the beginning of his messianic mission. Mk too begins his gospel at this point. The other evangelists preface theirs with a prologue, Jn on the pre-existent Word of God, Mt and Lk on the birth and infancy of Jesus, a subject on which the earlier writings are silent, but which reaches a full and luxuriant development later in the apocryphal gospels. Mt's infancy narrative is composed of five panels. Each of the five panels except the fourth begins with an indication of time; each is guided by a divine message (either through a divine messenger, an angel, or—in the case of the second—the star); and each concludes with a reference to a passage of scripture which is thereby fulfilled (cf note on vv 22—23).

1 Jesus Christ, son of David, son of Abraham— **b** The purpose of Mt's first ch is to show that Jesus the Messiah is descended from Abraham, the father of the people of Israel, to whom it was promised that in him all nations of the earth should be blessed (Gn 18:18, cf note to Mt 28:19a), and from David, for it was from David's line that the Messiah was to be born (2 Sm 7:12—16, cf § 734i). The difficulty will be that Jesus had no earthly father through whom his descent could be traced. **1.** 'A genealogy of' (lit 'book of the begetting of'). Mt, the careful teacher, brackets the genealogy by repeating at the end 'such was the begetting of Jesus Christ' (v 18). The expression is a biblical one, used also Gn 5:1. On the name 'Jesus' see § 712i. 'Christ' is the Gr. for the Aram. Mesiha', lit 'anointed'. It is primarily a title, not a proper name, and in Mt is regularly used with the article (Jesus the Christ), which shows that it retained this character; Mt uses it as a proper name only in this genealogy. On the Messiah and Jewish messianism cf § 617a—g. Because of the current political conception of the Messiah Jesus himself avoided using the title; when he is challenged by the high priest to accept or reject the designation of 'the Christ', he accepts it only with extreme reserve (cf § 761v).

2—17 The Ancestry of Jesus—The list is divided into **c** the three classic periods of Jewish history: Abraham to David (**2—6a**, cf 1 Chr 1:27—2:15), the period of the kingdom of Judah: David to Jechoniah (**6b—11**, cf 1 Chr 3:5—16), the period after the Babylonian captivity (**12—16**, cf for the first part, 1 Chr 3:17—19; Ez 3:2). The list is stylized into 14 generations for each period, perhaps in order to achieve a multiple of the sacred number 7. (In order to arrive at complete symmetry it is necessary to regard the Jechoniah of v 11 and the Jechoniah of v 12 as different people. The son of Josiah (v 11) is called in the OT Jehoiakim, not Jechoniah; but perhaps he was also called Jechoniah, as was his son, who enjoys in the OT two names, both Jehoiachin and Jechoniah.) In fact a number of generations are omitted for the sake of this symmetry, e.g. only three generations are given—Perez to Nahson—for the period of the

712c captivity in Egypt, which probably lasted considerably longer; between Joram and Uzziah 1 Chr places another three generations. But the Gr. *'egennēsen'* has a less strict sense than 'was the father of'; it can mean also 'was the ancestor of'. The four women, Tamar, Rahab, Ruth and Uriah's wife are mentioned with a purpose; there is something special about each of them (Gn 38; Jos 2; Ru 1—4; 2 Sm 11 respectively); the motherhood of each did not occur in the normal course of affairs, and was regarded—though no moral judgement is implied—as due to a divine intervention. This prepares for Mary's motherhood.

d **18—25 Jesus, Son of David**—The Messiah was to be son of David. It was not through Mary that Jesus was son of David, for in Jewish law ancestry was counted only through the father. There is, incidentally, no indication in scripture that Mary was of David's line. In any case Mt's genealogy is directed towards Joseph, not Mary; it is therefore through Joseph that Jesus was son of David. But it was not by generation that Jesus was son of Joseph and so of David. The purpose of the passage is not to defend the virginal conception of Jesus. This is, rather, its presupposition, for the whole argument to show how Jesus was incorporated by divine command into the house of David would have been unnecessary if Joseph had been Jesus' father by way of generation. The virginal conception is shown also, incidentally but clearly, by the different formula in v 16 (contrast vv 2—15) and by the expression 'virgin' in v 23. To the Jews generation was only one way of gaining a son; e.g. by the law of the levirate (Dt 25:5—10) a widow who has no son must be taken to wife by her brother-in-law and the eldest son of this union is the son, not of his natural father but of the dead husband of his mother. In Jewish law at the time of Christ a man may adopt a boy by a solemn declaration that he is his son; the boy is then, to all intents and purposes, his son (SB I. 35). It is this act, by which Jesus becomes a son of David, that is described in this passage, ending in the last words which form the climax and goal of the ch. The motif of these vv is that this adoption was no casual or wilful act on Joseph's part; it was done in obedience to God's command, which overcame Joseph's hesitation to intrude where the spirit of God was at work.

e **18b.** In Jewish law a girl was betrothed to a man (who then paid her father or guardian compensation for the loss of her, the bride price); henceforth she was in his power and he ranked as her 'Baal' (= 'lord, master, husband,' cf Hos 2:18—19). If she lay with another man it counted as adultery; she could be repudiated only by a bill of divorce; if he died she ranked as a widow. Only sexual intercourse between husband and wife was (probably) not permitted until the man formally 'took the wife to his home' (v 24); cf SB II. 372—99. It was before this event that Mary was found to be with child (perhaps only a solemn expression for 'conceived a child'). The spirit of God is in the OT that by which God acts in the world, destroying (Is 40:7), or more especially giving life (Gn 1:2; Jdt 16:14); it is in this sense that the expression is used here. The full implications are expressed in Lk's annunciation scene, (1:26—38), to **f** which Mt has no parallel. **19.** It has frequently been maintained that the purpose of the angel's message was to reassure Joseph, hitherto unaware of the divine origin of Mary's child, that she had not misconducted herself. Quite apart from the curious reflections which this implies as to the lack of openness and trust between the two spouses, it not only fails to account for many elements in the text, but even makes them inexplicable. If Mary had

committed adultery she was liable to the death penalty **712f** (Dt 22:23—24), and her husband would, according to Jos.Ant 4, 8, 23, have been bound to denounce her. Joseph was a *'just'* man; JB's 'man of honour' is tendentious, for the term *dikaios* has always a strictly legal, rather than primarily moral connotation (e.g. 9:13; 13:17; 23:29), related always to the Jewish law or its fulfilment in Christ (cf 5:17). (C. Spicq's claims, RB 71 (1964) 206—14, that it means something like 'good, decent, exemplary' are invalid; his examples are drawn from Jewish literature whose object is to persuade non-Jews of the value of Jewish observances). Joseph's 'justice' would not be exemplified by divorcing Mary, especially secretly, unless he knew her to be guiltless. It is clear from the sequel that his motive was a sense of his own unworthiness to take her to wife. It is mentioned in order to increase the force of the incident which follows. **20—23.** **g** The details of this passage show it to belong in the series of divinely-directed birth-stories of the OT (Gn 17:15—22; Jg 13:2—5, 8—20): God—in the parallel passages of later strands often replaced by 'the Angel of the Lord', seen in a dream—appears to a man and declares that his wife, who is barren, will have a child by divine intervention. He announces the son's name and declares his special mission. The difference in this case is that Joseph is to have a son not by begetting but by adopting. **20.** Alone of NT authors Mt, the most Jewish of the gospels, mentions dreams as a means of revelation (2:12, 13, 19, 22; 27:19). They occur frequently in rabbinic literature, though their revelatory value was disputed (SB I. 53—63). The most important parallel is the announcement to Moses' father that a son would be born to him who would free Israel from Egypt; but on the Jewish Moses-traditions cf § 713b. The opening words of the messenger recall that the purpose of the whole passage is to ensure Jesus' incorporation into David's line. The message itself has **h** been diversely interpreted. In the most obvious sense of both Gr. and Eng texts v 20bc is curiously lacking in punch; there seems no connexion between the reason given (the 'because'-clause) and the action commanded: why should Jesus' divine paternity be a reason for Joseph to take Mary to wife—unless, which we have already excluded (§ 712f), this remove his suspicions? But in both the Gr. (cf X. Léon-Dufour—'L'annonce à Joseph', *Mélanges A. Robert*, 1957, 390—7) and the underlying Aram. (M. Kramer, 'Die Menschwerdung Jesu Christi', Bib 45 (1964), 1—50) the sentence can well mean that Jesus' divine paternity should not make Joseph fear to take Mary to his home: 'Do not, because Mary has conceived by the holy spirit, be afraid to take her home as your wife. She will give birth to a son, and *it is for you to* name him Jesus'. Thus the message would provide the central point of what seems to be the purpose of Mt 1, that Jesus should be divinely incorporated into the house of David, in spite of the virgin birth. The Greek, it must be admitted, is awkward though not without parallel (Zerwick *Graecitas Biblica*, § 474—7); but, rather than base an interpretation on the frail evidence of Mt's use of particles, it is better to rely on the underlying Aram. expression (*di* for Gr. *gar*) which can bear equally well the sense which fits the whole passage as that which cuts across it. **21.** Naming a child is normally the prerogative **i** of the father, as part of his acknowledgement of his son (Gn 17:19; 1 Chr 22:9; Is 8:3); hence Joseph's act of naming the child is tantamount to adoption. The name given, especially when it has been predetermined by God, signifies the nature and mission of the child. **Jesus** (Heb. *Yešua'*, shortened form of *Yehošua'*) means 'the Lord saves' or 'the salvation of God'. In the OT it is God who

12i saves his people (Hos 1:7), but already in the pre-Christian Psalms of Solomon (c. 50 B.C.) this office has passed to the Messiah, though always through the power of God. We cannot therefore conclude from the name and its interpretation that the child is already given a divine prerogative; rather it signifies the intimate union of the boy with God and his interpenetration with the divine power. The salvation is to be liberation 'from sins'; this needed to be stated clearly from the first, for in current hopes the Messiah was to deliver Israel from the political domination of the Romans. In Mt Jesus is seen fulfilling this mission in 9:2—6 and especially by means of his blood, shed for the remission of sins and received in the eucharist (26:28, cf § 739j); thus his work is **j** to be continued in the Church (cf § 711f—h). **22—23.** The first of eleven occasions on which Mt explicitly quotes the scripture as being fulfilled (four times in Mt 1—2 alone). On all but two of these occasions, (2:17; 27:9), when it is Jesus' opponents who perform the action, Jesus or his parents are represented as acting precisely in order to fulfil the scriptures. Jesus had come to fulfil the scriptures cf 5:17. The position of the citation is significant: one might have expected it at the end of the passage; its occurrence already here indicates that all the stress is laid upon the divine ordination of Joseph's naming (cf § 712d). **23.** This text of Is 7:14 LXX is much quoted in early Christian literature (e.g. Justin Apol. 1:33; Dial. 43:8; 67:1); Mt's slight variation from our LXX version ('they will call', instead of 'you will call') suggests that he took the quotation from a book of texts collected for use by Christian apologists, especially since the exact LXX-text would have suited his theme **k** far better (cf note on v 19). The word 'virgin' is an interpretation by the LXX of the Heb. "almāh', which means only 'girl': this interpretation suggests that they were especially guided by the Holy Spirit (P. Benoit, p. 3—12), for the MT does not necessarily have this prophetic sense. This passage of Is was not recognized by the Jews to have any messianic significance. According to their expectations nothing was known of the Messiah's birth (cf 13:55; Jn 7:26—28); he was simply to appear from the desert (cf § 682e). In view of this it is absurd to say that the virgin birth was invented in order to fulfil the expectations of the Jews or the prophecies. 'Emmanuel, God with us' forms the key-note of Mt's Christology and ecclesiology (cf § 711b, f). **25.** This v contains no implication that Joseph and Mary had intercourse thereafter. The Gr. 'heōs hou' rather translates the Aram. ''ad di' (as Dn 2:34; 7:4, 9, 11; 6:25 LXX): in Dn and in rabbinic writings ''ad di' often introduces the clause where the emphasis lies, with a nuance of surprise at, or suddenness of, the event. Translate: 'before he had had (almost 'could have') intercourse with her, she gave birth to a son'. On 'the brothers of the Lord' cf §§ 663—4.

3a 2 The Infancy of Jesus—These stories correspond strikingly to contemporary Jewish legends, based on the Bible, about the patriarchs Abraham, Moses and Jacob. Jewish reflection on the significance of these figures expressed itself not in abstract theological statements but in stories about them which illustrate their importance. Jewish study of scripture, called midrash (from Heb. dāraś, 'to search'), was divided into two categories, halakah, rules of conduct drawn from the scripture ('hālak' = to walk), and haggadah ('higgid' = to tell, declare), narratives which interpret the significance of persons and events. Cf the categories 'moral' and 'dogma' into which Catholic theology was divided. The essential of midrash is not that it is fictional but that it is derived

from reflection on scripture; thus to define a narrative as **713a** midrash says nothing with regard to its historicity (cf M. Bourke 'Literary genus of Mt 1—2', CBQ 22 (1960), 160—75). Paul uses the technique of midrash to apply the lessons of the OT in Gal 4:21—31; 1 Cor 10:1—13. The version of the life of Moses used in Stephen's speech (Ac 7:22—32) owes much to the haggadah type of midrash. There can be no doubt that the NT writers accepted this manner of interpreting and using scripture as legitimate, and that Mt may therefore be employing it here. He deliberately tells stories about Jesus in the terms of the stories which were told about the patriarchs, in order to show his stature and to bring out his significance, cf § 711e. Therefore the effect of these narrations is largely dependent on the knowledge of the legends about the patriarchs; this may be assumed in Mt's original audience. The chief parallels are: to **Moses**: before Moses was **b** born his father had a dream predicting his greatness and his role as liberator of Israel from Egypt. In another version Moses' birth was foretold to one of Pharaoh's priestly scribes; Pharaoh and his court were filled with dread, and Pharaoh consulted his sages as to the interpretation and the course of action he should take, cf R. Bloch in Moise l'homme de l'Alliance 1954, 106—12. Further parallels between Jesus and Moses come from the Bible itself: the king's attempt to eliminate the child by slaughtering all male children (Ex 1:15—16), the flight into exile (Ex 2:15) and return at a divine command (Ex 4:19—20—but command given by an angel, according to rabbinic tradition, cf Ac 7:35). The star recalls **Abraham**, for legend tells that at his birth a star appeared to King Nimrud and his court; this was interpreted as a portent that Abraham and his descendants would gain everlasting power over the whole world (SB I. 77—78). This motif of a star appearing at a great man's birth is, however, common to many literatures; it is recounted e.g. of the birth of the emperor Nero (Suetonius, Nero, 36). Similarly the theme of a king who hears that he is to be supplanted by a child, whom he then tries unsuccessfully to kill, is found also of the Roman Romulus and Remus. The typology of Jesus as **the new Israel** also occurs (D. **c** Daube NTS 5 (1958/9), 184—7): according to a pre-Christian haggadah Jacob (also called Israel, and the father of the 12 tribes of Israel) went down into Egypt, warned by a dream, to escape the massacre of his sons by Laban (like Herod, half a foreigner and half a Jew), and received a divine command to return from Egypt when it was safe to do so. Two of Mt's scriptural quotations fit this typology best: the citation of Hos 11:1 (which refers to Jacob—Israel's return from Egypt) in v 15, and perhaps the mention of Rachel, Jacob's wife, in v 18. This symbolism of Jesus as being in himself the new Israel is present also in the account of the temptations (cf § 715b) and in the whole theme of the Suffering Servant (cf § 711d). For Mt it is especially important because of his stress that the Church is the new Israel (§ 733e) and that Christ is ever present in his Church (§ 711f). But in view of the wealth of themes which appears here, it would be a mistake to insist upon one to the exclusion of the others. Finally on the problem of the **d** **historicity of the stories in Mt** it is impossible to be dogmatic. The midrashic technique certainly occurs in the NT (§ 713a). The character of these stories differs widely from the rest of the gospel, in its constant admonitions in dreams and the general atmosphere of the marvellous (not merely the miraculous). The constant reference to the OT, and explicit quotations to explain each incident, could suggest that it is entirely modelled on scripture; in the rest of the gospel the OT references are much less dense, more

713d incidental. The events of the infancy narrative did not form part of the message of the earliest preaching, as seen in Ac, for this began only with Jesus' ministry. There is no echo of them in Paul, Mk or Jn, and the stories related by Lk 1—2 have only a limited number of points of contact with Mt 1—2. Hence J. L. McKenzie (*Dictionary of the Bible*, 1965, 387) writes without comment 'These features . . . have led modern scholars to suppose that the primitive Church possessed little or no living memory of the infancy and childhood of Jesus' and he believes that they 'were intended to be theological expansions of the bare data contained in the memory of the early life of Jesus'. This conclusion is delicately balanced. Some features are common to the tradition: the virginal conception of Mary, birth at Bethlehem, childhood at Nazareth. Herod's persecution is in character with what we know of his ruthless and bloody repression of possible rivals. A visit of Magi could have been occasioned by the messianic ferment of the times. But around the core of fact is a good deal of inspired embroidery, whose message is not to be learnt by feverish insistence on historicity of every detail.

e **1—12 Visit of the Magi**—Throughout the ch runs the contrast of recognition of Jesus by the gentiles and rejection of him by the Jews, which will form a major theme of the gospels (cf § 733e). Israel's recognition by all nations in the messianic age is a constant theme of the prophecies (Is 49:23; 60; Ps 72 (71):10—11), many of whose details are here fulfilled. **1.** Bethlehem, the home town of David, lies some 6 miles S of Jerusalem. Herod reigned in Judaea 37—4 B.C. The last years of his reign were marred by suspicion of rivals, and consequent judicial murder of most of his family, including wife, brother and three sons. Nevertheless he founded a dynasty, mention of whose members occurs frequently in the gospels. The 'wise men (*Magoi*, magi) from the east' (in later sources described as three in number and eventually dignified with the rank of king) may well come from 'Arabia', the strip of country running between the Jordan depression and the desert to the East, then flourishing under the Nabataean civilization; to the Jews it was proverbially the land of wise men (Jb 1:1; Jer 49:7). Elsewhere in the NT *magoi* are unfavourably portrayed: Ac 8:9—24 'Simon who had previously practised magic' ('Simon Magus') and 13:6—11 'Elymas the magician' (*magos*). From the frequent contemporary prohibitions of practising magic it appears that this was a real danger. Since myrrh and incense are normal components of charms (cf K. Preisendanz, *Papyri Graecae Magicae* I (1928), it is possible that Mt here symbolically represents the members of the profession as laying down their instruments and their profits at the **f** feet of the Messiah. **2—4.** The star, the terror of Jerusalem and consultation of the wise men are midrashic elements. The first gentiles to acknowledge the salvation of God in the Messiah journey to Jerusalem, thus fulfilling the prophecy of Is 2:2—3; 56:6—7; Tb 13:11. **5—6.** The second of the four scriptural quotations which articulate the narrative, showing the theme of fulfilment in Christ (cf § 712j). Jewish messianic predictions showed little interest in the birthplace of the Messiah; it is located to Bethlehem only in two 4th cent. A.D. texts (SB I. 83). This, one of the few points in the infancy narratives on which Mt and Lk agree, is certainly not invented to fulfil the prophecies. **10.** 'Delight' and joy are themes with which Lk's infancy narrative is shot through (e.g. 1:14; 2:10). Mt's sparing use of the term suggests that it had for him the special connotation of the joy of the last times; he uses it here, of the joy of heavenly reward (25:21, 23), and of the women's reaction to the message of **g** the resurrection (28:8). **11.** The reverence they pay to

Jesus is the *proskynēsis* properly due only to God; it is **713** often accorded to Jesus, especially in Mt, for whom it becomes one of the ways of showing his transcendent dignity **12.** The gifts are the products for which the East was famed (Ezek 27:2). Gold and frankincense are offered to God in the Bible (Is 60:6; Jer 6:20). Myrrh is interpreted by the Fathers as being an omen of Jesus' death—perhaps not without reason, for it occurs elsewhere in the NT only in this connexion (Mk 15:23; Jn 19:39).

13—15 Flight into Egypt—Another little tableau in **h** which events are directed by the message of God in fulfilment of the prophecies (cf § 712j.). There was in Egypt a large colony of Jews, especially at Alexandria and Heliopolis (where the tree under which Mary sat is still shown to the more intrepid and enquiring traveller). The journey on foot would take about a week from Bethlehem. But the kernel of the incident is the typology of Jesus as the new Moses or the new Israel (cf § 713c).

16—18 Massacre of the Innocents—This scene begins **i** abruptly, without the usual introductory temporal clause, suggesting Herod's ferocity. Significantly there is no divine command to guide the action this time (cf § 712a); only the final fulfilled prophecy. It is impossible to estimate the number of infants involved in this massacre; in the hamlet and outlying dwellings of Bethlehem there can hardly have been more than a dozen boys of this age. Human life, and especially that of children (cf Lagrange p. 34), was cheap in those days: such slaughter falls well within the bounds of Herod's capacities (cf note to v 1). The theme of the wicked king who tries to eliminate at birth possible rivals is common to folk-lore. But this does not mean that the incident was invented. There is again a reminiscence of the typology of Jesus as the new Moses or new Israel (cf § 713c). Added to this is the contrast between the gentiles' acknowledgement of Jesus and the Jews' rejection (cf § 733e). **18.** At first sight this citation **j** seems out of place, for Rachel's children were of the tribe of Benjamin, not Judah (in whose territory Bethlehem lies); D. Daube (NTS 5 (1958/9), 184—7) argues that the mention of Rachel is due to the typology of the new Israel, for she was wife of Israel-Jacob. More probably the reason is connected with the fuller context of Jer 31:15—17: Rachel is told not to weep, because her sons will return from exile in Babylon, as Jesus will return from his exile in Egypt. It was perhaps suggested also because Rachel's tomb is traditionally situated in Bethlehem.

19—23 From Egypt to Nazareth—The last of the five **k** panels in the infancy story is similarly directed by an angel (cf § 712a) but closes only with an obscure scriptural allusion, instead of the usual quotation. One of Mt's major preoccupations in this ch has been to justify by reference to scripture the places of Jesus' sojourning (cf also 4:13—15 and note). That he was brought up at Nazareth was one of the firmest data of tradition, and gave rise to the earliest appellation of those who were later called Christians (Ac 24:5; cf Mt 26:69, 71). **23.** The difficulties of Mt's allusion are two: firstly, Mt is vague about the text which he has in mind, saying only 'through the prophets'; thus it seems that he may be making a general allusion rather than a reference to a single prophet. Secondly, Nazareth is properly transcribed from semitic languages with a *s*, while the closest form to the Gr. *Nazoraios* has a *z*. Thus two allusions, neither exact, could be meant. Perhaps Mt refers to the expression *Naziraios* (cf Jg 16:17) a translation by the LXX for 'holy to God'; in this case he rejoins Mk 1:24 (Lk 4:34) and Jn 6:69 in calling Jesus 'the Holy One of God'. Perhaps the reference is to Is 11:1, where the coming Messiah is called a 'shoot' (neser) from the stock of Jesse. Either of these would be permissible to one

13k of Mt's exegetical principles as a pun on Nazareth (cf Stendahl, p. 191—9).

14a **3—4 The Manifestation of the Messiah**
3:1—12 John the Baptist heralds the Messiah (Mk 1:1—8; Lk 3:1—18)——John the Baptist appears, a prophetic figure announcing the arrival of the last times of the world, exhorting the people to prepare themselves by conversion, and finally pointing to Jesus as the Messiah who is to usher in this final period. His prophetic character is clear at once from his garb: a hair cloak is the mark of a prophet in Zech 13:4. This and a leather loincloth are sufficient to identify Elijah in 2 (4) Kgs 1:8; Elijah was the prophet awaited to herald the arrival of the last times (Mal 3:23), so by wearing this garb John identifies himself specifically with this prophet (denied by Jn 1:21, for a special reason; see note there). The remaining elements in the description suggest an association of John with the Qumran community, for they ate locusts (CD XII. 14) and used in connexion with their expectation of the Messiah (1 QS VIII. 14) the text of Isaiah quoted by John in v 3. His appearance in the desert——given more prominence by Mk, who uses the word 'desert' in vv 4 and 12 to bracket the whole section——was also a sign of the Messiah's arrival, for it was from the desert that he was expected to come. This was one of the chief reasons for the withdrawal of the Qumran sectaries to the desert to found a community to prepare for the Messiah: 1 QS VIII. 13; but also it was the place for other pseudo-Messiahs to appear (Mt 24:26, cf SB I. 86); Jesus fulfils this expectation by retiring to the desert after his baptism, and coming from there to begin his mission.

b The kernel of John's call to penance in preparation for the Messiah is his proclamation of the text of Is 40:3, recognized by Jesus' contemporaries and the later rabbinic writings (SB I. 96) as applying to the Messiah. This text is quoted also by Mk; but Mt fills out John's message with phrases from Jesus' own teaching: thus 3:2 reappears in Jesus' mouth in 4:17 (see § 715e), and phrases from 3:7—10 in 23:33 and 7:19. Mt insists on the parallelism between Jesus and his forerunner also by describing their audiences in largely similar terms (3:5 and 4:25), and by describing John's death in terms reminiscent of our Lord's (see 14:3—12 and notes); but he also throws into relief **c** the difference between them: 3:11. John proclaims that the time for conversion has come, using forceful metaphors of a rotten tree cut down (**10**) or chaff separated from grain (**12**); for both the fate is unquenchable fire. It is not enough to claim physical membership of Israel (**9**). Here already is Mt's theme of the true Israel, composed of those both Jew and gentile who enter the kingdom of heaven. The Israel of the flesh is to fail and be rejected, cf § 733e. For those who are not prepared to welcome him the day of the Lord's coming at the last time will be a visitation of wrath (**7**), as it will be a saving visitation for those who receive him. This is the constant message of the prophets, who especially use the figure of destroying fire (Is 33:11; Ezek 30:8; Zeph 1:18; Jl 2:3—5; Mal 3:19), and refining fire (Ezek 22:17—22; Mal 3:23). By using this imagery John proclaims that the day of the final visitation is at hand. It seems that John concentrated so exclusively on this aspect of a wrathful visitation that he was puzzled by Jesus' action, and needed special explanation to understand that there was another side to the Messiah's activity, see notes to 11:2—6.

d The response to John's preaching was an admission of sin and **baptism** for repentance (**6**). This creates a slight geographical difficulty. In Mk 1:4—5 John appears to be simultaneously in the desert and baptizing in the Jordan. This is an indication that the 'in the desert' is theological, rather than a piece of geographical information; it tells **714d** us more of John's function than of his location (cf § 714a). Mt perceives the geographical difficulty, and locates the preaching in the desert, the baptism at the Jordan. Lk, the careful historian, meticulously indicates a change of position (3:3). Ritual immersion was practised by the Essenes and at Qumran at this time, but in a manner very different from John's baptism. At Qumran it was a rite of **e** legal purification, not a sign of conversion of life; it was repeated daily, not made once and for all; it was a private, solitary act, not performed by a minister; it was not connected with admission to a community, as John's was a sign of preparation for the eschatological community. John's baptism was more akin to the Jewish baptism of proselytes, but there is no sure attestation of this practice at so early a date. John himself distinguishes his baptism from that of Jesus (**11**), in that it was only 'for repentance', whereas Jesus' was to be 'with the Holy Spirit and fire'. Mt, moreover, will not admit, as do Mk 1:4 and Lk 3:3, that John's baptism is 'for the remission of sins'; he reserves this phrase for Christ's blood in the eucharist (26:28). Thus John regards his baptism as only a sign of repentance, in preparation for the eschatological visitation of the Messiah, He promises that Christ's baptism will bring about that visitation in fire, a purifying initiation of each individual into the eschatological community of the last times, and an imparting of that new Spirit of God which was promised by the prophets for the last times (Ezek 11:19; 36:26). Though Jesus himself baptized during his earthly life (Jn 3:22) this was probably a baptism similar to John's, for the outpouring of the Spirit and the forgiveness of sins was to come only with his death (Mt 26:28; Jn 7:39).

John describes in two ways the gulf between himself **f** and the Messiah whom he heralds (**11**): first by means of a play on words in Aram. more clearly preserved in the version of Jn 1:30: Jesus comes behind John (the position of disciple to rabbi) but is in fact 'greater than me' (= rabbi). The reference to the Messiah's 'power' recalls Is 40:10, where the Lord Yahweh is said to be coming with power at his visitation. Secondly John uses a figure drawn probably from ancient court ceremonial: a slave is depicted carrying Pharaoh's sandal, e.g. on the Narmer palette: John says he is not worthy to perform even this menial task—— there could be no more forceful way of expressing the gulf in rank between two persons.

13—17 Baptism of Jesus (Mk 1:9—11; Lk 3:21— **g** 22)——This is the decisive point at which the signal for the beginning of Jesus' messianic mission is given, in the form of the manifestation and voice from heaven. In Mk and Lk the baptism itself is little more than the occasion of this manifestation. In Mt however the baptism has more importance. Jesus comes 'in order' to be baptized', and insists even against John's remonstrances. Vv **14—15** (proper to Mt) lay stress on Jesus' reasons for this. It has been supposed that these vv are intended to answer scruples on the part of the early Christians that the baptism implies that Jesus is either inferior to John (this could be a motif in Lk's account, for he carefully refrains from saying that Jesus——or indeed anyone——was baptized by John (cf note on Lk 3:21)), or at any rate not sinless. Barth (p. 140) holds that their point is to show that Jesus humbled himself and entered the ranks of sinners, though himself sinless. This would, however, be a mere pretence. In fact, John's baptism was a sign of entry into the community of those awaiting the Messiah (§ 714c), which was normally through an act of conversion. Jesus' submission to baptism makes sense psychologically only if it has this significance, that by it he aggregates himself to this

714g company, and by so doing makes the community properly
h messianic, inaugurates the messianic era. Thus Mt's phrase '*achieve* all that *the will of God* demands' (cf Barth, p.139), on which his whole emphasis lies, denotes both that by his action Jesus does what was required of a good Jew, and that his so doing is a completion or crowning. This sense of 'fulfilling' is most prominent in Mt: Jesus acts in order to fulfil the scripture (cf § 719*i*); he has come in order to fulfil the Law and the prophets (5:17); the antitheses of 5:21—48 aim to complete the interpretation of God's will as shown in the Law. For 'justice' see §§ 710*b*, 717*e*. Thus Mt teaches that the baptism is the moment of the decisive fulfilment of God's plan; it inaugu-
i rates the messianic era. **16.** The epiphany, consisting of the descent of the spirit and the voice, is variously recounted by the evangelists. In Mk it is said that Jesus saw the vision, without suggesting that anyone else did or did not; Mt, who certainly depends on Mk here, could only with difficulty be otherwise interpreted, Lk, also depen-ent on Mk, is the first to add carefully 'in bodily shape', thus emphasizing that the event was a public phenomenon, not confined to Jesus' consciousness. Jn 1:32 goes a stage further: the Baptist witnesses to it. This history of the text shows at least that for Mk and Mt the importance of the divine manifestation is as a sign to Jesus himself. It is a sign of the beginning of Jesus' mission as Messiah. This is made clear by the biblical language of the passage: the only places in the OT where the heavens are said to open in these words are Ezek 1:1 (the vocation of Ezekiel to his prophetic mission) and Is 64:1 (of the advent of the Messiah). In the significant prophecies of Is 11:2; 42:1; 61:1, the spirit of God rests upon the Messiah. The form of a bird suggests to some commentators the spirit hover-ing in Gn 1:2. The spirit of God in the OT is given always for a specific task, to enable the recipient to accomplish a specific vocation (Jg 3:10; 6:34; Nm 11:17; 2 (4) Kgs 2:9; Zech 7:12). In this case it is the anointing of Jesus for his messianic mission (cf Is 42:1; Ac 10:38). In a certain limited sense it could be said that it is from this moment that Jesus is Messiah, since from this moment he
j begins his work as Messiah. **17.** The voice is, in Mk and Lk, addressed to Jesus. Mt substitutes for 'you are' his favourite demonstrative phrase 'this is' (cf 3:3; 7:12; 13:19). His purpose is not to suggest that the voice was addressed to the bystanders but to underline the similarity of this scene with the Transfiguration (17:5). The words spoken suggest several OT texts (Is 42:1; 44:2; 62:4; Ps 2:7), indicating that Jesus fulfils the prophecies of the Suffering Servant of Isaiah (see § 461*k* and, especially, §§ 711*d*, 739*a*), and that he himself is the new Israel promised by God; cf the title son of man', where the individual personality and the members of the kingdom are also interchangeable (§ 719*k*). With this Suffering Servant Christology is combined the theme of the Son of God—a combination which is characteristic of the Christian message, not found in the OT or Jewish writings. On the title '**Son of God**', see § 677. Mt is far more free than Mk in his use of this title, in accordance with his tendency to emphasize the divine dignity of Christ, see § 711*b*.

715a **4:1—11 The Temptation** (Mk 1:12—13; Lk 4:1—13)—Here Mt combines Mk's very brief account of the tempta-tions, from which he derives much of vv 1 and 11, with the account given in Q, the source common to Mt and Lk (cf § 646). Since there were no witnesses to this scene it has been suggested that the account owes its origin to the early Church, 'edited under the influence of Hellenistic-Jewish scribes' (Bultmann p. 304). The account given, in the style of a rabbinic scriptural controversy, is certainly

highly formalized. It is not impossible that Jesus may **715** have recounted his temptations to the disciples; but it is also possible that, aware (cf Mk) that Jesus was tempted at this moment, the Q tradition gathered the elements of the temptations which beset him throughout his messianic mission into the account of these same temptations as they occurred to him now, at its beginning.

It is possible also (cf B. Gerhardsson, *The Testing* **b** *of God's Son*, 1966) that the form in which the tempta-tions are narrated is strictly midrashic, that is, that it brings out the significance of the events by describing them in terms of previous events described in the OT; this narrative certainly leans heavily on the OT account of the testing of Israel in the desert. One of the major themes of Deutero-Isaiah is that the phenomena of the exodus are to be repeated at the dawning of the messianic era. Mt is fond of representing Jesus as being himself the Israel of the last times, cf § 714*j*. It is as Son of God that Jesus is tested (v 3, linking with 3:17), an appellation which is used of Israel also, especially in connexion with the beginning of its life in the desert (Ex 4:22—23; Hos 11:1; Jer 31:9), when Israel was tested and disciplined by God as a son by his father (Dt 8:5). The lesson is emphasized by the fact that Jesus replies entirely in the words of Dt. But whereas Israel failed in the testing, Jesus overcomes the temptations. Gerhardsson holds that the three temptations correspond to the three clauses of the Shema (Dt 6:5), the text recited thrice daily by Jews, in which Israel is commanded to love God 'with all your heart, with all your soul, with all your strength'; Jesus rejects the temptation to fall in each of these ways, for in rabbinic terminology it is the *heart* which listens to God's word (v 4), the mortal danger of falling from the pinnacle of the temple is a danger to the life or *soul*, and *strength* represents possession of land and material goods.

1. Already echoes Dt 8:2; it is in terms of Dt 6—8 that the whole scene is described. Jesus' forty days of testing correspond to Israel's forty years (cf Nm 14:34; Ezek 4:5—6). The round number of forty occurs frequently in the Bible of an indefinite long period, especially a period of preparation, e.g. Ac 1:3, when the apostles are prepar-ing for their mission, as Jesus is now for his. Testing (or tempting—the original word has both senses) is, in the later books of the Bible, no longer a means by which God discovers whether Israel is faithful, but is a means of training, a privilege and sign of affection (Sir 2:1—6; Wis 3:1—6; Jn 15:2—8). Hence Jesus is led into the desert by the spirit, though the actual tempting is done by the devil (1, 5, 8, 11) or Satan (10). In Dt the testing is done by God himself. But in the Bible and Jewish theology from Jb 1:6 onwards there appears a professional tempter, so to speak, who at least in Jb is an emissary of God, called after his office 'the tester', 'the Satan', not just 'Satan'. His duty is also to dilate the faults of sinners to God (Jb 1:8—11, 2:3—5) and to punish them (SB I. 139—49). Mt's addition of forty nights to forty days (not in Lk) could be an allusion to Moses' fact, described in these terms in Dt 9:9, 18; cf v 8 below. **3—4.** The first temptation plays on Israel's murmuring **c** (Ex 16:2), as a result of which God gave them manna; Jesus replies with the words of Dt 8:3—the lesson taught by the manna—complete trust in God. **5—7.** The order of the latter two temptations differs in Mt and Lk. In favour of Mt's order it may be said that his first two temptations are linked by the devil's use of the title 'Son of God' (which is so crucial here), the temptation to perform a miracle and Jesus' scriptural reply; the tempter takes Jesus up on his profession of complete trust in God,

15c and suggests that he should demonstrate how well-founded it is. This order provides also an effective dramatic crescendo, and corresponds to the order of the events of the exodus alluded to. Perhaps Lk's motive in changing the order was to obtain a movement towards Jerusalem, which plays an important part in his gospel (cf § 765e). The 'parapet (literally wing) of the temple' cannot be identified with certainty. In Hegesippus' account of James' martyrdom James is thrown down from this point at the beginning of his stoning, which would suggest the S or E wall of the temple-enclosure, where there is a drop of some 120 feet into the Cedron valley. But Hegesippus is probably influenced by our pericope. The evangelist seems to be using a rare architectural term in order to suggest even more strongly the protection of God's wings; Jerusalem and the temple are the prime seats of God's protective watch over his own (cf the Pss). To the tempter's Ps 90 (89):11—12 Jesus replies with Dt 6:16; though God tests his people, it is a heinous lack of trust if man casts doubt on God's promises by testing **d** his fidelity. **8—10.** The third temptation is dramatically situated on a very high mountain. There is of course no mountain from which 'all the kingdoms of the world' can be seen; hence Lk avoids this element. But Mt is probably alluding again to the Moses-typology (cf § 711e): in Dt 34:1 Moses is led by God to Mount Nebo from where he sees all Israel as far as Dan, the Mediterranean and the Negeb, and (according to rabbinic legend) was tempted by the devil. It is impossible to see any of these three points from Mount Nebo, but clearly Moses sees a part of the land which stands for the whole. So now, except that the whole embraces all kingdoms and their glory. Since the 12th cent. the first and third temptations have been located respectively in a cave in, and on the summit of, Jebel Qaruntul above Jericho. This accords with the localization of John's baptism at the ford below Jericho, but does not necessarily follow from it. No indication is given by the NT beyond 'the desert'. The Moses-symbolism might suggest Mount Nebo, on the East side of the Jordan valley, but the mid second century author of the Gospel of the Hebrews (apud Jerome, In Mic 7:7) guesses that the mountain was Tabor (? in Galilee). This temptation is to sacrifice God's design of a humble and suffering Messiah for a world empire. The temptation parallels that of the Israelites (Dt 6:10—11) on entering the promised land to forget God before the blandishments of worldly prosperity and to turn to idolatry (which is often equated with devil-worship in late Jewish tradition). Jesus rejects it with the words of the warning of Dt at this temptation of the Israelites (Dt 6:13).

e 12—17 Return to Galilee (Mk 1:14—15; Lk 4:14)— The arrest of John (cf 14:3) marks the end of the period of preparation for the Messiah which it was his mission to preach. On receiving the news of it Jesus begins his mission as Messiah. Mt, who is so careful to show that even Jesus' geographical movements are intended to fulfil the prophecies (cf § 713k), explains that the move to Capharnaum too fulfils a prophecy. On Jesus' deliberate fulfilment of prophecies cf § 719i. While Nazareth is in the territory of Zebulun, Capharnaum is in that of Naphtali, on the 'way of the sea', understood by Mt as the main road which runs from Damascus round the North end of the sea of Galilee down to Egypt. Capharnaum is henceforth Jesus' home-town (cf 9:1), though he visits Nazareth once more, to be rejected there (Lk 4:16—30 advances this visit and rejection, in order to motivate Jesus' change of residence). **17.** 'From that moment' is used by Mt only three times (also 16:21 and 26:16) to mark the beginning of the significant periods

in Jesus' ministry (stressed here also by 'began', not in **715e** Mk). He proclaims the message put by Mt also in the Baptist's mouth: repentance (cf 3:2 and § 714b). The reason given is that *the Kingdom of Heaven* has come. The concept of the messianic kingdom, already used by **f** Mk (15 times) is given enormous prominence by Mt (used 52 times). While Mk uses the expression 'Kingdom of God', Mt prefers a current Jewish circumlocution of respect which avoids using the name of God by substituting his dwelling-place, though he retains the expression 'Kingdom of God' (drawn from his source) in 12:28; 21:31, 43. In the OT God himself is king over the world in virtue of creation (Ps 93—99 (92—98)), and more especially of Israel (Jg 8:23; 1 Sm 8:5—8). Gradually it came to be seen that this kingship of God was to be established in a special way by a messianic king (Is 9:1—7; Mi 2:13; Jer 23:5—6; Ezek 20:33; 34:23—31). Jewish speculation of our Lord's time was dominated by the concept of a messianic king according to the visions of Dn 2:44 and 7:13—27 (Enoch, 4 Esdr). The Pharisees concentrated on a reign of God to be established in men's hearts by the perfect observance of the Law (SB I. 172—8), emphasizing less the exterior and visible kingship (ibid 178—80). But in the popular imagination the Messiah was to be a conquering hero who would free Israel from the Roman yoke and establish a world empire (Jos BJ 6, 5, 4; Suetonius, *Vesp.* 4); it was this which led to the many Jewish messianic risings until the final disaster of the Second Revolt (A.D. 135). It was in this **g** atmosphere that Jesus proclaimed the **advent of the messianic kingdom**, a kingdom very different from that expected by the Jews, so that the main burden of Jesus' teaching was to correct the ideas on the subject both of the crowds and of his own disciples (cf their persistent desire for a glorious kingdom 20:21; Lk 24:21; Ac 1:6). Jesus proclaimed that the kingdom had arrived (4:17; 10:7; 11:12; 12:28). This proclamation is, for Mt, equivalent to the whole of Mk's 'announcing the Good News' (Mt 4:17 cf Mk 1:14). Jesus also showed this by many of his actions (cf § 719a and 21:1—9). But there is still expectancy, for it is also in some sense still in the future: its arrival can be prayed for (6:10); entry into it is promised for the future (7:21; 18:3; 21:31) after a judgement scene (25:34). This tension shows an aspect of the notion: it is to be conceived, not so much as a territorial kingdom which has been taken over, but as an actively-exerted kingship or rule of God through the Messiah. Hence it admits of degrees of totality, an inauguration which has taken place, and a consummation which is still to come, when the Son of man will come in his kingship (16:28), the disciples will sit on thrones of judgement (19:28), the members of the kingdom will be sorted into worthy and unworthy (13:24—30, 36—43, 47—50; 22:11—14) and the messianic banquet will be celebrated (8:11; 22:1—10; 26:29). But this triumph, expressed in current apocalyptic imagery (cf § 737a), concerns the future; it is in the **present character of the kingdom and the requirements for it** that the novelty of Jesus' message consists. Membership of Israel **h** does not automatically confer that of the kingdom (3:9—10; 8:11—12; 21:43 cf § 733e). Some statements show continuity with the rabbinic tradition (7:21; 13:52). But others show a radical novelty. The kingdom must be sought single-mindedly (6:33), though it is freely given by God (20:1—16). It belongs to the poor and the oppressed (5:3, 10—the beatitudes may be termed 'the conditions of entry into the kingdom'— 19:23—24), to those with the humility and trust of a child (18:1—5; 19:14), to the merciful (18:23—35).

715h Its king is no conquering destroyer, but the gentle king of Zech's prophecy (9:9, cf Mt 21:1—9; 11:28—30), cf § 711*d*. The kingdom itself is humble and unnoticed in its beginnings, though it has the presage of such greatness (13:31—32, 33; Mk 4:26—29). Indeed Mt considers the king and his kingdom to be equivalent, for he interchanges the terms (16:28; 21:9 and parallels). It is to the disciples that the profound knowledge of this kingdom (13:11), and the ministry (16:19) are imparted, so that it may be proclaimed to all peoples (24:14). It is the presupposition of Mt 13 and 18 that the kingdom is coextensive with the Church.

i **18—22 The First Disciples are Called** (Mk 1:16—20, cf Lk 5:1—11; Jn 1:35—42)—The first act of Jesus in his ministry is to begin to form his messianic community. The similarities and differences between the various evangelists in their accounts here are most instructive. Jn retains (1:39, 43) the direct call without any previous preparation. The *logion* of 'fishers of men' is given by Lk also in connexion with the call (5:10), accompanied by the full scenario of a fishing expedition (5:1—11) of which there is no trace in Mk and Mt. In Jn 21:4—17 the *logion* (vv 15—17), with a different imagery but bearing the same message, is again preceded by the same scenario. The time and circumstances of the delivery of the *logion* are neither discoverable nor of great importance; it is sufficient to know that the commission contained in it was an integral part of the vocation of Peter (and his brother), given by all four evangelists. Historically the commission to be fishers of men is more probable later; it would have been totally enigmatic at this early moment. Mk and Mt could have anticipated by giving it already here, in order to show that it is central to the apostolic vocation. Mt takes over the narrative of the scene from Mk practically **j** unchanged. With his customary pedantry he makes some improvements of logical order: he tells us before mentioning the names that each pair were brothers, instead of tacking it on as an afterthought (Mk); similarly Zebedee is introduced in a more timely fashion, instead of being mentioned only as his sons leave him. But by minute touches Mt also emphasizes the theological lessons: in Mk 1:20 Jesus 'at once' calls the second pair; Mt 4:22 transfers this 'at once' to their obedience, stressing, as in 4:20; 8:22; 9:9, the immediacy and unconditional character of the response to the apostolic call. He also makes clearer the renunciation involved (cf 19:21) by a crescendo: the first pair leave only their nets (there is no sign of a boat; they could have been fishing from the shore); the second pair leave the boat and their father. Thus Mt adumbrates a theology of the call to discipleship (cf § 711*g*).

k **23—25 Jesus preaches and heals the sick** (Mk 1:39; Lk 4:44; 6:17—18)—This summary of Jesus' activity (welded together from phrases found in Mk 1:14, 21, 28, 32—34, 39; 3:7*b*—8) serves as a transitional piece. It concludes the section 3—4 on the manifestation of the Messiah, and serves as an introduction to the next major section, on his teaching (5—7) and his messianic activity (8—9). **23** is repeated almost unchanged in 9:35 thus bracketing the section. On the significance of the healing and miracles see § 719*a*. The Good News of the Kingdom (cf Marxsen 77—101), the *evangelion*, seems to have been drawn by the early Christians from the hellenistic cult of sovereigns and emperor-worship; in that context it is used of the announcement of the birth, crowning or victories of the emperor (in the LXX it is used only three times, in 2 Sm, and then in the plural, which never occurs in the NT). The term is widely used already by Paul, of his proclamation of the risen Christ. It seems that Mk did not find it in his **715** source, but introduced it editorially. For Mk believing **l** (1:15), suffering for (8:35; 10:29) or preaching (10:29) the Good News is the same as believing, suffering for or preaching Christ; Christ is the Good News. Mt characteristically, with his ecclesial interests, shifts the emphasis from the person of Christ to his messianic kingdom: the Good News is not simply Christ as such, the Good News of God (Mk 1:14), but is 'the Good News of the kingdom' (4:23; 9:35; 24:14). **24.** Syria here denotes either the whole region of Syria—Palestine vaguely (as in current Roman terminology), or (as in Mk 1:28) 'the surrounding Galilean countryside'. **25.** The Decapolis was a league of ten largely hellenized city states in Northern Transjordan (except for Scythopolis, a few miles W of the river). The crowds gather from all around, to prepare an audience for the Sermon on the Mount.

5—7 Sermon on the Mount—The second major section **716** of the gospel is divided into a narrative part (3—4: the initial manifestation of the Messiah) and a discourse (5—7). The discourse constitutes the initial proclamation of the nature of the messianic kingdom; more exactly, it sets out the qualities required in its members, and by this means shows the nature of the kingdom. Lk has already given his first messianic proclamation of Jesus, on the occasion of his visit to Nazareth (Lk 4:16—30), and so can leave the 'Sermon on the Plain' until a later stage. The material is assembled here from various sources in the tradition; much is given also by Lk either in the 'sermon on the plain' (6:20—49) or in his account of the journey to Jerusalem (9:51—18:14); some occurs again elsewhere in Mt (e.g. 5:29—30 in 18:8—9; 5:32 in 19:9; 7:17 in 12:33—35) in a more original setting. Mt, the careful teacher, is always anxious to give the complete lesson, and for this purpose uses what material is apposite, even though he uses it also elsewhere. But **b** underlying each ch of the sermon a schema is discernible which Mt received, and developed by the insertion of additional teaching (cf Dupont):

Introduction: the beatitudes (5:3—12)
1. The Perfection of Justice
    (i) general statement (5:17—20)
    (ii) five antitheses: old and new justice (5:21—48)
2. Good Works
    (i) general principle (6:1)
    (ii) three applications: almsgiving, prayer fasting (6:2—18)
    Into this part is inserted the Lord's Prayer (6:7—15); after it is added a collection of sayings on single-mindedness (6:19—34)
3. Three warnings, each followed by a parabolic development:
    (i) on judgement (7:1—5), followed by various sayings (7:6—14)
    (ii) various sayings (7:6—12)
    (iii) on the two ways of the true and false disciple (7:13—27)

1—2 Introduction—Jesus is on a mountain, as was **c** Moses at the giving of the Law which he now brings to perfection, and as he will be for his final solemn mission to the world (28:16). He is enthroned, in the position of a rabbinic teacher. Mt says 'he *opened his mouth* and taught them', lending solemnity by this formal biblical expression. The place of the mountain is not indicated. The next localization given is Capharnaum (8:5); it is perhaps for this reason that the sermon is situated by tradition on a broad low hill a few hundred yards from the lakeside, about a mile W of Capharnaum.

16d 3–12 The Beatitudes (Lk 6:20–23)—The sermon begins with nine magisterial pronouncements in the solemn biblical form (cf Ps 1:1; 112(111):1; Prv 3:13): 'Blessed is he . . .'. Various indications combine to suggest that Mt has slightly changed the accent of his source. Lk has only four beatitudes (the poor, the hungry, those who mourn, the persecuted), so that his opening has the effect of a declaration in the tradition of Is 61:1–3: the Messiah has come to proclaim salvation to the oppressed. Mt, however, by his additions puts the accent on the moral requirements and the activity required for entry into the kingdom; this is characteristic of his homiletic interests, and a linguistic examination of the passage shows the shift to be the work of the evangelist.

e 3–4. The privileged position of 'the poor' in the eyes of God has a steadily increasing prominence in the post-exilic parts of the OT, especially in the prophetic tradition: Ps 22 (21):26; Is 61:1; Jer 20:13; Zeph 2:3; 3:11–12. It was for ruthless oppression by the wealthy that God destroyed the kingdom of Judah (Ezek 22:29). Thenceforth the poor of Israel in exile (Is 49:13), and eking out a precarious existence in Palestine, were compelled to depend more on God for survival. This is, however, primarily Lk's message, and it is central to his gospel. Mt explains 'poor *in spirit*', and adds the second beatitude, for the 'gentle'; this latter is not in Lk, but depends on Ps 37(36):11 rather than on the original version of the beatitudes; it is primarily an explicitation of the first **f** beatitude, making it refer unambiguously to a spiritual attitude. The expression 'poor of spirit' is used several times at Qumran (1 QM XIV 7; 1 QS III 8, IV 3) to denote the attitude of humble expectancy of God's mercy which characterized their spirituality. But in the Pss too the poor are blessed precisely because it is they who seek the Lord (Zeph 3:12; Ps 69 (68):32). The theme of 'gentleness' runs right through Mt's gospel: Jesus himself is gentle (11:29), the messianic king in gentleness (21:5), the suffering servant who accepts his death in patience and gentleness cf § § 711*d*, 739*b*; it is this quality which the follower of Christ must learn from Jesus (11:29, cf 722*k*). It is the reverse of roughness and inconsiderateness, best expressed in the terms of Is (Mt **g** 12:20), a spirit founded on love (1 Cor 4:21). **5.** In some texts and versions the blessing on those who mourn precedes that on the gentle but the gentle obviously pair with the poor in spirit; the transposition is most easily explained if this order was original (Dupont 252–3). The blessing on 'those who mourn' retains the overtones of the proclamation of the good news to the unfortunate (cf 11:2–5 and § 716*d*). **6.** The blessing on 'those who hunger and thirst' originally alluded to the same theme in the prophets (Is 49:10; 55:1–2; 65:13) of the filling of the poor with the overflowing plenty of messianic times. But Mt again, by adding 'for what is right', weaves in a moral theme; mere misfortune is not enough, the kingdom must be earned (cf 22:1–13). He adds this expression '*justice*' (on whose force cf § 717*e*) also to the eighth beatitude, thus forming two stanzas of four, and stressing the central importance of the new, Christian justice.

h 7. 'Mercy' is a quality whose importance is ever stressed by Mt: it sums up the attitude required of Christian leaders to their communities (18:33); lack of this quality condemned the Jewish leaders (9:13; 12:7; 23:23). It flows from the commandment of love, paramount in all relationships between men, cf § 734*g*, 25:31–46. **8.** It is not by ritual purity that entry to the kingdom is won, but by purity of heart (cf Ps 24 (23):4; 51 (50): 12). The prophets had already announced the insufficiency of ritual observance, circumcision of the flesh (Jer 4:4);

the theme will be developed by Paul (Rm 2:25–29). But **716h** Mt does not wholly reject all ritual observances; he merely subordinates ritual law to the law of love (cf § 726*d*). **9.** The blessing on peacemakers is a further example of **i** Mt's stress on active good works, and on the works of love, for it is the furthering of love between men. This good work occurs again and again in rabbinic writings as the most highly-prized of all the works of love (SB, 1, 215–8). Peace was to be the mark of the messianic age (Is 60:17; Ps 85 (84):10), and 'Peace' becomes the specifically Christian greeting (10:13; Rm 1:7; 1 Cor 1:3 etc). It is the gift of Christ (Jn 14:27; 2 Thes 3:16) through the Spirit (Rm 8:6; Gal 5:22), and is regularly paired by Paul with love itself (2 Cor 13:11; Gal 6:16). **10.** The eighth beatitude closes the second stanza, with its mention of '*justice*' (cf v 6), linking up also with the first beatitude by its blessing 'theirs is the kingdom of heaven'—a favourite bracketing process of Mt. It forms a summary of and transition to the next two vv, which are found also in Lk. **11–12.** The final beatitude, in the second instead of the third person, has a broader and less epigrammatic character. Persecution is the lot of the disciples, as of their master (cf § 721*h*); Mt stresses frequently that the Jews, in persecuting the Baptist (cf § 725*e*) and Jesus himself (§ 735*k*) stand in a series of murderers of the prophets (23:37).

13–16 Salt and Light (Lk 14:34–35; 11:33)—The **j** warning note of these two sayings jars somewhat after the previous joyful blessings on the disciples. But in fact they look forward to the contrast between the new justice of Christ and the insufficient justice of the Jews which is to be superseded; for both figures, salt and light, seem to concern the supersession of Israel and the succession of the disciples of Christ to its privileged position. **13.** In a highly allusive rabbinic conversation of c. A.D. 90, salt becoming tasteless seems to be a figure of the impossibility of the old Law losing its force (SB I. 236). In fact already Pliny, *Hist. Nat.* 91, 34, noted that impure salt from the Dead Sea (the easiest source in Palestine) easily loses its taste. **14–15.** In Is 60:3–5 it is Jerusalem that is the light of the world, to which all nations stream to learn the Law of God (cf Is 2:2); but now the disciples are to perform this function. **16.** Seems to clash with 6:2, 5, 16. These are in fact two sides of the same coin, but the lack of explanation suggests that 5:16 did not originally belong in the same context.

17–48 Fulfilment of the Law: Six Antitheses between **717a** the old Law and its perfection by Christ—The antitheses have a triadic structure; all begin with a sharp opposition between the narrow interpretation of an OT command and the wider application which Jesus enjoins; in some cases this antithetical structure seems to be due to Mt (31–32*a*, 38–39, 43) who prefixes to the teaching drawn from Q (cf § 646) a saying of the Law which, in these cases, is superseded: in the other three cases the old teaching is not superseded, but is given a more far-reaching application. There follow usually some practical examples and cases (22*bc*, 29–30, 34*b*–36, 46–47), in all but the last passage perhaps inserted by Mt for the sake of symmetry; in any case he often gives practical and casuist applications. Finally comes a positive command (23–24, 37, 42, 48). Dupont maintains (p. 156) that this triadic structure is due not to Mt, but already to his source, for he slightly obscures it by the addition of vv 25–26. The second and third antitheses have also only some elements of it. But both the striving after such neat literary structures, and several vv which here realize the structure are characteristically Matthean.

717b 17—20. The Principle—18—19. Probably additions, drawn by Mt from other occasions (Dupont p. 145); the principle is stated in 17 and 20. Both here and in ch 6 we are given first a general principle and then particular applications of it. The same form occurs in Lv 18:2—23; Eccl 3:1—8; it is common in the rabbinic writings, where the general principle is called *'ab* (= *ancestor),* and the applications *tolaḍa* (= descendant), cf Daube p. 63—65. **17.** Jesus' attitude to the Law, expressed in the antitheses which follow, can be understood only if it is realized that the recurring expression 'You have heard' at the head of each is a technical formula attested in rabbinic teaching as early as the beginning of the 2nd cent. A.D.; in this context it gives a strict, literal understanding to which the teacher then opposes a wider interpretation (Daube p. 55—62). It is in this sense that Jesus fulfils the c Law; he gives it the due, full interpretation. There is never a suggestion in Mt that the Law has been superseded: in 3:15 Jesus fulfilled all justice; in 12:5—6 he claims to be greater than the temple, but invokes the Law as a witness; in 7:12; 22:40 he implies its lasting validity under his new interpretation. Even the ceremonial law as such is never questioned in principle, though its application is made to depend on the law of love. For this reason rabbinic interpretations of the law are often rejected. It is clear that the Sabbath is still observed in Mt's community (12:1—14 and notes). The fulfilment of the prophets is less apposite here. A. Descamps (TU 73 (1959), 156—73) holds that 'or the Prophets' has been added by Mt; the pair certainly constitute a formula in Mt (7:12, 22:40). But fulfilment of the scripture, especially of the prophets, by Jesus' life and actions is a theme which runs throughout Mt; Jesus is often shown as acting deliberately in order to fulfil the pro- d phecies (cf § § 719*i*, 739*a*). **18.** The original purpose of this saying of Jesus could be a reply to the Pharisees who accused him of infidelity to the Law. The 'iota' means the smallest letter of the Hebrew alphabet, *yod* = i; the dot or 'little stroke', a serif or ornamental flourish on a letter. The final 'until *all* is achieved' is added by Mt, since it is not in Lk's version of the saying (16:17); if taken in a purely temporal sense, as in 24:34, it merely reduplicates the beginning of the v.; it is therefore probably to be interpreted (Barth p. 70) not as a limitation of the validity of the Law to a certain period, but of the goal aimed at, the total accomplishment of the Law. **19.** On greater and lesser commands of the Law see 22:36 § 734*g*. The v reinforces 18, being probably drawn from some controversy with the Pharisees over Jesus' legal observance ('these e commandments' has no reference). **20.** Mt now returns to give the principle proper of the antitheses which follow. The whole discourse is concerned with this fuller 'justice', 'righteousness' or 'virtue'; already Mt has added it twice to the beatitudes, in a key position at the end of each strophe: the rest of the ch gives the contrast between Christian and Pharisaic justice; the next ch how Christian justice should manifest itself and be sought (6:1, 33). Mt does use the term of observance of the old Law (1:19, 13:17; 23:29, 35), but indicates also elsewhere that such observance is insufficient (9:13; 23:28). f **21—26 First Antithesis: Murder**—The core of the antithesis comes in 21—22*b*: a narrow interpretation of the prohibition of killing is insufficient (see note on 17). As the last antithesis (43—48), so the first is concerned directly with love; here the negative action is forbidden as there the positive is enjoined. **22***bc.* A casuist's applications such as Mt often gives (29—30, 36; 18:15—17). The Aram. *'reqa''* means 'light-headed';

'moreh' is more serious: 'stubborn', or often 'impious' **717** (SB I. 278—80—the Gr. word used, *'mōros',* means 'fool', but Mt surely has the semitic root in mind). On *'Gehenna'* (.JB 'hell fire') see § 711*b*. **23—24.** The positive action demanded; this is already required by Sir 28:2 and Mk 11:25, though in general terms without Mt's vivid presentation in function of Jewish sacrifices. **25—26.** Probably inserted into the discourse here by Mt. The saying occurs in Lk (12:57—59), in the context of the imminence of judgement: there is little time to set one's affairs in order. Mt puts it here as a more general moral exhortation on the necessity of reconciliation; the application of a lesson, originally expressed in function of the crisis of the Messiah's coming, to the Christian life is characteristic of him (cf § 724*d*). Human prudence is part of God-given wisdom (cf § 358*b*). **27—30 Second Antithesis: Adultery**—To the kernel **g** of the antithesis expressed in 27—28 Mt adds (by association of the ideas 'look' and 'eye') 29—30, whose original context is 18:8—9, see § 729*d*. **31—32 Third Antithesis: Divorce**—This passage repeats the teaching of 19:9 (cf § 730*bf*). But linguistically v 32 is closer to Lk's formulation (Lk 16:18); the saying was probably preserved independently in Mk and Q. The antithetical formulation may well be due to Mt (cf § 717*a*). **33—37 Fourth Antithesis: Oaths**—The old Law's **h** prohibition of perjury (Ex 20:7) is insufficient; Jesus extends it to all oaths. The examples of oath-formulae given in **34***b***—35** were common ways of swearing by God without actually mentioning the divine name, since, towards the end of the pre-Christian era, Ex 20:7 was interpreted as forbidding any use of the divine name. The Jews therefore either used a passive (e.g. 'May you be granted . . .' for 'May God grant you . . .') or named some attribute of, or something closely associate with God (e.g. 'the kingdom of heaven' for 'God's kingdom'). **36.** A different sort of oath-formula, forbidden for a commonsense reason. Probably this, and perhaps also the previous examples of formula, are added by Mt here; he frequently inserts practical applications of Jesus' commands (cf note to 22*bc*); this v is in the singular, whereas 33—34*a* were plural. **37.** After the prohibition, a positive command is given (cf § 717*a*). The same command is found Jas 5:12; both formulations are so compressed that the teaching must have been well-known. Mt's sentence can be translated either 'All you need say is "Yes" if you mean yes, "No" if you mean no' (JB); or more literally, 'Say "Yes, yes" or "No, no"'. These doubled 'Yes' and 'No' seem to have been regarded as oath-formulae at least from the early 2nd cent. (SB 1, 336—7). **38—42 Fifth Antithesis: Retaliation** (Lk 6:29—30)— **i** The permission of the Mosaic law, which Jesus now abrogates, replacing imperfect justice by his fuller demands, was made in the context of a primitive society where men took the law into their own hands, before there was a central authority to deal with such injustices. The 'tit-for-tat' ruling authorized therefore legal action, not personal vindictiveness. It is against personal vindictiveness that Jesus now speaks out; he is not directly considering legal or police action. The antithesis is given **38—39***a*; then follow three examples (**39***b***—41**). The tunic is the normal garment still worn by Arabs, the cloak a loose outer garment in which the poor man wraps himself at night (Ex 22:25). Since the original action is considered unjust, the order to go one mile is probably not a requisitioning by the state, but a demand by a rabbi to his pupils, which was considered irregular

17i (SB 1, 344). This may be why Lk omits it. In each case the lesson is generous forgiveness of injury and an additional offering of love. **42.** Finally a positive counsel of spontaneous generosity (cf § 717*a*).

j 43—48 Sixth Antithesis: the Perfection of Love (Lk 6:27—28, 32—36)—As the first antithesis concerned the extreme example of lack of love, so the last treats of positive love. **43*b*** is not taken from scripture (43*a* is from Lv 19:18), and is perhaps a popular saying built by semitic parallelism on to 43*a*. In the OT the Israelites were required to love only fellow-Israelites and those who dwelt in the land (Lv 19:18, 34); the rabbis restricted the latter class to those non-Israelites who had become Jews by proselytism and circumcision (SB I, 354—5). Hatred of those outside their own community was regarded as a sacred duty by the sectaries of Qumran (1QS 1, 10). The extension of the commandment of love to all men, even beyond the brethren (**47**, used by Mt of fellow-Christians) is specifically Jesus' own, cf 22:40; Lk 10:29—37. In Mt it is especially stressed that this is the basis of all Christian action; cf § 734*g*. **48** therefore forms the conclusion both to this antithesis and to the whole series. The only other passage where 'perfect' is used is Mt 19:21, where it also concerns the commandment of love (cf § 731*a*). It denotes more than 'righteous', including a 'superabundance' (20, 47, at beginning and end of the antitheses). At Qumran it denotes a whole-hearted embracing of their interpretation of the law, a 'complete dedication to God' (Barth p. 98). It is all the more significant that the epithet 'perfect' is not applied to God in the OT: he is above perfection, but the structure of the v is a clear reflection of Lv 19:2 'Be holy, *as* I, the Lord your God, am holy'.

18a 6:1—18 Good Works in secret—After the principles which guide a Christian's action, examples are given of the practice of good works. The examples are characteristic of Jewish piety at the time of Christ: almsgiving, prayer and fasting. As in rabbinic writings, a general principle is given first (**1**), followed by its particular applications (cf note on 5:17—20). Each of the three applications has the same structure:
1. When you do this work, do not advertise it as the hypocrites (the Pharisees and scribes, cf 15:7; 22:18; 23:13 etc) do; they have their reward already (2, 5, 16)
2. But you must do it without drawing attention (2, 6*a*, 17). But 'Jesus does not condemn the practice of praying in public assemblies, Lk 18-19 the words of 6 are as hyperbolic as those of 3' (CCHS (1), ad loc), cf 5:16. What is condemned is not being seen, but acting in order to be seen.
3. Your reward shall be from your Father in heaven (4, 6*b*, 18).

After the second application are inserted two passages on prayer (7—15). **7—8** contains an opposition to the prayer, not of the 'hypocrites' (as 5—6), but of pagans. Examples of senseless repetition are not unknown in Jewish prayers (SB 1, 405—6), but directly envisaged by the saying are the endless, synonymous, repeated phrases of pagan prayers and e.g. the accumulation divine names to ensure that the god is addressed by the title which is pleasing to him.

b 9—13 The Lord's Prayer (Lk 11:2—4)—Lk's version comes at the beginning of a section (11:1—13) on the necessity of prayer. Mt's version is considerably longer and more solemn; this may well be due to liturgical expansion, and some of the elements are typical of Mt's gospel (Father in heaven, the will of God, heaven and earth, the evil one). Lk's context may well be the original one, for there is no reason why the mention of John

the Baptist and his disciples should have been added. **718b Our Father** sets the tone of the prayer: it is the prayer **c** of the Christian community ('our') made in filial confidence to a loving Father. Already in the OT God is regarded with filial intimacy as a Father who warmly cares for his beloved son Israel (Hos 11:1), who carried his child along the road out of Egypt 'as a man carries his son' (Dt 1:31), who can no more forget his son than a mother her child (Is 49:15; 63:7—16). But Israel did not acknowledge this Father (Jer 3:19—20; Mal 1:6), so was chastised with a father's chastisement (Dt 8:5). In later Judaism so much stress was laid on the transcendence and other-ness of God, and observance of a strict law, that his paternal affection receded into the background. Jesus showed again in his person the love of the Father (Jn 1:17—18; 1 Jn 4:9), addressing the Father with the intimate family name '*Abba*' (= 'papa': Mk 14:36)—an intimacy which struck the early Christians, and formed their attitude towards him (Gal 4:6; Rm 8:15; 1 Jn 3:1—2). It was perhaps this staggering intimacy which led Mt's community to add (not in Lk) 'in heaven'. The revelation of God's personal **name**, Yahweh, was refused **d** to the patriarchs (Gn 32:30), and was granted to Moses as a pledge of special intimacy and protection (Ex 3:13—20). To the semites a name always corresponds to the nature of that which is named, and Yahweh himself reveals that his name means tenderness and love (Ex 34:6—8—a passage which re-echoes down the tradition, Nm 14:18; Ps 86 (85):15; Is 48:9; Jer 32:18; Mt 9:13; 12:7; 23:23). God's name was defiled among the nations by the sins of his people (Am 2:7; Lv 18:21; 21:6) and by the exile to which he must subject them (cf Ex 20:22). It was to be held, i.e. acknowledged as, holy through the re-establishment of his people (Ezek 20:41; 36:23—24; Is 63:14), and by the recognition of his universal kingship (Zech 14:9). It is this that the first petition asks the Father to accomplish (the passive formula is less brusque, and is used out of reverence). **10.** It is for the full and **e** **final establishment of the messianic kingdom**, awaited by the Jews from OT times, that the second petition also prays (cf § 715*fh*). The third petition, absent in Lk, shows still more clearly in what the acknowledgement of the Father's kingship consists. 'He who does **God's will**' is a special Matthean definition of the disciple of Jesus (7:21; 12:50), and Jesus himself takes this petition on his lips in the agony in the garden (26:42). But the passive form ('your will be done') suggests that something wider is at stake, independent of man's co-operation; the same impression is given by its reaching to both heaven and earth. The Heb. '*rason*', which stands behind 'your will' here, has a wider connotation, denoting not only obedience by men to God's commands, but also the accomplishment of God's plan of salvation for man (Is 49:8; 60:10; 61:2), the complete satisfaction made to him by the Messiah (cf Ps 40 (39):7—8) and the perfect harmony between God and man, which unites heaven and earth (Ps 85 (84):10—13). **11.** After these three petitions for the **f** accomplishment of God's will follow three others for man's immediate needs. The expression translated '**daily bread**' puzzles commentators; normally the adjective means 'of tomorrow', but 'give us today our bread of tomorrow' is such an odd prayer that Black (p. 150—3) suggests that it is a mistranslation of the Aram. 'day by day', preserved by Lk (who has both 'day by day' and the puzzling adjective side by side) and by the apocryphal Gospel of the Hebrews. In later Jewish prayers (e.g. Berakoth 7:11) God is praised as the giver of

718f bread, which stands for all the necessities of life, but not luxuries. There seems to be no direct allusion to

g manna or to the Eucharist. **12.** Mt places special emphasis on this petition, since he returns to the subject as soon as the prayer is ended, in 14—15. His '**debts**' instead of Lk's 'sins', is probably original, since in the balancing second half of the v both have the notion of debt. Mt is certainly considering sin, but under the aspect not of a juridical transgression but of a personal debt to God. It is one of the chief lessons of the Law that man's generosity to his fellow-men must imitate that of God to Israel (Ex 23:9; Dt 15:7—10), especially in the matter of debt (Ex 22:25; Dt 23:20; 24:12). In the NT the same lesson sums up the instructions on life in community (Mt 18:23—35), cf Lk 6:36; 16:1—13.

h **13.** God can lead his people into temptation to test and purify them, as he did Abraham (Gn 22:1), Israel in the wilderness (Dt 8:2), and Israel tested and purified by the exile as metal in the crucible (Jer 6:27; 9:6; Ezek 22:17). But, though such a temptation successfully endured brings a blessing (Lk 22:28—30), and this testing is in itself a sign of divine favour (Jdt 8:27; Jn 15:2), the time of testing itself is a terrible one (Mal 3:2; Dn 12:1—12). In Gethsemane Jesus himself again tells the disciples to pray to be delivered from temptation. The time of the Messiah's coming is the great testing time (Mal 3:2; Jn 3:19), especially at the two moments of his triumph in the passion (Mt 26:41, 56; Jn 12:31) and of his final manifestation (Mt 24:15—30). It is above all from this testing that we pray to be delivered. In the last petition it is not immediately clear whether 'evil' or 'the **evil one**' is meant; in fact the tradition of the Eastern Church supports the former interpretation, that of the Western Church the latter. Mt uses 'evil' with the article to make a noun five times, all of which could be masculine and so personal; at least in 13:19, 38 a personal 'evil one' must be intended (also 1 Jn 2:13, 14; 3:12; 5:18; Eph 6:16). The petition is, then, to be saved from the same Enemy who is to oppose the coming of the kingdom in the last times (2 Thes 2:3—10). The final petition brings the prayer back to its starting point: a prayer that God's kingdom may be established on earth and in his community. The doxology which follows in some MSS has probably crept in from liturgical usage; it occurs already in the *Didache*. **16—18** returns to the theme of good words in secret (cf § 718a) which, unlike those of the Pharisees, will receive their reward from the Father.

i **19—34 On Single-mindedness**—This section is inserted here by Mt, drawing on Q (cf § 646); the various parts of it are found in three separate passages in Lk. Lk begins with a parable (omitted by Mt, who keeps his parables till ch 13), to which is linked the passage with which Mt concludes (25—33). But, since Mt has omitted Lk's introductory parable, he takes Lk's concluding vv, and sets them as a heading at the beginning of the whole section (19—21). After this he intercalates two short related sayings (22—23, 24). The theme of the whole accords with 6:1—18: generosity towards God with no other hope than the confident expectation of reward from the Father in heaven. **19—21 Treasures in heaven** (Lk 12:33—34)—Mt, in setting these vv as a heading for his whole section prefixes a negative formulation (v 19, not in Lk) which makes the lesson even clearer. This little saying is bracketed by the word 'treasure'. The metaphor of storing up treasure in heaven seems a general one; but to the minds of Jesus' hearers it had a precise connotation, for it is always used in the Bible (Sir 29:8—12; Tb 4:9) and con-

temporary Jewish literature (SB 1, 429—30) of generous **718** alms-giving. Practical love of the neighbour is a lesson to which Jesus, and especially in Mt, is always returning (6:43—48; 19:21; 24:36). **20.** In Palestine it is no excessively difficult task for thieves to '*dig through*' the mud walls of a house. **22—23 The light of generosity** **j** (Lk 11:34—36)—Lk gives this saying among others castigating the Pharisees for their spiritual blindness. This is its most obvious sense. But the expression 'malicious eye' is often used of jealousy or of a grudging giver (SB 1, 833—4; Mt 20:15). In Mt it is this which is opposed to a healthy, sound or faultless SB I. 431) eye. For Mt, then, the saying inserted here teaches once again that generosity is the great virtue. **24 A single master** (Lk 16:13)—This isolated saying of Jesus, attached by Lk to the parable of the unjust steward, challenges to a decision between two opposing standards of value. It makes use of a situation which could in fact arise, a slave being owned by two masters (e.g. Ac 16:16, 19), but which is obviously unsatisfactory. 'Mammon', Gr. *mamōna* is transliterated into Gr. from the Aram. for 'wealth'. **25—34 Confidence in the Father** (p Lk 12:22—31)— **k** Relying on their heavenly Father, Christians must devote their energies exclusively to the search for the kingdom. It is not that the birds and flowers are free of worry, but that they do not toil over household tasks. The wild flowers of Palestine are gay and colourful but short-lived; a few weeks after the end of the rains they wither and are mown for burning with the rest of the grass. **30.** The conclusion is drawn by the rabbinic argument *a minori ad maius*. By 'men of little faith' it is the confidence rather than the understanding of the disciples which is reproached, cf 8:26; 14:31; 16:8. This is the only meaning possible in this context. **33.** On 'righteousness, cf § 717e. **34** forms an independent saying, not given by Lk, with a slightly different point of view. **Ch 7.** On the arrangement, see § 716b.

1—5 On Judgement (Lk 6:37—38, 41—42)—The **l** general rule stated in **1—2** takes up the common OT and Jewish teaching. Especially in Wis 11:15—16; 12:24; 18:4—5 the punishment of the Egyptians fits their crime against the Israelites. But Jesus refers also to the Jewish doctrine of the two measures which may be used in judging: Justice and Mercy (Jeremias, *Parables*, 213). The 'hypocrite' of **5** shows that these sayings were first addressed to the Pharisees, against whom it is a constant reproach that they lack God's mercy and love in their judgement (cf note on 12:5—7). **3—5.** Lk, by inserting the saying on the blind leading the blind (Lk 6:39), interprets this vivid simile of the splinter and the plank which occurs also in Jewish literature, though not attested before A.D. 100 (SB 1, 446) of the guiding function of the religious authorities; Mt, however, of their role as judges.

6—12 Various sayings—**6.** Dupont (p. 171) suggests **m** that this saying was inserted here by Mt in order to qualify the absolute force of the prohibition of judging in 1—2: one may at any rate judge whether one's audience is capable of receiving a certain teaching. Both 'dogs' and 'pigs' are used in later Jewish writings of the gentiles, to whom the Law should not be divulged (SB I. 447—50), cf 15:26. The expression 'giving to dogs what is holy' may perhaps have originally been derived from the sacred meat offered in the temple (Lv 22:14; Ex 22:30). **7—11. Prayer** (Lk 11:9—13)—Mt returns to the theme of the generosity of God which underlies all this part of the sermon. After the exhortation to judge with mercy rather than justice comes a saying which shows how this mercy is found in God. The passives are 'theological', to avoid

8m naming God; but it is he who gives and opens. Lk gives the saying probably in its original context, as an explanation of the parable of the friend who is plagued into granting his friend's request; this gives a precise context **n** for the expressions of 7–8. **9–11.** There is no need to suppose with Jeremias (*Parables* p. 114–5) that the 'you, who are evil' indicates an originally polemical context e.g. against the Pharisees who query Jesus' proclamation of God's gifts to the poor. It is merely to provide a reasoning **a** *fortiori*; cf also 19:17. **12 The Golden Rule** (Lk 6:31)—This concludes the body of the sermon on the mount; there remain only final exhortations. The mention of the Law and the Prophets looks back to the same mention at the beginning of the development (5:17, cf § 717*c*). The 'Golden Rule' is found in negative form frequently in Jewish writings Tb 4:15, Ac 15:20, 29 (Western text), *Didache* 1:2. But the positive form seems to be due to Jesus. The rule only *specifies* the type of action to be done; it does not profess to give the motive for such action (Strecker, p. 135).

o 13–14 The Two Ways (Lk 13:23–24)—Perhaps the more primitive form of the saying is Lk's, where all the emphasis is on exertion to press in through the difficult entry before it is too late—a crisis-parable, on the moment of decision at confrontation with the Messiah. Mt's teaching, however, is more theoretical: v 12 concludes the expository part of the sermon on the mount; now Mt combines this saying with the Jewish teaching of the two ways (Jer 21:8; Dt 30:15; SB I. 460–4; *Didache* 1–6; cf 1 QS III. 13–IV. 26), to serve as introduction to the diptych of two contrasting reactions to the words of Jesus. Speculation was widespread in late Judaism on the relative numbers of saved and damned (this is the question which gives rise to Jesus' saying in Lk); but the terms 'many' and 'few' are stereotyped, and **p** should not be pressed; cf 1 Tm 2:4. **15–23. False Prophets** (Lk 6:43–46; 13:26–27)—Mt concludes the sermon with a characterization of false and true disciples. **15.** These false prophets have the appearance of Christian teachers, for this word for sheep is used eight times by Mt of the flock of Christ. The warning here and in 24:4–5, 24 suggest that they were a real danger. Similar warnings against false teachers occur in 2 Pt 2 (v 14 mentions their greed, as here) and Jude 5–19 (v 12 compares them to barren trees, as here). **16–20.** A method of identification (bracketed by 16*a* = 20). The criterion is originally applied to the Pharisees, and makes use of an OT metaphor (see note to 12:33–35). **21–23.** 'Those who call on the name of the Lord' is practically a definition of Christians (cf § 825*f*). But it is not sufficient simply to profess adherence to Christ, and to the Christian community; it is necessary to accomplish the Father's will, as it has been set out in the sermon. The necessity of good works, in addition to the initial answer to God's call, is emphasized also **q** by 22:11–13 (cf § 733*j*). **24–27 The Wise and the Foolish Disciples** (Lk 6:47–49)—Mt normally concludes his great discourses with promises and threats to the obedient and disobedient, often in parabolic form (10:40–42; 13:47–50; 18:23–35; 25:31–46). Lk's image suggests a house built near a river, which bursts its banks; Mt is more Palestinian; he envisages a house built on the sand of the dry bed of a wadi, washed away by the torrents following the winter rains. A similar image is used in Jewish tradition (SB 1, 469), of a man learned in the Law; his house is made of firm or destructible material by the presence or absence of good works. **28*a*.** Mt concludes each of his five great discourses

with the same stereotyped formula (11:1; 13:53; 19:1; **718q** 26:1). **28*b*–29.** The amazement of his hearers was justified, for the standard and sole approved method of teaching in Judaism was mere repetition of the opinions of the ancients. The weight carried by an interpretation was entirely dependent on the weight of the authorities quoted to support it. Yet Jesus is here teaching formally as a rabbi expounding the Law (this is the meaning of *didaskō* in Mt, cf Bornkamm, p. 38 n 1) and adduces no authorities to support his teaching. It is this teaching on his own authority which finally brings Jesus into conflict with the Jewish leaders (cf § 732*l* and also 9:1–8).

Chh 8–9 Ten Miracles—The third major section of the **719a** gospel consists of a narrative section (the ten miracles) and a discourse (the missionary discourse). The narrative looks back to the sermon on the mount, which showed the Messiah as a new Moses in his teaching, promulgating his fulfilment of the Law; the miracles show him as a new Moses by his action, balancing Moses' ten plagues by ten beneficial miracles. It also looks forward to the missionary discourse, for there the apostles are charged to work miracles (10:1, 8) as part of their mission of carrying on their master's work.

Jesus' miracles are signs that the messianic era has **b** arrived. To John the Baptist's question whether he is the Messiah (11:3), Jesus gives answer by calling his miracles to witness, with an allusion to the prophecy of Is (35:5–6) which they fulfil. Mt also, in his first summary of the miracles here (8:17), points out that they fulfil the prophecy. Particularly the casting out of devils is a sign that the messianic age has dawned, as Jesus says (12:28), for the end of Satan's reign is closely associated in Jewish thought (Ass Mos 10:1; Ethiopian Enoch 10:11–16) with the arrival of the Messiah. But the evangelist does not make any distinction between nature miracles, healings and casting out devils; all alike are signs of the Messiah's presence, without necessarily and always being contraventions of the laws of nature. It suffices that they should be startling actions which fulfil the prophecies. But the attribution to Jesus of the power to work miracles is not, as some have maintained, merely evidence of the faith of early Christians in him. The two *logia*, 11:4–6 and 12:28, show Jesus' own claim to this power. Paul similarly claims for himself the power to work miracles (Rm 15:18–19; 1 Cor 12:9, 10) in continuance of Christ's work (2 Cor 12:12). This claim is without parallel in contemporary Jewish literature; the nearest approach is a cure effected in answer to the prayer of R. Johanan ben Zakkai in *Bab. Berakoth* 34 (but Jesus acts by his own power). A rabbi at the end of the 2nd cent. A.D. heals a man who is *sick unto death* (SB 1, 560); but he is not yet dead. Nor have the fantastic cures claimed in hellenistic literature for certain shrines any analogy with the sober narratives of the gospels.

The ten miracles are gathered together here by Mt, **c** to illustrate nearly every aspect of Jesus' miracle-working. They fall into three groups: first three cures, followed by a summary of Jesus' healing activity and its significance (8:1–17). The last four also are miracles of healing, followed by a conclusion which sums up the whole section (9:18–37). The middle group, prefaced by two *logia* on the hardships of the apostolic calling (8:19–22), and followed by the call of Mt (9:9–13) concerns discipleship. It is not, of course, implied that Jesus worked all these miracles one after another; the collecting of them together and the ordering of them are Mt's own work, for Mk gives them in different places, to teach different points. Indeed the ninth miracle (9:27–31, q.v.)

719c is composed by Mt. himself, using phrases and themes from elsewhere in the gospels. The same is true of the tenth (9:32—34, see § 720r). For this last miracle 'the early Christians drew upon their store of generalized memory about Jesus' (Fuller p. 32), about the many miracles he performed, rather than upon knowledge of one specific miracle.

d Mt's stark and economical style is again in evidence here. He omits many of the lively, 'eye-witness' details of Mk, concentrating on the lesson which he wishes to teach. He stresses the faith in Jesus which is required for a miracle; in almost every case this is expressed (8:2, 5, 25; 9:18, 21, 27) or clearly implied (8:14, 16a; 9:2a, 32); even the demons at least recognize his power (8:29). Where faith was lacking he could not (Mk 6:5) or did not (Mt 13:58, in passage parallel to Mk) work miracles. The messianic kingdom does not impose itself but comes only to those who are willing to receive it. From the second group onwards the miracles are acclaimed also by all who witness them (8:27, 33; 9:8, 26, 31), save only the Pharisees, whose disbelief even after the tenth miracle stands out in strong contrast (9:34).

e 8:1—4 Cure of a leper (Mk 1:40—45; Lk 5:12—16) Mt sets this miracle at the head of his group of ten, disarranging Mk's order, because it both shows how Jesus fulfils the Law (cf 5:17) and presents a connexion between Moses and Jesus, the second Moses (cf § 719a).

2. Leprosy proper, still of high incidence in some parts of the world, was until recently incurable. But the word covers also various other skin diseases, described in Lv 13, sufferers from which were, after diagnosis by the priests isolated, to avoid contagion until they were declared free from the disease. When one so afflicted had been certified cured by the priests he had to offer a sacrifice of reparation (Lv 14). Mt stresses the leper's reverence for Jesus by adding over Mk's account 'bowed low' and 'Lord', both of which expressions are used normally only of God (cf Dt 6:13). **3.** He also lifts Jesus above the sphere of human emotion by omitting Mk's 'feeling sorry for him' and 'sternly', while similarly emphasizing that Jesus cures through an act of his own will. **4.** Mt stresses that Jesus has come that the Law may be fulfilled by concluding the episode on this note, omitting Mk's conclusion (1:45), which tells of the notice aroused by the cure. Also, according to Mt (cf § 719b), the wonder of the witnesses at these miracles increases gradually. The theme of the refusal of the authorities to acknowledge the miracles is already hinted at: evidence for the first miracle is presented to them specially, yet even at the end they remain unbelieving (9:34).

f 5—13 Cure of the Centurion's Servant (Lk 7:1—10; Jn 4:46—53)—For Mt the point of this incident is the contrast between the faith of the gentile centurion and the disbelief of Israel, as can be seen by comparison with the account preserved by Lk. It already shows that entry into the kingdom is to be won by all those who believe in Christ. Mt omits all details which do not serve to point the lesson of the faith and submission of the centurion. The centurion approaches Jesus personally instead of through intermediaries, so that there is no room for the (characteristically Lukan) recommendation of the gentile to Christ. The dialogue between the centurion and Jesus is retained, for it shows the former's complete recognition of Jesus' sovereign power of command. The final word of Jesus (13) underlines that the cure corresponds to the centurion's faith, and is instantaneous on the manifestation of this. **5.** The centurion is an officer commanding nominally one hundred men, presumably a detachment of auxiliary troops stationed at Capharnaum, the first town after crossing the border into Galilee from the Tetrarchy of **719** Philip. The word translated 'paralyzed' does not necessarily mean paralysis in the strict, modern sense. It is more general: 'laid low, disabled', whence it is worth adding that he is in great pain. **10.** It is not incompatible with our Lord's divine and messianic knowledge that he should also learn from men, and experience wonder; this belongs to the fulness of his humanity. Mt's 'nowhere in Israel' points the condemnation of Israel's faithlessness more sharply than Lk's 'not even in Israel'. **11—12.** The contrast between the gentile's faith and Israel's stubbornness **g** is pointed by a saying of Jesus. It is inserted here by Mt, for it is introduced by a turn of phrase which he alone uses, translated 'and I tell you that . . .'. Lk has the saying not here but in a different context (13:28—30), where it fits in perfectly. The theme of the rejection of Israel owing to its stubbornness, and the admission of the gentiles to God's promises, is dear to Mt. The gathering from the E and W is used in the OT primarily of the chosen people brought together again from the diaspora (Ps 107 (106):3; Is 59:19); so it is all the more shocking when Christ says that 'many' will come to partake with the patriarchs of Israel of the messianic banquet (for which see § 720m), while 'those to whom the kingdom belongs as of right' are excluded. But it is only after the Jews have finally rejected Christ that they lose their privileges, and the Church is thrown open to the gentiles, cf § 733e. **12b.** Is a favourite phrase of Mt, added by him as a conclusion at 13:42, 50; 22:13; 24:51; 25:30. Grinding the teeth is a typical reaction of the wicked before the just man, either in fury (Jb 16:9), derision (Ps 35 (34): 16), plotting (Ps 37 (36):12) or envy (Ps 112 (111):10).

14—15 Cure of Peter's Mother-in-Law (Mk 1:29—31; **h** Lk 4:38—39)—Mt, in his hieratic style, omits Mk's details which make a lively scene, that Andrew, James and John were there, and that they mentioned the sick woman to Jesus. He, who stresses so much the part of the head of the apostles, already puts his official title instead of his old name. A significant detail is that after she has been 'raised up' (perhaps an allusion that the cure is an earnest of the resurrection) she waits no longer upon the whole company (as in Mk, where this is merely proof of the complete and instantaneous cure), but specifically on Jesus—a more direct homage to him. Throughout the scene one has the impression of a direct confrontation of the two principal actors, Jesus in his power and the woman in her weakness, as though no one else were present—contrast Mk's lively crowd impression.

16—17 Summary of various cures (Mk 1:32—34; Lk **i** 4:40—41)—This summary concludes the first group of three miracles, giving the sense of them. As is clear from Mt's editing of Mk, he is less interested in the colourful aspect of crowds and diseases, stressing that it was by a mere word of command that Jesus cured and that he left none unhealed.

17. Jesus came to fulfil the promises (cf 5:17), and in seven places (2:23; 4:14; 8:17; 12:17; 13:35; 21:4; 26:56) Mt presents him acting in a certain way precisely in order to fulfil the scriptures (cf § 710c). In fact the cures appear to fulfil only the first half of this prophecy of the Suffering Servant of Isaiah (cf § 711e), 'he took our sicknesses'. But the deeper significance of this is brought out by the second half: it was by taking upon himself the expiation of our sins that he took away all our sicknesses. The physical cures are, then, only signs of the total cure which Christ brings.

18—22 Hardships of the apostolic calling (Lk **j** 9:57—60)—These two exchanges of Jesus with a would-be disciple and with a disciple are welded by Lk into the

719j beginning of the great journey to Jerusalem, just before the mission of the seventy-two disciples. Mt gives them here to set the tone for the second group of three miracles (cf § 719c), which all have some reference to the Church or evangelization. In the pre-gospel tradition they were probably handed down without a fixed context. It is Mt who makes the first interlocutor a scribe and gives him the characteristic form of address 'Master' or 'teacher' i.e. rabbi. Since the disciples of a rabbi followed behind him (SB I. 188), his offer is a formal offer to take Jesus as his rabbi. Jesus' reply, vivid with the freshness of the Palestinian countryside, is a challenge, leaving the man to make his own decision. This was Jesus' own method. Mt implies that he did not accept the challenge, for the title 'teacher' is never used of Jesus by his disciples; they usually say 'Lord'.

k The title **Son of Man** appears here for the first time in Mt. On the force of the expression, with its connotation of lowliness and of transcendent dignity, cf §§ 676k–n, 534c; in Mk the latter sense appears clearly only after Caesarea Philippi. Mt does not observe so strictly the two stages in the use of the title, employing it in his proper material both of Jesus' lowliness (8:20; 11:19; 12:40) and of his future triumph (10:23; 12:32; 13:41) before the scene at Caesarea Philippi. He also shows us the community dimension suggested by Dn 7:22, 27 by using it in passages where Christ is acting as head of the Church (13:37, 41; 16:13; 19:28).

21–22—In the narratives of the call of the disciples it is always stressed that their response is immediate and unconditional (4:19–22; 9:9); this is a condition of discipleship. Jesus' reply is puzzling; has a pun been mistranslated from the Aram. and so lost? Lagrange (*Luc* p. 288) suggests that Jesus is hinting that those who do not recognize him are spiritually dead (cf Lk 15:24); but this is too allusive.

720a 23–27 Calming of the storm (Mk 4:35–41; Lk 8:22–25)—The first of the middle group in the collection of ten miracles (cf § 719c). After Jesus' response to two candidates for discipleship Mt shows his power to protect those who follow him in faith, sensitively moulding Mk's miracle-story to bring out this lesson. From a mere miracle story, such as it is in Mk, it is transformed into an action-lesson of Christ's care for the disciples and so for the Church, and about the need for complete trust in him. Thus he alone mentions that Jesus is 'followed by his disciples'. Instead of Mk's '*Teacher*, do you not care?' it is the direct appeal 'Lord, save us', full of confidence and

b reverence. Mt uses the title 'Lord' not as an openly divine title, but consistently substitutes it for Mk's 'teacher' (also 17:4, 15; 20:33) when the disciples address Jesus, while Judas uses 'rabbi' (26:25, 49; and cf § 731c). The depths of its implications are seen finally when it is used of Jesus as judge at the Last Judgement (25:27, 44), cf Strecker, 123–5. While according to Mk Jesus reproaches the disciples *after* calming the storm for their lack of *faith*, according to Mt the reproach comes *before* the miracle and concerns only their lack of *confidence*. This is in accordance with Mt's tendency to spare the apostles (cf § 724e), and also gives the lesson that at least some faith must precede a miracle (cf § 719d). Consistently the amazement and questioning at the miracle cannot be attributed (as in Mk) to the disciples, who expected such an intervention, but to 'men' in general; each of this second group of miracles is acknowledged by the crowds.

c 28–34 The Demoniacs of Gadara (Mk 5:1–20; Lk 8:26–39)—Mt as usual files down many of the endearing elements in Mk's picturesque story, concentrating on essentials: the ferocity of the possessed (28b), their

contrasting acknowledgement of Jesus, his power over **720c** them, the recognition of the miracle by the whole city. This last element is brought out very strikingly: the whole city comes out (not Mk's indefinite 'they') to see Jesus (not the cured man). The language employed suggests the triumphal procession of homage made at the official reception of a hellenistic monarch. By contrast their final request to go away loses all the significance it had in Mk, atrophying into a mere stage direction. **28.** For the textual variants of the name and the location **d** of the place see § 752f. According to Mt there are two possessed men, though Mk has only one (similarly in 20:30, against Mk; and 9:27); this may be connected with the necessity of two witnesses for testimony valid in Jewish law (cf 26:60, against Mk). The change amounts, then, to stressing the objective reality of the miracle. **29.** For the title 'Son of God' see § 714j. The demons complain that it is 'before the time', thereby implicitly recognizing that the establishment of the messianic kingdom means the end of their power (cf 12:28). Though Satan's power is to be destroyed totally only at the end of days (Apoc 20:10) the decisive moment for the end of his empire is the passion and resurrection (cf Jn 12:31), which Jesus elsewhere calls 'my time' (Mt 26:18) or the time of harvest (13:30, 21:34). In Mk's theology it is the coming of Jesus as a whole which is regarded as the decisive moment (Mk 1:15). **30–31.** Mt shares the worries of modern com- **e** mentators about the propriety of Mk's story. Was it not unjust of our Lord to send the demons into the pigs and so deprive their owner of his herd? If the owner was a Jew it was illegal for him to keep pigs, an unclean animal (SB I. 492–3). But there is no indication that the owner was a Jew, and the district of the Decapolis was very largely hellenized. But according to Mt the demons '*kept pleading*' (imperfect denoting lack of success, against Mk's aorist of success). Jesus merely 'said to them "*Away with you*"', unlike Mk's 'gave them leave'. Thus Mt carefully avoids the implication that Jesus at least connived at the destruction of the pigs. This may also be the purpose of his indication that the pigs were 'some distance away', unless this is to spare Jesus from all possibility of ritual uncleanness.

9:1–8 Cure of a paralytic (Mk 2:1–12; Lk 5:17– **f** 26)—Mt's middle group in this collection of ten miracles now reaches its climax in the forgiveness of sins. But the conclusion shows that Mt is interested in the story most of all as a demonstration of the power of the Son of Man Remission of sin was to be one of the signs of the coming of the messianic age (Hos 14:5; Jer 31:34); but, though the Messiah was to be instrumental in this (Is 53:4–12), in the OT the power to forgive sins belongs to God alone. The claim made in 2, and more clearly in 6, is, then, more than a claim to be Messiah: it is a claim to a divine prerogative; this, rather than bald statement, was the way in which Jesus showed that he was God. In the explicit claim the title 'son of man' is used; this mysterious title was Jesus' way of rousing his hearers to reflection on his person and significance (cf § 719k). This is one of the occasions where it hints at superhuman powers. The title is especially apt here in Mt, for Dn's son of man, besides being an individual, also personifies the kingdom of his followers. So here 8b suggests that God gives the power to forgive sins not only to Christ but also to other men through him (cf 18:18; 28:18–20).

At first sight Jesus' conduct suggests that he accepted **g** the common belief that disease was the result of personal sin (attested later, SB 1, 495–6, and also Jn 9:2). The bed-ridden man (for this is all 'paralytic' means) is brought for a cure, and Jesus' answer to this implicit request is to

720g forgive his sins. In his reply to the scribes Jesus puts the visible and invisible cures parallel. Finally the visible cure is a proof of his invisible power. But since this attitude is brushed aside in Jn 9:2 the significance of the miracle is probably that cures from sin and from disease are alike signs and parts of the Messiah's mission to restore all things. Both forms of evil, sin and pain, are to be eliminated in the final manifestation of the messianic kingdom, cf Apoc 21:3—8.

h Bultmann (pp. 14—16) maintains on slender grounds that Mk 2:5b—10 (parallel to Mt 9:2b—6a) is a secondary interpolation, so that a saying about the forgiveness of sins, otherwise unparalleled for Jesus, would be inserted into a miracle story. But the combination occurred at least at the pre-evangelical stage of the tradition, for Mk puts the passage here among four other passages which feature controversy with Jesus' opponents. The controversy is, then, integral to the story.

i As usual Mt cuts out many picturesque elements in the story to concentrate on its catechetical lesson. Thus (2) the roof-incident disappears, making the bearers' faith much less obvious. But Mt inserts the exhortation 'Courage!', since it is often used to herald and promise the coming of the Messiah (Jl 2:21; Zeph 3:16). Jesus' penetration of men's minds is emphasized ('knowing' **4** instead of Mk's 'observing'). **6.** With his usual care Mt changes Mk's ambiguous 'authority to forgive sins on earth' to 'authority on earth to forgive sins'. **8.** He increases the 'astonishment' (Mk) of the by-standers into 'awe', emphasizing not only the reality of the miracle but also the hint of divine power.

j **9—13 The Call of Matthew** (Mk 2:14, 17; Lk 5:27—32)—Mt continues to follow Mk's order; in Mk this passage presents the second of five controversies with Jesus' opponents; in Mt it could be said to conclude his section on discipleship, cf § 719c. **9.** Relates the call of a disciple, closely modelled on the call of the first disciples (Mk 1:16—20, Mt 4:18—22), with the same stark elements: the direct call to follow Jesus, and the unhesitating acceptance. But the identity of the disciple is puzzling: Mk gives Levi son of Alphaeus here; but Levi does not figure in any list of the twelve (Mk 3:16—19 and par.), though they include a James son of Alphaeus. The description of Matthew as 'the publican' (Mt 10:3) stands in Mt alone. The usual explanation of the discrepancy here between Mt and Mk is that Levi and Matthew are two names for the same man (two names for one man, even two Semitic names, are not uncommon, e.g. 1 Mc 2:2—5); and that while Mt is not ashamed to admit his old opprobrious profession, the other evangelists conceal it out of respect for him. But this explanation, which stems from Jerome, surely forgets the lesson of 10—13. Could it be that the evangelist was moved by the absence of Levi from the apostolic lists to substitute the name of a known disciple, Matthew, for Levi (cf § 709e)? On tax-gatherers,

k see § 622b. **10—13.** Mt transforms Mk's story to make it a deliberate lesson. The Pharisees call Jesus a rabbi ('your teacher') and do not merely remark on his action (Mk), but ask for an explanation why he does it. But Mt makes Jesus's answer a lesson to all, not merely to the Pharisees, by omitting Mk's 'said to them'. Jesus' reply ends with a formula often used by a rabbi to his pupils as a final injunction to penetrate better the meaning of a text: 'Go and learn . . .'. It is not the legally 'observant' whom he has come to call. The text (Hos 6:6) which he exhorts them to meditate is a capital one for Mt. It is quoted also 12:7 and alluded to 23:23. The Heb. word contrasted with sacrifice is best translated 'love' (as it is in Lk's parallel to Mt 23:23). In Hos 6:4—6 and e.g.

Jer 2:2 it refers to the freshness of Israel's love for Yahweh **720l** when she was first betrothed to him in the ideal days of the desert. The need for a return from mere ritual observances to this is often stressed in Hos (e.g. 2:21) and the other prophets: Am 5:21—24; Mi 6:8. It is the basis of that fulfilment of the Law which Jesus proclaims in Mt (cf §§ 717c; 734g).

14—17 Discussion on Fasting (Mk 2:18—22; Lk **l** 5:33—39)—Before starting on his third group in the collection of ten miracles (cf § 719c), Mt continues to follow the order of Mk, who next gives the third of a group of five scenes of controversy between Jesus and his opponents. Mt makes only minor changes of wording over Mk, omitting several of the repetitions which in Mk still betray oral tradition (Hawkins' 'context supplements'). The only major change is that Mt refuses to associate the Pharisees with the disciples of John in asking the question (Mk).

Fasting as a pious practice became very common, especially in Pharisaic circles, among the Jews in the last centuries B.C. (Tb 12:8; Jdt 8:6; Ps Sal 3:8; Lk 18:12; cf SB 2, 241—4). The practice was adopted also by the early Church (Ac 13:2—3; Didache 8:1). In his reply Jesus points out that fasting ('mourning' in general according to Mt) is out of place in the messianic era. In **m** using the figure of a marriage feast to describe the messianic times Jesus was alluding to an idea well-known to his hearers (from Is 54:5; Hos 2:21; for rabbinic interpretations in this sense, cf SB 1, 517), and frequently used in the NT (Mt 22:1—12; 25:1—10; Jn 2:1—12; Apoc 19:9). Jeremias (p. 52) holds that Mk 2:20 (p Mt 9:15b) is not original to Jesus' saying, but is 'a product of the early Church', designed to justify their practice of fasting, which directly disobeys the original saying. The original saying then indicated only that the messianic times had begun, and the reference to the person of the Messiah is a product of the undeniable tendency (Jeremias 66—89) of the early Church to allegorize the parables. Jeremias holds that this particular piece of allegorization cannot stem from Jesus himself, since, in OT and rabbinic uses of the figure of a marriage-feast, the bridegroom is never the Messiah, though sometimes God. But in Jn 3:28—30 Jesus is clearly the bridegroom. This is then perhaps another allusive claim which would be understood by the hearers, not only that he is the Messiah but also that he is the divine spouse of Israel. There is also a veiled reference to the passion, the word for 'taken away' being an allusion to Is 53:8, the Suffering Servant-typology which plays such a large part in the narratives of the passion (cf § 739ab). **16—17.** A pair of **n** similes follows, both showing the foolishness of trying to integrate new with old. Each of these symbols is used elsewhere also of the messianic renewal (cf Jeremias 117—19): the new world is compared to a new garment in Heb 1:12, the time of the Messiah to that of vintage and new wine in Gn 49:11—12; Jl 3:13 etc. The lesson is that Christianity is not something which can be grafted on to Judaism; it is radically new.

18—26 Cure of the woman with a haemorrhage. Official's daughter raised to life (Mk 5:21—43; Lk 8:40—56)—Mt concludes his collection of ten miracles with a group of four cures, of which the first two are interwoven.

18—19. As usual Mt drastically simplifies Mk's **o** lively account to concentrate on the elements essential to his message: the faith of the official and Jesus' readiness to help. Since it does not add to the lesson he omits Mk's dramatic detail that the girl has died while they are on their way (the other miracle is perhaps placed on the

20o journey by Mk precisely in order to lengthen it dramatically), and in order to do this feels justified in altering the official's request to include the news he heard only later (both words 'just died' are characteristically Matthean); this is merely a process of telescoping, and does not affect the substance of the story. Mt also introduces here the disciples, who are mentioned only much later in Mk. The man is called indefinitely 'an official', though Mk and Lk give him an exact title and a name, Jairus. Mt is more concerned to emphasize his reverence for Jesus by a couple of details not found in Mk: he 'bows low', and insists that he must lay 'your hand' not just 'a hand' upon the girl (cf § 711c). **20—22.** Mt again greatly shortens the episode. Instead of Mk's jostling crowds once again, as in Mt 8:14—15, gains the impression of a solemn and solitary meeting between the woman and the Messiah. Her humility is stressed (in Mt she touches 'only' (21) 'the fringe of his cloak' (20)) as well as her faith. The immediacy of the cure is noted too. By two touches Mt draws attention to the deeper significance of this bodily cure: he inserts the messianic exhortation 'courage!' (cf 9:2 and note there), and says

p boldly 'from that moment the woman was *saved*'. **23—26.** The majesty of Jesus appears well in this incident. Instead of holding a conversation with the noisy mourners (Mk), Jesus simply orders them to go; he does not himself turn them out (Mk), they are 'turned out' without mention of human agency. On the phrase 'the little girl is not dead, she is asleep', see on Mk 5:39. **26.** Mk concludes the story with an injunction to keep silent (cf §§ 748 753i); by contrast Mt insists on the widespread acknowledgement of Jesus' messianic signs.

q **27—31 Cure of two blind men**—the last two miracles in Mt's collection of ten are not drawn from any specific passage of Mk. This passage seems to be Mt's own composition, though the healing recorded is probably that of Mt 20:29—34. Many of the expressions and themes are drawn from that passage. Strecker, however, maintains (pp. 199—200) that there are enough themes habitually avoided by Mt to exclude the possibility that he composed the passage without any clearly-defined basis; for instance Mt habitually avoids any evidence of emotion in our Lord, and does not transcribe the word used for 'sternly' (30) in his passages parallel to Mk 1:42 and 14:5. Similarly he habitually disregards Mk's commands to keep silence (see last note), but here includes one. The solution is perhaps that the conclusion of the similar miracle in 20:34 was inept here, so Mt substituted a verse which he had been forced for other reasons to leave aside, namely Mk 1:45 (omitted after Mt 8:4 in order to stress the fulfilment of Moses' law). The passage is centred on the declaration of faith by the two men cured (cf 8:13; 9:22), which they are brought to profess by Jesus' question, as in 20:33. It was already implied by their appeal to the 'Son of David' (on this title cf § 734j), but is brought out clearly by the dialogue.

r **32—34 Cure of a dumb Demoniac**—this last of Mt's collection of ten miracles is again without parallel in Mk, but very similar, even verbally, to the miracle by which Mk introduces the same reactions of crowds and of Pharisees (as here) for a second time: 12:22—24. For this reason it is probably put forward as a typical rather than as a particular miracle, completing Mt's Mosaic number of ten (cf § 719a) and provoking the reactions of crowds and Pharisees which typify their respective reactions to all the miracles. At any rate the miracle itself is reduced to the barest essentials, and its message lies in the reactions of the witnesses. The crowds acclaim the miracle as unprecedented in Israel (Mt's theme that Jesus is the

fulfilment of Israel); the Pharisees refuse credence, **720r** preparing for the total rejection of Jesus by official Judaism.

35—36 Conclusion—The collection of ten miracles is **s** rounded off with a summary and interpretation. **35** is closely modelled on 4:23, thus forming a pair of brackets round Mt's first double panel which shows the Messiah teaching (the sermon on the mount) and healing (the miracles), cf Fuller p. 78. For the expression 'Good News of the kingdom' see §§ 711a, 715fh. **36** stresses once more that by his activity Jesus fulfils the prophecies of the Messiah, the messianic shepherd; the v is here secondary, drawn from Mk 6:34, cf note to Mt 14:14.

37—38 The Need for Missioners (Lk 10:2; cf Jn **721a** 4:35—38)—With this saying both Mt and Lk introduce Christ's charge to his missioners before sending them out. The harvest is a frequent symbol of the great judgement which ushers in the messianic era (Jl 3:13; Is 63:1—6) and generally of a judgement by God (Is 17:5), used by John the Baptist (3:12) and in the interpretation of the parables (13:9, 24—30) and Apoc 14:15. Its reference has the same ambiguity as the arrival of the messianic kingdom, which in a real sense is inaugurated by Jesus himself on earth, but receives its full completion only later (cf § 715f). The apostles are the labourers who are to prepare the harvest for its garnering.

10 The Missionary Discourse—The third major **b** section of the gospel consists of a narrative section (chh 8—9), which showed Jesus' messianic work in his miracles, and of a discourse in which the Twelve are instructed to carry on this mission. As in the sermon on the mount, Mt has assembled material from various parts of the tradition in order to give in one instruction the fullest possible teaching on a subject. Thus he prefixes (2—4) the list of names of the Twelve, which both Mk and Lk give separately from their mission-charge.

1—4 Names and Mission of the Twelve (Mk 6:7; **c** 3:13—19; Lk 9:1; 6:13—16; cf Ac 1:13)—On the whole Mt shows less interest in the Twelve than the other evangelists; he is concerned more with the wider circle of disciples, and the implications of following Christ (cf § 711g); of Mk's ten mentions of the Twelve Mt omits four. But there is no doubt that in Mt as in the other gospels they form the foundations and patriarchs of the new Israel, as the twelve sons of Jacob were the patriarchs of the Israel of the Old Law (19:28). It is they who receive the final revelation of the Passion (20:17) and share (26:20) in the supper which forms the ratification of the new covenant. The term 'apostle' (= sent out), which was most commonly used of the Twelve by the early Church (outside the gospels), occurs in Mt only here (2); again he concentrates more on the mission of all followers of Christ. **1.** The twelve are given the same healing mission as Christ himself (4:23; 9:35); they provide an extension of his work. Their mission to preach is imparted in v 7. **2.** On the names of the apostles cf Mk 3. Mt alone adds 'the first' after Peter's name; he is always careful to stress his pre-eminence, cf §§ 679h; 711i.

5—16 Mission to Israel—All the synoptic gospels agree **d** in giving these instructions as referring to the activity of the disciples during Jesus' lifetime, whereas 17—39 are put later by Mk and Lk, and seem to refer to a wider mission-field. **5—6.** Mt, writing in a community sprung from Judaism, insists that the first mission historically was to the Jews, and that it is only since their definitive rejection of the gospel that the gentiles are called into the Church (cf § 733e). **7—8.** Besides preaching the arrival of the kingdom, as the Baptist (3:2) and Jesus himself (4:17, cf § 715eg), they are also to show its

721d arrival by working the miracles prophesied for the messianic age by Isaiah; this is the meaning of Jesus' miracles too (cf § 719b). **9—10.** (Mk 6:8—9; Lk 9:3; 10:4, 7). The spirit of the instructions is that the missioners should rely on God to supply their needs, through the generosity of the faithful, who have a duty to provide for the sustenance of missioners (cf Gal 6:6; 1 Cor 9:13—14). The details vary, Mk permitting them to take staff and sandals, which Mt and Lk disallow. The latter, stricter version may be due to a comparison in the matter of poverty with the 1st cent. Cynic itinerant preachers, who were recommended if possible not to wear even sandals (cf W. L. Knox, *Sources of the Synoptic Gospels* II (1957) p. 48), or Mk may have accommodated to

e Roman or W conditions. **11—15.** (Mk 6:10; Lk 9:4; 10:5—7a). Mt alone indicates that the preacher should first seek out someone 'worthy', and that the house similarly must be worthy. He stresses in this way also elsewhere that a certain goodwill is a prerequisite for receiving the message of Christ (10:37—38; 22:8), and that Israel lacked this goodwill. His stress on the qualification here is, then, a warning that it will not in fact be fulfilled in Israel (cf 15, with 11:24). In Mt more than any other gospel the threat of judgement looms constantly (cf § 738f). **13.** The normal semitic greeting is 'Peace', but in the Christian message this takes on a deeper sense. 'Peace' sums up the nature of the new covenant (Ezek 37:25—26), and the Messiah is to be prince of peace (Is 9:6—7; 11:6—9). Accordingly, in the missionary language of the early Church, the gospel is the good news of peace (Ac 10:36; Eph 6:15) cf Lk 2:14; Jn 16:33. The peace which they bring is Christ himself (Eph 2:14; Col 1:20; 3:14—15). To the Hebrew mind such a blessing is so palpable a force that, if not accepted, it can return to the

f giver. **14.** A Jew shook the unclean dust of gentile land from his shoes and garments before returning to the Holy Land, lest he defile it. By this gesture the preacher, then, shows that the city or house which refuses the message no longer forms part of God's chosen people, cf § 733e, and Ac 13:51. **15.** Sodom and Gomorrah are the stock type of sin punished by annihilation (Is 1:9—10; Zeph 2:9; Jer 23:14). The threat here made generally is applied to the coastal cities of Jesus' mission in 11:24. **16.** The faithful are often compared to sheep, as Christ is to the shepherd (cf Jn 10). The same contrast between sheep and wolves occurs 7:10, where the wolves are false prophets. The image of the dove probably refers not to their simplicity (cf Hos 7:11, used in an unfavourable sense) but to their innocence; of the possible meanings of *akeraios*, this alone occurs in the NT (Rm 16:19; Phil 2:15), with the sense 'uncontaminated by evil'.

g 17—25 Persecution of the missionaries (Mk 13:9—13; Lk 21:12—17, 19; 12:11—12; 6:40)—Mt now gives instructions for the wider mission to the world after the resurrection (hence the 'governors and kings' of 18), given by the other synoptics as part of the eschatological discourse. This transference is not merely for the sake of completing his missionary discourse; it underlines the eschatological character of the whole missionary activity of the Church. The thought of the **coming judgement** is always present (vv 15, 23, 28, 32—33, 41—42; cf 25:31—46); it is under the sign of the approaching end that the missionary works. The division between members of the same family also is a sign of the separation and judgement to occur in the last times of the Messiah's coming (SB 4, 978—9); Jn emphasizes that the coming of Jesus itself occasions this judgement, through the separation inevitable in the acceptance or rejection of Jesus' person; but Mt concentrates more on the division operated

by the acceptance and rejection of Christ's message as **721** handed on by missionaries (vv 21, 34—36). The theme of **imitation of Christ** is also prominent (vv 24—25, **h** 38, 40): as the master is persecuted, so will the disciples be. They will be flogged as Jesus (20:19), like him in his Passion brought before sanhedrin, governors (Pilate), and kings (Herod——this episode of the Passion is recorded only in Lk, who stresses this likeness of disciple to master also in the martyrdom of Stephen, cf § 829a). It is constantly stressed that the persecution (18) and the hate (22, 25, contrast 40—42) are directed to Christ; that it is the Spirit of the Father (sent also on Jesus at his baptism, cf § 714i) which speaks in them (**19—20**); that the Father himself protects them (29—31, cf 4:6—7 of Jesus).

17. '*their*' synagogues' is a decisive indication that by **i** the time Mt's gospel was written a final and definitive split had occurred between Christian and Jewish communities (also 4:23; 9:35; 12:9; 13:54; cf 23:34). The possessive is not certainly so used in Mk. Ac 28:21 shows that the split had not yet occurred in A.D. 62; but it is clearly shown by the Jewish imprecation on Christians, Birkath ha-Minim, to have been in operation by A.D. 85 (Kilpatrick 110—11) **19, 24—25.** These sayings on the **j** relationship of the disciple to the Spirit and to Christ himself are preserved also in Jn 14:26; 13:16 respectively (24—25 also by Lk 6:40). At least the latter seems to have come to Mt and Jn by independent channels, for the differences between the form of the saying are not typical of the evangelists' editorial work (C. H. Dodd, 'Some Johannine *Herrnworte*' NTS 2 (1955/6), 75—76). The disciples had been warned against vain anxiety and effort, when the Father (Mt uses his frequent 'theological' passive in 19) will provide (6:25—34). **23.** A further reminder of the lack of success of the mission to Israel (cf § 733e). The visitation by the Son of Man here threatened is usually interpreted not of the final judgement (§ 719k), but of the special visitation of Israel in judgement at the sack of the city (cf § 736). **24—25.** The basis of this saying may be a common Jewish proverb, since it occurs frequently in rabbinical writings (SB I. 577—8); but the application is nearly always, as here, religious: the lord stands for God and the slave for one of the patriarchs. Jesus' application to himself and his disciples would, then, constitute a striking claim to divinity. The Pharisees call out 'Beelzebul' to him in 12:24, q.v.

26—33 Open and Fearless Speech (Lk 12:2—9)— **k** This passage, drawn from the source Q common to Mt and Lk, continues the themes of 17—25 (see § 721g). Lk, however, uses it as polemic against the Pharisees. **26** is handed down independently in Mk 4:22. Jesus brings the fullness of revelation promised in the OT, cf § 722i. **27.** But during Jesus' lifetime, owing to the Jews' refusal, he could reveal himself only to a small group of disciples (cf § 725a); it is for them after his resurrection to spread to the world this revelation made in secret. **28.** The seeming opposition between body and soul here is impossible to a semite; the opposition is between the body and the whole person (*nepeš*, translated into Gr. *psuchē*). Men can kill, but not destroy someone wholly; God can allow someone's total destruction in hell. This latter possibility is stated energetically as though God imposed the destruction; in fact he only fulfils the destruction brought on themselves by the damned. On 'gehenna' see § 741b end. **29—31** returns to the theme of God's fatherly care (§ 718b). An *as* ('penny') was worth rather less than a halfpenny; it occurs often in proverbs to denote cheapness. **32—33.** The threat occurs also Mk 8:38; but here it is preceded by a balancing promise. The preacher

21k is only Christ's messenger to men, and is to be judged therefore on his fidelity to this task (cf § 721*i*).

l **34—39 Separation and Renunciation** (Lk 12:51—53; 14:26—27; 17:33)——For completeness Mt adds various sayings which he finds in the source Q, which he shares with Lk. The substance of **34—36** has already been given in 21. The mention of dissension within the family occasions the insertion of **37**, showing where the priorities lie. The renunciation involved attracts, in its turn, the saying of **38—39** which occurs also in 16:24—25 q.v.

m **40—42 Conclusion of the Missionary Discourse**——These sayings, for the most part, found also in 18:5 and Mk 9:41, form a final blessing for the missionary, a blessing on those who receive Christ in the person of his messengers. **40** envisages perhaps more docility and openness to the message, **42** more active co-operation, by which he who receives the missionary is associated with his work and receives his reward.

'22a **11—12 The Mystery of the Kingdom of Heaven**——This fourth major section of the gospel concerns the mysterious, hidden and humble nature of the kingdom (cf § 715*gh*). As usual it consists of a narrative section and a discourse. The narrative section (11—12) begins with John the Baptist's surprise at Jesus' way of acting (11:1—11), then comes the contrast between stiff-necked Israel and the disciples (11:12—30), and finally controversies with the Pharisees (12). All these serve to show the true nature of the kingdom.

b **11:1—6 The Baptist's Question** (Lk 7:18—23)——**1.** The missionary discourse ends with Mt's usual formula for the end of such discourses (7:28; 13:53; 19:1; 26:1). **2—6.** In this ch there is constant reference to Christ's works (2 and 19, serving as brackets to the section on the Baptist; 20, serving as link to the previous section). It is about these that John asks. For his imprisonment cf § 725*d*. 'The one who is to come' is a clear characterization of the Messiah both for the OT (Gn 49:10; Ezek 21:32; Dn 7:13) and the NT (Mk 11:9; 14:62 and, referring to the second coming 1 Cor 4:5; 11:26, Heb 10:37; Apoc 1:4). John's question about Jesus' messianic role is not a pretence or merely a way of teaching his disciples. The Messiah whose coming he heralded was one of fire and judgement (cf § 714*c*); when Jesus' action did not accord with this expectation John naturally asked questions. Jesus' reply is to point out, by describing his own action in a way full of allusions to Is 26:19; 29:18—19; 61:1, that his action does fulfil a quite different set of messianic prophecies. Jesus deliberately omits from his allusions to Is any which refer to anger or judgement. Lk, the meticulous historian, makes Jesus work some miracles on the spot to serve as evidence (and then say 'what you *have* seen and heard' instead of Mt's continuous present). He obviously reasons that they had not yet seen any of Christ's miracles, being absent at John's side. On the significance of Jesus' miracles cf § 719*ab*. The advent in judgement expected by the Baptist is reserved for the second coming. This distinction between two comings of the Messiah was a difficulty not only to John, but also to 2nd cent. Jews (Justin, *Dial.* 32) and still today.

c **7—11 Jesus looks back on the Baptist's role** (Lk 7:24—28)——Jesus first praises the Baptist's personal qualities (7—8), then his lofty function in God's plan (9—11*a*). This serves only to contrast the still greater present reality of the kingdom (11*b*). **7.** A reed is proverbial for weakness (1 (3) Kgs 14:15; Is 42:3), in contrast to John's fiery inflexibility; there is perhaps also allusion to the reeds of the Jordan where John baptized. **8.** This contrast is made more pointed by the knowledge that John was now not in the king's palace but in his prison. **9—11*a*.** Christ points out John's supreme role in preparation using the same quotation from Mal 3:1 as was used by Mk (who has no parallel to this passage) at 1:2. The quotation differs from the original version of Mal (according to both MT and LXX), which reads '*Look, I am going to send my messenger to prepare a way before me*'. All versions in the gospels substitute 'you' for 'me', making clear that Jesus' coming is the Day of the Lord prophesied. Since the same version appears twice independently, in Mk and in Mt–Lk, it is possible that this version was used by the early Church as a proof-text (though Justin, *Dial.* 50, quotes the LXX version). This identification of John with the promised prophet is strengthened by 14 where he is identified more precisely as the Elijah of Mal 3:22 (cf § 714*a*). But it is a testimony to the greatness and all-importance of the kingdom that, since, however great his personal merits and his function, he stands only on its threshold, the least in the Kingdom is greater than he.

722c

d **12—24 Opposition to the Kingdom** (Lk 16:16; 7:31—35; 10:13—15)——Mt passes to those who rejected his message (12—15) and that of Christ (16—19), and finally to a condemnation of them (20—24). The enigmatic **12** introduces the section. Lk's version (16:16) of Mt's vv 12—13 is probably original (Strecker p. 167), the order being reversed by Mt for the sake of an easier transition to 14, and to make 12 the key to the section. The 'violence' is probably intended in a derogatory sense, as usually with compounds of the Greek word (TWNT, 1 (1933), 613); so the last phrase means '*violent men are taking it away by force*', i.e. the opponents of the kingdom are making it inaccessible to others; but this sense is not certain. Lk's 'by violence everyone is getting in' is probably due to a misunderstanding of the Aram. (cf Black p. 84). **13—14** emphasizes once more the Baptist's function: the last of the prophets, the promised forerunner, he heralds the arrival of the kingdom, cf § 714*a*.

e **16—19 Condemnation of the present generation**——'This generation' is used uniformly in an unfavourable sense in the gospels (e.g. 12:39—45; 16:4; 17:17), of Jesus' contemporaries in general. In the rabbinic writings it is a commonplace that the generation of the Messiah will be an unworthy one (SB 1, 641). Jesus' parable uses the semitic way of naming extremes to express the whole intermediate range; so it means 'whatever is suggested . . .'. The vivid language and the recognition that he is strongly criticized are traces that the saying must stem from Jesus himself (Jeremias p. 160). He decries their perversity also in 17:17. **19.** Lk has 'wisdom *is* justified by all her *own* children', which concludes the parable better; but Mt changes 'children' to 'actions' to provide a link with 20. The wisdom of God is Christ himself, cf § 722*i*.

f **20—24 Lament over the Lake-towns**——Mt finishes off the first panel (12—24) of the diptych on reactions to Christ and their reward, by inserting here Christ's lament over Chorazin, Bethsaida and Capharnaum. This lament, drawn from Q, is given by Lk in a far more probable position, after the Galilean ministry has ended. It is transferred here by Mt, though historically it is still too early for Jesus to have abandoned hope for these cities, in order to provide a climax to this panel of the rejection of the Jews (cf §§ 733*e*; 742*c*). In view of the scriptural quotation in 23, and the contrast with 'children' in 25, we may deduce that it is precisely the pride of these cities which is reprobated. The day of judgement (22,

722f 24) is one of Mt's major preoccupations (cf § 738*f*). **20** and **23b–24** have no parallel in Lk and are formed by Mt to provide a frame to the lament, bracketing it with the word 'miracles', which serves also to bind the whole section 2–24 into a unity. **24,** which occurs almost identically in 10:15, adds little to 23*b*, but seems to be attracted simply by the mention of Sodom——an interesting example of Mt's use of mnemonics. The extensive basalt ruins of Chorazin (now Keraze) lie some 3 km. N of the lake. Bethsaida is commonly identified with the commanding hill et-Tell 2½ km. from the lake-shore, E of the Jordan, though no vestige of the buildings of the city have been found. Capharnaum is probably Tel Hum, on the shore 4 km. W of the Jordan. In accord with Jesus' lament, all three cities have been totally destroyed. Tyre and Sidon are used as a contrast because these great Phoenician ports were major enemies of the kingdom of Judah at the time of its final destruction (cf Ezek 26–28). There is a hint that the gentiles will be more willing to receive the message of Jesus than were the Jews, cf 8:10–12; even these proud and hostile cities would have humbled themselves.

g 25–30 Revelation to the Simple (Lk 10:21–22)—The lament over those who reject Christ's message is followed by a vividly contrasting hymn of thanksgiving for, and appeal to, those who welcome it. The warmth of tone here is in as strong contrast with the severity there, as is the humility of those here addressed with the pride of those who rejected Christ. The hymn is in three strophes (25–26, 27, 28–30) of which the first and third imply opposition to Christ's opponents, or more especially the Pharisees. Thus it continues the theme of division of the people into two parties, a division which is complete by ch 13 (cf § 724*e*). But it shows also a joyful return to contact with the Father, and with Christ's own, after the **h** struggle with his opponents. The original **occasion** of the pronouncement of the hymn cannot be recovered; as it stands, 'these things' (25) is without the reference to an antecedent which it must originally have had, and the third strophe is only loosely tacked on (the first two are connected by the theme of 'revelation'). In Lk the first pair of strophes occurs, aptly, at the return of the disciples from their missionary journey; Lk may provide the position of the first two strophes, though Mt's third is inept there and is not given by Lk. Bultmann holds (p. 163) that the whole hymn is the product of a Christian prophet of the early Church, though he admits (p. 160) that he can see no compelling reason for denying at least 25–26 to Jesus. But the Aram. colouring is unmistakable (in 25: the initial confessional 'I bless you', the expression 'Lord of heaven and earth'; in 26 the Aram. form of the vocative, the circumlocution of respect 'good pleasure has been such before you'; in 27 the 'theological passive'; in 30 'humble in heart'). The absolute use of 'the son' (27), in sayings which express the unique relationship between Jesus and the Father, is indeed typical of Jn in passages where Christ is speaking (5:19–26; 6:40; 8:36) as well as in editorial comments (1:18; 3:35–36), but it occurs also in Mk 13:32 and parallels. The hymn is rich in OT **i** tradition, sapiential, apocalyptic and prophetic. The sapiential background shows that Jesus here represents himself as the wisdom of the Father. Thus Jesus claims a unique relationship between himself and the Father, for wisdom —in Gr terms —shares the nature of God, cf Wis 7:22–26 and note there; Col 1:15. As in 27 the Father knows the Son, so in Jb 28:23; Sir 1:9 only God knows wisdom; as only the Son, and those to who the Son reveals him, know the Father, so in Wis 8:3–4; 9:9–18; Prv 8:22–36 only wisdom, and those to whom she reveals

herself, know God. In Sir 6:28; 51:27 it is in wisdom or in **722** accepting the yoke of the Law that man will find rest. Jesus transfers this promise to himself and to his own yoke. The **apocalyptic** overtones imply that the revelation **j** which Jesus gives is that of the 'kingdom which shall never be destroyed' (Dn 2:44): the word 'reveal' which forms the keynote of the hymn occurs 7 times in Dn 2, where this kingdom is prophesied; the revelation there (v 20 and 23), as here, begins with a thanksgiving to God for his revelation; in Dn 7:13–14, 24–27 all power and 'eternal sovereignty' is conferred on a son of man, as here upon the Son (cf Mt 28:18; Jn 3:35; 1 Cor 15:28). The power and the knowledge, then, conferred on the Son, and by him on those to whom he reveals himself, are those of the mystery of the kingdom (cf 13:11). But the combination of these notes with the **prophetic** theme is wholly new. In Dn 2:21–23 revelation is to the wise; in Sir 6:19–22 and Prv 1:22 the unlearned is reviled and true knowledge is accessible only to the elite. This is the predominant sense in the OT (TWNT IV (1942), 915–18). It is extremely rare in the OT that the 'simpleton' (25) is under God's special care and the recipient of his special revelation (Ps 19 (18):7; 116 (114):6; 119 (118):130; also Wis 10:21). The extension of the blessing on the poor (cf § 716*d*) also to the simple is Jesus' own innovation. Hence the novelty of the hymn, though hinted in **k** the first, lies chiefly in the third strophe. Implicit in this strophe is the contrast between the heavy yoke of legal obligations and the light yoke of Christ. From the earliest rabbinic writings the expressions 'yoke of the Law', 'yoke of the commandments', 'yoke of penance' are current (SB 1, 608–10), and already Sir 51:26 cf Ac 15:10. That this yoke could be a crushing one is seen from a touching story (SB 2, 728) even in a rabbinic work. The yoke Jesus promises releases from the burden of the Law: on Mt's attitude to the Law see § 710*b*. The lightness of Jesus' yoke comes from knowledge of him, as is clear from the sequence of thought. The word used for 'gentle' implies the opposite of roughness and overbearing, cf § 711*d*. Of the evangelists Mt alone insists on this quality of Jesus; in Mk and Lk it pales beside his divine power and in Jn beside his omnipotence (TWNT VI (1959), 649). But for Mt he is the messianic king in gentleness, cf 8:17; 12:15–21; 21:5—a quality which must be imitated by those who take his yoke upon themselves: 5:5; 2 Cor 10:1. In his promise to give 'rest', he is to fulfil the promise of the messianic times that 'God will give rest' (Is 25:10 LXX—MT and JB read differently), a promise repeated Heb 4:1–11. Jesus claims here, therefore, a divine prerogative.

12—This ch shows the **contrast between the 723a stubborn Pharisees and the gentle spirit of Jesus** in action (cf 722*a*). Three controversies are presented (with a quotation from the OT and its interpretation), leading up to a condemnation of the Pharisees' blindness. The first two controversies, on Sabbath observance, well illustrate Jesus' whole attitude towards the Law in Mt, subordinating it to the law of love, and so treating it with much more flexibility.

1–8 Picking corn on the Sabbath (Mk 2:23–28; **b** Lk 6:1–5)—Mt has taken the story from Mk, but subtly changed small details of the narration so that it becomes an object-lesson in his interpretation of the Law. It is clear from this and the following story that the Sabbath was still observed in Mt's community (on the general question of Mt and the Law, see § 710*b*). 'We may suppose that the ethics and institutions (of Mt's community) would be thoroughly Jewish, but that its Judaism was subordinate to its Christology.' (Kilpatrick p. 108).

23b Hence Mt is careful to point out that the disciples had a reason for their action, by adding the information that they 'were hungry' (**1**). The disciples were picking the corn-ears, and eating the corn, after rubbing them between their hands as a way of separating the husks from the grain (still done by Palestinians). This counted, according to a rabbinic interpretation, as threshing on the Sabbath, and so was forbidden (SB 1, 617). **2.** Mt slightly increases the malice of the Pharisees (cf § 724c): they no longer have even the goodwill to ask why the disciples are doing it (as Mk); they merely point out the fault. **3–4.** Jesus' reply is an argument from scripture to show that the Law can be broken. But what, for Mt, is the application intended? The obvious sense is that the Law may be broken in any case of need, and this is Mk's application. As his v 27 shows, he interpreted it to mean that Sabbath observance is at most of relative and limited value; but Mt omits this verse, which is at variance with his whole

c concept of the Law. His solution comes in 7. **5–7.** Are added by Mt (absent in Mk and Lk, and linked by his characteristic 'or again', cf 7:4, 9, 10; 12:33); they present two arguments interwoven, for 5–6 lead on to 8, while 7 draws the conclusion of the earlier argument in 3–4. The clue to Mt's conclusion is the favourite quotation, used also 9:13 and 23:23 against the Pharisees (cf § § 718l; 720k). Its meaning is clearest in 9:13; God requires not mere ritual but the freshness of love. To understand fully its use here it must be remembered that the word used for 'mercy' is used primarily of God's mercy to men, and in the mind of Israel was inseparably connected with the great revelations of God's 'kindness' (Ex 34:6–7; Jer 32:18; Jon 4:2 etc); he is a God of understanding love, not of rigid observance, and man must imitate this in his own conduct. But the only possible application of this principle to the case under discussion would be that the Pharisees should overlook the fault committed in need by the disciples. This is not the application intended by Mt, for he insists that they are 'blameless', not merely pardonable; to achieve this he combines the argument with the Christological one of 5–6 and 8: as the service of the temple is more binding than Sabbath observance, so the Son of man is greater than the temple, and Lord of the Sabbath. The first claim, to be greater than the temple, would be staggering enough to a Jew. But only God, who delivered the Law and—according to Jewish tradition—daily meditates the Law, is lord of the Sabbath. So Jesus, as often in his use of this mysterious title (cf § 719k), hints at his divinity and leaves his hearers to draw the conclusion.

d **9–14 Healing on the Sabbath** (Mk 3:1–6; Lk 6:6–11)—In this chapter, which contrasts Jesus' messianic activity and so the nature of his kingdom with the harshness of the stiff-necked Pharisees, comes a second controversy over observance of the Sabbath, also taken from Mk. Mt, as usual, cuts out what he considers irrelevant to the lesson of the story (Mk 4b–5a, repetitions and, characteristically, Jesus' anger; Mt tends to omit signs of emotion in Jesus), and makes it clear from the start that we are concerned with the general lesson of the story, not the particular question of the right course of action in this particular case (Mk 3:2). By his careful insertion of the rabbinic argument *a minori ad maius* in 11–12a he shows that he is not concerned with the abolition of Sabbath restrictions in general but with the interpretation of these restrictions according to the all-important law of love. As always, Mt retains observance of the Law, but with greater flexibility than rabbinic practice permitted; cf § 710b. Rabbinic interpretation permitted healing on the Sabbath only in cases of danger of death

(SB 1, 623), of which there is no question here. Mt's **723e** rabbinic-style argumentation (v 11, which is drawn from Q, and parallel Lk 14:5 show traces of a triple pun in Aram.; cf Black p. 126) presupposes a laxer ruling to be acceptable than was later current. But late in the 3rd cent. A.D. it was at least still disputed whether it were permissible to extract a beast from a ditch on the Sabbath. The great Rabbi then ruled that one might feed it and ease its position; and then 'if it gets out, it gets out!' (SB I. 629). In **14** Mt omits mention of the Herodians (Mk 3:6); by Mt's time the family and political supporters of Herod were things of the past cf § 709g.

15–21 Jesus the Suffering Servant (Mk 3:7–12; **f** Lk 6:17–18)—After these two confrontations with the Pharisees over Sabbath observance, Mt shows how the spirit of the kingdom there evidenced accords with the prophecies, cf § 710e. In **18** he adjusts the wording of the quotation to fit the divine voice at the baptism (3:17) and the transfiguration (17:5), suggesting that he considers the voice to be referring directly to this text. In **20** Mt introduces the word 'victory' (OT: 'till he has established true justice on earth'); his humiliation will issue in a triumphant reign.

22–30 Jesus and Beelzebul (Mk 3:20–27; Lk **g** 11:14–23)—A final encounter between Jesus and the Pharisees completes the picture of the distinction between the spirit of the Pharisees and that of the kingdom (cf § 722a) and the resulting division between their adherents. **22–24.** The occasion of the controversy is the cure of a possessed man, very similar to that recounted in 9:32–34, which results in a similar accusation. It is not in Mk, but Mt is here combining his two major sources, Mk and Q; it served therefore in Q (cf § 646) to introduce the controversy, and was perhaps transferred from there also to 9:32–34. **23.** The crowds hail Jesus with the popular messianic title 'son of David', for casting out devils was to be one of the signs of the messianic age (cf 8.29 and SB IV. 526–7). This title is much used by Mt, though Jesus' own attitude to such acclamation was reserved, owing to the political overtones which the title had acquired (cf § 734i). **24.** For Mk's 'scribes' Mt substitutes 'Pharisees'. On seven other occasions also he omits deliberately the opposition of the scribes (substituting the Pharisees at 22:34). In his time the opposition from the Jews was clearly centred in that of the Pharisees, cf § 709g. **25–30.** Jesus' reply is composed of three little comparisons: the divided kingdom, the divided family and the mighty warrior. According to Mk who has no parallel to Mt's 27–28, 30, Jesus merely leaves these ringing in his opponent's ears, challenging them to draw their conclusion. But Q (and so Mt) gives the interpretation, that in the person of Jesus the messianic kingdom has come; this is the meaning of all Jesus' miracles (cf 11:1–6 and § 719ab). Expulsion of demons was not unknown among the Jews, cf SB IV. 534–5.

31–50 Opponents and true Disciples—the division **h** between those who accept and those who reject Christ's kingdom has been gradually building up throughout these two chh (11–12). Finally before the revelation in parables to the disciples (13) these two groups are characterized: the brood of vipers or the evil and unfaithful generation (vv 31–45), and true brethren (46–50). **31–37.** In a symmetrical pattern, a chiasmus, constructed by Mt chiefly from combining Mk and Q, the **brood of vipers is characterized** as discernible by their fruits or their words. The centrepiece round which the structure is built up is 34a: blasphemous words (31–32, from Mk)—image of the trees and their fruit (33, from Q)—centrepiece (34a from Q)—interpretation of the image (34b—

723h 35 from Q)—judgement on blasphemous words (36—37, Mt's own composition). **31—32.** The 'blasphemy against the spirit' is a refusal to recognize that the spirit of God is manifested in Jesus' messianic actions. In the Synoptic gospels the Spirit is the power in which Jesus fulfils his mission (Mt 3:11, 16; 4:1; 12:18, 28; Lk 4:14, 18; 10:21) and later the disciples theirs (Mt 10:20; Mk 13:11; Lk 11:13). It was this spirit which Is (11:2; 42:1; 61:1) had foretold would rest upon the Messiah. The blasphemy is unforgivable because it opposes not the Son of man (here Jesus in his lowly condition, cf § 719*k*) but the offer of God itself. Jesus, characteristically, gives this teaching, leaving his hearers to apply it to them-

i selves. **33—35.** After their evil words have been noted, the conclusion that they themselves must be rotten follows through the intermediary of the figure of a tree and its fruit, already used in the OT (Is 3:10; Hos 10:13) and by Mt 3:10 (by John the Baptist against the Pharisees) and 7:16—20. The chiasmus is sustained: a^1, a^2, b, c, b, a^2, a^1. The imperative with which **33** opens is difficult (smoothed over in JB), and is probably a mistranslation of the Aram. (Black p. 148—149), which is rendered correctly in the parallel passages.

36—37. Finally the judgement—always a major preoccupation with Mt (cf § 738*f*)—in a v full of Matthean

j expressions. **38—45.** Next this 'evil and unfaithful generation' is threatened with the judgement of God (Lk 11:29—32, 24—26). The passives here are 'theological', respectful circumlocutions to avoid using the divine name. On the expression 'an evil generation', which brackets this section (39 and 45) see § 722*e*. 'Unfaithful' in the sense of 'adulterous' is an allusion to the figure of Israel as the spouse of the Lord (Hos 2; Ezek 16); their faithlessness consists in their infidelity to the covenant, conceived as a marriage-bond between the Lord and his people. **40.** The sign of Jonah which is the only sign (other than those already granted and disbelieved) to be granted to 'this generation' is of course the resurrection. In Jewish tradition, as in Lk 11:30, it is the freeing from the whale which was regarded as a sign of God's guarantee of Jonas as a messenger (TWNT 3 (1938), 413). Mt has slightly altered the content of the sign; for him it is the duration of the period in the belly of the whale, compared to that of Christ's in the tomb. The 'three nights'—not accurate of Jesus— is the result of literal quotation of the LXX, and causes no difficulty. **41—42.** As in 11:20—24 the condemnation of those who will not receive Jesus builds up to an unfavourable comparison of them to non-Jews, a presage of the passing of the inheritance of Israel to a new Israel composed of Jews and gentiles (cf § 733*e*).

k **43—45.** The condemnation is reinforced by another simile; it is Mt himself who makes the application explicit by adding 45*b*. Jesus' activity as a whole is compared to the expulsion of a demon with which the incident began. The time of his presence is a time of salvation in which evil is cast out; but, if his kingdom is not embraced, every kind of evil (the seven demons, being of a perfect number, represent every kind of devilry) enter in. As the Gr. of 44*b*—45 stands, the return of the demon seems inevitable; but the underlying Aram. was a conditional clause: '*If* it arrives to find it unoccupied, swept and tidied, *then* . . .' (H. S. Nyberg, 'Zum grammatischen Verstaendnis von Matt. 12, 44f' in *Arbeiten u. Mitteilungen aus dem ntlichen Seminar zu Uppsala*,

l 4 (1936), 22—35). **46—50. True brethren of Jesus** (Mk 3:31—35; Lk 8:19—21). Finally with Jesus' stubborn opponents are contrasted the true members of his kingdom (as in 11:25—30). Thus the presentation

of the two opposed groups (chh 11—12) is completed, **723** and a transition is made to the revelation in parables to the disciples (ch 13). Mt, as usual, simplifies, especially if **47** is to be omitted on the grounds that it is a harmonization to Mk and Lk, absent from several important MSS. The lesson is made more solemn by the OT gesture in **49***a*. It is also made clearer, for it is by no means certain that 'those sitting in a circle about him' (Mk) all fulfil the conditions of the last v. Mt makes the passage a formal lesson on discipleship by referring it to the disciples alone (v 49); the condition of discipleship, 'doing the will of my Father in heaven' is that stressed also in the solemn passage 7:21. 'The claims of physical relationship come after those of spiritual, cf 8:21f; 10:37', JB. On the brothers of the Lord see §§ 663—4; it denotes any close relation, not only brothers in the English sense. In the transferred sense of v 50 it is used of fellow members of many religious societies, including of course the early Christians (TWNT 1 (1933), 145—6).

13:1—52 The Discourse in Parables—as usual, the **724** fourth major division of the gospel consists of a narrative section and a discourse. The narrative section (11—12) has shown the division between the Pharisees who reject and the disciples who accept the message of the kingdom. Now the disciples receive further instruction in the mystery of the kingdom, delivered to the crowds in parables but explained to the disciples. Mk collected into his ch 4 three parables on the nature of the kingdom; Mt omits one (Mk 4:26—29) but adds five others, thus achieving the perfect number of seven, a favourite number with him.

The parable (Heb *māšāl*) is a favourite form of instruction with semites both in the OT (e.g. 2 Sm 12:1—10; 14:1—11) and in post-biblical Jewish writings. The term embraces 'figurative forms of speech of every kind' (Jeremias, *Parables* p. 20) e.g. similitude, allegory, proverb, riddle, symbol. In the NT *parabolē* can mean comparison (Mk 3:23), proverb (Lk 6:39), riddle (Mk 7:17), symbol (Heb 9:9), though Mt in fact uses it only of a lesson learnt by means of a comparison (13; 15:15; 21:33, 45; 22:1; 24:32). Dodd and, after him, Jeremias, have shown that the parables of the gospels have a double historical setting (Jeremias, *Parables*, 23ff): the original, concrete, historical setting in the life of Jesus, and their setting in the preaching of the Church. The lesson originally taught by Jesus through a parable often became inapplicable when the moment of his preaching was past, but the Church applied the message to its own situation and needs. It will often be possible to trace this process of transformation: cf § 733*g*.

1—9 Parable of the sower (Mk 4:1—9; Lk 8:4—8)— **b** **1—3.** The ch is set by the sea of Galilee; Mt's additional indication of 'the house' shows that he sets it at Capharnaum, for he uses this expression only five times, always in connexion with Capharnaum; it must be the house where Jesus dwelt in his adopted city (cf 4:13; 9:1). He solemnly takes his seat, in the posture of a teacher (cf 5:1; 15:29; 23:2—of the scribes; 24:3). **6—9. The parable**, as always, takes a scene familiar to the hearers; in the description of the sowing the stony and unproductive nature of Palestinian soil is evident, and the loss of much of the labour involved. Since in Palestine sowing precedes ploughing, the fallen seed being later ploughed in, seed would be sown both '*on the path*' (a track worn across the field) and on patches where stone was concealed beneath the surface. Hence a considerable loss of seed and effort (cf Jeremias, NTS 13 (1966), 38—43). In Mk the point of the story lies in the amazingly rich harvest (note the crescendo: 30—60—100); a hundred-

24b fold average yield on a field is unbelievably high, but here is meant a hundred grains in one ear, which is in fact recorded in the Decapolis at this period (Varro, *R.R.*, 1, 44, 2). By reversing the numbers Mt changes the delight at success into a warning and exhortation (Barth, p. 60 n. 1). As it stands this story could well find its setting in Jesus' life, as a result of his reflection of the only partial success of his preaching, the many who rejected it, and the rich increase among those few who accepted it (Jeremias, *Parables*, 150—1). On the harvest-time as a figure of the messianic times cf § 721*a*. Since Justin, *Dial.*, 125 and Clem., *Rec.*, 3, 14 interpret the story as an encouragement of the Christian preacher to perseverence, Jeremias suggests that their interpretation goes back independently, behind Mk 4:13—20 and parallels. But for the application of this parable in the gospels, see Mt 13:18—23 and notes.

c 10—17 Why Jesus speaks in parables (Mk 4:10—12; Lk 8:9—10; 10:23—24)—In order better to understand Mt we must first examine Mk. It is Mk himself who inserts this passage. It is indeed normal for the disciples to seek further explanations in private, as do other rabbinic pupils (cf § 757*a*), but the disciples' question originally concerned only the parable of the sower, not the whole principle of teaching in parables. Thus 11 and 13 both begin with Mk's own transitional formula 'and he said to them'. The vv themselves, however, are taken over by Mk from some source; they contain expressions quite untypical of him (cf Gnilka). The purpose of using parables is given: 'to those who are outside everything comes in parables so that they may . . . not perceive'. In fact this programme is carried out by Mk. He gives no great discourses to the people; the only teaching they receive is in parables (cf 4:34). This marked distinction between two groups stands firmly in the traditions of Jewish apocalyptic and of Qumran (Sjoberg p. 124). There was an inner group of the chosen of God to whom the inner mysteries were to be revealed, distinguished from the others, whose unfaithfulness to God, and even persecution of the chosen ones, excluded them from reception of revelation. They are to blame, not for their failure to understand the parables, but for their failure to show sufficient good will to be worthy of revelation. When this is not shown, the concealment is intended by God. Hence the constant veiling of the revelation of the mystery, especially strong in Mk (1:25, 34, 44; 7:33, 36). Of Mk's six parables only one is explained (4:13—20), and that only to the disciples; the rest remain mere images thrown down, on which the hearers themselves must reflect. Their lesson is, moreover, far less developed than the lessons of Mt's and Lk's parables; there are no parables of mercy or of judgement; there is no allegorization by Mk (4:13—20 comes from a source). They proclaim only, by means of arresting but traditional images, that the messianic times are here; even the identity of the Messiah is never clearly shown (Mk has no parallel to Mt 12:28), but must be deduced by the hearers' own reflection. And in fact the only result of the public parables recorded by Mk is the deepening of the enmity of his opponents to **d** Jesus (3:28—29; 12:12). **Mt's view** of the parables is somewhat different. Much more than Mk he is concerned to make everything clear to the reader. Thus he adds a sentence in explanation (e.g. 12:28), often giving an application to Church life (13:49—50; 18:14, 35; 22:14; 25:13, 30) or a complete allegorical interpretation (13:36—43). The same basic division between groups remains, and is stressed by the insertion here (v 12) of the saying given by Mk in 4:25, and by that of vv 16—17,

which builds a forceful contrast between those who cannot **724d** perceive or hear and the disciples, blessed for their hearing and perception (cf the contrasts of chh 11—12, especially 11:20—30; 12:31—50). But the rift is so much wider already that the parables are no longer a means of widening it (Gnilka p. 91). For Mk 4:12's 'so that', Mt can substitute 'the reason . . . is that' (v 13); the rift is a *fait accompli*. Their situation is indeed worse than it is in Mk (v 12); for there they may not perceive or understand, but do at least see and hear; but in Mt (v 13) they look without even seeing, and listen without even hearing. So also Mt, instead of his usual introduction of a scriptural passage ('*in order that* **e** the saying of the prophet *might be* fulfilled'), can use the unprecedented 'This prophecy of Is *is being* fulfilled'. This citation of Is must have played a large part in the reflections of the early Church on the rejection of Jesus by the mass of the Jews. The formula by which it is introduced here, wholly uncharacteristic of Mt, must have been copied by him with the quotation itself. Luke reserves the full citation till the final rejection of the gospel message by the Jews of Rome, with which he closes his work (Ac 28:26—27). (Yet the use of the text must be very old, for Mk's version follows the Palestinian Targum (Gnilka p. 16)). Throughout his gospel Mt constantly stresses the stubbornness of the Jews (8:11—12; 11:20—24; 12:42, 45, 49; 16:3*b*—4; 22:1—14; 23:31—35, 39; 26:5; 27:24—25; he even omits Mk 12:41—44 because of its hints to the contrary.) By contrast he stresses the understanding of the disciples, disregarding or softening any suggestion in Mk that they lacked understanding (Mt 13.51, 14.33, 16.9, 11, 17:4, 9, 13, 23; 19:23). They may lack trust (8:26; 14:31; 16:8; 17:20; cf 6:30 for meaning) but not understanding, as in Mk's parallels. All this prepares for Mt's greater theme, that the remaining privileges of Israel (the old Law) will be taken away from it, and given to a new Israel drawn from Jew and gentile alike (**12**, cf § 733*e*). **11**. The expression '**mystery**' occurs only here, **f** and parallels, in the gospels. Its primary meaning, both in the LXX and in pagan usage, is of a secret, usually a religious secret. More precise associations are provided by Dn 2: 18—19, 27—30; 4:6 and the texts of Qumran (where it occurs over 40 times); there it indicates the designs of God which are to be revealed in the last days. In the Pauline epistles the content of this revelation is salvation by means of the Cross (1 Cor 2:7), or, more generally, the whole of God's plan of salvation in Christ (Eph 1:9; 6:19). A wide sense is preferable here. The passives here, as in v 12, are 'theological'; it is God who reveals, who gives or takes away the privileges of the kingdom, but out of reverence the direct naming of God was avoided. **16—17**. These vv occur in Lk after the passage parallel to Mt 11:25—27, which could well be their original position. They are introduced here by Mt to complete the contrast with stubborn non-believers, cf § 724*d*.

18—23 Parable of the Sower Explained (Mk 4:13— **g** 20; Lk 8:11—15)—The explanation is universally acknowledged by scholars to stem, at least in form, not from Jesus himself but from the primitive Church (Jeremias pp. 77—79; Gnilka, p. 41). 'The word' becomes a technical term of the apostolic preaching, and is used in this sense only once more by Mk (2:2) where it is also due to the evangelist. The metaphorical use of the words for 'sowing', 'producing fruit', 'root' (of perseverance) occur only here in the synoptics, but are common in Paul. Further, the preoccupations which the explanation presupposes are rather those of the apostolic

724g community than those of Jesus at this early stage in his ministry: 'with the best will in the world the crowd by the Lake of Galilee could not interpret the parable in the way that Jesus according to Mk interprets it to his disciples' (Gnilka); particularly striking is the emphasis

h on persecution and failure under pressure of trial. A major difficulty of the interpretation is that the seed represents sometimes the gospel message, sometimes the response to it; these applications occur respectively in IV Esdras 9:31 and 8:41; but the combination of them is awkward and hardly spontaneous. The explanation must however be prior to Mk, since it contains many words foreign to his habitual vocabulary. We may suppose that it stood in his source for this ch. But the explanation is (cf A. George, 'Le Sens de la Parabole des Semailles', *Sacra Pagina*, 2 (1959), 163–9) in continuity with Jesus' own message in the parable; both reflect upon the checks undergone by the preaching of the kingdom and its success nevertheless—the parable in Jesus' own situation, the explanation in that of the Church. Mt, in accord with his insistence in v 13, underlines the importance of *understanding* the message, by adding the word in vv 19 and 23 (cf 13:51; 16:12; 17:13; omission of Mk 6:52; 8:17, 9:10, 32). 'It is precisely "understanding" which differentiates the disciples from the obdurate multitude'. (Barth p. 107).

i **24–30 Parable of the Darnel**—This parable, given by Mt alone, takes the place in Mt of Mk's Seed Growing Secretly (4:26–29). The substitution helps to show the lesson intended by Mt, though he also supplies an allegorical interpretation. It is the first of three parables which illustrate the paradoxical nature of the Kingdom in its various aspects: here that it is still composed of good and bad, until the time of the harvest (a symbol, in Jewish literature, of the eschatological manifestation of the Messiah, cf § 721a). Jeremias (*Parables* pp. 223–4) not improbably supposes it to be an answer of Jesus to some such accusation as is recorded in Mt 9:11, that Jesus makes his company with sinners. This is even more probable if the version preserved in the *Gospel of Thomas* (*logion* 57), which ends after the first phrase of v 30, is the original one. The elaboration of v 30 would then be a preparation for Mt's own interpretation (vv 36–43), and, as the latter, occasioned by his own special preoccupation with the final judgement (cf § 738f). **24.** The introductory formula 'The kingdom of heaven may be compared to . . .' is misleading (cf 18:23; 22:2; 25:1; 13:31, 33, 44, 45,

j 47; 20:1). Underlying this formula is the Aram. *l*ᵉ; literally this means 'to', but as an introduction to parables it is an abbreviation and should be fully translated 'It is the case with (the Kingdom of Heaven) as with . . .' (Jeremias pp. 100–101). E.g. here the Kingdom is compared not with the man but with the whole situation. **25–30.** Darnel, *lolium temulentum*, is common in Palestine, but 'until the ears appear the most experienced eye would scarcely manage to distinguish its blades from those of wheat' (Lagrange p. 266–7). The harvesting would in fact be quite simple, for wheat grows considerably higher than darnel, so could easily be cut first. For Mt's explanation of the parable see vv 36–43.

k **31–32 Parable of the Mustard Seed** (Mk 4:30–32; Lk 13:18–19)—To the Jews the mustard seed is proverbial for any very small quantity (SB 1. 669). I have seen in Galilee a willowy but luxuriant mustard plant, some dozen feet high, claimed to be only a few months old. The parable, the second of Mt's three concerning the paradoxical nature of the Kingdom (cf § 724i), illustrates its astounding growth from insignificant beginnings. There is (Dodd p. 190) perhaps also an allegorical reference to

Ezek 17:22–23, where a tree in which all kinds of birds **724** come and dwell is a figure of the Kingdom of the last times. In this allegorical sense the birds symbolize the people of all nations. (In Ezek they dwell in its shadow; but the tree is a cedar, and this would be less apt of a mustard plant). A tree sheltering birds is used of a kingdom and its subjects also in Ezek 31:6; Dn 4:11.

33 Parable of the Yeast (Lk 13:20–21)—The last of Mt's three parables about the paradoxical nature of the Kingdom concerns its unexpected and hidden intrinsic power. The vast quantity of flour involved (50 lbs.) would produce a meal for some 100 persons— far more than the normal housewife requires. In fact the quantity constitutes an allusion to Gn 18:6, where Abraham takes this quantity for his three celestial guests. So this is 'meant to tell us that we have to do with divine realities' (Jeremias p. 147).

34–35 Teaching in Parables Foretold (Mk 4:33– **l** 34)—Mt seizes the occasion of the end of Mk's chapter of parables here to show how Jesus' activity intentionally fulfils the prophecies; this he likes to do, especially in the middle of a similar series of actions (cf 8:17; 12:17 and § 719i). Ps 78 (77):2 in Mt and LXX reads '. . . *riddles of former times.*' Mt's 'things hidden since the foundation (of the world) has a far more apocalyptic and remote ring; it deals no longer with the banalities of history, but with the eternal designs of God.

36–43 Parable of the Darnel Explained—This **m** explanation, or rather key to the allegory, is composed by the evangelist; Jeremias (*Parables* pp. 82–84) counts 37 linguistic characteristics of Mt in the 8 vv. Strecker (p. 160 n. 2) maintains that it has a pre-Matthean basis, but on very slender grounds. If the original purpose of the parable was indeed (cf § 724i) to provide an answer to those who complained of Jesus' consorting with sinners, then Mt has made a significant shift of emphasis in the direction of one of the major preoccupations of his gospel (cf § 738f). The explanation is, however, in continuity with the original message of the parable, being merely an examination of the same problem under its eschatological aspect; Jesus showed how sinners could be in the kingdom on earth, while the early Church considers how this will be resolved at the consummation of the Kingdom (cf § 715fh). **36.** The explanation of the parable is given only to the disciples (cf § 724c). **43.** The shining light of glory is a metaphor drawn from Jg 5:31; Dn 12:3 and familiar in Jewish literature, cf SB I. 673. The consummation of the Kingdom is that the Messiah should hand it over to the Father; cf 1 Cor 15:24; Eph 1:22.

44–46 Parables of the Treasure and of the Pearl— **n** The central element in each of these parables is the overpowering joy of the unexpected discovery (Jeremias, *Parables* pp. 200–201). This joy leads the man to give up everything for his new-found treasure; giving up everything is an essential part of Mt's description of a disciple; cf § 711g. Hence these parables, addressed to the disciples (cf v 36), are intended to remind them of the joyful nature of their sacrifice.

47–50 Parable of the Dragnet—The parable is closely similar to that of the darnel (vv 24–30). This is confirmed by the explanatory conclusion (49–50), expressed in Matthean terms almost identical to the explanation of the Darnel parable (cf § 724m). Since it is included in this collection of three parables addressed to the disciples, it is perhaps intended by Mt as an encouragement and a warning. A dragnet is a band of net some 500 yards long by 3 deep, with corks at intervals to keep the top on the surface. Some members of the fishing-group stand on the shore paying it out, while the others in

724n a boat lead the other end round in a circle, till they close the circle by returning to the point of departure. The net is then pulled in, the bottom being first brought tight to prevent the fish escaping. This method is still used today on the Lake of Galilee, but the whole operation is from boats. The Kingdom is likened, not to the net itself, but to the entire process; cf § 724f.

o 51—52 Conclusion of the Discourse in Parables— 51. Mt stresses once again the understanding of the disciples, cf § 724h. **52.** A last little parable to characterize the Christian scribe (this seems to be an office in the community, cf 23:34 and Kilpatrick, p. 126). The word *matheteutheis* could be translated 'becomes a disciple of' (as JB), but the sense 'instructed in' fits the context much better (Trilling p. 145—6), since there is a question of understanding and passing on the message of the Kingdom, whose nature has been being revealed especially in this ch. The 'things both new and old' are perhaps the OT and the message of Jesus, perhaps the message of Jesus and its application in the life of the community; more probably it is the tradition composed of the OT and the sayings of the Lord, and the interpretation and continuation of these, which it was the function of the Christian scribe to give (cf Gerhardsson pp. 208—323).

725a 13:53—17:27 Training the Disciples—After this discourse on the nature of the Kingdom begins the fifth major division of the gospels, as usual composed of narrative, and discourse (18). In it, after a sharp bout of persecution (13.53—14.12), Jesus withdraws from the synagogues and begins to concentrate on the training of the disciples. First he brings them to a realization that He is the Messiah (16:16). Then he initiates them into the consequence of this: the Passion (16:21).

b 53—58 Visit to Nazareth (Mk 6:1—6; Lk 4:16—30)— After Mt's usual formula at the end of a discourse (53a, cf 7:28; 11:1; 19:1; 26:1), he tells of a visit to Jesus' original home town (cf 2:23). Bultmann (p. 31) holds that 'the present text derives from two originals—the saying and the scene of success' (i.e. 54—56) 'which then, in the light of later experience was turned into its opposite' (i.e. 57—58). But the scene is really a unity centred on the saying in v 57; this alone implies both that he was accorded some sort of recognition as a prophet, i.e. wonder at his teaching, and that they did not put faith in him. Lk puts the scene at the beginning of Jesus' ministry, not only to explain Jesus' move to Capharnaum (which Mt has already done 4:13—16), but also to give a scene typical of the Jews' rejection of the Messiah. By adding 56b Mt has structured the incident in a formal chiasmic pattern so that it runs: home-country (54a)— whence? (54b)—is not? (55a)—is not? (55b)— whence? (56b)—home-country (57b) (Léon-Dufour p. 159, cf note on 12:31—37). This serves not only art, but also as a mnemonic and to concentrate interest on the main points. **54.** It is chiefly by Jesus' 'wisdom' that they are surprised. About his education we know little; he could certainly read (Lk 4:16) and write (Jn 8:6). A Jewish father was obliged to have his son instructed in the Law (Dt 6:7), and for this 'at the time of the fall of the Temple there were private elementary schools in all the Jewish towns of Palestine, and the larger villages of Judaea also . . . . School attendance was, to judge from the evidence, quite general, although not compulsory' (Gerhardsson p. 59). But in these schools instruction was probably limited to reading, translation and memorization. It is highly unlikely that Jesus ever attended a higher rabbinic school where alone interpretation of the scriptures could be learnt; even then this consisted chiefly in memorization of interpretations (Gerhardsson pp. 85—

121). He would not, therefore, have been officially **725c** equipped to teach. **55.** Mt changes the accusation that Jesus himself was a manual worker (this is all *tektōn* means; the information that their craft was carpentry comes from an apocryphal source; any other village craft could also be meant) into an allegation that he was a manual worker's son; perhaps this was considered less injurious. But it is possible that Mk's text is now corrupt, and originally read as Mt (cf § 753a). The fact that Jesus was still thought to be Joseph's son is an interesting commentary on Joseph's care for his wife's reputation (cf 1:19). On 'the brothers of the Lord' see §§ 663—4; the term denotes any close relation. **58.** Mt makes two significant Christological changes here: instead of Mk's 'he could work' few miracles, Mt has 'he did not'. He makes clear that, though in fact Jesus never works miracles where there is no faith (cf § 719d), he is not unable to do so. Mt also omits Jesus' amazement (Mk), to accord with his hieratic presentation of Jesus' dignity and omniscience (cf §§ 711c).

14:1—12 Herod and John the Baptist (Mk 6:14—29; **d** Lk 9:7—9)—Mt severely prunes this whole section. **1—2.** Serves merely as an introduction. Mt corrects Mk; Herod Antipas was strictly only tetrarch of Galilee and Perea. The title of king is given either by popular carelessness or by confusion with his father Herod the Great. **3—12.** Mt discards all the colourful details of Mk's **e** account for which see § 753c, in order to highlight the one point which interests him: the execution of John has its place in a continuous line. John is murdered as the other prophets were by the Jews (cf v 15; 21:33—41; 23:37), and as Jesus himself will be. It is now Herod, not his wife (Mk v 19), who wants to kill John, as his father had wanted to kill Jesus (2:13). His reason for hesitation is no longer his own respect for John (Mk v 20), but his fear of 'the people who regarded John as a prophet'; the Jewish rulers later hesitated for the same reason to kill Jesus (21:46). (This makes Herod's grief in v 9 awkward). A further touch which suggests this theme of parallelism is that already in 4:12 the same word "was given up" is used of John's arrest, as is often used of Jesus'. The most significant point is the position of the story here (cf § 725a): in Mt it stands juxtaposed to the rejection of Jesus at Nazareth, with it forming the break between Jesus' mission to the crowds and his withdrawal to instruct the disciples. The parallelism is stressed by Mt also: 17:12.

13—21 Feeding of the Five Thousand (Mk 6:30—44; **f** Lk 9:10—17)—Now that the break from Jesus' open ministry to the masses has been firmly established (cf § 725a), there starts a section on the instruction of the disciples, which will lead up to Peter's profession of faith (16:16). L. Cerfaux ('La Section des Pains', in *Recueil L. Cerfaux*, 471—85) notes that the theme of bread runs through the section 14:13—16:12, or at least occurs at beginning, middle (15:32—39) and end, and e.g. 15:26. More significant is the constant aid and instruction of the disciples (cf §§ 725k; 726g, l).

The story of the feeding of the five thousand is theologically perhaps the most allusive of all the miracle stories. Not only are there allusions to the Eucharist, but also the story is carefully modelled, especially in Mk, to bring out its messianic significance. In the other story of a miraculous feeding (15:32—39 and parallels) this intention is less apparent. It is impossible to say whether the two stories are **different versions of the same g event**; the divergencies between them are less than those between many pairs of narratives which certainly record the same event (e.g. Gn 1 and 2; 15 and 17; Jg 4 and 5).

725g Such differences can be due to different authors, or different points of view and interests. The helpless surprise of the apostles on two separate occasions (14:17 and 15:33) is unlikely after Jesus' opening suggestion. We can hardly suppose that they had forgotten so significant an event—which they afterwards remembered in such detail! An argument for two events cannot be drawn from 16:9—10 for, since two stories had been included, the words of Jesus were naturally accommodated to this, without thereby guaranteeing their independence. From his omission of the second incident it seems that Lk considered it to be a doublet; he regularly omits doublets. One possibility is that Mt and Mk relate in two consecutive partial sequences what Jn relates in one complete sequence, thus:

Mt Mk	Jn
Feeding (Mt 14:13—21)	Feeding (6:1—15)
Walking on water (14:22—23)	Walking on water (6:16—21)
Feeding (15:32—39)	
Refusal of sign (16:1—4)	Refusal of sign (6:26—33)
Confession of Peter (16:13—20)	Confession of Peter (6:67—71)

See also § 755a.

h The miraculous feeding stands firmly in a **biblical tradition** (for what follows cf A. Heising, *Die Botschaft der Brotvermehrung*, 1966). Already Moses had miraculously provided food for God's people (Ex 16:13—14), as a sign of God's care for and presence among his people (Ex 16:7—8). Elisha too had fed a hundred men miraculously (2 (4) Kgs 4:42—44). At the time of Christ the Messiah was awaited as the last and greatest of the prophets (Jn 1:21, 25; 4Q Test 5—8) in accordance with God's promise to Moses to raise up a prophet like him (Dt 18:15—18). Many of the wonders of the Exodus were to be repeated especially that of miraculous **i** feeding with bread (Jn 6:30—31; SB II. 481). The synoptic account is shot through with **allusions to this expectation**. It is modelled most closely after Elisha's miraculous feeding in 2 (4) Kgs 4:42—44; Elisha orders his servant to feed the men (cf Mt v 16); the servant intimates the impossibility of this (cf Mt v 17); the order is repeated and the servant distributes the food (cf Mt v 19); they eat and have enough (cf Mt v 20). Only the numbers are different; instead of twenty loaves between a hundred men, it is five loaves between five thousand and there is plenty left over; but this shows that Jesus is so much greater than Elisha, and suggests the ungrudging plenty of the Messianic era. And now it is not, as in Ex and 2 (4) Kgs, God's word which is fulfilled, but that of Jesus. Further allusions to the OT background are not wanting: the miracle takes place 'in a *desert* place' (Mt vv 13, 15—not easy to find in those parts, but an allusion to the miraculous feeding in the desert at the exodus). The people are told to 'sit down on the green grass' (Mk v 39, cf Mt v 19), an allusion to Ps 23 (22):2: 'in meadows of green grass he lets me lie', in the prophecy of a feeding by the messianic shepherd.

The evangelists also bring out the continuity between this messianic feeding and **the Eucharist** by their use of phrases: blessed, broke, gave to his disciples (Mt v 19), where each word occurs in almost identical form at the account of the last supper, already then familiar to Christians from the liturgy (26:26, cf § 761*in*). Similarly 'all ate' (v 20) combines two elements of 26:26 and 27. These elements are not in themselves sufficient, since they could describe only features normal to a meal: they

occur also in Ac 27:35 which is certainly not a Eucharist **725i** (but it lacks also the important element of giving the bread). But Mt v 15 assimilates it directly to the Last Supper by changing Mk's time indication to 'when evening came' as in Mt 26:20, the sole time he does this. But Mk 6:41 has deliberately been remoulded to include the eucharistic phrases; cf 753*e*.

The question inevitably arises of the **historicity of j the account**, and the extent to which it has been shaped to express the messianic significance of the miracle. Mt certainly was unaware of the significance, since he omits elements (the green grass, and the divisions into hundreds and fifties) found in Mk, and shows that he misses the significance of the final 'five thousand men'—the messianic community in the Qumran sense included only men—by adding 'to say nothing of women and children'. Even Mk misses one element: according to Jn 6:9, 13 the loaves were of barley, a further point of contact with 2 (4) Kgs 4:42 omitted by Mk, unless this touch was added by Jn himself. It may be then that, Mk too, then, drew his account from an already existing account, whose allusions he did not fully appreciate, and was not responsible for the messianic, though perhaps the eucharistic, allusions. Two factors speak in favour of the basic historicity of the account: a similar miracle is recorded by Jn 6:1—13 though he explicitly denies its messianic significance (6:26—27), and some elements, e.g. the fish, seem to have no such significance. Nevertheless a large part must be attributed in the formation of the narrative to a desire to express its theological message. One may perhaps doubt whether the figure of 5,000 is intended literally; it is almost impossibly high; could they all hear him teaching (Mk v 34)? Could so large a number be fed by twelve men between 'evening' and nightfall? Would such a gathering be permitted by the suspicious and vigilant Romans?

Mt in addition makes two alterations, in accordance **k** with his preoccupation with the disciples here: in his anxiety to spare them from any slur (cf § 724*e*) he softens their rather tart rejoinder to Jesus (v 17, Mk v 37). Similarly he emphasizes their part in the distribution (v 19); already they are Christ's ministers, bringing his good things to men (cf § 725*f*).

22—33 Walking on the Water (Mk 6:45—52; **726a** Jn 6:15—21)—Mt and Mk now recount a second occasion on which Jesus calms a storm for the sake of the disciples sailing across the lake (cf Mt 8:23—27 and parallels). Lk omits this incident, probably considering it a doublet. But the emphasis, as well as the circumstances, are very different. In the former case the whole weight was upon the calming of the storm in response to the disciples' appeal in faith. Here the calming is a side-effect; the interest centres upon Jesus' sudden appearance. In common are only Jesus' command of the elements (a divine prerogative: Ps 65 (64):7; 89 (88):9; Jb 38:11) and the disciples' faith; on this occasion both these elements are more manifest than before, especially in vv 28—33, proper to Mt and lacking in Mk. **22.** On the geography see § 753*f*; by omitting the place-name Mt shows that he considers it unimportant. **24—25.** A vivid picture of the hopeless toil of the disciples far from land, far into the night (between 3 and 6 a.m., the last and most depressing watch of the night). **26—27.** Jesus' arrival is described in terms of a divine theophany. They thought it was a vision or just (neutrally) 'appearance'—the word used is wider than 'ghost'. The fear and terror are the invariable reactions to a divine visitation (Gn 3:6; Is 64:2; Ezek 30:13; Jon 1:16), and 'Do not be afraid' the response to this fear (Lk 1:13, 30; Apoc 1:17). It is doubtful whether the phrase 'It is I' (literally: 'I am')

726a has the same connotations as for Jn e.g. 11:25 (cf comm in loc). Peter's profession of faith in v 33 confirms the

b impression given by these vv. **28—33.** This first incident in which Peter plays a separate part was first written down by Mt, since it contains a number of literary peculiarities of his (Kilpatrick pp. 40—41); but it was not invented by him, for it is strongly reminiscent of the incident in Jn 21:7ff. It enables Mt to stress the growing understanding of the Apostles—if not yet their unwavering trust (this is the force of 'man of little faith', cf 6:30; 8:26) instead of the reproach with which Mk concludes the incident (cf § 724e). As always, the ecclesial interest is present in Mt: Peter, as Christ's representative in the Church, needs his help. This is the lesson of the passage in the education of the disciples, with which the whole section is concerned (cf § 725f). **31.** Peter 'hesitates' before this vision of Jesus: the word appears elsewhere in the NT only in 28:17, where the hesitation seems to be due to awe, cf § 743h. **33.** The disciples' profession of faith does not necessarily imply a recognition of Christ's divinity at this stage, though the title can bear this meaning (cf § 714j). The fullness of understanding of Christ came only after the resurrection.

c **34—36 Cures at Gennesaret** (Mk 6:53—56)—A brief summary, even more compressed by Mt till it shows only the outline of faith rewarded by miracles. The Gennesaret which gave its name to the Lake is, according to Jos BJ 3, 10, 8, the plain (which he describes in glowing terms) 4 miles along the lakeside by $2\frac{1}{2}$ deep, running W from Capharnaum. But this plain in turn takes its name from an ancient town located at Tell el-Oreme near its NE extreme. Either plain or town could be meant here.

d **15:1—20 Traditions of the Pharisees** (Mk 7:1—23)— This passage expresses more fully than any other Mt's attitude towards the Law and pharisaic tradition. Unfortunately its interpretation is hotly disputed: Kilpatrick (p. 108) maintains that the insertion of vv 12—14 indicates that the attack is directed more against the Pharisees themselves than against their interpretation. Strecker (p. 30—32) considers that it unequivocally rejects all Jewish ritual commands. Barth's view (pp. 80—90) is more subtle: Pharisaic tradition as such is not rejected, but only those elements in it which clash with a true interpretation of the OT (of which the principal criterion is the law of love: Mt 5:43—48), and so are false developments. Certainly in ch 23 (especially 23:3) this is Mt's attitude; from the discussions on Sabbath observance (12:1—8, 9—14) the same principle emerges (cf §§ 710b, 717b). Mt's discussion is more intricately constructed than Mk's series of three separate discussions. He omits Mk's vv 3—4, which explains the Jewish purification rites; obviously they were familiar to Mt's community already. The whole passage is then bracketed by the expression 'to eat with unwashed hands' (vv 2, 20); this is Mt's way of drawing attention to the formal point which he is teaching (cf 6:19, 21 'treasures'; 11:2, 19 'actions of Christ'), and is crucial for the interpretation, giving the heading and conclusion in relation to which the whole discussion must be understood. In his exposition Mt proceeds more deliberately than Mk; whereas Mk had loosely inserted vv 9—13, Mt uses these vv earlier in his argument (Mt vv 3—6). Thus his reply to the Pharisees' and scribes' question of v 2 is: (1) some at least of these traditions are contrary to God's law in the OT, so tradition is not invariably to be observed (3—8); (2) the particular tradition in question has no connexion with moral conduct

e and so need not be observed (10—11, 15—20). **2.** The prescriptions of ritual purification (for innumerable details of which cf SB 1, 689—705) were laid down by

oral tradition, which the rabbinic schools considered **726e** to stem from Moses; the oral Law and written Law were equally binding (SB 1, 692). **3—6.** Mt brings out the force of Jesus' counter-attack by a neatly symmetrical chiasmus (cf note on 12:31—37) 'transgress God's command by means of your tradition'—'God said' (stronger than Mk's version, which has only 'Moses said') ' "do your duty to your father and mother" '—'you say " . . . he shall not do his duty to father or mother" '— 'annul God's word by means of your tradition'. Thus he underlines that the tradition is clean contrary, not merely to the Law but to God's command. **5.** The usage to which Mt refers is this: by an oath a son might dedicate or 'offer up' to God his parents' enjoyment of the help which they were entitled to receive from him. Thus he lost nothing, but they were bound by his vow to 'offer up' (i.e. forgo) any assistance from their son. But, at least by the end of the 1st cent. A.D., the injustice of this was reconized, and there were ways and means by which the parents could get round it (SB 1, 716). The oath formula 'Qorban' is preserved by Mk, but translated by Mt, whose sentence becomes less clear in consequence. **10—20.** f Having cleared the ground by vv 3—9, Mt proceeds to answer the question of v 2 (cf § 726d). That his discussion, though verbally almost identical with Mk's, has a wholly different point, is shown by minute but careful alterations. Mk's discussion teaches that all culinary restrictions, e.g. the distinction of clean and unclean foods, have lost their force; it is not especially linked with the question of washing the hands before eating. But Mt restricts the discussion precisely to this question, deliberately refraining from any pronouncement on the larger issue. Firstly, the whole discussion stands under this heading, which reappears in the conclusion (vv 3, 20; cf § 726d); secondly, Mt v 11 carefully removes the all-embracing force of Mk v 15: instead of 'Nothing that goes into a man . . . ' Mt has 'it is not what goes into . . . '; thirdly, he omits from v 17 Mk's (v 19) 'Thus he pronounced all foods clean'. He does not intend to annul all culinary restrictions, but only the prescription concerning ritual purification of the hands. Other culinary restrictions are reaffirmed by the 'apostolic decree' of Ac 15:29, and remained in force generally among Christians till the end of the second century (RB 4 (1907) 57—58). It is manifest that neither version was handed down word for word from Jesus, for the question was still to be decided (and decided substantially in Mk's sense) by the vision to Peter in Ac 10:2, which presupposes that no decision on the matter could be quoted from the sayings of Jesus. The list of sins in v 19 (Mk vv 21—22) is reminiscent of the catalogues of vices common in Stoic and Hellenistic writings (and Paul) but rare in Judaism; it could be due to influences in the Diaspora. This does not imply that the whole discussion here is a fabrication, but only that we have two different expansions by the inspired authors, for different circumstances and different communities, of the saying of Jesus given in Mt v 11 (Mk v 15). The original force of the saying is hard to evaluate—it is after all a parable, cf § 724a—for the breadth of application intended depends largely on its lost context, whether it was a deliberate statement of principle or evoked by a particular situation.

Mt's discussion concentrates more on 'the mouth' g (which he inserts four times in three vv), perhaps to centre attention on the act of eating, with washed or unwashed hands, rather than on the food eaten, perhaps because most of the sins detailed in v 19 are sins largely of the mouth (the only one he adds is perjury). But the real principle of this list, cut down to Mt's favourite

726g number of seven, is that they all offend against love of one's neighbour, cf 22:39. **12—14.** Mt adds a condemnation of the Pharisees. V 14 is given separately by Lk (6:39), which suggests that vv 13 and 14 were originally independent sayings; v 13 hints at a condemnation of all Israel, for this is the meaning of a 'plant' in biblical (e.g. Is 5:1—7) and post-biblical Jewish terminology (SB 1, 720—1); it is also a favourite theme of Mt (cf § 733e). **15—16.** Public instruction followed by further explanation to the disciples is a process found often in rabbinic stories as well as in the gospels (cf § 757a). This whole section of the gospel is devoted to the special formation of the disciples, particularly of Peter, which will issue in Peter's profession of faith at 16:16 (cf § 727a). As usual Mt, who cannot here wholly remove, at least minimizes the disciples' lack of understanding by inserting a 'yet': 'Do even you not yet understand?' cf § 724e.

h 21—28 The Canaanite Woman (Mk 7:24—30)— Immediately after this rejection of the Pharisaic interpretation of the Law comes by contrast an example of the reward of a gentile's faith, thus illustrating what qualities are really necessary. Mt does everything possible to stress that the woman is a **Gentile** who nevertheless forms part of the new Israel. He adds that she is a Canaanite and that she 'came out' of the Gentile territory (symbolising her conversion?); but she calls on Jesus by a distinctively Jewish messianic title, 'son of David' (on which cf § 734i), and Jesus says that he is sent to the lost sheep only of the 'House of Israel'. It is by her **faith** alone that she obtains her reward. According to Mk v 29a it seems almost 'as though Jesus was outwitted by the adroit and nimble-tongued woman' (Barth p. 199); but Mt leaves no doubt that it is her faith that wins a reluctant acknowledgement from Jesus: this faith she manifests already in v 22. Jesus gives this as the reason for his compliance (28a) and the evangelist adds the instantaneousness of the cure as a confirmation (29b) cf 8:13; 9:22.

i 29—31 Cures near the Lake (Mk 7:31—37)—Mk relates the cure of one deaf-mute only, but Mt transforms this into a general summary of many kinds of healings and adds the solemn biblical note of Jesus enthroned on the mountain (cf 5:1). Here the mention, at the end, of 'the God of Israel' shows that this passage should be regarded perhaps as a pendant to the last (cf 24) in contrast still to the Pharisees and scribes of 1—20, and like the Gentile women, some at least of the Galileans are prepared to accept Christ's mission to 'the lost sheep of the House of Israel'.

j 32—39 Feeding of the Four Thousand (Mk 8:1— 10)—This account is based on a tradition from a Hellenistic milieu, whereas the feeding of the five thousand is on one from a Palestinian milieu (see § 755a). On the question whether the same event lies behind both see § 725g. On the messianic and eucharistic significance see § 725hi. Here Mt's primarily eucharistic interest can be seen in his omission of all mention of the blessing and distribution of the fish, since fish have no place in a eucharistic meal (Held p. 186).

We are still in Mt's section on the training of the disciples (cf § 725f), and they have by now realized that, as the ministers of Jesus, it is their duty to do something to help the people and carry out his wishes: 'Where could *we* get enough bread' (v 33, contrast 14:15). **39.** The location of Magadan is unknown, unless it is an alternative form of Magdala, as Magada is of Migdal in one version of the LXX at Jos 15:37 (Abel, *Géographie de la Palestine*, 2 (1938), p. 373).

k 16:1—12 The Yeast of the Pharisees and Sadducees

(Mk 8:11—21; Lk 11:29; 12:1)—**1—4** serve as an **726l** introduction to the following dialogue with the disciples, designed to present vividly the perversity of the Pharisees and Sadducees (only the former in Mk) which is about to be castigated. On the formation of the scene see § 755b.

5—12. The disciples are encouraged to reflect more **l** deeply on the person of Jesus. Mt has transformed Mk's pericope. This was a stern rebuke to the hardness of the disciples' heart, in which the initial saying about yeast formed only a link (cf § 755d). Mt radically modifies the reproach, as often (cf § 724e), by omitting Mk's sternest v (17b—18 and 21) and changing the subject matter. By repeating at the end the mention of yeast he shows that he intends the whole passage to refer to this, which he interprets, not in its normal Jewish sense of bad dispositions but as 'the doctrine' of the Pharisees and Sadducees. He also substitutes 'the Sadducees' for Mk's 'Herod'. Yet it is not easy to be sure what point of doctrine shared by these opposing schools is intended. Lk interprets it as hypocrisy (12:1). Kilpatrick (p. 120) suggests that in Mt, uninterested in the tenets of these schools as they actually were, the term 'Sadducee' 'embraces all non-Christian, non-Pharisaic Jews', so that 'Pharisees and Sadducees' means in general all non-Christian Jews; it is against their doctrine that the disciples are warned. Mt, here, at the end of the period of special instruction of the disciples, which is to issue in Peter's confession (cf § 725f) substitutes for Mk's reproach a statement that they finally understood.

13—20 Peter's Profession of Faith (Mk 8:27—30; **727a** Lk 9:18—21)—This section of the gospel concerning the special training of the disciples, which began in 14:13 (cf § 725f) here reaches its climax, issuing in Peter's acknowledgement that Jesus is the Messiah. This acknowledgement has its full force in Mk: until Mk 8:21 the disciples had failed to understand; then came the highly symbolic opening of the blind man's eyes (8:22—26), then immediately Peter shows for the first time his comprehension. In Mt this dramatic climax is dulled, since the comprehension of the disciples has several times been stressed (cf § 724e)—the incident of the blind man is consequently omitted, and Peter has already made a full profession that Jesus is the son of God (14:33). **13.** Caesarea Philippi, so named because it had **b** been rebuilt by the tetrarch Philip in honour of Caesar Augustus, was an old sanctuary of Pan situated in the pleasantly fertile area round the main source of the Jordan in the foothills of Mt Hermon. Perhaps Jesus withdrew here because it is a pleasant place in which to escape in summer from the torrid humidity of the Lake of Galilee. But the area has other associations which make it a suitable site for this scene: Hermon is traditionally a holy mountain, meeting-place of God and man, a fit background to this scene of revelation and solemn mission; the spring of the Jordan is, in Jewish legend (RB 62 (1955), 405), the opening to Hell (cf v 18). Mt inserts into Jesus' question the mysterious title 'Son of Man' which Jesus has been using to hint at his personality (cf §§ 676k, 719k). **14.** The common opinion was that **c** Jesus was 'a prophet', precursor of the Messiah, who was to be *the* prophet promised by Dt 18:15—18 (cf § 725h), and liberator of his people. On the role of the Baptist, and Elijah as precursor cf § 714ab. Jeremiah (Mt only) enjoyed great prestige in Judaism at this time, as protector of the chosen people; more especially it was he who was to put into the hands of the Messiah the sword with which he would free Israel from foreign oppression (cf 2 Mc 15:14; 2:1). The popular conception of the Messiah was indissolubly tied to political liberation;

27c Jesus' activity had not shown that he fulfilled this expectation, so he could be no more than the precursor. It is Peter's role, in a flash of revelation, to break through, beyond these political preoccupations. **15—16.** Jesus, as so often (e.g. 12:27; 16:8—11a; 20:15; 22:42—45), by questioning, forces his interlocutors to reflect and commit themselves. Peter responds to the challenge: he is the Messiah (on the title see note on 1:1). Mt adds 'son of **d** the living God', as in 14:33; cf 714j. But on the construction of these vv, see § 755g fin.). **17—19.** Before discussing the meaning of these vv, proper to Mt, we must discuss their **authorship** and original position. They were put in written form first by Mt: several expressions are characteristic of Mt ('father in heaven', 'so I', double 'whatever'—see concordances); v 19bc is repeated in 18:18, according to Mt's frequent habit of repeating important sayings. The whole passage is 'a highly elaborated aesthetic structure with a series of careful and deliberate interior balances' (Butler p. 132), in which in each case one member of the two is taken from Mk and the other supplied by Mt (see Butler's table, p. 132; it should be added that Butler is offering an argument for the priority of Mt; but it can be used equally well in reverse). But the underlying Aram. phraseology of these vv is undeniable (Strecker p. 202). Since Mt's community seems to have been ignorant of Aram. (Kilpatrick p. 105) we can only admit that the phrases stem from an earlier source. It would be of interest to know **when this promise to Peter was in fact pro-**
e nounced by Jesus. A similar promise is recorded by Lk 22:32 and by Jn 21:15—17 both in a eucharistic context; a similar confession by Peter is recorded by Lk 22:33 and by Jn 6:68—69, both again in eucharistic contexts, and associated with a mention of betrayal (Lk 22:21—22, 34; Jn 6:70—71; also present in Jn 21:20) which recalls Mt 16:23. But this combination of themes into a eucharistic context could well be due to the eucharistic theology and practice of the primitive Church: the Eucharist is the event where the hierarchical structure of the Church is clearest, where the profession of adherence to Christ is made by the Church and her representatives, where betrayal may occur (cf 1 Cor 11:27). This may act as a caution against too easily assuming (cf Cullmann p. 190—1) that Mt's material was drawn from traditions about the Last Supper. In any case the promise is most suitably placed here. Not only should the foundations of the Church be laid before the great discourse on the Church (ch 18); but also during the section leading up to this scene Peter has appeared as leader and spokesman of the disciples (14:28, 29; 15:15). Furthermore the Messiah was, to the Jews, inconceivable without a messianic community (cf § 715f); now Peter recognizes Jesus as the Messiah, and Jesus replies 'And **f** you are the foundation of the messianic community'. **17.** The promise to Peter is preceded by a solemn introduction: 'flesh and blood' is a common expression to signify man's limited and transitory powers in contradistinction to God's eternity (Sir 14:18; Rm 7:5; SB 1, 730—1). It is God alone who can reveal (cf 11:25—27; Dn 2:47; 4:15), God alone who can impart blessing (Dt 33:29; Jb 5:17; Ps 33 (32):12; Is 30:18—this shows that JB's 'You are a happy man' is too banal; God's blessing is more solemn and profound than this). Thus Jesus proclaims that God has taken a special hold of Peter; such a hold is always allied to a special mission. 'Jonah', a name rarely used in OT times of any historical person, cf 2 Kgs 14:25; Jn 1:42 and the Gospel of the Hebrews says that Peter's father was named John. 'John' was a rare abbreviation for 'Johanan', of which the

normal form was 'Johai'; perhaps this was the form given **727f** here, but was so unfamiliar that it was changed to 'Jona'; in either case Peter's father's full name would seem to have been Johanan. **18.** Jesus now, in his **g** divine capacity (this was the reason for Peter's profession under this title too,), imparts to Peter his mission. This function is contained in his name in Aram, *Kepha* (Jn 1:42; 1 Cor 1:12, 15:5; Gal 2:9), which even if not first given here (cf Jn 1:42) is here first explained. The giving of a name to correspond to a special function or mission in the history of salvation is a frequent occurrence in the Bible (Gn 17:5; 32:29; Mt 1:21; Lk 1:13, 31); God alone gives such a mission and the name which goes with it. The name 'Rock' is not known to have been used of any other person before, either in Gr. or in Heb. Its associations are drawn from Is 51:1 (Abraham, the rock from which Israel was hewn); Is 28:16, which is applied to Jesus himself in Mt 21:42; Dn 2:34—35, 44—45, where the stone stands for the new kingdom itself. This implies that Peter is more than a mere foundation, as the other apostles are Eph 2:20; Apoc 21:14, 19. The expression used for 'Church' is that normally used in LXX for the 'community or assembly of God', i.e. Israel as God's chosen people (cf Ac 7:38). In the hymns of the Qumran community (1 QH III. 37, VI. 24—28) it is God who builds the community of the last times on the foundation of a rock. These ideas are taken up; only now it is not God but Jesus who founds his own community of the last times, corresponding to the community of God in the OT, so again claiming a divine prerogative. The 'gates of the underworld' signify the powers of evil (Is 38:10; Ps 9:13; 1 QH VI. 24; III. 17). **19.** The giving of keys is, in both **h** ancient and modern ceremonial, the symbolic act by which authority is conferred (cf Is 22:22; 9:5; Apoc 1:18; 3:7). Peter 'is to lead the people of God into the resurrection kingdom' (Cullmann p. 210), unlike the scribes and Pharisees who lock the doors of the kingdom (23:13). The extent of his authority is defined by the semitic expression 'bind and loose'; this is a rabbinic technical term, expressing by mention of the extremes all the intermediate area. It is used both of admission to and excommunication from the community (this is the primary sense in 18:18) and in a wider sense of making any binding decisions (SB 1. 738—41). 'In Heaven' is a circumlocution of reverence to avoid using the divine name: 'in God's eyes'. **20.** The disciples have still not realized the full implication of Jesus' messiahship; until they have been instructed in this too they are bound to silence.

21—23 First Prophecy of the Passion (Mk 8:31—33; **i** Lk 9:22)—As soon as Jesus has brought his disciples to the acknowledgement that he is the Messiah he begins to show them what this means (cf § 725a): he is not the triumphant liberator of Jewish dreams but the Suffering Servant of the Lord. Mt marks this new beginning by 'from that time', an expression he uses only here, at 4:17 (the beginning of Jesus' preaching) and 26:16 (the preparation for the Passion). He also uses the solemn full title 'Jesus Christ' for the first and only time since 1:18. The Passion and Resurrection are three times solemnly foretold (also 17:22—23; 20:18—19) Bultmann (p. 152) says that these 'have long been recognized as secondary constructions of the Church', invented afterwards to explain the scandal of the cross. It is indeed possible that the details of the prophecies may have been influenced by subsequent events (e.g. Mt's 'on the third day' instead of Mk's 'after three days' accords more exactly with Hos 6:2 and the primitive preaching, as shown in Lk 24:7,46; Ac 10:40; 1Cor 15:4). We must

727i suppose that the disciples were amazingly obtuse or lacking in conviction to behave as they did at Jesus' arrest, if they had already heard three such clear prophecies of both Passion and Resurrection as 16:21, 17:22—23; 20:18—19. Hence the clarity of the prediction is no doubt the product of the disciples' post-Resurrection understanding. Even the triple repetition of the prophecy is probably a formal way of underlining the importance of the prophecy rather than historical.

But other sayings which show that Jesus reflected on the Passion are too veiled to have been invented for this purpose (9:15; Lk 13:33), or too discreditable to the revered apostles to have been invented at all by the community (20:22). V. Taylor has shown (NTS 1 (1954/5), 159—68) that the prophecies of the Suffering Servant of the Lord, who will be humiliated and will suffer to redeem his people, and eventually be raised up by God (cf § 461*l*). played a great part in the earliest Christology (e.g. the pre-Pauline hymn Phil 2:6—11; 1 Cor 15:3; **j** Ac 3:13, 26; 4:30; 8:26—40). But already by Paul's time this interest is on the wane; Mt twice quotes texts of the Suffering Servant (8:17; 12:18—21), but neither time in connexion with Jesus' suffering. There are other traces of this Christology in the gospels (cf § 711*d*), but it is so early and so foreign to the later theological preoccupations of the primitive Church, where the theology of the Suffering Servant is very rare, that it can be attributed only to Jesus himself. Jesus himself saw his future suffering in these terms, and as the fulfilment of the prophecy intended by God. Hence 'was destined', as 17:10; 26:54. **22.** Peter, in spite of his recognition of Jesus as the Christ, still holds firmly to a political conception of the Messiah (cf § 715*f*), and seems to suppose that Jesus is envisaging the possibility of failure. Hence his soothing 'God forbid' (literally: 'may God be propitious to you' SB 1, 748). Peter repeats the temptation of 4:8—9 (cf § 715*a*), and receives the sharp rebuke of the tempter.

k 24—28 Conditions of following Christ (Mk 8:34—9:1; Lk 9:23—27)—After this first announcement that Jesus is to suffer, the evangelist collects a series of sayings to show that following Christ means suffering for the disciple too. V 24 is a general heading of which the others are applications (the derivative version in 10:38—39 gives only heading and one application). In Mt (not in Mk) the sayings are addressed only to the disciples (v 24*a*), and fill out their understanding both of Christ's role and of their own discipleship. **24.** To take up one's cross is not used in Jewish literature of accepting suffering (SB 1, 587), and some have therefore supposed that this phrase is due not to Jesus but to the Church after the Crucifixion. But Jesus could have pronounced it on some such occasion as Jn 21:18—19; even before the crucifixion of Christ, crucifixions were a common enough sight in Palestine for the disciples to understand Jesus' meaning, and this bold metaphor would be thoroughly characteristic of him. **25—26.** These sayings are based on an Aram. word-play: *nepeš* means both 'self' and 'life'; the abnegation demanded is not only of the disciple's life but of his whole self. **27—28.** Mt, who so consistently stresses the theme of judgement and reward (cf § 738*f*) is not content with Mk's 'when the Son of man comes', and underlines: 'for the Son of Man is going to come . . .'. Here 'Son of Man' is used in the sense of the eschatological judge (cf § 676*n*). On the moment referred to by 'coming with his kingdom' see §§ 715*f*; 737*b*; perhaps here Mt intends a reference to the immediately subsequent scene of the Transfiguration, cf § 728*b*.

728a 17:1—8 The Transfiguration (Mk 9:2—8; Lk 9:28—36; cf Jn 12:27—30)—After the introduction of the

idea that Christ must suffer and be humiliated (16: **728** 21—23), three disciples receive a revelation of his glory. The revelation is, as the whole section of the gospel, directly related to the agony in the garden; it is given to the same three disciples who are present at the agony, also on a hill (26:30), where they also sleep (26:40 cf Lk 9:32) and are aroused by Jesus (26:40—41). The scene of glory here is to prepare them for the scene of humiliation there, to show them the reality of the Person who is to lead them through abasement to salvation. It is described in the gospels with a wealth of biblical imagery which recalls scenes of the OT, and so conveys the significance of the event. We are given not a snapshot but an artist's impression, the result of reflection on the scene by men whose imagination was formed by OT imagery, who can describe their experience adequately only by the use of these terms. 'His face shone like the sun' does not profess to give a light-meter reading. On the historical event which lies behind the account, see § 756*a*. The general features of the description are those of a **divine revelation**, such as those in Is 6, Ezek 1—2, Dn 7, 10, Apoc 1: there **b** is a heavenly being, a divine voice is heard, the visionary is terrified and falls on his face, is revived by a touch and an injunction 'Fear not'. The language is closest to that of Dn 10:5—10: his face shone, a voice, falling face to the ground, fear, the touch of a hand, 'Stand up', and 'Do not be afraid'. Thus Jesus is here seen clearly as the Son of Man of Dn's visions (7; 10; cf Apoc 1:13—17); the full glory of this figure is seen as it will be prophesied (24:30; 26:64; 16:28) but seen only at the last day (25:31); cf § 719*k*. The transformation into the light of glory is properly reserved till then (13:43; Apoc. Baruch 51:10). The white garments too have eschatological associations, cf 2 Cor 5:1—4; Apoc 7:15. Especially in Mt, there are also strong reminiscences of the *theophany* to Moses: the mountain, six days, three named companions, a voice from a cloud (Ex 24:12—16); after this vision Moses' face shone (Ex 34:29). The cloud which 'covered them with shadow' (v 5) suggests the cloud of God's presence which overshadowed the Tent of Meeting in Ex 40:34, and in its turn suggests that the function of the 'tents' in v 4 was to prolong the encounter with these numinous presences (but cf note on v 4). This imagery shows that Christ, as well as being seen as the Son of Man in his divine glory, is seen also as the new Moses, the new lawgiver (cf § 711*e*) and prophet promised by God to Moses (Dt 18:15—18, cf § 725*h*). The message **c** of the celestial voice, which forms the centre and climax of the scene, is that they should listen to him (Dt 18:15). In Mt this prepares for the discourse in ch 18, where Jesus will teach the way of life of his new people of God. The appeal to listen to Christ echoes the constant appeal of the Wisdom literature to listen to Wisdom (e.g. Prv 5:7; 8:33; Wis 6:1; Sir 6:35; 21:15). The mention of tents also may touch this theme, for wisdom has her tent on God's holy mountain (Wis 9:8; Sir 24:10). For Christ as Wisdom, cf § 722*i*. But as at the Baptism (Mt draws attention to the similarity by inserting the phrase 'he enjoys my favour', cf 3:17) Jesus is also shown to be the **Suffering Servant** of the Lord, since the words of the voice recall these prophecies, cf § 711*d*, and 714*j*. **1.** Peter again, as 14:28—29; 15:15; 16:16—23, plays **d** the leading role among the disciples. But instead of Mk's apology (v 6), Mt stresses Peter's understanding (cf § 724*e*): he uses the address 'Lord', and acknowledges Jesus' complete mastery of the situation by the parenthesis 'if you wish' (as 8:2; 15:32; 26:17; 27:34). The location of the scene is not given: in the gospels we have only the biblical phrase 'a high mountain' whose primary

'28d intention is theological (an echo of Ex 19:20). In the 4th cent. it was considered essential to locate every event of our Lord's life, and Tabor was picked on, a low but strikingly isolated hill (1850 ft.) in the plain of Esdraelon. There are, however, traces of a fortification of this time on the summit, which make it unlikely. A place suitable for its associations in the Jewish mind, and also geographically convenient, is Mt Hermon (cf § 727b). **3.** Moses and Elijah perhaps represent the Law and the Prophets testifying to Christ (so the Fathers); they too had received a vision of God on a holy mountain (Ex 33:19; 1 (3) Kgs 19:11—13). In Mk, Elijah is unexpectedly mentioned first, perhaps because the second Elijah is the forerunner of the Messiah (cf § 714a), while the Messiah himself is the second Moses; but Mt restores the two to their normal order. By their presence they show that Jesus completes and does not abolish the OT.

e 4. The suggestion of tents recalls the Feast of Tents, when all Israel dwelt in tents for seven days (cf Dt 16:13—15 and § ad loc); it was a feast of great joy in which light and illuminations played a great part. In later Jewish thought the final manifestation of God's kingship of the world was represented in terms of this feast (Zech 14). Here it is Christ's glory which evokes a response in the same terms: it is a glimpse of the final kingship of Christ. Peter's suggestion indicates then that he considers that the moment of final repose in God has come and would like to celebrate from now the eschatological Feast of Tabernacles; its lack of success shows that the period of trial is not yet over. Mt, characteristically, qualifies the unsuccessful request by 'if you wish' to soften Peter's misunderstanding. He also omits Mk's 'he did not know what to say', no doubt in order to spare the prince of the Apostles. Cf A Feuillet, 'Les Perspectives propres à chaque évangeliste dans les récits de la Transfiguration', Bib 39 (1958), 281—301, and M. Sabbe, 'La rédaction du récit de la Transfiguration', *La Venue du Messie* (1962), 65—100.

f 9—13 Question about Elijah (Mk 9:9—13)—On the descent from the vision of Christ in his glory the disciples are initiated still further into the meaning of Jesus' prophecy of his Passion (16:21). In Mk we still see Jesus' own teaching method: he makes them reflect and ponder by a mysterious statement (v 10) and a conundrum (vv 12—13). Mt omits the puzzled silence of the disciples, as often (§ 724e), and changes the conundrum in order to give a clear statement which they understand (v 13). In the whole passage Mt's didactic purpose is paramount. Mal 3:22—23 had prophesied that Elijah would precede the Messiah. Jesus now teaches that the prophecy was rather that his mission would be repeated (as it was by the Baptist, § 714a) than that His person would reappear. Mt characteristically stresses the stubbornness of the Jews (v 12, cf § 724e). He returns to the theme that John's death stands in the line of those of the murdered prophets, and so prefigures Christ's (cf § 725e).

g 14—21 The Epileptic Demoniac (Mk 9:14—29; Lk 9:37—43a)—A miracle story seems to be out of place here, in the section on the instruction of the disciples (cf §§ 725a; 756d). Mt, though he takes it over from Mk, transforms it into an object lesson on the necessity of faith. Gone are the lively details of thronging crowds, symptoms, and reluctant demon. Jesus, as often in Mt's miraculous cures (8:14—15; 9:20—22), is seen in majestic isolation with the suppliant; even the disciples seem to come close only afterwards (v 19). Of symptoms Mt gives barely enough for an identification of the trouble: '*He is an epileptic and is having an attack*' (15). Attacks of the intermittent affliction are as fickle as the moon, whence the ancient description 'moonstruck'. Mt was **728g** evidently not aware that an attack lasts at most only a few seconds (*A Textbook of the Practice of Medicine*, ed. F. W. Price (1966[10]); Mt leaves only an element which concerns faith: Jesus' reproach of their faithlessness (**17**—for the expression see § 723j). He stresses the **h** effortlessness and immediacy of the cure (**18**—no long command or final convulsion as in Mk). **20.** Finally he adds a v from Q (also in Lk 17:6, though the 'sycamore' of Lk is changed for the 'mountain' of Mk 11:23—uprooting a mountain is proverbial for doing the impossible, SB I. 759). It is not their lack of faith (in the sense of understanding) but rather their lack of trust that he reproaches (cf § 724e). A mustard seed is proverbial for the smallest conceivable quantity (SB I. 669), so we have here a furious paradox of clashing proverbs. **21** is missing in some MSS and is probably a harmonization to Mk v 29; it would be quite out of place after Mt's conclusion.

22—23 Second Prophecy of the Passion (Mk 9:30— **i** 32; Lk 9:43b—45)—The second of the three prophecies (also 16:21; 20:18—19) it is the most schematic, omitting all details. Mt stresses the voluntary nature of Jesus' sacrifice: '*The Son of Man shall be* (almost '*intends to be*') *handed over*' (cf § 731i). According to Mk the disciples did not understand and were afraid to ask for an explanation; but Mt, as usual (cf § 724e) passes this over.

24—27 The Temple-tax—This incident, given by Mt **j** alone, contains a number of typical Matthean usages and a number of usages quite foreign to him; it was therefore probably derived by him from oral tradition and first written down by him (Kilpatrick p. 41—42). A tax was levied on all male Jews aged twenty and more for the upkeep of the Temple (Ex 30:11—16; Neh 10:32—34); at this time the amount was two drachmas (Gr.) = two denarii (Roman) = ½ shekel (Jewish) = two days wages of a hired labourer (Mt 20:2). After the destruction of the Temple in A.D. 70 the *fiscus Judaicus* must be paid to the temple of Capitoline Jove in Rome, until it was abolished by Nerva (A.D. 96—98). Kilpatrick suggests that the story has been made up to provide a setting for a ruling of Jesus, as the similar story (where again Peter receives the ruling for the Church) in 18:21—22. Since the question and ruling became otiose after A.D. 97, the inclusion of the pericope indicates a date earlier than this for the final redaction of the gospel (cf § 709g). On the other **k** hand, in its present form, the passage displays a consciousness of separation between Christians and Judaism which is perhaps too clear for Jesus' life-time. It is possible that some saying of Jesus on the freedom of the sons of the kingdom (a semitism for 'citizens', cf 8:12; 13:38) has been adapted to this particular problem. The wider lesson of the story remains: to avoid the scandal which may be caused by insisting on one's rights; cf 1 Cor 10:31. **27.** The theme of finding valuables in a fish's mouth is common to Gr. (Herodotus 3, 42: Polycrates' ring) and Jewish (SB 1, 614, 675: two different stories of finding a pearl) folklore. It seems that this theme has been taken up as a final flourish to the story, showing Christ's control over the powers of nature. (Lagrange, p. 342, defends the literal truth of the account).

Ch 18 Discourse on the Community—After the narra- **729a** tive part (chh 14—17) of the fifth major section of the gospel, in which the gradual initiation of the disciples into the mystery of Christ's personality was seen, comes the corresponding discourse. As always in the discourse which form the second panel of the five central blocks of Mt, the evangelist assembles the sayings of Jesus on a particular point and himself welds them into a unity. This ch concerns the attitude and conduct of the leaders of the

729a community to their flock. The keynote is loving care of the 'little ones' of God: 2—4 are dominated by the notion of 'little child', 5—9 and 10—14 by 'little ones' and the figure of a shepherd and his sheep (frequently used by Mt of the faithful), 15—35 by open-handed forgiveness.

b **1—4 The Example of a Child** (Mk 9:33—37; Lk 9:46—48)—In Mk Jesus' reply arises out of a squabble about precedence among the Twelve. Mt, ever anxious to spare the disciples (cf § 724e), removes this unedifying element, and changes the message from a particular lesson on service (cf 756h) into a general lesson on the attitude required in disciples for entry into the kingdom. On what aspect of childhood does Mt most insist? It cannot be the innocence, for 12—22 presuppose sin in the member of the community. There is certainly no sweet sentimental view of children; Mt cuts out the only trace of emotion in Mk, Jesus' embrace of the child (Mk 9:36). Mt inserts here the teaching of **4** from another context in Mk, which suggests that humility is the most important quality; this does indeed play an important part in Mt's gospel, see §§ 711d; 715h; 732c, but is not stressed in the rest of the ch. Conversion is indeed required (**3** cf Jn 3:3—4), and a child is used to symbolize a new convert to Judaism in the rabbinic writings; but this too is only a passing re-

c ference in Mt. The main emphasis here seems to be on the helplessness of the child or sheep. Neither is given any active role; the child is an exposed prey to scandal (**5**); the sheep gets helplessly lost and must be sought out (12—14); the debtor has no means of his own at all (25—30). This accords with the further use of 'sheep' by Mt (9:36; 10:16; 12:11; 26:31); it is always entirely dependent on someone's care. The figure of a child immediately recalls that of a father (Rm 8:15). For Mt the father is always our heavenly Father in whom we may have complete confidence that he will provide (6:25—34; 10:20, 29—31; § 718k). The keynote of the lesson here given is, then, the confident dependence of the believer on God.

d **5—9 On Leading others Astray** (Mk 9:37, 42—48; Lk 9:48; 17:1—2)—The blessing for receiving a child in Christ's name is the same as that for receiving a missionary (10:40—42). But whereas Mk suggests that the original sayings referred literally to a child, Mt is careful to point out, by adding 'who have faith in me' (**6**), that he is concerned with believers, as in 1—4. The group of three sayings (**6—9**) is brought together under the heading of 'scandal'. A *skandalon* is literally a trap, e.g. the spring-board of a mousetrap (TWNT 7 (1964) 339), so an occasion of falling; the verb means 'to trip up'. The 'millstone' is presumably the upper millstone of the mill of those times. The lower stone was a fixed upright pillar, over which a heavy hour-glass-shaped stone was fitted. Into the top 'cup' was poured the grain, which emerged from the lower part ground by the friction on the two stones. A large mill-stone needed an ass to turn it. The saying of **8—9** is attached to the prohibition of even adulterous looks and thoughts in 5:28—29 (where the foot is omitted) the eye and the hand being possible means of sinning in this matter. But here the chief interest is on the possibility of being led into sin by other members of the community.

e **10—14 The Lost Sheep** (Lk 15:3—7)—In Lk 15:2 the context of this parable is given: it was addressed by Jesus first to Pharisees in order to justify his association with sinners; all the emphasis was on the joy of God at the return of a sinner. Mt applies it to teach the duty of Church leaders to bring back the sinner, who is now not 'lost' (as in Lk) but only 'astray'. As the Messiah was to be the Good Shepherd (Ezek 34:11—31; Jn 10), so the

disciples are to carry on this mission of his (cf note on **729e** 10:1). The passage is constructed as a chiasmus: little ones—father—astray—99—99—astray—father—little ones; thus the theme is again (cf § 729c) the helplessness of men and their complete, confident dependence on their heavenly Father. **10.** The doctrine that each man **f** had two angels allotted to him was widespread in late Judaism; usually one of these was held to be good, the other evil (SB 3, 437—9). At Qumran two spirits lead men in the ways of light or of darkness (1QS III 18—IV 6, cf 1 Jn 4:6); but here it seems that there are only two spirits altogether, one of Truth and one of Perversity, rather than one of each kind allotted to each man. In late Jewish tradition there is also an accuser (Apoc 12:10) and a defender in heaven (1 Jn 2:1), who accuse or defend man before God. In the Jewish tradition it is not certain whether the same pair of spirits performs both guiding and juridical function. Here, however, in Mt, it appears that the same 'guardian' angel also has the task of interceding or defending before God.

15—22 Fraternal Harmony—Four sayings: the first **g** (**15—17**) concerns fraternal correction. The fault committed is not necessarily against the brother who corrects it, though this is implied by the version of the saying in Lk 17:3, and by the textually doubtful '*something wrong against you*' (15). The expansion of the saying in **16—17** (not in Lk) concerns the stages leading to excommunication, whereas the original saying of 15 concerns more fraternal forgiveness (as in 21—34; cf 12—14, 19—20). It is the lesson of forgiveness which is Mt's primary concern; but, characteristically, he cannot forego the casuistical development which has become attached to it. The same stages of loving correction, private, public and then official are prescribed at Qumran (1 QS V. 24—VI. 1). **16—17** can hardly come from Jesus' own lips; they presuppose already an organized community; nor is the attitude towards pagans and tax-collectors Jesus' own (cf 9:10). Paul similarly prescribes the excommunication of a persistent sinner (1 Cor 5:9—11). The measure existed already in Judaism (SB 4, 293—333). **18.** The second saying applies to the Church the power which was given to Peter in 16:19. It is impossible to say which of the two, if either, was the original context of the saying; proabably it was a floating saying without context. The power and authority which Peter exercises in his own person are the power and authority given by Christ to his community. **19.** Any cell of the messianic community shares this privilege granted to the Church of obtaining infallibly from the Father (= 'in heaven', v 18) what they ask. **20.** The reason for the efficacy of the prayer of the **h** community is the presence among them of Christ, whose prayer the Father always hears (Jn 11:42). In Judaism the rabbis taught that God is present in power wherever a group of believers is gathered for the sake of the Law (SB 1, 794—5). In the new dispensation Christ takes the place of the Law; whenever a group is gathered for his sake ('in my name') he himself, the presence of God among men (1:22—23), is there. The abiding presence of Christ is a reality which forms the basis of Mt's ecclesiology (28:20 and note). **21—22.** This saying introduces the **i** final section of the discourse; the whole discourse has concerned generosity in forgiving. Mt's little dialogue is probably formed from the saying given by Lk 17:4. Peter is made the spokesman as in Mt 17:24 (cf § 728j); the introductory phrase is typically Matthaean. The number seven already means completeness, so that there can be no limit to the forgiveness (thus Lk); but seventy times seven (as in the contemporary *Test. Benj.* 7; SB 1, 797 but it may be seventy-seven) strengthens even this. While

729i in Lk the offender repents and asks forgiveness, even this condition is absent in Mt.

j **23—35 Parable of the Unforgiving Debtor**—The ch on relations between brethren is summed up by a parable on forgiveness, a lesson to which Mt often returns (6:12; 7:2). Underlying is the Jewish doctrine of the two measures by which judgement may be exercised, justice or mercy; it is the latter which Jesus constantly demands (cf note to 12:5—7). This free-handed mercy is a pale shadow of God's mercy to men. **23.** On the introductory formula cf § 724*j*. The circumstances envisaged by the parable are pagan, for in Jewish law sale of an Israelite for debt was forbidden, and sale of a wife for any cause. **24.** The sums of money involved are meant, not to be realistic, but rather to stagger by their difference and by the size of the first. Ten thousand talents (£3 million, $9 million) is six hundred thousand times a hundred denarii; the latter sum represents wages for a mere four months casual labour (20:2), but the former could never be repaid by an employee or minister, however exalted. The tribute of all Galilee and Peraea in 4 B.C. was one fifth of this sum, a mere two hundred talents (Jos.Ant.

k 17, 318). **26—27.** Thus there is barely more possibility of the servant fulfilling his promise than of man paying off his debt to God. **29.** The reaction of the lesser debtor and his plea are related in terms identical to those used for the first servant; this increases the contrast in the creditor's answer. **32.** '*Poneros*' ('wicked') has, in Mt especially, often the nuance of 'grudging', 'miserly', 'ungenerous' (6:23; 7:11; 20:15; 25:26), cf also the name of Satan 'the jealous one' (5:37; 6:13; 13: 19). It is this lovelessness and lack of generosity which appears as the worst of the vices in Mt (contrast 22:39 and note). **34.** Torture was forbidden in Israel, and regarded as the extreme of barbarity. This also indicates a pagan context, unless it is an expression of the boundless wrath of the king. **35.** Mt, the careful pedagogue, gives the application to the life of the Church. 'You each forgive your brother' is an Aramaism for 'You forgive each other'.

730a **19—22.** The narrative half of the sixth major division of the gospel is already preparing for the Passion. First it insists on the demands which the following of Christ makes (19—20): restraint in sexual matters, renunciation of wealth and position and service. Then at last the Messiah is manifested in Jerusalem, and a series of controversies follows, broken up by a group of parables, all of which show the bankruptcy of the official Jewish religious leaders.

1a. The normal formula at the end of Mt's discourses (cf 7:28, 26:1 etc) **2.** For Mk's 'teaching' Mt substitutes 'healing' as in 14:14; Mt portrays Jesus as 'teaching' almost exclusively in the great discourses.

b **19:3—12 Divorce and Celibacy** (Mk 10:2—12)—Mk's controversy, though couched in terms of a formal rabbinic

c exchange, took little account of Jewish law. **3.** Mt transforms this by putting the question in the context of contemporary legal controversy of the Jewish schools; the question concerns not (as in Mk) the *legitimacy* of divorce but what *reasons* are sufficient, assuming that it is at least sometimes permitted. On this matter there was, at the time of our Lord, disagreement between the schools of Hillel and Shammai about the interpretation of the grounds of divorce given in Dt 24:1: *erwat dābār* (literally 'a shameful thing'). The strict school of Shammai interpreted this to mean something in the order of a sexual offence (but again details are disputed), whereas the broad school of Hillel said it was sufficient that a man's wife should burn his food or even be less pleasing to him

than another woman (the great R. Aqiba c. A.D. 120). **730c** They interpreted the two words of Dt 24:1 as alternatives, so (literally '*a shameful or some thing*' (SB 1, 313); hence 'any pretext whatever' (3) would suffice. **4—9.** **d** Mk represents Jesus as making the Pharisees quote Moses, and then himself opposing their citation with the words of Gn. Mt significantly gives first the general principle in the words of Gn, next the Pharisees' quotation which allows an exception; finally he corrects their interpretation of Moses (8) and on his own authority cancels the exception (9). The order is more didactic, and shows Jesus perfecting the Law on his own authority (cf § 717*c*), though it destroys the formal rabbinic procedure given in Mk. **7—8.** Moses did not 'command' to give a writ of dismissal. In Dt 24:1—4 the only positive legislation is that '*if* he has made out a writ of divorce for her, and *if . . .* (various things happen—vv 1—3 all belong within the 'if'—clause), *then* her first husband may not take her back'. The legislation was designed to discourage a casual divorce by making it irrevocable. Thus the most they can claim is that Moses permitted divorce, not that he encouraged it. **9.** Mt has created a *crux inter-* **e** *pretum* by inserting in the v which he found in Mk (as also into 5:32, derived from Q) the clause '*I am not speaking of fornication*', or '*apart from the case of fornication*'. Various interpretations have been proposed: 1. Separation and re-marriage are permitted in the case of adultery (the classic Protestant view). Against this it must be urged that (a) No other NT evidence exists for this ruling; it is impossible that Mt could on his own authority so have interpreted his sources Mk and Q, improbable that he alone had access to a saying of the Lord which has perished without any other trace. (b) The ruling which had, when the gospel was written, already been given by Paul, who appeals for it to the teaching of the Lord, is that separation is permissible provided that there is no re-marriage (1 Cor 7:11). This is the practice of the Church in the early 2nd cent. (Hermas, 4, 1, 5—8). (c) This interpretation puts Jesus in the same position as the strictest lawyers of the school of Shammai. But in such legal questions as this he invariably cuts through the tangle of rabbinic interpretations to return to the principle on which the solution must be based (22:15—22, 23—33, 34—40). He claims to be doing this in 5:32 (cf 5:17), and appears to be doing it in 19:4—9 (cf § 730*d*). He cannot then lamely relapse into one of the recognized interpretations. (d) If Jesus gives an interpretation already current, the horror of the disciples in v 10 is unmotivated. 2. The **f** clause excepts from this ruling an incestuous union within the forbidden degrees, illicit to Jews. The Gr. word used translates the Heb *z^enuth*, as it does in 10 of the 39 occurrences in the LXX translation, and probably also in 1 Cor 5:1; Ac 15:28. Mt alone includes the words because only to his readers is this Jewish concept relevant (J. Bonsirven, *Le Divorce dans le NT*, 1948).

This interpretation is indeed possible, but (a) The Gr. '*porneia*' can bear the meaning, but does not *usually* do so, either in LXX or in NT. It would not be clear that the less usual and more restricted meaning is intended here. Mt is always careful to make his lesson clear, and would not leave himself so obviously open to misinterpretation. (b) It is an addition too banal to be worthwhile. Moreover it is no true exception from the rule enunciated, which concerns separation after marriage. Here there is question only of illicit union, which is a different question and one so obvious that it needs no ruling. **3.** The man who **g** separates from his wife for any reason other than her adultery, and any man at all who marries a second wife is

730g an adulterer (the classic Catholic view). Unlike Mk, Mt considers the matter only from the man's point of view, for while in Roman law a wife could divorce her husband, in Jewish law this was impossible. Mt inserts his restricting clause carefully, so that it applies not to re-marriage but only to separation. If he had intended to say that remarriage was not adulterous in the case of the wife's adultery, then he would have inserted the clause immediately before 'is guilty of adultery'. This is not by chance, for Mt is a careful and exact writer, often altering Mk on quite trivial points to avoid the possibility of misunderstanding, e.g. in 9:6 he changes Mk's ambiguous 'authority to forgive sins on earth' to 'authority on earth to forgive sins'; in 12:4 he changes Mk's 'the loaves which *are* not allowed to be eaten' to 'which *was* not allowed', to avoid the impression that some of the loaves might legitimately be eaten. Mt's ruling does not contradict Mk's and Lk's; they consider only the case of separation-with-re-marriage; he rules in addition (clearer in 5:32) that the husband who even separates for any other grounds than adultery commits adultery even though he does not himself re-marry, by driving his wife to adultery. Cf J. Dupont, *Mariage et Divorce dans l'Evangile*, 1959.

h 10–12. The surprise of the disciples, and their suggestion that it is for this reason better not to marry, are directly related to the severe ruling which Jesus has given. **11** must similarly refer back to this (well brought out by JB, '*what I have said*'). The gift which is granted is not, therefore, some special gift granted to some Christians and not to others. There is no hint elsewhere in the gospels of such a distinction within the Christian body (cf § 731*a*); the distinction is always between those to whom revelation is granted and those to whom it is not (cf 10:19; 13:11; Jn 3:27; 6:65) never in degrees of generosity in God's giving. It is therefore a matter of some being able to accept Christ's doctrine on divorce and **i** others not. St Paul of course does speak of special gifts within the Christian body, in particular that of celibacy, e.g. 1 Cor 7:7: 'I wish that all were as I myself am. But each has his own special gift from God, one of one kind and one of another'. Then comes the surprising statement about eunuchs. It uses a traditional form of saying, cf Prv 30:17–31. Two familiar things are mentioned and then the point comes in the third. Eunuchs are divided in rabbinic terminology into two classes, the impotent and the castrated (SB 1, 805–7). A third class is here added; their state is not to be taken literally as self-inflicted—a practice regarded with horror by the Jews—but as indicating, by a vivid form of statement, those who voluntarily embrace a life of celibacy 'for the sake of the kingdom of heaven'. The saying in 12 was inserted here by Mt, perhaps elaborating an original saying of Jesus, so that we cannot now recover its original context. In its present position it can perhaps be interpreted as indicating the state of those who, having separated from their wives, refrain from re-marriage. This interpretation however does not harmonize very well with the evidently voluntary nature of the state of life envisaged in 12. Almost all commentators take it as referring to the life of celibacy voluntarily embraced for the love of God as being a state in which one can serve him more single-mindedly than in the married state. Taking it in this sense many commentators then interpret *ton logon touton* of v 11 as referring to the disciples' comment of v 10 that 'it is not expedient to marry', rather than to our Lord's original command about marriage in v 9 (RSV 'this precept'). The concluding remark of v 12 'He who is able to receive this, let him receive it' appears to

support this interpretation. Although the ideal of per- **730j** manent celibacy was unknown among the Jews, Jesus' own celibacy 'for the sake of the kingdom' would have made it intelligible to his followers. It is moreover probable that John the Baptist was celibate, as well as Paul.

13–15 Jesus and the Children (Mk 10:13–16; Lk 18: **j** 15–16)—Jesus' teaching on marriage is completed by showing his blessing on children. In Mk the passage is an object lesson to the Apostles on being spiritually childlike. But Mt removes the v which gives this lesson and incorporates it in 18:1–5 (cf § 729*b*); he shows that he here wishes to concentrate on the children and the blessing they receive, by making them the subject (in Mk they form the object) of the introductory sentence, and by framing the incident with Jesus' gesture of blessing (13, 15*a*). Note Mt's presentation of Jesus as a noble, impassible figure (cf § 711*c*); both annoyance with the disciples and tenderness to the children are here cut out. On the Kingdom of Heaven cf § 715*fh*.

16–23 The Rich Young Man (Mk 10:17–24*a*; Lk **731a** 18:18–24)—A similar story is told of R. Eliezer to whom his pupils came asking him to tell them the way of life (SB 1, 808). He gave various special counsels, but Jesus just repeats the commandments. Mt clarifies the structure of the incident by the double challenge 'If you wish to enter into life' (17), 'If you wish to be perfect' (21). This has been interpreted to indicate two degrees of Christian perfection, to the second of which only a select few are called. But Barth (p. 96–97) this stratification is foreign to Mt's thought: (1) There is no sign of it elsewhere in the gospel (cf § 730*h*); rather the whole of Jesus' message is addressed indiscriminately to the disciples, in whom Mt sees the representatives of the whole Church. (2) V 23 shows that wealth is an impediment, not to a special position in the Kingdom, but to entering it at all. (3) In 5:48 the call to be 'perfect' (as v 21) is addressed to all Christians, and this perfection sums up the antitheses which distinguish the new Law from the old; it constitutes the essence of Christianity.

Mt's slight change of construction from Mk's '*One* **b** *thing is lacking to you*' into '*In what respect am I lacking*' suggests that the perfection he means concerns, not a new command, but a new way of fulfilling the command already given. The most important command for Mt is clearly that of loving one's neighbour: he has added it in v 19 to Mk's list, he makes it his principle for judging the value of Jewish observances (cf § 734*g*, 726*g*), and sets it at the climax of his six antitheses (5:43–48). The point of the giving to the poor which is a preliminary to following Jesus is therefore not so much self-denial as total generosity to one's neighbour. In the narratives of the call of disciples taken over almost unchanged from Mk (Mt 4:18–22; 9:9) and Q (8:18–21) giving up everything is a sign of the immediacy and unconditionality of the response. Perfection consists in active fulfilment of this command of love, and Mt brings out that the young man fails because in some respect he is not fulfilling it. 'Treasure in heaven' **c** is a circumlocution for 'reward from God' (cf 6:19 and SB 1, 430). **16.** Since he does not in the end become a disciple Mt will not allow the man to kneel to Jesus (Mk v 17), and lets him use the form of address which the disciples never employ: 'Teacher' (cf § 720*a*). Similarly Jesus does not conceive an affection for him (contrast Mk v 21)—but this may be due to the hieratic remoteness of Mt's presentation (cf § 711*c*). **17.** Mt changes Jesus' reply (Mk: 'Why do you call me good? . . .) perhaps fearing that it might imply a denial of Jesus divinity. **20.** Mt alone makes the man young; Mk rather implies the reverse (only

731c an older man would say 'from my youth' Mk v 20), and Lk interprets him to be a ruler.

d **24—26 The Eye of a Needle** (Mk 10:24b—27; Lk 18:25—27)—To the incident of the rich young man is appended a general lesson suggested by his case. See § 757f. Mt adds great emphasis to the saying and shortens it, concentrating only on the difficulty of the salvation of the rich, not on the more general (and more original) question.

e **27—29 The Reward of Discipleship** (Mk 10:18—30; Lk 18:28—30; 22:28—30)—A second appendix to the story of the rich young man. Mk already attached the saying corresponding to Mt v 29, to which Mt prefixes another, taken from Q. **28.** 'You who have followed me' (inexplicably omitted by JB) is the definition of a disciple (cf § 711g). The 'renewal', a term derived from Stoic language, was used already by Philo and Josephus to denote the transformation of the world in the last times (Apoc 21; SB 3, 840—7; TWNT 1 (1933), 685—8); this is equivalent to the moment of the final manifestation of the messianic kingdom (cf § 715g). The 'thrones' denote not condemnatory judgement of the old Israel, but rule over the new Israel (cf 1 Mc 9:73; Gal 6:16; Jas 1:1). Judgement proper belongs to the Son of Man

f himself: 25:31—46. The number of twelve thrones should not be pressed too closely (? Judas, Matthias, Paul?); but it does reflect awareness that the Apostles constituted a college of twelve (cf § 823d). **29.** Mt soberly reduces Mk's 'hundredfold' to 'manifold'; both he and Lk omit the repetition of the list detailing the individual benefits; Mt alone omits Mk's promise of reward already in this present time, though with persecution. For him, the last judgement is the time of rewards and punishments and it is to this moment that he defers the reward.

g **19:30—20:16a Parable of the Vineyard Labourers** (Mk 10:31, Lk 13:30)—cf Jeremias pp. 33—38. Mt takes the closing remark in Mk, and by repeating it (reversing the order of 'firsts' and 'lasts') frames the parable which he adds to illustrate the truth that at the manifestation of the kingdom—'pay day' for Mt, cf 738f—all earthly orders of priority will be turned upside-down. This was, however, not the original meaning of the parable. V 16 cannot be used to discover the original lesson, for such generalizing conclusions are often added to the parables (22:14; 25:29; Lk 13:30); the only link with this moral within the story is the unexpected order of payment (8b), which is in fact a minor element. More central to the story is the generosity of the master of the vineyard in giving beyond what has been earned; it is this element which really makes the continuity between the original lesson of the parable and its present situation. But the most prominent element is the sense of injustice of the first workers; it is on this also that the final double question of 20:15 fastens (Jesus' method of questioning to provoke reflection, as 12:27; 16:8—11a, 15—16; 22:42—45). The context in which the story was originally told may therefore well be some such as 9:10—13, in reply to objections that sinners are admitted to Jesus' company and kingdom, cf 13:24—

h 30, 47—50. **1.** 'Now with the kingdom of heaven it is like when . . .'; the two situations are compared, not the kingdom and the landowner, cf § 724j. An exact allegory is not intended, but the figure of the vineyard cannot but recall the comparison of Israel to God's vineyard (Is 5:1—7), so prominent in all Jewish thought. **2.** A denarius is a normal day's wage. **7.** Their excuse gives a vivid impression of the bazaar: 'an idle evasion, a cover for typical oriental indifference' (Jeremias p. 37). **13.** 'My friend' a term of warmth and intimacy, used in the NT only by Mt (11:16; 22:12; 26:50 cf Sir 37:2), contrasts with

the other's roughness, cf Lk 15:18—32. The owner of **731h** the vineyard is allegorized as the owner of the vineyard of Israel. **16b.** is missing in some MSS: it was subjoined very early (from 22:14), perhaps not by Mt but in any case in accordance with the tendency to add generalizing conclusions, cf § 731g.

17—19 Third Prophecy of the Passion (Mk 10:32— **i** 34)—for the third time the Passion is prophesied; thus Jesus' foreknowledge and willingness are declared (cf 16:21; 17:22—23). As in 17:12, 22; 20:22 Mt especially underlines Jesus' firm will by using the verb mellō which expresses a determined intention for the future. The details, handing over to the Gentiles, mockery, scourging and crucifixion, appear in this prophecy for the first time. On the basic historicity of these prophesies cf § 727i; if some details are given which are unlikely to have been understood and retained by the disciples, even if they were spoken on that occasion, this is in order to express Jesus' willingness to undergo the full horrors of the Passion.

20—28 A Request for the Sons of Zebedee and its **j** lesson (Mk 10:35—45; Lk 22:24—27)—on the origin and authenticity of this pericope see § 757i. This passage shows once again the difficulty which Jesus had in weaning even his closest disciples from the conception of the Kingdom as a wordly triumph (cf § 715g, 19:27; Ac 1:6) The lesson had to be repeated again and again. **21.** Mt spares the reputation of the two Apostles by putting the request not in their mouth (as Mk) but in their mother's; but the plural of 'You do not know what you are asking' (22) confirms that Mk's version is original. **22—23.** On the imagery of cup and baptism, see § 757j. The seats of the rulers in the manifestation of the Kingdom (cf 19:28) are apportioned by the Father, cf 13:43; 18:35; 25:34. **24—27.** The real point of the passage comes in the lesson to which it gives rise, one repeated 18:1—5; 23:11—12. **28.** This **k** is perhaps the fullest expression in the gospels of Jesus' conception of himself as the Suffering Servant of the Lord foretold by Is 53 (cf § 711d). The description of his death as a 'ransom' can well have occurred to Jesus. The expressions of this v are all thoroughly semitic (contrast 1 Tm 2:6) and pre-Pauline; the idea of the life of a martyr being offered as a ransom for others is suggested already by 2 Mc 7:37, by the contemporary 4 Mc 6:28, and is echoed in the rabbinic literature (cf J. Jeremias, 'Lösegeld für Viele', Judaica 3 (1947), 249—64); cf also 26:28. It may well therefore be Jesus' own description of his sacrifice. 'For many' is a semitism for 'for all', not excluding some, as the English expression may imply. The ransom is paid, if to anyone, to God cf Ex 30:12; but probably the metaphor should not be pressed in too great detail.

29—34 Two Blind Men of Jericho (Mk 10:46—52; **l** Lk 18:35—43). Mt has already told this story in 9:27—31, where he inserted it in his collection of ten miracles, perhaps in order to include a miracle of every kind. But he re-tells the story here as a preparation for the entry into Jerusalem, to which it is linked by the repeated and openly-broadcast messianic cry 'Have pity on us, Son of David' (30, 31; cf 21:9). As in the earlier version, there are two blind men (to Mk's one). But, whereas in 9:27—31 all the emphasis was on their declaration of faith, and they were forbidden to let the miracle be known, here all explicit mention of faith is omitted (contrast Mk v 52) and they immediately follow Christ among his disciples (hence their triple confession 'Lord', which Mt allows only to disciples: § 720a, 731c). Characteristically Mt reduces the role of the minor actors, crowd and disciples, to a minimum, in order to leave the stage to the principals. Reversing his normal practice (cf § 711c) he inserts an

731l expression of emotion in Christ, **34**, perhaps to balance his anger in 9:30.

732a **21:1—11 The Messiah enters Jerusalem** (Mk 11:1—11*a*; Lk 19:28—38)—The evangelist describes the scene of Jesus' entry into Jerusalem in such a way that every detail brings out its messianic significance. The key is given by **4**, in which Mt points out that it fulfils Zech's prophecy of the Day of the Lord. **1.** The village of Bethphage is the last on the road from Jericho before the descent into the Kedron valley. Mt, abnormally, gives the geographical precision because of its messianic significance: on the Day of the Lord 'his feet will rest on the Mount of Olives which faces (the same rare word as in Mt v 2) Jerusalem' (Zech 14:4) at the beginning of his cata
b clysmic manifestation. **2—7.** The detailed instructions to the disciples show the fulfilment of the enigmatic Gn 49:11 'He ties up his young ass to the vine, and to its stock the foal of his she-ass'; it is interpreted messianically already by Zech 9:9, and accounts for the mention of the tethering (v 2). Mt neglects the fact that the v is constructed on a semitic parallelism 'on a donkey and on a colt', so, to show the literal fulfilment of the prophecy, seems to make Jesus ride simultaneously on both beasts (v 7). The absence of any mention of a previous arrangement, and the stark order 'The Lord needs them' suggest divine power; here alone in Mt and Mk is the title 'The Lord' applied to Jesus—an appellation otherwise reserved for God.
c **4—5** indicate that Jesus fulfils the prophecy deliberately cf § 711*f*. This passage of Zech is interpreted consistently of the Messiah in Jewish literature, the humility and poverty of his approach are occasionally attributed to the unworthiness of Israel (SB 1, 842—4); this no doubt was Mt's interpretation too, cf § 724*e*, for in Mt Jesus is constantly stressed to be the humble king cf § 722*k*. His kingship is shown also by v 7*b* 'and he sat on them', for the same rare verb is used of the mounting of Solomon upon his steed for his enthronement procession (1 (3) Kgs 1:38, 44—accordingly perhaps read at v 7*b*, with Codex
d Sinaiticus, '*and they enthroned him*'). **8—9.** Here the crowd too seems to recognize Jesus as king, for they spread their garments before Jehu at his proclamation as king (2 (4) Kgs 9:13), and green branches at the triumphal return of Simon Maccabaeus (1 Mc 13:51). This last element, and the singing of Ps 118 (117):25—26 in v 9, suggest the feasts of the Dedication of the Temple or of Tabernacles; they formed an important part in the ritual of these feasts, see § 758*b*. The cry 'Hosanna' (more exactly in Heb. '*Hôšî'a-nā*') meant originally 'Pray, save' but passed from a cry for help into an acclamation. In the Ps quoted it is addressed to God; but Mt addresses it first to Jesus under his favourite messianic title 'Son of David' (cf § 734*i*) as well as to God (reverently avoiding the mention of God by 'Hosanna in the highest heavens', but for an alternative explanation of this phrase, see § 758*d*. By inserting 'to the Son of David' and omitting Mk's mention of 'the kingdom of our father David' Mt concentrates even more on the person of Jesus; it is he alone who is welcomed as the Messiah, coming 'as the
e Lord's representative'. **10.** 'The whole city was in turmoil' raises in its most acute form the problem of the fairness from the point of view of historicity of Mt's presentation. He consistently increases over Mk's account the element of crowd participation. Where Mk has only 'many people' (v 8) and 'those who went in front' (v 9), Mt transforms these into 'great crowds' (v. 8) and 'the crowds who went in front' respectively. These are now joined (v 10) by 'the whole city' (as 2:3). But such terms are vague interpretations of what in fact might have been a numerically small group, waving branches and singing round a man

on a donkey as, in accordance with the ritual, they went **732e** up to the feast. Thus the same facts, which, to a casual observer, might have seemed comparatively normal are, when interpreted against the background of the biblical prophecies of the Messiah, in reality of far-reaching significance, as the triumphant arrival of the messianic king.
12—17 Renewal of the Temple (Mk 11:11, 15—17; **f** Lk 19:45—46)—After Jesus' messianic entry into Jerusalem he proceeds immediately to reveal himself as Messiah in the temple, by fulfilling here too the prophecies of the Messiah. The positioning of this incident varies: Mk inserts between the entry into Jerusalem and the Temple incident the curse of the fig-tree; the two are connected as action and interpretation (cf § 732*k*), but Mt reverses the order to achieve the sweep from entry straight into the Temple, and to show more clearly the realization of the prophecies. On the divergence between the Synoptics and John, see § 758*g*.

12—13. Sacrificial victims were always for sale in the **g** outer court of the temple (SB 1, 850—2). In the month before the Passover the temple-tax had to be paid (cf § 728*j*), and since for this only the reliable Tyrian coinage was acceptable, money-changers set up *bureaux de change* in the temple (charging the reasonable sum of 4 per cent for exchange from often imperfect and under-weight coins into good coinage: SB 1, 763—5). For neither of these activities have we any evidence suggesting sharp practice. Rather Jesus is still fulfilling the prophecy of Zech 14 about the coming of the Day of the Lord; it concludes 'There will be no more traders in the temple of the Lord when that day comes' (v 21*b*—because on that day everything will be sacred and it will be unnecessary to buy special victims). Again (cf § 732*e*) the actual extent of Jesus' action need not be as great as El Greco and other artists suggest; Mk has only 'he *began* driving out . . .'
13. The sense of the contrasting quotations from Is 56:7 **h** and Jer 7:11 is not the contrast between prayer and robbery; both passages refer to the acceptability of sacrifices, which always depends on the fidelity of the offerers to God's covenant. Jesus is proclaiming the vanity of the Temple cult as it was carried out, and the barrenness of Israel (cf § 732*k*): whereas the cult should have been a focus of true worship (Is), their moral bankruptcy has made it valueless (Jer 7:1—11). It has also been suggested that Jesus is referring to their narrow nationalist concept of the Messiah, since the word translated 'robber' is frequently used (e.g. JosBJ 4, 3, 3) for the militant nationalist party of the Zealots (cf § 609*c*). **14—17.** The **i** blind and the lame were excluded from the temple by an ordinance attributed to David (2 Sm 5:8); but the 'Son of David' (again the messianic cry, § 732*d*, 734*i*) admits them and heals them from their disability; thus he declares a higher order than that of David and of the Temple. All miracles of healing are a sign of the Messiah, cf § 719*b*.
15—16. The contrast is pointed between the official representatives of Judaism, who should have received the Messiah, and the children who actually do so. Jesus' quotation of Ps 8 was intended to suggest perhaps the contrast between the acclamations of children and the crushing of God's opponents (Ps 8:2), perhaps the dignity to which God had raised man (Ps 8:5,6—here of Jesus).
17. On Bethany cf § 739*e*.
18—22 The Barren Fig-Tree (Mk 11:12—14, 20— **j** 24)—The cursing and its 'explanation' were probably not in fact originally connected. In Mk they are separated by the cleansing of the Temple; Mk vv 20—22*a* show clear traces of his redactional activity, and the sayings which make up the explanation are found independently (Mt v 21 = 17:20 = Lk 17:6; Mk v 25 = Mt 6:14). Mk has

32j used the opportunity to teach the lesson of trusting faith incorporated by Mt also in 17:20, but copied also here

k from Mk. The meaning of the curse is clear from its connexion to the preceding events: it is a prophetic action in the manner of the OT prophets (Jer 13:1–11; Ezek 4:1–3; also Ac 21:11–13). Israel is compared to a fig-tree on which God seeks fruit in vain (Jer 8:13). The metaphor of good works as fruit is frequent (3:8, 10; 7:17; 12:33); this is the fruit for which Jesus is hungry. Note that Mt, by omitting Mk's 'it was not the season for figs' removes the excuse of the Jews; Jesus had a right to expect fruit. By their rejection of him at this great messianic manifestation (1–17) they have forfeited all chance to bear fruit, and are condemned to barrenness, cf § 733e. Mt returns to this theme 21:28–22:10. **18.** By telescoping action and explanation Mt misses out a day according to Mk's timing (Mk 11:12, 20). He shows no interest in Mk's carefully-elaborated scheme of days.

l **23–27 Authority of Jesus Questioned** (Mk 11:27–33; Lk 20:1–8)—Mt turns Mk's general confrontation about Jesus' authority (see § 758hi) into a specific rabbinic examination about his authority to teach. A rabbi receives authority to teach only by the imposition of hands of another rabbi, his teacher; cf Daube, p. 217. Mt shows that he intends this specific point to be the matter in hand by representing Jesus as teaching (**23**, not in Mk); he also omits Mk's 'scribes', who have no authority in the matter, since their capacity is only an advisory one in matters of interpretation. **24–25a.** Jesus' reply invites them to admit that there exists a higher authority than rabbinic ordination; Jesus hints that as John possessed this, he too has it. Since they refuse to acknowledge this (**26**), he leaves them in the same position with regard to his own authority (**27**—Mt here uses for 'he retorted' the emphatic *ephē*, which he employs only for important pronouncements of Jesus). By this refusal to accept the possibility of the messengers of God entering in and breaking through their own institutions, the Jewish authorities show their stubborn deafness to God's voice. Mt adds two more parables to Mk's one to force this lesson home.

'33a **28–32 Parable of the Two Sons**—This little parable was first put in writing by Mt, for it contains over a dozen of his special literary characteristics. The sharp point is contained in the contrast between the son who claims to do the will of the father (as the Jewish authorities do, even in the control of teachers which they have just exercised) but does not do it, and those who make no grandiloquent claims (cf Sir 3:8). This is combined (principally by means of the Matthean v 31b) with the reminder that 'tax collectors and prostitutes' have repented. Finally the parable is bracketed to the previous passage 23–27, by a reminder of the successful mission to such people of this same John the Baptist whom they will not acknowledge. A number of textual variants further complicate the passage, but its principal meaning, condemnation of the self-righteous attitude of the Jewish authorities, is clear.

b **Parable of the Wicked Husbandmen** (Mk 12:1–12; Lk 20:9–19)——**33.** The metaphor of a vineyard immediately recalls Is 5:1–7 (here even quoted) in which Israel is the Lord's vineyard. The landowner is, then, God, and the husbandmen the rulers of Israel. **34–36.** Mt's language here '*when vintage time arrived*' vividly suggests the coming of the Messiah, often compared to vintage or harvest time. But in fact Mt assimilates the groups of servants to the earlier and later prophets sent to recall Israel to her fidelity to God. This is clear not only because he increases the single servants of Mk vv

3 and 4 (one is enough to collect revenue), but also because **733b** he makes them die the classic death of a prophet, stoning (2 Chr 24:21; Mt 23:37; Lk 13:34; Heb 11:37). **37–39.** **c** The son for his part is made more clearly the figure of Jesus: Mk v 6 calls him the 'beloved son', thereby recalling the voice heard at Baptism and Transfiguration. Mt and Lk achieve the same allusion by reversing Mk's order: instead of the son being killed within the vineyard and his body then thrown out, the son is now first thrown out of the vineyard before being killed, as Jesus was crucified outside the city. **40–41.** Jesus challenges his hearers to make the application themselves. The language 'when the Lord of the vineyard comes' suggests at first sight the final coming in judgement (cf 24:42; 25:31; 10:32), but 41b (added over Mk's version) shows that a period is envisaged after this event. The coming of the lord must therefore here be the coming of the Messiah. **42.** The text of Ps 118 (117):22–23 is added to conclude **d** with some mention of the Resurrection, and also some intimation of the new condition of the vineyard: Christ is the keystone of the arch, which completes and holds together the building (TWNT I (1933) 792–3), cf Eph 2:20. There is perhaps also a reminiscence of Dn 2:34, 44–45 (the stone which symbolizes a great and eternal kingdom, especially if v 44 (missing in some MSS, and perhaps added from Lk) is authentic. **43.** This introductory formula, the pair of theological passives 'taken away . . . and given to' (to avoid using the name of God with the active, cf 13:12), metaphorical use of 'fruit' (cf § 718p), kingdom (cf § 711a), are all characteristic of Mt. But, above all, the transference of the kingdom from Israel **e** to a new race is central to Mt's message. Not only does he make this ecclesiological aspect the point of the parable (by adding this v and 41b); he emphasizes constantly the Church formed of a new race, composed of Jew and Gentile. Mk teaches how the leaders of the people proved unworthy, and that their standards are not those of Jesus; but Mt is the first to stress that the inheritance of Israel, as a race, passes from them. Jesus' own mission was to the Jews alone (10:6; 15:24); he is primarily the Messiah who is the hope of Israel (1–2; 20:29–34; 21:1–17; notes ad locc and § 734i). But they persistently reject him (specially underlined by Mt, cf § 724e) until Israel shows itself to have forfeited its privileges as God's chosen people (21:18–19; 23:39 cf § 715h, 735l). Only after his own rejection, does Christ give to his Apostles the mission to preach to all nations (28:19; 24:14; cf 12:18–21). Now entry into the Kingdom will not follow from merely belonging to the chosen people, but will be won, by Jew and Gentile alike, through belief in Christ (8:5–13; 15:21–28 and notes). **45.** The authorities recognize that the parable is **f** directed against their stewardship of the vineyard. **46.** Here again in connexion with Jesus' death, Mt recalls that John the Baptist was a prophet; their deaths stand in a continuous line (35–39) of murders of the prophets by the Jews (5:12; 23:37; cf § 725e).

22:1–14 Parables of the Wedding Feast (Lk 14:16– **g** 24)—Mt has here united two parables, to embrace the whole history of salvation. The former underlines yet again the lesson of 21:33–46 that salvation is to pass from the Jews to others (1–10); the latter parable warns that even for Christians mere membership of the Church is not enough (11–14). **1–10.** Jesus is perhaps using a well-known Palestinian story (SB 1, 881). Lk interprets the parable as justifying the preaching of the gospel to the poor (cf Lk 14:13); this is also its sense in the apocryphal gospel of Thomas. It may well have been told originally by Jesus in some such

Q

733g situation as that of Mt 9:12. Mt's lesson differs slightly from Lk's, though in obvious continuity with it. In Lk the invitation passes from the leaders of the Jews to the poor: in Mt from the Jews to the Gentiles. Mt adapts the parable **h** to his own message by little allegorizing touches. **2.** Lk's simple 'man' becomes a 'king' in Mt, and his 'banquet' a 'marriage feast for his son'; thus the significance of the story is made unmistakable, for the figure of the messianic times as a marriage feast was a familiar one (cf § 720*m*). **3—6.** It was a custom, at least in Jerusalem, to invite guests to an important wedding twice (SB 1, 881); but here it is more a question of a remote invitation followed by notice that all was prepared. But the doubling of this notice by Mt and the maltreatment of the messengers (reasonable in 21:35—37, where they come to collect money, but here gratuitous) suggest accommodation of the story to reflect the earlier and later prophets of Israel and their maltreatment. Mt is harsher on the guests than Lk; they do not want to come (3), are *'not interested'* (5), **i** whereas in Lk they do at least make excuses. **7.** It has often been held that the excessive punishment of the murderous invited guests (while the food still waits to be eaten) is an allegorical trait reflecting the sack of Jerusalem, city of Jesus' murderers, in A.D. 70, and that consequently we have here an indication that the gospel was written after that date (e.g. Kilpatrick p. 6). But K. H. Rengstorf ('Die Stadt der Mörder, BZNW 26 (1960), 106—29) has shown that the burning of a city is a stock form of punishment in ancient literature (Jg 1:8; 1 Mc 5:28; Assyrian texts, Josephus and other contemporary Jewish works), a commonplace which could have been used without thought of any explicit historical reference. Moreover the Jews connected the destruction of Jerusalem much more with the sack of the temple and the end of its cult than with the burning of a whole city. An allusion to the historical event is, then, not merely unnecessary but even **j** unlikely. **8—10.** Since the Jews were 'unworthy' they are replaced by the Gentiles, cf § 733*e*. But the mixture of good and bad in the resultant community prepares the way for the next parable. **11—14.** This second parable, not found in Lk, carries on the allegorical history of salvation, representing the time of the Church up to the last judgement. It is surely an addition by Mt, who insists especially on the mixed character of the members of the Church (13:24—30, 36—43, 47—50) and the coming judgement (§ 738*f*). He wishes to show that mere faith, by which one adheres to Christ in his Church, is not enough; the works of love, too, are required (cf 5:43; 18:3 etc); this **k** is the lesson also of 13:18—23. A very similar parable was told c. A.D. 80 by Johanan ben Zakkai (SB 1, 878), who means by the garment the good works of penance— a virtue highly-prized in Pharisaic and rabbinic spirituality, cf § 720*l*. Mt in fact leaves open the exact meaning of the garment, cf Is 61:10; Apoc 3:4, 5, 18; it must be interpreted by the rest of his doctrine, in which love of the neighbour is so important. **14.** 'Many' in Aram. indicates no limitation whatsoever and could be translated 'all', 'the multitude'. Mt inclines to add explanatory or hortatory conclusions to his parables, cf § 724*d*; he is a preacher, and thus sums up the lesson of the double parable, the warning lesson of salvation history.

734a **15—46 Four controversies** (Mk 12:13—37*a*; Lk 20: 20—44)—These four controversies, given here by Mk and Mt, represent the great parting of the ways between Jesus and the Jews. In Mt this is especially clear, preceded as they are by the parables of the rejection of the Jews (21:28—22:14), and followed by the lament over the Pharisees, scribes (23:1—36) and Jerusalem (23:37— 39).

15—22 On Tribute to Caesar—The question is one **73** which might well have arisen between the two parties, for the Pharisees were content to work for the observance of the Law under the Roman government, and so would consider it permissible to pay the Roman taxes (for which cf on Lk 2:1), whereas the Herodians were probably the champions of the family of Herod, who campaigned to abolish Roman direct rule and return to independence under their native rulers. This poll tax was imposed when **c** Judaea had been incorporated into the Roman provincial system and was the symbol of subjection, so bitterly opposed by nationalists. There had been a revolt when it first had to be paid (cf Ac 5:37; Jos.Ant. 18, 1, 1), and Josephus suggests that it was one of the chief causes of unrest and nationalism. The 'malice' which Jesus recognizes (18—so Mt; Mk, 15, has more clearly 'hypocrisy') was to present Jesus with a question which might well involve him in unpopularity with one party or another. In spite of the fulsome compliment (16) they do not really want instruction on this point. But if Jesus answers against paying the tribute he will separate himself from the Pharisees; if he answers for paying it, he will lose the sympathy of the nationalistic Herodians. It might, however, be objected that it hardly amounts to a malicious trap if each party tries to get Jesus to side with them; only if a third party poses the question is it simply an attempt to catch him out. But this is slender grounds for saying that Jesus' opponents in the dispute were originally unnamed and only lated added. The controversy follows a recognized rabbinic pattern of question, counter-question, expected answer from the original questioner and *ad hominem* rejoinder; the pattern occurs also in 21:23—27; Mk 10:2—9 etc, cf § 757*a*. **19.** The denarius presumably bore the inscription 'Ti-(berius) Caesar Divi Aug(usti) F(ilius)'; the two fully written words give Jesus the terms of his answer—one can almost imagine him pointing to them in turn. As always in his answers to such legal questions, he cuts through the details to the underlying principle, leaving his interlocutors to reflect upon the conclusions to be drawn. He suggests that each party is preoccupied with irrelevancies, to the exclusion of the one essential.

23—33 The Resurrection of the Dead—cf § 759*c*. **d** The Sadducees, the aristocratic and priestly class in Judaism, possessed also in their theology that quality often associated with this class, conservatism. Thus they refused to accept the more recent progress of revelation, notably on the points of the normative value of tradition other than the written Law, the existence of angels and retribution after death (Ac 23:8; Jos.Ant. 18, 1, 4). The realization that there was an individual survival after death had come to the Jews only comparatively recently, cf on 2 Mc 7:9. The Sadducees present their objection in the form of what they hope to be a *reductio ad absurdum*. They quote in their favour the institution in the Mosaic Law of the levirate (clearly described in vv 24—27). Jesus' answer is double: (a) Their **e** conception of the after-life is too crude, based on the supposition that the after-life is basically similar to this life (30). There must be a trace of humour in our Lord's comparison of the life to that of the angels, since the Sadducees did not, of course, accept their existence! Jewish belief in the possibility of the use of marriage in Heaven is not attested earlier than Maimonides (A.D. 1135—1204; SB 1, 888), but may perhaps be presumed from their general supposition that the just man's life after death was a continuance of the more pleasurable aspects of life on earth. It is such views that Paul tries to correct in 1 Cor 15:35—53. (b) The doctrine of the

34e resurrection of the dead is contained in the scriptures (31—32). Jesus uses as his text a passage from the Pent, to which alone the Sadducees attributed full authoritative force (Jos.Ant. 13, 10, 6). His scriptural argument is not immediately clear to us, for the primary literal sense of the words of Ex 3:6 is '*I am God whom Abraham, Isaac and Jacob worshipped*'. But in current Jewish exegesis (F. Dreyfus, RB 66 (1959) 213—22) they were understood in the sense '*I am God, the protector of Abraham, Isaac and Jacob*', and great stress was laid upon the unceasing nature of this protection (e.g. in the psalm at the end of the Heb. version of Sir). Jesus argues, then, that God would not be the God of Abraham, Isaac and Jacob (in the fuller literal sense, as then understood) if they were 'dead' (in the sense in which the Sadducees understood 'dead'); His protection would have failed them, for God cannot be the unceasing protector of one who is no more.

f 34—40 The Greatest Commandment—The third of the four debates, cf § 759c falls under the rabbinic heading of *Derek 'Ereṣ*, or principles of living. Mk's presentation of this debate is markedly well-disposed towards the scribe, and shows also from its preoccupations that a Hellenistic environment has had some part in shaping its final form (cf G. Bornkamm 'Das Doppelgebot der Liebe', *Ntliche Studien für R. Bultmann* BZNW 21 (1957²) 85—93; Strecker p. 135—6. From comparison with Lk it is clear that Mt used also an independent source, Q; he is far more hostile to the questioner ('they got together' used also constantly in the Passion narrative of Jesus' enemies; 'testing him'; the title used only by Jesus' opponents 'Teacher'); Mt omits the mutual compliments of Mk vv 32—34; the lawyer belongs to the arch-enemy in **g** Mt, the Pharisees. The question asked again seems innocent enough: the 613 'commandments of the Law' were divided by the rabbis into greater and lesser commandments (i.e. whose transgression was more or less grave), with a considerable area of dispute as to which commandments belonged to which category. It is into such a dispute that the lawyer invites Jesus to enter, with his question 'What is a great commandment?' Christ's answer is wholly new. Various rabbis produced great general principles (*kelalim*) which were supposed to sum up the spirit of the Law, e.g. R. ben 'Azzai (c. A.D. 110) 'When God created Adam, he created him in the image of God' (SB 1, 907). But Jesus' terminology of the law and the prophets 'hanging' (40) indicates that they can be *derived from* these two commandments (SB 1, 908). No rabbi ever dared to cut through the tangle of equally binding observances to the principles on which all were based, but offered only didactic headings from which the various commandments could be logically deduced. Philo, however (*de spec. legis* 2:63) does offer these two commands as 'the highest principles of the law'.

h The first novelty of Jesus here is that he clears the ground, to return to essentials. Of the two commandments specified, the first is taken from the *Shema*, the prayer or profession of faith recited by every male Jew, morning, noon and night (Dt 6:4—9) Jesus' second novelty is, unasked, to put another commandment on a level with this; Mt insists that this is the principle on which all Christian interpretation of the Law must be based, cf 5:43—48; 7:12; 9:13; 12:7, 11—13; 19:19; 23:23 and notes.

i 41—46 Christ, Son but also Lord of David—The last in this group of four controversies (cf § 759c). Mt, as often (e.g. v 34), brings forward the Pharisees. In Mk, Jesus' interlocutors are unnamed, but Mt is primarily interested in the Pharisees (cf § 709g) and makes them

the ringleaders of Jesus' opponents. Here he insists on **734i** their hostility—the word used for 'gathered round' is often used in this sense—and on their discomfiture before launching into the attack of 23:1—36. He also retouches the exchange to leave no doubt that the Messiah is to be the son of David, for in Mk it is only reported that the scribes give him this title. In Mt we actually see the Pharisees acknowledge him as such. Mt, however, makes **j** especial use of the title, in function of his insistence that Jesus' mission was first and foremost to the Jews, that their rejection was not from lack of fidelity on God's part (cf § 733e). The whole of his first ch is directed to showing how, in spite of the virgin birth, Jesus was truly son of David (cf § 680bd). 'Help us, son of David' is the frequent appeal and acclaim in Mt (9:27; 15:22; 20:30—31); it is this cry which accompanies the messianic entry into Jerusalem and the Temple (21:9, 15). But Mt too is aware that Jesus' significance is not confined to Israel, and that he has a higher transcendent dignity which makes him also David's lord (cf Strecker p. 118—20). It is as a proof of this that Ps 110 (109):1, quoted here, is so frequently used in the NT and in early Christian literature.

23 The Hypocrisy of the Scribes and Pharisees (Mk **735a** 12:37b—40; Lk 20:45—47; 11:39—51; 13:34—35)— The sixth major section of the Gospel is, as all the central blocks, divided into two parts, narrative (chh 19—22) and discourse (chh 23—25). More exactly, there are here two discourses: 23 against the scribes and Pharisees, 24—25, the eschatological discourse. After a series of controversies with the religious authorities of the Jews (chh 21—22), Mt presents in one chapter a summary of Jesus' charges against them. The centrepiece is a sevenfold indictment (13—31), preceded by instructions on the attitude to Jewish religious teachers and to religious teachers in general.

1—7 Attitude of the Disciples to Scribes and Phari- b sees—Jesus does not here in principle reject the authority of the scribes and Pharisees. On the contrary, while condemning their behaviour he reaffirms the binding force of their teaching, at least in principle (3). The basic accusation against them which recurs again and again is that of hypocrisy, that their actions do not accord with their teaching, but are done simply to gain the good opinion of men. But this approval of their teaching is surprising after the correction of it in 15:1—20 and the general warning against it in 16:11—12. Jesus' interpretation of the Law, based as it is on the primacy of love, is frequently in conflict with the official Jewish position, e.g. 5:20—48; 12:1—14. Strecker (p. 16) even says that there is an irresolvable tension between 16:11— 12 and 23:3, and that the latter must be a saying taken over by Mt without his realizing this. But 4a also echoes 11:29—30, where the heavy yoke of the Pharisees is contrasted to the light yoke of Jesus. The conflict is resolved if we take 2—3a as referring originally to some **c** particular case or ruling. Alternatively the 'all' of 3a is a mere cliché, as at Qumran, where 'all' is 'often a purely customary addition' (Barth p. 72), especially in matters concerning the Law; it insists more on whole-hearted fidelity than on details of observance. **2.** The 'chair of Moses' appears to be a special chair of the teacher (SB 1, 909); one such has recently been discovered at Capharnaum. Metaphorically it means that they have the teaching authority of Moses. **5.** Phylacteries (= safeguards) or *tephillin* (Aram. = prayers) are small match-box sized cases containing the central texts of the Pent, viz Ex 13: 1—16; Dt 6:4—9; 11:13—21; they are bound on to the forehead and forearm in literal fulfilment of Ex 13:9, 16. Broader ones would be more ostentatious proof of the

735c wearer's observance. Tassels were prescribed to be worn on the hem of the garment by Nm 15:38; Jesus too followed this practice (Mt 9:20), but condemns overostentation here too. **6–7.** It is not these signs of respect which are condemned but over-insistence on and too great delight in them.

d 8–12 Warning to Christian Teachers—The intention of this passage is shown by the two sayings, 11 and 12, which Mt has added from elsewhere (they occur also Mt 20:26 and 18:4 respectively) at the end: the Christian teacher is a minister and servant of his flock, who must not take on the lordly airs of some rabbis. The prohibition of the two titles 'rabbi' and 'father' (often used of great Jewish teachers, SB 1, 918–19) must be seen against the background of the relationship between rabbi and pupils, for it is to this that Jesus objects, rather than the mere use of a name. The adulation accorded to a rabbi was so great that he became an obstacle to the realization of direct dependence on God as the unique father and authority, of whom men can only be representatives. The sayings of the rabbis were quoted as carrying weight independently; this is in startling contrast to Christianity (B. Gerhardsson, *Tradition and Transmission in Early Christianity* (Lund, 1964), p. 41–42): in spite of the reverence in which the Apostles were held, early Christian writings quote no sayings of or stories about them; Christ is the only authority and centre from whom all teaching
e is drawn. **8.** 'Rabbi' literally means 'my great one'; hence 11 is based on a pun. The title is, in Mt, never used even of Jesus by the disciples; he is so addressed only by Judas (26:25, 49); similarly he is addressed as 'teacher' only by his opponents (8:19; 9:11; 12:38; 22:16 etc). It seems that Mt felt this title to be insufficient, for the disciples call Jesus 'Lord'. **9.** The re-discovery of God as a father, though this doctrine was contained already in the OT, is a part of Jesus' message to which the NT, and especially Mt, constantly refer (cf § 718c). **10.** Uses a further title for a teacher, constituting a slight variant on 8.

f 13–31 Sevenfold Indictment—The seven charges, beginning 'Woe upon you' or 'Alas for you' are not, as is often supposed, curses invoking God's anger upon the scribes and Pharisees, but statements that this anger is already upon them, and lamenting it (cf Nm 21:29; Is 3:11; 1 Sm 4:7–8). Thus they are not the direct opposite of blessings, which ask God's favour upon someone as well as stating that it is deserved, since they include a lament for the situation they describe. To these seven charges there are two main themes: the first four denounce the harmful influence of the scribes and Pharisees on others, the last four their punctilious observance of externals at the expense of the more important intention behind them. Thus the two themes meet in the fourth charge, whose central position indicates that it is the crux of the accusations. It concerns the interpretation of the Law with love (cf § 735*i*). Each charge begins with the accusation of hypocrisy, a vice frequently found where there is an obligation to a minute observance of externals: the Pharisees themselves were aware of the danger, and the rabbinic writings contain a number of wry but humorous stories about pharisaic hypocrisy (SB 1, 921–3). **13.**
g *First charge: obstacle to the Kingdom*: this sums up their harmful influence on others; entry into the kingdom sums up for Mt the goal of true following of Christ (at beginning and end of the sermon on the mount 5:20; 7:21; cf 18:3; 19:23). **14** is missing in some MSS and is of uncertain position (before or after 13) in others. It is probably a later addition from Mk 12:40, for it makes eight charges instead of the perfect number seven, a

favourite with Mt. **15.** *Second charge: harmful proselytism*: the energetic efforts of the Jews to convert gentiles to their religion were a bye-word at this time; they are mocked by Horace and Seneca. 'Son of Gehenna' means 'fit citizen of Hell', cf 'sons of the kingdom' (13:38). On Gehenna see end of note to 27:3–10. **16–22.** *Third* **h** *charge: pedantic casuistry*: This particular distinction in the validity of vows is not attested in the rabbinic sources; but a similar example is that a vow made on the Law is invalid, while one made on what is written in the Law stands. As usual Jesus takes the dispute to the ultimate principle: it is the sanctity of God which makes things holy and therefore fit guarantors of a vow. 16–21 are built on an elaborate formal verbal pattern such as Mt loves: Temple-gold, gold-Temple; altar-gift, gift-altar; altar; Temple. **23–24.** *Fourth charge: false standards*: **i** This is the central accusation, both in position and in importance; they are scrupulously attentive to little things, while neglecting the greater commandments. 23 stands as a heading to the last three charges, while the 'blind guides' of 24 sums up the first three (cf § 735*f*). The command to give tithes of crops perhaps applied originally only to corn, wine and oil (Dt 14:22–23), but by the time Tb was written it had been considerably extended (Tb 1:6–8). In Jesus' time even the smallest seasoning-herbs must be scrupulously tithed. In this care for punctilious external observance, the principles which lay behind the Law were forgotten. In Mt Jesus is constantly stressing that the ritual laws and all the Law must be interpreted according to the law of love (cf §§ 716*h*; 726*d*; 734*g*). This is the loving 'mercy' and 'confidence' in God's loving mercy which must be shown in judgement'. **24.** This energetic hyperbole uses a play on words: gml (= camel), qlm (= gnat), qml (= filter); cf Lagrange p. 447. **25–26.** **j** *Fifth charge: impure purity*: Jesus takes up the accusation of the prophets, that their ritual observance, divorced from regard for fellow-men, is vain (Is 1:10–17; Am 5: 21–6:7). Especially 'extortion' was a fault to which the rulers in Israel were always prone (Is 3:14; 10:2; Ezek 22:27, 29). **27–28.** *Sixth charge: hypocrisy*, a variant on the fifth charge. Mt heightens the contrast given by Lk: in Lk the graves are unnoticed, but in Mt the exterior even appears attractive. In Palestine the low graves or grander 'bee-hive' tombs are still kept glistening in the sun with white-wash. **28** gives Mt's application, with a formal accusation of hypocrisy and Mt's favourite contrast between 'justice' and 'lawlessness'. **29–31.** *Seventh charge: murder of the prophets*: The exact charge here is somewhat obscure; it can hardly be that they build the tombs of the prophets, for this should be a good work. More probably it is a combination of their attitude to the dead prophets and to the present ones: they claim to make reparation for their ancestors' murder of the prophets, by building their tombs. Thus they admit to being sons of the murderers. But, in spite of their protestations, their present conduct proves them to be indeed true sons, following in their fathers' ways. **k**
32–36 Murder of the prophets and punishment— The murder of the prophets, of John the Baptist, of Jesus Himself and of his envoys, constitute one continuous line (cf 14:15; 21:33–41 and notes). This is emphasized here by the use of the same expressions, crucifixion, scourging and persecution, as are used in the prophecy of the Passion (20:19) and in the missionary discourse (10:17, 23). It is the retribution for all this persecution—the climax of the infidelities which the seven charges have castigated—which is now considered (bracketed by 'your fathers' and 'brood of vipers' in 32–33 and 'this generation' in 36). **33** recalls

35k the preaching of John the Baptist; but whereas there (3:7) it was 'Who warned you to flee from the retribution that is coming?', now the opportunity is passed: 'How will you escape?' **35.** The expression 'the blood of the just' looks forward to the expressions used of Jesus himself in the trial before Pilate (27:19, 24—25). The two examples taken are the first and last murders to be described in the Hebrew bible: Abel (Gn 4:8) and Zechariah (2 Chr 24:20—22). This Zechariah the priest is son not of Barachiah but of Jehoiada. The insertion of 'son of Barachiah' could be due to a copyist who was unaware of the wide meaning of 'prophet' (though Abel is not a prophet in any strict sense), and thought the minor prophet Zechariah was intended (cf Zech 1:1). **36** already prepares for chh 24—25.

l 37—39 Lament over Jerusalem (Lk 13:34—35)—The climax of the judgement on the barrenness of the official Jewish practice of religion, and on the rejection of the messengers sent to Jerusalem, dwells on Jesus' loving attempts to convert Jerusalem. He will now leave the Temple for ever (24:1) and announce its destruction. The 'how often' suggests that Jesus in fact made several visits to Jerusalem, as in Jn, though they are schematically presented as one visit by the synoptics. God's care of his people is compared to that of a mother of her children already in Is 49:15; it is more constant even than that. By his presence he shelters Israel as with the protection of a bird's wings (Ps 17 (18):8; 36 (35):7, etc). This divine care Jesus claims as his own. **39.** Has been taken as a promise of the final conversion of Israel which Paul promises (Rm 11:25). The quotation of Ps 118 (117):26 does suggest this, for it is used both in the original and in Mt 21:9 to welcome the Saviour. But the climax of the condemnation cannot end in a promise of salvation nor is there any sign in Mt of recognition of eventual conversion: contrast 8:12; 21:43; 22:7 (Strecker p. 114—15). This thought may perhaps not be excluded from the original intention of the saying in Jesus' mouth, but Mt sees in the cry only an acknowledgement of the coming judge.

36a 24—25 The Eschatological Discourse—The sixth major section of the gospel is concluded by Christ's teaching on the last times. For 24:1—36 the basic document was Mk 13; with this Mt combines other teachings found also in Lk, so derived from Q, cf § 646a,b, and some proper to himself alone. Mt's discourse falls fairly clearly into two halves: the former (24:1—44) concerning the divine judgement on communities, the latter that on individuals (24:45—25:46; but 24:37—44 could also be allotted to this half).

b 24: 1—44 The Last Times of the Community—Views on the authorship, divisions and interpretation of this passage vary widely. For a partial survey, see § 760a—e. Mt's emphasis here is less than Mk's on the positive value of the persecution of the Apostles, since he has already made this point in 10:17—21, to which, following his principle of grouping in one place all teaching on a single matter, he has removed Mk's material. According to Mt's arrangement three phases are portrayed; (a) **c** Prelude: apostolic preaching received with the hostility which will justify punishment (4—14); (b) Punishment of Jerusalem, but survival of the elect (15—28); (c) Victory of the Kingdom and its final establishment (29—31).

d 1—3 The Disciples' Question (Mk 13:1—4; Lk 21: 5—7)—Immediately after the charges against the scribes and Pharisees and the lament over Jerusalem, Jesus leaves the Temple for the last time (1). From the mount of Olives the full splendour of the Temple could be seen, with the gold plating of its roof and pinnacles glittering in the

sun; even today the Temple enclosure is a moving spectacle **736d** from there. But God would destroy it all (the awkward passives of **2** are 'theological', to avoid using the divine name). When Jesus has taken his seat on the mountain—the formal position of a teacher (5:1; 15:29; Mk 9: 35)—the disciples ask him their double question. The word for 'coming', *parousia*, is used by Mt alone of the evangelists. The word was introduced from pagan usage into Christian by Paul, but the idea of a divine visitation, the 'Day of the Lord', is a commonplace of the OT prophets, cf Am 5:18—20; Is 19:1; Zeph 1:15—18; Dn 7:13—27.

4—14 Prelude: preaching and persecution (Mk 13: **e** 5—13; Lk 21:8—19)—This section prepares for the punishment of Jerusalem by a recital of the traditional signs of the final world-cataclysm (SB 1, 949—51) which appeared in the decades before A.D. 70, and by a prophecy of the persecution of those who preach the gospel. War, plague and famine raged during these years (Tacitus *Hist.* 3, 2, 1; *Ann* 16, 13; Jos.Ant. 20, 2, 5; Ac 11:28), making a savage contrast to the preceding years of peace. But the vv are less an exact description of the events than general terms, reminiscent of the signs which, in prophetic and apocalyptic literature, precede the Day of the Lord (cf Is 8:21; Jer 21:9; Am 4:6—11 etc). Especially the metaphor of 'birthpangs' is used to describe the sufferings which are to precede the birth of the new era (Hos 13:13; Mi 4:9—10; 1 Thes 5:3; Apoc 12:2). This was a period when the appearance of self-styled Messiahs to lead rebellions against the Roman power in Palestine (cf § 715 f) both resulted from and raised to yet higher fever-pitch the hopes of the Jews for a new era of freedom (Jos BJ 2, 13, 4; 6, 5, 4). Several expressions here used occur also in 2 Thes 2:2—11, where Paul is similarly endeavouring to restrain his converts' expectation of an immediate end to the world. It is impossible to establish with certainty a direct connexion between the two passages; they may both be drawing on the same traditional material. B. Orchard has maintained (Bib 29 (1938) 19—42) that the Matthean version is more primitive. But his chief argument is that Mt's version is invariably fuller than Paul's; the conclusion does not necessarily follow. **9—14.** By his removal of **f** Mk 13:9b—13a to the missionary discourse (Mt 10:17—21) Mt alters the whole character of this passage. It is no longer, as in Mk, designed to give instructions and consolation to the disciples for the period of persecution, but rather to underline the guilt and lovelessness (the greatest of all vices to Mt) of the persecutors. **14.** No conclusion may be drawn from this v that the gospel must be preached to all men before the end of the world; the expression used signifies the 'inhabited world' of the hellenistic civilization of the time, centred on the Mediterranean basin. The spread of the gospel to 'the ends of the earth', i.e. to Rome, is a principal theme of Ac (cf 821*ef*). The related theme of the rejection of the gospel-message by the Jews throughout the world, stressed by Ac, may be suggested here; it would certainly be apposite as the climax before the destruction of Judaism. 'Witness to all nations' is not '*against* all nations' (Mt omits the phrase where it has this meaning: 10:14 (Mk 6:11)) but *before* all nations' (8:4; 10:18; cf Trilling p. 127—30). The universal preaching of the gospel will before the destruction of Jerusalem witness before all nations to the guilt of the Jews (cf § 733c).

15—28 Punishment of Jerusalem; Survival of the g Elect (Mk 13:14—23; Lk 21:20—24; 17:23—24, 37)—The destruction of Jerusalem is described in terms which make its meaning clear. **15.** The 'disastrous abomination'

736g of which Dn 9:27 spoke was the altar and statue dedicated to Olympian Zeus set up in the temple by Antiochus Epiphanes in 168 B.C. (2 Mc 6:2), to be a symbol of the destruction of the Jewish faith and people. It is the destruction which is to recur, rather than an exact recurrence of this particular act of defilement. The emperor Gaius did attempt to have his own statue set up in the Temple; but such strong representations were made against this that it was delayed, until his death in A.D. 41 enabled his subordinates to abandon the offensive **h** project. **16—17.** The flight and destruction are described in terms reminiscent of the punishment of Israel in Ezek 7:15—16. The flat roof-top was a favourite place for reading or sleeping. **20.** We may not conclude that Mt would regard flight on a Sabbath day as excluded by the limitation imposed by a 'Sabbath day's journey', for by this time canonists allowed flight to save life (SB 1, 952—3). Though Mt's community still observed the Sabbath, their observance was less, not more, tyrannical than that of their contemporaries (12:1—44 and notes). Perhaps Mt is thinking of the conspicuousness of the fleeing Christians before their opponents, the Jews (Barth p. 92). **21.** The 'distress such as there has never been' recalls the description of the sack of Jerusalem by the Babylonians (Lam 1:12; Bar 2:2) and the punishment of the persecutors and exaltation of the chosen prophesied by Dn (12:1). By means of these allusions the evangelist shows that the destruction which he predicts is similarly **i** a punishment on Israel's infidelity. **22.** The first clear indication that to the punishment is linked a saving deliverance. As at the first destruction of Jerusalem, a faithful remnant shall survive (Am 3:12; Is 4:2—3; 10:19—21; Ezek 6:8—10), God's chosen ones, who will now constitute his chosen people, after the purging away of the unfaithful. Paul already noted the repetition in the history of the Church of the OT situation (Rm 11:5—7). The new people of God is formed of a mere remnant of Israel onto which the Gentiles are grafted **j** (Rm 11:16—17). **23—24.** Seem to be largely a repetition of 5 and 11; hence Lk omits them. Besides false messiahs, false prophets and teachers are a recurrent feature of the NT period (2 Thes 2:3, 9; 2 Pt 2:1—3); since they really have power to work miracles and to prophesy, they can be discerned only by their fruits (7:15—20). **26—28.** Mt adds a short passage whose parallel in Lk (17:23—24, 27) refers to the punishment of Jerusalem. Unless it is simply attracted by the similarity between 26 and 23, it forms the climax of the passage on the judgement of Israel; it is to this that 'the coming of the Son of Man' refers here, as in 10:23 (DBS 6, 1353). Lightning is a feature of divine interventions (Ps 18 (17):14; 97 (96):4; Zach 9:14; Apoc 4:5). The mention of birds of prey indicates how radical is the destruction which God has wrought on a people (Is 18:6; Jer 7:33; 15:3; Ezek 29:5).

737a **29—31 Victory of the kingdom** (Mk 13:24—27; Lk 21:25—28)—After this great trial is described, again in the apocalyptic imagery drawn from the prophets, the establishment of the Kingdom in glory, in the power of the Son of Man. Since Jesus took for Himself the title of Son of Man he was not wholly averse to the use of the apocalyptic language current in his day, foreign though it may seem to us. Though it is not necessary to hold that Mt is here reporting *verbatim* the words used by Jesus, vv may well rest upon his own prediction of his ultimate vindication and that of his community expressed in apocalyptic terms. **29.** The cosmic significance of the event is brought out by means of the astronomical phenomena, used in the OT to describe the Day of the

Lord (Is 13:9—10; 34:4). The same language is used **737** (taken from Jl 2:2) in Ac 2:19—20 to describe the outbreak of the new era inaugurated by the resurrection. They are two different moments in the same event. **30.** The **b** 'sign of the Son of Man', also an astronomical phenomenon (cf v 27 and SB 1, 954—5, 161; Is 60:1), is the sign for the gathering together of his elect (cf Is 11:12). The 'peoples of the earth beat their breast' as a sign of repentance in the last times (Zech 12:10—14). The mention of 'all peoples of the earth' (only in Mt) is a reference to the promise that all nations will have a share in the salvation which stems from Abraham (Gn 12:3, cf Ac 3:25; Gal 3:8—9). Mt particularly stresses that, after the rejection of Jesus by the Jews, salvation will pass to a new chosen race composed alike of Jew and Gentile (cf § 733e). 'The Son of Man coming on the clouds of heaven is the sign predicted to the sanhedrin (26:67), as the sign of inauguration of his reign (cf § 739g). The language is here that of Dn 7:13—14. Since the members of the sanhedrin are themselves to witness it, the moment referred to cannot be taken exclusively as the end of the world, nor yet as the sequel of the destruction of Jerusalem in A.D. 70. As is clear from Jn (13:31; 17:1—4) and the speeches in the early parts of Ac (e.g. 3:13; 7:55—56), this glorification of the Son of Man, which inaugurates his kingdom, basically occurs at the resurrection. But there are successive stages of its manifestation. **31.** The 'loud trumpet' is also part of the **c** Jewish apocalyptic scenario of the Day of the Lord (Zech 9:14; SB 1, 959—60; 2 Thes 4:16) and the gathering of the elect (Is 27:19; 1 Cor 15:52). It is the sign for the re-establishment of Israel, gathered from all the earth into a new religious unity (Is 11:12; 27:13; Jer 29:14; Ezek 20:34, 41). Again Jewish apocalyptic did not envisage a period in which this newly reconstituted Israel would exist upon earth; it was simply the last times; all the emphasis was upon the finality of the divine intervention. A clear awareness of the duration of these last times of the earth was forced even upon the Christian consciousness only by the gradual realization that the world was not immediately to come to an end (cf § 672p).

32—44 Warnings to be on the Watch—The prediction of the outbreak of the last times is followed by four warnings to be on the alert for it, of which the first and last are parables.

32—33 Parable of the Fig-tree (Mk 13:28—29; **d** Lk 21:29—31)—Summer and its harvest is frequently used as a symbol of the messianic times (cf § 721a), a time of judgement and separation for reward or punishment. But it is not only dread of this judgement which is here suggested, but also a more optimistic note, for the shoots and leaves of the fig-tree in spring both naturally and in Jl 2:22 suggest hope, and promise of a fruitful harvest. Jeremias (*Parables* p. 119) suggests that this little simile was originally pronounced in another context, to draw the disciples' attention to the signs of the messianic age in Jesus' own ministry. The presence of the Son of Man 'at the very gates' can be both a threat (Jas 5:9) and an invitation (Apoc 3:20). **34—36. Three e Sayings** (Mk 13:30—32; Lk 21:32—33)—These three sayings, put together by Mk just before the conclusion of his eschatological discourse, were originally independent. The saying of v 34 occurs also Mt 16:28 in a slightly different form: v 35 also Mt 5:17, qq.v. They were, then, floating sayings which could be used to emphasize different teachings of Jesus. **34** cannot be taken to mean that Jesus thought the end of the world would come within a generation. 'All these things' refers globally to the manifestation of the kingdom pictorially described in

737e 4—31; this will begin at the resurrection. **36** has embarrassed the tradition to such an extent that a number of MSS omit it, in whole or in part. The Son's knowledge is put in a category of its own (cf 11:27), above that of men and angels. But, as man, he knew only what he had learnt in the normal human way, and those things which were revealed to him for the needs of his mission. It seems that the date of the final manifestation was not among these. Nor need the disciples know, for even in his glorious state after the resurrection he refuses them this information (Ac 1:8). Cf E. Gutwenger. 'The Problem of Christ's Knowledge', Concilium, 1 (1966) 2, 48—55. It might be urged that, since the original context of the sayings is unknown, the reference of 'all these things' and 'that day' in Jesus' words has similarly been lost; they may not have referred to the Parousia at all. But this merely transfers the problem to the level of the evangelist.

f **37—41 The Need for Vigilance** (Lk 17:26—27, 34—35)—Of these two sayings, given by Lk in his passage on the destruction of Jerusalem, the former indicates the suddenness with which the visitation will come. On the Matthean expression 'coming of the Son of Man' cf § 736d. The latter saying warns of the terrible and final division which God will effect at this judgement (the passives are 'theological' to avoid naming God). **42—44 Parable of the Burglar** (Lk 12:39—40)—A final warning of the suddenness of the impending crisis and the need to be always ready. Originally all the emphasis was on the suddenness of the event; there can have been no allegory intended; in 1 Thes 5:2, 4; 2 Pt 3:10 it is the Day of the Lord itself which is likened to the thief, though here and in Apoc 3:3 it is the Lord himself who is rather curiously allegorized as the thief. Jeremias (Parables, p. 48—51) suggests that Jesus used the case of an actual burglary as a warning of the imminent calamity. Digging through the mud wall is the simplest way of breaking into a Palestinian house.

g **45—51 Parable of the Good or Bad Steward** (Lk 12:42—46)—After the prediction of the punishment of Israel and establishment of the kingdom of the Son of Man, Mt gives three parables on the judgement of individuals (24:45—25:30). Like many of Jesus' parables of judgement, it was probably originally addressed to the leaders of the Jews; it was especially they who needed the warning. This application of the figure of the servant who is put in charge of his absent master's property would be immediately recognized (21.45, 23.13, SB 1, 714). The evangelists apply the parables to their own times and to the needs of their own communities (cf § 724a). Lk applies this parable to the duties of the leaders of the Christian community. **h** But in Mt the application is perhaps more general; instead of Lk's 'steward' he has 'servant', and insists that he is one among many 'fellow-servants' (not in Lk). This is perhaps also a hint of the need for love among fellow members of the community, a favourite theme in Mt. **48.** '"My master is taking his time"' does not imply that the evangelists feels any problem about the delay of the final coming, for other sayings in Mt imply its proximity (e.g. 10:23; 16:28). It is simply part of the picture of the parable, showing an additional factor in the servant's temptation to infidelity (Trilling p. 44).

738a **25:1—13 Parable of the Ten Bridesmaids**—From its position it is clear that Mt intends this parable to be a lesson on preparedness for the future judgement, but that of the individual (as all 24:45—25:46) rather than that of communities (as 24:1—44). A similar parable was told by R. Eliezer (c. A.D. 90) of the

necessity of being prepared for death: many guests are **738a** invited to a feast, but only those who hold themselves in constant readiness, wearing their best clothes, are admitted when the sudden summons comes (SB 1, 878). The concluding v 13 is Mt's own interpretation (cf § 724d), for 'staying awake' is not the sort of preparedness demanded by the story; all the girls fall asleep, even those who are praised. If any allegory is intended, it may be that oil stands for a virtue or good work, cf the wedding-garment of 22:11. As it stands, the whole story **b** seems to have been given an allegorical twist to fit the likening of the Messiah to a bridegroom; this comparison was perhaps Paul's own development (2 Cor 11:2), since it is not found in Jewish writings (TWNT 4 (1942) 1095); the comparison of the Messianic times to a marriage-feast was common, but it was God who was cast as bridegroom of his people Israel. But cf § 720m. The necessity for the sake of allegory of making the division between those who enter (the kingdom, cf 5:20; 7:21 etc) and those who are excluded, makes the lamps functionless in the story. They might be expected to be used for the torchlight procession which is still a feature of Palestinian weddings, to accompany the groom to his waiting bride; but we hear nothing of a procession, and the girls are waiting only to take their lamps into the house. **1.** The **c** word used for 'went to meet' suggests that it is no ordinary bridegroom, since its normal use is of the solemn procession to meet the emperor on a formal visit to a city. **5.** The delay is part of the story, and need not be allegorized of the delay of Christ's second coming (cf note to 24:48). **11.** The cry 'Lord, Lord' is more appropriate to Christ than to the bridegroom of the story; again the allegory shines through. It recalls Jesus' warning that calling on his name is not enough (7:21 and note).

14—30 Parable of the Talents (Lk 19:12—27)— **d** The last of Mt's three parables on the individual judgement, it is intended by the evangelist as an allegory: the 'master' (literally 'Lord') represents the Messiah at his second coming, the 'servants' Christians with their various gifts which they must use to the best of their ability, and the reward, 'your master's happiness' (the expression, 21, 23, can mean 'marriage-feast', a symbol of the kingdom of heaven: SB 1, 972—3; § 720m; Mt 25:1—13), the joys of heaven. But these elements are absent from Lk's version: the master is clearly described as a nobleman, the reward is an earthly one (power over ten or five cities) without any hint of a heavenly banquet or eternal damnation (as Mt v 30). The sums of money involved are more moderate, one mina (= 100 denarii, so wages for 100 days casual labour cf 20:2) instead of talents (= sixty minas). But the allegory breaks down at the character of the 'master', 'a hard man', reaping where he has not sown etc; this cannot originally have been intended of Jesus. Perhaps, as so many other **e** parables of judgement, this too was originally directed to the religious leaders, the administrators of God's patrimony, warning them that they were to be called to account. It is suggested that through their timid scrupulosity, based on the conception of God as a tyrannical and exacting task-master, instead of a loving father, they prevented his patrimony from bearing its due fruit. The evangelist legitimately applies this lesson to the situation of the Church (cf § 724a). **29—30.** As often, two generalizing conclusions as to the moral of the story are added (cf § 724d). The first must have been added at a pre-Matthean stage, for it occurs in Lk also here (as well as in Mt 13:12 and Mk 4:25, Lk 8:18). The second occurs also in Mt 22:13, and v 30b six times in Mt (cf note on 8:12b).

738f **31—46 The Last Judgement**—This passage constitutes the key-stone to the edifice of Mt's morality. After the three parables about the final judgement of the individual, warning Christians to be prepared for its unforeseeable occurrence, we learn the criteria by which this judgement will take place. Judgement and retribution have been ideals which recur at frequent intervals throughout the gospel; they are a major preoccupation in Mt more than in the other gospels (10:15; 11:24; 12:36—37; 13:36—42, 49—50; 16:27; 18:9; 19:28; § 717e; 721g), and often also under the heading of conditions for entry into the kingdom (5:20; 7:21; 18:3; 19:23; 23:13). Such judgement-scenes as this occur frequently in Jewish literature of about the time of Christ (SB 4, 1199—1212). J. A. T. Robinson has made an ingenious attempt ('The "Parable" of the Sheep and Goats', NTS 2 (1955/6), 225ff) to show that the scene is built by Mt himself from the little parable in 32b—33, fused with the sayings of Jesus which give the ground on which judgement is given. Introduction, parallelism and all references to separation and rewards or punishments are to be attributed to Mt himself. (This interpretation is, incidentally, dictated by this author's general view of Jesus' eschatology, according to which Jesus had no expectation of a second coming; all references to his second coming are due to the early community). It is certainly true that some traditions in the early Church laid more stress on the imminent second coming than the sayings of Jesus demand; but all references to it cannot
g be denied to Christ himself. It is also true that Mt frequently stresses the **transcendent qualities of Christ** in a way which reaches a climax here (cf § 711bc): in **31** the glory is Christ's and the angels too, whereas in 16:27 he is to come in the glory of the Father, and in Mk 8:38 the angels seem to be part of the Father's glory, not Christ's. Only in v 31 and in 19:28 in all the Bible, except Apoc 3:21, is the Son represented as enthroned; though this occurs in the apocryphal Book of Enoch (SB 4, 1200), the great R. Aqiba (c. 120) was decried for blasphemy for suggesting that the Messiah could be enthroned beside God (SB 1, 978—9). In 34 Christ is represented as king of the Kingdom, as is done only by Mt (13:41; 16:28); elsewhere the kingdom is the Kingdom of the Father ('the Kingdom of Heaven' means 'God's kingdom', cf § 715f). Elsewhere Christ seems to be only the witness of the judgement (10:32— 33; Mk 8:38), but here he is the judge himself—unless the evasion of Jeremias is adopted (*Parables* p. 207—8): Christ does not pronounce sentence but merely 'announces the judgement of the Father'. This representation of Christ the Lord and Judge of the world may well be due here to Mt; it is given by the thoroughly Matthean v 31 and by the insertion of the Matthean phrase 'of my Father' into v 34, by which the 'King' is designated as the Son. It is due to the profound understanding of the position already claimed by Jesus during his life (e.g. the
h claim before Pilate to be King: 27:11). Similarly the theme of **fraternal love** is one stressed especially by Mt, and the terminology of the key phrase **(40, 45)** 'I tell you solemnly, if so far as you did this to one of the least of these brothers of mine, you did it to me' is predominantly Matthean (*eph' hoson, adelphos, elachistos*). But the sentiment is amply attested by other sayings of Jesus (10:40—42; 18:5; Mk 9:42; Lk 10:16; Jn 13:20). The importance of the works of fraternal love has been stressed constantly throughout the gospel (5:21—48; 12:11—12; 15:18—20; 18:10—35; 19:17—22; 22:39— 40; 23:23). The fulfilment of this commandment now provides the sole criterion on which men are judged.

There is a close rabbinic parallel to this (SB 1, 1212), **738i** in which a man after death is judged by his practice of the works of mercy. But in none of the parallels does the central point, the presence of Christ in his members, occur. The realization that love shown to man, even only implicitly for the sake of Christ, is love shown to Christ himself, can come only from Jesus' own teaching. This again links up with another characteristic theme emphasized by Mt: the continued presence of Christ in his Church (cf § 711f). **32.** In Jewish judgement- **i** scenes the gentiles appear, if at all, only to receive punishment; but here all nations equally are gathered to be judged by the same criterion of love. A mixed flock of sheep and goats is common enough in Palestine; they must be separated at night, since goats are more sensitive to cold and need to be kept warm. Sheep often represent Christians in Mt (e.g. 10:16; 18:12), as the Messiah is a shepherd (9:36 and note). No reflection is implied on the character of goats: Arab children more often keep a kid than a lamb for a pet. **34, 41.** God calls all men to be saved (1 Tm 2:4). According to Jewish tradition (SB 1, 137—9) Satan, or Sammael, and the angels under his command were driven out of heaven as punishment for their part in the fall of man.

26—28 Passion, Death and Resurrection of 739a Christ—Unlike the rest of the gospels, made up from incidents and sayings preserved more or less independently, the narrative of the passion early formed a single whole, due to its central importance in Christian preaching. From the first these events were seen to be the accomplishment of the prophecies of the OT (e.g. already in the formula which was traditional as early as Paul's day, 1 Cor 15:3—5): Christ is said to have suffered 'in accordance with the scriptures'. The evangelists concentrate particularly on those incidents in the passion by which the prophecies are fulfilled; they are interested less in the narration of the actual events than in showing, by means of the scripture, their significance. The major **b** prophecy in showing the meaning of the passion is that of the suffering servant of the Lord in Is. This text, though seldom explicitly quoted, formed the background of Jesus' own thought on the passion (cf § 711c); it is alluded to already in 1 Cor 15:3 'for our sins' (cf Is 53:4—12) and lurks behind much of the gospel passion narrative. Of this prophecy the central theme is the final exaltation of God's servant through suffering. This servant is God's people and yet is an individual partially distinguished from God's people, since he takes their sins upon himself, and, by his atonement for them, leads the whole people of God with him to exaltation. It is from here that a biblical theology of the Passion must take its starting-point. Another nucleus of references in the passion narratives is to Ps 22 (21), which is constantly recalled, especially in Mt; on its message in this context cf § 762m.

26:1—5 Conspiracy against Jesus (Mk 14 1—2; Lk **c** 22:1—2)—The account of the Passion begins with a clear statement that the responsibility lies with the authorities of the Jewish nation. Mt here omits the scribes, included by Mk; he leaves them out of the Passion narrative also in vv parallel to Mk 14:43 and 15:1. It has been suggested that this is because Mt himself was a Christian scribe (cf 13:52) and wanted to spare his Jewish colleagues. But he does not do this in 5:20; 7:29; 8:19—20; 27:41, or the prophecies of the Passion (16:21; 20:18). It is simply that he has an exact idea of the function of a scribe as an expert legal adviser, and regularly removes them when there is no legal or exegetical question involved, but introduces them when there is (12:38;

39c 21:15—16). Here the reason for their omission may be that he thought their role as scribes was only advisory and that they had no authority to make decisions (similarly 26:47; 27:1). **2.** Mt prefixes yet one more intimation that Jesus expected and willingly accepted his Passion cf § 731*k*. The appellation 'Son of Man' was Jesus' own self-designation in this connexion, cf §§ 676*k—n*, 534*c*. **3.** Joseph Caiaphas was high priest A.D. 18—36. **5.** Mt increases their malice: they do not merely fear the possibility of a riot on Jesus' behalf (Mk); they are certain it would happen (cf § 724*e*).

d 6—13 Anointing at Bethany (Mk 14:3—9; cf Lk 7:36—50; Jn 12:1—8)—Daube p. 301 points out that the Passion narratives are anxious to show that a number of shameful defilements (*ninwul*) were avoided during the Passion, especially in connexion with Christ's burial e.g. disfigurement of the body by crushing of the bones (Jn 19:33*b*, 36), burial in the criminals' common grave (Mt 27:60), without proper grave-clothes (Mk 15:46) cf § 742*d*. This episode obviates the accusation that he was buried unanointed, though Mk at least is still uneasy about the validity of this explanation, since he shows the women attempting to anoint him on Easter morning (Mk 16:1—2—Mt omits it). The episode cannot, however, have been invented, since the early Church would surely have included some reference to the Resurrection (TWNT 5 (1954), 712). Nor need its positioning here, after the notice that 'It will be Passover in two days time', contradict Jn 12:1 ('six days before the Passover'); it is undated in Mt and Mk, but it is inserted here, after the notice that the decision which led to the crucifixion has already been taken, to link it as closely as possible to the burial. Since Mk and Mt relate that his head was anointed (unlike Lk and Jn) there may be an allusion here, on the threshold of the passion, to the Messiahship (Messiah = anointed) of Jesus. It also emphasizes Jesus' calm foreknowledge of his passion. In Mk and Mt all the interest centres on Jesus: the woman is not named (as in Jn), nor said to be a sinner (as in Lk's possible parallel). Mk does not even record the presence of the disciples, who are introduced by Mt (v 8). Mt also characteristically adds to the solemnity and calm dignity of the scene by removing Mk's 'she broke the jar' (which perhaps indicates her reckless generosity), 'they were angry with her' and **e** 'leave her alone'. **6.** Bethany, a village on the shoulder of the Mount of Olives, is about forty minutes walk from Jerusalem. Jesus was staying there during the week (21:17; Mk 11:11—12). It was the home of Martha, Mary and Lazarus (Jn 11:1—44). We do not know the relationship between this family and Simon the leper. The relationship between the incident of the anointing and Lk's account of the repentant prostitute is complicated; Jn 12:1—8 has possibly interwoven the two, but not entirely satisfactorily (cf comm. in loc.) We are not justified in concluding that the same woman performed both actions. **10—11.** Jesus does not belittle almsgiving but defends the woman by two arguments (a) Christological, that this service to Christ will not always be possible; (b) technical rabbinic, among recognized 'good works' burying the dead ranked higher than almsgiving.

f 14—16 Judas betrays Jesus (Mk 14:10—11; Lk 22:3—6)—In this short passage Mt again stresses the malice of the chief priests, by underlining their desire to pay (Gr. *thelō* in Mt always indicates determination). He sees in the price paid (thirty shekels, the price to be paid as compensation for a slave accidentally killed Ex 21:32) the fulfilment of scripture (Zech 11:12) 'Iscariot' is probably a corruption of '*iš sakariot* ('man of payments')

i.e. the treasurer, cf note on 10:4. It is fruitless to specul- **739f** ate on his motives; Jn (12:6) says that he stole out of avarice, but in a different connexion. His name and patronymic are both those of members of the Maccabee family, leaders of Jewish nationalism two centuries earlier. Judas is also the name of several nationalistic rebels in the first cent. It is therefore not impossible that Judas was a name chosen in nationalistic families, and that Iscariot, having joined Jesus in the hope of a nationalistic messianic movement, could not be converted to a true understanding of the nature of the Kingdom, and betrayed his leader. **16.** The third 'From that moment' (cf 4:17; 16:21) ushers in the supreme moment of the Passion.

17—19 Preparations for the Passover Supper g (Mk 14:12—16; Lk 22:7—13)—Mt gives only the barest outline, disregarding all Mk's practical details; thus he achieves the same impression of majestic command as at 21:2—6, leaving his reader to puzzle over the materialities if he will. The kernel of Mt's account is the commanding 'My time is near' (v 18). Jesus does not question or explain; he states, and goes forward to his passion with full knowledge and utter control.

The date of the last supper—The synoptics on the one **h** hand and Jn on the other give divergent accounts cf Mk 14:12 Jn 18:28, and A. Jaubert, *La Date de la Cène* (1957) and NTS 7 (1960/1) 1—30. The most acceptable solution is that Jn is following the official solar calendar of the temple authorities, and the synoptics the lunar calendar adopted by the Qumran sect and a number of others. The Last Supper, then, was celebrated on the Tuesday, and the crucifixion took place on the Friday, but the evangelists seem to represent in one cycle of 24 hours what in fact took place in three days; such foreshortening is, however, explicable on literary and liturgical grounds cf § 761*f—g*.

20—25 Treachery of Judas Foretold (Mk 14:17—21; **i** Lk 22:14, 21—23)—The passage underlines once again two points, cardinal for the evangelists, Jesus' foreknowledge, and so freedom, and (v 24) that the Passion fulfils the prophecies. **20.** The reclining posture is (Jeremias, *Eucharistic Words* pp. 48—49) a sign that it was a festive meal. Normally the Jews of this time ate sitting, but the Passover must be eaten reclining, as a sign of relaxation in freedom. The arrangement of the room was presumably (as in the Roman *triclinium*) in the form of three sides of a hollow square. **22, 25.** The two forms of address are significant: the other disciples say 'Lord', expressing their reverence, as always in Mt; Judas says 'Rabbi', a form used in Mt only by Jesus' opponents, cf § 711*b*. **23.** Mt here and in 25 makes Jesus identify Judas, whereas in Mk he spoke only of the heinous betrayal by an unidentified member of the Twelve. See § 761*h*.

26—29 The Institution of the Eucharist (Mk 14: **j** 22—25; Lk 22:15—20; cf 1 Cor 11:23—25). For a description of the character of the meal, see § 761*in*. In the only significant differences between the accounts Mt makes minor clarifications of Mk's version: he changes 'to them' (v 22) to 'to the disciples', inserts 'Take, eat' and 'drink' (for Mk v 23 'they drank'), explains 'for many' (v 24) as meaning 'for the forgiveness of sins', and adds 'until I drink *with you*' to v 25.

30—35 The Disciples' Denial Foretold (Mk 14:26—31; Lk 22:39)—Further evidence of Jesus' calm foreknowledge, and a reminder that the Passion fulfils the scripture (cf § 739*a*). **31.** 'You will all lose faith in me'; better 'I shall be a stumbling-block to you all'. Jesus is aware, at any rate by now, that his disciples are not yet to share his suffering (? contrast 20:22) **34.**

739j Mt has only one cook-crow (cf 74—75), against Mk's two.

k 36—46 Gethsemane: the Agony (Mk 14:32—42; Lk 22:40—46)—Mt's version differs from Mk's (see § 761gh) by slight expansion and clarification; He stresses (38, 40) that the Christian's watching must be with Christ by inserting 'watch with me'. His homiletic interest is also seen in that Jesus comes 'to the disciples' and addresses his reproach to them in the plural (40, cf 45) instead of to Peter alone as Mk v 37. In Mt the disciples represent all Christians, to whom the reproach is therefore conceived as indirectly addressed. **37b.** Mt moderates Mk's 'sudden fear', a far stronger expression in the Gr., into 'sadness'; he is habitually reticent in describing any emotion in Jesus (cf § § 711c, 729b). **42.** Jesus' complete acceptance becomes still clearer. The prayer is composed by Mt, using several sayings of Jesus: 'if this cup cannot pass me by (a more resigned negative form of the first prayer) without my drinking it (cf 20:22; Jn 18:11) Your will be done' (a phrase from the Lord's prayer, 6:10). There is surely also an allusion to Ps 40 (39):7—8.

l 47—56 Gethsemane: the Arrest (Mk 14:43—52; Lk 22:47—53)—For Mk's account, see § 761m. Mt considerably expands this opening scene of the Passion narrative, stressing—by inserting words to explain the actions—three points: the treachery of Judas, the majestic power of Jesus and his obedience to the Scriptures. **47.** Mt here and frequently in the Passion narrative omits the part played by the scribes. Is this because he was himself a scribe? **49—50.** Mt alone mentions Judas' greeting—probably the Hebrew 'shalom' = 'peace'—as he gives Jesus the kiss of respect accorded to a rabbi (SB 1, 995). Jesus greets Judas still with the warm and intimate greeting of a friend: perhaps there is a reminiscence of Sir 37:2; Jesus' next phrase to Judas (literally 'for what you have come') cannot be a question, and is probably to be translated 'Do what you have come for'. The arrest is carried out entirely by Jesus' permission; He remains in majestic control throughout the scene; only after His permission do they 'come forward' (v 50); Jesus prevents any attempt to deliver Himself, lest the scriptures remain unfulfilled (52—54, cf § 739a) stressing his continued union to his Father (53). **52—54.** Mt underlines Jesus' complete control of the situation, and his submission to the Father's will expressed in Scripture. Underlying 52b may well be a proverb (cf Apoc 13:10). **53.** The conception of angels, so common in Mt, is here peculiarly Jewish, attested also in the squadrons of angels so active in the War Scroll of Qumran.

740a 57—68 Jesus before the Sanhedrin (Mk 14:53—65; Lk 22:54—55, 63—71; cf Jn 18:12—14, 19—24)— The order of events and their significance are discussed § 761o—y. Mt as usual clarifies Mk's account. E.g. in **60—61** He removes the impression that the specific charge was false or that the witnesses did not agree, and states specifically that there were the two witnesses necessary for testimony to stand. The version of the saying here given is so close to that reported elsewhere in the Gospels as having been uttered by Jesus that Mt perhaps overlooked that Jesus never said he would destroy the Temple. In **62** Mt puts an adjuration in the High Priest's mouth which Jesus could not disregard without sacrilege; this is perhaps to explain why he breaks the silence which fulfils the scripture. In **64** Jesus' reply is much more cautiously phrased: Mt has 'You say that I am' (though this is also given by some texts of Mk). The words translated 'Moreover I tell you' mean literally 'except I tell you', and make the following statement clearly a qualification

of Jesus' claim. Mt is perhaps stressing that Jesus has **740c** not yet been 'proclaimed Son of God in all his power through his resurrection' (Rm 1:4; cf Phil 2:9; Ac 2:36). But by 'from this time onwards' he stresses also the immediacy of the vision of Jesus' triumph; another argument that it cannot refer to the Parousia. **67—68 Mockery.** Mt's addition to the text of 68 (which should read 'Play the prophet, Christ!' only) shows that his mockers are thinking of the Messiah as high priest, for the high priest has the gift of prophecy (Jos BJ 1, 68; Jn 11:51). At Qumran the tradition that the Messiah will be a priest is as important as the tradition that he will be king. For Mt this mockery is especially suitable since it implies that the councillors (among them priests) did the mocking. The version of Mk, Lk and Jn attributes it, with more probability, to others (attendants, Lk, Jn).

69—75 Peter's Denials (Mk 14:66—72; Lk 22:56— **b** 62; Jn 18:17—18, 25—27)—The emphasis placed upon this incident by the evangelists goes against Mt's usual tendency to spare the apostles (§ 724e) and especially Peter cf § 728j. Mt even increases the publicity of the denial 'in front of them all' (**70**). Mt removes some of the awkwardness left by Mk's join of the two narratives (see § 761z): he omits the cockcrow after the first denial, and makes the second servant-girl 'another' (**71**). Mt makes a fine crescendo in the denials: at first Peter merely pretends to misunderstand: then he denies with an oath; finally he calls down curses on himself. **73.** Mt explains how she knows that he is a Galilean. Their pronunciation of 'aleph, 'ayin and heth tended to be confused (SB 1, 517). **75.** Mt magnifies also Peter's repentance: 'he wept "bitterly"'.

27:1—2 Jesus Taken before Pilate (Mk 15:1; Lk **741** 22:66; 23:1)—**1.** The Gr. cannot mean 'met in council' (JB) but must, as always in the NT, mean 'took counsel'; this is indicated also by the run of the sentence. There is therefore no evidence for an official session of the Sanhedrin (cf § 761p—t). **2.** Pontius Pilatus was prefect of Judaea A.D. 25/27—35 (Mt gives him the correct title; the appellation 'procurator' was introduced only in A.D. 44). He is represented as harsh and rapacious by Josephus and Philo, but they both have axes to grind. He could not, certainly, understand the complicated and bitter Jewish religious prejudices. The mainspring of his activity in Judaea seems to have been a punctilious loyalty to Rome; it was this trait which the Jews played upon to secure Jesus' condemnation (cf § 741c). There is no reason to doubt that, as other governors, he resided when in Jerusalem at the erstwhile royal palace of Herod (now known as 'David's Tower') and exercised judgement there. It is at the highest point of the town (whence Mk 15:8) and similar scenes of the mob interceding there with the governor are recorded by Josephus. Cf Benoit pp. 316—39.

3—10 Death of Judas—An account of Judas' fate is **b** given also in Ac 1:18—20. Each rests on popular tradition, but unmistakably shows also the style of Mt and Lk respectively: they must have put the traditions in writing, and in slightly different form. At the basis of each is the conviction that Judas' death fulfilled the scriptures. Mt's version is influenced by two different texts of Zech 9:13 'Taking the thirty shekels of silver, I threw them into the Temple of the Lord, into the treasury' (Peshitto version, cf Mt vv 5—6) or '. . . to the potter' (MT, cf Mt vv 7—10). But the field of the potter seems to be a confused reminiscence of Jer 32:6—15 and Jer 18—19 (whence Mt attributes the quotation to Jer instead of Zech). The strained character of this reminiscence, and the firm traditional localization of

1b *Haqeldama* (Aram. for 'field of blood') in the potters' quarter of Jerusalem, suggest that the Jerusalem community knew that Judas was buried there, and were seeking to interpret this fact. It was the quarter of Jerusalem where refuse was commonly thrown (2 (4) Kgs 23:6, 13–14), whose perpetually burning fires and odours of decay suggested the fires of Hell or Gehenna (Enoch 26–27—a corruption of its name *Ge' Hinnom*). Judas' burial-place was then, full of associations. **5.** His mode of suicide recalls that of the Ahithophel (2 Sm 17:23) who had betrayed his master David, as Judas the Messiah.

c 11–26 Jesus before Pilate (Mk 15:2–15; Lk 23:2–5; 17–25; Jn 18:28–40; 19:12–16)—On the Markan account see § 762a–e. Mt increases the malice of both people and leaders. He removes Mk v 8 with its suggestion that the crowd was undecided for any particular prisoner and attributes the jealousy of handing over Jesus, to them all, not just to the leaders. They do not need to be persuaded by the chief priests. Their deliberate decision is stressed by the triple use of *thelō* (15, 17, 21) which normally in Mt emphasizes freedom of choice. On the other hand blame is shifted off Pilate by making their cry impersonal 'Let him be crucified' (22, 23) instead of Mk's 'Crucify him'. Mt's two insertions are in the same sense. 19, 24–25 are peculiar to Mt and contain many of his linguistic characteristics. They are more important for their theological than their historical value. The theme of the judge's wife who pleads for the accused is known elsewhere in Jewish literature (SB 1, 1032): the point is to contrast the gentile pleading for Jesus' release with the Jews urging his conviction (cf 2:1–18). It is unlikely, though not impossible that the Roman governor acted out his decision by carrying out the purely Jewish rite for washing away blood guilt prescribed in Dt 21:1–9. The biblical cry of the crowd in 25 contrasts by its complicatedness with the one-word shouts adopted from Mk's account. The verses, like 3–10, were probably first put in writing by him, on the basis of tradition (Kilpatrick, p. 96). Whatever the original sense of v 19 (Trilling, p. 67–68 suggests that it was to increase Pilate's guilt by showing him pronounce sentence in spite of a heaven-sent warning), Mt uses these two insertions, the Roman and Jewish sides of the coin respectively, to increase the guilt of the Jews: the Romans are prepared to acquit Jesus, and the Jews accept the guilt as a 'whole people' (Mt uses the expression which often signifies the chosen people of Israel, instead of the more casual 'crowd' of 15, 24; no doubt he has in mind the fulfilment **d** of their curse in the destruction of Jerusalem). **26. Scourging** normally followed sentence to death by crucifixion; the consequent weakness hastened the condemned's death on the cross. There were various degrees of severity possible: the mildest form could be imposed as a minor correction, or even as a warning if there were insufficient grounds for conviction (this was the form earlier suggested by Pilate: Lk 23:16). Under the more severe forms the victims often died; the *flagellum*, here employed, was used also to inflict the death penalty (Horace *Satires*, 1, 2, 41; Cicero, *Rab. Perd.* 4, 12).

e 27–31 Jesus Crowned with Thorns (Mk 15:16–20; Jn 19: 1–3)—For Mk's account see § 762f. Mt tidies up Mk's scene. There the disordered acts of mockery give an impression of riotous and light-hearted derision; Mt arranges the scene: first Jesus is robed and crowned, then there is an orderly succession, almost a procession, of acts of homage. **28.** There are two historical details more exact than Mk's account: Mt says Christ was first stripped, whereas Mk assumes that he was still naked **741e** after the scourging; Mt's version is more likely if in fact the mockery was at an earlier stage in the trial. In Mt he is clothed with a scarlet cloak, the normal cloak of a soldier; Mk interprets this as it was intended: to represent the emperor's purple.

32–38 The Crucifixion (Mk 15:21–27; Lk 23:26–34; **742a** Jn 19:17–24)—See § 762g–j. Mt changes few details of Mk's account: **32** he omits Alexander and Rufus, presumably not known in his community. **34.** He changes Mk's 'myrrh' to gall in order to make a reminiscence of Ps 69 (68):21 (cf § 739a). Jesus' complete freedom and control are emphasized: 'he did not wish to drink'. **35.** The actual horror of crucifixion is passed even more cursorily, with a mere participle. **37.** Mt gives the detail which tells us the shape of the cross, †. To the inscription he adds 'This is Jesus . . . ', but he frequently inserts this demonstrative (3:17; 12:23; 14:2) and the Holy Name.

39–44 The Mockery of Christ on the Cross (Mk 15:29–32; Lk 23:35–43; Jn significantly omits) also fulfils the prophecy Ps 22 (21):7; Jer 18:16. The dignity and divinity of Christ are here seen in paradoxical clarity: at the depths of his wretchedness they still recognize (twice 40, 43) that he claims to be Son of God—recognition found nowhere else, which constitutes at the same time Jesus' triumph and their self-condemnation, especially since their mocking quotation of Ps 22 (21):9 is to be fulfilled by the resurrection. By introducing twice the expression 'Son of God' Mt is surely referring to the testing of a just Son of God in Wis 2:13–20 which many phrases evoke.

45–50 The Death of Jesus (Mk 15:33–37; Lk **b** 23:44–46; Jn 19:28–30)—See § 762l–n. Mt gives the Heb. version of Jesus' cry, which makes the misunderstanding more easily intelligible; his community seem to be familiar, apart from Gr., only with Heb. (Kilpatrick, 103–5). **47–49.** Mt allows the gesture, a taunt according to Mk, to be understood as an act of kindness on the part of one individual (as Jn 19:29), for the gibe is uttered only by 'the rest of them'. They perhaps try to prevent him giving it, for Mt's imperative is singular: 'Wait! Let's see . . . ' against Mk's plural: 'Wait and see . . . '.

51–56 Effects of Jesus' Death (Mk 15:38–41; Lk **c** 23:45–49)—See § 762op. Mt adds vv 51b–53 to Mk's narrative, thus completing the picture of the effects of the crucifixion: the end of Judaism (51), the fulfilment of the promises of the OT and the beginning of the resurrection (52–53), the acknowledgement of Christ by the Gentiles (54), cf N. A. Dahl, 'Die Passionsgeschichte bei Mt', NTS 2 (1955/6) 28. **51a.** Earthquake is, in the Bible, the accompaniment of the Lord's visitation in judgement (Jg 5:4; Zech 14:5; Jer 51:29), especially at the fall of a nation; Mt then understands the rending of the veil primarily in this sense. **52–53.** The rebirth of Israel and the incorporation of the nations into Israel is to be accompanied at the last times by the rising of the dead from their tombs (Is 26:15–19; Ezek 37:1–14). The entry of the faithful of the OT into the holy city of Jerusalem ushers in the messianic era (Is 40–55 passim). The Jerusalem here envisaged is not primarily the earthly but the heavenly city (Apoc 3:12; 21:2–10; cf Heb 11:10; 12:22–23). **54.** In Mt not only the centurion but his men too become the first to acknowledge the great event and so be the first-fruits of the Gentiles who are to go to make up the new Israel (cf § 733e). Their 'great fear' is a recognition that the hand of God is at work; cf note on 14:26–27.

57–61 The Burial (Mk 15:42–47; Lk 23:50–56; Jn **d**

742d 19:38—42)—See § 762q—s. Mt is concerned especially to mitigate the shame of the criminal's burial: Joseph is a 'rich' man (this also perhaps fulfils Is 53:9) and a disciple of Jesus. He had himself hewn out a sepulchre (a more dignified word is used than Mk's 'grave'), which is now said to be new and his own. He notes also that the linen cloth was 'clean'. In this way the dignity of Jesus' burial and even temporary resting-place is shown.

e **62—66 The Guard at the Tomb**—A number of difficulties in this episode (first written down by Mt, and given by him alone) have led critics to describe it as 'an apologetic legend, invented later' (Grass, *Ostergeschehen und Osterberichte*, p. 23). Its theme is to refute the slander that Jesus' body was stolen by his disciples. The action of the chief priests and Pharisees is certainly unlikely on a Sabbath, though perhaps an exception to the Sabbath-regulations might be found to legitimize it. It is surprising that the Jews should have taken so seriously Jesus' prediction of three days, which had been uttered to the disciples often enough (though not understood by them), but in the presence of His opponents only in 26:61. The excuse which they later tell the guards to give (28:13), that they fell asleep while the body was stolen is so transparently self-contradictory that it is hard to believe that it was invented by lawyers. But in the earliest preaching of the Resurrection more emphasis was put on the positive evidence in the form of Christ's appearances than on the negative evidence of the empty tomb.

743a **28:1—10 The Resurrection** (Mk 16:1—8, Lk 24:1—12; Jn 20:1—10)—The problem of the divergencies between the accounts of the resurrection appearances in the four evangelists is notorious. The major difficulty is that with the exception of 28:9—10, they are located by Mt (28:7, 10, 16—20; 26:32), and presupposed by Mk (16:7; 14:28) to be in Galilee, while Lk 24 and Jn 20:11—29 locate them in Judaea and Jerusalem. (The enigmatic Jn 21 also mentions an appearance in Galilee; but this stands wholly isolated). Any attempt to harmonize is excluded: the frantic journeying between the two places required may not be quite impossible (a week's march each way); but certainly Mt does not envisage that the Twelve stayed in Jerusalem a whole week (Jn 20:26) before obeying the command of Mt 28:10; their journey then would, besides, be pointless. In Lk 24:49 the disciples are explicitly forbidden to leave Jerusalem. The earliest preaching (1 Cor 15:3—7—it is a summary formula to be learnt by heart: Gerhardsson p. 296—7) contains

b no reference to the place of the apparitions. A courageous solution is that of Koch in *Die Auferstehung Christi*: Galilee was in fact the place of the apparitions. But in order to express the unity of Christ's death and resurrection, a theme so prominent in Jn, who regards the two events as aspects of the one movement of Christ's glorification, they were dramatically located in Jerusalem (pp. 45—51). The actual place of the apparitions is important only in so far as it deepens our understanding of the message of Christ. Koch also points out (p. 44) that it would have been reasonable for the disciples to flee home immediately after Jesus' arrest (cf 26:56). But the predictions always insist that Jesus will 'go before' them into Galilee (26:32; 28:7, 10): this is required also by Jn 20:1—10.

c The **episode of the empty tomb** is strangely neglected in the preaching of the early Church; it appears nowhere in Paul or Ac, our two earliest witnesses to this preaching. All their stress on the reality of the Resurrection comes from the positive evidence of eye-witnesses of the risen Christ, rather than the negative evidence of the **74**: empty tomb (e.g. 1 Cor 15:3—7). Their silence on the episode of the empty tomb may be due to the fact that, at any rate in the synoptics, the witnesses are women, whose testimony was not valid in Jewish law. Others (e.g. Grass p. 23) say that the episode is a late and legendary invention (but it is admitted that apologetically the testimony of women had no value; it is hard to think of any other reason for its invention (cf Lk 24:11, 42—44); cf Bultmann p. 287). In Mt the purpose of the **d** account is to interpret the event and show why the disciples returned to Galilee; both of these elements occur twice. **1.** 'After the Sabbath': the expression refers to the period from sunset on Saturday till sunrise on Sunday; further precision is given by 'towards dawn'. The holy women, disciples of Jesus, come in Mt merely to see the tomb. This is better motivation than in Mk, where they come to anoint the body, unaware that Jesus was anointed already at Bethany (Mt 26:6—13), that in Palestine it is vain to anoint a body after so long (cf Jn 11:39), and forgetting that they had themselves seen the stone rolled into its socket (cf 27:61). In Mt it is just a visit of love. **2—4a.** Mk's 'young man' is, according to Mt, an angel with all the biblical panoply which authenticates a divine message. On earthquakes cf 26:51 and note; on the garment white as snow cf Dn 7:9; Apoc 1:14; the effect of such a divine apparition is prostration (Ezek 1:28; Dn 8:17; 10:9) and fear (cf 14:26—27 and note). An angelic interpreter is, in the later prophetic writers, the usual medium of divine revelation. All this serves to add weight to his message. **4b—8.** The point of the episode for Mt **e** is the message to the disciples, leading them to the meeting with Christ in Galilee. Mt omits all mention of proof that the tomb is empty; they do not even seem to accept the angel's invitation to 'see the place' (v 6b) before hurrying to fulfil their commission. Their obedience is stressed by its expression in the exact words of the command (8a, 7a) Mk ends his passage (v 8) with an emphatic statement that fear kept them from delivering the message. Perhaps he wished to emphasize that the witness of the disciples was entirely independent of the women. Mt removes this statement. **9—10.** Finally the command is reinforced by Jesus himself. The repetition of the command by Christ himself presumably overcame the fear which silenced them in Mk. But the vv are oddly casual compared with those describing the angel; they almost seem to be added simply in order to explain the execution of the command in contrast to Mk. The account of this appearance may be based on a different tradition of the appearance to Mary Magdalene alone in Jn 20:11—18.

11—15 Precautions by the Leaders of the People— **f** This passage is complementary to 27:62—66, and similarly problematic; cf § 742e. 15b shows that at the time of writing the break between the Church and the Jews was complete. Jn consistently uses 'the Jews' in this sense, Mt only here.

16—20 Mission to the World—The mission of Jesus on **g** earth was to Israel, but their mounting opposition to his call reached its climax in the rejection of the Messiah through the crucifixion. The significance of this act as the death-knell of the chosen people was shown in the manifestations which followed. Already then began the entrance into the Church of the Gentiles, in the persons of the soldiers at the foot of the cross (cf § 742e). Now, as the Son of Man to whom all sovereignty belongs (cf § 719k). Christ charges the disciples to continue his mission, which has now passed from Israel to the

43g world (cf § 733*e*) promising them his presence in the Church. These vv, full of Matthean expressions, do not so much rest on individual sayings of Jesus as sum up the message which he gave to his disciples after the resurrection. It is to this scene that the whole of Mt's **h** resurrection-story, indeed his whole gospel, tend. **16.** The purpose of the appearances at the tomb had been to lead the disciples to this meeting with their master in Galilee. He is now found on the mountain, position of authority (cf 5:1; 17:1; 24:3 and notes). **17.** Some pay him the reverence accorded properly only to God (*prosekunēsan*, as often to Jesus in Mt); others hold back in awe. This is probably the meaning of their 'hesitation' (cf Peter's hesitation at the divine appearance of Jesus on the Lake, the only other use of the word in the NT: 14:26–33). This hesitation, or failure immediately to recognize the exalted Lord, is common to almost all the appearances of Jesus after the resurrection (Lk 24:16, 31, 37; Jn 20:14; 21:4); he was in some way transformed. **i 18** recalls Dn's Son of man, to whom all sovereignty over the world is given (cf § 722*jl*); Jesus had adopted this title to hint at his true position, and by means of it has frequently recalled the position of authority to which he is entitled (esp. 11:27; 26:64; cf 25:31). But his authority far exceeds that of Dn's Son of Man, to include not only all nations but Heaven itself; it is God alone who is 'Lord of Heaven and Earth', a title familiar to Jewish ears (cf 11:25 and note). This title suggests especially the ever-present power and protecting guidance of God. Now God has given (the passive in Mt is a Jewish circumlocution of reverence, to avoid using the divine name) this authority to Christ (cf Phil 2:9–10). This is underlined by the fourfold 'all' in 18–20. **19a.** It is in virtue of this power ('therefore') that Christ sends his apostles to make disciples or followers of Christ (cf § 711*g*) of 'all nations'; by this expression Mt means not only gentiles but Jew and Gentile alike (12:21; 24:9;

25:32); the new Israel of God is composed of both **743i** elements. By embracing all nations this command finally fulfils God's promise to Abraham, that in him all nations of the earth shall be blessed (Gn 18:18 LXX; 22:18; cf Mt 12:21). **19b.** Entry into the Church is effected by **j** baptism. The classic trinitarian formula has been impugned as a later addition (Loisy); this view is now seldom found, so devoid is it of critical foundation. It is not impossible that the actual formula is drawn from the very ancient liturgical practice of the Church (perhaps already reflected in 2 Cor 1:21–22). Ac 2:38 might suggest that a different formula, 'in the name of Jesus', was used, but this is probably not the sense of the passage, cf note on Ac 2:38. '*into* the name' of something (as here) in Judaism signified incorporation into that thing, e.g. slavery or covenant-fellowship with God (SB 1, 1055). So here it means fellowship with the Trinity. It is 'baptism into the company of . . . ' cf Ac 19:5; 1 Cor 1:15; 12:13. Christian baptism presumably developed out of John's baptism (cf § 714*d*), Mt carefully avoids Mk's phrase (1:4) 'for the forgiveness of sins', lest it suggest that John's baptism of itself forgave sins; this phrase he reserves for the Christian sacrament of the eucharist (26:28) **20a. k** 'Teacher' ('rabbi') is a title often used of Jesus in Mt; only Mt regarded it as insufficient: the disciples always address him as 'Lord'. In more than any other gospel Jesus is shown as a teacher, by the five great discourses. The disciples too are to be teachers, but subordinated to him (13:52 and note; 23:8). **20b.** The gospel closes with a return to the prophecy of Emmanuel 'God with us' (1:23). With this phrase God promises his powerfully active assistance, no mere static presence, but a dynamic force for the accomplishment of a mission, as in Ex 3:12; Jos 1:5, etc. Mt returns constantly to the theme of Christ's ever-present power in the community; 11:29–30; 13:41; 18:20; he has (cf § 738*f*) always in sight 'the end of time'.

ST MARK

BY HENRY WANSBROUGH O.S.B.

744a Bibliography—(i) *Commentaries*: H. B. Swete, 1913[3]; J. Huby, BJ. 1953[2]; J. Schniewind NTD 1952[6]; V. Taylor, 1966[2]; J. Schmid, RNT, 1954[3]; E. Lohmeyer, *Meyer* 1937[10]; D. E. Nineham, Pelican, 1963; F. C. Grant, IB, 1951; E. Haenchen, 1966; E. P. Gould, ICC, 1896; M. J. Lagrange, EB, 1947[4]; S. E. Johnson, BNTC, 1960; A. E. J. Rawlinson, *Westminster Commentaries*, 1925. (ii) *Other Works*: P. Benoit, *Passion et Résurrection du Seigneur*, 1966; R. Bultmann, *The History of the Synoptic Tradition*, E.Tr., 1963; O. Cullmann, *The Christology of the NT*, E.Tr., 1959; D. Daube, *NT and Rabbinic Judaism*, 1956; J. Gnilka, *Die Verstockung Israels*, 1961; J. Jeremias, *The Parables of Jesus*, E.Tr., 1963; W. G. Kümmel, *Promise and Fulfilment*, E.Tr., 1957; R. H. Lightfoot, *History and Interpretation in the Gospels*, 1935; R. H. Lightfoot, *The Gospel Message of St Mk*, 1950; W. Marxsen, *Der Evangelist Markus*, 1959[2]; A. Richardson, *Miracle Stories of the Gospels*, 1941; J. M. Robinson, *The Problem of History in Mk*, 1957; E. Sjöberg *Der Verborgene Menschensohn in den Evangelien*, 1955. L. Cerfaux, *Jésus aux origines de la tradition*, 1968.

b Importance of Mk—In early times Mk was neglected among the gospels. With the exception of Bede none of the great Fathers of the Church wrote commentaries on this gospel (Lagrange, 9—10), for Mk was regarded only as the abbreviator of Mt (Aug, *De Consensu Evang.*, 1, 2). Indeed the material given by Mk alone is practically confined to two miracles (7:31—37; 8:22—26), and a parable (4:26—29). But since it has become overwhelmingly accepted, even among Catholics (cf *De Jésus aux Évangiles*, ed. I. de la Potterie, 1967), that Mk is the most primitive of the synoptics, on whom Mt and Lk build and whom they interpret, the study of Mk has come to hold a central position in gospel research, especially in matters concerning history. Mk, to be sure, being a theologian not a mere chronicler, himself forms and shapes his material, showing many of the same editorial tendencies as the later synoptists; but, if we wish to reach behind the gospels to the stage when the gospel material was circulating among the churches in oral and fragmentary form, and so come nearer to the very first Christians' understanding of Jesus and even to the personality of Jesus himself, it is through Mk that this may most easily be done. Similarly, comparison with Mk is the prerequisite of serious study of Mt and Lk, for only so can the passages which the latter draw from Mk be interpreted, through seeing the theological interests which have led them to remould their material.

745a Authorship of Mk (i) **External Evidence**—The tradition of the Church Fathers, at least in the W, agrees that this gospel was written by Mk, the follower of Peter. This agreement appears to stem from Papias, bishop of Hierapolis c. A.D. 110—30 (cf § 709c on his person and doubtful reliability in Eusebius' eyes). He quotes John the Presbyter as saying: 'Mk, the interpreter of Peter,

as far as he could remember, wrote down accurately but **745** not in order those things which had been said or done by the Lord', Eus. HE 3, 39. (From the rest of Papias' discussion it is clear that he is rebutting the charge that Mk is not well-ordered and further stressing his fidelity to Peter's message). The link with Peter is perhaps confirmed c. A.D. 150. by Justin (*Dial*, 106) who mentions the nickname Boanerges as occurring in the 'Memoirs of Peter'; in canonical writings this nickname is given only by Mk 3:17, but it is not excluded that Justin may be alluding to an apocryphal work of that title. Clearly dependent on Papias is the testimony of Irenaeus (c. 200) and Tertullian (c. 220). Clement of Alexandria (c. 210) adds the information that Peter authorized the gospel for use in the churches (Eus. HE 2, 15, 2). But he too may well be dependent on Papias.

(ii) **Internal Evidence**—Before going on to discuss the **b** link between the author and Peter we must consider the **evidence whether or not the gospel is derived from a single preacher, eye-witness of Jesus' actions**. Literary considerations show that much of the material has undergone considerable reworking e.g. in order to bring out its symbolic value and the fact that it fulfils the OT. In many cases what was handed down was only an isolated story, or a saying of Jesus (a collection of these sayings survived to be extensively used by Mt and Lk in composing their gospels, for which the framework was manifestly composed later without any more historical information than could be derived from the saying itself: 3:31—35; 13:1—4; In a number of these frameworks a certain stereotyped pattern of structure and language repeats itself so frequently that it may be seen to derive from the literary author of the gospel himself (e.g. the withdrawal into a house and further instruction to the disciples: 7:17; the stereotyped formula by which Mk adds on an additional saying: 4:11, 13). The arrangement of the material, grouped according to subject-matter (4:1—34; 12:13—36) or symbolic value (8:22—26) does not suggest the preoccupations of an eye-witness; nor does one independent **c** saying added to another pronounced in all probability on another occasion (9:28—29; 12:37b—40). Hence most contemporary scholars agree that in places Mk's '**material bears all the signs of having been community tradition** and cannot therefore be derived *directly* from St Peter or any other eye-witness. But once that admission has been made about some of Mk's material, it seems only logical to go on and make it about *all* his material, for all of it, without exception, seems to bear the characteristic marks of community tradition' (Nineham, p. 27). An objection to this view springs from the wealth of lively details, 'eye-witness touches', which are so characteristic of Mk's narratives. Some commentators, e.g. V. Taylor, still incline, where these occur, to attribute the story to the 'Petrine tradition', supposing that the details are derived from his eye-witness account. It would, however, be surprising if Mk had mingled elements so derived with items of community tradition; nor would it

45c even then accord with the statements of the tradition derived from Papias. Since, moreover, some of these 'eye-witness touches' come in passages which can hardly in fact be derived *in toto* directly from an eye-witness (4:1; 6:17—29), it seems best to put them down to Mk's own count. He had certainly the gifts of a graphic and gripping *raconteur*, as a comparison of his version of stories (5:1—20, 21—43; 9:14—29) with those of the other synoptists shows. But a good story-teller can make a story live and charm without distorting it, even though from the point of view of the vivacity of the story he considerably improves the material he has received.

d As to the **link with Peter**, it is true that Peter has a definite prominence. Though this is primarily due to his position as leader of the Apostles, it may be true also that Mk is especially concerned to show this prominence. In the passages parallel to 1:36; 11:21; 13:3; 16:7 his name is omitted by the other synoptists. On the other hand Mt also adds to his prominence in other ways (see § 711*i*). Another link with Peter would be provided if it could be shown that Mk wrote his gospel at Rome (see § 746*a*), but this is far from certain.

e (iii) **Conclusion**—Internal evidence does not corroborate the tradition derived from Papias, at any rate in the form in which he proposed it. But one would be loth entirely to discard this tradition, and Clement of Alexandria hints at a relationship between Peter and Mk which is perhaps more acceptable: Peter is the guarantor of Mk. K. Aland ('Problem of Anonymity and Pseudonymity in Christian Literature of the first two cent.', JTS 12 (1961), 39—49) has stressed the importance attached in the early Church to sheltering a Christian writing under the patronage of Apostles from whom it could derive its authority. Often this patronage was only fictitious (e.g. the *Didache*, which claims the authority of all twelve Apostles). There is perhaps room for reinterpreting the traditional connexion of Mk with Peter in this sense: though the material did not derive from Peter, the gospel circulated in the churches under his patronage as guarantor of its message.

46a Place of Origin—It has been widely accepted, following Clem. Alex. and Origen (but contrary to Chrys), that Mk was written at Rome. It was certainly written for readers who needed an explanation of Jewish customs (7:3—4; 14:12; 15:42), and reflects both much less understanding of the Jewish scene (10:2) and much less regard for the Jewish Law (2:23—28; 7:14—23) than Mt. Certain passages emphasize that Jesus' message is accessible to the Gentiles too (7:27; 13:10) or show that a pericope has been handed down by a Gentile community (8:1—10; 10:12). The author does not seem to have any detailed knowledge of Palestinian geography, cf § 752*g*. The linguistic evidence is equally vague; H. J. Cadbury (*The Making of Lk-Ac* 1927, 88—89) points out that many of the Latin words used in Mk are used also in the Talmud, Midrash and Targums, and so cannot be used to prove a non-Jewish origin; they were simply loan words common to the Mediterranean world. Cadbury's own suggestion that the linguistic evidence points away from rather than towards Rome, since 'the Latin words *census, centurio, denarius, legio* etc, are precisely those which would be adopted outside of Italy in any of the Greek-speaking **b** provinces', is, however, unjustified. A slight indication that Mk was not in circulation in Rome at the end of the first cent. is provided by I Clem, which shows no knowledge of the Gospel and seems to use only a collection of the Lord's sayings. Two passages in the NT have been taken as evidence for a Roman origin of Mk: the assumption that Rufus, who was at Rome in Rm 16:13, is known to the readers (15:21—but was it the same Rufus?) and **746b** the mention of Mk as present at 'Babylon' with the author of 1 Pt 5:13 (but was it the same Mk? and was 'Babylon' really a code name for Rome?). Cadbury even suggests that this passage, in conjunction with the ascription of 1 Pt to the apostle Peter, lies at the origin of the traditional connexion of Mk with Peter (p. 86). But not everyone now accepts the Petrine authorship of that epistle. While therefore the facts are compatible, on the whole, with a Roman provenance, it is far from being proved beyond question, and it seems better to refrain from any detailed localization. Let us say only that the gospel was written for a Gentile community of the Roman world outside Palestine.

Who was Mark? 'The Roman praenomen *Marcus* **c** was in common use among Greek-speaking peoples from the Augustan age onwards. The inscriptions offer abundant examples from every part of the Empire and from every rank of society', Swete, p. xiii. There is no need to dispute the name of the author; but who was he? If we accept the evidence for a Roman origin of the gospel we may identify the author with the Mk mentioned in Col 4:10 and Phm 24. Now Col 4:10 describes Mk as 'the cousin of Barnabas' and tradition has identified him with John Mark, the associate of Barnabas and Paul, Ac 12: 12, 25; 15:37—39. It is pointed out that John Mark was a native of Palestine and it is argued that this authorship could account for the knowledge of local conditions evident in the Gospel. Now one may admit that 'the general picture in the Gospel is remarkably true to the conditions of Palestine in Jesus' day, and from time to time Aramaic expressions are quoted in the original; but it is not clear how far all this is due to the Evangelist and how far to the tradition; and numerous vaguenesses and inaccuracies are most naturally explained if the Evangelist was *not* directly acquainted with Palestine' (Nineham, p. 40).

Mk was a man of little culture, as it was then understood, for his Gr. is essentially a non-literary Gr., full of roughnesses and semitisms 'the kind of Gr. which might be spoken by the lower classes at Rome (Rawlinson, p. xxxii). But his achievement was little short of staggering: not only did he evolve this completely new genre known to us as 'gospel'; but he also, as it will appear in the course of the commentary, had personally a large part in giving their present form to many of the pericopes included therein.

Date—Papias' 'as far as he could remember' perhaps implies that the gospel was begun after Peter's death, though Clement thought the opposite. But, if our interpretation of the tradition on this point is correct, not much weight can be placed on either of these for the purpose of dating. Mk must have been extant for some time when Mt was written, c. A.D. 80?; but the latest possible date for Mt is perhaps around the turn of the first cent. (cf § 709*g*). Much depends on interpretation of Mk 13:2ff. Is it a prophecy of future events, or has the sack of Jerusalem already taken place? (§ 760*d*). It has been argued that the ch appears to be more like a genuine foretelling of future events than the parallel passages in Mt and Lk, which, especially Lk, seem to be a recognition that the events of A.D. 66—70 are a fulfilment of our Lord's words. On the other hand, Mk 13:14, which appears to describe a definite historical situation, creates a difficulty and perhaps suggests a later date of composition, cf § 760*h*. If some date must be given, perhaps 65—75 would be the most probable, though somewhat wider limits cannot be excluded.

Theology: (i) Christology—The overriding emphasis **747a** in Mk is to present Jesus to the reader as **the Son of God**.

747a (On the connotations of this title to contemporary audiences, see § 677). In Mt, Jesus is presented as the Messiah, fulfilling the hopes and prophecies of Israel. In Mk this aspect is already present, especially through the healing activity of Jesus, a sign that he is the Messiah; cf § 754*d*. But—as might be expected from the impression of a Gentile Christian community which pervades the gospel (cf § 746*a*)—this aspect of Jesus' mission is less developed, and an aspect which had more obvious relevance in the Gentile world more prominent. The title 'Son of God' itself occurs seldom, but at crucial points in the narrative: the heading of the gospel (1:1), the trial (14:61—62), and the final recognition of Jesus on the cross by the centurion (15:39), which is the first move in the spread of Christianity to the nations. It occurs also in the mouth of the evil spirits, whose supernatural knowledge enables them to discern his true identity (3:11 (a Markan summary); 5:7), and whose testimony is therefore all the more weighty, especially since it is unwilling. Elsewhere they use an equivalent but more semitic title, 'the Holy One of God' (1:24). Especially significant are the two occasions when a voice from heaven is heard, proclaiming the same divine

b sonship (1:11; 9:7). But the message that Jesus is the Son of God extends far beyond the mere use of the title. It may be doubted whether the overtones of claims which for a Jew were tantamount to claims to divine prerogatives (to forgive sins, 2:5; to be Lord of the Sabbath, 2:28; to command the sea, 4:39—41; to raise the dead, 5:39—41) were fully understood against their OT background by Mk, as they were by Mt. But the air of command which Jesus bears is fully underlined: his incontestable authority in teaching (1:22, 27; 11:28—33), his irresistible and effortless control of the evil spirits (e.g. 5:1—20), his **calm foreknowledge and direction of events** (11:2—6,13; 14:13—15), his majestic power over the elements (6:45—52). All these serve, even for an audience unfamiliar with Jewish lore, to fill out and support the claims made by the use of the title.

c One way in which Jesus' power of command is seen in Mk is in the **conflict of spirits**. To contemporaries who were familiar with the idea that evil spirits were an ever-present menace, causing illness and disruption, this would have been most forceful. The conflict is seen at its clearest in two passages: in the introduction Jesus is anointed with the Spirit of God at his baptism (1:10) and is led by the Spirit to do battle with Satan (1:12—13; cf Ac 10:38). This passage must be considered highly significant because, being the introduction, it is 'the basis presupposed by the whole ministry of Jesus' (Robinson, p. 31). The pure form of the conflict is seen also in the debate about the spirit in which Jesus casts out Satan (3:23—27). But the opposition is seen working itself out in the exorcism stories, where the violence of the evil spirits (1:23; 3:11; 5:3—7; 9:18—26) is quelled by the masterly severity of Jesus' rebuke (1:24, 27; 3:12; 5:7; 9:25). The same presuppositions of diabolical influence are reflected also in other miracle accounts (1:43 see § 749*k*; 4:39; 7:35 'the *bond* of his tongue').

d In the telling of these stories the **contemporary idiom** is unreservedly adopted: the evil spirits cry out in words found in contemporary pagan stories where a devil about to be exorcised acknowledges the power of the exorcist: 'I know you', 'you are . . .' (O. Bauernfeind, *Die Worte der Dämonen im Mk evang.* 1927, p. 13—23); in 5:7 they even seem to attempt to drive out Jesus' spirit 'I exorcize you' (cf ibid, pp. 24—25). Hence it is the more noteworthy that Jesus uses none of the contemporary exorcist's rituals and spells, but simply expels them by the power of his command. For the modern reader this 'naïve', un-

questioning acceptance of demonic possession is not **747** without its difficulties. Any attempt to regard the cries of the evil spirits as vocalizations of what was in fact a more or less inarticulate shriek is foreign to the mind of the early Christian community, which freely accepted the notion that sickness was a form of possession by evil spirits. But the deeper significance of these stories is that Jesus inaugurates the final struggle against all evil, including physical and natural ill, and adumbrates the victory. Significant here is the peace (4:39; 5:15; 6:51), and awareness of a divine presence (1:27; 2:12; 5:15) which follow these works of Jesus. Perhaps it is not by chance that language is used which suggests the resurrection ('raised her up', 1:31; 5:40—41; 9:27).

(ii) **The Son of Man and Suffering**—On the Son of **e** Man in general see § 676*k—n*, 534*c*. Besides being Son of God, Jesus is also Son of Man. One of the chief connexions in which Mk uses this title is that of suffering, and Jesus' suffering plays such an important part that Mk has often been called 'a passion narrative with extended introduction'. Already by 3:6 the shadow of the cross is cast over the gospel in a very real sense; since 2:1 the disputes with the scribes and Pharisees had been leading up to the decision to put Jesus to death. The theme develops as Mk shows the gradually hardening opposition, and ominously inserts the story of the Baptist's fate (6:17—29). From 8:31 onwards it becomes a major preoccupation: the journey to Jerusalem begins, and is articulated in the three solemn and ever more detailed predictions of the Passion. The Jerusalem ministry itself is seen as leading inevitably towards this end (see § 758*a*). A **f** question which would certainly follow from the fact that the powerful and healing Son of God died a criminal's death at the hands of the highest religious and political authorities was how this could have occurred. Mk gives the answer in two ways, first by showing the genesis and gradual development of the attitude of stubborn refusal by the religious authorities to join the overwhelming mass of the people in acknowledging the quality of this unique person, and secondly by underlining that Jesus had foreknowledge of, and willingly accepted, this ignominious death, in view of the vindication by the resurrection in which it was to issue. By the allusions in the predictions of the Passion to the prophecy of the Suffering Servant in Isaiah (cf § 727*ij*), by the stress on the divine necessity of his suffering (8:31), and in the Passion narrative itself by the constant, though often implicit, allusions to the fulfilment of scripture it is shown that in going willingly to his death Jesus is only accepting the will of the Father as manifested in scripture. Another reason for Mk's **g** emphasis on the suffering of Jesus is seen from the way he links to it warnings that his *followers too must suffer*. The first and third predictions of Jesus' sufferings are immediately followed by sayings on the necessity of suffering in order to follow him (8:34—36; 10:35—45), and after the second prediction there is much teaching on the need for renunciation (9:42—47; 10:17—31). The 'little apocalypse' (13:5—37) is cast in a form often used to comfort those under persecution with the promise of future triumph (cf § 760*ab*), and this has suggested that Mk's reason for laying such stress on the value of Christian suffering is particularly that the community had recently undergone or were even then subject to persecution.

(iii) **The Messianic Secret**—The extraordinary fact **748** remains that Jesus was not acknowledged for what he was. In this connexion two series of texts are significant, one in which Jesus forbids men to reveal his identity, the other in which the inability of the Apostles to understand is

8a noted. Since the publication in 1901 of W. Wrede's *Das Messiasgeheimnis in den Evangelien* the so-called messianic secret has been one of the most discussed problems in Mk. Jesus attempts to prevent rather than encourage the revelation of his identity. A number of the texts where this occurs are integral to miracle-stories: in 1:25 Jesus bids the spirit to be silent as part of his exorcism (cf the same command to the sea in 4:39); in 5:37 the expulsion of, and in 7:33 and 8:23 the withdrawal from, the crowd seem to be merely for the sake of tranquil privacy for the accomplishment of the miracle.

b But other texts give **prohibitions of publishing the miracles**, addressed to spirits (1:34; 3:12) and to beneficiaries of miracles (5:43; 7:36; 8:26). These occur as epilogues to miracles and may well be (1:34 certainly is) due to the evangelist. Apart from the teaching included in the controversy-stories, a parable (4:1—9) and the brief saying in 7:14—16, all Jesus' teaching is imparted to his immediate followers, not to the crowds, or even only to the three apostles privileged to receive special revelations (9:2; 13:3; cf 5:37; 14:33). Repeatedly teaching is given 'in the house' or 'on the road' when these phrases suggest a deliberate withdrawal from the multitudes. At 4:11—12 Mk—who inserts these vv—clearly interprets Jesus as meaning that 'those outside' receive teaching only in figurative language (as 7:14—16) which they cannot at least fully understand. But the **failure of the apostles to understand** is similarly stressed: 4:13, 40—41; 6:37, 52; 7:18; 8:4; 9:6, 32; 10:35—40. Until the confession at Caesarea Philippi they fail to understand who Jesus is, after this they fail to understand that his mission is one of suffering. They too are commanded to keep the

c secret (8:30; 9:9). *Various explanations* of these puzzling phenomena have been offered. Wrede, followed by Bultmann p. 346, held that the whole theory was invented by Mk to explain why Jesus was not acclaimed as Messiah during his ministry: in fact faith in his messiahship began only at the resurrection, but the evangelist thought it necessary to draw a veil over this fact, and in the service of this veiling pretended that the only reason why he had not been acclaimed before was that he had done all he could to prevent it. This explanation does not, however, account for Mk's careful differentiation between the two stages of the Apostles' misunderstanding, before and after Caesarea Philippi. It is indeed clear, also from Jn's independent tradition, that the Apostles failed to understand much (and especially the necessity of suffering, death and resurrection) until after the Resurrection. But there is no reason to reject as fantasy such passages as the confession at Caesarea Philippi, which do at least show some comprehension. It may, indeed, be asked whether, if it were true that they recognized his dignity only at the Resurrection, it would have been necessary to

d conceal this fact. Certainly sparing the Apostles was not Mk's motive; he is so severe on them that Mt consistently tones down the rebukes. V. Taylor, p. 123 in his great commentary, interprets the Secret in terms of the nature of Jesus' messiahship: full revelation could not be made before Christ's victory because 'Messiahship is a destiny: it is that which he does, that which the Father is pleased to accomplish in him. The Messiah already, he would not be the Messiah until his destiny

e was fulfilled'. But even if distinctions such as those implied by Rm 1:4; Ac 2:36 can be applied to Jesus' messiahship, there seems no reason—on Taylor's own dogmatic assumptions—why what Jesus already was should not be revealed. A more common explanation is that Jesus prevented the publishing of his identity in order to prevent misunderstanding of his claim. If the

evil spirits had been allowed freely to proclaim him as **748e** Messiah the crowds would soon have put him up as a political liberator according to the current popular messianic hopes. Much of his teaching on the Kingdom (e.g. the mustard seed, 4:30—32) is directed precisely to correcting these misconceptions. There is considerable **f** truth in this theory, but it requires completion. **The moment of the resurrection is decisive** for the removal of the Secret (9:9) but also it is the Resurrection which lies at the centre of the Apostles' failure to understand (9:10). Until the Apostles understood Jesus' identity as Messiah they had nothing to reveal; but after this moment they must still be prevented from preaching Jesus, because they could not give a true picture of him owing to their inability to understand about his suffering, death and resurrection. It is at the announcements of this that Mk notes their failure (8:31—32; 9:30—32; 10:32—38). Only when this failure to understand has been dissolved by the actual accomplishment of the prediction can they publicly proclaim him. It is not without significance that the first human voice to acclaim Jesus as 'Son of God' does so immediately after his death (15:39).

It remains only to ask whether Mk invented the theory **g** of the Secret. Apart from the four passages 1:25; 5:37; 7:33; 8:23 (for which see above) it appears only in his editorial passages. In Mt 9:30 there is a formal repetition of the motif; but since this miracle-story is composed on the model of others in the gospel (cf § 720q), it cannot be regarded as independent nor probably as deliberate. There is, then, no other evidence for it in the gospel tradition. But nor is there any reason to suppose that Mk invented it without any basis in the tradition of his community. The whole apocalyptic tradition of Dn, the Qumran literature etc, is shot through with the idea that the ultimate revelation will be at first to a small and privileged group; the multitude of men will at first be excluded. This is in fact fulfilled because only the Apostles receive the full revelation. But this is not quite the same as the messianic secret discussed in these lines.

Plan of the Book—It has been said that Mk has no **h** plan, but is like a series of snapshots juxtaposed. It will, however, become clear that at least sometimes the material is in fact carefully arranged:

748h misunderstanding (the epileptic
demoniac), 9:2—29
Second Prophecy of the Passion,
squabble for precedence, sayings on
renunciation, 9:30—10:31
Third Prophecy of the Passion,
request for precedence, sayings on
service, 10:32—45
Public revelation: Bartimaeus, 10:46—52
2. *Ministry in Jerusalem*
Messianic entry and cleansing of
the temple, 11:1—25
Final confrontation with opponents
in Jerusalem, 11:27—12:44
Eschatological discourse: future
prospects, 13:1—37
3. *Passion and Resurrection*, 14:1—16:8
Appendix, 16:9—20

749a **1:1—15 Prelude: the Forerunner** (p Mt 3:1—4:17, Lk
3:1—4:15)—This passage sets the stage for the opening
of Jesus' ministry. Unlike Mt and Lk, with their emphasis
on the moral and other teaching of Jesus, Mk is concerned primarily with the person of Jesus, his proclamation of himself as the Messiah, and of the advent of the
last times awaited by the Jews. Thus for Mk the
Baptist's sole function is to point to Jesus, to introduce
him to the reader as the Messiah heralded by the
prophesied forerunner. His message of moral reformation
is entirely omitted. The passage is constructed on a
chiasmus, concentric circles centring on the contrast
between the persons of John and Jesus, and the double
witness to Jesus. This is made clear verbally: an outer
frame is formed by 'Good News' (vv 1, 15), an inner frame
by 'wilderness, proclaiming repentance' (vv 4, 12—15),
and the centre by 'and so it was, baptise, the Jordan'
(vv 5, 9) and in the one case John's witness onwards to
Jesus (v 7) and in the other that of the voice from heaven
(vv 10—11). The sense of the historical events is brought
out by allusions both to the OT (especially in vv 2—3,
5, 6, 10—11, 13 q.v.) and to the primitive Kerygma of the
early Church (especially in vv 1, 4, 14—15). Several
terms in these latter verses are characteristic of the
Kerygma: 'Good news' is Paul's standard term for his
message, still used fairly frequently by Mk, only four
times by Mt and never by Lk; the résumé here given is
very close to that of Rm 1:2—4, dwelling on the Scriptures,
the Son of God and the spirit (though not Jesus' Davidic
descent, as Rm). The purpose of the Kerygma was always
to bring the hearers to 'repentance' and baptism for
the remission of sins (v 4, cf Ac 2:38, 5:31; 13:38;
Rm 2:4; Eph 1:7). The traditional starting-point of the
Kerygma was John's preaching (Ac 1:22; 10:37).

b **1.** 'Good News': Mk retains the Pauline sense of this
expression: the whole of the Christian message, brought
by Christ and concerning him, whereas Mt uses it to
indicate particular elements of this message; cf § 715*kl*.
'Son of God' is missing in some good MSS; but it has
good MS support; it accords well with the kerygmatic
terminology of the passage and with Mk's practice of
using this title as key points only; cf § 747*a*. **2—3.**
The awkward introduction to this quotation and the
formal opening of v 4 suggests that it was Mk who inserted
the quotation, to emphasize the meaning of what follows;
from the very beginning the significance of the events of
Jesus' life is seen in the light of the OT and is interpreted
in terms of it. Here Mk shows that the Baptist is the
forerunner of the Messiah according to the prophecies. In
fact v 3 is not from Is but from Mal; since it was used of

the Baptist elsewhere in the tradition (Mt 11:10), Mk— **749**
or conceivably an early copyist—may have derived it from
a collection of texts about him in which it was preserved
together with the quotation from Is in v 4; attributing the
whole to Is. **4—6.** Here begins the gospel proper, with a **c**
formal opening phrase found at the head of several OT
books. Probably 4*b* and 6 were added to a more primitive
account (such as is preserved in the *Gospel of the
Ebionites*). The former fits on awkwardly: *ho baptizōn*
is a title 'the Baptist' (cf 6:14), but *kērussōn* is a real
participle, and the half-verse introduces the kerygmatic
motifs mentioned above. The latter v (**6**) is an awkward
afterthought, indicating that John's clothing and food
show him to be the second Elijah heralding the Messiah
(cf § 714*a*); Mt shifts it to an earlier and neater
position. **4. The Baptist**—The implication that he was
baptising, though in the waterless wilderness, suggests
that two traditions have been combined: baptism of
repentance in the Jordan, and the second Elijah in the
desert. Mt and Lk avoid the difficulty by slight adjustments. **5.** The specific mention of Judah and Jerusalem
could derive from Is 40:9, where the herald of the
Messiah proclaims his message to these two. The
baptism which John preaches may be related to the
baptisms of Qumran or to proselyte baptism (cf § 714*e*),
but it could also derive quite independently as a sign
of renewal e.g. from Naaman's washing in the Jordan (2
(4) Kgs 5:14) by which he was cleansed from his sickness.
7—8. The contrast between the two figures of John and **d**
Jesus is central to this pericope (the same contrast forms
a theme of Lk 1—2); the forerunner himself made a mark
(v 5; 11:32) but is entirely subordinated to Jesus. For
the first saying see § 714*f*. Power is such a regular
attribute of God (Dt 10:17; 2 Sm 22:32; Jer 39:18) and
of his Messiah (Is 11:2; 40:10; 42:13; Mi 5:1—3) that
'more powerful' is already a hint of the role of him who
comes after. The second saying is attributed by Ac 1:5;
11:16 to Jesus himself. Since the original audience could
hardly understand 'holy spirit' of the third Person of the
Trinity, the sense of this saying on the Baptist's lips may
have been a reference to the spirit of the messianic times
(Is 11:2—4). But in the early part of Mk the theme of
the conflict between the spirit of Jesus and the evil spirits
is so strong, and it is so emphasized that the spirit of
Jesus is more powerful than the evil spirits (cf § 747*cd*),
that Mk may have chosen these two sayings with this
conflict in mind. **9—11. Baptism of Jesus**—cf A.
Feuillet, 'Le Baptême de Jésus' RB 71 (1964), 321—52.
In the first central panel of the chiasmus on which the
introduction is built (see § 749*a*) John had borne witness
to Jesus. Now John retires into the background, and in
the second central panel the voice from heaven bears
witness to Jesus. The mention of the baptism itself serves
only as an occasion for the witness of the voice and the
dove (on which see § 714*ij*). Here Mk uses apocalyptic
language, such as will seldom appear again after the
introduction (the Transfiguration is an exception), to
show the true nature of the Person who will afterwards
be seen carrying out his mission in more everyday
circumstances. There are allusions to numerous biblical
passages and contemporary apocalyptic texts which show
the sense of the theophany: the opening of the heavens
(Ezek 1:1; Is 63:15; Jn 1:51; Ac 7:56; Apoc 4:1;
Apocalypse of Baruch, 22:1), the outpouring of the
spirit at the last times (Is 44:3; Jl 3:1; Pss Sal. 17:37,
42). The 'favour' expressed by the voice from heaven is
often mentioned in apocalyptic contexts (Mt 11:25—27;
Lk 2:14). Owing to the prominence which the spirit of
Jesus is to have, it is perhaps the element of the descent

49e of the spirit which is most important to Mk. **12—13. Temptation in the Desert**—The conflict with the Devil and the evil spirits begins immediately, instigated by the messianic spirit which has just come upon Jesus (cf § 747cd). Mk gives no details of this conflict but only names the two opposing forces: Satan in the wilderness, the traditional haunt of evil spirits, and Christ served by angelic spirits (there is no mention of fasting, and this angelic ministration could imply the very opposite). Jesus' association with the 'wild beasts' may well be an echo of Is 11:6; Hos 2:18, since harmony between all creatures is a sign of the messianic times (Ezek 34:25, 28), renewing the harmony of Eden (Gn 2:20). In Ps 91 (90):11—13 and *Test. Naph.* 8:4 the man who trusts in God is promised victory over evil, peace with wild beasts and the service of angels. This promise is here

f seen to be accomplished. **14—15. Summary of the Gospel**—Mk concludes his prelude by this summary of Jesus' whole preaching: the emphasis is not upon the Messiah himself, but upon the arrival of the last times foreordained by God, the breaking out of the messianic kingdom, and upon the necessity of personal decision and commitment to it. Although v 15 is couched largely in the terms of the preaching of the Apostles rather than that of Jesus himself, the challenge to a decision at the inruption of the Kingdom is characteristic of Jesus' own message, e.g. in the parables. The word for John's 'arrest' means literally 'handed over'; it is not the normal word for an arrest, but assimilates the Baptist's arrest to Jesus' own passion; the forerunner suffers just as the Messiah is to do, and the disciples after him (13:9; cf § 747g). The impression is given of close chronological succession in the events of the passage 1—15; they may in fact have occupied some time, but the point is that as a prelude to Jesus' preaching they form one entity, and the forerunner's mission must be finished before Jesus' begins.

g **16—20 Call of the First Disciples** (Mt 4:18—22, cf Lk 5:1—11; Jn 1:35—42)—There is both a literary and a theological propriety in placing this narrative here. literary, because there immediately follows the account of a day in Capernaum in which these disciples play an important part; theological, because it was the firm tradition of the community that the apostles had been with Jesus right from his baptism onwards (Ac 1:22; 10:37), and also because the Messiah would start forming his messianic community as soon as possible. The brief stories are laconic but lively, perfect examples of Mk's skill as a *raconteur*. He has no interest in the psychology involved, why they followed him without question; he does not tell us that they have had any previous contact with Jesus; Lk leaves the call until after some miracles have been performed to make it psychologically easier. The first story is built round the saying about fishers of men, and stresses their immediate response. The second stresses the totality of their renunciation. This was a most important element in following Christ; those who do not follow him are those who will not renounce all: 10:22; Mt 8:18—22 cf Ac 5:1—11. There is here probably a contrast implied with the call (1 (3) Kgs 19:20) of Elisha, who first returns home to kiss his parents. Jesus' call is even more demanding (cf Mt 8:21—22; 10:37). These form the kernel and point of the stories; some of the imaginative details are no doubt elaborations to make them more tangible.

h **21—34 A Day in Capernaum**—Mk begins his account of Jesus' ministry with narratives of four events which are located at the town of Capernaum, on the north shore of the Lake of Galilee, in the space of a day.

21—28 Jesus' Authority (Lk 4:31—37, cf Mt 7:28— **749h** 29)—The authority of Jesus is one of the dominant impressions of his personality given us by Mk. Later Jesus claims divine authority by forgiving sins (2:10) and by claiming jurisdiction over the sabbath (2:28). Here however his actions are not above those of a saintly Jewish teacher, though the account sees them already as examples of his messianic authority. The bystanders are struck by his authority in teaching and in casting out devils. In the former case it could be that they are merely contrasting Jesus, who proposes new interpretations as only a fully ordained rabbi might do, with the less qualified village teachers (this can be the sense of 'scribes') to whom they were accustomed in distant Galilee. As for the latter, examples of exorcism are not unknown in Judaism; what may be unusual is that Jesus uses no exorcist's formula (though it has been suggested that his words are part of such a formula, but on flimsy evidence). Historically, then, it could be as an extraordinarily authoritative rabbi that Jesus' reputation spread everywhere (v 28). But the Christian knows that the spirit of authority, of which Christ here gives the first public signs, is that of the Messiah. It is curious that the full acknowledgement of Jesus as the Holy One of God by the demons finds no echo among the people (similarly in 5:7) but this is characteristic of Mk's treatment of Jesus' secret revelation of his messiahship (cf § 748). Perhaps the words put into their mouth are those of the Christian tradition; the designation 'Jesus the Nazarene' is a favourite of the early community (Mt 2:23; Lk 24:19; seven times in Ac). On exorcism in Mk see § 747 ed. **24.** The semitic formula 'What to us and to you?' occurs several times in the OT (Jud 11:12; 2 Sm 16:10 etc); it deprecates interference in various ways, but its exact force—as with many popular proverbial expressions—can be derived only from the context. 'The Holy One of God' is a title closely similar to that of 'Son of God' (Lk 1:35; Jn 10:36); holiness is primarily a divine attribute. In the early Kerygma the title was associated with the designation of Jesus as the Just Servant of God (Ac 3:14; 4:27), but in Apoc the same expressions 'holy and faithful' are used of Christ (3:7) and of God (6:10). It is, then, almost a recognition of his divinity.

29—31 Peter's Mother-in-Law Healed (Mt 8:14— **i** 15; Lk 4: 38—39)—A miracle story of noble but graphic simplicity, showing Jesus' authority over other diseases too. Mk here has no suggestion of diabolic possession, but Lk introduces such a hint; Mt also heightens the wonderful element slightly. Bultmann (p. 345) supposes that Andrew, James and John, were added by a copyist under the influence of 1:16—20, since they occur in neither Mt nor Lk. There is no reason to suppose that Mk received the story directly from Peter (cf § 745cd), though it may well derive from him ultimately. The fact that as soon as she is cured she starts to serve Jesus and his followers is surely significant: those who are healed by Christ must serve his Church (or, in Mt's version, Christ himself).

32—34 Many Healings (Mt 8:16—17; Lk 4:40—41)—Mk ends his account of this 'specimen day' (Nineham, p. 82) with a report of Jesus' general healing activity, in order to show the extent of the power over both sickness and evil spirits, and of his saving mission as Messiah to cure every kind of ill. Note the repeated 'all' and 'many' (which in Aramaic does not have our English sense of excluding some). **32.** Only after the sabbath had ended at sundown was it lawful to carry the sick. **34.** On the secrecy imposed by Jesus see § 748.

749j 35—39 Jesus Extends his Mission to all Galilee— Lk 4:42—44)—Jesus' primary purpose in leaving Capernaum is to spread his proclamation to all Galilee. But there is also perhaps an undertone of disappointment that they were seeking him just as a healer, not as the Messiah. The disciples too show no deeper understanding of his mission. It is significant that Mt, ever more respectful of them (§ 724*e*), omits the passage and Lk substitutes 'the crowds' for 'the disciples'. Failure by the people and even by the disciples to understand Jesus are frequent themes with Mk. It is especially at moments of stress and important new departures in his mission that Jesus' prayer is mentioned (14:35; Lk 6:12; Jn 12:27).

k 40—45 Cure of a Leper (Mt 8:1—4; Lk 5:12—16)— This cure forms a significant stage in the crescendo of Jesus' miraculous activity, for in rabbinic literature leprosy is a special scourge from God and counts as a living death (SB IV. 750—1). A cure, then, shows a power approaching the divine. It is also significant that there is more than a physical evil involved; Jewish teaching is constant that leprosy is a punishment for sin and that a conversion is required before the patient can recover. In the gospels leprosy is always treated as a defilement to be cleansed (Mt 10:8; 11:5; Lk 4:27) not a normal disease to be healed: here Mk speaks of it as a case of possession by a demon which is to be cast out. It is, then, a hint that Jesus' healing mission transcends merely physical ills, for all Jesus' cures are prophetic actions whose sign-value exceeds their visible effects. This may account for the two puzzling references to Jesus' anger (v 41*a*, where JB reads *'feeling sorry for'* for the more probable text *'angry with'*, and v 43); it is directed to the demon, not the leper. Jesus' anger is perhaps symbolic of God's anger at sin. It is possible that both these vivid elements are additions made to a more primitive version by Mk himself; they occur neither in the independent version preserved in B.M. Egerton Pap. 2, nor in the parallel Lk 17:12—14. **44.** On the prescription of the Law see § 719*e*. The command to keep silence is characteristic of Mk (cf § 748); it is perhaps added by him to the primitive account, since it is lacking in the parallels. **45.** May refer wholly to Jesus (*'the man'* of JB is an interpretation of the Gr. *'but he'*), so we may not assume that the man immediately disobeyed Jesus' command; it may be merely a note that Jesus continued his mission, cf vv 38—39.

750a 2:1—3:3 Mounting Opposition—As soon as Jesus has made himself known Mk gives us a group of five stories of verbal duels between him and the recognized religious leaders, scribes and Pharisees. Jesus continues to heal, physically and spiritually, but, in contrast to the normal onlookers (2:12), the religious leaders obstinately refuse to recognize him. Already those who confront Jesus are being divided into two camps; it is only a few who will receive his message in parables (4:1—34); others are already plotting his death (3:6).

2:1—12 Cure of a Paralytic (Mt 9:1—8; Lk 5:17— 26)—The first controversy is linked to the previous stories in that the occasion is a cure by Jesus, and it shows that the meaning of the healings is the healing of all ill by the Messiah. But Mk's inclusion of it here shows that he is concerned in the miracle stories not primarily with the visible effect but with their importance as a sign. Here the interest lies not primarily in the cure but in that which it symbolizes, Jesus' power to forgive sins, a more than messianic power, since God alone can forgive sins. The vv 5*b*—10 which relate this claim are in some ways surprising here (no account of the scribes' reaction to the miracle—did they join in the general astonishment? 10 is almost the sole use of the title 'Son

of Man' at this early stage; the claim of Jesus to forgive **750** sin is paralleled only by Lk 7:47). Hence it has been suggested that the early Church, to justify its own claim to forgive sins, was led to attribute this activity also to Jesus. But even if a controversy over a claim has been inserted into a miracle story it does not mean that the controversy should not depend on a genuine, though different, recollection. **3—4.** 'Paralytic' could be used of anyone bedridden; it does not indicate paralysis in the modern sense. The scene presupposes the flat roof of a Palestinian house, constructed of beams, matting and beaten earth. The word for 'stretcher' is derived from the Latin term for a camp bed (Mt and Lk substitute a more elegant word); it would be easily portable. **10a.** On the mysterious title 'Son of Man' see § 676; Jesus uses it at this early stage of his ministry to provoke reflection, and as a hint of his more than human person (cf 2:28). 'Authority' and 'on earth' are direct allusions to Dn 7:14; Jesus here exercises his authority as universal judge.

13—17 Jesus with Sinners (Mt 9:9—13; Lk 5:27— **b** 32)—This second in Mk's group of controversies is in two parts, each of which shows Jesus associating with men usually shunned by the religious. The brief and stylized account of Levi's call (cf 1:16—20) is related not for itself, but only to introduce 16—17. Tax-collectors are frequently coupled with sinners in the NT (e.g. Mt 21: 31; Lk 5:30); they were excluded as unclean from the company of those who kept the Law strictly (SB I. 379). But it is such men whom Jesus calls to follow him (13—14) and accepts into the close fellowship of a shared meal (15—17). As its place among controversies about Jesus' person shows, Mk's passage gives no teaching on the validity for Christians of the ritual prescriptions of the Law (Mt's addition of 9:13 changes this). Mk is concerned only to show that Jesus is the physician who turns to, and is accepted by, religious outcasts, while being rejected by the respectable. **14.** Levi, son of Alphaeus, is not one of the Apostles, unless he is the James son of Alphaeus of 3:18. Since Jews often had two names, Levi may be James, or even Matthew (also a tax-collector) whom Mt here substitutes for Levi; but he would also be a disciple not among the twelve. The name seems to have puzzled both Mt and Lk, for each changes it in his own way. **17.** The point of the incident lies in the first member of Jesus' answer, a proverbial saying which occurs also in Hellenistic literature, expanded and explained in 17*b*.

18—22 Discussion on Fasting (Mt 9:14—17; Lk **c** 5:33—39)—The third in Mk's series of controversies with Jewish religious leaders gives the motive for Christian penance: conformity to Christ in his passion (18— 20). There follow two sayings, perhaps originally independent, which concern the wider question of the relationship of Christian to Jewish practices (21—22). It has been suggested that the Pharisees had no place in the original discussion, where the question was put by John's disciples who were mourning for the loss of their master, asking why Jesus' disciples (some of whom had been John's disciples) did not join them in this. Jesus answers with the figure of the marriage feast used of Jesus by the Baptist himself (Jn 3:28—30). Certainly the two mentions of the Pharisees could have been added to give the controversy its place in Mk's series; the phrase 'disciples of the Pharisees' is strange, since it was scribes, not Pharisees, who had disciples. Bultmann (p. 19 note) calls it a 'badly conceived analogy to "disciples of John" and "your disciples"'. **20.** Jeremias holds that this v is an addition to Jesus' primitive saying; Jesus would not

0c have been so concerned about details of Church practice (see § 720*m*). In any case it shows that the motive for Christian fasting is no longer observance of the Law, but is Christocentric. 21—22; cf § 720*n*.

d 23—28 Picking Corn on the Sabbath (Mt 12:1 8; Lk 6:1—5)—The fourth of Mk's series of controversies is again composite: 23—26 present a rabbinic-style argument, to which 27, or at least 28, is added. Picking ears of standing corn with the hand (not a sickle) on the way through another man's field is permitted by Dt 23:26. But the Pharisees considered this to be threshing, one of the works which violates the Sabbath. To judge from the number of allusions to it in the gospels, Sabbath observance must have been a burning issue in the primitive Church. The rabbis admitted that special need justified breaking such ritual laws (cf Mt 12:11); so Jesus cites David as a precedent that hunger constitutes a sufficient need. David, fleeing from Saul, went into the sanctuary at Nob and was given by the priest the loaves laid out each week as offerings (1 Sm 21:1—6). This was in fact during the highpriesthood of Ahimelek, not that of Abiathar his son (26)—a minor historical slip. **27** generalizes the lesson of 23—26; the introductory formula is one frequently used by Mk when he adds material from elsewhere (4:11, 13; 7:8; 9:1), but the occurrence of a similar saying on the lips of two different rabbis in the late 2nd cent. A.D. does not show that it was a 'rabbinical commonplace' (Nineham) at least in Christ's day. **28.** In Jewish tradition only God is lord of the Sabbath, so that this is tantamount to a divine claim: it is in this connexion that the pregnant title 'Son of Man' is used, cf § 747*b*. The ν is loosely tacked on by the awkward 'so', though it does not follow logically from v 27, and many consider it a saying of the early Church rather than Jesus himself; but the following story shows Jesus acting on this claim.

1a 3:1—6 Healing on the Sabbath (Mt 12:9—14; Lk 6:6—11)—This last in Mk's series of controversies with the Jewish leaders brings the situation to a climax. With deliberate bad will they refuse to acknowledge him and plot to kill him; henceforth the shadow of the cross lies over the gospel cf § 747*eg*. Mt, and to some extent Lk, make a rabbinic discussion out of the incident, but in Mk the question is wider. It was indeed forbidden to heal on the sabbath except in cases of danger of death (SB 1, 623), but this provision forms no more than the starting-point for Jesus' challenge in **4**, which is not confined even to healing, let alone danger of death. There is no suggestion that Jesus details the only two courses of action open to him, for he could refrain from any action, which could hardly be said to amount to 'killing'. Unless, then, his question is an energetic semitic way of expressing 'to do good or not' by means of antithetic parallelism, it must look forward to 6: Jesus saves a man, while they plot to destroy him, both on the sabbath. After 2:28 Mk feels no need for a detailed justification of Jesus' disregard of sabbath laws. The fact that it is a sabbath is relevant to him only as the occasion of their suspicion. The crux of the incident is the bad dispositions of Jesus' opponents. **6.** The Herodians, the political supporters of the family of the Herods, were probably working for a return of the client kingdom under the Herods, instead of direct rule by Rome; they would be opposed to any messianic movement because it might interfere with their aspirations by causing trouble with Rome.

b 7—12 Crowds follow Jesus (Mt 12:15—16; 4:25; Lk 6:17—19)—In contrast to the mortal opposition of the Pharisees to Jesus stands the acceptance of him by the multitudes. This is shown by a summary describing the

relationships between Jesus and the crowds, and by the **751b** nomination of his chosen group of disciples (13—19). Apart from the list of place-names 7—12 contain no new information, only gathering together threads and motifs which occur more fully elsewhere, e.g. the boat (4:1), many healings, exorcisms and prohibition to the spirits to make him known (1:32—34). Except for Galilee Jesus has not yet preached in any of the places detailed. Marxsen surmises that they are the places where Christian communities are later to be, so that these crowds represent future believers (p. 39). But it is rather a notice similar to 1:28, showing the spread of his fame.

13—19 Appointment of the Twelve (Mt 10:1—4; Lk **c** 6:12—16)—This is one of the turning-points of the gospel: after the authorities' rejection of Jesus, and his acclaim by crowds from far and wide, he selects the circle who are to form the nucleus of his community—the 12 foundation stones of the new Israel—to receive his intimate instruction and carry on his mission. **14.** The sacral character of their ordination is implied by the word used for 'appoint' (literally 'made' or 'constituted'), used in the LXX of ordination of priests: 1 Sm 12:6; 1 (3) Kgs 12:31; 2 Chr 2:17. **16.** Mk is probably using a list from here onwards (cf Mt 10:2), to which the unimportance or total non-appearance in the rest of the NT of some of the names adds verisimilitude; there would be no motive for inventing them. But the variations in the lists given by Mt and Lk suggest that it was the *number* of twelve rather than the *identification* of each member that was important to the early Church. Mk begins awkwardly 'And to Simon he gave the name Peter'; but the different circumstances of this naming in Mt 16:18 and Jn 1:42 show that it did not necessarily occur on this occasion. **17.** *James* (Jacob) and *John* (Johanan = the Lord favours) are, with *Andrew*, the first four called (1:16—20). The interpretation of their surname suggests that Boanerges may be a corrupt form of Bene-roges. The two share with Peter the experiences of the transfiguration and the agony in the garden. Traditionally this is the James martyred by Agrippa (Ac 12:1). John is traditionally 'the beloved disciple' (Jn 13:23), the evangelist. **18.** Philip is otherwise mentioned only in **d** Jn, where he seems to have been very close to Jesus (1:43—48; 6:5—7; 12:21—22; 14:8—9). *Bartholomew* (Bar, i.e. son of, Tolmai) is sometimes identified with Nathanael, who is associated with Philip in Jn 1:44, just as Bartholomew is here; but perhaps Nathanael was not one of the twelve. *Thomas* (Aram *te' oma*) = the Twin, as Jn (11:16; 21:2) notes. 'James of Alphaeus' is one of several designations for the Jameses of the early Church; James the Less (15:40), James brother of the Lord, who presides over the Jerusalem community (Gal 1:19; 2:9 cf Ac 15:13), are also mentioned. Traditionally these are regarded as three designations of the same person. Alphaeus is probably the name of James' father. Thaddaeus (Mk, Mt) has the place assigned by Lk to 'Jude (son) of James'; they may or may not be the same person. *Simon the Zealot* (literally 'Kananaios', from Aram. Qana'na') must have belonged to the militant nationalist party who aimed to shake off the Roman yoke by force of arms. These attempts were often associated with a pretended Messiah, and Simon may have been attracted to Jesus first by nationalist hopes. **19.** The name of *Judas Iscariot* has long puzzled scholars: it used to be considered to mean 'man of Qeriyoth' (a village in Judah mentioned only in Jos 15:25). But J. M. Allegro's recent suggestion may be correct: it is derived from *'iš sakariot* = man in charge of payments, i.e. treasurer (cf Jn 13:29).

751e **20–35 Jesus' true Followers** (Mt 12:22–37, 46–50; Lk 11:14–23; 12:10; 8:19–21)—The central block of this section is a further confrontation between Jesus and the religious leaders of the Jews concerning the nature of his authority to heal (22–30). It prepares for the chapter on parables, which are to be understood only by those who accept Jesus, whereas the leaders, with deliberate blindness, reject his claim. Hence the bridge is formed by the requirements necessary to be a true follower of Jesus (31–35). **20–21.** The section begins with a passage difficult to interpret. It has often been understood to show that even Jesus' family fail to understand him (as by JB); it then balances 31–35, where Jesus teaches that membership of his family is not in itself sufficient. But v 21 can equally well be translated. '*When his relatives heard this, they went out to bring it* (i.e. the crowd) *under control, because they said it was beside itself*'. Naturally, by the run of the sentence, the Gr. *auton* refers to the crowd. Further it is outside, while Jesus is inside (and the relatives go out). In addition, the verb for 'was beside itself/was out of his mind' normally in the NT and invariably in the gospels refers to the reaction of amazement to Jesus or (in Ac) to the Christian message; it is used of a single person only at Ac 8:13 in the NT. This passage, then, continues the Markan theme of contrast between the favourable reaction to Jesus of the common people and his rejection by its leaders.

f **22–30.** These scribes from Jerusalem seem to represent a highly official enquiry; the malevolence with which they immediately attribute Jesus' power to Beelzebul stands out in bleak contrast to the enthusiasm of the crowds. In the former group of five controversies (2:1–3:6) the point had been to establish the fact of Jesus' power: now it is to establish its source. Jesus replies by two simple illustrations: no kingdom where there is civil war can survive (24–26), the fact that a man is robbed of his property shows that he has first been overpowered (27). Though Mt and Lk point the lesson, showing how these parables apply by inserting two sayings about Jesus himself, Mk characteristically leaves the hearers to reflect on these figures themselves: if civil war in Satan's Kingdom is ruled out, Jesus' attack must be from outside: if evil spirits are deprived of their prey, it must be by a spirit stronger than themselves. Mk adheres rigidly to the rule (4:11, 34) that teaching, except to the inner circle of disciples, is in unexplained parables only. **28–29.** Jesus concludes with a warning, whose meaning is tolerably clear in Mk's version, though Mt's has a difficult contrast between two sorts of blasphemy. In Mk the 'Holy Spirit' is surely Jesus' own spirit or power in which he acts (1:8, 10, 12, cf 13:11), the spirit whose victorious conflict with the unclean spirits is so crucial in this early part of the gospel (cf § 747*cd*). **28.** 'I tell you solemnly' (JB) translates the curious semitic phrase 'Amen I say to you', which occurs frequently on Jesus' lips but nowhere else in literature; it must have been a characteristic expression of his. 'Amen' literally means 'So be it', but is normally used to express agreement with or acceptance of someone else's statement. **29.** Salvation is only through Christ, and hence refusal to recognize him inevitably cuts a man off from salvation. Mk expresses this by means of terms drawn from the stock rabbinic classification of the gravity

g of various sins. **31–35.** The lesson of the contrast which has been developing between those who accept and those who reject Jesus is summed up in this transitional passage before the parables, which are to give teaching explicable only to Jesus' followers. The close relations of Jesus (on his 'brothers' see §§ 663–4) are seen as representatives of Israel, the blood-relations of Jesus. Mere blood-relation-

ship is no guarantee of salvation. They stand 'outside' **75** which in view of 4:11 and Paul's constant usage of 'those outside' (1 Cor 5:12 etc.), must signify that they are outside the community of salvation. Hence the traditional interpretation of the passage (in conjunction with Lk 11:27–28), as showing wherein the true dignity of Christ's mother lies, is not its primary sense.

4:1–34 Parables—On parables in general see § **75** 724*a*. Mk here brings together four parables to answer the question which must by now be forming itself in the reader's mind: how the proclamation of the Kingdom of God can meet with so little apparent success. The section is composed of several different layers: the basis is formed by the three parables (3–9, 26–29, 30–32). To this have been added the allegorical interpretation (10, 13–20 and perhaps 33) and the explanation of why Jesus taught in parables (11–12, 34) with two other parables about the process of revelation (21–25). Finally the typically Markan introduction (1–2).

1–2. The introduction is distinctly Markan in vocabulary. This is one of the few occasions when Mk gives us any teaching of Jesus (e.g. at 1:22 we do not learn what he taught); but even here, though he says 'in parables' he gives only one parable before the change of scene in v 10. Mk seems less interested than Mt and Lk in imparting the content of Jesus' teaching; there is no equivalent to the Sermon on the Mount.

3–9 Parable of the Sower (Mt 13:3–9; Lk 8:5–8)— on this parable see § 724*b*. Since the 'punch-line' of such popular stories is usually the last, the point of the original story may well lie less in the continual disappointment at failure than in the joy and almost unbelievable fruitfulness where the preaching is accepted (note the rising crescendo: 30:60:100). If the first vv are not intended as an allegory, they form only a build-up to v 8.

10–12 Why Jesus speaks in Parables (Mt 13:10–15; **b** Lk 8:9–10)—It is Mk himself who inserts this passage. It is normal for the disciples to seek further explanations in private, as do other rabbinic pupils (cf § 757*a*), but the disciples' question originally concerned only the parable of the sower, not the whole principle of teaching in parables. Thus vv 11 and 13 both begin with Mk's own transitional formula 'and said to them'. The vv themselves, however, are taken over by Mk from some source; they contain expressions quite untypical of him (cf Gnilka). Jeremias (p. 16) suggests that *parabolais* (11) translates the Aram. word not for 'parables' but for 'riddles'. The original saying of Jesus might, therefore, not have referred to parables at all, but just have been a statement about the failure of outsiders to understand, inserted here simply due to the ambiguous translation. But G. H. Boobyer (NTS 8 (1961/2) 59–70) is probably right, that the term as used in vv 2, 10, 11, 13 has a wider sense, including all the sense of Heb *mašal* (see § 724*a*). The purpose of using parables is given: 'to those who are outside everything comes in parables so that they may ... not perceive'. But it must be noted that though the semitic expression is awkward, the theology remains supple. The language of 11–12 may not leave room for the permissive will of God, but the prophets, from whom the language is drawn, had no doubt that this direct causation by God of Israel's blindness in no way removed Israel's own guilt in the matter. In fact this programme is carried out by Mk. He gives no great discourses to the people; the only teaching they receive is in parables (cf 4:34). This marked distinction between two groups stands firmly in the traditions of Jewish apocalyptic and of Qumran (Sjöberg p. 124). There was an inner group of the chosen to whom the inner mysteries were to be

2b revealed, distinguished from the others, whose unfaithfulness to God, and even persecution of the chosen ones, excluded them from reception of revelation. They are to blame, not for their failure to understand the parables, but for their failure to show sufficient good will to be worthy of revelation. When this is not shown, the concealment is intended by God. Hence the constant veiling of the revelation of the mystery, especially strong in Mk (1:25, 34, 44; 7:33, 36). Of Mk's six parables only one is explained (4:13—20), and that only to the disciples; the rest remain mere images thrown down, on which the hearers themselves must reflect. Their lesson is, moreover, far less developed than the lessons of Mt's and Lk's parables; there are no parables of mercy or of judgement; there is no allegorization by Mk (4:13—20 comes from a source). They proclaim only, by means of arresting but traditional images, that the messianic times are here; even the identity of the Messiah is never clearly shown (Mk has no parallel to Mt 12:28), but must be deduced by the hearers' own reflection. And in fact the only result of the public parables recorded by Mk is the deepening of the enmity of his opponents to Jesus (3:28—30; 12:12). It has often been suggested that the early community invented the theory that the parables were intended by Jesus to conceal his nature from all but those of goodwill, in order to explain how the Jews can have rejected their Messiah. But in fact the gospels stress only that *full* understanding of the parables is granted only to a few. This is perhaps the consequence both of the transmission of the parables, already in the pre-gospel tradition devoid of their contexts (so that their exact application is not immediately obvious), and of the evangelists' view of the parables as allegories. In the climate of the times allegorical interpretation of every detail of a story (cf Philo's interpretations of Scripture) was so widespread that the attitude could not fail to affect the Christian community, until they demanded a sort of meaning from the parables which the parables did not contain. This demand is reflected in the allegorical interpretation of Mk 4:13—20; Mt 13:36—43, 49—50. Such a 'key, as it were, to the code' (Nineham p. 130) is given only to the disciples, but Mk recognizes that the parables were not entirely unintelligible to outsiders (12:12).

c 13—20 Parable of the Sower explained (Mt 13:18—23; Lk 8:11—15)—The explanation probably stems from the early Church rather than from Jesus himself, but it continues his lesson, only removing it from Jesus' own situation to that of the Church; see § 724gh. 'In the interpretation the parable has lost its original *eschatological* bearing; it becomes simply a warning and encouragement to Christians in conditions of persecution and worldly temptation. There is no suggestion that Christ is the sower. Any faithful Christian preacher is the sower' (Nineham p. 140).

21—25 Parables on Revelation (Lk 8:16—18)—These two parables are composed from four originally independent sayings given in various different contexts by Mt and Lk. Sayings of this proverbial stamp are always polyvalent, and it is impossible to recover their original force as used by Jesus (there are strong traces of Aram. e.g. in the theological passives of 24—25, and especially in 22). The passage seems to have been built up by 22 being added to 21 and 25 to 24 as explanatory comments. But the juncture of the pairs thus formed was not due solely to the similar word 'measure' in 21 and 24 (Nineham), for each pair is independently relevant to the theme of revelation, and so completes 11—20. Vv 11—12 showed that understanding of the parables was only for some; **21—22** explains, as though answering an

objection, that the light of revelation is indeed for all, and **752c** temporary secrecy is precisely to further this end (perhaps when men are more receptive). Lk (and JB in 22*a*) weaken the point by substituting a relative for what is in Mk a purpose clause. **22.** The saying forms an independent utterance, and need not necessarily have been said by Jesus with reference to parables. The application of it here is part of the evangelist's interpretation of the parables. The explanation of **24** by **25**, and their place here, suggest that Mk referred them to the allegory of 13—20: if you have goodwill (give good measure) God will give you even more return from it than you deserve; but if you have no good will you will lose all.

26—29 Parable of the Seed growing to Harvest— d Without the clue provided by a context it is hard to decide the central point of this parable. So soon after the parable of the sower Mk must surely mean the seed to be the word of God, intending to dissipate discouragement at lack of visible progress. The stress is then on 'he does not know': one cannot assess the invisible growth of God's word in man and society. But another lesson frequent in the parables could have been intended: in Jewish terminology harvest-time is a symbol of the Day of God's final visitation (Jeremias, p. 118—19). Jesus could be showing the suddenness and unexpectedness of the arrival of the kingdom, the unpreparedness of the Jews (cf Mt 21:33 22:13 etc). This gives full value to the superb contrast between the tranquillity of 27—28 (the present subjunctives could be translated 'goes on and on going to bed at night and getting up in the morning etc') with the startling suddenness of 29.

30—32 Parable of the Mustard Seed (Mt 13:31—32; Lk 13:18—19)—Mk's third parable, in which the seed represents the word of God. On its force see § 724*k*. The minor agreements of Mt with Lk against Mk show that they are combining another tradition of the same parable with Mk's version.

33—34 The Use of Parables (Mt 13:34)—These vv seem to be pre-Markan (Gnilka p. 60) and perhaps were attached originally to the parable of the sower. But they sum up the theory of the parables which we find in Mk, that they played a part in Jesus' plan of revealing himself fully only to an inner circle (cf § 748).

35—41 Calming of the Storm (Mt 8:23—27; Lk **e** 8:22—25)—What might have been a gripping story of danger at sea and unavailing attempts to master the storm (cf Jon 1:4—15) is filed down to a form which serves only to bring out the theological overtones of the incident provided by the OT. Here, and especially in the Pss, the sea is the location of destructive powers which are restrained only through the power of God (Jb 7:12; Ps 74 (73):13; 89 (88): 9—10). Calming of storm on the sea is one of the major proofs of God's love in Ps 107 (106):23—30. But here it is Jesus who plays the part attributed in the OT to God. There may also be further dimensions to the symbolic value of the scene: salvation from the evil powers is frequently described in the OT as freeing from deep waters (Jb 22:10—11; Ps 18 (17):4; 69 (68):1—2). Perhaps Jesus' sleep and the call to him to awake recall similar prayers to God: Ps 44 (43):23—24; 35 (34):23. But at the time the disciples had only an inkling of the full meaning of the event (cf § 748*b*). This is the first occasion where Jesus rebukes them for lack of faith (cf § 755*c*), so severely that both Mt and Lk mitigate the rebuke out of respect for them. But even after the miracle they do not get beyond a fear of the numinous and questioning wonder like that of the crowds (2:12).

752f 5:1—20 The Gerasene Demoniac (Mt 8:28—34; Lk 8:26—39)—A second story demonstrating Jesus' power, not this time over the forces of nature but over the powers of evil, this is the fullest account of the expulsion of demons in any gospel. It was popularly accepted by contemporaries that one of the most tangible ways in which the forces of evil manifested themselves was sickness (cf § 747cd). Such a violent and destructive form of illness as the mental derangement here described is a supreme test of the Messiah's power over evil; hence the symptoms and force of the sickness are described at length. But Jesus' cure is effortless: the demon acknowledges Jesus' power spontaneously; before he makes any move, it blurts out its name (which spirits normally concealed, since exorcists then had power over them by the invocation of their name), and is, after pathetic appeals, expelled without recourse to any of the formulae or incantations used by Jewish exorcists in similar stories. It is idle to deny that Mk accepts uninhibitedly the belief that such sickness was due to inhabitation by personal forces of evil; the dialogue of 7—13 and the pigs admit of no other explanation. The fate of the pigs has been explained as a stampede caused by fright either at the presence of strangers or at a final paroxysm of the hysteric, but at any rate in Mk's view it shows the destructive force of the evil over which Jesus has such absolute power. In Jewish eyes there was a certain fittingness that the unclean spirits should enter these unclean animals. There is no evidence that the owner of the pigs was transgressing the Law by possessing such a herd, and so deserved to lose them, for it is quite uncertain whether the owner was a Jew and whether Jews were at this time forbidden to keep pigs. But the humanitarian and moral objections sometimes raised are wholly alien to the story-teller's point of view.

g **1.** 'The country of the Gerasenes' has long caused difficulty, since the town of Gerasa is 30 miles from the Lake of Galilee. Mt has 'Gadarenes', which is scarcely better, for Gadara is still 6 miles away, a run which hardly accords with the impression given by v 13. Origen suggested 'Gergesenes', but the Kersa on the coast of the Lake which he had in mind is unsuitable, being on a level with the Lake and devoid of tombs (cf v 2). The localization is, then, at best very rough. Mk himself was probably unfamiliar with Palestinian geography (cf notes to 6:45; 7:31; 10:1, § 746a). **7.** The cry is similar to that in 1:24, except that for 'Holy One of God' the even more explicit title 'Son of God' is given. Such recognition requires supernatural insight, granted as yet neither to crowds nor to disciples (cf § 747ab). **9.** 'Legion' is a clever name, since it can be used in Aram. of either a single soldier (SB II. 9) or a detachment theoretically 6,000 strong. Similarly the spirit hovers between being one and many. **14—17.** As is normal with miracle stories, the account ends with a notice of the astonishment of the witnesses. The request to leave their territory is perhaps due to fear at such an awesome display of supernatural power (cf 4:41; Lk 5:8). **18—20.** Whatever the reason for Jesus' refusal to admit the man among his disciples—perhaps he was to prepare the way for a fuller mission to these parts—it is not the desire for secrecy (cf § 748). The conjunction 'and' at the beginning of v 20 shows that his proclaiming obeyed, not disobeyed, Jesus' command.

h **21—43 Jairus' Daughter and the Woman with a Haemorrhage Cured** (Mt 9:18—26; Lk 8:40—56)— This third full miracle story is double, the story of the woman with a haemorrhage being inserted between the two 'acts' of the story of Jairus' daughter. The purpose of this unique arrangement was perhaps to heighten the

dramatic effect by allowing the girl to die while Jesus **75** is on the way. In both incidents Mk's story-telling is at its best, almost making visible the oriental bazaar-crowds. A comparison with Mt's hieratic simplification is instructive: § 720op. **22.** For Jairus' rank of 'archisynagogos' see § 923a; it is important, as showing that in a case of dire need even high ranking Jews would humbly acknowledge Jesus (Nineham). **25—34.** The woman is presumably suffering from a menstrual flow which makes her ritually unclean (Lv 15:25—27). The didactic point of the incident is that, while she seems to treat Jesus after the Hellenistic fashion as a source of magic power, Jesus insists that it is only through her faith in him that she is healed, not by any automatic force emanating from him. This story then, serves as a corrective to others where the healing seems to be considered automatic (3:10; 6:56; Ac 5:15; 19:12). Faith is stressed also in Jairus' case **i** (**36**). **37.** Jesus takes with him only the three intimate disciples who will be with him also at the Transfiguration and the Agony in the Garden. The motive for clearing the room of mourners is (**40**) not necessarily secrecy. There was a feeling that such a miracle should be accomplished in private (cf Ac 9:40; 1 (3) Kgs 17:19; 2 (4) Kgs 4:33). **39.** 'The child is not dead, but asleep' cannot mean that she was not physically dead, for this would make nonsense of the story, and especially make the mourners' derisive laughter functionless. The same opposition between death and sleep occurs on Jacob in a rabbinic source (SB I. 523), to indicate that his death is not the end of everything for him. The Christian and NT use of the term serves to allude to the fact that the dead will rise again; this seems to be all the saying means. The miracle is a foretaste of Christ's power to raise the dead. **43.** A characteristic Markan secrecy command, cf § 748.

6:1—6a Visit to Nazareth (Mt 13:53—58; Lk 4: **75:** 16—30)—Intentionally Mk sets after three full miracle stories the account of Jesus' rejection by his own townsfolk, which typifies the rejection by all the Jews that is finally to bring about his death. Their initial reactions are right: wonder and enquiry after the source of his wisdom and power; but then (3) the attitude changes to a hostility founded on envy of one of themselves. On the hints about Jesus' early life see § 725bc. **3.** The original reading is uncertain; many MSS give 'the carpenter's son'. Mt and Lk are most easily explained from this reading, which is also presupposed by Origen's assertion (C. Celsum 6:36) that nowhere in the canonical gospels is Jesus said to have been a craftsman. The change to 'the carpenter, the son of' requires the insertion of a single letter, and could have been made to prevent the Nazarenes from impugning the virgin birth. **5.** This does not mean that he tried and failed to work miracles, as though the cures were by faith-healing. He worked miracles only in response to faith in himself, as signs of the kingdom. If this faith were lacking, the miracle would have no significance. He lacked, then, opportunity rather than power at Nazareth. **6a.** A valuable insight into our Lord's real human psychology.

6—13 The Mission of the Twelve (Mt 9:35—10:1, **b** 9—11, 14; Lk 9:1—6)—After the rejection by his people in spite of this second group of miracles, Jesus turns his attention to his special disciples. The shadow of the cross now deepens (it is emphasized still more by the insertion of the story of the Baptist's death in 14—29), as Jesus concentrates on instructing those who are to carry on his mission. This is a curious fragment almost without sequel: we hear nothing of the extent, success, failure or effect of the mission. The most notable feature of the charge to them is its simplicity and confidence in God's

53b providence: they are to take nothing superfluous; they are not even to search out suitable lodging. Mt's version is more developed (with the aid of other sources) and differs in some details (cf § 721*df*); similarly Lk. **12—13.** The content of their preaching was not the full post-resurrection message, but more akin to the Baptist's preparatory call to repentance (1:4; Mt 3:7—10; Lk 3:7—14), they did not themselves yet fully understand (§ 748). Their miracles, as those of Jesus, are signs of the arrival of the last times. Their use of oil as an element in the miraculous cures is no doubt at the origin of the sacrament of anointing of the sick (cf Jas 5:14).

c 14—29 Herod and John the Baptist (Mt 14:1—12; Lk 9:7—9)—Mk fills in the gap between the mission and return of the disciples with the ominous story of Herod's treatment of John. **14—16.** Serve as an introduction, composed by Mk. The opinions mentioned in v 15 occur also in 8:28, q.v. **17—29.** The story of John's death has all the characteristics of a popular tale, full of life and vivid details. It contains probably unconscious reminiscences of the biblical stories of Jezebel and Esther. It is not without minor inaccuracies, e.g. Philip was Salome's not Herodias' husband, while Herodias was first married to another Herod, the half-brother of Antipas (though he too may have been called also Philip; in this family a few names are used in many combinations; this inaccuracy is avoided by Mt. According to Jos.Ant. 18, 5, 2 it was for fear of his popularity and power to raise rebellion that Herod beheaded John. Although this may be due to Josephus' desire to whitewash Herod in Roman eyes, highlighting a scandal with a personal drama and neglecting deeper political causes is typical of the popular imagination which lies behind this story. The scene is (Jos.Ant. 18, 5, 4) Herod's fortress at Machaerus, above the E shore of the Dead Sea; though somewhat remote for guests, it was probably sumptuously equipped (cf the similar fortress of the Herodeion, recently excavated), and could well stage such a banquet.

30 34 Return of the Disciples and Crowds (Mt 14: 13; Lk 9:10—11)—The disciples had been sent out on their mission in vv 6—13, but nothing more is heard of this mission.

d Note on the arrangement of 6:35—8:26—Here begins a series of incidents which is curiously paralleled by another series (cf V. Taylor, p. 628—632):

Feeding of the 5000 (6.35—44)
Feeding of the 4000 (8:1—9)
Crossing of the Lake (6:35—44)
Crossing of the Lake (8:10)
Controversy with Pharisees (7:1—23)
Controversy with Pharisees (8:11—13)
The Children's bread (7:24—30)
The Leaven of the Pharisees (8:14—21)
Healing at the Lake (7:31; 37)
Healing at the Lake (8:22—26)

Apart from the story of the multiplication of loaves and fishes (cf § 725*g*), and perhaps the final healing (cf § 755*f*), there is no question that the incidents are the same, but there may well be some reason, not now apparent, for the same *order* of events being repeated. Whether it is due to Mk or not is similarly unclear; he certainly had a great part in the formation of some of the pericopes (he added on 7:9—23; his geography and vocabulary are apparent in 7:31—37; his preoccupation with the blindness of the disciples in 8:17—21); but he could still have received an outline of the whole from

elsewhere into which he incorporated much himself. L. **753d** Cerfaux has pointed out (*Receuil L. Cerfaux* (1954), I. 471—85) that all the incidents are somehow concerned with bread; does a eucharistic catechesis underlie this schema?

35—44 Feeding of the Five Thousand (Mt 14:15— **e** 21; Lk 9:12—17)—On whether this and the feeding of the four thousand are the same event see §§ 725*g*, 755*a*. The account is not a 'pure miracle-story' in Bultmann's sense, for it lacks the regular elements of an initial appeal for help and a final acknowledgement of Jesus' power (indeed they fail to understand: 6:52). Its meaning is brought out by biblical allusions, see § 725*hi*. In addition to those adopted by Mt, Mk has three overlooked by him: 'rest for a while' (v 31) may well have messianic connotations, as in similar uses in Is 14:30; 27:10; 32:16; Ezek 34:14, 15. Mk v 34 alludes explicitly to the messianic shepherd (Is 40:11; Ezek 34; Jn 10:1 18) who will provide food for his sheep (Ezek 34:13—14, 31; Ps 23 (22): 5; 78 (77): 70—71; Jn 10:9). Finally Mk v 39's groups of hundreds and fifties accord with messianic expectations, for these groupings were current in the would-be messianic community of Qumran (1 QS II. 22; 1 QM IV. 3; 1 QSa I. 14). It has been disputed whether the account contains allusions to the eucharist. For Mt this seems probable (cf § 725*i*), but already in Mk v 41 there are indications: the v seems disarranged, in that the 'two fish' occur awkwardly twice, and seem, unlike the bread, to be distributed by Jesus alone. B. van Iersel (NT 7 (1964), 167—91) suggests that the original reading was 'Then he took the five loaves and two fish and shared them out among them all', and that the middle portion was inserted at a pre-Markan stage to serve as a eucharistic catechesis. **37.** This somewhat sarcastic question of the disciples is toned down by Mt. In Mk they are often abrupt to Jesus, though he never rebukes them (5:31; 8:4; 10:26*b*); in Mt this is rare (19:10), and he usually softens such remarks out of reverence, cf § 724*e*.

45—52 Walking on the Water (Mt 14:22—33; Jn **f** 6:15—21)—Lohmeyer (130—1) sees in this story the fusion of two in which the emphasis lies on Jesus' walking on the water and on his calming the wind respectively. There are indeed some doublets (e.g. 'he came to them' and 'he was going to pass them by' 48; 49 = 50*a*; unprecedented doubling of 'courage' with 'do not be afraid'). But it is questionable whether these show more than Mk's pleonastic style (J. C. Hawkins, *Horae Synopticae* ('1909), 127—9, 139—42). In Mk it is merely the rowers who are 'worn out' (48) by the wind, whereas in Mt the boat is 'battling with a heavy sea' (14:24): this may be due to contamination from the similar incident of the calming of the storm (Mt 8:23—27). In Mk the emphasis is all on the quasi-theophany of Jesus. On the allusions common to Mt see § 726*a*; Mk's 'he was going to pass them by' is also suggestive of God's passing by in Jb 9:8—11; Ex 33: 19—22; 1 (3) Kgs 19:11. **45.** Bethsaida has caused commentators much difficulty: it is on the E side of the entry of the Jordan into the Lake, whereas Gennesaret, where they eventually put in (v 53) is some miles to the W of it. But Mk is not too sure of Palestinian geography (cf § 752*g*). **52.** Mk underlines the failure of the disciples to understand the mystery of Jesus until 8:28 (cf § 748*b*); 'their minds were closed' is a very strong expression, elsewhere used of the Pharisees (3:5; Jn 12:40).

53—56 Cures at Gennesaret (Mt 14:34—36)—The **g** same sort of generalized summary of Jesus' healing activity as at 1:32—34; 3:10, composed (as the vocabulary shows) by Mk without any specific basis in the

753g tradition. Nineham suggests that its insertion here is intended to point the contrast between the enthusiasm of the crowds and the attitude of their leaders (7:1–23), as Mk often does. **53.** On Gennesaret see § 726c.

754a **7:1–23 Traditions of the Pharisees** (Mt 15:1–20)— This is a composite section formed from three sayings about Pharisaic practice. It perhaps serves (Nineham) as a transition to Jesus' ministry to the gentiles.
1–8 Ritual purification—Our information about the customs mentioned is scanty and mostly late, but it suggests that at this time it was only priests who were obliged to wash ceremonially before eating. But there is evidence that outside Palestine where contact with unclean gentiles was unavoidable there may have been stricter rules of purification. All those mentioned by Mk may then reflect customs of the Diaspora; in any case 3–4 are clearly his own explanation. **3.** 'as far as the elbow': the Gr. word may be a mistranslation of the Aram. word meaning also 'with a purifying jug'. **5–8.** In the discussion itself Jesus characteristically goes back to the basic principles of the scriptures (as 10:1–9; 12:28–31). He does not impugn the practices as such, but merely shows that their priorities are wrong and their observance soulless and automatic (cf Mt 23:23 etc). Such is the sense of Is 29:13 (quoted in the LXX version, but the Aram. Targum text, though different, points the same lesson). V 8 is only an energetic semitic mode of expression (cf Lk 14:26), not yet suggesting that the purification rites themselves violate God's law.

b **9–13 Corban**—A second discussion, unrelated to the first. (Note the typical Markan transitional formula 'and he said to them' in vv 9 and 14). Here the practice sanctioned by the rabbis would clearly counter God's law, but see note to Mt 15:5.
14–23 Culinary Restrictions—This double scene presents a common rabbinic procedure: the rabbi delivers in public a short, pithy pronouncement, which he afterwards explains in private to his disciples (Daube p. 141–51; Mk often uses a house for this second part: 9:28, 33; 10:10). On the teaching of this section in Mk and Mt, and on the historicity of the passage, see § 726f.

c **24–30 The Syro-Phoenician Woman** (Mt 15:21– 28)—The most marked feature of this cure is its exceptional nature. The point of it lies in the dialogue of 17–28, in which Jesus makes clear that the Jews claim his own attention (stressed still more by Mt v 24). Even the 'first' of v 27 does not really harmonize with the next, more absolute, saying. The early Church was well aware that the Jews had had the first claim to the kingdom (Rm 1:16; Ac 13:46). So on this journey to the mountains of Tyre (which includes upper Galilee, only semi-gentile country, with a large Jewish population (J. Jeremias, *Jesus' Promise to the Nations* (1958), p. 36) Jesus does not preach, but avoids publicity, going immediately 'into a house'. The conversion of the gentiles begins only after his death (15:39; Mt 28:19). This cure is wrung from him only with difficulty, and it is perhaps symbolic that this and another cure of a gentile (Mt 8:5–13) are the only two recorded in the gospels at a distance. The mention of 'bread' (27, 28) suggests that the dialogue may have some reference to common participation between Jew and Gentile not only at the ordinary table but at the eucharist. The former had been hotly disputed (Ac 11:1–3; Gal 2:11–14). Although the door is thereby opened to the Gentiles with faith, the exceptional character of the miracle for Jesus' own ministry is strongly emphasized by the double appellation 'dog' (27, 28). This insulting term, evoking the mangy curs of Oriental cities, was used by Jews to express their contempt for gentiles

(SB I. 722–4). Even if Mk's diminutive is intended— **754** which is unlikely, for he uses diminutives at random—to soften this (cf JB's '*house-dogs*'), it cannot have stood in Jesus' Aram. words, for Aram. has no equivalent to this diminutive. Moreover the chiastic pattern of the pericope centres on it: Tyre (24)—into a house—devil (26)—out of the daughter—children (27)—bread— dogs— (28)—bread—children—out of the daughter (29)—devil—in the house (20)—Tyre (31). It is therefore stressed as much as possible.

31–37 Healing of a Deaf Man (Mt 15:29–31)—This **d** is one of the passages where the significance of Jesus' healing activity is clearest in Mk (cf Mt 11:2–6; Lk 7:18–23 and § 719ab). By means of allusions to OT prophecies it is shown to be the manifestation of the messianic era: Is 29:18; 32:3; Ezek 24:27; only in view of realization of the fulfilment of these prophecies is the extreme excitement of v 37 intelligible. But the clearest allusion is to Is 35:6, for the word used for 'who had an impediment in his speech' is used only in these two passages in the Bible. It is all the more significant because the nature of the complaint which is healed is thereby made unclear: is he dumb (32, 37), or only afflicted with an impediment (32, 35)? **31.** The geographical indications are confusing: Jesus starts off NW to arrive at a point which lies to the S, which he finally reaches from the E. Mk is perhaps giving a résumé of a long tour, but he would surely have provided some explanation, were he aware of the surprising route he gives. It is easier to suppose that his geographical knowledge is faulty cf § 746a. **33–34.** The actions here described 'are common to the technique of Greek and Jewish healers' (V. Taylor p. 354); for instance Vespasian healed a man by using spittle. Spitting and groaning are both widely used in exorcism rites (*Reallexikon für Antike u. Christentum* 7 (1966), 52). But, though Jesus uses these gestures, he gives them a new sense: they are no longer mechanical, automatic means of healing, but are signs of his messianic power (the touch) and of the divine power by which he heals (sighing and looking up to heaven). As in the sacraments of the Church there is no question of sympathetic magic, but the bodily gestures are made vehicles of God's healing. Some may consider that there is trace of superstition in Mk's preservation in the original Aram. of 'Ephphatha' (35), the 'operative word', if the purpose of this was so that it should not lose its effect. He does the same at 5:41. It may have been to avoid any suspicion of superstition that Mt omits these vv, and both Mt and Lk the 'operative words' at 5:41. **36.** On the command to remain silent cf § 748.

8:1–10 Feeding of the Four Thousand (Mt 15:32– **75** 39)—Since Augustine it has been normal, more for symbolic than for textual reasons, to explain this feeding as being for the benefit of the gentiles and the first that of the Jews. There are indeed linguistic reasons for supposing that this account developed in a hellenistic milieu (cf B. van Iersel 'Die wunderbare Speisung u. das Abendmahl' NT 7 (1964), 167–91). It contains only one possible semitism (in v 3), as opposed to six in the first account (cf V. Taylor, p. 66). In v 7 Jesus blesses the fish, a Hellenistic, not Jewish, phrase, for the Jews never bless objects, but bless (lit 'give thanks to') God for objects. In v 6 the word used for 'giving thanks' is not that used by Mk at the last supper (14:22) and therefore in 6:41, but that used in the account of the Eucharist in 1 Cor 11:24, drawn by Paul from a Hellenistic community. The expression 'from afar' (3), used of non-Jews in Jos 9:6, recalls the terminology used by the rabbis of Gentiles,

55a and familiar in this sense to Christians (Ac 2:39; 22:21; Eph 2:11—22). Finally, as the twelve baskets of fragments in the first account correspond to the twelve Apostles, so the seven baskets here may correspond to the colleges of seven ministers which seem to have existed in some Gentile communities (Ac 6:1—6 and note: 21:8). For the baskets themselves a normal Gr. word is used, instead of the word *kophinos* (6:43) which Juvenal uses (Sat 3:14; 6:542) for a basket evidently characteristic of Jews at Rome. Whoever, then, were in fact the beneficiaries of this feeding (it may well be a different account of the same incident, see § 725*g*) Mk (though cf § 753*d*) perhaps inserted this account to show the equal right of Gentiles to share the Eucharist (cf the disputes of Ac 11: 1—3; Gal 2:11—14). The same point is suggested less confidently by 7:28. On the *allusions* and *eucharistic symbolism* of the passage see § 725*hi*. **10.** Dalmanutha is quite unknown, but is a good Aram. formation. Various more or less known places have been suggested from which this name might have been corrupted, but none has much probability. Mt reads 'Magadan', which is perhaps Magdala.

b 11—13 The Pharisees Ask a Sign from Heaven (Mt 16:1—4; 12:38—39; Lk 11:29)—This little confrontation is fitted in somewhat awkwardly, for it does not really fit any geographical context, and v 13 virtually repeats v 10. But Mk is not interested merely in tracking Jesus' route, and inserts this as an introduction to the lesson of 14—21, showing vividly the perversity of the Pharisees who are there to be castigated—unless it is merely to preserve his enigmatic sequence, cf § 753*d*. The kernel of the scene is the saying in v 12; the rest merely provides a setting. The saying and the request are puzzling, since the whole point of the miracles is that they are signs that the messianic era has come in Jesus' person. They perhaps wanted some such sign as that promised by the pseudo-Messiah Theudas, that he would enable his followers to march through the Jordan dryshod (Jos.Ant. 20, 5, 1), or a voice from heaven. Clearly Jesus' signs were not such as to compel assent, but only to elicit faith. In the gospels, it must be remembered, they are recounted to and for believers. In Mk Jesus refuses absolutely (with an oath formula, literally 'If God grants this generation a sign [may such-and-such evil befall me]'), though the Q form preserved in Mt and Lk promises the sign of Jonah (cf § 723*j*). By biblical terminology Jesus suggests that their stubbornness is like that of Moses' followers (Ps 95 (94): 10; Dt 1:35; Nm 14:11). See also § 722*e*. Mt's version enriches this by 'adulterous' (cf § 723*j*). The notion of testing too (v 11) immediately recalls the occasion when the generation in the desert tested God (Ex 17:7; Ps 95 (94):9).

c 14—21 Understanding of the Bread-Miracles (Mt 16:5—12; Lk 12:1)—Here Jesus' sorrow at the failure of the disciples to understand comes to a head. It has been a recurrent theme since their instruction began cf § 748*b*. The next pericope will symbolize their enlightenment, and then they will make their profession of faith (8:29). But first their failure to understand is stressed (note the repeated 'Are you still without perception?', which brackets 17—21), in function of bread, which has featured so much in the section dealing with their instruction (cf § 753*d*), and especially of the great central sign, given so much prominence in all four gospels, of the miraculous feeding. Apart from v 15 it is possible that the passage was constructed by Mk to serve the purposes of his theme (cf § 748). The style of questioning to stimulate reflexion, which seems to have been characteristic of Jesus, is there (17, 18, 21), but much of the vocabulary is typically Markan, many of the phrases are **755c** drawn from elsewhere in the gospel (e.g. 4:12; 6:52; 7:18; the two miraculous feedings), the two feedings are presupposed though in fact it seems that they are two accounts of one event (§ 725*g*, 755*a*). The severity of **d** the rebuke is striking: v 15 is already stern, but in 17 their minds are said to be 'closed', with a word elsewhere applied only to the stubborn Jews and especially the Pharisees; the v quoted in 18 (Jer 5:21; Ezek 12:2) originally castigated the rebellious people of Israel who refused to be converted, and is reminiscent of the quotation of Isaiah in Mt 13:14—15 against the Jews who rejected Jesus. **15.** This saying serves to introduce the dialogue, and link it to what precedes. It is not organically connected with the rest of the passage, and in Mk seems to be forgotten (otherwise Mt). In Judaism yeast stands for bad will and dispositions (SB I. 729, IV. 468; 1 Cor 5:6—8; Gal 5:9). The bad will of the Pharisees has just been shown, and that of Herod earlier (6:14—29); it is against this, according to Mk, that Jesus warns his disciples, almost hinting here and in what follows that only such dispositions could prevent them from seeing the significance of his miracles. **16.** The JB translation is impossible, RSV better.

22—26 The Blind Man of Bethsaida receives e Sight—This cure is highly significant in Mk's structure: it brings to a close the long section about the instruction of the disciples which began in 6:35. Whereas in 8:14—21 their blindness to the significance of Jesus' miracles was underscored, in vv 27—30 Peter's understanding of the mystery of his personality is expressed, thus concluding the first part of the gospel which was concerned with the revelation of his identity as Messiah, and setting the stage for the revelation, in the second part, of his suffering role as Messiah. It is impossible not to see in this incident a parable of the gradual opening of the eyes of the disciples and in particular of Peter (who is also a man of Bethsaida: Jn 1:44), especially since the stages of the narrative correspond to the stages seen in vv 27—30: Jesus leads away from an inhabited area (23*a*, 27*a*), puts a question (23*b*, 27*b*) to which an insufficient answer is given (24, 28); Jesus again takes the initiative (25*a*, 29*a*) at which full sight is achieved (25*b*, 29*b*); Jesus then commands secrecy (26, 30). But the account also looks back to the cure of the deaf **f** man by the Lake in 7:31—37, to such an extent that it has been suggested that they are in fact accounts of the same incident: some unnamed people bring the sufferer, Jesus takes him aside, uses spittle in the cure (which occurs nowhere else in Mk), touches him again, and when he is cured enjoins silence. But there are sufficient differences to show that, rather than the incident being the same one, Mk wished to show that it was complementary. Each comes at the end of a parallel series of incidents (cf § 753*d*), and the healing of the deaf and the blind are often complementary in prophecies of the messianic era (see references given in § 754*d*, for which see also notes on this use of what appears to be a magical technique). **22.** On Bethsaida see § 722*f*; it was really too large to be called a 'village' (also 26), whence it has been suggested that Mk located there a story handed down without indications of place, chiefly for symbolic reasons (see above), and to correspond to the destination announced in 6:45. **23, 26.** Mk's motif of secrecy is shown here (cf § 748). Such miraculous healings are frequently accomplished away from the crowds for the sake of reverent privacy (see 5:37 and note, 7:33), but the final command of silence is not so explicable. In 26*b* a command not to return to the village would be extraordinarily

755f harsh, if not impossible of accomplishment; on textual grounds also the reading 'Do not tell anyone of it in the village' is preferable (C. M. Turner, JTS 26 (1924/5), 18).

g 27—33 Peter's Confession and Correction (Mt 16: 13—23; Lk 9: 18—22)—This passage is the great watershed in the gospel. During the first half of the gospel the question of Jesus' identity has been posed in various ways, by various people and with various answers. Some had refused the evidence of his teaching and signs of power; some had acknowledged him as a prophet, the Baptist or Elijah (6:14—15), fulfilling the predictions about an eschatological prophet in Dt 18:15—18 and Mal 4:5; the chosen disciples had shown awe and wonder, but, especially during the period of their special instruction, their blindness had been stressed (§ 755d, 748b) until the highly significant miracle of the opening of the blind man's eyes (vv 22—26); only the evil spirits had fully acknowledged Jesus for what he was. Now the disciples too proclaim him as Messiah—the triumphant conclusion of the first part of the gospel. But immediately the second part of their instruction starts, which will end only with the Crucifixion and Resurrection. Jesus replies to Peter's confession with a command to remain silent, for they do not understand what are the true nature and consequences of his messiahship, and cannot instruct others until they do. The popular conception of the Messiah concentrated so much on a political liberator that Jesus never describes himself as Messiah: he hints that the messianic title 'Son of David' is insufficient (12: 35—37); before the high priest (14:62) he immediately corrects the answer to the high priest's question; here he does not even express acceptance of the title. To describe his role and mission he preferred to use other titles and imagery, especially the Servant of the Lord and the Son of Man (see § 676i—p). It has recently been suggested (E. Haenchen 'Die Komposition von Mk 8:27—9:1' NT6 (1963), 81—109) that this section was artificially composed by Mk in function of his theological interests, using e.g. 6:14—15 to provide the answers of 8:28. Haenchen maintains that there was no reason for Jesus to ask what the opinion of either men in general or the disciples in particular was. He had already told them what he was (cf 2:10, 28). But, while there is undoubtedly some relationship between 6:14—15 and 8:28, it could equally well be the other way. The sayings in 2:10, 28 need not have been pronounced by Jesus on these occasions (see notes). The style of the double question and the vocabulary are, however, familiar

h features in Mk. **27—29.** On the details of setting and personalities see § 727bc. **31—33.** On the force and historicity of these vv see § 727ij. **32a** shows Christ as the model of the fearless Christian preacher of the cross. The terminology is that of the mission preaching of the Church; especially *parresia* (openness, confidence, fearlessness), which occurs only here in the synoptic gospels, is constantly stressed in Paul and Ac as a quality essential to preaching the word (Ac 4:13, 29; 2 Cor 3:12; Eph 6: 19). **33.** Here and in 30 Mk uses the same word for Jesus' reaction, which normally means 'remonstrate' (as JB in v 32). Mk continues to stress the blindness of the disciples, now not to Jesus' personality but to the nature of his office. Mt softens the rebuke both times (cf § 724e).

i 34—9:1 Conditions of Following Christ (Mt 16: 24—28; Lk 9:23—27)—A collection of sayings which show that the follower of the suffering Messiah must be ready for suffering; for its composition see § 727k. Mk stresses more than the rest of the tradition that per-

secution for the sake of Christ embraces also persecution **75** for the sake of the gospel (cf § 747g). It was probably Mk who introduced the expression 'gospel' or 'Good News' into the evangelic material from Pauline traditions (Marxsen, p. 82—83). In **35**, where Mk has 'for my sake and for the sake of the gospel', Mt and Lk both omit the second phrase. Similarly in the Q version of v **38** (Mt 10: 33 = Lk 12:9) 'and of my words' is lacking. By adding these phrases of explanation Mk teaches that what is done for the sake of the gospel is done for Christ's sake, because Christ is present in the preaching of the gospel. The same thought lies behind Mt 10:40—42; Lk 10:16.

2—8 The Transfiguration (Mt 17:1—8; Lk 9:28—36; **75** cf Jn 12:27—30)—Views on the historical occurrence which lies behind this story differ widely. Bultmann (p. 259) virtually assumes that the event behind it occurred after the Resurrection, following Wellhausen and Loisy (who maintained this simply because he could not see that the scene could have any meaning for the apostles during Jesus' earthly ministry: *Les Evangiles Synoptiques* II (1912), 39—40); this opinion is widely held, even by some Catholic scholars. But Mk certainly sees some sense in its position here, coming as it does with such forcible contrast at the beginning of his section devoted to the revelation of the suffering Messiah. M. P. Müller (ZNW, 51 (1960) 56—64) considers it a creation of the community to legitimize the position of Peter, James and John. But the major difficulty historically is to decide in what the phenomena consisted. It is perhaps most satisfactory to consider the account to be an attempt to describe a mystical (but not therefore unreal) experience by these disciples of Jesus' transformation when in union with the Father in prayer (Lk 9:29). It would not be without analogy in the experiences of the saints. This is one of the rare occasions after the introduction where apocalyptic language is used to show Jesus' person and dignity. For men of those times it was a mode of expression which came easily. For notes to this passage see § 728ae (Mt's version). There are only minor differences between the first two evangelists, e.g. Mt omits the reference to an 'earthly bleacher' (Mk v 3) which shows immediately the supernatural quality of the figure. **6.** (omitted by Mt, to excuse Peter) Mk's comment illustrates his theme of the misunderstanding of the apostles (§ 755cd). They do not yet understand that the goal is to be reached only after suffering. But Peter's reaction is due, not, as their failure to comprehend Jesus had been in 8:17—20, to spiritual blindness, but to the awe felt before divine mysteries.

9—13 Question about Elijah (Mt 17:9—13)—As an **b** appendix to the story of the Transfiguration two separate matters are treated. **9—10.** The command of silence which is so regularly imposed in Mk (cf § 748). This time we gain the valuable insight that the moment of full understanding, and so of full, open revelation, is the resurrection. Mk hints at the connexion between the disciples' understanding and open revelation by his v 10 (omitted by Mt); they cannot proclaim until they have understood, and they will not understand the mystery of Jesus' suffering and glory until after the resurrection. **10.** The puzzle was not resurrection of the dead as such, which was accepted by the majority of the Jews. Nineham suggests that they did not see how the figure they had seen in glory could die and so rise again. More probably they could not grasp the idea of a separate resurrection for the Son of Man before the general resurrection at the end of time. **11—13.** The saying of Jesus here **c** given may have been handed down without context, for it is introduced by a dialogue whose style and vocabulary

56c are typical of Mk. Its position here may be accounted for by the appearance of Elijah at the Transfiguration, unless it originally came straight after 9:1, and the Transfiguration is a later insertion. Mal 3:22—23 had prophesied that Elijah would precede the Messiah. Jesus hints that John the Baptist has already performed Elijah's function of preparation, but immediately turns to another aspect of his role as precursor: he is the precursor also in suffering at the hands of the Jews. But the abruptness and difficult sequence of 12—13 have led to the theory that 12*b* is a gloss on 13 which has slipped into the text. It is lacking in Mt, though it could also have been omitted by him for the sake of clarity. However the general sense is doubtless that understood by Mt, that the Baptist's sufferings are an earnest of those of Jesus. It is difficult to see what passage of scripture could be meant by 'just as the scriptures say about him in 13*b*; this may be the reason why Mt omits the phrase.

d **14—29 The Epileptic Demoniac** (Mt 17:14—21; Lk 9:37—43*a*)— Some explanation of the presence of this single miracle story in the part of the gospel concerned with Jesus' approaching sufferings seems required. It could have been drawn in by the mention of the failure of the disciples, whose lack of understanding is so constantly stressed (cf § 748*b*), or by the indication in Jesus' reproaches (19) of his coming departure. Nineham has assembled some indications that the evangelist had in mind a comparison between Moses' descent from the mountain encounter with God and Jesus' descent from the Transfiguration: some visible transformation of Jesus, such as that of Moses in Ex 34:29—30, would explain the otherwise unexplained amazement in 15; both find their lieutenants engaged in strife with the people; both pronounce a condemnation of infidelity. Commentators (e.g. Bultmann, V. Taylor) have pointed out that there appear to be two stories combined: in 14—19 and 28—29 the disciples hold the stage and the interest centres on their impotence through neglect of prayer, the father playing only a secondary part, while in 20—27 there is a normal miracle-story. But it would be better to speak of different emphases: the two main centres of interest are Jesus' reproach of lack of faith in 19, to which 14—18 leads up, and the father's cry in 24. Both these concern faith. It is all the more surprising that the lesson which Mk adds—as he appears to do—in 28—29 concerns prayer. Mt's exchange of this for a saying on the power of faith is only logical. Lk merely omits Mk's lesson, and substitutes the wonder at God's greatness usual after a miracle (9:43).

e **17—26.** The symptoms are those of procursive epilepsy: sufferers from this intermittent disease, found chiefly in children, may injure themselves by running into water or fire (22), and are liable to attacks of *le grand mal*; in this the patient falls to the ground (20) with convulsions and movement of the jaw (18), foaming at the mouth (21), often a cry (26), and finally lies in a coma (26), cf *A Textbook of the Practice of Medicine*, ed. F. W. Price (1966[10]). The only questionable feature in Mk's graphic description is 'goes rigid' (18), for in the final coma the body is limp, not stiff. Lk removes this element, but his whole description is more economical. **19.** Jesus' solemn reproach recalls those to Moses' generation Nm 14:27; Dt 32:5, 12; cf Mk 8:12. It is not clear to whom precisely it is directed, disciples, father, scribes, crowds, or all. **20.** The confrontation with Jesus distresses the powers of evil; we are reminded of the early stages of the conflict between the spirit of Jesus and the unclean spirits (§ 747*cd*). Lk will

not allow the boy to suffer even any passing discomfort **756e** from his contact with Jesus, and puts both these and the final convulsions of the cure earlier (cf Lk 9:39*b*). **24.** This cry expresses the complicated psychological **f** state of many; it is not an analytic theological statement. **25.** Commentators who hold that two stories are combined in this incident claim that the crowd, already mentioned in 17, appears here as if for the first time. This, as the JB translation, is incorrect; the compound Gr. word, used only here, should mean that an existing crowd was increasing. Jesus prefers privacy for his miracles (5:40; 7:33 etc). **26—27.** There is surely an echo here, audible to the Christian ear, of the resurrection of the dead. The Gr. of 26*b* suggests the overtones 'Jesus . . . raised him up, and he arose'; both verbs are frequently used of Christ's own resurrection. **28—29.** The *mise en scène* and vocabulary are typically Markan, which suggests that Mk has tacked on a saying, handed down without context, which applies here less aptly than the lesson of 23*b*.

30—32 Second Prophecy of the Passion (Mt **g** 17:22—23; Lk 9:43*b*—45)—see § 728*i*. The journey to Jerusalem is punctuated by a regular reminder that its goal is the passion. The atmosphere is subdued and threatening (v 30). Lightfoot has pointed out (*History*, p. 117—20) that each of the three predictions is followed by a scene where the apostles appear in an unfavourable light (8:32—33; 9:33—37; 10:35—45)—they still do not understand—contrasting with a (favourable) reference to someone outside the circle of the disciples (8:34; 9:38—41; 10:46—52), and some teaching on the greatness of renunciation called for, with always some mention too of the reward (8:34—9:1; 9:42—48; 10:42—45). This strengthens the impression that this triple repetition of the prediction is didactic rather than historical, cf § 727*ij*.

33—50 Various Instructions about Service (Mt **h** 18:1—9; Lk 9:46—50; 17:1—2)—The unity of this section is formed less by subject-matter than by verbal links: 33—37 concerns the greatness of service to little ones in Christ's name; 38—41 is linked on by 'in Christ's name', and 42—48 (whose internal coherence comes from the word *scandalon*) by 'little ones'; 49—50 contains three short sayings about fire and salt, drawn in by the incidental mention in 48 of 'fire'.

33—37 Greatness of Service—The point of this scene lies in the two sayings 35*b* and 37, for which the rest serves as a setting. Commentators complain that the sayings are badly chosen for Mk's purpose: Nineham would prefer the version in 10:43—44 to the saying in 35*b*, and V. Taylor finds Mt's parallel saying more apt than 37. Nineham also finds Mk's introduction inept (Jesus would not stay in Capernaum on a journey through Galilee in secret, cf 30; grown men do not behave as the disciples do in 33—34). Clearer understanding is possible if it is realized that Mk's angle is quite different to Mt's: Mt transforms into a lesson on spiritual childlikeness what in Mk was a lesson on the dignity of service: 35*b* states how true honour comes from service (cf also Jn 13:14—16—the saying has been handed down in many forms, a sign of frequent repetition either in the Church or by Jesus himself), 36 acts this out by means of a symbolic action in the style of the prophets, and 37 gives a reason for its dignity: it is service to Christ and to the Father. **33—34.** Further example of the disciples' failure to understand the true nature of the kingdom. Mk emphasizes this after each of the predictions of the passion (§ 748*b*). **36.** It has been suggested that this v is linked on by the word 'little child' because the same

756h Aram. word *talya* lies behind both this and 'servant'. But the roles are reversed, for in 36 the child is served not servant. **37.** 'In my name' is a semitism meaning either 'for my sake' or 'in my power' (as 38). In the early Church the Christian was baptized 'into the name of Jesus' (Mt 28:19; 1 Cor 1:13, 15), thus putting himself into the power of Jesus and taking upon himself the person of Jesus; i.e. the expression is the semitic equivalent of what Paul expressed in Gr. terms by the 'body' of Christ.

i **38–40 The Strange Exorcist** (Lk 9:49–50)—This was a problem which faced the apostles frequently enough later (Ac 8:18–24; 19:13–17). The story is here related not only because of the verbal link ('in your name') but also as another example of the disciples' failure through arrogance to understand the nature of their mission of service. Jesus' attitude is not in direct opposition to that of the apostles in Ac: Peter does not forbid Simon Magus to exercise power which he possesses, but refuses to confer power on him; the sons of Sceva are stopped by Paul, but battered by their own victims. **41.** A saying linked by 'in the name' (JB translates well 'because'). The present form of the saying derives from the apostolic Church, not from Jesus himself, since it uses 'Christ' without the article as does Paul, whereas the gospels and Ac have always '*the* Christ'. But Mt 10:42 provides a more semitic version. It reinforces the lesson of v 37. **42–47 Occasions of Sin**—For details see § 729*d*; Mt adds a v, and telescopes Mk's 45, making only two parallel sayings, instead of one each for hand, foot and eye. In context, however, Mt's attitude is slightly different: he is regulating life in the community (cf § 729*a*), whereas Mk is still insisting upon the need for renunciation, in the face of the disciples' inability to grasp the necessity of suffering. This is why Mk here concludes with the threatening 48–50. **47.** On 'hell' see § 741*b*. **50.** On tasteless salt see note to Mt 5:13.

757a **10:1–12 Divorce** (Mt 19:1–9)—This discussion is introduced by a difficult (v inf) note on the progress of Jesus' journey towards Jerusalem; but it is not easy to see why the subject is treated just here. Perhaps it continues the theme of self-denial for the sake of the kingdom which is prominent in this section where the shadow of the cross is so clear. Mk's account shows the formal schema of rabbinic dialectic attested for the earliest rabbinic writings: question (2)—counter-question (4)—*ad hominem* rejoinder which silences the original questioner (5–9). There sometimes follows in the rabbinic parallels a further question by the rabbi's disciples, later in private (as 10), and an explanation (11–12), cf Daube, 141–52. In this case the last element is constructed by Mk by means of his usual structure, entering *the* house (9:33 at Capernaum, cf 7:17), although it hardly fits the circumstances
b of the journey; it is a dramatic convenience. Mk's controversy concerns the legitimacy of divorce; the surprising thing here is that no Jews questioned the legitimacy of divorce, so that the Pharisees' question could only be a shot in the dark, unless they had already heard of Jesus' teaching on this subject. For the Jews the only question concerned sufficient grounds for divorce (as in Mt, cf § 730*c*). Is it possible that Mk, in his Roman milieu, was unaware of this, and formed the question to elicit most straightforwardly Jesus' answer? The exact starting-point of the controversy is of secondary importance, since in any case Jesus sweeps away the permissive legislation of Dt (on which see § 730*d*) to make an absolute prohibition of divorce. Thus, as in 2:25–28 and 7:14–23 on points of the ritual law, so here on a point of social law Jesus departs, not merely from the

customs of the Jews, but from the Mosaic Law itself. 75' On the other two occasions his rulings bring more freedom, but this change makes observance stricter. In each case his new ruling returns to the basic values which underlie OT teaching, in 2:25–28 and here making an explicit appeal to a text, in the rabbinic style.
   1. The geographical indication is self-contradictory, c for Judaea is on the near side of the Jordan. V. Taylor suggests that it indicates a journey through the country beyond Jordan to Judaea, with an inversion of the order of places as in 11:1, where Bethphage and Bethany are mentioned after Jerusalem, though they must have been reached first. But this is no parallel, for it is merely an instance of Mk's trick of giving first a wider, then a narrower datum (RF 1, 203). The oddity is better accounted for by Mk's ignorance of Palestinian geography, cf § 746*a*. **10–12.** The further explanation added by Mk, perhaps using an independent saying of Jesus, defines that divorce and remarriage is tantamount to adultery. V 11 introduces the interesting new legal concept that he commits adultery against his wife, whereas in Jewish law adultery could be committed only against a man (by a wife through intercourse with another man, or by a man through intercourse with another man's wife); now the woman's rights, too, are infringed. V 12 accommodates this teaching to Roman law. It would be impossible in a Jewish context, in which a wife cannot divorce her husband; at most she can sue for him to divorce her (SB I. 512). But in Roman law a woman could divorce. Mt omits this v as irrelevant to his audience. Some MSS read 'leaves' for 'divorces', but this makes the v pointless, since it would only repeat a well-known truth.
   13–16 Jesus and the Children (Mt 19:13–15; Lk d 18:15–17)—A typical little scene where Mk's powers of narration are seen at their best, it completes Jesus' teaching on marriage in the preceding pericope. The teaching of this pericope is primarily in the two sayings: Jesus will accept only those of a childlike disposition. He then is shown acting out this saying (16). It would be a mistake to enquire too closely into the reason for the disciples' prohibition; this and Jesus' indignation are related less for their inherent psychological interest than to form a background for the sayings. O. Cullmann (*Baptism in the NT* (1950), 71–78) discerns in the expression 'Do not stop them' a reflexion of a baptismal formula, some such question in the earliest Christian practice of baptism as 'What is to hinder so and so from being baptized?', of which reflexions may be seen in other NT passages concerning baptism (Mt 3:13–14; Ac 8:36; 10:47; 11:17). There might then be some connexion with questions of infant baptism in the first cent.
   17–31 The Rich Man and Renunciation (Mt 19:16– e 30; Lk 18:18–30)—Mk returns to the subject of renunciation with this story, to which two groups of sayings (23–27, 28–31) are appended. **17–22.** The description of the man's excited approach to Jesus and Jesus' initial reserve, combined with the man's eventual failure, suggest that his enthusiasm outran his generosity. The scene recalls those who cry 'Lord, Lord' ... (Mt 7:21). **17.** The exaggerated respect of this form of address is not necessarily ironical. In Jewish literature there seems to be only one parallel to it (SB 2, 24), and that from the 4th cent. A.D. As Jesus' answer shows, the primary association of 'good' for the Jew is with God; rabbinical literature has a regular formula for God: 'the Good who makes good' (TWNT 1 (1933), 13). Various suggestions about Jesus' meaning have been made, but the purpose of

7e his reply must surely be to turn the man's extreme reverence to God (ibid, 15). Since the Law too is called good as being the expression of God's will, and Jesus immediately quotes the Law, his more specific intention may be to turn the man's attention to the Law, suggesting that it is the divine teacher. This is at any rate Mt's interpretation, but he softens the reply, perhaps to avoid its possible implications against Jesus' consciousness of his divinity. These implications are not inescapable: Jesus could merely object to the combination of 'good' with the restrained appellation 'teacher', or be drawing the man on to acknowledge his divinity. **20b.** Mt changes this phrase, calling the man 'a young man', though Mk's phrase would sound more natural on the lips of an older man. In Lk (v 18) he is an official, which implies a certain age. **21a.** This touch of warmth occurs only in Mk. The aorist tense would normally imply a single action, so in this case a *gesture* of affection, rather than the mere feeling; but Mk's use of tenses cannot be pressed.

f **23—27 Difficulty of Entering the Kingdom**—This little section is more than usually pleonastic even for Mk: the repetition of the saying 'How hard it is . . .', first applied to wealth and then generalized, the return to the difficulty for the wealthy in 25, the double astonishment of the disciples are all difficult. Moreover, in view of 28 there is little reason why the disciples should be so dismayed by 23 or 25. Wealth was indeed considered a mark of God's favour, especially in the Wisdom Literature (JB), but the spiritual dangers of riches were a commonplace (SB I, 827—8). The conclusion in 27 has also more force if the saving power of God is praised in general, not only for overcoming the obstacle of riches. S. Légasse has therefore suggested (NTS 10 (1963/4) 480—7) that the dialogue originally started at 24b, and that 25 had no specific reference to 'a rich man'. The earlier part was added when Mk attached it to its present context. **25.** This figure of a camel is used also in later rabbinic literature (c. A.D. 260, SB I. 828) as an example of the impossible. Hence there is no need to posit either a gate called 'The Eye of a Needle' or a mistake (*camelos* for *camilos* = cable). This, with 27, contains the essence of all Paul's soteriology.

g **28—31 The Reward of Renunciation**—The saying of Jesus forms a second appendix to the story of the rich man, added on by the rather awkward 38. Mk is careful to balance sayings on the need for renunciation with promises of its reward (cf § 756g). Bengel notes that the items renounced are given disjunctively, those promised, cumulatively. As in 8:35 'for the sake of the gospel' is probably an addition by Mk (cf § 755i). **30.** It has been held that the word used in 'in this present time' denotes that for Mk the eschatological era has already arrived (cf 1:15; 12:2). But the usage of *kairos* is far broader than this cf J. Barr, *Semantics of Biblical Language* (1961), 225—6. It is here perhaps contrasted to the world to come, making use of the Jewish idea of two eras; Paul often uses it (as Mk here) with the connotation of a time of persecution and suffering (Rm 8:18; 11:5; 2 Cor 8:14). This v, with 17 which brackets the whole section, is the sole passage in the synoptics where the expression 'eternal life' appears; it is primarily a Johannine expression (cf on Jn 3:15), for which the synoptics usually employ the idea of kingdom.

h **32—34 Third Prophecy of the Passion** (Mt 20:17—19; Lk 18:31—34)—On the prophecies of the Passion and their sequels see § 756g. Here the details of Jesus' sufferings and death are given with such exact accuracy that it must surely be a 'prophecy after the event'. Two other new details are given which serve to intensify the **757h** expectation: the destination of Jerusalem is mentioned and the distress and fear of his followers.

35—45 A Request by the Sons of Zebedee (Mt **i** 20:20—28)—The prediction of the Passion is again immediately followed by a passage which shows that the disciples—or at least the privileged James and John— still failed to understand Jesus' mission and thought only of honours and glory (Mt spares them by making their mother ask the favour). Nineham tentatively suggests that they thought the glorious kingdom would be inaugurated at their arrival in Jerusalem (p. 283); but this perhaps depends too much on the present position of the pericope. It has been pointed out that an adequate answer remains in 40 if all reference to suffering (38b—39) is cut out. It has been suggested also both that 40 is a later invention of the Church to explain why two disciples so prominent in the gospels have no part in the government of the later community, and that 38b—39 is an invention of the Church after their martyrdom to show that Jesus foresaw it. Furthermore the cup and the baptism are said to reflect the later sacraments of Eucharist and Baptism. But evidence that John was martyred is extremely slender, a weak current running contrary to the main stream of the tradition. (A. Feuillet, 'La Coupe et le Baptême de la Passion', RB 74 (1967) 361—2). Certainly the story as a whole is unlikely to have been invented by the Church to honour these apostles, since—as Mt saw—it presents them in a far from favourable light. The saying of Jesus here reported is perfectly explicable in terms of OT and Jewish symbolism, and provides a valuable insight into his view of his future suffering, and his disciples' share in it. A *cup* is used in the OT as a symbol of **j** someone's destiny (Ps 16 (15):5 cf Mk 14:36) more especially in so far as this is brought by the wrath of God in punishment for sins (Hos 5:10; Is 51:17, 22; Jer 25: 15, 27—28; also in the first century Pss Sal 8:14—15; and at Qumran 1 QpH XI 10—15). It is clear that from his baptism by John onwards Jesus thought of his messianic role in terms of the Suffering Servant of the Lord in Deutero-Isaiah, who would (Is 53:4—11) take upon himself the punishment for sin deserved by his people. Here he expresses this consciousness in terms of the cup of God's wrath. *Baptism* or immersion in waters is a frequent symbol of misfortune in the OT (Ps 42 (41):7; Is 43:2; Jb 9:31); in Is 30:27—28 it is used specifically in connexion with punishment sent by God. This would rejoin the symbolism of the cup. But in the NT the many uses of the word all refer to a rite of purification. There is no need to suppose an anachronistic reference by Jesus here to specifically Christian baptism, for Jesus was familiar with John the Baptist's rite of purification (1:9—11; Jn 3:22; 4:1—2). By this symbol, then, he alludes to his Passion under the aspect of a purification of sin. When he invites James and John to share his cup and his baptism he is not necessarily inviting them to share his death. Their sharing could be understood—it is questionable whether Mk thinks of them as understanding it at all—in the sense which has been so constantly prominent since the first prophecy of the Passion (e.g. 8:34) of Christian renunciation (cf § 747g). **42—45.** Mk uses this occasion to append **k** some sayings on the dignity of service, and especially on Jesus' service in giving his life. A similar passage (9:36—37) followed the squabble about precedence (cf 35—41) after the second prophecy of the Passion. **42a.** uses formulas which Mk frequently employs to dovetail in further material (why should Jesus need to call them to himself now?), and 43—44 is manifestly an expansion

757k of the saying in 9:35. But **45** contains valuable new teaching, for which see § 731*k*.

l 46—52 The Healing of Bartimaeus (Mt 20:29—34; Lk 18:35—43)—This second of the two cures of blind men in Mk is highly significantly placed. Until now the blindness of the crowds, and even of the disciples, has been constantly stressed (cf § 755*c* for references). But in the next episode, Jesus is to be publicly acclaimed as Messiah. That this symbolic dimension of the miracle is not imagined is shown by the similar function of the other cure of the blind (cf § 755*e*). The nearness of Jerusalem is stressed by the double mention of Jericho (some 15 miles from Jerusalem), which they were leaving (46), and of the continued journey (52). The startling reversal of Mk's usual secrecy motif (see § 748) is underlined with all possible force. Usually it is Jesus who commands silence (1:43; 3:12; 5:19, 43, etc); here it is the onlookers who attempt to silence Bartimaeus' acclaims (hitherto only evil spirits have made such clear, public acknowledgements), while Jesus approves his words by effecting the cure. The form of the acclaim, too, looks forward to the mention of David in 11:10 (q.v.), and the 'hosanna' of 11:9 (which literally means 'Help!', as Bartimaeus' cry). The miracle is in itself significant, for opening the eyes of the blind is one of the chief works predicted for the Messiah (Is 29:18; 32:3; 35:5 etc), but its context makes it especially important.

758a 11—13 Ministry in Jerusalem—The gospel now enters its final phase, for Jesus' activity in Jerusalem leads directly up to his Passion. All the events recounted fit into this pattern: the messianic entry and cleansing of the temple (11:1—11, 15—19—with which is intertwined the symbolic withering of the fig-tree: 11:12—14, 20—25) lead to a direct challenge by the representatives of all the authorities (27—33) to which Jesus replies with a parable which forces them to a decision (12:1—12). Then comes a group of four controversies, an artificial collection representing Jesus' final confrontation with the leading parties of the Jews (13—37). A pendant to all this is provided by the diptych of the condemnation of the scribes and the praise of a poor widow (38—44). The die is now cast and it remains only to provide for the future after Jesus' death (13:1—37). Mk spans this activity over three days (11:1, 12, 19, 20) which perhaps correspond to the three days of the Passion and Resurrection. But this division, no less than the whole unit, is artificial. The third day is heavily overloaded; the postponement of the cleansing until the second day is unmotivated and curious. There are also possibilities that Jesus' ministry in Jerusalem was not confined to these three days: the 'day after day' of 14:49 implies it (in Mk he teaches only on one day); Jn certainly envisages more than one visit to Jerusalem; the group of four controversies is a standard unit in rabbinic literature, and it is unlikely that these groups of people succeeded each other as rapidly as Mk's account might suggest. Above all the development and fluctuations in relationships between Jesus and the authorities are improbably mercurial. But there is a certain didactic convenience in thus neatly assembling all the incidents at Jerusalem, which overrides the evangelist's very secondary (or indeed minimal) biographical interest.

b 11:1—11a The Messiah enters Jerusalem (Mt 19:1—11; Lk 19:28—38; Jn 12:12—18)—The Jerusalem ministry opens with a solemn entry and cleansing of the temple. Mk's allusive account of the entry shows that it was of the highest significance, though his account does no more than hint at this significance, leaving the other evangelists—notably Mt—to bring out all the significance by a series of minor adjustments. One of the **75** most striking differences between Mk and Mt is that in Mk there are none of Mt's great crowds; the scene could have been enacted and witnessed by the immediate followers of Jesus alone. It is historically interesting to recover the occasion of this scene, for if Mk's three days represent an artificial construction we cannot assume that it actually took place on 'Palm Sunday'. Much of the activity described fits the Jewish Feasts either of Tabernacles (October) or of Dedication (December). At both these feasts branches were carried in procession (primarily at Tabernacles) and Ps 118 (117), from which Mk 11:9 is drawn, was sung (composed probably for the Dedication). Of the two feasts that of the Dedication is more suitable, for the dedication was described as a cleansing of the temple (2 Mc 10:5, after its defilement by the Gentiles under Antiochus Epiphanes), and the cleansing of the Temple by Jesus is the direct sequel to this episode. But consequently, if the episode was regarded by the Christian community as a new dedication, some of the details of the procession may have been heightened to show this meaning. The *background* against which **c** the scene has its significance is given in § 732*a—e*; here attention is drawn only to Mk's special features. On the whole his account refers less obviously to the background: in **1** they are only 'close to' the messianic Mount of Olives, not on it. But in **2** the sacred nature of the procession is hinted by 'that no one has yet ridden'; a beast employed for sacral purposes must never have been used: Nm 19:2; Dt 21:3. In **4—6** the execution of Jesus' command is narrated in full, to show his mysterious incontrovertible authority (cf 14:12—16 and § 761*d*), but the passage from Zech which gives the colt its importance is not explicitly cited. Nor does Mk v 7 go to the same lengths as Mt to ensure that the prophecy is fulfilled literally in every detail. In **8—9** there is no sign of a crowd (the 'many' could refer merely to many of the disciples) unlike Mt's 'great crowds' or Lk's 'whole multitude' praising God at the tops of their voices. The shouts in **10** are difficult to interpret. It is clear that **d** the acclamation is directed to the messianic kingdom as such, and not to Jesus (as Mt) as king (explicit in Lk). But the expression 'our father David' is unprecedented; there was a rule that only Abraham, Isaac and Jacob should be given this title (SB II. 26). Accordingly F. C. Burkitt suggested (JTS 17 (1915/6), 144) that the cry was 'Kingdom of our Father! Kingdom of David' and the cry was telescoped. The Father would then be God, and the cry would hail God's messianic kingdom. Similarly, since 'Hosanna' seems to have lost its original sense of 'Help us!' and become either a mere shout of acclaim, or a name for the branches waved on such occasions (ibid 141), the final phrase could mean 'Up with your branches!'. The expression 'Hosanna in the highest' occurs nowhere else; it could, strictly, also mean 'Send help *from* heaven'. **11.** This v seems to be put in by Mk to enable him to insert the story of the fig-tree before the cleansing of the temple. It is perhaps not fanciful to see in Jesus' survey (though a very common word is used) a gesture by which he shows his control of the temple as Messiah.

12—14, 20—25 The Withered Fig-Tree (Mt 21: **e** 18—22, cf Lk 13:6—9)—Mk has previously sandwiched an incident between two similar ones (3:20—21, 22—30, 31—35) or two parts of a story (5:21—24, 25—34, 35—43). Here he sandwiches the cleansing of the Temple between the two halves of the action which is a symbol of it. Jesus' action is certainly an acted parable or prophetic action (for OT background, § 732*k*). But the

58e puzzling feature is the unreasonable expectation by Jesus, especially as it was not the time for figs (13). It has often been pointed out that this almost puts the miracle on a par with the unreasonable miracles of the non-canonical gospels. It is of course no solution to claim that the story was made up by the evangelist on some such basis as Lk's parable (13:6—9), or that the evangelist took over a story invented by the community to explain a barren fig-tree beside this road; this merely shifts the blame. The evangelist's note that it was not the season for figs shows that he was well aware of the unreasonableness, and that he was interested only in its symbolic value (similarly the unusual remark in 14*b* that the disciples noted his saying). The symbolic actions of the prophets in the OT are not by any means always reasonable (Jer 13:1—11; Ezek 4—5). The point of the fig-tree is that its leaves give the impression it is healthy, as the flourishing business of the temple gives the impression that Jewish worship is healthy; but a closer inspection reveals the barrenness of both. The proof of the one consists in the adverse reaction of the authorities to Jesus, in spite of the popular support, and of the other **f** in the actual withering. **22—25.** Instead of commenting on the sign (considering it perhaps too clear to need comment) Mk takes the opportunity of adding three sayings, linked by and centred upon 'faith' and 'prayer'. An alternative version of the first existed also in Q (Mt 17:20 = Lk 17.6). This and the second are inserted at the opportunity to show the strength of faith. Nineham notes that **24** shows the energetic manner of expression which so many sayings of Jesus possess (e.g. 9:43; 10:25; Lk 14:26): we cannot 'expect to receive literally "whatever" we ask, however selfish and contrary to God's will. Perhaps v 25 was added to guard against such a notion' (p. 300). **25** shows that Mk was aware of at least some of the material incorporated by Mt in the Sermon on the Mount, where this follows the 'Our Father'. He sometimes gives the impression of deliberately keeping silent (1:21). Standing in prayer is the normal position for a Jew, but kneeling or prostration could occur in times of stress.

g 15—19 Cleansing of the Temple (Mt 21:12—13; Lk 19:45—48; Jn 2:13—17)—The position of this incident is different in the synoptic and in the Johannine account, but each is best accounted for by theological reasons, neither providing a sure indication of when it actually occurred. Jn's account stands early, as a sign of the beginning of the new order, a manifesto or demonstration of what is to come in Jesus' ministry. For the synoptics it comes almost as the climax of his ministry. The renewal of Jerusalem, the holy city, and its temple was to be one of the most confidently expected and prominent events of the renewal of all things effected by the Messiah (Mal 3:1; Ezek 40—48; Pss Sal 17:30—31; Apoc 21:2—5, 22—24). This was to be accompanied (e.g. Pss Sal and Apoc) by an influx of the nations to receive salvation from Jerusalem; this is perhaps the point of Mk's phrase, omitted by Mt and Lk, 'for all the peoples'. **15, 17.** On the details of the account see § 732*gh.* **16.** (Mk only) A similar prescription is given in the Mishnah (SB II. 27) to safeguard the use of the sanctuary for sacred purposes only. The Temple was so positioned that it was a convenient short cut; the Temple enclosure is still so used. **18.** This reaction is both strangely dilatory and strangely violent. Swift action by the plentiful Temple police or the guards stationed overlooking the temple in the fortress Antonia would have been expected. We simply do not know the extent of the disturbance which he caused; the synoptic account gives a much less violent impression than Jn;

there is no whip, no wrath, no indication that he 'drove **758g** them *all* out of the temple', only that he made a start of it. Since the importance of the action lies mainly in its symbolic value, the disturbance may not have seriously exceeded that normal to an oriental bazaar. A similar answer may be given to those who point out forcibly that we have no evidence of general abuse in the practices either of changing temple money or of selling sacrificial victims, so that wholesale eviction would have been morally unjustified. **18b.** Nineham complains that Jesus' popularity was no reason for deciding to kill him (Lk's alteration presupposes the same point). But Mk often adds on an observation loosely by means of this particle 'for' (e.g. 1:22; 2:15; 5:42 etc); it should not, then, be pressed.

27—33 Authority of Jesus Questioned (Mt 21:23—27; **h** Lk 20:1—8)—This controversy begins the final show-down with the authorities, some members of each of the three groups within the Sanhedrin being represented. But Bultmann (p. 19—20) suggests that the controversy was not originally connected with the cleansing of the Temple (cf § 758*a,* on the artificial arrangement of this part of the gospel), although the cleansing in Jn too is followed by a similar discussion (2:13—22). The 'these things' of 28 has no obvious antecedent, and could refer to anything. Mt and Lk both supply an antecedent by showing Jesus teaching/preaching the Good News at the beginning of the pericope. Mt perhaps felt that such a rabbinic-style controversy about so precise a point as authority should refer to teaching authority (cf § 732*l,* Lk, however, writing for an audience unfamiliar with these points of law, makes them ask who is giving Jesus authority—quite a different question—and removes the precise legal formulation of Mk 29*b*). The mention and comparison with John's baptism leads Bultmann to conjecture that the question originally concerned Jesus' authority to baptize (Jn 3:22, 26). He also suggests that the original opponents are presupposed to accept John's authority, and that 31—33 are therefore a later addition. But his reasoning is not cogent. The cross-questioning follows the formal schema of a rabbinic controversy (cf § 757*a*): question (28), counter-question (29—30), expected answer (33*a*), *ad hominem* rejoinder (33*b*). Jesus still does not reveal his messianic secret, but, just as in 1:21—27, invites them to reflect. Much the same situation arises in Jn 5:19—47; 7:15—30; 8:13—20. The parable which follows is a further invitation to self-examination.

12:1—12 Parable of the Wicked Husbandmen (Mt **759a** 21:33—46; Lk 20:9—19)—For this parable Jesus uses a clear historical background: much of the land in Galilee was in the possession of foreign overlords and farmed for them by bailiffs. Perhaps also he envisages the law by which if a proselyte dies intestate his land can be claimed by anyone, and he who is in possession has prior claim; this could be the particular point of killing the heir. The parable clearly refers to Israel: the figure of Israel as the vineyard of the Lord could not but spring to the voice from heaven at the Baptism and Transfiguration. In this case the tenants must represent the authorities in Israel and the parable be a threat against them. But the question arises: how many of the details **b** were intended as allegorical? In Mt's version the allegory is widespread, and Mk's '*beloved* son' is clearly a reference to the voice from heaven at the Baptism and Transfiguration. But a Jewish audience would not understand the son to refer to the Messiah, since in pre-Christian Judaism he is never given the title of the Son of God (Cullmann, *Christology,* p. 272—5). Hence, even though it be granted

759b that the original parable contained no allegory, there is no need to suppose, as some have done, that in Jesus' original parable there were only three servants (a frequent number in popular stories), and that the son was added by Christian allegorizers. In addition the Christian community is unlikely to have added the son in this form, since the parable contains no possible allusion to the resurrection. The son, then, need not be excised as the product of later allegorizers, and remains to testify to the reckless depravity of the vine-dressers. But the version in the Gospel of Thomas is free from allegorical traits, which suggests that the gradual process of assimilation to the actual happenings of sacred history of the details of the story, which reaches its term in Mt (see § 733*bc*), did not originate with Jesus. **8.** The factor of throwing the body out of the vineyard, and so depriving the son even of burial, is intended to show the last depths of brutality. Mt and Lk reversing the order, use the trait to form an allegory of Jesus, led out of the city and then killed. **9—11.** See on Mt 21:40—42.

c 13—37a Four Controversies—These four last controversies between Jesus and the Jews form a group, similar to disputes on four parallel subjects in which R. Joshua ben Hananiah was interrogated at the end of the 1st cent. A.D. The subjects come under the headings of (1) *hokma* = wisdom concerning a point of law (2) *boruth* = ridicule, ridiculing a belief held by the interrogated (also in the example from the Talmud this is belief in the resurrection) (3) *derek 'eres* = fundamental principles of a good life (4) *haggada* = non-legal teaching, a conflict between texts of scripture. The gospel disputes may, then, correspond to a recognized schema (Daube, p. 158—63); whether Mk himself or a predecessor assembled them in this way is not now discernible. The questions also provide an occasion for a confrontation of Jesus with four principal parties among the Jews, Pharisees, Herodians, Sadducees and scribes. There is no good reason to suppose that they were added after the controversies were already formed, for the parties represented suit the subject of each dispute admirably (though cf § 734*c*).

d 13—17 On Tribute to Caesar (Mt 22:15—22; Lk 20:20—26)—see § 734*bc*. The story of Jesus' pronouncement on this matter would be carefully preserved, even where there was no obligation to pay this tax (e.g. the free cities of the empire) since the Christians' loyalty to Rome was constantly in danger of being called into question (cf Ac 17:7; Pliny, *Letters* 10:90). See also Rm 13:1—7.

e 18—27 The Resurrection of the Dead (Mt 22:23—33; Lk 20:27—40)—see § 734*de*. It has been suggested that the story originally ended at v 25, a brief and memorable answer, as is usual in such stories of controversy between Jesus and his opponents, and that 26—27 were added later. Bultmann's argument (p. 26) seems to be chiefly that Jesus would not use such a rabbinical argument, and this must therefore stem from the early Church. To Mk and his community, in a hellenistic milieu, the first reply (25) was perhaps the most important, as clarifying the nature of the after-life. To the Greeks the idea of resurrection of the body seemed crude and primitive. Thus Paul is mocked for mentioning resurrection at Athens (ac 17:31—32), and has to explain carefully what it means to the Corinthians (1 Cor 15:35—53). The Hellenistic Jewish writer Philo, in his attempt to make Jewish beliefs intelligible and acceptable to Greek minds, explains it as a mere setting free of the soul (*Q in Ex* 2:46). In rabbinic writings, too, about Alexandrian Jews, belief in the resurrection is seen

to be ridiculed for the same reasons (Daube, 159, **75** 162). **26.** Before the division of the Bible into chapter and verse this method of reference to a passage was necessary, (cf (perhaps) 2:26).

28—34 The Greatest Commandment (Mt 22:34—40; **f** Lk 10:25—28)—On the legal and rabbinical background of this discussion see § 734*f—h*. Mk uses a different source from that used by Mt and Lk, who probably depend on Q. It is remarkable among these four confrontations for its friendly atmosphere: the scribe approaches Jesus observing 'how well Jesus had answered' (28) and continues to approve his answer (32), while the pericope concludes with Jesus paying the scribe a high compliment (34*a*—somewhat at variance with the clearly Markan addition 34*b*). The lesson of the pericope in Mk seems to be, not the superiority of Jesus to his opponents, as in the first two controversies, but the agreement of Jesus' teaching on the right priorities in observance of the Law with that of scribes who have a deep understanding of it. It adumbrates the basic solution to the whole question of to what extent Christians should observe the law, in a far more sweeping way than the partial answers of 2:23—28; 7:1—23. There are a number of indications **g** that the pericope in Mk's form stems from a Hellenistic Jewish environment: the insistence on monotheism (29— not in the Q version, and necessary only in a polytheistic environment), and on reasonableness. This latter is a characteristic of hellenistic Jewish writings, e.g. Josephus, and Philo's exposition of the Law; it shows in the addition of 'with all your mind' in 30, the choice of the translation 'with all your understanding' in 33, and finally in 34 'how wisely (or 'with what understanding'—the word occurs only here in the NT) he had spoken'. A further indication is the reserved attitude towards the sacrificial cult, again characteristic of hellenistic Jewry, though also emphasized in the teaching of the OT prophets. All this is of major interest as evidence for Mk's own milieu and the nature of his sources in the Christian community (cf § 746*a*). **34.** At first sight the nation of the kingdom of God is different from that shown elsewhere in the gospels. It is not an eschatological entity which is to come or is approaching, but is already present. The idea is therefore suggested that the Kingdom is present in Jesus and his disciples. The scribe is on the right path, and has only to acknowledge Jesus to be admitted among his disciples and so to the kingdom.

35—37a Christ Son of David? (Mt 22:41—46; Lk **h** 20:41—44)—The last in this group of four questions (see § 759*c*) is raised by Jesus himself. Daube considers that this results from the pattern of a Passover *haggada*; according to this if the youngest son present at the paschal meal does not know how to ask the question which should give the father the cue for his explanation of the paschal ceremony, the father must take the initiative himself (p. 167). This is a possibility, since 34*b* has stated that 'no one dared question him any more', but it is not certain that this pattern really underlies the four questions. The title 'Son of David' for the Messiah is well founded in the OT (2 Sm 7:12—16; Jer 23:5; Ezek 34:23; Mi 5:1—6), at Qumran, and becomes the normal designation for the Messiah in rabbinical literature. But Jesus showed himself to be wary of this title, for it was too bound up with the Jews' expectation of a political Messiah, whose function was conceived purely in terms of the liberation of Israel from the yoke of Rome. In Mk it is used in only one passage apart from **i** this (10:47—8). It has accordingly been suggested (e.g. by Nineham, p. 330) that this passage 'implies, not that the Messiah was *not merely* Son of David, but that he was

59i not son of David *at all'*. But Jesus does not in fact refuse the Messiah this title; he only puts the difficulty, challenging his audience, as often, to further reflexion. Cullmann (*Christology*, p. 132) compares this passage with 3:31ff, where Jesus insists that physical descent is not the most important sort of relationship, without denying that his physical kinsmen are his kinsmen. Similarly here, Jesus does not deny that the Messiah is to be David's son, but merely sets the conundrum that he is in a more important sense David's Lord. By so doing he suggests that the Kingdom of this Davidic Messiah will not be a physical, terrestrial one in the normal sense. If Jesus had denied that he was of the lineage of David it is hard to see how the belief in his Davidic Messiah which was so important in early Christian theology arose, and long before Paul wrote Rm 1:3 (probably using earlier material). Physical descent from David was not a necessity for the Messiah, as is shown by the number of non-Davidic Messiahs who arose: Bar Kocheba was accepted as such in A.D. 132 even by R. Aqiba, the **j** greatest figure in all post-Christian Judaism. At the other extreme Bultmann claims (p. 136—7) that this controversy does not stem from Jesus at all, but is the product of the early Church. His main reason (and that of 'the majority of scholars (Nineham p. 331) who follow him) seems to be that Jesus cannot have had the consciousness that he was a pre-existent being. But this presupposes at least that the picture of Jesus given in Jn is worthless, a presupposition which can no longer be made. It is also difficult to see how a community which laid so much stress on the Davidic descent could have invented a saying which at least shows that it contained some theological difficulty. **36.** This quotation from Ps 110 (109) is frequently used in the NT of Christ (e.g. Ac 2:34; 7:56; Heb 1:3, 13; Eph 1:20; Col 3:1). The fact that David, the greatest figure since Moses, should address the Messiah as 'my Lord' and that he should sit at the right hand of Yahweh shows that he is more than a son of David, cf § 761y.

k 38—40 The Scribes Censured (Lk 20:45—47, cf Mt 23:1—36)—Jesus' ministry in Jerusalem ends with a diptych: the scribes are censured and a poor widow praised; this is as though to sum up the relations of Jesus with his people, indeed the whole moral message of the gospel. The two charges here made may well have been excerpted by Mk from a much larger source, such as is presented by Mt 23 and Lk 11:39—52. V 40 is not grammatically linked to what precedes, which suggests a random selection from a source which has not yet been worked into a carefully structured inventory such as that of Mt 23. It is possible that Jesus' relations with the scribes were not so uniformly negative as these vv suggest. The phrase in 38 *could* be translated 'those of the scribes who like . . .' and similarly in 40 'the ones *who* swallow up'; **32—34** and 35 show a more harmonious side. **38.** The 'robes' are an outer garment; that of the scribes was distinguished by its length (it often trailed on the ground) and voluminousness. There were special occasions when these were worn (at prayer, giving judgement, performing a vow, visiting the sick: SB II. 30—33) which could make them an especial means of self-advertisement. It is not necessarily the customs which are condemned but the vanity with which they are practised. **40.** Jos.Ant. 17, 2, 4 also mentions that the Pharisees made capital out of the gullibility or good will of pious old women. The abuse is not confined to the 1st cent.

l 41—44 The Widow's Mite (Lk 21:1—4)—This story stands by way of contrast to the preceding denunciation of the scribes; it is also linked by the catch-word 'widow'

(40, 42). There were several treasure-houses in the **759l** Temple-area, one of which was known as '*the* treasury'. The usual way of giving offerings was to put them in one of thirteen trumpet-shaped money-boxes labelled 'doves for holocausts', 'incense' etc (the various necessities of the temple services), SB II. 37—42. Jesus could not, therefore, normally be expected to know how much she put in. But in so brief a story there is no need even to appeal to Jesus' supernatural knowledge; nor does the exact sum affect his lesson. But because similar stories exist it has been claimed that a parable told by Jesus has been turned into a story about him. But the stories are not nearly similar enough to warrant such a conclusion. One such story, the most similar, is illustrative (SB II. 46): A woman brought a handful of meal as an offering, which the priest despised; but then in a dream he heard 'Do not despise it, for she is someone who has offered her life'. Here the word for 'life' means also 'self'; hence in 44 too we should perhaps translate 'she has offered her whole self'. **42.** The coin, a *lepton*, is the smallest in circulation; its name means 'tiny'. Mk tells us that two *lepta* make a *quadrans*; at Rome poor retainers might receive one hundred *quadrantes* in lieu of a meal (Juvenal, *Sat.* 1:20; Martial 10:75).

Ch 13 The Eschatological Discourse (Mt 24:1—36; Lk **760a** 21:1—40)—This chapter, the only extended passage in Mk besides the chapter of parables (4) where Jesus is shown teaching, concludes the narrative of his ministry, and prepares for his departure from this world by preparing the Apostles for events which are to come. It falls therefore into the genre of *farewell discourses*, a literary type especially common in the 1st cent. among the Jews, but also widespread at other times and in other cultures. Sayings of a great man are, with varying degrees of literal fidelity, gathered together to form, so to speak, his last will and testament, (e.g. Dt; Jos 23—24; 1 Sm 12; Ac 20:17—35; Plato's *Crito* and *Phaedo*). It falls also into the category of *apocalypse*, another literary type particularly common in Palestine at this time: this consists of a prophecy made in time of persecution, intended to strengthen and encourage the persecuted with assurance that their sufferings have been foreseen by God, and that they will ultimately be vindicated, usually by an intervention of God described in terms of a cosmic catastrophe, cf § 454. The chief examples of this type in the Bible are Dn (written during the persecution by Antiochus Epiphanes in 167 B.C.) and Apoc (written, at least partly, during Nero's persecution in A.D. 64). Hence the use **b** of imagery drawn from Dn in the important vv 14, 19, 29; cf B. Rigaux in Bibl 40 (1959). 675—83. The present discourse shows some affinity to and use of Jewish apocalyptic ideas, so that many have claimed that the evangelist based his work on a Jewish apocalypse rather than on Jesus' own words. Thus Lagrange in RB 3 (1906), 409, though he later abandoned this view; similarly as far as concerns vv 24—27 J. A. T. Robinson, *Jesus and his Coming* (1957), and for the major part of the chapter, Marxsen. On the other hand V. Taylor points out (p. 637) that even the most apocalyptic parts (7—8, 14—20, 24—27, 30—31) can 'hardly be called an apocalypse, since it lacks such characteristic ideas as the casting down of Satan, the Last Judgement, the punishment of sinners, and the blessedness of the righteous'. Kümmel complains (p. 98) that the Jewish apocalyptic broadsheet which is supposed to underlie it must have been 'extremely short and colourless', and he holds that it was at least partly constructed from detached sayings of Jesus. But the variety of opinions on the authenticity and origin of the discourse is too wide to detail here. **Catholic exegesis**

760b has tended to keep as authentic sayings of Jesus as much as possible, and has concentrated on the meaning which
c the evangelists saw in the discourse. On the question of **authorship** of the chapter as a whole it is impossible to give a clear answer. Some Catholics attempt to retain the integral authorship of Jesus. At the other extreme Kümmel says (p. 103): 'These texts drop out of the otherwise reliable tradition of Jesus' sayings. They also form an irreconcilable contrast with his refusal to search for apocalyptic enlightenment and for premonitions of the end'. But if, as will be suggested, we have only a description of Jesus' triumph and that of his community, couched in symbolic and apocalyptic language, there is no contrast with Jesus' refusal to give a date for the end (e.g. v 32; Ac 1:7), since it contains no time indications. The basic reason for the denial of these sayings to Jesus is often that those critics who deny it will not admit the possibility that Jesus had such knowledge of the future. The form of the discourse is also urged against attributing it to Jesus, for the protracted exposition is very different from the other sayings, which are either short and pithy sayings or memorable tales used as parables. Certainly in some parts (e.g. 9—13, see § 760g) there seems to be a combination of sayings of Jesus and their interpretation. It is possible also that the more apocalyptic parts (5—8, 14—27), though based upon sayings of Jesus—since he certainly assumed the apocalyptic title of Son of Man—
d have undergone considerable development. As for the **interpretation**, Lagrange finally held that Mk combined two discourses of Jesus, one concerning the destruction of the temple in A.D. 70 (vv 5—18, 28—32) and another concerning the second coming (vv 19—27). P. Benoit (JB, note *a* to Mt 24) holds that, in the unity created from these two discourses, the whole discourse 'operates on two levels' simultaneously, the destruction of Jerusalem in A.D. 70 being regarded as 'the inevitable forerunner and prefiguration' of the return of Christ at the end of time. The same richly symbolic language is used to describe, in the manner of the Jewish apocalyptic literature, both events, since the one prefigures the other. Feuillet's interpretation (DBS 6 (1960) 1347—50) is subtly different: directly, the discourse envisages only the destruction of Jerusalem, which it describes in metaphorical terms. But the significance of this event is that the old order is destroyed and the new messianic order thereby finally established. Only 'in this sense is it possible to speak of a true proclamation of the end of the world . . . This end is envisaged from the point of view of an event which constitutes its prelude' (col. 1349). Just as the triumph of Christ was to be achieved only by the seeming scandal of the Cross, so the triumph of Christianity is to be achieved only by the seeming scandal of the destruction of Jerusalem. The passage gives, then, a theological interpretation of the destruction, using the highly-coloured biblical language familiar to the Jews from the prophets' announcements of the des-
e truction of cities in the OT. Kümmel however (p. 97 n. 37) characterizes Feuillet's exegesis as 'monstrous'. The imagery is indeed so thickly used that it is difficult to discern what, if any, particular historical reality is intended by it. In any case the central message of the chapter is that of any other apocalypse, the promise of ultimate vindication after persecution; the difference from Jewish apocalypses lies in the positive importance attached to the persecutions, which provide an opportunity of following Christ and spreading his gospel, and in the central position of Christ in the vindication itself. But though the majority of terms used are purely symbolical, devoid of historical reference, it is possible

that v 14 does contain reference to definite historical **760** events. This would then give a historical correlative at least for the final period of trial before the vindication. It would, however, still not necessarily follow that 24—27 were thought of as being realized at the same time. The foreshortening of perspective familiar from the prophetic writings would still leave the possibility that the ultimate vindication should be separated by some considerable period from the climax of the tribulations. Nor indeed is it necessary that the climax of persecution should end with the destruction of Jerusalem; the time is shortened (20) but we do not know from how long. **Mk's version falls into two parts**: Vv 5—23 is built on a chiasmus in which the centre, and so the chief emphasis, is given by vv 9—13. Then follows the short apocalyptic passage on the coming of the Son of Man (24—27). Finally an appendix is given (28—37), made up of isolated sayings of Jesus warning of the sudden and unexpected character of his coming. Thus the accent is different from that of Jewish apocalypses, in that the emphasis is less upon the final vindication than upon the necessity of suffering which precedes it, cf § 747g.

1—4 The Disciples' Question (Mt 24:1—3; Lk **f** 21:5—7)—A saying of Jesus announcing the destruction of Jerusalem is given in various forms and on various occasions (14:58; Jn 2:19; Ac 6:14). Although Mk was to give it again at Jesus' trial, in the Passion-narrative which already existed as a coherent unit, he gives it here too to serve as an introduction to the things to come. The renewal of the Temple was a standing element in the expectation of the last times (SB I. 1003—5; Apoc 21:22—23; Ezek 40—44); this is perhaps the reason why Mk introduces his discourse by the question about the temple, although Jesus' reply does not directly answer the apostles' question. Mt seems to have perceived this difficulty, and fills out the question to make it fit the answer more explicitly. Similarly the scene is set on the mount of Olives perhaps because (Zech 14:4) 'it is the destined scene of the apocalyptic judgement' (Nineham, p. 342). Bultmann notes (p. 36) that 1—2a may well be constructed by Mk to introduce the saying. The same may be true of 3—4, which contain many stock Markan elements.

5—23 The Time of Persecution (Mt 24:4—25; Lk **g** 21:8—24)—V. Taylor asks (p. 499): 'Why do two sections, 5f and 21—23, speak of deceivers?' The sections on deceivers or false Messiahs, and those on the signs of the approaching end (7—8, 14—20), form an outer and inner bracket to centre the interest upon the kernel of this preparatory period, the persecution of the apostolic community. On the content and imagery of these brackets see § 736e, g—j. The core of the passage is formed by three sayings linked by the prediction that they 'will hand you over' (9, 11a, 12). The same word is used as that which describes Jesus' handing over to those responsible for his death (9:31; 10:33; 14:41 etc), thus emphasizing that the disciples follow their master. Many commentators point out that these vv reflect the preoccupations of the early community. Especially the energetic persecutions of Nero would have made these sayings important for the community in the empire. But there is no reason to suppose that they were invented on this occasion; there are enough sayings of Jesus whose clearly semitic character or veiled nature indicates that they are attributable only to him and not to the community (e.g. 8:34—35; 10:39) to show that Jesus insisted that his followers would take up their cross after him in this way. **10.** This is probably an expansion by Mk of the last words of v 9: the witness will consist in preaching the

0g gospel; arrest is seen as a positive opportunity. Lohmeyer, 269—70, points out that the sayings of 9, 11*a*, 12 all have the same rhythmical four-line structure, which the prosaic 10 and 11*b* interrupt. The vocabulary of 10 is also distinctively Markan. It does not imply a world-wide mission in the modern sense, for the evangelist is not looking beyond the confines of his own Mediterranean world (for which Mt, in his parallel passage 24:14, uses the technical term). 'First' is without any immediate point of comparison, but in the context of 5—23 must

h mean: before the coming of the Son of Man. **11.** 'When we remember that most of the early Christians were simple and unlearned people, for whom a speech in court would have been a terrible ordeal, we realize how much such a promise will have meant to them' (Nineham, p. 349). 11*b* gives the sole reference in Mk to the holy Spirit as possessed by the followers of Jesus. 'The phrases are more reminiscent of the Epistles and the Acts' (V. Taylor, p. 509). Mk may have felt that the theological passive 'whatever is given to you' for 'whatever God gives to you' needed expansion; but for the thought cf Lk 12:12; Jn 14:26. **12.** This form of the saying has a reminiscence of Mi 7:6. Informers were one of the chief agents in arrests in the 1st cent. A.D. Trajan (Pliny, *Ep.* 10, 97 cf 96) alludes to their activity against Christians. V. Taylor holds (p. 510) that the phrasing of 12—13 reflects that of the early Church rather than Jesus. 'Persevere' occurs only here in the gospels—the noun only Lk 8:15—but it is a virtue which is constantly stressed by Paul and the other epistles, written

i amid the stress and temptations of persecution. **14—20.** See § 736*g—i* for the significance conveyed by means of reminiscences of the OT. **14** has caused great difficulty. Firstly 'set up' is in the masculine instead of neuter as it should be after 'abomination', suggesting that the abomination was thought of as personal; perhaps it represents Anti-Christ (2 Thes 2:4; 1 Jn 2:18). Secondly, 'let the *reader* understand' betrays a literary tradition and cannot be Jesus' spoken word, cf § 760*c*. Whether inserted by the evangelist or taken over by him from his source, it may be a hint to the reader to penetrate the highly allusive language to reach the reality. S. G. F. Brandon (NTS 7 (1960/1), 126—41) suggests that the hint is to the Christians of Rome; they would know that the Emperor Titus had been acclaimed in Jerusalem after sacrifice to the Roman standards in the court of the temple (JosBJ 6, 316—hence the masculine with 'abomination') and would have seen the spoils of the captured city carried through Rome in triumph in A.D. 71. The hint encourages them to see the true significance of these events; but cf § 746*a*. **21—23.** See § 736*j*. These vv correspond to 5—6, and so conclude the chiasmus on persecution, cf § 760*g*.

j **24—27 Victory of the Kingdom** (Mt 24:29—31; Lk 21:25—28)—This is described by means of apocalyptic imagery, for whose details see § 737*a—c*. V. Taylor points out the difference in atmosphere from that of 14—23: the scene is set no longer on earth but in heaven; there is no further mention of the 'disastrous abomination', whose overthrow is never recounted. Hence he suggests that they are taken from different sources. But in any case some such break is to be expected between the description of the preparatory period of tribulation and persecution and that of the final vindication. As to the temporal succession of these two occurrences see § 760*e*.

k **28—37 Concluding warnings** (Mt 24:32—36; 25: 13—15; Lk 21:29—33; 19:12—13; 12:40, 38)—The chapter concludes with a series of originally isolated say-

ings, here collected by means of catchwords, to encourage **760k** a spirit of watchfulness. This in itself suggests that the happenings just described by means of images will not occur according to the literal sense of the description, for then they would constitute sign enough of the approaching end. It is impossible to recover the original context in which Jesus uttered these independent sayings; they are given a unity of purpose and sense by the evangelist. 30 is bound to 28—29 by the catchword 'happening/take place' (the same word in Gr.); 31 to 30 by 'pass away'; 33, 35 and 37 by 'be on your guard/stay awake'. **28—29 Parable of the Fig-tree**—for interpretation **l** see § 737*d*. **30—32 Three sayings**—see 737*e*. **33—37 The Watchful Servant**—Mk here combines material from several parables given more fully in Mt and Lk. Thus the charge to the servants (34*a*) comes from the parable of the talents (Mt 25:14—15), but the doorkeeper from the parable of return from a marriage feast (Lk 12:38). Commentators point out that orientals do not journey at night, so there can be no question of returning from abroad at 'midnight, cockcrow, dawn'. Further, the type of vigilance required of bailiffs entrusted with property and of doorkeepers is quite different. Mk joins the two elements in order to conclude his guidance for future attitudes with the combination of two lessons: the Christian must continue to work calmly (cf 2 Thes 3:6—15) but must live in a spirit of expectation (cf 1 Thes 5:1—11).

14—16 Passion, Death and Resurrection of 761a Christ—The central event of Christianity is the resurrection, but in the apostolic preaching of the Ac and Epistles the events of the passion are always linked to it, for the scandal of the cross is the obverse to the glory of the resurrection. Understandably, therefore, a continuous account of these events came into being far earlier than did developed stories about the earlier events of Jesus life, which are nowhere mentioned in the NT outside the gospels and Ac. It is significant that Jn, who elsewhere diverges considerably from the synoptic tradition, both in material and in treatment, here remains substantially close to it. The account of the passion naturally tended, as did the rest of the gospels, to show the meaning of the events related, by the incorporation into the thread of the narrative of reminiscences of the OT (see § 739*ab*); these are developed considerably by Mt and Lk, but were already at work in the formation of the account given by Mk. Another motif which is at work is the stress that, though he died a criminal's death, Jesus was innocent, condemned only through malice and illicit pressure on the Procurator by those who would not recognize him.

14:1—11 The Plot and the Anointing (Mt 26:1—16; **b** Lk 22: 1—6)—Thus Mk opens his account of the events leading up to the crucifixion with a contrast between the malicious schemes of the stiff-necked Jewish leaders and Judas, and the love for Jesus of the crowds and especially of this unnamed woman. Again we have a 'Markan sandwich' in which the story of the anointing is placed between two parts of a naturally continuous account of the conspiracy against Jesus.

1—2, 10—11 The Plot—It is unlikely that the Christians possessed any direct evidence of the negotiations between Judas and the authorities, but so much as we have here could easily be deduced from subsequent events. **1*a*.** On the Passover and the Feast of Unleavened Bread see R. de Vaux, AI. The time indication is imprecise, for the Passover was celebrated on the 14th Nisan, while the week of unleavened bread (originally celebrating the barley harvest when the corn was too fresh to have

761b fermented) ran from 15th—21st Nisan. **1b.** It is remarkable that the passion narratives contain no allusion to participation by the Pharisees, who hitherto had been Jesus' chief antagonists. But, scrupulosity and timidity being two of their most marked characteristics, it is possible that when it came to the point they could not bring themselves to act. Similarly the Pharisaic legal code was so hedged about with cautions that, even had it ever had practical force, it would have been virtually impossible to inflict the death penalty. **2.** Since there is no note that this intention was ever revoked it would normally follow that Jesus was not in fact arrested during the feast. This would imply that the Last Supper was before the Pasch began (cf § 761*fg*). But perhaps Mk's expression is careless; if the stress on trickery and the initial 'for' of v 2 are intended, he must mean that public arrest must be avoided. The prominent notice of Jesus' popularity stresses their blind malice, as does 'one of the Twelve' (1) Judas' treachery.

c 3—9 The Anointing at Bethany (Mt 26:6—13; Jn 12: 1—8; cf Lk 7:36—50)—see § 739*de*. Mk's picture is much more lively than Mt's hieratic presentation, with details which make the whole scene more vivid, e.g. 'he was at dinner when', 'she broke the jar'. He also tells us the type of ointment: spikenard; the word translated 'pure' is obscure, but it could also be a transliteration of the Aram. *pistaqa*, pistachio, which is 'extensively used as colouring material in confectionery' (*Encyc. Brit.*) and originates in Syria. Mk further gives its value, 300 days' pay (cf Mt 20:9). **10—11.** See above.

d 12—16 Preparations for the Passover Supper (Mt 26:17—19; Lk 22:7—13)—Various indications suggest that this narrative did not form part of the earliest accounts but was later added, perhaps by Mk himself. The men are consistently called 'the disciples', a term which occurs in Mk almost exclusively in his own editorial additions, instead of 'the Twelve' as in the surrounding narratives (vv 10, 17, 20) but it is not quite excluded that these disciples were not of the Twelve. The time indication is more likely coming from one who was unfamiliar with Jewish customs, for the lambs were killed on the afternoon of the 14th Nisan, and the Feast of Unleavened Bread began only at sundown (when the 15th began, according to the Jewish system of reckoning). The quasi-miraculous errand of the two disciples is narrated in terms which recall the similar procedure in 11:1—7 (cf the affinity between 7:31—37 and 8:22—26: § 755*f*). It is perhaps surprising that v 17 has no allusion to the errand (strictly 'the Twelve' there is incorrect, since two of them were probably already in the upper room). The question of authorship is important, for only in this passage is it clear that the last supper was to be a paschal meal; if the passage stems from Mk he may well be giving a later interpretation influenced **e** by Christian liturgical rites. The disciples' errand evokes that of Saul in 1 Sm 10:2—5. Since nothing is said of a previous arrangement the impression is given of messianic or divine foreknowledge and authority, and this is no doubt intended. **13.** A man carrying a pitcher would be distinctive; normally only women do so. **15.** The room is both large and well furnished: the word used 'describes the covering of couches with carpets and rugs' (V. Taylor). Preparations would include making ready the lamb, unleavened bread, sauces, wine, herbs and spices.

f Note on the Date of the Last Supper—Mk and Jn give divergent accounts of the date. Jn indicates that the passover was to be eaten on the following day (18:28), a Friday (19:31). Mk 14:12 leaves no doubt that the paschal victims were being killed on the afternoon of

the day (the 14th Nisan) preceding the Passion, to be **76** eaten that same evening (since the day was reckoned from sunset to sunset this was theoretically now the 15th Nisan). Theological reasons have been adduced to account for transference in either direction: Jn wishes to emphasize the parallelism between Jesus and the paschal lamb (Jn 19:36 and note), which could make him represent their being killed at the same moment. (But this parallelism is not certain even in Jn 19:36; the parallelism in the *moment* of death is never mentioned; it is hardly credible that Jn inserted the statement in 18:28 if it was historically false). On the other hand it has been suggested that Mk was misled by the paschal character of the Christian Eucharist and the paschal significance of the Last Supper into concluding that the supper took place at the time of the Jewish paschal meal. To show that Mk was mistaken, critics have pointed to certain actions on the day of the Passion which they allege to be illicit or impossible for the 15th Nisan, since the Sabbath day restrictions were in force on that day (e.g. purchasing the shroud, holding a Jewish capital trial). To support the synoptics, scholars have shown these actions to be in fact possible even on the 15th Nisan, and have indicated a number of incidental details in the narrative explicable only if Jesus and his companions were celebrating the Passover, and not to be explained by liturgical influence or paschal symbolism (e.g. spending the night within the sacred area of Jerusalem according to the paschal prescriptions instead of returning to Bethany; Judas going out 'to give alms' at night— a pious custom which kept beggars abroad even though the paschal meal was at night). **Solutions**—some **g** scholars (Jeremias, *Eucharistic Words of Jesus*, ET 1965, p. 26) abandon hope of a reconciliation of irreconcilables. Others suggest that Jesus anticipated the paschal meal on his own initiative and authority (JB). Recently opinion has been settling in the direction set by A. Jaubert (*La date de la cène*, 1957; 'Jésus et le calendrier de Qumran', NTS 8 (1960/1), 1—30; cf J. Carmignac, *Revue de Qumran*, 5 (1964), 59—79): two different calendars existed at this time in Palestine, the official, solar calendar of the temple authorities, and a lunar calendar, followed by Qumran and a number of groups, and indicated in arrangements found in some later books of the Bible. If Jn 18:28; 19:31 refer to the official calendar, but Jesus celebrated the Passover according to the lunar calendar, all details fall into place (but still see note to Mk 15:42). In this case the supper was celebrated on the evening of Tuesday, and the crucifixion took place on Friday. The chief difficulty remaining is that the evangelists then seem to represent in one cycle of 24 hours what in fact took place in three days.

17—21 Treachery of an Apostle Foretold (Mt 26: **h** 20—25; Lk 22:14, 21—23)—In keeping with the nature of the whole approach of the synoptic gospels no description is given of the Last Supper such as men of later days have desired. The evangelist concentrates only on specific points, the prediction of treachery and the institution of the Eucharist. If it is granted that this pericope consists of no more than a framework for the two sayings (and 20 could be another form of 18*b*), it follows that the original prediction need not have been uttered on this occasion. Jn gives the same prediction in another form at 6:70, also in a eucharistic context. But its tragic force here, showing Jesus' foreknowledge and command of the situation, is obvious, and could have occasioned its introduction here. In Mk and Jn Jesus does not even hint at the identity of the traitor among the Twelve, dwelling exclusively on the unspeakable nature of the crime, in

61h terms of betrayal of table-fellowship, to Semites a bond which is sacrosanct. In 18*b* it is described in terms which recall Ps 41 (40):9, one of the frequent hints of the fulfilment by Jesus of God's plan as expressed in scripture. Mt (v 23) makes the second saying more demonstrative and adds (v 25) the exchange in which Jesus identifies Judas. Lk (v 21) makes the dipping of the hand a sign for identification, when it was originally merely a semitic way of expressing table-fellowship.

i 22—25 The Institution of the Eucharist (Mt 26: 26—29; Lk 22:15—20)—The *character of the* account is unmistakably liturgical. It is one of the most firmly established results of the work of the school of Form Criticism that individual passages of the gospels were preserved in the pre-gospel tradition because they correspond each to a special need of the community. As in the present canon of the Mass, so in the earliest eucharistic anaphorae, the account of the institution of the rite was recited to give authority for, and explanation to, the repetition of the rite. Of the accounts so recited in the early Church we have two slightly divergent versions in the Nt, one in 1 Cor and Lk, the other in Mk and **j** Mt. Traces of liturgical influence can be seen: e.g. 'As they were eating' (v 26) is unnecessary in a continuous account after the same words in v 21, but in an independent fragment they formed a necessary introduction. 'Gave it to the disciples' (26, 27) and the instructions to eat and drink are absent from Paul (and much reduced in Lk); they seem to be later developments, rubrics incorporated into the text (Jeremias, *Eucharistic Words*, p. 113). This liturgical character of the accounts provides an explanation for the total absence from Mk and Mt of explicit mention of the Jewish paschal meal which provided the context for Christ's actions; this formed no part of the Christian eucharist, and so is lost in **k** silence; Paul retains only a trace, in 'after supper'. Of this meal, the commemorative celebration of the freeing of the Hebrews from slavery in Egypt, and their formation into God's chosen people, there were five stages:

1. The blessing of a cup of wine by the president to inaugurate the feast (mentioned only by Lk v 17).
2. All washed their right hands, and helped themselves to some bitter herbs dipped in a salty sauce, symbolic of bitter slavery in Egypt (cf Mt v 23).
3. In reply to a question by the youngest adult member of the gathering, the president explained the sense of the rite and its elements, unleavened bread, the lamb and the joyous wine. Then Ps 113 (112) was sung and a second cup of wine drunk. After this all washed both hands (which perhaps provided the occasion for the washing of the feet in Jn 13:3—11).
4. The president solemnly blessed, broke and distributed bread; the paschal lamb and the bread were eaten; a third cup of wine was blessed and drunk. It was this part of the rite which Jesus transformed into the rite perpetuated in the Christian Eucharist.
5. The joyful 'Hallel' (Pss 114—8 (113—7)) were sung in conclusion (cf Mt v 30), and a fourth cup of wine drunk. (Cf Jeremias, *Eucharistic Words*, p. 85—86).

l Four themes which the associations of this rite would have suggested to the Jewish participants may be mentioned:

1. The purpose of any such sacred meal was to initiate those who partook into more **intimate union with God**. This was the purpose of all the sacrificial meals of the OT. In this case the eating of Christ's body,

and especially the drinking of his blood, are obvious **76ll** means of union to God through Christ. This is particularly clear of the blood, for the Jews were forbidden to partake of the blood of any victim; it represented the life itself, and as such belonged to God. Partaking of the blood of Jesus means sharing his God-given life.

2. The most prominent elements in Jesus' words are thanksgiving (a blessing always has the form 'Blessed are you . . .' i.e., I thank you, and is addressed to God) **and the new covenant**. The latter gives the **m** sense of the former. The 'blood of the covenant' meant to a Jew either the blood by which the old covenant was ratified and Israel constituted God's people (Ex 30:8), or the blood of circumcision by which individuals were incorporated into this chosen people (SB I. 991—2). As the blood of the ratification of the old covenant was distributed to its members (by sprinkling), so also the blood which ratifies the new covenant. The rite therefore both constitutes the new, covenanted, people of God (prophesied by Jer 31: 31—34; Ezek 36) and incorporates into this people those who participate in it.

3. The thought of Jesus' coming sacrifice is ever in the background of this chapter, constantly recalled by word or gesture. In 28 it is gently alluded to by 'poured out for many for the forgiveness of sins'. This phrase recalls the prophecy of Is 53:11—12, of the **atonement for Israel** to be effected by the servant of the Lord. This prophecy was prominent in the thought, not only of the early Church, but of Jesus himself in his reflection upon his imminent suffering (cf § 711*c*). At this solemn moment he thus interprets the coming Passion, cf 1 Cor 11:26—27.

4. The saying of Jesus added immediately after the **n** rite by Mt (v 29) and Mk or before it by Lk (v 18), rejoins the allusion of Paul (1 Cor 11:26) to show that the Eucharist was celebrated by the early Christians in **joyful expectation of the final coming** of Christ and definitive establishment of the 'kingdom of the Father' (cf 1 Cor 15:24; Eph 1:22; Mt 13:43; 26:29), in which all things are renewed (Apoc 21:1—5, cf 'new wine'). For the banquet of the Messiah in the age to come, cf § 720*m*.

26—31 The Disciples' Denial Foretold (Mt 26:30— **o** 35; Lk 22:39, 33—34) These sayings were important to the early community—and were therefore preserved and included in the narrative as showing again Jesus' foreknowledge and acceptance of what lay before him, and as providing an explanation of the disciples' desertion: it was foretold by scripture. It is also a partial excuse: they retained their enthusiastic devotion to their master even though they failed at the critical moment. **30.** Cockcrow may be used here as the name of the buglecall which sounded the start of the fourth and last night watch (C. H. Mayo, JTS 22 (1920/1), p. 367—70). But this depends on the excision of 'twice' and of 'and a cock crew' in 14:68, which is supported by few MSS (but cf § 761*zz*).

32—42 Gethsemane: the Agony (Mt 27:36—46; Lk **p** 22:40—46)—Bultmann (p. 267) holds this scene to be an individual story of a thorough-going legendary character'. But its profound testimony to Jesus' natural human shrinking before death (cf Heb 5:7) cannot have been invented by the Church, for it runs clean contrary to its tendency to underline whenever possible his exaltedness and majesty (cf § 711*bc*). Furthermore the unflattering portrait of the disciples does not spring from the reverence in which they were held. On the other hand, like the

761p account in Mt and Lk of the temptation of Christ in the desert (cf § 715a), this passage makes no claim to be an eye-witness account in every detail. The disciples were asleep during the prayer, and (according to Lk 22:41) a stone's throw distant. The triple repetition of Jesus' action leaves Mk so short of material that it seems that the number may be due to stylization. Such a triple repetition is, of course, a recognized means of emphasis (three prophecies of the passion, three denials by Peter, three declarations of innocence before Pilate). Many of Jesus' phrases are found also in various places of the gospels, especially Jn, which suggests that details of the scene, especially of Jesus' words, may derive from the evangelists, who for this purpose made use of sayings uttered by Jesus at various times during his ministry. Two different theological themes are illustrated: Jesus' acceptance of the Father's will, in spite of his horror at his approaching suffering, and that his followers too must watch well. Benoit suggests (p. 30) that at one time two separate accounts were current in the community, each

q stressing one of these points. **32.** Gethsemane (Aram. *gat semānîm* = oil press) was a garden or orchard, according to Jn 18:1−2, on the E side of Kedron, which Jesus frequented often enough for Judas to know it. There were presumably many such plots on the Mount of Olives; This was distinguished by its oil-press. **33.** The three disciples who have received other special revelations (cf § 748b) are mentioned by Mk as witness here too. **34.** By the use of the words of Ps 42 (41):6 it is suggested that Jesus' grief fulfils the scriptures. **35−36.** Jesus' words here are strongly reminiscent of his sayings reported Jn 12:27; 18:11. Especially Johannine is the use here and 41 of 'the hour' in this sense. There may well be some contact between the two traditions. **38.** It has been suggested that this saying was originally independent (Nineham, p. 392); it is reminiscent of the sayings in 13:33−37. The antithesis of flesh and spirit here is not used in Paul's sense (e.g. Gal 3:3) of the spirit of God as opposed to man's fallen nature, but in the sense of man's own spirit, cf Jas 4:5; 1 QS V 20−24. **41b−42.** The final introduction to the Passion, cf Jn 12:23; 14:30−31.

r 43−52 Gethsemane: The Arrest (Mt 26:47−56; Lk 22:47−53; Jn 18:2−11)—Here begins the Passion narrative proper, the events to which the predictions referred: 9:31; 10:33. From now onwards the synoptic thread is followed much more closely by Jn, but it seems likely that Lk and Jn share a supplementary source unknown to Mk and Mt. No doubt at the time of the festival there were large numbers bivouacking on the mount of olives, so that in the darkness a special signal was needed to enable the Jewish militia (or especially Jn's Roman

s 'cohort', if it is correct) to distinguish their man. **45.** Judas' greeting is the normal kiss of respect accorded by a pupil to rabbi (SB I. 995); its treacherous nature here is much more stressed by Mt and Lk. **46.** Lk and Jn delay the arrest till after the slight affray and Jesus' reply recorded in 47−49. This is a more logical order, for in Mk they have no function; perhaps Mk anticipates. **48−49.** The prominence of this statement in Mk's account shows its importance: from the start of the affair it is clear that Jesus' opponents are not playing straight, but using underhand methods. But Jesus accepts because the scriptures show this to be the will of God. The word for 'brigand' is also used for members of the militant nationalist party of the Zealots (JosBJ 4, 3, 3); if this sense is intended Jesus means that he is no political Messiah. **51−52.** These vv, a lively Markan touch, are unparalleled in the other gospels. Christian

piety has identified the young man as the evangelist **76** himself, but cf § 746c.

53−72 Jesus before the Sanhedrin (Mt 26:57−75; **t** Lk 22:54−71; Jn 18:15−27—A **divergence** exists **between Mk/Mt and Lk** on the order and content of the elements in the Jewish trial of Jesus. Mk gives

1. Session of 'the whole sanhedrin (55) at the high priest's palace (54)

　　False witnesses (56−60)

　　High priest's question and Jesus' answer (61−62)

　　High priest's reaction, and decision that Jesus 'deserves to die' (63−64)

　　Mockery (65)

2. 'First thing in the morning' the members of the sanhedrin 'having got ready a plan' hand Jesus over to Pilate (15:1). Mt retains this order of events, though some details are modified (cf § 740). Lk, on the other hand, gives.

1. At the high priest's house (54) mockery by Jesus' guards (63−65)

2. 'When day broke' session of the sanhedrin (66)

　　High priest's question and Jesus' answer (67−70)

　　Claim, without any form of verdict, that the evidence suffices (71)

　　They hand him over to Pilate (23:1)

Jn's account differs still more widely:

1. At Annas' palace (13, 15) a private interrogation by Annas (19−21)

　　A slap in rebuke by an attendant (22−23)

2. Jesus 'sent to Caiaphas the high priest'—no details of proceedings (24)

　　Jesus led thence to Pilate praetorium (28).

The major divergencies are that Mk−Mt have a full **u** sanhedrin trial (with? verdict) during the night, followed (Mt) by a morning session to make plans. Lk has during the night only a mockery, then a full Sanhedrin trial in the morning without a verdict. Jn implies that during the night there was only a private interrogation, and gives no details of the morning session. There are difficulties about the Mk−Mt order: a session of the whole Sanhedrin is unlikely, as well as being irregular, during the night, especially if it was the night of the Passover. If they needed in any case to meet in the morning the night session would be superfluous. Of the various **solutions** proposed the most probable is that of P. Benoit *Exégèse et Théologie*, I. 290−313) that Mk had no record of what happened during the night session—not improbable if the ultimate source was Peter, who stayed 'down below in the courtyard' (66)—and filled in the gap with an account based on what happened in the early morning. In fact, then, Jesus was first taken for a preliminary private investigation to Annas, with perhaps members of the sanhedrin present; sometime during the night occurred the mockery; in the early morning there was a meeting of councillors to decide upon the procedure to be followed by Pilate. It has, however, been claimed that there was no **v** record of any proceedings available to the Christians, and that they composed an account, based on Jesus' saying about the Temple, the claim that he was Son of Man, a number of scriptural allusions etc, whose difficulties are such that it is manifestly unhistorical. Some difficulties cannot be denied, but these hardly go beyond such as should be expected from an account which is both popular and more interested in theology than in legal procedure. It has been much discussed whether the meetings included a *formal verdict*, or indeed a *formal trial* at all. This depends firstly upon the legal situation at the time. It is virtually inconceivable that the Sanhedrin had the right under Roman rule to pass a capital sentence.

1v Removal of this power was an obvious and universal practice in the empire to avoid disturbances and victimization of Rome's friends. Furthermore, since Jesus'

w execution was carried out by Romans and according to Roman Law, it was the result of a Roman sentence. Hence the question whether the Sanhedrin's decision to hand Jesus over to the Roman authorities amounted to a formal sentence or not becomes relatively unimportant. The primitive kerygma in Ac makes no mention of it (2:23; 3:13–14; 4:10; 5:30; 10:39; 13:27–29). The slight divergence between the gospels on this point may therefore be explained: Lk and Jn do not bother to record any formal sentence by the Sanhedrin because it would have no effect; the decision recorded in Mk and Mt was, even if intended as a formal verdict, ineffective. The making of a plan, mentioned in Mk 15:1; Mt 27:1, does not suggest that they considered the verdict passed (according to them) in the night to be formal and sufficient. Hence the alleged illegalities of the trial, even if real, become unimportant if the trial itself was no trial but only a preliminary hearing. The illegalities alleged by P. Blinzler and P. Winter in their works on the trial of Jesus suppose the later theoretical Pharisaic rules, which were never in force, and were certainly more hedged about with factors which could make a trial irregular than the Sadducean code then in operation. There is no mention of the Pharisees at any stage in the trial. **53.** In the accounts of the trial both Annas and Caiaphas are mentioned as high priest. In fact Caiaphas was high priest at this time, but his father-in-law Annas had held the office A D 6–15. Perhaps he still retained the title, by courtesy or abuse, especially since he was a man of great influence; five of his sons became High Priest. The Sanhedrin, a council of 71 members drawn from the chief priests, elders and scribes, and presided over by the ruling High Priest, was, under Roman rule, the native organ of government in Judaea. But it met in a public building in the Temple area, not in the High Priest's palace—an indication that this was not in fact a session of the Sanhedrin as such.

x **55–59 False witnesses**—From the beginning of the trial Mk makes it clear that there is to be no unbiased hearing: their object is to put Jesus to death. 57 and 59 curiously repeat 56a and 56b respectively, as though 57–59 were inserted. The precise charge rests on the saying reported in various forms, Jn 2:19; Mk 13:2; it cannot therefore be invented by the witnesses, and this may be the reason why Mt removes the implication that it is false. Strictly, however, it *is* false, for Jesus never said that he would himself destroy the temple. For the implications of the saying intended by Jesus see note on Jn 1:19–22. Accusation by false witnesses fulfils Ps 27 (26): 12; 35 (34):11–12 etc. **60.** Jesus' silence before his accusers is frequently mentioned during the trials (v 61; 15:4; Lk 23:9; Jn 19:9). His refusal to defend himself fulfils the prophecy of Is 53:7 'he bore it humbly; he never opened his mouth'.

y **61–62 Question and answer**—The title of Messiah has been given explicitly to Jesus only at Caesarea Philippi (8:29), that of Son of God only by the evil spirits, and on each occasion Jesus has forbidden its public proclamation. Jesus is again called Christ in 15:32, and Son of God by the centurion (15:39). This seems, then, to be the decisive moment of the breaking of the secret (cf § 748). But Jesus' reply is guarded: in Mt and according to some texts of Mk he says only 'You say that I am' and in any case he immediately explains in what sense he accepts this. He thus deliberately negates the political overtones of the title of Messiah as a political liberator which it bore in the minds of the common people. **761y** But in their charge to Pilate that he claimed to be King of the Jews the chief priests nevertheless deliberately play on these overtones. On 'Son of God' see § 677, in the High Priest's question it need not imply divinity. Jesus is thus compelled to clarify positively **in what his Messiahship consists**; this he does by means of imagery connected with the Son of Man of Dn (cf § 676*hp*), and Ps 110 (109):1. In Jn a claim analogous to this is made by Jesus earlier (1:51); it is hinted at by Mk 12:35–37. In what sense will the Sanhedrin 'see' this for themselves? The coming cannot be that of the end of the world, but rather that of the original sense of Dn: the Son of Man comes to God to receive power and honour. This is not necessarily connected immediately with the return to exercise judgement. Jesus, being a Palestinian of his day, did not hesitate to use current apocalyptic ideas and the terminology of Ps 110 to describe the vindication which would follow his Passion in the Resurrection, which the councillors will witness. He does not describe to them the factual details, but tells them the significance of it: it will inaugurate his glorious reign. **63–64.** The frantic **yy** oriental gesture of horror had been reduced to the ritual tearing of one hand's breadth of clothing. It is much disputed in what the blasphemy consisted. Perhaps in claiming to be the Messiah in such a state of abjection, he was considered to be insulting God; merely claiming to be Messiah was no blasphemy. Later what constituted blasphemy was minutely laid down (cf SB I. 1008–18), but we cannot be sure that these distinctions already held. But the great R. Aqiba, perhaps the most revered teacher of post Christian Judaism, was decried for blasphemy by his contemporaries (c. A.D. 120) for interpreting Dn 7:9–14 in the sense that the Messiah and David should have thrones beside God himself. The blasphemy perhaps consisted, then, in claiming that he, a man, should be enthroned at God's right hand. Neither of the texts to which Jesus referred could, taken separately, involve a blasphemy, for the son of man in Dn was not held at that time to be a divine figure, and the sitting at God's right hand of Ps 110 could be understood in a metaphorical sense of the king. But when they are combined they constitute a claim to sit in the Heavens on God's right. This was the blasphemy for which Aqiba was impugned. Cf P. Lamarche in *Recherches de Science Réligieuse* 51 (1962), 80. **64.** All statements that the sentence was unjustifiably severe, that condemnation upon the accused's word was illegal etc, rest upon the later and more lenient Pharisaic code of law, excogitated after A.D. 70. But in any case the decision of the Sanhedrin had not the force of a capital sentence (cf § 761*w*). **65–66 Mockery**—According to Mk the mockers are, **z** indefinitely, 'some people'; Mt seems to interpret that it was the councillors, but the independent tradition of Lk and Jn shows that it was the attendants. The textual tradition is confused, but it seems that the blindfolding has intruded from Lk's game of blindman's buff (the blindfolding has no sense without Lk's question 'Who hit you then?'); this game is attested in pagan sources, but not Jewish ones, so could well be an interpretation by Lk. In Mk the mockery keeps to OT ideas of Is 50:6; 1 (3) Kgs 22:24, so fulfilling the scriptures, e.g. Is 53:3–5.

66–72 Peter's Denials (Mt 26:69–75; Lk 22:56–62; **zz** Jn 18:17, 25–27)—Over against—or rather, through v 54, entwined with—Jesus' steadfast confession and suffering is deliberately set the contrast of Peter's cowardice and escape in fulfilment of Jesus' word. C. Masson (*Vers les sources de l'eau vive*, 1961, 87–101) holds that

761zz Mk has built up a triple denial out of two sources, one with a single, one with a double denial: his intention would be to make a triple recurrence for emphasis, as in the scene of the agony in the garden. Jn too, though his arrangement is highly literary, separates the first denial from the other two (18:15—18, 25—27). This joining would explain why Peter remains so almost incredibly insensitive after the cockcrow given by many MSS (probably correctly) in v 68. To effect the join Mk has merely contradicted the extremely strong 'he went outside' by adding 'into the forecourt' in 68, and by adding 'for the second time' in 72; but on the meaning of 'cockcrow' see § 761o. It is strange that there is no corresponding indication that the girl follows him. **68.** Benoit (p. 71) points out the clever effect of shocked stuttering given by 'I do not know, I do not understand'.

762a **15:1—15 Jesus before Pilate** (Mt 27:1—2, 11—26; Lk 23:1—5, 17—25; Jn 18:28—19:16)—The trial before Pilate would have been, in technical Roman terms, a *cognitio extra ordinem*. A provincial governor was 'not bound by the criminal law of the Roman state. There was no criminal code for the provinces ... the governor was free to make his own criminal rules', bound only by custom. The trial took place at the governor's *tribunal*; formal charges were normally made, the accused was free to defend himself, and the governor normally asked the advice of his *consilium* (A. N. Sherwin-White, 'The Trial of Christ', in *Historicity and Chronology in the NT* (1965), p. 100). Roman officials usually held their courts at dawn, beginning and ending their working day early (ibid, p. 114), whence the need for a decision on procedure

b by the Jews in the small hours of the morning. The attitude of both parties was governed by the reluctance of Roman officials to interfere in technical questions of the Jewish religion (cf Ac 18:12—16), and the consequent Jewish attempts to present their religious charges as political offences. Thus Paul too was arraigned at Thessalonica (Ac 16:20—21; 17:6—7) and before Felix (Ac 24:5) on the charge of exciting rebellion and disturbance of the peace. The accusation against Jesus that he claimed to be king of the Jews (Jn 18:33; Mk vv 2, 26—the charge for which he is executed) was precisely that; it followed from the political conception of a Messiah which Jesus vainly corrects before the high priest (14:62). Josephus (*Ant*, 17, 18) tells us that every rebel against Rome was immediately acclaimed king by his followers. According to Jn 19:12—16 Pilate was eventually induced to act by fear of an accusation of being accessory to such a

c rebel movement. The evangelists' account is, however, highly unsatisfactory from the legal point of view: Jesus is never charged, but Pilate seems suddenly to know the charges (v 2); there is no formal sentence but Jesus is just 'handed over' (again the word used in v 1, recalling Is 53:6 and therefore hinting at its fulfilment). Pilate is little more than a dummy, tossed to and fro between chief priests and crowd. But these are no arguments against the historicity of the scene, and there is no need to conclude with Lightfoot (*History*, p. 149) that the account was merely a deduction from the outcome of the trial and the title affixed to the cross. The evangelists were concerned to bring out the significance of the event for Christians. The account falls into two scenes: in the first (**2—5**) the accent is on the innocence and silence of Jesus; as in the Jewish interrogation, from which many of the phrases are taken, the silence fulfils Is 53:7. Here Pilate's reaction is the same as that of the crowds who witnessed Jesus' miracles, and amounts almost to an

d acknowledgement of his dignity. There is a strong contrast already between the gentile's respect and the wild

accusations of the Jews. The key to the whole trial is also **762** given in the title 'King of the Jews' (2); from now on Mk stresses that it is as king of the Jews, i.e. Messiah, that Jesus is rejected by the crowd and crucified (vv 9, 12, 18, 26, 32). In the second scene (**6—15**) the contrast is even stronger between the attitude of the Roman and that of the Jews as they both try to sway the crowd; Pilate is convinced of Jesus' innocence and three times attempts to set Jesus free (the triple repetition for emphasis again), while the chief priests are motivated only by jealousy (v 10). The crowd is not hostile, but irresponsible: they first go up without any particular prisoner in mind, merely asking that the amnesty should be granted. When the chief priests suggest to them Barabbas, they want only to avoid a rival candidate by getting rid of Jesus. In this way responsibility for Jesus' death is seen to rest fairly and squarely on the shoulders of the chief priests. It has been said that the Pilate here presented with his 'scrupulous concern for justice' (Nineham, p. 413) is very different from the Pilate of our Jewish sources (for his character and career see § 741a). But in this scene he could be motivated simply by a desire to thwart the chief priests' designs. This would fit well in the perpetual cold war waged between them. **1a.** In Mk it is not clear that there **e** was any formal meeting; this could refer simply to the decision already (according to Mk) made. So Mk does not perhaps imply two sessions in all. Mt, however, understands him to mean that they then at least took counsel. **6.** A similar amnesty is attested in Roman Egypt in A.D. 86—88 (*Papiri Fiorentini* 1 (Milan 1908), 113) whose administration was in many ways similar to that of Judaea. The paschal amnesty is nowhere else attested, but is quite possible as a gesture of the Roman government on this, the feast which commemorated the liberation from Egypt. **7.** Barabbas, presumably a hero of national liberation in the uprising, was a clever choice to oppose to Jesus. Some MSS of Mt call him 'Jesus Barabbas', and the awkward Gr. of Mk, literally 'Now a man *the one* called Barabbas', makes it possible that 'Jesus' has fallen out of Mk too, from reverence to Christ. **15.** On scourging see § 741d.

16—20 Jesus Crowned with Thorns (Mt 27:27—31; **f** Jn 19:1—3)—Jesus is mocked by the Roman soldiery as king, wearing the purple of the Emperor, as before Herod he had been mocked wearing the white robe of Jewish kings. But scourging was the immediate prelude to, or even the beginning of the process of execution, so that it is unlikely that the pause for this scene of mockery would be possible after it. It would be more likely in the middle of the trial (as in Jn), an attempt allowed, or ordered, by Pilate to show how ludicrous was the alleged claim to be king, by letting the crowd see this pitiable travesty of kingship, and so obtain Jesus' release. The scene again fulfils the mockery prophesied for the Suffering Servant in Is 53:3, 5; 50:6—7; but this is no reason to suppose that it was invented for the purpose. Other such mockeries of prisoners as kings before execution are known. A few years after this a very similar mockery was enacted in derision of Agrippa I's title of king of the Jews: a halfwit was carried in triumph and regal robes through the streets of Alexandria during Agrippa's visit (Philo, *In Flacc.*, 6:36—39). **16.** The cohort, theoretically 200—600 men, was no doubt the detachment which accompanied the governor from Caesarea to quell any possible riots during the feast.

21—27 The Crucifixion (Mt 27:32—38; Lk 23:26—35, **g** 38; Jn 19:17—24)—**21.** Simon was a Cyrenean Jew perhaps resident in Jerusalem; the mention of his two sons suggests that they were known to Mk's community (cf

32g § 746*ac*). 'Coming in from the country' suggests that he had been out to work in the fields, and was coming home early to prepare for the Passover. If this were the sole possible interpretation it would settle the question of the date (cf § 761*fg*). **Crucifixion** might be carried out in various ways, the crudest being that the victim was simply nailed to a tree (as the 6,000 slaves crucified after a slave revolt in 62 B.C. along the Appian Way). JosBJ 5, 451 tells how during the siege of Jerusalem in A.D. 68—70 some five hundred Jewish escapers a day were crucified by the Romans. The soldiers amused themselves by nailing them in a variety of positions. If an erected upright was used, the criminal usually carried the **h** crossbeam which was to be fixed to it. Mk is clear that Simon carried the beam alone; v 22 may suggest that Jesus needed assistance himself, for the word is used of the sick being carried or led to Jesus (1:32; 2:3; 9:17). Lk's 'behind him' suggests that they both carried it, as the disciple carries the cross after his master. Jn insists that Jesus himself carried his own instrument of victory by which he was to triumph; but his theological theme, strongly affected by anti-docetism, has coloured his presentation. **22.** The Aram. for 'skull', written *gulgolta*, was pronounced more simply *golgotha*. The place is firmly identified by tradition with an isolated rocky knoll rising some 15 feet, just outside the city gate beside the old road to Joppe (a road is suggested also by 'the passers-by' of v 29). It was usual to crucify criminals beside a road to increase their sufferings and provide a salutary example to others. **23.** Some aristocratic women used to charge themselves with the good work of giving condemned criminals on the way to execution a narcotic of wine mixed with incense to lessen their sufferings (SB I. 1037). Wine mixed with myrrh is unattested; it would refresh or perhaps inebriate and so lessen at least the consciousness of pain: but Jesus prefers to retain full **i** consciousness for his final action. **24.** Many shapes of cross were possible: X, T or +; from Mt v 37 it appears that the last was used for Jesus, for the *titulus* was fixed above his head. The victim could be fixed by nails or thongs; often a block of wood was used as a 'saddle' to support his weight, and the early Fathers speak of the throne on which Jesus was seated. Lk 24:39, 40 show that there were marks, presumably of the nails, in his feet as well as his hands. But Jn 20:20, 25 show no awareness of them. Lk is perhaps influenced by Ps 22 (21):16 in the Gr. version. But the evangelists do not dwell on the frightful tortures of crucifixion; their readers were familiar with this *crudelissimum taeterrimumque supplicium* (Cicero, *Verr.* 2, 5, 64) and they are more concerned to bring out the details which show how it fulfilled the scriptures. The soldiers' division of the clothes (their right at an execution, by analogy to the spoils of battle) is mentioned as a fulfilment of Ps 22 (21):18. The Romans normally crucified naked, but the prisoner was normally also led naked to execution. Perhaps, as Jesus was led to execution clothed, the Romans made some concession to Jewish susceptibilities on the cross also. **25.** Mk divides the last hours of Jesus' life into three-hour periods (14:72; 15:1, 25, 33, 34, 42). Jn 19:14 would have a slightly different chronology. Mk's artificial arrangement perhaps subserves some liturgical interest e.g. the traditional hours of prayer, cf Ac **j** 3:1; 10:9. **26.** A *titulus* was customarily affixed to the gibbet to warn passers-by of the consequences of the criminal's offence. It usually included notice of his name and place of origin (Jn 19:19). Mk concentrates again on the fact that it was specifically as Messiah that he was crucified (cf § 762*d*). It would not be the first time that

'King of the Jews' had hung on a cross to mock the claims **762j** of a messianic pretender. **27.** Lk 22:37 shows that the presence of two 'robbers' was regarded as fulfilling Is 53:12. The same point is made by the doubtfully attested Mk v 28. The 'robbers' may in fact have been rebels, less fortunate fellows of Barabbas, for Josephus uses this word of nationalist rebels.

29—32 The Mockery of Christ on the Cross (Mt **k** 27:39—44; Lk 23:35—37; Jn significantly omits). This also fulfils the scriptures, Ps 22 (21):7; Jer 18:16; Lam 2:15. The details are probably filled in by the evangelist, for the two explicit gibes are taken from the Jewish trial scene. Again the mockery is triple for emphasis. It is unlikely that the chief priests were among the mockers who passed by on the road, or that they came out for the purpose. If Jn is correct that Jesus died at the time the paschal lambs were being slaughtered in the temple, they should have been fully occupied there. But Mk intends to stress the continued and implacable blindness and hostility of the Jewish leaders, who are fully aware of Jesus' claims and refuse to recognize them. **29.** 'Aha!' is a cry of admiration (Epictetus 3, 23—24), here satirical.

33—37 The Death of Jesus (Mt 27:45—50; Lk **l** 23:44—46; Jn 19:28—30—As in the case of the fixing to the cross, the synoptics do not say much on the death of Jesus but hasten to interpret it. Each incident is rich in scriptural associations. **33.** The darkness over the land recalls the description of the Day of the Lord (Am 8:9; Jer 15:9; Jl 2:10), the great day of God's judgement when he will take vengeance on the sins and infidelities of Israel and finally establish his people. This element therefore sets the stage for the decisive saving event which is the death of Jesus. 'The land' is perhaps the land of Israel, on whom judgement is passed, rather than the whole world. There can be no question of an eclipse (at full moon during the Passover); there was perhaps some natural phenomenon such as the strong spring duststorm which makes the sky dark and lowering, but pitch darkness need not be presumed. Universal sadness at the death of a beloved teacher is often described in Jewish literature in these terms (SB I. 1041—2); but this is only part of its significance here. **34.** Jesus' cry is not **m** intended primarily to give an insight into his feelings, on which the evangelists are duly reticent; it is his own interpretation to us of the significance of his death. Some suggest that it is put into Jesus' mouth by the Christian community, since no Jew would have been allowed near enough to the cross to react by giving him the drink, and no Roman would understand it. But the passers-by were certainly within earshot, and it is not clear who gave Jesus the drink. Some early Fathers interpreted the cry as one of dereliction, but it must be seen in its context: it begins Ps 22 (21) of which the theme (though it mentions the jeers of the psalmist's persecutors) is confident trust in God's protection during affliction and certainty of eventual deliverance—the theme of the prophecies of the suffering servant of the Lord, which figures so prominently in Jesus' thought on his passion and death (cf § 711*d*). Most significant of all, the last part of the Ps tells how he who is now suffering will bring all nations to acknowledge the sovereignty of God. Curiously Mk gives the cry in its Aram. form (Mt in Heb.); Jesus could have quoted it in either language but the misunderstanding is more likely from the Heb. form; perhaps it was translated back into Aram. **35—36.** Those who so understand the cry must be **n** Jews, for Elijah figures in Jewish legend as the deliverer of prisoners from execution, especially at the hands of the Romans (SB IV. 770). The gesture seems in Mk to be an

762n inhuman taunt, for vinegar would act as a temporary reviver, perhaps intended to provide spurious relief, while prolonging the agony—a mocking substitute for deliverance. But the words used are a reference to Ps 69 (68): 21, and the beverage was probably the sour wine favoured by the lower classes at that time.

o **38–41 Effects of Jesus' Death** (Mt 27:51–56; Lk 23:45, 47–49)—These happenings show the significance of Jesus' death, a fitting climax to the story of the Passion. **38.** There were two great veils, one to the holy of holies, the other to the outer temple. The latter was of marvellous beauty, embroidered in four colours (to represent the four elements, according to JosBJ 5, 5, 4), and with the signs of the zodiac. A similar event is recorded as a portent by Jewish tradition: the great doors of the temple, which needed twenty men to close them, flew open one night (cf Ezek 10–11). By one source this prodigy is dated forty years before the destruction of Jerusalem in A.D. 70; but since the historian Josephus puts it in the year 66 (SB I. 1045–6) we can hardly bring it into relation with the death of Jesus, and must interpret the 'forty years' as 'an indefinite period'. The significance of the rending of the veil is multiple and perhaps should not be confined to one single aspect. The obvious sense is that the Jewish sanctuary and OT observance are abrogated. It perhaps shows the fulfilment of the prophecy in Jn 2:19 (cf Mk 14:58). In early tradition it is understood as showing the entry of all nations into harmony with and acceptance by God (Heb 9; 10:19–25), and also as breaking down the barrier between the chosen people and the nations (Eph 2:14–15) through their incorporation together into Christ. **39.** Hence the centurion's confession is of the highest significance at this moment, showing the first access of the Gentiles to Christ (the Gentile women in 7:24–30 was stressed to be an exceptional case). The Jewish mockers had challenged Jesus to show his divinity, but it is the Roman (representing also perhaps the whole empire) who acknowledges it. In his mouth the expression 'Son of God' would not have had the full sense of later Christian theology (cf § 677); but the evangelist legitimately allows it to have this sense for Christians. **40–41.** The terms in which the faithful women are described are barely complimentary, since they fulfil Ps 38 (37):12: 'My friends and companions shrink from my wounds; even the dearest of them keep their distance'. They also serve as witnesses to the veracity of the account (cf Jn 19:35), which is why their names are given at length. Mary of Magdala (on the NW shore of the Lake of Galilee) is mentioned before this scene only in Lk 8:2, though tradition identifies her with the woman of Lk 7:37.

p **42–47 The Burial** (Mt 27:57–61; Lk 23:50–56; Jn 19:38–42)—cf Daube, p. 310–12. The bodies of crucified criminals were left by the Romans to rot on their gallows. But Jewish law (Dt 21:23) prescribed the burial of criminals on the day of execution since their bodies defiled the land, and the Romans bowed to this susceptibility (JosBJ 4, 5, 2). Especially on the festal Sabbath day which began at sundown of Good Friday was it important to avoid this defilement. But criminals might not be buried in their family tombs until their bodies had lain for one year in one of the common graves belonging to the courts of justice; only then might their family come to gather up the bones (SB I. 1049). This burial of criminals was the duty of the lower Beth-Din (lower court of justice). Joseph of Arimathaea, a 'councillor' was presumably charged with this task by the council. 'His tomb' (Mt v 60—not Mk) would belong to the council rather than to him personally. The traditional **762** site of the Holy Sepulchre is within a few yards of the place of execution (cf Jn 19:41). Many tombs of this period are still visible in the vicinity of Jerusalem. They consist of an entrance shaft, whose outer opening is blocked by a millstone being rolled into a carved-out socket, and an inner chamber 6′–12′ square. Into the walls of the inner chamber run slot-shaped alcoves into which a body can be slid. The actual tomb of the Holy Sepulchre was cut away by Constantine from the rocky slope which it was let into, and thus made free-standing, but it was razed to the ground in the eleventh century. Just such a tomb may still be seen in the depths of the rock behind Constantine's rotonda. The evangelists are concerned with two apologetic themes: they wish to show that Jesus was really dead, and really buried there (the burial was one of the events mentioned in the earliest Kerygma—1 Cor 15:3–4—perhaps for apologetic reasons). They also wish to mitigate as far as possible the shame of a criminal's burial (cf § 739d). Thus Mk includes the notice (44–45) that his death was certified by the centurion (this was no doubt part of the procedure in handing over the body) in the face of Pilate's surprise. To stress that he was dead, Jesus' body is called by the most brutal term, which might be translated 'carcase' (43, 45—it is avoided by the later evangelists). And it is noted that the Marys saw where it was laid. Mt, Lk and Jn add that the tomb was new or that no one had yet been buried in it; they were presumably familiar with the burial customs, and, knowing that several bodies could be buried in the same chamber, wanted to point out that there could be no risk of mistake at the Resurrection, because the chamber had no other bodies in it. Mk's readers at any rate, seem not to have known the customs, for he explains (46) that the tomb was 'hewn out of the rock'. **42.** Mk as usual explains the Jewish nomenclature. The timing makes difficulties: if the sun had set the Sabbath had already begun; but if not, it was still the day of the Passover whose rules were almost as strict as those of the Sabbath; but perhaps exceptions were possible for such cases (cf § 761fg). **43.** Mk is anxious to show Joseph's sympathy with Jesus, though the phrase 'lived in the hope of seeing the Kingdom of God' expresses only the attitude of all pious Jews (e.g. Simeon, Lk 2:25, 38). Mt and Lk carry this further: Mt makes him already a disciple, and Lk remarks that he had not participated in the action of the Sanhedrin. **46.** From the synoptics we learn only that the shroud was 'a piece of fine cloth' in which Jesus was 'wrapped'. Grave-clothes could be very elaborate, and in A.D. 90 R. Gamaliel made a protest against this by being buried in a simple linen cloth; but of criminals' grave-clothes we know nothing. There is no mention of anointing, and Jesus' remark at Bethany implies that it did not occur; the whole purpose of telling of the anointing at Bethany was to show that Jesus was thus saved from the shame of burial unanointed (but contrast Jn 19:39). **47.** The holy women are not said to have assisted at the burial. This v could even imply that they arrived only afterwards and 'tried to see' where he had been laid', but other translations are possible.

The Conclusion of Mk—Informed opinion is united in **763a** considering Mk 16:9–20 as not stemming from the hand of the author of the rest of the gospel (e.g. Lagrange, p. 426–39). They do not accord with 16:1–8; e.g. vv 9–11 show no sign of what precedes. Their style is wholly different, being written as a sort of résumé devoid of Mk's usual lively and observant details of factual narrative. Finally they are lacking in the important MSS. B and S, and Eusebius speaks of accurate copies ending

3a at v 8. Some MSS have a shorter ending but the evidence for this is slight. The longer ending, though not by Mk, is accepted as canonical by the church. It has often been suggested that there must have been *some ending to Mk other than 16:1–8*—the author(s) of the additional vv had a right instinct—and this was lost. It is argued that (1) vv 1–8 do not provide an ending sufficiently joyful for the 'Good News' after the sombre account of the Passion. (2) 14:28 looks forward to Galilee in a way which 16:7 only reiterates without satisfying. (3) The last words, aptly translated by Nineham 'they were afraid, you see' (p. 440), are far too weak an ending for a primitive ancient book, whatever their qualities as the conclusion of a sophisticated modern work. But *how could this ending have got lost?* Mt and Lk a very few years afterwards clearly had copies which ended at 16:8. Recurrence must be had to improbable hypotheses to explain how it disappeared so soon and so completely: e.g. the last page was lost before the original MS had been copied, and Mk was by this time no longer available to supply the loss. It seems, then, that there is no alternative but to accept vv 1–8 as the original ending intended by Mk, and see if an exegesis can solve some of the objections raised. Cerfaux (p. 222) suggests that Mk breaks off so abruptly here simply because the report that the tomb is empty duly concludes the Jerusalem tradition about the passion, death and resurrection of Jesus.

b 16:1–8 The Resurrection (Mt 28:1–10; Lk 24:1–12; Jn 20:1–10)—In the early Church there is little emphasis on the apologetic of the empty tomb (cf § 743c). In Mt the women do not certify that the tomb is really empty as the angel says, and Mk does not report any apparition of Christ. He resumes the message of all this in the witness of the angel—angelic witness is far stronger than any human testimony—which at the same time shows that what has occurred is a supernatural event: the body was not stolen but is truly risen. Benoit suggests (p. 294–5) that Mk knew the story of the apparition to Mary Magdalene, but preferred to compose this biblical story of the angel to give an interpretation of the facts to serve as the finale of the gospel. After the matter-of-fact beginning the story is suddenly transformed by an atmosphere of awe at the marvellous happenings—hence the terror of the women in 5 and 6, and the note of awe on which **c** it ends (8). **1.** The motive of their journey is strange; even if it had been possible to buy spices on the sabbath or at sunrise, it would have been vain to attempt to anoint a body after so long in the tomb (cf Jn 11:39). It is odd also that they do not think of the stone until so late, although they themselves had seen it put in place. Mt—for whom the sealing of the tomb and the guards add further obstacles—has no suggestion of this purpose; they merely come, as was customary in Palestine, to visit the tomb. The element of the anointing is perhaps no more than a confused effect of the insistence that Jesus' body was not unanointed (cf § 739d). **2.** The time indications are slightly contradictory: 'very early' suggests before sunrise (cf 1:35), and most MSS have 'when the sun had risen'; one suspects that the reading of a few MSS 'when the sun was rising' may be a facilitating correction.

5. The 'young man' (the description of an angel in 2 Mc **763c** 3:26, 33 and Jos.Ant. 5, 8, 2) is shown by his clothes to be a heavenly being (cf 9:3; Apoc 7:9, 13–14). The reaction of the women is described by a term which denotes almost horrified fear (cf 14:28); it is a typical reaction to the supernatural (9:15; see note there). The *angelus interpres* is used in biblical literature to give the inspired explanation of an event (e.g. 2 Mc 3:33; Ac 1: 10–11; Apoc 17:1 etc); we need not hold that the imaginative details are intended as an exact historical report. **6.** As befits a heavenly being with so exalted a message, **d** he speaks 'with a marvellous lucidity, without connexions between the words' (Lagrange, 417). This v contains the kernel of his, and indeed of the Christian, message. After the solemn announcement of these facts, by an authorized and acknowledged messenger from heaven, there was no need for accounts of apparitions to guarantee the apostolic Kerygma. **7.** This v remains enigmatic. Clearly some mention of the Apostles is required, and especially some indication that Peter's denial was not a final desertion; it would have been unfitting if the gospel ended on an interpretation given to women (who could never play much part in evangelization, granted conditions of the time) without a glance at the future role of the Apostles. This accounts for what would otherwise be very strange, the giving of a message by one who knows it will never be passed on. But why Galilee? Some scholars (Lohmeyer, and especially Marxsen) have held that Galilee held some special place in the early Church's hope of the second coming. But this rests on too much conjecture and doubtful reconstruction. Is there a hint of some theme similar to Lk's double movement: towards Jerusalem for the climax of the Passion, away from Jerusalem for the spread of the faith? **8.** The gospel ends leaving this note of holy fear and reverence at the supernatural happenings still echoing.

9–20 Appendix—It was felt that the single passage **e** which Mk devotes to the resurrection was unsatisfactory as an ending to the gospel, and a later author added these vv, clearly in a different style from the rest of the gospel (§ 763a). They are quoted already by Irenaeus (3, 10, 6) (c. A.D. 180) so must have existed by then; and perhaps by Justin (perhaps *Apol* 1, 45 refers to v 15), which would bring them down to a date earlier than A.D. 140. One 10th cent. MS attributes them to the 'priest Ariston', meaning perhaps the Ariston whom Papias reports to have been a disciple of the Lord; but this merits little credence (Lagrange, p 436–7). In content these vv are 'résumés of stories and sayings already reported more fully in other written sources' (Nineham, p. 450).

Alternative ending—This two-sentence conclusion is given by a number of MSS either as an alternative to or before vv 9–20. The first sentence removes the paradox of the frustrated message with the help of Jn 20:1–2. The second describes a programme of universal evangelization. *The Freer Logion* (so called) from the quondam owner of the one MS, Washingtonianus, in which it occurs after v 14—an apocalyptic exchange between the Apostles and Christ about the tribulations which the faithful must suffer during 'the age of lawlessness'.

ST LUKE

BY W. J. HARRINGTON O.P.

764a Bibliography—*Commentaries*: A. Plummer, ICC, 1922[5]; M.-J. Lagrange, EtB 1927[4]; K. H. Rengstorf, NTD, 1962[9]; W. R. F. Browning, Torch, 1960; J. Schmid, RNT, 1960[4]; E. Osty, BJ, 1961[3]; G. W. A. Lampe, PC (2), 1962; A. R. C. Leaney, BNTC, 1966[2]; Earle Ellis, CBi[2], 1967; G. B. Caird, 1963. W. J. Harrington, 1968. S. M. Gilmour, IB, 1952; L. Marchal, PCSB, 1950[2]; *Other Literature*; L. Vaganay, *Le Problème synoptique*, Tournai, 1954; L. Cerfaux-J. Cambier, 'Luc', DBS 4 (1957), 545−94; A. Wikenhauser, *Einleitung in das NT*, Freiburg, 1956[2]; 145−62; X. Léon-Dufour, RF, 1959, 144−334; H. Conzelmann, *The Theology of St Luke*, E. tr. 1960; R. Laurentin, *Structure et Théologie de Luc I–II*, 1957; J.-P. Audet, 'L'Annonce à Marie', RB, 63 (1956), 346−74; A. Jones, *God's Living Word* 1961, 151−75; J. Jeremias, *The Parables of Jesus*, E.tr. NTL, 1963; W. J. Harrington, *He Spoke in Parables*, Dublin, 1964; J. Dupont, *Les Béatitudes*, Bruges, 1958; P. Benoit, *Exégèse et Théologie*, I. 1961; id *Passion et Résurrection du Seigneur*, 1966.

Authorship

b 1. The testimony of tradition—Marcion in his *Apostolicon* accepted one gospel only—a mutilated Lk. Irenaeus (end of 2nd cent.) says: 'Lk, the companion of Paul, wrote the latter's gospel in a book' (*Adv. Haer* 3, 1, 1); 'Lucas creditus est (= 'was judged worthy') referre nobis evangelium' (ibid 3, 14, 1). The text of the *Muratorian Canon* (end of 2nd cent.), with some grammatical corrections and conjectures, reads: 'Tertium evangelii librum secundum Lucam. Lucas iste medicus post ascensum Christi, cum eum Paulum quasi ut iuris studiosum secum adsumpsisset, nomine suo ex opinione conscripsit; Dominum tamen nec ipse vidit in carne, et ideo, prout assequi potuit, ita et a nativitate Johannis incipit dicere.' The *Anti-Marcionite Prologue* (c. 160−80) gives details of the evangelist: 'Lk, a Syrian of Antioch, doctor by profession, was the disciple of the Apostles. At a later date he was a disciple of Paul until the latter's death. Having faultlessly served the Lord, and without marrying and begetting children, he died, full of the Holy Spirit, in Boeotia, aged eighty-four. As gospels had already been written by Mt in Judea and by Mk in Italy, Lk, under the impulse of the Holy Spirit, wrote **c** his gospel in the region of Achaia. In his prologue, while admitting that other gospels had been written before his, he explained that it was necessary to present to the faithful converted from paganism an exact account of the economy of salvation, lest they should be impeded by Jewish fables or caused to stray from the truth by the deceit of heretics.' Tertullian (*Adv. Marc.* 4, 5), Clem. Alex. (*Strom* 1, 21, 145; V, 12), Origen (*In Matth.* I) and Euseb (HE, 3, 4, 6) are witnesses to the same tradition, summarized by St Jerome: 'Thirdly, Lk the physician, by nationality a Syrian of Antioch, whose praise is in the gospel (cf 2 Cor 8:18), and who himself was a disciple of the Apostle Paul, wrote in the region of Achaia and Boeotia, seeking material from the ancients **76** and, as he admits in his prologue, writing rather from hearsay than as an eyewitness.' (*Comm. in Mt*, prol.). The main points of the impressive traditional witness come to this: the author of the third gospel is Lk, a companion of St Paul and a doctor. Present-day scholarship, generally, is satisfied to accept the tradition. It follows that Lk is also the author of Ac for Lk and Ac are demonstrably two volumes of the one work.

2. The New Testament Witness to St Luke—In the **d** Pauline epistles Lk is named three times: 'Lk the beloved physician and Demas greet you' (Col 4:14); 'Epaphras, my fellow prisoner in Christ Jesus, sends greetings to you, and so do Mark, Aristarchus, Demas and Luke, my fellow workers' (Phm 23f); 'Lk alone is with me' (2 Tm 4:11). Thus, according to Col and Phm, **Lk was with Paul in Rome during the latter's imprisonment (61−63)** and according to 2 Tm he was with him also during a second Roman captivity (67), (cf § 822f−g). In Col 4:10−14 the collaborators of Paul are divided into two groups: (a) Aristarchus, Mark and Justus 'the only men of the circumcision among my fellow workers'; (b) Epaphras, Luke and Demas who, by implication, are of pagan origin. The designation 'beloved physician' reveals that Lk belonged to an educated class and also that his services were appreciated by Paul. In this context we might mention that, though Hobart (*The Medical Language of Luke*, Dublin 1882) and Harnack (*Lukas der Artz*, Leipzig 1906) have sought to demonstrate that the language of Lk and Ac proves that the author was a doctor, Cadbury (*The Style and Literary Method of Luke*, I, Cambridge 1919, 39−64) seems to have shown that his vocabulary is no more coloured by a knowledge of medical terms than that of a cultivated contemporary like Josephus or Plutarch. But this means only that the tradition cannot be confirmed by a literary argument and, indeed, the presence of medical terms has a special significance in view of the tradition.

In the **'we-passages' of Ac** (16:10−17; 20:5−15; **e** 21:1−18; 27:1−28:16) **the author**—who, beyond all reasonable doubt, is Lk—**writes as an eye-witness** (cf § 822e,g). We learn that Lk met Paul at Troas during the latter's second missionary journey (50−52). He went to Macedonia with him, to Philippi, where Paul founded a church (16:10−17). Lk appears to have remained at Philippi because the next 'we-passage' occurs in the context of the third missionary journey (53−58). Lk joined Paul at Philippi about 57 (20:5−15) and went with him to Jerusalem (21:1−18). On this occasion Paul was arrested and spent two years as a prisoner in Caesarea (58−60). This afforded Lk time and opportunity to search out sources, oral and written, both for his gospel and for Ac. He accompanied Paul on the journey to Rome 60−61 (27:1−28:16); there Lk could have met the people mentioned in Col 4:10−14 and Phm 24—especially Mk. The data of the Pauline epistles and of Ac are in perfect accord and it is clear

64e how a disciple of Paul came to know the Palestinian tradition.

f Destination and Date—St Luke dedicated his gospel (and Ac) to a certain Theophilus. The title given to him (*kratiste*, 'Excellency') indicates a man of some social standing. According to ancient custom the man to whom a book was dedicated was expected to promote its circulation. **Lk certainly wrote for Gentiles**—this is evident from a study of his gospel. Thus he consistently avoids many matters which might appear too specifically Jewish. He omits whole passages: the traditions of the ancients (Mt 7:1—23), the return of Elijah (Mk 9:11—13) the antitheses (Mt 5:21f, 27f, 33—37). Sometimes, instead of suppressing a passage he rearranges it or omits details. E.g. compare Mt 5:38—48 with Lk 6:27—36; Mt 7:24—27 with Lk 6:47—49. He is also careful to omit or play down anything that might shock his Gentile Christian readers: sayings liable to be misunderstood—'Of that day or that hour no one knows . . . nor the Son' (Mk 13:32) and the cry from the Cross—'My God, my God, why hast thou forsaken me?' (15:34); sentiments of Christ like anger, indignation, sorrow—compare 'And he looked around at them with anger, grieved at their hardness of heart' (Mk 3:5) with 'And he looked around on them all' (Lk 6:10). (Cf Lk 19:45f and Mk 11:15—17; Lk 22:39—46 and Mk 14:32—42); anything which might seem to cast doubt on the omnipotence of Christ—compare 'And he could do no mighty work there (in his own country) . . . and he marvelled because of their unbelief' (Mk 6:5—6) with Lk 4:25—30 (cf Lk 4:30—Mk 1:34; Lk 5:15f—Mk 1:45). Lk also omits or changes details that do not redound to the credit of the Apostles: he has omitted Mk 4:13; 8:22f; 9:10, 28f, 33f. Elsewhere he has modified the text of Mk. See Lk 8:24f and Mk 4:38, 40; Lk 18:25f and Mk 10:24—26; Lk 22:31—34 and Mk 14:27—31.

g Some scholars would date Lk between 65 (the probable date of Mk) and 70. Many others would put the composition of Lk in the decade 70—80. Their main reason for doing so is based on the detailed form of the prediction of the destruction of Jerusalem (19:43f; 21:20, 24; 23:28—30). Where Mt 24:15 and Mk 13:14 have 'abomination of desolation' (cf Dn 9:27; 11:31; 12:11) Lk 21:20 reads: 'When you see Jerusalem surrounded by armies, then know that its desolation has come near.' V 24 adds that the inhabitants of the city 'will fall by the edge of the sword, and be led captive among all nations; and Jerusalem will be trodden down by the Gentiles until the times of the Gentiles are fulfilled.' These would seem to be a *ex eventu* clarification of the veiled prophecy of the destruction of Jerusalem in 70. The argument is not conclusive, however, because the expressions, general in themselves, may well have been suggested by the OT (cf Dt 28:64; Hos 9:7; Zech 12:3). Lk may have been written **shortly before 70** but in the long run the exact date of the gospel, apart from being uncertain, is hardly a vital question—it has no bearing,

direct or indirect, on matters of faith or morals. In the course of the commentary we shall suggest that a date after A.D. 70 is probable. **764g**

Sources—It is universally recognized that **Lk has used Mk as a source**, indeed that Mk is his chief source, and he has manifestly followed the order of Mk. We may put the relationship between them in schematic form (X. Léon-Dufour, 233). **765a**

(See table below.)

The chief differences that meet the eye (apart from the omission of Mk 6:45—8:26) are the **additions made by Lk**—6:20—8:3 and especially 9:51—18:14. It is instructive to see how this last section has, in fact, been inserted into the order of Mk. In Lk 9:18—10:50 and Mk 8:27—9:40 the sequence of events is: profession of faith by Peter; the Transfiguration; the epileptic; the second prediction of the Passion; who is the greatest; use of the name of Jesus. At this point Lk makes the **insertion comprising some nine chh**, and at the end of it (18:15) he takes up the plan of Mk again, almost where he had left off, so that in Lk 18:15—43 and Mk 10:13—52 the sequence is: Jesus and children, the rich young man, the danger of riches, detachment rewarded, the third prediction of the Passion, the blind man at Jericho.

While it is undoubtedly, and indeed obviously, true **b** that Lk follows Mk, he does not, by any means merely reproduce his source. We may classify the changes he makes under the general headings of *omissions additions and retouches*, and *transpositions*. Many of these changes are due to the theological plan of Lk.

Omissions—Lk has **omitted Marcan passages** which might not be understood by his readers, such as specifically Jewish matters (Mk 7:1—23; 9:9—13; 10:1—12) or which might raise difficulties for them (Mk 3:20f; 7:24—30; 11:12—14, 20—25; 6:45—52). Lk avoids Marcan passages that occur in another context in his gospel—Mk 1:16—20 (Lk 5:1—11); Mk 3:22—30 (Lk 11:14—23), Mk 4:30—32 (Lk 13:18—21), Mk 6:1—6a (Lk 4:16—30) Mk 8:11—13 (Lk 11:29—32); Mk 9:42—48 (Lk 17:1f); Mk 9:49 (Lk 14:34f); Mk 10:35—45 (Lk 22:24—27); Mk 12:28—34 (Lk 10:25—28). He also avoids the repetition of closely related narratives and so omits: the parable of the seed growing secretly (Mk 4:26—29), Jesus walking on the waters (6:45—52), the second multiplication of loaves (8:1—10), the anointing at Bethany (14:3—9), the first appearance before the Sanhedrin (14:55—64), the episode of the wine mingled with myrrh (15:23). Further omissions are motivated by reverence towards Jesus: passages in which his human sensibility appears to be too boldly expressed (Mk 1:43; 3:5; 9:36; 10:16, 21, 14; 14:33f) or where his knowledge seems to be limited (Mk 13:32; 15:34); and, of course, Mk 3:21. Similarly, the Apostles are spared by leaving aside the passages—Mk 4:13, 38; 5:31; 9:10, 28f, 33f; 10:35—45; 14:50. In general, Lk omits the picturesque

	Luke	Mark
Prologue	1—2	—
	⎰ 3:1—6:19	1:1—3:19
		3:20—35
A. In Galilee 3:1—9:50	⎰ 6:20—8:3	—
	8:4—9:50	4:1—6:44 + 8:27—9:40
	—	6:45—8:26
B. To Jerusalem 9:5—19:27	⎰ 9:51—18:14	
	⎱ 18:15—19:27	10:13—52
C. In Jerusalem	19:28—24:53	11:1—16:8 (20)

765b but unessential details of Mk's narrative. Finally certain topographical data are omitted in view of the theological plan of the gospel (cf § 766f—g).

c Additions and retouches—These are variously motivated by Lk's desire for clarity and by his literary and religious sensibility. So, Lk 4:31; 5:1; 8:24; 19:37; 23:51 (geographical data), 6:15 (explanation of an Aram expression), 4:1, 40, 43; 8:18, 30f, 53, 55; 9:9; 22:51, 69 (varied). Especially notable are 21:20, 24. See also 22:45, 47f, 41. **The favourite themes of Lk frequently make their appearance**—Lk 5:25; 18:43; 19:37; 23:47 (praise), 3:6—cf Mk 1:3 (universalism), Lk 3:21; 6:12; 9:28; 23:34 (prayer), 5:11, 28; 14:26; 18:22, 29 (detachment), 4:14; 10:21; 11:13 (the Holy Spirit).

d Transpositions—Again the motives are varied. The arrest of the Baptist (3:19f; cf Mk 1:14; 6:17—20) emphasizes the fact that the Baptist now fades into the background. The **expulsion from Nazareth** (4:16—30; cf Mk 6:1—6a), placed by Lk at the beginning of the ministry, symbolizes Israel's rejection of Jesus. The **call of the first disciples** (5:1—11), placed after the first miracles at Capernaum, and not before as in Mk 1:16—20, makes their immediate response more understandable. The introduction of **the Sermon** (6:17—19) follows **after the choice of the Twelve** (cf Mk 3:7—19) so the discourse itself (6:20—49) can follow immediately and naturally. In **the passion and resurrection** narrative (22:1—24:53) the transpositions seem to assure a more correct literary presentation. The institution of the Eucharist is placed before the announcement of the betrayal and after the Jewish pasch (22:14—23) in a logical order (cf Mk 14:17—25). The announcement of Peter's betrayal is placed at the supper after another admonition of the Apostles (22:31—34) and not on the way to Gethsemane (Mk 14:26:31). For the same reason the question on precedence (cf Mk 10:42—44) and the recompense promised to the Apostles (cf Mt 19:28) have been added here (Lk 22:24—30). The narrative of the arrest of Jesus (22:47—53; cf Mk 14:43—50) has been rearranged in a better literary style.

These examples give, at this stage, an idea of Lk's freedom in regard to his sources; his approach will be remarked throughout the commentary. It should be noted, however, that **though Lk does follow Mk** there is perhaps room for qualification since **both may have used a common source.** This could be a Gr. version of the Aram. gospel traditionally attributed to St Matthew: a schematized form of the Palestinian catechesis, the apostolic gospel preaching (Vaganay). It may be that some of the changes of Lk with respect to Mk are due to the order of this (hypothetical) source. On the other hand, Lk has no knowledge of Mt (cf Leaney, 12—16).

e Another, and very important, **source of Lk** comes to light when we analyse **the long section 9:51—18:14** which has been inserted into the plan of Mk. In this part of his gospel Lk has grouped 'under the sign of Jerusalem and the Passion', and in no strict chronological order, **a great bulk of material** which did not come to him via Mk or the Aram. gospel, whereas (and this is the significant point) many of these elements are found in Mt also. The only reasonable explanation is that, besides Aram. Mt, **another common** (or partly common) source was known to **Mt and Lk**—the source Q of the critics; cf § 646a. The passages common to the two evangelists make up, in the main, **a collection of sayings and parables**; these Mt has distributed throughout his gospel while Lk has grouped most of them in the long section under review. The **principal sources**, then, of Lk are: Mk, (perhaps a

Gr. translation of Aram. Mt) and the special source **765j** common (more accurately in part common) to himself and Mt.

But Lk is not confined to these. We know that he had ample time (the two years 58—60) for personal research in Palestine and not only his own prologue ('having followed all things closely for some time past') but a study of his gospel, afford proof that he did not waste his time. First of all there is the **Infancy-narrative (1—2)**, which is proper to Lk and independent of Mt's first two chh. The colouring of Lk 1—2 is highly Semitic; it has been suggested that this section is based on a Gr. translation of an Aram. source, while some contend that these chh were first written in Heb. Perhaps the most satisfactory explanation is this: Lk may have had Aram. sources, but he has written chh 1—2 of his gospel in a Gr. that is modelled on the style of the LXX. These chh show the hand of Lk but, manifestly, he has followed a source of some sort. It is conceivable that our Lady may have been his informant; the two references to her meditation on the things that concerned her Son (2:19, 51) would seem to indicate as much. At any rate, most of the information must have come from her ultimately.

Not only in the Infancy-narrative but throughout his **f** gospel Lk presents to us the fruits of his research. One is quite surprised to discover how much that we had learned to take for granted is owed to Lk alone. The passages proper to him will be noted throughout the comm. Lk shows certain **affinities with Jn**, notably in the Passion and Resurrection narrative. He cannot have known Jn (did Jn use Lk?); the contacts are there, numerous and varied (cf Comm. Jn § 793f). It seems that Lk would have known the Johannine tradition before it had taken final shape in the fourth gospel.

Language and Style—Lk has **the best Gr. style 766** among the evangelists and that language is certainly his mother-tongue. Jerome testifies: 'Lucas . . . inter omnes evangelistas graeci sermonis eruditissimus fuit' (Epist 19, 4, *Ad Damasum*, PL 22, 378). He often avoids the literary faults he finds in his sources; he chooses more exact Gr. words and he usually suppresses foreign words and expressions. It is, however, true that he does not carry out these improvements consistently, and, not infrequently, he reproduces his sources just as he finds them. This makes for an unevenness in the style of the gospel that is something of a mystery. For instance, though he regularly corrects Mk, we find that the *metemorphōthē* of Mk 9:2 becomes in Lk 9:29 *kai egeneto. . . to eidos tou prosōpou heteron.* More curious still, in Lk 9:42 *daimonion* replaces the hebraistic *pneuma* of Mk 9:20, but the v then goes on to speak of *pneuma akatharton.* The problem which emerges is not so much Lk's paucity of aramaisms and his frequency of Gr. expressions in relation to Mk as the inconstancy of his stylistic changes (cf Léon-Dufour, 231—3).

Though Lk has preserved traces of the Aram. originals **b** of his sources **as a rule he avoids aramaisms** and translates Aram. words. E.g. instead of 'Rabbi' (Mk 9:5; 10:51) he has 'Master' (9:33) and 'Lord' (18:41); and instead of 'Abba' (Mk 14:36) he has 'Father' (22:42). On the whole, though aramaisms are less frequent than in Mk and Mt, they are nonetheless more in evidence than is commonly suggested and witness to the Semitic substratum of the gospel.

On the other hand, **true hebraisms** are found almost exclusively in Lk. E.g. *egeneto . . . kai:* 5:12, 17; 8:1; 9:51 etc; *eleusontai hēmerai:* 5:35; 17:22; 21:6 etc; *kai idou:* 2:25; 5:12; 8:41 etc; *enōpion:* 1:15, 19, 76; 12:6, 9; 15:6 etc; *Hierousalēm* instead of the grecized

66b form *Hierosolyma*. The presence of these hebraisms is almost certainly due to the influence of the LXX; it seems that Lk has consciously imitated the style of the Gr. Bible. This viewpoint is not infrequently contested, however, especially with regard to the Infancy narrative.

c   An interesting feature of Lk's style is his habit of rounding off one subject before passing on to another; it is a characteristic that might easily lead to misinterpretation. When he says, 'Mary remained with her about three months and returned to her home' (1:56), and goes on to tell of the birth of John, he does not mean to imply that Mary had departed before this event. He merely wanted to complete the episode of the Visitation before taking up another matter. In ch 3 he ends his account of the preaching of the Baptist by stating that Herod had John cast into prison (3:19f), and then immediately tells of the baptism of Jesus (3:21f); in other words, he finishes what he has to say about the ministry of John before going on to that of Jesus.

In the same way he indicates well in advance matters that will be dealt with later and so ensures the unity and flow of the narrative. In 1:80 he mentions the sojourn of the Baptist in the desert and later we learn that it was in the desert that the divine call came to him (3:2). At the close of the temptations the devil departed from Jesus 'to return at the appointed time' (4:13 (BJ)), that is to say, the hour of his arrest: 'this is your hour and the power of darkness' (22:53; cf 22:3). In 8:2f we are told of the women who accompanied our Lord on his journeys and these reappear, quite naturally, and with no need of any explanation of their presence, as those who prepare the spices and ointments for the body of Jesus (23:55f). We may also consider 3:20 and 9:9; 5:33 and 11:1; 9:1–6 and 10:1; 9:9 and 28:8; 18:31 and 24:25f; 20:19 and 22:2; 20:25 and 23:2; 21:27 and 22:39.

d   It is certainly true that the author of the third gospel is **the most versatile of the NT writers**. Left to himself his Gr. is excellent but it is less good when he wishes to be faithful to his sources and, lastly, he can imitate, perfectly, the style of the LXX. The language and style of the gospel reveal a Christian who is **familiar with the OT** and an author familiar with **the Gr. literary style of his time**. If the style of the third gospel is complex it is, in great measure, because Lk is undoubtedly a poet. According to a late tradition he was an artist and he is credited with the first painting of our Lady. It is easy to see how the legend could have grown out of the word-picture he has drawn of her in his Infancy narrative. And surely it is because of its poetic depth that the same story has inspired, dominated indeed, Christian art. At the other end of the gospel we find the charming story of the two disciples and the unknown Traveller on the road to Emmaus—while in between there is so much beauty. We should be thankful to Lk not only for the treasures he has searched out for us and so carefully preserved but also for the artistry that went into the setting of these pearls of great price.

e **The Minister of the Word—1. The historian—** Lk's careful wording of his prologue and his dedication to the 'excellent Theophilus' introduce a work that does not purport merely to tell us about the Good News; his object is to establish the **soundness of the catechetical teaching** and, for that reason, his express intention is to weigh his sources. In view of this he shows **care in presenting historical data.** By the detailed synchronisms prefixed to his narrative of the birth of Jesus (2:1–3) and of the ministry of John (3:1f) he sets these events in the framework of general history. He can, on occasion, correct the chronology of his sources. Thus,

while in Mk we are told that the Transfiguration took **766e** place six days after Peter's profession of faith at Caesarea Philippi (Mk 9:2) Lk quietly modifies the statement and says: 'about eight days after' (9:28); and he regularly qualifies round numbers by adding 'about' (1:56; 3:23 etc). He speaks of Herod as 'tetrarch'—his correct title—(9:7) and not, as he was popularly described, as 'king' (Mk 6:14). Similarly, he speaks of the 'lake of Gennesareth' (5:1) rather than of the 'sea of Galilee' (Mk 1:16). He mentions contemporary facts: the massacre of Galileans by Pilate (13:1–3) and the fall of the tower of Siloam (13:4f). It is in the same spirit that he has had recourse to new sources.

We may not, however, judge the work of Lk as we would that of a modern historian; **his gospel is not scientific history, nor** is it, any more than Mt and Mk, a **biography of Jesus**. Even though he has retouched his sources in this respect, he has scarcely anything of the modern passion for precise chronology and detailed topography. He is interested in historical facts but he does not have our regard for 'history'. If he does promise to write an 'orderly account' that **order is primarily theological** for his concern is with the things delivered by those who were not merely eyewitnesses of events but 'ministers of the word' (1:2) cf § 708d.

2. The evangelist—Lk himself is, first and foremost, a f 'minister of the word', an evangelist, and his work is, in the strict sense, a 'gospel'. That is why he has remained faithful to the general plan of Mk, the consecrated plan of the apostolic *kerygma*. For in the NT itself the word 'gospel' means the *preaching* of Christ and the evangelist is a *preacher* (Ac 21:8; Eph 4:11; 2 Tm 4:5). When, in the 2nd cent., *euangelion* came to designate the written account of the life and teaching of our Lord, these writings were still regarded as filling a missionary need and served the same purpose as the spoken word: to waken and strengthen faith (cf Jn 20:31). Similarly, the evangelist, too, is a preacher and behind him stands **the whole teaching activity of a living Church**; of that Church he is a spokesman. **His work is kerygmatic**, in the proper sense of that overworked term; to herald Jesus Christ, his works and words. And because this is so an evangelist has, necessarily, a care for the historical and a certain biographical interest: the Good News that he preaches is all concerned with a Person who lived and moved among men and taught them, a Man who died at a given time and place, and rose from the dead. The person of Jesus, seen and interpreted in the light of the Resurrection, is the very centre of *Heilsgeschichte* and the presentation of his words and deeds is necessarily theological. While Lk, no doubt because of his Gr. background, is somewhat more meticulous than the other synoptists about historical data, his intention remains, fundamentally, kerygmatic and theological.

The Purpose of Lk—To appreciate the overall purpose g of Lk one must take his second work too into consideration. Then one can see that his object is to present the definitive phase of **God's saving intervention, from the birth of the Baptist to the proclaiming of the gospel** in the capital of the Gentile world. His theme is the progress of the Good News from Jerusalem to Rome; it is above all a message of salvation to the Gentiles. Simeon had seen in Christ 'a light for revelation to the Gentiles' (2:32) and Paul's last words to the Roman Jews are: 'Let it be known to you then that the salvation of God has been sent to the Gentiles: they will listen' (Ac 28:28).

All of this follows, in the plan of God, on Christ's rejection by Israel, for that rejection led to his death and exaltation and to universal salvation (Lk 24:46f). It is

766g indeed a **constant (theological) preoccupation of the evangelist to centre his whole gospel around Jerusalem,** for Jerusalem is for him **the holy city of God** and the theatre of the great redemptive event, the passion and triumph of Christ. In Jerusalem the gospel begins (1:5) and in Jerusalem it closes (24:52f). The Infancy-narrative has two significant entries into the holy city (2:22—38, 41—50) and it is this same interest that explains why, unlike the natural climax of Mt (4:3—10), the culminating temptation of our Lord in Lk is at the pinnacle of the Temple (4:9—12). The long central section (9:51—18:14) is presented as a journey to Jerusalem and, to heighten the effect, all other place-names are omitted. The journey outside of Galilee (Mk 6:45—8:26) is not given and Caesarea Philippi is not named as the place of Peter's profession of faith (9:18—22). It is this concern too that explains why Lk has no mention of an appearance of Christ in Galilee. Jesus had come to Jerusalem and there had suffered and died and risen from the dead, and it was from Jerusalem that he was to ascend, finally, into heaven; a departure from the holy city would, in Lk's plan, be an anti-climax. And, consistently, when he came to write his second book he took care to show the christian message radiating from that same centre: 'You shall be my witnesses in Jerusalem and in all Judea and Samaria and to the ends of the earth' (Ac 1:8).

h Lk, we have seen, is an evangelist rather than an historian; here we may go further and describe him as a **theologian of salvation-history.** For him that *Heilsgeschichte* falls into three periods: (i) the period of Israel; (ii) the period of Christ; (iii) the period of the Church. The OT is the time of preparation for the culminating event of Christ's coming: 'The law and the prophets were until John; since then the good news of the kingdom of God is preached' (16:16). Yet, though this is true, the period of Christ is pre-eminently that of his ministry and the time since the Ascension is that of the Church, looking back to the period of Christ and forward to the Parousia. In this perspective the Ascension, followed by the sending of the Spirit, is more the beginning of Ac than the close of Lk, (Conzelmann, 13—17; 202—6).

All this is more understandable, and the outlook of Lk is clearer if we see it in a wider perspective. In the OT view the midpoint of time is marked by the future coming of the Messiah. **For Christians** this is no longer so: **the midpoint of time is now in the past, in the historical life and work of Jesus Christ.** There is another difference. For Christians the midpoint of time does not coincide with the Parousia (as it did in the OT perspective); there is a space of time between Christ and the Parousia. These factors account for a certain tension that we find throughout the NT writings. There is still an expectation, a looking to the future, as there was in the OT, but that future event (the Parousia) is no longer the centre of salvation history; that centre is found in an historical event. The NT outlook is based on 'the thoroughly *positive* conviction that the mighty Christ-event has given a new centre to time, and so its roots are in the faith that the fulfilment has already taken place, that it is **no longer the Parousia but rather the cross and resurrection of Christ that constitute the middle point and meaning of all that occurs.**' (Cullmann, *Christ and Time*, 1951, 81—86). Lk, in his gospel, is concerned with that midpoint of salvation history, the Christ-event, which he sees as the climax of the preceding period of Israel. In Ac he deals with the opening moments of the time between the great saving event and the Parousia, the period of the Church.

767a **Structure of the Gospel**—Lk, like Mk and Mt, has followed the original four-fold gospel plan: (i) Preparation **767** and Baptism in Judea, i.e. the preaching of John the Baptist and the inauguration of the public ministry of Christ; (ii) Ministry in Galilee; (iii) Journey from Galilee to Jerusalem; (iv) In Jerusalem: Passion, Death, Resurrection. However, he has made two important changes in this order and so has given his gospel quite a different bias. By placing at the beginning the long Infancy narrative (1—2)—which balances the Passion and Resurrection narrative—he has presented the story of Jesus in perfect equilibrium. By his insertion of the long section (9:51—18:14) he has fitted cleverly into the gospel narrative a very important collection of episodes and sayings which are entirely absent from Mk and only partially represented in Mt. This Lucan section is dominated by the perspective of the Passion and the journey to Jerusalem is seen as a journey to death (cf 9:51; 13:22; 17:11). In Lk, then, the story of Jesus falls into three parts: (i) From the Temple to the Close of the Galilean Ministry, 1:5—9:50; (ii) The Journey from Galilee to Jerusalem 9:51—19:27; (iii) The Last Days of the Suffering and Risen Christ in Jerusalem, 19:28—24:53.

Doctrine—1. Universalism—Lk wrote his gospel for **b** the Gentile Church and so he stressed **the universal import of the Good News.** This intention is already present in the Infancy narrative, despite its marked semitic character. It is expressed in the canticle of the angels ('peace among men with whom he is pleased' 2:14) and Simeon saw that the Child would be a light to the Gentiles. In his genealogy of Jesus Lk does not stop at Abraham (as Mt does) but goes back to Adam, the father of all men. The Baptist, in his preaching cites the prophecy of Is: 'all flesh shall see the salvation of God' (Lk 3:6; cf Is 40:5); Lk 2:30—32 refers to another universalist text of Second Isaiah (52:10). Jesus' charge to the Twelve, not to go among the Gentiles or Samaritans (Mt 10:5f) is not recorded by Lk. The Jews are warned that they will be supplanted at the Messianic Feast by men from every land. And the last commission of the Risen Lord is that the gospel should be preached to all nations (24:47; cf Mt 28:19f).

Apart from these clear pointers, the universalist bearing of the gospel is also indicated by several deft touches which open up a wider perspective than the original Palestinian one. The Pharisees tithe not only mint and rue but 'every herb' (11:42; cf Mt 23:23). Not only the fig tree (Mk 13:28) but 'all the trees' (21:29) herald summer. In the parable of The Two Builders (6:47—49; Mt 7:24—27) Lk has wholly changed the details so that the story might be readily intelligible to his non-Palestinian readers. The omissions and explanations we have noted (§ 764f) have the same effect: the gospel for all men is presented in a way that all men can understand.

2. The Saviour—Each of the gospels has its own charac- **c** teristics, its own peculiar quality; and these depend, to a large extent, on the manner in which each evangelist presents the person of our Lord. **For Lk Jesus Christ is the Saviour of men.** He uses the title once only in his gospel, in the words of the angel to the shepherds: 'to you is born this day a Saviour' (2:11). The title is not repeated, it is true, but it is significant that the evangelist has drawn attention to the name given to the child at his circumcision—Jesus (2:21). At any rate the Christ of Lk is throughout, and before all else, a Saviour who is full of compassion and tenderness and great forgiveness. And the gospel of Lk is **a gospel of mercy.**

Lk has a gentle soul; it is because of this that he sees so clearly the tenderness of Christ. It is characteristic of him that he has omitted the cursing of the fig

7c tree (Mk 11:12—14; Mt 21:18f) and has given instead the parable of The Barren Fig Tree (13:6—9)—'let it alone this year also'. In the same vein of tenderness and mercy he has assembled the three parables of ch 15: The Lost Sheep, The Lost Coin, The Prodigal Son. Mt, too, has the first of these but the others are proper to Lk. We are told that God rejoices at the repentance of a sinner (15:7, 10); we are shown the love of the divine Father for the prodigal child (15:20). The three parables of ch 15 are addressed to Pharisees and scribes, critical of our Lord's association with sinners (15:2f); a high proportion of Jesus' parables were spoken to the same audience. They witness in a striking way to his solicitude for those blind guides. He sought by every means to open their eyes, for he had come that they too might have life—if they would.

Perhaps nowhere else as in the wonderful passage on the 'woman of the city who was a sinner' (7:36—50) do we see Christ as Lk saw him. The Lord does not hesitate between the self-righteous Pharisee and the repentant sinner and his words are clear and to the point: *'And so, I tell you, her great love proves that her many sins have been forgiven'* (7:47 (NEB)). Lk alone records the words of Jesus to the 'good thief' (23:43) and his prayer for his executioners: 'Father, forgive them, for they do not know what they do' (23:34). He alone tells of the look that moved Peter so deeply (22:61). Everywhere, at all times, there is forgiveness. It has been well said that the gospel of Lk is the gospel of great pardons.

d It is typical of Lk that in his gospel he has paid **special attention to women**, for in the world of his day the position of women was degraded; and his insistence is all the more striking when we compare his gospel with Mt and Mk. Among the women introduced by Lk are: Elizabeth, the mother of the Baptist (1:39—58), Anna the prophetess (2:36—38), the widow of Nain (17:11—17), the repentant sinner (7:36—50), the women of Galilee who accompanied Jesus on the public ministry, notably Mary Magdalen, Joanna and Susanna (8:2f)—who were with him at the end (23:55f), the sisters of Bethany, Martha and Mary (10:38—42). There are, also, the woman who declared the mother of Jesus blessed (11:27f) and the women of Jerusalem who met Christ on his way to Calvary (23:27—31). We find, besides, two parables proper to Lk in which women figure: The Lost Coin (15:8—10) and The Unjust Judge (18:1—8). Finally, it is impossible not to recognize that the person of our Lady is shown in a vivid light in the Infancy-narrative. God deigns to inform her of the great thing he is to do in her and the lingering echo of the angel's 'Rejoice! O Favoured One' is heard already in the *Magnificat*.

The gentle heart of Lk beat for the distressed, the poor, the humble. His sensitive soul perceived the tenderness of Christ. His gospel of mercy and pardon is the gospel of the supreme Physician of souls who has told us that 'the Son of Man came to seek and to save the lost' (19:10). And if the Lord at his birth was hailed as Saviour (2:11) it is also true that the last message of Christ to his disciples is a message of repentance and forgiveness: "Thus it is written, that the Christ should suffer and on the third day rise from the dead, and that repentance and forgiveness of sins should be preached in his name to all nations' (24:46f).

e **3. The Holy Spirit**—Jesus as Messiah is the bearer of the Holy Spirit—this is a truth emphasized by Lk. After the Baptism and Temptation it is 'in the power of the Spirit that Jesus returned to Galilee and began his Messianic work (4:14), and his very first words were a quotation of Is 61:1f—'The Spirit of the Lord is upon me, because he has appointed me to preach the good **767e** news to the poor' (Lk 4:18). **The whole public ministry is thus put under the sign of the Spirit** and all the works and teaching of Christ must be seen in the light of this introduction.

In the early part of the gospel Lk has named the Holy Spirit very often, but in the later chh such references are rarer; yet there are a number of significant texts. In 10:21 Christ 'rejoiced in the Holy Spirit' at the manifestation of his Messiahship to the unworldly. The Holy Spirit is, in the estimation of Jesus, the 'good thing', the gift *par excellence* (11:13). Finally, the Risen Christ guaranteed that he would send the 'promise of the Father', the 'Power from on high', upon his disciples (24:49; Ac 1:8) for the Holy Spirit is the gift of the Risen and Ascended Lord (Jn 7:38f; 14:26). From Pentecost onward the Spirit is the guide and motive power of the Church's mission. The Spirit which moved the Messiah is now poured out by the Risen Lord upon his Church (Ac 1:8; 2:4) and the prophecy of Joel (2:28—32) was fulfilled (Ac 2:17—21); for, indeed, the gift of Pentecost is not for the little circle of disciples only but for all who believe in the name of Christ (cf 2:38f; 10:44f).

Almost all the persons mentioned in Lk 1—2 are said **f** to be moved by or filled with the Holy Spirit: John the Baptist from his mother's womb (1:15, 18), his parents Zachary (1:67ff) and Elizabeth (1:41ff) as well as Simeon (2:27ff) and Anna (2:36). In all these cases the Holy Spirit is the spirit of prophecy, and throughout Lk the Spirit is presented as a supernatural divine power. Perhaps the clearest text is 1:35 where Mary is told: 'The Holy Spirit will come upon you, and the power of the Most High will overshadow you'. The parallelism indicates that here Holy Spirit = Power of the Most High. In other words, Lk shows us the activity of the Spirit rather than the divine Person himself. Jn, however, tells us that the Holy Spirit is a Paraclete, an Advocate, just like the Son (Jn 14:16) and throughout the discourses after the Last Supper it is manifest that the Spirit is a Person, sent by the Father and the Son. But this more developed doctrine of the Trinity is not elaborated in Lk.

4. Prayer—Lk is the gospel of prayer and the sup- **768a** reme example of prayer is given by Jesus Christ himself. This fact is not neglected by Mt and Mk. According to the three synoptists Christ prayed in Gethsemane; he prayed after the first multiplication of loaves (Mk 6:46; Mt 14:23); he prayed in Capernaum after he had cured many (Mk 1:35). But Lk speaks of the prayer of Christ in eight further circumstances. He prayed at the Baptism (3:21), he retired into the desert to pray (5:16) and before choosing his Apostles he spent the whole night in prayer (6:12). He prayed before the confession of Peter (9:18) and later he told Peter that he had prayed specially for him (22:32). He prayed at the Transfiguration, and it was the sight of him in prayer that moved his disciples to ask to be taught how to pray (11:1). He prayed on the Cross for his executioners (23:34). Indeed, we might add that the surrender of his soul to the Father was a prayer (23:46).

Our Lord often recommended prayer to his disciples: persevering prayer like that of the importunate friend (11:5—13) or of the widow before the unjust judge (18:1—8). They must pray to obtain the Holy Spirit (11:13) and, in short, they ought to pray at all times (21:36). Their prayer must be true prayer, like that of the publican (18:13).

Prayer is necessary for all men, for the in- b dividual Christian, but it is the special office of the Church to give glory to God. It is, perhaps, not always

768b recognized that the third gospel has furnished the Church with her canticles of praise: the *Benedictus* at Lauds, the *Magnificat* at Vespers, the *Nunc Dimittis* at Compline and the theme of the *Gloria in Excelsis* in the Mass. But it is not surprising to find these canticles in Lk for the whole of the gospel sheds an atmosphere of joy and peace.

c 5. Joy and Peace—The coming of the Saviour has created an atmosphere of joy and Lk is keenly aware of it. The annunciation of the birth of John includes a promise of joy (1:14), a promise that is fulfilled (1:58) and the yet unborn child leaps for joy in the womb at the presence of the mother of the Messiah (1:41, 44). At the greater annunciation the angel bids Mary rejoice (*Chaire* = 'Rejoice!') and her thankful joy finds expression in the *Magnificat* (1:46—55). The birth of Jesus is an event of great joy for the angels who proclaim it and for the people he had come to save (2:10, 13f). Later, the crowds rejoiced at the works they had witnessed (3:17). The 72 disciples returned, rejoicing, from their mission and Jesus pointed out to them the true motive of joy (10:20) and he himself 'rejoiced in the Holy Spirit' (10:21). Zacchaeus received Jesus joyfully (19:6). The disciples rejoiced on the occasion of the entry into Jerusalem (19:37) and after the Ascension they returned to the city with great joy and praised God in the Temple (25:52). The parables of ch 15 depict the joy of God at the repentance of a sinner.

Peace follows on joy, the peace which Jesus gives (7:40; 8:48), the peace that came into the world at his coming (2:14, 29). The canticle of the angels celebrating the birth of the *Rex pacificus* (2:14) is echoed by the disciples when the King of peace enters the holy city in triumph (19:38)—the city that did not receive the message of peace (19:42). It is this same gift of peace that the Risen Christ gave (24:36), the peace which the disciples spread throughout the world (Ac 7:26; 9:31; 15:23). But peace and joy, both, are the fruit of prayer, of close personal union with Jesus Christ the Saviour.

d 6. Rich and Poor—If we were to speak of Lk in modern terms we might describe it as **the 'social' gospel**. The preaching even of the Baptist is given this character, and he points out to the tax-collectors and soldiers what their social duty is (3:10—14). But **the beatitudes offer the clearest case** in point and the differences between Lk and Mt are instructive. Mt speaks of the 'poor in spirit' (5:3) Lk of the 'poor' (6:21). Mt has 'blessed are those who hunger and thirst for righteousness' (5:6) while Lk has 'blessed are you that hunger now' (6:21). In both cases Mt uses the term 'poor' and 'hungry' metaphorically but Lk speaks of the really poor and of real hunger.

We must, however, keep the context in view. The poor are not worthy of the kingdom of God by the mere fact of being poor; Lk is careful to indicate that the poor in question are disciples (6:20) and, therefore, **they are poor who put their trust in God.** The poor who hunger in this life will be satisfied in the next: this is the thought of Ps 107 (106):9—'He satisfies him who is thirsty, and the hungry he fills with good things'. And the *Magnificat* announced the great social upset that the gospel will bring about: 'He has put down the mighty from their thrones, and exalted those of low degree' (1:52).

e Lk has many warnings against the danger of riches and he is much more emphatic than the other evangelists on this score: 6:24—26; 12:13—21; 14:33; 16:9, 11, 19—31; 18:22. It is not the possession of wealth as such that is condemned, rather it is the selfishness of the rich that is severely censured. The parable of The Rich Fool (12:16—21) is given the moral: 'So is he who lays up treasure for himself, and is not rich toward

God.' A choice must be made, for no man can serve God **76** and mammon (16:13). On the positive side there is the fact that the life of Jesus was lived among the poor. At his birth it was shepherds who came to visit him (2:8; cf Mt 2:1—12). His mother and Joseph gave the offering of the poor (Lk 2:24). In short, it is above all in the humble birth of the Son of God and in the penury of his life that poverty is exalted: 'Foxes have holes, and the birds of the air have nests; but the Son of man has nowhere to lay his head' (9:58). And this example was efficacious, for Simon and James and John—and so many others—left everything and followed him (5:11).

It is to be expected, then, that **Lk insists on renunciation.** Confidence is not to be placed in riches (12:13—21) but on God who will provide (12:22—32): 'sell your possessions and give alms' (12:33). The follower of Christ must renounce all: 'whoever of you does not renounce all that he has cannot be my disciple' (14:33) and so the ruler who comes to him is bidden: 'Sell all that you have and distribute to the poor . . . and come, follow me' (18: 22). In both these texts and in 5:11, 28 Lk, unlike the other evangelists, stresses the completeness of the renunciation (cf Mk 10:21; Mt 19:21). He, too, is the only one of the synoptics who includes the *wife* among the possessions of this world which call for renunciation or detachment on the part of the perfect disciple (14:26; 18:29); here speaks the disciple of St Paul (1 Cor 7:7, 26).

7. The Influence of St Paul—We are assured that Lk **f** was a disciple of St Paul (cf § 822e) and the influence of Paul can indeed be traced in the third gospel. This is not so much a matter of vocabulary—though there are resemblances—or of traditions—though in the account of the institution of the Eucharist (Lk 22:19f; 1 Cor 11: 23—25) both follow a similar tradition—as of **a common atmosphere of thought and sentiment.** Both, for example, insist on the theme of the universality of salvation (Lk 2:30f; 3:23, 38; 13:28f; 14:23; 24:46f; Rm 1: 16; 1 Tm 2:4; Ti 2:11). This is not to say that the other Synoptics do not make it clear that salvation is offered to all men (and not to the Jews only) but that it is more emphatically the view of Lk as it is of Paul.

The atmosphere of joy that we have noted in Lk is like that of the Pauline epistles. In both we find frequent invitations to serve the Lord in thanksgiving and joy (Lk 5:25f; 10:17; 18:43; 19:37; 24:52f; Phil 4:4; 1 Thes 5:16; Rm 12:12 etc). In both we find the same pressing exhortation, by word and example, to have recourse to prayer (Lk 3:21; 5:16; 6:12; 9:18, 28f; 11:1—13; 18:1—5, 9—14; 22:32; 33:34, 46; 1 Thes 5:17; Col 4:2; Eph 6:18; Phil 1:3—6 etc), and the same manner of indicating the action of the Holy Spirit on the conduct of life (Lk 3:16, 22; 4:1, 14, 18; 10:21; 11:13; 12:10, 12; 24:49; Gal 3:2—5, 13f; 5:22; 1 Cor 6:11; 12:13; 2 Thes 2:13; Rm 8:2, 9; 14:17 etc).

Lk, alone among the synoptists, gives Christ the title *Kyrios*—7:13, 19; 10:1, 39, 41; 11:39; 12:42; 13:15; 16:8; 17:5f; 18:6; 19:8; 22:61; 24:3, 34. In the LXX 'Yahweh' was rendered *kyrios*, and the early Christians, from the first, gave this same divine title to Christ. 'Lord', for us has lost its very specific meaning, but the definite signification it had in the primitive Church is brought out by such texts as these: 'if you confess with your lips that Jesus is Lord. . . you will be saved' (Rm 10:9), and 'every tongue should confess that Jesus Christ is Lord' (Phil 2:11)—in both cases the divinity of Christ is professed. And when Lk uses the title he is writing as a Christian firm in his faith and so applies this christian title to the Saviour—for Jesus was not

68f addressed as 'Lord', in this full sense, during his lifetime.

g It is not necessarily the influence of Paul only that has moved the evangelist to use the title 'Lord' so frequently, for many of the concepts in the epistles go back beyond Paul to the primitive tradition. Such are the divine Sonship of Jesus, the universality of salvation and the importance of faith as a condition of entry into the kingdom of God. It is precisely these, and similar, ideas that we find in Lk, and not as part of the preaching of the Apostle, but as they figured in his own written sources. Doubtless, in reproducing these concepts, he was influenced by the teaching and expressions of his master. But despite his origin and his education, despite his close contact with Paul, despite the Gentile-Christian readers to whom his gospel is addressed, Lk reproduced, substantially, the primitive catechesis, the tradition of the Apostolic Church.

1: 1–4. PROLOGUE

769a In the manner of the Gr. writers of his day Lk dedicates his book to a patron, at the same time setting out the occasion, method and purpose of the work. He does this in a flawless and elegant Gr. that contrasts sharply with the style of the following chh. It is probable that this prologue was meant to introduce both parts of Lk's work, and the brief reference in Ac 1:1 marks the link between both volumes and suggests the continuity of the whole. **1f.** 'Many', while not to be taken too literally, must mean more than a few: there had been several narratives of the gospel events, some perhaps of no great extent. Among these documents we must surely number Mk, and the special source common to Lk and Mt—and perhaps as well the Gr. version of Aram. Mt. The authors of the documents—and Lk is in the same position—had recorded the traditions authoritatively handed on by the 'eyewitnesses and ministers of the word' i.e. the Apostles, or, at least, these in the first place; the 'word' = the gospel (cf 8:13, 15; Ac 4:4; 6:4; 8:4; 11:19). **3f.** Lk has himself decided to write a gospel and so he has carefully studied these things 'from the beginning' (rather than 'for some time past') i.e. going beyond the starting-point of the Apostolic *kerygma*, the Baptism of Jesus, to the infancy of Jesus and of his Precursor; in other words, he has done careful preparatory research. His work will be 'orderly', with a theological rather than a chronological order. The book is not written for Theophilus but is dedicated to him as its patron. Addressed as 'Most Excellent' he is a man of some social standing who will help to circulate the work. He himself can learn from this gospel an appreciation of the solid historical foundation of the teaching he had received: in this very Gr. phrase *logoi* stands for 'teaching' rather than 'things' and *katēchēthēs*, while it can mean 'informed', most likely means that Theophilus had been 'instructed' as a Christian.

1:5–2:52 THE INFANCY NARRATIVE

b The Literary Form of Lk 1–2—Like Mt, but independently of him, Lk prefaces his gospel with a narrative of the infancy of Jesus; he alone treats of the infancy of the Baptist. This whole section is notably more Semitic than the rest of the gospel and it has been seriously argued that a Semitic (Heb. or Aram.) original underlies these chh. In point of fact there is wide divergence among scholars as to the extent and character of source material, and regarding the personal contribution of Lk. The different viewpoints may be reduced to three—

though, admittedly, at the price of over-simplifying the **769b** situation.

(1) These chh are based on **a written Heb. source** which, presumably, was known to Lk **in Gr. translation**; thus are explained the many notable hebraisms throughout the Infancy narrative. In this view the editorial work of the evangelist would be quite restricted.

(2) The whole is **a free composition of Lk** who deliberately, and successfully, imitated the style of the LXX. Since that version abounds in hebraisms their presence in these chh is to be expected. A strong point of this argument is Lk's undoubted knowledge of the LXX and his penchant for reproducing the flavour of it.

(3) Lk has drawn on sources—**Gr. versions of Aram. traditions.** But these have been rewritten by him, and the **whole arrangement** of the carefully constructed Infancy narrative **is his work.** In the process, he has not only turned to biblical models but has written 'biblical' Gr., and has kept himself deliberately within the framework of the OT.

While it is not possible to make an unqualified choice, the third theory seems more satisfactory than the others. For one thing, it takes seriously Lk's assurance that, in his desire to go behind the traditional opening-point of the gospel (the ministry of the Baptist), he sought out existing, trustworthy material (1:1–4). Then, by means of his carefully cultivated OT style, he has reproduced the atmosphere of that moment before the emergence of Christianity. It is a brilliant achievement on the part of one who himself enjoyed the fulness of Christian revelation, but our evangelist is capable of such artistry. In brief, the position taken here is that **Lk, while leaning on a Gr. form of originally Aram. traditions, has himself written chh 1–2 of his gospel, and in a style redolent of the LXX.**

Whatever theory of literary construction one adopts, the question of literary form remains and must be faced. It has become fashionable to describe Lk's Infancy narrative as midrash. The use of the term does at least recognize the influence of OT texts on the form of the Infancy gospel and acknowledges the presence of a distinctive method, but the designation, applied to Lk 1–2, or to any part of it, is unfortunate. These chh are not midrash, and it is not helpful to characterize them as such.

The fundamental principle of midrash is the actualization of a biblical text. If this were to be verified in Lk 1–2 we should have to say that these chh—or certain episodes—have grown out of specific biblical texts. In fact, what we do find is that the author, starting with episodes in the infancy of John and of Jesus, has described them in terms of OT analogies and in OT language. Where midrashic development flows from the biblical text, Lk has used biblical language to illustrate, and interpret, the events with which he deals. The procedure is very different in each case. And even if, as is probable, the Baptist infancy story is Lk's own composition, he modelled it on his narrative of Jesus—this is not midrash. But how might we describe the literary form of Lk 1–2? The verdict of a recent scholar, at the close of a long study of midrash, is very sound. 'Perhaps the best classification of our material is simply *infancy narrative*, for **these chh seem to have been written in the tradition of infancy stories, biblical and extra-biblical, sharing with them many of their motifs'** (A. G. Wright, 'The Literary Genre Midrash', CBQ 28 (1966), 456; cf ibid, 105–38, 417–57).

Throughout his Infancy narrative, even more than in the rest of his gospel, **Lk is concerned,** not with facts

769b only, but, in a special way, **with the meaning of the facts.** In the Introduction we have noted his theological preoccupations and will have cause to draw attention to these throughout the Commentary. But what are we to say on such matters as the nature of the apparitions to Zechariah and to Mary? Did Gabriel really appear in both cases? Perhaps—but it is more likely that Lk (as, no doubt, his sources had done), has presented genuine spiritual experiences in a traditional and consecrated style. What we do learn is that Zechariah received intimation of the birth of a remarkable son. And we do accept that Mary was called by God, and knew herself to be called, to play an essential role in God's plan of salvation, to be the mother of his Messiah. This is the essential factor; the manner in which God's will was made known is secondary. *A fortiori*, the angelic announcement to the shepherds is to be understood in the same manner as the other two annunciations; and the canticle of the angels, like the other canticles of the narrative, is meant to bring out the spiritual significance of the episode.

It was Lk's express intention to compile a narrative of 'the things which have been accomplished among us' (1:1); he assures us that he is dealing with facts. We should take him at his word, while keeping in mind that his concern is the significance of the facts. It was his intention to write history, but we must not forget that, in the Infancy narrative above all, he is writing history in the biblical manner. And **to the Hebrews, history was the mighty acts of God, the God who is Lord of history.** Faith was the background of history and events were the inbreaking of spiritual purpose and power upon the day to day affairs of men (See Caird, 47f).

The Literary Construction of Lk 1:5—2:52—Lk's Infancy narrative is composed in the form of a diptych and has two phases: before the births of John and of Jesus (1:5—38) and the accounts of the birth of both (1:56—2:40). Each of these phases has a complementary episode: the Visitation (1:39—56) in the first case and the Finding (2:41—52) in the other (Laurentin, 32f). There are seven episodes in all.

1. Diptych of Annunciations 1:5—56

I. Annunciation of the Birth of John 1:5—25
Introduction of the parents
Apparition of the angel
Zechariah troubled
'Fear not . . .'
Annunciation of the birth
Q. How shall I know?
A. *Reprimand* by the angel
Constrained silence of Zechariah
Departure of Zechariah

II. Annunciation of the Birth of Jesus 1:26—38
Introduction of the parents
Entry of the angel
Mary troubled
'Fear not . . .'
Annunciation of the birth
Q. How shall this be done?
A. *Revelation* by the angel
Spontaneous reply of Mary
Departure of the angel

III. Complementary Episode 1:39—56
Visitation
Conclusion: Return of Mary.

2. Diptych of Births 1:57—2:52.

IV. Birth of John 1:57—58
Joy at the birth with canticle element
Circumcision and Manifestation of John 1:59—79

Manifestation of the 'Prophet'
Canticle: *Benedictus*
Conclusion:
Refrain of growth, 1:80

V. Birth of Jesus, 2:1—20
Joy at the birth
Canticle of angels and shepherds.

VI. Circumcision and Manifestation of Jesus, 2:21—35
Manifestation of the 'Saviour'
Canticle: *Nunc Dimittis*
Supplementary episode: Anna, 2:36—38
Conclusion:
Refrain of growth, 2:40

VII. Complementary episode, 2:41—52
The Finding in the Temple
Refrain of growth, 2:52

A glance at the plan of the Infancy narrative, as it appears in schematic form, brings home to one the intention of Lk. John the Baptist and Jesus are compared and contrasted but the greatness of Jesus is emphasized even by the more developed account of his earthly origins. Within the parallel narratives the same point is made. Mary is clearly shown to be far superior to Zechariah and, more explicitly, the Son of Mary is set on a pedestal and towers above the son of Zechariah. The parent cell of these two chh is the infancy of Jesus and, more precisely, the Annunciation, while it may well be that the infancy of the Baptist is no more than a prelude, composed by Lk, in order that the Messiah may be introduced by his Precursor as in the primitive gospel; cf Lk 3 (Benoit).

Theology of Lk 1—2—These chh are dominated by **the** c **idea of messianic fulfilment.** The different scenes build up the climax of the entry into the Temple, for Lk saw in that event the formal manifestation of Jesus the Messiah. He has achieved his effect, in large measure, by his use of Dn 9—10 in the annunciations to Zechariah and to Mary and by his use of Mal 3 in the annunciation to Zechariah, the *Benedictus* and the Presentation. Taken together with the pregnant *eplēsthēsan* (1:23, 57; 2:6, 21f) this use of messianic texts underlines the arrival of the messianic age. These chh are a religious history written in the biblical manner. Lk has rethought the facts and has recounted them in terms of scriptural precedents— hence a constant echoing of Scripture. This gives rise to what we may term an 'allusive theology' that lies beneath the surface throughout.

When the chh are read on this deeper level it emerges that Lk has wished to present Jesus as a transcendent, divine Messiah. The titles given to him (Great, Holy, King, Light, Glory, Son of God, Saviour, Christ the Lord, Lord), when taken together, point in that direction. In short we might say that the assimilation of Jesus to Yahweh is 'the final word of the christology of Lk 1—2' (Laurentin, 130). We should note, too, that the transcendent dignity of Jesus sheds a reflected glow on Mary. As mother of the Messiah she is the true daughter of Sion where God has come to dwell among his people—a truth brought out by the use of Zeph 3 and Mi 4—5 (Laurentin; P. Benoit, RB 65 (1958), 427—32).

1:5—25. Annunciation of the Birth of John—5. d Herod the Great reigned from 37 to 4 B.C. 'Judea' is to be understood in a broad sense: Herod's territory included Idumaea and Samaria. The division of Abijah is the eighth of the 24 divisions of priests (1 Chr 24:10) who carried out, in turn, the daily service of the Temple. **6f.** Zechariah and his wife are Israelites who faithfully observed the commandments of God. Elizabeth was barren like Sarah (Gn 16:1ff), Rebekah (25:21), Rachel (30: 22), the mother of Samson (Jg 13:2) and Anna the mother

9d of Samuel (1 Sm 1—2), while, like Abraham and Sarah, she and her husband were elderly and, humanly speaking, must remain childless. Hence the child to be born is in a special way the gift of God, a child of grace like Isaac, Samson and Samuel. **8—10.** The gospel begins, as it closes (24:53), in the Temple. Each division of priests served for a week at a time. Because of their number the chief offices were assigned to them by lot. To Zechariah had fallen the highest priestly duty of tending the fire and burning fresh incense on the golden altar which stood before the Holy of Holies. Though the offering was made both morning and evening, the presence of a whole multitude, in the outer courts, suggests the evening offering. **11f.** It was an auspicious moment for a divine message, and the messenger of the Lord, Gabriel, suddenly appeared in the place of honour at the right hand of the altar. Zechariah's spontaneous reaction to the heavenly apparition was fear; Lk often refers to similar religious awe: 1:29f, 65; 2:9f; 5:26; 7:16; 8:37; 9:34;

e Ac 2:43; 5:5, 11; 19:17; cf Dn 10:7. **13f.** The angel reassures him (cf 1:30; 2:10): God has heard his prayer (cf Dn 10:12). The remainder of the v makes it clear that the object of the prayer was, indeed, the birth of a son; though, in view of v 18, this had not been a recent prayer of the old priest. God announces beforehand (cf 1:31; Gn 17:19; Is 7:14) the significant name of the child: John = 'Yahweh is gracious'; and John will indeed herald the age of grace (cf Jn 1:6). So it is that the natural joy of the father will be transformed into a greater joy and many others (and not only the neighbours of 1:57f) will rejoice when, in due time, he will stand forth as the greatest of the prophets of Israel. **15f.** John will be great not only by human reckoning but in God's eyes (cf 7:28); his true greatness is indicated by the role he plays in God's plan. Like the Nazirites (Nm 6:23; Jg 13:4f; 1 Sm 1:11) and the Rechabites (Jer 35), the great ascetics of Israel, John will abstain from strong drink. He will be filled with the Holy Spirit 'from his mother's womb'—it is not clear whether the phrase means 'from his birth' or 'already in the womb'. Here, as almost everywhere in the Infancy narrative, the 'Holy Spirit' is the spirit of prophecy, and the meaning is that John is called to be a prophet from (or before) birth, like Jeremiah (Jer 1:5) or the Servant of Yahweh (Is 49:1,5). The v offers no support for the common view that John was freed from original sin in the womb (cf 7:28). Filled with the prophetical spirit he will win back many Israelites from the ways of sin to

f their God (cf 3:1—20). **17.** It was widely believed (Mal 3:23; Sir 48:10f; Mt 17:10 parr; Jn 1:21) that the messianic era would be preceded by the return of Elijah; here it is shown that John is the Elijah who is to come (cf Mt 17:12). The v is a—rather free—citation of Mal 3:23f. John's preaching of repentance will leave the people well disposed for the coming of the Lord—*Kyrios* is the Lord of the OT. Though the evangelist is aware that John is the forerunner of the *Messiah* he, in these chh, remains faithful to the OT perspective and represents the new Elijah as the forerunner of Yahweh; such, at least, is the general view. However, it appears to follow from a closer study of the narrative as a whole that the 'Lord' whose way the Baptist prepares is Jesus himself. The dominant idea is that of messianic fulfilment, which is realized at the entry to the Temple. We may observe the influence of Dn 9—10 and Mal 3 in the present passage. **18.** Abraham (Gn 15:8), Gideon (Jg 6:37) and Hezekiah (2 Kgs 20:8) requested signs in similar circumstances and were granted them without reprimand; Zechariah's demand betrays a certain scepticism which will be punished (v 20). **19f.** Gabriel is named in Dn 8:16; 9:21. Like Raphael (Tb

12:15) he is one of the seven 'angels of the Face' of **769f** Jewish tradition, who stand in the presence of God. He is sent by God to bring this 'good news'—*euangelizesthai* is a favourite word of Lk (10 times in the gospel and 18 times in Ac). The sign that Zechariah receives is also a punishment; he will be dumb (and deaf—v 62f) until the good tidings are fulfilled. **21f.** The ceremony of offering incense was a simple and brief one and the people who awaited the priestly blessing were wondering at the delay. When he did come forth he was able to convey to them, by signs, that he had seen a vision. **23—25.** Zechariah was not one of the priests who lived in Jerusalem and he left the city when his term of office was over (*eplēsthēsan* has certain theological overtones— 1:57; 2:6, 21f). We are evidently to understand that the child was conceived in the normal way, but it is due to a special intervention of God that it does happen despite sterility and old age.

26—38. Annunciation of the Birth of Jesus—The **770a** close parallel between this and the foregoing passage is obvious from a glance at the plan. Both annunciation narratives, involving an angelic message, are presented in a distinct literary form (Audet, 350—5). We find OT examples of the form in the messages to Hagar (Gn 16:7—15), to the wife of Manoah (Jg 13:3—20) and to Gideon (6:11—24). In these cases, and wherever the form occurs, we find that always the initiative is God's. Always too, though certain difficulties crop up in the dialogue, the message is taken to be sufficiently clear before the messenger departs. **26f.** In the sixth month of Elizabeth's pregnancy (1:24, 36) Gabriel was again sent by God, with tidings of joy, to a 'city' called Nazareth; for the benefit of his Gentile-Christian readers Lk specifies that it is a village of Galilee (cf Mt 2:23). The angel was sent to a 'virgin'—*parthenos* is best taken in its current sense of a young girl of marriageable age; though Lk is aware that Mary is a virgin in the strict sense (v 35), he is not here insisting on this. She is already betrothed and betrothal was, in Jewish law, a fully valid and binding contract. Yet not until the bridegroom had taken the bride to his home (cf Mt 1:24)—by custom a year after the espousals—did the couple live as man and wife. In the case of Mary and Joseph this final step was not taken until some time after the birth of John: from Judah Mary returned to *her* home (v 56). Joseph belonged to the house of David and so the legal Davidic descent of Jesus is assured. It cannot be shown that Mary was of the family of David, though it is reasonable to think so; she was certainly related to Elizabeth who was of Aaronic descent (v 36). **28.** The occurrence, in such a **b** semitically coloured narrative, of the Gr. formula *chaire* in place of the Semitic 'Peace!' is so surprising that one hesitates to accept it at its face value. On closer inspection we find that Lk has a specific OT passage in mind: Zeph 3:14—17 (cf Jl 2:21—27; Zech 9:9f): 'Sing aloud, O daughter of Sion; Rejoice . . . O daughter of Jerusalem!' The word 'Rejoice'—also occurring in Jl and Zech and nowhere else in the LXX—is *chaire*, the same term used by the evangelist. Since that messianic passage of Zeph underlies Lk 1:30f, *chaire* must have the meaning 'Rejoice!'—an invitation to rejoice at the advent of messianic times (for Gabriel's message does herald the new age). RSV rendering of *kecharitōmenē* ('favoured one') is preferable to the *gratia plena* of Vg. Here, in view of the cognate literary form, the episode of Gideon (Jg 6:11—24) is instructive. It is striking that Gideon is **c** not addressed by his proper name; indeed it is obvious that the angel's opening words ('Yahweh is with you, Valiant Hero' v 12) are anything but a conventional

770c greeting. The angel of Yahweh speaks words of hope and promise and Gideon is designated as the chosen vehicle of that promise, so 'Valiant Hero' is a new name which already indicates something of the whole purport of the message. And the accompanying phrase, 'Yahweh is with you', is the guarantee that the promise will be efficacious: the Lord who has chosen Gideon will accomplish his purpose. On the basis of the close parallel between Jg 6:12 and Lk 1:28 we must see that the opening words of Gabriel cannot be just a conventional greeting. Nor can *kecharitōmenē* be, primarily, a reference to the personal holiness of Mary, a compliment. The context is messianic, and she is present in her messianic rôle. What Gabriel announces is that she has been chosen to play an essential part in God's plan, so, very much better than 'full of grace' is the portentous name 'Favoured One'. This title not only preserves all that 'full of grace' might imply of personal sanctity (Mary is endowed with grace in a permanent fashion) but points to the source of that fulness, for the favour that will make of Mary the Favoured One *par excellence* is the messianic motherhood, the divine maternity. And now, too, the statement 'the Lord is with you' falls into place. Coming after 'full of grace'—as this is commonly understood—it is unnecessary, even banal. But once it is recognized that the new name designates a function allotted by God then the assurance that the Lord will be with the chosen one is a guarantee of the effective accomplishment of the divine purpose. Gideon, we may recall, received just such an assurance. **29.** Mary was 'greatly troubled', not like Zechariah (12) by the appearance of the angel, but at his
d words. The common view, that Mary's humility was disturbed, is not satisfactory—her humility is seen in her unhesitating *Fiat* and in her *Magnificat*: serene and direct, quite forgetful of self. The best explanation is the obvious one: Mary is 'troubled', perplexed because she does not yet understand for what purpose and to what extent she has been favoured by God. **30f.** The angel proceeds to enlighten her: the Favoured One is to conceive and bear a son, and she will give to this son the name of Jesus. The text of Zeph is again enlightening: 'The King of Israel, the Lord, is in your midst (lit in your womb) . . . Fear not, O Sion . . . the Lord, your God, is in your midst (in your womb)' (3:15-17). We notice the same reassuring 'fear not' and the parallel also explains the tautology of Lk: 'you will conceive *in your womb* (cf 1:13)—it is an echo of a phrase (*beqirbeh*) which occurs twice in the passage of Zeph. Like the mother of Immanuel (Is 7:14) Mary will impose the name on the child; 'Jesus' meaning 'Yahweh is Salvation' summarizes Lk's presentation of Christ (cf § 766g). **32f.** The angel describes the son and his destiny in terms borrowed from the OT, especially from the oracle of Nathan (2 Sm 7:12-16; cf Is 9:6; Dn 7:14). In view of the background, the title 'Son of the Most High' and the reference to an everlasting kingdom do not look beyond the Jewish horizon; but Lk will go on to explain (35) that the intervention of the Holy Spirit will mean that Jesus must be named 'Son of God' in an entirely new sense.
e **34.** Like Zechariah (18) Mary asks a question—and her words have embarrassed countless commentators. A common (Catholic) view is that Mary had made a vow of virginity and had entered into a compact with Joseph to that effect. This interpretation, which cannot be traced back beyond Ambrose, seems unsatisfactory on many grounds. Admittedly, the question is unexpected but the problem it has set is due in large measure to the fact that our understanding of it has been clouded by the intrusion of later ideas. To state that our Lady had made

a vow of virginity surely betrays a later (Christian) **77** mentality and the anachronism is not very effectively redeemed by the substitution of 'intention' or the like. This approach to the text is ultimately due to a preoccupation that is apologetical rather than theological, a care to uphold the doctrine of the virgin birth. But this is not Lk's preoccupation. V 35 shows that he takes the virginal conception for granted, but his interest does not bear on it directly. We have to look at things from his point of view and keep the OT background in mind. We should consider that Mary was a young Jewish girl with her people's high regard for marriage. Moreover, she was already betrothed, and so was about to enter the married state; but she was not yet living with Joseph (cf 2:5—note). Now here precisely is the point of Mary's question. She had understood that the conception of which the angel spoke was to take place without delay, and not only the parallel with Gideon but the context too indicates that she had understood correctly. As one betrothed she naturally felt that it would come to pass in the normal way; her perplexity is due to the fact that she is not yet married. And that is just what her question implies: 'How can this be since I am not in the married state?' (Schmid, 42f; Jones, 174).

Another solution is to regard the question as a **f** literary technique of Lk: it marks the change from the OT level of 32f and opens the way for the explanation (45) that what is about to happen is something entirely new. In this view the v tells us nothing about Mary's understanding of the mystery, J. Gewiess, 'Die Marienfrage, Lk 1:34', BZ 5 (1961), 221-54. Since we take the position that the Infancy narrative, as it stands, is the work of Lk, we have no difficulty in accepting 34 as an editorial link-v. But the evangelist has put the question into the mouth of Mary and it should be interpreted as a question of hers. It does indeed serve as a transition to the further elucidation by the angel but that is not its only role; it still needs to be explained and we have ventured an explanation. Leaney (20—27), who sees an open contradiction between vv 27 and 34 postulates two sources, one of which knew nothing of a virginal conception.

35. Holy Spirit and Power of the Most High stand **g** in parallelism; the Spirit is the divine power or energy. Already in Gn 1:2 the Spirit of God hovered over the waters about to perform the great work of creation; here that divine power overshadows Mary, about to perform a new and wonderful creation, a conception wrought by the direct action of God (cf Jn 1:14). It is possible that there is an allusion to Ex 40:35—the overshadowing Spirit and the presence of the Child in the womb of Mary recall the cloud that abode upon the tent of meeting and the glory of Yahweh that filled the tabernacle. But is this to read too much into *episkiazein* the one word common to both texts? In 35*b hagion* causes some difficulty— RSV rendering seems the best of a number of possible translations; the same word occurs, also unexpectedly, in 2:23. The presence of the word is due to the influence of Dn 9 in the one case and of Mal 3 in the other. In Dn 9:24 the messianic times will be marked, among other ways, by the consecration of a Holy One. (While it is not clear whether Dn refers to the consecration of a holy place or of a holy person, Lk was entitled to choose the second sense which, moreover, seems to have been a current Jewish interpretation). It is this 'Holy One' he has in mind in v 35, and thus insinuates that the angel's message was the signal for the inauguration of the messianic age. In 32 we have noted that 'Son of the Most High' is a title within the Jewish messianic perspective and does not necessarily imply divinity. Here

70g the situation is quite other; *dio kai*, 'that is why', points back to the action of God: the Holy One will be Son of God in an entirely new sense, because he will be conceived by the power of God alone. **36f.** In accordance with the literary form of angelic message, Mary, like Gideon and like Zechariah, is given a sign, a guarantee of the authenticity of the message—though, in her case, the sign is unsolicited.

h **38.** In Mary's consent we may see the true pattern of her humility. If she had been troubled and if she had asked a question it is because she had been perplexed. Now that she knows the divine purpose, she accepts that purpose unhesitatingly and with perfect simplicity. Mary now knew the divine purpose—but did she *understand* it? Above all, did she realize that the Child to be born of her would be divine? If we look to the essentials of Lk's narrative we find that his attention first bears on the child whose birth he announces, then on the motherhood of Mary and lastly on the manner of her maternity. In other words, the central fact, and the source of the others, is the Incarnation and this, by definition, means that God became Man. It forms the kernel of the angel's message and if Mary had not grasped this she had not really understood the message. But, according to the principles of the literary form in question, she ought to have understood the message before the departure of the angel, and Lk's treatment of the matter implied that she had. We may maintain, therefore, not gratuitously but with sound reason, that at the moment of the Incarnation, Mary knew that the child then and there conceived in her womb was divine. This, however, is not to claim that she was fully enlightened (cf 2:50; 2:19, 51); and we are told that her *Fiat* was essentially an act of *faith* (1:45)—which included, in its object, the divinity of Christ, but seen in the darkness that is a necessary feature of faith.

771a **39–56 Complementary Episode: 39–45, The Visitation—39.** The 'city of Judah', in view of the determination 'hill country' must be in the neighbourhood of Jerusalem; a tradition, going back to the 6th cent., points to Aïn Karim, 5 m. W of the city. The 'haste' of Mary was inspired by friendship and charity; the journey would have taken some four days. **40f.** At Mary's greeting Elizabeth felt the infant move in her womb; as an inspired prophetess ('filled with the Holy Spirit') she understood that he had leaped for joy at the presence of the mother of the Messiah (44). It does not follow that John enjoyed the use of reason or that he was then and there cleansed of original sin (cf 15). **42–45,** Enlightened by the prophetic spirit, Elizabeth is aware of Mary's secret: she is the mother of her 'Lord' i.e. of the Messiah; that is why she is 'blessed among women', a hebraism (cf Jdt 13:18) meaning more blessed than all women. Elizabeth's expression of unworthiness at the signal honour of this visit echoes that of David in the presence of the ark of Yahweh (2 Sm 6:9); but the influence of the passage (6:2–11) on the Visitation narrative and Lk's consequent presentation of Mary as the true ark of the covenant, must remain doubtful.

b **46–56 The Magnificat—**Three Old Lat MSS (a b l), some texts of Irenaeus and Origen and Nicetas attribute the *Magnificat* to Elizabeth, all other witnesses attribute it to Mary. In form a thanksgiving psalm, it is a catena of OT reminiscences and leans especially on the canticle of Hannah (1 Sm 2:1–10); hence it is even more Semitic in tone than the rest of these chh. It is unlikely that the hymn represents the *ipsissima verba* of Mary and may well be Lk's interpretation of her mind. Since there is no clear reference to the messianic birth it is possible

that it is his adaptation of an existing Jewish psalm, from **771b** the milieu of the 'poor of Yahweh'. Lagrange (54) warns that the literary quality of the canticle has too often been exaggerated. Whatever its origin, the attribution, by an inspired writer, of the *Magnificat* to Mary gives us an assurance that it truly represents her sentiments. **46–48.** Elizabeth had blessed Mary as mother of the Messiah; Mary gives the glory to God in joyful thanksgiving (cf 1 Sm 2:1; Hb 3:18; Ps 35 (34):9). God has regarded her position as his handmaid i.e. her entire submission to him (cf 1 Sm 1:11). The fruit of that submission, that unselfish humility, redounds to the everlasting glory of Mary. **49f.** Immediately, she turns her attention to the Almighty, the holy and merciful one (cf Dt 10:21; Ps 111 (110):9). **51–53.** The manifestation of God's power, holiness and goodness (cf Ps 118 (117):15; 89 (88); 103 (102):17; 147 (146):6; Sir 10:14; Ez 21:21; Ps 107 (106):9). **54f.** These vv, in the mouth of Mary, point to the last great help, the fulfilment of the promise made to Abraham (cf Is 41:8f; Ps 98 (97):3; Mi 7:20). **56.** Typically (cf 1:64–67; 3:19f; 8:37f) Lk rounds off one theme before passing on to another. Consequently, it does not follow that Mary had departed before the birth of John. She returned 'to *her* home' i.e. she had not yet begun to live with Joseph.

57–80. The Birth and Manifestation of John— c 57f. The birth of John marks the fulfilment of the angel's message to Zechariah. The completion (*eplēsthē*) of Elizabeth's term of pregnancy suggests, too, the fulfilment of messianic times (cf 2:6, 21f). The rejoicing of the neighbours and kinsfolk is already an accomplishment of the promise of v 14.

59–66 Circumcision and Manifestation of John— 59–62. Circumcision was prescribed for the eighth day after birth (Gn 17:12; Lv 12:3). It had become the custom to name the child on that day and to celebrate the occasion by a feast to which relatives and neighbours were invited. There is no need to suppose that Elizabeth had learned the name by revelation, for Zechariah, though deaf as well as dumb (62) could still have managed to inform her (cf 63). **63f.** Zechariah, confirmed his wife's declaration. Thereupon he found himself able to speak again and his first words were a hymn of praise i.e. the *Benedictus*. **65f.** Before giving the text of the canticle Lk, in his usual style, rounds off the episode. The closing remark of v 66 (cf Jer 26:24; Ac 11:21) is a reflection of the evangelist (cf v 80; ch 3).

67–79 The Benedictus—67. Zechariah, like so many **d** others in this narrative, is inspired by the Spirit of prophecy. His canticle, like the *Magnificat*, is a chain of OT quotations and reminiscences and gives an even stronger impression of being a pre-existing psalm put, by Lk, in the mouth of Zechariah. This is true especially of the first part (67–75) which is markedly Jewish in tone; the remainder may be a composition of Lk. Yet, 78f might be considered the natural conclusion of the original psalm, in which case, 76f forms an insertion of the evangelist. It is noteworthy that if the canticle were removed v 80 would fit smoothly after v 66. At any rate, the inspired writer has judged that the canticle reflects the mind of the old priest at that moment. As it stands, the first part of the canticle (68–75) praises God's great actions in the history of his people; the second part (76–79) turns to the son of Zechariah and foreshadows his office and his preaching. **68–71.** The hymn opens, like many of the psalms (cf 41 (40):14; 72 (71):18; 106 (105):48) and like later Jewish prayers, with the praise of God. 'Visit' is a biblical term which indicates a—generally favourable—intervention of God

771d (Ex 4:31; Ru 1:6; Ps 65 (64):10; 80 (79):15; 106 (105):4). In the present context the visitation and deliverance refer to the sending of the Messiah, the 'horn of salvation'—horn is the symbol of strength (cf 1 Sm 2:1, 10; Ps 18 (17):3; 75 (74):5)—of the house of David in accordance with the prophecies (cf 2 Sm 7) who, in his divine strength, will save his people from their enemies (cf Ps 18 (17):18; 106 (105):10; 2 Sm 22:18). 72—75. Then will be the overflowing of God's great mercy (Mi 7:20) when, in remembrance of his covenant (Ex 2:24; Ps 105 (104):8f; 106 (105):45) and of his oath to Abraham (Jer 11:5) his people can serve him, unmolested **e** and without fear, all their days. **76f.** These vv, addressed to the infant Baptist, point to his vocation of Prophet and Precursor. As in 1:16f he goes before Yahweh, not the Messiah. Whereas this may be an archaic touch, the influence of Mal 3 here, at 16f and in the Presentation story, suggests rather the assimilation of Jesus to Yahweh and so his transcendence. John will declare, going beyond the perspective of the first part, that true salvation consists in the forgiveness of sins. Salvation in terms of remission of sins is a favourite theme of Lk and strongly supports the view that these vv were inserted by him. **78f.** This could very well be the conclusion of 68—75. As it stands, v 78 indicates that the true salvation is the fruit of the loving mercy of God, and will be brought from on high by the 'rising Sun'—*anatolē* (Mal 3:20; cf Is 60:1) i.e. the Messiah or messianic age. *Episkepsetai* (p⁴ B S W O sy sin bo sa arm) is preferable to *epeskepsato* (the others). Better than RSV is BJ rendering of 78*b*: *qui nous amènera d'en-haut la visite du Soleil levant.* The 'shadow of death' is thick darkness (Is 9:1; 42:7) the darkness of sin which will be dissipated by the messianic light (cf Jn 1:5). That same Sun will guide men along the right way of true peace, the faithful service of God (74f). **80.** The infancy story of the Baptist closes with a 'refrain of growth' (2:40, 50) indicating his physical and spiritual development (cf Jg 13:24f; 1 Sm 2:26). In typical Lucan style, reference to John's sojourn in the desert prepares the way for his next appearance (3:2). The 'wilderness' is that of Judea, in the neighbourhood of the Dead Sea and suggests a possible link between the Baptist and the Essene establishment of Qumran.

772a 2:1—20. The Birth of Jesus—So far Lk's narrative has remained rigidly within the Jewish world, but when he comes to the birth of him who is 'a light for revelation to the Gentiles' (2:32) his perspective opens on the Gentile world. **1.** Augustus was Emperor 30 B.C. to A.D. 14. The general census of the Roman Empire ('all the world' = the *orbis Romanus*) was a means to tax assessment; Lk sees it as the providential means of ensuring that Jesus would be born in Bethlehem. There is evidence for a census in Gaul in 12 B.C. and there was provision for the taking of a census in Egypt every 14 years; the series seems to have begun 10/9 B.C. According to Tacitus (*Annals,* 1, 11) a *Breviarium Imperii* in Augustus' own hand found at his death gave not only the number of regular and auxiliary troops and the strength of the navy, but provided statistics on the provisions of dependent kingdoms, direct and indirect taxation and recurrent expenditure; this information must have resulted from a general census which, of course, need not have been carried out simultaneously in all parts of the Empire. The possibility of a Roman census in the domain of Herod the Great has been questioned. But Augustus knew that Herod, a puppet king, must bow to his wishes and, besides, there was a distinct coolness in their relations following Herod's unauthorized campaign against the Nabataeans 9/8

B.C. In view of the evidence it is reasonable to suppose **772** that Lk is standing on sound historical ground when he refers to the edict of Augustus. **2.** The celebrated chrono- **b** logical difficulties raised in this v are still unsolved; cf § 707*a*. It is widely accepted, on the sole authority of Jos. (Ant. 17, 13, 5; 18, 1, 1; BJ 7, 8, 1) that a census was held A.D. 6/7 when Publius Sulpicius Quirinius was legate of Syria, and was resisted by the Zealots under Judas the Galilean (Jos.Ant. 17, 10, 5; cf Ac 5:37). If this dating is accepted we must look for an earlier census carried out by Quirinius. On the evidence of inscriptions from Venice, Tivoli and Antioch of Pisidia it has been argued that he was legate of Syria between 4 and 1 B.C. and also that he had a special commission to carry out a census in Palestine 10—8 B.C. Tert (*Adv. Marcionem* 4, 19) attributes the nativity census to Sentius Saturninus legate of Syria 8—6 B.C.; he could well have completed a census begun by Quirinius. The truth of the matter is that the **available evidence is an inadequate basis for any firm conclusion**; but, by the same token, it is too scanty to convict Lk of historical inaccuracy—a charge that has often been levelled at him (Lagrange, 65f; G. Ricciotti, *Vita di Gesù Cristo,* 1941, 195—202; Schmid, 66—70). **3.** This was not the Roman method. Egyptian papyri tell of a Roman census carried out in an analogous fashion in that country, and specify that married women, too, had to present themselves for enrolment (cf v 5). **4f.** Joseph, of the house of David, went **c** from his home in Nazareth to the birth-place of his ancestor (1 Sm 16:1). Although Joseph had taken Mary to his home (cf Mt 1:24), and she was therefore his wife in the full legal sense, Lk, in referring to her as 'betrothed' delicately hints that Joseph was not the father of Jesus. The reading 'wife' of it sy sin and the harmonizing reading 'betrothed wife' of many MSS are presumably meant to account for Mary and Joseph travelling together. **6f.** No indication is given of the time spent in Bethlehem, nor does the text necessarily mean that Joseph had taken his wife on the long journey just when she was about to give birth to her child. The term 'first-born son' has in mind the law prescribing the consecration of the first-born male to God (Ex 13:12; 34:19; cf Lk 2:23); an only son is 'first-born' in this technical sense. Most likely because of an exceptional influx of travellers due to the census the *khan*—a hostelry in which men and beasts settled themselves down side by side as best they could—was full. Since we are told that the new-born baby was laid in a manger, we learn that Joseph and Mary at last found shelter in a stable of some sort—a tradition going back to Justin Martyr (*Dial,* 78) specifies a cave. **8—20 The Annunciation to the Shepherds**—In 7:22 **d** one of the signs by which the Baptist might know that Jesus is indeed the Messiah is that 'the poor have the good news preached to them'. So it was that the first announcement of his birth was made to simple shepherds: these, the poor and humble, accept the revelation which the leaders of Israel reject. **8.** Bethlehem lies at the edge of the desert of Judah and the shepherds in question, living in the open, were nomads. The shepherds recall David (cf 1 Sm 17:34f). **9.** The 'glory of the Lord', an expression frequent in the OT (cf Ex 13:21; 16:10) accompanies a theophany. Fear was the natural reaction to this manifestation (cf 1:12, 29; Mk 16:5). **10—12.** Again the encouraging 'be not afraid' (1:13, 30). The angel's announcement is a 'gospel' (*euangelizomai* is a favourite word of Lk) of good tidings and joy to all the people of Israel—the universalist note is not yet struck. 'This day'—the long-awaited day of Israel's salvation has dawned; a new-born child is the Saviour (*sōtēr* occurs

2d here only in Lk; cf Ac 5:31; 13:23) who has brought salvation. This Saviour is 'Christ the Lord'. *Christos Kyrios* occurs once only in the OT (Lam 4:20—LXX) and nowhere else in the NT. It would seem that Lk, in the context of an angelic message and the manifestation of the divine glory, insinuates the divinity of Christ; cf Ac

e 2:36 (Laurentin, 127–30). **13f.** The short canticle is closely related to the acclamation of the crowd at Christ's triumphal entry into Jerusalem (19:38); it differs from the latter in not being addressed to the Messiah but to God who had sent him. It would seem that 'Glory to God' is not to be understood as a wish ('let God be glorified') but as a statement, as a recognition of the significance of the hour (Schmid, 72). In 14 *eudokias* (S A B D W vet. lat sa) is to be read instead of *eudokia* (the majority). However, the Vg rendering *bonae voluntatis*, referring to human goodness, does not give the true meaning; RSV 'with whom he is pleased', BJ *qu'il aime*, pointing exclusively to the divine benevolence, suit the term and the context. **15f.** The shepherds, having set out immediately for Bethlehem, found that the facts (*hrēma* in the sense of *dābār*) were just as the angel had described. **17f.** Naturally, they spoke of the things the angel had told them; we do not learn whether the wonder of the hearers led to an acceptance of the angel's words. **19.** Mary pondered these words and all these happenings (*rhēmata*); cf the almost identical observation in v 51 (cf Gn 37:11; Dn 7:28). Lk is perhaps reminding us that Mary is the ultimate source of his Infancy narrative.

f 21–35. Circumcision and Manifestation of Jesus— The Circumcision—21. This is closely parallel to 1:59–63, the circumcision of John, and here, too, the emphasis is on the bestowal of the name. Born under the Law (Gal 4:4), Jesus submitted to the observances of the Law.

g 22–28 The Presentation of Jesus in the Temple— Lk has combined two requirements of the law: the purification ceremony after childbirth, and the consecration of the first-born to the Lord, and so he can, somewhat loosely, speak of 'their' purification i.e. of Mary and Jesus. It is convenient to consider these apart. **22a, 24.** According to Lv 12:2–4 a mother was purified 40 days after the birth of a son; she was required to make an offering of a lamb for a burnt offering and of a young pigeon or a turtledove for a sin offering—a poor woman could substitute another pigeon for the lamb (Lv 12:6–8). The 'purification' concerned strictly legal uncleanness and did not, of course, imply a moral fault in childbirth. Mary, like her Son, fulfilled the observances of the Law, even to the

h making of a sin offering. **22b–23.** It was in view of the presentation of Jesus in the Temple that Lk has mentioned the purification of Mary. The first-born son belonged to the Lord (Ex 13:2, 12) but was redeemed, bought back, by the payment of five Temple shekels (Nm 18:15f). It is nowhere laid down that the child should be brought to the Temple and presented there, yet the fact that Jesus was so presented is obviously of great importance for Lk, who appears to have in mind the dedication of Samuel (1 Sm 1:11, 22–28). We should note that *eplēsthēsan* (2:22; cf 1:22, 57; 2:6, 21) has more than the banal significance of the completion of a specified period of time and, in the context of the Infancy narrative, suggests the arrival of the messianic age. In v 23 *hagion* is unexpected (cf 1:35b). The v is a rather free citation of Ex 13:2, 12; but Lk has inserted the word 'holy'—it does not occur in the Ex text. The procedure of the evangelist becomes clear only when we realize that behind his description of the Presentation lies Mal 3. Since in 1:16f and in the *Benedictus* he presents the Baptist as the messenger, the Elijah, who will prepare the way of Yahweh (Mal

3:1, 23), it must follow that the 'Holy One' who is **772h** presented in the Temple and awaited by Simeon is none other than the Lord: 'Behold, I send my messenger to prepare the way before me, and the Lord whom you seek will suddenly come to his Temple' (Mal 3:1). Simeon, a pious Israelite, awaited, with faith and patiently, the fulfilment of the hope of Israel, its 'consolation' (Is 40:1; 49:13; 51:12; 61:2). He, too, like so many others in these chh, had received the Spirit of prophecy. The same Holy Spirit that had assured him that he would not die until he had seen the Messiah (the anointed one of the Lord) (cf 4:18) now inspired him to visit the Temple and revealed to him that the infant at that moment being presented there was indeed the longed-for Messiah.

29–32 The *Nunc Dimittis* is the third canticle given i to us by Lk alone and, like the others, it is used daily in the liturgy. In 29 *despotēs* is best rendered 'Master'. Simeon realizes that in view of the fulfilment of the promise (26) death must be near; but he can die in peace, like Abraham (Gn 15:15). His cup of joy has been filled to overflowing because he has gazed upon the 'salvation of God' (cf 3:6; Is 40:5), the Messiah whom God had sent to save his people; and not his own people only: salvation is destined for the Gentiles too (cf Is 52:10; 2:1ff; 42:6; 49:6). This messianic salvation is not only a beacon which shines before the nations but is a light which dissipates the darkness and enlightens them (cf Jn 1:5, 9). But since this salvation comes from Israel (cf Jn 4:22) and was made manifest through the chosen people, it redounds to the glory of Israel. In this passage for the first time in the Infancy narrative, we look beyond Jewish limits to a universalist horizon; but the perspective is that of Second Isaiah.

33–35 The Prophecy of Simeon—The field is again j limited to Israel. **33.** The prophetic words of Simeon are a manifestation of divine power and so meet with astonishment, the customary reaction throughout Lk and Ac (1:63; 2:18, 33; 4:22; 8:25; 9:43; 24:12, 41; Ac 2:7; 3:12; 4:13; 7:31). Here (cf 2:27, 41, 43, 48) Lk names Joseph as the father of Jesus; in view of 1:26–38 he can manifestly mean no more than legal paternity. **34f.** Simeon blessed Mary and Joseph—the privilege of age—and spoke again prophetically, addressing his words to her whose mother's heart would feel most keenly the fate of her Son (35a). Though the infant has come as the Saviour of his people (11) he will be rejected by many of them (cf Jn 1:11), for he will stand as a sign of contradiction, a stone that can be corner-stone or stumbling block (Is 8:14f; 28:16; Ps 118 (117):22f) according as men accept him or turn their backs on him (Lk 20:17f; Ac 4:11; Rm 9:33; 1 Pt 2:6–8). In his presence there can be no neutrality, for he is the light that men cannot ignore (Jn 9:39; 12:44–50), the light that reveals their inmost thoughts and forces them to take part for him or against him. V 35a is a parenthesis which associates Mary with the sad and painful aspect of the career of the Messiah, a veiled presage of the great sorrow that was to be hers in full measure when she stood at the foot of the Cross (Jn 19:25–27).

36–38 Anna the Prophetess—After a prophet, a k prophetess—the delicate hand of Lk—and, once again (implicitly this time) the spirit of prophecy. Anna, now 84, having lost her husband seven years after an early marriage, had remained a widow—a decision that was highly regarded in Israel (Cf Jdt 8:4ff; 16:22ff). She practically lived in the Temple, so uninterrupted were her prayers; a typical saint of the OT, one of the 'poor of Yahweh' she is also an example to Christian widows (cf 1 Tm 5:5, 9).

772l **39f Return to Nazareth**—The return to Nazareth serves to round off Lk's narrative. This typically Lucan literary feature and the independence of the two Infancy narratives are sufficient to account for the apparent discrepancy with Mt 2:1—21. V 40 is parallel to 1:80, another 'refrain of growth'. The growth and development was not only physical but intellectual as well: he is not only 'full of wisdom' but grew in wisdom daily (cf 2:52— note); his wisdom is exemplified in the next scene.

m **41—52 Complementary Episode**—This episode forms an epilogue to the Infancy narrative proper. It is the only incident we are allowed to learn of the hidden life and has for Lk a significance beyond that of evidence of the increasing wisdom of Jesus (40).

41—50 Jesus in the Temple—**41f.** The Law obliged all men who had reached the age of puberty to go to the Temple three times yearly—for the feasts of Passover, Pentecost and Tabernacles (Ex 23:14—17; 34:23f; Dt 16:16f). Women and children were not bound by the law (but women did freely accompany their husbands) and the law itself was not literally observed by those at some distance from Jerusalem: an annual journey to one feast sufficed in practice. The rabbinical ruling was that a boy was not bound to make the pilgrimage before the completion of his thirteenth year; but it was customary for the parents to take him up at an earlier age. The text does not necessarily imply that this was the first visit of Jesus to the Temple (apart from 2:22). **43—45.** It was not obligatory to remain for the whole term of the feast (here the seven days of unleavened bread), but most pilgrims did remain until the end. As a Jewish boy of twelve Jesus was well able to look after himself and his parents would naturally have taken for granted that he was with one of the scat-

n tered groups of the returning Nazareth caravan. It was usual to set out late in the day and the first stage would have been a short one, of, perhaps, some three hours (Lagrange, 95)—the 'day's journey' (44) need not be taken too literally. **46f.** 'After three days' i.e. on the third day (cf Mk 8:31). Here we have to do with a discussion among a group of rabbis, one which naturally attracted some attention. The intelligent questions of Jesus won him a hearing and these 'teachers of Israel' (cf Jn 3:10) were soon lost in wonderment at the unusual wisdom of this twelve-year-old boy. **48.** The relief of the parents was intense: *exeplagēsan*—'ils furent saisis d'émotion' (BJ)—and Mary's reproach is the spontaneous expression of the pain she had suffered. **49f.** Jesus' reply, the first and only words of his recorded in these chh, might be paraphrased: 'Where would you expect a child to be but in his father's house?' (Ginns). (The phrase *en tois tou patros mou*—lit 'in the things of my Father'—could mean my Father's affairs but here, without doubt, means 'my Father's house'). The significance of the reply is that Jesus declares that God is *his* Father (in contrast to his legal father: v 48). It follows that the claims of this Father must over-ride all other demands; his mission will break the natural ties of family (cf Mk 3:31—35), but the full implication of his words unfolded itself gradually.

51f The Hidden Life—The hour for the breaking of family ties was not yet; until the beginning of his public ministry Jesus was to remain quietly in Nazareth, humbly obedient to his earthly parents. Joseph is never again mentioned and, apparently had died before Jesus set out on his mission. Mary's pondering on 'all these things' (cf 19) surely brought a growth in her understanding of the mystery of her Son. The 'refrain of growth', an echo of 40, underlines the complementary nature of the Finding in the Temple (cf Jn 20:31; 21:25); the v is practically

a quotation of 1 Sm 2:26. Lk has very clearly marked the **772** physical development of Jesus: *to brephos* (2:16), *to paidion* (40), *Iesous ho pais* (43), *Iesous* (52) (Plummer, 78). Here (cf 40) we learn that his human mind, too, developed. And God looked with complacency on his Son who also attracted the favour of men (cf Prv 3:4). Thus the Infancy narrative, which has subtly intimated the divine nature of the Messiah, closes with an emphatic assertion of the reality of Christ's humanity.

3:1—4:13 PREPARATION FOR THE MINISTRY

The prologue has introduced the Messiah and his **773** herald and has indicated a first manifestation of both; now the time has come for a public manifestation, a proclamation that the age of fulfilment has begun. So John steps forward to prepare the way, to open the hearts of men.

3:1—20 Preaching of John the Baptist (Mk 1:1—8; Mt 3:1—12)—**1f.** Lk is at great pains to date exactly the ministry of the Baptist; his real purpose is thereby to date the beginning of our Lord's ministry. His elaborate synchronization serves to set the gospel event in the framework of world history (cf 1:5), and describes the political situation in Palestine. The reign of Tiberius began on 19 Aug, A.D. 14; the 15th year would be—in the Roman system—19 Aug 28—18 Aug 29. It is more likely that Lk follows the Syrian calendar with its year beginning on Oct 1. In this case the short period 19 Aug—30 Sept would be reckoned as the first year of Tiberius and the 15th year of his reign would be 1 Oct 27—30 Sept 28. Thus it seems that we can put the preaching of the Baptist, and the beginning of the ministry of Jesus, in the years A.D. 27—28. Pontius Pilate was procurator 26—36; his territory included not only Judea but also Idumea and Samaria. Herod Antipas, son of Herod the Great and Malthake, was tetrarch of Galilee (and Peraea) 4 B.C.—A.D. 39. Philip, son of Herod the Great and Cleopatra (not the Egyptian queen) was tetrarch of Ituraea, Trachonitis, Auranitis, Batanaea and Gaulanitis—territories NE of the sea of Galilee—4 B.C.—A.D. 34. Lysanias (not of Herod's family) was tetrarch of Abilene (NW of Damascus) until c. A.D. 37; two inscriptions have shown that Lk had not erred in respect of Lysanias. Caiaphas was High Priest 18—36; he was son-in-law of Annas who had been High Priest 6—15. The latter's influence was very great (five of his sons and his son-in-law had been high priests) and that is why Lk can associate him with Caiaphas and speak of 'the high priesthood of Annas and Caiaphas' (cf Jn 18:13—24; Ac 4:6). In the manner of the OT prophets John (who had already been marked as a prophet, 1:15) is now solemnly called to his mission (cf Jer 1:1, 5, 11; Hos 1:1; Jl 1:1.

3—6. John is presented as an itinerant preacher **b** whose message was repentance with a view of forgiveness of sins, an anticipation of the christian message (24:47). Lk, unlike Mk and Mt continues the quotation of Is on to v 5 (Is 40:3—5) and so introduces a universalist note ('all flesh'); cf 2:30—32.

7—20 The Preaching and Witness of the Baptist (Mt 3:7—10)—**7—9.** These vv agree almost word for word with Mt 3:7—10. The audience, however, is different: Lk has 'the multitudes' in place of 'the Pharisees and Sadducees' of Mt. **10—14.** A passage peculiar to Lk which explains the character of the repentance required as a preparation for the kingdom: it is a thorough-going conversion finding expression in the observance of the

73b commandments and in works of charity. The recommendation to tax-collectors and soldiers (most likely troops of Herod Antipas in whose territory John was preaching) is more specific in view of the special temptations of their way of life. **15.** Peculiar to Lk. The common opinion that John was the Messiah, a view explicitly rejected by the Baptist, is also referred to in Jn (cf 1:19f; 3:28); both Jn and Lk emphasize the subordinate role of the Baptist. **16f.** Almost textually the same as Mt 3:11f, but in Lk the preceding v has turned the statement into

c a disclaimer of messianic dignity. **18—20.** Following a summary account of John's preaching—he 'evangelized' the people—comes a typically Lucan conclusion: before turning to Jesus he closes the ministry of John. He thereby suggests that the last spokesman of the OT had finished when the preaching of Jesus began (cf Mk 6:17—29; Mt 14:3—12). The period of Israel is ended; now begins the period of Christ.

21f The Baptism of Jesus (Mk 1:9—11; Mt 3:13—17)—Jesus is baptized as one of the people so, perhaps, identifying himself with the people of Israel. John is not mentioned (20) and Jesus holds the stage. He prays as (in Lk) he does at all the decisive turning-points in the gospel. V 22 adds that the Holy Spirit descended 'in bodily form'—Lk underlines the reality of the theophany.

23—38 The Genealogy—In juxtaposition to his relation of sonship to God Lk now presents Christ's human ancestry. Since he is taken to be, and is legally, the son of Joseph his ancestry is traced through Joseph. This intention is unmistakably expressed in v 23 and those who, disturbed by the dissimilarities with Mt's genealogy (1.1—17), have sought to show that Lk traced the descent of Jesus through Mary, have had to do violence to this text. While Mt does not go beyond Abraham, Lk, with his universalist view, goes back to Adam: Jesus is Saviour not only of the chosen people but of all mankind. Lk has 77 names (against Mt's 42). Those from Jesse to Adam he could have worked out from the LXX but for the first part of the list, which traces the Davidic ancestry of Jesus through David's son Nathan (2 Sm 5:14; 1 Chr 3:5; 14:4; Zech 12; 12) he must have had a special source.

d 4:1—13 Temptation in the Wilderness (Mt 4:1—11; Mk 1:12f) **1f.** Lk agrees with Mt in giving a description of the temptations of Christ, but with Mk (unlike Mt) he declares that Jesus was tempted during the 40 days—the three temptations given here are the climax of the trial. The Holy Spirit had descended on Jesus at the moment of his baptism (3:22) and it is 'full of the Holy Spirit' and led by the Spirit that he goes into the wilderness. It is not implied that he received the fulness of the Spirit only at the baptism—the Spirit descended on him, not in him (3:22)—and he was 'holy' (1:35) from the moment of his conception. Lk shares the Johannine view that Jesus was the bearer of the Spirit in an unique sense and that he bestowed this Spirit only after his 'glorification' (Jn 7:39)—hence the emphasis on the action of the Spirit throughout Ac. **3—12.** Lk is very close to Mt except that he inverts the order of the last two temptations, cf § 715a. Mt's order is more logical and it can scarcely be doubted that Lk has deliberately changed the order so that the series may end at Jerusalem; this is in keeping with his special theological interest in the holy city. In v 5, in contrast with Mt, the mountain is not mentioned though it is suggested in the expression *anagagōn*; perhaps because in Lk 'the mountain' seems to have a fixed meaning. 'It is the place of prayer, the scene of secret revelations, of communication with the unseen world. No temptation can take place on it nor any public

preaching' (Conzelmann, 29). The addition proper to **773d** Lk 'for it has been delivered to me, and I give it to whom I will' (6) echoes the opinion of Jn on the dominion of Satan, the 'prince of this world' (Jn 12:31; 14:30; 16:11). **13.** *Syntelesas panta peirasmon*—the temptation ends decisively, and the devil departs. Henceforth there will be no temptation in the life of Jesus—until the moment indicated by *achri kairou*, the moment of his Passion (22:3, 53). 'A period free from Satan is now beginning, an epoch of a special kind in the centre of the whole course of redemptive history. What is now beginning, therefore, is not the last times, but the interval between the period of the Law, or of Israel, and the period of the Spirit, or of the Church' (Conzelmann, 28).

4:14—9:50 THE GALILEAN MINISTRY **774a**

In this section of his gospel Lk follows Mk 1:14—9:41 closely—apart from the omission of Mk 6:45—8:26 and the addition of Lk 6:20—8:3.

14f The Beginning of the Galilean Ministry (Mk 1:14f; Mt 4:12—17)—these vv are a heading for what follows: they provide a survey of the whole of the first period of the ministry of Jesus. The 'power of the Spirit' has reference to the miracles that Jesus will work (cf 4:36; 5:17; 6:19; 8:46). Jesus' preaching in the synagogues sets the pattern for the constant practice of Paul (cf Ac 13:5; 14, 44; 14:1 etc).

16—30 Jesus in Nazareth (Mk 6:1—6a; Mt 13:53—58)—At this point Mk (1:16—20) gives the call of the first disciples; Lk instead deals with the preaching of Jesus in his own village (cf Mk 6:1—6a) and his rejection. His intention is to trace symbolically the course of Christ's mission: he preaches the good news and his own people refuse to accept him. The inaugural scene has been composed by Lk from different sources. Vv 16—22 concern a visit like that of Mt 4:12f; 23f deal with the same episode as Mk 6:1—6a and Mt 13:53—58 while 25—30 refer to the close of the Galilean ministry (Osty, 60). **16f.** 'Where he had been brought up' looks back to 2:29, 51 and forward to v 24. As a faithful Israelite he had regularly attended divine service in the synagogue each sabbath. The service consisted of prayers, and readings (with commentary) from the Law and the Prophets. The readers were well-instructed members of the community or visitors known to be versed in Scripture. **18f.** Lk cites **b** (freely) Is 61:1f from the LXX; Jesus would have read the Heb. text and then given an Aram. version since Heb. was no longer understood by the great majority of the people. At the beginning of his mission Jesus is consecrated by an anointing, not with oil like the kings and priests of the OT, but with the Holy Spirit (cf Ac 10:38). The text of Is effectively sketches the work of Jesus, the works of the Messiah (cf 7:22). The 'year' is the jubilee year *par excellence* (cf Lv 25:10—13), the messianic era, the age of salvation. **23f.** Most probably this reply of Jesus answers an objection raised by the people of Nazareth on a later visit—hence the reference to miracles at Capernaum which does not, obviously, fit in the context of an inaugural appearance. In its present situation 23 refers to a demand that Jesus should back his claim by miracles and 24 explains why he cannot do this: he shares the fate of every prophet—rejection by his own people. **25—27.** The passage 25—30, with its description of the violent reaction of the people really belongs to the close of the Galilean ministry. Not accepted by his own people Jesus, like his great prophetic predecessors, will turn to the Gentiles who, by implication, will receive him. **28—30.** The fate of Jesus at the hands

774b of his own people is foreshadowed, but his hour is not yet come (cf 9:51; Jn 7:30, 45; 8:59).

c 31—44 Ministry at Capernaum (Mk 1:21—39; cf Mt 4:23—25; 7:28f; 8:14—17)—At v 31 Lk takes up the thread of Mk's narrative. 'The spirit of an unclean demon' = a spirit who was an unclean demon. **36f.** Since Lk gives the call of the first Apostles after the Capernaum episode, and not before it as Mk does, he here omits the names Andrew, James and John (cf Mk 1:29); for that matter, Simon is introduced abruptly. 'They besought him for her' replaces Mk's 'they told him of her': Jesus does not need to be informed (cf 9:47). **40f.** Reference to imposition of hands is proper to Lk. At 41 (cf 35) we have evidence of the 'messianic secret'; 'Son of God' is evidently equivalent to Messiah ('Christ') cf Mk 3:11.

42—44. Lk cannot mention the 'Simon and those who were with him' of Mk 1:36 since he has not yet given the call of the disciples, so he speaks of 'people' who sought Jesus and wanted to keep him with them. Curiously, contrary to his general tendency, Lk omits the Marcan detail that Jesus prayed in the 'lonely place'. Lk further specifies that this preaching is the 'good news (*euangelizomai*) of the kingdom of God' (cf Mk 1:38). He also clarifies the ambiguous phrase of Mk: 'that is why I came out'—from the Father? from Capernaum?—by the emphatic 'I was sent for this purpose'.

d 5:1—11 The Call of the First Disciples (Mk 1:16—20; Mt 4:18—22)—Lk has left until now the call of the first four disciples, which Mk has at the very beginning of the ministry (1:16—20); their immediate response, prepared by the rumour of his ministry (4:14, 44) is psychologically more understandable. The passage is composite and we may distinguish three elements: (a) a description of a discourse of Jesus in a detailed setting (1—3) parallel to that of Mk 4:1—2; (b) a miraculous catch of fish (4—10a); (c) the call of Simon (10b—11) related to Mk 1; 17, 20. (Osty, 54). **1—3.** 'Lake of Gennesareth' is Lk's more precise designation of the popularly named 'sea of Galilee' (cf Mk 1:16; 7:31). Throughout Lk the lake is more a 'theological' than a geographical factor. It is the place of manifestations which demonstrate the power of Jesus (Conzelmann, 42). **4f.** Simon's words underline the miraculous nature of the subsequent catch: if the night, the proper time for fishing has yielded nothing this daylight attempt is, humanly speaking, doomed to failure. **6f.** The 'partners' are named in 10. The great catch prepares the way for the promise to Peter in 10. **8f.** 'Simon Peter', here only in Lk, is typical of Jn (cf Jn 21:2, 3, 7, 11). Peter addresses Jesus as 'Lord' instead of 'Master' (5); it does not follow that he, at this stage, recognized Jesus as Messiah. The reaction of Peter, who had already witnessed the miraculous healing of his mother-in-law (4:38f) has seemed strange to some who have not recognized, or do not admit, that the present scene is not in its proper **e** chronological setting. **10f.** The symbolism of the miraculous catch is now made clear: henceforth Peter will be a fisher of men; already he stands forth as the leader. The implied call is, however, not addressed to him alone (11). Lk specifies that they left 'all' (cf 5:28; 11:41 etc).

12—16 The Healing of a Leper (Mk 1:40—45; Mt 8:1—4)—Here Lk takes up again the thread of Mk which he had dropped in order to insert 5:1—11. He omits the very human sentiments of Jesus (Mk 1:41, 43) and carefully avoids stating that Jesus could no longer openly enter a town (Mk 1:45). On the other hand he adds, characteristically, that Jesus withdrew to pray (cf Lk 5:16).

5:17—6:11 Conflict with the Scribes and Phari- 774f sees—Lk, following the exact order of, and departing little from, the text of Mk 2:1—3:6 gives a series of five disputes between Jesus and his adversaries: on forgiveness of sins (5:17—26); on eating with publicans and sinners (27—32); on fasting (33—38); concerning the plucking of ears on the sabbath (6:1—5); concerning healing on the sabbath (6—11). These are arranged in progressive order. At the cure of the paralytic the opposition is latent, the scribes and Pharisees 'question in their hearts' (5:22). During the meal in the house of Levi they addressed the disciples, though they were really attacking Jesus (30). With regard to fasting they questioned Jesus about an omission of the disciples (33) but in the case of the ears on the sabbath the charge is a direct violation of the law (6:2). In the last episode the adversaries spy on Christ (v 7) and then meet together to plot his destruction (11).

17—26 Healing of a Paralytic (Mk 2:1—12; Mt 9:1— **g** 8)—Throughout, Lk has omitted the vivid details of Mk. Characteristically in 19 he substitutes a tiled roof (more intelligible to his readers) for the earthen roof of a Palestinian house (Mk 2:4). More logically he mentions the presence of Pharisees and scribes at the beginning (30) and not later as in Mk 2:6. It is less easy to explain the presence of Pharisees and scribes from Judea and Jerusalem; but then the climax of the conflicts (6:11) points to a time very much later than the early stages of the Galilean ministry. In 17 *auton* (B S W) is unquestionably the original reading; *autous* (Vg *eos*) is a correction, perhaps because *kyrios* was taken to refer to Christ. The sense is that the power of God enabled Christ to work miracles (cf 6:19; 8:46).

27—32 Call of Levi; Eating with Sinners (Mk 2:13—17; Mt 9:9—13)—Mt, in the parallel passage, names this man 'Matthew' (9:9). Typically, Levi is said to have left 'everything' (cf Mk 2:15). Lk delicately speaks of 'tax collectors and others' (cf Mk 2:15); it is the Pharisees and scribes who describe these others as 'sinners' (30). Lk adds (32) that sinners are called 'to repentance' (cf Mk 2:17): the following of Jesus demands a sincere conversion.

33—39 A Question concerning Fasting (Mk 2:18— **h** 22; Mt 9:14—17)—**36.** This manner of introducing a parable is peculiar to Lk (cf 13:6; 14:7; 18:1; 20:9). He has quite changed the parable: Mk (2:21) says that the patching of an old garment with a piece of unshrunken cloth will only make the tear worse; in Lk the piece is torn from a new garment, so it is the new that suffers. He thus assimilates the first parable to the second. **37f.** In the parable of the new wine Lk follows Mk closely: the new is destroyed by contact with the old. The parables illustrate a contrast between the old spirit and the new—there can be no question of taking something from the gospel and adding it to Judaism (the one would suffer without profit to the other), nor can the gospel be contained within the framework of Judaism—there must be new wineskins for the new wine. **39.** Peculiar to Lk. It does not fit the context and is best considered as an independent logion here by means of the catchword (*oinos*) *neos* (37f). While its original sense is not clear, Lk would appear to understand it as the sad reflection of Jesus that the new wine he offers is not to the taste of those who have drunk the old wine of the Law.

6:1—5 Plucking of corn-ears on the Sabbath (Mk **775a** 2:23—28; Mt 12:1—8)—**1.** *Deuteroprōtō* 'second first' (A C D etc lat) is omitted by S B L W etc copt eth ar got, and is to be regarded as a secondary reading. The rubbing of the ears was, in rabbinical casuistry,

75a interpreted as reaping and so as an infringement of the sabbath. **4.** Lk omits the inexact detail 'when Abiathar was high priest' of Mk 2:26 (cf 1 Sm 21:1—6; 2 Sm 8:17); he also omits Mk 2:27. **5.** Codex Bezae transfers v 5 after v 10, and in its place makes the interesting insertion: 'On the same day, seeing one working on the sabbath, he said to him: "Man, if indeed you know what you do, blessed are you; but if you know not, you are accursed and a transgressor of the Law".' The saying shows the influence of Pauline doctrine (cf Rm 14:14, 23).

6—11 Healing on the Sabbath (Mk 3:1—6; Mt 12:9—14)—**8.** Again Lk goes beyond Mk (3:3) in stating that Jesus knew their thoughts. **10.** On the other hand he plays down the reactions of Christ (anger and grief)—Mk 3:5. **11.** Mk 3:6 certainly refers to the close of the ministry (the whole conflict passage is a literary unit reproduced as such by Mk); Lk softens this impression by suggesting less specific action against Jesus.

b 12—16 Choice of the Twelve (Mk 3:13—19; Mt 10:1—4)—Lk has switched about two Marcan passages (3:7—12 and 3:13—19) so that the choice of the Apostles, followed by a concourse of the people, sets the scene for the inaugural discourse (6:20—49). **12.** He emphasizes the importance of the choice of the Twelve by the night-long prayer of Jesus (cf 9:28f; 11:1; 22:41); throughout Lk 'the mountain' is a place of prayer or revelation. **13.** Instead of Mk's 'to be with him and to be sent out to preach' (3:14)—thus describing their function Lk declares that Jesus named the Twelve 'apostles'; it seems, however, that *apostolos* as a title was of later origin and the evangelist is reflecting Christian usage. **14ff.** Lk gives a list in Ac 1:13—so we have four lists altogether. While no two agree in the exact order of names all of them set out the Apostles in groups of four and the same name always appears at the head of each group: Simon Peter, Philip and James of Alpheus, *Ioudas Iakōbou* would normally be 'Judas, son of James', but 'brother of James' is possible (cf Ac 1:13); by Mk and Mt he is named 'Thaddaeus'.

c 17—19 Crowds come to Jesus (Mk 3:7—12; Mt 12:15—21)—Where Mk gives a summary description of the great crowds which attended the ministry of Jesus, Lk sets the stage for the Sermon. Jesus came down from the mountain—the place of prayer or revelation where he is alone or with a privileged few (cf 9:28)—and went to meet the people (cf 9:37). This 'level place' is no longer beside the lake (cf Mk 3:7, 9). The confession of the unclean spirits and Jesus' rebuke (Mk 3:11f) have been anticipated by Lk in 4:41, since they would be out of place immediately before the Sermon. The power of God which was in Jesus (5:17) healed those who so much as touched him (cf 8:46). At this point Lk leaves the plan of Mk, which he picks up again at 8:4. The following section (6:20—8:3) is, in this respect, an insertion of Lk.

d 20—49 The Sermon on the Mount (Mt 5—7)—Jesus formulated the special character of the kingdom of God in a discourse which Mk has omitted and which Mt and Lk have preserved in widely different versions. The name 'Sermon on the Plain' sometimes given to the Lucan version—because of the 'level plain' of v 17—suggests that the discourse here recorded is distinct from the 'Sermon on the Mount' of Mt. In fact, because of the special symbolical value of 'the mountain' in Lk— a place where the people do not come—the evangelist has changed the setting. This is entirely a literary device and it is best to keep the same title for both

versions. The discourse in Mt is much longer than that **775d** in Lk but, on the other hand, many of the passages found in Mt 5—7 occur elsewhere in Lk, in chh 11, 13, 14 and 16. It can be shown that Lk has omitted, as being of little interest to his Gentile readers, what concerned Jewish law and custom (Mt 5:17—6:18). In general, we may say that whereas Mt, borrowing from other sayings of our Lord, has added to the original Sermon, Lk has omitted some of it.

The discourse is introduced by the beatitudes and **e** woes (20b—26). Only a very small part of the matter dealt with in the antitheses of the Sermon (cf Mt 5:21—48) is included—the recommendations of the fifth and sixth antitheses of Mt; but this is sufficient to prove that Lk had known the series of antitheses and had deliberately omitted all the rest. He has combined two sayings by introducing into the middle of the positive part of the sixth antithesis the corresponding part of the fifth:

$$\text{Mt } 5:43\text{—}48 = \text{Lk } 6:27f \quad + \quad \text{Lk } 6:32\text{—}36$$
$$\text{Mt } 5:39\text{—}42 = \qquad\qquad\quad \text{Lk } 6:29f$$

Lk 6:27—36 then becomes an instruction on the love of enemies. The whole section, beginning with the commandment, 'Love your enemies' (27a)—repeated in the conclusion (35a)—is a unit that is rounded off by 36.

Lk 6:37—42 also forms a unit. The warning not to pass judgement on others, the parable of the mote and the beam, and the other elements are all linked together. Here it is no longer a question of love of enemies (as in the previous passage) but of love of the brethren. The last part of the discourse (6:43—49) regards the necessity of proving good dispositions in action and the necessity of putting into effect the teaching one has received. As a result of these changes the plan of the discourse in Lk takes on the following form (Dupont, 189—203): Introduction: Beatitudes and Woes (20b—26); Part I: Love of Enemies (27—36); Part II: Fraternal Charity (37—42); Conclusion: Necessity of Good Works (43—49).

20—26 The Beatitudes and Woes (Mt 5.1—12)— Mt **776a** has nine beatitudes while Lk has four only, paralleled by four 'woes'. The beatitudes of Lk correspond to four Mt's, yet with notable differences. Mt's beatitudes—except for the ninth (5:11)—are in the third person; those of Lk are in the second person. A study of *macarisms* ('beatitudes') in the OT and in Jewish literature shows that the third person is normal, while a study of Lk's style shows his preference for the second person plural—direct style (cf Mk 2:16; Lk 5:30; Mk 2:19; Lk 9:15, etc). The 'poor'—without the qualification of 'in spirit' (Mt)—are the really poor in the literal sense. But they are not worthy of the kingdom of God by this fact alone; we must keep the context in sight. Lk (20a) is careful to point out that the poor in question are disciples; and close behind *ptōchoi* stands *'anāwîm*, the 'poor of Yahweh', with all the religious association of the term (cf Zeph 2:3; 3:11f; Ps 130). Jesus assures the poor who have become his disciples that their hope will not be groundless; it is already realized, for the kingdom of God is theirs. The reign of God has already begun and they participate in it—with the hope of entering into the Kingdom.

21a. (Mt 5:6). The textual differences here are **b** notable. Mt speaks metaphorically of hunger and thirst; Lk speaks of real hunger and omits reference to thirst— since it is implicitly contained in hunger, and also in view of the corresponding woe. The poor who hunger in this life will be satisfied in the next: it is the thought of Ps 107 (106):9. **21b** (Mt 5:4). The beatitude of Mt is addressed to 'mourners', that of Lk to 'weepers'; according to Mt the mourners will be 'comforted' and according to Lk the

776b weepers will 'laugh'. The terms of Lk are more realistic, more universally human; those of Mt are more traditional and biblical. Weeping is the lot of the servants of God here below because evil is so much more in evidence than good. But they will be consoled—this promise lights up their sorrow with a ray of happiness. The promise extends to all who suffer, on condition that they are disciples of Jesus. **22f.** (Mt 5:11f). The degrees of maltreatment are better ordered in Lk: first hatred, then exclusion, next outrages and defamation; in Mt this order is not evident. In both, the beatitude is addressed directly to the disciples. *Aphorizō* 'exclude' is a technical term = excommunicate (cf Is 56:3; Jn 16:2; 1 QS II, 16; V, 18; VI, 25 etc). 'Cast out your name as evil' means to defame, to speak falsely against (cf Dt 22:13f, 19)—it is a juridical term. 'On account of the Son of Man' (Mt 'on my account')—the presumption is that 'Son of Man' is original (cf Lk 12:8; Mt 10:32; Mk 8:31; Lk 9:22; Mt
c 16:21). In 23 *skirtaō* 'leap for joy' is typical of Lk (1:41, 44). This fourth beatitude is more particularly addressed to the disciples: they will not have to wait long to experience persecution and the supernatural joy which follows it (Ac 5:41). 'On account of the Son of man' is the characteristic note of the beatitude: it is because they preach the doctrine of Christ that the disciples will be maltreated. They must rejoice not in spite of persecution but because of it; not, of course, because of persecution as such but in so far as it is a guarantee of recompense. Jesus introduces the notion of merit, but the Kingdom of God is not the reward of service rendered to God, it is gained by the practice of the humble virtues taught in the beatitudes.
d **24—26 The Woes**—The four *vae* are attached to the beatitudes by the conjunction *plēn* ('however', 'but') characteristic of Lk. After the *vae* the transitional phrase, 'But I say to you that hear' (27) brings the discourse back to the disciples; this phrase scarcely smoothes the brusque change from invective aimed at the rich to the recommendation of love of enemies (27—31). The difficulty seems to be caused by the addition of the woes. Lagrange (192) remarks that 'v 27 would follow better on v 23. After saying that the disciples will be hated, Jesus teaches them to love their enemies: the context is excellent.' It seems impossible that Lk could have substituted the Woes for the Beatitudes of Mt which he himself does not have. He may, possibly, have found them in his source, but the simplest solution is that he has inserted them here. **24.** The *vae* is addressed to rich who enjoy their riches and aspire after nothing else. Absorbed in the pleasures which this wealth procures they have no desire for the kingdom of God. **25.** Is the antithesis of 21, with the same contrast between the present age and the time when each will be treated according to his deserts. **26.** While shorter than the corresponding beatitude (22f) it is still parallel to it. The end of the v is the exact counterpart of 23, except for the qualification of 'false' prophets. It forms an *inclusio* which rounds off, and relates the series of beatitudes and woes.
e **27—36 Love of Enemies** (Mt 5:38—48)—Of the six antitheses of Mt 5:21—48 Lk has preserved only the two last (in part). He has built a new unit by combining two sayings and in doing so he has even reproduced the difference in person of these sayings: Lk 6:27f, 32—36 = Mt 5:43—48 (2 p.pl); Lk 6:29f = Mt 5:39—42 (2 p.s.). The inspiration behind Lk 6:27—36 is clear; it is an instruction on the love of enemies. **29.** The parallel (Mt 5:39—41) is more developed and more biblical (cf Ex 22:25f; Dt 24:13); besides, Mt refers to judicial action and Lk to aggression. **32—34.** In place of the 'tax col-

lectors' and 'Gentiles' of Mt 5:46f Lk has 'sinners'; 34 **776e** is a third example added to Lk. **35.** S W sy. sin read *mēdena apelpizontes*, 'despairing of no man', but the MS evidence is overwhelmingly in favour of *mēden*, 'expecting nothing in return'. **36.** In Mt 5:48 the perfection of the heavenly Father is somewhat intimidating; characteristically Lk stresses the mercy of 'your Father'.
37—42 Fraternal Charity (Mt 7:1—5; cf Mt 10:24f; **f** 15:14)—The warning not to pass judgement on others (37), the parable of the mote and the beam (41f) and the other elements are artificially linked. It is no longer a question of love of enemies but of love of the brethren. **38a.** Peculiar to Lk. It is clear that 6:38b follows logically after v 37 (cf Mt 7:1—2); 38a, an independent logion, has been added by means of the catchword 'measure'—it is manifestly secondary. *Kolpos* (RSV 'lap') is the fold formed by a loose garment overhanging a cincture; this was often used as a pocket (cf Ru 3:15). **39ff.** In Mt the warning not to judge others (7:1f) is followed, logically, by the parable of the mote and the beam (3—5); Lk, however, inserts two sayings between them and, consequently, these (Lk 6:39f) are not really at home in their present context. Mt 15:14 gives the true context of 39; it has been added in Lk because of a certain vague association of ideas: blind—mote or beam in the eye. In Mt the saying refers to the Pharisees, here it is applied to the disciples. The saying of 40 has two parts, clearly distinguished in Mt 10:24—25a. It is inserted in Lk because of the vague link with 39: a teacher is one who leads the blind (cf Mt 15:14; 23:16 24).
43—49 Necessity of Good Works (Mt 7:15—27; cf 12— **g** 23—35)—The saying about the two trees (43f) instead of illustrating a warning against false prophets (Mt 7:15) has become a recommendation addressed to the disciples. **45.** We have here two sayings which are found, in inverse order but in a similar context, in Mt 12:34f. In Lk's context they are secondary because the fruits of 43f are 'good works' and those of 45 are 'words'; the addition was made on the ground of the recurrence of 'good' and 'evil'. **47—49.** The opening phrase of 47 is reminiscent of Jn (cf Jn 5:40; 6:35; 37, 44f, 65; 7:37). Lk has modified the Palestinian colouring of the concluding parable (cf Mt 7:24—27). In Mt the contrast is between the house built on rock and one built on sand; the causes of destruction are heavy rain which brings torrents of water beating on the house, and a violent wind. These conditions are typically Palestinian. Lk has changed the details so that the parable might be more readily intelligible to his non-Palestinian readers. His concern is not the situation of the house but whether or not it was given a sound foundation, and the flooding is caused not by torrential rains but by an overflowing river. The wise man and the foolish man are alike disciples, both of them have heard the words of Jesus, but only one of them acts accordingly. At the last judgement (and in times of trial) the doers of the word, and they alone, will stand firm.
7:1—10 Cure of a Centurion's Servant (Mt 8:5— **777a** 13)—It is sufficiently clear that Lk and Mt have not followed an identical source but have found different versions of the incident. **3—5.** The centurion sent 'elders', distinguished members of the Jewish community of Capernaum, to Jesus (cf Mt 8:5f). He is, obviously, like Cornelius, a *phoboumenos ton theon* a 'God-fearer' (Ac 10:1f), one of the numerous class of Gentiles attracted to Judaism, but distinct from the proselytes who took on full Jewish observance. The saying of Mt 8:11f is given by Lk in another context (13:28f).
11—17 Raising of the Widow's Son—Peculiar to Lk **b** who has inserted the miracle here as a preparation for

77b the reply to the Baptist ('the dead are raised up', 22). **11.** Nain lies about 8 m. SE of Nazareth, on the slope of the Little Hermon. **12f.** The added poignancy of the death of a widow's only son moves Jesus to compassion. *Ho kyrios* henceforth appears regularly as a title of Jesus: 7:19; 10:1, 39, 41; 11:39; 12:42; 13:15; 16:18; 17:5f; 18:6; 19:8; 22:61; 24:34 (but once only in a parallel passage of Mk and Mt: Mk 11:3; Mt 21:3). It is a Christian title (cf Rm 10:9; Phl 2:11), implying divinity, and Jesus was not addressed as 'Lord', in this full sense, during his lifetime. **14f.** The body lay on a stretcher, without a coffin; life was restored by the mere word of Jesus. **16.** 'Fear' is the normal reaction to a manifestation of divine power (cf 1:12, 65; 2:9; 5:26; 8:25, 37), quickly followed by praise of God (cf 2:20; 5:25f; 9:43; 12:13; etc). The people see in Jesus a great prophet (cf 24:19) like Elijah and Elisha who also raised people from the dead (1 Kg 17:17—24; 2 Kg 4:18—37); his deed is a merciful intervention of God in favour of his people (cf 1:68, 78). **17.** 'Judea' is used in its wide sense of the land of the Jews—Palestine (cf 4:44).

c 18—23 The Baptist's Question (Mt 11:2—6).—**18—20.** John's question was prompted by the fact that he shared the ideas of his time about the nature of the coming Messiah—an apocalyptic figure (cf 3:9, 16f); Jesus' approach was so different. **21.** Proper to Lk—superfluous after 18a. **22.** These are the works of the messianic age (cf Is 26:191; 35:5f; 61:1)—John can draw his own conclusions.
24—30 Panegyric of John (Mt 11:7—15)—**24—28.** Almost identical with Mt 11:7—11. **29f.** Lk has omitted Mt 11:12f (he has the sayings in another context—16:16) and Mt 11:14 (he has already dealt with the return of Elijah—1:17). Instead, he has inserted 29f—found in another context in Mt 21:32—which prepare the way for 35.

d 31—35 Judgement of Jesus on his Generation (Mt 11:16—19)—The parable of the Capricious Children is set squarely in its context by Lk (29f)—the attitude of the scribes and Pharisees is criticized. The point is the frivolous captiousness of these children—the conduct of the scribes and Pharisees is no better. At the moment of crisis, when the last messengers of God had appeared, they criticized and sulked: they hearkened neither to the preaching of repentance nor to the preaching of the Good News. **35.** Lk's 'by all her children' (and not Mt's 'by her deeds'—11:19b) would seem to be the original text. The 'children of wisdom', the wise ones, are the people and the tax collectors (29f) who have recognized and accepted the works of God; they have heard both John and Jesus and have heeded them.

e 36—50 The Pardoned Sinner—Proper to Lk. Nowhere more clearly than in this passage, the story of the 'woman of the city who was a sinner' do we see Jesus as Lk saw him. The context, too, is admirable: here indeed is the 'friend of sinners' (34). **37f.** Though 'sinner' is of wider connotation, the impression is that this was a woman of loose morals and was well-known as such. Lk has courteously refrained from naming her, and she must remain anonymous; there are no grounds for identifying her with Mary Magdalene (8:2), or with Mary the sister of Martha (10:38—42). Her action was an extraordinary display of gratitude for the mercy she had already received (47) and her tears, too, were tears of thanksgiving. **41—43.** The moneylender (*daneistēs*) of the parable is hardly typical of his calling. It is manifest that close behind him stands a God who is ready to forgive any debt. In the parable, and throughout the narrative, 'love' means 'thankful love', 'gratitude'; so the question of Jesus would

run: 'Which of them would be the more grateful?' **44—47.** **777e** Simon is told: This woman, despite her sinful past, is nearer to God than you, for she has, what you lack, gratitude. **47.** While 47a, by itself, could mean that her sins were forgiven as a result of her love, the context (the parable and v 47b) excludes this sense. It must be taken the other way about: her loving gratitude is a consequence of forgiveness—'*her great love proves that her many sins have been forgiven*' (NEB). **48f.** These vv do not quite fit the context, since only now does Jesus declare the woman free from sin. They form a literary doublet (cf 5:20f) and have been added here by association of ideas—forgiveness of sins. **50** too, really in place in 8:48, is loosely attached here; hence the sudden switch to 'faith' from the 'love' theme of the whole passage is no longer a problem, (Schmid, 149f).

8:1—3 Women Disciples of Jesus—Peculiar to Lk. **778a** **1.** Jesus is fulfilling the declaration of 4:43. **2f.** It is typical of Lk that he took care to introduce these women disciples of Jesus. Faithful to the end, they are present at the foot of the Cross (23:49) and at the burial (23:55f) and become witnesses of the Resurrection (24:1—11). Their role is restricted to ministering to the needs of Jesus and the disciples, but even in this he had broken with Jewish tradition. Mary Magdalen (from Magdala) on the W shore of the lake of Gennesareth) had been possessed by many ('seven') demons; this has to be understood in the same way as other cases of possession related to the gospels. It does not mean that Mary had lived an immoral life—a conclusion reached only by means of a mistaken identification with the anonymous woman of 7:36—50.

4—8 Parable of The Sower (Mk 4:1—9; Mt 13:1— **b** 9)—At this point Lk takes up again the thread of Mk. **4.** A vague description replaces the picturesque setting of Mk 4:1. **5—8.** In 5 Lk has added 'his seed' and the fact that the seed 'was trodden upon'. This last factor and his 'rock' for Mk's 'rocky ground' abstract from Palestinian conditions: he depicts the seed as falling on a roadway or on rocks bordering a field—not on a casual path and on stony ground. He underlines the astonishing abundance of the harvest, omitting the thirtyfold and sixtyfold of Mk. In spite of everything, the Kingdom of God will grow and develop.

9—15 Explanation of The Sower (Mk 4:10—20; Mt 13:10—23)—**9f.** In Mk 4:10 Jesus is asked, privately, why he speaks in parables; here he is asked openly for the meaning of 'this parable'. Lk has somewhat softened the impact by cutting short the text of Is 6:9 (cf Mk 4:12). The saying of 10 originally referred not to the parables but to the Lord's teaching in general. It concerned the 'secrets (Mk "secret") of the kingdom' which is revealed to the disciples and not to all; i.e. that the kingdom is already present in Jesus and in his works. **11—15.** It is obvious that the application of the parable is somewhat forced: the point of interest is no longer the abundant harvest but the word and the hearers' reception of the word, and the parable has become an exhortation to converts to examine themselves and test the sincerity of their conversion. In order to do this the parable has been allegorized. It is sufficiently clear that the interpretation—at least in the form in which it has been transmitted—is the work of the primitive Church; the linguistic argument is compelling (Jeremias, 65—67). However, the fact that all three synoptists have attributed it to Jesus is surely significant. We may conclude that the explanation now found in our gospels goes back to an interpretation of our Lord, but one that has been considerably adapted to meet a new situation. **11.** By

778b 'word of God' Lk understands the preaching of Jesus—the seed is the gospel preaching. **12.** In the parable the seed (i.e. the Kingdom) held the centre of interest throughout; in the application the seed has become the word and the influence is on the reaction of men to the gospel preaching. Consequently, the seed has to represent both the word *and* the hearers. *Ho logos* used absolutely is a technical term for the gospel widely used in the primitive Church (cf Ac 4:4; 6:4; 8:4; 10:36, 44 etc); it is significant that 'the word' is found in the mouth of Jesus *only* in the interpretation of The Sower (8 times in Mk, 5 times in Mt and 3 times in Lk)—and, apart from Mk 2:2, the designation occurs nowhere else in the Syn. **13f.** The seed represents the hearers of the word or, perhaps, more accurately, the failure of those who hear it; the parable envisages the kingdom triumphing over all difficulties. **15.** These hearers, at last, hold the word fast. **16–18 The Lamp** (Mk 4:21–25; cf Mt 13:12)—**16.** Repeated in 11:33 (cf Mt 5:15). **17.** Repeated in 12:2 (cf Mt 10:26). Lk omits Mk 4:23, 24*b*. **18.** By writing 'what he thinks that he has' instead of 'what he has' (Mk 4:25) Lk has softened the paradox.

c **19–21 True Kindred of Jesus** (Mk 3:31–35; Mt 12:46–50)—Lk has judged that this passage will form an excellent conclusion to his short treatment of the parabolic teaching of Jesus and so he has changed it from its Marcan context.
22–25 The Stilling of a Storm (Mk 4:35–41; Mt 8:18, 23–27)—In Mk the incident occurred on the evening of the day of parable teaching; Lk has simply 'one day'. Throughout he has improved the style, but he has sacrificed the picturesque touches of Mk.
26–39 The Gerasene Demoniac (Mk 5:1–20; Mt 8:28–34)—Lk has stylistically improved, and shortened, Mk's version. In 26 and 37 'Gerasenes' (B D lat sa) is to be preferred; variants are 'Gadarenes' and 'Gergesenes'. On this occasion only, in Lk, does Jesus go beyond Jewish territory and the lake.
40–56 The Daughter of Jairus and the Woman with the Flow of Blood (Mk 5:21–43; Mt 9:18–26)—Lk improves the style of Mk, but notably abbreviates his version. **42.** Lk adds that this was an only daughter and mentions her age at the beginning of the story; Mk has it almost as an afterthought (5:42). **43.** The majority of MSS add: 'and had spent all her money upon physicians'—better omitted with B D sy. sin sa arm as due to harmonization with Mk 5:26. **45.** Peter is the spokesman; cf Mk 5:31—'his disciples'. **54.** Lk omits the Aram. phrase of Mk 5:41; cf Ac 9:40f.

d **9:1–6 The Mission of the Twelve** (Mk 6:7–13; Mt 10:5, 8, 9–14)—Lk leaves aside the passage Mk 6:1–6 (Jesus in Nazareth) because he has already (4:16–30) dealt with the reception of Jesus there. Otherwise he follows Mk closely. **3.** Agreement with Mt 10:10 on the prohibition of a staff, against Mk 6:8. **6.** 'Preaching the gospel' for Mk's (6:12) 'preached that men should repent'.
7–9 Herod and Jesus (Mk 6:14–16; Mt 14–1–2)—An excellent example of Lk's editorial liberty. Herod (Antipas) the tetrarch (Mk: 'king') is sceptical on the subject of prophets coming back from the dead: 'John I beheaded' i.e. that accounts for him! (cf 'John, whom I beheaded, has been raised' Mk 6:16). His express wish to see Jesus (9) prepares the way for the meeting of 23:8. Lk omits the account of John's execution—it would interrupt the flow of events.
10–17 Return of the Twelve; the Multiplication of Loaves (Mk 6:30–44; Mt 14:13–21; Jn 6:1–13)—**10f.** In Mk (6:31) Jesus took the returned Apostles to a 'lonely place' and only after the multiplication of loaves **778c** did they cross to Bethsaida (6:45) on the NE of the lake. Lk has taken the place-name from the Marcan incident of the walking on the waters (6:45—52) which he has omitted. **12–17.** Lk follows, and re-writes to a certain extent, Mk 6:35–44.
After 17 Lk omits Mk 6:45–8–26—the so-called 'great omission'. He may have done so in order to keep his work within definite limits. It is noteworthy that the first and last episodes of the Marcan section are set at Bethsaida (6:45—52; 8:22—26); we might say that Lk has omitted a journey of Jesus which began and ended at Bethsaida.
18–21 Peter's Profession of Faith (Mk 8:27–30; Mt **e** 16:13–20)—Lk gives no indication of the setting of this incident. Typically, he refers to the prayer of Jesus (cf 3:21; 5:16; 6:12). In 20 the 'Christ of God' (in place of Mk's 'the Christ') is an OT expression (cf 2:25; 1 Sm 24:7, 11; 26:9)—the one whom God has anointed. **21.** The 'messianic secret' is not something peculiar to Mk.
22. First Prediction of the Passion (Mk 8:31–33; **f** Mt 16:21–23)—With Mt (16:21) Lk changes Mk's 'after three days' to 'on the third day'. Lk has omitted the intervention of Peter and the rebuke of Jesus.
23–27 The Following of Jesus (Mk 8:34–9:1; Mt 16:24–28)—As in Mk the invitation is addressed not only to the Apostles but to all disciples. **23.** The 'daily' taking up of the cross indicates a spiritual interpretation (by the early Christians) of a saying of Jesus which originally pointed to martyrdom (cf Mk 8:34). **26f.** These vv represent distinct sayings linked by a vague association of ideas. The first refers to the final coming of the Son of Man; the other concerns the establishment of the kingdom of God on earth, marked unmistakably by the destruction of Jerusalem in A.D. 70—an event which underlined the passing of the old dispensation.
28–36 The Transfiguration (Mk 9:2–8; Mt 17:1– **g** 8)—The Transfiguration has greater significance for Lk than for Mk, and he departs rather freely from the latter. It is a typical mountain-scene, where Jesus is separated from the people (28, 37) and involving a special manifestation; the geographical situation (Tabor or Hermon) has no relevance for Lk. The purpose of the heavenly revelation is to show that the Passion is something decreed by God. It also serves to corroborate Peter's profession of faith and is a means of strengthening the disciples for the road that lies ahead (Conzelmann, 57–59). **28.** 'Almost eight days' in place of Mk's (and Mt's) 'after six days'. Jesus prays as on other major occasions (3:21; 6:12; 9:18; 22:41). **30f.** Moses and Elijah represent the Law and the Prophets. Lk gives the theme of the conversation: the 'departure' (*exodos*—2 Pt 1:15; Wis 3:2; 7:6 = 'death') of Jesus at Jerusalem. **32f.** Peter's offer of three booths is meant to prolong the moment ('as they were parting from him'). **34f.** Lk specifies that they 'entered into the cloud'; their fear is due to their recognition of the OT value of the 'cloud'—the accompaniment of a theophany. *Ho eklelegmenos*, 'My Chosen'—P⁴⁵ B S L it sy. sin bo sa arm (cf 23:35; Is 42:11). The majority reading *ho agapētos*, 'My Beloved', is manifestly due to harmonization with Mt and Mk. **36.** The 'messianic secret' is implied.
37–43a Cure of an Epileptic (Mk 9:14–29; Mt 17:14–21)—Lk drastically shortens Mk; he has altogether omitted: Mk 9:14*b*–16, 20*b*–24, 25*b*–26, 28f. On the other hand he adds that the child was an only son (38) and describes the impression on the crowd (43).
43b–45 Second Prediction of the Passion (Mk 9: **h**

78h 30—32; Mt 17:22f)—Lk departs from Mk in many respects. He says nothing of a rather furtive journey through Galilee but, instead, emphasizes the wonder of the people at the deeds of Jesus. The difference of approach is explained by the place the passage occupies in each gospel. For Lk Jesus is still at the height of his success; but in Mk the Galilean ministry is over and Jesus, accompanied only by his disciples, is journeying to his death. **44.** The disciples are warned that they must not be led astray by the momentary enthusiasm of the crowds. **45.** Their total failure to understand is emphatically stated. They will not be able to understand until after his resurrection (24:25—27, 44—46).

46—50 Dispute about Precedence: the Strange Exorcist (Mk 9:33—50; Mt 18:1—5)—The passage is all that Lk has preserved of the original ecclesiastical discourse underlying Mk and Mt (18:1—35) (Vaganay, 361—404). Lk has omitted any indication of place; also the question of Jesus (Mk 9:34). The disciple who acts as the least by becoming the servant of a child (a type of the humble) in the name of Jesus is, in fact, the greatest; and, in acting so, he serves Christ himself. **49f.** Lk abbreviates Mk, omitting Mk 9:39b, 41. Here ends the Galilean ministry of Lk.

779a **9:51—19:27 THE JOURNEY TO JERUSALEM**
The long section (9:51—18:14) has been inserted by Lk into the plan of Mk. The sayings and narratives of this section are grouped together and the whole is fitted into the framework of a journey to Jerusalem, a journey which ends at 19:27 (or 19:46). On examination it can be seen that the arrangement is artificial. It is a striking fact, for instance, that though the chh are supposed to describe a journey from Galilee, **all topographical reference to any place other than Jerusalem is suppressed.** The journey is explicitly indicated in 9:51: 'When the days drew near for him to be received up, he set his face to go to Jerusalem'. The Samaritans would not receive him 'because his face was set towards Jerusalem' (9:53), and so he went on to 'another village' (56). In 10:1 there is reference to 'every town and place' where he was to go and, in 10:38, while on his way he entered 'a village'. In 11:1 he prayed 'in a certain place'. In short, we may say with Lagrange (xxxviii): 'In vain do we try to discover where he is; we know only that he is still in the land of Israel because there is no indication that he has left it. Apart from references to Jerusalem there is no indication of place; the scene is always just "somewhere".'

A reference in 17:11 removes any doubt that the framework is artificial. Though he had begun his journey from Galilee in 9:51, and had been on his way ever since, we are now told: 'On the way to Jerusalem he was passing along between Samaria and Galilee'—he is still at the starting-place. In 18:31—33 he tells his Apostles plainly that the journey to Jerusalem is a journey to his death, and from now on the tempo speeds up remarkably and other place-names appear to mark the final stages of the journey.

The intention of the evangelist is manifest: **to present dramatically the last journey of our Lord to Jerusalem.** The over-all effect is striking, especially the mounting tension of the final chh. But he has obviously used this same journey to frame, and give a certain unity, to, an important collection of sayings and parables; and the framework does set these sayings of Jesus in relief and gives them an added solemnity. The plan of this long section is only one expression among many of a constant preoccupation of the evangelist—to centre his whole gospel around Jerusalem (cf § 766g).

51—56 Unfriendly Samaritans—51. This v is the **779b** title of the journey section. The *analēmpsis* ('taking up') of Jesus comprises his death and resurrection as one event in the same way as the Johannine terms 'glorification' (Jn 7:39; 12:16; 13:31f) and 'elevation' (3:14; 8:28; 12:32, 34). **54.** James and John, living up to their reputation as 'sons of thunder' (Mk 3:17) expect Jesus to act like Elijah (2 Kg 1:10—12). **55.** Jesus rebukes them: his way is one of mercy not destruction. **56.** Most likely another Samaritan village.

57—62 The Demands of Discipleship (Mt 8:19— **c** 22)—The first two sayings are common to Mt and Lk, the third is proper to Lk. **57f.** According to Mt the man is a scribe. The disciple of Jesus must be, like him, a homeless wanderer. **59f.** In Mt the second questioner is a disciple. Others who are 'dead', insensible to the call of Jesus, will take care of the man's obligation to his father (cf 14:26). Lk adds the commission to proclaim the kingdom of God, (cf 4:43; 8:1; 9:2; 16:16)—discipleship implies missionary activity. **61f.** Like Elisha (1 Kgs 19:19—21) this man wants to return to take leave of his people; Jesus is more demanding than Elijah. The sayings teach, in forthright language, that sacrifice and total self-committment are demanded of a disciple of Jesus.

10:1—16 Mission of the Seventy-Two—A discourse **d** parallel to that of 9:1—6. Mt has (9:35—10:16) combined elements of both discourses—though he does not mention the 72. It seems best to regard 9:1—6 and 10:1—16 as *one* sending: Jesus addressed not only the Twelve but a wider circle of disciples. It is understandable that the emphasis should have been brought to bear on the mission of the Twelve; cf Mt (Schmid, 183f). **1.** 'Seventy-*two*' (B D M R a c e lat sy. sin sy. cur arm) is preferable to 'seventy' (the majority) a change to a round number. **2f.** Cf Mt 9:37f; 10:16—obviously distinct sayings; taken together they reflect the experience of the first missioners: their own zeal and the opposition they encounter. **4.** Cf 9:3 — Mk 6:8f; Mt 10:9f. The warning not to waste time on civilities (cf 2 Kgs 4:29) underlines the urgency of the mission. **5f.** Cf Mt 10:12f. Lk gives the Jewish greeting: 'Peace'; Mt has 'salute it'. 'Son of peace' is a hebraism = one worthy of peace. Clearly, the greeting is meaningful, a blessing. **7.** Cf 9:4; Mk 6:10; Mt 10:11. Food and shelter are not alms but wages, cf 1 Cor 9:14; 1 Tm 5:18. **8f.** Cf Mt 10:7. The mission is not private but is a public proclamation of the Kingdom. **10f.** Cf 9:5; Mk 6:11; Mt 10:14. **12.** Cf Mt 10:15. The unreceptive town will not go unpunished; 'on that day'—on the day of judgement (cf Mk 13:32). **13—15.** Cf Mt 11:21—24. In Mt the saying refers to the rejection of the preaching of Jesus; here it is added because of the similar theme of 12. **16.** Cf Mt 10:40, Lk 9:48; Mk 9:37; Jn 13:20.

17—20 Return of the Seventy-two—Proper to Lk. **e** **17.** The ability to cast out demons had, understandably, made a deep impression on the disciples. The power has come to them from Jesus (v 19; cf 9:1) and it is by their faith in him that they have succeeded. **18.** The real cause for rejoicing is that the Kingdom has come (cf 11:20; Mt 12:28); for Satan it is the beginning of the end—his fall will be lightning fast. **19.** The disciples have received power over the enemy of mankind in all fields; serpents and scorpions (though these may have a spiritual sense, cf Ps 91 (90):13) exemplify evils in nature, the works of Satan. (Cf Ac 28:3—6). **20.** The assurance of being numbered among the elect is the ultimate reason for rejoicing.

21—24 The Thanksgiving of Jesus (Mt 11:25—27)—

779e **21f.** 'In that same hour'—Lk, unlike Mt, gives an excellent psychological explanation of the joy of Jesus: he had just witnessed the power of God at work through his disciples. 'Rejoicing in the Holy Spirit' is characteristic of Lk (cf 4:1, 14, 18). For the rest the saying, so reminiscent of Jn, and so clearly expressing the unique relationship of Father and Son, is the same as Mt. **23f.** Cf Mt 13:16f.

f **25–37 The Principal Commandment; The Good Samaritan—25–29** (cf Mk 12:28–31; Mt 22:34–40). In Mk the scribe is sincere and is praised by Jesus and his question is about the principal commandment; in Lk he seeks to trap Jesus and asks about eternal life. It is reasonable to suppose that in the passage 10:25–37 Lk follows a distinct source. The original question was meant to embarrass Jesus but he, adroitly, puts the onus on his questioner. The lawyer tries again and asks for a definition of 'neighbour'. This was a much-discussed problem. **30.** It is implied that the man who had been waylaid was a Jew. His nationality is not expressly mentioned because the point of the parable is that the lawyer's question is not going to be solved in terms of nationality. **31f.** The priest chanced to be going along the same road and carefully avoided the wounded man. We are to take it that he did not want to get involved; the Levite took the same selfish course. **33–35.** The Samaritan has been designedly chosen (the traditional enmity of Jew and Samaritan) to bring out the essential unselfishness of love. **36.** In 29 the lawyer had asked: 'Who is my neighbour?', while the question that Jesus asks in 36 is rather: 'To whom am I neighbour?' The lawyer was concerned with the object of love and his question implies a limitation; Jesus looked to the subject of love: which of the three has acted as neighbour? The lawyer's question is not answered because it is a mistaken question; the point of the parable is that a man's neighbour is any man who needs his help. **37.** The lawyer had learned his lesson and answered correctly. Significantly, Jesus bids him *act* accordingly.

g **38–42 Martha and Mary**—Proper to Lk. **38f.** From Jn 11:1 we know that the village was Bethany, on the E slope of the Mount of Olives—so much for Lk's 'journey' to Jerusalem! In Jn 11:1–44 the sisters have the same contrasting temperament. **40.** The familiar relationship between Jesus and the family of Bethany, explicitly indicated in Jn 11:5, is here strikingly exemplified. **41f.** There is textual confusion with regard to 42*a*: 'few things are needful, or only one' (B S L some minusc. bo sa); 'one thing is needful' (P[45] C P etc vg). The longer reading, impressively attested, refers to the needless preparations of Martha—'one dish will suffice'. The shorter reading, however, may well be authentic: Martha is told that the one thing necessary is the seeking of the kingdom (cf 12:29–31)—Mary, drinking in the words of Jesus, has chosen the good portion. In support of this interpretation is the fact that 42*b* must be understood in a spiritual sense.

780a **11:1–4 The Lord's Prayer** (Mt 6:9–13)—Lk has undoubtedly given us the circumstances in which the Saviour spoke the prayer. Mt has placed it in the context of the Sermon on the Mount, but this is clearly secondary. On the other hand, Lk has a shorter version and it is generally held that in this respect he is very close to the original. **2.** Nonetheless, there is little doubt that Lk's 'Father' (Mt: 'Our Father who art in heaven') is primitive. The expression 'Father in heaven' is typical of Mt: it occurs 20 times in Mt, once in Mk (11:25), never in Lk. Besides, in the other prayers of Jesus recorded in the gospels, he addresses God simply as 'Father'

(cf Mt 11:25f = Lk 10:21f; Mt 14:36; Lk 23:34; Jn **780** 17:1–26). *Pater* stands for the Aram. *Abba*. The title *Abba* given to God by Jesus (and taken over by the primitive Church—Rm 8:15; Gal 4:6) is intimate, familiar and was never used, with reference to God, by the Jews. The address to the Father is followed by a number of petitions, seven in Mt, five in Lk. 'Hallowed be thy name'—the precise meaning of this petition is disputed; it is not clear whether the one who hallows is God or man. It may mean that God is sanctified, glorified, by the conduct of men; but in the OT it is God who sanctifies himself, who glorifies his name (Ez 36:23), and the notion that the name of God is glorified by men is secondary. It is only when the reign of God is manifest and his power and holiness are finally revealed that the first petition will be fully answered. 'Thy kingdom come': this is the primary and central petition of the prayer. Desire for the prompt coming of the kingdom of God is a leading feature of Jewish piety. Only God knows the day and the hour of this happening (Mt 24:36); yet we can and must pray for the final coming of God's reign for, by so doing, we enter into God's plan and, so to say, make God's business our concern too. **3.** Lk omits the third petition of Mt (6:10*b*). Here he has: 'Give us each day our daily bread' for Mt's: 'Give us today our daily bread'. **4a.** Lk has substituted the more precise *tas hamartias* 'sins' (cf 5:20; 7:47) for the *opheilēmeta* 'debts' of Mt—he has retained *opheilonti* 'debtor' in the second part of his own petition. **4b.** The word 'temptation' has acquired a certain pejorative sense and so we may paraphrase: 'do not allow us to succumb to temptation.' But *peirasmos* signifies no more than 'trial' (cf Jas 1:2); it is a prayer to be preserved from occasions of sin. Lk does not have Mt's last petition (6:13*b*).

5–8 The Friend at Midnight—Peculiar to Lk. In the **b** passage 11:1–13 Lk gives a synthesis of Jesus' teaching on prayer; in this context the parable has to do with persevering prayer—we shall see that originally it did not have precisely this meaning. **5f.** The phrase *tis ex humōn* regularly, in the NT, introduces questions which invite the emphatic answer: 'Impossible!', 'Nobody!' or 'Of course!', 'Everybody!' (cf Mt 6:27; 7:9; 12:11; Lk 11:11; 12:25; 14:5, 28; 15:4; 17:7 etc). The phrase may best be rendered: 'Can you imagine that any of you would . . .?' Here 5–7 should be regarded as one rhetorical question (Jeremias, 138). **7.** The house consisted of a single room and the 'bed' was a mat, laid on the floor, on which the whole family slept—the opening of the door would involve disturbing the children stretched on the floor. **8.** Though the refusal of the request is regarded as unthinkable—a blatant breach of the code of hospitality—yet, for the sake of argument, Jesus supposes that if the man is to be moved neither by friendship nor by the demand of hospitality he will at least grant the request in order to be rid of the other. As he spoke the parable, the centre of interest was not the action of the man who came to ask but the attitude of the other. The lesson is obvious: if this man acts so, how much more will God hearken to those who call upon him. Jesus insists that prayer must be *trustful*—one must have unshaken confidence in the goodness of God—and if Lk finds in the parable a teaching on perseverance in prayer, is not perseverance the consequence of trust?

9–13 The Efficacy of Prayer (Mt 7:7–11)—These **c** sayings of Jesus—placed in the Sermon on the Mount by Mt—were not originally a sequel to the parable; their present position is due to Lk (or to his source). The introduction: 'I tell you' is emphatic—Jesus speaks in his own name and with authority. **9f.** The passive form

780c stands in place of the divine name: 'Ask and *God will give you . . .*' **11f.** Where Mt (7:8f) has 'stone' and 'serpent' Lk has 'serpent' and 'scorpion', showing a development in the direction of the unlikely (cf 5:36)—the scorpion can only be the black Palestinian species which no one could mistake for an egg (Lagrange, 327). **13.** 'Holy Spirit' in place of Mt's 'good gifts': the Holy Spirit is, therefore, the gift *par excellence.*

d 14—26 Jesus and Beelzebul (Mt 12:22—30, 43—45; 9:32—34; Mk 3:22—30)—**14f.** Jesus casts out a dumb demon (cf Mk 9:17); in the parallel passage (Mt 12:22) a blind and dumb demoniac is healed. Lk (Mt also) avoids the suggestion that Jesus himself was possessed (cf Mk 3:22). **16.** Anticipates 29—32 (cf Mt 12:38). **17—20.** Cf Mt 12:25—28; Mk 3:24—26. In 20 we have 'finger of God' in place of Mt's 'Spirit of God'. **21f.** The figure is that of a duel; in Mk 3:27 and Mt 12:29 it is a question of armed robbery. The contest is decisive: Satan has been overcome by a mightier than he. **23.** (cf Mt 12:30). A warning to his adversaries: they cannot remain neutral. The apparently contradictory saying of 9:50 is explained by the different context. **24—26.** (cf 12:43—45)—a passage added here by means of catchwords: 'unclean spirit', 'demon'.

e 27f The True Blessedness—Proper to Lk (but cf Mk 3:31—35). The episode is admirably in place after the malicious charge against Jesus and his defence: *Une femme lui donne raison avec son coeur de mère* (Lagrange, 335). The idea is Jewish: a woman's joy in her son, especially a distinguished son (Gn 30:13; Prov 23:25). For 28 cf 8:21—those who live according to the preaching of Jesus truly belong to the family of God.

f 29—32 Seeking for Signs (Mt 12:38—42; cf Mt 16:1—4; Mk 8:11—13)—already introduced in 11:16 this passage, except for 30, is textually very close to Mt 12:39—42. **30.** In Mt 12:40 the resurrection of Jesus, typified by the miracle of Jonah, will be the only sign he will give, but a decisive one. Lk gives an early Christian adaptation of the same saying, which now refers to the Parousia: Jonah had been a warning of ruin to the Ninevites, Jesus at his coming will be a sign to those who have rejected him, a sign *ad condemnandum* (Schmid, 207f).

33—36 The Light (Mt 5:15; 6:22f; Mk 4:21 = Lk 8:16)—**33** is essentially the same as the parallel texts. In its Lucan context the light is Jesus himself (cf Jn 1:5; 8:12); no further sign is necessary. **34f.** In another context by Mt these sayings are superficially linked to 33. Here they imply that undistorted vision is required to see the light of Jesus. Those who seek signs, or perversely misrepresent his works (15f), are, in fact, blind. **36.** Not in Mt, this saying is related to 34. Its meaning would seem to be: 'When a man, through the *inner* light of sound eyes is full of light and has no trace of darkness (evil), then and only then will the light *from without*, the God-enkindled light of Jesus, enlighten him wholly' (Schmid, 209).

g 37—54 The Pharisees and Lawyers Denounced (Mt 23:1—36)—While Lk places the denunciation as a climax to the discussion on signs, Mt puts it, more suitably, at the close of the Jerusalem ministry. The two versions differ widely; Mt, as might be expected, is longer. **37f.** Jesus did not observe the extreme punctiliousness of the Pharisees in the matter of ritual purification before meals (cf Mk 7:2—4). **39.** (Cf also 23:25f) At first the Pharisees only are addressed. This v does not reply to the unspoken criticism of the Pharisee; Lk, using his setting of a meal, refers to the cleansing of table ware; i.e. the link with 38 is redactional only. **40.** Not in Mt. The sense

of this apparently banal question would seem to be: **780g** Because God is not only the Creator of 'outer' visible things but also of the things within, i.e. the heart of man from which good and bad ('clean' and 'unclean') come (Mk 7:15), it is a grave error to set store by ritual cleanliness to the neglect of moral cleanness (Schmid, 212). **41.** Cf Mt 23:26. The v might be rendered: '*Give alms according to your resources*'; in the light of 40 the sense is that true cleansing is effected by almsgiving. **42—44.** Three 'woes' addressed to the Pharisees—all paralleled in Mt, with some differences. The idea of 43, not in *vae* ('woe') form, is found at the beginning of Mt's discourse (23:6), and, closer to Mt's form, in Lk 20:46. For 44 cf Mt 23:27; both sayings depict the hypocrisy of the Pharisees—the whitewashed tombs (Mt) and the hidden graves (Lk) which can occasion ritual impurity (Nm 19:16). **45—52.** Three 'woes' addressed to **h** the lawyers. In Mt the series of woes is addressed to the 'scribes and Pharisees'; in Lk the doctors of the Law feel themselves particularly affronted by the reproaches against Pharisaism in general (45). V 46 is paralleled by Mt 23:4 (though not in *vae* form). Where Mt 23:29—31 is straightforward, Lk 47f is ironical; by building the tombs of the prophets the lawyers imagine that they can repair the crimes of their ancestors—while all the while they are disposed to kill the prophet *par excellence.* **49.** Cf Mt 23:34—the 'Wisdom of God': perhaps 'God in his Wisdom'; or the plan of God revealed by Jesus. Lk has 'apostles' instead of 'wise men and scribes' (Mt). **50f.** Lk does not state that Zechariah was 'son of Barachiah' (Mt 23:35) and so avoids the difficulty raised by that detail. The warning is addressed not to the lawyers only but to 'this generation'. **52.** Cf Mt 23:13. Where Mt has 'kingdom of heaven' Lk has 'knowledge'. The lawyers will permit none except themselves to explain the Scriptures. Yet they do not possess that true understanding of the Scriptures which would reveal to them the plan of God. Worse still, they, by their authority, prevent others from professing faith in Jesus. **53f.** From now on the opposition against Jesus hardens: 19:47; 20:19f; 22:2. The text of these vv exhibits an unusual number of variations; the RSV rendering is supported by S B C L 33 boh. Vg reflects readings of other Gr. MSS.

12:1—12 Exhortation to Fearless Preaching (Mt **781a** 10:26—33; 12—32; 10:19f)—The passage is composed of various sayings loosely linked; almost all occur in Mt, in a different context. **1.** Though surrounded by a multitude (a Lucan touch, cf 14:25; 18:36; 19:3; 20:45; 21:38) Jesus first addresses his disciples. He bids them avoid the hypocrisy of the Pharisees which is a pervasive evil influence. **2f.** In Mt 10:26f (cf Mk 4:22 = Lk 8:17) the sayings refer to the gospel preaching. But the sense here is that a man's true dispositions cannot remain hidden forever. **4—9.** In 8f 'the angels of God' is a circumlocution = 'before God' (cf Mt 10:32f; Mk 8:38 = Lk 9:26). **10.** Cf Mt 12:32; Mk 3:28f. Linked to the foregoing by the catchword 'Son of man'. Vv 9 and 10 were originally distinct sayings and the apparent discrepancy between 9 and 10*a* is due solely to their artificial juraposition. Where 9 envisages disciples only, 10 contrasts those who do not know Jesus for what he is and may be excused, with disciples who deny Christ and so, sinning against the light, blaspheme the Holy Spirit. **11f.** (Mt 10:17—20; Mk 13:11 = Lk 21:12—15). The saying has been added here by the catchword 'Holy Spirit'.

13—21 The Rich Fool—Proper to Lk. Though the **b** parable begins at 16 the immediate context is necessary for an understanding of it. **13—15.** The Jews were

781b accustomed to submit similar questions to their rabbis for a practical decision. The presentation of the case, and the title *didaskale* 'Teacher', strikingly indicates the standing Jesus had won with the people. He formally declines to arbitrate; he will not seem to condone an attitude of absorption in this world's goods. **16—19.** The rich man is providing for the coming years when his crops may not be so abundant. 'Soul' means the seat of the appetites, the seat of life; and at the moment that his plans are laid God will take away this life from him. **20.** Rightly is the man called 'fool'—in OT usage one who, in practice, denies God (cf Ps 13:1)—for he had not only forgotten that his life was a loan which must be restored, but he had forgotten God, so absorbed had he become in his possessions. **21** has all the appearances of a generalizing conclusion and is, in fact, omitted by D it; it serves to underline the truth that the man is indeed a 'fool' and to emphasize the worthlessness of worldly possessions.

c **22—24 Trust in Providence** (Mt 6:25—33)—**22—31.** This passage is very like Mt 6:25—33, but the context is different: Mt has it in the Sermon; here it is addressed to the disciples as a development of the parable's message. In 24 'ravens' ('unclean' birds, Lv 11:15; Dt 14:14; cf Jb 38:41; Ps 147 (146):9) is more likely to be original than Mt's 'birds of the air'. In 27 *they neither spin nor weave* (D it sy. sin sy. cur) is preferable to 'they neither toil nor spin', a majority reading, but suspect of harmonization with Mt 6:28. **32.** This v has been added by means of the catchword 'kingdom'. A 'little flock' (cf Jn 10:2, 11f, 14, 16; 21:16, 18) in a hostile world. **33f.** (cf Mt 6:20f). In 33 Lk has rewritten a saying that must originally have been close to Mt's version (6:20).

d **35—48 Watchfulness and Faithfulness** (Mt 24:43—51; Mk 13:33—37)—The passage is a compilation of parables and sayings on the common theme of judgement; Mt has much of the same material in his Parousia discourse.

35—38 The Waiting Servants—This is best considered to be another version of Mk 13:33—37 (cf Mt 25:1—13); both evangelists have understood it in terms of the Parousia and allegorical additions in Lk have heightened the application. **35.** Lk's introduction to the series of parables (36—48): an exhortation to constant vigilance. **36—38.** In 37*b* Lk has an addition which points to the identity of the Master: unlike any earthly master (cf 17:7f) he himself will serve the faithful servants (cf 22:27; Jn 13:14). The coming of the Son of Man will be unexpected and watchfulness must characterize the attitude of the disciples who wait for his return.

39f The Thief at Night (Mt 24:43f)—This little parable points to the uncertainty of the hour at which the Lord will return—he will come 'like a thief in the night' (1 Thes 5:2; Lk 17:24; 21:34f). Therefore, the moral, expressed in 40, is not so much vigilance as before, but preparedness: The Son of Man will appear as Judge at an unexpected moment.

e **41—48 The Servant: Faithful or Unfaithful** (Mt 24:45—51)—**41.** The question is absent from Mt and its style betrays the hand of Lk; it refers to the preceding parable of The Waiting Servants (36—38). **42—46.** The steward faithful or unfaithful in his Lord's absence. At 46*b* the parable has been allegorized: it is no longer an earthly master who stands there but the Son of Man who has come as Judge. Moreover, the parable has been re-applied. As Jesus spoke it, the servant set in authority represented Israel's leaders (cf Mt 23:2; Lk 11:46—52). The early Christians interpreted it as a warning to the Church's leaders—a perfectly natural extension of its meaning. The

new interpretation is neatly brought out by Peter's question. **781** **47f.** These vv (not in Mt) have no more than a loose link with the parable; they introduce the fresh idea that the punishment of disobedience will be in proportion to knowledge of the master's will. Though now referred to the disciples the saying would originally have contrasted the scribes' culpable rejection of Christ with the far less culpable rejection by the ordinary people 'ignorant of the Law' (Jn 7:49). V 48*b* stands on its own; though perhaps originally addressed to the religious leaders of Israel it can easily be applied to the leaders of the new Israel.

49—53 The Moment of Truth (Mt 10:34—36)—The f coming of Jesus marks a time of decision, a crisis in which none can be neutral. **49f**—these may be considered independently of their context. The fire which Jesus so wishes to see kindled is that which purifies souls, a fire lighted on the Cross (cf Jn 12:32). The 'baptism' is the Passion which will 'plunge' Jesus into a sea of suffering. He looks with desire (22:15) to that event which will inaugurate the new age (Osty, 106). **51—53.** (Mt 10:34—36). Jesus is 'set for the fall and rising of many in Israel' (2:34): men will be for or against him. The description of family dissension (an emphatic presentation of the division he brings) is based on Mi 7:6.

54—59 The Signs of the Times (Mt 16:2f; 5:25f)—**54—56.** The images of Mt 16:2f are different but the idea is the same. In Palestine the SW winds bring rain, and the SE wind is the sirocco. **57** is Lk's link between the discernment of signs and the following parable. **58f.** The little parable has been inserted by Mt in the Sermon (5:25f). The Jews are in the position of the plaintiff: they must settle with God, repent, without delay.

13:1—9 The Call to Repentance—The urgent need **782a** for Israel to take immediate action is illustrated by tragic incidents (1—5); a parable further emphasizes the last chance that is being offered. **1.** The episode is otherwise unknown. The Galileans, come to offer sacrifice in the Temple, had caused some disturbance; Pilate was capable of such ruthless methods (Jos. Ant. 18, 3, 2; 4,1). **2f.** The Galileans who suffered thus were not necessarily greater sinners than others; but their fate is a warning to all Jews, a call to repentance. **4f.** 'Tower in Siloam' i.e. a tower built near the Pool of Siloam, S of the Temple area; foundations unearthed in 1914 may be those of the tower in question. The incident is otherwise unknown. The massacres and destruction of A.D. 70 are foreshadowed.

6—9 The Barren Fig Tree—Lk, who has omitted the cursing of the fig tree (Mk 11:12—14; Mt 21:18—22) is alone in giving this parable. The fig tree symbolizes Israel (cf Hos 9:10; Jer 8:13) and, as in Jer, a sterile Israel. If, in the short moment left, Israel does not bring forth the fruits of repentance the time of grace will have run out. Throughout, the urgency of the hour is stressed and the warning is plain.

10—17 Healing of a Woman on the Sabbath— b Proper to Lk. The emphasis is not on the miracle as such but on the ensuing discussion, cf 6:9—11; 14:1—6. There is no real link between the episodes of this ch. **10—13.** The 'spirit of infirmity' does not imply that the woman was possessed but, rather, attributes her disease to Satan who can afflict men (16). Without being asked (cf 6:8; 14:4) Jesus cured her. **15f.** The same legalistic and carping outlook blinds the rulers of Israel to the significance of the works of Jesus.

18—21 The Mustard Seed and The Leaven (Mt 13:31—33; Mk 4:30—32)—**18f.** The phrase 'it is like a grain of mustard seed' represents a rabbinical introduction formula which should really be rendered *It is the case with*

82b it (the Kingdom) *as with a grain of mustard seed*. It follows that it is not the seed itself but what happens to the seed that is significant, and the Kingdom is like the tree that grows out of the seed (Jeremias, 85f). **20f.** Mk does not have 'The Leaven' but in Mt and Lk it is a companion parable to 'The Mustard Seed'. Here again the Kingdom is not being compared to leaven but to what happens when leaven is placed in a mass of dough prepared for baking; ultimately, the kingdom is like the leavened dough (cf Rm 11:16).

c **22—30 The Closed Door** (Mt 7:13f; 25:10f; 7:22f; 8:11f)—In this passage various sayings of Jesus— which may be found isolated in Mt—have been built into a parable. It is unlikely that the fusion is due to Lk; it is much more probable that the evangelist found the passage in his source and that he reproduced it as he had found it. **23f.** The question was a current one and the regular answer was that all Israel would have a place in the future kingdom; even the ordinary people, though 'ignorant of the Law' (Jn 7:49) would not be excluded— only tax-collectors and suchlike, 'sinners', would be debarred. Though the question is concerned solely with the salvation of Israel it is still one that Jesus refused to answer directly. **25—27.** In 25 we are dealing no longer with a narrow door but with a closed door, and the image is now that of the messianic banquet. A comparison with Mt 25:10f indicates that the master here is Jesus himself. The Jews had not accepted him, they had not entered into the Kingdom while they had the chance; now it is too late, the door is firmly closed. **28f.** Their chagrin will be all the greater when they see not only their own great ancestors, but the Gentiles, too, present at the Banquet. **30** is a familiar secondary conclusion (cf Mk 10:31; Mt 19:30; 20:16) added here in view of the contrast between Gentiles and Jews (28f).

d **31—33 Herod**—**31.** Jesus is still in the territory of Herod Antipas (cf 3:1) and, more probably in Galilee than in Perea. The 'warning', significantly brought by the Pharisees, is more probably a ruse of 'that fox' (32) to get Jesus out of his territory—he did not want a disturbance sparked by messianic hopes. **32f.** Jesus will continue to do his great works for a short while yet ('today and tomorrow'); then, in due time ('the third day') he will finish his task (cf Jn 19:30). Nevertheless, Herod need not worry, for Jesus must soon be on his way to Jerusalem—that is the fate of a prophet (cf 2 Chr 24:20—22; Jer 26:20—23; 2 Kgs 21:16). Until then, however, his hour has not come (cf Jn 7:30; 8:30). **34f Lament over Jerusalem** (Mt 23:37—39)—In Mt this apostrophe forms the conclusion of a series of 'woes' against the scribes and Pharisees. Here it has been added because of 'Jerusalem' in 33.

e **14:1—24 A Meal in the House of a Pharisee**—The following four episodes, the first three proper to Lk, are set in the context of a meal to which Jesus had been invited. This setting is editorial and the link vv betray the hand of Lk (Schmid, 242).
1—6 Healing of a Man with Dropsy—**1.** Once again Jesus receives and accepts an invitation from a Pharisee (cf 7:36; 11:37). **2—4.** Following E custom, the man was free to enter. Jesus, knowing the thoughts of those who watched him so jealously (1), anticipated their objection and went on the offensive (cf 6:6—11; 13:13—17). **5f.** Cf Mt 12:11; Lk 13:15. The reading *huios*—'son' (P^{45} A B W sy. p sa) is preferable to *onos*—'ass' (S L K it vg sy. sin bo arm). Cf CD 11, 16f.
7—11 Places at Table—**11** is the key to the passage. This saying also occurs at 18:14—as a generalizing conclusion to The Pharisee and the Publican—here,

however, is its proper place. The scribes and Pharisees **782e** are quietly warned that they may be fortunate to get the lowest place in the kingdom.
12—14 The Choice of Guests—No more than the preceding parable is this passage meant as practical advice. Rather, Jesus teaches that a limited and interested love is worthless in the sight of God (cf 6:32—34). The passage is a commentary on 6:35. **14b.** Those who act from motives of disinterested charity will receive their reward at the resurrection.
15—24 The Great Feast (Mt 22:1—10)—**15.** The **f** exclamation follows the mention of recompense in 14b; the feast is a common Jewish figure for the Kingdom (cf 12:37; Mt 22:1f). **16—24.** This is a straightforward parable and must be very close to the original Aram. form. Mt 22:1—10 represents a later version. **21—23.** The double summoning of the ultimate guests would seem to be an allegorical development. Those within the city (21) are doubtless the publicans and sinners, and so we have the familiar contrast between them and the rejected leaders of the people; the invitation to those outside the city (23) can refer to the Gentiles. **24.** The essential point of the parable is, very clearly, the refusal of the invited guests and their replacement by others. The parable is addressed by Jesus to his critics and opponents.
25—35 The Cost of Discipleship (Mt 10:37f; 5:13; **g** Mk 9:50)—Lk has set the two parables (28—33) in the context of self-renunciation. **25.** This link-verse is a Lucan composition (cf 12:1). **26f.** (Cf 9:23 = Mk 8:34; Mt 10:37f). The exhortation is couched in its strongest terms ('hate' here means detachment). **28—32.** The twin parables drive home the lesson that discipleship does involve commitment; it cannot be undertaken thoughtlessly. **33** was very likely added by Lk, in the light of 26f, and is a practical consequence of the parables rather than their moral. **34f.** In Lk's context the saying warns of the fate of a disciple who has lost the spirit of total commitment to his Master.
15:1—32 The Parables of Mercy—**1—3.** Lk has **783a** explicitly established the original *Sitz im Leben* of the three parables of this ch.
4—7 The Lost Sheep (Mt 18:12—14)—The moral of the story is stated in emphatic terms: God will rejoice ('joy in heaven' is a circumlocution) that, together with the just, he can also welcome home the repentant sinner. That is why Jesus seeks out sinners, while the scribes and Pharisees, by cavilling at his conduct, are criticizing the divine goodness.
8—10 The Lost Coin—Peculiar to Lk. This parable is parallel to the other; it is typical of the evangelist that he has brought a woman into the picture. Ten drachmas ('silver coins') was a modest sum, but the loss of even one coin is of great concern to a woman in humble circumstances. She had to light a lamp because the small windowless house—the only opening being a low door— was in near darkness. The phrase 'before the angels of God' (10) is a doubly periphrastic rendering of the divine name: (1) 'the angels' (those who stand 'in the presence of' God); (2) 'before God' (Jeremias, 118); the meaning is that God rejoices when a sinner repents (cf 7).
11—32 The Prodigal Son—Peculiar to Lk. This, the **b** most widely known and best-loved parable might be better named The Loving Father. **11f.** The parable speaks of two sons, a point sometimes overlooked. **13.** 'Gathered' (*synagagōn*) is better rendered 'realized'—the younger son turned his portion into cash. **20—24.** The return. The son could get through the first part only of his little speech for the father hastened to clothe him in fine garments and had a signet ring (an indication of rank)

783b put on his finger. Similarly, he was given shoes, for he was no barefoot servant but a son of the family. **31f.** The father gently pointed out to his elder son that he remained his heir; he should enter into the spirit of the occasion and rejoice at the return of his brother.

The parable is two-pronged (11—24; 25—32) and the emphasis falls on the second point; both parts conclude with almost identical words (24, 32). The younger son and the father thinly veil the sinner and his God. The sinner goes his unthinking way and is brought up short only when his world breaks in pieces about him; but a loving God is looking for his return. So is God, Jesus says, so incredibly good. In the context, the elder son represents the scribes and Pharisees who cavil at the goodness of God.

c 16:1—31. Parables on the Right Use of Money (with the exception of vv 16—18 which concern the Law and Divorce).

1—8 The Unjust Steward—This parable has always proved difficult to interpret and to link up with its context in the Gospel: Where does the parable end? Who is the *kyrios* of 8*a*? and, Why is seemingly reprehensible conduct held up for approbation? J. D. M. Derrett considers that the answer is to be sought first in treating the parable as an (imaginary) account of 'how people behave' rather than to fit it to a lesson it may be supposed to convey. Further, the story must be seen against its background of contemporary Palestinian law and custom. Like the unjust judge (18:1—5), the steward is called dishonest because of his past conduct; it does not necessarily follow that his action in the parable is dishonest. In Jewish law, the steward or agent fully represented his master, who was obliged to honour his agent's business transactions. If the agent swindled him, dismissal was his only recourse. But before this took effect, the agent had to render an account of the state of the property and until this had been done he remained his master's legal representative. Also of great significance is the law governing usury. This forbade the taking of interest on loans to Jews (Ex 22:25; Lv 25:36; Dt 23:19f) but ways had been found of evading the law. It was argued that it only applied to the destitute and was meant to protect them from exploitation. If one could prove the borrower was not without some of the commodity he wished to borrow and was under no compulsion to acquire it, a loan could be allowed. In this way commercial transactions were concluded, by a legal fiction, without infringing the letter of the law. Wheat and oil were especially liable to this kind of treatment, since most people could be assumed to have at least the minimum of both commodities—to light a lamp or bake a cake. But apart from the fact that oil could be adulterated, the interest on oil was greater than that on wheat, a point reflected in the parable, cf vv 6 and 7. Thus the steward, casting around for some way of earning the good opinion of people outside after his dismissal, realizes that his master has been evading the law and decides to rectify this situation with a view to gaining support for himself. He hands back to the debtors their promissory notes which undertook the payment of principal plus interest and tells them to write new ones specifying repayment of the principal only. His master opportunely decides to take to himself the credit for a just action which he did not initiate. The meaning then is that one who knows his moral duty but who has neglected it for worldly advantage may be forced by circumstances to change his conduct and seek the good opinion of those whom he has hitherto neglected. 'Worldly people know how to utilize worldly goods to do righteous acts and to obtain the reward of righteousness while those who fancy themselves as the " 'Children of

light' " are either narrow mindedly refusing to soil their **783d** hands with tainted earnings or are devising means whereby service to God can be mixed with service to worldly purposes. They are carefully watering down the prescripts of God so as to enable piety and comfort, fear of God and prestige among men to go hand in hand', p. 365 of 'Fresh Light on St Luke', NTS 7 (1961) 198—219, 364—80.

While this explanation does indeed throw light on certain aspects of the story and enables us to give a more rational solution of the link with its setting it seems more probable that Luke did not understand it this way. For him the *kyrios* was Jesus and this is vital to the interpretation. The steward accused of malpractice is about to be dismissed. Rejecting honest procedure, he devises, with total lack of scruple, a way of safeguarding his own future at the expense of his master. The verb *dexontai* (4) is not impersonal ('people') but refers specifically to the debtors of 5 ('that they may receive me'). **5.** 'one by one'. The plan had to be carried out very discreetly to avoid detection. **6.** The *batos* or *bath* (RSV 'measure') was about 5 imperial gallons. **7.** The *koros* or *cor* (RSV 'measure') was about 6 bushels (or 50 gallons), a very much larger quantity than a *bath*, but as the price of oil was higher than that of wheat, the difference in terms of monetary value was not so considerable, cf § 86*e—h.* **8.** Here we come to the crux of the interpretation. The precise meaning of *kyrios*, 'Lord', 'master', determines the limit of the parable proper and affects the interpretation. The more usual practice has been to take *kyrios* in the parable as the steward's master and then the v 8 is part of the parable. In that case 9 brings out the moral. But in Lk *kyrios* almost always means Jesus himself, and it seems preferable to take it in that sense here, cf Lk 18:6—8f: 'The Lord said' (6), 'I tell you' (8). The parable therefore, on this view, ends at 7 and describes a rascal who, faced with ruin, finds a drastic remedy. His method, though unscrupulous, is clearly effective. In 8*a* we have Jesus commending the dishonest steward for his resolute action and in 8*b* explaining that the commendation is restricted to the cleverness of worldly men ('sons of this world') in their dealings with one another. 'sons of light' is a Johannine phrase which is also found at Qumran. Like the steward, the hearers of the parable are faced with a crisis which they must resolutely meet. It is significant that in 14 Lk numbers Pharisees among the audience and it is especially to such that the parable is addressed. In the person of Jesus the kingdom of God has come among them; it is the decisive moment and, in effect, they are being urged to take the bold step of accepting him before it is too late.

9—13 The Right Use of Money—The parable is **d** difficult and these appended vv—added by the familiar technique of catchwords—show how the early Christian teachers wrestled with it. The links are 'unrighteous mammon' in 9 and 11 and 'mammon' in 13; while vv 9—11 are further linked by the repetition of *adikos* (unrighteous). **9.** In 8 we have the original application of the parable; now we find a different application. The meaning seems to be: 'Do good works with the unjust mammon that when it passes away, God may receive you into eternal dwellings' (in rabbinical terminology good works are 'friends'—they speak on one's behalf; the impersonal 'they may receive' avoids the divine name—Jeremias, 35). **10—13.** These vv are meant to answer the difficulty raised by the steward's unscrupulous conduct: how can he be in any sense an example? V 10 states a general principle of conduct with regard to honesty or

783d dishonesty in unimportant matters; in **11f** the principle is applied to mammon and to everlasting riches. In view of the parallelism it is clear that 'that which is another's' and 'your own' of 12 mean respectively, the material wealth that must remain external to a man and the true spiritual riches which are his own. The problem of the steward's conduct is solved: he is no longer an example but a warning. **13** occurs in an entirely different context in Mt 6:24; it epitomizes the obligations and the unending struggle of the christian life.

14f The Pharisees and Money—The Pharisees realized that the parable had them in mind, and they scoffed (lit 'turned up the nose') at him. The sayings prepare for the parable of 19–31.

e 16–18 The Law and Divorce (Mt 11:12f; 5:18, 32)—These three sayings break the link between 14f and the following parable. **16.** The saying appears, in inverse order, in a very different context of Mt. The OT ended with John; now Jesus preaches the good news of the kingdom which is open to all who force their way into it. **17.** Cf Mt 5:18. The old economy has come to an end and the new age has dawned, but the Law, as a norm of morality, still stands intact. **18.** (Cf Mt 5:32; Mk 10:11f). An example which shows that the gospel has not abrogated the Law but has, instead, brought out the spirit of the Law.

f 19–31 The Rich Man and Lazarus—Proper to Lk. **20f.** The dogs, wild scavengers, add to his misery since he is unable to keep them at bay. **22.** The contrast between the two men in the next life is far more pronounced—but they have exchanged rôles. Death was currently described as 'going to Abraham' or 'being gathered to Abraham', a modification of the OT phrase 'gathered to the fathers' i.e. the patriarchs (cf Gn 15:15; 47:30). Lazarus is given the place of honour at the right hand of the patriarch; the phrase 'to Abraham's bosom' is explained by Jn 13:23. **23f.** In speaking to Jews Jesus followed the prevalent notion of life beyond the grave. Throughout most of the OT *Sheol*, a dark, gloomy place, is the abode of all the dead, where good and bad lead a vague, unhappy existence. When, eventually, the doctrine of resurrection, and retribution after death, had evolved—not until well into the 2nd cent. B.C.—this idea of Sheol necessarily underwent a change. Now it was thought to have two compartments: in one the just quietly awaited the resurrection, while in the other the wicked were already being punished. Though these two sections were rigidly separated (26), it was commonly believed that both parties were in sight of each other. **25f.** Abraham does not disown the rich man: as a Jew he is, according to the flesh, his son, but this is not enough to save him. **27f.** This is one of the two-pronged parables (cf 15:11–32) and, true to form, the greater emphasis is on the second point (27–31). The reaction of the rich man is described **g** from an ordinary human point of view. **29.** Cf Ex 22:25; Dt 24:6, 10–13; Am 6:4–7; 8–4; especially Is 68:7. **31.** (Cf Jn 5:46f). There can be little doubt that the parable was originally aimed at the Pharisees. Elsewhere (cf 11:29f) Jesus had refused to grant a like request: they will receive no sign but the sign of Jonah; any other sign would leave them unmoved and unconvinced. Lk, however, has taken it as addressed to the disciples (cf 16:1; 17:1)—the common reapplication of a parable—and sees it as a warning about the danger of riches.

784a 17:1–6 Teaching on Scandal, Forgiveness and Faith (Mt 18:6f; Mk 9:42; Mt 17:20; 21:21; Mk 11:22f)—The passage 17:1–10, instruction to the disciples, is a mosaic of sayings. **1–3a.** In practice it is inevitable that there should be scandal, but the man who deliberately leads astray the 'little one' will be severely punished. The **784a** warning, 'Take heed to yourself' puts the disciples on their guard against involuntary scandal (cf Rm 14:21; 1 Cor 8:13). **3b–4.** In Mt these vv frame a series of sayings on discipline (18:15–22); in Lk the fault is a personal matter involving two brethren; his emphasis on repentance is typical. **5.** The request (proper to Lk) has no connexion with the foregoing. **6.** A little faith can achieve great things.

7–10 Unprofitable Servants—Peculiar to Lk. **7.** The phrase *tis ex humōn* means: 'Can you imagine that . . .?' (cf 11:5); and expects the rejoiner: 'Certainly not!' Jesus draws out the moral in 10. In the context *achreios* has the meaning 'poor', 'humble'—there is no suggestion that mens' works are useless (cf Mt 25:31–46).

11–19 The Ten Lepers—Peculiar to Lk. **11.** Lk again **b** (cf 9:51; 13:22) reminds us that Jesus is journeying to Jerusalem; the indications of this v (still at the starting-point) prove that the journey is a literary construction. **12–14.** The lepers remain at a distance as the Law demanded (Lv 13:45). The command of Jesus (cf Lk 5:14) implied the granting of their request—the priests would verify the cure and authorize them to return to normal life (Lv 14:1–32)—but was also a test of their faith. **15f.** One only, a Samaritan, returned to thank him (cf 2 Kgs 5:14f); by implication the others were Jews (mutual hatred (cf 9:53) was forgotten in their common misery). **17f.** The nine, sons of Abraham had apparently accepted the miracle as a matter of course; but Jesus praises the gratitude of the 'foreigner' (one of the mixed Samaritan race). Already the contrasting attitude of Jews and Gentiles to Jesus and his gospel is foreshadowed. **19.** A stereotyped phrase (cf 7:50; 8:48; 18:42). **20f. The Coming of the Kingdom**—The *entos humōn* of 21b cannot, in the context—the words are addressed to Pharisees—mean 'within you'. Rather, Jesus tells them that the kingdom is 'in the midst of you'; in his person it has come quietly and unnoticed (cf Jn 1:10).

22–37 The Day of the Son of Man—Proper to **c** Lk—though certain passages occur in the eschatological discourse of Mt 24:1–36 parr. The change of audience indicates that the passage is distinct from 20f. **22.** The hebraism *eleusontai hēmerai* (a favourite expression of Lk, cf 19:43; 21:6; 23:29)—it has influenced the phrasing 'one of the days of the Son of man', vv 24, 30—reproduces the introductory formula of an oracle of woe (cf 1 Sm 2:31; Am 4:2; 8:11; Jer 7:32; etc): in their trials the disciples will long for the Second Coming of Christ—but the Parousia will be delayed. **23f.** (Cf Mt 24:23–27). Two examples from the OT illustrate the unexpectedness of the Coming and the unpreparedness of many for such the Parousia will be a catastrophe. Mt has the first example (24:37–39; cf Gn 6–8), the second is peculiar to Lk (cf Gn 18:20–33; 19:24f). **31–33.** These vv which interrupt the link between 30 and 34f have been inserted by Lk into the original discourse. Mk 13:15f refers to flight before the threatening disaster of A.D. 70, here v 31 refers to the urgency of preparation for the manifestation of the Son of Man. In Lk's eyes such preparation is found in flight from worldly goods, in detachment; one must not 'turn back' to such things as Lot's wife 'looked back' to (cf Gn 19:26). Only so can one win salvation, 33 (cf 9:24; Mk 8:35). **34f.** (Cf Mt 24:40f). Again, two examples illustrate an idea. In both examples two persons, closely associated, are suddenly separated: one is taken for the Kingdom, the other is left—the interior dispositions of each is the basis of distinction. After 35 many MSS (incl. D vg) insert v 36, borrowed from Mt 24:40. The disciples' question seems to refer to the place of judgement rather than to the place of the assembly of the elect. In Mt the reply of Jesus is that men will gather to the Son of Man as instinctively as

784c vultures (*aetei*—rather than 'eagles') gather to a dead body, whereas Lk understands it to mean: Wherever men (= a body) are, there will the judgement take place (Schmid, 278).

d 18:1—8 The Unjust Judge—**1.** Lk makes clear his understanding of this parable (proper to him): the disciples should pray at all times and persevere in it (cf 1 Thes 5:17). In reality, like The Friend at Midnight (11:5—8) the parable originally had a different emphasis. **2f.** It is implied that the widow has right on her side, but the judge is not interested in the rights of a penniless plaintiff. **4f.** But, in the face of continued pestering he gives in. 'Wear me out'—lit 'hit over the head'—'she will end by hitting me over the head'. **6—8a.** Jesus ('the Lord') draws attention to the words of the judge; as he spoke the parable the emphasis lay on the judge rather than on the widow's entreaties. The lesson is confidence in prayer; the lesson of perseverence is easily drawn, but is secondary. **8b.** This sentence is not part of the original parable; it is surely an isolated saying of Jesus added here by Lk. In its present context, spoken to the disciples (1), its meaning appears to be: will the Son of Man, at his coming, find men like them, will he find faith on the earth? (cf Mt 24:12).

e 9—14 The Pharisee and the Publican—This parable (like the foregoing, proper to Lk) is distinct from the other; they are set side by side because both concern prayer. **9.** The people so described can be none other than Pharisees. **10.** From the first the parable maintains a dramatic contrast: the Pharisee, taking his stand on minute observance of the Law, is the embodiment of Jewish faith and morality; the tax-collector, by his office one who does not observe the Law, scarcely merits the name of Jew. **14a.** The verdict of Jesus: the tax-collector was justified—his sins were forgiven (cf Ps 51 (50):19); he had asked for pardon and his prayer was heard. The Pharisee was not justified (the better rendering is: 'This man was justified, the other not'), his sins were not forgiven—because he had not asked for pardon. Jesus strives to bring the Pharisees to see themselves as they really are. **14b.** This is not part of the parable (cf 14:11; Mt 23:12) but has been added to it as a secondary conclusion.

15—17 Jesus and Children (Mk 10:13—16; Mt 19:13—15)—At this point Lk returns to the plan of Mk which he had dropped at 9:50. In this context the children are contrasted with the self-righteous Pharisee; Lk omits Mk's conclusion.

f 18—30 The Rich Ruler (Mk 10:17—31; Mt 19: 16—30)—Differs in detail only from Mk's version. **18.** The 'man' of Mk has become a 'ruler' (*archōn*) a favourite word of Lk (cf 12:58; 14:1; 23:13, 35). **21.** Lk has omitted the striking observation of Mk: 'And Jesus looking upon him loved him.' **22.** Lk, typically, insists on the completeness of the renunciation: 'sell *all*'. **30.** Lk has rewritten Mk 10:30.

31—34 Third Prediction of the Passion (Mk 10: 32—34; Mt 20:17—19)—**31—33.** Lk omits Mk 10:32 since the indication is superfluous after 9:51; 17:11. Lk alone refers to the fulfilment of Scripture (cf 24:25, 27, 44; Ac 3:3:18; 8:32—35; 13:27; 26:23). **34.** (Cf 9:45)—an emphatic statement, proper to Lk, on the disciples' failure to understand.

g 35—43 The Blind Man at Jericho (Mk 10:46—52; Mt 20:29—34)—In Mk and Mt the miracle takes place as Jesus was leaving Jericho (Mt has two blind men). Lk, for purely literary reasons (cf 4:5—12) has put it at the entry to the town because he wants to fit in the episode of Zacchaeus, which takes place at Jericho, and the parable

of the Pounds, which he sets in the context of departure **784i** for Jerusalem (19:11). Lk is substantially the same as Mk. **19:1—10 Zacchaeus**—Proper to Lk. **1f.** Zacchaeus held high position at an important customs post and had turned it to good account. **3f.** Curious to see a man with such a reputation, Zacchaeus forgets his dignity. **5.** It was Jesus who saw Zacchaeus; he 'must' come to the house of the tax-collector, he who had come to seek out 'the lost' (10). **6f.** The joy of Zacchaeus is matched by the murmuring of those who did not understand the goodness of God (cf 5:30; 15:2). **8.** Touched by the gracious approach of Jesus, the tax-collector is a changed man—he is more generous than the ruler (18:23). Henceforth he will give half of his goods in alms; moreover, he will make fourfold amends (the requirement of Roman law in the case of *furta manifesta*) if he can ascertain that he has defrauded anybody. **9.** Jesus turns to the murmurers: Zacchaeus is a son of Abraham and has as much right to his mercy as any other Israelite (cf 13:16). **10.** This is very likely an independent logion which echoes the theme of the parables of ch 15—and indeed of the whole gospel; the episode is a striking illustration of it.

11—27 The Pounds (Mt 25:14—30)—Despite notable **h** differences, the Pounds and the Talents (Mt) are versions of the same parable. However, Mt's merchant becomes in Lk a nobleman who went abroad in order to make sure of his right to a throne (12). Though an embassy of his own people tried to forestall him (14) he did return as king; he set about rewarding his friends (17, 19) and punishing his enemies (27). These features, admittedly foreign to The Talents, are the bones of an originally independent parable which we might name The Pretender. Lk, finding The Pounds and The Pretender already fused, treated the whole as a single parable. **11.** In a v that shows manifest traces of his style, he has told us how he understood this new parable for, by placing it in the context of the entry to Jerusalem, he related it to the Parousia. **12—14.** While 13 is part of the main parable, the other vv recall an episode of 4 B.C. when, on the death of Herod the Great, his son Archelaus went to Rome to be confirmed in his possession of Judea. A deputation of Jews attempted to block his claim but Archelaus won and, on his return, took a bloody revenge on those who had opposed him (cf 27). This secondary parable, The Pretender, would have been a warning to the Jews, a parable of judgement. **13.** Each of ten servants received a small sum—the *mina* = c. £6—and were bidden to trade with it; Mt (25:15) has three servants who receive very much larger sums. **20.** The man should have taken the elementary precaution of burying the money (cf Mt 25:18)—in rabbinical law the man who buried a deposit as soon as he received it was free of blame, but he who merely wrapped it in a cloth was held responsible for its loss (Jeremias, 53). **24.** The seam, not noticeable elsewhere, may be seen here: the pound, a relatively insignificant sum, was given to a man who had just become governor of ten towns! **26.** This is an isolated saying of Christ (cf 8:18; Mk 4:25; Mt 13:12) added to widen the application of the parable (27 is part of The Pretender).

19:28—21:38 THE MINISTRY IN JERUSALEM.

28—40 The Entry into Jerusalem (Mk 11:1—11; **785a** Mt 21:1—11; Jn 12:12—19)—Lk follows Mk, but with some omissions and additions. **38.** Lk, thinking of his Gr. readers, omits the exclamation 'Hosanna'; he has rewritten Mk 11:9b—10 on the model of the angel's canticle (2:14). The entry of Jesus into Jerusalem, as messianic King is the sign that the peace, the salvation, decreed by God ('in heaven' cf 15:7) is at hand; by that fact

35a God glorified his name i.e. manifests his power (cf Mt 6:9). **39f.** Not in Mk; but cf Mt 21:15f. The Pharisees obviously fear that the general enthusiasm may lead to a disturbance. But the moment is more significant than they suspect—if men were silent nature itself would proclaim this event (cf Hb 2:11).

41—44 Lament over Jerusalem—Peculiar to Lk (cf 13:34f). **42.** Unlike the disciples (37—40) the city does not recognize the message of salvation. Because they have not accepted Jesus as Messiah (cf 13:34), God (i.e. the passive 'are hid') has punished the unbelieving Jews with blindness (cf Jn 12:37—40); the wish of Jesus will remain unfulfilled. **43f.** The ultimate punishment of the faithless city—which had remained unaware of the divine favours (44*b*; cf 1:68, 78)—will be terrible. The siege imagery echoes OT texts (cf Is 29:3f; Hos 14:1; Na 3:10; Ps 137 (136):9); hence the passage is not necessarily written after A.D. 70, though it may well have been (cf 21:20—24).

b 45—48 The Cleansing of the Temple (Mk 11:15—19; Mt 21:12—17; Jn 2:13—17)—By his omission of the cursing of the fig tree (Mk 11:12—14) Lk is able to present the Cleansing of the Temple at Jesus' first entry. **45f.** Lk has much abbreviated Mk's account. The Lord had taken possession of his Father's house (2:49). **47f.** Lk (cf 20:1) creates the impression of a fairly long period of activity, of a third epoch of Jesus' ministry comparable to the two earlier ones. It is characterized by the absence of miracles and by a special kind of teaching (Conzelmann, 77). Lk naturally omits Mk 11:20—25—a discussion based on the episode of the fig tree.

20:1—8 Question about the Authority of Jesus (Mk 11:27—33; Mt 21:23—27)—Lk has somewhat abridged Mk's version but, otherwise, has followed it closely. In 1 the 'one day' gives the impression of a notable length of time and the expression 'preaching the gospel' is distinctive.

c 9—19 The Wicked Vinedressers (Mk 12:1—12; Mt 21:33—46)—From a comparison of the three versions of the parable it emerges that originally the narrative must have described the sending of three successive servants as in Lk; in Mk the third is followed by 'many others'; Mt has two groups of servants who are maltreated or killed. On the other hand, in Mk 12:8, the son is murdered in the vineyard and his body is cast out of it; in Mt (21:39) and Lk (20:15) he is killed outside the vineyard. Otherwise the three versions are much the same—allegorical traits are present in all. **9.** The hearers must have recalled Is 5:1—7; this vineyard is Israel and the vindressers are the leaders of Israel (cf 19). **10—12.** The servants represent the long line of prophets sent by God to his people. **15.** This detail (cf Mk 12:8) underlines the identification of the son with Jesus, who died outside the walls of Jerusalem (Jn 19:17; Heb 13:12)—the secondary nature of the change is clear from the fact that the vineyard has become Jerusalem. **17.** The three synoptists conclude by quoting Ps 118 (117):22, a v which does not really fit the meaning of the parable. In early Christian preaching it was regularly applied to the resurrection of Christ (cf Ac 4:11; 1 Pt 2:4—7) and it owes its insertion here to the fact that 'the early Christians could never speak of the death of Jesus without proclaiming his resurrection' (George, 1161). **18.** Lk alone has this comment (Mt 21:44 is not authentic) which has in mind two OT sayings. In Is 8:14 Yahweh will become for Israel 'a stone of offence and a rock of stumbling'; in Dn 2:34f; 44f the kingdom of God is a 'stone cut out from a mountain by no human hand' which will break in pieces all world empires. The evangelist sees in Jesus the fulfilment of these messianic texts: those who collide with him, like the unbelieving Jews, will be broken and when he comes again, as the great Judge, he will crush them.

20—26 Tribute to Caesar (Mk 12:13—17; Mt 22:15—22)—The scribes and chief priests, having decided to attack Jesus (19), plan to bring a political charge against him. Lk omits mention of Pharisees and Herodians (Mk 12:13) and speaks of specially chosen agents.

27—40 The Resurrection of the Dead (Mk 12:18—27; Mt 22:23—33)—**34—36.** Lk has omitted Mk 12:24 and has entirely rewritten v 25. He distinguishes two ages. Marriage is an institution of this age, necessary for the continuation of the race. But in the next world there will be no marriage. The reason is that those who have risen are like the angels, immortal—there is no longer any need for marriage. **39f.** Lk has omitted the question on the greatest commandment (Mk 12:28—34)—he has dealt with it in 10:25—27—but reproduces Mk's conclusion (cf Mk 12:34).

41—44 David's Son (Mk 12:35—37*a*; Mt 22:41—46)—This passage, independently transmitted by Mk, has been attached by Lk to the foregoing discussion; he abridges and stylistically improves the text of Mk. 'In the Book of Psalms' (42) cf Ac 1:20.

45—47 Warning against the Scribes (Mk 12:37*b*—40; cf Mt 23:1—36)—Lk has addressed the warning to the disciples; otherwise his text is almost verbally the same as Mk.

21:1—4 The Widow's Mite (Mk 12:41—44)—The incident illustrates the theme of the gospel that the poor and outcast are nearer to God than the self-sufficient rich. Lk, unlike Mk, does not give the Roman equivalent (*quadrans*) of the two *lepta* (Gr.).

5—36 The Apocalyptic Discourse (Mk 13:1—37; Mt 24:1—51)—In 17:22—37 Lk treated of the Parousia, the glorious return of Jesus; here he takes up the same subject but this time, like Mk and Mt, in close association with the question of the destruction of Jerusalem. He follows Mk but with more changes than usual. This fact, and the clear distinction (much more obvious than in Mk/Mt) between the destruction of Jerusalem and the End, are most satisfactorily explained on the assumption that Lk wrote after A.D. 70. If this is granted, it is obvious why the eschatological terms of Mk 13:14—20 are translated into the plain language of Lk 21:20—24. It explains, too, why in 8—11, 25—33 Lk follows Mk more closely than elsewhere: these events still lie in the future; but the prophecy of the destruction of Jerusalem, vague for Mk, has been clarified for Lk by the course of events. In short, Lk manifestly handles two distinct themes: one historical, the destruction of Jerusalem and the victory of the gospel; the other eschatological, the End of this age and the Parousia of the Son of Man (Schmid, 301—3).

5—7 The Destruction of the Temple (Mk 13:1—4; Mt 24:1—3) 'The days will come'—cf 17:22. The question of 7 (cf Mk 13:4) concerns the destruction of the Temple; the reply of Jesus refers to the end of the world: the fall of Jerusalem will not mark the End.

8—11 The Signs of the End (Mk 13:5—8; Mt 24:4—8)—Lk follows Mk closely. In 8 the addition of 'the time is at hand' points to the end of this age and the coming of the Kingdom (cf Dn 7:22). The warning not to follow the false Christs echoes 17:23. In 9 'the end will not be at once' is a stronger expression than Mk's and emphasizes the delay of the Parousia: these events preceded the fall of Jerusalem, but they do not herald the End. **10f.** The insertion 'then he said to them' marks off these authentic signs of the End from the other signs of 8f. Lk omits Mk's 'this is but the beginning of the

785c
d
e
786a
b

786b sufferings' (13:8) because he sees the beginning in the persecution of the disciples (12—19). This persecution is no longer in an eschatological context as in Mk but in an historical context. The sequel of 10f is 25—28.

c **12—19 Persecution of the Church** (Mk 13:9—13; Mt 24:9—14; 10:17—21)—Lk certainly follows Mk but handles his source with considerable freedom. The tone of Lk is optimistic, reflecting the atmosphere of Ac. **12.** The introductory phrase, 'before all this' distinguishes the following from the signs of 10f; the persecution belongs to the epoch of 8f—the time before the fall of Jerusalem. Lk omits Mk 13:10 because the gospel has been preached to the ends of the earth (Ac 1:8; 28:30f). **13.** Confession of faith in such circumstances will be the supreme testimony to the gospel (cf Mk 13:9c). **14f.** Lk has rewritten Mk 13:11, to avoid a repetition of 12:11f. **18f.** The two vv follow on 14f (16f may be regarded as a parenthesis): steadfast, supported by Christ, the disciples will come through the persecution (cf Apoc (Rev) 3:10)—16*b* refers to a small minority. The picture is that of Ac; but Lk intimates that Christians must anticipate a long period of tribulation.

d **20—24 Siege of Jerusalem** (Mk 13:14—20; Mt 24: 15—22)—The text of Mk is here drastically rewritten: in 20 the 'desolating sacrilege' (Mk 13:14) in the Temple has become the siege of the holy city; 21 replaces Mk 13:15f (already used in 17:31) and 22 is a new addition. A vivid description of the fate of the city (23f) replaces the vague prophecy of Mk 13:19f; reference to the Christian remnant (Mk 13:20) is omitted. The most reasonable explanation of this procedure is that Lk worked over the text of Mk in the light of the historical fate of Jerusalem. The suggestion that Lk wrote before this event but cleverly used biblical texts relevant to the siege of Jerusalem in 587 is undoubtedly a serious one and has much in its favour; but it is quite the manner of Lk to be guided by biblical parallels and to imitate OT language (Schmid, 308f). **20.** The opening phrase echoes Mk 14:1, the rest is Lk's composition; as clearly as 19:43 the siege of Jerusalem is described. **21.** In the initial stages of the siege there is yet possibility of flight. **22.** Proper to Lk—gives the reason for the flight of the disciples: the fate of the city is sealed. **23.** Mk 13:17 refers to the difficulties of flight. Lk (23*a*) applies the *vae* to those in the doomed city; in 23*b* he adapts Mk 13:19 to fit the fate of the Jews. Mk 13:18 has been omitted, perhaps because of its obscurity, but, more likely, because the siege did not take place during winter but in April—Sept., A.D. 70. **24.** The merciful shortening of the days of wrath (Mk 13:20) is left aside; doubtless because the prophetic doctrine of the Remnant would be unfamiliar to Lk's Gr. readers. The fate of Jerusalem is summed-up in three points: part of the inhabitants will be slain; the rest will be sold into slavery (cf JosBJ 6, 9, 3 § 430); the city will be 'trodden down' by the Gentiles (Titus stationed the 10th Legion on the site of the ruined city—cf JosBJ 7, 1,2 § 5; 1, 3 § 17). Lk may well have been aware of all this. 'Until the times of the Gentiles are fulfilled': Lk has set, between the destruction of Jerusalem and the End (25ff) an undetermined period. The fall of Jerusalem makes manifest to all that the 'time of Israel', which really ended with the ministry of Christ and the founding of the Church, had indeed come to an end.

e **25—28 The Coming of the Son of Man** (Mk 13:24—27; Mt 24:29—31)—This passage—resuming the theme of 10f—concerns the end of the 'time of the Gentiles' and the judgement of mankind. **25f.** Lk's apocalyptic description, based on Mk 13:24, has been

influenced by Is 13:10 and Ps 65 (64):8; more clearly, 786f too, the whole world is involved (26). **27.** Cf Mk 13:26—the fulfilment of Dn 7:13f. Lk leaves aside Mk 13:27. **28** looks back to the signs of 25f. The cosmic events that will terrify the nations will indicate to the followers of Christ that the time of persecution is ending: their 'redemption' (a Pauline word, cf Rm 3:24; 8:23; Eph 1:7) is *drawing near*. These signs before the End do not contradict 17:20f; 21:34f—the End will be preceded by signs, but yet the Son of Man will appear like lightning.

29—33 The Coming of the Kingdom (Mk 13:28—31; f Mt 24:32—36)—The introductory formula (29*a*) is proper to Lk; otherwise the three passages are in close agreement. Yet it seems that Lk's interpretation, or application, differs widely from that of Mk (his source). The latter is referring to the fall of Jerusalem and while Lk, going back beyond 25—28, may have in view the signs of 20—24, it is surely more natural that the parable and its comment agree with the immediate context, 25—28; 34—36. It is true that, strictly speaking, 32 will not suffer this interpretation; but Lk may well have taken 'this generation' in the broad sense of 'mankind'—for his statement has no temporal value but, like 33, underlines the constancy of God's design. Thus he has omitted Mk 13:32 with its reference to time.

34—36 Watchfulness—Lk has replaced the passage Mk 13:33—37 (cf Lk 12:35—40) with an admonition to watchfulness (cf 1 Thess 5:1—11), one influenced by his realization of the delay of the Parousia.

37f Jesus' Last Days—This summary statement links up with 19:47. Jesus spent the nights, not in Bethany (cf Mk 11:11), but at the Mt of Olives (cf 22:39, 47). The wording suggests a fairly long period of activity (cf 19:47). There is an undeniable literary contact with Jn 8:1f; significantly, a few cursive MSS have inserted here the passage on the Woman taken in Adultery (Jn 7:53—8:11).

22:1—23:56. THE PASSION.

Lk here still follows Mk, but not as closely as elsewhere. 787 To a notable extent he has arranged the order of events to give a clearer and smoother account and here, as elsewhere, his theological ideas give a personal colouring to the narrative. Ultimately, however, the more satisfactory arrangement is due to the fact that he is evidently following a special source, one related to the Johannine tradition.

22:1f The Plot of the Sanhedrin (Mk 14:1f; Mt 26: 1—5)—Very close to Mk. Lk omits Mk's 'not during the feast' because, in the synoptic view, Jesus was crucified on the feast (cf § 739*h*). He omits the anointing at Bethany (Mk 14:3—9), doubtless because he has described a similar incident in 7:36—50.

3—6 The Betrayal (Mk 14:10f; Mt 26:14—16)—Apart from 3, Lk has slightly retouched the text of Mk, notably by the explanatory addition in 6. But his explicit attribution of Judas' action to the influence of Satan (3) is a new and powerful theological insight (cf Jn 13:2, 27). At the beginning of the Passion narrative it is made clear that the machinery now set in motion against Jesus is guided by the Adversary.

7—14 Preparation for the Passover (Mk 14:12—16; b Mt 26:17—19)—Lk differs from Mk in having Jesus take the initiative; he also specifies that the two disciples were Peter and John. He has placed the announcement of the betrayal at the close of the meal (21—23) and not at the beginning, as in Mk/Mt. Thus he achieves as uninterrupted sequence and more effectively presents the institution of the Eucharist as the climax of the Paschal meal.

87b 15—20 The Lord's Supper (Mt 14:22—25; Mt 26:26—29; 1 Cor 11:23—25)—The first problem that presents itself is a celebrated textual one: the choice of 'longer' or 'shorter' text—depending on the acceptance or rejection of 19b—20. The longer text is represented by the majority of MSS and versions; vv 19b—20 are missing from D it; v 20 is omitted by syr. cur. syr. sin. The matter cannot be decided on textual grounds alone, and internal evidence strongly supports the authenticity of 19b—20. In favour of the longer text we may note its symmetrical structure—two parallel panels, 15—18 and 19f, each composed of two corresponding elements: Passover of 15f and bread of 19; cup of 17f and cup of 20. The shorter text, on the other hand, appears to be due to a misunderstanding of Lk's purpose and literary construction. The presence of two cups (17, 20), over which Jesus had pronounced a blessing, disconcerted certain copyists. To judge from the MSS evidence, the first cup was regarded as being sufficiently eucharistic and the other was set aside. It is also likely that the words of 17 were closer to the liturgical formula which was familiar to the scribes in question

c (Benoit, 167—172). **15—18.** It is often argued that Lk here follows a special source. In fact, it is far more likely that he has rewritten Mk 14:25—there are clear traces of Lk's style. The eschatological saying, placed by Mk after the institution of the Eucharist, is better situated before that event; but its new situation is due to Lk's deliberate arrangement. His literary construction is dominated by a theological idea: the Eucharist is the Christian Passover, so, before describing the institution of the Eucharist he gives a schematized description of the paschal meal. The juxtaposition of the two rites sets up an opposition between them: the old rite must be 'fulfilled' (16b) by something new in the Kingdom which is to come (18b). But now the outlook is no longer purely eschatological as in Mk 14:25; in its Lucan context the 'kingdom of God' (16, 18) suggests the domain in which the new paschal rite will find expression i.e. the Church. Significantly, Lk does not speak of 'new' wine (Mk). In implying that Jesus will again eat and drink in the Kingdom he has in mind the post-Resurrection meals which he (24.00, 41ff, Ac 10:41) and Jn (21:9ff) alone mention (Benoit, 197—99). **19f.** Literary dependence on 1 Cor 11:24b—25a (more accurately, on the liturgical tradition which Paul has reproduced) is undeniable. The minor retouches of Lk are meant to achieve a better parallelism and are also

d suggested by the text of Mk. While RSV margin has 'is given' and 'is poured out' it seems that the participles *didomenon* and *ekchunnomenon* refer to the immediate future; hence *qui va être donné; qui va être versé* (BJ): Jesus announces his approaching death and presents it as a sacrifice, like that of the victims whose blood sealed the Sinai covenant (Ex 24:5—8)—but a redemptive sacrifice. For, in speaking of blood 'poured out for you' (Mk 'for many') in view of a 'new covenant' Jesus had in mind the Servant of Yahweh whose life had been 'poured out' and who had borne the sins of 'many' (Is 53:12); God had given him as 'a covenant to the peoples, a light to the nations' (Is 42:6; cf Lk 4:17—21). Jesus is about to inaugurate the new covenant which Jer had foretold (31:31—34). 'Do this in remembrance of me': it is not a mere commemoration but the renewal of a rite by means of which the sacrifice of the living Christ is made actual in bread and wine. The gestures, the words, will be repeated, but the reality will persist unchanged: the sacrificial offering of the Body and Blood of Christ made once for all.

e **21—23 Announcement of the Betrayal** (Mk 14:17—21; Mt 26:20—25; cf Jn 13:21—30)—Lk has avoided the difficulty, present in Mt and Mk, that Judas still remained on for the meal after he had been unmasked. **787e 21.** Suggested by Ps 41 (40):10, but changed to fit this context. In 22 Lk emphasizes the divine preordination of events and omits the terrible saying of Mk 14:21c.

24—30 Greatness in the Kingdom (Mt 20:20—28; Mk 10:35—45)—While Mk and Mt have the journey to the Mount of Olives immediately after the institution of the Eucharist, Lk adds some farewell words of Jesus in the supper room (24—38)—thus anticipating the discourse of Jn (13:31—14:31). **24—27.** Mk and Mt have this episode after the demands of the sons of Zebedee. Lk has it here, in the context of the paschal meal, because of the reference to sitting at table (27). **25.** The title Euergetes (benefactor) was assumed by many of the Ptolemies and Seleucids. **26.** In the kingdom of Jesus those who hold authority must be the servants of those whom they govern: the principle of authority is admitted but the manner of its exercise is bluntly characterized as service. **27** is not a veiled reference to the feet-washing of Jn 13:4—17; it is a simple example by way of answer to the question of 24. **28—30.** Proper f to Lk—though 30b occurs, in another context, in Mt 19:28—the passage seems to be a combination of two sayings (28, 30b and 29, 30a) and is added here by means of the catchword 'table' (30, 27, 21, and the general context of the paschal meal). **28.** In its present context the saying probably has in mind the betrayal of Judas: the others are those who have remained faithful. **29f.** In virtue of the royal power which Jesus already possesses he can make provision for his faithful Apostles: they will have part with him in the messianic feast (cf 14:15—24) and, for the earthly phase of the kingdom of Christ, they will participate in his authority over all its subjects. Another, and perhaps more satisfactory, interpretation is to regard the passage in the light of Lk 24:26—as Christ through suffering entered into his glory so the disciples, the companions of his trials (28), will share his glory; that is their reward.

31—34 Peter's Denial Foretold (Mk 14:27—31; Mt 26:31—35)—Originally two distinct sayings (31f proper to Lk and 33f Marcan), cf the change of names (31, 34). **31f.** Unlike Mk and Mt the scene is still the supper-room (cf Jn 13:36—38). Satan makes his final onslaught not only against Jesus (22:3) but against his Apostles for whom the Passion will be a 'sifting', a profound spiritual trial. Simon will stumble and deny his Master, but the prayer of Jesus will sustain him; deep down, his faith in the Messiahship of Jesus had not failed. When Peter will have 'returned', will have come to his senses (cf 22:62) he will become the strong support of his brethren. **33f.** Substantially the same as Mk 14:29—31, but rather freely re-written.

35—38 The Testing Time—Peculiar to Lk. The sayings g have been influenced by the experience of the Christian community. **35** looks back to the time before the hour of trial. The reference is to 10:4, the sending of the seventy-two, and supports the view that 9:1—6 and 10:1—16 are not distinct discourses. **36.** The hostility they will have to face is depicted in symbolical terms: a purse, in order to buy food (no longer given freely), a sword, to win it by force. **37.** The reason is that the disciples will share the fate of their Master. Jesus quotes Is 53:12 and thus explicitly identifies himself with the Suffering Servant of Yahweh. For him, the decisive moment has come. **38.** The disciples, still 'slow of heart' (24:25) take the words of Jesus literally. The phrase, 'It is enough', does not refer to the swords but closes the discussion.

39—46 At the Mount of Olives (Mk 14:26, 32—42; **788a**

788a Mt 26:30, 36—46)—Lk abridges Mk more drastically than usual but, at the same time, makes his own contribution from another tradition. **39.** Only now do Jesus and the disciples leave the supper-room to go, 'as was his custom' (cf 21:37; Jn 18:2) to the Mount of Olives. At this point Lk omits the prophecy of the disciples' desertion and the promise of a post-Resurrection appearance of Jesus in Galilee (Mk 14:27f); he has anticipated the foretelling of Peter's denial which Mk puts on the way to the Mt of Olives (Mk 14:29—31). **40—46.** In Lk's presentation Jesus seeks no human comfort; instead, by his repeated warning (40, 46) he seeks to fortify his disciples; prayer is the weapon against temptation. It is an angel that strengthens Jesus for the hour of death. **43f.** These vv, proper to Lk, though missing from A B W φ sy. sin sa bo Marc Clem Or, are, nonetheless, authentic. Their omission can be easily explained on theological grounds: the Lord strengthened by an angel and the too human details of the agony; for the same reasons it is inconceivable that they should be a later insertion. It is the soul of Jesus that is troubled in the first place, an anguish that reacts on his body (44) and so the 'strengthening' is primarily spiritual. How this was achieved, and why by means of an angel, remain God's secret (Lagrange, 560). The extreme spiritual anguish of Jesus affected his body: his sweat became *like* great drops of blood. The expression may indicate the intensity of the sweat; it does not necessarily imply that it is a sweat mixed with blood—though this is, perhaps, the more natural and the more generally accepted interpretation.

b 47—53 The Arrest (Mk 14:43—52; Mt 26:47—56; Jn 18:2—11)—Lk follows Mk more closely than in the preceding passage. Yet he cannot bring himself to state that the traitor actually kissed Jesus and, he also omits reference to the desertion of the disciples (Mk 14:50). Jesus is not at once seized (cf Mk 14:46) and, as in Jn (18:4—11) is perfectly in command of the situation. The healing of the servant's ear (the *right* ear, cf Jn 18:10), given by Lk only, is a gesture that this evangelist could not overlook. **52f.** It is surprising, to say the least, that the chief priests and the elders should have been present in person at the arrest. On the other hand, the saying of 53 (cf Mk 14:49; Mt 26:55) strikingly resembles the answer of Jesus made before Annas (Jn 18:20), a saying that could have been addressed only to the Jewish authorities. It is likely that a reply of Jesus made at the appearance before Annas (not recorded by the synoptists) is anticipated at this point (Benoit, 305).

c 54—62 Peter's Denial (Mk 14:66—72; Mt 26:69—75; Jn 18:15—18, 25—27)—**54.** The high priest is not named but, very likely, Annas is meant (cf Jn 18:13). Lk names Annas before Caiaphas in 3:1 and Ac 4:6 and it is altogether credible that the influential old man would have been popularly called high priest, and may have been regarded as still the legitimate high priest: his deposition by the Romans would have seemed invalid. **60f.** A typically Lucan touch is the look that moved Peter so deeply. **63—65 The Mockery** (Mk 14:65; Mt 26:67f)—On the assumption that the high priest of 54 is Annas, those who mock Jesus are the guards who, after an interrogation (cf Jn 18:19—23) have charge of him until the morning session of the Sanhedrin.

d 66—71 Jesus before the Sanhedrin (Mk 14:53—64; 15:1; Mt 26:57—66; 27:1f)—Mk and Mt speak of two sessions of the Sanhedrin, one at night which they describe in some detail (Mk 14:53, 55—64; Mt 26:57, 59—66), the other in the early morning, which they

mention briefly (Mk 15:1; Mt 27:1). Lk speaks of one **788e** session only, and places it in the morning (22:66—71). During the night he has the denials of Peter and the mockery of Jesus by his guards. Mk/Mt's presentation is frankly unlikely: a night assembly of the Sanhedrin is hard to imagine and it is difficult to believe that the members of the Sanhedrin, so conscious of their dignity, would, immediately after the judging of Jesus, have taken part in the crude mockery scene. In Lk this last is shown as the guards' way of passing the night. In short, it can scarcely be doubted that Lk owes his better arrangement to a personal source distinct from Mk. Comparison with Jn not only confirms the order of Lk but helps to explain the presentation of Mk/Mt. Above (54—65) we have suggested that the high priest in question is Annas. Lk omits the interrogation before him (cf Jn 18:19—23) but sets the mockery at the courtyard of his house where Jesus was confined until morning. Mk/Mt, on the other hand, speak of two sessions, because there were two sessions, but they have substituted for the private interrogation of Annas, held at night, the official process of the Sanhedrin held next morning. The discrepancy between Mk/Mt and Lk/Jn is explained by this simple displacement—one that easily happened in the oral tradition. **66.** The morning session was that of the *presbyterion*, the 'assembly of elders' i.e. the Sanhedrin, whose main components were the chief priests and scribes. **67—71.** This passage is based on Mk 14:61—64, **e** with the customary Lucan modifications. Lk has omitted the saying about the Temple (Mk 14:57f). The course of the trial has been schematized; the examination of witnesses has been omitted as being superfluous. **67—69.** This first question (67a) regards the messianic dignity of Jesus. The first part of his reply (67b), proper to Lk, is Johannine in tone: cf Jn 10:25 which comes after the same question. Cf Jn 3:12; 6:36, 64; 8:45. The 'power of God' (69) explains the Jewish expression 'Power' (Mk 14:62). Lk avoids saying that the Sanhedrites 'will see' the Son of Man (Mk 14:62). 'From now on' (cf 1:48; 5:10; 12:52; 22:18; Ac 18:6) the Son of Man is exalted to the right hand of God (Ps 110 (109):1) because his imminent death is the entry into his glory (cf 24:26; Ac 2:36). Jesus is the Messiah—but seated at the right hand of God, equal to God. **70f.** The second question seeks to clarify this point: is Jesus claiming divine sonship? Though Lk omits the term 'blasphemy' (Mk 14:64) the reaction of the Sanhedrites shows that they regarded him guilty of that crime: he, a man, had 'made himself the Son of God' (Jn 19:7). More clearly than Mk/Mt, Lk has brought out the reason why Jesus was condemned to death.

23:1—5 Jesus before Pilate (Mk 15:1—5; Mt 27:11—**789a** 14; Jn 18:28—38)—The Sanhedrin had decided that Jesus must die; it was necessary to have sentence of death pronounced by the Roman procurator: the *ius gladii*, or power of execution, was reserved to Rome (cf Jn 18:31) as in all the provinces of the Empire. **1.** The place of judgement was perhaps the fortress Antonia which dominated the Temple; but more probably it was the palace of Herod, in the NE of the city (Benoit, 316—39). **2.** If Jesus were to be condemned by Pilate the charge against him would have to be a political one, not a religious issue. **3f.** Pilate's reaction to the enigmatic reply of Jesus presupposes a longer conversation similar to that of Jn 18:35—38. Lk emphasizes Pilate's testimony to the innocence of Jesus (cf 23:15, 22). **5.** The charge is reiterated. Judea = Palestine (cf 4:44). For the range of the ministry cf Ac 10:37.

6—12 The Sending to Herod—Peculiar to Lk. **6f. b**

39b Mention of Galilee (s) suggested to Pilate a means of evading this troublesome affair. Herod Antipas (cf 3:1) would have been in Jerusalem for the Passover. **8–10.** For Herod's curiosity, cf 9:9; his question seeks to satisfy it. This is not a trial, though the chief priests and scribes attempt to make it one. The 'gorgeous apparel'—doubtless a cast-off princely robe—would mark him as 'king'; it is a practical recognition of the baselessness of the charges. This scene of mockery is strangely like Mk 15:16–19; Mt 27:27–30, where Jesus is mocked by the Roman soldiers, an episode omitted by Lk. It is likely that the Romans had played their part when the prisoner had returned from Herod. **12.** The enmity had been caused or aggravated by Pilate's massacre of Galileans (cf 13:1). Now, each was flattered by the recognition of the other.

c **13–25 Again before Pilate** (Mk 15:6–15; Mt 27:15–26; Jn 18:38b–19:16)——**13–15.** Pilate, forced to re-open the case, again professes his conviction that the prisoner is innocent; he can add that Herod shares the same view. **16.** The 'chastisement' (scourging, cf Jn 19:1) was a compromise suggestion. Here some MSS (S W D it vg sy. sin sy. cur) add 17 (cf RSV margin) which appears to be an explanatory gloss based on Mk 15:6; Mt 27:15. **18–25.** Lk omits Mk 15:6–11 so Barabbas appears abruptly. For the third time (22) Pilate bears witness to the innocence of Jesus—in contrast to the blind hate of the Jews (21, 23), who preferred a murderer to their Messiah (25). Lk lays the blame squarely on the Jews (cf Jn 18:38; 19:4, 6) while he tends to minimize the culpability of Pilate (cf Jn 19:11). This fact, and the omission of any reference to outrages by the Roman troops (cf Mk 15:16–20), suggest that Lk has sought to present the rôle of Rome in the crucifixion in as favourable a light as possible.

d **26–32 The Road to Calvary** (Mk 15:20b–23; Mt 27:31b–34; Jn 19:17)——**26.** Jesus is led away by Roman soldiers (cf 36, 47). The rest of this passage is proper to Lk. **27.** A morbidly curious crowd follows the three (cf 32) condemned men. The women are not those mentioned in 8:2f (cf 23:49); they are, perhaps, women who had known Jesus or women who habitually attended to the last needs of condemned criminals, and especially prepared the spiced wine (cf Mk 15:23). **28f.** Jesus is moved by thought of the sufferings that lie in wait for these women and their children, in the war of 66–70 (cf 21:20–24). **30.** Cf Hos 10:8; Apoc (Rev) 6:16. **31.** If the innocent ('the green wood' = Jesus) suffers so what will happen to the guilty (the 'dry wood' = the Jews)?

e **33–38 The Crucifixion** (Mk 15:22–32; Mt 27:33–43; Jn 19:17–24)——**33.** A combination of Mk 15:22, 24a, 27. **34a.** MSS evidence for (S A C λ φ Koine it vg sy. c sy. p Iren Orig) and against (B D W Θ sy. s sa bo) seems evenly balanced; on internal grounds the v is to be accepted. Cf Ac 7:60. Its omission can be explained on the grounds of apparently excessive indulgence towards the Jews and because it seemed to contradict other sayings (cf 20:16; 21:24; 23:31). These words of forgiveness are not primarily for the soldiers who are merely obeying orders but for the Jewish leaders. These cannot be absolved from guilt in their calculated rejection of Jesus and in the manner in which they engineered his death. But they were motivated by fierce zeal for their religion (as Paul was to be) and they did, sincerely, believe Jesus guilty of blasphemy (22:70f). Above all they were not, subjectively, guilty of deicide—as Paul explicitly acknowledges (1 Cor 2:8). **35–37.** Lk divides the spectators into three categories: the people who looked

on (cf 27); the rulers who mocked Jesus; the soldiers who **789e** joined in the raillery. **38.** The title on the cross is the climax of this mockery.

39–43 The 'Good Thief'—Proper to Lk. **39.** In place f of Mk's (15:32f) brief statement that the two crucified men also reviled Jesus, Lk declares that one only acted so. **40f.** The other acknowledges the innocence of Jesus. **42.** Further, he recognizes Jesus as the Messiah. He asks to be remembered when Jesus comes in (not 'into') his Kingdom (or kingly power) i.e. when he comes to inaugurate the messianic age, an event that, in Jewish belief, would involve the resurrection of the dead. **43.** 'Paradise': the heavenly dwelling-place (cf 3 Ez 4:7f).

44–49 The Death of Jesus (Mk 15:33–41; Mt g 27:45–56; Jn 19:25–30)——**44f.** If Lk adds that the sun was eclipsed (cf RSV margin) he uses the expression in a wide sense, as a rough description of the phenomenon. The rending of the Temple veil, placed after the death of Jesus by Mk/Mt is given here by Lk as a companion sign—the transposition is made on literary grounds. **46.** Lk, who omits the citation of Ps 22 (21):2 (cf Mk 15:34), doubtless because it might be misunderstood, here gives as the cry of Jesus (Mk 15:37) another psalm-text (Ps 31 (30):6; cf Ac 7:59f). **47.** Yet another witness to the innocence of Jesus. The term *dikaios*, especially after the praise of God, indicates that the centurion has seen in Jesus the perfect man whose martyr's death is a glory for God; the word has replaced Mk's 'a son of God'. **48.** Lk adds this moving description of the repentant crowd.

50–56 The Burial of Jesus (Mk 15:42–47; Mt 27:57–61; Jn 19:38–42)——**50–52.** Lk adds that he was a 'good and righteous man' (cf 2.25, Ac 11.24) who had taken no part in the action against Jesus. The surprise of Pilate and his questioning of the centurion (Mk 15:44f) are omitted. **53.** Lk specifies that the tomb had not been used (cf Jn 19:41). **54–56.** The women of 49 saw the tomb and the body of Jesus laid in it; thus they are important witnesses of the Resurrection (cf 24:3f). The preparation of spices and ointments before the sabbath began (Mk 16:1—'when the sabbath was past') is very likely a literary arrangement which enables Lk to get right on with the resurrection narrative in 24:1.

24:1–53 AFTER THE RESURRECTION

24:1–12 The Resurrection (Mk 16:1–8; Mt 28:1– **790a** 10; Jn 20:1–18)——Lk differs from Mk most obviously in avoiding mention of appearances of Jesus in Galilee. Textually, this ch is remarkable for the number of possible 'Western non-interpolations' i.e. shorter readings that may reflect the original text. **1f.** Lk abridges and alters (in the light of 23:56) Mk 16:1f, 4 and omits 16:3. **3.** 'Of the Lord Jesus' is absent from D it Iren Eus and in part from sy. In favour of authenticity, apart from the majority MSS evidence, is the use of the title in Ac 1:21; 4:33; 8:16. **4—6a.** Where Mk has 'a young man' (16:5) and Mt (28:2) 'an angel of the Lord', Lk speaks of 'two men' and Jn (20:12) of 'two angels'. The women are filled with religious awe (cf 1:12; etc); the rhetorical question implies the resurrection of Jesus. D it omit 6a; it is possibly an assimilation to Mk 16:6; yet it is not an exact assimilation and the weight of MSS evidence is in its favour. **6b—8.** This is perhaps the most striking example of Lk's editorial freedom. Since, in his theological plan, the climax of his gospel must be in Jerusalem he cannot, without bringing about an anti-climax, record the appearances in Galilee. So he rewrites Mk 16:7 and changes the promise of an appearance in Galilee into a prophecy made by Jesus 'while he was still in Galilee'.

790a 9. Lk apparently contradicts Mk 16:8; the discrepancy is no doubt explained by the abrupt ending of Mk (cf Mt 28:8). **10f.** Instead of Salome (Mk 16:1) Lk names Joanna (cf 8:3). For the incredulity of the Apostles cf Mk 16:14; Mt 28:17. **12.** This v is missing from D it (cf RSV margin). It is argued that it is an interpolation, based on Jn 20:3—10, intended to illustrate 24 and 34 and to bring these vv into harmony with 11. But a later interpolation would surely agree more closely with the text of Jn.

b 13—35 On the Road to Emmaus—This delightful narrative is proper to Lk. **13.** It is impossible to identify the site of Emmaus with any certainty. The problem is complicated by a variant reading: '60 stadia' (A B C etc), '160 stadia' (S and some dozen Gr. MSS); however, on the evidence and from the details of the narrative (cf 33) 60 stadia (c. 7 m.) is preferable. Emmaus was most likely the home of one or both of the disciples. **17f.** Cleopas (possibly the Clopas of Jn 19:25) was probably Lk's source. **19f.** Once again responsibility for the crucifixion is placed squarely on the shoulders of the Jewish leaders. The disciples acknowledged that Jesus was a mighty prophet (cf Ac 7:22); as such his violent death was not exceptional (cf 11:47—51; 13:34). **21.** But they had seen in him something more—the Messiah, though their expectation was thoroughly Jewish. In 21*b* their disillusionment is forcefully expressed: before the death of Jesus they could still hope for a divine intervention. **22—24.** The situation had been aggravated by the report of some women (cf 3); momentary hopes were dashed when some of the disciples (cf 12; Jn 20:3—10), investigating the matter, had found only an empty tomb.

c 25f. The disciples, like the Jews, in general, had not accepted *all* that the prophets had spoken: they had closed their eyes to the suffering of the Messiah (cf 18:31; Ac 26:23); that is why the death of Jesus had been a fatal stumbling block. But, in God's design, the way to glory was the path of suffering (cf 9:22; 22:69). Christ had suffered and so *had* already entered into his glory (cf Jn 20:17, 19—23). **27.** The statement is general—he need not have touched on *all* the messianic texts—but it is a precious testimony to a Christian interpretation of the OT. It is noteworthy that 19f and 25—27 echo the theme and the very words of the *kerygma*, the mission preaching of the primitive Church, as we find it in the discourses of the early part of Acts (cf Ac 2:22f, 29—36; 3:14f, 22—24). **28f.** 'He appeared to be going further'—not a feigned action; rather, everything depended on their invitation. In fact, they 'constrained' him, i.e. oriental etiquette (cf Gn 19:3; Ac 16:15). **30f.** The breaking of bread is the occasion of their recognition of him. The expression 'breaking of bread' is a technical term for the Eucharist (cf Ac 2:42, 46; 20:7, 11; 27:35; 1 Cor 10:16). While it does not necessarily follow that here (and in 35) the Eucharist is meant, it is clear that Lk has deliberately used eucharistic language: Jesus *took bread, blessed, broke it, gave to them* (cf Lk 22:19). And his lesson is that as the two disciples recognized Jesus in the setting of a meal shared with him, so Christians, in the eucharistic meal, make the same real encounter with their Lord, (cf Dupont, *The Eucharist in the NT,* 1964, 105—121). **35.** Again Lk draws attention to the 'breaking of bread'—he is determined that his readers will not miss the significance. The whole passage, centred around the 'liturgy of the word' (19—27) and the eucharistic meal (30f) has a marked liturgical colouring. It is an early catechesis, in a liturgical setting, highlighting the encounter with the Lord in the Eucharist.

d 36—43 Appearance of the Risen Christ in Jeru-

salem—This time Jesus appears to a greater number **790c** and goes out of his way to emphasize the reality of his resurrection. **36.** Doubtless the same appearance as that of Jn 20:19—23. The phrase 'and said to them, Peace be to you,' omitted by D and it, is very probably an interpolation after Jn 20:19; Jesus begins to speak in 38. **37.** The disciples are startled by his sudden appearance 'the doors being shut' (Jn 20:19). Their reaction is not inconsistent with 34; Lagrange (612) observes 'On leur avait dit que le Seigneur était ressuscité, mais qu'est-ce qu'un ressuscité?'. **39.** Cf Jn 20:20, 25, 27. V 40 is missing from D it, syr. sin syr. cur; the suggestion that it is an interpolation from Jn 20:20 leaves unexplained the substitution of 'feet' for 'side'. **41—43.** 'They disbelieved *for joy*' surely means no more than 'they could not believe their eyes'. (The Vg addition, *et favum mellis*—perhaps referring to a baptismal rite—is certainly not authentic). A glorified body does not require food—but this is not to say that it cannot assimilate food. We might paraphrase Lagrange's question: 'What is a glorified body?'

44—49 Final Instructions (Ac 1:3—8)—At the close **e** of his gospel Lk summarizes the last commission of Jesus to his Apostles; this he repeats in a more developed form at the beginning of Ac. **44.** 'Moses the prophets and the psalms' stand for the Law, Prophets and Writings, the Jewish threefold division of the OT. 'While I was still with you': Jesus has entered into his glory (cf 26) by his exaltation to the Father (Jn 20:17); his relations with the disciples are not what they were before his glorification. **45—48.** He gives them a new understanding of the OT, an insight that will enable them to see how and where it 'bears witness to him' (cf Jn 5:39). This reinterpretation of the OT is the basis of the primitive *kerygma*: the suffering of the Messiah and his resurrection on the third day; and in consequence of this, the proclamation of repentance and forgiveness of sins to all men. The message of salvation will go forth from Jerusalem, preached by the Apostles who are witnesses of the fulfilment of the prophecies (cf Ac 1:8). The Good News is the straightforward proclamation of events that manifestly followed a pattern traced by God, the fulfilment of a divine plan. It was inevitable that this proclamation, couched in terms of the OT, should itself become a new ch in the word of God. Lk has shown us, on the authority of Christ, that our preaching of Christ must be, first and last, scriptural. **49.** Jesus assured the Apostles that he would send upon them 'the promise of the Father' (cf Ac 1:4) i.e. the promised Holy Spirit (cf Jl 3:1—4; Ac 2:16—21). Hence, they are bidden to stay in the city until 'baptized with the Holy Spirit' (Ac 1:4f). This is perfectly in accord with Lk's plan: in order to end his gospel at Jerusalem he studiously avoids mention of the appearances in Galilee (cf 24:6). In this final charge Jesus looks to the future. His work is done; now begins the work of his disciples, the mission to the world.

50—53 The Ascension (Ac 1:9—14; cf Mk 16:19)— **f** Lk has undoubtedly given the impression that all the events of ch 24 had taken place on Easter Sunday (cf 1, 13, 33, 36, 44, 50). This arrangement is redactional and the passage 44—53 is a telescoped version of Ac 1:3—14. Though it is true that Jesus did ascend to his Father on Easter day (cf Jn 20:17) it is clear that the Ascension in question here is the same as that of Ac, the final, visible departure of Christ, forty days (Ac 1:3) after the Resurrection (Benoit, 363—411). **50f.** 'As far as Bethany'; in Ac the place of ascension was 'the mount called Olivet' (1:12)—Bethany lies on the E slope of the Mt of Olives. With his hands raised in blessing (cf Lv

'90f 9:22; Sir 50:22) Jesus parted from them (cf Ac 1:9). Though missing from S D it syr. sin, 51*b* is authentic; its omission can be explained on the grounds of apparent discrepancy with Ac (ascension after 40 days). **52f.** The phrase 'having worshipped him' (cf RSV margin) is missing from D it syr. sin Aug; it may have been omitted for the same reason as 51*b*. The joy of the Apostles, at the moment of parting, though at first sight surprising, is explained by the realization that 'the Lord has risen indeed' (34). And they have his assurance that, very soon, they will be 'clothed with power from on high' (49).

Their minds have been opened to understand the **790f** Scriptures: now they have grasped the plan of God and they realize that Christ, their Lord, has triumphed. Thankfully, they hastened to glorify God in his Temple. Lk has closed his gospel as he began it, in the Temple; yet all is 'changed, changed utterly'. He has shown the 'time of Israel' yield to the 'time of Christ' and now, about to begin his description of the word of salvation going forth from Jerusalem to the end of the earth (Ac 1:8) he leaves us at the beginning of a new age, the 'time of the Church'.

ST JOHN

BY DOM RALPH RUSSELL

791a Bibliography—*Commentaries*: Orig PG 14, 21–829; Chrys PG 59, 23–482; Cyr Alex PG 73, 74, 9–756; Aug PL 35, 1379–1976; Bede PL 92, 635–938; B. F. Westcott, 1908; M. J. Lagrange, EtB 1936[5]; J. H. Bernard, ICC 1928; G. H. C. McGregor, 1928; W. Bauer, HNT 1935[3]; F. M. Braun, PCSB 1962[2]; E. C. Hoskyns, 1947; D. Mollat, BJ 1953; C. K. Barrett, 1955; L. Bouyer, 1955; R. H. Lightfoot, 1957; R. Bultmann, 1959[3]; H. Strathmann, NTD 1951[6]; A. Wikenhauser, RNT 1961[3]; R. E. Brown AB (chh 1–12) 1966; R. Schnackenburg 1, 1965; E. tr. 1968; J. Marsh, 1968 J. N. Sanders —
b B. A. Mastin, BNTC, 1968. *Other Literature*; C. F. Burney, *The Aramaic Origin of the Fourth Gospel*, 1922; A. Gordon Smith, *St John and the Synoptic Gospels*, 1938; F. R. Hoare, *The Original Order of St John's Gospel*, 1944; P. H. Menoud, *L'Evangile de Jean, d'après les recherches récentes*, 1947; E. Ruckstuhl, *Die Literarische Einheit des Johannes-evangelium*, 1951; A. H. N. Green-Armytage, *John who Saw*, 1951; H. E. Edwards, *The Disciple who Wrote these Things*, 1953; R. A. Edwards, *The Gospel according to St John*, 1954; W. F. Howard, *The Fourth Gospel in Recent Criticism and Interpretation* (ed. C. K. Barrett), 1955; F. M. Braun, *Jean le Théologien et son Evangile dans l'Eglise ancienne*, 1959; id. *Jean le Théologien; les grands Traditions d'Israel*, 1964; X. Léon-Dufour, *Les Evangiles et l'histoire de Jesus*, 1963; W. J. Leahy, *An Historical and Exegetical Study of Luke-John Relationships*, 1964; RF, E.tr. 1965; W. G. Kümmel, *Introd. NT*, E.tr. NTL, 1966; J. Dupont, *Essais sur la christologie de S. Jean*, 1951; C. H. Dodd, *The Interpretation of the Fourth Gospel*, 1953; F. M. Braun, *La Mère des*
c *Fidèles*, 1954; M. E. Boismard, *The Prologue of St John*, 1957; id *Du Baptême à Cana*, 1956; O. Prunet, *La Morale Chrétienne d'après les écrits johanniques*, 1957; F. L. Crosse (ed.) *Studia Evangelica*, TU, 1957; B. P. W. Statherr-Hunt, *Some Johannine Problems*, 1958; W. Grossouw, *Revelation and Redemption, an Introd. to the Theology of St John*, E.tr. 1958; H. van der Bussche, *Le Discours d'Adieux de Jésus*, 1959; F. X. Durrwell, *The Resurrection*, E.tr. 1960; P. Benoit, *Exégèse et Théologie*, 1960; M. F. Wiles, *The Spiritual Gospel*, 1960; O. Cullmann, *Early Christian Worship*, E.tr. 1962; J. A. T. Robinson, *Twelve NT Studies*, 1962; O. Betz, *Der Paraklet*, 1963; J. Delorme and others, *The Eucharist in the NT*, E.tr.1964; W. F. Albright, 'Recent Discoveries in Palestine and the Gospel of St John' in *The Background of the NT and its Eschatology, Studies in Honour of C. H. Dodd*, 1964; A. Feuillet, *Johannine Studies*, E.tr. 1964; G. M. Behler, *The Last Discourse of Jesus*, E.tr. 1965; J. Crehan. *The Theology of St John*, 1965; N. Lazure, *Les Valeurs morales de la théologie johannique*, 1965; R. E. Brown, *NT Essays*, 1965. For articles, see commentary.

792a Introduction—A gospel proclaims the Good News of salvation, cf Jn 20:31. Like the others, Jn's starts with the Baptist's preaching and recounts miracles and teaching from the life of Jesus, his Passion, his Resurrection

with some appearances, and the Apostolic mission. It **792** therefore belongs to the traditional teaching of the ancient Church. It implies that it is the work of an Apostle-witness (Ac 1:22), present with Jesus from the Baptism of John, who saw him after his Resurrection, Jn 13:23; 15:27; 17:20; 20:20. In place of the synoptists' collection of episodes and words of Jesus, it presents a small number of scenes closely knit together. With concentrated dramatic power it moves progressively from the first revelation of the 'glory' of Jesus (2:11) to its final manifestation in his 'Hour'. As the light grows, the darkness of rejection becomes ever more implacable. John's 'actuality' is concerned not only with events as historical (which are recorded with care), but as decisive for his readers and for us. The Word has come into the world and enlightens every man (1:9); whoever believes in him has eternal life; he who rejects him is condemned (3:16–19). Again, John claims to see things under the retroactive influence of the Spirit. The Apostles did not understand at the time (e.g. 2:22; 12:16; 20:9), and could not until Jesus had been glorified and sent the Spirit, 7:39; 14:25f; 16:7–14. That is why Jn reveals his secrets only at the end, mingles his exposition with the words of Jesus, and projects upon Jesus's actions and words experience from the life of the Church.

The purpose of the gospel has been interpreted in **b** many ways: the 'Spiritual Gospel', written to give Christians a deeper understanding (Clem.Alex., ap. Eus. HE 6, 14, 7); primarily to show Hellenistic non-Christians how the Eternal life it offers fits their previous interests and experience (Dodd, *Int.*, 9); perhaps to satisfy himself, but also to re-affirm the fundamental convictions of the Christian faith in the crisis of early eschatology and Gnosticism (Barrett, 114–7); for the Christian community, with some defence against Jews, Gnostics and disciples of the Baptist (Feine, Michaelis); to show that the Christ of the Church is the historic Jesus and that its sacraments and mission come from him (O. Cullman, *The Early Church*, 186). The elements of truth in these views will be apparent as we proceed.

But the Gospel affirms its own purpose. Luke states **c** his in his preface, Lk 1:1–4. John leads, like a guide to a panorama, to the doubter's profession of faith (Jn 20:29), and ends (ch 21 is an appendix): 'Jesus did many other signs in the presence of the disciples, which are not written in this book; but these are written that you may believe that Jesus is the Christ, the Son of God, and that believing you may have life in his name', (30f.). Let us analyse this (W. C. Van Unnik, 'The Purpose of St John's Gospel', *Studia Evangelica*, TU 18 (1959), 382–411; J. A. T. Robinson 'The Destination and Purpose of St John's Gospel', *Twelve NT Studies* (1962). 'Believe' present subjunctive (best MSS), means 'persevere in believing', and so refers to existing Christians; the verb 'believe' (§ 799d), repeated thrice in 20:25–31, occurs constantly in the Gospel (never the noun: the act of believing is what matters). **'The Christ'** means the

92c Messiah, § 676. 'Christ' in Jn is never a proper name, as with us, unless in 'Jesus Christ', 1:17; 17:3. It takes us at once into the Jewish sphere where alone the title was still significant, like that of 'King of the Jews', 1:49; 12:13; 18:33 37; 19:12, 15, 19ff. Commentators, fascinated by theories of the 'Logos', have given little or no weight to 'the Christ', and in searching for Hellenistic parallels, have failed to notice those from the NT. Paul argues before Jews that Jesus is the Christ, and that he had to suffer and rise again, e.g. Ac 9:20, 22 (same terms as Jn); 13:26ff; 18:5, 28, cf 17:7 'another king'. Therefore this Messiah-formula is rooted in the Christian mission among the Jews, to which John's activities had been directed (Gal 2:9), and where it continued as the standard, decisive topic; cf Just., *Dial.*

d The Jews wanted to know **the relation of the Messiah to the OT**, Jn 1:45; 5:39; Ac 17:11. So throughout the Gospel Jesus is shown to be the Messiah (21 times in Jn to Mt's 17). What he says and does fulfils and transcends the Messianic hopes of his People: he cleanses his Temple, (Jn 2:13—22), is 'the prophet like to Moses' (6), heals the lame and the blind (5 and 9; Is 35:5f), and sets free (61:1; Jn 8:36); he is the Light of the world, that men may not remain in darkness (Jn 1:5, 9; 8:12; 12:46; Is 9:1, 60. 1), the fountain of living water giving drink to his People (Jn 7:37ff; cf ch 4; Ex 17:1—7; Is 55:1; 58:11), the true Shepherd-King (Jn 10; Ezek 34), and he who quickens the dead (Jn 11; Rm 4:17 (a Jewish name for God, SB 1,523t, 593), 'Can this be the Christ?' (4:29).

e Signs—bring or strengthen belief in Jesus. The meaning (Dodd's definition, 'symbols of an unseen reality', is too Platonic), is seen in the OT and in the missionary activity of the early Church. Signs are given by God to point beyond themselves, to manifest his presence and power to save, as symbolic anticipations of a greater reality, or to authenticate a mission, e.g. Ex 3:12; 4:8, 17; 1 (3) Kgs 13:3; Is 8:18; Ezek 4:3; 'signs and wonders' confirm the preaching of the Gospel, e.g. Ac 14:3; 2 Cor 12:12; Heb 2:4. Signs are frequently mentioned in Jn up to 12.37, and lead Jesus's disciples to believe, 2:11. Nicodemus acknowledges that 'no man can do these signs unless God is with him', 3:2. At a deeper level (Ch 5 onwards), they are called 'works', which Jesus shares with his Father. Man's response should not stop at the 'wonder' (4:48), but look where the sign points and so come to believe, 12:37; 15:24. John knows of many more signs (2:23; 3:2; 6:2; 7:31; 11:47), but those he has selected are enough, 20.01.

f **The Son of God** was a Jewish title for the Messiah (1:49) and if they once acknowledge him as Messiah, they can come to believe him when he says he is the Son of God, and that the more from the works he is able to do as the Son of the Father, 5:36f. But his claim to be the divine Son is their greatest stumbling-block 5:18. The transition from 'the Christ' to 'the Son' begins in Ch 5. His assertion of his special relationship with the Father who sent him (e.g. 7:28f; 8:16—19, 26ff, 36ff; 10:30, 36ff) brings on attempts to stone him for blasphemy. The Gospel begins and ends with witness to the Son, §§ 677, 678, 679.

g **Witness** is part of the NT definition of the Apostolic office, Mt 24:14; Lk 24:48; Ac 1:8, 22; 2:32; 1 Cor 1:6. John knows the OT intimately, refers to 'the law', 'the Scriptures', and 'it is written', and shows, like Syn., mostly in the Passion narrative, how Scripture is fulfilled, Jn 12:38; 13:18; 15:25; 17:12; 18:9; 19:24, 36. But mainly he uses the approach of witnesses, which is more direct and accords with Jewish legal mentality. Probably Jn, like Jesus (18:20) and Paul, often argued and preached

his Gospel in synagogues (he is interested in those put **792g** out of them, 9:22; 12:42; 16:1), before setting it in writing. Juridical terms abound: judge, judgement, advocate (Paraclete), convict, accuse, truth as opposed to a lie or a false witness. In the 'trial' which the Gospel seems to present, (cf § 793i), the Baptist's role is simply to witness to Jesus, 1:7, 15, 19ff; 3:26ff; 5:33ff. The Samaritan woman, 4:39, the OT, 5:39, the crowd, 12:17, bear witness. In Jesus's disputes with the Jews a central point is that while a man cannot bear witness for himself, Jesus has that of his Father through the works which he does in his name, 5:31—36; 8:17f; 10:37; 14:10f. In their turn the Apostles, the Beloved Disciple, the guarantors of the Gospel and above all the Paraclete continue the witness, 15:26f; 19:35; 21:24; 1 Jn 1:2; 4:14, cf also on Jn 1:6.

Destination—There are arguments for the view, so **h** different from those held till recently, that the Gospel was not written for pagans, nor in the first place (except perhaps Jn 13—17) for Christians, but for Jews of Palestine or the Diaspora (Unnik, art cit; Robinson, art cit). This 'most Hebraic book in the NT, except perhaps Rev' (J. B. Lightfoot, *Biblical Essays*, 135), 'smells of the soil of Palestine'. Jesus is often called Rabbi (Lk omits the title); Nicodemus, 'the teacher in Israel', is conspicuous, Jn 3; 7:50; 19:39. Jn is concerned with Jewish social and geographical divisions: between the common people and the authorities, the Sanhedrinites and the Pharisees, Jews and Samaritans (e.g. 4:9; 7:13, 25—32, 45—52; 9:22; 12:42), despised Galilee (7:52) and Judaea. He is not concerned with divisions between Jew and Gentile. In the Syn. Jesus is 'a light for revelation to the Gentiles' (Lk 2:32), and even in Mt and Mk we are conscious of them from first (Mt 2:1ff) to last, Mk 15:39. But in John the name 'Gentile' is not mentioned. The Baptist's mission is to reveal Jesus to Israel, Jn 1:21; instead of the Phoenician woman (Mk 7:26ff) and the centurion (Mt 8:10; Mk 15:39), there are the Samaritan woman ('our father Jacob', Jn 4:12) and the court official, reproached as a Jew would be, 4:46ff. There is no favourable comparison of Gentiles with Jews (Mt 11:21), no statement (even in Jn 11:48) that Israel's heritage will go to the Gentiles (Mk 12:9), no mention of the disciples appearing before Gentiles (Mt 10:18), but rather of their being expelled from synagogues, Jn 16:1. Jesus, a Jew (4:9), distinguishes Jews from Samaritans as 'we' and declares 'salvation is from the Jews', 4:22. The many Jews who believe in him (2:23, 7:31, 8:31; 10:42; 11:45; 12:11), if they 'abide in him' and follow him (8:31; 10:27) become the true Jews (Rev 2:9; 3:9), sons of Abraham not by the flesh, but by birth from above, from God Jn 3:58. Just so Paul speaks of true Jews, true sons of Abraham (Rm 2:17—29; 4:9—22), when he is asking what is involved for a Jew in becoming a Christian.

Then it is Jewish ideas and institutions which Jesus **i** transforms and transcends: the Law's word of wisdom into the eternal Word Incarnate (Jn 1:1—17), the water of Jewish rite into the abundant wine of the Gospel (2:10), the Temple into the sanctuary of his body (2:21), birth from Abraham into birth from on high (which admits to a Kingdom, unlike that of Jewish apocalyptic, 'not of this world', 1:12; 3; 8:33; 18:36f), the unsatisfying waters of Jacob's well into the living water of the Spirit enabling true worshippers to adore, no longer at Jerusalem, but 'in spirit and in truth' (4:13f, 20—24; 7:37ff), perishable manna into bread from heaven giving eternal life, 6: 49—58.

Then why are 'the Jews' (66 or 67 times in Jn) **j** generally the enemies of Jesus? This is no Gentile

792j triumphalism. The term, as used for those who reject the Messiah, envisages especially the rulers on whom rested the chief blame, cf 7:13, with 25—32, 48f; 9:22, cf 12:19. That the rulers of the Jews rejected Jesus through malice, but the people through ignorance, and that God decreed the death of their Messiah to open salvation to all, was a Christian theme (Ac 2:23; 3:13f, 17ff; 13:26ff; Jn 11:50ff; 18:38—19:16), and persecutors are called 'the Jews', even in Judaea, 1 Thes 2:14. That Jesus comes 'to his own' (Jn 1:9) and is delivered by them to death (18:35), is the tragedy. But if John's Gospel was first preached in Judaea and the Diaspora, the non-converted would be called 'the Jews'; further, in Jn the ever-contemporary enemy becomes 'the world', 1:10; 7:4, 7; 14:19, 22; 18:20; 1 Jn *passim*.

k For Jn is completely universalistic and certainly in its final form the Gospel is for all. Jesus is 'the Lamb of God who takes away the sin of the world' Jn 1:29, 'the light that enlightens every man', who 'gave power to all who received him to become children of God' (1:9, 12, exactly as Rm 3:22), 'the Saviour of the world', Jn 4:42. The effect of his redemptive death is universal. Lifted upon the Cross, he draws to himself all who 'see' him and believe in him as their Saviour, 'for God so loved the world that he gave his only Son that whoever believes in him should . . . have eternal life', 3:14—17; 12:32, cf 6:40; 11:51f; 1 Jn 2:2. Those who believe in the word of the Apostles are to be one 'that the world may believe that thou hast sent me', Jn 17:21. Even if the 'Greeks' of 7:35; 12:20ff were Diaspora Jews (H. Windisch *Hellēn*, TWNT 2, 506, but K. L. Schmidt *Diaspora*, 102 leaves open that they might be Gentiles), the word meant 'pagans' when the Gospel was finally written down. Their solemn introduction illustrates 'the whole world has gone after him' (12:19ff), and occasions Jesus' declarations on the glorification of the Son of Man and the dying grain of wheat bringing forth much fruit. Finally, Jesus brings 'the other sheep that are not of this fold' not into the Jewish fold but into the flock which he leads to eternal life, 10:18, (BJ). Of the universalism of 1 Jn there is no doubt.

l Therefore Jn shows signs both of being directed to Jews and of universalism. The latter is re-inforced by the translation into Gr. of elementary words such as Rabbi (Jn 1:38), and Messiah (1:41), and of the name Cephas, (1:42); by the explanation of Jewish ways of purification (2:6), burial (19:40), relations with Samaritans (4:9) and the Passover as the feast of the Jews (6:4), besides topographical details in Jerusalem: Bethesda (5:2), Lithostrotos, 19:13. The hypothesis which does justice to both factors is that there are various strata in the Gospel. It was for long preached 'among the circumcision' (cf Gal 2:9). It was finally written down, probably in the traditional site of Gr.-speaking Ephesus, and for everyone.

793a **A Liturgical and Sacramental Gospel** took shape as preached in these early communities. Jn addresses them directly: 'that believing you may have life in his name' (20:31), 'there came out blood and water. He who saw it has borne witness . . . that you also may believe', 19:24f, cf 1 Jn 1:1—4; 5:6ff. The Gospel showed them Jesus, not only as Messiah and Son of God, but as present in their communities by word and sacrament, the same historical Jesus who by the paschal mystery of his death and resurrection is the Mediator of God's plan of salvation in the OT, in his time on earth, and now in the Church (F. X. Durrwell, *The Resurrection*, 13ff; O. Cullmann, *Early Christian Worship*, 37—119 and R. Brown, 'The Johannine Sacramentary', *NT Essays*, 51—76 for criteria). In selected events, without surrender of historic truth

(which would have contradicted his witness), Jn brought **793a** home to his hearers their sacramental life as it came from the Jesus whom they did not see but in whom they believed. Syn. recount the commands to baptize and to repeat the Supper; Paul connects both sacraments with the Redemption; Jn links their origins with events in the life of Jesus, the significance of which he interprets by the light of the Spirit.

(a) **Connections with the OT** are sometimes explicit **b** (e.g. 12:15f) but more usually inferred. Gn lies behind the first part of the Prologue (Gn 1:1—5; Jn 1:1—5) and behind the real, if hidden opposition between Jesus and the 'prince of this world', liar and murderer from the beginning (Jn 8:44; Gn 2:17; 3:4, cf Rev 12:9), cast down (Jn 12:31) at the hour when the Seed of the Woman (Gn 3:17) wins the final victory, with which the 'Mother of all the living' is associated, 3:20; Jn 19:26f; Rev 12. The second part of the Prologue and thereafter the whole Gospel are set against the backcloth of Ex. The Word made flesh '*tabernacled amongst us*' (Ex 25:8); 'we saw his glory, full of grace and truth' (33:18; 34:6). The Son's revelation is contrasted with Moses and the Law, and with 'no man has seen God', 33:20. Like the brazen serpent, Christ must be lifted up (Jn 3:14; Nm 21:4—9); like the manna, he comes down from heaven as food (Jn 6:25—58, note 'murmuring', Ex 16); like the rock, he gives drink (Jn 7:37ff; Ex 17:1—7); like the pillar of fire, the Light leads them (13:21f; Jn 8:12; 12:35). He manifests himself to them (14:21; Ex 33:18f) as 'I am', (Ex 3:14); Jn *passim*. He enacts the real Passover, the 'Passage of the Lord' from captivity to liberty (Jn 8:31—36), from death to life, when having given 'a new commandment' (13:34; Ex 20), he 'passes from this world to the Father', (13:1; 16:28;) as the Paschal Lamb he dies, (19:36; Ex 12:46).

(b) Jn signposts the dynamic movement of **the c Paschal theme**, repeated and perfected **in the life of Jesus**, by the three 'Passovers of the Jews': the first (Jn 2:13ff) connects Jesus's cleansing of the Temple with the prophecy that after his death it will be succeeded by the sanctuary of his risen Body; the second is 'at hand' (6:4) when the feeding of the five thousand and the discourse on the Bread of Life (Jesus's flesh offered for the life of the world), presage the paschal Mystery and the Supper; the third, mentioned continually from 11:55 onwards, is Jesus's 'Hour', when, lifted upon the Cross, he will draw all to himself (12:31f), receive back the glory which he had given up during his time on earth (17:1, 5) and grant eternal life to all who believe in him, 3:14ff. These Passovers provide the setting and indicate the themes of principal activities and discourses of Jesus, as do also 'a feast of the Jews'. (probably Pentecost), Tabernacles and Dedication, 5:1; 7:2ff; 10:22. The Jewish liturgical framework is reinforced by the images used (lamb, water, wine, temple, bread, shepherd, vine), and by the drama in conflict of God and the world, light and darkness.

(c) **The sacraments** are facts of salvation particularly **d** relevant to the selected 'signs'. Jn takes great interest in water. A line goes from the baptism administered by John and Jesus's own baptism to the baptism given by Jesus and baptism in the early communities. There is no baptism of John independent of Christ's (cf Ac 19:3f) and the Baptist, who is no more than a witness to Jesus (Jn 1:8), himself declares that it is Jesus who takes away the sin of the world and baptizes with the Holy Spirit, 1:15, 25—33. The changing of the water of Jewish purification into wine at the wedding at Cana is a Messianic sign presaging Christ's 'hour' (2:4), and probably the Eucharist. Allusion to baptism in ch 5 is

793d doubtful: in place of occasional healing in miraculous waters, Jesus, the giver of life, by a resurrectional word (5:1, 8, 21, cf 25—39) cures 'the whole man' (7:21, 24) and warns him not to sin again, 5:14. However, in ch 9, traditionally associated with baptism, (the 'Enlightenment', Heb. 6:4; 10:32), the Light of the world (8:12; 9:5) gives light by healing the man born blind through washing in Siloam ('Sent', standing for Jesus); the baptismal ritual is suggested in the dialogue between Jesus and the man, and it is perhaps implied that those who humbly acknowledge their sins, receive baptismal forgiveness (35—39). One of the two interpretations of the washing of the feet is baptismal (cf on 13:1ff). The Eucharist is certainly envisaged in ch 6, the allegory of the Vine in the Last Discourse, with its constant mention of 'abiding' in Jesus (15:1ff), corresponds closely, and the atmosphere is conveyed in the new commandment of love. The Sacerdotal Prayer asks that the Apostles too may be consecrated in truth (17:19), and the Holy Spirit, promised at the Supper (14:16, 26; 16:7ff), and figured in the water flowing from the Crucified (19:34, cf 7:39), is given to them after the Resurrection, together with the power to remit sins, 20:22f. On Bultmann's elimination of the sacramental passages from the Gospel, cf § 794b and R. Brown, *Jn* (Anchor Bible), xxix—xxxii.

e Jn and Syn.—Jn's symbolism used to be contrasted with the historicity of Syn., of which he was supposed to be ignorant. For: (a) The episodes of Jn 1—4 are missing from Syn. But in 3:24 the Baptist is still at liberty and the Syn. account of Jesus's Galilaean ministry starts after his arrest (Mk 1:14); besides, the Apostles' previous meetings with Jesus alone explain their immediate answer to his call, Mt 4:18—22, paral. (b) Jn omits the preaching of the Kingdom and the parables. But he knows of them, Jn 3:3; 16:25, 29. (c) Jn centres Jesus's activity in Judaea and Jerusalem, Syn. in Galilee. But Jn supplies the motive for Jesus leaving Judaea, 4:1ff, and Syn. pre-suppose frequent preaching there (Lk 4:44, best reading, cf 7:17) and in Jerusalem (Mt 23:37ff, par.) before the Passion. (d) In Jn Jesus appears to reveal himself at once to believing disciples (Jn 1:41), whereas in Syn. the 'Messianic Secret' is important. But Jn 10:24 implies it, Jesus breaks it only in Samaria (cf on 4:26), and perhaps to an outcast (9:35ff), and the disciples are slow to believe. In fact, Jn assumes that his readers know the Syn. tradition, e.g. he omits the baptism of Jesus, the choice of the Twelve (6:70; 15:16; 20:24), the manner of Judas's treason (6:64; 12:6; 13:2, 27), and lets pass Jesus's supposed origin, 1:45; 6:42; 19:19. Other allusions or transpositions are: Christian baptism (3:5), the institution of the Eucharist (6), the Transfiguration (1:14; 12:28ff), the judgement of the Sanhedrin (7—8), the agony (12:27), the Ascension, 20:17.

f Nowadays the question is whether Jn depended on Syn. His direct knowledge of them was denied by P. Gardner-Smith, and affirmed by e.g. R. H. Lightfoot, Hoskyns (87), Barrett, for Mk (34), H. F. D. Sparks (JTS 3 (1952), 58—61), for Mt. But 'behind Jn lies an ancient tradition independent of the other Gospels' (Dodd, HT, 423). Since the rise of Form Criticism, others hold that Jn knew Syn. not in writing but in tradition. 'Jn is both a gospel in its own right and also a master-commentary on an existing and familiar tradition about Jesus' (H. Balmforth, 'The Structure of the Fourth Gospel', *Stud. Ev.* 2, TU 87 (1964), 25—33, who holds that direct literary dependence on Mk, whose structural themes Jn maintains, cannot be proved or disproved). L. Dufour concludes an exhaustive study on the relation of Jn with Syn. in the Passion narrative ('Passion', DBS, 6, 1438—

44): Jn knew Syn. not in writing but in tradition (perhaps **793f** partially edited), he wrote with complete liberty, his contacts with Mt-Mk, especially Mt, are not negligible, but he is much closer to the Lk tradition. In fact the many points of contact, literary, historical and theological, with Lk (more than 40 in the Passion narrative, E. Osty, in *Mél Lebreton*, 1, 146—54) seem to show that it was Lk who knew the Joh. tradition (Lk 1:2 'eyewitnesses'), cf W. K. Leahy, *An Historical and Exegetical Study of Luke-John Relationships* (Rome, 1964); so the influence came from Jn, cf Mollat, BJ, 37—40; F.-M. Braun, *La Mère des Fidèles*, 27—30; H. Laurentin, *Structure et Théologie de Luc I—II*; P. Benoit 'Marie-Madeleine et les Disciples au Tombeau selon Jn 20:1—18', *Judentum Urchristum* **g** *Kirche*, 141—52.

But we hold that the final author of Jn took account of Lk, for where they overlap, he often adds details as from an eyewitness, e.g. they alone mention Martha and Mary, (Lk 10:38f; Jn 11:1; 12:1f, adding Bethany); Satan's part in Judas's treachery (Lk 22:3; Jn 13:2, 27, with details); the traitor denounced after the Eucharist (Lk 22:21; Jn 13:18, 'who ate my bread', cf 6:54, 70); Jesus's custom to go to the Mt of Olives (Lk 22:39; Jn 18:2, 'frequently', 'Judas knew the place'); the right ear (Lk 22:50; Jn 18:10, Peter and Malchus); Annas as high priest (Lk 3:2; Ac 4:6; Jn 18:13, 'the father-in-law of Caiphas'); the official trial held elsewhere (implied, Lk 22:66; explicit, Jn 18:24, 28, 'bound'); Pilate's triple declaration of Jesus's innocence (Lk 23:4, 14, 22; Jn 18:38; 19:4, 6, with much detail); the tomb where no one had yet been laid (Lk 23:53; Jn 19:41f, 'in the garden', 'close at hand'); also Lk 24:12, 24 and Jn 20:3—10, etc. This, together with Jn's contacts with Mt and Mk, seems to make impossible the view of M.-É. Boismard that Lk was the final redactor of Jn, (RB (1962), 185—211; etc). Jn 4:44f (? editorial) cites the saying of Jesus at Nazareth in Gr. which echoes Lk 4:24, but also Mt 13:57; Mk 6:4. The anointing of Jn 12:1—8 seems written in terms of Mk 14:3—7; Lk 7:38. The Prologue suggests Lk's Infancy Gospel: the surprising insertion on the Baptist and his name (Jn 1:6ff) corresponds to Lk 1:13ff; 'the light that enlightens every man' and 'glory' (Jn 1:9, 14) call to mind Lk 2:32; 'his own received him not' (Jn 1:11) could refer to Lk 2:7; the probable allusion in Jn 1:13, (cf 1 Jn 5:18b), and '*the Word . . . pitched his tent amongst us . . . glory as of an only Son*' suggests Lk 1:34f

The Historicity of Jn is taken more seriously now; **h** it is seen that the Syn., while historically based, are theologically organized and owe much to transmission. They cannot be taken as a yardstick to measure Jn, who sometimes shows signs of being the more primitive. Beneath the surface resemblances show signs of being deeper than differences; cf J. A. T. Robinson, 'The New Look on the Fourth Gospel', *Stud. Ev.* TU 73 (1959), 338—50; R. E. Brown, 'The Problem of Historicity in John', CBQ 24 (1962), 1—15.

But the **differences** are obvious. The concrete, living images of Christ's teaching in Syn. change to abstract, doctrinal language. Everything is brought to its essential point. The Kingdom is seen from the inside in terms of light, life and truth (Jn 18:37). Jn knows of the legalistic discussions with the Jews on e.g. Sabbath-breaking (5:16; 7:23f), but the crucial topic is belief in Jesus as sent by the Father and Son of God. The 'works of God' are reduced to one: belief in him (6:28f); the commandments to 'love one another as I have loved you', 15:12. Jn knows of many miracles (6:2; 12:37; 20:30) but selects a few, and they not as 'wonders' (4:48) but 'signs' or 'works' manifesting the sending of Jesus by the Father and

793h his 'glory', e.g. 2:11; 3:2; 5:36; 11:4, 40; other actions, like the cleansing of the Temple, are equally 'signs'. The portrait of Jesus, tender and human though it is (4:6; 11:5; 13:4ff, 23) concentrates upon the final reality of his Person.

i **But Jn is not only a theological meditation,** Jesus's life in symbolic form, cf D. Mollat in BJ: (1) This Gospel sets out to prove by 'signs' that Jesus is the Messiah, the Son of God, 20:30f. Were the 'signs' un-historical, the design would be contradicted. (2) Jn, like 1 Jn, is opposing those who denied the Incarnation. He must show the Word made flesh really involved in human history. (3) The value of the claim to witness (19:35, cf 15:27) depends on having seen what really happened. (4) The arguments between Jesus and his opponents are authentically Jewish, e.g. over action on the Sabbath Jesus cites the uninterrupted divine activity discussed in the rabbinic schools (5) and appeals to the admitted exception for circumcision (7:23); the true sons of Abraham (with Palestinian colouring: 'You are a Samaritan', 8:31—59); the Scriptural arguments of 3:14; 6:31, and the rabbinic one of 10:32—36. (5) **The Gospel is a kind of vast law-suit** between the Jews (or 'the world') and Jesus. Starting with the commission of enquiry (1:19ff), it unfolds the story. Chh 5, 7, 8 specially are like a judicial process: the Jews prosecute Jesus for claiming to be the Son of God (5:18; 8:13—18), and Jesus reverses the situation, so that Moses accuses the Jews (5:45ff), who are proved no true sons of Abraham, 8:39ff. Before Jesus is finally con-demned, 'according to the Law' (19:7), he has declared the condemnation of the world with its prince (12:31), his own victory (16:33) and the coming of the Spirit to overturn the world's judgement, 16:7—11. The Gospel is thus a kind of re-trial after an unjust sentence, Jn putting in as witnesses the Baptist (1:20—28; 3:26ff; 5:33f; 10:41), the 'works' of Jesus showing his divine origin (5:32, 36f; 10:25, 37f; 14:10f), the Scriptures (e.g. 5:39) and himself (19:35), all under the Spirit's guidance. A judicial process in reverse is also suggested in the Judgement made actual by the presence of the Son of Man, which starts from the House of God (2:13—22) and continues through the Gospel. In all this, unhistorical testimony would be irreverent folly.

j **Jn's space indications** illustrate his combination of fact with symbol (D. Mollat, 'Remarques sur le vocabulaire spatial du quatrième évangile', *Stud. Ev.*, TU 5, 18 (1959), 321—8). Precise, geographical, and confirmed on various points by archaeology (Aenon near Salim, 3:23, Bethesda, 5:2, Lithostrotos, 19:13), they are often introduced by 'this happened in', (e.g. Cana of Galilee, 2:1; 4:46; 21:2, showing Jn knew of another Cana; Bethany near Jerusalem 'about 25 stades away', 11:18). Yet they acquire theological meanings. Nazareth and Galilee stand for the 'scandal' of the misunderstood reality of the flesh contrasted with Jesus's real origin, 1:45; 6:38, 42; 7:28f, 41, 52; 18:5—8 (the contemptuous 'Jesus of Nazareth' and the glory of 'I am'); 19:19 (The Nazarene, the king of the Jews). The Jordan valley, where John baptized and witnessed, and Jesus ended his public life, 'and many believed in him there' (10:40ff), confronts Jerusalem's infidelity. Samaria, with its heretic village below Gerizim, where Jesus declares that the conflict of temples will be ended by adoration in spirit and truth (4:23f) and the ripening fields of corn betoken the coming harvest (35, 42), is symbol of the non-Jewish world. In sinister Judaea, Jesus's native land which rejects him, his life is in danger; he will go thither when his 'moment' is come, 4:3, 44; 7:1—8; 11:7—16. Jerusalem, centre of Israel, and Messianic (12:12—19) city of un-peace,

sends out its embassy to the Baptist (1:19f; 5:33) and **79** makes its great refusal. Jesus goes forth from its Temple (8:59) and from its walls to Calvary, 19:17. The Temple, 'house of my Father' (2:16), 'place' (11:48) of OT ador-ation, where Isaiah saw Jesus's glory (12:41), whence has come salvation (4:22), whither the world assembles and hears Jesus's revelation not made 'hiddenly' as in Galilee (7:4; 12:19f; 18:20), must give way to the glorified body of Jesus, 2:19f. The living waters of the Spirit will flow from the crucified Saviour (7:37ff; 19:34; Zech 14:8f) into the whole world, the new Johannine space of which Jesus is the Light (3:19; 8:12; 12:46), which will go after him (12:19) when, lifted from the earth, he draws all to him-self, 32.

Jn's time indications are also precise: 'About the **k** tenth hour' (1:39), 'about the sixth hour' (4:6; 19:14); the 46 years of the building of the Temple, cf on 2:20; his dating of the Passover is now more usually accepted. But again there is symbolism: 'it was winter' (10:23); 'it was night' (13:30).

The historical setting is that Palestine which was **l** blotted out in A.D. 70: Jews and Samaritans with their mutual hatred (4:9; 8:48), despised Galilee under its king (4:46; 7:52), its crowds ready for a Messianic adventure (6:14f), pilgrims and pious proselytes going up to the holy city for the feasts (11:55; 12:20), the partly built Temple with its money-changers and merchants (2:13ff, 20), the Pharisees disdainful of the crowd 'who do not know the Law' (7:49), the Romans' yoke, 18:28—31. It is the Jewish world with its religious customs, purifications (2:6; 3:25; 11:55), and burials, 11:38, 44; 12:7; 19:31, 40 (BJ).

Yet Jn's historicity has limits, for he is not writing **m** a history but a Gospel. He omits much, 20:30f. Thus we cannot be sure of a chronology based on Jewish feasts—except for the three Passovers—for we do not know what may be omitted. Again, when Jn puts the cleansing of the Temple at the beginning of Jesus's public life (2:13, contrast Syn.) the chronology is probably correct, but not certainly, for he may have put it there for theological reasons. There is theological intention in the order of chh 5, 6 and 7, but this probably involves breaking off the discourse of ch 5 and continuing it in ch 7. Finally, a disciple editor may have inserted some pieces where he could, e.g. 2:12; 4:44.

The Discourses in the Synoptics group sayings **79** together, Jn takes definite themes: the living water (4), the unity in action of the Father and the Son (5), the Bread of Life, 6. They are closely bound to facts: Jacob's well, the cure of the paralytic, the multiplication of bread, the feast of Tabernacles, etc. In Syn. Jesus is not inter-rupted, though there must have been interruptions from unintelligent disciples or enemies. In Jn he is often inter-rupted by crassly material or malicious questions which conform to literary type and keep the dialogue going: The scheme: first revelation—question—second revel-ation, is found in apocalyptic literature (e.g. Dn) and in the explanation of parables, cf L. Cerfaux, 'La connaissance des secrets du royaume d'après Mt 13:11 et par.', NTS 2 (1955—6), 238—49. Jn has the enigmatic saying, the misapprehension (by 'the flesh', human intelligence with-out the Spirit, sometimes refusing, sometimes on the way to the Light), and the explanation, cf 3:3—13; 4:10ff, 32ff; 5:17—23; 6; 7:33ff; 8:21ff, 31—59; 14:4ff (cf *idem*, 'La thème littéraire parabolique dans l'Évangile de saint Jean', ConjNT 11 (1947), 15—25). Yet the speeches are not simply Jn's speculation. He was far too intent on the Word of God to want to do other than give the deep meaning of Christ's acts and sayings, mediated

94a under the influence of the Spirit and preached during a long life. No ancient author would have tried to reproduce the words exactly, but there are pithy, lapidary phrases of Jesus in the same vein as in Syn.: 2:19; 5:17 ('my Father is working still and I am working'); 10:11; 12:24; 13:16; 16:21; 20:29, cf C. H. Dodd, 'Some Johannine *Herrnworte* with Parallels in the Synoptic Gospels', NTS 2 (1955), 75—86. However, Jesus more often speaks a different, doctrinal language, and that not only to theologians but with the same depth and in much the same way to simple people, 4:7—26; 6; 12:23—36. This is also the language of the Baptist (1:29ff; 3:27—30) and of 1 Jn. It is natural to conclude that Jn lends Jesus his own way of expression. Yet now that we know from Qumran that this way was not Hellenism but in use in Palestine, it becomes the more likely that he caught his Master's accents and style. At the least, if we accept Jn as the Beloved Disciple (see § 796b), privileged witness and interpreter, we shall not think that he misunderstood his meaning, or easily attribute the most sublime sayings to the disciple rather than to the Master, cf RF, E.tr. 1965, 654—6. The Discourses are ascribed by Bultmann to an originally Gnostic source of 'revelation discourses' which the evangelist modified and adapted to his purpose, see § 794b. Nevertheless the Johannine stamp on them is so clear that the question of sources must remain unresolved. Does the Johannine character disprove the use of sources or prove that Jn thoroughly assimilated his material? Perhaps the solution lies, as Kümmel suggests, in thinking of oral tradition as a source rather than written documents apart from the Syn. see *Introd. NT*, 152—4. Kümmel however appears to go too far in saying 'the Gnostic language of the Johannine Jesus-discourses makes impossible the composition of John by an eyewitness', ibid 170.

b Literary Criticism of the Gospel (see M. Laconi, 'La Critica letteraria applicata al IV Vangelo', Angelicum 40 (1963) 277—312). Additions to the primitive text are generally recognized to be:

(1) **The Woman taken in Adultery** (7:53—8:11). This is omitted by most old Gr. MSS and the most ancient versions; it is marked in some MSS as of doubtful authenticity or placed at the end of the Gospel or even put after Lk 21:38. The Gr. Fathers do not comment on it; Tert. and Cyp. seem not to know it; the text has many variants; the irony is Johannine but the style and language nearer to Luke. Its wide acceptance (D, many cursives, Boh, Vg, and among early writers, Papias (apparently, Eus.HE, 3 39) Amb., Jer. and Aug.) points to its being an authentic part of the Gospel tradition, perhaps omitted (Aug., De Conj. Adult. 2.6) because Jesus seemed too lenient. The Council of Trent implied canonicity without deciding authorship. Lk could be the author.

(2) **The angel moving the waters** (5:3b—4). This passage is omitted by the best Gr. MSS and many others. 4 is regarded as a gloss ('Je n'aime pas cet ange-là,' Lagrange is reported to have said) and 3b is doubtful at best, see § 806b.

(3) **Ch 21**, though never separate in the MSS and of fully attested authenticity, is **an appendix** and may be an editor's addition, cf § 820a. Apart from these, is the Gospel an integral unity or can it be dismembered and analysed into sources? **Bultmann**, in particular, distinguished, first, a miracle or *semeion* source containing accounts of various miracles and signs wrought by Jesus, secondly, a source of 'revelation discourses' which formed the basis for Jn's reports of Jesus's speeches, and thirdly, a collection of passion and resurrection narratives, see

§ 794a above and comments there. But E. Schweizer **794b** (*Ego Eimi*, 1939) found 33 literary formulae in all sections corresponding to Bultmann's sources and, continuing Schweizer's work, P. H. Menoud and E. Ruckstuhl showed 51 well-marked characteristics covering all the Sections (summarized, Braun, *Jean le Théologien*, App. 1). Thus the Gospel's literary unity receives support from the very work endeavouring to dissect it (C. H. Dodd, JTS 44 (1943) 88—90). These results are confirmed by the development throughout the Gospel of characteristic doctrinal themes: light, life, truth, witness, belief, love—as opposed to darkness, blindness death, the lie, refusal to believe, hatred.

The importance of numbers in binding the Gospel **c** together is doubtful. Take the number 7. There are seven days from the Baptist's witness to Cana, 7 miracles, 7 testimonies (i.e. of the Baptist, Jesus, works, Bible, the Father, Apostles, the Paraclete), 7 journeys in Palestine, and certain phrases or words occur 7 times: e.g. 'love', 'I am'. But some of these figures can be queried (Braun, op cit 13—16; Van den Bussche, art cit 67—76; Barrett, 242, 282): the 7 days are not sure and not stressed; walking on the water may be joined to the multiplication of loaves to make only six miracles; 'I am' with predicate occurs 7 times but absolutely in 6:20—and note 8:24, 28; 13:19. Deeper study is needed on all this, and perhaps on the symbolism of 6 (7—1 = imperfection, 2:6), 8 (7 + 1 = plenitude, Christ rises on the 8th day of the new week, 12:1—20:1), 3 (resurrection symbol) and even 153 (J. A. Emerton, JTS 9 (1958) 86—89). Jn gives his work consistency by more evident methods.

Inclusion is a literary form setting limits to a **d** passage by a repetition or antithesis which relates its end to its beginning. This key to interpretation recurs in little sections (e.g. the Prologue, 1:1—18, the Baptist's witness, 19—34, the sign of Cana, 2:1—11, the cleansing of the Temple, 2:13—23, the healing of the official's son, 4:43—54 and of the blind man, 9:1—41), in big blocks ('Cana of Galilee', 2:11—4:46, the beginning and end of the public life, 1:28—10:40), the whole Gospel ('God', 1:1—20:28, 'life for those who believe in his name', 1:4, 12—20:21) and in group-inclusions in the less strict sense of early texts given full meaning at the end ('the Lamb of God', 1:29—19:36, 'he who baptizes in the Holy Spirit', 1:33—20:22, 'the mother of Jesus . . . woman . . . my hour—his mother . . . woman . . . from that hour', 2.1, 4—19.25ff).

Further, **events are bound together** 'like tiles on a **e** roof', e.g. the Baptist's witness is anticipated, 1:6f, 15, and recalled, 3:28; 3:23 is recalled by 4:1, 2:23 by 4:45, and 4:14 by 7:37; 7:21ff refers to 5:9 and 7:50 explicitly to 3:1ff; 10:21 goes back to ch 9; the Good Shepherd allegory (10:1—18) re-appears in 10:26—29; the mention of Lazarus and the witnessing crowd links 11 with 12:1, 17; 13:33 refers to 7:34 and 8:21; 18:14 to 11:50; 19:19 recalls the Nazareth and royalty themes, cf 12:12—15; 18:33—37.

Yet **incoherences and difficulties** show this unity to **f** be far from rigid: the Gospel ends at 20:31 but continues in 21 with a second epilogue; after 'arise, let us go hence' (14:31) the Supper Discourse contains 15—17, Jesus going forth only at 18:1; the Good Shepherd discourse re-appears after some months (10:27ff); Jesus hides in 12:36 and 37—43 concludes the first part of the book, but in 44—50 he speaks again; the discourse in 5 would normally conclude with 7:19—24; there are apparent contradictions: Jesus baptizes and does not (3:26; 4:2); 'who is seeking to kill you?' and 'is not this the man

794f going?' and 'none of you asks me, "where are you going"' (13:36; 16:5). For particulars, cf commentary. The overall picture is a human composition with **a long formation**. The first oral teaching would be enlarged and deepened to accumulate later material. Probably the discourses were composed first (perhaps growing from 'I am' sayings) and Bultmann rightly distinguishes their origin from the episodes with which they are sometimes artificially united (3:31—36). Though the style is Johannine throughout, there are traces (*kai* in 1, 2, *oun* in later chh, (Boismard, RB 59 (1952), 427) of evolution here too. Thus the Gospel reflects the teaching of a life-time with 're-touches, additions, complements, resumptions, diverse editings of the same teaching' (Mollat, BJ, 26). Moreover some vv, sections and chh which seem to break an already formed text, appear to be *editorial additions*, made perhaps after Jn's death, to preserve (since ideas and form remain Johannine) other parts of the tradition. Chief among these is 15—17, inserted between 14:31 and 18:1, 16 being another version of 14; cf also 4:43—45; perhaps 12:24—26; 18:19—22; 20:2—11. Editorial too may be brief explanatory notes, e.g. 4:2, 9*b*, 25; 11:2; 19:13, 31, and the back references mentioned above, e.g. 4:45; 18:14.

g But unless the style differs (5:4; 11:2) **the editor could be Jn himself**, working out later layers of his own sacramental tradition (3:5; 13:1—15) or realized eschatology (5:25 and 28f). This holds e.g. for the doublets in 3, 5, 7—8 which are deliberately composed to enrich each other: in 3:11—18, 31—36 either doublet is basically three little strophes of which the former two criss-cross (11 with 32, 13 with 31) and the third corresponds directly (15—33), while in 5:21—25, 26—27, 21 corresponds to 26, 22 to 27, 24—25 criss-cross with 28—29, etc. (Láconi, art cit; cf further, Brown, XXIV—XL). The personal meditations of Jn, penetrating deep into the sayings of Jesus, are a highly important element in the formation of the Gospel. In view of all this, the dislocations of text supposed, against the MSS, by Bultmann and others, need sturdier proof, as does the view (F. R. Hoare) that the original sheets got displaced.

h Language and Expression—The view that the Gospel was originally written in Aram. (C. F. Burney, *The Aram. Origin of the Fourth Gospel*, 1922; C. Torrey, 'The Aram. of the Gospel of Jn', HTR (1923) 305—44), though it has not won general acceptance, has gained a new argument for certain passages, especially words of Christ, where the textual variants seem different translations of one Aram. original (M. É. Boismard, 'Importance de la critique textuelle pour établir l'origine araméenne du quatrième évangile', *L'Év. de Jean* 1—57). This is another clue to the gradual formation of the Gospel. But Jn's generally correct, simple Gr. is not like a translation. He uses terms and double senses which have no Aram. equivalents, and his alleged mistranslations from Aram. are not proved. However he was accustomed to think in Aram. as well as in Gr. He translates words like Cephas and Gabbatha into Gr. He is fond of Semitic constructions, e.g. parataxis ('he spat . . . and made . . . and anointed . . . and said', 9:6), or the redundant pronoun after a relative (13:26—though these also occur in the *Koine*). He uses Aram. and Heb. parallelism (e.g. 6:35), and the strophic arrangement and assonance of Aram. poetry, e.g. in 3:29f (M. Black, *An Aram. Approach to the Gospels*, 109). Most significant is his vocabulary, especially when echoing his Master: 'Truly truly I say to you', 'What to me and to you' (2:4), 'see' as 'rejoice in' (3:3; 8:52); 'answered and said' (2:18, etc), 'walk' of

moral conduct (8:12, etc), 'come in and go out' (10:9), **794** 'sons of' (12:36), 'give' in a wide sense (3:35; 5:36; 7:22), especially of God's gratuitous love (15 times in the Priestly Prayer), 'name' (17:11, etc), 'hand' for power (3:35; 10:28f), 'put into the heart' (13:2), 'the flesh', 'flesh and blood', 'flesh and spirit', 'be lifted up', 'have no part in', 13:8, etc (J. Bonsirven, 'Les aramaïsmes de S. Jean l'Evangeliste', Bib 30 (1949), 405—432).

Jn's ways of expression differ greatly from ours. **i** His words are comparatively few and ordinary, his favourites recurring constantly. We use conceptual, abstract terms. He works with representations which have not lost their concreteness. 'God is unlimited perfection, the source of all grace' becomes 'God is light and in him there is no darkness' (1 Jn 1:5) and 'I am the vine, you the branches', Jn 15:5. 'The truth' is not a logical concept, but the realization of God in Christ. Our syllogistic Gr. reasoning develops in a linear direction. Jn, a Semite and a contemplative, does not reason, he bears witness; he sets his reader directly in front of Christ and moves around this central point (concentric thinking), trying to approach ever closer (spiral thinking), e.g. 6:52—57. His images representing the total Christ are not sharply delineated, as in abstract thought, but open to many shades of meaning (e.g. 'light' in 3:19ff) and interchangeable ('the light was the life of men', 1:4), (W. Grossouw, *Revelation and Redemption*, 8—17).

The Gospel of the Spirit—Because Jn knows that both **j** he and his readers are inspired by the Paraclete (14:26; 16:12ff; 1 Jn 2:20, 27), he sees, and expects them to see, the saving meaning of the events he selects. Sometimes he states explicitly that the disciples did not understand until after Christ's glorification (2:19, 22; 12:12—16; 20:9), when the Spirit was given, 7:39. Exegesis of Jn must take account both of events and of their relation to God's ever-present, saving work. The original witnesses really did see (11:15; 19:35; 20:8; 1 Jn 1:1), but bodily sight is not enough unless followed by believing, 6:30, 36, 40; 7:3, 5; 11:45f; 20:29. It is possible to 'see and not see', 9:39; 14:9, 19f. Inversely, 'if you believe, you will see the glory of God', 11:40, cf 1:14, 51; so for hearing: the voice comes from heaven for the sake of the crowd, but they hear only the sound, 12:28, 30.

The double or multiple sense of words in Jn is **k** involved in this. His spatial vocabulary (Mollat, art cit), expresses the 'coming forth from God' of the Incarnate Word (1:11; 8:42; 13:31; 16:27f; 17:8), who knows 'whence he comes and whither he goes' (8:14), and will come again in his risen apparitions (20:19, 26), with his Father (14:18—24) and at the Parousia, 14:3; 21:22. He comes into the world as the Light (12:46), as the Son of Man and the bread of life who descends from heaven, 3:13; 6:33—58. The Spirit comes down from heaven and abides on him (1:33), and the angels ascend and descend upon him, 51. His own ascent will be a lifting up (3:14; 8:28; 12:32), a return, a passing to his Father (13:1; 17:11ff) and he himself will be the 'door', the 'road' to his Father's house, 10:9; 14:6. Then again 'follow' is literal in 1:37, shades into attachment to Jesus in 1:40, 44, comes to mean going after him to the Father (13:36f) and finally rings the changes between the literal meaning and discipleship even to death, 21:19—22. Jn's favourite 'abide' (*menō*) passes from where Christ is staying (1:38f) to the mutual abiding of Christ and the communicant (6:56), to permanent abiding in him (15:4—7) and to that of the Father and the Son in the man who keeps Jesus's word, 14:23, cf 1 Jn 2:24, 27f; 3:24. Other double senses: 'blind', physically and spiritual-

94k ly (9:39ff), 'end', for end of life and final accomplishment (13:1; 19:28, 30), *anōthen*, meaning 'again' or 'from above', 3:3ff. 'Living water' is water from a spring and the Holy Spirit (4:10, 14; 7:39, cf 3:5, water of baptism); 'be lifted up' refers to the brazen serpent, the Cross and the Ascension (3:14; 8:28; 12:32, 34); 'bread of life' (6) means ordinary bread, manna, Christ, and Christ in the Eucharist; in 11:23ff present bodily resurrection is sign of the risen life which Christ's resurrection makes real for believers, with a double sense of 'live' and 'die', and also resurrection at the Last Day.

95a The Background of Jn—Though it becomes ever clearer that the Gospel was worked out from the Apostolic Kerygma (Dodd, *Int.*, 384—386), it is written in a language and with a sensibility such as to fulfil aspirations traversing the ancient world, cf F.-M. Braun, 'L'arrière-fond du quatrième Évangile', *Év. de Jean*, 179—196. Its **relation to these currents of thought** has been stated in many ways, often one-sidedly. Jn was considered to have hellenized Christianity under the influence of **Judaeo-hellenic syncretism** (Philo), or of **the Mystery Religions**, or, more recently, of **Gnosticism**; today attention turns to later Judaism. But Jn's spiritual originality and atmosphere make it impossible to identify him with any one system.

b (1) **Biblical Judaism** is the principal background. The Christ is set in the perspectives of the OT. To the twenty or more explicit references are joined implicit allusions, e.g. to the Messianic king and his banquet, to the prophet to come, and to classic themes: the Word, Light, Life, Temple, Shepherd, Vine. Jn offers not a mosaic of texts but an assimilation of the deepest meaning of the Scripture, the whole OT fulfilled in Jesus. For Gn and Ex cf § 793d. Again, the Messiah will be he upon whom the Spirit rests (Is 11:2; 42:1; Jn 1:32f), and he will establish the Davidic royalty, 12:12—16; 18:33—39;

c 19:1—22. Jn goes deeper in naming Jesus **the Word**. The expression **Logos**, occurring ceaselessly among the Gr. philosophers from Heraclitus to Philo and the Hermetic writings is 'the pillar for the theories that Jn hellenised the Gospels' (Braun, art cit, 182; H. Kleinknecht, 'Der Logos in Griechentum und Hellenismus', *TWNT* 4, 76—89). But though Jn may be conscious of its value for contemporaries, the context leads to the Heb. 'Word', (§ 679f—k; G. Kittel, TWNT 4, 89—138; J. Dupont, *Essais sur la Christologie de Saint Jean*, 13—58; M-E. Boismard, *St John's Prologue*, 82—124; R. Brown, App. II, 519—24). 'In the beginning was the Word' (Jn 1:1) refers to Gn 1:1ff, 'In the beginning God created the heavens and the earth . . . God said . . .'. God's Word is his creative power, the theme expressed by Ps 33 (32):6, 'by the word of the Lord the heavens were made' and developed by Jn in line with the Wisdom literature, cf further on Jn 1:1ff.

d (2) **The extra-canonical books** (§ 88) were in a literary 'genre' which influenced, e.g., Rev. Jn sets Jesus's message in apocalyptic (§ 454) terms when he presents him as the revealer of heavenly things which only he can know because he comes down from heaven, Jn 3:12f, 31ff; but for the more usual apocalyptic contrast of the present with the future world, with judgement, resurrection and eternal life at the last day, Jn substitutes 'heavenly' and 'earthly', 'from above' and 'from below' (8:23), and eternal life offered already, 5:24, cf 8:21. Prominent in this literature is the figure of the **Son of Man**, founder of the endless kingdom of the Last Days (Dn, Enoch), who being essentially glorious, cannot die, cf the Jews' astonishment on being told that the Son of Man must be 'lifted up', 12:31f. Jesus will

refer to him when belief is difficult, e.g. 3:15; 6:62; **795d** and cf on 1:51.

(3) **The Qumran texts** (DSS, § 610), belong to this **e** apocalyptic milieu, cf F. H. M. Braun, 'L'arrière-fond judaïque du quatrième évangile et la communauté de l'alliance', RB 72 (1955), 5—44; R. Brown, 'The Qumran Scrolls and the Johannine Epistles and Gospel', CBQ 17 (1955), 403—419; *NT Essays*, 102—31. Though words like darkness, light, life, truth and spirit are the common fund of contemporary Judaism, the conceptual resemblances and significant diversities between DSS and Jn are so striking as to confirm the hypothesis of at least an indirect connexion between Qumran and the Baptist— with his disciple Jn. Jn himself records that the first five of Jesus's disciples were of the Baptist's circle, that Jesus stayed with him beyond the Jordan and—through his disciples—baptized, 3:22, 36; 4:2. So Christianity began as a baptising movement which plunged its roots not only in Jewish land, but in that part of the *élite* of Palestinian Judaism where, brought to life by the rite' preached by the Baptist, 'the expectation of the Messiah put forth its most ardent flame' (Braun, *Jean le Théologien*, 309). The Baptist's menace of vengeance, his preaching of penitence and administration of a baptism to which men submitted, confessing their sins, accord with the Manual, as do the expectation in the question 'are you the Prophet', and the answer, 'a voice crying in the wilderness. Make straight the way of the Lord', Jn 1:21ff; Mt 3:3; Is 40:3; 1QS 9, 10; 8:13f. This does not prove him a member of the sect, for their exclusiveness and method (the study of the Law), are far from his open, universal appeal. But Zachary his father was a priest of the Zadokite class so esteemed by the 'sons of Zadok', and the 'Benedictus' is analogous to the final 'Benedic tion' of the Manual, Lk 1:68—79. 80; 1QS 11.

The doctrine of DSS and Jn—(a) Both share the **f** Jewish belief in God's creation. 'All that is, he established by his purpose, and apart from him, nothing was made' (1QS 11, 11) with its positive and negative form equals Jn 1:3. (b) Both see men in opposing camps of light and darkness, each with a personal leader: For Qumran, the Angel of Light, 'spirit of truth, prince of lights, holy spirit' (1QS 3, 18—24; CDC 7, 19) and Mastema (same root as Satan), 'prince of the sons of darkness', 'the angel of destruction', 1QS 3, 19, 21—24; 4, 12; CDC 2, 4. These angels are the basis of every act; they struggle in equally appointed measure for the hearts of men till the final age, 1QS 3, 15; 4, 26. But for Jn there is no angel of light; the Light is Jesus, Jn 1:9; 8:12; 12:46. The 'sons of light', who 'do the truth' (cf 1QS 1, 3) come to the light and follow him (Jn 3:21; 12:35f, cf 1QS 1, 5; 8, 2). Jn's 'prince of this world' (Jn 12:31; 14:30; 16:11, cf Rev 12:9) is not created evil, but 'murderer and liar from the beginning' (Gn 3:3f), his 'sons' love darkness rather than light, not by predestination but because their works are evil (Jn 3:19; 8:44; 1 Jn 3:8). (c) The 'Two Ways' of light and darkness (1QS 4, 3—13) are not in the Gospel (unless by 'walking' in light or darkness, 8:12; 11:9f; 12:35) but appear in 1 Jn 1:6f; 2:9f with the same contrasts of light and truth, darkness and the lie as in 1QS 3, 18; 5, 24; 6, 17. The closest literary paral. is 1 Jn 4:1—6 (two rival groups, led by the spirits of truth and error, and the testing of the spirits). The spirit of truth who opens the right ways of truth' (1QS 4, 2) suggests Jn 16:13. (d) A fatalist (cf Jos.Ant. 13, 5), probably Zoroastrian, trend combines at Qumran with the Hebrew doctrine of reward and punishment for free actions. Jn's dualism is moral. Qumran's angels do not fight each other. Jesus is attacked, but not overcome

795f (Jn 1:5) by the Darkness. His triumph on the Cross casts down the 'prince of this world' (12:31; 14:30; 16:11) and takes away the sin of the world, 1:29; 1 Jn 3:5. He appeals to men to come to him, the Light, 6:35; 7:37; 12:32, 35. Their culpable refusal is the basis of their

g judgement, 3:39; 9:41. (e) The basic difference is Christ. Qumran's 'son of light' follows the Law in the community, Jn's believe in Jesus, 12:36, 46, cf 8:12 'the light of life' as 1QS 3:7. Both must continue to walk as such, (cf Eph 5:9), but Jn adds that Jesus's blood cleanses from sin all who walk in the light, 1 Jn 1:7. For Qumran victory in the War will come in a great battle (1QM); for Jn, Jesus has already conquered (Jn 1:5; 12:31); 'the darkness is passing away and the true light already shining', (1 Jn 2:8) and victory is assured: 'Take courage. I have overcome the world', Jn 16:33; 1 Jn 2:18; 4:4. Both urge men to confess their sins and trust in divine mercy, e.g. CDC 1, 8f; 1QS 1, 25; 1 Jn 1:8ff; but for Jn we have an Advocate with the Father, the expiation also for the sins of the whole world, 2:2; 4:10. (f) The rites and symbolism of water interest both deeply. The Manual insists also on interior dispositions (1QS 3, 4—6) and the purifying action of the spirit of truth (4, 20ff). Jn leaves ritual purifications (Jn 1:26, 33; 2:6; 3:25) for birth from water and the Spirit (3:5), whose gift water symbolizes,

h 4:13ff; 7:38ff; 19:34; 1 Jn 5:6ff. (g) The Manual's 'kindness-and-goodness' (*ḥesed*) (1QS 4, 5, etc) seems a first sketch of Jn's *agapē*, love. Qumran's high community ideal aimed at perfection and fraternal love with 'communion' of goods (1QS 1, 11ff; 5, 1—6). But their community was closed and had to hate all the sons of darkness and have no relation with them, e.g. 1, 10; 2, 5—18; 5, 7—20. Their ideal, transformed into terms of the Christian community, aims (1 Jn 1:1—7) at fellowship with Jesus and love of one another according to his command (2:7—11). They too are separated, 'not of this world' (Jn 17:14 cf 1 Jn 1:6f 'light and darkness'; 2:19 'they went forth from us'), which, with its sin, evil tendencies and errors, all from the devil, they are not to love (1 Jn 2:15ff). But whereas 'the world' hates the Christians (3:13), they are to love all men, sinners included, for 'God so loved the world as to give his own Son . . . the expiation for the sins of the whole world' (Jn 3:16; 1 Jn 2:2). Their community, too, is to be open, for Jesus does not pray that they be taken from the world but kept from the evil one, and sends them into the world (Jn 17:14—18). (h) Qumran expected two Messiahs 'from Aaron and from Israel', the latter, 'the spring of David', being the lesser. The Baptist knows only one, the 'stronger than he', whose coming is immediate (Mt 3:10), 'the Lamb who takes away the sin of the world' (Jn 1:29, 36). To prepare for his coming, he preaches a conversion-baptism offered to all, whereas at Qumran sinners were not allowed the baths of purification, 1QS 5, 13. (i) The Doctrine of renovation by the Spirit (cf Ezek 36:35ff) is common to Qumran, the Baptist and Jn. For 1QS 4, 18—22, the present imperfect cleansings (cf 3, 6ff) will be followed in the last time by a supreme lustration, when God will radically purify his chosen by the spirit of holiness and truth as by lustral waters (Braun, 316—310; J. Coppens, 'Le Don de l'esprit d'après les textes de Qumran et le Quatrième Évangile', *Év. de Jean*, 215—23). The Baptist compares the baptisms of water and the Spirit. Jn continues the theme with birth from water and the Spirit (Jn 3:3—8) and the 'torrents of living water' which are the gift of the Spirit, 7:38f. The Baptist's profound, original addition is that baptism in the Spirit will be the work of the Messiah, and Jn develops this into a favourite theme: it is from Christ's sacrifice that the pouring

forth of the Spirit will come (7:39; 19:34; 20:22), **795** and he is a Divine Person, the Paraclete, the Spirit of Truth, who will lead into all truth (14:16f; 16:13f) those within whom he will be the life-giving principle (4:14, 23f; 6:63).

So the Baptist and Jn modify Qumran's doctrine in **i** identical ways: over dualism (of which the Baptist shows no trace), the one Messiah, the immediacy of his judgement, salvation offered to all through him (not through study of the Law), over baptism and the Spirit. The 'desert' background of the Gospel, the connexion between the Baptist and the ideas of Qumran, the discipleship of Jn to the Baptist and the originality of the Christian message are thus confirmed. Moreover, the resemblances in thought and vocabulary between Qumran and Jn are such 'that we do not need to look outside Palestinian Judaism for the soil in which the Johannine theology grew' (M. Burrows, *The Dead Sea Scrolls*, 339f).

(4) **Gnosticism**, with the importance it gives to **j** knowledge, has been claimed as principal source of Jn (especially by Bultmann, who however has to cut out passages disagreeing with his theory). But the recent find of a Gnostic library at Nag-Hammadi in Egypt has demonstrated that the relation is that of dependence on Jn. Was Jn in contact with a pre-Gnosis, orthodox because without metaphysical dualism and genealogies of 'aeons'? From what we can infer about it and a study of the use of 'the name' in Jn, this may be implied (G. Quispel, 'L'Évangile de Jean et la Gnôse', *L'Év de Jean*, 197—208). Of literary contacts between the **Hermetic writings** and Jn there can be no doubt but they too are later. However, since Hermetism as a 'spiritual *koinē*' was spread through the Hellenistic world before Christianity, it is possible that Jn felt some of its influence.

While it is idle to seek outside Palestine for close **k** influences upon Jn, it does not follow that he who preached 'the Light which enlightens every man' was inattentive to the aspirations of religious paganism, though another alternative is that his disciple editors may have enriched his style from e.g. Alexandrian philosophy and mysticism. If so, he used them, not to hellenize the Apostolic Kerygma but to show souls seeking truth that Jesus is the Way, the Truth and the Life.

Author and Date—As Kümmel points out, much of the **79** heat generated over the question of the Johannine authorship is due to misunderstanding. Defenders of it believed that the apostolic authority and historical trustworthiness of the Gospel depended on its being ascribed to the apostle John, the son of Zebedee. Attackers were equally sure that by destroying this tradition they would be able to deny all historical reliability and apostolic authority to the Gospel and regard its theological teaching as a later production of doubtful value. In fact neither of these conclusions is true. What are the facts? In the first twenty chh of Jn the author is not named. But in 21:24, an appendix to the Gospel, we read, 'This is the disciple (i.e. the 'disciple whom Jesus loved' referred to in v 20) who is bearing witness to these things and who has written these things. This disciple is referred to several times earlier in the Gospel, e.g. 13:23 at the Last Supper, 19:26 at the foot of the Cross, running to the tomb with Peter, 20:2—8. But apart from having a close connexion with Peter, no further clue is given as to the identity of the Beloved Disciple. We are told however something more about him. He was an eyewitness of the death of Jesus, 'He who saw it has borne witness—his testimony is true and he knows that he tells the truth—that you also may believe' (Jn 19:35). Since no other disciple is

96a mentioned as present it may reasonably be assumed that the person referred to in 35 is the disciple mentioned in 26. The same disciple may well have been an eyewitness of much else in the Gospel. But did he write it? 19:35 only asserts that he was a witness and makes no mention of writing. Indeed many commentators affirm that v 35 makes a distinction between the Beloved Disciple and the author of the Gospel. This, however, is not so clear as some writers suggest. On this hypothesis we have the author saying of the witness (the beloved Disciple) 'He who saw it has borne witness—his testimony is true'. That seems enough, one would think, though one could add 'and I (we) know it is true'. That is to say—'insofar as we have a good deal of corroborative evidence'. But in fact v 35 adds *he* knows it is true' which, to say the least, has little if any significance on the supposition that the writer is distinct from the witness. But if the two are the same person, this sentence assumes a meaning and is an emphatic reaffirmation of the truth of what he has just said. A great deal has been written about the exact significance of *ekeinos* in this v, most of it inconclusive. Suffice it here to say that, if writer and witness are the same person, *ekeinos* adds emphasis—'I am absolutely sure of the truth of what I say'; but written of himself in the third person. Turning now to ch 21 we have to keep in mind that this, in the view of many commentators, is a later addition to the Gospel which seems to end so decisively at ch 20:30. It seems to have been written after the death of the Beloved Disciple (v 23), but not much later than the rest of the Gospel for it is a fully authenticated part of it, being present in all MSS. In v 24 it is declared that the Beloved Disciple (cf vv 20–23) was both the witness *and* the writer of 'these things', i.e. the Gospel. This however is not accepted by many modern commentators as a statement of fact in face of the absence as they see it of any reference to such authorship in chh 1–20, and is regarded as one more instance of that pseudepigraphy of which the early cent. afford us so many examples, cf M. R. James, *The Apocryphal NT*. But apart from our interpretation of 19:35 as given above, there is another difficulty in accepting this view. Pseudepigraphy usually requires time to elapse between the date of the person to whom a writing is to be attributed and the date of the writing itself. Such a period of time would be lacking in this case. Ch 21 could hardly have been written later than A.D. 100; probably within a decade of the Gospel chh 1–20. It seems improbable that a ch added so soon to the Gospel by the early Christian community could have ascribed the authorship of the Gospel with such emphasis if it were not in fact correct.

b **Who is the Beloved Disciple?** (1) One of those present in ch 21: Peter, Thomas, Nathanael, the sons of Zebedee (James and John) and possibly two others, 21:2. (2) His place 'close to the breast of Jesus' (13:23) points to one of those three privileged to be present on special occasions, Mk 5:27; 9:2; 14:33, cf 1:29; 13:3, namely Peter, James and John. Peter and James are out of the question. James was killed A.D. 44, Ac 12:2 by Herod Agrippa. (3) 'Just as in Jn, six out of the seven incidents about the beloved disciple' (including 1:35; 18:15, omitting 19:26) 'show us Peter associated with him, so in every mention of Jn in Ac his name is coupled with that of Peter' (H. J. Chapman, 'Names in the Fourth Gospel', JTS 30 (1929), 19–20, cf Ac 3:1–11; 4:1–23; 8:14ff. This association is also in Lk 22:7. (4) Had the author of the Gospel wished to enhance his reputation by passing himself off as an Apostle, he would, like the apocryphal

writers, have given himself a name (Braun, op cit, 303). **796b** The number of times names of Apostles (apart from Peter) occur in Syn. is: John 20, James 18 (including 'sons of Zebedee'), Judas 9, Andrew 4; in Jn, Philip 12, Judas 8, Thomas 7, Andrew 5, John 0, James 0, sons of Zebedee 1 (probably editorial); the names of Salome (mother of the sons of Zebedee, cf Jn 19:25) and of Mary the Mother of Jesus are also omitted. The only 'John' is the Baptist, named without addition, though the Gospel carefully distinguishes people who might be confused (Chapman, 21). The only 'I' (21:25) is probably editorial. (5) But if John is so modest and is also the author of Apoc, why does he name himself there (Apoc 1:9)? Prophets had to give their names to guarantee their mission. And why in the Gospel does the Beloved Disciple effectively sign himself? He must guarantee his own witness to Jesus (Jn 19:35; 1 Jn 1:1–4); but he will go no further, and with the humility of a humble soul, recalls only that he has been loved (Lagrange, xx). It is highly probable that he is also the 'other disciple known to the high priest', Jn 18:15f.

How do the sons of Zebedee fit this picture? Jesus **c** nicknamed them 'Boanerges', that is, says Mk 3:17, 'sons of thunder'. They wanted to call down fire from heaven upon an inhospitable Samaritan village (Lk 9:51–56), and John stopped a Jewish exorcist using the name of Jesus because he did not follow with the Apostles (Mk 9:38ff; Lk 9:49f). The brothers tried to steal a march on the others by getting their mother to ask Jesus for them to sit on his right and left hand (Mt 20:20–23; Mk 10:35–40). Young ardent natures make good lovers. John was to learn love from intimacy with Jesus (Jn 13:23) and his Mother (19:25ff). But love is not soft, and it is a son of thunder that the Johannine writings show. Zebedee was a fisherman, probably at Bethsaida, sufficiently well-off to have paid helpers. Salome must follow and minister to Jesus (Mk 15:40; 16:1) Syn recall how, on being called by Jesus, the brothers left father and boat and followed him (Mt 4:21f; Mk 1:19f; Lk 5:1–11). The apparently astonishing suddenness is explainable from the previous initiation which we hear of from Jn. John's having been a disciple of the Baptist explains his information on his master's altercation with the Jerusalem envoys and his words about the sign of the Spirit resting on Jesus, on the dispute raised later by his disciples (Jn 1:19–28, 32f; 3:22–26; 4:1–4) and the relation of both to the doctrines of Qumran. So the Beloved Disciple fits the Gospel picture of John son of Zebedee, disciple of the Baptist and Apostle of Jesus. Views that he was a wholly ideal figure, or an unknown young man, or Lazarus, must be brought to the touchstone of this evidence.

All that the Beloved Disciple tells of his subsequent **d** life concerns the Mother of Jesus: 'from that hour the disciple took her to his own', 19:27. Ac relate how Peter and John faced the Sanhedrin boldly, and the latter's surprise at the Scriptural knowledge of such 'illiterate, amateurish men' (G. Lampe, PC (2) on Ac 4:13) which may mean simply that their education was not rabbinical. St Paul (Gal 2:9) mentions him as one of the Apostolic 'pillars' at Jerusalem, and that he would 'go to the circumcision', i.e. at that stage at least to missionary activity among the Jews. Tradition names him as author of Apoc while in exile on Patmos, of the three Epistles, and at Ephesus, in extreme old age, of the Gospel.

Many critics would now agree that much of the **797a** Gospel's material comes from the Beloved Disciple, but deny that he wrote it, as Jn 21:24 appears to say. It has been objected (a) that John the son of Zebedee was killed with his brother James by Herod c. A.D. 44. This has no

797a support in Ac 12:2f, and rests on the supposition that 'drink my cup' and 'be baptized with my baptism' (Mt 20:20ff; Mk 10:35—40) must refer to simultaneous martyrdom, and on the 'flimsiest' late evidence of George the Sinner (9th cent.), the epitomiser (7th or 8th cent.) of the bungling Philip of Side (c. 450), a Syrian martyrology (c. 411, but martyrologies grouped saints) and 'some hardly relevant odds and ends' (Dodd, HT, 12; Braun, op cit, 375—88). (b) Old critical positions ascribed a late date to the Gospel (the Tübingen school to c. 160—70). This has become untenable. (c) The most weighty and respectable reason for denying John's authorship (not only reasons for which cf Jn 12:43), has been the difficulty of ascribing a gospel with supposedly Gr. sources to a Galilaean fisherman. We now know that the sources are Palestinian. (d) J. N. Sanders' thesis (*The Fourth Gospel in the Early Church*, 1943) has been revived by C. K. Barrett (54, n. 2, 92, 97): 'The fact that the Gospel attained publicity so slowly and was first used (so far as we know) by Gnostics, does not support Apostolic authorship' (PC (2) 845).

b   To this view Père Braun's *Jean le Théologien* replies. He sets out to show that the thesis rests on too narrow a basis, taking no practical account of the Egyptian papyri, the Roman cemetery frescoes and much else which prove the ancientness of the Gospel and its authority in orthodox circles.

c   (a) **Egypt.** The famous papyrus fragment **P. Rylands 457** (*recto*, Jn 18:31f—*verso*, 37f) discovered by C. H. Roberts (*An Unpublished Fragment of the Fourth Gospel*, Manchester, 1935) dates from the first half of the 2nd cent., and since the Gospel had to reach Egypt, points to its existence around the beginning of the century. If Jn knew Lk, as is most probable, then Jn could hardly have been written before 80—90. It is commonly agreed today that Jn was written near the end of the 1st cent. Egerton pap. 2 (H. I. Bell and T. C. Skeat, *Fragments of an Unknown Gospel*, 1935), dates c. 150, contains indubitable extracts from Jn and 'would seem to have emanated from a circle which held the Fourth Gospel to be authoritative' (Dodd, NTS (1953), 42). P. Bodmer II, c. 200, contains all the Gospel except 6:11—35, 21:9b—25. The text of these three papyri, though very similar, probably does not go back to one original, testifies to the early diffusion of the Gospel in Egypt and shows no trace of Gnostic influence.

d   (b) **Rome.** The Gospel's authority is shown by the frequency of its themes in the catacomb frescoes, probably as material for the earliest catechesis (Lazarus 53 times). The striking of the Rock (68 times), connected with baptism, alludes to Jn 7:38f; 19:34f. So does Just. (*Trypho*, 69, etc), and the frequency of the parallels between him and Jn makes impossible Barrett's view (93f) that it is not proved that he had read him, e.g. 'his blood, not born of man's seed but of the will of God' (*Trypho*, 63) echoes Jn 1:13, seven passages show that when he thinks of the Incarnation, he refers to Jn's Prologue, he takes the Logos doctrine for granted (*1 Apol.* 32, with Jn 1:1, 14), and echoes Jn 3:3f, *Apol.* 63. Hermas (c. 141—49) depends on Jn or his teaching, cf 'the door', *Sim.* 9, 12, 6 with Jn 10:9; baptism, *Sim.*, 9, 12, 3; 11, 16, 4 with Jn 3:5, 18, etc. Earlier still, 1 Clem shows, whatever the reason, the Roman community, c. A.D. 95, 'in possession of a theology closely related to that of Jn and living by it' (Braun, 170—80). So the Gnostics appealed to Jn because he was already established in the hearts of Christians, (100—21).

(c) **Syria.** Ignat.'s (martyred c. 115) anti-docetism, **797** realism about the flesh, inner mysticism, vision of unity at all levels, intimacy with the Father, overwhelming love of Christ and desire to bear him witness, are closer than any other ancient text to Jn and 1 Jn; they sometimes include reminiscences. e.g. 'the living water which murmurs (? leaps) in me, saying within me "Come to the Father" . . . I long for the bread of God which is the flesh of Jesus', *Rom.*, 7, 2f, cf Jn 4:10; 6; 7:38; 14:12. Some of these testimonies, especially 1 Clem, may come from a Joh. tradition. But the unanimous MSS, the papyri and statements now to be examined show a written Gospel accepted as authoritative. So when the Roman priest Gaius (c. 200), to combat its use by the Montanists, rejected its authenticity, he was opposing tradition. His sect—if such there was—called 'The Unreasonables' (*Alogi*) and 'a feeble reptile' by Epiphanius (*Haer.*, 51, 34—35) was 'not an oak but a mushroom' (Lagrange, lv—lxi).

The tradition of antiquity, maintained by the **f** Muratorian Canon (c. 200) which says that the Gospel was written by the eyewitness John by the persuasion of a group of disciples who guaranteed it, by Orig. (Eus.HE 6, 25), Clem.Alex. (ib, 14), Tertull. (*Adv. Marc.*, 4, 2, 5), and by 'everybody' (Lagrange), is thus stated by Iren. (Adv. Haer. 3, 1, 1) c. 180: 'John, the disciple of the Lord, who also rested upon his breast, he himself published his gospel while staying at Ephesus in Asia'. Iren. vividly recalls (3, 3, 4 and ap. Eus.HE 5, 20, 5—8) his youthful Asian memories of Polycarp, bishop of Smyrna, recounting his intercourse with John and the others who had seen the Lord, and the words of these 'eyewitnesses of the Word of Life' (cf 1 Jn 1:1). To Pope Victor he argues that the Asian date of Easter was kept 'by Polycarp who lived with John the disciple of Our Lord and with the rest of the Apostles' (Eus.HE 5, 24, 16); 'and all the presbyters who in Asia met John the disciple of the Lord, bear witness that John has transmitted his doctrine; for he stayed among them right up to the time of Trajan' (*Adv. Haer.* 2, 22, 5). In deriving authority from those who lived with the Lord, he is taking John as an Apostle in the strict sense. His first-hand witness for Polycarp is not invalidated if he is mistaken in saying that Papias also was a 'hearer of John' (5, 33, 4; Eus.HE 3, 39, 2). Polycrates of Samos also appeals to John's authority in writing to Pope Victor: among the 'great stars' buried in Asia was 'John, who rested upon the breast of the Lord, who was priest and wore the 'petalon', who was martyr and teacher' (3, 31, 3; he refers probably to Apoc 1:19, and to the 'petalor,' proper to the Jewish high priest, as meaning that he was head of the Asian churches). Of his burial in Asia he is sure.

So is Eusebius; he cites Clem.Alex.'s story of John **g** re-converting the young man turned robber, and has no doubt that he wrote the Gospel 'which is recognized by all the churches under heaven'; he adds the informative tradition that John used oral preaching all his life and was led to write to fill the gap left by the other Gospels for the time before the Baptist's imprisonment (3, 23—24). What he does query is whether John wrote Apoc. This he conjecturally assigns to another John, 'the Presbyter', for 'they say' that there are two tombs at Ephesus, each said to be John's (7, 16, 25). Besides, Papias mentions the name of John, once among the Apostles and once among the presbyters, and that after the name of Aristion: 'If anyone came who had been in the company of the presbyters, I used to inform myself of the words of the presbyters: what Andrew or Peter

7g said, what Philip or Thomas or James or John or Matthew or any other of the disciples of the Lord, and what Aristion and John the Presbyter, disciples of the Lord, are saying' (3, 39, 2—6). Eusebius (who wants to discredit Apoc) is not disinterested, and the main difficulty against his interpretation of Papias is the repetition of 'disciples of the Lord' (all Gr. MSS, but not Syr. trans.). Some, with H. J. Chapman, *John the Presbyter*, identify Apostles and presbyters, cf 1 Pt 5:1; 2 Jn 1; 3 Jn 1. But at the end of the Apostolic age, the word had a technical sense, as in Iren., 'hearers of the Apostles'. Probably an ancient, or presbyter, called John, existed (Braun, 362). But there is no 'positive evidence in favour of the view that he wrote the fourth gospel or was in any way connected with it' (Barrett, 92), nor ancient authority for identifying him (Bernard) with the 'Presbyter' author of 2 Jn and 3 Jn. 'The Old Man' was a natural name for John to give himself. Besides, to accept another John as author of the gospel or epistles is to postulate two Jewish Christians called John, probably Palestinians, spiritual geniuses of the first order, close contemporaries, of great authority among the churches of Asia. 'Such a situation of Tweedledum and Tweedledee is exceedingly hard to swallow', A. H. N. Green-Armytage, *John Who Saw*, 128—9. Moreover, 'nobody seems to have noticed these coincidences at the time' and is it credible that if the Presbyter got his information from the Apostle, he should ignore his existence and hint that he is the author? Besides, what happened to the son of Zebedee, so important in Ac? Finally, the authority of the Gospel points, not to an obscure presbyter, but to the great Apostle.

h The discovery by Austrian archaeologists of the reputed **Tomb of St John at Ephesus** (Braun, 365—374), object of continuous veneration, supports the literary evidence. Such a tomb was an argument for the tradition and doctrine of the place—as at Rome. So of John's stay in Asia—confirmed by Rev's mention of the exile in Patmos—there can be no reasonable doubt. But it is possible that **only the final Gospel was composed at Ephesus**. Ephraim (*Comment. on Diatessaron*) places its composition at Antioch; Jer. and the 4th or 5th cent. *Acts of the Martyrdom of Ignatius* say that he as well as Polycarp was a disciple of John, and perhaps Ignatius's *Letter to the Ephesians* mentions Paul but not John because he was not wholly theirs (Lagrange, lxvi).

98a **Doctrine—The Mystery of the Incarnation** is basic to the Gospel with its ceaseless question 'Who is Jesus?'. It is the key to the 'birth from on high' (3) and to 6. Its consummation in **redemptive love** (13:1) is expressed in the great themes of the Last Discourse: the love between the Father and the Son shared in unity with the disciples, the summit being the Priestly Prayer, 17. Then Jesus in the hour of his glorification, lifted on the Cross, draws all men to himself (3:14; 8:28; 12:32; 17:1—5) and confirms them as his brothers in the Resurrection, 20:17. 'I came forth from the Father and am come into the world; again I am leaving the world and going to the Father', 16:28.

This doctrine is expressed in the messianic, saving work of Jesus (J. Giblet, 'Jésus et le Père', *L'Év. de Jean*, 111—30). At the heart of the Good News is that mysterious point where we meet God in Jesus and make our choice, 5—11. In 5:18—22 Jesus justifies his sign of power in curing the paralytic on the Sabbath by going straight (as the Jews see) from action to being. As he does the same divine works as his Father, he is uniquely the Son; his Person is in the unity of God, yet not independent of, but totally dependent on his Father. So

it is in the name of his Father and not his own (5:34, **798a** cf 7:28) that he '**comes**' to do his messianic work, to save (12:47), give life (10:10), exercise judgement, 9:39. Though 'he who comes from above is above all' (3:31), he consistently says that he has been **sent** by his Father (e.g. 5:36; 6:57; 11:42; 20:21), whose words he proclaims (3:34; 6:29; 17:3), whose work he does, 9:4. This mission implies consecration (10:36) and a share in divine life so complete that to honour, believe in and see the Son, is to honour, believe in and see the Father, 5:23f; 12:44f; 14:9, cf § 679*f—k*.

'**I am**' (E. Stauffer, *Egō*, TWNT 2, 347f, 350—2; A. **b** Feuillet, *E. Joh.*, 80ff) is the supreme OT title of the One, active, saving God, e.g. Ex 3:14; 10:2; Is 42:8; 43:10—13; Ezek 6:7. In Jn the great 'I am' sayings reveal Jesus's divine being, usually as source of salvation: 'I am the bread of life' (6:35), 'the light of the world' (8:12; 9:5), 'he who bears witness to myself' (8:18), 'the door of the sheep' (10:7), 'the good shepherd' (10:11, 14), 'the resurrection and the life' (11:25), 'the true vine' (15:1—5), 'king' (18:37); without predicate (8:24, 28, 58; 13:19), with overtones (? 4:26; ? 6:20; 18:6); Apoc 1:8, 17; 21:6; 22:13. Though these expressions would appeal to 'the cosmopolitan society of a great Hellenistic city such as Ephesus' (Dodd, *Int.*, 9), Jn's brief formulae, basing promises of salvation and followed by conditions on which to attain it, are quite unlike e.g. the Isis hymn, and take their structure from OT praises of divine Wisdom, Prv 8—9; Sir 24.

'**The Light**' (22 times in Jn, 6 in 1 Jn), mentioned **c** in the Prologue, develops in 8—10 (the festival of Lights, the blind man). In OT light accompanies God's presence, Is 60:19f; Ezek 1:4; Dn 7:9ff, cf Rev 21:23. The Messiah is 'the light of the nations', Is 42:6; 49:6, cf 9:1f. The Christians pondered these texts (Lk 1:79; Ac 13:47; Eph 5:14), and as 'children of the light' in a moral sense, 'walk in the light', Rm 13:12f, 2 Cor 6:14; Eph 5:6—9, cf DSS. In Jn this is simply to follow the light which is God revealed in Jesus with whom it came into the world (1 Jn 1:5ff; Jn 3:19ff; 12:46), and from whom it shines as from 'the true light that enlightens every man', 1:9; 12:35f. Thus Jn breaks through the Jewish, Messianic function of light-giving to concentrate everything upon 'the Light of the world' (8:12; 9:5) and that Light's reflection in brotherly love, 1 Jn 2:8ff. The Gospel's tragedy is the opposition of the Darkness to the Light, which effects the Judgement in the spirit of man, Jn 1:5ff; 3:19ff; 9:13-30. For DSS background of § 795*f*. Jn's images are so subtle that the Light can also be the Life, 1:4; 8:12.

Life or 'live' occurs 55 times in Jn. This dominant **d** theme, introduced in the Prologue (1:4), develops especially in 3—7, 10—12 and expresses the purpose of the Gospel, 20:31. In OT God is essentially Living and source of life, Ps 36 (35):10. In late Judaism's eschatological vision the just will live again (Dn 12:13), cf the tree, water, book, crown of life in Rev. In Jn the Father who has life in himself has given the Son to have life in himself (5:26; 6:57) as 'the life eternal who is with the Father', 11:25; 14:6; 1 Jn 1:2. The Son himself comes to give life and that abundantly, Jn 10:10, 28; 17:2. He gives himself as the bread of life (6:47—50, 57) and source of the living waters of the Spirit, 7:37ff; 19:30, 34. For earthly life Jn uses (Gr.) 'soul' in 10:15ff; 12:25 and 'live' only in 4:50—53. But the life which the living, risen Lord gives (14:19) is eternal life, e.g. 3:36; 1 Jn 1:2. It is 'to know thee the only true God and Jesus Christ whom thou hast sent', 17:3, cf 1 Jn 1:2. It is the inside of the Kingdom, Jn 3:3, 5 with 16, 36. Being divine, it is realized in us now and being exempt from death is

798d the foundation of the resurrection life, in which it will reach its fullness, 5:24—29; 6:40, 54; 11:25f. It is God's gift to those who believe in his Son (3:15f, 36; 20:31; 1 Jn 5:10ff), brought from on high by the sacraments which well up into eternal life, Jn 3:3ff; 4:14; 6:53ff. Those who thus pass from death to life do not incur condemnation, 5:24. The proof that they have passed is that they love the brethren, for life expands by giving, 1 Jn 3:14, 16f, cf R. Brown, 505—8.

e **The unique Trinitarian relations** are expressed by the Word's 'presence towards' (*pros*, usually translated 'with God'), Jn 1:1; 1 Jn 1:2. He is 'the Only-Begotten Son', whose sight of the Father founds his work as revealer, Jn 1:14, 18; 3:16, 18; 1 Jn 4:9. At the Gospel's end the risen Jesus shows the difference between himself and his brothers: 'I am ascending to my Father and your Father, to my God and your God', 20:17. Identity of nature ('I and the Father are one, 10:30; 17:21ff) goes with reciprocity in life and being: 'the Father is in me and I am in the Father', 10:38; 14:10—20. The Son's mission into the world is no separation: 'He who sent me is with me; he has not left me alone', 8:29; 16:32. This is no local presence but 'abiding in love', 15:10. The Father's love for the Son, (3:35; 5:20; 10:17; 15:9), shown by putting everything into his hand (3:35; 13:3) and giving him power over all flesh (17:2), fills Jesus with joy which he transmits to his disciples, 15:9ff; 17:23f. It calls forth his own love for his Father shown by total acceptance of his word, will, command, pleasure, even to death; this passion of his life is the food that nourishes him, 4:31—34; 8:55; 10:18; 14:13, etc. He awaits his 'hour', his 'time', fixed by his Father (7:30; 8:20) to pass out of this world in glorifying him, 12:24, 27f; 13:1; 17:1. Their total existence for each other is source and model of the communion of knowledge, love and life between Jesus and his friends and between those friends themselves: The Father knows the Son and the Son the Father, 10:15; the Father is in the Son and the Son in the Father, 14:10f, 20; 17:21, 23; the Son knows and is in men, men know and are in the Son, 10:14; 14:20; 17:23, 26; men know and are in the Father and the Son, 14:7ff; 17:21. This is also expressed in terms of glory.

f **Glory** (G. Kittel, G. von Rad, TWNT 2, 235—58; J. Dupont, *Essais*, 235—93; W. Grossouw, 'La glorification du Christ', *L'Évang de Jean*, 131—45) occurs 18 times and 'glorify' 22 in Jn. Heb. *Kabôd* denotes weight, real value, importance, then the manifestation of God's being by miraculous signs (Ex 14:18; 16:7) or in shining radiance, 15:10ff; 1 (3) Kgs 8:10f. LXX translates by *doxa* which in ordinary Gr. stands for 'what seems', opinion, reputation (good or bad), cf Est 4:17; 1 Thes 2:6. Syn. and Paul attach Christ's glory to his *parousia* (e.g. Mt 25:31) and to his Resurrection, e.g. Rm 8:17f; Phil 2:11. But Jn starts from the Incarnation, where 'glory as of the only Son from the Father' (1:14) describes the glory hidden by the 'flesh' from unbelievers (9:41), but seen by the disciples as inseparable from the Father's. Cana is the first instance (2:11). In the debates with the Jews Jn first plays upon the Gr. meaning of mere, human honour: 'I do not receive glory from men' (5:41, cf 7:18); 8:50, 54. Then he introduces the verb 'glorify', first in the usual sense of Jesus glorified by the Resurrection (7:39; 12:16). Finally, he applies the glory of Yahweh directly to Jesus (12:41), contrasts it with the Gr. sense of honour from men (43) and then insists that the glorification of Jesus, begun by signs, culminates in a death accepted in love, as the very act by which the Father glorifies him and he the Father (12:20—33). Introducing the Discourse (13:31f), Jesus sets the same

idea in relation to his 'Hour'. It culminates in ch 17, which **79** is enfolded by inclusion in 'glory' (17:1—5 . . . 22, 24). Jesus's glorification consists in dying and so passing to a heavenly existence of glory with the Father by the Resurrection and Ascension (17:5, 24, cf 3:14 and e.g. 1 Tm 3:16). This involves not only the state of being honoured as the Son but active power (as with the *Kabôd* Yahweh) over all flesh (17:2) to give eternal life. Thus the 'glory' of 1:14 is finally shown in its achievement. Jn mentions no Transfiguration; all Jesus's actions are full of glory apparent to faith (Dodd, *Int.*, 207).

Finally (17:20ff) Jesus gives his glory to **his Church**. **g** His own, living still in this world under sorrow (11—16; 16:20), will by their unity in the power of the Spirit manifest in mystery and to faith the glory of the Father revealed in the Son, until the day when, being with him and contemplating his glory, they share in it perfectly, 17:24, exactly as 1 Jn 3:2. Thus **Jn reveals the Church from the inside**, as when he speaks of the life of the Spirit given by baptism (3:5) and the eternal life of those fed on the Eucharist (6). But he does not omit the sending of the Apostles as witnesses to Jesus (15:8, 16, 27; 17:18) with power to remit or retain sins (20:21f), and Jesus's setting Peter over his flock in a shepherd's office of love, 21:15ff. All this will come about through the assistance of the Spirit, the Paraclete, who will continue Jesus's work within the Church.

The Holy Spirit (D. Darrieutort, 'Esprit de Dieu', **79** VTB) is revealed with the Father and the Son, but in a way proper to himself. He has no name suggesting a human figure, but one (Heb. *rûah*, Gr. *pneuma*) from the wind or human breath, which, like his other great symbols, water or fire, suggests a presence: 'You do not know whence he comes or whither he goes', 3:8. In OT the Spirit of God is a divine force, transforming human personalities to make them capable of exceptional actions: judges and kings (Jdt 3:10; 1 Sm (1 Kgs) 16:13), prophets (where he is seen connected with the word of God and knowledge of him and the power to bear witness, 1 (3) Kgs 19:12f; Is 11:2; Ezek 2:1f), the Messiah especially, the Servant of the Lord whom the Spirit sanctifies for his sacrificial role (Is 42:1; 53:11; 61:1ff), finally the whole people, Ezek 37. In Jn 'God is Spirit' expresses his life-giving activity as sender of the Spirit, Jn 4:24. As the Spirit always acts by transforming another, he is known from within: 'You know him, for he dwells with you and will be in you', 14:17; 1 Jn 2:27. From the time when he rests upon Jesus at his baptism (1:32f) Jesus 'baptizes in the Holy Spirit' (1:33) and manifests him in all that he does; but, until he is about to leave his disciples, not as One distinct from himself. For only after his redemptive death and resurrection will the Spirit whom he will send forth from the Father be poured forth in his fullness, 7:39; 15:26; 16:7. He will **b** take Jesus's place as **The Paraclete**; cf O. Betz, *Der Paraclet*; R. Brown, 'The Paraclete in the Fourth Gospel', NTS 13 (1967) 113—32. The word is used in Jewish writings (certainly by the 2nd cent. A.D., e.g. *Pirke Aboth*, 4, 11) as a loan from Gr. meaning Advocate. In the OT background are (a) those who take the place of others who have died; Joshua is filled with Moses's spirit and Elisha with Elijah's, Dt 34:9; 2 (4) Kgs 2:9, 15; (b) the spirit who comes upon the prophets that they may interpret what God does in history, (c) angels who explain revelations and defend God's people, e.g. Dn 9:22ff; 10:13; Zech 1:1—5; this is worked out in DSS, e.g. IQS 3, 18ff, 'Spirit of truth'. The Paraclete in Jn is the same as the Spirit (Jn 14:16f, 26), and his functions are similar to those of the Spirit in the rest of the NT, e.g.

99b Mt 10:20; Lk 12:12; Ac 5:32; 6:10. He is (1) basically, the Advocate (J. Behm, TWNT, 5, 798—812), the Spirit of Truth who witnesses about Jesus (Jn 15:26) and like a prosecuting counsel reverses the sentence of condemnation which the world passed upon him, 16:8—11; (2) the spokesman for the absent Jesus (also 'Paraclete', 1 Jn 2:1) to teach the disciples and guide them in a moral sense into all truth concerning him, and so bear evidence through them, 14:26; 16:13f, cf 1 Jn 4:6; (3) though he is not called the Comforter, he does console (16:6f), and the active joint witness of the Spirit and the disciples in Christian preaching (Jn 15:26f) will give the consolation (*paraklèsis*) of the Messianic age, Is 40:1; 57:18f; 66:10—14; Mt 5:4; Lk 2:25; Ac 2:40; 9:31, cf C. Barrett, 'The Holy Spirit in the Fourth Gospel', JTS 1, n.s. (1950) 1—15. He is distinguished from Jesus and yet what is said about Jesus is said about him: Jesus is the Paraclete, the Holy Spirit 'another' (1 Jn 2:1; Jn 14:16); both come forth from the Father, Jesus in the Father's name, the Paraclete in Jesus's name (5:43; 14:26; 15:26; 16:28), for the Father who gave and sent the Son will give and send the Paraclete at Jesus's request, 3:16f; 14:16; Jesus is the Truth and the Holy One of God, the Paraclete is the Spirit of Truth and

c the Holy Spirit, 6:69; 14:6, 17, 26; 16:13. So the Paraclete is the Spirit of Jesus, who rested upon him (1:32) and whom he breathes forth upon his disciples, 20:22; ? 19:30. He will come back to them through the Paraclete, 14:16ff. As he will remain in and with them and make his dwelling with them (14:20, 23; 15:4f, 7), so the Paraclete will be in them and they will know him as they know Jesus, 14:7, 9; 16:17. He will remind them of what Jesus taught, and glorify him, 16:14, as Jesus speaks what the Father taught him and glorifies him, 8:28; 12:27f; 14:13; 17:4. As the world did not know or accept Jesus, so it cannot see or know the Paraclete, 7:28; 8:14, 19; 14:7; 16:3. Jn may be insisting that the Paraclete carries on the witness to Jesus after the death of the eyewitnesses who formed the visible link with him, and in spite of the delay in the Parousia. His 'reminding' will represent to each generation in a living way what Jesus said and did. Jn's own Gospel is an example of his ever-active presence, so was the kerygmatic preaching of the Twelve, and he continues to dwell in all who love Jesus and keep his commandments (14:15ff; 1 Jn 2:20, 27) and to lead them into all truth, 14:26. But this he does in his own way: 'He will not speak on his own authority . . . . He will take what is mine and declare it to you', 16:13f.

d To believe (Lazure, 161—206, 97 times in Jn, 9 in 1 Jn) is the vital step required from man confronted with Jesus, the condition for receiving God's gift of life. Chh 1—12 focus upon it (74 times), each episode ending with an act of belief or disbelief. Jn's purpose is to bring his readers to this 'work of God' (6:29), which is accorded his only Beatitude, 19:35; 20:29, 31. The drawing to belief is the Father's (6:44, cf 1 Jn 4:19), the invitation Jesus's (Jn 12:36), but it is for man to open himself and receive Jesus (1:11f; 5:43), to come to the light and break with sin (3:21; 8:24; 12:46), the Syn. 'conversion'. 'Believe' by itself takes its meaning from the context. 'Believe' with dat. expresses giving faith to what is said (Dodd), to God's revelation manifested in Jesus (4:21), or his words (2:22; 5:46), or statements about him, 14:11. **'Believe' with *eis* and acc.** (39 times in Jn), with its para. 'come to' (6:35) means not merely accepting Jesus's doctrine but giving oneself to him, to his allegiance (12:11), setting the whole of one's life in movement towards him, 11:25f. The expression probably

comes from a Heb. root meaning to entrust oneself to **799d** someone who is sure, cf 14:1, where Jesus, to keep their hearts in peace, demands the same belief in himself as in Yahweh. Believe 'in the name of Jesus' is to believe in the divine reality manifested in his Person, 1:12; 3:18. Belief has many degrees: from the crowd's more or less superficial openness to Jesus (2:23f; 7:31; 8:30f) or from belief that fears to 'confess' him (12:42f) to whole-hearted gift of self to him, 9:36ff; 20:29. In impersonal sayings 'he who believes' (*ho pisteuōn*, art. and pres. part, often with *pas*, 'everyone who believes') is the Christian (e.g. 11:26), and he is made promises which go with themes of eternal life, resurrection (3:15ff; 6:40) and fruitfulness in Apostolic works, 14:12. Though Jn does not go in for abstract definitions, the content of belief is objective: the heavenly doctrine, the revelation of the Father in Jesus, Messiah and Son (3:12, 33—36; 7:16f), the saving work which he comes to accomplish, which the Spirit will reveal, 8:28; 14:9, 26. It is all synthesized in the Eucharist, food of believers, bread of life, redemptive sacrifice of the world, presence on earth of the Lord who has ascended into heaven, 6:35f, 50ff, 57, 62f. The free decision to believe in Jesus or to 'disobey' (3:36), to come to the Light or remain in darkness (18—21), to pass from death to life or not to believe and die in sin (5:24; 8:24), operates the division among men, **the judgement**, 12:44—48. And wilful incredulity is shown in all its malice as satanic opposition to the Father (8:40f, 44), spiritual self-sufficiency and inexcusable rejection of the Light, bringing divine wrath, 5:44; 9:41; 12:43, 47f. To believers 1 Jn insists rather on fraternal charity and the richness of their vocation: 'that you may know that you have eternal life', 1 Jn 5:13. But they must persevere in authentic faith (2:22f; 4:15), the Father's commandment (3:23), and its dynamism has become the source of a new moral life, victorious over the forces of evil, 4:2ff; 5:4f

Belief commonly goes with '**seeing**' in the sense of vision, which is contrasted with physical sight, 6:36, 46; 20:25—29, cf 'see his glory', 1:14; 11:40. This is why 'he who has seen me, has seen the Father', 14:9. Ultimately we, God's sons, will 'see him as he is', 1 Jn 3:2. With 'to see' goes '**to know**' (14:7ff, 19f) in Heb. sense of an existential, personal relation, concrete experience of God in his works and willing response to him. God knows his People by loving choice, Am 3:2. But the world does not 'know' God, Jn 1:10; 8:55; 17:25. Jesus knows his own, and they him, and this Jn compares to the full, mutual, loving knowledge between the Father and the Son, 10:14f. This knowledge is a 'communion' (1 Jn 1:3), a sharing in the same life, a perfect union in truth and love which involves keeping Jesus's commandments, Jn 14:19ff; 17:26, cf 1 Jn 2:3f; 3:16. It is 'to enter the great current of life and light which comes from God and leads back to him' (J. Corbon, A. Vanhoye, 'Connaître', VTB, cf § 955e-g).

Truth (*alètheia*, 25 times in Jn) in the Covenant **e** context of Jn 1:14 may mean 'fidelity', but normally (I. de la Potterie, 'L'Arrière-fond du thème johannique de vérité', *Stud. Ev.*, TU 18 (1959) 277—94; 'Verité', VTB) takes its meaning from the Sapiential and apocalyptic sense of '*emet* (e.g. Jn 5:33; 17:17; 18:37): 'The Truth' is wisdom (Prv 23:23), a mystery revealed (Tb 12:11; Wis 6:22; Dn 11:2) and often in DSS a term of revelation, e.g. 1 QH 11, 7—10. Its sources being neither Gnostic (Bultmann) nor Hellenistic (Dodd), it can stand for the Law with a moral side shown in the entirely un-Gr. expressions 'to do the truth' (Jn 3:21; 1 Jn 1:6; 1QS 1, 3), 'to walk in the truth', 2 Jn 4; 3 Jn 3f. As revelation,

799e Truth is not conquered by an effort of thought but 'heard' (Jn 5:24; 8:26, 40, 43, 47; 14:24; 15:15) and synonymous with 'the word', e.g. 8:31; 17:17, cf 14:25 with 16:13. So 'The Truth' is the definitive revelation, the Word himself perfectly revealing the Father (14:6), contrasted with the OT revelation of the Law to Moses (1:17), and understood through the witness and inspiration of the Spirit of Truth, the Paraclete, 14:17; 15:26; 16:13; 1 Jn 4:6; 5:6. Believed, it becomes the interior, transforming principle of moral life (2 Jn 1f; 3 Jn 1), of liberty (Jn 8:32), of holiness (17:19) and of adoration, 4:23f.

f   Law and Commandments (Dodd, *Int.*, 75—86; Brown 504—5; Lazure, 123—45). Law (*nomos*) in Jn is OT *Torah* and denotes prescriptions for administering justice (7:51; 8:17; 18:31; 19:7), or the Pentateuch (1:45), or all the OT (10:34; 12:34, Pss), or the whole divine teaching at the base of the religious and moral life of Israel, 1:17; 7:19, 23, 49. It was a gift of God (1:17) to guide to Christ, 5:46. So in the mouth of Jesus 'your law' (8:17; 10:34) and 'their law' (15:25) are not hostile expressions, for they refer to Scripture, and it is just because of the continuity of the new revelation with the old, that to refuse Jesus is to contradict the OT. But they do mark the break. For **the Law has given place to Jesus** (1:17), the new 'way', 14:6 (contrast Dt 5:33—6:1; Ps 119 (118):1). Jn's proclamation of the pre-existent creative Word in the bosom of the Father, the Wisdom Incarnate whose glory we see full of grace and truth (Jn 1:1—14) confronts what the Rabbis said of the Torah; so do the 'real light of the world' (1:9; 8:12, cf IQS 2, 26) and the real bread from heaven, 6:32. It is not the words of the Torah but his words which are spirit and life (6:63), life given by him, not by knowledge of the Scriptures, 5:39f, cf 24; 1QS 8, 10. Not the Law but Jesus makes men sons of God (1:12) and gives them peace, 20:19f. So 'Law' in Jn never refers to the new salvation brought by Jesus. That is ruled by the **'New g Commandment'**, '**My Commandment**' (*entolē, entellesthai*) 'to love one another as I have loved you', 13:34; 15:12. This is not a code of laws but a way of love, perhaps best translated as a 'mandate', interiorly embraced, to share in God's loving work of salvation, cf 15:5 'much fruit'. Five texts concern the commandment(s) of the Father to the Son (10:18; 12:49f; 14:31; 15:10) and five of the Son of his disciples, 13:34; 14:15, 21; 15:10, 12. In both cases the command is to love even to giving one's life, 12:25f; 1 Jn 3:16. The relation between the Father and the Son is, as usually in Jn, in continuity with that between Jesus and his disciples. It is Jesus's last discourse which (like the Patriarchs' last words containing injunctions to their sons) contains this his testament, a mark of confidence bringing his disciples into his work, cf Mt 28:20. The sing. or pl. ('commandment(s)') may be interchangeable (Bultmann), or the sing. express an aspect of the Father's or the Son's will (Lazure), or the sing. show that love is the unifying factor of moral obligations (Brown, cf Mt 22:40; Rm 13:10). There is equivalence with 'keep my word(s)' (Jn 14:21—23), which confirms that this is no catalogue of precepts but the revelation of the divine will. This revelation is a 'gift' of the New Covenant ('give', 12:49; 13:34; 1 Jn 3:23; 'has', Jn 14:21; 1 Jn 2:7; 2 Jn 5), eternal life (12:50) to those who 'keep' (*tērein*) the commandment(s) by active love, 15:10; 1 Jn 5:3. 1, 2 Jn ('commandment(s)' 18 times) show in the life of the Christian community that the observance of the joyous message (*angelia*, 1 Jn 3:11) commanding brotherly love manifests the victorious dynamism of the new life

of the children of God, 2:4—8, 12ff. The 'New Commandment' is a way of faith, hope, love, adoration of the Father, and practice of justice and truth, directed by Jesus and the impulse of his Spirit, which follows his Person, life and words through the Cross to the Resurrection; it is 'new' because a reality of eschatological times, and 'not burdensome', 5:3.

Love (Lazure, 207—51; verb *agapan*, 37 times, noun **h** *agapē*, 7 times; in 1, 2, 3 Jn verb 31 times, noun 21; *philein* 13 times, probably synonym, Brown, 497ff) is essentially religious, all-embracing, practical. God is love, for love is from him, a love of gratuitous universal giving, whereby he has first loved us and sent his Son as propitiation for our sins (3:16; 6:37; 17:2; 1 Jn 4:7—10, 19). The Father loves the Son and the Son the Father (Jn 3:35; 5:20; 17). We have known love because Jesus has given his life for us (1 Jn 3:16), and his love is the source of the self-forgetful love (Jn 14:28) whereby we 'abide' in communion ('fellowship') with the Father and Jesus (15:4, 7; 17:21ff; 1 Jn 2:24) through the indwelling of the Spirit (3:24; Jn 14:15—20) and on condition that we prove our love for Jesus by obeying his command to love one another, 8:42; 14:21, 23f. This divine love of fellowship creates a community of life between God and man and a new community between men themselves, 1 Jn 1:3. The Father loves his Son's disciples (Jn 14:21, 23; 17:23), and the Son loves his own as the Father has loved him, and loves them even to the end, and in this love we are to abide, 13:1, 34; 15:9. Besides, Jesus loves the Beloved Disciple (13:23) and Martha and Mary and Lazarus (11:5), and we too are invited to be his friends to whom he reveals his secrets, 15:14f. This good news is also proclaimed by the formulae of reciprocity frequent in Jn: we are to share the love between the Father and the Son by the love between Jesus and ourselves and between each other, 6:57; 10:14f; 17:26.

The OT background is the Covenant love of Yahweh **i** for his People, calling forth and requiring an active response by observance of the Commandments, cf Dt *passim*. Jn takes the love of God for granted (5:42) without directly mentioning it (cf 1 Jn 4:20f; 5:2 and Syn.) but expresses it in terms of adoration, seeking the Father's glory, prayer to him. The Gospel is concentrated on Jesus the Mediator, cf 14:6. Further, it reflects the life of the Christian community who, in the midst of a hostile 'world', share the divine love uniting the Father and the Son. This picture goes with Jn's 'dualism' and resembles the intense brotherhood of Qumran, without its 'hate', 1QS 1, 10; 5, 4. It needs completing by the universal aspect of love envisaged by the rest of the NT and by 1 Jn, e.g. 2:2; 3:17; 4:20f.

So we are to love one another as Jesus has loved us **j** by a self-sacrificing practical love to our brother whom we see, not only in the rare case of laying down our lives for him, but in humble service, in loving sympathy and almsgiving, in hospitality, Jn 13:34; 15:12f; 1 Jn 3:16ff; 4:20f; 3 Jn 5ff. In its perfection love knows no fear, 1 Jn 4:17f. It is to be the one distinctive sign of Jesus's disciples, Jn 13:55.

Eschatology, cf § 672*n*.   **k**

Plan of the Gospel—Every kind has been proposed. **80** Most illuminating is Dodd's 'each several episode contains in itself the whole theme of the Gospel' (*Int.*, 385), yet even so each is in tension before the 'Hour'. To find Jn's plan we must look for his own simple, semitic criteria: inclusions, introductions and conclusions marking divisions, sub-divisions and sections dominated by the same theological theme, indicated perhaps by a constantly

00a repeated term which would not strike us (H. van den Bussche, 'Structure de Jean I—XIII, *L'Év. de Jean*, 61—109). His structure for Jesus's public life 'makes one think of a mounting of selected close-ups', but there is perspective and principle. A strong break is made between the hidden glory and the hour of glorification.

b **Chh 1—12 First Part of the Gospel: Signs and Works.**

1:1—18 The Prologue.

   1:19—51 Introduction: from the Baptist to Jesus.

Chh 2—4 The section of Signs (from Cana to Cana):

   2:1—12 The wine at the marriage.

   2:13—22 The sign of the Temple.

   2:23—3:36 From imperfect faith to birth from the Spirit and Jesus's baptism witnessed by the Baptist.

   4:1—42 The gift of God and the living water.

   43—54 Believe Jesus and live.

Chh 5—10 The section of Works:

   5 A healing and the works of the Son.

   6 The Messiah's banquet and the Bread of Life.

   7—8 The rejection of the Son, Light and refreshment of the world, at Tabernacles.

   9 Light to the blind.

   10:1—21 The noble Shepherd.

   22—31 Rejection at the Dedication.

   32—42 Inclusions on Works and the Public Life.

Chh 11—12 The ascent to the Passover:

   11:1—54 Lazarus: Life from death.

   55—12:19 The anointing and entry of the Messiah.

   12:20—36 The coming of the Gentiles; Jesus faces death.

   37—50 Meditation on the blindness of the Jews. Epilogue.

Chh 13—21 Second Part of the Gospel: the Hour of Glory.

13:1—17:26 The Supper:

   13:1—30 The washing of the feet. The traitor goes forth.

   14 Consolations.

   15—16:3 The Vine and the Branches; love and hate.

   16:4—33 The work of the Paraclete (= 14).

   17 Jesus's Priestly Prayer.

Chh 18—19 The Passion:

   18:1—27 The hour of darkness: betrayal and denial.

   18:28—19:16 The trial of the King-Judge.

   19:17—37 Jesus, lifted up on the Cross, fulfils all things, and, dying, gives the Spirit, the water and the blood.

Chh 20—21 Resurrection:

   20:1—29 Resurrection and Ascension in the garden. Jesus sends forth his brethren. Belief without seeing.

   21 Appendix. Peter and John. Second conclusion.

1:1—18 THE PROLOGUE

801a   **The Prologue** summarizes and interprets the Gospel. Its balanced rhythm probably shows that it is based on an ancient Christian hymn, but it resembles that of 1 Jn. The whole is set within an inclusion; see § 794*d*.

From the eternal presence of the Word with God, the movement passes to his creation of all things (3), then to his coming into the world to give life and light to men (4, 5) and to his own people granting to all who receive him to become sons of God (9—12) through his finally becoming flesh and dwelling amongst them (14). Then (with the antithetic structure of semitic v), after manifesting his glory as Son and his gifts of truth and grace which form us into a new, divine creation (14, 16f) he brings us back with him to the bosom of the Father whom he reveals (18). Jn is transposing the OT theme of Wisdom

existing with God, coming forth from him in creation, sent **801a** to dwell among his Chosen People, and bringing benefits to those who seek her; cf Prv 8:22—31; Wis 7:22—28; 9:9—12; Sir 24:1—22, and especially Is 55:10f, 'my word that goes forth from my mouth shall not return to me empty, but shall accomplish that which I purpose', cf Jn 8:42; 16:28, 'I came forth from the Father and have come into the world; again I am leaving the world and going to the Father'; 17:8. Vv 6—8 and 15 on the Baptist break the sequence of ideas, are in prose introduced by the OT formula 'there was a man' (e.g. Jg 13:2), and use subordinate clauses instead of the simple 'and'. Some (e.g. Boismard, R. Brown) think them inserted by a disciple-editor. Yet they balance each other (if they are not original, their insertion is hard to account for) and the allusion to future developments is Johannine. Perhaps vv 6, 7 originally stood before 19ff. As it is, Jn seems to follow and comment upon Lk: vv 13, 14 on Lk 1:35; 11 possibly on Lk 2:7, and 6—8 to summarize Lk 1:13—17, 57—80. The Prologue's central ideas become themes in the Gospel: the Word, life, light, darkness, witness, the Baptist, believe, genuine, the world, know, sons of God, born, flesh, glory, truth, the Law, see, the Son, the Father. As Gn 1 forms the background to 1—8, so does Ex to 14—18: the Shekinah, presence of Yahweh tented among men, is now the Word made flesh, the OT divine glory becomes the glory of the Son, the Law given through Moses, grace and truth given through Jesus, the passage to the Promised Land, the passage to the Father led by Jesus.

1—8 The Word with God and in creation—1—2. Four **b** simple sentences, the first three joined by 'and'; 'The Word' being the subject and 'was' the verb. The Gr. order is Word-Word . . . God-God, like 'a spiral flight to the Godhead' (Jn is traditionally 'the eagle' of Apoc 4:7). 'In the beginning', cf Gn 1:1; Prv 8:22. 'Was' contrasted with 'came to be' (aorist, vv 3, 6, 14) implies eternity, cf Ex 3:14f; Jn 8:58. **The Word**, cf § § 795c, 679*f—k*. Jn assumes that his readers will understand the name, cf 1 Jn 1:1; Rev 19:13. The OT word of God is his revelation expressed by creation (Gn 1:3; Wis 13:1), by the Law (Ex 34:27; Ps 119 (118)), the prophets (e.g. 2 Sm 23:2; Jer 1:9), and action, cf Is 55:10; this Word, like Wisdom, was personified; there was also God's avenging word, Is 11:4; Wis 18:14ff (cf Rev 19:11—16. In the NT the word becomes the message of or about Jesus (e.g. Mk 4:14—20; Ac 18:5). In Jn the word of God is what Jesus says and is, and cannot be separated from him, Jn 5.38. Jesus's own word is 'life' (6:53) and it purifies those who receive it (15:3), judges those who reject it (12:47f) and gives eternal life, 5:24. Jesus, not the Scriptures, gives life (5:39f), and is himself the Word of Life, 1 Jn 1:1f. Thus Jn 1:1—4 in the manner of sapiential Judaism gives a new interpretation of Gn's account while introducing the new creation. Jesus is God's creative Word and also the Word in substitution for the Jewish idea of the Law existing at the creation, cf Ps 33 (32):4—9; Jn 1:17. Jn has realized that Jesus, whose pre-existing role in creation Christianity had already proclaimed (Col 1:15f; Heb 1:1—3), is in his Person that Wisdom, Law, Word. Though he calls him Word because of his creative and revealing function, this is founded on the very nature of the Only Son (Jn 1:13, 18) whose relations with the Father, are now described (Dupont, Boismard). *Pros ton Theon* marks distinction but intimate presence, cf 10:38; 14:11; no English preposition ('with' God) can render the dynamic Gr. 'towards': 'looking towards God', E. A. Abbott, *Joh. Grammar*, n. 2308, and

801b cf on *eis*, v 18. 'God' with the article is the Father, as mostly in NT, cf 2 Cor 13:13; 1 Jn 1:2.

c But the Word was also God. There is no article before 'God', and this avoids personal identification with the Father, or the Hellenistic sense of a second God. But that it does not imply simply a divine being ('god') is shown by the inclusions (§ 794*d*) with 1:18 and 20:29, and by 10:30 and ch 17; indeed 'the whole Gospel will go on to reveal this mystery of the distinction of Persons within the divine unity' (BJ); 'John intends that the whole of his Gospel shall be read in the light of this v' (Barrett). **2.** Inclusion and summary, cf 17:5. **3.** Transition to the Word's relation to the world: all else 'came to be' through him, God's Personal Word, cf 1 Cor 8:6; 'and not-one-thing came to be apart from him'. The division we adopt suits the rhythm and is borne out by 1QS 11, 11. **4—5.** Structure, rhythm and chain words as in 1f. Until the Arians abused the text, 'that which was made' was universally joined to v 4. 'All that came to be was alive with his life' (NEB). The best MSS have 'is', but 'was' is probably right from parallelism with 4*b*. All life has its source in the Word (BJ), cf 1 Jn 5:11ff. This Life communicates itself as Light. **5.** Light and Darkness form a major theme in Jn (Gn 1:2f and cf DSS). 'has not overcome it'; lit did not overtake it, cf Jn 12:35. The verb has the idea of seizing or grasping after a pursuit, cf Rm 9:30; Phil 3:12f, but, in the present context, with the implication of overcoming or quenching, cf Wis 7:30; 1 Jn 2:8; *Odes Sol.* 13:6. It should not be taken as 'understand' (not Semitic), nor 'welcome' (contrast *parelabon*, v 11). 'Darkness' in Jn never means men as such, but Satan's world in which they are plunged.

d **6—8. Anticipatory parenthesis** in Jn's manner, cf above. He is called simply 'John' ('God has given grace') as the remembered Master. '**Witness**', key word in Jn, who uses the verb 33 times (Mt 1, Lk 1, Mk 0); it has affinity with truth, faith and light, and means not only to attain the historic truth of Jesus but to have 'contemplated his glory' (Jn 1:14) revealed only to the believer, 11:40; 'he who believes in the Son of God has the testimony of God in himself', 1 Jn 5:10; cf TWNT 4, 504 (Strathmann); for the principal witnesses, cf § 792*g*; for the light Jn's treatment sheds on modern philosophy, cf J. C. Hindley, 'Witness in the Fourth Gospel', ScotJT, 18, iii, (1965) 319—37. 'Witness to the Light', needed because veiled by 'the flesh'; the Baptist saw and brought others to believe, Jn 1:34—37; 'all', he has a universal mission; 'not the light', but a lamp, 5:35. Jn is insisting that he was not the Messiah, cf Ac 19:1—5.

e **9—11 Rejection of the Light**—'The Light', cf § 798*c*. 'True' (*alēthinos*), real, genuine, usually as fulfilling its OT type (Crehan, 31ff), which here is the light of Gn 1:3, cf 1 Jn 2:8. So used for the bread from heaven contrasted with manna (6:32), the Sender (7:28), the vine (15:1), God (contrasted with idols), the Son (with Israel, Ex 4:22; Jn 17:3; 1 Jn 5:20), worshippers (Jn 4:23); the witness (Apoc 3:14); *alēthēs* means truthful, correct. Translate: '*He was the real light that enlightens every man and was coming into the world*'. 'Coming' could be (a) masc. accus., referring to 'man' as 'him who comes into the world' (*Lev. R.* 31, 6), but this is pleonastic; (b) periphrastic imperf. (Barrett), but 'was' is emphatically first and 'coming' separated from it, so both should have their full force; (c) neut. nom. agreeing with 'light', cf Jn 3:19; 9:39; 13:46. Christ's action as the Light is 'a constant, continuous coming . . . advancing towards the Incarnation by preparatory revelations' (Westcott), as Creator (10), among the Jews (11), at the Incarnation

(14). 'Every man', not only the Jews. **10.** Again three **80** short sentences joined by 'and' (last is Heb. adversative). **The world** (*kosmos*) is part of creation, the world of men, cf 3:19; it is loved by God; Jesus, its Saviour and Light, gives his flesh for its life (3:16f; 9:5, cf Mt 5:14; Jn 6:51) and sends his disciples into it, 17:18. But men's opposition to the Light (3:19) makes of 'the big world' (7:4) a 'negative counterpart of "kingdom"' (Crehan, 115), with Satan for prince, 12:31; 14:30; 17; 18:36; 1 Jn 5:19. For this world Jesus does not pray (Jn 17:9), nor may his followers love it, 1 Jn 2:15. **11.** 'To his own' People (through the Law, the prophets, the Incarnation). Yet they did not receive (essentially 'believe', cf 3:11f) him.

12—13 Welcome to the Light—Hinge of the Prologue. **f** 'Received him not . . . received him', semitic way of speaking; probably the Jews are first in mind, then the 'remnant'; perhaps a summary of the two parts of the Gospel: The Book of Signs in which Jesus is rejected, 1—12, and the Book of Glory, in which he forms his own as believing Christians, 13—20 (Brown). 'Who believed in his name', omitted by many Fathers, could be a conflated text (BJ, Boismard), but is typically Johannine. 'He gave power to' prob. here translates Aram. *natan*, 'grant', on the root OT idea that to give life belongs to God (Bultmann, Boismard); elsewhere 'power' is authority over judgement, life and death, 5:27; 10:18; 17:2; 19:10. 'Children of God', born from on high by baptism, 3:5. 'Who was born' is the reading of a number of versions and very early Fathers (Aug. and Amb. knew both readings) adopted by Boismard ('Critique textuelle et citations patristiques', RB 57 (1950) 406f), Burney, Dupont, Mollat, etc. But all Gr. MSS, both Bodmer papyri and most ancient versions read 'who were born' and a Christological text is unlikely to have been altered; J. Schmid, ('Joh. 1:13', BZ 1 (1957) 118—25), Barrett, Bultmann, Brown opt for the pl., which refers to baptismal regeneration. The sing. may have arisen from Jn's strong triple negative, prob. alluding to Jesus's virginal birth as pattern for the birth of Christians (Barrett), while undersigning Lk 1:26—38, cf 1 Jn 5:18 where Jesus's virginal birth is combined with baptismal re-birth. He empowers others to be what he is himself, cf Jn 11:25; 12:35f; 14:12. 'Blood', human generation, cf Wis 7:2; 'flesh', man in his weakness; our text may be conflated— some Fathers read simply 'neither blood nor flesh'.

14—18. 'The Word became flesh' introduces the **g** Second Part of the Prologue (contrasted by inclusion with the first): The Word who 'was with God in the beginning' (v 1), now 'became' historically 'flesh', the whole man in his weakness (Gn 6:3; Is 40:6; Jn 3:6) in complete contrast with God, cf Phil 2:5ff. Jn may also be refuting the Docetists, cf 1 Jn 4:1ff; 2 Jn 7. 'And dwelt', lit 'dwelt in his tent' (*eskēnōsen*), as God among his People under the sign of the Cloud and the Glory, Ex 33:9f; 40:34. His presence (*Shekina*, same consonants as Jn's Gr. word 'dwell in a tent') continued in Sion (1 (3) Kgs 8:10f; Jl 3:17—21) especially as Wisdom dwelling in Israel through the Law, Sir 24:1ff. It is now realized in magnificent fullness by the humanity of Jesus who becomes God one with his People, cf Lk 1:35; Rev 21:3. 'We saw his glory' (as eyewitnesses) enuntiates Jn's theme of the **Glory** of the Son (§ 798*f*) against the background of Yahweh's manifestations of his glory (Ex 24; 33:18ff; Is 6:1), pointing on to the miracles and probably the Transfiguration (Mt 17:1—9 and pars), and culminating in ch 17 and the Passion and Resurrection. 'Glory as', not 'like' but 'as being', cf Mk 1:22; Lk 6:22 (Chrys.); 'from the Father' could refer to 'glory' (cf Jn 17:22; 2 Pt 1:16f)

1g or to 'Son' with a further idea of 'sent', cf Jn 3:16f; 1 Jn 4:9. A key doctrine in Jn is that Jesus is the Son proceeding and sent from the Father. 'Full', possibly nom. referring to the Word, but probably gen. (*koinē* form) agreeing with Son. 'Grace and truth' in the Covenant context are God's *ḥesed* (kindness, goodness to someone) and *'emet* (fidelity in this merciful love), e.g. Ex 34:6; Nm 14:18; Hos 2:16—22; Ps *passim*; so here Boismard translates 'fidelity' and Brown 'enduring love', cf Rm 15:8. But for Truth in Jn generally cf § 799*e*.

h **15.** 'John bears witness (pres.) and has cried' (perf.)—his witness is present and complete (Westcott). This is the Baptist's first witness (repeated v 30) to the Word's pre-existence. The image of two runners later passes into one of dignity, cf ? 20:4ff; 'before me he was', cf 8:58. **16** follows on from 14. 'Of his fullness', of the divine life filling him which he communicates to us, cf v 14 and Col 2:9f. 'Grace upon grace', *anti* expresses opposition or substitution. The Gr. Fathers held it to be the grace of the Gospel substituted for the Law, but then (v 17) the Law is not 'grace' for Jn; so best: grace corresponding to the fullness of grace in the Word (Bernard, Braun, etc). **17.** The comparison of Moses and the Law with Christ is implicit throughout the Gospel cf § 799*f*. The whole Mosaic revelation, expression of God's wisdom (Sir 24:23ff; Bar 4:1), divine gift to Israel (cf Jos.Ant., 7, 338), is contrasted with the New Covenant which comes to us through Jesus. 'Grace and truth' here must be what Christ from his fullness creates in us (for they 'came to be' cf v 3), cf Col 2:9f; Orig. 'Grace' is Christian grace, the free, interior principle of love (Westcott, Braun). The word appears four times in the Prologue but never again, although the 'spiritual Gospel' is entirely penetrated with the doctrine and with alternative formulae (Bonnetain, 'Grâce', DBS, **i** 716). Perhaps Jn is saluting the NT expression. **18.** 'No one has ever seen God' in this life, cf Ex 32.20, Jn 6.46, 1 Jn 3:2; 4:12. Then three readings: 'Only Begotten God', the commonest, is awkward for the Son as revealer and probably adopted against the Arians; 'Only Begotten Son' attested by ancient versions and many Fathers, fits with Jn 3:16, 18; 1 Jn 4:9; 'Only Begotten' (Tat., Orig. (once) Epiphanius, Cyr. Jer.) is shortest and perhaps best, well rendered by 'the only Son'. 'Who is in (*eis*) the bosom of the Father' expresses intimate union and active intercourse, forms an inclusion with v 1, which it deepens, and is parallel with 1 Jn 1:2, 'the eternal life which by its very nature was turned towards the Father', not just divine life but filial divine life. The real translation is 'into the bosom'. I. de la Potterie ('L'emploi de *eis* dans S. Jean et ses incidences théologiques', Bib 43 (1962), 366—87) has shown that Jn never uses *eis* (into) for the static *en* (in), cf also E. A. Abbott, *Joh. Grammar* (1906), 2305—23, 2706—13. 'Into' has a dynamic sense 'a combination (as it were) of rest and motion, of a continuous relation with a realization of it' (Westcott). By a surely intended contrasted likeness the Beloved Disciple is 'in (*en*) the bosom of Jesus'. So the text does not directly concern consubstantiality (as Gr. Fathers, Aquin.) and yet expresses more than a psychological intimacy. It suggests the eternal generation of the Only Son (*ōn*, pres. part.). Always object of his Father's love (cf Jn 17:5), he is always 'turning towards the bosom of his Father', eternally conscious of receiving all his divine **j** life from him, cf 6:57. This interior penetration balances and goes beyond v 1, and is important for the living relations of Father and Son. The Prologue's theology is more than 'functional': it describes not only 'the Logos

turned to the world' (O. Cullmann), but 'the Logos who **801j** is God turned towards God' (L. Malevez, 'Nouveau Testament et théologie fonctionelle', RSR 48 (1960), 258—90). Hence the Son shares the secrets of the Father, cf 13:23ff; 'he has made him known': *exēgēsato* (Vg 'enarravit'), a term for description and explanation (cf Lk 24:35; Ac 10:8, etc) and so for revelation (TWNT 2, 910, F. Büchsel), is here used without complement in its full amplitude. Jesus reveals the Father with all the riches of his life to be communicated to us, cf 1 Jn 1:2; Jn 1:4. The Son 'looks towards the Father and then towards us and "speaks the Father forth", cf 14:16' (Martindale). The word can also mean 'led out, and Boismard ('Dieu dans le sein du Père', RB 59 (1952), 23ff) argues from some MSS and Fathers to an original text 'the Only Son is he who has led into the Father's bosom'. As the Pillar of Fire led the Israelites into the Promised Land, Jesus who fixed his tent amongst us, goes before us to illumine our way to the Father, cf Lk 16:22. This interpretation can also claim inclusion with v 1.

PART I. SIGNS AND WORKS. 1—12.

1:19—51 From the Baptist to Jesus—Many hold that **802a** Jn here presents seven days, inaugural week of the new creation, the birth of the Church's faith, cf Gn 1. Vv 19—28 first day, the Baptist's witness before the Jews; 29—34 'the next day', 'behold the Lamb of God'; 35—39 'the next day', the first disciples follow Jesus; 41—42 'in the morning' (possible reading), the call of Peter; 43—51 Jesus starts for Galilee, call of Philip and Nathanael; 2:1ff 'on the third day', the marriage at Cana (Boismard, *Du Baptême à Cana*). Jn also marks out Jesus's last week, cf on 12:1. For another view, H. Van den Bussche, 'Structure de Jean 1—12', *L'Év. de Jean*, 61—109. Jn assumes the Syn. account of the Baptist, the baptism of Jesus and the theophany. He confines himself to one point: the Baptist's testimony (19), already summarized (6—8, 15). He is simply the bridge between OT and NT, the pointer to the Light. **19—28 John's Witness—19—20.** 'And', the Prologue is **b** not detached from the Gospel and passes to the Baptist's actual witness. This 'opens the dramatic trial which in Jn encloses the life of Jesus' (BJ). 'The Jews', the official heads of the nation at Jerusalem, standing for opposition to Jesus, cf § 792*i*; 'priests and Levites', a delegation of experts sent to enquire about a baptizing movement which might be Messianic. 'Who are you?', a normal question to the originator of an unauthorized movement; 'Are you the Messiah?' would be too pointed. The reply is put positively, then with solemn negative, then positively again. 'I am not the Christ' points to another; they were asking the Gospel's great question of the wrong person. **21.** The Jews, taking literally Mal 3:23f (cf Mt 16:14; 17:10, para.), thought that Elijah would prepare the Messiah's coming (cf Just., *Dial.* 8, 4) and John had appeared in the desert like him in dress and character, Mk 1:4ff. 'I am not' Elijah in person. Jesus identifies their roles, Mt 11:14; 17:12. 'Are you the prophet?' awaited (Jn 6:14, cf Dt 18:15—18; cf also Qumran, 1QS 9, 11). 'No', still more curt, John will not be taken for any great religious figure. **22.** The delegates 'want something for their dossier' (Van den Bussche); John simply describes himself as the unknown 'voice crying in the wilderness' (Is 40:3), once heralding Israel's deliverance, and now preparing a new Exodus, cf Mt 3:1f; IQS 8, 13ff; 'make ready' is changed into 'make straight'; 'as . . . said' may be Jn's addition.

802b **24—25.** 'from the Pharisees' (RSV) is strange, for the authorities and most priests were Sadducees, unless Jn is using 'Pharisees' for Jesus's enemies. Better 'some *Pharisees who were in the deputation*' (NEB, BJ alternative), for some priests were Pharisees (Oxyrh. pap. 840; Lagrange, RB ns 5 (1908), 538ff) and these add their own aggressive thrust: What right has a nobody to create a new rite of purification and Messianic preparation, cf Ezek 36:25; Mk 1:4—8? **26—27.** To these indiscreet enquirers John does not mention the revelation made to him (33); simply, to the rite of water he opposes the person of one who should have aroused their curiosity, for the Messiah would remain unknown until his public manifestation, Jn 7:27; Just., *Dial.* 8, 3. 'You do not know' suggests the theme of the Jews' blindness (e.g. 8:19; 9:29), and they take no notice here. To untie the thong of a sandal was not a Jewish servant's, but only a slave's office. **28.** Jn solemnly marks the place of the Baptist's witness and makes of it an inclusion for Jesus's public life, cf 10:40. 'Bethany' is the better attested reading, though it cannot be identified geographically. 'Bethabara' which occurs in some MSS is probably due to Origen, who looked for Bethany and could not find it by the Jordan, but did find a Bethabara where a local tradition existed that John had baptized there, *In Joannem*, 6, 40. 'Bethany' must be accepted as the reading in 1:28, though the alternative is attractive. 'Bethabara' is attested by some MSS which may not depend on Origen and possibly go back to Tatian, cf Boismard, 37f. Bethabara means 'Place of Passage', Orig. had at least heard of such a place, (see Jg 7:24) and as Père Abel noted (RB n.s. 10 (1913) 240 citing the Talmud), it is unlikely that no place would have commemorated the Israelites' passage of the Jordan, Jos 3:14—17. Perhaps Jn sees Jesus as the new Joshua. The deputation evidently left.

c **29—51 From John to Jesus**—Some of Jn's key words keep recurring here: 'See' or 'look at' (14 times), 'find' (5), 'stay' or 'abide' (*menō*, 5), 'follow' (4) or 'come to' Jesus. Note the titles given to Jesus: 'Lamb of God' (vv 29, 36), 'he who baptizes in the Holy Spirit' (33), 'the elect of God' (34), 'Rabbi' (38), 'the Messiah' ('the Christ') (41), 'he of whom Moses wrote in the Law' (45), 'Jesus of Nazareth, the son of Joseph' (46, in an objection), 'Son of God and King of Israel' (49), 'Son of Man' (51) (Boismard, 21ff). **29.** 'The next day' the Baptist, hitherto curt, becomes expansive, for now he points to Jesus. Jn assumes from Syn. (and cf v 33) that Jesus has come from Galilee to be baptized, then gone into the desert and now returned, probably staying in a hut by the Jordan. 'There he is!' The audience are presumably disciples. 'Lamb of God' is traditionally interpreted of the Paschal Lamb, and Jesus dies to take upon himself the sins of the world. But the Baptist had not gone beyond an avenging Messiah (cf Mt 3:11f) and the Lamb does not 'bear the sins' but 'does away with the sin'. This is a function of the Jewish Messiah apart from any thought of a redemptive death, e.g. Is 60:21; Ezek 36:25ff; *Test. Levi*, 18, 9 (Dodd, *Int.*, 237); also 1QS 27, 4—6. It is the sense of 1 Jn 3:5—9: Jesus has received the Spirit (Jn 1:32) and communicates it to men as a divine seed which gives them the power to walk in God's Law (cf Ezek 36:26f), and so he 'takes away sin' (Boismard). But why 'Lamb of God'? The Baptist, conscious of being the unknown prophet of Is 40:3 (Jn 1:23), thinks in terms of Is 53:7; 42:1f, cf the reading 'Chosen One', Jn 1:34. The silence and obscurity of the Lamb-Servant is what he is conveying about Jesus (cf Van den Bussche). Later, at the Cross, Jn will see a deeper sense and make the Lamb

one of his main symbols (19:36; 1 Jn 2:2; Rev 5:6—12, **80** cf Ac 8:32; 1 Cor 5:7; 1 Pt 1:18ff). **30.** Repeats 15. The Baptist may be thinking of an Elijah-like figure (J. Robinson, *Twelve NT Studies*, 28—52). But Jn can hardly fail to see the pre-existence of the Word in 'he was before me', and yet his vocabulary is Messianic: 'A man' translates *anēr* (husband), the Messianic bridegroom (cf 1:13; 4:16ff; 6:10; Rev 21:2). **31.** 'I myself did not know him' is possible in the literal sense if he had been in the desert from childhood. But it may mean 'as Messiah' (cf however Mt 3:14), or as the one who would baptize with the Spirit. **32—34.** Jn adds to Mk 1:10 that the Spirit 'remained' (*menō*) on him, sign that he had the Spirit in fullness, Is 11:2; 42:1; 61:1, cf Jn 3:34. 'As a dove', omitted by some versions and set in different places by others, may have come in from Syn. Dodd (HT 259, n.) suggests 'as the flight of a dove'. Not 'Son of God', but 'the Chosen one of God' is the better reading (Sin., etc), cf Is 42:1; Lk 9:35; 23:35.

35—51 The first disciples—'A personal souvenir, **d** caressed in the memory, simple and graceful' of the origin of the Christian Church (Bengel). **35—40.** 'The next day', a new stage: John standing with his disciples, Jesus passing by. John looks hard at him and repeats the words which may 'yesterday have startled but today spur on to action' (Martindale). The two disciples 'follow' (from curiosity, but the word will deepen into 'follow as disciples'; so with 'seek' and 'stay', (*menō*). Jesus's welcoming frankness overcomes their shyness. Jn still remembers the word 'Rabbi', a mere title of politeness, translated for Gr. readers. 'Where are you staying?' hints that they want to meet him. 'Come and see' has Rabbinic parals (SB 2, 371). The vivid, banal 'around four o'clock' is Jn's signature (cf 4:6; 18:28; 19:14). According to oriental hospitality, they would have stayed the night (Chrys., Cyr.Alex., Aug.). The unnamed disciple is either undistinguished—but then why mentioned and allowed to fade out?—or the author (Chrys.), never named, but indicating his witness by a detail, cf 13:23ff; 19:26; 20: 2ff; 21:7, 20. **41—42.** Readings: 'The first thing he did was to find his brother' (best attested); 'was the first to find his brother'—and the other disciple found his; 'at daybreak' (3 Latin MSS and syr. sin.). 'Looked', same word for intense gaze as v 36. 'Simon', Gr. form of Chimeon, son of John; 'Cephas'. Graecized form of Kepha, 'Rock', Gr. *Petros* as Jn notes. To change a name was an authoritative act corresponding to a change in situation or function, Gn 17:5; 32:28; Is 62:2. Jn records the occasion, the list of Apostles (Mk 3:16; Lk 6:14) the fact, Mt 16:18 the reason. **43—44.** The mention **e** of Jacob's ladder suggests that the route was W to Bethel and then along the N highway through Samaria. Apparently it is in Galilee that Jesus finds Philip; and Nathanael sounds at home under the fig tree. 'Follow me', cf Mt 4:19, 22; 8:22; 9:9. Bethsaida-Julias, NE of the Lake of Tiberias (modern Et-Tell), was a Hellenized town; Philip ('Lover of horses') and Andrew ('Manly', also in Talmud) have Gr. names, cf on Jn 12:20ff. **45—46.** Nathanael ('Gift of God'), from Cana (21:2), is not **f** named in the lists of the Apostles, and patristic tradition does not know him as one. But he is among them in Jn 21, and 1:51 implies that he is a principal witness of the glories of Jesus. He is usually identified with Bartholomew, whose name follows Philip's in the lists (cf U. Holzmeister, 'Nathanael fuitne idem ac S. Bartholomaeus Apostolus?', Bib 21 (1940), 28—39). 'Moses wrote', cf Dt 18:18f; Philip gives the popular view of Jesus's parentage. Nathanael's spontaneous objection may be about a rival town (? with a bad reputation, Mt 13:54—48, parals),

02f but Nazareth and Jesus's supposed origin are stumbling-blocks throughout the Gospel, for the Messiah must be from Bethlehem, Jn 7:41f. Nathanael accepts the good method of coming to see for himself (contrast the Pharisees' prejudice against a fact). **47.** 'An Israelite worthy of the name' (NEB), cf Is 44:5; 'guile', not a lie but the sin of irreligion (e.g. Hos 12:1; Zeph 3:13; Rev 14:5), whereas Nathanael admits that he is a sinner (J. Jeremias, 'Die Berufung des Nathanael', Angelos 3 (1928), 4). 'Israelite' prob. taken here as 'a man who sees God' (contrast Jn 8:39—47). **48—49.** Nathanael will not be taken in by a compliment. Jesus shows knowledge of perhaps some crisis in his secret heart. The straightforward sceptic becomes the enthusiastic believer. The Messianic titles given Jesus (cf Ps 2:6f) illustrate the disciples' deepening knowledge of him during his whole ministry, cf Mk 1:22; 4:40f; 8:29; 15:39 (Brown,

g 77f). **50—51.** 'The man who sees God' will see greater things, usually seen as miracles in the wider sense of Christ's glorification, but also his glorification at the Cross, Resurrection and Ascension (2:11, 18—21; 6:62) and the Last Coming, Mt 26:64. 'Truly, truly' is 'Amen, amen', Jesus's solemn assertion, 20 times in Jn. **'The Son of Man'**, the Messianic figure of glory, (§ 676k—p), incorporates in himself the People of God and indeed humanity as the Second Adam (cf 19:5) and in Jn is bound up with exaltation and glorification, 3:14; 8:28; 12:23—34, cf Ac 2:33; 3:13. Dn 7:13f is especially in mind and related also to Jn 3:1ff; 6:62. The narrative of the call of the disciples has worked up to this title, into which Jesus changes those given him by Nathanael, and to the promise of the vision. It will now reach a first fulfilment.

2—4 THE SECTION OF SIGNS

03a **2:1—11 The Marriage at Cana**—**1.** On the 'third day' (probably reckoned from 1:43, there could be resurrectional symbolism), Jesus 'manifests his glory' (2:11) by this abundant gift of wine, first of the 'signs' of his Paschal Mystery. His 'Hour' includes the Eucharist (13:1), the Cross and the Resurrection on the Third Day, and in it his Mother will have a special part, 19:25f. 'Marriage' must recall the marriage of Yahweh and his People, and so now that of Jesus the Bridegroom (3:39), bringing new wine (Mk 2:19—22), cf NT parables of the marriage feast, Mt 22:1—14; 25:1—13. Cana, Kefr Kenna, 4 m. NE of Nazareth, or Khirk-t Qânâ, 9 m. N, is distinguished carefully from Cana not far from Tyre, Jos 19:28. 'Mother of Jesus' was the most honourable way of naming a woman who had had a son; Mary's name, like those of others connected with himself, is never mentioned in Jn. A kind of inclusion ('Mother . . . Woman . . . hour') joins these first manifestation of glory to her presence at Jesus's glorification in death and 'suggests a whole Marian theology' (BJ). **3.** 'Wine' rejoices the heart of man (Ps 104 (103): 14), and its abundance, a principal OT sign of blessing, will mark the Messianic restoration, Gn 49:11f; Is 62: 8f. The changing of water for Jewish purification into this wine has for background the wine of Wisdom's banquet (Prv 9:1—5; Is 55:1) and the water of the Law replaced by Christ's teaching (Orig., In Jn, 10, 31; Cyr. Alex., PG 73, 229, Dodd, Boismard). It could not fail to suggest a sacramental significance (Cullmann, etc) as the early Christians saw when they depicted this miracle as the counterpart of the multiplication of the loaves. Marriage festivities could last a week and with poor people it was easy for wine to run short. Mary's

kindly eye sees the embarrassment. 'They have no wine' **803b** could be a simple observation or a discreet request, (cf 11:3, 21). **4.** 'Woman', a polite and normal title but very strange from a son to his mother, is clearly linked with 'woman' in 19:26, and the natural reference is to Eve (Gn 2:23; 3:15, 20). Literally 'what to me and to thee'? This means 'what is there in common between you and me?' (e.g. Jg 11:12; 2 Sm 16:10; 19:23; 1 (3) Kgs 17:18; Mt 8:29; Mk 1:24; Lk 4:34; 8:28). Interpretations such as 'leave it to me' are without support in scripture or the great line of tradition, e.g. Iren., Chrys., Aug. (PL 35, 1455, 9), Aquin. (In ev. Jn, 79), Bernard (PL 183, 160). Jesus belongs wholly to his Father's will, and now that his public life has started, the bonds of blood, however dear, are suspended, cf Mt 12:48f; Mk 3:33f; Lk 2:34f, 49; 11:27. Indeed 'woman' seems to abstract from his being her Son (Braun, La Mère des Fidèles, 50). 'You have no claims on me—yet' (Barrett). The words could be softened by tone of voice or a smile. 'My hour' has been taken as that of public miracles, but almost always refers in Jn to Jesus's Passion and glorification, cf 7:30; 8:20 (our phrase); 12:23, 27; 13:1; 17:1, and especially 19:27 'from that hour the disciple took her', cf Aug., op cit, 1456, 1950. Clearly similar is Jesus's refusal to his brethren to go up to Jerusalem because his 'time' has not yet come, 7:6, 8. In Jn Jesus always keeps the initiative over miracles, e.g. 4:47, 50; 11:3, 21. But he implies that when his 'Hour' has come, the separation will be at an end (J. H. Newman, Letter to Pusey, 72), and in spite of his declaration, Mary gives the order to the servants which initiates his action. Jesus, who never resists humble faith, grants an outstanding miracle to his Mother before his 'Hour'. **6.** There is contrast with the New Dispensation, cf Mk 7:3f; Jn 3:25. The jars held about 9 gallons each. **7.** 'This v makes it impossible to regard v 4 as a refusal to take any action. Jesus has not changed his mind in the interval, though he has indicated his independence' (Barrett). **8.** The 'steward', probably 'toast-master', perhaps a local expert, is patronizingly 'knowing'. **11.** 'Signs', cf § 792e. 'Glory', cf § 798f. 'believed', their belief is confirmed by a 'sign' which completes their initiation.

12. The short stay at Capharnaum makes a transition **c** to the next tableau. 'Went down' from about 1,500 feet above sea level to 680 feet below. Later Jesus made the town (probably Tell Hum, NW shore of the Sea of Galilee) his headquarters (cf Mt 9:1, 'his own town'). Caravans would be forming there for the Paschal journey to Jerusalem. 'His brethren', cf §§ 663—4. But other MSS read 'and the brethren' i.e. the disciples, in which case 'and the disciples' (omitted by S. and others) could be a doublet.

13—22. The Sign of the Temple is a diptych to the **d** Sign of the Water made Wine. Jesus manifests himself as Messiah in the Temple and proclaims that he will take its place as centre of worship. To the faith of the disciples (2:11) corresponds the incredulity of the Jews. This is the first of Jn's three Passovers, cf 6:4; 11:55. Mk, followed by Mt and Lk places the Cleansing of the Temple in the last week of Christ's life, Mk 11:15—19; Mt 21:12f; Lk 19:45. Perhaps he is putting all his Jerusalem material together at his only Passover and Jn's is the more accurate chronology as his are the more vivid details. But if Jn used Mk it is possible that he has changed the position of the cleansing, for theological rather than chronological reasons. Thus, after the witness of the **e** Baptist, it is appropriate that the Messiah should come to his Temple to cleanse it. Besides it seems more likely that Jesus would precipitate a crisis of this kind at the end of his public life rather than at the beginning,

803e (Barrett). **13.** 'went up': a technical term for pilgrimage to Jerusalem, but possibly 'to the hilly country', may be an intended contrast with the Christian feast or an ex-
f planation for Gentiles. **14—16.** 'In the Temple', i.e. the outer court of the Gentiles. This marketing meant uproar and cheating. Foreign money was changed into the half-shekel coin of the tribute (Mt 17:24); only Jn mentions the whip made of small cords—easy to pick up in a market. The men were driven out first, then the slower moving beasts; pigeon sellers had their chairs overturned and were told to be off (Mk). 'My Father's house' implies special relationship, cf Lk 2:49. **17.** Note the presence of disciples. They remembered Ps 69 (68):9, seen as prophecy: the zeal of Jesus for his Father's house will lead to his death; the ps is often cited in relation to the Passion (e.g. Jn 15:25; 19:28). **18.** After the Baptist's witness the authorities may suspect something, Mal 3:1ff. They demand a sign to justify his action, cf Mk 11:28, and for a wrongful demand for a sign, Mt 12:38ff; Jn 4:48; 6:26. **19.** Cf A. M. Dubarle, 'Le Signe du Temple', RB 48 (1939), 21—44. 'Destroy' stands for a future condition: 'if you shall destroy', cf Is 37:30; 'temple', the sanctuary, *naos*, the most sacred part, including the Holy of Holies. To those in bad faith Jesus gives a sign not clear at the time, cf Mt 16:4. However they should have understood something: Jer 7:11—14 foretold that the evil-doing of the people would destroy the Temple, and Tb 14:7—10; Zech 14:20ff spoke of an ideal Temple in which no commerce would be tolerated, cf also Is 56:7. So if the Jews destroyed the Temple by defiling it, Jesus would raise up the Messianic Temple
g (Brown). **20.** But, as usual in Jn, the Jews understand only materially. How can he so quickly re-build what has taken 46 years to build? If Herod started re-building the Temple in 20—19 B.C., we are at the Passover of A.D. 28. **21.** Instead of the Syn. word 'build', Jn uses 'raise up'. The new place of divine presence (1:14), centre of the worship 'in spirit and in truth' (4:23f), the spiritual Temple from which the living waters of the Spirit will flow (Ezek 47; Jn 7:38) will be the sanctuary of the risen body of Jesus. As his Spirit dwells in us, our bodies too will be temples of God, 1 Cor 3:16; 2 Cor 6:16. The substitution of Christ for the Temple is one of Jn's symbols, Rev 21:22. The presence of God, once filling the Temple, has become flesh in Jesus. **22.** But the disciples had to await the Resurrection and the Paraclete to understand. Though no miracle occurs, Jesus's intervention in the Temple is a sign, an action revealing his Messiahship (cf Mal 3:1; Zech 14:21).

804a **23—25 Imperfect Faith**, which Nicodemus instances, is based on 'signs' (23 and 3:2, cf 4:48). There is no break before ch 3 (read 'him' in 3:2); 'believe' (2:23f) with 'believe' 7 times in 3:12—18, unifies the passage. 'In his name': they believe (imperfectly) what is in him; 'see' (*theōrein*) is used, at least at the outset of the Gospel, for superficial or inferior 'beholding' (Abbot, *Joh. Vocab.* n. 1598). 'Trust himself' (Gr. 'believe' with dat.), confide himself to their enthusiasm (Brown). For Jesus (Joh. theme) knows men.
b **3.** Unified by 'cannot see the kingdom' (3), 'will not see life' (36), has two episodes: the meeting with Nicodemus (1—12) and the witness of the Baptist (22—30), followed by two meditations on the Redemption (13—21, 31—36), homogeneous in style and doctrine and inwoven with the narrative.
c **1—21 Christian faith comes by birth from the Spirit**—Jn's way of working is to take an episode, like many in Syn., and an instruction of Jesus's. After the giving of the Spirit (7:39), he has so penetrated these

'words of spirit and life' (6:63) as to develop from them **804**
'the heavenly things', in a sense the whole Gospel (cf I. de la Potterie, 'Naître de l'eau et naitre de l'Esprit', ScE 14 (1962), 417—43; F.-M. Braun, 'Le Don de Dieu et l'Initiation Chrétienne (Jn 2—4)', NRT 86 (1964), 1023—48). Some distinguish Jesus's words to Nicodemus from Jn's, but the one discourse represents alike the thought of Jesus and Jn's ecclesial experience. Its scheme is frequent in Jn: first enigmatic revelation by Jesus (3:3), misunderstanding and objection (4), new revelation (5—8), second difficulty (9), leading to the longest, most important exposition (11—21); the three short discourse are each introduced by 'Truly, truly, I say to you' and linked by several inclusions (e.g. 'Rabbi' and 'we know' (2) reversed by Jesus's 'the master in Israel' and 'you do not understand' (10)) and by a series of progressive key words. The subject is that true faith requires birth from the Spirit. The words 'of water' (5), certainly authentic (in all MSS and Fathers), refer to water baptism (Dz 858). But what could Nicodemus have made of this, even if Ezek 35:25ff is the background? Besides, 'of water' does not fit into the progressive word-structure. Finally, Syn. express the conditions for entering the Kingdom as becoming a child (Mt 18:3, parals.), or conversion and believing (Mk 1:15), and Jn himself speaks of believing, of the Spirit and of the word, Jn 1:13; 1 Jn 5:1, 4—10. Hence some Catholic scholars hold that 'of water' was inserted by Jn from Jesus's post-Resurrectional teaching and within the wider baptismal context of 1:25—33; 3:22—26; 4:1f. The primitive teaching to Nicodemus was of birth from the Spirit. Jn's emphasis bears upon this together with progressive transformation from the 'fleshly' to the 'spiritual' man, 6, 8, 34, 36; 8:30ff; 1 Jn 5:5f. The 'master in Israel' should have recognized the Messianic interior renewal by the Spirit, Is 59:21; Jer 4:4; Ezek 36:25f; Jl 3:1f, cf 1QS 4, 21ff. Jesus implies that the New Covenant is being accomplished and that birth into the Chosen People is unimportant.

1—12 Nicodemus (Gr. name used among high-class **d** Jews), Pharisee and member of the Sanhedrin (7:50; 12:42), represents ('we', 2) the imperfect faith of a sincere, cautious intellectual. He comes timidly by night, from the darkness to the Light, 3:19ff. **2.** He begins respectfully, 'Rabbi'; the 'signs' show that God is with Jesus as with Moses, Ex 3:12; 4:1—9. **3.** Jesus cuts this short. He has to shake Nicodemus's presuppositions. 'Flesh' cannot reach a divine level; OT religion cannot just evolve into the Kingdom of God without a supernatural begetting, Jn 1:12; 1 Pt 1:3, 23; Ti 3:5; 1 Jn 2:29, etc; *anōthen* means 'from above' in Jn 3:31; 19:11, 25, but can mean 'again', as Nicodemus takes it; 'see', enter into (5), experience. 'Kingdom of God', only here and v 5 in Jn, who uses instead 'eternal life', 15f, 36 (17 times altogether). **4.** Understanding on a merely human level and so misunderstanding (13), Nicodemus, shocked, turns to ridicule. **5.** Jesus replaces 'from above' with 'of water and Spirit' (cf above). **6.** No contrast between body and soul: 'flesh' is man limited to his own resources, 'spirit' is the divine, cf 4:24. **7—8.** A little parable to help Nicodemus. The Heb. and Gr. words mean both 'wind' and 'spirit'; we believe in the wind without knowing its origin or destination (Eccl 11:6), and so is the Spirit in his fathomless goings and comings, cf Ign. Ant. *Philad.* 7, 1. **9—10.** Nicodemus will not surrender and **e** receives a gently ironic comment, reversing the 'teacher' in v 2. Jesus may mean: 'The teacher' of the People of God ('Israel'), with an official rank which I have not, should know about the coming birth from the Spirit. **11.** 'We' because Jesus associates his own knowledge and

04e vision with the witness of the Church; or he simply picks up 'we know' from Nicodemus, v 2; 'you' (pl.) perhaps again referring to v 2, or because he envisages the wider audience represented by this half-believer, cf 12:37—50; 15:18—21. The word for 'speak' (*laleō*), often reserved by LXX for prophetic utterance, recurs 59 times in Jn, almost exclusively when Jesus speaks and constantly in the Last Discourse; it can often be rendered 'proclaim the word', 'publish a divine message' (J. Dupont, *Essais*, 20). **12.** The best of many views on the meaning of the 'earthly' and 'heavenly' things, seems to be that they are the parables about birth and the wind contrasted with the revelation now to be given. Nicodemus fades out.

f 13—21 The Heavenly Revelation shows how the birth from on high is guaranteed by the Son of man whose heavenly origin and right to be a witness is proved by the Ascension; add 'who is in heaven', omitted by too exclusively Egyptian MSS, probably as difficult after 'descended' and if spoken to Nicodemus; but Jn knows that the Word incarnate, who must be believed because he has seen, is in the bosom of the Father, 1:18. **14—15.** The re-birth finds its explanation (cf v 9) and source only in the Person of Christ crucified, risen and ascended, cf Rm 6. As Moses lifted up the brazen serpent that those bitten by the serpents might see it and live (Nm 21:4—9; Wis 16:6f), so the Son of Man 'must' (Mk 8:31) be 'lifted up' (Jn's double-meaning word for Jesus's crucifixion and glorification, Jn 8:28; 12:32ff). Read 'whoever believes' ('sees', 19:37) 'may have in him eternal life'; this is the life of those begotten of the Spirit, cf § 798d. **16.** The role of God the Father now becomes prominent. 'Loved', cf § 799h. 'Gave' showed his practical love by sending his Son at the Incarnation, and 'gave him up' (double sense, cf the sacrifice of Isaac, Gn 22:2, 16, for background, and Rm 8:32) to death, leading to the glorified life which he shares with believers, 1 Jn 4:9f. 'Believe in him', cf § 799d. 'Perish' (*apollunai*) can be transitive (6:39) or intransitive, 'suffer destruction' (6:27; 10:28; 11:50; 17:12), as do all who, refusing salvation, incur the apocalyptic judgement, Is 65:15; Mt 25:31ff; Jn 12:25; Rev. **17—18.** 'Sent' (*apesteilen*), practically 'gave' (16) introduces the important idea of **mission** or **apostolate**. For the Messiah-Judge foretold by Jewish apocalyptic writings Jn substitutes the Messiah-Saviour, Jn 4:42; those who believe incur no judgement (condemnation), 5:24; Rm 8:1; those who refuse belief in the name (person manifested) of the Son, have set themselves in a state (perf., cf 3G) of judgement, division, condemnation (*krisis*). **19—21.** The Light is Jesus, Jn 1:4, 9; 8:12; 9; 12:46ff. The refusal to come to Jesus of those who prefer the dark, is their judgement. Those who 'do what is true' (1 Jn 1:6; 1QS 1, 3), i.e. conform their conduct to divine truth (BJ), come to the light that the spring of their action may be shown to lie in God (Westcott, cf Aug., *In Joann*. 12, 13). The Gospel will illustrate all this 'realized eschatology', and cf the paral. 12:46ff. On the paral. and contrast with Qumrân, cf §§ 795f, g, h.

g 22—30 The Baptist's last witness—22. After the pilgrims left, Jerusalem was perhaps no longer safe. Jesus moved 'into the Judaean land', cf Mk 1:5. 'Baptized', cf Jn 4:2: Jesus did not baptize but his disciples. Many commentators since Trent. have held that this was only John's baptism, since the Spirit was not yet given (7:29); others (Aug. against the Donatists; Aquin.) argue from 1:32f that Jesus gave his own baptism through his disciples. Neither explanation wholly satisfies. Jn cannot be denying all previous activity to the

Spirit in 7:39, or setting the baptism of John and of **804g** Jesus on the same plane in 1:33; 3:27ff; yet the great outpouring of the Spirit (Is 32:15; Ezek 11:19f; Jl 3:1f) cannot precede Jesus's glorification. Maybe Jesus's own baptism in the Jordan is the source of Christian baptism (Ign.Ant., Tert., Clem.Alex., Cyr.Jer., Amb.) but should be regarded as the beginning of Christian initiation to be consummated by the gift of the Spirit which is the Messianic baptism (Braun). **23—24.** The Precursor continues his baptizing role. 'Aenon' ('Wells') near Salim, probably in Samaria near Shechem, site of Jacob's Well, cf 4:5 (Albright). 'John not yet in prison' ties in with Mk 1:14 and explains why Jn 1—3 is outside the scope of Syn. **25—26.** 'A Jew' and 'Jews' are well-attested variants; attractive (without MS support) is 'with the disciples of Jesus'. The turn of the sentence shows that John's disciples began the 'meticulous dispute' (1 Tm 6:4, Bernard), probably over baptism and Jewish purification, cf 2:6. They are loyally but petulantly jealous because Jesus, whom their Master's ('Rabbi') witness had started on his career, is drawing the crowds. **27—30.** The Baptist's chance for his final witness; **h** Jesus's presence has changed this austere man, now profoundly humble, full of love and joy. 'Receive', lay hold of, the work God gives him must content a man, cf 19:11. With gentle tact (Chrys.) John consoles them by getting them to rejoice with him, the bridegroom's friend ('best man'), whose unselfish joy is now complete. Jesus as the bridegroom (cf Mt 9:15; Mk 2:19) turns the marriage of Yahweh and his People (Ex 34:14; Is 54:5f; Jer 2:2; Ezek 16; Hos 2:18ff) into **the Messiah's marriage**, Mt 22:1ff; 5:1ff, parals. This theme, developed by Paul, also the bridegroom's friend (2 Cor 11:2; Eph 5:22ff), culminates in the marriage of the Lamb, Rev 19:7; 21:2. The marriage is being inaugurated as Christ gathers his Church, Jn 2:1—11. 'This joy of mine is now full', favourite theme with Jn, 15:11; 16:24; 17:13; 1 Jn 1:14. 'Increase . . . decrease', 'the fullness of religious sacrifice' with 'an ever-germinant fulfilment' (Westcott).

31—36 The Heavenly Witness—Themes interlock with **i** 1—21 and also form an appendix to 22—30; John is essentially a witness (1:7, 15, 32, 34); the witness theme, recurring twice in 3:11 of Jesus and of John in 26, is repeated three times of Jesus the heavenly witness in 32f. **31.** 'He who comes from above' (cf 3, 6, 12), contrasts with 'he who is of the earth' (cf 8:23; Gn 2:7; 2 Cor 15:47); he speaks of washing and repentance, but of the Spirit only by promise which another must fulfil, omit 'is over all' (with Sin., Bez., Tert., Orig.) which repeats 31a. Read 'he who comes from heaven bears witness'. **32.** Goes with 11; 'no one', hyperbole, (33, 36, cf 1:11). **33—34a.** 'Has set his seal' (cf 6:27b), as in contracts to attest the truth of a statement. To accept Jesus's witness is to attest God's truth, because he speaks the words of God, cf 5:19; 1 Jn 5:10. **34b.** Either God gives the Spirit to Christ not by measure (as to the prophets), cf 'all things' (35) and 1:32f; or Christ gives the Spirit—which goes with the run of the sentence and the Messianic sign (20:22; Orig.; Clem.Alex., Lagrange); B, syr. sin. omit 'the Spirit'. **35—36.** Go with 16, 18. Between the Father who gives and the Son who receives all for man's salvation, the deepest relationship is love, Mt 11:27; 28:18; Jn 13:3; 17:2. The ch's themes conclude with the ultimate division.

4:1—42 The Gift of God

1—4 To Galilee through Samaria—1—3. The **805a** sentence, with three subordinate clauses one within the other, the awkward parenthesis of v 2 and some un-Joh.

805a expressions ('the Lord'—most MSS—is probably not used by Jn before the Resurrection), may be editorial transition (Dodd, *HT*, 236ff). The Baptist has probably been arrested. The Pharisees' hostile interest turns to the still more influential work of Jesus. He withdraws (Mt 4:12; Mk 1:14) beyond their immediate power into Galilee; 'only his disciples' qualifies the statement here and in 3:22; 'left Judaea' suggests 'to itself' (16:28) as if his ministry would otherwise have been there; 'again' distinguishes (unlike Syn.) the visits to Galilee. **4.** The Galilaeans' ordinary route to Jerusalem was through Samaria (Jos.Ant. 20, 6; BJ 2, 232), but Jesus was coming from the Jordan valley; perhaps he 'had to' take it to avoid the Pharisees' interference in spite of possible molestation from the Samaritans § 67*cd*. They were considered idolaters and then schismatics, especially those of Shechem (Sir 50:25f) after Manasseh established a rival temple there (Jos.Ant. 11, 7, 2) destroyed by the high priest Hyrcanus 129 B.C. (13, 255f). They were despised (Lk 10:53; 17:16) and hatred was mutual, 9:53; Jn 8:48.

b **4—42 'A masterpiece of composition'** (J. Bligh, 'Jesus in Samaria', HeyJ 3 (1962), 329—46): The meeting at the well with the woman (5—9) and dialogue (The Gift of the Living Water, 10—18), worship in Spirit and Truth, central 19—26) balanced by the dialogue with the disciples (the Food and the Harvest, 27—38), all summed up by the Samaritan 'chorus' (Dodd): 'The Saviour of the World', 39—42. These furnish the ch's great themes. The Gospel is advancing from the new birth (3:3—8) to the water of the Spirit welling up continually from within the believer into eternal life (4:14), and from the Temple theme (2:13—22) to worship in spirit and in truth, 4:23ff. **'The gift of God'**, Jesus's expression for the living water of the Spirit (10) is exactly that used for the gift of the Spirit, equivalent of Pentecost's, in Samaria by Peter and John following the baptism conferred by Philip; Ac 8:20 (cf 10:45, 47; 11: 15, 17; 15:8). This makes the more probable O. Cullmann's view ('La Samarie et les origines de la mission chrétienne. Qui sont les *alloi* de Jean iv, 38f?' *Annuaire de l'Ecole Pratique des Hautes Études* (Paris, 1953—54), 3—12) that the ch refers forward to that first apostolic mission outside orthodox Jewry (cf Braun, art cit). Questions might have arisen: Could the converts still adore on Mt Gerizim, or must they cut themselves off from their people by going to Jerusalem (W. L. Knox, *St Paul and the Church of Jerusalem*, 69—75)? Should the evangelization be put to the credit of the Hellenist deacon's baptism or to the gift of the Spirit by the Hebrew Apostles (cf Jn 4:36ff)? Perhaps this ch was preached by Jn as Jesus's answer. Again, the nuptial theme of Jn 2:1; 3:39 is not absent. The preliminaries to the marriage of Isaac (Gn 24) form a closely par. background and an equally striking contrast between the pure Rebecca and the sinful woman needing the world's Saviour (Braun, 1038f). This is the crown of Biblical poetry about places for water (e.g. Gn 2:10ff; 26:14ff; Ex 15:22—27; 17:1—7) and a woman met there (Gn 24, 29; Ex 2:15ff); the woman is a real character, and yet this 'daughter of Samaria' is, as usual in Jn, representative, and may even suggest Ezek 17:45—61. Jesus guides the discourse throughout; the woman and the disciples, in Jn's manner, misunderstand materialistically a mysterious saying, which leads to an explanation (cf 3:4; 4:33; 6:34; 8:22).

c **5—18 The Well of Living Water—5—6.** The place, Sychar, ancient Shechem, Aram. Sichara, shown by E. Sellin's excavations to be at Balatah, so near as to explain

why the woman came thence for water, is rich in memories **805** of the patriarchs, Gn 12:6; 33:18ff (Jacob); 48:21f; Jos 24:32. The well is over 100 ft deep, and though 'the spring of Jacob' flows into it, the water is far down. The very human Jesus is tired by his hot climb from the Jordan valley. Chrys and P, "Bodmer 2 read 'sat simply as he was upon the ground'; sixth hour', midday, cf 19:14. **7—9.** Jesus opens by asking for a drink (a favour never refused), 'for' his disciples (who perhaps have a pail) are not there. She recognizes him as a Jew, perhaps by the fringe on his cloak (Mt 9:20; Mk 6:56) or his Galilaean accent, Mt 26:73. Translate *'for the Jews do not use the same vessels as Samaritans'* (D. Daube, 'Jesus and the Samaritan woman, the meaning of *synchraomai*', JBL 69 (1950), 137—47), probably a custom codified by *Niddah* 4, 1, A.D. 65—66. **10. Water** in OT, especially **d** 'living' (running) water, symbolizes God's saving gifts (Is 12:3; 55:1; Jer 2:13; Ezek 47:1—12; Zech 14:8; 1QH 8), often the Law and its wisdom (e.g. Sir 24: 21—29; 1 Enoch 96, 6; CD 3, 16; 19, 34, 'the well which the princes dug', 6, 3), and the Spirit of God (Is 44:3; Jl 3:1; 1QS 4, 21), cf A. Jaubert, 'La Symbolique du Puits de Jacob', *L'homme devant Dieu* (1963) 63—73. So here water can be both **Jesus's revelation and the Spirit**, to be given by the Messiah (7:37—39; 19:34; Rev 7:17; 22:17; cf Heb 6:4; 1QS 4, 21) in line with the prophetic theme of interior transformation and renewal of the People of God by the Spirit in Messianic times (Is 32:15ff; Jer 31:33; Ezek 11:19f; Zech 12:10; 1 Jn 3:24; 'living', cf 'the bread of life', 6:35, 48, 51). **12.** 'Greater than Jacob', cf 8:51; 'and his cattle', Jn's irony. **13—15.** 'Will never thirst', because he has his own spring within himself; this goes beyond the prophets and 3:5f. Though still misunderstanding, she asks for water, cf 6:34 and perhaps Mt 7:17. **16—18.** So now Jesus **e** touches her conscience without requiring an explicit avowal, and twice, with gentle irony, praises her. The five husbands are real (29, 39), like all Jn's 'signs', but some think they represent the five religions (seven gods, but two in pairs, and Josephus reckoned five, Ant. 9, 288) brought to Samaria by the foreign settlers, and the sixth the syncretized Yahwehism ('whom you do not know'), practised by the 'daughter of Samaria', 2 (4) Kgs 17: 28ff; others (Lagrange, Bernard) protest that by Jesus's time the Samaritans worshipped only one God and that the allegory would make the five gods legitimate and Yahweh not. **19—20.** Surrendering, she skilfully turns away the 'prophet's' attention to the burning local question of the legitimate place for worship, Dt 12:5, 11; 'our fathers' are contrasted with 'you' (modern Jews). Samaritan tradition gave itself antecedents in the altars set up by Abraham and Jacob at Shechem (Gn 12:7; 33:20) and by Joshuah on Mt Ebal (Dt 27:4), transformed into Mt Gerizim in the Sam Pent. Even after 129 B.C. the Samaritans continued (and continue) to use Mt Gerizim for their rites. **21—22.** Jesus associates himself with the Jewish race ('we') from whom comes salvation, cf Is 2:3; Jn 10:16 'other sheep'; St Paul says nothing stronger of their privileges, Rm 3:2; 9:4; 11:17—24. **23—24.** But already the 'hour' of that **f** salvation has outdated the dispute. The new, universal worship comes (like the new birth, Jn 3:5) from the Spirit, 7:37ff; 'genuine' worship 'in truth' comes from the dynamism of the Father's revelation made in Jesus, centres upon his glorification (on the Cross, where blood and water flow from his pierced side, and in the Resurrection, 3:14f; 19:34; 1 Jn 5:5ff) and issues in personal and public worship in the Christian community (cf Jn 9:38; 1 Cor 14:25; Heb 1:6; Rev 4:10; 5:14, etc; cf H.

05f Greeven, *proskyneō*, TWNT 6, 759—67, and on Qumran, R. Schnackenburg in BZ 3 (1959) 88—93). This 'decisive word in the history of humanity' (Largrange) contradicts, not sacramentalism (Jn 3:5, 8; 6), but materialistic localization in the 'fleshly' liturgy of the Temple) Heb 9:13f). The Father 'seeks for' such worshippers by sending his Son, Jn 3:16f; 1 Jn 4:10. 'God is spirit' (like 'God is light', 'God is love', 1:5; 4:8, 16) does not define his immaterial essence but expresses his life giving activity as sender of the Spirit into the hearts of believers, Jn 3:5—8; 6:63; 7:38f, cf § 799e. **25.** Said perhaps with a shrug. 'Messiah' (no article, like a proper name): the Samaritans too (Just., *1 Apol.* 53) expected 'him who returns' (*Ta'eb*) as a second, lesser Moses (Dt 18:15) to explain things; 'who is called Christ', added for Gr. readers. **26.** Summit of the meeting. 'I am he' is not yet 'the style of deity', but cf Is 52:6. What of the 'Messianic secret', Mk 8:30? In Samaria the title was predominantly prophetic and would not cause political trouble, cf J. Macdonald, *The Theology of the Samaritans* (1964), 362.

g **27—38 The Food and the Harvest**—**27—30.** Public speech with a woman was thought undesirable for a Rabbi (SB 2, 438). The awe of the disciples reflects an eyewitness, as does the detail of the woman leaving her water-jar. She recounts her great adventure with some female exaggeration; but though her belief is still hesitant (contrast 1:41), she brings the men of Sychar to Jesus. **31—33.** Meanwhile Jesus talks with his puzzled disciples (cf 11f). **34.** People whose spiritual hunger is satisfied may not feel hungry. Jesus goes far beyond Mt 4:14; Dt 8:3; his food is continually to do his Father's will (5:30; 6:38; 14:41, cf 7:17; 9:31), thus bringing to perfection the work given him (5:36; 17:4; 19:30), the salvation of men, 3:17; 4:36; 6:39f; Heb 10:7. **35—36.** He may be quoting a country proverb, 'it is no use hurrying'; but probably his saying springs, as usual, from the situation, and bids them lift their eyes to the fertile fields (golden with us, white in dry Palestine); if so, we are in May—June after the Passover of March—April (2:23; 4:45) and before the ? Pentecost of 5:1. In the spiritual order, faith ripens quickly, and the approaching Samaritans are the harvest (Mt 9:37f; Lk 10:2 are close pars.). Spiritually too, the sower went to sow in sorrow without sharing the reaper's joy (Ps 126 (125):5) and the reapers will rejoice together. Who is the sower? Not Jesus, for he does the sending; perhaps Moses but especially the Baptist, if 'Aenon near Salim' (Jn 3:23) is near Shechem (cf J. A. T. Robinson, 'The "Others" of John 4:38', *Twelve NT Studies*, 61—66); in 3:29 the Baptist rejoices with Jesus. **37—38.** What is true in the saying is that sower and reaper are different persons: a lesson in humility and disinterestedness in Apostolic work. 'I sent you' (Jesus has not yet sent them and, when he does, forbids them to go to the Samaritans, Mt 10:5), is probably prophetic future, cf Jn 17:18 with 20:21; as the same word (from which comes 'apostle') is used in Ac 8:14 for the sending of Peter and John to Samaria, Philip could be thought of as labouring there first.

h **39—42 The Faith of the Samaritans** is in contrast with the disbelief of the Jews. The woman is the first 'witness'. But when Jesus at their earnest request 'abides' with them two days (Jn's time-precision, cf 11:6), living contact with his word (contrasted with her 'speaking') brings many more to 'believe in' him (the aorist, 6 times in Jn, suggests a definite, though not necessarily lasting movement of faith), and recognize him not only as 'king of Israel' (1:49) but 'saviour of the world'; for Jn's universalism, cf § 792k. Here, then, is the message to the early Church: The old barriers of Judaism are down;

the spring of living water has flowed from Jerusalem and **805h** is to refresh the whole world. The Well from which it flows is present everywhere the Word is carried. Those sent to preach it will, like Christ, draw strength from carrying out their task. But, that done, they must not be possessive. God will assign the rewards to everyone together (Bligh).

43—54 Jesus's Word gives Life—There may be **i** editorial work here (M. E. Boismard, 'Saint Luc et la redaction du quatrième évangile' (Jn 4:46—54), RB 69 (1962), 185—211). But basic expressions (e.g. triple repetitions) are Johannine and essential ideas primitive: Jesus gives life even at a distance; his word must be believed. Some (Dodd, Feuillet, J. Bligh, 'Jesus in Jerusalem', HeyJ 4 (1963), 115—34) attach the passage to ch 5, to which it does serve as prelude. But 'Cana in Galilee' (46, cf 54), making pointed inclusion with the repeated 'Cana in Galilee' of 2:1, 11, groups it firmly among the six 'signs' of universal renewal of the old order: the water changed into wine, the new temple, the new birth, the new baptism, the new worship, and now the gift of new life to one 'at the point of death' (Braun, 1043f). 'Live', thrice repeated (50—53) marks both a culmination (living body, 2:21f, eternal life, living water) and a rehearsal for the gift of life to Lazarus (ch 11), preluding the Resurrection (Lightfoot). The life of the Spirit is spreading (as it would later) from unbelieving Jerusalem, and finds a welcome among heretics ('believe', thrice, 4:39—42) and perhaps, if the offical was one, pagans ('believe', thrice, 48—53). **43—44.** Some think **j** Nazareth is 'his own country', others, Galilee; but 'own' (1:11, cf especially 4:3; 7:1) may indicate Judaea, the Galilaeans' welcome, though superficial, being contrasted (45); or (R. Brown, CBQ 24 (1962) 13f) 44 is editorial, recalling the rejection at Nazareth (Mt 13:57; Mk 6:4; Lk 4:24), while 48 characterizes the Galilaeans' faith as based only on signs (*terata* is *hapax* in Jn and the *oun* of 45 follows naturally on 43). **46—47.** Iren. and many others identify the royal official with the centurion of Mt 8:5—13; Lk 7:1—10, and literary contact between Lk 7:3, 6 and Jn 4:47, 50f is certain (Boismard, 197—200). Yet in Syn. all happens in Capharnaum, and the centurion, a Gentile, does not approach and is praised. In Jn we are in Cana, the official approaches and is rebuked, the reproach suggesting rather a Jew (Robinson). Perhaps we have, not an original story differently developed, but a different one, deliberately chosen by Jn, where the official's faith is not as great as the centurion's, but that 'of Israel' Mt 8:10ff. **48.** Why so harsh to a father pleading for his son's life? Editorial, or a test, partly addressed over his head (plur.) to the Jews, which Jesus uses to call out deeper faith when asked for a miracle, Jn 2:4, 11. The emphasis on signs and 'wonders' (only here in Jn) and on 'see' marks distrust for belief based on sight which fails to penetrate to the divine, 2:23f; 20:29. **49.** When the father speaks simply from love of his 'little' son, he is heard. **50—53.** Now he believes Jesus's word without seeing. One o'clock is the heat of the day, the 'hour' (thrice repeated) least likely to get rid of a fever (Bligh). 'Official' becomes 'man' in 50 and 'father' in 53 (Lightfoot). 'Believed' means Christian conversion in Ac, but in Jn can mean 'become disciples'. The father might be Chuza, Herod's steward, Joanna's husband (Lk 8:3). Jn's readers are to believe without seeing, on the word of the risen Jesus, that he does not need to 'come down' to give life. 'Life' is eternal life in Jn, except here, where, as with Lazarus, the physical miracle is the sign that Jesus is 'the resurrection and the life' (11:25).

805k This cure, a parable in act, introduces the great discourse of ch 5, which starts from another 'resurrection-al' miracle done by Jesus's word 'rise', 5:5. It attributes to the 'voice' of the Son of Man the spiritual resurrection of believers at this present 'hour' (5:25) and their corporal resurrection at the last 'Hour', 28f.

5–10 THE SECTION OF WORKS

806a 5 The Works of the Son—The Gospel now passes to a new plane, much deeper than the liturgical setting of a feast, 5:1. The 'signs' are seen to be the 'works' of the Father and we are initiated into the secret of the Person of Jesus not only in its Jewish Messianic aspect but also in his relationship with his Father as joint source of these 'works' (5:17–20, 36; 7:21; 9:3; 10:25, 32, 37f; 14:10f; 15:24). The revelation of the Father is reflected in the consciousness of Jesus. This points to the final revelation when the Father will be manifested in the person of the glorified Jesus. Henceforth the title 'Christ' disappears from key passages. Though used in contexts of doubt, imperfect faith and opposition, it seems inferior, and Jesus never employs it (cf 7:26f, 31, 41f; 9:22; 11:27, 39; 12:34); 'Christ' in 20:31 leads up to 'Son of God' (Van den Bussche, 88f).

b 1–9 The Cure in Jerusalem—**1.** 'After this' a vague transitional note of time as in 6:1; 7:1. 'A feast', better than 'the feast'. Probably Pentecost, the giving of the Law, cf 5:22, 30 (Christ judge), 46f (Moses witness); 'The feast' would be Passover, but cf 6:4. **2–3.** Archaeologists have identified this pool a little N of the Temple with porticoes on four sides and another across the middle (cf J. Jeremias, *The Rediscovery of Bethesda*, E.tr. 1966). The ruins are now in the grounds of the Church of St Anne. **2.** The problem here is to know if *probatikē* (sheep) is to be taken with *kolumbēthra* (pool) or whether we should suppose a noun with which it agrees, e.g. *pulē* (gate) cf Neh 3:1; 12:39 ('Sheep-Gate'). There are no accents in the Gr. MSS to determine the question and the references in Neh suggest an attractive solution. RSV adopts this: 'There is in Jerusalem by the Sheep-Gate, a pool . . .'. This interpretation is further supported by the fact that the pool would have been difficult of access for sheep and moreover had been for a long time a centre of healing. Nevertheless, against this we have the whole weight of ancient tradition which connects *probatikē* with *kolumbēthra*; (cf Vg: Est autem Ierosolymis probatica Piscina) and no writer before A.D. 1283 understands *probatikē* as referring to a gate. If we take *probatikē* with *kolumbēthra* in accordance with tradition, then we have the following words *hē epilegomenē* without a substantive to agree with. A word has to be supplied and we may translate 'There is in Jerusalem by the Sheep Pool, (a building) called in Hebrew . . .' (see Jeremias, op cit). Each solution has its difficulties, but the latter has more evidence in support of it.

What is the name of the pool or the building attached to it? The chief variants are, according to the MSS: Bethzatha, Bethesda and Bethsaida. Bethzatha 'house of olives' has Sinaiticus in support of it and the name is like Bezetha, the name of that district. But MS evidence is stronger in favour of the other readings, and it is hardly likely that the same name would be given to district and pool. 'Bethsaida' though well supported in MSS is also less likely as it is otherwise unknown in the vicinity and the name may be transferred here from the town of similar name on the Sea of Galilee. 'Bethesda' 'house of mercy' is more probable, but Jn gives no translation (contrast 9:7) to suggest that meaning. But it is strongly supported in the MSS and is a suitable name for a place of healing. The right etymology however may be *Beth-esdatayin*, 'house of the two springs' (J. T. Milik, 'Le Rouleau de cuivre de Qumran', RB 66 (1959), 347f). **806**

3b–4. The passage: 'waiting for the moving of the water;[4] for an angel . . . whatever disease he had' (see RSV footnote) is not found in the best MSS and it seems likely that it was added as an explanation of v 7. Moreover the language of 4 is not Johannine. **5.** The number 38 need not be symbolic nor, for that matter does it say that the man had been lying there for 38 years. The *Acts of Pilate* 6.1, mention a man claiming to have been cured by Jesus after being ill for 38 years but this story may simply be dependent on Jn and dates only from the 4th cent. **6.** Jesus, touched with pity, and knowing or 'learning' he had been there a long time, asked him if he wanted to be cured; a surprising question but it would help to focus the man's attention—unless we understand it as symbolic: Christ will force no one; each must desire baptism for himself. **7.** A contrast with the paralytic in Mk 2:3–5; this man has no one to help him and there is no special manifestation of faith. The crowding at the pool effectively prevented the man from trying the waters. There is no need to accept the further elaboration of v 4 ('whoever stepped in first . . .'). 'When the water is troubled'. The excavations at St Anne's provide no evidence of any intermittent spring at that place, nor is there any independent tradition of such a phenomenon at any other pool in the area of Jerusalem. Perhaps further research will provide the solution. **8.** The similarity to Mk 2:11 is remarkable and suggests dependence. **9.** The word of Jesus had instantaneous effect. The man picked up his mat (aorist) and began to walk about (imperfect tense), proving the reality of the cure.

9b–16 The Word of Jesus and the Sabbath—Jn **c** tersely underlines the point of the coming controversy—it was the Sabbath when Jesus cured him (cf Mk 2:23–3:6). Jer 17:21 (cf Neh 13:19) forbids carrying burdens in and out of the city on the Sabbath. The Mishnah (*Shabbath*, 7, 2) forbids moving an object from place to place and (10, 5) allows moving a living man on a bed, but not an empty bed (SB 2, 454–61). The Jews (i.e. the authorities) call the delinquent to order. **11–13.** He is quite a different character from the sturdy blind man of ch 9, and throws the responsibility on his benefactor. The authorities, who should have attended to the healing, 'sign' of God's working, are only interested in the 'fellow' who dared to give the man the order to carry his bed. Jesus, not yet known to everyone, has slipped away in the crowd. **14.** He seeks out and finds (1:43; 9:35) the man in the Temple (where he may have gone to give thanks) in order to complete his saving work by warning him that his cure must bring conversion of heart if something worse is not to happen to him, cf 5:24; Mt 9:2–8. The case, different from 9:3, suggests that sin lay behind his trouble. Christians might see the command to avoid sin after baptism (Rm 6; Heb 10:28f; Cypr., *Test.*, 3, 27). **15.** We are not told his motive. **16.** Jn sums up the original cause of the Jews' quarrel with Jesus (e.g. Mt 12:9f): 'used to persecute . . . used to do' are Gr. imperfects. At the same time, these cures on the Sabbath enabled Jesus to set out his claims.

17–30 The Work of the Son—Jn passes to the divine **d** plane. **17.** 'This very important v is the seed out of which the discourse which fills the rest of the ch grows' (Barrett). How God could 'rest' (Gn 2:1f) and yet

06d continue his providential government exercised the rabbis. They distinguished the end of the process of creation from his activity as giver of life and as judge who rewards good and punishes evil—which continues on the Sabbath. Jn sees God always as creative, and Jesus is stating that when he himself heals, he is working as his Father does even on the Sabbath, cf Mt 12:8; or 'still' (better 'until now', Gr. CV) may show a new concept of divine rest justifying the Sabbath's suppression: when, his 'works' accomplished, Jesus enters into his rest (9:4; Heb 4:9f), there will be a new Sabbath, the 'Day of the Lord', both the final new creation and the Day celebrated by the Christian community (Apoc 1:10 (Cullmann)). **18.** The Jews now have three reasons for killing Jesus: Sabbath breaking (the inferior offence), calling God his 'own' Father, and making himself equal with God. He makes his claim to be God's 'own' Son not simply by calling God his Father (cf 2:16; 6:32 which arouse no special opposition) but by asserting that he is above and exempt from the Sabbath Law, like his Father, and possesses what the Jews correctly consider to be proper to God alone: the power to give life and to pass judgement. It is of faith that Jesus is equal to the Father in his divine nature, but in Rabbinic teaching a rebellious son 'made himself equal to his father', and for Jn as for Paul (Phil 2:6), 'equal to God' seems to suggest rivalry and independence, like Adam's (Ex 15:11; Ps 89 (88):7; Is 14:14; 40:25), whereas Jesus says 'the Father is greater than I' (Jn 14:28). Jn is emphasizing (5:19; 10:30) the Son's unity with the Father in action. That is how Jesus goes on to explain that his claim does not infringe monotheism (Dodd, Bligh, 125f). These Jerusalem Jews understand Jesus's claim and their opposition is on the religious plane, whereas the Galilaeans will stick at human, material difficulties, 6:41ff, 52. The main shock of encounter comes first at Jerusalem. That is one of the reasons why ch 5 has to come before ch 6, which presupposes it and makes an advance upon it (6:37—40), even though ch 5 continues in ch 7 (Van den Bussche,

e 91f; Dodd, *Int.*, 340). **19 20.** Perhaps originally a parable from a son inheriting his father's trade: 'God is my Father, for I do things which only he can do; loving his Son (3:35), he has shown me all the secrets of his trade'; this explains 'sees'; the hierarchic tone would be Jn's, (P. Gaechter, 'Zur Form von Joh 5:19—30', *NT Aufsätze* (Festschrift für Josef Schmid, 1963), 65—68; Bligh, 176). As Son, Jesus is completely dependent on his Father, with no sight save for what he does (cf 2 Cor 5:19). Hence his ministry is a complete revelation of the Father. **21—22.** The 'greater works' are the divine prerogatives of giving life (2 (4) Kgs 5:7) and judging, (which includes vindicating the good, At 32:36; Ps 43 (42):1 as well as condemnation Jn 3:17—21), now publicly proclaimed as belonging to Jesus. **23.** The fundamental, revolutionary consequence, doubtless drawn later by Jn, is that no one can honour the Father while refusing honour to his Son. Jesus is the centre of Christian

f liturgy. **24.** 'Truly, truly' (cf 1:51) introduces an important summary. 'Hear', 'believe in' and 'keep my word' mean adherence of mind and will to Jesus and through him to the Father. By this welcome (10:27; 18:37) of 'the words of eternal life' (6:63, 68), a man possesses it; instead of going towards 'judgement' (separation, condemnation), he has crossed from death into life. **25.** Another 'truly, truly' expands 24. 'The hour is coming', cf 4:21; 'and now is' (cf (4:23), contrasting with 5:28, indicates present, resurrectional life, as when a man believes and is baptized. The spiritually dead (not in the tombs, 28) rise to life by listening

to the voice of the Son of God, cf Rm 5:1f; 6:4f; 8:1f. **806g**
26—30 are another version of 19—25. Their final eschatology and mention of the Son of man may show an earlier stratum in the Gospel tradition (Boismard, Brown). **26—27.** 'Just as', repeats 21. The Father, source of life (Ps 36 (35):10) grants his Son to be source of life and to judge as Son of man (the Gr., with no articles, directly recalls Dn 7:13), who is thus identified with the Son of God, v 25. **28—30.** Jesus's claim to judge ('marvel' repeated from v 20), is the same as in Syn., e.g. Mt 25:31ff. Jn, in spite of his realized eschatology, holds, like the rest of the NT (e.g. Ac 17:30f; Rm 2:16), a final judgement (not made on faith alone but on good and bad actions, cf Mt 25), and bodily resurrection, cf Jn 11:23ff. Strictly speaking (as in v 24) the just are not submitted to judgement but rise to life. The condemnation of those who exclude themselves from salvation (3:36) is contained in their resurrection, Dn 12:2. An inclusion (cf 19) ends this part of the discourse.

31—39 Witnesses to the Son—We may suppose a **h** Jewish objection (cf 8:13): 'Who bears witness to your claim?' Jesus cites four, all aspects of the witness of 'Another': the Baptist, 'sent by God' (cf 1:16f); the 'works', given by the Father to the Son; the Father's word in their hearts; the Scriptures. Here is a developed apologetic to persuade Jewish Christians to leave the Synagogue and profess faith in Jesus (Brown). **31—32.** That no one can testify for himself was a general principle (Dt 19:15; SB 2, 466, cf on Jn 8:13—16). 'Another' is the Father. **33.** His hearers would think of the Baptist (cf 1:19ff); Jesus sums up his reply 'You' is emphatic **34** So is 'I'; Jesus needs no human witness (8:18); he has said that John was a 'kindled' (not 'burning') lamp, shining with real but derived light (1:8f; Sir 48:1). The Jews preferred this brief religious excitement to faith in him to whom John bore witness. **36.** The 'greater testimony' is Jesus's works, his Father's gift, divine seal on his mission (6:27) which they authenticate (5:20; 9:3f; Ac 17:31). **37—38.** 'And' (consecutive, 'so that') the Father bears witness about his Person. For what follows, cf 1 Jn 5:9f. The Jews cannot hear God's voice (12:29), or see him (1:18, contrast 14:9) or recognize the witness of his word abiding in them, because they refuse to believe Christ. **39.** So again, for all their searching, they fail to find eternal life in the Scriptures (cf 2 Cor 3:16), for Christ and the Scriptures must be accepted together; they point away from themselves to Jesus (e.g. 1:45; 5:47; 20:9). Though doubtless grounded in Jesus's apologetic, 37ff show post-Pentecostal Church development. The Christian experience and the Scripture's full testimony could not be known till Christ had died and risen, and to these testimonies the Christians appealed, cf Rm 3:21f.

40—47 Why the Jews will not come to Jesus—This **i** is the tragedy of the rejection of the Messiah by the Messianic race. Jesus's poignant sorrow is not wounded pride. He does not seek from them the 'glory' which he has from his Father, Jn 1:14; 8:50; 1 Thes 2:6; he knows from experience that the reason why they will not accept him or his witnesses is that they have not the love of God in them; (not so much man's love for God (1 Jn 5:3) as God's love for man (Jn 3:16; 1 Jn 2:15; 4:16) refused; in Jn our love for God and one another is God's love freely accepted, 1 Jn 4:10f). 'In the name of my Father' (7 times in Jn) expresses personality; so not only as representative but as Son revealing the Father, cf 14:26. Jesus's immense claims go with complete self-effacement. 'But', (*kai* adversative) 'you do not receive me' is their condemnation (3:19). The Fourth Gospel is

806i in one aspect 'the Gospel of the Rejection' (cf 1:11; 3:11, 32; 12:37ff (Bernard)). 'Another', a false Messiah who comes in his own name, they accept because he is like themselves (Mt 24:5, 24, pars; Ac 5:36ff; Jn 7:18). **44.** The root of their refusal to believe is their seeking approval from their fellow-men rather than from God (12:43; Rm 2:29; 1 Cor 4:5). Basking in the righteousness accorded them as sound, religious men, they are unwilling to believe in a Saviour whom they need to reconcile them to God (Bligh). They cannot 'believe', not in the sense of crediting God's existence, but of giving him their complete answering love and obedience, like a child, cf Mt 18:3, pars. **45—47.** Jesus is universal judge (22) but will not accuse them before the Father; their accuser will be Moses (Dt 31:26) who they pretended would commend their loyalty in the Judgement if they refused belief in Christ, cf 9:28f. Disbelief in Christ's words means disbelief in Moses's writings, for it was of Christ, centre and end of Scripture, that he wrote.

j **The Order of Chh**—Many exegetes defend the order 4, 6, 5, 7, holding that the present one is due to an editor or misplacement of sheets, and shows inconsistencies such as Jesus being said to cross over 'to the other side of the sea' (6:1) when he was last in Jerusalem, and the allusion to the healing of the lame man in 7:21—24, made as if no interval had elapsed. But the MSS show no trace of transposition, and Jn is interested, not in itineraries as such, but in theological themes, whose development seems to require that the teaching of the relationship of Jesus to his Father, as shown in his works in ch 5, should precede its concrete fulfilment in ch 6.

807a **6:1—72 I am the Bread of Life**—The 'sign' (the meal given by Jesus, followed by his walking on the water, 1—21) leads through a prologue, describing the place and circumstances (22—25), to its interpretation in the Discourse (26—59). An epilogue contains judgement through faith or disbelief in the Word and the Bread of Life, 60—71.

b **1—15 The Messiah's Banquet**—The vivid, eyewitness account can be compared with Mt 14:13—21; Lk 9:10—17, but especially with Mk 6:30—44 and 8:1—21, 27—33; this reproduces another eyewitness, Peter, and shows a sequence resembling Jn's: multiplication of the loaves, walking on the sea, then (after Mk's second multiplication) demand for a 'sign', discourse on bread, faith of Peter, Passion theme and 'Satan'. Jn with complete independence omits, adds and takes just the touches he wants from events to set in relief the person of Christ. 'After this', vague time indication before a fresh tableau; 'to the other side' does not show an inversion of chh, for we are being led by a witness who **c** also mentally crosses the Lake in vv 17, 22, 25; 'sea of Tiberias' (cf 21:1) from the city founded by Herod Antipas in A.D. 26 and called after the Emperor Tiberius; the name came to prevail over 'Sea of Galilee' in Gr. and may be used by Jn for the sake of his readers. **2—3.** The crowd 'used to follow him'; Jn pre-supposes numerous miracles. The mountain occupies all the E shore. **4.** Syn. wording shows that they thought of the multiplication of bread as anticipating the Last Supper; in Jn 'the Passover, the feast of the Jews was near' suggests that it will be replaced, as at the first Passover he suggests that the Temple will be replaced (2:19—22). **5—7.** Omitting the teaching, the miracles (Mt) and the disciples' representations, Jn goes straight to Jesus's initiation of the meal; 'coming to him' suggests in Jn 'disposed to believe in him' (35); Philip, who being from Bethsaida knew the district (1:44), 'although curious to ask questions because he wanted to know the answer, was not very quick at a

generous appreciation of what fitted the divine', Cyr.Alex., **807** cf 14:8. To Jesus's test of his confidence (cf the testing in the desert, Ex 16:4) he replies after meticulous calculation (cf Mk 6:37b) that it would take 200 days' wages (cf Mt 21:2) 'for each of them to get a bit' (Jn's addition). **8—9.** The practical Andrew (Jn 1:41; 12:22) has found a lad hawking barley loaves (food of the poorest, perhaps contrasted with 'food from heaven', and cf 2 (4) Kgs 4:42ff) and fish, salted perhaps at Taricheae, 'Salt Fish City' on the SW corner of the Lake. **10.** 'Much grass', cf Mk 6:39 'green grass'; it was spring. **11.** Omitting **d** Jesus's looking up to heaven and breaking the bread (Mk, but cf 'fragments', v 13), Jn describes his actions almost exactly as in Lk's (22:19) account of the Institution: 'he *took* the loaves and *having given thanks* (*eucharístesas*) *gave* them for distribution' (cf Mk 14:22f; 1 Cor 11:23). That Jesus distributes marks his initiative again (cf Jn 21:13) but does not exclude the Apostles' ministry (Mt, Mk, Lk). Each receives not Philip's 'little bit' (7) but as much as they wish, 'and of the fish too'. **12—13.** When the Israelites 'gathered' (LXX *synagō*) the manna, there was no surplus (Ex 16:16—21); now more was left over than there had been originally (cf 2:7, 10). Jn alone mentions Jesus's order to 'gather' the fragments (as Christians did carefully at the eucharistic *synaxis*); 'lest anything perish' leads on to 'the food that perishes' and 'I should let nothing perish' (27, 39); the manna perished. Filling the twelve baskets is in Mk 6:43 (cf 2 (4) Kgs 4:44); Jn interested only in the bread, omits the fish. Christ's gift of inexhaustible food (himself, as the Discourse shows) will be gathered by the Church. **14.** **e** The crowd realize that this banquet provided in the wilderness is Messianic and apparently identify 'the prophet who comes' (Dt 18:15ff; Ps 118 (117):26) with the Messiah. Qumran (and cf Jn 1:21) distinguished them. **15.** Probably their conferring together showed their design. It is Jn who explains why Jesus 'compelled' (Mk 6:45) his disciples to go off in the boat: the crowd's Messianic excitement was heady. He went alone into the hills to pray: his kingdom is not of this world, Mt 4:8ff.

16—21 It is I. Be not afraid—**16—19.** The Apostles set **f** off at evening (cf Mk 6:47) in the direction of Capharnaum; Jn adds 'dark' to Syn. 'late'; 'Jesus had not yet come to them' reflects their distress and longing. With strong contrary (Mk) wind and rising sea, they had rowed 3 or 4 miles. Jn omits the 'ghost' (cf Jn 20:19 with Lk 24:37)—perhaps an anti-Docetist trait—but says they feared (contrast 1 Jn 4:18). **20.** 'It is I' is the simple meaning (Mk 6:50, cf 13:6; Jn 9:9), but since the words are also the divine 'I AM' and God walks on the waters (Jb 9:8; Ps 77 (76):20), Johannine overtones are likely. Here is the highlight of the story. 'Do not be afraid' is not in syr. cur. and may have come in from Syn.; Jn omits the calming of the sea. **21.** Probably 'therefore' (recovering from fright) 'they decided' (*ethelon*, cf 1:43; 5:35; 8:44a) 'to take him into the boat'; Jn omits that they did; *eutheōs* means 'directly' rather than 'immediately', so while it enhances the miracle (Chrys.) it makes unnecessary another one, which Mt 14:32ff; Mk 6:51ff seem to exclude; Ps 107 (106):30; Jn 14:5f; 15:4f may be in Jn's mind (Lightfoot). 'This is exactly the kind of story that we might expect from John the son of Zebedee, a fisherman with experience of the lake in all its moods, well accustomed to its sudden storms, and knowing the distance from one point to another' (Bernard).

22—25 Prologue to the Discourse—The text may be **g** confused, but gives clear sense if the verbs are taken as pluperfects. As they had seen the disciples go off without Jesus in the only boat, he must be nearby. Next day, still

07g failing to find him, some doubtless returned on foot and others took advantage of boats coming up from Tiberias and were ferried to Capharnaum. On account of the winds, boats never pass the night on the E shore but come back again from Tiberias in the morning (Lagrange). **23.** 'After the Lord had given thanks', though in most MSS, is probably to be omitted with D, etc. 'The Lord' is not Johannine until after the Resurrection. **25.** They apparently find Jesus at the synagogue (60) which he and his disciples, after a busy morning of miracles (Mt, Mk), could have reached for the start of the Sabbath at 6 p.m. 'Rabbi' is respectful. 'When did you come here?' asks for an explanation; they suspect something.

08a **26–59. The Discourse** has had its meaning disputed since the time of the Fathers: Clem.Alex. and Orig. tended to a purely spiritual interpretation (eating by faith) to avoid a gross, material eating of Christ's flesh; Chrys. was realist; Aug. referred the ch to the Eucharist but with not very clear spiritual explanations which influenced the Middle Ages and Cajetan. The Council of Trent refused to decide between the spiritual and realist interpretations, the majority opting for both together (F. Cavallera, RHE (1909), 687–709). Discussion continues: Is the Discourse entirely about faith in the Person of Jesus or entirely about the Eucharist, or is the Bread of Life Jesus first as Word (calling forth faith as introduction to the Eucharist) and then as Eucharist, and if so, where does the eucharistic development start? Again, is the Discourse a unity, and if vv 51–58 are properly eucharistic, are they a Christian addition or inserted from a discourse of Jesus at the Last Supper where their sacramentalism would be in place rather than before a Galilaean audience (Lagrange, 195f)? For various opinions cf X. Léon-Dufour, 'Le mystère du pain de vie', RSR 46 (1958) 481–523; E. J. Kilmartin, 'The Formation of the Bread of Life Discourse', Scr 12 (1960) 75–78; T. Worden, 'The Holy Eucharist in St John', Scr 15 (1963) 97–103; 16 (1964) 6–16; D. Mollat, 'The Sixth Chapter of St John', *The Eucharist in the NT*, 143–56; R. Brown, *NT Essays*, 77–92; *Jn* in AB, 268–304.

b **Biblical Themes**, also familiar in Syn., lie behind all the parts of the discourse. A. Feuillet, (*Johannine Studies*, 53–128, with bibliographies) finds three: (1) **The Manna**, symbol of spiritual food (OT 'bread from heaven', e.g. Ex 16:4; Neh 9:15; Ps 78 (77):24f) is constantly in mind, (Jn 6:31f, 49f, 58) with the background of the feeding in the wilderness and the murmuring of the Jews (41, 43, 61; Ex 15:24; 16:2, 7; 17:3). The Messiah was expected to renew the miracle (e.g. *Orac. Syb.* 7, 148f), and as condition of believing, the Jews demand a sign not inferior (as they think) to the manna coming down from heaven (Jn 6:30f, cf Mt 16:1–4; Mk 8:11f for a similar demand). Jesus is fully in the line of Dt 8:3 (cf Wis 16:26 and especially 'Man does not live by bread alone', Mt 4:4) in trying to raise them from materialism by asserting the eternal life given by his food and the sign or 'seal' value of his miracle, Jn 6:27.

c (2) **The Messianic Banquet** had sources in the Covenant meal in God's presence (Ex 18:12), in the manna and the water from the rock, and especially in the joyful, sacred meals in a sanctuary, the food being a victim sacrificed (e.g. Dt 12:7; 14:23, 26; 15:20; 27:7); this is linked (Is 25:6ff) with destruction of death and with resurrection and the promise of no more hunger and thirst (49:9f; 55:1ff); 65:13. It is Jesus's constant way in Syn. of describing the Kingdom of Heaven (e.g. Mt 8:11ff; 22:1–14; 25:1–13). Moreover Syn. accounts of the Last Supper tally with Jn 6: 'This is my flesh', as

Jesus probably said (J. Bonsirven, '"Hoc est corpus **808c** meum", Recherches sur l'originel araméen', Bib 29 (1948) 205–19), with 'eat my flesh' (Jn 6:53ff), 'my body given for you' (Lk 22:19, cf 1 Cor 11:24) with 'my flesh for the life of the world' (Jn 6:51) and Judas's treason with 6:70f. 'The bread of life' (which gives life) does not connect with the manna but with the Tree of Life, Gn 2:9. The promises of Jn 6:37, 50f, 58 are the contradictory of man's condemnation (Gn 3:22ff, cf Rev 2:7; 22:2). (3) **Wisdom's Banquet d and Disciples.** From the Wisdom literature (Sir 24; Bar 3:29–38; Wis 9:1–18) with which Jn is connected (cf on the Prologue and Jn 8:25) derives (perhaps more than from the manna) the idea that Jesus has come down from heaven (6:33, 38, 41f, 50f, 58; otherwise only 3:13). 'I am' (6:35, 41, 48, 51) is OT structure on Wisdom personified as divine source of salvation (Prv 8:12–21; Sir 24:1–21) and in Jn 6, after the pattern of Wisdom's appeals, always goes with an invitation to believe or come to Jesus or be fed by the heavenly food which is himself. But while Wisdom's disciples ever hunger and thirst for more (Sir 24:19ff), those of Jesus have all aspirations satisfied (Jn 6:35, cf 37, 44, 65; Is 55:1ff; 65:13). Sir 24:17ff recurs in the Allegory of the Vine (Jn 15). Wisdom and Christ promise themselves as food to disciples called 'sons' or 'children' (e.g. Prv 8:32; Sir 4:11; Jn 13:13). Jesus, unlike the rabbis, requires no intellectual preparation but only belief that he is sent by the Father who draws them to him, Jn 6:29, 44. By this belief the disciple opens his whole being to the Lord who 'comes', and he is led to the banquet of the New Covenant (Jer 31:33f; Mk 14:24), in which man's movement towards Christ is met by Christ's sacramental initiative towards man. Hence communion of faith with Christ (Jn 6:35–50) precedes the messianic gift of the spiritual manna, when their Master, Wisdom Incarnate, in marvellous intimacy, offers them at his banquet himself as food and drink. Jesus thus appears as the fulfilment of all the hopes of Israel, of all Scripture, historical, prophetical, sapiential, liturgical. At the same time he crowns the simple, religious aspirations of man, as himself the food which satisfies all hunger, quenches all thirst, raises to communion with God, brings a life which, conquering death, will rise and live for ever (Mollat). The presence of these themes throughout shows that the discourse in its final form is a unity.

Literary Structure—The opening dialogue (26–34) **e** closely resembles ch 4: Surprise at Jesus's presence or request brings a question (6:22–25; 4:10ff), and a mysterious word of his, a new question (6:26f, 30f; 4:10ff); Jesus reveals that the bread gives life to the world (6:32f; 4:13f) and the request for this bread (6:34; 4:15) leads to a deeper revelation. Many divisions of the discourse have been proposed. Barrett makes three: 27–40, 41–51, 52–58. Léon-Dufour has two parts (35–47; 48–58) preluded by a quotation in this order of words: 'bread from heaven' (A) 'he gave them to eat' (B) (33), and introduced by the repeated 'I am the bread of life', 35, 48. As before (ch 3), Jesus's revelations arouse objections which leads him to develop them further. That of v 60 recapitulates the discourse, to which the answer provides the key. Brown divides the parts as 35–50, 51–58, marked by inclusions; this we adopt.

Was Jesus's original discourse **a Haggadic Midrash f** (§ 607e), apparently used in Galilaean synagogues in Paschal (4) time? By setting Ex and the Passover in relation to the Messianic banquet Jesus could be preparing

808f men's minds for the Eucharist. Jn for his part may be using this literary form derived from the Synagogue or from a Christian Paschal liturgy modelled on the Jewish of which there seem to be traces (Ac 20:6; 1 Cor 5:6ff; Iren). Texts of the Jewish Paschal Haggada show a tri-partite form: significant gesture (the meal), questions by four sons, explanations by the father, and fourfold use of 'I am' to show God's saving activity, cf Ex 12; Jn has the significant gesture (feeding with bread), four questions asked during the discourse, Jesus's explanation and the fourfold 'I am' for his saving activity, cf B. Gärtner, 'John 6 and the Jewish Passover', Conj NT, 17 (1959); E. Kilmartin, 'Liturgical Influence on Joh. 6', CBQ 22 (1960), 183—91.

g But was Jesus's discourse spoken as one? If, as is increasingly acknowledged, vv 53—58 are sacramental, how could the Galilaeans and the disciples be blamed for failing to understand the reference? We mention three solutions: Léon-Dufour's is that to the original hearers the whole discourse concerned faith in Jesus, the contrast between the parts being between Christ as the 'bread from heaven' (the Incarnation) and as vowed to death (51, the Redemption), while 'eat my flesh' and 'drink my blood' would stand for adherence to his Person. But Jn's con-temporaries, in the context of the Messianic meal, by the guidance of the Spirit and their own Christian experience, could not but see, as he intended, the eucharistic meaning, not only in 48—58 but in the whole discourse in the light of the Incarnation (first part), the Redemption (second) and the Ascension (third). In the first part faith in Christ's Person ('believe in me . . . come to me') is distinct and yet inseparable from the Eucharist for which it prepares; vv 51*b*—58, the sustained climax of the whole, leave no doubt on the

h realism of eucharistic belief. R. Brown argues strongly that 51—58 are exclusively eucharistic: eating Jesus's flesh and drinking his blood cannot be metaphors for accepting his revelation, for in the Bible eating someone's flesh means hostile action (Ps 27 (26):2; Zech 11:9) and drinking blood, brutal slaughter, Jer 46:10. So these vv are a later addition, but Johannine and harmonized with 35—50. They are Jn's re-thinking of the discourse (which already had eucharistic overtones) in the light of the Last Supper, and his substitute for an account of the sacramental Institution. Mollat shows that in Jn the Incarnation, 'the Word made flesh' (1:14), finds comple-tion in the redemptive gift of the Eucharist ('my flesh for the life of the world . . . eat my flesh'). At the same time, it is only in faith in Christ, the living bread come down from heaven to give life to the world, that the Eucharist makes sense. The whole mystery will be revealed at the Ascension of the Son of man (62), when he enters into the fullness of the Spirit even in his body, which becomes the overflowing source of risen life for the world. Such is the heavenly food and drink. The fundamental ideas are Jesus's, but mention of the blood drunk seems to suppose Calvary, the Institution and the Liturgy.

i 26—34 Opening Dialogue—**26.** Before saying that he has come from heaven, Jesus tries to raise their interest above free bread (cf 4:14) to the heavenly bread to which the sign pointed. **27.** A basic idea: to work, not for perishable food (Semitic contrast, cf Mt 6:33), but for the food (*brōsis*, twice, and v 55) which remains for ever, cf 4:13f. The Son of man, usually mentioned in difficult teaching (1:51; 3:31f; 5:27) is the figure enfolding the discourse, 6:33, 62. The Father (source of the whole ch) attested him ('sealed', cf 3:33) chiefly by the 'signs', cf 5:36. Though they ought to 'work' (cf 28—30), this bread is the Son of Man's gift (key word,

repeated 31—33); 'will give' (better reading) is euchar- **808** istic, but could be a correction of 'gives'. **28.** True to type, they ignore the 'gift' and ask what 'works' God requires. **29.** Jesus cuts short legal notions. The work which God looks for (Rm 3:28; 1 Jn 3:23) is to go on believing (pres.) in him whom he has sent. **30—31.** We must see you (emphatic) do a sign to believe you (dat., 'believe your words'), cf 2:18. 'What work', cf 28f. They demand not just bread multiplied but Moses's 'bread from heaven' (another key phrase) which the Messiah was to renew; 'our fathers' (cf Ex 16:1ff; 1 Cor 10:1). **32—34.** Jesus contrasts Moses with his Father and the manna from the sky with the genuine (Dt 8:3) bread from heaven which his Father is now giving (pres.): he who (they understand 'that which') comes from heaven (pres. part. characterizing Jesus, 3:31; 6:62; 8:23); 'gives life to the world', reappears vv 49—51. The bread of life is Jesus. They ask for continuous supplies (cf 4:15).

35—50 Come and Believe in Me—(35—40 is a unity, **j** 35f going with 40*b* and 37 with 39*b*). **35.** 'I am the bread of life' (repeated v 48) is the first certain 'I am' (§ 798*b*). 'Bread of life', 'living bread' (51) includes power to give life, 33. Jesus is inviting to his banquet, (§ § 808*cd*; 'comes to me', the same as 'believes in me'). **36** answers v 30 and links with v 40. **37—40.** The Son's tender invitation turns on the Father's will that all pass to him through the Son. The Son will never cast out one whom the Father gives him, cf Mt 8:12; 'not my own will', cf Mt 14:36, parals.; 'lose', let perish, cf Jn 6:12. The Son gives him eternal life now and will raise him up at the last day, 5:24—29. The text is not about predestin-ation, but God's initial gift and man's free 'coming' by faith. **41—42.** The now hostile crowd (henceforth 'the Jews') 'murmur' as Ex 15:24, etc. The rock of scandal is the Incarnation. 'Son of Joseph', ironical—Jn knows of the virgin birth, cf on 1:13 and 2:1ff; Mk 6:3. **43—45.** They should not be stiff-necked murmurers like their fathers, for it is God they have to deal with. They need his help if they are to come to Jesus (Aug., quoting 'trahit sua quemque voluptas,' *Eclogues*, 2:65). The Father's 'gift' (cf 37, 65) is an attraction; all are taught by him; all who listen and learn are drawn by him to Jesus (the prophets' 'teaching in the heart', Is 54:13; Jer 31:33f). **46.** Not the self-sufficient, but only he who is 'from the presence of God' has seen his Father, cf 1:18; 7:29. **47.** Summary so far: A man has eternal life by believing in Jesus 'the bread from heaven'. This the Galilaeans could understand. Jn's contemporaries would see Eucharistic teaching in the banquet offered (35) and the manna perpetuated but requiring faith (33, 43ff), and could pray 'Lord, give us always this bread', 34, **48—50** form inclusion with 35, and the themes of 31—33; for spiritual death, cf 12:25.

51—58 Eat my flesh, drink my blood—This part is **k** paral. to the last but with new developments; the bread from heaven is 'living' and it must be eaten to possess eternal life; it is Jesus's flesh sacrificed for the life of the world. Jesus's mysterious saying (51) brings an objection (52) which leads to full revelation, 53—58. Key words are now 'give', 'eat', 'drink', 'flesh', 'blood'. **51.** The 'living' theme culminates v 57; 'will live for ever', Gn 3:22. Best reading, 'The bread which I shall give is my flesh for the life of the world'; 'give', 'flesh', 'on behalf of' (cf 10:15) show the sacrificial sense. The Word become flesh (1:14) gives up his flesh as food and source of life for men. In the words of consecration Jesus said 'This is my flesh' (Bonsirven, art cit); the eucharistic sense is one with 1 Cor 11:24 (cf on Lk 22:19); only, in Paul the Eucharist proclaims the death of the Lord until

08k he comes, whereas Jn evokes the Incarnation ('flesh') while re-stating the sacrifice which is its redemptive end. **52.** In this Jewish objection against the Saviour's gift, Christians would see an objection against the **l** Eucharist; 'how can', cf 3:4. **53—58.** In Jesus's answer 53—54 go together, and after the affirmation of 55, so do 56—57; 58 forms inclusion with 51. **53—54.** Instead of explaining away, Jesus insists ('Truly, truly') on the necessity of this eating and drinking, only hinting at its personal character by adding his blood. In Heb. 'flesh and blood' mean the whole man. Drinking blood was forbidden, for it stood for life sacred to God, Gn 9:4; Lv 7:26f; 17:14. Jesus calls men to share that life—his own. Léon-Dufour holds that since 'eat and drink' are parallel to 'come to me, believe in me' (Jn 6:35) and 'flesh and blood' to 'me' and 'this bread' (57f, cf Mt 16:17), the Jews could understand them as Jesus sacrificed (blood is expiatory, Lv 17:10—14) and find life by faith in his Person and Redemption. Christians would see sacramental realism and the duty to share Christ's sacrifice by communion. Jn uses a realist word for eating (*trōgō*, almost 'munch') four times here and also in 13:18 where it substitutes for *esthiōn* in Ps 41 (40):10. Bodily resurrection is the consequence, cf Ign. Ant. *Eph.* 20:2, 'breaking one bread who is the medicine of immortality'. **55.** 'Indeed', 'true', insists on the efficacy of this food and drink (cf Jn 6:35b; Ruckstuhl, 235—42). **56.** 'Abide', word for eucharistic union with Jesus (Jn 15:4—7). Note the order: first we are incorporated in his fulness, then he makes his home in us. **57.** Climax: either, as the living Father is source of Jesus's redemptive life, so Jesus is the source of life for those who eat him, cf 5:26; 1 Jn 4:9—this life being a mutual indwelling (most moderns); or, 'as I, sent by the Father, live for him, so he who eats me will live for me' (ancient versions, Lagrange); Aug., Aquin. give both. **58.** Inclusion and summary. **59.** Lit 'in synagogue', the Sabbath teaching rather than the building, cf 18:20.

m 60—71 The need for faith—60—62. The third objection is from the disciples (also 'murmurers'), who seem to think of cannibalism. Instead of retracting, Jesus leads deeper into the mystery of the Son of Man's Ascension, cf 3:12f, corresponding to 'descend', 6:33, 38, 50f, 58. He can hardly be removing the scandal from his immediate hearers (as Aug., BJ). Jn's remedy for these deserters would not be a re-assuring vision but deeper faith (4:48; 20:29). But the Ascension, making a heavenly reality of Jesus's presence, is essential for the Christian understanding of the Eucharist, which contains the three great mysteries of the Son of Man: Incarnation, Redemption, Ascension. However R. Brown would solve the difficulty by suggesting that vv 60ff originally stood after v 50: the disciples cannot bear to listen to Jesus saying that he came down from heaven, and Jesus asks what they will think if they see him ascending. **63.** 'The flesh' (*not* 'my flesh' (53ff). ('Jesus does not contradict his own realism') is Biblical for human judgement without faith (8:15; 3:6 Rm 8:4). The mystery of the heavenly bread is only open to the life-giving Spirit (Gn 2:7; Ezek 37; Jn 3:6; 4:24) resting upon Jesus (1:32f) whose words become life-giving too (5:24). In the era of the Spirit (7:38f) Jesus's total revelation is expressed by union of word and sacrament (cf Dodd, *Int.*, 342, n. 3) and the life given by his body is received, not magically, but through personal faith and charity animated by the Spirit (Léon-Dufour, 518ff). **64—65.** Jesus's words effect the 'separation', the 'judgement', cf 3:16—21, etc. By emphasizing that he always knew their hearts, Jn brings the mystery of refusal again within the deeper mystery

of grace, cf 44; 3:27. The Son always effaces himself **808m** behind the gift of the Father. **66—67.** 'After this' or 'in consequence of this', perhaps both meanings, cf 19:12. Jn assumes that his readers know the Twelve. 'Will you take this or leave me'? **68—69.** Peter answers for all, cf Mt 16:17ff. 'Words of eternal life', cf 63. Knowledge has come from belief; 'the Holy One of God', his elect, consecrated emissary, cf 17:19. **70—71.** Christ called them (Mt 10:1; Mk 3:14; Lk 6:13), and he deliberately called Judas; even becoming one of the Twelve does not prevent a man making himself a devil. The ch on the Bread of Life ends in anticipation of the Last Supper.

7—10 The Refusal to believe—At the end of 6 the **809a** stage is set for the tragedy. Jesus is left with the Twelve of whom one is a traitor as in 13. Yet he must continue his mission (9:4; 11:9; 12:35) in face of the growing opposition of his enemies. Ch 7, though marked as a unity ('Galilee', 1, 52) harks back to 5 and is united by another inclusion ('hidden', 7:4, 8, 'hid himself', 8:59) with 8. After the interlude of 9, the subject continues into 10 (10:32, 37f repeat the theme of 5:17f) until Jesus's return beyond the Jordan (10:40) concludes the great debates and (inclusion with 1:19) the public ministry.

The polemics which fill these chh are not haphazard **b** but move in dramatic progression, controlled (though the Jews do not think so) by Jesus until the 'Hour' fixed by his Father for him freely to give up his life. Their constituent elements, most of which occur in the introduction (7:1—9) may be summarized (cf Van den Bussche): **The murderous intention of the Jews** penetrates the narrative (7:1, 13, 19, 25, 30, 32, 44; 8:37, 40, 59). The central subject is still Jesus's **Works**, but as seen from different points of view: his 'brethren' want to show them off to the big 'world'; Jesus, who will not seek his own glory or do anything of himself, regards them only as the works that please and come from his Father (8:28; 10:32) bearing witness to their unity of action (10:25, 37f); the Jews refuse to acknowledge them and declare Jesus possessed by the devil (7:20; 8:48, 52) and try to stone him (8:59; 10:31). **The works of the world** are inspired by the devil (7:7; 8:40) who now appears more openly and is denounced by Jesus 8:33, 41, 44, cf 1 Jn 3:8, 10; Gn 3:15. To his relations Jesus speaks of his '**moment**' (*kairos*) of manifestation (Jn 7:6, 8) until which he must stay **hidden** (Jn 7:4, 10), coming to the Temple incognito and avoiding attempts to get an avowal that he is the Messiah (7:26, 31; 10:24f); this hiddenness unifies 7:4—8:59. Deeper is the growing **c** interest in the '**Hour**' determined by the Father before which the Jews cannot kill Jesus (7:30, 32, 44—52; 8:20, 59; 10:31, 39). The 'Hour' is set in the framework of the **Jewish Feasts** which both sustain attention (cf Jesus's hint that he will go up for another feast, 7:8) and show the Jewish liturgy fulfilled in Jesus: Tabernacles with its water ceremonies ('Come to me and drink, 7:27) and illuminations ('I am the light of the world', 8:12) and the winter Dedication when amid cold hostility Jesus declares himself consecrated by the Father (10:22, 36). No disciples appear (except for 9) from 7:10 to 10:42. The foreground of a kind of double stage (Dodd, *Int.*, 347f) is often occupied, with or without Jesus, by the thoroughly alive **Jewish crowd**, impertinent and impressed, but not knowing how to decide and looking for a line from **the authorities**, who are secretly plotting in the background. When the crowd are prepared to believe that Jesus may be the Messiah, they send agents to arrest him. The debate continues front stage until there is division in the crowd (7:43f) when backstage the impressed

809c agents report. Then, the attempt to arrest him having failed, Jesus speaks anew (8:12ff), this time in the Treasury of the Temple, until an attempt to stone him (8:59, Dodd, ibid). In 10 Jesus is again with a crowd, now more hostile, until their final attempt upon him (10:39). **The discourses** during which Jesus is constantly interrupted and Jewish objections to his Messianic claims are dealt with, appear (at least in 7 and 8) to be a whole: 7:16 is taken up in 8:28; 7:20 in 8:48, 52; 7:28 in 8:42; 7:29 in 8:55; 7:33f in 8:21 (Dodd, ibid).

d In these chh Jn gives full play to his **irony**, both in the dialogue with the relations ('manifest yourself to the world' suggests the manifestation of the Messiah to Israel, of the Redeemer to mankind and of the eternal Logos to the Cosmos) and in the polemic with the Jews, e.g. 7:33ff, 41f, 52; 8:19, cf 22, 27, 33, 57 (H. Clavier, 'L'ironie dans le quatrième évangile', *Studia Ev.*, 272).

e **7:1—13 To Jerusalem**—'After this' is indefinite but may cover from the second Passover (6:4) to Sept.— Oct. Mk 9:30f; Mt 17:22 show Jesus spending time training his disciples. 'For he had not the power to go about in Judaea' is the harder reading (Chrys., cf 10:18), understandable in human terms, cf Aug. **2.** 'Scenopegia', the **Feast of Tabernacles**, (Ex 23:16; 34:22; Lv 23:33ff, 39—43), originally the autumn thanksgiving festival, celebrated the miracles of the Exodus, during its seven days with an eighth closing day, the people lived in shelters made of branches in memory of their fathers' tents in the desert. This joyful and most popular of Jewish feasts (Jos.Ant. 8, 10) had taken on a prophetic and eschatological sense, proclaiming the royalty of Yahweh and those living waters flowing from Jerusalem, the joys and blessings of Messianic times, Ezek 47; Zech

f 14:8f, 16—21. **3.** 'His brethren', cf 2:12. This group of probably elder cousins, sceptical but becoming impressed (contrast Mk 3:21) are patronizingly ready with sound advice: He must convince Jerusalem. 'Your disciples', perhaps those whom Jesus had made in the capital and Judaea, (cf 2:23; 3:26; 4:1) with whom he might recoup the losses of 6:66. **4—5.** Worldly wisdom cuts across the obscurity and humiliation involved in the Messianic Secret and the Cross, Mt 4:5ff, etc; Jesus, who does not take glory from men (Jn 5:41), never manifests his glory to the world which, like his brethren, is incapable of understanding him, 14:22ff. The brethren 'continued not believing in him' (imperf.), i.e. had not true faith, cf 2:24; 6:26; 8:30ff. **6.** 'This is not the moment for *me* to go to Jerusalem; you are free to do as you like' (Martindale); his *kairos*, the moment to manifest himself, is at his solemn entry into Jerusalem (12:12—19), rather than the 'Hour' of the Passion. **7.** 'The world', here the Jews of the capital, cf 7:1; 'cannot hate you', 'you' is emphatic—it would hate the Apostles (15:18f); 'I testify that its works are evil', for his whole life denounces unbelief and its moral causes, 5:42—45. **8.** 'I am not going up to this feast': the readings inserting 'yet' or omitting 'to this feast' seem due to v 10, but the difficulty is not felt by Jn. Jesus may refer to joining an organized pilgrimage, or mean that *this* is not the feast for him to 'go up' (cf 3:13; 6:62; 20:17) to his Father; anyhow the 'moment' will be that of his decisive entry. As in 2:4; 11:3ff he refuses to act on merely human advice. **10.** 'In private', cf Mk 9:30; 'as it were' is probably a gloss. **11—13.** 'The Jews', the hostile leaders (1:19) 'were seeking him', a word recalling Mal 3:1*b* and so leading up to v 14 when the Messiah appears suddenly in his Temple. In the crowd 'whispered comment' (CV) of different groups

describes Jesus either as 'good' or as seducer of the 809 people, cf Jn 7:47; Mt 27:63; Just., *Trypho*, 69, 108; 'for fear of the Jews', cf Jn 9:22; 12:42; 16:2. Only those who, being drawn by the Father (6:44), believe in Jesus and abide in his word, really know him, 7:31; 8:30, cf Mk 10:17f.

14—52 The Feast of Tabernacles is half over (4th or g 5th day) when Jesus suddenly appears in the Temple (Mal 3:1) teaching like a Rabbi in the centre of official Judaism. Jn keeps emphasizing that this is a new phase of his ministry (hitherto he has only answered objectors) by mentioning that his teaching is in the Temple and by using the word for a prophetic oracle, 'proclaimed' (*krazō*) for the essentials of his revelation (Jn 7:28, 37, cf 8:20; 18:20). **15.** The Jews 'began to express astonishment', 'letters', here the Scriptures, cf 5:47. As he has never 'learned' at the feet of the Jerusalem Rabbis, his teaching must be 'his own', innovating, seductive, cf 7:12, 47. **16.** This implied charge Jesus answers: My teaching is not my own, for I am an envoy, cf 8:28; 12:49; 14:10. **17—18.** Two criteria: (1) The man who wants to do God's will (Ps 40 (39):8, cf Jn 4:34; 8:29) will recognize by sympathetic understanding (like a friend's instinct for the half-expressed, or 'connaturality' (Aquin.) in mystical knowledge) that its source is not an individual's notions but God, cf 1 Cor 2:14; contrast Jn 8:44; (2) the man who treats himself as the fount of knowledge seeks his own honour, but Jesus seeks only (5:30, 41ff; 8:50, 54) that of him who sent him; such humility should attest his truth and honesty. **19.** Since Ps 40 (39):8, which he has just h quoted, continues 'thy law is within my heart', Jesus tells them that they do not understand because, for all their boast of Moses and the Law, they do not keep it (cf Jn 5:45); and he asks them straight out why they are seeking to kill him, cf 8:37. **20.** The crowd, gaping at this dispute with the Rabbis and ignorant of the intentions of the authorities, break in; 'you have a devil' means as yet hardly more than 'you have persecution mania', contrast Mk 3:21f. **21.** Disregarding their question, Jesus fastens on the original ground of their hostility. They had concentrated, 'puzzled' (Jn 3:7; 4:27), or 'scandalized' (Sir 11:21), upon the one 'work' of his (healing the lame man) done in apparent violation of the Sabbath (cf Ex 31:15; 35:2; Jn 5:17). **22—23.** As the Law required a child to be circumcized on the eighth day, he must, if born on the Sabbath, be circumcized on the Sabbath (SB 2, 487). Either Jesus is giving a proof that the Sabbath law is not inviolable, or an instance of 'Moses wrote of me', 5:46: Moses gave the right to circumcize on the Sabbath as assurance of the complete healing to be effected by Christ (5:6, 9, 14), which displaces the Sabbath rest (Hoskyns, Lightfoot). Mention of the patriarchs (cf Gn 17:10; 21:4; Rm 4:11) carries circumcision back to the great ideas before the Mosaic Law; or it could be an insertion for Gentile readers. **24.** The just Messianic judgement was made not 'according to the flesh' (Jn 8:15) but by the wide spirit of the lawgiver and by charity, looking to 'the accomplishment of the redemptive purpose to which the Law had pointed' (Barrett), cf Is 11:3ff; Zech 7:9f and the Sermon on the Mount.

25—36 Whence comes the Messiah?—The occasion i may be different, cf 28 'in the Temple'. **25—27.** 'Some of the people of Jerusalem' (cf Mk 1:5), being 'in the know' about the plot to kill Jesus, are surprised that his speaking 'openly' (cf Jn 7:4; 18:20) is tolerated. Variants, 'the authorities', 'the high priests', 'the ancients' and the silence of Chrys point to there having been no precise word in the original: 'Surely they could not (*mēpote*) have acknowledged that he is the Messiah?' The idea is dis-

809i missed on the ground that Jesus's Galilaean origin is known (cf 7:41f) but that of the Messiah would be hidden. They state the belief correctly; it has Biblical (Mal 3:1; Dn 7:13) and apocalyptic sources, e.g. 1 Enoch 48, 6; 4 Ezra 13, 51f, cf Just., *Trypho* 8, and further Mt 24:26f; Jn 7:10. What they misunderstand is the nature of the Secret. **28—29.** This challenge and opportunity Jesus must meet by a solemn proclamation. In their sense they know him and whence he comes, and yet (cf 'and' in v 30) he has not come self-commissioned but from one with a right to send (genuine, *alēthinos*), and if they knew him, they would not be rejecting Jesus, cf 8:42. He himself (a claim he makes throughout, e.g. 6:46; Mt 11:27; Lk 10:22) knows him uniquely. **30.** Realizing the gravity of this denunciation, they 'kept on seeking' to seize him, but ineffectually, for his 'Hour' had not come, cf Jn 8:20; no miracle need be meant. **31.** But in the crowd Jesus divides his hearers as usual. Many are sufficiently impressed (cf 2:23; 8:30) to incline to believe him the Messiah; but they reason, like his brethren (7:4) by adding up miracles, not by looking to the meaning of the sign.

j 32—36 Whither goes the Messiah?—Intelligence of this swing in Jesus's favour alarms the Pharisees. 'They' (some versions and Chrys.; variants probably come from v 45) send the Temple police to arrest him. The Pharisees are prime movers (cf v 47; 11:46f; 12:19), but the Sanhedrin could not have ordered his arrest without the consent of the chief priests, who later appear as the principal agents, 11:47ff, 57; 18:3. The police did not arrest him because they were so impressed (46) and heard no blasphemy from him, and because his 'hour' had not come. **33.** Then Jesus urges his hearers to make the most of this 'little while' (probably six months) he would be with them. 'I go to him who sent me', a favourite expression of Jn's, suggests going home rather than death and would be mysterious to the Jews but lucid and consoling to Christians. **34.** God's threat to his faithless people (Is 55:6; Hos 5:6; Prv 1:24—28); 'seek find', important theme with variations: now they seek him to arrest him; after their Messiah has gone, they will seek him but not be able to come 'where I am'; those who really seek him, cannot come to him in this life, but have him with them and will eventually follow him (8:21; 12:26; 13:33, 36; 14:1ff; 17:24). **35—36.** Puzzled, the Jews repeat among themselves 'all save the key words'— that he was returning to him who sent him' (Martindale). 'Among the Greeks', lit 'of the Hellenes': some think these too are Diaspora Jews, but to Jn's Greek readers they must be the pagans among whom the Jews lived. To teach them is the climax of absurdity in Jewish eyes, and just what Jesus will do, cf 12:20.

k 37—39 Come to me and drink—As Tabernacles was originally a festival to pray for rain, water was daily carried in a gold vessel from Siloe (9:7) and poured forth in memory of the water from the Rock (Ex 17:6). Is 12:3, all or part of the Hallel Pss (cf Ps 114 (113):8) and possibly Ps 105 (104):41 (1 Cor 10:4) were sung exultantly: 'he who has never seen the joy of the *Beth ha-She'ubah* ('Place of the drawing') has never in his life seen joy', *Sukkah*, 4, 9. The festival also foreshadowed the Day of the Lord, Yahweh's royal reign over all the earth, the messianic age with the ingathering of the harvest of the nations. The reading of Zech 14 proclaimed under images of continuous daylight (cf Jn 8:12; Rev 21:23) and of spring water flowing from Jerusalem the spiritual renewal of Sion. In Rabbinic tradition the pouring forth of the water symbolized the pouring forth of the Spirit in the days of the Messiah. **809k** With this liturgy goes Jesus's invitation to drink. Its literary and theological form (J. Blenkinsopp, 'The Quenching of Thirst', Scr 12 (1960), 39—48) is similar to the sayings about the Temple (Jn 2:21f) and the Messianic entry (12:16): an action communicating symbolically the Messianic presence of Jesus, deepened by a Scriptural quotation and understood only later through the gift of the Spirit. Wisdom and the Torah personified as 'water' and 'living water' are sapiential commonplaces (for 'stood' and 'proclaimed', cf Prv 1:20; 8:2; 'they who drink of me will yet thirst', Sir 24:21, 30f; 15:3). Symbolic action combines with sapiential saying to make a sign which for Christians would stand for Jesus, Wisdom in Person (contrasted in Jn with the Torah) and for the element into which they were baptized, to drink with deep and lasting satisfaction from union with the living God **37.** Some MSS omit 'the great day', others (perhaps better) 'the last day'; so either on the 7th (when the libations were probably increased) or on the 8th day (when the rite was over) Jesus 'stood up' (contrast Mk 4:1; 9:35; Jn 6:3) and 'proclaimed', cf 7:28. **38.** Two **l** interpretations make Joh. sense: (1) 'He who believes in me, as the Scripture says, from within him': the believer, who has drunk from Christ, communicates the Spirit to others (Orig., etc). (2) 'If any one thirst, let him come to me, and let him drink who believes in me. As the Scripture says: From within him . . .'. The Spirit flows from Jesus (The earliest Fathers, cf H. Rahner, 'Flumina de ventre Christi', Bib 22 (1941), 269—302, 367—463). Christ is more naturally the source of the Spirit (v 30) than is the believer, the parallelism is typically Hebraic, and whereas 'Scripture' in Jn usually means a particular text, no one text describes the Spirit as coming from believers, but a number (Is 48:21; Ps 105 (104):41) speak of the water from the Rock. Thus this Christian midrash summarizes the prophetic significance of the Mosaic miracle. Christ, the spiritual Rock, (1 Cor 10:4) and the Temple (Ezek 47:1ff) is the source of the waters of the Spirit, from which the People of God drink, Zech 13:1, cf Rev 22:1. 'Belly' could mean 'person' (SB 2, 492) or 'heart' (Chrys.), since in LXX both words translate Heb. *beten*. **39.** A key v. Read 'for there was not yet Spirit', not 'the' personal Holy Spirit, but the Spirit given; the pouring-forth of the life-giving Spirit (6:63) following upon Jesus's glorification (14:26; 16:7; 19:30) marks the Gospel's turning point; Jn writes in the age of the Spirit, 1 Jn 2:20f, 26ff.

40—52 Christ divides men—'Schism' among men **m** comes from their attitude to Christ (cf 7:12; 9:16; 10:19; Lk 12:51ff). 'Descended from David' (2 Sm 7:12ff; Ps 89 (88):4f); 'Bethlehem' (Mi 5:1f); Jn's irony, cf 6:42. **45— 46.** The Temple police return to the top plotters (after four days, or this is Jn's arrangement of scenes), convinced by Jesus's simple words (not now by 'signs', Jn 4:48). **47—49.** The Pharisees, with snobbish contempt for the accursed, Law-ignorant (Jer 5:4f) 'people of the land' (SB, 2, 494—519), ask if a single member of 'order and religion' (Lightfoot) has believed in him. **50—52.** Thereupon Nicodemus, Sanhedrinite and doctor of the Law (Jn 3:2, 10), 'one of them' (but some MSS omit), though still too cautious to defend Jesus, appeals to the Law's requirement of a fair hearing (Dt 1:16f; 17:4). At this inconvenient intervention in front of the police, the Pharisees rudely tell him 'search the Scriptures', cf 5:39; 'is to rise', not 'has risen', for Jonah and others were from Galilee; however the two Bodmer papyri have 'the prophet', cf 1:2.

810a 53—8:11 The Woman taken in adultery—This beautiful story, though canonical and inspired, is interpolated here, cf § 694*b*; its irony has the Joh. bite; but the vocabulary resembles Lk's; Jn never mentions the Mount of Olives, scribes, 'condemn' (*katakrinō*), 'all the people', *orthrou* for 'early', nor joins all sentences by *de*, etc. **8:1.** In Lk 21:37f Jesus spends the night on the Mount of Olives and comes to the Temple again in the morning. **3.** The woman is set in the midst of a ring of onlookers. **5—6.** Death for an adulterous wife (Lv 20:10), death by stoning for an engaged girl (Dt 22:21—24) and cf Ezek 16:38ff. 'You' is emphatic: if, as they expected, he was for mercy, he set himself against Moses; if for stoning, he could be denounced to the Romans for inciting to murder, Jn 18:31f. Jesus was perhaps sitting on some low stool or cushion and leant forward. **7.** It has been suggested that he was writing down their sins (Jer., PL 23, 553), or refusing to look these shameless men in the face (J. R. Seeley, *Ecce Homo*, ch 9) or (J. Jeremias, T. W. Manson, ZNW (1950—1) 145—50; (1952—3) 255f) that imitating a Roman judge, Jesus first wrote down and then read aloud a sentence (which they could not carry out); 'without sin', cf Mt 23:28; Rm 2:1. The legal point was that a prosecution might only be instituted by persons free from malice (cf J. D. M. Derrett, 'Law in the NT: the Story of the Woman Taken in Adultery', NTS 10 (1963—4) 1—26). **9—10.** 'The eldest', deeper in sin or quicker to see defeat. When the last accuser (not the crowd) has gone, Jesus and the woman are alone in the midst: 'relicti sunt duo; misera et misericordia', Aug. **10—11.** With delicate sympathy Jesus evokes her one gleam of hope—and wins her. He who has come not to judge but to save (Jn 8:15) does not deny her sin but pardons completely. 'Sin no more' implies contrition and resolution for the future.

b 12—59 The Son of God rejected by his own—The Gospel now takes us beyond the Messiahship of Jesus. Ch 8 does not mention it. The themes now are his divine Person and origin, and the witnesses, not Moses or the Baptist (cf Jn 1:30; 5:35f), but (since only God can reveal God, 1:18), the Father and the Son himself, who alone knows his heavenly origin and eternal home (8:14, 35f) and existed before Abraham came to be, 52—58. As we reach the revelation of the Light (8:12), the surrounding darkness grows thicker, the mockery more bitter, the denunciation sterner. The 'unrighteousness' of the Jews (implied, 7:18) becomes the opposite of what Jesus is: they are from below (8:23), with not Abraham but the devil as their father, and liars and murderers like him, 8:37ff, 44, 55; 'you cannot come where I am' (7:34) has become 'you will die in your sins', 8:21, 24. As they refuse the knowledge and freedom of the truth (8:32), their attempts to arrest (7:32, 44) become attempts to stone, 8:59; 10:31ff. Key words are extended in meaning by allusion, e.g. 'judge', 5:22, 30—7:24—8:15f, cf 12:48; 'find', 7:34f—8:21f; 'a devil', 7:20—8:48, 52. The crowd seems to have disappeared (with the ending of the festival or dramatically with the increased tempo). Interruptions from the Pharisees, who are now present (8:13; contrast 7:32), from the 'Jews' (8:22, 25, 33, 39, 48, 52f, 57) condition and direct the discourse (Hoskyns). Since 7:53—8:11 is interpolated, we are still in the atmosphere of Tabernacles. There are three sections: 12—20, introduced by 'again' and unified by inclusion (*elalēsen*, the word for revelation); 21—30, 'again'; 31—59 a new audience.

c 12—20 The Light his own Witness—12. 'I am the Light of the World' (§ § 798*bc*) probably alludes to the huge candelabra lit at Tabernacles in the court of the women to represent the Pillar of Fire ('follows', cf Ex 810 13:21f; Wis 18:3f). Its illumination (*Sukkah*, 5, 2—4), almost turning night into day (Zech 14:6) was said to be so brilliant that every courtyard in Jerusalem was lit by it (SB 2, 799—805). The great light of Messianic salvation in OT and primitive Christian symbolism (Is 9:1; 42:6; 49:6; Mt 4:14ff; Lk 2:32) comes from Jesus, the guiding light, not of one nation only, but of 'the world' (cf Jn 1:4, 9; 3:19; 9:5; 12:46); 'follows me' suggests action, movement, progress (Westcott); 'the light of life', because this saving light has life in itself and gives life (Jn 1:14); disciples who abide in him (15:4) will themselves be 'the light of the world' (Mt 5:14). 'Light', although not mentioned again till ch 9, suitably introduces the real subject of the ch: the divine origin and witness of Jesus; for light cannot but bear witness to itself and is authenticated by its source (Barrett). **13—14a.** The Pharisees quote against Jesus the principle behind 5:31 (which meant that he could not witness independently of his Father). His reply drops the human witnesses (the Baptist and Moses), for only he can know whence he comes and whither he goes (cf 5:33f; Rev 3:14). **14b—15a.** The Jews cannot know, for they judge (and condemn) according, not just to appearance (as Jn 7:24) but to 'the' flesh (article unknown in LXX and almost in NT), i.e. that taken by the Word (1:14) which in this sense is of no avail, 6:63; 2 Cor 5:16. **15b—16.** Digression: Yet Jesus for his part condemns no one (cf Mt 7:1, 'judge not'; Jn 3:17; 12:47); if he does condemn (typical Joh. 'contradiction', cf 5:30), his judgement will be correct (*alēthēs*, cf Papyrus Bodmer 2), for his Father who sent him will be with him and one with him, cf 10:30; 16:32. **17.** He clinches the witness theme: 'your Law' d (7:51; 10:34; 15:25) provided for them an irrefutable argument; nor could they accept it as their own and refuse their Messiah. Dt 19:15 (cf J.-P. Charlier, 'L'Exégèse Joh. d'un précepte légal', RB 67 (1960), 503—15) requires two witnesses for an accusation, cf 17:6; Mt 18:16; 2 Cor 13:1; 1 Tm 5:19; *a fortiori* they suffice for a private discussion; but Jn has changed 'witnesses' to 'men', showing the answer to the difficulty that if Jesus does not count (13), he is producing only one witness, the Father. The clue is 'the testimony of God is greater', 1 Jn 5:9ff. This Jesus now asserts. **18.** 'I am he who bears witness', an 'I am' proclamation, shown in Gr. by the article and the periphrasis, and in the context by the words 'true' and 'genuine' which usually accompany these revelations, 6:32, 35; 15:1; cf 14:6; Rev 3:14; the 'light' is 'genuine', Jn 8:12; 1:9. The two witnesses are the Son and the Father (through the Baptist, the works, the Scriptures and his presence in the Son (5:32, 36—39; 14:10f), as later in the Church the Son and the Spirit, before whose witness that of men fades (1 Jn 5:6—9). **19.** There was no appeal to a witness who was not visible, and the Jews demand that Jesus produce his father. His reply means that their ignorance is culpable and comes from refusal to recognize him. **20.** The Treasury must here be the place where gifts were offered (cf Lk 21:1f) in the court of the women, Mk 12:41. 'Spoke' makes an inclusion with v 12.

21—30 Who is Jesus's Father?—The place indication e in v 20 and 'again' suggest a detached discourse. Basically it is still about the origin and destiny of Jesus, but the prophecy becomes more precise and the opponents more aggressive. **21.** Cf 7:34; but 'you shall die in your sin' goes further, cf 9:41; 15:22; Dt 24:16; Ezek 33:12—20; to reject Jesus is sin against the truth (Jn 8:40, 45f; Heb 10:26—31; 1 Jn 5:16); 'where I am going', to the Father, cf Jn 13:33; 14:2—6. **22.** The Jews' idea

810e differs from 7:34; irony, for Jesus will lay down his life for the world at their hands, 10:11–15. **23–24.** Cf 3:31. 'Your sins', individual acts; 'unless you believe that I am', the 'Yes or No' concerning Jesus; in the context it could mean 'what I am telling you, from above', but the reference to the OT divine name (Dt 32:39; Is 43:10f) sets Jesus on a level with God. **25.** 'Who are you?', the eternal question, asked in hope of blasphemy. Jesus's answer avoids the trap but is a famous difficulty: RSV is favoured by P[66], Bodmer 2; 'the beginning who am speaking to you' (Vg) is grammatically impossible and the real reading 'quia' (WW) unintelligible; 'absolutely what I tell you' (cf Bernard, BJ); 'how is it that I even speak to you?' (Gr. Fathers, Lagrange, NEB) is unlike Joh. and Biblical usage; 'at the beginning' (*tēn archēn* as in LXX, e.g. Gn 41:21) 'I am what I tell you', i.e. that Wisdom which exists from the beginning (Jn 1:1f; 1 Jn 1:1; 2:13f)— a Joh. riddle, which revelation will explain (Hoskyns,

f Lightfoot, Feuillet). **26.** Expands v 16 and anticipates vv 40, 45; 12:48f, cf 18:20: Jesus does not bring out the many things he could say to their condemnation (for such reserve, cf 16:12; 2 Jn 12; 3 Jn 13), for he keeps within his Father's mandate to be Saviour and not judge (Chrys., Cyr.Alex.); but he who sent him understands the case (Jn 7:18); so Jesus, however it riles the Jews, will go on proclaiming truth to the world. **27.** In v 18 he was more explicit, and they understood something; but here, nothing. **28.** Climax, and answer to 'who are you?'; 'when you have lifted up the Son of man' must mean crucified the Messiah, cf 3:14; 12:32; the divine 'I am' goes with acts of power which will show who Jesus is—we are not told how, but cf 19:37; Rev 1:7; 1 Cor 2:8. **29–30.** Then Jesus applies to himself in a deeper sense the OT assurance 'I will be with you' (Ex 3:12, etc) while his human will is given at every moment to his Father's pleasure—a glimpse of his interior life priceless to all who from afar desire to follow him to perfection (Braun), cf 5:30; 6:38. So profound a conviction rallies many to him; it is an unstable impression (2:23), but he follows it up. There is an inclusion with 21, 'said' . . . 'spoke'.

g 31–51 The Word of Jesus brings the freedom of true sons of Abraham—This passage of vivid contrasts is unified by an inclusion (31, 51); in the first part (31–45) Jesus reveals to the Jews who will not believe in his word that they are not sons of Abraham but of the devil; the second part (46–51) concerns the Person of Jesus who cannot be convicted of sin (46) and whose word preserves from death (51); 52–58 will then be the climax: Abraham and Jesus. There may be gradation between those who 'believed in Jesus' (30) and 'the Jews who gave him credence' (dat. in 31, Westcott); still it seems ungracious that those who had shown some sign of believing should be so soon accused of murderous intentions (37, cf 7:19), and unlikely that even unstable converts would change so suddenly. Possibly vv 30, 31 are editorial (Brown), or perhaps the answer lies in the structure of the whole discourse: 6 mysterious words of Jesus (31f, 37f, 41, 46f, 51, 56) bring 6 Jewish objections (33, 39, 41, 48, 52f, 57) leading to 6 answers (34ff, 39f, 42–45, 49f, 54f, 58); perhaps too the touchy interruptions come not from those who believed but from those who did not (Aug.); besides, vv 31–37 form a whole marked by the triple inclusion 'abide', 'free', 'my word'. They contain an encouragement to all would-be converts to be steadfast which is not deflected but expanded by the description of real freedom (35f). It is only in v 37 that Jesus turns upon those who objected that they were the seed of Abraham, a group in whom his word 'has no place', and exposes their murderous intentions. The subsequent,

increasingly bitter polemic thus falls into place. The **810g** passage is rich in themes: **Freedom** (not mentioned after 36); **the word of Jesus**, given no hearing by some (37, 43, 47b) but bringing those who abide in it, hear it, keep it to eternal life (31, 47a, 51); **the truth** which Jesus hears from God and speaks will set free those who are 'truly' disciples (31f, 40, 46); **the lie** (not just lies but the denial of Jesus) uttered by **the devil**, murderer and liar like his followers who has not truth in him; Jesus is then accused of having a devil (44, 48, 55); **Abraham and his seed**, introduced by the Jews (33), taken up by Jesus (37), and given moral and spiritual meaning (39f), recur with great force to reach the climax 'before Abraham was made, I am' (52–58); the Jews' boasts 'our father is Abraham' and 'we have one Father, God' (33, 39, 41b) meet with Jesus's comments 'if you were the children of Abraham . . . if God were your Father' (39c, 42) and the terrible 'you do the works of your father . . . the devil' (40a, 44) and are in contrast with **divine fatherhood and sonship** (35f, cf 42, 49, 54).

C. H. Dodd ('A l'arrière plan d'un dialogue johannique', **h** RHPR 37 (1957), 5–17, on 7:33–47) suggests that the 'Jews' here take the place of early Judaizing Christians who pretend to believe in Jesus while remaining attached to the Mosaic economy. He also notes the universal perspectives, for Christians of all times may claim to have God for Father and yet not hear his words. **31–32.** 'Abide', not merely continue, but live in and by my word as inspiring all your life, cf 15:4, 7, 9; 1 Jn 2:6, 24, 27; 2 Jn 9. Progress in this loving knowledge (especially that 'I am', 28) brings freedom from the enticements of evil— Jn's mysticism condensed in a few words. **33.** Objectors retort that as the seed of Abraham (Gn 15:5; 22:17, cf Mt 3:9; Lk 3:8) they have never been slaves to anyone— never lost freedom of soul—and are racially confident that they need no liberator (cf Mk 2:17; Jn 9:40f; Gal 4:31). **34.** This Jesus solemnly ('Truly, truly') contests, for whoever practises sin is a slave, cf Rm 6:16, 20; Aquin. Omit (NEB) 'of sin' with D, Clem.Alex., etc. **35–36.** The Jews too are slaves who can be turned out of Abraham's house (Gn 21:10, Gal 4:30). To become free, they must have recourse to the Son who abides there always and who is the Truth (cf 14:6; Rm 6:18, 22). **37–40.** The best commentary is 1 Jn 3:4–15, e.g. 'he who does sin is of the devil', 'the Son of God came to destroy the works of the devil', 'Cain', 'he who hates his brother is a murderer', 'abide', cf 4:20 'liar'. Physically they are the seed of Abraham, but they are plotting to murder the Son (cf Mt 21:33–46, para.) who tells them what he has seen when with his Father (cf Jn 1:1; 5:19), and so they are doing what they have heard from their father, being no sons of the faithful and obedient Abraham (cf Gn 15:6; Mk 3:9; Lk 3:8; Rm 4:11–17; 9:7f; Gal 3:7). **41.** The Jews now claim God as their **i** Father, cf Ex 4:22; Dt 32:6; Is 63:16; Mal 2:10, thereby protesting their fidelity to the God of the Covenant, as against the accusation of the prophets who because of their infidelities had already called them sons of prostitution (Jer 2:20; Ezek 16:15ff Hos 1:2, 9–2:4 (BJ)). If there is a hint that Jesus is illegitimate, he ignores it. **42–43.** (cf 1 Jn 5:1); 'I came forth' (without leaving him, 7:28f) by the Incarnation, and 'am come' into the world, and his coming has nothing of self in it. They cannot understand, cf Rm 8:7. **44.** (Gn 2:17; 3:19; Wis 2:23f; Rm 5:12; 1 Jn 3:8), the liar whose very being is refusal of the truth (BJ, contrast Jn 18:37d; Eph 4:21) and when he tells a lie (cf Gn 3:4f), speaks his own language (NEB). **45.** 'But I' (emphatic). They have identified themselves with the mind of the Liar, cf Jn 3:19f. **46.** The direct

810i question of 16:8; Is 53:9; 2 Cor 5:21; 1 Pt 2:22. Such righteousness must come from Truth. 'Why do you not believe?' shows his audience are not the new believers, **47.** The final reason is that they are no true sons of God (cf 1 Jn 4:6). These terrible, hard-seeming words, (paralleled e.g. Mt 23:15) are addressed to spiritual leaders whose obstinate pride is about to thwart God's merciful design for his People and lead them to murder his Son.

j Had they not to be warned? (Lagrange). **48.** In fury the Jews evade reply by insult. 'Samaritan' (cf Jn 4:9) as belonging to the bastard, apostate race, or as possessed, like their famous magicians, cf Ac 8:9; but 'have a devil' is practically 'to be mad', cf Jn 7:20; 10:20. **49–50.** Jesus's mild reply ignores the Samaritan charge (cf Lk 10:33ff; Jn 4:21); he claims to honour his Father in heaven and not seek his own glory (cf 7:18); insults do not touch him, cf 5:23, 44; 8:54. The Jews seek for and judge Jesus and will put him to death, but it is really God who is judging (12:47f) those who reject his Son, and they are under sentence of death, 8:21, 24 (Hoskyns). **51.** 'Judge' suggests reward too, and Jesus solemnly ('Truly, truly') rounds off (cf 31) and reaches the summit of his discourse: Those who keep his word (14:23f; 17:6) will never see real death, cf 5:24; 6:50; 11:25; 1 Jn 3:14. The contrast between Jesus and the devil, between Christians and unbelievers, is complete: Jesus brings the opportunity for eternal life (6:51), the devil brings certain and permanent death (cf Hoskyns). The theme of the relationship of the Jews to Abraham is also exhausted—they are children of the devil.

k 52–59 Abraham and Jesus—52–53. 'Whom', cf 5:18c; 10:33; 19:7. **54.** Jesus replies that it is his Father who is in process (pres. part.) of glorifying him: the 'witness' to Jesus (so frequent in the early chh of Jn, e.g. 5:32–37) is gradually (10:25; 15:26) replaced by references to the coming glory, 7:39; 11:4; 12:28; 13:31f, etc (Lagrange). Here Jesus formally identifies his Father with the God of Israel. **55–56.** Cf 1 Jn 2:4; silence here would be a lie. 'I keep his word', cf Jn 15:10; 17:6c; Jesus's 'knowledge' is characterized by the same active devotion to his Father as that of the believer to him, **56.** 'Abraham exulted (5:35) at the thought of seeing "my day",' my coming, OT 'Day of the Lord', cf Lk 10:24; he saw it 'afar' (Nm 24:17; Heb 11:13) in a prophetic event (cf Jn 12:41), probably the birth of Isaac. Abraham's 'laughter' (Gn 17:17; 21:6) then was interpreted as great joy, e.g. Jub. 16, 19; Philo, *De Mut. Nom.*, 131. Jesus declares himself the true object of the promise made to Abraham and the real cause of his joy, the spiritual Isaac. **57.** The Jews are scornful; 'fifty', a round number. **58.** Solemn ('Truly, truly'); 'before Abraham came into existence, I am' (cf Jn 1:1ff, 6; Ps 90 (89):2) not 'I was', for it is the name of God (e.g. Ex 3:14). **59.** In their eyes, this is blasphemy; the punishment was stoning (Lv 24:16). But they cannot anticipate his 'Hour', and Jesus (by a miracle, or Providential help?) evades them; 'hid himself' joins 7:14, 10 by inclusion. He goes forth from the Temple, cf 19:17.

811a **9:1–41. The Light** (1:6ff; introduced in 8:12 and repeated 9:5 as key to this ch) described in its dramatically different effects its **judgement** (a) (3:19ff) on the blind disciple (cf 1:12) and (b) on the sons of darkness, 8:21, 24; 9:41. **The beggar** comes to recognize 'the man called Jesus' (9:12), whom he has never seen (36f, cf 14:9) as a prophet (9:17, cf 4:19) who comes from God (9:33), and finally, when himself rejected by his judges and enlightened by Jesus, as 'Son of man' and 'Lord', 34–39. **The Pharisees**, after separation (16, cf 7:43; 10:19) from those inclined to believe, have already made up their minds (24) and progressively blind themselves by **811** attempts to disprove or ridicule the miracle (17, 19, 24–30, 34), until Jesus, Advocate for his follower, pronounces judgement on them, 39ff.

Gospel healings of the blind indicate the coming of **b** the Messiah (Is 29:18; 35:5; 42:7) and the enlightening of his followers. This 'sign' points to Jesus, sent from God as Light of the world, Jn 9:3–7. But Jn is especially interested in the brilliant scene with the laconic 'he went and he washed and he came back seeing' (7, 11, 15) and the successive interrogations (8–12, 13–17, 18–23, 24–34). There is also baptismal symbolism (5, 7, 39). The ch is a unity, marked by inclusion ('blind', 'sin', 2, 3, 41) but with extension to 10:41; narrative and dialogue are followed by monologue (Truly, truly, 10:1) as in 3:11; 5:19; 12:24 (Dodd).

1–2. 'As he passed by (cf Mt 9:9, 27; Mk 1:15), **c** apparently from the Temple; 'from his birth' (cf Ac 3:2; 14:8) explains the disciples' question (Chrys.); 'that' is 'so that'; that all pain is punishment was a common Jewish idea; contrast Ezek 18:20. **3–4.** 'We must work . . . who sent me' is the right (hard) reading: Jesus associates the disciples with his work, cf 3:11; 4:38; 14:12. The 'day' of life is the time for work, (Ps 104 (103):23); 'night', cf 11:10; 12:35. **5.** Connects with 8:12; 1:4. The Light of the world must be seen during his earthly life. **6.** Jesus shows this by actions forbidden on the Sabbath: spittle (cf Mk 8:23) was held to transfer a part of the spitter's life with medicinal value (Tacitus, *Hist.*, 4, 81). Iren. (*Adv. Haer.*, 5, 15, 2), Chrys, etc see the Creator's gesture (Gn 2:7) but the connexion may be with baptismal anointing and 'Ephpheta'. **7.** By interpreting Siloam (Neh 3:15; the Jews refused its water, Is 8:6) as 'Sent', Jn identifies it with Christ, the 'sent' (3:17, 34; 5:36d, etc). Fathers (Iren., loc cit 3, Chrys., Aug.) and catacomb frescoes rightly see allusion to baptismal enlightenment (Heb 6:4) through the sacramental waters (cf Jn 3:5), and perhaps the insistent 'from birth', 9:1, 19, 32. **8–16.** Division **d** caused by Christ's action first among the neighbours, then among the Pharisees. It was forbidden to make clay on the Sabbath. **17.** 'A prophet', sent by God with power of wisdom and healing, cf 4:19; not '*the* prophet' (1:21; 6:14). **22.** Cf 12:42; 16:2; full excommunication cut off from the community, cf Lk 6:22; this could be a milder form (SB 4, 293–333). This v may reflect the situation around A.D. 90 when Christians were formally excommunicated from the synagogues, and Jn would be appealing to the hesitant to come out and follow Jesus (Brown). **24.** 'Give glory to God' put a man on oath to speak the truth and so repair an offence to God (Jos 9:19). Ironically, he does give this glory. **28.** Moses and Jesus contrasted, cf 1:17. **29.** 'We do not know', irony again. **31.** E.g. 1:15; Ps 35 (33):12–16; Prv 15:29. **34.** Contrast 6:37. **35f.** 'The Jews cast him out of the Temple, the Lord of the Temple found him', Chrys.; for Jesus 'finding', cf 5:14. 'Son of man' (not 'Son of God', an easier correction), the great Messianic judge of Dn 7:13ff, cf Mt 26:64 and parallels, Jn 1:51; 6:62; 12:34. **37.** 'You have seen him' shows the purpose of the miracle (to open the eyes of the blind to the true light, cf 1:9), and reveals its intended symbolism, BJ; 'is he', emphatic, cf 4:26. **38–39.** Sin., P[75], Tatian, etc omit from 'he said' to 'Jesus said'. If these words stand, and if 'worshipped' in Jn's context expresses real adoration (cf 4:20ff; 12:20; Rev 4:10), he was given light to adore the Son of God, Orig., Lagrange, Hoskyns. Then Jesus sums **e** up: 'Judgement', the discrimination of 3:18–21; 'those who do not see', the humble who, like the blind man (12,

811e 25, 36), confess their ignorance; 'those who see', the 'know-alls' (16, 22, 24, 29, 34, cf 5:39; Is 6:9f; Jer 5:21; Ezek 12:2) whose smug satisfaction destroys their spiritual vision, cf Mt 23:16; Mk 4:12; Rev 3:17f. **40.** Some Pharisees hear and sneer 'surely *we* are not blind?'. **41.** 'An overwhelming answer' (Bernard): If you were simple, you would have no sin (cf Rm 4:15; 5:13), but your arrogant claim to see (cf Mt 6:23) involves sin against the light, and because of your wilful ignorance, your guilt remains, cf Jn 15:22; 1 Jn 5:16f. This terrible judgement rounds off the story, cf 3:36; 12:48; Mt 15:14; 23:16f. Sin is the cause of spiritual (not physical) blindness.

f **10:1—21 Jesus the Door and the Good Shepherd—** (Cf Feuillet, *Joh. Studies*, 129—47; J. A. T. Robinson, *Twelve NT Studies*, 67—75). This parable, perhaps a fusion of two original ones about the gate-keeper (1—3*a*) and the shepherd (3*b*—5), does not wholly fit the theme of ch 9, but is closely connected in Jn's intention. For 'Truly, truly' (Jn 10:1) never introduces a wholly new episode but a fresh movement in an argument (e.g. 8:34, 51, 58) or transition to monologue, 3:11; 10:21 is joined by inclusion to 9:1, and 10:19ff refers back to 9; finally, Jn deals with the relationship of the Jewish rulers to Israel's flock only in 9. Their condemnation is naturally followed by a parable recalling the polemic of Ezek 34 against false pastors. There, Yahweh dispossesses them, brings back the scattered sheep and gives them the Messianic shepherd king, David (cf also Jer 2:8; 10:21; 23:1—6; Zech 11:3—9, 15ff). But Jn's shepherd gives his life that his sheep may have eternal life, Jn 10:28. All this is summed up in the great declaration: 'I am the Good Shepherd'.

g The 'parable' is a Palestinian pastoral. The sheepfold, a courtyard or simple enclosure, contains by night sheep belonging to various shepherds. There is a door and a guardian. Thieves (like Judas, 12:6) and robbers (like Barabbas, 18.40), try to climb in another way. A genuine shepherd enters in the morning by the door. He knows the sheep individually and they know him. Jesus's development of the key ideas, door (7—10), shepherd (11—18), his own sheep (26—30), becomes not just a polemic against the Pharisees but a teaching on the whole work achieved by his voluntary death and a prophecy whose import will be realized in the Church.

h **6.** 'Figure', ('parable', CV) Jn's *paroimia*, is equivalent to Syn. *parabole*, but accentuates the enigma, cf Jn 16:25, 29. In LXX either word translates *mashal*, whose original meaning, 'proverb' (Prv 1:1, cf 2 Pt 2:22) developed into parable, a figurative, symbolic word-picture needing interpretation. The Pharisees, not being of his sheep, do not understand. **7.** 'Truly, truly' introduces the interpretation. 'I am' (§ 798*b*) 'the door' through which the sheep and genuine shepherds must pass, cf 21:15ff for Peter. **8.** 'All' cannot mean the Patriarchs, but claimants to be 'the door', false Messiahs. **9.** Cf 3:17; 1 Jn 2:28; Ac 1:21. The security and freedom of the whole Christian community—sheep and shepherds—are conditioned by the all-embracing 'through Jesus' (Hoskyns). **10.** 'Destroy' is just what Jesus will not do, Jn 6:39; 18:9. 'I came' (aor.) contrasts 'the single unparalleled fact' with the universal presence of the powers of destruction (Westcott); 'life' is eternal life (28), given by Jesus abundantly, Lk 6:38; Rm 5:15; 2 Cor 1:5. **11.** The climax: 'I am the good shepherd', not just kindly, but noble, splendid (*kalos*), with all the name denotes: self-sacrifice, tenderness, even sternness; 'lays down' is Joh. ('give', Mt 20:28; Mk 10:45) for Jesus's voluntary death, Jn 15:13; 1 Jn 3:16,

cf Jn 13:37f. **12—13.** 'wolf', their traditional enemy, **811h** Is 11:6; Sir 13:17; Ac 20:29; 'scatters', Ezek 34:5; Zech 10:2; 13:7; Mt 26:31. **14—15.** Repetition of 'the **i** good shepherd' to stress the mutual, loving knowledge between shepherd and disciples (cf Jn 15:15), not only like but rooted in the loving mutual knowledge of the Father and his incarnate Son, cf Mt 11:27, par. Jn 17:23—27. By laying down his life for his sheep, Jesus creates the new flock and gives it increase. **16.** 'This fold' is Israel, some of whose sheep belong to Christ and some do not, 5, cf Mt 15:24; 'other sheep' are the scattered Gentiles (cf 11:52; 12:20ff), brought, not into the Jewish 'fold', but into the one 'flock' which Christ leads to eternal life; 'hear my voice', cf 3:39; 5:25; 18:37; Ac 28:28; 'one flock, one shepherd', the new Israel, the Church universal and one, cf 11:52; 17:11, 21; Jer 23:3; Ezek 34:23; Mi 2:12; Eph 2:14—18; 4:4ff. **17—18.** The obedient love with which Jesus lays down his life for men according to his Father's design, calls forth his Father's love, cf Jn 3:35; 5:20; 8:29; 17:4f. He willed all this only that Jesus may take up his life again at the resurrection, cf Phil 2:9; Heb 2:10; 12:2. With complete freedom (constantly emphasized, cf Jn 18:4; 19:30) Jesus accepts death and brings about his own resurrection (cf 2:19; attributed to the Father, e.g. 2:22; 21:14; Ac 2:24; Heb 1:4) by his Father's command. The words 'commandment' and 'command' will henceforth be frequent, as also in 1 Jn, 2 Jn, cf § 799f. **19—21.** Again (cf 9:16) division and so judgement, cf Ezek 34:17. The scene ends in suspense.

22—42. The Dedication (*Hanukkah*, 'Renewal') **j** resumes the sequence of Jewish feasts. In mid-December it celebrated the purification of the Temple by Judas Maccabaeus and the dedication of a new altar after the profanations of Antiochus Epiphanes (1 Mc 4:36—59; 2 Mc 1:9; 10:5f). The point of reference is to the consecration or dedication of Jesus by the Father, Jn 10:36, cf 17:19. The cold incredulity ('it was winter') of those who refuse to be of Jesus's flock (26f) connects with the previous episode, probably three months earlier. The trap question 'Are you the Messiah?' would follow Jesus's claim to be the shepherd 'David' of Ezek 34. **22—23.** Read 'then'; some time has elapsed, perhaps **k** filled by Lk 10—13. But the discussion continues (cf 26—29) from 10:21. Solomon's portico (Ac 3:11; 5:12) on the E of the Temple demesne gave protection from the cold desert winds. **24—25.** This most direct question so far about the 'Messianic secret' (cf 2:18; 8:25) is close to Lk 22:67, and this section may be Jn's counterpart to the trial scene. 'No' would discredit Jesus and 'Yes' would enable them to denounce him to the Romans; and yet he has told them (e.g. 5:39; 8:56); and they would believe if their hearts were right, cf 6:69. He avoids their trap by appealing again (cf 5:36) to his works, e.g. 3:2; 9:31ff; 14:11. **26.** The root reason why they will not listen to his voice is that they are 'of this world', not 'of God', 8:23, 47: 'not because I am not a shepherd but because you are not my sheep' (Chrys.). **28—29.** Eternal life is Jesus's gift, cf 6:39; 17:12; 18:9; Rm 8:36—39. No one will snatch the sheep from the hand of the Son because no one can snatch them from the Father, with whom he is one; 'my hand' and my 'Father's hand' are clearly equivalent; but readings vary; RSV's may be a simplification of '*as to my Father, what he has given me is greater than all*', i.e. his gift of souls (cf 6:37, 44; 17:6, 9, 11f) is more precious than anything else. **30.** The direct **l** meaning is the unity of power of Jesus and his Father, but the Jews sense the deeper mystery (33): the unity in Godhead indicated by 'one' and the distinction of Persons

811i by 'are', cf 14:9; 17:11, 22. 'If the power is the same, so is the being', Chrys.; 'non dividat arianus "unum", *non deleat sabellianus "sumus"'*, *Aug* **31.** 'Again', cf 8:59; literally 'they started to carry away stones' (cf 20:15), i.e. from the open since the portico was paved (note the eyewitness). Orientals would be quite ready to halt such a movement for an argument (Lagrange). **32.** With splendid irony Jesus offers many 'noble' (cf 11) works proving that he acts in the power of his Father, cf 5:36. **33.** These the Jews neither concede nor deny. For their charge, cf 5:18. Jesus has not directly called himself God, he has preserved monotheism by saying he is one with the Father, and has offered the proof of his works to **m** lead them to a greater knowledge of his Person. **34—36.** He seeks to make them more cautious; 'your law', Scripture (cf 7:49; 12:34; 15:21; 1 Cor 14:21; Ps 82 (81):6) calls judges 'gods' because the word came from God to them (cf Dt 1:17; 1 Sm 15:10; Ps 58 (57):1; 82 (81):6). Scripture cannot be set at naught, cf Jn 5:18; 7:23; Mt 5:19; therefore the Word made flesh, consecrated and sent to his task by the Father (Jer 1:5; Jn 3:16f; 17:17, 19) cannot be accused of blasphemy for saying 'I am the Son of God'. The reasoning is not only a Rabbinic *a fortiori* (SB 3, 223f). It rests on the Scriptural intuition (now perfectly fulfilled) of a presence of God in any man acting in God's name. The 'consecration' (cf Nm 7:1) marks Jesus on this Consecration feast as the new Temple. **37—38.** To convince them of his intimate union with the Father he makes a final appeal to his works (cf 5:19, 30; 14:10f; 17:21) which take away all excuse, 12:27f; 15:24. On the now explicit title 'Son of God' (5:25; 11:4, 27) will depend the fate of Jesus, 19:7; 20:17, 21 (BJ). **39.** As he has retracted nothing, they try again to seize him, perhaps (for Scripture has been cited) to take him before the competent tribunal. **n 40.** Jesus returns (inclusion with 1:28) to the place of his first beginnings in Peraea where the Baptist's testimony lingers. Probably he stayed three months (read imperf.). Jn (cf 11:54) accurately describes moves of Jesus which in Mt 19:1; Mk 10:1 look as if he were coming from Galilee. **41—42.** Jesus's witness is greater than John's (cf 5:36), yet John prophesied truly. At least beyond Jordan there are humble hearts ready to give Jesus peace and consolation.

To Jerusalem and the Passover 11—12

812a A series of **facts**: the raising of Lazarus, the anointing at Bethany, the triumphal entry into Jerusalem (11—12:19), and then a series of **discourses** commenting upon them (Feuillet). To see how facts and discourses correspond, we must watch for what is the essential meaning of the facts for Jn.

b 11:1—53 Life from Death—The resurrection of Lazarus is the last and greatest sign: Jesus is the source of eternal life and resurrection for all. He does not 'go' (11) to his death against three protestations from the Apostles (8, 12, 16) simply to do an act of kindness to the family he loves (5), for he waits until Lazarus is dead and even rejoices that he will arrive too late (15). The key theme in which 'word and action form an indivisible whole' is Jesus 'the Resurrection and the life' by virtue of his self-sacrifice (Dodd, *Int.*, 363, 368). His death, like Lazarus's illness (4), will be for the glory of God manifested in the Son. As Lazarus will die again, this instalment of the resurrection life (cf 5:21, 25, 28f) is not its final fulfilment. The ch stresses the resurrection of Jesus himself and the eternal risen life, victory over death, which will flow from him, cf 6:54. The cost to

the Good Shepherd is underlined in the opening dialogue **812** with the disciples and after the miracle by the appended report of the consequent Sanhedrin meeting when he is handed over to death (45—53). It is the surrender of his own life in order to give life to the world. Thomas's remark in 16, while characteristic, will be read in the light of 12:24ff or Rm 6:8: we too must die with Christ if we are to live with him (Lightfoot). The 'sign' of the natural life restored, pledge of the risen life to be given by the glorified Christ, concludes the 'Book of Signs and Works' and introduces the 'Book of Glory'.

1—44 The Raising of Lazarus—1. The name (short- **c** ened from Eleazar) seems borrowed by Lk 16:19—31. Bethany where Jesus stayed before the Passion (Mk 11) was on the E slope of Mt Olivet, some 2 miles from Jerusalem. Jesus was now again near Peraean Bethany (Jn 10:40). Mary is put before Martha (contrast 11:5, 19; Lk 10:38ff, who leaves their home unnamed, cf Mk 14:9). **2.** Probably editorial: 'the Lord' for Jesus and *ēsthenei* for *en asthenōn* are not Johannine (Bernard). The past tense could allude to 12:3; Mk 14:3f from the reader's point of view, but if he knew Lk 7:36ff he would be made confused unless she was also the sinful woman (Bernard). **3.** 'sufficit ut noveris; non enim amas et deseris', Aug. But as in 2:3; 7:3, Jesus's answer shows he must do what pleases his Father (8:29): in this case, delay (Lightfoot). **4.** The hint that death would not be the end (cf Mk 5:39; 1 Jn 5:16f) appears to mean that he would not die. God's glory (cf Jn 11:40) is one with the glory of his Son (cf 13:31f; 14:13) glorified by the miracle (cf 1:14) and by his death which follows from it (11:46—53; 12:20, 32). This is the key to what follows. **5—6.** 'Jesus loved' shows his delay was not indifference (15). **6.** The mention of the time marks his deliberately free action and the greatness of the miracle. **7—8.** 'Into Judaea', not just to Bethany but to danger; 'are you going there again' (cf 8:59; 10:31) shows they do not propose to face it with him, cf Mk 10:32. **9—10.** Cf 9:4f; the Jewish day had twelve equal hours; the statement that a man must journey by day and can do so safely while light lasts is connected with the thought that he who walks by the light of the world (8:12) has the light 'in him', cf Mt 6:22f, par.; 1 Jn 2:10f; 'without other light or lamp save that which in my heart was burning' (St John of the Cross). **11—13.** Jesus pauses for them to volunteer. Silence. 'Our friend' and 'I go' are reproachful. 'Sleep' is often used for being dead, e.g. Mt 27:52. The frightened disciples fasten on the word: 'sleep will make him well'. **14—15.** Jesus tells them plainly; cf by contrast vv 21, 32; 'believe': 'faith is always growing if it be alive' (Bernard), cf Lk 17:5. **16.** The doggedly loyal sceptic Thomas (Heb. 'twin', Gr. 'Didymus'), so like his modern counterparts, is an important figure in Jn, cf 14:5; 20:24—29; 21:2. He rallies the disciples and calls on them to die with him. **17—20.** The journey would take at **d** least a day; funerals were normally on the day of death (cf Ac 5:6, 10). The proximity of Jerusalem and the presence of Jews from the capital account for the publicity of the miracle there, Jn 11:45ff; 12:9ff, 17—19. Martha is the same active person as in Lk 10:40. **21—22.** Her regret shows faith, and she hardly dares to hope for what is to come. **23—24.** She takes 'Your brother will rise' for the usual orthodox consolation (cf Lk 14:14; 20:35), and desponds. **25—27.** 'I am' (cf § 798b) 'the resurrection' here and now, contrasts with 'will rise', cf 5:19—30, which is the commentary on this whole miracle, and 1 Jn 3:14; 'and the life' is probably to be omitted with P⁴⁵, Sin. Syr., Cypr.; 'whoever' believes in Jesus (not only Lazarus), though he go to the grave, will come to

812d eternal life, and whoever receives the gift of life through belief in Jesus will never die a spiritual death, for this life *is* eternal life (Dodd). The Jews did not know that the Messiah would bring about the resurrection; Martha is asked to believe this of Jesus. She makes her act of **e** faith. **28—31.** Mourning lasted a week. **32.** Falling at Jesus's feet, Mary uses the same words as Martha—words which the sisters must often have said to each other. **33.** 'Deeply moved', the word *enebrimēsato* expresses groaning with indignant anger (Dn 11:30; Lam 2:6; Mk 9:30; Mk 1:43; 14:5), probably because he was face to face with the realm of Satan here represented by death (Brown). 'He was troubled', (lit 'troubled himself'), as at Jn 12:27; 13:21, for he knew that this miracle would precipitate his Passion. **35—37.** The sorrow which makes Jesus weep silently (*edakrusen*) cannot be caused, as the Jews suppose, by the loss of a loved friend, since he is about to raise him to life, and yet in his grief and suffering the love of God is manifested, so that 'See how he loved him' (cf 3:16; 13:1) is true (Hoskyns), cf Lk 19:41. **38.** The tomb may have been a vertical shaft with a stone upon it, or horizontal, closed with a stone rolled against the entrance and having a little porch. **39—44.** Jesus takes complete control. He sweeps aside Martha's protests (the fourth day was reckoned to bring permanent corruption, cf Hoskyns), cf 2:11; 11:4. Jesus truly prays as man, but knowing the harmony of his will with his Father's, can already thank him for granting his prayer; he prays aloud so that the result may show the people that he has a mission from God, cf 20:21.

f **44.** The Jews buried in a shroud or the flowing clothes of daily use. 'His feet and hands bound with bands and his face tied about in a shroud'; not 'bandages' (RSV); *keiriai* are not Egyptian swathing bands but thongs (Prv 7:16; Aristophanes, *Birds* 816 with scholiast) or surgical tapes (Liddell-Scott) which would hold the feet together and the hands against the sides; Lazarus could **g** only shuffle; the 'sudarium' ('cloth', RSV, CV) could be a chinband folded over the face or the shroud itself folded over the head and body and tied at the neck, cf 19:40; 20:5, 7 (E. A. Wuenschel, 'The Shroud of Turin and the Burial of Christ', CBQ 7 (1945), 404—37; 8 (1946), 135—78. Here Jn ends the story and goes on with his theme.

h **47—53 The Life must die—45—46.** As ever, division: many of the Jews believe; some report to Jesus's chief enemies. **47.** 'A', not 'the', council, so an informal meeting of the principal members, cf 7:32. 'What are we doing?', i.e. nothing, or 'what are we to do?' 'Signs', here miracles. **48.** The Sadducees' exclusively political angle: if Jesus is left free the people will acclaim him Messiah and the Romans will destroy us; 'place' could be Jerusalem but probably the Temple (Jer 7:14; 2 Mc 5:19); irony: this happened from crucifying Jesus; and cf 12:32. **49—50.** Caiaphas, high priest A.D. 18—36. 'That year' (thrice, 51, 18:13) of the crucifixion; 'one of them', not presiding as the meeting was unofficial. Sadducees were notoriously rude (Jos.BJ 2, 8, 4); 'for the people' is omitted by Sin., Chrys., Theodoret, Aug.; the sense is unaffected. For this cynic Jesus must die to preserve the nation politically (cf 18:14); in God's plan he must die for mans' salvation, cf Is 53:6; Jn 10:11; 15:12f. **51.** The Jews ascribed prophetic powers to the high priest, cf Ex 28:30; Nm 27:21; SB 2, 546. **52.** cf 3:16; 10:16; 12:24, 32. **54.** Jesus's hour has not quite come; he withdraws to a yet more remote spot (? Et-Taiyibeh, 20m. N of Jerusalem). **55—57.** Thrice Jn stresses the on-coming Passover and so its relation to the death of

Jesus, cf 2:13ff; 6:4. Ceremonial purity was required for **812h** the Jewish feast, cf 18:28; Nm 9:6—13; 2 Chr 30:17f. Jesus's disciples are made clean in another way (13:1—11; 15:3). Pilgrims gossip: 'Will he come or not?' (BJ).

12:1—11 The anointing for burial—1—3. Saturday **i** the 8th Nisan; Jn marks out the last week of Jesus's life as perhaps the first (1:19—2:1; 12:12; 13:1; 18:28; 19:31, BJ). The supper is at Simon the Leper's, Lazarus is a guest, Martha helps with the serving, the same occasion as Mt 26:6ff; Mk 14:3ff. Jn uses, (3, 5, 8) the same words as Mk (14:3, 5, 7) ('very precious' as Mt 26:7), but makes his own additions: Martha, Mary and Lazarus are named (the earliest tradition perhaps feared danger for the family, cf Jn 12:10 and 18:10 for Peter's name); Jesus's 'feet' are anointed ('head', Mk); Judas is grumbler and thief, 'wherever the gospel' (Mk 14:9) is replaced by 'the house was filled with the fragrance' (cf Ign.Ant., *Eph.* 7, 1), both accounts stress the prodigality of the gift and Mary's act associated by Jesus with his burial. The event is very different from Lk 7:36ff—a neglectful Pharisee host (also called Simon, but Jn's is 'the Leper'), a harlot washing Jesus's feet with her tears and justified by Jesus in quite another way. But Jn 12:3 seems written in terms of Lk 7:38 and has 'the feet'. This likeness and unlikeness to Lk is explainable (with Bernard, cf on Jn 10:2) if Mary of Bethany is the sinful woman (there is no evidence to associate her with the Mary Magdalen of Lk 8:2; 'seven devils' are not sins). She repeats for Jesus (now her brother's Saviour too) an act full of memories for her. She buys specially fine ointment (not in Lk but featured in Jn) and by using her hair as a towel reproduces the former scene. Anointing on the head would be taken for granted (Lagrange) and 'my body' (Mk 14:8) implies more; here the feet, as exceptional, suggest the burial rite (BJ). For another account, but accepting two basic scenes, cf A. Legault, 'An Application of the Form-Critique Method to the Anointings in Galilee and Bethany', CBQ 16 (1954), 131—41, and Brown, 449—54. **4.** In Mt, Mk several disciples protest; Jn goes to the root; the traitor is sharply contrasted with Mary, cf 6:70; 13:2, 21—30; 17:12. **5—6.** 300 days wages, cf 6:7. 'He used to take' what was put in the money-box, cf 13:29. He would not have sold his Master had not his love of money led him to lesser sins (Chrys.). **7.** Best taken as an ellipse (cf 1:8; 6:30, 50; 9:3): 'Let her alone; (she did not sell it) *to keep it for the day of my burial*' (Lagrange, Hoskyns, Feuillet); her anticipated symbol of his burial (the sense of Mk 14:8 also) is joined to his burial at the end of the week (19:38ff, BJ). **8.** Omitted by D, S, etc and identical with Mt 26:11. **9.** 'The large crowd' apparently came on the Sabbath evening. **10—11.** The priest-politicians have taken control and the Pharisees are not mentioned; 'began to go away', leaving their party to join Jesus, cf 6:67; 11:45.

12—19 The Triumphal Entry into Jerusalem— j Jn's account is close to Mk 11:1—10 with approximations to Mt 21:1—9; Lk 19:29—40 ('king'), but has important, independent features: the triumphal procession originated with the crowd who had heard of the miracle of Lazarus; they carried palm branches, symbols of triumph (cf 1 Mc 13:51; 2 Mc 10:7; Rev 7:9), and applied the ritual acclamation 'Hosanna' (Ps 118 (117):25f) to Jesus as 'King of Israel'. It was to counteract this merely political enthusiasm (the sinister word 'crying' occurs again in Jn 18:40; 19:6, 12, 15, when they 'yell' for Jesus's death) that Jesus acted out Zech 9:9f, riding on a donkey as the humble king who brings peace. **12.** This is Sunday; the crowd up from the country (cf 4:45) hear

812j 'Jesus is coming into Jerusalem', and go out to meet him; another crowd accompanies him (17). **13.** Jn is precise: 'branches of palm trees'; 'Hosanna' is a shout of joy, cf 2 Sm (2 Kgs) 14:4; 'Blessed in the name of Yahweh is he who comes', i.e. the Messiah, cf Mt 11:3; Jn 11:27; 'the king of Israel' (addition to Ps 118 (117):26) preludes the title 'king' in the Passion; not 'of the Jews', but 'of Israel', so the Messiah, heir to David's rights, cf 1:49. Here is the foundation of the charge before Pilate (Bernard). **14–15.** Jn omits the finding of the donkey; he quotes Zech 9:9f freely: 'fear not', instead of 'exult' emphasizes the peacefulness of the coming. **16.** 'This', the true Messianic meaning of the event and the prophecy it fulfilled, cf 2:22; 7:39; 16:4; 20:9. **19.** Cf Lk 19:39f; irony, for 'the world' (*tout le monde*) is also the whole human race which Christ came to save, 3:17.

k **20–36 The Coming of the Gentiles**—This 'climactic scene' (Brown) marks the end of the first part of the Gospel and presages the universal extension of Jesus's mission and kingship. It stirs Jesus to the depths as he envisages the harvest of souls to come from his death. Jn's Gentile readers will recognize themselves, and realize that they have now reached his presence effectively. **20.** Not Hellenists (Gr.-speaking Jews, Ac 6:1; 9:29), but Gentiles of non-Jewish birth, 'those who feared God' (e.g. 1 (3) Kgs 8:41ff; Ac 10:2), attracted to monotheism and some Mosaic observances, who have come to the festival. Whether their actual motive for wanting to see Jesus went beyond curiosity we are not told, cf Lk 8:20; 9:9. **21–22.** Respectfully ('Sir') they approach the cautious, slightly dull Philip (1:46; 6:7; 14:8) and he Andrew, who is resourceful and very close to Jesus (cf 6:9; Mk 13:3). Both come from Gentile Bethsaida Julias, have Gr. names and probably talk Gr. (cf on 1:44); together they speak to Jesus. The scene, as often, melts into Jesus's discourse. The crisis is here, and it seems this is no time for interviews, but Jesus looks beyond the crucifixion to a spiritual conversation with all men who will believe through the word of his disciples, 17:20. **23.** 'The hour' (cf 2:4; 7:30; 8:20) of his immolation and glorification (13:31f) has come at last; 'Son of Man', **l** cf 1:51. **24–26.** 'Truly, truly' asserts that to win universal redemption Jesus must die, as must the grain to re-appear in a full field of wheat, cf Mk 4:3–9, 26ff, 31f; Mt 13:24–30; 1 Cor 15:26ff. This key note of the discourse sums up the Syn. doctrine that Jesus 'must' suffer, Mk 8:31; Lk 17:25; 'bear fruit', cf Jn 15:1–8. 'The law of nature is the law of the word of God' (Hoskyns). The fruit of Jesus's isolated ('alone', and cf 16:32) death will be the disciples' faith. And for the disciple to 'serve' Jesus is to follow him in self-sacrifice, even to giving up his life. Thus 24–26 contain three illustrations of the paradox of life through death, of glory through the Cross, the essential Gospel teaching of Mt 16:21–25 and paral., cf for our text Mt 10:39; Lk 17:33. In Jn 'hate' (the Semitic 'non-preference') is added and explained by 'in the world' and 'for eternal life', and the sweetening thought of following and serving Jesus and being where he is (cf 14:3; 17:24) comes not before but after. Note that the Father may 'honour' us as he honoured Christ, cf 23. **m** **27.** Jesus anticipates his Agony. Jn, who omits the Gethsemane event though he knows of it (18:11), supplies this account instead. His words are close to Mk 14:34ff with the anguish, the Hour, the appeal to the Father's pity, the acceptance of the sacrifice, the comfort from heaven. But here Jesus is standing in a crowd though his Father's words are not communicated to them. 'Now', at last, cf 23; 'is in anguish', cf 11:33; 13:21; Ps 42–43

(41–42):6, 12; how human! cf Heb 5:7ff; Cyr.Alex. The **812** deliberative question 'What am I to say?' is followed by another, 'Father, save me from this hour?' But this could be a prayer, cf Mk 14:36. He rejects the idea in favour of the obedience which is his life's purpose, cf 18:37. **28.** 'Glorify thy name', i.e. Person as manifested, cf 17:6; Is 63:14. In this perfect example of 'hallowed be thy name' (Bernard, Mt 6:9), Jesus offers himself for death to accomplish the redemptive work which will glorify the Father in manifesting his love for the world, cf Jn 3:16f; 1 Jn 4:9f (BJ). The heavenly voice came as the Father's witness to Jesus at the two other great moments of his Baptism and Transfiguration, Mk 1:11; 9:7; cf Ac 11:7; Rev 10:4; 'have glorified', by Jesus's works done in his Father's name (e.g. Jn 11:4, 40), perhaps including the 'Hour' now begun, 13:31f; 'will glorify again' in the resurrection of Jesus, the continuance of his work (14:12f), the sending of the Spirit, the founding of the Church and every Christain triumph. **29–30.** Only Jesus and perhaps the disciples **n** hear the words; some of the crowd suppose thunder ('the voice of God', 2 Sm (2 Kgs) 22:14), others an angel's voice, cf Ac 23:9; none understand (9:7; 22:9), and yet the voice came to assure, not Jesus but the crowd of the Father's approval, cf Jn 11:42. **31–33.** Jesus explains: the third 'now' (cf 23, 27) shows that with the 'Hour' has commenced the judgement on the 'world', on those who, refusing their Saviour, are self-condemned (e.g. 3:19f; 5:29; 1 Jn 2:15ff), and on its prince, Satan (14:30; 16:11), Qumran's 'prince of darkness', St Paul's 'god of this world' (2 Cor 4:4) is 'cast down' (so prob. read with θ, Chrys., etc) cf Lk 10:18; Rev 12:7ff; 20:1–6. But Jesus, once 'lifted up' (which Jn 'this he used to say') explicitly refers to the crucifixion) will draw all men to himself, cf Jn 3:14f; 8:28. The day of a national religion is over. The answer to the Greeks is the universal religion which, as for the Jews (8:28), stems from the cross, 19:37. **34.** The crowd, expecting a glorious 'Son of Man' for Messiah (Dn 7:13f, cf Ps 89 (88):36; Mk 14:61f; 1 Enoch 41:1) fail to see the prophecy of glory and stumble at what they rightly see to be a prophecy of death, cf 1 Cor 1:18–25; Gal 5:11. This ends their welcome of Jesus as 'King of Israel', and they pass from the scene asking their question, cf 18:38. **35–36.** But first in his last public words to them Jesus gives the warning that the Light is among them but a little while (7:33) and they must walk by it (11:9) lest the darkness overcome them (1:5; 1 Thes 5:4; 1 Jn 2:11); if they yield themselves to the Light present among them, they will become 'sons of light' (Eph 5:8; 1 Thes 5:5). Qumran expressions here reach fulfilment. 'Hid himself': 'It is the end of Christ's public ministry. The Light withdraws. The faithless are left in darkness' (Dodd).

37–43 Evaluation—'His own received him not', 1:11. **o** **37.** 'They did not believe in him' is Jn's account of the result of Jesus's working 'so many' signs (though some did believe, 10:16; 11:52; 12:19f, 24, 32). Non-belief brings judgement by the Light, refusal of whom blinds, 12:35f, 40. **38.** 'In order that' means for a Semite that Is 53:1 showed God's knowledge of the future, not that it caused disbelief; 'arm', power, cf Lk 1:51. **39–40.** Not positive reprobation but an explanation: The Jews' obstinacy, which Jn has amply shown to be their own fault (and cf Jn 3:20; 12:42), is no obstacle to God's mysterious design which it realizes, cf Rm 9–11. Is 6:9ff (God foresaw that the prophet's merciful appeal would result in obstinate resistance and yet ordered it) is used by Jesus and Christians (Mt 13:14f; Mk 4:12; Lk 8:10; Rm 10:16; Ac 28:26f) to show that rejection by his People does not

12o disprove his claim. Jn cites freely from the Heb. **41.** Jn interprets Isaiah's vision (Is 6:1—4) of the glory of Christ, identified with Yahweh, cf 8:56; MSS differ between 'when' and 'because'. **42—43.** 'Many', relative, but Nicodemus and Joseph of Arimathea were not alone, cf Ac 6:7; 'out of the synagogue', cf 9:22; 16:2; 'glory of man . . . glory of God', cf 5:44; 12:23—33. Jn's last, sad comment, valid for all time.

p 44—50 Epilogue to Jesus's ministry—Far from being transposed, e.g. from after 36 (Bernard), this is a recapitulation; the ancients used direct speech and here no time, place or audience is mentioned. But Jesus was already hidden (36) and this may be a Jn fragment with editorial work shown by slight vocabulary changes (M.-E. Boismard, 'Le caractère adventice de Jn 12:45—50', Sac. Pag. II, 188—92). The terse, epigramatic sentences sum up the salient features of Jesus's discourses on belief, light, judgement and life. The passage is included within words for loud, solemn proclamation (*krazō, lalō*) and asserts authoritatively that in rejecting Jesus the Jews did not merely fulfil prophecy but denied God (Hoskyns). **44—45.** 'Cried out', cf 1:15; 7:28, 37; contrast the obsequious silence of 42f; 'believe not in me but . . .', belief cannot stop at Jesus who is in the Father and the Father in him, 10:38; 14:10f; 17:21; to come to him is to come to the Father whom he reveals, 1:18; 13:20; 17:6; 'sees me' spiritually, cf 6:40; 14:7ff. **46—47.** 'Light into the world . . . not judge but save' are closely par. to 3:16—19, cf 9:5; 'not keep them', cf 8:31; Mt 7:26; 13:18ff. **48—50.** The Christian form of what Moses proclaimed, and echoing Dt 18:18f; 31:19, 26; 32:46f (Brown). The 'word' (*logos*), sum of the 'words' (*rhēmata*) spoken, is personified as judge; the 'word of eternal life' (6:63, 68; 8:51; 1 Jn 2:25) becomes condemnation to him who refuses it, Jn 8:37, 47. The word of the Incarnate Christ is absolute because it is the Father's, 7:16ff; 8:28; 14:10, 31. Jesus's ministry is finally summed up as proclamation (*lalō*) of the Father's command which is eternal life, cf 3:15. The inclusion ('word') with 1:1 marks the end of the first part of the Gospel.

PART II THE HOUR OF GLORY. 13—21

813a 13—17 The Last Supper forms the introduction to the Passion. The Passover (§ 180f) is the liturgical background. Jesus is celebrating his 'passing' (13:1) from this world to the Father, a 'going' he constantly re-affirms, 14:28; 16:5, 10, 28; 17:11, 13. On the way he gives his disciples the bread from heaven (ch 6, cf Ex 16) and his own new commandment of love (13:34; 15:12, cf Ex 20) until he shall take them to be with him in his Father's house, to see and share his glory, 14:2f; 17:24. The cosmic background is the death struggle between Satan, 'prince of this world', the 'darkness', with his human agents, and Jesus, cf Gn 3:15; Lk 22:3f, 53; Jn 6:70f; 12:31; 13:2, 27; 14:30; 1 Cor 2:8; Rev 12. In this Hour, Jesus, fully conscious of his sovereign dignity and power, manifests by gesture and word the meaning of his love for his own and for all men which he will express most fully when he lays down his life in obedience to his Father, 13:34; 15:9, 13; 17:23; 19:30; 1 Jn 3:16. The words 'life' and 'live' (50 times in 1—12) and 'light' (24 times) give place to 'love' (31 times in 13—17; 'life' 6; 'light' 0; Dodd). The inaugural, public Sermon on the Mount is balanced by this talk of intimate love at a supper (cf Plato's *Symposium*). It illustrates Jn 1:12f, recalls Jesus's private instructions to the disciples, and has been confided to the Beloved Disciple to reveal. Note the serenity: Jesus disregards himself and his sufferings to

come, and shows only love for his own and compassion **813a** for their future trials. His words, mingling tenderness, restrained melancholy and triumphant certainty of victory (Rebstock), are set between two actions, one of humble service (13:1—11), the other of prayer, ch 17. The institution of the Eucharist is omitted, but the Discourse (especially 15:1—17) tells of its permanent significance and effect in terms of mutual love. The problems put to Jesus by the disciples and the way they behave forecast the ways we speak and act, and his replies show his care for subsequent generations of believers.

13:1—17 The Washing of the Feet is, as Jesus says **b** (13—17), his way of teaching humility and brotherly love. Is it also related to baptism? This commentators have denied or affirmed since Chrys. and Cyr.Alex. Again, is the passage homogeneous, or made up of two episodes? M.-E. Boismard, 'Le caractère adventice de Jn 12:45—50' argues convincingly: The washing of the feet (4f) has two introductions, moral (1, 2) and baptismal (3), and two interpretations, baptismal (6—10) and moral (12—17) with their respective conclusions, 'you are clean, but not all . . .' (11), 'blessed are you if . . . I speak not of you all' (18). In the sacramental interpretation, the fact of being washed and purified by Christ gives 'part' in him; in the moral, washing the feet of others, loving them to the death according to Christ's example, makes the disciples blessed. These aspects are complementary, but 12—15 could be joined to 4—5 without modification of sense, and the baptismal part appears to be a later addition.

1—3 The Introduction, solemn and profound, shows **c** its composite character by its repetition: 'knowing that', (1 and 3), 'pass to the Father' and 'go to God' (1, 3); 27 is also a doublet to 2. **1.** 'Before the feast of the Passover', i.e. on the 13th Nisan, (see Com. on Mk). 'Knowing', Jn constantly underlines Jesus's knowledge (e.g. 6:6, 61, 64; 16:19, 3)) especially of his death, 18 4; 19 28. 'Hour', the supreme hour for Jesus and for all history, 2:4; 12:23, 27; 19:27. 'Pass from this world to the Father'—Jn's beautiful description of Jesus's being 'lifted up' in death and resurrection to the right hand of the Father is expressed in Paschal Terms. 'Having loved' characterizes his whole work as one of love, cf 3:16; 1 Jn 4:8. 'His own', not the Jews (as Jn 1:11), but the friends who belong to him, cf Mk 4:34; Jn 10:3f; 'in the world', cf 17:6, 11; 'to the end' of his life, but much more 'to the uttermost', 'to perfection', cf 15:13; 19:30; Phil 2:8; 1 Thes 2:16. **2.** 'During', not 'after'. What was striking was that he did it during, not before, the meal. 'The devil having already' (perf.): with Semitic love of drama and contrast, Jn opposes the great Adversary (Mt 13:39), murderous instigator of the Passion (cf Jn 8:44), to Jesus's consciousness of his origin and destiny (cf 3:35; 17:2), and Judas's devil-inspired crime to his meek, winning charity.

4—11 'To have part with me'—The washing may **d** follow the dispute on precedence, Lk 22:24—30. The detailed, precise account and dramatic Gr. present tenses suggest an eyewitness. 'When Christ serves, he serves perfectly' (Westcott). He girds himself for a task from which Jewish slaves were exempted, cf 1 Sm 25:41; Suetonius, *Caligula*, 26; SB 2, 557. **6.** Peter's emphatic 'you . . . my' suggests that Jesus came to him first. **7.** 'afterward you will understand' must refer, not to 13ff, but (as always in Jn, and cf 13:36f) to the time of the Spirit (Epiphanius, Chrys.), and so to baptism. **8.** 'Have no part', cf P. Dreyfus, 'Le Thème de l'héritage dans l'Ancient Testament', RSPT 42 (1958), 3—49: the OT idea of inheritance (e.g. Dt

813d 10:9 for Levi), spiritualized (e.g. Ps 73 (72):26) into man's eschatological destiny (e.g. *Eccl. Rabba*, 3, 9), passes to the NT, e.g. Lk 22:29f; Rm 8:7. To be washed by Christ, giver of life (Jn 13:3) is necessary in order to have part with him in eternal life, cf 14:2f; 17:24; 1 Jn 3:2f. **9.** 'The one thing Peter cannot do is to leave the Lord alone to act as he pleases' (Temple). **10.** Sin., Vg (WW), Orig, Tert., rightly omit 'except for the feet', which misses the point. This is, one of Jn's 'literary parables', cf 2:19; 3:3; 16:16. Christians would recognize 'bathed' and 'clean' as usual NT words for baptism, Eph 5:25f; Ti 3:5; Heb 10:22, cf Jn 3:3ff. The word and blood of Jesus also cleanse, 15:5; 1 Jn 1:7, cf Dodd, *Int.*, 402. **11.** But the blot is the traitor, whom Jesus warns but will not unmask, cf Jn 6:64, 70.

e **12–17 Serve like your Master—12–15.** 'Do you know?', cf 7. Jesus proclaims 'the first article of a charter of apostolic life: the apostle (and every Christian) vows himself to the service of his brethren' (Hauret), cf Lk 22:24–27. 'The Lord, the Master', articular nom. for voc., emphatic; humility is not incompatible with authority. The Great Servant (from Is 53) gives his life for all. The Maundy Thursday washing of the feet takes Jesus's command literally, but any service of humble charity fulfils it. 'An example', 'the example of Christ is always offered in connexion with some form of self-sacrifice' (Westcott), cf Mt 11:29; for his example of love, cf Jn 13:34; 15:12; Rm 15:1–7; Phil 2:5–8; Eph 5:2. **16.** Emphasizes ('Truly, truly') humble service as the essence of Christian authority, but as the v breaks the sequence of vv 15, 17, reproduces Mt 10:24, and uses the un-Joh. 'apostle', it is probably editorial. **17.** To what is easy in theory but vital and hard in practice (cf Mt 7:21–27; 23:3ff; Jn 12:47f) Jesus gives a 'blessing' (also 20:29, frequent in Syn.), corresponding to 'have part in me' in v 8.

f **18–30 The traitor** who has already cut himself off from their fellowship must be dismissed before Jesus can open his heart in full intimacy. **18.** He knows the characters of those he has chosen (Orig., cf 6:70) but has allowed a traitor among them to fulfil his Father's will expressed in Scripture, i.e. Ps 41 (40):10; 'who ate my bread' means my friend (Lk 22:30); for 'ate' Jn uses *trōgō* as in 6:54, 58; this, with the flash-back to 6:70f, suggests that Judas received Holy Communion, cf Lk 22:21; 'lifted up his heel' implies a vicious kick, but also suggests the serpent of Gn 3:15. **19.** Jesus tells them now, so that when the betrayal takes place it may actually steady their faith in his divine claim, cf Dt 18:21f; Is 44:8; Jn 8:24, 28, 58; 14:29; 16:4. **20.** Resembles Mt 10:40 and may be editorial. **21–22.** Deeply moved (*etarachthe*) Jesus at last makes his solemn denunciation (*emarturēsen*), cf 18:37. The Apostles did not of course yet know (though the reader does) that there was a traitor among them. In Mk 14:18; Mt 26:21ff each asks 'Is it I **g** Lord?' This is the moment of da Vinci's picture. **23.** 'The disciple whom Jesus loved' (cf 19:26; 20:2; 21:7, 20) is one of the Twelve who alone were present, cf 13:18; Mk 14:7; Lk 22:14. They would recline on carpets or cushions, resting on the left elbow, the right hand free to take food; the disciple was on Jesus's right, his back turned to him, his head at the level of Jesus's breast (place of a trusted friend, Pliny, *Ep.* 4, 22, 4). As Jesus is in the bosom of the Father, so his own are in his bosom, cf 14:20; 15:4; 17:21ff, Orig. The place of honour on Jesus's left had probably been taken by Judas to whom he could speak without being overheard, 27; Mt 26:25. **24.** Peter 'always boiling over' (Chrys.) cannot stand the suspense, but perhaps intimidated by his rebuff (Jn 13:8ff), signs and

whispers to the Beloved Disciple, probably on his left, **813g** to ask Jesus. **25.** He has only to turn back his head, 'leaning back like this' (cf 4:6) towards Jesus's breast (or possibly 'reclining as he was'). **26–27.** Clarifies Mt 26:23; Mk 14:20. With the courteous gesture of an oriental host Jesus dips a morsel in the dish and gives it to Judas. This last proof that he is discovered and loved only hardens the traitor, who by taking the morsel contracts the sacred union among those who eat together. Satan, who had tempted him to his treason (Lk 22:3f; Jn 6:70; 13:2), 'then' finally takes complete possession. 'Do more quickly' (literally), perhaps 'than you intended', is not a command to do evil but 'the last word of a discouraged friend' (Lagrange), wanting to be alone with his loved ones (cf Epictetus, 4, 9, 18). Thus serenely and freely Jesus gives the signal to begin the work of Redemption (Orig., Aug., Cyr.Alex.). **28–29.** So delicately has he screened the traitor that not even John and Peter realize the immediate import of these words. The Passover was next day; alms were of obligation for it; Judas was bursar, 12:6. **30.** Three terrifying monosyllables, which we translate 'it was night' (cf 1 Cor 11:23) show that outside the lamplighted room darkness had come down (cf Mt 22:13) suggesting the reign of its prince, cf Lk 22:53. As he left 'the light of the world' (Orig.) to plunge into the darkness (Jn 3:19; 8:12; 9:4) 'ipse qui exivit erat nox' (Aug.).

31–38 Prelude to the Last Discourse—The story of **h** rejection (1–13) is closed, and the judgement, the 'sifting' of the Twelve, finally made. Jesus, alone with his faithful remnant, can speak freely of the blessedness of 'those who receive him', 1:12 (Dodd). The themes keep recurring in 14–17: the glory of Jesus and of his Father, the separation from his disciples into whose hearts he instils his new commandment of love, their imminent failure. **31.** The repetition of 'gone out' conveys the change of atmosphere. The Light is shining, 1:5. 'Now' the work of salvation has begun. Jesus can speak (Heb. aorists for prophetic futures) of his triumph as accomplished, cf 16:33c; 21:19. The Son of Man, already glorified by miracles (2:11; 11:4) has as supreme glory to be 'lifted up' on the throne of the Cross and so ascend to his Father, cf 3:14; 8:28; 12:32f (Cyr.Alex.). He has always sought his Father's glory (7:18; 8:50; 11:4, 40; Heb 10:5ff) but will give him perfect glory by the obedient, loving sacrifice of his life, Jn 8:29; 12:28. 'In' has often a causal meaning, 'through him'. **32.** Many MSS omit 'if God is glorified in him', possibly through similarity of endings, but it fits Jn's redundant style: 'He will glorify him in himself', after the Passion the Father will take the Son of Man into his own glory, 17:5, 24, 20; Ac 3:13. 'At once': at the Resurrection and Ascension, which are very near. The departure of Jesus is near too. 'My little children' (7 times in 1 Jn) shows by its tenderness that the warning given them is not a rebuke, as it was to the Jews (7:33f; 8:21). Concentrating upon going away, he does not yet mention his return, cf 14:2f; 'a little while', recurring motif (7:33; 12:35; 14:19; 16:16–19). **34.** A dying father leaves **i** his most intimate thought to his children (33). Jesus gives to his 'family' which is to live by his spirit when he has left them, a '**commandment**' (Lat. 'mandatum', whence 'Maundy'), cf § 799g. The Father's commandments which Jesus lovingly obeyed (15:10) embraced all the work of his life with the Passion as its summit (10:18c; 12:49f). Jesus's commandments are identical with his 'word' (14:15, 21 and 23; 1 Jn 2:3–5; 3:22f; 2 Jn 4–6), the whole revelation of God's love by his life and death inspiring fraternal love as the rule of life of his disciples, Jn 15:12; 1 Jn 4:11. 'Love your neighbour

813i as yourself' (Lv 19:18; Mt 19:19; 22:39; Lk 10:27—37) is superseded by 'love one another as I have loved you', a love new in source, spirit, model and measure, for it is unto death (Jn 15:9—17; Eph 3:19). **35.** This love, between Christians first (1 Jn 1:3, but also 4:20f), inaugurates a new age, and is the mark by which Jesus's disciples are to be recognized, cf Ac 4:33; 'See how these Christians love one another', Tertull., *Apol.* 39, 7, (PL 1, 534). Charity, 'the face and image of Christ the Saviour in us' (Clem.Alex.), opens hearts and wins them to the truth more than miracles (Chrys.). It comes from God who is love, and his Spirit of love and is manifested in doing good with self-sacrifice, 1 Jn 3:16; 4:7—10; Rm 5:7f; 1 Cor 13; Eph 5:1f; Rev 1:5. In extreme old age, John's only sermon was 'my little children, love one another' (Jer., *ad Gal.* 6, 10). **36—38.** Since Jesus said he was going away, Peter has attended to nothing else. Now he explodes; 'Domine quo vadis?'; cf the legend of his martyrdom (*Acta Pauli*, 4, 72). Jesus's consoling words ('will follow me' means through death to glory, 21:18ff, contrast 7:33ff; 8:21f) make no impression. 'I will lay down my life' is imaginative heroism; Jesus will first lay down his life for him, cf 10:11. Jesus allowed Peter's fall that when he became head of the Church he might know how to be humble and have pity on sinners (Aquin; Ste Thérèse); so much for fine resolutions without a prayer for help (Cyr.Alex.); cf Phil 4:13. Mt 26:33ff; Mk 14:29ff put the prediction on the way to Gethsemane. Lk 22:33f and Jn perhaps bracket it with Judas's apostasy.

814a **14—17 The Last Discourse**—In this most sublime of farewells, Jesus, on the eve of his visible departure from this world, consoles and strengthens his own, and through them, us. Jn wrote in and for the Christian community after experiencing for more than half a century the wonders done by the disciples in the name of their Master (14:12), the fraternal charity marking the brethren (13:25, etc), the persecutions endured for Jesus and the death of Peter (15:18—21; 13:37; 21:18f), and above all the coming of the Paraclete and the unity of the Church prayed for by Jesus, 14:16ff, 25ff; 16:13ff; 17:20ff. There are no logical divisions, no systematic developments, but always the same spiral, circling movement of the eagle, the same recurring thoughts ('the Father', some 40 times, going to the Father, coming-seeing-knowing-believing-loving-the Spirit-life-truth-abiding-peace-joy-fruitful-prayer-persecutions from the world-unity-glory) progressively strengthened and deepened. Jesus is as one still in the world and yet not of it. He speaks of the heights of spirituality: the life and action together of the Divine Persons, the intimate relations between them and believers, between himself and the Paraclete, and again between them and the Christians of the future. The other speeches in Jn are to hostile audiences; this alone is to intimate friends. Like Mt in his Sermon on the Mount Jn may have grouped material from other sources and at least 16:7—11 could come from after the Resurrection. But the bulk belongs here. Ch 14, which is one composition (cf the inclusions 'let not your hearts be troubled' and 'believe', **b** 1—27c, 29), enunciates themes developed in other chh. 'Arise, let us go hence' (30f) suggests that it is the completed discourse. Yet chh 15—17 follow and the end comes with 18:1. Various explanations have been proposed: (1) 15—17 are to be taken as spoken elsewhere; this is highly unlikely. (2) Re-arrangements of material; these are without MSS support, and 14, with the questions (5, 6, 22) and opening mention of the Paraclete, is in its natural place. (3) Best is the redactional solution: Jn (or editors, but cf the masterly inclusion on love,

13:1—17:26) added to ch 14 (or 13:31—14:31) the comple- **814b** mentary matter in chh 15, 16, probably delivered orally over a period of time: 16:4b—33 corresponds substantially to 14; 15:1—17, with theme and language close to ch 6, goes with the Institution of the Eucharist; 15:18—16: 4a with the eschatological discourse of Mt 24:1—23 (Braun).

14:1—31 Words of Consolation—The disciples have **c** been told that Jesus will leave them and will be betrayed by one of themselves. We may suppose a sad silence. Then Jesus goes straight to the **confident faith** (*leitmotiv* of all his encouragement) which they must have in God and in him. Next he raises their troubled minds to his Father's house, whither he goes to prepare them places and whence he will come to bring them with him (1—4); the way is himself (4—11); he will enable them to do greater things than he has done (12—14), will send the Paraclete to them (15—17) to guide them (25f), will himself be living and present to all who love him (18—24) and will give them his peace and joy, 27—29. **1.** 'You **d** believe in God' is a possible translation, but 'believe in God, believe also in me' goes better with the command 'let not your hearts be troubled'; faith in God is always growing and is one with faith in Jesus, cf 10:28ff; 16:32b. **2.** This essential basis of faith and trust once set, Jesus gives the most comforting reason for his departure: he is going before them ('fore-runner', Heb 6:20). In his Father's hospitable house there are many 'rooms' ('abiding places', cf 23, cognate to 'abide', *menō*, which comes 40 times in Jn, 23 in 1 Jn); the point here is not degrees in heaven but plenty of room; otherwise, to spare them so cruel a deception, he would have told them; the rooms really await them for he is going to prepare them a place. '*Were it not so, I should have told you*' is a parenthesis, and *hoti* means 'because' (Barrett, BJ, CV, NEB), rather than 'if it were not so, would I have told you that . . .?' (RSV). By his Passion, glorification and sending of the Spirit, the Son of the house (8:35f) prepares eternal life for them, cf Rev 12:6; Aug., Aquin. **3.** Departure is the condition of return. 'I will come again': no time given; the Parousia indicated (cf 21:22; 1 Jn 2:28) is simply 'the consummation of all "comings"' (Westcott); 'take you to myself' suggests death. Jesus is always 'coming'. The promise that we shall be 'with' him (cf 17:24; 1 Thes 4:16f; 1 Jn 1:3) evokes the eager Church's 'Maranatha, come Lord', 1 Cor 16:22; Rev 22:17, 20. **4.** 'the way' draws out the disciples, cf 6. Literal minded Thomas thinks of a journey, cf 7:35; 13:37. **6.** 'I am', cf § 789b, 'the way', the only way to the Father whom he reveals (1:18; 12:45; 14:9; cf Eph 2:18; Heb 10:20) because he is the Truth (§ 799e) and the Life (§ 798d). Outside him, the one Mediator, the 'door', no one can give divine truth and life, 3:13—16; 10:7, 9; Ac 4:12; 1 Tm 2:5. **7.** '*Since you know me, you will also know my Father*', a consolation (S, D); not 'if you knew', a reproach as 8:10, cf 'from now you are beginning to know him' and 1 Jn 2:13. **8.** Philip (cf 6:7; 12:22) wants a theophany, cf Ex 24:9ff; 33:18. **9.** An affectionate reproach for being too slow of faith to penetrate Jesus's mystery yet, cf Jn 12:45; Col 1:15; Heb 1:3. **10.** 'This unity of Father and Son is the very being of Jesus' (Lebreton), but only faith can discern 'the glory of God on the face of Christ' (2 Cor 4:6). Both his words and his works, revelatory and full of power, are his Father's, for his Father is in him, 5:17—26, 36; 7:16f; 8:26, 28; 12:49f. **11.** 'Believe' (plur.) 'me' (dat.) i.e. what I say. Jesus wants the knowledge of himself that comes from love and trust whereby a man 'has the witness in himself', 1 Jn 5:10; but better to believe through Messianic

814d works such as miracles than not at all, 3:2; 9:33; 10:25, 38.

e **12—14 Comfort in their apostolic work—12** is joined, Semitic fashion, to 11 by 'works' and 'believe'. 'Truly, truly', solemn and unexpected: if only a man believes in me (result of 'believing me'), he will do greater works (e.g. in the spread of the Gospel, Ac 1:8; 2:41), because Jesus, now triumphant Lord with his Father, will be in him, cf 10:16; 12:32; Eph 4:7—16. **13—14.** Prayer 'the soul of every apostolate'. To pray in Jesus's 'name' (the Person manifested, cf 17:6, 26) is to pray in full faith as to who he is, his revelation about himself and his relations to us, cf 'pray in me', and 15:7. As what they here ask 'in my name' concerns the apostolate, it accords with his will, 1 Jn 5:14. Henceforth the Lord whom they ask, will not only intercede for them (Rm 8:34; 1 Jn 2:1) but act himself, so continuing his work for the glory of his Father. The early Church prayed this wholly new prayer (Ac 3:6; Rm 10:13; Phil 2:10).

f **15—25 Coming of the Divine Persons—**If we keep the commandments of love, they will dwell in us. This theme is applied to the Spirit (15—17), Jesus (18—22), the Father and Jesus, 23f (Brown). **15—16.** Love, shown by keeping 'my' commandments (Jesus is obeyed as God is), now succeeds faith as key condition, 1 Jn 2:3f. **The other Paraclete**, 'given' by the Father, sent by him and by the Son (26; 16:7), is a living Person, distinct from Jesus. The name, masculine and personal (contrast 'spirit' in 7:39, which in neuter) means 'Advocate' in Gr. cf § 799*b*. **17.** As 'the Spirit of truth' (Jn 15:26; 16:13), he reveals the whole religion of Jesus (4:23f; 2 Cor 4:2; 1 Jn 5:6, cf 1QS 3, 18f), teaching (Jn 14:26), witnessing (15:26), 'taking' what is Christ's and declaring it, 16:14, cf 2:22; 12:16. As 'the Spirit of prophecy' (frequent rabbinical name), he will speak in the Apostles. 'The world', in Jn's bad sense (1:10; 7:7; 12:31, some 30 times in this Discourse) is Qumran's 'darkness', blinded to the Spirit by its love of what passes and by its lying (1 Cor 2:14; 1 Jn 2:15ff; 4:6). The disciples' reception is contrasted; 'with you' suggests the Spirit in the Church, 'in you' in believers; 'is', rather than 'will be', cf Rm 8:16. **18.** Yet Jesus knows that what they want is their beloved Master back, and he consoles them again. 'I am coming back to you' (NEB) refers here most naturally to his mystical indwelling in their hearts, cf Mt 28:20. **19.** 'A little while', after his death and burial. The unbelieving world will see him no more 'for their hearts are without the Spirit' (Cyr.Alex., cf Jn 7:34; 8:21). But the disciples will see him in glorious life and share it with him, 20:29; 6:57. **20.** 'Day', prophetic formula for great divine interventions, e.g. Is 2:17; 4:1f; primarily the day of the Resurrection, but the sun will never set on it (Lagrange, cf 16:23). Pentecost is dawning too, and by the Spirit they will understand the presence of Jesus in the Father and in them, cf 14:10; 17:21. **21.** Again, love proved by keeping Jesus's commandments, cf Ex 20:6; Dt 5:10; 1 Jn 5:3; Aquin., ST 2—2, q. 23, a.1; 'by my Father', whose love for the Son will extend to him and draw him into the divine family. The Son will show his love by manifesting himself **g** to him, cf Ex 33:13,18. **22.** 'Manifest' catches the attention (cf Jn 7:4) of 'Judas', cf Lk 6:16; Ac 1:13, prob. Thaddaeus of Mt 10:3; Mk 3:18; why then not to the public but only to the hearts of the disciples? Cf Ac 10:40 **23—24.** The reply is fundamental. 'Quaesierat de Christi manifestatione et audivit de dilectione et mansione' (Aug). The divine presence can be known only by one who loves; when the Son has returned to the Father, both will come and (together with the Spirit, 16f) make 'abode' with him in delightful, permanent intimacy (Prv 8:31; **814** Is 62:5; Aquin). In Jn 6:56 the abiding is Eucharistic, in 14:2, heavenly, here mystical, requiring no qualifications save sincere love of Jesus (Lagrange), cf 1 Jn 4:13, 16; Eph 3:17. God's dwelling with his People is completed, Ex 25:8; Lv 26:11f; 2 Cor 6:16. But 'the world', which does not love him or keep his words (Jn 8:37, 42f, 47, cf 7:16f) cannot receive a manifestation. **25—26.** 'These things I have spoken to you' (solemn refrain, 7 times in the Discourse, cf Heb 1:1f) shows that Jesus's doctrinal mission is ending. But the Father will send the Paraclete (called Holy Spirit in OT language, Ps 51 (50):13; Is 63:10, to suggest the interior master) not just 'in my stead' but 'in my name' to reveal the Son, as the Son came in his Father's name to reveal the Father, 5:43. He will teach (Ps 25 (24):5, 9; 1 Jn 2:27) no new truths, but the inner meaning and hidden riches of the words and deeds of Jesus (Jn 16:13ff, cf 2:22; 12:16), who will thus continue to teach the Church through his Spirit, e.g. Mt 23:10; Ac 11:16; Eph 3:16f; Cyr.Alex.

27—31 Epilogue: Peace, Joy, Confidence—Inclusion **h** with Jn 14:1. **27.** Transforming the Eastern farewell (e.g. Mk 5:34), Jesus bequeaths them **peace** (Nm 6:26; Ps 122 (121):6f), 'my' peace, the perfect Messianic gift: love of God and each other, individual and collective hope, harmony, happiness (Is 11:6ff; Ezek 37:24ff; Jn 14:1—4; 16:33; Gal 5:22; Eph 2:14). It is not the world's, Jer 6:14; Lk 12:51; 1 Thes 5:3. It makes hearts confident, for Christ's army wants no cowards, (Dt 31:8; Jos 1:9; Mt 8:26; 1 Tm 1:7; Rev 21:8). **28.** Their friend is going; but instead of selfish sorrow, there should be self-forgetful joy for his sake (Jn 14:3, 18; 16:5f)——as at the Ascension, Lk 24:53. 'Greater than I' does not deny equality in the Trinity (cf Jn 1:1; 5:17ff; 10:30), for in the context Jesus is in the humiliation of 'the flesh', cf 1:14; Mk 13:32; Phil 2:7f; the return to the Father will be return to the glory of the Son of God, cf 1 Cor 15:27f; Cyr.Alex. **29.** By foretelling the scandal of his death, he will lead them to believe in the divine plan, cf Jn 13:19; 16:4. 'Believe' makes inclusion with 14:1. **30.** Time presses; Satan himself (cf 12:31; 16:11), using Judas, Caiaphas, Pilate and the rest, is at hand for the final combat, cf Lk 4:13; 22:53; 'against me he can do nothing' who am 'not of this world', 8:46; 17:11; 18:36; Heb 4:15. **31.** Serenely, freely, to prove utter obedience to his Father, Jesus goes to his Passion, cf 4:34; 5:19, 30; 6:38; 12:49f; 15:10. The last words recall Mt 26:46; Mk 14:42. On why three more chh follow, cf § 814*b*.

15:1—16:4. Love and Hate.

15:1—17—The Vine and the Branches is an allegory **815a** (cf 10:1—18) about the intimate union of love between Jesus and his own, permeated with the Eucharistic spirit and closely resembling ch 6: 'abide' 11 times (cf 6:27, 56), 'love' 9, 'friends' 3, 'in me' 5, 'fruit' 8 (elsewhere only 4:36; 12:24). The Father, who gives the bread of life in 6:32, is here the vinedresser. The fidelity in faith and confidence insisted on in ch 14 has deepened into a communion of life with Jesus and one another bearing its fruit in love, 'an epitome of the Christian religion' (Hoskyns). **1.** 'I am the vine', cf § 798*b*; this recalls **b** 'the fruit of the vine' and the wine of the Eucharist, making them one with Jesus, cf Mt 26:29; Mk 14:25; Lk 22:18; 'true', 'genuine', distinguishes Jesus from Israel, noble but degenerate vine or vineyard (Hos 10:1f; Is 5:1—7; Jer 2:21; Mt 20:1—16; Mk 12:1—11, pars). But these accusation formulae, in which the OT Vine never gives life, cannot be the unique source of so life-giving a symbol. Practically non-existent Mandaean analogies are unnecessary, for in Sir 24:17—20 the fruitful vine is

15b Wisdom (Feuillet). Here Jesus, the Father's perfect planting (Mt 15:13, cf *Did*. 9, 2), is the 'total Christ', one with his disciples, Head of his Body, or the Body itself, 1 Cor 12:12—27; Eph 4:15f; Col 1:18. On how both allegories show the giving of grace for meritorious acts, cf Dz 809. **2.** To be 'in me' is basic for Christian life and for fruitfulness in that love of each other which is the essence of discipleship. The sterile branch not 'in me' is cut off by the vinedresser (Is 27:3) who 'prunes' (Gr. also means cleanse; a play on *airei* and *kathairei*) the good branch to make it more fruitful, Rm 11:16—22; Ign. Ant. *Phil*. 3, 1. **3—5.** They are already cleansed by 'the word' (the whole revelation of Jesus as dynamic principle, cf 6:63; 12:48; 13:10*b*; Rm 1:16, etc) but their reciprocal (Jn 15:4, 5, 7) union with Jesus must continue if they are to bear fruit. Here is the law of spiritual fecundity. 'Without me you can do nothing' (cf 1:3; 21:6) refutes all Pelagianism, cf Gal 2:20; 1 Cor 4:7; 15:10; Dz 105, 108. Because he first abides in them, they abide in him, cf 1 Jn 4:10. **6.** Separation from Jesus is by free decision, cf 2:19; 'fire', cf Ezek 15:2—6; Mt 13:30, 40; repentance is not in the perspective; 'aut vitis aut ignis', Aug. **7.** Union with Jesus (the same as abiding in his words, cf Jn 5:38; 14:10) makes prayer according to his will infallibly effective, cf on Jn 14:13; 16:23; 1 Jn 5:4. **8.** 'The fruitfulness of his vine is the joy and glory of the vine-grower' (Keppeler); all ends, as it began, with the Father, v 1; cf 14:13*b*; Mt 5:16; 1 Cor 10:31. 'My' disciples are

c necessarily apostolic. **9—10. Love and Joy.** The Father's love for his Son made man (3:35; 5:20; 10:17; 17:26) is source and model of Jesus's love for his own, 13:1, 34; 15:12; in this love they must abide 'as in an atmosphere of light and joy which will envelope and penetrate them entirely' (Huby, cf 1 Jn 4:16), allowing themselves to be loved, and corresponding by solid fidelity in action—the spirituality of a Ste Thérèse (Braun, cf 4:34; 8:29; 10:17). **11.** 'Nothing causes so much joy as to be loved' (Lagrange), and Jesus desires to enlarge their hearts by the fullness of joy, 3:29; 16:24; 1 Jn 1:4; 2 Jn 12; 'the delightful divine merriment of the Christians, which originates in the Son and is deposited in his disciples (Jn 17:13) is matured and perfected as they love one another, undergo persecutions and readily lay down their lives for the brethren', 1 Jn 3.16 (Hoskyns). **12—10.** Form inclusion with 17; 'my commandment' (summarizing them all, 10) is the 'new' one of 13:34, cf § 799*g* **14.** 'Friends' suggests 'my friends'. Abraham was 'the friend of God', Is 41:8. Now Jesus, Divine Wisdom (Wis 7:27), makes them his friends provided they are loyal to the mission confided to them, cf 14:15. **15.** Progressive intimacy: slaves (13:13—16), friends, 'my brothers', 20:17. As distinguishing mark of friendship (Gn 18:17f), Jesus makes known to them (in principle, Jn 16:21) all that he has heard from his Father, 1:18; 14:7; 16:25—30. **16—17.** His choice of them, a pure gift, invests them with a mission to take his place ('you', emphatic) by virtue of his Passion (*thē*, 13, *ethēka*, 16, cf Ac 20:28; 1 Cor 12:18, 28) and 'go' (Mt 28:19; Jn 12:24) to bear fruit. Apostolic prayer in union with him will make the fruit lasting, cf 14:13f. Here the vine image finds its key and its close, and all the instructions are summed up by mutual love.

d 15:18—16:4. The Hate of the World is in opposition to their love. Even here Jesus consoles: they will be sharing his lot; they are not to be surprised that the world never ceases to hate Christians (1 Jn 3:13), for like their Master who has chosen them out of the world, they are not of it (Wis 2:41f; Jn 7:7; 8:23; 17:14). 'Christianity is not talk but power when it is hated by the world',

Ign. Ant., *Rom*., 3. Vv 18—27 are very like the persecution **815d** sections of the 'mission sermon', Mt 10:18—25 (which 24:9; Mk 13:9—13; Lk 21:12.19 set at the end of Jesus's life, Brown). **20—22.** Cf Mt 10:22—25 rather than Jn 13:16; the Christian persecuted 'for my name's sake' is identified with Christ (Ac 9:4, 16); suffering becomes his joy, Lk 6:22f; Ac 5:41; 1 Pt 4:12ff. The persecutors' ignorance is the fundamental culpable refusal to recognize the Father's revelation in the Son, Jn 8:19ff, 54f; 14:7, 17; 16:3, 9. Even culpable ignorance can extenuate in the charitable eyes of Jesus in Lk 23:34, but here he notes the enormous guilt of voluntary self-blinding (cf Lagrange). **23.** Hate is of the 'world's' essence (contrast 1 Jn 4:8, 16). It is directed against the light, Jesus and his disciples (3:20; 7:7; 15:18; 17:14; 1 Jn 3:13) and so against the Father who sent him (cf 5:23; Lk 10:16; 1 Jn 2:23) and who reveals himself in Jesus as Light and Love, TWNT 4, 695—6 (Michel). **24—25.** To his words (22) Jesus has added works; 'seen' cf 9:40f. 'Their Law', Scripture, cf 8:17; 10:34; § 799*f*. Even this enters the redemptive plan. Jesus recognizes his prophetic image in the just man persecuted without reason, Ps 35 (34): 19; 69 (68):5. **26. But the Paraclete will come**, the Spirit of **e** true witness, whom Jesus glorified will send from the Father's side, 14:16f, 26; 1 Jn 5:6*c*; § 799*g*. The context of 'comes forth from the Father' concerns directly the role of each Person in the work of revelation, cf Rev 22:1. **27.** The Spirit and the disciples will continue the work of Jesus, he in them (1 Jn 4:13; Mt 10:20; Ac 1:8), they as qualified ocular witnesses, Jn 1:14; 1 Jn 1:1—4; Lk 1:2; Ac 1:2f. **16:1—4 The Persecution theme returns** to warn them and all Christians that the world's hatred will be masked as the love of God, lest they be 'scandalized', i.e. give up their faith, cf Jn 6:61; 1 Jn 2:10; Rev 21:8; Pliny, *Ep*. 10, 96, 6. **2.** Cf Jn 9:22; 12:42; 'an hour' (4:23; 16:25, not 'the Hour' but like it) will come for them too, cf 4; Ac 26:9ff and NumR 21, 4 on Nm 25:13 'every one who sheds the blood of the godless is like one who offers a sacrifice'. Pagans too called Christians atheists. **3—4.** Cf Jn 15: 21; on the persecutors' 'hour' cf Lk 22:53. Before this Jesus would not sadden them and drew the attacks on himself.

5—00 Same themes as ch 14 The disciples' sorrow, **f** where Jesus is going (14:1—5), the coming of the Spirit-Advocate (16f, 26), the disciples' misunderstanding (19—22; 16:16f), Jesus's peace (14:27; 16:33), prayer (14:13f; 16:23f). This may be a complementary draft, but (Lightfoot) the thought seems to progress, cf 14:20f with 16:23f; 14:16f with 16:7ff.

5—12 The Spirit as Advocate—5—6. Perhaps ironic **g** (they had asked twice, 13:36; 14:5): 'Do you not ask me now but only grieve selfishly over my going?', cf 14:28. **7.** Yet his going will benefit them, for the Paraclete will come only after his glorification, 7:39; Aquin., ST 3, 57, 1 ad 3. **8—11.** 'The world' which has Satan for prince, 12:31; 14:30; 'convict', expose to the light (cf 3:20; Eph 5:11ff), not 'convince', for the world as such is never persuaded, Jn 14:17. Think of a 'trial' bearing on the **h** guilt of one party and the innocence of the other and ending with a condemnation. The 'world' claims to have condemned Jesus (e.g. 9:24; 18:30; 19:7), and the Apostles will be faced with the weight of that judgement. But the Advocate, speaking in and through them, will reverse the verdict: the sin is not with Jesus (cf 8:46) but with the world's monstrous disbelief (3:18ff, 36; 8:24; 15:22; 1 Jn 5:10, 19); the 'just one', he who wins the suit (Ps 50 (49):6*b*, Bultmann), is not the world but Jesus, Jn 9:29; Ac 3:14; 7:52; his going to his Father proves his right to

815h call himself the Son of God, Jn 6:62; 13:1; 20:17; 10:33; 19:7; his disappearance (? the empty tomb) is his vindication, 16:17ff; the condemnation falls on the arch-plotter (Gn 3:15; Jn 8:44; 13:2; 14:30), who, in contriving the death of Jesus, has met his own defeat, 12:31f; 16:33. The Spirit's witness, ringing through the Kerygma (cf Ac) will reveal the true meaning of Jesus's death. It will reverse many a verdict of the 'world' in history, e.g. St Joan of Arc.

i **12—15 The Spirit as Teacher** will complete the Apostles' education. Jesus, the Father's Word, has revealed everything to them (1:14, 18; 15:15), but the Spirit of Truth will guide (not 'teach', Vg; it has a moral sense, Ps 25 (24):5) them into the height and depth of these riches, Jn 14:26; 1 Cor 2:10—15; Eph 3:18f; Col 2:3. His guidance is sure, for like the Son (Jn 7:17; 12:49; 14:10) he will not speak of himself. **13.** 'The things that are to come', the new order which springs from Christ's death and resurrection, his mystery in the Church (Col 3:11) and events in which the Spirit of prophecy discerns his working (e.g. Ac 20:27; Rev 1:19; 2:7). **14—15.** He will glorify Jesus, as Jesus does his Father (17:4) by communicating the mystery of the Son who has his source in the Father, 3:35; 5:20—26; 8:26—40; 13:3; 17:3. Revelation is one: it comes from the Father through the Son and is completed in the Spirit to the glory of the Son and the Father, BJ.

816a **16—33 'A little while'**, recurring 7 times. Though Jesus's death and resurrection are directly in view, there are further implications with regard to the Ascension and the life of the Church. **16.** Omit 'because I go to the Father' (Vg) which is not in the best MSS and obscures the sense. **17—19.** Some disciples find novel and puzzling 'not see' (physically) followed by 'contemplate' (*opsesthe*, cf 1:50f; 11:40), and 'a little while' which seems to contradict 'because I go to the Father', 16:5, 10. Jesus puts their question for them but does not answer it in their terms. **20.** Have no illusions: my death will plunge you in sorrow (e.g. Mk 16:10; Lk 24:17) while the world triumphs in evil joy (cf Rev 11:10). He thinks of them rather than of himself (Aquin). **21.** He takes the theme of the birth-pangs of a new order (Is 26:18ff; 66:7—14, cf Rm 8:22), but underlines the joy of childbirth, cf 1 Pt 4:13; 'hour', cf Jn 13:1, etc. **22.** 'I will see' (contrast 17) because it is he who will come. The one note expressing the situation is Joy, the ineradicable Paschal joy of Jesus himself (17:13; 20:20, cf Is 66:14) which is to be the dynamism of the Church (Ac, *passim*; Phil 1:25; 1 Pt 1:8). **23—24.** In the serenity of 'that day' (cf on Jn 14:20; Ac 2:18) the disciples will ask him no more busy questions (nor do they, Jn 21:12, except to meet rebuke, 21:21f; Ac 1:6). Instead ('Truly, truly' bringing a new modulation) they will use the free access of prayer to their Father, 'in my name' (7 times in the Discourse), a name they had not hitherto mentioned in prayer, for Jesus was with them and not glorified, 14:13f; contrast Eph 2:18; Heb 10:19ff. But now 'keep asking' (pres.), 'so that your joy (6 times) may be full', cf on Jn 15:11. This entirely new type of prayer, far above the formulae reminding God of the Patriarchs, can be made to Jesus himself (14:14), and even when made to the Father is **b** heard by him as well (Durrwell, 206). **25.** 'Parables' exactly describe 16:19—22, but extend to his sayings in general; note link with Syn., and for Jn cf 3:8; 10:6; 15:1ff. But now his whole life, as he approaches his glorification will speak directly of the Father (6:45, cf Jer 31:33f; 1 Jn 5:20) whom they will see in him by the revelation of the Spirit, cf Jn 14:26. **26—27.** 'That day' is the 'hour' of v 25. There is no distinction between a

merciful Son and a just or angry Father! The Father is **816** himself within the circle of love, 15:9f, 13ff (Barrett). They pray in Jesus's name (and so rely on his priestly intercession, Heb 7:25; 1 Jn 2:1). But instead of waiting on the threshold for him to intervene (cf Lk 4:38, Lagrange), they enter and look into the Father's eyes; faith and love are all they need. **28.** Perfect summary of this Christian faith: 'I came from the Father' (cf 13:3; 17:4f; Is 55:10f) refers directly to the Incarnational mission. Earliest Christianity appealed to the Resurrection, cf Jn 16:10. Jn embraces the whole divine scheme: the ascent proves the descent, the return, the origin, 1:51; 3:14; 6:60ff; 16:5 (Van den Bussche). **29—30.** The **c** Apostles think that nothing could be plainer (contrast 18), and this before the coming of the Spirit! They base their 'more enthusiastic than solid' faith (Huby) on the correct but flimsy foundation that Jesus divines their thoughts, cf 19. **31—32.** But Jesus welcomes it, though with gentle irony: 'now' could mean 'none too soon' or 'only for the moment'. Reciting the Creed is one thing, living it another. 'An hour' (cf 25) is upon them when, for all their assurances, they will scatter (Zech 13:7, set by Mt 26:31; Mk 14:27 on the way to Gethsemane) and leave him alone (Jn's addition); and yet (Jn's point) he is not alone, for the Father is with him, cf 8:28f and the contrast with Mt 27:46; Mk 15:34 (Ps 22 (21):1). **33.** The seventh solemn 'These things I have spoken to you' seems to refer to the whole discourse; 'peace' sums up 14:27; 'tribulation', 15:18ff; 16:21; but Jesus's victorious cry (cf 14:27—31) raises their hearts: he has decisively conquered the world (12:31; Rev 5:5; 17:14) and so in him will they (1 Jn 2:13f; 4:4; 5:4f; Rev 3:21; 12:11; Rm 8:37; 1 Cor 15:57).

17:1—26 Jesus's Sacerdotal Prayer for Unity, **d** which owes its title to the Lutheran David Chytaeus (d. A.D. 1600; cf already Cyr.Alex.) is the Priest-Victim's oblation-intercession on the eve of his sacrifice (19), asking that his work may continue through those whom the Father has given him in a unity of charity that shares the unity of the Father and the Son (20—23), a unity holy, apostolic, universal (19f) to be consummated in eternal love (24). This 'preface' to the historical sacrifice of the Cross is chanted by the Son as he is about to pass the threshold of eternity and enter upon his glory in the bosom of the Father, cf 1:18. He speaks at times as if still in the world (17:13, 19), at times as if his ministry were past (11f, 18). The spirit of this longest of Jesus's prayers resembles that of the short prayers recorded in Jn (11:41f; 12:27f) and in Syn. (e.g. Mt 11:25; Lk 22:42; 23:34, 46), above all of the Our Father: 'Father' in the intimate sense, Jn 17:1, 5, 11, 21, 24, 25; 'hallowed be thy name', 6, 11, 12, 26; 'thy kingdom come', cf 1f; 'on earth as it is in heaven', 4, 5; 'lead us not into temptation', 12 ('I kept, I guarded them'); 'from evil' (or 'the evil one'), 15 (F. H. Chase, 'The Lord's Prayer in the Early Church', TSt 1 (1891) 111). The sweating victim falling face to earth in the prayer of the Agony (Mt 26:39; Mk 14:35) is in striking contrast to the majesty of the Son lifting his eyes to heaven. But the Priest-Victim speaks in both, Jn 17:19.

This is no short-hand report, but a synthesis which **e** may have had in view the eucharistic celebration of Jn's day. Yet a prayer accompanied the Paschal supper, and the fundamental elements of this prayer go back to the historic event: namely the references to the 'Hour', the contacts with the Bread of Life discourse, Jesus's care for his own who are to remain in the world, his allusions to the treason (12), the mission of the disciples (18) and to his self-consecration to death (Van den Bussche).

816e Besides, 'the tenacious memory of an old man recalling the greatest days of his youth' (Bernard) would preserve Jesus's last prayer in the presence of his disciples. This prayer has teaching value for the Church in every age (Aug., Aquin., cf 11:41f). Taking its origin from the act of salvation (1—5), it passes through the medium of the Apostles (6—19) to all generations (20—23) and the end of time (24). In the flight of the Spirit Jn's gaze—as in the Prologue with which there are many contacts—embraces the eternity of the beginning and the eternity of the consummation (Van den Bussche). Proper to the ch, and marked by inclusion, is the theme of glory (1—5 . . . 22—24). There are three parts: Jesus prays for himself (1—5), his Apostles alone (6—19), those who will believe through their teaching (20—26).

f 1—5 Jesus prays for himself—1. Having spoken, Jesus prays; 'lifted his eyes' as in manifestations of his Father's glory, 11:40f; cf Mk 6:41; 7:34. 'Father', title of loving intimacy, introduces the three petitions (5, 11, 21) and the two parts of the close of the prayer, 24, 25; 'the hour', cf above; 'glorify thy Son', not egotistic (cf 7:18; 8:50): divine acceptance of his sacrifice will redeem men to the glory of the Father, whose glory is one with his, 13:31; Phil 2:9ff; **2.** The Son was sent to 'all flesh' (all men), to give them life, cf Jn 3:35f; 10:10; 'all whom thou has given him' (cf 6:37, 39; 10:29; 17:6, 8, 24), not strict predestination; but no one comes to faith save through grace (6:44, 55) and the Father has confided this little seed-ground to Jesus for his mission. **3.** The joy of the early Church shines out in Jn's description (not definition) of eternal life; it has sapiential roots (cf Wis 15:3; contrast Gn 2:17); 'know' implies intimate, loving union (cf Jn 14:7; 1 Jn 4:8) continuously growing (pres. tense, cf Hos 6:3); 'true god', not an idol (1 Thes 1:9; 1 Jn 5:20f). Revelation being no longer founded on the Law, it is equally eternal life to know the glorious Son whom the Father sent to reveal him (Jn 1:17; 6:68; 14:1; 1 Jn passim); 'gloria Dei vivens homo; vita autem hominis visio Dei', (Iren. Haer. 4, 20, 5). **4—5.** Jesus has achieved his life's aim of glorifying his Father (Jn 4:34; 5:36; 13:1; 19:30) by completing the work of our redemption which he was sent to do. He asks in recompense (1 Sm 2:30) that his suffering humanity may achieve, in the Father's bosom, the glory which the Father eternally decreed for him in the Incarnation (1:14), or that which belongs to his eternal existence as Son (cf 8:58).

g 6—19 Jesus prays for his Apostles—6—8. He presents to his Father those to whom he has 'manifested' (Ps 22 (21):23; Heb 2:12) his 'name' (cf Ex 3:13f; Jn 1:18; 10:38; 14:7—11): 'not that name by which you are called God, but that by which you are called my Father: a name which, without the Son's own manifestation, could not be manifested' (Aug., cf Cyr.Alex., Aquin). These 'men of God' (8:47), chosen from the world, and so given a mandate to witness to the revelation they have received (cf Dt 4:5; Jn 15:15) have loyally kept his, and therefore his Father's word (7:16; 8:51; 14:23) and recognized that everything in Jesus is from his Father (3:35; 8:40; 12:49). For they accepted the sayings (rhēmata) which Jesus gave them from the Father, and so have known in faith that it is from the Father he comes forth as emissary. **9—11a.** This prayer is for his Apostles alone, his friends, 15:15. The world as such is impervious to prayer (8:43; 14:17; Jas 4:4) but later he prays for those others with whom they will have contacts, in the world which he has come to save, Jn 17:21ff; cf 1:10; 3:16; 1 Jn 4:9. On behalf of his Apostles he urges three motives: they now belong more intimately to the Father, since they are

the Son's very own; and Son and Father have all in **816g** common, 16:16; cf Lk 15:31; he has been and is (perf.) glorified by them and they will spread his glory, cf Jn 6:68f; 15:8; 16:14; 17:22; they will now be left alone in the world. **11b.** 'Holy' (Lv 11:44; Is 6) expresses separation **h** from the profane and in God the highest perfection of purity. 'Holy Father' introduces the prayer for the disciples to be guarded from contagion (11b, 15) and consecrated, like Jesus, to God's service and love, 17, cf Did. 10, 2. 'Keep them' safe as being your own, cf Jude 1; 'in thy name', by the power (cf Prv 18:10 and for the divine name giving protection, Jn 18:6f; Ac 4:12); this name is incarnate in the Son; the divine nature possessed in common by Father and Son is to be source and model of the disciples' unity with God and with one another, cf Eph 4:3—6. **12.** Up to now, Jesus himself strove to keep (imperf.) his little ones (cf Mt 23:37; Lk 13:34) around him (Jn 6:39; 10:28) and guarded them as their shepherd; 'none of them perished save the son of perdition', has a play on Gr. words and a semitism for which cf 12:36; 2 Sm 12:5; Mt 23:15; 2 Thes 2:3. The fulfilment of Scripture shows that the divine plan took account of Judas's free action, cf Ps 41 (40):10; Jn 13:18. **13.** Jesus prays aloud that the disciples may share to the full his joy as he returns to the bosom of the Father. **14.** His gift of the cleansing 'word' (15:3) opposes the hate of the world for those who receive it, cf 7:7. Like him, they are not of the world, for he has chosen them out of it, 8:23, 44 47; 15:18f; 1 Jn 5:18f. **15.** Those with a mission to the world must be in it as leaven and not in ivory towers; but Jesus knows the danger they run and prays that they be not infected; 'from the evil one' rather than 'from evil', since Jn sees evil not as impersonal but as diabolic in origin (Jn 12:31; 13:27; 14:30; 16:11; 1 Jn 2:13f; 5:18f). **16.** Repetition of 14 to introduce the idea of consecration. **17—18.** 'Sanctify', set them apart and consecrate them; 'in the truth', God's revelation, his 'word' (Ps 119 (118):142), penetrating and transforming them (Sir 45:6; 1 Thes 5:23). Consecration prepares them, as it does Jesus (Jn 10:36) for mission into the world, cf 20:21. **19.** Jesus consecrates himself as a sacrificial victim (Ex 13:2) for them (Is 53:4f; Jn 6:51; 11:50ff; 15:13; Heb 10:5ff) that they too may be consecrated by a total commitment in and to the full revelation of Jesus (Jn 13:1—5; Rm 15:16; Heb 2:11; 1 Jn 3:18).

20—26 Jesus prays for those to come—20—21. 'Jn **i** never forgets his readers'. He makes vital contact with them and every age of the Church to whom the word of men transmits intact the Word of God; hina thrice leads up to the parallel vv 22—23 (hina thrice). 'Through their word', cf Mt 28:30; Rm 10:17. Jesus prays that these others may have the same grace of unity ('all' juxtaposed emphatically with 'one') as the Apostles (11), that they may have unity in the Divine Persons (cf 15:9; 1 Jn 1:3f) and that through seeing this unity the world may go on believing (pres., best reading) that he was sent by the Father (cf Jn 10:38; 14:10f; 1 Jn 2:24). He must be praying for the visible unity of his Church. His prayer does not fail, though our witness to him by love does fail, Jn 13:35. **22—23.** 'Glory' (cf § 798fg) given to the Incarnate Son and by him to men, is to be the principle of a unity like that of the Divine Persons. 'I in them', cf 6:56; 14:20; 15:4f; 2 Cor 13:5; Gal 2:20; 'thou in me', Jn 14:10f, 20; this current of continuous divine life, reflecting the unity of the Father and the Son (10:38), consummates the unity of Christians in doctrine and love (cf 1 Jn 2:5; 4:12, 17f), so that according to Jesus's repeated desire the world may at last recognize (cf 14:31) that the Father sent him

816i and has loved men with the same love as he loves his Son (cf 3:16; Rev 3:9c).

j 24—26 The vista on eternity—24. 'Father', ardently, pressingly, the prayer reaches its supreme moment, ending, as it began, with two invocations of the Father, cf 1, 5. Lit. 'what thou hast given me' (neut. sing.) includes all in a single body. Since they now belong to the Son as the Father's gift (6:37, 39), he wants them to be with him. 'I will', 'the ordinary language of prayer breaks down' (Barrett), for Jesus has received all power to do judgement (5:22—30) and knows that his will coincides with his Father's (4:43; 5:30; 6:38; cf 5:21). Great friends of God sometimes speak like this. His demand that they be with him (an inclusion with 14:3; cf 12:26; Lk 23:43), reverses the original situation when he came into the world to be with them (1:9f (Van den Bussche)). 'Non ei satis fuit dicere "volo ut ubi ego sum, et illi sint," sed addidit "mecum". Esse enim cum illo, magnum bonum est' (Aug). 'My glory' is that of the Word incarnate (the uncreated Son's glory is not said to be 'given' (cf Phil 2:6; Col 1:15; 2 Cor 8:9) (Schanz)) So far we see it only in faith's obscurity (Jn 1:14; 1 Cor 13:21) but 'we shall see him as he is' (1 Jn 3:2); 'to see is to have a share, to see is to enjoy . . . That will be the perfect consummation of the work for which Jesus Christ has come' (Bossuet). 'Before the foundation of the world', 'the beginning and the end of time are here brought together to find their meaning in the historical mission of Jesus and its results' (Barrett). **25.** 'Just Father', for judgement is concerned, cf Jn 8:26. Jesus asks no more. He summarizes the substance of the Gospel and contemplates the justice of the Father towards the world which has refused to know and love him. But Jesus knew him by perfect, reciprocal knowledge (7:29; 8:55; 10:15; Mt 11:25f; Lk 10:21), and the disciples have at last recognized that Jesus has been sent by the Father. **26.** 'I have made known thy name' (cf 6, 'manifested' thy inner nature) and will make it known by the Spirit in the future Church, 16:12, 25. 'That the love . . . and I in them' (14:20) is Jesus's supreme goal and final desire. This love (coming from the knowledge he gives) is to be in us too as his members, loved when the whole Christ is loved (Aug. Cyr.Alex). 'By his use of inclusion (cf 13:1) the Beloved Disciple has chosen to set all these chh under the *leit-motiv* of love' (Behler); cf 15:9; 17:23. 'I in them' is the last aspiration of Jesus for his own before he sets forth to meet death. In these words alone, everything is said (Bernard, Van den Bussche).

18—19 THE PASSION

817a **Jn and Syn.** sequence, closely related from the entry into Jerusalem, is almost identical from the arrest onwards. On their relationship, cf § 793efg. Jn has dealt with the Agony (12:27), the treachery, denial and abandonment (13:1f, 21—32, 36ff; 16:32) and with the judgement given already (5; 7—10; 11:49—53). Allusions are enough, and he stresses above everything else the progress of Jesus towards his Cross and ultimate glory. Even ill-treatment is dignified by Jesus's (18:22f) and Pilate's (19:1—5) interpretations. Before Pilate, Jesus shows who is the real judge, especially if he sits on the judicial bench (19:13). In the account of the crucifixion, Jn omits the humiliations: Simon's help, the thieves, mockeries, darkness, cry of desolation, and also the rending of the veil of the Temple. He underlines the meaning of the carrying of the cross, the royal title, the seamless tunic, Jesus's words to his Mother and Disciple, his initiative in asking for a drink, the prophecies concentrating upon his 'Hour', the grandeur in dying with all accomplished and in giving the Spirit, the coming forth of the blood and the water, the faith in him whom they pierced. The Son sent into the world as weak flesh, leaves it in triumphal ascent to his Father. Jn **817a** penetrates to the inner meaning and links up the mystery of the Cross with the mystery of glory. He shows himself as the witness who lived through it; not a young man fleeing into the darkness (Mk) but the disciple whom Jesus loved, standing beside him and attesting the facts (18:15); 19:26, 35 (X. Léon-Dufour. 'Passion', DBS 6, 1419—91, closely followed).

18:1—12 Arrest—His words ended, Jesus goes forth **b** with his disciples over the torrent Kidron ('Blackwater'), crossed by David fleeing from Absalom, 2 Sm 15:23. The garden, doubtless private and enclosed by a low, drystone wall, Gethsemane (Mt, Mk) on the Mount of Olives, was at Jesus's disposal as a rendezvous, where he 'often' gathered with his disciples for the night (Lk 21:37; 22:39). So Judas 'who was in the act of betraying him' (cf Mk 14:44), knew the place and Jesus was not hiding. The agony is only alluded to, v 11 (cf 12:27f). **3.** The band Judas was guiding included a 'detachment' (maniple, 200 men if at full strength) of Roman soldiers, probably auxiliaries, under their tribune (12), sent to help the Temple police in case of trouble; only Jn mentions these Gentiles; their presence suggests Pilate's complicity; if the Paschal moon was clear, the reference to the (army regulation, Dion. Hal., 11, 40, 2) 'lanterns' and 'torches', needed no more than arms (Mt 26:55) to find the Light of the World, may be ironical. They closed in for the arrest (12), presumably acted as escort to Annas's palace and then returned to barracks, 18. **4—6.** With full knowledge and free will, Jesus comes out from the garden (cf Mk 14:42), and this makes Judas's sign (Mk 14:44) unnecessary. Jn notices the traitor standing with the party. 'Whom do you seek?': contrast Jn 1:38; 20:15; 'Jesus of Nazareth' describes him (Mk 10:47; Lk 18:37) with a touch of contempt, cf Jn 1:44; 19:19. 'I am (he)' means 'the man you want' (cf 9:9). Some of the party perhaps awed by his majestic bearing started backwards in surprise and this made others stumble and fall.

7—9. Repetition underlines Jesus's authority; he uses it to save 'these' ('my disciples' would have compromised them). Jn recalls Jesus's saying (17:12, cf 6:39), and sees him defend their liberty with the same loving care with which he preserved them from moral destruction (cf 10:11ff). Perhaps at this point Judas gave his traitorous, now futile kiss (Mk 14:45). **10.** '*The* servant of the High Priest' implies that he led the police; perhaps he laid hands on Jesus. Peter, who had one of the two swords (Lk 22:38), could now strike and die for his Master, Jn 13:37; Jn, like Lk 22:50, mentions the 'right' ear but avoids several details and adds new facts: Peter's name (safely revealable after his death) and Malchus's (? a later convert, cf Lk 22:51). **11.** Cf Jer 47:6; Is 51:22; this is the cup of the Agony, Mt 26:42 and pars.

12—27 Jesus before Annas. Peter's denials—Either **c** there were three events: a short, unofficial hearing before Annas, a night session of the Sanhedrin (with Peter's denials in the courtyard) and a hurried daybreak session to give an appearance of legality to the decision arrived at in the night; or Syn. may have run together the unoffical night inquiry before Annas, during which Jesus is ill-treated and Peter denies him, and the offical morning trial by Caiaphas before the Sanhedrin, which Jn assumes (18:29; 19:7, cf Mk 14:53—64 and pars). All the Gospels put Peter's denials at night, and Jn repeats 'Peter was standing and warming himself' before (18) and after (25) the inquiry before Annas. The third denial could be followed by Jesus's 'looking on Peter', Lk 22:61. **12.** 'All combined to take the willing prisoner' (Westcott); 'captain', 'chiliarch', strictly the commander of a cohort (Ac

17c 21:31); the binding was normal; the Fathers compare Isaac, Gn 22:9. **13.** Annas was still formally high priest since the office was for life (Lk 3:2; Ac 4:6; Jos, BJ 5, 506). His position was patriarchal, for though deposed by the Romans in A.D. 15, he was succeeded by his five sons and his son-in-law Caiaphas (A.D. 18—36). Rabbinic sources and Jos. Ant. (20, 179—81) describe the priestly aristocracy as noted for intrigue, bribery and love of money. As if clearing up a misunderstanding, Jn records that Jesus was brought to Annas 'first', perhaps a courtesy and to extract material for formal accusations. **14.** Cf Jn 11:
d 49f; the case was pre-judged. **15.** Peter 'was following' Jesus; Jn tells how he got in; 'another disciple', almost certainly Jn, who conceals his name thus, is usually with Peter, has also come from the Garden and is the obvious source for the eyewitness details. Others (e.g. Braun, *Jean, Evangile*, 307f) argue that 'known' to the high priest means familiar friend (Ps 55 (54):14; for a contrary view, see A. Schlatter, *Der Evangelist Johannes*, 332) and he must be a 'notable' (Jn 12:42), not an illiterate man, Ac 4:13. Yet Annas and Caiaphas 'recognized' Peter and John as having been with Jesus; social relationships in the East are like those between a Highland chief and his humblest clansman, John (son of Salome, perhaps sister of the Mother of Jesus and so cousin to Elizabeth, Lk 1:5, 36) may be connected with a priestly family; and notice the tone of the portress. **16—17.** She cannot resist a dig: 'another of this fellow's disciples?' Peter's 'Oh no', might be called a small lie to avoid embarrassment, but to go back on it will be hard. **18.** Standing (Jn) warming themselves at the brazier, for in Jerusalem nights are often very fresh in early April, are the servants and the police. Hoping to avoid attention, Peter stands and warms himself with them. **19.** The high priest is here Annas. It was natural to ask Jesus about his accomplices and his projects if he was to be accused of an anti-Roman plot (Lagrange). **20—21.** Of his disciples Jesus says nothing (cf 8), but as his teaching has been open (7:4, 26; 11:54) he has no conspiratorial accomplices; the saying is in place here rather than in Gethsemane, Mk 14:49 and par. Jesus then demands that instead of trying to trap him in speech, proper witnesses be heard. **22—23.** As this just (23) plea would embarrass the high priest, one of his officers curries favour by striking (illegal in a regular court, Ac 23:2) Jesus with a stick (the meaning, rather than 'with his hand'). This would be the signal for the general mockery recorded by Syn. **24.** 'To Caiaphas', with 'from Caiaphas' (28) implies the Sanhedrin's meeting either in his palace or in their building (Mt 27:1f; Mk 15:1; SB 1, 1000). This coherent account (from P. Benoît, 'Jésus devant le Sanhedrin', *Exégèse et Théologie*, I 290—311; cf X. Léon-Dufour, art cit 1461) makes unnecessary the transposition of v 24 to after v 13 on slender MS evidence. **25—27.** 'Standing and warming himself' picks up the story from v 18; the climax is a question from a relative of Malchus (10); Jn omits Peter's cursing and swearing (Mk); 13:38 is fulfilled.
e **28—19:16 The Trial of the King—28.** 'The praetorium' was the official residence of the Governor when in Jerusalem, outside which Pilate set up his tribunal 'at a place called the Pavement (Lithostrotos) and in Heb. Gabbatha', 19:13; 'pavement' could describe the small tesserae of a mosaic or large paving blocks. P. Benoît (RB 59 (1952) 531—50) holds that the praetorium must be the Governor's normal residence, the former palace of Herod the Great to the W of the city (cf Jos BJ 2, 30); so far no excavations have been made which could reveal a 'pavement' here. But they have shown one of great stone blocks in the court of the Antonia, fortress and first palace

of Herod, which Pilate may have made his praetorium in **817e** troublous times. This site is accepted by L.-H. Vincent, RB 42 (1933), 83—113; 46 (1937), 563—70; 61 (1954), 87—107 and W. F. Albright, *The Background of the NT*, 158f; cf J. Starcky, 'Lithostroton', DBS 5, 398—405. 'Early'; Roman name for the 3—6 a.m. watch. Legal impurity (ironical!) was contracted by entering a pagan's house (cf Ac 11:2f), but why it could not have been removed by a bath, is not clear; 'eat the passover', this is Friday 14th Nisan (cf 13:1, 29; 19:14), April 7th A.D. 30, or April 3rd A.D. 33. **29. Pilate**, prefect (JBS 81 **f** (1962), 70; 'procurator', Tacitus, *Ann.* 15, 44, seems anachronistic) of Judaea since A.D. 26, whose cruelty, furious temper, illegal killings and implacable hatred of the Jews are attested by Philo (*ad Gaium*, 302) and Jos (Ant. 18, 3; BJ 2, 9, 2—3), need not be a judge anxious to be just, partly conquered by Jesus and trying to defend him. He seems rather to be indulging his war to the knife against the Jews; Jesus, whose innocence he proclaims, bears the cost. He resists their attempt to force his consent to a bad case, but with no regard for justice in his shifting expedients. He takes continual pleasure in mocking them in the person of their inoffensive king. Finally, beaten by the threat of a report to Rome and unwilling to compromise his career for an innocent man, his regret is to have to capitulate before his enemies. He does this with sustained insult which does not free him from his share in responsibility (P. Benoît, 'Le procès de Jésus', op cit, 284). In Jn's terms this judge, in the presence of the Light (Jn 15:22) and borne down by the 'the world' (3:19; 7:7; 19: 6), falls step by step under the same condemnation as the Jews, Rm 3:19f. 'What accusation?' He was doubtless **g** apprised of Jesus's arrest but his haughtily correct question perhaps takes the Jews unawares. **30—32.** Wheedling rather than insolent: we should not have handed over one of our brethren to you if he were not guilty (Lagrange). Pilate jeers that as they present the case as judged, they should deal with it. The Jews (now first named, the crowd has not yet come, Mk 15:8) explain (as in no other Gospel) why they have come to Pilate. 'It is not lawful for us to put any man to death' expresses Rome's policy in all her provinces, at least in the sense of requiring the governor's confirmation, (cf Jos, BJ 2, 117 for Palestine's first governor, Coponius). This would hold good in spite of some irregular stonings (cf Jn 8:50. 10:31; Ac 7:58) and possibly (Jos, ibid 6, 126) the case of a Gentile trespassing beyond the barrier into the Temple. The contrary arguments of P. Winter, *On the Trial of Jesus* (1961) expanding H. Lietzmann's paper *Der Prozess Jesu*, are considered by A. N. Sherwin-White, *Roman Society and Roman Law in the NT* (Sarum Lectures, 1960—1), 24—47. He concludes that there is no historical improbability in Jn's account. At the same time, if the Sanhedrin could not put to death, the alleged irregularities in their 'trial' of Jesus, already suspect as evidence derived from the later Mishnah (H. Danby, JTS 21 (1919—20) 51—76), do not apply. A Roman condemnation meant crucifixion, as Jesus had anticipated, Jn 3:14; 12:32f; Mt 20:19. The religious Messianic charge levelled against Jesus by the Sanhedrin is now changed into a political one for Pilate's benefit. Among the treason charges made (Mk 15:2; Lk 23:2), that of being king prevails. **33.** The Roman soldiers **h** now take charge of Jesus. Dramatically (cf chh 7 and 8) the front scenes of the trial occur before the praetorium with alternating back scenes between Pilate and Jesus. For Jn to give his own version of these would accord with the literary forms of the times, but one who did not share the priests' scruples and wanted to hear what was going on could presumably have entered the hall of inquiry

s

817h (Bernard). 'Are *you* the king of the Jews?' Pilate picks out the vital point, scornfully expecting 'No'. **34—35.** '*Is that your own idea?*' (NEB): in the Roman sense, Jesus is not a king; in the Jewish, Messianic sense, he is. Pilate is irritated: '*Of course the Jews started it: the chief priests representing your Sanhedrin handed you over to me. What have you done?*'. **36.** Jesus's kingdom (though in and extending over the world, 17:11) does not come from it, 8:23; otherwise his 'officers' (contrast 18:3) 'would now be striving' (imperf. and cf Lk 13:24) to prevent his falling into the hands of those who are in fact his enemies. **37.** 'So you are a king?' cf Mk 15:2 and par. ' "King" is your word' (NEB, cf Dodd, HT, 99, n. 1). His kingship goes with his whole life's mission to reveal the divine truth of which he, the Incarnate Word, is himself the revelation, cf 14:6 (BJ); 'witness', cf 1 Tm 6:13 Rev 1:5; 3:14, §§ 799*e*, 792*g*. As the Stoics spoke of wise men as kings, the idea of a kingdom of those 'who draw from truth the inspiration of their life' (Westcott, cf 1 Jn 3:19) should not have been incomprehensible to a
i Roman. **38.** Pilate has no use for 'truth', but he does see that this philosopher or dreamer is no dangerous political character. He declares Jesus innocent for the first of three times, cf 19:4, 6; Lk 23:4, 14, 22. The Herod episode can be inserted here, Lk 23:6—12. **39—40.** Jn is condensing. In Mk 15:6ff (cf Mt 27:15ff) the crowd arrive to make their usual request. This is Pilate's chance to make the first of his three attempts to free Jesus (cf 19:4, 12) and yet it is his first downward step. His sneer 'king of the Jews' would provoke the crowd to fury, egged on in any case by the Pharisees, Mk 15:11; 'again', Jn is condensing (Mk 15:13) or reminiscing. 'Robber' (curt irony), cf Mk 14:48; Josephus's word for a bandit resistance leader; a murderer (Mk 15:7; Lk 23:19, 25; Ac 3:14) but (cf art. before his name) 'notable', Mt 27:16. The type we know. Of the 'custom' nothing is known, but it fits the Passover, feast of liberation, and cf Livy, 5, 13, 8; Dion. Hal., 12, 9 for the Roman *Lectisternia*.
j **19:1—3. The scourging and mockery** are recorded by Mt 27:26ff; Mk 15:15ff in connexion with the death sentence; scourging would normally precede crucifixion, but Jn (cf Lk 26:16) deliberately places them at this point, and Pilate would not have troubled about injustice in his next downward step, cf Ac 5:40. It was the soldiers, who now took Jesus inside (cf v 5) and started to mock him; perhaps getting the idea from Herod (Mk 15:16ff; Lk 23:11). Jn uses the word for scourging, not as in Mt but as in Jesus's prophecy (Mk 10:34), and omits the sceptre, reed and spitting. 'Crown of thorns'. It has been suggested that the soldiers tried to imitate the crown depicted on coins, the royal *diadema* which had overtones of divinity: this might appear to be suggested by the 'knelt in homage', Mk 15:19, cf H. St J. Hart, 'The Crown of Thorns in Jn 19:2—5,' JTS 3 ns (1952) 66—75. This suggestion however may be a little too subtle and the soldiers are more likely to have had in mind the laurel wreath of the Emperor often given to royal persons in recognition of military prowess. For this, they would have taken the nearest plant to hand, which happened to be a thorny one, perhaps the Spina Christi, which still grows in the neighbourhood. The word used here for 'crown', *stephanos*, properly indicates the wreath rather than the royal diadem, cf Mk 15:17. **4—5.** Pilate makes his second declaration of Jesus's innocence and brings him out, doubtless faint from the scourging and wearing the mock-royal insignia. 'Behold the man' cf Lk 23:4, 6, 14. Pilate means '*Look at the fellow. How can you expect me to take this scarecrow seriously?*'. For the believing Christian it means 'Behold the Lamb of God', Jn 1:29. **6.** The yelling (by

the chief priests and their officers) for the first time of **817** 'Crucify him' riles Pilate, who retorts 'Crucify him yourselves', knowing they cannot do it, 18:31, and for the third time declares Jesus innocent of the charge against him; indeed he goes further: 'I find no crime in him'. Contrast this with the Jews' retort that his death is required to fulfil the Law, cf 11:50f (Hoskyns). **7.** The Jews change their **k** attack in view of Pilate's intransigence, and claim that Jesus is a blasphemer and their Law (which Rome respected) required that he should die (Lv 24:16). This was a reference to the trial before Caiaphas and to a charge on which Rome was not competent to pronounce, cf Mk 14:55—64 (cf Jn 5:18; 10:33). But they now (contrast Mt 26:63) use the phrase 'a son of a god' (as does the pagan centurion, Mt 27:54; Mk 15:39). This would suggest to Pilate a wonder-worker claiming divine origin (Dodd, *Int.*, 251f; HT, 114). **8—9.** Hence his superstitious fear; 'the more' refers most naturally to the fear caused by his wife's dream, Mt 27:19. Hence too his question, 'Where are you from?' (he knew he was from Galilee, Lk 23:5f): the eternal question, for the mystery of Jesus is the subject of the Gospel, Jn 1:13; 16:28; 17:25 (BJ). But Pilate has refused the truth (18:28), and (a Passion motif, Is 53:7) before insincerity or mere curiosity Jesus is silent, e.g. Mk 14:60; Mt 27:14. **10.** Irritated, Pilate explains the Law (cf *Digest*, L, xvii, 37, Lagrange) with Roman precision. **11.** Cf Rm 13:1ff; Pilate thinks the authority to be his, but it comes from above, cf Jn 3:27; 'therefore' probably shows Jesus to mean, not that Pilate's was the lesser guilt (though doubtless it was), but that, in that case, Caiaphas, in using divinely delegated authority for his wicked ends, was more guilty than if he had used an irresponsible executioner (Wetstein, Bernard). 'He who gave me over to you' is Caiaphas as head of the Sanhedrin (18:30, 35), though Judas too 'gave him over' (6:64; 12:4; 13:2, 11, 21; 18:2). **12.** 'Upon this' marks a positive endeavour to release Jesus. Seeing their prey in danger of escaping, the Jews yell their threat to report Pilate to the ultra-suspicious Tiberius (Suetonius, *Tib.*, 58) as tolerating a pretender to kingship; 'friend of Caesar', a 'notable political term', enforces their point (Sherwin-White, 47). **13—15.** Pilate is impressed. There are two **l** views over his action at this dramatic moment: (1) He sat on the magistrate's seat and gave judgement. (2) He sat *Jesus* on the judge's bench (I. de la Potterie, 'Jesus King and Judge according to Jn 19:13,' Scr. 13, 24 (1961), 97—111, trans. of Bib 41 (1960), 217—47, which has documentation): 'sat' can be transitive (1 Cor 6:4; Eph 1:20), is so taken here by Just. *1 Apol.* 35 and 'Gospel of Peter' 7, and must be, for the two verbs combine in one movement, '*Pilate brought Jesus out and sat him on a bench at a place . . .*', cf *idem*, 'L'emploi dynamique de *eis* dans S. Jean', Bib 43 (1962) 371f; that no pronoun follows is not an objection, for the common direct object of two verbs is placed between them 17 times in Jn; 'bench' (no article) is not the curule chair but either a temporary one or the meaning is 'install as judge', 'set on the bench', on the semi-circular platform; far from pronouncing judgement, Pilate mockingly proclaims Jesus 'your King' and Judge. Finally (M. E. Boismard, 'La royauté du Christ dans le quatrième évangile', LumVi 57 (1962) 43—63), Jn deliberately contrasts Jesus, seated on an ass, making a royal entry acclaimed by the Jews as king (12:12—19) with him sitting as King and Judge before them as they yell 'away with him'. All else (vv 2, 3, 5) leads up to this supreme sign, the real proclamation of the trial. Because rejected as their King, Jesus, now that the Hour has come (12:23, 31; 19:14), faces them as their Judge, cf 5:22, 27. The judgement is their own refusal of the Light, the

817l saving Word of truth (1:11; 3:19; 5:24; 12:48): 'Away with him' who takes away (same word, 1:30) the sin of the world. Jn adds dramatic force by two circumstances of place and two of liturgical significance: if Gabbatha comes from 'high', Jesus was proclaimed 'on the height' at 'the Preparation of the Passover' (not just the eve) which began at the sixth hour with the burning of the old leaven (1 Cor 5:7); Judaism was ended (Lagrange); the Passover of the world's salvation had begun. 'About the sixth hour', cf on Mk 15:25. The high priests in rejecting Jesus reject God as their King (Jg 8:23; 1 Sm 8:7) for the pagan **m** Caesar. **16.** For Jn (cf Lk 23:35) Pilate handed over Jesus to those really responsible, the high priests, though the soldiers took charge. On responsibility for the death of Jesus, cf Léon-Dufour, art cit, 1488—91; Benoit, 'Le procès; 285—91. The thesis that the initiative was Pilate's, helped by some quisling Sadduccees, does not stand critical examination (Sherwin-White, 24—27). Pilate was juridically (and morally) responsible, but the principals were Caiaphas with his high-priestly clique and the Sanhedrin with the violent, hostile Pharisees and the cynical, opportunist Sadduccees. On subjective conscience, cf Rm 2:1. The Pharisees had convinced themselves (which does not excuse sin against the light) that they were serving God in refusing a Messiah who transformed the letter into the spirit and made divine claims. Even for them ignorance can be pleaded, Ac 3:17; Lk 23:34. The crowd had such responsibility as belongs to crowds; other contemporaries, none, nor sons for their father's sins (Ezek 18:2ff; Jer 31:29). Everything falls within Israel's own prophets' account of God's saving design, Jn 19:30; Ac 3:18. Jn's verdict (coinciding with Ac 3:13ff; 4:10) on the sin of 'the Jews' is not racial. Besides the original faithful few there were Jews who 'looked on him whom they had pierced' (Jn 19:37; Zech 12:10, cf Lk 23:37; Ac 2:37) and became the new Israel. Rather, (cf § 792j) Jn uses 'the Jews' for all who reject Jesus crucified and risen, 'the world' (Jn 7:4, 7; 14:17, 22; 17:25; 1 Jn 3:1) which hates him in his disciples also, 15:18—25.

818a **17—37 The Crucifixion**—Jn omits much in order to concentrate on five Messianic events in which by direct quotation or implication Scripture is seen fulfilled, the first two marked off by inclusion: (1) The King proclaimed ('wrote... written'), (2) the garments divided by lot and the coat without seam ('soldiers . . . soldiers'), (3) Jesus's words, 'Behold your son . . . behold your Mother', with 'Hour' (4) Jesus's cry 'I thirst', and giving up his Spirit, (5) the water and the blood from the Lamb's pierced side.
b **17—18.** Lit. 'bearing the cross for himself', emphatic (cf Mk 8:34 and par.); it was outside the city (Mt 27:32; Mk 15:21) that Simon had to take it for the exhausted Jesus; 'went out', cf Nm 15:35f; Heb 13:12. Jn says only that Jesus was crucified in the midst between two others, recalling Is 53:9, 12 and preluding v 32. **19—22.** The King of the Jews 'lifted up' on the throne of the Cross is proclaimed to all mankind in three languages (of the people, of culture and of government); 'title', the Latin word, only in Jn; 'Nazareth' (cf Lk 23:6), the scandal of lowliness, cf 1:45f; 18:5; 'the king of the Jews' is the charge affixed, worded to mock them; Jesus's royal claim was Pilate's only extenuation (such as it was); with imperial brevity he refuses to forgo it or his revenge. **23—24. c** The soldiers, a unit of four (cf Ac 12:4) with their centurion (Syn.), had the clothes as perquisites (*Digest*, 48, 20, 6). Jn's fuller account suggests an eyewitness by the cross all the time (Bernard); 'woven from top to bottom' is his own detail; otherwise he describes the tunic, the seamless undergarment, in the terms of the high priest's (cf Jos.Ant., 161; Philo, *Fug.* 110—12), perhaps suggest-

ing Christ's priestly sacrifice, cf 17:19; Rev 1:13. The **818c** Fathers since Cyp. see it as type of the unity of the Church coming from that sacrifice, and 'tear' is Jn's word for divisions, 7:43; 9:16; 10:19, cf 1 Cor 1:10, 13 (Hoskyns, Lightfoot). **Jn recalls Ps 22 (21):19 (LXX), implicit in** Syn., seeing in its parallelism of garments and clothing an inspired forecast. **25.** Omitting all else, he concentrates **d** on a contrasted group beneath the cross whom Mt 27:55f; Mk 15:40 (without mentioning Jesus's Mother) speak of as standing afar; perhaps they came near as the crowds thinned. If Jn means that four women were present, 'his mother's sister' could be Salome (Mk 15:40), apparently the mother of James and John (Mt 27:56), which would account for her being unnamed; or she could be Mary, the mother of James the Little and Joseph, Mk 15:40. We need not suppose two sisters of the same name, for 'sister' can mean cousin or sister-in-law. If Jn mentions only three women (omitting his mother altogether), then Mary is the wife of Clopas, whom Hegesippus (Eus. HE 3, 11, 2) calls brother of Joseph, Jesus's foster-father, cf § § 663—4. Mary Magdalen's name appears for the first time in Jn. **26—28.** A kind of triple inclusion links Cana, 'the begin- **e** ning of signs' (Jn 2:1—11) with this scene: 'The Mother of Jesus . . . Woman, what have you to do with me? My hour has not yet come' becomes his 'Mother . . . Woman, behold your son . . And from that hour'. All history converges upon Jesus's Hour, and 'all was now finished' (28) points to Scripture fulfilled here too, cf E. Hoskyns, 'Genesis 1—3 and St John's Gospel', JTS 21 (1920), 210—18; F. M. Braun, *La mère des fidèles*, 77—129; Lightfoot, *in loc*. That more is involved than simple provision for his Mother is suggested because Jesus first confides the disciple to her care, not her to his. 'Woman' with 'mother' goes naturally back to Gn 2:23; 3:15, 20. The enmity between the woman and her seed on the one hand (Jn is probably thinking of the LXX where it is masculine) and the serpent (cf Rev 12:9; 20:2) and his seed on the other (Jn 8:44; 1 Jn 3:8ff) has reached the 'Hour' when Jesus is 'lifted up' and 'the ruler of this world is cast down', Jn 12:23—33, cf 16:8—11. Beside Jesus stands the Woman, his Mother, who as the new 'mother of all the living' (Gn 3:20) is told 'Behold your son'. Persons in Jn represent groups (Nicodemus) and in 'the disciple whom he loved' the article can be used in the Heb. collective sense (GK, 126d), i.e. Jesus loves all who keep his commandments (14:15, 21, 23) and they are his friends, his beloved disciples, 15:13ff, 17. For the same theme, with the woman ambivalent symbol of the Church and Mary, her Son, the serpent and 'the rest of her seed', cf on Rev 12. The Fath- **f** ers call Mary the Second Eve for restoring at the Annunciation what the first woman had lost. At Calvary, her motherhood acquires a new dimension from her place by her crucified Son. So, though Orig. (*In Joann.*, 1, 4, 23) was the only precursor of Rupert of Deutz (PL 169, 790) in deriving her universal motherhood thence, the doctrine has a Scriptural basis. 'Received her as his own' rather than 'took her to his own house' (RSV), for in Jn *lambanō* of persons or divine gifts means 'welcome', 'receive', (e.g. 1:12, 16; 3:11; 14:17) and *eis ta idia* 'into his own possession' (1:10) or 'into his own way' (16:32), but 'into his house' is *eis oikian*, 2 Jn 10. **28—29.** Jn stresses **g** Jesus's knowledge and initiative; 'all accomplished', his Father's work (4:34; 5:36; 17:4) and Scripture. Thirst (cf 4:7) was one of the worst agonies of crucifixion; Jn explicitly recalls Ps 69 (68):22, cf 22 (21):16; 'vinegar', the soldiers' sharp *posca* and the action perhaps not unkindly; a sponge was used as stopper for flasks; Mt (27: 48). Mk (15:36) say it was 'placed around' a reed or cane. Jn (alone) mentions hyssop, a fern-like plant. But this

818g would be too pliable and does not provide canes or strong stalks on which to place a sponge. The Gr. has *hyssōpō perithentes* unequivocally. Hyssop was dipped in the blood of the Paschal lamb to sprinkle the doors of Jewish houses (Ex 12:22; Heb 9:19; cf Jn 1:29; 10:7) but this symbolic parallelism does not suit (Dodd). An 11th-cent. cursive MS no. 476 reads *hyssō perithentes* and this may provide the clue to our text, which could be due to a scribe writing *hyssōpō* instead of *hyssō*. *Hyssos* (Latin *pilum*) is the javelin carried by Roman soldiers. Jn, the eye witness, knew that the '*kalamos*' or cane of the Synoptists was in

h fact a spear (Bernard). **30.** 'It is finished': the prophecies fulfilled, the sacrifice offered, the salvation of the world achieved. Jn does not record the cry of dereliction (Mt 27: 46; Mk 15:34). He confines himself to recording the main event in all its dignity (cf Lk 23:46). The Fathers see the Church, the new creation, coming forth from the side of Christ as Eve from the sleeping Adam (Tert *De Anima*, 43). He 'gave up his spirit' is the initial pouring forth of the Spirit (Jn 1:33; 3:34; &c) and is connected with what follows. **31.** 'The Lord's work is finished but the world continues on its way' (Lightfoot). Dt 21:23 forbade bodies of criminals to be left on the gallows after sunset, cf Gal 3:14, JosBJ 4, 5, 2, and the next day was the Sabbath.

i **32—34** Breaking the limbs with a heavy mallet ended the tortures of the crucified who might otherwise linger for days (cf Mk 15:44). To make sure, one soldier pierced the right side of Jesus with a spear; *nyssein* can mean to prick but is also used for a spear-thrust——'to run through' thereby becoming equivalent to *ekkentein* (37), cf Jg 9:54, Dodd HT, 135, 2. The coming forth of the blood and water (serum) is physiologically possible. Jn is stressing the sign: the blood shows the reality of the Lamb's sacrifice for the world's salvation (Jn 6:51, 53ff; Rm 3:25; 1 Jn 5:6ff; Rev 1:5), the water, the Spirit in his purifying force and fecundity as eternal life, Jn 4:14. Both flow 'as rivers of living water' out of the heart of the Saviour (7:38) bringing literally 'from above' (3:3, 5) the new birth in the Spirit to the infant Church, the little group beneath the Cross (Hoskyns, *art. cit.*). The Fathers see Baptism and the Eucharist coming from Christ's sacrifice, cf 3:5, 14f. **35.** Against the Docetist teaching that Jesus had no true body to suffer, the Beloved Disciple (it must be he, in spite of the third person, cf 9:37), bears 'genuine' witness as his master the Baptist did at the start (inclusion with 1:34) lest their Christian belief he deceived by false mysticism, cf also Dz 480. 'He' (*ekeinos*) 'knows', could refer to the witness (cf the formula, 3:11) or to Christ (as 1 Jn 2:6; 3:3, 5, 7, 16; 4:17), thus providing the required additional witness, Jn 8:13—18; 21:24; 3 Jn 12 (Hoskyns). **36—37.** Fusion of 'you shall not break a bone of it' (Ex 12:46, cf Nm 9:12: Jesus the Paschal Lamb, cf Jn 1:29; 1 Cor 5:7) with 'not one shall be broken' (Ps 34 (33):20: Jesus the persecuted Servant, Is 53) (BJ). 'They shall look on me whom they have pierced' in Zech 12:10 (Heb, not LXX) is eschatological lamentation 'as for an only son, a first-born' (cf Jn 1:18) whose mysterious death Jn sees as a figure of the Passion (Rev 1:7 applies it to Christ coming in Judgement, cf Just., *Apol.* 1, 52; *Tryph.* 32, 64).

j **38—42 The burial—38.** Jn rejoins and condenses Syn.; Joseph, a secret disciple (12:42), now made his bold (Mk) request. **39.** Nicodemus (Jn's addition), perhaps too cautious to approach Pilate, arrived next with a princely gift (cf 2:6) of 72 lbs of spices; for 'mixture' read 'roll' or 'packet' (*lectio difficilior*): myrrh (sweet-smelling gum), aloes (aromatic wood), crushed into powder; there was no time to wash or anoint the body (cf Lk 23:56). **40.** For 'bound', Theodoret, etc read 'wrapped'; 'in linen cloths',

not swathing bands, the pl. (like Heb. *takhrikhim*) can 818j stand for the shroud of Mt 27:59; Mk 15:46 with the bands to secure hands and feet, the spices being sprinkled in the linen 'as is the Jews' custom to prepare for burial' (Gn 50:2, LXX; Mt 26:12), cf on 11:44. **41—42.** Joseph's (Mt) tomb, in the nearby garden (Jn) was hastily chosen; the Sabbath, which was also Passover (19: 14, 31) was upon them at sundown.

20—21 RESURRECTION

On 'the first day of the week', the darkness (20:1) 819a passes and the true Light shines, 1 Jn 2:8. These chh are closely related to the Last Discourse and to the inner life of the Church of the Risen Christ, cf 1 Jn. Jesus 'comes' again to be with his own (14:18), and brings with new sight of him peace and joy never more to be lost (14:27; 16:16, 22; 20:19f) and the gift of the Spirit to pass on his redemptive mission (7:39; 17:18; 20:21ff). In this fresh creation, starting in a garden (Gn 2:7f; Jn 20:15, 22), all things are made new (Rev 21:5) and familiar characters are transformed: the contemplative Mary, who stays while the men go away (Aug.) becomes apostle to the Apostles; the impulsive (20:4; 21:7, 21), puzzled (20:6f) Peter, now humbled and deeply loving, becomes Shepherd and follower to death (21:15—22); the good-hearted doubter (11:16; 14:5) makes the Gospel's supreme declaration of faith (20:24—28).

20:1—10 The Empty Tomb—1—2. Jn takes for gran- b ted the great stone and the other women ('we', 2); 'while it was still dark' sets the atmosphere and accounts for Mary not looking into the tomb; she had gone straight there; the others went to buy spices and arrived after sunrise, Mk 16:1f. At her discovery she sets off running, with one thought in her mind, to Peter and 'the other disciple' (18:15f, here combined with 'whom Jesus loved', 13:23); 'and to' suggests they were not together. **3—5.** The younger outruns Peter, peeps down into the tomb, but (eyewitness detail) stands back to allow Peter to pass (Lk 24:12 mentions only Peter but (24) he was not alone; Lk may show early Joh. tradition). **6—7.** Peter notes exactly; not 'napkin' (so to cover the face was not contemporary Jewish custom, at least in a hasty burial) but chin-band or probably the shroud which had been folded over his head, cf on 11:44; 19:40. There had, then, been no theft. But he is slow to understand, Mk 9:5f. **8—10.** The Disciple 'saw' and by a flash of spiritual insight believed in the Resurrection before knowing Scriptural testimonies (cf Ps 16 (15):8—11; 1 Cor 15:4).

11—18 The Meeting in the Garden—cf Mt 28:9f. c Jn is not concerned with the Synoptic kerygma based on the empty tomb so much as on the new spiritual glory of Jesus. **11b—14a.** 'As she wept' may introduce an editorial join-up with Syn.: the angels are as Lk 24:4, but ask only why she weeps (doublet of Jesus's question, 15); her answer reproduces v 2; 'one at the head and one at the feet' expands Mt 28:6; Mk 16:6; 'turned', unless she had turned back again, is a doublet of v 16, cf P. Benoît, 'Marie-Madeleine et les disciples au tombeau selon Joh 20:1—18', *Judentum Urchristentum Kirche*, Festschrift für J. Jeremias, (1964), 141—52. **14b—15.** Pure Jn again: she sees (cf 14:9) but does not recognize, Cf Lk 24:16. 'Whom do you seek', cf Jn 1:38, etc. '*The keeper of the garden*' is her natural guess, but Jn may be thinking of the new creation in this 'garden' (18:1; 19:41, twice, *kēpos*, synonym for Paradise in Aquila and Theodotion) and its new Keeper (cf Gn 2:15; 3:23) sinless and having overcome in a garden his betrayer's prince (Jn 14:30; 18. 3) he now in the cool of the day converses not with the

19c fallen but with the redeemed (Hoskyns, art cit, 214f). 'I will take him away' fits 'the audacious Mary Magdalen' (St Teresa) who thinks of only one 'him'. **16.** '*Mariam*', the well-remembered Aram. word, is the best reading. 'Rabboni' (Mk 10:51), familiar form of 'Rabbi', 'my dear **d** Master', often used later to address God. **17.** Take the whole v together and cf Mt 28:9f (? borrowed from Jn's tradition, Benoit, 145f); not 'do not touch me' (CV) but 'do not keep on holding me' (pres. imper.); 'for I have not yet ascended to my Father' seems a playful 'I've not gone yet', but some think he defers intimate union until the relationship of faith. Instead, he has a mission for her: 'my brethren' in this new spiritual context can hardly be relations (as Dodd, comparing 'I am ascending' with 7:8) but his disciples, the new 'sons of God' (Ps 22 (21):23; Mt 12:48; 28:10; Jn 1:12; 1 Jn 3:1). Though 'my Father and your Father' distinguishes his sonship from theirs, they are his brothers for whom the promises of Jn 14:2f, 16–23; 15:26; 16:5–24 are being realized. 'I am ascending': the Resurrection includes the Ascension (3:14f; 12:32); it is from the Father's side that Jesus in glory sends the Spirit and gives the disciples their mission, 21ff; Mt 28:18ff; forty days later the apparitions are ended by the 'Ascension', cf P. Benoît, 'L'Ascension', RB 56 (1949), 161–203. **18.** Magdalen was not believed (Syn.).

e 19–23 The Sending of the Apostles—Christ 'whom the Father consecrated and sent into the world' (10:36), his self-consecration completed, has returned to the Father. He sends his Apostles to continue his mission (17;17ff), breathing into them his Spirit (Gn 2:7; Ezek 37:9f; Jn 1:33) that they in turn may re-create men in the Spirit, save, judge, divide (F. X. Durrwell, *The Resurrection*, 306–8). **19.** Late that Sunday evening, through doors shut to exclude Jewish intruders after the empty tomb report, Jesus 'came' (14:18); 'Peace be with you', the Jewish greeting, repeated (21), conveys the peace he promised (14:27; 16:33). **20.** Lk mentions hands and feet, Jn hands and side (19:34), marks for recognition and signs of the victory (16:33) in the power of which he now commissions and consecrates them (17:18f). Their joy he had promised also (16:22f; cf Lk 24:41); Jn omits the rebuke and the food (Mk 16:14; Lk 24:42f). **21.** As Jesus has already spoken of sending the Apostles as the Father has sent him (Jn 17:18, cf 13:20; 15:9), this naturally refers to them (cf Mt 28:16ff) even with Thomas absent and possibly (Lk 24:33, 36) others present. **22.** The glorified (7:39) Jesus breathes (Gn 2:7) upon them the promised Paraclete (14:16f; 16:7 13) who will effect (and complete at Pentecost) the transition from his life to the life of the Church and continue her in his saving work; remission of sins includes conversion and baptism (Lk 24:47) but the par. with Mt 16:19; 18:18 and the power to retain sins show that the Apostles are to judge the sins of believers, Dz 894, 913. Thus the Gospel ends with the sending forth of the Church to save. There is a corollary:

f 24–29 Seeing and Believing—24–25. Thomas, who believes only what he sees, shows his despairing sorrow by the neurotic brutality of his conditions; 'the Twelve', name of the Apostolic College. **26–27.** 'Eight days' includes both, so next Sunday. Jesus offers just the proofs this modern man asks. His reply is the climax of the Gospel, not an exclamation (for not a vocative) but a profession of faith 'honouring the Son as the Father' (5:23, cf Hos 2:23) and making inclusion with Jn 1:1: 'You are my Lord and my God' (cf 1 Jn 5:20; Rm 9:5). **29.** Perhaps said with a smile and not reproachfully, for the Disciple (8) and Magdalen believed when they saw, and without

seeing there is no witnessing and no Christian faith, e.g. **819f** 1:18, 50f; 4:45; 9:37; 14:9; 19:35. But all Christians who, without seeing, believe the apostolic witness (1 Pt 1:8) are reached by 'the last and greatest of the Beatitudes' (Westcott, cf Mt 5:3).

30–31 First Epilogue on the scope and purpose of **g** the Gospel is shot through with its themes. Lagrange would remove it to after 21:23, but the almost identical 1 Jn 5:13 does not end the Epistle. Jn is always sparing of words, 2 Jn 12; 3 Jn 13. Read 'that you may continue to believe' (S, D); 'the Christ', for Jn's audience the Messiah is now expressed in Gr. alone, cf Ac 2:36; 'the Son of God', cf 'Believe in Jesus and have life' is the Gospel's central message, Jn 1:12; 3:15f; 6:47, cf 19:35; 'in his name', through and in union with him, 14: 13f; 15:16; 16:23–26; 1 Jn 5:1ff. For in him is life (Jn 1:4) and he has come that men may have it, 5:40; 6:53f; 10:10.

21 In Galilee—An Appendix, cf the two epilogues. It **820a** was published with the Gospel and completes its teaching on the Church, perhaps on its catholicity (153 fishes!), certainly on Peter as fisherman and shepherd, adding a prophecy of his martyrdom and a note on the end of the Beloved Disciple. Joh. traits abound. 'Simon Peter' (usual in Jn), Nathanael, Thomas called Didymus; the Disciple whom Jesus loved (only in Jn); v 2 'of his disciples two' = 1:35 (Gr.); 4b resembles 20:14b; 13, 6:11; 19, 12:33 and 18:32; 24, 5:32; *own* is used 8 times in Jn's resumptive way, etc. But M.-E. Boismard, 'Le chapître xxi de S, Jean', RB 54 (1947) 473–501, argues that though written under the more or less direct influence of Jn, the work of a disciple-editor is shown by a style resembling Lk's. His evidence for this is impressive, but ably criticized by E. Ruckstuhl, *Die Literarische Einheit*, 146–9. The ch's symbolism is drawn from facts described by an eyewitness. Nor is it 'unthinkable' (Barrett) that after the apostolic charge of ch 20 former fishermen should take again to a night's fishing, or in uncertain light fail to recognize their Master hailing from the shore as if he wanted to buy fish. The paras with Lk 5:4–11 are striking, the differences considerable. Perhaps Lk, having no Galilaean appearances, supplied the call of 'the fishers of men' by a similar scene.

1–14 The Catch of the Fishermen—1–3. 'After **b** this', vague. 'Sea of Tiberias', cf 6:1. Jn has both Judaean (Lk) and Galilaean (Mt) appearances. Nathanael from Cana fits Jn 1:45–2:1. 'Sons of Zebedee', editorial gloss on the 'two others of his disciples', whose anonymity at the end of a list suggests that as usual Jn is concealing himself and his family. The little band is hanging about; Peter says 'I'm off to fish'; 'the boat', probably their usual one. **4–5.** The Risen Jesus manifests himself when he **c** wills, 20:14; Lk 24:16. In the half-light, about 100 yards from shore (8), the pre-occupied disciples might not recognize an unwonted 'Lads, have you caught anything', lit 'to go with bread'; the question is doubtful (4:29; 8:22) rather than expecting No (18:35). It receives the unsuccessful fisherman's curt 'No.' **7–8.** The Beloved Disciple is first to penetrate the meaning of the sign, Peter first to act, Mt 14:28; Jn 18:10; 20:8. He has been fishing naked or with only an under-garment; in one movement he girds his fisherman's cloak around him and is in the sea (deep here) swimming to land. The rest row, towing the net which, since the fish would crowd to the end of it, is very heavy. **9–10.** With practical love Jesus has a fire ready and fish cooking so that they can start without delay. He tells them to add some of their own catch. **11.** The net is the kingdom of heaven (Mt 13:47ff) and fishing

820c for men the mission of the Apostles (Lk 5:4—11; Mt 4: 19; Mk 1:17; Ezek 47:10), directed by Peter (vv 15, 17), while 'the Church (the un-rent net) remains one in spite of the number and variety of its members, (Barrett). For Gr. zoologists there were 153 kinds of fish (Jer., PL 25, 474). **12—13.** Full of kindness, Jesus again (6:11) gives bread and fish (early eucharistic symbol) to his awed (4:27; 16:23) disciples; 'third time' to them collectively.

d **15—19 Peter, Shepherd and Martyr**—What has been symbolized for the Fisherman, Jesus gives the Shepherd. The passage is full of subtle references to the Gospel. **15—17.** 'Simon son of John' echoes 1:42. Instead of reproaching Peter, Jesus gives him the chance to repair his triple denial and boastful claim to be more loyal than the rest (Mt 26:33; Mk 14:29; Jn 13:37; 18:17, 25ff) by a triple declaration of humbled, sorrowing love which takes Jesus as his only judge. In terms of this greater love, necessary in his delegate both towards himself and towards the sheep he will serve, Jesus entrusts to Peter his whole flock to feed and tend in his place, cf Mt 16: 17ff; Lk 22:31f; Dz 1822; the other Apostles are here part of the flock. Most commentators think that the pairs of Gr. words for 'love', 'sheep', 'feed and pasture' and 'know' express the same meanings; others that there is gradation marking the universality of the charge. **18—19.** Peter too will lay down his life for the sheep, Jn 10:11—18; 'girded yourself', cf v 7; 'stretch out your hands', 'another gird and lead you' are taken in v 19 and by early writers as describing crucifixion (e.g.

Artemidorus, *Oniv.* 1, 76; *ep. Barnabas*, 12; Just., **820** *Tryph.* 90f) and applied to Peter (Tert., *Scorp.* 15); 'show by what death', cf 12:33; 18:32; 'glorify God', 13:31f; 1 Pt 4:16; 'follow' (double meaning, 1:43, in death, 12:24ff); Peter could not follow earlier (13:36f); now he takes the invitation literally.

20—23 The Beloved Disciple, ever close to Peter **e** (13:23ff; 18:15ff; 20:2, 6), wants no invitation. Peter turns, sees him following too, and asks with impulsive naturalness: 'What about him?' '*If it should be my will*' (NEB); 'until I come' at the Parousia (1 Cor 11:26; Rev 1:7; 22:7, 20) or 'while I am coming', cf Jn 9:4; 12:35f; Mk 6:45; 1 Tm 4:13; 'remain' (double meaning, Jn 1:33, etc) cf 1 Jn 3:24. The question rebuked, cf on 16:23. The need to remove the misunderstanding suggests that the Disciple was near death or lately dead.

24—25. Second Epilogue: Witness to the Author, f necessary on Jn's canon of evidence (5:31f; 8:13—18; 19:35; 3 Jn 12). **24.** 'Has written' can mean 'caused to be written'; 'these things', probably the whole gospel; 'we', in Jn the disciples, (e.g. 1:14; 1 Jn 1:1—4; 3:2) could refer to the collegiate witness of the Apostles, which Jn, the last of them, cites as one with his own (Hoskyns, 559f, Crehan, 17f); or be added by a group, cf Clem.Alex. (Eus. HE 6, 14, 7) and the Muratorian Canon 10—15; 'testimony true', cf 1:7, 14. **25.** Resembles 20:30; 'I suppose' (contrast 24 'we know') might come from the editor as Jn never uses first singular, or (Westcott) be Jn's recorded words.

ACTS OF THE APOSTLES

BY HENRY WANSBROUGH O.S.B.

821a Bibliography—*Commentaries*: L. Cerfaux and J. Dupont, BJ, 1958[2]; H. Conzelmann, HNT, 1963; E. Haenchen, Meyer, 1961[4]; C. S. C. Williams, BNTC, 1964[2]; J. Munck, AB, 1967[2]; A. Wikenhauser, RNT, 1956[2]. *Other literature*: H. Conzelmann, *The Theology of St Luke*, E. tr. 1960; M. Dibelius, *Studies in the Acts of the Apostles*, E. tr. 1956; C. H. Dodd, *The Apostolic Preaching and its Development*, 1936; J. Dupont, *Les problèmes du livre des Actes*, 1950; id *The Sources of Acts*, E. tr. 1962; B. Gärtner, *The Areopagus Speech and Natural Revelation*, 1955; B. Gerhardsson, *Memory and Manuscript*, 1961; J. Gnilka, *Die Verstockung Israels*, 1961; A. N. Sherwin-White, *Roman Society and Roman Law in the NT*, 1963; M. Wilcox, *The Semitisms of Acts*, 1965; J. P. Charlier, *L'Évangile de l'Enfance de l'Église*, 1966; L. E. Keck and J. L. Martyn, (ed), *Studies in Lk-Ac*, 1966; J. Dupont, *Études sur les Actes des Apôtres*, 1967. *Orientis Graeci Inscriptiones Selectae*, ed W. Dittenberger, 1903—5 (abbreviated OGIS); F. H. Foakes Jackson and K. Lake, *The Beginnings of Christianity*, IV & V, 1933.

b Composition and Sources—The hand of one author is visible throughout Ac, not merely in the style (q.v.) but in the way in which the material is handled. In Lk's gospel it is possible to isolate Lk's own editorial work by comparing Lk to Mk and Mt. But for Ac we have no such measure of comparison, and can divine what underlies it only on internal grounds. It is, however, unlikely that any such extensive source was available for Ac as for the gospel; for the Christian message and preaching concerned primarily Christ, not his apostles.

Throughout Ac we can discern certain interests (cf §§ 821e, 823b) and methods of working which seem to stem from the author himself. This gives us some indication of the way in which he would treat his sources, and so indirectly of the sources themselves. E.g. from a comparison of the three narratives of Paul's vocation (in 9, 22 and 26) it is clear that Lk permitted himself considerable **liberty in moulding his sources** to enable the narrative to express his message in each particular passage. **In the account of Pentecost** (and perhaps all ch 1, cf Charlier) **Lk is using** a **midrashic technique** familiar from the infancy narratives of the gospel. **He brings out the significance of events by relating them in images and terms drawn from the OT.** Another instructive passage is the introduction to the Areopagus speech (17:16—21), which is assembled from literary rather than witnessed data; it is intended to create an atmosphere, though it seems to relate history. The final scene at Rome (28:17—31) corresponds so exactly with Lk's theological message, rather than with the historical situation that we may deduce that it is Lk's own elaboration, intended specifically as the final climax of many converging themes. Most clearly of all, the 'summaries' about the life of the primitive Jerusalem **821b** community in the early chh of Ac are general descriptions rather than a detailed record.

Haenchen has written of Lk, 'It is not as a dogmatic **c** theologian but as a dramatist that he teaches' (*Zeitschrift für Theologie und Kirche* 22(1955) p. 212); he presents little scenes, often seemingly unconnected, by which he impresses his message on the imagination of the reader, instead of expressing it in a dry analysis. It is a **pictorial way of imparting theology, in which historical chronicle and theological comment are interwoven**. What may seem to the untrained ear to be 'straight' chronicle is found, by an insight into Lk's method of working, to be a plastic presentation of theology. But this does not mean that Lk dreamt up the contents of Ac. Divers sources have been proposed (for an historical survey see J. Dupont, *Les Sources du Livre des Actes*, 1960). The most widely-accepted is Dibelius' 'Itinerary': at least in the second and third missionary journeys of Paul there is a certain recurring pattern of detailed information: the routes taken, the towns visited, houses in which Paul stayed, usually a note about length of stay and names or number of converts. This could well stem from notes taken at the time for practical use if the journey were to be repeated. From this sort of information stand out clearly other types, anecdotes such as the conversion of the gaoler at Thessalonica (16:25—34), incidents such as the appearance before Gallio at Corinth (18.12—17) or the demonstration at Ephesus (19:23—41), which could well have come to Lk from memories of those concerned in them. It has recently been shown beyond all doubt by Sherwin-White that the historical details concerning **Roman officials, law and procedure in this part of Ac correspond exactly to what we know of this period** from other sources. The reliability of Ac's sources is the more firmly established in that often the conditions described obtained for a short period only in the mid 1st cent. The accuracy can be due only to eye-witness accounts.

Another source, proposed by Harnack and advocated **d** by Bultmann, is the 'Antiochene Source'; this is represented as a chronicle of the community at Antioch, from which Lk drew his information not only about the community there but also about the divisions and persecutions which led to its foundation, and perhaps also about the first missionary journey. Most scholars, however, while admitting that the community at Antioch probably provided Lk with a good deal of information, do not see the need to postulate a written source here. Less easy to assess are the narratives of the early community at Jerusalem. Some clearly depend on individual memories, such as the stories of Ananias and Sapphira (5:1—11) or of Peter's escape (12:6—17). But it is in this early part that Ac is at its most semitic, and comes closest to the OT way of writing history; it is often difficult to discern the 'brute facts' behind the biblical language and images in which they are narrated (cf 634d, 641c). But this very

821d semitic character is an indication that the ultimate sources are stories current in the community itself.

It is, then, from many and varied sources that Lk composed his book, moulding them all into a great unity to subserve a well-defined plan.

e **Purpose and Plan**—The second part of Lk's gospel is a journey towards Jerusalem, where Christ is to perform his central act of redemption. In Ac we see the corresponding movement away from this centre, the diffusion of the redemption so won. In 1:8 Christ himself sends out his apostles to be his **witnesses in the power of the Holy Spirit**; they accomplish his instructions, as he commanded, **first in Jerusalem** (chh 1—5), **then in Judea and Samaria** (6—8), **then to the ends of the earth**, i.e. **Rome** (9—28). It is particularly in this last stage that the guidance of the Holy Spirit is evident: history is forced by the divine hand. Lk is concerned to impress ineradicably on his readers that **the mission to the gentiles is the clearly-expressed will of God**: thus multiple interventions of the Spirit force Peter to abandon his Jewish culinary restrictions and to receive the first gentile into the Church (10), and Paul to accept his mission to the gentiles (9). It is by the Spirit that Paul is sent on his first missionary journey (13:2—4), which raises the problems of gentile Christianity, settled at the Council of Jerusalem (15:1—29). It is the Spirit which leads Paul willy-nilly to Greece (16:6—9), and finally on the journey which ends in captivity and his goal, eternal Rome (20:23). The triumphal expansion of Christendom is directed at every step by the Spirit.

f The first corollary of this geographical expansion all over the world is that **the heritage of Judaism passes over to the gentiles**. It is not till the Jews have rejected the message that the missioners pass to the gentiles. Once by Stephen (7, esp. 7:51—53) and three times by Paul (13:45—47; 18:6—7; 28:24—28) is the stubborn resistance of the Jews solemnly declared. Three times Paul continues by proclaiming salvation to the gentiles, while the first gentile Christian community results from the persecution of Stephen (11:19). But Lk is for ever stressing that Christianity is no falling away from, but is the true successor of Judaism, centred as it is on the hope of resurrection in Christ, a hope shared (even if only implicitly) by Judaism (23:6—8; 26:5, 30—31; 28:20). Only the Jews will not accept the fulfilment of their hopes.

g Another corollary of the mission by Christ to all men is that there can be **no cause for opposition to Christianity**. Any opposition which is recorded is excused as due to lack of understanding (23:29; 25:18—19; 26:24). The dignity—and so the reliable judgement—of converts is carefully noted (17:4 and note). Particularly important is the relationship of the Church to the authorities of the Roman empire. From its first contacts with the Roman world in the person of Cornelius (10) Lk is at pains to show the acceptance, indeed the protection, of the Church by Rome and its representatives. Thus Paul's first proclamation is before a Roman proconsul, who owns himself convinced (13:7—12). The fact that Paul is imprisoned at Thessalonica by the magistrates quite vanishes in the excitement of his release amid their profuse apologies (16:19—24, 35—40). When Paul is brought before Gallio it is his accusers who receive a rebuke (18:12—17); when there is a rising at Ephesus the power of Rome intervenes on Paul's behalf, but the rising is cowed into dispersal (19:23—41). Especially in the last part of Ac the protection and favour of Rome is paradoxically but constantly being shown: it is almost a pure accident that Paul is taken to Rome under the familiar and benevolent care of a centurion, who imposes on him none of the restrictions normal for prisoners awaiting trial (28:7—10 and note). Finally the impending trial is quite forgotten, and the reader sees Paul's journey to Rome only as a providential means to enable him to preach the gospel at the centre of the known world.

Noting Lk's interest in showing the favour which **h** Paul, and so the Christianity which he represents, enjoys with the Roman authorities, many critics have concluded that one of Lk's chief aims is to produce an apologetic for Christianity (perhaps for use at Paul's trial in Rome). But Ac was intended to be read not by Roman but by Christian readers. The theological purpose is much deeper: nothing can, or can want to, stand in the way of Christianity. It is this theologico-apologetic purpose which determines the end of Ac. Many have been puzzled that the book seems to end inconclusively, with the accusations still hanging over Paul's head at Rome. But to have related the trial or release of Paul would only have complicated the story and clouded the issues which Lk wished to put before his readers. As it stands, the final scene is the climax of the book, for Ac is the history of the expansion of Christianity in the power of the Holy Spirit to all lands and all classes of men, presaging the universal acceptance of the Kingdom.

For the modern reader the **speeches of Ac**, which **822** form one quarter of the book, pose a problem. In Greco-Roman historians the speeches put into the mouth of the characters made no pretentions to being *verbatim* reports of what was said. Their basic function was to provide the historian's comment, showing the issues at stake and the historical moment of the situation. But they should also conform to the character and views of the speaker (Thucydides I 22). Success in this may vary widely; thus in two different works Josephus can put in the mouth of Herod two wholly different speeches on the same occasion (BJ 1.19.373; Ant. 15.5.127); on the other hand Tacitus delights to reproduce the tedious antiquarian meanderings of the emperor Claudius which were so mocked by the emperor's contemporaries. Lk certainly uses speeches in a number of places to convey to the reader the meaning of a particular event or the moment of a particular situation, often a turning-point in the history of the Church; e.g. Peter's speech at Pentecost (2), Stephen's speech (7), Paul's speech in the Temple (22), see notes ad loc. Lk, as the preface to his gospel shows, deliberately conforms to the style of hellenistic history. 'This is symptomatic; the first Christian generation had been waiting for the approaching end of the world. Now, however, the Church is compelled to come to terms with a prolonged existence in this world' (H. Conzelmann in Keck & Martyn, p. 218). There can be no question that Lk reproduces in Ac the words of his characters. The case is wholly different from that of the gospel, where the 'speeches' of Jesus are based on individual logia carefully memorized and handed down by the community. The communities had no cause to treat the words of the apostles in the same way, and in any case the speeches given to us by Lk are of a wholly different, literary, type, unlike the *sententiae* memorized in the rabbinic schools. Many of the speeches cannot have been delivered in the form in which they are presented; some would be unintelligible to the hearers because, directed primarily to the reader, they presuppose earlier parts of the narrative (28:17—20); others impart information to the reader already familiar to the hearers (1:16—20). A number of important speeches purporting to have been delivered

22a in Aram. rest on a proof of scripture which can be drawn only from the Gr. text used, not from the original Heb. or the Aram. version which could have been used in such a speech (cf 15:1—35 note).

b On the other hand, and much more important, the **speeches bear the stamp of the early Church**. C. H. Dodd (cf note to 2:22—36) has pointed out that the Christological kerygma of the early part of Ac is based on a certain schema which reappears in all the sermons in chh 2—13. This centres on the use of proofs from scripture, a method which is not only used widely elsewhere in Lk (Lk 24:46—47; Ac 26:22—23; 28:23) but also contributed to the formation of the gospels themselves (e.g. especially the Passion narratives), and conforms to the rabbinic method of instruction whose continuity with Christian methods has been fully shown by Gerhardsson. The primitive character of many of the Jerusalem speeches is further underlined by an abundance of semitic material (see Wilcox), and rabbinic methods of arguing and proving. Stephen's speech and Paul's at Lystra (13) have a feature distinctive of synagogue teaching, that they start with a résumé of Jewish history. Dibelius maintained that the sermons of Peter and Paul were examples of catechesis to Jew or gentile as Lk, rather than Peter and Paul, considered it should be done; but recent research has shown that they are too impregnated with Jewish and rabbinic characteristics to have been invented by Lk. The final product may stem from Lk, but he too is formed by tradition.

c A further question concerns the extent to which the **speeches catch the thought of the individual speakers**. In the matter of style Lk is punctilious in accommodating the speech to the occasion (e.g. the Areopagus speech, 17:22—32; the apology before Agrippa, 26:1—23); it is *a priori* probable that he would show the same sensitivity in reproducing the characteristics of the speaker. In Peter's speeches are found words which occur elsewhere in the NT only in 1 Pt, and perhaps a hint at Christ's descent into hell (2:24), which is attested elsewhere only in 1 Pt 3:19. For Stephen's speech the case is clear; it represents a current of opposition to the temple attested by other sources (O. Cullmann, *L'opposition contre le temple*, NTS 1958/9 (5), 157—73), which explains the persecution raised against him. Paul's speech on the Areopagus has been compared to Rm 1:18ff with diametrically opposed conclusions, but modern research overwhelmingly confirms its fidelity to Paul's thought (Gärtner, Nauck, op cit ad loc). Similar conclusions have been reached with regard to the speech at Antioch (13:32—37, cf Lövestam, op cit ad 13:16—41). This is not to deny that there are some differences between the Paul of the epistles and the Paul of the speeches in Ac (cf 822f). But in assessing these divergencies it is essential to bear in mind that the epistles were written to communities already Christian, whereas the majority of speeches given in Ac were addressed to non-Christians; a certain difference of approach would be expected. But in addition there is a difference in emphasis between Paul's theology and that of Ac, e.g. on Christology and on the redemptive value of Christ's death (823c, 836g); Paul's message is inevitably seen through Lk's eyes. But he does make a real effort to represent the characteristics of this message, e.g. it is only in a speech of Paul that there occurs any mention of the distinctively Pauline doctrines, not elsewhere found in Ac (823c).

Thus, while we cannot speak of the verbal authenticity of the speeches in Ac (as though a tape-recorder had been used), we can rely on the speeches with which Lk

interprets events and provides the catechesis, to re- **822c** produce an authentic picture of apostolic Christianity.

Date—Owing to the excellence of the sources of Ac, **d** both for the history and for the teaching of the early Church which it contains, the question of its date is of secondary importance. But this excellence itself makes a late date unlikely; the stories would not have survived in oral form without adaptation of some of the historical details to the conditions of a later period, nor would the primitive semitic elements in methods of teaching and in the texts of the OT used. A number of similarities of expression to those of 1 Clement (c. 90), and the occasional appearance of themes popular in the sub-apostolic age (see note to 24:25) make a date fairly near the end of the century probable. On the other hand the lack of any trace of the monarchical episcopate (Ac 20:28) suggests that Ac is earlier than the Pastoral Epistles (cf 1 Tm 3:2; Ti 1:7). Similarly 2 Tm 3:12 strongly suggests that the author of Past was acquainted with Ac (see note there). The traditional date of 62/3 is founded on a misinterpretation of the conclusion of Ac; it was argued from the 'sudden breaking off' that Lk could not have omitted the result of Paul's trial had the trial already taken place. But an understanding of the function of the conclusion of Ac in the structure of the whole shows that Lk had quite other reasons for ending when he did (see § 821e).

Author—Traditionally the author has always been **e** regarded as **a companion of Paul**. This has been accepted as proved beyond all doubt by the 'We-Passages'. Four passages in the book (16:10—17; 20:5—16; 21:1—18; 27:1—28:6) are written in the first person plural, which certainly implies to the modern reader that the author of the book accompanied Paul on these parts of his journeys. Various hypotheses have however been suggested to account in other ways for the use of this 'we' (see J. Dupont, *Sources*, ch 6). Of these the most recent and most powerful is that of Haenchen (p. 430, 536); he regards it merely as a trick of style whose implications to the ancient reader we cannot now discover, perhaps a means of 'drawing the reader into closer contact with the story' (but why, just in these unimportant accounts of a mere journey?). This suggestion is unsupported by any reference to ancient literature. In the many biographies and accounts of journeys which have come down to us from hellenistic times the use of the first person always constitutes at least a claim that the author was present. Haenchen's agnosticism on this point is unjustified.

The real reason for doubt whether Ac could have been **f** written by a companion of Paul is the difference in the outlook on several points of its author from the Paul of the Epistles. Their concept of what constitutes an apostle is different (but see notes to 1:20b—26; 9:10—19a; 14:14). Their view of the relationship between Christians and the Jewish Law is, at least on the surface, at variance (see note to 21:15—26). But these differences of theological opinion do not exclude the possibility that they travelled and even worked together. Each of these differences is linked in Ac with a particular purpose. Lk uses the concept of an apostle in function of his theme that the Church is in continuity with Christ's earthly life; the Twelve provide the link between the Church and the earthly Christ. Lk gives more prominence to Paul's observance of the Law for the sake of charity and fraternal harmony than to his polemic against the claim that the Christian is bound to its observance as a means to salvation; this is because one of the principal themes of Ac is the continuity of Christianity with Judaism (see § 821e). A third point of difference between Ac and Paul lies in the

822f importance which they attribute to Paul's collection among the Churches of Greece and Asia Minor for the community at Jerusalem; but this is perhaps explained by the result of the collection (see note to 24:17). Thus all the difficulties adduced for refusing the authorship of Ac to a companion of Paul have other explanations.

g As to the **name of this companion** of Paul there is no conclusive evidence. The internal evidence of the NT gives us little indication. We know from Col 4:14 that Lk was among Paul's companions when Col was written. This was probably at Rome during his 'first' captivity. The 'We-Passage' 27:1—28:6 shows that the author of Ac went to Rome then with Paul. There is moreover a striking similarity between Ac 26:18 (speech of Paul) and Col 1:12—14. But it would still be possible that Ac was written by another of those who were present with Paul in Rome at this time. Irenaeus argued (*adv. Haer.* 3.14.1—2) from 2 Tm 4:10—11, 'Lk alone is with me' (in captivity in Rome) that the author must be Lk; but since 2 Tm was not written during the captivity mentioned in Ac we have no evidence that the author of Ac was present when 2 Tm was written, and Irenaeus' argument falls to the ground. Other somewhat untrustworthy attempts to narrow the field down to Lk have been made by eliminating all companions of Paul mentioned in Ac, who for some reason or other are adjudged unsuitable for the authorship of Ac. But some companions (e.g. Titus, never mentioned in Ac) have not been satisfactorily eliminated; there may also have been other unnamed companions from whom the author is drawn.

The one point which is certain, from the combined evidence of prologue, Ac 1:1, plan, vocabulary, style and theology is that the author of Ac is also the author of the third gospel. The **tradition** of the Church from about A.D. 180 (Irenaeus, Canon of Muratori) ascribes both of them to 'Lk the follower of Paul'.

823a **Style**—The style of Ac shows that the author was a more literary man than any other NT writer (with the possible exception of the author of Heb). His vocabulary is large (but this is partly due to varied subject-matter), and his use of language supple. He can write a prologue conforming to the literary conventions of the day, or speeches which follow contemporary rhetorical practice (e.g. those of Tertullus and Paul before Felix and Agrippa, 24—26) with scarcely a flaw. His talent for suiting his style to the occasion contributes in no small measure to the attraction of the book, e.g. the humour of Peter's escape (12:6—17), the Alfred Hitchcock suspense of 23:12—35, the warmth of Paul's farewell (20:18—38). But even with this flexibility there is an underlying stability of vocabulary and style (see Haenchen p. 67—68) which marks the work as that of a single author. C. C. Torrey (*Composition and Date of Ac*, 1916) developed the thesis that Ac 1—15 was translated by the author from an Aram. document, with some mistakes and a definite residue of semitic idiom. But M. Wilcox has finally shown that such semitic expressions as exist in Ac probably came to the author already translated into Gr.; they, and many of the scriptural quotations which correspond neither to MT nor to LXX, must have formed part of the Christian tradition at the time. The use of these specifically Christian technical terms and expressions and a frequent deliberate modelling of the mode of expression on the LXX show that Ac was not intended for a pagan audience.

b The **teaching on Christ** given in the early part of Ac is at a very primitive stage of development. Explicitly it is centred on the Messiahship of Jesus; it is this which the speeches of Peter set out to prove. His chief concern is to remove the scandal of the crucifixion by showing that it was foretold by scripture that the Christ must suffer **823** and so enter into his glory. To this purpose he uses especially Isaiah's prophecies of the Suffering Servant (Ac 3:13, 26; 4:27—30—used also by Philip in 8:32—33); reference to these passages of Isaiah is implicit also in the title 'the Just One' (3:14; 7:52; 22:14). Ac uses 'Christ' only to show that Jesus is the Messiah, not yet as a personal name but as a title (cf O. Cullmann, *Christologie des NT*, ³1963 p. 135). The early chapters of Ac are shot through with the joy of the understanding that the crowning event of Jesus' passion and resurrection manifests him as the Messiah, not only suffering (4:24—30) but also triumphant, inaugurating the new age of the Spirit. Thus he accomplishes the promises to the Fathers, and fulfils the hope of Israel (3:21—26; 24:15; 28:20; cf § 821e).

But besides this Messiah-Christology Ac contains also **c** a clear though implicit realization that Jesus enjoys the divine powers and prerogatives. He is called 'Son of God' only twice, and both times (9:20; 13:33) by Paul, for whom this title is so important. But his divinity is shown in a way far more forceful to the semitic mentality than mere predication. He is invoked by the title 'Kyrios', reserved in the OT for God. Indeed in Ac this name refers to Jesus rather than to God the Father, so that in Paul's vision in the temple (22:17—19) it is Jesus who appears, thus arrogating to himself the Temple of God. He also calls Paul to be his tool, in just the same way as God called the prophets in the OT (see note to 9:3—9). It is by calling on the name of Jesus that men are to be saved (2:21), as in the original passage of Joel it is by calling on the name of God; 'those who call on the name of Jesus' becomes indeed a designation of Christians. This phrase is itself a hint of Jesus' divinity, recalling as it does the OT blessing by calling on the name of Yahweh.

A clear difference from Paul's Christology is that Jesus is conceived as being away in heaven, an exalted individual; the Spirit is his substitute in the Church. For Paul Christ is present in his Church; the Spirit is the mode by which he is present (C. Moule in Keck and Martyn, p. 180). Nevertheless Ac itself shows traces of the other view, in Peter's speech (4:2), and in three accounts of Paul's conversion (9:4—5; 22:8; 26:15). Another striking difference is that for Lk Christ's death is principally a prelude to his resurrection; there is no redemptive interpretation of it in Ac—except, on Paul's lips, in 20:28.

The perspective in which Ac views the new Messianic **d** age is different from that of Paul, at least in his early period (cf § 672c—h). For Lk the inauguration of 'the last times' implies not the imminent end of the world (this is hinted at only in 3:20—21), but the beginning of the **age of the Church**, in which the Church witnesses to Christ, carrying his work to the ends of the earth (1:7—8). There are certain clear parallels between incidents in the life of the Church and incidents in Christ's life: Philip (8:26—39) gives the same catechesis as did Christ (Lk 24:18—27); Peter's miracles parallel those of Christ; Stephen's martyrdom corresponds in many details with that of Christ. The Church is ruled and directed by **the Spirit** promised by Jesus (1:8), whose descent constitutes the beginning of her mission to the men of the whole world gathered together (2). It is the Spirit who directs every step in the expansion of the Church (see § 821e), who fills the ministers of the Church (4:8; 6:5; 7:55; 9:17; 11:24) as he filled the OT prophets (1:16; 28:25). But the Spirit fills all those who belong to the Church; the manifestations of the Spirit are the sign that men are accepted into the community of believers (10:44—47; 11:17).

23d But the Spirit is normally imparted through the ministry of **the Apostles** (8:15) or other ministers (8:39; 19:6). For there is also a visible authority in the Church. At the centre are the apostles. As a body they form the link with the Christ of history and the patriarchs of the new Israel, and must therefore be made up to the number of Twelve, even before the coming of the Spirit. We glimpse them acting too as a college, sending their representatives (8:15), conferring authority on Stephen (6:6), accepting Paul (9:27), as well as bearing witness, teaching and healing generally. The only individual apostle, however, of whom any special incidents are related is **Peter**. John is present with Peter on three occasions, but only as a lay figure. It is Peter who speaks at Pentecost; he is the first to work a miracle (3), and to suffer persecution for Christ's name; he is the judge of Ananias and Sapphira (5). Most significant of all, it is Peter who takes the responsibility, immense in Lk's eyes, of carrying out the vital step of accepting the first gentile into the Church, of justifying this step before the community (10—11), and of defending the independence of gentile Christians at the Council of Jerusalem (15). We cannot perhaps speak of a primacy of jurisdiction, but it is certain that Lk regards Peter's authority as an irrefutable guarantee. But authority is seen to be possessed also by the community itself; it is they who elect and present Stephen and his fellows (6:3—5), and they who confirm the decision of the apostles and elders at the Council of Jerusalem (15.22).

e As time goes on we find a supplementary authority appearing in the Church, **the elders**. These appear first at Jerusalem (11:30), where they are later (21:18) in charge of the community, under James, when the apostles have disappeared. Paul establishes them in all the communities which he founds on his first missionary journey (14:23). It is to the elders of Ephesus that his pastoral charge is addressed: they are the 'guardians of the flock', established by the Holy Spirit to guide and protect it in Paul's absence (20:28—30). Since the office of elder is not mentioned until the Pastoral Epistles, whose Pauline authorship is disputed, Haenchen (p. 077) assumes that Lk is here reading back the conditions of his own time. But Paul was simply establishing for the Christian communities the same organization as the Jewish communities of the Diaspora possessed; each synagogue had its own board of elders. How these elders worked together we do not know; apart from Jerusalem, where James has some special authority (already 12:17, perhaps by prolepsis; 21:18; cf Gal 2:12) there is no sign of any institution which will later develop into the monarchical episcopate.

The most striking feature in Ac's picture of the Church is provided by the summaries and editorial remarks of the early part of Ac, where Lk depicts the peace, simplicity and joy which characterize the messianic community of the new Israel (see notes to 2:41—47; 4:32—35; 5:12—16). These tableaux are supplemented by frequent editorial remarks in which Lk notes the fraternal harmony, mutual generosity and growth of the community. These features are certainly a major preoccupation with Lk, and combine to give us an ideal picture of the early community.

f Although the Spirit can be given without the mediation of the Church (10:44—47), the normal means of incorporation into the community is by **baptism**. We can already glimpse the baptismal practice of the Church in its primitive stage. There always precedes instruction, normally represented by a sermon directed to showing that Jesus is the Messiah of Scripture, in whom alone there is salvation, and to arousing repentance and belief. In the liturgy of the sacrament itself there seems to be a question whether any impediment to baptism exists (cf **823f** note to 8:36—38), a profession of faith, and baptism with water. The neophyte calls upon the name of Jesus, or perhaps the name of Jesus is called upon him; in either case the neophyte is thereby appropriated to Jesus (2:38 note). In two passages there is a separate ceremony of imposition of hands, which has been regarded as an adumbration of a separate ceremony of **confirmation**; but the explanation of this is quite other, see notes to 8:14—17 and 19:1—7. For the ceremony by which the Seven are **ordained**, see notes to 6:6. About the **eucharist** we gain little detailed information from Ac; it was part of the Christian way of life even when they were still taking part regularly in the temple liturgy (2:42, 46); there is perhaps an allusion to it just before Paul's shipwreck (27:35 note). But the only scene in which we get any picture of the Christian eucharistic assembly on the first day of the week (20:7—11) concentrates all attention on the sermon which precedes the eucharist, and the miracle connected with it on this occasion.

Text—Of all the textual variations of the NT those in **g** Ac fall most clearly into a definable pattern. The text is preserved in two forms, the 'Eastern' or Alexandrine text and the 'Western'. These names do not strictly correspond to the origin of the MSS and citations, but may serve as technical terms. Within the W tradition falls the Codex Bezae, a Gr. text with Latin translation, originating c. A.D. 500. It is liberally sown with errors of transcription, largely due to dictation in the undifferentiated pronunciation of the day, and with some mistakes of translation; but it contains also some variants which are of interest. The differences between the E and W texts are such that scholars at one time proposed the theory that Lk himself had published two variant editions. There is however a type discernible among the Western readings: they smooth awkward transitions or small illogicalities, make explicit obscurities, add picturesque details; one interesting theological tendency is to increase the prominence and honour of Peter (cf Lagrange, *Critique Textuelle II, livre II* (1935), p. 391). Although on the whole the readings of the W text are secondary, there remains the possibility that readings which do not fall into the pattern just indicated merit some consideration.

1:1—5 Prologue—Lk's introduction to his second book **824a** links it to his first by a short résumé of the contents of the gospel. Its elevated style indicates that we are to expect a history written after the model of Hellenistic histories, for Lk's appeal was to an educated audience, cf § 823*a*, though only to one which was already conversant with the Bible and Jewish practices; Ac would be unintelligible to pagans. For Theophilus, cf Lk 1:3. A second introduction does not necessarily mean that Ac forms an independent work, for an introduction could be placed at the beginning of a second volume of a single work (as Jos, CAp); some have accordingly claimed that Lk-Ac originally formed a single work. But the genres of the two books are too distinct, and the genre of gospel too well-defined to admit of a second volume being added.

2. 'through the Holy Spirit' is not linked by either **b** grammar or sense to the phrases on either side of it. Although Christ appeared to many others after his resurrection (1 Cor 15:5), Lk here concentrates on the special preparation of the apostles for their special rôle in the Church; he wishes to emphasize the part played in this by the spirit, as he will constantly stress its part in their mission, cf § 821*e*. **3.** Since a prime function of the apostles is to bear witness to the resurrection, Lk notes that they received many proofs of it. The forty days may be understood as a round number; it is common in biblical

824b language to signify any considerable period (e.g. Elijah and Jesus in the desert), especially a period of preparation for a work (Ex 24:18; 1 Kgs 19:8; Mk 1:13) or before a significant intervention by God in the history of salvation (Gn 7:4; Nm 14:34). Here there may be a particular allusion to the forty days spent by Moses on Mount Sinai receiving instruction from God (Ex 24:18); the apostles' instruction is complete after a similar period, cf P. H. Menoud, 'Pendant Quarante Jours'. NTSuppl VI (1962), 148—56. Other texts tell of an ascension on or soon after the day of Easter itself. But Lk's interest is not in the immediate exaltation of Christ after his resurrection, but in his final and definitive parting from his apostles, cf P. Benoit, 'L'Ascension', RB 1949 (56), 161—203 (also in his *Exégèse et Théologie*). **4.** Jerusalem
c is the turning-point of sacred history for Lk; the last part of his gospel is a journey to Jerusalem for the Passion which must (Lk 9:22; 13:33) take place there. So after the resurrection Jerusalem forms the centre from which the faith spreads, and to which the missioners constantly return for strength and guidance, cf § 821e. The promise, as **5** makes clear, is of the spirit, promised in Jn 14:16; its coming at Pentecost will enable the Twelve to fulfil their mission. This non-sacramental sense of baptism by the spirit is used also 11:16.
d **6—12 The Ascension**—**6—8** The apostles' question seems to show that they still shared the hopes of their contemporaries for the establishment by the Messiah of a worldly kingdom, cf Jn 6:15; and so in spite of the forty days' instruction on the kingdom they still radically misunderstood its nature until the coming of the spirit. But Lk gives the question rather for the sake of its answer, which contains two important teachings: **7** (a logion found also Mk 13:32) a prohibition of hoping for an imminent second coming of Christ, cf §§ 670—72; Lk carefully damps this expectation, concentrating on the era of the Church which is now beginning. **8.** The kingdom is not to be confined to Israel; this verse gives a programme for Ac; the diffusion of the gospel starts at Jerusalem (chh 1—7), spreads from there to Judea and Samaria (8—9), then to the rest of the world, finally reaching Rome, which is described also in the 1st cent. Ps. Sal. 8:15 as the end of the earth. Thus Christ's final instructions
e set in action the whole movement of Ac. **9—11.** The ascension itself is described in the simplest terms; the emphasis is not on Christ's entry into glory or on the emotions of the apostles (as in the apocryphal gospels) but on the separation. Both cloud and angels are conventional; a cloud frequently intervenes in the departure from this world of heroes in both pagan and Jewish apocalyptic literature (refs in Conzelmann, *Apg*. p. 23). The angels appear to give an inspired interpretation of what has happened, as at the resurrection, Lk 24:4; Charlier (p. 66) says they are only a 'literary personification of divine inspiration', guaranteeing the truth of the message. Their prohibition of remaining gazing into heaven is another warning against waiting in idleness for the second coming, cf 7; 2 Thes passim e.g. 3:10—11.
f **12—14.** The apostles return because it is at Jerusalem that the mission just entrusted to them must start. The Mount called Olivet is on the way to Bethany (thus there is no contradiction with Lk 24:50), five furlongs from the city (Jos.Ant. 20:169), so one furlong within the six permissible on the Sabbath. The place is especially significant, because it is from here that the glory of Yahweh left Jerusalem (Ezek 11:23)—a hint of the divinity of Christ—and hither that it will return in the last times (Zech 14:4, cf 710e, Ac 1:7). **13.** 'The upper room' (with the definite article) suggests a well-known place, perhaps

a regular meeting-place of the community. Epiphanius **824** says that when Hadrian visited Jerusalem in A.D. 130 he found a little church on the site of the upper room. Only since the 6th cent. have the room of the last supper and the house of John Mark's mother (12:25) been located with it on Mount Sion, see C. Kopp, *The Holy Places of the Gospels* (ET 1963), 323. The minor variations in the lists of the apostles given by the evangelists (Lk 6:14 par.) show that the essential point remembered was that they numbered twelve; it is for this reason that their number must be made up. **14.** The first of the summaries of the life of the Church in Jerusalem given periodically by Lk, see note to 2:43. Mary, mother of the Saviour and mother of the Church, is present (cf § 661p).

15—26 The choice of Matthias—Lk shows the impor- **g** tance of the apostolic office by depicting this scene alone between the Ascension and Pentecost, and by giving us Peter's speech on the qualifications and duties of an apostle (on the historicity of speeches in Ac, see § 822a—c). Their chief duty is to witness to the resurrection (2:29ff, 3:12ff, 4:10 etc), but also to provide a thread of continuity between Christ's lifetime and the era of the Church. They must be twelve in number as the patriarchs of the new Israel, cf Lk 22:29—30; one function of the account is therefore to stress that initially the apostles still hoped to convert Israel, turning to the gentiles only when this hope was disappointed, cf K. H. Rengstorf, 'Die Zuwahl des Matthias', StudT 1961 (15) 35—67, cf § 821e. The number 120 is given perhaps because this was the minimum number required for a sanhedrin to have jurisdiction; it therefore indicates the legitimacy of the **h** election. **16—20a.** The versions of the fate of Judas given here and in Mt 27:3—10 seem to be based on popular oral traditions from which it would be a mistake to expect precision on every historical detail. They have in common the name of the place and the conviction that Judas' violent death fulfilled the prophecies. The details vary in the two accounts, those here being drawn from the description of the death of the persecutor of the just man (a title of Jesus 3:14) in Wis 4:19. Mt tells us the field was bought only after Judas' death, but in Ac the field belonged to Judas himself, in order to fulfil Ps 69 (68) more exactly, cf P. Benoit, 'La mort de Judas', in *Synoptische Studien Alfred Wikenhauser* (1954) (also in *Exégèse et Théologie*). The passage is typical of Lk in style and vocabulary; it cannot have been spoken in its present form in Aram. by Peter, for it provides information for the reader which would have been superfluous to his hearers (18—19), and required the Gr. version of Ps 69 (68) for the quotation to be relevant (*he who* lives in it *be annihilated*—RSV carelessly translates the Heb. OT, not Ac). **20b—26.** The **i** second quotation (also according to the Gr.) introduces the appointment of Matthias itself. The twelfth member is to be a witness to the resurrection, but, to secure the historical continuity, must also have been present during the whole time of Jesus' earthly ministry (semitically expressed 'went in and out'). Paul is not, therefore, in this sense an apostle. The necessity of replacing Judas arises perhaps also from the rôle of the apostles as the 12 patriarchs of the new Israel (cf 823d); it therefore results rather from his desertion than from his death, and need not be repeated at the death of each apostle. **23.** Neither of the candidates appears again in the NT; this shows both the historicity of the names (since Lk can have had no reason to invent them) and that their function is to make up the number of the Twelve. **24—26.** Lk **j** underlines that it is Christ who makes the choice, by verbal reminiscences of Christ's first choice of the Twelve in Lk 6:12—14, by the prayer to Christ ('Lord' in Ac has this

24j sense), and by the casting of lots, which leaves full play to the divine initiative.

25a **2:1—13 The coming of the Spirit**—Lk depicts the coming of the Spirit upon the apostles and the beginning of their world mission vividly by means of allusions which are clear in the light of late Jewish literature. Pentecost (lit the fiftieth day) was, at least in the second century, the feast of the giving of the Law on Sinai. The existence of this feast is attested as early as the book of Jubilees, but we have no evidence for the day on which it was kept before the 2nd cent. According to Philo, *Decal.* 33, at the giving of the Law God sent a mighty invisible sound (the same word as Ac 2:2) which turned to fire and gave forth a voice proclaiming the Law. Thus the day was (Dt 4:10; 9:10) known as the Day of the Assembly (*ecclesia*, in Christian terminology the Church), since on this day it was formally constituted. Because of the spread to all nations the Assembly or Church is shown to be essentially missionary in its very foundation. According to another tradition (SB 3, 48—49) this voice split into seventy tongues so as to be understood by all the nations of the earth (seventy in Jewish lore). The nations listed in Ac 2:9—11 also represent all nations, for the list is founded on a list of countries corresponding to all the signs of the zodiac, so 'every nation under heaven' 5; cf S. Weinstock, 'The Geographical Catalogue in Acts 2', JRS 38 (1948)

b **43–46.** Lk heightens both these elements. In **2** he likens the sound of the spirit to that of a rushing wind, thus producing a play on the Gr. words *pnoē-pneuma* (but cf also Jn 3:8, where the spirit is likened to a wind). In **3** he similarly puns on *glōssa*, which can mean both 'tongue' and 'language', so that languages are divided (the same Greek word as that used for the division of the nations after Babel in Dt 32:8) among them. The fire has here also the sense of ushering in the last times, as frequently in the NT, especially in connexion with baptism in the spirit (Lk 3:16 and 3:9); for Lk Pentecost is the

c beginning of the last times, the era of the Church. **4.** The account is no slavish copy of the Jewish Sinai tradition, for that has no parallel to the filling of the members of the community with the spirit (conversely Lk has no Law-giving). This is the immediate prelude to, and strengthening of the apostles for, their mission, cf Jn 20:22. In the OT it is the spirit which enables God's representatives to fulfil their office of teaching and guidance e.g. 1 Sm 16:13 (at David's anointing), Is 11:1ff (the Messiah). At Jesus' baptism (Lk 3:22 par.) the Spirit comes down to give him power for his messianic mission. **5.** At first the mission of the disciples is only to the Jews of the world. Even after the crucifixion they are given a second chance to bring salvation to the world according to the promises Is 2:3; Ps 87 (86), etc, until they repeatedly refuse, cf § 821*e*. **7.** It is a characteristic of Lk's dramatic style to put in the mouth of his characters explanations which a modern author would himself give, e.g. 1:18—19; but here and in

825c 12 the 'saying . . .' would be more exactly rendered 'as though to say . . .', cf Gn 30:6—13, Lk 1:63 etc; it interprets their thoughts.

14—40 Peter's Proclamation—Lk tells how Jesus, **d** after he had received the spirit at baptism, began his ministry by proclaiming himself Messiah at Nazareth (4:16—30). So now Peter, having received the Spirit, proclaims that the promises for the last times have been fulfilled. There is some foreshortening of historical perspective in the presentation of the scene (Haenchen, p. 151), for one may doubt that the Church elaborated so quickly either the proofs from messianic texts of scripture or the rites of baptism; indeed the texts quoted require, to be relevant, the LXX version in 21, 27, 28, qq.v., so cannot have been used in Aram. But there are clear traces of Aram. formulae which have been used, e.g. in 14. But Lk's message is not concerned with development of doctrine; rather it concerns the power and efficacy of the spirit poured out on the apostles and on the Church. The scene falls into three sections:

14—21 Explanation of the speaking with tongues— **e** This serves to introduce the message itself, by a preliminary proclamation that the extraordinary phenomena show that the last days of universal salvation have come. **14.** The semitic parallelism of the two pairs of phrases and the formula, 'let it be known to you', awkward in Gr. but frequent in contemporary Aram., show Lk's link with the primitive Palestinian tradition (Wilcox p. 90—91). **15.** Drinking at 9 a.m. is castigated by Cicero *Phil* (2 41, 104) as unbelievably debased. **17—20.** Lk adduces as **f** evidence not only the visions and dreams frequently recounted in Ac but also cosmic phenomena; but a divine intervention in history is automatically expressed by the Heb. in these terms, Jg 5:4, Mk 13:24—27, cf § 737*a*. **21.** The sense given by the original Heb. is inapplicable here, since the word used for 'the Lord' refers invariably to God, not to Christ, as here. But the phrase, 'whoever calls on the name of the Lord', is an early formula, practically a designation of the Christian Rm 10:13; 1 Cor 1:2; 12:3, and 5 times in Ac, cf 2:36; Jas 2:7 suggests that it was a baptismal formula.

22—36 Proclamation of salvation in the risen **g** **Christ**—The proclamation of the risen and exalted Christ dominates the message of Ac. C. H. Dodd, *The Apostolic Preaching and its Development* (1936), has shown that the same schema underlies all the apostolic proclamations of Christ in the early part of Ac:

1. 'The age of fulfilment has dawned through Jesus':
(See Table below)

The chief divergencies from Paul's kerygma are that Jesus is not called 'Son of God', and that forgiveness of sins is not connected specifically with his death. **22—24.** Some **h** authors point out Jesus' subordinate position with regard to God in these verses and conclude that Lk's Christology was 'subordinationist' in the strict sense, or that these

ministry	2:22	3:22				10:38	
death	2:23	3:13—14	4:10	5:30		10:39	13:27—29
resurrection	2:24—31	3:15	4:10	5:30		10:40	13:30
(witnessed	2:32	3:15		5:32		10:41	13:31)
exaltation	2:33—36	3:13	4:11	5:31		10:36; 42	13:33
2. Witness of							
spirit	2:33			5:32			
3. Appeal to repent and turn to Christ							
	2:38—39	3:17	4:12	5:31			13:26; 38.

825h are primitive formulae deliberately inserted to retain the archaic theology of the first years of the Christian move-
i ment; cf § 821*b*–*d*. **25–31.** The scriptural proof is intended to remove the scandal of the Cross by showing that it was pre-ordained with a view of the resurrection and exaltation of Christ. Lk 24:46–47 shows Christ himself giving an example in this use of scripture to explain the meaning of his life, death and resurrection. The early Church naturally took over the principles of exegesis current in their time among the Jews, which perhaps carry less conviction today, cf P. Bonsirven, *Exégèse rabbinique et exégèse paulinienne* (1939). **27, 28** In Heb. the expressions translated 'corruption' and 'ways of life' have not the sense required for the argument here, cf § 822*a*–*c*.

j 37–40. The call to repentance which is the invariable conclusion of the apostolic sermons is here introduced by a short dramatic dialogue. The purpose of these sermons is to awaken in the hearers a sense of guilt for the crucifixion (or, in the case of pagans, for idolatry), and of the need for Christ. **38.** The exact sense of the formula 'in the name of Jesus' is not clear, cf TWNT 5 (1954) 274–5. Apart from this passage and Ac 10:48, baptism is said to be '*into* the name of Jesus'. It seems that the name of Jesus was called over the baptized, thus appropriating him for Jesus. The chief consequences of baptism, here mentioned, are forgiveness of sins and reception of the spirit. **39.** The universalist Lk (cf § 766*g*–*h*) ends with an indication that salvation is for all men.

k 41–47 The primitive messianic community—These verses contain the first of three major summaries of the life of the Jerusalem community (also 4:32–35; 5:12–16), all of which are composed by Lk from scattered sources and remarks. P. Benoit, 'Remarques sur les "sommaires" des Actes 2:42 à 5' (*Mélanges Goguel*, 1950, 1–10), holds that each contains a non-Lukan interpolation drawn from the others. That they are non-Lukan is refuted by Haenchen (p. 156f), who maintains that their function is to separate scenes of Peter's activity and give the impression of lapse of time. Each trait corresponds to Lk's ideal of the messianic, eschatological community, cf J. Schmitt, 'L'Église de Jérusalem ou la "Restauration" d'Israël' RSR 27 (1953), 209–18. **41.** As always (Lk 24:30, Ac 8:38; 10:48) the reception of the sacrament follows that of the word. The growth of the community is constantly noted (2:47; 5:14; 6:1, 7; 9:31; 11:21, 24; 16:5); it exemplifies the silent growth of the messianic community,
l cf Mk 4:26ff. **42–47.** In listening to the apostles' teaching they listen to the word of the Lord. 'Breaking of bread' is a technical term for the Eucharist. Other elements of this description are stressed by Lk in his gospel; he emphasizes the importance of prayer (3:21; 11:1; 18:1–14), joy and praise (1:14; 2:10; 10:17) and internal peace (2:14; 19:38, cf Is 11:6ff for messianic community). He notes also of Jesus that he enjoyed the favour of men (2:51), a point on which he is sensitive (14:10; 16:3). On community of goods see note to 4:32–37. The chief value of the description is the representation of the virtues which make up the ideal of the Christian community. According to Benoit, 43–45 are out of place because they interrupt the description of the community life.

826a 3:1–10 Peter heals a lame man—Peter shows that Christ continues in the Church by working in his name just such a miracle of healing as Jesus himself worked during his life. In Lk 9:6 the power to heal diseases is given to the apostles (not in Mk's version), and in Lk 10:9 to the disciples when they are sent out. Commentators

have noted that the miracles performed for the Jews by **826** Peter (healing here, raising the dead 9:36–41) are performed by Paul for the gentiles (14:8–10; 20:9–12). But the parallelism is not stressed by the author; the interest is rather in the continuance by both apostles of the messianic mission by healing in the power of Christ. John's silence throughout this episode, and various slight awkwardnesses of the Greek, suggest that the story originally mentioned only Peter; Haenchen suggests, p. 162, that John was added so that there should be two witnesses, as required in Jewish law for valid testimony, mentioned in 4:20. Lk often associates these two apostles (Lk 22:8, Ac 8:14, etc). **2.** The Beautiful Gate is not mentioned in any Jewish description of the temple, but **b** it is unlikely to have been the (misnamed) Golden Gate with which tradition identifies it. This is on the East side of the temple, leading directly into the valley, whereas a beggar sits at the gate leading in from the market. Further localizations are mere conjecture. **6.** Lk again insists that the primitive community practised poverty, cf note to 2:42. The formula, 'in the name of Jesus', probably used in baptism cf note to 2:38, implies profession of faith in the saving power of Jesus, for faith is always a prerequisite for miracles, cf 16, and note to 4:8–12.

11–26 Peter's address in the Temple—The cure **c** serves as an occasion for presenting the power of Jesus, in whom alone salvation is to be found. The speech may be divided into three sections. **12–16.** After an introduction Peter contrasts the rejection of Jesus by the Jews with the honour shown to him by God in raising him from the dead (to which the apostles bear witness) and by granting a cure to a believer in his name. For the schema underlying this section see note to 2:22–36. The version of scripture quoted in 13 (and again 7:32) is the Samaritan version, which connects the use of the quotation with the Palestinian community; but the text quoted in 25 requires, in order to be relevant, the LXX version used. This, and the Greek-style rhetorical contrasts in 13–15 (glorified—denied, holy—murderer, murderer—author of life, killed—raised) suggest that the speech was composed by Lk, though from traditional material, cf § 822*a*–*c*. The doctrine on Christ contained in these verses reflects the prophecies of the Suffering Servant of Isaiah, rejected of men but glorified by God; to this 'glorified', 'servant', 'righteous one' are allusions, cf Is 52:13; 53:11. These prophecies are a major source for the Christology of Ac, cf. § 823*b*.

17–21 Exhortation to conversion in view of the d second coming—**17.** If this mention of the ignorance of the Jews and their rulers is intended to excuse them, the passage is unique in Ac; in Lk 23:34 the Roman soldiers are excused on these grounds, but nowhere are excuses given for the action of the Jews (2:23; 4:10, 27; 5:28); Lk's account of the Passion rather emphasizes their responsibility. The word used here for 'ignorance' always implies rather guilt, and in the LXX translates five different Heb. words, all of which mean sin or guilt (Gärtner, *The Areopagus Speech* . . .). Peter's purpose is to arouse repentance, and he is persuading rather than excusing. **18.** This verse serves as a résumé of Peter's theme in 2:25–31. **19.** For 'repent and turn again' see note to 26:20. **20–21.** Dodd, *Apostolic Preaching*, p. 33f, points to these verses as the sole passage in Ac where there is the sense of urgent expectation of the second coming of Christ so prominent in other parts of the NT (cf §§ 670–72). But there is little sign of urgency even here; the thought is rather allied to Rm 11:25–27, that the end of the world is delayed until after the conversion of Israel. It also comes close to Paul's announcement

6d (Eph 1:10) of the final restoration of all things in Christ and his rule over the whole universe.

e **22—26 The true Israel consists of the adherents of Jesus, the prophet and Messiah foretold**—This reinforces the appeal to conversion, but arouses the fury which puts an end to the speech. (The interruption of speeches in Ac may be regarded as a dramatic convenience, since it occurs always as they reach their climax, thereby lending special emphasis to this climax). The expectation of the Messiah as a prophet similar to Moses was widespread in first century Israel; its fulfilment in Jesus is constantly stressed by Mt and Jn (see §§ 711e and 809i—m respectively). It is hinted at already in Ac 3:13, for Moses too was rejected by his people and yet made their leader (cf 7:35—37). Peter now insists that it was of Jesus that Moses foretold that those who did not listen to the prophet to come would be cut off from Israel ('the people' is **f** the people of God). **25—26.** No opportunity is missed to stress that it is to the Jews first, and through them to the gentiles, that salvation was promised. In the quotation of Gn 22:18 even the LXX 'races' is altered to 'families' to avoid the directly universalist overtones of that word. Only after the refusal of the Jews do the apostles turn to the gentiles, cf § 821e.

g **4:1—22 Peter and John before the Sanhedrin**—On account of various difficulties in this account (e.g. the Sadducees as such have no right to arrest anyone, especially not for merely believing in the resurrection, vv 1—2) Haenchen, pp. 179—83, and Conzelmann, pp. 135—7, refuse it all historical foundation. Haenchen characterizes it as 'one of those dramatic scenes with which Lk, instead of a dry dogmatic exposition, puts before the reader's eyes the Christian's duty . . . to bear fearless witness to his Lord'. No doubt the scene does illustrate in practice Mt 10:17—20 (especially Ac 4:19—20), that Christians will be dragged before the Sanhedrin and scourged (not until Ac 5:40), and that the spirit of God will bear witness in them (Ac 4:8). This may account for its inclusion in Ac, but there are not sufficient grounds for concluding that it was invented for this purpose. E.g. it is the captain of the temple who carries out the arrest in his capacity as the high priest's delegate for preserving order in the temple; the charge is proclaiming not the resurrection of the dead, but resurrection in Jesus, cf note to 5:17—42.

h **1—4. The arrest** was no doubt instigated by the Sadducees, whose denial of a general resurrection made them more averse to Christianity than were the Pharisees, who accepted this doctrine. Since the ruling priestly families were all drawn from the ranks of the Sadducees they had ample power to persecute, and in fact all the persecutions in Ac (apart from those of Saul, which were at least under their authority) are instigated by them. The more timid and cautious Pharisees, who took no part even in Jesus' execution, tend to restrain them (5:34; 23:8f); at this trial they are not even present (5). In view of the lack of interest which Lk's gospel shows for the parties within Judaism, this is excellent evidence for his fidelity to a source here. **4.** This note, cf 2:41, is effectively placed here: in spite of the arrest, the numbers of believers went on increasing.

i **5—22 The trial**—**6.** Annas was in fact deposed from the office of high priest in A.D. 15 but continued to have considerable influence through his son-in-law Caiaphas (A.D. 17—36) and later his sons; even if he did not retain the title of high priest, the confusion is understandable. **7.** The two halves of the question are virtually synonymous, for to the semites the name is the expression of a person's power and qualities (Ex 34:6, Phil 2:10, Heb 1:4). **8—12.** The ques-

tion gives Peter occasion for a short proclamation on the **826i** saving power of the name of Jesus (= God saves); he uses a miniature version of the schema which serves all the apostolic speeches, see note to 2:22—36. The formula 'Jesus the Nazarene' was probably used in professions of faith in the early Church (O. Cullmann, *Earliest Christian Confessions*, 1943 E.tr. 1949, 23—25), both at baptisms (cf note to 2.38) and in connexion with healings and exorcisms (Mk 1:24; 10:47, Ac 3:6; Justin Dial. 30:3), as a profession of faith in his saving power. Peter is 'filled with the Holy Spirit', as was promised Mt 10:20. **11. j** This verse of Ps 118 (117) is used of the Messiah in Jewish literature (SB 1,876), and is recognized by the Pharisees in Mt 21:42 to imply a messianic claim. **13.** The 'boldness' or 'fearless *outspokenness*' of the apostles was one of the notable characteristics of their preaching, cf 4:29, 31; 28:31; 2 Cor 3:12, Col 2:15, after the model of their Master Mt 7:29, Jn 5:19ff. The authorities are amazed that '*illiterate*' men can speak so, for study was in their eyes the only passport even to respectability (Jn 7:15; 9:34, and many rabbinic passages SB 2, 494—519). But since at least in cases of blasphemy it was forbidden to punish offenders who were unaware of the evil of their crime, and those who had not studied the Law were presumed in law to be ignorant of this, they could at a first offence be warned (4:18—21, cf 5:40).

23—31 Prayer for strength under persecution—The **k** apostles have been warned and can expect only persecution to follow their intended disregard of the prohibition to preach. Hence the reference to the pre-ordination of Christ's suffering and its inevitable fulfilment, together with the mention of the threats just made, and soon to be fulfilled (29, cf 17 and 5:28). The call upon God's creative power implies confidence in his control of the situation. We have here what may well be a very ancient prayer of the Church, still modelled on the OT prayers (Is 37:16—20). Several expressions reflect the prayer-style of the early Church. 'Sovereign Lord' occurs in the NT only here and in the prayer of Simeon (Lk 2:29), but also frequently in prayers in the early Fathers (TWNT 2,44 n, 13); the formula 'God's servant' occurs almost exclusively in liturgical prayers until A.D. 160 (Wilcox p. 71f). **31.** The closest parallels to an earthquake signifying an answer to prayer are pagan (Ovid, *Metamorph.* 15:619ff, Virg, *Aen.* 3:88ff), but there are analogies also in the Bible: Ex 19:18, Is 6:4, Jn 12:29.

4:32—5:16 The life of the community two sum- **827a** maries separated by an example.

32—37—The second of three major summaries on the life of the apostolic community (also 2:42—7; 5:12—16), this passage concentrates on community of goods as evidence of unity of heart. Therefore Benoit (see note to 2:41—47) regards v 33 as an insertion drawn from the other summaries. In his gospel Lk stresses more than the other evangelists the dangers of owning property and the beatitude of poverty (6:20, 24; 16:13, 19—31). Poverty was highly esteemed in contemporary Judaism (cf Zeph 2:3) as part of the ideal of the messianic community, as well as by Hellenistic moralists. The poverty practised by the Essene communities caught the imagination of all observers (Josephus, Pliny, Philo); but total community of goods was practised by them only among certain groups or at certain periods, viz that of the Rule of the Community, but not that of the Damascus Document. Haenchen, p. 190f, maintains that Lk exaggerates the degree of community of goods for the sake of his ideal, that he generalizes from Barnabas' action (36—37), which was in fact recorded precisely because it was exceptional, and that 5:4 shows such pooling of funds to have been optional.

827a **36.** Attempts to account for the meaning of 'Barnabas' have been unsuccessful; it has been pointed out that 'son of encouragement' fits better the name of Menaen who is mentioned with Barnabas in 13:1. The abundance of details given about Barnabas in Ac suggests that he may have been Lk's source for much of his information about the communities of Jerusalem and Antioch, and about Paul's first missionary journey. The description of the **b** common life leads on, by way of contrast, to **5:1—11 Ananias and Sapphira**—the severity and immediacy of their punishment (contrast Mt 18:15) has often shocked commentators. The story contains allusions to the sin of Achan (Jos 7) who committed sacrilege by keeping back for himself booty which had been dedicated to God; but the precise nature of the sin is perhaps made clearer by the parallel from Qumran (1 QS 6:24), where deception in matters of property declared to the community is severely punished, though not with death. The couple's sin consists in deceiving the Holy Spirit who rules the community in the attempt to gain the regard due to generosity without suffering the discomforts involved. The opposition of Satan and the holy spirit (3) is also frequent at Qumran, and the enigmatic 'young men' (6, 10) perhaps reflects the term used for junior members of the Qumran community (1 QS 6:16—21), cf J. Schmitt, in *Les manuscrits de la Mer Morte* (1957) 93—109. The classic explanation of the story (already Jer, *Ep.* 130, 14) is that the punishment of one couple serves as instruction for many. The story is certainly catechetical in purpose; the scandal of Peter's seeming harshness is best explained by appeal to the schematic and oversimplified nature of the story, due to its transmission through popular oral tradition. There are traces of an Aram. background, and some improbable details (the apostles seem to sit frozen with the money at their feet for three hours; Ananias is carried off to burial without his wife being informed); reduplication (1—6/7—10) for emphasis is a feature of such popular stories.

c **5:12—16 The third summary, the miracles of the apostles**—12*b*—14 treats the themes of assembly and growth given in the first summary, cf note to 2:41—47. But they serve also as a bridge between the motifs of reverent fear at the miraculous power at work in the community (5:11) and of opposition which is to break out again (5:17ff). In his general healing Peter shows the continuance of Christ's own work (Mk 6:56) as will Paul in Ac 19:12.

d **17—42 The apostles before the Sanhedrin**—In the same way as the account of the persecution of Peter and John in 4:1—22, this account also has been denied all historical foundation. Dibelius, p. 123—37, holds that the first persecution of Christians was that directed against the Hellenists (chh 6—8). The purpose of this story is again to paint vividly the fearless confession of Christ, this time not merely by two but by all of the apostles, the special divine protection which they enjoyed, and the favourable attitude of the greatest figure of contemporary Judaism. But to discover an author's interests in telling a story is not to prove that he invented it. Nor may we conclude to its inauthenticity simply from its similarity to 4:1—22 or from the *crescendo* in many of its details (all apostles, not two—punishment, not threats), though this has led many critics to see in it a mere literary doublet of the former persecution. Some details are improbable, e.g. the miraculous escape is passed over by the court in silence; but this may be ascribed either to mere simplification or to Lk's desire not to attract too much attention to it lest he detract from the similar incident fully described in 12:6—10. But for this very reason he would not have

included the incident if it were not an integral part of the **82*** tradition; he is merely practising selective reporting. The **e** details of history mentioned in Gamaliel's speech have been queried; but they do not affect the substantial historicity; the caution he shows is typical of the Pharisees, and his breadth characteristic of the liberal school of Hillel of which he was the foremost representative. The strongest argument for the historicity of the incident is J. Jeremias' ('Untersuchungen zum Quellenproblem der Apg' ZNW 1937 (26) 208—13), that in accusations on capital charges and even for scourging the uneducated may at a first offence only be warned (as 4:18) if he can be unaware of the gravity of his offence, and may be punished only at a second offence (as 5:40). Bo Reicke (*Glaube und Leben der Urgemeinde*, 1957, 108—9) points out that the extension of the warning to cases involving scourging is attested only for the Talmud, and was far too impractical to have been applied in practice (the Talmud is mere theorizing in this matter). He therefore regards the two passages as different recensions of the same incident, both based on a reliable source.

19. The motif of miraculous release from prison recurs **f** 12:6—11; 16:26—27. Here the release seems to have had oddly little influence on the rest of the affair. It could well be a doublet of the release due to Gamaliel's intercession, a popular version (for the theme is typical of popular stories, cf note to 16:25—34), expressing that the release was due to the special intervention and protection of God. In any case we need not conclude that these proofs of divine protection and guidance involved any bodily appearances; God's messengers are real beings, but spiritual forces; they do not necessarily require bodies; cf notes to 8:26; 12:8. **20.** 'Words of life' is used by Peter in Jn 6:68 also to describe the message of Christ, 'Life' sums up the gift of Christ to men also Ac 3:15; 11:18. **21.** This pompous enumeration of the elements of the court makes their disappointment the more comic. **29—32.** Peter's little sermon uses the same themes as his previous ones, see note to 2:22—37. Three details may be noted: 29*b* is very close in form to Plato, *Apol.* 29*d*, probably a literary allusion on Lk's part. In 31 the same word is used of Christ (RSV 'leader') as in 3:15 'author of life'; Peter fulfils the command of v 20 to the letter. 32 again stresses the apostolic office of witness (cf 2:8, 22, 29, etc), and the presence of the holy spirit in the apostles (Jn 15:26, Mt 10: 20, Ac 4:8). **34—39.** Gamaliel the Elder, according to **g** Jewish tradition the greatest religious authority of his generation (SB 2, 636ff), and Saul's master, restrains the Sanhedrin, cf note to 4:1—4. Many stories in the Mishnah illustrate his love of men and his pithy humour. But in this case his attitude accords also with the caution and aversion to decisive action characteristic of the Pharisees. **36.** A certain Theudas led a revolt in c. A.D. 45 (Jos.Ant. 20, 5), a decade after the date of Gamaliel's speech, and some fifty years after that of Judas the Galilean which it is said (37) to have preceded. But revolts and messianic uprisings were so frequent in the century before A.D. 70, and our knowledge of the earlier part of this period so meagre, that it is quite possible that another Theudas led another revolt. There were two revolts led by two Judases of Galilee. We cannot accuse Lk of putting incorrect history on Gamaliel's lips. **40— 41.** The first suffering for confessing Christ's name, prophesied in Mt 10:17, is followed by the joy promised to the persecuted in Lk 6:22 par.

6:1—8:3 Persecution of the Hellenists—this section **82** is all-important in the plan of Ac, marking the first advance of Christianity beyond Jerusalem, and setting the stage for its expansion to the world (cf 1:8 and § 821*e*).

8a It also reveals a difference of opinion and practice within the community.

6:1—7 The election of the Seven—Lk's interest in this election is limited to introducing Stephen by the explanation of how another group of seven officials came to exist alongside the Twelve. This he cannot do without revealing a dissension within the community which casts a shadow on his ideal picture of fraternal harmony. But it has long been noticed that his account of the affair is far from satisfactory; he does not make clear who the Hellenists were, what office the Seven held, what was the root cause of the dispute.

1. The Hellenists were of course Jews (the gentile mission had not yet started), generally supposed to have been speakers of Gr rather than the Aram.-speaking 'Hebrews'. O. Cullmann and M. Simon, however, maintain with good grounds that they were Jews strongly influenced by Greek ways of thought (cf 2 Mc 4:13). It has also been claimed that they were connected with the sectaries of Qumran, but the link has not been satisfactorily established. But they were a well-defined group, since they alone were expelled as the result of this persecution (11:18, and cf note to 8:1).

b 2. According to 6:1—4, the Seven are concerned with material ministrations (whence their usual appellation of 'deacons' from the Gr. 'to serve'; but Ac does not call them deacons, distributors of poor relief, who thereby spare the Twelve from being distracted from prayer and the 'ministry of the word'. But elsewhere it is clear that the Seven are full of the spirit (6:3), work miracles (6:8), evangelize and baptize (8:12, 38; 21:8) just as the apostles do; nor do they take charge of the collection sent up to the Jerusalem community in 11:30. Therefore it has been suggested that the Seven formed a hierarchy for the Hellenist element in the community, ordained by, and loosely subordinated to the Twelve; cf note to vss 3, 6. M. Simon suggests that they may have existed before the disagreement, but have secured recognition only now.

c 3. It was a pious custom among Diaspora Jews to come to Jerusalem to spend the evening of their lives in the holy city; there were therefore a number of old people of slender resources who relied on a weekly distribution of alms. We hear that the Hellenist widows were being neglected in a daily distribution, a practice which is unknown in Jewish sources; this suggests that they, at any rate, were no longer in receipt of the official Jewish alms. Conversely the Hebrew widows, having no such complaint, may be presumed to be still beneficiaries of it. At any rate this neglect was surely the symptom of a deeper cleft which divided the Hellenists from the Hebrews. The appointment of a board composed exclusively of Hellenists (as the names 6:5 show) suggests that they were not intended to look after the Hebrews, because these latter enjoyed other means of support. **2b** suggests that the crisis had only just arisen, and the Twelve refused to undertake a new burden, not that they wanted to be relieved of an old one. **3.** The same qualities are required for the 7 as for Joshua, the successor of Moses: the spirit (Nm 27:18) and wisdom (Dt 34:9). This suggests **d** some parity of office with the apostles. **4.** This 'ministry of the word' which, with prayer, forms the Twelve's chief duty may be not preaching, but—analogously with the Jewish 'ministry of the Law' (SB 2, 647)—study of the word, and care for the preservation and transmission of the oral tradition of Christ's message (cf B. Gerhardsson, 240—5). **5.** This list must come from a source, probably written. **6.** This is the first case in the NT of the conferring of an office by imposition of hands. This was common in the OT (Nm 27:23; Dt 34:9). It was a real leaning on,

by which the personality of the ordainer was poured and **828d** pressed into the ordained. Since this sort of imposition of hands was used later only for the ordination of rabbis, not other representatives, this is a further argument that the seven were no mere distributors of poor relief. Jesus laid on hands only for blessing and healing (Mk 10:16; Lk 4:40), not to confer offices (similarly it was not used to make Matthias an apostle, Ac 1:26) D. Daube (*NT and Rabbinic Judaism*, 1956, 236—7) suggests that this was because there could be no second Jesus. Ordination by imposition of hands is the normal practice by 1 Tm 4:14; 2 Tm 1:16.

8—7:1 Stephen's arrest—In the summary of Stephen's **e** activity only miracle-working is mentioned, but the accusations show that he had been teaching too. The mention of Cyreneans both among his followers and among his opponents (11:20; 6:9) suggests that his missionary activity had split his own community (Haenchen p. 220); Hellenists are mentioned also among Paul's opponents at Jerusalem (9:29). It is the Hellenists who arouse the persecution. Ac shows here the definitive break between Christians and Judaism by showing the persecutions mounting to a climax here (warning in 4:17, scourging in 5:40, stoning to death 7:58), by the subsequent scattering of Stephen's followers from Jerusalem (8:1), and especially by reserving until now the accusation of opposition to the Law and that symbol of Judaism, the temple (6:11, 13f). Lk had omitted the charge of threatening to destroy the temple from his account of Jesus' trial (cf Mk 14:55—61), presumably to increase its decisiveness here. The wit- **f** nesses of 6:13 clearly speak the truth, for the chief burden of Stephen's speech is an attack on the temple and its institutions; so their description as 'false' witnesses is either carried over from the account of Jesus' trial in Mk 14:56, or represents the conventional theme—Ps 27 (26):12; 35 (34):11; Prv 14:5—that all persecutors of the just are false. The account underlines that Stephen was acting under divine inspiration by its reference to divine power (1), to the invincible spirit (10—a deliberate allusion to Lk 21:15—and 7:55), and to Stephen's appearance as a messenger from heaven (15). Thus Stephen's arrest and trial are shown to constitute the turning point in the emancipation of Christianity from Jewish law and practices, preparing for its diffusion to the gentiles.

9. An inscription of the 1st cent. A.D. found in Jerusalem **g** relates to the founding of a synagogue by a certain Vettenius. Since his family was presumably freed by the Vettenia family in Rome, the synagogue could conceivably be the synagogue of the Freedmen here mentioned, cf RB 30 (1921) 237—77.

2—53 Stephen's speech—Stephen begins with a peace- **h** ful, neutral account of the history of God's guidance of Israel: **2—7** Abraham, **9—16** Joseph, **17—34** Moses; in vain have commentators searched for some apologetic or polemical link with Stephen's own situation, for he neither replies to the charges made against him nor attacks his opponents. This early part of the speech is akin only to the didactic histories of Israel which occur in the OT, e.g. Ps 105 (104):12—43; Neh 9:7—31. It must depend on some Palestinian tradition, for it shows links with various Palestinian versions of the Bible text in vv 3, 4, 5, 10, 32 (see Wilcox). There is only one phrase, added to the LXX in 27, which hints at the parallel which is to be drawn between the rejection of Moses, the lawgiver of Israel, and the Righteous One (52). Only in **35** does apologetic begin; he points out how Israel rebelled against Moses, God's emissary, (with a clear rhetorical style—5 times the demonstrative 'this' of Moses in three vv—the

828h Christian catchword translated 'refused' in 35, and the
i Christian text—used also 3:22—in 37). In **39–50**
Stephen outlines the story of idolatrous worship in Israel,
from the golden calf (whose lesson is rammed home by a
quotation from the LXX which cannot have been used
before the Sanhedrin) till Solomon's construction of the
temple, against God's will as it was revealed to David.
Thus the accusations against Stephen are substantiated
by his speech; he does indeed attack the temple and the
Jews' attitude to Moses (cf 6:14), maintaining that in
this they are but following their fathers' infidelity. This
attitude of Stephen's can be traced back for the one point
to Christian teaching that Jesus fulfilled the Law of Moses
as the Jews did not (e.g. Mt 5:17–48; Jn 5:45–46), and
for the other to a tendency to reject the temple in favour
of a spiritual worship (Jn 4:21–24; Ac 17:24) attested
also for the Jewish Diaspora (Just. *Dial.* 117,2). Thus,
after the manner of Hellenistic historians (cf § 822*a*–*c*),
at this turning-point in the history of the development
of Christianity, Lk underlines its significance by putting
in Stephen's mouth a speech which, though at least its
earlier part would hardly be apposite in the speaker's
situation, gives the reader a full historical perspective
of the issues at stake: Israel is a stiff-necked people who,
by rejecting Christianity in the person of Stephen, only put
the seal on their age-old rebellion against God's provident
guidance.

829a **7:54–8:3 Stephen's martyrdom and the subsequent
persecution**—The deliberate parallelism between
Stephen's martyrdom and the Crucifixion seems intended
to show both a Christian martyr following his Master (a
trait which is imitated by the later accounts of the
martyrdoms of James and Polycarp), and the Jews of
Jerusalem rejecting their final chance a second time, just
as at the Crucifixion they rejected Christ himself (cf §
821*e*). The Sanhedrin is again moved to action by a vision
of the Son of Man, they again drive their victim outside
the city; just as did Jesus, Stephen forgives his executioners and commends his spirit to God. Haenchen and
Conzelmann, ad loc, detect two distortions by Lk:

b 1. Stephen was really lynched by a mob, for (*a*) The
stoning is not according to the rules laid down in the
Mishnah (SB 2, 685), by which the bound victim is
pushed off a ten foot ledge so that his neck is broken, and
then, if necessary, finished off by a rock being dropped on
his chest by the chief witness. (*b*) A private grave and
mourning were forbidden by law after stoning. (*c*) The
Roman authorities would have interfered, for the
Sanhedrin had no right of execution.

Hence the Sanhedrin had originally no part in the
martyrdom; it was simply introduced by Ac to increase the
solemnity of the occasion, and give the opportunity for
Stephen's speech. But (*a*) Ac's description is merely
vague, not incorrect; it does not exclude the prescriptions of the Mishnah (even if these were already in
force, which is not proved). Some hints make sense only
if the stoning was conducted according to these rules,
e.g. the prominent part played in the execution by the
witnesses at the trial. (*b*) Stephen's burial by 'devout men'
may still have been in a criminals' tomb, as Jesus' probably was (cf § 722*h*). The mourning is yet another sign
of the break between Christianity and Judaic customs.
(*c*) The Sanhedrin may have taken advantage of Pilate's
recall in A.D. 36 to arrogate to itself the right to condemn
to death, as it did during another interregnum in A.D. 62.

c 2. Paul's part in persecuting Christians is exaggerated,
here and elsewhere. In the insertion by Lk in 58*b* (which
made necessary the awkward repetition in 59 of 'they
began to stone him') he is only a 'young man'. Yet in

8:3 he is already leading the persecution. This is a **829**
legendary trait due to a desire to paint him in the
blackest possible colours, in order to make his conversion
appear more wonderful. Paul, it is claimed, would surely
have mentioned his presence here himself. But in fact
the disparity between 7:59 and 8:3 is not fatal. Christ's
reproach in 9:4–5 must have had some foundation. Paul
may not have mentioned his presence here because to
him Stephen's execution was only one among several.

55–56. Various attempts have been made to explain **d**
why Jesus is standing and not, as is usual, sitting at the
right hand of God. He rises to greet Stephen? A subordinationist Christology by which Jesus is only among the
angels who stand before God? (Haenchen) He rises to
pronounce sentence on the Jews? (R. Pesch, *Die Vision
des Stephanus*, 1966). Since there is no emphasis on
his stance Dodd is probably right in saying (*According
to the Scriptures*, 1952, p. 35 n. 1) that the verb translated 'standing' means here only, as often, 'situated'.
For the sense of the vision see note to Mk 14:62. **58.** Luke
binds together his story by introducing characters who
are later to play an important part, e.g. Barnabas 4:36,
John Mark 12:12. **59.** Although the title 'Lord' is not
of itself sufficient to indicate belief in the divinity of
Christ, this is shown by the parallels cf § 678*a*. In other
occurrences of this prayer (Ps 31 (30) 5; Lk 23:46) the
spirit is commended to God.

8:1. 'Except the apostles'; the exception surely includes **e**
their adherents, the Hebrew Christians. 11:19–22 shows
that it was primarily the Hellenists who were persecuted
and scattered; the others continued to live in peace at
Jerusalem, still continuing to attend the temple rites.
The mention of Samaria prepares the second section of
Ac (cf note to 7:58).

4–25. The Mission to Samaria (cf note to 1:8) **f**
follows immediately on the rejection by the Jews of
Jerusalem. Ac presents four scenes: **4–8** a general description of the work of the apostles, showing how they
bring the blessings of the messianic times: harmony,
casting out of devils, healing, joy, as did Christ himself
in the gospel. **5** '*the* city' poses the problem: which city?
(RSV avoids by translating 'a city'); but in fact the Gr.
for 'city' in vv 5, 8, 9, as in Lk 1:39, is a mistranslation
of the Aram. for 'region' (Wilcox). Thus for this section
Lk had an Aram. tradition as a source.

9–13. Simon's conversion is specially mentioned. He
was universally revered by the Samaritans of Justin's
time (mid 2nd cent.; *Apol.* 1, 26, 3) as God, or—as his
title 'great power of God', and his later reputation as
founder of Gnosticism would indicate—an emanation
of God. Hence his conversion is presented as a signal
proof of the impressiveness of the missionaries.

14–17. Since reception of the holy spirit is normally **g**
an immediate consequence or part of baptism (1:5; 2:38;
9:17–19), v 16 indicates that Philip's work was incomplete. Peter and John (who maintains his usual silence, cf
note to 3:1–10) are sent down by the apostles at Jerusalem
to complete it and thereby give apostolic sanction to this
new departure in the mission-field. Since imposition of
hands is not attested as a formal part of baptism before
Tert., we may assume that it is an *ad hoc* gesture to solve
the abnormal situation created by the need to stress the
unity of all mission works under the direction of the
apostles.

18–25. Simon the magician tries to buy (whence
'simony') not Philip's power to heal, but Peter's power
to impart the spirit. Thus he acknowledges that this is
a greater miracle still. Peter curses him roundly in biblical
terms before exhorting him to repentance (RSV 'if possible'

29g is unduly pessimistic; the Gr. has no such doubt of the possibility of his conversion).

h **26—40 Philip baptizes the Ethiopian**—a second story of the spread of the faith beyond Jerusalem. Ac does not represent the Ethiopian as a gentile (this would anyway interfere with the plan of the work § 821*e*); the indications, a pilgrimage to Jerusalem and reading of the scripture, are in the opposite directions. It has been suggested that the Ethiopian must be a gentile (so that this would be the first conversion of a gentile), because (Dt 23:1) a eunuch could not be counted among the chosen people; but the Gr. word can mean also 'a high official'. What then is the significance of the story, and why is the divine guidance stressed at each step (an angel sets Philip on the road, the spirit brings him near at the moment the official happens to be reading a messianic passage, they come to water on this desert road just when it is needed)? Some hold that the story originally constituted the first conversion of a pagan, and that Lk has concealed this for the sake of his plan, but left the divine warrants whose original purpose was to legitimize the step. But, by analogy with the conversion of Samaria, we may see in the story merely the geographical progress of the faith far beyond the reach of the mother-Church of Jerusalem, though still within Judaism, an expansion which required the divine warrant. The story, told with such exquisite art, must stem from the same source as the similar story in Lk 24:13—35; there is the same unexpected appearance of a companion to a traveller preoccupied with religious subjects, the same explanation of the scriptures leading to a deeper understanding of Jesus and a sacrament, the same final disappearance.

i **26.** Ac seems to make no difference between the two ways in which Philip receives divine guidance here and 29, cf note to 5:19. **27.** Candace was not a personal name, but the official title of the queens of the kingdom of Napata (roughly N Sudan). **31.** Lk makes this high official speak a fittingly exalted style of Gr., putting on his lips two classical constructions not commonly used in speech at this time.

32—35. The doctrine taught from this passage of scripture would be that of Christ as the suffering servant of God, as 2:23—31; 3:18, cf § 680*e*.

36—38. O. Cullmann (*Urchristentum und Gottesdienst* 1950[2], p. 27f) points out that this question about impediments to baptism occurs regularly enough (also 10:47; 11:17) to suggest that it formed part of the baptismal ritual of the early Church. It is perhaps from the same source that v 37 has intruded into the text of one manuscript tradition; on the other hand Cullmann prefers to think that it may have been original and have been excluded from most manuscripts precisely because it does not correspond to any known formulary of the second and third centuries.

40. Azotus (ancient and modern Ashdod) is a Jewish port some 20 miles N of Gaza, Caesarea a Gr. port built by Herod the Great some 50 miles further N.

80a **9:1—19*a* The Conversion of Paul**—Paul is to dominate the last part of Ac, and his conversion is related three times, to impress it ineradicably on the reader's mind. The only other event which receives this attention is the conversion of Cornelius, also three times recounted. Both gain their significance in the author's eyes as proofs of the divine warrant for the mission to the gentiles. This is to be described in the latter part of Ac, and the stage is already being set for it. Ac stresses the special divine guidance which intervenes at each stage of this process.

1. It is highly unlikely that the high priest had any legal authority over the Jews of Damascus (Haenchen

p. 268 n. 4 for evidence); these letters are therefore no **830a** more than letters of recommendation, in spite of 22:5. **2.** The 'way' designates the whole Christian way of life, for it is not merely a doctrine, or the community itself; it is used only in Ac, but is not without analogies with the usage at Qumran, where the community's way of life is called 'the right path' (1 QS 8:17ff).

3—9. Since the Jews saw the religious significance **b** of events by constant reference to previous religious history as recounted in the Bible, and represented it in these terms, it is difficult for the modern historian, eager to penetrate to 'what actually happened', to separate the two elements in this highly significant event. What is allusion and what is 'brute fact'? Since the mentality which gives rise to this question would be regarded by the author as impoverished and short-sighted, his account does not readily yield an answer. Whatever actually happened, the two chief types in function of which the author saw the event are the conversion of Heliodorus and the vocation-narratives of the OT. In the former incident (2 Mc 3:24—40) Heliodorus, the persecutor of God's people, is struck down by a shining vision and blinded; he has to be lifted up by his companions, and is converted to the true faith; by the same means Saul is converted from the same enmity to the same obedience. But inserted in this narrative is **c** an account of a divine vocation, whose stylized form recalls e.g. Gn 31:11—13; 46:2—3; 1 Sm 3:4—14 (introduction—double call—divine question—question by visionary—answering self-identification and commission). The effect upon Saul's companions varies in each version given (9.7, 22.9, 26.14); but the details are not to be harmonized, for Lk was well aware that he was providing elegant variations to enliven the thrice-told tale (G. Lohfink, *Paulus vor Damaskus*, 1965, p. 81—85); all the details are different ways of expressing the shock of a divine apparition, cf Dn 10:5—9. Similarly Lk feels himself at liberty to give different accounts of the words of Jesus; in 26:14, before a hellenized audience, a Gr. proverb is added, though the Lord is speaking in Aram., to lend distinction and explain by allusion; but in that account Jesus himself gives the full commission which in the other two versions is received only through the mediation of Ananias (cf note to 10—19*a*). On the other hand all reference to blinding and healing is omitted from the third version. Thus with the help of biblical allusions Lk brings out the significance of the event on the road to Damascus: as were OT persecutors of God's people, so Saul too is struck down and converted by a vision of the Lord, who at the same time calls him for a special mission, as God called the OT patriarchs and prophets. The nature of this mission we have yet to learn.

4. Because of the parallel to the OT vocations we may **d** see here an indication of the divinity of Christ; only God so appears and calls (cf § 823*c*). The v is also a major source for the ecclesiology of Ac, § 823*d*: Christ is present in his members; it is worth remarking that the other evangelists give only blessings for those who help the disciples (Mt 10:40; 18:5 etc), while Lk treats also of those who persecute them (10:16).

10—19*a* The Mission of Ananias—the precise names, **e** Ananias and Judas, show that the author was using a carefully-preserved tradition; but he also employs literary figures to bring out his teaching. Ananias' vision of Paul having a vision (12) presents the motif of a vision within a vision, a way well-known in Hellenistic literature of showing a very special guidance of God (e.g. Pap. Oxyrrh. 2, 1381, 2). The function of Ananias in the story of Paul's conversion (he drops out in ch 26) is to show that Paul's mission as witness before the gentiles as well as the Jews

830e was sanctioned by God's special intervention, but at the hands of the members of the Church. Thus in Lk's view even Paul comes under the line of jurisdiction stemming from the Twelve, who therefore still remain the sole link between the Church and the earthly Christ. Paul's view of the significance of this event was different; he considered the vision to be in the line of the resurrection appearances (1 Cor 15:8—9, whereas for Lk these definitively ended with the Ascension) and to have constituted him an apostle (1 Cor 9:1, a title Lk never gives to Paul, though cf note to 14:14).

f **13—15.** Ananias' nervousness is less to show his hesitation to obey than to emphasize the magnitude of the change which must have come over Paul (cf 21:26). The answer stresses the onerous nature of the missionary task, and the persecution which is always prominent in Lk's thinking (cf 4:1ff; 5:23ff); on 'the name' cf note to 4:7. **18.** The 'scales' are not a pseudo-medical detail, but an indication, by an allusion to Tob 11:12 that the restoration of sight is by divine power.

g **19b—30 Paul in Damascus and Jerusalem**—Lk shows how immediately after his conversion Paul begins his mission of preaching; already at Damascus it is the Jews who, as always (cf § 821e), plot to expel him. This, however, gives him the opportunity of returning to the centre of the mission at Jerusalem (cf note to 1:4) and of making contact with the apostles. The difference of this account from that of Gal 1:17—20 is marked: Ac mentions no stay in Arabia, does not mention the Arabian ethnarch's part in the expulsion from Damascus (2 Cor 11:32), does not give the impression of a three year gap before the visit to Jerusalem, and indicates a longer and more active stay in Jerusalem than the fortnight of private consultation with Peter described in Gal. The simplest explanation is doubtless that Lk had only very sketchy information about this period of Paul's activity. But this is only with difficulty reconcilable with the theory that the author was a companion of Paul's later travels. Alternatively he may have deliberately omitted the mission to Arabia, since he had not yet recounted the legitimation of a mission to the gentiles, and because a mission to Arabia interrupts the movement to Rome. After this omission the Arab's part in Paul's expulsion would seem pointless, and could also be omitted. The presentation of the Jerusalem visit is ruled by the authors' different interests: whereas Lk sets out to show Paul's friendly contact with the mother-Church of Jerusalem (28), Paul himself wishes to stress the independence of his authority from that of the Judeo-Christians; the two aspects, though different, are not incompatible.

h **20.** The title 'Son of God', so typical of Paul's preaching, is used in Ac only here; there is a reference to it, in a sermon by Paul, in 13:33. **21, 26.** The author continues to underline Paul's former ferocity (cf note to 13—15). **23.** This 'many days' could leave room for the three years' gap of Gal 1:18. **27.** There is no particular reason why Barnabas should have had this special rôle, or have had any special contact with Paul. It is really that he was Lk's informant **28** 'went in and out' a biblical formula expressing familiar converse, as 1:21. 'Preaching boldly': for this characteristic of the apostolic teaching see note to 4:13. **29** for the Hellenists see note to 6:1—7; naturally not all became Christians.

i **31—43 Expansion of the Church in Palestine**—After the summary report (cf note to 2:41) of the well-being of the Church in Judea, Galilee (whose evangelization has not been reported) and Samaria, we are given two stories to represent the evangelization of the coastal area W of Jerusalem (hence the optimistic hyperbole of v 35). Thus

the whole of Palestine between Azotus and Caesarea **830c** (8:40), and as far East as the Jordan, has been covered, and it is possible to embark further afield. The two stories show the power of Christ (34) acting in his apostle, as he had promised Jn 14:12. The second particularly was modelled, especially in its original Aram. form, on Christ's miracle in Mk 5:38—41 (mourners, spectators ejected, one letter only changed between 'Talitha, arise' and 'Tabitha, arise', he gives her a hand, he gives her back). There are also firm allusions to the similar miracle worked by Elisha in 2 (4) Kgs 4:32—35 (upper room, turning, opening the eyes). **36.** Dorcas' (her name means 'gazelle') alms-deeds are a particularly Lukan trait; it is a virtue he often recommends (Lk 3:11; 6:30; Ac 10:2, 4, 31).

10:1—11:18 The Conversion of Cornelius—This **831** also, as Paul's conversion, is recounted three times (chh 10, 11, 15); its significance is thereby stressed as the first entry of a gentile into the Church. Thus the actors are moved at each step blindly (1—20), if not positively unwillingly, by the intervention of the Holy Spirit. The acceptance of the gentile into the fellowship of the Spirit is witnessed and acknowledged by a group of Christians in the company of the leader of the apostles himself (21—48), but the mother-Church at Jerusalem also must be persuaded to recognize in this God's warrant to admit all men into the Church (11:1—18), cf § 821e.

1. The name Cornelius was common in the Empire since the mass enfranchisements by L. Cornelius Sulla; his new citizens took his name. The *Cohors II Italica* is attested in the E from at latest A.D. 69 onwards. Roman auxiliary troops were permanently stationed at Caesarea, the Roman capital of Palestine. It is not by chance that the first gentile to be accepted into the Church has these excellent Roman qualifications; Lk is always careful to show the compatibility between Christianity and the Empire (cf § 821e). W. L. Knox (*Acts of the Apostles*, p. 33) suggests that, since many were converted with Cornelius, we may have here the foundation story of the Christian community at Caesarea. **2.** Cornelius is des- **b** cribed as possessing all the virtues of a pious Jew (note especially the Lukan ones of prayer and almsgiving), thoroughly worthy to be received into the community. 'Who feared God' is a technical term, signifying that he was a proselyte. **3—6.** The first intervention of divine instructions, which sets one side in motion, as Peter's vision will the other; its importance is underlined by triple repetition (22, 30—32; 11:13—14). The possibility of illusion is carefully ruled out by 'clearly' and the time of day, mid-afternoon. As Peter in 21 and 23, Cornelius obeys blindly (**7**); God's purpose is not made clear till 44.

9—16 Peter's vision, also underlined by double re- **c** petition (28; 11:5—10), presents certain problems: (1) It is apposite only indirectly, being concerned with unclean food, not unclean races of men. (2) Peter's reaction is illogical (14), for he could legitimately kill and eat at least some of the animals. (3) It remains incomprehensible (17), and must be reinforced by another indication by the spirit to Peter (19—20; 11:12). Thus it plays no organic part either in explaining the situation or in prompting action. (4) It makes the discussion in 15:6—29 superfluous. Hence Dibelius (pp. 109—22) considered that the vision did not originally belong in this context; originally it was connected with the controversy over eating regulations, such as Paul reports at Antioch (Gal 2:11—14); it was awkwardly brought into this connexion by Lk. Lohfink (op cit in note to 9:3—9) points out that this motif of two visions corresponding to each other serves in hellenistic literature to indicate the very special guidance of God.

31c If this view is accepted, then 27—29a also must be regarded as a Lukan insertion into the story, since it refers to the vision; the insertion of these vv also accounts for the double reference to entry into the house (25, 27).

d 34—43 Peter's speech—The opening again points out the importance of the occasion. The speech differs from Peter's other speeches (cf note to 2:22—36 § 825g) in three important points:

(1) There is no exhortation to repentance; this is because the Holy Spirit had already come upon them right at the beginning of (11:15), or at any rate during the speech (10;44; Lk postpones its mention here to avoid breaking in on the speech, and to employ his stylized interruption-motif, cf note to 3:22—26). Some of the audience were in any case already converted (10:23; 11:12).

(2) The usually prominent proof from scripture is reduced to a mere allusion in 43a.

(3) The description of Jesus' earthly ministry is expanded, making the fullest description given anywhere in Ac. It closely resembles Lk's gospel in many respects (U. Wilckens, 'Kerygma und Evangelium bei Lukas', ZNW 49 (1958) 223—37).

Wilckens therefore suggests that Lk gives here a model of Christian preaching not to Jews (as usual, cf § 822a—c) but to Christians. As in the gospel, he presupposes an elementary knowledge ('You know' 36, cf Lk 1:1), but emphasizes two elements stressed equally in the introduction to the gospel: the ordered movement of events (from Galilee to Jerusalem), and the trustworthiness of the apostolic witness. **45.** The Christians, who have in

e fact been brought along as witnesses, do not miss the universal significance of this miracle. Peter points out (11:15) that it exactly parallels the outpouring of the Spirit at Pentecost. The holy Spirit produces the effect of baptism directly, without human intervention (just as at Jesus' baptism according to Lk v 38, cf Lk 3:21)—again the divine initiative (as 3, 9)—Peter could not but recognize it by baptizing them! **47.** For the question about impediments to baptism cf note to 8:36—38; for baptism in the name of Jesus cf note to 2:38.

f 11:1—18 The Jerusalem community confirms the propriety of this new departure. Their attack is represented not as directly against the reception of the gentiles (this was effected by the Spirit itself, so could hardly be queried) but against Peter's mixing with them. It seems they did not yet recognize the full implications of Christian fellowship (cf Gal 2:11—15). Peter answers the Judaeo-Christians with valid rabbinic arguments: visions (5—10, 13—14), a miracle (15), the authority of a rabbi, Jesus (16—17), cf Gerhardsson, p. 231. To enliven this now oft-heard tale, the author makes slight variations; v 14 would hardly be sufficient explanation to anyone who had not heard the story already.

g 19—30 The Founding of the Christian Community at Antioch—After the legitimization of the mission to the gentiles Ac recounts the founding of the first gentile community. Antioch on the Orontes was the fourth greatest city of the empire, the one-time capital of the Seleucid empire, with a large Jewish community among its half-million inhabitants. Its significance was as an ideal centre for the mission to the Hellenistic world, both from its geographical position (with its neighbouring port of Seleucis) and from its cosmopolitan population—witness the plethora of place-names which create the atmosphere of **19—20.** Lk stresses that, as usual, the missionaries preached first to the Jews, but that here for the first time

there was a mission also to the Greeks (the parallelism **831g** excludes the alternative reading 'Hellenists' in **20,** for the Hellenists were a party among the Jews). It was at Antioch that the name 'Christians' was first given (**26**), a momentous recognition that Christianity was not **h** merely a faction within Judaism but a separate entity; it was at Antioch that Christianity must have become conscious of this, and felt free to develop independently of Judaism. The paucity of precise information on such an important foundation and the general character of the report, composed entirely of Lukan theological themes and words, shows that Lk had only general information with which to build, no material for the lively vignettes he loves to give. The reading of the Codex Bezae 'when *we* had come together' in **28** results from a mistaken identification of the Antiochene Lucius of 13:1 with Lukas, the author of Ac. But the author is careful to point out the two-way traffic which bound this first gentile community to the mother-Church at Jerusalem: Barnabas and Agabus come down from Jerusalem (**22, 27**), and the filial affec- **i** tion of the new community leads them even to contribute money to the support of the mother-Church (**29—30**). In fact there must be some confusion here; Paul insists that he made only one journey to Jerusalem before his visit to the 'apostolic council' (Ac 15:2ff; Gal 1:17—20), and this journey has already been mentioned (9:26—29). The journey with the collection was probably in any case the visit to the council, for it was at that date (A.D. 48) that the famine which afflicted many parts of the empire in those years reached its height at Jerusalem (J. Jeremias, 'Sabbatjahr und ntl. Chronologie', ZNW 27 (1928), 98—103), and the community would be most in need. The Antioch community must have been founded long before this. Hence the 'in these days' of **27,** joining the prophecy **j** and its result to the foundation of the community, must be interpreted very elastically; Lk exaggerates the immediacy of the event in favour of his motif of unity between the Churches, cf note to 24:17.

12 The persecution of Herod Agrippa—This grand- **832a** son of Herod the Great, after a misspent youth at Rome, was granted much of his grandfather's territory at the accession of his crony, the Emperor Caligula, in A.D. 37. He was king of Judaea from 41 till his death in 44. Of all the Herods he alone won the friendship of the strict Jews by his careful observance of Jewish law while in Judaea, though his behaviour outside the district was openly pagan. His persecution of Christians to tickle the fancy of the Jews is quite in character.

3—18 Peter's Arrest and Release—The story is **b** delightfully told, with a mixture of reverence and humour quite unlike Lk's usual edifying and serious style. The wonderful character of the unhoped-for release is underlined at each stage: the prayer of the community, Peter's resigned sleep, doubled guards to increase the difficulty, Peter's passivity, the amazement of Rhoda and the community. At the same time the energetic action and detailed instructions of the angel (as if to a sleepy child) and the amusingly startled reaction of the Christians are strongly reminiscent of many later Jewish stories. From all this, three elements stand out as Lk's own: v 11 is wholly Lukan in vocabulary and expression; by a common Lukan turn of style one of the characters speaks information which Lk wishes to convey to the reader; thus Lk points the moral that it is Christ who has freed Peter, and from those permanent persecutors of Ac, the Jews. The other two touches are introductions of characters who are later to play important parts (cf note to 7:58): John Mark (12, cf 25; ch 13) and James (17, cf 15:13; 21:18). Stories of miraculous liberation of prisoners are not rare as proofs

832b of divine favour and protection in antiquity. We have already had one—often considered to be a doublet of this—in 5:19, cf also 16:26—27. **8.** There is nothing in the angel's action to make necessary a physical presence, cf note to 5:19. **12.** For the location of this house see note to 1:13.

c 19—23 The death of the persecutor—The final scene of Agrippa is described in detail by Jos.Ant. 19.8.2.: he appeared in the theatre at Caesarea, for the games in honour of the emperor, clad in a glittering robe which caught the sun's rays, so that the people hailed him as the incarnation of the sun-god—a claim made also by other contemporary oriental monarchs. At this impiety there appeared an owl of ill omen (the Hellenistic equivalent of Ac's biblical destroying 'angel of the Lord'). Within a few days he died of some internal disease, which Ac describes in biblical terms as being 'eaten by worms', the classic death of the persecutor of God's people (2 Mc 9:9). By this his death is seen to be the punishment for his treatment of the Christians. **20.** This affair of a commercial mission from Tyre and Sidon is so condensed from Ac's source that it becomes enigmatic.

d 24—25. This characteristic editorial note by Lk sets the stage for Saul's first missionary journey. The missioners set off direct from Jerusalem, cf note to 1:4. But in fact (cf note to 11:19—30) a journey of Barnabas and Saul to Jerusalem here is the result of a misconception, as P. Benoit, 'La Deuxième Visite de S. Paul à Jérusalem', Bib 40 (1959) 778—92, has shown. **25.** The reading 'to Jerusalem' makes nonsense, unless the Gr. word be taken to mean 'in Jerusalem', as it can in hellenistic Gr., and be taken with the following phrase 'their mission in Jerusalem'. But the word-order would be strained.

13—20. MISSIONARY JOURNEYS

e 13—14 The First Missionary Journey—In the plan of Ac this journey begins the mission to the gentile world, and sets the problem to be resolved in ch 15. Conzelmann holds that Lk had no information about Paul's route, which he constructed arbitrarily, and in fact this journey 'substitutes for the thirteen years of missionary activity of Gal 1:21—2:1' (Conzelmann, p. 72).

f 13:1—3 Barnabas and Saul sent out—The opening of the mission is depicted in all solemnity. The mission is attributed to the initiative of the Spirit, but through the community. It is the Spirit who chooses the missioners (in the list of v 1 they are separated as widely as possible to emphasize that it is the Spirit who joins them); the choice is preceded by fasting, the preparation for a revelation; the Spirit speaks during a solemn liturgy (the LXX word for the solemn temple liturgy is used); the words 'set apart' and 'work' recall the appointment of Levites by the Spirit in Nm 8:11—15. Further fasting and prayer precede the solemn delegation by the community, and the Spirit leads them off (4). But the Spirit works through the community; its charismatic ministers are listed, and it is presumably through one of the prophets that the Spirit speaks. The gesture of laying on of hands constitutes the missioners representatives of the community; it was used in rabbinic Judaism of the ordination of a rabbi by another rabbi, signifying the passing on of his authority, cf note to 8:6. It is fruitless to ask which sacrament was imparted; our seven sacraments had not yet been systematized.

g 1. Menaen, the *'foster-brother'* of Herod Agrippa is commonly supposed to be Lk's source for his information about the Herods, given by his gospel alone. This list of ministers must derive from a source. It is uncertain

whether the prophets are to be distinguished from the **832** doctors.

4—12 Paul and Barnabas in Cyprus—Their journey **h** follows the usual routes. The kernel of Ac's account is the strife before the proconsul, which illustrates various themes: (1) The triumph of Christianity over magical powers, as 8:9ff (Simon Magus), 19:13—17 (exorcism at Ephesus). Magic was rife in late Judaism, and even Jesus himself was accused of it (Mk 3:22). Thus there may be an apologetic motive when Ac describes Christian triumphs over it. It illustrates also Lk's theme of the superiority of Christianity to Judaism (Conzelmann, *Theology . . .* p. 142); the punishment which Elymas receives (11) is that of those who will not obey the voice of God (Dt 28:29). (2) The first man to believe as a result of this missionary journey is a high-ranking Roman; this shows again the favour which Christianity enjoys in the empire (cf note to 10:1 and § 821*e*). Since there is no mention of baptism and since 'believed' (12) does not necessarily imply embracing Christianity we cannot speak of the conversion of the proconsul; but at least he receives the message with favour and reverence. A Paulus, proconsul of Cyprus, is attested by inscriptions (e.g. *Corpus Inscriptionum Graecorum* 2361); as usual Lk is exactly informed about the officials of the places visited. (3) The miracle provides the occasion of bringing Paul **i** to the fore; hitherto Barnabas has always been named first, with the hint that he is the leader cf 13:13; but from now onwards the relationship is reversed (perhaps artificially, for at Lystra Barnabas is called Zeus, the supreme god, but Paul only Hermes, his messenger: 14:12). It is perhaps due to this that Saul's other name Paul is first mentioned here, though this may have other causes as well, the affinity of the name to that of the proconsul, and especially the appropriateness of the Gr. name in the context of the gentile mission. It was common for Jews in the hellenistic world to have also a Gr. name (e.g. Dorcas: 9:36). The name Paulus could have been adopted by Saul's family at receiving Roman citizenship through a Roman general of the same name; but since none of the three Roman families of that name seems to have been active in the East before our period it is unlikely that Paul's family received their citizenship from a Paulus. The name may have been chosen merely because of its similarity in sound to 'Saul' (Sherwin-White, p. 153—4).

13—52 Evangelization of Pisidian Antioch—The **j** journey to Antioch, the capital of Pisidia, is quickly told. Perhaps Lk chooses Antioch as the place at which he presents this example of Paul's teaching to the Jews because of its importance. There was a large Jewish community, settled there by the Seleucid kings as a bulwark against the tribes of the hinterland; it was also a Roman colony. After some initial interest by the Jews, they reject the message of Christ, and merit the first of the three great gestures in which Paul turns from them to the gentiles. **13.** No reason is given for the departure of John Mark, but Lk does not gladly delay over anything which disturbs the harmony of the ideal early days of the community. **14—15.** The synagogue service ended with a sermon preached by one whom the president invited, cf Lk 4:16—17.

16—41 Paul's Sermon—Some elements in this sermon **k** are characteristic of Lk rather than Paul, e.g. the diction throughout, the stress on John the Baptist (24f; he is never mentioned in Paul's letters), the clear distinction between the witness to the resurrection by the apostles and Paul's own preaching (31f; Paul numbers his vision of Christ among the resurrection appearances, 1 Cor 15:8, cf note to Ac 9:10—19*a*). Other elements seem

32k to indicate Paul's thought; his mention of Saul and Benjamin (he was himself of the tribe of Benjamin: Rm 11:1), and the theme of the inability of the Law to justify (39). But Lk could be expected to make some accommodation to his speaker; we do not need to postulate that he had before him notes on the speech (cf § 822a—c). The speech is dominated by the idea that the covenant and promises to David are fulfilled, cf E. Lövestam, *Son and Saviour* (1961).

l **16—25.** The speech begins with a **résumé of Jewish history**, as does Stephen's speech (cf note to 7:2—53); but the point of view is different: it lays special stress on the leaders of Israel, with their climax in David. **16.** The address is to Jews and proselytes, with differing results; it is only the former who are said to reject Christ (45). **20—21.** The figures are not those of the Bible, and no doubt depend on some rabbinic calculation. **22—23.** Only here in the historical part is there a foretaste of the theme of the fulfilment of promises in Jesus. The ambiguous 'raised up' in 22 (cf 3:22), a technical term for the resurrection, hints that David is a type of the Messiah. But his main rôle is as recipient of the messianic promises. **24—25.** John the Baptist is regarded by Lk as belonging to the old dispensation (Conzelmann, *Theology . . .* p. 22—27); here too he is separated from the time of fulfilment by the new address in 26. These two vv may represent polemic against the sect of John the Baptist (cf § 836a), since they so heavily stress his subordinate rôle.

m **26—37.** The centre of the speech is the **proclamation of the age of salvation** (for *schema* see note to 2:22 36). The content is much the same as in Peter's speeches. **27.** But Paul notes that the Jews themselves recognized Jesus' innocence, not Pilate only (as 3:13); the failure to recognize him is not intended to excuse them (cf note to 3:17—21). But the guilt is carefully limited to 'those who live in Jerusalem and their rulers'; the Jews of the Diaspora have, as yet, a clean slate. **30—31.** The contradiction of the crucified Messiah is, as always, explained by reference to the prophecies and appeal to the resurrection, witnessed by the apostles. But since these elements have been fully treated in other earlier speeches, they are only alluded to here. **32.** The 'we' strongly distinguishes Paul from the witnesses of the resurrection (cf note to 16—41); Paul's part is not to witness to the resurrection, but as a missionary to announce the good **n** news that the promises to David are fulfilled. **33 37.** The promises to David (2 Sm 7) are seen, by the constant allusion to them in the OT, to have been always prominent in Jewish thought (e.g. Sir 47:11; 1 Mc 2:57; Lk 1:68—70, cf Ps-Sal 17:4). They were regarded as constituting a permanent covenant, whose blessings, to be given to Israel through the Messiah, would include freedom from assault by their enemies and a world kingdom (cf Col 1:15—20). It is these promises which Paul says are fulfilled, by applying to Jesus the two recognizedly messianic passages Ps 2:7 and Is 55:3. The promises are not to the Messiah only but to his people also (cf ecclesiology). **36—37.** Are to show that the promises were not fulfilled to David himself, for he died; but Jesus rose from the dead, and therefore they are fulfilled in him (cf 2:25—31).

38—41. With an Aram. formula of solemn proclamation (cf note to 2:14) Paul warns his hearers; the threat is almost as if he expects them to fail.

o **42—52 Initial success of the appeal followed by expulsion**—the presence of 'almost the whole city' (a Lukan hyperbole) excites the envy of the Jews at their own failure to attract such crowds. The proselytizing zeal of the Jews is mocked both by Cicero and by Seneca. **832o** Ac will allow them no worthy motive for refusing the message. **45—47.** At three places on his missionary journeys, one each in Asia Minor, Greece and Rome, Paul solemnly turns from the Jews to the gentiles, always described with the same movement: (1) Their resistance is noted (13:45; 18:6a; 28:24); (2) Paul pronounces judgement on the Jews (13:46; 18:6b, 28:25—27); (3) He turns to the gentiles (13:47; 18:7; 28:28) cf J. Gnilka, *Die Verstockung Israels* (1961). On this first occasion he attests his obligation to preach first to the Jews (46), as Ac shows him doing so perseveringly and with such little success. Then he proclaims the universal mission of preaching Christ to all men which was so dear to Lk (cf § 767b). **48—52.** **p** Presents a strong contrast between the joy of the new Christians (48, 52), the spread of the gospel (49), both characteristics of the ideal messianic community (cf notes to Church and 2:41), and the scheming of the Jews. Finally in 51 the missionaries leave the city with the symbolic biblical gesture which Jesus told his disciples to make when their message was rejected.

14:1—7 At Iconium—The stay at Iconium contrasts **833a** markedly with those which precede and follow it, Antioch and Lystra. Lk has no special incident or even name to relate, and therefore gives only the bare bones, the pattern of events which occurred in every place: bold preaching, partial success, opposition aroused by the Jews, and expulsion. The expressions used ('together', 'a great company', 'a long time') are favourites, as well as the theological themes: boldness in preaching, divine confirmation by signs and wonders, division for and against the preachers. Was, then, Lk's information about Iconium no fuller than the tradition contained in 2 Tm 3:11 'what befell me at Antioch, at Iconium, and at Lystra, what persecutions I endured'? **2.** The transition from v 1 is so abrupt that the Codex Bezae, not realizing that we have here only an unadorned skeleton, smooths it with a description of how the opposition arose. **4.** For the appellation of Paul and Barnabas as apostles, contrary to Lk's normal practice, see note to 14: 14. **6.** The mention of Derbe is premature, since 8—18 has still to relate an incident at Lystra, and the move to Derbe is again related in v 20. Therefore Dibelius (p. 21) considers 8—18 to be drawn from a separate source.

8—20 Paul and Barnabas hailed as Gods at **b** **Lystra**—Haenchen considers this incident to be a Lukan composition. The reaction of the people and their priest in hailing the missionaries as gods is out of all proportion to their simple miracle of healing. O'Neill (*Theology of Acts*, 1961, p. 150—1) suggests that Lk is caricaturing the worship of pagan deities, using the myth that Zeus and Hermes appeared in this region (Ovid, *Metamorph.* 8, 611—724), in order to show its absurdity compared with the true religion. But the incident is so curious and uncharacteristic that Lk can hardly have invented it. The missionaries' activity for once does not begin with preaching to the Jews; they seem to have made no further attempt to convert their hearers to Christianity, directing their speech solely to restraining them; Lk does not tell us what the interest of this ludicrous situation is. Dibelius (see previous note) has shown that the incident is inserted from elsewhere into the narrative; but it must be drawn from some local tradition rather than from Lk's own invention. **8—10.** The healing of the lame man has **c** the classical features of a miracle story. Its similarity to the miracle by Peter in 3:2—10 is due to this rather than to any desire to establish a parallel between Peter

833c and Paul. **11.** Paul's initial failure to stop the attempt to worship is explained by his failure to understand their intentions, expressed in the local dialect. But they must have understood his Gr. as well. **12—13.** Haenchen holds that the tradition that Zeus and Hermes visited Phrygia is purely Hellenistic (Ovid), not Phrygian, but without evidence. The two gods do appear together on local monuments (refs in Conzelmann, p. 80). **14.** Only here and in v 4 is the term 'apostle' applied by Ac to Paul; otherwise it is confined to the Twelve. This is one of the major differences between the Pauline and the Lukan points of view (cf notes to 1:20*b*—26 and 8:10—19*a*). Here it presumably slipped in unnoticed from

d Lk's source. **15—17.** A first example of Paul's preaching to the gentiles, of which a complete version is given in 17:22ff. This speech intends only to prevent the sacrifice by showing that one God is over all, not to give the full Christian message. Many of its expressions are taken from Jewish monotheistic propaganda, with which Paul was of course familiar. Especially v 17 is of a fine literary style (with litotes, onomatopoeia and alliteration) quite unfitting for the barbarous Lycaonians. **19—20.** This is no doubt the stoning referred to in 2 Cor 11:25. Ac in no way suggests that his recovery was miraculous.

e **21—28 Return to Antioch**—The story is told entirely in Lukan generalities, which suggests that Lk had no information about the return journey, but had to get the missionaries back to Antioch somehow. Hence Haenchen (p. 377) assumes that Lk had no warrant for introducing the appointment of elders, whom he holds not to have existed in Paul's time, and simply to have been transposed by Lk from Church organization in his own day; but cf § 823*e*. **26—27.** A final reminder of the significance of the journey; from beginning to end it was directed by God, not by man; it was God who had opened to the gentiles the door to faith.

f **15:1—35 The Council of Jerusalem**—This is the turning-point of Ac, almost exactly central in the book, the last appearance of the apostles as a body, the last appearance of Peter; it is a last confirmation of the legitimacy of the mission to the gentiles and of their freedom from the Law, before Paul finally takes the centre of the stage and sets off on the missionary journeys which are to lead him to 'the ends of the earth'. In Lk's mind it is of cardinal importance. The problem of Lk's sources and editorial work has received widely differing solutions. That suggested by BJ (1958[2], p. 135 note c) has won wide acceptance among Catholics: the author joins two different controversies and their decisions, one (presided over by Peter) about obligation of the Law as a whole, the other (presided over by James) about various legal obligations. In favour of this it is argued:

g (1) The origin of the controversy is given twice (v 1, 6) independently. (2) v 6 gives the impression of a meeting of the leaders only, vv 12 and 22 of the whole community. (3) Paul shows no knowledge later of the 'decree' (23—29) though it is here given to him. In Gal 2:6 he insists that no obligations were laid upon the gentiles at this meeting. Therefore the 'decree' must have originated on another occasion. (4) Gal 2:1—10 describes a controversy at Jerusalem about the obligations of gentile Christians towards the Jewish Law, which issues in a guarantee of their freedom. The controversy about relations between Jew and gentile within the Church originates at Antioch (Gal 2:11—14), probably later; but this later controversy must precede the discussion which issues in the 'decree'. Thus to the controversy over circumcision before Peter, reported also in Gal 2:1—10, Lk has joined a decision

made and promulgated on a different occasion under 833 James' presidency, at which Paul was not in reality present.

Haenchen's solution is more radical: he denies all h historical worth to both Council and letter; the former is 'an imaginary construction which does not correspond to any historical reality' (p. 405). His argument is based upon two points: (1) Peter's speech is a Lukan composition without historical worth. It is inconceivable that the community which had made such a fuss about the conversion of Cornelius should so soon have forgotten the principles involved, and need to be reminded of the whole case. In fact it was Lk who made such a major issue out of the Cornelius episode; hence the full reference to it here also is due to his hand. (But this is an argument for, not against, the historicity—if not of Peter's speech—at least of the incident as a whole; if the significance of the Cornelius episode was realized and portrayed only by Lk, the Jerusalem community could still raise objections at least against the general admission of gentiles.) (2) James' speech cannot be authentic. He is represented as speaking Aram., as would be expected (the Aram. form 'Symeon'). But, although 'a people for his name' is a phrase applied to Israel frequently in the Aram. Targum (and only here boldly transferred to the new Israel of the Church), his scriptural argument requires the LXX text 'the rest of men', instead of the MT 'the rest of Edom'; without the Gr. version his whole argument falls to the ground.

Since the whole scene, Haenchen argues, is a fabrica- i tion of Lk's, who loved to express doctrinal points by such lively scenes, there can be no question of the historicity of the apostolic decree. But at least the prohibition of eating blood lasted till the end of the second century (Tert., *Apol.* 9:13), and presumably the other prescriptions were still in force in Lk's day. He therefore thus 'described a living tradition which already in his day was considered to have an apostolic origin' (p. 412).

The explanations of BJ and Haenchen share the conviction that the regulations about common life have no essential historical connexion with the earlier scene; but vv 12—18 is joined by Haenchen to the earlier scene, by BJ to the regulations; Haenchen's division seems preferable. But his scepticism over the historicity of the discussion is excessive; no doubt the speeches come from Lk's pen, but Gal 2 shows that some such discussion, involving Peter and James, took place.

1—5 Introductory—1—2 According to Benoit ('La j deuxième Visite', Bib 40(1959) p. 778) these vv are editorial; originally, before the insertion of chh 12 and 13—14, 15:3 followed 11:27—30. They are also inept, for the controversy then arises twice independently, once at Antioch (which is unlikely) and once in Jerusalem; the emissaries, on the other hand, say no word about the problem whose solution they were sent to ask (2*b*), but only recount the success of their missionary journey (4*b*). The fact that Paul and Barnabas were sent up by the community (2), by no means excludes the version of Gal 2:2 'I went up by revelation', cf Ac 13:1—3. **3.** Haenchen points out that this prepares the ground for the Council: most of those who heard of the conversion of the gentiles were delighted; it was only a minority at Jerusalem who were to object. **5.** The trouble is here stirred up by the Pharisees, not merely 'some men' as at Antioch (v 1). The Pharisees, being the strictest sect, of course put most worth on the exact adherence to the Law. **6—18 Controversy over circumcision**—The whole k community gathers (not just the leaders, as BJ holds, for 'all the assembly' (12) implies a large crowd, and there

33k is no break in the text before then). Peter gives his opinion first, both as head of the apostolic college and as the witness to the divine election of the gentiles and to the divine testimony of the outpouring of the spirit upon them—both references to Cornelius, as the reader will easily perceive, but Peter's audience could hardly divine! The reason which he adds (**10**), that even Jews cannot fulfil the obligations of the Law, must stem from Lk, for it would be an argument for the abolition of the obligations of the Law for Judaeo-Christians too, which would never have occurred to Peter. The missionaries add a further argument (**12**), by recounting the divine approval of their work as shown in signs and wonders, a valid proof according to rabbinic rules. It will be noted that Paul does not push himself forward here, but remains in the background though so much is at stake for him; the decision must be due not to his persuasion but to the will of God. Finally James, the head of the Judaising party himself, clinches the matter with a rabbinic argument from scripture (**13–17**).

l 19–29 Regulations for a *modus vivendi*—Immediately after the decision that gentile converts shall be free of the Law, restrictions are introduced. Is not this both paradoxical and contradictory to Gal 2:6 (as to Ac 21:25, see note ad loc)? In fact these four prescriptions hardly count as a limitation beside the plethora of regulations which make up the Law. Another reason why Paul does not mention them in Gal could be that they are not enjoined as having value in themselves, as did the works of the Law, but only to make a common life possible. These are the four conditions prescribed by the Law as binding on gentiles so that Jews may associate with them (Lv 17:8–18:18) The importance of the ruling to Lk is stressed by its triple repetition (Ac 16:4; 21:25). The Western text adds to vv 20 and 29 the so-called 'Golden Rule': 'and they should not do to others what they do not wish to be done to themselves', thus giving a simple saw which includes much of Christian morality It is, however, wholly out of place in this discussion of points of specifically Jewish Law. It was perhaps added when the purely ritual prescriptions had lost their interest, and some moralizing was thought to be needed. **22.** The solemnity is increased by the letter being not merely sent but carried by publicly elected **m** envoys. **23.** The address to Syria and Cilicia as well as Antioch is not intended as a restriction of the ruling to those areas, as some have held, in an attempt to explain Paul's silence about them to Corinth and Rome (1 Cor 8–10, Rm 14). Rather is it an extension beyond the bounds of Antioch, where the question arose, to the whole of the then Christian world. The Churches of Paul's first missionary journey are not included in the address of the letter, but he nevertheless promulgates the decree to them (16:4). **28.** The letter employs the usual formulae of greeting and farewell, but the now classic formula, 'it has seemed good to the Holy Spirit and to us', would have been a striking change to contemporary readers. Imperial and other decrees often began 'it has seemed good to me and my council'. Lk introduces the Holy Spirit characteristically to stress that the action, as all others in the Church, is directed by the Spirit.

n 30–35. The decree delivered at Antioch—a typically Lukan scene of joy and peace in the community. The source of their joy is obedience to the mother Church. **34** is given only in the Western textual tradition, and is obviously a characteristic attempt to harmonize with v 40, where Silas is still/again in Antioch; but the resultant clash with v 33 is more jarring.

**15:36–20:38 Paul's Great Missionary Journeys 834a
36–41 Preparations and departure**—Ac attributes at least the beginning of the quarrel between Paul and Barnabas to a difference over John Mark (Barnabas' nephew). Haenchen believes this to be a guess, made when the controversy over common meals between Jewish and gentile Christians, in which Barnabas opposed Paul (Gal 2:11–15), had been forgotten; this would constitute an argument for the late date of the book (cf § 822*d*). But there is no evidence that it was Barnabas' weakness on this occasion which caused the definitive break between **b** him and Paul. But we have already seen that Lk tends to play down elements which reflect disharmony between Christians (6:1; 13:13 and notes); he could well have deliberately omitted to record this controversy, which hardly enhances Paul's prestige. It is unlikely that the true nature of the quarrel would have been simply forgotten, either here or in 13:13, for the course of a quarrel is remembered far more easily than its place. As it is, Lk is careful to point out that the Church suffered no loss from the division, but rather gained, for Barnabas and Mark worked in Cyprus, while Paul went to other fields at the same time.

16:1–5 Derbe and Lystra: Timothy circumcised— c Here the faithful companion of Paul appears for the first time, though he is already a Christian, presumably converted on Paul's first journey. That he should be circumcised at this stage has puzzled commentators. Some hold the story for a fabrication, others for a confused memory of Titus' circumcision (Gal 2:3—Titus is never mentioned by Ac). One solution is that it was merely to make Timothy acceptable in the synagogues; by Jewish law the son of a Jewish mother is a Jew, and so bound to circumcision. But if circumcision had no longer any religious significance in Paul's eyes would this not be hypocrisy? On the whole question of Paul's Jewish observance according to Ac see note to 21:15–26.

6 10 Asia Minor: Divine Intervention—Ac tells **d** little of the long journey between Lystra and Troas. Paul must have engaged in some missionary activity in the course of it, for it must have been now that he founded the communities in Galatia (which already exist in 18:23), where he was also delayed by an illness (Gal 4:13). But all this is omitted to avoid distraction from Lk's main point: that Paul was led westwards to Greece by the direct guidance of God, blindly or even against his own plans. The triple divine intervention (vv 6, 7, 9) recalls that granted to Peter at another critical moment in the expansion of Christianity (10:9–20). Lk realizes the significance for all subsequent history of the Church of this first move from Asia into Europe. **10.** The first appearance of 'we' in the narration, starting the first of four passages in Ac narrated in the first person plural, as though the author had been present. For the question whether this indicates a different source, see § 821*b*.

11–40 Philippi: Suffering and Success—The ac- **e** count of the stay at Philippi is composed of highly diverse materials. Vv 11–15, 19–24, 35–40 present the familiar story: preaching, conversion, opposition, expulsion; with this thread are interwoven two others: the driving out of a spirit (16–18), and the miraculous liberation and the conversion of the gaoler (25–34), which are of a very different stamp. We shall treat these successively.

Narrative—The itinerary (cf § 821*b*) provides **f** much factual information about the journey, places visited, and hosts in each place. As always, the details of cities and constitution are exactly accurate. **12.** Philippi was

834f 'the leading city of the *first* district of Macedon', for Macedon was divided into four numbered administrative districts. In origin it was a colony of Roman veterans, governed by *duoviri* (Sherwin-White p. 92—95). **13.** The missionaries do not seem to have made contact with the Jews before the sabbath, or they would know about the place of prayer. **14.** Lydia was so called because she came from the region of Lydia, in which Thyatira, famed for its purple-dyers, lies. Since purple is an expensive commodity she must have been a woman of moderate wealth. Paul's acceptance of her hospitality was the beginning of the special bond which he felt towards the

g community at Philippi (Phil 4:14—19). **19—21.** The first clash between Paul and the Roman authorities. The accusers cannot of course bring before the magistrates the charge of expelling a spirit (so that the details of this incident remain irrelevant to the trial), but bring two charges, creating a disturbance and proselytizing. Theoretically a Roman citizen was forbidden to practise an alien cult not publicly sanctioned, but in fact many Roman citizens were proselytes, and a blind eye was usually turned to this. Sherwin-White suggests (p. 81) that the partial success of the accusation in this case may be connected with the recent discouragement of proselytizing by the emperor Claudius (cf 18:2). **22—24.** Roman magistrates had powers of inflicting minor punishments on non-citizens by summary jurisdiction. But this power was not extended to cover untried Roman citizens until a later data; at this date (though not for long afterwards) citizenship was still significant enough to make the magistrates tremble at the maltreatment of a citizen (38). **35—40.** The power of magistrates to expel undesirables is not otherwise attested till much later, but a provincial governor already possessed the corresponding power (Sherwin-White p. 77). Presumably the magistrates did not consider the case worth further proceedings. By this (modified) expulsion the incident at Philippi is closed, with no allusion to the other two episodes; only the gaoler's specifically Christian farewell 'Go in peace' shows that he has been converted.

h 16—18 Driving out the spirit—The story has considerable affinity with many similar stories in the synoptic gospels. The base motives for bringing the charges against Paul do much to overshadow the fact, unpalatable to Lk (cf § 821*e*), that Paul came into vigorous conflict with the Roman authorities.

i 25—34 Miraculous liberation from prison and conversion of the gaoler—The kernel of this story is the conversion by Paul of his gaoler. Some details are conventional ways of expressing divine protection of God's witnesses under persecution and the triumph of God's message even through persecution. A miraculous liberation from prison is a commonplace of Hellenistic literature (already twice in Ac, 5:19; 12:6ff), and an earthquake, a conventional manifestation of God's presence, especially in answer to prayer (cf 4:31 and note there). In addition

j there are some surprising features. It is odd that the gaoler does not even look to see if the prisoners are still there before deciding on suicide (though he would hardly be held responsible for the consequences of an earthquake). How did Paul perceive his resolve from the 'inner prison'? Further, his submission to Paul and instruction is, at best, foreshortened (between prison and house, meeting his household somewhere on the way). The silence over the events of this unquiet night in the sober record of the morning's activity is strange. These inconsistencies in the story and the conventional motifs are typical of the stories of folklore, handed down by popular repetition, and not diminishing in the telling—a wholly

different genre from the exact historical recording which **83** provides the narrative framework. A real incident has been described in a highly literary manner. But at the base of the story is the evidence of God's protection of his own, seen in the unexpected, sudden release of the prisoners, and the marvellous conversion of their gaoler.

17:1—9 Thessalonica: Persecution from the Jews— **83** Paul continues along the Roman trunk road, the Via Egnatia, to Thessalonica, the most important harbour town of the coast, then as now, in its sheltered gulf. **1—2** Thes show that he must have stayed far longer than the three weeks mentioned before the opposition began (2), for time would be required to instruct them, especially since Paul and presumably his companions were earning their keep at the same time (1 Thes 2:9), whence he preaches only on the Sabbath, a workless day. Phil 4:16 states that the Philippians sent him financial help several times during his stay in Thessalonica; such journeys, and the collections required beforehand, would not be made every week. But Lk is interested only in the pattern of preaching, conversion, opposition, expulsion, and generally neglects such commonplace matters as total length of stay or how Paul supported himself. **3. b** The explanation from the scriptures of the paradox in Jewish eyes that the Messiah must suffer is the theme of all preaching to the Jews (Lk 24:26f, 45f; Ac 8:32—35; 2:25—31 and note and § 680*a—e*). It was presumably through such preaching that the evangelical passion narratives, heavy with scriptural allusions, came into being. But in this case, as in the case of Jesus' own teaching, it was not sufficient to rule out the accusation (vv 6—7) of preaching a political Messiah, a king to rival Caesar, according to the current Jewish Messianic hope which Jesus so carefully corrected (cf § 651*a—c*). **4.** Lk is always careful to point out the dignity of those who embrace Christianity; Christianity was not exclusively the religion of slaves (also v 17, cf 2:47 and § 821*e*). He seems to be personally sensitive on the matter of social standing (Lk 14:10; 16:3; 23:50). **5.** The identity of this Jason is unknown; it was the Gr. name often assumed by Jews called Joshua, on account of its similar sound. **6—7.** As at Jesus' own trial the charge brought before the magistrates (as always Ac gives them the correct title) must be a political one, though motivated by religious grounds.

10—15 At Beroea—The same pattern of events repeats itself, save that initially the Jews show themselves to be more open-minded.

16—34 Paul at Athens—Some commentators remark **c** how lifelike and realistic is this episode; others, as A. D. Nock (Gnomon, 25 (1953) 506): 'it makes on me the impression of being based on literature rather than personal experience'. Paul's attitude on his arrival at Corinth (1 Cor 2:1—5) is certainly consonant with an immediately preceding unsuccessful attempt to translate the message of Christ into terms intelligible to the educated pagan. But Lk also used the opportunity of Paul's visit to the centre of Gr. wisdom, still basking in its old intellectual glory though now rather dowdy materially, to stage a grand confrontation between the gospel and the wisdom of the Greeks. The features he mentions at Athens are all ones well-known in the ancient world: their intellectual curiosity (19—21) and religiosity (22), the rival philosophical parties of Epicureans and Stoics (18), the disputing with passers-by in the market place (17), and the court of the Areopagus (19), now shorn of its former power but still possessed of some degree of influence. All these are mentioned to create an atmosphere for the speech—the last two providing a

35c delicate parallel to the trial of Socrates—so that it is idle to probe into the exact meaning of 'Areopagus' here (hill or court or committee?) and its location.

d 22–31 Paul's speech—The main burden is a demonstration that all the attributes of divinity which the Greeks recognize in fact belong to the living God. They therefore worship him all the time without knowing it. This is a favourite theme with Jewish apologists and propagandists vis-à-vis Hellenistic religion. Philo and Josephus also take passages and ideas from classical authors to show that in fact the Greeks adhere to the true faith and recognize what the Jews too value. Paul's skill in this is rewarded by the uncomplimentary epithet translated (18) 'babbler', which is used of 'a fellow who picks up scraps everywhere and parades them as his own' (Gärtner, p. 48). In the speech itself, though the ideas are drawn from the OT and Jewish apologetic, (cf W. Nauck, 'Tradition und Komposition in der Areopag-rede', *Zeitschrift für Theologie und Kirche* 55 (1956) 11–52), the terms and expressions used lend them the colouring of Gr. philosophy. The same schema, drawn from Jewish apologetic, is used also in Rm 1:18ff, q.v. **22–23.** Paul takes as his point of departure one of the many dedicatory altars which lined the roads. Commentators delight in remarking that, while many dedications 'to the unknown gods' are known, none has yet been found in the Gr. word in the singular; no doubt the change was made to fit the speaker's monotheistic purpose.

e 24–26. The universalism of God's rule pervades the speech (note the frequency of 'all' and 'every'). It is he who is responsible for the spread of peoples and for all history, cf Gn 1:28. This universalism permits a polemic against temples and sacrifices—an attack never made in Jewish literature, but introduced as a Christian theme by Stephen's speech (7:48–50); thus the speech is not entirely modelled on the lines of Jewish

f propaganda. **27–28.** The idea that even the pagans seek and hope to find God is a theme of Jewish apologetic (Wis 13:6; Philo, *Spec. Leg.* 1, 36), recommended to the audience by the reference to a Gr. author, probably Dio Chrysostom. The pessimism of 'in the hope that they might feel after him' (the verb means 'stumble like the blind') is close to that of Paul on the gentiles' lack of success in finding God (Rm 1). The following statement (28*b*), justified by the quotation from Aratus (which had already been used by the Jewish apologist Aristobulus: Eusebius, *Praep. Evang.* 13, 12, 3), must therefore be taken as a statement of the state of affairs as it should be, precluding from sin and the consequent need of redemption before union to God in Christ can be achieved. It is not equivalent to the statements in Paul about the Christian's life in Christ (Gal 2:20; Phil 1:21). **29.** A further polemic against idolatry: as our father, God is a living God, and so cannot be found in lifeless matter. This is reinforced by a quotation from Aratus, used already by the Jewish apologist Aristobulus (apud

g Eusebius, *Praep. Evang.* 13:12:3). **30–31.** Finally Paul introduces the familiar motifs of repentance, judgement and resurrection (cf 2:33, 38; 3:19–21, etc). The speech closes with a reference to ignorance, as it began with one to the unknown god—only one of the literary artifices of which it is full. It is often argued (e.g. Haenchen p. 463) that the leniency of **30** is un-Pauline: in Rm 1:20 he says the pagans are 'without excuse' for their failure to recognize God, while here God is willing to 'overlook' their ignorance. But Gärtner p. 246 shows that the word used for 'ignorance' here always implies guilt; and there is also the call to repentance to escape judgement. It is the doctrine of the resurrection which

makes the objections of the audience break out. They had **835g** realized that Paul preached 'Jesus and Resurrection' (18), but had probably taken this to be a pair of divinities, since the word is feminine, and gods often went in pairs. Though the immortality of the soul was commonly enough held, this was considered to consist precisely in liberation from the bonds of the flesh, so that the resurrection of the whole man seemed an absurdity. The stress on the resurrection and silence on the redemptive value of Christ's death are characteristic of the theology of Ac. There is certainly a difference of emphasis here from Paul's thought (cf § 822*bc*). **34.** The narrative takes up the thread again, with the customary notice of success, which was slight, though one of the converts is of high standing (cf note to v 4). Later legend made him first bishop of Athens, but in reality nothing more is known of him.

18:1–17 At Corinth—The Greek city of Corinth was **h** destroyed by the Romans in 146 B.C., but refounded as a Roman colony a century later by Julius Caesar. Due to its position on the isthmus, whose crossing avoided the dangerous sea voyage round the Peloponnese, it quickly rose again to be a flourishing commercial centre with a cosmopolitan population and a correspondingly lurid reputation. It was also the seat of the Roman governor of the province of Achaea. Thus it is not by chance that Ac records here the second of the three great gestures of turning from the Jews to the gentiles (6 7, cf note there) at Corinth, and that it forms the furthest point of expansion on the second missionary journey. It was a significant stage on the road to Rome. The story is told in a *crescendo*. First Paul works at his trade during the week, preaching to the Jews on the Sabbath only (3–4). When his companions arrive with funds from Macedonia (2 Cor 11:9) he is freed to preach continuously, which occasions the clash which issues in conflict (5–6). He then moves house, has considerable success, and receives a vision of encouragement (7–11). Finally the Jews attempt to prosecute him, but he emerges victorious and they discomfited (12–17), so that Paul stays some time longer and departs at his leisure. **2.** Some Jews **i** were, according to Suetonius also (*Vita Claudii* 25), expelled from Rome in A.D. 49/50 for causing disturbances 'at the instigation of Chrestus'. The measure cannot have been very energetic, for there is no gap in the archaeological evidence for the Jews at Rome, and even Aquila and Priscilla are soon found again in Rome (Rm 16:3). Lk uses 'all' very freely. Suetonius' notice shows that Christianity played a part in the expulsion, and Aquila and Priscilla were probably already Christians at Paul's arrival, since he did not baptize them (1 Cor 1:14), and yet they are leading a missionary effort soon afterwards (Ac 18:26); they later headed a congregation at Ephesus (1 Cor 16:19). It is not impossible that their expulsion from Rome was due to disturbances consequent on their active apostolate. **3.** Paul habitually earned his keep (1 Thes 2:9). He was by profession rather a '*leather worker*' than a 'tentmaker', cf Jeremias ZNW 30 (1931) 299. **6.** The solemn turning from **j** the Jews of Greece to the gentiles proceeds by the three steps noted at 13:45–47. Here the solemnity is lent not, as in the other two occasions, by a quotation, but by the biblical terms of the description. **8.** Crispus' title (as Sosthenes', v 17) means only that he had an honoured position, for it could be conferred on many members of the same community, and even on children. But his conversion seems to have been most influential; Paul baptized him personally (1 Cor 1:14). The conversion of one of the chief Jews after the account of the definitive

835j break with the Jews in v 6 suggests that the dramatic *crescendo* analysed above is somewhat artificial; it serves Lk's theme of 'no progress for Christianity

k within the bosom of Judaism' cf § 821*e*. **9–10.** The Lord Jesus encourages Paul in the terms in which the Lord God encourages his messengers, Isaiah (Is 41:10) and Jeremiah (Jer 1:8). **12.** Gallio's proconsulship provides us with the only certain date in Paul's career. An inscription at Delphi (CIL 3.1977) shows that at some time between January and August 52 he was in office. The year of office began in April (Dio Cassius 60.17.3), but the hypochondriac Gallio left Corinth as soon as the summer heats and consequent danger of fever began (Seneca, Ep. 104:1). Therefore this incident must have occurred in spring 52. But we do not know at what moment in Paul's year and a half at Corinth (11) it

l occurred. **13.** The Jews try to bring the same charge as at Philippi (cf note to 16:19–21). But Gallio deliberately interprets their charge as referring not to 'the (i.e. the Roman) law' (12) but to 'your own (i.e. the Jewish) law' (15), and refuses to take cognizance of the case (using the legal formula). His reply is usually taken to imply that the Jews had some internal jurisdiction recognized by Rome; but, apart from the special case of the Jewish community at Alexandria, this is not attested. **17.** It is uncertain to whom 'they' refers; was it the Jews or the Romans who beat Sosthenes? If the former, they were asserting their right to internal jurisdiction (Sherwin-White p. 101–4)—rather pointlessly since Gallio had just admitted it. If the latter, they were showing the depths of their anti-Semitism, or Lk is stressing the low opinion Romans have of Jews, especially those who stir up trouble for Christians.

m 18–23 Second to Third Journeys—A highly condensed section of travel notes. **18.** It is possible that Paul sailed for Syria via Ephesus because Priscilla and Aquila were now moving house to Ephesus (where they are in 1 Cor 16:19), and took Paul with them, perhaps paying his journey. The ceremony at Cenchreae, the E port of Corinth, is wholly enigmatic, for, on the supposition that the vow mentioned is that of the Nazirate, such hair-cutting could be done only at Jerusalem. It is conceivable either that he was now cutting his hair before undertaking the vow (which included leaving the hair uncut until it was absolved), or that the vow in question was a private vow; but both of these practices are unattested. BJ (p. 163 note a) suggests that there is some confusion with the end of the third voyage (21:26), Haenchen (p. 482) that Lk invented the vow to show Paul's Jewish piety. But the note gives the impression of being taken over from a source without much emphasis or understanding. In any case the vow must be somehow connected with the successful conclusion of the journey.

n 19–21. Ac is anxious to show that it was Paul who founded the Church at Ephesus, by at least a token appearance. However at any rate by his return there is some sort of Christianity established (cf 19:1–7). **22.** Before returning to base at Antioch, whence he started out (15:35), Paul pays his respects to the mother-Church at Jerusalem (cf note to 1:4); 'went up' is a Jewish technical term for the pilgrimage to Jerusalem. **23.** The third missionary journey opens with a summary notice; the author is hurrying on to Ephesus.

o 24–28 Apollos—In all but vv 25*c*–26 Apollos appears as a successful and independent missionary. It is thus also that he appears in 1 Cor 3:4–4:6, where he seems to have delivered at Corinth a teaching over and above that of Paul, of which (quite apart from the dissensions it aroused) Paul is suspicious; it is too much associated

with worldly wisdom for Paul, as one might have expected **83** of this cultured man from the centre of Hellenistic learning which Alexandria was. It is for these qualities that Apollos is considered by some to be the probable author of Heb (q.v.). But with the 'instructed in the way of the Lord' and 'taught accurately' of 25*ab*, the limitations noted, and made up by Aquila and Priscilla, (25*c*–26) are oddly at variance. Especially strange is that he is called 'fervent in the Spirit' though knowing only the baptism of John, when in 19:1–6 the Spirit seems to be precisely the element lacking from those who were baptized only with John's baptism. v 26 is intended to show that even Apollos owed something, albeit indirectly through Aquila and Priscilla, to the teaching of Paul, the hero of Ac; but it could be that on the details there is some contamination from the next incident.

19:1–7 The disciples of John—The continued **83** existence of disciples of John is suggested also by a careful devaluation of the Baptist's rôle by several passages of the gospels, which may therefore have a polemical intention, e.g. Lk 3:21 etc (in Lk John is nowhere said to have baptized Jesus, but rather disappears from the scene before his baptism), Jn 1:8 (the traditional connexion of John with Ephesus may be significant in connexion with our passage), Ac 1:5. All this suggests that the disciples of John formed a sect which rivalled Christianity. Our passage represents them less as rivals than as retarded Christians, who are lacking in the fullness of Christianity, notably the knowledge and gift of the spirit. Paul remedies this deficiency. Thus, as in the case of Apollos (cf note above) we see how Paul's influence extends to all Christianity in these regions (cf also note to 18:19–21). **4.** John's baptism **b** was only a baptism of repentance, preparing the people for the dawning of the messianic era, cf § 749*c*.

8–10 Mission in Ephesus—Ephesus, a rich and beautiful city, was the political capital of the Roman province of Asia; hence Paul stayed here over two years. Ac sketches in the usual pattern of rejection by the Jews and turning to the gentiles, but gives only a summary notice (10*b*) to the widespread missions for which Ephesus formed a centre. He passes over in silence both the danger which Paul underwent during this period (1 Cor 15:32; 2 Cor 1:8–10) and the dissensions at Corinth with which Paul had to deal now (2 Cor), cf life of Paul. **9.** In taking this lecture hall Paul models his teaching method on that of wandering philosophers. The W text adds that he preached between 11 a.m. and 4 p.m., i.e. during the siesta period, when he and other workers were free.

11–12 Paul's miracles—Such a miracle of healing is **c** told of Jesus also (Mk 5:27–31) and similar ones of Peter (Ac 5:15). For Paul, miracle-working is only one of the signs of the presence of the Spirit.

13–17 Paul's imitators discomfited—The contrast between Paul's success and the failure of his Jewish imitators brings even greater honour to him and shame to them. Jesus himself did not forbid others to cast out devils in his name (Mk 9:38), and even a pagan magical papyrus has been found in which Jesus' name is used (PG 4, 3019f). **14.** No high priest named Sceva existed; either the Western text's 'priest' is to be preferred to 'high priest' (but *lectio difficilior potior*), or he was merely a member of a high-priestly family. In any case the high position of his sons makes their failure all the more significant.

18–20 Magical Books—Ephesus was famed for its **d** magic formularies, so much so that 'Ephesine writings' was a common name for any magical formularies. Hence it is all the more striking that, at the very centre of magic,

36d they should be destroyed. Since a 'piece of silver' is a day's wage for a labourer (Mt 20:2), fifty thousand is a vast sum. These and other details may be embellishment, cf § 642a.

21—22 Paul's Plans—They are mentioned here to show that Paul already had a journey in mind and was not forced to leave Ephesus against his will. Ac gives no indication of the purpose of Paul's journey to Jerusalem, which was to deliver the collection made by the communities of Greece to supply the needs of the mother-Church—a surprising omission, cf note to 24:17. Paul's intention to go to Rome, mentioned for the first time now, is corroborated by Rm 1:10, written not long after this.

e 23—40 The Silversmiths' Demonstration—This final scene of Paul's stay at Ephesus is treated by Haenchen (p. 511—14) as an apologetic invention of Lk's to show the impact of Christianity, which threatened even so influential a cult as that of Artemis of Ephesus, the respectability of Paul, who is a friend even of such important officials as the Asiarchs, and the triumph of Christianity, which remains unhurt while the demonstrators eventually disperse in cowed submission. All these motifs are indeed present, but do not prove that Lk invented the scene. The historical details are too exact to be the invention of a later writer (Sherwin-White p. 85). Perhaps 'the city was filled with confusion' (29) need not be taken too literally; they seem to quieten down easily enough when the authorities take a hand.

f 24. Artemis of the Ephesians was a goddess of fertility whose cult was one of the greatest in the Hellenistic world; her shrine was one of the major monetary banks of the East. She is entitled on inscriptions 'the great goddess', as in 27. Pottery models of her temple, brought back by pilgrims, have been found in many places, but none in silver, for the metal is too precious to escape rapacious hands. The manufacture of them must indeed have been lucrative. A 1st cent. inscription (*Brit. Mus. Anc. Gr. Inscr.*, 2.578) mentions a Demetrius at Ephesus, the overseer of the fabric of the temple; but it was a common name, and need not be the same man. **26.** Paul's preaching has affected all Asia, cf note to vv 8—10. The theme attributed to him corresponds exactly to that preached in 17:29.

g Perhaps the words are Lk's. **29.** The great theatre at Ephesus, with a capacity for 24,000 men, was the regular meeting place of the popular assembly (OGIS 480,9), but the Town Clerk will not recognize this demonstration as a legitimate assembly (39). It is certainly odd that Demetrius, the original organizer, simply disappears from the scene (Haenchen p. 511); perhaps he thought this demonstration would be sufficient to induce the authorities to act. **30.** Paul saw an unsurpassed opportunity of bearing witness to Christ. **31.** The Asiarchs were 'the annual presidents, and perhaps the ex-presidents, of the provincial council of Asia' (Sherwin-White p. 90); thus Paul had friends in very high places. **33—34.** Alexander's intention is matter for conjecture; perhaps he wanted to explain that the Christians, not all the Jews, were responsible; but the anti-Semitic prejudices of the Ephesians (cf Jos.Ant. xiv, 10, 25) were too strong.

h 35—41. 'Town clerk' is the title enjoyed by the chief magistrate at Ephesus. He affirms that the cult of Artemis is far too famous and sacred to be in danger, and (40) that this unruly demonstration will only excite the wrath of the Roman authorities. At this date the public assemblies of the Gr. cities were fast being deprived of their constitutional powers by the Romans, due to their irresponsibility. The 'sacred stone' is presumably a meteorite, whose celestial origin often earned them veneration in the ancient world. **38.** He 'refers the disputants either to the proconsular assizes, if they have a private judicial dispute, or to the regular assembly of the city, if they are after something more than a private lawsuit' (Sherwin-White p. 83).

20:1—6 Visit of inspection in Europe—Paul makes a **837a** final visit to strengthen his communities in Macedon and Greece (in the course of which, at Corinth, he wrote Rm). Names are not mentioned and the report is summary (Dibelius, p. 178) in order not to distract attention from the pressing movement towards Jerusalem and Rome. **4.** The companions mentioned are perhaps the delegates of the various communities who are bringing their contributions to Jerusalem for the collection over which Ac is so strangely silent (cf note to 24:17); the list is limited to 7 names as the perfect number, but this does not imply that there were only 7 cities represented. **6.** The second of the four passages in the first person plural (cf note to 16:10) begins here, according to Haenchen, because the author wishes to draw attention to the group travelling together, taking his spotlight off Paul, but cf § 821b.

7—12 The raising of Eutychus—Paul's sermon was so **h** long because he was taking leave of them, cf 18—35. His way of raising the dead man is modelled on that of Elijah (1 (3) Kgs 17:21) and Elisha (2 (4) Kgs 4:34), and his reassurance on Jesus' in Mk 5:39. The similarity to Peter's raising of Tabitha (Ac 9:39—41) is not pronounced; there is no intention to build a parallel between the two events, rather it is a farewell-miracle, a final encouragement as Paul goes off to Jerusalem and captivity. **7.** The celebration of the Eucharist on a Sunday at this early date is suggested also by 1 Cor 16:2.

13—16 Journey to Miletus—A plain record, apart from **c** the reason given for not visiting Ephesus, which gives only one aspect of the matter: fetching the elders from Ephesus to Miletus would mean at least three days' delay; another motive for not putting in to Ephesus would be the desire to avoid needless danger and perhaps the delay of imprisonment (cf 19:23—40; 1 Cor 15:32; 2 Cor 1:8—10).

17—38 Paul's farewell—The speech is Paul's fare- **d** well not only to the elders of Ephesus, but through them to the whole of his own mission-field and to his free apostolate. It forms a spiritual testament, corresponding to a well-defined biblical and Jewish literary model. It is very close in spirit to the Pastoral Epistles, giving us a portrait of Paul as the great Church leader, model of future pastors. Paul presents himself as a model also (1 Cor 4:16; Gal 4:12). The speech may be divided up either formally, by the 'and now's of vv 22, 25, 32 (Haenchen p. 527), or, better, according to content (Conzelmann, *Apg*, p. 117). For its authenticity, see § 822a-c.

18—21 Personal apologia—A summary of past **e** conduct is a regular element in such farewell speeches (e.g. 1 Sm 12:2—5; *Test. XII Patr.*). Paul stresses the virtues of the apostle, service and steadfastness in trials, as well as the element so prominent in Ac: opposition of the Jews. **20** hints at a theme which is underlying throughout (26—27, 29—31): Paul has done everything possible to inculcate the Christian message, so cannot be held responsible for the errors which will spring up (cf, in this type of speech, Jn 17:4—15; *Test. Joseph* 20:1, and also 1—2 Tm, Ti passim). Such errors in the Churches of Asia appear already in Apoc 1—3; Lk was presumably aware of them.

22—27 Paul's own future trials—He must be refer- **f** ring to warnings given through the prophets in each

837f community (cf 1 Cor 12:10). He acknowledges that persecution is the lot of an apostle, cf Phil 1:21—23; 2:17. Ac does not recount Paul's martyrdom, but, as Dibelius says (p. 136) 'here, in a way, puts the martyr's crown upon his head'. It is hard to reconcile this certainty and the definitiveness of the parting (35) with the historical data of the Pastoral Epistles, that Paul returned to Asia Minor after being released from a first captivity in Rome, but cf note to 28:30—31.

g **28—31 Exhortation**—Paul charges the elders who are to take his place as pastors using the biblical metaphor for a ruler, underlining their appointment by the Holy Spirit, cf § 823*d—f*. The warning against wolves (cf Mt 7:15) is felicitous after the metaphor of pastors, but similar warnings are a feature of farewell speeches. The Gr. for 'guardians', *'episkopos'*, has not yet the technical sense of 'bishop', for many are envisaged in the same community.

h **32—35 Testament and blessing**—This section especially is couched in biblical terms: the blessing Paul gives them is inspired by Jr 12:14—16; the attestation that he has not used his ministry for profit follows 1 Sm 12:3 (but also see Ac 18:3; 2 Cor 11:7—9; and contrast, for false teachers, Ti 1:11). **35.** Paul shows his fidelity to his Master by ending with a logion of the Lord. In fact this logion is not found *totidem verbis* in the gospels; though a wholly Christian sentiment, the verbal parallels to it begin with Thucydides 2, 94, 4, and are common in contemporary pagan philosophers. Lk puts another such pagan logion in the Lord's mouth in 26:14c.

21—28. ARREST AND IMPRISONMENT

838a **21:1—14 Journey to Caesarea**—This section is full of the presage of Paul's coming arrest. Lk uses his data to form a dramatic *crescendo*. At Tyre the disciples try to dissuade him (4—their knowledge is 'through the Spirit'; Ac does not intend to convey that their dissuasion is a divine order; it merely shows Paul's steadfastness) and bid him a solemn farewell; as yet Paul makes no comment. We may surmise what Philip's daughters prophesied (9), but Ac withholds the climax until after Agabus' prophetic gesture (10—11). Only then does Paul proclaim his willingness to suffer for Christ (13). The parallel with Christ himself is marked: the same knowledge of future suffering, the same action of the Jews in delivering him up to the gentiles (somewhat forced, for the Romans rather rescue Paul from the Jews), the same words to express acceptance as Christ uses on the Mount of Olives (Lk 22:42). **8.** Philip the deacon arrived at Caesarea in 8:40; it may have been on the visit here related that Lk learnt about the events of 8:26—40. **10—11.** Agabus prophesied also in 11:28. His mime here recalls the prophetic actions of Jeremiah (Jer 13:1—11) and Ezekiel (Ezek 4).

b **15—26 Reception at Jerusalem**—A shadow is cast over Paul's reception by the community by rumours that he has preached apostasy to the Jews; he is required to show that he recognizes the value of Judaic practices by purifying himself and by paying the heavy expenses attached to the performing of the vows of four poor Nazirites. There is in fact no record of his preaching such apostasy; but his vehement plea to the Galatians that they should not accept circumcision could be misconstrued in this sense. The reason, however, why the Law is a stumbling-block to them is that they are tempted to seek justification through the Law (Gal 2:16—21). It is this which Paul combats; he does not go so far as to say that the practices of the Law are in themselves reprehensible. Paul's own principle of conduct is stated 1 Cor 8:9—13; 9:19—23: the only rule is charity. Thus though not bound to observance of the Law, he knows himself free to observe it (as, presumably, an act of devotion) if this will conduce to the salvation of others. Hence he can have Timothy circumcised (16:3) and can observe a vow at Cenchreae (18:18). The difference between Paul's attitude towards the Law in his letters and in Ac has been considered one of the chief arguments against the authorship of Ac by a companion of Paul. Certainly Lk is far more concerned than Paul to stress Paul's fidelity to the Law; he is determined to show that Paul was faithful to Judaism and turned away from the Jews only because they forced him away. But it must be remembered that all the pronouncements on the relations between the Christian and the Law which we have from Paul's pen were the result of polemic against those who insisted that observance of the Law was necessary to salvation. 'The fact that he did not demand obedience to the Law does not imply that he opposed any and every observance of the Law among Jews' (G. Bornkamm in Keck and Martyn p. 205). **18.** The Twelve have disappeared from the scene, and the Church at Jerusalem is now presided over by James, the brother of the Lord, with a body of elders. **19.** Paul's purifica- **c** tion and the 'purification' of the four Nazirites are quite different rites. Paul must undertake the purification from the uncleanness inevitably incurred by moving among the gentiles, whose rites are prescribed Nm 19:12. The Nazirites must absolve their vow, by a ceremony described in Gr. by the same general word, translated 'purification'. Thus in v 26 Paul performs the rite prescribed for himself and gives notice of the rite prescribed for the Nazirites, who accompany him. **25.** Paul hardly needed informing of the letter whose instructions he had been promulgating (16:4). Lk uses this opportunity, at a moment when Paul's conduct might be taken to imply general validity of the Jewish Law, of stressing to the reader for the third time (cf note to 15:19—29) that the gentiles are bound only to those prescriptions required for common life between Jew and gentile. Lk often puts in the mouth of his speakers information intended not for their hearers but for his readers, e.g. 1:18—19.

27—40 Paul's Arrest—It is Paul's old opponents, the **d** Jews of Asia Minor, perhaps come up for Pentecost (cf 20:16), who stir up the trouble; only they would know that Trophimus the Ephesian was a gentile. Death was the penalty for gentiles who penetrated into the Temple beyond the court of the gentiles (cf *Orientis Graeci Inscriptiones Selectae* ed. W. Dittenberger, 1903—5). So they set about lynching Paul, the cause of the defilement (but not within the *'sanctuary'* (30), where human blood should not be shed). Haenchen (p. 548) suggests that the reason why Paul is carried (35) is that he is too weak to walk after the attempted lynching, but that Lk must conceal this in order to leave room for the speech of 22:3—21. **31.** The garrison was stationed in the Antonia fortress overlooking the temple, in case of such disturbances, especially the religious-inspired liberation movements, which were liable to break out at the great festivals (cf note to v 38). It must have comprised well over 500 men (23:23). **37—39.** Lk brings together various types of **e** messianic movements of revolt (cf § 74*b*) which filled the years before the outbreak of the Jewish Revolt in A.D. 66. The Egyptian, according to Jos BJ 2.261ff with his usual inflated numbers, led out 30,000 men on to the Mount of Olives in the expectation that the walls of Jerusalem would fall down. The Assassins formed a nationalist movement constantly active in this period. Since the Messiah was to appear in the desert (cf Mt

8e 24:26; Mk 1:2—4 and note there), such messianic revolts often began with a march into the desert. The centurion immediately perceives that Paul is no Egyptian because he is free of their distinctive accent (cf Lucian, *Navig.* 2). This immediate trust in Paul by the Roman authority on the spot, and exculpation from any part in rebellious movements (so that he even allows him to address the mob in a language unknown to himself), is excellent propaganda for Christianity with the Romans (cf § 821*e*). It is unlikely that the raging mob would listen peacefully. But the conventions of Hellenistic historical writing permit Lk to insert at this important junction a speech which shows the significance of the occasion, cf § 882*a—c*.

8a 22:1—21 Paul's defence to the Jews—It has often been remarked that Paul makes no reference to the charge of bringing a gentile into the Temple (21:28*c*). Instead his defence is an explanation of why Christianity has been compelled to admit gentiles as a whole to the Church (Dibelius p. 158—60), and incidentally an answer to the charge (21:28*b*) concerning his teaching. Therefore he stresses his Jewish upbringing (3), his zeal for the Law (4—5), the divine compulsion at his conversion (6—16) and at his mission to the gentiles (17—21). His purpose is to show that it was not of his own will: his hand was forced by a divine power at each stage. **3.** The triad 'born, brought up, educated' is classical in ancient literature; the middle term invariably refers to infancy and primary schooling (W. C. van Unnik, *Tarsus or Jerusalem*, 1962 p. 19—29). Therefore Gamaliel, the great rabbi (cf note to 5:34—39), was concerned only with the third period. This v should also exclude the common opinion that Paul came to Jerusalem only after spending his early years at Tarsus (cf history of Paul). But perhaps Lk exaggerates to stress his thorough Judaism; it is hard to see how he would have acquired his hellenistic culture, or why he always uses the **b** Gr., not the Heb. Bible in his letters. **6—16.** The account of Paul's conversion is fully discussed at 9:3—12. The variations in this version are either for variety to entertain the reader or to bring home Paul's thesis to his hearers, e.g. Ananias' fidelity to the Law and good repute with the Jewish community are underlined (12), and his speech (14—16) is in Jewish terms, using the biblical expressions 'God of our fathers', 'the Just One'. **17—21.** The vision in the Temple is recounted to show that the God of the Jews (the divine title is used: 19) appeared in his own temple to command the mission to the gentiles because the Jews would not listen. This is the point of the speech; the hearers do not miss it, and, as always in Ac, interrupt just as the climax has been reached. **17.** Paul did not return to Jerusalem for three years after his conversion (Gal 1: 17—18); but this does not affect the argument, and is omitted. **18.** He left Jerusalem because of a Jewish plot (9: 29—30); the vision therefore showed him the larger significance of this plot. **19—20.** The sense is: if Paul per-**c** secuted Christians it must have required divine pressure to bring about such a change; the Jews should have recognized this.

22—29 Paul Examined by the Tribune—**23.** No exact parallel to these antics has been found; they seem to be merely gestures of uncontrollable fury. **24.** The tribune has still no notion of the cause of the riot against Paul. Scourging was a normal adjunct in the examination of slaves and provincials, but for Roman citizens was forbidden by the *leges Julia* and *Porcia*. **28—29.** We can only guess how Paul's family acquired citizenship. The large sum paid by the tribune was presumably a bribe to get his name enrolled on the list of candidates for enfranchisement (Sherwin-White p. 154—5); his name, Claudius

Lysias, shows that he received his citizenship from the **838c** emperor Claudius.

22:30—23:11 Paul before the Sanhedrin—This whole **d** scene has been impugned as an invention by Lk owing to various difficulties, of which the most serious is Paul's failure to recognize the high priest (5). The tribune could well have permitted the investigation in order to discover the rights and wrongs in the case, or even the charges. The account is clearly simplified, e.g. Paul's opening remark is impossibly truculent as it stands. The quarrel he sparks off between Pharisees and Sadducees is naively represented (6—10); but it is far from impossible that they eventually ranged themselves on one side or the other according to the differences of belief of v 8. As v 28 makes clear, the scene serves the apologetic purpose of showing that the Jews had no valid case against Paul in Roman eyes; he was being lynched for a theological difference of opinion, in which one party was in fact on his side. **12—35 The Jews plan an ambush**—In this suspense- **e** filled episode Lk is at his best as a story-teller. Haenchen (p. 573—8) regards it as a device of Lk to transform the routine journey of an accused Roman citizen to the governor's tribunal into a lively story, at the same time stressing the unscrupulous enmity of the Jews and the benevolent protection of the Romans. Conzelmann (*Apg* p. 129) merely remarks that the anecdote on which it is based clashes with the report of the session of the Sanhedrin, because the Pharisees defended Paul. But the Pharisees are not in fact said to have had a part in the plot; at least the chief priests, and perhaps the 'elders' too (14), would have been Sadducees, who had opposed Paul. It must be admitted that, as the story stands, the tribune is remarkably kind to (19) and trusting in Paul's nephew, and that the almost continuous march of 76 miles to Antipatris and back (31—32) is out of the question for foot-soldiers. Further, Lysias would be unlikely to send an escort of over half his garrison troops (23) all the way to Antipatris when the forty plotters contemplated no more than a swoop in the back streets of Jerusalem (15). But these are only incidental details, which do not discredit the main story; Lk must be allowed to add colour to such a promising plot. **25.** This letter is the *libellus* enjoined by military regula- **f** tions to be sent to the governor to explain the circumstances of the arrest (Sherwin-White p. 54—55). It is not quite true that Lysias was already aware of Paul's citizenship when he rescued him (27), nor that he had already ordered his accusers to take their charges to the governor (30—this would have removed the whole point of the cloak-and-dagger escape). **26.** For Felix see note to 24:27. **34.** Felix asks this question because an offender could be tried either in the province of his offence or in that of his domicile. Felix rejects the latter alternative because at that time Cilicia was not yet organized as a province, and the case would have had to be tried by the imperial Legate of Syria, who 'was not to be bothered with minor cases from Judaea' (Sherwin-White p. 56). **35.** The praetorium is called 'Herod's' because the residence of the governor had been built by Herod the Great as his own palace.

24:1—23 Trial before Felix—This is the only hearing **g** when we have both sides, the Jews' charges and Paul's defence, presented in speeches. The charges are two: (1) Paul is an agitator throughout the world (5). This charge was particularly topical, resembling even verbally the letter of Claudius to the Alexandrians a few years before, in which he accuses the Jews of being 'agitators throughout the world' (Pap. Lond. 1912). It is as 'ringleader of the sect of the Nazarenes' that he does this. Hence, as Sherwin-White points out (p. 51) the difficulty

838g of the case: 'the charge was political . . . and yet the evidence was theological'. (2) He tried to profane the temple.

h Paul replies by (1) Denying that he stirred up any trouble at Jerusalem (11—12—he omits to mention the disturbances outside Judea, as he had every right to do, since they were not within Felix's jurisdiction); 2) Claiming that 'the Way' (cf note to 9:2) is perfectly in accord with Jewish belief: it accepts the 'God of our fathers' (a biblical expression), the scriptures, and a hope in the resurrection shared by the accusers (14—16, 21). There is perhaps an apologetic motive on Lk's part visible here: as the true form of Judaism, Christianity should enjoy the tolerance granted by the Roman state of Judaism. But more important is the theological motif, which rings throughout the NT: Christianity does not make sense except as the fulfilment of the OT promises; (3) Rejecting the charge of the Jews of Asia Minor in the absence of his accusers (17—19). Here again there is a contemporary note, for the emperor Claudius had recently concerned himself with legislation against just such accusers who did not appear to pursue their charges (Sherwin-White p. 52). Thus Felix had no alternative but to adjourn the case until some concrete evidence was presented (22). **1.** Tertullus, **i** a professional orator, is not a Jew (cf 8). **2—4.** He opens his speech in the normal way, as does Paul too (10), with a *captatio benevolentiae*. To judge from the assessment of Felix by Josephus and Tacitus these compliments are highly exaggerated for such an unscrupulous rogue. But their condemnation is motivated by deeper political reasons, and is highly untrustworthy (see my article, *Suffered under Pontius Pilate*, Scr. 18 (1965) 84—86). He hardly succeeded, however, in bestowing 'peace' (2) for his term of office was marred by intense activity on the part of the *sicarii* or Assassins (cf 21:38). There is no other evidence than Ac that he had any special interest **j** in Christianity. **17.** The sole indication that the purpose of Paul's visit was to bring alms. From 11:29—30 also we gather that Lk was aware of a visit of Paul's to Jerusalem bringing alms; but for other reasons it is clear that this visit is chronologically misplaced. Haenchen (p. 322) maintains that Lk did not know when this took place: 'in the course of oral tradition Paul's collecting journey had got mixed up with his other journey to Jerusalem'; but this view is contradicted by the present passage. Paul's concern for this collection is clear from 1 Cor 16:1— 4; 2 Cor 8—9; Rm 15:26. But the only mention of Paul handing over any money at Jerusalem is 21:24, 26, and even this he was prevented by his arrest from actually paying. Perhaps the community at Jerusalem made a condition of accepting the money from the gentile communities that it should be, so to speak, purified by being partly used for the payment for the performance of the Nazirites' vows. Thus there was perhaps never in fact a solemn payment of the sum, and Lk thought it best to be silent about the whole collection, which did not in fact form the bond of charity which had been hoped for.

k 24—27 Paul and Felix—The similarity of this scene to that between John the Baptist and Herod (Mk 6:17— 20) is no reason for rejecting it. It again shows the respect of Roman authorities for Christianity, cf § 821g. **25.** The subjects of Paul's instruction are common themes in the sub-apostolic age (e.g. *Acta Pauli et Theclae*), but would also be apt for Felix. He had shocked Jewish opinion by marrying Drusilla, a Jewess and already married, though he himself was a gentile. **26.** Bribery of Roman provincial governors was perfectly normal. **27.** 'When two years had elapsed'; from his appointment or from Paul's arrest? Felix's desire to do the Jews a favour was not idle.

The provincials could, and frequently did, prosecute retir- **83** ing governors at Rome; in fact, though his two immediate predecessors had been prosecuted for maladministration, he escaped this charge (Jos.Ant. 18,4,2; 20,6,3; BJ 2,16. 6—7). It was unusual for a governor deliberately to deal with all outstanding cases before departure (Jos.Ant. 20.9.5).

25:1—12 Paul appeals to Caesar—Festus takes up **84** the case again with admirable dispatch, cleverly or luckily avoiding another perfidious Jewish trick (3). The charges and defence are repeated unchanged. Then suddenly Festus offers Paul a trial at Jerusalem and Paul appeals to Rome. Most probably Festus sees that there is no charge against Paul valid in Roman law, but does not wish to acquit him for fear of offending the Jews. If he is so sure of his innocence (8), let him clear himself before the Jewish authorities! He dare not hand over a Roman citizen against his will. But Paul insists that he is to be tried by Roman law (10a); his reason for appealing to Rome (11) could be that he sees that Festus is no impartial judge; Festus himself admits later that he could have been released (26:32). Festus' consultation with his *consilium* (12) does not imply that he was at liberty to disallow appeals; this was a right given to Roman citizens by the *lex Julia de vi*; but it was probably the first time such a case had occurred in his term of office. **1.** Josephus praises **b** sent by Rome (Ant. 20.182). This could well be due to his favourable attitude towards the Jews (v 9). **8.** This can only be a general protestation of innocence; if the third element were a denial of an accusation of high treason Festus would never have offered to transfer the case to the Jews. **9.** 'before me' can mean either that Festus would preside or that he would merely hold a watching brief. But in the former case the mere change of place would be pointless.

13—22 Agrippa visits Festus—We can hardly suppose **c** that Lk had a source for this private conversation; he is using the liberty of hellenistic historians to depict the issues at stake by a speech (note the minor variations, for the sake of variety, in the presentation of the details here and below), cf § 822a—c. We see how upright has been Festus' handling of the case—a useful counterbalance to the impression left by vv 1—12—and how incapable he is of seeing the real issues involved. Thus he is personally exonerated, and yet his refusal to absolve Paul is no bad mark against Paul. Agrippa II of Chalcis, in spite of his dubious relationship with his infamous sister Bernice, was well-qualified in Festus' eyes to give a second opinion from the Jewish angle, for he was superintendant of the Temple, with right to nominate the high priest. But he was in fact qualified for these positions more by his friendship with emperors than by his piety or knowledge of Judaism; he had been brought up at Rome, and his principate was in Syria. **19.** BJ (p. 202 note a) remarks on the 'Roman contempt for theological disputes'. The word translated 'superstition' is well-chosen (as in 17:22); it can convey contempt, but need not do so. **23—27 Paul presented to Agrippa**—This solemn **d** scene introduces Paul's final, public vindication, before as many notables as can be mustered; after this he is carried off to Rome. The legal basis for it is given in vv **26—27**: the procurator is obliged to send an account of the case to Rome with the prisoner. To omit this would be not merely 'unreasonable' (27) but irregular. But Festus considers the case so involved and opaque that he profits from the visit of the neighbouring Jewish monarch to pay his respects at the beginning of his term of office, in order to get a judgement from someone who

40d should understand the Jewish questions involved and be able to translate them into terms intelligible at Rome.

e **26:1—32 Paul's defence before Agrippa**——The clue to the understanding of this last apologia of Paul is given at its beginning and its end: it is an appeal to the Jews. **3.** conveys that anyone thoroughly conversant with Judaism will turn a sympathetic ear to Paul's plea; **27—29** that a sympathetic hearing will soon lead to conversion, for Agrippa goes as far as he can without actually submitting; it is merely due to lack of time to consider the matter that he does not follow Paul. The theme of the speech is that Christianity provides the logical conclusion of Judaism (cf note to 24:1—23): Paul belongs to the strictest party of the Jews (**5**), is on trial for the hope in the resurrection shared by all Hebrews (**6—8**), was naturally so disinclined to believe that he needed a vision from heaven to convince him (**9—18**), preaches only what was prophesied by Moses **f** and the prophets (**22—23**). At this climax comes, as usual, the interruption, which also serves to show again the inability of Romans to understand what is at stake in this theological difference between Jews and Christians. Paul then turns to a second point: these are no parochial trifles, but of world-wide importance (**26**). Lk has been at pains to show the place of Christ in world-history ever since his careful dating of the beginning by world-dates (Lk 2:1—2; 3:1). This was the significance of the witness of the world at Pentecost (2:9—11), of the constant encounters with high officials, the approval of Sergius Paulus on Cyprus (13:7), the proclamation at Athens (17:22ff), the protection of the Asiarchs at Ephesus (19:31), the final move to Rome. Christianity is a force to shake the world. The scene ends with a total vindication of Paul (**30—32**) both by Agrippa and his retinue and by Festus, representing the highest authorities of Jews and gentiles. Thus another motive of the speech is to claim for Christianity the tolerance accorded by the Roman authorities to Judaism, for Christianity is what Judaism should be!

g **2—3.** The speech begins with the classical rhetorical *captatio benevolentiae*, as in 24:2—3, 10. The style of the whole speech is the most elevated in Ac, as befits its distinguished audience. It abounds in classical and cultured turns of phrase (see Conzelmann, *Apg.* p. 137—40). A purely Gr. proverb (originally in Euripides *Bacchae* 794f) is put into the Lord's mouth (14), though he is represented **h** as speaking in Aram., cf note to 20:35. **4—18.** Most of the events related are already familiar to the reader. For commentary see notes to 9:3—19. To avoid boredom Lk expresses them differently, often with a slight heightening of colour, e.g. **10**, generalization of his part in Stephen's death; **11**, 'foreign cities' instead of Damascus alone; **12** 'commission from the high priests', not merely 'letters from the high priest' as formerly; **14** 'all' fall to the ground. But the mission from Jesus (**16—18**) is given no longer through Ananias, as in the two previous accounts of the conversion, but directly: Ananias falls out because the immediacy of the command is now more important than the intervention of the pious Jew (22:12 and note). The vocation narrative (cf note to 9:3—9) is here (**16—18**) modelled upon those of Jeremiah (Jer 1:7) and the suffering servant of Isaiah 42:7, 16, sent to enlighten the **i** blind. But to the song of David asking deliverance from the gentiles (17*a*, as 1 Chr 16:35) is significantly added deliverance from 'the people' (always a designation of Israel), for they too rejected Paul. The description of the salvation which Paul proclaims (**18**) has indeed a strongly Pauline ring: 'from the power of Satan', 'forgiveness of sins' and 'a place among those who are sanctified' appearing close together also in Col 1:12—14; thus the speech is not a completely free composition by Lk. On the other hand the themes of repentance and turning to God (**20**) **840i** are characteristically Lukan, reappearing again and again in both Lk and Ac (cf baptism and J. Dupont 'Repentir et Conversion' (ScE 12 (1960) 137—73)). For the proofs from scripture mentioned **22—23** see notes to 2:22—36; 2:25—31. **28—29.** Haenchen (p. 618) points out that Agrippa's slightly humorous retort, 'In a short time *you will persuade me to play the* Christian' is aptly answered by Paul's wry allusion to his chains.

27:1—44 Journey to Rome: Shipwreck——The theo- **841a** logical theme of this chapter is Paul the rescuer. Though Paul is himself a prisoner, all owe their safety to him and his divine mission. The bulk of the story falls into a recognized type. The passages in which Paul appears are quite different in character, and can be cut out of the narrative, leaving a neutral story of a sea voyage terminating in a shipwreck. We will examine these passages first:

9*b*—11 Paul forewarns disaster——We need not sup- **b** pose that Paul, a prisoner among prisoners, was called to a formal consultation with the centurion and the two ship's officers (neither of whom in fact appears again in the account). There is nothing improbable in the supposition that the centurion had noticed him and grown to respect him. The dating is given by Jewish reckoning perhaps suggesting that Paul even now kept the 'fast' of the Day of Reconciliation——as October 10th. This was already a month after the safe season for sailing was over, though shipping still plied until early November, when it stopped altogether until March (Vegetius, *De re militari*, 4.39).

21—26 Paul promises safety on account of his own **c** **mission**——Paul encourages the crew by pointing out that, though his advice had been disregarded——delicately hinted at by repeating his words of v 10 'injury and loss'——all are to be saved because he has received a heavenly reassurance that he is to fulfil his task of witnessing to Christ before Caesar (cf note to 26:26). This vision confirmed the prophecy of 23:11. In giving Paul's speech, made at the nadir of despair, such a set form, Lk follows the conventions for the literary description of such disasters.

31. Paul intervenes——It is by Paul's words, prompting the soldiers to action, that the shipwreck is made inevitable. The anchors must be laid out from the boat; when the boat was gone there was no way of getting ashore.

33—36, 38*a* Paul presides at a meal——Paul again **d** seems to be in a commanding position. It is not clear that Lk intends to depict a Eucharist in the full Christian sense. The blessing could be the normal Christian and Jewish blessing before a meal; but the phrase 'took bread and giving thanks. . . he broke it' has a definite eucharistic ring. In addition eating to satisfaction is often mentioned in eucharistic texts (e.g. Mk 6:42 and note there). A Eucharist to strengthen Paul for the coming trial would not be out of place. **43*a*.** 'wishing to save Paul': Paul is the centre of Lk's story; he is the centurion's sole concern. As the whole ship's crew in the storm, so now the prisoners owe their life to his presence among them. the remainder of the story falls into a recognized type of story about sea voyages, of which the most similar is Arrian's *Periplus Maris Euxeini*; others are quoted by Conzelmann, p. 152f. It is surprising that friends were allowed to travel with the prisoner. Dibelius (p. 204—6) holds that Lk has inserted the Pauline passages into a preexisting literary account of a voyage and shipwreck; but there are perhaps enough literary characteristics of Lk to support Haenchen's contention (*Acta 27* in *Zeit und Geschichte, Dankesgabe an R. Bultmann*, 1964,

841d 235–54) that Lk composed it without direct use of any literary model.

e **1.** Paul is only one of a number of prisoners sent to Rome under escort. A *Cohors Augusta* is attested at Caesarea for just this period (OGIS 421). **2.** The party has to take what shipping the centurion can find. The route followed is the normal one (cf *Sailing Directions for the Mediterranean IV*, U.S. Hydrogr. Office, 1942, 32f). **17.** This manoeuvre is obscure: the word for 'undergird' can mean merely 'overhaul' (but this is usually done in harbour) or perhaps 'rig a hogging truss' (a rope over the deck binding stem to stern to prevent the ship breaking amidships—but this is not attested for Greek and Roman shipping, cf H. J. Cadbury, in Jackson and Lake, V: 345ff). In any case the word is used only of warships.

f **30ff.** Manoeuvres such as letting down an open boat, eating, opening the hold to throw out the wheat, suggest that the storm had abated. The last-mentioned was a measure to get the ship as far inshore as possible before beaching, made necessary by the loss of the boat (v. supr., note to 31. **42.** A regulation of Justinian's makes a soldier answerable with his life for his prisoner; thus they had grounds to fear their escape.

g **28:1–10 Paul on Malta: Two miracles—1–6.** The first miracle has shocked critics because Paul does not (in 6) correct the 'natives' (the word is applied to all who do not speak Greek or Latin, without any directly contemptuous ring). The story is related perhaps to illustrate Lk 10:19 'I have given you authority to tread upon serpents and scorpions . . . nothing shall hurt you'. **7–10.** The second miracle-story shows Paul diffusing well-being around him even on his journey as a prisoner. The final stages of the journey become, indeed, almost a triumphal progress towards the goal. The guards quite disappear until 16*b*.

h **11–16 Malta to Rome**—The journey continues as though Paul were a free man (see note above), e.g. 14. **11.** Three months wintering from October (cf note to 27: 9*b*–11) makes a very early start in the shipping season; but no doubt the figure is not intended to be exact. The cult of the Dioscuri or 'Twin Brothers', the 'patron saints' of mariners were especially popular in Egypt, so there is a double reason that they should serve as figureheads for this boat. **13.** Before Ostia was dredged and improved by Claudius, Puteoli (now Pozzuoli) was the chief seafaring port of the coast; from there it was possible to reach Rome in 5 days on foot by the Viae Campana and Appia. **15.** Forum Appii is 40 miles, Tres Tabernae 20 miles from Rome. The escort of the brethren increases the impression of a triumphal progress. This is the sole mention of the Christian community in Rome (see next note).

i **17–31 Paul in Rome**—This is a grand finale to which Lk has been leading us. Paul has reached the 'ends of the earth' (cf 1:8 note). There again his missionary experiences are repeated: though Christianity is only the logical conclusion of Judaism (17–24), the Jews reject Paul's message and he turns to the gentiles (25–28). **84** Ac closes with a glimpse of free unhampered preaching to the gentiles, which promises the limitless spread of the Kingdom. To achieve this theologically fitting conclusion, which both rounds off the book and opens further endless vistas, Lk must drastically select and simplify. As always, he presents his theological message by means of a captivating, memorable vignette; but to paint this vignette he must improve on the historical situation. According to the presentation which he offers us here, this seems to be the first appearance of a Christian preacher in Rome; there are a few brethren in Rome (v 15), but we do not hear of any organized Church for Paul to make contact with; the Jews have heard of Christianity only remotely. But we know from secular historians that already in A.D. 49 there was some disturbance among the Jews of Rome due to Christ (see note to 18:2). Rm **j** also reflects a flourishing Christian community, and some controversy with the Jews. It is also surprising that the 'leaders of the Jews' (17) should never have heard of Paul (contrast 21:21), and should come so obediently to a prisoner awaiting trial, and that they should be so easily satisfied by Paul's protestations (17–20). These are of course directed not to the hearers but to the readers of Ac; they are a summary of what Lk will have us take away as the dominant impression from the series of trial scenes: that Paul is a true Jew, whose message centres on the hope which is theirs too, that he was vindicated by the Romans, that he bears no enmity to the Jews—leaving the puzzling impression that no one condemns him.

But vv 17–22 are only the *mise en scène* for the **k** final confrontation between Paul and the Jews. As in Asia Minor and Greece, so here in Rome, by a solemn action in three movements, he proclaims their resistance and blindness, pronounces judgement on them, and turns to a more receptive audience (see note to 13:45–47). It is the Jews, not Paul, who are condemned, and in fulfilment of the scriptures (cf § 821*e*). **23.** Paul uses the habitual method of preaching about Jesus, as fulfilling the OT, cf notes to 2:22–36, 25–31; and 26:22–23. He tries 'from morning till evening'; it is due to no lack of effort on Paul's part that they fail. **24.** The same division **l** results as in the Sanhedrin (23:6–10); this underlines the continuity of Paul's doctrine with that of Judaism, for some at least are sympathetic. But eventually all are condemned (26–28). **26.** This text of Is bulked large in Christian apologetic to the Jews, cf Mk 4:12; Jn 12:40; Rm 11:25; and J. Gnilka. **30–31.** Finally we are left with the picture of Paul preaching unimpeded to the gentiles at the centre of the world. No word is breathed of the charges against him. Lk has already hinted that Paul is to die a martyr's death for Christ (see note to 20:22–27). He does not see fit to enlighten us about the details of Paul's trial, release or death (for which see § 704*e–f.*), but prefers to leave us with this picture of crowning success in the mission.

ROMANS

BY A. THEISSEN

REVISED BY P. BYRNE S.M.

841a Bibliography—Origen, PG 14; Chrysostom, *Homilies*, PG 60; Aquinas, *In omnes S. Pauli Epistolas Commentaria*; Estius, *In omnes D. Pauli Epistolas Commentaria* (1614–6); R. Cornely, CSS 1927[2]; W. Sanday–A. C. Headlam (abbr. to SH), ICC 1907; A. Jülicher, 1929[4]; M.-J. Lagrange, EtB 1931[4]; H. Lietzmann, HNT 1933[4]; C. H. Dodd, Moffatt, 1932; A. Viard, PCSB 1948; A. Nygren, E.tr. SCM 1952; K. Barth, E.tr. 1933; S. Lyonnet, BJ 1953; J. Knox–G. Cragg, IB 1954; O. Michel, Meyer Komm. 1955; C. Barrett, BNTC 1957; J. Huby–S. Lyonnet, VS 1957; T. W. Manson, PC (2) 1963; F. J. Leenhardt, CNT 1957, E.tr. 1965; P. Althaus, NTD 1959[9]; P. Boylan, 1934; Sickenberger, BB 1957; O. Kuss, RNT 1950.

b Theme—The doctrinal section centres about the subject of salvation by faith; 1:16–17, announces the theme to be developed. The gospel assures salvation to believers; it carries the revelation of God's justice to be obtained by faith, and, once justified believers are assured of salvation. This theme is worked out in 1:18–8:39.

A secondary but related topic is the defence of the teaching on justification against objections from the Jews, who rejected the doctrine as an innovation contrary to the Torah. The new economy based on faith seemed to be opposed to the OT promises of salvation for Israel. In chh 9–11 Paul demonstrates the unity of God's saving plan, comparing Israel as a national entity with the Gentiles who believed.

Plan—The main divisions are clear, but commentators differ on the relative importance of some passages and on the development of the argument. The plans given in manuals either show the logical connexions between the ideas or take into account the underlying laws of oral composition in the letter. Recent studies on the subject, *e.g.* A. Feuillet, RB 57 (1950), 336–87, 489–529; J. Dupont, RB 62 (1955), 365–97, Suitbertus a Joanne a Cruce, VDom 34 (1956), 68–87, are valuable examinations of the composition of the work, but their variety suggests that a constructed sequence of thought is not to be looked for. The letter is not a composition after our rules of logic or rhetoric; the themes or motifs are set forth by juxtaposition rather than interconnected. Throughout the work Paul has in mind at once God's revelation of himself in history and the consequences of this for each person: grace and moral obligations.

c A. 1:1–17 INTRODUCTION.
B. 1:18–11:36 THE DOCTRINAL SECTION.
  I. 1:18–3:20 The need for the salvation of the Gospel.
  II. 3:21–4:25 The way to this salvation.
  III. 5:1–8:39 Effects of this salvation:
    (1) 5:1–21 Hope of eternal glorification,
    (2) 6:1–23 A complete break with sin,
    (3) 7:1–25 Christ the New Law,
    (4) 8:1–39 The indwelling of the Holy Spirit.

  IV. 9:1–11:36 The present exclusion of Israel from **841c** this salvation:
    (1) 9:1–29 The divine attributes of faithfulness and justice are defended,
    (2) 9:30–10:21 Israel's fault is exposed,
    (3) 11:1–36 Several other aspects of the problem of Israel's present exclusion from the salvation of the Gospel are mentioned.
C. 12:1–15:13 THE MORAL SECTION.
  I. 12:1–13:14 General exhortations.
  II. 14:1–15:13 Exhortations to the weak and the strong in Rome.
D. 15:14–16:27 CONCLUSION.

Authenticity—Paul's authorship has never been seriously questioned. The letter is incontestably the expression of his thought. For the evidence internal and external, see W. G. Kummel, *Introd. to NT*, 222; Lusseau-Collomb, *Manuel d'études bibliques* V (i) 1938, 523ff.; Lagrange, lxiff. The depth of thought, the agreement **with Gal, and the stylistic evidence argue against a** major role by Tertius in the composition (16:22); cf O. Roller, *Das Formular der paul. Briefe*, (1933), 22ff.

Purpose—The primary purpose must have been to ex- **d** pound in the form of instructions and exhortations the necessity and the gratuitous nature of the salvation brought by the preaching of the Gospel to Jews and Gentiles. Paul planned to go to Spain when his work in the E. was complete (15:25–27), and Rome was to be a stage on his journey. He takes the opportunity to prepare the faithful there for his coming, and, by giving an *exposé* of his thought, to forestall possible objections and difficulties. The importance of the subject of salvation by faith in Christ, the leisure Paul had at the time for mature reflection on the theme and the prestige of the Christian community in Rome would account for the length and the theological depth of the epistle.

Date—From details in Rm 15–16, Ac 19:21–21:19 the letter can be dated with tolerable precision. It was written during the winter 57–58 from Corinth, when Paul was on the point of leaving with the funds collected for the poor of Jerusalem, see § 704a–c.

Addressees—Apart from scattered references in Suetonius and Tacitus, little is known about the origin of the Christian community in Rome. The first Christians there were converts from the Diaspora. However affected by the edict of Claudius in 49 expelling the Jews, the community continued to exist, and was soon augmented by converts from paganism; cf Lebreton and Zeiller, *The History of the Primitive Church* 7 (1942), 240–2. It is hard to say which element was preponderant when Paul wrote; one can only conjecture. Certain details: Paul's **e** use of his title of 'Apostle of the Gentiles' 1:5–6, his addressing the Romans as converts from paganism 1:13, the contempt of the Christians for Israel 2:17–25, could be explained if the converted pagan element were in the majority. Although the contrary hypothesis cannot be ruled out, the arguments adduced in favour of a Church

1103

841e of converts from Judaism are not conclusive, e.g. Fahy IrTQ 26 (1959) 182ff; cf also Huby—Lyonnet, 9—16. There is no direct evidence on the social status of the Christian community in Rome; but the names listed in 16:3—15 may shed some light on their condition. They are for the most part names of slaves or of freedmen; some are of Jewish, others of Greek origin; most are to be found also on Roman inscriptions of 1st cent. A.D. The treatment of Israelite themes (especially chh 9—11) reflects Paul's standpoint on the Christian revelation and the Law rather than the social make-up of the community to which he was writing.

The Founder of the Church in Rome—Since Rome was a meeting place for all creeds and nationalities, it is likely that Christians met there early on. Consequently the beginning of Christianity in Rome need not be the work of any one individual. While it is widely accepted that St Peter resided in Rome and was martyred there (cf U. Holzmeister, *Com. in Epistulas SS. Petri et Judae*, CSS, 1937, 40—71), it is less certain that he preached in the city before Paul wrote his letter. Lyonnet (*Quaestiones in Epistolam ad Romanos*, I Series, Rome 1955, 25—43) examines the evidence available, and concludes that though the tradition has some data in its favour, it is not established with any certainty. Lack of any reference to Peter in Rm would be hard to explain if he were then in the city, but not in the case of a temporary absence.

f The Text—For a good introduction to the critical problems of the text see Lietzmann 1—18. The standard edition of the Greek text is H. v. Soden, *Die Schriften des NT, Text und Apparat*, 1913. This has been used for the present commentary. For a select list of textual variants see Westcott—Hort, *The NT* II (1882) 108—14. The standard edition of the Vg text is J. Wordsworth and H. J. White, *Novum Testamentum . . .* II i, Oxford, 1913.

Integrity—The MS tradition shows a short recension of Rm, omitting chh 15 and 16, while other MSS, retaining these, place the doxology 16:25—27 after ch 14. The respective MS evidence can be found in the critical editions of the text and in the larger commentaries. On the whole, the case seems to be far from clear. But there is agreement on the following points: (1) The best attested text is Rm 14:23; 15:1—16:27; so ℵBC etc; bo, sah; vet lat, Vg; pesh. (2) Marcion was the first to omit 15:1—16:27, partly because the contents contradicted his doctrine, 15:14—16:27. (3) The omission of 15:1—16:27 in some MSS may be due partly to the influence of Marcion, partly to the influence of church lectionaries. A list of names was not suitable for reading in church. (4) The theory that Rm 16 is a fragment of a letter addressed not to Rome but to Ephesus can quote no external evidence in its favour. On the internal evidence alleged cf. § 866*j*. On the whole question see R. Schumacher, *Die beiden letzten Kapitel des Röm.* NtAbh, 14, 4 (1929); Lietzmann, 130f.

842a 1:1—7 The Opening Salutation—St Paul begins his letter according to contemporary Jewish, Greek and Roman usage with the threefold statement of sender, addressee and greetings. Examples which illustrate this convention of ancient letter-writing are plentiful. A similar formula is still used in many papal and episcopal encyclicals. For a different salutation see the seven letters in Apoc 2—3.

The most obvious characteristics of the salutation in Rm 1:1—7 are its length and period style. The conventional superscription was short and formal; see Jas 1:1 which, of all letters in the NT, best preserves the stereo-

typed formula of an ancient letter. St Paul was the first **84** as far as we know to break away from the traditional formula by expanding it and filling it with Christian ideas.

The practical importance of Rm 1:1—7 lies in its doctrinal content. Nearly all the prominent articles of the early Christian faith are gathered together here in one sentence: (1) the Gospel as the fulfilment of the OT, 2; (2) the descent of the Messiah from the family of David, 3; (3) the glorification of Christ, 4; (4) the origin, purpose and range of Paul's apostolate, 1, 5, 6.

1. '*doulos* = servant': contains a confession of faith. **b** The phrase is not found in the gospels (contrast Jn 15: 15) but occurs frequently in the Pauline and the Catholic epistles. All agree that it expresses the Apostle's allegiance to Christ, but opinions differ on the definition of this allegiance. The main explanations are: (1) = slave or bondman of Jesus Christ, 1 Cor 7:22; i.e. Paul who claimed his rights as a Roman citizen before the Roman authorities, Ac 16:37; 22:25; 25:10, regarded himself as a slave of Christ. Older commentators insist on this literal translation. (2) = servant or minister of Jesus. This interpretation avoids the idea of slavery by explaining the phrase as an hyperbole. As such it would be in accordance with the oriental convention of calling even high officials 'slaves' with reference to their higher authorities, esp the king; 2 Kgs 5:6; Cowley, *Aram. Pap.* 1923, nn. 17, 30, etc. This explanation would come near the idea in Jn 15:15, and could be supported by the stress Paul lays on his apostolic authority in this context. *Doulos* would be synonymous in NT with *diakonos, therapōn, oikonomos, hupēretēs*, which are all different words for servant or minister. (3) = worshipper of Jesus Christ. This meaning is based on OT usage in which 'servant of God' is commonly used for those whose life is dedicated to the worship and service of God; e.g. Abraham, Ps 105 (104):6; Moses, Jos 14:7; Joshua, Jos 24:29, David, Jer 33:21; the just = the saints of OT, cf Lk 1:38, 2:29. The doctrinal significance of this explanation lies in the implicit confession of Jesus as Lord. As the OT saints were called 'servants of God', Paul called himself 'servant of Jesus Christ'. In NT the expression designates all Christians, Ac 4:29, 1 Pt 2:16, and is current in early liturgical prayers.

'Called to be an apostle'. Paul saw his experience on **c** the road to Damascus rather as an efficacious call by God to be an apostle than as a conversion in our sense of the word. **2—4.** Describe the Gospel which Paul preaches. (1) It is a Gospel promised in the Bible long ago, 2; (2) its central figure is Jesus Christ, 3—4. What is said of Christ can be summarized under two points: (1) Jesus Christ, the son of David; (2) Jesus Christ, the Son of God. **3.** For the descent of the Messiah from the house of David see 2 Sm 7:12—16. Davidic lineage was one of the principal marks of the Messiah. The phrase underlines Christ's human aspect as opposed to the divine aspect. **4.** The structure of this sentence has been disputed. Vg has 'praedestinatus', following, perhaps, a different reading. The resurrection brought a change in the condition and status of Christ. The general meaning is that Our Lord's resurrection is for him the source of a new state of being and a new function. The expression 'Son of God' does not imply an assertion of the metaphysical nature of Our Lord; Paul is not referring to the union of two natures in one Person, but has in mind the concrete person of Christ.

The precise definition of the state of being and the **d** function in the context depend on whether *en dunamei* is taken to qualify *huiou horisthentos*. It is of small moment whether *horisthentos* has a declarative or a con-

42d stitutive sense, since in biblical language to receive a name implies to be actually what is connoted by the name; cf K. Schmidt, *horizō* TWNT 5, 454ff. Boismard RB 60 (1953) 5–17, and LumVi 1953, 75–100, taking with 'designated' 'in power' interprets the passage as meaning that Christ was raised up by divine intervention and power, and received the title of 'Lord', that is, was installed as ruler of creation with dominion over men according to Ps 2:7. Certainly Paul conceives the resurrection of Christ as a work of divine power (Eph 1:18–21); but in his thought the Father also communicates this power to the Son with the additional capacity of communicating it in turn to believers; cf Phil 3:10. Taken where it occurs in the text, 'in power' would seem to indicate a quality possessed by 'Son', and mean therefore that at the resurrection the Son received the full powers proper to the Son of God, with the mission of sanctifying men. 'spirit of holiness', a hebraism for 'holy spirit', or 'holy-making (i.e. sanctifying) spirit'. By contrast with 'according to the flesh' the term implies directly something inherent in Christ, and would indicate the divine nature. The person of the Holy Spirit is, however, indirectly insinuated, since the Son's mission of sanctifying mankind is exercised by conferring a new life the principle of which is the Person of the Spirit, cf 8:9ff.

e Many scholars, e.g. O. Cullmann: *Les Premières Confessions de la foi chrétienne*, (1948), 45ff; see in the passage 3–4 an early formula, a pre-Pauline profession of faith in Jesus as Lord. The profession would centre on Jesus' divine sonship in its Davidic lineage and in its final manifestation at the Resurrection. According to this way of understanding the text, the promise to David in 2 Sm 7:14 is realized in his scion Jesus by the Resurrection; one of David's line is Son of God in a way surpassing all the promises, sharing in the divine power and glory, cf 2 Tm 2:8. Doctrinally it is clear that there is no essential difference between the various interpretations. For a suggestive study of the parallels between Rom 1:3–4 and Lk 1:35 see L. Legrand in RB 70 (1963) 161ff.

5. 'obedience of faith', the obedience involved in the assent by the virtue of faith, i.e. subjective genitive, rather than the obedience to the gospel message. **7a.** 'Called to be saints', the Apostle is not implying that the Christians of Rome were of extraordinary virtue. What he has in mind is that God has called (= chosen) them to be set apart for him in a special way. In this sense 'saints' is a common name for the Christians: Rm 8:27; 12:13; 15:25, 31; 16:2, 15; 1 Cor 1:2; 6:1f; 14:33; 16:1, 15; 2 Cor 1:1; 8:4; 9:1, 12; 13:12; Eph 1:1; 2:19, etc. The origin of this idea is to be found in the OT usage in which 'saints' refers to Israel as God's *chosen* people, cf Ex 22:31; Lv 11:44; 19:2; 20:7; Deut 7:6; 14: **f** 21; 16:19; 28:9, etc. In virtue of the call by Yahweh Israel belonged to God, and became a holy people, separated from other nations. In like manner by their faith and baptism Christians are consecrated to God. Eph 1:13. cf also *Recueil Lucien Cerfaux*, 2, 389–413. **7b** ends the salutation with greetings as was customary. But in the wording of his greetings Paul keeps neither to the Jewish nor to the Greek custom. The Jewish form was *šalôm* = peace (cf SB 1, 380–5), the Greek *chairein* (cf Jas 1:1). Paul instead used the formula *charis kai eirēne* except in 1 and 2 Tm. There are two main interpretations. (1) It can be taken as uniting the Jewish and the Greek formulas. Then it has to be translated 'greetings and peace (= happiness)' = 'all best wishes'; (2) The two nouns can be taken in their specific Christian sense. 'Grace' refers to all that God has given us through Christ,

and 'peace' is the tranquil possession of God's friendship **842f** and blessings.

8–17 Introduction—In accordance with the usage of ancient letter-writing the salutation is followed by an introductory paragraph enlarging on the Apostle's interest in those to whom he is writing. He praises the good repute of their faith, 8; he assures them of his prayers, 9; and finally expresses his desire to visit them and the hope that his visit will be for their mutual edification and for the benefit of the Gospel. The whole paragraph may well be called a *captatio benevolentiae*. The only letters of St Paul in which a similar introduction is wanting are Gal; 1 Tm; Ti; cf P. Wendland, *Die urchristl. Literaturformen* 1912, 413f. **9.** 'Serve with my spirit': Paul sees his apostolic ministry as a spiritual cult. cf A. Denis in RSPT 42 (1958), 401–36, 617–56.

16–17 The Theme of the Epistle—From the literary point of view these two verses clearly belong to the introduction, 8–17, since they explain Paul's statement in the previous sentence, 15, 16a, that the delay of his visit to Rome is not due either to fear or to shame. On the other hand, 16f are commonly set apart as a special paragraph because they contain the main thesis of the epistle. The points of this thesis are: (1) in the Christian Gospel God really offers men salvation; (2) this salvation is to be obtained by means of faith; (3) this salvation through faith is offered to all men without any of the traditional distinctions between races and cultures; (4) this salvation is not an innovation that contradicts but is in full agreement with what is written in the OT. It is impossible to sound the depth of these thoughts in one reading or in a short explanation. A brief exposition of the principal terms and phrases, however, may be useful.

16. 'The Gospel, the power of God for salvation'. **g** The gospel message contains a divine efficacy; by means of it God can save men. *sōteria* = salvation is one of the most comprehensive terms used in the NT to describe the whole purpose of the Incarnation, or to cover the whole range of Christ's mission on earth. Every attempt to define salvation has to start from the root-meaning; deliverance, safety, security, well-being. Paul is evidently thinking of deliverance in the religious or spiritual sense. But this can again be understood negatively, as deliverance from the death of sin; or positively, as the imparting of a new spiritual life. In either case the deliverance can be past, present or future. Thus, we have been saved through the Incarnation, Ti 3:4f; Eph 2:8; we are being saved through Christ in us, 1 Cor 1:18; we hope that we shall be saved at the resurrection from the dead on the Last Day, Rm 10:1; 13:11; 1 Thes 5:8f; Phil 1:19; 2:12. Paul has in mind here the definitive phase of salvation, in eternal life. The appeal which the word salvation had for Paul's readers can be gathered from its frequency in the OT and in the Graeco-Roman usage of the time. Among the many synonyms for deliverance in the OT (cf HRCS II 1328; HDB IV 357), *sōteria* had become more and more a technical term for the salvation expected from the Messiah, so that Messiah and Saviour could be used interchangeably, cf Mt 1:21. In the Graeco-Roman world 'the cry for salvation was loud, persistent, and universal'. Heroes and kings as well as gods were given the title Saviour and the mystery religions developed elaborate theories and rituals of salvation under the patronage of several oriental deities; cf S. Angus, *The Mystery* **h** *Religions and Christianity*, 1925, 225–30. To bring out the main differences between the Christian doctrine of salvation and that of the pagan cults, stress is to be laid (1) on the historical character of Christ the Redeemer,

842h and (2) on the moral obligations of the Christian faith, cf Prat II 385—90.

'To everyone who has faith', the emphasis seems to lie on the verb, because of the parallelism with 17*b*. Without faith neither the privileges of Israel nor the wisdom of the Greeks are of any avail; cf 1:17*b*; 5:1; Gal 3:8; Jn 3:36; 7:38; Council of Trent, sess VI cap 8 (Dz 801) 'Fides est humanae salutis initium, fundamentum et radix omnis iustificationis, sine qua impossibile est placere Deo (Heb 11:6) et ad filiorum eius consortium pervenire' = 'Faith is the first step in man's salvation, the foundation and root of all justification; without which (*sc.* faith) it is impossible to please God and to obtain fellowship with his sons.' On the fundamental necessity of faith for salvation, here clearly stated by St Paul, all Christian theology agrees. The differences of opinion begin with the definition of this faith.

843a **17*a*.** 'the righteousness of God', as it stands, independent of the context, could mean that justice communicated to men, a created quality intrinsic to the believer; what is called the state of grace; cf Phil 3:9 where it is opposed to a justice based on personal merits. The connexion with faith in the present context as the means by which God's gift is offered to us, would support this opinion. It could, however, also be understood according to its OT usage, where it is a technical term for God's saving activity, and is paralleled to fidelity to the divine promises. In texts such as Pss 85 (84):4—6; 98 (97):2—3; 103 (102):17; 143 (142):1—2, the term describes that activity by which God delivers his people from their enemies and sets them up in their inheritance. By this use Paul's meaning would be that in the gospel message God's saving act is revealed which had been promised for the Messianic era. The acceptations are not radically opposed, and some commentators, such as Nygren and Leenhardt try to harmonize them. They understand the divine righteousness as a quality inherent in God, but not as a static reality, rather made manifest in a concrete and an active way, affecting individuals. On the whole idea of the justice of God, consult A. Descamps and L. Cerfaux in DBS 4 (1949) 1417—1510; S. Lyonnet in Bib 35 (1954) 480—502, 36 (1955) 202—12. On the history of the interpretation of the term in Rm 1:17 see S. Lyonnet in VDom 25 (1947) 193ff. On the text under consideration see H. Cazelles RB 58 (1951) 169—88; S. Lyonnet VDom 25 (1947) 23—34. 'through faith for faith': the meaning is not very clear. The sense could be either the justice acquired through ever increasing faith, or that faith is the source and the term of salvation, that is to say, faith sets us on the way of salvation and salvation is attained by perseverance in faith. Thus essentially the meaning is the same. In the biblical sense faith is a commitment of the whole person to God, and therefore implies a way of life with knowledge and obedience. Cf A. Lemonnyer, 'Justification', DTC 8 (1925), 2061ff.

b **17*b*.** 'he who through faith is righteous shall live': Hb 2:4 in a general way contrasts the Chaldeans glorying in their own resources with the Israelites who place all their reliance on Yahweh alone and receive life for their fidelity. The just by their faith in God are assured of God's protection, for absolute confidence in God's word was the conditon for the salvation of Israel. The midrashic commentary on Habakkuk from Qumran defined this faith as fidelity in following the teachings of the Teacher of Righteousness, 1QpHab 8:1—3. For St Paul it is primarily faith in the redemptive value of Christ's work. Though the salvation envisaged in OT was originally of a temporal order, it foreshadows the more spiritual conception of

Messianic salvation. The sentence could be understood **843** in two ways: by faith the just man shall live, or: he who is just through faith shall live; in either case the text does not refer to the way justification is effected, but to the conditions under which the just shall be saved: fidelity, perseverance in their state is required of them.

1:18—3:20. All Men need the Salvation revealed in the Gospel, because all men are sinners (3:23) and therefore live under the shadow of the wrath of God. This is true of the highly civilized Greeks = Gentiles, 1:18—32, as well as of Israel, God's chosen people, 2:1—3:20. To prove the universal need for salvation is the Apostle's first point in the section 1:18—11:36, the dogmatic part of the epistle.

The Apostle's actual proof of the universal need for salvation in 1:18—3:20 is based on the thesis that all men have been caught in the net of sin. See Gen 6:5. Similar texts from non-biblical literature can be found in Lietzmann 33, 35f; Deissmann 31ff. It is usually **c** taken that Paul is painting the gradual degradation of divine cult by a survey of the phases in the decline. The sequence and the themes follow those of the plan in Wis 13—14; but Paul's viewpoint is rather the attitude of mankind to God and the divine law; cf G. Castellino *Analecta Biblica* 17—18, 2, 255ff. Outside the gospel there is place only for God's wrath revealed throughout history by the increase in sin (1 Thes 2:16). OT juxtaposed the manifestation of God's saving justice and that of his wrath against evil-doers particularly on 'the day of Yahweh' evoked in Paul's text; cf Mi 7:9 Ps 69 (68): 25; Zeph 3:1ff.

Plan. It is customary to distinguish two major steps in the argument: (1) 1:18—32 dealing with the Gentiles; (2) 2:1—3:20 dealing with the Israelites. Another arrangement is: (1) 1:18—23 the case of those guilty of gross idolatry; (2) 1:24—32 the case of those guilty of obvious immorality; (3) 2:1—3:20 the case of those who condemn both idolatry and immorality and yet are guilty themselves. Of these two the former analysis is undoubtedly in closer agreement with the whole trend of the Apostle's argument. In the world of Paul there was a clearly marked distinction between Gentiles and Israelites, and every Israelite was proud of it. It must, however, be admitted that St Paul passes from the one to the other in 2:1 without any of the literary devices commonly used to indicate the beginning of a new topic. Moreover, it seems he deliberately avoided referring directly by name to the Gentiles in 1:18—32, and to the Israelites in 2:1—3:20. The result is a certain vagueness as the different commentaries show. But if this indefiniteness is intended for the purpose of ensuring a better hearing in both groups, it cannot be used as an argument against the former analysis, which is followed in this commentary.

1:18—32 The Gentiles' Need for the Salvation of the d Gospel—To show the need of the pagan world for the salvation of the Gospel Paul enlarges (1) in 18—23 on the folly of pagan idolatry; (2) in 24—32 on the moral corruption of pagan life. For a more detailed analysis see A. E. Garvie, CBi 96.

18—23 The Gentiles' Need for the Salvation of the Gospel in view of their Idolatry—The Gentiles know God, yet they do not honour him accordingly. Their worship is not religion but idolatry. Such folly, however, cannot possibly lead to the blessing of peace which every soul expects from God. On the contrary, their whole religion is patently stamped with the indelible marks of God's curse and wrath.

The term idolatry, not actually used in the text, is here understood in its primary theological meaning, in which it

3d stands for all misinterpretations and misrepresentations of God's attributes, i.e. for faulty natural theology in general, cf 1:23, 25. Only in this wide meaning can idolatry be said to be the beginning of the false and broad way that makes men sink lower and lower in their morality. And this is evidently the point which Paul wants to make here.

Further, idolatry in the restricted sense, in which it refers to various superstitions practised in connexion with actual idols, would not deserve the first place in this arraignment. For hideous and harmful as many of those superstitious practices may have been, they were hardly as hideous as the perversities referred to in 1:24—27. See also the list of sins in Gal 5:20 where fornication ranks first and idolatry fourth. Similar attacks on pagan idolatry are frequent in the OT, especially in the prophetical and sapiential literature; cf Ex 20:2—6 = Dt 5:6—10 (the first of the Ten Commandments); Is 44:9—20; Jer 10:3ff; Bar 6:3. That according to 1:18—23 the pagans' failure to attain salvation was due chiefly to their false religion or idolatry is a point worth emphasizing.

e **18.** The revelation of the wrath of God is considered as being in progress. This follows from the present tense and from the context, 1:24, 26, 28. It is God's wrath working itself out in human history by turning the paths men take to get away from God into paths of depravity, degeneration and decay. The evidence is the manifest folly of idolatry, 1:22f, and the moral corruption of pagan life, 1:24—32. As applied to God, anger is a metaphorical expression which in OT designates God's reaction to the sin of man. Sin is considered as provoking God, so the image underlines the incompatibility between God and sin and the consequences of opposing God. Its effect is death in the sense of loss of salvation; cf *Con. Gent.* 1, 91. Really God does not reject man, but man by his sin freely rejects divine love and separates himself from God. 'suppress the truth': the Greek can mean (1) who hold down = hold back the truth through their immorality; (2) who hold fast or possess the truth but with immorality, 1:32. In either case Paul says that the religious failure of the Gentiles is due not to insufficient knowledge of God but to inefficient moral principles. The truth of which he speaks is the true knowledge of God such as is accessible to human reason, 1:19—23.

f **19.** What can be known about God = what man can know about God by applying his natural faculties, is clear to them in their mind and conscience. Another possible rendering is: manifest among them. **20.** 'Creation' takes *ktiseos* in an active sense. Paul's vocabulary in this whole passage has several words unknown elsewhere in NT, drawing, perhaps, on extrabiblical Jewish literature. That through created beings man by means of his intellectual faculties can and ought to come to know God as Creator is common biblical doctrine, Ps 8:3; Is 42:5; 45:18; Wis 13:1, 5; 14:22. The same was defined as dogma by the First Vatican Council (Dz 1785). For references to the idea in Greek philosophy cf Lietzmann. Wis 13:1—9 expounds the same thought: God can be known from created things; cf F. Ceuppens: *Theologia Biblica* I, 3—11. Whereas Wis attributes the moral disorder to ignorance, Paul sees its root in the wilful perversion of knowledge of God; he asserts that the pagans have in fact had knowledge of God. On the use of this text by the Council see R. Aubert in LumVi 14 (1954) 21—52; on the history of the interpretation, S. Lyonnet in *QQ in Ep. Rom.*, Iª Series, 96ff. Vatican I (Dz 1785) was referring only to the capacity of human reason to acquire knowledge of God.

g **21** cites the two attitudes by which Scripture sums up man's duties towards God. The pagans have refused **843g** to acknowledge that everything has come from God and to show gratitude for his favours, but ascribed all to their own abilities. cf Lk 17:16—18; Ac 12:21—22. **22.** Some editions and commentators, following E. Klostermann, ZNW 32 (1933), 1—6, see the whole passage 22ff as three parallel periods of protasis and apodosis, beginning at 22, 25, 28, emphasizing that all vices are consequences of the basic sin of idolatry. But to begin the threefold period at 24 gives the same interpretation: Israel is delivered over to her desires, and moreover brings out clearly the divine intervention. cf S. Lyonnet, Bib 38 (1957), 35—40. **23.** The description is taken from OT, cf Dt 4:16—18; Jer 2:5ff.; but explicit allusion is made to the golden calf, Ps 106 (105):19—20. The significance of idolatry in the present text is the same as that seen by OT in the worship of the calf: the search for a God proportioned to the human understanding and amenable to human aims.

24—32 The Gentiles' Need for the Salvation of the Gospel proved from the Immorality of Pagan Life— From the Gentiles' idolatry Paul passes on to their immorality. Immorality must here be taken in the general sense of sins against the second part of the decalogue as distinguished from the sins forbidden in the first three of the Ten Commandments. The Apostle verifies his accusation of general immorality in pagan life with a list of 23 vices. They are arranged in three groups: 24f, impurity; 26f, unnatural vice; 28—32, a catalogue of twenty-one miscellaneous sins. Each of these groups is marked as such by the same introductory formula *paredōken* = *tradidit*, Vg = God gave them up to.

24, 26, 28. The triple repetition 'God gave them **844a** up' evokes a solemn promulgation of the divine judgement. A Semitic way of expressing the causal influence of God in sin and the effects of divine anger, the formula recurs in Jg, e.g. 2:14; 3:8; cf also Ps 106 (105):41. It highlights the connexion between culpable religious error and moral and social disorder: sin has within itself its sanctions and its consequences; Wis 11:15—16; 12:23—27. In the manner of Jewish apologetic method the assessment is of civilizations not of persons, of whom God is the sole judge, 1 Cor 5:12—13. St Paul treats immorality as a regular consequence of idolatry, and in this sequence he sees a divine arrangement or divine law. According to this text it is God's order that the first commandment is the cornerstone of all religious and moral life. Without it the other commandments are a building that has no foundation. This implication is clearly stated in 28. To explain *how* this divine order is reconcilable with the absolute goodness of God is part of the general problem of evil rather than of the exegesis of Rm 1:24. For a special note on the relation between idolatry and immorality see Lagrange 36—41. **24f** 'impurity'. This can refer, generally speaking, to any sin as staining man's character. But the context of 24f makes it necessary to think here of sins of fornication. For the use of the word impurity in this sense cf 6:19; 2 Cor 12:21; and contrast the Christian reverence for the body in 1 Cor 6:12—20. **26f** single out from the sins against the sixth commandment two particularly humiliating types, namely, unnatural vice. **27c** refers to the vices of 26, 27ab, which are here considered not so much as sins in themselves but as punishment for the sin of idolatry described in 18—23. **28.** 'base mind': their moral judgement is debased because it has not been used rightly.

29—32. This is a summary charge of general im- **b** morality in form of a list of 21 (23 Vg) common sins.

844b Similar lists by Paul can be found in Rm 13:13; Gal 5:19—21. These lists may have their model in the OT, e.g. Ex 20; 21:1—23:19; 34:14—26. For a number of references to similar catalogues in classical (Stoic) and patristic literature see Lietzmann 35. All attempts to discover a systematic order in Paul's enumeration have failed. The later Greek MSS and Vg have two additions which are probably not genuine: 'fornication' in 29; and 'without fidelity' in 31. On the whole subject see Lagrange RB 8 (1911) 534ff. **32.** In one respect this is but another sin to be added to the previous list, viz the sin of applauding and encouraging wrong-doing. On the other hand, Paul has obviously set it apart and marked it as the climax of all the depravity mentioned before. This is no exaggeration. For to abet and to applaud evil is doing the devil's own work.

2:1—3:20 Israel's Need for the Salvation of the Gospel—Continuing his evidence of the universal need for the salvation revealed in the Gospel, Paul here takes up the case of Israel, the Chosen People. But there is no indication in the text of this change of subject. To make such an abrupt transition intelligible, commentators refer to Nathan's conviction of David in 2 Sm 12:1—9. As David wholeheartedly condemned the man of Nathan's parable, 2 Sm 12:1—5, so every Israelite would wholeheartedly join in Paul's condemnation of paganism in 18—32. But there follows in each case the unexpected 'thou art the man' 2 Sm 12:7 = Rm 2:1—3:20.

c The progress of thought in 2:1—3:20 is not easy to follow. The subdivisions proposed in the various commentaries differ widely. The difficulty arises mainly from the various objections with which the Apostle repeatedly interrupts the course of his argument. In addition, the actual objections are not stated in the text, but must be inferred from his answers. The objector is, of course, imaginary; cf SH 69f, on 3:1ff.

2:1—2 A General Statement introducing Israel's Case with regard to the Salvation of the Gospel—Without mentioning a name Paul here introduces the case of a man who condemns the idolatry and immorality depicted in 1:18—32 but is nevertheless guilty himself. Self-complacent he sits in judgement over the religious and moral life of others, but in reality he needs the salvation of the Gospel as much as they.

1a. So far Paul has addressed himself clearly to all those who were guilty of gross idolatry, 1:18—23, and immorality, 1:24—32. But these apart, there evidently remained a large group of men who condemned idolatry and immorality as much as Paul did, e.g. the followers of stoic philosophy and, much more numerous and out-**d** spoken than they, the whole of Israel. Hence the question, did Paul here think only of Israelites or did he include also the so-called good pagans? Both possibilities are defended by different commentators. The opinion that Paul thought exclusively of Israelites has in its favour that in 2:17 he actually mentions 'the Jew' by name, which he seems to have deliberately avoided before, in order to obtain a better hearing. Moreover, the whole description is said to fit the typical Israelite of the time who was proud of his higher religious and moral standards, cf 2:17—20; Lk 18:9—14. On the other hand, there is much to be said in favour of the opinion that here at the beginning Paul is still speaking generally, and includes everybody who fits the description, no matter whether Jew or Gentile. This opinion presents the wider view in every respect. After all, there were good pagans, then as now, and they could not reasonably be said to fall under the accusation of 1:18—32. Hence if they are not included in 2:1—3:20 they escape the Apostle's argument for the universal need of the salvation revealed in the Gospel. This may not be **84** impossible, but there can be little doubt that with 2:1—3: 20 he intended to close the ring of his evidence so as to let no one escape from the accusation of being under sin and therefore in need of the salvation of the Gospel. The division between Jew and Gentile in the text is not a hard and fast one: the Jews are explicitly referred to only in 2:16ff, and characteristic sins of each overlap in the indictment. It is almost as if in Paul's thought two epochs of history illustrated the divine plan and the working of God's relations with mankind; cf X. Léon-Dufour in Studiorum Paulinorum Congressus, *Analecta Biblica* 17—18, 2, 309—15, and A. Viard in RSPT 47 (1963) 14—24, where the question is put in focus.

1bc. This is Paul's summary reply to those who would **e** claim exemption from the previous charges of idolatry and immorality. As can be seen from his later explanations, he does not mean to say that those who belong to this second category are, in spite of their protest, guilty of all the sins enumerated in 1:18—32. But as far as the dominion of sin is concerned they are in the same position as those whom they condemn. For in principle they act in the same way, i.e. they, too, do not live according to their knowledge of God; and that is where their sin begins. Their guilt may be less evident owing to their higher knowledge of God, or because their religious and moral life is more refined, but this does not exempt them from the dominion of sin. They are caught in the net of sin like all the rest. This is no doubt a hard argument and one can well understand that the Apostle takes a long time over explaining it, 2:2—3:20. But, in all he says, nowhere does he go back on his word. Again and again he repeats it: all are under sin. There is no exception. Those who judge others, thereby speak their own judgement, cf Jn 8:7; 1 Jn 1:10. The practical conclusion which the Apostle wants to be drawn from it all evidently is: living in sin 'you will also die in your sin', Jn 8:21, unless you accept the salvation offered in the Gospel.

3—10 A First Objection—Do not God's kindness, forbearance and patience give a sufficient guarantee that the threatened punishment of men's sins will be averted, 3—4? To this St Paul sternly replies that such a hope is foolish. On the day of God's judgement his justice alone will rule, giving everybody his due according to his works, cf Ps 62 (61):12f; Prv 24:12. On that day God's goodness will certainly not declare sinners to be saints.

11—24 A Second Objection—Will the Torah, the Law **f** of Sinai, not protect Israel from the wrath of God? Paul's reply is substantially the same as before. On the day of God's judgement it is not God's law that will be weighed in the balance but men's works. On that day sin will be punished as sin, without any respect of persons, no matter whether it was sin against God's will as read in the Torah or as voiced in man's conscience, 11—16. **16.** Some connexion with 15 must be inserted, e.g. [as will be evident to all] on the day when God judges. The whole sentence seems to have been added here by Paul to answer the excuse that the voice or law of man's conscience is something which it is difficult to prove as it is hidden and secret and that it therefore should not be used in a discussion of this nature. Paul replies: this may be true for the present, but it will not be so on the day of God's judgement. Then all will have to confess that they had God's law written in their hearts. The law in 12—16 designates the norm of moral conduct intended for all men. Gentiles, without the help of a positive revelation, but acting according to conscience, would receive from God the graces necessary for salvation. The Torah was in itself only a guide for men, not a principle of salvation.

44f For a survey of the interpretations of 14—16 see J. Riedl in *Stud. Paulin.* I, 271—81.

g **17—24.** The Apostle follows up his first answer with an *argumentum ad hominem*. After a solemn introduction in 17—20 which enumerates all the alleged prerogatives of Israel (but is left without a proper apodosis), he instances in 21—23 the 7th, 6th and 1st commandments against his objector. With reference to these three accusations it would no doubt be an exaggeration to think that Paul regarded every Israelite as a thief, an adulterer, or a temple-robber. His point is rather that these sins were committed by Israelites, though they were expressly forbidden in the Torah, cf SB 3 108—15. The Law, therefore, has not saved Israel from sin in the past nor will it save Israel from the wrath of God on the day of judgement. **22.** This is commonly understood of pagan temples, cf Dt 7:5; Ac 19:37; Jos.Ant. IV 8, 10. The incentive to such theft seems to have been the great wealth stored up in many pagan temples. Others understand the phrase of defrauding the revenues due to the temple in Jerusalem. **25—29 A Third Objection**—Is not circumcision, Israel's first sacrament, a sufficient guarantee for her salvation? Paul's answer is that circumcision does not make a man holy before God, if he does not keep the law of God; cf Dt 10:16; 30:6; Jer 4:4; 9:26; Ez 44:7. And Israel has not kept the law. **28.** What gives an act value in the sight of God is the motivating principle. Paul reacts against the formalism in contemporary Jewish morality to affirm an interior religion. Later in 8:2ff he says that the Holy Spirit is the principle of interior renewal.

45a **3:1 8 A Fourth Objection** If the Law and circumcision cannot save Israel, what then remains of Israel's so highly-praised privileges? Paul's reply begins as if he intended to answer with a long description of Israel's privileged position as in 9:4. In fact, however, he does not get beyond the first point, that she has been entrusted with the Scriptures. **2.** 'The words of God' can mean: (1) the whole OT; (2) the Messianic promises in the OT, because of v 3. What is the use of the Scriptures, since according to Paul's own argument God is no longer bound to his promises after Israel has broken the covenant by unfaithfulness to her obligations? Paul answers as in 2 Tim 2:13; cf also Rm 9:6; Jer 31 (38 LXX): 32. True as it is that God's relation to his people is a bilateral covenant, yet this is not all. God's truthfulness and faithfulness to himself are above any changes which man may introduce. Man's untruthfulness and unfaithfulness only serve to bring out the opposite attributes of God all the more clearly. The words have been understood (1) of Israel's 'unbelief' in Jesus of Nazareth as the Messiah; (2) of Israel's unfaithfulness to the covenant of Sinai referred to in 2:11—24, 25—29. The second explanation is recommended by the contrast with God's 'faithfulness' in the context and by the same thought in 2 Tim 2:13. But **b** one cannot be quite dissociated from the other. If our unjustness (= sinfulness) serves to make God's justice stand out the more clearly, why are we still threatened with his wrath, and urged to seek justification? Is God not unjust in punishing such sinfulness? Paul's reply in 6—8 is difficult to follow. It seems to consist of three points, each meant to lead the objector *ad absurdum*. (1) According to such reasoning God could not judge the world at all, and yet we know that he will judge everyone, and that his judgements will be true, cf 2:2, 6—8; Ps 119 (118):137; Job 34:10—12, etc. (2) According to such reasoning the Jews could not condemn me (Paul) as a sinner = an apostate, but should rather acquiesce in my apostasy as a means of manifesting and glorifying God's truth in the possession of Israel. Yet the objector, being a Jew, must know very well how harshly Paul is judged by his former coreligionists, 7. So Jülicher. (3) According to **845b** such reasoning it would be right to teach as some maintain that I (Paul) do 'do evil that good may come'. Yet, such a doctrine is evidently abhorred by all, 8. **7** is taken by most commentators as a further objection, in which case it is but a weakened repetition of v 5. **8.** 'Do evil that good may come': is a malicious misinterpretation of Paul's doctrine of justification by faith and not by works, cf 6:1, 15.

The argument in 1—8 is worked out in a dialogue style reminiscent of the synagogal discussions, and is based on a parallelism between fidelity, veracity and justice, practically synonymous in OT, in contrast to infidelity, falsehood and injustice; cf P. Benoit in RB 47 (1938) 508 n.3. Because of the unfaithfulness of the Jews, their privileges are devoid of value, but God's oracles have not lost their force, for man's infidelity cannot nullify the divine promises, but only throw them into stronger relief. Yet this **c** will not save sinners from divine wrath, nor *a fortiori* excuse their sin. In 4 Paul quotes from Ps 51 (50):6 according to LXX; but even in MT where the situation is David's admission of guilt, to proclaim God's justice is an act of faith in the divine fidelity to the promises, cf Ps 89 (88):31—38; Dn 9:7—16; and S. Lyonnet in VDom 25 (1947), 118—21; Bib 36 (1955), 209.

9—20 Concluding Statement of Israel's Need for the Salvation of the Gospel—The Apostle returns from the various digressions in 2:3—3:8 to the principal question of 2:1—2: is he who claims exemption from the charge of idolatry and immorality in 1:18—32 (esp Israel) entitled to regard himself as 'just' before God, or in such a privileged position that he does not need the Christian justification? Paul's concluding answer is an uncompromising No. The Jews as well as the Greeks, i.e. Israel, the Chosen People (= the Church of old), as well as the pagan world, all are in the bondage of sin, as the Scriptures prove. The Apostle's proof from the Scriptures in 10—18 is a free combination of the following texts from LXX: Rm 3:10—12 = Ps 14 (13): 1—3 = Ps 53 (52).2—4; Rm 3:13a—b = Ps 5:10; Rm 3:13c = Ps 140 (139): 4; Rm 3:14 = Ps 10 (9):28; Rm 3:15—17 = Is 59:7f; Rm 3:18 = Ps 36 (35):2. **9.** *proechometha* = have we Israelites then still any advantage over the Gentiles? According to this translation the Greek middle is here used for the active, cf Lagrange, Boylan. If the Greek form is taken as passive, the meaning is 'are we Israelites then in a worse position than the Gentiles?' 'No, not so' = (1) not altogether, (2) not at all. In either case, Paul does not deny that Israel has privileges, but she has none as regards the need for the salvation of the Gospel which is the point here under discussion. **20.** Law convinces man of sin (cf 7:7—12) **d** but does not produce justness or salvation, cf Jn 1:17. Human nature by its innate forces cannot be justified in the sight of God. The Law is understood here as a set of precepts given by God as a means for our justification; and Paul contends that knowledge alone of these precepts as an external norm of conduct can only make man more conscious of sin, while mere observance irrespective of interior dispositions is useless.

Application of 1:18—3:20—Paul's argument for the universal need of the salvation revealed in the Gospel is still practical and convincing. For laws are still insufficient to make men saints, no matter whether we consider the laws of conscience, or the laws of the various systems of moral philosophy, or the laws of Christian moral theology. All these systems agree in showing the ideal more or less clearly, but they do not produce the longed-for justness—righteousness—salvation, because in practice

845d no one lives in complete accordance with all these laws. Because of sin men needed the salvation of the Gospel in the days of Paul, and because of sin they still need it today. The need for that salvation is the result not of religious speculations but of hard realities.

846a **3:21—4:25 The Way to the Salvation of the Gospel—** In this second part of the dogmatic section of his letter Paul sets out to describe the means by which the salvation of the Gospel is obtained. The logical connexion with the previous discussion, proving man's need for it, is self-evident. The two sections belong together as man's need and God's answer. At the same time it is easy to notice a gap in the argument. Between man's need for salvation and the way to the salvation of the Gospel one expects a discussion on the nature of this salvation. According to the dogmatic textbooks of today such a discussion would have to deal first with Christ's work of redemption, then with the negative side of salvation = justification = remission of sins, and finally with its positive side = sanctification = infusion of sanctifying grace. St Paul in his exposition of the way to salvation, 3:21—4:25, and of the effects of salvation, 5:1—8:39, does cover the ground of such a modern discussion on the nature of Christian salvation, but in a way that is not systematic according to our standards; cf Prat I, 171; II, 50—53.

Plan. According to the most common opinion 3:21—4:25 can be subdivided as follows: (1) 3:21—30 the way to the Christian salvation is faith in Christ; (2) 3:31—4:25 the Scriptural evidence in favour of this doctrine. Another arrangement is: (1) 3:21—26 the way to the Christian salvation; (2) 3:27—31 some practical conclusions; (3) 4:1—25 the case of Abraham as proof from Scripture for the Christian doctrine of salvation by faith.

b **21—26 The Way to the Christian Salvation is Justification by Faith in Christ—**In a picture which is very different from that in 1:18—3:20 Paul here gives a summary description of the new salvation which he is preaching and defending. Unfortunately for us, the description is so brief and compact that it becomes difficult to understand. The negative picture in 1:18—3:20 is much fuller and easier to analyse. The outstanding importance of the passage, however, is generally recognized. The characteristics of the Christian salvation singled out in this description by Paul are: (1) it is a justification which does not come by way of any law, 21; (2) it is obtained by faith in Christ, 22a; (3) hence it is open to all, without distinction, 22b, 23; (4) it has its ultimate origin in the propitiatory death of Christ, 24—26. See the similar description in 1:16f; and the detailed analysis in Prat I, 204—6.

c **21** The law in its various forms (be it conscience, or moral philosophy, or OT Scriptures) offers salvation to all who abide by this law and keep it in every point. From this system of justification the salvation of the Gospel must be clearly distinguished. They are worlds apart. Man's failure in the one is God's opportunity in the other. Another possible explanation translates Law as Mosaic Law, e.g. WV, Boylan. 'Justice' here is the divine attribute of fidelity by God to the promises of salvation. The Law shows only what must be done without giving any help to carry it out. Paul's aim is not so much to show how this justice has been manifested as to insist that there has always been only one divine plan for the salvation of mankind. **22.** The justness which the Gospel promises is obtained by way of faith in Jesus Christ. The law-fulness of the former system of salvation has been replaced by faithfulness; cf Council of Trent, sess VI, cap 8 (Dz 801). On the suitability of faith for playing such an important part in the process of salvation see Prat I, 172f; Gifford 89.

To accept God's justifying act man must respond to the 84 divine call in an act of faith. This is a conscious, deliberate and free act, and implies an admission of personal insufficiency and submission to the work of God within the individual. For an accurate delineation of the ideas of justification and salvation and their OT setting see S. Lyonnet in *Analecta Biblica* 17—18, i, 95—110.

23. The glory of God = the perfection of God. In this context it is evidently the justice of God as it was meant to be shared by men, therefore = justness = sanctifying grace. Others explain *doxa* (= glory) here as high opinion, honour, praise, favour from God, which leads to the same idea. All have sinned and thereby lost God's good opinion of them = his favour = his grace. Cornely understands it of eternal life as in 2:7; 8:18, 21. In OT the term referred to the majesty and power accompanying the presence of God, and connotes therefore the divine presence itself among the people and experienced by them, Ex 24:16. One of the special favours of the Messianic age was held to be the participation of the divine glory. cf Ez 43:2ff; Is 60:1ff. On Paul's use of the expression in a soteriological context see H. Schlier in *Analecta Biblica* 17—18, i, 45—56 with bibliography; G. Kittel in TWNT (1935) 2, 236—56. All men are one in that they have sinned and are unable to free themselves; there is only one way open to salvation: justification through the grace of God. No human act prior to justification can be taken into account as a cause.

24—25. The Christian justification derives its existence e ultimately from the propitiatory death of Christ, which the Council of Trent, sess VI cap 7—8 (Dz 799, 801) called 'the meritorious cause of our justification'. That this central thesis of all Christian doctrine of salvation—justification—sanctification (soteriology) is clearly expressed in our passage is beyond any doubt, and the differences of opinion which exist on the exact meaning of this or that term here employed by Paul should not be allowed to obscure this fundamental doctrine of the passage; cf Prat II, 181, 184; I, 380—4; SH 91—4, note after 3:26.

24. *apolutrōsis* = redemption. Does this term imply the idea of a ransom being paid, the ransom being the blood of Christ? This question cannot be decided for certain. The word *apolutrōsis*, redemption, taken by itself, need not carry the idea of a ransom, for LXX uses it for the 'deliverance' from Egypt; and the NT uses it in the same general sense of 'deliverance' six times out of ten; Lk 21:28; Rm 8:23; 1 Cor 1:30; Eph 1:14; 4:30; Heb 11:35. On the other hand it has the meaning of 'ransom' in Col 1:14; Eph 1:7; Heb 9:15. To these references we must add the passages in the NT in which the idea is clearly expressed that the Christians have been 'bought for a price', 1 Cor 6:20; 7:23; Gal 3:13; Apoc 5:9; cf also Mt 20:28; Mk 10:45; Ac 20:28; 1 Pt 1:18f; Prat II 181. But in the present setting of OT 84 concepts, the background of this and cognate expressions would be the deliverance of the chosen people from Egypt by an act of God, and this event is in OT associated with the Alliance on Sinai whereby Israel was made into a new people, the special possession of God, cf Ex 19:5ff; Dt 7:6—8; in NT 1 Pt 2:9; Ti 2:14. This interpretation would emphasize the motive for the redemption—God's gratuitous love. S. Lyonnet in LumVi 36 (1958) 35—66; VDom 36 (1958), 129—46, 257—9, brings out the close biblical connexion between the ideas of redemption and acquisition. In this light Paul would have in mind that messianic deliverance by God through a new alliance, making of all mankind a special, 'purchased' people. **25.** *hilastērion* = propitiation. There can be b

47b no doubt that this term describes our Lord's death as propitiation = expiation of our sins. But does it define our Lord's death as a propitiatory *sacrifice*? The doctrine that Christ's death was a sacrifice for men's sins = a propitiatory sacrifice, follows clearly from such texts as Mt 26:28 and parallels; 1 Cor 11:24f; 15:3; Eph 1:7; 5:2; Col 1:20; Heb 10:12—14; 1 Pt 1:18f; 3:18, etc. The question whether this doctrine is also expressed in Rm 3:25 must be left open, for the word *hilastērion* (= propitiation) taken by itself cannot be shown to have had the meaning 'propitiatory sacrifice'. According to etymology it signifies 'something connected with reconciliation, propitiation or expiation'. LXX uses it 25 times for 'the lid of the Ark of the Covenant' = the mercy-seat or propitiatory; cf Ex 25:17. So also Heb 9:5. The only other text in the NT where it occurs is here, where its exact meaning is consequently largely a matter of conjecture. The main explanations that have been put forward are: (1) a means of propitiation = a propitiatory = a mercy-seat; (2) a propitiator (taking the adjective as masculine which is possible in the Greek); (3) a propitiatory sacrifice. The last of these explanations is favoured in our context by the phrase 'in his own blood',

c 25. Cf Prat I, 42f; II, 180—8; SH 91—4. Many modern commentators, e.g. Nygren, Leenhardt, Kuss, see in the term a reference to the sacrifice of expiation, Ex 25:17—22; Lv 16:13—21. In virtue of its role as the place where God communicated his precepts, and in the ritual of expiation for the collective sins of the people, the mercy-seat in the minds of the Israelites was the place of God's presence and of his saving justice. The application to Christ is obvious: he is in the fullest sense the locus of the presence of God (Col 2:9), the Word of God (Heb 1:1), and by his blood effects the true remission of sins. According to the then prevalent conception, the people's sin was thought to have driven God from among them, but by the rite of blood the divine presence was brought back and good relations with God were restored. In contrast to the OT rite performed in secret, Christ is manifested to all men, since at his sacrifice the veil of the Temple was torn away (Mt 27:51). Furthermore, in OT, expressions for placating the divine wrath are not used. God is said to pardon, wipe away sin, and objects or places are purified, cf S. Lyonnet VDom 37 (1959) 336—52. Expiation has, then, rather the sense of intercession which depends for its value and force on the interior attitude of the worshippers. Essentially (Wis 18:21—25) it consists in recalling God's promises, and becomes thereby an act of faith in divine fidelity. See S. Lyonnet in Bib 40 (1959), 885—901; VDom 38 (1960), 65—75. On the theological development of this thought cf Aquin. *Summa Theol.*, 1, 23, 5; J. Lécuyer RTh 55 (1955), 339—62.

25—26. The structure of this sentence is: God set up Jesus Christ as a propitiation . . . 25*a*: (1) *with the intention* of showing his justice, 25*b*; (2) *the reason being* his having passed by the sins of the past in patience, 25*c*, 26*a*; (3) *with the intention* of showing his justice in the present time, 26*b*; (4) *with the intention* that he may be found just himself and justifying those who believe in Jesus, 26*c*. Nos. 1, 3,

d 4 form a clear and continuous line of thought. But how are we to fit in no. 2? It is evidently closely connected with no. 1 and at the same time there is a contrast with no. 3. Accordingly there are two explanations. (1) If the connexion with no. 1 is stressed then it seems inserted to explain why God manifested his justice with such severity in the death of Christ, 25*a*, 26*c*. The Apostle warns against interpreting God's

forbearance with man's sins in the past as a proof that **847d** God's punitive justice had fallen into abeyance for ever. The cross is the true measure of the rigour of God's justice in punishing sin. (2) If the contrast between no. 2 and no. 3 is stressed, i.e. the contrast between past and present, then no. 2 seems intended to show that God in the past merely passed by sin but did not justify = sanctify = save the sinner, as he has decided to do in the present time. The choice between these two possibilities depends on the interpretation given to 'the justice of God' in this paragraph; cf note on 25*b*. **25*b*—26*b*.** 'The justness of God' = his communicated justice, as in 3:21. This explanation has the advantage of consistency and simplicity. It does away with the necessity of remembering the distinction between justice of God as it is in God and as it is in man; and it concentrates on the main idea of the whole section 3:21—4:25 which is man's justification according to the Gospel. From the practical point of view, therefore, this explanation is certainly the easiest to follow. But it must be admitted that this is not the only possible explanation. In view of the respective contexts many commentators maintain that Paul's usage of the term 'justice of God' is not consistent in this paragraph. The different meanings are (1) = God's justice in man = communicated justice = justness, in 21; (2) = justice in God, in 25; and that with the emphasis on the special meaning of justice as punitive justice, the reference being to God's punitive justice as revealed in the terrible death of Christ for man's sins; (3) = the justice in God, in 26; but with the emphasis on the general meaning of justice = the whole moral perfection of God, as revealed in Christ's propitiation and in the justification of man. The context would, however, seem to **e** argue a strictly biblical notion of divine justice: God's saving activity operative in virtue of his promise. Because of his fidelity to his promises Yahweh was pledged to restore his people and re-establish them in the promised favours. In short, God's justice is his salvific act by which he delivers man from sin; and the sacrifice of Christ shows this act in operation. Before that the saving activity was not manifest to all. Sin had changed man's whole orientation and deprived him of 'life'. The process of justification, then, consists essentially in God's delivering man from sin, a painful experience since it involves reorientation by renouncing egoism, and conferring on him the promised favours. Such an interpretation fits into the thought of Paul for whom the initiative in the redemption lies in God's love for men. By the very fact of justifying mankind God carries out his promises. Aquinas, commenting on Rm, understands the word as referring to God's fidelity to his promises. **25*c*—26*a*.** According to the best editions of the Greek **f** text, *paresis* meaning praetermission rather than remission. There are two explanations of the idea here expressed. (1) In the past God only passed by man's sins in his patience (cf Ac 14:15) but there was no real justification of man, as this was reserved for the present time. Such must be the thought if the justice of God in 25*b* = justness. (2) God showed his justice so severely in the death of Christ, 25*ab*, because of his having apparently overlooked man's sins in the past by showing patience. To avoid this patience being misinterpreted as indifference to sin on God's part is one purpose of the terrible death of Christ for man's sins. This must be the idea if the justice of God in 25*b* is the punitive justice of God. As a substantive the word occurs only in Hellenistic literature where among other meanings it has that of remission of a debt or of guilt. The verb does not mean

847f 'pardon' alone, but implies also the idea of controls so that sins are not committed, cf Sir 23:2 and commentaries on this text. Likewise, it can mean 'omit' or 'set aside', but this is not to leave sin unpunished, nor does it suggest not remitting it. cf S. Lyonnet VDom 25 (1947), 138—42. In Paul's mind throughout is the conviction that true redemption is brought about only by means of the blood of Christ, which manifests the working of God's saving act. But the sacrifice of Christ also shows the real value of the old rituals as prefiguring that to come. In particular the remission of sins on the Day of Atonement did not justify the participants, but it did herald the future, true, justification, in view of which God could overlook the sins and accord a provisional pardon, a sort of non-imputation, orientated to the definitive remission. The attempt to convey the notion of a qualified pardon accounts for Paul's use of a rare term. See S. Lyonnet Bib 38 (1957), 40—61; and for a somewhat different interpretation

g T. Fahy IrTQ 23 (1956), 69—73. Summarily: the fidelity of God to his promises is manifested now, in the Messianic age, justifying mankind, delivering the race from sin on condition that the proffered gift is accepted and appropriated by faith. Some commentators, O. Michel and O. Kuss among the more recent, understand 'redemption' in 24 in reference to the historical event of the crucifixion, and similarly take 'expiation' in 25 as designating Christ's historical sacrifice, as an instrument working the effect. The contrary view would take both concepts in a subjective acceptation, and speak of the actual effectiveness with the individual person of Christ's redemptive act, and of the actual removal of sin in the believer through the sacrifice of Christ. K. Wennemer in *Analecta Biblica* 17—18, i, 283—8 summarizes both positions. Though there is, perhaps, some over-conceptualization of Paul's thought in pressing the distinction, the passage does stress the role of faith in the process of justification. The value of Christ's sacrifice remains active in him, and this fund of merit is appropriated by faith, the giving of oneself to Christ. But, since justification is gratuitous, even that faith is from the divine initiative. In short Paul's thought is that God's fidelity to his promises has been manifested in the work he has done through our Redeemer, which frees each person from sin and communicates divine life in so far as each one corresponds to and accepts this work by an act of faith of which Christ is the object and the source.

848a 27—31 Three Practical Conclusions from the Christian Doctrine of Justification by Faith— These vv throw further light on the way to salvation by means of three conclusions from its previous description in 21—26. (1) The Christian doctrine of justification by faith excludes all that boastful self-sufficiency and self-complacency which the various claims to superiority in law and lawfulness had spread and always will spread among men. In the Christian doctrine of salvation, law and lawfulness have been dethroned from the first place in the process of man's salvation, and their place of honour has been given to faith in Jesus Christ, 27f. (2) The Christian doctrine of justification by faith supersedes the old distinction between Israelites and Gentiles based on circumcision. All attempts to retain that distinction in the question of salvation are in vain. For faith in Jesus Christ cannot be made dependent on circumcision or descent from Abraham. And it is this faith which is henceforward the one and only condition for salvation required on the part of man, 29f. (3) The Christian doctrine of justification by faith is in complete agreement with the Scriptures = the Law of Moses =

the Pentateuch, 31. The proof of this follows in **848** ch 4.

27. 'boasting' *kauchēsis* in LXX describes the **b** characteristic attitude of the wicked opposed to that of reliance on God, Ps 74 (73):4; 49 (48):7. For Paul it designates the attitude of those Jews who set store on their conduct, 2:17—18, and of those who would attempt to realize a supernatural destiny by innate natural powers. The opposition here, then, is not between the economy of the OT and that of the New, but between a régime founded essentially on works and on a law as an extrinsic norm of conduct, and one built on faith and a law which is an interior dynamic principle, conferring the capacity to carry out what the law requires, cf Aquin. *in Rm*; *Sum. Theol.* 1—2, q. 106, a.2.

Faith for St Paul is a fully human and personal act in which man acknowledges his insufficiency by assenting to truths on the authority of God; so it is a submission to and an acceptance of God's justifying act. Theologically speaking, faith is the first act worked by God in the subject, what is now described as 'living faith'. cf Gal 5:6; Eph 2:10.

28. Christian justification is obtained by faith; **c** no one can earn it by works according to this or that system of law, whatever the name or character of that law may be: be it the law of Israel, or the law of the Gentiles; be it natural, moral or ceremonial law; cf 3:20—22; Dz 801, 1793; Prat I, 180f. Already Origen uttered a warning against the false conclusion that according to this v works *after* justification are of no account. To draw such a conclusion would be to overlook two important points: (1) Paul is here concerned not with the Christian life after justification, but with the way of obtaining justification. 'Initial justification' = the beginning of justification, is his point. (2) When Paul does speak of the life after justification has been obtained, he leaves no doubt that works are necessary to retain the justification obtained by faith. The evidence is to be found in his many exhortations, e.g. Rm 12—14. Among the more popular references to the same effect are Mt 25:34ff; 1 Cor 3:8; Gal 5:6; Jas 2:14, 17, 24—26. But St Paul would call these works 'works of faith' and not 'works of law'. Thus there is no contradiction. Faith leads to virtue, but virtue need not lead to faith (Greg, *Hom. 19 in Ez, cf* Estius). The necessity and meritorious character of good works after justification had to be defended by the Council of Trent, sess VI, cap 7, 10; Dz 800, 803, 834, 842.

Another conclusion from 28 that had to be rejected **d** by the Council of Trent is, that *before* justification only faith is necessary as a preparation and no other works. To prove such a conclusion it would be necessary to show that Paul considered here not only the immediate preparation for justification which is admittedly faith, but also the possibilities of a more remote preparation and deliberately excluded any such steps before the decisive act of faith. Such a proof is impossible and other texts show that we must leave room for such a more remote preparation. The Council of Trent, sess VI, cap 6 (Dz 798, 819), mentions: fear of God's punishment of sin, Sir 1:28; Heb 11:6; hope of his forgiveness for Christ's sake, Mt 9:2; Mk 2:5; love of God = hatred of sin, 1 Jn 3:14; repentance, Lk 13:3; Ac 3:19; the resolution to receive the sacrament of baptism and to keep the commandments Mt 28:19; Ac 2:38.

Verse 28 has also become famous through Luther's translation 'by faith alone' = *sola fide*. The adjective 'alone' was not in the text from which Luther translated, since no MS or edition has it. He may have added it for

48d the purpose of bringing out the sense of the passage more clearly. In fact, however, the addition has led to the false conclusion that—faith excepted—all other works both before and after justification are of no account according to Paul's doctrine of salvation. This so-called *sola-fides* doctrine was rejected by the Council of Trent, Dz 819, 798, 803f.

e But the Council condemned the interpretation given by the Reformers rather than the expression itself, which did not originate with Luther. While Bellarmine could appeal to the Fathers for the phrase, Aquin excluded even moral conduct as a source of justification. See the Excursus in S. Lyonnet, *QQ in Rom.*, Iª Series, 142—50. **30.** 'by faith' . . . through faith': stylistic variation seems to be the most natural explanation of the difference in the preposition; so Boylan, differently SH. There is also the widespread literary technique of multiplying prepositions to bring out the complexity of the relations between God and creation. **31.** It seems best to take 'law' without the article here in the sense of 'régime of law'; faith gives man a new principle, and thereby enables the goal of any régime of law to be attained: the justification of man.

349a **4:1—25 The Justification of Abraham as a Scripture Proof for the Christian Doctrine of Justification by Faith**—The purpose of this digression into OT history is to illustrate and prove the three previous conclusions, 3:27—31, esp the last, 3:31, that in teaching justification by faith and not by the observance of the Law, the Gospel asserts a doctrine which is not against, but in complete agreement with the Scriptures = OT, esp Pent. Paul also has the aim of correcting Jewish thought on Abraham as the type of justification through 'works'. Contemporary Judaism based salvation on the principle of distributive justice: a promised reward for upright conduct; thus the call of Abraham was considered to be the recompense for his devotion to the true God. The same tendency is reflected in OT, e.g. Sir 44:19—23, where the promise to Abraham is the reward for his faith. cf J. Bonsirven: *La Bible Apocryphe* (1953), 93ff. The covenant was viewed as a bilateral contract, and the Law, given to Israel on her merits, had an instrumental **b** function in the performance of good works. These were the presuppositions of that attitude and conduct impugned by Christ: self-sufficiency, e.g. Mt 3:9, and formalism, ascribing a positive value to the observance of the precept rather than to the motive, e.g. Mk 7:10—13. That this was not the universal Jewish way of thinking is seen from the Qumran writings which testify to sentiments in the best tradition of Jewish piety—looking to God alone for justification, e.g. 1QS 11:10—22. Paul in turn appeals to a conception of salvific justice, that is to a divine act in which God shows his fidelity to the promises, in other words a unilateral and gratuitous pact, while stressing the identity of the divine plan before and after Christ.

Note: theological speculations on the theme of Isaac's expiatory and meritorious sacrifice were current at the time of Christ, but the extent of their influence on and how they coloured Paul's soteriology is disputed. See W. Davies, *Paul and Rabbinic Judaism* (1948), 237ff; R. Le Déaut in *Analecta Biblica*, 17—18, ii, 562—74.

c The argument consists of the following 5 points: (1) 1—8. 'Abraham believed God, and it was reckoned to him as righteousness', Gn 15:6 LXX, Vg: this is the proof-text. It has a positive and a negative side. The former is the emphasis on Abraham's faith, the latter consists in the omission of any reference to his works. Both aspects must be taken together to make Abraham a suitable type of the justification of the Gospel by faith without works, 3:27f. (2) 9—12. Abraham's justifica- **849c** tion by faith, Gn 15:6, took place *before* his circumcision, Gn 17:9—14, 23—27. The typical significance of this justification of Abraham, therefore, must not be limited to the children of the circumcision (= Israel) only. It is a lesson and example for all. Abraham is first of all 'the father of the faithful', and that is an older and wider title than 'the father of the circumcision', 3:29f. (3) 13—17 continue the proof of the last point: the typical universality of Abraham's justification by faith. The new turn of the argument is the use made of the promise given to Abraham, that he will be the father of many nations, 13, 17. Abraham received this promise, Gn 12:3; 15:5; 18:18; 22:17f, in view of his faith and not in connexion with any law or commandment. The children of Abraham according to this promise, therefore, are those who are Abraham's children by sharing his faith. Thus, from the very beginning the promise given to Abraham was founded on faith and grace, and this can indeed be regarded as a secure basis of justification. Had it been otherwise, had the promise given to Abraham been made dependent on the observance of a law, there would today be no plea for the fulfilment of the blessing promised to Abraham, because the Law had admittedly been broken, cf Dt 11:26—28. (4) 18—22 are not essential to the argument; but to pass them by would mean losing one of the best descriptions of faith in general, and of Abraham's faith in particular. (5) 23—25 apply Abraham's justification by faith as a scriptural type of the justification by faith according to the Gospel and so bring this 'proof from Scripture', 4:1—25, to a close.

1—8. According to MT Yahweh accounted Abraham's **850a** act of faith, trust in the divine promises, as good; it is not, therefore, the transition from sin to the state of grace: Abraham is already held as just, cf de Vaux, BJ, *Genèse*, 82. Paul argues in the present passage from NT revelation to the adumbration of the truth in OT; where Jas 2:21—23 cited the text from Gn à propos of the sacrifice of Isaac, Paul re-sets it in its proper context, where Abraham is justified through faith before any covenant was made, contrary to Jewish thinking at the time. He thus establishes an OT connexion between justice and faith. Paul's conception of faith agrees with that in OT as the assent or commitment of one's whole being to the work of God. P. Michalon in NRT 75 (1953), 587—600. The text of **3** makes an equiparation between justice and faith, but this is variously explained. So God as it were sets down Abraham's faith as justice. Arguing in this way from the meaning of *logizomai*, faith, in the Pauline sense of living faith, is made part of justice, cf Aquin, *STh.* 1—2, q. 113, a.4. Others take the term as implying a judgement of value by God rendering man fully just in his eyes. Reasoning along these lines some modern Protestant commentators think in terms of a change in the human situation or the establishment of new relations between God and the believer, and stress the life of faith or total self-commitment to God rather than the initial encounter. cf H. Küng: *Rechtfertigung* (1957), E.tr., *Justification*, 1964; J. Jiairni, in VDom 46 (1968), 169—74.

13—17. The argument that the promise given to **b** Abraham ranks higher than the Law is repeated in Gal 3:15—18. There is this remarkable difference, however, that in Gal the superiority of the promise is based on the simple fact of its being 430 years older than the Law. **23—25.** There is admittedly a difference between the object of the faith of Abraham and the faith of a Christian. Abraham had to believe that God would

850b give him a son; the Christian has to believe that God grants redemption and justification through the death and the resurrection of Jesus Christ. The difference is no doubt substantial. But this difference is not St Paul's point. His point is rather that in either case it is faith and not works on which man is found to be just = justified. Paul has been demonstrating that the justification of Abraham by his faith in God's power and fidelity to the divine promises is a type of our justification. Associating as is his wont Christ's death and resurrection, he sees our justice as a first participation in the life of the risen Christ. More profoundly, in line with the preaching of the early Church, e.g. Ac 2:33; 3:13, he sees an intrinsic bond between the resurrection of Christ and the redemption; cf 6:3—4, and 1 Cor 14:45, where it is insinuated that Christ is able to give life to all by communicating the Holy Spirit, and it is precisely the resurrection which puts him in that position. The redemptive work of Christ is visualized as a return of mankind to God worked first in Christ, 1 Cor 15:20, i.e. what is called 'objective redemption', and then in each Christian following Christ's passion in baptism, 'subjective redemption'. Each one participates in that return by a free personal act—faith and baptism. Christ's death and his resurrection are in reality two aspects of the same mystery. cf B. Vawter in CBQ 15 (1953) 17—23. On the causality of the resurrection in our redemption see J. Lécuyer in *Doctor Communis*, 1953, 91—120; S. Lyonnet in *Gregorianum* 39 (1958), 294—318.

c 5:1—8:39 Some Immediate Effects of Christian Salvation, or the Fruits of Christian Justification—After the description of the means by which salvation according to the Gospel is obtained (Christ's redeeming death and man's faith, 3:21—4:25) Paul now recommends this salvation by praising some of its immediate effects, its present blessings. The same subject is treated in modern textbooks of dogma under the title: the formal effects of sanctifying grace, or sanctification. As such fruits we normally enumerate: (1) the forgiveness of sin, unless this be considered rather as the essence of justification; (2) divine adoption, 1 Jn 3:1; (3) the indwelling of the Holy Ghost, 1 Cor 3:16f; (4) the gifts of the Holy Ghost; (5) the implanting (infusion) of supernatural virtues, esp of the three theological virtues: faith, hope and charity.

Plan. Paul's method of treating the effects that follow in the soul upon the acceptance of the salvation offered in the Gospel in 5:1—8:39 is neither systematic nor complete. But the present chapter-division is generally acknowledged to separate the main points: (1) 5:1—21 he who is justified in the sense of the Gospel enjoys a triumphant hope of heavenly glory; (2) 6:1—23 he has ceased to live under the dominion of sin; (3) 7:1—25 he is free from the Law; (4) 8:1—39 he possesses the life and rights of an adoptive son of God. This last chapter can also be taken as a summary presentation of the blessings and principles of the Christian life. **5:1—21 The Salvation of the Gospel gives Hope of Final Salvation** = eternal glorification—That Paul in this chapter no longer speaks of faith leading to justification, but of sanctifying grace working in the justified, is beyond any doubt. But it is not so easy to see how many effects of this sanctifying grace (= initial salvation) he meant to single out for his description. On the whole it would seem that the argument centres on 'the hope of heaven' as the main point of the passage.

Many commentators prefer to call ch 5 a discussion of *the certainty* of the Christian hope of final salvation, because this particular aspect of the Christian hope of **85(** heaven is given by far the greatest space and prominence in 5—21. Others for the same reason go a step further and treat ch 5 as a section by itself and separate it from 6:1—8:39. For a consideration of the literary structure of the ch see X. Léon-Dufour in RSR 51 (1963), 83—95.

Plan. If the hope of heaven is taken as the main **d** point, then the argument has three parts: (1) 1—4 the hope of heaven as the first fruit of salvation; (2) 5—11 the certainty of this hope proved from God's love for us as revealed in the redemption through Christ; (3) 12—21 a second proof for the certainty of this hope of heaven: Christ the anti-type of Adam.

1—4 A First Fruit of the Salvation revealed in the Gospel: the hope of final salvation = of eternal glory in heaven—Paul begins his praise and recommendation of the salvation which he preaches by dwelling on the triumphant hope of final salvation hereafter as the consequence of initial salvation here. Initial salvation is the same as justification = sanctification = the obtaining of sanctifying grace = reconciliation with God. Strictly speaking, the first fruit of salvation here enumerated by Paul is 'peace with God', 1. But as this is only touched upon here, its full explanation can be left to other passages, e.g. 2 Cor 5:18—21; Eph 2:11—22; see also Rm 5:10f; 8:6; 15:33; 16:20; 1 Cor 14:33; Col 1:20; 3:15; 2 Thes 3:16; Lk 1:79; 2:14, 29, etc.

Paul describes the elements of the Christian experience: **851** peace or friendship with God, and hope, both pledges of final salvation. In Jewish thought of the time, justification and salvation were to be brought about simultaneously in an eschatological judgement. Paul dissociates the two events: justification is a reality already acquired, and is connected with Christ's first coming, whereas salvation is still in the future; it is a judgement, will include the resurrection of the body, and is associated with the second coming of Christ cf S. Lyonnet in *Recherches Bibliques* 5 (1960), 166—84. **1.** 'We have peace with God'. The indicative can be defended on external and internal evidence. **2a.** Is a relative clause to be connected with 1. Its purpose is to remind us that our peace with God which is the first effect of salvation according to v 1 is no more our own doing than our 'introduction to the faith' (= to Christianity). Both are the work of Christ. It should be noticed that the sentence does not introduce a new fruit of salvation. **2b.** 'and we rejoice **b** in our hope of sharing the glory of God': unlike those without hope, Eph 2:12; 1 Thes 4:13, the justified can rejoice, looking forward to the glory to come. It is the hope which we usually call the second theological virtue. Its main, though not only, object is final salvation = eternal life = beatific vision. Paul calls it 'glory of God'. Fuller descriptions of it can be derived from 3:23; 8:18; 1 Cor 2:9; 15:43; 2 Cor 4:17f; Phil 3:21; Col 3:4; 2 Tim 2:10. From the grammatical point of view 2b is the second part of the relative clause begun in 2a from which it cannot be separated without doing violence to the text. But the unfortunate result of this grammatical connexion need not be denied. It is not in accordance with the rules of clear writing to introduce in a second relative clause the point which finally turns out to be the centre of the whole passage.

3—4. Is a parenthesis like 2a. It forestalls the common objection that the Christian hope of heaven is a sign of weakness leading to inactivity and indifference here on earth. According to 3—4 the Christian hope of heaven has the opposite effect: it makes men strong in tribulation which is the time when this hope is being

1b tested and tried, cf Mt 5:4; Rm 8:37; 2 Cor 1:3—11; Jas 1:3f. **3.** 'more than that'. Probably = We do not rejoice in the hope of the future glory only, but we rejoice also in the present tribulations, knowing that these tribulations strengthen that hope. They are a source of security because they compel us to look for support to God. 2 Cor 12:9—10.

c 5—21 The Certainty of the Christian's Hope of Final Salvation in the Glory of Heaven—In this paragraph Paul dwells on one characteristic of our hope of heaven, its certainty. This he bases on two foundations: (1) on God's love for us as shown in his Son's death for us, 5—11; (2) on a comparison between the effects of Adam's sin and Christ's redemption, 12—21. In both cases the argument takes a form which follows the first of Hillel's seven rules for the interpretation of Scripture, usually translated as the conclusion from the minor to the major = the conclusion from the less important to the more important; cf 5:9, 10, 15; SB ad Rom 5:9f. The certainty of such a conclusion must not be identified with that of a categorical syllogism in logic. Its value is rather like that of an emphatic assertion based on an objective similarity and a subjective intuition. Such an assertion has the authority of the speaker, and that is in the case of Paul the authority of his inspiration. The originality of Paul in both arguments can be seen from a comparison with the treatment of hope in the OT and in modern theology. The OT keeps repeating that he who puts his trust (hope) in God will not be put to shame (cf Ps 22 (21): 5; 25 (24):20; Is 28:16, etc), and it is a general theologoumenon today, that the certainty of our hope rests on God's faithfulness to his promises. Such statements are so frequent that they have become commonplace. But how daring is their application by Paul to the greatest problem of all, the reaching of heaven; cf Prat I, 237—49.

d The doctrine of the Church on the question of individual certainty of final salvation was briefly stated by the Council of Trent, Dz 805, 825, 826. According to Catholic doctrine no one while on earth can be certain of his final salvation without a special divine revelation. In comparing this doctrine with Rm 5:5—21; 8:28—30, it should be remembered that the Council of Trent had to check exaggerations whilst Paul had to encourage beginnings. All the same, Paul's teaching on the certainty of final salvation in 5—21 needs a corrective, and this corrective follows in ch 6 with its emphatic warnings against sin. This addition by the Apostle himself proves beyond any doubt that the certainty of final salvation stressed in ch 5 is not an unconditional certainty that follows irrevocably on baptism or conversion. Even in Rm there is a condition attached to it, and this condition according to ch 6 is that the Christian convert must live the life demanded by the Gospel.

e 5—11 God's Love for us as the First Proof for the Certainty of our Hope of Final Salvation—The Christian's hope of eternal glory is no illusion. It is firmly based on God's love for men as revealed in the fact that his Son died for us though we were then still sinners, and therefore, 'children of enmity or wrath', cf 1 Jn 4:10. Starting from this as an acknowledged fact, Paul arrives at his conclusion—the certainty of the Christian hope of final salvation—as follows: If when still sinners (= at enmity with God) we received the grace of initial justification from God's love in view of Christ's death on the cross, how much more can we not now as his friends (= justified by responding in faith to his first love) expect to receive the grace of

final salvation from his love in view of Christ's life **851e** in heaven? The whole passage is difficult, the main thought being obscured by too many details. It can be reduced to this: If God's love justified us on the day of our conversion though we then stood before him as sinners, how much more will not the same love save us on the day of the last judgement when we shall stand before him as saints = such as have been justified and redeemed by his Son?

5b. Is a stray thought as regards the main argument. Before enlarging on the objective evidence of God's love for us in Christ's death (6—8), the Apostle inserts in 5b a subjective proof to the same effect by appealing to the readers' personal experience and realization of that divine love in the voice and witness of the indwelling Holy Ghost. God's love for us is envisaged as a reality present within us, while the Holy Spirit, described as a gift to us, is a witness to that love by his active presence. Taken in conjunction with parallel texts 8:15; Gal 4:6, it can be read as the participation of the Christian in the life of the Trinity, in other words 'sanctifying grace'.

6. 'For why ...?': the interrogative sentence of Vg is better read as a categorical statement in accordance with many Gr. MSS, cf Boylan. This has been explained in two ways: (1) Christ died for us when we were not only sinners but also remained such for a time. (2) Christ offered himself for us at that time in history which had been appointed by the Father; cf Rm 3:26; 2 Cor 6:2; Gal 4:4; Eph 1:10; 1 Tm 2:6; 6:15; Ti 1:3. The 'right **852a** time' would mean when mankind had become aware of its dependence on God, being made to realize that by natural abilities alone it could contribute nothing to a supernatural destiny. **9.** Elsewhere salvation is conceived as a process already begun, e.g. 11 3:4—7. In point of fact in Paul's mind salvation, together with other OT concepts, such as redemption and the kingdom, is seen in a twofold aspect, present and eschatological, that is, as having an inchoate and a perfect state. The process of salvation and of liberation begins in the present life, but attains full stature only with the resurrection of the body. The salvation worked by Christ, then, will produce some of its effects in this life, i.e. a change of heart or a new way of life. cf G. Didier in NRT 75 (1953) 1—14. 'the wrath of God' refers here to God's attitude towards those who are finally impenitent on the day of the Lord. We have been reconciled with God in that sin, the barrier between men and God, has been removed. Such reconciliation is definitive because based ultimately on God's love for us, and its effects are a foretaste of the joys of salvation.

11. 'Not only so': is an ellipsis, cf 5:3; 8:23; 9:10; **b** 2 Cor 8:19. The most probable completion would seem to read: we shall not only be saved on the day of the last judgement, but even now, at this present hour with all its afflictions, we glory in God through Jesus Christ, rejoicing in his love for us; cf 5:3.

12—21 Adam understood as a Type of Christ, another proof for the certainty of the Christian hope of Final Salvation = Eternal Glory in Heaven. Our physical connexion with Adam brings us sin and death with undeniable certainty; in a similar way and with a similar certainty our spiritual connexion with Christ brings us justification and final salvation. In other words, Adam's fall is the beginning and cause of our sin and death; Christ's redemption is the beginning and cause of our justification and final salvation in heaven. The comparison could also be arranged in this way: Adam → Sin → Death; Christ → Grace (=justification) →

852b Eternal Life. For further details see Prat I, 438ff; II, 171—9.

c This parallel between Adam and Christ and the description of the consequence of Adam's fall as typical of the fruits of Christ's redemption is in biblical theology peculiar to Paul. Before Rm he had already used it in 1 Cor 15:22, 45—49. But there as here he puts it before his readers without any proof whatever, taking it evidently for granted that they would follow and accept his argument. Thus the idea is not likely to have been entirely unknown to his contemporaries. For attempts to trace it in rabbinical theology see Prat II, 171; SB III, 477f (on 1 Cor 15:45). At all events, the whole argument of 12—21 stands or falls with the existence of this parallel between Adam and Christ. If Christ were not the antitype of Adam in God's economy of salvation, then Paul's second argument for the Christian confidence of reaching eternal glory in 12—21 would collapse.

d What then is the proof value of this parallel between Adam and Christ? Reason alone, excluding the doctrine of inspiration from the argument, cannot prove that Paul's typical interpretation of the story of Adam is necessary from the OT point of view. But once it is pointed out—and in this Paul seems to be original—reason cannot deny that this parallel between Adam and Christ is full of meaning and beauty. Ultimately, however, our acceptance of the Apostle's argument as a true doctrine must be based on our belief in NT (Pauline) inspiration, cf. § § 852c, 860h.

In most commentaries on 12—21 much space is given to the discussion of the evidence for the Christian doctrine of original sin in this passage. That the idea of original sin is presupposed in the argument of 12—21 can safely be taken as certain; but it is only one of several side issues. Paul's aim is to show that Christ is the sole source of life for us because he has removed, root and branch, the obstacle to our reconciliation. He points to a bond between sinful mankind and Adam, and to that between restored man and Christ. The leading idea in his mind is the achievement of Christ rather than the fact of original sin; but he uses the fact of the universality of sin to throw into relief the universality of redemption by drawing an antithetical parallel between the work of Adam and the reparation by Christ. He sees in mankind a state of sin transmitted from Adam, but does not explain how this takes place, as it lies outside the ambit of his argument, cf A. Dubarle: *The Biblical Doctrine of Original Sin* (E. Tr. 1966) 142ff. The essentials of the doctrine of original sin are contained in the passage: the human race was deprived of eternal life as a result of a relation with Adam's sin; it is able to recover it only in Christ by a gratuitous favour. On this see P. Grelot in NRT 90 (1968), 337—62, 449—78.

e Contemporary Jewish reflection, as deduced from writings of the time, e.g. 4 Esd, attributed the universal corruption of mankind, material and spiritual, to the causal influence of Adam's sin. This conception supposed that his sin involved posterity, so that his disobedience is at the source of the misery in the world including death and the inclination to evil. cf J. Bonsirven: *Le Judaisme Palestinien*, (1934), 2, 12—23. **12—14** is an anacoluthon. The thought is continued in 18*b* and 21*b*. From the experience of man redeemed and at peace with God Paul concludes that Christ has destroyed the great obstacle to salvation, i.e. sin and death; the assurance we have of salvation holds for all believers since all have been **f** redeemed from the effects of sin. In this way, following the trend of thought in 4 Esd, he leads to the source

of sin in the world. 'Sin' here is not the personal offence **852** of Adam, but a personified force for evil in opposition to God which has taken possession of mankind and separated it from God. 'Death' is understood not just in its physical sense of separation of soul and body, but in the sense of spiritual and eternal death, i.e. loss of salvation and definitive separation from God; physical death without the resurrection of the body is a sign of this. Paul has in mind the narrative of Gn 3 as reflected in Wis 2:23—24, where death is viewed as the loss of salvation and as opposed to supernatural and eternal life. The meaning, therefore, is that all men lost salvation and regained it only through Christ. **12***d* eph' hō pantes **g** hēmarton: is ambiguous and has been differently translated. Vg *In quo omnes peccaverunt*: 'in whom . . . ; death spread to all men through Adam.' This understands the cause of original sin as the inherited consequences of Adam's sin in the individual soul. In this sense the Latin text is quoted in the decree of the Council of Trent on original sin, Dz 789. But this rendering is philologically inadmissible. The Council of Trent quoted the passage according to Vg in defining that all men separated from Christ are under sin. The Council was impugning the opinion that in Rm 5 no allusion whatever is made to original sin. Any interpretation contradicting the meaning given by Trent would be contrary to faith; but a definitive interpretation of the Greek text was not given. cf A. Vanneste in NRT 87 (1965) 688—726; 88 (1966) 581—602. Another translation is: 'because all sinned', the common rendering of the Greek text, taking it to refer to actual sins. The death which came with Adam's fault affects all men not alone because of Adam's sin, but because all men have in fact sinned. Paul implies that death is inherited from Adam, thus holding for a causal link between Adam's sin and those of the race. However, it is not here asserted that a state of sin is inherited. The phrase can also indicate the condition attached **852** to a contract, 'on condition that . . .', and so the exact meaning must be determined from the context. The Greek Fathers understood it here as introducing a condition which has already been fulfilled, i.e. 'given that . . .' The personal sins of each, the consequences of Adam's offence for which we are fully responsible, ratify the disobedience of Adam. The causality of personal sin is secondary to that universal causality in Adam's, which, without redemption by Christ, involved the whole race in definitive separation from God. The implication of personal responsibility in the death introduced by Adam enhances the parallel with the saving work of Christ; in both cases there is a role for liberty, since we must participate in Christ's redemptive work by an act of faith. In short, the force of sin brought in by Adam produces its full effect of eternal death through the personal sins of each, so confirming Adam's rebellion. For a full investigation of the expression see S. Lyonnet in Bib 36 (1955), 436—56.

13—14 Following the development of 4 Esd treating **b** of the history of sin in the world, Paul thinks of human history as divided into periods: Paradise, from Adam to Moses (Law), from Moses to David, and from David to the Temple. In the epoch between Adam and Moses the law was not yet promulgated; hence there could be no violation of a positive divine precept. In that case an offence was not imputable, cf 4:15, and therefore death, i.e. eternal separation from God, could not be incurred. Paul meets this objection by the example of biblical history: the period in question was an era of sin and of exemplary chastisement—witness the deluge and the destruction of Sodom, as evoked in 4 Esd. Thus to incur death, in the

53b full sense of the word, it was not necessary to have violated a positive command to which the sanction was attached.

c **15—17** The antithesis is between the respective acts of Adam and Christ, contrasting the universal effects of their influence on the race. 'Many', from the context stands for totality, all men. **16.** 'Judgement', the sentence of a judge in condemnation. 'Justification', the real gift bestowed by Christ. The actual sins of man are taken as constituting one with the sin of Adam, all set in opposition to the work of Christ. **17.** Grace and righteousness are received by contact with Christ through faith and baptism. Throughout this entire passage Paul seeks to convey his thought more effectually by deliberate use of assonance. **18.** 'Life', participation in the life of the risen Christ, starting on earth but reaching full development after our resurrection. Just as all men inherit human nature and total death from Adam, they derive their supernatural state and life from Christ. **19.** 'Obedience' points to the interior aspect of the act, and lays stress on the satisfaction rendered in Christ's death. The obedience could be applied to the whole life of Christ, but his death was the supreme expression of his love for us and of his submission to his Father. cf Aquin. *In Rom* 5, 1, 5.

d 'Many shall be made righteous': MSS as well as commentators have tried to turn this future into a past tense. To do so is necessary if the whole passage, 12—21, is understood of Christ's justification as it works itself out in the Christian life on earth, i.e. before the Last Judgement. But if the whole passage is understood as referring to the Christian's final justification in the Last Judgement, then the future tense causes no difficulty. The adjective 'righteous' has a meaning wide enough to be used also for the state of 'final' salvation. But Paul thinks of justification as something already acquired by those reconciled to God. **20.** 'Law', the régime of law, referring to the period of history between Moses and David, v 14. The law did not put an end to sin or death; on the contrary it gave a fresh impetus to sin in giving a clearer knowledge of personal obligations without the strength to carry them out. In the Semitic concept of divine causality nothing happens without the authority of God; God permits evil effects in order to turn them to good. Exegetical aspects of Rm 5 are treated by S. Lyonnet in RSR 44 (1956) 63—84; Bib 38 (1958) 27—36; A. Dubarle RSPT 40 (1956) 213—54; RTh 56 (1956) 567—619; S. Lyonnet DBS 7 (1963) 524—66.

The conclusive argument for original sin is what is implied in the truth that Christ died to save all men, namely that all have sinned. Paul's centre of interest in Rm 5 is the redemptive work of Christ, not to explain the rule of sin in the world. It is not his explicit teaching that sin is transmitted through physical generation from Adam. Theological reflection has deduced this interpretation from the biblical texts, but it was not the point of the definition by Trent. cf J. deFraine: *The Bible and the Origin of Man* (1962), pp 68ff. It is difficult, but perhaps not impossible to see how sin as an ontological condition of the person belonging to the sphere of religion, can be transmitted by a biological process, e.g. the line of reasoning followed by Fr O'Doherty IrTQ 34 (1967) 115ff.

Though Paul asserts a causal link between Adam's sin and the sins of the race, and implies that death is inherited from Adam, solidarity in Adam's sin is only a figure of our solidarity with Christ the Redeemer. cf H. Cazelles DBS 8 (1967) 107ff. Paul would not, therefore, be affirming a teaching on an historical Adam

as an individual parent of the human race. Trent would **853d** have taken for granted that all happened as described in Gn 2—3, so that the question of the historicity of the narrative of the Fall would not have arisen. Since the point of reference in the biblical text is a judgement on the present situation, the explanation of original sin is not be tied to any scientific or pseudo-scientific theory of monogenism or polygenism. It may be shown that a polygenetic view of human origins can allow for original sin in the accepted sense of the term. cf K. Rahner in *Concilium*, vol 6, n.3 (June 1967) 30—35.

6:1—23 A Second Effect of Justification: the **854a** Christian's break with sin. Christian justification implies an irretrievable rejection of sin and the beginning of a new and holy life.

Paul here passes on to another immediate and major effect of Christian justification: the complete break with sin in and after obtaining justification = sanctifying grace. With us today, it is rather the forgiveness of sins that comes to our mind when the effects of justifying grace as regards sin are to be enumerated. But the forgiveness of sins is not Paul's subject here. All the weight of the passage is concentrated on the Christian's break with sin. The ensuing victory over sin is discussed in 8:1—8.

Object. The connexion of ch 6 with the previous **b** ch and the precise object of the Apostle in discussing this subject here are disputed. Was his intention to continue the enumeration of the effects of Christian justification begun in 5:1? Or was his purpose to refute lax conclusions from his doctrine, esp from 5:20f? Or did he intend to insert here, as the spirit moved him, a pressing exhortation to a holy life? Each of these possibilities has been and can be defended. Those who regard Rm 6 as the description of another effect of justifying grace can quote in their favour, besides simplicity, a long exegetical tradition. It is an explanation which gives the chapter a place in the whole epistle that can easily be remembered. The second opinion which treats 1—23 as a refutation of morally lax conclusions falsely drawn from Paul's teaching is supported by the two introductory questions, 1, 15, and by the fact that such false conclusions have actually been drawn from his doctrine. He himself refers to them in 3:7f (cf Gal 5:13). The third opinion treating 1—23 as an exhortation can appeal to the admonitory and exhortatory tone which runs through the whole chapter, cf 2, 3, 11, 12—14, 19. The obvious objection is that Paul clearly begins his exhortations proper with ch 12. It is difficult to choose between these possibilities. Perhaps the true solution lies in the combination of all three. The context demands doctrine; the subject matter could hardly be expressed without exhortation; and to think here of a kind of self-defence on the part of Paul is taking account of what we know from the history of this doctrine.

Characteristic. Paul's way of arguing in 1—23 has **c** often been criticized as difficult and complicated, as concealing the real issue under too many words and metaphors and as lacking clear progress of thought. From a literary point of view these objections are not without some foundation. But it must also be remembered that one cause of the difficulty lies in the subject, the problem of sin in life. For it is self-evident that the only straightforward solution of the problem of sin in life is *sinlessness*. But to be henceforward without sin is not among the effects of Christian justification. Sanctifying grace is a gift but also a task. The task it sets is the sanctification of daily life, and in this task Christians can and do fail. That is so today and was **d**

854d so in the days of Paul. But he believed, as we believe, that the fact of justifying grace makes a great difference to the power of sin. To describe, illustrate, and engrave upon the memory of everyone this new Christian counter-power to sin was the Apostle's first object. But leaving terminology and style alone, can we today really quote any stronger counter-forces to sin than the two here singled out by Paul: the mystical union with Christ, 1—11; and the hope of eternal reward after a life in the service of Christian holiness, 15—23?

Plan. To prove his thesis that Christian justification brings liberation from the dominion of sin St Paul employs two arguments: (1) 1—14 the Christian's break with sin in the sacrament of baptism; (2) 15—23 the Christian's break with sin because of the punishment of sin on the one hand, and because of the reward of of holiness according to Christian doctrine on the other.

e 1—14 The Christian's Break with Sin in the Sacrament of Baptism—Paul, arguing in 1—14 that there is no more room for sin in a Christian life, bases his argument on the (mystical) union with Christ which is the primary purpose of baptism. In baptism the Christian is created, as it were, by being united with Christ. Henceforward, therefore, the Christian's attitude to sin must be the same as that of Christ himself. He must die to sin, as Christ died to sin; he must be holy as Christ was holy.

f This is the substance of the argument in 1—11. But to drive his point home Paul proceeds to demonstrate or prove the existence and the nature of this union with Christ from the two baptismal ceremonies of immersion and emersion. According to Paul's own exposition the former of these two ceremonies represents the Christian's death and burial with Christ, the latter his resurrection with Christ. When in baptism the catechumen is *immersed* beneath the water, he is thereby, as it were, buried with Christ, sharing his being dead to sin; and when the Christian *emerges* from beneath the water he thereby rises, as it were, with Christ from the tomb, sharing the new life of the Risen Lord. The theological principles underlying this way of arguing in 1—14 are three: (1) the symbolical meaning of the ceremonies used at baptism; (2) the sacramental efficacy of baptism; (3) a real (mystical) union, incorporation, identification of the Christian with Christ as an effect of the sacrament of baptism.

What makes the argument somewhat complicated is the fact that two lines of thought are constantly crossing each other: (1) baptism as dying to sin; (2) baptism as the beginning of a new life. In a systematic treatment the two aspects would be kept separate and discussed as the negative and the positive effects of baptism. The real difficulty of St Paul's argument, however, is the character of the new life instilled in baptism. For in reality this new life remains far behind its ideal, the life of the risen Christ. With this difficulty St Paul wrestles in 5—9. On the one hand he insists on the fact of this new life being instilled in baptism; otherwise his whole argument would fall to the ground. On the other hand, he changes from the past to the future tense in describing the transformation worked in the Christian by the infusion of this new life in baptism: 'we *shall* certainly be united with him in a resurrection like his',

g 5; 'we *shall* also live with him', 8. Contrast Col 2:12; Eph 2:5. The result is that this new life is represented as a life which begins in baptism, 4, but is to be completed in the future, reaching its fullness after death in heaven, 5, 8. This way of presenting the case which is undoubtedly the true one may be compared with 'prophetical com-

penetration'. But a satisfactory grammatical explanation **85** of these future tenses does not seem to exist.

Plan. There are two clearly marked paragraphs: 1—11 doctrine; 12—14 corresponding exhortation.

1. Paul introduces his new point, the banishment of sin from Christian life, with an objection suggested by what he had said on sin and grace in the previous sentence 5:20f, or by the false conclusions which he knew had been drawn from his doctrine; cf 3:8; Gal 5:13; 1 Pt 2:16; Jas *passim*. If in the past man's sin provided the opportunity for God's grace, why not continue in sin to provide further opportunities for God's grace? The same objection is repeated in 15. **2.** '*We who died* to sin': is a metaphor for complete separation from sin. In a more detailed explanation account must be taken of the application of the same metaphor to our Lord in 10. In either case there is agreement that 'to sin' is dative and not ablative. The dative is then explained as a 'dative of reference', so that one could paraphrase Paul's thought as follows; as far as sin is concerned we have died; we have done with sin, we have finished with sin. The comparison with death in this metaphor would seem to lie in the complete change and absolute separation from all that was before.

3a. 'We who *were* baptized *into* Christ Jesus': introduces the sacrament of baptism into the discussion, and thereby the Apostle's first proof for his thesis that there is no longer any room for sin in the life of a Christian, 2. But how far can baptism be said to have this effect? This is briefly explained in 4—5 and then further developed in 6—10. As these explanations show, Paul, speaking of baptism into Christ Jesus, was here thinking not of the formula of baptism, but of baptism as 'immersion' into Christ. To combine the idea of baptism and immersion is strange to us, but was natural to Paul and his readers for two reasons: (1) the Greek verb *baptizein* means to plunge into; (2) in the early Christians this idea was kept alive through the ceremony of immersion in their baptism. **3b.** 'We *were* baptized *into* his death': if baptism is immersion into Christ, 3a, it must include immersion into his death as much as into any other work of his redemption, e.g. resurrection, ascension, etc. Why then does St Paul here single out the death of Christ; and which is the particular aspect of Christ's death that he has in mind? The answer is given in 10: Christ's death was his final settlement with all that concerned sin, and baptism is meant to be the same for every Christian.

The expression 'baptized into Christ Jesus' means **855** that we are incorporated into, become part of him. Baptism is not thought of as a rite operative independent of faith; so the same effect of uniting the person to Christ crucified and risen can be ascribed now to one, now to the other, e.g. Gal 2:16—20. Though we are united to the risen and glorified Christ, he is the same Christ who died, and so we share in the effects of his death and resurrection in being associated with him at the moment in which he became the Saviour. So far Paul has insisted on the negative aspect of our 'dying to sin', symbolically represented in the baptismal ceremony of immersion reminiscent of Christ's death and burial; now he turns from the negative to the positive aspect, the beginning of a new life, symbolically represented by the baptismal ceremony of emersion, which is reminiscent of Christ's rising from the tomb. The new Christian life, therefore, should be a life concerned only with heavenly things, like the life of the Risen Christ; cf Col 3:2; Phil 3:20.

Our new life will attain full stature at the resurrection, **b** but at present is manifested in moral conduct of which the Spirit is the motivating force, cf Col 3:1—4. 'Glory'

855b is communicated to the human nature of Christ, who is then empowered to communicate it to men. **5.** 'United', the verb used has the sense of 'growing together'. By uniting us to Christ baptism transforms our mode of existence and consequently our conduct. Conformity with Christ, begun with baptism, will attain its term with our resurrection. Paul's idea is that we are liberated from sin by a process of death and resurrection through which we are assimilated to Christ. **6.** 'old self' before baptism, in the state of sin. 'Sinful body' not referring to the organism as such, but as the instrument of sinful activities. That efficacy has been removed through baptism, Col 3:9. **7.** Death itself, as such, cannot expiate sin; if Christ redeemed us by his death, it was because that death was the expression of his love. The expression 'he who has died' occurs elsewhere in Paul's writings in reference to the person of Christ; 8:34; 2 Cor 5:15; 1 Thes 5:9. There is an analogous text in 1 Tm 3:16 referring explicitly to Christ as one who 'was justified', which critics take as a citation from an early profession of faith. Given the similarity in form between all these passages, it is possible to see in 6:7 a reminiscence of some such formulary, and to conclude that Paul was referring to Christ. Christ had in some sense come into contact with sin by the Incarnation, 8:3; but liberated himself by his death, and is now definitively established in that state of liberation. This is the conclusion of C. Kearns in *Analecta Biblica* 17—18, i, 301—7 cf also M. Boismard in RB 64 (1957), 183. **8.** It is only in our faith that we are made aware of the new life we have started. **9.** Because Christ's resurrection marks his entry into glory.

c **10.** That Christ died to atone *for* men's sins is the general Christian doctrine of the Cross. But this aspect of the death of Christ does not fit into Paul's argument here, where Christ's dying *to* sin is quoted as the model of our dying to sin. If the meaning of the metaphor 'dying to sin' from v 3 is to be kept, then Paul must here be thinking of the Cross as Christ's final settlement with regard to all that concerned sin in his life. On Calvary sin's claims were settled once and for all; henceforward God's claim alone was of practical importance to him. Death to sin on Calvary is followed by a life for God alone beginning with the resurrection. The application to the Christian life is easy. As Christ settled his account with sin of Calvary, so does the Christian in baptism, **11.** That Christ's account with sin was of a very different character from ours does not affect the argument.

d The presupposition underlying Paul's assertion is his view of redemption as a return of mankind to God, 3:21. Christ has brought this about by assuming human nature which then passed into the glorified state for good and all, 2 Cor 5:21. This was a real event, and not a piece of juridical fiction or a mere moral reparation. Those who are baptized have been grafted onto Christ, and so they share in the effects of his death and in his new life. This union entails moral obligations of maintaining their state, as in the present life sin could recover the dominion.

15—23 The Christian's Break with Sin once more—The Apostle returns to the question of sin in the life of a Christian raised in 6:1 and shows once more that there is no longer any room for sin in a Christian life. The subject is important enough to bear repetition. The passage can be summarized as follows: the Christian is bound to avoid sin and pursue holiness in his life in view of their respective wages according to Christian doctrine, death being the wages in the service of sin, eternal life the wages in the service of holiness. The connexion with

1—14 is disputed. Some would connect it with ch 7 which **855d** discusses the liberation from the Mosaic Law and regard it as a third effect of Christian justification; cf SH. The wording of the introductory question in 15 can rightly be quoted in favour of this view, but the trend of the argument speaks against it.

16—22. Develops the parable that man is a servant = **e** slave either under the rule of sin or under the rule of holiness. **16b.** 'Servants . . . of obedience unto *justness*': what one expects in the antithesis is: servants of justness (or of the Gospel, or of God) unto life. This conclusion actually follows in 22f. From the strictly logical point of view therefore 16b—21 forms a digression. Its object is to impress the necessity of obedience. The simplest proof is the vocabulary: obedience, 16 (twice); to obey, 16, 17; slave, 16, 17, 20; to be enslaved, 18, 22. It is, however, possible that in 16b obedience is but a synonym for Gospel, cf 1:5; 15:18. **17.** The normal phrase would be, the form of teaching that has been delivered unto you. In any case, it is clear that the phrase presupposes a set of dogmas in early Christianity. On the question what these principal doctrines were, cf Prat II, 28—35. **19.** cf Gal 3:15; Rm 3:5. Paul apologizes for using the obedience of a servant or slave to illustrate the Christian's obedience in the service of God. For in other respects to be a Christian is to have found true freedom, cf Gal 5:1, 13; 1 Cor 9:19; 2 Cor 3:17; Rm 8:15, 21. But see also Mt 11:29; 1 Cor 7:22; Rm 1:1; 7:25; 14:18; Eph 6:6; Phil 1:1; 2:22.

20—22. The life of 'the slave of sin' and of 'the **f** slave of God' are compared once more. **21.** The punctuation is uncertain. Many commentators translate: 'What fruit did you reap then? Such as you are now ashamed of . . . death'. **22.** 'Now . . . sanctification'. a difficult phrase because the common meaning of *hagiasmos* = sanctification, does not fit easily into the context. If this meaning is kept, the Apostle's thought is: now you have your fruit in such things (virtues, cf Gal 5:22f) as lead immediately to sanctification and thereby finally to life everlasting. But does the structure of the sentence bear such an interpretation? Many commentators prefer to translate: 'now you have your fruit *in* justness' And this is what one expects in the context: now you have your fruit (= reward) in the possession of justness (= sanctifying grace) for the present, and in the hope of eternal life for the future. **23.** 'For the wages of sin is death, but the free gift of God is eternal life', sums up the whole passage 15—23. Both the death and the life of which Paul speaks are eternal, cf Mt 10:28; Gal 6:7f; 2 Cor 5:10; but it would be a mistake to think that therefore they do not begin till after the grave, cf 6:4; Col 2:12; Eph 2:5; Jn 17:3. Sin as a principle of disorder inevitably leads to final separation from God, even in this life it begins to receive its due exactly as the just man has the pledges of the Spirit.

7:1—25 A Third Effect of the Justification revealed 856a in the Gospel: Christ the new principle of life in the place of the Old Law; or the Christian's New Law—There is no conversion without obvious changes in essential religious convictions, and there can be no such changes without the need of defending them against the charges of apostasy. These are the two general truths which form the background of this ch. The Christians addressed in Rm were baptized converts and the change defended in ch 7 is their new attitude to the Old Law. Our Lord touches on the same problem in Mt 5:17—48: '. . . *it was said . . . but I tell you*'. Paul takes it up both in Gal and Rm 7. For us today the main points in such a discussion are the fact that the Christian convert was taught a new attitude to the Old Law, and the content of that teaching.

856a In this respect, however, Rm 7 is no great help, because Paul takes the new Christian attitude to the Old Law for granted, and all his labour goes into defending it, just as the fact and doctrine of baptism are taken for granted in ch 6; cf the similar method in modern apologetic treatises.

b Natural as this apologetic method no doubt was in the days of Paul, it makes his argument in Rm 7 difficult for us unless we begin, as his first readers did, with a real and true conception of that new Christian attitude to the Old Law according to the mind of the Apostle. This new Christian attitude to the Old Law, therefore, may here be briefly stated. For the Christian the Old Law is no longer the first ruling principle in life. This first place of honour and importance the Old Law must yield to Jesus Christ who for our salvation (which is to be obtained in union with him) descended to earth and after his death and resurrection ascended again to heaven. This doctrine is the Christian's first ruling principle in life, and since two cannot be first the Old Law must give way. In other words the centre of Christianity is Christ, not Law.

c The point in this doctrine which needs explanation is the term 'Old Law'. We are accustomed to make clear distinctions between the natural moral law and the Mosaic Law; and again between the moral and the ceremonial law of the OT. Which of these laws then was Paul thinking of when writing Rm 7? This question draws attention to a serious difficulty in the explanation of this ch. The ultimate cause of the difficulty is the ambiguity of the term 'law' used by Paul. Taken by itself, 'law' can have any of the four meanings quoted above, and commentators do not agree in their choice. At first it seems clear from ch 7 that the Apostle was thinking of the Mosaic Law. But if the whole epistle, addressed to Gentile as well as Jewish Christians, is taken into account, it would be oversimplifying his teaching in ch 7 if we limited it to the discussion of the abrogation of the ceremonial law of the OT. For what reason is there to think that Paul did not apply the principles of Rm 7 also to the natural moral law of the Gentiles, which, if codified, would have all the advantages and the disadvantages of the Mosaic Law pointed out in this ch: the law is good but man does not keep the law. In view of the whole epistle therefore it seems better to accept the wider interpretation of 'law' in Rm 7, i.e. the Apostle was thinking first of the Mosaic Law = the Torah, but as representative of and including all other law. The sum total of the argument, then, is that for Paul the Christian's union with Christ superseded all that philosophy or theology had ever taught; he excepted nothing, not even the Torah of Moses, much less any other law.

Plan. Ch 7 falls into three paragraphs: (1) 1—6, for the Christian the law is no longer the first guide in life; (2) 7—12, the refutation of a first misinterpretation; (3) 13—25, the refutation of a second misinterpretation.

d 1—6 For a Christian the Old Law is no longer the First Rule in Life, or 'the transition from Law to Grace', SH—It is no superficial objection against Christianity from the OT or rabbinical point of view to argue that speaking of a New Testament law is as precarious as speaking of a new natural law. What was 'divine law for ever' in the days of God's revelation at Sinai must remain so till the end of this world. And yet it is clear Christian doctrine that there is a New Testament = a New Law. 'Nova sunt omnia'. How is this possible, and what are the practical consequences?

Plan. Paul bases his argument on the legal principle that the binding force of law ceases for the individual at death, 1. This principle is first illustrated by an example

from marriage law, 2—3; and then applied to the Christian **856** attitude to the Old Law in 4—6.

1. No one will question Paul's premise that death makes law irrelevant. It is a commonplace truth. What gives colour to its quotation here is the fact that it was used in rabbinical theology to denote a unique privilege of the Mosaic Law. According to rabbinical theology only death could set the Israelite free from the laws of the Torah. With regard to the Torah there was neither dispensation nor abrogation; cf Targum to Ps 89 (88):6; Wetstein and SB on Rm 7:3. Paul keeps the principle but turns it against the Torah by introducing the Christian's sacramental death in baptism. **2—3** make a digression. Instead of at once applying the principle of 1 to the point **e** under discussion, the Apostle illustrates his principle with an example taken from the law of marriage. A married woman bound to her husband under the penalty of adultery becomes free to re-marry after his death. Here then is a clear case in which death cancels law, cf Ruth 1:9. As long as 2—3 are taken as no more than an illustration of this principle generally stated in 1, the argument is simple and clear. The difficulties begin when these two vv are understood further as an allegory applied in 4—6. To quote 2—3 as direct NT evidence for the doctrine of the indissolubility of marriage (because of the omission of any reference to the possibility of divorce according to Dt 24:1ff) is perhaps basing too much on an *argumentum ex silentio*; cf Lagrange.

4—6 contain (a) the application of the principle of **f** 1; (b) the application of the illustration of that principle in 2—3; (c) the positive description of the New Law = the new dispensation.

(a) The application of 1 in 4—6 is clear. The Christian, having died with Christ in baptism, 6:1—11, has in this mystical death the charter which sets him free not only from the dominion of sin but also from every allegiance to the Old Law. The result is that he can enter into the new union with Christ without feeling guilty of any disloyalty or apostasy since 'death' frees man from old obligations. The point which deserves special attention in this argument is the reality of the union with Christ through baptism presupposed in this application. How deeply conscious must the early Christians have been of their union with Christ to accept such an argument! To a student of rabbinical theology it cannot have meant anything. To him it must have been sheer hair-splitting folly to dispose of the Torah by a ceremonial-sacramental death in baptism. The sacramental effects of baptism behind the argument of 4—6, therefore, cannot be stressed too much.

(b) The explanation of 4—6 becomes much more com- **g** plicated as soon as these vv are understood as an application not only of the principle of v 1 but also of the illustration of that principle in 2—3. The main difficulty is that the example, 2—3, speaks of two persons where the application, 4—6, has only one. In the example it is the husband who dies whilst the law ceases for the widow so that she is free to re-marry. According to the application, 4—6, however, it ought to be one and the same person, for it is one and the same individual who dies in baptism and is then free to enter into a new union with Christ. Now, to make two persons = one, or one = two, is evidently not in accordance with the rules of grammar or logic. A summary of present-day exegesis would seem to be: (1) To acknowledge that 7:2—3 is both an illustration of v 1 and at the same time a parable or allegory applied in 4—6. (2) To admit a certain amount of inconsistency in detail between parable and application which no one explanation can dispel. (3) To limit **h**

56h the interpretation of the parable to what is essential in Paul's own application, i.e. (α) death sets aside law, and so does the death undergone in the sacrament of baptism, (β) once this death has taken place the Christian is free to transfer his loyalty to Christ in the same way as a widow is free to marry again.

(c) The description of the New Dispensation = the New Law in 4—6 must be the third point in every explanation of this passage. And it is the most important point for us, since for us the liberation from the Old Law (esp in the sense of the Mosaic Law) is no longer a practical question. But even in the days of Paul nothing could be gained by an abrogation of the OT Law. All depended on what was to take its place, or what use was to be made of the freedom obtained. The answer in 4—6 is very clear. The law is not so much abrogated as superseded. The freedom obtained in baptism is intended to make room for a new principle, viz union with Christ risen from the dead; cf Gal 2:19. The comparison is between two situations, to illustrate that the binding force of a law ceases with death. In the application Christians are freed from the law; they participate in the life of Christ, who at his resurrection acquired a glorified body. By their union with him believers pass likewise to a spiritual condition of existence, and therefore can no longer be subject to an extrinsic law.

57a   **4.** This union with Christ as the new guiding principle of life instead of the Old Law is first described as marriage with Christ, risen from the dead, cf 2 Cor 11:2; Eph 5:25, 29. The metaphor is in agreement with the illustration used in 2—3. But it may be true that it should not be pressed. What Paul stresses most, is that it must be a union which bears fruit, and thereby proves its superiority over the former state. '*By their fruits you shall know them*', Mt 7:16f; Gal 5:22. **5.** The fruits of the pre-Christian time are then reviewed by way of contrast. That was the time of the 'old man' = the man in sin, or in the flesh, the man under the law, cf 6:6; 7:7—12; 8:13; Gal 2:19; 5:17; Eph 2:3; 4:22; Col 2:11; 3:9. **6.** But all this has passed in the death with Christ; and in the mystical-sacramental union with him, risen from the dead, there is the 'new man'. In him all is new, and his works must bear it out; cf 7:22; Eph 4:24; Col 3:10; Gal 5:25.

b **7—12 The Refutation of a First Misinterpretation**— The new Christian attitude to the Old Law must not be misinterpreted as if the Old Law were identified with sin. The doctrine that the Christian is no longer under the Old Law, 1—6, has always been liable to misunderstandings. Already in the days of Paul there were misinterpretations which he had to correct. Here he takes up one of them. Instead of quoting the actual misinterpretation, however, he puts it in the form of a question: 'Is then the law sin?'. To explain the problem in Paul's mind the following paraphrase may be helpful: if, on the one hand, it is so important for a Christian to get away from the Old Law as is suggested in 1—6 and if, on the other hand, the Law is so closely connected with sin as is maintained in 5:13, 20; 7:5, then the logical conclusion would seem to be that the law itself is sin. This conclusion is evidently absurd. The objection does not go very deep, and Paul's refutation is easy to follow. If the law applauded sin, it would indeed have to be identified with sin. But, in fact, as everybody knows, the law clearly forbids sin, so that there can be no disputing that the law is good and holy, 12. But at the same time, there can be no question of withdrawing the former statement, 5:13, 20; 7:5, that there is a close connexion between sin and law. True as it is that the law forbids and exposes

sin, it is equally true that the law at the same time stimul- **857b** ates man's attraction (concupiscence) to sin.

The proof is to be found in the experience of tempta- **c** tion, 7—11. The passage constitutes a defence of the law, and at the same time shows its part in the divine plan of salvation. As an institution it was not intended to justify men, but it allowed the whole force of sin to be expressed in transgressions, and so clearly showed all men their true condition of hostility to God. The régime of law was necessarily temporary, and had to yield place to an economy of faith and grace in which justice could be acquired and maintained.

For the purpose of tracing some of the details of **d** Paul's analysis of temptation in 7—11 it may be helpful to treat his description as a scene with four actors: (1) the Law 7, 8, 12 = the Commandment 8, 9, 10, 11, 12. (2) Sin 7, 8, 11. (3) Ego or Self 7, 8, 9, 10, 11. (4) Concupiscence 7, 8. The central figure is Self, whose service both Law and Sin are equally anxious to win. The discussion is opened by Law = Commandment, exposing sin as sin so that Self is left in no doubt as to the character of the next speaker, Sin. Nevertheless, the Law loses its suit, thwarted by Concupiscence in man. The result is that Self enters in service of Sin, which means he loses the life promised by the Law, Ez 18:5—9, to earn the wages of Sin, which are misery and death, Rm 6:23; Sir 21:11. The main question of theological interest in this paragraph are: (1) Who is the Ego or self? (2) What law is Paul referring to? (3) What does he mean by Sin? (4) What is meant by Concupiscence?

(1) Who is the Ego or Self? It is characteristic of **e** this and the following paragraph, 13—25, that Paul argues in the first person. The natural conclusion is that he relates his own experience. On the other hand, to argue from a purely individual experience is out of place in such a general discussion as is developed in Rm. This forces upon us the further conclusion that Paul regarded his own experience in this case as typical. And since he speaks in the past, obviously referring to the time before baptism, it can be further described as typical of the pre-Christian time. Then the question arises whether it is to be considered as a typical experience of Israelites and Gentiles alike or only of the former. The answers differ. All who limit the theme of Rm 7 to a discussion on the Mosaic Law must limit the typical value of Paul's experience accordingly, because it is the basis of the whole argument. On the other hand, Rm is addressed to a Christian community consisting of convert Israelites as well as of convert Gentiles (cf 1:18—3:20) and there is no evidence that in our ch Paul is speaking to the former only. In view of the addressees, therefore, it seems more natural to think that he looked upon his own experience in the matter as generally typical of the time before becoming a Christian. Recent scholars, e.g. Prümm, **f** Leenhardt, Michel, find an allusion to the narrative of Gn 3 behind Paul's argument. In this view he is outlining a history of salvation beginning with the situation before sin. What is true of Adam, designated as 'I', holds for all men, since Adam is taken as the representative of mankind.

(2) The law of which Paul speaks here has been identified with the natural moral law, the Mosaic Law, and both together. The last is the most satisfactory answer. That he had the Mosaic Law foremost in mind follows from the fact that he speaks in the first person. At the same time he must have included the natural moral law because of the former Gentiles among his readers. The simplest solution therefore is to take the law here as the Mosaic Law but as typical of the natural moral

857f law in the same sense as the first person in this description is meant to be typical of man in general, Israelite and Gentile alike. This wider interpretation of 'law' is not contradicted by the commandment 'Thou shalt not covet', 7. This is a quotation from the Decalogue, but so free (cf Ex 20:17; Dt 5:21) that it fits the natural moral law as well. Nor can it be urged against this explanation that it entails the abrogation of the natural law which is clearly against Christian doctrine. The point of the whole ch is not the abrogation of the law, but 'who is to be given first place', Christ or the law? When he speaks of 'law' Paul refers to its moral content, as embodying the divine plan for human conduct. Contemporary Judaism knew this wider concept of the Mosaic Law which covered every precept given to mankind, cf, Sir 17:1—12, where the law is summed up in one precept comprehending all commandments to men: 'Avoid all evil'. He argues, therefore, from a concept of law rather as the whole system of salvation than as a specific set of precepts, 6:14. The constituent notes of this concept are that it was given by God as a means of justification. In the way of thinking prevalent in Judaism there was no other way to justification than observance of divine commands.

g (3) The sin is not a specified sin against such or such a commandment, but sin in general or sin personified. At the same time it is sin resident in the speaker, 9, 18; and that, before it is shown up as such by the law. 'When the commandment came, sin revived' *anezēsen*, 9. All this combines to describe it as 'original sin personified' resident in the speaker, i.e. in Paul as in everybody else. If so, it must be remembered that Paul is analysing the pre-Christian state of the soul and that we have here the fact of original sin rather than a definition. 9 would apply to Adam better than to any other person. Indeed from a reading of the Gn account, particularly as narrated in Jub 3:15—17, no reference is made to a precept before the temptation; according to Gen 3:1 the woman is made aware of an external injunction only at the serpent's instigation. The appeal to the example of Adam is appropriate, because, far from deriving life from observance of the law, he lost it when the divine command was used by the devil as a means for his destruction. The verb *anezēsen* can also mean simply 'came to life', and so does not suppose renewal of an earlier state. Paul presents sin as a power extrinsic to the individual, but finding its way within and rousing the desire 'to be like gods'.

(4) As to the concupiscence of 7, 8, Paul is evidently using the term *epithumia*, in the sense of evil desires or inclinations towards the forbidden. Moreover, he seems to be thinking of concupiscence as that state in which it becomes or already has become sinful.

h In OT the sin of covetousness describes the crime of those who reject dependence on God, e.g. Ps 78 (77): 30; 106 (105):14. Thus in 1 Cor 10:6 it can sum up all the sins listed later. 'You shall not covet' sums up the injunction of Gn 2:17, and can evoke any sin including the first, cf Gn 2:9; 3:6. We come to know what sin is through experiencing its effects on us. In this sense the law gives us knowledge of sin inasmuch as sin is made manifest in the form of a transgression of a divine command, and is in that way brought to our consciousness as a power inimical to God and leading us to separation from him. On the passage 7—13 see S. Lyonnet in VDom 40 (1962), 163—83.

858a **13—25 The Refutation of a Second Misinterpretation—** The new Christian attitude to the Old Law must not be misinterpreted as blaming the law for the con-

sequence of its transgressions = death. According to 7— **858** 12 there would be no death without sin, and no sin without law. The logical conclusion would seem to be, that according to such doctrine it is after all the law which causes all the trouble, including death. The purpose of this conclusion is again (as in 7) to lead the Apostle's doctrine to absurdity. This second objection does not go any deeper than the first in 7. Paul's reply in 13—25 is substantially the same as in 7—12. The law is good, 14—16; sin frustrates the good intentions of the law, 13, 23. The proof is again taken from the experience of temptation. The description of temptation in 13—23, however, is much more detailed than that in 7—12. In this more detailed analysis of temptation lies the importance of the passage.

For a closer study of Paul's analysis of temptation in 13—25 it may again be helpful to treat it as a scene with four speakers: (1) Sin 13, 14, 17, 20 = the other law in 23 = the law of sin in 23, 25. (2) The carnal Self 14, sold under sin 14 = the flesh 18, 25 = the body 24. (3) The Law 13, 14, 16 = the law of God, 22, 25 = the law of my mind 23. (4) The better Self 15, 19, 21 = the inner man 22 = the mind 25. The conflict **b** takes place between 1 and 2 on the one hand and 3 and 4 on the other, with the result that 3 and 4 are defeated. This means the death of the better Self = the inner man; and it establishes the rule and sovereignty of Sin and its satellite, the carnal Self. Thus the analysis of temptation and sin necessarily leads to the question: whence is man to expect help and deliverance from this state? Paul answers: not through the Law but 'through Christ, our Lord', 24f. This is the point he wants to drive home, and the practical conclusion to which the whole discussion is meant to lead.

The peculiar and most noteworthy features of Paul's analysis of temptation in 13—25 can be studied under the following four questions: (1) What is the origin of the idea of 'the divided Self' (= the carnal Self *versus* the better Self) which is the most striking addition to 7—12 in 13—25? (2) Is Paul here speaking of the time before or after his conversion? (3) Is his description of the combat between Sin and Law =between the carnal Self and the better Self, historically true? (4) Is not his picture of man's inability to resist Sin in 13—25 so gloomy that it almost appears as if man were possessed by Sin, so that he is no longer responsible for his actions? There are rabbinical as well as Greek and Latin parallels; cf SB 3, 238—40; 4, 1, 366—83 (excursus on *yēser hārā'*); Wetstein ad 7:15. On the other hand literary dependence on the part of Paul on any of these sources cannot be proved, and the experience seems too general to call for such an explanation. Moreover in this context the divided Self might be but a development of the *epithumia*, concupiscence in 7, 8, to which Paul strangely does not refer again in 13—15 under that name.

(2) Modern commentators agree that both context and contents point decisively to the time before conversion. It is the characteristic experience of the soul before conversion to be unable to carry out its higher aspirations, 15, 18, 23, 25b. To regard this experience as remaining after conversion is against the whole line of the argument, cf 6:6, 9, 12—14, 17, 22; 7:6; 8; and also against all the moral exhortations in Paul's epistle. Nor is it necessary to understand the picture as a reflexion of the Apostle's own state of soul because he uses the present tense. There is no reason against taking this as an historic or graphic present to denote what is past, so that there is no real change of tense between 7—12 and 13—25. However, the Latin commentators of earlier **c**

58c centuries did commonly refer 13—25 to the time after conversion and baptism. This was due to the influence of Augustine who used this passage in the Pelagian controversies as an illustration and proof-text for the Christian struggle towards perfection. Details in Cornely, 373—6.

(3) Was the power of sin so overwhelming and was the law so unable to make men carry out its commandments before Christian faith and grace came to their help? To begin with, history can rightly object that the natural moral law as well as the Mosaic Law, the Roman law as well as the law of any other state have prevented millions of sins and crimes long before Christianity and that they still do so today. And as regards the Mosaic Law the Bible is full of praise for it (cf Ps 19 (18); and 119 (118)), and the Pharisees have never been worried about the failures of the *Law*. Against these objections Paul can be defended by pointing to the other sins which all those laws taken together did not prevent, cf 1:18—3:20. Nor does Paul's description stand alone. There is confirmatory evidence from Israelites as well as

d Gentiles. The Israelites read pictures just as dark in the Prophets and the Pss; cf Is 1:2f; Jer 17:1, etc; Pss 14 (13) = 53 (52); 51 (50), etc further the rabbinical saying on the *yēser hārā'*, the evil impulse. SB 3, 238—40; 4, 1, 466—83; Lietzmann, 75 ff. The confirmatory evidence from Greek and Latin literature, too, is plentiful, e g Ovid, *Metamorph*, VII, 19ff; Epictetus, *Enchiridion* II, 26, 4; see Wetstein ad 7:15. Finally it must be remembered that Paul would necessarily view life under the law from the glorious height of his newly gained Christian ideals and that as an outstanding saint. This, too, will help in comparing his view of the weakness of human nature with the more optimistic pagan view.

(4) Paul's object was to show the insufficiency of the law. He wanted to show that the law had proved a failure in the real issue of life, which is not merely to forbid but to prevent and overcome sin. And in this respect he argues, sin has ruled up to now in spite of the law; and all he expects from his readers is to admit this failure of the law as an historical fact. Bent on scoring this point Paul could and did abstract from the question of free will. Man's responsibility as the result of his free will has its place in other discussions. And if we want to find the Apostle's ideas on free will and man's full responsibility for sins committed against the law, we must consult those other passages, e.g. 1:18, 20, 21; 2:1, 9. There is plenty of evidence that Paul did hold the sinner

e responsible for his sins. Inasmuch as it is given by God the law must be good with a role in the economy of salvation. As a mere norm of conduct it cannot justify man, that is, bring about a transformation of heart. But as long as the present imperfect condition endures, a guide to conduct is necessary. Even the new law as an extrinsic written code of morals cannot have effective value unless it is identified with the interior activity of the Holy Spirit, cf Aquin. *Sum. Theol.* 1—2, q. 106 a.2. Sin, here personified and described as entering the world and dominating every descendant of Adam, is the real and the only cause of death; law is the occasion by making men more acutely aware of the power of sin to cause separation from God. On the place of law see S. Lyonnet, *St Paul. Liberty and Law* (1962); for a critical survey of interpretations of ch 7 see the same author in Bib 43 (1962), 117—51.

f **8:1—39 More Effects of Justification = Sanctifying Grace**, or the indwelling of the Holy Spirit—'Blessings of the spiritual life' expresses the topic of Rm 8, though Paul himself does not use those words. His own descriptions of what we usually call the spiritual life vary al- **858f** most from sentence to sentence. These must be taken together whenever we think of the spiritual life in the sense of Paul, and even then we must add the contrast to the natural life which is there like a cross-current all the time. On the different meanings of 'spirit, spiritual', etc, in Paul's letters see Prat II. 405—7; on the union with Christ in the spiritual life, cf P. de Jaegher, *One with Jesus*, 1937.

A general characteristic of the effects of justification or sanctifying grace enumerated in this chapter is the *positive* presentation of the doctrine of redemption, whereas all that Paul has said so far on the benefits resulting from redemption was expressed in a form which may be called negative. In ch 5 it was redemption or deliverance from the wrath of God; in ch 6 from the rule of sin; in ch 7 from the rule of the law. In ch 8, however, it is the life and power and triumph of the indwelling Holy Spirit. The doctrine of the indwelling Holy Spirit which is generally recognized as another characteristic feature of ch 8 should not be studied without bearing in mind the place which it holds in Paul's theology as a whole; cf 5:5; 8:9, 11; 1 Cor 3:16; 6:19; 2 Cor 1:22; 6:16; Eph 1:13; 4:30; also Jn 14:17, etc and Prat II, 406f.

The saving work effected by Christ is realized in **g** Christians by the interior activity of the Spirit making them sons of God. In ascribing the new life to the action of the spirit Paul was influenced by OT texts on the spirit of God as the creator of a new people of real inner holiness, e.g. Ez 36:26—28. OT conceived the spirit of God as the divine action within certain chosen individuals, Jg 3:10; Is 42:1.

1—8 The Victory of the Indwelling Spirit over the Flesh—Paul speaks of victory over Satan and sin: he is looking at the conflict between the spirit of Christ and the spirit of sin or of Satan in every man's own heart. Hence it is the internal victory over Satan and sin rather than the external results on which 1—8 throw light. It becomes a victory over the flesh or the carnal Self.

The force from which this victory over the flesh first came and still comes, according to 1—8, is Christ. To begin with, it was the very purpose of the Incarnation to conquer sin. What was not only unheard of but impossible before Christ has since come to be a fact. Sin has been overcome and it was Christ who set the first example. But not only that, it is part of God's economy of salvation that Christ's victory over sin should continue by means of that same spirit of Christ dwelling in men's hearts. Hence all who have that spirit of Christ can be sure of their victory over the flesh. They will not be spared the conflict between the spirit of Christ and the spirit of Satan in their own souls, but the victory of the spirit of Christ is as certain for the future as it is proved for the past, for the spirit of Christ is neither dead nor changeable.

A special feature of this passage is the contrast between *sarx* and *pneuma*, the flesh and the spirit. In this Paul may have been influenced by the rabbinical discussions on the *yēser tōb* and the *yēser hārā'* = the good and the bad instinct, cf SB 4, 1, 466—83.

A practical difficulty in this passage is the certainty **h** with which Paul speaks of the victory of the spirit over the flesh. Did he not know our Lord's warning, 'the spirit is willing but the flesh is weak', Mt 26:41? And does the Apostle not speak here as if in a Christian the inclination to sin (*fomes peccati*) had been extinguished by the grace of justification? Such conclusions could indeed be drawn, if 1—8 stood alone. But there is plenty of evidence in other parts of Paul's epistles that he, too, was

858h kept well aware of the fact that the victory of the spirit over the flesh can by no means be taken as a matter of course in Christian life, cf 1 Cor 5:1—6:20. His many exhortations show the stress which he laid on co-operation with the spirit of Christ dwelling in us. But in 1—8 Paul is not concerned with the duty of co-operation with grace but with the actual victory of those who are in fact guided by that spirit of Christ. Here, his point is, that the spirit of Christ is by its very nature a spirit of victory over the flesh; cf Council of Trent, sess V, *Decretum de pecc. orig.* (Dz 792).

Plan. There is no agreement among commentators as to the divisions to be made in 1—11. Many regard 1—11 as one paragraph combining the victory over the flesh and over death, cf v 2. Others separate 1—4 (5) and 5 (6)—11.

Style. The exact sequence of thought in detail is difficult to ascertain, cf the use of the connecting particles: *gar* 2, 3, 5, 6, 7; *de* 8, 9, 10, 11.

859a **1.** 'Therefore now': has been explained (*a*) as introducing a summary of chh 5—7; (*b*) as indicating the connexion with 7:24, 25*a*; (*c*) as taking up 7:6; (*d*) as referring back to 5:11. 'Condemnation': has been taken (*a*) as a sentence of condemnation, cf Council of Trent, sess V (Dz 792); (*b*) as the punishment inflicted in the sentence of condemnation; (*c*) as the consciousness of being under condemnation. This last meaning would suit the context best. 'To be in Christ': is a phrase which is essential for the study of Pauline mysticism. On its use and meaning see Prat II 391—5, note M. **2.** States the theme developed in 1—13. It is important but difficult to find a suitable rendering. Though some inclination to good can be experienced while in the state of sin, yet men are powerless to carry it out. But when they are united to Christ, the vivifying spirit becomes a principle of activity within the believer. A new régime has been ushered in, and its permanent principle of conduct is the Holy Spirit communicated by Christ. **3.** States necessity, mode and fruits of the Incarnation (Thomas Aq.). The sentence can be explained (*a*) as an anacoluthon: what the law could not effect, God [carried out; and] sending ... he condemned ... ; (*b*) as an apposition in the nominative or accusative: God condemned sin in the flesh, which the law could not do. '*In the likeness of sinful flesh*': so the Greek text against Vg, cf Lagrange; notice the bearing of the text on the pre-existence of Christ. *peri hamartias* (*a*) on behalf of sin; (*b*) as sin offering. 'Condemned': according to the context = God made sin stand condemned in the life of Christ, cf Jn **b** 12:31f. By the Incarnation Christ took on a full human condition; 'flesh' here not in the sense of instrument of sin, but connoting mortality, and so emphasizing Christ's resemblance to the human race. By his death, the great act of his love for us, Christ passed into a spiritual existence, destroying the rule of sin. Now Christians united to Christ by baptism pass into the same spiritual condition. **4.** The purpose of the Incarnation is to make obedience to the law of God possible for those whose life is spiritual. In their new spiritual state believers can attain the whole aim of law summed up in the commandment of love, Gal 5:14; Mt 22:40. **5.** Paul contrasts the two principles of flesh and spirit; the opposition is based on their respective attitudes towards God. Flesh, as nearly always in Paul, has a pejorative meaning: those tendencies inclining to sin and thence to separation from God. Spirit in the context is the Holy Spirit communicated to Christians. Through their union with Christ, the Spirit is within believers transforming the rational faculties, cf 9, where the ex-

pression indicates how much grace or sin can become **85** part of the person.

9—11 The Victory of the Indwelling Holy Spirit c over Death, or the indwelling Holy Spirit as the pledge of the resurrection of the body—From the victory of the spirit of Christ over the flesh in the present life Paul passes on to the victory of the same spirit over death, in the resurrection of the dead body. The pledge of our participation in that resurrection is the indwelling spirit of Christ. This step from the victory of the indwelling Holy Spirit over the living body, 1—8, to the victory of the same Spirit over the dead body, 9—11, which the Apostle's argument here implies is tremendous, and the wide gulf that separates the two should not be overlooked because Paul takes it in his stride.

The characteristic of 9—11 lies in the precise wording of the doctrine of the resurrection of the body with the emphasis on the indwelling of the spirit of Christ as the bond of our union with Christ. The body that has been the temple of the spirit of Christ will be raised from the dead by God as he raised Christ from the dead: cf 1 Cor 6:14; 15:20, 23; 2 Cor 4:14; Phil 3:21; 1 Thes 4:14. The value of this argument from the resurrection of Christ to the resurrection of every Christian must be judged not by the rules of logic but by the specific Christian and Pauline doctrine of every Christian's mystical-sacramental union with Christ, the living head of the living Church.

Connexion. The beginning of a new paragraph with **d** 9 must appear arbitrary from the literary point of view. But it has the advantage of a clear distinction between the two victories of the Spirit (*a*) in life, (*b*) in death, cf v 2.

10. 'Dead' = mortal, cf v 11. 'your spirits are alive' = the soul in the state of sanctifying grace, cf Lagrange. **11.** The text is uncertain. It can be: *through* or *because of* his spirit dwelling in you, i.e. the indwelling spirit is either efficient or meritorious cause of the resurrection. The body is doomed to die, but animated by the vivifying Spirit, will become spiritual itself. Through the might of his Spirit God will do for the believer what he did for Christ—transform the entire individual for a new mode of existence.

12—17 The Victory of the Indwelling Holy Spirit e for all Eternity, or the indwelling Holy Spirit as the pledge of a glorious inheritance in heaven—A life on earth according to the spirit of Christ will be followed after death by a life of eternal happiness and glory with Christ glorified.

The first distinctive feature of Paul's argument is that he calls those who have the spirit of Christ not servants or slaves, but sons of God, 14, or children of God, 16f. The proof which he quotes is the very nature of the spirit received, and its utterance in prayer. The Christian who acts according to the spirit of his baptism knows from experience that he has the spirit of the true children of God, 13; cf Jn 7:17; 8:31f against Jn 8:44. And again when the Christian prays it is to God as his Father.

The second characteristic feature of Paul's argument is that he calls the Christian's eternal glorification not his reward but his inheritance, 17. This follows logically from the former characteristic. For the servant's reward is his pay, but the child's remuneration its inheritance. The Christian as the child of God becomes the heir of God his Father, and the joint heir with Christ his brother, with the right to share in the possessions of the Kingdom; and the one possession here singled out and put before us is the glory of Christ into which he entered as his inheri-

9e tance on the days of his resurrection and ascension. That adoption is followed by heirship is nothing out of the ordinary in the natural order. What must astonish, however, is Paul's conclusion that the one will follow the other also in the supernatural order. This application defies logical explanation. As in the question of the resurrection of the body the whole argument presupposes a union between every Christian and Christ which is above and different from any even spiritual union known to us in time and space. Its existence and character must simply be accepted as one of the mysteries of God revealed in the Gospel.

f **12—13** can be taken as conclusion to 11 or as introduction to 14ff. The sense is not affected. There remain dispositions within the Christian which could bring him again under the power of the flesh; to be always open to the influence of the Spirit these must be curbed. The Spirit becomes the interior principle of our activity and transforms human conduct, Gal 2:20. **14.** 'Sons of God': is a title used in the Bible (a) for the angels, Job 1:6; 2:1; 38:7, etc; (b) for the Israelites, Ex 4:22f; Dt 14:1f; 32:6—10; Hos 11:1—4; Is 1:4; 30:9 etc; (c) for the just, Sir 23:1—4; 51:10 (MT); Wis 2:13—18; 5:5; (d) for the Christians, 2 Cor 6:16ff; Gal 3:26; 4:6; Phil 2:15; Jn 1:12f; I Jn 3:1f; 5:1, 4f. From these metaphorical usages (the meanings of which differ only in degree) must be distinguished the metaphysical use implying preexistence and divinity which the name has when applied to Christ in such passages as 8:3, 32; Gal 4:4; cf Prat II, 140—2. **15b.** 'Spirit of sonship' = state of sanctifying grace, cf Dz 790.

g **15c.** 'Abba! Father!': The repetition has been explained (a) as a Greek translation of the Aramaic Abba = father, cf Gal 4:6; Mk 14:36; (b) as a figure of speech (anadiplosis) for emphasis; (c) as a relic of an ancient bilingual liturgical (Aramaic-Greek) prayer or ejaculation. The meaning of the phrase cannot be that to pray to God as Father was a Christian innovation or privilege. To think and speak of God as Father is a custom that can be found also in non-Christian religions. For the OT see Ex 4:22; Dt 32:6; Is 1:2; 63:16; 64:8; Jer 31:9, 20; Hos 1:10; 11:1; Mal 1:6; 2:10; Sir 23:1, 4; 51:10 (MT); Wis 2:16; 11:10 (11 Vg); 14:3; 18:13 (LXX); Tb 13:4 (LXX). Here add the OT proper names compounded with 'Ab' =father, of which G. B. Gray, *Studies in Hebr. Proper Names*, 1896, counts 31. For the same idea in the OT apocrypha see Jubilees 1:24f, 28; 19:29; 3 Macc 5:7; cf 7:6; 6:3, 8; Test. Jud. 24. For the same usage in rabbinical literature, including the '*Shemone Esre*' in which two petitions are addressed to God as Father, see SB 1, 393—6, on Mt 6:4; but here it should be remembered that Abba about this time became also a title of the Rabbis, cf JE I, 29—35. Apart from Israel, the idea of God as Father was known also in other Semitic religions, cf Lagrange, *Études sur les religions sémitiques*, 1903², 110—18. For the same usage in the religion of primitive races see W. Schmidt, *The Religion of Earliest Man* (CTS Studies in Comparative Religion, no. 2),

h 17. Against false conclusions from the study of comparative religion, however, it is worth pointing out that to speak of God as Father is much more common in the NT than anywhere else. No less than 263 references in the NT are tabulated by J. Drummond, *Via, Veritas et Vita*, 1894, 175. At all events the full meaning of the phrase 'Abba! Father!' in 8:13 is not to be found by insisting on the form (which is common to many religions), but must be derived from the spirit in which it is used in Christianity. The gift of the spirit constitutes our adoption, and in adopting us God gives us a participation

in the sonship of Christ. The Christian can then speak to **859h** God in the very terms used by Christ. Uttered under the influence of the spirit, the prayer of the believer is a proof that God loves him as he loves his own Son, and that the Father is the centre and the end of the Christian's prayer and of his life. **17.** The glory is more than the reward of our labours, but follows on the necessary connexion established by God between Christ's suffering and his glorification. Our way of life must, too, be modelled after that pattern, cf G. Didier, *Le Désintéressement du Chrétien* (1955), 127ff.

18—30 The Indwelling Holy Spirit and the Present 860a Longing for Glorification = Perfect Happiness, or the certainty that the Christian life will lead to the glory of heaven——From the height of his contemplation of the Christian's inheritance in heaven, 12—17, Paul is forced back to earth by the contrast between those things to come and things present. In spite of all that he has said in praise of the salvation revealed in the Gospel the present life seems a life of tears everywhere. Nature, animate and inanimate, groans under a law of corruption and longs for the time of its freedom from pain and its full measure of happiness, 19—22; and the very same feelings and longings still linger in the Christian soul, in spite of all that the grace of justification may have changed, 23—25 (27).

It is necessary to limit the discussion to the kind of suffering which Paul has in mind. He is not speaking of this or that suffering in particular, this or that physical pain, this or that social or political evil. He is thinking of the general suffering, the absence of full happiness, or the universal want of glory, the general longing for glorification or the universal hope and desire for greater things one day to come. But if Christianity does not **b** remove even this 'spiritual suffering', what then is the immediate use or benefit of the indwelling Holy Spirit, or of the salvation of the Gospel in general? The simplest and today most common Christian answer is the general rule, that suffering is the path to glory. The best proof is the life of our Lord, cf Lk 24:26, 46; Ac 17:3; 26:23; Heb 2:9f. For the same rule in the life of the Christian cf Mt 10:38; 16:24; 20:22f; Mk 8:34f; 10:38; Jn 12:24—6; Rm 8:17c; 1 Cor 12:26; 2 Cor 1:5; 4:10; 13:4; Gal 6:17; Phil 1:29; 3:10; Col 1:24; 2 Tm 2:12; 1 Pt 1:6, 11; 2:21; 3:14, 17, 18; 4:13; 5:1.

The points to be noted in St Paul's reply to this universal cry of suffering rising from the earth are the following three: (a) He makes no attempt to deny the existence of this suffering or to belittle its painfulness. (b) He answers that this spiritual suffering is not against the indwelling Holy Spirit, but rather its very own voice and expression, 26f. The reason is that the present indwelling of the Holy Spirit is only the beginning of the Christian life, 23; it is only the pledge of the complete glory to come, cf 2 Cor 1:22; 5:5; Eph 1:14. It is by its very nature a spirit of hope, 23f. Those as **c** yet unfulfilled longings in nature as well as in the Christian soul, therefore, are like the pains foreboding and preceding the world's new birth = the final and general glorification of the sons of God, 21f. In the meantime, i.e. in the present time of want and suffering, nature as well as men must and can hold out in this hope of final glorification supported by the indwelling Holy Spirit. (c) The Apostle anticipates the objection: is not this hope of unseen glory to come just one more empty promise to the harassed souls of men? Far from it! It is the hope that God will carry out to the end his work of redemption, a hope that is as certain as any hope can be, inasmuch as God is certain to complete the work he has begun, 28—30.

860c For a deeper appreciation of 18—30 it would be useful to pursue the question, in what does the 'glory that is to be revealed to us' here discussed consist? St Paul himself does not develop this question. The answer can be found in the explanations of 'eternal life', in the last article of the Apostles' Creed.

Object. The explanations of the Apostle's object in 18—30 differ considerably. Some maintain that his purpose was to enlarge on the greatness of the Christian justification by adding a further triumph of the indwelling Holy Spirit over a practical difficulty in life: the universal want of happiness. This explanation has the advantage of showing progress of thought in accordance with the main argument in ch 8. But others see in 18—30 a new discussion on the certainty of the Christian hope of glorification, cf ch 5. In this case 18—30 becomes a kind of scholion or digression to the heavenly inheritance discussed in 12—17. The former explanation is followed in this commentary.

Plan. The commentators who take the certainty of the Christian hope of eternal glory as the keynote of 18—30 gain an easy division of the passage into four paragraphs according to the four proofs for this certainty. They are the witness (1) of creation, 19—22; (2) of the Christian soul, 23—25; (3) of the Holy Ghost, 26—27; (4) of God's economy of salvation, 28—30. If 'the victory and triumph of the indwelling Holy Spirit' is taken as the keynote, the following plan may be followed: (1) the victory of the Spirit over the suffering (longing) of irrational nature, 19—22; (2) the victory of the Spirit over the suffering (longing) of the Christian soul, 23—25 (27); (3) the certainty of this victory, 28—30. The difficulty of this plan lies in placing 26f.

d 19—22 The Longing of Irrational Nature for Glorification and the Holy Spirit dwelling in the Christian Soul—It is unusual for Paul to give his attention to irrational nature. But when in 19—22 he voices its agony under the burden of its age-long curse we need not think of a sudden flight into poetry. The ideas here expressed are biblical throughout. That irrational nature was affected by man's (first) sin is clearly stated in Gn 3:17f; and its share in man's redemption follows no less clearly from such messianic prophecies as Is 65:17—25; 66:22. For the same idea in the NT see Mt 19:28; Ac 3:21; 2 Pt 3:13; Apoc 21:1. Rabbinical parallels are collected in SB 3, 840—7, on Rev 21:1. There remains however something original and unique in the way in which Paul here personifies these two Biblical doctrines and argues from them to the greatness of the Christian glorification as that 'divine event to which the whole creation moves'.

What is the burden from which irrational creation longs to be redeemed? Paul calls it her enforced submission to *mataiotēs* = purposelessness, 20. This has been understood (a) as its physical mutability; (b) as its physical corruption, decay, death; (c) as its moral abuse by sinful man; (d) as the absence of fullness of harmony and order = the consequences of original sin. Of these explanations the last seems the most satisfactory, because the third is too narrow, and the first two raise points of natural science which were hardly in the mind of Paul. For there is nothing in his letters to support the idea that he regarded nature as free from mutability and death before man's fall.

e What will the glory to come bring for irrational nature? Paul answers with 'the glory of the children of God', 21. But Paul's wording is negative and may be compared with the negative definition of our redemption = freedom from the curse of sin. Hence, the various speculations on the way in which nature will eventually obtain her freedom

from the curse of Gn 3:17 cannot claim the authority **860** of Paul. By sin the harmonious relations between the human race and the rest of creation were thrown into disorder. The hope expressed could be an allusion to the protoevangelium Gn 3:15ff, in which contemporary Judaism saw proclaimed the victory for the posterity of the woman in the Messianic age. As man's sin involved all other creatures, the rest of creation will also be affected by his transformation. Various interpretations of the text are discussed by A. Viard in RB 59 (1952), 337—54, and by A. Dubarle in RSPT 38 (1954), 445—65. What has the longing of irrational nature for glorification, 19—22, to do with the Holy Spirit dwelling in the Christian soul, 23—27? The two voices agree in the longing they express, and thus become supplementary to each other.

23—27 The Longing of the Christian Soul for Glorification and the Indwelling Holy Spirit—In spite of all that Paul has said in praise of the effects of justifying = sanctifying grace from 5:1 onward, and esp in ch 8, there still remains a big gap to be filled in the soul. However highly the praises of justification or sanctification on earth may be sung, experience teaches that the soul longs for greater things still. It is with this that Paul is dealing in 23—27. The commonly accepted term for the object of this desire of the Christian soul is glorification or heaven. Neither term is used in 23—27, but see 18, 21. The terms used in 23—27 are (the full) adoption of the sons of God, and the redemption of our body, 23. For practical purposes, however, it simplifies matters to keep to the established distinction between sanctification and glorification, or between sanctifying grace and glorifying grace. But it must be remembered that the latter distinction is not a distinction in essence but only in time and degree, i.e. sanctifying grace is the beginning of glorifying grace, 23; cf 2 Cor 1:22; 5:5; Eph 1:14.

An important point in the explanation of 23—27 **f** concerns the distinction between the voice of the Christian soul, which has the Holy Spirit, 23—25, and voice of the Holy Spirit in the Christian soul, 26f. In either case it is evidently the voice of the indwelling Holy Spirit, i.e. of the Holy Spirit dwelling in the soul through sanctifying grace. The difference then seems to be but a difference of intensity in prayer. In 26f most commentators think of the charisma of tongues or glossolalia, Mk 16:17; Ac 10:46; 1 Cor 14:1—23. But this may be too narrow or too exact an interpretation. Ecstatic prayer in general satisfies the text.

Plan. Two points can be distinguished: (1) the voice of the Christian soul, 23—25; (2) the voice of the Holy Spirit, 26f. **23.** 'as we wait for adoption' = the fullness of the blessings conferred on us as sons of God. The context and the comparison with 14—17 make it necessary to insert some noun like: fullness, manifestation, realization, consummation. Some MSS and editors omit *huiothesian*. Adoption is a definitive **g** act and not susceptible of development, in contradistinction to the notions of 'salvation' and 'redemption', which imply the idea of progress. The Christian in the present life has already begun the process of salvation; its full term is attained only at the glorious resurrection of the body. Cf P. Benoit in RSR 39 (1951), 267—80. **24.** 'In hope': cannot be *dativus instrumenti*, because it is by faith that we are saved and not by hope. Hence it is commonly taken as *dativus modi* = with hope, i.e. we are saved with the hope (of glorification) as a part in the present state of justification = sanctification, but cf SH. **26.** 'Weakness': i.e. of our prayer. 'As we ought': can be connected with either verb: (a) we know not . . .; (b) we should pray. The former is the better

60g connexion, because the context leaves no doubt as to what we ought to pray for——our final glorification. But we are far from knowing the form, contents, etc, of this glorification as we might wish or ought to know.

h 28—30 The Christian's Longing for Glorification is certain to be fulfilled——The longing for glorification described in 19—22, 23—27 implies not only a vision of still greater things to come but also an element of hope, 23f. Now hope always needs encouragement to prevent the inevitable thought of possible disappointment from weakening it. The normal form of such encouragement is a reassurance that the object hoped for will materialize. Such a reassurance of the Christian hope of glorification in heaven is the subject of 28—30. The reason on which Paul bases this reassurance is 'the chain of Providential care with which God does accompany the course of his chosen', SH 214. Providence has started our Christian life on earth; Providence will also lead it to perfection in heaven, cf Phil 1:6.

The first point in Paul's argument is the design of Providence exhibited in the Christian life here and now. Paul enumerates four turning points in this life which bear evident traces of divine Providence, 29f: (*a*) God foreknew us; (*b*) he predestined us; (*c*) he called us; (*d*) he justified us. The second point in the argument is the conclusion that these four steps are but four steps before a fifth, which is to be the last and final step, i.e. our glorification in heaven. 'Whom God has justified (= sanctified) he will also glorify', 30. What is the logical value of this conclusion? Paul's conclusion in 30 that there must be this fifth step after the previous four is not meant to be a logical deduction. The Apostle presents it as faith based on the works of Providence in the past, 29f, and on the nature of God who is love, 28.

Does Paul teach in 28—30 that every Christian can be certain to reach his final salvation and glorification in heaven? The question can and must be answered in the affirmative for every true Christian. The Apostle made this condition in the numerous and urgent exhortations that fill his letters. Once this condition of a true Christian life, however, is accepted, the *uncertainty* of final salvation for the individual follows as an inevitable practical consequence, cf 5:5—21; Dz 825.

i 28a. The translation depends on what is considered to be the subject of the verb. The form of the text allows (a) *theos*, God; (b) *panta*, all things; (c) *pneuma*, the spirit, from 26. In any case the content is a general theological principle; 2 Tm 4:8; Jas 1:12, etc. Four parallels from Greek literature are quoted by Wetstein; for rabbinical sources to the same effect, cf Wetstein and SB. **28b.** 'Those . . . who are called according to his purpose' = those who love God in 28*a*, cf Eph 1:11; 3:11; 2 Tm 1:9. It connects the general statement in 28*a* with the application in 29f. Discussions on absolute predestination ought never to have been built on such an *obiter dictum*. Paul reminds the faithful that their call to faith has come by the initiative of God in accordance with his plan to confer the gift. God's loving design for mankind is the glory of the elect; their call to faith, their justification in baptism have meaning only in relation to the end God intends for them. The acts enumerated are not successive in God; but in the historical realization of the divine aim one must precede the other.

861a **29—30** give a summary description of the process of salvation, apparently in the order of time, cf Eph 1:3—14; 2 Thes 2:13f. **29.** 'Foreknew': cf 1 Cor 8:3. As a rendering of the OT *yāda'* it may also have the meaning of the verbs: prefer, choose. At all events Paul puts it down as the first stage in man's salvation. The distinction between *ante* and *post praevisa merita* belongs to later theology. 'Predestined to be made conformed to the image of his Son': at the general resurrection, cf 8:17; Phil 3:21; 1 Cor 15:49. **30.** 'Called': refers to the moment of becoming a Christian, cf Jn 6:44. 'Those . . . he also justified': cf 1:17; 3:21—30. This fourth stage in the process of man's salvation coincides temporally with the previous 'call'. 'Them he also glorified': refers to the future glory in heaven. The past tense is a prophetic perfect (aorist). **861a**

31—39 A Concluding Paragraph summarizing the blessings of the spiritual life in the assurance of God's love for us in Christ——Coming to the end of his exposition of the Christian life Paul seems to have felt that his explanation (like all later ones) must leave a great number of doubts and difficulties unanswered or untouched. For it lies in the nature of human life that no doctrine can in advance dispose of all difficulties that may arise in practice. But in so far as these difficulties belong to the religious sphere, the Christian life has one general answer which can never fail. All these personal difficulties become insignificant as soon as our eyes turn away from them to contemplate that one great act of the love of God in which he did not spare his own Son for our Salvation, cf Jn 3:16. No one who believes and **b** considers this truth can doubt that God wills his best under all circumstances. It is true that there will be an examination after death of which we are all afraid, but sanctified by God, 30, we need fear no accusation, 33. There will be a judgement, but redeemed and defended by Christ we need fear no condemnation from his lips, 34. Before that there may be sufferings and violence, but the love of Christ for us will remain unaffected as the sun remains unchanged by the clouds that may hide it for a while. Christ will not forsake us, 35. It may even come for us to a choice between life and death; to a struggle with the evil spirits and devilish powers; to battles with enemies known or still unknown, from above the earth or below the earth, yet all combined they will not be able to wipe out or mar in our souls the picture and reassurance of the love which God has shown us in Christ. However dark the earth may turn, God's love for us in Christ will remain undisturbed and continue to reign above like the spirit of God above the turbulent seas, Gn 1:2. And in his love we are eternally secure, 38f.

Connexion. The opening question 'what then shall we say?', 31, does not here introduce an objection as in 3:5; 6:1; 7:7; 9:14, but a summary, cf 9:30. God has given his elect the victory over sin and death, 1—8, 9—11; he has adopted them as sons and heirs, 12—17; he will fulfil their longing for glorification in heaven, 18—30: what more can be said? Paul has come to the end of his argument and **c** looks for a fitting conclusion. The thoughts which occur to him centre round God's love for us in Christ. Thus the passage becomes a summary of ch 8, and at the same time the description of another and last blessing of the spiritual life. This explanation of the connexion between 31—39 and 1—30 is not accepted by all commentators. Some see in 31—39 merely the continuation of 28—30 and therefore treat it as a further, i.e. a fifth, reason for the certainty of final salvation. Others regard it as the summary of the whole doctrinal part as the beginning of which they quote 1:16 or 3:21 or 5:1. The truth probably lies in the combination of these opinions. Here as so often Paul shows very little concern to follow the rules of classical composition.

Characteristic. When Paul concluded the first part of his letter with praise of the love which God has shown us in Christ, he did not intend to give a comprehensive or systematic treatment of the subject, cf 1 Cor 13. His object

861c in writing so far had been to recommend and preach the Christian life by presenting to his readers its greatness, benefits and glory. To crown these praises with a hymn on God's love for us in Christ was a fortunate choice.

Plan. The progress of thought in 31—39 is clearly marked by the four ascending rhetorical questions (Lagrange speaks of four stanzas): (*a*) 31f Who shall be against us, if God is for us? (*b*) 33 Who shall accuse us? (*c*) 34 Who shall condemn us? (*d*) 35—39 Who shall separate us from the love which Christ bears us?

d 32. 'All things': all the Christian needs to obtain the glory of heaven. Paul could allude to the sacrifice of Isaac, Gn 22:16, to which certain contemporary trends attributed expiatory value, and still others connected with the feast of the Passover. At all events Paul takes Christ's sacrifice as the most cogent proof of God's love for us. **33, 34a.** The punctuation is uncertain. Consequently the translations vary. (1) Who shall accuse the elect of God, when it is God himself who acquits them? Who shall condemn them, when it is Christ Jesus who died for them . . .? (2) Who shall accuse the elect of God? When it is God who justifies, who will condemn? [Certainly not] Christ . . . who died for them? Of these translations 1 is the most symmetrical but 2 has the support of Is 50:8, a passage which may well have been here in the Apostle's mind. The sense of the argument is not affected. **35.** 'From the love of Christ': has been understood (*a*) as an objective genitive = our love for Christ; (*b*) as a subjective genitive = the love which Christ bears us. The context which discusses the certainty of the glory to come decides in favour of *a*: 'Tribulation', etc: for similar lists of temptations in Stoic literature cf Lagrange. **36.** The Ps quoted describes the persecution of the faithful Jews and the triumphs of their forebears. In all trials Paul sees a proof of love because they herald the time of salvation from God, 1 Thes 3:2ff, and because the strength received to endure them is a sign of support from God. **38.** 'Nor angels nor principalities' can mean: (*a*) good spirits, Gal 1:8, and bad, Eph 6:12; Col 2:15; 1 Pt 3:22, or (*b*) evil spirits of two different kinds; or (*c*) spiritual and temporal powers = earthly authorities *dunameis = fortitudo*, Vg.

e 9:1—11:36 The Present Exclusion of Israel from the Salvation revealed in the Gospel—The problem which Paul sets himself in these three chapters is the failure of the Gospel to convince Israel. How can the Gospel be the true fulfilment of the Messianic promises, when its central doctrine declaring Jesus of Nazareth to be the Messiah is rejected by the very Israel to whom God had promised the Messiah. The Apostle discusses the exclusion of Israel as a whole from the salvation of the Messiah and that only here and now, i.e. in the Church on earth. It would lead to grave misunderstandings to think that his subject is Israel's exclusion from heaven at the Last Judgement, which judgement, needless to say, is not collective but individual; cf Prat I, 250; A. Charue, *L'Incrédulité des Juifs dans le NT*, 1929, 283ff and 343—52 where an extensive bibliography on the whole subject can be found.

The connexion of the subject with the preceding parts of the epistle is not stated in the text. Probably its importance at the time was responsible for its place here, cf Gal. Of the commentators who look for definite points of connexion some go back as far as 1:16; cf 2:9; others point to 3:1f, the privileges of Israel; and others to 8:30, divine election.

f Importance. In the days of Paul the theological problems raised by the separation of the Church from Israel and *vice versa* were probably the subject of daily conversations among Christians, cf Ac; Gal; Charue, **861** viif. Compared with Israel the Christians were but a small minority, with all the external advantages (power, organization, scholarship, tradition, money) on the other side. In this situation Paul more than anyone else, as far as we know, set himself to defend the Christian cause in a scientific, theological way; and Rm 9—11 is his most complete effort that has been preserved. The primary importance of these chapters, therefore, is that they present the first scientific vindication of the Christian cause in combat with the theology of the synagogue. They are the first chapters of early Christian apologetics. The terms 'scientific' and 'theological' must, of course, be taken here in accordance with the methods used at the time in the world of Paul, cf Philo and rabbinical theology. Apart from this apologetic aspect of the question which was no doubt foremost in Paul's mind, these chapters remain important for theology also because of the principles employed by the Apostle, especially those concerning the problem of evil and divine election or predestination to salvation within the Church. Why are the Gentiles in the Church and Israel is not?

Plan. Chh 9—11 can be divided as follows: (*a*) 9:1—5, **g** introduction; (*b*) 9:6—29, the vindication of God's justice and faithfulness in the present exclusion of Israel from the salvation revealed in the Gospel; (*c*) 9:30—10:21, this exclusion is Israel's own fault; (*d*) 11:1—36, other points of view from which light can be thrown on the problems raised by Israel's present unbelief and rejection. The new economy based on faith seems to be opposed to the Old Covenant. Israel, once the chosen vehicle of salvation for all mankind, has given place to the Gentiles, and so the Gospel message seems to be at variance with God's word. The problem to be faced, therefore, was how the divine promises can be kept intact when taken from the Chosen People and transferred to the old enemy the Gentiles.

9:1—5 Introduction of the New Subject, Israel's **h** exclusion from the salvation of the Messiah—This paragraph is evidently meant to be the introduction to a new topic. Nevertheless it does not state in one clear sentence what this new topic is. As so often in Paul's letters, the real problem becomes apparent only as the argument proceeds. In this case it is the problem created by the exclusion of Israel, the chosen people of old, from the blessings of the Gospel.

Connexion. There is none according to the rules of literary composition. Instead of connecting the new topic with what precedes the Apostle begins by expressing his deep sorrow over the fact that Israel as a whole has not accepted Christ and his Gospel of salvation. Thus 1—5 becomes a kind of *captatio benevolentiae*.

The first characteristic feature of this passage is the list of Israel's privileges, 4f. This list is without a biblical parallel, though the Bible is full of references to this or that prerogative of Israel. The purpose which the list fulfils in the context is twofold. 'It explains the Apostle's grief, and reveals the importance of the problem before us' (SH). The prerogatives of Israel enumerated in 4f are: (1) the name 'Israel'—a title of honour and divine favour, cf Gn 32:28; Gal 6:16. (2) 'Adoption, as sons of God'—cf Ex 4:22; Hos 11:1. (This adoption is different from that of Rm 8:15f.) (3) 'The glory'—of God manifested in his special presence at Sinai, Ex 16:10; 24:16—18; in the tabernacle, Ex 40:32, 34. (4) 'The covenants'—made with the Patriarchs, Gn 15:18; Ex 2:24, etc. (5) 'The Law'—of Moses or the Pentateuch. (6) 'The worship'—the liturgy according to the law of Moses in the tabernacle and later in the temple

51h of Jerusalem. (7) 'The promises' concerning the Messiah. (8) 'The patriarchs'—Abraham, Isaac and Jacob, Ac 3:13, etc. (9) 'The Christ'—who is of their race.

i A second feature of this paragraph is the statement of the divinity of Christ in 5. The different opinions as to its historical meaning are shown in the different punctuations of the text, cf SH 233—8. The first explanation punctuates: 'Christ according to the flesh, who is over all things, God blessed for ever, Amen', DV. In this form the meaning of the passage is clear and the sequence of thought natural. Besides being the most natural, this explanation has also the support of Christian antiquity. For other doxologies addressed to Christ, cf 16:27; 1 Tm 3:16; 2 Tm 4:18; Eph 5:14, 19; Prat II, 130. The second explanation argues that the explicit use of the name 'God' for Christ is without a parallel in Paul's letters and that this makes it necessary to avoid such a usage here if that is at all grammatically possible. Those who accept this argument find a corresponding interpretation by inserting a full stop after 'flesh' or after 'all things'. The remainder of the sentence (5c) then becomes a praise (doxology) not of Christ but of God: 'God, who is above all, be blessed for ever'; or 'God blessed for ever, Amen'. This is the exegesis among others of Wetstein, Tischendorf (1869), Jülicher, Lietzmann. Its main weakness is its artificiality which betrays itself in the far-fetched arguments necessary to make it plausible. More specific reasons which can be urged against it are: (a) 5c has not the recognized form of a biblical doxology which is 'Blessed (be) God', and not 'God (be) blessed', cf Lk 1:68; 2 Cor 1:3; Eph 1:3. (b) It is against Pauline usage to begin a doxology with a new sentence; cf 1:25; 2 Cor 11:31; Gal 1:5; 2 Tm 3:18, etc; Lagrange. (c) What is ultimately gained by this exegesis is less than the extent of the controversy suggests. For the first explanation remains at least equally possible and the doctrine of the divinity of Christ remains unimpaired because it is clear from other texts of Paul. Jewish literature reserved doxologies for God the Father; but Paul addresses some to the Father and Christ together; cf Phil 2:6ff—Christ as the equal of the Father, and 2 Tm 4:17, 22 on the application of *kurios* to Christ. The tenor of the passage argues a doxology to Christ, and the doctrine of his supremacy occurs elsewhere in Paul's writings, Phil 2:5—11; Eph 1:22. **3.** Paul is not making an assertion, but expressing heartfelt grief; cf the prayer of Moses, Ex 32:32, who, though guiltless, wishes to share the lot of his offending people. The privileges of Israel should have saved her from infidelity; now they rather make her disloyalty a veritable scandal. *euchomēn*: imperfect instead of potential optative denoting what is only thought.

62a 6—29 The Vindication of the Divine Attributes of Faithfulness and Justice in the Present Exclusion of Israel from the Salvation of the Gospel—The argument in this section is apologetic. The difficulties to be solved are objections against God's faithfulness, 6—13, and justice, 14—29, in the case of Israel and the Gospel. God has promised Israel the Messianic blessings. If they have now come with no share for Israel, then God has broken his solemn promises. This being impossible, the only alternative is that the Messiah has not yet come and that the salvation offered in the Christian Gospel is a heresy which Israel rightly rejects.

Characteristic. The passage 6—29 is difficult. But the difficulties are doctrinal—dogmatical, not textual or exegetical. They centre round the terms: election and predestination; grace and free will. For history of **862a** exegesis see SH 269—75.

6—13 The Vindication of God's Faithfulness in the Present Exclusion of Israel from the Salvation of the Gospel—The objection tries to refute Christianity by arguing that if the Gospel were true, then God would not have kept his Messianic promises to Israel. In his reply Paul tacitly admits that since the Messianic promises were given to Israel, their fulfilment also must have come to Israel. Nevertheless there is a fallacy in the objection. The mistake lies in the popular definition of the Israel to whom the divine promises were given. The divine promises were **b** not given to all the lineal descendants of Abraham. The Scriptures insist on the additional principle of God's free election as the examples of Ishmael, 6—9, and of Esau, 10—13, prove. Both were descendants of Abraham, and yet both were excluded from the blessings of Abraham their father, and of Isaac and Jacob their younger brothers. And these two cases cannot be set aside as exceptions, for they are typical of the Messianic times like the whole of the OT, cf Gal 4:23ff. As in the case of Abraham's and Isaac's children, so also in the history of the Chosen People, it is God's election that constitutes the true Israel of the Scriptures.

Besides this main argument, 6—9, Paul finds in the case of Esau and Jacob a further illustration of his thesis that God acted freely in electing whom he wished to the membership of Israel. According to Gn 25:23 Jacob was chosen and Esau rejected before either was born. If the election of the one and the rejection of the other had taken place later in their lives, their moral conduct might have been made responsible for the distinction. As it is, the lesson which that Bible record wants to drive home can be none other than the freedom of God's election, irrespective of descent from Abraham and also irrespective of works, 10—12.

The final conclusion to be drawn from St Paul's **c** reply to the Synagogue is: we must distinguish between the Israelites who are Abraham's children only by physical descent and the Israelites who are Abraham's children by God's special election, like Isaac and Jacob. Only the latter, irrespective of their number, constitute the true Israel. Hence the self-exclusion of the majority of national Israel from Christianity does not put the Gospel in contradiction with the divine and unchangeable promises of the OT.

A false interpretation. Paul's argument in 6—13 has **d** been wrongly quoted as scriptural evidence in favour of absolute predestination in the sense that each individual's eternal destiny is predetermined by an unalterable divine decree. Against such a false conclusion it must be remembered: (1) the two Scripture texts quoted in 13f are concerned not with the eternal salvation of Esau and Jacob but with their earthly life; and again Paul himself is discussing the election to the Messianic promises of Israel, not the election to heaven or hell; (2) the expression 'I have hated' in 13 is not to be pressed since it is part of a quotation. And further, when contrasted with 'I have loved', it may be taken as a Hebrew idiom and translated 'I have loved less' = I have not chosen, cf Gn 29:30f.

A slightly different form of the same misinterpretation **e** uses Paul's subsidiary argument in 10—12 to prove a false doctrine of predestination to heaven or hell in the specific sense of predestination 'independently of works', i.e. independently of merits or demerits, because Esau was rejected before there could be any works against him. Some commentators have tried to meet this difficulty by introducing the idea of God's foreknowledge of Jacob's

862e and Esau's later sins and virtues. The distinction between predestination before and after the prevision of merit (*ante vel post praevisa merita*) is no doubt right and helpful, but was it in the mind of Paul when writing 10—12? It seems simpler, and more in accordance with what the text actually says, to disown any theological speculations in 6—13 on predestination to heaven or hell as outside the scope of the argument. Paul is disputing Israel's claims to the Messianic promises as a nation; and he does not carry the discussion beyond the limits set to it by this immediate object. The exclusion of (Ishmael and) Esau from the Messianic promises proves these claims false and that is all the Apostle wants to prove. Paul did not intend to prove that Esau could not save his soul because he did not belong to the Chosen People. And there is no evidence to that effect anywhere else in the Scriptures.

f The texts quoted by Paul speak of a miraculous intervention in virtue of a promise. But, whereas the election of Isaac could be attributed to his mother's status or to Abraham's faith, the sole reason for the preference of Jacob to Esau is the gratuitous love of God. Jacob's posterity are the children in virtue of the divine promise, while that of Esau, the Edomites, came to be the type of all hostile to the Chosen People. Mal 1:2ff does not refer to the eternal salvation or damnation of Jacob and Esau, but to groups of peoples; cf Gn 33:3—15 on Jacob's deference to his brother. On these scriptural quotations see A. Feuillet in RB 57 (1950), 492ff.

g 14—29 The Vindication of God's Justice in the Present Exclusion of Israel from the Salvation of the Gospel—The objection to be refuted in this paragraph is based on Paul's reply to the first. It argues: if Christianity appeals to divine grace as the one and all-important condition for belonging to the Elect = the Church, then a terrible injustice is done to all those who are left standing outside. Such a doctrine of grace in the fundamental question of belonging to the Church is a doctrine of divine favouritism which contradicts God's justice.

Plan. This objection raises a serious theological difficulty and the Apostle argues the point at some length. The following four points may be distinguished in his reply: (1) 14—18, an answer from God's sovereignty; (2) 19—21, the answer from God's sovereignty repeated; (3) 22—24, another possible explanation; (4) 25—29, the answer of the Scriptures.

(1) An answer from God's sovereignty, 14—18. The objector has appealed to the divine attribute of justice; Paul replies with God's omnipotence. The two Scripture texts which he quotes as his evidence are, if possible, even more 'predestinarian' than those used before in 12f. The one, Ex 33:19, is taken from the story of Moses; the other, Ex 9:16, from the story of Pharaoh. God is the sovereign Lord, and as such can choose for his **h** elect whom he likes. God's act, being wholly gratuitous, is not unjust; the divine intention is the fulfilment of the promises, that is, the salvation of mankind. Moses claims that God answered his prayer out of divine mercy; in like manner the favours shown to his people are due to God's benevolence only. The infidelity of Israel does not run counter to God's justice; on the contrary, it has a place in the divine plan of salvation. Israel forfeited her privilege as God's chosen people, and Paul looks for the reason why God in his providence and justice so disposed events that the call was transferred. Far from being prejudicial to the divine plan, the infidelity of Israel rather promoted the conversion of the Gentiles, for these could have hesitated to come into a Church

of Jews. In this way God's justice is maintained in the **862i** realization of the divine promises. Hence Paul's reference to the example of Pharaoh is apposite: in the salvation of the race he was like Moses an instrument in the hands of God; even in resisting, he showed God's omnipotence active for the people of Israel, Ex 7:5.

In the context of Ex 9:16 the question of Pharaoh's eternal fate is not raised, but that of the role assigned him in history. He is represented as a recalcitrant instrument of God in contrast to the docility of Moses. The aim is to show how God used Pharaoh to further the work of salvation, and in this the divine glory is especially made manifest, cf Is 55:10—13.

(2) The answer from God's sovereignty repeated, **i** 19—21. The dispute with the objector continues. If the sovereignty of God's omnipotent will is to be stressed to such an extent, why then does God still accuse and punish men for their unbelief, disobedience and sinfulness? The Scriptures are full of such accusations and punishments. Surely God cannot be called just and yet, as in the case of Pharaoh, punish men for doing what is nothing but his own omnipotent will. In his reply (20f) Paul repeats his previous argument: God is the Sovereign and as such can treat man like the potter his clay. By using this well-known scriptural simile (cf Is 29:16; 45:9f; Jer 18:2—6; Wis 15:7), the Apostle goes beyond his first answer, 14—18, in that he specifies the sovereignty of God as that of the creator, and man's dependence as that of the creature. The evident conclusion is that man as God's creature has no more right than clay to question his maker's designs, plan or actions.

(3) Another possible explanation, 22—24. Paul's answers so far have been suppressing more than solving the difficulty. Now he introduces the idea of God's mercy mitigating his sovereignty. Unfortunately the sentence remains unfinished. Most commentators complete it in the form of a rhetorical question: 'But what would you say if God with such patience endured vessels prepared (= due) for destruction, intending to express his wrath and display his power, and to make known the wealth of his glory in vessels of mercy which he had made for glory, among whom he called also us both from Jews and Gentiles? The answer would seem to be that God's forbearance, giving time for repentance, can set everything right. But then obviously the same divine mercy must be applied also to Israel. And this application indeed follows in ch 11. The passage is connected **j** with 17—18, where Pharaoh's obstinacy is referred to the revelation of the divine glory consisting in the salvation of mankind. What is said of Pharaoh is applied now to the faithless people of Israel. The punishments inflicted by God on sins are in accordance with his saving plan corrective. Sapiential texts considered such punishment both on the chosen people and on their foes as proof of God's forbearance, because intended for their conversion; Ps Sol 8:30—35; Wis 12:10ff. Paul, therefore, can interpret Israel's infidelity as a manifestation at one and the same time of God's anger, that is, his absolute opposition to sin, of his power in being able to show mercy to all men, Wis 11:23, and of his patience in allowing opportunity for repentance when by their sins men had deserved death.

Parallelism with 15—18 demands a manifestation of God's anger against Israel and of his mercy towards the elect. Israel's infidelity is intended in the mind of God for their future salvation, and thus his anger shows itself in his forbearance. Irrespective of textual alterations by omitting or retaining *kai*, the sin of Israel can be intended in God's view for the conversion of the people

62j and for that of the Gentiles. cf S. Lyonnet in VDom 34 (1956), 193–201, 257–71.

k (4) The answer of the Scriptures, 25–29. The divine forbearance with vessels of wrath mentioned in 22 is as so often with Paul no more than a thought thrown in but not followed up. Without even finishing the sentence, 22–23, he seizes on another point in 25–29. However serious the intellectual difficulty from the point of view of justice may be, it is at all events definite scriptural doctrine that the members of the Church in the Messianic time are to come (a) from all the Gentiles, and (b) only from a remnant of Israel. Hence, whatever the Synagogue may say, the Church, as she is with but few converts from Israel, is in full agreement with the Scriptures. Things have come to pass as they were foretold. The failure of the Gospel to convince the majority of Israel is no argument against Christianity. Thus the argument is brought back to the point from which it started in 6. The Scripture texts which Paul quotes are: (a) for the conversion of the Gentiles Hos 2:23; 1:10 (LXX ed. Swete) = 2:25, 1 (LXX ed. Rahlfs); (b) for only a small number of converts from Israel, Is 10:22f; 1:9. All these texts are used by Paul in a typical sense. For Paul's purpose it is not necessary that Hosea intended to foretell the call of the Gentiles. The point at issue is whether God in OT showed his intention of calling a people without any right by a covenant on their part. In the oracles of Hosea Israel is in precisely the same position as the Gentiles are in Paul's time, called without any right to the choice. The call of the pagans, therefore, fits in with the salvific plan of OT.

l **18.** There are two opinions. The Thomist school explains this statement by means of the distinction between sufficient and efficacious grace. God's grace in such a case is sufficient but not efficacious. Because of bad disposition God does not add what would be necessary to make this grace efficacious (*non apponendo gratiam*.) According to the Molinists the grace God gives is sufficient, but man does not co-operate. According to man's reception this grace is either efficacious or merely sufficient. In either case the real problem remains, viz the beginning of evil. Cf 1 Kg 18:37; Is 6:10.

m Though Paul's words could be applied to the doctrine of predestination, he does not raise the problem. To do so, as Aquinas does in his commentary, requires distinctions unfamiliar to Paul and unnecessary to his purpose and argument. Certainly he makes God's causality explicit, and so implies more than mere permissive will; but even the OT texts are not concerned with Pharaoh's personal guilt.

22 refutes the false conclusion of an 'arbitrary' omnipotence. To bring out the importance of the clause it may be helpful to separate it from its adjuncts which are: (1) 'to show his wrath ...' (a first subordinate final clause); (2) 'to show the riches of his glory . . .' (a second subordinate final clause); (3) to give time for repentance (a third clause added by commentators to complete the thought of Paul). 'made for destruction' = (a) made for; (b) prepared for by themselves (Chrys. Cornely); (c) due for (Lagrange). To be 'a vessel of wrath' means to be the object of divine anger, and thereby to proclaim the incompatibility of God and sin, but not necessarily to be condemned to perdition. Similarly to be 'a vessel of mercy' is to proclaim by example the mercy of God. Though the objects of divine wrath are 'made for' destruction, it is not said that they actually perish; and indeed by tolerating them God shows that he does not will their loss.

25. 'Not my people' = *Lo-'ammi*, which was the symbolical name of a son of Hosea, cf Hos 1:9 . . . 'Her

who was not beloved' = *Lo-ruhamah* = no mercy, which **862m** was the symbolical name of a daughter of Hosea, cf Hos 1:6. **27.** 'Remnant': cf Is 1:9; 6:13; 10:20–2. From the verbal forms used the writer has future events in mind; and elsewhere the expression serves to announce the Messianic expectations of Israel, Gn 22:17.

27–29. Among the prophecies recalling Israel's infidelity, Paul selects two insinuating their salvation, citing both texts from Isaiah in favour of Israel. The second of these, Is 1:9, announces the salvation of a 'remnant'. The original context and the sense of the first, Is 10:22–23, are uncertain, see H. Cazelles in RB 58 (1951), 176–82; but taken in its present position, as Paul found it, it does proclaim the salvation of the people, while supposing their infidelity.

9:30–10:21 The Present Exclusion from the **863a** **Salvation of the Messiah is Israel's Own Fault**— Paul continues his debate upon Israel's exclusion from the salvation of the Messiah begun in 9:1 but from another point of view. If the blame for Israel's present position outside the Church cannot be laid on God, 6–29, it is natural to raise the question, who then is to blame? This is the question now taken up and the blame is put on Israel herself. Thus Israel, hitherto the plaintiff in the discussion, now becomes the accused.

Plan. The argument proceeds by three steps: (1) 9:30–33 contains the summary statement of the accusation of Israel; (2) 10:1–13 gives the main proof; (3) 10:14–21 refutes various objections.

9:30–33 Summary Statement of Israel's Fault— Israel's fault is her mistaken idea of 'justness' = sanctification. Trying to attain to justness by fulfilling the law, Israel finds herself with no room for Jesus, the Messiah, who demands faith. As a result the Messiah has become for her a stone of stumbling rather than a rock of salvation, as foretold in the Scriptures.

30. 'Pursue . . . attained': metaphors taken from the race course, cf 9:16; 1 Cor 9:24; Phil 3:12; 1 Tm 6:11f. **33.** The phrase is taken from Is 8:14 and from Is 28:16. **b** The same two texts from Is appear together in 1 Pt 2:6–8. Since Rm 9:33 and 1 Pt 2:6–8 agree in textual variants against LXX, a common source has been suggested in the form of an early Christian anthology similar to the testimonies of Cyprian, cf SH 281f. 'The stone' refers (1) to YAHWEH in Is 8:14; (2) to Christ in Rm 9:33; 1 Pt 2:8, cf Ps 118 (117):22; Mt 21:42; Ac 4:11. In Is 28:16 many commentators take the stone in reference to the Messiah, while the Qumran sectaries applied it to their own community, 1QS 8.7. Paul applies both to the Messiah, quoting the first oracle, originally a threat, in the light of the second which is in the context of promised salvation. In this way he combines two ideas: Yahweh as the stumbling-block, and the prophecy of the rejected stone becoming the corner-stone; in his thought Christ is both the stone against which the Jews fell and the corner-stone.

10:1–13 Israel's Fault is Explained—The argument **c** is not carried further, for Paul merely enlarges on the mistaken idea of 'justness' already stated in 9:31f as the cause of Israel's stumbling. The main line of thought presents no difficulty. In the introduction, 1f, the Apostle shows once more (cf 9:1–5) how anxious he is to avoid the impression that his argument is coloured by prejudice or antagonism. In 10:3f he repeats 9:31f, i.e. the point which he wants to prove: Israel strives after justness in her own way, but her way is not the way of God, who makes justness dependent on faith before works. In 5–13 the two ways of striving after justness are further contrasted. The first, v 5 = Lev 18:5, is that of the law, discussed

863c at length in 1:18—3:21. The second, 6—13, is that of faith, fully explained in 3:21—4:25, but here once more summarized in a series of free quotations from Dt 30:11—14; Is 28:16; Jl 2:32 Vg = 3:5 MT, LXX. The main purpose of the OT quotations in 6—13 must in this context be to show that justness according to the Scriptures is to be obtained by faith, cf 9, 10, 11, 13. At the same time they evidently have the further object of impressing upon the reader that the new way of faith is superior to the old because less difficult, 6—11, and open to all, 12f. The vivid language used to express this second object easily obscures the first and main point, that Israel's guilt is her neglect of the theological principle of faith.

d A question of general interest on which commentators disagree is the use of the OT in 6—8, where Paul quotes Moses against his own law. The simplest solution of this difficulty is that the Apostle is not using here Dt 30:11—14 as scriptural evidence for his thesis, but that he has no further intention than to clothe his own thoughts in scriptural language. This solution is based on the Gr. text in which there is no change of subject at the beginning of v 8 (against Vg, DV) so that personified justness is speaking throughout 6—8. If this explanation be accepted then we have here an example of what is called in Hermeneutics 'the accommodated sense', cf Bar 3:29. So Cornely. For the opinion that Paul uses these texts in a 'typical sense' see Lagrange, Boylan; cf also SH 302—7. To illustrate his argument in 6—7 and not in the process of the argumentation Paul applies Dt 30:11—14 to the Incarnation and the Resurrection of Christ. Contemporary Jewish exegesis had already paved the way for such use of OT texts, as Targum paraphrases of Dt 30 allude to Moses and to Jonah, both of whom are taken in NT as types of Christ. By this technique Paul can use Dt 30:12 in reference to Christ's conferring the Spirit on the new people of God, like a new Moses, after, like Jonah, going down to Sheol and death. His argument in 8 is based on a quotation from Dt 30:14; the 'word' referred to is the commandment to love God above all. By taking the passage in the light of its wider context Paul can find in the allusion to the Mosaic law a real foreshadowing of the New. The precept of loving God was a revelation, an unheard-of possibility, and so its realization is envisaged as a gift of God, who will create in man the capacity for such love. cf Dt 30:6; Jer 9:24ff. S. Lyonnet in *Mélanges Bibliques* (1957), 494—506. The circumcision of the heart, a characteristic of the new régime, is presented as the work of God in person, making the whole individual participate in the Covenant and so attached interiorly and not only juridically to himself. Pursuing the trend of OT tradition Paul can show that justice based on faith is proclaimed in OT.

e Another question in 1—13 is the meaning of the title Lord given to Jesus in 9: *ean homologēsēs ... kurion Iesoun*; cf 1 Cor 12:3; Ac 11:20; Phil 2:11; 1 Jn 4:2. In general Boylan explains well: 'The title 'Lord' includes all that was preached and believed concerning Jesus—His divinity, Incarnation, Work of Redemption, Resurrection and Glorification'. For a more detailed exegesis the following main interpretations may be mentioned. 'Lord' when used as a title of Jesus Christ by Paul has been taken: (1) for Hebrew YAHWEH, because LXX often translated the tetragrammaton in the OT with *kyrios*, cf HRCS II 800; and be ause Paul often applied such texts to Christ, cf note on 13. So Lattey, *Paul*, 1939, 54. (2) For Aramaic *mari* = my Lord;

maran(a) = our Lord, found in early Christian prayers **863** to Christ, cf 1 Cor 16:22; Apoc 22:20; *Didache* 10:5; G. Dalman, *Worte Jesu*, 1898, 276; Boylan 169. (3) In opposition to *kyrios, kyria* in the contemporary cults of hellenistic-oriental syncretism; so W. Bousset, *Kyrios Christos*, 1913, 113—25; Deissmann, *Licht vom Osten*, 1923, 298f. (4) In opposition to *kyrios* in the Roman Caesar cult, cf *Martyrol. Polycarpi* 8:2. Of these four explanations the first two seem preferable because more in agreement with the continuity of apostolic doctrine. But it may well be granted that according to circumstances the other connotations were stressed; e.g. the divine king against the Roman emperor cult; the one Lord of all, of Israelites as well as Gentiles, against the pagan cults of the time, cf Rm 10:12; 1 Cor 8:5. In any case Paul's usage of the title 'Lord' for Jesus clearly implies the divinity of Christ and so does every one of the above four explanations if logically thought out. On the whole question cf Prat II, 117—24; 437f; L. de Grandmaison, *Jésus-Christ*, Engl. Tr. III (1924) 379—83; TWNT, *s.v.* Kyrios; Lietzmann 97—101 on Rm 10:9; H. J. Cadbury, *Beginnings of Christianity* V (1933) 360—2.

2. Zeal not based on exact knowledge of God's love. **f** Paul contrasts two attitudes towards justification: that in which it is seen as obtainable by personal unaided activity, and that in which it is conceived as a grace accepted through faith in Christ. **3.** 'God's righteousness' = justness, justification, cf 1:17; 3:5, 21ff; 9:31f; Phil 3:9; 2 Cor 5:21. **4.** *telos nomou* = the end of law: can mean (*a*) the fulfilment of the law, cf Mt 5:17; Gal 3:24; (*b*) the abolition of the law, cf 6:14; Eph 2:15; Col 2:14. 'The law': has here been understood (*a*) of all legal systems; (*b*) of the Mosaic Law. The latter is more in keeping with the context, cf 9:31f; 10:3f. **6f.** In Dt 30:13f as a metaphor for something impossible. Paul's application of the second part to the resurrection of Christ, 7, contains a noteworthy reference to Christ's descent into limbo, cf Ac 2:27; 1 Pt 3:19; 4:6. **8.** 'But what does it say': *scil.* the justice = justness of v 6f. **9** develops the metaphor for something near and easy quoted in 8 from Dt 30:14. The sequence 'mouth-heart' is therefore not to be pressed. In the process of justification faith comes before outward profession, cf 10. Exterior profession of faith and conformity of life should correspond to the interior assent of the rational faculties. Faith is a personal decision, and as such is not separable from life. **10.** A clear text against any theory that faith of the **g** heart alone is sufficient. The profession of faith here demanded is the practice of faith in everyday life. There is no reason for limiting it to times of persecution. 'Justnes ... salvation': appear to be parallel. **12.** 'The same is Lord of all' = Christ, not YAHWEH; because of context, cf 9ff; Mt 28:18; Ac 10:36; Eph 2:14ff; Phil 2:11. **13.** 'Lord' here refers to Christ, but in Jl 3:5 (= 2:32 Vg) it refers to YAHWEH. Similar examples of YAHWEH texts applied to Christ are 1 Cor 1:31 = 2 Cor 10:17 = Jer 9:23f. In the formula of definition for a Christian Christ is given the place ascribed to Yahweh in the definition of a Jew, cf Ac 9:14.

14—21 Israel's Fault is further Explained—There is no change of subject here. The discussion of Israel's guilt continues. The Apostle's object, however, is no longer merely to show the fact of Israel's fault as in 1—13, but rather to prove that she is also fully responsible for that fault. The conditions necessary for the Jews to **h** believe in Christ were all realized.

The four excuses that might be made, 14—15*a*, 16*a*, 18*a*, 19*a*, are not convincing. First excuse, 14—15*a*: Where, in the case of the Gospel, is the authority which

34e Final—From the present, 1–24, Paul turns his attention to the future. The time will come when the present problem of Israel's exclusion from the salvation of the Messiah will cease to exist because of her conversion, which will follow upon the conversion of the Gentiles.

The final conversion of Israel could not be known to Paul from any natural source. He himself calls it a mystery, 25, cf Mt 13:11; 1 Cor 2:7; Eph 3:3f. Nevertheless he does not claim a special revelation as the authority for his statement but argues the point. The reasons which he advances are taken (1) from the Scriptures, (2) from Israel's history, (3) from the divine plan of salvation. (1) The evidence from Scripture, 26f, is the prophecy of Israel's restoration in Is 59:20f, plus the concluding clause 'when I take away their sins' from Is 27:9. See also Jer 31 (38):31–34. (2) The reason from Israel's history, 28f, is the election of the Patriarchs. This is a dogmatic-historical fact which cannot be undone. The promises made to the Patriarchs must one day be fulfilled in every respect, because God is unchangeable, cf Dt 4:31. (3) The reason from the divine plan of redemption, 30–2, is taken from the doctrine that salvation is the gift of God's mercy (= grace) after man's failure to obtain 'justness' (= holiness) by his own efforts. In this divine plan, therefore, man's failure becomes Mercy's opportunity. So it has been in the case of the Gentile Christians, so it will be in the case of the now disobedient (= unbelieving) Israelites. 'God has consigned all men to disobedience that he may have mercy upon all'.

f **25.** 'Mystery'. Lagrange, *Ev. selon S Luc* 1927, 396, on Lk 13:35 finds this mystery already revealed by our Lord himself. 'Full number of the Gentiles': need not be pressed so as to mean every individual, nor, **26,** 'all Israel'. The mystery is hidden, but to be revealed, and is a part of the divine saving plan, therefore a supernatural reality. Contemporary writing, e.g. 1QS 3:23 uses it in reference to God's plan for salvation, cf E. Vogt in Bib 37 (1956), 247–57. **26.** Prophecy is understood by the light of faith. Paul sees by faith that the prophecy is already realized in part by the conversion of the Gentiles, and this implies that of Israel also. The Israelites remain ever dear to God because of the bonds between him and their ancestors; his promises to them are unalterable, Ac 3:13; C. Spicq, RB 67 (1960), 210–19. **31.** 'mercy': is dative in the Gr., and as such can be explained: (1) as causal dative to 'they have now been disobedient', i.e. the salvation of the Gentiles has become the cause of Israel's unbelief; (2) as instrumental dative, to 'that they also may receive mercy', i.e. when roused to jealousy through mercy shown to the Gentiles. No. 2 yields a clear sense but strains the structure of the sentence; no. 1 follows the natural structure of the sentence but yields a sense which many reject because it would be contradicted by the fact that Israel disobeyed the Gospel before the conversion of any Gentiles. When Paul wrote Rm the mercy shown to the Gentiles *was* a **g** cause that stiffened the resistance of Israel. **32.** The purpose of the divine plan is to show that salvation is not acquired by one's own efforts, but is gratuitous. **33–36 Epilogue**—Election as well as rejection are facts in Israel's history, and one may call either predestination. But nevertheless Israel's election as well as her present rejection are both part of a wonderful plan, designed by God's mercy, wisdom, understanding and omnipotence for the salvation of all. God is free and can do as he chooses, ch 9; Israel is responsible for her failure, ch 10; the salvation of Gentiles and Israelites alike is God's ultimate aim in all his ways, ch 11.

33–36 develop v 32, cf the similar conclusion in **864g** 8:35f. **33.** Three co-ordinated genitives. 'The riches': *scil.* of his mercy, cf 10:12. 'Judgements': passed on Jews and Gentiles in the course of history to bring them to a realization of their misery and their need of divine assistance, Boylan. **35** is taken from Job 41:3 MT. The sense is: no one can earn the grace of salvation, so that he can claim it as his right. That Paul is not thinking here of meritorious works and their reward follows from the context and from such passages as 2:5f; 1 Cor 3:8; 2 Cor 11:5; Gal 6:7f; 2 Tm 4:8, etc. **36a.** God is the efficient, sustaining and final cause of all. The appropriation to the Father, the Son and the Holy Ghost, is not in the text but common in the commentaries of the Latin Fathers after St Augustine, cf Cornely 633f. Alleged parallels in stoic literature are collected by Lietzmann 107, e.g. M. Aurelius IV 23.

12:1–15:13 The Moral Section of the Epistle = **h** Exhortations—The purpose of these chapters evidently is to conclude the epistle with counsel for the Christians of Rome in their daily life.

Plan. None of the various plans that have been drawn up to present the contents of these chapters in the form of a logical scheme has found general consent. The reason seems to be that the Apostle passes from one point to the next as he pleases without following any prearranged plan. It may, however, be convenient, to distinguish: A. 12:1–13:14, general exhortations; B 14:1–15:13, exhortations to the Strong and the Weak at Rome.

12:1–13:14 General Exhortations—These two chapters contain a series of exhortations which cannot be brought under one heading. But it is customary to treat them together as a separate group because of what follows, 14:1–15:13. This long discussion of the relation between the Strong and the Weak evidently stands out as a section by itself.

Plan. No more than a separation of the main exhortations can be attempted. The arrangement followed in this commentary is: (1) 12:1–2, the Christian's service of God; (2) 12:3–8, the various functions in the Church; (3) 12:9–16, various precepts, (4) 12:17–21, love your enemies; (5) 13:1–7, the Christian and the State; (6) 13:8–10, charity; (7) 13:11–14, vigilance.

12:1–2 The Christian's Service of God, or con- **i** secration of body and soul to the service of God—The Apostle begins with an exhortation which many commentators would like to treat as Paul's one basic moral principle.

The main idea is, no doubt, the consecration of body and soul to the service of God. This idea is not new, cf 6:12–23; 8:12–17. Its expression in 1–2, however, is of special interest because of the liturgical language employed in 1. Serving God with one's body (and soul?) is here described as the Christian's sacrifice and worship. This worship is then further recommended as 'spiritual' and the sacrifice as 'living, holy and acceptable to God'. On the other hand, this liturgical presentation of our moral duties must not be exaggerated so that it becomes the one and only true Christian sacrifice and worship; cf A. Keogh, *The Ministry in the Apostolic Church*, WV III, 224–42. It must be remembered that this liturgical language is metaphorical as in Phil 2:17; 4:18; 2 Cor 2:14, 16; Rm 15:16. A mere dictionary interpretation easily reads too much into the text.

1. The meaning of this verse is often limited to the body exclusively, so that it becomes an exhortation to purity, like 1 Cor 6:12–20; 1 Thes 4:3–5. This interpretation is unnecessarily narrow; cf 6:12–23; 7:4–6; 8:11f. The 'body' for Paul designates the whole person

864i in its visible aspect. cf J. Robinson, *The Body. A Study of Pauline Theology* (1952).

j To be a sacrifice that is 'living, holy and acceptable to God', all spheres of life must be included. *logikēn*, the exact meaning depends on the contrast intended. This contrast some would find in the forms of worship observed by Israel according to the OT. But these forms cannot be called *un*-reasonable. Others, therefore, see the contrast in the forms of worship observed by the pagans of the time. This explanation implies that Paul regarded the pagan liturgy as *un*-reasonable, which is quite plausible. For history of exegesis see Cornely and Lietzmann. The prophets had reminded the people that interior worship alone was pleasing to God, Hos 6:6; Mt 9:13. **2.** If the wider interpretation of v 1 be accepted then 2 becomes parallel to it.

3—8 Let Everybody be Content with his Function in the Mystical Body of Christ, i.e. the Church—Every Christian must be content with that position, function or work that has been assigned to him in the Church through his 'measure of faith', the special grace, charisma or talent, given to him by God. All who argue differently lack sobriety—moderation, temperance and humility. They forget that the Church is a community and as such like a human body in which the perfect service of every part, small and great, is necessary for the welfare of the others. The allotment of the different functions (= *charismata*) in the Church is the work of God. The Christian's duty is to fulfil his task as best he can.

k **Connexion.** The reason for this exhortation may have been Paul's vivid recollection of the recent disturbances in the church of Corinth dealt with in 1 Cor 12:1—14:40.

Plan. The sequence of thought can be made easier by distinguishing (1) 3—5, the Mystical Body of Christ as the principle on which all community spirit in the Church is to be based; (2) 6—8, the application of this principle to seven different activities in the Church.

The doctrinal importance of the passage is its bearing (1) on the *charismata = gratiae gratis datae*, and (2) on the unity of the Church. The larger commentaries discuss here also (3) the relationship between the charismata of 6—8 and the regular early Christian Ministry, e.g. SH 358—60.

5. The human body is frequently used by St Paul as an image of the Christian community = Church, cf 1 Cor 12:12—14, 27. The expression brings out the mutual dependence of Christians rather than their identification with Christ. **6—8** contain the application of the principle of the Mystical Body laid down in 3—5; cf 1 Cor 12:27—30 as the application of 1 Cor 12:12—26. The same idea also in 1 Pt 4:9—11. The structure is difficult because of a double anacoluthon. Hence the additions to the text in the translations. **6.** *kata tēn analogian tēs pisteōs = secundum rationem fidei*, Vg; is a very much discussed phrase. There are two main interpretations: (1) = according to the rule of faith, DV. Then the meaning is, let prophecy be checked by what is established Christian doctrine (= *fides quae creditur*) and there will be no occasion for subjectivism. (2) = as far as the measure of his faith will let him (*scil.* the prophet). Then the meaning is, let every prophet keep to the measure of the faith (charisma) assigned to him by God (= *fides qua creditur*), and say nothing except what his charisma of faith prompts him to say. Both explanations agree that Paul's object is to encourage the right use of the gift of prophecy and to check abuses. The first explanation suits this purpose better, because the rule of faith, the doctrine or contents of the faith, offers an objective means for checking

any extravagant prophecy, cf Gal 1:8; 1 Cor 14:29; **864** 1 Thes 5:21.

9—16 Further Precepts of Christian Morals—It is a **l** common and tempting suggestion to regard this paragraph, in view of its beginning in 9, 10*a*, as a treatment of the commandment of charity. But the precepts which follow this beginning vary so much that they cannot easily be brought under any one heading; and the commandment of charity is more fully treated in 13:8—10.

The style of 9—16 is aphoristic and elliptic. The free transition from participles to imperatives, to infinitives and then to imperatives again is not in accordance with the rules of syntax. **10.** On *philostorgoi* cf C. Spicq RB 62 (1955), 497—510. It has the idea of preoccupation with and care for others. **11c.** On the inferior reading 'serving the time', cf H.A.W. Meyer and Lietzmann. **13.** On the virtue of hospitality, cf Ti 1:8; Heb 13:2; 2 Jn 10f; Hasting's *Dictionary of the Apost. Church* I (1915) 586. **14** cannot be a quotation of Lk 6:28, but it may be a reminiscence of our Lord's words, cf 13:9f; Mt 5:44; 1 Cor 4:12; Lietzmann.

17—21 Conduct towards Enemies—From duties **m** towards neighbours in general, 9—16, Paul passes on to conduct towards unfriendly neighbours in particular. Whether the enemies whom the Apostle has here in mind were Christians or non-Christians cannot be decided for certain, nor would it seem necessary to make this distinction. The rules of 17—21 apply in either case.

Similar views on conduct towards enemies. The topics of anger, envy, etc, figure largely in all parts of the Bible. For a collection of references see K. Vaughan 177—81. The main parallels to the Christian teaching in the OT are Ex 23:4f; Prv 25:21. Every Christian discussion of the subject must start from the relevant passage in the Sermon on the Mount, Mt 5:38—48. To this St Paul's short treatment here adds nothing new, except his proofs from the OT, Dt 32:35; Prv 25:21f. The rabbinical theology of NT times does not seem to have had a clear and authoritative teaching on the subject 'love thy enemy', cf SB I, 368ff on Mt 5:44; III, 301f on Rm 12:20. A parallel from classical literature that may be quoted is Plato, *Rep.*, I, 335. For more but doubtful parallels see C. T. Ramage, *Scripture Parallels* 1878, 280—3. To avoid wrong conclusions from 17—21 it must be remembered generally that Paul is concerned with the Christian's private conduct towards his enemies. The right and duty of the State to punish and control what is evil, is not in his mind. With this he deals in the next passage, 13:1—7.

20. 'burning coals': have been understood as a meta- **n** phor (1) for the feelings of remorse, (2) for God's judgements. The quotation is from Prv 25:21—22 LXX. The exact rendering of MT and the interpretation by LXX are disputed. Cf M. Dahood in CBQ 17 (1955), 19—24; F. Vattoni in *Analecta Biblica* 17—18, I. 341—5.

13:1—7 The Duty of Obedience to the Authority of the State—The Apostle passes on to summarize the Christian's duties towards the State. He first insists on the duty of submission and obedience to the ruling government as a divine law. Leaving all questions of the natural law aside he proves this divine law from the fact that no government could obtain or retain power without God's will. Every citizen therefore is bound to render submission and obedience to the *de facto* government because disobeying would be disobeying a divinely appointed authority, 1—2. In 3—4 the Apostle gives a brief description of the government as it should be, its main function being to support all good and suppress all evil. After this the way is clear for the conclusion which follows in 5. The submission and obedience due to such a government is a

4n matter of conscience, i.e. the Christian is to obey for God's sake, and not for fear of being found out and punished. The laws of such a government are not merely penal laws but moral laws. The law of taxation, 6, serves as an example. Finally, in 7, the Apostle concludes with a summary which is reminiscent of the words of our Lord in Mt 22:21 'Render to Caesar the things that are Caesar's'.

5a It is usually understood that Paul's teaching in this section is independent of circumstances, both of place and of time; but the context deals with love of one's neighbour and serious Christian duties, and civil society is the normal setting for a life in accordance with natural tendencies in association with one's fellow men. Paul could take the opportunity of explaining to the Christian community in Rome the practical importance of the State. cf the discussion by J. Kosnetter in *Analecta Biblica* 17–18, I. 347–55.

Paul had suffered at the hands of government authorities before this, cf Ac 16:37; 2 Cor 11:25. His attitude remained the same later, 1 Tm 2:1–7; Ti 3:1. The early Church remained true to the same principle during the persecutions, cf 1 Pt 2:13–17. The government of Rome is judged from a different point of view in Apoc 17:6, but this does not contradict Paul's principles in 1–7.

For a favourable description of the Roman government at the time see SH xiii–xviii. The evidence to the contrary comes mostly from the administration of the provinces. In any case Paul is not here discussing the grievances of Roman subjects, but stating every citizen's duty of obedience to the State. The kind of government he has in mind can be seen from 3–4. The duty of obedience to the government is clearly stated to be imposed by God, 1–2, 5, and as such is a precept of the moral law, while opportunism is ruled by circumstances and selfishness. A Christian may honestly regard and respect as divinely appointed every *de facto* government even when it is resented as usurping, enforced, foreign, tyrannical, pagan, anti-religious or anti-Christian in view of God's justice and providence; cf Ex 9:16; Rm 9:17, see also Aquinas *Sum Th* 1, q19 a9. Everyone by natural law has the right to resist injustice even when done in the name of a government, but the means used must be in accordance with the moral law; here in many cases conscience will be the final arbiter for the individual, cf Boylan on 13:2. Paul is concerned with the duties of subjects to their government. The terms used are general, and the contrast is between government, law and order on the one side, and anarchy, the ruin of every State on the other

b **8–10 Exhortation to Charity**—From loyalty to the government Paul passes to charity towards one's neighbour. The special feature is the stress on the place charity should be given among the commandments. Paul puts it first for the reason that he who loves his fellow man will be anxious not to wrong him. A difficulty arises that Christ in Mt 22:39 puts love of one's neighbour second. Some commentators in defence of Paul refer to 1 Jn 4:20 and Gal 5:14 arguing that in practice the love of one's neighbour implies the love of God, cf Cornely 683ff. A simpler solution is that Paul called charity the first of the commandments ruling our conduct towards men. This means abstracting from the love of God, which then does not come into the question: (1) because the context deals with man's duties towards man; (2) because the examples are taken from the second table of the decalogue only; (3) because Christ's words in Mt are clear and, if not actually quoted here, seem to have been in Paul's mind.

c **11–14 Exhortation to Vigilance and Sanctity**—It is difficult to find one name for the Christian ideal described in this short paragraph. St Thomas calls it 'honestas', sense of honour. It is described both negatively and positively by a series of metaphors mainly taken from time. On the one hand we have sleep, night, and the works of darkness: feasting and drinking, fornication and lewdness (wantonness), wranglings and jealousies; all these are to be shunned and cast off. On the other hand, there are the marks of a Christian life: vigilance, the light of day, and—one would expect—the *works* of light. But the metaphor is changed to 'the *armour* of light' which the Christian is to put on. The 'time' could refer to the eschatological era ushered in at Christ's death and resurrection. By faith and baptism the Christian is a child of day, with a share in God's kingdom, Col 1:13, and his new condition of life implies a new moral order, 6:3ff. Before his conversion the Christian belonged to the age before Christ; now he has the pledges, first instalments of the Spirit, 8:24. **865c**

Connexion. Some commentators do not regard 11–14 as a paragraph by itself but as an afterthought to 8–10. Then the meaning of the passage is: let the thought of the coming day of judgement be a further motive to fulfil all the demands of charity set out in 8–10; cf Cornely. **d**

The metaphors of 11–14. On their understanding depends the appreciation of the passage. But the exact meaning of some is difficult to ascertain. (1) The sleep from which the Roman Christians are to rise, 11, must be the state of their spiritual life at the time. Perhaps we are allowed to go further and think of that carelessness which often follows when the first fervour has spent itself, Apoc 2:4f; 3:15f; so Cornely, who speaks of *socordia, ignavia, tepiditas*. But it would certainly be exaggerating to interpret this sleep as the soul's sleep of death or state of mortal sin; cf Rev 3:1ff (against Estius). (2) The vigilance to which Paul exhorts in 11 is the same as that of Mt 24:42. (3) The night that is far gone, 12, has been explained (*a*) as the whole period of human history before the day of the Last Judgement, (*b*) as the readers' life on earth looked upon as the night that precedes the day of their glorification in heaven, (*c*) as the 'dark ages' of pagan morals, so Lagrange. (4) The day that is near, 12, has been interpreted (*a*) as the day of the Last Judgement (Parousia), (*b*) as the day of the readers' glorification, (*c*) as the period of Christianity (Christian morals) enlightening the darkness of heathendom. (5) The works of darkness, 12 = all manner of sin. (6) The armour of light, 12, which the Christian is to wear is amply illustrated in the list of Christian virtues in 1 Thes 5:8; Eph 6:10–17.

The nearness of the Parousia or the Second Coming of our Lord, 11. Paul refers to it in 11c when reminding his readers that the day of their final salvation is nearer now than when they were baptized. The purpose of the reminder is evidently exhortation to vigilance, cf Lk 12:37; 1 Cor 7:29; Heb 10:25, 37; 1 Pt 4:7. The modern discussions, however, turn round the question whether this text proves that St Paul regarded the Parousia as imminent. Inspiration covers no more than what the sacred author actually wrote and with this limitation 11c offers no difficulty. The case seems well put by SH 378: 'The language is that befitting those who expect the actual coming of Christ almost immediately, but it will fit the circumstances of any Christian for whom death brings the day'. **e**

11. 'Salvation is nearer to us than when . . . ' What the Apostle means is the final salvation or glorification. 'When we first believed': Aorist = when we became believers, or Christians, cf C. J. Vaughan. **14.** 'Put on Christ': here in the moral sense, cf Eph 4:24; Col 3:12. The same phrase

865e is used in Gal 3:27 in a dogmatic sense for the sacramental effects of baptism.

f **14:1—15:13 Exhortations to the Weak and the Strong in the Church of Rome**—Peace and unity in the church of Rome are the subjects of this long exhortation. But this time it is peace and unity in one particular point. Paul has heard of Christians at Rome who abstain from meat, 14:2, and wine, 14:21, and have fixed days set apart for special religious purposes, 14:5. On the other hand he knows that there are others who regard these formalities as having been made unnecessary by the Christian doctrine of salvation, and who therefore judge those who continue to set a great value on their observance as weak in the faith. The Apostle fearing that their differences of opinion might grow into serious disturbances of peace and harmony uses the opportunity of exhorting to unity and mutual tolerance. He is concerned with the consequences of the present situation, and with the maintenance of charity between Christians of divergent views. He applies the same principles as in 1 Cor 8—10, being aware that Christians can have different attitudes to the implications of faith in ordinary life.

Connexion. Most commentators see the connexion in the contrast with 13:13. It is equally possible that the Apostle left this exhortation last on purpose. The general exhortations in 12:1—13:13 are well suited to prepare the way for the discussion of what was evidently a delicate problem.

Plan. The whole section can be divided into three parts: (1) 14:1—12, avoid mutual criticism; (2) 14:13—23, avoid giving scandal; (3) 15:1—13, avoid selfishness.

Difficulties. The general outlines of the situation which the Apostle has in mind are clear. But as soon as attempts are made to reconstruct the argument in detail commentators begin to differ widely. The main controversies centre round these questions: (1) Who were the Weak? (2) What is meant by the observance of special days? (3) Why does Paul not treat the Weak in Rm in the same way as the Weak in Gal?

g (1) Who were the Weak of Rm 14:1—15:13? Six answers have been given: (a) Converts from the Synagogue who in these matters continued to live according to the Mosaic Law and Jewish custom, cf Col 2:16. (b) Converts from Essenism, a Jewish religious body with very severe rules of abstinence. (c) Another type of the Weak in 1 Cor 8, who refused to eat meat that had been offered to idols. The Weak of Rm then are understood to have gone a step further and abstained from meat and wine altogether to avoid every possibility of taking meat of this kind; cf Cornely 692ff. (d) Converts from some form of Orphic-Pythagorean mystery-religion, in which these practices were in vogue at the time; cf Lietzmann 114f. (e) Christian ascetics, who for various reasons regarded such mortification as the sign of a good Christian life; cf Lagrange 335. (f) Christians of 'excessive scrupulousness'. The complete abstinence from meat and wine, and the observance of special days are in this case no more than illustrations; cf SH 401f. Each of these six answers assumes a particular type of religious practice at Rome in the days of Paul. But none of them can be shown by independent historical evidence to have existed in the Christian community of Rome in those days, and it is easy to raise objections against each of them. (a) Complete abstinence from meat and wine was never enjoined in the synagogue. (b) The existence of Essene communities outside Palestine cannot be proved, Schürer II (1907) 656; nor can abstinence from meat and wine be shown to be characteristic of Essenism, Schürer II 664. (c) The situation in 1 Cor 8 is clear and Paul's exhortation

essentially the same as in Rm 14:1—15:13. But all this 86 does not explain the 'exaggeration' in Rome and the observance of special days. (d) Orphic-Pythagorean influence is possible but difficult to prove in this particular case. (e) Strong ascetical tendencies no doubt existed in early Christianity, cf Ac 4:32—5:11; 1 Tm 5:23; Col 2:16; Didache 8; scrupulousness is a common spiritual disease. But can complete abstinence from meat and h wine and the observance of special days be reasonably regarded as typical examples of what we call scrupulousness? They may have been such under the circumstances, but then they are more than mere illustrations, cf 1 Cor 8. Further, the concessions which Paul makes to the Weak of Rome cannot be applied to the scrupulous in general. In view of so much uncertainty most modern commentators refuse to decide in favour of one of the above six explanations. Instead they prefer to speak vaguely of a combination of various influences and tendencies known to have existed at the time. Briefly, as far as we know, Jewish as well as pagan current tendencies, pre-Christian as well as Christian thought, may have contributed to the complicated situation presupposed in Rm 14:1—15:13; cf SH 399—403; Lagrange 335—40; Boylan 211f.

(2) What is meant by the observance of special days in 14:1—15:13? The only reference to this practice of the Weak is 14:5. But it may be implied in 14:21c. St Paul's description is so vague that one can only discuss the possibilities. (a) The special days observed by the Weak may have been holy days = feast-days. In this case the holy days of the OT calendar (Sabbath, New Moon, etc) would seem to be meant, cf Gal 4:10f; Col 2:16f. This opinion is naturally held by all who regard the Weak as converts from the Synagogue, cf Cornely 702. But if they were holy days, one can also think of Christian holy days, e.g. Sunday, Apoc 1:10. (b) The special days of the Weak more probably were fast days. This explanation is based on the context in which abstinence is the predominant feature. So Lagrange, Boylan. The two extreme pos- i sibilities which the text theoretically allows, that the Weak fasted every day, and the Strong never, can safely be neglected.

(3) Why does Paul not treat the Weak in Rm in the same harsh way as the Weak in Gal? The difference in Paul's attitude to very much the same question is beyond any doubt. In Gal the Weak stand clearly condemned as being in the wrong; in Rm Paul pleads for sympathy and understanding. The difference cannot be explained as a change in the Apostle's doctrine, because the doctrine of justification by faith and not by observance of law is essential to his teaching and to Rm in particular, cf 3:21; 4:3f; 5:1. The true explanation then can only be found in the different circumstances. The Weak of Gal tried to enforce circumcision with all its subsequent observances as a sacrament necessary for salvation. Thus the observance or non-observance of the Mosaic Law became a matter of dogma, heresy and excommunication. On the other hand, though the Weak of Rm also had a j high opinion of their observances, there is no indication that they regarded them as necessary for salvation. For them as well as for their opponents these observances were a matter of opinion and practice, comparable with pious customs of today. That they preferred to associate with those who shared their views and mode of life was only natural. At all events the Apostle's positive teaching on this point in 14:1—15:13 does not go beyond the conclusion that whenever this or that rule of life comes to be considered as the more perfect, its acceptance or non-acceptance becomes a matter to be decided by the conscience of the individual in question. But that does not

65j make it a matter of dogma, heresy or excommunication in the Church at large. In brief, there is no contradiction between Gal and Rm 14:1—15:13.

k **14:1—12 Let the Strong and the Weak avoid criticizing each other**—The Apostle admonishes to mutual tolerance but does not deny the existing difference between the Weak and the Strong. The reasons which impose the self-restraint necessary for this mutual tolerance are: (1) 4—9, the Weak as well as the Strong are Christians and as such belong to Christ. As long as this bond of allegiance to Christ as the one Lord of all exists, no Christian can without trespassing on his Master's rights take it upon himself to condemn a fellow servant who belongs to Christ as much as he himself. (2) 5c, besides dogma there is in Christian life also a large province in which it must be left to each Christian to make sure of his own conviction and to follow his own conscience. (3) 10—12, one day each man's conduct will be judged before the tribunal of God; then each will have to give an account of himself, not of his fellow Christian. (4) Condemning each other in matters of practice and conscience endangers peace and unity. This fourth reason is derived from the trend of the whole exhortation.

1. 'Weak in faith': has been explained (1) as weak in the theological virtue of faith; (2) as weak in the comprehending of the Christian doctrine of faith; (3) as weak in applying the faith; (4) as weak in conscience; (5) *'him who is weak receive in faith'*, Sahidic version. Of these no. 4 is the simplest and perhaps the most practical, but no. 3 philologically the more accurate. For, whatever the context, faith is wider than conscience. **5c.** If he acted against his own conviction, he would commit sin, cf 14:23. The phrase must not be understood as being satisfied with one's own mind. **7f** is a Christian principle of fundamental importance, cf 2 Cor 5:15; Gal 2:20.

l **13—23 Let the Strong avoid scandalizing the Weak**—Paul passes on to the positive duty of mutual edification. This exhortation he addresses to the Strong, excepting perhaps 20, 22f. In brief: sympathy is Paul's way of meeting the scrupulosity of Christians who are still so weak in their faith that they cannot forget their inherited pious customs through which the kind of food they eat has become part of their religious life, cf 1 Cor 8:7—13.

Plan. The Apostle's thoughts flow backwards and forwards. But studying the reasons with which he tries to persuade the Strong to sacrifice their rights for the benefit of the Weak will help to trace the main sequence of thought. These reasons are: (1) 15b, 20—23, the commandment of charity which forbids giving scandal = endangering anyone's supernatural life. (2) 15c, 20a, the disproportion between the gain of a dish of food and the loss of a soul for which Christ has died. (3) 16, 18, the good reputation of the Christian faith. (4) 17f, the spiritual character of the kingdom of God, which lies not in the freedom from this or that ceremonial law, but in its supernatural graces and virtues. (5) 19a, the duty of preserving peace and unity in the Church. (6) 19b, the duty of mutual edification.

m **13b.** *skandalon* occurs first in LXX Lv 19:14, in Vg Ex 10:7; cf Aquinas, *SumTh* II 2, q 43 a 1. **14.** is important in the discussion whether and why the Mosaic Law of clean and unclean foods in Lv 11 has been abrogated. As Paul here clearly says, the authority for this abrogation is 'in Christ', cf Mt 15:10f. This v has also been quoted in defence of indecent art, literature and amusement, cf 1 Tm 4:4. These are said here to be sanctioned for those who resemble the Strong in faith of 14:1—15:13. But this argument would overlook the evident fact that 14:1—

15:13 is concerned with the importance of pious customs **865m** not with border cases of immorality. And further, even where pious customs are concerned, in 14:14—23, the Strong are clearly admonished not to insist on their opinion. **19.** The metaphor 'to build up, to edify' is frequently used by Paul for the growth and progress of Christian life, cf 1 Cor 3:9f, 16; 8:10. There were occasions when Paul 'pursued peace' along different lines, cf Ac 15:1f; Gal 2:3f. **22b.** 'He who': can be (1) the **n** Strong, whose conscience must condemn him if he chooses to go his own way regardless of the scandal to others; (2) the Weak, who is advised to follow his own conscience in this matter of foods regardless of the stronger faith of others; (3) anyone without a scrupulous conscience. **23b.** It is generally acknowledged that faith here does not mean abstract dogmatic faith, but personal conviction. **23c.** The doctrine can be expressed in the form of two possible translations. (1) *'All that is done in bad conscience is sin'*. In this form the v states a principle which is true for all men. (2) *'All that is not the outcome of faith is sin'*. In this form the principle is true only of Christians. For whatever a Christian does must be in accordance with his faith. To let every action be the outcome of his faith is the Christian's ideal of sanctity according to Paul, cf 1 Cor 10:31; 2 Cor 10:5; Col 3:17. This second explanation is to be preferred because of the context, which is concerned with Christians only, and not with pagans. This v therefore should never have been applied by later theology to the actions of pagans. **23** *fin.* is followed by 16:25—27 (doxology) in some MSS.

15:1—13 Let the Strong in their Relations with the **866a** **Weak imitate Christ's Example of Unselfishness**—Paul continues his exhortation to the Strong, 1, 8—12; but there are sentences in this paragraph which can be applied also to the Weak, 7a, 2? 4—6? The ambiguity arises from the main object of this exhortation which is to impress the duty of preserving peace and unity in the Church, 5, 6, 7a, 13; cf 14:19. Enlarging and insisting on this duty, the Apostle could hardly exclude the Weak, but there can be no doubt that he puts the main burden on the shoulders of the Strong.

In addition to the reasons given in 14:13—23 let the Strong remember the example of Christ's humility during his earthly life, 1—6. He did not follow the principle of pleasing himself, but submitted for our salvation to all kinds of humiliations. Now, if Christ acted thus to save and help us, though we were infinitely inferior to him, we too ought to do the same to help those who are weaker than ourselves. No doubt, it is humiliating for the Strong to humble themselves and live like the Weak. But it is equally true that this kind of humiliation is hallowed by Christ's example, 3, approved of by the Scriptures, 4, and deserves to be blest in prayer, 5f.

In particular, 7—12, let the Strong bear in mind the unselfishness of Christ in submitting to circumcision and all it implied, 8a, though his mission was not only for Israel, 8b, but also for the Gentiles, as the Scriptures abundantly prove, 9—12. Christ submitted to circumcision and lived according to the law of Moses in order to work for the greater glory of God among the Israelites as well as among the Gentiles—among the Israelites by making them see the faithfulness of God to his promises; among the Gentiles by causing them to acknowledge and praise the mercy of God. Thus, by aiming at the greater glory **b** of God in everything rather than by thinking of his own ease and pleasure, Christ overcame the difference between Israelites and Gentiles, a difference much greater than the difference between the Strong and the Weak in Rome. If the Strong follow this example and go the humbler way,

866b making the honour of God their rule as Christ did, then the present trouble between the two parties at Rome will soon pass. In brief: as in Phil 2:5—11 our Lord is described as the model of obedience, so in Rm 15:1—13 as the model of all peace-making by unselfishness and charity to the greater glory of God.

The connexion with what precedes is so close that the beginning of a new paragraph at first must seem more disturbing than helpful. On the other hand, 1—13 could stand by itself without 14:13—23. What binds the passage 1—13 together is the new motive on which Paul dwells in this exhortation to peace and unity, viz the example of Christ's unselfishness.

One of the more important points on which commentators disagree in this paragraph concerns the place which the difference between Israelites and Gentiles in 8—12 holds in the main argument. Some assign to it a central place in the discussion by taking Israelites and Gentiles as the true name for the Weak and the Strong in the whole section 14:1—15:13. Others treat it as no more than an illustration of the argument for peace and **c** unity beginning with 15:1. The Israelites are saved through God's veracity in carrying out his promises, the Gentiles through his mercy. Truth and mercy are complementary attributes summing up the divine perfections, e.g. Ps 25 (24):10. As Christ accepted the Gentiles, Christians should show the same dispositions to all who do not think in the same way. Their attitude should be inspired by Christ's love for all men. Cf J. Dupont in *Analecta Biblica* 17—18, 1. 357—66.

3b. (1) The OT text recommended itself as a suitable summary of all the relevant historical facts in our Lord's life; (2) since a Christian cannot be expected to imitate Christ in everything, Paul, by quoting the OT, gained the scriptural proof that imitating Christ in this matter is an indisputable duty of every Christian. To consider Christ in OT prophecies is to see him in God's plan; this traced throughout OT gives strength and comfort in tribulations.

5. 'In accord with Christ Jesus': has been explained as in accordance with Christ's (1) precept, (2) doctrine, (3) example, (4) union with us. No. 3 suits the context best, cf 15:3, 7. **7.** 'Therefore' = (1) because of the principle stated in 15:1f and explained in 3—6; or (2) in view of the example of Christ; or (3) for the sake of unity in the Church, stressed in 6. **8f.** The simplest construction of this difficult sentence is: Christ submitted to circumcision (1) that he might confirm the promises of the fathers, (2) that the Gentiles might glorify God for his mercy. **9—12.** The purpose of the four quotations is to prove the statement of 9a from the Scriptures. Though Christ lived like an Israelite, he aimed at and achieved the glory of God among the Gentiles.

d 15:14—16:27 Conclusion—In the matter of greetings, 16:3—16, 21—24, the conclusion of Rm follows the custom of the time. The rest is peculiar to this epistle. Its chief interest lies in what it tells us about Paul personally.

Plan. (1) 15:14—21, Explanatory comments to avoid misunderstandings. (2) 15:22—33, The immediate purpose of this letter. (3) 16:1—2, Recommendation of Phoebe. (4) 16:3—16, Greetings. (5) 16:17—20, Warning against heresies. (6) 16:21—24, Greetings. (7) 16:25—27, Concluding sentence.

15:14—21 A Retrospect with Apologies and Explanations—Paul has come to the end of his letter and he begins the customary conclusion by looking back on what he has written, and to whom he has written.

Plan. Distinguishing the explanations which Paul here gives for writing such a letter to Rome will help to analyse the sequence of thought. (1) 14: This long letter does not imply any criticism of the Christians at Rome. On the contrary, Paul shares the widespread admiration of their strong faith and their exemplary Christian life, cf 1:8. (2) 15: Bold though the language of this letter may be in parts, Paul makes no claim to have said anything new. His intention does not go beyond 'refreshing their memories' on essential points of Christian doctrine, which is the intention of every Christian preacher. (3) 16: What he has written he has written as the Apostle and 'the priest' of the Gentiles in accordance with his particular mission in the Church. (4) 17—19: There is another reason which he could use to defend the authority assumed in writing such a letter to Rome. It is based on his achievements in setting up new missions from Jerusalem to the Adriatic coast (Illyria). (5) 20f: What follows describes **e** in scriptural language the character of Paul's missionary activity. If looking back on his achievements he speaks with more than usual confidence, it is at all events not the empty boasting of one who had the good fortune of reaping what others had sown. In preaching the Gospel it has been one of his constant principles to go where the name of Christ had not as yet been heard. **16** is remarkable because of its liturgical (sacrificial) language in three terms: priest, sacrifice, offering. The essential point in every explanation is to realize that the sacrificial terms used here are metaphorical, and that therefore this **v** cannot be quoted against the existence of a specially consecrated priesthood in the Church when Paul wrote, cf Prat I, 342ff. The difficulties lie in the analysis of the metaphors. How can the conversion of the Gentiles become St Paul's sacrifice? Cornely works out a solution by introducing the idea of baptism in which every convert dies with Christ and thus may be said to participate in Christ's sacrificial death. Most commentators rightly maintain that the exact method or manner of Paul's offering the Gentiles as his sacrifice is not contemplated in the metaphor of v 16. To bring the Gentile world as a worthy sacrifice to the altar of God is probably all that Paul meant to say, cf Is 66:19f. The apostolate is viewed as a liturgical office, 1:9. Christ, by his mandate to the apostles, offers men to God, effecting their return to him.

17—19. Is an involved sentence owing to two intentions **f** in the Apostle's mind: (*a*) to defend his authority, for which purpose he appeals to all he has achieved in spreading the Gospel; (*b*) to avoid the impression of vainglory, for which purpose he transfers all the honour of his achievements to Christ. The main difficulty is the connexion of the second negative in 18. That appealing to his labours and achievements for the Church is not out of keeping with Paul's character can be seen from the similar passages: 2 Cor 11:1—12:18; Gal 6:17. **19.** 'Fully preached', i.e. make the Gospel, God's saving power produce its effects.

22—33 Paul's Programme for the Immediate Future: Journey to Jerusalem-Rome-Spain—It is not before he comes to the end of his letter that the Apostle states the special occasion which caused him to write. The immediate occasion of this letter, therefore, is Paul's wish to prepare for his proposed visit, 22—24. There has to be, however, a delay on account of a collection from the churches in Macedonia and Greece for the church in Jerusalem. For Paul is determined to be personally present at Jerusalem when this token of communion, goodwill and gratitude on the part of the Gentiles is handed over to the mother-church in the Holy City, 25—29. At the same time he is under no misapprehension of the dangers such a visit implies. For the majority of the inhabitants of Jerusalem his return will mean the return of an apostate of a particularly dangerous kind, and for

866f many of his own brethren in the faith he is still suspect on account of his battles and victories for the rights of the Gentiles in the Church. Nevertheless Paul is determined to go to Jerusalem, but realizing the dangers he **g** asks for prayers at Rome, 30—33. Paul conceives the collection as the symbol of the union between the Jewish and Gentile elements in the Church. He feared a split between these, since the Gentiles, unlike the Judaeo-Christians, had no links with the past. The special points are: (1) the Christian community of Rome not Paul's foundation, cf 20, 24, 28; (2) his collection journey to Jerusalem, cf 25—29.

23f. An anacoluthon which can be remedied with the *textus receptus* by adding the apodosis here given in brackets: 'and having been intent on coming to you for many years [I will now do so] when I make my journey to Spain. For I hope, as I pass . . .' **24.** 'Spain': cf 28; the earliest references in Christian literature to Paul's actual visit to Spain are Clem Rom, *Cor* 5:6f; Muratorian fragment, l. 35—9. **26.** Is important for fixing the date when Rm was written. It must have been after 2 Cor 8—9 when the collection for Jerusalem was still in full progress (A.D. 57) and shortly before his journey to Jerusalem, Ac 20:1—21:16. **28.** 'have delivered' = have sealed, which is a metaphor that can mean e.g. (*a*) authenticated, (*b*) completed, (*c*) safely delivered; cf Lagrange, Boylan. **h 30—33.** Paul asks for prayers at Rome. For similar requests cf 2 Cor 1:11.

16:1—2 A Note of Introduction for Phoebe—About to finish his letter with greetings to his friends at Rome and from his friends in Greece (Corinth or Cenchreae) Paul remembers first from among the latter a Christian lady named Phoebe. He gives her what may be called a note of introduction. Its purpose is to secure for her the welcome and the help of the Christians at Rome on her arrival. But it is an ancient conjecture that he intended to use her journey as an opportunity for sending his letter by a personal carrier; cf the subscription in many MSS, Tischendorf, NT II (1872) 457.

Phoebe is described by Paul (*a*) as *diakonos*, deaconess or helper in the church of Cenchreae; and (*b*) as *prostatis*, patroness or benefactress of many Christians, Paul himself included. The exact meaning of both titles **i** is disputed. The corresponding masculine nouns are official titles—the first signifying the office of deacon in the church, cf Ac 6:1—6; and the second signifying the office of a president, patron, or legal representative in Jewish as well as Greek and Roman religious organizations. Cf TWNT. On the other hand, the feminine use of these titles is found nowhere else in the NT. Further, the second remains unknown in the organization of the Christian Church during the following cent. And for deaconesses the four earliest references are: (*a*) Pliny the Younger, *Epist.* X 96, 8, written c. A.D. 112; (*b*) *Didascalia*, chh 9 and 16, ed. R. H. Connolly (1929), 88, 146—8 = *Apost. Constitutions*, ed. Funk II, 26, III, 12, written c. 3rd cent; (*c*) *Apost. Constitutions* VIII, 28, written c. 4th cent.; (*d*) Ps-Ignatius, *Letter to Antioch*, 12:2, written c. 4th cent. Under these circumstances the less technical interpretation of either description remains at least possible if not more probable, cf Vg.

3—16 Greetings—Having recommended Phoebe especially, Paul sends greetings to no less than 26 individual Christians and two households at Rome. Many of these names are well known from Gr. literature; others are Latin. It is not necessary to think that Paul knew personally all those to whom he sends special greetings. The names and importance of some can have been known to him from hearsay. The number of women in this list has

often been commented on. They are eight or nine apart **866i** from those that may be included in the two households. Commentators differ as to the number of groups = house- **j** churches, that can be distinguished in this list. Some distinguish three: (1) the house-church of Prisca and Aquila, 3—5*a*, with its members in 5*b*—13; (2) the house-church of Asyncritus, etc, 14; and (3) that of Philologus, etc, 15; Sickenberger distinguishes four groups: 3—5*a*, 5*b*—13, 14, 15. These house-churches are regarded as the beginning of the Christian parish-organization, cf Ac 12:12; Col 4:15; Phm 2. The religious interest of this list lies in the indisputable evidence which they give of the personal and human side in Paul's missionary activity. The mention of so many names in a town which Paul had never visited proves an extraordinary interest in personal contacts.

The attempts of archaeologists to identify the names of 3—15 concentrate on the inscriptions of the Roman columbaria from the 1st cent. Nearly all have been found there. But the discovery of a name in a sepulchral inscription does not reveal the identity of the person. The Ampliatus whose name is inscribed over a cell in the Domitilla Catacomb need not be the Ampliatus of Rm 16:8.

Is Rm 16:3 part of a letter to Ephesus? The theory that it was so originally is based mainly on the following argument. Paul lived at Ephesus for more than two years, Ac 19:8—10. Writing to Ephesus, therefore, one may well expect him to remember a great number of Christians personally, whilst it is difficult to imagine how he could know so many at Rome where he had never been. Cf Lagrange 370ff; A Feuillet in RB 57 (1950), 527—9; V. Taylor, JBL 67 (1948), 295ff. The arguments are not decisive, and do not solve the difficulties. cf Huby-Lyonnet, 492ff.

17—20 Warning against Heresies—This is a digres- **k** sion which may have been caused by the reference to 'all the churches' in 16. If so, this mere reference to 'all the churches' was enough to call to Paul's mind the persistent attempts to distort the true doctrine of the Gospel which he had everywhere to fight, cf 2 Tm 3.

What heretics the Apostle had in mind the text does not say. The charges are quite general: battening on doctrinal novelties, 17; material self-interest, 18*a*; and deceitful oratory, 18*b*. Commentators think of Judaism as in Gal 3:1 or of Antinomianism as in Rm 3:8; 6:1; Phil 3:17—21. Whether these false teachers were already at work in Rome or are here considered merely as a possible future danger is another question on which commentators differ, cf SH and Lagrange. On the whole it does not seem likely that Paul would leave the treatment of an immediate danger to a parenthesis in the conclusion of his letter, cf 16:19.

21—24 Greetings from Corinth—These greetings from Paul's companions continue the greetings from 'all the churches' in 16. Most of these names occur in Ac or elsewhere in the Pauline epistles. But the same name need not mean identity of person. The only exception is Timothy, 21. All are agreed that he is the Timothy whose history we can follow from his joining Paul at Lystra, c. A.D. 50 (Ac 16:1) to his episcopacy at Ephesus, c. A.D. 65.

25—27 Concluding Sentence—Paul finishes not as is **l** his custom with good wishes but with a doxology similar to 11:33—36; Clem Rom, *Cor*, 65:2; *Martyrdom of Polycarp* 22, 3. Of all these doxologies, however, 25—27 is the most elaborate. Nearly all the main points of the whole letter seem to be gathered here in one powerful finale: the power of God unto salvation; the revelation of God's plan of

866l salvation in the Gospel; salvation by faith in Jesus Christ; the Christian salvation offered to all; the Apostle's divine mission; the continuity with the OT. As the Gr. text stands in the modern critical editions the whole epistle ends in an untranslatable anacoluthon. The effect in the Gr. text, however, is a threefold doxology: (*a*) to God the Almighty, 25f; (*b*) to God the All-Wise, 27*a*; (*c*) to Jesus Christ, 27*b*.

The following analysis may be helpful in tracing the somewhat complicated sequence of thought.

m Glory be to God

(I) Who is able to strengthen you [so as to persevere] 25:
- (1) in accordance with my Gospel,
- (2) which is the same as the preaching of Christ,
- (3) which in turn is the same as the revelation of a (divine) mystery.

(II) This mystery is [God's plan of man's salvation]:
- (4) which was veiled in silence for eternal ages 25,
- (5) which however has now become manifest [through the Incarnation] 26,

- (6) and which has [already] been promulgated **86** by the Apostles 26.

(III) This promulgation means 26:
- (7) that it has been preached to the Gentiles,
- (8) to make them obedient to the faith = Gospel,
- (9) in accordance with a command from God,
- (10) with the help of [the evidence from] the prophetical writings.

The genuineness and textual history of 25—27 have **n** been the subject of much dispute. The difficulty arises from the differences in the MSS. A few omit the passage completely: D (Claromontanus) F^gr (Augiensis), G (Boernerianus). A number of MSS have the passage after 14:23: c. 200 minuscules, mainly von Soden's K = Antiochian recension of Lucianus. The oldest MSS as well as our modern critical editions place it after 16:23: ℵ (Sinaiticus) B (Vaticanus) C (Ephraemi rescriptus), etc. A few have it twice, after 14:23 and after 16:23: A (Alexandrinus) P (Porphyrianus)? etc. The confusion is nowadays generally traced back to the influence of Marcion who according to Origen-Rufinus X 43 interfered with the text of Rm 15—16 as early as the 2nd cent.; cf Lagrange 280—6; Boylan 256—61; Lietzmann 131.

9b of a synagogue in Corinth. The naming of a co-author or co-authors is a common practice in Paul: e.g. Timothy (2 Cor 1:1; Phil 1:1; Col 1:1; Phm 1), Timothy and Silvanus (1 Thes 1:1; 2 Thes 1:1). What the function of these men was cannot be determined, if there was one; certainly the fact that two are mentioned at times would seem to preclude the possibility that they were secretaries. **c** Sosthenes' name is Gr. **2.** 'To the church of God which is at Corinth' can be understood as referring to the local church or preferably to the local manifestation of the universal church; if this be correct, Paul already stressed the radical unity of the church. The designation shows the nature of the Church as the new people of God, for the term corresponds to the OT description of Israel as the *qehal Yhwh* The baptized person is called to be a. saint effectively, i.e., he is made a saint by the Sacrament. He is joined not only to the members of the local church but also to all believers by Baptism, who indeed acknowledge Jesus as Lord, that is God; for Paul uses of Jesus **d** the Christ the OT designation of God. **3.** Grace means every objective divine favour; peace is possession of everything needed for one's essential well-being. Paul combines the usual Gk. and Heb. greetings to manifest a religious truth.

e 4—9 Thanksgiving—Note that Paul does not praise the Corinthians for their charity; this is most significant, showing that the spirit of fraternal charity was lacking in many of the members of the community. **6.** 'of Christ' can be taken objectively or subjectively; the latter seems preferable (cf 1 Tm 6:13; 2 Tm 1:8). **7.** 'revealing': the Parousia, a main point in the Pauline teaching, for then salvation will be most definitive. **9.** God's fidelity is the motive for our hope.

f 1:10—6:20 Divisions and scandals—The apostle treats here some of the disquieting things which he has heard about the church in Corinth. It is a section marked by expressions of anger, sarcasm, and great affection, all of which shows the apostle's concern for those whom he had brought to Christ.

g 10—17a Factions—Cf introduction. **11.** Who Chloe was is otherwise unknown; it would seem that she was a Christian, whose servants informed Paul of the disorders in the church. Hers is a Gr. name. **12.** 'Each one' is a rhetorical exaggeration; it is patent from the whole letter that not every member of the community was at fault. While the name Apollos is Gr., the man was a Jew. Paul usually uses the Aram. form of Peter's name. **13.** **h** The words are angry and sarcastic. 'Is Christ divided?' is a theme which will be developed later (12:12—27). This sentence, together with the rest of the paragraph, is an example of how one must examine the whole context before deciding what is meant exactly by a statement of the apostle. Paul does not depreciate baptism; rather he is happy that no one can claim as a reason for the divisions the fact that Paul administered the sacred rite **i** to him. Baptism is important; who administers it does not matter. Crispus: cf Ac 18:8; Gaius: cf Rm 16:23; these are Latin names. Stephanus was one of the Corinthians' messengers to Paul; cf 16:15—17, his name is Gr. The mention of a household may indicate positively that children were baptized (but cf 7:14 and comment). **17a.** One must hear God's word before it can be accepted and one can be baptized (cf Rm 10:17; Mt 28:19—20).

j 17b—3:4 Worldly Wisdom and Christian Wisdom— There is here a diptych of antithetic assertions: Christianity is not wisdom but offends wisdom (17b—2:5); Christianity truly contains wisdom (2:6—3:4).

17b—2:5 Worldly Wisdom—17b. '*Wisdom of speech*' means that special competence in speaking which comes from a study of rhetorical arts and forms. Paul's preaching **869j** was of such a simple nature that the conversions effected through his labours could not be attributed to his skill but to the crucified Christ. **18.** 'Word of the cross' is not **k** only preaching about the cross of Christ but also the sermon which the cross in itself is. 'Who are perishing', 'who are being saved' (RSV): the participles are present and express therefore continuing action. They are those who are on the road either to damnation or salvation; the former by refusing Christ have made their condition worse, and the latter are now already inchoatively saved. The humility of the Christian religion with its crucified Lord and Saviour was the foolishness that most offended pagans. **19.** 'It is written' is a common introductory **l** formula for a citation from the OT. The citation is from Is 29:14 and is in fundamental agreement with the form found in LXX, whereas the Heb has the third person referring to wisdom which becomes dull and perception which becomes obscured. According to LXX God destroys wisdom which is purely worldly. **20.** The verse begins with words taken from Is 19:12 and 33:18. The implication is that purely human wisdom, whether that of the Jewish scribe or that of the Gr. 'debater' or philosopher, avails not at all if those who have it do not trust in God and believe his teaching. 'World' is to be taken **m** pejoratively as meaning what in our universe is opposed to God; since *kosmos* was 'order' and 'right' for the Greeks, the union of this word with 'debater' makes the statement extremely sarcastic to a Gr. reader. Because the liberation promised in the context of Is 29 is a liberation of the Chosen People, we are concerned with a type of the great liberation worked in Christ. As the foolish 'wise men' of old rejected salvation, so do their counterparts in Paul's lifetime. **21.** 'In the wisdom of God' **n** refers to the salvific will of God; 'through wisdom' refers to purely human wisdom; 'did not know' is to be taken in the Semitic sense of knowing and attaching one's self to. There is no contradiction to Rm 1:18—20, which treats of some knowledge of God's nature considered in itself, not of his positive salvific acts. God does not cause sin, but sin cannot thwart God's ultimate purposes (cf Rm 11:30—31). The preaching of the cross, not the teaching of Gr. philosophers or Jewish scribes, was directly conducive to salvation. **22.** Many Jews expected signs that **o** would manifest the power and glory of the Messiah; this expectation Jesus had often to combat (cf, e.g., Mt 16:4; Jn 4:48; 6:30), though not leaving himself without the testimony of signs. 'Greeks' means the Gentiles in general. The Gentiles, especially the Greeks, sought 'wisdom', i.e a philosophical system, attainable by purely human reason, which system would explain the whole universe and fulfil all the desires of the human heart. **23.** The preaching, the public proclamation, of a crucified Saviour was a stumbling-block to the Jews who did not expect a suffering Messiah, much less one who would appear as accursed (cf Dt 21:23); for the Greeks it was foolishness, if not insanity, to think that a god would submit to crucifixion. **24.** For Paul those 'who are called' are those who **p** hear and heed the divine vocation. Christ is the 'power of God' made manifest sensibly as it were; in him we have our salvation and will have our glorious resurrection (cf Gal 6:14). He is the 'wisdom of God' in this that God's salvific counsel is made manifest in him. **25.** For the Greeks **q** especially only a foolish or a weak god would have attempted to use a crucified man to accomplish his will; but the one and only God did just that, accomplishing by his 'foolishness', literally 'foolish act', and 'weakness', literally 'weak act', what was impossible to human wisdom and might (cf Lk 1:50—51). **26—29.** These sentences are **r**

869r replete with irony. Those things which count by worldly standards are not possessed by many: worldly wisdom, material power, noble birth; yet it was not from among those who possessed these that God chose those who were to share in the Messianic blessings; thus those who had been sanctified showed that their call and consequent status had come from God alone. This argument is directed against the pride of the Corinthians who considered themselves wise in a sense that was not wholly Christian, for in truth they were in worldly eyes 'contemptible' and 'things that are not', i.e. so insignificant

s as to be considered as non-existent. **30.** 'Justice and **sanctification' are in apposition to 'wisdom'. Jesus is our** wisdom for he makes us truly wise, and this in accordance with God's salvific counsel. **31.** The citation is a paraphrase of Jer 9:23—24. Authentic piety recognizes one's dependence upon God. Inasmuch as 'Lord' usually refers in Paul to Jesus, some see here an application of Jer's text to show the divinity of the Saviour. **2:1.** God gave testimony in Christ; this is what Paul preached. **2.** This statement is to be taken with a grain of salt since Paul does emphasize also the Resurrection of Jesus in his

t preaching (cf, e.g., 15:3—4). **3.** This stylized expression (cf 2 Cor 7:15; Eph 6:5) is not to be taken too literally; nevertheless, when Paul arrived in Corinth after his failure at Athens (Ac 17:32—18:1), he must have been troubled. **4.** 'Spirit and power' is an example of *hendiadys*; thus the power of the Spirit, the Holy Ghost, who in an inexplicable fashion instills faith into those who heard the apostle's words, and who worked signs and wonders in confirmation of his preaching (2 Cor 12:12). **5.** Faith is not the fruit of purely human reasoning nor the natural result of a preacher's eloquence.

870a **2:6—3:4 Christian Wisdom—6.** By change of number, 'we speak', Paul associates the other preachers to himself. 'Wisdom' is the 'meat' of 3:2, that knowledge of God and things divine possessed by those mature in the faith. The Gnostics abused this verse to give a foundation to their doctrine concerning the two classes of people: the perfect who possessed the secret knowledge about God, and the rest of mankind. Members of the modern *Religionsgeschichtlicheschule* also have tried to show that Paul changed the ethical dotrine of Jesus into something similar to the Gr. mystery cults. While Paul could have taken words from the vocabulary of the mystery sects without subscribing to their teachings, it is not proved

b that he did. Regarding the present question it must be noted that he never uses *teteleios* 'perfected', which in the mysteries signifies those fully initiated into the meaning of the rites; rather the apostle uses *teleios*, and generally in opposition to *nēpios* 'baby'. This suggests that Paul purposely avoided the vocabulary of the mysteries in this regard. Moreover, *teleios*, though used in reference to knowledge (13:11; 14:20; Eph 4:13; Heb 5:14), often has reference not to speculative but to practical know-

c ledge. Thus those who are 'perfect' or 'mature' are those who have attained some degree of perfection in the faith and its practice and who are thereby capable of obtaining a more sublime knowledge of God. This perfection differs from that of the Gnostics, for they divided mankind into those capable of receiving God's revelation and those incapable of it; for Paul the way to perfection is open to all. The 'princes of this world' are either the whole of human authorities or rather the bad angels (cf 15:24f; Eph 6:12; Lk 4:6; Jn 12:31; 14:30; 16:11); it is also

d possible that both groups are meant. **7—8.** The apostle likes to insist upon the mysterious character of God's salvific plan which was hidden but is revealed in the crucifixion and resurrection of Jesus. By calling Jesus

'Lord of glory' Paul places him implicitly on the same level **8** as Yahweh, for in the OT 'glory' is God's splendour and power which he communicates to no one. There is no reference here to any such outlandish theme as that of the tricked devil, or that found in the apocryphal *Ascension of Isaiah* and among the Gnostics that Jesus hid his dignity from the angelic powers when he became incarnate. What is meant is that the minions of Satan knew that Jesus was an extraordinary being but they did not understand anything concerning his life and especially his death (cf Eph 6:12; Col 2:15; Lk 22:3). **9.** 'It is written' **e** causes some difficulty, for this expression whenever it occurs is apparently intended to introduce a citation from the OT; but the words which follow are not found as such in any OT passage. Paul seems to have given a paraphrase of Is 64:4 with some influence felt of Is 65:17. Some **f** commentators hold that the citation is from the apocryphal *Apocalypse of Elijah*. In itself this view is not impossible for a citation from the apocrypha is found in Jude 9 and what is allowed to one NT author cannot be denied *a priori* to another; yet it would be a singular occurrence in Paul. 'Nor the heart of man conceived' means that man never had any desire for this, for it was too great to be imagined; one can only desire what is considered as at least remotely possible. **11—12.** Just as only a man's own **g** mind can know his innermost secrets, so only the Spirit of God, the Holy Ghost, knows the secret wonders of God. This Spirit has been given to all believers, and in those who are mature in the faith he has effected a greater realization of what God gives to those who have shown faith in him. **13.** *Synkrinontes* causes difficulty. Among **h** proposed translations are: 'comparing spiritual with spiritual' (CV), 'interpreting spiritual truth to those who possess the Spirit' (RSV, similarly NEB), 'showing the accord of things spiritual for those having the Spirit' (Allo), 'expressing in terms of the spirit the realities of the spirit' (BJ), 'adapting spiritual things to spiritual men' (Jacono), 'matching what is spiritual with what is spiritual' (K), 'comparing spiritual things with spiritual' (DV). It seems better to accept DV's rendering because of the basic meaning of the verb and the lack of the article with *pneumatikois*; the meaning then is that the Christian preachers compare spiritual things with spiritual things to come to a better understanding of them and thus to be able to arouse a deeper understanding of the spiritual realities in those who hear them. **14.** The 'natural' **i** *psychikos* man is he who does not possess the Spirit, who relies on natural resources only. **15.** The 'spiritual' *pneumatikos* man is he who possessing the Spirit cannot be judged in a condemnatory manner regarding things spiritual insofar as he acts in accord with the Spirit. In part at least this v is polemic: Paul is not to be judged by the Corinthians who are not as spiritual as he is (3: 1—3); moreover, since they too possess the spirit they should not allow themselves to be judged by non-Christians, especially in pagan courts (cf 6:1—11). **16.** **j** This begins with words taken from Is 40:13 in LXX, which here renders the Heb. well; in Rm 11:34 the first and second parts of the v are cited while here the first and third. When no introductory formula is found, it can be questioned whether Paul, or any other author wants the words to be taken as a citation. Paul's argument is that just as no one would give God a lesson so no one should want to give a lesson to him who thinks and speaks according to the teaching of Jesus. **3:1—4.** The Corinthians are as yet babes in the faith, still needing much instruction. **3:5—16 The True Position of Preachers—5.** **k** 'Ministers' *diakonoi* gives almost a definition of the role of the ordained ministers in the church: their prime duty

0k is to serve both God and other men (cf Y. Congar—B. Dupuy, *L'Épiscopat et L'Église Universelle*, 1962, 67—99). **6.** Each of the ministers contributed to the well-being of the Corinthian church in his own way, but the primary cause of sanctification of the Corinthians was God. **7—8.** From this two conclusions can be drawn: if the preachers are compared to God, they are nothing; if they are compared to one another, there can be found no opposition among them as long as they are truly doing their duty. Each preacher will receive a reward in propor-**l** tion to his own labors. **9.** 'God's fellow-workers', RSV Catholic edition's rendering of *Theou synergoi* seems better than RSV's 'fellow workmen for God' because the genitives in the latter part of the v are clearly possessive. Thus we have another expression of the unity of effort existing between Paul and Apollos. There is also expressed the dignity of the preacher who works under God's impulse. 'God's field', 'God's building': in Semitic fashion Paul passes quickly from one metaphor to another. **m 10—11.** 'Foundation' means the whole structure of a building without its ornamentation. Paul laid the foundation by his preaching of Jesus, that is by bringing Jesus, the foundation of the Church, to them. No human being, other than Christ, can serve as the foundation of his Church. (Patently this v causes no trouble for the teaching concerning the primacy of Peter, for Mt 16:16—18 is considering another, albeit essential, aspect of the Church. There Jesus indicates who will be the foundation-stone for his Church, who will serve as principle and sign of **n** external unity.) **12.** The materials are somewhat symbolic. There is a diminuendo according to their ability to withstand fire. **13—15.** 'The day' is the time of the general judgement at the second coming of Christ. The 'fire' is the judgement. The preacher will be judged according to the quality of his work; if it was poor that alone will cost him anguish and sorrow, though he himself as a true though imperfect teacher will be saved. It seems quite likely that the apostle teaches here that the special reward promised to preachers will be made up of the number of those who came to belief and virtue through his preaching and who will surround him as his crown or auréole in heaven. (cf W. Pesh in *Neutestamentliche Aufsätze*, Fs Schmid, **o** Regensburg 1963, 199—206). **16—17.** 'Temple': *naos* generally designates the innermost part of a sacred precinct, the small building in which in the pagan temple areas the statue of the god was found; the word applied to the Jewish centre of worship would signify the temple building and would point to the Holy of Holies, the most sacred part of the temple, in which God had his special dwelling place. The Holy Spirit is said to dwell in the church of Corinth. Those who attempt to destroy the unity of the Corinthian church attempt to destroy God's temple; thus they will be punished, if they succeed, for desecrating a sacred place.

71a 3:18—4:13 Conclusions regarding Wisdom—19—20. The wisdom of the world is that which is founded on purely natural things and which so concerns itself with them as to render any one who is satisfied with it incapable of attaining to God. The citations are very free ones of Job 5:13 and Ps 94 (93):11, both of which are adapted to the present context. In Job Eliphaz speaks of the wise wicked ones whose designs are rendered null. They who believe that God is ignorant of their plans against his people have, according to the Psalmist, vain thoughts, for God knows them and will bring them to naught. Paul adapts these expressions to declare that purely human knowledge is folly since it does not of itself bring men **b** to consider what is their proper goal. **21—23.** God disposes all things for the good of those who believe in him, for they belong to Christ who belongs to God. **4:1.** Another **871b** description of the Church's ministers; they are 'servants' *hypēretas* of Christ, that is his assistants, and 'stewards' *oikonomous*, those who oversee and dispense the goods, the 'mysteries of God', which are all the treasures of doctrine and of life-giving practices revealed and given to men by God. Among the practices may be mentioned baptism (1:15) and the celebration of the Eucharist (11:23—26). **2.** Just as human masters demand that **c** servants act for their good, so does God demand similar service and devotion from his servants, his ministers. **3.** The apostle is well aware of the powers of self-deception latent in each human being. This saying shows the apostle's true humility. **4.** It is the judgement of the all-knowing **d** God which really counts. **5.** God judges not only deeds but intentions. **6.** The first part means that the case of Paul and Apollos illustrates a more general truth, namely the nature of the apostolate which possesses basic unity. It is obvious from this and 3:5 that the principal factions or at least the principal quarrelsome factions, were those which claimed as their patrons Paul and Apollos respectively. The second part of the v is literally translated '*that you learn in us the not beyond what are written that no one be inflated concerning the one against the other.*' Evidently Paul's expression is difficult to understand. **e** Thus various translations are proposed based upon what '*not beyond what are written*' is assumed to mean. RSV has 'live according to the Scriptures'; RSV Catholic edition 'not to go beyond what is written', which was also the translation of RV; BJ inserts a word 'maxim' before the expression. Among the interpretations of the expression we may note these: a rabbinic precept which inculcated attachment to the Jewish law alone (Osty), the OT (Grosheide), a commercial or legal proverb (Allo), an *agraphon* or unwritten saying of Jesus (Chrys), the citations in 1:19—31; 3:19 (Luther). Whatever else may **f** be said it seems obvious that Paul is quoting a saying known to his readers (cf ... M. Hooker, NTS 10 (1963/64) 127—32). The saying is clearly directed against factionalism: ... member of the community should be proud that he has been particularly influenced by one preacher or the other, by Paul or by Apollos. **7.** The Corinthians are what they are on account of God's grace, not by reason of their own human efforts. **8.** Paul now uses irony. **9.** The apostles are, as it were, reserved for **g** the last place on the programme of a Gr. amphitheatre, as were slaves who were to die to give delight to onlookers. To all creatures the apostles would appear as unfortunate fools. **10 11.** Paul was undoubtedly thinking of the various trials and tribulations which marked his career at Antioch of Pisidia (Ac 13:13—50), Iconium (14:1—6), Lystra (14:8—20), Philippi (16:19—24), Thessalonica (17:1—9), Beroea (17:13f), Athens (17:32f). This same theme will be treated in 2 Cor 11:23—29. **12.** Greeks and Romans despised those who worked with their hands; this attitude was not shared by Jews.

14—21 Admonitions—15. There is hyperbole in the **h** number of guides, *paidagōgous*. In the strictest sense slaves who performed such duties were not teachers but rather had charge of the children of a household. Paul here shows his love for the Corinthians in an almost plaintive fashion; yet at the same time the figures he uses to describe himself and others show that he still considers them as most immature in the faith. **16.** This is not an appeal that all become members of the faction of Paul; rather they should imitate him whom they have known in the flesh that they may follow Christ whom they did not see or hear, for Paul imitates Christ. **17.** Timothy was known to the Corin- **i** thians (cf Ac 18:5). It is clear from 16:10 that Paul was

871i not sure that Timothy had reached Corinth again, a normal uncertainty in those days. Paul shows great affection for his disciple and manifests great confidence in his skill as a teacher. **18.** The tone changes; Paul writes harshly. Evidently some of those who were speaking perversely in Paul's absence would not have the courage or the effrontery to oppose the apostle face to face. They thought **j** that Paul would never return to Corinth. **19.** Certainly the apostle intended to visit the community at Corinth again. (For the question about a journey between this letter and 2 Cor cf § 886e; if 2 Cor 12:14—15 is taken in isolation from other questions, a second journey seems almost certain.) If he comes, Paul will show that their talk is nothing, that they are weak and lacking courage. **20.** 'The kingdom of God' here means at least in part its terrestrial manifestation which is in and is the Church. **k** The signs of a true Christian life are not mere words but are progress in the life of grace; this progress shows itself in the good order and the good works of the members of the community. **21.** Cf 2 Cor 13:2 for similar words.

l **5:1—13 The case of the Incestuous Man—1.** It is obvious from the context and the expression used, 'father's wife', that the woman is the step-mother of the sinful man. That she was not then married seems brought out by the use of *porneia* 'fornication' to describe the relationship; this is not brought out well by RSV's 'immorality', its usual translation of *porneia*. It must be admitted that *porneia* and its cognates are thought by many to indicate all types of sexual immorality and those who practise it respectively (cf MMV *sub vocibus*). This remark should be remembered elsewhere (5:9, 10, 11; 6:9, 13, 18). Inasmuch as the woman is not the object of the apostle's condemnation, it would seem that she was not a believer.

m Marriage with a widowed step-mother was prohibited by the Mosaic Law (Lv 18:7—8; Dt 22:30); among the Greeks and Romans such unions were also condemned generally (the exceptions found in certain royal unions do not derogate from this, since dynastic considerations were often thought to have overriding force); Roman law **n** prohibited such unions. Since Corinth was subject to Roman law it seems that the union was one that had no civil effect; on the other hand Paul appears to be speaking of some kind of more or less stable relationship. It is also probable that the man's father was dead. Perhaps the sinner believed, as evidently did other members of the community (cf 7:10—15), that many laws regarding social relationships no longer bound Christians; moreover, there was a licentious element in the community (cf 6:12—20).

o **2.** Yet another sarcastic condemnation of the pride of the members of the Corinthian church. The power of excommunication resided in the local church. It is not explicitly stated here if there were ministers in the community who should have acted. **3.** Paul expresses his authority over the Corinthians even though he is not present among them. **4.** All power in the Church is derived from Jesus and is exercised in his name. 'With the power of our Lord Jesus' probably goes with what follows and thus is the beginning of Paul's decree concerning the **p** punishment of the sinner. **5.** 'To Satan for the destruction of the flesh' has been interpreted in many ways. Seemingly the expulsion from the community was itself handling over to Satan; cut off from the community which is subject to Christ, the sinner is thereby subject to Satan. 'For the destruction of the flesh' gives part of the purpose of the punishment: the destruction of the sin in the man; 'flesh' is accordingly the sinful aspect of man; 'spirit' is the man under the aspect of his having been sanctified. **q** Thus the punishment is intended to move the sinner to remorse, so that he will be saved at the general judgement;

if he is thus saved, the purpose of the imposition of the **87** penalty will be fulfilled. The penalty is therefore not vindictive but medicinal; furthermore this shows that according to Paul someone guilty of grave sin after baptism could receive forgiveness. If 2 Cor 2:6—7 refers to the same event, it is seen that the punishment had salutary effect before the death of the sinner. In any case the principle derived from these vv must be complemented by the teaching contained in 2 Cor 2:6—7: punishment is not to be such as to drive the one punished to despair. **6.** Again Paul speaks out against the pride of the Corin- **87** thians. The figure of the leaven is also used in Gal 5:9; it recalls the teaching of our Lord in which the same figure is used (Mt 13:33; 16:6 etc). **7—8.** 'Unleavened bread' is an apt symbol for those who are holy and pure since it is bread made from the simplest kind of dough. The figure of speech found here is based on a physical impossibility, for it is impossible to make unleavened dough from that which is leavened. The figure is drawn from the **b** Jewish Paschal precept which forbade the presence of leaven in the houses of the people (Ex 12:19; 13:7). 'Paschal lamb' literally 'Passover' (cf also Lk 22:7). Christ is our Paschal lamb, the effective sign of our liberation from bondage, as the Jewish rite commemorated the exodus of the Jews from slavery in Egypt (Dt 16:1—4). This is an example of how OT realities were seen by the nascent Church as types of Christ. This appellation, 'Christ our Paschal lamb' was already one of the traditional appellations of Jesus; it expresses the sacrificial and redemptive aspects of his death. The reference to **c** celebrating the feast seems to show that the comparison was suggested to Paul by the time of year when he wrote. If this is correct, the teaching here is connected with Paul's Eucharistic teaching, and the appellation was taken from the Christian Paschal liturgy. **9.** 'I wrote': certainly a reference to a previous letter. **10.** Christians must **d** associate with non-Christians; it is not the vocation of Christians to withdraw into a ghetto or to lie down and die. **11.** 'Brother': one who has been baptized. 'Not even to eat' shows what is meant by the prohibition to associate with a sinner of the type mentioned. In antiquity, just as now, to eat with another implied a certain degree of intimacy: thus here a close relationship with such a sinner is prohibited. Furthermore, if the context have Eucharistic **e** overtones, the eating together which is forbidden would be that associated with the Eucharistic celebration. This was not strictly part of the Eucharistic service but was separated from it by what it signified, if not by time. Paul does not accuse the Corinthians here of allowing the sinful brothers to partake of the Eucharist (contrast 11:19—29); yet they perhaps did not exclude them from the *agapē*, which ideally was highlighted by the Eucharistic celebration. **12—13.** The community should concern itself **f** with the public conduct of its members, but it should not concern itself with the actions of non-Christians. Note that the punishment ordered for the sinners considered in the latter part of the ch is not as severe as that ordered to be inflicted upon the incestuous man, even though the final command is given with the same solemn words as are used in the OT where expulsion from the people of God is prescribed (Dt 13:6; 17:7; 19:19; 22:24).

6:1—11 Cases before Pagan Tribunals—1. **g** 'Against a brother' means another member of the Christian community. The members of the pagan tribunals are called unrighteous because they do not possess that justification which can only be had by members of the Church. Paul is not stating or implying that the administration of civil justice at Corinth was corrupt or

2h venal. **2–3.** All Christians are identified with Christ as his members (6:15; 12:12) and thus will share in his prerogatives, including that of being judge of the world (cf Jn 5:22, 27; Lk 22:30; 2 Pt 2:4; Jude 4; Apoc 20:4). Since Christians are to have a part in such a judgement, they should be able to act as judges in lesser matters. **4.** Paul becomes sarcastic. The inference is that such problems should not arise among Christians who are brothers. **5.** The sarcasm continues. The Corinthians thought themselves wise and yet could not find any 'wise men' capable of acting as judges or arbiters of disputes among the **i** members of the community. **7.** 'Defeat' *ēttēma* probably means here the loss of a case in court. Christians have already lost the case when they have such disputes because they are not acting truly as Christians if some injustice has been done; there cannot be a case unless some injustice has been committed or someone desires what is unjust. Rather than cause scandal or cause greater dissension, they would do better to suffer the wrong. From the context it is apparent that Paul is giving a counsel and not a **j** precept (cf v 5). **8.** Lawsuits of necessity presuppose that at least one party to the case has inflicted a wrong on the other or desires to do so; these are opposed to the spirit of the gospel. **11.** Note the Trinitarian presentation of thought. 'Washed', 'sanctified', 'justified' are in reality synonymous, but each presents one aspect of the total concept of the effect of baptism. 'In the name': by the power of the person.

k **12–20 Fornication—12.** 'All things are lawful for me' was undoubtedly a saying of the laxists—in the present instance, the libertines among the Corinthian Christians. To have had any force in justification of their conduct the saying must have been one used by Paul himself, though in a different context. Most likely the apostle meant that the Mosaic Law's ritual and dietary regulations did not bind the members of the Christian communities. 'Not all things are helpful': *sympherei* here means 'are helpful' in the sense of being useful or expedient. This seems to be another saying of Paul's (cf 9:20) quoted by the laxists to explain why they did not always follow their inclinations; but not everyone admits this interpretation (cf puncuation **l** ation in RSV). **13–14.** 'Food for the stomach and the stomach for food': a further argument used by the libertines who held that fornication was merely fulfilling a natural desire or was merely making an indifferent use of a bodily function. Since eating in itself is an indifferent act, so too, according to them, is fornication. This idea would have been in accord with ancient pagan views that fornication was not wrong provided no fraud or force was employed. For RSV's 'immorality' as a translation of *porneia*, cf comment on 5:1. The apostle replies that food and the stomach as a receptacle for food will be destroyed, for in the life of the glorious body eating will have no **m** place. The body is destined for a glorious resurrection similar to that of Jesus, not for fornication; the Christian's body belongs to Christ, not to a prostitute. For Paul the active role in the resurrection is always attributed to God the Father. **15a.** Paul recalls to the minds of the Corinthians something which they already know. In no other place is the dignity of our fleshly bodies so loftily expressed; we are members of Christ in our complete beings, not just in respect of our souls. This statement of Paul's is another indication of the depth of the teaching **n** given to early Christians not yet long in the faith. **15b–16.** '. . . members of Christ and make them members of a prostitute'. Nothing is more horrible than this statement (Chrys). Some place the force of the apostle's argument in this that in fornication one is joined to a vile person; others think that the argument is that in fornication a man

surrenders himself soul and body to sinful pleasure and **872n** thus the soul is made flesh. From the context the former interpretation seems preferable. Paul's use of Gn 2:24 is **o** rather bold for that verse concerns marriage and, seemingly, more than just the aspect of coition; nevertheless in any type of sexual intercourse there can be an absorption, as it were, of each person into the other, according to their sentient natures, and they are physically united. In his accommodation of the text from Gn, if indeed it should be distinguished by that term, Paul places emphasis on 'flesh', which for him usually has a pejorative meaning. It must be noted that the apostle's argument is completely valid only in cases of fornication with a prostitute, the specific type of fornication which he is considering. **17.** **p** To the degrading union of a man with a prostitute Paul opposes the Christian's union with Christ, which is effected at baptism and which makes us one spiritual entity with him; in this union our bodies are not 'flesh' but 'spirit' being animated by the soul in whom the Spirit dwells and which is destined for heavenly life. **18.** 'Every other sin . . . is outside the body': oratorical exaggeration is evident; nevertheless fornication (and adultery, etc) more profoundly engage the body than do sins opposed to other virtues than chastity. **19a.** Cf 3:17; 2 Cor 6:16. **19b–20.** Christians do not belong to themselves but to God. The price was the death of Jesus on the cross. Before this salvific redemption the Corinthians could have been compared to slaves, who according to civil laws were not considered as persons, as truly human beings, but as things.

7:1–40 Marriage, Virginity, and Celibacy—It 873a should be noted that Paul is not writing here a treatise on marriage and virginity; he is answering questions which have been proposed to him by members of the Corinthian church. He does indeed extol virginity and celibacy; at the same time it is not his intention to disparage the married state. Thus he exhibits that tension which besets any writer who treats two opposite subjects, both of which are good, but of which one is better than the other. The apostle **b** attempts to influence his readers towards the one, in the present case the embracing of the state of virginity, which demands the renunciation of marriage; yet he does not want to cause problems for those who cannot for one reason or another accept that state. Furthermore, it is apparent that some of the Corinthians were confused by pondering over his previous teaching, about which they now sought clarification. Undoubtedly his preaching had caused some who were married at the time of their entrance into the Church to consider living apart. The **c** chief points of his reply are: (1) as a general principle one should remain in that state of life in which one was when called to the faith; (2) virginity for those not yet married is preferable spiritually to marriage; (3) marriage is a protection from concupiscence and should therefore be embraced by those who feel themselves incapable of assuming the burdens which virginity entails. His main purpose, perhaps surprisingly, seems to have been to declare that marriage was licit for those yet unmarried and that the use of marriage was permitted to those married, indeed was advocated for them.

1–11 Advice to Married Persons—1. Paul affirms the **d** principle which he has taught, namely that the state of celibacy is a good thing; and from the following vv it appears to be a *better* state. **2.** Clearly he does not want to detract from the principle enunciated in v 1; so he considers marriage under a correct but less favourable aspect. He does not mean that the only reason for marrying is fear that otherwise one would fall into fornication. **3–5.** 'Debt' *opheilēn*: what is owed in justice; here it obviously

873d refers to the act of copulation. Apparently something new is taught here: the absolute parity of husband and wife
e in respect of the marriage act. The wife's equal rights were either not held by the pagans or ignored by them in practice. Moreover, ordinarily, husband and wife each have an obligation approaching one of justice to engage in intercourse. If they decide to abstain, it should be by mutual consent, for a short time, and for a spiritual purpose: 'that you may devote yourselves to prayer', i.e. give themselves over completely to prayer, *scholasēte*. While this is perhaps not the only good reason for sexual abstinence, it would seem that Paul's teaching is normative in most circumstances for most couples, lest they expose themselves to temptations against the chastity which is
f proper to the married state. This temptation is ascribed to the devil, who is the father of sin (cf Gn 3:1—5) and who thus can be described as the source of all temptation. Sexual abstinence for periods of special prayer was an OT ideal (cf, e.g., Ex 19:15; 1 Sm 21:5). **6—7**. Paul is not giving a universal command that all should marry, for he would prefer that all unmarried Christians should embrace the state of virginity; but this ability to renounce matrimony is a gift given by God only to some, and can be
g refused. It is not Paul's thought that the institution of marriage is a concession to sinful tendencies; rather, celibacy is a better state but one which lacks the normal outlet for the sexual appetite. It may be stated here that marriage is also a divine favour. 'That which is capital in the present passage . . . is v 2, the counsel given to the Corinthians to marry, although perfect continence remains in itself a superior state which Paul certainly does not wish to forbid to those who are capable of it' (Allo). Paul obviously was not married at the time when he wrote this
h epistle. **10—11**. Paul is addressing here Christians who are married to Christians. The 'charge' of the Lord means the teaching of Jesus regarding the indissolubility of marriage (Mt 5:32; 19:9; Mk 10:9; Lk 16:18). 'Separate' is said of the woman in juridical language because she would be presumed to be living in her husband's house; 'divorce' is said of the husband's action since it is presumed that he would force his wife to leave his house; thus the words are used of the juridically weaker or stronger parties
i respectively in a case of divorce. In Jewish, Roman and Greek law there was no 'separation from bed and board'. Paul, following the oral teaching of Jesus, forbids divorce though he allows a separation provided that neither remarries.
j **12—16 A Special Case: Marriage with a pagan**. But there is an exception to the previous teaching. The question asked the apostle was whether it was licit for a Christian to live with an unbaptized partner. Clearly when Paul wrote an 'unbeliever', he meant a person who had not received Christian baptism. The Corinthians seem to have shared Jewish ideas that marriage with non-Jews
k should be broken (cf Ez 10:11) *mutatis mutandis*. **12—13**. 'I say': The apostle is acting directly on his own authority; by his apostolic authority Paul could declare the force of the teaching of Jesus and derogate from it in a particular case. (This may be an indication that the excepting clause in Mt does derive directly from Jesus' teaching; cf HeyJ 6 (1964) 299—302). The general rule is that those who are married are to stay together, whether or not both
l parties are baptized. While some commentators do not think that Paul gives a command here, it is most difficult to see how *aphietō* 'let him (her) put away' can be taken otherwise, for it is an imperative. Paul speaks of the prohibition affecting both the Christian man and the Christian woman in the same way: neither is to 'divorce' the unbelieving partner; the term in which the command is

couched is significant, for in the mixed marriage the **87?** baptized party is juridically the stronger one in Paul's eyes. **14**. 'For the unbelieving husband is consecrated . . .': **m** For Jews the uncleanness of the non-Jewish partner, i.e. lack of holiness owing to non-membership in the people of God of the Old Covenant, was such as to defile the Jewish partner and the community. For Paul the cleanness, the holiness, of the believing partner overcame the unbelieving partner's lack of holiness, by close association with the community of 'saints' (cf 1:2) due to relationship to the believing partner. This is a sign of the superiority of **n** the New Covenant over the Old. 'Otherwise your children would be unclean': this is not an unequivocal indication that children were baptized at that time; the apostle's arguments would seem to have greater force if they were not: no one doubts that the children of baptized persons belong to the community by reason of their relationship to baptized parents; why then doubt that the unbelieving partner belongs in some way to the Christian community? (For the question of children's baptism cf J. Blinzler in Fs Schmid, 23—43; J. Jeremias, *The Origins of Infant Baptism*, London 1963). **15**. If the unbeliever 'desires **o** to separate' the believing partner is no longer bound by the marriage, or possibly is not to seek a reconciliation with the unbelieving partner. The latter interpretation, defended by some (e.g., P. Subau, CBQ 13 (1959), 146—52), does not seem to be in harmony with what follows, for it is stated that the believer 'is not bound' when the unbeliever departs. The Christian has been called 'to peace', i.e., to the possession of all those things necessary for his or her salvation. **16**. The unbeliever is not **p** sanctified internally by his or her matrimonial bond to a Christian. In general this v seems to be an exhortation to Christian husbands and wives to remain with their unbelieving partners so that they may possibly help to convert them. This passage seems to provide the basis for The Pauline Privilege of canon law; cf The Jurist 15 (1955) 132—37.

17—24 No Change of Status to be Sought—17. **874** 'Only' *ei mē*: normally this expression means 'unless'; however, in the NT it often signifies opposition and equals *alla* (cf F. Blass, A. Debrunner, R. Funk, *A Greek Grammar of the NT and Other Early Christian Literature*, Cambridge and Chicago 1961, §§ 376, 448 (8)); DV 'But' is excellent here (contra RSV, CV). The general principle is enunciated: the Christian should remain in that state of life in which he was called to the faith; while an imperative *peripateitō* is used, the context shows that Paul is giving a counsel and not a command in the strictest sense. This **b** general recommendation is not intended for the Corinthians alone, for it is taught by Paul everywhere. **18**. 'Let him not seek uncircumcision': this is a rhetorical figure intended to bring out the basic meaning of the passage that the Christian was not to seek to change his status; there is no reason to suppose that Paul had in mind the practice of some Jewish athletes who attempted to conceal the marks of their circumcision when they competed with pagans. **19**. 'Circumcision counts for nothing': as a **c** purely outward sign circumcision means nothing; moreover, with the establishment of the New Covenant one did not have to become a Jew in order to be a member of God's people. **21**. This v can be understood in two ways according as one interprets *mallon chrēsthai*, DV 'use it rather'. While some (e.g., WV, RSV, NEB) take it as meaning that a slave should take advantage of any opportunity of obtaining his freedom; it would seem that the context requires one to understand the meaning to be that the slave should take advantage of the opportunity of remaining a slave. **22—23a**. Various aspects of the **d**

d same Christian truth can serve as consolation to some members of the Church and as a reminder to others of their status as subjects of God. All Christians are free men of the Lord; their liberty from the servitude of sin was purchased with the death of Jesus upon the cross; at the same time all Christians are slaves of Jesus who acquired them for himself by his death, and who is now their Lord **e** and Master. **23b.** Christians must not allow themselves to become so attached to men that they no longer fully serve Christ. Is this a possible further reference to the factious spirit of the Corinthians?

25–35 The State of Virginity—25. There is no command from Jesus that anyone or everyone is to embrace the state of virginity, though Jesus certainly extolled that state (Mt 19:10–12). Paul now gives his counsel concerning virginity anew, speaking of himself in a somewhat deprecatory manner, which is a useful **f** oratorical device. **26–27.** 'The impending distress' is the object of many interpretations: 'the thousand worries of married life' (Osty); the imminent persecutions 'which an unmarried person is better able to bear' (Rees); the imminence of the end of the world; these are the last days of the existence of this world in which we should be preparing ourselves for the return of Christ; the last age is upon us, no matter how long it may last, with its special trials and tribulations. This last interpretation seems preferable (cf L. Legrand in Scr 12 (1960), 101–5; E. Maly in *Marian Studies* 13 (1962), 54–60; E. **g** Neuhasler in BZ 3 (1959), 43–60). It cannot be held that Paul taught that the *parousia* was to come in a matter of months or of a few years. These times are such that a new mode of life would of necessity be distracting. The only part of the teaching, therefore, that is limited to the then conditions in Corinth is that concerning converts of recent vintage as converts. **28.** 'Worldly troubles' (RSV) renders Gr. phrase which literally = '*tribulation of the flesh*' that is the cares and sufferings experienced in man's sensitive being (cf Gn 3:14) which will be accentuated for **h** those who realize, as Christians should, that they are in the final age of the world and thus should be preparing for the second coming of Christ in as perfect and undivided manner as possible. **29a.** 'The time has grown very short': This is the last age of the world. **29b–31.** Christians should be preoccupied with making proper preparation for the return of the Lord as judge. Hence those cares, sentiments, activities which normally mark men's lives and distinguish one man from another should insofar as this is possible become the object of but **i** secondary consideration. 'From now on': *to loipon* is better understood in this way, although another understanding is possible 'it remaineth' (DV). 'This world' as we know it subject to evil influences is passing away and will finally yield place entirely to the glorious age of Christ. **32.** Paul wants the Corinthians to be able to prepare in the best manner possible for Christ's coming; thus he wants them to have less care. This state is achieved more readily in one who can devote himself entirely or almost entirely to the things which pertain directly to God. **33.** A married man just by his status as husband must be concerned with what will please his wife; this is of obligation. Hence he is divided, if he have the proper understanding of the nature of the present age, by his concern for the things that pertain directly to God and by this concern for the things which pertain directly to **j** his wife. **34.** A similar situation exists for women. **35.** Paul gives his reason for extolling the state of virginity; one can devote oneself more completely to prayer in that state. His direct intention is not to remove Christians from entrance into marriage; rather he wants them to embrace

that state which of itself is more noble and permits more **874j** easily fuller devotion to Jesus. Both *euschēmon* and **k** *euparedron* 'noble' and 'constant', hence proper and devoted, while in the positive degree, should be understood as comparatives; this is not an uncommon rhetorical use. It would be a grave error to take the apostle's praise of virginity to imply that the direct opposite is to be said of the married state; it would be at least an equal error to take his description of the virgin's quest for holiness of body and spirit as implying that the matron could not have a similar quest.

36–38 A Special Case—These vv have become the **l** object of much discussion during the past century. RSV, NEB, Kleist—Lilly make interpretative translations, though the three are not in accord. The vv have been interpreted as referring to (1) a father and a daughter, (2) a man and a *virgo subintroducta* or persons in a somewhat similar relationship, (3) a man and his fiancée, (4) persons who should enter into a levirate marriage (cf J. M. Ford, NTS 10 (1963/64), 361–5), (5) a patron and a poor girl who had been practically indentured to him (cf G. Castellino in Fs Tisserant I, 31–42), (6) a man and his female slave. Regarding (1) to call a man's daughter his virgin is, to say the least, a strange way of **m** speaking or writing about her. While a father could not under Roman law force his daughter into a marriage, he could expect that his wishes would count for much and that in point of fact they would usually be obeyed. At least the same is to be said of the rights of a Jewish father in the first Christian cent. On (2) a *virgo subintroducta* **n** was a Christian maiden who fictitiously entered into a marriage as a device for protecting her virginity. This practice was known in the 3rd cent., but there is no earlier evidence for it unless here. This interpretation seems impossible when one takes into account the apostle's pastoral wisdom, as is shown in 7:5. Re (3) Betrothal **o** in a Roman city would not have created any social pressure for the concluding of the marriage; Jewish customs, however, would have; but one may ask whether such a Jewish opinion would have had much weight in the Corinthian church; v 1 seems to imply that it was nothing Judaic which was causing the problems treated in this ch. Re (4) while it may be true that occasionally *parthenos* was used in a broader sense, two reasons militate against this opinion: the problem does not seem to have been of Judaic origin; was the levirate marriage common among Jews of the first century? On (5) and (6) these opinions are not **p** far apart. However, the relationship existing between a master and his slave makes the appellation 'his virgin' sound quite natural (cf CBQ 20 (1958), 292–8). 'Above the age' would mean, if such be the proper rendering here of *hyperakmos*, that the woman in this case was somewhat beyond the usual age for marriage; according to Plato this age was twenty; among the Jews and many other peoples of antiquity it was from twelve to fifteen. *Gamizō* certainly means 'give in marriage' and it has not been established beyond all doubt that it can mean 'marry', the meaning which it must have in opinions 2 and 3 and in RSV. We should not think over harshly of what were **q** the prerogatives accorded to a father or master (if either be the subject of the power of giving in marriage in this passage) since they would have been in accord with the social usages of that era. Paul normally did not attempt to subvert the social order when no basic principle was at stake. Most women would have been content to follow the usual customs concerning entrance into marriage.

39–40 Concerning Widows—39. This actually re- **r** states the doctrine of the indissolubility of marriage. At the same time the lawfulness of remarriage for widows is

874r declared. 'Only in the Lord': either 'She must take a Christian husband' (Osty) or she must marry in accordance with the principles of Christian morality. The latter interpretation seems preferable. 'It does not appear that the condition that the new partner be a Christian is absolutely necessary' (Jacono); thus even if the prior interpretation is held, Paul's words apparently admit

s of exception. However, a widow who remarries will be less blessed in the same sense that in her new marriage she will be in a state which is less conducive to the fullest attention to the things of God (cf v 34f). Later the apostle will advise young widows to remarry (1 Tm 5:14); there is no contradiction, for experience will have shown him that many young widows had difficulties in preserving chastity (cf vv 2, 9 above). Paul then closes this section with a very mild assertion of his own authority (cf v 25).

875a **8:1—11:1 Concerning Things Sacrificed to Idols—** Greco-Roman religion was an unending series of rites and practices. Every phase of human life, whether public or private, gave occasion for some type of sacrifice. Moreover, the flesh which was immolated to false gods was only in part given to the idols or their priests; part was often returned to those who had provided the offering; this portion was then eaten at a sacred banquet. Much of what had been offered was sold in the public markets, generally at a cheap price. The Corinthian Christians were troubled as to the consequences of their living in the midst of a pagan people: Should they accept an invitation to one of the sacred repasts, which often were considered more as social than as strictly religious affairs? Should they buy in the markets meat which had come from sacrifices?

b Should they remain at table and eat if they discovered that what was being served had come from a sacrifice? It can be seen that negative answers to all of these questions would make social intercourse with non-Christians most difficult; moreover, they would place a heavy burden on the poor who bought much of the cheap meat which originally had been sacrificed.

c **8:1—6 General Principles—1.** Knowledge can be a source of pride; the Corinthians had thought themselves particularly wise. Knowledge of the true nature of meat which had been sacrificed is not the sole determinant for action; one must above all act in accord with charity, that love for others, which leads to the building up of the Church, its expansion among non-Christians and the increase of all virtues among those who have already been baptized. Thus the Christian must have concern for the views of others, even when they are mistaken. **3.** He who loves God is 'known', i.e., in the Hebraic sense of the word,

d loved by God. **4—6.** Idols are in reality nothing; thus in no way can they affect the nature of something natural such as meat. While the pagans had a plethora of gods and lords, there is in truth but one God and one Lord. There is here an implicit assertion of the divinity of Jesus. 'Through whom are all things, and we through him': a reference to the function of Jesus in creation and redemption. We have here a theme considered peculiarly Johannine (cf Jn 1:3, 12—13).

e **7—13 Practical Applications: Charity Must Reign—7.** There is a textual problem here. While most commentators accept a Gr. text which can be translated as in RSV and WV, there are those who accept a text producing the translation found in Vg (and DV), BJ, CV. Although the latter reading produces an intelligible meaning (*contra* WV's note); nevertheless the reading with *synētheia* 'habit' seems preferable because of the rarity of the word, and thus one should agree with RSV, etc. Although there can be some degree of doubt about its cor-

rectness (as is noted in: Aland, ed., *The Greek New* **8** *Testament* (1966) RSV's 'accustomed to idols' renders a Gr. phrase which literally would be translated 'in the habit of the idol'. Notwithstanding the fact that they had once **f** been worshippers of idols, if all had true knowledge, they would know that eating meat had no significance, even though the meat had been sacrificed to an idol, since an idol is nothing (v 4). Since this knowledge is not possessed by all, some think that they partake of idolatrous worship by eating meat already offered in pagan sacrifice. 'Con- **g** science' *syneidēsis* means here the faculty or power to make a passing judgement concerning one's relationship to God (cf J. Stelzenburger, *Syneidesis im NT*, Paderborn 1961, 68—71, 95, who, however, gives a somewhat different interpretation; C. Pierce, *Conscience in the NT*, 1955, 79—90, does not agree). **8.** In themselves eating and drinking are nothing. **9—10.** One should avoid doing anything which, though proper in itself is not necessary, if the action is likely to lead others to sin owing to their ignorance of the true nature of the action. Thus one **h** should abstain from things sacrificed to idols if there is fear that some other Christian might take part in an act which for him would be idolatry. **12—13.** If scandal can be avoided, it must be avoided. Christ demands that we act charitably towards others; that we respect their weaknesses. This is the true sense of the dictum already cited by the apostle in 6:12a. If one causes another to sin by an act which is indifferent in itself, one sins against Christ. That other is wounded in conscience because he thinks that what he has done has brought him into an incorrect relationship to God. This teaching must be complemented by that contained in Gal 2:11—21. This can be considered as following naturally after the preceding: Paul does not make use of all the liberties which are his. If this is so he is carried away soon by the theme of the authenticity of his apostolate. This is perhaps the more natural understanding of his mind. However, he may rather be returning to the themes of the opening chapters which demand a defence of his apostolate.

9:1—14 Paul's Rights as an Apostle—1. Paul's **87** vision of Jesus is the apostle's title to that office in a special sense; cf 15:8. A similar defence will occupy much of 2 Cor. 'Are you not my work': cf 3:6—10. **2.** If Paul **b** has not preached to others, he could be said by them not to be their apostle, i.e. one sent to them from God; however, he has preached to the Corinthians and hence was one sent to them. This is a play on the etymology of the word 'apostle'. They are the 'seal' of his apostleship because their existence as Christians authenticates his claim to have acted in accordance with a mission imposed upon him by Jesus the risen Lord. **3.** The tone becomes sarcastic **c** as Paul begins to show that he has not taken advantage of all his rights and privileges as an apostle and minister of Christ. **4.** 'To eat . . .': i.e. at the expense of the community. **5.** It seems clear that many of the apostles were accompanied by pious women or their wives during their missionary activity (Cf RSV CE note). Pious women ministered to Jesus during his public life (cf Lk 8:2f). Elsewhere in the NT little is said of the activity of the Twelve save that of Peter. 'A sister' would indicate that such a woman was a believer. The order of the Gr. words *adelphēn gynaika* would seem to show that they should be translated 'a sister, a wife', even though *gynē* has the more generic meaning of 'woman'. Non-dogmatic tradition **d** has been almost universally opposed to this interpretation. Allo proposes a compromise understanding of the expression: those apostles who had believing wives still alive took them along; the others had pious women to minister to them. There is no support in the text for this view.

6e Thus some commentators (e.g. J. Bauer, BZ 3 (1959), 94–102) hold that believing wives accompanied some of the apostles; indeed it has been proposed that Paul himself had been married but that his wife had not become a 'sister', a believer, or was dead. In part this view is based on the practice usual among rabbinical students, who were expected to marry by their twentieth year (cf X. Leon-Dufour in Fs Gelin, Le Puy and Lyons 1961,
f 321, n. 4); however, given the undoubted influence of Qumran or related teaching on some of the students in Palestine in the 1st cent. and the fact that some exceptions to the general practice are known, it seems most likely, if not certain, that Paul had never married. 'The brothers of the Lord'. On this see § 664. It would seem that the mention of them here indicates that they were apostles, for they are placed between 'the other apostles' and 'Cephas'; obviously Cephas-Peter was a member of the
g Twelve. From Mt 13:55 we know the names of four: James, Joseph, Simon and Jude; of these names three are found in lists of the apostles. (Regarding the translation here of *adelphoi* by 'brethren' cf RSV CE note to Mt 12, 46; K. W. Clark, JBL 85 (1966), 8). Tradition is unanimous, apart from Heliodorus, that these men were not the sons of Mary. The position of Cephas in the numeration shows that he held a special place in the early Church. **6.** Barnabas was the early collaborator of Paul (cf Ac 11: 25*f*; 13:2 14:28); the two separated after the dispute about Mark (Ac 15:36 39). It would seem that they had reunited their efforts. **7.** Paul wrote at a time when gentlemen soldiers did not exist. Undoubtedly this does
h not affect the argument. **8–9.** Paul cites the OT to support his claim that preachers of the gospel should be supported by those whom they evangelize. Dt 25:4 is also cited in 1 Tm 5:18, preceded there as here by an introductory formula. Here the word order is the same as that found in LXX but a change is made in one word; in 1 Tm LXX's words are used but in a different order. The meaning is substantially the same as that found in the Heb, though 1 Cor's is a bit closer to it than is LXX (and 1 Tm). The argument is made according to the first rule of Hillel (c. 30 B.C.), *qol wᵉhomar*, that is *a fortiori*. **12.** Cf 2 Cor 11:7–21. Especially at Corinth Paul refused any material
i assistance offered to himself. **13.** According to Nm 18: 20–32; Dt 12:22–29 priests and levites were to receive their support from the offerings of the people, including a portion of some of the sacrifices. If the ministers of the Old Law were to receive material support from the people, then certainly the ministers of the New Covenant might also receive support. It is perhaps suggested here that the ministers of the New Law, especially the apostles,
j had functions which were specifically cultic. **14.** Cf Lk 10:7, which, however, states that support should be offered to the minister, not necessarily accepted by him. Since Paul did not consider himself in any way disobedient, it is obvious that the command of the Lord referred to here was either the same command or was to be interpreted in the same way; however, it seems implied that ordinarily the ministers of the church were to accept **support from members of the community and thus not to** engage in other activities. Paul, himself, did at times accept such support (cf Phil 4:15).
k 15–27 Reason for Not Using his Rights—15–16. Paul has received a divine calling to preach the gospel; in this he cannot glory since it was given on account of no merit of his; however, his refusal to accept support from the Corinthians is beyond the call of duty. There is a touch of humour in his 'I would rather die than have anyone deprive me of my ground for boasting'. **17–18.** Paul's reward is to preach without recompense. This somewhat

paradoxical statement is also a bit humorous, though **876k** bitingly so. **19–22.** Paul strove continuously to bring **l** as many as possible to Christ. Paul was a free man, a Roman citizen, and as a Christian not subject to the law of sin or to the prescriptions of the Mosaic Law (cf Gal 2:19; Rm 7:4). **23.** 'Partaker' *synkoinōnos*: i.e., with others; Paul desires that others share with him in the good things effected by Jesus. **24.** Examples drawn from sporting life were particularly effective among the Corinthians, who lived in the city which was the site of the Isthmian Games. Every Christian should deny himself, **m** as does Paul, for the crown of glory. **25.** Athletes deny themselves for a small reward; the Christian should therefore be more than willing to do so. **26a.** Paul has a definite goal. **26b–27.** 'I do not box as one beating the air': Paul is not engaged in mere practice; he truly fights. 'I pummel' (RSV) or 'I chastise' (CV): *hypōpiazō* literally means '*I beat in the region beneath the eyes*'. 'The term is technical, but it must have been current' (Osty). 'Subdue **n** it': Perhaps the figure is taken from Greek pugilistic practices: the victorious fighter led his vanquished opponent around as a slave. Paul practises bodily penance so that the body, that part of man from which much sin comes, may be brought under the subjection of virtue.
10:1–13 Lessons from Israel's Past—1–2. 'Our **877a** fathers': Christians are the true sons of Abraham (Gal 3:7; Rm 9:6). 'Under the cloud': The cloud guided the Israelites during the beginnings of the exodus from Egypt (Ex 13:21) and protected them from the heat (Ex 14:19). The crossing of the Red (or Reed) Sea was a great part of the work of deliverance (Ex 14:22). 'Baptized into Moses': i.e., they were intimately united to him to form no longer a conglomeration of tribes but a people; this interpretation is demanded by the use of *eis* before the name of the leader in contrast to the use of *en* before the names of the things. Paul sees the cloud and the crossing of the sea as types of baptism, which unites us to Christ, forming thus the new people of God, while liberating us from the bondage of sin. **3–4a.** 'Spiritual **b** food': the manna (Ex 16:4–35); 'spiritual drink'. the water flowing from the rock (Ex 17:5–6; Nm 20:7–11). In these the apostle sees Eucharistic typology. The gifts given to the Jews are called 'spiritual' because they were prophetic or prefigurative of the Eucharistic food and drink (cf Apoc 11:8 for a similar use of *pneumatikos*). **4b.** 'Allusion to a rabbinic legend according to which the rock from which Moses made water come forth accompanied the Israelites across the desert' (Osty). Perhaps **c** this interpretation is correct, but it rather seems that Paul has somewhat switched the symbolism of the rock, applying now the figure of the rock to the person of Christ, who, though not yet born according to the flesh at the time of the exodus, was the source of the Israelites' deliverance. In the OT the figure of the rock was often used to describe Yahweh (e.g., Dt 32:18; Ps 18 (17):3). **5.** Most of the Jews who left Egypt died in the desert because of a condemnatory judgement of God (Nm 14:16–29); only Caleb and Joshua, of those who left Egypt, were to enter the Promised Land (Nm 26:64*f*). **6.** Notwithstanding the **d** Christian's possession of baptism and the Eucharist, he can suffer loss of the Messianic blessings, just as many of the Israelites lost their chance of entering Canaan. **7.** Here begins an enumeration of some of the sins committed by the Israelites during the journey from Egypt to the Promised Land. Similar sins are to be avoided by Christians during their journey towards their heavenly home. The first sin was that of constructing the golden calf and honouring it; the Scriptural reference is to Ex 32:6, a verse from the description of that event. This **e**

877e citation is one of the many examples which show that Paul often intends that his readers remember a whole context when he cites but a part of it; the citation serves as an *aide-mémoire*. 'To play' means to participate in cultic dances. The names of those who sin will be struck out of the book of life. **8.** The event referred to is related in Nm 25:1—9; the OT gives the number of fallen as 24,000; obviously there is no deviation from the funda-

f mental meaning when round numbers are used. **9.** This event is narrated in Nm 21:5—6; the Jews tempted God by complaining about the hardships which they had to endure during the journey through the desert. The implication is that the Christian must be ready to accept hardship with patience and fortitude. **10.** Nm 16:1—17:3 narrates this event. 'Destroyer' should be written with an initial capital letter, for it is the name of the avenging angel mentioned in connexion with the tenth plague (Ex 12:23), whose name is not mentioned in the actual account of the punishment inflicted on the Egyptians.

g The Israelites who murmured against divinely constituted authority are equated with the Egyptians who opposed God's salvific action on behalf of his people. The Christians are to obey the authorities in the Church. The final age in the history of the world was introduced by the death and resurrection of Jesus. **12—13.** One's assurance in time of temptation comes from God's fidelity to his word, not from one's native powers.

h 14—22 Idolatry and the Eucharist—14—15. In contrast to 4:10, *phronimoi* 'sensible' is used here without pejorative overtones. Christians should flee, not only avoid, idolatry. **16.** Obviously the reference is to the Eucharist. 'The cup of blessing': it is a source of blessing for us. 'We bless': i.e. pronounce a blessing over (it) in imitation of our Lord at the Last Supper (cf 11:25 and comment). 'Partaking of the body': in receiving the Eucharist we are united in union with one another to the sacrificial victim, who is Christ. 'Breaking of the bread' became an almost technical term for the whole Eucharistic

i rite of the bread-body, cf § 790c. The switch of the usual order, body-chalice, may be significant, illustrating that among some the sacrificial aspect of the Eucharist was seen with reference more to the blood than to the body, something apparent in the formulas of consecration found in Mk/Mt when compared to 11:25 and Lk (cf besides Neuenzeit, H. Schürmann, *Der Einsetzungsbericht*, Münster Westf. 1955, 73—133); this would accentuate the covenant notion, which was marked by the blood of a victim (cf Ex 24:8; Zech 9:11; 1 Cor 11:25), while not bringing out the notion of the suffering servant directly (cf Is 52:13—53:12) which is apparently mentioned in

j 11:25/Lk 22:19. **17.** There is but one Eucharist, which makes stronger, and thus in a sense effects, the unity among Christians already brought into existence by baptism; it is also a sign of the unity which exists among members of the Church, who partake of the same victim. **18.** *Israēl kata sarka*, '*Israel according to the flesh*' (DV) 'the Jews of our own day' (Phillips): the physical descendants of Abraham; Christians are the Israel of God (Gal 6:16). RSV 'the practice of Israel' seems to miss this point. Those who partake of a thing sacrificed as sacrificed are united in a special way to the altar of sacrifice and hence to God. **19—20.** Of course an idol is nothing if not a representation of Satan and his minions, for idolatry is sin and hence the work of the devil; thus to partake of a thing sacrificed to an idol as a thing sacrificed to an

k idol is to sin, to enter into communion with Satan. **21.** A true Christian cannot attempt to reconcile the impossible. **22.** To provoke the Lord to jealousy was an OT expression for one of the aspects of sin. It seems that jealousy should

be taken as expressing the exigencies of the divine love, **87** moving him to punish the beloved one who has sinned so that he will become once more the worthy object of God's love (cf S. Lyonnet, *De Peccato et Redemptione* I, Rome 1957, 46—51). To be guilty of idolatry would certainly be an apt way of provoking this divine jealousy. Men do not have the strength of God; thus they should fear his punishment, even though they proceed from God's love. **23—11:1 Practical Directions—23.** 'All things are **87** lawful': cf 6:12. 'Edify': cf 8:1, 10; here the reference would seem to include both the individual Christian and the whole Church. **24.** Charity for others should be primary in the concern of the Christian. **25.** After a thing has reached the market place it is to be considered as profane; thus nothing should prevent a member of the community from buying such meat; this advice explains to what extent one is to explore the possibilities of causing scandal. 'On the ground of conscience': Most **b** take this to mean that in this case a man should not let his conscience be bothered by scruples, with conscience understood as the ethico-religious power of discernment. **26.** The words are from Ps 24 (23):1. In themselves the things of nature are not impure, but are God's workmanship. **27.** 'Conscience' here seems to mean one's awareness. One is not to ask questions which could cause concern when there is no apparent reason for so doing. Obviously the meal in question here is a merely social affair or one which appears to be principally social. **28.** 'Someone': he would seem to be a Christian who would be troubled at seeing a fellow Christian eating with pagans what had been sacrificed to idols. Conscience here **c** means that man's mistaken awareness of the nature of the act. Scandal is to be avoided. **29.** The implied answer to the question is 'for the sake of charity' (cf 8:7—13). **30.** The implied answer to the question is 'because I have caused scandal'. Even if the act is of such a nature that, considered in itself, one could offer thanks to God for reason of one's ability to do it, it should be omitted if scandal would otherwise result. The custom of saying prayers at even ordinary meals is more than implied here. **31—33. d** Everything should be done to bring glory to God; especially should a Christian consider how his example can influence those outside the Church for the good. Paul has shown by his own actions how others should act (cf 9:19—23). **11:1.** 'Imitators of me': cf 4:16; Phil 3:17; 1 Th 1:6; 2 Th 3:7, 9. Christ is to be the model for all.

11:2—14:40 Order in Religious Gatherings—Here the apostle takes note of some things which were occurring during the various gatherings of the community; some of these things were causing scandal; others were causing disorder.

2—16 The Conduct of Women—2. Paul seemingly is **e** not sarcastic here; rather he attempts to gain his audience by telling them that they for the most part observe what he has handed down to them. Undoubtedly he 'reproduces under the form of an encomium an assurance which the Corinthians had given to Paul in the letter which they had addressed to him' (Spicq). **3.** Here we have a schematic presentation of the ideal relationship of mankind to God. Christ as man is subject to the Father; all males are subject to Christ (cf Phil 2:5—11, which contains an early hymn of praise); women are subject to men according to the order of creation (cf Eph 5:22f). Perhaps the part of the v concerning women's role can be understood as being completely valid only under the social conditions of the times. The Gr. allows the interpretation that Paul is **f** concerned directly here with a husband and wife relationship (RSV). **4.** Prophesying means to speak out under the influence of the Holy Ghost to exhort or to edify others;

78f sometimes it includes the forecasting of the future; prophesying is an extraordinary function while praying is an ordinary one. 'Dishonours his head': this can be taken as meaning that the man's own head is dishonoured or Christ is; probably no metaphor is intended. It seems that ordinarily men did not cover their heads in public **g** gatherings in Greece or Italy, soldiers excepted. **5.** Every woman who puts aside the veil denies her dependence vis-à-vis man, or, as seems more likely, her husband. Among the Jews a woman accused of adultery had her head shaved (Nm 5:18); among the Greeks and the Romans no similar practice is known. At Rome certain classes of women, who ordinarily were equated with prostitutes even if they were not truly such, had at certain times to wear their hair quite short; but to what extent such regulations were obeyed is open to question. **h** Corinth was subject to Roman law. However, Paul, whatever may have been the prevailing custom at Corinth when he wrote, evidently considers the actions of the women here under consideration as unbecoming one who is a Christian. In point of fact in the Greek world of the period women were not ordinarily veiled at pagan cultic gatherings. It appears correct to say: 'The Corinthian women had introduced this usage in Christian assemblies contrary to the practice of other places. Paul perhaps would not have had occasion to speak against it if he had not seen in it a dangerous tendency to total emancipation, pursued undoubtedly under the pretext of "evangelical freedom"' (Allo). Perhaps there is some connexion with this v and 7:10. 'Only an unveiled woman would dare to **i** speak in an assembly' seems to be Paul's thought. **G.** A Christian woman must act like a true lady or suffer the consequences. All of the verbs regarding 'a woman' are to be taken as middle forms. **7–9.** Man was made to God's image and likeness directly (Gn 1:27a); woman, being taken from man (Gn 2:20) is directly an image of man (Gn 2:20b, 23) and thus only mediately an image of God. She was created for man as his helpmate. Actually the argument is based in part on an accommodation or something similar, for Gn 1:27 is concerned with the creation of mankind as a species and Gn 1:27b specifically shows that woman is included in what has been created to the **j** image and likeness of God. Paul is using a rabbinic procedure, taking 'man' ('$i\check{s}$) in its more specific sense while in fact it was employed in the passage of Gn to which reference is made in its generic sense. **10.** Woman is to have an *exousian*, literally 'power', on her head, i.e. a symbol of the power to which she as a wife is subject; hence a veil. It has been proposed that the authority symbolized by the veil is that which is given to woman in the church to pray and prophesy (cf v 3); by the veil she in turn does not reflect the glory of her husband (cf M. Hooker, NTS **k** 10 (1963/64) 410–16). 'because of the angels', i.e. those angels that were believed to be present during divine worship (cf J. Fitzmyer in NTS 4 (1957/58), 48–57 for Qumran affinities) 'in the example of the angels who (according to rabbis) veiled themselves also before God Is 6, 2 and who are believed to be present at cult cf 4, 9; Ps 138, 1' (M. Zerwick, *Analysis Philologica NT Graeci*, Rome 1960²). There is no evidence for the opinion that the veil was looked upon at that time as a safeguard against evil spirits or the devil. **11–12.** Man and woman are created to live in close relationship and harmony not only, though especially, in marriage (Gn 2:24) but also **l** in general (Gn 1:27f). According to Gn the first woman was taken from the first man, but each subsequent man is born of a woman. The comparison is such that at first sight it appears to justify the interpretation that the preceding vv are concerned with men and women in general; however, cf 7:39–40 which apparently indicates **8781** that a woman is not bound to the law of a man if she is not married. Here Paul wants to prevent husbands from becoming overbearing in their relationship with their wives (cf also Eph 5:23–33). **14–15.** 'Argument in the Stoic **m** manner, whose value time has enfeebled' (Osty). A male is not to be effeminate; women, especially wives, should not imitate men. **16.** No one is to cause strife in the community. The mildness of the remark only accentuates its coldness.

17–33. The Agape and the Lord's Supper—The **n** agape is treated in vv 17–22; the Eucharist, in vv 23–32; v 33 serves as a conclusion to both sections. It would seem that at Corinth the two celebrations were ordinarily joined together, but Paul insists that less emphasis be given to the *agapē* because of the abuses which have crept in (cf also 5:11). **17–18.** Apparently the subject of the misconduct of some during the cultic meals was not brought up in the letter sent by the Corinthians to the apostle. 'Divisions': as will be seen, these resulted from the lack of charity found in some members of the community. **20.** For some the *agapē*, the meal commemorating **o** the Last Supper, had become for all practical purposes the more important part of the gathering together of the members of the community; thus they did not have proper regard for 'the Lord's Supper', the strictly Eucharistic part of the celebration. The term 'the Lord's Supper' is found only here in the NT. The Eucharistic celebration is here clearly distinguished from the meal proper which preceded it since some of the Corinthians were in no condition to discern the Lord's body and blood when the Eucharistic celebration took place. It seems that normally at that time the fraternal meal, the *agapē*, and the properly Eucharistic celebration were joined together in imitation of what happened at Our Lord's Last Supper. **21.** Instead of sharing their food with the poorer **p** members of the community, some kept all of their food for themselves. This is another indication that one does not become perfect overnight. Some even went so far as to become drunk. Thus a combined rite which should have been a bond of unity among the members of the church had become an occasion of division and of scandal. **22.** 'Church': Is this an indication that the building in which the community gathered was already set apart for divine worship? 'humiliate': The poorer members had nothing to contribute to the feasting of the others.

23–25. 'I received': Paul taught to them what he **879a** himself had been taught, a traditional Eucharistic formula. It is not necessary to take 'from the Lord' as indicating an immediate revelation of the Eucharist given by the risen Jesus to the apostle. 'This is my body': Obviously the subject is identified with the predicate. 'Which is for you': This can be taken to mean that Jesus died for our salvation (Rm 5:6–8; 14:15; 1 Cor 15:3), that he died in our place (Gal 3:13), or that he is given to them; the last interpretation seems most unlikely. Given what seem overtones of Is 52:13–53:12 in the expression, both of the other ideas seem included. Liturgy is often pregnant in its meaning. 'This cup is the new **b** covenant in my blood': The blood of Christ is that which seals the new covenant between God and man, which was foretold in the OT (Jer 31:31). Like the Old Covenant (Ex 24:8), it is a pact in blood, one therefore marked by a sacrifice which is both a sign of the pact and a cause of it, subordinate of course to the primary causality which is God's. 'As often as you drink': This restrictive clause not found with the similar command 'do this in remembrance of me' found with the bread formula suggests the possibility that at times the communicants received only

879c the bread. 'The remark of 1 Cor 11, 25b ... emphasizes the cup. According to Schürmann, the phrase excluded other drinking from the *agapē* connected with the Eucharist and thus betrays a certain anxiety to ward off possible impropriety. It could mean, however, that Paul is emphasizing the necessity of using wine in the Lord's Supper. ...'

d (E. Kilmartin in CBQ 24 (1963), 43.) The Eucharist is a symbolic reenactment of Jesus' sacrificial death and recalls its various aspects. As the eating of the Paschal lamb was a reminder to the Israelites that God had freed them from servitude in Egypt (Ex 12:1–13:9), so the Eucharist recalls to Christians that God had liberated them from slavery to the devil and sin (cf Jn 19:36).

e 26. The previous thought concerning the meaning of the formulas is continued. The announcement is contained in the Eucharistic celebration, the meaning of which is known to the Christians; by their partaking of the Eucharist they show their faith and proclaim its object, namely the meaning of our Lord's salvific death and his resurrection (cf J. Audet in RB 65 (1958), 371–99). 'Until he comes': The rite is to be repeated until Jesus returns at the Parousia; thus the rite also proclaims belief in the second coming of Jesus and in the general resurr-

f ection. 27. The whole Christ is received under either kind alone. 'Or': This is another indication, it seems, that at times participants received but one species. 28. 'Prove himself' *dokimazetō heauton*: i.e. put himself to the test to show to others that he is worthy to partake of the Eucharist; this is shown by the use of an active verb with a reflexive object. The rest of the v seems to mean that if he did not discern the body of the Lord it was due to his being in no condition to do so, hence drunk.

g 30. It is not implied that those who became ill or died were themselves guilty; 'to sleep' is not used in the NT for the death of the impious. 31. If they—note ('we') Paul's nice touch in joining himself to them—had examined their conduct, they would not have suffered such loss and suffering; suffering and death are a result of sin (Gn

h 3:16–19). 33–34. Jude 12, and perhaps 2 Pt 2:13, is also a reaction against abuses in the celebration of the *agapē*. 'About the other things ...': We do not know what they were.

i 12:1–14:40 Charisms and the Overriding Excellence of Charity—From a theological viewpoint this section is most important, especially for the teaching about the Church as body of Christ (12:12–30). The general subject, charisms, is always actual since men endowed with special gifts will never be lacking in the Church.

j 1–11 Charisms, Their Diversity and Unity—1. 'Spiritual gifts': *Pneumatikōn* could also be understood as masculine; however, from the context it is almost certainly neuter (cf especially 14:1ff). 2. The words allude to the violent and orgiastic activities associated with some

k of the Gr. cults. 3. Evidently some thought that *any* extraordinary event was a good thing; this would have resulted from their background of association with mystery cults. But it is inconceivable that the Holy Spirit would move anyone to curse Jesus, just as it is inconceivable that the Holy Spirit would move anyone to curse Jesus, just as it is inconceivable that anyone could come to belief, and continue in that belief, without the

l grace of the same spirit. Thus the statement is an assurance to the Corinthians that their profession of faith comes from God's spirit (cf K. Maly, BZ 10 (1966), 94f). 'Jesus be cursed' lit 'Anathema': Originally it meant a votive offering; in LXX it usually translates *haram*, which can mean either consecrated to or accursed by God;

m in the NT (and later) it has the latter meaning. 4–6. The Trinitarian presentation in the passage seems

impossible to deny (cf B. Schneider in Bib 44 (1963), **87** 358–69). 7. 'for the common good': i.e. for the good of the community. To each, *hekastō* is to be understood as designating those who receive any of the special graces or gifts mentioned in the preceding vv. It does not mean that every member of the community receives one or more of them. 8. 'Wisdom' is the gift of expounding the deepest Christian truths (cf 2:6–13). 'Knowledge' is the faculty of teaching the elements of faith. (These gifts seem to be mentioned in Heb 6:1.) 9. 'Faith' is not theological faith, **n** though it is obviously presupposed; rather it is that which sees that here and now God wishes to work a miracle; it is the 'faith to move mountains' (13:2). 10. 'Prophecy' is the gift of acting as a divine spokesman (cf 11:4). 'Discernment of spirits' is the ability to discern the origin of extraordinary phenomena (cf 14:29). 'Various kinds of tongues' is here the gift of praising God with words unintelligible in themselves when one is under the influence of the Holy Spirit in a more or less ecstatic state; this was the most prized gift in the opinion of many of the Corin- **o** thians (cf 14:1–6, 18, 23, 29) because it most closely approximated to the extraordinary phenomena associated with the Gr. mystery cults. False mysticism is a rather common happening, easily induced in those inclined to hysteria. 'Interpretation of tongues' is the ability to interpret the sounds uttered by those having the gift of tongues.

12–31 The Body of Christ—12. 'So it is with Christ' **88c** (RSV, BJ, CV, WV): actually *Christos* is in the nominative. Recently this expression has become the object of some dispute. The following are some opinions: 'This is exactly the same formula as in Rm 12:4ff, except that the construction is reversed ... to bring into relief the efficacious part played by Christ in the unity of the community ... The human body brings into unity all of its many members; and so also Christ. The clause should continue: So Christ has many members and brings all **b** Christians into the unity of the body ...' (Cerfaux, *Church*, 268). Cerfaux asserts that Paul refers not to the Mystical Body but the risen body of Christ, (similarly J. Reuss in BZ 2 (1958), 109f). The more common exegesis is that 'Christ' here means the risen Jesus and those who believe in him, his members, who are mystically united to him, hence the Church. The difficulty of the **c** latter opinion is that 'body' (*sōma*) cannot be shown to have had collective signification at the time when Paul wrote, save in a few texts where Latin influence can be suspected; in favor of the opinion is the fact that shortly after the close of the apostolic age *sōma* did have a collective meaning (cf J. Havet, 'La Doctrine Paulinienne du "Corpus du Christ"', *Littérature et Théologie Pauliniennes*, Bruges 1960, 206f); perhaps it may be noted that Corinth was a Roman colony. Nevertheless, it may be doubt- **d** ed if there is really as much opposition between the views as is sometimes claimed. No one is claiming that the members of the Church are physically identified with the risen body of Christ. There may be an OT basis, at least a conceptual one, for the use of 'body' here (cf M. Adinolfi in *Studiorum Paulinorum* ..., 333–42). 13. 'Were made to drink': The Spirit is the internal **e** principle of unity in the Church; we have been made to drink of it at baptism. Some see here a reference to Confirmation or to the Eucharist. 17–18. The human body requires members with different functions; so too the Church. In the Church God's free choice determines the offices offered to the various members. 20–21. The parts **f** are mutually dependent. Unless a body can move the area of vision is restricted; without eyes the feet cannot be guided. 22. We do not know which members of the human

30f body are meant here. **23.** Paul regards clothing or covering
g as an 'honour'. **24—25.** Here Paul intends to humiliate
the Corinthians: if they receive more gifts of a charismatic
nature than do others, they have no cause for pride; it is
because they are weaker than others. This may indicate
that in point of fact the special effusions of the Spirit
were rather common in the Corinthian church, and that
some gloried in them. In predicating of God the clothing
of the body, Paul uses a Heb. expression in which secondary causes are ignored. 'have the same care': Here we
h may recall those beautiful words: 'The ear sees in the
eye; the eye hears in the ear. The eye can say the ear hears
for me.' (Aug, *Enarratio in Pss 130*, 7, PL 37, 1707).
Differences in the respective conditions of the various
members of the community can and should make more
manifest the unity that should exist among its members.
28. 'Apostles': the Twelve and Paul; 'prophets': those
i who have the gift of prophecy. 'Miracles' are signs which
lead to faith or confirm the believer in his faith. 'helpers':
those giving themselves to works of charity. 'administrators': those administering the churches. The order
should be noted; the first three constitute something of
a hierarchy; then comes the working of miracles, while
the rest are not ranked. There is nothing to be derived
from this list against the hierarchical order in the Church.
j While in the early apostolic age the organization of the
Church was in a stage of development, it does not follow
that there was not already existing at Corinth some
skeletal ruling organization; moreover, some to the gifts
mentioned here are in fact part of the office of those who
form the actual hierarchical order in the Church, especially
that of bishops, who by sacramental ordination are
teachers with the duty of giving assistance and rulers;
moreover, they share in the prophetic charism. **31.** This
thought is developed in the v to follow.
k 13:1—13 The Supreme Importance of Love—The
theme throughout is that love (charity) is important
for every one and is much more important than any
l charism. **1.** Whatever the speaker says for the good of
others would be belied in a sense by his lack of love for
them. Christianity is a message of love which can only be
effectively preached by those who manifest love for others.
m 3 Philanthropy is not necessarily a sign of true love. It
is not Paul's thought that a person would sacrifice his life
without having charity. **4.** Love bears the shortcomings
of others. **5.** Love allows scope to the beloved's wishes;
he who truly loves does not manifest annoyance at the
idiosyncrasies of the one loved nor resent the beloved's
n good fortune. **6.** He who loves does not relish the misfortune of those whom he loves; he rejoices in their good
fortune. **7.** The true lover does not allow the imperfections
of the beloved to destroy his love; when possible, he interprets the actions of the other in a good light. He even
tolerates harm done to himself by the beloved, hoping
that the latter will be transformed. **8—10.** All our knowledge in this life will pass away because of its imperfection
when we see God face to face. At that time there will be
no need of spokesmen. But love as a fundamental attitude
o will remain. **11—12.** Our knowledge of God on earth is
imperfect. There is no need to dwell at length on the
simile of the mirror, since the apostle's thought is clear.
However, in the ancient mirror the reflection was not as
clear as in our modern ones. **13.** Faith, hope, and love are
not gifts in the same sense that the others are, for these
three are given to all. They remain while the other gifts
will pass away; they are thus a part of the complete
p realization of the eschatological period. Love is the
greatest of these because it already attains to God as he
is and to one's neighbour in God. Faith and hope have

effective meaning when conjoined to love. They remain **880p**
in a perfected state at the consummation of this world
(cf F. Dreyfus in *Studiorum Paulinorum . . .*, 403—13).
14:1—25 Hierarchy of the Charisms in View of the **881a**
Common Good—In particular a comparison is made
between charity and the charisms in the restricted sense,
and then between prophecy and the other charisms. Above
all else the religion of Christ is a religion of love. **1.** As
has been noted, the Corinthians had a predilection for the
gift of tongues. **2.** This gift, of itself, does not contribute **b**
to the well-being of others though it may help the one
who has the gift. **3.** Paul implies that one should desire
those gifts especially which would help others; of these,
prophecy is the most complete. **5.** Paul does not wish to **c**
exclude the exercise of any gift; he wishes them to be
completely satisfied; he realizes that they will not all be
gifted with every charism (cf 12:4—31). **6.** Even Paul,
who is their father in the faith (4:15), will be of no further
good to them if he utters only unintelligible words. **7.** **d**
Music demands a variety of sounds if different times are
to be recognized. **11.** Language is of use for communication only when a knowledge of the same language is shared
by the speaker and the listener. **12.** The desire for extra- **e**
ordinary gifts should be directed to those gifts which
directly benefit others. **13—15.** The gift of tongues does
not even instruct the one so gifted; thus he should ask
God to give him the gift of interpretation so that both
he and others may be benefitted both in mind and heart.
16. A person can only say 'Amen', 'so be it', to what he
understands. He should be thankful that the speaker
or the one who prays has cause to be thankful. **17.** Know- **f**
ing why the other is thankful gives him cause for edification. **19.** 'In Church' *en ekklēsia*: perhaps better 'in a
gathering'. When with others Paul does not desire that
what was given for his consolation be made manifest;
rather his love for others leads him to wish that he be
able to say something useful to them. **20.** The Corinthians **g**
should become mature in their thought and recognize that
the gift of tongues is of little practical importance. **21—25.**
The citation is from Is 28:11—12; Paul quotes in the first
person, whereas it is a third person statement in both
the Heb and LXX; the apostle accommodates it to his
purpose: speaking in tongues may serve as a sign to **h**
unbelievers, namely that Christians are insane. This
statement is directed against a carry-over from the Corinthians' pagan days, for in the Greece of that day religious
mania was considered as something desirable, cf § 630h.
24. Paul's statements in the indicative would be under- **i**
stood by them as showing but a possibility, since Paul
was a prophet and he had not converted all to whom he
had preached, something well known to the Corinthians.
Conversion is effected by prophecy because the hearer
understands what is said.
26—39 Practical Rules Concerning the Use of **j**
Charisms—**26.** The mention of a hymn, better 'a psalm',
seems surprising; apparently some species of prophetic
utterance is meant. Any charismatic manifestation should
tend to edify the other members of the community.
27—28. This is yet another expression of Paul's desire **k**
to counteract their excessive attachment to this gift. It
was not Paul's thought that all prayer should be communal,
much less liturgical. **29.** Not too much of anything was to
be made known on a given occasion. This is a sound
pedagogical approach, perhaps not always followed by
Paul himself. **31.** Prophets have it within their power **l**
to remain silent; they never have an excuse for causing
the disruption of good order. **33a.** 'The golden rule which
has remained dear to the Church' (Osty). God's peace
means lack of discord and disorder. **33b—35.** The

881l reference to the Law is actually to Gn 3:16; this gives yet another indication that Paul was concerned **m** with married women in 11:1—16. There does not seem to be any opposition between what is stated here and in 11:5 (*contra* Osty). **36.** Cf 1:2. **37—38.** If any one dares to contradict Paul's teaching, let him know that his claim to be a prophet is false; he will be ignored by God, i.e. no longer enjoy God's friendship.

n 15:1—58 The Resurrection of Jesus and the General Resurrection—It was not Paul's purpose to construct a defence of the resurrection of Jesus, even though he does give in outline form the argument which is classical: the testimony of knowing and truthful witnesses; he does not descend to particulars, however, for it is given only as an introduction to his teaching concerning the general resurrection of the just, which was denied by some members of the community at Corinth. This teaching complements that given in 1 and 2 Thes.

882a 1—11 The Fact of Christ's Resurrection—**1.** The resurrection of Jesus was contained in Paul's initial teaching to the Corinthians, as it was in the earliest Christian proclamation (cf Ac 2:22—24). **2.** The apostle affirms that there is no uncertainty about what they believe—and it will save them—unless their belief were **b** vain. He goes on to explain. **3—4.** Paul preached to the Corinthians what had been revealed to him on the road to Damascus and what had been taught to him later. The content of this teaching is probably given here in the form of an early credal formula; something of the order of a catechism answer. If this be correct, *logos* (v 2) may indicate a grouping of doctrinal elements in didactic form; and so (v 1) 'in what terms' (RSV, WV) should be taken as meaning 'in what formula', in Gr. the gram- **c** matical construction is an indirect question. 'For our sins': Christ's atoning death is no Pauline invention; this teaching was already contained in the traditional teaching given to him. The OT is referred to generically; among the texts which could have been cited as referring in some way to the death and resurrection of Jesus are Is 52:13—53:12; Ps 17 (16): 9—15; Hos 6:1—3; Jon 2:1—2. **4.** 'On the third day': This appears to have been meant both by Paul and in the original formula as a chronological indication (cf B. Prete in *Studiorum Paulinorum . . .*, 413—31), though some take it as meaning 'but a short time', i.e. that Christ would be 'but a visitor in the house of the dead and not a permanent resident therein' (B. Metzger in JTS 8 (1957), 123; **d** cf J. Dupont in Bib 40 (1959), 7410762). **5—7.** The list of appearances may continue the primitive, i.e. early, credal formula, but it would seem that it is not in the strictest sense a part of it though some continue the formula so as to include 'the Twelve' (cf E. Schweizer in W. Klassen—G. Snyder, *Current Issues in NT Interpretation*, Fs Piper, 1962, 166f); nevertheless it did constitute a formalized portion of Paul's earlier teaching at Corinth. **e** As it stands there is nothing polemical about the list or about what precedes (contrast Ac 2:23f; 3:13ff; 4:10; 5:30; 10:39f; 13:29f); this is an indication that it is a development, or better an adaptation, of the Palestinian proclamation. Given its schematic nature, it seems futile to attempt to relate these appearances to those narrated in the Gospels (but cf E. Bishop in CBQ 18 (1956), **f** 341—4). Notable is the listing of the appearance to Peter first. The Twelve is the technical term for the college of apostles, and thus it is no indication of the number to whom Jesus appeared at a given moment. The mention of a separate apparition to James has led some to believe that this man is not to be identified with any apostle of **g** the same name (but cf 9:5 and comment). **8.** For Paul this appearance was the foundation of his title of apostle **88** (cf also 9:1); there is no good reason for separating this vision from Paul's experience on the road to Damascus (Ac 9:1—9; 22:4—16; 26:9—18). **9.** For Paul's persecuting the nascent Church, cf Ac 7:58—8:1; 9:1f. **10.** Cf 2 Cor 11:5—23; 12:9f. **11.** The tradition preached by Paul and the others is the same. (For the whole question cf Cerfaux, *Christ*, 21—30; C. Martini, *Il Problema della Risurrezione negli Studi Recenti*, Rome 1959, 29—33.)

12—20 Necessary Relationship between the Resur- h rection of Jesus and that of the Faithful—Paul's argument is not that any Christian showed himself sceptical about the fact of the resurrection of Jesus. He argues that anyone who doubts about or denies the possibility of the future resurrection implicitly questions or denies the possibility of the resurrection of Jesus, and consequently of his power to save. Hence no one can call himself a **i** believer and deny or doubt the future general resurrection. **16.** 'Are not raised' is to be understood as referring to the future (cf v 23); *egeirontai* should be translated as a passive, given Paul's usual attribution of the positive act in Christ's resurrection to God the Father. **19.** 'Hope' **j** here means without fulfilment. **20.** He is the first-fruits because he was the first to rise in glory and is thus the promise and the sign of the later fruits—our resurrection—to come. The offering of first-fruits was a means of consecrating an entire harvest to God (cf Rm 11:16; Nm 15:18—21); thus our resurrection is consecrated to God by that of Jesus.

21—28 The Resurrection of the Faithful and the 88 Final Triumph of Christ—**21—22.** Cf Rm 5:12—20. In Paul's antithesis of death and resurrection each is regarded as being caused by two men set in opposition to each other. Death includes the notion of physical death but means more: separation from God of which physical death is a consequence and a sign. The glorious resurrection is a consequence of Christ's saving death and is a sign of its efficacy. All who accept Christ and his teaching **b** will share in the glorious resurrection. Paul uses comparison Adam—Christ again (vv 46—49; Rm 5:12—21). **23.** The general resurrection will take place with the second coming of Christ. Paul is not denying here the resurrection of *all* the dead; he does not speak directly of those who are not in Christ; rather he considers it only from the aspect of faithful Christians. **24.** 'Then' *eita* **c** can also be translated 'afterwards' (DV); logical or temporal sequence can be understood here. 'The end' *to telos* can be taken to mean 'the rest', i.e. non-Christians; *eita* is then temporal in signification. *To telos* can also mean 'finally'; it can mean furthermore 'the end', i.e. the consummation of the old. This last seems preferable; the first interpretation would mention, quite *en passant*, something important; the second would introduce an unusual grammatical construction. If the third interpret- **d** ation is correct, *eita* has logical signification. The consummation of the world is concomitant with the general resurrection of the just (cf 1 Thes 4:13—18). (For the whole question cf J. Leal in VDom 37 (1959) 225—31.) At the end of the world all elements hostile to Christ will have been destroyed and he will be able to present what he has gained to the Father. There is an allusion to Ps 110 (109):1, a messianic Ps (cf Ac 2:34; Eph 1:20; Col 3:1). **26.** With the general resurrection death and all its effects **e** will be finally conquered. **27.** The citation is from Ps 8:7; the introductory formula is implied in the beginning of the explanation. The Ps, a lyric contemplation of Gn 1:26, is applied to Christ in a special sense; that is, he is the most excellent member of mankind. This Ps is **f** associated with Ps 110 (109) in Eph 1:20—22. Clearly

3f God the Father is not made subject to the God-man, who as man is inferior to God. **28.** The reign of Christ in the earthly kingdom, which began to manifest itself at his resurrection and ascension, will cease with the end of the world, which will mark the end of that kingdom; from the moment of the Parousia, Jesus will cease to reign over this world for it will disappear and become part of the **g** heavenly kingdom. Christ as man is subject to God; in the heavenly kingdom as God he is associated with the other persons of the Trinity in the rule of God, for he is God. Thus one can explain the apparent differences between this passage and Eph 6:8–11; Apoc 7:17; 22:1–3. (Cf R. Schnackenburg, *God's Rule . . .*, 284–317.)

h 29–34 Confirmation of the Doctrine—29. Regarding **baptism for the dead** more than forty opinions have been advanced among those who take baptism other than metaphorically; in addition at least twenty other interpretations have been proposed. It should be noted that Paul does not condemn the practice, but uses it as an argument against those who deny the general resurrection. **i** If a distinction can be made in the passage between *hoi nekroi* 'the dead (Christians)' and *nekroi* 'dead persons (in general)', the v may refer to pagans who had themselves baptized in order to be united in the resurrection with their deceased Christian relatives and friends. If there is no resurrection, they have been baptized for the sake only of resting among the dead. (Cf M. Raeder, ZNW 46 (1956), 258–60; J. Jeremias in NTS 2 1955/56), 155f; J. Collins in ThS 17 (1957), 504.) Another opinion is that Paul is asking if we have been baptized only to **j** be among those who die and do not rise again. (Kürzinger, cf also K. Staab in *Studiorum Paulinorum . . .*, 443–50, who shows that this opinion was supported by some of the Greek Fathers and that none of them thought of any type of vicarious baptism.)

Nevertheless many ancient and most modern writers understand this as a vicarious baptism received by baptized Christians on behalf of deceased catechumens. The obvious difficulty is that Paul does not appear to offer any objection to this practice, so prevalent later among heretics. But, as Allo suggests, such a ceremony could be regarded as a symbol or even a sacramental, added to prayers for the dead.

k For other opinions cf B. Foschini in CBQ 12 (1950), 260–276, 13 (1951), 46–78, 172–98, 276–83. **30–32.** Paul refers to his sufferings and tribulations; most take his fighting with beasts as a metaphor. If there be no resurrection, why does he bear such perils and hardships? The concluding words are found in Is 22:13. If there is no resurrection one is foolish to submit to **l** privation and danger. 'fought with beasts'. Some have understood this literally (including Luther and Calvin) and find support for their interpretation in 4:9; 2 Cor 11:23; 2 Tm 4:17 (considered even by P. Harrison as a Pauline statement); but this is improbable since Paul was a Roman citizen. Others interpret the saying as a metaphor describing the apostle's troubles or indecision, cf J. Hunkin ExpT 39 (1927/8), 281f. This is much more likely. Paul was given to using metaphors, cf Tit 1:12; 2 Tm 4:17 for similar ones. But it is hard to determine **m** the exact trouble. It could not have been the tumult caused by the silversmiths because Paul is still at Ephesus, cf 16:8. He is thinking perhaps rather of the troubles with the Jews at the beginning of his evangelization at Ephesus, Ac 19:9; 20:19, (Allo). This interpretation has received some support from the Qumran comm. on Habakkuk 2:17, cf R. Osborne, JBL, 85 (1966), 225–30. **33.** The concluding words are from the play *Thais* by Menander, a Greek playwright of the 4th cent. B.C. The use of these words does not prove that Paul was well- **883m** educated in the classics. The apostle's thought is that **n** even a pagan author teaches that one must be cautious in treating with those who profess evil. In a sense this saying, which is almost an aside, shows how one is to understand 5:9–13 (cf also 2 Cor 6:14—7:1). **34.** Again Paul reacts against those who thought themselves wise amongst the Corinthians.

35–44a The Qualities of the Risen Body—There **884a** is only one difficulty: how will the dead rise? The speculative difficulty raised doubts among members of the Church. Everything else is a particularization of the same difficulty. Paul answers that the resurrection of the bodies of those who die is possible by reason of the infinite power of God. **36.** Cf Jn 12:24. The apostle, as did our Lord, speaks in accordance with popular beliefs: the seed dies that the plant may have life. Is there here a recollection **b** of and a generalization of a saying of Jesus: The Christ had to die that he may rise? We must die in order to rise. 'The oriental mind includes both beginning and end in its purview, seizing the paradoxical element in both cases, the two successive, yet fundamentally differing, situations. It is no mere coincidence that in the Talmud . . ., in Paul . . ., in John (12, 24), in I Clement. . ., the seed is the image of the resurrection, the symbol of mystery of life out of death. The oriental mind sees two wholly **c** different situations: on the one hand the dead seed, on the other, the waving corn-field, there, through the divine creative power, life' (J. Jeremias, *The Parables of Jesus*, 1963, 148). **39–41.** The divine omnipotence is abundantly manifest. God can do even more marvellous things. **43.** The body which died was already subject to putrefaction; the risen body will be incorruptible. **44a.** **d** 'spiritual' because it is completely under the influence of the glorified soul in whom God's Spirit dwells; the body takes on the properties of the soul and hence cannot die. (Much material of interest can be found in J. Guitton, *The Problem of Jesus*, 1955, 120–239; M. Dahl, *The Resurrection of the Body*, 1962, but with reservations; cf, e.g., CBQ 25 (1963), 154f).

44b–50 The Risen Christ is Second Adam, Proto- e type of Those Who Will Rise—44b–45. The apostle continues here the thought contained in 37–38. The spiritual body is no less a body. The first Adam became a *nepeš hayyah* (Gn 2:7), a *psuchē zōsa*; the second Adam who is Christ becomes a cause of our resurrection, of our glorious life. Christ is called the last Adam because in his glorified humanity human-kind has attained the zenith of perfection. This v and the following develop the antithesis already mentioned in 20–21. **46.** While **f** some consider this v difficult, it seems merely to bring out the thought of 37–38: in the present order of salvation—the only one after sin—bodies subject to death must in time precede bodies no longer subject to death. Paul is in no way here writing in the terms of a professional philosopher. First we must share in the mortality of the first Adam before we can share in the immortality of Jesus, the second Adam; we share in the sinful nature of the former before we share in the sinless nature of the latter. **50.** Cf Jn 1:12–13. Only those who share in the life- **g** giving principle which is the Spirit can enjoy a glorious eternal life; 'flesh and blood', human nature with its imperfections and weaknesses, if left to itself, cannot. **51–53 Not All Will Die but All Will Be Trans- h formed—**(Vg, followed by DV, has an incorrect reading here.) There is no denial of the universality of death (v 22; Rm 5:12–13). Although those who are survivors at the time of the second coming of our Lord will not die, there will be in them the guilt of death but the punishment

884h will not be inflicted by God (Aquin, *SumTh*, I II^æ, q. 81, a. 3, ad 1), or, perhaps better, a few exceptions do not detract from the general rule.

i **54—58 Expression of Triumph and the Conclusion—54—55.** The citation is from Hos 13:14 preceded by (in Gr.) five words from Is 25:8. The Isaian section as given approaches the words of LXX, but is closer to the Heb., which LXX mistranslated; however, in Heb. 'God of armies' is the subject and 'death' the object of the sentence. Paul's use accords with the general meaning of the passage, for it treats of God's delivering his people from **j** utter destruction in the Messianic period. The words from Hos only approximate to those found in LXX, which paraphrase the Heb.; however, the words are contained in a comminatory passage. Thus Paul uses them contrary to their original meaning, either as an accommodation or possibly in the sense of fulfillment through opposition: then death could win, but at the resurrection it will be **k** rendered powerless. **56.** It is grammatically possible to hold that 'of death' is an epexegetic genitive in the first part of the v, but this is not possible in the second part. **What is meant is that sin, the manifestation of the power** of death, will be no more at the general resurrection. Law is said to be a power of sin because of itself law does not provide the means for its observance, yet, when it is disobeyed, it makes sins manifest; and thus in a sense law increases sin, renders sin more powerful because sins are made more numerous, sins which are **l** violations of law. Without a law there is no offence, no sin (Rm 7:8; cf also Rm 3:20; 4:15; 5:13, 20; 7:10, 13; Gal 3:19).

m **16:1—24 Conclusion**—A number of secondary matters are treated. The final ch is but an epilogue to the whole epistle and it touches explicitly only a few of the points treated in the body of the letter.

1—4 The Collection—The collection for the members of the Jerusalem church, which is made up of the those who can be called 'saints' *par excellence* by reason of the place in which they are found, the site of the greatest acts in our redemption, was considered of the greatest **n** importance by Paul (cf Gal 2:10; 2 Cor 8—9; Rm 15: 26—28; Ac 24:17). Because of his fears that some among the Corinthians might not trust him, or, perhaps better, because of a fear that the fractious element might use the occasion of the collection to slander him, the apostle orders that their own messengers be used to carry it to Jerusalem with testimonials of their belonging to the **o** Corinthian church. Later Paul was in fact attacked because of his concern for this collection (cf 2 Cor 8:18—24). The apostle does not use the term 'alms' for the collection but rather he calls it a 'grace', a notion which he develops in 2 Cor 9:5—15; it is a favour to the Corinthians. He states that if his missionary labours permit it, he will go to Jerusalem with the agents of the Corinthian **p** community. There can be no doubt that Paul saw in the collection a manifestation of the unity of belief uniting the predominantly Gentile churches outside of Palestine with the Jewish Jerusalem church, a sign of unity notwithstanding their different customs. (For the whole question cf A. Ambrosiano in *Studiorum Paulinorum . . .*, 591—600.)

q **5—12 Paul's Plans**—The Apostle, who is writing from Ephesus, hopes to make a quick journey through Macedonia and then to stay with the Corinthians; this is an expression of his special regard for them. However, he feels that he must remain at least some more weeks in Ephesus, where he hopes to gain many to Christ, a number of enemies notwithstanding. **10—11.** For Timothy cf 4:17. Apparently he had a small company with him.

Timothy was young (1 Tm 4:12) and timid (2 Tm 1:7), **8** qualities not the best for dealing with a number of the members of the Corinthian church. Paul's words about Apollos show that there is no opposition between them, and are a deft way of showing that Apollos in no way countenances the factionalism found in the Corinthian church.

13—24 Final Admonitions and Greetings—13—14. **8** A Christian must be firm in his faith and he must be charitable, i.e. loving towards others. **15—16.** Cf 1:16 for Stephanas. He and his household had given themselves over in a special manner to the service of the community. It is perhaps here stated that Stephanas and other men were ordained ministers of the community. **17.** Stephanas, **b** Fortunatus, and Achaicus were seemingly the bearers of the letter sent to Paul (cf 7:1). Achaicus is a Gr. name; Fortunatus, a Latin one. **18.** This is a nice touch. After berating them he lets the Corinthians realize that he knows that there are many among them who are a cause of joy to him, and that the fact that the three men were able to see their father in God brings joy to them. **19—20.** **c** Ephesus was the capital of the Roman province of Asia. These final salutations are typical of Paul's letters; usual also is the association of others with him in the farewell. It is noteworthy that Sosthenes, named as a co-sender of the letter (1:1) is not mentioned in the final greeting. Aquila and Prisca (or Priscilla, which is the diminutive form of the same name) are among Paul's closest friends (cf Ac 18; Rm 16:3; 2 Tm 4:19). Their names are Latin, **d** though they were Jews. It is evident that their house was either the seat of the Ephesian church or that it constituted an element of it, one of the 'house-churches'. **21.** As a sign that the letter truly came from him the apostle writes a small section in his own hand to serve as a sort of signature. Obviously some among the Corinthians must have known what Paul's own handwriting looked like. It is also clear that, whatever may have been the contribution of Sosthenes to the letter, the thing which really counted was that the letter came from Paul. **22.** Because **e** *philei* is used instead of *agapa* for 'love' many feel that Paul uses here a statement from the Eucharistic liturgy. Even though this interpretation is not certain, it is true that normally Paul used *agapan* instead of *philein* (33 times against 2; in 1 Cor, however, 2 against 1, which makes any conclusion in the present case somewhat tenuous, for a man's style can change). It is surprising **f** to see an epistle so much given over to discourse on fraternal charity closing with a malediction. 'accursed' lit 'Anathema': cf 12:3 (for the verse cf C. Spicq in NT 1 (1956), 200—4). **23.** The Aramaic expression *maranatha* can be read *marana tha* 'Our Lord, come' (cf Apoc 22:20) or *maran atha* 'The Lord comes' or 'has come'. Some see this as a part of the Eucharistic liturgy **g** also: a command that Jesus be present in the Eucharist or a statement that Jesus is present among those gathered for the celebration. It seems that there is no parallel to a Eucharistic understanding in 2 Tm 4:1 (cf C. Moule in NTS 6 (1959/60), 307—10), which seems to be eschatological. It does seem that we are concerned here **h** with Our Lord as Lord, i.e. as God and judge, not only in a Gr. church but in the Palestinian as well, and at a period long antedating any part of the written NT. It is impossible to decide whether the expression is a command or a profession of belief in Christ's redemptive act and its consequences (cf Scr 13 (1961) 24—26). **24.** A beautiful conclusion showing the great **i** affection which Paul, a man of strong emotions, felt for those whom he was instrumental in bringing to Jesus.

2 CORINTHIANS

BY TOMÁS O'CURRAOIN S.P.S.

6a Bibliography—*Commentaries*: E. B. Allo, EtB 1956²; J. Héring, CNT 1958; E. Osty, BJ 1959³; A. Plummer, ICC 1925; C. Spicq, PCSB 1951; R. H. Strachan, 1948; C. S. C. Williams, PC(2) 1962; F. V. Filson, IB 1953; H. D. Wendland, NTD 1954⁶; O. Kuss, RNT 1940; R. P. C. Hanson, Torch 1954; H. Windisch, Meyer, 1924⁹. *Other Literature*: J. Cambier, RF, 1959², E.tr. 1965; A. Feuillet, DBS 36 (1961) 183—95; J. Cambier, 'Le *Critère* Paulinien de l'apostolat en 2 Cor. 12:6s', Bib 43 (1962) 481—518; W. D. Davies, *Paul and Rabbinic Judaism*, 1948; id *Christian Origins and Judaism*, 1962; J. Dupont, 'Le Chrétien, miroir de la gloire divine d'après 2 Cor. 3:18', RB 56 (1949) 392—411; A. Feuillet, 'La demeure céleste et la destinée des Chrétiens' RSR (1956) 161—92, 360—402; K. Prümm, *Diakonia Pneumatos*, 2 vols, 1960, 1962; id 'Die katholische Auslegung von 2 Kor in den letzten vier Jahrzehnten . . .', Bib 31 (1950) 316—45, 459—82; Bib 32 (1951) 1—24; W. Schmithals, *Die Gnosis in Korinth*, Göttingen, 1956; B. Schneider, 'The Meaning of St Paul's Antithesis "The Letter and the Spirit"', CBQ 15 (1953) 163—207; W. G. Kümmel, *Introd to the NT*, 1966. J. A. Fitzmyer, 'Qumran and the Interpolated Paragraph in 2 Cor 6:14:7:1', CBQ 23 (1961) 271—80.

b Authenticity—It was known to Polycarp of Smyrna, quoted by Irenaeus and by name, used by Theophilus of Antioch, Clem. Alex., Tert., named in the Muratori fragment, and accepted by Marcion. Internal evidence points overwhelmingly in the same direction. The innumerable allusions, which are so obscure to us, yet so obviously known to the writer and addressees, the naturalness of the details, the credibility of the autobiographical details, the very complicated situation which is presupposed, are all evidence of genuineness. Above all the relations of thought and diction with other great Pauline epistles of this period, and the manner in which the writer lays bare his soul, exclude the possibility of forgery. It is Paul's epistle par excellence.

Date and Place of writing—The place is Macedonia, cf 2:13; 7:5; 8:1; 9:2—4. The time is the end of Paul's third missionary journey, when he had left Ephesus and 'departed for Macedonia' (Ac 20:1). This missionary journey lasted from A.D. 53 to the beginning of 57, and the composition of this epistle can be placed in the second half of A.D. 57. A very early subscription of the epistle in some MSS gives Philippi as the city in which the letter was written, and this is quite possible. The time-interval between 1 Cor and 2 Cor is more difficult. The vast difference between the states of the Church at Corinth, as suggested by 1 Cor and 2 Cor respectively, seems to demand a relatively long interval—say a year and a half (Jülicher, Allo). This view is supported by the number of events which 2 Cor mentions or hints at as having occurred in the meantime—all of which seems to demand an earlier date for 1 Cor than 57,—at least a year earlier. However, many do not agree.

Intermediate Events, Historical Problems—Any 886c interpretation of 2 Cor depends to a considerable extent on our understanding of the historical situation which led up to it; and our knowledge of this situation must be based entirely on what we can glean from the epistle itself. The difficulty of reconstructing that situation arises from the obscurity of so many of the allusions, so that we are forced to decide, by a balance of probabilities, as to what actually happened. Four problems call for special attention and decision: (1) the 'intermediate letter'; (2) the 'intermediate visit'; (3) the 'grave offence'; (4) the visits of Titus.

1. The 'Intermediate Letter'—Paul mentions in 2:3, **d** 4, 9, and 7:8, 12, that he wrote the Corinthians a letter. The universal opinion until the 19th cent. was that it was 1 Cor; (Chrys said that 2:3—4 referred to 2 Cor). But since then an increasing body of scholars holds that it must be a letter written by Paul between 1 and 2 Cor. The reasons advanced are the terms in which Paul describes this letter: he wrote it 'out of much affliction and anguish of heart and with many tears' (2:4); it was written to test their obedience (2:9); and it caused the addressees such grave pain that Paul for a time regretted having written it (7:8f). Now the letter described in such terms is far removed from 1 Cor, which—though lively, indignant and emotional at times—is a marvellously noble and consoling letter, in which Paul is serenely master of the situation. In addition this letter was written after a change of plans about a voyage (1:23; 2:1—3)—a circumstance which finds no place in 1 Cor; and was written to deal with an 'offence' committed at Corinth which cannot be the case of incest dealt with in 1 Cor 5:1—6 (cf below), and which is in any case no adequate explanation for the writing of 1 Cor. It may be taken as certain then that this severe letter was a distinct letter, written between 1 and 2 Cor; so that Paul wrote four letters to the Corinthians; our two canonical epistles, the one mentioned in 1 Cor 5:9, and this severe 'intermediate letter'. The further problem as to whether this letter has been wholly lost, or whether it, or part of it, is preserved in 2 Cor 10—13, will be discussed in the section on 'Unity'.

2. The 'Intermediate Visit'—The words of Paul in **e** 12:14a and in 13:1a, if they mean anything, mean that Paul had visited the Corinthians twice already; in other words, in addition to his sojourn when he founded the Church, and to the visit which he paid them after this letter, he visited Corinth for some other intermediate period. Chrys was almost alone among ancient and medieval scholars in accepting the reality of this intermediate visit; however, the vast majority of modern scholars accept it as historical. This visit was one of sorrow and humiliation caused by the Christians of Corinth, (cf implications of 12:21; 2:1; 1:23), and cannot therefore be identified with Paul's first sojourn in Corinth which, though begun in weakness (1 Cor 2:3), was a missionary triumph. Paul must have paid a second visit to Corinth, before he wrote

886e 2 Cor. He could have paid this visit only during his third missionary journey, and most likely from Ephesus; and it ought probably to be placed after the writing of 1 Cor, since there is no mention in that letter that Paul had personally witnessed any abuses; (not all would agree). Why he should have gone, or what occurred during that visit, can only be the subject of conjecture, which may be illuminated by e.g. the remark of 10:10, by the adversaries whom we find unmasked in 2 Cor, and by the 'grave offence'.

f 3. **The 'Grave Offence'**—We learn that a member of the Christian community outraged another by some deed (7:12); the offender was a definite individual (2:5—7, 9), though part of the community was not guiltless (2:9). The offence was grave (2:1—4), and it was considered a personal offence against Paul (2:5, 10)—at least as a form of disobedience. Traditionally this fault has been identified with the crime of incest mentioned in 1 Cor 5:1—5; of the ancients only Tertullian disagreed, for his own rigorist reasons. Nowadays it is generally agreed that they cannot be identified. In the first place the 'offence' was chiefly against the person of Paul (2:5—10), whereas the incest was above all a crime against God, and against the honour of the Church—even in the eyes of the Gentiles (cf 1 Cor 5:1ff). Secondly the procedure was different: in the case of the incest, Paul alone in virtue of his apostolic power imposed sentence of excommunication, the community being given no option but to promulgate his sentence; in the case of this 'offence', the community judged, the majority decided (2:6) on a punishment which Paul regarded as sufficient, and in 2 Cor he merely counsels the Church to allow, after another official decision by them, the punishment to cease (2:8, 10). It would be a strange way for Paul to remit the excommunication against the incestuous man; and strange if part of the community were to favour him against Paul, as is implied here (2:6). It seems certain that a quite different offence is in question.

g As to when this grave offence occurred opinions differ: many are of the opinion that Paul was insulted to his face during his intermediate voyage. It is, however, difficult to see how the community would have tolerated this; and it is certainly not in character for Paul to run away from an insult to his apostolic authority. Much more likely the offence occurred in his absence, probably after his intermediate visit, and affected Paul indirectly through some representative of his at Corinth; and it was not repressed firmly enough. It was this, when Paul heard of it, that made him write the 'severe letter'.

4. **Missions of Titus**—The number of these accepted is closely connected with the view taken of the unity of the epistle; they are taken in the order in which they are mentioned. *First Mission* (2:13; 7:6ff; 7:13—15)— Titus appears as the man for delicate negotiations. Paul sent him to Corinth, either as bearer of or at the same time as the 'severe letter' (7:7ff). Once arrived he acted for Paul, studied the situation (7:13; 8:6, 23); he made a favourable impression, and brought the painful affair to a successful conclusion; 7:6ff, 2:5—11 tell of the results of Paul's letter and of Titus' activity. He returned to Paul in Macedonia to tell him of the happy outcome (2:13; 7:6ff).

h *Second Mission, the Collection*—Titus was sent back once more by Paul in company with two others (8:17, 18—23), this time to organize and finish the Collection for the Church at Jerusalem. This collection held a very important place in Paul's thinking and strategy. He mentions it four times: Gal 2:10; 1 Cor 16:1—4; 2 Cor 8, 9: Rm 15:25—27; (cf Ac 24:17). The Church in Jerusalem was in dire economic straits, and to come to its aid was a deeply-felt need of a man of such national **88** piety as Paul. In addition this aid was urged on him by the 'pillars' of the Church (Gal 2:9—10). He had, however, a further reason for insisting on it. Many Judaeo-Christians were violently opposed to his Universalism and to the liberty of Gentile Christians from the Mosaic Law which he preached. He needed therefore to give public proof of the solidarity of the Gentile Christians with the Judaeo-Christians, of their veneration for the stock of Israel. This public manifestation was to consist in the generous contributions of the new Christians for the relief of the poverty of the Jerusalem Church—an ecumenical act to end all dissensions (9:12—14).

At the time of writing of 2 Cor it had become urgent **88** to bring this plan to realization; it had been broached in Galatia, at the beginning of the third missionary journey, urged on the Corinthians (1 Cor 16:1ff; cf Gal 2:10); had been very successful in Macedonia (2 Cor 8:1—7), but had been unduly delayed in the Corinthian Church (cf 8:10—11; 9:2—5). It was now time for Paul to leave for the W Mediterranean (Rm 15:17—19, 23; cf 2 Cor 10:15—16). But first of all Corinth, a rich Church and a key-city of the E Mediterranean must be brought under his control and into harmony with Jerusalem. If he could complete the collection there, and bring from Corinth the massive contributions from all the Churches, this city would stand out as a centre of charity and unity even to the Judaeo-Christians. The failure of the collection there would both slow up the execution and lessen the impact of Paul's strategy.

Accordingly Titus, with two 'brothers', was sent back **b** to Corinth by Paul to complete the collection (8:16—24). Had he already gone back when Paul was writing these lines? The most common opinion is that Titus was still in Paul's company, that the aorists used in these vv are 'epistolary'. If that be true, chh 10—13 can hardly belong to the same letter, due to 12:17—18 (cf below). However the opinion adopted here is that he had already gone back when Paul was writing; he is not mentioned in the salutation (1:1), and the aorists refer to the real past (cf Commentary).

Titus and the 'brother' (of 8:22) are mentioned again in 12:17—18. The view favoured by some [e.g. Plummer, F. F. Bruce in PC (2)] is that this refers to an earlier, first, visit of Titus to Corinth—so that our 'first' and 'second' visits were, respectively, 'second' and 'third' visits; this is in line with the theory that chh 10—13 are the 'severe letter', written prior to chh 1—9 (cf below, 'Unity'). But how explain the mention of the 'brother', which certainly recalls 8:16—24? Moreover 7:13—15 give the impression that Titus had not been acquainted with the Corinthians before his disciplinary visit. Windisch holds that these words were probably written *after* the return of Titus to Paul from this collection—mission; it certainly favours his theory that chh 10—13 are a fifth letter of Paul to the Corinthians (cf below 'Unity'). The opinion adopted here is that Titus is still at Corinth (12:17 'I *have* sent'); the collection has given rise to opposition which Paul has heard about through Titus—and which he repels in the following lines.

By the time that Paul wrote Rm, from Corinth in **c** the winter of 57/58, we gather that the collection had been successful. Rm 15:25—28, 30—32, and Ac 24:17ff tell the sequel—the failure of the strategy, triumph of Paul's enemies.

Unity—Many scholars claim that 2 Cor was not originally one letter, but its unity is questioned in a great variety of ways. It must be pointed out in the first

7c place that there is no support in the textual tradition or in the Fathers for such hypotheses; external evidence entirely supports the unity and integrity of the epistle. Theories that 2 Cor is composite are based wholly on internal evidence. This evidence bears especially on three sections of 2 Cor:
(a) **6:14—7:1**—It breaks the sequence of thought between 6:12—13 and 7:2, so that the thought would run more smoothly if it were omitted. It deals with the problem of paganism—of which there is no question before or after. In addition it has a less Pauline appearance (5 NT hapax legomena occur). It appears to advise the Corinthians to flee contact with paganism, and thus to contradict the advice of Paul in 1 Cor 5:9ff; 10:27ff. There is a marked **similarity to Qumran terminology**. Hence some have suggested that it is an adaptation of an Essene paragraph, cf J. A. Fitzmyer. Others suggest that it is (part of) the precanonical letter of Paul mentioned in 1 Cor 5:9ff,—which caused the misunderstandings which we might expect this text to cause. Windisch suggests that a textual dislocation occurred—he would place the passage after 5:21 or 6:2.

d Against these conjectures stands the unanimous witness of the texts. What is more, this pericope is always found in this same place; it seems odd that a redactor should insert the pre-canonical letter or Essene paragraph precisely where it did not fit; and the notion of textual dislocation presumes too many coincidences e.g. that leaves were used, that the complete section corresponded exactly to the size of the page. Moreover the break with the context is not quite so violent: (1) it can be seen to draw the moral consequences of the doctrine of 5:14—21; (2) Paul wants the Corinthians to be open with him (6:12—13; 7:2), and a major cause of constraint between them is their continuing compromise with paganism (6:14—7:1). The overall style is Pauline enough—the unusual words could result from an unusual topic and emotion. There is no contradiction with 1 Cor 5:9ff—Paul is talking about religious compromises with paganism, not about merely social relations. Finally the existence of Qumran parallels is adduced by other scholars to prove Essene literary influence on Paul. All in all, despite its abruptness, it appears to be in its proper place.

e (b) **8—9** (The Collection)—A number of scholars suggest that ch 9 is a doublet of ch 8, that it was addressed to the Churches of Achaia recommending the collection to them, and that it found its natural place here when the Corpus Paulinum was formed (Semler, Osty in BJ). The reasons advanced are: first, the repetitions in 8:7—15 and 9:6—14, in which the motives for generosity are treated twice and developed differently; secondly, in 9:1 Paul speaks of the collection as if it had not been previously mentioned; thirdly, in 8:1—5 Paul cites the example of the Macedonians to urge the Corinthians to generosity, whereas in 9:1—6 we are told that the Macedonians were aroused to generosity by the example of Achaia. It is suggested that a mere interruption is not sufficient to explain how Paul could write such inconsistent passages in the same letter to the same Church on the same topic.

However, the inconsistencies are more apparent than real: firstly, the motives presented in 8:7ff and 9:6ff are not the same—in fact the latter complement the former. Secondly, these chapters have been badly divided—9:1—5 is not an introduction to a new subject, but an explanation of Paul's action announced in 8:16—24. Third, it is not said in 9:2 that Achaia had been generous—merely that it had made preparations,

and that this had aroused the Macedonians to act; **887e** whereas in 8:1ff the actual generosity of the Macedonians is used to get the Achaians (and Corinthians) beyond the merely preparatory stage. In fact the themes are complementary; and in any case Paul did not separate the small scattered churches of Achaia from the parent Corinthian Church. Finally the whole section has a unity too marked to justify a separation.
(c) **10—13**—The problem of the relation of these chh **f** to the rest of the epistle is much graver. **The sudden change of tone from general confidence and affection to menace is extraordinary.** It is extraordinary from the psychological view-point, because normally one would expect the reproaches and threats to come first, and the conciliatory words to follow; as it is, many claim that the tone of these chh would destroy the good effects of the early chh. They are especially strange as immediately following upon the request for money. In addition a number of logical inconsistencies have been asserted, of such a kind that the reverse order would be logical; e.g. various references in chs 10—13 (10:6; 12:16—17; 13:2, 10 etc) seem to be taken up again in more friendly fashion in chh 1—9 (2:9; 4:2; 7:2; 1:23; 2:3 respectively); and in general the great joy of Paul and his praise (7:4, 14—16; 8:7) give way to reproaches about corruption (12:20—21), about the welcome given to intruders who take away the Corinthians' liberty and money (11:3—4, 20—21). As a result a number of scholars detach chh 10—13 from chh 1—9.

The theory of Hausrath (1870), followed by many **g** others, is that chh 10—13 are the 'severe intermediate' letter', written prior to chh 1—9, and they are Paul's outburst at the height of the crisis; chh 1—9 are the final words of reconciliation. This theory has many points in its favour. However, it is not accepted here; firstly, because there is no allusion in these chh to that which formed at least a main topic of the severe letter—the 'grave offence'; and to suggest that this was omitted when the letters were later joined by a compiler is, in Osty's words, to explain 'obscurum per obscurius'. Secondly, wrath and indignation are primary in these chh rather than anguish and sorrow. Thirdly, it does not really harmonize the logical inconsistencies: e.g. 13:2, 10 deal with a visit to be made soon, while 1:23, 2:3 speak of a letter which Paul wrote in order not to make a visit. There are other reasons given later.

Krenkel, Windisch, Osty (in BJ) have suggested that chh 10—13 are a later letter—the fifth in fact— of Paul, written to the Corinthians after chh 1—9 had been constituted and sent. The harmony reported in chh 1—9 was short-lived, and due to new events—the difficulties encountered by Titus, and the resumption of attacks by the adversaries—Paul sent off this stormy letter to bring the Community finally to heel. This hypothesis has much to support it—especially the progress of events in the epistle, the reference to Titus and the brother in 12:17—18. However it labours under the difficulty that it introduces still another fall from fervour in the Corinthian Community (i.e. between chh 1—9 and 10—13), which must have developed extraordinarily fast. In addition the projected voyage at the end of this supposed letter (12:19—13:10), and the final words of salutation and benediction (13:11—13), go at least as well with the earlier chh as with the last four. They suggest certainly that chh 1—13 are one letter; and if not, what has happened to the end of Paul's fourth letter (chh 1—9), and to the beginning of the 'fifth' letter?

Other, more positive, reasons seem to demand that **h**

887h we accept the integrity of 2 Cor. There is, first, the unanimous evidence of the texts. Secondly, the break between chh 1—9 and 10—13 is not quite so absolute as sometimes asserted; the aims of Paul in writing are to be found consistently all through the epistle: to destroy the opposition of 'some'—whose traits are hinted at all over the epistle, and some of the most marked traits earliest (e.g. 3:1; 3:6, 10; 4:1—5 etc); to vindicate his claim on the community's obedience—the apologia for his apostolic status certainly reaches a climax in chh 10—13, but it is there from the beginning (e.g. 1:12ff; 2:14; 4:1—6; 6:4—10; 5:12, 14; 7:2—4 etc). His aims cannot be assigned exclusively to any one section, they are present all over. Thirdly, if we separate the two parts of the epistle, all these polemical allusions remain in the air: a build-up of tension can be detected, a laying of theological foundations (chh 3—7), which prepare for more precise applications. We can feel that Paul is building up his courage for a difficult venture, so that by the end of ch 7 he has 'perfect confidence' (v 16), and can now attack more difficult and personal matters.

i It seems best then to hold to **the integrity of the epistle**. At the same time it is necessary to allow that the epistle took some time to write. Merely to dictate and write such a long letter took time; and a break should be admitted after ch 7, and after ch 9. And during a long dictation—often interrupted,—Paul would hear more bad news (e.g. 12:17—18), which would cause greater severity in his reproaches. But fundamentally the problem to be faced is the same; it is one epistle.

Sequence of Events—Granted the reliability of the foregoing, the following reconstruction of events leading up to the writing of 2 Cor can be suggested: Paul sent Timothy to Corinth, (there is no evidence that he got there), wrote 1 Cor, which was effective—at least doctrinally. Itinerant preachers arrived in Corinth (cf next section), and soon an underground campaign against Paul's person and authority was in progress. Having heard disquieting reports Paul paid a short unexpected visit to Corinth from Ephesus, found an atmosphere of intrigue and suspicion, and coldness from the Community. He could not stay long, but warned that a future visit (1:15—16) would find him more ready to deal with delinquents (13:2). But his general diplomacy convinced his opponents that he was a man of paper (10:10), and some grave public insult took place—after his departure? When Paul heard of it he cancelled his planned visit (1:15—17, 23), and wrote instead a severe letter (2:1ff) to deal with the affair, sending Titus at the same time to do what he could. Titus dealt with the affair very successfully, the majority of the Community expressed their sorrow for his negligence, and punished the offender (7:7ff). (Did Titus begin to organize the Collection at this time?). But he was not able to come to grips with the intriguers, and aware of the resistance of a minority—who now had added fuel because of Paul's non-appearance and his severe letter—he returned to report to Paul. He had impressed the general community deeply (7:14ff, 8:6ff).

j Paul meantime had left Ephesus (Ac 19:21—20:1), and gone to Troas (2:12). (Did he suffer a deadly attack of illness in Asia at this time? 1:8—11). He was so anxious about the success of Titus' mission that he pushed on into Macedonia (1:16), met Titus (7:5ff) and learnt with great joy the extent of his success. He sent him back with two brethren to complete the Collection (8:6ff, 16ff). He began to write this epistle—to express his confidence in the Community, to rouse it further to deal with delinquents and intruders. But word of the increased **88** activity of the intruders came back from Corinth, even of calumnies occasioned by the Collection (12:17—18); and this possibly decided the all-out attack and total apologia of the last 4 chh.

The Nature of the troubles in Corinth, Paul's 8§ Adversaries—Basically it is Paul himself who is in the dock in 2 Cor. His authority has been called into question because his apostleship has been called in question; but even more because his character has been attacked—his disinterestedness, honesty, courage, humility. He has therefore to defend his good name and re-establish his apostolic authority over the Community. He does this at three levels:

(a) Over the Corinthians as such he demands his rights as a loving father who expects great things from them. **Family misunderstandings** have arisen between them, but the Community is the bride of Christ (11:2). The community has been negligent, however, firstly in not being free from dissensions (12:20), and in not being energetic in dealing with its own sinful members (12:21)—but more especially in its weak tolerance of intriguers (11:19—20), which has resulted in danger to the faith (11:4), and in dishonour to Paul, their father (cf 12:11). But he hopes for much more energy from them in future (10:6, 15; ch 13).

(b) Concerning **bad Christians of the community** **b** Paul speaks with unconcealed menace of how he proposes to deal with them in his forthcoming visit (cf 12:20—13:2; 6:14—7:1). It seems certain that these are moral laxists, libertines, of pagan antecedents, who are still not convinced that all is not permissible to them (12:21; cf 1 Cor 6:12; 10:23). There are clear allusions in 1 Cor to such people, who abuse the Christian freedom of sons by claiming freedom from all moral restraints (cf 1 Cor 6:9ff; chh 8—10). It appears that these 'paganisers', although they do not now publicly profess erroneous doctrines (2 Cor 1:24), have not been reformed in their moral lives at all (12:21).

(c) Far more dangerous is a **group of intruders,** who have invaded Corinth and are **destroying Paul's authority**. Our knowledge of these is based on inferences from what Paul says, but a fairly accurate general picture of them may be drawn. Paul calls them derisively 'superlative apostles' (11:5; 12:11), who claim the title of apostle for themselves (11:15), while refusing it to Paul (12:12). They present themselves as ethnic Hebrews (11:22), 'servants of righteousness' (11:15), 'servants of Christ' (11:23). They came as itinerant teachers with letters of recommendation (3:1), certainly not from the Twelve (there is no hint of this in the epistle), probably from other Churches. They appear as Jewish Christians, but also as Greek-speaking Hellenists—as witness their demands for eloquence (10:10; 11:6). There is no mention of circumcision, but Moses seems to be exalted, and the true spirit of the gospel is veiled from them (chh 3—4).

Probably these were prejudiced against Paul from **c** the beginning, and after arrival in Corinth they intensified their attacks on him, (having discovered Gentile converts practising pagan vices? 12:21). So for them Paul is no apostle, he is a poor preacher; in their character they attack him as a double-dealer (1:17—18), a tyrant when far away (10:8, 10), but a coward who did not dare to show his face now (1:23; 13:2); he ran away from Corinth (2:1; 13:2). The fact that he accepted no support proved that he was no apostle (11:7—9; 12:14), but he obtained it by trickery through his agents (7:2; 12:17—18); did he even embezzle the Collection funds? (8:20—21). Yet

8c he is constantly praising himself and his successes (3:1; 12:1, 17), asserting his authority (4:5); he is out of his mind (5:12—13).

It is no wonder that Paul's authority was gravely compromised, especially in view of the community-leaders' failure to combat such calumnies. **So Paul attacks them mercilessly as ministers of Satan** (11:14—15), fraudulent pedlars (2:17; 4:2), who use their influence like tyrants to maintain themselves (11:12, 20); whose so-called zeal is expended in fields worked by others to take the credit for themselves (10:15—16). They preach 'another Jesus . . . a different spirit . . . a different gospel' (11:4; cf 3:5—10). It is not easy to determine the content of this 'different gospel'; for Plummer they were 'Judaizers who insisted on the Law to an extent which was fatal to Christian freedom' (p.1). But why no mention of circumcision (as in Galatians)? For Allo they are rather Hellenized Judaizers of the Diaspora who preached 'probably a species of Judaeo-pagan-Christian-gnosis' (2 Cor, p. 272), Christians in whom 'the remains of a liberal Judaism became mixed with more or less conscious gnostic tendencies . . .' (op cit, p. 272). For Schmithals (*Die Gnosis in Korinth*, Göttingen, 1956), their doctrine is simply Gnosticism passed through a Jewish filter, and preached as a means of union with Christ. This last seems to force the available evidence too much. The truth probably lies somewhere between the three.

d Finally it may be remarked that all this turmoil presupposes a great deterioration in personal relations between the community and Paul as compared with 1 Cor, where, though moral and doctrinal aberrations were many, Paul was confident of his fatherly control and of their filial submission. He writes his apologia to restore that harmony, and to destroy those who are undermining it. **Theme and Plan**—2 Cor is a very personal and impassioned letter, and it is not easy to provide a cut-and-dried analysis of its contents. However, a theme and single aim of Paul may be detected, namely: the re-establishment over the Church of Corinth of his Apostolic authority which appeared gravely undermined, by regaining their confidence and showing his status as apostle. In the early chh this apologia is more general, proving the apostolic excellence in the light of the Truths of Revelation; later he descends to his particular and personal defence.

e A tripartite division of 2 Cor is provided: *General Apologia*—1:12—7:16, *Collection for the poor of Jerusalem*—8:1—9:15. *Personal and particular Apologia*—10:1—13:10. With an Introduction (1:1—11) and Conclusion, 13:11—13.

f Value of the epistle—Its value lies, first, in the information it gives us about the history of Paul—his evangelization of Troas (2:12—13), his immense labours, his sufferings exterior and interior, his dealings with Christian communities and particularly with the Corinthian crisis. Secondly, the epistle gives us insights into the life and growing pains of the early Church—especially the tensions existing between Jewish and Gentile Christians—, the public aspects (cf 2:6—8; 8:19ff), its public prayer (cf 1:20). Thirdly, it contains important developments of Paul's theology: Jesus is wholly central, and the sufferings and virtues of his earthly life (4:11—12; 1:5—7; 8:9; 10:1) are the model for the apostolic sufferings, through which the power of the risen Christ operates. There are frequent allusions to the role of the Holy Spirit (cf 3:3, 18; 13:14 etc), the Holy Trinity (especially 13:14). There are special details in his eschatological doctrine (5:1—10), on the relation of the old and new Alliance (chh 3 and 4), on the transformation of the

Christian (3:13; 4:16ff; 6:1—10), on the Communion of **888f** Saints (cf 1:1—11), which forms a kind of atmosphere for the epistle. An entire theological vocabulary is waiting to be appreciated—Spirit, Letter, Power, Authority, Glory, Grace, Image etc . . .

Possibly its greatest gift to us is the insight it gives us into Paul himself, and in this it is unique. Paul lays bare his soul in a tumult of conflicting emotions. His richly endowed personality—intellectual, sensitive, visionary, practical, womanly in tenderness and inflexible in decisiveness—is displayed for us as belonging totally to Christ and totally to men.

1:1—2 Address—Paul is apostle by God's special will; **889a** Timothy just one of the brethren, Paul's spiritual son. Addressees: not only the Church at Corinth, but all those holy by vocation in small communities of Achaia; the gospel has spread since Paul's departure. **2.** Wish: objective favour of God (grace), and consequent internal and external peace; source is God our Father and Lord (divine title) Jesus—equality of rank of Father and Jesus.

3—11 Gratitude for a benefit conferred on Paul—**3.** May blessing be given to the God of and Father of Jesus (Creator of his Humanity and Father of the Second Person); he is merciful and source of every kind of 'comfort' (*paraklēsis* recurs as verb and substantive 10 times in 5vv; Paul's emotion expresses itself rhythmically in vv 3—6). This comfort, consolation, gives power to act manfully. **4.** The experience of God given comfort, enables the apostles to comfort, sympathize; and the communion of saints makes all consolation a common possession, Christ. **5.** As the sufferings which Christ suffered overflow into them in their sufferings which complete his (Col 1:24), so by balance of cause the effect they receive a superabundance of consolation through Christ. **6.** Apostles are intermediaries of the divine comfort for Christians—both when they suffer and when they are comforted; and the comfort they communicate 'shows its efficacy' in the endurance by the faithful of the same kind of tribulations as Paul himself suffers. **7.** Paul's confidence is sure, 'for we know' **b** that, as the trials and contradictions of their daily lives in a wholly pagan city are an entry into fellowship with the sufferings of Christ, so there is a common sharing of the comfort brought by Christ. This solidarity makes for full intimacy between Paul and his Corinthians. **8.** Makes his motive of thanks more precise, at the same time appealing for sympathy, by recalling the intensity of his affliction. It was a determinate trial, known to the Corinthians as having occurred in Asia, (province in which Ephesus situated); he stresses its intensity—death seemed the inevitable outcome. **9.** 'We had received' the judicial response of death. Allo says an acute, apparently mortal, attack of a grave malady with permanent effects is in question; Paul is preoccupied with his physical state and with death in 2 Cor (cf chh 4, 5; 12:7—10). Others speak of a continual persecution, e.g. by Jews of Ephesus,—or refer to 1 Cor 15:32, Ac 19—20. However, suffering has another purpose—to teach us our helplessness, and to trust in God only, 'who raises the dead'. **11.** Paul lays down a condition whose obscurity possibly reflects his anxiety about the Corinthians; the text has many variants, but the general sense is that Paul counts on their prayers for his continued deliverance from death—an act of faith in the communion of saints and the power of prayer.

1:12—7:16. *Part One* **general apologia**

12—14. These vv form a transition to his aim—to **c** establish perfect mutual understanding. His title to glory and claim on their sympathy is the testimony which his

889c conscience gives of the sincerity of his conduct towards them especially. He feels the need to stress this, for his letters have been accused of double meaning. He has learnt (from Titus?) that the Community knows in a certain measure what he is; he hopes that with this letter they will come to know 'fully' that he is someone they can be proud of, just as he is sure they will provide him with matter for pride at the Last Day.

15–23 Change of plan of voyage was not due to fickleness but to consideration—15–16. With this assurance of mutual trust he had resolved upon a voyage, first of all to Corinth, thence to Macedonia, and back 'again' to Corinth—as a second mark of his consideration and esteem; (this is not the same plan of voyage as that given in 1 Cor 16:5–18, but a second plan—made known to the Corinthians). He did not fulfil it. **17.** He has obviously been accused of duplicity and

d inconstancy because of the change of plans. **18.** His answer is to strike for the summits: God's fidelity is the guarantee and source of the apostles' constancy. **19–20.** For this faithful God's Son, preached by the authoritative preachers, is no Christ of compromise, he is definitive, permanent—'yes' has been realized in him. He is God's affirmation to man's highest hopes, the fulfilment (i.e. the 'yes') of all God's Promises. As a parenthesis Paul explains that this is why in the liturgy, it is through Christ that 'Amen' (= yes, perfect confidence of realization) is said by the people to God; and our confidence of being heard gives glory to the Father. **21–22.** It is this God who strengthens the apostles continually so as to remain always in Christ; to ensure that constancy he 'anointed' them (once for all consecration), 'sealed' them as Christians as a further security, and gave the Holy Spirit as a first instalment, earnest of final glory, to be in their hearts. A clear reference to the Trinity, and probably to rites connected with baptism and confirmation. At any rate all these things guarantee constancy.

23. His true reason for not coming 'once more, (any more)' was consideration for them. He wanted to give them time to be reconciled; if he had gone, he would have had to adopt a painful course of action.

e **1:24–2:11 Paul's motives in the 'severe letter' and the 'grave offence', and final counsels—24.** It was not in the matter of the faith that Paul has to exercise his authority over them; from that point of view 'you stand firm'. **2:1.** How then was he considerate? 'I made up my mind', definitively and with no levity, for his own benefit, 'not to make you another painful visit'; this appears as the preferable meaning, due to the order of the words, and other passages (cf 12:21). The first allusion to a painful, intermediate visit. Others read: 'not to go to you again, (this time) in sorrow' i.e. the first time was the foundation voyage. **2.** The principal anguish would have been Paul's own; he would have saddened the only ones who could cheer him. **3.** So instead he wrote as he did; i.e. the intermediate letter. Convinced as he was about their community of sentiments, he decided that the letter would expose them to less danger of estrangement than a personal meeting in such conditions. **5.** In the next three vv is a definitive ironing out of misunderstandings. 'Someone' (whom there is no need to name) caused trouble, (the grave offence—cf. Intrdn.— which gave rise to Paul's letter) not only to Paul, but to the whole community, (Paul has learnt this from Titus, cf 7:7, 12ff). **6–7.** On receipt of Paul's letter, after deliberation, the majority of the Community inflicted a severe punishment; it appears that a minority was opposed to this. We gather too that the guilty one repented

and submitted. So Paul expresses the opinion that the **88** punishment was sufficient. So he counsels indulgence for the man, but an implication of displeasure for the minority; (Plummer interprets differently). **8.** Paul f had not made the first decision, (as he did in the case of the incestuous man, 1 Cor 5:1–5); so now he merely invites them to restore the man officially to the communion of the Church. **9–11.** He had written to test the quality of their obedience; now that this had been proved by their communal action against the person, there is no need for further punishment. Satan might gain an entry if they denied charity. Paul feels himself at grips with the adversary in 2 Cor (cf 4:3–4; 6:15; 11:3); 'for we are not ignorant of his designs'— is Paul thinking of the false apostles (11:3; 11:13–15)?

2:12–17 Experiences in Asia and Macedonia; God's triumphs in his apostolic instruments—Troas (in NW Asia Minor, N of Ephesus, a few miles S of ancient Troy). **13.** Paul experienced no relaxation in his soul because (causal dative) he did not meet Titus, who had been sent to Corinth to deal with the painful affairs there (cf 7:5–7, and Introdn.). So, tormented, Paul bade good-bye to the rich possibilities, and went on to meet him in Macedonia—such was his solicitude for the Church of Corinth. **14.** The thought of the result over- g whelms him with gratitude to God who, like an emperor in a Roman procession 'leads' the apostles like captives 'around in his triumph'; like captives they are publicly exposed 'in the Christ' (a phrase, occurring 50 times in Paul, which expresses for him the essence of the gospel). They are the instruments by whose preaching God spreads abroad everywhere that perfume (like the incense during the triumphal parade?) which is the knowledge of Christ. **15.** In doing so, the apostles are 'the aroma of Christ' (i.e. a sacrifice pleasing) to God; and no one can be indifferent. **16.** For the believers, who are on the road to salvation, the perfume of the preaching vivifies, and intensifies that life; for those who are on the road to perdition, who prefer darkness and death (Jn 3:20–21), the preaching drives deeper into evil and death. Paul fires off an abrupt question: whose capacity is proportionate to such responsibilities of the apostolic ministry? **17.** The answer, given in 3:5–6, is implied here—'we are'—for Paul speaks as member of Christ, under the gaze of God, the word which is the gospel of God, out of that sincerity and divine inspiration which authenticates; he and his fellow-workers are not like 'those many' who are adulterating that word with outworn Jewish or with Gnostic elements. The polemic has begun, and the section which follows—3:1–6:10—is a glorification of the splendour of the apostolic ministry, of which Paul is authentic representative, (cf Plan).

3:1–3 The Corinthian Church is his letter of re- 89 commendation—1. The false evangelists obviously reproached him for attaching too much importance to himself; 'as some do'—a disdainful allusion to the strangers who have come to Corinth with such letters, obtained probably from other Christian communities (cf Ac 18:27). **2.** But Paul needs no such letters; he carries one everywhere which all men can read, namely the existence of a strong Christian community in the corrupt city of Corinth, which guarantees Paul more than any letter. **3.** It is manifest to all that Christ furnished this letter through the authentic ministry of Paul; and the content of this letter is their faith in Christ graven by the Spirit of God on their hearts. Again there is reference to the Trinity; and there is a clear recalling of the Old Alliance (Ex 24:12), and the New (Jer 31:33; Ezek

0a 23:26), the contrast between which will furnish the theme for the following pericopes.

b **3:4—11 God alone made Paul capable of such a ministry of the Spirit, which far outshines the ancient ministry of the Letter— 5.** God alone (El Shaddai, in popular false etymology the 'Sufficient Being'? cf Ru 1:20; Jb 21:15ff), has chosen, and has of course 'made us sufficient' so as to be ministers of a new *kainē*—new and superior to the old) Covenant. This Covenant is characterized by the Holy Spirit, who is active in it. It is not limited to a written code, such as the decalogue, which could remain external. Such a code without the Spirit is ineffectual, because it commands and forbids, without giving the power to accomplish; it kills because it makes conscious of evil, without enabling to do good. But the Spirit, who informs the new convenant ministered by Paul, vivifies, transforms men, makes them live the new order of things. **7—11.** He develops an argument *a fortiori* in three stages: the dispensation confided to Moses 'came' in such glory (Ex 34:29—35) that his very features were physically illuminated, and the people were unable to gaze at him, on account of this physical glory which was indeed already gradually disappearing. **9.** If God marked with such glory a ministry which, apart from the New Alliance which it prepared, was a dispensation of death and condemnation, (cf Rm 7:1ff), external, instituted in letters and engraved on stones, and which was transitory,—much more would the dispensation, which has the Holy Spirit for its principle be attended by (v 8) eschatological glory; the ministry which is a communication of righteousness, of life in a new creation, the permanent gospel which is and shall be in glory. **10.** The affirmation is intensified: the dispensation of Moses, which has been glorified 'to the extent mentioned above, cannot be said to have any glory in the light of the supereminent glory of the new covenant. The ministry of the gospel is the ministry of glory, with which the old cannot compare.

c **3:12—4:6 Bold freedom and sincerity are the duty of the ministers of the New Dispensation—** The possession of such a hope (in the eschatological permanence of the gospel glory, vv 8—11) inspires great boldness and frankness in speaking to men, by contrast with Moses. Ex 34:33—35 says that Moses, having delivered his message, veiled his face until he next went to talk with God. His intention was to hide the glorious irradiation of his face; but in reality, interprets Paul, what he hid from the Israelites was the gradual extinction of the illumination. The evanescence of the glory on Moses' face is a symbol of the transience of the Old Dispensation, and the veil on his face a symbol of the concealment of this transience. **14—15.** In the Jewish assemblies, where Moses is still speaking to them, the 'same veil' remains,—now on their hearts—during (or 'as to the meaning of') the reading of the ancient covenant, 'it not being revealed' (absolute accusative) to them that this ancient alliance has been absorbed in Christ and in his definitive Revelation. **16.** Paul varies the words of Ex 34:34 (LXX) to make the physical act of Moses the type of the hoped-for interior conversion of the Jews: as often as Moses went in to Yahweh he took off the veil; likewise, if any Jew is converted internally to the Lord (*ho Kurios*), the Source of the Law, then the veil is taken away from his heart, (and he will recognise that the old alliance

d has been absorbed in Christ, v 14c). **17.** Now who is that 'Lord' of whom Exodus is speaking? He is the Holy Spirit (*to Pneuma*), of whom Paul has been speaking in 3:3, 6, 8. And he is the Spirit of Christ our Liberator, he is the Spirit of Revelation, and therefore whoever turns

to him shall see the Truth unveiled, and the Truth shall **890d** set him free—especially, in the context, from the slavery of the Law (cf 3:7—11). [This verse has received innumerable interpretations; cf K. Prümm, S. J., 'Die Katholische Auslegung von 2 Kor 3:17a . . .' in the Bibliography, for a summary. His interpretation, that of many Greek Fathers, is followed here. Allo takes 'Lord' in 16—17a to be Christ, and the 'Spirit' of 17a to be the divine sense of the Scriptures, which vivifies the letter.] **18.** Concludes exultantly: there is no veil to hide Christ from us believers, the true Israel, or to hide us from men; for with faces unveiled we contemplate Christ, and 'reflect like a mirror' the Glory of the Son of God, which excels that of Moses. So we are being continually transformed into the image of Christ (who is the Image of God 4:5). This divinization cannot fail, for it takes place under the action of the Spirit of the Lord Christ, to whom such transforming efficiency is proper.

4:1—6 Paul's fidelity to the Ministry committed to **e** **him—**Takes up the thought of 3:12: having by God's Mercy been made competent for such a ministry, he does not yield to defeatism; he has renounced once for all any false shame which would hide part of the message, all unscrupulous behaviour, or any fallacious interpretations of the word of God. There may be such people at Corinth, but Paul is not like them. **3—4.** To some his gospel is hidden (cf 3:14ff),—to those on the way of perdition— whom the 'god of this world' (cf Jn 12:31), Satan, the usurper, maintains in the blindness of their thoughts, to which their own culpable infidelity has led them. As a result the luminous radiance from the gospel which unveils the Glory of Christ, as the Perfect Image of the Father (cf Col 1:15), does not shine out for them. There is then a superhuman factor, as well as a culpable human one, in their blindness. But especially to be noted is the consubstantiality with the Father of Christ in his Divinity expressed in the terms 'Glory' and 'Image' (RSV 'likeness'). **5.** (Cf 1 Cor 3:22; 9:19—22). **6.** The preachers are **f** nothing, it is God who uses them as heralds. He who in Creation commanded light to shine out from the dark (Is 9:1), has shone out in their hearts (and Paul's particularly, cf Gal 1:15—16; Ac 26:13, 18), so that the knowledge grew lightsome in them of that Glory of God (the Father) which was made visible in the face and Person of Christ (i.e. the knowledge in faith of Christ as Incarnate Son of God—which is the foundation of christian transformation, cf 3:18). The glory in his face exceeds and absorbs the reflected glory of Moses and the Law.

4:7—15 Supernatural Significance of the apostolic **g** **sufferings —**This divine illuminating glory has been entrusted by God to beings so fragile that their surpassing efficiency is a positive proof that the power of God is active in them. **8—9.** Paul describes rhythmically the misery of their lives,—probably using the imagery of the chase: *'pressed upon, but not ferreted out; deprived of a way, but not entirely without escape; pursued, but not headed off; grounded but not lost utterly.'* **10.** Their vocation is to suffer in order to re-enact in the world the 'putting to death' of Jesus—i.e. all his trials ending in his Death; but this occurs in order that Christ who lives gloriously forever may manifest simultaneously his power to save them so that they can accomplish their mission to the end. **12.** Sums up the sense of the spectacle presented by the apostles; death operates in them to assimilate them perfectly to Christ; but the life of Christ which they reproduce is poured out more intensely on the hearers. The doctrine of the Communion of saints is here in its fulness. **13.** Such a life demands

890g a living faith: Paul's faith in the action of Christ in him is that of the Spirit who inspired the psalmist in Ps 116:10 (Ps 115:1 LXX version quoted); because of his faith he does not fear to speak out boldly.

891a **4:16—5:10 The Attitude of the Christian to Death**—Paul allays the fear of death by affirming the certainty of bodily resurrection, and the union of the **b** separated soul with Christ. **18.** The source of this courage is the glimpse which faith gives of the future goal, invisible but already virtually attained; this glimpse closes our eyes to present misery which is but a fleeting shadow. **5:1.** Even if the present 'psychic' body be gradually dissolved—this earthly dwelling which is but a tent, and like a tent movable—'we know' certainly (as he told them in 1 Cor 15) that we have hold by hope on an indestructible dwelling—the 'spiritual body' which God's Omnipotence prepares for our heavenly state. **2—5.** Present immense problems of interpretation; one interpretation only can be presented here. The Christian existence and Christian virtues receive their ultimate crowning at the Parousia. Paul places himself in the ranks of Christians (first person plural), for whom the natural fear of death is opposed by the desire for the Parousia before their death—an event which is certain (cf 1 Cor 15:51ff; 1 Thess 4:17), but which may not be verified in the case of many Christians. The mortal body is imaged as tent, garment, exile; the soul is 'clothed with' (*enduō*) the body; death is an 'unclothing' (*ekduō*) by which the soul is left 'naked'; those still alive at the Parousia will be 'over-clothed' (*ependuō*) with the glorious body. **c** (Cf K. Prümm). **2.** The firmness of our hope (cf v 1) finds expression in our ardent desire for the Parousia (Rm 8:23) in which we may be 'overclothed' with our heavenly habitation, i.e. put on directly our glorious body without dying. **3.** At least if (*ei ge*) it be our destiny to put on the glorious body over our mortal body (*kai*), which will be verified only if we are found alive (clothed) at the Parousia, and are not dead (naked). (This verse is variously interpreted: Allo understands concessively 'although assuredly' we ought not to fear such a transitory state, for we shall certainly put on a glorious body at the Last Day, and shall not be left bodiless forever. Others—Menzies, Plummer,—as a conditional affirmation; sure that this putting on of it will secure us from being found at Christ's coming without any house at all.) Spicq (PCSB), Prümm, Cornely favour the first, adopted here. **4.** A deeper reason for our desire for the Parousia is our will to avoid death; we will our mortal frame to be swallowed up by the life of glory without dying. **5.** It is God who inspires this desire for avoiding death, and for the Parousia—(a good desire therefore, possible though not certain of fulfilment for us); and he has given us the Holy Spirit as first instalment (Rm 8:23) to dwell in us and spiritualize us. **6—8.** Changes to individual eschatology. Having the Holy Spirit, our whole desire is for union with Christ, to which life in this body is an obstacle. The metaphor now is of the voyager far from his destined home. **8.** So between death and resurrection of the body the separated soul possesses essential beatitude with Christ, Phil 1:21—23. **9.** Paul draws the moral conclusion. **10.** For all—those still alive at the Parousia, those already dead,—must be manifested before the judgement-seat of Christ, who is God; and then the existence and extent of our union with him will be seen to be the due recompense for what each has done, good or evil, during bodily life. (Universal Judgement, and recompense according to works done in this life).

d **5:11—21 The Redemptive Incarnation is the**

Ultimate Root of the Apostolic Ministry—The **89** thought of the judgement (above) arouses a fear of the Lord which keeps him from straying, even when he has to use diplomacy. His sincerity is clear to God, whom alone he wishes to please; he hopes it is equally apparent to his readers. **12.** He defends himself once more against the accusation that he is always commending himself (3:1); the aim of his apologia is the profit of the Corinthians, so that they can answer the hypocritical pretensions of Paul's critics, by explaining—as they should have done already—that the basis of their glorying is their experience of Paul (cf 11:15ff). **13.** There is no selfishness: his whole life is covered by his zeal for God and for his converts; his enthusiasm and transports, (which have aroused accusations of insanity? cf Ac 26:24), are between him and God; his prudent daily teaching is for the benefit of his converts. **14—15.** The theological foundation for his selflessness: Christ's love in him possesses and controls him, since first, having visioned the Truth on the road to Damascus, he decided once for all that One Man, Christ, underwent death as representative of the human race, so that in Law all died; and that he rose to a glorious life so that all men might live that life effectively, and no longer be enslaved to egoism (Gal 2:20 6:14; Rm 6:6—12). **16—17.** In the past Paul may have evaluated the historical Christ in a human fashion (i.e. before Damascus he judged Jesus a Messianic pretender, a condemned and accursed failure); but what counts now is the knowledge of and union with the Risen Son of God, whose life we live. **18—19.** God is **e** the Source of this new order of creation. **21.** This reconciliation is possible and urgent because for our profit God made the man, Christ, who had no personal experience of sin, to be the very personification and carrier of sin, and treated him as such (Gal 3:13); in virtue of the solidarity of Christ and humanity, when he was killed, sin (our sin) was killed; and the aim was that the Justice of God which was in him might be communicated to us by our union with him. He became our sin to die; so that we acquire his holiness.

6:1—10 Life of the ambassadors of reconciliation, f human weakness and divine power—**1.** Paul is afraid of infidelity among his Corinthians. **2.** In a parenthesis, which reinforces his appeal from the OT, he emphasizes that the favourable time of universal redemption promised by God to his servant in Is 49:3 is now—these last messianic days which began with the redemptive work of Christ; and these days are short. **3—4a.** His co-operation (v 1) is described: *negatively*—he acts in such a way that no man of good faith has any reason to be scandalized, or find fault with his behaviour; *positively*—the fact that in every circumstance he acts as befits a minister of God is recommendation enough of his authenticity. **4b—10.** Paul describes all that the apostles have to endure as Christ's ambassadors, in a masterly lyrical passage, in which rhythm, balance, assonance, alliteration, antithesis, abound: (1) **4b—5 g** deal with their abundant endurance, shown in nine situations—three general situations; three inflicted by hostile men; three in part self-imposed for the sake of the mission. (2) **6—7a** describe the interior gifts by which the apostles endure and conquer—whence result preaching of the Truth in loyalty to the Revelation, and the divine power which guarantees success. (3) **7b—8a.** He acts as befits an apostle during attack ('the right hand'), or in defending himself ('the left') in circumstances of honour or ignominy, of ill-repute or good-repute. (4) **8b—10.** Finally in seven antithetical pairs Paul ironically opposes the opinions people have of him to what he is in reality.

1g It is the paradox of divine strength in human weakness, summed up at the end; despised as having nothing— but in fact the absence of possessions frees him to master the whole world for Christ; above all he possesses God, and in him everything (cf 2:17; 1 Cor 3:22). Such is Paul, the authentic minister, as the Corinthians can see for themselves.

h 6:11—7:4 Appeal for return of affection—11—13. He has revealed himself frankly; his heart is open wide in love for them. But they are restricted and reserved in their affection for him. Let them respond. **6:14—7:1** arrive abruptly (cf § 887c), but they fit in to the general context as revealing a major cause of the coolness which has risen between the Corinthians and Paul; in this pagan city many Christians desire more accommodations with the pagan world. He refuted in 1 Cor the theoretical basis of these compromises—the appeal to Christian liberty (cf 1 Cor 6:12ff, 9:1ff, 11:23ff); but the practical danger of repaganization remains. He commands these 'libertines' of Corinth not to 'become mismated' i.e. have moral community with paganism, which is incompatible with membership of Christ. As proof he cites Lev 26:12, Ezek 37:27. So he commands the libertines in the words of Jer 51:45 'come out from them' (v 17), i.e. from the demoralizing contact with paganism. The attempt to efface the distinction between Christian and pagan in daily life is disastrous. Paul does not forbid all contact with pagans, (cf 1 Cor 5:9ff; Eph 5:11), but rather religious or moral fellowship with paganism, whose morals are dominated by Satan. **10.** Only thus will they be God's sons, (Paul, quoting Is 43:6, adds 'and daughters', indicating the evangelical care to raise the moral and religious status of women, who were in such danger in Corinth).

i 7:1. He appeals to these 'beloved' sinners. **2.** He returns to his plea of 6:11—13; and he alludes for the first time to calumnies which must have been current in Corinth against his disinterestedness (to which he will return).

2a 7:5—16 Mutual confidence re-established by the Mission of Titus—5—6. Even after his arrival in Macedonia (cf 2:12—13, to which he returns after his long 'digression'), his suffering humanity had no repose: conflicts against pagans and hostile Jews; internal fears about the success of Titus' mission. **8—10** take up gingerly the affair of 'that letter' again, (the 'intermediate letter', cf § 886d, and 2:3, 4, 9). The letter caused pain; and Paul had had misgivings about its effect; but now he is reassured. Godly grief produces a salutary repentance which one does not regret, whereas worldly discouragement produces only self-pity and despair which may end in **b** spiritual death. **11.** Paul, overjoyed, seems to exaggerate their merits—earnestness in setting things right, eagerness to exculpate themselves, indignation at the hurt done to the Church, fear of God's judgement and Paul's anger, desire to renew relations with him, zeal in condemning the wrong, requital for the offence. He assures them they have done everything to establish themselves, that they are now free from all complicity 'in the matter' (the 'grave offence'—cf Introdn., and 2:5, 7, 12). In fact their 'self-exculpation' and 'fear' show that they had not been innocent—there had at least been passive complicity by tolerating the outrage. **12—13.** So Paul wrote the 'intermediate letter', not vengefully, but in full consciousness of his responsibility to them before God, in order that their own real sentiments towards him, which had been partly obscured, might become plain to themselves (cf 2:9). All this had brought him consolation. **13bff.** Paul comes back to speak of Titus, to recommend him

warmly in view of his new mission (cf 8). **14.** It would **892b** appear that Titus had not been to Corinth previously, and Paul, sending him on the repressive errand, had encouraged him by boasting of the many good qualities of the Corinthians; (the troubles then were due more to unthinking tolerance than to rebelliousness). **15.** He **c** stresses Titus' special affection for the Corinthians in order to make it easier for him to complete his new task among them (cf 8:16—17). **16** concludes the first part of the epistle, and appears to provide a springboard for the two major offensives which follow; the Collection (8—9); the polemic against disturbers (10—13). Paul presumes that the reconciliation with the Community as such is complete. Without all the previous apologia and expressions of esteem, the hard things which he is about to write might not be accepted submissively.

8:1—9:15. *Part Two.* **Collection for the Poor at Jerusalem.** (Cf Introdn. for discussion on unity, Pauline strategy, and missions of Titus.) The whole can be divided into three sections:

8:1—15 Paul arouses them to emulate the example d of the Macedonians' generosity—In his new-found courage (7:16) he draws their attention to the effects of the 'grace of God' displayed, even yet, in the Churches of Macedonia: **3—5.** The generosity of the Macedonians (cf 1 Thes 4:9ff; 2 Thes 3:13; Phil passim), was shown in that voluntarily, they contributed even beyond their means; and when Paul had not asked them due to their poverty, (probably temporary, due to persecutions,) to contribute, they begged earnestly 'the favour of taking part (hendiadys) in the service' of the Christian brethren at Jerusalem by their alms; and even more they offered their services, to help Paul accomplish the task of collecting. **6.** 'as he had already made a beginning' (by his pacification of the Corinthian Church? or by collecting in other regions? or by collecting in Corinth? the first seems more likely). **7.** A second motive for being generous: as the Corinthians excel in so many ways, he hopes they will excel in generosity in giving also (they are obviously lacking in it). **9.** A third motive, introduced casually, **e** is the supreme and pressing 'graciousness' of Christ. **10.** Paul is therefore giving 'advice', not commanding; such a procedure 'accords with' the dispositions of such as the Corinthians, for even 'since last year' they were ahead of Paul's formal invitation, not only in acting (which has ceased) but in intending to give alms (which will-act still presumably continues). **12—13.** No **f** community can be expected to reduce itself to poverty in order to provide easy living for others. **14—15.** The aim is to achieve equality, of a real though proportionate kind, as Ex 16:18 shows to be the intention of Providence; the sharing of material goods with the Christians of Jerusalem will merit increased sharing of spiritual goods, of which the latter have a primary share.

8:16—9:5 Paul recommends Titus and two other approved delegates—16—17. He describes the eagerness of Titus to take up the task; his voluntary offer and Paul's request came together in this official commission. The question arises as to whether Paul is now sending Titus (i.e. is the aorist (*exēlthen*) epistolary?), or whether Titus has already left again for Corinth at the time of writing (i.e. does the aorist refer to the real past?). The latter supposition finds support in 12:17—18, and is accepted here and in vv 18, 22, 23; the former has in its favour the phrase 'who is giving' (v 16, which however expresses merely a temporal continuity). **18—19.** As a colleague 'we sent' (cf v 17) that brother '*whose fame in the gospel-preaching*' has spread through all the Churches; he had been '*chosen by*

892f *vote*' by the Churches (of Macedonia, Galatia?) to travel with Paul in the 'gracious work' of the collection. Many guesses have been made as to his identity—Luke, Barnabas or one of the seven of Ac 20:4? but they are

g only guesses. As to why Paul did not name him, Allo's suggestion seems best: it is because they have already gone to Corinth, and it is for Titus to present him; Paul need only stress his merits. **20—21.** In a revealing passage Paul explains the reason for the presence of this colleague: he is '*taking precautions*' lest anyone question his honesty in the handling of this large sum of money; 'for we aim at what is honourable' (his reputation) before men, as well as before God (cf 7:2; 12:6—18). That he persists with the collection despite such suspicions proves its importance for him. **22.** A third member of the commission, again unnamed, more closely associated to the work of Paul than the former brother—'we have often tested'—he seems to be Paul's personal choice, and is mentioned again in 12:18. **23.** Abruptly he sums up their qualifications. **24.** He asks them bluntly to prove that his confidence in them is well-founded.

h **9:1—5** continue the explanation as to why the delegates have been sent. It is superfluous to be writing about the necessity or advantages of the collection to these Corinthians. **3—4.** But now, due to the postponement of practical measures, 'I sent' (cf 8:17) the delegates to ensure action. And he challenges their local patriotism. **5.** He wants the collection to be ready when he arrives, but gathered in such fashion that it deserves to be called a free gift, and not something extorted from unwilling givers. He wants to hear no complaints about undue pressure.

893a **9:6—15 The benefits of generous giving**—He uses the motive of divine recompense to rouse them (cf Mt 6:4, 6, 18). The good grace with which they give is more important in God's eyes than the amount given, (quoting LXX addition to Prv 22:8). **8—9.** God is so rich that he is able to reward almsgiving with temporal gifts; he can make every blessing (external goods as well as interior grace) abound in the generous—so that they have self-sufficiency, and can thus accomplish all good works (i.e. give more alms), which enrich further the interior life. Such a man fulfils the role played by the man of right conduct in Ps 112 (111):9. **10—11.** God is not less generous in the supernatural than in the natural order, in which he supplies seed and bread in such profusion; he will recompense even temporally the resources of the almsgiver—to serve in advancing him further spiritually, by increasing his capacity to be generous. Such simple liberality in the present case will cause many Christians

b to thank God. **12.** The supreme characteristic of the collection—it is a sacred service, a liturgical act, which not merely 'fills up by addition' (to what others give) the wants of the poor Christians, but overflows in the acts of gratitude it causes to be offered to God. It is a communal act of love, and a service of love to God: 'the service which this liturgy is'. **13.** This service will attest for the Jewish Christians the genuineness of the Corinthians' Christianity, and they will glorify God for this, as well as for the generosity with which the Corinthians expressed their communion with them. So the collection, whose success is presumed, is an inspired ecumenical strategy, to bring into harmony the Jewish and Gentile Christians. **14.** For their part, Paul hopes, the Judaeo-Christians will pray for their new Christian brothers who have received such abundant favours from God (issuing in their generosity), and will desire to enter into loving relations with them; full union will be accomplished.

Chh 10—13. *Part Three.* **Personal defence against** **89** **detractors**—Paul reaches unmatched heights of polemic eloquence in an inspired self-defence whose aim is to destroy the influence of his enemies in Corinth, and to force the Church to take an energetic initiative against the intruders, preparatory to Paul's own imminent disciplinary visit to Corinth.

10:1—6. A warning about the nature of his intended visit, and an answer to the change of cowardice—He emphasizes that what is to follow is a purely personal statement; and begs that the meekness and '*unfailing fair-play*' displayed in the human life of Christ may characterize the reform of the Corinthian Church. **2.** The Corinthians can make his task easier by initiating the reform before he comes; otherwise 'some' enemies, who consider that Paul always acts according to carnal principles—of cowardly cunning—are going to encounter his audacity. **3—5.** With God's arms he will 'take captive' every machination of his opponents, so as to make them obedient to Christ, the Truth who sets free. (So his victory will benefit even the vanquished?). **6.** As well as combating doctrinal errors, he will combat and punish disobedience. He counts on re-establishing perfectly by means of this letter and his visit his full authority over the Community; then he can deal with intruders.

10:7—18 His apostleship proved by his success in **d** **Corinth; the adversaries are mere intruders**—The opening phrase may be taken as statement or question. Some teachers claim a special relationship with Christ, (claiming a special gnosis? a special vocation? or special earthly links?); a group rather than an individual is meant (cf 11:23). Paul claims with ironic humility to be no less a man of Christ, and he will prove it. **8—11.** These official powers were conferred on him by the Lord for the building up of the Corinthians and not for their ruin, (which is what his adversaries are effecting). The reference to terrifying letters is to his correspondence in general, in particular the 'intermediate letter'.

12—13. He does not dare to 'class or compare' himself **e** with his critics; their standard of excellence is what they do i.e. subjective. But Paul's measuring line has been set for him by God, he will not go beyond that assignment—but that line has reached as far west as Corinth (and they have experienced his efficacy). **14.** The facts support him: the intruders may strain uncertainly to influence and control the Corinthians, but Paul is not overextending himself, because he arrived first—and with all the transforming efficacy of the good news—as far as the Corinthians' hearts. **15—16.** He does not claim credit for labour done by others—as his adversaries do. He is the founder of the Corinthian Church, and hopes for great things once his influence is re-established: first, the increase of their faith, which will vastly increase his apostolic prestige; then from Corinth the extension of his evangelical activity to lands west not yet evangelized, (Rm 15:23—24). **17—18.** A person is not proved genuine by the fact that he recommends himself (Jer 9:23—24); only those whom the Lord recommends are proved genuine—because only to such does he give the supernatural successes; and such is Paul.

11:1—6 Jealous love compels to the folly of boast- **f** **ing**—He has just scorned the intruders for self-praise (10:18); now he begs leave to imitate this folly. His motive is jealousy—the Corinthians are his, and he has the right to make a scene about their frivolous behaviour. 'God's own jealousy' (Ex 20:5; Ezek 16:8ff) is in him. As a father his daughter, Paul proudly betrothed them to 'one Man', Christ, and wants to present to Christ at the Parousia a virgin-bride (Is 54:5—6; Ezek 16:23—33). But this new

93f Creation is imperilled, as was the first, by the craftiness of the serpent (Gn 3:1–6, 13); and the source of Paul's jealousy are his misgivings that now the New Eve, the Church, may be corrupted and fall from that devotion and and simple adherence which is due to Christ. **4.** He has good reason for jealousy in the weak tolerance by the community of intruders. **5–6.** He claims at least the same tolerance for himself, because he can claim, with ironic modesty, to have been in no way inferior to these 'superlative apostles'; the reference is certainly not to the Twelve, who are nowhere in context, but to the intruders. Paul admits sarcastically that he is no professional rhetorician—as probably some of these were and disliked his vehement directness and absence of polish. But he is no way inferior in that knowledge of God which is worth having, which knowledge he had manifested to the Corinthians, hiding nothing.

g 11:7–15 Repels criticisms about the gratuitousness of his ministry—8–9. His 'plundering' of other churches is obviously hyperbole—he could not have refused the Macedonians' gift without grave discourtesy; he wants to shame this fairly wealthy community. **10–11.** The fame of his disinterestedness aids his success everywhere; and he swears he is not going to renounce this in Corinth or Achaia, in order to please critics, or to avoid being called an amateur. **12.** He gives his reason, appropriate to the polemic; he has higher motives (cf 1 Cor 9),—but they are irrelevant here. His refusal of maintenance 'undermines the claim' of his rivals, who boastfully claim apostolic status, and therefore would like to see Paul accepting payment like themselves. His refusal of money is an undeniable mark of his authenticity,—a mark which the intruders will never dare aim at, and which they counter by calumny (12:16–17). **13–15.** Paul describes them; the disguise of apostles which they adopt is natural to men who are servants of Satan, the arch-disguiser. He threatens them with eternal damnation. Only the existence of a very grave situation in Corinth could justify such language.

94a 11:16–33 Apologia in detail; boasting about his natural advantages, his labours and sufferings for Christ—17–21a. He is ashamed, boasting is not Christian. But this glorying about worldy and external advantages is what impresses the Corinthians, so he will boast, with a fury which makes him merciless. **21b–22.** He too can validate his claims, can 'dare' where anyone dares. He puts himself at his adversaries' level; from the viewpoint of the national-religious heritage, he can claim at least equality with them—ethnically he is Hebrew, by religion one of God's people, a sharer in the promises made to Abraham. **23.** From the viewpoint of the ministry, if they are 'servants of Christ', as they claim (v 15), Paul is a better one (*huper*), and will prove it by his sufferings: these are God's favours, which establish the authenticity of his mission (cf 4:7–12; 6:4–10). The great miracle is his survival amid such experiences; the power in Christ's, and the boasting is in fact a confession of his 'weaknesses'—fatiguing labours, imprisonments, beatings beyond measure, dangers of death. **24–25.** Five scourgings from Jewish synagogues, which still exercized penal jurisdiction over Jews; three beatings with rods—the official torment for condemned Romans (cf Ac 16:22–23 for one); stoning once,—at Lystra by the mob (Ac 14:19); three shipwrecks—all prior to the one mentioned in Ac 27; 'a night and a day I have been adrift at sea'—clinging to floating wreckage. **26.** The perils of his long journeys, especially overland; from the rivers of Anatolia, the brigands of the Taurus, from Jews and Gentiles; in the city, in mountain fastnesses, at sea, or from false brethren (Gal 2:4). **28–29.** Other things **894b** he passes over to go on to the daily interruptions and disturbance—arising from administration, visits, letters etc,—and the tension imposed by his anxiety for the Churches he has founded, and the extreme dissipation of forces which these cause. Paul is no stoic, he is weak, constantly burnt up by a fever of disquiet if a brother is enticed into sin. **30–32.** He pushes his boasting about his weakness to comic proportions: his escape from Damascus in a basket was possibly known and regarded as shameful, and Paul boasts of it; for the power is Christ's. The incident itself raises problems: psychologically and even grammatically it comes with bizarre suddenness, (which has given rise to theories of interpolation, which can be discounted),—probably explained by Paul's being tired of the heroic, and now choosing suddenly a humiliating misadventure from his early days. Historically there is the problem of the jurisdiction of the Nabatean king, Aretas IV, over this Roman city; possibly due to a concession given by Caligula—which would place the occurrence between A.D. 37 and 40 (cf Ac 9:25; Gal 1:17–18; the date of Paul's conversion is also involved).

12:1–10 Glorying about a great Revelation, and a c thorn for his flesh—Visions and revelations are in fact reduced to one (or two?), and certainly Paul had more (cf Acts, 1 Cor 14:6, 18). They are probably mentioned in opposition to revelations claimed by his adversaries; the veiled manner suggests they were unknown until now. **2–4.** He speaks with great sobriety and reserve: '*a man (who lived) in the Christ*'—in the 3rd person,—he can scarcely believe he was that man, so many labours since then. As with the prophets, the date is given—14 years previously—which suggests the period of Ac 11:25, before the missionary journeys. He was 'caught up', i.e. though conscious of an ascension, he was wholly passive under an external power. It is disputed whether v 3 and v 4 describe the same event, or two events; it seems much better to regard it as one event, (possibly in two stages). Paul does not give details—'things that cannot be told' due probably to the incapacity of the human intellect to conceptualize and express the content. The visions were probably spiritual, but he employs the contemporary imagery—'Paradise', 'third heaven' i.e. the heavens *par excellence*, where God dwells. A supreme mystical experience. **5–6.** Paul could boast **d** 'on behalf of that man'—himself as passive recipient of extraordinary favours; but refrains from drawing arguments from these favours for asserting his authority. He wants to be judged on the basis of his public activity—what one 'sees in me or hears from me'; therefore of his normal life he will boast only of his 'weaknesses', as described. **7.** The text and punctuation present as insoluble problem; it is probably better to accept the reading of Vg, BJ, RSV; (but cf J. Cambier, Bib 43 (1962) 481–528). The opening words recall the greatness of the revelations, as basis for the following experience: 'for that very purpose', lest he be tempted to pride, God provided a companion, 'a messenger of Satan', to remind him of his weakness, who continually buffets him, seeking to destroy his capacity to work. It is 'a pointed stake (or splinter) for the flesh' to suffer, i.e. certainly not temptations to carnal pleasure; a common modern opinion, as also the most ancient, is that there is question of a chronic humiliating malady, with acute attacks (marsh fever? cf 1:8ff; Gal 4:13–14). This is the humiliating experience he boasts of now. **8–9a.** 'About this' afflicting presence Paul in his agony begged the Lord Jesus three times (like Jesus in Gethsemane?) that it might depart; but he 'has replied', and this answer is still effective:

894d his supernatural strengthening is sufficient to guarantee Paul's apostolic success; for it is when human strength fails that the Power of God realizes itself to perfection (4:7, 12). **9b–10.** Most gladly will Paul rather glory in these weaknesses than ask for their removal, 'in order that the power of Christ may *make a dwelling in* me' (the Shekinah?). This experience no rivals will dare emulate.

e **12:11–18 The Corinthians are to blame for his outbreak of folly: defends his disinterestedness—** **11.** Paul admits he has become a fool, but the Community which failed to defend him drove him to it, lest they be led astray. **14.** He is going to act just as independently during his projected third visit (cf 13:1, and Introdn.); and a new reason (cf 11:10–12)—his fatherly love for them. He seeks their souls not their possessions; children ought not to 'accumulate money' for their parents, but vice-versa. **15–16.** He affirms his limitless devotion; is he to be loved less in exchange for his love which surpasses that of fathers? and he quotes another calumny of his critics. They cannot deny that he personally accepted no maintenance; but, they say, he is so crafty that he trapped them by guileful use of his agents, intending to keep part of the Collection for himself (8:20–21). **17–18.** Do they seriously suggest that those whom he 'has sent',—'Titus . . . and the brother' (8:17, 22),—or Paul through them, exploited them? the mere mention, of Titus especially, is enough to scotch such an absurd charge. N.B. use of perfect 'I have sent': the collection-mission is in progress in Corinth, and has occasioned the calumnies which Paul has heard of and now answers. But he has defended himself enough.

f **12:19–13:10 Admonitions concerning his next visit—20–21.** The vices he lists comprise those against unity and harmony—the relics of the factions of 1 Cor, aggravated by the agitators. He fears too lest God should again humiliate him, (as during the intermediate visit?), by the disgrace of their moral collapse; their sexual **894** libertinism (cf 1 Cor) is still very much a problem (cf 6:14ff). He fears to come up against incorrigibles; he may be driven to extreme measures against them—even excommunication. **13:1.** The natural interpretation is that Paul is about to pay his third visit to them (cf Introdn.), during which the power of the Church will be exercised according to the judicial forms (Dt 19:15): cases must be proved by witnesses. **4.** Christ has united **g** his apostles to his human weakness, but also to his power, to enable Paul now to deal vigorously with the Corinthians (4:7–14). **5–6.** It is not Paul they should be testing, but themselves continually, to see if they have the vitality of an operating faith. Let them face up to the demands of this faith,—surely they realize that Jesus is in them to help them; unless it be—which Paul refuses to believe—that they are forced to recognize themselves as Christians of bad alloy. **7–9.** He has no desire to prove his apostolic quality by rigorous punishment; so he prays that they do what is morally beautiful, even if his authority should remain unproven and disregarded as a result. He is delighted if ever they are strong in moral truth, and need no correction, and he himself left powerless to punish. And in addition (to v 7) he prays for their continuing improvement. **10.** His reason for writing sharply—so as not to be forced to act 'sharply' when he comes.

13:11–13 Conclusion—The stormy epistle ends in **h** exhortations adapted to the recipients' needs: 'be in joy', let them work their way to perfection, and live in peace and harmony; if they do, God, who sustains the least effort, will dwell among them with the gifts of love and peace of which he is Author. Having read this letter, let them express the restored mutual love by the liturgical custom of the kiss of peace. **13.** Ends with a benediction, the fullest of all Paul's references to the Triune God, and its scope unlimited—'with you all'.

GALATIANS

BY DOM BERNARD ORCHARD

5a **Bibliography**—*Commentaries*: B. à Piconio, E.tr. 1890; J. B. Lightfoot, 1884[8]; W. M. Ramsay, 1900[2]; M. -J. Lagrange, EtB 1925[2]; E. D. Burton, ICC 1921; H. Schlier, Meyer, 1962[12]; J. Steinmann, 1935; A. Viard, SBib 1964; F. Amiot, VS, 1946; R. T. Stamm, IB 1953; H. W. Beyer—P. Althaus, NTD 1962[9]; K. Grayston, 1958; O. Kuss, RNT 1940; Lyonnet, BJ 1959[2].
Other Literature: J. Chapman. 'St Paul and the Revelation to St Peter, Mt 16:17', RBen 29 (1912) 133—47; F. Prat, *Theology of St Paul*, E.tr. 1942[4]; Kirsopp Lake, *The Earlier Epistles of St Paul*, 1930[2]; W. L. Knox *St Paul and the Church of Jerusalem*, Cambridge, 1925; J. B. Orchard, 'A New Solution of the Galatians Problem', BJRL 28 (1944) 154—74; E. Tobac, 'Galates', DTC; B. Rigaux, *St Paul et ses Lettres*, 1962; J. Dupont, 'Pierre et Paul dans les Actes', RB 64 (1957) 35—47; C. H. Buck, 'The Date of Galatians', JBL 70 (1951) 113ff; W. G. Kümmel, *Introd to the NT*, E.tr. NTL, 1966.

b **Authenticity and Genuineness**—The Epistle itself and its attribution to St Paul have been accepted by all the ancient ecclesiastical writers and by all modern critics, save certain radical members of the Dutch School of Bauer and his associates, and by Loisy in his later years. It is certainly quoted by Ignatius of Antioch, Polycarp and Justin, it is explicitly attributed to St Paul by Irenaeus, and is already found in the Muratorian Canon and in all the catalogues drawn up by the earliest Councils. Moreover the internal evidence reveals in every line the unique hand and personality of St Paul.

c **Galatians** by race were Celts who had settled in the centre of Asia Minor during the 3rd cent. B.C. Their territory centred on the valley of the Halys. In 25 B.C. the Romans made a province of the territory, but including Pisidia, and parts of other regions such as Lycaonia, Phrygia and Pontus. The boundaries varied from time to time, and the province had no official name but was known as Galatia.

Date and Destination of the Letter—Who were the Galatians to whom it was addressed? Those who were Galatian by race or those who were of different race but lived in the S part of the province of that name? Kümmel rightly points out that we should not speak of the 'north and south Galatians' theories, but of the 'territory and province theories': *Landschaftshypothese* and *Provinzhypothese*. The former theory was put forward by St Jerome, who admittedly did not suspect any alternative because at the end of the 3rd cent. A.D. the province was divided by Diocletian and 'Galatia' was confined to the N part. The latter theory was first mooted by Johann Schmidt (1748) but is best known in connexion with the name of Sir William Ramsay. Ac 16:6 refers to the 'region of Phrygia and Galatia' and 18:23 mentions the presence of disciples on the third missionary journey 'in the region of Phrygia and Galatia'. In favour of the 'South-Galatians' or Province theory, it is urged that Paul

did not visit N Galatia on his first missionary journey **895c** (Ac 13—14) and the later narrative of Ac (16:6—8; 18:23) does not suggest that he did so on his 2nd or 3rd journeys. Again, it is said, Paul refers to the different lands he passed through by their Roman provincial names, rather than the territorial names. Further, in Ac 20:4 there are Christians from the province Galatia (Derbe, Lystra) among the delegates chosen to carry the alms to Jerusalem but none from the 'territory' further N, even though (1 Cor 16:1) a collection was made in Galatia. Opponents of this view urge that Paul does not always use the provincial names in referring to territories; Gal 1:21 Syria, 1 Thes 2:14 Judaea, Gal 1:17 Arabia. As for Ac 20:4—there are also no delegates from Achaia, although there had been a collection there too. Furthermore it is said that if Paul had sent Gal to the S Galatians evangelized on the first missionary journey, he would surely not have written 'I went into the regions of Syria and Cilicia', Gal 1:21, without adding 'and visited you'. Lastly—could Paul have called Pisidians 'foolish Galatians' (Gal 3:1) an improbable designation for those not Galatian by race? The arguments for each position seem to be fairly evenly balanced and perhaps other considerations may be brought in to decide the destination of the letter. The question of the circumcision, debated and settled at the Council of Jerusalem, A.D. 49—50, Ac 15, is so central to Gal that it is difficult to suppose it was written after that event. On the other hand the only Galatians made Christian by that date were those of S Galatia on Paul's first missionary journey. It is true that Paul chose to utilize and expand some of the same thoughts in Rm some six or seven years later, but this only proves that Judaizing tendencies were still active at that time in Rome and Corinth; the similarities in no way compel us to relegate the composition of Gal to the time of the writing of Rm. For a development of the argument, see the commentary. Nevertheless, because of certain similarities of mood and tone and parallels in phraseology with 1 Cor and Rm, many commentators with Benoit, ascribe Gal to a date about the same as Rm, i.e. c. A.D. 56.

The internal evidence of the letter favours the **d** view that it is dealing with the same controversy over circumcision as occurred at Antioch in A.D. 48—49—all, that is, except Gal 2:3—5 which seems to be a reference to Paul's third visit to Jerusalem at the time of the Council. If we accept this reference at its face value then of course we must date the letter after the Council, with all the attendant difficulty of explaining e.g. why there is no reference to the decrees of the Council in the letter. If, however, we take Gal 2:1—10 as an account of events during Paul's 2nd visit to Jerusalem (Ac 11:29—30) with parentheses and a reference to 'false brethren' (2:3—5) inserted in view of the controversy raging when he wrote the letter just before his 3rd Jerusalem visit then there is no longer any serious objection to accepting an early date for Gal (A.D. 49).

895d The view adopted here, therefore, is that Gal was addressed to the converts of St Paul's first missionary journey, being despatched probably whilst on his way up to Jerusalem for the Council in A.D. 49, cf Ac 15:3. (For details, see the article in BJRL listed in Bibliography). Gal would thus be the earliest of St Paul's epistles.

e Occasion and Object—The occasion of the Epistle was the news that his Galatian converts (mostly Gentiles, as it would appear from Ac 13–14; Gal 4:8) were being won over by certain 'false brethren' to the doctrine that circumcision and the Mosaic Law were as necessary to salvation as faith in Christ, 2:16; 5:2. Acceptance of this doctrine would logically result in the conclusion that faith in Christ, and therefore the redemption on the Cross, was insufficient to justify a man without adherence to the Law of Moses; in other words, all converts to Christianity were bound to Judaize i.e. live as Jews. This would have been a mortal blow at the universality of the Church and clean contrary to the teaching of Christ and the subsequent instruction to St Peter, Ac 10–11.

These Judaizers, Ac 15:1, 5, 24, had gone down to Antioch and there, it seems, had wrongly alleged the authority of the Apostles for their doctrine. Not content with causing mischief at Antioch, some of them had secretly, 2:4, gone into S Galatia to attempt to win over Paul's converts to their way of thinking.

f Their chief argument was the agreed fact that the Law of Moses was divinely instituted and that Christ had said he came 'not to abolish but to fulfil the Law' Mt 5:17. To overcome any scruples of the Galatians they declared that their teaching had the support of the Twelve whose authority was in any event superior to that of Paul, who (they claimed) was probably also in agreement in his heart of hearts. Paul's reaction was swift and violent. Stirred to his depths and quivering with just indignation he at once dictated this passionate vindication of his apostolic authority and crushing denunciation of their wicked error and of all who followed or favoured it. He put the true issue to the Galatians with unmistakable force and clarity: 'If you receive circumcision, Christ will be of no advantage to you' 5:2. We know that in the main his appeal succeeded because not only did the Council of Jerusalem fully endorse his policy and action but there is also no hint of any dissidence when a short time afterwards he again passed through the S Galatian region delivering 'to them for observance the decisions which had been reached by the Apostles and elders who were at Jerusalem', Ac 16:4.

g Doctrine—The main teaching of the epistle concerns the general economy of **salvation for all, Jew and Gentile**, based on faith in God's promises, and the relation of the Law of Moses to it. It has been well said that the starting point of this epistle as of St Paul's theology is his vision on the road to Damascus of the glorified Christ his saviour, who came to redeem both Jew and **h** Gentile. The Judaizers, however, insisted that in order to participate in the benefits of the redemption every catechumen must observe the Law of Moses, including the rite of circumcision, and asserted that salvation was impossible without it. Now these Christian Pharisees were affected by the strongest school of thought in contemporary Judaism, the school that esteemed the Law of Moses as eternal and immutable, even, it would seem, identifying it with the divine wisdom and regarding it as the source of grace and life, of joy and peace (J. Bonsirven, *Le Judaisme Palestinien*, 1934, I, 302–3). But though he admitted the Law to be divinely given,

3:19, Paul refused to allow it any redemptive power or **89** power to justify, for that would be to put it in the place of the unique and all sufficing sacrifice of Christ on the Cross, 3:21. The error was fundamental and had to be instantly crushed, for compromise was impossible without nullifying the Cross of Christ, 2:21. So in this Letter, while showing that for all men for all time salvation has been, is, and always will be based on belief in Christ and his justifying grace, he devotes more space to showing the Galatians why the Law cannot justify and what is its true place in the economy of salvation.

For St Paul there are three stages in the religious **89** life of the world from the time of Abraham, the founder of the Jewish race: (1) from Abraham to Moses: during which justification came through faith in God's promises, without any positive law properly so-called (circumcision being only the sign of God's covenant with Abraham, Gen 17:11); (2) from Moses to Christ: during which justification came through faith in the promises, but with the obligation besides of keeping the Law positively given on Sinai (faith, not Law, justifying); (3) since Christ: justification by faith in him and at the same time by observance of the Gospel (which is much more than a new and improved edition of Judaism).

Christianity is not so much an addition to and **b** completion of the imperfect OT regime as a positive religion of pardon, justification, salvation and life through Christ and in Christ, prolonging beyond the interlude of the Law of Moses the covenant concluded by God with Abraham and his posterity. In this Letter the transitory character of the Mosaic Dispensation clearly appears. It is emphasized by the fact that the Law was promulgated by the mediation of angels and of Moses and under the form of a bilateral contract which the apostasies of the Jewish people could render inoperative. The promises, on the contrary, were made to Abraham directly and unilaterally; they are by way of favour, are without any condition (circumcision was only imposed later as a sign and seal of the covenant) and concern all the peoples of the world. For St Paul the essential thing for every human being is the establishment and promotion of the divine life in the soul through union with Jesus—which cannot be done by adherence to the Law, 3:20, 21. This divine life Abraham received by faith in God's promises independently of the works of the Law and by a pure favour of God, 3:6–9. Justifica- **c** tion (*dikaiosunē*), which means for St Paul the passage from the state of enmity with God resulting from original and actual sin to the state of sonship in which we possess the divine life of Christ in ourselves, is always the free gift of God to us in virtue of the gift of faith. Christians, whether Jew or Gentile, are now the true sons of Abraham and heirs of the promises because they too have received justification by faith in the Son of God, likewise entirely out of God's liberality. Christ by dying on the Cross as the representative of mankind satisfied for the sins of the whole human race whether committed explicitly against the Law of Moses or against the natural law. Like Christ the Christian must die to the Law through the Law of Faith so that he may live to God, 2:19. This rebirth which the Christian undergoes in baptism makes him live on a new plane in which he 'walks by the Spirit,' 5:25f, and so is no longer under the Law, 5:18. This liberty of the sons of God comes from the doing to death of the vices and concupiscences of the flesh; he is a new creation, 6:15, whose life, being the life of Christ, of whom he is a member and also of whom he is a temple, 2:20; 1 Cor 6:15, 19, shows forth

3c the fruits of the Spirit, 5:22—23, against which there is no law.

d **The True Nature of the Law of Moses**—Since justification has never at any time in the religious history of mankind come through the observance of the Law but only through faith in the promises, what is the position of the Law in the history of the Jews?

The Law imposed a 'curse' on all who were subject to it, yet failed to keep it, but did not supply the means to keep it; it merely provided a standard or code by which the Jews were judged and by which their transgressions were revealed (and even increased because of their failures to keep the Law), 3:19. The Law was like a prison, for it revealed the unhappy servitude of the human race and itself offered no means of escape 3:22; but it did at the same time perform the useful function of isolating the Jews from pagan vice and idolatry, did in fact keep them together and directed them towards the future Messiah, 3:22. In this sense, before the coming of Christ, mankind was a minor and a pupil, and the Law was his pedagogue and tutor, 3:24. Now that Christ has come, the task of the pedagogue has ended; the Jews are no longer under its authority but are to enter into full sonship and inheritance, 4:5—6. Thus the part of the Law in the history of the Jews was that of a provisional and transitory dispensation suitable for the adolescence of the human race and destined to pass away when the coming of Christ inaugurated its full maturity. There is now in consequence no distinction between Jew and Gentile, 3:28.

e Paul gives the following **indications of the abrogation of the Law of Moses** and of its powerlessness to justify, 2:16—21: (1) The Apostles and faithful have always acted on the assumption of its powerlessness; (2) Scripture itself declares it, Ps 143 (142):2; (3) the abandonment of the Law on the strength of the sufficiency of the redemption would, if the Law still retained its obligatory character, be sin, the blame for which we should have to place upon Christ—which would be blasphemous; whilst on the contrary those who are putting themselves again under the yoke of the Law must admit the sin of having abandoned it in the first place; (4) the Christian, has died to the Law with Christ; (5) since the death of Christ, which is the source of all graces, has infinite value, to set up another means of arriving at perfect justice is to deny the redemptive power of the Cross of Christ (cf Prat, op cit, I, 198—9); (6) the characteristics of the regime of Law are incompatible with those of the Promise; for whereas the Promise is the source of freely given spiritual goods, the Law always offers a *quid pro quo*, a measured recompense for a measured service, 3:12; (7) Christ by his death on the Cross, in which 'he became a curse for us', 3:13, redeemed us from the curse of the Law by fulfilling in his Person all the requirements of the Law perfectly and at the same time making complete and perfect satisfaction for all the transgressions of the Jews (and mankind in general) against the Law. The Law thus satisfied has no further claims on him nor on the rest of the human race in so far as they are united to him by baptism. The Law therefore has no further power over him or over us and hence Paul can say 'For I, through the Law died to the Law, that I might live to God', 2:19.

f (8) To conclude his argument Paul gives the famous allegory of Hagar and Sarah, representing the two testaments. Hagar the slave represents the synagogue; Sarah the freewoman, symbolizes the Church. Their respective sons take after the condition of their mothers. Therefore those who wish to Judaize rank themselves with Ishmael, the son according to the flesh, and renounce the patrimony given to Isaac, the son of the promise, which is also that **896f** of Christians who are the true spiritual heirs of Abraham. The point of the comparison is that the lesser and imperfect testament must give place to the new and perfect one, for the two are incompatible, and cannot co-exist: 'Cast out the slave and her son: for the son of the slave shall not inherit with the son of the freewoman', 4:30; Gen 21:9—13. Paul uses OT texts in the rabbinical way to back his arguments. They do not always appear convincing to us. This is one of the better examples of the use of the spiritual sense of Scripture to support a thesis, cf Amiot, op cit 202, note 1: J. Bonsirven, *Exégèse Rabbinique*, 275, 309—10, Prat, op cit I, 221—2; Lagrange, op cit 118—22. But throughout the discussion Paul is a Rabbi arguing with Rabbis.

1:1—2:21 Vindication of his Apostolic Autho- **g** **rity**—The abruptness of the opening indicates not merely the impetuosity and haste with which Paul takes up the challenge of the Judaizers in Galatia, but also his determination to vindicate his preaching authority.

1:1—5 Introduction—1. From the first word Paul claims the fullness of the apostolic authority, for his, too, is from God (unlike that of false apostles which is 'from men'); and like the Twelve he has been commissioned not by the mediation of men ('from man') but directly by Jesus Christ, (Ac 9:3f), and so by God the Father, who thus constituted Paul a true witness of the Resurrection. **2.** 'All the brethren who are with me' probably refers to his small band of companions. 'The churches of Galatia' refer to the local churches founded during the first missionary journey, Ac 13:14f, the omission of all commendation of them is pointed. **3.** These words of greeting are found in all the epistles of St Paul save Hebrews, and they show Paul's teaching of the complete equality of the Son with the Father. *Kurios* (Lord) is always a divine title with St Paul (cf J. Lebreton, *Histoire du Dogme de la Trinité*, 1927[7], I, 368, and I Cor 8:6). **4.** Paul will later show them that their readiness to accept circumcision demonstrated their failure properly to value the atoning death of Christ. **5.** Doxology. The everlasting character of God's Kingdom is contrasted with the present evil age.

6—10 A Stern Rebuke for their Apostasy—6. **h** According to the view of the date and occasion of the Epistle taken above no more than a few months had elapsed since Paul had left them; cf Ac 14:22f. Lightfoot notes that this is the sole instance in which St Paul omits to express his thankfulness for their faith in addressing any Church, substituting for it this indignant expression of surprise 'him', i.e. God. **7.** There can be no other gospel: it is merely a matter of certain men (Judaizers) presenting a false teaching utterly incompatible with the true gospel. **8.** Any such teacher should be regarded as given over to destruction, utterly excluded from the Kingdom of God (anathema), and hence by inference excommunicated also. The Church in its Councils has taken over the use of this same formula. **9.** His solemn anathema underlines the authoritative element in his teaching. **10.** Clearly his Judaizing opponents had falsely accused him of compromising and of lack of consistency in the past; cf 5:11.

1:11—2:21 His Mission is from God the Father **897a** **Himself**—The Judaizers of Galatia maintained that their gospel came from Christ through the Twelve Apostles, but Paul declares that the Gospel of Jesus Christ was directly revealed to him by God the Father in the same way that St Peter himself received it, Mt 16:16f, Gal 1:16 (cf Chapman, RBen 29 (1912) 133—47); hence his gospel is as authoritative as that of Peter and identical with it. **11—12.** His gospel is not a man-made doctrine, nor

897a has it been transmitted through a man but it came, as Chapman says, 'by a revelation of Jesus Christ, which taught me who He is' (rather than Lightfoot's subjective genitive, 'by a revelation from Jesus Christ'). **13f.** He begins explaining in detail how his Gospel teaching has always been independent of, though fully in accord with, that of the Twelve.

14. Cf Phil 3:5—6. He advanced more quickly in knowledge and authority than any of his contemporaries, because of his greater zeal for the traditions (added to the Law by the Pharisees); cf Mt 23 passim. **15.** There is perhaps here a play on the meaning of the word 'Pharisee'. Paul, already 'a Separated One' from his birth, had been in a more profound sense 'separated' or pre-destined before his birth (cf Jer 1:5) to his Christian vocation. **16.** Read 'in me' with CV. The reference here is primarily to his conversion, Ac 9:3f. 'Immediately I conferred not with flesh and blood': stresses his independence of Jerusalem. He did not originally get his gospel from the Twelve.

b **17—24.** He now gives a list of his movements in subsequent years to prove that his few contacts with the Twelve had not been for the purpose of obtaining authorization of his mission from them. **17.** 'Those who were apostles before me', i.e. the Twelve, chosen in point of time before him. 'Arabia' probably means the country S of Damascus, the kingdom of the Nabataeans, rather than the district of Sinai. We have no record of what happened during these three years, but while the opinion of the Fathers is that he immediately started preaching, many now prefer to think that he devoted himself to a life of prayer and meditation similar to that of St Benedict at Subiaco. **18.** 'After three years', i.e. three years from his conversion according to the Jewish mode of reckoning; cf Mt 16:21. On the date of St Paul's conversion, cf § 708a. 'to visit', *historēsai*, to make the direct official acquaintance of Peter, cf Ac 9:26—30. **19—20.** Paul declares on oath that of the Twelve he saw only Peter and James on this visit. 'James' is most probably James the Less, the first bishop of Jerusalem, a relative of Jesus, cf § 664f. **21.** Paul next evangelized the regions near his native city of Tarsus in Cilicia and around Antioch in Syria; cf Ac 9:30; 11:25. **22—24.** Outside Jerusalem he was not known in Judaea at that time save by reputation, though he was to become much better known to the Churches of Judaea during his next visit.

c **2:1—10**—The complicated question of the identification of this visit to Jerusalem with the corresponding visit in Ac has been briefly discussed in § 895d. The visit recorded here is therefore taken to be identical with the famine relief visit of Ac 11:29—30; cf also Chrys., *Hom.* in Ac 25:2 (PG 60, 193). **1.** 'After fourteen years': St Paul is still pursuing the same line of argument as in the latter part of the preceding chapter; he means 'fourteen years' from his conversion according to Jewish reckoning, i.e. anything between say $12\frac{1}{4}$—14 full years after his conversion. As Peter however was still at liberty in Jerusalem (cf 2:9) this visit 'after fourteen years' must have been made before his imprisonment by Herod, who died in the summer of A.D. 44, cf Ac 12:20—23. St Paul's conversion would therefore seem to have taken place not long after the Resurrection, perhaps in A.D. 31. Thus this Famine Relief Visit would have been in A.D. 43—44, shortly before Peter's imprisonment and Herod's death, but cf § 708b. 'Titus' was one of St Paul's early Gentile converts. His name is not mentioned in Ac, but several times in 2 Cor.

2. Paul's going up to Jerusalem in obedience to **897** 'revelation' is quite compatible with his other purpose of taking the famine relief. Indeed, it is not forcing the text to make it mean that he went up in response to the 'revelation' made to Agabus (Ac 11:18). But if we take it as a special revelation made to himself, then in this revelation he was instructed to compare his teaching privately with that of the Twelve not for the purpose of reaching an agreement (which already existed), nor for their approbation, but for mutually confirming their complete doctrinal harmony and in order to forestall future possible sources of disagreement over matters of practical policy between him and Peter, James and John, i.e. lest he had, or should, 'run in vain'. 'but privately *before the authorities*'; *tois dokousin* is a term of honour, not of depreciation. This action of Paul was therefore taken to safeguard unity, and in view of the storm that arose in Ac 15 it was well to have secured in advance the full trust of, and complete accord with, the leaders of the Twelve.

3—5 from a parenthesis that interrupts Paul's **e** account of his private conference with Peter, James and John; what happened at their conference and what resulted from it is told in 6—10. **3.** We have seen that on this visit Paul brought with him the Jew Barnabas and the Greek Titus, both his friends and helpers. This v begins a parenthesis as Paul suddenly introduces a new consideration, viz that in tacitly approving of Titus as a collaborator, uncircumcised Gentile though he was, the Apostles showed that they were already committed in principle to the admission of uncircumcised Gentiles into the Christian fellowship. The question of circumcising Titus never arose at all; the question, St Paul means, was not raised on that occasion, though it would have been, if the Apostles had ever accepted the views of the Judaizers. Forgetful of grammatical coherence Paul's impetuous flow of eloquence proceeds to contrast the reasonable attitude of the 'men of repute' towards the uncircumcised Titus with the present narrowness of these perverters of the Gospel (1:7). These 'false brethren' in an underhand way have already undermined his authority both in Galatia and Antioch and have altered his basic teaching. **4.** The freedom of the Gentiles from the yoke of the Law of Moses has been jeopardized by these men. In the context the addition of a subject and its verb (both lacking in the Gr.) is required to complete the sense of the sentence beginning 'But . . . because of false brethren . . . who . . .' The words that are most natural to supply and which also illuminate the whole passage are: 'But *your liberty is now endangered* because of false brethren . . . cf Orchard, art cit supra.

These 'false brethren' are the persons mentioned in Ac 15:1—2; they had done their destructive work before Paul heard of it. 'into bondage', viz by insisting on the necessity of circumcision and the observance of the Mosaic Law by all Gentile converts. **5.** Sums up the resistance described in Ac 15:2f, and concludes the parenthesis. Far from being thought up to differentiate Gal 2 from Ac 15 (as Benoit holds, Bib 40 (1959) 778—9) this explanation of the passage is forced upon us by the logic of the fact that Gal 2:1—3, 6—10 clearly refer to the visit of Ac 11:30, whilst the parenthesis of vv 4 and 5 equally obviously refer to the situation of Ac 15:1—5. This solution in fact fairly meets and solves neatly all the major difficulties of the text and makes good sense of the whole as well as of the parts.

6. Resumes the description of Paul's private con- **f** ference. The authorities, i.e. the three apostles, imparted

f no fresh knowledge to him, saw nothing defective or incorrect in his teaching, but on the contrary heartily recognized his mission as being directly from God. 'But *from those who are looked up to as authorities*': Paul is depreciating not the Twelve themselves, but the extravagant and exclusive claims set up for them by the Judaizers, viz the fact that the Twelve knew Jesus in the flesh before his Resurrection did not give them any special advantage over him, for God does not judge according to this. Both he and they are apostles in the fullest sense and God does not regard the difference between him and them in the circumstances of their call. While admitting fully their apostolic authority his own is not dependent on their approbation. **7.** The revelation made to Paul in Ac 9:3f is comparable only with that made to Peter in Mt 16:16f; cf Chapman, art cit supra. **8.** 'He who worked for Peter', by making his apostolate fruitful in respect of the Jews, 'worked for me also in respect of the Gentiles'. 'The gospel of the uncircumcision' means 'the uncircumcised Gentiles as the object of the apostolate' (Lagrange). This mission of Paul to the Gentiles must not be understood in any exclusive or monopolistic sense, but he himself had been called in the designs of God primarily for work among the Gentiles. Peter as the chief of the apostles and the centre of unity had the responsibility of welding the Jewish and Gentile elements in the Church into one whole and because of his closer contact with the mother-church of Jerusalem and of his pre-eminence among the Apostles (cf Roiron RSR (1913) 501—4) he personifies for Paul the principal agent in the conversion of the Jews, at this particular time at any rate. Of course St Paul never renounced, nor did St Peter ever confine himself to, the evangelization of the Jews; cf Ac 10—11; 1 and 2 Pet **g** passim. **9.** 'the grace', i.e. of the Gentile apostolate; cf Rom 1:5, 'James and Cephas and John'. Lightfoot (in loc) remarks that when Paul is speaking of the missionary office of the church at large, Peter holds the foremost place, 7, 8: when he refers to a special act of the Church of Jerusalem, James is mentioned first, as here; cf Ac 12:17; 15:13; 21:18. On Paul's relative use of Cephas and Peter, see Chapman, art cit 143. 'Who were reputed to be pillars', a statement without any touch of irony or depreciation. The accord here made between the Three Pillars and Paul on the latter's second visit to Jerusalem was to be renewed on his Third Visit to the Holy City, Ac 15 passim. In all probability they agreed on a territorial delimitation of their spheres, the Pillars retaining the evangelization of Palestine, whilst Paul kept to the westward; cf also Rm 15:20. **10.** 'Only they would have us remember the poor; which very thing I *had also been careful* to do.' The aorist *espoudasa* can bear here a pluperfect sense. The reference is clearly to the famine relief collection, Ac 11:29—30. Paul's constant solicitude for the welfare of the mother-church in Jerusalem is also seen in 1 Cor 16:1—4; 2 Cor 8—9; Rm 15:26—27; Ac 24:17.

h **11—21 Paul opposes Peter at Antioch**—It seems that the incident at Antioch took place either immediately before or immediately after the first missionary journey of Paul. **11.** Cf also 14 infra. This avowal implies that Paul both recognized and venerated the authority of Peter as being superior to his own (Lagrange); there is no ground for the assumption that Paul considered himself superior to Peter. The use of the title *kēphas* and its contrast with *petros*, 7—8 show that he was fully aware of Peter's position as The Rock; cf v. McNabb, *The NT Witness to St Peter*, 1928, 43—46. **12.** 'The men from James' may be those 'men from Judea' Act 15:1, but less probably. St Peter was scandalizing Gentile Christians. It is

clear from this v and from Ac 10:5—10 that Peter now **897h** made no distinction between clean and unclean foods. It is also clear from Ac 15:24 that the emissaries from Jerusalem must either have exceeded their powers or abused them. It was presumably for the sake of peace and to avoid serious friction that Peter '*withdrew gradually*' from taking meals with the Gentile converts in Antioch, and therefore presumably from sharing the Eucharistic Meal with them. Peter's authority led the rest of the Jewish Christians and even Paul's own lieutenant, Barnabas, to follow his example. **13.** Though Peter's attitude was negative, it was nevertheless 'hypocritical' in the sense that his action was not in conformity with his convictions, and the truth of the Gospel and the liberty of the Gentiles (not to mention the Jews as well) from the Mosaic Law would very soon have been endangered.

14—21 sum up Paul's speech on this occasion to **i** Peter and to the faithful of Antioch. **14a.** 'the truth of the Gospel', i.e. liberty of conscience with respect to the ritualistic prescriptions of the Mosaic Law. Paul reproaches Peter not with a doctrinal error, but with not holding firm in the principle which he recognizes, 'conversationis vitium, non praedicationis' (Tert., *De praescript*. 23). 'before them all', i.e. before a formal gathering of Jewish and Gentile Christians. **14b.** Peter is accused of exerting a moral pressure in favour of Judaizing since the Gentile Christians would feel themselves bound to submit in order not to be separated from the chief of the Apostles. (N.B. For the local compromise agreed on for the storm-centre areas of Syria, Cilicia and Galatia, see Ac 15:28—29.) No word is said there about Jewish Christians and the Mosaic ritual, but Gentile converts are merely to observe four prohibitions, which seem to be identical with those formerly imposed in the OT upon Gentile minorities in Jewish territory, for the sake of peaceful living, cf Lv 17:8, 10, 13, 18:26. **15.** 'Gentile sinners'—a common expression. Said perhaps with a slight touch of irony, but it emphasizes the special privileges of Israel as a race possessing a rule of conduct vastly superior to anything found among Gentile nations. **16.** Gives the essence of Paul's position. Cf Ac 15:11 Jews as well as Gentiles need redemption through Christ. 'Justification' in St Paul means an interior purification by which a man's sins are utterly blotted out and he is made acceptable to God in virtue of faith with charity, and good works, cf § 896c, and Rom 2—5. The last part of the v is a free quotation of Ps 143 (142):2; no one under the Old Dispensation was justified, not even by the works of the Law, save by the foreseen merits of Christ, and through faith in God's promise of Redemption. It would seem that Paul is in fact using this text in an accommodated sense, cf RB (1938) 503—4.

17. A difficult v, which seems to mean: seeing **898a** that in order to be justified in Christ it was necessary to abandon our old ground of legal righteousness and to become 'sinners' (i.e. to put ourselves in the position of heathen), may it not be argued that Christ is thus made a minister of sin? (Lightfoot). 'Heaven forbid that anyone should teach that justification by faith without the Law makes a man a sinner; for Christ would be responsible'. **18.** But to put oneself back again under the Law after having abandoned it would indeed be 'to make oneself a transgressor of it'. This v seems to hint at the possible consequence of Peter's action. Renunciation of the Law is then absolutely imperative. If the Jew who abandons it apparently makes himself a 'sinner', he does it in reality in order to be at once justified in a marvellous participation of the life of Christ. He will have gained infinitely more than he has lost.

898b **19.** He died to the Mosaic Law through faith and baptism, by which a Christian puts on Christ and is united to his death; cf Gal 3:29; Rm 6:3. 'Through the law' is a difficult phrase, and is easier, perhaps, to understand as 'through the law of faith', cf 6:2, than 'through the Law of Moses', which, in causing as it were the death and Resurrection of Christ, does the same for us in virtue of our solidarity with him. Being freed from the bondage of the Law by this mystic death, the Christian now lives with the life of God and in union with him.

c **20.** 'With Christ *I was and am concrucified*': the perfect tense of the Gr. indicates that the state acquired by a man on the day of his justification by baptism still endures. (For further development of the idea of 'concrucifixion', cf Gal 5:24; 6:14; Rm 6:6.) 'And it is no longer I who live, but Christ who lives in me'. These words have inspired a great mystical literature which has attempted to draw out their meaning. 'Walking in the spirit' (5:25) the Christian is 'another Christ' in virtue of his mystical union with him. His present physical life since his conversion is a life elevated and animated by faith in Christ. **21.** To return to the practice of the Law of Moses would be to spurn this incomparable gift of divine life. If justification could be gained through the Law then the Redemption was unnecessary and a mockery. Doubtless not all of Gal 2:15—21 was said to Peter. Paul has wandered off into his own thoughts.

We are not told the effect of his words on Peter, but obviously Paul would not have related the incident unless the issue had been favourable to him and Peter had seen his mistake. At the subsequent Council of Jerusalem, Ac 15:6 f, the conditions laid down for the fraternization of Gentile Christians with the rest of the Church (in which Peter concurred) marked a complete victory for St Paul on all the essential points.

d **3:1—5:12 The Gospel of Paul agrees with the Promises of the Old Testament**—Paul, having established fully the independence and authority of his teaching and the fact of its full acceptance by the other Apostles, including Peter, now demonstrates its full harmony and continuity with the doctrine of the OT. The Judaizers had misunderstood the relation between Christianity and the OT, so he draws out the doctrinal basis of his doctrine of the liberty of the Gentiles from the Mosaic Law, by showing that they are the heirs of the promises and of the blessing given to Abraham before the Law and before circumcision. The New Dispensation is not merely superimposed on the Old Dispensation, nor an enriched edition of it. The two are incompatible, the New driving out the Old. Here is the familiar paradox. The New completes yet supersedes the Old, cf § 717*bc*.

3:1. 'Jesus Christ . . . crucified': these words show the important place held by the Passion in the preaching of Paul. **2—5.** He tells them to recall to mind that it was the wonderful and beneficent activity of the Holy Spirit among them that had transformed their lives, and not adhesion to the Mosaic Law; cf Ac 13—14. **2.** 'hearing with faith' means 'faith which has come **e** through hearing'. **4.** 'experience' ('Suffered' CV); the reference is to the magnitude of their supernatural experiences. **6.** The answer to the question put in 5, viz 'By faith of course', is omitted by Paul as being too obvious to require statement. The sense is 'And so it was with Abraham who believed . . .'; cf Gn 15:1—6. Abraham was justified because of his faith in God who had just promised him a numerous posterity (and ultimately the Messiah) at a time when humanly speaking it was impossible for him or Sarah to have a

son. The comparison between Abraham and the Christian **89** rests on the fact that in both cases it is faith in God's promises and not the works of the Law that makes them pleasing to God. **7.** The only true sons of Abraham are those who imitate his faith. The virtue of faith brings the Gentiles closer to Abraham than carnal descent brought the Jews. The Scripture blessed the Gentiles in and with Abraham because it foresaw that faith would play the same part in their salvation and bring them the same blessings. Abraham was justified by faith fifteen years before ever the law of circumcision was imposed; cf Ramsay, op cit § xxxi. **9.** Those who rely on faith in Jesus Christ for their justification shall be blessed with the faithful Abraham.

10. But everyone who is under, or who puts himself **f** under, the Law is morally obliged to keep it in its entirety under pain of malediction, Dt 27:26; 28:15f. It is true that for a Jew, before Christ, faith also required the faithful observance of the Law. **11.** But this is no longer so; since Christ abrogated the Law, faith in Christ alone suffices, since there is no inherent sanctifying power in the works of the Law. The quotation from Hb 2:4 refers in its original context to the faithfulness (rather than the faith) of the just man. The NT concept of faith could develop from this. It may be translated either 'the just man shall live by faith', i.e. in virtue of faith, or 'he who is just by faith shall live.' **12.** The Law, as such, has not faith for its principle. The quotation from Lv 18:5 proves that the Law is concerned solely with works and with nothing else. Paul means that the vivifying principle even in OT observance of the Law was faith. **13.** But now redemption through Christ has taken away all value from legal observances. The Law could only reveal the deficiencies of human conduct; it would not cure them or atone for them. This Christ himself did in redeeming us by the sacrifice of the Cross. As regards Dt 21:23 it is clear that in the case of Christ the curse is only apparent and in the common estimation of men, 2 Cor 5:21. But he took upon himself all the penalties due to the human race for its transgressions of God's Law, and atoned for them by his death, thus completely negating the curse. **14.** And because Christ is God as well as man, 'the blessing of Abraham' (which is justification by participation in the life of God through the Holy Spirit, the Spirit of Jesus) is given alike to Jew and Gentile through his death and resurrection.

15—29 The Blessings of Abraham are inherited g solely through an indefectible Promise—15. He institutes a comparison from human affairs. 'A man's will, if it be valid, no man annuls or adds fresh clauses to it'. **16.** Cf Gn 13:14—17; 17:5—8. Paul, with the Jewish rabbis, takes the promise of the possession of the land of Canaan symbolically of the glorious and eternal Messianic Kingdom. '"and to his offspring!" It does not say: "and to offsprings"'. A well-known crux. It has been argued that Paul's proof rests on a grammatical error. The plural of *zera'* ('seed') could not be used anyway here as it is only used for grain or crops. But perhaps, as Lightfoot suggests, the expression supplies the answer too. For it is just as unnatural to use the Gr. *spermata* in this sense. It appears, then, that Paul is not stressing the actual word used but the fact that a singular noun, a collective term, is used, where some plural e.g. *tekna*, might have been substituted. But a plural noun would have excluded the interpretation given; the singular, though it allows a plurality, at the same time involves the idea of unity. The point is thus one, not of grammar but of theological interpretation. Doubtless the collective meaning came first ('seed of

98g Abraham') but this typified other meanings—(1) Christ was the true 'seed of Abraham' and in him the race was summed up. Israel typified Christ and in this sense Paul uses the term here. (2) But also 'Israel according to the flesh' was a type of the 'Israel according to the spirit' as Paul points out in Rm 4:18, 9:7 and of course above, Gal 3:7: 'it is men of faith who are the sons of Abraham', Lightfoot, in loc. **17–18.** The Law coming 430 years later did not in any way modify the testament of the inheritance by God's free promise. Paul follows the LXX dating; cf Ex 12:40 and § 145*f.* **19.** 'because of transgressions' i.e. to reveal sins. Jewish tradition held that the Law was given to Moses as mediator by means of angels. **20.** Though this v might mean that the Law is inferior to the Promise because it comes from God indirectly whilst the Promise comes without intermediary, Paul probably means that the Mosaic covenant was a bilateral alliance involving a mediator (Moses) and the possibility of the covenant failing through the transgression of the Jews, whereas God's Promise was unilateral, unconditonal, indefectible, and could not be modified by the Law. **21.** The Law could only be against the promises if it could give life. **22.** 'has *shut up all under* sin' as in a prison—the Scripture is here represented as doing that which it declares to be done; cf Dt 27:26. **23.** 'faith' i.e. the object of our faith, Christ. **24.** 'custodian' (CV *tutor*) or pedagogue was a superior slave entrusted with taking a boy through the streets to his schoolmaster. **26.** The coming of the faith means the fulfilment of the Promise, and all who believe become sons of God. **27.** Baptism is the consequence of the act of faith, and the newly baptized are as it were clothed with Christ, nay more (28) they are one person with him. A magnificent proclamation of the unity and spiritual equality of all human beings. **29.** The Christian is the true seed of Abraham and true heir to the Promise; Christians are the true 'Israel of God'; cf 6:16.

h **4:1–11 At Christ's Coming the Period of Tutelage gives place to that of Full Worship of God—3.** Better to read with CV 'elements of the world', probably signify ing those imperfect rules of conduct which held humanity in a kind of slavery—for the Jews their legal observances, for the Gentiles their pagan rites and customs. 'Elemental spirits' suggests a backsliding to the pagan worship of the powers thought to inhabit stars, stocks and stones, that seems less appropriate in the context. **4.** A very important v from which we learn of the pre-existence of the Son, of his taking flesh from a Woman, at a time predetermined by God, and of his further condescension in his submission to the Law, cf Lk 2:21. 'Fulness of time' CV, the time fixed by God for the ending of the minority of the human race, cf Eph 1:10, also Heb 1:1. 'born of a woman': the only direct mention of the Blessed Virgin in the Pauline writings; the Gr. *genomenon* 'made', is practically synonymous with *gennōmenon* 'born'. 'born under the law': subject to the Mosaic Law. **5.** The two-fold object of the divine plan, to redeem the Jews from the Law and to confer divine sonship on all. **6.** The Holy Ghost, the Spirit of Jesus, gives the Christian this sonship and the intimate conviction thereof. 'Abba' is the actual Aramaic word our Lord spoke. **7.** Sonship gives inheritance of God's kingdom. **8–10.** 'by nature; i.e. in reality. These vv imply that most of the Galatian converts were Gentiles; nevertheless they have already started to observe the Jewish calendar. **11.** He fears lest his work among them may have utterly failed.

i **12–20 A Digression Revealing his Anxiety Con-**cerning their Lapse—**12.** Just as he had previously **898i** freed himself from these Jewish practices so let them now imitate him by doing likewise. 'You did me no wrong' may allude to an incident of which there is no record. **13.** It is possible that this illness (?malaria) came upon him while at Perga and that it may have had some connexion with John Mark's desertion at that time, Ac 13:13. 'at first' *to proteron* more usually means 'on the former of two occasions', but can also mean 'previously'; if the former, it could imply that he had already visited the Galatians twice before he wrote this Epistle, though the return half of his First Missionary Journey might legitimately count as a second visit to each of his Galatian city churches, cf Introd. **14.** 'not scorn or despise', did not diminish their welcome. **15.** '*Why has your friendliness now turned into enmity?*' This change of attitude is all the stranger because at one time they would have given him their eyes. Some think this v hints at Paul having some disease of the eyes. **17.** '*They pay court to you for bad motives; and they would hatch you out*' (in order to exploit you, cf JTS, 40 (1939), 149–51), '*so that you in turn may pay court to them*'; **18.** '*But it is always good to be courted for a good motive*', i.e. by Paul himself. **19.** Owing to their lapse he has again to go through the labour of begetting them in Christ.

4:21–5:12—concludes the proof that the New Dispen- **j** sation of the Spirit replaces the Old Dispensation of the Law (**Allegory of the Two Covenants**, 4:23–5:1), and sums up the reasons why circumcision is not merely unnecessary but wrong for Christians.

4:21–5:1—The Law itself proclaims its temporary character. **21–23.** In Gn, we find Abraham as the type of faith. Of his two sons, Ishmael the son of Hagar the slave-girl, is the type of the Jew, and Isaac the son of Sarah, the freewoman, by the free promise of God and beyond all natural expectation, is the type of the Christian. **24–26.** The two mothers, Hagar and Sarah, likewise represent the Old and the New Dispensation respectively, the former the present Jerusalem, that subjects itself to the slavery of the Law, the latter the heavenly Jerusalem, the home and mother of the Christians who rejoice in the freedom of the Gospel. Hagar and Ishmael are both connected historically with Sinai the source of the Old Covenant; but not so Abraham or Isaac. **27.** The quotation is from Is 54:1, q.v. with which the Rabbis connected Is 51:2 with its reference to Abraham and Sarah, who though long sterile eventually through Isaac brought forth a nation. **28–29.** Draw the conclusion that the Christians, like Isaac, are the true children of the Promise, and that in suffering persecution as he did from the Ishmaelites their position as children of the Promise receives further confirmation, cf Gen 21:9. **30–31.** Paul quotes Sarah's words in Gn 21:10 as the Lord's own decision, viz that the inheritance is now only for the son of the free woman, i.e. the Christian. **5:1.** CV, DV and KV, with some good MS support prefer **k** to read '*in virtue of the freedom wherewith Christ has set us free. Stand fast therefore . . .*' 'Slavery' i.e. of Judaism and the Law. **5:2–12**—Receiving Circumcision cuts them off from Christ. **2.** Adherence to Christ and not to the Law of which circumcision was the sign, can only give salvation and righteousness. Clearly the Judaizers must have taught the Galatians that circumcision was necessary for salvation, cf Ac 15:1. **3–4.** Those who receive circumcision not only bind themselves to keep all the OT regulations, but in relying on the law for salvation they really reject Christ. **5.** 'The hope of righteousness' i.e. the good things to

898k be received through our justification. **6.** Faith working through charity, as he explains in the next section is all-sufficing.

7–12. An Indictment of the Judaizers—Paul is confident that the Galatians will return to his way of thinking despite the insidious activity of his opponents that is capable of ruining the Galatian Church. **11.** It appears from this v that the Judaizers claimed Paul as at least a secret supporter of circumcision for Gentiles. His reply is that if he were such (1) he would not be persecuted as he is, and (2) that also what is for them the 'scandal of the cross' would—'per impossibile'—be set aside. **12.** A strong sarcasm. If they are so interested in the question let them go a step further than circumcision!

l 5:13–6:10 Christian Liberty is not Licence and Requires Good Works done in Charity—The danger that freedom from legal observances may lead Christians into excesses of other kinds can only be guarded against by the practice of Christian charity. The Christian is bound by the higher Law of Love. **13.** 'the flesh' here and in 16 signifies simply unredeemed man, man in his natural state. **17–18.** Form a slight digression. **17.** By 'the spirit', St Paul means the intelligence and will of a man when guided by the Holy Ghost; by 'the flesh', the same powers divorced from the guidance of the Holy Spirit and so leading to evil. **19–23** contrast the works of the 'flesh' with the fruits of the Spirit. **19.** 'immorality' signifies sexual irregularity in general. **21.** 'carousing' i.e. sacred orgies. **23.** Cf 18 supra. The Law was largely negative; there is now no limit to the practice of virtue under the influence of the Spirit. **24.** The Christian by his baptism has died to all the works of the 'flesh'. **25.** Yet the complete victory over ourselves is not yet ours, but will be if we follow the Spirit.

m 6:1–10. Practical Advice for Good Living—**1.** 'is overtaken'. i.e. is found out. **2.** i.e. help the sinner to throw off the burden of his sin and shame. **4.** Let each man examine his own conscience and not make (odious) comparisons. **5.** Every one is responsible for his spiritual life and problems. **6.** Let him who receives instruction repay spiritual benefits by temporal support. **7–10.** Since we cannot deceive God as to our real worth, it is only good sense to acquire real worth in his eyes by well-doing to all, but especially to those who are united to us in Christ in the Church.

n 11–18. Autograph and Epilogue—**11.** 'See with what large letters'—It is generally held by modern commentators that at this point, Paul adds the concluding words with his own hand, cf 1 Cor 16:21, either **898l** as a precaution against forgeries, cf 2 Thes 2:2; 3:17, or (as often done) by way of ending a letter otherwise written by a scribe, as today one might add a few words by hand to a typewritten letter. It is true that *grammata* is sometimes used for a letter (epistle) though not by Paul elsewhere, e.g. Ac 28:21; but 'to write a letter' would be *grammata graphein*, not, as here, *grammasin* which could only mean letters of the alphabet. But why should Paul draw attention to the *large* letters he makes? Because he was handicapped by defective eyesight? There is no positive evidence of this, though if it were so he could have made a joke of it. Or was it because he was unable to write elegantly? But Paul was well educated and his normal use of a scribe would hardly influence his handwriting. But were large letters in any case inelegant? There is nothing in the expression *pēlikois grammasin* to suggest that the letters were badly formed. There is no reference in Gr. texts to a large or small hand but there is a passage of some interest in a Coptic life of a saint. It relates that St Symphronius, as a small boy, learned first the 'small hand' and six months later the 'large hand'; which certainly suggests that in Coptic, very similar to Gr., the large hand was more difficult, W. Till, *Koptische Heiligen-und Martyrerlegenden, Orientalia Christiana Analecta*, 102, Roma, 1935, vol. 1, p. 57. Perhaps the correct answer is to be found in the length of the final paragraph, as contrasted with the few words with which Paul usually concluded, in his own hand. Here he sums up the lesson of the epistle and writes in bold characters to stress its importance, cf Lightfoot, in loc. Lagrange observes that in the papyri the more important parts are often written larger, Comm. in loc.

12. Fear of persecution by the synagogue was therefore a leading motive in the Galatian movement towards circumcision. **14.** '. . . by which the world has been crucified . . .' **15.** All that matters now is to be 'a new creation' transformed by baptism into a Son of God, being made one with Christ by the seal of the Holy Spirit. **16.** 'The Israel of God', i.e. the Church in general. **17.** Paul orders that there be no further disputes on these matters. 'The marks of Jesus' are almost certainly the marks of the ill-treatment he had already received in Galatia during his first missionary journey; cf Ac 14 passim.

18. Sums up the teaching of the epistle: it is by 'grace' that we are saved and not by the Law; cf Ac 15:11.

EPHESIANS

BY LIONEL SWAIN

99a Bibliography—*Commentaries*: B. F. Westcott, 1906; J. Armitage Robinson, 1922²; T. K. Abbott, ICC 1922⁴; J. Huby, VS, 1947¹⁵; M. Dibelius-H. Greeven, 1953³; F. W. Beare, IB 1953; C. Masson, CNT 1953; H. Schlier, 1957; E. K. Simpson, NIC 1957; P. Benoit, BJ 1959; F. F. Bruce, 1961; H. Chadwick, PC (2) 1962; H. Conzelmann, NTD 1962⁹; K. Staab, RNT 1959³; G. Johnston, 1967; G. H. P. Thompson, 1967.

Other Literature: W. Kümmel, *Introd. to NT*, NTL, 1966; L. Cerfaux, RF, 1965; E. J. Goodspeed, *The Meaning of Ephesians*, 1933; W. L. Knox, *St Paul and the Church of the Gentiles*, 1939; E. Percy, *Die Probleme der Kolosser- und Epheserbriefe*, 1946; H. Schlier & P. V. Warnach, *Die Kirche in Epheserbrief*, 1949; J. A. T. Robinson, *The Body*, 1953; C. L. Mitton, *The Epistle to the Ephesians*, 1951; F. L. Cross, ed. *Studies in Ephesians*, 1956; H. J. Cadbury, 'The Dilemma of Ephesians', NTS 5 (1958–9), 91–102; L. Cerfaux, *The Church in the Theology of St Paul*, E.tr. 1959; id *Authenticité des épîtres de la Captivité, Littérature et Théologie Paulinlennes, Recherches Bibliques*, 1960; J. Dupont, *Gnosis*, 1960; M. Barth, *The Broken Wall*, 1960; B. Rigaux, *St Paul et ses lettres*, 1962, 143–8; P. Benoit, 'Épître aux Ephésiens', DBS 7 (1966) 195–211; D. Guthrie, *NT Introd.* 1966²; J. Cambier 'La Bénédiction d'Eph. 1:3–14'; ZNTW 54 (1963) 58–104; id 'Le Grand mystère en Eph. 5:22–33', Bib 47 (1966) 43–90; 223–42.

b Literary Form—Apart from the address and initial greeting: 1:1–2, and the brief personal note and final greeting: 6:21–24, Ephesians has little that belongs to the recognized literary form of a letter or epistle. Its two main parts: 1:3–3:22 and 4:1–6:20 comprise principally the literary forms of prayers and paranesis respectively, but there are also possible traces of pre-existing prayers, hymns and exhortations which could have been borrowed from the practice of the early Church. Thus Ephesians is more an elaborate homily or discourse than a letter in the generally accepted sense of that term. In this respect, it is very similar to Hebrews and I Peter, with which latter it has the most striking resemblances.

c Language, style and composition—This conclusion about the 'epistle's' literary form is confirmed by a consideration of its language, style and composition. Both the language and the style reflect a principally Semitic background with strong Asianic overtones. The style, in particular, is often liturgical, at times hieratic and the author has a predilection for long, tortuous sentences and phrases, an accumulation of nouns and genitives, and repetition. In the light of the author's possible sources: Christian hymns, prayers, elements of catechesis and paranesis, the unified composition of the work is truly remarkable, the author displaying a full mastery of all the well known literary techniques of his time: parallelism, chiasm, inclusion, the use of link words. All of these observations hardly point to an epistolary literary form.

Destination—According to the title and the address **899d** (1:1) the work was directed to the faithful at Ephesus. However, the former is non-authentic and non-canonical, dating from the 2nd cent. at a time when the NT Canon was established, and the latter is more commonly recognized as an addition to the text, dating from the end of the 4th cent. In fact the phrase 'in Ephesus' is missing from the best MSS and its addition is more intelligible than its omission from the original. Moreover, as a consideration of its literary form has suggested, Ephesians does not appear to have been sent to a particular community, since it contains very few personal elements. Also, on the supposition of a Pauline authorship, it is extremely improbable that a 'letter' sent to Ephesus would omit references to known individuals in the community. These considerations have led virtually all scholars to reject an Ephesian destination. But there is little agreement about an alternative. Some identify Ephesians with the document sent to the Laodiceans (Col 4:16), while others hold strongly to the hypothesis of a circular letter, sent to the Churches of Asia Minor. None of the arguments so far adduced on this point is conclusive.

Author—Ephesians is explicitly ascribed to Paul **e** (cf 1:1; 3:1). Moreover, ancient tradition, from the time of Iren. and Clem. Alex., has firmly attributed it to the apostle of the Gentiles. Nineteenth-cent. criticism, however, elaborating the insights of Erasmus (16th cent.) and of Evanson (18th cent.) questioned this traditional view and today there is division among exegetes.

The arguments levelled against the Pauline authorship are of two kinds: theological and literary, none of which is fully conclusive.

From the theological viewpoint, it is claimed that the thought of Ephesians represents a marked development, and, is some instances, an opposition *vis à vis* the thought of the genuine Pauline epistles. This, it is maintained, is so even in the case of Colossians, which, on the hypothesis of Pauline authenticity, must have been produced just before Ephesians. Is it possible that Paul's thought could have developed so considerably over such a comparatively short space of time? Further, and the argument affects also the authenticity of Colossians, the climate of thought appears to be different in Ephesians from that in the Great Epistles. Ephesians seems to be bathed in the Hellenistic gnostic atmosphere of the end of the first cent., especially with reference to such terms as 'mystery', 'wisdom', '*plērōma*', 'body', 'head', the 'New Man', and to the marriage image of the union between the Church and Christ, a replica of the gnostic syzygy theme.

As far as the development of thought is concerned, **f** it can be answered in favour of Pauline authorship, firstly that the observation of a development of change of perspective is a matter of exegesis, and that not all scholars agree about all these supposed changes of meaning; secondly, that once a development has been observed, it can be satisfactorily explained by Paul's

899f changed historical situation. Most scholars accept the Pauline authenticity of Colossians and it is widely agreed that his perspective is noticeably different in this epistle from that in the Great Epistles. This new perspective is clearly explained by the concrete problem which Paul is here facing: the Colossian heresy. In the light of the latter he was forced to re-think and re-formulate the mystery of Christ in cosmic terms which were comprehensible to his readers. What was to prevent Paul from writing at the same time or immediately after Colossians, but this time in a less polemical and more contemplative frame of mind, a synthesis of his new insights gained in the Colossian episode? Being a creative literary genius there was no need for him to confine himself to a parrot-like use of the terms already used in Colossians. Thus Eph would be related to Col as Rm to Gal. Further, the 'originality' of Eph *vis à vis* the Great Epistles can too easily be exaggerated. Many of the epistle's main themes are found already in the Great Epistles, at least in embryonic form: predestination to divine sonship, the relationship between Jews and Gentiles, the gratuitousness of salvation, the gift of the Holy Spirit, the Church the body of Christ and the bride of Christ; baptism as union with Christ. Also. the two main parts of Eph: the prayer and exhortation, both have their more simple antecedents in the Great Epistles. Many scholars today try to explain the phenomenon of Eph along these lines.

g Regarding the thought atmosphere of Eph it is too facile to appeal directly to gnosticism or the Hellenistic mystery religions as the source of the author's ideas. The discoveries at Qumran have shown the existence of an incipient form of first-cent. Jewish gnosticism and there are many possible contacts with the thought represented at Qumran and Ephesians: the sapiential apocalyptic idea of 'mystery', the oppositions: light—darkness, truth—deceit, the idea of holiness, the notion of the community as a living temple, but the first clear instances of 2nd-cent. gnosticism are far too late to prove any influence of this movement of thought on Eph. This is particularly true of the gnostic Urmensch-Saviour myth. Indeed it is relevant to ask whether the influence is not in the other direction. Could the insights of Col, Eph not have influenced gnostic speculation? Certainly the respective controlable dates would seem to suggest a positive answer. Greater emphasis needs to be put on Paul's creative theological genius. Granted that in his time there existed a certain form of gnosticism known to his readers, who were also familiar with the Hellenistic mystery cults, it is possible that Paul used its vocabulary as a vehicle for the Christian message. The ultimate source of his theology, however, is situated, beyond the Christian revelation, in the OT. His idea of *plērōma*, for instance, is possibly a reflection of his meditation on Is 6:1—4, while his notion of Christ as the New Man, incorporating the whole Church was doubtless prepared by the Danielic Son of Man (Dan 7) and the Heb. concept of corporate personality.

h From the literary standpoint, it is indeed remarkable that Eph appears to use Paul's undisputed works, especially Col, more than these works themselves use Pauline sources. It is argued that this phenomenon is best explained on the hypothesis of a plagiarist who is drawing on Paul's epistles and presenting a new work under his name. However, all these sources are not assembled in the familiar fashion of the plagiarist, but they are blended together in a general way which evinces a powerful theological mind having complete control of his sources. To confirm this we only have to read the recognized apocryphal Epistle to the Laodicaeans.

The particularly close contacts with Col can be explained **899** by the proximity of the two works. As far as vocabulary is concerned, the proportion of new words and *hapax legomena* in Eph is not significantly greater than in any of Paul's epistles. In order to explain certain clumsy constructions, reflecting a contact with Col which could hardly be due to Paul himself, some scholars (e.g. P. Benoit) have suggested that Eph in its present form is the work of an inspired secretary who was working under Paul's instructions and with particular reference to Col.

In fine, the burden of proof lies with those who would reject Pauline authorship, but, so far, no conclusive evidence has been adduced. In any case, whether by Paul or not, Eph is a masterpiece of inspired Christian literature, and cannot but be the fruit of a genius of at least Paul's stature.

Place and date—If Eph is Pauline and the references **900** to imprisonment refer to Paul's captivity the obvious place of origin is Rome some time towards the end of his first captivity, i.e. about 63. If, however, Pauline authorship is ruled out, the *terminus ad quem* would have to be the first decade of the 2nd cent., to coincide with Ignatius' obvious allusion to it. In this hypothesis, it would probably have been written in Asia Minor, due to the affinities with Col.

Theology—Apart from the development and the deepen- **b** ing of the key Pauline themes already mentioned, Eph has the originality of expounding the mystery of Christ in extra-temporal and cosmic terms. This mystery is essentially trinitarian and the author, in several passages, underlines the trinitarian structure. The Father has revealed his redemptive love for men through Christ and this redemption is appropriated by Christians in the Spirit. The author's Christology is essentially triumphant. It is the glorious Christ enthroned as Lord of the universe and filling the whole of creation by his influence that is constantly in the background of the author's thought. By baptism and the life of faith the Christian already shares in Christ's Kingdom. This Kingdom is expressed in vivid images: the vital head—body relationship, the cultic stone-temple relationship, the loving wife—husband relationship. The eschatology of Eph is also remarkable: Christ's Kingdom is already here, but it has yet to be fully realized. The Parousia theme of the earlier epistles has been replaced by the concentration on present Christian existence, although there is still place for a futuristic aspect. This eschatology is very similar to that of Heb and Jn. The present Christian condition is seen as a fundamental response to God's initiative through Christ in the Spirit, culminating in prayer. For the author, the whole of Christian morality has its source and motivation in God's gift. Finally, Eph is the epistle of unity, that most profound but elusive of all human hopes. Christ, the New Adam, already uniting in himself the whole of creation is the unique source of human unity, which is to be attained not by mere human endeavour but by ever deepening penetration in the Spirit into the mystery of Christ. This unity is itself eschatological: already present in Christ it is still the aim of constant and eager striving.

Plan:

A. Address and greeting 1:1—2
B. Prayer 1:3—3:21
   I. Blessing 1:3—14
   II. Thanksgiving and Intercession 1:15—2:22
   III. Intercession and Doxology 3:1—21
C. Exhortation 4:1—6:20
   I. Universal Exhortation 4:1—5:21

d A. Address and Greeting 1:1—2 (Col 1:1—2)—
1. The epistle is explicitly attributed to Paul, who insists on his apostolic authority (cf Gal 1:1—2). As in Gal, Rm and Pastoral epistles, no collaborator is mentioned. 'The saints' is a technical term for all Christians who, by baptism, have received the dignity and privileges of God's chosen, consecrated people (cf Ex 19:6). The common reading 'in Ephesus' is absent from the best MSS and the most ancient quotations. Its appearance in the majority of MSS is best explained on the hypothesis of a late addition. Its exclusion from the original text, however, poses the problem of 'who are also'. Did this phrase figure in the original, as the mass of manuscript evidence seems to suggest, or was it also added at a very early stage in the manuscript tradition? Some scholars hold that it was in the original, followed by a blank space in which could be inserted the names of the different churches to which this encyclical letter was sent. Such a practice, however, is totally unknown in the ancient Middle E. Others, beginning with Origen, see in the phrase the pregnant meaning of 'to be', i.e. 'to exist'. Yet others take it as a reinforcement of 'the saints', i.e. 'those who are truly holy'. It is probably best understood in connexion with 'faithful' (cf Col 1:2), i.e. 'to those who are also faithful, or believing'. 'In Christ Jesus' announces a major theme of the epistle, Christ's mediating role and the union of all Christians, indeed the whole of creation, in him (cf 1:3, 4, 6, 7, 9, 10, 11, 12, 13, 20; 2:6, 7, 10, 13, 15, 18, 21, 22; 3:6, 11, 12, 21; 4:21; 5:20; 6:10).

e **2.** As in the Pauline epistles, the conventional opening greeting of the letter is charged with the quintessence of the Christian gospel and thus contains, in germ, the message of the whole work. It is more a prayer than a greeting, the author interceding for what, paradoxically, he knows is already given in Christ: grace (cf 1:6, 7; 2:5, 7, 8) and peace (2:14—18; 4:3). The source of these blessings is God our Father and the Lord Jesus Christ (RSV) or, possibly, God who is both our Father and the Father of our Lord Jesus Christ (cf Jn 20:17). In this latter rendering the Father's initiative in the work of redemption, so clearly pronounced in the main part of the epistle, is already adumbrated. In any case, the whole phrase strikingly evokes two of the epistle's most abundant themes: the Fatherhood of God (1:3, 5, 17; 2:18; 3:14; 4:6; 5:1, 20; 6:23) and the dominion of Christ (1:3, 15, 17, 21—22; 2:21; 3:11; 4:10; 4:17; 5:10, 17, 19, 20, 22; 6:1, 4, 7, 8, 9, 10, 21, 23, 24). The title God (*theos*) refers to the Father and the title Lord (*kyrios*), although not without a certain obscurity, to Christ. Since this latter title is the Gr. translation of Yahweh its so frequent application to Christ cannot but be an oblique reference to his divinity. Thus, by an ingenious use of words, the author implicitly asserts both an identity of nature between God and Christ (theos-kyrios) and a distinction of persons (Father—Son, cf 4:13).

f B. Prayer 1:3—3:21. I. Blessing 1:3—14—The first of the three prayers forming the first main part of the epistle is a blessing, doubtless based on the Jewish form of Berakoth (cf Lk 1:68—79; 2 Cor 1:3—6; I Pet 1:3—5). The style is both typically semitic and evocative of the cultic hymns of Asia Minor. It is also possible that the author is borrowing a pre-existing Christian hymn, although his own rich, tortuous and redundant style is evident throughout. Vv 3—10 present the longest

sentence of the NT. The structure of the whole hymn **900f** is essentially concentric, the author's mind moving in constantly decreasing circles over the same ideas expressed in different terms. In this way he inculcates his message less by logic than by sheer repetition. It is, however, possible to detect a real progress in his thought. Interior to the whole hymn in its present form, 3—10 are clearly to be considered as a literary unit distinct from 11—14. In the first section (3—10), after v 3 which resumes the whole hymn, the author moves from a contemplation of God's plan in eternity (4—6) to a description of its accomplishment in time (7—8) and then back to a consideration of God's eternal plan (9—10), v 10b rejoining v 3, after the manner of semitic inclusion. This structure places v 7 at the centre of the picture—which corresponds to the author's apparent principal preoccupation: to express the fact of redemption (*apolutrōsis* v 7) in supra-temporal and cosmic dimensions. In 11—14 the author covers essentially the same ground as in 3—10, though this time considering the 'mystery' of salvation from the viewpoint of mankind's two distinct compartments: the Jews (11—12) and the Gentiles (13—14).

3. The recurrence of 'God ... Father ... our Lord **g** Jesus Christ' links the hymn to the address and greeting (1—2). A 'blessing' is essentially an explicit recognition given to God of a 'blessing' received from him. This is clear from the threefold mention of the idea in v 3. Given this, it naturally follows that prayer of blessing includes a description of God's blessing. Thus 4—14 contain a *résumé* of the whole epistle. Also, the idea of blessing characterizes the author's entire attitude, not only in the prayer section of the epistle which is so permeated with the atmosphere of gratitude, but also in the paranetic section where the author emphasizes that the Christian life is basically and essentially a response to God's initiative. He therefore achieves an admirable synthesis between prayer and morality: the summit of the Christian life is the explicit and conscious recognition of God as he who blesses (1:3, 16; 2:14; 6:18—19) while the leading of the Christian life is itself a most eloquent response to that blessing (4:1; 5:1, 21). 'In Christ'. This formula, frequent in Eph, here has **h** both a mediatory sense, i.e. 'through Christ', and a local sense, i.e. in union with Christ. It is because Christ, by his resurrection and ascension, is himself in the heavenly places (cf 1:20; 2:6; 3:10; 6:12), that Christians being, by baptism, in Christ, are themselves blessed in those heavenly places (cf 6:24). Thus right at the beginning of the epistle the author evokes the image of the heavenly enthroned Christ. It is Christ's resurrection and ascension that forms the main background to his thought (cf 1:10, 20—23; 2:5—6; 4:8—10). 'Every spiritual blessing' contrasts the blessings communicated in Christ with mere material blessings and, possibly, the blessings of the New Covenant with those of the Old (Dt 28:1—14). It may even be an oblique reference to the promise made to Abraham, Gn 12:2f: it is in Christ that this promise is fulfilled, and in a way which transcends all its preparations in the OT (cf Gal 3:14). It could also contain an allusion to the Holy Spirit (cf v 13), who resumes in himself all of God's blessings (cf Lk 11:13 and Mt 7:11). V 3 would therefore contain a reference to each of the three Divine Persons. This trinitarian perspective is a marked characteristic of the author's thought (cf 1:13, 17; 2:18, 22; 3:4—5; 4:4—6; 5:18—20). The rest of the hymn (cf 'even as', **i** v 4) and indeed the whole of the epistle is a commentary on this v 3. **4.** The verb 'to choose' emphasizes the freedom of God's initiative and the phrase 'before the

900i foundation of the world' suggests both the eternal character of this plan and the pre-existence of Christ. In v 3 the author emphasized the transcendent aspect of God's blessing in relation, probably, to the promise made to Abraham. Now he intimates that God's plan transcends his 'choice' of Abraham and his seed. The plan of redemption is now given a supra-historical dimension. Thus the tension expressed in Rm 9—11 is greatly relieved, the 'chosen people' being now placed in a much less absolute position. The 'us', as in vv 3, 5, 6, 7, 8, 9, is the Church, the New Israel. 'Holy and blameless before him in love'. This is the aim of God's choice. Both 'holy' and 'blameless' are basically cultic terms (cf also 5:27; Col 1:22) but here they have been spiritualized by the qualification 'in love' (*agapē*). The Church, as Israel before it (cf v 1; Ex 19:6) is called to be holy and blameless, but not by means of the cult considered as an external performance of certain rites. Rather the source of the Church's holiness is in the existential quality of love which, according to the prophets of the OT, was the soul of the liturgy (Hos 6:6). The RSV reads 'in love' with v 5, but it is better kept in its original position, modifying 'holy and blameless'

901a in v 4 (cf Jn 17:17—19). **5.** Parallels v 4, the verb 'to pre-destine' emphasizing more than 'to choose' the divine intention (cf Rm 8:29). 'To be his sons' (lit 'into sonship') is a very rare expression (cf Gal 4:5; Rm 8:15, 23). This relation of sonship consists of love (*agapē*, v 4; cf 'the beloved', v 5) and *vice versa* (5:1—2). Although it is hardly necessary, the author insists that this is according to the purpose of God's will (cf 9, 11). **6.** Expresses the ultimate purpose of redemption: the recognition (cf 3) and 'the praise of God's glorious grace' (lit the glory of his grace) (cf 12, 14), and underlines the supreme freedom (cf 4) of God's choice (cf 2:5—10). **7.** From the contemplation of God's eternal plan (4—6) the author moves to its historical realization and experienced reality: 'we have'. The vocabulary 'redemption' (*apolutrōsis*), 'blood', 'remission of trespasses' evinces the sacrificial, cultic aspect of Christ's death and possibly reflects the twofold tradition of baptism and the Eucharist. In apposition to 'redemption', the phrase 'forgiveness of trespasses' shows in what sense this 'redemption' is to be understood in the present context: not as the final achievement of union with God (cf v 14; 4:30), but as its radical beginning. The modification 'according to the riches of his grace' (cf v 6; 2:7) assures that, despite the use of the forensic term '*apolutrōsis*', the 'redemption' is, above all else, the work of God's grace and does not involve his vindictive justice (cf Rm 3:21—26).

b **8.** The cultic-forensic idea of '*apolutrōsis*' is further spiritualized by the expression 'in all wisdom and insight' (cf Col 1:9) which properly belongs to 8 and not to 9 (RSV). The climax of God's redemptive love lies less in the fact of Christ's death than in the revelation of its meaning. After all, this death would have been of small value had its meaning as an expression of God's grace not been revealed. Throughout the epistle the author stresses this revelatory and noetic aspect of redemption (cf 1:17, 19; 3:9—10, 18, 19). **9.** The thought now rejoins the perspective of vv 4—6. God's choice (v 4) and pre-destination (v 5) constitute 'the mystery of his will' which has now been 'made known' in the Christ-event. In this context the 'mystery' means 'secret' (cf 3:9; 5:32; Col 1:26). This revelation of the mystery is not the privilege of a chosen few, as in the 'mystery' religions, but is destined for all. Further, this revelation is itself part of God's 'purpose which he set forth

in Christ' (cf 3:9—11). **10.** Since God's secret involves **9(** a certain 'working out' or 'disposition' it is rightly called a 'plan' or 'economy' (*oikonomia*) (cf 3:9). The phrase 'for the fullness (*plērōma*) of time' could refer simply to a future moment, but, in accordance with the general eschatology of the epistle, it more probably refers to the Christ-event considered as an eschatological reality (cf Gal 4:4), although still susceptible of a future final fulfilment (cf vv 7, 14). 'To unite (*anakephalaiōsasthai*) all things in him': the verb used here means 'to resume' (cf Rm 13:9) or 'to sum up', with the possible nuance of 'again' in the '*ana*' (cf v 7). The choice of the root '*kephalaion*' may be an intended reference to Christ as 'head' (*kephalē*) (cf 1:22; 4:15; 5:23). 'Things in heaven and things on earth'. This is an expression of totality (cf 'all things' in the same v), but it also serves to recall v 3. In raising Christ from the dead God has established his power over the universe. Here the author's universalistic perspective widens yet further to embrace not only all men (vv 4—5) but the whole of creation. This cosmic dimension of Christ is one of the epistle's most striking characteristics (cf 1:22; 3:10; Col 1:15—20). Christ is thus presented as the summit and king-pin of the whole of creation. It is possible that the author is here interpreting the creation accounts of Gn 1—2 in the light of Christ, the whole of creation thus being considered as receiving its full meaning and consistency in him (cf 2:10, 15; 4:24; Col 1:15 and Gn 1:26).

11—14 Judaeo- and Gentile Christians—After **d** contemplating the vast canvas of God's universal saving plan (3—10), the author delays on its reference to the two ethnic groups within the Church: the Jews (11—12) and the Gentiles (13—14, cf 2:11—22). This best explains the otherwise curious transference from 'we' (12) to 'you' (13). As distinct from in 3—10 the first person plural refers to Christians of Jewish origin, contrasted with those of Gentile stock. **11—12.** The verb 'to pre-destine' (*pro-orizō*, cf 5) and the relative 'in whom' (RSV 'in him') link 11—14 with the previous section. The RSV translation disturbs the order and the meaning of the v. The two verbs (RSV 'destined' *pro-orizō*, and 'appointed' *klēroō*, 12) belong to 11 and not to 12. It should therefore read, more correctly: 'In whom both we (cf the contrast in 13) have become heirs (or an inheritance, cf Dt 9:29) having been pre-destined, according ... his will, to be those who previously hoped (lit 'pre-hoped' cf 2:12) in Christ, for the praise of his glory'. Thus the 'pre-hoping' in Christ is not simply a description of the Judaeo-Christian, it is the object of the divine predestination. Similarly, the refrain 'for the praise of his glory' (cf vv 6, 14) is not the object of the divine predestination (RSV), but the end of the 'pre-hoping'. This translation brings out more the striking parallel between 11—12 and 13—14. The Jews were heirs of God's Kingdom (cf 5:5) in so far as they 'pre-hoped' in Christ—and for this they were pre-destined (cf v 5) by God. **13—14.** The Gentiles, on the other **e** hand, are heirs (v 14 '*klēronomia*', forming an inclusion with '*klēroō*' v 11) in so far as they have been sealed with the Holy Spirit of the promise (not 'promised Holy Spirit' RSV), through believing in the Gospel (or in Christ RSV). Thus the Gentiles are not in any position of inferiority *vis à vis* their Jewish colleagues. By their faith in Christ they participate in the Spirit of the promise (Gal 3:8—14; Rm 4:13—22; Acts 2:15—21, 33). The mention of 'sealing' (cf also 4:30) is possibly an implicit reference to the baptismal rite (cf 2 Cor 1:22). The Holy Spirit is described (v 14) **f**

01f as 'the guarantee' (*arrabōn*, cf 2 Cor 1:22) of our inheritance until we acquire possession of it (lit 'for the redemption (*apolutrōsis*, cf v 7; 4:30), of the possession'). The Gr. word '*arrabōn*' means a first instalment in kind of what is later to be completed. This underlines the futuristic aspect of redemption (cf 10). It is already achieved (7), but it is not yet fully realized (10, 14). The blessing of God in Christ (3) is not a static object but a dynamic reality capable of considerable development and growth. This dynamism of the Christian existence is another dominant note of Eph (cf 2:21—22; 3:16—19; 4:13—16). With the explicit mention of the 'Holy Spirit' (13) the author completes the trinitarian structure begun in 3, and the third, final reference to 'the praise of God's glory' (14; cf 6, 12), re-emphasizes the God-orientated character of his thought: just as everything comes from God, so it must return to him. He is the Alpha and the Omega.

02a **II. Thanksgiving and Intercession 1:15—2:22.**
15—16 Thanksgiving—The author's prayerful attitude is underlined by the fact that he begins his work not only with a blessing (3—14; cf 2 Cor 1:3f; 1 Pet 1:3f) but also with a prayer of thanksgiving (16; cf 1 Thes 1:2f; 2 Thes 1:3f; Rm 1:8f; Col 1:3f; Phil 1:3f; Phm 4—5). Indeed he appears so lost in prayer that he forgets that what he has recounted in 3—14 was in the context of a 'blessing': 'for this reason' (15). This phrase, together with the mention of 'faith' (cf 13) links the two prayers together. If the reference to 'love' ('*agapē*' missing from some witnesses, cf Col 1:4) were original, it would corroborate this link (cf 4). Without it the passage is certainly difficult to understand, unless the faith ('*pistis*') is taken in the sense of 'faithfulness'— which would be unusual in this context. On the other hand, the reference to 'love towards all the saints' suggests the famous collection which Paul organized for the poor of Jerusalem, the 'saints' *par excellence* (cf Gal 2:10; 2 Cor 8—9; Rm 15:25—27) which contributed considerably towards the union in faith and love between the Gentile and Jewish Christians (cf 2:11—22). Some scholars see in v 15 an intimation that the author did not know his readers personally and, therefore, either he could hardly have been Paul or his readers could hardly have been the Ephesians (cf Ac 20:31). But this argument seems very flimsy (cf Col 1:3; 1 Thes 1:2; 2 Thes 1:3; Phm 4—5). **16.** The phrase 'I do not cease' stresses the intensity and the constancy of the author's prayer (cf 6:18; Col 4:2; Phil 1:4; Col 1:3; 1 Thes 5:17; 2 Thes 1:11).

b **17—19 Prayer of Intercession—17.** The author's prayer moves imperceptibly from thanksgiving to intercession, the link being in 16b. The request is introduced by 'that' ('*hina*') (cf 3:16, 17; 6:19) and is essentially a demand for God 'to give' (cf 3:16; 6:19). There is a remarkable parallel between the substance of the prayer and the plan of redemption as outlined in 3—14: address to God (17, cf 2, 3), the Father of glory (6, 12, 14), 'spirit of wisdom and revelation in the knowledge of him' (17; cf 3, 8, 9), hope (18, cf 12), 'his glorious inheritance in the saints' (18, cf 11, 14, 15). Thus the prayer is not without a certain paradox: it is a request for what is already given (3—14) and, therefore, a recognition of God's gift, the prayer of intercession rejoining the prayer of thanksgiving (16). The emphasis, however, is clearly on the noetic aspect of redemption: it is a prayer for wisdom, revelation, knowledge (cf 8—9). In this respect there is a progress in relation to 3—14: it is a prayer not for redemption itself, but for the knowledge of redemption. There is progress also in the substance of **19**: the power

(*dynamis*) at work in the believer (cf 14). The trinitarian **902b** structure of the author's thought can be detected in v 17.
20—2:10 Description of God's might—20. The power c now at work in the faithful is that which God displayed in raising Christ from the dead and enthroning him at his right hand in the heavenly places (cf 3). The resurrection is the work of the Father in Christ (cf 1 Thes 1:10; 1 Cor 6:14; 15:15; 2 Cor 4:14; Gal 1:1; Rm 4:24; 10:9; Ac 2:24; 1 Pet 1:21). The celestial coronation of Christ has two principal consequences: he transcends all (v 21); everything is, therefore, submitted to him (v 22).

21. The cosmic beings mentioned here also figure in Col but in a more polemic context, Paul being there preoccupied with showing, in face of the Colossian heresy, that Christ transcends all the cosmic powers (cf Col 1:16; 2:15). Here, however, there is little or no polemical note, the author simply wishing to affirm Christ's universal supremacy (cf Phil 2:9). **22a.** This is an application of Ps 8:6 to Christ's exaltation (cf 1 Cor, 15:24). **22b.** The climax of God's power is manifest in the creation of the Church. God has given Christ, who has dominion over the whole cosmos, to the Church as its head. Pronounced as the cosmic aspect of redemption is in Eph, it is only accidental to the central theme: the union of all men with Christ in the Church. The fact that Christ transcends the whole of creation is a striking proof of God's love for the Church in giving Christ to it as its head. It is interesting to notice that Christ is not the 'head' of all creation, but only of the Church. The head-body image applies only to the relationship between Christ and the Church and not between Christ and creation (cf Col 2:10). Here lies an d essential difference between this image and the Gnostic Urmensch myth which is often adduced as the source of the author's thought. Further, the earliest clear references to this Saviour myth in the Gnostic literature are of a much later date than Eph. It is also noteworthy that here the term 'church' (*ekklēsia*) denotes not a particular assembly as it does usually in the undisputed Pauline epistles (cf 2 Cor 11:28) but the transcendent community of all believers (cf 5:23—33; Col 1:18, 24; 2:19), the universal Church. **23.** The term 'head' (v 22) is ambivalent. Possibly reflecting the Hebrew '*rōsh*' it can mean both the principal, the superior, and the head, in the physiological sense. The author resolves all doubt by describing the Church in Christ's body (*sōma*). This image is found in the indisputable Pauline literature, but there it is used either to express the Church's social character (1 Cor 12:12—13; Rm 12:4—5; cf Eph 4:25) or its Eucharistic aspect (1 Cor 10:17), or to provide a basis for sexual morality (1 Cor 6:15—20), without any explicit distinction being drawn between the 'head' and the 'body', the one being considered as just a part of the other. Here, however, because of the context, such a distinction is clear (Col 1:18). For all his transcendence, however, Christ is also dependent upon the Church as the head upon the body. In other words, the 'whole Christ' is both head and body. Christ is both transcendent (head) and immanent (body). It is this active immanence of Christ e in the faithful that is God's power (v 19; 3:17), the principle of growth (2:21) and, therefore, of all Christian behaviour (4:23). The 'body' is further qualified by the difficult term 'fulness' (*plērōma*; cf 3:19; 4:13; Col 2:9—10). The most probable sense of the whole clause is that the Church is itself the fulness, i.e. the fullest manifestation, the completion of Christ who himself, by his resurrection and ascension, fills everything (cf 1:10). The Church, in other words, is God's masterpiece, the end of redemption. The effect of this notion of '*plērōma*'

902e is to underline the dynamic character of redemption: accomplished once and for all in Christ, it develops in so far as its completion involves the assimilation of more men into Christ's body, and to the extent that these respond to their new God-given existence (cf Col 1:24). The expression 'all in all', as 'plērōma' itself, is very probably a borrowing of Stoic terminology.

f **2:1—10.** Having already (1:22—23) raised the subject of mankind's incorporation into Christ by redemption, the author now proceeds to elaborate it. The links between this section and the previous one are obvious, the Christian's baptism being expressed in the same terms as Christ's resurrection and heavenly exaltation. It is also remarkable how vv 9—10 rejoin and resume 1:22—23. **1.** Against the background of Christ's redemptive death and resurrection (1:7, 20—23) the previous sinful state of the Gentiles (cf 1:7) is seen as a living death. **2.** This condition is fostered by human behaviour: 'in which you once walked', itself influenced by evil and malignant forces: 'following . . . disobedience'. This condition is thus the exact opposite to that of Christians, who must now behave (lit 'walk', cf 4:1) in justice and truth (cf 4:24) in the Holy Spirit (cf 2:22) as a child of God (5:1). In raising Christ from the dead, God had conquered the 'world' and radically incapacitated the 'power of the air' (cf 6:11—12), that is, the space between earth and heaven, considered by ancient cosmology as the abode of demons. But in so far as men are not yet incorporated into Christ by baptism, that is, in so far as they are still 'sons of disobedience' they are still under the demons' sway (cf 6:10—17).

g **3.** The Jews too were involved in this previous sinful condition. The double reference to 'flesh' ('body' RSV) is possibly a touch of irony (cf 11). 'By nature children of wrath' does not refer to the doctrine of original sin, but to a factual situation and also to the seemingly 'natural' proclivity to sin. **4.** To the state of rebellion incurring God's wrath is now strikingly contrasted his undeserved 'love' (agapē, cf Rm 5:6—11). **5—6.** By baptism the Christian is inserted into Christ. He therefore shares in Christ's destiny (cf 1:3). **7.** As in 1:6, 12, 14, the final aim of redemption is the revelation of God's 'grace'. **8.** (cf v 5b) In a typically Pauline strain (cf Rm 3:24; 9:6; Gal 2:16), the author stresses the absolutely gratuitous character of the redemption.

9—10. The ultimate extent of God's power at work in Christians (cf 1:19) is that they should be 'created in Christ Jesus' (cf 1:22—23), not only in their being but also in their activity. It is this new creation in Christ (cf 2:15; Gal 6:15; 2 Cor 5:17; Col 1:15) that is the basis and principle of all Christian morality (cf 4:1f). Christian activity consists less in man's action than in God's action in man through Christ. Man's role is to respond to that action.

h **11—22 Union between Jews and Gentiles**—Since redemption involves the re-creation of mankind in Christ (v 10; cf 1:10, 22—23; 2:15), the old division between Israel and the Gentiles no longer has any meaning (cf 1:11—14). The author now draws out the consequences of his cosmic and creative view of redemption for a new understanding of the relationship between Jews and Gentiles (Gal 3:6—29; Rm 9—11; Ac 15:1—29). The abolition of all essential difference is doubtless the greatest sign of God's power still active in Christ.

11. There is a note of irony here: the distinguishing mark of the Jew was circumcision, made in 'the flesh'. He was therefore no less 'carnal' than the Gentile (cf 2:3). To this merely accidental, superficial and fleshly difference will be opposed the profound, essential and spiritual

unity of all men in Christ and the Spirit (cf vv 15, 18, **902** 20—22). **12.** The author does recognize, however, the privileged position of Israel before Christ (cf 1:12; Rm 9:4—5) and the relatively unprivileged situation of the Gentiles.

13—18. Here the unifying and pacifying aspects of **i** Christ's death (cf 1:7) and resurrection are emphasized, 13 and 17 being an application of Is 57:19 to the Christ-event. The Gentiles have not had access to God through becoming Jewish proselytes. Christ's religion is a New Religion. The Jewish law is considered in its pejorative aspect, as being a dividing wall of hostility, symbolized, probably, by the wall in the Temple which separated the Court of the Gentiles from the Court of the Jews. A reference here to the Gnostic idea of a heavenly wall (Schlier) is less probable. There are no longer two sections of humanity, because Christ, by his death and resurrection, has destroyed the Jewish law, in so far as it was a dividing factor (cf Gal 3:13; Col 2:14), and united all mankind in himself, so establishing peace. It is interesting to notice that, for the first time in the epistle, the initiative is here given to Christ (vv 14, 15, 16, 17). The 'new man' (v 15; cf 4:24) is a reference back to 1:10, 22—23; 2:9). The 'one body' (v 16), because of the immediate connexion with 'the cross' seems to be Christ's individual body, but it also evokes the Church (1:23), since it is through the cross and resurrection that the whole Christ (1:23) is created and so reconciled to God. V 17 may contain a reference to the tradition recounted in Jn 20:19—23. The trinitarian character of this new unity is clearly pronounced in **18.**

19—22. In and after the Christ-event the lot of the **j** Gentiles has changed. In the present context, 'the saints' (19) may refer to the Jews, or at least the Jewish Christian communities (cf 1:1), but it could also refer to the citizens of heaven (cf Gal 4:26). **The members of the Qumran community considered themselves as fellow-citizens of the angels. The mention of 'God's household'** leads the author to another powerful image—that of a sacred building (cf v 20; 1 Cor 3:10; 2 Cor 6:16; Rm 15:20). The 'foundation' of the apostles and prophets doubtless refers to the first preaching of the Gospel which is the basis of faith (cf 3:5). The 'prophets' in question are more probably those of the NT (3:5; 4:11; Rm 12:6; 1 Cor 12:28; 14 etc) than those of the Old. The 'corner stone' could be the foundation stone, but it is more probably the stone which crowns, completes and holds together the whole building (cf Pet 2:4). This would be an evocation of 1:10, 22—23; 2:10. **The image of a building imperceptibly blends with that of the body (v 21;** cf 4:12, 16). The community, the Church, is now the New Temple of God (cf 14), another concept which is found in the Qumran literature. Finally (22) the trinitarian structure of the building is expressed (cf 18).

III. Intercession and doxology 3:1—21—The **903** author has never really left his prayer, but in 3:1 he gives the impression of making a fresh start (cf 1:15).

1. Despite appearances Paul (cf 1:1) is a prisoner neither of the Jews nor of the Romans, but of Jesus Christ. Further, his captivity, far from being a hindrance to his apostolate, is an integral part of it (cf v 13).

2—13 Parenthesis on Paul's apostolic role (cf Col **b** 1:24—29)—**2.** Is frequently adduced as an indication that the author was unacquainted with his readers (cf 1:15). But this is by no means clear. It could simply be his rhetorical way of introducing his description of the apostolate which he obviously considers important and is certainly no mere digression. Further, the same Gr. expression introducing the v recurs in 4:20 and this passage

3b could hardly suggest that the readers had not heard about Christ! Also the author is not so much affirming the fact of his apostolate as outlining its 'disposition' or 'plan' ('*oikonomia*', cf 1:10) which even his closest acquaintances need not have known. Just as in 1:3—14 he was intent on describing the plan of redemption, so now he wants to describe the plan of his vocation and mission (cf Gal 1:11—16). The term '*oikonomia*' (RSV 'stewardship'), therefore, is used in the same sense as in 1:10, but designates a different reality. It would be best rendered by 'plan' or 'blue-print'. Correspondingly, 'God's grace' which was given to Paul is not the 'grace' of 1:6; 2:5, 7, 8 but the charism of the apostolate to the Gentiles (cf vv 7, 8; 4:7—13; Rm 1:5; 15:15f; 1 Cor 3:10; Gal 2:9; Phil 1:7; Col 1:25).

c   **3—5.** Clearly evoke 1:3—14 and 2:1—22, the previous descriptions of the 'mystery' (1:9; 3:3, 4), the mention of writing and reading in 3 and 4 most probably referring to these passages. **3.** 'by revelation' (cf 1:17) is possibly a reference to the episode on the Damascus road (Ac 9:15ff; Gal 1:16). **4.** The idea of 'revelation' is deepened by that of 'insight' (cf 1:8), that is, the personal appropriation of the revelation (cf 1:17f). The author thus claims for himself what he demands for others. **5.** The 'mystery' has been revealed to the whole Church (cf 1:8—10, 17f) but first and foremost to the 'apostles and prophets' (cf 2:20). These are described as 'holy', an epithet which, some scholars say, Paul would hardly have applied to himself. It is, however, to be understood not in the moral sense, but in the sense of 'sacred', 'consecrated' (cf 1:1, 4), meaning 'dedicated' or 'chosen' (cf Jn 6:69; 10:36; 17:17—19). The apostles and prophets (cf 4:11) are the channels of God's revelation to the whole Church. It is in this sense that they are its foundation (cf 2:20). The 'Spirit' (1:17) is the instrument of revelation to the apostles and prophets (cf 1 Cor 2:10—13).

d   **6.** Succinctly resumes the content of 2:11—22. 'The gospel' (*evangelion* cf 1:13; 2:17; *evangelizomai*), is both 'the good news' of redemption itself and the means whereby the Gentiles are incorporated into Christ's body.

7—13. Explain the apostle's communicatory role. **7.** The term 'the gospel' forms a link with what precedes. The apostle is essentially a 'minister' (*diakonos*) of the gospel, that is, an instrument in its communication. The apostolate is a charisma (cf vv 2, 8; 4:7—13) and an aspect of God's power at work in the Church (cf 1:19—20; Gal 2:8; Col 1:29; Phil 4:13). **8.** The sentiment of humility is strikingly reminiscent of 1 Cor 15:8—11; 1 Ti 1:12—17). The apostle's function is essentially that of a preacher, of a proclaimer of the 'good news'. He is thus a representative of Christ (cf 2:17). The phrase 'unsearchable riches of Christ' recalls 1:18; 2:4, 7.

e   **9.** This preaching is an illuminating process (cf 1:18; 5:7—14), the apostle now being depicted as a revealer, after the manner of the initiator in the mystery religions (cf 1:9). 'The plan (*oikonomia*, cf v 2) of the mystery' evokes 1:9—10. The idea of God as creator (cf 2:10, 15) reinforces the transcendence of the mystery.

10—11. The final end of redemption is the universal and cosmic manifestation of God's wisdom (cf 1:6, 12, 14; 2:7). This has been achieved by Christ's resurrection and heavenly exaltation (1:3, 10, 20—23) which finds its fullest development and expression in the 'Church' (cf 1:22—23). The term 'purpose' evokes 1:5, 11. **12.** This irrevocable triumph of Christ is the guarantee of the apostle's final victory and the source of his confidence (cf 6:19—20). **13.** The apostle's afflictions are the climax of his role (cf the inclusion 'for you', vv 1 and 13, also 2 Cor 6:3—10; 11:21—12:10; Phil

1:14; 2:17; 3:10; Col 1:24; 2 Ti 1:12; 2:9; 4:6). He **903c** is thus presented throughout this section (3:1—21) as an intercessor (cf v 1, v 14f), a preacher (vv 8, 9) and a sufferer (vv 11—12). These are three essential aspects of the apostolate.

14—19 Intercession—14. After the parenthesis 2—   **f** 13, the author resumes his prayer. As in 1:3f and 1:17f it is directed to the Father. As the latter prayer, it is a subtle blending of adoration: the bending of the knee (cf Is 45:23; Phil 2:10) and intercession: '*hina*', vv 16, 18, 19 (cf 1:17; 6:19, 20). **15.** The word 'family' (*patria*), apparently a play on the word '*pater*', designates a social group which derives its existence and unity from one ancestor. The author's intention is clearly to emphasize the Father's transcendent causality (cf 1:21; 3:9) as a starting point and motivation of his prayer.

16—19. Express the object of the intercession. As in   **g** 1:17f it is essentially a prayer for God's gift (cf 'grant', v 16). But, seen in the context of the whole epistle, it is clearly a request for a blessing which God is already granting (cf 1:19—2:22). For the Christian, even the prayer of intercession is essentially a response to God's initiative. **16.** For 'the riches of his glory' cf 1:7, 18; 2:4, 7. For 'strengthened with might' cf 1:19. The 'inner man' is the Christian in so far as he is re-created in Christ (cf 2:10, 15; 4:24). The preposition 'in' (into, RSV 'in') brings out the dynamic aspect of the Christian life (cf 1:23), and the mention of the Spirit underlines the trinitarian aspect (cf 1:3, 14, 17, 2:18, 22, 3:4—5). **17.** In 2:20—22 the Christians are considered as being a temple in Christ. Here Christ is seen as having a dwelling place in them. 'Being rooted and grounded in love' modifies more 'dwell in your hearts' than 'have power to comprehend' (18). 'Faith' and 'love' (cf 1:4, 13, 15; 2:8) are the media of Christ's indwelling. Again the dynamic aspect is emphasized, the author praying not simply that his readers may have love, but that they may be 'rooted and grounded' in it.

18. Here the notion of power (*ischus*, cf 1:19) is related   **h** to comprehension (cf 1:18). For 'the saints' cf 1:1, 4, 15; 2:19. The phrase 'breadth and length and height and depth' is doubtless derived from Stoicism (cf 1:22—23) and is intended to designate the universal and all-embracing character of Christ's love (cf v 19; 1:23).

19. The 'love of Christ' is both the love which Christ has for the Church (cf 5:1, 25) and that which the Father has manifested in Christ (1:3—14). To 'know' that love is to have experienced contact with it in a way that transcends mere intellectual awareness. The final 'that' (*hina*) of this intercession could denote either the consequence of this knowledge of Christ or be yet another request (cf 16 and 18). It clearly forms a climax to the prayer and corresponds to the meaning of redemption (cf 1:22—23). What God has achieved already in Christ (cf 1:20—23) still has to be fully realized. The eschatology here evokes 1:13—14.

20—21 Doxology—The 'prayer' part of the epistle ends   **i** fittingly with the finest of all prayers: praise of God. Thus is made explicit what has been implicit throughout the whole of this part: the end of redemption is God's glory: 1:6, 12, 14; 2:7; 3:10. Characteristically, this prayer takes up several of the themes found in the first part: the superabundance of God's gift (v 20; cf 1:8, 19; 2:7; 3:19); God's power at work within the Christian (v 20; cf 1:19; 4:16); the parallel between Christ and the Church (v 21; cf 1:22—23; 3:10) and 'glory' (v 21; cf 1:6, 14, 18; 3:16). God has manifested his glory in Christ and in the Church, his body. It is the Christian's highest duty to recognize, and to respond to, this

903i revelation in the prayer of praise. At the end of this part, therefore, the author resumes the sentiments expressed at the beginning (1:3—14).

904a **C. Exhortation 4:1—6:20**—The second main part of the epistle: 4:1—6:20, as the first: 1:3—3:21, forms a clear literary unit in the form of an exhortation, itself comprising three distinct exhortations: to all Christians: 4:1—5:21, to specific classes of Christians: 5:22—6:9, to all Christians again: 6:10—20. Also, just as the first part is contained within an inclusion: 1:3—14 and 3:20—21, so is the second: 4:1 and 6:20. However, many of the ideas and expressions of the first part recur in the second and both are explicitly linked together by 'therefore' (*oun*) (4:1). This literary connexion expresses a more profound theological relationship. In 4:1—6:20 the author suggests that the Christian life is a response to God's revelation, and, therefore, is itself a prayer (cf 1:3). Moreover, the author, for his part, has hardly changed his prayerful attitude, since now he is interceding with his readers.

b **I. Exhortation to all the Faithful 4:1—5:21—4:1. The General Principle**—The content of the previous section is immediately evoked: 'prisoner of the Lord' (cf 3:1), 'to lead a life' (lit 'to walk'; cf 2:2), 'call' (cf 1:18).

2—16 Unity. The Essence of the Christian's vocation, described in 1:3—3:21 is unity: unity among men (cf 2:13—17) established by union with the Father, through Christ, in the Spirit (2:18). This 'ontological' unity is now transposed on to the moral plane, the faithful being exhorted to realize it in their own community. The emphasis is thus placed, as throughout most of this part, on the social aspect of Christian behaviour.

c **2.** 'in love' (*agapē*) (cf 1:4, 15; 4:15, 16; 5:2, 25, 28, 33) sums up the social attitude demanded of the Christian (cf Col 3:14). **3.** 'unity of the Spirit' and 'peace' have been given already in Christ (2:13—18). It is for the Christian to 'keep' them. Despite the absence of polemic, the background to this exhortation is probably at least a threat of disunity similar to that which had existed in Corinth (cf 1 Cor 12—14). **4—6.** Give the 'ontological' basis for this 'moral' unity: in terms which obviously refer back to the first part of the epistle: 'one body' (cf 1:23; 2:16; 3:6), 'one Spirit' (cf 2:18, 22), 'called' (cf 1:18), 'one hope' (cf 1:18; 2:12); 'one Lord' (cf 1:2, 3, 15, 17; 2:21; 3:11) 'one faith' (cf 1:13, 15, 19; 2:8; 3:12; 4:17) 'one baptism' (cf 1:13), 'one God and Father' (cf 1:2, 3, 17; 2:18; 3:14). The author typically qualifies God with the notion of transcendence and omnipresence (cf Jer 23:24; 1:20—24; 3:9, 15) and evinces the trinitarian structure of his thought (cf 1:3, 14, 17; 2:18, 22; 3:4—5).

d **7—16 Diversity in Unity**—This unity, however, is not uniformity. The thought here is very similar to that found in 1 Cor 12 and Rm 12:3f, the diversity of the one body being explained.

7. The 'grace' in question here is, as in 3:2, 7, 8, a particular role of function, a 'charism', given to the different members of the Church. As in 2:15 it is Christ himself who has the initiative, here being the person who gives. **8—10.** In typical rabbinic fashion the author uses Ps 68:18 in order to illustrate Christ's resurrection, heavenly exaltation and subsequent effusion of the Holy Spirit (cf 1:3, 14; Ac 2:33), the principal of all the charisms (cf 1 Cor 12:1—13). 'The lower parts of the earth' (v 9) is a reference either to the nether regions to which Christ descended after his death, or to the world itself to which Christ descended in the Incarnation. To this descent is opposed Christ's ascension through all the heavenly spheres by which he established his universal dominion (v 10; cf 1:3, 10, 21—23; 2:6; 3:10; 4:6). **11.** In his translation of Ps 68:18, possibly reflecting a contemporary targum, the author found already related the ideas of ascension and giving. He now develops this second point. The 'officials' of the Church are Christ's gift (cf 1 Cor 12:28; Rm 12:6—8 for other lists of charisms): 'Apostles and prophets' (cf 2:20; 3:5). 'Evangelist' (cf Ac 21:28; 2 Ti 4:5) 'Pastors and teachers' (cf Ac 13:1; 20:28). True to his emphasis on the revelatory or noetic aspect of redemption (cf 1:8—9, 17—18; 3:8—9), the author mentions only the charisms connected with teaching (cf vv 13, 14).

12. These charisms are all orientated essentially towards the service of the whole Church. In the present context 'the saints' (cf 1:1, 4, 18; 2:19; 3:5) probably refers to the immediate beneficiaries of these charisms (cf 3:5, 7) but it could also include a reference to all the members of the Church who, in different ways, share in 'the work of the ministry' (3:7). The phrase 'building up the body of Christ' evokes and combines two major ideas of chh 1—3: the building (cf 2:20—22; 3:17) and the body (cf 1:23; 2:16; 3:6.)

13—16. Elaborate this double image, emphasizing the **f** dynamic, developmental character of present Christian existence (cf 1:10, 14, 19; 2:21—22; 3:16—19). Christians are in Christ, have one faith, as a living body which grows and develops and, therefore, they have not yet achieved full maturity in Christ. Paradoxically, the Church both 'is' the fullness (1:23) and has 'not yet' attained it (v 13). This full maturity consists in 'knowledge' of the Son of God (v 13), possibly implying the full realization of what and who Christ is. It is obvious, therefore, that this full development will have as a necessary negative consequence the elimination of error and falsehood (v 14). Again (cf v 3) there is a possible allusion here to a real danger, this time from false teachers. Contrasted with these latter, the Christian's vocation (cf v 11) is 'to speak the truth' (v 15). This fundamental opposition between the children 'of deceit' and 'of truth' is also found at Qumran. The RSV **g** rendering of the verb '*alētheuein*' weakens its original meaning: 'to be true'. The means of this truth and the principle of growth is 'love' (cf v 2). The concentric structure and the movement of thought in vv 15—16 themselves give the impression of both dynamism: 'into the head (cf 1:22), Christ . . . from whom the whole body (cf 1:23) . . . upbuilding itself in love', and of the mutual dependence between Christ and the Church (cf 1:22—23). The image evoked in v 16, very close to that of 1 Cor 12:14—26 and Rm 12:4—8, stresses, by the use of precise anatomical terms, (cf Col 2:19) the intimately close and harmonious union existing between all the members of the Church (cf v 25).

17—24 The meaning of true conversion—v 1 was an **90** exhortation to positive behaviour (*peripatein*); 17, on the contrary, is an exhortation to abandon Gentile behaviour. Clearly the term 'Gentile' is used here pejoratively, somewhat differently from in 2:11; 3:1, 6, 8. The phrase 'no longer' is a reminder of the readers' previous condition (cf 2:1—2, 11—12), only here the emphasis is placed on the noetic aspect of that condition: 'the futility of their minds' (v 17; cf 2:3; 4:22), obviously in opposition to the essentially revelatory character of redemption.

18. This condition consists in 'darkness of understanding' (cf 1:18; 3:9) and 'alienation from God's life' (cf 2:12f), having their root cause in 'ignorance' and 'hardness of heart'. This latter phrase clearly suggests the mysteriously culpable character of the Gentile's ignorance—an important note in a work which so stresses the

5a noetic character of redemption. In the final analysis, Christ's redemption is not simply an ontological liberation, it is a moral salvation. It is essentially a redemption from sin (cf 1:7; 2:1). In this lies a major difference between the author's Christianity and Gnosticism, despite possible contacts of thought and expression. **9.** It is because of this profound perversity of mind and heart that the Gentiles have abandoned themselves to a vicious behaviour. Here the thought is strikingly reminiscent of Rm 1:18–32, although in this latter passage it is God who has abandoned men to their vices (1:24). The note of abundance in 'greediness' contrasts glaringly with the abundance of redemption (cf 3:20).

b 20–21. The Christian revelation is radically opposed to such behaviour, again with attention paid particularly to its educative aspect. The simple mention of 'Jesus' (v 21) is possibly an advertance to the historical character of this revelation: God has revealed his saving truth in the man Jesus (cf v 13).

22–24. Christian conversion is a profound and interior transformation of the whole man. The imagery of divestiture and investiture, probably reflecting the early baptismal ceremony (cf 1:13; Gal 3:27; Rm 13:14) in which the changing of clothes symbolized a transformation of life, vividly emphasizes man's active role in justification: he rejects (v 22) and he accepts (v 24). However, the Gr. original for the RSV 'nature' (vv 22, 24) is 'man' (*anthrōpos*) and cannot but refer to 2:15 and 3:16, that is, the whole Christ. Baptism involves a new creation by God (cf 2:10, 15; 2 Cor 5:17; Gal 6:15) effected through the justice and holiness 'of the truth' (v 24, not merely 'true', RSV), that is, the truth which is 'in Jesus' (cf v 21) communicated in the Gospel (cf 1:13). As in 14–15, there is a basic opposition established between deceit (v 22) and truth (v 24). Thus these vv (22–24) combine admirably both the objective aspect of redemption: new creation in Christ, and the subjective aspect: the personal, responsible assimilation of the new creation by each individual Christian.

c 4:25–5:5 Exhortation concerning particular virtues and vices—This section is neatly linked with the preceding vv by the verb 'to put away' (25, cf 22). In form and content it is typical of contemporary Jewish paraenesis, particularly as witnessed in Qumran, but it is original in its basis and motivation: mutual membership (25; cf 1:23; 2:16; 3:6; 4:4, 16; 5:30), the sealing with the Holy Spirit (30; cf 1:13–14), inheritance in the kingdom of Christ and of God (v 5; cf 1, 14, 18, 3.0) and, particularly, the imitation of God and Christ (v 32–5:2; cf 4:24). Once more, the trinitarian structure of the author's thought is clearly pronounced. **32.** Evokes Lk 6:30, although the verb 'to forgive' (*charizomai*) suggests more immediately Eph 1:6. Further, the expression 'beloved children' (5:1) evokes, by way of opposition, 'sons of disobedience' (2:2; 5:6) and 'children of wrath' (2:3; cf 5:6). The most perfect example of this filial comportment (*peripatein*, 5:2) in love (cf 4:1, 15, 16; Jn 15:12) is Christ's love (5:2; cf 4:13: the Son of **d** God; Jn 15:12). This love was expressed in Christ's self-abandonment to his Father. Thus, whereas the Gentiles' ignorance and hard-heartedness (cf 4:18) moves them to abandon themselves (*paredōkan*, v 19) to vice, the Christian's love, as that of Christ, inspires him to surrender himself to God in worship and to his fellow-men in service and kindness (5:2). This v clearly contains a reference to Christ's death (cf 1:7), although here, as in 2:14–18 and in 4:7–11, Christ's active role in redemption is emphasized: he 'gave himself' (cf vv 25–26; Gal 2:20). Since this gift is a sacrifice (cf Ps 40:7;

Ex 29:18) he, the giver, is here presented as both priest **905d** and victim.

6–17 Exhortation to general attitudes—After the **e** particular exhortation of 4:25–5:5, the author returns (cf 4:22–23) to a comparison between the respective states of the Gentiles and the Christians.

6. The reference to deceit (cf 4:14, 22) suggests the danger of heretical teachers. 7–14 emphasize the radical incompatibility existing between pagans and Christians (cf v 5; 2 Cor 6:15). The symbolism of opposed light and darkness (cf 1:18; 3:9; 4:18) is common in the early Christian literature and also occurs at Qumran (cf 4:15). Here again, however, (cf 4:25–5:5) a familiar Jewish theme is christianized, as the reference to 'the Lord' (vv 7, 10) and, particularly the quotation from an early Christian hymn (v 14) clearly show. The whole section vv 8–14 suggests an original baptismal context (cf 1:13–14; 2:1–6; 4:22–24).

15–17 are an exhortation to wise behaviour (*perip-* **f** *atein*) (cf 1:8, 17), which consists in the knowledge of the Lord's will. The word 'will' (*thelēma*, v 17) is not God's plan of redemption (cf 1:5, 9, 11) but the norm of Christian action manifested by God in Christ, the Lord (cf 4:32; 5:1–2, 10, 22–6:9). The eschatological, almost apocalyptic urgency in v 16 (cf Col 4:5) finds a parallel in the eschatology of Qumran (cf 6:10–17).

18–21: Exhortation to particular attitudes—Now **g** the author reverts to further specific forms of Christian behaviour (ct 4:1–16, 25–5:5). **18.** Is virtually a pun (cf Ac 2:1–13). Repletion (cf 1:23; 3:19; 4:13) with the Spirit is opposed to debauchery. **19.** The effect of this 'inspiration' is prayer and praise. Thus the 'Spirit' is seen to be the source of Christian prayer (cf 1:3; 1 Cor 12:3; Rm 8:26–27). This is one of the rare texts of the NT in which there is mention of prayer addressed to Christ the Lord (cf 1:2). **20.** On the other hand, expresses poignantly the more common structure of Christian prayer to the Father, through Christ, in the Spirit (cf vv 18, 19). The universality and constancy of this 'thanksgiving' evokes 1:16.

21 belongs more immediately to 4:1f than to 5:22f, since it concludes the exhortations addressed to all the faithful, the phrase 'being subject to one another out of reverence for Christ' forming an inclusion with 'forbearing one another in love' (4:2). The connexion of this v with the preceding vv also emphasizes that, for the Christian, the praise of God is inseparable from the service of men (cf 4:32–5:2).

II. Exhortation to specific categories of Christians h 5:22–6:9 (cf Col 3:18–4:1)—Throughout this whole section, the principle of Christian morality is presented, as in 4:1–5:21, as God's will made manifest in Christ. **22–33 Wives and husbands**—Previously two images **i** have helped the author to express the relationship between Christ and the Church: the head and body (1:22–23; 2:16; 3:6; 4:15–16) and the holy building (2:20–22; 4:12, 16). He now uses a third image: marriage. From the context it is clear that his immediate aim is to promote domestic morality, by showing that the relationship wife–husband, and *vice versa*, parallels the relationship the Church–Christ. But it is also obvious that, in the continuation and fulfilment of the familiar prophetical theme (cf Hos 1–3; Jer 2:2; 3:1, 6–12; Ezek 16; 23; Is 50:1 etc, 2 Cor 11:2; Apoc 12; 21:2, 9) he also intends to express the relationship between Christ and the Church in terms of marriage (cf v 32). Thus the revelation of the true meaning of Christian marriage and the manifestation of the Church's mystery are here interdependent.

905j **22—24 Wives—22.** Although 21 concludes the preceding section, it also forms a link with what follows, so that in the original Gr. (as against the RSV) there is no repetition of the verb 'to subject' in 22 (cf 24). Thus the 'subjection' of wife to husband is but one particular example of the more general mutual subjection within the Church. **23.** The contemporary sociological structure of marriage (cf 1 Cor 11:3) according to which the husband was the 'superior' of his wife (cf 1:23), evokes and is corroborated by the dominion which Christ has over his body, the Church (cf 1:22—23). The notion of Saviour (cf 1:13; 2:5, 8) applies more exclusively to the Christ—Church relationship.

906a **25—33 Husbands—25.** Recalls Christ's sacrificial love (cf 5:2) for the Church, considered here as pre-existing the actual work of redemption. **26.** As in 5:2, the cultic character of Christ's death is emphasized and he is again portrayed as a priest (cf Heb 9:13; 13:12; Tit 2:14; Jn 17:17—19). The mention of 'washing of water with the word' could be a reference to baptism, but is more probably an allusion to the sanctifying and purifying power of the Gospel which communicates Christ's redemptive mystery to the Church (cf 1:13; 3:6; Jn 17:17—19). In the background is probably the ancient middle-eastern custom of the ritual bathing and preparation of the bride before the wedding. **27.** Christ is presented not only as the husband but also as the friend of the bridegroom who presents the bride to the bridegroom (cf 2 Cor 11:2). The picture painted here is very similar to that in Apoc 21:2. It is remarkable that whereas in 1:4 the Church is depicted as being 'holy' and 'blameless' before God, here it is 'holy and blameless' before Christ. This v shows the source of the church's holiness (cf 1:1) to be in Christ as both priest and sacrificial victim.

b **28.** As in 23, there is here a projection of the Christ—Church relationship on the husband—wife relationship: if Christ is the head of the Church, and the Church his body (cf 1:22—23), then since the husband is the head of the wife (cf v 23), his wife is likewise as his body. It is interesting to observe that the distinction between husband and wife is much clearer ('as' (*hōs* cf v 33) their bodies) than that between Christ and the Church, which *is* his body (cf 1:22—23). **28b** is even more of a simile. In **29—30** the author avoids stating that the wife is either the husband's flesh or a member of his body, but does not shrink from asserting this of Christ and the Church. This observation is probably the clue to the meaning of v 32. The 'mystery' here could refer to the 'mystery' of 1:9; 3:3, 4, 9, considered as being summed-up in the Church. But it more probably refers to the hidden meaning of Gn 2:24, and v 31 which the author sees revealed in the union between Christ and the Church. This is a typical rabbinical exegesis (cf 4:8—10). Manifestly man and wife do not become literally 'one flesh', hence the 'mystery' of this passage. But the Church *is* the body (1:22—23), the flesh (29) of Christ, hence this passage refers to Christ and the Church. The union between husband and wife, however perfect in itself, is only a more or less perfect image of the union between Christ and the Church. **33.** Thus the real basis for the husband's love for his wife and the wife's respect for her husband is not simply the institution text of Gn 2:24 (cf Mt 19:5) but the sacrificial love which Christ has for his Church and the respect which the Church bears towards Christ.

c **6:1—9 Other Social Categories—**The basic principle of 5:21 is now applied to the remaining categories of the contemporary social structure. In each case: children (1—3), parents (4—5), slaves (5—8) masters (9) the readers are exhorted to contemplate their social status **906** in the light of Christ and to see in their social relationships a profound relationship to Christ (cf 1 Cor 7:17—24) and a responsibility towards him.

III. Exhortation to all Christians 6:10—20—The **d** final exhortation is in the form of a call to arms for a spiritual battle. **10.** Recalls the vocabulary of 1:19 and 3:16, with the emphasis here being placed on the Christian's active role (cf 4:22—24). **11.** The clothing which the Christian must now put on (cf 4:24) is God's armour. The impression given by 1:10, 20—23 is that God's battle is over (cf 2:3). It is now clear, however, that the dynamic growth of the Christian (cf 4:13) involves him in a real conflict. The theme of a spiritual war is common in Jewish apocalyptic (cf 1 Thes 5:8; 2 Cor 6:7; 10:4; Rm 13:12) and is especially noticeable at Qumran. Here the enemy is explicitly named as the 'devil' (cf 2:2, v 16), who is seen as operative in the malevolent spiritual forces of the universe. **12.** (cf 1:21; 2:2). The mention of 'the heavenly places' recalls Christ's triumph in 1:3, 20; 2:6; 3:10, the apparent contradiction involved being explained by the essentially eschatological character of the Christian life. Although they are already triumphant in Christ, the Christians of each successive age must, in Christ, attain their own triumph over the force of evil. **13.** 'The evil day' may refer to the Parousia, considered as the moment of the final encounter, but more probably it refers to the Christian's present situation (cf 5:16).

14—17 God's armour—All the elements of this armour, **e** except the shield of faith (v 16) have antecedents or parallels in the Bible: 'the girdle of truth' (Is 11:5), 'the breastplate of righteousness' (Is 59:17), the equipment of the gospel of peace (Is 52:7), the helmet of salvation (Is 59:17), the sword of the Spirit the word of God (Is 11:4, 51; 16; Hos 6:5; Heb 4:12), although they are always related either to God himself (Is 59:17) or his Messiah (Is 11:4). The significance of the present passage is that all these arms are available to the Christian, who, in assuming them, is invested with God's own power (cf 6:10). Moreover, all of these items are found already in Eph: truth (1:13; 4:21, 23), righteousness (4:24), the gospel of peace (1:13; 2:14—18; 3:6, 7; 4:3), faith (1:13, 15, 19; 2:8; 4:13), salvation (1:13; 2:5, 8; 5:23), the Spirit (1:3, 13, 17; 2:18, 22; 3:5; 4:4, 30; 5:18), the word of God (1:13; 5:26). They are already given to the Christian, but not as so many objects to possess, rather as influences at work within him (cf 1:19) and to which he must positively and urgently correspond if he is to come to the fulness of Christ (cf 4:13) unscathed by the assaults of God's enemy. **18.** In the original Gr., does not begin a new sentence **f** (RSV), but completes v 17 and, very possibly, the whole development of vv 14—17. In the early Christian tradition prayer itself was considered as an eschatological warfare or struggle (cf Rm 15:30; Col 4:12, 16; Lk 22:44) and it is certainly in prayer that the author of Eph situates the Christian's most profound response to God's gift (cf 5:19—20). As in 1:16 and 5:20 the intensity, constancy and universality of the prayer are underlined, together with the mention of the Spirit. In 18b the author widens the scope of his readers' prayer to embrace 'all the saints'. **19—20.** Finally, he requests prayers for himself, the **g** formula he suggests is strikingly reminiscent of his own prayers for the faithful, 'that . . . may be given' (cf 1:17; 3:16), and the object of the prayer corresponds remarkably to the essence of his mission: 'to proclaim (lit make known) the mystery of the gospel boldly' (cf 3:7—13). Instead of losing heart over his sufferings (3:13) his readers are to pray for him (6:19—20) in his role as

6g an apostle. Their prayers will contribute to his mission, just as his sufferings are their glory (3:13). There is thus a mysterious interaction of prayer and apostolate not only in the one apostle (cf 3:7—13) but also on the level of the Church as a whole (cf 4:16). It is interesting to observe that the body of the epistle ends, as it began, on this note of prayer. **20.** The explicit mention of the author's imprisonment forms an inclusion with 4:1 (cf 3:1).

h D. Personal news 6:21—22—21—22 are parallelled by Col 4:7—9 although here there is no mention of Onesimus. The phrase 'you also may know' suggests that others, possibly the Colossians, had already been informed about the author's condition. Tychicus was a close companion and assistant of Paul (cf Ac 20:4; 2 Tm 4:12; Ti 3:12). In the hypothesis of the Pauline authenticity of Eph it is possible that he delivered this epistle at the same time as he delivered Col.

i E. Final greeting 6:23—24—As the initial greeting, the final words of the epistle evoke and are loaded with the fundamental message of the whole work: peace (v 23; cf 1:2; 2:14—18; 4:3; 6:15), love (vv 23, 24; cf 1:4, 15; 2:4; 3:17, 19; 4:2, 15, 16; 5:2, 25, 28, 33), faith (v 23; cf 1:13, 15, 19; 2:8; 3:12, 17; 4:5, 13; 6:16), God the Father (v 23; cf 1:2, 3, 17; 2:18; 3:14; 4:6), the Lord Jesus Christ (vv 23, 24; cf 1:2, 3, 15; 3:11; 4:5; 6:1, 4, 7, 10, 21), grace (v 24; cf 1:2, 6, 7; 2:5, 7, 8). The **906i** Gr. original of the RSV phrase 'with love undying' is 'in incorruptibility (or immortality '*aphtharsia*')' (cf Rm 2:7; 1 Cor 15:42, 50, 53, 54; 2 Tim 1:10). From the literary viewpoint it could be a complement of 'grace', 'love' or 'our Lord Jesus Christ'. The first seems preferable. The epistle began with a description of God's grace to us in Christ, consisting in our share in Christ's heavenly exaltation (1:3f; cf 2:1—7). The last word of this epistle corresponds to this theme. By his insertion into Christ's resurrection, in baptism, the Christian already shares Christ's incorruptibility. But, for the present, this is only in seed (cf 1:13—14) and is directed to a fine flowering (cf 2:21—22; 4:13). Thus it can be the object of hope and, above all, of prayer.

PHILIPPIANS

BY JOHN J. GREEHY

907a Bibliography—*Commentaries*: Chrys PG 62; a Lapide, 1908; F. Badcock, 1937; K. Barth, E.tr. 1962; F. W. Beare, BNTC, 1959; P. Benoit, BJ, 1959[3]; P. Bonnard, CNT 1950; M. Dibelius, LHNT 1937[3]; G. Friedrich, NTD 1962[9]; H. G. C. Herklots, 1946; J. Huby, VS 1947[2]; J. B. Lightfoot, 1908[2]; E. Lohmeyer, Meyer, 1956[11]; R. P. Martin, 1959; A. Médebielle, PCSB 1946; J. H. Michael, Moffatt 1948[5]; W. Michaelis in *Theol. Handkomm. zum NT*, Leipzig, 1935[3]; H. C. G. Moule, CBSC 1918; A. Péry, Neuchâtel, 1958; A. Plummer, London 1919; P. Rees, Grand Rapids, 1964; E. F. Scott, IB, 1955; K. Staab-J. Freundorfer, RNT 1959[3]; F. C. Synge, Torch, 1951; R. Vincent, ICC, 1902; W. C. Vine, 1956.

Other literature: L. Cerfaux, RF, 1959, 2, 477—87; G. S. Duncan, *St Paul's Ephesian Ministry*, 1939, G. Gaide, OSB, in Evangile 46 (1962), 5—78; A. W. Heathcote, *An Introd. to the Letters of St Paul*, 1963; C. F. D. Moule, *Birth of the NT*, 1962; H. C. G. Moule, *Philippian Studies*, 1928; J. Murphy-O'Connor O.P., 'Epître aux Philippiens' in DBS, 1211—33; B. Rigaux, O.F.M., 'St Paul et ses lettres', état de la question', *Studia neotestamentica* (subsidia 2), Bruges, 1962; D. M. Stanley, *Christ's Resurrection in Pauline Soteriology*, Rome, 1964[2]; A. Wikenhauser, *NT Introduction*, 1958.

The commentary of F. W. Beare contains good general and particular bibliographies, also bibliographical notes on special studies: (a) on the Time and Place of Writing, (b) on the Interpretation of ii. (5), 6—11, (c) on Paul and Stoicism, (d) on the City of Philippi. For an extensive bibliography on such studies, as well as on the subjects of Integrity and particular vv, cf J. Murphy-O'Connor in DBS.

On 2:6—11 cf in particular L. Cerfaux, 'L'Hymne au Christ—Serviteur de Dieu', in *Recueil Lucien Cerfaux II*, 1954; P. F. Ceuppens, O.P., *Quaestiones Selectae ex Epistulis S. Pauli*, VI, 'Christus, Deus et Homo (Phil 2:6—11),' 189—97. Torino 1951. P. Henry, 'Kénose', DBS 5 (1957), 7—161. A. Feuillet, RB 1965, 352—80; 481—507. R. P. Martin, *Carmen Christi: Philippians 2:5—11 in recent interpretation and in the setting of early Christian worship*. Cambridge, 1967. This book surveys the researches of European scholars into this passage during this century; discusses authorship (majority prefer adaptation of a pre-existing hymn), origin (the interesting possibility of Stephen is mooted) and gives detailed exegesis of the text.

Note also B. M. Ahern, *The Power of his Resurrection and Fellowship in his Sufferings*, Rome, 1958. (Summary in VDom 37 (1959) 26—31; and 'The Fellowship of his Sufferings' Phil 3:10), CBQ 22 (1960) 1—32.)

Authenticity and Canonicity—From the 2nd cent. up **90'** to the 19th we find the Pauline authorship, and consequently canonicity, of this epistle generally accepted. From 1845, F. C. Baur and his Tuebingen school, the Tendency critics, raised the first doubts regarding the authenticity of all the Pauline corpus, with the exception of four major epistles. The case against Phil, however, has received no support from recent authors. The witness for a Pauline writing is as old as Polycarp. In his *Philippians* (3:2), which may be as early as 135, he speaks of letters (note the plural!) which Paul wrote to them, when absent, to build up their faith. Marcion accepted it, and the Muratorian fragment also names it among Paul's epistles. Iren (*post* 150: PG 7, 1026; 1158), Tert (2nd—3rd cent.: PL 2, 826; 863), Clem Alex (do., PG 8, 312; 408; 557) all quote the epistle as Paul's. 'The style, diction, and spirit are characteristically Pauline, and it is now universally accepted as an authentic composition of the great Apostle of the Gentiles.' (F. C. Beare, op cit, 1). Recently, with the growth of the science of cybernetics, an argument has been advanced 'from the computer' which would support the old Tuebingen thesis. Apart from the well-attested practice of using an 'interpres' (scribal redactor), there are many factors which would weaken any study based on word-usage alone, such as: the psychological and doctrinal development in Paul himself, the new problems which he had to meet, and the different surroundings with varying cultures in which he found himself.

Integrity—In recent years, **arguments for the composite nature** of the epistle have become more frequent. The following division is suggested: (1) 4:10—20. A letter of thanks. (2) 1:1—2:30; 4:2—9, 21—23. A letter entrusted to Epaphroditus on his return to Philippi. (3) 3:1 or 2—4:1. A third letter, or an interpolation in the second letter, warning the Philippians against Jewish claims. Now, while Polycarp's 'plural' may have referred simply to 1, 2 Thes, or even to other letters written specifically to the Philippians which were not preserved, internal arguments also can be adduced to support the claim that Phil is a collection of disparate documents. The most famous is that drawn from the sudden transition of 3:1—2. Yet, one wonders whether this could really be the work of any skilled redactor, who would surely endeavour to make the work appear more convincing, in that the point has been reached in the letter where Paul attacks the judaizing faction who consistently opposed him. Psychological reasons may also explain why the letter was not written according to the more usual scheme, where a moral exhortation follows a dogmatic section. Many authors still uphold the unity of the letter, despite contrasting literary data. While this type of study

907b on integrity does not throw much light on the epistle's interpretation, it could, if the 'collective' hypothesis were accepted, provide a possible solution to the complex question of place and date. One could then suggest that separate parts were written in various places at different times. This would be the position of Beare, whereas Murphy-O'Connor places the writing of all three letters at Ephesus around the same earlier date.

c Philippi and the Philippian Christian Community—The early Krenides ('little fountains') was re-founded and named by Philip II of Macedon in 356 B.C. It had easy access across Mt Pangaeum to the fine harbour of Neapolis (less than ten miles away), and the gold mines in the neighbourhood were of enormous value to Philip, in his acts of war and diplomacy. After the Roman conquest of 168 B.C. it became part of the first Macedonian district. In 42 B.C. it became famous as the battleground where Antony and Octavian (later Augustus) defeated Brutus and Cassius. Some of the victorious veterans were settled there and it became a Roman colony. With the settlement of another Latin-speaking colony in 30 B.C., Octavian gave it the name *Colonia Augusta Julia Philippensis*. The city thus acquired the *Ius Italicum*, with the right of proprietorship according to Roman law, and exemption from poll-tax and land-tax. It had its own supreme magistrates called *strategoi* (generals) Ac 16:19, 35—39. After most of a century, the Latin families had been influenced by their Eastern environment and, of course, the city always contained a native Thracian population. Since it was the first station on the Egnatian Way, which linked Asia with the West, traders from many parts of the Mediterranean world would also be found in the city.

In Ac 16:11—40 we get an account of Christian beginnings at Philippi which is instructive for our present purpose. After the events so vividly narrated there, Luke seems to have been left in charge of the new foundation as the 'we' narrative ceases until the departure from Philippi towards the end of the third missionary journey Ac 20:5—6. Paul's insistence on an apology from the magistrates by whose orders Silas and himself had been beaten and imprisoned (Ac 16:37—39) must surely have been due to the necessity of ensuring that the newly-founded religion should be placed on a secure footing. The people, seeing the perturbation of the magistrates, would think more of this new doctrine. We know from Phil 4:15—16 that the community sent gifts to Paul, and that he looked on it with particular favour.

908a Place and Date—Phil has been classified traditionally with Eph Col Phm as one of the Captivity epistles, and the imprisonment involved has been commonly accepted as Roman. In 1897 Adolf Deissmann suggested an earlier, Ephesian, captivity for their date of composition. In 1929, G. S. Duncan adhered to this view. Even though there is no mention of such a captivity in Ac, an increasing number of scholars incline to this earlier writing of Phil, while rejecting the hypothesis in the case of the other epistles. The 19th cent. opinion in favour of Caesarea (later supported by Lohmeyer) has received little support from the authors. Two possibilities only are now regarded as worthy of serious consideration. (1) The epistle was written at Ephesus around 56—57. (2) It was written at Rome between 61—63. This second view is ancient (the oldest evidence is Marcion's prologue), but in its origins may have been only guesswork. Arguments in favour of an Ephesian location may be found in the following works cited in the bibliography: Duncan; Stanley, 66—67 comes down in favour of the view; Benoit, 11—13 considers the hypothesis attractive, Wikenhauser, 434—6 presents

the arguments in favour of the 'Roman' position. A critical **908a** analysis of the 'Ephesian' argumentation is to be found in Beare, 15—24. He concludes 'Taking everything into account, the ancient hypothesis that Philippians was written from Rome must be allowed to hold the field. A precise date cannot be established. We must be content to place it between 60 and 64, probably towards the later date'.

Since the burden of proof probably lies with the more **b** recent view, we present a summary of the arguments brought forward in its support, with some critical comments which can be made against them. (1) From Phil 4:10, 16 it would seem that Paul had received no alms from the Philippians since he was in Thessalonica on the second missionary journey. Yet he had twice visited the Philippian Church before his Roman imprisonment, when we would have expected him to receive renewed support. Surely his reference to lack of opportunity is not sarcasm. If this was written at Ephesus in 56, however, then all is explained since he had not been among them up to that time. One might counter that 4:10 could mean that the Apostle had not needed their help again until the costly Roman sojourn, or that, due to their own pressing needs, they had been unable to renew their support until this later date. (2) The epistle presupposes four journeys, and three others are shortly contemplated—those of Epaphroditus, Timothy, and even Paul himself. The time for any one journey between Rome and Philippi would be seven or eight weeks, as against about ten days in the case of Ephesus. Since the Roman captivity lasted two years, this 'placing', however, is still possible. (3) When Paul wrote to the Romans (15:24, 28) he announced his intention of visiting them on his way to Spain. Why has he changed his mind, telling the Philippians (2:24) that he hopes to come to them shortly? In fact, the mission of Timothy and Paul's post-Ephesian activity (Ac 19:21—22; 20:1—2) would fit in very well with the 'Ephesian' hypothesis. One must, however, note the possibility of a psychological difference between the Paul of 57, and the Paul of 63 who had been five years in some type of captivity. He could easily have changed his mind about an immediate Spanish journey, and desire to see and encourage his communities in Macedonia after his long absence. We might add that the inference from Phil 1:26, 30; 4:15f. that Paul had not revisited the community since he founded it, and therefore wrote this before Ac 20:1f. seems very weak indeed. (4) The argument based on the cause of arrest in Phil may also seem less convincing to many. In Phil 1:7, 12—13 the motive is given as defence of the Gospel. From Ac 21:28; 24:6; 25:8 we know that the alleged defilement of the Temple was the reason given for the Roman imprisonment. An examination of the texts, however, must surely show that the real reason lay in the fact that he was a leader of the sect of the Nazarenes, who spoke against the Jewish religion. Again, one may remain unconvinced by the argument that the attack on Judaizers, be they Jewish-Christians or Jews, fits in only in the period before Galatians. Such tendencies were to continue in the Church after the death of the Apostle. (5) The theological argument pointing out the similarities between Phil and the major epistles, (cf particularly the considerable treatment of Murphy-O'Connor), can be countered by pointing to resemblances with the later epistles. Thus, compare Phil 3:8 with Eph 3:19 and Phil 3:10 with Eph 1:19f. Phil is primarily a 'situational' letter rather than a 'theological' epistle, and thus cannot be readily placed in the Pauline corpus using doctrinal arguments.

908c Was there ever, in fact, an imprisonment at Ephesus? We have no proof of it, but we must hasten to add that 2 Cor 11:23 presupposes a number of imprisonments not mentioned in Ac. The phrase in 1 Cor 15:32 'I fought with beasts at Ephesus' can hardly be taken literally. A Roman citizen was not liable to such punishment, and furthermore Paul was still alive! If he did undergo imprisonment at Ephesus, it would still have to be long enough for the 'comings and goings' of which we read in the Epistle. Again, would this imprisonment have been of the less stringent 'Roman' character, which allowed free access to Paul, and considerable activity on his part?

An interesting case has been made by Professor Manson, supported by A. W. Heathcote, against the tradition that Paul wrote from prison. This would remove a primary objection to Ephesus. While this position is just arguable from the bare text, nevertheless the whole context (as e.g. the repeated references to 'chains' or 'imprisonment', also 2:17) is more in keeping with the tradition that the epistle was written at the time of an actual captivity.

Lastly, it can be pointed out that: (1) The references to the 'whole praetorian guard' and 'Caesar's household' 1:13; 4:22 are more easily applicable to Rome than to Ephesus. (2) The situation of 1:15–17 would be certainly true of Rome, but such 'partisanship' would hardly be the case at Ephesus. (3) The significance which Paul attached to his imprisonment would be better explained in a Roman captivity. (4) Would the dangerous journey of Epaphroditus bringing alms from Philippi be really necessary at Ephesus, the centre of a flourishing Pauline Church? It would be most useful in distant Rome. We might conclude that while a number of arguments for Ephesus are plausible, and the hypothesis itself most stimulating, one may still remain unconvinced and refuse to abandon a 'Roman' Philippians.

909a Doctrine—Eleven times in this epistle, the characteristic note of Christian joy is sounded. This is due to our fellowship with God and one another, through the Spirit of Jesus. We find such a *koinōnia* already exists in the 'summaries' of Ac 2:4. From his first contact with the Philippians up to this latest manifestation of their partnership with him in the Gospel, they had given him every proof that they were filled 'with the fruits of righteousness which come through Jesus Christ'. The centre of Paul's doctrine on Christian suffering is contained in 3:8–11. Our salvation does not come from our own merits or from the Law. True righteousness comes through faith in Christ, which is itself a gift of God. This means a unity with Christ in his passion and death, so that from being crucified with him we partake also in the newness of his risen life, 3:10–11, 20–21, a theme expounded with fuller emphasis in Eph 2:1–10; 3:14–19; 4:15–16, 22–23; Col 2:6–13; 3:3–11. While Christians are to work out their salvation with fear and trembling, 2:12, they have every reason to hope for final union with Christ through their sharing in Christ's sufferings. The link between Christian suffering and Christ lies in the fact that we live in him. All such suffering, borne in the cause of Christ, and so abundantly exemplified in Paul himself, will help in the spread of the Gospel and the attainment of the final stage of heavenly citizenship.

b The 'Hymn' to Christ 2:5–11—(Murphy–O'Connor offers a bibliography up to 1965 on this passage, as a supplement to the abundant list already found in P. Henry, art cit col 158–61). It should be noticed that in this passage on the divinity of Christ, Paul has no intention of teaching his readers anything new. It presupposes the doctrine as already known in order to exemplify from Christ's saving action the type of mind which should be **909** found in a Christian. The idea is that Christians must be prepared to sacrifice their rights for the benefit of the community, and they have Jesus as example, who gave up his own divine prerogatives and, in obedience of his Father, underwent the death of a slave. Each strophe of the hymn presents a different stage in the mystery of Christ. **6.** The divine dignity. **7.** The 'emptying' of the Incarnation. **8.** The final humiliation of the cross. **10.** The exaltation. **11.** The worship of all creation. **12.** The confession of Jesus Christ as Lord.

Many authors now agree that this passage is a hymn, and various strophe-divisions have been suggested. The question of authorship immediately arises. One can view with more than considerable scepticism any assertion which claims here an adaptation of a Gnostic hymn or Iranian myth. Categorical statement should always be supported by convincing arguments. Cerfaux supports Pauline authorship and suggests it was probably intended for use in the liturgy. He points to the similarity with 2 Cor 8:9. A number of authors, like Jeremias, speak of a pre-Pauline composition. We would then have in Phil the oldest proof of the teaching regarding the three modes of Christ's existence. The arguments for non-Pauline authorship seem to fall under two main headings. (1) The soteriology fits in more with the primitive *kerygma* which we find in the Jerusalem church of Ac rather than with Paul's, e.g. Paul never considers the glorification of Christ as a reward for his obedience in suffering. (2) The Servant of Yahweh theme, as applied to Christ, is typical of the Jerusalem church. (This is not necessarily a Jewish hellenistic contribution, as some authors hold. Surely the application could be due to the Master himself). In Paul's letters, he himself appears as the servant. One could suggest, then, that the ideas come from Jerusalem to Antioch, where they receive a hymnic form, and thence were brought to Philippi by Paul, delegated for work among the uncircumcized by that Church, Ac 13:1–3. The Philippians would immediately recognize such an ingenious use of a popular hymn. (We may hear well-known hymns so used in present-day sermons).

Even though such a hymnic background for Phil 2:6– **c** 11 makes a very enticing hypothesis, one feels obliged to consider also the carefully chosen words of C. F. D. Moule, 25–26, 'Many other passages have been claimed as hymns: Phil 2:6–11; Col 1:15–20; 1 Pet 1:3ff. to mention only a few. But in actual fact the criteria are inconclusive. These passages may or may not be strophic—i.e. symmetrical and balanced in their lines or their rhythms: nobody has conclusively demonstrated that they are. Even if they are not, as a matter of fact, they might still have been sung, just as Psalms and other irregular or metreless pieces in English can be sung. But who is to prove that they were hymns? Prose and poetry, adoration and statement, quotations from recognized liturgical forms and free, original composition, mingle and follow one another so easily in the mind of a Christian thinker that, without some external criterion, one can never be certain how much or how little of "common prayer" one is overhearing.'

1:1–2 Greeting—1. Saints are those to whom God **910** has given his own life (grace) in the church of Christ. Bishops were as yet equivalent to presbyters (cf Ac 20:17, 28 and also § 923a). These ruled the churches, and were visited at intervals by the Apostles themselves, or by 'Regional Apostles' such as Timothy and Titus. We find a somewhat similar institution in the 'overseership of all the camps' found in DSS; CD 14. The deacons were administrators of church property, which also involved alms-

0a giving. **2.** Christ is placed on an equality with the Father. **3—8 Thanksgiving—** 5—7. Their 'partnership' with Paul in the grace of the Gospel is exemplified in the material aid they have sent him. This present grace is a pledge of their future glory at the Second Coming. **9—11 Intercession**—Paul prays that their charity may increase, along with a developed moral insight. They will then follow the more perfect way, filled with the supernatural life which comes through Jesus Christ. They will live, therefore, for the glory of God, and thus work out their salvation for the day of Christ. **12—14 The Furtherance of the Gospel—12.** Paul expresses his thoughts on the present situation (imprisonment). **13—14.** It has advanced the cause of Christ through the talk of the soldiers, and confirmed the brethren so that they preach the Gospel without fear. **15—18 Though with Various Motives—** Whether this is done out of good-will or jealousy (cf 1 Cor 1:11—12) Paul is unworried, as Christ is being proclaimed in either case. **19—26 The Apostle's Own Mind— 19** quotes Job 13:16 (LXX). He is assured of salvation through the help of the Holy Spirit, invoked by the prayers of the faithful. **20—24.** Paul's dilemma was to be often repeated in the lives of saints; the burning desire to be united forever to the glorious Christ in heaven, with the realization that they may yet be needed on earth on account of their brethren. **25—26.** He knows that he will come again to the Philippians, and help in the progress of their faith, through the power of Christ working in him. **27—30 Begins Advice to the Philippians—27.** politeuesthe. Live according to the laws which govern heavenly citizens. Let there be no dissensions among you. **28.** Work for the Gospel, and your own salvation, despite opponents (pagans or Jews) who condemn themselves. **29.** The gift of faith brings with it suffering for Christ's sake, which they can see from Paul's life, both past and present.

b **2:1—4 Appeals again for Unity—1.** Four phrases, no verb, many interpretations! Paul is looking for motives which will encourage them to unite. Herewith a possible paraphrase: '*If there is anything that can exhort (move) you in Christ, anything that can appeal to you in your experience of the Father's love, if there is any fellowship in the Holy Spirit among you, or any affection or sympathy (in response to my own plea) . . . 2. then fill up my joy through your mutual charity.*' **3.** Through humility, they should remove all selfishness and vainglory so that. . . **4.** each one will look not merely to his own interests or even right to honours (perhaps due to special gifts, 1 Cor 12), but also to those of others. **5—11 The Hymn to Christ** (cf § 000b) **5.** Introductory verse. Either '*Have this mind in you which was in Christ Jesus (before you)*' or '*Have this mind in you which you ought to have due to your intimate union in Christ Jesus*'. The second version seems more in harmony with the general subject of the ch which concerns the implications of life 'in Christ'. **6. Form,** morphē. This word describes the divine sphere, in which Christ dwells, before taking up the condition of a servant. All the passage recalls Is 53, esp. vv 3, 8, 12. Christ was entitled, then, to all the divine prerogatives. **A thing to be grasped** (harpagmon): this is better understood in the passive sense of a great prize to which a man clings tenaciously. Thus, though Christ was divine and remained so, nevertheless he did not insist on the external honour which was due to this dignity, but rather. **7.** 'emptied himself, taking the form of a servant, being born in the likeness of men'. The emptying (kenosis) regards the method of the Incarnation. He now adds to his divine dignity the condition of a human being, and this serves to conceal the prior mode of being, to which glory is due (cf this theme also in 2 Cor 8:9; Heb 5:8; 12:2).

Born (genomenos): the new state of Christ began, like **910b** that of any man, in time, and he was similar to all men in his servant-condition before God. (Even though the hymn is directed towards the salvation-event primarily, nevertheless the doctrine which concerns Christ's being can be drawn from it. It gave a basis for future theological thought. Christ is divine from all eternity, and, while retaining this prior mode of existence, becomes a man, like ourselves, at a point of time). **8. Human form:** the Gr. word (schēma) indicates the external appearance of anything. Christ became in every way as other men. This emphasizes the reality of Christ's abasement from a human viewpoint. This self-humiliation of Christ goes still further. His obedience (the mark of a servant) leads to the death of a slave on a cross. With this death, he reaches the depths of abasement, farthest removed from his divine dignity. (There can be little doubt that such obedience is stressed in contrast to the disobedience of men. Authors disagree as to whether an Adam—Christ comparison is also present).

We now begin the ascent in the exaltation of Christ. **c** Attention is drawn to the style of an enthronement, including the acts of mounting the throne, proclamation of new dignities, genuflection and acclamation. **9.** Because of his deepest humility, God has given him the highest glory (through the Resurrection, and Ascension of his right hand in heaven, cf Eph 1:20—22). He receives the divine **name** (and authority), which is Yahweh, translated in the LXX by kurios, rendered in English as **Lord.** **10 11a.** We have a clear reference to Is 45:23. This title of kurios, applied to Jesus, means that divine cult is to be paid to his Person, and this on the part of the whole universe. We should note that, at the Resurrection, Christ is exalted as Lord even in his human nature. The crucified Jesus is Lord (Ac 2:36). He returns to the Father, who invests him with the powers of governing, judging, and saving (cf Jn 17:1—5). We might add that the Catholic custom and rubric of giving external sign of reverence to the name, Jesus, is not essentially based on a particular interpretation of this v. The expression of the 'material' name occasions an acknowledgement of the meaningfulness of the Person which it represents. **11b.** 'Jesus Christ is Lord': the confession of faith in the divinity of Christ (which will glorify his humanity) is to be found also in the short formula 'Jesus is Lord' (cf 1 Cor 12:3 and Rom 10:9). This confession will redound to the glory of the Father, in whom the work of Christian salvation originates.

A Note on kenōsis. Cf TWNT, E.tr. Vol. 3, 661—2. ' What is meant is that the heavenly Christ did not selfishly exploit His divine form and mode of being, but by His own decision emptied Himself of it or laid it by taking the form of a servant by becoming man.' The subject of ekenōsen is not the incarnate but the pre-existent Lord. There is a strong sense of the unity of His person.

Theology: cf Appended note by Professor Fairweather to Dr Beare's commentary: the 'Kenotic' Christology.

The kenotic theories in general involve 'some real modification of the divine attributes as a necessary condition of the true and personal entrance of the Son of God into human history and human experience'. Thus, for Gess, the Father would cease to beget the Son. In the opinions of Forsyth and Mackintosh the divine attributes would be reduced from act to potency. The Godhead, in all such theories, must depart, or in some way be diminished, if any human life of the Word is to be possible. 'There are, in fact, two presuppositions whose influence can be clearly traced in the development of the Kenotic speculation. The first of these is the peculiar variety of "monophysitism" characteristic of Lutheran Christology, while the second

910c is the tendency, typical of much modern philosophy, to define personality in terms of the natural activity of consciousness. The convergence of these two trends results in a disposition to construe unity of *person* as a functional unity of *nature* (or principle of action), and so to telescope the divine and human natures of the incarnate word into one. When this disposition is linked to the Kenoticists' dual concern for the full recognition of Christ's humanity, the predictable outcome is an emphasis on the human functioning of Christ as defining his incarnate personality and, as an inevitable consequence, a virtual suppression of the divine nature'.

Over against any idea of a 'diminution' or a 'depotentiation' of deity, we can amass a wealth of evidence of theologians from the Fathers, through St Thomas Aquinas ('He emptied Himself, not by laying down the divine nature, but by taking up human nature'. Comm. on Phil) to Karl Barth ('He humbled Himself, but He did not do it by ceasing to be who He is'. *Church Dogmatics* 4, i, Edinburgh 1956, p. 180). Again, cf Barth's commentary p. 66 '. . . he who was abased and humble even to the obedience of death on the cross is also the exalted Lord. Notice that there is no mention of any reassumption of the "form of God". . . .' If the Christ has not the unalterable deity of God, then doubt is thrown immediately on his power of atonement.

The aspect under which the *kenōsis* of Christ should be viewed is that of *purposeful renunciation*. He voluntarily took upon himself the lowliness of the human condition for our sakes. He has thus provided us with an ideal of 'poverty' which all Christians are called upon to follow. This idea was particularly emphasized by St Theodosius (d. in 1074), and has always been found subsequently in Russian spirituality. We find it constantly repeated at the Second Vatican Council. Thus, the Dogmatic Constitution on the Church, paragraph 8. In paragraph 41 we read 'In the various types and duties of life, one and the same holiness is cultivated by all who are moved by the spirit of God. . . . These souls follow the poor Christ, the humble and cross-bearing Christ, in order to be made worthy of being partakers in His glory' (trans. from Abbott edition); cf also Decree on the Missions: *Christian Witness*, § § 11—12. The kenotic ideal is set before every Christian . . . 'Bishops' 15, 'Religious' 13, 'Priests' 17, 'Laity', 4.

12—18 An Appeal—12—13. After such an example, Paul now exhorts his Philippians to filial obedience before God, who will use them in his designs, and bring them, consequently, to salvation. **14.** Grumbling or questioning i.e. asserting oneself; thinking only of what oneself may gain out of an action. **15.** Cf Dt 32:5. **16.** Their loyalty to the Gospel will demonstrate Paul's fruitful work. **17.** Just as in Jewish and pagan sacrifices, he is prepared to make a drink-offering to God (one which will be his own blood), and this will be an addition (?) to the sacrifice involved in their faith.

19—30 Future Plans—21. He is possibly thinking of the attitude of those mentioned in 1:15—17. **25.** Epaphroditus is not to be confused with the Epaphras of Colossae (Col 4:12). **30.** 'risking his life'. The word is taken from the language of gambling. He completes their service (note the 'priestly' terminology) by his personal attentions to Paul.

d 3 Warning against Jewish Propaganda: The True Way of Salvation—The Judaizers attacked here may be the Christian-Jews of the early Palestinian church, who caused considerable trouble among Paul's gentile communities, but they are more likely to be non-Christian Jews. **2.** Beware of the scavenging dogs! **3.** He distinguishes between Jewish circumcision, now to be regarded **91** as mere mutilation, and the true circumcision of the spirit (cf Ac 7:51). **4—6.** Paul himself is more Jewish than they. Although he was a persecutor of the Church, he was blameless according to 'legal' standards of righteousness. **7—10.** In describing the 'gain' of his conversion, Paul brings out the 'gains' which every Christian can claim. The ultimate 'gain' is to be the resurrection of the just at the Parousia. This hope for final union with Christ pervades all the epistle. Those who have a righteousness not based on the law, but which is through faith in the risen Christ (cf theme of Gal—Rm) will achieve this complete conformity to the risen Christ through living and suffering in the Christian way. All apostolic Christians living in the body of Christ share in his sufferings, and thus contribute to the growth of that body. This death to the world, assisted by the Spirit, is a continuation of our baptism when we were brought to a state of union with the suffering and dying Christ. **12—15.** Paul presses on, like an athlete in a race, to his goal, which is complete possession of Christ. He exhorts them to do likewise. Note that the RSV translation of 3:12 'to make it my own' rather than **him** would refer back to the 'resurrection from the dead'. It seems better to suggest that Paul is thinking of Christ Jesus as the prize offered by God to those whom he has called into his service. **16.** Whatever truth we have attained, let us order our lives by that. **17.** He proposes himself as a model for their conduct. (He imitates Christ, 1 Cor 11:1). **18—19.** The reference is to those who glory in dietary laws and circumcision (both now obsolete), rather than in the cross of Christ. **20—21.** Christians, however, having turned from the things of earth, become citizens of heaven, awaiting the coming of the Lord Jesus, when he will glorify their bodies, making them like his own glorious body (cf 1 Cor 15). The humiliation-exaltation theme of the Christian in this passage is closely related to 2:5—11.

4:1—9 The Dissensions—1—3. He entreats them to **e** live in this way of the Lord, addressing particularly two rival women (one of whom may be the Lydian woman of Ac 16). These seem to be the root of some disharmony in the church. *Syzygus* may be a proper name, but more probably means 'yoke-fellow' (RSV). Since he must have been a man of some influence, Silas or Luke have been suggested. *Clement* was quite a common name. **4.** *chairete:* imperative of 'rejoice', the Gr. 'Hello' or 'Good-bye'. The translation 'rejoice in the Lord' can be justified by (1) the fact that such an undertone may lie beneath the literal sense as 'God be with you' under 'good-bye'; (2) the theme of joy which runs through the epistle; (3) the emphatic repetition of the verb. Goodspeed's translation seems satisfactory: 'good-bye, and the Lord be always with you'. (*Problems of NT Translation*, Chicago 1947. 174f). **5.** Show Christian courtesy to all. '**The Lord is at hand**'. Inevitably two interpretations. (a) Expectation of a proximate Coming. 'Come, Lord Jesus', Apoc 22:20. (b) Nearness of God's abiding presence as Ps 119 (118):151. **6—7.** Trust in God, and his peace will protect us. **8.** Paul baptizes a list of natural virtues: *aretē* is the most comprehensive Gr. term for moral excellence. **9.** Let them imitate Paul, and God will be with them.

10—20 He thanks the Philippians—Note the delicate way in which Paul expresses his appreciation of their gifts, without using any words of thanks. **10.** The second part of the sentence removes any possible interpretation of reproach in the first. **11—13.** The indifference of a true Christian towards wealth or poverty. '**I have**

0e **learned the secret**' employs 'mystery' terminology. This is not an attitude of Stoic independence, but is caused by the strength received through union with Christ. **14—16.** He refers to their partnership or fellowship with him in the early days of evangelization in the Graeco-Roman world. **17—19.** He uses technical 'business' terms to acknowledge receipt of their gift. The verb *apecho* occurs also in the Sermon on the Mount, Mt 6:2, 5, 16. Paul then changes into the language of sacrifice (cf Gn 8:21; Ex 29:18). God will repay their generosity with his gifts, according to their needs. This will be done through his mediator, Christ Jesus. **20.** This section **910e** (which *may* be an earlier letter of thanks (cf § 907*b*) ends with an acclamation of praise to the eternal Father. **21—23 Final Greetings—21.** One presumes that the presbyters, in reading this letter to the community, would convey such greetings. **22.** The Christian brethren with Paul join in the greeting, and particularly all those in the Emperor's service. The term 'Caesar's household' applied to such officials in any part of the Roman Empire. **23.** A last blessing, which Paul may have written in his own hand as a kind of signature.

COLOSSIANS

BY JEROME MURPHY-O'CONNOR O.P.

911a Bibliography—*Commentaries*: T. K. Abbott, ICC, 1922[4]; F. W. Beare, IB, 1955; M. Dibelius—H. Greeven, LHNT, 1953[3]; C. H. Dodd, Abingdon, 1929; J. Huby, VS, 1947[15]; J. B. Lightfoot, 1890[9]; E. Lohmeyer, Meyer, 1953[9], with a Beiheft by W. Schmauch, 1964; C. F. D. Moule, CGTC, Cambridge, 1957; F. F. Bruce, 1957; H. Conzelmann, NTD, 1962[9]. *Other literature*: P. Benoit, 'Corps, Tête et Plerôme dans les ép. de la captivité, RB, 63 (1956), 5—44; id. 'Rapports littéraires entre les ép. aux Colossiens et aux Ephésiens', Fs J. Schmid, Regensburg, 1963, 11—22; id. 'Paul. ép. aux Colossiens', DBS 7 (1966), 157—70; A. Feuillet, *Le Christ, Sagesse de Dieu dans les ép. pauliniennes*', 1966, 163—273; 'E. Percy, *Die Probleme der Kolosser-und Epheser-briefe*', Lund, 1946; id. 'Zu den Problemen des Kolosser-und Epheserbriefes', ZNW 43 (1950—51), 178—94; J. A. T. Robinson, *The Body*, 1953; J. Schmid, *Zeit und Ort der paulinischen Gefangenschaftsbriefe*, Freiburg im B., 1931. M. Bogdasavich, 'The Idea of *Pleroma* in the Epp. to the Col. and Eph.', DowR 83 (1965) 118—30; H. Gabathuler, *Jesus Christus, Haupt der Kirche, Haupte der Welt. Der Christushymnus Col 1:15—20 in der theol. Forschung der letzten 130 Jahre*, Zürich 1965; W. Foerster, 'Die Irrlehrer des Kolosser-briefes', *Fs T. C. Vriezen*, Wageningen 1966, 71—80; A. van den Heuvel, *These Rebellious Powers*, 1966; E. P. Sanders, 'Literary Dependence in Col', JBL 85 (1966) 28—45; *Paul and Qumran*, ed. J. Murphy-O'Connor, 1968.

b Colossae—The site of the town lies about ten miles E of the modern town of Denzili in Turkey. Situated on the banks of the river in the unusually fertile but earthquake-prone Lycus valley, it has never been excavated, and is known simply as 'the hill' (*Hüyük* = Arabic *tell*). At the time of Paul its former glory (Herodotus, 7, 30; Xenophon, *Anabasis*, 1, 2, 6) had already begun to wane under competition from the growing political power of Laodicea (2:1; 4:15—16) and the rising religious popularity of Hierapolis (4:13); it was just a minor town on the trade-route from Ephesus to the interior, whose chief source of prosperity lay in the trade of dyed woollen goods. The majority of the population was certainly pagan, but the epistle supposes the presence of a Jewish colony. In 62 B.C. there were at least 11,000 adult male Jews in the district of which Laodicea was the capital (Lightfoot, 20), the descendants of the 2,000 families transported from Babylon and Mesopotamia by Antiochus III (Jos. Ant., 12, 3, 4).

Colossae was not evangelized by Paul himself (2:1), but by Epaphras, who was probably converted by Paul during his long ministry at Ephesus (Ac 19). Due to the uncertainty of the MS tradition of 1:7 it is impossible to say whether he was Paul's delegate in this mission, or whether it was simply his own fervour which motivated him to spread the Good News among his fellow-countrymen (4:12). However 1:2 weighs the balance in favour of the latter.

Authenticity, Date, and Place of Origin—A strong **91** presumption in favour of the authenticity of Col is established by the fact that on a number of points the relation of the writer to his readers corresponds to that of the undoubtedly genuine letter to Philemon. In both epistles **Epaphras, Aristarchus, Mark, Luke and Demas** send greetings (Col 4:10ff; Phm 23ff); in both there is talk of sending Onesimus (Col 4:4; Phm 12); and in both Archippus is addressed (Col 4:17; Phm 2). Nonetheless authenticity is denied by such eminent scholars as Bultmann, Bornkamm, and Käsemann on the grounds of theological content, language and style. The style is cumbersome and verbose, many new terms are used (e.g. 'Fullness'), several noted Pauline themes are missing (righteousness, justification, Law, etc), and Pauline concepts are presented in a different way (e.g. the Body of Christ). All these points, however, can be satisfactorily accounted for if the purpose of the letter is kept in mind. It is essentially a polemic treatise directed to countering the influence of false teachers. We should expect, then, (i) that Paul's thought evolved under the pressure of new difficulties, (ii) that he should emphasize only what was relevant to his purpose, and (iii) that he should to some extent adopt the terminology of his adversaries. Hence Col, which was probably used by Justin (*Dial.* 85, 2; 138, 2), and which is listed in the canon of Marcion, is to be taken as authentically Pauline.

Col was written at a time when Paul was a prisoner **d** (4:3, 10, 18) which limits the place of origin to Ephesus, Caesarea or Rome. If as seems most probable (but see § 908a—b), Phil was written towards the end of an Ephesian imprisonment (DBS 7 (1966), 1216—20) Col must have been written at a later date, because otherwise it becomes impossible to explain the doctrinal development. Caesarea has some eminent partisans (Goguel, Lohmeyer, Dibelius), but offers a much less satisfactory explanation of certain data than does Rome. The close connexion between Col and Philem has been noted above. They were certainly contemporary, and written at a time when the fugitive slave Onesimus constituted one of Paul's minor problems (Col 4:9; Phm 12). It is intrinsically more probable that a fugitive slave would make for Rome. Moreover, at Caesarea Paul was contemplating an appeal to the Emperor (Acts 25:11ff; 26:32). In such circumstances it is unlikely that he would express the hope of seeing Philemon soon (Phm 22). The Roman imprisonment is dated A.D. 61—63.

The Errors Combated—All that we know of the **e** Colossian heresy comes from Paul's refutation. Hence its reconstruction is a very delicate matter, and cannot be based on the naïve assumption that what Paul denies the heretics asserted and vice versa, because Paul was capable of seeing implications in their doctrine that they themselves did not perceive. It is clear that certain observances were proposed to the Colossians concerning the calendar (2:16b), dietary regulations (2:16a, 21—23), and possibly circumcision (2:11). Their obviously Jewish character is confirmed by Paul's state-

1e ment that they are but shadow compared to the 'reality' which is Christ (2:17; cf Gal 4:8). From Paul's insistence on Christ's superiority to all angelic beings (1:16; 2:10) we are entitled to infer that these latter were given a prominence that amounted to an attack on Christ's role as the unique mediator of salvation. From the apocryphal writings we know that at this period certain circles within Judaism exhibited an exaggerated interest in angelology. The combination of legalistic rigorism and esoteric speculation indicates that the heretics did not come from the mainstream of Judaism, but the evidence is far too slight to warrant their classification as 'Gnostics'. This tendency, typified by the work of Bornkamm and Käsemann, disregards the complete absence in Col of such specific characteristics as the ontological dualism in which matter is opposed to spirit. Lightfoot's intuition that the heresy was in some way associated with Essenism has been remarkably borne out by the discovery of the Dead Sea Scrolls (cf on 2:10; 2:16ff and P. Benoit, DBS 7 (1966) 161–62; S. Lyonnet, Bib 37 (1956) 27–38).

f Doctrinal Teaching—The kernel of the epistle is to be found in 1:15–20, which represents the high-point of Pauline Christology. This hymn evokes a number of themes which made their appearance in previous letters: Christ is the image of God; God created the world through him; the Church is his Body. But it also contains new elements: all has been created 'in' and 'for' Christ; He is the 'Head' of the Body; the 'Fullness' dwells in him; the reconciliation effected by Christ has a cosmic dimension. Stoicism made a minor contribution to this rich and varied synthesis whose principal source was the sapiential literature, but the key insight which gives the structure harmony and unity was the identification of Christ with the Wisdom of God. As Wisdom Christ is the 'beginning' of all things in every sense of the term. As Wisdom all things are in him. Consequently his role in both Creation and Re-creation has a cosmic quality.

g A major consequence of this insight is a new emphasis on the collective aspect of salvation. In distinction to previous epistles in which the believers are presented as 'members' of Christ, they here appear simply as 'the Body'. The new creation effected by Baptism is described in function of the theme 'old man-new man' (3:9) whose corporate associations are clear from the contrast drawn in 1 Cor 15:45–49 between the two epochs of salvation in terms of 'the earthly man' (Adam) and 'the heavenly man' (Christ). In this perspective special attention is accorded to the Gentiles, for the mystery of salvation being realized by Paul is 'Christ among you' (1:27). In him there is no longer any distinction between Greek and Jew, between barbarian and Scythian, between slave and free man (3:11). Humanity with its sin-caused divisions has been absorbed into Christ, who is 'all in all' (3:11b).

In Christ the believers have 'the hope of glory' (1:27). The revelation of the splendour of this union remains for the future (3:4), but instead of an anxious expectation of the end we find in Col the calm conviction that the essential of Christ's work is to be found in the present. This realized eschatology appears most clearly in Paul's theology of baptism: we have already risen from the dead.

912a 1:1–2 Greeting—**1.** Departing from epistolary custom which demanded only the name of the sender (e.g. Acts 23:26), Paul adds a phrase which underlines his authority. He has been chosen and sent by God. 'Timothy' was Paul's favourite assistant, cf Ac 16:1ff; Phil 2:19–22; 1 and 2 Tim *passim*. **2.** When writing to communities he has founded Paul normally addresses the greeting to the Church (1 Cor 1:2; 2 Cor 1:1; Gal

1:1). Phil constitutes an exception to this rule, which is **912a** perhaps to be explained by the extremely cordial relations between the Apostle and this community. Writing to the Romans he addresses the individuals who make up the Church. Col falls into this category. 'Saints' is an abbreviation of the formula 'saints in virtue of a divine call' found in Rom 1:7; 1 Cor 1:2. 'Dedicated' would be a better translation, for in the OT *kadhôsh* did not connote personal virtue but separation from the profane in view of complete consecration to God. 'Faithful' = steadfast, and suggests that some members of the community have fallen away.

3–8 Thanksgiving for the Past—**4.** As always in **b** Paul, 'faith' implies complete commitment. Yet 'in Christ' does not simply indicate its object (cf M. Zerwick, *Graecitas Biblica*, Roma 1953³, 88). The 'in' evokes the whole sphere of faith, and the best image is that of an electromagnetic forcefield. Col never speaks of 'love' as directed to God. In a divided community Paul stresses its unitive effect (3:14; cf Gal 3:27). 'Hope' = that which is hoped for. **5.** 'Heard before' (RSV), i.e. prior to the advent of the false teachers. The object of the letter is to confirm the Colossians in their first belief, which was '*the truth*'. **6.** Suggests the intrinsic dynamism of the word of God, cf 3:16; 1 Thes 2:13; 1 Cor 1:18; Rom 1:16. The unusual inversion, fruit-bearing *before* growth, has a parallel in the Markan version of the parable of the Sower (4:8). **7.** The MS tradition is almost equally split between the readings 'on our behalf' (i.e. Paul and his associates) and 'on *your* behalf' (i.e. the Colossians). Intrinsically, either suits the context, but the extrinsic evidence rather favours the former reading.

9–11 Prayer for the Future—This liturgically cad- **c** enced petition is for (i) a sensitiveness to God's will consisting in a grasp of what is spiritually valuable, (ii) the overflow of this knowledge into external activity, and (iii) the strength required to do this. **9.** If the Colossians are filled with a profound awareness of God's will they will be less likely to crave the merely human speculation (2:8), which is the root of the trouble at Colossae. **10.** 'Bearing fruit'. The same phrase is used of the power laden word in v 6; cf 1 Thess 2:13: '*God's word is made operative in you*', a theme which leads naturally into **11.** 'The might of his glory,' i.e. perhaps 'the power which belongs to God as he has revealed himself to men' (Moule). As applied to God in the OT, 'glory' (*kâbôd*) suggests a manifestation of God's being characterized by radiant splendour and rendered accessible to human experience by the accompanying action. In Paul it is sometimes a synonym for salvific power (Rom 6:4).

12–14 Conversion—**12** may be the conclusion to the **d** petition, or the introduction to what follows. The former is more natural, but *eucharistountes* is frequently found as a liturgical introduction (cf G. Bornkamm, Theol. Bl. 21 (1942) 61), and nowhere else does a Pauline intercession pass over into thanksgiving. **12b–13.** The redeemed and the unredeemed are symbolized by light and darkness respectively. This contrast appears neither in the OT nor in the Rabbinic literature, but was a basic theme at Qumran. 1QS 3:13–4:26; 1QM 13:9–12 have many contacts with our passage. See also Acts 26:17–18 and 2 Cor 6:14–7:1 (J. Fitzmyer, CBQ 23 (1961) 271–80). 'Saints' = angels, cf Wis 5:5–6. The 'kingdom of his beloved Son' could be a synonym for the Kingdom of God (cf Eph 5:5), but it is more probable that it designates the interim period between the Resurrection and the definitive appearance of the Kingdom (cf 1 Cor 15:24–28; L. Cerfaux, *L'Eglise*, 1965³, 345), i.e. the time of the Church.

913a **15—20 The Christological Hymn**—Italicized words are additions made by Paul to the original hymn. The translation differs somewhat from RSV.

15a Who is the Image of the invisible God
  b First-born of all creation
16a For in him were created all things
  b *in heaven and on earth*
  c *visible and invisible*
  d *whether thrones or dominations*
  e *or principalities or powers*
  f All things through him and to him have been created.
17 *And he himself is before all things and all things in him con-sist.*
18a *And he himself is the head of the body, the Church.*
  b Who is the Beginning
  c First-born from the dead
  d *that he might in everything himself become pre-eminent*
19 For in him willed all the Fullness to dwell
20a And through him to reconcile all things to him
  b *making peace by the blood of his cross through him*
  c *whether those on earth or those in heaven.*

b The hymnic character of this section is generally recognized. There is agreement that the passage is a two-strophe hymn depicting the cosmological and soteriological roles of Christ to which Paul has made additions, but on the detail of the strophic arrangement opinions differ widely (for a good summary cf Lohmeyer—Schmauch, *Beiheft*, 48—52). The position adopted here is a modification of that of J. M. Robinson (JBL 76 (1957) 270—87). *Original hymn:* Strophe I—vv 15, 16*af*; Strophe II—vv 18*bc*, 19, 20*a. Pauline additions:* vv 16*b*—*e*, 17, 18*ad*, 20*bc.* The original hymn exhibits literary and doctrinal affinities with previous Pauline letters, and if it was not originally composed by Paul on another occasion (the opinion of Lohmeyer, Benoit, Feuillet), it must be the work of a charismatic deeply imbued with Pauline theology. Käsemann's suggestion that the hymn is prechristian and gnostic in origin fails to recognize that the principal source on which the author drew was the sapiential literature: Jb 28; Ps 38; Prv 8; Sir 24; Wis 7. Nonetheless he is probably correct in proposing that the hymn formed part of a baptismal liturgy, which Paul evokes in order to recall the Colossians to the original profession of faith which they are now in danger of abandoning (*Essays on NT Themes*, 1964, 149—68). The Pauline additions draw out implications of the hymn which are specially relevant for the situation at Colossae. On hymns in the primitive Church, cf Col 3:16; Eph 5:18—20; and D. M. Stanley, CBQ 20 (1958) 173—91.

c **15—17 Christ and Creation**—No clear distinction is made between the pre-existent and the incarnate Christ. **15a.** In Wis 7:25—26 Divine Wisdom is 'the pure emanation of the glory of the Almighty . . . the reflection of eternal light, the untarnished mirror of his active power, the image of his goodness'. These themes are already associated with Christ in 2 Cor 3:18—4:6. For the biblical writers an 'image' is not merely a faithful copy, but a visible reproduction, a radiant impression in which the being of the original is exteriorized. In Paul it is closely linked with the idea of 'glory' (cf above v 11; 1 Cor 11:7). **15b.** Many exegetes understand 'First-born' as a Messianic title (e.g. Abbott), but it is much more probable that the allusion is to Prv 8:22, because *rēšit* can mean both 'first-fruits' and 'first-born'. In this perspective the meaning would appear to be that it was in Christ that God contemplated

the plan of the universe. **16af.** If the previous v appeared **91** to range Christ among creatures here we find his transcendance emphatically affirmed. Though the formulae have a Stoic ring the thought is again sapiential (cf Job 28:23—27), with the exception of the idea that Christ is the goal towards which all creation tends. Cf 1 Cor 8:6 and the note by F. M. Sagnard, ETL 26 (1950) 54—58. **16b—e.** Paul draws out the implications **d** of 'all beings' (v 16a) in order to make it clear that the angelic beings on which the heretics laid such stress were created in Christ and were therefore subordinate to him. The past tense here contrasts with the future in 1 Cor 15:24. The Essenes considered themselves the eschatological community of the saved and attributed a key role in this process to angels, and in particular to their chief, Michael, cf 1QS 3:20, 24; 11:8; 1QM 13:9—10; 17:6—7; CD 5:18. **17** is a summarizing conclusion to the first strophe. It is difficult to decide whether 'before all things' is a reference to rank or to time. Possibly both are intended (cf Sir 1:4; 24:9). The Universe owes its cohesiveness to Christ. Cf Sir 43:26 'all things hold together by means of his [God's] word'. According to Heb 1:3 Christ sustains the universe through his word.

18—20 Christ and the New Creation—18a. The **e** introduction of the idea of the Church at this point disturbs the equilibrium of the two strophes, and it is best to consider this v as a Pauline introduction to the second strophe. The gradual development of the theme of the Church as the Body of Christ which can be traced through Gal 2:26—29; 1 Cor 6:13—17; 10:14—21; 12:12—27; Rm 12:45 (cf B. Ahern, CBQ 23 (1961) 199—209) here reaches its climax. 'The Body' has become an accepted designation of the universal Church, and by the introduction of the theme of 'Head' the whole Christ is more adequately distinguished from the individual Christ. In this epistle 'head' is used with two connotations (i) dignity and authority (1:18a; 2:10); (ii) source of vitality (2:19). Allusions to these two aspects are perceptible in v 18d and v 18b respectively. **18bc.** The structure corresponds exactly to v 15. **18b.** The presentation of Christ as 'the Beginning' (Prv 8:22) implies that he has a real influence on all that happens subsequently. Compare Prv 8:35 with Ac 3:14. Cf Is 44:6; Apoc 1:5, 17. **18c.** For the close connexion with the preceding title cf Gn 49:3; Dt 21:17. We have here allusions both to the physical resurrection of Christ (1 Cor 15:20; Rm 8:29) and to the spiritual resurrection effected in baptism (2:13; 3:1) of which it is the type and cause (Rm 4:25). **18d.** It is a characteristic of Pauline theology that the resurrection marked a new beginning not only for humanity but also for Christ. Through his resurrection he was 'constituted Son of God in power' (Rm 1:4) and 'became a life-giving Spirit' (1 Cor 15:45). These texts, however, are immediately concerned with the advantages accruing to humanity—a theme that appears in v 20a. Here we find a polemic emphasis on the position of Christ (cf Phil 2:9—11). **19.** 'One of the most obscure **f** and disputed vv in the Pauline letters' (Feuillet). 'Fullness' (*plērōma*) is taken by some to designate the Church (Theodoret, J. A. T. Robinson), but nothing in the context supports this interpretation. The majority of scholars understand it as the plenitude of divinity (note the gratuitous addition 'of God' in the RSV), but this opinion is based ultimately on the technical value of *plērōma* in Gnostic texts written much later than Col (cf H. Jonas, *The Gnostic Religion*, Boston 1963[2], 181). More satisfactory is the view of Dupont

3f (*Gnosis*, 1949, 461—8) and Benoit (RB 63 (1956) 31—40) who trace the concept to both the OT and Stoicism. The Stoics conceived the cosmos as a unified diversity in which the divine spirit compenetrated material reality 'filling' it with its universal presence and in turn 'being filled' with it. It is impossible to see this materialistic immanentism reflected in this hymn, but purified of its pantheistic associations it rejoins the OT theme of the close bond linking the Creator with his creation, e.g. 'Do I not fill heaven and earth?— it is Yahweh who speaks' (Jer 23:24; cf Is 6:3; Ps 49:12; 71:19; 88:12; etc). There is here a sense of the divine omnipotence which easily lent itself to expression in Stoic terms when this philosophy came into contact with biblical revelation, e.g. 'The spirit of the Lord fills the whole world' (Wis 1:7). In this perspective *plērōma* is the plenitude of being and englobes both the divinity and the material world. Understood in this sense this v takes up the thought of the corresponding line of the first strophe (v 16*a*) while at the same time opening up new perspectives. This interpretation makes it clear that the subject governing 'willed' is not *plērōma* but 'God' (understood). For the same absolute

g use of *eudokein* cf Lk 2:14; Phil 2:13. **20a**. The phrase depends on 'God willed' of v 19. In the OT man had to take the first steps to reconcile himself with a wrathful God (2 Mac 1:5; 7:33; 8:23). Paul, on the other hand, stresses that the initiative lies exclusively with God whose unlimited love (Eph 2:4—6) moves him to establish peaceful relations with a sinful humanity which had made no effort to propitiate him. Cf J. Dupont, *La réconciliation dans la théologie de saint Paul*, Bruges— Paris 1953. The initial 'and' may be consecutive, but more probably explicative. It is by reconciling a sin-divided cosmos through Christ that God makes it to dwell in him. That the thought remains on the cosmic level is confirmed by the Pauline interpretation of 'all things' in v 20*c*. **20b**. Paul automatically associated 'reconciliation' with 'the Cross', for in his theology the effects of redemption are attributed either directly to the blood of Christ (Rm 5:9) or to his violent death (1 Thes 5:10; 1 Cor 6:20; etc). The 'through him' is repeated for the sake of emphasis. Reconciliation is exclusively through Christ. All other beings are beneficiaries of his work.

h 21—23 Participation of the Colossians in Salvation—Vv 20—23 reflect the same thought-pattern as 2 Cor 5:18—19. **21**. 'You who were once strangers and enemies through your evil thoughts and deeds' (BJ). If, as Gentiles, they were enemies of God it was due to personal sin and not to an accident of birth. **22**. On the two stages of the process of reconciliation cf 1 Cor 3:10—11. 'Body of flesh' is a polemic emphasis on the physical body of Christ directed against the role attributed to incorporeal angels by the heretics. Lacking bodies they could not share our mode of being, and in consequence could do nothing to reverse the situation of fallen man. **23**. 'In the whole of creation', rhetorical exaggeration. At this stage the Gospel had been preached in all the great centres of the Empire cf Rm 15:19—23.

914a 24—2:5 The Apostle's Role in the reconciling work of God in Christ—Before beginning his explicit polemic in 2:6 Paul attempts to dispose the Colossians to accept it by demonstrating (i) his divine commission and the zeal with which he carries it out (v 24—29), and (ii) his solicitude for the churches of the Lycus valley and the confidence he has in them. The community is bound not only to its confession of faith (evoked in the baptismal hymn), but to the apostolic office as the

guardian of truth. **24**. Absolutely speaking the genitive **914a** in 'the sufferings of Christ' can be objective (sufferings borne for Christ), qualitative (sufferings like those of Christ), subjective (sufferings undergone by Christ), or mystical (sufferings undergone by the members of Christ's Body). A survey of the history of interpretation reveals that no compelling solution has emerged (cf J. Kremer, *Was an den Leiden Christi noch Mangelt*, Bonn 1956), but what we know of Paul's mind as revealed by the parallel texts, Rm 8:17—18; 2 Cor 1:4—5; 4:8—10, makes it very probable that 'the sufferings of Christ' here means the concrete sufferings of the Apostle as viewed in the perspective of the intimate union that obtains between the Risen Christ and those in whom his Spirit is operative. 'Christ', then, is not the historical Jesus but the Lord as living in his members. The Gr. verb *antanaplērō*, which appears in the phrase 'to complete what is lacking', implies a duality which excludes the complete identification of the sufferings of Paul with those of the whole Christ. This immediately implies that others also have a role to play. But in what sense? The answer is suggested by Paul's assertion that his sufferings are 'for the sake of the Church'. Until the end of time the Church will be imperfect in **b** the sense that it must continually develop both intensively and extensively (Eph 4:10—13). In virtue of their baptism all Christians are called to contribute to filling up this gap between the actual and the potential, the real and the ideal. This they do simply by living as authentic Christians which inescapably involves suffering. Pain is always a condition of growth. This interpretation is confirmed by Phil 3:10 in which Paul says that his personal sufferings have won him a place in the immense 'fellowship of Christ's sufferings', i.e. that they contributed but a share in the vast afflictions of the mystical Christ which all Christians must bear in order to bring the Body of Christ to full measure. Cf B. Ahern, CBQ 22 (1960) 1—32. **25—27**. 'According **c** to the divine commission given me in your regard (which is) to fulfil the word of God, the mystery . . . which is Christ among you'. Eph 3:1—9 is the best commentary on these vv. The revelation, through preaching, of the divine plan of salvation ('the mystery') brings it to fulfillment as regards the Gentiles ('you'). The power-laden word (1:6) realizes a presence of Christ among them in so far as it encounters faith, which leads to baptism by which they are incorporated into Christ, and thus inherit the promises of salvation hitherto reserved to the Jews. **29**. Human gifts do not suffice for the apostle. He must be made 'competent' by an infusion of divine power, cf Gal 2:7—9; 2 Cor 3:6; 1 Tim 1:12; 2 Tim 1:6—7. **2:2**. Even if they are not authentic, the words 'of Christ' (RSV with the better MSS) accurately interpret the meaning of 'the mystery of God'. He *is* the mystery in as much as hidden in him are all the treasures of wisdom and knowledge. Polemic overtones are not difficult to detect. The Colossians have no need of any other teacher. Christ is the all-sufficient Wisdom in which they have been trained (1:27; 3:11). This presentation of Christ as Divine Wisdom makes explicit what is latent in the titles of the Christological Hymn (1:15—20).

2:6—3:4 Warning against Errors—2:6—7. The **d** structure of this introductory phrase is typical of a Pauline exhortation—a dogmatic indicative followed by a moral imperative. The former is amplified in v 9—15, the latter in v 16—3:4. **6**. 'You receive Christ [as] Jesus the Lord' (Lightfoot, Benoit). The true doctrine of Christ consists in (i) the acceptance of the historical

914d person of *Jesus*. Only rarely does Paul use 'Jesus' alone and always in a context which evokes the historical events of the passion and resurrection; (ii) the recognition of this Jesus as *Lord*, i.e. as Messianic saviour. With their interest in spiritual beings Paul's adversaries presumably stressed the latter at the expense of the former. **7.** If they are rooted in Christ the Colossians should be *progressively* built up in union with him, and *progressively* reinforced in their Christian conviction.

e 8. First explicit allusion to the Colossian heresy. It is a 'philosophy' which Paul describes as 'empty deceit' because it gives the central place not to Christ but to the 'elements of the world' (*stoicheia tou kosmou*). In the eleven instances of the phrase *stoicheia tou cosmou* in profane literature it means the constituent elements of the physical world—fire, water, air, and earth (cf J. Blinzler, *Stud. Paul. Cong. Internat. Cath.*, Romae 1963, II, 440—2). While perhaps appropriate here, this meaning is incompatible with 2:20. The way out of the dilemma is suggested by Paul's use of *kosmos*. Frequently it means not the material universe, but the sphere of human activity constituted by interpersonal relationships (cf R. Bultmann, *Theology of the NT*, 1965, I, 254—9). In this perspective the *stoicheia* would be the factors that condition human existence without Christ (2:20). In Rm 7 these factors are Sin and Death, and their ancillaries the Flesh and the Law (with which angelic powers were closely associated, cf Gal 3:19; Heb 2:2). If this interpretation is correct, *stoicheia tou kosmou* (cf Gal 4:3, 9) is not a formula used by the heretics, but Paul's understanding of the implications of their teaching.

f 9—15 Christ the Unique Head of Men and Angels— 9a. For a summary of the various opinions, cf Moule, 92—94. 'Fullness' has the same sense as in 1:19, but its components are expressed analytically by means of the adverb and the genitive, viz 'God' and 'the cosmos'. In Stoicism 'body' was a current designation of the universe in its diversified unity. **9b.** If the plenitude of all being is englobed in Christ those who are 'in him' participate in this fullness, so that they themselves are filled with the divine life, some of whose manifestations are mentioned in 2 Cor 4:7; Rm 15:13—14; Phil 1:11. **10.** This use of the term 'head' with the connotation of authority probably suggested to Paul the application of this theme to the Body (cf Benoit, RB 63 (1956) 22—31). As united to Christ the Christian is superior to all angelic beings. **11.** In Paul's view the 'flesh' was the avenue whereby Sin gained dominion over man. Jewish circumcision, which was 'made with hands' (Eph 2:11), only removed a tiny particle of flesh. Its Christian correspondent, Baptism, has a much more radical effect. By destroying the whole body-person viewed precisely as 'flesh' (in the pejorative sense, i.e. the self as the willing servant of sin) it breaks completely the tyranny of sin. In the phrase 'the circumcision of Christ' there may be an allusion to Christ's literal laying aside of his body on Calvary, which is described **g** as a 'baptism' (Mk 10:38; Lk 12:50). **12—13.** Paul sees the rite of immersion as an . . . inclusion in what happened to Christ. From this insight it was but a short step to seeing baptism as a participation in the two events which are linked by the tomb of Christ, his death and resurrection. Paul's principle is: what happened to Christ happens to all Christians. Compare the kerygmatic proclamation of 1 Cor 15:3—4 ('Christ *died* . . . was *buried* . . . was *raised*') with Rm 6:3—4 ('baptised unto his *death* . . . *buried* with him . . . in order that as Christ was *raised*'). By comparison with

Rm, Col lays greater emphasis on the present character **91** of the Christian's resurrection. Baptism is not a magical rite, because 'faith' on the part of the recipient is an essential prerequisite, cf Gal 3:26—27.

14. '*Having completely wiped out our bond [to subscribe]* **h** *to the ordinances, which stood against us; he set it aside nailing it to the Cross*'. For this translation, cf J. A. T. Robinson, *The Body*, 43 note 1. 'Ordinances' is deliberately vague so as to cover both cases: Jews who were bound by the Law, and Gentiles who were bound by their consciences (Rm 1:32; 2:12—16). For a good example of a 'bond', cf Phm 19. Though having signed an undertaking by their very existence as creatures, men had consistently failed to fulfil their obligations. Yet God 'blotted it out' through Christ's expiatory death in which we are included by baptism. An IOU cannot be urged against a dead man (cf Rm 7:1). 'The metaphor is so violent as to practically rupture itself' (Moule, 98). **15.** '*Having divested himself [of his flesh], he boldly displayed in public the principalities and powers, leading them in triumphal procession on the Cross*'. The dying Jesus like a king divests himself of that 'flesh' which is the tool and medium of the powers of evil, thus reducing them to impotence. BJ and RSV translate *apekdusamenos* by 'having despoiled (disarmed)', but according to Lightfoot it is impossible that the verb could be so used in the middle voice, and in fact no examples of such a use have been found (cf Blass—Debrunner, § 316, 1).

16—23 Against False Asceticism—16—17. External **915** (Jewish) observances are no longer of any value. Christ is the only 'reality', and the preparatory role that they played with regard to him has now ended (Gal 2:24—25). The Essenes of Qumran believed themselves to be the recipients of a special revelation concerning the calendar (CD 3:13—15; 6:18—19; 16:3—4), and manifested an extreme rigorism with regard to the observance of the sabbath (CD 10:14—11:18) and dietary regulations (CD 12:12—15). **18.** 'Crowded with problems of interpretation' (Moule). 'Impossible to translate' (Conzelmann). Paul stigmatizes his opponents for offering '*service* to angels'. This service (*thrēskeia*, cf Ac 26:5; 4 Mac 5:7) consisted in certain ascetic practices (*tapeinophrosunē*, cf v 16, 21) based on 'visions' considered to have been transmitted by angels (cf v 16 above. The Essenes were men who 'saw the holy angels, received revelations, and heard profound mysteries' 1QM 10:9—11). Apropos of these 'visions' Paul uses the rare verb *embateuō*, which literally means 'to enter', and metaphorically 'to enter into a subject = to examine'. Paul perhaps used it deliberately because of the technical cultual value it had at Claros, a pagan sanctuary 30 miles N of Ephesus. To readers aware of this, the effect would have been to assimilate the doctrine and practices of the heretics to a particularly abhorrent idolatrous cult. He employs a similar technique in Gal 5:12. Cf S. Lyonnet, Bib 43 1962) 417—35. **19.** Here 'head' appears as the source **b** of the Body's vitality and growth, and is a necessary complement to 'head' as authority (1:18a) if Christ's relationship to his members is to be accurately expressed. **20.** 'Elements of the world', cf on 2:8. In Christ the believer is no longer subject to the Law (Rm 7:4), to Sin (Rm 6:10), or to Death (Rm 6:9). 'Living in the world' i.e. an inauthentic existence centred on anyone or anything other than Christ (cf 3:2). **3:1—4.** These vv are the positive counterpart to 2:20—23, and serve to introduce the exhortatory section (3:5—4:6). **1.** The Christian shares the life of the Risen Christ here and now. **2.** 'The things that are above' i.e. matters of

b ultimate concern as contrasted with trivialities. What Paul is attacking is a materialistic type of superstitious ritualism. **4.** The splendour of the believer's vital but hidden union with Christ will one day be made manifest.

c 3:5—4:6 The Practical Implications of Faith—5. Become what you are! The vices characteristic of the 'old man' are essentially self-centred. **9.** The terminology 'putting on' and 'taking off' (cf v 10, 12), which originally referred to clothes, was suggested by the believer's unclothing before immersion and reclothing in new garments after it. **10.** The underlying allusion is to Gn 1:26ff. Man, created in the image of God, deviated by seeking knowledge of good and evil in a way opposed to the will of God. Recreated in Christ (Eph 2:15), who is the perfect image of God (1:15), he is now in a position to attain true moral knowledge. The theme 'old man—new man' refers primarily to the condition of the individual, but also carries corporate associations inasmuch as it forms part of Paul's presentation of the Gospel in terms of 'the earthly man' (Adam) and 'the heavenly man' (Christ), cf 1 Cor 15:45—49. Note 'You have put on the new man ... *where* there can be no distinction between Greek and Jew'. Cf J. A. T. Robinson, *The Body*, 64 note 2. **14.** 'And on top of all the other "articles of clothing"—in addition to the rest—put on love, which holds them together and completes them' (Moule, 123). Note that Christ is both the principle of cohesiveness (1:17) and the embodiment of love (Titus 3:4). **15.** This admonition has particular force when we recollect how divided the community at Colossae must have been. **16.** The indwelling of the power-laden word (cf 1:6) has a twofold effect each introduced by a prepositional phrase which is followed by a participle (against RSV): (i) 'in all wisdom teaching ...'; (ii) 'in gratitude singing ...'. The didactic value of hymns is admirably exemplified in 1:15—20.

d 18—4:1. Pagan prototypes for this type of instruction were current. As taken over by Paul they underwent a radical modification not only in the emphasis laid **915d** on the reciprocal nature of the duties, but especially with regard to the motive for which they were performed. 'In Christ' is *the* new factor. Col gives special prominence to slaves, presumably because of Onesimus (cf Phm). A Christian slave who acts as Paul advises 'adorns' the word of God (Titus 2:9—10). **2.** Is Paul perhaps thinking of the sleep of the disciples during the Agony in the Garden (Mt 26:40ff)? **3.** As a prisoner Paul had only limited opportunities to preach. **5—6.** Cf 1 Thes 4:11—12; 1 Tim 3:7. These passages, which are devoid of any religious motivation, reflect the sociological situation of the early Church, which was that of a minority group in an environment which might turn hostile. Paul's concern is to preserve harmonious relations.

4:7—18 Personal News and Final Salutations— e 7. 'Tychicus' (Ac 20:4), the bearer of this letter as well as Eph (Eph 6:21) and Phm 11b. The Jewish Christians mentioned previously are distinguished from the names which follow. This is how it is known that St Luke was a Gentile (v 14). **15—16.** 'Laodicea' was the most important city in the region and situated about 10—15 miles from Colossae. Relations between the two were very close, and Paul no doubt had reason to fear that the heresy that had got a grip on Colossae might also infect Laodicea. 'The letter which will come to you from Laodicea', which may perhaps be Eph (cf Lightfoot, 272—98), was presumably written by Paul with this in view. **17.** 'Archippus' may have been the son of Philemon and Apphia (cf Phm 2). **18.** Paul had the custom of authenticating letters written at his dictation by adding a few words in his own hand, cf 2 Thes 3:17; 1 Cor 16:21; Gal 6:11. Forgeries were not unknown (cf 2 Thes 2:2). 'My chains'. Paul does not appeal for sympathy with his sufferings but for obedience to the Gospel. He who is suffering for Christ has a right to speak on his behalf (Lightfoot).

1 AND 2 THESSALONIANS

BY DOM BERNARD ORCHARD

916a Bibliography—Chrys PG 62; John Damascene PG 95; I. Knabenbauer, CSS 1913; J.-M. Vosté, 1917; C. Lattey, WV 1927²; J. Steinmann, BB 1935; F. Amiot, VS, 1946; B. Rigaux, EtB 1956; K. Staab, RNT 1959³; L.-M. Dewailly—B. Rigaux, BJ 1960²; P. Rossano, SacB 1965—6; J. B. Lightfoot, *Notes on the Ep. of St Paul*, 1895; G. Milligan, 1908; J. E. Frame, ICC 1912; A. Plummer, 1918; J. W. Bailey, IB 1955; W. Neil, PC (2) 1962; Ch. Masson, CNT 1957. A. Feuillet, 'Parousie', DBS.

b Thessalonica—Thessalonica, was founded by Cassander in 315 B.C. and was named after his wife the stepsister of Alexander the Great. The city became the chief naval station of the Macedonian kings, and the advantages of its situation for commerce and naval warfare secured it a rapid and increasing prosperity. It was perhaps the most important city of the Roman Province of Macedonia and became the place of residence of the proconsul and virtually its capital. Its situation on the Via Egnatia, the highway connecting Rome with her E Provinces increased its importance. In the Second Roman Civil War the city took the side of Octavian and Antony, and in reward was made a Free City, ruled by its own assembly and magistrates, who were called politarchs (Ac 17:5—6). In the time of St Paul, therefore, the city was important, populous, and a strategic centre for the spread of the Faith in Macedonia. Its population was chiefly Greek, but on account of its commercial advantages, many other nations were represented, especially the Jews, who formed a large and powerful community possessing a synagogue. Apart from the Jews, its inhabitants were as licentious as those of any other seaport population of those days.

c   The Church in Thessalonica at the time of the Epistles consisted of a few Jewish converts and a large number of convert pagan Greeks (Ac 17:4; 1 Thes 1:9). Though the account of Paul's visit in Ac would lead us to assume that he only spent three weeks there on his second missionary journey, most commentators agree that the flourishing state of the Thessalonian Church at the time of the Epistles presupposes a fairly long residence, during which he converted a great number of Gentiles and set up a system of Church government (1 Thes 5:12—14). It was in fact his great success with the Gentiles that roused the envy of the Jews (Ac 17:5) and led to a riot. Though they failed to find Paul, the situation was sufficiently menacing to cause the brethren to send him and Silas away by night to Beroea. From there the relentless persecution of the Jews of Thessalonica drove him down to Athens (Ac 17:15), where Timothy rejoined him. Being anxious to know how his recent Thessalonian converts were facing up to the bitter persecution of the Jews, he despatched Timothy to find out and report back to him (1 Thes 3:2).

d Occasion—1 Thes is the result of the favourable report brought back by Timothy to Paul who in the interval had moved on to Corinth (Ac 18:5). Along with the good news of their spiritual progress and of their patient endurance of persecution, Timothy also, it seems, informed Paul that the Jews were trying to discredit the authority of the three missionaries. He also brought two questions, possibly in writing, that required immediate answer as they were disturbing the minds of some in the Thessalonian Church, one concerning **the date of the Parousia** or Second Coming, and the other **the fate of those of their brethren who, by their premature death, could not possibly be witnesses of the Parousia**. The Apostle's answer to the latter question satisfied them, but his clear statement of his own and every one else's ignorance of the date of the second coming of Christ did not convince some of the Thessalonians and necessitated the Second Letter in which he reaffirmed the total ignorance of all men of the date of the Parousia and calmed their fears of its nearness by stressing that certain things must happen first.

Date, Place and Genuineness—Both letters were **e** accepted very early as genuine writings of Paul—1 Thes is included in Marcion's Canon c. A.D. 140 and 2 Thes by Polycarp, *Ep. XI*, 24, c. A.D. 120. The situation reflected in **1 Thes** is that **Silvanus** (Silas) and Timothy are with Paul who has left **Athens** whence he despatched Timothy to Thessalonica (1:1, 3:1, 6). The predominant view is that the letter was written from Corinth, see Ac 18:1. As Gallio seems to have been resident in Corinth as proconsul during the latter part of Paul's stay (Ac 18:11, 18) in the spring of A.D. 51 or 52, 1 Thes may have been written between autumn 50 and spring 52, cf §§ 706i, 708c. Arguments for a later dating are based on (1) the fact that the attacks on Paul are the same as those in 2 Cor, (2) the need for more time since the founding of the Church in Thess. to enable the situation to develop, and (3) the silence of Ac 17—18 on the presence of Timothy at Athens, whereas 1 Thes 3:1 suggests he was there. The conclusion from this would be that 1 Thes was written later, perhaps during the third missionary journey. But it may be replied that (1) though the charges are similar they may be made by different people; in the case of 1 Thes, by Jews not Judaisers, (2) the time required for developments is uncertain and unpredictable; moreover Paul writes in 1 Thes as if the memory of their foundation is still fresh, and (3) silence is not contradiction. We may accept 1 Thes as evidence that Timothy was at Athens in advance of Silas who rejoined Paul only when he had reached Corinth (Ac 18:5).

2 Thes must have been written soon after 1 Thes. Silvanus (1:1) was with Paul only on the second missionary journey and the situation appears to be roughly the same as in 1 Thes. It was probably written, like 1 Thes, from Corinth. The authenticity of 2 Thes has been doubted since 1801 by a number of writers. It is said that the warnings and details about the Parousia and the antichrist are not Pauline (2:1—12) and were composed by a later

6e writer who set them in a Pauline framework. The 'mark' of Paul referred to in 3:17 is also regarded as a sign of pseudepigraphy. Yet, is the contrast between 2 Thes 2:1—12 and 1 Thes 4:13ff really so sharp? see § 914d. The Lord comes like a thief in the night (1 Thes), yet this is not incompatible with a historical preparation; and it should also be recalled that 2 Thes 2:1—12 is clothed in apocalyptic language. As for the reference to his 'mark' this may have been occasioned by a rumour that spurious letters were circulating purporting to be by Paul. The language too is thoroughly Pauline, apart from a few individual words which are not enough to upset the general impression of authenticity. Lastly, both Letters are written throughout in the 1st pers. pl. (except the final vv) on account of the part played by Silas and Timothy in converting Thess, cf Kümmel, *Introd. to the NT*, in loc.

f Doctrinal Content—1 and 2 Thes are notable for the glimpse they give us of the personality of Paul and his love and friendship for the brethren and his converts in particular. He often thanks God for their progress in the Christian way of life and praises them for being an example to all in the province of Macedonia (1 Thes 1:3—8). The Thess. are his brethren for whom his love is so intense that he would gladly communicate not only the Gospel but also his soul, thoughts and feelings; indeed his very life (1 Thes 2:8). Though they had been brethren so short a time he cannot continue for long without news of their progress. He 'lives again' when he learns not only that they are doing well but that they are as eager to see him again as he to see them (1 Thes 3:6—8).

The fundamental Pauline teaching on our union with God in Christ, the Son of God, and his full divinity and equality with God the Father is made clear in the first salutation of both epistles. All the main doctrines found in the other epistles are in 1 and 2 Thes, e.g. the redemptive work of Christ, his resurrection and the resurrection of all faithful believers into eternal life with him, sanctification through the Holy Spirit, grace; whilst the laws of Christian morality, are taken for granted in many passing allusions. Special emphasis is laid on the importance of work, of earning a living soberly and of avoiding idleness. Sexual indulgence is especially to be avoided since all Christians are temples of the Holy Spirit. There is an interesting reference to a group of rulers of the Church in 1 Thes 5:12—14, and though they are given no name we may assume that they are similar to the clergy ordained previously in S Galatia (Ac 14:22); the people are to reverence and obey them.

g The most important teaching in the Letters is, however, usually held to be the teaching on **the Second Coming or the Parousia**. The present writer believes that our present Gr. Mt was one of the principal sources of the eschatological teaching of these epistles, cf Orchard 'Thessalonians and the Synoptic Gospel' Bib 19 (1938), 19ff. The great majority of exegetes however today maintain a different view.

At this stage the notion which dominates Christian thought is the expectation that Christ will soon return to bring about the consummation of all things. This must have been a leading motif in Paul's instruction at Thessalonika, for it had given rise to the problem which he answers: Christians at Thessalonika had died, and this had come as a shock to the community, posing the question whether the dead were thereby excluded from the triumph of Christ. Paul replies that, alive or dead, we are all united to Christ, and those who have died in Christ will also rise and go to meet him when he comes in his glorious return.

[All the language which Paul uses suggests that **916h** Christ's return is to be at no very distant date. It is not only that he writes 'those of us who are left alive at the Lord's coming' (1 Thes 4:15—17). This could be merely a dramatic way of expressing 'those Christians who are left alive' or a mere hypothesis '*if* any of us are left alive', and thus make no suggestion that the Lord's coming would be within his generation. But the whole accent of the letter is upon waiting for the Lord's coming. Apologists have carefully pointed out that Paul may *hope* for the coming of the Lord soon, but he does not formally *teach* that he will come in the near future or within a generation. Strictly this is correct; his aim is to stress the unexpectedness of Christ's coming, rather than its nearness; "the day of the Lord will come like a thief in the night", 1 Thes 5:2. As time goes on and the Lord does not appear the vivid hope fades and is replaced by a deeper understanding Phil 1:20ff. It is hardly surprising that the Thessalonians were stirred to a fever pitch of expectation—probably aided by another, spurious, letter (2 Thes 2:2)—and that Paul has to add a corrective and complement to his teaching, warning them that the Lord's coming will not be immediate, 2 Thes 2:3. To explain this he uses the ideas current in Jewish apocalyptic writings about the glorious coming of the Messiah. This was to be preceded by certain preliminaries: the Great Revolt or Apostasy is to take place. The Rebel or the Enemy (the Anti-Christ of Jn) is to appear openly, since 'what is holding him back' is to be withdrawn, allowing him full play. Prophets of doom in every age have attempted to provide historical counterparts to these phenomena, but the attempt shows a fundamental misunderstanding of Paul's meaning. Paul is using terminology which was already conventional in the OT.

The Rebel or Enemy is described by means of phrases **i** used originally of the classic persecutor of God's people, Antiochus Epiphanes. One expression used (2 Thes 2:4) occurs in both Is and Ezek of foreign kings, the type of proud independence of God, who will enjoy a brief moment of glory and then be toppled from their exalted positions. The Great Revolt, though not explicit in the OT, is already implicit in OT teaching about the purging out of a remnant, and is a prominent feature of Jewish writings in the first century about the coming of the Messiah; this is to be preceded by a mass apostasy of the faithful. Many of the expressions used here occur also in Mt 24. The exact relationship between these two documents is disputed, but, since most scholars reject the view that Mt was written—at least in its entirety—before Thes, the most probable solution is perhaps that both Paul and Mt are drawing on stock phrases of current Jewish apocalyptic, or possibly on some common element in the original apostolic catechesis.

The problem which is discussed in Thes arises from **j** the new element introduced into Jewish-based thinking on the last times by the coming of Jesus as man to die an ignominious death. The Jews looked forward to a messiah who would inaugurate the last times by his coming, which was to be a coming in triumph and majesty. Jesus' coming did indeed inaugurate the last times, but the coming in triumph and majesty was still in the future. But in Jewish thinking the last times were always considered as a series of events (many of which are described in 2 Thes) which occur in quick succession, almost forming one composite event. With this background it was natural that Christians should presume that once the last times had been inaugurated the end could not long be delayed, and so to look forward to an imminent final coming of the Lord.

916k What is true and important in this is that the Christian's life must be lived in expectation of the Lord's coming (whether this is to take the form of a coming similar to that expressed in the Jewish apocalyptic imagery of the Day of Judgement, or whether it is only the meeting of the individual with the Lord at his death). This is the lesson stressed in 1 Thes. But, lest it be thought that this means that the Christian should *merely* wait for the Lord's coming, Paul underlines in the second letter that the Christian must continue to carry out his ordinary occupations. In the last analysis all that Paul says about the date of the final coming is that it is not so near that one can just sit down and wait for it; he reinforces this teaching by an appeal to the popular conception of events which are to precede the end. [*General Editor's Note.*]

1 THESSALONIANS

917a **1:1—2a Greeting**—Although the Epistle is entirely his own composition St Paul associates Silvanus (Silas, Ac 15:22) and Timothy (Ac 16:3), his two chief assistants on his second missionary journey, with his greetings and message throughout. This v shows that he had taught the Thessalonians the equality of Jesus Christ with God the Father.

b **2—10 Thanksgiving for their Conversion**—**3.** Basing all their hope on Christ, they had fruitfully exercised the Theological Virtues. **4.** In this behavior he sees their active response to God's gift of Faith by which they were chosen (elected) members of Christ's Kingdom. **5.** God's favour to them was shown by the efficacy and fulness of St Paul's preaching amongst them on the one hand, and by the sincerity and depth of their conversion on the other—'our gospel'; the 'glad tidings' of salvation through Christ as proclaimed by St Paul—'in power': either 'by miracles' or 'efficaciously'. **6.** 'imitators', cf 1 Cor 4:16; Phil 3:17. **7—8.** These vv favour a residence of some months in Thessalonica, during which, and afterwards, the praise of their life sounded forth in all directions. **9.** 'they themselves': the inhabitants of Macedonia and Achaia—'from idols'; implying that the majority had formerly been pagans, not Jews. **10.** Paul urges them to order their life towards the Second Coming and to look forward to it; he does not say that they will live to see it—cf § 916*k*. 'the wrath to come': the judgement of condemnation on the wicked at the Parousia, cf 5:9; 2 Thes 1:8.

c **2:1—12 A Defence of his Conduct Amongst Them**—The apologetic character of this description of his preaching is apparent in the praise of his own work and life among them. **1.** 'not in vain': neither hollow nor lacking in sincerity. **2.** Cf Ac 16:19f. This preaching at Philippi was 'with much stress' (*Agōni*) viz his scourging and imprisonment. **3.** His motives for preaching were entirely pure and disinterested. He taught neither error nor indulgence of sexual passion nor did he use guile or deceit to attract converts. **5.** He was neither a flatterer nor secretly avaricious, nor seeking notoriety. **6.** They might have claimed either 'special honour' or the expenses of their board and lodging, cf the proverb 'honos propter onus'. **7.** The balance of textual evidence is slightly in favour of the Vg 'Babes' (*nēpioi*) as against 'gentle' (*ēpioi*); the Vg reading involves a sudden change of metaphor, by which Paul first describes himself as a babe and then in the next line as a nursing-mother; such a change would however be characteristically Pauline—'a nurse': he loves them like a mother and teaches them like a father (v 11). The true punctuation of 7—8 is uncertain. **9:** cf Ac 18:3 Phil 4:15f. **12:** cf Gal 5:21; 1 Cor 6:9; 15:24,

50; 2 Thes 1:5—'kingdom': the kingdom of the Messiah **9** whose glory will be revealed at the end of the world. This kingdom consists in an invisible sharing of the divine nature on earth, a sharing that will become visible and glorious in the definitive and eternal phase of God's kingdom.

13—16 Praise of their Behaviour: Condemnation of d the Jews—**14.** They became 'imitators' by suffering the same sort of persecution from their fellow-citizens and countrymen in Thessalonica; it was indeed an honour for them to suffer in such good company. The Judaean persecutions in question are probably those referred to in Ac 8:1f; 9:1—2; 12:1. **15—16.** This outburst against the Jews, i.e. the Jewish authorities, is not paralleled elsewhere and seems to have been evoked by their opposition to his work at Corinth as formerly at Thessalonica and Beroea—'the prophets': cf Mt 5:12; 23:34—they oppose all men precisely because they do all in their power to prevent him preaching to the pagan world. Nothing was so repugnant to them as the proclamation that they no longer had a monopoly of the Messianic Kingdom. 'to fill up': cf Mt 23:32. When the pre-ordained measure of their sins has been filled to capacity (the process has been long drawn out) then retribution will fall suddenly. While the time God allows to all men is, for those who repent, a time for acquiring their measure of grace, for the stiff-necked it is by their own fault a time for filling up the measure of their sins. 'The wrath of God' is either the Day of Judgement, or the destruction of Jerusalem, the consequence of their rejection of Christ as he foretold (Mt 24). The latter is more likely—'has come upon them completely'. The verb is proleptic, i.e. St Paul is so sure of the terrible penalty awaiting the Jews that he speaks as if it has already come upon them to the utmost.

17—3:10. His intense desire to see them again, his **e** frustration and anxiety about them until relieved by Timothy's return, perhaps because he may have been accused of neglecting them. **18.** 'Satan hindered us': For Paul Satan is an active and evil personality ever seeking to thwart the servants of God, cf 3:5, i.e. Paul and his companions. **19.** 'Coming': the Gr. *parousia* (lit presence) signified the coming of a king to mark a new era, and is the regular NT term to indicate the coming of Christian glory and judgement, cf Mt 24:3f.

3:2. 'God's servant': another reading, 'fellow-worker of God', is also well attested; cf 1 Cor 3:9. **3—4:** cf Ac 14:21. **5.** The Tempter is Satan; cf Mt 4:3. **6—10.** Timothy's favourable report filled him with joy and gave him fresh life. **10.** 'supply what is lacking in your faith': i.e. to complete their catechetical instruction so abruptly broken off, cf Ac 17:5.

11—13. A Prayer for the Thessalonians—He prays God not only to bring him to them but to enlarge their charity and keep them in readiness for the coming (parousia) of Christ. **11.** 'direct': this verb is singular in the Gr. thus showing that the two Persons, Father and Son, share the same divine nature. **13.** Christians are to direct all their attention to preparation for the Last Judgement, of which the Particular Judgement at the hour of death is in a sense merely the anticipation. 'his saints': probably the angels, cf Zech 14:5; Mt 25:31; the souls of the just do not seem to be included under the term.

4:1—11 Exhortations to Purity (1—8) Love of the f Brethren (9—10) and honest Work (11)—Paul here affirms certain precepts of the Christian moral code that he had already explained at Thessalonica. **3.** The first principle of this code is that God expects all Christians

7f to be holy, i.e. attached to God, and so separated from sin. They are to preserve their holiness or sanctity (*hagiasmos*) by keeping God's marriage laws, i.e. by abstention from every form of sexual vice (*porneia*). Among the ancient heathen, as with the modern pagan, the commonest and greatest obstacle to a holy way of life was extramarital sexual indulgence, which was regarded as practically inevitable and was treated almost as a matter of course like eating and drinking. Hence the necessity of giving stringent charges against it to Gentile converts. **4.** Render 'how to control his own body in holiness and honour'. Commentators, both ancient and modern, are about equally divided between taking '*skeuos ktasthai*' to mean either (1) to acquire or gain possession (control) of his own body, or (2) to acquire (i.e. marry) his own wife. The former explanation would lay emphasis on personal chastity, and the latter on chastity in marriage. **6a.** RSV text is preferable to footnote c. **6b—8.** The reasons for these prohibitions. The appeal to the indwelling of the Holy Spirit is his supreme argument in his exhortations to purity; cf 1 Cor 6:19. **9—10.** Still, they are not lacking in love for one another. **11—12.** Apparently certain weaker-minded brethren, obsessed by a belief in a speedy return of Christ gave up earning their living, thus drawing the ridicule of non-Christians and even becoming a charge upon the community, cf 2 Thes 3:10f.

18a **4:13—5:11 The Second Coming**—This passage is remarkable for the large number of similarities to Mt. He here answers two questions conveyed to him through Timothy concerning:
(a) 13—18 The Lot of Those who die before the Parousia—13: cf Mt 27:52; Jn 11:11. The Thessalonians knew their dead would rise again but apparently feared that they would not find them in Christ's retinue at the time of his glorious return. **14.** St Paul assures them that their dead will indeed be there by the power of Jesus; CV, with DV, prefer to read 'slept through Jesus', a unique phrase, equivalent to 'the dead who are in Christ' of 15, cf Rm 1:17 8. **15.** 'By the word of the Lord' must either mean 'on the direct authority of a personal revelation of Christ to Paul himself', or it must refer to some saying or teaching of our Lord not recorded in the Bible, since nowhere in the Gospels did he touch on this precise point. 'we who are alive . . .': this much discussed phrase is either (1) a quotation from the words of the question put by the Thessalonians, or (2) a literary device, common in St Paul, by which he puts himself in the place and state of mind of his correspondents, and ranks himself among those, whether now living or yet unborn, whom the Lord will find alive at his return. As it is clear from his answer to their second question (5:1—12) that neither he nor anyone else knows the time of the Second Coming, these words need not and ought not to be understood to imply that he believed the Parousia would come in his own lifetime. But at this time, he seems to have believed it possible, and certainly welcomed the thought. But his thought and statements remain in full conformity with the teaching of Christ in Mt 24, cf § 916i.

b **16.** The details of the description of the Second Coming are of course metaphorical and drawn from various OT theophanies, cf Ex 19:16; Zech 14:5; Is 27:13. cf Mt 24:31; 1 Cor 15:52. This command will re-establish the holy dead in full equality with those living at the last day. **17.** Then will take place, both for those newly raised from the dead and for those who are alive, the mysterious transformation that will make their bodies incorruptible and immortal and enable them to

enjoy the beatific vision and union. There is no indication here or elsewhere of an interval for a millennary terrestrial reign of Christ before his heavenly reign begins, as Schweitzer thought. **18.** Since those who have already died in Christ will therefore be at no disadvantage in the Resurrection of the Just, there is no ground for anxiety, but only for consolation.
(b) 5:1—11: The Unknowableness of the Time of the c Parousia—Having explained the identical destiny of the living and of the dead at the moment of the Parousia, Paul now deals with the second question: Is the Parousia close at hand?

1. He refers to his having given previous adequate instructions in this matter; the substance of Mt 24:36—43 must have been included since it reappears here. **2—3.** The Parousia will be 'the day of the Lord', will be as catastrophic as the Deluge and as unexpected as the burglar or the birth-pangs. In the OT 'the day of the Lord' means the time when he will vindicate his saints and restore a just world order. **4—8.** No one can escape the visitation, but it is possible to be ready for it whenever it comes. (Note that all the warnings and illustrations about watchfulness in Mt 24:36—25:13 are present here in abbreviated form).

As Christians belong to the light and to the day and not to the darkness of sin they will confidently await 'the day of the Lord', provided they have been ever watchful and sober and have put on the armour of the three theological virtues. **9—11.** Knowing God's salvific will in their regard they have no ground for uneasiness about the future, or for idleness in the present.
12—14 Exhortations to Clergy and Laity—12—13. d The laity are invited to respect and love the hierarchy appointed by St Paul to work among, rule over, and advise them. 'Be at peace *with them*', i.e. those set over them, is a preferable reading with CV, to 'among yourselves'. **14.** 'admonish the *disorderly*': cf 2 Thes 3:6. The Gr. '*ataktos*' literally refers to a soldier who breaks ranks. The hierarchy in Thessalonica are to be conscientious, patient and universally charitable. **15—18.** Four general directions, summarising the Christian life, for the practice of charity, joy, prayer and thanksgiving. **19—21.** Brief advice on the treatment of charismata at liturgical assemblies, cf 1 Cor 12 and 14, where he treats 'prophesying' and the 'speaking with tongues', etc, at much greater length. 'Do not quench the Spirit'; do not suppress such manifestations of the Holy Spirit, though they should always be tested.
23—28 Final Prayers and Requests—23. 'May c your spirit and soul and body be kept sound and *free from all defect* . . .': This passage does not prove that Paul believed in a trichotomy or threefold division of the human being, as opposed to the dichotomy or twofold division he follows elsewhere, cf Prat, *La Théologie de Saint Paul*, 1925[12], II, 61, 173—, 490—2. He simply means 'the whole person'. **26.** Probably, the origin of the liturgical kiss of peace cf Rm 16:16, 1 Cor 16:20. **27.** He demands that the epistle be publicly read so that it may reach the ears of all in the Thessalonian Church.

II THESSALONIANS.

1:1—2 Greeting; Cf 1 Thes 1:1. **919a**
3—12 Thanksgiving and Encouragement—This thanksgiving and warm appreciation of their spiritual progress is intended to prepare them for the rebuke to follow.
4. They have well understood and faithfully carried out the principal teachings of St Paul, especially in

919a their endurance of external and internal trials. **5.** Their present suffering is a sure sign of their future reward. **6–10.** A digression on the rewards and punishments to be meted out respectively to the just and to sinners at the Parousia, by a complete reversal of the fortunes of persecutors and persecuted. **8.** Two classes of wicked: (1) those who have failed to keep the natural law of God, (2) those who have heard the Gospel and rejected it. **9.** The wicked shall suffer the pain of loss of God; whereas for the just there will be the beatitude of eternal union. **10.** 'on that day': the day of the Parousia. **11b.** i.e. make fully efficacious every delight (of yours) in goodness and activity inspired by faith. **12.** The 'name' of Christ is put for the Person according to the usual biblical manner of expression.

b 2:1–12 The Parousia and the Antichrist—This pericope contains very much matter the interpretation of which still remains very obscure. Paul not only borrows words and phrases from the apocalyptic passages of the OT and NT but speaks elliptically as well. He develops further the teaching of 1 Thes 4:13ff. The basis of his teaching is, however, to be found in Mt 24 and Daniel 11; cf § 916i.
1. 'And as regards the coming of our Lord . . ., we beseech you'; cf Mt 24:31, Mk 13:27. The Apostle proceeds to answer two questions that have been put to him about the coming of the Lord and the gathering together of the faithful to Christ. **2.** Some members of the Thessalonian Church had clearly been under serious misapprehension but Paul does not seem to know whether it was as the result of a false revelation ('by Spirit') or by some word of his misunderstood ('by word'), or by some 'letter' forged in his name. In any event, some had not only ignored his previous letter (1 Thes) but had even falsely invoked his authority for spreading a rumour that the Day of the Parousia was actually 'dawning'. **3.** 'that day will not come', these words are rightly added by RSV to complete the sense. Two events must happen first, neither of which is yet verified, viz (1) '**the rebellion (apostasy)**' against Christ (which itself presupposes the conversion of a large part of the world) and, (2) the revelation of '**the man of lawlessness**, the son of perdition', i.e. the man who is not only destined to perdition but brings perdition (as Christ brings salvation).
c 4. The phraseology is apocalyptic and need not be taken literally: the meaning is that the opposer (whom we may justly equate with the Antichrist of 1 Jn 2:18, etc) will endeavour to substitute himself for the true God and to obtain full divine honours from men. **5.** It is clear that when St Paul was personally instructing them he had expounded carefully and at length (cf 1 Thes 5:2) the apocalyptic teaching which we find recorded in Mt 24 and Dn 7:25ff, 11:36ff, cf §916i. **6.** The meaning seems to be: 'And now you yourselves have had experience of the working of the withholding or restraining power which keeps the Man of Lawlessness in check until his appointed time'. The revelation of the Man of Lawlessness is dependent on the removal of a mysterious obstacle that is described in 6 as *tò katechon* (what withholds) and in 7 as *hò katechōn* (he who withholds). Among the many suggestions as to the nature of this obstacle, the following seem to be the most plausible; (a) Tertullian's view that it is the Roman Empire seen as 'a restraining power of law and order'; (b) the view (proposed by Buzy, and followed by Amiot) that it is the 'collectivity' constituted by the sum total of the preachers of the Gospel; and (c) the view of Prat that it is the Archangel Michael who appears as the champion against the forces of evil

in Dn 12:1 and Apoc 12:7–9; 20:1–3, 7, where the angel **91** binds and looses Satan.
There is no sure tradition of the Church on this point **d** to assist us to decide. **7.** 'Mystery' here means 'a secret to be revealed'. 'the mystery of lawlessness' probably denotes the present secret and partially ineffective activity of the Man of Lawlessness; cf Buzy, RSR (1934) 404f. This v confirms the statement of 6. The lawlessness is at present working secretly on account of the check imposed, but 'only until he who now withholds be taken out of the way'. **8.** 'and then the Lawless One will be revealed', only to find himself destroyed by the mere breath of the Lord's mouth, imagery borrowed from Is 11:4. **9–11.** A description of the Parousia of the Antichrist, the Man of Lawlessness. The removal of the withholding or restraining power will permit the parousia of the Antichrist, a lying counterpart of the true Parousia of Christ that will follow it and immediately destroy the Lawless One. **11.** 'To believe *the Lie*'. **12.** 'but *consented to* unrighteousness'.
The Character of 'the Man of Lawlessness'—Is he **e** to be an individual or a collectivity? Most modern commentators consider him to be a mere personification of the evil forces that will, it seems, get the upper hand at the end of the world. According to Paul the activity of the Man of Lawlessness is already taking place, although he is not yet revealed. He certainly cannot be Satan himself as he receives his powers from him. As this activity has been going on for nineteen centuries, the Antichrist would seem to be an apocalyptic personification of the powers of evil let loose. Moreover in the Gospels (esp Mt 24) our Lord nowhere speaks of one Antichrist, but of many false Christs and false prophets. With this agrees St John's teaching in his Epistles, whilst in the Apocalypse he symbolizes the sum total of persecuting political powers and false prophets by the two beasts who are the emissaries of Satan. On the other hand, the teaching of St Paul on the Antichrist is quite compatible with his being a single person, and the manner in which all the Sacred Books from Dn to Apoc, speak of him, as a man incarnating all the forces of evil and as the false counterpart of Christ himself in the last days of the world, does not permit us to lay aside as improbable the view that the Antichrist is indeed an individual; cf Rigaux, *L'Antéchrist*, Paris, 1932.
12–3:5 Further Encouragement and Exhortation— **f 13.** 'as first fruits' CV; but RV, RSV 'from the beginning' has slightly more MS support. Revealed truth is transmitted both by oral and written tradition, as the Church has always taught. **15.** The traditional character of St Paul's own teaching in the matter of the Parousia is discussed in § 916h. **3:2.** Read '*for not to all does the faith belong*' with CV. **3.** '*from the evil one*'; there seems to be a reminiscence of the Lord's Prayer in this and the preceding v.
3:6–15 A Special Exhortation to Work—Cf 1 Thes 5:14. All are bidden to act in accord with the Apostle's teaching and to get on quietly with their daily work, and to avoid vain idling in view of the supposed imminence of the Parousia. **11b.** The play of words in the Gr. is preserved in the well-known rendering 'doing no business but being busybodies'. **13–15.** A special word to the main body of loyal followers of the Apostle. The offender is to be subject to a minor excommunication to bring him to a more reasonable frame of mind.
16–18 Conclusion—As a sign of authenticity (in view of 2 Thes 2:2) St Paul here pointedly directs the attention of his correspondents to his custom of autographing the final salutation in every epistle of his.

THE PASTORAL EPISTLES

1 AND 2 TIMOTHY, TITUS

BY HENRY WANSBROUGH O.S.B.

21a Bibliography—*Commentaries*: C. Spicq, EB 1947; M. Dibelius—H. Conzelmann, ³1955; P. Dornier, BJ ²1958; C. K. Barrett, 1963; J. N. D. Kelly, 1963. *Other Works*: P. N. Harrison, *The Problem of Past.*, 1921; *Paulines and Past.*, 1964; O. Roller, *Formular des paulinischen Briefe*, 1933; P. Benoit, *Exégèse et Théologie*, 1945 II, 232; C. Spicq, DBS (1961) 'Past.'; C. F. D. Moule, *The Birth of the NT*, 1962. *Abbreviation*—Past. = Pastoral Epistles.

b Name—The letters to Tm and Ti form a group homogeneous in matter, theology and style, differentiated to some extent by these elements from the other traditionally Pauline epistles. They received the designation 'the Pastoral epistles' from Berdot and Anton of Halle in the early 18th cent., with reference primarily to their subject matter: What sort of man a pastor should be, what and how he should teach.

c Authenticity—Since the possible citation of 1 Tm 1:16 under Paul's name by 2 Pt 3:15, antiquity did not seriously question the attribution of Past. to the apostle. In modern discussion, however, the question of their authenticity has assumed unwarranted proportions. The **arguments** which have been put forward **against their Pauline authorship** may be summarized: (i) Historical: the data of Past. are impossible to fit into the life of Paul as known from Ac; if these are historical we must suppose that Paul was released from captivity in Rome after two years, made an extended tour of the East and returned again to Rome as a captive. But there is nothing impossible in this: it was early accepted by Christian tradition (Euseb. *H.E.* 2, 25, 5). (ii) Church structure and the heretical tendencies shown in Past. are said to correspond to conditions of the 2nd cent. rather than to Paul's lifetime. This is a weak argument, for their Church structure is certainly less developed than that attested at the turn of the 1st cent. (cf § 923 *ac*), and the heretical tendencies cannot be sufficiently clearly determined to **d** warrant any conclusion (cf § 923*d*). (iii) Doctrinal: this argument is based on an alleged fundamental difference of attitude from that of the Paul of the earlier letters. His dynamic Hebraic personality, ever developing new theological syntheses, has given way to a flat and tired Hellenistic mentality. He continually stresses the need for fidelity to tradition and grasps at formulae. Instead of the bold demands of celibacy we have mistrust of power to persevere, and what has often been described as a 'bourgeois morality' of good deeds, moderation and piety. These changes have been accounted for as the result of age and imprisonment: Spicq (pp. lxxxix—xciv) paints a convincing portrait of the old man, broken by hardship and years, fearful for the future, unable any longer to think through to his magnificent old doctrinal formulations, concerned only to instruct his two beloved 'sons' in the preservation of doctrine and structure of the Church after his fast-approaching death. But specific differences of doctrine are not lacking: the cross and the Spirit, so

prominent in the earlier letters, barely feature. The phrase **921d** 'in Christ' which was earlier so characteristic does indeed occur seven times; but always as a quality, not the Christian himself, which is in Christ; the personal union of life in Christ has disappeared. The teaching on the Law (see note to 1 Tm 1:8) hardly fits that of the earlier letters. (iv) Differences of style and vocabulary, Spicq, cvii—cxix, **e** are the most immediately striking. The former are difficult to evaluate, for an author's style may evolve considerably (Plato and Shakespeare are given as parallels); in e.g. the scarcity of metaphors, rare in the early letters, most frequent in the 'great' epistles, becoming rarer again in the captivity epistles, Past. merely continues the known tendency (V. Heylen, ETL 12 (1935) 253—90). The vocabulary, however, is indubitably un-Pauline, one-third of the words used not occurring in his accepted letters. However tricky the use of word statistics, this is impressive.

In face of this evidence **three types of solution** have **922a** been proposed: (1) *Pseudepigraphy*: An anonymous writer, convinced that he was teaching the message of Paul, expressed it in the form of letters purporting to be from his pen. This was a recognized literary convention of the period. The personal reminiscences, news and greetings at the end of the letters, are forged to add verisimilitude. To this it must be said that pseudepigraphical ascription to a great figure of the past certainly occurs in Jewish literature of about this time (the 'Psalms of Solomon', the Testament of the XII Patriarchs, cf the Shepherd of Hermas etc); but this sort of forgery for verisimilitude is not a part of it. Furthermore the scraps are too 'artless, and in some ways pointless' (Barrett, p. 11) to be contrived for this purpose; and 1 Tm has none **b** of them; why should it lack this sort of authentication? (2) *The Fragment Theory*: an author writing between A.D. 90 and 175 incorporated in his 'Pauline' compositions some genuine fragments of letters of Paul. P. N. Harrison, the protagonist in this century of the theory, gave a list of these genuine fragments in 1921, which he revised in 1956 (NTS 2, 250—61) to three notes, Ti 3:12—15 (written from Macedonia or Illyricum in 56), 2 Tm 4: 9—15, 20, 21*a*, 21*b* (written from Nicopolis in 56) and 2 Tm 1:16—18; 3:10—11; 4:1—2*a*, 5*b*—8, 16—19, 21*b*—22*a* (written from Rome in 62). This theory leaves unanswered a number of questions: Why were such tiny fragments preserved and collected, or indeed written? Why were they interwoven in such a curious fashion? Why was 1 Tm left without any? But above all, it seems brutal and callous to include such hopeful plans as those given in 2 Tm 4:17, 21 after their frustration by Paul's martyrdom. There remains (3) *Recourse to a secretary*. **c** Roller showed (pp. 19—20, 306—42) that conditions of Roman imprisonment were such as to exclude the possibility of writing a letter or of dictating it in the modern sense of dictating. The prisoner was chained in cramped semi-darkness, and would hardly be allowed to dictate a letter of the length of 2 Tm while his scribe wrote it out in

922c longhand (Gr. shorthand is not attested till after 150). On the other hand, authors could be said to dictate even if they gave merely general lines and left the expression of their thoughts and the formation of whole paragraphs to the secretary. It could well be that Past. are the work of a secretary to whom, for some reason, Paul at the end of his days left more liberty than he had given to other secretaries. The especially un-Pauline character of 1 Tm and its lack of final greetings would alike be explained if it had been hurriedly sent off, before Paul had checked the draft and added his personal messages. C. F. D. Moule (BJRL 47 (1964/5 430—52) has suggested that a mumber of linguistic peculiarities point to the evangelist Lk (cf 2 Tm 4:11) as this secretary. Several of the differences of doctrine detailed in § 921*d* are found also in Ac (cf §§ 822*c*, 823*c*, 838*b*). Cf id *The Birth of the NT*, 175. The linguistic argument for Lukan authorship is put very strongly by A. Strobel, 'Schreiben des Lukas? Zum sprachlichen Problem der Pastoralbriefe', NTS 15 (1968/9), 191—210.

923a The Ministry—Past. form the *locus classicus* in the NT for the ministry, but discussion has been bedevilled by controversy, each exegete wishing to find his own particular Church structure therein. It must be said from the outset that we should not hope to find the exact equivalent of bishop, priest and deacon in the ministers of Past. There is clear evidence in Ignatius of Antioch (c. 109) of the monarchical episcopate, at least in some communities (cf P. Camelot, *Ignace d'Antioche*, 1944, 32—4). The triple ministry is attested already by 1 Clem 40 (c. A.D. 95), but the position in Past. is less easy to assess. The position of Paul himself, who has complete authority as the founder-apostle, and of his delegates Tm and Ti, is extraordinary and of less interest, since they are above and outside the normal communities; it is the ordinary structure of the community at this time which is of overriding interest. In Jewish communities of the Diaspora towards A.D. 100 authority was held by a council of elders (*presbyteroi*), presided over by an *archisynagōgos*; since the inscriptions show many *archisynagōgoi* who held the office several times, this official was presumably appointed only for a period. At Qumran similarly there was a council of elders, with a *meqabber* (CD) or *paqid* (1QS) at its head; it is not clear whether he was permanent or not. In Ac (cf § 823*e*) there are elders in each community, though there is no mention of any presiding officer except James at Jerusalem (but his authority had special reasons). In Ac 20:17—28 these elders are called both *presbyteroi* and *episkopoi*, and are said to have care of the flock; no differences in rank are apparent, but any council must have its president. *Episkopos* is the word used by the LXX to translate *paqid* (the president at Qumran) or words derived from this root. All the data of Past. fit this situation. There are *presbyteroi*, some of whom preside (*proestōs*—used in secular documents of the mayor of a village), some of whom preach and teach (1 Tm 5:17—18), in every town (Ti 1: 5). Not clearly differentiated from them, but always mentioned in the singular, there is an *episkopos* (1 Tm 3:1—7; Ti 1:7—9—in this passage the transition from plural 'elders' to singular 'episkopos' would be abrupt if there could be more than one *episkopos*, but perhaps not wholly impossible). Their office is somewhat similar, since much the same qualities are required for each official. It is, however, only the *episkopos* who must have the ability to manage a household (1 Tm 3:4), who is called 'steward of God's household' (Ti 1:7—but cf note to Ti 1:6) and who teaches. In the light of the other documents, then, it is reasonable to conclude that the com-

munity was guided by a council of *presbyteroi*, one of **92:** whom perished as *episkopos*. If, as seems likely, the instructions of 1 Tm envisage only one community, then the office of *episkopos* is not yet permanent, since several elders are envisaged as filling it, with varying diligence and reward (1 Tm 5:17); on whether this reward is financial cf § 925*h*. Benoit (p. 240) holds that the *episkopoi* themselves formed a sort of executive committee in the council of *presbyteroi*; but this leaves unexplained why *episkopos* is always singular.

In addition the community has **deacons**. They are not **b** yet deacons in the later technical sense; both verb and abstract noun from the same root ('serve' and 'service') are used in the NT generally of any service to the community. Both Paul (Eph 3:7) and Christ himself (Rm 18:5) are described as 'deacons' i.e. ministers. Stephen and his six colleagues, generally regarded as the first deacons, are never in fact so called; their ministry is not much different from that of the apostles themselves (cf 828*b*); although the author suggests (Ac 6:1—2) that it was connected with the distribution of relief to widows, this has been widely considered to be an anachronistic interpretation. The chief argument in its favour is that Jewish communities had a developed relief organization, which (1 Tm 5:3—8) seems to have existed also in the early Church. No more can be said than that the qualities required of deacons and (probably, cf note to 1 Tm 3:11) deaconesses are consonant with an office more concerned with provisions and money than with teaching and directing (1 Tm 3:8—13).

Of **appointment** of ministers we learn little. A pre- **c** vious examination to determine their fitness is mentioned only for deacons (1 Tm 3:10), but it was normal practice in the Hellenistic world before the assumption of any public office. Responsibility for their appointment is laid squarely upon Tm (1 Tm 5:22); no part seems to be played by the people. In the appointment of Paul and Barnabas as missioners by the Church of Antioch (AC 13:1—3) some part in their designation was played by prophets, and several people laid hands on them. In Tm's own appointment, however, though again prophets took part (1 Tm 1:18), the imposition of hands seems to have been done by Paul alone (cf note to 1 Tm 4:14). It could however be argued that, although Tm thus received the dignity of an elder, he was being appointed as Paul's own representative, and that this ceremony tells us nothing of the appointment of other ministers.

One of the chief concerns of the author of Past. is **d preservation of traditional teaching**. This is no doubt to be seen against the background of the erroneous teaching which he regards as so pernicious. The hints of Past. do not enable us to construct of these errors any coherent whole, nor even to see clearly the direction in which the doctrines are tending. Such reconstruction would be possible only if we possessed fuller documentation of the mental climate of the communities for which the letters were intended. It is clear, however, that much of the teaching was Jewish in origin (1 Tm 1:7—11; Ti 1:10—16 and note). There may also be signs of the mentality which was later to emerge in Gnosticism (cf § 924*c*), or perhaps the myths of mystery religions (cf § 630*g—j*).

To oppose this the author stresses the Church's function of upholding the truth (1 Tm 3:15); he constantly returns to the reliability of certain major soteriological formulations (1 Tm 1:15 and note), or the healthiness of certain doctrines (1 Tm 1:10 and note). He specifies repeatedly that Tm and Ti must teach uncompromisingly what they have been taught (1 Tm 6:20: 2 Tm 1:13—14;

d 2:24; Ti 3:8), and that they must appoint *episkopoi* who can hand on this doctrine intact (1 Tm 3:2; 2 Tm 2:2; Ti 1:9). By his use of '*parathēkē*, deposit' (1 Tm 6:20; 2 Tm 1:12, 14) the author shows that he regards this tradition as a body of doctrine, to be handed down after the Jewish manner of memorizing a *corpus* of oral tradition (cf B. Gerhardsson, *Memory and Manuscript*, 1961). This is also the attitude of Paul in 1 Cor 11:23; 15:3).

e Nevertheless in practice Past. provide us with a prime example not of senseless repetition of old formulae but adaptation of the unchanging message to a new idiom. The language of Past. already shows accommodation to the Hellenistic world. In both understanding of the Christian message and guidance of conduct there is a deliberate attempt to use the idiom of this milieu (cf § 924*d*). Thus salvation is the key-concept of teaching on God and Christ, and is the centre of all the quasi-credal formulations of doctrine (note to 1 Tm 1:15) which recur in Past. Only twice elsewhere does Paul use the noun 'saviour' but in Past. it is used 5 times of God, 3 times of Christ. God's grace becomes 'saving' (Ti 2:11); and it is in 1 Tm 2:4 that the statement of God's universal salvific will is found. This concept of salvation receives its prominence, though not its origin, from the prevalence of various mystery cults in the Hellenistic world, all promising salvation (cf § 630*g*). There are also clear connexions with the language, and opposition to the reality, of the cult of a saviour-emperor (cf 928*d*).

In the matter of conduct the Christian message is presented largely by means of, and in the terms of, the ideals of popular moral philosophy of the day. This has led to gibes against the 'bourgeois morality' of Past. But it is a genuine attempt to show that the highest standards of non-Christian morality were also those of Christianity (cf § 928*c*).

I TIMOTHY

24a Introduction Tm, a convert from Lystra (Ac 16:1), joined Paul early on his second journey, and remained his constant companion, being frequently mentioned in Paul's letters (Rm, 1–2 Cor, Phil, Col, 1–2 Thes). I Tm 1:2 tells us that Paul left him at Ephesus on his way to Macedonia (? in 66) to continue his work. The letter falls basically into two parts: the ordering of the community, the assembly and its officials (1–3), and advice to Tm on his personal conduct (4–6), though this latter part contains also regulations for two more official positions, those of widow and elder.

1:1–2 Address—Paul begins all his letters with the type of formula usual at the time in official letters, naming the writer and the recipient, and giving a greeting. But he innovates by dwelling on the Christian quality of the recipient, and by substituting for the normal profane greeting (used also in Ac 15:23) a specifically Christian one. The greeting always comprises grace and peace, but in 1–2 Tm he adds 'mercy', the word used in the LXX to express God's generosity to his people, far beyond that required by his covenant relationship to Israel. His designation of himself as 'apostle . . . by the command of God' indicates from the outset his right to lay down regulations to Tm, who is also his pupil (for which 'son' is a rabbinic technical term, SB III, 643). The address already contains two hints that Past. are to be seen against a background of rivalry with the religions of the pagan world: God is called 'our saviour', a title used rarely of Christ and never of God in the earlier letters. However God is frequently called the Saviour of his people in the OT; the resumption now of this title is **924a** perhaps due to the numerous 'saviour-gods' of the hellenistic environment (cf § 923*e*). The blessing ends with 'Christ Jesus our Lord' instead of the usual 'the Lord Jesus Christ', perhaps to contrast him more forcibly with the emperor, who also claimed the title of Lord.

3–20 Opening charge—Paul's concern is with faith **b** and love, words which recur constantly in this section. To Paul faith is no intellectual act but is the total acceptance in hope of Christ's message and of its implications, among which the chief is love. (In Past. the obedience-aspect of faith is particularly stressed, preoccupied as they are with preserving traditional doctrine, cf § 923*d*). So Paul first castigates preoccupation with side-issues of doctrine propagated by pretended doctors of the Law (3–7), then shows why the Law is irrelevant (8–11), which leads him to break out into thanks that he was called from the Law to Christ's service in faith and love (12–17). Finally he briefly encourages Tm (18–20). **6.** The exact character of the irrelevant doctrines cannot **c** be determined. Hellenistic tales of gods and heroes, Gnostic pedigrees of emanations from the principle of the good, rabbinic genealogies (such as in the Book of Jubilees), even excessive interest in genealogies such as are included by Mt and Lk in their gospels, all have been suggested. In any case it seems clear from vv 7–15 that they were of Jewish origin (cf Ti 1:10–16 and note). **8.** The treatment of the Law here is somewhat flat; it is regarded simply as a penal code which will not affect the Christian (this is the meaning of 'people who are good' cf Rm 5:10). Elsewhere (Gal, Rm) Paul fills this out by teaching that the Law leads men to Christ by showing them their sins and inability to do right by fulfilling the Law, whence their need for a different justification, in Christ. The reasons for the irrelevance of the Law are therefore different in the earlier letters and here (cf § 921*d*): in those it is because the Law has already done its job of leading men to Christ, here it is merely because the justified Christian will not in fact fall foul of its prohibitions. **9–10.** The first of four lists of vices in Past. **d** (also 1 Tm 6:4–5; 2 Tm 3:2–5; Ti 3:3); these lists are common in Paul's letters (e.g. Rm 1:29–31), and are probably largely drawn from catalogues of vices in contemporary and synagogal moral teaching; many of the words do not occur elsewhere in Paul, and there are rhetorical word-plays, assonance, etc, which are not typical of him. Often they represent the vices of every age, without any particular connexion with the context; here he merely takes a selection of 14 (— 7 × 2). **10.** Desire for security of doctrine is characteristic of Past., whence the recurrence of the expressions 'sound doctrine' (1 Tm 6:3; 2 Tm 1:13; 4:3; Ti 1:9, 13; 2:1, 2) and 'a saying you can rely on' (1 Tm 1:15; (3:1); 4:9; 2 Tm 2:13; Ti 1:9; 3:8). This reflects the struggle with unorthodox and untraditional tendencies; the contrast between this attitude and Paul's earlier adventurous thinking could be due (if Paul is the author) to the timorous conservatism of old age (cf § 921*d*). **11.** The 'glory of the blessed God' is Christ, the revelation of God's nature, which thus shows itself to men in his love and tenderness (Jn 1:14; 17; 2 Cor 4:4; Ti 2:13).

12–17. The aorist tenses here refer to Paul's conver- **e** sion on the road to Damascus, an experience which is constantly recurring to Paul's mind in his letters, as the decisive moment when Christ took possession of him. It was this event which freed him from subjection to the Law. **15.** 'A saying you can rely on' (cf note to v 10) each of the five certain uses of this expression refers to a major formulation of doctrine of Christ as the saviour, a point

924e especially stressed in Past. by contrast with the claim of Hellenistic cults to grant salvation (cf § 923e). Each time this formulation is presented as grounds for hope. **18.** These prophecies are no doubt the words by which the prophets of the Christian community designated Tm as a missioner cf 4:14; Paul himself was designated in a similar fashion (Ac 13:1—3). **19—20.** The military metaphor is a favourite with Paul (1 Cor 9:7; 2 Cor 10:3—4; 2 Tm 2:3); here again the language of Hellenistic cults exercises an influence, for their initiates were said to enter the *militia* of the god (Apuleius, *Metamorph.* 11:15). **20.** Hymenaeus is mentioned also 2 Tm 2:17; this Alexander may be the coppersmith of 2 Tm 4:14. Their punishment, of which excommunication is an element (1 Cor 5:2—5), is intended to bring them back to the true way; deliverance to Satan is not meant as an abandonment of the offenders.

f Chh 2—3. The letter now comes on to its primary purpose, the ordering of the community, and 'first of all' of the assembly for prayer, firstly its purpose (2:1—7), then various classes: men (2:8), women (2:9—15), the president of the assembly (3:1—7), deacons (3:8—13).

2—7 Prayer for the salvation of all men—As so often in Paul's letters, practical instructions are founded on and lit up by the proclamation of a truth central to the Christian message. The polemical context of the passage is the Hellenistic assumption that there exist many saviour gods and many mediators (cf § 923e), usually superhuman, whether the author has in mind the mystery cults with their mediators such as Mithras, or Gnostic-type religions, with a chain of emanations from the principle of the good which eventually form a bridge to man, or judaic theories, in which the angels act as mediators (cf Gal 3:19). Men put themselves under the patronage of any, or simultaneously of several, of these saviours. Paul counters that there is only one saviour—God who offers salvation to all.

g **1—2 The primacy of prayer** in the Christian life demands that it be treated first in the regulation of the community. Prayer for kings and secular authorities was a regular feature of synagogue services (Philo, *In Flaccum*, 49), taking the place of worship of them in pagan cults. This duty holds also when there is, as at the date of this letter, at least a real danger of persecution. The religious benefits to be derived by the community by those prayers are expressed in typically Gr. terms, showing that translation of the Christian messages into the terms of its Hellenistic environment which is a feature of Past., cf § 923e. In the terms 'piety' and 'decorum' Paul's old fire is less apparent, which has given rise to the charge of 'the bourgeois Christianity of Past'. The longing for 'peace and quiet' in the turbulent second half of the first century is attested by innumerable texts.

h **4.** The tangled problem of the 'universal salvific will of God' is outside the perspective of our passage, which is concerned to teach only that the unique way of salvation, which is barred to nobody, is through the Christian God. If it be asked how the NT can elsewhere envisage that not all men in fact are saved, thus implying successful opposition to the will of God, appeal may be made to the distinction sometimes apparent between *thelein*, (used here) meaning to wish in a non-effective way, and *boulesthai*, meaning to will or decide upon (Spicq 58); thus God would wish, but not definitively decree, the salvation of all men, still leaving room for the action of human free will in accepting or refusing the offer. The author is more concerned to show that the one way of salvation is not through any superhuman intermediary but through the historical act of Christ: he insists that it is in virtue of his solidarity with men that he pays the ransom for all.

6. This metaphor of 'ransom' has roots both in the **i** Jewish and in the Hellenistic world. Among the Jews it was the duty of the next of kin to redeem for his relation (i.e. buy back for him) land which he had been forced by poverty to sell (Lv 25:25). In the same way Yahweh was to redeem his people from the nations which oppressed them (Dt 7:8; Jer 50:34). In both these usages the idea of kinship, by blood or by the covenant, between redeemer and redeemed plays an important part. But in Yahweh's redemption of his people a ransom-price does not feature; rather the reverse (Is 45:13). This may be the reason why the expression occurs only once in Jesus' prophecies of his sacrifice (Mk 10:45 and par.; but is the wording here Jesus' own?). Indeed the metaphor of 'redemption' seems to have come into use more in Hellenistic than in Jewish Christianity (four times in Lk-Ac, once each in Ti, 1 Pt, Heb, Apoc only); in the Hellenistic world it gained its appeal from the usage of ransoming prisoners of war or freeing slaves. As later theologians discovered, the metaphor must not be pressed too far; much ink was spilt on the question of to whom the ransom was paid. The last phrase of the v is obscure; it is not clear to what Christ's death bears witness; presumably to God's love of all men, cf Jn 17:23, 26. **7.** The mission of an apostle is to herald Christ's salvation, but only here (and identically in 2 Tm 1:11) is the apostle called a herald, though the message is often called a herald's proclamation. Similarly only in these passages is Paul described as a 'teacher', which elsewhere is the name of one of the offices within the community.

8 Men—The chief point of this instruction is the inter- **j** ior, not the exterior attitude of prayer (the normal position in Judaism, and shown in many early Christian paintings and sculptures). 1 Cor 11:17—33; Jas 2:2—4 show that it was not superfluous.

9—15 Women—The attitude of the early Church is uncompromising: women may give great material help (Ac 9:36; 16:15; 1 Cor 16:19), they may even give some instruction (Ac 18:26), but in church they must be self-effacing (1 Cor 14:34—35); it is however, envisaged that they may prophesy (1 Cor 11:5). The reasons which Paul adduces—quite apart from the curious rabbinic argument here, vv 13—14—are more arguments of propriety to justify a *status quo* than real theological arguments (1 Cor 11:3, 7, 10; Eph 5:22). Women always remained far less emancipated within Judaism (even today they are confined to an upper storey in the synagogue) than in the Hellenistic world, where prophetesses, priestesses and at least titular women magistrates are not uncommon. With this emancipation went also a good deal of libertinism, which did not commend the change. Paul recognizes in principle that each sex is equally necessary to the other (1 Cor 11:11—12). But here devoted motherhood and all it stands for is woman's way of salvation.

3:1—7 President of the Assembly—On his function **92** and position cf § 923a. Here described are the requisite qualities. **1.** The common text has 'here is a saying you can rely on', as 1:15 q.v.; but the saying which is introduced is so unlike that at the other occurrences of the phrase that the alternative of one group of MSS may be correct: 'There is a *popular* saying'; this was lost by assimilation to the other, commoner phrase. Though the word *episkopē* is found only twice in profane literature, *episkopos* is used commonly of magistracies and other offices. The saying would well accord with the attitude to magistracies in the empire by this time: it was becoming a ever harder to find candidates to undertake this comparatively arduous, costly and unrewarding service to the community; this was one of the symptoms of the degeneracy of society. Similarly our author stresses how worthwhile is the task of presidency, though it ranks low in all the lists of charisms (1 Cor 12:28; Rm 12:6—8; Eph 4:11), arranged perhaps according to the honour they carry. The *Didachē* (15) also needs to say that *episkopoi* are not to be despised. **2.** A number of the qualities here required for the president are demanded also by the 1st cent. writer Onosander for a general (*Strategicus*). Here and in the corresponding Ti 1:6—9 the list is not specifically Christian: only a generally good moral character, with some ability to command and teach (but no brilliance), is demanded. The pairing and assonance of the lists suggest a rhetorical origin, and the author may well have drawn his list from profane philosophical lists. 'Husband of one wife' can mean that a second marriage after the death of a first wife is forbidden. A widower's fidelity to his first wife is praiseworthy, but a second marriage is not generally reprehensible; indeed it is prescribed in some cases (5:14), and there is no obvious reason why the same should not hold for a bishop. The phrase could merely prescribe monogamy; this would seem to go without saying, but then so should 'not a drunkard' (a strong word is used). The Christian teaching on monogamy was so uncompromising and unusual (SB III, 647—50) that it could bear repetition.

b **6—7.** The phrase translated by JB '*condemned as the devil was condemned*' means literally '*incur the judgement of the slanderer, or accuser*'. The Gr. and Heb. name for the devil is 'the Accuser' since his prime duty was to delate men's sins at God's judgement-seat as well as to test them (Jb 1.6—2.7). In Past. the normal sense of 'accuser' is of human accusers (3:11; 2 Tm 3:3; Ti 2:3 as against 2 Tm 2:26). This sense certainly fits well here, where it is a question of good repute. So the apostle could be warning against 'condemnation occasioned by a slanderer' rather than that condemnation (for pride) incurred by the devil.

c **8—13 Deacons**—Their title means simply 'ministers', but it is not clear in what exactly their ministry consisted. From the epistles and from the *Didachē* and 1 Clem it is clear that they were in a subordinate position to the heads of the communities. Lk certainly considered their ministry to consist in the administration of material goods for the sake of the poor (Ac 6:1, cf 828*bc*). The Jewish synagogues had special officers for the distribution of alms and the qualities here required of deacons would fit this duty, cf § 923*b*. **10.** An examination normally preceded appointment to any public office in the ancient world. **11.** The women here meant may be the deacons' wives (but why were no qualities demanded of the presidents' wives?), but more probably the office of deacon was filled by both men and women (Rm 16:1; Pliny, *Ep* 10:96); the latter merely need a special caution on some points. **13.** The reward here promised could be either heavenly standing (cf Lk 16:10—12) or earthly; in the latter case the exhortation parallels v 1 to presidents.

d **14—16 Summary and Transition**—The author summarizes his instructions for conduct in the Church, advancing by way of the mystery which it guards to the necessity of faithful teaching. He uses the metaphors 'pillar and foundation of the truth', indicating that it is the Church which is the guarantee of truth preventing its collapse or overturn. The dignity of the mystery which the Church guards is the reason for the need for a high moral standard among its members. 'Pillar' had been used

already of the three chief apostles (Gal 2:9), and 'founda- 925d tion' is probably equivalent to the word used for the seniors of the Qumran community (1QSa I,12). **16.** The expression 'mystery' is used by Paul to denote God's plan of salvation for all men in Christ, hidden from all ages and revealed now in these last times (1 Cor 2:7; Rm 16:25—26; Eph 3:3—9); this use has its roots in the OT, especially Dn 2, but may have been used by Paul particularly because of the popularity at that time of various mystery cults (cf § 923*e*). The v contains a hymn in three couplets founded on a typical Hebrew balance: flesh-spirit (contrast), seen-proclaimed (complementary), world-glory (contrast). It is difficult to see how the statements form a chronological progression (as Barrett holds), or represent the three stages of an ancient oriental enthronement chant (exaltation, presentation, enthronement—so Jeremias and Spicq).

4:1—5. Here begins the second part of the letter, e personal advice to the recipient on his pastoral conduct. It begins, as did the first part (1:3—7) with a warning against false teachers, this time in the matter of practice rather than of belief. Again it is difficult to discern his target precisely; the prohibition of marriage reappears among the 2nd cent. Gnostics. But prohibition of certain foods suggests Judaic legalism, though it might also spring from a Gnostic mistrust of all material things, which he rejects in v 4 (cf Gn 1:31; Ac 10:15). In short there is the same atmosphere as in 1:3—7. **4—5.** The custom of saying a blessing, in the form of a thanksgiving, over food was strictly observed in Judaism (SB I, 685—7), cf 1 Cor 10:30. The expression 'the word of God' does not necessarily imply that the blessing was scriptural; the genitive could be objective (as also in the only other NT use of the phrase without the article: 1 Thes 2:13) meaning 'mention of God'; every Jewish table-blessing began: 'Blessed art thou, Jahweh our God . . .'.

6—16 Tm's own conduct—Significantly the personal f instructions to Tm for his mission begin with counsels for his own sanctification; he must be 'constantly nourished' by sound doctrine and must keep himself in training (a favourite athletic metaphor in Paul). **9** must refer to what precedes, since v 10 begins 'for'; cf note to 1:15. **12.** Tm's timidity is mentioned also 1 Cor 16:10—11, cf 2 Tm 1:6—2:7); some commentators find this remark artificial and evidence of pseudepigraphy. Though at a pinch Tm could be called 'young' till the age of 40, he joined Paul in A.D. 49 (Ac 16:1—3) and would have a dozen years' experience as a missionary by the supposed date of writing. **14.** The laying on of hands refers to Tm's designation or ordination. In 2 Tm 1:6 the grace is attributed to the laying-on of Paul's hands alone; in 1 Tm 5:22 Tm is given instructions for doing it himself. It seems, therefore, that the rite was performed by one man. '*The laying-on of hands of elders*' therefore means the conferring of the authority possessed by elders (D. Daube, *The NT and Rabbinic Judaism*, 244—5). This rite is therefore closer to the ordination by one rabbi of his pupil, making him his representative and successor by imposition of hands (cf Nm 27:23), than to the ceremony of Ac 13:1—3. Daube remarks 'we have here the first reference to apostolic succession'.

5:1—6:2 Ministry to various classes—First general g advice on how to behave towards different groups (1—2), then special instructions for the ministry as regards widows (3—16), elders (17—25), slaves (6:1—2).

3—16. Widows are considered largely from the point of view of the assistance due to them, as in Ac 6:1. For the ancient world a widow was the epitome of the lonely and helpless; so this passage constitutes a major text on

U*

925g the treatment of the unwanted in society. The writer is aware of both virtues (v 5) and vices (v 6, 13) which may accompany this precarious state. The synagogue already had a developed organization for the distribution or relief to the needy, which seems to have been early adopted by Christians (Ac 6:1; 9:39, 41). But this is to be invoked only if the widow has no family, to whom first the duty of caring for her falls (vv 4, 16). **9.** *'Enrolment as a widow'* shows that there was a constituted register; but, since the requirements for enrolment include a high past record of Christian service and a firm purpose of perseverance, it may be that enrolled widows constituted some sort of active charitable organization. There would be a number of widows who needed help, yet would be excluded by these conditions. **11, 14.** This anxious mistrust, especially of the young, is characteristic of Past. contrasting markedly with the confidence of 1 Cor 7, whose advice in the matters of marriage and celibacy is clean contrary to this passage. Is it a sign that the writer is a prey to the anxieties of old age, or an indication that the first fervour of Christians is already beginning to wane? cf § 921*c*–922*b*.

h 17–25 Elders—17–18. A difficult passage: it envisages at least three groups: elders, elders who preside well, elders who are assiduous in preaching and teaching. Does the 'consideration' euphemistically include financial reward (as in v 3)? If so, is this to be double that of widows or double that of other presbyters? In the Jewish communities of the diaspora there was a body of elders under a temporary president; this arrangement was no doubt adopted by Christian communities, for elders appear in Jas 5:14 and frequently in Ac, though not in the earlier Pauline epistles. It seems that of the presidents some played a fuller part in the ministry than others. It is hard to believe that 'consideration' really means 'pay'; little experience of administration is required to make it obvious that such vague prescriptions would raise more dissension than they would settle; nor does it appear that the corresponding synagogue officials received any emolument. On the other hand all difficulties vanish if it is granted that the word is to be taken in its literal sense 'honour' (as in 6:1); the writer would be returning to the theme of 3:1 (q.v.). Concern for the good name of those who accept the exposed and vulnerable position of Church leadership is the theme of the whole section. The mercenary interpretation results from an application of the two quotations of v 18 in the same sense as the former is used in 1 Cor 9:9; but this is not the sole possible sense; an application to honour would well accord with Pauline use of scripture. **18***b*. This saying is quoted as scripture; it occurs nowhere in the OT, but in Lk 10:7. It is, then, the first instance of the gospels being cited as scripture. Whether it was drawn from our canonical gospel or from an earlier written version, Past. have clear links with Lk, cf § 922*c*. **22** counsels against ordaining anyone untried, cf 3:10. It has been taken as a reference to the imposition of hands at the reconciliation of a penitent, but this practice is unattested till the third century. **23.** A curious interjection here; but this advice is given by many contemporary medical works (Spicq s.v.).

i 6:1–2 Slaves—For slaves of pagan masters an additional motive of service is witness to Christianity; for slaves of Christian masters, fraternal respect. At this period the treatment of household and other slaves in the city was sufficiently humane not to make slavery of Christians to Christians any more incompatible with the equality of all men declared by Christ than is the position today of servants in a Christian household. It was perhaps this which led Paul to accept the institution of slavery without question. The condition of agricultural and mining slaves was far less tolerable, but Christianity **9** was at first confined mainly to cities.

3–21 Conclusion—Much of this is taken up with a renewed warning against false teachers (3–10, 17–21, cf 1:3–7; 4:1–5) and against a mercenary approach to religion. **10***a*. A popular proverb, much used also by contemporary non-Christian moralists.

11–16 Final Exhortation to Tm—The motives pro- **j** posed are fidelity to his vocation and profession of faith, imitation of Christ and expectation of his second coming. His profession 'before many witnesses' seems to refer to a definite occasion. The witnesses were not necessarily hostile, as in the case of Christ's witness (v 13), and the occasion could be at some Church assembly. Since it is linked with his vocation, this may well be at baptism, when he was called to be a Christian (the normal sense of 'the call' in the NT), though it might also, perhaps, refer to his ordination as a minister. The second motive refers to Jesus' own witness to his dignity, Jn 18:37. The third leads in to a final hymnic doxology. The term 'Epiphany' is adopted in Past. instead of Paul's usual 'Parousia' to refer both to the first manifestation of Christ at the incarnation (2 Tm 1:10) and to his final manifestation. This, as several terms of the doxology (vv 15–16), was used in the hellenistic cult of kings and emperors as manifestations of the divinity; they are adopted here to oppose these claims, cf § 923*e*. **20.** Tm's Christian heritage is summed up as a 'deposit', an expression which had exact overtones at that time. In Roman law one who received a deposit from a friend for safe keeping was bound to preserve it intact, making no personal use of it till the friend required its return. Just so Tm and Paul himself (2 Tm 1:12, 14) have received the faith as a sacred trust; they are its ministers who may not use it for their own advantage, and must keep it intact for him who entrusted it to them.

II TIMOTHY

Introduction—The letter presents Paul as a lonely **92** prisoner; as he sees his martyrdom approach he warns Tm of the difficulties and opposition ahead, and encourages him to imitation of his own steadfastness.

1:1–2 Address—On the formulae cf § 924*a*; Paul's authority as receiving his apostleship by the will of God is again stressed. **1***b*. Literally: 'according to the promise of life in Christ Jesus'. That the Christian lives in Christ is a major theme of 2 Tm (3:12, cf 1:9; 2:10), as it was with Paul ever since his experience of Christ on the road to Damascus (Phil 1:21; Col 3:4).

2–5 Thanksgiving—Commonly in Greek letters the address is followed by some good wish or blessing. In most of his letters Paul gives such a blessing, usually connected with the matter of the letter. Here, in the only one of Past. to contain such a blessing, the theme is Paul's anxious care for Tm; much of the letter is given up to reassuring and encouraging him. **5.** The Greek 'first' could suggest that Tm's grandmother was a convert to Judaism, but in popular Greek 'first' was often confused with 'formerly'. From Ac 16:1 we learn that Tm's father was a Greek, hence his omission here.

6–14 The Spirit which Timothy has received—Paul **b** encourages Tm by reminding him of the power of the Spirit received at his ordination, the strength in which he himself endures imprisonment. On Tm's ordination cf note to 1 Tm 4:14. For Paul the spirit of Christ which dwells in us is primarily a source of strength and power (Rm 9:17; 15:13, 19; 2 Cor 12:9; Eph 1:19; 3:7) in which the Christian can fulfil his vocation, as distinct from

6b others who give the appearance of piety but lack power (3:5). It is received not only in baptism but also by ordination—the germ of a theology of the sacrament. It is in confidence in this strength that Tm is to proclaim the gospel, in spite of his natural timidity (cf 1 Tm 4:12 and note). **9—10.** The vocabulary and balanced phrases of this summary of the Christian vocation and message suggest a liturgical origin. The 'call with a sacred vocation' refers to God's call of a man at baptism. **10.** Here the 'Appearing' of Christ is his incarnation (as in Ti 2:11; 3:4) though elsewhere (1 Tm 6:14; 2 Tm 4:1, 8; Ti 2:13) it refers to his final coming. The term was used in the hellenistic world of visits and other manifestations of semi-divine rulers, and especially of their birth. **11** = 1 Tm 2:7, q.v. **12.** The 'deposit' may be taken either as entrusted by Paul to God or vice versa; in view of 1 Tm 6:20 (q.v.) and especially 2 Tm 1:14, the latter is more likely.

15—18. Desertion and Fidelity of Christians— Nothing more is known of persons and events here mentioned (except that Onesiphorus is mentioned again 4:19). **15.** The Gr. has 'all those in Asia' (the Roman province of Asia, of which Ephesus was the chief city). Since the letter seems to be written from Rome to Ephesus (cf 1 Tm 1:3), and the defection would be on such a large scale, some commentators take the phrase to designate Asians in Rome. **18a.** Some of the awkwardness of this phrase is avoided by regarding the first 'Lord' as referring to Christ, the second (without article, as in the LXX) to God.

c 2:1—13 Further Encouragement to Tm 1 2. In the strength which comes from living in Christ (cf note to 1:1b) Tm is to pass on the deposit which he has received, in order that they too may pass it on. The same word is used for this handing on as for the 'deposit' of 1 Tm 6:20 (q.v.), 2 Tm 1:12, 14. Already a chain of witnesses to the oral tradition, as in the rabbinic schools of Judaism, is envisaged. The author is clearly conscious of the importance of exact fidelity to tradition. The phrase 'in public', literally 'through many witnesses', may contrast Paul's teaching with secret gnostic instructions, or this may be mentioned to assure Tm that others can confirm the exactitude of his message. **3—7.** Three metaphors, all common in rhetorical and moral writing of the period, to spur on Tm to whole-hearted concentration on his task; they suggest that Tm was distracted by other cares. **8—13.** Spicq (p. 350) considers vv 8, 11—13 to form a baptismal hymn, vv 9—10 being a gloss by Paul. Such sudden illumination by the theological basis of activity is typical of Paul's Christocentric thought. So are the example of his own sufferings (Phil 1:13—18) and the rhetorical figure of a sorites in vv 11—13 (cf Rm 5:4—11). But other elements (Christ's Davidic descent, mentioned by Paul only Rm 1:3, the static perfect tense of 'risen') point to a non-Pauline origin. The purpose of these vv is to set before Tm the prize to be won by the exertions of vv 3—6. They are shot through with the hope and confidence which is so characteristic of Past. (see note to Ti 1:2); hence the typical 'here is a saying that you can rely on' (v 11 cf note to 1 Tm 1:15). The proper object of this hope is 'eternal glory' (v 10), which sums up all the divine gifts brought by Christ. This glory is properly the inaccessible glory of God, which man cannot see and live (Ex 33: 20), but which was made manifest in Jesus (Jn 1:14) and is to be shared by his followers (Rm 8:18; Col 3:4). It is Paul's way of expressing the Christian's share in the divine life itself.

d 14—3:9 Two Cautions—Tm is now warned against two dangers, erroneous teaching and moral corruption.

14—26 Attitude towards erroneous teaching— 926d Here again appear the vain philosophical speculations of 1 Tm 1:3—7; 4:1—5; here at last we learn one specific point of their teaching: that the resurrection has already occurred (v 18). Resurrection of the body seemed so absurd to the Greeks (cf Ac 17:32) that they were tempted to hold that resurrection affects the soul only, and that this has already taken place at baptism (cf Rm 6:1—11). **17.** No more of these two is known. **19—21.** How some can fail without the whole structure being damaged is explained with two Isaian images (Is 28:16; 29:16) already used by Paul (Eph 2:20; Rm 9:21). **19.** In Isaiah the foundation stone is the promised remnant of Israel (cf Mt 16:18), inscribed according to the practice of 'sealing' a temple with an inscription stating its specific dedication to God. The two inscriptions on this stone show that mere membership of the Church is not enough; the former citation (of Nm 16:5) refers to the occasion when certain levites were cut off from Israel for their sin; the latter recalls the baptismal ceremony (cf note on Ac 2:21) and stresses the necessity of fidelity to it. **20—21.** This metaphor of dishes made for different purposes regularly occurs to explain—or to legitimate the refusal of an explanation—how some of those called by God fail to answer the call. **22—26.** The kindly correction of a pastor. **3:1—9 Moral Corruption—**The second of two warnings **e** which form the main body of the letter is against the decay of morals which is to occur in the last times. According to Jewish tradition the messianic times were not to be born without birth-pangs (SB IV, 977—86); by Christian tradition this is applied to the final manifestation of the Messiah, which will be preceded by a complete breakdown of standards (2 Thes 2:3—8; 1 Jn 2:18—19). This is expressed also through the apocalyptic imagery of Mk 13 and parallels (cf § 715ad). The corruption is to occur within the Church too (v 5, 1 Jn 2:19). The list of vices here given (cf § 924d) suggests a predominance of sheer wilfulness, rejection of all law and convention in favour of what each man wants to do, for the first two and last two are compounded with philo (lover of). **8.** Jannes and Jambres are the names given by Jewish tradition to the Egyptian magicians who competed with Moses in Ex 7.

10—17 Tm to stand firm—in the face of the two **927a** dangers mentioned in 2:14—3:9, false teaching and failing morals, Paul strengthens Tm by mentioning his own endurance (10—13) and the sound training which Tm has received (14—17); the remedies are given in reverse order to the dangers, forming a chiasmus. **11.** For the persecutions at Antioch see Ac 13:50—52, at Iconium Ac 14: 2—6, at Lystra Ac 14:19. Just afterwards (Ac 14:22) the apostles make the same comment as v 12 here. In view of the way Ac was composed (cf § 821b) it is hard to avoid the conclusion that the author of Past. is here using Ac rather than his own reminiscences. We would then have the earliest witness to the existence of Ac. But it has been suggested that Paul used Lk as his secretary for Past. cf § 922c. **14.** The combination of oral and written tradition on which both synagogue and Church are founded. The Jewish child should begin to learn the scriptures at the age of five or six (SB III, 664—5). **15.** The common apostolic theme that it is through knowledge of God's promises in the OT that one is led to knowledge of their fulfilment in Christ: much of the apostolic preaching is devoted to showing that Christ's ministry, death and resurrection were the inevitable outcome of the OT prophecies of the Messiah (cf §§ 678c, 825i). **16.** Two translations are possible: 'all scripture is inspired by God and . . .' or 'all divinely-inspired scripture is also . . .'. The latter is perhaps more likely, presupposing rather

927a than affirming the inspiration of scripture (which no Jew would doubt), by the very terms used, SB IV, 435—50), for if the adjective were intended predicatively the noun would have the article, according to NT usage (except 1—2 Pt). The formulation 'divinely-inspired' is an excellent example of the adaptation in Past. of OT ideas into Hellenistic categories (cf P. Benoit RB 70 (1963), 343; TWNT 6 (1959), 452), cf § 923e.

b **4:1—5.** A solemn charge to Tm to fulfil his mission of proclaiming the message of Christ, in spite of the opposition it will arouse (vv 3—5, as 2:14—3:17). **1.** The liturgical language could suggest that these phrases are part of some liturgical formula; 'judge of the living and the dead' was early incorporated in the Creed. On the 'Appearing' of Christ see note to 1 Tm 6:14. **4.** On these **c** myths see notes to 1 Tm 1:6; 4:1—5. **6—8 Paul's own course**—as so often in Past. (1 Tm 1:12—16; 2 Tm 1:8; 2:9) and in the earlier letters Paul uses the example of his own apostolic labours to strengthen his followers. **6.** Libations of wine and oil accompanied some Judaic sacrifices (Nm 28:7), but it was an especially common sign of reverence to the Greek or Roman gods to pour out a libation of wine to them; the metaphor is therefore rather an adaptation to the hellenistic environment, as are the two following, cf § 923e. **7—8.** Two final metaphors of an athletic contest and a race (cf 1 Cor 9:25; 1 Tm 4:10; 6:12); in the Hellenistic world life was often compared to these two sports. The crown is primarily the victor's prize, but becomes in pagan funeral art the symbol of immortality (adopted already in Wis 4:2).

d **9—22 Personal Epilogue**—Authorities are agreed on the Pauline authorship of this passage, more than any other in Past.; it is too disordered and inconsequent to be the work of a literary forger. But not necessarily all of it was written as one single note (see § 922). **9—15, 19—21. Greetings and requests**—**9.** 'Galatia' the Gr. word for the province in modern Turkey and for Gaul were at this time the same; if the latter is meant (as some MSS already interpret it) we have an interesting indication of the spread of Christianity. **11.** Perhaps the Evangelist Lk, cf Col 4:14. He may have acted as Paul's secretary, cf § 922c. **13.** The 'cloak' may be the heavy *paenula* (from which the chasuble is derived) or possibly a wrapping-cloth for books (hardly important enough). **16—18 News of Paul's Trial**—**16** is the sole information we have about Paul's trial, too meagre to lay any construction on it, especially since the Gr. means only 'no one stood by me'. **22.** Instead of the usual brief 'Farewell' of profane letters, Paul concludes with a specifically Christian greeting, from which is derived the greeting used in the Mass. The exact sense of 'spirit' is obscure.

TITUS

928a **Introduction**—Titus was a gentile, probably a convert of Paul's (1:4), who had been working with Paul since before the Council of Jerusalem (Gal 2:1—3), and was later sent on a mission to Corinth during the crisis in the community there (2 Cor 7:13—15; 8:16—24). According to the letter he was left in Crete during an otherwise unknown journey of Paul's to complete the organization of the community there (1:5). The letter which is to guide him naturally covers much of the same ground as 1 Tm: general rules of conduct, qualities requisite for elders, warnings against false teachers, and encouragement to Ti himself.

1:1—4 Address—on the formulae and their force cf § 924a. Here Paul calls himself the 'servant of God', as he was 'sevant of Christ' in Rm 1:1 and Phil 1:1; in oriental courts the title of servant of the King implied high office, so this too is a term of dignity and of mission. **2.** The core of his mission is said to be that hope which is such a mark of Past. (1 Tm 6:12—16; 2 Tm 1:12; 2:9—11; 4:8; Ti 2:13; 3:7—8)—also a strong overtone in the use of 'faith', which is an acceptance of Christ in the hope of his salvation, and in the frequently-mentioned endurance under trial. **3—4.** Here and in 3:4—6 both God and Christ are called saviour. In the earlier Pauline epistles the title is used only twice (Eph 5:23; Phil 3:20), both times of Christ. In Past. however, it is frequent, a formulation sprung from rivalry with pagan saviour-cults; cf 923e.

5—16 Organization of the community—This consists **b** in the appointment of ministers (5—9) and the silencing of erroneous teachers (10—16). **5—9.** On his missionary journeys Paul appears to have appointed elders some time after the preliminary evangelization (Ac 14:23). Nevertheless v 5 does suggest a longer stay than would appear from Ac 27:7—8. On the position and function of elders and president, cf § 923a. On the qualities required see note to 1 Tm 3:2. The requirement (**6**) that his children should be believers suggests that their other qualities are considered more from the point of view of peace and unity in the family than for their reflection on the father's power of command. Here his adherence to the tradition he receives is also stressed (cf note to 1 Tm 1:10), and leads on to Ti's second duty. **10—16.** The danger of myths, vain speculations and desertion of sound doctrine is everpresent in Past. (1 Tm 1:3—7; 4:1—5; 2 Tm 2:14—24; 4:2—4). It is not easy to get any clear idea of the character of the errors in circulation (cf 924c), but in the present passage it is connected with Judaism (vv 10, 14). Probably also vv 15—16 constitute polemic against Judaic ritual observances, following the theme familiar in the prophets that observance without commitment is empty. All compulsion to observe the ritual laws of purity now becomes a denial of Christ and ignorance of God, since only commitment to him in faith is needed. The theological objections are reinforced by gibes against the Cretans commonplace in the ancient world. It was proverbial that Cretans were liars—the verse here quoted stems from Epimenides, c. 500 B.C.—and avaricious: probably neither accusation need be taken too seriously, though the latter finds its echo in 1 Tm 6:6—10.

2:1—3:2 Moral Ideals—**1—10 For various classes**. **c** Similar instructions to various classes of ordinary people occur also Eph 5:22—6:9; Col 3:18—4:1; but in those cases they are classified according to positions in the family instead of, as here, by age and sex. The virtues recommended are not specifically Christian; only the motive which should lead Christians to keep to them (2:11—14; 3:3—8; cf 1 Tm 3:15—16). The behaviour itself is constantly recommended in Hellenistic popular moralizing and in that of the Jewish Diaspora. But the advice is not otiose; the backgrounds of some Christian converts were highly dubious (e.g. 1 Cor 1:26—28; 6:9—11), and slaves seemed to have figured prominently among them, whose moral instruction would not have been too complete or careful. Furthermore they might need guidance on how much of the contemporary non-Christian standards of conduct should be left behind and how much retained. The two key-notes of the passage are reserve or moderation, and a good example to be seen by those outside the Church.

11—15 The Grounds of Christian Living—The **d** author breaks off his instruction to give its motive: The Christian life is founded on the salvation which has appeared in Christ, as in Col 2:6—3:4. But here, as

927b (margin, top right)

so often in Past., these truths are translated from the semitic into the Hellenistic idiom. The terms in which the saving act is described are drawn from the Hellenistic cult of rulers whose advent was hailed as the apparition of a saviour-god. Outside Past. and Apoc such terms are avoided, perhaps as being debased by their usage (C. F. D. Moule in JTS 10 (1959), 262), but in Past. the technical terms 'epiphany' and 'saviour' are frequently used, to show that it is Christ who is the true saviour-God, by opposition to other claimants (cf Dibelius, 74—78, 108—10), cf § 923e. **11.** The 'grace of God' here is not sanctifying grace but rather 'graciousness', his loving-kindness, exceeding even that required by fidelity to the OT covenant; it is extended not just to the Jews but to all men; the expressions here too are common in saviour-cults. **12.** The earlier Paul considered God's gift more as setting men free from bonds (Rm 6; Gal 4:1—11; Col 2); but now it is seen that God's graciousness spurs on to training in good behaviour—again a theme of Greek moralists and ascetical writers; this is more cautious than the dynamic earlier attitude of Paul. The virtues mentioned are again the Hellenistic ones of moderation and piousness. **13.** The motive of confident hope, the key-note of Past. (cf note to 1:2).

e 'Our great God and Saviour Jesus Christ' probably refers only to Christ, not to God *and* Christ, thus constituting an explicit affirmation of his divinity. This is required both by Gr. grammar and by the Hellenistic usage of these terms; a double apparition simultaneously of Yahweh and his Messiah is unknown in Jewish apocalyptic. **14.** The metaphor of Christ giving himself as a ransom is based on Jesus' words in Mk 10:45, (cf note to 1 Tm 2:6). In the OT God is frequently said to ransom his people; it is by this means that he won Israel to be his own; this belonging to Jahweh means that Israel must be holy as Jahweh is holy (Ex 19:5; Dt 26:18). Similarly the people which Christ has won for himself (Ac 20:28).

f 3:1—2 Moral Ideals for all Christians—after instructions to various classes of Christians regarding their behaviour to each other (2:1—10) and a digression on its motive (11—15), the author completes his guidance **928f** by instructions on behaviour to outsiders and to the secular power.

3—8 Renewal in Christ—again (cf note to 2:1—3:2) **g** the grounds for Christian action are given as the salvation brought by Christ: it was only by God's kindness (again a politico-religious term drawn from Hellenism, cf 928d) that we were taken out of the mass of sinners. **5.** A rich statement of how the salvation won by Christ is applied to the individual. It begins with a contrast between man's own useless deeds and God's generous mercy; this is not the Pauline contrast, familiar in Gal and Rm, between justification by faith and by works of the Law; the problematic is here different, and does not envisage the Jewish propaganda so prominent there. The 'cleansing water of rebirth and renewal of the holy Spirit' (the whole phrase probably belongs together so) again presents a new angle on baptism. The Pauline imagery had been chiefly in terms of dying with Christ and rising in him (Rm 6:4). The fact that it is in Christ is now not explicit. The term 'rebirth' is merely a philosophical term, drawn from the Pythagorean doctrine of transmigration of souls, to express the new life of the risen Christian. This rebirth is a renewal in the Spirit, as 2 Cor 5:17; Rm 8:1—2; Gal 5:16—24. From both these figures it is clear that baptism is only a beginning; the renewal works itself out progressively, cf 2 Cor 4:16. **7.** For Past. 'eternal life' is a thing of the future not, as often in Paul and John, already acquired and awaiting only its manifestation, cf § 921d; this is the reason for the constant expectant hope of Past. (cf note to 1:2). **8.** Cf note to 1 Tm 1:15. **9—10.** A final **h** warning against idle speculation, cf § 924c. As in 1:16 knowledge of God is seen as a whole: errors in belief lead to depraved action. **12—15.** Greetings and conclusion— Artemas and Zenas are not mentioned elsewhere, but Tychicus is known from Ac 20:4 as a travelling missionary, and Apollos may be the prominent preacher of Ac and 1 Cor. Hospitality, especially of missionaries, is an important charge in the NT (Mt 10:11—15; 1 Tm 3:2; 5:10; Ti 1:8).

PHILEMON

BY JEROME MURPHY O'CONNOR O.P.

929a Bibliography—In addition to the commentaries noted in § 912*a*. R. H. Barrow, *Slavery in the Roman Empire*, London, 1928; P. Benoit, 'Philemon (Epître à)', DBS 7 (1965), 1204—11; P. R. Coleman-Norton, 'The Apostle Paul and the Roman Law of Slavery', *Festschrift A. C. Johnson*, Princeton, 1951, 155—77; P. N. Harrison, 'Onesimus and Philemon', ATR 32 (1950), 268—94; J. Knox, *Philemon among the Letters of Paul*, New York, 1952² (cf H. Greeven, TLZ 79 (1954), 373—8); T. Preiss, *Life in Christ*, London, 1952, ch 2; M. Roberti, *La lettera di S. Paolo a Filemone e la condizione giuridica dello schiavo fuggitivo*, Milan, 1933; U. Wickert, 'Der Philemonbrief. Privatbrief oder apostolisches Schreiben?', ZNW 52 (1961), 230—8. J. Murphy-O'Connor, 'The Christian and Society in St Paul', *New Blackfriars*, Jan 1969, 174—82.

b Introduction—On the basis of the close contacts between Phm and Col noted in § 912*c* it is clear that the two letters were written at the same time and by the same individual. Hence those authors who deny the authenticity of Col are forced logically to deny the Pauline character of Phm. This has rightly been regarded as one of the worst blunders of the Tübingen school, for the whole letter is redolent of the spirit of the great apostle. The vast majority of scholars are convinced that in this perfect example of the letter-writer's art we hear the authentic voice of Paul at its most personal.

c The letter concerns a fugitive slave, Onesimus, who has been persuaded by Paul to return to his master. J. Knox has suggested that this master was Archippus (Col 4:17), who was also the host of the Church at Colossae. Nothing in the letter, he claims, demands that we assume Philemon to have been the master. It is more likely that Philemon was the overseer of the Lycus valley churches and resident at Laodicea, and that Paul involved him in this affair because he did not know Archippus personally. This ingenious theory, however, does not merit the sympathy accorded it by H. Greeven. That the real addressee should only be mentioned in third place (v 2) is without precedent in the letters of Paul, and while grammatically 'the church in your house' (v 2) could refer to Archippus, it is most naturally taken as a reference to the first mentioned, Philemon. Moreover, it is not natural to understand the frequent 'you' as meaning Archippus. Hence the traditional reconstruction remains the most probable. Philemon apparently lived at Colossae, since Onesimus was a native of that place (Col 4:9). That Apphia was his wife and Archippus his son are suppositions which the text neither refutes nor supports. The fact that the community assembled in his house does not necessarily make him its head. He was certainly one of its outstanding members, perhaps because he had been a collaborator of the Apostle (v 1, 17) by whom he had been converted (v 19) possibly during the ministry at Ephesus (Acts 19:10).

d Doctrinal Teaching—Phm is an intensely personal communication, but behind it one senses the authority of an apostle, and there is latent in it a doctrinal message of universal import, viz the attitude of the primitive Church to slavery. Paul touches on this problem in 1 Cor 7:20—24; Col 3:22—4:1; Eph 6:5—9; 1 Tm 6:1—2; Ti 2:9. These passages give offence to many because they seem to give tacit approval to an institution which is the antithesis of belief in an individual's right to be treated as an end in himself. Even in Phm Paul is more concerned with getting Onesimus as an assistant than with his affranchisement which is not mentioned explicitly at all. We would like a flat denunciation of slavery such as Philo attributes to the Essenes (*Quod Omnis Prob.* 79). However, we should not permit ourselves to be misled by statements such as 'Everyone should remain in the state in which he was called' (1 Cor 7:20). By affirming the principle that *all* are equal before the one Master, Christ, Paul had taken a step which would eventually undermine the whole system. Men and institutions interact and influence each other. Paul was faced with the alternative of influencing men through a violent change in a social institution, or of changing men who would then from conviction abolish the institution. The fallacy underlying the former procedure has been made clear to us by the progress of the Russian revolution, and Paul could not have been unaware of the horrible consequences of the three slave revolts. Hence he decided to apply the more subtle solvent of transformation of attitude. It is true that this solvent has worked far too slowly, but does the blame for this attach to the principle, or to the Christians who were supposed to live it?

1—7 Greetings and Thanksgiving—5. The structure **e** seems to be chiastic (*a b b a*). Hence 'love' is directed to the 'saints' (cf on Col 1:2), and 'faith' to the 'Lord Jesus'. Cf Col 1:4. **6.** 'Notoriously the most obscure v in this letter' (Moule). A possible paraphrase, 'that the fellowship which is an essential element of the faith you profess may be activated through effective recognition of all the good deeds in our power, which bring us into union with Christ'. The fellowship that Philemon is being asked to manifest englobes all the members of the community, and thus, by implication, Onesimus.

8—21 Petition on behalf of Onesimus—8. '*Although* **f** *it is within my power to command . . .*'. **9.** The translation 'ambassador' (RSV) reinforces v 8, but 'old man' (JB) is not impossible. **10.** Cf 1 Cor 4:15; Gal 4:19. **11.** A pun on the name Onesimus which means 'useful, beneficial'. Cf v 20. **13.** If Paul expected imminent release (v 22) he must have wanted Onesimus as an assistant in the spread of the Gospel. It is quite possible that the ex-slave became the bishop of Ephesus addressed by Ignatius (*Ad Eph* I, 1). **16.** Because of Onesimus' conversion a new relationship has been set up both on the ordinary human level—as a man—and on a specifically religious level. He is a 'brother' in the full sense underlined by Rm 8:29 (cf 1 Cor 5:11). 1 Tm 6:2 shows that this **g**

g doctrine gave rise to certain practical problems. **18.** Onesimus may have provisioned himself for his flight at Philemon's expense. **19b.** V 14—15 make it clear that Paul was quite aware that it might not be Philemon's intention to permit Onesimus to return to him. Hence he applies a little discreet pressure. **20.** The 'I' may be emphatic (Lightfoot, Lohmeyer). In which case Paul is more concerned with the use Onesimus would be to him than with his legal status. **21.** Only here is it hint- **929g** ed that Paul hopes that Onesimus will return a free man. **22.** Cf Ac 28:30. According to Roman law if the accusation against a prisoner had not been substantiated within two years he was automatically freed. At the time of writing of Phm this period must have been nearing its end, and Paul's accusers had not yet appeared.

HEBREWS

BY DOM AELRED CODY O.S.B.

930a Bibliography—(a) *Commentaries*: Chrys, John Damascene, Oecumenius, Theodoret, Theophylact; F. Bleek 1828–40; J. Bonsirven, VS, 1943[4]; F. F. Bruce, NIC 1964; J. Héring, CNT, 1954; O. Kuss, RNT 1953; O. Michel, Meyer, 1960[11]; J. Moffat, ICC 1924; H. Montefiore, BNTC, 1964; A. Nairne, CBSC, 1957; A. C. Purdy IB 1955; W. Manson 1951; E. Riggenbach, Zahn, 1922[2–3]; C. Spicq, EtB 2 vols 1952–3, BJ 1957[2]; Teodorico da Castel S. Pietro, SacB, 1952; B. F. Westcott, 1903[3]; H. Windisch, LHNT, 1931[2]; W. Neil, Torch, 1955.

(b) *Recent Special Studies*: E. Käsemann, *Das wandernde Gottesvolk*, Göttingen 1938, 1961[4]; M. Dibelius, 'Der himmlische Kultus nach dem Hebräerbrief', *Theologische Blätter* 21 (1942), 1–11; J. Jeremias, 'Hbr 5:7–10', ZNW 44 (1952/53), 107–11; F. J. Schierse, *Verheissung und Heilsvollendung*, Munich 1955; C. K. Barrett, 'The Eschatology of the Epistle to the Hebrews,' *The Background of the NT and its Eschatology* (C. H. Dodd Fs), Cambridge 1956, 363–93; C. Spicq, 'L'Epître aux Hébreux, Apollos, Jean-Baptiste, les Hellénistes et Qumran', *Revue de Qumran* 1 (1958/59), 365–90; C. E. Carlston, 'Eschatology and Repentance in the Epistle to the Hebrews', JBL 48 (1959), 296–302; A. Wikgren, 'Patterns of Perfection in the Epistle to the Hebrews', NTS 6 (1959/60), 159–67; A. Cody, *Heavenly Sanctuary and Liturgy in the Epistle to the Hebrews*, St Meinrad 1960; F. F. Bruce, '"To the Hebrews" or "To the Essenes"?', NTS 9 (1962/63), 217–32; A. Vanhoye, *La structure littéraire de l'Epître aux Hébreux*, Paris 1963; J. A. Fitzmyer, '"Now this Melchizedek..." (Heb 7:1)', CBQ 25 (1963) 305–21; E. Grässer, *Der Glaube im Hebräerbrief*, Marburg 1965; J. Swetnam, 'A Suggested Interpretation of Heb 9:15–18', CBQ 27 (1965) 373–90; A Vanhoye, '"Par la tente plus grande et plus parfaite..." (Heb 9:11)', Bib 46 (1965) 1–28.

There is an almost exhaustive bibliography in C. Spicq's commentary, I, 379–411, brought up to date by the same author in DBS 7 (1962), 272–5. A valuable survey and analysis of work done in the last quarter of a century is presented by E. Grässer, 'Der Hebraerbrief 1938–63', TRu 30 (1964) 138–236.

Authorship and Canonicity—The question of the authorship of an anonymous document like Heb has to be approached both from internal evidence and from external ascription. In what follows we propose to analyse briefly the internal similarities and differences between Heb and other documents of NT times, then to review the history of Heb's inclusion in the canon and of its extrinsic attribution to St Paul, concluding each of the two parts with a summary of what we are justified in saying about its authorship in the light of the knowledge we have at the present day.

An investigation of the **internal evidence** reveals that Heb has similarities with many other writings of NT times,

but that it also shows marked divergences from each of **93** them. The details of the life and work of Christ used by Heb are simply those recorded by the Gospels—often by the Synoptics without parallels in Jn. But the theological interpretation of those elements is often that found in Jn rather than in the Synoptics (C. Spicq, I, 109), and there are elements of Christology stressed by Heb and Jn which are found less, or not at all, elsewhere—especially those elements in Heb 2:5–18; 5:6–10. Both have much to tell us of the priesthood of Christ (cf Jn 17). Both share a love of antithesis and a fondness for the more highly 'spiritual' aspects of the *kerygma* they announce. For both the transcendent world is the true world, and their eyes are turned towards a Christ who is exalted in glory after his very human sufferings on earth, and yet neither comes near laying as much emphasis on the Resurrection of Our Lord as do St Paul and the Synoptics. So the author of Heb knew both the stream of early Christian catechesis set down in the Synoptics and the Johannine catechesis, perhaps even Johannine texts, with which he shares the same spiritual climate. And yet more often than not he has his own proper interpretations to give to the elements received from the catechesis.

Both Heb and 1 Pt speak of the sacrifice of Christ made **b** once and for all (Heb 7:27; 9:26f; 10:10; 1 Pt 3:18), with sprinkled blood (Heb 12:24 with 9:22–24; 1 Pt 1:2), resulting in the forgiveness of sins (Heb 9:28, etc; 1 Pt 2:24), and both are concerned with priesthood, but for 1 Pt it is the general priesthood of the Christian people, while for Heb it is always that of Christ. W. Manson, *The Epistle to the Hebrews* (1951) has pointed out a number of similarities between the traditions of the Jerusalem Hellenists (attached to Stephen and Philip) in Ac 6–8 and Heb. The point is easily understandable—presuming that these traditions can really be assigned to Jerusalem Hellenists—for the Jerusalem Hellenists were at the origins of the spread of Christianity into the Diaspora.

Most important for our consideration, of course, **c** because of the long-standing attribution of Heb to St Paul, is the question of the similarities and dissimilarities between Heb and the Pauline *corpus*. The omission of Paul's favourite words and expressions by Heb and *vice versa* is an initial indication of difference, although this is a delicate factor to weigh in questions of authorship. But we cannot help being struck by the difference between Pauline style, dashing ever onward, breaking off involved sentences without ever finishing them, continually inserting parenthetical remarks, leaping from subject to subject, and Heb's beauty of form and elegance of expression, turned out with all the care and technical ability employed in composing a sonata or a symphony; or between Paul's headlong impetuosity and Heb's quiet control, even when he is writing the direst of threats. These differences, to be sure, could be accounted for by postulating a writer giving literary form to ideas offered by Paul.

c This, in fact, has been the usual compromise sought by those who felt great difficulties in attributing the letter to Paul but were uncertain what to do with the customary Pauline ascription. There are certainly many 'Pauline' ideas found in Heb (e.g. on Christ exalted in glory, on stages of perfection, on the danger of not co-operating with divine grace), yet we could hardly expect not to find Pauline ideas in a NT document written after the great work of St Paul and aiming, like the other works in the Pauline *corpus*, at giving doctrinal and practical instruction to a primitive Christian community. But if Paul is to be reckoned the true author of the epistle, he must directly have provided the substance of the material contained therein, leaving only the literary composition to an amanuensis or literary reviser. Almost all serious scholars today, both Catholic and Protestant, find that after allowance is made for the natural, general debt owed to St Paul by an author who knew Paul's work and the Pauline traditions spreading through the Church, the differences between Heb and the rest of the Pauline *corpus*—especially the 'great' Pauline epistles (Rm, 1 and 2 Cor)—is too great to allow more than a remote possibility of real collaboration between the author of Heb and Paul in the writing of our epistle (cf Spicq, I, 144—68; Moffatt, lvi—lxiv; Kuss, 18; Michel, 9—16; J. Coppens, 'L'état présent des études pauliniennes', ETL 32 (1956), 363—72). This is not to say that there are contradictions, but there are considerable variations of concern and aspect, not to speak of approach and presentation.

d Looking beyond the canonical books of the NT, we find great similarities between Heb and the Alexandrian Jew Philo, especially in the axiological dualism of the heavenly and the earthly worlds, the related notion of the two sanctuaries (heavenly and earthly), the importance of the divine oath, the importance of 'perfection', and a general doctrine of the *logos*. Even more important is the idea they share of a heavenly high priest, seen against the shadowy figure of Melchizedek, free from sin, divine, entering the sanctuary, and interceding there for sinners. The author of Heb, of course, Christianizes all these ideas and gives them a radically different direction, but we can safely say that while the substance of his doctrine depends on the traditions brought down from Christ and developed in the theologies of Jn and Paul, his own elaboration of this doctrine is made in the philosophical, religious and exegetical style proper to Alexandrian Judaism.

Finally, the readers of the present day will want to know something about Heb and Qumran. For some (e.g. Y. Yadin, H. Kosmala) the similarities of concept and idea between Heb and Qumran are more striking than between Qumran and any other NT book. For others (e.g. J. Schmitt) they are, on the contrary, less striking than between Qumran and the other NT books. As usual in these matters the truth lies somewhere between the extremes (cf C. Spicq in *Revue de Qumran* 1 (1958/59), 365—90; J. Coppens in NRT 84 (1962), 128—41, 257—82; F. F. Bruce in NTS 9 (1962/63) 217—32). There are parallels of expression and analogies of thought between Heb and the DSS, but almost without exception they are of the kind that can be simply explained by a community of cultural background rather than by close dependence, and it is not yet certain that many of these ideas do not themselves belong to a wider circle of Palestinian Judaism than that of the Qumran sectaries or of the Essenes alone. Indeed just as many, if not more, parallels with Heb can be found in traditions found in Rabbinic literature and in Jewish apocryphal works.

We cannot conclude that the author of Heb was a **930c** Palestinian sectary.

Our brief examination, then, of the internal evidence has succeeded only in revealing that Heb shares many things with many writings. Evidence of identity of literary hand is to be found nowhere. Theological similarities are to be found between Heb and both the Johannine and Pauline writings, philosophical similarities between Heb and the Hellenistic Jew Philo. Heb shares Christian material with the catechesis underlying other NT writings and shares Jewish traditions with both rabbinic and non-rabbinic Judaism. The parallels from these various religio-cultural environments certainly throw light upon the interpretation of Heb, but the student must always be alert to the original twists and new directions Heb itself gives them.

The questions of **canonicity** and of **extrinsically 931a ascribed Pauline authorship** have been discussed over the years. The author of Heb does not tell us his name, so there is no question of intrinsic authenticity. The question of canonicity is a dogmatic one with an historical aspect, but that of authorship is historical, not dogmatic. Yet, it is the confusion of the two problems which has led to the difficulties with the question of authorship, and to a great extent the history of both has gone hand in hand. So we must begin by examining the history of the question.

Heb was used very early in the W by Clement of Rome (c. 96) and Hermas (c. 140), and we find it somewhat later in Alexandria with Pantaenus (c. 180) and Clem. Alex., who suggests, in a fragment of his *Hypotyposeis* preserved by Eus. HE 6, 14, 2, that Paul wrote the epistle in Heb., while Lk translated it into Gr. Orig. held that the epistle's thought (*noēmata*) is Pauline, but not its writing (in Eus. He 6, 25, 13). By the 3rd cent. Heb was definitively inserted in the Pauline epistolary *corpus* in the E, although the fluctuation of Heb's location in the earliest NT codices and the Chester Beatty papyrus P⁴⁶ shows that its Pauline authorship was accepted only after that of the other 13 epistles.

But the story is different in Rome and the W. Here, in the earliest stage (c. 96–c. 140) Heb is used and valued, but there is no indication of Pauline attribution. Next (c. 150–c. 350) we see its use actually declining in the W. Tert, writing c. 220, holds it to be a work of Barnabas and gives the impression that he does not hold it to be canonical (*De pudicitia* 20). It is not found in the Muratorian Canon, or in the writings of Cyprian or Iren. Hippolytus seems to have esteemed Heb highly without saying whether or not he held it to be canonical, but he did hold that it was not written by Paul (cf PG 103, 404 and 1104). In the next stage (after 350) the W begins to accept the idea of Pauline authorship, because of the unanimity of the E, which enjoyed theological leadership in the Church at the time. But Zeno of Verona and Ambrosiaster still attribute only 13 epistles to Paul. Jer. (*De viris illustribus* 59) and Aug. (*De civitate Dei* 16:22), impressed by the weight of tradition in the Orient for including Heb in the canon, accepted it as canonical, while remaining aware of the doubts about its Pauline authorship. The regional councils of Hippo (393) and Carthage III (397) added Heb to the 13 Pauline epistles known to them as traditional. In the succeeding centuries, the hesitation gave way to general acceptance of that authorship.

But the new learning of the Renaissance, with its **b** awakening to matters of style and its restoration of patristic study, opened the question again. Erasmus and Cajetan rejected Pauline authorship, and the latter even

931b rejected Heb's canonicity before the Council of Trent (EnchB 59) decided its inclusion in the canon; they were followed by Luther, Calvin, Melanchthon, and Beza. After a period in which the question of Pauline authorship was not raised, the critical studies of the 19th cent. considered it on the basis of the obvious differences of viewpoint, doctrinal interest, presentation, and style between Heb and Paul, and, as scientific method became better balanced and its results more certain, the anti-rationalist fears in orthodox circles subsided, so that the number of scholars maintaining Pauline authorship has dwindled to the vanishing point.

What do we learn from these facts? From an early date Heb began to be accepted as an inspired book, before the question of authorship arose. Sometime in the early 2nd cent., as the churches began to seek criteria for including individual books in the canon or excluding them from it, a cogent criterion came to be authorship by an Apostle. The feeling grew that a NT document accepted as inspired should have an Apostolic pedigree. In this situation the E took Heb, received as inspired and therefore *de facto* canonical, and ascribed it to Paul, on the basis doubtless of 13:22—25 and of certain affinities with other epistles in the Pauline *corpus*. The Alexandrians saw that it also had marked differences, Orig. clearly seeing that Paul could not actually have written the work, but not hesitating on that account about calling Paul the author as distinct from the writer. But the less sophisticated and more 'fundamentalist' W, knowing nothing of any tradition of Pauline authorship, was not subtle enough to take this step; Pauline authorship was not part of the tradition, and this, probably, was the reason for Heb's eclipse in the W. The unnecessary connexion established between inspiration—a matter of utmost doctrinal significance—and authenticity of apostolic authorship—a matter of historical interest but not of doctrinal importance—probably led the Latins to question the inspiration of the epistle.

c We see the same confusion in the interpretation which some have wished to give to two more recent documents of the teaching office of the Church. The decree of Trent, which defines the Canon of the OT and NT, gives '14 epistles of the Apostle Paul', each of which it then lists by name, and '*ad Hebraeos*' is at the end of the list (EnchB 59). But we know from the acts of the Council that certain bishops, aware of the position of Cajetan and Erasmus and of many Protestant Reformers, tried to have some phrase inserted in the text of the decree which would settle the Pauline authorship, but the *pars sanior* of the Council rejected the idea and let the text stand as it was prepared (cf *Concilium Tridentinum* ed. Societas Goerresiana 5 (1911), 70, 76—78, 91). Authenticity was not a matter of faith or morals, and the decree was deliberately limited to the doctrinal question of canonicity.

Again, in the early 1900s, the Biblical Commission issued responses dealing with the authorship and composition of Heb (EnchB 416—18). The first of the three questions answered by the Commission clearly distinguishes between Heb's canonicity, defined as *de fide*, and its Pauline origin, which remains open to the research of the scholar. It is worth noting, too, that the text of the first two questions does not directly touch the substance of Heb's origin, but asks about the weight of evidence. In 1914 people were hesitant to make a judgement that would seem 'new' to Catholics deeply concerned with preserving the 'old'. We are now at the point where we can confidently say that, although the influence of Paul's thought is in evidence in Heb, the epistle was composed and written by someone else.

Various names have been proposed: Barnabas, Luke, Clement of Rome, Prisca, Silvanus, and Apollos—most of them little more than names. There is really no way of determining the author's identity from the evidence we have. He is an early Christian of some authority, well educated, well versed in the Scriptures, in Jewish tradition, the doctrine of the Apostles, and the learning of Alexandria, a man of somewhat melancholy temperament and a sense of harmony and quiet beauty, with warm and living faith, who has given us a moving and in many ways original expression of the mysteries of Christianity. If we conclude with Orig. that 'in truth God alone knows who wrote the epistle' (cf Eus. He 6, 25, 14), we can add with Jer. that 'it matters not who wrote it, for he is a man of the Church' (*Epist.* 129, 3).

Destination—The superscription 'To the Hebrews' was already known to Pantaenus, Clem.Alex. and Tert around the year 200. For many centuries the epistle was accepted without question as addressed to Jewish Christians, because of the wealth of reference to Jewish institutions and thought and the frequent comparison of the old Mosaic order of salvation with the new one in Christ. It was presumably on the basis of this that the superscription itself originated. The author himself does not name the people to whom he is writing. It was not the Church at large but a particular community which he hoped to visit presently (13:23). It was hardly the community at Jerusalem, a poor community to which Paul himself brought aid (Ac 24:17), because we read that, on the contrary, it has itself often helped others and continues to do so (6:10). There are no clear indications which would enable us to determine what community of the Diaspora it might be. Many have been suggested. Those scholars who maintain that the readers are converts from Judaism argue that the abundance of reference to the OT presupposes a knowledge which Gentile readers would not have had, and that the detailed programme showing the superiority of the heavenly liturgy of Christ over the earthly liturgy of the OT ordinances is intended to forestall the relapse of converts into their former Judaism.

These arguments, however, are not conclusive. While there may well have been many converts from Judaism among the addressees, Rm and Gal provide evidence that Paul felt the OT could be used quite effectively in writing to Gentile converts (cf the difficult passages of Rm 4 and Gal 3). The comparison Heb makes between the OT order and that of the NT is not a matter of apologetics but of his fondness for antithesis—here an antithesis between less perfect OT shadows and perfect NT realities. He propounds a positive Christian theology by taking OT texts and ideas as the basis of a set of transposed analogies. Furthermore, the four passages dealing with apostasy (3:6—4:13; 6:4—8; 10:26—31; 12:16—17) are concerned with total apostasy; there is no indication that they have a lapse or relapse into Judaism in mind, and none of them occurs in a context which puts the OT order as such in an unfavourable light. Where it is a question of distinctively Palestinian Jews tempted to relapse into a distinctively Palestinian Judaism, there is even more to give us pause. The director of the Swedish Theological Institute in Jerusalem, H. Kosmala, in his *Hebräer, Essener, Christen* (1959) has suggested that the addressees of Heb are former Essenes tempted to relapse into a Palestinian Judaism with properly Essene characteristics, or even as Essenes not yet Christians whom the author of Heb hopes to convert. But, apart from the unlikelihood that the content of Heb is directed toward Essenes (cf J. Coppens, NRT 84 (1962), 128—41, 257—82; F. F. Bruce, NTS 9 (1962/63), 217—32), we

a can doubt whether a work like Heb, written in Gr. (a Hebrew or Aram. original is next to impossible) and couched in thoroughly Hellenistic categories, could be expected to persuade men who were completely devoid of non-Semitic language and culture, like the sectaries of Qumran. Much the same thing can be said of the suggestion that the addressees were former Jerusalem priests, converted to Christianity but tempted to relapse out of nostalgia for their past. The hypothesis is attractive, but it remains faced with the general objections to a theory about addressees tempted to relapse into Judaism rather than to commit total apostasy, and with the unlikelihood that the highly nationalistic Palestinian-Jewish priesthood of NT times would be much moved by a letter coming from a hellenistic Jewish convert, couched in Alexandrian categories, and written in Gr.

b Today there are more exegetes in favour of Rome as the destination of the epistle than any other place. Their principal reasons are these: (1) the earliest evidence of knowledge of the epistle is in the writings of the Romans, Clement and Hermas, and the title *hēgoumenoi* for superiors (Heb 13:7, 17, 24) is found also in 1 Clement 1:3 and the *Shepherd* of Hermas, Vis. 2. 2, 6; 3. 9, 7 (*proēgoumenoi*); (2) the 'brethren from Italy' of 13:24 would not be likely to make a point of having their greetings sent to a community other than that of Rome (but on the 'brethren from Italy' cf comm. on 13:24); (3) the Roman community was well known for its generosity to others (cf Eus. HE 4:23), a point which makes 6:10 applicable to Rome just as Ac 24:17 seems to exclude it from Jerusalem.

Most of the scholars who accept Rome consider the addressees to be a Gentile community; but, without admitting that there was danger of lapse into Judaism, we may hold that a number of converted Jews may very well have been among the addressees, and that their presence may have entailed a certain danger of syncretism (cf 13:9—13). Rome itself contained one of the three great Jewish communities of the Diaspora in NT times, and we know that the Jewish community of Rome was deeply Hellenized (cf H. J. Leon, 'The Gr. Inscriptions of the Jews of Rome', *Greek, Roman, and Byzantine Studies* 2 (1959), 45—49). Many possibilities are open, but the balance of the evidence indicates addressees somewhere in the Diaspora, and the community of Rome has most in its favour.

Date—The absolute *terminus ad quem* is afforded by its use in 1 Clement, which was itself written c. 96, and we have to allow a certain lapse of time for knowledge of Heb to spread before it could be used in another work; this lapse would be comparatively brief if Heb were written to a Roman community, longer if it had to spread to Rome from an original destination elsewhere. 8:13 and 9:9 might at first sight seem to imply that the Temple ritual was still being carried out in Jerusalem so that one might infer the epistle was written before the destruction of the Herodian Temple by the Romans in the year 70. But the inference is not necessarily justified, because the author's entire handling of the Temple and its ritual is a symbolic, parabolic thing, quite atemporal, and because his descriptions are based not on the Herodian Temple and its practice but on the norm for sanctuary and liturgy set down in the Pent. The only internal evidence we have is 2:3, which tells us that the author and his readers belonged to the second generation of Christians, so that the epistle could hardly have been written much before 65. If it was written to the Romans, then 10:32 would suggest that it was produced several years after the persecution of Nero in 64. The majority opinion proposes a date between 80 and 90, but some competent scholars (e.g. Spicq) prefer a date shortly before 70.

932b

Literary Nature and Purpose—It has often been **c** claimed that Heb is less an epistle than a sermon, written down and dispatched to an audience which would read it instead of hearing it, or even that it is a theological treatise, with the brief conclusion (13:22ff) tacked on later to give it enough of an epistolary appearance to allow its inclusion in the Pauline *corpus*. Those who hold that it is a sermon argue, apart from the document's content and organization, that the author himself never refers to his work as 'writing' but as 'speaking' (2:5; 8:1; 9:5). Both those who hold that it is a sermon and those who hold that it is a theological treatise argue that the regular epistolary introduction, with the name of the writer and his addressees and a salutatory formula, is completely lacking.

But in other epistles too we find the author referring to his own epistolary activity as 'speaking' rather than 'writing' (cf Rm 3:5; 6:19), and more recent research has revealed that the absence of the ordinary epistolary introduction, even in the Hellenistic world, does not necessarily mean that the document in question is not a letter. O. Roller, *Das Formular der paulinischen Briefe* (1933), 213ff, has isolated in the profane literature of NT times a particular type of letter form, originating in the Semitic Near E, in which the epistolary introduction is regularly lacking. Heb does not fit this form perfectly, and its conclusion is of a pure Hellenistic type; but the fact of this form's existence shows that the omission of an introduction in Heb (and in 1 Jn) does not of itself mean that the document is not an epistle. Everything seems to indicate, however, that 13:22ff was added after the body of the work as a whole had been completed (cf the comm. in loc.). It is impossible to say with certainty whether these vv were added by the author of the body of the work or by another. But it is clear from 13:22 that the author of those concluding lines considered the whole work as an epistle and was sending it off as such. The work, despite its homiletic style, was certainly not originally a sermon delivered extempore and later set down in writing. Its extremely complex and well planned structure, with literary 'inclusions', and vast symmetrical construction throughout, reflects laborious and carefully written composition, and we have no reason to believe that it was not, from the very outset, meant to be read rather than heard.

Our author himself calls his work a 'word of exhortation' which he has sent to his readers (13:22). His doctrinal exposition itself serves, in the whole context of the epistle, to converge toward the same end as his hortatory and encouraging words. The 'main point' of his theological doctrine is that 'we have a high priest one who is seated at the right hand of the throne of the Majesty in heaven' (8:1). And the main purpose of his exhortation and encouragement is to support the faith of his readers, a faith which must be directed toward heaven, the place of things hoped for and things not seen (11:1). The Christian life is represented as a pilgrimage toward heaven: Christ is our forerunner (6:20), and the main reason for our keeping the faith and avoiding apostasy is that we may enjoy a salvation which consists in approaching the heavenly Jerusalem where his blood speaks for us (12:22—24). So Heb is a work of high literary quality, but unlike the other NT epistles it has a single but complex theme in which all the others are co-ordinated: Christ exalted in the heavenly sphere at the conclusion of his sacrifice, thereby inaugurating

932c a new and eternal covenant in which the eschatological fruits of that sacrifice are actually available to those who persevere in the Christian community. In this respect it is not unlike a sermon. But its theological exposition does not make it a theological treatise as such; its ultimate purpose is to encourage a certain Christian community to remain steadfast in the faith, and its theological exposition serves to give its members profound motives for doing so.

933a **The main divisions** given here are those **clear from the epistle itself**, as established by A. Vanhoye, *La Structure littéraire de l'Epître aux Hébreux* (1963), but a number of minor divisions have been made to help the reader find his way.

1:1—4 Prologue—The ordinary epistolary introduction is lacking (cf § 932c), and in its place stands a prologue which announces the great themes to follow: the superiority of the new order of revelation to the old which it perfects, the divinity shared by the Son and manifested to us in him, his place in the cosmos, his rôle in achieving salvation for us by his Passion and *transitus* to the heavenly world, his superiority to the angels.

1—2a The Old and the New—The revelation God gave in the old dispensation is contrasted with the superior revelation in the new. In the old, God spoke 'many times and in many ways' (e.g. through visions, dreams, promises, symbolic actions, the interpretation of historical events), and the very multiplicity of occasions and forms is a sign of its imperfection (cf 7:23; 10:1—2, 11—12). 'Fathers' and 'prophets' are words chosen for their power to evoke memories of a long history; all the spiritual ancestors of the New Israel are 'fathers', and the record of revelation is found not only in the strictly prophetical writings but also in the historical books, which the Jewish canon includes among 'the prophets', for it was often in the vicissitudes of history that God manifested his hidden ways. 'In these last days': the Gr. is basically a formula often used by LXX to express Heb. *beahᵃrît hayyāmîm*, whose connotation of the Messianic Age had been growing more pronounced in late Judaism; Heb, by adding 'these', makes it plain that in his perspectives of inchoative eschatology that age has already arrived. The Gr. has no article in the phrase 'in Son'; the omission evokes the Gr. tragic style and we cannot capture its grandeur in English. It bespeaks nature and character, all the depth and breadth of what that Son is in relation to the Father. Heb. will show God speaking, i.e. manifesting himself, through the Son's coming to earth, obedient suffering, and exaltation in glory, rather than through anything spoken in words.

b **2b—4 Essential Christology**—**2b.** When Heb says God made the Son *heir* of the universe, his perspective is still that of eschatology already begun; when he goes on to say that through the Son God *made* the worlds, his gaze turns back to the other end of time. The first attribute belongs primarily to Christ's humanity, the second to his divinity. The divine Son was not 'made' heir, for the universe belongs to him from eternity, but Christ as man actually came into possession of his dominion over the universe when he entered the heavenly world in glory (2:8; 10:12f; Rm 1:3f; 1 Cor 15:24—27; Phil 2:5—11). Rather than 'the world' the Gr. plural *aiōnes*, 'worlds', should be kept. Jewish apocalyptic literature knew a plurality of superimposed worlds, but Heb takes the Jewish idea of two 'ages' (also *aiōnes*, Heb. *'ōlāmîm*)—one of historical time, the other of a future eschatological state replacing the first—and, without entirely abandoning the Jewish perspective, crosses it with an Alexandrian perspective of two worlds, one that of our

historical, visible world, and the other that of trans- 93 cendental, celestial existence which, through the glorified Christ, is already eschatologically shared by Christians. Heb, like Jn and Paul—always in doxologies or passages of great solemnity—presupposes an Alexandrian *theologoumenon* or theological principle of interpretation which attaches all the functions of Wisdom to the Son (here Wisdom's creative function). The idea had probably been spread through liturgical hymns in the very early Church, even before the NT writings had taken final shape. The author stresses complementary aspects with a unifying principle behind them: (1) God, author of the old revelation and the new; (2) Christ, God and man; (3) Christ as the one in whom creation finds its first beginning and its final consummation, his '*protological*' and eschatological rôles. **3a.** The divine Son's relation c to the Father is expressed as a 'reflection' (*apaugasma*) of the Father's glory and a 'stamp' or 'imprint' (*charaktēr*) of his nature. *Apaugasma* has been variously interpreted in an active sense ('radiation, emanation' of light) and in a passive sense ('reflection' of a luminary's light on another surface). The active sense was the one commonly accepted in early exegesis, with conclusions at times orthodox, at times pantheistic or gnostic, but the parallel with *charaktēr* indicates that it is the passive sense which is intended by our author. *Charaktēr* is the imprint of a seal, the mark of one thing found in something else. 'Glory' is the form of God's manifestation (Ex 24:16; 33:18; 40:34; cf Jn 1:14), and in late Judaism often meant God himself. *Hypostasis* is essence, substance, nature; to try to make the clear-cut metaphysical or speculative distinctions of a later theology is out of place; the word is chosen on the basis of theological imagery and metaphor. Without pressing these images further than the author intends, we may say that 'reflection of his glory' denotes the Son's divine origin and perfect similarity to the Father, and 'stamp of his nature' that similarity qualified by his distinction from the Father. 'Upholding the universe by his word of power': *pherōn* has the double sense of maintaining the existence of creation and of governing, directing the course of history. The 'word' here is the dynamic OT 'word' which produces physical or historical effects, and 'word of power', of course, is a Semitism for 'powerful word'. **3b.** Christ's suffering and entrance into the world of glory. The humanity of Christ returns to the fore. The verbal forms are aorist, and express action at a single moment of past time; the reference to the purification from sins, therefore, is not to the cleansing of our personal sins, which continues in the present, but to that objective restoration of the relations between God and the created world which had been wrecked by sin, i.e. to the objective redemption achieved by the saving action which began with the Passion, to be completed by the Session in glory (cf 5:7—10; 9:13f, 26). 'The Majesty' is a reverential expression signifying God. In this prologue Christ has appeared as prophet (1:1), priest (purification from sins, to be developed later on in Heb), and Messianic king (sitting at the right hand of God). **4.** The prologue concludes with mention of Christ's superiority to the angels, which is to be the subject of the section immediately following. 'Name' has its Jewish connotation of ineffable and inalienable dignity attached directly to the person.

FIRST PART. 1:5—2:18: The son Superior to the 93 **Angels**—(1) a proof of the Son's superiority, made up of a chain of OT texts (1:5—14); (2) an exhortation based on the Son's superiority (2:1—4); (3) an answer to the implicit objection that Christ was 'a little less than the angels' (2:5—18).

a **5–14 The Son's Superior Dignity**—The inferiority of the angels is 'proved' by texts concerning them (1:6 = Dt 32:43 LXX or Ps 97 LXX (96):7; 1:7 = Ps 104 (103):4) and the superiority of the Son by texts whose original literal sense applied to God (1:10–12 = Ps 102 (101):25–27) or to a Messianic figure (1:5*a* = Ps 2:7; 1:5*b* = 2 Sm 7:14; 1:8f = Ps 45 (44):7f; 1:13 = Ps 110 (109):1). The dialectic methods of rabbinic exegesis are evident, but Heb is inspired to see a Christian sense in these texts which was not theirs literally in the OT. Dialectically the texts 'prove' the thesis, although not in our logical sense. Theologically they are looked upon as conveyors of mysteries which only now in the fullness of time are unveiled by God, the author of both orders of revelation. The modern reader may wonder why Heb takes such pains to show Christ's superiority to the angels. In the world of late Judaism the angels were present at the creation of the historical cosmos and had a rôle in its government; they were called collectively 'sons of God', and in Alexandrian Jewish theology the *logos* was called 'archangel' and 'firstborn of the angels'. These notions make it opportune to establish Christ's transcendence. But even more important is the notion held in Jewish circles of NT times that the OT was given to men through the mediation of angels; one of the principal components of Heb's theme is that of Christ as mediator of a new and better covenant, and this becomes clear for the first time in 2:3, for which the preceding vv prepare. **5.** Two OT texts used to show the sonship of Christ. The argument: God himself has proclaimed Christ alone—never an angel—as his Son; hence the Son's superiority. Ps 2:7 was often given a Messianic interpretation in late Judaism, and 2 Sm 7:14 has recently been found applied to the Messiah of Qumran (cf JBL 75 (1956), 176f). Ps 2:7 is applied to Christ's Baptism in Mk 1:11 and parallels, to his Transfiguration in Mk 9:7 and parallels. Heb would seem to have particularly in mind the Session in glory, when Christ in his humanity became fully heir of the universe (cf *supra* on 1:2*b*), without excluding the Incarnation and other moments of glorification in the historical life of Christ. 'Today' in the exegesis of Philo refers to an entire age, and Heb may have in mind the eschatological age introduced with Christ. The Christian exegetes of the Alexandrian School interpreted 'today' as eternity and saw in our v the eternal generation within the Trinity, but this is not likely to be the sense in Heb itself. The citation from 2 Sm 7:14 stresses the continuity of relations between Father and Son, while that from the Ps bespeaks rather a declaration of Sonship (the ancient declaratory formula 'thou art'). **6.** The argument: if the angels must adore the Son, they are inferior to him. Theologically, the bringing of the first-born into the universe seems to refer to the Incarnation, but many see a reference to the *parousia*. These are ambiguities in the Gr. **7.** The argument: the angels are wind and fire—elements unstable; the Son is above change and lasts forever (1:8–12). The angels are servants, but the Son is royally enthroned (1:8f). Speculation on the nature or incorruptibility of the angels is completely foreign to the author's concern. **b** **8–9.** The text is from a royal enthronement psalm. In Heb's argument the citation contrasts the Son's divinity and permanence with the servitude and impermanence of the angels in 7. The two vocatives 'God' were not in the primitive Heb. text of the psalm, but by two separate errors in the MS tradition they appeared, then went into the Gr. text, and now fit Heb's Christian exegesis; the hand of God inspiring can also be behind a copyist's

error. In his historical life on earth Christ showed himself to be a lover of justice and hater of iniquity (the **934b** aorists show particular past time) and this contributed ('therefore') to his joyful anointing as king of righteousness when he ascended into glory to reign forever. The Messianic hallmarks of sinlessness, regal splendour, and power will be in evidence at the *parousia* (cf 9:28; 10:27; Mt 24:30; 26:64). If Heb really intends the 'comrades' of the psalm to be taken formally in his exegesis, he could have Christ's human brethren in mind (cf 3:14, where the same word *metochos*, here translated 'comrades' or '*fellows*', is CV's '*partakers*' and underlies RSV's 'we share'), or possibly the angels. **10–12.** More on the permanence of the Son contrasted with the limitations of the angels, but the theological sublimity now leaves the dialectic almost forgotten. The passage on the divine aspect of Christ follows one on his human aspect, as in 1:2f. Christ the Lord precedes the historical universe in whose creation he had a hand, and he will continue unchanged long after the historical universe has come to an end. His timelessness is stressed by the contrast between future and present tenses: 'they will perish, but thou remainest'. The image of a used garment applied to perishing creation is used in the OT (Is 51:6; Sir 14:17), and there are rabbinic texts which interpret the heavens as the dwelling of angels (SB III, 680). A parallel with the Grecian mythical idea of the starry heavens as a cloak worn by some divine being has been suggested here, but none of Heb's images in this section, so redolent of Judaism, are drawn from the pagan world. **13.** Ps 110 (109):1 is applied to Christ, the Messiah and victorious eschatological 'Son of Man', enthroned at God's right hand, with the enemies of his justice beneath his feet. **14.** In conclusion, while the Son is divine and even in his glorified humanity reigns in victory and dominion, the angels are, without exception, 'ministering spirits' (a Jewish concept of angels serving God), continually sent (present participle) to be of service to God in bringing men to the eschatological salvation which the Son has won for them in the world of heavenly realities (2:10; 5:9; 9:28; 12:22–24).

2:1–4 Exhortation Based on Christ's Superiority c to Angels—The actual exhortation is in **1**. 'What we have heard' is the *kerygma* of the NT revelation announcing salvation in Christ and the duties incumbent on those who would seek it. **2–4.** The reason is given in the form of an argument *a fortiori*. If the OT and its order of salvation, mediated by the angels, provided for just punishment of failure to accept it and live in accordance with it, so much more will a failure to accept the new order of salvation, mediated by Christ, bring punishment on those who do not take it seriously and conform to its requirements. The idea of angels as mediators of the OT was common in Judaism of the 1st cent. The new order of salvation was announced by Christ himself (cf 1:2), transmitted to others by witnesses who heard him, and corroborated by the eschatological wonders and effusions of the Spirit which were a mark of the primitive Church—strong reasons for believing and acting.

5–18 A Paradox: Jesus for a Time Less than the Angels—In 1:5–14 the Son's dominion over the universe was emphasized, but he became man and suffered ignominiously in an historical world which in NT times was thought to be subject somehow to the angels. **5.** Heb now makes it clear however that he is really concerned not with this world but with 'the world to come', i.e. the eschatological world of heavenly realities, already inaugurated, but not to be completed until the *parousia* (5:8;

934c 9:28; 12:18—29; 13:14). **6—8a.** Citation of Ps 8:5—7 in a messianic-apocalyptic sense (Son of Man). **8b—9.** Exegesis of the text cited. The universe without exception is subject to the dominion of Christ, but not yet totally subjected in actual, concrete fact. Here we have the tension between eschatology already inaugurated and eschatology not yet realized. The consummation of Christ's dominion will occur at the end of history. The phrase 'for a little while made lower than the angels' (*brachu ti*, which meant 'a little bit' in the Gr. Psalter, is given a temporal sense: 'for a little while') is applied to the humiliation of Jesus in his earthly life, Passion, and death, and 'crowned in glory' is applied to his exaltation; his humiliation was only temporary (cf Phil 2:5—11). 'By the grace of God' could be an 'easier' reading substituted for an original 'without (or "apart from") God', a reading which was known to the Patristic writers and could refer to the abandonment of Christ on the Cross, but actually the present reading fits the context far better and is far better attested in the MSS; the poorly attested variant can easily be explained as an anti-Patripassian theological attempt to insist that it was only in his human nature—not his divine—that Christ suffered death. The argument thus far: Christ's humiliation was a necessary step toward his exaltation, and his exaltation was required for bringing the universe into

d subjection (and men to salvation). **10—11a.** Reasons for Christ's suffering. The expression 'it was fitting' can imply necessity arising from a given set of circumstances (here God's freely ordained plan of salvation). Heb's theology sees a thorough correspondence between Saviour and saved, Son and 'sons', 'sanctifier' and 'sanctified', between a leader or chief (RSV's 'pioneer' in 2:10) entering into the heavenly world (9:11—28) and those who follow him into heaven (6:20), between Christ glorified by God (2:9) and sons led by God into glory, and now between suffering Christ and human brethren. It is, then, for his office of Saviour that Christ is made 'perfect' by suffering. **11.** 'Have all one origin': the simple Gr. phrase *ex henos* is ambiguous. Many commentators see a common origin of descent from Adam or Abraham, but Heb, always consistent in his use of prepositions, would express that by *aph' henos* (cf 11:12). Others see a common origin in God. This is quite possible, but the context makes it probable that the phrase refers to a community of nature rather than of origin. This, too, is linguistically possible for *ex henos*. The translation then would be 'have all one nature'. **11b.** 'He is not ashamed': this expression is a peculiar Palestinian idiom used of public avowals. It is a declaratory formula, not the expression of a mood (cf O. Michel in *Glaube und Ethos* (Fs G. Wehrung, 1940), 36—53). **12—13.** OT texts invoked as witnesses. **14—15.** Two parallel series of antitheses: devil-sin-death, and Christ-salvation-life. By becoming man and dying, Christ mystically undoes the death of sin and the power of Satan, and gains eschatological life for himself and his brethren (Rm 6:3—11), for whom physical death no longer causes the anguish which is 'bondage'. **16.** The verb means 'come to the aid of, take an interest in'. Use of the phrase 'descendants' of Abraham rather than 'men' recalls the ancient promises. **17—18.** Conclusion: Christ had to be like his brethren (cf *supra* on 2:10), tempted and tried like them, and compassionate with them. The theme of Christ the High Priest is announced.

935a **SECOND PART. 3:1—5:10: The High Priest, Faithful and Compassionate**—(1) Fidelity towards God (3:1—4:14); (2) Compassion towards men (4:15—5:10). **3:1—4:14 Fidelity**—Christ is supremely faithful, even

more than Moses (3:1—6); Christians should be much **93** more faithful than the Jews and follow Christ in his fidelity into the promised rest of heaven (3:7—4:14). **1—6 Moses, a Type of Christ's Fidelity—1.** 'Heavenly because belonging to the order of heavenly reality and because of its goal (beatitude in heaven). 'Apostle', i.e. one sent from God (Jn 17:3; 1 Jn 4:10). 'Of our confession': the priesthood of Christ and his mission from God are part of the object of faith and its expression ('confession'). **2a.** 'Him who appointed him' probably refers to God appointing Christ 'apostle and high priest' (3:1). **2b—6a.** Another argument *a fortiori*, with Nm 12:7 as implicit starting-point: Moses was faithful in the house of God (i.e. the Chosen People) as freely willing servant and witness 'to the things that were to be spoken later' (until the ultimate word came through the Son, 1:1f); but he who establishes the house is greater than he who serves in it, so Christ, the Son of the God who established it is greater than Moses the servant, and his fidelity is greater. **6b.** We Christians are now the Chosen People, if we are faithful, i.e. if we do not abandon our religion (viz the assurance it gives, and the hope). The two ideas of fidelity and of our fulfilment of the type constituted by the Chosen People will be developed in what follows. **7—19 Exhortation to Personal Fidelity**—The fidelity of Christ should be followed by the fidelity of his brethren. A complex typological moral exegesis is employed from here to 4:13. **7—11.** The text (Ps 95 (94):7—11) serving as basis of the applied exegesis. **12—19.** A warning to the new Chosen People against repeating the infidelity of the Israelites in the desert. The typological theme is explicitly given in v 15. **12.** 'Unbelieving': not so much a lack of faith as a refusal of fidelity, a disobedience, a 'hardness', that apostasy (6:4—6) by which one 'falls away from the living God'. **13.** 'As long as it is called "today"': a peculiar turn of phrase resulting from a stylistic predilection for words of the same stem in the Gr. text. The sense is 'as long as "today" is with us'— 'today' in a Jewish exegetical sense of 'a time of decision'. **14.** 'First confidence': the strong faith had immediately after conversion. 'Confidence' is the Gr. *hypostasis*, translated 'assurance' by RSV in 11:1, q.v., but the concept expressed by the English words 'confidence' or 'assurance' is less objective than that expressed by *hypostasis*, which is almost 'the grounds for confidence'. **16—18.** The rhetorical questions and answers bring out those points in the typology of the Israelites in the desert which are important for Heb's exposition: the general sin of the people led by Moses and their exclusion from the promised rest because of their disobedience. **19.** 'Unbelief': cf 12.

4:1—14 Heavenly Rest—The promise of rest at the end **b** of their journey was denied the Israelites for their infidelity. The rest promised to them was to have been in an earthly place, but now the members of the new Chosen People are given the promise of a rest which is in heaven, if they remain faithful to an all-knowing God. **1.** 'Remains', i.e. as long as it is open to us in the 'today' of decision (3:13; 4:7). RSV's 'to have failed to reach it' translates *hysterēkenai* here better than CV's 'wanting'; cf *infra* on *hysterein* in 12:15. **2.** There are four variant readings of this v, three of which yield differences of sense. The reading reflected in RSV is not the most widely attested but may well be the original. The reading preferred by the majority is 'because they were not joined in faith with the hearers (i.e. Moses and Joshua)'; the difference is one of a single Gr. letter (*-menous* for *-menos*), and the latter reading can easily have been a very early scribal error (false agreement with the immediately

b preceding *ekeinous*), perpetuated in the majority of MSS. **3.** 'Have believed': the Gr. would indicate *'have come to believe'*. We 'enter' (present), yet we are encouraged to enter as not having done so (4:11)—the double aspect, present and future, of early Christian eschatology. CV's *'shall* enter' loses this nuance. **3c–4.** The 'rest' is likened to the repose of God after the work of creation, which had given rise to the Rabbinic concept of a Messianic Sabbath. **5–7.** The Israelites in the desert failed to reach the promised rest, but God has set another 'today', another time of decision, in which Christians can accept or reject the promise. **8–10.** The rest which Joshua gave the Israelites by leading them into Canaan was not the rest of the promise in Heb's typological exegesis, for it was a worldly rest, not the heavenly rest **c** with God. **11.** The hortatory conclusion. **12–13** are poetic, with strophe and antistrophe. **12.** The strophe: power of God's word, evoked with image and metaphor. The word is, again, the dynamic OT *dābār*, full of vital force, almost ineluctably producing extrinsic effects; here it is admirably used to express God's vital immanence in the world of man. The reader should not try to interpret the cluster of metaphors here in a material, physical sense. **13.** The antistrophe: creation faced with God's word. 'Open': a translation based on the parallel 'laid bare', but the real meaning of the Gr. verb *trachēlizō* is obscure. A study of its use in Gr. authors would indicate something like 'lay prostrate' (from the vocabulary of the prize ring, used allegorically by Philo) as a better sense here. CV's translation (with Syr.) of *pros hon hēmin ho logos* as *'to whom we have to give account'* is better than RSV's 'with whom we have to do'; the idiom is known from patristic Gr. **14.** Sectional conclusion. Jesus the high priest who has entered the heavenly sanctuary (6:20; 7:26; 8:1; 9:11) is a motive for holding fast to the faith we confess.

4:15–5:10 The Compassionate High Priest—15–16. The heavenly high priest, in sympathy with our miseries (2:17f) is a source of confidence; let us turn to him in need. 5:1–10 lends itself to a division: (1) a description of the function and calling of a high priest (1–4); (2) a demonstration of Christ's fulfilling this description (5–10), which is also a theological exposition. The author looks toward the OT and its types to find reflected therein images of Christ and the New Covenant already formed in his mind. Much of his handling of OT liturgical and cultic ideas here and elsewhere in his work shows colouring from the Hellenistic Judaism of the Diaspora. **1.** The Gr. word *archiereus*, 'high priest', entered Jewish Gr. quite late and was originally the title of an official in the Seleucid administration. In the LXX it occurs almost exclusively in 1 and 2 Mc. Heb seems to have chosen it because it becomes the dignity of Christ better than simple 'priest', and because of the OT type he will establish (9:7, 25). A priest or Levite was to be chosen from the people he represented (Ex 28:1; Nm 8:6), but Christ represents all mankind, so it is 'from among men' that he must be chosen, and Heb, with Christ in mind, puts this among his general principles. In rabbinic thought all gifts and sacrifices came to have value as sin-offerings, and this is where Heb prepares to lay the emphasis in the priestly work of Christ (for the atonement of sin). **2. d** 'Deal gently' (RSV) does not convey the idea of *metriopathein* adequately (nor does CV's simple 'have compassion'). To the Hellenist mentality *pathos*, 'feeling', was unseemly for great men because it could easily become maudlin. But Heb evidently finds the opposite *apatheia*, 'lack of feeling', which the Stoics especially held desirable, too severe for Christ (all the more so in a literary work

seeking to console people and exhort them to carry on **935d** under trial), so he uses *metriopathein*, which could be translated here 'have a measure of compassion toward'. Such an idea is nowhere to be found for priests in general: Heb is thinking of Christ. 'Ignorant and wayward': terms for sinners not hardened in their sin (contrast 6:4–8). 'Beset with weakness' because human. **3.** Priests generally are sinners (7:27), but Christ is sinless (4:15). **4.** 'Honour' (*timē*) has its sense of (honourable) office or position. This section on priesthood in general closes with its only concrete reference to the OT: Aaron's call by God (Ex 28:1; Lv 8:1; Sir 45:7). **5–6.** The application to Christ begins. The divine calling of Christ to the priesthood is shown by two psalm citations, the first already given in 1:5 and the second to be the *leit-motiv* of ch 7. In the Apostolic Age Ps 2:7 was understood as applying particularly to the glorified Christ of the Ascension and Session (cf J. Dupont, 'Filius meus es tu', RSR 35 (1948), 522–43), and this is the Christological sense it is given in Heb (cf also 1:5); but here Heb wishes to point out the relation between this exaltation and Christ's priesthood, so he immediately complements Ps 2:7 with Ps 110 (109):4, where priesthood is mentioned explicitly. Both citations contain the declaratory formula 'thou art': it is the glorified Christ who is at last formally declared priest by God. The priesthood of Christ flows not from his Passion alone but from his Passion crowned with his exaltation, for both belong to the heavenly sacrifice in which his priesthood was perfected (cf *infra* on 9:24). **7–10.** Exegetes have usually seen only the Passion of Christ's humanity in these vv, but it is important to note that the aspect of his exaltation in glory and its rôle in his priesthood are here too (cf J. Jeremias in ZNW 44 (1952/53), 107–11). Our Saviour, confronted with imminent suffering and death, prayed to his Father, 'who was able to save him from death', but according to Jn 12:27f, 32; 17:5; Ac 2:25–31 this deliverance from death went beyond deliverance from tasting death to deliverance from the grip of death in resurrection and glorification. 'Although' Christ 'is Son' and, as such, obedient, 'he learned obedience' humanly in his accepted suffering, and because of this obedient reverence of his toward his Father's will (the sense of the Gr. behind RSV's 'godly fear') he 'was heard' and exalted in glory, thereby being 'made perfect', becoming a 'source (or cause) of eternal salvation', and 'being designated by God a high priest'. All of these result from his glorification and establishment in dominion, with his Passion and death a prerequisite. It is in this light that the quotation of Ps 2:7 and the phrase 'Christ did not *exalt himself* to be made a high priest' in 5:5 find their significance. The verb *teleioun*, 'to make perfect', is that used by the LXX to refer to the conferring of priestly power. In the context of 2:10 it was applied to suffering, here to suffering crowned by exaltation, and it is practically equivalent to 'being designated by God a (high) priest'. But by putting the double sense of the word *teleioun* to good use Heb can present Christ 'designated a priest' in his Passion-and-exaltation and at the same time 'perfected' so that he can 'perfect' others (10:14 with 2:10). The salvation is 'eternal' (*aiōnios*) because in Heb's vertical Alexandrian axiology it belongs to the perfect reality of the heavenly world (*aiōn*) in which our high priest is glorified and in which we too shall come to glory (cf 9:12, 14, 15).

THIRD PART. 5:11–10:39: Jesus the High Priest. 936a 5:11–6:20 Preliminary Exhortation—The author, aware of the difficulties of the central part of his epistle and the torpor of his readers (5:11), begins with a

936a preamble designed to make them aware of the seriousness of Christian engagement and to stir them to more enthusiastic hope.

11–14. The readers are rebuked for remaining at a level of Christian infancy when they should by now have advanced to an adult stage of doctrinal knowledge, able to help others in their initiation in the mystery of Christ. **6:1–3.** An exhortation to leave this elementary stage for the adult stage and to pay heed to the difficult doctrine which is to follow. 'Dead works' are those which lead to spiritual death, or at least which do not lead positively to life. In the first alternative there would be a question of repentance for sin, in the second of initial conversion to the way of life which is Christianity. The Gr. plural *baptismōn* (RSV 'ablutions') is enigmatic, for Christians knew a single baptism. Perhaps the reference is to an instruction on the difference between Christian baptism and that of John the Baptist or certain Jewish ritual ablutions like those we know to have been practised at Qumran. 'The laying on of hands' in Judaic background had to do with the conferment of an office and the giving of the spirit (cf Ac 8:17–19; 19:6; 1 Tm 4:14; 5:22; 2 Tm 1:6). The topics listed in these vv must have constituted some sort of catechesis of neophytes in the primitive Church.

b 4–20 Failure or Hope?—The readers have just been faced with the choice of remaining children or becoming adults. Now they are faced with a choice of apostasy and ultimate failure or of perseverance and hope. **4–6.** Once a man has become a Christian and then fallen away he cannot be restored again to repentance. The text does not deny the possibility of repentance for sin generally, but supposes the case of a man who has deliberately turned away from the light with positive disobedience and hardness of heart (3:16, 18; 4:6, 11), scorning the salvation brought by Christ (cf 10:26–31). Basically the apostasy here is the sin against the Holy Spirit in the Synoptics (Mt 12:31f; Mk 3:22–30; Lk 12:10). Such a man cannot be restored again to repentance because he himself is unwilling; his free will is opposed to grace. These few vv of Heb have weighed heavily in controversies on the theology of repentance and the practice of readmitting apostates to the Church. In evaluating the real sense of the passage we have to replace it in its historical situation and to distinguish Heb's inspired pastoral rhetoric from his theology. The author is writing to Christians faced with active persecution. In Greco-Roman times the officials of a persecuting civil government made an effort to assure apostasy by eliciting from the apostate some positive public action against his former religion, e.g. the eating of forbidden foods by Jews (cf 2 Mc 6–7; Jos BJ 2, 152) or, from Christians, acts of cult before images of the emperor and the pagan gods, accompanied by a curse against Christ himself (cf Pliny the Younger, *Epistulae*, 10.96, 5f). It is probably this curse against Christ which lies behind Heb's reference to 'crucifying the Son of God' and 'holding him up to contempt' in 6 (cf also 10:29). In the Roman administrative mind the reason for requiring these acts was the desire to have an external, legally valid proof of the suspect's abjuration of Christianity; cf Trajan, *apud* Pliny op cit, 10.97, 1. Pagan sacrifice with a curse of Christ was irreconcilable with Christianity, and the Romans knew it

c (ibid, 10:96:5). Heb is deeply concerned to prevent such apostasy, and uses strong language to attain this end. The result is rhetorically somewhat overdrawn, but this need not lead us to conclude that repentance is theologically and practically impossible for a man who freely repents of his apostasy. Inspiration and inerrancy meet the inten-

tion of the sacred author, and Heb's intention here is a **9** practical, pastoral, not a theological one. **4.** 'Enlightened' i.e. with a spiritual illumination which shines upon the elect (Rev 21:23; 22:5), and which comes through Christ (Lk 11:36; Jn 1:9; Eph 5:14) and the Gospel (2 Cor 4:4). In the DSS the just were 'sons of light', generations of truth 'springing from a fountain of light' (1QS 3:14–25; 1QM *passim*). 'Heavenly gift' is roughly equivalent to grace. **5.** The 'powers of the age to come' are the wonders produced by the Holy Spirit which announce the Messianic Age (2:4; Ac 2:11ff; Gal 3:5). The 'age to come' (*mellōn aiōn*) is the future Messianic Age of Judaic Messianism, which has become the heavenly *aiōn* or world already present spiritually in Heb (cf the 'heavenly gift' already tasted). **6.** 'Commit apostasy': RSV translates the sense accurately but there are untranslatable nuances. The verb *parapiptein* means 'to fall outside' and in Gr. usage has a noticeable connotation of failure. The rhetorical contrast in 4–6 is well made—the evocation of the joy and enthusiasm and realized hopes of the Christian, followed by the dark failure of the apostate. **7–8.** The contrast illustrated by a similitude. **9–12.** Now that the readers have been presented with the sorry lot of the apostate, they are given assurance of the author's confidence in them on the basis of what they have already done, with hope for perseverance into a brighter future. **13–20.** God's unfailing promise gives the firmest grounds for Christian hope. **18.** The 'two unchangeable things' are God's promise and the oath by which he has sworn. **19–20.** What is behind the 'curtain' or 'veil' is the inner sanctuary which is heaven (9:24ff); the image is based on that of the curtain which divided the Holy from the innermost Holy of Holies in the Temple of Jerusalem (9:3). The anchor of faith keeps the Christian moored to his goal, the heavenly sanctuary into which Jesus has gone before (4:14–16). Now that the author has finished bringing his readers to an earnest frame of mind, he is ready to take up his more arduous doctrine.

7:1–28 Jesus, High Priest after the Order of 93 Melchizedek—The purpose is to show the sublimity and transcendence of Christ's priesthood. The method used is a combination of rabbinic exegesis and Christian typology. In the first part (7:1–10) the priesthood of Melchizedek is shown to be superior to that of the Levitical priesthood by a double argument *a fortiori*: he who receives a tithe is greater than he who pays it, and he who blesses is greater than he who is blessed; but the Levitical priests, greater than their fellow Israelites because they received tithes from them, themselves paid tithes to Melchizedek implicitly in their ancestor Abraham and were blessed implicitly by Melchizedek in him; therefore, Melchizedek is greater than the Levites and, by implication, his priesthood greater than theirs. In the second part (7:11–28) Christ the High Priest is shown to be the antitype of Melchizedek, and theological conclusions are drawn. The basis of the typology is laid in v 3. **1–3.** The figure of Melchizedek, with only those traits drawn which will be useful for Heb's argument. The OT material is from Gn 14. **2.** 'King of righteousness' is the translation of the Heb. name Melchizedek (philologically, '*My king is righteousness*' is more probable). 'King of peace': 'peace' is Heb's translation of Salem, which, however, is really a place name. **3.** 'Without father or mother or genealogy': since Gn gives no genealogical data for Melchizedek and no indication of his death, Heb uses this as an argument *e silentio* to conclude (with Christ in mind) that he had an ancestry which was mysteriously supernatural and a life which did not end. 'Resembling the Son of God':

7a this phrase shows Heb's intention: Melchizedek is a type of the Son of God, and his priesthood a type of Christ's eternal priesthood. The spirit of all this is typically rabbinic, and to our way of thinking proves nothing. But the Christian typology of Heb is not really meant to give a rigorous proof of anything. The mysteries of Christianity are marvellously foreshadowed and illustrated by OT figures. **4 10.** Melchizedek, Abraham, and the Levites. We have given the sense and purpose of the passage above in introducing this section. **11—14.** The priesthood of Christ is not a continuation of that of Aaron and the Levites; it is of another order. Heb 'proves' this by pointing out: (1) that Christ is of the non-priestly tribe of Judah; (2) that his priesthood is not 'after the order of Aaron' but after that of Melchizedek. This change was necessary because of the imperfection of the old priesthood. The perfection of Christ's priesthood and its consequences will be shown in 8:1—10:18. **12** contains an important principle: priesthood and (covenant) law go together; when one changes, the other must change as well (cf 8:6—13; 9:15—18). **15—28.** More arguments **b** for the transcendence of Christ's priesthood. **17.** The old priesthood was based on heredity, but Christ's is based on life without end (exegesis of Ps 110 (109):4 and typology from 7:3). **18—22.** The old priesthood and covenant ('law') did not avail unto salvation, because the old covenant did not belong to the eternal, heavenly world of genuine spiritual efficacy (cf 13:20). In addition, the psalm v says God swore in declaring the Messiah priest, but since there is no mention of such an oath for the Levites (argument e silentio) only Jesus' priesthood (and covenant) are backed by the value of divine oath. **23—24.** For Heb, multiplicity and change are marks of imperfection, oneness and permanence, of perfection (cf 1:1f, 10—12; 10:1). The idea is Hellenistic. The old priests were many and they died; Christ is one and his priesthood remains forever. **25.** The salvation brought by Christ is not transitory but permanent (and therefore marked with perfection). The 'intercession' mentioned in this v should be understood in relation to Christ's appearance in the presence of God and its expiatory value (cf 9:24 and commentary). **26—27.** Christ's sanctity, heavenliness, permanence, compared with the sinful nature of the earthly high priests of the OT and the multiplicity (hence, imperfection) of their sacrifices. **28.** Summary.

8:1—9:28 Jesus, the Perfect High Priest—After a brief introduction (8:1f) a negative part (8:3—9:10) shows the failure of the old priesthood and covenant (the two being inseparable, 7:12), then a positive part (9:11—28), theologically rich and compact, shows the perfect priesthood of Christ. **1.** 'The point': really the main or principal point (kephalaion). **2.** The sanctuary and tent are the heavenly, true sanctuary, as will appear from what follows.

3—9:10 The Failure of the Old.

c 3—5 The Old Priesthood and Liturgy were Earthly—Christ would not be an earthly priest because there was no lack of earthly priests, who had a monopoly of earthly sacrifices ('something to offer'). The argument is logically specious, but, as always in Heb, it is not the logic of the argumentation but the point of the conclusion that counts. A sanctuary where sacrifice is valid must belong to the heavenly sphere, the realm of spiritual realities, but the priests of the Old Law served only a 'copy and shadow' of this sanctuary, not the authentic heavenly sanctuary. The old cultic order was not totally without value, but that value was only a shadow-value, derived from the plenitude of the celestial reality (cf 10:1 on the

idea of 'shadow'). The end of 8:5 cites the LXX of Ex 25: **937c** 40, which depicts God showing Moses the plan or pattern of the desert tabernacle on Sinai. Allegorizing texts of Philo in his Platonic tradition, with its doctrine of subsistent ideas (rather than in his Stoic tradition, where the notion of a temple of the soul comes into play) had envisaged the pattern of Moses' earthly sanctuary as an archetype in the sense-perceptible world. Jewish apocalyptic literature, on the other hand, had developed the notion of a heavenly temple corresponding somewhat materially to the earthly one (cf the traces of this in Rev 11:19; 15:5f; 16:1). Heb draws from the two currents to arrive at the notion of a sanctuary in the heavenly world of perfect value, from which the earthly one derives its shadow-value.

6—13 The Old Covenant is Replaced by a New One—In keeping with the principle enunciated in 7:12, covenant and priesthood go together; when one is changed the other must change also. The nature of this new covenant and of the 'better promises' underlying it is shown by the quotation of Jer 31:30—33 (LXX 38:31—34), the eschatological prophecy of a covenant whose norms will be in the very mind and heart of man rather than in an external law, and whose terms will be carried out by initiative which comes from willing, personal responsibility rather than from fearful, reluctant compliance. **7—8.** The deficiency of the old covenant is evident from the very need for a new one, but the formula introducing the quotation from Jer, 'he finds fault with them when he says', seems to lay the blame on the people subject to the old covenant. **13.** The power of the unfailing word of God is the ultimate basis for the passing of the old covenant. RSV obscures this nuance slightly. The sense of the Gr. is that by the very act of uttering the word 'new' (i.e. in the oracle of Jer: cf 8:8) God has made the first covenant obsolete.

9:1—10 The Old Sanctuary and its Liturgy— **938a** These vv, the end of the negative part of the section, have a double function: (1) to provide types for the heavenly sanctuary and liturgy of 9:11—28; (2) to prepare the contrast between the old order of salvation, with its sanctuary and liturgy, and the new transcendent and efficacious order. **1—5.** A description of the 'earthly sanctuary' of the old Covenant, i.e. the desert tabernacle, drawn from the LXX of Ex 25—26, with the golden urn and Aaron's rod from Ex 16:33; Nm 17:2—5. The most important detail is the division of the desert tabernacle into two tents: a first, outer one (the Holy Place) and a second, inner one (the Holy of Holies). The other details will not be important for Heb's exposition, as he states in v 5. **6—10.** The ritual of Yòm Kippùr, the Day of Atonement (Lv 16), is introduced, and the transitory, imperfect, earthly nature of the old liturgy is maintained. **6—7.** Ordinary priests entered the outer tent daily to see that the lamps were burning, to offer incense morning and evening, to change the bread of the presence weekly, but only on the Day of Atonement did the high priest— and he alone—enter the Holy of Holies to consummate the sacrifice of expiation for his own sins and those of the people. The continuity of the ordinary priests' activity bespeaks the imperfection of their functions (cf 7:23f), and this is the main reason for Heb's mentioning them. But the singularity of the liturgy of the Day of Atonement and the fact that it was performed by the high priest, with blood, for the sins of the people, provide types for the atoning work of Christ the High Priest in 9:11—28. **8—9a.** These prescriptions of the Law had a meaning not immediately evident from the OT. But only the Holy Spirit makes this meaning clear—an

938a important point for the theological basis of typology. Under the Old Law with its earthly liturgy access to the sanctuary was closed to the people at large; in 10:19 we shall learn that as a result of Christ's heavenly liturgy of the new covenant all of us have access to the heavenly sanctuary, the place of eternal (heavenly) salvation (cf 5:9). Yet the translation of RSV and CV ('the way into the sanctuary was not yet open') is not a faithful rendering of the Gr. here. Heb says it was not yet 'manifested' (*pephanerōsthai*): the way into the new, celestial sanctuary needed not only to be opened by Christ but to be manifested by Christ, for even when it is opened we still need to have it made known to us in the completion of revelation brought by the Son (cf 1:1f). Unlike the earthly 'copy', the heavenly sanctuary is not divided into two parts, and *ta hagia* in 9:8, 12, 24f—perhaps because of 10:19—refers to the sanctuary as a whole, rather than to the outer 'Holy Place' as in 9:2. RSV's 'as long as the outer tent is still standing' is not exact here. The *prōtē skēnē* is, to be sure, the 'outer tent' in 9:2, 6, but here *skēnē* is the whole tabernacle, and the *prōtē skēnē* is the 'first tabernacle', i.e. the earthly tabernacle of Mosaic institution (9:5), distinguished from the new, celestial sanctuary. This 'first tabernacle' is a symbol whose reference is to the 'present age', the age of earthly history, distinguished from the 'coming age' of Jewish eschatological writings, which for Heb is also the heavenly age, already here, but yet to arrive completely at the end of earthly life and ultimately at the end of earthly history. This eschatological age has another tabernacle or sanctuary—the heavenly one—into which Christ has already gone (9:11—14, 23—27), but toward which the Christian people must still be tending (10:19—25) until the *parousia* (9:28; 10:25). **9b—10.** 'According to this' (this symbol? this tabernacle? either is possible in the Gr. text; CV avoids the dilemma with its '*inasmuch as*')—i.e. according to the old order of salvation symbolized by the desert tabernacle—gifts and sacrifices were offered which had no effect on the innermost man. The dispositions of the old covenant, typified by those having to do with food and drink and washings which stopped at the flesh, remained in a material order outside the realm of the spirit, but the new covenant will penetrate the depths of man (cf 8:10), and the liturgy of Christ will cleanse consciences (9:14). The '*critical moment*' (A. Nairne, commentary, ad loc.) of 'reformation' has arrived with Christ's saving actions, but the reformation will not be completed until the end of time.

b **11—28 The Perfect Priesthood and Liturgy of Christ**—The perfection of Christ's priesthood and liturgy is contrasted typologically with the imperfection of the old, and in a framework of typology and imagery drawn from the OT a theology of the saving work of Christ is propounded. The great barrier to the access of men to God is sin, and Heb uses details of the ritual of the Day of Atonement, in which the OT high priest worked toward a reconciliation between God and sinful people, to draw typological parallels with the 'heavenly liturgy' of Christ, i.e. his work of salvation (cf A. Cody, *Heavenly Sanctuary and Liturgy in the Epistle to the Hebrews*, 1960, 168—202). The three divisions correspond to those of the negative part (8:2—9:10), but in inverse order: sanctuary and liturgy (11—14), covenant (15—23), the heavenly-earthly polarity (24—28).

11—14 Christ the High Priest Enters the Heavenly Sanctuary—In the old Day of Atonement the high priest would slaughter the victim outside the sanctuary, then take its blood and enter the Holy of Holies to sprinkle the propitiatory to bring about a reconciliation between God and the people (Lv 16:3, 5—11, 15f). Christ, the high **93** priest of the new covenant and its order of salvation, was himself killed as victim on earth, then in his Ascension he entered the heavenly sanctuary, the heavenly world, as priest, to bring about a reconciliation which was totally efficacious. **11.** 'The good things that have come': the numerical majority of the MSS read *mellontōn*, 'to come'; others read *genomenōn*, 'that have come'. The MSS which read *genomenōn* include the two most ancient MSS containing Heb (P⁴⁶, B), and a number of Gr. codices and ancient versions noteworthy for their relative independence. The reading *mellontōn* is most probably a harmonization of this v with the 'good things to come' of 10:1, where the temporal aspect is that of the OT, when the good things were yet to come. In 9:11ff the time element is that of the new age, and the good things have already come (we have already 'tasted the powers of the age to come', 6:5). So the evidence favours 'that have come'. What is the 'greater and more perfect tent not made with hands'? Opinion varies. Some see **c** a reference to the upper cosmic heavens through which Christ passed, but the Hellenistic texts which provide partial parallels seem to indicate that the upper cosmic heavens *were* considered 'made with hands' and of 'this creation'. Some recall Ac 7:48; 17:24, which refer, however, not to the upper cosmic heavens but to the heaven which is God's dwelling place. Others see a reference to the body of Christ or a symbol of his humanity, 'not of this creation' because of its subsistence in a divine person (cf Oecumenius, PG 119, 376), and the Gr. *dia* would then have its instrumental sense ('by means of') rather than—or along with—its local sense 'through'. This appears more plausible in the light of God's 'pitching his tent' among us in Jn 1:14 and of the texts relating Jesus and the Temple (Jn 2:19; Mk 14:58) or indicating the body of Christ as mysteriously divine and glorious even on this earth (cf Jn 1:14; 2:19, 21; Col 2:9). The reason for this puzzling phrase may be that if the old high priest went through a tabernacle (the whole desert sanctuary or the outer tent) to reach the Holy of Holies, Heb felt that the imagery should be carried over in his antitype and did so, charging it with a theological concept: the old high priest reached the place of God's presence through (*dia* in a local sense) the outer tent, a part of the sanctuary 'made with hands'; but Christ the new high priest entered heaven by means of, or with (*dia* now in an instrumental or modal sense), his glorified body, risen after three days and 'not made with hands' (Mk 14:58). It is because of the glorified mode of existence acquired by his body—indeed by his human nature—in the Resurrection that Christ has taken up his station at the right hand of the Father in heaven. **12.** The old high priest entered the Holy of Holies with the blood of animals, but Christ entered with the blood of his own human nature, united to the Godhead. (Blood here is a symbol required by the OT type. 10:10 makes the important observation that it is Christ's obedient *will* that has pleased God.) The old priests entered year after year, achieving a redemption that remained extrinsic (9:6f; 7:27), but Christ entered the heavenly sanctuary (rather than 'Holy Place'; cf supra on 9:8) once and for all, achieving an objective salvation which, when applied to individual men, cleanses consciences (v 14). It is 'eternal' because it belongs to the celestial, eternal sphere of perfect validity. It is most probable that Heb means the eternal redemption was found *in* the unified act of Our Lord's death, Ascension, and Session rather than before his Ascension; the Gr. aorist participle says nothing about time relative to a main verb. **13—14.** **d**

8d Argument *a fortiori*: if the old liturgy with only animal victims could achieve a reconciliation with God which affected the 'outer man', so much more will the effects of Christ's liturgy with himself as victim reach the 'inner man'. 'Eternal spirit' is certainly the correct reading, rather than the variant 'holy spirit', which is a scribal attempt to give a simpler reading for the more difficult original. 'Eternal spirit' is not the Third Person of the Trinity but a quasi-personal expression of divine power and sanctity, taking hold of Christ's human nature (cf L. Cerfaux, *Christ in the Theology of St Paul*, 1959, 294). This spirit is the divine principle behind Christ's saving work, the spirit which has raised the humanity of Christ to the plenitude of glory and in virtue of which Christ is priest 'not according to the law of a fleshly precept but according to the power of an indestructible life' (7:16). And it is this same 'eternal spirit' permeating the saving work of Christ which is the ultimate reason for that work's being able not only to cleanse the 'flesh' of men like the liturgy of the old 'fleshly' ordinances but to bring about that internal, spiritual renovation of conscience and newness of heart (8:10) which enable us to come to celestial glory, for what is 'fleshly' has limited, earthly value; what is 'spiritual' has the 'eternal', 'heavenly' value of perfection. An interesting parallel is 1QS 3:7, which says that it is by 'holy spirit' that a man 'can be cleansed from all his sins'; but the meaning of 'holy spirit' is not the same as Heb's 'eternal spirit', and in 1QS 4:21 it is the flesh that the 'holy spirit' will clean, while for Heb the great difference in the new cleansing is that it will clean not flesh but conscience. On 'dead works' cf 6:1.

939a **15—23 The New Covenant**—Christ is the mediator of the covenant built on 'better promises' than the old (8:6). In 9:11—14 the theological emphasis is on Christ's *transitus* to the heavenly realm and in 9:23—28 on his work after that *transitus*, but here it is on the importance of his death. **15—17.** The argument is this: a last will and testament (*diathēkē*) has no validity until the testator has died; but Christ, whose legacy is the New Covenant, has by his death made that covenant (*diathēkē*) valid. The argument depends on the double meaning of the Gr. *diathēkē*, which means both 'last will and testament' and 'covenant'. This double sense of *diathēkē* is used to show that the 'eternal covenant' is: (1) the new, 'eternal covenant' (13:20); (2) a legacy of Christ actually given to us as a result of his death. **18—21.** The use of blood in ratifying the old covenant provides a type for the need of blood in ratifying the new. **22.** The principle enunciated in Lv 17:11 on the use of blood in making atonement for sins is broadened to a general principle that without bloodshed there is no forgiveness of sins (there are rabbinic parallels). Heb never really uses OT or Jewish texts and institutions to prove *a priori* the necessity of this or that element of the Christian mysteries. Rather he uses them to show the fittingness of the new dispositions. The point he wishes to make here is simply that without Christ's death and glorification (cf 9:24—26 and 12:24 in context) we should not have had that total forgiveness of sins (9:14) now made available to us in the new covenant 'in his blood' (Lk 22:20). The argument is rhetorical, but the point is theological, and even the argument has a theological presupposition: the perfect realization of the old order's

b shadows in the new. **23.** A bridge-verse which carries forward the preceding notion of purification but attaches it to the idea of sacrifice in the sphere of heavenly realities which is to follow. The purification of 'heavenly things' has been explained in various ways. The two most common are: (1) that the v has in mind the victory of Christ over Satan and the powers of evil, whose realm was thought

to be somewhere in the sky (e.g. Héring, Michel); (2) **939b** that the dedication or inauguration of the heavenly sanctuary is meant (e.g. Riggenbach, Bonsirven, Spicq). Yet, 2:14 places the victory of Christ over Satan in direct relation with the death of Christ, while the present v is more of an introduction to the following vv on Christ in heaven than a conclusion to the death-and-covenant vv preceding; and the purification of the temple in 2 Mc 2:16, 18; 10:3, 5 was made in view of the previous profanation by pagan rites and was not sacrificial, while the sacrificial dedication pertained to the rebuilt altar rather than to the sanctuary and was not considered a purification (1 Mc 4:52—59). The Gr. expression *ta epourania*, 'the heavenly things', would seem to be related to the general celestial 'realities' (*ta pragmata*) of 10:1, of which the OT institutions were 'copies' (*hypodeigmata*), and the immediate sense is that of another *a fortiori* argument, made implicitly: if a purification had to take place in the old earthly 'shadow' arrangements, so all the more should a purification take place in the heavenly sphere (*ta epourania*), where the effects would have the value of perfection. But the mention of 'sacrifices' and the fact that this v is a structural parallel to 8:5, where the 'copy' (*hypodeigma*) is a copy of the heavenly sanctuary, indicates that the completion of the ritual of atonement in the heavenly sanctuary is already in the author's mind as he approaches the following vv. In the OT the sanctuary was the focal point of the relations between God and Israel. If the people sinned, God abandoned the sanctuary (cf Ezek 10:18f; 11:22 with the rabbinic interpretation found in Midrash Rabba on Lam 2:8), but if the sanctuary was purified with the determined rite, the sins of the people were expiated objectively (Lv 16:16, 34), and God returned to the sanctuary (cf Ezek 43:2—5; 44:4). This is the background of the v and those which follow. It should not be forgotten that the imagery is improper metaphor: the fact to be expressed is not that heaven itself is purified but that our consciences are cleansed (9:14, 16; 10:2).

24—28 The High Priest Established in the Heavenly **c** **Sanctuary** The suffering and death of Christ correspond to the slaughter of the victim in the Day of Atonement ritual, his *transitus* to the heavenly world (9:11—14) corresponds to the passage of the high priest into the Holy of Holies, and now there remains the theology based typologically on the blood-sprinkling by the high priest when once he has arrived in the Holy of Holies. **24.** 'Made with hands': belonging to the earthly, created sphere of existence (cf 9:11). It was the blood-sprinkling by the high priest in the Holy of Holies which was the actual rite of expiation in the old ritual (Lv 16:14—16), and what preceded this rite was only a preparation for that climax. By analogy, the consummation of Christ's saving work has taken place in the heavenly Holy of Holies, i.e. at the term of his glorification in the heavenly world. Heb uses three images to express the work of Christ in the heavenly sanctuary: (1) the purification of the sanctuary on the Day of Atonement, which reconciles God and the people (9:23); (2) appearance in the presence of God (9:25f); (3) 'intercession' (7:25). The first expresses the result of his work——the 'eternal redemption of 9:12. The reality behind the second and the third is really only one, for later Jewish religion (Wis, Philo, Targums) had come to see expiatory activity in the OT (and particularly in the Day of Atonement ritual) as an 'intercession' (cf S. Lyonnet, 'Expiation et intercession: à propos d'une traduction de St Jérôme', Bib 40 (1959), 885—901). All three images are combined in 12:24, which mentions the 'sprinkled blood' of Jesus

939c in heaven, 'speaking more graciously than the blood of Abel'. The theological reality behind these images is that of the presence of the glorified humanity (once a suffering humanity) of Christ with God, and the value of that confrontation in reconciling God and the new people of a heavenly calling. **25—26.** A recapitulation of ideas expressed in 7:23f, 27; 9:12, 24. The saving actions of Christ need never be repeated, for they have eternal value. These actions make up an eschatological event that has *already* taken place at 'the end of the ages'; 28 will speak of an eschatological event *yet* to take place. **27- 28.** The moments of man's destiny: death and judgement of the individual man, Christ's single sacrifice of atonement for the sins of all after his first coming in the Incarnation, and his return for the final moment of destiny at the end of time. Without forcing or paraphrasing the simple 'without sin' of the Gr. in 28 we can perhaps best interpret the sense in the light of 1:8f (the justice and sinlessness of the Messianic, eschatological Son of God) and 7:26 (the sinlessness of Christ the High Priest). The phrase is an eschatological attribute of the heavenly high priest in his *parousia*. So CV's 'with no part in sin' is better than RSV's 'not to deal with sin'.

940a **10:1—18 Eschatological Fruits of Christ's Liturgy**—The material in this section has been handled in the two preceding ones. But the formal aspect here is that of the eschatological arrival of the good things of salvation foreshadowed by the Law. **1a.** The Law, i.e. the whole old order of salvation, was a 'shadow' of the good things to come. But the new order of salvation in Christ possesses the 'true form' (*eikōn*) of the celestial realities (*ta pragmata*) of which the old institutions and the old salvation were shadows. The Gr. word *eikōn* (RSV: 'true form'; CV: 'exact image') has a number of subtly varied meanings. It can mean 'copy' or 'model', but that meaning does not fit here, because the *eikōn* is contrasted with the OT shadows and copies. It can mean something like 'substance', but not in a purely Aristotelian sense. The meaning here is probably that of a form through which the nature or essence of a thing is made manifest so that it can be grasped by the senses, the intellect, or the spirit. The new order of salvation makes the eternal realities present to us in such a way that we can actually take hold of them and share in them in a mystical way. **1b—3.** It is because the old sacrifices were made in an order which did not have this *eikōn* by which celestial realities already cross over to the earthly sphere that those sacrifices could not perfect consciences like the celestial sacrifice by which Christ 'cleansed' the heavenly sanctuary—the focal point of relations between God and people in the sphere of real validity (9:14, 23—27). **4.** Cf 9:12—14. **5—10.** Ps 40 (39):7—9 is cited to illustrate the inability of the OT sacrifices to placate God, and to state that it is the obedient will of Christ which has pleased God and brought about the reconciliation between God and the people in Christ's sacrifice. It is by making and expressing this willingness that Christ has actually undone the old order and inaugurated the new. (On the effective power of the spoken word cf supra on 8:13.) **11—14.** Again, the multiplicity of futile actions is contrasted with the single, permanently effective action of Christ. Vv 12 and 13 add a new dimension to the texts of 9:23—28 (which were determined by the literary necessity of remaining consistently in the ritual metaphors): the heavenly high priest's 'presence' before God is that of the messianic, eschatological figure in 1:5—13, and the interval between the beginning of messianic eschatology with Christ's exaltation and the realization of that eschatology in his future second coming is characterized by the incomplete

subjection of the universe to his dominion (cf 2:8). **14. 94** Now that Christ is 'perfected' as priest (5:9), the 'sanctifier' has 'perfected' those 'who are sanctified' (cf supra on 2:10f). **15—18.** The new order is presented in terms of covenant. **18.** This maxim is made in the realm of objective redemption. The sacrifice of Christ has been made once and for all, and the forgiveness it achieved has been achieved once and for all. There is no more sacrifice to be made for sins. There remains only to apply the sacrifice of Christ to individual men through the sacramental order, from the time of Christ's death and exaltation until his *parousia*— 'proclaiming the Lord's death until he comes' (1 Cor 11:26).

19—39 Epilogue to the Third Part—This section is one of Heb's exhortations to fidelity and constancy, based on the doctrine he has presented.

19—25 Divine Acts and Christian Endeavour as b Grounds for Confidence—**19—20.** The 'sanctuary' is heaven, the focal point of union between God and man, and the goal of our pilgrimage toward salvation (12:22). The 'blood of Jesus' is a theological symbol for his saving work and its fruits (9:12, 22; 12:24). The 'curtain' is that which separated the Holy of Holies from the outer sanctuary (9:3); here, as in 6:19, it is a symbol of the barrier which separates heaven from what is without. The problem here is that of deciding whether the phrase 'that is, his flesh' explains 'curtain' or 'way'. The curtain is surely an image of a barrier rather than of an entrance, and if Christ's flesh is the curtain the allusion would then be to the Pauline opposition between flesh and spirit, so that the fleshly aspect of Christ would be something that had to be transcended before we could have access to heaven through his spiritual aspect. But it is far better to attach the phrase to 'way': it is precisely because he has taken on our flesh and blood that Christ has been enabled to become the way that leads his brethren into heaven (cf 2:14 with context; 9:11; Jn 14:6). **21.** The theme of 3:1—6. **22.** The readers can take confidence if they hold to their qualifications for drawing near to God: a sinless heart and fullness of faith. The expression 'our hearts sprinkled clean ... and our bodies washed with pure water' certainly refers to their baptism. Allusions to sprinkling, washing of flesh, pure water, and water of truth occur in connexion with the ritual ablutions of the Qumran sectaries (1QS 3:4, 9) and with the eschatological cleansing which God will perform at the end of the time of trial (1QS 4:21). There are essential differences between these cleansings and baptism. The Qumran ablutions of the flesh had to be united with a just and humble spirit (1QS 3:8f), but Heb's insistence on a cleansing of consciences in a transcendental order is absent (cf *supra* on 9:14 and DSS). Furthermore, the regular Qumran ablutions were repeated often, while Christian baptism is not (the Gr. perfect participles 'sprinkled' and 'washed' here in Heb denote a single action in the past, with enduring effects). But the similarities of terminology between Heb and the DSS (and there are others in this section) indicate that Heb is dependent on an early Christian catechesis which shares certain material elements with nonconformist Jewish thought. **23.** The themes of promise, hope, and entrance into heaven, which are found more fully developed in 6:13—20. **24—25.** Exhortation to a strong community sense. The author shares the expectation of an early return of Christ ('the Day') which was general in the primitive Church. In these vv (22—25) faith, hope, and charity appear under the eschatological sign of Christ's return.

26—31 Warning against Apostasy—The perspectives c

0c are those of 6:4—8, q.v. In this passage the completeness of the apostasy as a positive turning away from God is evident in more detail: it is done 'deliberately' and with full knowledge of the truth; those who turn away are positive 'adversaries' who have 'trampled upon the Son of God' and 'insulted the Spirit of grace'. For such men 'there no longer remains a sacrifice for sins' because the unique sacrifice of Christ has achieved an objective salvation which is already sufficient for the forgiveness of all sins (9:12, 26; 10:15—18); it is the apostate's own final, hard-hearted turning away from God which prohibits him from sharing in the fruits of that sacrifice, and if he will not share in the all-sufficiency of *that* sacrifice there is no sacrifice that can help him. **32—39.** Just as after the terrible warning of 6:4—8, the author reassures his readers of his confidence on the basis of the constancy they have already shown in the face of persecution, and again they are reminded of the promises of God as the best encouragement to the necessary endurance. On 'enlightened' in v 32, cf supra on 6:4.

FOURTH PART. 11:1—12:13: Faith and Endurance—When Heb writes about faith, it is regularly with a strongly eschatological outlook that he does so. So it is that in 10:22 we are urged to move onward in faith through all our trials toward the great moment of our definitive arrival in heaven and the presence of God. So too, here 11:1—40 deals with the faith of the OT patriarchs, with the reminder that faith is necessary for those who move onward to draw near to God (11:6); then 12:1—13 exhorts readers to the perseverance necessary to reach the goal of faith.

11:1—40 Faith—Examples of enduring faith are marshalled from the traditions of the patriarchs. The beginning and end of the section (11:1, 39f) put this patriarchal faith (and our faith) in the eschatological dimension specified by the beginning and end of another section (10:1, 15—18): the *values* of the OT look forward to something not yet attained, but in the NT age between Christ's first coming and his return in the Parousia those realities toward which the patriarchs looked in faith are already attained—though not yet perfectly on earth. The exegesis of the patriarchal traditions is midrashic in tone. Historical facts are reported and then contemplated in such a way that valid insights which transcend the historical details are placed upon them. It is not historically true, for example, that Rahab the harlot (11:31) was an example of faith in God's promises, but Heb sees the details of her action in this light. Our author may even be using elements of some Jewish midrash known to him, giving them a new Christian direction. **1.** Heb's definition of

1a faith. It is a descriptive definition, based on metaphor, and it is 'existential' rather than 'essential', i.e. it is concerned not with articles of faith which must be believed, with God as the formal object of faith, or with the components of intellect and will and grace which go into the making of an act of faith, but with the assurance which suffering, persecuted Christians have that faith is a guarantee of the unseen realities in which they hope, the celestial homeland which they are approaching (11:6, 14). Indeed the definition's existential approach here blends faith and hope into one another, but faith stands out as the basis of hope. 'The assurance (*hypostasis*) of things hoped for': *hypostasis* here has not the meaning 'substance, nature' it has in 1:3 but rather '(objective) assurance' or 'guarantee', a sense it often bears in the LXX and in various Hellenistic writers of NT times (Polybius, Diodorus Siculus, Josephus) as well as in Heb 3:14, where, however, the context specifies it differently. But to grasp the effect the word would have on the epistle's

941a readers we can turn to its use in the ordinary common speech of the Hellenistic world, where the papyri show it to indicate actually possessed landed property, or, more significantly for us, 'the whole body of documents bearing on the ownership of a person's property, deposited in the archives, and forming the evidence of ownership' (Grenfell and Hunt, cited in MMV, s.v.). For Heb's readers, then, whom we may presume to have been reasonably familiar with colloquial Hellenistic usage, the definition would have particular resonances: faith would be that by which they already had a title of possession to the things they hoped for (an idea theologically clarified by 6:5; 10:1), so that if they kept their faith they would have an unshakable assurance, based on God's own promise (10:36; 6:17—20), of those things when the term of their earthly trials arrived. 'The conviction (*elenchos*) of things not seen': *elenchos* here has its sense of 'proof'. The more subjective conviction of the individual believer derives, strictly speaking, from the objective 'proof' given by faith. For the true believer the 'things not seen' need no rational proof; his faith based on God's promise provides all the 'proof' he needs of the reality of those things (cf supra on 10:1 for the connotation of reality in the Gr. word *pragmata*, here translated 'things', there 'realities'). The 'things not seen' of 11:1 are the celestial 'realities' of 10:1, towards which the holy people of the OT looked but which are already shared by us on earth, though in an invisible way (faith as *hypostasis* in the sense suggested by the papyri; the *eikōn* of the realities in 10:1). Faith anchors us firmly in the things to which we have a title in the heavenly world (6:18—20) and gives us a firm conviction of that world's reality, proved despite its invisibility. **2.** An introduction to the examples of the OT heroes.

3—7 Faith before Abraham—**3.** Not an example of **b** the faith of a particular patriarch but of OT faith in what preceded historical times. In this ch faith is regularly directed: (1) towards the future; (2) towards things unseen. Here the temporal aspect is thrown backwards to the beginning of time, but the solid relation between the visible world and the invisible world, a relation sustained by God himself, remains in evidence. The 'word' of God is the dynamic, effective 'word' as in 1:3a, the word which made the visible cosmos and sustains it in being; but it is also the word of God's promise which assures us of our own solid relations with the invisible world—relations grounded on faith (11:1). **4.** An old Jewish tradition held Abel to be the 'father of the just', and a trace of this appears also in Mt 23.35. The blood of Abel 'speaking' is a midrashic interpretation of Gn 4:10 which will be carried further in Heb 12:24. **5.** In the mysterious seizure of Enoch by God without the intervention of death (Gn 5:24) Heb sees a relation between faith and the statement of the Gn text (LXX) that Enoch was pleasing to God. **6.** Enoch's example gives rise to the dictum that without faith there is no pleasing God. And since without pleasing God there is no 'drawing near' to him (personal salvation in Heb being envisaged as the arrival in the celestial presence of God toward which we make our way through earthly life, 4:16; 7:25; 10:22), faith is a requisite for salvation. If faith is treated from a more existential point of view in the definition of 11:1, here an 'essential' aspect appears: the fundamental object of faith, viz God's existence and just providence. Without at least a vague admission of these facts no one can arrive in the presence of God. A man without faith lacks what is absolutely necessary for reaching the presence of God, but it is only the man who has positively turned against God who merits 'the fury of fire' (10:27). **7.** In Heb's midrashic exegesis

941b Noah's obedient building of the ark was a 'condemnation of the world' ('world' being taken in the sense of mankind set against God), and it was also an act of faith which led to his justice in God's sight.

8—22 Faith from Abraham to Joseph—In Jewish tradition it was with Abraham that faith in the distant future was first given, along with hope founded in God's promise (cf Gn 12). In the same circle of Jewish traditions there were legends in which God rewarded Abraham's faith with visions of the future in this world and the next of (cf SB II, 525). Heb draws heavily on Abraham for his examples of OT faith. **8—10.** The faith and trust Abraham placed in God, leaving the Upper Mesopotamia he knew for an unknown land at God's bidding, 'not knowing where he was to go'. Abraham had never seen his goal, but he had God's word that it existed and that it would one day be his. Thus, he was a type of our pilgrimage toward heaven, a land unseen and unknown to us, but in whose existence we have grounds for confidence, with an assurance that one day it will be ours (6:13—20; 11:1). Abraham 'sojourned in the land of promise as in a foreign land', and we who already share in the promised gifts are like pilgrims in a foreign land as long as we are on earth. The allusion to Abraham's dwelling in tents is a symbol of the impermanence of this life, where 'we have no lasting city' (13:14), and just as Abraham 'looked forward to the city which has foundations', 'we seek the city which is to come' (ibid). **11—12.**

c Faith is seen as the reason for Sarah's conception of Isaac when she was past the age of child-bearing. Of course, this goes against the OT account of Sarah's attitude (Gn 18:12—15), but that makes no difference in Heb's midrashic interpretation; the OT material is being used to show the possibility of wonders resulting from faith in God's power. 'And him as good as dead' translates the idiomatically used *nenekrōmenos*, literally 'put to death'. In Hellenistic Gr., *nenekrōmenos* was used in the sense of 'worn out', 'impotent', especially of persons who no longer enjoyed the full use of their faculties. **13—16.** An interlude in which the author makes some general observations on the examples he has proposed. **13a.** The author begins with the phrase *kata pistin*, which RSV translates 'in faith', construing it as though it modified the verb 'died'. But for this sense Heb's style would probably use the dative *pistei*. *Kata* here has its sense of 'with respect to' or 'in relation to', and the phrase modifies not the actions of the patriarchs but the interpretation Heb gives in these 4 vv, i.e. 'with respect to faith' or 'in the light of faith' we see the holy men of the OT dying without receiving the promises but awaiting better ones, etc. 'Having seen it and greeted it from afar' seems to be an allusion to Moses who saw the promised land and greeted it from afar without ever entering it. **13b—14.** The patriarchs did not actually acknowledge that they were strangers and exiles on the earth (as distinguished from heaven), but Heb sees the wandering and exiled patriarchs as figures of our exile from the heavenly country (cf 16). **15.** Argument from the unreal to the real. The argument is not particularly relevant for us, and the conclusion in 16 is the important thing. The 'land from which they had gone out' is Mesopotamia (11:8). **16.** For the patriarchs' desiring a better, heavenly, country cf supra on 11:13b—14, and for God's 'not being ashamed' cf supra on 2:11b. The city God prepared is the heavenly city

d of 12:22—24. **17—22.** A return to personal examples, from Abraham to Joseph. A certain thematic unity is given by the elements of imminent death and of concern for the future with its posterity in each of these examples. **17—19.** Abraham's faith in the promises God had made

to him about a numerous posterity was so great that he **9** was undaunted even by the immediate prospect of losing his only son at God's bidding, for it was coupled, in Heb's exegesis, with a faith in God's wonder-working power by which he could raise the dead to life again. 'Hence, figuratively speaking, he did receive him back' (RSV); 'Hence he did receive him back, and this was a symbol' (RSV, Catholic edition): there was a Palestinian Jewish tradition that represented Isaac as actually having been killed and then brought back to life (SB III, 746). This is also Heb's viewpoint, and it helps to explain the use of the perfect in the opening clause of 17: 'Abraham offered up Isaac'. We question the RSV's translation 'figuratively speaking' for the phrase *en parabolē*. In Heb *parabolē* is a symbol or type or figure of another reality (cf 9:9 and *Epistle of Barnabas* 6:10). In the *Epistle of Barnabas* 7:3 Isaac is a type of the sacrifice of Christ on the Cross, and a bond between Isaac and the future also appears in 1 Clement 31. Something like this is doubtless what Heb has in mind here and we prefer the Catholic edition's 'as a symbol' i.e. as a symbol of the Resurrection (?). Cf also CV. **20.** Hope and futurity are mingled (10:1 with 11:1). **21.** Hope in God's promise of posterity remains the theme. 'The head of his staff': Heb follows LXX which depends upon a vocalization *matteh* ('staff') rather than (MT) *miṭṭāh* ('bed') in the Heb. text. *Matteh* is also capable of meaning 'tribe', and the double meaning lent itself to popular Jewish legends associating a patriarchal staff with Israelite posterity. Both the Vg's *adoravit fastigium virgae eius* and CV's 'bowed in worship *towards* the top of his staff' are mistranslations of the Gr. **22.** Allusions to the Exodus and to Joseph's provision for his mortal remains recall the movement of the Israelites toward the promised land, implicitly a type of Heb's favourite theme of our deliverance and movement toward the promised land of heaven.

23—31 Faith from Moses to Joshua—The element **9** of faith, historically speaking, is rather weak in the examples cited, but there was a general faith in the lives of Moses, his family, and the wandering Israelites, and Heb wishes to carry his examples as far as the approach to the promised land. **23.** Really an act of Moses' parents rather than of Moses himself. **24—26.** Examples of detachment from the pagan world and attachment to the community of believers, with constancy when tempted to accept the fleeting enjoyment of worldly comfort whose price would be apostasy. The lesson drawn from the examples is directed at the readers, faced with persecution. So, too, is the rather surprising statement that Moses 'considered abuse suffered for the Christ greater wealth than the treasures of Egypt'; the author is not reproducing historical sentiments of Moses but providing a figure to be imitated in the minds of persecuted Christians who might be tempted to prefer better relations with the imperial government to the abuse inflicted on them for their faith. Thus the 'reward' laid up for Moses is a type of the 'reward' proposed to the persecuted readers of the epistle in 10:35. **27.** RSV's 'he endured as seeing him who is invisible' is characteristic of all translations made so far. But recently W. Bauer in ConjNT 15 (1955), 28, has discovered that in hellenistic Gr. *kartereō* (in itself 'endure') + a participle is an idiomatic construction in which the action or state signified by the participle is that in respect of which someone is 'enduring' or 'continuing'. For this v Bauer suggests something like 'he had him who is invisible constantly before his eyes'. The reference is to faith's grasp on the unseen (11:1). **28—31.** These vv call for no comment other than that given before 11:1 and 11:23.

2a 32—40 Faith of Israel in General—The author breaks off his detailed series of particular actions and continues with a more general picture of the exploits and hardships of the Israelites from the time of the Judges onward. **32—33.** 'Conquered kingdoms': e.g. the Judges, David, Solomon. 'Stopped the mouths of lions': Samson (Jg 14:6), David (1 Sm 17:34—37), Daniel (Dn 6:22f; 1 Mc 2: 60). **34.** 'Quenched raging fire': the three young men in the fiery furnace (Dn 3:49f; 1 Mc 2:59). **35—36.** 'Women received their dead by resurrection': the son of the widow of Sarepta, restored to life through the intervention of Elijah (1 Kgs 17:17—24), the son of the Shunammite woman through Elisha (2 Kgs 4:32—37), and cf the words of the mother of the seven martyrs in 2 Mc 7:29. The next examples are quite general. **37—38.** Sawing in two is a torture and death not mentioned in the OT, but it is found in legends of the death of Isaiah preserved in BaTal and the apocrypha (pseudepigrapha). Who were the homeless wanderers clad in skins? Elijah and Elisha, David and Ezekiel, the Maccabees perhaps, or even Jewish sectaries (cf John the Baptist). **39—40.** Despite the heroic faith of the holy people of the OT, attested by God himself, their awaiting the promise was an eschatological awaiting. But now that 'these last days' (1:2) have arrived with Christ, the believers who persevered during the days of the old covenant have their hopes fulfilled along with Christians. The idea of solidarity in salvation returns here (cf supra on 2:10—11a): our perfection depends on the perfection of our Saviour, our sanctification on his sanctifying power, and our entrance into the heavenly sphere where salvation and the promises are realized depends on Christ's having opened the way before us (8:19f, 10,19f). The patriarchs, too, had to wait until Christ opened the way to heaven, and now they enter with Christians, sanctified by the same sanctifier, to take their place among the 'spirits of just men made perfect' in the heavenly Sion (12:23).

b 12:1—13 Endurance—After turning his gaze to the past to survey the OT figures of persevering faith, the author returns to the present to exhort his readers to perseverance in their own faith, no matter what hardship it costs. Christian existence in this world is likened to a school of endurance and toughening in hardship, in which the training and formation are divine.

1—3 Persevering Endurance in the Footsteps of Christ—1. The 'cloud of witnesses' is that made up of the OT witnesses to faith presented in ch 11. Their very multitude should encourage the perseverance of the man beset with trials. 'Weight, and sin which clings so closely' are images to be taken with that of the race to be run; sin and moral torpor are things which encumber and impede the Christian life, just as excess baggage and closely clinging clothes do the runner. **2.** 'Jesus, the pioneer and perfecter of our faith': cf supra on 2:10; 11:39—40. Jesus as 'pioneer' ('chief', 'leader'—not 'author' here) of our faith is one who himself provides an example of faith strong enough to enable him to endure the sufferings of his whole life, sufferings brought to a climax on the cross, knowing that the reward of divine exaltation awaited him afterwards in heaven (cf also 5:7—10). As such, he is an example—greater than the entire 'cloud' of OT examples—for Christians who suffer in this world but are assured in faith of the promised reward awaiting them in heaven (11:1, 13—16). 'Who for the joy that was set before him endured the cross': there are many commentators who by taking the preposition *anti* to mean 'instead of (the joy)' interpret this in the light of Phil 2:6f, so that Christ would be enduring the cross instead of the celestial joy he abandoned in becoming man, or instead of the 'joy' of

an earthly life without suffering. But, quite apart from **942b** the fact that neither the concept of Christ's celestial pre-existence as a 'joy' nor the idea of a possible earthly life free from suffering is found at all in primitive Christian thought, such an interpretation is made unlikely by the context in Heb, where the joy actually present in the author's mind is that of his exaltation after death. Rather should one take *anti* to mean not 'instead of' but 'for the sake of', just as it does a little farther on in 12:16, where Heb speaks of Esau, 'who sold his birthright for (*anti*) a single meal'. The more general context of this section requires this interpretation, too: Christ endured the Cross for the sake of exaltation afterwards in heaven as an example of our enduring our lesser crosses for the sake of salvation afterwards in heaven. And the verb *prokeimai* ('set before') is used normally in Gr. of offering rewards. **3.** The author's reasons for proposing the example of Christ are made clear: if Christ endured so much at the hands of his sinful adversaries, we ought to take heart from his example and remain firm in the face of our own adversaries.

4—13 Divine Training for the Contest—The author **c** continues to speak of Christian life and endeavour in terms of a contest or struggle. Like any athlete putting himself in shape for a contest or a period of hardship, the Christian must prepare himself by strenuous training and discipline, and the programme of training (*paideia*) is drawn up and given him by God. **4.** 'Sin' here is probably the sin of apostasy especially, but not necessarily to the exclusion of other sin. 'You have not yet resisted to the point of shedding your blood': it is difficult to determine whether the author is referring to actual history in which his readers have not yet had to shed their blood for the faith or is using a fixed expression from athletic terminology meaning something like 'you have not yet had the worst of it' or 'you have not yet put up a very good fight'. The latter alternative seems more likely. In either case it may be the sufferings of Christ on the Cross which led to the choice of the expression: the readers have not yet had to suffer that much. **5—6.** The exhortation is the word of God, i.e. Holy Scripture, in Prv 3:11f. God deals with us paternally, and the disciplined training he gives us is designed in love to help us grow to personal maturity. 'Discipline' here and in the following vv is the Gr. *paideia*, which expresses the whole process of education, training, discipline by which young people are helped to shape themselves in those qualities of mind and body which characterize the real adult, strong, sober, and able to cope with the problems that life will bring his way. The verbs 'discipline' (RSV) and 'correct' (CV) are *paideuō*, which expresses the giving of *paideia*. **7—8.** Brief exegetical orientation of the citation from Prv. Every father who admits his paternity sees to it that his son receives *paideia*, and so must it be with those who have God as their father. The training in which the readers 'all have participated' is the regimen of hardship into which they have entered. The very fact that they have these hardships should not be a source of discouragement but of consolation; it is a sign that they are under God's paternity. **9.** Argument *a fortiori*. If the readers respect their fleshly fathers for the training they give in preparation for life, so all the more should they respect God, their spiritual father, for giving them the trials they are undergoing; by submitting to the regimen of trials they will live, in the life of the spirit. **10.** Explanation of the preceding v. Earthly fathers give training that is good for the short space of life on earth (or, the Gr. could mean that the actual giving of *paideia* lasts only a short while), and they give it as they see fit; the results are not always satisfactory.

942c But God submits his children to just the training they need to reach the goal, which is a sharing in his holiness. If in the first clause *pros oligas hēmeras* does mean (in paraphrase) 'good for the space of life on earth', then we have a contrast with 'sharing in his holiness' in the sentence's chiastic structure. And if this is the case, the sharing in his holiness takes on an eschatological note, for it is something that is realized after this life, in heaven. **11.** *Paideia* is painful while it is being experienced (and so, by analogy, are the trials of the readers), but there is consolation in the thought that endurance of the hardships will lead to an enjoyment of the 'peaceful fruit of righteousness', the celestial tranquillity and security of the man who is disciplined. **12—13.** Conclusion of the exhortation to discipline and endurance. V 13 is somewhat difficult. The 'straight paths' are evidently an image of a well disciplined, well directed, and constant moral life (cf Prv 4:26 in the LXX), but does the verb *ektrepō* after 'what is lame' mean 'turn away, get out of line' with respect to the paths, or 'be dislocated' to balance with the following 'be healed'? Both meanings are attested for the verb, and it is hard to say what the author has in mind.

943a FIFTH PART. 12:14—13:19: Sanctity and Peace— This includes a number of suggestions and admonitions meant to help his readers along in that holiness of life which will bring them to that 'peaceful fruit of righteousness' he mentioned in 12:11.

14—17 Admonitions—14. The *leit-motiv* for the entire section. The Christian life consists in striving for peace with our fellow men on earth and for a share in God's own holiness (12:10). The eschatological overtones are included, too. Why should we be holy? That we may see the Lord. In that simple phrase all the longing of a Christian is found. **15.** But the road to God is not easy, and those who set out upon it must be urged to unremitting diligence on the way. 'Fail to obtain' (RSV; CV 'be wanting in') 'the grace of God': *hysterein apo* is an idiom meaning 'to be left out of something (here the grace of God) because of a negligently late arrival'; cf the parable of the Wise and Foolish Virgins (Mt 25:1—13). So the real sense implied here is that a Christian must not dally with distractions and diversions along the way. The elements of the phrase 'root of bitterness springing up' are in the LXX of Dt 29:18 (MT 29:17), where the context has to do with the presumption of the man who decides to 'walk' without God. It will be seen that both of the images in this v have been chosen because of the idea of walking along the way of life. 'Cause trouble' actually has a double subject in the Gr: (1) the man who is left out of God's grace, (2) the 'root of bitterness'. Both kinds of men, the dallier along the way and the man who thinks he is sufficient for himself without God, have evil effects on the whole community, for there is a question of bad example and of social responsibility involved. **16—17.** The use of Esau as an example of sexual immorality (the adjective *pornos*) and godlessness is less surprising when we remember that late Jewish literature, both Palestinian and Hellenistic, had built up a strong tradition of Esau's loose morals, out of midrashic and allegorical interpretation of certain phrases in Gn. It may be that Heb has in mind the relation of the Christian to God as father (12: 5—10, 23) and a certain depreciation of 'food' (13:9) in mentioning the exchange of paternal birthright for food as an example to be avoided. The continuation of the example of Esau—his rejection and failure to find a chance for repentance—has to be interpreted like 6:4—6. **b 18—24 Sinai and Sion—**The heavenly city, goal of the Christian's pilgrimage, at last appears in detail. At the

same time the contrast of the two covenants, two orders **94** of salvation, is made with the symbolism of two mountains—Sinai, the mountain where the old covenant was made, and Sion, the mountain of the heavenly Jerusalem. **18—21.** The making of the old covenant is evoked exclusively in images of fear and dread, drawn partly from the Pentateuchal accounts but embellished with elements which figure in the midrashic fashion of later tradition. The midrash aims precisely at expressing the significance of dread in the relations between God and man under the old covenant. **22.** The contrast found in the heavenly Sion begins. The imagery is apocalyptic and eschatological. Rabbinic Judaism made much of a restored Jerusalem, which was at the same time a 'Jerusalem of the coming age' and a 'Jerusalem above' (cf SB III, 532 and 573; Apoc 3:12; 5:11; 14:1; 21:2, 10; Gal 4:26). In Heb's perspectives this Jerusalem belongs to the heavenly world of valid spiritual realities (not a mountain that 'can be touched', 12:18) and of man's meeting with God. It is also the Jerusalem which belongs to the eschatological age which for the OT was the coming age, but which is now the Messianic age already ushered in by Christ. And again, in Heb's double perspective of the eschatological age as an age which is, and at the same time is yet to be, we have *already* come to the heavenly city, according to the v we are now examining, because we share already in the reality of the good things brought by Christ (10:1), but at the same time we are *still* on the way to the heavenly city 'which is to come' (13:14; cf also 10:19—25). **23.** The 'firstborn who are enrolled in heaven' are the elect in general, and we may surmise that the author has in mind both the first generation of Christians and the elect of the OT. The idea is drawn from that of the 'Book of Life' or 'Heavenly Book' in which the names of the just (and in some traditions those of the unjust as well) are written. That the 'firstborn' are a class of angels has been suggested, but the idea of angels registered in the heavenly book is unknown, and it is only in later Gnostic writings that angels are called 'firstborn' (for reasons having to do with Gnostic systems of divine emanation). 'Spirits of just men made perfect': the just men of the first generation of Christians, now gone to their heavenly rest, and those of the OT, for whom God has provided 'that apart from us they should not be made perfect' (11:40). **24.** The literary and theological climax of this eschatological scene. The first part of the scene evoked the covenant of Sinai; this second part has evoked the new covenant symbolized by the eschatological Sion, and Christ now appears as the mediator of the eschatological covenant (7:22; 8:6—13; 9:15—23). These previous texts dealing with Christ and covenant were set plainly in the context of Christ's heavenly liturgy, and the connexion reappears here, with the 'sprinkled blood speaking' before God,—i.e. in the symbolism drawn from the liturgy of the Day of Atonement—realizing the reconciliation between God and sinful people (cf *supra* on 9:23—24). This reconciliation and union through the blood of Christ (cf also Ac 20:28; Rm 5:9; Eph 1:7; 2:13; Col 1:20; 1 Pt 1:19; 1 Jn 1:7; Apoc 1:5; 5:9) is the consummation of that 'peace' and 'holiness' which Christians strive after as their goal (12:14).

25—29 Heaven and Earth—The perspectives remain **c** apocalyptic and eschatological. **25—26.** He who 'is speaking' now is God. He who 'spoke' or 'warned' is probably Moses, the spokesman of the old covenant. If those who refused the old covenant did not escape punishment, still less will those who refuse the new. The heaven at the end of 25 is the dwelling-place of God, but the heaven of 26 is the cosmic heaven with the sun and moon and stars, to be

43c caught up in the great cosmic upheaval at the end of world history, when Christ will appear in definitive judgement (9:27f). In the theophany of Sinai (12:18—21) only the earth was 'shaken'. **27.** When Heb writes 'this phrase indicates' he is introducing his exegesis (today we might be inclined to say rather 'transferred application') of the OT text he has just cited (cf 9:8). CV's translation of what follows: 'the removal of things which can be shaken—created things—' is accurate, and clearer than RSV's translation. The removal or destruction of the cosmic heaven and earth as they now exist, i.e. in the imperfect realm of the 'earthly', will have as one of its results the manifestation of the perdurability of those things which belong to the 'heavenly' realm of unchanging, eternally valid ('unshakable'), and perfect realities. **28—29.** A hortatory conclusion to what has immediately preceded. The earth was shaken at Sinai, both heaven and earth will be shaken at the end of time (12:26), but the transformation of movable, transitory things is already accomplished in the new and eternal order established by Christ, in which we are already receiving our unshakable kingdom. The Gr. *echōmen charin, di' hēs latreuōmen* is troublesome. Literally translated it reads '(receiving a kingdom that cannot be shaken) let us be grateful, *through which let us offer worship*'. Although the phrase *charin echein* regularly means 'to be grateful' (or, in Ac 2:47, followed by *pros*, 'to enjoy favour'), *charis* can also mean grace (a sense not unrelated to *charin echein pros* in Ac 2:47, where the favour, however, is human favour). Broadly speaking, commentators either (1) take *echōmen charin* to mean 'let us be grateful', and interpret the rest '*and by being grateful let us offer worship*'; or (2) take *echōmen charin* to mean 'let us have (i.e. acquire, take hold of) grace', continuing '*through which* (i.e. grace) *let us offer worship*'. The first alternative is not difficult to admit philologically, if *di' hēs* is understood as 'in circumstances of gratitude' or 'by means of gratitude', but the resulting sense would be rather strange. 'Because of gratitude' or 'out of gratitude', though, would require the accusative after *dia: di' hēn*. The second alternative runs into more serious difficulties with its interpretation of *echōmen charin*. If the phrase were to mean 'let us acquire' (or 'let us take hold of') 'grace' we should expect the subjunctive to be aorist rather than present. The present could express a nuance of holding fast to grace, but then both Gr. usage and Heb's particular style would require either the compound *katechein* (cf 10:23) or another verb, e.g. *kratein* (cf 4:14). It is probably as a way out of this difficulty that a scribe, or certain scribes, altered the subjunctive to an indicative: 'we have grace'—a reading given by certain Gr. MSS, followed by the Lat. versions, and reflected in CV. But Heb's style would indicate another solution. Heb is fond of putting to good use the variety of meaning which a word or phrase can have. We need but recall the very clear example of *diathēkē* meaning 'last will and testament' and *diathēkē* meaning 'covenant' in 9:15—18, or the complex significations of 'first tent' in 9:2, 6, 8—9*a*, or the double sense involved in *teleioun* in 5:9. Thus *charis* here, by that paronomasia or word-play dear to the more literary-minded ancients, can mean both 'gratitude' and 'grace', so that the sense would be: '*Therefore as we receive an unshakable kingdom let us be grateful, and through grace let us offer worship to God.*' But our share in the kingdom, though already given us, should not be taken lightly, for we can still lose it by turning away from God who speaks to us (12:25): our worship should be made in 'reverence and awe', for if we fall away we may know that 'God is a consuming fire' (cf 12:18).

13:1—6 Particulars of Christian Morality—1—2. **944a** Concrete practices of charity. A particular species of the more general charity is 'brotherly love', which is directed at those who are members of the Christian community (the 'brethren', often in the NT). Hospitality to strangers was especially important in the ancient world, because travellers were usually obliged to find lodging with families because of the lack of inns and hostelries. Examples of reception of angels can be found in Gn 18 and 19; Jg 13; Tb 12. **3.** Charity towards prisoners was all the more important for Christians in the Roman Empire because of the anti-Christian policies of the imperial administration. **4.** The 'immoral' are *pornoi*, the sexually immoral in general. **5—6.** That a man should be free from love of money (*aphilargyros*) and content with what he had was an ideal found among the Stoics, but also in OT wisdom (e.g. Prv 30:8) and rabbinic thought. NT parallels are Mt 6:34; Phil 4:6; 1 Tm 3:3 (also *aphilargyros*); 6:6; 1 Pt 5:7). The ideal in early Christianity had as its special motive a freedom from earthly cares so that the Christian might occupy himself better with the things of the coming heavenly world, and it was grounded in a trust in God's loving providence. Hence the two Scriptural citations insisting on this providence. The first is practically equivalent to Dt 31:6, but in the LXX text of Dt the verbs are spoken to God, in the third person; Heb's text is found verbatim in Philo—an indication that both were using a Gr. text differing slightly from our LXX. The second citation is Ps 118 (117):6.

7—19 Fidelity to Orthodox Teaching and Worship— **b** Exhortations made, no doubt, in view of the situation of the readers. **7.** 'Leaders' (CV 'superiors'): it is not clear just what classes of men were included among these *hēgoumenoi*, or what kinds of authority they exercised. In any event, they preached the authentic Gospel and provided examples of perseverance in faith until the end. CV misses the sense of the Gr. here by making two co-ordinated clauses with the verbs 'consider' and 'imitate' and by paraphrasing *ekbasis tēs anastrophēs* by 'how they ended their lives'. *Ekbasis* can mean the 'end' of physical life, but *anastrophe* has the nuance of a 'way of life' (cf *anastrephesthai*, 'to live' or 'to act' in 13:18), indicating that *ekbasis* here has its added connotation of 'outcome'. And the participle 'considering' in the Gr. text is subordinated to the imperative 'imitate'. RSV's 'consider the outcome of their life and imitate their faith' (i.e. the faith they showed throughout their life until the end when the outcome is weighed) is good. **8.** In this declaration the divinity of Christ resounds. From ch 2 onward the humanity of Christ has been uppermost in the thought of the author—sometimes a suffering humanity, sometimes a glorified one, always a humanity acting in the power of eternal spirit (9:14). But Jesus Christ who in the stages of his life, suffering, death, and glorification was subject to the changes of historical development and, ultimately, of glorification, is also Jesus Christ, the Son of God, timeless and unchanging, transcending the world of past, present, and future, in the sphere of eternal existence which belongs strictly speaking to God alone. What is the function of this affirmation in the immediate context? Faith (v 7) is based on the word of God, and the word of God in the new dispensation is brought by the Son of God (1:2), whose word enjoys the immutability of eternity; the varied and contradictory teachings of others (v 9) are not worthy of belief. **9—11.** Doctrine and worship which are not of Christ. **9.** 'Strange' **c** not in the sense of 'peculiar' or 'novel' but of 'foreign' (*xenai*), i.e. coming from outside authentic, orthodox Christianity. Genuine holiness and 'truth of heart' (10:22)

944c come from spiritual grace, not fleshly foods (9:9f). **10.** 'Those who serve the tent' are those who serve 'the first tent', the tabernacle of the desert, symbol of the old order of salvation (9:8—9a), hence, those who carried out liturgical functions according to the Mosaic Law. Such people are excluded from our altar, because in the primitive Christian catechesis which Heb presupposes, the altar of the Lord's Supper was the sign of unity in the Church; he who was excluded from the one was excluded from the other (cf Ign. Ant., *Ad Ephesios* 5:2; *Ad Magnesios* 7:2; *Ad Trallianos* 7:2; *Ad Philadelphenses* 4), in each of which unity with those having authority is also stressed, as in Heb 13:7, 17). Some commentators see an identification of this altar and the body of Christ on the cross, but it is doubtful whether Heb has this primarily in mind, if it has it in mind at all. Some, however, have carried this line of interpretation even further and made 'those who serve the tent' those who preside in the new Christian liturgy, so that the text would be a condemnation of the new liturgy in favour of the sufficiency of the cross and its sacrifice, without benefit of Christian liturgy (e.g. J. Behm in TWNT 2, 690; 3, 182f). The violence thereby done to the text is obvious, and most commentators have rightly rejected this view along with its polemic background. For more light on this verse cf infra on 13:15. **11.** The ritual of the Day of Atonement which figured so prominently in ch 9 is taken up again, this time with a new element needed for the typological contrast to be made with Christ's liturgy: the burning of the victims' bodies outside the Israelite camp (Lv 16:27). **12—16.** The genuine liturgy of Christ and our participation therein. **12.** 'In order to sanctify the people through his own blood': cf 9:11—14, 23—26; 12:24. Christ died on Calvary, at that time still outside the gates of Jerusalem (Jn 19:17, 20), somewhat as the OT expiatory victim's body was destroyed outside the encampment belonging to the Israelites. The reason for this somewhat artificial typological *rapprochement* is to be found in the exhortation which follows. **13.** The readers have already been told in vv 9—10 that sanctification is not to be had in the earthly liturgy of the OT but in the (liturgy of) grace, the heavenly liturgy of Christ's saving acts (9:11—28). The preceding vv have suggested the symbolic identification of the 'camp' with the religious world of Israel and its institutions. Now the readers are urged to unite themselves with Christ 'outside the camp', i.e. outside the religious world of Judaism, taking part in Christ's sacrifice, bearing the reproach he himself bore ('his abuse' rather than RSV's 'abuse for him'), and, implicitly, sharing in the fruits of that atoning liturgy, which, unlike the Mosaic liturgy, really cleanses consciences from the barrier of separation from God (9:14). The 'camp' is a symbol of the cohesive and exclusive religious world of Judaism, the 'altar' of v 10 of the no less cohesive and exclusive religion of Christianity. A man can find himself within the one or the other, but not in both. Heb seems to be giving a warning against some sort of Judaeo-Christian syncretism (cf 13:9). **14.** The earthly city in these vv is a composite of the two related symbols: (1) the earthly Jerusalem outside of which Christ was crucified; (2) the earthly camp of the Israelites, with its first, earthly, tabernacle and earthly liturgy which the people served under the old covenant, according to 13:10. It is not a lasting city, and it is not our city; we have left it with Christ. We 'strive for' (the meaning of *epizētein*) the eschatological city which is to come, and which, in keeping with Heb's double aspect of eschatological future and celestial present in one and the same reality, is also the celestial Jerusalem to which we have already come

(12:22). **15.** 'Sacrifice of praise' (*thysia aineseōs*) is **9** the way the LXX translates the Heb for 'sacrifice of thanksgiving'. The description of the sacrifice of thanksgiving in Lv 7:12—15 includes food offerings which fall to the lot of the priests. But Heb 13:10 has just said that those who carry out liturgical functions according to the Mosaic Law cannot eat of the altar of the Christian community, so this sacrifice of praise of which Heb is speaking is a new kind of sacrifice, in which the 'praise' is to be taken literally as the 'fruit of lips that acknowledge' (*homologounta*, i.e. 'publicly declaring praises to') 'his name'. We have a glimpse here of the sacrificial theology of the Apostolic Age. The expiatory sacrifice itself is the sacrifice of Christ (9:11—28; 10:8—17), who sanctifies the people with his own blood (13:12); this sacrifice has been made once and for all, never needing to be repeated because the forgiveness of sins it achieved is totally sufficient (10:18, with comm.). Christians living in the space of historical time between this historical sacrifice of Christ and his return at the end of time associate themselves personally with this sacrifice (13:13), but they have something of their own to bring to their celebration of this mystery: a liturgy of praise. Unlike the single and unique sacrifice of Christ, this liturgy of praise continues throughout the age of redemption (RSV 'continually', CV 'always') and is the same kind of liturgy as that of the angels and the elect in heaven: praise sung to the glory of God and the saving work of Christ (Rev 4:6—11; 5:6—14; 11:15—17; 14:1—5; 15:2—4; 19:1—8). But even this rôle of creatures in the sacrifice is carried out in power and virtue which come through the grace of Christ ('through him'; cf also 12:28). The historical sacrifice of Christ—his Passion and death, Ascension and Session—is all-important and all-sufficient; the liturgy of Christians is derived from it and made in its power, and the rôle proper to Christians in that liturgy is one of praise—'sacrifice' only in an extended sense. We have already seen (commentary on 13:10) that unity of altar went hand in hand with unity within the Church and unity with those having authority in the Church. But Heb says nothing of a priesthood other than Christ's high priesthood, whether an institutional priesthood or the general priesthood of 1 Pt 2:9; Rev 1:6; 5:10; 20:6. The DSS use the phrase 'sacrifice of lips' (1QS 9:4—6, 26; 10:5f, 8, 14; 1QH 11:5). But unlike Heb, for whom this 'sacrifice of praise, fruit of lips' is to be made in virtue of the power of a mediating Christ, the theology of Qumran admitted no mediator in *cultic* activity (cf 1QH 6:13). **16.** Sacrifice **b** in an even further extended sense. The two things the readers are urged not to forget are *eupoiia* ('doing-good') and *koinōnia* ('community sense, fellowship'—especially Christian fellowship—but here, as in 2 Cor 9:13, a generosity based on that sense of fellowship). Perhaps these terms refer to particular forms of beneficence in the early Church, but if so we do not know what they were. Already in both rabbinic and Hellenistic Judaism, and in pagan Stoicism, the material cultic concepts of the ancients were being sublimated to what was often a transfer into the moral order (cf H. Wenschkewitz, 'Die Spiritualisierung der Kultusbegriffe Tempel, Priester und Opfer im NT', *Angelos* 4 (1932), 70—230). We have an example of this trend here. **17.** For the 'leaders' or 'superiors' cf on 13:7. Heb urges obedience to them on the part of the subjects, but at the same time he calls attention to the cares and responsibilities of those in authority. **18.** The end of the last theme. The author seems to situate himself among the 'leaders' of the Church by asking his readers to pray for him and by alluding to the way he has been living, because the v forms a

45b structural 'inclusion' with 13:7, where the readers are urged to remember the leaders, with allusion to the leaders' way of life and its outcome. **19.** The sudden change from the majestic plural to the simple first person singular, the unaccustomedly terse style, and the sentiment itself (an insistence on that of v 18) suggest that this v was added to v 18 just as the epistle was being made ready for dispatch. Cf infra on vv 22—25.

20—25 Epilogue and Conclusion—20—21. The epilogue, in the form of a blessing terminated by a doxology. In v 20 we find the only explicit reference to the Resurrection of Our Lord in this epistle. The phrase 'in virtue of the blood of the eternal covenant' syntactically must modify 'bringing back from the dead'. The Gr. *en* (RSV 'by'; CV 'in virtue of') is probably the LXX's *en* representing a Heb *beth* of association (LXX examples followed by the word 'blood': Gn 9:4; Zech 9:11). The scope of such constructions is wide, and the association can be one of logic or intention, so that the action expressed by the main verb (here: bringing Christ back from the dead) is made in consideration of, or with a view toward, the object of *en* or the Hebrew *be* (here: the blood of the eternal covenant). Of the two LXX examples just cited, this is clearly the case in Zech 9:11; there are several examples in Heb (cf GK § 119*m—n*, p. 380). Here, then, the idea seems to be that God raised Christ from the dead, and this resurrection itself, whether actively or passively taken, is connected with, or occurred with a view toward, the actual establishment of the new and eternal covenant made with Christ's blood (9:15—22). For Heb the Resurrection, like the Ascension and Session, is an integral part of the sacrifice of Christ through which the new covenant was ratified (cf § 939c).

c **22—25.** Here, as in 13:19, the first person singular is used instead of the first person plural used throughout the epistle ('and what more shall I say' in 11:32 is a fixed expression not deriving from the author's own style). The **945c** body of Heb comes to a structural and logical conclusion with the doxology in 13:21. The style of these concluding vv is brief, terse, and concerned with minor matters. These observations suggest that the 'word of exhortation' which is the body of the epistle runs from 1:1 to 13:21, and that 13:19 and 13:22—25 were added as more personal afterthoughts just as the work was about to be dispatched to its addressees (cf A. Vanhoye, op cit, 220—2). **22.** 'Word of exhortation': the emphasis is on the exhortation, whether in a spoken discourse (Ac 13:15), in ordinary conversation, or in various kinds of written word. The verbal parallel with Ac 13:15 cannot be used to argue that our epistle was originally meant to be a sermon. The author asks his readers to bear with what he has written, adding rhetorically that he has written 'briefly', although, in fact, he knows that his missive is rather long. **23.** 'Timothy' is probably the companion and disciple of Paul. Such matters as the imprisonment and release of the leaders of the early Church must have been of great interest to Christians in general, faced with the same hard realities of faithful living. **24.** The greetings of epistolary **d** conclusion. The term 'saints' is one of many terms used of the early followers of Christ, not yet known generally as Christians. The distinction between Christians in general (the 'saints') and the leaders having authority in the Christian community is worth noting. 'Those who come from Italy': in Hellenistic Gr. *hoi apo* + the name of a place refers to birth and origin; hence, it can be applied here either to Italians in Italy or to Italians who have left Italy. The original readers would know very well who were meant, but we have no way of solving the ambiguity. **25.** The epistolary conclusion ends with a prayer for grace for the readers, just as at the end of all the epistles in the Pauline *corpus* except Rm. This little v is sublime in its very simplicity.

JAMES

BY K. CONDON C.M.

946a **Bibliography**—*Commentaries*: J. Chaine, 1927; M. Meinertz, BB 1932⁴; J. Charue, PCSB 1938; J. Michl, RNT 1953; T. Garcia ab Orbiso, Rome 1954; R. Leconte, BJ 1961²; P. De Ambroggi SacB 1949²; F. Mussner, Herder, 1964; J. B. Mayor, 1913; J. H. Ropes, ICC 1916; H. Windisch–H. Preisker, LHNT 1951³; M. Dibelius–H. Greeven, Meyer, 1959³; L. E. Elliott-Binns, (PC(2); Bo Reicke, AB 1964; B. S. Easton, IB 1957; J. Marty, Paris, 1935;
Other Literature: J. Cantinat, RF, 2, 559–76; J. Bonsirven, DBS 4, 1949, 783–95; A. Meyer, *Das Rätsel des Jak.*, BZNT 10 1930.

b **Literary Form**—The address to the 'twelve tribes in the Dispersion' (see on 1:1) puts the epistle in the category of the catholic or general epistles of the NT canon. But apart from 1:1 nothing indicates that this is meant to be a letter: there are no personal allusions (contrast St Paul), no reasons given why it is written, no epistolary conclusion. And yet the author of the opening verse was also the author of the rest (cf the word-play *rejoice-joy* in 1:1f). What follows is not a letter but a series of homely, practical sermonettes, very Jewish in character and inspired by Jewish wisdom literature. More accurately, one might speak of *proverb-sequences*, for the proverb—in the imperative mood, as used by a teacher to his disciples (see on 3:1)—is the basic literary unit. The didactic-proverbial sequences of Ben Sira and the logia sequences of the synoptic gospels form a parallel. Briefly, Jas is above all a Jewish-Christian *paraenesis*, or exhortation.

Argument—As in the synoptic gospels, James's proverb-instructions follow each other rather loosely, on the basis of association of ideas. Sometimes the proverbs are quite independent of the context (cf 3:18; 4:17; 5:12); sometimes they constitute loose sequences (1:2–18 on trials and temptations; 1:22–27 on doing as opposed to hearing; 3:13–17 on false as distinct from true wisdom; 4:1–10 on strifes and their cause; 4:13–16 on the deception of worldly interests; 5:1–6 on the unscrupulous rich; 5:7–11 on patient endurance; 5:13–20 final admonitions). The kernel of the epistle is in three longer, more self-contained passages, all bearing on *doing* rather than mere *hearing*: 2:1–13 on one's attitude to the poor and the rich; 2:14–26 on faith and works; 3:1–12 on the tongue's potency for evil.

c **Doctrine**—James's doctrine is conditioned by his theological approach which, because it is different from that of Paul, gives rise to a sharp polemic on faith and works. Whereas for Paul faith is a commitment to Christ consequent on acceptance of the kerygma of the Christ-event, for James, on the other hand, faith is the acceptance of a doctrine and the doing of it, viz (as allusions to the sayings of Jesus indicate) the precept of love as inculcated by Jesus himself. Whereas, therefore, for Paul the very notion of faith necessarily includes love and works of love, this is not so for James. In his insistence on *doing* rather than mere *hearing*, which presupposes a teacher's doctrine, James is more in the tradition of the wisdom of the OT or the sayings of Jesus in the Syn. gospels (cf Mt 7:21 = Lk 6:46) than in that of Paul. Again as in the *logia* of the Syn.

'so speak and so act as those who are to be judged under the law of liberty'. He therefore inculcates an 'eschatological' (rather than 'supernatural') outlook in respect of various aspects and circumstances of life: trials, poverty, works of love, sins of the tongue, etc (cf 1:12, 20f; 2:5, 13, 14–26; 3:1, 18; 4:9f, 11; 5:1ff, 7ff, 12, 14ff). His prevailing doctrine is that mere hearing or mere faith is not enough, that works of love must be done, if one is to be saved from judgement: 'judgement without mercy to him that shows no mercy, but mercy triumphs over judgement' (2:13; cf Mt 25:31–46. On the anointing of the sick see § 949a–c).

Jewish or Christian—The style, the outlook, the failings alluded to (e.g. ambition to be teachers, boasting in one's faith, frequent swearing), the phrases used (*synagoga, Abraham our father, the Lord of Sabaoth*)—all give a very Jewish character to this work. Conversely, the name of Jesus occurs only twice (1:1; 2:1). Whence the thesis (F. Spitta, A. Meyer) that James was originally a Jewish document, later made Christian by minor changes and interpolations. But the Christian features are so entwined in the woof of the epistle as to rule out an interpolation theory. Thus no other work of the NT has so many echoes of the Synoptic (especially Matthaean) tradition e.g. 2:5—Mt 5:3–5; 2:8–11—Mt 22:39f; 2:13—Mt 5:7; 2:15—Mt 25:35f; 3:12—Mt 7:16; 5:12—Mt 5:34ff). Other Christian features: 1:18 (*first-fruits*); 2:7 (*the noble name invoked upon you*); 2:14–26 (*faith and works*); 5:9 (*the parousia of the Lord*); 5:14 (*the elders of the Church*—not *synagogue*!); also 1:25; 2:8, 12 (*attitude to the law*. See *ad loc.*)

There are also striking verbal affinities with other Christian writings: with Rm and Gal, on faith and works; also 1 Pt (cf 1:6f; 2:11; 4:8; 5:5–9) as well as 1 Clement and the *Shepherd* of Hermas. These affinities (apart from the Pauline contact) probably mean no more than that all are drawing on a common fund of traditional material. But can James then be very early?

Author—In 1:1 he presents himself as 'James, the **d** slave of God and of the Lord Jesus Christ'. Three names have to be considered: (1) James the son of Zebedee, Apostle (Mk 1:19, 29; 3:17; 5:37; 10:35, 41), beheaded by Herod Agrippa in the early forties (Ac 12:2), who cannot therefore have been the author. (2) James the son of Alphaeus, also an Apostle (Mk 3:18; Ac 1:13*b*). (3) James 'the brother of the Lord' (Mk 6:3; 15:40?), who was granted to see the risen Christ (1 Cor 15:7) and was head of the Jerusalem community (Ac 12:17; 15:13; 21:18), a 'pillar' of the Church (Gal 2:9), later stoned by the high priest Ananus II (A.D. 62; cf Jos.Ant. 20, 9, 1). Our James must be identified with the last-named. Whether he is also to be identified with the son of Alphaeus, who was an apostle, is another matter. See § 664.

From Gal 1:19; 2:9, 12; Ac 15:13–29 we gather that, while James gave to Paul 'the right hand of friendship' and was not an extremist in the Jew-Gentile controversy, yet he himself as head of the Jerusalem church must have remained a strict observer of the Jewish ritual and was not a little feared by Paul (cf Rm 15:31; Gal 2:12). Turning to the epistle we find that—apart from the

6d Jew-Gentile controversy, of which there is no trace (see on 1:26f)—the style and themes fit well with what we know elsewhere of James.

Destination—Since the epistle is so Jewish, and no allusion is made to Gentiles or their failings, it is probable that the 'twelve tribes in the Dispersion' (1:1) means the Jewish Christian church. In view of the affinities between James and Mt (especially in respect to the 'poor' and the new Christian 'justice') the readers were probably communities in the Syro-Palestine area.

Canonicity—The epistle came late into the Canon. The earliest undoubted scriptural citation from it is from the 3rd cent., and the earliest writer to mention James, by name, as author, is Origen. Eusebius lists the book among the *antilegomena* (disputed books). But by 350 in the East, and by 370—80 in the West, all seven catholic epistles were accepted as Scripture. (Cf § 20 *a—b*).

e **Date and authenticity**—The date is variously assigned by critics: (a) before *Romans* and the Council of 49 (Meinertz, Kittel, Michaelis, Zahn); (b) after Rm, in late 50's or early 60's (Chaine, Bonsirven, Behm); (c) in the late first or early 2nd cent. (so most non-Catholic critics today). Pointers to an early or very early date are as follows: (a) the absence of the title 'brother of the Lord' in the inscription, not to be expected if the letter were pseudonymous; (b) a letter to Jewish-Christian communities would seem to presuppose a date prior to A.D. 70, when such communities still existed; (c) echoes of the Synoptic tradition, which is never formally cited, would point to a date when oral tradition had not yet been replaced by scriptural citation, (d) as in all early NT works, Parousia expectation is vivid. (So G. Kittel in ZNW 41, 1942, 71—105; cf also ZNW 43, 1950/51, 54—112).

On the other hand there are indications of a later date (c. 100 or later): (a) the late date at which the epistle was received into the canon; (b) complete absence of reference to Jewish laws of purity (contrast Gal 2:12 and see on 1:26f); (c) while the author says much about faith *versus* works, he does not touch at all on a much deeper issue in the early decades—the place of *works of the law* in the Christian economy. Moreover, the epistle shows the law of Judaism to have been supplanted by the law of the Christian gospel (Gutbrod, TWNT IV 1073—75; see on 1:25) and this points to a late date; (d) finally, apart from Semitisms, no letter of the NT is written in more cultured Gr. (To explain this many postulate that James was helped by an educated Hellenist.)

To conclude, the 'enigma of James' (Meyer) remains unsolved by the critics. The work is either very early or relatively late. A middle date (late 50's, early 60's) is difficult to maintain in view of 2:14—26, q.v. A late date and authorship within the Palestine region by a disciple writing in James's name cannot be ruled out on intrinsic grounds. (Against Kittel, cf K. Aland in TLZ, 1944, 97—104 and E. Lohse in ZNW 48, 1957, 1—22).

7a **1:1 The Greeting**—Following the simple Hellenistic pattern (cf Ac 23:26), James introduces himself as 'servant of God and (of) the Lord Jesus Christ'. In the Bible, God is the one absolute Lord and the one who serves him is his 'slave' (thus, frequently, the prophets, and Paul of himself and his fellow-workers). As well as humble service, the title also connotes an exalted office in the Church. The 'twelve tribes in the dispersion' means in the proper sense the Jewish race in exile, but here can only be a metaphor for the new Israel, the Church (cf Gal 6:16; 1 Cor 10:18; Phil 3:3; Apoc 7:4—8; 21:12), in this case the Jewish-Christian church (see above, § 946d). The

concluding '*hail*' (*chairein*, RSV 'greeting') gives the cue **947a** for the opening words (*chara*, 'joy' in v 2).

1:2—4 The blessing of trials—(The first proverb-sequence really extends from v 2 to v 18, the first half on trials from without, the second on temptations from within. But catch-word contexts induce several themes, which are here treated separately). Note the climax in v 3f and the striking parallels in Rm 5:3—5 and 1 Pt 1:6f. **2.** By 'trials' he means not open persecution but irking social circumstances; later he uses the same word of internal temptations (1:12ff). **3.** Trials serve to test or prove faith (i.e. confidence in God) and bring about, not patience in a passive sense but 'steadfastness', tinged with a certain heroism. **4.** Literally, 'let steadfastness achieve a perfect work', by which he probably means not perfection in the moral sense but that constancy and perfection which save one in judgement: *usque in finem* (Estius). It is this eschatological motivation which leads James to say (1:12) that these trials are crowned by *eternal* life.

5—8 Praying for wisdom—Linked with the preceding by the catch-word 'to be lacking'. **5.** Wisdom is a gift of God—not wisdom in the Gr. sense of man's capacity to attain truth by reason, but in the biblical sense of the insight given by God which enables one to judge rightly on the things of life (here 'trials'). For this wisdom one should ask of God 'who gives to all *without reserve and without cavil*' (cf Mt 7:11). **6.** But God's good will must be met on man's part by 'faith', i.e. in God's power and God's promises (cf 5:15; Mk 11:23f). Without it one is a 'waverer', like a billow '*storm tossed and driven back and forth*'. **7f.** '*A man of two minds*, unstable in all his ways' (i.e. torn between hope and fear of not being heard) *cannot hope to* receive anything from the Lord' (= God). The fault lies in his lack of faith, not in God's will (cf Eph 4:14).

9—12 The poor and the rich—A new antithesis, **b** tenuously linked with the foregoing. **9f.** The 'lowly brother' is a Christian (cf 1 Cor 1:26ff), the rich probably a non-Christian (see on 2:7). In the new era worldly priorities are reversed. **11.** Illustrates the point by a figure from the sun-baked lands of the East (cf Job 14:2; Ps 90 (89): 5f; Is 40:6f). James's attitude to the poor is very like that of certain circles in Judaism, for whom the poor, the oppressed, the lowly—but faithful—ones would be the first to experience God's saving help in the era to come (cf Enoch 94—105; 1QM XI, 9, 13; XIII, 14; 1QH V, 13—22). So too, Jesus pronounces a special blessing on the poor as a class (Mt 5:3—11 = Lk 6:21—23). **12.** A concluding *beatitude* on trials, reverting again to vv 2—4 and leading to the next section (13—18). The man who has stood the test of trial will obtain 'the crown of life which God has promised to those who love him'—*love* being the driving force. The figure 'crown of life' comes from the Greco-Roman games, in which the victor was crowned with a garland. Here 'life' is the eternal life of the 'kingdom which God has promised to those who love him' (2:5).

13—18 Temptations and their origin—From external trials he passes to internal temptations. **13.** The Jew, brought up in a strict monotheism which excluded all causality other than that of the one God, easily entertained the view that God was also the source of temptation and evil (cf Ex 4:21; 15:25b; 1 (3) Kgs 22:22f; Jdt 8:25). Whence 'God *is outside the reach of evil, neither does he himself tempt any one*'. **14.** Sin comes rather from within man himself, from his own evil desire (= the *yeser hara*' of the rabbis), which, it is implied, in its power to lure and captivate is like a wanton woman. **15.** '*Then desire conceives and breeds sin, and sin, when it*

947b *has reached its term, brings forth death*', i.e. eternal exclusion from fellowship with God. The figure of generation and birth illustrates the dread link between concupiscence, sin and death, but teaches nothing of the origin of concupiscence (cf Rm 5:12—14). **16f.** First admonishing them (in the style of the Stoic diatribe), James emphasizes the fatherly goodness of the unchanging God (cf Mt 7:11), in a v that reads as a hexameter and may have come from a lost Hellenistic-Jewish work. Every good gift and endowment is from God—therefore, *not evil*. All good 'comes down from the Father of lights'— probably an echo of the creation narrative of Gn 1 (God created the 'lights' of heaven; God saw that everything was 'good'; cf 1QS V, 17f; Apoc. Mos. 38). Therefore no evil, certainly no moral or demonic evil can come from him. But, unlike the heavenly bodies, there are in God *'no phases of change or lengthening shadows'*: the former would be (for instance) alternating day and night, light and darkness; the latter (literally, 'shadow due to turning') would refer to the respective shortening or lengthening of shadows as the orb approaches its zenith. (So Mussner. Technical and non-technical terms are juxtaposed— whence the textual variants). Again it follows that if God suffers no change he cannot be the source of evil (cf 1QS III, 15—17). **18.** A double contrast: unlike the working of sin through evil desire, and unlike the ever-moving heavenly bodies, 'of his own free will he *begot* us through the word of truth (i.e. the preached gospel; cf Eph 1:13; 1 Pt 1:23) so that we should be a kind of first fruits of his creatures'. Born anew through the gospel, Christians are the 'first-fruits' of a new creation which, it is implied, will ultimately extend to the whole cosmos.

c **19—27 On hearing and doing**—Coming to his main theme, James opens with an appeal, 'know my beloved brothers', then enunciates a rule for Christian life: 'be quick to hear, slow to speak, slow to anger', a frequent theme of wisdom (cf Prv 10:19; 14:29; 16:32). **20.** 'For the anger of man does not work the righteousness of God'. Whatever contravenes the law of love is incompatible with God's justice. **21f.** 'Therefore'—apparently ignoring v 20 and reverting to the 'be quick to hear' of 19—'put away all *filth and evil excess* and receive with meekness the implanted word which is able to save your souls' (i.e. from judgement). Whence *doing* rather than mere *hearing*; works of love rather than mere faith. **23f. An illustration.** A man observes his natural appearance (Vg. *vultum nativitatis*) in a mirror . . . then goes off and forgets how he looked—not having done what was necessary. **25.** On the other hand, to look into the law of liberty, taking stock and observing what one sees and *doing* it, is to be blessed. The 'perfect law of liberty' is the 'word of truth' (18), the '*implanted word*' (21), the 'word' (23)—i.e. the Christian gospel, called a 'law of liberty' (in contrast to that of Judaism) because of the freedom and power which accompany it (see on 2:8; 4:11f). For James, as for Jesus (Mt 5:17—19), the interior grace of the gospel perfects and fulfils the law of Moses. **26f.** The qualities of 'true piety', first negatively: a man cannot be truly religious 'while not bridling his tongue' (see on 3:1—12); then positively: true religion consists, firstly, in looking after orphans and widows (the biblical types of neediness) and, secondly, in keeping oneself unspotted from the world. *Thrēskeia*, piety or the fulfilling of one's duty towards God, would connote in Jewish ears above all the observance of ritual and cultic laws. James, following the teaching of the prophets and of Jesus (cf Mk 7:1—23), makes it clear that mere formal ritual observance is worthless; that

love of the neighbour and interior moral purity belong **94** to the essence of religion. (See § 452*dg*;) Hos 6:6; Is 1:11.

2:1—13 Against respect of persons—1. Faith in Jesus Christ, 'our Lord of glory' is incompatible with social snobbery. 'Our Lord of glory', as we translate it, would imply that as we believe in the *hidden* glory of Christ, so we must respect the hidden worth of the poor. **2f.** An illustration, the point of which is the *different* treatment of the rich man and the poor on entering the 'synagogue', which here means the 'congregation', not the place of congregation. At the time, Christians had their own assemblies, but not necessarily their own places of worship, like the synagogues of the Jews. **4.** By so doing they make wrongful discrimination and 'become judges *on the basis of evil considerations*'. **5f.** 'Has not God chosen those who are poor in the world to be rich in faith (see on v 1) and heirs of the kingdom which he has promised to those who love him' (i.e., in effect, eternal life; see on 1:12; also Mt 5:3; Lk 6:20). On the other hand, the rich '*tyrannize over*' them and 'drag' them before the courts. Since court administration was in the hands of the rich and powerful, the poor had no redress. (A similar situation in the prophets: cf Is 5:8ff; Am 6; also Enoch 92ff. But James also idealizes—see on 1:11). **7.** He adds a third note: the rich blaspheme 'the name'—of Christ—invoked upon his readers in baptism, by which they are Christians. The rich therefore would be unbelievers, probably Jews (so too in 4:13—5:6 and, possibly, in 2:2—3). **8f.** Thus to discriminate in favour of the rich (9) is to commit sin and be convicted by the law, the *law* being the 'royal law' of love of the neighbour (8) in so far as it epitomizes the law of Moses (cf Mk 12:31). **10.** Corroborates this statement by the rabbinic principle: 'whoever keeps the whole law but fails in one point has become guilty of all of it.' Since the 'law'— here the Mosaic legislation, especially the decalogue— represents the will of God, which is one, to transgress one precept is, in a sense, to transgress all. **11.** An illustration, based on the 6th and 5th Commandments. Why these two? And in this order? Probably because James has in mind the case he presented above (2:2ff). Wooing the rich would be a form of infidelity or adultery, while sins against the poor are a form of murder (so Mussner; see on 4:3). **12f.** On this verse see § 946*c* and cf Mt 25:31—46.

2:14—26. On Faith and Works—Both the subject and **94** the vivid polemic, in the manner of the Stoic diatribe, show this to be the kernel of the epistle. James's message is that one's faith in God must show itself in works of love to one's fellow-men. The former cannot exist without the latter; faith alone will not save one from judgement (14*b*). He then gives a graphic illustration, the point of which lies in the question 'What is the use?' (16), followed by the answer in **17**: faith without works is useless; dead. **18** is difficult. Indeed Dibelius calls it one of the most difficult passages in the NT. Objections from an opponent are a feature of the Stoic diatribe, cf Rm 3:1, 9, 9, 27, 31; 4:1; 6:1, 15; 7:7, 13; 9:14, 19 etc, but esp. 1 Cor 15:35 'But someone will say (*alla erei tis*). But who is 'someone' (in Jas 2:18) opposing? The 'But' (*alla*) would suggest an objection in support of faith without works. This however would seem to require a transposition in the succeeding sentence: '*You have works and I have faith*', the implication being that 'to one who does not work but trusts him who justifies the ungodly, his faith is reckoned as righteousness', Rm 4:5. To this James replies '*Show me your faith without works*' (an impossibility because it cannot exist), 'and I by my works will show you my faith'.

48a This makes good sense—on the apparent contradiction with Paul, see below—but the only textual support for this transposition of 'faith' and 'works' is the Old Latin: 'tu operam habes, ego fidem habeo', which is perhaps hardly enough to justify it. Another solution is possible. James, in v 18, introduces an independent witness, the 'man in the street' so to say, possibly a Gentile Christian, who corroborates James's argument thus: 'You have faith, you say, and I have works, but not as you suggest, without faith. Show me your faith, apart from works—which you cannot do—and I by my works will show you my faith'. James implicitly makes this argument his own by the fact that he introduced it at this point. It is as if he said 'Any ordinary man would argue "You say you have faith (but don't prove it because you cannot) while I have works, though not without faith. But let us put this to the test. Prove the reality of your faith without works and I will prove the reality of my faith by my works"'. One difficulty in this explanation appears to be the word 'But' (*alla*) in v 18. But the word *alla* can be taken to introduce a further argument reinforcing a previous one or a statement stronger than the preceding, e.g. 'They will put you out of the synagogues, *indeed* (*alla*) the hour is coming when whoever kills you . . .', Jn 16:2 (RSV), cf F.-M. Abel, *Grammaire du Grec Biblique*, 346. No solution, however, which retains the text as it stands appears to be fully satisfactory. **19.** Also ironic. Even the demons have a knowledge of God divorced from love 'and (they) shudder', i.e. before God's judgement (cf Mk 1:24; 5:7). **20—26.** Proves his thesis from Scripture, again to the conventional objector (*O homo inanis*). Only when Abraham offered his son (21) was the word of Gn 15:6 fulfilled (cf v 23), because it was only then that faith showed itself to be 'active along with his works and faith was completed by works' (22). Gn 15:6 actually refers to Abraham's faith in God's *promise* of a numerous posterity, which is also the way Paul understands it (Rm 4); in linking this text with the 'works' of Gn 22, James is following a later Jewish tradition (cf 1 Mc 2:52; Sir 44:20). **24.** The 'justice' credited to Abraham in Gn 15:6 only came into effect when his faith issued in the works of Gn 22, therefore 'you see that a man is justified by works and not by faith alone'. **25.** So too, by her carrying out the will of God and saving Joshua's messengers, Rahab was, in the eyes of later Jewish tradition, 'justified' before God (cf Jos 2:1ff; also Heb 11:31—her *faith!*) **26.** Concludes: like the body without the life-giving spirit, 'so faith apart from works is dead'.

Faith, works and justification, in James and in Paul—*Justice* and *justification*, *right* and *righteousness*, are legal terms. They imply a juridical relationship between man and God, both in the OT and in the NT, without at the same time excluding a relationship of grace. The covenant between God and man implies a mutual bond, mutual promises, mutual obligations. God is the supreme Judge, to whom man is beholden. When the supreme Judge (and Creator) 'justifies', he pronounces a verdict, declares a man 'right', while at the same time his creative word makes him 'right', *effects* justice within him. Hence justification involves on the part of God a declaratory verdict, and on the part of man a new state of being, a new 'justice' relative to the divine Judge. While **the justifying verdict** is yet to be pronounced definitively in final judgement (cf Jas 2:12), yet it **has its effect** in man here and now **in his present life and its activity**; and it is this present activity of man that **James has in mind**. God's justification reveals itself here and now in a man's works of love. Even if a man 'believes' in God, yet his faith is empty unless it is fulfilled in the good works which reveal his justice and must necessarily **948a** follow on faith.

Paul, on the other hand, is concerned with how a man becomes just before God, becomes the beneficiary of God's saving verdict, *in the first instance*. His Jewish opponents would hold that one must first observe the 'works *of the law*'. This meant that Gentiles who did not observe the law of Moses would be excluded from the salvation of Christ. Paul's repudiation of this Jewish legalism is the essential theme of Rm. For him, the sole basis, whereon man avails himself of the saving verdict pronounced by God in the death of Christ on the cross, is faith in Jesus Christ, without the works of the law (Rm 3:21f). But that this faith must issue in works of love, since faith for Paul involves a total commitment to Christ, is a no less essential tenet of the latter than it is of James (cf esp. Rm 2:6; Gal 5:6). There is no fundamental conflict between them.

Why then should an apparent conflict have arisen? Paul certainly had not read Jas when he was writing Rm and Gal. Almost equally certainly James had not read Rm or Gal. James's polemic is not against Paul, but against some misunderstanding of Paul. But how could James have misunderstood Paul, whom he knew and had met (Gal 1:19; 2:9)? Therefore, either the work is very early (before 49), or it is relatively late and by an author who is remote from the original controversy; see § 946e.

3:1 12 On Sins of the Tongue—Two points: (1) the **b** responsibility of teachers; he warns against the ambition to be teachers, 'knowing that we shall receive the severer judgement'. (2) The potency of the tongue for evil (3—12), introduced by the observation 'if anyone makes no mistakes in what he says he is a perfect man', (v 2; cf Sir 22:33ff). **3—5.** Like the bit in the horse's mouth (3) or the rudder that guides a big ship (4), 'so the tongue is a little member and boasts of great things. How great a forest is set ablaze by a small fire!' **6.** Following the catchword *fire*: '*So also is the tongue a fire! There it is, set among our members, the quintessence of wickedness, staining the whole body and setting ablaze the whole course of existence, with a flame breathed forth by hell!*' The text is uncertain and, as it stands, ungrammatical. '*World of iniquity*' is a sort of cliché, as though the tongue were itself an evil cosmos, pouring out its infection over the whole man, setting ablaze the whole '*wheel of life*'—another cliché, originally probably a term of Indian religious philosophy which passed into Gr. mystery cults and then, as a hackneyed term, into Judaism (cf 1QH XII, 5—8 on the 'divinely established cycle' and the 'parturition of time'). The tongue itself is set ablaze by *gehenna*, here apparently regarded as the abode of Satan, which is unusual. **7f.** Every 'kind' of animal (according to the popular four-fold classification) can be tamed by 'human kind', but not the tongue! **9f.** From the same mouth come forth both blessing and curse, an anomaly illustrated by three proverb examples (v 11f; cf Mt 7:16 par.)

3:13—18 On false and true wisdom—Wisdom reveals itself in the way one lives (see on 1:5), in meekness (13b) and peaceful relationship with one's fellow-men (14—18). It is unlikely that James is attacking Gnostic ideas when he contrasts wisdom that is 'not from above'—'earthly, sensual, devilish'—with God-given wisdom which is 'first pure, then peaceable, gentle, open to reason, full of mercy and good *works*, undivided, unfeigned'. **18.** A loosely appended proverb: 'the harvest of righteousness' (i.e. the reward which consists in God's justification in judgement) 'is sown in peace by *the peacemakers*'. *Peacemakers* probably means no more than

948b 'those who live peacefully'. (A similar eschatological outlook in Mt 5:9).

c 4:1—10 On strife and its causes—(Catch-word 'strife', 3:14, 16). **1.** 'Whence wars and struggles among you?' Does James envisage a real situation (e.g. lowly Christians in conflict with wealthy overlords)? Or does he by hyperbole seek to show the extremes to which greed and passion can lead? The latter seems more probable. On 'the passions that are at war in your members' cf 1 Pt 2:11. **2.** *'You covet but do not possess. You rage murderously and jealously but cannot get what you want. You fight and make war. The reason you do not possess is because you do not ask'. You murder* can be understood literally, if James does not envisage a real situation; otherwise one must understand it in the broad sense of hatred and mordant abuse (cf Mt 5:21f). The correction to *you crave* (*phthoneite* for *phoneuete*) is not justifiable. **4.** *'Adulterers!'* (RSV 'unfaithful creatures')—since love of the world entails infidelity to God—'do you not know that friendship with the world is enmity with God?' **5f.** Two difficulties: the first, a minor *crux interpretum*, is that the quotation in 5*b*, introduced as 'Scripture' in 5*a*, does not in fact occur in Scripture. But the words read as a hexameter and may have come from some lost florilegium based on Scripture. This may be what James quotes from as 'Scripture'. Second: which is the subject of 'yearns' in 5*b*, *God* or *the spirit*? The RSV presumes the former, the Vg the latter, which is preferable (cf Gn 2:7; 6:3; Eccl 12:7—of the inordinate, evil concupiscence of the human spirit). Translate: '*Do you think the Scripture speaks vainly* (when it says): "*with yearning does the spirit crave which he has made to dwell in us*"—*but he* (God) *gives the greater grace'*. **7—10.** A call to penance in the vibrant language of the prophets (cf Is 1:16f; Jl 1:8ff).

4:11—12 Again on detraction and judging—Cf 3:1—12. Here sins of the tongue are regarded as sins of pride which call for the penance of which he has spoken (vv 6—10). **11.** Detraction (not necessarily calumny) is an offence against *the law* (i.e. the law of love; see on 2:8). If one refuses to bow to God's will as set forth in the law, one becomes a 'judge' over the law. **12.** 'Now there is one lawgiver and judge . . . And who are you that you *become judge over* your neighbour?'

4:13—17 On the deception of worldly interests—A new subject. Cf *Come now!* both here and in 5:1, introducing in both cases examples of the love of the world condemned in 4:1. **14—17.** On the improvident plans of the rich, cf Lk 12:16ff.

949a 5:1—6 On the unscrupulous rich—describing in vivid terms the fate of the rich 'in the last days' (3). **2f.** Their riches have 'rotted'; their garments are 'moth-eaten'; the rust of their gold and silver 'will be for testimony against them'. Their present hoarding of wealth, which should have been distributed to the poor, will witness against them on the day of judgement. The 'rust' of accumulated treasure 'will eat their flesh like fire' (where he passes from a concrete to a half-figurative sense). Then the climax: '*you have piled up treasures in* (not 'for'; cf RSV) the last days', i.e. in spite of the urgency of forthcoming judgement with the 'coming' (*parousia*, v 7) of the Lord cf §§ 670—72. Here again the rich are godless and enemies of the Christian faith (cf 1:9f; 2:1—13), while the poor (cf 5:7) are the pious ones, like the *'anawim* in the OT and Judaism. **4—6.** Echoing many OT texts he castigates the luxury of the rich, who have fattened their hearts 'in a day of slaughter' (cf Jer 12:3), who 'have condemned and killed the righteous one and he does not resist'—a grim but factual picture of the exploitation of helpless poor masses by **949** unscrupulous rich in the ancient world. (It is improbable that the 'righteous one' alludes to Christ and 'the day of slaughter' to his crucifixion). Vv 5—6 show that the whole passage is an enlargement of v 3*b*: already broken are the 'last days', the 'day of slaughter'. Christians are living in the end-era, which has been inaugurated with the Christ-event and the consummation of which may be ushered in at any moment (see on v 8).

5:7—12 On patient endurance and on swearing—Turning from the rich, he comforts the suffering brethren. The coming judgement will bring a reversal of their lot. **7f.** They must wait patiently the 'coming of the Lord', just as the peasant looks forward to the grain harvest (June in Palestine), 'being patiently over it till it receives the early and the late rain' (the *early* in November, the *late* in late March or early April). In common with early Christendom (cf Mk 9:1; 13:30; Rm 13:11f; Phil 4:5; 1 Pt 4:7; Apoc 22:6f, 12, 20 et al) James looks to the consummation soon of the kingdom of God and the establishment of its justice through the coming of Christ in glory, which is 'at hand' (8). **9.** In view of this proximate coming of the Judge, 'do not *sigh* against one another'—even an inarticulate sigh is a judgement!—'so that you may not be judged'. The Judge is 'at the doors'! **10f.** As an example of patience he points to the 'prophets who spoke in the name of the Lord' (a concise definition of the essential function of a prophet), singling out Job (11), in whose case they have seen 'the outcome (lit, 'end') of the Lord', since, after many trials of faith which Job had to suffer, the Lord finally had pity on him and rewarded him, showing that he is 'compassionate and merciful'. Again here it is unlikely that the 'end of the Lord' refers to the patience of Jesus in death (cf v 6).

12. Quite unexpectedly and very emphatically James proceeds to warn against swearing, in a saying very similar to that of Mt 5:34—37. In both cases there is a polemic against the Jewish prevalence of swearing by God, or by substitutes for the name of God, and a Christian ideal is presented of a truthfulness such as would render oaths unnecessary. But, since such an ideal cannot be fully realized, oaths have always been permitted for adequate reasons.

5:13—20 On prayer, the anointing of the sick, the b confession of sins, the conversion of sinners—Counsels for various circumstances of life. **13.** If any one suffers, 'let him pray'; if one is in good spirits, 'let him sing praise'. **14f.** 'If any one is sick among you'—i.e. with bodily sickness, not sickness of the soul or sin, even if in the Jewish mind the former often was linked with the latter—'let him call for the elders of the Church . . .' 'Elders' (Gr., *presbyteroi*) is a word which, like 'senator', connotes dignity rather than mere age. In the Jewish world, towns and villages were ruled over by colleges of elders. So too, Paul appointed 'elders' to rule the churches which he had established in Asia (cf Ac 11:30; 14:23; 15:2, 4, 6, 22f; 16:4; see § 923). That it is the *elders*, and not any other group that is to be called, shows that the power of healing belongs to them *as* elders, that what we have here is not quite the same as the 'charismatic healings' of 1 Cor 12:9. [Note: It would follow that the elders had what we call the 'power of order'. This is confirmed by 1 Tm 4:14 ('the gift given you . . . *by the laying on of the hands of the presbyteral college*') and by the fact that the elders, and not the charismatics—whose function pertained solely to the proclamation of 'the word' (e.g. in 1 Cor 14)—must have presided over the eucharistic meal (cf 1 Cor 11:18ff).

9b Therefore, while our word 'priest' is derived from *presbyter*, and the proper Gr. word for priest, *hiereus*, is not used in the NT of those who officiated in the Christian cult, nevertheless sacerdotal functions are not excluded from the NT usage of the term 'elders'.] 'And let them pray over him'—*over* probably in a descriptive sense, not intercessory; in Mk 16:18 and in Origen's allusion to the rite there is mention of an imposition of hands. 'Anointing him with oil *of olives*': the prayer and the anointing go together as a single rite, more analogous to the Catholic conception of a sacrament than to the exorcistic rituals practised in the Jewish world. In these, too, olive oil (the universal healing medium of the ancient world) was used along with a prayer-formula or adjuration in order to remove sickness, or a 'spirit of sickness' (Lk 13:11). 'In the name of the Lord' (i.e., more probably, *of Christ*): in the NT the phrase means either *at the behest of* or *by the power of* (cf Lk 10:17; Mk 9:38f; Ac 3:16). Therefore, by the power of his invoked name—not by their own power. (Cf 15*b*: 'the Lord—the glorified *Kurios*—will raise him up'). **15.** First, a qualification: it must be a prayer of *faith*. Jesus, too, demanded faith as an essential condition before his miracles could take effect (cf Mk 5:34; 16:17f et al; also Jas 1:6). Then the effect: 'will save the sick man and the Lord will raise him up'—not *two* effects (a 'saving' of his soul and a restoration of his body), but one effect brought about by the double element of the rite, the outer prayer of the elders and the inner, hidden power of God. 'Saving' and 'raising up' would therefore mean the same thing. Elsewhere James uses the verb to 'save' of salvation from final judgement (1:21; 2:14; 4:12; 5:20), but in the present context he more probably means salvation from sickness and death (so frequently in the gospels), and this is confirmed by the second verb, to 'raise up', which, apart from final resurrection of which there cannot be question here, is regularly used of restoration to health and well-being. (The Vg *alleviabit* should read *allevabit*). **15b.** 'And if he has committed sins he will be forgiven'. As well as healing his sickness the sacrament can also heal his sins. By sins he means not merely daily faults (cf 3:2), but also grave offences; he also implies that sickness does not necessarily presuppose sin, as was commonly held by Jews. The anointing, therefore, is a sacrament of healing in a concrete sense, a healing of the whole man, both in body and in spirit.

c **Note on the 'sacrament of the sick'**—The background of James's healing ritual is the saving ministry of Jesus. The casting out of demons, the healing of the sick, as preludes to and signs of the spiritual healing of the remission of sins: these were the essential marks of the irruption of the kingdom of God with the ministry of Jesus (cf Mt 12:28 par). Similarly the Twelve, when sent on their mission, 'went out and preached that men should repent, and they cast out demons, and anointed with oil many that were sick and healed them' (Mk 6:12f). Later on, in the situation of the Church, there were charisms of healing (cf Mk 16:18; 1 Cor 12:9), and in the present text of James this power of healing is linked with the office of the elders. In the course of later history the motivation of the anointing of the sick underwent development. There is evidence that during the first seven centuries the primary object of the rite was the healing of the sick, as is still the case in the Greek Church. From the 10th cent. onwards, due largely to the systematic theology of the seven sacraments as signs of sanctifying grace, on the one hand greater emphasis was put on the spiritual effect of the unction, while on the other hand it came to be regarded more as an immediate preparation for death than as a saving medium against sickness. The Council of Trent **949c** defined that 'extreme unction' is a sacrament instituted by Christ and promulgated by James; that it confers grace, remits sins and comforts the sick; that its rite and use conform to the mind of James and therefore should not be changed; that the elders of the Church mentioned by James are priests ordained by a bishop. (DzS 1716—19).

Catholic exegetes are not at one in their interpretation of v 14f. Many understand both verbs in 15*a* ('save', 'raise up') to refer to bodily restoration (Belser, Bardenhewer, Chaine, Michl, Mussner). Others take one verb ('save'—De Ambroggi, Charue, d'Alès) or the other ('raise up'—Estius; cf Mussner) or both (Garcia ab Orbiso, Meinertz) to refer to the spiritual grace or comfort imparted to the soul by this sacrament. The above exposition follows the normal meaning of the biblical words. 'Will save' can only refer either to salvation of the body from death, or to salvation of the whole man from eschatological judgement. 'Spiritual salvation' in the sense of securing here and now the salvation of one's soul after death is not a meaning of *sōzō*; moreover such salvation can only be conceived of in the context of salvation from sin, and James only mentions sins hypothetically in 15*b*. Nor is *sōzō* used in the Bible of God's comforting grace, or of an 'increase of sanctifying grace'. 'Raise up', in the context, can only mean bodily restoration, although spiritual alleviation and comfort are not necessarily excluded (cf Estius, Mussner; also Vg *alleviabit*). It is a question, therefore, of the concrete healing of a sick man (not a dying man!). If later theology apportions the effects of this healing to both soul and body, and to the former in the first place, this can be explained as a normal theological development. That Trent was condemning contemporary errors rather than defining the meaning of James's words in their context is confirmed by the Liturgical Constitution of the 2nd Vatican Council, which ordains that 'extreme unction, which may also and more fittingly be called the *anointing of the sick*, is not a sacrament reserved for those who are at the point of death' (No. 73; contrast Dz 1698 and see also *Instr. ad exsec. const.de sac.lit., no 68*). The true sacrament of the dying is *viaticum*.

Further reading: H. Schlier, TWNT I 230f; A d'Alès, DBS III 262—71; T. Garcia ab Orbiso, VDom 31 (1953) 70—82; P. F. Palmer, ThS, 19 1958 309—44; C. Davis, CleR 18, 1958 726—46; K. Condon, Scr 11, 1959 33—42; LTK, 6 585—91; Poschmann, *Penance and the Anointing of the Sick*, 1964, 233—57.

16. 'Therefore confess . . .' Why *therefore*? Presumably **d** the sick man also made a confession of sins. Such mutual, public confession was highly esteemed by the Jews (cf Ac 19:18; 1 Jn 1:9; Didache 14:1) and still survives in the liturgical *Confiteor*. (One cannot conclude to the practice of sacramental confession). 'That you may be healed': *healed* probably in a total sense, i.e. extends to both body and spirit (cf 1 Cor 11:30). 'For the powered prayer of a righteous man *has great effect*'. **17f.** An example of such 'powered' prayer. The 'three and a half years' ($7 \times \frac{1}{2}$) follows a tradition different from that of 1 (3) Kgs 17:1; 18:1 (cf also Lk 4:25). **19f.** Final words: A Christian who brings back a fellow-Christian who has 'wandered from the truth (i.e. the right practice of Christian life) will save his soul from death (i.e. eternal death; cf 1:21) and will cover a multitude of sins'. Whose soul? and whose sins? Probably those of the person who has erred from the truth. Thus God can use others as instruments of his salvation (cf Rm 11:14; 1 Cor 9:22; 1 Tm 4:16*b*; Jude 23).

1 PETER

BY W. J. DALTON S.J.

950a Bibliography—*Commentaries*: (on 1 and 2 Pt except where otherwise stated.) C. Bigg, ICC 1901; W. Wrede, BB 1932[4]; A. Charue, PCSB 1938; H. Windisch—H. Preisker, LHNT 1951[3]; R. Leconte, BJ 1961[2]; K. H. Schelkle, TKNT 1961; J. Schneider, NTD 1961; Bo Reicke, AB 1964; J. Michl, RNT 1953; A. M. Hunter, IB 1957. F. J. Hort, 1 Pt 1898; E. G. Selwyn, 1 Pt 1947; F. W. Beare 1 Pt 1958[2].

Other Literature: O. Cullmann, *Peter, Disciple, Apostle, Martyr*, 1962[2]; F. L. Cross, *1 Peter, a Paschal Liturgy*, 1954; C. F. D. Moule, 'The Nature and Purpose of 1 Peter', NTS 3 (1956), 1—11; T. C. G. Thornton, '1 Peter, a Paschal Liturgy?' JTS 12 (1961), 14—26; K. Gschwind, *Die Niederfahrt Christi in die Unterwelt*, Münster, 1911; Bo Reicke, *The Disobedient Spirits and Christian Baptism*, Copenhagen, 1946; M. E. Boismard, 'Une Liturgie baptismale dans la Prima Petri' RB 63 (1956) 182—208; 64 (1957) 161—83; id, *Quatre hymnes baptismales dans la première Epître de Pierre*, 1961; W. J. Dalton, *Christ's Proclamation to the Spirits*, Rome, 1965.

b Literary Genre and Purpose—Up till modern times, it was taken for granted that 1 Pt was a letter. From the time of Harnack, however, it has been suggested that the epistolary beginning and end are additions, that the work was originally a sermon, or, more specifically, a baptismal homily (Perdelwitz, Bornemann). Support for these views was given by later scholars (Hauck, Windisch). Preisker, in the third edition of Windisch's commentary, carried the hypothesis further, maintaining that 1 Pt was originally a baptismal liturgy, in which baptism was conferred after 1:21. Cross agreed substantially with Preisker, suggesting that 1 Pt (apart from its later additions) was originally the part of the celebrant in the baptismal rite performed at the Easter vigil. General approval of this hypothesis was given by Beare, who makes much of the supposed break between 4:11 and 4:12. Meanwhile, Boismard investigated the possibility that 1 Pt, while not being a continuous baptismal liturgy, nevertheless contains substantial fragments of such a liturgy.

The hypothesis that 1 Pt is a baptismal homily or liturgy is not convincing. We know too little of the liturgy of the apostolic church to be able to find its traits here. For detailed criticism, cf the articles of Moule and Thornton. This is the verdict of Schelkle, p. 5. It seems more reasonable to take seriously the account which 1 Pt gives of itself in 1:1 and 5:12: that it is a letter of encouragement to Christians facing persecution. There is considerable internal evidence of its being a literary unit. In particular, the break in thought between 4:11 and 4:12 has been much exaggerated. On the other hand, while one would hesitate to go as far as Boismard in his reconstruction of liturgical fragments and hymns, it seems evident that precious elements of primitive Christian catechesis and possibly liturgy are woven into the text.

Content and Plan—1 Pt, despite the various topics **95** treated in its development, is essentially an exhortation in time of persecution. The note of suffering for Christ is sounded at the very beginning (1:6), repeated in the exhortation to slaves (2:18—25); the last section of the letter is devoted to preparing the readers for persecution, first by a calm discussion of the attitude to adopt (3:13—17), then by providing the doctrinal ground for this attitude (3:18—4:6), finally by bringing them to face the actual rigours and sufferings of persecution with courage and even joy (4:12—19). In this setting of persecution (5:1, 8—10), the letter ends with an exhortation to the Christian leaders, the younger men and to the general body of the faithful (5:1—11). The following plan may be suggested:

1:1—2: *Address and Greetings*. Announcement of three themes: A. The foreknowledge of God the Father. B. Sanctification by the Spirit. C. Obedience to Jesus Christ and sprinkling with his blood.

I. 1:3—2:10: *The Dignity of the Christian Vocation and its Responsibilities.*
    1. 1:3—25: The Christian vocation.
        A. 1:3—12: Salvation wrought by the Father, through the Son, revealed by the Spirit.
        B. 1:13—25: Exhortation to holiness.
    2. 2:1—10: Responsibilities of the Christian Vocation.
        A. 2:1—6: Exhortation: Put away malice, come to the living stone.
        B. 2:7—10: The new Christian priesthood. **d**
II. 2:11—3:12: *Duties of Christian Life.*
    1. 2:11—12: Conduct in the pagan world.
    2. 2:13—3:7: Traditional catechesis on various aspects of conduct.
    3. 3:8—12: Above all, charity, humility.
III. 3:13—5:11: *The Christian and Persecution.*
    1. 3:13—4:11: Persecution viewed in calm detachment.
        A. 3:13—17: Christian confidence in persecution.
        B. 3:18—4:6: Basis for this confidence.
        C. 4:7—11: Christian life in view of the parousia.
    2. 4:12—5:11: Persecution faced realistically.
        5:12—14: *Personal Note. Greetings.*

Author, Destination, Date, Place of Composition— **e** From the time of Irenaeus until comparatively recent times, there has been unanimous agreement among scholars that the author of 1 Pt was Peter the Apostle. This view is still held by the majority of modern Catholic commentators and by some non-Catholic scholars. However in modern times the view has arisen that a later writer used the name of Peter to present apostolic teaching to the persecuted churches of Asia Minor. The main objections to the Petrine authorship are: (1) The literary *genre* of the document, which is taken to be essentially a homily or liturgy (cf § 950b). (2) The persecutions alluded to in the letter, directed against the Christians as such (4:16), could not have

50e occurred before the time of Domitian or even Trajan. This, however, is by no means clear. Even though it can be admitted that the Christians suffered in pagan courts (3:13–17; 4:15–19) and were even punished on occasion merely for their adherence to this sect (4:16), it does not follow that the state itself had unleashed a general and systematic persecution of Christians. The situation can better be explained by the hostility and calumny of private citizens and the cooperation of prejudiced and conniving magistrates. (3) The style and content of the letter, it is alleged, cannot be attributed to Peter. The style reveals a mastery of the Gr. language impossible in a Galilean fisherman. The citations from the OT are regularly taken from the LXX. In addition the letter has many affinities with Pauline writings (particularly Rm and Eph) and with Jas. In reply to this difficulty, it can be urged that the text itself points to a solution. In 5:12, it is implied that Silvanus (Silas) is more than a mere copyist or messenger: he has cooperated actively in the composition of the letter. This solution, proposed by St Jerome, has had particular support in modern times from Selwyn (7–38). Silvanus cooperated in the apostolic work of Paul and was associated with him in the writing of 1 and 2 Thes. In addition, he belonged to the circle of the brethren at Jerusalem (Ac 15:22, 27, 32) where James became leader. While the activity of Silvanus may be offered as a solution to the difficulty raised above, it is very probable that much of the matter common to 1 Pt and other NT documents derives from the common fund of catechetical instruction developed in the primitive Church (cf Selwyn, 363–466). Further evidence for Petrine authorship is offered by the comparison of 1 Pt with the speeches attributed to Peter in Ac (cf Selwyn, 33–36).

f It must be admitted that the Silvanus hypothesis is not regarded as satisfactory by many modern scholars (cf Beare, 188–92). In his recent commentary, Schelkle leaves the question open (p. 15). It is important to note that the value of the letter as an inspired document does not depend upon Petrine authorship. Given the literary customs of the times, it is not necessary to suppose dishonesty or unworthy motives in pseudonymous literature (cf Schelkle's essay on 'Biblical Pseudepigraphy', 245–8).

The five provinces to which the letter was sent comprise the whole of Asia Minor N and W of the Taurus mountains. Scholars are divided in opinion about the composition of the Christian communities: some assume from the address ('exiles of the dispersion') and from the frequent citations of the OT that they were largely of Jewish origin; others find in 1:14, 2:9–10; 4:2–4 indications of pagan origin. It seems best to suppose that the communities contained converts from both the Jewish and pagan world. There is no indication that the writer of the letter was personally known to his readers.

There are indications of the letter's Petrine authorship. The fury of the Neronian persecution, in which Peter died, had not yet been unleashed (July, 64): note the difference in attitude towards the state and the emperor in Apoc and 1 Pt 2:13–17. On the other hand, Asia Minor had been evangelized, and Rm, Eph and Jas had been written. Hence we may set the composition of 1 Pt between 62 and 64.

g The 'Babylon' of 5:13 is almost certainly a reference to Rome (cf Apoc 14:8; 16:19; 17:5; 18:2, 10, 21). This is supported by the fact that Peter, Silvanus and Mark are found in this city at the same time. That Peter was in Rome and that here he suffered a martyr's death under Nero is solidly supported by literary evidence

from the end of the 1st cent. (cf Cullmann, pp. 71–123). **950g** This evidence is corroborated by the recent excavations beneath St Peter's basilica, cf J. Toynbee—J. W. Perkins, *The Shrine of St Peter*, 1956; M. Guarducci, *The Tomb of St Peter*, E.tr. 1960.

Canonicity—There has never been any doubt about the canonical standing of 1 Pt. It was cited liberally in the early Church from the time of Clement of Rome, and has been listed in every official account of the canon. The one exception is its omission from the Muratorian Fragment. This omission, given the abundant testimony of the second century to the canonical nature of the letter, is clearly accidental.

Doctrine—This letter is essentially a message of encouragement to those facing the rigours and perils of persecution. This encouragement takes the form, not merely of an explanation of the point and value of persecution (2:21–25; 3:13–4:6), but of an exposition of the dignity of the Christian vocation and of its fulfilment in daily life. Thus, although the Church is not mentioned by name, it provides the setting of the whole letter. With this in mind, we offer the following synthesis: Salvation begins with the call of God (1:2, 15), who is merciful (1:3), holy (1:15), Father (1:17), the faithful creator (4:19), judge (1:17; 2:23; 4:17), powerful (5:6), saviour (5:10). In keeping with this call, men are rescued from sin (1:18; 2:24; 3:18; 4:3) through his Son, who was 'destined before the foundation of the world' (1:20), whose Spirit inspired the prophets (1:11), the 'Lord' (2:3; 3:15).

Man's salvation, effected by the passion of Jesus **h** Christ (1:2, 19; 2:24; 3:18) and his resurrection (1:3; 3:18, 21, 22; 4:11; 5:10), is gained by entry into the Church through regeneration by obedience to Jesus Christ (1:2), through sanctification of the Spirit (1:2), by acceptance of the word of God (1:23), through baptism with its pledge of loyalty (3:21).

Thus the people of the new covenant is formed (1:2; cf Ex 24:8), the new spiritual temple with Christ as corner stone (2:4–8), 'a chosen race, a royal priesthood, a holy nation, God's own people' (2:9), offering God spiritual sacrifices (2:5), a chosen few, saved like Noah and his family, through water (3:20–21). The members of this new Israel are called 'Christians' (4:16), a universal brotherhood (5:9; cf 5:12), a flock united around Christ, their chief pastor (2:25; 5:4), under the visible guidance of their community leaders (5:1–3) and of Peter himself (1:1; 5:12).

The life must be one of holiness (1:15), of fraternal charity (1:22; 3:8–12; 4:8–11), obedience to all who have authority from God (2:13–3:7), avoidance of pagan vices (1:4; 2:1, 11; 3:16; 4:2–3, 15).

Suffering in imitation of Christ is an essential aspect of the Christian vocation (1:6; 2:19–21; 4:1; 5:9), a cause of blessing (1:7; 3:9, 14; 4:13). Thus the Christian should face persecution with confidence (3:14–17), even joy (4:13–14), knowing that Christ has won the victory by his passion and resurrection (3:18), a victory proclaimed to the powers of evil at work in the unbelieving world (3:19, 22; cf 5:8–9), shared by the Christian through baptism (3:21) and faith (5:9).

The sufferings of the moment are the beginning of judgement (4:17), involving the purification (1:7; 4:12), leading to the final glory (1:4–5, 7, 9; 3:9; 4:6, 13; 5:4, 10) of the faithful Christian; for the unbeliever a day of reckoning (2:7–8; 4:5, 17–18). This manifestation of the chief shepherd (5:4), this revelation of Jesus Christ (1:13) is at hand (1:5–6; 4:5, 7; 5:10).

951a **1:1—2 Address and Greetings**——The letter is addressed to 'the exiles of the Dispersion' in Pontus, etc. The Church is the new Diaspora: to Christians life on earth is an exile (1 Pt 1:17; 2 Cor 5:6); they are strangers (1 Pt 2:11; Heb 11:13); they seek a city to come (Heb 13:14; Phil 3:20; Col 3:1—4). Note the trinitarian reference and its development in 1:3—12 (see plan). Salvation begins with the initiative of the Father (cf Rm 8:29; 9:11; Eph 1:11). 'Sprinkling with his blood' introduces the theme of the Exodus as the type of Christian salvation: the people pledge obedience (Ex 19:5; 24:7), and are sprinkled with the blood of the covenant victim (Ex 24:8). This theme is developed in the Christian Law of Holiness (1:13—2:10).

3—12 Salvation wrought by the Father, through the Son, revealed by the Spirit——This section introduces a passage on the Christian vocation (1:3—25) and the first of the three great divisions of the letter, 1:3—2:10. **3.** The writer adapts the Jewish form of blessing (cf Ps 66(65):20; 2Mc 15:24). Christian salvation is the result of God's activity in giving us a new birth, entry into new divine life (cf Jn 1:13; 3:3; 1 Jn 2:29; 3:9; 4:7; Ti 3:5). This new birth is ascribed to 'the living and abiding word of God' in 1 Pt 1:23—25 (cf Jas 1:18). In 1:3 the writer may be thinking of baptism, but more probably he is referring to the whole process of entry into the new divine life. He strikes the note of 'living hope' which dominates the letter (1:13, 21; 3:15). Re-**b** birth comes 'through the resurrection of Jesus Christ from the dead' (cf 1:21; 3:18, 21). **4.** Christian salvation is also an inheritance. The inheritance promised to Abraham and the people of Israel was the land of Canaan, but the Christian inheritance is the Kingdom of God (cf Mt 25:34), fully realized only in the life to come. Unlike an earthly inheritance, this cannot be devastated by enemies or defiled by the sins of the people. **5.** Salvation can be regarded as a present possession (Ti 3:4—5), or as a coming eschatological reality as here (cf Col 3:1—4; Phil 3:20; 1 Jn 3:2; Rm 8:18; 1 Pt 1:20). **6—7.** The theme of rejoicing linked with that of suffering trial and purification by fire is echoed at the end of the letter in 4:12—13. This 'inclusion' seems to indicate the literary unity of the letter. Joy in suffering is the Christian's share of the mystery of the passion and resurrection of Christ (cf Mt 5:11—12; Lk 6:22—23; Rm 5:3—4; 2 Cor 6:8—10; Jas 1:2—3, 12).

8. This v seems to indicate that the writer *had* seen Christ (cf Jn 20:29; 1 Jn 1:3). **9.** Faith and love lead to vision (cf 1 Cor 13:12). The translation, 'salvation of your souls', is misleading. As usual in the NT, 'soul' indicates the whole person, not just the incorporeal element in man; just as 'flesh' indicates not simply the physical body but the whole man in his weaker aspect, especially as subject to sin and death.

10—12. Early Christian catechesis insisted on the role of the OT prophets in announcing the mysteries of the Christian faith (cf Ac 3:18; 7:52; Mt 13:17; Lk 10:24; 24:26—27; Heb 11:13, 39—40). Even the angels did not receive this divine revelation (cf Heb 2:16): to them the mystery of Christ is revealed in the Church (cf Eph 3:10). 'The Spirit of Christ' in 1:11 is more probably the Holy Spirit (cf 1:12) than the pre-existing Christ (cf 1 Cor 10:4). The OT formula, 'the spirit of the Lord', is thus applied to Christ. For the role of the Holy Spirit in the prophecy of the OT, cf 2 Pt 1:21.

c **13—25 Exhortation to Holiness**——The living hope of the Christian demands from him a new way of life, a holiness showing itself in obedience (1:14), fear of God

(1:17) and sincere love of the brethren (1:22). Such **951** a life is based on the holiness of God himself (1:15—16), on reverence for him as Father (1:17), on the redemption wrought by the blood of Christ (1:18—19), on the re-birth effected by acceptance of the gospel preaching (1:23—25). In this passage, the theme of the Exodus is applied. Like the Israelites at the Passover (Ex 12:11), the Christians gird their loins, leave their former ignorance and promise obedience to the word of God (Ex 19:5—8), to the Law of Holiness (Lev 11:44; 19:2; 20:7). Like the Israelites they are ransomed not by silver and gold (cf Is 52:3) but by the blood of the Paschal victim (Ex 12:22—23; 15:13). **18—19.** The central thought is liberation from captivity rather than that of payment of a price (cf Ex 6:6; Neh 1:10). Christ is the true paschal lamb (cf Jn 1:29; 19:36; 1 Cor 5:7; Apoc 5:6, 12), the true expiatory victim (Ac 8:31—35; Heb 9:1—14; cf Is 53:7; Lev 14), the true covenant victim (Heb 9:15—28; cf Ex 24:3—8). The Eucharist, as the Christian paschal rite, fulfils these OT images (Mt 26:26—28; Lk 22:14). **22.** As in the Law of Holiness (Lev 19:18), so in the new Christian life, fraternal charity is essential (Gal 5:14; Jas 2:8; Rm 12:9—10; 13:8—10; Col 3:14; 1 Jn 2:8—10; 3:10—11).

23—25. The idea of a new birth is taken up again from 1:3, but here more precisely attributed to the 'living and abiding word of God', 'the good news which was preached to you'. Probably 'living and abiding' is to be taken with 'word' rather than with 'God' (cf 1:25a). We have here a hint of the theology of the Word of God developed in the prologue of St John (cf Apoc 19:13).

2:1—6 Put away malice: come to the living stone—— **d** 2:1—10 together with 1:3—15 forms the first main division of the letter. 2:1—10 deals above all with the responsibilities of the Christian vocation. **1** recalls a common catechetical formula of renunciation found in a similar context in Eph 4:25 (cf Selwyn, pp. 393—400). **2.** The comparison is between the desire of newly born babes for their mothers' milk and the longing of the Christian for 'the pure spiritual milk'; this longing is not restricted to the newly baptized, and there is no contrast between milk and adult fare as in 1 Cor 3:2—3 and Heb 5:12—14. 'Spiritual' seems to be the best rendering of *logikon* (cf Rm 12:1). **3.** '*Surely you have tasted that the Lord is good*' (NEB). **4—6.** The verbs are probably to be taken as imperatives: 'Come . . . let yourselves be built.' The idea of Christ, the living stone, comes from the Christological interpretation of Ps 118 (117):22 (cf Mk 12:10; Mt 21:42; Lk 20:17; Ac 4:11), Is 28:16 (cf Rm 9:33; Eph 2:20—22) and Is 8:14 (cf Rm 9:33). **4.** Christ is the *living* stone, not merely because he is a person, but because as risen Lord, he is endowed with new life (cf 3:18). **5.** Christians are to grow continually in their union with Christ, to share his life as 'living stones', forming with him a spiritual temple (cf Jn 2:19—21), which is the Church. The image changes a little to present the Church as a consecrated priesthood, offering to God through Jesus Christ a spiritual sacrifice, which is a life based on Christian faith (cf Phil 2:17; 4:18; Rm 12:1; Heb 13:16; 2 Tm 4:6; Apoc 8:3—4). **6.** The cornerstone is to be understood as the great foundation stone set at the corner of a building and holding the walls together.

7—10 The New Christian Priesthood——The term **e** 'believe' is taken up again in v 7 to introduce a further development of the idea of the new spiritual temple. Citing Ps 118 (117):22 and Is 8:14, the writer insists that men cannot be indifferent to Christ: he brings salvation

1e to the believer, but to the unbeliever he is the occasion of ruin. In vv 9—10 the titles of Israel in the OT are applied to the Church, and also Israel's role of bearing witness to the mighty works of God (Ex 19:5—6; Is 43:20—21). The reference to Hos 2:1, 23 (cf 1:6—9) points to the explanation of God's creation of the Church, his gratuitous love. **8b.** Unbelief as well as belief has its place in the over-all plan of God. For a fuller treatment of this topic (as applied to the Jews) cf Rm 9:11. **9.** In the LXX version of Ex 19:6, *basileion* ('kingdom') is a noun in apposition with 'priesthood' (cf 2 Mc 2:17; Apoc 1:6; 5:10); it should probably be taken in the same way here.

11—12 Conduct in the Pagan World—This passage introduces the second main section of the letter, 2:11—3:12. **11.** The Christian is by vocation an alien and exile on this earth (cf Gn 23:4; Ps 39 (38):13; Heb 11:13; 1 Pt 1:1, 17). 'Soul' here refers to man's true (supernatural) life. 'Flesh' designates human nature in so far as it is opposed to the guidance of the Spirit; there is no emphasis on sexual morality. **12.** 'The day of visitation' refers more probably to the last judgement. The good life of the Christians, it is hoped, will be the means of the pagans' salvation.

13—17 Obedience to Civil Authorities—This and the following two sections present traditional catechesis on various aspects of Christian behaviour. Other passages on civic duty are Rm 13:1—7; 1 Tm 2:1—3; Ti 3:1—3. Christians are to be dutiful citizens 'for the Lord's sake' (v 13), to fulfil God's will (v 15), not under constraint, but with the freedom of the sons of God. It is licence, not freedom, when legitimate authority is disobeyed (v 16; cf 1 Cor 7:22; Rm 6:18, 22). **17b** recalls but modifies Prv 24:21.

f 18—25 Obedience of Slaves to Masters—This passage recalls Col 3:22—4:1; Eph 6:5—9 (cf 1 Tm 6:1—2; Ti 2:9—10). The writer does not attack or question the institution of slavery. He simply directs Christian slaves to serve God with inward freedom despite their humiliating condition. This was the only practical attitude for the tiny Christian Church in a world which took slavery for granted, cf 1 Cor 7:21. **19.** As in 3:16, 21, *syneidēsis*, does not mean 'conscience'; here it could be translated by 'loyalty' to God, (RSV 'mindful of'). **21—25.** Christian slaves are to find inspiration in the innocent and patient sufferings of Christ. The theme of Christ's role of the suffering servant of Is 53, hinted at in Peter's second speech in Ac (3:13, 26), belongs to the primitive theology of the passion of Christ, and is here applied effectively to the situation of slaves. In v 24 the thought goes beyond the example of Christ to the salvific efficacy of his passion. Note the echo here of Rm 6:11 (cf 1 Pt 4:1b).

3:1—7 Husbands and Wives—There is special emphasis on the attitude of the believing wife towards her pagan husband. According to civil law, a wife was completely subject to her husband, hence the obvious difficulties of a Christian wife with a pagan husband. Following the example of the good women of the OT, especially Sarah (cf Gn 18:12), she should try to bring her husband to Christ by the testimony of Christian virtue and by the inward beauty of *'a gentle and quiet spirit',* (RSV: 'reverent and chaste behaviour'). **7.** Normally the wife would be converted with her husband; hence there is no reference to a believing husband with a pagan wife. Despite her subjection in the family and her physical weakness, the wife is a 'joint heir of the grace of life', to be treated with courtesy and honour. Cf 1 Cor 7:1—7.

8—12 Charity, Humility—This section echoes the **951g** teaching of Christ (Mt 5:39, 44; Lk 6:28) and Paul (Rm 12:14—18). The Christian is called by God to bless his enemies and thus to inherit the blessing of God himself. The whole section on Christian behaviour (2:11—3:12) concludes with citation of Ps 34 (33):12—17. The long life on this earth envisaged by the psalmist becomes the eternal life of Christian revelation.

13—17 Christian Confidence in Persecution—With this section the third great division of the letter is introduced (see plan). **13.** No real harm can come to those who are 'zealous for what is right'. **14.** The 'if' clause here does not necessarily indicate that persecution is merely a remote possibility. The construction is used rather to introduce a painful topic in a gentle and indirect manner. **15.** 'Reverence Christ as Lord', as the glorious risen Lord of Christian confession. The 'defence to anyone who calls you to account' is probably a reference to defence in a court of law. **16.** The Christian's loyalty (*syneidēsis*) to God should be so unswerving that his very calumniators may be put to shame. **17.** Cf 2:20.

3:18—22 Basis for Christian Confidence: Christ's Victory Shared in Baptism—This is an extremely difficult passage. It has given rise to a great number of interpretations. Only the more important can be mentioned here.

St Augustine (PL 33, 708—16) and almost all Western **h** commentators up till the time of Bellarmine understood the text to say that Christ, in his pre-existent divine nature, preached repentance to the sinners of the flood through the person of the just Noah, 'the herald of righteousness' (2 Pt 2:5). This interpretation is now entirely abandoned.

Bellarmine made popular another view, which has dominated Catholic commentators until very recent times. According to him, Christ's soul descended in the *triduum mortis* to the abode of the dead to announce salvation to the souls of those men who had sinned at the time of Noah but who had repented before dying in the waters of the flood (cf above all Holzmeister).

The more common view of Protestant commentators is that, in this descent of Christ's soul, he preached *to convert* the sinners of the flood. This was the interpretation of Clem.Alex. (PG 9, 268—9) and of Orig. (PG 11, 206, 864; 13, 1780).

These last two groups commonly link 3:19 and 4:6, seeing in the second text a more general presentation of the same theme.

Another interpretation (best expounded by Selwyn) is that, in the *triduum mortis*, Christ's soul proclaimed final defeat to the evil spirits who sinned before the flood and then instigated the human sin which provoked God's punishment.

The interpretation offered here is that of this writer's **952a** *Christ's Proclamation to the Spirits,* in which there is a full treatment of the history of the exegesis of 3:19 and 4:6 and of the exegetical problems arising from these texts. In this view, Christ, after his bodily resurrection, ascends through the heavens. In this ascension he confronts the wicked angels, who in Jewish tradition sinned by an unholy alliance with the 'daughters of men' (Gn 6:1—4), and then induced men to sin, thus provoking the punishment of the flood. These wicked spirits, whose influence lay behind the aberrations of the pagans and especially of the sin of unbelief, were definitively conquered by Christ's death and resurrection. Christ himself proclaimed to them his victory on the occasion of his ascension. In this victory of Christ lies the basis of Christian confidence in time of persecution, since the

952a unbelieving persecutors are the visible expression of the powers of evil now conquered by Christ. The sacred author finds in the salvation of the just Noah and his family a type of Christian salvation. Christ's victory is communicated to men by baptism. Through the power of his resurrection they, like Noah, are saved by water.

This interpretation seems to suit the context (providing the ground for confidence in persecution; cf Jn 16:33). More than any other solution it does justice to the individual terms of the text and to the background of Jewish tradition. The following commentary, with its references to fuller treatment in *Christ's Proclamation to the Spirits*, will endeavour to substantiate this interpretation.

b **18.** 3:18, 22 is probably the whole or part of a Christian hymn (cf 1 Tm 3:16; *Christ's Proclamation*, 87–102). The point of the introductory 'for' is to indicate an explanation, not of the preceding v (which is obvious and needs no explanation), but of the whole preceding passage. The more probable reading is '*suffered*', not (RSV) 'died'. The contrast of 'flesh' and 'spirit', in keeping with NT usage, has nothing to do with the distinction between 'body' and 'soul'. It refers to two spheres of reality, one human (with its mortality and weakness), the other divine (represented by the presence or action of the Holy Spirit). See *Christ's Proclamation*, 124–34. This v presents the common doctrine of the NT that Christ 'brought us to God' by his bodily death and especially his bodily resurrection. **19.** 'In which' refers naturally to the 'spirit' of the preceding v. Christ, then, as risen Lord 'went and made proclamation to the spirits in prison'. It is true that normally in the NT *kērussein* means 'to preach the gospel'. This is due to the general context. In itself the word means simply 'to make proclamation' (cf Lk 12:3; Apoc 5:2). Here Christ is presented as the new Enoch. This patriarch (cf Gn 5:21–24), who figures largely in Jewish apocryphal literature, received the commission from God to proclaim their doom to the evil spirits who instigated men to sin at the time of the flood (cf 1 Enoch, chh 12–16, etc). In the early Christian presentation of the same tradition (2 Enoch, ch 7), Enoch confronts the angelic sinners in the second heaven (cf *Christ's Proclamation*, 163–84); In strikingly similar fashion, Christ proclaims his victory to the hostile angelic spirits. His 'going' is that of the ascension (cf 3:22). This picture of Christ's victory is in keeping with Paul's presentation of his triumph over the 'principalities and powers' (Col 2:15; Eph 1:20–22; cf 1 Cor 15:24); these hostile powers are allied to 'the spiritual hosts of wickedness in the heavenly places' (Eph 6:12) and to 'the prince **c** of the power of the air' (Eph 2:2). This Pauline doctrine is recalled in 1 Pt 3:22 (cf *Christ's Proclamation*, 190–201). **20.** The 'disobedience' of 'the spirits' is to be identified with the sin of 'the sons of God' (angels) of Gn 6:1–4, which, according to Jewish tradition, was the cause of the moral chaos which ensued among men. Noah and his family are delivered from this world by means of water. The fewness of those saved (Gn 7:13; 2 Pt 2:5) is stressed to point the comparison with the Christian Church, a tiny minority in the great pagan world. Cf *Christ's Proclamation*, 204–10. **21.** Another very difficult v. Noah was saved by means of water, and a new era began with the covenant between God and him (Gn 9:9–17); thus the flood is a fore-shadowing of Christian baptism. In addition, the writer is probably thinking of the flood as a type of eschatological judgement (cf Mt 24:37–39; 2 Pt 2:5, 9; 3:5–7). The first part of the description of baptism is generally understood as

'not a mere external washing of the body', but it more **95** probably refers to circumcision: the phrase, literally '*putting away the filth of the flesh*', corresponds remarkably with the picture of circumcision found in the OT, the NT, and Jewish writings. The contrast between circumcision and baptism would thus be similar to that of Col 2:11–12. The second part of the description can be translated, '*but a pledge made to God to maintain a right attitude*'. This understanding of *eperōtēma* is supported by Gr. usage, and by the rite of baptism as known in the NT and in the early Church. For this interpretation of *syneidēsis* cf 1 Pt 2:19; 3:16. For a full discussion of this v, cf *Christ's Proclamation*, 210–34. **22.** The theme of Christ's ascension and of his subjection of hostile spirit powers is taken up again, this time in language akin to that of Paul.

4:1–6 The Share of the Baptized Christian in the d Victory of Christ—This section is linked with the previous one as a practical application to life of the ideas on baptism. **1.** 'Suffering in the flesh' is the equivalent of 'dying'. The writer recalls the thought of Christ's death from 3:18, and applies it to the baptized Christian. The *hoti* of v 1*b* introduces an explanation of the 'same mind' and is better translated as '*that*', (RSV: 'for'). This explanation refers briefly to the doctrine, expounded by Paul in Rm 6:1–11, of the Christian's share in baptism of the death of Christ. Christ 'died to sin, once for all' (Rm 6:10), and the Christian who has died (in baptism) is 'freed from sin' (Rm 6:7). **3–4.** Cf Wis 2:7–17 for a similar situation, that of the just man persecuted by the wicked. For full treatment of 4:1–4, cf *Christ's Proclamation*, 238–63. **5.** Christ will vindicate the faithful Christians and judge their persecutors at the coming Parousia. 'The living and the dead' are those physically alive and dead at the moment of the Parousia. **6.** A much disputed v. More commonly authors understand it to refer to Christ's announcing the good news of salvation to the souls in the abode of the dead during the *triduum mortis*. In this view it would refer to the same event as 3:19. We have seen that 3:19 does not refer to the activity of Christ's soul, but to his proclamation of victory, as risen Lord, to the hostile spirits. There is good reason for thinking that this v, also, has nothing to do with the descent of Christ's soul to the abode of the dead.

The context requires that Christian faith should be **e** vindicated against the attacks and ridicule of its persecutors. These could point out that it was in vain that Christian converts believed the gospel message, since they, like other men, could die. Where is their hope of immortality? The sacred author replies that, even though some of the converted Christians have died, the preaching of the gospel to them was not in vain, since, despite their physical death, they are destined to 'live in the spirit', to rise again in glory. The background of the text is that of the lively expectation of the Parousia among the early Christians, and of the problem raised by the realization that death could occur for some of them before the coming of the Lord.

Christ is probably to be taken as subject of *euēngelisthē* since he is more probably the judge mentioned in 4:5 (cf Ac 5:42; 8:35; 11:20; 17:18; Gal 1:16; cf also 1 Cor 15:12; 2 Cor 1:19 and especially 1 Tm 3:16). If this is so, then Christ is not the person who did the preaching. 'The dead' refers to those who, in their lifetime, heard and accepted the gospel, but who have since died. They seemed to believe in vain, since they will not be alive at the Parousia (cf 1 Thes 4:13–18). Although '*in the eyes of men*' (especially the pagan unbeliever) 'they

2e were judged in the flesh' (they suffered the lot of death as frail human beings), still '*in the eyes of God*' (who sees reality) they were destined to 'live in the spirit', to share at the Parousia the resurrection of Christ. Note the 'inclusion' with 3:18*b*: the experience of Christ, 'put to death in the flesh, but brought to life in the spirit', becomes that of the Christian through the preaching of the gospel (4:6*a*) and baptism (3:21; 4:1*b*), cf *Christ's Proclamation*, 263—77.

f 7—11 Christian Life in View of the Parousia—Here, as in 1:5; 4:17; 5:10, the writer expresses the common belief in the imminence of the Parousia (cf Phil 4:5; Jas 5:8; 1 Jn 2:28; Apoc 22:12). For the correction of a too wooden understanding of its proximity, cf 1 Thes 5:1—3; 2 Thes 2:1—12; 2 Pt 3:3—10. Cf §§ 670—2. **8b.** The reference seems to be to the sins of others (cf Jas 5:20; Prv 10:12), but the thought may go further to the expiation of sins effected by charity (cf Ps 85 (84):2; 32 (31):1). **9.** Cf 3 Jn 5—8. **10—11.** Cf Rm 12:6—8; 1 Cor 12:4—11. The doxology of v 11 does not mean that the following vv must be taken as a later addition. Of the 26 doxologies in the NT, only three, Rm 16:27; Jude 25; 2 Pt 3:18, come at the end of a letter.

12—19 Joy and Confidence in Actual Persecution—In 4:12—5:11, the second half of the section on persecution, the tone of the letter changes. Having prepared his readers by instruction and exhortation, the writer now brings them face to face with the severe ordeal before them. **12.** The idea of persecution as a purification by fire has already been introduced in 1:7. **13.** Suffering with and for Christ (2:20; 3:17) leads to joy, which is a foretaste of the final joy of the resurrection (cf Mt 5:12). **14.** The Spirit of glory, that is, the Spirit of God, rests on those who are reproached for the name of Christ, thus anticipating the glory of final fulfilment (cf 2 Cor 4:17; Col 3:4; 1 Pt 5:4). **16.** For the name 'Christian', cf Ac 11:26; 26:28. As in 3:15, the supposition seems to be that Christians are being brought to the public courts. **17.** Cf 4.7 on the imminence of the Parousia, and 2:5 on the image of the house of God. The Church will be purified by the sufferings of the last times (1:7; 4:12; cf Mal 3:1), but the lot of the culpable unbeliever will be terrible (cf 2 Thes 1:5—10). **18.** Prv 11:31 (LXX) is cited, and applied to the eschatological judgement. **19.** 'Their souls': cf note on 1:9.

g 5:1—5 Exhortation to Leaders and the Faithful—This section goes naturally with the earlier exhortations of 2:13—3:7. Possibly this appeal to leaders and faithful is kept to the end to stress the need for unity and mutual understanding in the face of persecution. **1.** The term *presbuteros* means lit 'elder', and is used in the NT to designate local church leaders (cf Ac 20:17, 28; 1 Tm 3; Ti 1:5—7, where *presbuteros* and *episkopos*

seem to refer to the same persons). Cf § 923. They are **952g** presented as men of authority and teachers; that they presided at Christian worship can reasonably be understood (cf Jas 5:14). 'Witness' may mean 'eye-witness', but could also mean one who bears witness by suffering for Christ ('martyr'). 'Partaker in the glory that is to be revealed' could refer to Peter's experience at the transfiguration (cf 2 Pt 1:16—18), or to the glory which will come to those who suffer for Christ (cf 1:5, 13; 4:7—17; 5:10; Col 3:4). **2.** 'Tend the flock of God' recalls Peter's commission of Jn 21:15—17 (cf vv 3—4). 'Not for shameful gain': cf 1 Cor 9:14; Ti 1:7; 1 Tm 3:8. **3.** '*Not tyrannizing over those allotted to your care*' (NEB): cf Mk 10:42. For similar exhortations to good example, cf 1 Tm 4:12; Ti 2:7—8. **5.** 'You that are younger' could refer to the simple faithful, but probably the thought glides to a comparison of age, not authority. For exhortations to the young, cf 1 Tm 5:1; Ti 2:6; 1 Jn 2:12—14. The citation, from Prv 3:34 (LXX), is found also in Jas 4:6.

6—11 Final Exhortation: Humility, Watchful- h ness—'The mighty hand of God' is a common OT expression for the power of God: cf Dt 9:26, 29; 26:8. For the exaltation of the humble, cf Lk 14:11; Jas 4:10. **7.** Cf 4:19; Mt 6:25—34; Lk 12:22—31. The first half of the v is a citation from Ps 55 (54):22. **8.** 'Your adversary the devil': behind unbelief and persecution it is the devil and the powers of evil who are at work (cf Eph 2:2; 6:11—12; Apoc 12:7—17, etc). This is in keeping with the explanation given above of the proclamation to the spirits of 3:19. **9.** The phrase 'throughout the world' means rather 'while they are in the world' (cf Jn 16:33). **10.** The body of the letter concludes with an emphatic summary of its message, first introduced in 1:6—7. For the theme of suffering leading to glory, cf Rm 8:18; 2 Cor 4:17.

12—14 Personal Note. Greetings This ending was probably added personally by Peter (cf 1 Cor 16.21, Gal 6:11; Col 4:18; 2 Thes 3:17; Phm 19). **12.** 'I have written through Silvanus': this implies that Silvanus is more than the bearer of the letter, but does not determine his degree of cooperation in the actual writing. For Silvanus, cf 1 Thes 1:1; 2 Cor 1:19; he is probably the same person as Silas in Ac 15:22, 32, 40. **13.** 'She who is at Babylon': the church at Rome (cf Apoc 14:8, 16:19; 17:5; 18:2, 10). 'My son, Mark': a term of affection for Mark the evangelist (cf 1 Ti 1.2, 18). Mark was with Paul in Rome (Col 4:10; Phm 24), and was summoned by Paul to his side just before his death (2 Tm 4:11). **14.** 'Kiss of peace': a sign of Christian brotherhood which had possibly become already a liturgical rite (cf Rm 16:16; 1 Cor 16:20; 2 Cor 13:12; 1 Thes 5:26).

2 PETER

BY W. J. DALTON S.J.

953a Bibliography—*Commentaries*: as for 1 Peter; and in addition: J. Chaine EtB 1939; A. E. Barnett IB 1957; *Other Literature*: J. A. Sint, *Pseudonymität im Altertum*, Innsbruck, 1960; A. Wikenhauser, *NT Introduction*, 1958, 509—19; J. Cantinat, in RF, 2, 1959², 590—661; W. G. Kümmel, *Introd. to the NT*, E.tr. NTL, 1966, 302—5; E. Testa, *Introd. al NT*, Brescia, 1961, 529—39.

b Relationship of 2 Peter to 1 Peter—The author of 2 Pt refers in 3:1 to an earlier letter he had written to the same readers. Is this letter 1 Pt? The only two letters in the NT canon associated either in reality or by literary device with Peter the apostle are 1 Pt and 2 Pt. It is natural to suppose that the earlier letter referred to in 2 Pt is none other than 1 Pt. While there is a notable difference in style and vocabulary between 1 and 2 Pt (e.g., the second coming of Christ is called his 'revelation' in 1 Pt, while it is described as his 'visit', '*parousia*', in 2 Pt), still there is evidence that 2 Pt was written with 1 Pt in mind. The opening salutation, 2 Pt 1:2, reproduces almost exactly that of 1 Pt 1:2. Again, the development of thought in 2 Pt 1:3—11 recalls very much that of 1 Pt 1:3—9. It seems reasonable to suppose that the author of 2 Pt, in claiming to recall the traditional teaching of the Church, 1:12, 15; 3:2, is referring to the catechesis of 1 Pt. He reminds his readers of apostolic teaching, 1:12, to be recalled after his death, 1:15. They are to 'remember the predictions of the holy prophets, and the commandment of the Lord and Saviour through your apostles', 3:2: these witnesses are listed in 1 Pt 1:10—12. In keeping with this, the OT is invoked as witness in 1 Pt 1:16; 2:6—8; 3:10—12; 5:5, while Christ is proposed as example in 2:21—25. The author of 2 Pt seizes on those elements which bear on his principal purpose: to uphold belief in the second coming of Christ, upon which the false teachers have cast doubts, 1:16; 3:4.

Relationship of 2 Pt to Jude—Ch 2 of 2 Pt has such manifest similarity with Jude that it is almost certain that there is between the two epistles a direct relationship of dependence. It is much more likely that 2 Pt depends on Jude. Cf § 959*c*.

Authenticity and Canonicity—It is of great importance to distinguish the two questions of authenticity and canonicity. Its canonicity has been established in the various declarations of the Church; cf § 20*a*, and see below § 953*c*. However, the authenticity of the epistle presents a real problem.

c Up till recent times, Catholic scholars have not made the necessary distinction between canonicity and authenticity. Being bound to defend the former, they felt obliged to find reasons to establish the latter. If one excludes *a priori* the possibility of pseudonymous literature in the NT (all modern scholars admit this for the OT), then one can attach undue importance to evidence from ecclesiastical writers who ascribe the writing of the

letter to the apostle Peter. This evidence is of little **953** value unless it can be shown that the writers concerned were aware of the problem of authenticity and intended to make a decision against pseudonymity. In general, it is clear that they merely repeat, without further reflection, the simple statement of the letter that it derives from 'Simon Peter, a servant and apostle of Jesus Christ' (1:1).

Faced with the alternative of Petrine authenticity or rank forgery, these scholars have tried to find internal evidence to support the former. Of course, one can find similarities between 1 Pt and 2 Pt: there is no doubt that 2 Pt was written with 1 Pt in mind. But once the possibility of pseudonymity is admitted, the internal evidence will be assessed very differently. It will not be used to support an *a priori* dogmatic position, legitimate in itself, which would exclude deliberate forgery from the authors of the Bible: it will be assessed critically simply on its own merits. The scholar is free to accept the evidence or to reject it.

To the end of the 2nd cent., there is no clear case of reference to 2 Pt in the ecclesiastical writings of the time. The first explicit reference is made by Origen. He accepts 2 Pt as authentic, but admits that this is controverted, PG 14, 188—9; cf PG 12, 437, 857; 14, 1179. The epistle is not included in the Old Latin or Old Syriac, or in the Muratorian canon. In the 3rd and 4th cent., it is more widely used and commonly associated with Peter, yet some doubts remain. For example, Euseb. puts 2 Pt among the disputed books, and himself doubts its authenticity, PG 20, 216—17, 269. Jer., while accepting 2 Pt as canonical, notes that its authenticity is controverted, PL 23, 638. However, it is included in the canon drawn up by the Council of Carthage in 392, Dz 92, and formally accepted as canonical scripture by the Council of Trent, Dz 784.

The Council of Trent did not touch the question of the authenticity of 2 Pt. Although in Christian tradition the two factors have been intimately linked, so that 2 Pt was accepted as canonical precisely because it was believed to be the work of Peter the apostle, still it is possible to accept the Church's verdict on its canonicity, without regarding the discussion of its authenticity as closed. It is the dogmatic conclusions which are binding, not the implicit reasoning which precedes them.

Actually, it is very difficult indeed to accept the **d** Petrine authorship of this epistle. The difficulty does not lie principally in the style. This is very different from that of 1 Pt, though admittedly the apostle could have used the services of different secretaries. But this is the only NT document where the problem of the *delay* of the Parousia appears, 3:4. This indication of late composition is supported by other evidence. The false teachers say: 'Ever since the fathers fell asleep . . .', 3:4, indicating that the early Christian teachers are dead. The almost slavish use of Jude points, not merely to a date later than that of Jude, but to a dependence

953d which would be strange in the leader of the apostles. Add to this the reference to 'all the letters' of Paul, 3:16. It would be unwarranted to see here a collection of the whole Pauline *corpus*, but the term implies a substantial collection of his letters and so a relatively late date. Other less cogent arguments can be added to these. When all are put together they provide a formidable case against authenticity.

It is not necessary to conclude that 2 Pt is merely a forgery. No one suggests that the Books of Wisdom or Ecclesiastes are forgeries, although both are admitted to be pseudonymous. It is possible that the author of 2 Pt was a disciple of the apostle and wished to invoke his authority in insisting on the orthodox tradition of Christian belief. This view, expressed with various modifications, is becoming more common among Catholic scholars. For a discussion of pseudonymous writing, cf J. A. Sint, *Pseudonymität im Altertum*, Innsbruck, 1960.

e *Destination and Purpose*—We can hardly conclude from 3:1 that the readers of 2 Pt are the same as those of 1 Pt. Of the former we know very little, except that they were once pagans, cf 2:18, 20—22. We may take it that the letter was addressed to a particular group of Christians placed in the special circumstances described in it; one can only guess about their location.

The letter is written to preserve the readers in the orthodox faith in spite of the influence of false teachers, who, like those castigated in Jude, have fallen into antinomian errors and resultant immorality. They seem to have gone further than Jude's adversaries: they ridicule the second coming of Christ and the judgement, 3:3ff, and misinterpret both OT prophecy, 1:19—21, and the orthodox testimony of the NT, found in the gospel tradition, cf 1:16—18, and the letters of Paul, 3:15—16.

Time and Place of Composition—In the light of the evidence given above, the letter must have been written at a date considerably later than that of Jude. It is difficult to be more precise. A reasonable date would be towards the end of the 1st cent. There seems to be no need to put it as late as A.D. 140, a period favoured by a number of commentators. There is no evidence to determine the place of composition.

Theme and Analysis—The writer, speaking in the name of Peter, recalls to 'those who have obtained a faith of equal standing with ours in the righteousness of our God and Saviour Jesus Christ', 1:1, the certainty of Christ's return and the judgement which follows it. Hence they must grow in the knowledge of the truth and in the practice of Christian virtues if they wish to gain 'entrance into the eternal kingdom of our Lord and Saviour Jesus Christ', 1:11.

f **The structure of the epistle is loose**, but the following indicates its content and development. After the initial greeting, 1:1—2, the author exhorts his readers to fulfil their vocation to **holiness of life**, 1:3—31: after the exhortation itself, 1:3—11, he states his desire to remind them, before his coming death, of the basic truth of the second coming of Christ, 1:12—15. This he can do with assurance, since he was an eye-witness of the Transfiguration, 1:16—18, which guarantees the teaching of the prophets on the second coming, 1:19—21.

Then follows a **warning against the false teachers**, 2:1—22: first they are described and their judgement foretold, 2:1—3; their judgement is as certain as that of the notorious sinners of the past, 2:4—10a; their sinful conduct is more fully described, 2:10b—22.

The writer comes to his chief topic, **The Day of the Lord**, 3:1—10: he recalls the teaching of the prophets and the command of Jesus Christ handed on by the apostles, 3:1—2; the false teachers, who deny the **Parousia**, **953f** are refuted, 3:3—10.

The epistle concludes with a fervent exhortation to a life of holiness in expectation of the Day of the Lord, in keeping with the doctrine of Paul, which the false teachers misinterpret, 3:11—18a. The last words are a doxology to Christ, 3:18b.

Doctrinal Content—The religious doctrine of 2 Pt **g** centres around **Jesus Christ**. Quite unusually in NT terminology, he is called God (the more probable interpretation of 1:1; cf Rm 9:5; Jn 20:28). His is the 'divine power', 1:3, and the 'divine nature', 1:4. He is the Son of God, 1:17, and Saviour, 1:1, 11; 2:20; 3:2, 18, Redeemer, 'the Master who bought them', 2:1, eternally glorified, 3:18, a glory anticipated at the Transfiguration, 1:16—18. His most frequent title is 'our Lord', 1:2, 8, 11, 14, 16; 2:20; 3:2, 15, 18. He is the object of knowledge through faith, 1:2—3; his is the eternal kingdom, 1:11. His coming, *Parousia*, is certain, 1:16; 3:4, 12. Belief in this is based on its anticipation at the Transfiguration, 1:16—18 and on 'the prophetic word', 1:19. The Day of the Lord is delaying, but will surely come, 3:3—7, in God's good time, 3:8—9, and suddenly, 3:10.

There is evidence of the Christian tradition of **The Trinity** implicit in the mention of the three persons, Father and Son, 1:17, and Holy Spirit, 1:21. The Father is Creator, 3:5, the just Judge, 2:4—9; he is the 'Majestic Glory', 1:17. The angels, also called 'the glorious ones', 2:10, are divided into those 'greater in might and power' than men, 2:11, and those who have sinned, 2:4; cf Jude 6; these latter have been punished and await the final judgement.

Man has been redeemed, 'bought', by Jesus Christ, 2:1. He is to live a life of faith, in response to the apostolic preaching of the gospel, 1:12; 3:1—2, which leads to 'knowledge of God and of Jesus our Lord, 1:2; cf 1:3, 8. Faith involves acceptance of Christ's promises, 1:4; 3:4, 9, the sharing of his 'divine nature', 1:4. It shows itself in a life of Christian virtue, 1:5—8; 3:11, 14, 18, and is fulfilled by 'entry into the eternal kingdom of our Lord and Saviour Jesus Christ', 1:11, on the day of his coming, 3:9, 14.

The **false teachers**, who 'deny the Master who bought **h** them', are doomed to destruction, 2:1. Their vices lead them to a state worse than that before conversion, 2:20, and final condemnation, 2:3, 9. The Day of the Lord is delayed to give them time to repent, 3:9.

To offset the arbitrary interpretation of the OT by the false teachers, the author offers a valuable comment on the **inspiration of scripture**; 'No prophecy ever came by the impulse of man, but men moved by the Holy Spirit spoke from God.' For this reason prophecy must not be twisted to suit private caprice (1:20—21). Under this heading of 'scriptures' comes a collection of Paul's letters (3:15—16).

Text and Style—The newly discovered P 72 (Papyrus Bodmer VII), which is commonly dated from the 3rd cent., indicates that 2 Pt was at this time accepted by the Church in Egypt. However the new text does not throw much light on the interpretation of the epistle. Many variants are due to obvious errors. Possibly in 3:10 it presents an original reading 'the earth . . . will be found dissolved', (*heurethēsetai luomena*), cf Schelkle p. 183.

The style of 2 Pt is very different from that of 1 Pt. For a full discussion of the former's style, cf Bigg, 224—32, and Chaine, 14—18. Jer. suggests that two different secretaries were used by Peter. While the mere differences in style could be explained by this hypothesis, there are

953h deeper differences of thought and attitude which can scarcely be explained in a satisfactory manner along these lines.

954a **1:1—2 Salutation**—'Simon', Gr. '*Symeon*', an archaic form no doubt to stress the author's claim to give the apostolic teaching of the primitive Church. The readers are simply designated 'those who obtained a faith of equal standing with ours'. Faith here, unlike the general Pauline usage, is 'fides quae creditur'. Also the 'justice' of God here is not the same as the Pauline term, but rather the moral quality of one who gives 'faith of equal standing' to apostles and faithful without acceptance of persons. The terms, 'our God', and 'Saviour, Jesus Christ', are preceded by the one article. Much more probably (despite the separation in v 2) they are both to be applied to Christ. The title, 'Saviour', applied to Christ, is a favourite one in 2 Pt, as it is in the Pastoral Epistles. Both titles indicate a later rather than an early date of composition. The first half of v 2 is identical with the wish expressed in 1 Pt 1:1.

3—11 Exhortation to Spiritual Progress—Calling attention to the very great blessings which they received through faith, the writer points out that earnest effort is required to correspond with such a gift. **3.** It is the divine power of Christ which lies behind the whole Christian life, which enables a man to know Christ by faith. It is better to understand v 3b: 'called us *by* his own glory and excellence'. The 'glory' of Christ is shown in his miracles and above all, in our context, by his transfiguration. **4.** Through this 'glory and excellence' Christ has founded Christian hope. The Christian, now by faith, later in the fulfilment of the Parousia, is a 'partaker of the divine nature'. No doubt the reference is to the divine nature as possessed by Christ, parallel to his 'divine power' mentioned in v 3. The expression, 'partakers of the divine nature', uses the terminology of Hellenistic philosophy, but the idea is biblical. Already, even before the Parousia, the Christian enjoys intimate union with Christ and with his Father, Jn 14:20—23; 17:21—23, and with the Holy Spirit, Jn 14:16f. Thus, the Christian has fellowship with the Father and his Son, Jesus Christ, 1 Jn 1:3.

b To secure this divine gift, it is necessary to 'escape from the corruption that is in the world because of passion'. Cf 1 Jn 2:16. Christians should be 'dead to sin' but 'alive to God, in Christ Jesus our Lord', Rm 6:2, 11. **5—7.** For similar lists of virtues, cf 2 Cor 6:6; Gal 5:22—23; 1 Tim 6:11; Apoc 2:19. Here, as elsewhere, Christian love takes first place. The author insists, like Jas 2:14—26, that faith must develop into a virtuous Christian life if it is to be fruitful. 'Knowledge' here and in v 8 is a practical knowledge; 'godliness' is a general term, covering the whole of a Christian's life. 'Brotherly affection' is restricted to the circle of the community. True Christian 'love' embraces all men in Christ. The author is merely repeating the teaching of Jesus, cf Mt 5:43—48. **8.** All is directed towards the 'knowledge of our Lord Jesus Christ'. It is in this knowledge that the false teachers are wanting. **9.** These have not been true to their baptismal programme, which involves an ever deeper knowledge of Christ. From the point of view of style, the phrase, 'blind and short-sighted', is awkward; one would expect the order of the two terms to be reversed. **10—11.** This call and election to faith must be confirmed by a life in keeping with the faith, if we would enter the eternal kingdom of our Lord.

1:12—15 Apostolic Witness—This witness, as appears later, is to the Second Coming of Christ. It is presented as a sort of last testament of the apostle Peter. He **954** is depicted as aware of his imminent death through revelation from Jesus Christ. This can hardly be the saying of our Lord recorded in Jn 21:18, since there is no indication here of the *time* of Peter's martyrdom. More likely we have here a literary device in keeping with the pseudonymous nature of the letter.

16—21 Certainty of Christ's Return—16. Changing **c** now from the first person sing. to the plural, cf 1:1, he implies that the second coming of Christ is the general apostolic tradition. Unlike 'the cleverly devised myths' of the false teachers, this tradition is firmly founded. There can be hardly any doubt that the 'coming', '*Parousia*', mentioned here refers to the Second Coming. Peter was eye-witness of Christ's glory on the mountain, the same glory which will be publicly revealed at the Second Coming. It is of interest that in all three synoptic accounts of the Transfiguration, the preceding vv deal with the coming of Christ in glory, Mt 16:28; Mk 9:1; Lk 9:27. **17.** The transfiguration of Christ, cf Mt 17:1—9 and par., is cited as proof of the singular glory which belongs to him, a sort of foretaste of the Parousia. **19.** The experience of the apostles at the time of the Transfiguration gives further security to the testimony of the OT prophets to the Second Coming. This prophetic word, backed by apostolic teaching, should be to the readers 'as a lamp shining in a dark place', that is, a sure guide in the present dark times which will terminate with the Second Coming. The 'morning star' is Christ, cf Apoc 2:28; 22:16. He will rise 'in your hearts', a strange expression to describe the Parousia, normally presented as a cosmic event. Here we have rather the reaction of the faithful at the coming of Christ. **20—21.** The false teachers have evidently provided their own interpretation of the OT prophecies about the Day of the Lord. The author insists that 'no prophecy of scripture is a matter of one's own interpretation', that is, that there is an objective meaning of scripture, which should not be distorted to suit the views of a private individual. The apostles, who have been given by Christ the task of preaching the gospel and have the guarantee of the Spirit, are the appointed interpreters of OT prophecy.

Another, but less likely, interpretation runs: 'No **d** prophecy of scripture is derived from private interpretation, that is, prophets do not make up their own prophecies, but receive them from God.' In v 21, we have a summary of the doctrine of biblical inspiration supposed in both the NT and in Jewish teaching. The true prophet is one who, 'moved by the Holy Spirit, spoke from God'. Since the prophecies of the OT derive not from mere human insight but from the Holy Spirit, they are to be interpreted, not on mere human authority, but on the authority given by the Holy Spirit to the apostles. The writer does not consider the further question of the interpretation of scripture in the post-apostolic Church. In keeping with his principles, one would expect to find a continuance of the living apostolic authority, guided by the Holy Spirit, capable of giving an authentic interpretation of scripture. This is the teaching of the Catholic Church, as found in the Tridentine profession of faith, Dz 995.

2:1—3 Warning against False Teachers—The severe denunciation contained in this ch is similar to that of Jude 4—16. Since Jude is more spontaneous and less reflective, it is usually considered to be the earlier, cf § 959c. The author puts his Christian readers on guard against certain deceitful teachers, who by their evil lives and their spirit of avarice are luring some to destruction. **1.** 'False prophets among the people'

54d recalls the false prophets among the people of Israel, castigated by the true prophets of the OT. The writer, using the future tense, refers to the false teachers, who in NT catechesis will appear at the Last Times, cf 1 Tim 4:1—3; 2 Tim 3:1—8; Mt 24:24. These 'deny the Master who bought them', practically, by living unchristian lives, theoretically, by denying essential elements of the Christian gospel, such as the Second Coming. Christ 'bought them' with his precious blood, cf 1 Pt 1:19; 1 Cor 6:20; 7:23. **2.** 'The way of truth', called simply 'the Way', Ac 9:2, or 'the way of righteousness', 2 Pt 2:21, or 'the way of the Lord', Ac 18:25, or 'the way of salvation', Ac 16:17, refers to the Christian community or religion. **3.** For the greed of the false teachers, cf Jude 11, 16. 'Their destruction has not been asleep': cf Rm 2:5.

e **4—10a Examples of Divine Judgement**—Three instances of God's punishments are given: (1) the rebel angels; (2) the sinners at the time of the flood; (3) the inhabitants of Sodom and Gomorrah. From the fate of these three classes, one may conjecture what God will do to the false teachers. **4.** For the sin of the angels, cf Jude 6—7; Gn 6:1—4. **5.** 'The ancient world' is the race of men before the flood. Noah is called 'the herald of righteousness'. For Jewish tradition on this point, cf SB 3, 769. By his building of the ark, Noah proclaimed the coming punishment of his contemporaries; cf Heb 11:7. It is possible that the phrase should be translated 'the righteous herald', in the same way as 'the righteous teacher' (rather than 'the teacher of righteousness') of the Dead Sea texts. **6—8.** The destruction of Sodom and Gomorrah, Gn 19:24ff. Lot, like Noah, was righteous, and thus stood out in contrast to his wicked contemporaries. His righteousness, together with that of Noah and Abraham is celebrated in Wis 10:4—8. **9.** The lesson is directed towards the present scene: God will rescue the godly, but he will condemn the false teachers to hell, where they will await their final condemnation at the last judgement, cf Lk 16:19—31. **10a.** The two chief sins of the false teachers are mentioned: their immoral life and their rejection of Christ. They 'despise authority', lit, 'lordship'. This abstract term probably stands for 'Lord', the most common title of the risen Christ. This is the same sin as that of denying the Master, mentioned in 2:1; cf Jude 8.

f **10b—22 The Wickedness of the False Teachers—10b.** 'The glorious ones', lit, 'glories': these are the angels, cf Jude 8—9. In the following v, our author makes a distinction between these and the good angels. It seems, then, that the 'glories' are the wicked angels of 2:4. **11.** The good angels, in reverence before God, leave the judgement to him, cf Jude 9. **12.** Cf Jude 10, which is modified to bring out more clearly the comparison with wild animals. **13.** NEB has 'Suffering hurt for the hurt they have inflicted', recalling Rm 6:23: 'The wages of sin is death.' Others understand: 'being deprived of the reward they hoped to gain from their wrongdoing', like Balaam, cf 2 Pt 2:15; Nm 24:11. Others, again, follow the less likely and easier reading, *Komioumenoi* 'receiving'. 'To carouse is broad daylight' (NEB) is better than Goodspeed's 'They find pleasure in the indulgence of the moment'. Since the chief meal of the day was in the evening, to revel in the daytime was doubly reprehensible, cf Is 5:11. The occasion of this revelry may have been the Christian love-feast, cf Jude 12; 1 Cor 11:17—34. 'Revelling in their dissipation': better, 'because they revel in their own deceptions', NEB. The reading best attested is *apatais*. The other reading, *agapais*, supported by B and early versions, corresponds to Jude 12. It is possible that the writer of 2 Pt, who had the text of Jude

before him, deliberately modifies the word *agapais*, to **954f** indicate that these were no true love-feasts but 'deceptions'. **15—16.** Balaam 'loved gain from wrongdoing', cf Nm 22:2—24:25, Dt 23:4—5; Jude 11; Apoc 2:14. Balaam was misled by avarice to disregard the command of God in undertaking to prophesy against the Israelites. The better attested reading, 'Bosor', is probably a mistake for 'Beor'. Note the contrast between 'the right way', cf 2:2; 2:21, and 'the way of Balaam', cf Jude 11.

17—18. These vv recall Jude 12—13, 16. 'Men who **g** have barely escaped', that is, recent converts from paganism. These are the 'unsteady souls' of 2:14. **19.** 'They promise them freedom': probably distorting the Pauline doctrine of Christian freedom, cf 3:16; Gal 5:1. Paul was aware himself of this possible misunderstanding, and anticipated the condemnation given in this v of such aberration, cf Rm 6:14—16. 'Slaves of corruption', cf Rm 8:21; 2 Pt 1:4; Gal 6:8. **20.** Of whom is the writer speaking, the false teachers, or those whom they have corrupted? Commentators are divided. More probably this severe verdict is directed against the former. They are the subject of the preceding v, 'the slaves of corruption'. Those who are ill instructed and recently converted from paganism would scarcely merit such severity; but Christians of long standing, like those equally condemned in Heb 6:4—8; 10:26—31; cf 1 Jn 5:16—17, who fall into apostasy, are much more open to condemnation. We are reminded of Christ's words on the return of the unclean spirit, Mt 12:43—45. 'The knowledge of our Lord and Saviour Jesus Christ' is the heart of the Christian religion, cf 1:2, 8, 21. 'The way of righteousness', cf 2:2, 15. 'The holy commandment delivered to them': this is 'the faith which was once for all delivered to the saints', Jude 3. For the Christian faith as a 'commandment', cf 1 Tm 6:14; 1 Jn 3:23. **22.** The picture of the false teachers is concluded with two parallel proverbs, both concerning animals regarded as unclean, cf Mt 7:6. The first is taken from Prv 26:11 (not from the LXX), the second is otherwise unknown.

3:1—10 The Day of the Lord—The writer returns to **h** the chief topic of the letter, 'the power and coming of our Lord Jesus Christ', 1:16, and essential Christian belief which he defends against the false teachers. **1.** 'The second letter', a probable reference to 1 Pt. This does not imply that Peter is the actual author of 2 Pt, cf § 953b. It does provide a very ancient testimony to the Petrine authorship of 1 Pt. **2.** 1 Pt also appeals to the testimony of prophets and apostles, 1:10—12, and stresses the Second Coming as central to Christian belief, 1:4—7; 4:5—7, 13, 17—18; 5:4, 10. For 'commandment', cf 2:21. **3—4.** The false teachers scoff at belief in the Second Coming. 'The last days', the period preceding the end of the world. Such false prophets are foretold in texts such as Ezek 12:27f; Mal 2:17; 1 Tm 4:1—3; 2 Tm 3:1—5; 4:3. 'Where is the promise of his coming?': the early Church lived in the fervent hope of the proximate coming of Christ. The false teachers base their objection, first of all, on the fact that Christ actually has not come. 'The fathers fell asleep': 'the fathers' are the first generation of Christians; a considerable time has passed since their death. The death of the first generation of Christians posed a problem in the church of the Thessalonians, cf 1 Thes 4:13—18. The second argument of the false teachers seems to be a philosophical one, the essential immutability of the universe. **5.** The writer refutes this scepticism. He accuses the false teachers of bad faith. Their supposition of the immutability of the universe is contradicted by what has happened in the past, in the Flood. Similarly, God can and will effect another change

954h in the world, this time by fire. 'By means of water' is not clear. The Genesis account of creation presents the emergence of the earth as due to the movement of the waters, first the separation of the upper from the lower waters, then the collection into one place of the lower waters, **i** Gn 1:2, 7, 9. **6.** The author seems to suppose, from the parallel with 'the heavens and earth' of v 7, that the whole universe, not just the earth, was ravaged by the Flood. This is in keeping with the P tradition, which represents the deluge as a return to original chaos, Gn 7:11. Cf Enoch, 83:3—4. **7.** The parallel between the deluge and the end of the world is drawn by our Lord himself, Mt 24:37—39; Lk 17:26f. Fire is associated with God's judgement in Pss 50:3; 97:3; Is 66:15; Zeph 1:18; Mal 4:1; 1 Cor 3:13; 2 Thes 1:7. The belief that the universe would be finally destroyed by fire is found in Jewish tradition, SB 3, 773; 1QH 3:31—36. The inspired author uses these cosmological ideas, prevalent at his time, to draw the lesson of God's mastery over the universe. They are to be understood in the same way as those which lie behind the flood narrative. Thus we should not conclude from this text that we are bound to hold, on the authority of Scripture, that the universe will actually be destroyed by fire. **8—9.** Here we have the basic reply to the false teachers. With God there is no time element; everything is present to his mind, and such distinctions of time as we make have no meaning in the divine plans. For a similar explanation, cf 1QpHab VII, 13—14. Whatever delay there may be is proof of God's patience. He wills that no one shall perish, but that all be brought to repentance, cf 1 Tm 2:4; Mt 18:26—27; Rm 2:4; 9:22; 1 Pt 3:20; cf also Ps 90:4, 'For a thousand years in thy sight are but as yesterday when it is past, or as a watch in the night'. **10.** Despite the delay, the saying of Jesus, Mt 24:42f, will be fulfilled, cf 1 Thes 5:2. The author interprets this as the coming of the world conflagration, as in v 7. The 'elements', mentioned between the heavens and the earth, are probably the stars. 'Will be burned up': the better attested reading is *heurethēsetai*, 'will be laid bare', NEB. The recent P 72 reads *heurethēsetai luomena*, 'will be found dissolved', which is possibly the original reading.
j **11—18a Exhortation to Watchfulness—12.** 'Hastening the coming of the day of God': since God delays the Parousia because of men's sins, 3:9, it follows that **95** the holiness of men will cause it to come sooner, cf Ac 3:19—21. It was the fervent prayer of the early Church that the Lord should come, Apoc 22:17, 20; 1 Cor 16:22. **13.** 'New heavens and a new earth': cf Is 65:17; 66:22; Apoc 21:1; Rm 8:19—22. The author does not link the old universe with the new. In keeping with Rm 8:19—22, it seems reasonable to think of the material world as sharing in some way the transformation of the glorious body of the risen Christ and that of his faithful followers. **14.** Cf Jude 21, 24. **15.** 'So also' probably refers to both 3:14b and 3:15a. 'Our beloved brother': the author, writing in the name of Peter and no doubt aware of the differences between Peter and Paul, cf Gal 2:11—14, insists on their brotherly union as apostles of Christ. 'To you': the author could be referring to some particular letters of Paul written to Asia Minor, cf 1 Pt 1:1; 2 Pt 3:1. These could be Col and Eph. Or more probably at a later date, the letters of Paul, already collected into a group, were considered as addressed to Christians everywhere. The passages dealing with Christian expectation of the Parousia could be any of Rm 13:11—14; 1 Cor 7:29—31; 1 Thes 5:4—11; 2 Tm 3:1—5; Ti 2:12—14. For 'the forbearance of our Lord', cf Rm 2:4; 9:22f. **16.** 'All his letters', that is, a group of letters known to the writer. The letters of Paul have been treasured in the various churches to which they were sent, brought together into a collection, and are now accepted as of equal standing as 'the other scriptures', more probably the inspired writings of the OT. Thus we have here the first explicit mention of the formation of a Christian canon of scriptures. 'Things . . . hard to understand', probably connected with Christian liberty: cf 2 Pt 2:19. The false teachers misunderstand the nature of scripture, cf 1:20f. **17—18a.** Final exhortations, one negative, the other positive. The writer finishes with the second member of an 'inclusion' which enfolds the whole letter: 'grace and knowledge of our Lord and Saviour Jesus Christ', recalling 1:2. **18b.** Doxology to Christ, unlike that of Jude 25, which is directed to God. Cf 2 Tm 4:18. 'The day of eternity': this could be the same as 'the day of the Lord', the parousia, or possibly mean simply 'eternity', corresponding to 'for ever' in Jude 25, cf Sir 18:10.

1, 2 AND 3 JOHN

BY DOM RALPH RUSSELL

55a **Bibliography**—*Commentaries*: B. F. Westcott, 1905[8]; A. E. Brooke, ICC 1928; A. Charue, PCSB 1938; J. Chaine, EtB 1939; J. Bonsirven, VS 1954; P. de Ambroggi, SacB 1949[2]; F.-M. Braun, BJ 1953; A. N. Wilder, IB 1957; J. Schneider, NTD 1961; J. Michl, RNT 1953; C. H. Dodd, Moffatt 1961[4]; R. E. Brown, 1960; R. Schnackenburg 1962[2]. *Other Literature*: W. G. Kümmel, *Introd. to NT*, 1966; A. Feuillet, RF (E.tr.) 1965, 670—89; R. Leconte, DBS 4 (1949) 797—815; J.A.T. Robinson, 'The Destination and Purpose of the Johannine Epistles,' NTS 7 (1960—61), 56ff.

I JOHN

b **Author**—held to be John the Apostle by Iren. (*Adv. Haer*, 3, 16, 5 and 8); Clem.Alex., 2, 15, 66; 3, 4, 32 and 5, 44); Orig. (Eus.HE 6, 25, 10); Tert. (*Adv. Prax.*, 15; *Scorp.*, 12); Dion. Alex. (Eus.HE 7, 25, 7—8); Mur. Canon, etc. Papias used it (Eus.HE 3, 39, 17), Polycarp, (*Phil.* 7, 1) clearly cites 1 Jn 4:2f and prob. Justin, *Dial.* 123, 9, 1 Jn 3:1, 22. Resemblances to the Gospel in vocabulary, style and doctrine are many, close and deep, e.g. light, life, love, come in the flesh, do the truth, witness, born of God, of the truth, of the devil; then cf 1 Jn 1:1—4; 2:4, 11, 27; 3:14; 4: 9, 12; 5:9 with Jn 1:1—14; 8:44; 12:35; 16:30; 5:24; 3:16; 1:18; 5:34 (lists in Brooke and Chaine). Christ is preached as Logos and as God (1:1; 20:29, 1 Jn 1:1; 5:20), with emphasis on the Incarnation (1:2; 4:2; Jn 1:14); eternal life comes through belief and knowledge, making us one with the Incarnate Son, 17:3; 20:31; 1 Jn 1:2f; 5:10—13; the opposing 'world' is darkness, death, and characterized by unbelief, hate, the lie, murder, e.g. 1:6; 2:22f; 3:12ff; Jn 1:5; 3:18f; 8:44; 15:18ff; love is defined by the practical side of fulfilling the commandments of God and of Christ, e.g. 14:23f, 31; 15:10, 14; 1 Jn 2:4; 3:23f; there are the same formulae of mystical immanence, such as 'abide in'. 'The onus of proof is on those who deny **c** common authorship', G. Johnston, PC (2). But C. H. Dodd (BJRL 21 (1937), 128—56 and his commentary) has argued from the absence of certain Gospel key words, a more monotonous and less dramatic and Semitic style, paucity of allusions to the OT, and more primitive teaching on the Second Coming and the Paraclete, etc, to a different author. W. F. Howard and W. G. Wilson, JTS 48 (1947), 12—25; 49 (1948), have shown that these arguments are not so strong as to weigh against ancient tradition and the author's solemn insistence that he is an eyewitness. Though the Gr is faultless *Koine*, it is packed with Semitisms. A letter addressed to already formed Gentile Christians would not have much comment on the OT, nor the Gospel's drama, nor the splendour derived from Jesus's own words as nucleus of the Discourses. But it has its own beauty and great sayings. Teaching on the Second Coming, the Paraclete and the Atonement is essentially the same as the Gospel's, (Jn 6:39f and ch 8; 1 Jn 3:24; 4:13 and cf 1 Jn 3:5; 4:9f; 2:2 with Jn 1:29; **d** 3:16). But Professor Dodd's arguments make a point. The general presentation is more primitive than the Gospel's: **955d** the terminology less precise, (cf 1 Jn 1:1—3 with the Prologue), Trinitarian relations and the Personality of the Holy Spirit less clear; passages could refer to the Father or the Son (e.g. 2:20; 3:2, 24); the Second Coming is more emphasized (with perhaps a transition to realized eschatology in 2:18), DSS parallels and vocabulary more marked, e.g. 1:6f; 3:8ff; 4:1—6. Probably, then, the Epistle preceded the Gospel, and yet passages (e.g. 2:7f; 3:8—15; 5:9f) require its fuller treatment. This is explainable if the Gospel, and especially the Last Discourse, were already in formation.

True Knowledge To understand 1 Jn some idea of **c** **the heretics** is necessary. They come originally from pagan rather than Jewish circles, have left the Church, and appear to form one body and to have success among the pagan 'world'. They combine the Christological 'lie' (denial that Jesus is the Christ and the Son of God come in the flesh) with errors in morals, 1:5—2:11, 22f; 3:4—24; 4:2f, 20—5:3, 5. Their outlook and terminology show a Gnostic orientation. They claim special knowledge of God (2:4) and to be sinless (1:6, 8, 10) without keeping his commandments; they do not love the brethren, but hate them, 2:3f, 9; 3:10, 15. Iren. (*Adv. Haer.* 1, 26, 3) thought Jn had in mind Cerinthus, who taught that the spiritual Christ came upon Jesus at his baptism and left him at his Passion, cf 2:22; 4:3; 5:5f. It may be safer to speak of an early form of Gnosticism.

To combat them, Jn relies chiefly on positive, **f** doctrinal exposition and practical exhortation. But the Christians have to be put on their guard, encouraged and especially reassured that they know God. '**Know**' comes continually, makes the climax: 'That you may know that you have eternal life' (5:13) and is then repeated six times, 15—20. This principal aim of the epistle has been obscured by failure to realize that we must ask what 'know' means, not for a Greek, but for a Semite. To '**know God**' (cf M. E. Boismard, 'La connaissance dans l'Alliance nouvelle d'après la première lettre de S. Jean', RB 56 (1949), 365—91) is to recognise and experience his power and effective presence, Ex 6:6; 7:5, 17; 29:45f, and especially Ezek, e.g. 25:5; 39:28f. It requires corresponding service and love in man (e.g. Jer 9:2, 5; Hos 6:6) by keeping his commandments and walking in his ways, e.g. 1 (3) Kgs 14:8. Not to do this is not to 'know' him, Jer 9:2, cf 1 Jn 2:3ff. When the Israelites broke the Covenant, God through Jer and Ezek proclaimed a new one, in which he would himself change the hearts of all of them by his Spirit to 'know' him and keep his commandments. Jn is **g** sure that this has been realized and is what he wants to describe, e.g. 1 Jn 2:27 'you have no need that any one should teach you' (Jer 31:34), 4:13 'he has given us of his own Spirit (Ezek 36:27), 5:20 'The Son of God has given us understanding to know him who is true, cf Jer 24:7. This spiritual knowledge is manifested by signs, constantly expressed as 'by this', 1 Jn 2:3, 5; 3:10, 19, 24; 4:2, 6, 13; 5:2. While '**belief**' in 1 Jn concerns Jesus as Messiah

955g or Son of God, or his 'name', or God's witness to him (like 'confess'), and is the sign of the true Christian (2:23; 4:15f; 5:1, 10, 13), 'know' (with 'see') reaches the living Person of God or of Jesus, 2:3f; 3:1f, 5f; 5:20. It manifests itself by keeping the commandments, by holiness, belief, brotherly love, 2:3f; 3:23; 4:6ff. We have it through being 'born of God' or being 'of God', by the divine, dynamic seed of life set in us to make us act like God, 2:29—3:10; 4:7f. It goes with that abiding in God and God in us, that presence of the Spirit which is a share in the divine life and principle of manifestatory action, above all of love, 2:5f; 3:6, 24; 4:4, 12ff, cf Jn 15:1—5 'he who abides in me and I in him, he it is that bears much fruit, for apart from me you can do nothing'. Thus the OT experimental knowledge of God, issuing in service, expands in faith and love now that we know God who is Love, who has sent his Son to save us and to abide in us by active presence.

h Literary Character and Unity of the Epistle—1 Jn has none of the usual marks of a formal letter. There is no opening address nor concluding greeting or blessing so characteristic of the letters of Paul. There are no contemporary proper names or references to concrete historical situations, apart from the rather vague allusions to antichrists and false prophets. Many scholars are of the opinion that it is a tractate written for all Christians in general—a kind of encyclical letter. Granted that the historical background presupposed by the references to heretics imposes certain chronological limits, it may be doubted if the remarks addressed to the readers of the letter tell us anything specific about them apart from the fact that they are believers.

Attempts have been made (e.g. Bultmann) to demonstrate that the letter is of composite character, distinguishing for example, a number of antithetical couplets said to be from another writer. Apparent contradictions too (1:8f; 3:6ff) have been cited to prove the same point. But diversity of style does not necessarily prove diversity of authorship. Thus one recognizes polemic, poetic and homiletical passages without being in any way obliged to abandon the unity of the epistle. In particular Jn may have used material from his own catechesis (cf on 4:13ff) and added 14—21 to his ending in 5:13. On the *Comma Johanneum*, see § 958a. The many divergent views on *the plan of the epistle* show that there is no logical one. Parallelisms, repetitions and returns to the same theme come naturally to Jn, Semite and contemplative. But after the preface (1—4) there are progressive developments; God is Light (1:5—2:28), God is righteous (2:29—3:24) and (after the digression on the discernment of spirits, 4:1—6), God is love (4:7—5:3). Then 5:4—12 shows that belief in Jesus, Son of God, rests on divine witness. Conclusion: We know that we have eternal life, 5:13—21.

956a 1:1—4 Preface: From witness to communion—Best understood from Jn's Prologue of which it seems like a first sketch. V 2 being a parenthesis, v 3 resumes v 1. **1.** Jn is assuring his readers, menaced by the false teachers, that their belief is true and reliable. 'We', not here all Christians (Dodd), but the Apostles' original, authoritative witness, differing from 'you' and real: 'our eyes', 'our hands'. 'That which' (neut, but often standing for masc. e.g. 1 Jn 5:4f), best taken as like 'his glory' in Jn 1:14; 'was' (imperf.) 'from the beginning', prob. not the creation, but the eternal life (1 Jn 2:13f) become incarnate; 'we have heard . . . have seen', perfs. of continued effect; 'looked upon and touched', aorists, pass by 'a wonderful crescendo' (Chaine) to the resurrection experiences, Lk 24:39; Jn 20:27f. 'The Word of Life' is

taken by RSV (no caps), Westcott, Dodd, as the Gospel, **956** cf Phil 2:16; but the article shows it stands for the fullness of God's life (gen. of quality,cf Jn 8:12) in the preexistent and then incarnate Word, cf 1a. **2.** 'The life', a **b** main theme of the epistle: the Word embodies for men eternal, divine life (cf 1 Jn 2:25) which he bestows on all who believe in him, 5:11f; Jn 11:25; 14:6; 'made manifest', the unseeable God appeared in the Person of Christ (aorist, showing the Incarnation, e.g. 1:31; 1 Jn 3:5, 8; 4:9). 'Saw, testify, proclaim', the apostolic function of bearing witness, § 666; 'the eternal life', he is the life he brings; 'was with the Father' cf on Jn 1:1; 'to us', cf 1:14. **3.** 'With us; and our fellowship', union with the Church brings union with God (Bede), cf 17:20ff; this is to 'have' the Son and through him the Father, Jn 2:23; 5:11f; 'fellowship', Gr 'communion', sharing in the fullness of eternal life which is that of the Father and the Son, Jn 3:16, 36; 14:6ff, cf 15:1—11, a branch in Christ the Vine. Jn aims to keep his Christians in the life of this communion, based on true belief in Jesus Christ, 1 Jn 5: 13, cf 2 Jn 9. **4.** Read 'our joy'; Jesus revealed himself to his own that this, his own joy, might be perfected in them, Jn 15:11; 16:24, 17:13 (BJ), cf the sower's joy, 4:36; and 2 Jn 4; 3 Jn 3f.

5—2:28 God is Light. Walk in the Light.

5—2:2 Light and Darkness—**5.** 'God is light', one of **c** Jn's great sayings, with 'God is spirit' (Jn 4:24), 'God is greater than our hearts', (1 Jn 3:20), 'God is love', 4:16. 'Light is taken in a moral sense of holiness and purity (Brooke). The light-darkness (cf 2:8f; Jn 1:5) corresponds to the Truth and the Lie, 3:21; 8:44; 1 Jn 2:21f, and is close to DSS, cf § 612b. **6—10** work out the implications: Three slogans of the false teachers 'if we say' (6, 8, 10) are progressively answered. If we claim union with God but are morally indifferent, we lie, and do not carry out the truth of revelation (6); if we deny our guilt after sinning, we are responsible for our self-deception (8); if we say that we have not sinned personally, we call God a liar and cease to hear his voice, for he has revealed that all men sin, cf Gn 8:21, etc. But 'if we walk in the light', (7), i.e. keep his commandments, (cf Jn 14:15ff), 'we have fellowship with one another', (we expect 'with God', but Jn insists that this means fellowship with the brethren); and Christ's redeeming blood (which the 'sinless' heretics deemed unnecessary), cleanses us as nothing else can from sin's active power, cf 1 Jn 2:2; 4:10; Eph 5:26f; Ti 2:14; Heb 9:13f, 22f. If we confess our sins **(9)**—how is not **d** said, but they are personal and concrete, cf Mk 1:5—God the 'faithful and just' (Ex 34:6f; Dt 32:4; Jer 42:5, keeping to his merciful Covenant) remits our sins. God's justice and mercy are not opposed. **2:1—2.** Tenderly the old Apostle (cf the young robber story, Eus.HE 3, 23) warns (cf Rm 6:1) his 'little children' not to sin (aorist, the single act); but he adds as a realist 'if any one sin' (aorist, so one act against the tenour of his life, 1 Jn 1:7), 'we' (setting himself amongst sinners) 'have', as divine gift (cf 2:23; 5:12), 'an advocate' (cf Jn 14:16 'another Paraclete' and Heb 7:25 for Jesus's heavenly intercession); 'the righteous', who perfectly fulfills all law, 1 Pt 3:18; 1 Jn 1:9. He 'is the expiation', (cf 4 Mc 6:28f; Rm 6:10; Heb 9:12; 1 Jn 4:10) eternally valid and universal, Jn 1:29; 3:16f; 4:42; 12:37; 'the whole world' marks the end of the sin-theme.

3—11 We know God if we keep his command- e ments—**3.** Know', cf § 955f. **4.** Negative development against the heretics, with contrasts; three more slogans: 'he who says', cf 6, 9; 'the truth', here the pre-requisite for knowledge. **5—6.** The sign that we are 'in him' and, still more permanently, 'abide in him', is that we 'walk',

56e not by a code of laws, but as Christ lived and died, Jn 14:31. From him we 'know' brotherly love, 1 Jn 3:16f. **7—8.** 'Beloved': Jn expresses his own love when speaking of love or with special tenderness, cf 3:2, 21; 4:1, 7; 3 Jn 2, 5, 11. 'Old', the original Gospel message (2 Jn 5) bears truth's seal and is ever the same. 'Again' (cf Jn 16:28), this commandment is 'new' (13:34): Love as Jesus did; 'true', really manifested 'in him and in you', 15:13; 1 Jn 3:14. 'Already' Christians experience sin's darkness passing away before the shining of the true light, Jn **f** 1:9; 8:12. **9—10.** To show up heretical morality ('he who says'), Jn introduces his great theme of brotherly love, cf 3:10ff, 23; 4:7, 11, 20f; 5:1f; for him not to love is to hate. 'No cause for stumbling in it', love (RSV), or 'in him' of scandal for others (BJ). **11.** Very close to Jn 12:35, and cf DSS. The dark, impenitent self-excuse blinds, cf Is 6:9f; Jn 12:40 (Schnackenburg). The meaning of 'brother' (e.g. Mt 5:22ff; Ac 2:29, 37) deepens in Jn to involve the same begetting from the Father and attachment to Jesus and his ways, Jn 20:17; 1 Jn 3:10, 16; 5:1f. Brotherly love is envisaged by Jn as spoken of by Jesus to his intimate disciples (3:11ff; Jn 13: 34; 15:12, 17) but it goes out also to all, 1 Jn 4:20f. DSS say that the 'sons of light' must 'hate' the sons of darkness; Jn only that these hate the Christians, 2:9ff; 3:10—15; Jn 15:18ff.

g 12—17 Do not love the world—12—14. In two lyrical, symmetrical passages Jn first comforts, strengthens and reassures all the Christians ('children') that (not 'because') their sins are forgiven 'for his sake', lit 'his name', cf 20:31; 1 Jn 3:22ff; 5:13; then the old men that they 'know him', lit 'have known'; 'from the beginning,' cf 1.1, and the young men—for whom the fight is hottest and whom Jn seems to care for specially—that they are strong through the word of God that abides in them, cf Jn 8:31; 17:14, contrast 5:38; 1 Jn 1:10; or through the Word, (parallel with 'him who is from the beginning'). **15—17.** A model of early Christian exhortation, with double antithesis (15 *a—b*—17 *a—b*), triple rhythm (16) and effective motivation (Schnackenburg). 'The world', not God's creation, but the work of its prince the evil one, 13f; Jn 12:31, cf Jas 4:4; DSS, § 611*i*; in the concrete it may be thought of as surrounding pagan society; to love the world is incompatible with love of the Father, cf Jn 5:42; 'flesh', cf Jn 1:13 and Paul's 'desires of the flesh', Gal 5:16f (not only sexual). Passions are aroused by the eyes, 'the windows of the soul'; 'pride of life', better 'of possessions' as 3:17 *bios*: the vulgar arrogance of riches. This brittle world passes; he who does God's will (which includes the right use of all that answers to it, Rev 4:11, Westcott), abides for ever, cf Jn 8:35; 12:34.

h 18—28 Beware of antichrists: Abide by the Spirit in Christs' teaching—18—19. 'Last hour', no Gr. article, suggesting 'the character of the period rather than its relation to the end' (Westcott). 'Antichrist', (cf 4:3; Mk 13:14; 2 Thes 2:3ff) has no article and is here a collectivity, not the Antichrist before the Parousia; Rev 2:6—3:10 may show these antichrists at work. 'They went out' (aorist, one action), but 'used not to be of us', did not draw their life from ours (Westcott, contrast 1 :3). Is he thinking of Judas going out from the room? 'That it might be plain'. God thus provided against interior evil influences. **20—21.** Lit 'an anointing': Jn is using an OT term in all its width, but it points principally to the Holy Spirit. He anoints the Christ and so Christians, Is 11:2; 61:1; Ezek 36:27; Lk 4:18; Ac 10:38; 27*b* shows he is meant personally and Jesus (Jn 14:17,26; 15:26; 16:13) ascribes the same efficacy to the Spirit of truth, the Paraclete. Christians 'have' (possess) him and he leads them to true knowledge; 'you all know'

is the better reading, cf 19. Every Christian is given a **956h** saving knowledge of the truth, cf Rm 15:14f; 1 Thes 4:9; *Lumen Gentium* on the People of God. Translate either 'because' (RSV) or 'not *that* you do not know the truth but *that* you know it, and know'. **22.** 'The liar', no mere error, but Satan's dark dangerous deceptions, cf Jn 8:44. 'The Christ' stands no longer simply for the Jewish Messiah (Jn 20.31) but for the Saviour Son, cf 1 Jn 3.23; 5:1. Some Gnostics held that 'the Christ' descended on Jesus at his baptism and left him at the Passion. **23.** Jn's denial (negative, then positive) of any **i** communion with the Father save through confessing the Son, echoes Mt 10:32f; 11:27f, cf Jn 12: 44f; 14:6—11. **24—25.** To abide in Christ's word (the message received when their Christian life began), as objective standard and living power (Jn 5:38; 6:63; 8:31) is to abide in him (15:7) and through him in the Father, 17:21ff. 'Eternal life', cf § 955*f*; the promise throws the emphsis on the future, cf 12:25; salvation has not yet reached fullness, 1 Jn 3:13; 4:5. **26. He lifts his beloveds' eyes to the future;** warning begun v 18, cf 2:1. **27.** carries on from 20f; the Spirit's inspiration went with the message received from the Apostles, 1:3, 5; 2:7, 24; 4:13. **28.** A last urging to abide in Christ carries the thought to the Parousia, in which a good conscience will make them free, trustful and candid. This ends the section started in v 18.

29—3:10 God is righteous. His children and the 957a Devil's—An inclusion marks the section as a unity and shows that its themes are birth from God and the eschatological opposition between the forces of good and evil (10) which will be manifested fully at the Parousia but can be seen now by moral signs. **29.** Transition; 'righteous' for Jn includes holiness but adds keeping God's commandments of belief and love, 3:3f; 'he' is Jesus; one expects 'every one who abides in him must do righteousness', but the thought supervenes that the righteous are begotten of the Father ('him', cf Jn 1:13). This leads to **3:1.** Against these heretics in morals Jn brings in the love of the Father, who by an unmerited gift ('given', cf Mt 5:9) calls us his children; the name is not enough: 'are' his children (Jn 3:5f), safe from the world; 'does not know', treat as its own, love; the deep reason is that it does not know our Father, 15:19; 17:25, cf 10:14f, 27; 1 Jn 3:13; 4:5. **2.** He lifts his beloveds' eyes to the future; he does not tell us what we shall be; he is interested in the present fact and the future glory to be revealed, cf Jn 17:24; Rm 8:29f; Col 3:1—4; 'as he is', the unveiled sight of God as eschatological fulfilment, cf Rm 8:19; 1 Cor 13:12. **3.** This hope stirs us to be pure like Christ; 'purifies', not by Jewish ceremonial (Ex 19:10; Jn 11:55) but by Christ' purity, Heb 10:10, 14. Purity leads to the sight of God, Mt 4:8. **4.** 'Lawlessness', though Biblical synonym for sin, is here emphatic: eschatological enmity, dominated by Satan, opposed to Christ and the Kingdom, cf 2 Thes 2: 3, 7; I. de la Potterie, 'Le péché, c'est l'iniquité', NRT (1956), 785—97. **5.** To sin Jn opposes **b** the sinless Christ who 'appeared' (Jn's word for the Incarnation), to take away sins (pl., but probably alludes to the Baptist's saying, Jn 1:29, cf 1 Cor 15:3). **6.** Fellowship with Christ is inconsistent with sin, cf 1 Jn 1:6; 'seen', come to know, cf 3 Jn 11. This against heretical slogans. **7.** 'Little children'; their peril calls forth Jn's tenderness (Westcott); 'is righteous', goes with 2:29. 'It is all very white and black. It had to be so, if the readers were to be sufficiently warned' (Dodd). **8.** The works of the devil which Jesus came to destroy are sins; 'from the beginning', cf Jn 8:44. **9.** Cf I. de la Potterie, 'L'impeccabilité du chrétien', *L'Év. de Jean*, 161—77. The holiness and sinlessness of the elect at the end of time is

957b already a theme of Is 60:21; Dn 7:18; Ezek 36:27f. It is due to docility to wisdom, the Law, God's word, Sir 24:22; Ps 37 (36):30f; 119 (118):11. For NT cf Gal 5:16; Jas 1:21, 25; 1 Pt 1:22f, 'incorruptible seed'. The men of Qumran confess their sins, but as the Messianic community, purified by the spirit of sanctity and truth (1QS4, 20—23), are of perfect holiness, 1QH 1, 25; CD 20, 2, 5, 7. So here, though he who says he is sinless is a liar (1 Jn 1:5—10), the sons of God are opposed as eschatological **c** group to the sons of the devil, cf 5:18f. For Jn resurrection, judgement, victory are eschatological realities aleady present in Christ, Jn 11:25; 12:31; 16:33; 1 Jn 5:4; so is impeccability, privilege of those who have passed from death to life (3:14), from darkness to light, Jn 3:21. 'God's nature', lit 'seed', another wide OT concept, taken by most as the Holy Spirit, citing 3:6; 1 Jn 3:24; 4:13, but these are not real parallels; others interpret 'the offspring of God' (his posterity, or Jesus), but this would require the Gr. article, as in Gal 3:16; Rev 12:17; others, the word of God, the dynamic, cleansing principle of new life, cf the 'seed' of Mt 13:19ff; 1 Cor 4:15; Jas 1:18; 1 Pt 1:23; Jn 15:3f; 1 Jn 2:14, 24; 2 Jn 2. 'Abides' (favourite word of Jn, 67 times) can be used from the human point of view hortatively and conditionally (Jn 8:31; 1 Jn 2:24), or from the divine point of view of the divine reality as a fact, as here, cf 2:14; if docile to this, we do not sin (Jn 6:45; Gal 5:16) until in heaven we become incapable of sinning, Rev 21:27. This solution is essentially that of the Gr. Fathers. **10.** Summary, inclusion with 2:29 and introduction to the positive idea of brotherly love.

d 11—4:21 God is Love.

11—24 Love one another—'Jn is never more strongly un-gnostic' (Schnackenburg). 'For' binds with v 10 and introduces the summit theme. To neglect the message (a command, Jn 13:34; 15:12; 1 Jn 3:23) known from the beginning (2:7) is innovation; love is for the brethren first, but not exclusively, vv 13—15. **12.** 'Not as' (cf Jn 6:58). A Christian midrash on Cain's devil-inspired hate, cf 8:44; 'his deeds were evil', exactly 3:19. **13—15.** 'Brethren', only here as address, implies their mutual affection. The world's hate (15:18—25) takes the same moral line as the murderer's and is incompatible with eternal life. Not to love is to stay in the sphere of death. But love of the brethren has already brought us from it to the sphere of life (elsewhere in NT the work of faith and baptism). 'Love and life are convertible terms' (Westcott). **16.** True love means action; its measure is Jesus ('he') dying for us, 10:10—15; 'we ought' suggests 'as I have loved you', 15:12f. **17.** But lofty imaginings are easy. The real, homely test is 'the imperious duty of compassion' (BJ) for a brother in distress, cf Lk 6:38; Ac 2:44f; Jas 2:15f; the world's' marks their transience, cf 1 Jn 2:17. **18.** 'Little children' introduces the affectionate warning: beware the heretics' fair words, **e** love is selfless, practical service. **19—20.** 'By this' refers back, cf 2:5b; 4:6; 'of the truth', so belonging to God, Jn 8:47; 18:37. What follows, a crux, is best taken (RSV, BJ, Dodd), as motive of confidence: 're-assure' (cf Mt 28:14), overcome self-accusation of past, repented sins, for 'God is greater than our heart' and the wide, divine outlook (cf Jn 21:17) forgives the falls of those who love— the confident doctrine of Ste Thérèse or Brother Lawrence. **21—22.** Those whose heart does not condemn (or who have peace in spite of it, Brooke) have free, frank access to God (16:26f), and all their prayers are answered. Jesus's promise (15:7—10) has become present reality for Jn, cf 1 Jn 5:14. For, like Jesus (Jn 8:29), we do what pleases the Father. **23—24.** Central themes return to

round off the whole exhortation from 2:18: God's command **95'** is to believe in Jesus (1 Jn 2:22f), i.e. give ourselves to him, and love one another; 'the name', the Person; this belief becomes a creed, Phil 2:9; brotherly love flows from belief in Jesus, for he has commanded it, Jn 13:34; 15:12, 17; communion with God flows from fulfilling the commandment, ('abide', cf 1 Jn 2:5f). Jn can now pass on to Christ's gift of the Spirit. The love, freedom and joy he brings (cf Rm 5:5; 8:14ff; Gal 4:6), show our communion with God (Bonsirven).

4:1—6 But test the spirits—This is close to DSS on the **f** spirits of truth and lying and their testing, 1QS 3, 13f, 18f; 5, 20f. **1—2.** A true or lying spirit spoke in prophets, Mi 3:5—8; for NT cf Mt 7:15ff; Mk 13:22; 1 Thes 5:21; the test is from what they say of Jesus, 1 Cor 12:3, cf Hermas, *Mand.*, 11. 'In the flesh', anti-Gnostic formula for the Incarnation, like 2:22; 4:15; 5:1; 2 Jn 7. **3.** 'Does not confess Jesus' (Gr. MSS), or *'dissolves Jesus'* (Iren., Clem.Alex., Tertull.), makes naught, precisely anti-christ's spirit. Polycarp, *Ad Phil.*, 7, has 'confess'. **4—6.** Still encouraging his 'children', Jn contrasts the groups in their root difference: 'from God', 'from the world', cf Jn 3:31; 8:23; 'he who is in you' (Jesus) not 'he who is in the world' (Satan); they have conquered (16:33; 1 Jn 2:13f), for Jesus is greater, Jn 12:31f; 14:30; 16:11. But the heretics are successful in the pagan world around. 'Listens to us', the test of hearing the Church. 'The Spirit of truth', cf 14:17; 15:26; 16:13; that of error is from Satan. After this warning parenthesis:

7—5:4 Love is of God—This longest discourse on love, **g** deeper than 3:11ff, makes no difference between love of God and of neighbour. The Bible's God shows what he is by what he does. He is Love because he has sent his Son with gratuitous love. **7.** Love is of God, and the criterion of knowing God (§ 955f). The Christian is a lover, and thereby born of God. **8—10.** For 'God is love' (Jn's greatest saying), shown by sending his only (or Heb. 'beloved') Son among us (Jn 1:14, 18), 'that we might live through him', dominant note of Jn's Good News, 3:16; 20:31; 1 Jn 5:13. Love begins not from us, but from God's free initiative, its high point is sending his Son as expiation for our sins, cf Rm 5:8; 1 Jn 2:2; 3:16. **11—12.** So let us love one another. Communion with God who cannot be seen (cf Jn 1:18, prob. also against the visionaries), is conditioned and perfected by loving others; 'his love', prob. divine love (gen. of quality, cf 1 Jn 3:17) rather than God's love (subjective) or love to God (Dodd). In this life we come closer to God through love than through knowledge, Aquin. (Brown). **13.** Comes **h** in oddly and is like 3:24b; perhaps the phrase of a long-practised teacher, wont to impress definite ideas: love (12), faith (15), possession of the Spirit witness to communion with God (Schnackenburg). **14—15.** Also digress, returning to 1:1—4. As bases for communion with God, faith and love are inseparable. 'Son of God' combines for Jn Christology and soteriology, cf 5:5. **16.** Returns to the theme of love and Jn sets together his thoughts on love. 'We' (all Christians), 'know and believe' (here almost synonymous). 'God is love' means he is a lover who gives what he holds dearest to redeem men; if we abide in a reciprocal love which refracts his, he abides in us and we in him. This is the high point of Jn's contemplation of God and the fullest expression of his message. **17—18.** Love reaches its highest sovereignty and power in us who still live under threat of judgement by giving free confidence before our judge (cf 2:28), because (or 'that') we are following him as best we may, cf Jn 4:34; 15:9f. The fear is of damnation, separation from God, cf Jn 3:18. Jn is saying, not that the world should

57h not fear, but that servile fear and full love do not co-exist. Such people trust too little; communion with God overcomes their fear. Filial fear, not to love God enough,
i is a higher form of love. **19—21.** 'We love' (RSV), better than 'let us love'. Jn works this out in practice, cf 1 Jn 3:16ff. 'If anyone says' and 'liar' show the heretics are in mind, cf 2:4. Jn pre-supposes that it is easier to love a person seen continually (perf.) than one not seen. He who loves his brethren shows that he loves God, for he keeps his commandments, e.g. Mt 22:37ff; Jn 13:34; 1 Jn 2:7ff. **5:1.** The emphasis is not yet on 'believes' but on 'child of God'; being born of God, he loves his Father, loving his Father, he loves his other children. **2—3.** 'By this' probably refers to what precedes, as 2:5, etc; 'commandments', all summed up in loving the brethren, Rm 13:9f; Gal 5:14; 'not burdensome', cf Mt 11:30, another encouragement. **4.** He overcomes the world's allurements (2:13f) by the indwelling (4:4) power of belief in Christ's all-sufficing victory, Jn 16:33; Rev 3:21; 5:5. 'Our faith' makes transition.

58a 5—12 Belief in Jesus to whom God witnesses— 5—7. 'Overcomes', links with 4. Jn's concern is now right belief as key to victory. 'Son of God', the world's Saviour (4:14f), bringing eternal life (5:20) by his death, 4:10. **6.** 'Came' must refer to the unique event when blood and water issued from Jesus's side; of this Jn is the insistent witness, Jn 19:34f. (Most MSS omit 'and Spirit', though Sin and A have it.) 'Not with the water only' probably rebuts heretics (? Cerinthus) who regarded Jesus's baptism as alone significant for giving the Spirit, omitting his bloody death. 'The Spirit is the witness' to Jesus as Son and Redeemer in his life and now in and through the Church, 1:32ff; 15:26; 16:8ff; for he is 'the truth' (16:13; 1 Jn 4:6), who disposes of and shares out God's truth. **8.** 'Three witnesses', cf Jn 8:17. Probably the water and blood from Christ's side showed for Jn his redemptive death as source of the life giving power of the Spirit (also symbolized by water) and of baptism and the Eucharist, cf 3:6; 6:63; 7:38f. These sacraments as 'visible words' confirmed the prophetical word inspired in the Church by the Spirit (Dodd). To later generations the three work together to witness the saving nature of Christ's death. **The Comma Johanneum**—After 'three witnesses' Vg inserts 'in heaven, the Father, the Word and the Holy Spirit and these three are one; and there are three who give testimony on earth'. This passage occurs in no Gr MS before the 14th cent. and is absent from the earliest Vg MSS. A Trinitarian interpretation of 'the spirit, the water and the blood' can be traced back as far as Cyprian (A.D. 258). Augustine gives the same interpretation suggesting that by his time (c. 400) it had become an established marginal gloss. Vigilius of Thapsus (c. 490) regards it as an authentic part of the Vulgate. In the Vg MSS in which the passage first occurs as part of the text, the 'earthly' witnesses appear before the 'heavenly', thus seeming to confirm the interpretative nature of the passage. The transposition of the 'heavenly witnesses' to the position in front of the 'earthly' appears to have taken place in the 14th cent.
b **9—12.** To strengthen his point (supra, v 8), Jn contrasts the witness of men (which should be accepted if worthy of belief, Dt 17:6; 19:15) with that of God, (cf Jn 5:31—47—36 'greater than John's'). 'God has borne witness to his Son' in Jesus's time on earth (perf. 5:37) and now in the Church. Dodd refers this to the three witnesses, God adding (Bonsirven) the inner testimony of belief. Refusal of belief is insult to God. Belief brings eternal life, cf 1 Jn 1:4. Vv 9, 10 and 11 end with 'his Son'. **12.** Climax with antitheses: 'To have' the Son

is to have life (2:23; inclusion with 1:1—3); not to have **958b** the Son is not to have life, cf Jn 3:15, 36.
13—21 Conclusion—13. Closely resembles the original **c** end of the Gospel (20:31) but here the aim is 'that you may know'. In the additional encouragement which follows no word so dominates as 'we know' (6 times). To keep away dangers Jn relies chiefly on the positive contemplation of their victory in Christ and happiness in Christian communion, cf 2:12—17, 21, 27. They are to know that as they have the faith, they have eternal life. **14.** 'According to his will' shows early Christian reflection on Jesus's promises in which he bases sureness of attaining the object of prayer on communion with God, cf Jn 14:13f; 15:16; 16:23—26 'in my name'; 15:7 'if you abide in me'. This prayer must be confident, cf Mk 11:24 'believe that you have got it'; 1 Jn 3:21f. **16.** Prayer for the sinner is the great example of brotherly charity. As he has to recover supernatural life, RSV's 'mortal sin' has more than our meaning. 'Sin to death', originally sin punished by death, here brings eternal death, antithetic to 'life', cf Jn 5:24; 8:51. Jn's readers knew what sin he meant; it is not so easy for us; perhaps it is that of the anti-christs, whose hate has broken with the faith and attacked God, Christ and their brethren. Jn does not forbid prayer for such, but makes no promise that it will be heard. **17—19.** **d** Jn has returned to prayer for the sinner. 'Born of God' and so continuing (perf.); 'does not sin', ideally, and overcomes sin through Christ, 1 Jn 2:1; 3:9. **18.** 'He who was born of God' i.e. Christ, cf on Jn 1:13; Rm 8:29. 'keeps him' (Jn 17:11f, 16; Rev 3:10, BJ); this seems better than 'the Christian holds fast to God' Schnackenburg. 'Does not touch', cf Jn 14:30. 'We are of God' gives assurance amid surrounding unbelief and hate originating from the world's prince, 12:21; in this they live, not separated as at Qumran, but like Christ and by his power, 17:15; 1 Jn 4:4, 17. **20.** Jubilant confidence of salvation past (perf.) and present by living communion ('we know') with the one true God (Jer 24:7; Jn 8:42; 17:3) through the life-giving mediator; in him, divine being come on earth is open to believers, 1:14, 16. 'Jesus Christ' is emphatically placed, and 'this' must be Jesus. As at the start, his Godhead shines forth at this pinnacle of the epistle, cf Jn 1:1; 20:28. 'Life' as in 1:4 and (inclusion) 1 Jn 1:1ff. **21.** Last affectionate down-to-earth warning. Idols are always with us too.

II and III JOHN

Character—That these are letters appears from **e** formulae which occur often in papyri. They have the form of the Hellenistic private letter (Kümmel). This is borne out too by the close-fitting handling of concrete fragments and the reference to individuals, 1, 9, 12 (3 Jn). They are fresh and primitive in style but they do not treat of the personal concerns of the addressees but of matters that pertain to the life of the Christian community. 2 Jn is to a community and 3 Jn to an active Christian about a community. The 'elect lady' (kuria) of 2 Jn could indeed refer to an individual, but the tenor of the epistle indicates rather a community. The 'lady' is joined by the bond of mutual love with 'all who know the truth'. Her 'children' likewise are (cf the elder's children in 3 Jn 4) not physical but spiritual children. Gaius in 3 Jn is not otherwise known. It is clear from the letter that he is a prominent member of his community.
Author—Both letters have the same author. The lan- **f** guage and style are the same, and both are written by 'the elder', ho presbuteros. It is not likely that the term indicates one of the familiar elders or presbyters but rather

958f the venerable age and position of the writer. The connexion with 1 Jn is close. The ideas in 2 Jn: right belief, and love, are again leading themes and cf 5, 6, 9, 12 respectively with 1 Jn 2:7; 5:2f; 2:23; 1:4. 3 Jn, besides the title of 'elder', has also about the same length, style and eschatology as 2 Jn. Both letters are closely connected with the Gospel of John: cf 'know the truth' (2 Jn 1) 'which will be with you forever' (2), 'as we received commandment from the Father' (4), 'that you may receive a full reward', (8), 'abide in the doctrine of Christ' (9) with Jn 8:32; 14:16f; 10:18; 4:36; 8:31, and 3 Jn 12 with Jn 19:35; 21:24. The same deep expressions recur: 'to be of', 'to know', 'to abide in'. If all four Johannine writings are to be ascribed to the same author then the identity of the writer of these letters must be tested by the arguments for the authorship of the Gospel, but conversely we can also ask how suitable the title 'elder' is to the author of Jn and 1 Jn. The title 'elder' is certainly not used in 2 and 3 Jn to hide the identity of the writer. The implication is that the readers would at once know from whom it came, as in the case of many other well-known men in history familiar to contemporaries as 'the old man'. Just as there is nothing to suggest that the title indicates a presbyter in the technical sense, so there is no evidence to connect 'the elder' with the 'John the elder' (or presbyter) referred to by Papias in connexion with the Apocalypse, cf Eus.HE 3, 39, 4. The attitude of the 'elder' as evidenced in these letters is more patriarchal than jurisdictional—such as could be only if he had real authority. Tradition is not unvarying with regard to the identity of the author. Iren (PG 7, 633, 927) cites 2 Jn as from the Lord's disciple; Clem.Alex (8, 1004) implies it; the Muratorian Canon accepts one letter, perhaps both; Dion. Alex accepted both, as do Orig., Eus.HE and Jer, but they say Jn's authorship is contested (Eus.HE 6, 25, 10; 3, 25, 3). Jer adds that some attributed the letters to Presbyter John (*De Vir. Illust.* 9, 18; *Ad Theol.* 75, 3, etc). C. H. Dodd tentatively makes Presbyter John, a disciple of the Evangelist, the author of these letters cf § 955c. The Syrian Church accepted them only in the 5th cent. The Councils of Hippo (A.D. 393) and of Carthage (A.D. 397) held them to be inspired, and subsequently their canonicity was universally admitted.

g **Place of origin, Date and Purpose**—The place is generally agreed to be Asia Minor. There is little evidence for fixing a date. 3 Jn may reflect a time before the monarchical episcopate and open heresy and possibly precedes 2 Jn which shows doctrinal troubles endangering a particular Church at a time when more radical condemnation was called for (BJ). One may think of a date at the end of the 1st cent. for both letters but there is really no firm evidence on which to base an opinion.

II JOHN

h **The aim** (as in 1 Jn) is first to strengthen brotherly love and true belief and then to ward off false teachers who may arrive to spread their poison. Soon 'the elder' hopes to make a visit. The 'elect lady' beloved of the elder and all true Christians, of whose children some live with her and are greeted, some (? not others) are good Christians, but none are named, must be a church, like her 'elect sister', whose children greet her from the place where the letter is written 13, cf 1 Pt 5:13.

1—3 Greeting—Letter-form and expressions are Jn's: 'the elder' (no need to name himself), 'love', 'know', 'the truth' (the eternal reality revealed in Christ Jesus as opposed to the 'knowledge' of the Gnostics); 'for ever', cf Jn 14:16. 'Grace, mercy, peace', as 1, 2 Tm, but here the blessing is assured; 'and from' shows

the equality of the Son, thought of as bearing salvation. **958i**
4—6 The Commandment of Love—Some who have visited him 'follow' ('walk in', Semitism) the truth, cf 1 Jn 1:6; Eph 5:2; DSS 'walk in the light'. Was the church divided? He begs all to love one another; 'from the beginning', cf 1 Jn 2:7f; love of others is love of God.

7—11 Antichrists and avoiding them—'For' shows he **i** already had them in mind; same errors as 4:1f; 'coming', pres. part. for the timelessness of the Incarnation; 'the antichrist', cf 2:18ff; 'look to yourselves', eschatological warning; 'you', better reading; 'worked for' by believing, 'full reward', eternal life, cf 2:25; Jn 6:27ff. 'Goes ahead', heretical slogan, or Jn's reproach for leaving apostolic doctrine; 'of Christ', about him, or, deeper, subj. gen., 'Christ's', cf 7:16; 18:19; 1 Jn 2:22f. Refuse guest friendship rather than have your faith poisoned by the entry of this lying spirit of error, 1 Jn 4:6, cf Jud 23; Did 11f; Ign. Ant., *Eph.* 7, 1; the greeting meant a blessing, Mt 10:13. 'These words are to be interpreted with the limitations suggested by the character of the "coming"' (Westcott), cf 2 Cor 11:4.

12—13 Ending—Same as 3 Jn 13; 'our joy', cf 1 Jn 1:4.

III JOHN

Here is the charm with which a person in authority in **j** the early Church speaks with a friend. Characters stand out: 'each personal trait speaks of a fullness of knowledge behind, and belongs to a living man' (Westcott). Gaius 'keeps truth and love'; he has been charitable to stranger-brethren, probably itinerant preachers sent by Jn. As they would not ask money from the pagans to whom they preached, they relied on the charity of the brethren, who thus contributed to the spread of the faith. But the jealous Diotrephes, head or ambitious to be head of the local church, would cut off the community from the elder himself and these life-giving outside influences, and bully those who offer hospitality. The elder will come and deal with him. He warmly commands Demetrius, perhaps a preacher and bearer of the letter, and hopes to see Gaius soon. The *Apostolic Constitutions*, 7, 46, make Gaius (? later) bishop of Pergamum and Demetrius of Philadelphia, but this evidence is late.

1—3 Greeting and praise of Gaius—1—4. 'The elder', **k** cf 2 Jn 1; Gaius, common name, e.g. 1 Cor 1:14; 'soul', cf Jn 10:24 (Gr.); 12:27; 'some brethren arrived', 'follow the truth', cf 2 Jn 4; 'my children' shows the elder as universal father, cf 1 Cor 4:15. Gaius, praised for his hospitality to the missionaries ('before the church', the local community, cf Rev) is exhorted to help them on their way; 'for his sake', Christ's, lit 'for the name', Jn 1:12; 1 Jn 3:23; 5:13; unlike heathen begging priests, they took no collection, cf Paul's example, 1 Cor 9:15ff. By helping them the 'old' Christians share their apostolate, Mt 10:10; 1 Cor 9:14; 1 Tm 5:18.

9—12 Misbehaviour of Diotrephes. Demetrius recommended— 'Something', like perhaps the Rev letters, hardly 1 Jn; the presumptuous, arrogant Diotrephes is probably opposed to the central mission; he makes personal charges against the elder, whose arrival will be decisive. 'Stops . . . puts out' may be pres. expressing only the attempt: 'tries to stop . . . put out' (Westcott, Schnackenburg), cf Jn 10:32. By contrast, Demetrius is testified to by 'every one', by 'the truth' (his own acts, 3, 4, or Jesus (Jn 14:6) or the Gospel) and by the elder himself, just as 19:35; 21:24.

13—15 End—very like 2 Jn; 'peace', the Semitic greeting, 2 Jn 3; Jn 20:19. Gaius will transmit the letter to the elder's friends.

JUDE

BY W. J. DALTON S.J.

959a **Bibliography**—Commentaries: as under 1 and 2 Peter.

b **The Author**—In the inscription of this short epistle we read: 'Jude, a servant of Jesus Christ and brother of James'. In the list of the apostles two are named Judas, cf Mt 10:3; Mk 3:18; Lk 6:16; Ac 1:13; one is called Judas the Iscariot, who betrayed the Lord, the other is called 'Thaddaeus' or 'Lebbaeus' or 'of James'. However, it is more likely that the James and Jude who are the authors of the two Catholic epistles do not belong to the twelve apostles. For the discussion of James, 'brother of the Lord' and leader of the church at Jerusalem, see § 664. The well known James, mentioned in the inscription of our epistle, is almost certainly this person. Jude is here the 'brother' of Jesus mentioned in Mk 6:3. He does not give himself the title of 'apostle', and in v 17 he seems to distinguish himself from 'the apostles of our Lord Jesus Christ'. On the 'brethren of the Lord', cf § § 663—64

Because of the Gnostic nature of the heresy attacked in the epistle, it has been urged by some critics that it is the product of an anonymous writer of the 2nd cent. who invoked the name of Jude to give authority to his work. While on dogmatic grounds such a solution should not be ruled out, there seems to be no convincing critical ground for such a view. The Gnosticism attacked does not show any characteristics which require such a late date. Nor does the correct Gr. of the epistle rule out Jude as author. We know too little of him to pass judgement on the sort of Gr. he could write. Besides there always remains the possibility that he used the services of a hellenistic Jewish convert in the actual redaction of the letter. All in all, it seems more reasonable to accept simply the evidence of the letter's inscription, and to ascribe it to Jude, the 'brother' of the Lord.

c **Canonicity**—This epistle is placed on his list of disputed books by Eusebius, HE 3, 25, 3. Jerome gives the reason why not all accepted it as an inspired writing: 'Jude has left us a short epistle, which is one of the seven Catholic Epistles; but since he quotes the apocryphal Book of Enoch it is rejected by many. Yet it deserves a place in the Holy Scripture because of its antiquity and the use that is made of it' (*De Vir. Illust.* 4). Early Christian writers of the 3rd cent. who defend its authenticity and quote it as Scripture are: Clem.Alex., *Paedag.* 3, 8; *Strom.* 3, 2; Orig. *Com. in Mt* 10, 17 and 17, 30; *In Ep. ad Rom* 3, 6; 5, 1; Tert., *De Cultu Femin.* 1, 3. It is found in the canons of the Muratorian Fragment, of Athanasius (PG 26, 1176), Cyril of Jerusalem (PG 33, 500), Damasus (Dz 84), Innocent I (Dz 96), of the Councils of Hippo, Laodicea and Carthage III (Dz 92).

The Relation between Jude and 2 Pt—See § 953b. Both letters were written to warn certain Christian communities of a grave danger to faith and morals propagated by false teachers. There is, however, a closer connexion between the two epistles that arises from a common purpose. There is great similarity of thought **959c** and language, as may be seen by comparing Jude 3—18 with 2 Pt 1:5; 2:1—18, so much so that direct literary dependence is indicated. Which letter was written first? It is much more likely that it was Jude. 2 Pt 2:4—7 corrects the order of Jude 5—7, giving the chronological order of the examples of God's punishment. 2 Pt omits elements which are strange: the nature of the angels' sin, Jude 6f, the dispute of Michael with the devil, Jude 9, the reference to the 'wandering stars', Jude 13, the citation from the Book of Enoch, Jude 14f. Finally, the section in 2 Pt which deals with the false prophets, ch 2, while modified somewhat to suit the intentions of the writer, seems to break into the general theme of the epistle (Christian expectation of the Parousia). This also points to its derivation from the epistle of Jude.

The Relation between Jude and the Book of d Enoch—As Jerome pointed out, Jude makes considerable use of the apocryphal Book of Enoch. Apart from the citation of vv 14—15 (which corresponds almost literally with an extant Gr. translation), he recalls passages from the same book in his references to 'wandering stars', v 13, and to the punishment of the angels, v 6; cf Enoch 1:9; 10:4—13; 18:13—16. Jude, of course, does not pronounce on the inspiration of this book. He uses it as an authority recognized by his readers to confute the heretics whom he attacks.

Destination and Purpose—The letter is addressed 'to those who are called, beloved in God the Father and kept for Jesus Christ' (1), which might apply to any Christian community. From the tone of the letter it seems to be directed to a definite church or group of churches in a definite locality. It is not clear whether the heretics are converts from Judaism or from paganism. The ample use of Jewish tradition, the fact that James, and, we may suppose, his brother Jude, were chiefly concerned with the Palestinian Jewish converts, both point to a possible Jewish origin of the converts. On the other hand, the flagrant immorality of the heretics is more in keeping with Gentile converts. Nor can we rule out a background of Hellenistic Judaism, in which heterodox and pagan influences were all too evident. No indication is given about the locality of these Christians, and there is no point in guessing.

The dangerous heresy attacked by Jude was threatening e to undermine the Christian life and belief of his readers. The heretics still belonged to the Christian community, vv 4, 12, 22, 23. They seem to be imbued with an incipient form of Gnosticism, in which Christian liberty was misunderstood so as to give rise to unbridled licentiousness. Not merely do they lack respect for the angels, v 8, but they 'deny our only Master and Lord, Jesus Christ', v 4, probably seeing in him a being of subordinate rank. It seems unwarranted to set the epistle in the 2nd cent. because of the Gnostic nature of the heresy attacked. Sporadic and undeveloped forms of Gnosticism existed from the time of Paul.

959e Time and Place of Composition—Nothing definite is known about either. 2 Pt, which is dependent on Jude, can only with difficulty be ascribed to the apostle Peter. Nor can anything certain be derived from the fact that the destruction of Jerusalem is not mentioned among the examples of God's punishment. On the other hand, there are indications, cf vv 3, 17, 20, of a rather late date. Possibly some date about A.D. 80 would not be far wide of the mark.

f Analysis—After the greeting, 1—2, the writer gives the occasion for his writing, the presence of false teachers among his readers. He deals with these heretics, 5—16, describing first the punishment which awaits them, 5—7, the blasphemies of which they are guilty, 8—11, and their abandoned wickedness, 12—16. Then follows an exhortation to fidelity, 17—23, based on the teaching of the apostles, 17—19, and on the love of God and of one's neighbour. The epistle closes with a doxology to God the Father.

Text and Style—The variants in the Gr. text are not many and are of little importance. The recently discovered P 72 (Papyrus Bodmer VII), commonly dated from the 3rd cent., has many careless mistakes. In v 5 it reads *theos Christos*. While this is probably not the original reading, it indicates an early interpretation of *kurios*. The style of Jude is impassioned, somewhat vague, picturesque and vigorous.

960a 1—2 Salutation—As in the case of Jas 1:1, the author is content to call himself 'a servant of God and of our Lord Jesus Christ', with no reference to his status as 'brother of the Lord'. The expression, 'beloved in God the Father', is strange. It refers to God's love (not Jude's) for the readers. 'Kept for Jesus Christ' is also strange; it seems to refer to the complete union with Christ which will be theirs at the Parousia. V 2 recalls and amplifies the prayer of 1 Pt 1:2; cf 2 Pt 1:2.

3—4 Purpose of the Letter—It seems probable that Jude had planned to write a general letter about what is most necessary for salvation, cf vv 20—21, but that a sudden danger caused him to send instead a warning plea, urging the faithful to preserve unchanged the deposit of faith which had been transmitted to them by the apostles. **3.** 'Saint' here simply means 'Christian', cf Ac 26:10; Rom 12:13; 1 Cor 14:33. **4.** First description of the heretics: 'who pervert the grace of our God into licentiousness', an error similar to that rejected by Paul, Rm 3:5—8; 6:1; 'and deny our only Master and Lord, Jesus Christ', not only by immoral conduct, but probably by reducing his dignity to that of an inferior being, cf v 8.

b 5—7 Warning Examples—**5.** Jude takes up traditional doctrine: already polemic against heretics was part of common Christian instruction. The first example is taken from Nm 14:1—36, cf 1 Cor 10:5; Heb 10:26—30. There are a number of variant readings for 5b: 'Jesus', 'the Lord', 'God'; the recent P 72 reads *theos Christos*. 'The Lord' is probably to be preferred, and is to be understood of the pre-existent Christ, cf Jn 12:41; 1 Cor 10:4, 9; 1 Pt 1:11; Heb 11:26. **6.** The second example is the fall of the angels, taken from Gn 6:1—3, developed in Jewish tradition, especially in the Book of Enoch. 'The sons of God' of Gn 6:2 were unanimously understood as 'angels' in both Jewish and Christian tradition until the 3rd cent. A.D. **7.** The third example is that recorded in Gn 19:1—29. It is parallel to the second because of the attempt of the people of Sodom upon the angels who came into the city in the guise of men, Gn 19:1—11. 'Eternal fire': cf Wis 10:7; Apoc 19:20; 20:10; 21:8.

c 8—11 The Blasphemies of the Heretics—**8.** Now

follows the application of the preceding examples to **960** the false teachers. 'In their dreamings': possibly in the revelations they appeal to in order to justify their conduct. 'Reject authority': literally 'lordship', referring probably to Christ the Lord, cf v 4; 'glorious ones', literally 'glories': this term refers to the angels. In the parallel passage of 2 Pt 2:10, they are angels hostile to God. **9.** The dispute between Michael and Satan over the body of Moses is taken, according to Clem. Alex., *Adumbrat. in Ep. Iud.*, and Orig., *De Princ.* 3, 2, 1, from the apocryphal work, *The Assumption of Moses*. The words of Michael recall Zech 3:2. The restraint of Michael, who leaves condemnation to God even in the case of the devil, is contrasted with the revilings of the heretics. **10.** The false teachers know nothing of spiritual things. They are destroyed by yielding to their sensual passions and natural cravings, in which they do not rise above the level of brute beasts. **11.** Next, Jude likens the false teachers to three notorious sinners mentioned in the OT: Cain, Balaam and Korah, cf Gen 4:3—15; Nm 16; 22—24; Dt 23:5. For other triads cf 1, 2, 4, 5—7. 'The way of Cain': in Jewish tradition Cain was a type of lack of faith, cf Heb 11:4, of treachery, avarice and lust. 'Balaam's error': he was bribed by Balak, and perverted the youth of Israel, Nm 22—24; 31:16; Neh 13:2; Jos.Ant. 4, 6, 5—9; Korah rebelled against the authority of Moses, Nm 16:1—35.

12—16 Their Abandoned Wickedness—**12.** 'Blem- d ishes': the Gr. *spilas* commonly means 'reef'; here it seems to have the same meaning as that of *spilos*, 'blemish'. 'Love-feasts': the liturgical banquets of the early Christians, at the end of which the Eucharist was celebrated, cf 1 Cor 11:20—22; Ac 2:46. The false teachers spoiled these occasions by their presence and selfish excesses. 'Waterless clouds': cf Prv 25:14. 'Fruitless trees in late autumn': when they should be bearing fruit, they are fruitless. 'Twice dead': they are apostates, cf Heb 6:4—6; 10:26—27; Apoc 20:14—15; 21:8. 'Uprooted': no longer rooted in Christ, cf Col 2:7, but separated from him, cf Mt 13:28—30; 15:13; Jn 15:1—10. **13.** 'Wild waves': cf Is 57:20. 'Wandering stars': borrowed from Jewish apocryphal literature, where the wicked angels are pictured as stars, cf Enoch 18:12—16. **14—15.** The heretics come under Enoch's prophecy of judgement. The prophecy of Enoch is not contained in the OT, but is found almost verbatim in the apocryphal Book of Enoch, 1:9. This book was held in great esteem in the early Church. Jude simply cites the book as an authority which his readers would accept. For similar use of apocryphal tradition, cf 1 Cor 10:4; 2 Tim 3:8. 'The holy myriads' refers to the angels. **16.** 'Loud mouthed boasters': from Dn 7:8, 20. 'Flattering people to gain advantage': cf v 11 above; Jas 2:1—9.

17—23 Exhortation to Fidelity—**17—18.** The faithful e should recall the predictions of the apostles. That false teachers and seducers will appear 'in the last days' and will resemble in character the men here described as 'mockers walking according to their own desires in ungodliness', is foretold in Ac 20:29—30; 1 Tim 4:1; 2 Tim 3:1, cf Mt 24:11. The warning against heretics became part of traditional Christian catechesis. Jude can refer to 'the predictions of the apostles' as something belonging to an earlier period. By implication, he does not regard himself as belonging to this group. **19.** 'Worldly people, devoid of the Spirit': literally 'psychic people'. The same distinction between 'psychic' man, man viewed in himself, apart from the grace of the Spirit, and 'pneumatic' man, man transformed by the presence and power of the Spirit, is found in 1 Cor 2:13—15; cf 1 Cor

60e 15:44—46. **20—23.** The exhortation becomes a positive appeal to growth in faith and Christian love. **20.** 'Build yourselves upon your most holy faith': cf 1 Cor 3:9—17; Eph 2:20—22; 1 Pt 2:5. 'Faith' here as in v 3 is regarded as an objective system, 'fides quae creditur'. Prayer 'in the Holy Spirit' is the necessary means of providing this growth: cf Rm 8:15—26; 1 Cor 12:3; Gal 4:6; Eph 6:18. **21.** Love of God, showing itself in love of neighbour, cf v 22, is the substance of Christian life. Jude returns to the thoughts with which the epistle opened in v 2. 'Waiting for the mercy of our Lord Jesus Christ', above all in his final coming. **22—23.** The Gr. text is rather uncertain. Probably the shorter and more difficult reading of B is to be preferred: '*There* **960e** *are some doubting souls who need your pity; snatch them from the flames and save them. There are others for whom your pity must be mixed with fear; hate the very clothing that is contaminated with sensuality*' (NEB). Of the two classes, the first is not yet lost and is open to help. The second is to be the object of pity, but must be treated with fear, lest the believing Christian be contaminated.

24—25 Concluding Doxology—This doxology, very similar to that of Rm 16:25—27, is probably liturgical in origin. 'Through Jesus Christ our Lord' can be taken either with 'Saviour' or with 'be glory'.

REVELATION (THE APOCALYPSE)

BY JOHN J. SCULLION S.J.

961a Bibliography—*Commentaries*: E.-B. Allo, EtB 1933³; M.-E. Boismard, BJ 1959³; J. Bonsirven, VS 1951; W. Bousset, 1906⁶; G. B. Caird, BNTC 1966; L. Cerfaux–J. Cambier, LectDiv 1955; R. H. Charles, ICC 1920; A. Farrer, Oxford 1964; A. Gelin, PCSB 1951³; T. S. Kepler, Oxford 1957; M. Kiddle—M. K. Ross, Moffat, 1940; E. Lohmeyer, LHNT 1953²; E. Lohse, NTD 1960; R. H. Preston—A. T. Hanson, Torch 1951; J. Rohr, BB 1932⁴; E. Schick, EchB 1952; H. B. Swete, 1909³; C. C. Torrey, Oxford 1959; A. Wikenhauser, RNT 1959³, W. J. Harrington, 1969.

b *Special Studies*: F.-M. Braun, *Jean le Théologien*, EtB 1959; C. Brütsch, *Clarté de l'Apocalypse*, Geneva 1955⁴; J. Comblin, *Le Christ dans l'Apocalypse*, 1965; 'La Liturgie de la Nouvelle Jérusalem' ETL 29 (1953) 5—40; G. Delling, 'Zum gottesdienstlichen Stil der Johannes-apokalypse' NT (Leiden), 3 (1959) 107—37; A. Farrer, *A Rebirth of Images: The Making of St John's Apocalypse*, 1949; A. Feuillet, *Etudes Johanniques*, 1962; *The Apocalypse*, 1964; P. Gaechter, 'Semitic Literary Forms in the Apocalypse and their Import', ThS 8 (1947) 547—73; cf ThS 9 (1948) 419—52; ThS 10 (1949) 485—521; S. Giet, *L'Apocalypse et l'histoire*, 1957; P. Haring, *Die Botschaft der Offenbarung des hl. Johannes*, Munich 1953; T. Holtz, *Die Christologie der Apokalypse des Johannes*, TU 85 1962; E. Käsemann, 'Zum Thema der urchristlichen Apokalyptik', ZThK 59 (1962) 357—84; J. Michl, 'Apokalypse', 'Apokalypsen', LTK²I 690—703; H. P. Müller, 'Die Plagen der Apoka-c lypse. Eine formgeschichtliche Untersuchung', ZNW 51 (1960) 268—78; J. Munck, *Petrus und Paulus in der Offenbarung Johannes*, Copenhagen 1950; A. T. Nikolainen, 'Der Kirchenbegriff in der Offenbarung des Johannes', NTS 9 (1962—63) 351—61; B. Rigaux, 'L'interprétation apocalyptique de l'histoire', in *Los géneros litterarios de la Sagrada escritura*, Barcelona 1957, 245—74; M. Rissi, 'Das Judenproblem im Lichte der Johannes-apokalypse', TZBas 13 (1957) 241—59; J. Sanders, 'St John on Patmos', NTS 9 (1962—63) 75—85; H. Schlier, *Die Zeit der Kirche. Exegetische Aufsätze und Vorträge*, Freiburg 1956, 16—29, 265—74; J. Schmid, *Studien zur Geschichte des griechischen Apokalypse-textes* (3 Bände), Munich 1955—56; 'Unbeachtete und unbekannte griechische Apokalypse-handschriften', ZNW 62 (1961) 82—86; E. Schweizer, 'Die sieben Geister in der Apokalypse', EvT 11 (1951) 502—12; A. van Hoye, 'L'utilisation du livre d'Ezéchiel dans l'Apocalypse', Bib 43 (1962) 436—76. G. Vermes, *The Dead Sea Scrolls in English*, Harmondsworth, 1965². See also below, § 968b.

d **Author**—The author of the Apoc names himself, John, four times 1:1, 4, 9; 22:8. Christian tradition of the 2nd cent. identifies him with the Apostle. Justin wrote in Rome c. 155 that 'a man of our company called John, one of Christ's apostles, foretold in a prophetic communication made to him, that those who believed in our Christ would live for 1000 years in Jerusalem'. *Dial.* 81 (PG 6, 669). 961⁣ Irenaeus, writing some 20 years later in Lyons, speaks of what 'John, a disciple of the Lord, meant in the Apocalypse,' *Adv. Haer.* 5, 26, 1. (PG 7, 1192). Both Justin and Iren. had lived at Ephesus. This same tradition is witnessed to by Tert. c. 160—222, *Adv. Marc.* 3, 15; 4, 5, (PL 2, 366); Origen c. 185—255, *Comm. in Ioh.* PG 14, 100, 116; Clem. Alex. c. 150—215, *Quis Dives* 42 (PG 9, 648—9); Hippolytus of Rome c. 200, *de Anti-Christo* PG 10, 770, 785 and *passim*. Add to these the Marcionite prologue to Luke, c. 160—80, cf RBen 40 (1928), 198. It was the Roman priest Caius who, at the beginning of the 3rd cent., first declared the Apoc to be a forgery of the heretic Cerinthus because of its gross millenarianism, Eus.HE 3, 28. Epiphanius of Salamis, c. 315—403 records that a group of opponents of Montanism ascribed the Apoc to Cerinthus on the grounds of its containing statements contradicting the other apostolic writings PG 41, 945. The greatest opponent of the Johannine authorship in the early Church was Denys, bishop of Alexandria, d. 264. He granted that the Apoc was written by a holy and inspired man, but not by the apostle John; the style was so different from the gospel and epistles. And the name John was too common among the faithful to admit of any identification, Eus.HE 7, 25, 14. Eusebius is himself hesitant, but would follow Denys (HE 3, 39, 7). He tells us too that at the end of the 1st cent. a Christian of Asia Minor named John was appointed Bishop of Ephesus by John the Apostle. This would account for the name, the authority of the writer, his knowledge of the religious situation of Asia Minor. Cyril of Jerusalem and Gregory of Nazianzen do not count the Apoc among the inspired writings. Chrys. does not mention it. It does not appear in the Syr. versions. But this negative judgement comprises only a fraction of the testimony so that one can say that the almost unanimous tradition of the early Church acknowledges the Apostle as the author of the Apocalypse. Such witness cannot be set aside lightly; nor can we presume that these men, especially Justin and Irenaeus, did not know what they were talking about. Opposition to Johannine authorship at that time is based not on a contrary tradition, but on exegetic, stylistic and dogmatic grounds.

The arguments against John the Apostle being the e author are: (i) the author distinguishes prophets and apostles, but does not call himself an apostle; (ii) the differences in manner of speech and style from the gospel and epistles; (iii) the absence of some leading gospel themes. Taking each of these briefly: (i) in 18:20 and 24 the author mentions the important position of the apostles in the Church; he does not include himself among them. But Paul does the same in 1 Cor 12:28; Eph 4:11. As well exclude him from apostleship. (In *other* places Paul insists on his apostleship, e.g. 1 Cor 15:9.) The author of the Apoc is merely describing in broad terms the structure of the Church. (ii) It has been proposed that

961e the general differences in style and expression and grammar would be due to the apocalyptic *genre* in which the author speaks. However neither this nor the recourse to the after effects of being 'taken up by the Spirit' would account for the grammatical and morphological vagaries. The Gr. of the Apoc differs from the Koine in many ways; despite its irregularity in detail it shows a striking regularity when seen as a whole. Cf J. Schmid, op cit, t. 2. (iii) Some leading gospel ideas are indeed absent, Light, Darkness, Truth. But many are found in both, Vine, Shepherd, Lamb, Bride, Water of Life, Christ as Victor, as the Word, the use of Zech 12:10 in Apoc 1:7 and Jn 19:37. Taking the very strong external evidence of tradition together with the internal difficulties it would seem reasonable to put the Apoc and the other Johannine writings under the aegis of the Apostle John; and this in a manner *analogous* (every analogy is deficient) to the position ascribed by the Biblical Commission to Moses as author of the Pent., 'his great share and profound influence as author and legislator'. EB[3] 580. But John is incomparably nearer in time to the final edition of the Johannine corpus than was Moses to the Pent. as we have it.

The question of authorship is quite distinct from that of canonicity or its inclusion in the Canon of Sacred books. Despite an individual out of step from time to time, the Church has maintained its canonicity, and the decree of the Council of Trent on the Canon settled the matter, cf § 20a.

962a Nature of an Apocalypse—RGC[3] I, 464–9; LTK[2] I, 696–705

(a) General—In general an apocalypse is a speculation which explains allegorically the course of world history; it reveals too the end of the world. It occurs especially in those religions which have a developed eschatology, i.e. theology of the last things, death, judgement, reward, punishment. Such speculations in the religion of India have influenced Iranian religious thought; this in turn had its influence on the OT—Ez was written near Babylon during the exile and parts of Is are generally regarded as late-exilic and post-exilic.

(b) Jewish—cf § 88d. This type of writing grew up in Judaism in the period c. 200 B.C.—A.D. 100. Of its essence is the presentation of the two eras, (i) that in which the forces of evil wield unbridled power, though history is in God's hands and his plan must prevail; (ii) the new era, the coming of the Messiah and the kingdom. The deeply religious Jew was very conscious that God's promises had not yet been fulfilled. Prophecy had now ceased, i.e. there was no authentic communication from God 1 Mc 4:46; 9:27; 14:41. For centuries the chosen people had been under the foreign yoke—Babylonian, Persian, Hellenistic, Egyptian, Syrian, and Roman. But the apocalypse directed the people's gaze to the happy messianic future. God must be faithful to his promises. The apocalyptic writings are rooted in a deep faith in the fidelity of God. The idea content and imagery is taken almost completely from the OT. The authors often understand the OT prophetic writings quite literally. Apocalypse may be considered as a continuation of Prophecy; it is often difficult to draw a sharp line of distinction. Communications are made in dreams and visions—part of the apocalyptic *genre*. Symbolic numbers are normal, there is a characteristic vagueness in describing visions—'as it were'. But its purpose is always comfort and encouragement. The cosmic upheavals, so characteristic of the prophets and taken up both in the apocalyptic writings and in the NT, are merely this literary *genre's* way of

saving that an era is at an end or beginning—usually **962a** both.

Apocalypse too arises out of an historical context **b** from which it cannot be separated. B. Rigaux op cit 252 puts three questions regarding the apocalyptic use of history: (1) In the material used, what is the proportion which is really historical? (2) What laws govern the choice and classification of facts? (3) In what way have the events been transformed?

The following are some individual NT pieces of apocalyptic writing: Mk 13; 1 Thes 4:13—5:6; 2 Thes 1:4—10; 2:1—12; 2 Cor 12:1—9; 1 Pt 3:19ff; 2 Pt 3:10—13; Ac 10:9—16. In biblical apocalypse the vision can be a literary fiction; inerrancy remains untouched. The revelation granted by God is one thing; its mode of expression another. The truth contained in an apocalyptic message does not depend on subordinate circumstances, actual or fictional.

Interpretation—'The book of Revelation is simply the apostolic *kerygma* transferred into the apocalyptic key in order to provide a theology of history for the Church. Its basic message is that the risen Christ, identified with Jesus of Nazareth, is lord of this world's history.' D. M. Stanley CBQ 25 (1963), 388. The interpretation of the Apoc begins with the author's conviction in faith that the gloriously reigning Christ has enlightened him. What is essential is the revelation received. The symbols and numbers will be interpreted in a Jewish sense, in an OT background. As Christ has gone through suffering to victory over the powers of evil, so must the faithful. This is necessary. 'Was the Messiah not bound to suffer thus before entering upon his glory?' Lk 24:26. 'If they persecuted me, they will persecute you' Jn 15:20. So the conflict is not accidental, a mischance; it is between two utterly irreconcilable powers. But 'why fear?' exhorts the seer. Christ has already won. It is with this victory as the source of strength and the constant point of reference that the faithful press on. The Apoc too is an unravelling of the OT prophecies in the light of the NT. There is scarcely a verse which does not contain an OT allusion. It is composed in '*le style anthologique*', 'i.e. the working of OT expressions and phrases into the very fabric of the composition . . . It is well known that a book like the Apoc, which does not contain a single explicit quotation from the OT, abounds nonetheless in OT allusions.' J. A. Fitzmyer, NTS 7 (1960—61), 298. Such a style involves, at least implicitly, an exegesis. Hence it is absolutely essential for an understanding of the Apoc to read carefully the OT references given in the commentary and to examine the use which the seer makes of them. It is this constant re-interpretation of the OT that makes one of the difficulties in the Apoc.

The people of God, the *qᵉhal Yahweh*, Israel, pre- **c** figured the Church of God, the *ecclesia Dei*. Through those historical and theological facts which constitute the primitive *kerygma*, Jesus crucified and risen, Christ Redeemer and Judge, the people of God becomes the Church of God, ch 12. The victory of the Messiah, the Lamb, was to be the triumph of Israel. It was to this that Israel was moving. This victory, both timeless and accomplished in time, is the key to the real, religious history of mankind. It is therefore put at the beginning of the prophetic section, chh 4—5. The sufferings of the people of God prefigured those of the Church of God. This would explain the parallelism of chh 4—9 and 12—19. The author has coloured *both* descriptions with his own background, immediate and remote. The Church is born amid the Messianic 'woes'. Though the Messiah has

962c come and won, these 'woes' are to continue until he comes again.

But the Apoc is not thereby a prophetic sketch of the history of the world or of the Church. It deals with the end of one era and the beginning of a new. With the Incarnation-Passion-Resurrection-Ascension cycle Christ *has* triumphed, the new era *has* begun—but only begun; it has not yet reached its consummation. This is the tension of the Apoc, the tension of the NT. The faithful live united to Christ in a state of victory, a victory which has yet to be completed. They are still exposed to persecution. Such must be until Christ comes again. And this is the Christian philosophy, or theology, of history. The powers of evil will *always* rise up against God, simply because they *are* evil and God *is* God.

Though timeless, the Apoc is yet bound to time. It is not without relation to the events of the epoch in which it was written; from these events the author received many an impulse. The wars in Palestine were just over, the temple of Jerusalem destroyed and Jewry scattered, the new people of God had been persecuted. The faithful needed encouragement. It was into this definite situation that the timeless message of the Apoc was written. *'But courage! The victory is mine; I have overcome the world.'* Jn 16:33 (NEB).

d Hypothesis of Two Texts—It was proposed in the 19th cent. that the Apoc is based on a Jewish writing(s) that had been Christianised. Some two or three apocalypses, usually of Jewish origin, were rather ineptly joined together by a Christian writer. Later however scholars were struck by the unity of style throughout; hence they tended to look to a single redactor who had assimilated previous writings to his own style without any attempt to iron out the discrepancies due to the different sources. Discrepancies do indeed exist: to explain them M.-E. Boismard has proposed his hypothesis of the two texts, RB 56 (1949), 507—41; BJ 1959[3]. Three sets of data are to be considered:

1. Doublets—almost every vision or episode is duplicated: 7:2—8 and 14:1—5, the one hundred and forty four thousand; 7:9—17 and 15:2—5 the blessed in heaven; 8—9 and sixteen the plagues; 13:1, 8 and 17:3, 8 the beast with seven heads and ten horns; 17:9—10 and 17:12—14, 16—17 symbolism of the seven heads and ten horns; 14:8 and 18:2—3 proclamation of the fall of Babylon; 18:9—19 and 18:22, 23 lamentations over the fallen city; 19:1—5, 18:20 and 16:5—7 the cries of joy that accompany the fall; 19:11—20 and 20:7—10 eschatological struggle against the pagan nations; 20:12 and 13 the last judgement; 21:1—8 and 21:9—22:5 the new Jerusalem of the future; 21:8—22:15 the final rejection of the impious. These doublets must be explained. (Note the strict parallelism between chh 4—9 and 12—19.)

2. Persons or things appear apparently for the first time, though they have already been adequately explained—17:3, 4 *a* beast—cf 13:1; 14:1 *a* Lamb—cf ch 5; 15:2 *a* sea of crystal—cf 4:6; 20:11 *a* throne of God—cf chh 4—5. In addition there are the following incoherencies: (a) 11:14—18, the seventh trumpet announces the third disaster, but the disaster does not materialize; (b) 17, the judgement upon the great prostitute is announced, but a description of the beast follows; (c) the heads of the beast symbolize the Emperors, 17:10, and the seven hills 17:9; the beast symbolizes the Roman Empire and is therefore alive 13:1, 3, 8, yet it symbolizes the Emperor Nero who is already dead 17:8; 13:18; (d) 20:12 and 13 the dead are gathered and judged before the sea and Hades have yielded up those whom they contain. These incoherencies require explanation.

3. Passages out of context—18:14, abrupt transit **e** from third to second person; 18:21—24, 21 and 24 belong logically together, but are separated by 22—23.

In view of these difficulties Boismard suggests that the prophetic section of the Apoc, chh 4—22, comprises two different apocalypses, originally independent, combined together into one text. They have the same literary characteristics and so the same author, but were composed at different times. Separating the visions that form doublets and uniting those that complement each other, two primitive texts can be established.

(See Table below)

The general theme of both texts is the Day of **f** Yahweh. The prophets announced the perspectives of salvation to the dispersed people. The enemies of the people will experience the divine wrath; the people of God, gathered to Sion under the ideal shepherd, the Messiah, will experience an era of imperishable prosperity and fidelity to God's law. Cf Jl 3—4; Mal 4:1—6; Zeph 2:1—15; Zech 12—14; Is 34—35; Ezek 38—39, plus the many citations in the commentary. The

	Text I	Text II
The Small Book		10:(1), 2*a*, 3—4, 8—1.
Satan against the Church	12:1—6, 13—17.	12:7—12
Preludes to the 'Day of Yahweh'	4—9; 10:1, 2*b*, 5—7; 11:14—18.	13—16.
The Day of Yahweh		
Babylon	17:1—9, 15—18; 18:1—3.	17:10, 12—14.
Fall of Babylon	18:1—3.	(cf 14:8)
Elect Saved		18:4—8.
Lamentations	18:9—13, 15—19, 21, 24.	18:14, 22, 23.
Songs of Triumph	19:1—10.	18:20 (cf 16:5—7).
Messianic Kingdom	20:1—6.	
Final Combat	20:7—10.	19:11—21.
Judgement	20:13—15.	20:11, 12.
New Jerusalem	21:9—22:2; 22:6—15.	21:1—4; 22:3—5; 21:5—8.
Appendix		11:1—13, 19.

2f author has combined the ideas of the Day of Yahweh as affecting the nation in general and the Roman Empire in particular. Text I follows Ezek more closely.

Text II would have been composed under Nero, shortly after the persecution c. 65, and ch 11 added after the martyrdom of Peter and Paul. Text I, with the temple of Jerusalem no longer a point of reference, would point to the time of Vespasian or the beginning of Domitian's reign. The letters to the Church are considerably later and correspond quite well to Domitian's rule, before the persecution of 95. These three different parts come from the *same* hand. They would have been put together about 95. This hypothesis would account for the two different Christian traditions, one of an Apoc written under Nero, the other of a composition in Domitian's reign. The hypothesis is ingenious and well worked out. Only time and deeper study of the apocalyptic literary *genre* will show to what extent it is valid. Perhaps insufficient account is taken of the fact that the symbols can and do bear different meanings, and that apocalyptic writings are notorious for sudden changes of scene and repetition of themes.

g Symbols and Numbers—As indicated in the commentary, it is important to remember that the visions are conceptual, intellectual, not visible, imaginable. How distribute the ten horns on the seven heads? The great scenes of chh 4—5 represent the transcendence of the ever-active divinity and the eternal intercession of the victorious Christ in whom all is brought into unity. The cosmic events sound the death knell of an era and the beginning of another.

Eyes symbolize knowledge—hence many eyes are the fullness of knowledge; the horn symbolizes power, a long robe the priesthood, a crown royalty; whiteness indicates joy, purity, victory, etc. The numbers too are symbolic. The four: 7:1; 9:14, the four angels bound at the Euphrates; 20:8 the ends of the earth; 4:6, the four beings. The number is related to cosmic order. The twelve is *originally* connected with astral religion, though for both the OT and the NT this no longer had significance; 12:1, symbol of completion (?); 7:5—8 and 14:1—5, the twelve tribes, 12 by 12 by 1000, making up the people of God; 21:12, 14, 21, the twelve gates of the city and twelve precious stones; 21:6 the new Jerusalem is a square, twelve thousand stades each side. The number contains some notion of fulness. (Cf *comm. ad loc*.) It is seven that occurs most: 1:4, 11 the seven Churches; 1:4; 4:5; 5:6 the seven spirits; 1:12, 20; 2:1 the seven lamps; 1:16, 20; the seven stars; 5:1 the seven seals; 8:2 the seven trumpets in the hands of seven angels; 1:3 the seven thunder-claps; 15:1, 7; 16:1, the seven plagues in seven bowls. In the ancient world the seven symbolizes perfection. In Babylonian astrology seven stars, venerated as divinities, determined the course of the cosmos. Though Babylon and her astrology may well be the remote origin of the symbolic number, nothing of its speculations enters into the biblical writers' mentality. In Judaism the astral bodies were regarded as God's creatures. For the three and a half, cf comm. on ch 11.

3a Theology: *(a) God*—The God of the Apoc is indeed the transcendent God of the OT, *Kyrios ho theos*, 1:8, alpha and omega, everlasting and almighty. These truths are presented again in the symbolism of ch 4 where the *trisagion* of Is is sung. He is the creator of all, 4:11, and the source of the new creation, 21:5. He is also the master of history; it is he who permits the plagues to the end that men may repent, 9:20; it is he who passes judgement on Babylon, 18:1, 8 and who will judge all. God is the

beginning and the end 21:6, and it is he who gives his **963a** children a draught from the springs of life 21:6—7. He, together with the Lamb, is the new temple 21:22. He is the light of the eschatological kingdom in its fullness.

(b) Christ—Christ is presented as fulfilling the Messianic prophecies, as the Lion of Judah and the Root of David 5:5; 22:16. As prophesied in Ps 2:9 he will come and 'shepherd' his people with a rod of iron 2:27; 12:5; 19:15. He is 'coming soon', and 'those who pierced him' shall see him 1:7; 3:11; 22:7. So he comes as a man of flesh and blood, as Dn's Son of Man 1:12ff. Yet he is not a man simply as other men; he is given attributes that belong to God alone. Like the Father he is alpha and omega, first and last, beginning and end 1:17; 2:8; 22:13. Christ is King of Kings, Lord of Lords 17:14; 19:16; he is the everlasting one 1:18, the all-knowing one 2:23. In his first coming he has given his blood in sacrifice to redeem men from sin 2:8; 5:9—14 (cf comm.); 7:14; 12:11. He has died and risen again 1:5; as the Lamb slain and alive his very presence before the throne is his intercession 5:6, 9; 13:8. As first born from the dead 1:5, he, before the throne 3:21; 7:17; 22:1, 3, will bring the faithful to their resurrection; for only those written in his book can enter the new Jerusalem 21:27. Here the Lamb, with the Father, is the altar of the new city, the lamp that gives it light, the source of eternal life and blessedness 21:22, 23. He is the judge on whose decision hangs admission to this life 19:11; 14:1. As God's word he is faithful and true 19:11, 14, i.e. he is the complete expression of God's fidelity to his promises.

(c) Holy Spirit—the Holy Spirit is represented by the **b** seven spirits, the fulness of God's spirit at work in the Church 1:4; 3:1; 4:5. In 1:4 the seven spirits are before the throne of God; in 4:5 the seven are the seven spirits of God. In 3:1 it is he who has seven spirits that speaks; in 5:6 the Lamb has seven horns and seven eyes 'which are the seven spirits of God which have been sent (*apestalmenoi*) into the whole world'. The seven spirits, the Holy Spirit, is God's and the Lamb's. One recalls, 'But when your Advocate has come, whom I will send you from the Father—the Spirit of truth that issues from the father—he will bear witness to me' (NEB) Jn 15:26. There is certainly a *basis* for the Spirit proceeding from the Father and Son. It is the Spirit who speaks to each of the seven Churches at the close of the letters. And the Spirit joins with the blessed in the petition for the second coming.

(d) The Church—The birth of the Church, the new people of God, is the climax of the Apoc ch 12. The Church is presented as an uninterrupted continuation of the people of God of the OT (cf comm. *passim*). It is a 'kingdom of priests' 1:6; 5:10, constituted as such by the blood of the Lamb. Though certainly of earth, the Church is not purely so; the dead, the martyrs especially, are united to their suffering brethren on earth 6:9—11; 19:2. The relation of the Church to Christ is expressed through the traditional biblical marriage image, 19:7; 21:2, 9. Christ is ever active in his Church, 1:13—16, ever directing it. His union with her will reach its consummation in the joy of the Parousia.

(e) Eschatology—For Judaism the eschatological event **c** remained in the future. For Christianity it has taken place in the Christ event. This is God's definitive, final intervention in history. The last age has begun, but has not been consummated. There is a direct relation between a share in the final eschatological glory 20:6; 21:1—4, and decision in the face of Christ and Satan

963c in this life. The eschatology of the Apoc is both communal, the new Jerusalem, and individual, 21:6; 14:1. (cf § 51*a–h*).

(*f*) *Judgement*—This is certain both for the good and the wicked. The seven letters assure victors of their share in the divine life 2:1–3:22; but to achieve it the Christian must be sober and watch 3:2–4. The reward is described in terms of Messianic fulfillment in chh 21–22. But severe judgement will come upon those who have aligned themselves with Satan. Theirs is eschatological death, definitive separation from God 2:11; 20:6; 21:8.

d Liturgy—The beginning and the end of the book of the Apoc frames it in a liturgical setting. The very Christian greeting '*charis*' of 1:4 is taken up again in 22:21. A Pauline formula is 're-worked'. The whole is quite permeated with references to the liturgy. The liturgy of Israel centred around the Exodus event by which the seed of Abraham became the people of God; witness Pss 78 (77); 80 (79); 105 (104); 106 (105); 114 (113*a*); 136 (135). The liturgy of the Church of God, naturally, will centre about that event which made it such, the redemptive work of Christ. And this appears in hymnic form throughout 1:4–7; 4:8, 11; 5:9–14; 7:9–17; 11:15–18; 12:10–12; 15:2–4; 19:1–8. With the Amen, '*that is true*', the community makes its own the sentiments expressed in 1:7; 5:14; 7:12; 19:4; 22:20. In 19:1, 3, 4, 6 the Hallelujah, the call to praise God, is raised. Some of the standard formulae of the confession of belief recur, e.g. that Christ has redeemed us through his blood. The 'Amen. Come Lord Jesus' of 22:20 is the cry with which the community began its service. The liturgical prayer of the worshipping and suffering Church on earth is projected into the heavenly liturgy, e.g. 4:11, 5:9. The two liturgies are bound together. And they are quite cosmic, as ch 5 witnesses. The pericope 21:22–22:5 seems to allude to the liturgy of the feast of the Tabernacles. On the first evening of this feast the temple court was brilliantly illuminated; there were the golden candelabra with four golden bowls on each of them and four ladders leading up to each. Four young priests fed the lamps with oil. There was dancing by pious men with torches in their hands; there were trumpets, cymbals, lyres; Pss 120–34 (119–33) were sung. In the morning there was a procession to the pool of Siloam. Water was brought back to the temple and poured upon the altar with a libation of wine. But in the new Jerusalem, the temple is God and the Lamb; God is the light, the Lamb is the lamp. Not merely Israel, but all the nations come to worship. And the water is no longer drawn from Siloam; it flows from the throne of God and the Lamb down the streets of the city. The letters to the Churches, the liturgical responses, the many hymnic sections indicate that it may have been intended to read sections of the Apoc at the assemblies of the worshipping community.

e Text—The outstanding work on the text tradition of the Apoc is that of J. Schmid, cf § 961*c*, and especially Part 2 of the work, '*Die alten Stämme*'. The oldest papyrus with the Apoc is Chester Beatty, P[47], from the 3rd cent.; it contains Apoc 9:10–17:2 with insignificant gaps. The text appears fully in Sin. (S), 4th cent., Alex. (A), 5th cent., and Ephraim Rescriptus (C), 5th cent. The whole of the Gr. tradition of the Apoc text is divided into four branches, AC, P[47] S, An (the text of Andrew of Caesarea in Cappadocia, written c. 563–614) and K (Koine). The two latter are recensions, each with its own peculiarities, due mainly to corrections. The branches AC and P[47] S are the older. In a number of places AC alone has preserved the original reading.

Division

Introduction—1:1–20.

Part 1—2:1–3:22 The Exhortation; 2:1–3:22 Letters to the Seven Churches.

Part 2—4:1–22:5 The Prophecy; 4–5 The Overture; 6:1–11:14 Act 1. Preludes to the Eschatological Drama; 11:15–20:15 Act 2. The Definitive Struggle between God and Satan for Lordship of the World; 21:1–22:5 Act 3. The New Creation with the New Jerusalem at its Centre.

Close of Book—22:5–21.

The drama simile should not be understood 'theatrically'. The Christian is not a mere spectator at this event. He participates. Because he is committed to Christ, the convinced Christian must act and suffer personally in this drama which is now taking place and involving him, and which will continue until Christ comes again.

1:1–20 Introduction—*apokalypsis* means an unveiling, a revelation. 1–3 **Title**—**1**. Jesus Christ is revealer and is himself the revealed as the centre of world history, as in Eph 1:2–14. The revelation is made 'to his servants', the prophets of the new era, 10:7; 11:18; 22:6. 'Surely the Lord does nothing without revealing his secret to his servants, the prophets' Am 3:7; cf Dn 2, 19, 22, 28. 1QpH[ab] 7, 4 teaches that God has made known to the teacher of righteousness, who instructs the pious in the scriptures, all the secrets of the words of his servants, the prophets. 'What must soon take place', is God's providential plan of Salvation. **2**. Angels play an important role as interpreters of visions in the apocalyptic writings. The 'witness', *martyria* was for Israel an acknowledgement, in the presence of the nations, of God, who alone is God, and who has chosen her cf Is 43:10–12; 44:8. The Christians bear witness to Christ, Ac 1:8; 10:39–40; and above all to his resurrection, Lk 24:48; Ac 1:22; 2:32; 3:15; 10:40ff; 13:31. In Ac 1:9; 6:9; 12:17; 19:10, the witness is the public proclamation of the truth. Ac 22:20 is the only occasion where *martyria* is used of the suffering and death of a Christian. In Apoc the witnesses, *martyres*, are those who have sealed their confession with blood, 2:12; 11:3; 17:6; 18:24. Christ is *the* witness, 1:5; 3:14, *the* proclaimer of revelation. **3. The 1st of 7 beatitudes**, cf 14:13; 16:15; 19:9; 20:6; 22:7, 14. The book is to be read at the liturgical assemblies.

4–8 Greeting and Benediction—a tissue of OT reminiscences, Ps 89 (88); Is 54–55; Zech 12; Dn 7. These passages concentrate on the solemn enthronement of the King-Messiah who is to reign over the people of God by virtue of the promises made to David. A major theme of Apoc BJ[3] 28. **4a.** The seven churches, i.e. the whole **b** Church in Asia Minor. **4b.** 'Grace and peace', refer to that one event in which God has come to his people; a typically Christian, Pauline, Oriental form. (For the Gr. form of greeting, *chairein*, cf Ac 15:23; 23:26.) Lit '*From the Being, the Was and the Coming*'. The preposition, *apo*, which governs the genitive, here takes the nominative. In Ex 3:14 God reveals Himself to Moses as 'I am Who am', LXX 'I am the Being'. The Jerusalem Targum 1 commenting on Dt 32:39 has: 'I am the one who is here and who was, and I am the one who will be here, and there is no other God but me' (SB 3, 788). John identifies the God of OT with Christ 'the Coming' of the NT. The number seven applied to the 'spirits' expresses rather the fulness of the spirit of God who in John and Paul is the dynamism of the Church. **5a.** The Messiah is the 'faithful witness', cf Ps 89 (88):28; Is 55:4, and 2 *supra*. With Christ the first-born, *prōtotokos*, 1 Cor 15:20; Col 1:18, the resurrection from the dead has begun. 'And I will make

4b him my first-born, the highest of the kings of the earth' Ps 89 (88):27. 'Ruler of kings on earth' cf Dn 7:14. **5b.** Doxology, 'to him who *is loving* us . . .' (pres. part., continuing action). It is because of this love that he has freed us by his blood, cf 5:9—14; Gal 3:13; Eph 1:7; Ti 2:14; Ac 20:28; 1 Pt 1:19. **6.** '*a royal house to serve as priests* . . .' Ex 19:6. The people of the new covenant will be priests, i.e. united to Christ the priest they will offer the whole universe in a sacrifice of praise. **7.** A combination of Dn 7:13, and Zech 12:10. He who has been put to death by mankind will appear at the end as the divinely appointed judge, Mk 14:62; his enemies will repent too late. **8.** Because God is God, the promises will be fulfilled. *pantokratōr*, 'almighty', applied here to God the Father, in 22:13 to Christ. The first eight verses are dense with theology: Trinity, Incarnation, Redemption, Church, Judgement.

c 9—20 Introductory Vision—Cf Ezek 1. **9a.** John shares the suffering of those to whom he writes; his exhortation is to perseverance, an important message of the book cf Rm 5:3; 2 Tm 2:12. **9b.** Patmos is one of Sporades, W of Miletus. Pliny the Elder 4, 23 describes the island as a place of banishment. The climate is mild. This may indicate that, rather than punish, the authorities wished to prevent John exercising his apostolic ministry. **10.** His being caught up by the spirit may be but part of the apocalyptic literary form cf 4:1—2a. **11.** If not the whole Church, at least the Church of Asia Minor. The cities formed more or less a circle, each on the great Roman roads along which passed the Imperial post. **12—15.** The 7 lamps represent the 7 churches v 20. 'One like a son of man' Dn 7:13; 10:6. Christ is active in his Church. The Messiah appears in his role of eschatological judge. His priesthood is represented by a long robe, Ex 28:4; 29:5; Zech 3:4; royalty by a cincture of gold, 1 Mc 10:89; 11:58; eternity by white hair, Dn 7:9; knowledge by blazing eyes, 2:18; stability by feet of 'burnished brass', Dn 2:31—35; 10:6. The Gr. *chalcolibanon*, found only here, is rendered in Vg by *aurichalcum*, *orichalcum*, cf Verg Aen. 12, 87. It is an alloy, the nature of which is uncertain **16.** Cf 20 infra The two-edged sword, the word, is the only weapon of the rider in 19:15ff. **17—18.** The epithets could only apply to God made man. He has power over life and death, can call the dead to a resurrection. Death and Hades cf 6:8; 20:13. **19.** This is the revelation to be given him. **20.** What (who) are the 'angels' of the seven Churches? Many see them as the angels that protect the communities. According to Jewish beliefs, angels presided not only over the material world, cf 7:1; 14:18; 16:5, but also over persons and communities, cf Dn 10:13, 20; 12:1. But how write to angels, urge them to penance? Hence some understand these 'angels' as the bishops. But the word is never used of a human being in Apoc. Lohmeyer understands the whole v as speaking of the Church; 'the angels of the Churches' symbolize the religious aspect, the 'Churches' the historical aspect. Christ holds the seven stars in his right hand; he controls them. The combination of seven angels, seven lamps, seven stars would indicate the Church in general, the angels, perhaps as protectors of the communities, standing as symbols for the individual Churches.

d Part I 2:1—3:22 Exhortation.
2:1—3:22 The Letters to the Seven Churches—It is the Apoc such as we have it now that is the inspired book, whatever its sources, its mode of composition. Of this book the seven letters form an essential part. They follow a pattern: address to the 'angel' of the Church;

Christ speaks of himself by some title; the Church is **964d** praised—except Sardis and Laodicea; the Church is admonished—except Smyrna and Philadelphia; an encouraging promise is made to the 'conqueror' under some symbol. The evils condemned are universal, but geographical and historical circumstances permit them to be attached appropriately to definite cities. The seven Churches represent the Church in Asia Minor, the whole of the primitive Church, the Church at any time confronted with ungodliness.

1—7 Ephesus—The capital of the Roman proconsular province of Asia and, after Alexandria, the largest port in the E, 'lumen totius Graeciae' (Cicero). It was an early seat of emperor-cult; in A.D. 29 a temple was erected to the worship of Roma and later to the deified Julius Caesar. Paul stayed two years at Ephesus on his second missionary journey, Ac 18:23—21:16. The amphitheatre seated some 50,000; population c. 250,000. In Domitian's reign, 81—96, Ephesus was the main seat of the emperor cult. Tradition has it that Timothy, John and Mary had lived there. However critical history may judge this, it shows the significance of Ephesus in the early Church. **1.** Christ active in his Church. **2—3.** Paul had warned the Ephesians against false teachers Ac 20:29; 1 Tm 1:7. Ignatius praises them for shutting their ears to false teachers, *ad Eph.* 9, 1. **4.** Perhaps an orthodox legalism had quenched fraternal charity. **5—6.** Repent! Nicolaitans, cf 15, 20 *infra*. Gnostics? **7.** The glorified Christ possesses the spirit in its fulness and through the spirit directs the Church. 'The Lord is the Spirit' 2 Cor 3:17. The victor: a word of encouragement, cf Jn 16:33 which expresses the spirit of the exhortation of the Apoc. The tree of life theme Gn 2:9; 3:22. Wisdom is a tree of life Prv 3:18; 13:12; 15:4. The reward is the same in all the victory promises—eternal life, a share in the heavenly reign of Christ.

8—11 Smyrna—Some 30 m. N of Ephesus, the main **e** city of Lydia. In 195 B.C. the city had dedicated a temple to the goddess Roma. In A.D. 26 Smyrna alone of Asian cities at the time was granted the privilege of erecting a temple to honour Tiberius, Livia and the Senate. The city had a reputation for loyalty to Rome, and for the natural beauty of its setting. Behind it the rich Hermes valley stretched into the interior. Tradition was that Paul founded the Church there. The Jewish community was very influential. **8b.** Christ's titles are those of 1:17—18. 'Poor', in contrast to the material wealth of the city, 'penniless, we own the world' 2 Cor 6:10. **9.** Paul suffered much from certain elements in the Jewish communities who often arraigned him before the civil magistrates. Such do not deserve the honourable name of Jew, Rm 9:4. Not an assembly of God, but of Satan! The true Israel acknowledges Christ, Rm 2:28; Gal 6:15. **10.** The ten days—symbolic of a short period? Gn 24:55; Dn 1:14. The crown is the symbol of victory and eternal life, 2 Tm 4:8; 1 Pt 5:4. The sons of truth shall receive 'every everlasting blessing and eternal joy in life without end, a crown of glory and a garment of majesty in unending light' 1QS 4, 7 (VDSS). **11.** The second death, cf 20:6, 14; 21:8.

12—17 Pergamum—Pergamon, about 44 m. NE of Smyrna, a religious centre of all forms of pagan worship. Pliny, NH 13, 21, praises the city: (i) because of its excellent library of parchment rolls; the name parchment comes from *pergamene charta*; (ii) because it was a centre of emperor cult; (iii) on the hill overlooking Pergamon, 1000 ft. high, were temples to Zeus, Asclepius, Athena; (iv) the Roman governor there had the *ius gladii*. In 29 B.C. a temple had been erected to Augustus and Roma.

964e **12.** Eumenes II, 180—160 B.C., built a large altar of white marble and had it dedicated to Zeus. Deissman, *Light from the Ancient East*, London 1927[4], 281 n. 3, who saw the altar *in situ*, remarks that 'Satan's throne' could only be this altar. **13.** Nothing known of Antipas. **14—15.** Balaam, cf Nm 22—24; 31:16; 2 Pt 2:15; Jude 11. Philo, *Moses*, 1, 294ff, and Jos.Ant. 4, 6, 6; 126ff, explaining the texts of Nm, say that Balaam advised the Moabite women to give themselves to the Israelites on condition that these turn to their gods and take part in the sacrifices,

f cf Nm 25:1. The prophetic 'fornicating after strange gods' meant a falling away from loyalty to Yahweh. Association in false worship and immorality went together at Pergamon, as elsewhere. Some, Boismard, BJ[3] 33, Wikenhauser, 41, see in the Nicolaitans Jewish-Gnostic speculators such as Paul attacked in Eph and Col. Others, Lohse, identify, them with the adherents of Balaam; just as he once seduced the Israelites, so now the Nicolaitans have won over some of the community of Pergamon. **16.** Perhaps an oblique reference to the *ius gladii*. **17.** (i) the hidden manna: for the tradition from 2 Mc 2:1—8, cf 11:19. Elsewhere in NT the manna is mentioned only in Jn 6 and Heb 9:4. The manna played an important role in rabbinic writings, SB 2, 481ff. At the end, it was to come down from heaven where it was hidden and nourish the faithful. (ii) The white stone: there was a wide spread practice in the ancient world of carrying protective amulets inscribed with some magic secret name; the bearer who understood the name was protected against evil spirits. Christ's amulet is symbolic: white—heaven; new—of the new creation. 'Both images have the same meaning; care and protection from dangers of those on the pilgrimage to final glory' (Lohmeyer). **18—19 Thyatira**—The least important of the 7 cities, lay some 40 m. SE of Pergamon in the fertile valley between the rivers Hermes and Caiacus, on the road to Sardis. It was military outpost of Pergamon and was well-known for its workers' guilds; cf Ac 16:14 where Lydia at Philippi was from Thyatira and was a dealer in purple fabric. Membership of the guilds involved festal meals in temples. **18—19.** For description cf 1:14.

g **20—23.** A modern Jezebel leads the Thyatirans to fornication and false worship. For the prototype cf 1 (3) Kgs 16:31ff; 2 (4) Kgs 9:22, 30ff. This woman claims to be a prophetess. (For the functions of prophets in the early Church cf Ac 13:1; 1 Cor 12:28; Eph 2:20; 4:11.) Her lovers are those who have been led away by the false teaching without fully adhering to her; their repentance is hoped for. Her spiritual children are like the mother, eternal death is their lot. The divine intervention will teach all that no sin escapes God's sight. **24.** Christ speaks to the community. 'the deep things of Satan': perhaps some Thyatirans believed that one must experience Satanic power to be independent of it. Irenaeus describes the Gnostics as 'profunda Dei adinvenisse se dicentes', *adv. Haer*. 2, 22, 3. **26—29.** The victor will receive a share in the messianic reign; cf Ps 2:8, which is used of the Messiah in 12:5; 19:15. In 22:16 Jesus refers to himself as the 'Morning Star'. In the Orient the morning star was a symbol of power and domination. Likewise here. It may well imply the idea of Resurrection and Ascension in glory, as Christ reigns by virtue of his Resurrection, Ac 2:32—36; Phil 2:9—11, and the passage means '*I will make the victor a sharer in my Resurrection*'. Speaking of the Parousia, 2 Pt 1:19 exhorts the readers to attend to the message of the prophets 'until the day breaks and the morning star rises to illuminate your minds'. And in the *Exsultet* of the Easter Vigil: 'May the Morning Star find its (the

candle's) flame alight; that Morning Star which never **96** sets; which, returned from the underworld (*ab inferis*) sheds its clear light on the human race.'

3:1—6 Sardis—about 30 m. SSE of Thyatira, and once **96** the capital of Lydia. Under Croesus, 6th cent. B.C., it had been proverbial for its wealth. Its citadel, Mt Tmolus, was 1500 ft. high and regarded as impregnable; but it was twice taken by surprise, by Cyrus in 546, Herodotus I, 84, and by Antiochus in 195. Hence the point of the admonition to watch. At the time when John wrote, it was a provincial city, a centre of wool industry. **1.** Cf 1:20. The community is alive in name only and not in spirit. **2.** Spiritual sleep and death cf 1 Thes 5:6; Rm 13:11; Lk 15:24; Rm 6:13. **3.** The thief in the night was a standard simile in early Christian tradition, Mt 24:43; 1 Thes 5:2; 2 Pt 3:10. **4—6.** The white garments are the symbol of purity, joy, victory, 4:4; 6:11; 7:9, 13. He whose name is written in a city's book is a citizen cf 20:12. These Christ will acknowledge at the judgement. **7—13 Philadelphia**—some 28 m. SE of Sardis was founded by Attalus II Philadelphus of Pergamon with the express purpose of being an 'open door', v 8, for Gr. culture to the hinterlands of Lydia and Phrygia. In A.D. 17, Philadelphia (and other cities) was destroyed by an earthquake, the tremors lasting intermittently some three years more. Tiberius rebuilt it with the name of Neo-Caesarea, and under the Flavians it called itself Flavia. Hence the allusions, 'pillars' and 'name' in v 12. **7.** Key of David, is a messianic reference, Is 22:22; Christ, the son of David, decides who shall or shall not enter the kingdom. The 4th Advent antiphon reads: 'O Key of David and sceptre of the house of David! You open and no man closes; you close and no man opens. Come, deliver from the chains of prison him who sits in darkness and the shadow of death'. **8.** Some see the open door as a reference to ultimate entrance into the kingdom which Christ alone can give; others understand it as describing the missionary activity, a meaning witnessed by Ac 14:26—27; 1 Cor 16:9; 2 Cor 2:12; Col 4:3. **9.** Trouble with Jewish community, cf 2:9. Ignatius refers to difficulties with Judaizing Christians, *ad Phil*. 6, 1. The Jews shall bow to the people of God. **10—11.** 'I am coming soon' is typically apocalyptic; God *will* intervene. **12.** The 'pillar' was a common rabbinic expression, often applied to Abraham, SB 3, 537; cf Gal 2:9; 1 Tm 3:15. Three names shall be written on the victor, God's, the city of God's, Christ's. He is the property of God, of Christ, a citizen of God's kingdom cf Nm 6:27.

14—22 Laodicea—named after Laodice, wife of Antio- **b** chus II, 261—244 B.C. and lay on the S bank of the Lycus river some 40 m. SE of Philadelphia and 80 m. E of Ephesus. An industrial and commercial centre, with a flourishing medical school, the city produced woollen garments—one, a tunic, called the Trinita—and was well known for its ointments for the eyes and ears. Opposite, on the N side of the river, was Hierapolis with its mineral springs and white cliffs. Laodicea was destroyed by earthquake in A.D. 60, but was able to rebuilt without outside assistance, Tacitus, *Ann* 14, 26, **14.** 'Amen' is immediately explained as 'the faithful and true witness'. Christ points to his trustworthiness as witness to his divine message. In Is 65:16, 'Amen' appears as a divine name, *be 'lohe 'amen*, 'by the God of truth'. Christ is the perfect 'Amen', 'be it so', to the Father's plan. '*He is the prime source of all God's creation*', (NEB) cf Prv 8:22; Wis 9:1; 1 Cor 8:6; Col 1:16; Heb 1:3; Jn 1:3. **15—16.** The spiritual state of the city is contrasted with its wealth—it is flabby. The point of comparison is this: a beverage must be hot or cold; if luke warm it is un-

5b pleasant. One must be spiritually acceptable—hot or cold, not revolting (lukewarm). All note the allusion to the hot springs of Hierapolis which are but lukewarm by the time they have flowed to Laodicea. **17–18.** John contrasts the material wealth of the many banks of Laodicea with true riches, its violet woollen tunics with grace, its eye ointment with true spiritual perception. **19.** Cf Prv 3:12. **20–22.** Sharing a meal in the orient expressed union and harmony, signified obligation. In the bible it is a symbol of messianic fulness cf Is 25:6; Mt 8:11; 22:12; 25:10. '. . . that you may eat and drink at my table in my kingdom' Lk 22:29–30. Apoc 3:20 seems to take up Song 5:1–2, where the Covenant doctrine is expressed in the language of human love.

Part II 4:1–22:5 The Prophecy.

The Eschatological Drama   Overture and Three Acts.

c **Chh 4–5 Overture**—The essential, permanent background against which the drama is played and to which the seer constantly refers 7:11; 11:16; 12:5; 14:3; 19:4; 20:11; 21:5. It is magnificently represented in the splendid altar-piece of Prof. Georg Meistermann in the Church of St Alphonsus, Würzburg.

4 The eternal worship of God by all creation—OT background Ez 1 and 10. **1–2a.** 'I looked' and 'at once I was in the Spirit' may be no more than a literary device characteristic of apocalyptic writing cf Testament of Levi, 2, 6 (CAP 2, 304); Enoch, 1:8 (ibid 432). Heaven is conceived as a solid vault with swinging doors which give access. For the open heaven cf Is 64:1; Mk 1:10; Ac 7:56. **2b–3.** See Ezek 1:20, cf Ezek 10:1. Rainbow: as a symbol of mercy? Gn 9:12. 'God is light' 1 Jn 1:5. **4.** Twenty-four elders. The function of the elders is to praise and worship 4:10; 5:9; 11:16–17; 19:4, to offer the prayers of the faithful 5:8. The throne is a sign of government, the long robe of priesthood, the whiteness of victory, the crown of royalty. What do they themselves symbolize? It has been suggested: (i) the twenty-four classes of priests 1 Chr 24:1–9, (ii) the twelve patriarchs or tribes and the twelve apostles, (iii) the angels, Mt 18:10, '. . . I (Raphael) . . . was offering that prayer of thine to the Lord,' Tb 12:12, (iv) the Old and the New Law. More probably the twenty-four elders are just part of the concrete imagery in a description of the heavenly court: '. . . and before his elders he will manifest his glory' Is 24:23. We have lost the clue to the number twenty-four which probably had its origin, though this does not come into the consciousness of the seer, in Babylonian astronomy; twenty-four astral divinities of the zodiac, twelve in the N, twelve in the S, Diod.

d Sic. 2, 31. **5–6a.** Fire and thunder are normal accompaniment of an OT theophany Ex 19:16ff; Ezek 1:13. The seven flaming torches are the seven spirits of God cf 1:4; 3:1; 5:6. Some see here the 'angels of the face', the highest in the angelic hierarchy Tb 12:15. Perhaps this fire in the whole context of fire but symbolizes the fulness of the dynamic reality which is God cf Baruch Apoc 21:6 (CAP 2, 293). Sea of crystal, Ex 24:10, part of heavenly furnishing: '. . . who hast laid the beams of thy chambers upon the waters' Ps 104 (103):3. It is not accurate to say that the author of Apoc never uses any detail as merely decorative, but *always* as symbolic. He is, after all, in the full stream of apocalyptic tradition.

6b–11 The 'beings' and the adoration of the heavenly court—Ezek 1:4–21. It is impossible to explain the position of the 'beings', *zōa*, in relation to the throne. If the position of the beings, the location of the eyes, the number of the wings is somewhat different from Ezek, the message is essentially the same. Nothing is gained by

conjuring up a phantasm. The imagery is conceptual. **965d** Lion—nobility, man—wisdom, ox—strength, eagle—mobility; 'eyes in front and behind', i.e. nothing escapes their gaze. These attributes are God's in an infinite degree. The number four is a symbol for the cosmos. The beings belong originally to astral mythology, though this is not foremost in the seer's mind. The ox introduces spring (April), the scorpion-man autumn (October), the lion summer (July), the eagle near the waterman winter (January). Iren., *Adv. Haer.* 3, 11, 8, first made the application of the 4 to the evangelists. **8b–11.** The doxology is inspired by Is 6. The function of the whole court is to praise God. The elders lay their crowns before the throne. Tacitus, *Ann.* 15:29 relates that Tiridates, the Persian king, laid his crown at the feet of Nero's statue. The elders sing: '. . . *ho kyrios kai ho theos hēmōn*', 'our Lord and God'. So had Domitian let himself be called, Suetonius 13. It is God alone who is Lord and Master, Creator of all, who holds the threads of history in his hands. The attributes point to his absolute perfection. Compare the doxologies to the Lamb 5:10, 12–13. In ch 4 God is Creator, in ch 5 he is Saviour.

5 The scroll and the Lamb—The ch continues without **e** interruption from the foregoing. **1.** The scroll is of papyrus, written on both sides as was that of Ezek 2:9. In the Ancient E a document drawn up on clay was at times fitted with a cover and the same message repeated on the other side to guard against falsification. Later this practice was sometimes adopted when papyrus was used. A string was passed around the scroll and it was sealed. The seven seals indicate the supreme importance of the message; seven symbolizes fulness and the scroll, as we shall see, untolds God's essential plan not merely for the chosen people and the Roman Empire, but for the whole time that the powers of evil will assault God's Church, i.e. until the Lord Jesus, 22:20, comes again. **2–5.** The breaking of the seals does not make known the written content of the book; it accomplishes God's plan of salvation history (*Heilsgeschichte*). It is the Messiah alone who makes this plan intelligible. He is 'the Lion from the tribe of Judah' Gn 49:9, 'the Root of David' Is 11:1, 'the Root of Jesse, the one raised up to govern the Gentiles' Rm 15:12.

6–8 The Lamb—Again the symbolism is conceptual. The Lamb is, literally, 'in a state of having been slain'; 'for I died, and behold I am alive for evermore' 1:18. The Lamb is a peculiarly Christian title for the Messiah; Is 53:7 is taken up in Ac 8:32; cf Jn 1:29, 36; Heb 9:14; 1 Pt 1:19. The seven horns and the seven eyes symbolize fulness of power and knowledge respectively. The eyes are 'the seven spirits of God sent out into all the earth' cf 1:4; 3:1; 4:5; Zech 4:10; the fulness of the divine *dynamis* which effects the mystery of salvation Rm 1:16. In 4:5 the 7 spirits belong to God the Father; here to the Lamb. The Lamb has the right to take the scroll and break the seals because of his victory over Satan by his death and resurrection. The Saviour is Lion and Lamb, dead and alive. The Lamb 'slain' before the throne recalls, theologically, the Jesus 'who is always living to plead on our behalf', cf Heb 7:25.

9–14 The Hymn of Praise—The elders, the angels and **f** the whole of creation take up in succession the paean of praise for the salvific work of the Lamb. The song is 'new', a characteristic word of the Apoc. Elders: The context is the covenant with Israel Ex 19, 24:4–11. By the sprinkling of the blood—'for the life of the flesh is in the blood' Gn 9:6; Lv 7:26–27; 17:11; Dt 12:23—the people of Israel were united to God, they became his people. By the blood of the New Covenant, Christians are united to God

965f in Christ in a new life. He has made us his own people. There is no question of the blood being paid to anyone. Cf S. Lyonnet VDom 37 38 39 (1958—59—60). The people of the New Testament now reign as a kingdom of priests, 1:6, over the earth. Angels: the Lamb receives 'power and wealth'. The whole of creation: a sign of the universal message of the Apoc which is restricted neither by time nor place. With the 'Amen' of the four beings and the elders prostrate, the heavenly liturgical stage is set. In its light a message of firmest hope can be presented: '*But courage! the victory is mine! I have overcome the world,*' Jn 16:33 (NEB). The overture now moves without interruption into the first act.

966a **Act 1 6:1—11:14 Preludes to the Eschatological Drama.**

6:1—8:1 The Seven Seals

6:1—8 The first four seals: the four hosemen—the whole of this ch is similar in language, imagery and spirit to the synoptic apocalypse, Mk 13:5—27 and paral.; Lohmeyer HKNT 58. The immediate OT imagery and literary affinities are Zech 1:8—10; 6:1—7. But there seems to be no intrinsic relation between the visions of prophet and seer. The threats of scourge by war, hunger, plague, wild beasts are often on the lips of the prophets Ezek 6:11—12; 7:15; 12:16; Jer 14:12; 15:2; cf also Lv 26:21—26; Dt 32:33—24. **1st Seal: White Horse.** The rider on the white horse holds a bow and rides out to conquer and conquer again. Wikenhauser RNT 59 sees the Parthian wars of A.D. 62 as the background of the riders. Likewise Lohse NTD 41—2. Without denying that the seer may have had all this in view, it would seem to be secondary to his main thought which is to typify by means of OT imagery the history of the people of God and their oppression *at all times*. The first horseman does not represent, as he does in 19:11—13, Christ or the victorious march of the gospel, pace Giet op cit 151. The meaning is to be understood in the context of the whole ch. 3—4. **2nd Seal: Red Horse.** A symbol of war. Cf Mk 13:8, 'nation will rise against nation, kingdom against kingdom'. **5—6. 3rd Seal: Black Horse.** A symbol of famine. The scales are a symbol of shortage of food with corresponding rise in price. '. . . I will break the staff of bread in Jerusalem; they shall eat bread by weight and with fearfulness . . .', Ezek 4:16. Cf Lv 26:26. A *choenix* was a dry measure, almost a quart; a quart of flour was a daily ration for one man, Herodotus 1, 187; Diog. L. 8, 18. *Krithē*, barley used in the cheaper sort of bread. Rather than give modern equivalents, call the *denarius* a day's wage; cf Mt 20:12. 'But *spare the olive and the vine*, (BJ) suggests three possible explanations: oil and wine, (i) essential foodstuffs, are spared from the plague, (ii) because of liturgical association are sacred and represent those who will be spared, (iii) are to be used sparingly because of rationing in famine, (more likely). An inscription from Pisidian Antioch testifies to a food shortage under Domitian. **7—8. 4th Seal: a Horse 'Sickly Pale'** (NEB). Death with Hades, the underworld, as his page comes to gather up the dead. Hades always appears with Death in Apoc, 1:18; 20:13—14. Christ holds the key of Death and Hades. Martindale aptly: 'Extension of godless power; this involves war; this creates terrible decline in "standards of life" which, unless arrested, brings about famine and epidemic.' CCHS (1).

b **9—11 5th Seal: the Martyrs' Cry for redress**—The martyrs are under *the* altar; that of 11:1? In the temple of Jerusalem the blood of animal sacrifices was poured at the foot of the altar; the life is in the blood, *supra* 5:9—14. They cry to God who is 'holy and true', to show himself faithful to his promises in the victory of the

anointed which is the judgement upon the world Jn 12:48; **96** 16:11. White robes: a sign that victory is assured Jn 16:33. '. . . and will not God vindicate his chosen who cry out day and night, while he listens patiently to them?' cf Zech 1:12; Ps 79 (78). I would see in the martyrs *all* those who have shed their blood as witnesses to the word, and particularly the great ones of the OT: 'Jerusalem, Jerusalem *still murdering* the prophets . . .', Mt 23:37—39. The martyrs of the OT are longing too for the kingdom. The Christians addressed in the Apoc would see here the martyrs under Nero. But the time has been fixed by God, the Lord of history; it must run its course.

12—17 6th Seal: the cosmic upheaval—Here we have the whole of the apocalyptic imagery in concentrated form. These cosmic signs are part of the prophetic tradition which announces the unleashing of a divine judgement. None can escape it. Such images often announce the end of an era and the emergence of a new; cf synoptic apocalypse Mt 24:15—31; Mk 13:5—27; Lk 21:8—28. Earthquake Am 8:8; sun as sackcloth and black Is 50:13; Am 8:9; Is 13:10; moon as blood Jl 2:31 (RSV); falling stars, heaven as a scroll Is 34:4; mountains moved Jer 4:24; islands disappear Na 1:3—4. The cosmic catastrophe of Apoc 6 is a prelude to the great eschatological drama. Through Judaism and its sufferings the Messianic age is to be born. Read Is 13; Na 1—3, for the end of Babylon and Nineveh. From this upheaval men think that the end is near. They hide in caves Is 2:10, 19; they call on mountains to fall on them Hos 10:8. This latter is part of the traditional imagery of despair Lk 23:30. It need scarcely be said that a literal interpretation misses the point. Parallels in apocalyptic literature: Assumption of Moses 10:3—6; Apoc of Baruch 70:8; 4 Ezra 6:14, (CAP 2, 421—22, 517, 576).

7:1—17 Interlude The sealing of the one hundred **c** **and forty four thousand; the elect of every nation, tribe people and language**—**1.** Behind the imagery is the old notion that the earth was flat and cornered (Ezek 7:2; 37:9). The angels of the winds: cf 14:18; 16:5, for the angels who preside over the other elements. Zechariah's four chariots go off to the four winds of heaven (Zech 6:5), and Dn 7:2 sees the four winds stirring up the great sea. It was a Jewish view that favourable winds came from the four sides, harmful winds from the four corners. **2.** The angel who presides over the fire, 14:18, over the waters, 16:5. **3.** The incident has its forerunner in Ezek 9. Those who are sealed belong to God. In the context it means that those so signed will endure to the end and with supernatural strength when human strength fails. The seal does not protect them from physical evil and pestilence: (*contra*, BJ³ 46; they will be preserved from scourges as in Ezek 9; Ex 12). **4.** 12 by 12 by 1000, i.e. a huge number. The seer cannot count this throng, he 'heard' the number. They are the elect of God at any moment of history. The Church is the New Israel, the eschatological people. Jas 1:1 addresses 'the twelve tribes dispersed through the world', and Paul speaks of the Israel of God Gal 6:16. But one must not exclude the just of the OT; on the contrary, the true Israel is continuous and really forms one, cf 14:1—5, the ideal realization of this passage. Those signed with God's seal (9:4; 14:1; 22:4) are opposed to those who bear the mark of the beast (13:6; 14:9, 11; 16:2; 19:20; 20:4). Not the seal of the sacraments of initiation, baptism-confirmation, though it may have helped prepare the ground for this terminology. **5—8.** Judah first because it gives the Messiah? Manasseh is substituted for Dan; because of the Rabbinic tradition that the antichrist would come from Dan? cf Iren. *Adv. Haer.* 5, 30, 2. **9—17.** Those who have come through the

c 'great tribulation' Dn 12:1 and owe their victory to the blood of the Lamb. They share in Christ's victorious death. Imagery from Gn 49:11. The author encourages the Christians pointing to what will be theirs. **10.** Victory is **d** through God and the Lamb, instrumental dative. **13–14.** Dialogue sequence, Ezek 37:3; Zech 4:2; it is a literary device 'to introduce with greater impact the message to be given' (Heidt). **15.** God will dwell with them, *skēnōsei*; the word occurs only here and in Jn 1:14. God 'pitches his tent' among his people, just as he did in the wilderness. The imagery and language which describe the heavenly liturgy or bliss come direct from the OT, and are repeated in ch 21. 'They shall *never again* hunger . . .' cf Is 49:10; 'the Lamb . . . will be their shepherd . . .' Ps 23 (22); 'God will wipe away every tear from their eyes,' Is 25:8.

8:1 The 7th Seal The great silence in heaven—the silence is a solemn prelude to the ever increasing catastrophes. Silence before the Day of the Lord cf Hb 2:20; Zeph 1:7; Zech 2:13.

8:2–9:21 The Seven Trumpets
e **2.** The seven angels who stand in the presence of God. Tb 12:15, LXX B, reads: 'I am Raphael, one of the seven holy angels who present the prayers of the saints and have access to the glory of the holy one' cf Is 63:9; Mt 18:10; Lk 1:19. The trumpet heralds a divine intervention Ex 19:16; Is 27:13; Jl 2:1; (Zech 9:14. In NT it heralds the Parousia, 1 Cor 15:52). 1 Thes 4:16; Mt 24:31. **3–6.** *libanōtos*, censer, incense-shovel (?) BJ³ 48. These words of comfort to the suffering people of God assure them that their prayers reach the throne of God and are heard, cf Ps 141 (140):2. The angel takes the coals and scatters them on the earth as in Ezek 10:2. The earthquake and storms are preludes to a divine judgement. **7–12.** The first four Trumpets. The first four plagues form a unity. Plagues of Egypt are the literary background. The one third to be destroyed in each case is a standard part of prophet language, Ezek 5:12–13; Apoc 12:4 First plague against the land = seventh plague of Ex 9:24–27; second plague against the sea water = first plague of Ex 7:20 31; third plague against sweet water, cf Jer 9:13–15; 23:15; Am 5:7; 6:12. Wormwood perverts justice; the star is called 'Wormwood' because it corrupts. Fourth plague against the heavens = ninth plague of Ex 10:21. Utter disorder has been thrown into the cosmos. **13.** An eagle, flying high in the heavens so that all can see it, proclaims three woes against the *katoikountes epi tēs gēs*, i.e. those who do not belong to the God fearers, cf 3:10; 6:10; 8:13; 11:10; 13:8, 14; 14:6; 17:8 For the eagle as a sign cf Mt 24:28; 4 Ezra 11:1–35, CAP 2, 609ff. The triple woe means that something more dreadful is about to befall mankind. Giet understands them as the three periods of the Jewish war, *infra*. In 9:12, the first woe is past; in 11:14, the second; 'the third is soon to come', though we hear no more of it.

f **9:1–12 The Fifth Trumpet**—The plague has its forerunner in the eighth plague of Ex 10:14. But it is not a question of the fearsome locust plagues that occur in the E from time to time. **1.** The 'star': one opinion sees it merely as an angel sent down by God to open the abyss; reference is made to 20:1 and 1:20; it is God who controls the plagues. But the verb 'fallen', *peptōkota*, expresses a state, and the key is *given* to him. Better, one of the fallen angels, Lucifer Is 14:12–15. The abyss is the place where the demons live 11:7; 17:8; 20:1–3. **2–5.** The classic and even more fearsome description of a plague of locusts is in Jl 1–2. The locusts are to harry those who belong to Satan, 4b, i.e. those who have not been sealed. The locusts bring spiritual and physical suffering, and they do so for five months. It has been suggested that this five

months is the life span of a locust; it may well be just part **966f** of the picture as in Mt 25:15; Lk 12:6, 52; 14:9; 16:28; 1 Cor 14:19. Perhaps we have lost the clue—or there isn't one! **7–10.** For illustrations of composite monstrous figures in the Near E cf ANEP 644–71. The mingling of images symbolized the combined ferocity, devilishness, intelligence (human faces) of the scourge. The poisonous sting of the scorpion was proverbial in OT and NT, cf Lk 10:19. **11.** Abaddon: in Jb 26:6 Abaddon is in parallelism with Sheol, in Ps 88 (87):12, with 'the grave'. The leader of the host is the 'Destroyer'. 11c of Vg does not appear in the Gr.

13–19 The Sixth Trumpet—13–16. The author stresses that the plagues are completely under divine control; only when God speaks—here from the altar—is the scourge loosed. The four angels, cf 7:1, are they the leaders of the hosts of v 16? or simply symbolic of God's might? or God's instruments? we are not certain. The two hundred million is obviously symbolic of countless hordes, (16) **17–19.** Here, as in 7–10, the author mingles the **g** fear of the Parthian invaders, whose border was the Euphrates, with Middle Eastern mythology and OT prophetic imagery. There are many of the qualities of the beasts of fable and legend, e.g. Job's description of Leviathan, 41:18–21, with fire and sulphur coming from mouth and nostrils. **20–21.** The purpose of the plagues is to bring about the repentance of the heathen from idolatry and the depravity that usually accompanies it. How stupid is idolatry is shown from the stuff from which the images are made cf Is 44:9–20; Ps 115:4–8 (113:12–16). But the history of salvation repeats itself—man does not repent, cf Am 4:6–11.

The Jewish War and the Apocalypse—S. Giet, *L'Apocalypse et l'Histoire*, Paris 1957, understands the three woes of the eagle, 8:13, as corresponding to the three stages of the Jewish war. The 1st stage under Gessius Florus lasted five months, May–June 66 to 25 Sept 66. This would explain the five months of the locust plague 9:5, 10. This is the first woe. The second stage of the war, and second woe, follows at once, Oct–Nov 66. This campaign was directed by Cestius, governor of Syria who led four legions—four angels—from the region of the Euphrates. It was a particularly devasting and murderous campaign, Jos BJ II, xix, 4:520. The third stage and woe was the series of Flavian campaigns, 25 Apr 67 to 26 Sept 70. It lasted three and a half years. The Jewish war, its preludes and shattering spiritual consequence, is certainly a background fresh in the mind of the writer and on which he draws. Whether the Apoc follows its course exactly is questionable, especially in the light of the fluidity and timelessness of apocalyptic imagery.

10:1–11:14 Interlude An Angel with the 'little **967a** **book': the Two Witnesses**—The title of these two chh could well be 'Children, it is the last hour' 1 Jn 2:18. The end is near, but its actual coming can be postponed indefinitely. This paradox of early Christianity calls us to see something other than date in the nearness of the end. OT background is Ezek 2:8–3:3. The opinion which discerns two texts in the books allots them: 1–1, 2b, 5–7: 2–(1), 2a, 3–4, 8–11.

10:1–11 The angel and the book—1. The angel was 'wrapped in a cloud'; part of the traditional imagery of those moving between heaven and earth cf Ps 104 (103): 3; Dn 7:13. For the rainbow, cf Gn 9:12–17 where it is the sign of the covenant after the deluge. **2.** 'He had a little scroll open in his hand'. It is the essential message of the NT. The scroll with the 7 seals, 5:1, looked primarily to the destiny of the chosen people which was to shed light on the nations through the *ecclesia Dei*. The

967a object of the small scroll is limited to the 'time of the nations'. The book is open, its message clear. 'Sea and land' in the OT signify the entire world, Ex 20:4, 11; Ps 69 (68):35. It is the terrestrial globe; the angel's mission is universal. Now comes the paradox: 3—4, universal judgement is still far off; 5—7, the end is nevertheless near cf Dn 12:2—9. Daniel receives the order to seal up the revelation he has received; the man clothed in linen raises his right hand to heaven and swears that the accomplishment will only take place after a certain time. Here, John himself seals the scroll; the angel raises his right hand and swears there shall be no delay. The author is expressing a paradox of the highest importance. With the triumph of Christ in his passion-resurrection-ascension the 'end time' has come and judgement has been passed; but judgement is consummated only at the end of this 'end time', the time of the Church, with the second coming cf 11:13—14.

b 3—4. In the vigorous prophetic imagery even Yahweh roars like a lion, Jer 25:30; Hos 11:10; Am 1:2; 3:8. Thunder is the sign of the voice of God, seven times mentioned, in Ps 29 (28):3—9. In Jn 12:28 a voice like thunder announces the judgement on the world. The thunder here seems to announce to the seer a revelation which he must keep secret. 5—6. The angel, swearing by him who created the universe, touches its three parts. For the same gesture when taking an oath, cf Gn 14:22; Dt 32:40. 7. 'There *shall* be no more delay,' NEB. It is not a question of the suppression of time and its replacement by eternity. When the seventh trumpet is sounded then will the hidden purpose of God, *tò mystērion tou theou*, have been accomplished; at this moment the hour of the kingdom, the eschatological plan for the whole of humanity, begins. The 'mystery' cf 1:20; 17:5, 7. For Paul the mystery is the inclusion of the Gentiles in the Church and the return of Israel through the conversion of the Gentiles Rm 11:25; 16:25—26; 1 Cor 2:1; Eph 1:9—10; 3:3, 9; Col 1:26—27; 2:2; 4:3; 2 Thes 2:6 **7c.** cf Am 3:7, 'Surely the Lord God does nothing, without revealing his secret to his servants the prophets.' 8—10. Cf Ezek 3:1—3. It is a type of prophetic investiture; the seer is to transmit the contents when he has assimilated them. The scroll is sweet, because it announces the triumph of the Church; bitter, because of the persecutions which necessarily accompany the Gospel. 11. '*They said*'. Presumably the seven thunder claps. His prophecies concern *peoples, nations, languages, kings* cf 13:7; 14:6; 17:15. Like Jer 1:5, 10 John's investiture is to nations and kingdoms; the future Church goes 'far unto the Gentiles'. The Apoc is essentially a *religious* interpretation of history, a theology of God's dealings with man. Proceeding from the data of the text we must bear in mind (i) that it is Christian, (ii) that it has many distinctly Jewish traits.

c **11:1—14 The measuring of the Temple: the Two Witnesses—1—2.** Cf Ezek 40:1—43:17; Zech 2:1—5. The measuring symbolizes preservation cf 2 Sm 8:2*b*; Ezek 40:1—6; 42:20; Zech 2:5. The seer is given a rod to measure the temple, altar and worshippers. How measure worshippers with a rod? We are in the presence of pure symbol; the true adorers, who stem from Israel, will enjoy divine protection always. The outer court, representing Jewry, 'Will be *trampled down by foreigners until their day has run its course*' Lk 21:24. It is the opposition between the Church and the synagogue. **2a.** *ekbale exōthen*: some translate '*have nothing to do with . . .*', NEB; '*laisse-le*', BJ³. Perhaps better understood in the light of Lk 13:28; Jn 15:6; Mt 8:12. The religion of Israel was the outer court of, the approach to, the Christian Church. The refusal of the Jews as a nation, in the person

of their leaders, to believe in Christ caused their definitive **9d** exclusion. Another opinion, Cerfaux-Cambier, sees the whole of the Church here represented—the outer court, the Church externally persecuted; the inner temple, the hidden interior life before God. *Forty-two months* occurs in 11:2; 13:5; *twelve hundred and sixty days* in 11:3, 12:6; three and a half days in 11:9, 11; three and a half in 12:14 (a time, two times and half a time). cf Dn 7:25; 9:27; 12:7. Antiochus' persecution June 168—Dec 165 B.C. lasted three and a half years. The third stage of the Jewish war A.D. Apr 67 to Sept 70 was three and a half years. Lk 4:25 and Jas 5:18 refer to the three and a half years drought in the time of Elijah, 1 (3) Kgs 17 (where the drought is three years). The number is symbolic, its usage proverbial; the symbol emphasizes suffering, persecution, not duration of time which may be long or short. That it marks the period of the Church to the Parousia does not exclude reference to events in history.

3—14 The Two Witnesses—3. The witnesses are **d** Enoch and Elijah (Hippolytus and Tert.), Moses and Elijah (many ancients, Lohse), Peter and Paul (Munck, Giet, Boismard), two prophets martyred under Titus (Gelin). **4.** Zech 4:3, 11—14, probably refers to Joshua and Zerubbabel, heads of the priesthood and royal house. The olive trees symbolize witness to God. **5—6.** Allusions to Jer 5:14, to Elijah 1 (3) Kgs 17, to Moses Ex 7:17—20. More probably the two witnesses are but one symbol, not so much of the preaching of the gospel in general (Wikenhauser), but of the Church faced first with Judaism, which does not believe, and then with the Roman empire, the beast of v 7. The Church contains in her gospel the law and the prophets, Mt 7:12; 22:40, which do not cease giving witness to Christ. Oblique reference to historical personages is not excluded. **7—10.** This is the first appearance of the beast, ch 13, who is opposed to God and his Church. Many see Rome clearly indicated as the 'great city', cf 14:8; 16:19; 17:5; 18:2, 10. Some, Boismard and Giet, would then consider 8*c* as a gloss. Babylon is the code name for Rome. But the whole setting here is Jerusalem, which is taken as typical. The history of the Church is synthesized in the history of the martyrs. Every place of martyrdom is Sodom, Egypt, Babylon, Jerusalem 'who kills the prophets'—not the true and holy Jerusalem. The death of Jesus is reproduced in the martyrs (Cerfaux—Cambier). **11—13.** The resurrection of the witnesses echoes the language and thoughts of Ezek 37:10, the valley of dry bones: Israel in captivity prefigures the Church. Martyrdom, death, glorification are in the best gospel tradition; the Church reproduces in herself the lot of her founder. The witnesses went up to heaven in a cloud—as did Jesus Ac 1:9, an external sign that their sacrifice had been accepted by God. The seer looks to the culmination of the process of salvation history—with the Church rising in glory, the end of an era is at hand. The repentance of the inhabitants of Jerusalem would signify that the Jewish people will in the end accept Christ, Rm 11:25—27. (So too Wikenhauser and Lohse.) The earthquake and numbers are part of the apocalyptic apparatus. The first part of the Apoc ends with a judgement.

Act 2 11:15—20:15 The Definitive Struggle between 96 God and Satan for Lordship of the World.
11:15—19 Overture and introductory chords—15. The scene is heaven. Christ's triumph has already taken place. This is what the seventh trumpet signifies. **18.** 'prophets', both of OT and NT Lk 13:34—35; Heb 11. 'those who fear thy name': in Ac the 'God-fearers' were those who sympathized with the Jews, shared their beliefs and moral principles, but were not integrated into the

8a community by circumcision. **19a.** 2 Mc 2:4—8 records the tradition that Jeremiah, warned by God hid the tabernacle, ark of the covenant and altar of incense in a cavern on Mt Nebo. The place was to remain unknown 'until God gathers his people together again and shows his mercy'. The seer is probably referring to this. The moment for the full flowering of the covenant has come. **19b.** Part of apocalyptic apparatus. It is not necessary to suppose that the author saw this. It is the accepted convention in this literary form for drawing attention to the most important event which is to come. The background of ch 11 is the disaster of A.D. 70——the Church and synagogue definitively separated. But the seer is immediately concerned with the spiritual signification of all this.

b 12:1—14:5 The Attack of the Powers of Evil against the Church.
12:1—18 The Dragon and the Woman——B. J. Le Frois, *The Woman Clothed with the Sun (Apoc 12). Individual or Collective?* Rome 1954; A. Kassing, *Die Kirche und Maria. Ihr Verhältnis im 12. Kapitel der Apokalypse,* Düsseldorf 1958; P. Prigent, *Apocalypse 12. Histoire de l'exégése,* Tübingen 1959; A. Feuillet, RB 66 (1959) 55—86; J. Michl, 'Die Deutung der apokalyptischen Frau in der Gegenwart', BZ 3 (1959), 301—10. This important ch may be divided thus: (i) 1—4a, a diptych which presents the two symbolic persons, the woman and the dragon; (ii) 4b—12, birth of the child, Messiah, attack against him, his victory; (iii) 13—18, persecution of remainder of woman's offspring. The woman is presented with all the qualities of the ideal Sion. She, the true spiritual Sion, the people of God as sung by the prophets, gives birth to the Messiah, to Messianic salvation. 'But the Jerusalem above is free and she is our mother', Gal 4:26. The anguish and trials of her labour ushers in the Messianic era, '. . . the birth pangs of a new age begin' cf Mk 13:8. The dragon, 'who is called the Devil and Satan', v 9, is now faced with the decisive conflict. The struggle is won through Calvary, the necessary condition for the triumphant Resurrection and Ascension, all forming the one great redeeming action; through this one mystery the q^ehal Yahweh becomes the ecclesia Dei. The direct line from OT to NT is preserved. Christ, the Messiah, has won the victory, 'Now is the judgement of this world, now shall the ruler of this world be driven out', Jn 12:31. But the woman, the Church, flees to the desert; her trial is for the symbolic twelve hundred and sixty days, three and a half years, the time that has yet to run to the Parousia, *supra* 11:2. Michael's triumph over the dragon corresponds to the triumph of the symbolic woman; vv 7—10 are a parallel to what has gone
c before. The best commentary is our Lord's: 'I saw Satan fall, like lightning, from heaven' Lk 10:18. Satan then turns his fury against the woman's offspring, the loyal members of the Church till the end of time. But the dragon and his violence are an allusion to Gn 3:15, 'I will put enmity between you and the woman and between your seed and her seed'. It is with the coming of the Messiah that the enmity reaches its climax. Eve is 'the mother of all living', Gn 3:20. As early as Iren., before A.D. 200, Mary appears as the second Eve. The woman of the Apoc appears in a context which evokes Eve in Gn; she too, like Eve, has further offspring. In Jn 19:25—27 Jesus gave Mary as mother to the beloved disciple. The Apoc is in the same theological tradition as the Gospel. Also, 'God sent forth his Son, born of woman' Gal 4:4; and the child born in Apoc 12 is clearly the Messiah. It is by such legitimate theological allusion, deduction, argumentation, and remembering that Mary is a type of the Church (cf § 662i)

that one may endeavour to see her in the great sign of the **968c** Apoc. She is not immediately and directly evident. It is not sufficient to ask, 'how could John not have thought of her?' The question is: what is John here trying to convey?

A selection of opinions in the history of interpretation——Hippolytus (c. 230): the woman symbolizes the Church clothed with the Logos. ' "The woman clothed with the sun" very clearly symbolizes the Church clothed with the Father's Word who shines more brilliantly than the sun. "The moon beneath her feet" shows that she, like the moon, is adorned with heavenly glory. "A crown of stars on her head", signifies the apostles through whom the Church **d** was founded. *"She was pregnant, and cried out in the anguish of her labour to be delivered"* means that the Church never ceases begetting from her heart the Word who is being persecuted by the unbelievers of the world.' PG 10, 780. Victorinus of Pettau (Steiermark in Austria, d. 304): the woman is the Church of the Fathers. Methodius (d. 312): the woman is the Church, the child is Christ born spiritually in the hearts of the faithful. Augustine (d. 430): CSEL 40, 968: the woman is the ancient city of God, the child is Christ. Greg (d. 604): PL 79, 1113—14, 1410—12, and Quodvultdeus, bishop of Carthage (d. c. 450) both understand the woman as the Church. For Ambrosius Autpert (wrote c. 758—67) the woman is a figure of the Church who daily gives birth to new people and so forms the body of the mediator. Oecumenius (6th cent.): the woman is Mary, a citizen of heaven, though of the same nature as we. For Bonaventure (1221—74) the woman is mystically the Church and literally Mary. The 16th and 17th cent. saw the rise of the so-called Jesuit interpretation of the Apoc, fathered by F. Ribeira (1578): the woman is the Church at the end of the times who then bears children to God. There is no Marian interpretation. Of the moderns, L. Fonck, M. Jugie, taking the Encyclical of Pius X, *Ad Diem Illum Laetissimum,* 4 Feb 1904 (AmER 30 (1904) 402—15) as starting point, 'Nullus autem ignorat, mulierem illam, Virginem Mariam significasse, quae caput nostrum integra peperit', ib 412, read primarily a Marian interpretation. Others, H. Rahner, J. J. Weber, F. M. Braun do not consider the Marian and ecclesiological interpretations mutually exclusive. B. J. LeFrois sees the woman as simultaneously an individual and a collectivity: **Mary and the Church** in its final stage of perfection on earth, i.e. when the Church of the Consummation has acquired the full likeness of the ideal Virgin-Mother. For A. Kassing the panorama of the first four vv is much vaster than Mary; it is the people of God bringing in the Messiah and the messianic age. It is as a member of this people of God, the new people continuous with the old, that Mary in v 5 gives birth to Christ. The Mariological meaning is *part* of the *whole* meaning which is ecclesiological. Mary is not merely a symbol of the people of God——she belongs to it. Hence the woman is the people of God, but in the birth in v 5, Mary——the birth is a concrete event, not an abstraction—— and with her all others as members of the community and in their various relations to this event.

1—2. A sign, *sēmeion,* appeared: not a miracle, but a **969a** phenomenon illustrating a truth cf Song 6:10; Is 60:1—3, 19—20, the dawning of the messianic splendour. The 12 stars, in their origin, may well derive from the traditional imagery of Babylonian astronomy. But cf Gn 37:9; the writer may have in mind the twelve tribes. The cries amid the pangs of childbirth have their prophetic setting Is 26:17; 66:7—14; Mi 4:9—10, the trito-Isaiah reference being particularly apposite. The pains and the cries symbolize the coming of the messianic era——but somehow too the birth of the new people of God is without the

969a pains of child-birth. **3—4a.** Red is the colour of the Egyptian Tryphon, a monster of the deep. Is 27:1 speaks of Leviathan the fleeing serpent, the twisting serpent, who appears in the literature of Ugarit with seven heads cf G. R. Driver, *Canaanite Myths and Legends*, Edinburgh 1956, 103. The seven diadems are symbols of power. The fourth beast in Dn 7:7 has ten horns. 'he swept down a third of the stars', refers to the dragon's fury, not to the fall of the angels. **4b—12.** The reference is to the Messianic Ps 2:9. The birth at Bethlehem is not in question, nor does the predatory beast stand for Herod. **5b.** The resurrection and the triumph of the Messiah. **6.** The woman nourished by God in the desert is the Church nourished by Christ as it 'wanders' Israel-like to its home. **7—9.** 'in heaven'. Here, as in vv 1 and 3 heaven is the region of the upper air as in Eph 6:11—12 where the Jewish apocalyptic tradition saw the strife between the angels. Not a reference to the primeval revolt. **10—12.** May be an early liturgical hymn cf Is 66:10—11 and the rejoicing there. The dragon is conquered by the blood of the Lamb and knows that it is the last hour: he redoubles his attack on the Church. **13—18.** The eagle's wings recall Ex 19:4; 'how I bore you on eagle's wings and brought you to myself', cf Dt 32:11. And Is 40:31, 'but they who wait for the Lord . . . shall mount up with wings like eagles'. **16.** How the earth helped the woman is not clear. **17.**
b It is the Church which the dragon now attacks. **18.** The dragon faces westwards, to the Roman empire, the power it serves. Some, Dupont-Sommer, Delcor, see in 1QH 3, 6—18 (VDSS 157) a Messianic reference and a parallel to Apoc 12. Others, Betz, Lohse, deny this. Whatever the resemblances, they demonstrate only that similar traditions or scriptural sources may be the background to both. Conscious use of the Python-Leto-Apollo and Hathor-Isis myths is, I think, unproven and unnecessary. It has been proposed, however, that the Hellenistic world in which the author wrote was familiar with these legends; the author may have taken over the legends and reworked them (Lohse, 64—65). With ch 12 the mystery of salvation has burst into history. Christ has conquered. His victory is permanent. It is to be carried on in and through him in his Church.

13:1—10 The Beast from the Sea—The dragon of 12:3 has seven heads, seven diadems, ten horns; cf Dn 7 where the four beasts are the embodiment of the pagan world empires Babylon, the Medes, Persia, Alexander and his successors—all opposed to the people of God. The qualities of Dn's four beasts are here fused into one which symbolizes Satanic powers, found in any state at any time which makes an absolute claim on man. For the seer and his audience that power was the Roman empire. **1—2.** For the symbolism of the heads, crowns, the head that was 'slain', cf 17:9—14. The beast is invested by the dragon; it is a diabolical creature. **3—4.** One of the heads was *hōs esphagmenēn* 'as though it had been slain'—as was the Lamb in 5:6, a terrible parody. The world worships the empire, amazed at its power and strength. The words of awe parody the cry of triumph of Ex 15:11, at the wonder of the Red Sea and Ps 35 (34):10. In 2 Thes 2:4 the enemy *'rises claiming to be a god himself'*. **5—6.** The fourth beast of Dn 7:8 had a small horn of which the mouth spoke 'great things'; so also the beast blasphemes. Dn's beast, 7:25, shall speak words against the Most High, and shall wear out the saints of the Most High for a time, two times and half a time. So too the beast. **7—8.** All this is but permitted by God, who controls history. Only those whose names are in the book of the Lamb, written there since the world was made, hold back from this false worship. **9—10.** An exhortation to be firm,

Christians must not rise up against the beast nor must **9€** they worship it. They must stand firm against its claims on God and Church, even if this means persecution and prison. 'Here the fortitude and faithfulness of God's people have their place'.

11—18 The Beast from the Land—11—12. Externally, **c** like a lamb, internally like the dragon: it 'spoke like a dragon'. This beast is in the service of the power that the first beast symbolizes; it is named as the first beast's prophet 16:13; 19:20; 20:10. False prophets were spoken of by Christ Mt 24:24; Mk 13:22, and by Paul 2 Thes 2:9. The background is the oriental emperor worship. **13—15.** The reference is to the miracle of Elijah 1 (3) Kgs 18:38. Emperor 'worship' had been known in the Hellenistic world since Alexander the Great. Later, Augustus tolerated the erection of temples in his own honour in Asia Minor and the offering of sacrifice. He neither demanded nor originated it. In the course of the 1st cent. of the era the emperor cult was encouraged by Rome as a bond of unity. Domitian, 81—96, was the first to demand divine honour in his life-time, Suetonius 13. A temple was built at Ephesus in which his more than life-size statue was honoured. In Pliny's Bithynia, A.D. 112, those denounced as Christians had to offer wine and water before the image of the Emperor. The seer is referring in these vv to the charlatan priests in some of the pagan cults. A belief in statues that spoke and worked wonders is well documented from antiquity. In the early Church, the Spirit produced prodigies as a guarantee of the apostolic preaching and to help faith in the risen Christ. So the second beast parodies the Spirit. In the historical context the second beast symbolizes the priesthood that serves the imperial cult. **16—17.** In antiquity soldiers and slaves were suitably marked; the devotees of a god would have his image or name tatooed on themselves; cf 22:4, 3:12, where the citizens of the new Jerusalem bear the name of God on their forehead, and 7:3; 14:1, where the elect receive the seal of the Lord as a symbol of His protecting hand. Worship the beast—or be deprived of the means of livelihood.

18 The number of the beast—The NEB renders, 'Here **d** is the key; and anyone who has intelligence may work out the number of the beast. The number represents a man's name, and the numerical value of its letters is 666'. The letters of the Heb. and Gr. alphabets were also used for numbers—aleph and alpha for one, bet and beta for two etc. The system of adding the numbers symbolized by the letters of a name was called Gematria (cf G. R. Driver, *The Judean Scrolls*, Oxford 1965, 335ff). The walls of Pompeii preserve: 'I love her whose number is 545' cf *Sibylline Oracles* 5, 12 (CAP 2, 397). In such a system many names can add up to any given number. Who is the man whose name is 666? Iren. knew three candidates. In later times Leo X, Luther, Knox, Napoleon have been proposed for this dubious honour. If one starts with A = 100, B = 101 etc, then Hitler fills the requirements! But a modicum of sanity must prevail. Seven is a symbol of perfection or fulness and is well attested as such. Six falls short of this; three times six points to complete imperfection. In the author's eyes this could well look to Nero. Taking the *Hebrew* consonants of Nero Caesar, NRWN QSR, we have as total 666; or dropping the final N of the first word, 616, a number known to Iren. The general explanation of 'complete imperfection' with the actual application to Nero is the least unsatisfactory, but by no means certain, explanation. (For Nero Redivivus cf 17:9—14). Using the *Greek* alphabet, *Kaisar theos* = 616. Taking the first letter of the *Greek* names for the Roman emperors

d from Caesar to Vespasian inclusive (Augustus = Sebastos); G only for the three Galba, Otho, Vitellius of the year A.D. 69, *or* the letter O = 70 representing Otho, Vitellius, Vespasian together, each of whose name begins with O in Gr., we have 666. 'Here is the key'. Perhaps we have lost it.

The manuscripts discovered in the Judean desert have shed a little light on this puzzle. Papyrus Mur 18 (DJD 11, 101, Mur 18. Wâdi Murabba' at is 15 m. directly SE of Jerusalem and about 11 m. S of Qumrân Cave 1) is introduced '. . . in the second year of Nero Caesar . . .' Nero Caesar is written NRWN QSR. The date of the papyrus is A.D. 55—56, the language is Aram. Substituting the current numbers for the letters we get 666. This does not prove that the beast of the Apoc is Nero. It merely shows that in the Aram. of that time Nero Caesar was spelled in that particular way, cf D. Hillers, BASOR 170 (1963) 65; J. A. Fitzmyer, 'The Bar Cochba Period' in *The Bible in Current Catholic Thought* (ed. J. L. McKenzie) New York 1963, 134 n. 6.

a 14:1—5 The Lamb and the One Hundred and Forty Four Thousand—Sion is, prophetically, the traditional place where the remnant will assemble as the kernel of the Messianic kingdom cf 2 (4) Kgs 19:30—31; Jl 2:32 (3:5); Obad 17; Zeph 3:12—13. Here it is not the geographical Sion, but the ideal place of refuge for the people of God. For the one hundred and forty four thousand cf 7:4; the people of God has reached its goal, whatever the prophetic idealization. **2—3.** Only the elect are sensitive to the 'new song'. No words of it are written here cf 19:1—10. **4—5.** The elect are those who, (i) 'did not defile themselves with women, for they have kept themselves chaste'; *parthenoi gar eisin*, 'for they are virgins'. The reference is neither to a particular state of life in the Church nor to the unmarried. It is to be understood in the traditional prophetic sense of those who have not succumbed to false worship, as in Jer Ezek Hos cf 14:8; also the bridal metaphors of 19:8; 21:2; 2 Cor 11:2; Hos 2:14—21; (ii) 'follow the Lamb wherever he goes', (iii) have been redeemed as the first fruits of humanity for God and the Lamb' cf 5:9—14. For Israel as the first fruit cf Jer 2.3.

b 14:6—20:15 The Divine Judgement on the Powers of Evil.

14:6—13 Proclamation of the hour of judgement— 6—7. The first angel proclaims *an* eternal gospel; not specifically Christian; a call to penance and to the worship of the one true God cf early missionary preaching Ac 14:15; 17:24; 1 Thes 1:9. **8.** The second angel proclaims the fall of Babylon cf Is 21:9; Jer 51:7. Babylon, the symbol of moral and religious degradation is now the symbol of Rome. Here 'fornication' is the false worship and the immorality connected with it. **9—12.** The third angel proclaims the ultimate fate of those who turn to the beast and its worship. The imagery is from the destruction of Sodom and Gomorrha Gn 19:24; Is 30:33. The cup of God's wrath is a prophetic symbol of divine chastisement cf Is 51:17; Jer 25:15; 49:12. This fate is without end cf Is 34:9; 66:24. In face of this there is a final exhortation to stand firm in the faith. **13. Second Beatitude,** cf 1:3. Primarily addressed to the Christians who are to die as martyrs. The 'beatitude' has, of course, universal application. In the best Jewish tradition, good works are seen as an obligation arising out of faith—for the Jew, out of commitment to the Torah. Unity of works and faith Jas 2:14—26. The translation could be: 'Happy are those who henceforth die in the Lord! Yes, says the Spirit . . . , *or* 'Happy are those who die . . .' 'Henceforth' (or assuredly), says the Spirit . . .' The Holy Spirit? or the Christian conscience?

14—20 The final judgement in anticipation under 970c the image of harvest and vintage—14—16. The presentation of the judgement as the reaping of a harvest Is 17:5; 27:12; Mt 3:12; 13:30, 39, or as the treading of the wine press Is 63:3—6; Jer 25:30, is traditional. In Jl 3:13 (4:13) both images occur together. The image of the son of man is that of Dn 7:13—14; it is the fulfillment of Apoc 1:7. The son of man appears as the middle one between two groups of three angels. The crown of gold symbolizes a king and conqueror, the sickle a judge. Why an angel should call to the son of man is not clear. But the angel comes from the temple; so it is God alone who determines the hour of judgement. The Parousia is fully described in 19:11—21. **17—18.** The sixth angel, the angel of the fire, cf 7:1; 16:5, comes from the altar where the souls of the martyrs wait crying for vengeance 6:10. **19—20.** The wine press was trodden outside the city. According to an old Jewish tradition God will hold the last judgement over his enemies in the valley of Jehoshaphat, outside Jerusalem, cf Jl 3 (4) 2, 12; Zech 14:4; *Sibylline Oracles* 3, 663—97; Baruch Apoc 40, 1; 4 Ezra 13, 35 (CAP 2, 390, 501, 618). The sixteen hundred stades, 4 by 4 one hundred times, is symbolic rather than geographic—the blood covers the whole world. Many see in the harvest the gathering of the elect, and in the treading of the grapes the punishment of the wicked. Is 63 would point to this. Not so Jl 3:13—14; the heathens who have harrassed the people of God are as ripe for judgement as is the harvest for the sickle, the juicy grapes for the wine press. The end is near.

15:1—16:21 The Vision of the Bowls, d 15:1—8 The sea of glass where the victors sing of the Lamb—1. Another sign cf 12:1—2. The wrath of God is consummated. After the vision of the bowls the judgement on Babylon takes place; then, with the coming of Christ the old era passes into the new. **2.** cf 4:6. Here the crystal sea is mingled with fire, a sign of the judgement at hand. **3 4.** From four OT passages, Dt 32:4; Jer 10:7; Ps 86 (85):9; Am 4:13, scarcely altering a word, the author has made a unified hymn. Many passages from the Psalms are echoed too. God's dealings are 'just', i.e. he is faithful to his promises. **5—8.** The phrase *hē skene tou martyriou*, 'the tent of the testimony,' is from LXX, Ex 40:24. The angels are dressed like priests cf 1:13; 19:14. They receive their bowls from one of the beings. The smoke is a symbol of the glory of God. In 2 Mc 2:4—8 the apparition of the tabernacle and the glory of God as in the time of Moses, Ex 40:34—35, and Solomon, 1 (3) Kgs 8:10, was to effect the messianic times and the restoration of the people of God. As long as the cloud remained over the tabernacle none could approach; so here none can step into the Holy Place to intercede till the plague-bowls have been emptied.

16:1—21 The Seven Bowls—The vision of the bowls is a remarkable parallel to, though no slavish imitation of, the vision of the trumpets in chh 8—9.

Trumpets	Bowls	971a
1. Hail, fire, one third of vegetation burnt 8:7.	1. Poured on earth; ulcers on all 16:2; Ex 9:8—12.	
2. One third of sea becomes blood, one third of living beings destroyed 8:8.	2. Sea becomes blood, all life is destroyed 16:3. Ex 7:20—24.	
3. One third of rivers and waters turned to wormwood 8:10.	3. All rivers and waters become blood 16:4; Ex 7:14—24.	

971a

4. One third of sun and stars are destroyed 8:12.

5. Shaft of abyss is opened; locusts darken sun and cause anguish to mankind 9:1—12.

6. The four angels on the Euphrates set free 9:14.

7. Lightning, Uproar, thunder, earthquakes, hail 11:9.

4. The sun scorches mankind 16:8—9. (for opposite, 7:14; Is 49:10).

5 Kingdom of beast is darkened; anguish comes upon mankind 16:10; Ex 10:21—23.

6. Bowl is poured on the Euphrates 16:12.

7. Lightning, uproar, thunder, earthquakes, hail 16:17—21; Ex 9:13—35.

The apocalyptic literary *genre* hammers home the same truths by the repetition of standard symbols and phrases. The plagues from the bowls affect the whole earth and are directed specifically against the unrepentant heathen world, vv 2 and 10. Their goal is to achieve repentance. Key vv are 7 and 21. **5.** The angel of the waters: in 7:1 and 14:18 we meet the angel of the winds and the angel of the fire. Part of the apocalyptic *genre*? **12.** For the drying up of the Euphrates and Nile cf Is 11:15; Jer 51:36; Zech 10:11. The Euphrates is the boundary of the Parthians; the sixth bowl proclaims a punishment for **b** Rome at their hands. **13—14.** Probably suggested by the plague of frogs in Ex 8:1—15. The frog was an unclean animal to the Heb., Lv 11:10. Three foul spirits like frogs came out of the mouths of the 'unholy trinity' (Heidt). The great day is that on which the enemies of God gather together to fight against him and are destroyed. It is graphically described in 2 Pt 3:12. **15. An interruption.** The 'keeping on of the clothes' signifies readiness. **Third Beatitude.** A homiletic addition? some set the v after 3:3*a*. **16.** The 'they' are the frogs. The Gr. *harmagedòn* most probably represents the Heb. *har megiddo*, a phrase not found in the OT where we read of the 'Plain of Megiddo' Zech 12:11; 2 Chr 35:22, and the 'Waters of Megiddo' Jg 5:19. Megiddo is on the S edge of the plain of Esdraelon, commanding the entrance to it. Here Sisera was slain by Jael, Jg 4—5, and Josiah fell in battle, 2 (4) Kgs 23:29. Is it a name from apocalyptic tradition, no more understood? Here it is some terrible place where the last conflict will be played out. Lohmeyer sees here Mt Carmel. **17—21.** A typical apocalyptic description and preview of the ultimate fate of all powers opposed to God, and typified in the Babylon——Rome association. The seventh bowl is poured upon the air. Universality? No parallels. The cosmic upheaval is 'like none before it in human history' cf Dn 12:1; Mk 13:19. Part of the *genre*. It is vain to search historically for such events or to measure the three parts into which the city fell. It is a prelude to the complete destruction of the anti-God forces described in ch 18. The cataclysm is the last attempt to bring the godless to repentance before the end.

c 17:1—19:10 Judgement on Babylon.
17:1—6 The Prostitute of Babylon—1—2. The image of the prostitute to designate godless cities is standard prophetic expression cf Is 23:15 (of Tyre); Na 3:4 (of Nineveh). Jerusalem and Samaria are so described in Hos 4:12; Is 1:21; Ezek 16 and 23. Israel's 'fornication' was a violation of her betrothal to Yahweh cf Hos 2. Babylon is described as 'you who dwell by many waters' Jer 51:13, and Is 23:17 speaks of Tyre as playing 'the harlot with all the kingdoms of the world upon the face

of the earth'. For the heads and horns, *infra*. **3—4.** The **9** whole of the beast on which she rides is covered with blasphemous names. She is dressed as becomes her profession with her name written on her forehead as Roman Law required of prostitutes. **5.** From the beginning of salvation history, Gn 11, Babylon had been a symbol of revolt against God; even after her destruction her name lived on into the final panorama of salvation in Apoc. A mystery——how could there be such wickedness? A significant name, understood only by the initiated? Babylon is here the Roman might——and all in history that stands opposed to God. **6.** She is drunk with the blood of prophets and martyrs cf 6:10; 18:20, 24; 19:2, a sure sign of her opposition to God.

7—18 The Beast, the seven heads, the ten horns, 9 the Nero saga—7—8. The beast who was once alive and is alive no longer is a parody of 1:4, 8; 17:8. It is the symbol of that political power which is opposed to God; though it wins the plaudits of the godless, it must of its very nature pass away; in v 10 one of its representatives reigns 'for a little while', in v 12 the ten kings share authority with the beast 'for one hour'. **9—12.** 'Here is the clue for those who can interpret it' (NEB). The seer, and his readers, were perhaps more fortunate than we: cf 13:1—4. The seven heads are seven hills; this is a well known descriptive formula of Rome, Verg., *Aen.* 6, 782; Hor., *Carm. Saec.* 7. The seven heads are also seven kings. Throughout the Apoc the number seven is used symbolically, why not here? the summation of anti-religious might? The nations against whom Isaiah 13—35 and the other prophets spoke their oracles——Babylon, Moab, Egypt, etc——passed away; so must, ultimately, all who arraign themselves against God. From Dn 7:7—8 the beast must represent an empire. Lohse 87 thinks that the difficulty in identifying the kings is such as to force the conclusion that the question is not one of pure chronology. The author is interested in an eighth king who will soon come; though like his predecessors, he yet surpasses them. As God's opponent he apes the Lamb's death and resurrection so as to draw all power to himself. This is satisfactory—— but what of the five who have fallen? With which of the emperors does one begin to count? Caesar, Augustus, Claudius are candidates. And the calculation will depend on whether the author is considered as actually living in the time of Domitian or Vespasian or writing, by literary fiction, as if he were living in the time of Vespasian and/or Nero.

The following is no more than an explanation. cf **b** Giet op cit 48, 83, 224—5; Feuillet op cit 270ff. Josephus counts the emperors from Caesar to Vespasian; Nero is then the sixth, Vespasian the tenth. This is at least a non-subjective criterion. He does not give the title of emperor to Nero's three successors of A.D. 69, Galba, Otho, Vitellius. Josephus lists ten rulers, seven of whom he calls emperors. The ten horns bear ten crowns, 13: 1—2; but there are only seven heads with blasphemous names. Why? Because three of the ten had not been the object of cult in Asia Minor, nor had they opportunity to use the titles saviour, benefactor, lord etc. Five are no more, Caesar to Claudius; the seventh, Vespasian, is reigning; the sixth, Nero, *was, is not*, has not yet returned. He will be the eighth, yet one of the seven. In v 11 he is identified with the beast. This introduces the Nero Saga, witnessed by Suetonius 57; Tacitus, *Hist.* 2, 8; *Sibylline Oracles* 4, 119—22, 137—9; 5, 143—8, 361—70 (CAP 2, 395—6, 400, 404 respectively). Soon after Nero's death the rumour spread widely that he had neither committed suicide nor been murdered; he had fled to the Parthians, whence he was to return at the head of

2b a Parthian army to avenge himself on his enemies. When this did not eventuate towards the end of the century the saga took the form that Satan would return as anti-Christ in the form of Nero, and that Nero would come to life again (Nero Redivivus), through a miracle of Satan's. This tradition, some claim, would lie behind the present pericope. But there are many other explanations. **13–14.** The single purpose of all such powers is anti-God. But they are doomed to failure because of the victory of the Lamb. **15–18.** The language recalls Ex 23:25–29. The ten horns rise up against the 'prostitute'. These horns have been seen as vassal kings, kings of the E, kings of the earth, the forces of Armageddon. The revolt may express an aspect of Mk 13:8–9. 'For God put it into their hearts to carry out his purpose . . .'. God is always the director of history.

c **18:1–8 The Fall of Babylon**—When a godless, idolatrous city opposed to the people of God falls, there is a traditional way of describing this event. From the standpoint of religious history something momentous has happened—an enemy of Jerusalem, hence of God, has fallen; the enemy is Babylon, Rome, any power which stands against God. It is a cosmic event. **1–3.** Background is Is 13:19–22; 21:9; Jer 51. Wild beasts and jackals shall dwell in her cf Jer 50:39; Is 34:11–15 (Edom); Zeph 2:13–15 (Nineveh). Fornication (essentially false worship), surplus wealth, international commerce—these are her attractions shared by the world cf Is 23:17, where Tyre plays the harlot by her trading. **4–8.** Evil has reached its full. Exhortations to flight are part of the apocalyptic genre Jer 51:6, 9, 45; Mk 13.14. 'Pay her back in her own coin' Jer 16:18; 17:18; Is 40:2. 'The prophetic command is to be understood spiritually; we are to flee this earthly city, setting out for God with the steps of faith' Aug., *Civ. Dei* 18, 18.

3a Prophetic proclamation on the city's fall—it is in imitation of Ezek 26:15–27:36, the fall of Tyre. **9–10.** The future. **11 17a. The present.** Practically all the costly articles of trade mentioned in Apoc are here listed. The passage is symbolic of the luxury of Rome rather than a description of Rome as a port of commerce. The description fits an E port better. **17b–19.** Utter destruction from every aspect. **20.** Addressed primarily to the martyrs. If Babylon (21) is Rome, we have, according to Wikenhauser, the earliest witness to the martyrdom of Peter and Paul there. **21–24.** Cf Jer 51: 60–64. This is the definitive end of Babylon. No music or song Is 24:8; Ezek 26:13; no sound of mill, no lamps Jer 25.10; no joyous shout at the marriage feast Jer 7:34; 16:9. The sorcery of her traders is the baneful influence they had on the peoples of the earth. But her worst fault was the shedding of the blood of God's prophets and people. 'Babylon must fall for the slain of Israel, as for Babylon have fallen the slain of the earth,' Jer 51:49.

b **19:1–10 The heavenly triumph at the fall of Babylon**—**1–2.** God's definitive sentence on the powers of evil now begins to take effect. *Hallᵉluyāh* = praise God; it is a Jewish liturgical response, common in the Psalms. The hymns of praise which go right through the book are here brought together 4:11; 5:9–14; 7:9–17; 11:15–19; 12:10–12; 14:1–5; 15:3–4. 'The blood of his servants' has been avenged cf 2 (4) Kgs 9:7; the cry of the martyrs, 6:9, has been heard. **3.** As a surety of the dreadful judgement cf Is 34:10. **4–5.** The elders' hymn of praise, 11:16–18. **6–8. Fourth Beatitude.** God enters victoriously into his reign; the promise of 11:18 is fulfilled. The marriage image as an expression of the union of God with His people is common in OT cf Is 54:6; Hos 2:16;

Ezek 16:7; in the last two, the marriage image is an expression of the covenant. In NT, 2 Cor 11:2; Rm 7:4; Eph 5:25, 32 it expresses the most intimate bond between Christ and the people which he has made his own by his blood. The era of salvation is like a marriage feast Mt 22:1; Mk 2:19; Jn 3:29. The glittering of the bride is in contrast to the gaudy colours of the whore. It symbolizes grace *given by God*. **9–10. Fifth beatitude.** The angel **973b** is a fellow servant, and the servants who bear witness are to possess and carry about as something living God's revelation and to proclaim it to others.

11–21 The judgement on the beast and false prophet c—the stage has been set for the decisive combat. It was an OT idea that Yahweh would make war on and annihilate Israel's enemies before setting up his kingdom Jl 3:1–3, 11–15; Zech 12; Ezek 38. Many facets of the Messiah's redemptive work, already mentioned in Apoc, are here brought together. **11.** Faithful and true are two constant OT qualities of Yahweh. He judges with righteousness cf Ps 96 (95):13; Is 11:4–5. He is faithful to his promise. **12–14.** Many crowns, because he is the real king, a contrast to the dragon and the beast 12:3; 13:1. The 'name' for the Semite stood for the person; it pointed to his essence. None knew the name. 'No one knows the Son but the Father . . ., Mt 11:27. He is 'the Word of God'; only here and in Jn 1:1; 1 Jn 1:1; 2:14. The name is a sign of Christ's commission; through him God speaks to man; he is revealer and the word of God become man. '. . . *garments drenched in blood*', cf Is 63:1, where Yahweh returns from the chastisement of his enemies like one who has trod the wine press. The angels and the martyrs make up his army, cf Mk 13:27; 2 Thes 1:7; 1 Cor 6:2. **15–16.** (i) Christ's only weapon is his sword-like word cf 1:16, 2:12; Is 11:4; 2 Thes 2:8. In Wis 18:15ff, the eternal word comes down like a stern warrior to execute God's decrees. (ii) the Messiah will rule with a sceptre of iron, Ps 2:9; Apoc 12:5. (iii) Wine press, *supra*. His name is written on his sword belt. **17–18.** Ezek 39:17–20; is the source. Obviously not to be pressed literally. **19–21.** The battle is not described, only the outcome. Wherever the Lamb does battle, he conquers 17:14; and with the word only. The beast and his prophet are handed over to eternal damnation, 14:10; 20:10, and their followers destroyed.

20:1–10 Judgement on Satan: the Thousand **974a** **Years**—**1–3.** Satan is the power behind the beast and his prophets; it is now his turn to be vanquished. The binding of the powers of darkness, and confining of them, is a common *motif* in ancient theology, Is 24:21–22; Enoch 28:16; Baruch Apoc 40; (CAP 2, 200, 501). In Enoch the wicked are bound for ten thousand years. It has been suggested (Heidt) that in 2, 3b, 7, the author is taking a stand against millenarianism, a doctrine according to which there would be a long period of peace and prosperity between the setting up of the kingdom of Christ and the Parousia. This is ridiculed by 'letting the devil loose', hypothetically, 'to foul things up'.

I have no satisfactory explanation to offer for the millennium and the loosing of Satan at its conclusion. The thousand years recalls 2 Pt 3:8, 'with the Lord one day is as a thousand years and a thousand years as one day' cf Ps 90 (89):4. God is timeless; it is not that he is 'slow' in bringing about the Parousia. Satan is bound and loosed; this is done by God through his angel. God is above history and time, above Satan and his minions; yet all is under his control. **4–6.** Boismard, BJ³ 80, considers v 4 unintelligible, and would redact it: 'and I saw the souls of those who had been beheaded for the sake of God's word and their testimony to Jesus; they

974a have come to life again and have reigned ...'. The remainder, inserted by an editor, is from Text II. For the thrones of judgement, cf Dn 7:9, 10, 22; for the faithful as judges, cf Mt 19:28; Lk 22:30; 1 Cor 6:2. The millennium and the first resurrection are the difficulties, perhaps having their origin in an attempt to make the events of the vision successive, Martindale

b CCHS (1). Satan is bound for a thousand years; but he is in a state of defeat, he has been driven out, Jn 12:31. The millennium runs from the time of the defeat, from the Incarnation with its consummation in the Resurrection-Ascension to the Parousia. So Aug. and Jer. Aug. sees baptism as the first resurrection cf Rm 6:1—10; Jn 5:25—28. Those who have remained loyal to Christ to the shedding of blood have won the right to share in the messianic rule; they live, supernaturally, with Christ. This is the first resurrection. The remainder have not been 'alive' in this way during the millennium; but they ultimately become alive to a living death— definitive, eschatological separation from Christ, the second death, which cannot touch those who have died just. These are reigning as priests in accord with the eschatological vision of Is 61:6.

Millenarianism—the concept of a messianic 'millennium' is rather late in Judaism. There are three periods, the present, the time of the Messiah, the end time; for modifications and presentation, cf Enoch 93; *Sibylline Orac.* 3, 652; Baruch Apoc 29, 2; 40, 3; 4 Ez 7, 28 (CAP 2, 262, 390, 497 and 507, 582). An early tradition, found in Papias, Justin, Iren., Tert., Hippolytus, interpreted the millennium literally; after a first resurrection Christ would come to reign on earth a thousand years with the faithful. This has never been in favour in the Church, and as recently as 1944 the Holy Office pronounced that a form of 'mitigated millenarianism' might not be safely taught; 'mitigated', i.e. that before the final judgement, with or without a previous resurrection of many of the just, Christ would come to reign visibly for a time on earth, AAS 36 (1944) 212.

c 7—10 Gog and Magog—The king of Gog in the land of Magog in the area near the Caspian Sea, Ezek 38—39. In Ezek are many contemporary characteristics of the campaigns of the Scythian hordes who c. 630 B.C. moved to the border of Judah. In Apoc the names symbolism, Ex 32:32; Mal 3:16. The Book of Life, Lk for the final campaign against Christ. **9.** The 'beloved' city: not in OT, but recalls passages which speak of God's love for Jerusalem, Ps 78 (77):68. **10.** Satan, the source of all strife, is defeated; all is now ready for establishing the eschatological reign.

11—15 General Resurrection and Last Judgement—God himself is judge. Heaven and earth disappear to make way for the new, 21:1; cf Rm 8:19ff. Between vv 11 and 12 Boismard BJ³ would insert v 4, cf *supra*. **12—13.** The books are opened; traditional symbolism, Ex 32:32; Mal 3:16. The Book of Life, Lk 10:20; Phil 4:3; Heb 12:23; Apoc 3:5; 13:8; 17:8; 21:27; 22:19. The great truth is expressed that man cannot attain salvation merely by his own efforts. He must be chosen, but his life must correspond to his calling. **14—15.** 'the last enemy to be destroyed is death,' 1 Cor 15:26; Is 25:8. Hades, cf 6:8. The sea of fire is the second death; only that man definitively dies, i.e. is separated from God and the divine life, who incurs it. Death is the enemy of God, who is Life.

Act 3 21:1—22:5 The New Creation with the New Jerusalem at its Centre.

975a 21:1—8 The new creation—The author is speaking as an eschatological theologian, not as a geo-physicist. **97 1—2.** The heavenly Jerusalem of Gal 4:26 is presented either as a community, Heb 12:22, or as a city built in heaven. Again Is is the source of the imagery, Is 65:17—19; 66:22. For the new Jerusalem of the apocalyptic writings, cf 4 Ezra 7:26; 8:52; 10:27, 50 (CAP 2, 582ff). For the marriage of Jerusalem and the joy, cf Is 61:10; 62:4—5; 65:18. The prophecies are fulfilled. Judgement has passed, the sea has disappeared. Why? it was the habitat of the dragon, the primeval chaos. **3—4.** Now is fulfilled the prophecy of the most intimate sharing of life between God and his people, Lv 26:12; Jer 31:31—34; Ezek 37:27; a constant OT theme. The new earth will be like the garden of Gn 2 cf Is 25:8. The 'presence' is characteristic of the covenant, Ex 23:12; 40:34; fulfilled in the Incarnation, Jn 1:14; 17:22, it is the era of peace and joy, Is 12:6; Zeph 3:15—17. 'If anyone is in Christ he is a new creation; the old has passed away, behold the new has come,' 2 Cor 5:17. BJ³ would insert 22:2—3 here. **5—6.** God speaks for the first time in Apoc. The seer is to write a surety that God has fulfilled his promises. God is alpha and omega, the creator and the goal. Water as a symbol of life is characteristic of the messianic times, Is 12:3; 41:18; 44:3—4; 55:1; Ezek 47:1. In NT water is a symbol of the Spirit, of the new era, Jn 4:10—14; 7:38—39. **7a.** Like the cry of victory at the end of the seven letters. **7b.** As was David, 2 Sm 7:14. Christ fulfilled the promises concerning the King-Messiah by his Resurrection; all the faithful are called to share this kingship, Ac 2:26—28; 13:33. **8.** Catalogue of sins, as in the epistles, Rm 1:29; 13:13; 1 Cor 5:10 etc.

9—22:5 The New Jerusalem—As the author of Gn 2 **b** described the garden in terms which were the opposite of his experience, so does the seer, up to a point, exclude from the new paradise the unpleasantnesses which confront him in life. The surpassing beauty and peace symbolize the inheritance of the faith of those who have persevered in trial. Obviously he did not *see*; e.g. v 23. The model is Ezek 40—48. **9—14.** The city is square, three doors on each side bear the names of the twelve tribes which have become the *ecclesia Dei*; the new Jerusalem has within it the people of the New Covenant founded by Christ on his Apostles cf Eph 2:20—22.

15—21. Measuring, Ezek 40:3; Apoc 11:1. The city was square. According to Herodotus I, 178 and Diodorus Siculus I, 3 Babylon and Nineveh were square, a symbol of perfection for the Greeks. The length is 12,000 stades, c. 1500 m. (one stade = 202 yds. approx); 1000 times the twelve tribes, symbol of plentitude. Obviously only a building could be cubic. The inner sanctuary of Solomon's temple was cubic, 1 (3) Kgs 6:20. The comparatively low wall, 144 cubits, c. 216 ft., merely indicates a boundary. The materials out of which the city is made recall the description of Is 54:11. The precious stones correspond generally to the stones on the breast-plate of the high priest, Ex 28:17; 39:10. They bear the names of the tribes. The foundation stones are the apostles, v 14 *supra*. Again, the direct line from the *qᵉhal Yahweh* to the *ecclesia Dei*. **22—27.** The rapturous, calm, yet brilliant messianic peace of Is 60 is here fulfilled. **22.** God the almighty, *ho pantokratōr*, and the Lamb are, equally, the Holy of Holies. **23.** They are the sun and the moon. God is in no wise hidden, as he was in the temple of old. **24—26.** Is 60:11, echoed in 1QM 12, 13: '... keep your gates ever open that the hosts of the nations may be brought in. Their kings shall serve you.' (VDSS). The seer modifies the passage from Is; when God's kingdom comes with the new earth, there will be no longer people inimical to him. **27.** There will be nothing unclean in the new city.

c 22:1—5 The city of divine life—cf Ezek 47:1—22; Jl 3 (4):18; Zech 14:8. **1—2a.** The waters symbolize the messianic plenitude. **2b.** In the garden was the tree of life Gn 2:9; 3:22. The vv have a parallel in 1QH 8, 20ff; 'No (man shall approach) the well spring of life or drink of the waters of holiness with the everlasting trees, or bear fruit with (the planting) of heaven, who seeing has not discerned, and considering has not believed, in the fountain of life, who has turned (his hand against) the everlasting (bud)' (VDSS); cf Jn 4:10—12; 7:37—39. **2c.** The divine anathema, *katathema*, which destines a city to destruction. **3—5.** There we shall see God, a privilege not granted to mortals in this life, cf Ex 33:20; Jn 1:18; Mt 5:8; Heb 12:14; 1 Jn 3:2; 1 Cor 13:12. Happiness is eternal.

Close of the Book—Three persons speak, the angel, Jesus, John. It is not always clear where one begins and the other ends. As it is very difficult to follow the sequence of the vv, Boismard, BJ[3] suggests that 8—9, 6a, 10—11, 13, 17c, 14—15, 18—19 form the conclusion of Text I; 16, 12, 17ab, 20—21 should include the letters to the seven Churches; 6b—7 would be editorial additions.

22:6—9 The revealing angel assures John that the message is trustworthy—**6.** 'trustworthy and true' cf 19:9; 21:5. The next phrase is, literally, 'the Lord, the God of the spirits of the prophets', i.e. God, through his spirit, intimates to the prophets what they are to proclaim. John is numbered among them v 9 **7a.** The v looks back to the opening 1:1, 3 and to the whole content of the book. **7b—9. Sixth beatitude.** John is overcome by the greatness of the revelation.

975c

10—17 Jesus proclaims that his coming as judge is near—**10—11.** Contrast to Dn 8:26; 12:4, 9. The prophecy is to strengthen the Christian community. **12—13.** Cf Is 40:10; '*to requite everyone according to his deeds,*' 2:23; 20:12; Mt 16:27; Rm 2:6. Christ now says of himself what God has already said of himself, alpha and omega, 1:8, 21:6; the beginning and the end, 1:17; 2:8. 'My Father and I are one,' Jn 10:30. **14. Seventh beatitude.** Through the gift of the spirit the faithful have a right to the tree of life lost at the beginning of salvation history. **15.** Cf Phil 3:2; a term of abuse for those who are tainted with paganis. **16.** Christ pledges for what has been written in the book. He of the line of David, his son and heir. The Morning Star, cf 2:28. 'a star shall come forth out of Jacob' Nm 24:17 was understood in a Messianic sense in Judaism Test Levi 18, 3; Judah 24, 1, (CAP 2, 314, 323); 1QM 11, 6. **17a.** The spirit and the spouse, i.e. the living Church. **17c.** What God gives is a pure gift.

976a

18—21 Threat to those who would distort the message—**18—19** Dt 4:2. This is divine revelation, it must remain intact. **20—21.** Three times repeated in these last vv. 'Come, Lord Jesus', *Maranatha*, cf 1 Cor 16:22; *Didaché* 10, 6. This prayer has liturgical context; the ending too is liturgical, indicating, perhaps, that the prophecy was to be read at the liturgical assemblies of Asia Minor.

INDEX

the Israelites work at making, 176b, 178f
BRIDE, Israel as a, 281a, 412f, 542fg, 543cd, 544efij; see also ADULTERY, Apostasy
the Church as Christ's, 686c, **689d—f**, 899f, **906a**
the, of the Song of Songs, 426j—q, 427a, 428ij
BRIDE GIFTS, PRICE, 166b, 265h, 430d, 618f, 712e
paid by Christ for the Church, 430f
BRIDEGROOM, Jesus as the, **738bc**, 803a, 804h, **906a**
BRIDESMAIDS, the parable of the ten, **738a—c**
BRIDLE, the symbol of the, 473f
BRISTOW (R.), 34a—c
BRITISH MUSEUM, 312b
BRITISH SCHOOL OF JERUSALEM, 80l
BROAD WALL, the: see JERUSALEM, top
BROOK OF EGYPT, the: see RIVER OF EGYPT
BROOM, charcoal made from, 407b
BRONZE, 81i, 146c, 246c, 510e
used in the Temple, 188p, 190bh
BRONZE AGE, the, in the Near Egypt, **81ei**, 120b
the middle, **81e, 59c—60b**
the late, **81e**, 256c
BROOKE-MACLEAN-THACKERAY, 352c
BROTHER, the Lord's, 946e
BROTHERHOOD, Christian, true, 656l, 872d, 929f, 950h, 954b, 956f, 957d
true, 417b
BROTHERS, of Jesus, the **660de**, **663—664**, 725e, 809f, 875fg, 946d;
the true, 723l, 959b, 960a
BROTHERLY affection, love, 950h, 951c, 954b
BROWN (R.), N.T. studies by, 638b, 659fg
BRUNNER (G.), on Judith, 349e
BRUNS (J.E.), on Judith, 349f
BRUTUS, Decius, 70h, 907c
BUBASTIS, 517g
BUBONIC PLAGUE, 294h
BUFFALO, 385c
BUHEN, 162b
BUILDING METHODS, ancient Palestinian, 89f—h
BUL, the month, 85d, 87g
BULL CULT, the, 64g, **103h**, 121c, **187a—d**, 188a, 283f, 288bf; see also BAALISM
BULLOCKS, sacrificed, 192h, 522c, 523g
BULLS, sacrificed, **1041**, 105d, 211c; see also ATONEMENT, the Day of
BULLS OF BASHAN, 385c
BULRUSH(ES) used in the Ark of Moses, 176f
BULTMANN (R.), N.T. studies by, **96b**, **97d**, 628d, 632afg, 634eg, 635abd, 636abe, **651b—f**, 652dk, 655e, 658g, 659a, 665c, 670a, 674d
BUNYAN (J.), 32d
BURIAL CUSTOMS, Egyptian, 172e
and rituals, Jewish, **84ab**, 165gh, 449a, 474k, 491l, 556i, **739de**, **742k—m**, 812df
BURIAL, Honorable, the importance of, 114g, 337f, 339c, 341cd, 351j, 423h
BURIAL OF JESUS, the, 739d,

742d—m, 762q, 789g, **818j**
BURNEY (C.), biblical studies by, 259e, 647f, 648d
BURNT OFFERINGS, **104h**; see SACRIFICES
BUR-SAGALE, 124e
BUSAIREH, 556g
BUSH, the burning, 177h
BUTLER (B.C.), N.T. studies by, 709f, 727d
BUZ, 165f
BUZY (D.), 421c
BYBLOS, 79f, 81kl, 252b
role in the development of writing, 22h
BYZANTIUM, Byzantines, 88l
and Palestine: see HISTORY OF PALESTINE

C

CABUL, 287a
CACTUS, 55m
CAESAR, Paul's appeal to, **840ab**
the household of, 908c
tribute to, in Jesus' teaching, **734bc**, 759d, 785d
CAESAR, JULIUS, 70gh
CAESAREA, capital of Judaea, 53c, 54i, 58c, 74i, 80m, 649a, 830i, 840n, 841e, 908a
Colossians written from (?), 911d
Jews massacred at, 74e
Paul at, 838a
Paul sent to, 704c, 764e
recensions of the school of, 29ei
CAESAREA PHILIPPI, 54n, 55e, 58c, 73b, 727b
Peter's confession at: see CONFESSION OF JESUS
CAESURA: see POETRY, HEBREW
CAFFIYEH, 257f
CAIACUS RIVER, 061f
CAIAPHAS, Joseph, High Priest, 739c, 761w, 773a
and the raising of Lazarus, 812h
at Jesus' trial before Pilate, 817km
Jesus' trial before, **676ej, 817cd**
the house of, 80i
CAIN, 142c, 147a, **154a—e**, 155a, 435i
false teachers compared to, 960c
founds cities, 154de
the mark of, 154c
CAIN AND ABEL, the narrative of, 142ce, 147a, **154a—c**, 957d
CAINITES, the history of the, 142ce, 154ad, 156a—c
CAIRO, 14f, 53n, 79c, 517g
the Geniza of: see GENIZA
CAIUS OF ROME, on the Apoc., 961d
CAJETAN (Card.), on canonicity and inspiration, 17a
on Hebrews, 931bc
CALAH, 159d
CALAMUS, 189q, 516f
CALEB the KENNIZITE, 57d, 61c, **210fgik**, 226k, 449e, 877c
and Hebron, 245d, 252g, 256b
the tribe of, 56g, 57b, 275g, 276b
CALEB the son of JEPHUNNEH, 299de, 300a
CALENDAR, the Babylonian, **85d, 87g**
the Canaanite, **85d, 87g**
the Jewish, **85d, 87g**, 193e, 202k, **204a—c, 216ab**, 318c
the Maccabean, **85d**, 87i, 124c
the N.T. Christian, 911e, 915a

the O.T. festal, **105, 233f—i**, 523gh
the QUMRAN, 611h, 612e
CALF, the Golden, 318g, **187a—d, 188a**
CALF of Horeb, the, 400u
CALVES, worshipped in Baalism, 542k
worshipped under Jeroboam I, 288b, 293j; 547bk; see also BULL CULT
CALIGULA, GAIUS, Emperor, 832a, 894b
Alexandrian Jews received by, 613c
Damascus given to Aretas by, 708a
supposed divinity of, 629h
CALL, CALLING, Divine, 869p, 950g, 954b, 959d
of Apostles and disciples, 687a, **711g, 715ij, 719ck, 720jk, 721c, 748g, 749g, 750b, 757c, 765d, 774cd, 802a, 808m**
of Gideon, 270a
of Israel, 381s
of sinners to repentance, 691k
to prophecy, 270c, **271e—g**, 452ab; of Amos, 554d, 556a; of Ezekiel, 507f, 510fg; of Isaiah, 460b, **464a—g**; of Jeremiah, 487l, **488b—e**; of Moses, 177adgh, **178a—cg i**; of Paul, 830a—f; see also PAUL, conversion; of Samuel, 270a, **271e**
CALL UPON THE NAME, to, 553b
CALL UPON THE NAME OF JESUS, to. **678cd, 718p**
CALLIRRHOË, 159c
CALLIRRHOË RIVER, 55d
CALVARY, 80g, 84c, **789d—g**, 855c
Mary at, **662f—i**
CALVIN (John), biblical teachings of, 17b, 33d, 91e, 931b
CAMBYSES I, King of Persia, 67c, 127c, 310g
CAMBYSES II, King of Persia, 310g, 317e, 331l, 335c, 337t
CAMEL(S), 55q, 162b, 179h, 312i, 364c, the gnat and the, **735i**
the needle's eye and the, **757f**
unclean, 200c
CAMP, the, in Hebrews, 944c
CANA, 511, 01c
Jesus and Mary at, 661r, **662a—f, 802u, 803ab**, 805ij
CANAAN (person) 158cd
CANAAN, the land and people of, 53of, 59c, 60ab, 61a, 88k, 103f, 159de, 581k, 585a
Abraham's relations with, 145bc
and the Wisdom Movement, 411h, 414c
early history of, the, 79d, **120b—e**
Egyptian influence in, 60b, 162d
in the laws of the Pentateuch, 223c, 255i, 287d
Israelite conquest of, 60a, 61ce—g, 103g, 145d, 205c, 215e, 225ab, 241c, 245c, 246g, **247n—251e**, 254cd, 255dfg, **256**, 318g
language of, the, 22efh, 468f
lists of place names in, 79ad
original population of, the, **61a—c**, 159e
place in the Kingdom of the, 898g
religion of, the, 64fg, 103gh, 104h, **120—121**, 162f, 270g, 272m, 278i, 282d, 542h; and the patriarchs, 103g; and Yahwism, **452e**; psalmody in, 386e; sacrifices of, 104h;
sexuality in, 203g;
suppressed, **232bce**; the serpent in, 153b

society of, **120–121**
spies sent into, **210a–f**
CANAANITE, meaning, 380d
CANAANITES, the, 61ag, **120–121**,
162c, 351ab
Israelites' relations with the surviving,
217b, 223c, 245c, **251ab, 255d–i**,
256e, **257a–h**, 264a, 287d, 445d
CANAANITE WOMAN, declares faith in
Jesus, 726h
CANAL, 377b
CANDACE, Queen of Ethiopia, 829i
CANDAULES, King of Lycia, 354j
CANDLESTICK(S) of the Temple, 103k,
305g
the seven-branched, 103k, 577lm
CANNIBALISM, 237d, 290q, 436d, 503f,
505e
CANON LAW, 643e, 669k
CANON OF SCRIPTURE, the, **13b**, 14d,
88bc, 422a, 641e, 946d
and progressive revelation, 21c
history of the, **13–21, 90p**, 336g, 931c
N.T., history of the, **18–21c**, 606e,
669k, 914e, 930b
O.T., history of the, 14a–h, 15a, 241b,
298a, 349f, **453a–454b**, 606e
O.T., history of the Christian, **15bc,
16a–e, 17a–c**; history of the Sama-
ritan, 14b
CANTICLES, Habakkuk's, 570cd, 571pr
Judith's, 347b, 351hi
Mary's: see MAGNIFICAT
Simeon's, **767b**; see also NUNC DI-
MITTIS
the Angelic, **767b, 769b, 772de**
Tobit's, 345c
Zechariah's, 768b, 769b, **771de**; see
also HYMNS
CAPELLUS (L.), 91g
CAPER (capparis spinosa), 201h
CAPERNAUM, (CAPHARNAUM), 54lm,
55f, 57f, 80e, 82a, 716c, 725a
Jesus at, performs miracles at, 687l,
715e, **749g–i**, 757a, **774b–g**,
803c
Jesus' lament for, 722f
CAPHTOR, 500e, 560j
CAPHTORIM, the, 159d
CAPITAL CRIMES, punishment for, in
the O.T., **184m, 185a**, 618g; under
the Romans, **608b**
CAPPADOCIA(NS), 161c, 350d
CAPTIVITY EPISTLES, the, 643d, 704e,
908a (see also COLOSSIANS,
EPHESIANS, PHILEMON,
PHILIPPIANS)
CARAFA, Card., 30h
CARAVANSERAI, 83h
CARBUNCLE (gem stone) 304c
CARCASSES, of clean animals, disposal
of, 200i
of unclean animals, disposal of, 200g
CARCHEMISH, 79j, 160d, 466i
the battle of, 116h, 119i, 487bc, 488f,
494o, 495j, 499b, 507c, 570e
CARE, Divine, for all, a psalm of, 409a–e
CARLETON, 34c
CARMEL, Mount, 53l, 54djk, 55c,
57b, 80hm, 170c, 285d, 350g, 429e,
474h, 556b, 560i, 568b
Elijah's challenge at, **298de**
CARNAIM, 589d
CARNIVAL, 354c
CARPUS OF TROAS, Paul's visit to,
704f
CARTHAGE, sacrifices at, 104hj

CARTHAGE, the Council of: see
COUNCILS
CASAUBON (I.), on paganism and Chris-
tianity, 628c
CASE LAW, in the Pentateuch, 133c
CASEL (Dom O.), on Christian and Pagan
rites, 628e
CASIPHIA, 310e, 315e
CASIUS, 180m
CASPIAN SEA, the, 350a
CASPIN, 599c
CASSANDER the COMPANION, 535d
CASSIA, Oil of, 189q, 380k, 516f
CASSITES, the, 159d
CASSIODORUS, the Latin recension of,
30c
CASSIUS, Dio, 70h, 706h, 907c
CASSUTO, on the Flood, 157d
CASTLE, the governor of the, 318a
CASUISTRY, of the Pharisees and Scribes,
607g, 735h
CATACOMB OF DOMITILLA, 866j
CATACOMBS, the Ark of Noah depicted
in, 157a
CATECHESIS, primitive Christian, 16c,
641e, **646f, 666gh**, 704g, 768h,
936ab, 940b, 950bde, 951b, 953b,
960e
corrupted by false teachers, 953bdfh,
954bce, 959cf, 960c–e
formulae of renunciation in, 951d
CATHERINE, the monastery of St, 28g
CATHOLIC EPISTLES, the, 19b, 640ab,
644a–d, 946d, 959c
CATTLE RUSTLING, laws concerning,
184uw
CAULDRON, Ezekiel's symbolic use of a,
512kl, 515lm
CAUSALITY, O.T. views of, 513f, 558b
CAVALRY, 285g, 593j
CAZELLES (H.), 348d
CEDAR TREE(S), 55o, 386f, 427g, 446d
used in construction of altars, of temple,
120c, 187o, 286acd
CEDAR TREE, Egypt so called, 517hi
of the Messiah, 509a
CEDAR WOOD, used on purification rites,
201h
CELIBACY, Christian traditions of, 32b,
730b–i (passim), 867g, **873a–cg**
Jeremiah's, 493d, 494ij
Jewish Qumranic, 611bc, 612d
CELTS, 71e
CENACLE, the site of the, 80i
CENCHREAE, 835m, 866h
CENDEBEUS, General, defeated by the
Jews, 586i, 593j
CENSERS, 211l
CENSUS, David's, 57g, **282l, 302hi, 303i**
Moses', 190i, **205c, 206a–djl**, 215cd
Nehemiah's, 309f, 318a
Roman, 72b, 605l, **707a, 722ab**
Solomon's, of non-Hebrew residents,
305e
CENTRALISATION OF YAHWISTIC
CULT, the, 103gl, 223c, 224h, 225c,
232a–i, 234cd, 235c, 254b, 283ef,
288bef, 294a, 295bce, 297dg
superstitions arising from, 491c–f;
see also AMPHICTYONY, JOSIAH,
DEUTERONOMIC REFORM
CENTURION, the, at Jesus' Cross, 742c,
747a, 748f, 762p, 789g, 818c
guards Paul, 840k–m
the servant of a, healed by Jesus, **719fg**,
777a
CEPHAS, 19a, 727g, 802d, 876fg; see

also PETER
CEREALS, offered in sacrifice, 104j,
194d, 195f
CERFAUX (L.), 18b, 880ab, 909b
CERINTHUS, 642f, 955e, 961d
CESTIUS GALLUS (Legate), besieges
Jerusalem, 74e, 966g
CEUPPENS (F.), 665b
CHAFF, as symbol, 573e
CHAINE (J.), on Bethel, 167c
on the historicity of Genesis, 146c
CHAIR, SEAT of Moses, the, 735c
chaire(in), chairete, 661a, 842f, 910e,
947a
CHALCOLITHIC PERIOD: see PRE-
HISTORY OF PALESTINE
CHALDAEA(NS), 136h, 159f, 161b,
310g, 350ab, 467e, 515k, **527bc**,
570e, 571c
letters and language of the, 572bc
Nebuchadnezzar's edict against the,
527h
CHALLONER, DR R., 35c
CHAMPIONS, the judges as, 255c
CHAMPOLLION, 78b
CHAOS, **148af, 149ab**, 471f; see also
ABYSS
the final disappearance of, 975a
the flood as a return to, **157ei**,
952a–c, 954i
CHAPHENATHA, 592h
CHAPHI, 592e
CHAPTER DIVISIONS of the Bible, 602d
charakter, 933c
CHARIOT OF YAHWEH, the, 290f, 507f,
510a–e, 512dij, 966c
CHARIOTS, a vision of four, 578d
introduced into Egypt, 170i
iron, 61f, 63a, 287c
charis, charein, 943c, 963d
CHARISMATA, 21a, 667cd, 669j, 864jk,
867g, **904de**
in I Cor., **879–881**
CHARISMATIC LEADERSHIP, 255c,
271h, 272cel, 273j
CHARITY, 339ac, 687j, 850c, 865bcl,
875eh, 878ac, 880k–p, 881a, 885a,
910ab, 915e, 916d, 944a, 950dh,
951cg, 952f; see also ALMSGIVING
CHARLES (R.H.), 88m
CHARY (T.), 575h, 583g
CHASIDIM, the, **70d**; see HASIDIM
CHASTISEMENT of Christ, the 789c
of the Nations, 546k, 580g
CHASTITY in marriage, 873e
Jewish views of, 348e, 618g
pagan teaching on, 626b
CHEDORLAOMER, 162d
CHEEKS of peace-offerings, 197l
CHELUB, 300a
CHELUBAI, 299d, 300a
CHEMOSH, the cult of, 213g, 215a, 261d,
266b, 500g
CHENOBOSKION PAPYRI, the, 79e
CHEOPS, Pharaoh, 79f
CHEPHIRAH, 250c
CHERETH(ITES), 276bf, 284c, 516c,
573f
CHERUB(IM), 105i, 152cd, **510ac**, 512i
God rides upon, sits among the, 384d,
396b
in Solomon's temple, 103dk, 189ab,
286de, 305f, 396b
CHESED, see HESED
CHESTER BEATTY, 19e; see also
MANUSCRIPTS
CHIASM(US), scriptural examples of,

INDEX

FORNICATION, 446b, **730ef**, 844a, 871l, **872k–p**
idolatry so called, 203b, 970b, 971c, 972c; *see also* ADULTERY; APOSTASY; IDOLATRY
FORTIFICATIONS, and town development, 83a–d, 306b
FORTRESS, the captain of the, 318a
FORTUNATUS of Corinth, 867h, 885b
FORTY DAYS, the great, **824b–d**
FOTHERINGHAM, N.T. studies by, 706f, 707cd
FOUNDATION(S), 383c
Christ as the Church's, 870m
of truth, 925d
FOUNDLING, Israel as a, 514b
FOUNDRY, 580f
FOUNTAIN, the, flowing from Ezekiel's temple, 553g
FOUNTAIN GATE: *see* JERUSALEM, topography
FOUR EMPERORS, the years of, 74f
FOURTH GOSPEL, the, 636ef, 638b; *see* JOHN
FOXE, *The Book of Martyrs*, 32b
FOXES, 55q, 427n
FRAGMENT THEORY, 922b
FRANCISCANS, the, and Palestinian Archaeology, 80g
FRANKINCENSE, given to Christ, **713g**
offered in sacrifice, 104j, 195df
symbolism of, 204d
FRANZELIN (J.B.), on Inspiration, 406d
FRATERNAL CHARITY, 738h; *see* BROTHERLY LOVE, CHARITY
FRATERNAL HARMONY, **729g–i**
FRAUD, condemned, 560f, 567p, 571l
to be expiated, 196g
FREE WILL, 433b, **445c**, 924h; *see also* EVIL INCLINATION; FALL
FREEDMAN (D.N.), biblical studies by, 36d, 90j
FREEDMEN, 184s, 625i, 841e
the synagogue of the, 828g
FREEDOM, human moral, 608d, 615i, **810gh**
Christian, **810gh**, 705h, 855e, 888b, 709f, 746c, **766ef**
history, **14c**, 133fg, **143a–e**, **144a**, 146d, **224a–d**, 241–244, 246a, 255fi, 264a, 298f, **310a–d**, 311e–g, 587a, **641c**, 642e
homiletics and didactics, 269d, 356d, 950e
hymns: *see* POEMS, PSALMS AND SONGS
laments, 501c, 559a
'last words' (farewell discourses), 269b, 760a
legal, **14b**, **133c**; *see also* LAW
legends, 634g
logia of Jesus, 634g, **673de**, 674d, 752c, 822a
midrash, 432e
New Testament, general, **641–644**, 665d, 674d, 822a
of the Lukan Infancy Narratives, 769b
proverbs and parables, 157f, 269c, 356d, **357a–d**, 411bc, 426o–q, 946b, 947a; *see also* PARABLES
poems, psalms and songs, 241g, **257e–h**, 356mn, 363c, 381j, 426eh, 567r, 592b; *see also* POEMS AND SONGS
prayers, **899bc**
prophecy, 14b, 451–454
riddles, 357c
speeches, **822a–c**

891h, 901a, 951e
FREER LOGION, the, 763e
FREEWILL OFFERING: *see* SACRIFICES
FRIEND of Jesus, the apostle, Christian, disciple as a, 815c
FRIENDSHIP, false and true, 417ab, 419f, 447b, 448a
for/of Yahweh, 381q, 382gh, 383f, 405f
FRIDAY, in Jewish liturgical tradition, 226b
FROGS, 971b
the plague of, 179e
FRUIT TREE, Judah a barren, 492c
FRUITS, 605f
of justification, 691i
of the Spirit, 669f, 898l
of Wisdom, 435f
FRUSTRATION, 421h
FUCHS (E.), N.T. studies by, 652ef
FUGITIVES, asylum given to, 190d
ful, 55n
FUL (geog.), 80e
FULFIL(MENT) of righteousness, 714h
of the scriptures, 712j
FULL OF GRACE, the, **661bc**, **662pq**, **770bc**
FULKE (W.), 34bc
FULL MOON, Passover a feast of the, 105e
FULLER (R.H.), N.T. studies by, 657b, 658d
FULLER'S FIELD, the: *see* JERUSALEM, top.
FULNESS, Jesus Christ as the, 628h, 911cf, **913f**, 914f; *see also* PLEROMA
of time(s), 672c, 898h
FUNCTIONS, diverse, in the early church, **879–880**; *see also* CHARISMATA
FUNERARY RITES, PRAYERS, 232c, 343b; *see also* MOURNING
FURLONG, a, 85a, 86c
FURNACE, 286n
of the Three Children, 529cfj
FURNITURE, Roman, 626g
FUTURE, the, is unknowable, 424ac, 425a

G

GAAL, 260f
GABAEL, son of GABRIAS, 341c, 344d
GABINIUS, Governor of Syria, 70f
GABLER, O.T. studies by, 633g
GABRIEL, 526r, 535h, 536e, 616a
his annunciation to Mary, 769b, **770a–h**
his annunciation to Zechariah, **769bd–f**
GAD, son of Jacob-Israel, 172c, 252d, 298q, 486d
the chronicles of, 241j
the tribe of, 300cd, 524d; in Moses' blessing, 239d; territory of, 57g, 205c, **216l–p**, 247c, 252cd, 285d
GAD the SEER, 275j, 304e
the ACTS of, 298d
GADARA, 54o, 55d, 58d, 720c–e
GADD (C.J.), 569i
GADDI, 587i
GADYTIS, 500e
GAHAM, 165f
GAIUS (in III JOHN), 644d, 958jk
GAIUS CALIGULA, Emperor, 73cd, 75d
gal, 281d
GALAAD, 300c
GALAADITIS, 58c
GALATIA, 895ce, 927d
Paul's mission to, 703a, 704a, 834d, 887a

GALATIANS, the EPISTLE to the, 13b, 19a, 643cd, 649a, 704a, **895–898**, 946d
and the Gentile Controversy, 692bf–**693c**, 833gh, **895cd**, **897g–i**, **898a–g**, 908b
date, destination and purpose, 895c–e
justification in, **692bf–693c**
relation to other N.T. works of, 708b, 841c, 895d, 946c, 947a
the death of Christ in, 681e
the mother of Christ in, 660c
GAL'AZU, 58a
GALILEANS, assassinated in the temple, 782a
massacred by Pilate, 766e
GALILEE, 53chl, 54bl–o, 57f, 58d–f, 70abf, 72a, 73a, 74f, 79c, 245c, 253d, 256d, 285d, 341a, 351g, 568b, **675a–cj**
in N.T. times, 71a, 72a, 73ad, 74f, **605dghi**, **675a–cj**, 770a
Jesus' journeys and preaching in, 715e, **749j–751b**, **774a–778h**, 802e, 804c, **805a–k**
Jesus' resurrection appearances in, **743ab** (cf 763d), **820a–e**
Maccabean campaigns in, 589b–e
taken by Assyria, 293f, 466ab, 547c
the first Christian mission in, 830i
GALILEE, the SEA of, 54m, 341a, 744d
GALILEO, 422f
GALL, 345a
GALLING (K.), 421d, 422j
GALLIO, Proconsul of Achaia, 706i, 708c, 835kl, 914e
examines Paul, **821cg**
GALLOWS, 353i, 355h
GAMAD, 516f
GAMALIEL I, Rabbi, Paul's teacher, 701c, 704c, 839a
speech in *Acts*, **827eg**
GAMBLING, 625g
GANGES RIVER, 151e
GAOLER, a, converted at Philippi, **834e–j**
GARBANZOS, 55n
GARDEN, a, the bride as, 428h
the, of Paradise, and the heavenly Jerusalem, **975a–c**; *see also* EDEN; PARADISE
of the Lord, 480c, 483l
GARDENS, the sacrifice of, 486b
GAREB, Mount, 498f
GARIZIM, 53h, 57e
GARLAND, the victor's, 484i, 947b
GARMENT, the Wedding, the parable of the, **733k**
GARMENTS, clean and soiled, symbolism of, 577i
ceremonial, of the scribes, 759k
divided by lot, 385c
leprous, 201f
spread before Jesus on Palm Sunday, **732d**
taken as pledges, 557c
torn for blasphemy, **761yy**
GARSTANG, archaeological work by, 80dk, 126c
GASTER on *Tobit*, 336d
GATES, city gates, uses of, 83e, 267a, 366e, 418df, 435a
GATES of HELL, 727g
GATES of JERUSALEM: *see* JERUSALEM, top.
of the Temple, 521d
GATH, 54ef, 80m, 271l, 278i, 300j, 556b, 559h, 573f

LIST OF MAPS

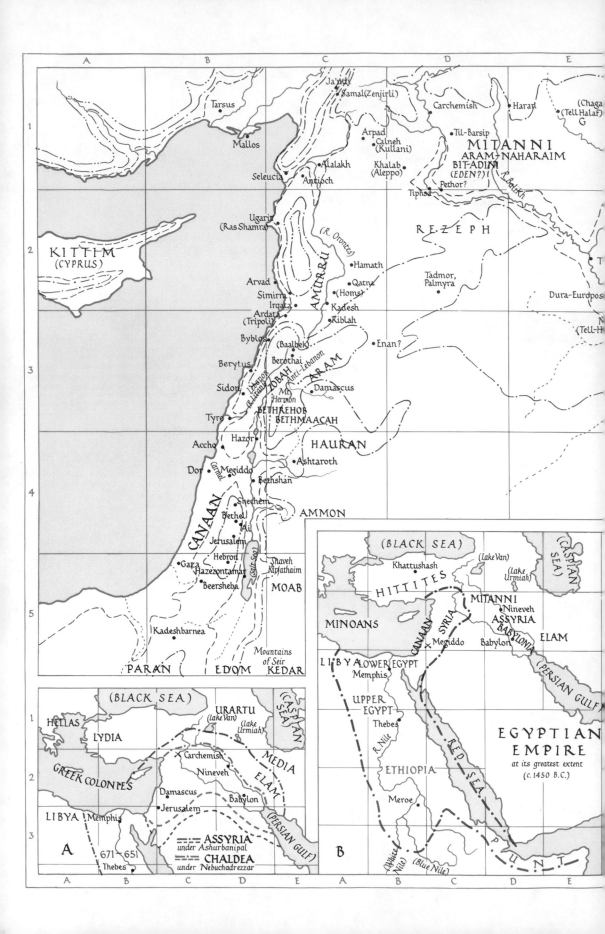

Main map labels:

A B C D E

1

Tarsus

Ja'di
Samal (Zenjirli)
Carchemish · Haran · (Chaga Tell Halaf) G

Mallos

Arpad
Calneh (Kullani)
MITANNI
ARAM-NAHARAIM
BIT-ADINI
(EDEN?)
Til-Barsip

Seleucia
Alalakh
Khalab (Aleppo)
Antioch
Pethor?
Tiphsa
R. Belikh

KITTIM
(CYPRUS)

2

Ugarit
(Ras Shamra)

REZEPH

Hamath
Tadmor, Palmyra
Dura-Europos

Arvad
Simirra
Irqata
Ardata (Tripoli)
Qatna
(Homs)
T

AMURRU
(R. Orontes)
Kadesh
Riblah
Byblos
(Baalbek)
N
(Tell-H

Berytus
Berothai
Enan?

ZOBAH
ARAM

3

Sidon
Mt. Hermon
Damascus

Tyre
BETHREHOB
BETHMAACAH

Accho
Hazor
HAURAN

Dor
Megiddo
Ashtaroth

Bethshan

Shechem
AMMON

Bethel
Ai

Jerusalem

Hebron
Shaveh Kirjathaim

Gaza
Hazezontamar

Beersheba
MOAB

CANAAN

4

Kadeshbarnea

Mountains of Seir

PARAN
EDOM
KEDAR

5

Inset A:

(BLACK SEA)

HELLAS
LYDIA
URARTU (Lake Van)
(Lake Urmiah)
(CASPIAN SEA)

GREEK COLONIES
Carchemish
MEDIA
Nineveh
ELAM

Damascus
Babylon

Jerusalem

LIBYA Memphis
(PERSIAN GULF)

A
671–651
Thebes

ASSYRIA under Ashurbanipal
CHALDEA under Nebuchadrezzar

Inset B:

(BLACK SEA)
(CASPIAN SEA)

Khattushash
(Lake Van)
(Lake Urmiah)

MINOANS
HITTITES
MITANNI
Nineveh
ASSYRIA
ELAM

CANAAN SYRIA
Megiddo
BABYLONIA
Babylon
(PERSIAN GULF)

LIBYA LOWER EGYPT
Memphis

UPPER EGYPT
Thebes
R. Nile

ETHIOPIA
RED SEA

EGYPTIAN EMPIRE
at its greatest extent
(c. 1450 B.C.)

Meroe

(White Nile) (Blue Nile)
PUNT

B

A B C D E

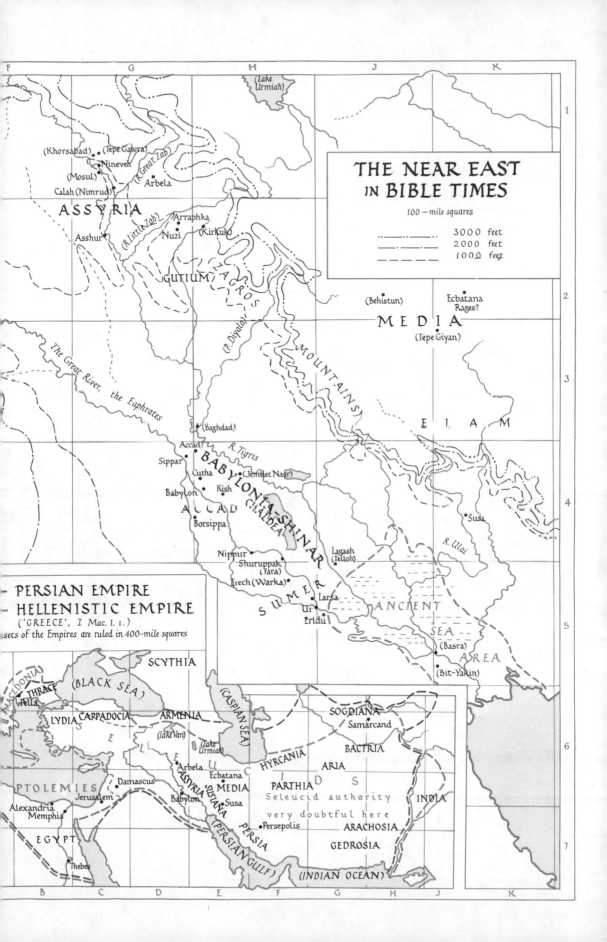

THE NEAR EAST
IN BIBLE TIMES

100 – mile squares

———————— 3000 feet
——·——·—— 2000 feet
—— —— —— 1000 feet

F   G   H   J   K

1

2

3

4

5

6

7

(Lake Urmiah)

(Khorsabad)   (Tepe Gawra)
Nineveh
(Mosul)   R. Great Zab
Calah (Nimrud)   Arbela
ASSYRIA
Asshur   R. Little Zab   Arraphka
Nuzi   (Kirkuk)
GUTIUM   ZAGROS
(R. Diyala)
MOUNTAINS
(Behistun)   Ecbatana Rages?
MEDIA
(Tepe Giyan)
The Great River, the Euphrates
ELAM
(Baghdad)
Accad?   R. Tigris
Sippar   Cutha   (Jemdet Nasr)
Babylon   Kish
BABYLONIA-SHINAR
ACCAD   CHALDEA
Borsippa   Susa
R. Ulai
Nippur   Lagash (Telloh)
Shuruppak (Fara)
Erech (Warka)   SUMER   Larsa
ANCIENT
Ur   SEA
Eridu   (Basra)   AREA
(Bit-Yakin)

PERSIAN EMPIRE
HELLENISTIC EMPIRE
('GREECE', I Mac. 1. 1.)
...sets of the Empires are ruled in 400-mile squares

B   C   D   E   F   G   H   J   K

SCYTHIA
(MACEDONIA)
THRACE   (BLACK SEA)
Pella
LYDIA   CAPPADOCIA   ARMENIA   (CASPIAN SEA)
(Lake Van)   SOGDIANA
Samarcand
(Lake Urmiah)
Arbela   BACTRIA
HYRCANIA
PTOLEMIES   Damascus   Ecbatana   ARIA
ASSYRIA   MEDIA   PARTHIA
Jerusalem   SUSIANA   Susa   Seleucid authority   INDIA
Babylon   very doubtful here
Alexandria
Memphis   Persepolis   ARACHOSIA
PERSIA
EGYPT   GEDROSIA
(PERSIAN GULF)
Thebes
(INDIAN OCEAN)

i

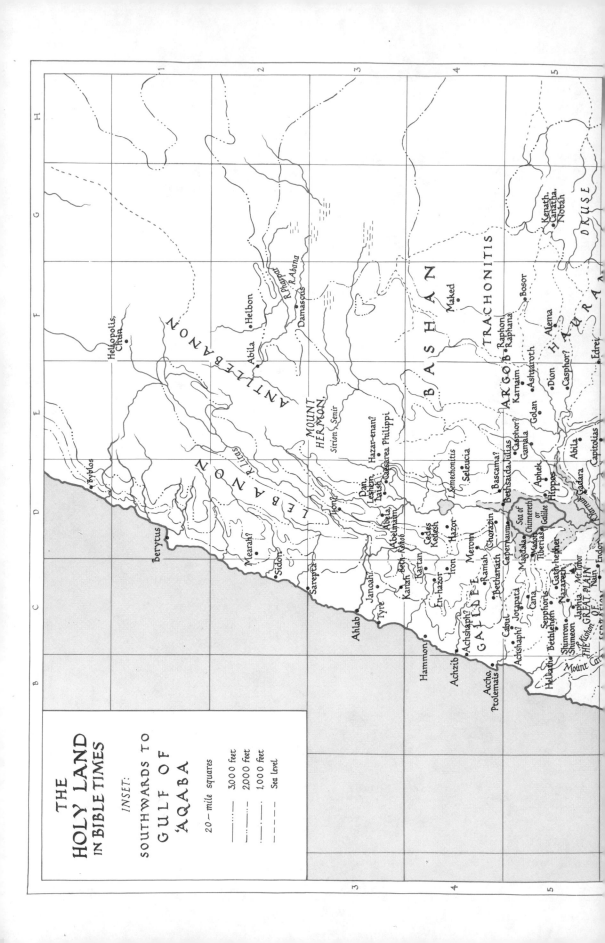

THE
HOLY LAND
IN BIBLE TIMES

INSET:

SOUTHWARDS TO
GULF OF
'AQABA

20—mile squares

——— 3000 feet
—··— 2,000 feet
—···— 1,000 feet
—— — Sea level

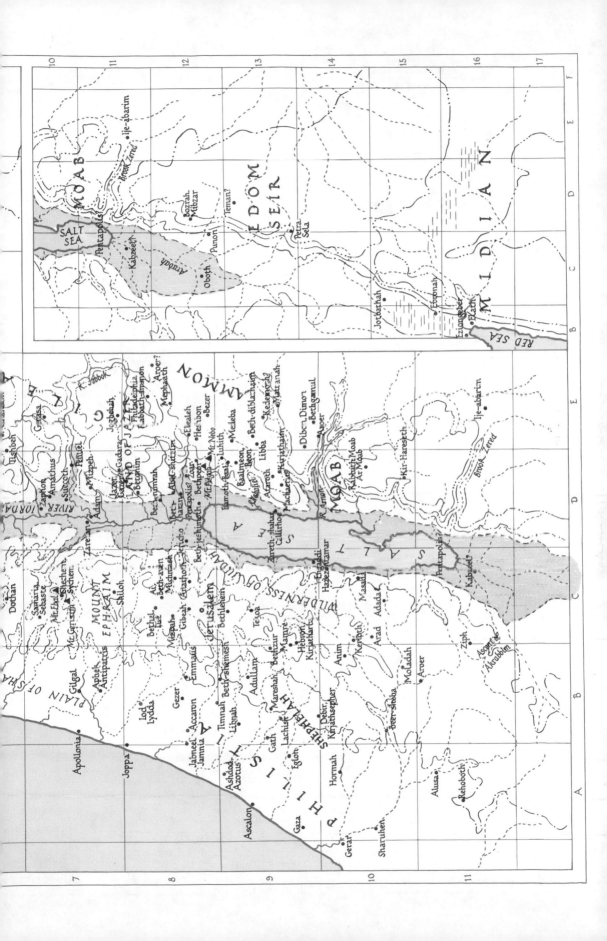

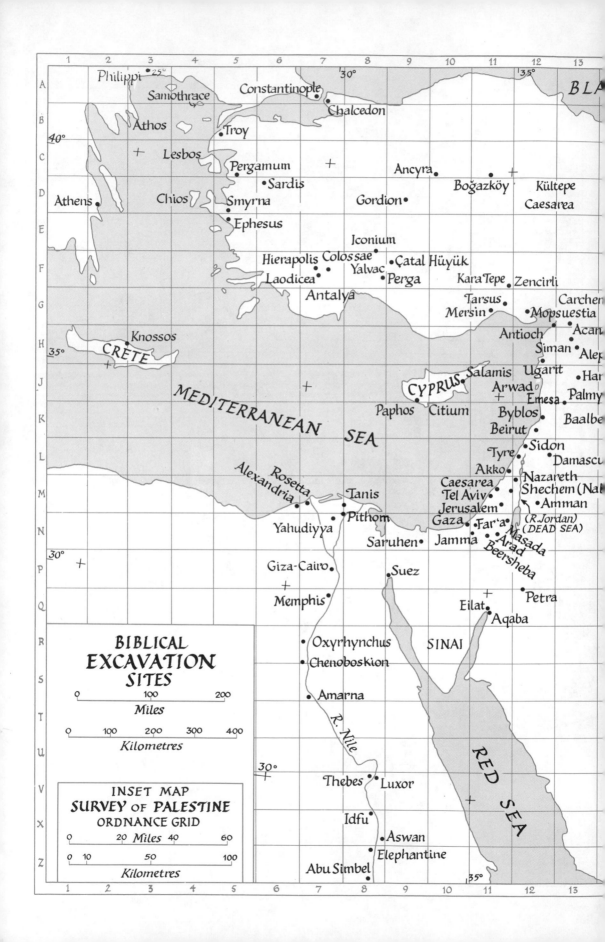

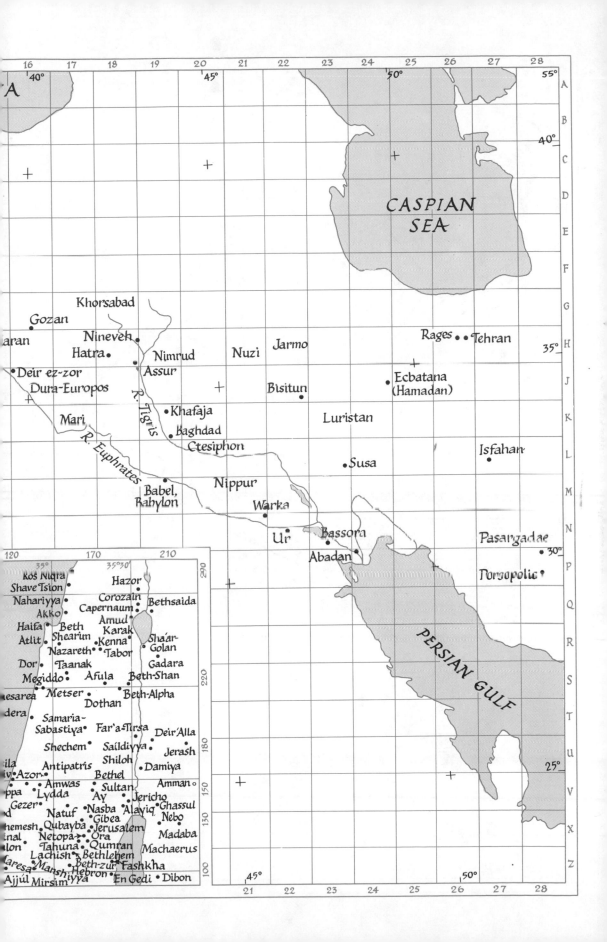

CASPIAN SEA

Gozan
Khorsabad
aran
Nineveh
Hatra
Deir ez-zor
Dura-Europos
Nimrud
Assur
R. Tigris
Nuzi
Jarmo
Khafaja
Mari
R. Euphrates
Baghdad
Ctesiphon
Babel,
Babylon
Nippur
Warka
Ur
Bassora
Abadan
Bisitun
Ecbatana
(Hamadan)
Luristan
Susa
Isfahan
Rages
Tehran
Pasargadae
Persopolis

PERSIAN GULF

40°
45°
50°
55°
40°
35°
30°
25°

Kos Niqra
Shave Tsion
Nahariyya
Akko
Haifa
Atlit
Dor
Megiddo
Caesarea
dera
la
y
ppa
Gezer
d
hemesh
nal
lon
aresa
Ajjúl
Hazor
Corozain
Capernaum
Bethsaida
Amud
Beth
Shearim
Karak
Kenna
Nazareth
Tabor
Shaʿar-Golan
Taanak
Gadara
Afula
Beth-Shan
Metser
Beth-Alpha
Dothan
Samaria-
Sabastiya
Far'a-Tirsa
Deir 'Alla
Shechem
Saildiyya
Jerash
Shiloh
Antipatris
Bethel
Damiya
Azor
Amwas
Sultan
Amman
Lydda
Ay
Jericho
Natuf
Nasba
Alayiq
Ghassul
Qubayba
Gibea
Nebo
Netopa
Ora
Jerusalem
Madaba
Tahuna
Qumran
Machaerus
Lachish
Bethlehem
Mansh
Beth-zur
Fashkha
Mirsim
yya
Hebron
En Gedi
Dibon

120
170
210
35°
35°30'
290
220
180
150
130
100
45°
50°

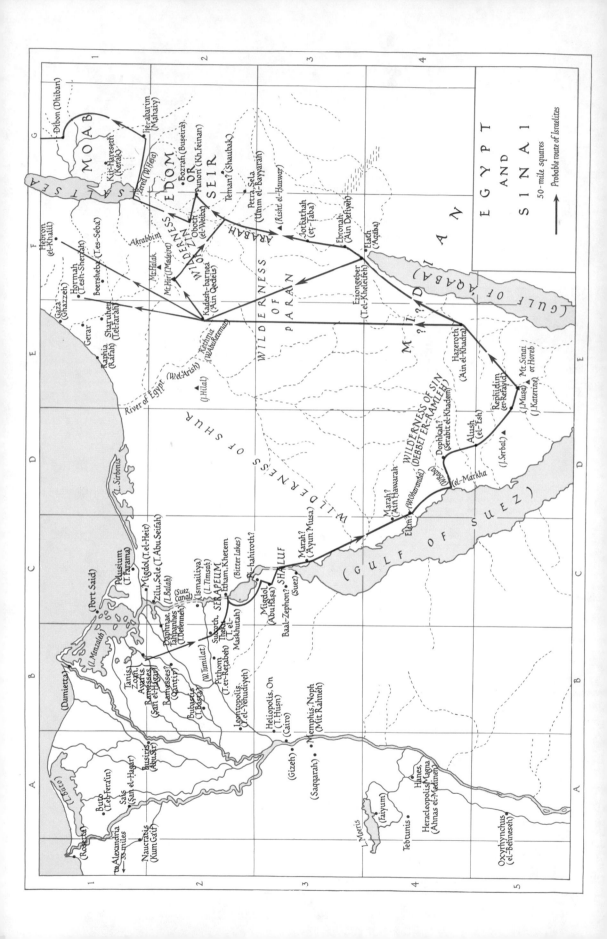

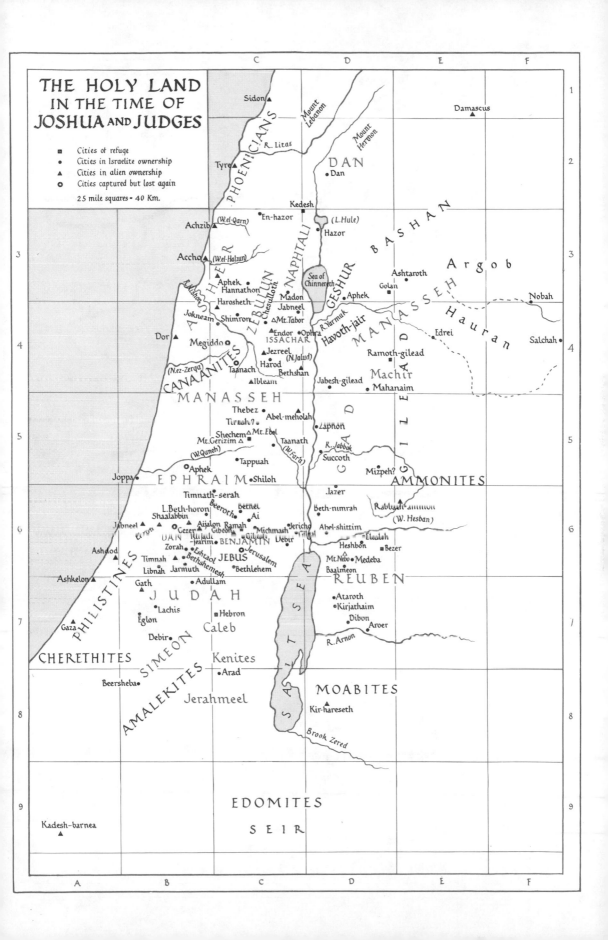

THE HOLY LAND
IN THE TIME OF
JOSHUA AND JUDGES

- ■ Cities of refuge
- • Cities in Israelite ownership
- ▲ Cities in alien ownership
- ○ Cities captured but lost again

25 mile squares = 40 Km.

C   D   E   F

Sidon

Damascus

Mount Lebanon

Mount Hermon

PHOENICIANS

R. Litas

Tyre

DAN

Dan

Kedesh

(L. Hule)

En-hazor

BASHAN

Achzib (W.el-Qarn)

Hazor

Accho (W.el-Halzun)

NAPHTALI

GESHUR

Ashtaroth

Argob

Aphek

Golan

Nobah

Hannathon

Chesulloth

Madon

Aphek

ASHER

ZEBULUN

Jabneel

MANASSEH

Hauran

Harosheth

Jokneam

Shimron

△ Mt. Tabor

R. Yarmuk

Edrei

Salchah

Dor

Endor Ophra

Havoth-jair

Megiddo

ISSACHAR

Jezreel (N. Jalud)

Ramoth-gilead

CANAANITES

Harod

Machir

(N. ez-Zerqa)

Taanach

Bethshan

Jabesh-gilead

Mahanaim

△ Ibleam

MANASSEH

GILEAD

Thebez

Abel-meholah

Tirzah?

Zaphon

Shechem △ Mt. Ebal

Mt. Gerizim △

Taanath

R. Jabbok

(W. Quneh)

(W. Fara)

Succoth

Tappuah

Mizpeh?

AMMONITES

Joppa

Aphek

Shiloh

EPHRAIM

Jazer

Timnath-serah

Beeroth bethel

Rabbath-ammon

L. Beth-horon

Ai

Beth-nimrah

(W. Hesban)

Shaalabbin

Aijalon Ramah

Michmash Jericho

Jabneel

Gezer Gibeon

Debir

Heshbon

Elealeh

Ekron

Kirjath-jearim

Gilgal

Bezer

Ashdod

DAN

Zorah

BENJAMIN

Mt. Nebo Medeba

Eshtaol

JEBUS

Baalmeon

Timnah Bethshemesh

Jerusalem

REUBEN

Ashkelon

Libnah Jarmuth

Bethlehem

Gath Adullam

Ataroth

PHILISTINES

Kirjathaim

JUDAH

Dibon

Lachis

Hebron

Aroer

Gaza

Eglon

Caleb

R. Arnon

Debir

CHERETHITES

SIMEON

Kenites

MOABITES

Beersheba

Arad

AMALEKITES

Jerahmeel

Kir-hareseth

SALT SEA

Brook Zered

EDOMITES

Kadesh-barnea

SEIR

A   B   C   D   E   F

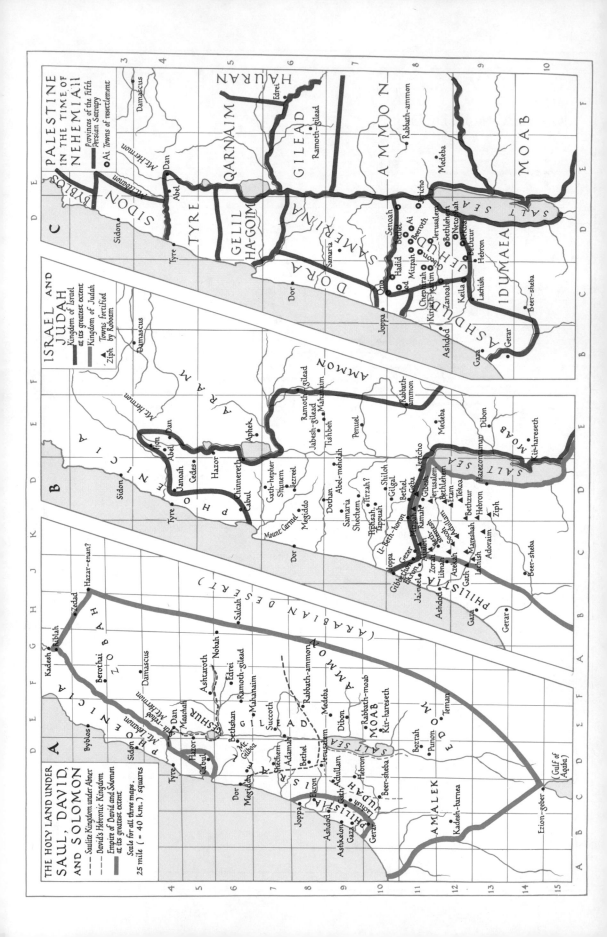

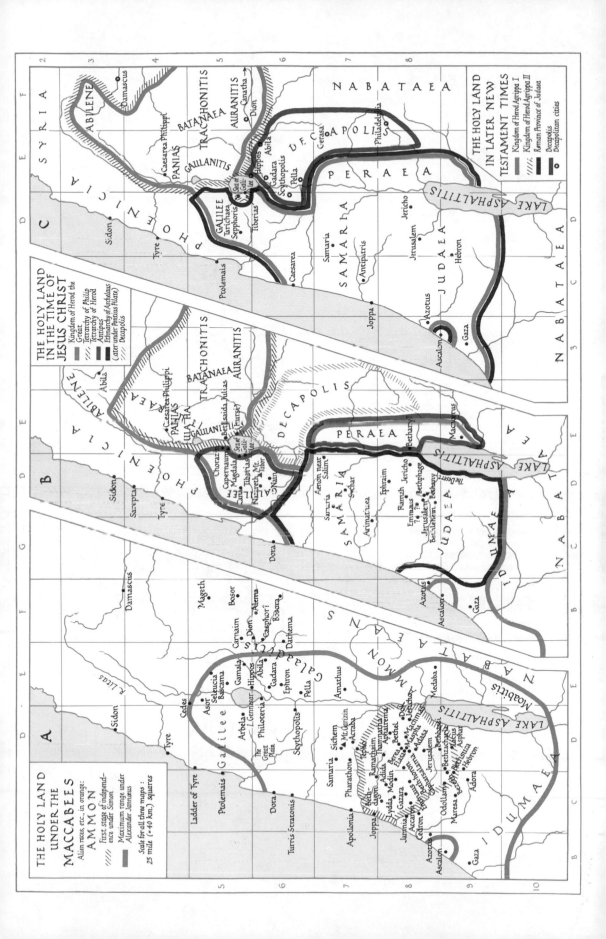

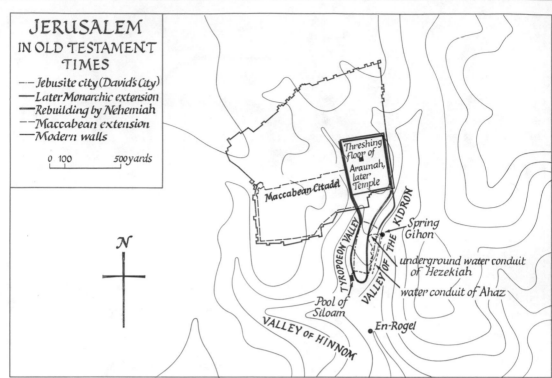

JERUSALEM
IN OLD TESTAMENT TIMES

- ·–· Jebusite city (David's City)
- —— Later Monarchic extension
- ▬▬ Rebuilding by Nehemiah
- – – Maccabean extension
- —— Modern walls

0 100   500 yards

N

Threshing floor of Araunah, later Temple

Maccabean Citadel

TYROPOEON VALLEY

VALLEY OF THE KIDRON

Spring Gihon

underground water conduit of Hezekiah

water conduit of Ahaz

Pool of Siloam

En-Rogel

VALLEY OF HINNOM

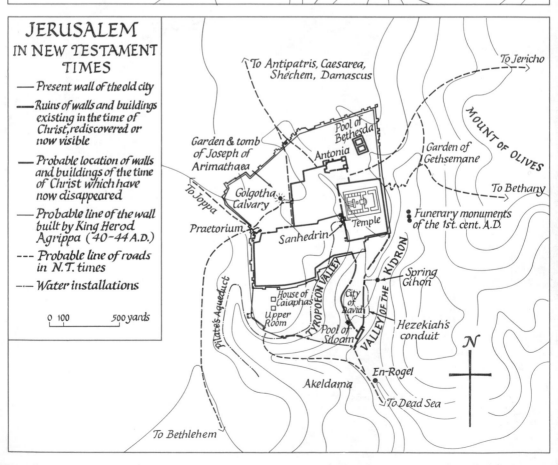

JERUSALEM
IN NEW TESTAMENT TIMES

- —— Present wall of the old city
- ▬▬ Ruins of walls and buildings existing in the time of Christ, rediscovered or now visible
- —— Probable location of walls and buildings of the time of Christ which have now disappeared
- —— Probable line of the wall built by King Herod Agrippa (40–44 A.D.)
- – – – Probable line of roads in N.T. times
- ·–· Water installations

0 100   500 yards

To Antipatris, Caesarea, Shechem, Damascus

To Jericho

Pool of Bethesda

Garden & tomb of Joseph of Arimathaea

Antonia

Garden of Gethsemane

MOUNT OF OLIVES

To Joppa

Golgotha Calvary

To Bethany

Praetorium

Funerary monuments of the 1st. cent. A.D.

Sanhedrin

Temple

VALLEY OF THE KIDRON

Spring Gihon

Pilate's Aqueduct

House of Caiaphas

Upper Room

City of David

TYROPOEON VALLEY

Pool of Siloam

Hezekiah's conduit

N

Akeldama

En-Rogel

To Dead Sea

To Bethlehem

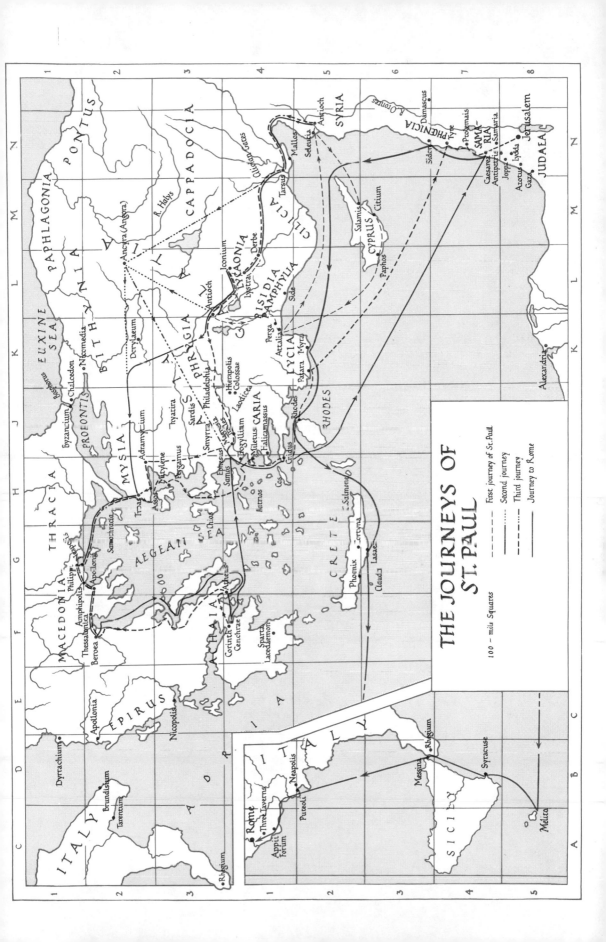

THE JOURNEYS OF
ST. PAUL

100 — mile Squares

- - - - - First journey of St. Paul
--------- Second journey
·········· Third journey
- — - — Journey to Rome